Subject Collections

Subject Collections

A guide to special book collections
and subject emphases as reported by
university, college, public, and
special libraries and museums
in the United States and Canada

Sixth Edition
Revised and Enlarged

Compiled by
Lee Ash
Library Consultant, Bethany, Connecticut
and
William G. Miller
Watertown Public Library, Connecticut

With the collaboration of Barbara J. McQuitty

Volume 2
M – Z

R.R. Bowker Company
New York & London, 1985

Published by R. R. Bowker Company
205 East Forty-second Street, New York, NY 10017
Copyright ©1985 by Xerox Corporation
All rights reserved. Reproduction of this work, in whole or in part,
without written permission of the publisher is prohibited.
Printed and bound in the United States of America.
International Standard Book Numbers:
Set 0-8352-1917-8, Vol. 1 0-8352-1967-4, Vol. 2 0-8352-1968-2

*To My Wife
Marian Neal Ash
of whom I am so proud
and continue to owe so much
– from the First to the
Sixth Edition and Beyond*

and

*To My Mother
Elsie Ann Eklund
for whose love, support,
and understanding I am
forever indebted.*

– WGM

Preface

The Sixth Edition of *Subject Collections* has been a pleasure to compile because, after several problems were confronted and then solved, the computers really did their work. The problems were major ones, and one of my rewards has been the publisher's faith in the book that encouraged them to underwrite it at much greater cost than had been planned.

Once again we followed the same questionnaire system used for the Fifth Edition, although in a somewhat different format: printouts were sent to libraries covering all entries submitted for the Fifth Edition or described from my notes accumulated between editions. Libraries were asked to return the forms with revisions, deletions, and new additions. We believe that nearly (but not quite!) 100 percent of these changes have been noted, with some subject headings altered to conform to the Library of Congress or to our own authority lists; notes have been revised to correct ambiguities and the like. Some subject headings have been changed for clarity or modernization, and we have, I hope, cross-referenced all of the old forms to the new and added many more *see* references; as usual, we have not used *see also* references.

This Sixth Edition continues our practice of including from the previous edition all entries formerly sent by libraries that did not respond to the current questionnaire. These and entries I have made from my between-edition notes, without reconfirmation from the institution, are marked with a dagger (†).

We have not attempted to guess at the number of entries other than to recognize that there are certainly at least 6,500 new ones and that over the years, every week we have discovered new and unusual collections that enhance opportunities for reference or research in additional subject fields. One observation that seems interesting is the continuing increase in collections of materials by or about individual persons.

Many more libraries have reported to us, and some of the larger ones have literally hundreds of additional entries. As noted in the Fifth Edition, very few libraries eliminated entries, a few small libraries (mostly industrial or commercial) were dissolved, and a few – mainly small ones – asked not to be included. A number of collections were transferred to other libraries, which we noted when made aware of the transfer. Once again, in spite of repeated requests by mail or telephone, a few libraries, including some large ones, did not respond at all to our efforts or, for one reason or another, did not report fully.

The growing number of antiquarian booksellers who made use of *Subject Collections* is well known to us. It is for this reason (they quote materials for possible sale to libraries) that we continue to list smaller as well as large special collections. To repeat for emphasis – as from edition to edition – librarians should read the Preface to the Third Edition before criticizing the qualitative differences between collections. Similarly, to those who want an index to an expanded *American Library Directory,* the description of the genesis of *Subject Collections* recorded in the First Edition (1958) must suffice.

ACKNOWLEDGMENTS

My enjoyment in undertaking this compilation since 1958 is appreciated on two levels: first, as a professional contribution in which I take pride through the frequent use of the book in libraries around the world; second, and even more pleasurable, is the recognition of the friendly sacrifice of time and effort that literally thousands of librarians have put into the book. I have said this before and it continues as the greater reward.

I am especially proud to have had Bill Miller as my associate in editing the Sixth Edition. He has helped me on different editorial projects and with other work since he was thirteen. During his last year in high school, Bill took charge of all cross-references in the Fourth Edition and he did the same for the Fifth Edition in his last year of college. Then he went to library school at the University of North Carolina, and here he is now as a colleague of whom I am very proud! I look forward to many years of working with him on this and other projects.

This edition of *Subject Collections* could not have been made into a book without the careful and accurate attention of Barbara J. McQuitty and her staff at the Jaques Cattell Press in Tempe, Arizona. Our continual interfacing by mail and telephone and her expert solutions of difficult computer and editorial problems (compounded by my dreadful handwritten entries) are only partial recognition of what she had to face. My debt to her and her co-workers is immeasurable.

My "Sharon workshop" at our summer base has grown up. All of the teenaged boys who helped with other editions have gone away, except Bill Miller, but my indebtedness, acknowledged by name in previous editions, continues. My reliance upon them and their assistance in manipulating cards – sorting, alphabetizing, and other things, some done now by computer – were always an encouraging factor leading to another edition because I knew they would be there to help. They all remain close friends and the friendliest computer cannot replace them.

Louis A. Rachow of the Edwin Booth/Walter Hampden Memorial Library, The Players, New York City, continues to be a major contributor to references about new collections not reported directly to me or noted in the library press. Similarly, Philip Weimerskirch at The Burndy Library, Norwalk, Connecticut, has given me lists of libraries with new or unrecorded collections. Additional help has come from assistance by Michael Cahill (formerly of Sharon), Bruce Hescock, and Lee Brockett, who have taken special interest in their assignments over the past two years.

Gary Ink, at the Bowker Company, has been my special connection and supervised *Subject Collections* as a project for the publisher. He has been very easy to work with and to enjoy as a new friend. I am gratified by his support and interest in the book. Everyone at Bowker and at the Jaques Cattell Press has been remarkably patient with me and ever so helpful, for which I am humbly appreciative.

Most of all, the continuing devotion and advice of my wife, Marian Neal Ash, must be recognized. Her tolerance level for the mess of notes, cards, printouts, and correspondence that flows over from my study to the library, porch, and dining room have tested her, and she has always been patient. More than that, her work as a senior university press editor always helps me to solve problems. Dedication of all editions of *Subject Collections* to her is only a partial expression of appreciation and love.

Six editions of *Subject Collections* in twenty-six years is an encouraging record that prompts plans for the Seventh Edition. As I have written before, however, the compiler of any standard reference work has a responsibility to do the best for those who use the book. I hope that our errors are few and I apologize for them. I am anxious that we may know what to correct in the future. Therefore, I welcome any suggestions that could make the book a better one and more inclusive, so that future scholars, librarians, antiquarian booksellers, and others may know more about the collections that have been preserved for them.

Lee Ash

Bethany, Connecticut
September 1984

Introduction

INCLUSIVENESS

What we said in the Fifth Edition remains true for the Sixth: "Virtually all libraries included in this book are listed in the *American Library Directory;* however, not all libraries listed there are included in *Subject Collections,* either because the libraries did not return their questionnaires, or because their replies were unusable."

Once again *museums* were questionnaired, and returns for this edition were better in number and quality than the previous edition. We must continue to urge these institutions to report their holdings more explicitly, however, because they are often unique or extensive and should be a part of the corpus of research materials available to scholars or students. We hope to continue to improve our efforts among them. United States government libraries still report poorly, except for the careful coverage at the Library of Congress. It seems that we must again "emphasize that we have expended our best efforts to include all the material that has been submitted but have no legal responsibility for accidental omissions or errors in any listing."

EXCLUSIONS

Generally, in this edition, as in the previous ones, local history collections have not been listed. The public library and/ or historical society in any town are usually prime sources for these materials, as well as for genealogical reference work; however, we have not been quite as exclusive of these collections as in the past. In future editions, as descriptive notes concerning these local history collections become more explicit, it is likely that more collections of this type will be listed.

I have not tried to complete listings of college and university departmental libraries when these were not reported; neither are listings of medical, nursing school, or law libraries complete. (These are available on Bowker mailing lists or in other directories.) For law, I have arbitrarily excluded the smaller county libraries, too. Unspecialized U.S. Department of Agriculture field libraries and teachers' college professional libraries also are not all listed.

OTHER SOURCES

There has been no effort to duplicate material in the *National Union Catalogue of Manuscript Collections* or in similar directories at the state or regional level, but it must be remembered that *Subject Collections* and *NUCMC* are complementary to one another. *Subject Collections* stands, similarly, in relation to other standard guides such as Downs' *American Library Sources: A Bibliographical Guide* and its supplements; the Special Libraries Association's *Directory of Special Libraries,* as well as local guides compiled from time to time by the Association's various state and regional chapters; Hamer's *Guide to Archives and Manuscripts in the United States* (still useful and greatly in need of its planned updating). Many new local and regional guides have been published since the previous edition of *Subject Collections.* All, though they vary in character, can be helpful to the researcher who is careful enough to search them out. New special collections are frequently described in library, book trade, and historical publications such as *College and Research Libraries News, AB Bookman's Weekly, Publishers Weekly, Library Journal,* and publications of "Friends" of libraries groups, the scholarly press, and the daily newspapers.

ARRANGEMENT

Subject headings are alphabetized and based, with some adaptation, on the most recent edition of the Library of Congress list and its supplements. Following each subject heading, entries are arranged alphabetically by state name abbreviated and designated in boldface type. The abbreviated state names, including the District of Columbia (D.C.), are listed first, followed by Puerto Rico and other U.S. territories, then Canada. Within each of these *geographical divisions,* the arrangement is alphabetical by *city,* then alphabetical by the *name of the library.*

Abbreviations and Symbols. Where reported, I have indicated that a collection is cataloged (Cat.), that manuscripts are included in the collection (Mss.), and that there are pictures (Pix). Other abbreviations used are self-evident. **Parentheses.** If parentheses enclose the number of volumes or budget dollars, this indicates that the enclosed figure represents the total for the library or collections, *not* the amount for the specific subject. **Parallel Lines** (//) following the number of volumes indicate that the collection is no longer being enlarged. Sometimes the double virgule appears alone, signifying that the number of volumes was not reported and that additions are not being made. **The Dagger** (†). The dagger symbol has been explained above, as it relates to the compiler's notes about unreported collections.

LOAN AND PHOTOGRAPHING FACILITIES

Most libraries permit interlibrary loans or have institutional or local facilities for photographic reproduction – photocopying or microform; therefore, I have not cited such facilities. Instead, I noted exceptions imposed by resource libraries which limit these commonly accepted privileges. Users of interlibrary loans should be aware of the new copyright restrictions which are in force everywhere.

Abbreviations

The names of the subject collections in the text are preceded by the two-letter abbreviations used by the U.S. Post Office for the various states. A list of such abbreviations follows for anyone who may be unfamiliar with them.

AMERICAN STATES AND TERRITORIES

AK	Alaska	LA	Louisiana	OR	Oregon
AL	Alabama	MA	Massachusetts	PA	Pennsylvania
AR	Arkansas	MD	Maryland	PI	Pacific Islands
AZ	Arizona	ME	Maine		(Incl Guam, Western Samoa,
CA	California	MI	Michigan		Samoa, Mariana Islands,
CO	Colorado	MN	Minnesota		Wake Island)
CT	Connecticut	MO	Missouri	PR	Puerto Rico
CZ	Canal Zone	MS	Mississippi	RI	Rhode Island
DC	District of Columbia	MT	Montana	SC	South Carolina
DE	Delaware	NC	North Carolina	SD	South Dakota
FL	Florida	ND	North Dakota	TN	Tennessee
GA	Georgia	NE	Nebraska	TX	Texas
HI	Hawaii	NH	New Hampshire	UT	Utah
IA	Iowa	NJ	New Jersey	VA	Virginia
ID	Idaho	NM	New Mexico	VI	Virgin Islands
IL	Illinois	NV	Nevada	VT	Vermont
IN	Indiana	NY	New York	WA	Washington
KS	Kansas	OH	Ohio	WI	Wisconsin
KY	Kentucky	OK	Oklahoma	WV	West Virginia
				WY	Wyoming

CANADIAN PROVINCES

AB	Alberta	NF	Newfoundland	PE	Prince Edward Island
BC	British Columbia	NS	Nova Scotia	PQ	Quebec
MB	Manitoba	NT	Northwest Territories	SK	Saskatchewan
NB	New Brunswick	ON	Ontario	YT	Yukon Territory

Subject Collections

M

MABBOTT, THOMAS OLIVE

NC —DUKE UNIVERSITY, William R
Perkins Library, Jay B Hubbell Center for
American Literary Historiography, Durham,
27706. Erma Whittington, Librn
Notes: 77,312 items, including manuscripts,
pictures, clippings, and correspondence. "The
objective of the Center is to gather the
papers and materials of significant scholars
and critics in American literary history." The
Center is a part of the Perkins Library
Manuscripts Department.

MACABRE TALES

RI —BROWN UNIVERSITY, John Hay
Library, 20 Prospect St, Providence, 02912.
Mark N Brown, Cur Mss
Holdings: Vols (600) Cat Mss Pix
Phonorecords Audiotapes
Notes: Howard Phillips Lovecraft Collection
of books, amateur and professional
magazines, plus mss/typescripts by and
about Howard Phillips Lovecraft, incl first
and subsequent editions of Lovecraft's work
in 12 languages; complete runs of *Weird
Tales, Marvel Tales, The Californian,
Driftwind, Rainbow, Leaves,* and *Amateur
Fantasy Correspondent* plus scattered issues
of 50 amateur and professional magazines;
1500 letters written by Lovecraft to more
than 200 correspondents, 270 mss/
typescripts of his essays, fiction and poetry
plus over 3000 mss/typescripts of essays,
fiction, letters, and poetry written by his
correspondents. Photocopying of mss is
restricted.
WI —UNIVERSITY OF WISCONSIN, LA
CROSSE, Murphy Library, 1631 Pine St, La
Crosse, 54601. Edwin L Hill, Special
Collections Librn
Holdings: Vols 1000 Cat
Notes: The Paul W Skeeters Collection of
science fiction, fantasy, and horror literature.
Complements the library's complete
collection of Arkham House books, which
contains many titles autographed by August
Derleth, and H P Lovecraft's complete
fiction and poetic works.

MCAFEE, BYRON

CA —UNIVERSITY OF CALIFORNIA, LOS
ANGELES, Research Library, Dept of
Special Collections, 405 Hilgard Ave, Los
Angeles, 90024. Edward Shreeves,
Chairman, Bibliographers Group; David S
Zeidberg, Head
Holdings: Mss
Notes: 6.5 linear feet of mss,
correspondence, and photocopies of material
relating to the Nahuatl language.

MCALMON, ROBERT

CT —YALE UNIVERSITY, Box 1603A, Yale
Station, New Haven, 06520.
DE —UNIVERSITY OF DELAWARE, Hugh
M Morris Library, S College Ave, Newark,
19711. T Stuart Dick, Special Collections
Holdings: Cat Mss Pix
Notes: Manuscripts, etc, incl literary
correspondence.

MCANENY, GEORGE, 1869-1954

NJ —PRINCETON UNIVERSITY, Library,
Manuscript Collection, Nassau St, Princeton,
08540. Jean F Preston, Cur
Holdings: // Mss
Notes: Incl 45 scrapbook volumes; 79 letter
boxes; 34 cartons of papers.

MACARTHUR, CHARLES

MA —HARVARD UNIVERSITY LIBRARY,
Cambridge, 02138.
Holdings: Cat Mss

MACARTHUR, GEN. DOUGLAS, 1880-1964

VA —MACARTHUR MEMORIAL, Library &
Archives, MacArthur Sq, Norfolk, 23510.

Ellen E Folkama, Asst Archivist
Holdings: Vols (4000) Cat Mss Maps Pix
Slides Phonorecords Audiotapes 16mm
Films Microforms
Notes: Everything relating to the life and
related activities of MacArthur. The
Archives of the collection consist of 600
shelf-feet of documents from Gen
MacArthur's official headquarters files over
the period 1941-1951. These papers pertain
to all matters with which his various
commands were involved: military, naval
and air matters; international relations;
political science; Japanese occupation; peace
treaty and Constitution, etc. Each Record
Group is indexed. The indexes are retained
here since they are being expanded. They
are available for researchers.

MCARTHUR FAMILY

ME —BOWDOIN COLLEGE, Library,
Brunswick, 04011. Dianne M Gutscher, Cur
of Special Collections
Notes: Besides a general collection of 13,000
volumes relating to the State of Maine, there
are also many ms collections touching on
political, economic, and social history of
Maine. These incl the McArthur Family
Papers; 8000 pieces from this Limington,
Maine, family, 1795-1810.

MACARTNEY, GEORGE
MACARTNEY, EARL

CT —YALE UNIVERSITY, Box 1603A, Yale
Station, New Haven, 06520.
Notes: Papers concerning his embassy to
Russia, 1764-1767.
NY —CORNELL UNIVERSITY LIBRARIES,
John M Olin Library, Wason Collection of
China & the Chinese, Ithaca, 14853. James
Cole, Cur; Paul P W Cheng, East Asia Librn
Holdings: Cat Mss
Notes: 10 vols of manuscripts.

MCAULIFFE, FRANK

MA —BOSTON UNIVERSITY, Mugar
Memorial Library, Special Collections Dept,
771 Commonwealth Ave, Boston, 02215.
Howard B Gotlieb, Dir
Holdings: Mss

MCCAA, DAVID G.

PA —FRANKLIN INSTITUTE LIBRARY,
Dept of Historical Programs, 20th St and
Parkway, Philadelphia, 19103.
Notes: Notebooks and other papers.

MCCABE, ROBERT KARR

MA —BOSTON UNIVERSITY, Mugar
Memorial Library, Special Collections Dept,
771 Commonwealth Ave, Boston, 02215.
Howard B Gotlieb, Dir
Holdings: Cat Mss
Notes: Mss, correspondence, etc collected in
depth; incl publications by or about.

MCCAGUE, JAMES P.

MA —BOSTON UNIVERSITY, Mugar
Memorial Library, Special Collections Dept,
771 Commonwealth Ave, Boston, 02215.
Howard B Gotlieb, Dir
Holdings: Cat Mss Correspondence

MCCALL, MONICA

MA —BOSTON UNIVERSITY, Mugar
Memorial Library, Special Collections Dept,
771 Commonwealth Ave, Boston, 02215.
Howard B Gotlieb, Dir
Holdings: Cat Mss
Notes: Mss, correspondence, etc collected in
depth.

MCCAN, WILLIAM

DC —GEORGETOWN UNIVERSITY,
Library, Special Collections Div, 37 & O Sts
NW, Washington, 20057. George M
Barringer, Special Collections Librn;

Nicholas B Sheetz, Mss Librn
Holdings: Cat Mss Pix
Notes: Panama Canal, and papers of Tomas
Herran, Earl Harding, Thomas E Martin,
William McCan, Clark Thompson, Leonor K
Sullivan, and Capt Miles Duval.

MCCARTER NAIRNE AND PARTNERS

AB —UNIVERSITY OF CALGARY,
Libraries, Special Collections Div, 2500
University Dr, Calgary, T2N 1N4, Can.
Holdings: Cat Mss Pix
Notes: 22,300 pictures; 15 cm mss.
Collection consists of original working
drawings, blueprints and renderings, as well
as reports and photographic albums by one
of Vancouver's oldest and most important
architectural firms, McCarter Nairne &
Partners, 1961-date. Incl are the Marine
Building, Georgia Medical-Dental Building,
the original David Spencer Department
Store and the Canadian Services College
HMCS Royal Roads. The collection incl
many fine full-scale detail drawings for
stone, wood, metal and plaster work. Pre-
dating the firm's establishment are original
drawings by Thomas Hooper, Architect, for
the Winch Building (1908), the Milne
Warehouse, and the Morris Office Building
(1911). The collection is supported by tape
and transcript of an oral history interview
conducted by Dr Harold D Kalman with
John Young McCarter, founder of the firm.
Inventories will be availableshortly.

MCCARTHY, EUGENE J.

DC —GEORGETOWN UNIVERSITY,
Library, Special Collections Div, 37 & O Sts
NW, Washington, 20057. George M
Barringer, Special Collections Librn;
Nicholas B Sheetz, Mss Librn
Notes: The Division has received the
complete collection of materials generated
by Senator Eugene McCarthy's 1968 bid for
the Presidency, ca 600 linear ft, incl photos,
audiotapes, videotapes.
MN —MINNESOTA HISTORICAL
SOCIETY LIBRARY, 690 Cedar St, Saint
Paul, 55101. Patricia C Harpole, Chief of
Reference Library; Bonnie G Wilson, Head
of Special Libraries
Notes: Materials by such well-known figures
as Hubert H. Humphrey, Eugene J.
McCarthy, Orville L Freeman, Maurice H.
Stans, Donald M Fraser, Albert H Quie,
Clark MacGregor and John A Blatnik. A list
of these holdings is on file in the Audio-
Visual Library, the tapes are housed in the
MHS Research Center, 1500 Mississippi
Street, St Paul, Minn.
NY —CORNELL UNIVERSITY LIBRARIES,
Collection of Regional History, Dept of
Manuscripts and Univ Archives, Ithaca,
14853.
Notes: Oral History Interview, 1969, of the
Eugene McCarthy Project.
NC —NORTH CAROLINA DIV OF
ARCHIVES & HISTORY, 109 E Jones St,
Raleigh, 27611.
Notes: The Euticus Renn Collection of
Eugene McCarthy Campaign Materials.

MCCARTHY, GEN. FRANK

†VA —GEORGE C MARSHALL
RESEARCH FOUNDATION AND
LIBRARY, Drawer 920, Lexington, 24450.
Royster Lyle Jr, Cur Collections
Holdings: Cat Mss Maps Pix
Notes: Papers, incl personal correspondence,
etc, especially with regard to service during
World War II.

MCCARTHY, JOSEPH

ME —MARGARET CHASE SMITH
LIBRARY CENTER, Skowhegan, 04976.
James C MacCampbell, Dir
Notes: Papers of Senator Margaret Chase
Smith; considerable on Senator Joseph
McCarthy.
WI —STATE HISTORICAL SOCIETY OF
WISCONSIN, Archives, 816 State St,

MCCARTHY, JOSEPH (cont.)

Madison, 53706. Harold L Miller, Reference Archivist
Notes: Papers of Eugene and Peggy Dennis, Communist Party activists, 1926 - date. He was national head, CP, USA. Papers trace development of CIO in '30s, Farmer-Labor-Progressive Federation, and other Wisconsin and national political groups. Much on Senator Joseph McCarthy.

MCCARTHY, SHAUN

MA —BOSTON UNIVERSITY, Mugar Memorial Library, Special Collections Dept, 771 Commonwealth Ave, Boston, 02215. Howard B Gotlieb, Dir
Holdings: Mss

MCCARTY, DWIGHT

IA —STATE HISTORICAL SOCIETY OF IOWA LIBRARY, 402 Iowa Ave, Iowa City, 52240. Darold J Brown, Librn
Holdings: Cat
Notes: Thousands of individual items and smaller collections. Two hundred larger collections incl the papers of Cyrus C Carpenter, Jonathan P Dolliver, Gilbert Haugen, W W Waymack, Ephraim Adams, A C Dodge, Dorothy Houghton, Jesse Macy, Agnes Samuelson, Donald Johnson, Jack Miller, Ruth Sayre, Samuel Kirkwood, Thomas McKnight, Robert Lucas, Dwight McCarty, William Larrabee. Includes church, school, company and organization records, Civil War materials.

MCCARTHY, MARY THERESE

NV —UNIVERSITY OF NEVADA, RENO, University Library, Special Collections Dept, Reno, 89557. Robert E Blesse, Head
Holdings: Vols (71) Cat
Notes: Includes individual works by author in all editions including translations; also prefaces, introductions, published correspondence, appearances in anthologies, periodicals, etc. Bibliographical research collection, part of Modern Authors Collection. Other appearances 205 cataloged.

MCCAY, WINSOR

OH —OHIO STATE UNIVERSITY, Library for Communication and Graphic Arts, 242 W 18th St, Columbus, 43210. Lucy S Caswell, Curator
Notes: Original cartoons by Winsor McCay, John T McCutcheon, Dick Moores, Ned White, Walter Berndt, Jim Larrick, Carl Rose and Bill Crawford.

MCCLARY, JANE

VA —UNIVERSITY OF VIRGINIA, Alderman Library, Manuscripts Dept, Charlottesville, 22901. Edmund Berkeley Jr, Cur
Notes: Letters of many other Virginia authors, such as Sherwood Anderson, Hawthorne Daniel, Murrell Edmunds, George Cary Eggleston, John Fox, John Pendleton Kennedy, Katie Letcher Lyle, Julian Rutherfoord Meade, Thomas Nelson Page, Virginius Dabney, Clifford Dowdey, Jane McClary, Peter Taylor, and others.

MCCLELLAN, GEORGE B.

DC —LIBRARY OF CONGRESS, Manuscript Division, Washington, 20540. John C Broderick, Chief
Holdings: Cat Mss Pix
Notes: Mss, papers, records, etc.

MCCLELLAN, JOHN L.

AR —OUACHITA BAPTIST UNIVERSITY, McClellan Hall, Arkadelphia, 71923. Jan Savage, Research Librn
Holdings: Mss Maps Pix Audiotapes Videotapes
Notes: Room in McClellan Hall is dedicated to the papers and memorabilia of US Senator John McClellan (1942-1977). Local copying facilities are available. Research by appointment only.

MCCLELLAND AND STEWART, LIMITED

ON —MCMASTER UNIVERSITY, Mills Memorial Library, Div of Archives & Research Collections, Hamilton, L8S 4L6, Can. G R Hill, Univ Librn
Holdings: Mss
Notes: The archives of McClelland and Stewart Ltd (1955-1980) and Macmillan of Canada (1907-1980), consisting of executive correspondence, editorial files, publicity, author correspondence, some art work.

MCCLENDON, MARY

MI —WAYNE STATE UNIVERSITY, Walter P Reuther Library, Archives of Labor & Urban Affairs, Detroit, 48202. Philip Mason, Dir
Holdings: Mss
Notes: Papers, correspondence, etc.

MCCLINTOCK, SIR FRANCIS LEOPOLD

BC —UNIVERSITY OF VICTORIA, McPherson Library, Victoria, V8W 3H5, Can.

MCCLOY, HELEN

MA —BOSTON UNIVERSITY, Mugar Memorial Library, Special Collections Dept, 771 Commonwealth Ave, Boston, 02215. Howard B Gotlieb, Dir
Holdings: Cat Mss
Notes: Mss, Correspondence, etc collected in depth; incl publications by or about.

MCCLUNG, NELLIE LETITIA (MOONEY), 1873-1951

BC —UNIVERSITY OF VICTORIA, McPherson Library, Victoria, V8W 3H5, Can.

MCCLURE, MICHAEL, 1932-

NY —STATE UNIVERSITY OF NEW YORK, STONY BROOK, Melville Library, Dept of Special Collections, Stony Brook, 11794. Evert Volkersz, Head
Holdings: Cat Mss
BC —SIMON FRASER UNIVERSITY, Library, Burnaby, V5A 1S6, Can. Percilla Groves, Special Collections Librn
Holdings: Cat Mss Pix Videotapes
Notes: Complete archive incl correspondence, mss, photographs, first editions, memorabilia, 1955-1982.
BC —UNIVERSITY OF VICTORIA, McPherson Library, Victoria, V8W 3H5, Can.
Notes: Poet, playwright. Letters to Michael Horowitz (New Departures, England), John Martin (Black Sparrow Press, Los Angeles); ms fragment from *Dark Brown*; 1 page holograph "I suspend my wait;" corrected typescript of an application for a Guggenheim Foundation Fellowship.

MCCLURE, SAMUEL SIDNEY, 1857-1949

IN —INDIANA UNIVERSITY, Lilly Library, Seventh St, Bloomington, 47405. William R Cagle, Librn
Holdings: // Mss Pix
Notes: Business and family papers and correspondence of editor/publisher S S McClure, 1865-1949. Incl letters and papers of his wife, Harriet Sophia (Hurd) McClure, 1855-1929. Much of the material concerns specific publications such as *McClure's Magazine, The American Magazine, The Evening Mail*, etc 24,069 items, incl several hundred photographs.

MCCLURG, A. C., AND COMPANY

IL —NEWBERRY LIBRARY, 60 W Walton St, Chicago, 60610. Diana Haskell, Cur of Modern Mss
Holdings: Cat Mss
Notes: Stresses publishing history as it relates to bibliography and the history of printing. Incl partial archives of A C McClurg and Company, Stone and Kimball; other Chicago publishing history.

MACCOLL, HUGH FREDERICK

RI —BROWN UNIVERSITY, John Hay Library, 20 Prospect St, Providence, 02912. Mark N Brown, Cur Mss
Holdings: Mss
Notes: Papers of William O Fuller (1828-1910), music teacher of Providence, comprising letters 1848 from Europe, incl a letter from Franz Liszt; papers of Johann Christian Gottlieb Graupner (1767-1836) and John Rowe Parker (fl 1820s) collected by Horace Mason Reynolds, relating to the music-publishing business in Boston, 1802-1838; papers of the American folklorist Mellinger Edward Henry (1873-1946) relating to his research and publications on American folk-songs 1910-1942; papers, 1912-1948, of Providence composer Hugh Frederick MacColl (1885-1953); papers of Frances Herriot Sargent, stage manager for "Porgy" and "Porgy and Bess", relating to productions of these, 1928-1942.

MCCORD, DAVID

MA —HARVARD UNIVERSITY LIBRARY, Cambridge, 02138.
Holdings: Cat Mss

MCCORD, HOWARD

DE —UNIVERSITY OF DELAWARE, Hugh M Morris Library, S College Ave, Newark, 19711. T Stuart Dick, Special Collections
Holdings: Cat Mss Pix
Notes: Manuscripts, etc, incl literary correspondence.

MCCORMACK, JOHN W.

MA —BOSTON UNIVERSITY, Mugar Memorial Library, Special Collections Dept, 771 Commonwealth Ave, Boston, 02215. Howard B Gotlieb, Dir
Holdings: Cat Mss
Notes: The John W McCormack Collection of papers, documents, memoranda, correspondence, background files and memorabilia covering all Administrations from President Coolidge to President Nixon, primarily 1957-11970. Three to four million pieces.

MCCORMICK, LEANDER H., 1859-1934

KS —MENNINGER FOUNDATION, Archives, 5600 W Sixth St, Box 829, Topeka, 66601. Alice Brand, Librn; Mark West, Archivist
Notes: 15 boxes, 1894-1933. Consists of diaries, correspondence, research notes.

MCCORMICK, LEANDER J., 1819-1900

IL —CHICAGO HISTORICAL SOCIETY, Library, Clark St at North Ave, Chicago, 60614. Robert L Brubaker, Librn
Notes: Papers.

MCCORMICK, WILFRED

MA —BOSTON UNIVERSITY, Mugar Memorial Library, Special Collections Dept, 771 Commonwealth Ave, Boston, 02215. Howard B Gotlieb, Dir
Holdings: Mss Correspondence

MCCULLERS, CARSON

NV —UNIVERSITY OF NEVADA, RENO, University Library, Special Collections Dept, Reno, 89557. Robert E Blesse, Head
Holdings: Vols (39) Cat Other appearances 70 Cat
Notes: Includes individual works by author in all editions including translations; also prefaces, introductions, published

MCCULLERS, CARSON (cont.)

correspondence, appearances in anthologies, periodicals, etc. Bibliographical research collection, part of Modern Authors Collection.

NC —DUKE UNIVERSITY, William R Perkins Library, Manuscript Dept, Durham, 27706. Ellen Gartrell, Cur of Mss
Holdings: Cat Mss
Notes: Papers, correspondence, etc.

MCCULLOCH, HUGH, 1808-1895

IN —INDIANA UNIVERSITY, Lilly Library, Seventh St, Bloomington, 47405. William R Cagle, Librn
Holdings: Mss
Notes: Papers of Hugh McCulloch, US Comptroller of Currency 1863-65, US Secretary of the Treasury, 1865-69, Oct 1884-March 1885. Incl business and family correspondence, scrapbooks, letterpress books, and some US Treasury related correspondence. 15,749 items.

MCCUTCHAN, KENNETH P.

IN —INDIANA STATE UNIVERSITY, EVANSVILLE, Library, 8600 University Blvd, Evansville, 47712. Gina R Walker, Acting Archivist
Holdings: Cat Mss Pix
Notes: Typescripts, art proofs, correspondence, diaries, journals, etc for his published work and his unpublished book on the history of Saundersville. Several original sketches for *Adventures of Isaac Knight* and *From Then Til Now*. Restricted use: noncirculating.

MCCUTCHAN, ROBERT GUY

CA —CLAREMONT COLLEGES, Honnold Library, Ninth & Dartmouth, Claremont, 91711. Tania Rizzo, Special Collections Dept Head
Holdings: Vols 3500 Cat Mss Periodicals Phonorecords
Notes: Card index by Mr and Mrs Robert Guy McCutchan, donors. Mainly American, 17th century to present. Most complete for Methodist hymnbooks. Donor was editor of 1935 edition of Methodist Hymnal. Scrapbooks of McCutchan's life, accomplishments, and tributes, compiled by his widow.

MCCUTCHEON, GEORGE BARR

MA —HARVARD UNIVERSITY LIBRARY, Cambridge, 02138.
Holdings: Cat Mss

MCCUTCHEON, JOHN T.

IL —NORTHWESTERN UNIVERSITY, Library, Special Collections Dept, 1937 Sheridan Rd, Evanston, 60201. R Russell Maylone, Cur
Holdings: Cat
Notes: John T McCutcheon drawings of political cartoons from the *Chicago Tribune*. 560 original drawings.
IN —INDIANA UNIVERSITY, Lilly Library, Seventh St, Bloomington, 47405. William R Cagle, Librn
Notes: Contemporary with and depicting Lincoln; the War of 1812 and other periods. Incl significant mss of the modern cartoonists and caricaturists Ardizzone, Beerbohm, Fontane Fox, Kin Hubbard, Charles Bacon Jackson, McCutcheon, Messick, Nast, Rothenstein, Sendak, and many miscellaneous items.
OH —OHIO STATE UNIVERSITY, Library for Communication and Graphic Arts, 242 W 18th St, Columbus, 43210. Lucy S Caswell, Curator
Notes: Comic strip artists Hal Foster, Dudley T Fisher, Jr, Mark Szorady, Edwina Dumm, Jim Baker have original works in the library. Also new collections of original cartoons by Windsor McCay, John T McCutcheon, Dick Moores, Ned White,

Walter Berndt, Jim Larrick, Carl Rose and Bill Crawford. Also a large collection of the work of illustrator Will Rannells. The Shel Dorf Collection incl historic comic strips and related materials. A small but growing collection of comic books, especially those featuring *Katy Keene*, is available in the library.

MCDAVID, RAVEN IVOR

NC —DUKE UNIVERSITY, William R Perkins Library, Jay B Hubbell Center for American Literary Historiography, Durham, 27706. Erma Whittington, Librn
Notes: 77,312 items, including manuscripts, pictures, clippings, and correspondence. "The objective of the Center is to gather the papers and materials of significant scholars and critics in American literary history." The Center is a part of the Perkins Library Manuscripts Department.

MACDIARMID, HUGH (CHRISTOPHER MURRAY GRIEVE), 1892-1978

CO —UNIVERSITY OF COLORADO, Libraries, Special Collections, Boulder, 80309. Nora J Quinlan, Head
Holdings: Vols 97 Cat Mss
Notes: Incl 47 ms pieces.
DE —UNIVERSITY OF DELAWARE, Hugh M Morris Library, S College Ave, Newark, 19711. T Stuart Dick, Special Collections
Holdings: Mss
Notes: Incl Scottish literary renaissance drafts, typescripts, articles, book reviews, sketches, miscellaneous memoranda by Christopher M Grieve (Hugh MacDiarmid), when he was in London (1931-32). Also incl are autograph notes, plays, prose, verse, and correspondence for Sydney Goodsir Smith.
IL —NORTHWESTERN UNIVERSITY, Library, Special Collections Dept, 1937 Sheridan Rd, Evanston, 60201. R Russell Maylone, Cur
Holdings: Vols 20,000 Cat
Notes: First, limited, special editions, works about and ephemera of the major authors of the 20th century as well as representative minor writers. Incl English, American, French and German authors and to a lesser extent Italian, Spanish and other European writers. Extensive collections of Lawrence Durrell, T S Eliot, William Faulkner, Robert Graves, Ernest Hemingway, James Joyce, Karl Kraus, D H Lawrence, Hugh MacDiarmid, Henry Miller, Anais Nin, Ezra Pound, Gertrude Stein, H G Wells, W B Yeats. 15,000 "little magazine" titles (exclusive of runs in the general library collections).
NV —UNIVERSITY OF NEVADA, RENO, University Library, Special Collections Dept, Reno, 89557. Robert E Blesse, Head
Holdings: Vols (94) Cat
Notes: Includes individual works by author in all editions including translations; also prefaces, introductions, published correspondence, appearances in anthologies, periodicals, etc. Bibliographical research collection, part of Modern Authors Collection. Other appearances 425 cataloged.

MACDONALD, GEORGE

CT —YALE UNIVERSITY, Box 1603A, Yale Station, New Haven, 06520.
Holdings: Cat Mss
IL —WHEATON COLLEGE, Library, Marion E Wade Collection, Irving & Franklin Sts, Wheaton, 60187. Lyle Dorsett, Cur; Marjorie Mead, Associate Cur
Holdings: Vols (6500) Audiotapes Videotapes
Notes: Extensive Marion E Wade Collection of seven British authors incl an excellent library of the books of George MacDonald.
MA —HARVARD UNIVERSITY LIBRARY, Cambridge, 02138.
Holdings: Cat

MCDONALD, GREGORY

MA —BOSTON UNIVERSITY, Mugar Memorial Library, Special Collections Dept,

771 Commonwealth Ave, Boston, 02215. Howard B Gotlieb, Dir
Holdings: Mss
Notes: Mss, correspondence, etc collected in depth; incl publications by or about.

MACDONALD, JOHN

CO —UNIVERSITY OF COLORADO, Libraries, Special Collections, Boulder, 80309. Nora J Quinlan, Head
Holdings: Vols Uncat Audiotapes
Notes: Over 1000 vols of all the works of the American mystery writer John MacDonald as well as audiocassettes of some of his more popular works. A fascinating gathering which is both an example of one of America's most successful popular writers as well as a look at the history of the paperback (most of the books are in paperback).

MCDONALD, RUTH SEELY BERRY, 1913-

NY —CORNELL UNIVERSITY LIBRARIES, Collection of Regional History, Dept of Manuscripts and Univ Archives, Ithaca, 14853.
Notes: Incl papers, 1850-(1936-59); two drawings, two watercolor sketches, scrapbooks, photos, obituary notices, and other clippings of both the Berrys and the McDonalds.

MACDONALD, THOREAU

ON —UNIVERSITY OF TORONTO, Thomas Fisher Rare Book Library, 120 Saint George St, Toronto, M5S 1A5, Can. Richard G Landon, Head
Holdings: Vols 350 Mss
Notes: Thoreau MacDonald Collection of books and pamphlets designed by Thoreau MacDonald, Canadian artist and illustrator, and works containing illustrations by him. Some manuscript items, including original sketches and drawings. Gift of Mrs Margaret E Edison. Collection described in Edison, Margaret E, *Thoreau MacDonald* (Toronto: University of Toronto Press, 1973).

MCDONOGH, JOHN, 1779-1850

LA —TULANE UNIVERSITY, Howard-Tilton Memorial Library, Special Collections Div, 7001 Freret St, New Orleans, 70118. Wilbur E Meneray, Librn
Holdings: Mss
Notes: Correspondence, business papers and legal documents of New Orleans businessman and philanthopist John McDonogh including his interest in the emancipation of slaves.

MCDONOUGH AND PAYNE

LA —NEW ORLEANS PUBLIC LIBRARY, Louisiana Div & City Archives Dept, Louisiana History Collection, 219 Loyola Ave, New Orleans, 70140. Collin B Hamer Jr, Head
Holdings: Vols Mss
Notes: Private mss collection covers the period 1795-date, incl the following separate collections: James H Dakin (architect, ca 1834-47, 217 items); Walter E Easey (engineer, 1907-79, 22 cubic feet); McDonough & Payne (merchants, 1801-04, 200 items); ERA Club (women's group, 1914-19, 2 items); Neville Levy (civic leader, ca 1891-1963, 1 cubic foot & 11 vols); and Robert Tallant (author, 1945-57, 3 cubic feet & 10 vols). 92 vols scrapbooks; 100 mss vols, 55 cubic feet.

MACDOUGALL, THOMAS BAILLIE

NY —AMERICAN MUSEUM OF NATURAL HISTORY, Library Services Dept, Central Park W & 79th St, New York, 10024. Nina J Root, Chairwoman; Mary Genett, Asst Librn for Reference Services
Holdings: Cat Mss Maps Pix Slides 16mm Films
Notes: Manuscripts, diaries, correspondence,

MACDOUGALL, THOMAS BAILLIE (cont.)

artifacts, some art work, and collected materials. Not all cataloged as of 1983.

MCDOUGALL, WILLIAM, 1871-1938

†NC —DUKE UNIVERSITY, Archives, 341 Perkins Library, Durham, 27706.
Notes: Incl psychic phenomena, the plight of emigres and the growth of the police state in Nazi Germany, euthanasia and eugenics, behaviorism and John Watson, and such figures as Aldous Huxley and C G Jung. 1800 items and 24 vols. Correspondence with individuals significant in the fields of psychology, psychic research, and social sciences.

MCDOWALL, RODDY

MA —BOSTON UNIVERSITY, Mugar Memorial Library, Special Collections Dept, 771 Commonwealth Ave, Boston, 02215. Howard B Gotlieb, Dir
Holdings: Cat Mss Pix
Notes: Mss, correspondence, etc collected in depth; incl publications by or about.

MACDOWELL, EDWARD ALEXANDER

DC —LIBRARY OF CONGRESS, Washington, 20540.
Holdings: Cat Mss Pix
Notes: Autograph mss and letters.
NY —COLUMBIA UNIVERSITY LIBRARIES, Rare Book & Manuscript Library, 801 Butler Library, 535 W 114 St, New York, 10027. Kenneth A Lohf, Librn
Holdings: Cat Mss Pix
Notes: Papers, manuscripts, publications, etc. 2000 items. Restricted use.

MACDOWELL, KATHERINE SHERWOOD (BONNER)

MA —HARVARD UNIVERSITY LIBRARY, Cambridge, 02138.
Holdings: Cat Mss

MACDOWELL COLONY

DC —LIBRARY OF CONGRESS, Washington, 20540.
Holdings: Cat Mss Pix
Notes: Records of the MacDowell Colony, Peterboro, New Hampshire. Approx 21,000 items, with additions expected, from 1896 to 1968, with the bulk in the 1945-1965 period. Administrative files, correspondence, etc.

MACEDONIAN LANGUAGE AND LITERATURE

MA —HARVARD UNIVERSITY LIBRARY, Widener Library, Slavic Collections, Cambridge, 02138. Hugh M Olmsted, Slavic Dept Head
Holdings: Cat
Notes: Virtually complete collection; see Widener Library Shelflist, 18-31 (1971) and Harvard Library Bulletin, XVII (1969): pp 425-433.

MACEDONIAN LANGUAGE AND LITERATURE (MODERN)

NY —NEW YORK PUBLIC LIBRARY, Slavonic Div, Fifth Ave & 42 St, New York, 10018. Edward Kasinec, Chief
Holdings: Cat Microforms
Notes: See New York Public Library, Dictionary Catalog of the Slavonic Collection (Boston: G K Hall, 1974), 44 vols.

MACEDONIANS

NY —NEW YORK PUBLIC LIBRARY, Slavonic Div, Fifth Ave & 42 St, New York, 10018. Edward Kasinec, Chief
Holdings: Cat Microforms
Notes: See: New York Public Library, Slavonic Div, Dictionary Catalog of the Slavonic Collection, 2nd ed, rev and enl (Boston: G K Hall, 1974), 44 vols; and New York Public Library, Dictionary Catalog of the Research Libraries (New York, 1972-).

MACEDONIANS IN THE U.S.

MN —UNIVERSITY OF MINNESOTA, Immigration History Research Center, 826 Berry St, Saint Paul, 55114. Susan Griegs, Cur
Holdings: Vols (35,000) Mss Maps Pix Phonorecords Audiotapes 16mm Films Microforms
See also entry under US - Emigration and Immigration

MCELHENY FAMILY

NY —CORNELL UNIVERSITY LIBRARIES, Collection of Regional History, Dept of Manuscripts and Univ Archives, Ithaca, 14853.
Notes: Incl papers, 1846-1907; 2 reels microfilm, diaries, letters and a microfilmed genealogy of the McElheny and related families.

MCELROY, FR. JOHN

DC —GEORGETOWN UNIVERSITY, Library, Special Collections Div, 37 & O Sts NW, Washington, 20057. George M Barringer, Special Collections Librn; Nicholas B Sheetz, Mss Librn
Notes: Historical archives of the Maryland Province. Incl the letters of Abp John Carroll and Fr John McElroy.

MCELWAIN SHOE COMPANY (1894-)

NH —MANCHESTER HISTORIC ASSOCIATION, Library, 129 Amherst St, Manchester, 03104. Elizabeth Lessard, Librn
Notes: McElwain Shoe Company (1894-): Materials related to Massachusetts Institute of Technology, Trade Associations in the leather and shoe manufacturing industry, and personal correspondence of executives including J F Mcelwain, founder (2 document boxes and 1 Hollinger storage box).

MACEWAN, (J. W.) GRANT, 1902-

AB —UNIVERSITY OF CALGARY, Libraries, Special Collections Div, 2500 University Dr, Calgary, T2N 1N4, Can.
Holdings: Mss
Notes: The holdings consist of Grant MacEwan's correspondence, personal diaries, financial records, research, scrapbooks, newspaper clippings, and photograph albums.

MCFARLAND-RUSSELL FAMILY

TX —STEPHEN F AUSTIN STATE UNIVERSITY, Ralph W Steen Library, Special Collections Dept, Box 13055, SFA Sta, Nacogdoches, 75962. Linda Cheves Nicklas, Special Collections Librn
Holdings: Mss Maps Pix
Budget: ($5000)
Notes: Incl personal and business papers, letters, diaries, and other records of East Texans and East Texas institutions and businesses. Major collections incl papers of Karl Wilson Baker, George L Crocket, Bennett Blake, McFarland-Russell family, Orton family, Samuel E Asbury; and records of Nacogdoches University, East Texas Historical Association, Kelly Plow Company and many local organizations; 60 Thomas J Rusk letters. Indexes, calendars and inventories are available. Description: SFASU, A Guide to Special Collections, 1980.

MCFEE, WILLIAM

CT —YALE UNIVERSITY, Box 1603A, Yale Station, New Haven, 06520.
Holdings: Cat Mss

MCGAFFIN, WILLIAM

MA —BOSTON UNIVERSITY, Mugar Memorial Library, Special Collections Dept, 771 Commonwealth Ave, Boston, 02215. Howard B Gotlieb, Dir
Holdings: Cat Mss
Notes: Mss, correspondence, etc collected in depth; incl publications by or about.

MCGHEE, GEORGE CREWS, 1912-

DC —GEORGETOWN UNIVERSITY, Library, Special Collections Div, 37 & O Sts NW, Washington, 20057. George M Barringer, Special Collections Librn; Nicholas B Sheetz, Mss Librn
Holdings: Mss Cat Maps Pix
Notes: The papers of George Crews McGhee (1912), geologist, oil producer, and diplomat. The papers incl files from McGhee's United States ambassadorships to Turkey (1951-1953) and Germany (1963-1968) as well as his extensive involvement in numerous organizations and committees incl the Combined Raw Materials Board, the Bilderberg Group, the Draper Committee, the Committee for Economic Development, and the Business Council for International Understanding, among many others. Also incl are 264 volumes from the 17th to early 20th century relating to Turkey.

MCGILL, RALPH EMERSON

GA —EMORY UNIVERSITY, Robert W Woodruff Library, Special Collections Dept, Atlanta, 30322. Linda M Matthews, Head Special Collections; Virginia J H Cain, Processing Archivist; Richard H F Lindemann, Reference Archivist
Holdings: Cat Mss Pix Slides
Notes: Papers, ca 1927-1969, of Ralph E McGill, journalist and author, editor of the Atlanta Constitution, 1938-1960, publisher, 1960-1969. Collection incl personal and professional correspondence, writings, scrapbooks, photographs, memorabilia, and personal books. Description and index available in repository. 200 boxes.

MCGILL PHYSICAL SOCIETY

PQ —MCGILL UNIVERSITY, McLennan Library, University Archives, 3459 McTavish St, Montreal, H3A 1Y1, Can. Martha Caya, Archivist
Holdings: Vols (7) notebooks
Notes: The papers of the McGill Physical Society, 1897-1959. Original mss and handwritten work available for Scholarly research only. Microfilm available to public.

MCGIVERN, WILLIAM P.

MA —BOSTON UNIVERSITY, Mugar Memorial Library, Special Collections Dept, 771 Commonwealth Ave, Boston, 02215. Howard B Gotlieb, Dir
Holdings: Cat Mss Pix Audiotapes
Notes: Mss, correspondence, etc collected in depth; incl publications by or about.

MCGONIGLE FAMILY

AZ —NORTHERN ARIZONA UNIVERSITY, Special Collection Library, CU Box 6022, Flagstaff, 86011. Peter M Whiteley, Coordr/Archivist; William Mullane, Librn
Notes: Ed McGonigle Family Collection. Incl files on the McGonigle Lumber Company, Flagstaff; Flagstaff Lumber Company and Oatman Amalgamated Gold Mining Company. Also Incl hundreds of early 1900's post cards of holidays and places.

MACGOWAN, KENNETH, 1888-1963

CA —FRANCIS BACON LIBRARY, 655 N Dartmouth Ave, Claremont, 91711. Elizabeth S Wrigley, Dir
Holdings: Mss Pix
Notes: Arensberg's miscellaneous correspondence with American literary figures (1920's-50's) including Bruce Bliven, Catherine Drinker Bowen, Kay Boyle, Witter Bynner, Edwin Corle, Helen A Keller, Lysander Kemp, Kenneth Macgowan, John

MACGOWAN, KENNETH, 1888-1963 (cont.)

Macy, Henry Miller, Lewis Mumford, Clifford Odets, Kenneth Patchen, Irving Stone, and William Carlos Williams.

CA —UNIVERSITY OF CALIFORNIA, LOS ANGELES, Research Library, Dept of Special Collections, 405 Hilgard Ave, Los Angeles, 90024. Edward Shreeves, Chairman, Bibliographers Group; David S Zeidberg, Head
Notes: 34 linear feet of mss and correspondence, primarily concerned with the American theater, but also relating to his activities in moving pictures, university teaching, anthropology, and archeology.

MCGRAW FAMILY

NY —CORNELL UNIVERSITY LIBRARIES, Collection of Regional History, Dept of Manuscripts and Univ Archives, Ithaca, 14853.
Notes: Incl papers, (1854-90)-1956; many letters, 2 diaries, photos, a handwritten scroll, 3 drawings on linen, and obituary clippings and printed items concerning the family and Cornell University.

MACGREEVY, THOMAS

MO —WASHINGTON UNIVERSITY, Libraries, Special Collections Dept, Campus Box 1061, St Louis, 63130.
Notes: A small but significant collection.

MACGREGOR, CLARK

MN —MINNESOTA HISTORICAL SOCIETY LIBRARY, 690 Cedar St, Saint Paul, 55101. Patricia C Harpole, Chief of Reference Library; Bonnie G Wilson, Head of Special Libraries
Notes: Materials by such well-known figures as Hubert H. Humphrey, Eugene J. McCarthy, Orville L Freeman, Maurice H. Stans, Donald M Fraser, Albert H Quie, Clark MacGregor and John A Blatnik. A list of these holdings is on file in the Audio-Visual Library, the tapes are housed in the MHS Research Center, 1500 Mississippi Street, St Paul, Minn.

MCGREGOR, JOHN

AZ —NORTHERN ARIZONA UNIVERSITY, Special Collection Library, CU Box 6022, Flagstaff, 86011. Peter M Whiteley, Coordr/Archivist; William Mullane, Librn
Notes: John McGregor Collection; correspondence, papers, and class lectures of McGregor, an archaeologist. Correspondents incl A E Douglass, University of Ariz, and James Griffen, University of Michigan. Also incl reprints of articles about archaeology in Ariz, the US, and many foreign countries, 1881-1975.

MCGRANERY, JAMES P.

DC —LIBRARY OF CONGRESS, Manuscript Division, Washington, 20540. John C Broderick, Chief
Holdings: 32,500 Items
Notes: Papers.

MCGREEVEY, JOHN

IN —INDIANA UNIVERSITY, Lilly Library, Seventh St, Bloomington, 47405. William R Cagle, Librn
Holdings: Cat Mss
Notes: Papers of television writer John McGreevey, 1922- , who began as a radio writer for radio station KTAR in Phoenix, Arizona, 1944-52. He also produced scripts for Armstrong Circle Theatre of Today, Cavalcade of America, Dr Christian, and Suspense, the original scripts of which are in his collection. 1645 items.

MCGUANE, THOMAS

NY —UNIVERSITY OF ROCHESTER, Rush Rhees Library, Department of Rare Books and Special Collections, Rochester, 14627. Peter Dzwonkoski, Librn
Holdings: Vols Cat Mss
Notes: Manuscripts, drafts, proofs, notes, correspondence, relating to the publication of his books.

MCGUFFEY, WILLIAM H.

DC —LIBRARY OF CONGRESS, Rare Book & Special Collections Div, Washington, 20540. William Matheson, Chief
Notes: The *McGuffey Readers,* a series of textbooks which fused moral instruction with the teaching of language skills.

OH —OHIO UNIVERSITY, Vernon R Alden Library, Department of Archives and Special Collections, Athens, 45701. Gary A Hunt, Head
Holdings: Vols 130 Uncat
Notes: Examples of McGuffey's Readers, 1846-1925, incl Spellers, Primers, Juvenile Speakers, Word Lists, and Readers One through Six.

OH —MIAMI UNIVERSITY, King Library, Walter Havighurst Special Collections Library, Oxford, 45056. Helen Ball, Cur of Special Collections
Holdings: Vols (300) Cat Mss
Notes: Collection includes many editions of various McGuffey Readers. A related collection of 3500 volumes of 19th century American textbooks includes history, geography, spelling, rhetoric, elocution, and music books.

MCGUIRE, BIRD SEGLE

OK —UNIVERSITY OF OKLAHOMA, Bizzell Memorial Library, Western History Collections, 401 W Brooks, Norman, 73069. John Ezell, Cur
Holdings: Mss
Notes: US Representative. His papers. Guide available.

MACHA, KAREL H.

IN —INDIANA UNIVERSITY, Lilly Library, Seventh St, Bloomington, 47405. William R Cagle, Librn
Holdings: Vols (400)// Cat
Notes: First editions and later printings of Karel H Macha (100 vols) and Vladimir Vasek (300 vols).

MACHEN, ARTHUR, 1863-1947

CA —CLAREMONT COLLEGES, Honnold Library, Ninth & Dartmouth, Claremont, 91711. Tania Rizzo, Special Collections Dept Head
Holdings: Vols 146 // Cat Mss
Notes: First and special editions, by or about, or edited by Machen; journal contributions; 38 ALsS from Machen to Paul Jordan-Smith, donor; Mr Smith's correspondence with the Arthur Machen Society; and ephemera.

CT —YALE UNIVERSITY, Box 1603A, Yale Station, New Haven, 06520.
Holdings: Cat Mss

IL —ILLINOIS STATE UNIVERSITY, Milner Library, Dept of Special Collections, Normal, 61761. Robert Sokan, Librn
Notes: First editions, limited editions, ephemera, etc.

OH —OHIO UNIVERSITY, Vernon R Alden Library, Department of Archives and Special Collections, Athens, 45701. Gary A Hunt, Head
Holdings: Vols 33 Cat
Notes: Mostly first editions.

MACHIAVELLI, NICCOLO

CA —UNIVERSITY OF CALIFORNIA, BERKELEY, University Library, French and Italian Collections, Berkeley, 94720. Donald G Williams, Librn
Notes: Research collection with special strengths in early Italian literature (to 1400), and Italian literature of the Renaissance. Strong holdings for such authors as Dante, Petrarch, Boccaccio, Ariosto, Machiavelli, Tasso, and many others. The collections in the Main Library are complemented by significant incunabula, rare books and ms holdings in the Bancroft Library.

MACHINE DATA STORAGE AND RETRIEVAL see Computers; Information Storage and Retrieval Systems

MACHINE LANGUAGES see Programming Languages (Electronic Computers)

MACHINE SHOP PRACTICE

SC —SUMTER TECHNICAL COLLEGE, Library, 506 Guignard Dr, Sumter, 29150. Fanny M Davis
Holdings: Vols (20,000) Cat Mss Maps Pix Slides Microforms
Budget: ($500,000)
Notes: Incl 200 books on machine shop practices.

WI —BLACKHAWK TECHNICAL INSTITUTE, PO Box 5009, 6004 Prairie Rd, Janesville, 53547. Grace M Sweeney, Librn
Notes: Machine shop, automotive; Avianics; Drafting.

MACHINE SHOPS

MI —GENERAL ELECTRIC COMPANY, Carboloy Systems Department, Library, Box 237, GPO, Detroit, 48232.
Holdings: Vols (4500) Cat Maps Slides 16mm Films Filmstrips Microforms
Budget: ($5000)
Notes: Collection covers cemented carbide cutting tools, powder metallurgy, metal cutting, metalworkings, machining, and related subjects. Also numerical control, statistics (related to the cutting tool industry) and general management. Incl 500 maps, 4000 slides, 61 films, 261 filmstrips, 700 microfiche, 7000 patents, and 300 periodical titles.

NC —TECHNICAL INSTITUTE OF ALAMANCE, Learning Resources Center, Jimmy Kerr Rd, PO Box 623, Haw River, 27258. Ron Plummer, Coordr
Holdings: Vols 137 Cat Audiotapes Filmstrips Microforms

SC —HORRY GEORGETOWN TECHNICAL COLLEGE, Library, Hwy 501, Box 1966, Conway, 29526. Barbara Brittain, Librn
Holdings: Vols (20,000) Cat Slides Microforms

MACHINE TOOLS

NH —NEW HAMPSHIRE VOCATIONAL TECHNICAL COLLEGE, Library, 277 R Portsmouth Ave, Stratham, 03885. Nancy L Dodge, Librn
Holdings: ($9500)

OH —PUBLIC LIBRARY OF CINCINNATI & HAMILTON COUNTY, Science & Technology Dept, 800 Vine St, Cincinnati, 45202. Rosemary Gaiser, Head
Holdings: Vols (250,000) Cat
Notes: Pure and applied science. Incl over 1600 periodicals and serial titles and more than 100 abstracting and indexing services in major fields of science and technology.

OH —CLEVELAND PUBLIC LIBRARY, Science & Technology Dept, 325 Superior Ave, Cleveland, 44114. Jean Z Piety, Head
Holdings: Cat
Notes: Extensive collection of books and journals; old and current catalogs and manuals.

MACHINE TOOLS—HISTORY

PA —SWARTHMORE COLLEGE, Library, Swarthmore, 19081. Michael J Durkan, Librn
Holdings: Vols 959 Cat Mss
Notes: This was the collection belonging to Greville Bathe. It is comprised of books on machines and steam engines published from the 16th-20th century. Also works on military engineering.

MACHINE WORKERS UNION see United Electrical, Radio, and Machine Workers

MACHINERY—HISTORY

MA —OLD STURBRIDGE VILLAGE, Research Library, Sturbridge, 01566.

MACHINERY—HISTORY (cont.)

Theresa Rini Percy, Librn
Holdings: Cat
Notes: History of machinery making, New England, to 1860.

PA —SWARTHMORE COLLEGE, Library, Swarthmore, 19081. Michael J Durkan, Librn
Holdings: Vols 959 Cat Mss
Notes: This was the collection belonging to Greville Bathe. It is comprised of books on machines and steam engines published from the 16th-20th century. Also works on military engineering.

MACHINERY, AGRICULTURAL see Agricultural Machinery

MACHINERY, TEXTILE see Textile Machinery

MACHINES see Machinery—History

MACHISMO

CA —CALIFORNIA STATE UNIVERSITY, FULLERTON, Library, Box 4150, Fullerton, 92634. Alfredo H Zuniga, Coord
Notes: Some materials on the subject; not maintained as a separate collection.

MCHUGH, ARONA

MA —BOSTON UNIVERSITY, Mugar Memorial Library, Special Collections Dept, 771 Commonwealth Ave, Boston, 02215. Howard B Gotlieb, Dir
Holdings: Cat Mss

MCHUGH, FRANCIS DODD, 1903-

NY —CORNELL UNIVERSITY LIBRARIES, Collection of Regional History, Dept of Manuscripts and Univ Archives, Ithaca, 14853.
Notes: Papers, 1907-70; 26 ft. City planner.

MACINNES, COLIN

NY —UNIVERSITY OF ROCHESTER, Rush Rhees Library, Department of Rare Books and Special Collections, Rochester, 14627. Peter Dzwonkoski, Librn
Holdings: Vols 30 Cat Mss
Notes: Collection incl books, notebooks, drafts, typescripts, proof copies of Macinnes' novels; correspondence.

MACINNES, HELEN

NJ —PRINCETON UNIVERSITY, Library, Rare Books Dept, Princeton, 08544. Stephen Ferguson, Cur
Notes: Mss and material for 14 novels incl letters, photos, etc.

MCINTOSH, JOHN, 1930-1970

MA —BOSTON UNIVERSITY, Mugar Memorial Library, Special Collections Dept, 771 Commonwealth Ave, Boston, 02215. Howard B Gotlieb, Dir
Holdings: //Cat Mss

MACINTYRE, C. F., 1890-1967

CA —UNIVERSITY OF CALIFORNIA, LOS ANGELES, Research Library, Dept of Special Collections, 405 Hilgard Ave, Los Angeles, 90024. Edward Shreeves, Chairman, Bibliographers Group; David S Zeidberg, Head
Holdings: Vols 15 Mss Pix
Notes: Incl 8 linear feet of mss, correspondence, and photographs.

MCINTYRE, THOMAS J.

NH —UNIVERSITY OF NEW HAMPSHIRE, Dimond Library, Durham, 03824. Barbara A White, Special Collections Librn
Notes: Senatorial papers, Thomas J McIntyre, (D-NH, 1962-78), incl correspondence, speeches, legislation, voting

records, campaign materials, reports to New Hampshire, and other papers dealing with the state.

MACIVER, ROBERT MORRISON

NY —COLUMBIA UNIVERSITY LIBRARIES, Rare Book & Manuscript Library, 801 Butler Library, 535 W 114 St, New York, 10027. Kenneth A Lohf, Librn
Holdings: Mss Pix
Notes: Incl the papers (5000 items) of Professor Robert Morrison MacIver: correspondence, notes, drafts of mss, etc on sociology, political power and juvenile delinquency, incl his participation on the City of New York Juvenile Delinquency Evaluation Project, on which he served after his retirement from Columbia University. Restricted use.

MACK, CONNIE

KS —SAINT MARY COLLEGE, Library, Leavenworth, 66048. Therese Deplazes, Special Collections Librn
Notes: Holographs of American personalities, mostly of Colonial, Revolutionary, Confederacy periods, and 19th Century. Incl ms letters, deeds, petitions, wills, slave papers. Holographs of Col Philip Marsteller (one of George Washington's pall bearers), family papers of Richard, Mary and Edward Cutts; love letters to Mary "Polly" Carter, Frank Ellery (grandson of William Ellery, signer of the Declaration of Independence), letters of Connie Mack and Babe Ruth, of some American authors.

MACK, TED

DC —LIBRARY OF CONGRESS, Motion Pictures, Broadcasting and Recorded Sound Div, Washington, 20540.
Notes: The *Amateur Hour* Collection consists of original radio recordings of the Major Bowes series (1935-1944) and disc, tape, and television coverage of the Ted Mack series (1948-1968). Incl applications to appear on the program and accompanying correspondence and news clippings.

MACKALL, LEONARD L.

MD —JOHNS HOPKINS UNIVERSITY, Milton S Eisenhower Library, Charles & 34 Sts, Baltimore, 21218. Ann S Gwyn, Assistant Dir for Special Collections
Holdings: Vols Cat Mss Microforms
Notes: Standard bibliographical reference works. Also the personal library of bibliophile Leonard L Mackall, plus 46 drawers of his letters and correspondence.

MCKAY, CLAUDE

IN —INDIANA UNIVERSITY, Lilly Library, Seventh St, Bloomington, 47405. William R Cagle, Librn
Holdings: Cat mss
Notes: First editions, many of which were presentation copies to Max Eastman. Ms include correspondence with Max Eastman, 1919-1948(103 items)
MA —HARVARD UNIVERSITY LIBRARY, Cambridge, 02138.
Holdings: Cat Mss

MCKAY, WILLIAM, M.D.

OR —UMATILLA COUNTY LIBRARY, 214 N Main St, Pendleton, 97801. Barbara L Bishop, Dir
Holdings: Vols (675) Cat Mss Pix Audiotapes 16mm Films Microforms
Notes: Oregon history, especially Umatilla County. Lee Moorehouse photos (glass negatives)--1004 negatives, use restricted to professional photographers, copies may be made on premises only, also 3 rolls of microfilm of Moorehouse photos. Dr William McKay papers, 1830-1900, 14 folders, uncataloged, letters, coroner's reports (1885-86), miscellaneous papers, notes, memos and rough drafts, Army

statements, receipts, accounts and business and personal receipts, accounts, 8 letters written by Donald McKay, one letter written December 7, 1880, by William F Cody. Early brands of Eastern Oregon, 1/2 reel microfilm. Some cassette recordings of interviews with early pioneers.

MACKAYE, PERCY WALLACE

MA —HARVARD UNIVERSITY LIBRARY, Theatre Collection, Cambridge, 02138. Jeanne T Newlin, Cur
Notes: One of the largest existing collections of playbills, programs, prints, photographs, promptbooks, and other materials relating to the performing arts, the scope is worldwide; resources on the English-speaking stage of the 18th and 19th centuries are unequalled. Incl materials on ballet and modern dance, the circus, magic, minstrel shows, cinema, and pantomime. For description, see *Harvard Library Bulletin,* VI (1925): pp 281-301. Also, papers of Robert E Sherwood (1896-1955), John Mason Bowers, George Pierce Baker, Edward Sheldon, Percy Mackaye; Angus McBean collection of photographs of the London Stage, 1937-1965; Alix Jeffry collection of photographs of the Off-Broadway Theatre; and others.
MA —HARVARD UNIVERSITY LIBRARY, Cambridge, 02138.
Holdings: Cat Mss

MACKAYE FAMILY

NH —DARTMOUTH COLLEGE, Baker Memorial Library, Hanover, 03755.
Holdings: Cat Mss
Notes: Family papers of Steele, Percy, James, and Benton.

MCKEE, HARLEY JAMES

NY —SYRACUSE UNIVERSITY LIBRARIES, Ernest S Bird Library, George Arents Research Library for Special Collections, Syracuse, 13210. Carolyn A Davis, Manuscripts Librn; Amy S Doherty, University Archivist; Mark F Weimer, Rare Book Librn
Notes: The George Arents Research Library for Special Collections at Syracuse University contains the papers of Harley James McKee, Lorimer Rich, Frederick Lear, Max Abramovitz, James I Arnold, Pietro Bulluschi, Claude Bragdon, Marcel Breuer, William Lescaze, Skidmore Owings & Merrill, Ralph Walker, Eric Fisher Wood, Minoru Yamasaki, Joseph Louis Young, and Archimedes Russell.

MACKENZIE, COMPTON

DC —GEORGETOWN UNIVERSITY, Library, Special Collections Div, 37 & O Sts NW, Washington, 20057. George M Barringer, Special Collections Librn; Nicholas B Sheetz, Mss Librn
Holdings: Mss Pix
Notes: The papers of Christopher Sykes, biographer, journalist, and novelist; containing mss, letters, photographs, and drawings. With extensive correspondence from Harold Acton; Angela, Countess of Antrim; Sir John Betjeman; Ivy Compton-Burnett; Alick Dru; T S Eliot; Max Beerbohm; Graham Greene; John Hayward; Lord Patrick Kinross; Compton Mackenzie; Nancy Mitford; Anthony Powell; Dame Flora Robson; Cecil Roth; Sir John Russell; Osbert Sitwell; John Sparrow; Freya Stark; James Stern; and Evelyn Waugh, among others. Also, considerable research material about Evelyn Waugh, Adam von Trott, Robert Byron, Lady Nancy Astor; and the foundation of the state of Israel.

MACKENZIE, DONALD

MA —BOSTON UNIVERSITY, Mugar Memorial Library, Special Collections Dept, 771 Commonwealth Ave, Boston, 02215. Howard B Gotlieb, Dir
Holdings: Cat Mss

MCKENZIE, R. TAIT

PA —LLOYD P JONES GALLERY, Gimbal Gym, Walnut & 37th St, Philadelphia,

MCKENZIE, R. TAIT (cont.)

19104.
Notes: Incl 83 works of art by R Tait McKenzie.

PA —UNIVERSITY OF PENNSYLVANIA, Archives and Records Center, North Facade - Franklin Field, Philadelphia, 19104. Mark Frazier Lloyd, Archivist
Notes: R Tait McKenzie's personal papers, and the J William White Collection of personal papers--sealed until 2016. Incl materials relating to McKenzie's sculpting and the sports medallions and medals which he sculpted. Biographical and reserved materials for two books about him. Incl 39 cu ft.

ON —R TAIT MCKENZIE MEMORIAL MUSEUM, Tait McKenzie Research Library, PO Box 268, Lanark, K0G 1K0, Can. Pamela Scheel, Curator
Holdings: Cat
Notes: Letters and papers by or about Tait McKenzie, surgeon, sculptor, and educator. Open in May and September.

MACKENZIE VALLEY PIPELINE

MB —UNIVERSITY OF MANITOBA, Elizabeth Dafoe Library, Government Publications Section, Winnipeg, R3T 2N2, Can. June Dutka, Head
Holdings: Vols 1300 // Uncat Maps Pix
Notes: The collection, which dates from 1975, consists of written direct testimonies and responses with supporting exhibits from over 100 oil and gas companies, Indian and native associations and concerned citizen groups. The content of these documents incl construction plans, financial statements, alternate corridors, and describes the social and economic impact of the Arctic Gas Pipeline in northern Canada. The *Biological Report Series* offers vital information on soils and vegetation, movements of porcupine, caribou herds, bird distribution and fisheries research. An index listing the various company exhibits accompanies this collection.

MCKEOWN, THOMAS DEITZ

OK —UNIVERSITY OF OKLAHOMA, Bizzell Memorial Library, Western History Collections, 401 W Brooks, Norman, 73069. John Ezell, Cur
Holdings: Mss Documents
Notes: US Representative. His papers. Guide available.

MCKIM, MEAD, AND WHITE

NY —MUSEUM OF THE CITY OF NEW YORK, Photo Archives, Fifth Ave & 103 St, New York, 10029. Esther Brumberg, Librn
Holdings: Mss Maps Pix
Notes: All aspects of New York City-- history, costume, social life and customs, etc. Also, Byron Collection--about 10,000 prints, 1880-1930, of views of New York, commercial interiors, interiors and exteriors of private residences, social events, shipping, immigration; Wurts Collection--15,000 glass negatives, 1890-1940, mostly architectural; 100,000 Wurts Architectural Photographs, to be cataloged. Underhill Collection--about 900 glass negatives, mostly architectural, 1896-1936; McKim, Mead & White Collection--1000 glass negatives of the work of the firm, 1880-1915; and Berenice Abbott Collection, Changing New York--about 350 negatives taken by Miss Abbott for the Federal Arts Project, 1930s. Other FAP photographs incl a series on Coney Island, one on Harlem, Sewing Project, and Sabbath Studies.

MACKINAC ISLAND

MI —MACKINAC ISLAND STATE PARK COMMISSION, Library, Bos 30028, Lansing, 48909. Keith R Widder, Cur
Holdings: Vols (1000) Cat Mss Maps Pix Slides Audiotapes
Budget: ($2500)
Notes: Mackinac area history-research

collection: archaeology, historic preservation, etc. Great Lakes ships and shipping.

MCKINLEY, CHARLES

OR —UNIVERSITY OF OREGON, Library, Eugene, 97403. Kenneth W Duckett, Curator
Notes: Papers of Prof Charles McKinley, incl files of correspondence, minutes, reports, position papers concerning (largely) public administration and planning.

MCKINLEY, WILLIAM

DC —LIBRARY OF CONGRESS, Manuscript Division, Washington, 20540. John C Broderick, Chief
Notes: The Presidential Papers collection incl the papers, etc, of numerous Presidents.

OH —RUTHERFORD B HAYES LIBRARY, 1337 Hayes Ave, Fremont, 43420. Watt P Marchman, Dir
Notes: Correspondence in the Lyman-Lincoln Collection.

MCKINNON, BARRY

BC —SIMON FRASER UNIVERSITY, Library, Burnaby, V5A 1S6, Can. Percilla Groves, Special Collections Librn
Holdings: Cat Mss
Notes: Mss for published and unpublished works, plus a complete collection of published books, chapbooks and broadsides by Canadian and American writers, plus correspondence and business records of the British Columbia Press run by poet and teacher Barry McKinnon from 1972 to 1980.

MCKINNON, EDNA (RANKIN), 1893-1978

MA —RADCLIFFE COLLEGE, Arthur & Elizabeth Schlesinger Library on the History of Women in America, 3 James St, Cambridge, 02138. Patricia Miller King, Dir; Eva Moseley, Cur of Mss
Notes: Books, pamphlets, clippings; also oral history interviews in the Family Planning Oral History Project, and numerous mss collections, espec those of the Birth Control League of Massachusetts, Mary (Steichen) Calderone, MD (1904-), Edna (Rankin) McKinnon (1893-1978), and Florence Clothier, MD (1903-).

MCKNIGHT, THOMAS

IA —STATE HISTORICAL SOCIETY OF IOWA LIBRARY, 402 Iowa Ave, Iowa City, 52240. Darold J Brown, Librn
Holdings: Cat
Notes: Thousands of individual items and smaller collection. Two hundred larger collections incl the papers of Cyrus C Carpenter, Jonathan P Dolliver, Gilbert Haugen, W W Waymack, Ephraim Adams, A C Dodge, Dorothy Houghton, Jesse Macy, Agnes Samuelson, Donald Johnson, Jack Miller, Ruth Sayre, Samuel Kirkwood, Thomas McKnight, Robert Lucas, Dwight McCarty, William Larrabee. Includes church, school, company and organization records, Civil War materials.

MCKOWN, ROBIN

MA —BOSTON UNIVERSITY, Mugar Memorial Library, Special Collections Dept, 771 Commonwealth Ave, Boston, 02215. Howard B Gotlieb, Dir
Holdings: Mss Pix
Notes: Mss, Correspondence, etc collected in depth; incl publications by or about.

MCLANE, LOUIS, 1784-1857

DC —LIBRARY OF CONGRESS, Manuscript Division, Washington, 20540. John C Broderick, Chief
Notes: The Louis McLane Family Papers.

MCLANE, ROBERT MILLIGAN, 1815-1898

DC —LIBRARY OF CONGRESS, Manuscript Division, Washington, 20540. John C

Broderick, Chief
Notes: The Louis McLane Family Papers.

MCLANE FAMILY

DC —LIBRARY OF CONGRESS, Manuscript Division, Washington, 20540. John C Broderick, Chief
Notes: The Louis McLane Family Papers.

MACLAREN, JAMES see Macdiarmid, Hugh (Christopher Murray Grieve), 1892-1978

MACLAREN-ROSS, JULIAN

CO —UNIVERSITY OF COLORADO, Libraries, Special Collections, Boulder, 80309. Nora J Quinlan, Head
Holdings: Cat Mss
Notes: Incl 36 ms pieces.

MCLAUGHLIN BROTHERS, PUBLISHERS

†NY —COLUMBIA UNIVERSITY LIBRARIES, Butler Library, Rare Book and Manuscript Library, 535 W 114 St, New York, 10027.

MACLEAN-HUNTER PUBLICATIONS

ON —MACLEAN HUNTER LIBRARY, Maclean Hunter Bldg, 777 Day St, Toronto, M5W 1A7, Can. Theresa Butcher, Librn
Holdings: Vols 1500 Cat Pix
Notes: Mainly a resource for the journalists of the *Financial Post*, Canada's foremost financial paper. The library is basically made up of vertical files divided into (1) general subject files, (2) Canadian public companies, (3) biographical (maintly photgraphic). The *Financial Post* (weekly) is completely clipped. The Toronto *Globe* and *Mail* (daily) and other Canadian publications are selectively clipped. In addition, the library houses all Maclean-Hunter publications (over 80 and constantly growing). The *Financial Post* is indexed by the library staff.

ON —UNIVERSITY OF TORONTO, Thomas Fisher Rare Book Library, 120 Saint George St, Toronto, M5S 1A5, Can. Richard G Landon, Head
Holdings: Vols 6535 Uncat
Notes: Maclean-Hunter and Southam Press Collections contain periodicals issued by these two Canadian publishers. These are largely trade journals. Many long and complete runs of items like *Canadian Footwear, Electrical News and Engineering; Gift Buyer; Canadian Home Journal; Chatelaine; Macleans;* etc. Many runs originate in 1880s and 1890s. Also include current publications. Approx 268 titles. Fisher Library designated the official archives for published material by Maclean-Hunter and Southam Press.

MACLEISH, ARCHIBALD, 1892-1982

CT —YALE UNIVERSITY, Box 1603A, Yale Station, New Haven, 06520.
Holdings: Cat Mss

DC —LIBRARY OF CONGRESS, Manuscript Division, Washington, 20540. John C Broderick, Chief
Notes: Correspondence in the J Robert Oppenheimer Collection.

MA —UNIVERSITY OF MASSACHUSETTS AT AMHERST, Library, Amherst, 01003. Siegfried Feller, Assoc Dir for Collection Development
Holdings: Vols Cat
Notes: First editions, some signed, some inscribed; few mss.

MA —HARVARD UNIVERSITY LIBRARY, Cambridge, 02138.
Holdings: Cat Mss

MA —GREENFIELD COMMUNITY COLLGE, The Archibald MacLeish Collection, One College Dr, Greenfield, 01301. Margaret E C Howland, Cur
Holdings: Vols 1662 Cat Mss Pix Slides Phonorecords Audiotapes Videotapes
Notes: The only authorized collection in the

MACLEISH, ARCHIBALD, 1892-1982 (cont.)

world devoted exclusively to the study of Archibald MacLeish, the man, his works, and his life. Contains all his published works plus clippings, galley proofs, letters, memorabilia, playbills and programs, posters, etc. Separately housed. Open by appointment.

NV —UNIVERSITY OF NEVADA, RENO, University Library, Special Collections Dept, Reno, 89557. Robert E Blesse, Head
Holdings: // Vols (93) Cat Other appearances 650 Cat
Notes: Includes individual works by author in all editions including translations; also prefaces, introductions, published correspondence, appearances in anthologies, periodicals, etc. Bibliographical research collection, part of Modern Authors Collection.

MACLENNAN, HUGH, 1903-

AB —UNIVERSITY OF CALGARY, Libraries, Special Collections Div, 2500 University Dr, Calgary, T2N 1N4, Can.
Holdings: Cat Mss
Notes: Correspondence, manuscripts, public addresses, book reviews, and published articles of Hugh MacLennan, one of Canada's leading literary figures.

MACLEOD, CHARLOTTE

MA —BOSTON UNIVERSITY, Mugar Memorial Library, Special Collections Dept, 771 Commonwealth Ave, Boston, 02215. Howard B Gotlieb, Dir
Holdings: Cat Mss

MAC LEOD, MARGARET ARNETT, 1878-1966

MB —UNIVERSITY OF MANITOBA, Elizabeth Dafoe Library, Archives and Special Collections Dept, Winnipeg, R3T 2N2, Can. Richard E Bennett, Dept Head; Corrado A Santoro, Reference Archivist
Notes: This collection traces the geneaology of a pioneer family and describes the growth of the Hudson's Bay Company in Manitoba in the mid-nineteenth century. 7 boxes of materials.

MCLUHAN, MARSHALL

MB —UNIVERSITY OF MANITOBA, Elizabeth Dafoe Library, Archives and Special Collections Dept, Winnipeg, R3T 2N2, Can. Richard E Bennett, Dept Head; Corrado A Santoro, Reference Archivist
Notes: Newsclippings, book reviews, interviews, articles and publications of and about Marshall McLuhan. Three boxes.

MACMAHON, ALINE

NY —NEW YORK PUBLIC LIBRARY, Performing Arts Research Center, Billy Rose Theatre Collection, 111 Amsterdam Ave, New York, 10023. Dorothy L Swerdlove, Cur
Holdings: Cat Mss Pix
Notes: Papers, scrapbooks, mss, photographs, memorabilia, etc.

MCMANUS, GEORGE, 1884-1954

CA —UNIVERSITY OF CALIFORNIA, LOS ANGELES, Research Library, Dept of Special Collections, 405 Hilgard Ave, Los Angeles, 90024. Edward Shreeves, Chairman, Bibliographers Group; David S Zeidberg, Head
Holdings: Mss Pix
Notes: 1.5 linear feet of drawings, mss, and scrapbooks of the creator of *Maggie and Jiggs.*

MCMANUS, JOHN

DC —LIBRARY OF CONGRESS, Rare Book & Special Collections Div, Washington,

20540. William Matheson, Chief
Notes: See description of McManus-Young Collection under Houdini, Harry.

MACMILLAN, ADM. DONALD BAXTER, 1874-1970

ME —BOWDOIN COLLEGE, Library, Brunswick, 04011. Dianne M Gutscher, Cur of Special Collections
Holdings: Mss Maps Pix
Notes: The collection consists of Admiral MacMillan's personal library of about 4000 books relating to arctic exploration, several volumes of clippings, numerous scrapbooks, ms diaries and journals, photographs, maps, and other records.

MACMILLAN, EDWIN

CA —UNIVERSITY OF CALIFORNIA, BERKELEY, Bancroft Library, Manuscripts Division, Berkeley, 94720. James D Hart, Dir
Notes: Papers and research notes relative to the history of nuclear science and the Lawrence Berkeley Laboratory.
See also entry under Cyclotron.

MACMILLAN, SIR ERNEST

ON —NATIONAL LIBRARY OF CANADA, 395 Wellington St, Ottawa, K1A 0N4, Can. Andre Preibish, Dir
Holdings: Vols 35,000
Notes: Includes 2000 pieces of Canadian sheet music (mostly 19th century imprints), 40,000 cylinders, discs, tapes; over 600 serials titles devoted to music; 200 archival collections of composers, musicians and conductors, eg papers of Healy Willan, eminent composer; Glen Gould, well-known pianist; Sir Ernest MacMillan, conductor, director and composer. Since 1950 the Canadian imprints have been received on legal deposit. Intensive purchases aim at a comprehensive collection of Canadian music.

MCMILLAN, HUGH (ARCHITECT)

AB —UNIVERSITY OF CALGARY, Libraries, Special Collections Div, 2500 University Dr, Calgary, T2N 1N4, Can.
Holdings: Cat Mss Pix
Notes: Collection consists of about 2500 architectural drawings, office files, records, correspondence for projects from 1960 onwards, of the architectural firm of Hugh McMillan Architect Ltd, Calgary. It is similar to and complements the collection of Long Mayell & Associates (qv), and includes numerous projects for the Calgary Public and Separate School Boards, the City of Calgary, Alberta Department of Public Works, and a considerable number of townhouse and apartment designs for Calgary Development Companies. Project list is on hand. 25.5 meters documents.

MCMILLAN, THOMAS FORSYTHE

AZ —NORTHERN ARIZONA UNIVERSITY, Special Collection Library, CU Box 6022, Flagstaff, 86011. Peter M Whiteley, Coordr/Archivist; William Mullane, Librn
Notes: Thomas J Flemming Collection; copies of biographies of Thomas Forsythe McMillan, early settler of Flagstaff, Ariz, written by his daughter, Mamie McMillan Flemming, 1941, 1952.

MACMILLAN OF CANADA

ON —MCMASTER UNIVERSITY, Mills Memorial Library, Div of Archives & Research Collections, Hamilton, L8S 4L6, Can. G R Hill, Univ Librn
Holdings: Mss
Notes: The archives of McClelland and Stewart Ltd (1955-1980) and Macmillan of Canada (1907-1980), consisting of executive correspondence, editorial files, publicity, author correspondence, some art work.

MACMORRIS, DANIEL

MO —UNIVERSITY OF MISSOURI-KANSAS CITY, General Library, State

Historical Society of Missouri Manuscripts, 5100 Rockhill Road, Kansas City, 64110. Kenneth J LaBudde, Dir; Gordon Hendrickson, Assoc Dir
Holdings: Mss
Notes: Western Historical Manuscript Collection incl papers of Charles B Wheeler, Jr, Charles N Kimball, Arthur Mag, Oscar D Nelson, Lou B Holland, J C Nichols, Perry Cookingham, Blevins Davis, Daniel MacMorris, and the records of the Kansas City Board of Trade.

MACMURRAY, JOHN VAN ANTWERP, 1881-1960

NJ —PRINCETON UNIVERSITY, Library, Manuscript Collection, Nassau St, Princeton, 08540. Jean F Preston, Cur
Holdings: // Cat Mss Pix
Notes: Incl 259 boxes of papers. The collection has some family papers dating back to 1715. A typescript guide (44 p) is available for consultation.

MCMURTRIE, DOUGLAS CRAWFORD, 1888-1944

AL —SAMFORD UNIVERSITY, Special Collections Library, 800 Lakeshore Dr, Birmingham, 35229. Annie Ford Wheeler, Acting Head Librn
Holdings: Vols 420 Cat
Notes: Albert T Scroggins Collection. Many limited editions.
IL —NEWBERRY LIBRARY, 60 W Walton St, Chicago, 60610. Diana Haskell, Cur of Modern Mss
Holdings: Cat Mss
Notes: Very strong collection. Includes Imprints Inventory material on cards as used by McMurtrie and A H Allen.
IL —NORTHWESTERN UNIVERSITY, Library, Special Collections Dept, 1937 Sheridan Rd, Evanston, 60201. R Russell Maylone, Cur
Holdings: Vols 482 // Cat //
IN —INDIANA UNIVERSITY, Lilly Library, Seventh St, Bloomington, 47405. William R Cagle, Librn
Holdings: Vols 300// Cat
Notes: Materials by and about McMurtrie.
MI —MICHIGAN STATE UNIVERSITY, Libraries, Special Collections Div, East Lansing, 48824. Jannette Fiore, Librn
Holdings: Mss
Notes: Outstanding collection of over 100, 000 items, including Douglas C McMurtrie's published pamphlets and monographs, with manuscript, typescript, galleys, etc, material for the unfinished *History of Printing in the United States,* and his vast correspondence on printing and its history. Supported by a collection of works on printing.
OH —OHIO UNIVERSITY, Vernon R Alden Library, Department of Archives and Special Collections, Athens, 45701. Gary A Hunt, Head
Holdings: Vols 52 Cat
†PA —UNIVERSITY OF PITTSBURGH, Graduate School of Library & Information Sciences Library, L I S Bldg, Third Fl, Pittsburgh, 15260. Jean Kindlin, Librn
Holdings: Vols 250 Cat
Notes: Incl works by McMurtrie and some examples of his design work. No photocopying.
TX —EAST TEXAS STATE UNIVERSITY, James G Gee Library, Special Collections Dept, East Texas Station, Commerce, 75428. James Conrad, Dept Head
Holdings: Vols 74 Cat
Notes: McMurtrie imprints.
TX —UNIVERSITY OF HOUSTON, M D Anderson Memorial Library, University Park, Houston, 77004. David Farmer, Cur, Special Collections; Jean Jackson, Assistant Cur
Holdings: Vols 225 Cat
Notes: The collection follows, to a degree, the checklist prepared by Charles Heartman in 1942 (supplement, 1946), but contains many items not included by Heartman.

MCMURTRY, LARRY

AZ —UNIVERSITY OF ARIZONA, University Library, Special Collections,

MCMURTRY, LARRY (cont.)

Tucson, 85721. Louis A Hieb, Head
Holdings: Vols (7000) Cat Mss Microforms
Budget: ($30,000)
Notes: Incl the belle lettres of the American Southwest. The collection covers the complete scope of works by Southwest authors and those works which are set in the Southwest. The major authors are Edward Abbey, Coolidge, Eastlake, Fergusson, Garfield, Horgan, King, McMurtry, Nichols and Rhodes.

TX —NORTH TEXAS STATE UNIVERSITY, Rare Book and Texana Collections, NT Station Box 5188, Denton, 76203. Kenneth Lavender, University Bibliographer
Notes: Larry McMurtry Collection. 64 typescripts; proofs; signed editions; ephemera. Typescripts incl undergraduate and graduate papers, drafts, notes.

TX —UNIVERSITY OF HOUSTON, M D Anderson Memorial Library, University Park, Houston, 77004. David Farmer, Cur, Special Collections; Jean Jackson, Assistant Cur
Holdings: Vols 25 Cat Mss
Notes: Incl a series of early letters, drafts to several novels, short (some unpublished) and other related materials. Use is restricted. *See also* entry under Authors, Texas.

MCNARY, CHARLES L.

DC —LIBRARY OF CONGRESS, Manuscript Division, Washington, 20540. John C Broderick, Chief
Holdings: Cat Mss Pix
Notes: Mss, papers, records, etc.

MCNAMARA, PATRICK V.

MI —WAYNE STATE UNIVERSITY, Walter P Reuther Library, Archives of Labor & Urban Affairs, Detroit, 48202. Philip Mason, Dir
Notes: The politics of 20th century America are mirrored in the collections of Patrick V McNamara, US Senator; Charles Diggs, US Representative from Michigan; Ofield Dukes, aide to Vice-President Hubert H Humphrey; and George and Grace Brewer, Socialist Party workers and assistants to Eugene V Debs.

MACNAUGHTON, CLARA AND MARY

CA —UNIVERSITY OF SAN FRANCISCO, Richard A Gleeson Library, The Countess Bernardine Murphy Donohue Rare Book Room, San Francisco, 94117. D Steven Corey, Special Collections Librn
Holdings: Mss
Notes: Papers and correspondence of Mary MacNaughton (Mrs Arthur Powell Davis) and Clara W MacNaughton ca 1890-1910. One box of materials.

MCNEER, MAY

DC —GEORGETOWN UNIVERSITY, Library, Special Collections Div, 37 & O Sts NW, Washington, 20057. George M Barringer, Special Collections Librn; Nicholas B Sheetz, Mss Librn
Notes: The papers, files, art work, etc of Lynd Ward and his wife, May McNeer.

MACNEICE, LOUIS, 1907-1963

NV —UNIVERSITY OF NEVADA, RENO, University Library, Special Collections Dept, Reno, 89557. Robert E Blesse, Head
Holdings: Vols (54) Cat Other appearances 575 Cat
Notes: Includes individual works by author in all editions including translations; also prefaces, introductions, published correspondence, appearances in anthologies, periodicals, etc. Bibliographical research collection, part of Modern Authors Collection.

†NY —COLUMBIA UNIVERSITY LIBRARIES, Butler Library, Rare Book and Manuscript Library, 535 W 114 St, New York, 10027.
Notes: The Louis MacNeice Collection.

BC —UNIVERSITY OF VICTORIA, McPherson Library, Victoria, V8W 3H5, Can.

MACNEIL FAMILY

CA —AZUSA PACIFIC COLLEGE, Marshburn Memorial Library, Citrus & Alosta, Azusa, 91702. Edward Peterman, Librn
Holdings: Vols (1000)// Uncat Maps Pix
Notes: Macneil Family Collection on Local History. These items relate to the Slauson, Macneil and Wilcox families, incl photographs, diaries, letters, maps, books, and financial and legal documents.

MCNEILL, ROBERT B.

MA —BOSTON UNIVERSITY, Mugar Memorial Library, Special Collections Dept, 771 Commonwealth Ave, Boston, 02215. Howard B Gotlieb, Dir
Holdings: Cat Mss
Notes: Mss, correspondence, etc collected in depth; incl publications by or about.

MACNELLY, JEFF

†VA —UNIVERSITY OF VIRGINIA, Library, Charlottesville, 22901.
Notes: Bernard Meeks original cartoons and drawings collection, 326 items incl some original comic strip art. Fred O Seibel collection of ca 6000 original drawings, and cartoonists' working papers and files. Additional collection of editorial cartoons by Oscar Cesare, Jeff MacNelly, Art Wood, etc. Examples of almost all political and many comic artists working in he mid-20th century.

MCPHEE, COLIN

CA —UNIVERSITY OF CALIFORNIA, LOS ANGELES, Music Library, Schonberg Hall, Los Angeles, 90024. Stephen M Fry, Music Librn
Notes: Mss.

MCPHERSON, JAMES LOWELL

MA —BOSTON UNIVERSITY, Mugar Memorial Library, Special Collections Dept, 771 Commonwealth Ave, Boston, 02215. Howard B Gotlieb, Dir
Holdings: Cat Mss Correspondence

MCRAE, EDNA L.

IL —NEWBERRY LIBRARY, 60 W Walton St, Chicago, 60610. Carolyn A Sheehy, Administrator
Holdings: Cat Mss Pix
Notes: Extensive holdings in the areas of dance history (including important first editions) and dance music. Newly formed Midwest Dance Archive contains the papers of Ann Barzel, Walter Camryn, Diana Huebert and Edna McRae.

MCRAYE, WALTER J., 1876-1946

†ON —MCMASTER UNIVERSITY, Library, Hamilton, L8S 4L6, Can.
Notes: Letters and mss collected by Walter McRaye, addressed to him from Canadian writers, such as Charles G D Roberts and Bliss Carmen.

MCREYNOLDS, JAMES CLARK

VA —UNIVERSITY OF VIRGINIA, Alderman Library, Manuscripts Dept, Charlottesville, 22901. Edmund Berkeley Jr, Cur
Holdings: Cat Mss Pix
Notes: Personal, political, and business papers.

MCSHANE, JAMES

MA —JOHN F KENNEDY LIBRARY, Columbia Point, Boston, 02125. Henry J Gwiazda II, Cur
Notes: The Burke Marshall papers, 50 archives boxes re civil rights, 1961-1964 and the Bedford-Stuyvesant Development and Restoration Corporations; the Joseph Dolan papers, 1 box; the Thomas Johnston papers, 3 boxes; the James Mc Shane papers, 2 boxes; the Frank Mankiewicz papers, 15 boxes; and the Scott Rafferty papers, 4 boxes.

MCSHANE, MARK

MA —BOSTON UNIVERSITY, Mugar Memorial Library, Special Collections Dept, 771 Commonwealth Ave, Boston, 02215. Howard B Gotlieb, Dir
Holdings: Cat Pix Mss Correspondence

MCVITTIE, G. C.

NY —AMERICAN INSTITUTE OF PHYSICS, Center for the History of Physics, Niels Bohr Library, 335 E 45 St, New York, 10017. John Aubry, Librn
Notes: The Sources for History of Modern Astrophysics documents the history of 20th-century astrophysics. Incl some 400 hours of oral history interviews with astronomers, such as Bart Bok, S Chandrasekhar, Martin Schwarzschild, and A E Whitford. The project also organized and cataloged the papers of Henry Norris Russell, Frank Schlesinger, Otto Struve, Ejnar Hertzsprung, Harlow Shapley, Charles Young, Robert Atkinson, Seth Chandler, Theodore Dunham, Jr, and G C McVittie.

MCWHORTER, LUCULLUS VIRGIL

†WA —WASHINGTON STATE UNIVERSITY, Library, Manuscripts, Archives & Special Collections, Pullman, 99164. John F Guido, Head
Holdings: Vols Cat Mss Maps Pix Microforms
Notes: Ms resources for the study of Pacific Northwest Indians incl the papers of historians William Compton Brown, Carl Parcher Russell, and Lucullus Virgil McWhorter; and missionaries Henry Harmon Spalding, Elkanah Walker and Marcus Whitman. A few of these publications: *William Compton Brown: A Calendar of His Papers in the Washington State University Library* (Pullman, 1966); *Carl Parcher Russell: An Indexed Register of His Scholarly and Professional Papers, 1920-1967, in the Washington State University Library* (Pullman, 1970); *The Papers of Lucullus Virgil McWhorter*, compiled by Nelson A Ault (Pullman, 1959).

MCWILLIAMS, CAREY, 1905-1980

CA —CLAREMONT COLLEGES, Honnold Library, Ninth & Dartmouth, Claremont, 91711. Tania Rizzo, Special Collections Dept Head
Holdings: Vols 60 // Cat Mss Pix
Notes: Incl 40 serial titles, often incomplete, some in Japanese, from War Relocation centers, 1941-1945. One document case of miscellaneous newspaper clippings and pamphlets; 8 document cases, part of a Carey McWilliams collection, incl press releases, private agency and governmental reports, newspaper clippings, pamphlets, and over 150 pieces of correspondence, 1942-1945, to and from McWilliams, correspondence, 1942-1945, to and from McWilliams, some with evacuees. Restricted use.

CA —UNIVERSITY OF CALIFORNIA, LOS ANGELES, Research Library, Dept of Special Collections, 405 Hilgard Ave, Los Angeles, 90024. Edward Shreeves, Chairman, Bibliographers Group; David S Zeidberg, Head
Holdings: // Uncat Mss
Notes: 17.5 linear feet of personal papers, clippings, and reports relating to migrant farm labor, the problems of the Mexican American, 1930-1940, and on the Zoot-Suit Riots.

MCWILLIAMS, HARRY

NY —MUSEUM OF MODERN ART, Dept of Film, 11 W 53 St, New York, 10019. Eileen

MCWILLIAMS, HARRY (cont.)

Bowser, Cur
Holdings: Mss Pix
Notes: Papers, correspondence, scrapbooks, pictures, etc. Partially cataloged.

MACY, ANNE SULLIVAN

NY —AMERICAN FOUNDATION FOR THE BLIND, M C Migel Memorial Library and Information Center, 15 W 16 St, New York, 10011. Diane Wolfe, Head Librn & Info Ctr Coordr; Marguerite Levine, Supvr Archives
Holdings: Mss Pix Slides Audiotapes 16mm Film
Notes: Helen Keller's papers in Helen Keller Archives. A collection relating to Helen Adams Keller. Incl are correspondence with friends and admirers, speeches, literary mss, legal and genealogical material, photographs, sound recordings, and one film: about Helen Keller, her teacher Anne Sullivan Macy, her companion Polly Thomson, and John Albert Macy, husband of Anne Sullivan Macy. Among the subjects represented are work on behalf of the blind, deaf-blind, and deaf; children and women in factories; planned parenthood; labor movements; peace; and suffrage.

MACY, JESSE

IA —STATE HISTORICAL SOCIETY OF IOWA LIBRARY, 402 Iowa Ave, Iowa City, 52240. Darold J Brown, Librn
Holdings: Cat
Notes: Thousands of individual items and smaller collections. Two hundred larger collections incl the papers of Cyrus C Carpenter, Jonathan P Dolliver, Gilbert Haugen, W W Waymack, Ephraim Adams, A C Dodge, Dorothy Houghton, Jesse Macy, Agnes Samuelson, Donald Johnson, Jack Miller, Ruth Sayre, Samuel Kirkwood, Thomas McKnight, Robert Lucas, Dwight McCarty, William Larrabee. Includes church, school, company and organization records, Civil War materials.

MACY, JOHN ALBERT

CA —FRANCIS BACON LIBRARY, 655 N Dartmouth Ave, Claremont, 91711. Elizabeth S Wrigley, Dir
Holdings: Mss Pix
Notes: Arensberg's miscellaneous correspondence with American literary figures (1920's-50's) including Bruce Bliven, Catherine Drinker Bowen, Kay Boyle, Witter Bynner, Edwin Corle, Helen A Keller, Lysander Kemp, Kenneth Macgowan, John Macy, Henry Miller, Lewis Mumford, Clifford Odets, Kenneth Patchen, Irving Stone, and William Carlos Williams.
MA —HARVARD UNIVERSITY LIBRARY, Cambridge, 02138.
Holdings: Cat Mss
NY —AMERICAN FOUNDATION FOR THE BLIND, M C Migel Memorial Library and Information Center, 15 W 16 St, New York, 10011. Diane Wolfe, Head Librn & Info Ctr Coordr; Marguerite Levine, Supvr Archives
Holdings: Mss Pix Slides Audiotapes 16mm Film
Notes: Helen Keller's papers in Helen Keller Archives. A collection relating to Helen Adams Keller. Incl are correspondence with friends and admirers, speeches, literary mss, legal and genealogical material, photographs, sound recordings, and one film: about Helen Keller, her teacher Anne Sullivan Macy, her companion Polly Thomson, and John Albert Macy, husband of Anne Sullivan Macy. Among the subjects represented are work on behalf of the blind, deaf-blind, and deaf; children and women in factories; planned parenthood; labor movements; peace; and suffrage.

MADAGASCAR

DC —HOWARD UNIVERSITY, Moorland-Spingarn Research Center, 500 Howard

Place NW, Washington, 20059. Clifford L Muse, Jr, Acting Dir
Notes: Malagasy Democratic Republic.
OH —CLEVELAND PUBLIC LIBRARY, Fine Arts and Special Collections Department, 325 Superior Ave, Cleveland, 44114. Alice N Loranth, Head
Holdings: Vols 500 Cat Maps
Notes: Notable in the collection is the periodical literature, dating back to the 19th century.

MADDOX, LESTER

GA —UNIVERSITY OF GEORGIA, Libraries, Special Collections Division, Athens, 30602. Vesta Lee Gordon, Asst Dir for Special Collections
Notes: Collection contains 1394.8 linear feet of mss: papers of US Senator Richard B Russell; US Congressmen John W Davis, Maston O'Neal, Robert G Stephens Jr, John L Pilcher, Dudley M Hughes; Governors Hoke Smith, Lester Maddox, Carl Sanders.

MADDUX, RACHEL

MA —BOSTON UNIVERSITY, Mugar Memorial Library, Special Collections Dept, 771 Commonwealth Ave, Boston, 02215. Howard B Gotlieb, Dir
Holdings: Cat Mss
Notes: Mss, correspondence, etc collected in depth; incl publications by or about.

MADER, CLARENCE

CA —UNIVERSITY OF CALIFORNIA, LOS ANGELES, Music Library, Schonberg Hall, Los Angeles, 90024. Stephen M Fry, Music Librn
Notes: Mss.

MADERO, FRANCISCO

CA —CLAREMONT COLLEGES, Honnold Library, Ninth & Dartmouth, Claremont, 91711. Tania Rizzo, Special Collections Dept Head
Holdings: Cat Mss Pix Scrapbooks
Notes: Correspondence, mss, documents, clippings, photographs, and ephemera, 2200 pieces, some in carbon copies, of Jose Maytorena, from 1882-1947. Important correspondents incl Venustiano Carranza, Francisco Madero, and Alvaro Obregon, among many others. Guy T McCreary, *A Primary Study of the Revolutionary, Governor, General, Jose maria Maytorena and the Mexican Revolution 1910-1916* (thesis, 1967) based on this collection. Restricted use.

MADISON, JAMES

DC —LIBRARY OF CONGRESS, Manuscript Division, Washington, 20540. John C Broderick, Chief
Notes: The Presidential Papers collection incl the papers, etc, of numerous Presidents.
MA —HARVARD UNIVERSITY LIBRARY, Cambridge, 02138.
Holdings: Cat Mss
NJ —PRINCETON UNIVERSITY, Library, Manuscript Collection, Nassau St, Princeton, 08540. Jean F Preston, Cur
Notes: The James Madison collection, which fills 10 ms boxes, also includes material on Dolley Madison. An unpublished typescript guide (27p) is available in the library.
NY —NEW YORK PUBLIC LIBRARY, Rare Books and Manuscripts Div, Fifth Ave & 42 St, New York, 10018. William L Joyce, Asst Dir; Susan E Davis, Cur of Mss
Holdings: Mss
Budget: ($7161)
Notes: Incl personal and literary mss, papers, etc.
VA —UNIVERSITY OF VIRGINIA, Alderman Library, Manuscripts Dept, Charlottesville, 22901. Edmund Berkeley Jr, Cur
Holdings: Cat Mss
Notes: Papers, chiefly from post-presidential years and many regarding the establishment of the University of Virginia.

VA —VIRGINIA STATE LIBRARY, 12 & Capitol Sts, Richmond, 23219.
Holdings: Vols 510 Cat Mss Maps Pix

MADISON, RUSS

MA —BOSTON UNIVERSITY, Mugar Memorial Library, Special Collections Dept, 771 Commonwealth Ave, Boston, 02215. Howard B Gotlieb, Dir
Holdings: Cat Mss

MADONNA see Mary, Virgin

MADRAS

WI —UNIVERSITY OF WISCONSIN, MADISON, Memorial Library, South Asian Collection, 728 State St, Madison, 53706. Jack C Wells, Bibliographer
Notes: Madras history sources. Filmed collections of 112,000 documents (400 reels of positive microfilm) from the Revenue, Public, Judicial, Ecclesiastical, Political, Military, and Financial Departments of the Madras Presidency. Public and private papers of Governors of Madras: George Hay Tweedale (1842-1848); John Elphenstone (1837-1842); William Bentinck (1803-1807), Thomas Munro (1761-1827). District gazetteers and manuals. Survey and settlement reports of selected districts. Administrative reports of the Revenue Department (1892-1926). Madras Native Newspaper Reports (1877-1921). South of India Observer, 1864-1887; Madras Times, 1858-61, 1863-69, 1871-77.

MADRID, SPAIN

CT —UNIVERSITY OF CONNECTICUT, Library, Storrs, 06268. R H Schimmelpfeng, Dir of Special Collections
Holdings: Vols (1650) Cat Mss Maps Pix
Notes: Collection incl all aspects of the history, social life, politics, economics, etc, of Madrid. Core of collection was property of Jose Luis Oliva Escribano.

MAETERLINCK, MAURICE

MS —UNIVERSITY OF SOUTHERN MISSISSIPPI, William David McCain Graduate Library, Box 5148, Southern Sta, Hattiesburg, 39406.
Holdings: Vols 23 Uncat Mss
Notes: Various editions of Maeterlinck's works (some signed), correspondence, literary mss (1 cubic foot), articles, essays and other publications (circa 1920-1950) by and about this Belgian born Nobel Prize winning author.

MAG, ARTHUR

MO —UNIVERSITY OF MISSOURI-KANSAS CITY, General Library, State Historical Society of Missouri Manuscripts, 5100 Rockhill Road, Kansas City, 64110. Kenneth J LaBudde, Dir; Gordon Hendrickson, Assoc Dir
Holdings: Mss
Notes: Western Historical Manuscript Collection incl papers of Charles B Wheeler, Jr, Charles N Kimball, Arthur Mag, Oscar D Nelson, Lou B Holland, J C Nichols, Perry Cookingham, Blevins Davis, Daniel MacMorris, and the records of the Kansas City Board of Trade.

MAGALHAES, FERNAO DE

MA —BRANDEIS UNIVERSITY, Goldfarb Library, 415 South St, Waltham, 02154. Bessie Hahn, Dir
Notes: McKew-Parr Collection on Magellan and the Age of Discovery. Approx 4000 books relating to Magellan and Columbus and other voyagers of the 15th and early 16th century. A card catalog to the collection is located in Special Collections.

MAGAZINES see Periodicals—Collections

MAGIC, BLACK see Black Magic

MAGIC, COPTIC

AZ —WORLD UNIVERSITY, Library, 711 E Blacklidge Dr, Tucson, 85719. Howard John

MAGIC, COPTIC (cont.)

Zitko, Cur
Holdings: Vols (15,000) Cat Mss Maps
Audiotapes
Notes: Collection concerns what are
generally called the "frontier sciences." No
interlibrary loan.

MAGIC AND MAGICIANS

AZ —WORLD UNIVERSITY, Library, 711 E
Blacklidge Dr, Tucson, 85719. Howard John
Zitko, Cur
Holdings: Vols (15,000) Cat Mss Maps
Audiotapes
Notes: Collection concerns what are
generally called the "frontier sciences." No
interlibrrary loan.

CA —FRANCIS BACON LIBRARY, 655 N
Dartmouth Ave, Claremont, 91711.
Elizabeth S Wrigley, Dir
Notes: Collection incl witchcraft and magic
from early times to the 20th century. Many
17th century volumes.

†CA —UNIVERSITY OF CALIFORNIA LOS
ANGELES, Center for the Study of
Comparative Folklore and Mythology, Los
Angeles, 90024.
Notes: Archive, consisting of nearly 500,000
entries and cross-references, developed by
Prof Wayland D Hand over the past 40
years as part of his monumental *Dictionary
of American Popular Beliefs and
Superstitions*. Entries have been drawn from
both field collections and from printed and
published sources. Analytical data stress
both the historical component and the
comparative approach. Of special interest is
the emphasis on magical medicine, although
natural and botanical medicine are also well
represented.

DC —LIBRARY OF CONGRESS, Rare Book
& Special Collections Div, Washington,
20540. William Matheson, Chief
Holdings: Cat
Notes: The Houdini Collection of Magic and
Spiritism consists of over 4000 vols of
printed works and a large number of
scrapbooks containing clippings, programs,
catalogs, posters, etc. The McManus-Young
collection of 1076 vols, as well as mss,
prints, and organized scrapbooks on
Houdini, the history of magic, and related
fields.

IL —UNIVERSITY OF ILLINOIS,
URBANA/CHAMPAIGN, Library,
University Archives, 19 Library, 1408 W
Gregory Drive, Urbana, 61801. Maynard
Brichford, University Archivist
Holdings: Vols (5000) Cat
Budget: ($7000)
Notes: The Mandeville Collection in
Parapsychology and Occult Sciences. Titles
in the Merten J Mandeville Collection are
purchased by funds from an endowment
provided specifically for the collection on its
establishment in 1966 by Merten J
Mandeville, Professor Emeritus of
Management, who donated 400 vols from his
personal library as the nucleus of the
collection. There are currently about 5000
titles in the collection, supplemented by
related materials in the general collection.
Topics include astrology, extrasensory
perception, yoga, magic, satanism, faith
healing, hypnosis, Eastern religions,
witchcraft, fortune telling, reincarnation,
flying saucers, ghosts, dreams, numerology,
graphology, and mysticism. Biographies and
reference books are a part of the collection
as are journals devoted to the scientific study
of parapsychology.

MD —JOHNS HOPKINS UNIVERSITY,
Milton S Eisenhower Library, George
Peabody Collection, 17 E Mt Vernon Place,
Baltimore, 21201. Lyn Hart, Peabody Librn
Notes: Noncirculating.

MA —HEBREW COLLEGE, Jacob & Rose
Grossman Library and Lawrence Jay &
Anne Cable Rubenstein Library, 43 Hawes
St, Brookline, 02146. Maurice Tuchman,
Librn
Holdings: Vols 600 Cat Mss
Notes: Hassidic and Cabalistic literature.

MA —HARVARD UNIVERSITY LIBRARY,
Theatre Collection, Cambridge, 02138.
Jeanne T Newlin, Cur
Holdings: Cat Mss Pix Slides Microforms
Notes: One of the largest existing collections
of playbills, programs, prints, photographs,
promptbooks, and other materials relating to
the performing arts, the scope is worldwide;
resources on the English-speaking stage of
the 18th and 19th centuries are unequalled.
Incl materials on ballet and modern dance,
the circus, magic, minstrel shows, cinema,
and pantomime. For description, see
Harvard Library Bulletin, VI (1925): pp 281-
301.

NJ —PRINCETON UNIVERSITY, Library,
Rare Books Dept, Princeton, 08544. Stephen
Ferguson, Cur
Notes: The nucleus of the Library's magic
collection is that put together by Carl W
Jones '11 and presented by his wife. For
particulars refer to: James Holly Hanford,
"The Magic Collection of Carl W Jones '11"
in the *Princeton University Library
Chronicle* XX, 1 (autumn, 1958) pp 47-53.
Checklist of the Jones collection with call
numbers for the books is incl in the
Collections File. See also: Trevor Hall. *A
Bibliography of Books on Conjuring in
English from 1580 to 1850* (Minneapolis,
1957) (Ex Z6878.c7xH2) The Ex copy has
been checked for the Library's holdings.

†NY —COLUMBIA UNIVERSITY
LIBRARIES, Butler Library, Rare Book and
Manuscript Library, 535 W 114 St, New
York, 10027.
Notes: 76 vols of diaries of Lynn Thorndike,
1902-63. A record of his daily reading,
progress in research and writing, European
travels, relations with scholars and librarians,
and other personal matters.

NY —NEW YORK PUBLIC LIBRARY,
Performing Arts Research Center, Billy Rose
Theatre Collection, 111 Amsterdam Ave,
New York, 10023. Dorothy L Swerdlove,
Cur
Holdings: Cat
Notes: Approx one-third of the book
collection is a private collection housed by
the Theatre Collection but under the aegis of
the Society of American Magicians. Use of
the material is limited to the membership of
the Society. Permission for use must be
secured from the Secretary of the Society.

RI —BROWN UNIVERSITY, John Hay
Library, 20 Prospect St, Providence, 02912.
Mark N Brown, Cur Mss
Holdings: Mss
Notes: Two collections relating to the occult
sciences: The Mary Ann Smith Atwood
Collection--English theosophist and writer
(700 items); and the S Foster Damon, 1893-
1971, Collection--poet, dramatist and
Professor of English at Brown University,
(more than 15,000 items), unprocessed.

RI —PROVIDENCE ATHENAEUM, 251
Benefit St, Providence, 02903. Sally Duplaix,
Dir
Holdings: (152,000) Vols
Notes: Material available on interlibrary loan
under certain conditions.

RI —PROVIDENCE PUBLIC LIBRARY, 150
Empire St, Providence, 02903. Lance J
Bauer, Special Collections Librn
Holdings: Vols 2500 Cat Mss Pix
Notes: The John H Percival Magic
Collection. The reference library of a
practicing magician, this collection is one of
a handful of collections devoted exclusively
to conjuring located in American libraries.
Contains books on conjuring, many out-of-
print, some rare on conjuring from 18th to
20th century. Contains conjuring periodicals,
pamphlets, programmes, photographs and
mss holdings. Several scrapbooks. Material
must be used in-house. Photocopying of a
limited nature when condition permits.

VA —UNIVERSITY OF VIRGINIA,
Alderman Library, Tracy W McGregor
Collection, Charlottesville, 22901. William H
Runge, Cur
Holdings: Vols 2500 Cat Mss
Notes: This collection was gathered by
William Gwinn Mather, a direct descendant
of the New England Mathers. It is one of
the 3 important Mather collections in the

world. Excellent collection on magic and
witchcraft in America. Collection incl 20th
century imprints. Thomas J Holmes used
this collection as a basis for his monumental
biographies of Increase Mather, Cotton
Mather and the minor Mathers.

PQ —CONCORDIA UNIVERSITY
LIBRARIES, Vanier Library, 7141
Sherbrooke St SW, Montreal, H3G 1M8,
Can. Martin Cohen, Collections Coordinator
Holdings: Vols 350// Cat Mss
Notes: About 200 titles and 150 books of
ritual; emphases on history, ritual,
encyclopedias, biography, magic. Incl North
American and European works.

MAGIC AND
MAGICIANS—PICTURES,
ILLUSTRATIONS, ETC.

MI —AMERICAN MUSEUM OF MAGIC,
107 East Michigan Ave, Marshall, 49608.
Robert Lund; Elaine Lund
Notes: The Irving Desfor Collection of 40,
000 photographs of magicians. In addition to
the Desfor photographs, this collection
consists of approx 250,000 books, magazines,
newspaper clippings, letters, programs,
advertising material, posters, films, authors'
manuscripts, paintings and prints, apparatus,
coins and tokens, toys, phonograph records
and tape recordings, statuary, sheet music,
costumes and other material, all on the
subject of magic and magicians. The
collection is privately owned by Robert and
Elaine Lund.

MAGIC MANUALS see Grimoires

MAGIC SQUARES

RI —BROWN UNIVERSITY, John Hay
Library, 20 Prospect St, Providence, 02912.
Mark N Brown, Cur Mss
Notes: The Royal Vale Heath Collection of
about 200 of his designs, drawings, models,
ocular, and verbal descriptions of
simultaneous solutions to linear Diophantine
equations in such examples as magic squares,
Platonic solids, etc. These curious designs
often were devised as talismans in ancient
India and were first developed as
mathematical problems by the Chinese.

MAGNES, JUDAH L.

DC —LIBRARY OF CONGRESS, Manuscript
Division, Washington, 20540. John C
Broderick, Chief
Notes: Papers of Hannah Arendt; now
unrestricted, except for the Judah L Magnes
correspondence.

MAGNETIC MEMORY (ELECTRONIC
COMPUTERS)

CA —INTERNATIONAL BUSINESS
MACHINES RESEARCH LIBRARY, 5600
Cottle Rd, San Jose, 95193. Phil Grincewich,
Mgr Technical Information
Holdings: Vols (13,500) Cat
Notes: Principally electronic computer
storage system architecture. Incl 21,000 vols
of 770 journals. On-line search facility. Vols
are divided into three libraries, Technical
Research, Technical Information, and
Programing. Not open to public.

MA —MASSACHUSETTS INSTITUTE OF
TECHNOLOGY, Institute Archives, Special
Collections, Cambridge, 02139.
Notes: The materials in the Magnetic Core
Memory collection assembled in support of
MIT during the patent litigation over the
magnetic core memory. Invented in 1947 by
Jay Forrester during the development of the
Whirlwind Computer, magnetic core
memory set the stage for the development of
high-speed digital computers. Though
Whirlwind was originally begun as an
aircraft simulator project during World War
II, the computer which resulted became the
prototype for most large scale general
purpose computers. The collection dates
mostly from the 1940s and 1950s.

MAGNETIC NEEDLE see Compass

MAGNETIC RESONANCE
ACCELERATOR see Cyclotron

MAGNETISM

CA —INTERNATIONAL BUSINESS
MACHINES RESEARCH LIBRARY, 5600

MAGNETISM (cont.)

Cottle Rd, San Jose, 95193. Phil Grincewich, Mgr Technical Information
Holdings: Vols (13,500) Cat
Notes: Incl 21,000 vols of 770 journals. On-line search facility. Vols are divided into three libraries, Technical Research, Technical Information, and Programing. Not open to public.
NY —ENGINEERING SOCIETIES LIBRARY, 345 E 47 St, New York, 10017. S Kirk Cabeen, Dir
Holdings: Vols 250,000 Cat Maps 16mm Films Microforms
Notes: One of the largest, most comprehensive engineering libraries in the world. Covers all engineering disciplines; particularly strong in electrical and electronic, mechanical, mining and metallurgical, petroleum, chemical, industrial, air conditioning and refrigeration engineering. Incl Wheeler Collection of early materials on magnetisn and electricity. 125,000 bound periodical volumes; 10,000 maps; 5000 serial subscriptions (many foreign-language). Virtually all materials abstracted in *Engineering Index* (1884-date) are incl in Library. Noncirculating, except to members of professional engineering societies which support the Library. See *Engineering Societies Library, New York, Classed Subject Catalog and Index* (Boston: G K Hall, 1963); and *Supplements*, 1-10, 1964-1973.
PA —FRANKLIN INSTITUTE LIBRARY, 20 & The Parkway, Philadelphia, 19103. Miriam Padusis, Dir; Charles Wilt, Readers Servs Librn
Holdings: Vols (300,000) Cat Maps Pix Microforms
NS —CANADIAN COAST GUARD COLLEGE, Library, PO Box 4500, Sydney, B1P 6L1, Can. David MacSween, Librn
Holdings: Vols 50 Cat

MAGNETISM—HISTORY

MD —US NAVAL ACADEMY, Nimitz Library, Annapolis, 21402. Alice S Creighton, Assistant Librn for Special Collections
Holdings: Vols (1150) Cat
Notes: Park Benjamin Collection incl works published 1488 to 1905.

MAGNETISM, TERRESTRIAL

NY —US MERCHANT MARINE ACADEMY, Schuyler Otis Bland Memorial Library, Steamboat Rd, Kings Point, 11024. Stephen R Wiist, Acting Chief Librn
Notes: All aspects of maritime affairs.
ON —ENERGY, MINES & RESOURCES CANADA, Earth Physics Branch Library, Ottawa, K1A 0Y3, Can. W M Tsang, Chief Librn
Holdings: Vols (4500) Cat Maps Pix Slides Microforms

MAGNETOHYDRODYNAMIC (MHD) GENERATORS

TN —UNIVERSITY OF TENNESSEE, Space Institute Library, Tullahoma, 37388. Helen B Mason, Librn
Holdings: Vols (14,000) Cat Microforms
Budget: ($50,000)
Notes: Incl NASA, DOE, and other series of technical reports.

MAGNETOHYDRODYNAMICS (MHD)

MA —AVCO EVERETT RESEARCH LABORATORY, INC, Library, 2385 Revere Beach Parkway, Everett, 02149. Lorraine T Nazzaro, Librn
Holdings: Vols (24,000) Cat Maps Microforms
Budget: ($150,000)
Notes: Incl 50,000 reports.

MAGNETOSTRICTION

MA —HARVARD UNIVERSITY LIBRARY, Cambridge, 02138.
Notes: The papers of George Washington Pierce (1898-1955).

MAGNETS

PA —COLT INDUSTRIES, Crucible Research Center Library, Box 88, Pittsburgh, 15230. Patricia J Aducci, Technical Librn

MAGNUSON, DONALD

WA —UNIVERSITY OF WASHINGTON LIBRARIES, Suzzallo Library, Manuscripts Section, FM-25, Seattle, 98195. Karyl Winn, Librn
Notes: Incl 27 linear ft, circa 1953-63.

MAGNUSON, SEN. WARREN

WA —UNIVERSITY OF WASHINGTON LIBRARIES, Suzzallo Library, Manuscripts Section, FM-25, Seattle, 98195. Karyl Winn, Librn
Notes: Senator Warren Magnuson's official papers, incl personal books, government and other publications, awards, photographs, correspondence, and other items. Some not processed and not open for use as of 1984.

MAGRUDER, CALVERT, 1893-1968

MA —HARVARD UNIVERSITY LIBRARY, Law School Library, Langdell Hall, Cambridge, 02138. Erika S Chadbourn, Cur of Mss
Holdings: Cat Mss
Notes: Judicial and personal papers. Typed inventory in repository. Inclusive dates: 1920-1965.

MAGUIRE, JOHN MACARTHUR, 1888-1978

MA —HARVARD UNIVERSITY LIBRARY, Law School Library, Langdell Hall, Cambridge, 02138. Erika S Chadbourn, Cur of Mss
Holdings: Cat Mss
Notes: Professional papers. Typed inventory in repository. Inclusive dates: 1924-1973.

MAGYAR LANGUAGE AND LITERATURE see Hungarian Language and Literature

MAHAN, ALFRED THAYER

RI —US NAVAL WAR COLLEGE, Historical Collection & Museum, Newport, 02841. Anthony S Nicolosi, Dir; Evelyn Cherpak, Cur
Holdings: Mss
Notes: The Alfred Thayer Mahan Papers consist of personal letters and copies of official letters to Sir John Knox Laughton; research notes and lectures at the Naval War College which formed the basis of his work, *The Influence of Seapower on History;* journals, scrapbooks and diaries. Mahan was a noted naval historian and second president of the Naval War College, 1885-1888.

MAHLER, ANNA

†NY —SYRACUSE UNIVERSITY LIBRARIES, Ernest S Bird Library, Syracuse, 13210.
Notes: Louis Krasner Collection, with original scores by classic composers, also an original death mask of Alban Berg made by Anna Mahler.

MAHLER, GUSTAV

CT —YALE UNIVERSITY, Beinecke Rare Book & Manuscript Library, Osborn Collection, New Haven, 06520. Stephen R Parks, Cur
Holdings: Mss
DC —LIBRARY OF CONGRESS, Music Division, Washington, 20540.
Notes: Papers and recordings of composer Arnold Schoenberg. Extensive correspondence with other composers, writers, etc.
PA —UNIVERSITY OF PENNSYLVANIA, Van Pelt Library, Rare Books Collection, 34 & Walnut Sts, Philadelphia, 19104. Daniel Traister, Special Collections Librn
Holdings: Cat Mss
Notes: "Note on the Alma Mahler Werfel Collection," by Adolf Klarmann and Rudolf Hirsch (University of Pennsylvania), *Library Chronicle*, vol 35, no 1 and 2, 1969. Also, 24 holograph mss of Werfel's works, some in two versions.

MAHORKA see Tobacco

MAHRATTA LANGUAGE see Marathi Language and Literature

MAHRATTI LANGUAGE see Marathi Language and Literature

MAIDEN, WILLIE

TX —NORTH TEXAS STATE UNIVERSITY, Audio Center, Box 5188, NT Station, Denton, 76203. Morris Martin, Music Librn
Notes: More than 1600 manuscript jazz compositions, (incl scores and parts, alternate versions, expanded arrangements) by Stan Kenton, Johnny Richards, Joe Coccia, Lennie Niehaus, Pete Rugolo, Willie Maiden, Bob Curnow, Ken Hanna, Gene Rowland, Bob Graettinger and others, used by the Stan Kenton Band and given to North Texas State University in 1962 and at Kenton's death in 1979. Unpublished catalog: Breeden, Leon, *Stan Kenton Music in the NTSU Jazz Studies Library and the NTSU Music Library*, Denton, 1983 (99 pages).

MAIDS see Servants

MAIL ORDER CATALOGS

IL —SEARS, ROEBUCK & CO, Merchandise Development & Testing Laboratory Library, Sears Tower, Dept 817, Chicago, 60684. Mary M McCarron, Librn
Holdings: Cat Pix Microforms
Notes: Microfilmed sets of Sears, Roebuck catalogs have been placed in more that 100 libraries in key geographic locations. Contain catalogs from 1888 to date.

MAIL SERVICE see Postal Service

MAILER, NORMAN

NV —UNIVERSITY OF NEVADA, RENO, University Library, Special Collections Dept, Reno, 89557. Robert E Blesse, Head
Holdings: Vols (127) Cat
Notes: Includes individual works by author in all editions including translations; also prefaces, introductions, published correspondence, appearances in anthologies, periodicals, etc. Bibliographical research collection, part of Modern Authors Collection. Other appearances 350 cataloged.

MAINE

ME —BOWDOIN COLLEGE, Library, Brunswick, 04011. Dianne M Gutscher, Cur of Special Collections
Holdings: Cat
Notes: A collection of the works of Henry Beston, naturalist and author.
ME —UNIVERSITY OF MAINE AT PRESQUE ISLE LIBRARY, 181 Main St, Presque Isle, 04769. Anna McGrath, Technical Services Librn
Holdings: Vols 700
Notes: Aroostook County.
ME —BIGELOW LABORATORY FOR OCEAN SCIENCES & MAINE DEPT OF MARINE RESOURCES, Library, McKown Point, West Boothbay Harbor, 04575. Pamela Shephard-Lupo, Librn
Holdings: Vols Cat Mss
Budget: ($55,000)
Notes: This library presently serves two institutions. The Maine Dept of Marine Resources has maintained the library since 1957 and thus the majority of our holdings are geared to their needs, ie fish biology and stock assessment on a local, national and

MAINE (cont.)

international level. In 1973 Bigelow Laboratory for Ocean Sciences came to West Boothbay Harbor and began to contribute to the library with a very specialized collection on the Gulf of Maine marine chemistry, phytoplankton and nutrient cycles.

MAINE—GENEALOGY

ME —MAINE STATE LIBRARY, Special Collections Dept, Cultural Bldg, Station 64, Augusta, 04333. Shirley Thayer, Librn
Budget: ($2,500,000)
Notes: An extensive collection of Maine genealogy with a good representation of all New England. Non-circulating.

ME —MAINE HISTORICAL SOCIETY, Library, 485 Congress St, Portland, 04101.
Holdings: Vols (60,000) Cat Mss Maps Pix
Notes: The Society's holdings cover all Maine, with special emphasis on the Portland region.

ME —SANFORD LIBRARY ASSOCIATION, Louis B Goodall Memorial Library, 238 Main St, Sanford, 04073. Ken Scott, Librn
Holdings: Vols (2000) Cat Maps Pix Slides Phonorecords Audiotapes Filmstrips
Notes: Sanford history and Maine history. Incl Sanford's vital records, town newspapers, obituary index from *Biddeford Maine Journal Tribune*, Dec 1978-date.

ME —OLD YORK HISTORICAL SOCIETY, Library, PO Box 312, York, 03909. Eldridge H Pendleton, Dir of Collections
Holdings: Vols (3950) Cat Mss Maps Pix Clippings
Budget: $250
Notes: Maine history; York County Town Histories, Town of York Genealogies.

MA —AUBURN PUBLIC LIBRARY, Court & Spring Sts, Auburn, 04210. Nann Blaine Hilyard, Dir; Lois C Wagner, Ref Librn
Holdings: Vols (5000) Cat Mss Pix

MA —NEW ENGLAND HISTORIC GENEALOGICAL SOCIETY, Library, 101 Newbury St, Boston, 02116. Ralph J Crandell, Dir
Holdings: Vols (250,000) Mss Maps Microforms Pix
Notes: New England genealogy. Especially strong Massachusetts, Maine, and New Hampshire, although all states are well represented, as are the relevancies of each subject listed in this volume with regard to British antecedent and contemporary history. Special strengths in local history and biography, obituaries, etc, incl parish registers, censuses, British and American. 3125 linear ft of mss.

MAINE—HISTORY

CT —LEE ASH, (personal collection), 66 Humiston Dr, Bethany, 06525.
Holdings: Mss Maps Pix

ME —MAINE STATE LIBRARY, Special Collections Dept, Cultural Bldg, Station 64, Augusta, 04333. Shirley Thayer, Librn
Holdings: Vols Cat Mss Maps Pix
Budget: ($2,500,000)
Notes: Maine history, incl much on the Northeastern Boundary controversy, papers of Gov Percival Baxter, a very large photograph collection (incl glass slides), Maine music, mss, and an extensive collection of town histories.

ME —MAINE MARITIME MUSEUM, Library and Archives, 963 Washington St, Bath, 04530. Nathan R Lipfert, Asst Cur
Holdings: Vols (5000) Cat Maps Pix Slides
Notes: The collection is limited primarily to shipbuilding in Bath, Maine, and to a lesser extent Maine as a whole. The unique aspects of the collection are a large collection of photographs of wooden shipbuilding and related trades, photographs of the vessels themselves, and a large collection of papers of a shipbuilding company in Bath active throughout the 19th century.

ME —BOWDOIN COLLEGE, Library, Brunswick, 04011. Dianne M Gutscher, Cur of Special Collections
Holdings: Vols 13,000 Cat Mss Pix
Notes: Besides a general collection of 13,000

volumes relating to the State of Maine, there are also many mss collections touching on the political, economic, and social history of Maine. These include: Chase-Johnson Papers, 8000 mss relating to these two Brunswick families; Fessenden Family Papers, containing ca 4000 mss for the period 1801-1908; Hale-King Papers (700 letters 1787-1880) concerning these two Maine families and incl letters of Gov William King, first governor of Maine; Hubbard Family Papers, 12,000 pieces relating to the this Maine family, and incl extensive files of letters to and from Gov John Hubbard (1794-1869), governor of Maine, 1849-1853; McArthur Family Papers, 8000 pieces from this Limington, Maine, family, 1798-1810; Shepley Papers, 1000 items 1802-1910; Thacher Family Papers (400 letters) 1782-1892; Joseph Williamson Papers, 125letters of this Maine biographer; William Willis Papers (350 items) 1862-1869, of a president of the Maine Historical Society.

ME —RICE PUBLIC LIBRARY, 8 Wentworth St, Kittery, 03904. Hope B Neilson, Librn
Holdings: Cat Mss Pix
Notes: Items of regional and Maine history.

ME —LEWISTON PUBLIC LIBRARY, 118 Park St, Lewiston, 04240. Muriel P Landry, Actg Dir
Holdings: Vols 1547 Cat Mss Maps Pix
Notes: Collection comprised mostly of histories of Maine towns and cities. There is also much material on Maine writers. Local history is a special concern.

ME —UNIVERSITY OF MAINE AT ORONO, Raymond H Fogler Library, Special Collections Dept, Orono, 04469. Eric S Flower, Head
Holdings: Vols (9000) Mss Maps Pix Microforms
Budget: ($4000)
Notes: State of Maine Collection. Books by Maine authors; Maine-related subjects and Maine imprints. Index to *Maine Times*, vol 1 to present. Index to *Down East*, vol 1 to present. Collection incl 6500 state documents dated 1820 to present; 2000 maps; postcards. Telephone inquiries welcomed (581-1686).

ME —MAINE HISTORICAL SOCIETY, Library, 485 Congress St, Portland, 04101.
Holdings: Vols (60,000) Cat Mss Maps Pix
Notes: The Society's holdings cover all of Maine in its scope, with special emphasis on the Portland region.

ME —PORTLAND PUBLIC LIBRARY, 5 Monument Sq, Portland, 04101. Edward V Chenevert, Library Dir
Holdings: Vols 8500 Cat Maps Pix Microforms
Notes: State of Maine Collection. Books by Maine authors or about Maine-related subjects, and Maine imprints. Maine and Portland government documents dating back to 1829. Collection strong in Maine history and Maine literature and poetry.

ME —WILLIAM A FARNSWORTH LIBRARY & ART MUSEUM, 19 Elm St, Rockland, 04841. Marius B Peladeau, Dir
Holdings: Vols (4000) Cat Pix Mocroforms
Notes: Emphasis on American and European fine and decorative arts of all periods (largely modern). Other areas include marine history and Maine history (local); illustrated books and rare books also a part of our collection, which has its own catalog. Also, Louise Nevelsen, N C Wyeth Archives.

ME —SANFORD LIBRARY ASSOCIATION, Louis B Goodall Memorial Library, 238 Main St, Sanford, 04073. Ken Scott, Librn
Holdings: Vols (2000) Cat Maps Pix Slides Phonorecords Audiotapes Filmstrips
Notes: Sanford history and Maine history. Incl Sanford's vital records, town newspapers, obituary index from *Biddeford Maine Journal Tribune*, Dec 1978-date.

ME —PENOBSCOT MARINE MUSEUM, Library, Church St, Searsport, 04974. Charles Howard, Librn
Holdings: Vols (4000) Cat Mss Maps Pix
Budget: ($5000)
Notes: Maine maritime history, log books, journals, diaries, marine charts, ships registers, photographs, archives & mss, and

books relating to world navigation. The greatest emphasis is placed on the Penobscot Bay region.

ME —COLBY COLLEGE, Miller Library, Colby Archives, Waterville, 04901.
Holdings: Mss
Notes: Family papers or other correspondence.

ME —OLD YORK HISTORICAL SOCIETY, Library, PO Box 312, York, 03909. Eldridge H Pendleton, Dir of Collections
Holdings: Vols (3950) Cat Mss Maps Pix Clippings
Budget: $250
Notes: Maine history; York County Town Histories, Town of York Genealogies.

MA —AUBURN PUBLIC LIBRARY, Court & Spring Sts, Auburn, 04210. Nann Blaine Hilyard, Dir; Lois C Wagner, Ref Librn
Holdings: Vols (5000) Cat Mss Maps Pix

MA —NEW ENGLAND HISTORIC GENEALOGICAL SOCIETY, Library, 101 Newbury St, Boston, 02116. Ralph J Crandell, Dir
Holdings: Vols (250,000) Mss Maps Microforms Pix
Notes: New England genealogy. Especially strong Massachusetts, Maine, and New Hampshire, although all states are well represented, as are the relevancies of each subject listed in this volume with regard to British antecedent and contemporary history. Special strengths in local history and biography, obituaries, etc, incl parish registers, censuses, British and American. 3125 linear ft of mss.

MA —STATE LIBRARY OF MASSACHUSETTS, 341 State House, Boston, 02133. Gaspar Caso, State Librn
Holdings: Vols 2000 Cat Maps
Notes: Especially strong in pre-1820 history.

MA —OLD STURBRIDGE VILLAGE, Research Library, Sturbridge, 01566. Theresa Rini Percy, Librn
Holdings: Cat Maps
Notes: To 1900.

MAINE—IMPRINTS

ME —BOWDOIN COLLEGE, Library, Brunswick, 04011. Dianne M Gutscher, Cur of Special Collections
Holdings: Vols 800 Cat
Notes: Imprints to 1835.

ME —MAINE HISTORICAL SOCIETY, Library, 485 Congress St, Portland, 04101.
Holdings: Vols (60,000) Cat Mss Maps Pix
Notes: The Society's holdings cover all of Maine, with special emphasis on the Portland region.

MAINE—INDIANS

MA —COLLEGE OF THE HOLY CROSS, Dinand Library, College St, Worcester, 01610. James M Mahoney, Cur of Special Collection
Holdings: Uncat Mss Pix
Notes: The John J Williams SJ collection contains correspondence, notes on history of Passamaquoddy tribe; (86) letters and copies of documents concerning Maine Indians from 1778-1913; pictures and 3 notebooks. Restricted use, noncirculating.

MAINE—NATURAL RESOURCES

ME —BIGELOW LABORATORY FOR OCEAN SCIENCES & MAINE DEPT OF MARINE RESOURCES, Library, McKown Point, West Boothbay Harbor, 04575. Pamela Shephard-Lupo, Librn
Holdings: Vols Cat Doc
Budget: ($55,000)
Notes: This library presently serves two institutions. The Maine Dept of Marine Resources has maintained the library since 1957 and thus the majority of our holdings are geared to their needs, ie fish biology and stock assessment on a local, national and international level. In 1973 Bigelow Laboratory for Ocean Sciences came to West Boothbay Harbor and began to contribute to the library with a very specialized collection on the Gulf of Maine marine chemistry, phytoplankton and nutrient cycles.

MAINE—POLITICS AND GOVERNMENT

ME —BOWDOIN COLLEGE, Library, Brunswick, 04011. Dianne M Gutscher, Cur of Special Collections
Holdings: Mss Pix
Notes: (1) The Chamberlain Papers consist of 1900 mss pieces of correspondence, addresses, lecture notes, diaries, and clippings relating to Chamberlain's career in the United States Army (1862-1865), as governor of Maine (1867-1870), and as president of Bowdoin College (1871-1883). (2) The Fessenden Family Papers contain 4000 mss for the period 1801-1908 and incl almost 1300 letters written by William Pitt Fessenden, US Senator from Maine, 1854-1869, and Secretary of the Treasury, 1864-65. (3) The Hubbard Family papers contain more than 12,000 pieces of correspondence and other mss materials relating to the Hubbard Family, for the period 1794-1915. Of principal interest are extensive files of letters to and from John Hubbard (1794-1869), governor of Maine, who signed the "Maine Law" (prohibition law) in 1851, and was a commissionerunder the Reciprocity Treaty with Great Britain. (4) The Thomas Brackett Reed Papers contain 200 pieces of correspondence, primarily relating to his career in the House of Representatives, incl his terms as Speaker. Two large scrapbooks of newsclippings are also part of the collection.

ME —MARGARET CHASE SMITH LIBRARY CENTER, Skowhegan, 04976. James C MacCampbell, Dir
Notes: Senator Margaret Chase Smith's papers, her home and property in Skowhegan, donated by her to Northwood Institute, a business education college headquartered in Midland, Michigan. Also information on Senator Joseph McCarthy.

MAINE AUTHORS see Authors, Maine

MAINE COMPOSERS see Composers, Maine

MAINE MUSIC see Music, Maine

MAINE NEWSPAPERS see Newspapers, Maine

MAINE SEACOAST ISLANDS

CT —LEE ASH, (personal collection), 66 Humiston Dr, Bethany, 06525.
Holdings: Cat Mss Pix
Notes: Mss, notes, letters pictures, memorabilia, ephemera, etc, especially about Monhegan Island.

MAIZE—DISEASES AND PESTS

OH —OHIO AGRICULTURAL RESEARCH & DEVELOPMENT CENTER, Dept of Plant Pathology, Madison Ave, Wooster, 44691. Richard M Ritter
Holdings: Vols 2000 Papers Journal Reprints
Notes: Maize viruses and corn stunt. The Maize Virus Information Service (Mavis) was started in 1971 and aims to become the world center for this literature. The collection aims to be exhaustive for all true virus diseases affecting the maize plant (corn) and for corn stunt, which is caused by a mycoplasma, but was once thought to be caused by a virus. A preliminary list (500 refs) was published in 1971, with yearly supplements.

MAJAKOVSKII, VLADIMIR

MA —HARVARD UNIVERSITY LIBRARY, Widener Library, Cambridge, 02138.
Holdings: Cat Mss Microforms
Notes: For account of microfilms of manuscripts, see *Harvard Library Bulletin* IX (1955), 285-287.

MAJOR, HERMON S., 1876-1961

KS —MENNINGER FOUNDATION, Archives, 5600 W Sixth St, Box 829, Topeka, 66601. Alice Brand, Librn; Mark West, Archivist
Notes: 2 boxes, 1904-45. The collection contains photographs, clinic records, certificates, and miscellaneous materials.

MAKEUP (COSMETICS) see Cosmetics

MAKHORKA see Tobacco

MAKLAKOV, VASILII ALEKSEEVICH

CA —HOOVER INSTITUTION ON WAR, REVOLUTION & PEACE, Stanford University, Stanford, 94305. Milorad M Drachkovitch, Archivist
Holdings: // Mss
Notes: Papers, 1917-1923, of Vasilii Alekseevich Maklakov, ambassador to France, appointed by the Russian Provisional Government, 1917, and member of the Russian Political Conference, Paris, 1919. Diplomatic correspondence, reports, memoranda and notes relating to the activities of anti-Bolshevik groups, to questions of interest to White Russian groups before the Paris Peace Conference and to events and conditions during the period of civil war in Russia. The records are from the Russian embassy archives in Paris. 9 ft.

MALABAR LANGUAGE see Malayalam Language

MALACOLOGY see Mollusks

MALAGASY DEMOCRATIC REPUBLIC see Madagascar

MALAGASY LANGUAGE

NY —NEW YORK PUBLIC LIBRARY, Oriental Div, Fifth Ave & 42 St, New York, 10018. E Christian Filstrup, Chief
Holdings: // Cat Mss Microforms
Budget: ($56,455)
Notes: Published catalog of holdings.

MALAMUD, BERNARD

NV —UNIVERSITY OF NEVADA, RENO, University Library, Special Collections Dept, Reno, 89557. Robert E Blesse, Head
Holdings: Vols (57) Cat
Notes: Includes individual works by author in all editions including translations; also prefaces, introductions, published correspondence, appearances in anthologies, periodicals, etc. Bibliographical research collection, part of Modern Authors Collection. Other appearances 65 cataloged.

MALANGA, GERARD, 1943-

CA —UNIVERSITY OF CALIFORNIA, LOS ANGELES, Research Library, Dept of Special Collections, 405 Hilgard Ave, Los Angeles, 90024. Edward Shreeves, Chairman, Bibliographers Group; David S Zeidberg, Head
Holdings: Vols 40 Mss
Notes: Incl 15 linear feet of mss and correspondence.

MALARIAL FEVER

MD —MEDICAL & CHIRURGICAL FACULTY OF THE STATE OF MARYLAND, Library, 1211 Cathedral St, Baltimore, 21201. Joseph E Jensen, Librn
Holdings: Vols (10,000) // Cat Mss Maps Pix
See also entry under Medicine - History and Historic

TX —UNIVERSITY OF TEXAS, DALLAS, Health Science Center, Reference Dept & History of Health Sciences Dept, 5323 Harry Hines Blvd, Dallas, 75235. Helen Mayo, Head
Holdings: Vols (10,000) Cat Pix Slides Audiotapes Videotapes Microforms
Notes: History of Medicine collection contains ca 10,000 vols. This total is comprised of pre-1900 journals, primary materials in the History of Medicine and the History of Science, and secondary studies in these two areas. The major strengths of this collection are in the areas of epidemics and plagues, military medicine, and collected works of famous medical pioneers. Incl in this collection are the medical journals published by the county medical societies in Texas, local publications by Dallas County medical organizations, and ephemeral material in a similar vein. The university archives contain all theses and dissertations form UTHSCD and miscellaneous institutional documents circulated by the school's administration.

MALAWI

DC —HOWARD UNIVERSITY, Moorland-Spingarn Research Center, 500 Howard Place NW, Washington, 20059. Clifford L Muse, Jr, Acting Dir

WI —SEVENTH DAY BAPTIST HISTORICAL SOCIETY, Library, 3120 Kennedy Rd, PO Box 1678, Janesville, 53547. D Scott Smith, Historian
Holdings: Uncat Mss Maps Pix Slides
Notes: Nyasaland (Malawi) Collection. These materials (1895-1914) deal with the founding of Baptist work in Central Africa by Joseph Booth, his influence on John Chilembwa and others in the Blantyre area and in the northern provinces of the country. Founded by Seventh Day Baptists, the mission was sold to Seventh-Day Adventists and then later (1947) reopened with the help of native leaders who had remained Seventh Day Baptists. Incl correspondence, reports, ledgers, deeds. NUCMC - MS 72-1226.

MALAY LANGUAGE see Malaysian Language and Literature

MALAY-POLYNESIAN LANGUAGES see Malaysian Language and Literature

MALAYA see Malaysia

MALAYALAM LANGUAGE

MO —UNIVERSITY OF MISSOURI-COLUMBIA, Ellis Library, Ninth and Lowry, Columbia, 65201. Murari Lal Nagar, Librn
Holdings: Vols 100,000 Maps Microforms
Notes: The South Asia Studies Program at the University of Missouri-Columbia, is an interdepartmental, multi-disciplinary area studies program on India, Pakistan, Bangladesh, Sri Lanka and Nepal. Depository for the PL480 Program of the Library of Congress in many languages from South Asia. There are library resources in Sankskrit, Hindi, Bengali, Panjabi, and Malayalam. The library is particularly strong in Baroda, Bengal and the Punjab.

NY —NEW YORK PUBLIC LIBRARY, Oriental Div, Fifth Ave & 42 St, New York, 10018. E Christian Filstrup, Chief
Holdings: Cat Mss Microforms
Budget: ($56,455)
Notes: Published catalog of holdings.

MALAYSIA

CA —UNIVERSITY OF CALIFORNIA, LOS ANGELES, Research Library, Indo/Pacific Collection, 405 Hilgard Ave, Los Angeles, 90024. Edward Shreeves, Chairman, Bibliographers Group; Charlotte Spence, Indo/Pacific Bibliographer
Holdings: Vols Cat Mss Maps Pix Microforms
Notes: The Southeast Asian collection has been developed on a combination of the research and teaching levels; it focuses on the cultural, economic, political and social history of the area from ancient times to the present day. Although all the individual countries of the region are represented, some priority is given to Malaysia, Singapore, Indonesia and the Philippines. The majority of the materials is in Western languages except for a collection of several thousand books in Thai, and a smaller collection of

MALAYSIA (cont.)

materials in Vietnamese, Indonesian, Malaysian, and the Philippine languages.

HI —UNIVERSITY OF HAWAII, Library, 2550 The Mall, Honolulu, 96822. Joyce Wright, Head, Asia Collection; Masato Matsu, Head, East Asia Vernacular Collection
Holdings: Vols 331,620 Cat Microforms
Notes: The Asia Collection holds materials from and about Southeast Asia: Brunei, Burma, Cambodia (Kampuchea), Indonesia, Laos, Malaysia, Philippines, Singapore, Thailand. Large contemporary Indonesian language collection. Several thousand vols in Thai and in Vietnamese. Minimal holdings in Burmese, Khmer, Lao languages. Social sciences and humanities emphasis for the post-World War II period. Western language coverage supplemented by retrospective holdings in the main library collection.

IL —CENTER FOR RESEARCH LIBRARIES, 6050 S Kenwood Ave, Chicago, 60637. Donald B Simpson, Dir; Esther Smith, Collection Development Librn
Notes: Selected monographs, serials and government documents received on NPAC 1971 forward.

IL —NORTHERN ILLINOIS UNIVERSITY, Founders Memorial Library, Southeast Asia Collection, Normal Rd, De Kalb, 60115. Lee S Dutton Dr, Cur
Holdings: Vols (34,000) Cat Maps Microforms
Notes: An extensive collection of books, periodicals, newspapers, maps, and microforms from or about Southeast Asia. Areas of concentration incl Thailand, Malaysia, Indonesia, Singapore, Brunei, Philippines, Laos, and Burma. Holdings (except rare books, maps, and microforms) are housed in a separate area collection within the Founders Library. A departmental card catalog and specialized reference collection support reference services. A Thai collection of several thousand vols is the largest vernacular component. Extensive Malaysia, Indonesia, Singapore, and Brunei holdings have been acquired through the NPAC program. A collection of Filipino-American newspapers, and a growing collection of children's literature in common and uncommon Southeast Asian languages are available. Resources are accessible to borrowers through OCLC.

MI —UNIVERSITY OF MICHIGAN, Harlan Hatcher Graduate Library, Ann Arbor, 48109. Susan Go, Librn
Holdings: Vols (250,000) Cat Mss Maps Pix Slides Microforms
Notes: Incl in the Michigan Historical Collections (primarily archival material) are papers of Michiganders in southeast Asia, mostly the Philipines, eg papers of Joseph R Hayden, Frank Murphy and G Mennen Williams, also, on film, the selected papers of Philippines president Manuel Quezon. All aspects of the countries, cultures and peoples of Brunei, Burma, Khymer, Indonesia, Laos, Malaysia, Philippines, Singapore, Thailand, Portuguese Timor and Vietnam. Also the Malayo-Polynesian (Austronesian), Mon-Khmer (Austroasiatic), and Sino-Tibetan language groupings.

NY —CORNELL UNIVERSITY LIBRARIES, John M Olin Library, John M Echols Collection on Southeast Asia, Ithaca, 14853. Giok Po Oey, Curator
Holdings: Vols (167,000) Cat Mss Maps Pix Microforms
Budget: ($90,000)
Notes: Additions published in the collection's monthly accessions list (Ithaca: Cornell University, Southeast Asia Program, 1959-). Holdings through December 1980 listed in *Cornell University Libraries Southeast Asia Catalog* (Boston: G K Hall, 1976, First supplement, 1983), 10 vols.

OH —OHIO UNIVERSITY, Vernon R Alden Library, Southeast Asia Collection, Athens, 45701. Lian The-Mulliner, Head
Holdings: Vols (68,000) Cat Maps Slides Phonorecords Videotapes 16mm Films Filmstrips Microforms
Budget: ($35,000)
Notes: Emphasis on Indonesia, Malaysia,

Singapore, Brunei and the Philippines. Incl language and literature, history, civilization and culture, art, medicine, philosophy and economic conditions. Separate catalog.

MALAYSIAN LANGUAGE AND LITERATURE

CA —CLAREMONT COLLEGES, Honnold Library, Ninth & Dartmouth, Claremont, 91711. Tania Rizzo, Special Collections Dept Head
Holdings: Vols 150 // Uncat
Notes: Grammars and dictionaries (some dual-language with French or Dutch) of mainly Malayo-Polynesian, some Sino-Tibetan, and other languages, dating from the late 19th to mid-20th centuries. Checklisted.

CA —UNIVERSITY OF CALIFORNIA, LOS ANGELES, Research Library, Indo/Pacific Collection, 405 Hilgard Ave, Los Angeles, 90024. Edward Shreeves, Chairman, Bibliographers Group; Charlotte Spence, Indo/Pacific Bibliographer
Holdings: Vols Cat Mss Maps Pix Microforms
Notes: The Southeast Asian collection has been developed on a combination of the research and teaching levels; it focuses on the cultural, economic, political and social history of the area from ancient times to the present day. Although all the individual countries of the region are represented, some priority is given to Malaysia, Singapore, Indonesia and the Philippines. The majority of the materials is in Western languages except for a collection of several thousand books in Thai, and a smaller collection of materials in Vietnamese, Indonesian, Malaysian, and the Philippine languages.

NY —NEW YORK PUBLIC LIBRARY, Oriental Div, Fifth Ave & 42 St, New York, 10018. E Christian Filstrup, Chief
Holdings: // Cat Mss Microforms
Budget: ($56,455)
Notes: Published catalog of holdings. Currently collected in Western language materials only.

MALEMBA LANGUAGE see Congo Languages and Literature

MALET FAMILY

NC —DUKE UNIVERSITY, William R Perkins Library, Manuscript Dept, Durham, 27706. Ellen Gartrell, Cur of Mss
Holdings: Cat Mss
Notes: Incl 50,000 items, 18th-20th centuries, representing the political, diplomatic, military, ecclesiastical, and economic affairs of Great Britain and the British Empire. Incl papers of William Wilberforce, William Smith, John Wilson Croker, John Backhouse, Malet Family, etc.

MALFORMATIONS see Deformities

MALGACHE LANGUAGE see Malagasy Language

MALI

DC —HOWARD UNIVERSITY, Moorland-Spingarn Research Center, 500 Howard Place NW, Washington, 20059. Clifford L Muse, Jr, Acting Dir

MI —MICHIGAN STATE UNIVERSITY, International Library, Sahel Documentation Center, East Lansing, 48824. Eugene deBenko, Librn; Learthen Dorsey, Librn
Holdings: Vols (5100) Cat Mss Maps Pix Slides Phonorecords Audiotapes Videotapes Microforms
Budget: ($8000)
Notes: See description under The Sahel.

MALINA, FRANK

CA —CALIFORNIA INSTITUTE OF TECHNOLOGY, Robert A Millikan Memorial Library, Archives, 1201 E California Blvd, Pasadena, 91125. Judith R Goodstein, Archivist
Notes: Interviewed for the Oral History

Program of the Archives. Microfiche publication of his scientific and literary correspondence.

MALINA, JUDITH

CA —UNIVERSITY OF CALIFORNIA, DAVIS, Shields Library, Dept of Special Collections, Davis, 95616. Donald Kunitz, Head; C Danial Elliott, Asst Head
Holdings: Vols 1700 Cat Mss Pix Phonorecords Audiotapes Videotapes
Notes: Archives of the Living Theatre founded by Julian Beck and Judith Malina incl directing, lighting, and master scripts; correspondence; contracts; original art; programs; posters; reviews; photographs by Mantegna and Lissinger; performance notes an diagrams; music; Malina's diaries; published texts; financial records.

MALING, ARTHUR

MA —BOSTON UNIVERSITY, Mugar Memorial Library, Special Collections Dept, 771 Commonwealth Ave, Boston, 02215. Howard B Gotlieb, Dir
Holdings: Cat Mss

MALINOWSKI, BRONISLAW

CA —UNIVERSITY OF CALIFORNIA, SANTA CRUZ, University Library, Special Collections, Santa Cruz, 95064. Rita Bottoms, Special Collections Librn; Margaret Felts, South Pacific Collection Bibliographer
Notes: South Pacific Collection. His personal library and collection of material on the South Pacific Region and Antropology of the South Pacific.
See also entry under Islands of the Pacific.

CT —YALE UNIVERSITY, Box 1603A, Yale Station, New Haven, 06520.
Holdings: Cat Mss
Notes: Bronislaw Malinowski's correspondence, 1914-1939; also his writings, lectures, research notes, etc.

MALLARME, STEPHANE

MO —SOUTHWEST MISSOURI STATE UNIVERSITY, Duane G Meyer Library, 901 S National, Box 175, Springfield, 65804. Robert D Harvey, Dir
Holdings: Cat Mss
Notes: Incl material by and about Stephane Mallarme over 200 items.

MALLETT, JANE

†ON —METROPOLITAN TORONTO LIBRARY, Theatre Dept, Toronto, M4W 2G8, Can.
Notes: Copies of papers and scripts selected from private collection of Jane Mallett, Canadian actress. Originals will be deposited with the Public Archives of Canada.

MALLETTE, REV. DANIEL J.

IL —CHICAGO HISTORICAL SOCIETY, Library, Clark St at North Ave, Chicago, 60614. Archie Motley, Manuscript Librn
Notes: Papers of Roman Catholic priest and social activist.

MALMED, LEON, 1881-1956

MA —RADCLIFFE COLLEGE, Arthur & Elizabeth Schlesinger Library on the History of Women in America, 3 James St, Cambridge, 02138. Patricia Miller King, Dir; Eva Moseley, Cur of Mss
Notes: More than 500 letters written by Emma Goldman, most to Leon Malmed (1881-1956), a comrade in the anarchist movement and for a time her lover; also photographs, writings, pamphlets, etc.

MALOFF, SAUL

MA —BOSTON UNIVERSITY, Mugar Memorial Library, Special Collections Dept, 771 Commonwealth Ave, Boston, 02215. Howard B Gotlieb, Dir
Holdings: Cat Mss
Notes: Mss, correspondence, etc collected in depth; incl publications by or about.

MALTA

MN —SAINT JOHN'S ABBEY &
UNIVERSITY, Hill Monastic Manuscript
Library, Collegeville, 56321. Julian G Plante,
Dir
Holdings: Vols (5500) Cat Mss Slides
Microforms
Notes: A systematic program to microfilm
mss of collections in Mdina (Cathedral,
Museum), and other Maltese collections. In
addition to the microfilmed body of primary
source materials, published secondary source
materials are being regularly added to the
collection.

MALTA, KNIGHTS OF see Knights of Malta

MALTESE LANGUAGE AND LITERATURE

NY —NEW YORK PUBLIC LIBRARY,
Oriental Div, Fifth Ave & 42 St, New York,
10018. E Christian Filstrup, Chief
Holdings: Cat Mss Microforms
Budget: ($56,455)
Notes: Published catalog of holdings.

MALTWOOD, KATHARINE EMMA

BC —UNIVERSITY OF VICTORIA,
McPherson Library, Victoria, V8W 3H5,
Can.
Notes: Sculptress. Mss, correspondence,
illustrations and clippings concerning the
Glastonbury Temple of the Stars;
photographs of the artist's sculptures and
personal photographs.

MALTZ, ALBERT

MA —BOSTON UNIVERSITY, Mugar
Memorial Library, Special Collections Dept,
771 Commonwealth Ave, Boston, 02215.
Howard B Gotlieb, Dir
Holdings: Cat Mss Pix
Notes: Mss, correspondence, etc collected in
depth; incl publications by or about.

MALUKU see Indonesia

MAMMALS AND MAMMALOGY

CA —UNIVERSITY OF CALIFORNIA,
BERKELEY, Museum of Vertebrate
Zoology, Grinnell-Miller Library, Berkeley,
94720.
CA —UNIVERSITY OF CALIFORNIA, LOS
ANGELES, Biomedical Library, Center for
Health Sciences, Los Angeles, 90024. Louise
Darling, Biomedical Librn
Holdings: Vols (4000) Cat
Notes: Incl the Donald R Dickey Library of
Vertebrate Zoology. Classics of ornithology
and mammalogy and related materials.
CA —CALIFORNIA ACADEMY OF
SCIENCES, J W Mailliard Jr Library,
Golden Gate Park, San Francisco, 94118.
Ray Brian, Librn
Notes: Downs No 2160.
DC —SMITHSONIAN INSTITUTION
LIBRARIES, Natural History Branch,
Washington, 20560. Sylvia Churgin, Chief
Librn
Holdings: Vols 1450 Cat Maps Slides
FL —ARCHBOLD BIOLOGICAL STATION,
Library, Rt 2, Box 180, Lake Placid, 33852.
Fred E Lohrer, Librn
Holdings: Uncat VF
Notes: Physiological ecology of vertebrates.
Incl 3 vertical files of reprints, etc. Extensive
and growing cataloged collection on Florida
mammals also. (Library is no longer
enlarging reprint collection.)
IL —FIELD MUSEUM OF NATURAL
HISTORY, Library, Roosevelt Rd & Lake
Shore Dr, Chicago, 60605. W Peyton
Fawcett, Librn; Benjamin W Williams, Assoc
Librn
Holdings: Vols (210,000) Ca
Budget: ($100,000)
Notes: Extensive collections--publications of
learned societies and institutions and

monographic works--in all fields of natural
history, with emphasis on taxonomy and
evolutionary biology; and on museum
publications, American and foreign:
anthropology, especially archaeology and
ethnology of the Americas, Africa, East
Asia, and Oceania; botany, particularly
strong for the Americas; geology, chiefly
paleontology and meteoritic studies; and
zoology, worldwide (birds, fishes, insects,
mammals, mollusks, reptiles and
amphibians).
IA —IOWA STATE UNIVERSITY, College of
Veterinary Medicine, Veterinary Medical
Library, Ames, 50011. Sara R Peterson,
Librn
Holdings: Vols (17,000) Cat Microforms
Notes: Incl comparative and veterinary
medicine with emphasis in the fields of
mammalian anatomy and physiology,
laboratory animal medicine, pathology,
toxicology, biomedical engineering and
clinical veterinary medicine. Inc 2000
uncataloged German theses.
MI —UNIVERSITY OF MICHIGAN,
Museums Library, Ann Arbor, 48109.
Patricia B Yocum, Librn
Holdings: Vols 6000 Cat
NY —NEW YORK ZOOLOGICAL SOCIETY
LIBRARY, Bronx Zoo, Bronx, 10460.
Steven P Johnson, Archivist and Librn
Holdings: Vols (6000) Cat Mss
Budget: ($50,000)
Notes: Collection consists primarily of
journals in captive management of animals,
vertebrate zoology, and veterinary medicine.
Primarily intended for the scientific staff, the
collection is open to the public on a
noncirculating basis, by appointment, (212)
220-6874.
NY —AMERICAN MUSEUM OF
NATURAL HISTORY, Library Services
Dept, Central Park W & 79th St, New York,
10024. Nina J Root, Chairwoman; Mary
Genett, Asst Librn for Reference Services
Holdings: Vols (385,000) Cat Mss Maps Pix
Slides Microforms
Notes: Nearly all collections are outstanding
for depth of coverage and international
range. Early and historic works, rare books,
colored illustrations, and relevant serial
publications supplement the modern
scientific publications necessary to the
researches of the scientific staff and the
work of the educational division. Open to
the public.
PA —ACADEMY OF NATURAL SCIENCES
LIBRARY, 19 Benjamin Franklin Parkway,
Philadelphia, 19103.
Holdings: Vols (180,000) Cat Mss Maps Pix
Slides Microforms
Notes: Incl (250,000) mss. Described in
*Academy of Natural Sciences of
Philadelphia: Catalog* (Boston: G K Hall,
1972); *Guide to the Manuscript Collections
in the Academy of Natural Sciences of
Philadelphia*, by Venia T Phillips
(Philadelphia: Academy of Natural Sciences,
1963).
PA —ZOOLOGICAL SOCIETY OF
PHILADELPHIA, Library, 34 & Girard
Ave, Philadelphia, 19104. Alyssa N
Scheuermann, Librn
Holdings: Vols (1000) Cat
Notes: Photocopying with permission,
collection filed by order.
PA —CARNEGIE LIBRARY OF
PITTSBURGH, Science & Technology Dept,
4400 Forbes Ave, Pittsburgh, 15213.
Catherine M Brosky, Dept Head
Notes: Subject of secondary interest with
emphasis on North America. Covers
paleobotany, vertebrates and invertebrates,
foraminifera, mollusks, fish, reptiles,
mammals. Abstracts, indexes, catalogs,
bibliographies, journals, continuations,
federal, state and society publications
available.
ON —NATIONAL MUSEUMS OF
CANADA, Library Services Directorate,
Ottawa, K1A 0M8, Can. Valerie
Monkhouse, Director
Holdings: Vols (90,000) Cat Mss Microforms
Budget: ($81,000)
Notes: Emphasis on Canadian and
circumpolar natural history. Collection incl

botany, herpetology, ichthyology,
invertebrate zoology, malacology,
mammology, mineralogy, ornithology,
paleobiology, zooarchaeology. Exceptional
collections in lichenology, bryology,
malacology, ornithology. Research
collection, interlibrary loans available, public
may use on the premises.
ON —ROYAL ONTARIO MUSEUM, Main
Library and Archives, 100 Queen's Park,
Toronto, M5S 2C6, Can. Julia Matthews,
Head Librn
Holdings: Vols (85,000) Cat
Notes: Since January 1977, acquisitions have
been entered in UTLAS.

MAMMOTH CAVE, KENTUCKY

KY —WESTERN KENTUCKY
UNIVERSITY, Kentucky Library, Bowling
Green, 42101. Riley Handy, Head, Special
Collections; Connie Mills, Maps & Music
Librn; Nancy Baird, Photographs Librn;
Nancy Solley, Conservation Librn
Holdings: Vols (25,000) Cat Mss Maps Pix
Microforms
Notes: Besides Kentucky history, other
strengths are Mammoth Cave, South Union
Shakers, Kentucky religion; and steamboat
photos (3300 cataloged pictures); 8000
Kentucky postal cards, etc.

MAN—ORIGIN see Humanoids—Origin

MAN, FOSSIL see Fossil Humanoids

MAN, PRIMITIVE see Primitive Societies

MAN AND WIFE see Husband and Wife

MAN POWER see Manpower

MANAGEMENT

AL —UNIVERSITY OF ALABAMA, Business
Library, Box 2937, University, 35486.
Dorothy Eady Brown, Librn; Linda Suttle
Harris, Ref Librn and Data Base Searcher
Holdings: Vols (103,000) Cat Microforms
Budget: ($60,000)
Notes: Incl 90,000 corporation reports and
38,500 microforms.
CA —UNIVERSITY OF CALIFORNIA,
BERKELEY, Institute of Transportation
Studies Library, Library, 412 McLaughlin
Hall, Berkeley, 94720.
Holdings: Vols (82,000)
Budget: ($215,000)
Notes: US Department of Transportation
depository through NTIS.
CA —KAISER FOUNDATION HOSPITAL,
Management Effectiveness Library, 4747
Sunset Blvd, Los Angeles, 90027. Marilyn
Crawford, Librn
Holdings: Vols (1000) Cat Maps Slides
Audiotapes
Notes: Small, selective management,
business, and health care collection, with
many US and state health-related reports
and a few health newsletters. Internal index
to printed materials and audiotapes.
CA —UNIVERSITY OF CALIFORNIA, LOS
ANGELES, Graduate School of
Management Library, UCLA Campus, Los
Angeles, 90024. Robert Bellanti, Head Librn
Holdings: Vols (128,000) Cat Mss
Microforms
Notes: The
CA —UNIVERSITY OF SOUTHERN
CALIFORNIA, Crocker Business Library,
Hoffman Hall, University Park, Los Angeles,
90007. Judith A Truelson, Head Librn
Holdings: Vols (100,000) Cat Microforms
Notes: The Roy P Crocker Library of
Business Administration, located in Hoffman
Hall, houses more than 100,000 volumes and
regularly receives approximately 1500 trade,
financial, economics, labor, and general
business periodicals and newspapers. The
areas of subject concentration include
business economics, finance and investments,
general management/management theory,
international business, finance and
management, marketing/food marketing, and
quantitative business analysis.
CA —HUGHES AIRCRAFT CO, Solid State
Products Library, 500 Superior Ave,

MANAGEMENT (cont.)

Newport Beach, 92663. Barbara Squyres, Librn
Holdings: Vols (4500)
Budget: ($17,000)
Notes: Incl 2600 journal vols and 500 microforms.

CA —ALAMEDA COUNTY LIBRARY SYSTEM, Business & Government Library, 2201 Broadway, Oakland, 94612. David Lewallen, Manager
Holdings: Vols (10,000) Cat Maps Microforms
Budget: ($50,000)

CA —PASADENA PUBLIC LIBRARY, Business-Technology Division, 285 E Walnut St, Pasadena, 91101. Anne Cain, Librn for Reference Services
Holdings: Vols (19,000) Cat Microforms
Budget: ($35,000)
Notes: Investment and financial services (current and historical); trade and industrial directories; corporate annual reports; current economic statistics in business services and in state and federal government publications. Special index to directory collection.

CA —CONTRA COSTA COUNTY LIBRARY, 1750 Oak Park Blvd, Pleasant Hill, 94523. Lyn Talme, Business Specialist
Holdings: Vols (7000)
Notes: Incl 76 periodicals, 1000 corporate annual reports, and 316 telephone directories.

CA —CUBIC CORP, Technical Library, 9333 Balboa Ave, PO Box 85587, San Diego, 92138. Maxine Moser, Mgr Tech Librn; Ann Viera, Librn
Holdings: Vols (2500) Cat Maps Microforms
Budget: ($60,000)
Notes: Incl about 20,000 microforms and 1000 bound periodicals, technical reports, technical memoranda. On-line search service for employees, including DIALOG, BRS, SDC, DTIC/DROLS, NASA/RECON, RLIN, DMS.

CA —HOOVER INSTITUTION ON WAR, REVOLUTION & PEACE, Stanford University, Stanford, 94305. Milorad M Drachkovitch, Archivist
Holdings: Mss
Notes: Stenographic transcripts of the minutes of the First and Second National Industrial Conferences of 1919-1920. 15 ms boxes.

CT —UNIVERSITY OF CONNECTICUT, HARTFORD, School of Business Administration, Library, 39 Woodland St, Hartford, 06105.
Holdings: Vols (17,000) Cat Audiotapes Microforms
Notes: Incl 8 vertical file drawers of pamphlets, etc; 60 of annual reports.

CT —YALE UNIVERSITY, Social Science Library, 140 Prospect St, New Haven, 06520. Billie I Salter, Librn
Holdings: Vols (40,000) Cat Microforms
See also entry under Social Sciences

CT —STAMFORD'S PUBLIC LIBRARY, Ferguson Library, Adult Services Dept, 96 Broad St, Stamford, 06901. Ernest A DiMattia Jr, Dir; Doris Goodlett, Head Adult Servs
Holdings: Vols (29,500) Cat

DC —AMERICAN SOCIETY OF ASSOCIATION EXECUTIVES, Information Central, 1575 Eye St NW, Washington, 20005. Cathy L Lalush, Mgr of Research and Info
Notes: Information regarding association management. Resources are designed to provide the association executive with the background knowledge for management decisions through case studies, research and statistical reports, bibliographies, and articles.

DC —INTERNATIONAL LABOR ORGANIZATION, International Labor Office, Washington Branch Library, 1750 New York Ave NW, Rm 330, Washington, 20006. Karen J Mark, Librn
Holdings: Vols (13,500) Cat Pix 16mm Films Monographs
Notes: Wide range of titles dealing with worldwide labor and social matters. The library contains ILO publications and documentation only, dating back to 1919. Also, a collection of ILO films and photos. See Subject Guide to Publications of the ILO, 1919-1964 and ILO Catalogue of Publications in Print, 1982 (ILO).

GA —ATLANTA PUBLIC LIBRARY, Ivan Allen Jr Dept of Science, Industry & Government, One Margaret Mitchell Square, Atlanta, 30303. William D Munro, Head
Holdings: Vols (15,000) Cat Microforms
Budget: ($180,000)
Notes: This collection incl on microform annual reports and Securities Exchange Commission 10-K reports for some 11,000 companies from 1976 to date; current and retrospective stock quotations, stock reports, corporate and industry records and directories and supporting looseleaf services; information file on Atlanta's largest 15,000 with annual updates; and current plat maps for the five county Metro-Atlanta area. Atlanta and Georgia business history sections are being developed. Most material on this collection is noncirculating.

IL —CHICAGO PUBLIC LIBRARY, Business/Science/Technology Div, Science/Technology Information Center, 425 North Michigan Ave, Chicago, 60611. Lynda Sanford, Head; John R Moore, Environment Collection Coordinator & Engineering Librn
Holdings: Vols 60,000
Budget: $205,000
Notes: Collection incl all subject areas of business within HB-HJ Library of Congress classifications scheme. Emphases are on current materials in management, careers, investments, and reference. Collection is also strong in labor history. 2200 periodical titles; 60,000 vols monographs.

IL —CONTINENTAL ILLINOIS NATIONAL BANK & TRUST CO OF CHICAGO, Information Services Division, 231 S LaSalle St, Chicago, 60697. Susan J Montgomery, Mgr
Holdings: Vols (27,700) Cat Microforms

IL —ILLINOIS BELL TELEPHONE CO, Library, 225 W Randolph St, Chicago, 60606. Marguerite J Krynicki, Head Librn
Holdings: Vols (11,000) Cat

IL —LESTER B KNIGHT & ASSOCIATES, Library, 549 W Randolph St, Chicago, 60606. Clarita M Generao, Librn
Holdings: Vols (10,000) Cat Maps Slides
Notes: Collection is both technical and nontechnical; incl reports of the studies for our client companies, which incl European firms.

IL —LIBRARY OF THE AMERICAN HOSPITAL ASSOCIATION, Asa S Bacon Memorial, 840 N Lake Shore Dr, Chicago, 60611. Eloise C Foster, Dir
Holdings: Vols (39,000) Cat
Budget: ($95,000)
Notes: Literature on non-clinical aspects of health care administration, planning and financing of hospitals and related health care institutions; administrative aspects of the medical, paramedical, and prepayment fields. Special Collection: Ray E Brown Management Collection. Hospital Literature Index prepared by the Library of the American Hospital Association in cooperation with the National Library of Medicine; Catalog of the Library of the American Hospital Association, published by G K Hall, Boston.

IL —NORTHERN TRUST COMPANY LIBRARY, 50 S LaSalle St, Chicago, 60675. Marianne Lee, Head Librn
Holdings: Vols (2500) Cat Audiotapes Microforms

IL —ARCHER DANIELS MIDLAND CO, Library, 4666 Faries Parkway, Decatur, 62525. Richard E Wallace, Manager, Information Services; Karen E Perman, Librn
Holdings: Vols 8000 Cat Maps Slides 16mm Films Microforms
Notes: Economic, scientific and technical aspects of food.

IL —NORTHWESTERN UNIVERSITY, Library, 1935 Sheridan Rd, Evanston, 60201. Patricia Bush, Management Librn
Holdings: Vols Cat
Notes: Library has a current and historical collection of 5600 bound vols of corporation annual reports representing coverage of 2500 corporations, primarily industrials. Many date to beginning of the 20th century. Annual reports for 1200 corporations are currently received. Also available since 1973 is a microfiche collection of annual reports to shareholders and 10-K reports of corporations listed on the New York Stock Exchange.

IN —INDIANA UNIVERSITY, Business-School of Public and Environmental Affairs (SPEA), Bloomington, 47405. Michael Parrish, Dir
Holdings: Vols (100,000)
Budget: ($200,000)
Notes: Collection covers all phases of business, public administration and environment.

IN —MILES LABORATORIES, Library Resources and Services, 1127 Myrtle St, PO Box 40, Elkhart, 46515. Allam Hagopian, Mgr
Holdings: Vols (16,500) Cat Audiotapes Microforms
Notes: Incl files of pharmaceutical product advertising pieces, extensive literature files on company related drugs; domestic and international marketing files. 32,000 bound periodicals.

IN —CENTRAL STATE HOSPITAL, Medical Library, 3000 W Washington St, Indianapolis, 46222. Aurella S Baker, Librn
Holdings: Vols (10,400) Cat Audiotapes
Budget: ($41,000)

IN —INDIANA LAW ENFORCEMENT ACADEMY, David F Allen Memorial Learning Resources Center, Rd 700 E, PO Box 313, Plainfield, 46168. Donna K Zimmerman, Librn
Holdings: Vols (4500) Cat Slides 16mm Films
Budget: ($8500)
Notes: Concentrated in the areas of police science, criminology, and law.

IN —PURDUE UNIVERSITY LIBRARIES, Graduate School of Management, Krannert Library, West Lafayette, 47907. Gordon Law, Librn
Holdings: Vols (142,727) Cat Microforms
Budget: ($69,700)
Notes: There is an extensive collection of corporate reports and labor information material (some 115,000 items). Over 2500 periodicals are currently received.

†LA —TULANE UNIVERSITY, Graduate School of Business Administration, New Orleans, 70118.

MA —BANK OF NEW ENGLAND, 1 Washington Mall, Boston, 02108. Helen Mavareaf, Librn
Holdings: Vols (4500) Cat Microforms
Budget: ($18,000)
Notes: Annual reports of largest US banks; corporate financial reports on microfiche; Banking School theses from Stonier and Pacific Coast; industry studies.

MA —HARVARD UNIVERSITY, Graduate School of Business Administration, Baker Library, Soldiers Field, Boston, 02163. Mary V Chatfield, Librn; Florence Bartoshesky, Cur of Manuscripts and Archives

MA —RAYTHEON SERVICE CO, Library, Spencer Laboratory, 2 Wayside Rd, Burlington, 01803. Jean C Cameron, Librn
Holdings: Vols (1400) Cat
Notes: Collection emphasizes business and management.

†MA —MASSACHUSETTS INSTITUTE OF TECHNOLOGY, Cambridge, 02139.
Notes: Archival collections and papers at MIT.

MA —BOSTON COLLEGE LIBRARIES, Thomas P O'Neill Library, Chestnut Hill, 02167. John D J Slinn, Librn of the Central Library
Holdings: Vols 62,000 Cat Maps Audiotapes Filmstrips Microforms
Budget: ($120,000)

MI —GENERAL ELECTRIC COMPANY, Carboloy Systems Department, Library, Box 237, GPO, Detroit, 48232.
Holdings: Vols (4500) Cat Maps Slides 16mm Films Filmstrips Microforms
Budget: ($5000)
Notes: Collection covers cemented carbide

MANAGEMENT (cont.)

cutting tools, powder metallurgy, metal
cutting, metalworking, machining, and
related subjects. Also numerical control,
statistics (related to the cutting tool
industry) and general management. Incl 500
maps, 4000 slides, 61 films, 261 filmstrips,
700 microfiche, 7000 patents, and 300
periodical titles.

MI —WESTERN MICHIGAN UNIVERSITY,
Business Library, N Hall, Kalamazoo, 49008.
David H McKee, Head
Holdings: Vols (71,977) Cat Phonorecords
Microforms
Notes: Incl 14,570 vols of bound periodicals,
33,041 monographs, 14,605 government
documents, 1796 microfilm and 7u965
microfiche/microcards. Large collection of
corporate annual reports is separate.

MI —NORTHWOOD INSTITUTE, Strosacker
Library, 3225 Cook Rd, Midland, 48640.
Catherine Chen, Head Librn
Holdings: Vols 3000 Cat Maps Microforms
Budget: $30,000
Notes: Business and management, incl
economics and economic history.
Audiovisual materials are located in the
Griswold Communications Center.

MI —OAKLAND COUNTY REFERENCE
LIBRARY, 1200 N Telegraph Rd, Pontiac,
48053. Phyllis Jose, Library Dir
Holdings: Vols (11,000) Cat
Budget: ($34,000)

MN —MINNESOTA DEPARTMENT OF
TRANSPORTATION, Library, Information
Services Section, B-10 Transportation Bldg,
Saint Paul, 55155. Jerome C Baldwin, Librn

NH —NEW HAMPSHIRE COLLEGE, Harry
A B and Gertrude C Shapiro Library, 2500
N River Rd, Manchester, 03104. Richard
Pantano, Dir
Holdings: Vols (66,000) Cat Maps Slides
Audiotapes Videotapes 16mm Films
Filmstrips Microforms
Budget: ($133,173)
Notes: Library is a selective US Government
Documents depository, and New Hampshire
State Documents depository. Subscribe to
microfiche SEC 10K reports to AMEX and
NYSE (1975-), as well as AMEX and NYSE
company annual reports (1977-); AICPA
publications and cassettes. Strong collections
in accounting; business; business education;
computers; hotel and restaurant
management; and social service.

NJ —STEVENS INSTITUTE OF
TECHNOLOGY, Samuel C Williams
Library, Castle Point Sta, Hoboken, 07030.
Jane G Hartye, Special Collections Librn
Holdings: Vols (180) Cat Pix Slides
Budget: ($1500)
Notes: Frederick Winslow Taylor is known
as the "father of scientific management," and
we have in our collection volumes of
correspondence relating to the introduction
of this system into industry, government, the
army and navy, etc. This collection also
includes many personal items belonging to
and used by Mr Taylor. Our collection is the
most complete one on the subject of
scientific management.

NJ —RUTGERS, THE STATE UNIVERSITY
OF NEW JERSEY, Institute of
Management & Labor Relations, Ryders
Lane & Clifton Ave, New Brunswick, 08903.
Bernard F Downey, Librn
Holdings: Vols (18,530) Cat Slides
Phonorecords 16mm Films Filmstrips
Budget: ($4800)
Notes: Separate card catalog for collection.
Particular emphasis on dispute settlement.
Strong collection on public sector labor
relations, emphasizing New Jersey
publications.

NY —KEY BANK N A, 60 State St, Albany,
12207. Joy Pauline Longo, Librn
Holdings: Vols 200 Cat

NY —BROOKLYN PUBLIC LIBRARY,
Business Library, 280 Cadman Plaza W,
Brooklyn, 11201. Sylvia Mechanic, Business
Librn
Holdings: Vols (107,000) Cat
Notes: Library received about 1800
periodicals, 3000 serials, 2700 directories,

1600 telephone books from all over the
world with a complete back file on microfilm
for greater New York. Library is a selective
US Government Documents depository.
Subscribes to microfiche SEC 10K reports
for AMEX, NYSE and OTC from 1976 to
date; annual reports for earlier years.
Transnational annual reports, on fiche from
1982-to date. 78 vertical file trays; Sanborn
maps for Brooklyn, special collection of
corporation histories. Publish monthly
newsletter, *Service to Business and Industry*
with our Science Division.

NY —BERNARD M BARUCH COLLEGE
(CUNY), Library, 156 E 25 St, New York,
10010. Alan Weiner, Head of Reference

NY —CONFERENCE BOARD, Information
Service Library, 845 Third Ave, New York,
10022. Tamsen M Hernandez, Dir
Holdings: Vols 25,000 Cat Microforms
Notes: Heavily directed to collection of
government materials and corporate data.

NY —NEW YORK PUBLIC LIBRARY,
Research Libraries, Economic & Public
Affairs Div, Fifth Ave & 42 St, New York,
10018. Edward DiRoma, Chief
Holdings: Vols (l,5000,000) Cat Microforms

NY —RESEARCH INSTITUTE OF
AMERICA, Editorial Library, 589 Fifth
Ave, New York, 10017. Jamie Russell, Librn
Holdings: Vols 3500
Notes: Not open to public.

NY —SALES & MARKETING EXECUTIVES
INTERNATIONAL, Marketing Information
Center, 330 W 42nd St, New York, 10036.
Alayne J Ambrogio, Dir
Holdings: Vols (600) Cat
Budget: ($1500)
Notes: Extensive collection incl many
textbooks. For members only.

NY —YWCA NATIONAL BOARD, Library,
726-730 Broadway, New York, 10012.
Elizabeth Norris, Librn
Holdings: Vols (3000) Cat Mss
Notes: Emphasis on non-profit organizations.
Collection focuses on women and their
contemporary interests.

NY —UNIVERSITY OF ROCHESTER,
Graduate School of Management Library,
Rush Rhees Library, Rochester, 14627.
Edward Wass; Janet Prentice; Datta Kharbas
Holdings: Vols (108,000) Cat Microforms
Budget: ($84,500)
Notes: Incl a reference collection, a
geographical file on economic conditions, an
industry file of statistics and trends, research
reports and working papers, more than 2600
hardcopy annual reports. Several microfiche
or microcard Collections of Corporate
reports dating from the 1950s to the present
and over 900 management and economics
periodicals.

NY —GENERAL ELECTRIC CO, Main
Library, One River Rd, Schenectady, 12345.
Julia Hewitt, Mgr
Holdings: Vols (56,000) Cat

NC —NORTH AMERICAN YOUTH SPORT
INSTITUTE, 4985 Oak Garden Drive,
Kernersville, 27284. Jack Hutslar, Exec Dir
Notes: A private management consulting and
training firm for adults who are involved
with school age youngsters in community
sport, recreation and physical education.

OH —AKRON-SUMMIT COUNTY PUBLIC
LIBRARY, Business, Labor & Government
Div, 55 S Main St, Akron, 44326. William G
Johnson, Head
Holdings: Vols (10,000) Cat Microforms
Budget: ($20,000)

OH —PUBLIC LIBRARY OF CINCINNATI
& HAMILTON COUNTY, Government
and Business Dept, 800 Vine St, Cincinnati,
45202. Paul T Hudson, Head
Holdings: Vols 120,000 Cat
Notes: Department receives over 1200
periodical and loose-leaf service titles, 1500
serial titles and over 1500 telephone
directories. Subjects include political science,
especially foreign relations, economics, law,
public administration and business
management. Dept houses Murray
Seasongood collection of local government.
Dept has extensive census material from
1790. Library is a full depository for US
Government Publications, 1884 to date.

OH —CLEVELAND PUBLIC LIBRARY,
Business, Economics and Labor Department,

325 Superior Ave, Cleveland, 44114. Joan
Sorger, Head
Holdings: Cat
Notes: Currently receiving over 1700
periodicals and 1300 serial titles; 1000
individual trade, industrial and professional
directories, worldwide; 324 file drawers
annual reports of old companies, many local;
24 drawers historical information on
Cleveland companies. Annual reports, 10-
K's, Proxy Statements (disclosure SEC
filings on fiche); over 200 loose-leaf services;
1700 current telephone and city directories.
Emphasis on current material. Areas of
special strength are banking, investments,
marketing and management. Also strong
insurance, accounting, real estate and
transportation collections. Computerized
sources available incl Dow Jones News
Service and a variety of Dialog business-
related databases.

OH —OHIO STATE UNIVERSITY, Home
Economics Library, Campbell Hall Rm 325,
1787 Neil Ave, Columbus, 43210. Neosha
Mackey, Librn
Holdings: Vols (14,000) Cat Microforms
Notes: Separate catalog. Also, book catalog:
Catalog of the Home Economics Library
(Boston: G K Hall, 1976), 3 vols.

OR —US DEPT OF ENERGY, Bonneville
Power Administration Library, 1002 NE
Holladay St, PO Box 3621, Portland, 97232.
Karen Hadman, Chief of Library Branch
Holdings: Vols (2000) Cat
Budget: ($185,000)
Notes: Emphasis is on Federal and Pacific
Northwest law and in subject areas of
interest to the Departments of Energy and
Interior.

PA —DREXEL UNIVERSITY LIBRARIES,
W W Hagerty Library, 32 & Chestnut Sts,
Philadelphia, 19104. R L Snyder, Dir
Holdings: Vols (66,500) Cat Microforms
Budget: ($10,800)
Notes: Incl 25,000 microforms of annual
reports of companies traded on the NYSE
and the ASE.

PA —UNIVERSITY OF PENNSYLVANIA,
Lippincott Library of the Wharton School,
Philadelphia, 19104. Michael Halperin, Librn
Holdings: Cat
Notes: Incl labor management.

PA —UNIVERSITY OF PITTSBURGH,
Graduate School of Business Library, 138
Mervis Hall, Pittsburgh, 15260. Susan
Neuman, Head Librn
Holdings: Vols (36,000) Cat Microforms
Budget: ($40,000)
Notes: Incl material to support graduate
programs in business administration, as well
as faculty research. Reflects strongly the
interest of business in the behavioral, social,
and international aspects of management. 19,
000 microfiche cards, 1000 microfilm reels.

PA —SCRANTON PUBLIC LIBRARY, Vine
& N Washington Sts, Scranton, 18503.
Thomas McHale, Dir
Holdings: Vols (975) Cat
Budget: ($6000)

RI —BRYANT COLLEGE, Edith M Hodgson
Memorial Library, Rte 7, Douglas Pike,
Smithfield, 02917. John P Hannon, Dir
Holdings: Vols (103,000) Cat Phonorecords
Audiotapes Videotapes 16mm Films
Filmstrips Microforms
Budget: ($175,000)
Notes: Incl 6000 bound periodical vols, 250
phonorecords, 220 audiotapes, 120
videotapes, 30 16mm films, 150 filmstrips
and 7500 microforms.

TX —SOUTHERN UNION CO, Library,
Inter-First II, Suite 1800, Dallas, 75270.
Charles Woodard, Research Librn
Holdings: Vols 175 Cat
Notes: Incl periodicals (43 subscriptions),
and annual reports (1500).

TX —FORT WORTH PUBLIC LIBRARY, 300
Taylor St, Fort Worth, 76102. John R
McCracken, Manager
Holdings: Vols (7000) Cat
Budget: ($21,000)

TX —ECTOR COUNTY LIBRARY,
Department of Business and Technology,
321 W 5th St, Odessa, 79760. Pat Jones,
Dept Head
Notes: 25,000 Corporate Annual Reports

MANAGEMENT (cont.)

microfilmed reports are complete from 1978-1983. 200 vertical files, 30 periodicals. Collection includes the subjects of Business, Management, Real Estate Accounting, Land Economics, Labor Economics, Finance, Personal Finance and Environmental Economics. Also included are stock and dividend reports, commodities and bond reports as well as business rankings. All items are referenced and cataloged.

TX —UNITED SERVICES AUTOMOBILE ASSOCIATION, Library, USAA Bldg, San Antonio, 78288. Fran Day, Librn
Holdings: Vols (3600) Cat
Notes: Principally property and casualty insurance. 300 subscriptions.

VA —CENTRAL STATE HOSPITAL, Medical Library, PO Box 4030, Petersburg, 23803. P D Upadyaya, Medical Librn
Holdings: Vols (300)

WA —PUGET SOUND NAVAL SHIPYARD, Engineering Library, Code 202.5, Bremerton, 98314. Carol J Swanson, Engineering Librn
Holdings: Vols (1000) Cat

WI —UNIVERSITY OF WISCONSIN-STOUT, Library Learning Center, Menomonie, 54751. Philip Sawin Jr, Coll Develop Librn
Notes: Supports the Packaging concentration of the Master's Degree in Industrial Management. Concentration was authorized at the graduate level in 1974, but specialized collection since 1965.

WY —US AIR FORCE INSTITUTE OF TECHNOLOGY, Library, Dept 9 Bldg 831, FE, Warren AFB, 82001. Patricia A Johnson, Librn
Holdings: Vols (7000) Cat Microforms
Budget: ($9000)
Notes: The Library supports graduate programs for students (Air Force Missile-Combat Crewmen) seeking a Master of Business administration degree. Civilian students and other military personnel are also admitted.

MB —UNIVERSITY OF MANITOBA, Faculty of Administrative Studies, Administrative Studies Library, Winnipeg, R3T 2N2, Can. Judith Head, Librn
Holdings: Vols (15,000) Cat Microfiche
Notes: Actuarial science and management sciences; accounting; finance; public policy. Incl 11,000 microfiche, cataloged; annual reports of 800 companies.

ON —CANADA, DEPT OF EMPLOYMENT & IMMIGRATION LIBRARY, Ottawa, K1A 0J9, Can. P E Sunder-Raj, Dir Library Services
Holdings: Vols (15,000) // Cat

ON —CANADIAN HOUSING INFORMATION CENTER, Canada Mortgage and Housing Corp, CMHC Annex Bldg Ground Floor, Montreal Rd, Ottawa, K1A 0P7, Can. Leslie Jones, Mgr
Holdings: Cat

ON —INSTITUTE OF CHARTERED ACCOUNTANTS OF ONTARIO, The Merrilees Library, 69 Bloor St E, Toronto, M4W 1B3, Can. Theresa Wolak, Librn
Holdings: Vols 397 Cat

ON —METROPOLITAN TORONTO LIBRARY, Business Dept, 789 Yonge St, Toronto, M4W 2G8, Can. Patricia Dye, Head
Holdings: Vols (63,682) Cat Microforms
Notes: Economics and business management. Concentration on small businesses. Extensive current and historical information on Canadian corporations. Collection of domestic and international trade directories. Statistics collection. Approximately 1000 current periodicals and up-dating services. "A Focus on Business and Finance Libraries," in Special Libraries Association, Business and Finance Division, *BFD Newsletter*, no 44, Winter 1977, 99 13-15.

ON —ONTARIO MINISTRY OF TREASURY & ECONOMICS, Library Services, Frost Bldg N, Queen's Park, Toronto, M7A 1Y8, Can. Barbara Weatherhead, Head Librn
Holdings: Vols (100,000) Cat Microforms
Budget: ($76,500)
Notes: Index to Ontario regulations.

MANAGEMENT, GAME see Wildlife Management

MANAGEMENT, INDUSTRIAL see Industrial Management

MANAGEMENT, INSTITUTION see Institution Management

MANAGEMENT, WILDLIFE see Wildlife Management

MANAGEMENT, WOMEN IN see Women in Management

MANCHU LANGUAGE AND LITERATURE

MD —JOHNS HOPKINS UNIVERSITY, Milton S Eisenhower Library, Charles & 34 Sts, Baltimore, 21218. Ann S Gwyn, Assistant Dir for Special Collections
Holdings: Vols 1000// Cat Mss
Notes: Incl numerous rare texts and unusual pamphlets. History, politics, geography, philosophy. Chiefly in German, also French and English. Incl more than Buddhist texts.

MA —HARVARD UNIVERSITY LIBRARY, Harvard-Yenching Library, 2 Divinity Ave, Cambridge, 02138. Eugene W Wu, Librn
Notes: Strong in translations of Chinese Confucian classics, literature, history, and works on government and original Manchu publications on Manchu institutions.

NJ —PRINCETON UNIVERSITY, Library, Gest Oriental Library & East Asian Collections, 317 Palmer Hall, Princeton, 08544. D E Perushek, Cur
Holdings: Cat Mss
See also entry under China

NY —COLUMBIA UNIVERSITY LIBRARIES, C V Strarr East Asian Library, 300 Kent Hall, New York, 10027. James Reardon-Anderson, Librn
Holdings: Vols 644 Cat
Notes: Manchu and bi/tri-lingual books (with Chinese and/or Mongol), published in the Ch'ing Dynasty (1644-1911).

MANCHURIA

AZ —ARIZONA STATE UNIVERSITY, Library, Tempe, 85287. Marilyn Wurzburger, Special Collections Librn
Notes: The A T Steele Collection is a unique compilation of articles and documents dealing with events in China from 1932-49. The collection is divided into five parts: dispatches, newspaper clippings, pamphlets and books, original documents of the Communist Party (ca 1945) and memorabilia, written and/or collected by American journalist A T Steele. Dispatches cover events in China from 1940-49 land are mostly first-hand experiences of Steele. These dispatches, not all of which have been published, often contain details absent in the final copy. Post-war topics incl truce negotiations between the Nationalists and Chinese Communists and the "Manchurian Question." Index available. 12 linear feet of materials.

CA —UNIVERSITY OF CALIFORNIA, BERKELEY, University Library, Slavic Collections, Berkeley, 94720. Edward Kasinec, Librn
Notes: Russian Pacifica collection, the best on the West coast, incl materials in the folowing areas: Russian exploration and settlement of the North American continent; Russian exploration and settlement and colonization of Siberia; Russian exploration of the Pacific; Russian communities in Manchuria and other parts of the Far East. While many items pertaining to the geographical area are found in the Main Library's stack collection, the bulk of Russian Pacifica holdings is concentrated in the Bancroft Library. The Bancroft collections contain the greater number of items listed in the two major bibliographies of Russian Pacifica: Valentin Lada-Macarski's *Bibliography of Books on Alaska Published before 1868* (Yale Univ Press, 1969), and V I Mezhov's *Sibirskaia bibliografiia* (S Petersburg: Semenov, 1903). During 1983-84, with the assistance of Title II-C funding, a major project of collection evaluation and development was undertaken in the area of Russian Pacifica, resulting in the acquisition on microfilm of several hundred items, incl a part of the holdings of the Museum of Russian Culture in San Francisco relating to Siberia and Russian communities in China.

IL —FIELD MUSEUM OF NATURAL HISTORY, The Berthold Laufer Library, Roosevelt Rd & Lake Shore Dr, Chicago, 60605. W Peyton Fawcett, Librn
Holdings: Vols (12,000)// Cat Mss Maps
Notes: The part of the museum's collection of Berthold Laufer (1874-1934), Curator of Anthropology, dealing with the peoples of the pre-19th century Chinese Empire (incl Manchuria, Mongolia, Sinkiang and Tibet); their anthropology, art and religion; influences upon their cultures by those of India, Siberia, Japan, Indonesia, and Oceania--and vice versa. Incl about 500 books in Tibetan. About 2/3 of the collection is cataloged.

MANCHURIAN INCIDENT, 1931 see Mukden Incident, 1931

MANCINI, HENRY

CA —UNIVERSITY OF CALIFORNIA, LOS ANGELES, Music Library, Schonberg Hall, Los Angeles, 90024. Stephen M Fry, Music Librn
Notes: Mss.

MANEY, RICHARD

NY —NEW YORK PUBLIC LIBRARY, Performing Arts Research Center, Billy Rose Theatre Collection, 111 Amsterdam Ave, New York, 10023. Dorothy L Swerdlove, Cur
Holdings: Cat
See also entry under Theatre - History.

MANFRED, FREDERICK

SD —AUGUSTANA COLLEGE, Mikkelsen Library & Learning Resource Center, Center for Western Studies, Sioux Falls, 57197. Ronelle Thompson, Dir Library
Notes: The Center for Western Studies, located in the Mikkelsen Library, is an archival and research agency of Augustana College. Dedicated to the history and culture of the Great Plains and the Trans-Mississippi West, the Center collects and preserves materials relating to Plains Indians, immigrant settlers, Norwegiana, Western Americana, Herbert Krause, Frederick Manfred, Donald Parker, Richard F Pettigrew, Augustana College, the Episcopal Diocese of South Dakota, the South Dakota District of the American Lutheran Church, the South Dakota Penitentiary and Minnehaha County.

MANGLES, J. H.

OH —OHIO UNIVERSITY, Vernon R Alden Library, Department of Archives and Special Collections, Athens, 45701. Gary A Hunt, Head
Holdings: Vols 372 Cat
Notes: A comprehensive collection of Tennyson's published works, in first and later editions, incl a few mss and related material. Incl 22 different sets (1870-1908) of collected editions; some 30 editions (1878-1913) of the one-volume *Works;* many editions of each of the individual titles; and the ms journal (1870-1872) of Tennyson's neighbor, J H Mangles, recording or summarizing many conversations with the poet. All editions of all titles are collected, except those published posthumously.

MANGON, JOHN SHERRY

DE —UNIVERSITY OF DELAWARE, Hugh M Morris Library, S College Ave, Newark,

MANGON, JOHN SHERRY (cont.)

19711. T Stuart Dick, Special Collections
Holdings: Cat Mss Pix
Notes: Manuscripts, etc, incl literary
correspondence.

MANHATTAN PROJECT

IL —UNIVERSITY OF CHICAGO
LIBRARY, Dept of Special Collections,
1100 E 57 St, Chicago, 60637.
Holdings: Mss
Notes: Argonne National Laboratory deposit
of 46 linear ft of materials dealing with the
construction of Argonne and the Manhattan
Project at the University of Chicago.
MA —BOSTON UNIVERSITY, Mugar
Memorial Library, Special Collections Dept,
771 Commonwealth Ave, Boston, 02215.
Howard B Gotlieb, Dir
Notes: Papers of Stephane Groueff.

MANIFOLDING see Photocopying Processes

MANIGAULT, GABRIEL, 1809-1888

SC —COLLEGE OF CHARLESTON
LIBRARY, Special Collections Dept,
Charleston, 29401.
Notes: Incl manuscript copy of Manigault's
article on the black whale captured in
Charleston Harbor, January, 1880.

MANION, CLARENCE

IL —CHICAGO HISTORICAL SOCIETY,
Library, Clark St at North Ave, Chicago,
60614. Archie Motley, Manuscript Librn
Notes: Papers of conservative spokesperson
Clarence Manion.

MANITOBA

MB —UNIVERSITY OF MANITOBA,
Elizabeth Dafoe Library, Government
Publications Section, Winnipeg, R3T 2N2,
Can. June Dutka, Head
Holdings: Uncat Maps Pix Microforms
Notes: The Canadian National Energy
Board's Polar Gas Project documentation
provides an extremely useful source of
information describing the proposed
construction of the pipeline route which
would generally pass from the Arctic Islands
through the Northwest Territories, northern
Manitoba and into Ontario, Canada.

MANITOBA—HISTORY

MB —MANITOBA MUSEUM OF MAN &
NATURE, Library, 190 Rupert Ave,
Winnipeg, R3B 0N2, Can. V Hatten, Librn
Holdings: Vols (20,000) Cat Maps Slides
Audiotapes Videotapes Microforms
Notes: Human and natural history of
Manitoba.
MB —UNIVERSITY OF MANITOBA,
Elizabeth Dafoe Library, Archives and
Special Collections Dept, Winnipeg, R3T
2N2, Can. Richard E Bennett, Dept Head;
Corrado A Santoro, Reference Archivist
Notes: Papers and photos of the Liberal
Party in Manitoba, bulk of material falls
between 1960 and 1975. Papers of the
Consumers' Association of Canada
(Manitoba). Also some branch materials
from Winnipeg and Fort Garry.
MB —UNIVERSITY OF MANITOBA,
Elizabeth Dafoe Library, Icelandic
Collection, Winnipeg, R3T 2N2, Can. Sigrid
Johnson, Librn
Holdings: Vols (22,500) Cat Mss Maps Pix
Audiotapes Microforms
Notes: Material mostly in Icelandic, some in
other Scandinavian languages. All subject
areas incl with primary emphasis placed on
language, literature and history of Icelanders
in Canada, especially Manitoba (incl mss);
early publications of sagas and religious
literature; numerous periodicals and
newspapers, incl Islandske Maanedstidender,
1773, the first Icelandic periodical, and
Framfari, 1877, the first Icelandic newspaper

in North America; collections of Icelandic
music, such as S K Hall Collection
(published and mss); Gutturmur J
Guttormsson and Stephan G Stephansson
Memorial Collections; Vilhjalmur Stefansson
publications. Cited in, Saunderson, H H, *The
Chair of Icelandic Language and Literature
at the University of Manitoba.* Winnipeg:
University of Manitoba, 1961.
MB —UNIVERSITY OF WINNIPEG, Library,
515 Portage Ave, Winnipeg, R3B 2E9, Can.
W R Converse, Chief Librn
Holdings: Vols 225 Cat Microforms
Notes: Histories of the towns and districts of
the Province of Manitoba.

MANITOBA—PICTURES, ILLUSTRATIONS, ETC.

MB —UNIVERSITY OF MANITOBA,
Elizabeth Dafoe Library, Archives and
Special Collections Dept, Winnipeg, R3T
2N2, Can. Richard E Bennett, Dept Head;
Corrado A Santoro, Reference Archivist
Holdings: Pix
Notes: Barkwell Collection. 37 photographs
of Treherne, Manitoba and environs taken in
the early part of the 20th century. Also,
World War I photos and some portraits.

MANJU LANGUAGE see Manchu Language and Literature

MANKIEWICZ, FRANK

MA —JOHN F KENNEDY LIBRARY,
Columbia Point, Boston, 02125. Henry J
Gwiazda II, Cur
Notes: The Burke Marshall papers, 50
archives boxes re civil rights, 1961-1964 and
the Bedford-Stuyvesant Development and
Restoration Corporations; the Joseph Dolan
papers, 1 box; the Thomas Johnston papers,
3 boxes; the James Mc Shane papers, 2
boxes; the Frank Mankiewicz papers, 15
boxes; and the Scott Rafferty papers, 4
boxes.

MANLY FAMILY

†AL —UNIVERSITY OF ALABAMA, Amelia
Gayle Gorgas Library, PO Box S,
University, 35486.
Notes: The Alabama Collection contains
books about Alabama; by Alabama authors;
scrapbooks, pamphlets, newspapers. Such ms
collections as the Manly Family, Papers,
1819-1930; Samuel Townsend, Estate papers,
Gorgas Family, papers 1821-1920.

MANN, ARTHUR

DC —LIBRARY OF CONGRESS,
Washington, 20540.
Holdings: Cat Mss Pix
Notes: The Arthur Mann papers, incl
correspondence, 1923-1962, clippings and
drafts and notes for books and articles, by
the noted sports writer and baseball
authority.

MANN, HORACE

MA —NORTHEASTERN UNIVERSITY
LIBRARIES, Special Collections, 360
Huntington Ave, Boston, 02115. Nieves F
Farin, Head Collection Development Librn
Holdings: Vols 65 Cat Mss
Notes: Contains 3 ft of ms notes and
documents compiled by Louise Hall Tharp
as a basis for her book *Until Victory: Horace
Mann and Mary Peabody* (Boston: Little,
Brown, 1953); also, works by Mann and
other works used as source material (65
vols).
OH —ANTIOCH COLLEGE, Olive Kettering
Library, Livermore St, Yellow Springs,
45387. Nina Myatt, Cur
Holdings: //
Notes: Assembled by Antioch alumnus
Robert Staker, now deceased, in preparation
for writing a definitive biography of Horace
Mann. The book was never written. Material
well indexed. 34 vols arranged
chronologically, from 1607. Material,

compiled from many sources, covers Mann's
life, times, and related issues.
RI —BROWN UNIVERSITY, John Hay
Library, 20 Prospect St, Providence, 02912.
Mark N Brown, Cur Mss
Holdings: // Mss
Notes: Papers of Horace Mann, lawyer,
legislator, educator, and founder and
President of Antioch College. About 150
items for the period 1829-1856, of which
130 are correspondence with the Messer
family (qv).

MANN, MARY PEABODY

OH —ANTIOCH COLLEGE, Olive Kettering
Library, Livermore St, Yellow Springs,
45387. Nina Myatt, Cur
Holdings: Vols 14// Mss
Notes: Letters of the Peabody, Mann,
Hawthorne and related families. Collected by
Robert Straker from many sources arranged
in chronological order and well indexed.

MANN, THOMAS

CT —YALE UNIVERSITY, Box 1603A, Yale
Station, New Haven, 06520.
Holdings: Cat Mss
DC —LIBRARY OF CONGRESS, Music
Division, Washington, 20540.
Notes: Papers and recordings of composer
Arnold Schoenberg. Extensive
correspondence with other composers,
writers, etc.
IN —INDIANA UNIVERSITY, Lilly Library,
Seventh St, Bloomington, 47405. William R
Cagle, Librn
Holdings: // Cat Mss Pix
Notes: First editions of publications. Mss
incl correspondence and ms items from the
files of Mann's publisher S Fischer Verlag.
Most of the later correspondence, ie, 1932-
55, was published as *Thomas Mann
Briefwechsel Mit Seinem Verleger Bermann
Fischer* (S Fischer, 1973). The earlier
correspondence with S Fischer and Frau
Hedwig Fischer has not been published. 400
letters and 19 mss.
NJ —PRINCETON UNIVERSITY, Library,
Rare Books Dept, Princeton, 08544. Stephen
Ferguson, Cur
Holdings: Mss
Notes: Incl a collection of unpublished
letters, 1901-1941.
PA —BIBLIOGRAPHICAL CENTER OF
GERMAN LITERATURE, University of
Pittsburgh, Dept of Germanic Languages &
Literatures, 102 Loeffler Bldg, Pittsburgh,
15260. Klaus W Jonas, Dir
Holdings: Cat Mss Pix Microforms
Notes: Center for the development of
collections and bibliographical control of the
record of publications, mss, correspondence,
etc, by or relating to modern German
authors. Special sections have been
developed for Mann, Rilke, Hauptmann,
Hesse, Broch, Sachs and others. Described
by Professor Klaus W Jonas's "The German
Literature Center in Pittsburgh,"
Stechert-Hafner Book News, vol 24, no 8,
April 1970; "Documentation in Modern
German Literature: A Progress Report,"
Jahrbuch fuer Internationale Germanistik,
vol 4, no 2, 1972, and in *German and
Austrian Contributions to World Literature*
(1890-1970). Department of Germanic
Languages and Literatures, University of
Pittsburgh, 1983. 96 pp.

MANN, WILLIAM HODGES

VA —UNIVERSITY OF VIRGINIA,
Alderman Library, Manuscripts Dept,
Charlottesville, 22901. Edmund Berkeley Jr,
Cur
Holdings: Cat Mss
See also entry under Virginia - History

MANNERS see Etiquette

MANNERS AND CUSTOMS

CA —LOS ANGELES PUBLIC LIBRARY,
History Dept, 630 W Fifth St, Los Angeles,
90071. Mary Pratt, Principal Librn
Holdings: Vols 35,000 Cat Maps 16mm

MANNERS AND CUSTOMS (cont.)

Films Filmstrips Microforms
Notes: Extensive collection of travel books, designed to cast light on the customs and life of the people in all countries during all periods of history. The collection is planned to provide background materials for writers, and for the motion picture, radio, and television industries.

CA —LOS ANGELES PUBLIC LIBRARY, Philosophy & Religion Dept, 630 W Fifth St, Los Angeles, 90071. Marilyn C Wherley, Librn
Holdings: Vols 200 Cat
Budget: ($60,000)
Notes: Comprehensive coverage of all aspects of etiquette. Particular strength in manners of various historical periods.

IL —NEWBERRY LIBRARY, 60 W Walton St, Chicago, 60610. Diana Haskell, Cur of Modern Mss
Holdings: Vols 1550 Cat
Notes: See: Virgil Heltzel's *A Checklist of Courtesy Books in the Newberry Library,* 1942; and, Bell and Howell's microfilm package of *English Courtesy Books,* 1571-1773.

MI —APPLE TREE PRESS, Library, Box 1012, Flint, 48501. W D Chase, Editor/Librn
Holdings: Vols (1200) Uncat Mss Maps Pix Microforms

MN —MINNEAPOLIS PUBLIC LIBRARY & INFORMATION CENTER, Sociology Dept, 300 Nicollet Mall, Minneapolis, 55401. Eileen Scwartzbauer, Dept Head
Holdings: Vols (90,000) Cat Phonorecords Audiotapes Microforms
Budget: ($69,890)
Notes: Special collections: Foundation Center Regional Collection; college catalogs on fiche; adult basic education collection. Separate department catalog.

OH —CLEVELAND PUBLIC LIBRARY, Fine Arts and Special Collections Department, 325 Superior Ave, Cleveland, 44114. Alice N Loranth, Head
Holdings: Vols (41,050) Cat Mss Microforms
Notes: Part of the Folklore Collection. One of the large folklore collections in the US. Incl folk tales, riddles, proverbs, folk songs, ballads, fables, chapbooks, medieval romances, works on superstition, magic, witchcraft and studies of folk habits, beliefs, manners and customs. Described in Cleveland Public Library, White collection of folklore and Orientalia; *Catalog of Folklore and Folk Songs* 2nd ed (Boston: G K Hall, 1978), 3 vols; introduction by Alice N Loranth.
See also entry under Folklore

PA —TEMPLE UNIVERSITY LIBRARIES, Special Collections Dept, Contemporary Culture Collection, Philadelphia, 19122. Patricia J Case, Cur
Notes: The Contemporary Culture Collection. See full entry under US-Social Life and Customs.

MANNES, MARYA

MA —BOSTON UNIVERSITY, Mugar Memorial Library, Special Collections Dept, 771 Commonwealth Ave, Boston, 02215. Howard B Gotlieb, Dir
Holdings: Cat Mss Pix
Notes: Mss, correspondence, etc collected in depth; incl publications by or about.

MANNIN, ETHEL

MA —BOSTON UNIVERSITY, Mugar Memorial Library, Special Collections Dept, 771 Commonwealth Ave, Boston, 02215. Howard B Gotlieb, Dir
Holdings: Cat Mss Pix
Notes: Mss, correspondence, etc collected in depth; incl publications by or about.

MANNING, ELEANOR see O'Connor, Eleanor Manning, 1884-1973

MANNING, HENRY EDWARD, 1808-1892

DC —GEORGETOWN UNIVERSITY, Library, Special Collections Div, 37 & O Sts NW, Washington, 20057. George M Barringer, Special Collections Librn; Nicholas B Sheetz, Mss Librn
Holdings: Mss Cat
Notes: A portion of the papers of Bishop William Bernard Ullathorne (1806-1889), incl correspondence to and from other English prelates such as Nicholas Cardinal Wiseman (1802-1865) and Henry Edeward Cardinal Manning (1808-1892).

GA —EMORY UNIVERSITY, Candler School of Theology, Pitts Theology Library, Atlanta, 30322. Channing Jeschke, Librn; Anita K Delaries, Curator
Notes: 10 linear feet of ms and printed material (1822-92) documenting the life of Cardinal Henry Edward Manning (1808-92). The most notable items are his sermons, sermon notes and speeches; items on Archdiocese of Westminster. Finding aid available.

MANNING, JAMES, 1738-1791

RI —BROWN UNIVERSITY, John Hay Library, 20 Prospect St, Providence, 02912. Mark N Brown, Cur Mss
Holdings: Mss
Notes: Papers of James Manning, Baptist clergyman and first President of Brown Univesity. More than 300 letters, documents, and mss for the period 1759 to 1794, about half of which are written or signed by Manning. Subjects incl the early history of Brown University, the Baptist religion in England and American, the College Library, and the American Revolution. Register available.

MANNING, REG

AZ —NORTHERN ARIZONA UNIVERSITY, Special Collection Library, CU Box 6022, Flagstaff, 86011. Peter M Whiteley, Coordr/Archivist; William Mullane, Librn
Notes: Carol Jones Collection. Scrapbooks belonging to Mrs Jones, her mother, and grandmother, 1880's-1940's. One scrapbook contains World War II Reg Manning cartoons appearing in the *Arizona Republic.*

MANNING, WARREN, AND FAMILY

MA —UNIVERSITY OF LOWELL, Library, One University Ave, Lowell, 01854. Martha Mayo, Special Collections Librn
Holdings: Cat Mss Maps Pix
Notes: Warren H Manning was a founding member of the American Society of Landscape Architects. This collection contains his personal and professional papers incl project and client lists, business records, correspondence, plans, and photographs.

MA —ESSEX INSTITUTE, James Duncan Phillips Library, 132-34 Essex St, Salem, 01970. Prudence K Backman, Manuscript Librn
Holdings: Mss
Notes: Papers, incl documents relating to Nathaniel Hawthorne.

MANNY, CHARLES, 1890-1962

ON —METROPOLITAN TORONTO LIBRARY, Theatre Dept, 789 Yonge St, Toronto, M4W 2G8, Can. Heather McCallum, Head
Notes: Collections of playbills, clippings and correspondence document the career of Charles Manny (1890-1962) in both England and the United States; interviews and reminiscences on tape are available for the first all-sister act in vaudeville, the Canadian born O'Conner Sisters.
See also entry under Theatre - Canada.

MANOR, FREDERICK SIMHA, 1911-1982

MB —UNIVERSITY OF MANITOBA, Elizabeth Dafoe Library, Archives and Special Collections Dept, Winnipeg, R3T 2N2, Can. Richard E Bennett, Dept Head; Corrado A Santoro, Reference Archivist
Notes: Published editorials by the author that appeared in the *Winnipeg Free Press* from 1964-78; unpublished mss.

MANPOWER

DC —INTERNATIONAL LABOR ORGANIZATION, International Labor Office, Washington Branch Library, 1750 New York Ave NW, Rm 330, Washington, 20006. Karen J Mark, Librn
Holdings: Vols (13,500) Cat Pix 16mm Films Monographs
Notes: Wide range of titles dealing with worldwide labor and social matters. The library contains ILO publications and documentation only, dating back to 1919. Also, a collection of ILO films and photos. See *Subject Guide to Publications of the ILO, 1919-1964* and *ILO Catalogue of Publications in Print, 1982* (ILO).

IL —UNIVERSITY OF ILLINOIS, URBANA/CHAMPAIGN, Institute of Labor and Industrial Relations, Library, 504 E Armory, Champaign, 61820. Margaret A Chaplan, Librn
Holdings: Vols (11,597)
Budget: ($7500)
Notes: Collection incl four subject areas within industrial relations: collective bargaining and labor-management relations; manpower and labor economics; international and comparative labor movements; and organizational behavior. There is an extensive vertical file containing information on individual labor unions. The resources of the library which are relevant to the study of labor history are described in "Labor History Resources of the University of Illinois," by Patricia Wilson Onsi, *Labor History,* vol 7, Spring 1966, pp 209-215.

MA —HARVARD UNIVERSITY LIBRARY, John F Kennedy School of Government Library, Manpower and Industrial Relations Collection, Littauer Library, Cambridge, 02138. James C Damaskos, Librn
Holdings: Vols (120,000) Cat
Notes: Major strength is in publications of labor unions and government documents relating to labor.

MI —MICHIGAN STATE UNIVERSITY, Labor and Industrial Relations Library, East Lansing, 48824. Martha Jane Soltow, Librn
Holdings: Vols (55,000) Cat Microforms
Notes: All aspects of employer/employee relations.

ON —CANADA, DEPT OF EMPLOYMENT & IMMIGRATION LIBRARY, Ottawa, K1A 0J9, Can. P E Sunder-Raj, Dir Library Services
Holdings: Vols (35,000) Cat
Notes: Also have 1800 current journals and serials.

ON —ONTARIO MINISTRY OF LABOUR, Library, 400 University Ave, Toronto, M7A 1T7, Can. Jean Collins-Williams, Librn
Holdings: Vols (80,000) Microforms Films

MANSBRIDGE, ALBERT, 1876-1952

†ON —MCMASTER UNIVERSITY, Library, Hamilton, L8S 4L6, Can.
Notes: Letters, postcards, and correspondence cards, primarily addressed to Leonard Clark from Albert Mansbridge.

MANSBRIDGE, JOHN

CA —UNIVERSITY OF CALIFORNIA, LOS ANGELES, Theater Arts Library, Los Angeles, 90024. Edward Shreeves, Chairman, Bibliographers Group; Audree Malkin, Head, Theater Arts Library
Notes: John Mansbridge (art director) Collection: approx 5000 set stills and photographs of sketches of productions made at RKO Studios, 1932-1957; photographs from a variety of other studios; personal research photographs.

MANSFIELD, KATHERINE

IL —NEWBERRY LIBRARY, 60 W Walton St, Chicago, 60610. Diana Haskell, Cur of Modern Mss
Holdings: Vols 480 Mss
Notes: Autograph manuscripts, incl some

MANSFIELD, KATHERINE (cont.)

unpublished works, correspondence, journals and diaries, photographs, and memorabilia.

NV —UNIVERSITY OF NEVADA, RENO, University Library, Special Collections Dept, Reno, 89557. Robert E Blesse, Head
Holdings: // Vols (56) cat Other appearances 175 Cat
Notes: Includes individual works by author in all editions including translations; also prefaces, introductions, published correspondence, appearances in anthologies, periodicals, etc. Bibliographical research collection, part of Modern Authors Collection.

NY —HOFSTRA UNIVERSITY, Library, 1000 Fulton Ave, Hempstead, 11550. Charles R Andrews, Dean of Library Services
Notes: Strong collection. Incl some mss.

ON —VICTORIA UNIVERSITY, Library, 71 Queen's Park Crescent, Toronto, M5S 1K7, Can. Robert C Brandeis, Chief Librn
Holdings: Vols Cat
Notes: A collection of first editions and others of Virginia Woolf and Bloomsbury writers: Clive Bell, Roger Fry, E M Forster, V Sackville-West, K Mansfield, etc. Contains a significant collection of Hogarth Press books, and many of those handprinted by the Woolfs.

MANSFIELD, MICHAEL J.

MT —UNIVERSITY OF MONTANA, Library, Missoula, 59801. Katherine Schaefer, Special Collections Librn
Holdings: Mss
Notes: 2178 linear feet. Correspondence, photos, scrapbooks, sound and video recordings and memorabilia.

MANSFIELD, RICHARD

CT —CONNECTICUT COLLEGE, Library, Mohegan Ave, New London, 06320. Brian Rogers, College Librn
Holdings: Vols (382,000) Cat Mss
Notes: Also have bronze bust of Mansfield.

MANSLAUGHTER see Assassination; Homicide

MANTELL, ROBERT BRUCE

NY —HAMPDEN-BOOTH THEATRE LIBRARY AT THE PLAYERS, 16 Gramercy Park, New York, 10003. Louis A Rachow, Librn/Cur
Holdings: Vols 9 Uncat Mss Pix
Notes: The Robert Bruce Mantell Collection, incl 9 playscripts, several with holograph stage directions, correspondence, personal mementos. Indexed. Described in *Theatre & Performing Arts Collections* (New York: Haworth Press, 1981).

MANTOUX, PAUL

CA —HOOVER INSTITUTION ON WAR, REVOLUTION & PEACE, Stanford University, Stanford, 94305. Milorad M Drachkovitch, Archivist
Holdings: // Mss
Notes: Papers, 1916-1931, of Louis Loucheur, French industrialist, diplomat and public official. Correspondence, speeches, notes and other papers. Incl reports (1916) from Loucheur as an industrial adviser to Russia, papers relating to reparations negotiations (1921-1924), an interview (1924) with Konrad Adenauer, the Loncheur-Coudenhove-Kalergi correspondence (1927-1931) and notes taken by Paul Mantoux on the conversations armistice negotiations with the Germans. 5 ft. Index in the repository.

MANUAL SKILL see Motor Ability

MANUFACTURERS

OH —AKRON-SUMMIT COUNTY PUBLIC LIBRARY, Business, Labor & Government Div, 55 S Main St, Akron, 44326. William G Johnson, Head
Holdings: Vols (10,000) Cat Microforms
Budget: ($20,000)

PA —CARNEGIE LIBRARY OF PITTSBURGH, Science & Technology Dept, 4400 Forbes Ave, Pittsburgh, 15213. Catherine M Brosky, Dept Head
Holdings: Vols (380,000) Cat Maps Microforms
Budget: ($240,000)
Notes: General information acquired in various subject areas especially those relating to iron and steel and other metals, rubber, leather, pulp and paper, textiles, glass, petroleum and coal tar by-products, lumber, plastics, etc. Manufacturers directories, including old editions, standards and specifications, trade catalogs, basic periodicals, indexes, and bibliographies. *See also* entry under Technology.

MANUFACTURERS AIRCRAFT ASSOCIATION

FL —EMBRY-RIDDLE AERONAUTICAL UNIVERSITY, Regional Airport, Daytona Beach, 32014. M Judy Luther, Dir of Learning Resources

MANUFACTURES

TX —ECTOR COUNTY LIBRARY, Department of Business and Technology, 321 W 5th St, Odessa, 79760. Pat Jones, Dept Head
Holdings: Vols 100 Cat
Notes: Incl 15 periodicals, 6 Major Manufacturing Directories.

MANUFACTURES—HISTORY

DE —HAGLEY MUSEUM AND LIBRARY, Eleutherian Mills-Hagley Foundation Inc, PO Box 3630, Greenville, 19807. Richmond D Williams, Dir; Heddy A Richter, Imprints Librn
Notes: National Association of Manufacturers Records (1910-1975; 1000 cubic feet) incl minutes of adminstrative committees, reports, correspondence, and printed material.

IN —PURDUE UNIVERSITY LIBRARIES, Graduate School of Management, Krannert Library, West Lafayette, 47907. Gordon Law, Librn
Notes: An important resource at the Krannert Library is its Special Collection of Business and Economics, consisting of some 8000 rare pre-20th century strengths in books, journals, tracts and pamphlets covering primarily the early literature of economic thought and business practices in America and abroad, 1500-1870. A catalog was issued in 1979.

NJ —PASSAIC COUNTY HISTORICAL SOCIETY, Lamhurt Castle, Valley Rd, Paterson, 07503. Helen D Hamilton, Dir
Holdings: Vols (5000) Cat Mss Maps Pix
Notes: Material on the Society for the Establishment of Useful Manufacturing (founded) by Alexander Hamilton, papers relating to John Holland, who developed the submarine, the industrial magnates of the area who were active in the manufacture of locomotives, Colt revolvers, and textiles, especially silk.

MANUFACTURING ENGINEERING see Production Engineering

MANUFACTURING PROCESSES

TX —ECTOR COUNTY LIBRARY, Department of Business and Technology, 321 W 5th St, Odessa, 79760. Pat Jones, Dept Head
Holdings: Vols 100 Cat
Notes: Incl 15 periodicals, 6 Major Manufacturing Directories.

UT —EIMCO TECHNOLOGY & RESEARCH CENTER, Process Machinery Div, Technical Library, 414 W 300 S, Salt Lake City, 84110.
Holdings: Vols (1450) Cat

MANURES see Fertilizers and Manures

MANUSCRIPT CATALOGS see Catalogs, Manuscript

MANUSCRIPT SOCIETY

DC —GEORGETOWN UNIVERSITY, Library, Special Collections Div, 37 & O Sts NW, Washington, 20057. George M Barringer, Special Collections Librn; Nicholas B Sheetz, Mss Librn
Holdings: Mss Pix
Notes: Archives and records of the Manuscript Society and its publication, *Manuscripts*. Material dates from the founding of the National Society and Autograph Collectors in 1948. The name of the society and the journal, *Autograph Collector's Journal*, changed in 1953. On deposit.

MANUSCRIPTS

IN —INDIANA STATE UNIVERSITY, Cunningham Memorial Library, Dept of Rare Books & Special Collections, Terre Haute, 47809. Lawrence J McCrank, Head
Notes: The reference collection of the Rare Books and Special Collections Department holds bibliographies and reference works related specifically to the department's collections in lexicography, Indiana local and regional history, education, travel and discovery, etc, and on the book arts, eg, printing, typography, paper making, illustration, conservation and binding. Incl several facsimile editions of famous codices.

NC —DUKE UNIVERSITY, William R Perkins Library, Rare Book Room, Durham, 27706. John L Sharpe, III, Cur
Notes: Greek mss, 87 in number, dating from the 10th to the 12th centuries, incl 24 New Testament mss.

MANUSCRIPTS (PALIMPSESTS)

NY —COLUMBIA UNIVERSITY LIBRARIES, Rare Book & Manuscript Library, 801 Butler Library, 535 W 114 St, New York, 10027. Kenneth A Lohf, Librn
Holdings: Mss
Notes: Books and speciments in the history of papyrology and epigraphy. Incl 250 papyri fragments of Egyptian origin. 700 items.

MANUSCRIPTS (PAPYRI)

CT —YALE UNIVERSITY, Beinecke Rare Book & Manuscript Library, Osborn Collection, New Haven, 06520. Stephen R Parks, Cur
Holdings: Mss

DC —HARVARD UNIVERSITY, Center for Hellenic Studies Library, 3100 Whitehaven St NW, Washington, 20008. Jeno Platthy, Librn
Holdings: Vols (42,000) Cat Maps
Budget: ($76,824)
Notes: In addition to a large collection of editions of ancient Greek authors, the library is well equipped to cover every aspect of ancient Greek civilization from prehistoric times to about AD 200. The subject fields covered include epigraphy, paleography, papyrology, history, literature, philosophy, religion, mythology, archaeology and art. A small collection of works on Patristics as well as all important Latin authors complete the Center's holdings.

DC —LIBRARY OF CONGRESS, General Reading Rooms Division, Microform Reading Room, Washington, 20540.
Holdings: Cat Mss Maps Pix Microforms
Notes: Microform materials only in this LC Division. Works of individual authors; holdings of collections; archival records, etc, press releases and translations.

FL —FLORIDA STATE UNIVERSITY, Robert Manning Strozier Library, Special Collections Dept, Tallahassee, 32306. Opal M Free, Head, Special Collections
Holdings: Vols 83 // Uncat
Notes: Babylonian clay tablets (2100-2300

MANUSCRIPTS (PAPYRI) (cont.)

BC), 25 items. Papyri, 26 fragments, with Greek text. Ostraka, 32 items, 29 in Greek text, 3 in Latin text. Noncirculating.

IL —ORIENTAL INSTITUTE, 1155 E 58th St, Chicago, 60637. John Larsen, Archivist
Notes: The Bernhard Moritz Collection. Fine examples of bindings as well as of Islamic calligraphy and writing materials-- papyrus, parchment, papers, etc. Extensive collection is also in the Beatty Library in Dublin, Ireland; Victoria and Albert Museum in London; Libraries in East and West Germany.

MI —UNIVERSITY OF MICHIGAN, Library, Dept of Rare Books & Special Collections, Ann Arbor, 48109. Robert J Starring, Head
Notes: About 6200 items, largely documentary although some literary and biblical texts incl, dating from the 3rd century BC to the 8th century AD. The majority in Greek, but some in Latin, Coptic, Arabic, Hebrew and Egyptian (hieratic and demotic). Described by A E R Boak, The Building of the University of Michigan Payrus Collection, *Michigan Alumnus Quarterly Review*, vol LXVI, no 10, December 5, 1959, pp 35-42. Said to be the largest collection of papyrus mss in the Western Hemisphere (AB, 22/30 April 1976, p 988).

MN —SAINT JOHN'S ABBEY & UNIVERSITY, Hill Monastic Manuscript Library, Collegeville, 56321. Julian G Plante, Dir
Holdings: Cat Mss Microforms
Notes: Microfilms of 100,000 papyri from the Austrian National Library and 46 papyri from the University Library of Graz. Bibliographical aids to the Collection: *Mittheilungen aus der Sammlung der Papyrus Erzherzog Rainer*, Jg 1-6 (Wien: KK Hof-u Staatsdruckerel 1887-1897); *Mitteilungen aus des Papyrussammlung der Nationalbibliothek in Wien* (Papyrus Erzherzog Rainer), Neue Serie: Folge 1-.

NJ —PRINCETON UNIVERSITY, Library, Manuscript Collection, Nassau St, Princeton, 08540. Jean F Preston, Cur
Holdings: Mss
Notes: The collection consists of 400 items. See *Princeton University Library chronicle*, v 3, p 140-44, and *Papyri in the Princeton University Collections* (Baltimore: Johns Hopkins Press, 1931; Princeton: Princeton University Press, 1936-42), 3 vols.

NY —COLUMBIA UNIVERSITY LIBRARIES, Rare Book & Manuscript Library, 801 Butler Library, 535 W 114 St, New York, 10027. Kenneth A Lohf, Librn
Holdings: Mss
Notes: Books and specimens in the history of papyrology and epigraphy. Incl 250 papyri fragments of Egyptian origin. 700 items. Restricted use.

NY —PIERPONT MORGAN LIBRARY, 29 E 36 St, New York, 10016. Herbert Cahoon, Librn
Holdings: Mss

NC —UNIVERSITY OF NORTH CAROLINA, CHAPEL HILL, Wilson Library, Rare Book Collection, Chapel Hill, 27514. Paul S Koda, Cur of Rare Books
Holdings: Vols 1000 Cat Mss
Notes: The Hanes Collection of the History of the Books consists of Sumerian and Babylonian clay tablets, papyri in Egyptian and in Greek, stone inscriptions, 24 olas, manuscripts, and 600 items of 16th, 17th, and 18th century printing, incl many landmarks in the history of printing. It also contains many books about books, incl some rare bibliographies, histories of presses and technology, and books on collecting.

NC —DUKE UNIVERSITY, William R Perkins Library, Rare Book Room, Durham, 27706. John L Sharpe, III, Cur
Notes: Papyri collection. Several thousand fragments (in Greek, Latin, Coptic, Hieratic and Arabic). Greek manuscripts, 87 in number, dating from the 10th to the 12th centuries, including 24 New Testament manuscripts.

PA —UNIVERSITY OF PITTSBURGH, Hillman Library, Pittsburgh, 15260. Glenora

E Rossell, Head
Holdings: Vols (11,550) Cat
Notes: The classics collection is particularly strong in Greek and Latin literature, Greek and Roman history, Greek philosophy, Greek and Latin language, and Greek epigraphy, In combination with the Frick Fine Arts collection it has a good collection in Greek and Roman art and archaeology. The collection of journals is also quite strong in these areas. There has been an emphasis in collecting books by and about Homer, Aristotles, Euripides, Vergil, Cicero and Petronius. It has a unique collection of unpublished PhD dissertations and Master's theses on Petronius. It has a basic collection on Greek and Latin paleography and papyrology.

†UT —UNIVERSITY OF UTAH, Marriott Library, Salt Lake City, 84112.
Notes: Collection of Professor Aziz S Atiya, mostly in Arabic languages.

WI —UNIVERSITY OF WISCONSIN, MADISON, Memorial Library, Rare Books Collection, 728 State St, Madison, 53706. Gretchen Lagana, Cur
Holdings: //
Notes: The collection of non-literary, commercial and official documents consists of 83 items. The papyri are Egyptian, primarily written in Greek, with a few in Latin, and date from the 3rd century BC to the 8th century AD. The majority stem from the first three centuries AD. See P J Sijpesteijn, *The Wisconsin Papyri I* (Leiden, 1967). Housed in the Dept of Rare Books and Special Collections. No photocopying.

MANUSCRIPTS—CATALOGS

MN —SAINT JOHN'S ABBEY & UNIVERSITY, Hill Monastic Manuscript Library, Collegeville, 56321. Julian G Plante, Dir
Holdings: Cat Mss Slides Microforms
Notes: Incl catalogs of mss of all periods and languages, with emphasis on Medieval and Renaissance mss. Restricted use: non-circulating.

NY —COLUMBIA UNIVERSITY LIBRARIES, Rare Book & Manuscript Library, 801 Butler Library, 535 W 114 St, New York, 10027. Kenneth A Lohf, Librn
Holdings: Vols 5000 Cat
Notes: 5000 vols of catalogs of ms collections in the US, Europe, Great Britain, France, Germany, Italy and other countries of the Western World.

OH —CLEVELAND PUBLIC LIBRARY, Fine Arts and Special Collections Department, 325 Superior Ave, Cleveland, 44114. Alice N Loranth, Head
Holdings: Vols 700 Cat Mss
Notes: Printed catalogs and some ms listings of ms holdings of American and foreign libraries. Oriental, Latin, Greek languages and chess mss holdings are emphasized. Of special interest is the collection of more than 300 titles listing Oriental and Middle Eastern materials. The library holdings of Istanbul and Skutari are described in a unique collection of 45 vols. Rare titles and first editions are incl. Described in part in Material for Oriental Research in Cleveland, by F E Sommer, *Journal of the American Oriental Society*, vol 166, no 3 (July-Sept 1946); pp 261-264; and The John Griswold White Collection by D M Schullian, *Classical Philology*, vol 34, no 3 (July 1939): pp 253-254.
See also entry under Manuscripts - Collections.

MANUSCRIPTS—COLLECTIONS

AL —SAMFORD UNIVERSITY, Special Collections Library, 800 Lakeshore Dr, Birmingham, 35229. Annie Ford Wheeler, Acting Head Librn
Holdings: Vols 3000 Cat Mss Maps Pix
Notes: Alabama literature and history; ms collection exceeds 200,000 pieces, chiefly of Joseph J Willett papers and Bledsoe-Kelly Collection. Representative collection of maps, some pictures.

AK —TONGASS HISTORICAL SOCIETY, Library, 629 Dock St, Ketchikan, 99901.

Marjorie Anne Voss, Librn
Holdings: // Uncat Mss
Notes: Ketchikan Spruce Mill ms collection.

AZ —NORTHERN ARIZONA UNIVERSITY, Special Collection Library, CU Box 6022, Flagstaff, 86011. Peter M Whiteley, Coordr/Archivist; William Mullane, Librn
Holdings: Cat Mss Maps Pix Slides Audiotapes Microforms
Notes: Northern Arizona history and Arizona economic history. Depository of Forest History Society of America; custodian for Northern Arizona Pioneers Historical Society Manuscript Collection, center for the collections development of the Colorado Plateau Research Center. Also, Arizona newspapers and periodicals. Various other collections, incl (1) John Bury Collection; correspondence, mss, notes, subject files, oral history tapes, collected in writing 1975 NAU doctoral dissertation *Historical Role of Arizona's Superintendent of Public Instruction*. This collection is especially valuable for studying the history of education in Arizona. (2) Faye and Faith Hill Edgerton Collection; mss and notes of the translation of the New Testament into the Apache and Navajo languages, 1940's-1960's. (3) Guy and Doris Monthan Collection; mss, notes, correspondence, and other datafor the book *Art and Indian Individualists*, 1972-1975.

AZ —UNIVERSITY OF ARIZONA, University Library, Special Collections, Tucson, 85721. Louis A Hieb, Head
Budget: ($40,000)
Notes: The collection incl Arizona general periodicals and fiction, and books of the history, biography, travel, Indians, the arts, physical and natural resources, politics and government, business and industry, and social problems of Arizona. There are also over 450 processed ms collections varying in size from a single volume to hundreds of boxes. Also, incl are the Arizona photograph and pamphlet collections.

AR —UNIVERSITY OF ARKANSAS, Library, Special Collections Dept, Fayetteville, 72701. Michael J Dabrishus, Cur
Holdings: Vols (40,299) Cat Mss Maps Pix Phonorecords Audiotapes Microforms
Notes: Material pertaining to the political, governmental, economic, social, cultural, educational, religious, scientific and literary history of Arkansas, its people and its institutions, incl the natural history, anthropological development, and folk traditions of the area, from prehistoric times to the present. Holdings described in: Samuel A Sizer, *A Guide to Selected Manuscript Collections in the University of Arkansas Library* (Fayetteville, Ark, 1976) and in supplementary catalogs, inventories, indexes and other unpublished finding aids in the library.

CA —AZUSA PACIFIC COLLEGE, Marshburn Memorial Library, Citrus & Alosta, Azusa, 91702. Edward Peterman, Librn
Holdings: Vols 5000// Maps Pix
Notes: Azusa Foothill Citrus and local History collection is related to the genesis of Azusa, the citrus industry, the Slauson and Macneil families, and such companies as the Azusa Land and Water Company, Azusa Electric Lighting and Power Company, Azusa Foothill Citrus Association, Azusa Agricultural Water Company, and the Azusa Foothill Citrus Company. Includes letters, ledgers, etc.

CA —UNIVERSITY OF CALIFORNIA, BERKELEY, Bancroft Library, Manuscripts Division, Berkeley, 94720. James D Hart, Dir
Holdings: Cat Mss Maps Pix Slides Microforms
Notes: The mss of the Bancroft Library number over 32,000,000 items. Centering on diverse aspects of California and Mexico, they also incl papers of persons prominent in literature, politics, journalism, law, science, business, and other activities of many regions. Partial description of holdings in *A Guide to the Manuscript Collections of the*

MANUSCRIPTS—COLLECTIONS (cont.)

Bancroft Library, Vol I and II; unpublished guides for many of the major collections.

CA —CLAREMONT COLLEGES, mss Honnold Library, Ninth & Dartmouth, Claremont, 91711. Tania Rizzo, Special Collections Dept Head
Holdings: Uncat Mss
Notes: Incl 60 medieval, renaissance, 16th-18th century western European mss; 3 Korans; 2 Slavonic; miscellaneous authors; California and Western US history; papers of faculty and trustees of the Claremont Colleges. About 50,000 pieces. Card files and lists available. Published catalogue of medieval and renaissance mss in preparation.

CA —CALIFORNIA STATE UNIVERSITY, HAYWARD, Library, Hayward, 94542. Melissa Rose, Dir
Holdings: Vols (14,000) // Cat Mss Pix
Budget: ($7408)
Notes: Jensen Family Papers (about 3000 leaves) consisting of letters, journals, original watercolors, are the papers of a pioneer German family (Jensen-Hensen) who settled in the 1860s in the Hayward-Castro Valley, Calif, area. Covering the approx period 1830-1920, the collection incl both sides of the correspondence, a large part of which is written in German script.

CA —UNIVERSITY OF CALIFORNIA, IRVINE, Library, Irvine, 92664. Roger Berry, Dept Head
Holdings: Cat Mss Maps Pix Slides
Notes: The Meadows Collection, an extensive collection of Californiana. Rich in material on the history of Orange County, Southern California and Baja, California. Incl more than 3500 vols, thousands of pieces of printed ephemera, over 10,000 mss items, significant runs of California historical periodicals and of rare early Orange County newspapers, maps and several hundred local historical photographs.

CA —UNIVERSITY OF CALIFORNIA, SAN DIEGO, Central University Library, Mandeville Dept of Special Collections, La Jolla, 92093. Lynda Corey Claassen, Head
Notes: Materials range widely in subject and date: a 13th century treatise on orthography: family correspondence from the American Revolution and the Civil War; literary manuscripts of the 19th and 20th centuries; the papers of Nobel scientists Harold Urey and Maria Goeppert Mayer; the correspondence and writings of composer Ernst Krenek and musicologist Peter Yates. The papers of physicist Leo Szilard are located in the department; special arrangements are required for use.

CA —UNIVERSITY OF CALIFORNIA, LOS ANGELES, Research Library, Dept of Special Collections, 405 Hilgard Ave, Los Angeles, 90024. Edward Shreeves, Chairman, Bibliographers Group; David S Zeidberg, Head
Holdings: Mss
Notes: 18,000,000 items in 1300 collections, emphasizing humanities and social sciences; particular strength in British and American literature and California history, but incl 125 medieval mss, part of the Orsini family archive, and 10,000 Arabic, Armenian, and Persian mss in 6000 volumes, and 94 linear feet of Turkish mss, mostly uncataloged.

CA —UNIVERSITY OF CALIFORNIA, LOS ANGELES, Biomedical Library, Center for the Health Sciences, Los Angeles, 90024. Alison Bunting, Acting Biomedical Librn; Victoria Steele, Head, History & Special Collections Div
Holdings: Vols (21,000) Cat Mss Pix Slides Microforms
Notes: The History and Special Collections Division owns 11 mss dating to before 1600 as well as 9 later ones. They are described in: Ferrari, Mirella, *Medieval and Renaissance Manuscripts at The University of California, Los Angeles,* Los Angeles; Center for Medieval and Renaissance Studies, 1978.

CA —CALIFORNIA INSTITUTE OF TECHNOLOGY, Robert A Millikan Memorial Library, Archives, 1201 E California Blvd, Pasadena, 91125. Judith R Goodstein, Archivist
Holdings: Vols (3000) Uncat Mss Maps Pix Slides Phonorecords Audiotapes Videotapes 16mm Films Microforms
Notes: Over 70 collections (1830s-present) relating to history of 19th-20th centuries science and technology and the history of the Institute. Included are personal and professional papers of Caltech scientists and administrative officers; divisional records and faculty committees; over 5000 photographs of American and European scientists. Mss collections documents more than a century of American political, social, and intellectual history; the development of the physical sciences, aeronautics, molecular biology, and seismology in the US and abroad; and social and political conditions in Europe between the two World Wars. There are also family letters relating to 19th century American life before and during the Civil War (the Morley and A G Throop papers); to 19th century social conditions in Russia and Hungary (the Paul Epstein papers and Theodore von Karman papers); and to the development of 20th century Italian mathematics.

CA —POMONA PUBLIC LIBRARY, Special Collections, 625 S Garey Ave, PO Box 2271, Pomona, 91766. David Streeter, Librn
Holdings: Uncat Mss
Notes: 165 linear feet of Pomona Valley business records incl 16 water companies and 28 citrus companies; diaries; clubs and organizations; Laura Ingalls Wilder.

CA —A K SMILEY PUBLIC LIBRARY, 125 W Vine St, Redlands, 92373. Larry E Burgess, Archivist
Holdings: Vols (3500) Mss Maps Pix Phonorecords Microforms
Budget: ($45,000)
Notes: Emphasis on San Bernadino County and the Redlands area. Especially prized is *The Citrographic,* 1887-1908 (bound vols and microfilm) edited by Scipio Craig, prominent in state, national, and newspaper circles. The ms collection (250,000 pieces) incl the Smily Family papers, much on water development, and onthe citrus industry. The photograph collection (over 5000) covers the history of the area; there are many stereographs and glass slides. The collection on Indians of California and the Southwest was begun from a special gift by Andrew Carnegie honoring his friend, Albert K Smiley.

CA —CALIFORNIA HISTORICAL SOCIETY, Schubert Hall Library, 2099 Pacific Ave, San Francisco, 94109. Bruce L Johnson, Library Dir
Holdings: Vols (50,000) Cat Mss Maps Pix
See also entry under California - History

†CA —UNIVERSITY OF SAN FRANCISCO, Richard A Gleeson Library, The Countess Bernardine Murphy Donohue Rare Book Room, San Francisco, 94117. D Steven Corey, Special Collections Librn
Notes: Some highly specialized materials.

†CA —HUNTINGTON BOTANICAL GARDENS LIBRARY, 1151 Oxford Rd, San Marino, 91108. Ann Ravenscroft, Secretary
Holdings: Vols (8000)
Notes: Emphases on history of botanical science; papers and notes of American botanists and naturalists of The West; botanical illustration, etc. Subtropical horticulture, incl cacti and succulents of Australia, South Africa, and Mexico.

CA —STANFORD UNIVERSITY LIBRARIES, Cecil H Green Library, Stanford, 94305. Michael T Ryan, Cur
Holdings: Cat Mss Pix Audiotapes
Notes: Manuscript Collections incl over a half million pieces of Californiana, incl papers of the Progressive period in California; papers of New Almaden quicksilver mines; papers of J Arthur Younger (office records); comprehensive collection of personal, business and legal papers of Goodwin J Knight. Farm lbor materials incl papers gathered by Ernest Galarza, Fr Victor Salandini's records of farm labor activities, and a nearly complete run of Ignacio Lopez' newspaper *El Espectador.* Correspondence and literary mss of numerous British and American authors, incl John Steinbeck, Jack London, Ambrose Bierce, Bruce Bliven, John Galsworthy, Wallace Stegner, Janet Lewis (Mrs Yvor Winters), Somerset Maugham, and D H Lawrence. Collections in such fields as western American history, railroad transportation, the American Civil War(incl the papers of General Frederick Steele), the French Revolution and the Napoleonic era, and Mexican history during the French interventions in the 19th century.

CA —THE HAGGIN MUSEUM, Petzinger Library of Californiana, 1201 N Pershing Ave, Stockton, 95203. Diane Freggiaro, Librn/Archivist
Holdings: Vols (7000) Cat Mss Maps Pix Slides Audiotapes 16mm Films
Notes: The Petzinger Library is open by appointment only. Special emphasis on Stockton and San Joaquin County and Valley area, local biography, agriculture, agricultural history, industrial history, farm machinery (especially Holt Manufacturing Co, Stockton). There is a photograph collection of 8500 pictures, and extensive manuscript holdings (about 17,000 pieces).

CO —UNIVERSITY OF COLORADO, Libraries, Western Historical Collections, Boulder, 80309.
Holdings: Cat Mss Maps Pix
Notes: This repository of Colorado economic development, political and social action holds more than 500 ms collections ranging in size from more than 700 boxes to a few pieces and occupies approx 20,000 shelf feet. It also maintains the University Archive incl printed and manuscript materials. The most useful collections in this category incl the following: (1) Hardrock mining industry at Aspen, Central City, Leadville: D R C Brown Papers (1880-1920); Henry M Teller (1861-1877); Harper M Orahood; (1880s and 1890s) J J Blow, Henry Moody, W W Old, and Henry R Pendry; (2) Union (Greeley, Colorado) Colony and the Chicago-Colorado (Longmont, Colorado) Colony Papers-both successful agricultural experiments of the 1870s; (3) James P Maxwell Papers, pioneer Colorado businessman and developer; (4) David H Nichols Papers, pioneer Colorado military and political figure; (5) Jesse SRandall Papers, pioneer Georgetown, Colorado, newspaper publisher and civic leader; (6) Thomas J O'Donnell Papers (1880s-1924), prominent Denver attorney and Democratic party leader; (7) Hal Sayre Papers (1860s-1920), pioneer mining engineer and developer; (8) John C Bell Papers, western Colorado congressman and Populist leader; (9) Warren F Bleecker Papers, Colorado mining promoter and political leader in the 1920s; (10) J Sidney Brown and Brothers Papers, records of a large mercantile chain with branches throughout Colorado, New Mexico, and Wyoming; (11) George Bull Papers, civil engineer and water problem consultant in the West; (12) Samuel W DeBusk Papers, southern Colorado pioneer and business leader; (13) Leopold H Guldman Papers, Denver department store owner and operator; (14) James A Ownbey Papers, southern Colorado mining promoter; (15) A R Wilfley Papers, miningequipment inventor and manufacturer; (16) Edgar Chenoweth Papers, (1937-1964), concerning the activities of that US Congressman on behalf of his constituents in southeastern and southern Colorado; (17) Edward Keating papers (1910-1960), containing informed comments on national events by that former US Congressman (1913-1918) and later editor of the Labor newspaper; (19) Robert Rockwell Papers (1915-1950), relating to that former US Congressman's (1941-1949) business and political career representing Colorado's Western Slope and its range cattle industry. Typescript inventories or published guides available for each of the named collections.

CO —COLORADO HISTORICAL SOCIETY, Research Collections, 1300 Broadway, Denver, 80203. Catherine Kane, Head Public Service and Access
Holdings: Mss
Budget:
Notes: Approx 1000 collections relating to

MANUSCRIPTS—COLLECTIONS (cont.)

Colorado and western history. Calendars available for some. Indexed descriptive guide available on request. 8,000,000 mss.

CO —DENVER PUBLIC LIBRARY, Douglas Collection of Fine Printing, 1357 Broadway, Denver, 80203.
Holdings: Cat Mss
Notes: Miscellaneous collection, incl the Mahabarata on palm-leaves. Also, the Douglas Collection of Fine Printing.

CT —CONNECTICUT HISTORICAL SOCIETY, One Elizabeth St, Hartford, 06105. Christopher Bickford, Dir
Notes: Over 70,000 books and periodicals, 3500 bound vols of newspapers, and thousands of broadsides, maps, prints, and photographs pertaining to Connecticut. Also, more than 1 1/2 million historical mss; incl personal correspondence, diaries, account books, business records, and town materials dating from the earliest settlement. Extensive genealogical holdings, incl nearly 4000 printed genealogies and New England town and county histories.

CT —MYSTIC SEAPORT, MUSEUM, G W Blunt White Library, Greenmanville Ave, Mystic, 06355. Gerald E Morris, Librn
Holdings: Vols (40,000) Imprints Microforms
Budget: ($100,000)
Notes: American maritime history. The library is also a government depository for maritime materials with a subscription to 184 line items. Incl 400,000 mss, 4000 maps and charts, 30,000 ships' plans. Open to the public.

CT —NEW HAVEN COLONY HISTORICAL SOCIETY, Whitney Library, 114 Whitney Ave, New Haven, 06510. M Ottilia Koel, Librn & Cur of Mss
Holdings: Vols 25,000 Cat Mss Maps Pix Microforms
Notes: 25,000 printed books and pamphlets; ca 15,000 linear feet of manuscript material including historic manuscripts, records of education, maritime and harbor industry, private papers, business and family records; 40,000 photographic images; maps and microforms relating to the early settlement and subsequent history of New Haven and vicinity.

CT —YALE UNIVERSITY, Sterling Memorial Library, Latin American Collections, New Haven, 06520. Lee H Williams Jr, Cur
Holdings: Vols (300,000) Cat Mss Maps Pix Slides Phonorecords 16mm Films Filmstrips Microforms
Notes: Collecting policy is to collect in depth (about 5000 vols a year) in the humanities and social sciences over the whole continental and Caribbean area without emphasizing any one country or subject area. Science and medicine are collected only as they relate to the historical development of the area. Monographs, periodicals, newspapers, pamphlets, government publications, mss, broadsides, posters, photographs, films, musical recordings, maps, and pre-Columbian artifacts form part of the collection. Areas of unusual strength are 19th century Mexico and Peru, Castro Cuba, the Allende period in Chile, and Central America, with recent gift of some 5000 items from Frederick R Mayer, Yale 1950, along with the earlier gift of Central American documents from Lindley and Charles Eberstadt. The Manuscripts and Archives Collectioncontains the following collections related to the Latin America area: (1) Latin American Manuscripts Collection, with 170 bound volumes, and 130 boxes of manuscripts relating primarily to the civil and religious history of Peru and Mexico from the 16th through the 19th centuries; (2) the Puebla Archives Collection, 50 boxes of legal manuscripts relating to church and state affairs of the Mexican state of Puebla; (3) the Columbus Collection, containing briefs, documents and mss covering the lawsuit initiated by Columbus's descendants to determine who was entitled to his estate; (4) a number of smaller collections

DC —HOWARD UNIVERSITY, Moorland-Spingarn Research Center, 500 Howard Place NW, Washington, 20059. Clifford L Muse, Jr, Acting Dir
Holdings: Vols (106,086) Cat Mss Maps Pix Slides Phonorecords Audiotapes 16mm Films Filmstrips Microforms
Budget: $854,753
Notes: *The Glenn Carrington Collection: A Guide to the Books, Manuscripts, Music and Recordings* (DC MSRC, 1977). *Dictionary Catalog of the Jesse E Moorland Collection of Negro Life and History,* 9 vols and Supplement, 3 vols (Boston: G K Hall, 1970, 1977). *Dictionary Catalog of the Arthur Spingarn Collection of Negro Authors,* 2 vols (Boston: G K Hall, 1970). Guide to Processed Collections in the Manuscript Division of the Moorland-Spingarn Research Center (DC, MSRC, 1983). The Moorland-Spingran Research Center is recognized as one of the largest and most comprehensive repositories in the world for the collection, preservation and dissemination of historical materials documenting from antiquity to the present the history and culture of Black people in Africa, Europe, the Caribbean and the US. Since 1973, the Research Center has greatly expanded its facilitiesand resources and currently provides research services in all aspects of library and archival research, including manuscripts, oral history, music, prints and photographs and general library materials. The Research Center also maintains professional zerographic, micrographic, photographic and similar reproduction laboratories.

DC —GEORGETOWN UNIVERSITY, Library, Special Collections Div, 37 & O Sts NW, Washington, 20057. George M Barringer, Special Collections Librn; Nicholas B Sheetz, Mss Librn
Holdings: Mss Pix
Notes: Archives and records of the Manuscript Society and its publication, *Manuscripts.* Material dates from the founding of the National Society and Autograph Collectors in 1948. The name of the society and the journal, *Autograph Collector's Journal,* changed in 1953. On deposit.
containing handwritten journals, family papers and log books touching all periods of Latin American history. Of special interest are the personal papers of important diplomats and statesmen, such as Henry L Stimson, Edward M House, James Rockwell Sheffield, and Arthur BlissLane. For a partial listing of Chilean imprints in the collection for the years 1970-1973, see: *The Allende Years, A Union List of Chilean Imprints, 1970-1973,* "in selected North American Libraries, with a Supplemented Holdings List of Books Published Elsewhere for the Same Period by Chileans or about Chile or Chileans", comp by Lee H Williams, Jr (Boston: G K Hall, 1977).

DE —UNIVERSITY OF DELAWARE, Hugh M Morris Library, S College Ave, Newark, 19711. T Stuart Dick, Special Collections
Holdings: Cat
Notes: The personal and business papers of many prominent Delaware Valley politicians, merchants, lawyers, engineers. A few of those represented are the Latimer Shipping Papers, David Lenox (qv), John Lukens (see Lukens Family entry), Samuel Meredith (qv), George Messersmith (qv), and Willard Saulsbury (qv). Among the literary papers are collections of personal correspondence, holograph manuscripts of poetry, short stories and novels. Those represented include, among others, John Malsolm Brinnin, Erskine Caldwell, Waldo Frank, Elizabeth Jennings, Robert Underwood Johnson, Donald Justice, Walter Lowenfels, Howard McCord, Arthur Mizener, Ulrick O'Connor, Ishmael Reed, Carl Sandburg, Gilbert Sorrentino, Kurt Vonnegut, Tennesse Williams, William Carlos Williams, Edmund Wilson, Louis Untermeyer, William Butler Yeats, the *Pagany* archives, *Signature* archives, and Proscenium PressPapers.

DELAWARE, Library, 505 Market St Mall, Wilmington, 19801. Barbara E Benson, Library Dir
Holdings: Vols 1500 Cat Mss
Notes: Catalog complete for secondary sources, mss indexed. Photographs: 50 linear feet plus 55 linear feet of glass plate negatives. Maps: 400. Microfilm: 300 reels. Excellent collection of Delaware. Newspapers: 1750 linear feet of Delaware and other newspapers. Manuscripts: 120 linear feet. There is no printed catlog for the ms section with the exception of a listing of ms books (130 linear feet) published in *Delaware History* Vol XI, No 1 (April, 1964), pp 65-82. The collection includes the papers of such prominent Delawareans as George Read, the Rodneys, Commodore John P Gillis. Also part of the collection are the papers of the Bank of Delaware, the Chesapeake and Delaware Canal and the New Castle and Frenchtown RR. We have Delaware census material on microfilm.

DC —LIBRARY OF CONGRESS, Manuscript Division, Washington, 20540. John C Broderick, Chief
Notes: Collections of the papers of most of the Presidents from George Washington through Calvin Coolidge, of many other statesmen, military, scientific, and literary leaders of numerous enterprises and institutions, totaling more than 35,000,000 pieces, organized in more than 10,000 collections. Among them: Records of the Virginia Company of London, the American Colonization Society, the American Psychological Society, the League of Women Voters, *Harper's Magazine,* the American Council of Learned Societies, Moral Re-Armament, Inc, the National Association for the Advancement of Colored People, Russian Orthodox Greek Catholic Church records from Alaska, Harkness Collection (Mexican and Peruvian), Hendon-Weik Collection (Lincolniana), Hans P Kraus Collection of Hispanic American Manuscripts, papers of Joseph and Stewart Alsop,Henry H Arnold, Hannah Arendt, Newton D Baker, Nathaniel P Banks, Clara Barton, Alexander Graham Bell and family,

MANUSCRIPTS—COLLECTIONS (cont.)

Edward Bernays, Albert J Beveridge, Nicholas Biddle, Hugo Black, Gutzon Borglum, Irving Brant, Huntington Cairns, Truman Capote, Andrew Carnegie, Caleb Cushing, Charlotte Cushman, Josephus Daniels, Jo Davidson, Frederick Douglass, James A Farley, Peter Force, Felix Frankfurter, Benjamin Franklin, Daniel Chester French, Sigmund Freud, Arnold Gesell, Lillian Gish, William F Halsey, Alexander Hamilton, John Hay, Oliver Wendell Holmes, Benjamin W Huebsch, Charles Evans Hughes, Cordell Hull, Harold Ickes, John Paul Jones, Ernest J King, Henry A Kissinger, Frank Knox, Robert M LaFollette and family, Robert Lansing, George B McClellan, James P McGranery, Charles L McNary, Eugene and Anges Meyer, Edna St Vincent Millay, Ogden Mills, William (Billy) Mitchell,Samuel F B Morse, Louise Chandler Moulton, Reinhold Niebuhr, Frederick Law Olmsted, J Robert Oppenheimer, George S Patton Jr, John H Pershing, Gifford Pinchot, Joseph Pulitzer, Whitelaw Reid and family, Elliot Richardson, Elihu Root, Henry R Schoolcraft, Carl Schurz, Eric Sevareid, Carl Spaatz, Arthur B Spingarn, Edwin M Stanton, Robert A Taft, Joseph M Toner, Booker T Washington, Daniel Webster, Gideon Welles, James McNeill Whistler, William Allen White, Walt Whitman, Harvey W Wiley, Owen Wister, Wilbur and Orville Wright, National Urban League, and Mary Church Terrell. Also reproductions of mss in European archives that relate to American history. An important guide to ms collections acquired in the 19th and early 20th centuries is US Library of Congress, Manuscript Division, *Handbook of Manuscripts in the Library of Congress*, Washington: Govt Print Office, 1918 xvi,750 p Z6621.U55. Many ofthe Library's mss collections are described in *The National Union Catalog of Manuscript Collections*, Washington: Library of Congress, 1959/61 Z6620.U5N3. For an overview of the division's holdings, see US National Historical Publications Commission, *A Guide to Archives and Manuscripts in the United States*, New Haven: Yale University Press, 1961 xxiii, 775 p CD3022.A45, edited by Phillip M Hamer, p 85-121.

DC —LIBRARY OF CONGRESS, Geography and Map Division, Washington, 20540. John A Wolter, Chief
Holdings: Cat Mss Maps Pix Slides Microforms
Notes: *Cartographic Materials.* One of the largest cartographic collections in the world, all-inclusive in coverage. Early original manuscript maps, navigation charts by Italian, Portuguese, and Spanish 15th, 16th, and 17th-century cartographers; the Hummel & Warner Collections of rare manuscript and printed maps and atlases of China and Korea from the 17th, 18th, and 19th centuries; manuscript and printed maps of colonial America, the Revolutionary War, the War of 1812, the Civil War, and wars of the 20th century; individual sheets of large and medium-scale set maps and charts published in the 19th and 20th centuries, including official topographic, geologic, soil, mineral, and resource maps, and nautical and aeronautical charts for most countries of the world; special subject maps of the world and its various political entities; maps of the United States and the separateStates; county maps and plans of cities and towns, and the Sanborn Fire Insurance Maps, dating back to 1866 for some 13,000 cities in the United States. Atlases include earliest printed editions of Ptolemy's Geography (1482), and representative volumes of leading atlas publishers of the last five centuries covering individual continents, countries, states, counties, cities, and the world. Total: 3,800,000 maps, 49,000 atlases, 400 globes and 2000 relief models. See *The Geography and Map Division: A Guide to Its Collections and Services*, rev ed, 1975 (LC 5.2:SE6/975).

DC —LIBRARY OF CONGRESS, General Reading Rooms Division, Microform Reading Room, Washington, 20540.
Notes: Microfilm (378,000 reels and strips): Mss in St Catherine's Monastery on Mt Sinai and in the libraries of the Greek and Armenian Patriarchates in Jerusalem and selected monasteries on Mt Athos; Modern Lanuage Association reproductions of mss and rare books mss of American interest filmed by the American Council of Learned Societies' British Manuscripts project; Inventories of Latin ms books from numerous German, Austrian and Italian archives and libraries; Pandects of the Notaries of Genoa to 1300; selected inventories (relating to American history) from the Archives Nationales (Paris); books printed in English before 1640; early English and American literary periodicals; English parish registers 16th to 19th centuries (Challen typescripts); early Latin American imprints; Mexican provincial and local archives from Jalisco, Oaxacca, Parral, Puebla and other cities;early editions of Petrarch and Ronsard; 16th and 17th century Russian imprints; papers of Simon Bolivar; League of Nations documents; official gazettes of India and Pakistan and their states and of certain other countries; press translations from Mainland China, Indonesia, Japan and Yugoslavia; underground newspapers; preservation microfilm of books from the Library's general collections; doctoral dissertations and misc items. *Microfiche* (133,000): US city directories to 1860; US corporation annual reports; US Office of Education ERIC reports; State labor reports 1865-1900; British radical periodicals; Black journals (US and British); social and economic plans of developing countires; orgainzation of American States documents, amd misc items. *Microprint* (297,000 cards): American imprints to 1810; English and American plays 1516-1830; Journalsand Sessional Papers of the British House of Commons; Index to early American periodicals; US non-depository documents and UN documents.

DC —LIBRARY OF CONGRESS, Music Division, Washington, 20540.
Holdings: Cat Mss Maps Pix Slides Microforms
Notes: Probably the largest collection (more than 3,500,000 items) of music and music literature in the world. Incl. autograph mss. and letters of Bach, Hayden, Mozart, Beethoven, Weber, Schubert, Mendelssohn, Schumann, Liszt, Brahms, Wagner, Delibes, Schoenbert, Bartok, Hindemith, Stravinsky, MacDowell, and others.

DC —NATIONAL GEOGRAPHIC SOCIETY, Library, 1146 16th St NW, Washington, 20036. Susan Fifer Canby, Dir
Holdings: Vols (63,000) Cat Mss Maps Pix
Notes: Material concerning land, sea, and space exploration--past and present. All fields of anthropology, natural history, geography, etc.

DC —SOCIETY OF THE CINCINNATI, Library, 2118 Massachusetts Ave NW, Washington, 20008. John D Kilbourne, Dir of Museum & Library
Holdings: Vols (12,000) Cat Mss Maps Pix Slides Microforms
Budget: ($65,000)
Notes: Because of the French connections of the Society of the Cincinnati, a particular effort is made to incl information about the French contribution to the American Revolution. The collection is also rich in biographical materials concerning the officer personnel of the American and French armies of the American Revolution. There are two significant sub-sections of this collection: The George Rogers Clark Collection concerning the history of the Old Northwest (to 1820); and the Member-Author collection, writings of members of the Society of the Cincinnati in various fields. It is advisable to make an appointment for use of the collections.

FL —UNIVERSITY OF FLORIDA, Libraries, Special Collections, W University Ave, Gainesville, 32611. Sidney Ives, Librn & Rare Books
Holdings: Cat Mss Maps
Notes: This collection, of manuscripts only, deals especially with Haiti, revolutionary period and after. Also a very large group of notaries papers useful for research in trade and slavery, etc.

FL —FLORIDA STATE UNIVERSITY, Robert Manning Strozier Library, Special Collections Dept, Tallahassee, 32306. Opal M Free, Head, Special Collections
Holdings: Uncat Mss
Notes: Most of the 378,580 mss and papers relate to Florida history and development but some are of other interest. Some are papers of prominent families; some of obscure persons. Some account books and other business records, some papers of state officials.

GA —UNIVERSITY OF GEORGIA, Libraries, Special Collections Division, Athens, 30602. Vesta Lee Gordon, Asst Dir for Special Collections
Holdings: Vols (75,000) Cat Mss Maps Pix
Notes: Materials on Georgia history, incl approx 3,000,000 items in 2000 collections of mss; 1200 maps; 6000 pictures and over 200 pieces of sheet music.

HI —HAWAIIAN MISSION CHILDREN'S SOCIETY LIBRARY, 553 S King St, Honolulu, 96813. Mary Jane Knight, Librn
Holdings: Vols 15,000 Cat Mss Pix
Notes: Missionary period of Hawaiian history, 1819-1880, incl a general collection of Hawaiian history and travel, an outstanding collection of early voyages to the Pacific, and an almost complete collection of early Hawaiian imprints, ie, publications in the Hawaiian language during the 19th century. Ms material incl letters, journals and reports of the Protestant missionaries who came to Hawaii (the Sandwich Islands) under the auspices of the American Board of Commissioners for Foreign Missions. The material is for research only; the stacks are closed. Unpublished papers may be examined by qualified researchers on application to the librarian. Published material is cataloged. Hawaiian imprints are cataloged, except for the Dewey classification 300's which are mainly governmentdocuments. Ms collections are cataloged or in the process of being completely arranged and cataloged.

ID —IDAHO STATE UNIVERSITY, Library, Pocatello, 83209. Gary Domitz, Social Science Librn
Holdings: Cat Mss Maps Pix
Notes: Extensive collection.

IL —SOUTHERN ILLINOIS UNIVERSITY, CARBONDALE, Delyte W Morris Library, Special Collections Dept, Carbondale, 62901. David V Koch, Cur of Special Collections; Louisa Bowen, Cur of Manuscripts
Holdings: Cat Mss Pix Microforms
Notes: Estimated 460,000 pieces: Southern Illinois history; theatre (particularly political theatre); expatriate authors; Irish literature; philosophy; and other major collecting areas which are noted in this volume.

IL —CHICAGO BOARD OF TRADE, Library, 141 W Jackson Blvd, Chicago, 60604. Darlene Appleman, Librn
Holdings: Vols (4000) Cat Microforms
Notes: Incl materials on commodity exchanges, commodities that are traded on futures exchanges, finance, and agricultural economics. *Commodity Futures Trading, A Bibliography* is published annually. The archives of the Chicago Board of Trade are located in the Manuscript Collection at the University of Illinois at Chicago Circle Campus. A published catalog, *The Archives of the Chicago Board of Trade, 1859-1925*, is available from the Chicago Board of Trade.

IL —CHICAGO HISTORICAL SOCIETY, Library, Clark St at North Ave, Chicago, 60614. Archie Motley, Manuscript Librn
Notes: About 4,000,000 items (9000 linear ft). Personal papers and archives of organizations, primarily those active in the Chicago area. Most pertain to the 20th

MANUSCRIPTS—COLLECTIONS (cont.)

century, but there are substantial holdings for the 19th and some for the 17th and 18th centuries. Some significant manuscripts on the early history of Illinois, the Old Northwest, Abraham Lincoln, the American Revolution and the Civil War. For more complete description of holdings, see entries for Chicago Historical Society under the following subjects: US - History; US - Politics and Government; Illinois - History; Illinois - Politics and Government; Presidents - US; Legislators - US; Blacks - History; Business - History; Labor - History; Trade Unions - History; Public Welfare - History; Social Service; Civil Rights; CommunityLife.

IL —NEWBERRY LIBRARY, 60 W Walton St, Chicago, 60610. Diana Haskell, Cur of Modern Mss
Holdings: Cat Mss Pix Microforms
Notes: The Midwest Manuscripts Collection of about 100,000 items, is devoted to the papers of local literary, political and socially prominent figures. Restricted use: noncirculating.

IL —ORIENTAL INSTITUTE, 1155 E 58th St, Chicago, 60637. John Larsen, Archivist
Notes: The Bernhard Moritz Collection. Fine examples of bindings as well as of Islamic calligraphy and writing materials--papyrus, parchment, papers, etc. Extensive collection is also in the Beatty Library in Dublin, Ireland; Victoria and Albert Museum in London; Libraries in East and West Germany.

IL —UNIVERSITY OF CHICAGO LIBRARY, Dept of Special Collections, 1100 E 57 St, Chicago, 60637.
Notes: Bacon Collection of papers and manorial records regarding estates in Norfolk and Suffolk.

IL —NORTHERN ILLINOIS REGIONAL HISTORY CENTER, Sven Parson Hall, Northern Illinois University, De Kalb, 60115. Glen Gildemeister, Dir
Holdings: Cat Mss Maps Pix Slides Phonorecords Audiotapes 16mm Films Microforms
Notes: "A research center for advanced research in the humanities. This northern area of Illinois (excluding Cook County) has been virtually untouched by collecting agencies and we hope to fill that void. We will be strong in agribusiness, agricultural implement business, and hybrid farming mechanics....Will be primarily a ms repository, but [have] already taken responsibility for many artifacts and books, some rare."

IL —NORTHWESTERN UNIVERSITY, Music Library, 1937 Sheridan Rd, Evanston, 60201. Don L Roberts, Head Music Librn
Holdings: Vols (140,000) Cat Mss Phonorecords Audiotapes Microforms
Notes: Main emphasis is on the documentation (incl 2000 ms pieces) of 20th century music. Broad acquisitions of mss, books, music and recordings relating to 20th century music. Library contains a portion of the Moldenhauer Archive and the John Cage "Notations Collection".

IL —ILLINOIS STATE HISTORICAL SOCIETY, Library, Old State Capitol, Springfield, 62706. Roger D Bridges, Head Librn
Holdings: Vols (146,000) Cat Mss Maps Pix Microforms
Budget: ($40,000)
Notes: Incl 8 million mss, nearly 2000 maps, 180,000 pictures and 60,000 microfilm reels. Downs 2546, 2606, 2612, 187, 188. See also *Guide to the Microfilm Edition of the Pierre Menard Collection in the Illinois State Historical Library.* Separate catalogs (card) for printed material, mss, broadsides.

IL —UNIVERSITY OF ILLINOIS, URBANA/CHAMPAIGN, Library, University Archives, 19 Library, 1408 W Gregory Drive, Urbana, 61801. Maynard Brichford, University Archivist
Holdings: Uncat Mss Maps Pix Slides Phonorecords Microforms
Notes: In addition to the university archives

and the collections of academic and administrative staff, the archives have numerous other series of institutional and personal papers. Published guide to the collections is available: *Manuscripts Guide to Collections at the University of Illinois at Urbana-Champaign* (University of Illinois Press, 1976). Control cards and ADP control on 3644 record series; 5132 pages of supplementary finding aids. Probably the largest ms collection in the state. Holdings on the history of librarianship and faculty and student life are particularly strong.

IN —INDIANA UNIVERSITY, Lilly Library, Seventh St, Bloomington, 47405. William R Cagle, Librn
Holdings: Mss Pix
Notes: Lilly Library has approximately 5,000,000 ms items in 985 collections, with major concentrations in English and American literature of the 19th and 20th centuries, and Indiana history and literature. Collections are growing in French and German literature. Also, illuminated books, mss, etc.

IN —INDIANA UNIVERSITY, Institute for Sex Research Library, 416 Morrison Hall, Bloomington, 47401. Douglas Freeman, Collections and Services Librn; Joan Brewer, Information Services Librn
Holdings: Vols (62,000) Cat Mss Pix Phonorecords Audiotapes Slides Films Microforms
Budget: ($20,000)
Notes: One of the greatest and most extensive collections on sexual behavior, the library collects materials on all aspects of sex activity, with special emphasis on behavioral and social aspects. Also collects erotic literature and sexual ephemera. Incl 105 audiotapes, 23 vertical file drawers, 108 phonorecords, 55,000 pictures, 5000 slides, and 1700 films. Rich in French, German and American sources; also much Oriental. Semitraditional erotic poetry and song of 17th-18th century England. Bawdy limericks, double-entendre, puns, slang, erotic literature, graffiti, slang and special dictionaries, proverbs and sayings, epigrams and research materials of the Kinsey Studies, etc. Contact information Service for: literature serching, preparation of bibliographies, permission to use collection. Limited photocopying.

IN —INDIANA HISTORICAL SOCIETY, Library, 315 W Ohio St, Indianapolis, 46202. Robert K O'Neill, Dir
Holdings: Cat Mss Maps Pix Slides Microforms

IA —IOWA STATE UNIVERSITY, Library, Dept of Special Collections, Ames, 50011. Stanley M Yates, Head
Holdings: Mss Pix
Notes: Collections incl papers of Iowa Bankers Association; Louis H Pammel, botanist; Paul Errington, zoologist; Christian Petersen, sculptor; Austin Adams family; Robert E Buchanan, bacteriologist; Nils A Olson, Chief of Bureau of Agricultural Economics, USDA; George Henry von Tungeln, rural sociologist; Roswell Garst, farmer; J B Davidson, organizer of the American Society of Agricultural Engineers; Iowa Academy of Science; National Farmers Process Tax Recovery Association; Poultry Science Association; Weed Science Society of America; Agribusiness Accountability Project; Jim Hightower; Iowa Farm Bureau Federation; Iowa Farmers Union; Ralph K Bliss, director of the ISU Extension Service; Lauren K Soth, editor of the Des Moines *Register and Tribune*; Frederic Leopold, ornithologist; American School of Wildlife Protection; Dwight Isley, entomologist;and Frank Rinehart Everly, editor of Des Moines *Register and Tribune*.

KS —UNIVERSITY OF KANSAS MEDICAL CENTER, College of Health Sciences & Hospital, Clendening History of Medicine Library, Rainbow Blvd at 39th, Kansas City, 66103. Robert P Hudson, Chmn/Cur
Notes: Strong in all fields of medical history. Incl incunabula and serials. Mss incl Jakob Henle, 1809-1885, papers (ca 4050 items); Howard Atwood Kelly, 1858-1943, correspondence (ca 90 items); Joseph Lister,

1827-1912, letters (7); Florence Nightingale, 1820-1910, letters (20); and Samuel Jay Crumbine, 1862-1954, papers (ca 2365 items).

KS —UNIVERSITY OF KANSAS, Kenneth Spencer Research Library, Special Collections Dept, Lawrence, 66045. Alexandra Mason, Librn
Holdings: Cat Mss Maps Pix
Notes: Some 1100 linear feet of 9th-20th centuries, mostly 14th-19th. Noncirculating. Unpublished catalog in repository. Major holdings: About 650 mss and documents before 1500, incl 5 Mandevilles, glossary fragments, Anglo-Saxon, English and Scottish manorial documents, some vernacular mss (especially French and Italian), classical texts, liturgical and devotional works, histories and chronicles, legal documents and cartularies. Renaissance historians and humanists; renaissance (especially Italian) historical, commercial, economic, political sources; Poland-Vatican diplomatic relations; counterreformation; law. Sources for British and European, especially Italian, economic history, 1400-1800. Documents and correspondence pertaining to British overseas trading companies. 18th century English governmental records.Travel diaries and mss (about 120). 18th century British politics. Japanese falconry. A reasonable selection of humanists and church fathers. British, French and Italian land records, mediaeval to 18th century. Portuguese and Brazilian politics and history (Boehrer Collection, ca 4000 mss). Varied collections in English (little little magazine publishers). Miscellaneous sample letters of litterateurs and scholars. Ms maps (17th-19th centuries). Neurology (C Judson Herrick papers, George Ellett Coghill papers, Paul Gibbons Roofe papers). Natural history (15th-19th centuries), especially strong in ornithology (Chinese paintings, Japanese falconry, over 2000 drawings and paintings of John Gould, and miscellaneous letters of various ornithologists-some 50 writers and artists) and botany (Rafinesque, William Darlington, Laurent Garcin).

KS —MENNINGER FOUNDATION, Archives, 5600 W Sixth St, Box 829, Topeka, 66601. Alice Brand, Librn; Mark West, Archivist
Notes: 30 boxes. Contains hundreds of unpublished mss that relate to mental illness.

KY —WESTERN KENTUCKY UNIVERSITY, Kentucky Building, Folklore, Folklife & Oral History Archives, Bowling Green, 42101. Patricia M Hodges, Archivist
Holdings: Cat Mss Audiotapes Videotapes
Notes: Archive contains manuscripts of field collection projects done by students and faculty. There is a large folk song collection in manuscript and tapes of local performers of traditional songs and music. Materials generally relate to Kentucky and surrounding areas; or to country music and traditional music. 3500 tapes; 135 linear ft of manuscripts.

LA —AMISTAD RESEARCH CENTER, 400 Esplanade Ave, New Orleans, 70116. Clifton H Johnson, Exec Dir; Florence E Borders, Senior Archivist
Holdings: Vols (10,000) Cat Mss Pix Audiotapes Microforms
Budget: ($315,000)
Notes: In addition, 8,000,000 ms pieces, 10,000 pictures, 3500 microforms, and 500 audiotapes. Amistad Research Center is an historical research library devoted to the collection and use of primary source materials on the history of America's ethnic minorities, with particular emphasis on Afro-Americans, American Indians, and immigrant groups. Among the larger institutional collections held are the archives and records of the American Missionary Association, the American Home Missionary Society, the Race Relations Dept of the Anti-Defamation League, the Catholic Committee of the South, and the National Association of Human Rights Workers, (formerly NAIRO, National Association of Intergroup Related Officials). Also, private papers of the Harlem Renaissance poet,

MANUSCRIPTS—COLLECTIONS (cont.)

Countee Cullen; educator and civil rights leader, Mary McLeod Bethune;20th century civil rights lawyer, Alexander P Tureaud; 19th century Black attorney and judge, George Ruffin; founder and director of Operation Crossroads Africa, Dr James H Robinson; and over 70 others.

LA —LOUISIANA STATE MUSEUM, Louisiana Historical Center, 400 Esplanade Ave, (Mailing add: 751 Chartres St, New Orleans, 70116). Edward F Haas, Chief Cur
Holdings: Mss Maps Pix
Budget: ($1,200,000)
Notes: Archives and Manuscripts Collections. Special guides and indices are in preparation. The single most important collection in this section is the Louisiana Colonial Archives, consisting of the judicial records of the French Superior Council in Louisiana and the Spanish Cabildo in Louisiana dating from 1714 to 1803. There are approximately 500,000 pages of documents in this collection. Also 19th century collections of personal papers, plantation records, business ledgers, etc. Incl 3500 maps and 15,000 pictures.

LA —TULANE UNIVERSITY, Howard-Tilton Memorial Library, Latin American Library, New Orleans, 70118. Thomas Niehaus, Dir
Holdings: Vols (150,000) Cat Mss Maps Pix Microforms VF
Budget: ($67,000)
Notes: Catalog of the Latin American Library (Boston: G K Hall, 1970, suppl. 1973,1975,1978); Downs 5338-41; suppl (1961), 2727, 2737. The Latin American Library is a general collection, but specializes in Central American, Mexican, and Brazilian materials. The disciplines which are most strongly represented are history, anthropology, and archaeology. The Viceregal Ecclesiastical Mexican Collection contains manuscripts from the colonial period. The France V Scholes Collection contains a large number of photoprints and microfilm of colonial documents from the archives of Spain and Mexico. The Merle Greene Robertson Rubbings Collection contains nearly five hundred rubbings of relief sculpture from Mayan archaeological sites in Mexico and Guatemala. The Photographic Collection contains photos of archaeological sites inMeso-America, of pre-Columbian Peruvian architecture, and a general group of historic photos from Latin America.

LA —TULANE UNIVERSITY, Howard-Tilton Memorial Library, Special Collections Div, 7001 Freret St, New Orleans, 70118. Wilbur E Meneray, Librn
Holdings: Cat Mss Pix Slides Audiotapes Videotapes 16mm Films Microforms
Notes: The majority of the 2000 plus collections relate to 18th, 19th and 20th century New Orleans, South Louisiana and South Mississippi. See Brief Guide to the Manuscripts Section of the Special Collections Division Tulane University Library (New Orleans, 1977).

ME —MAINE STATE LIBRARY, Special Collections Dept, Cultural Bldg, Station 64, Augusta, 04333. Shirley Thayer, Librn
Holdings: Mss Cat
Budget: ($2,500,000)
Notes: Maine history, biography, personal papers, genealogies, diaries and a few mss of Maine authors. Also copies of deeds, surveys, vital records, legal and business papers and letters. Incl several thousand mss.

ME —MAINE MARITIME MUSEUM, Library and Archives, 963 Washington St, Bath, 04530. Nathan R Lipfert, Asst Cur
Holdings: Vols (5000) Cat Maps Pix Slides
Notes: The collection is limited primarily to shipbuilding in Bath, Maine, and to a lesser extent Maine as a whole. The unique aspects of the collection are a large collection of photographs of wooden shipbuilding and related trades, photographs of the vessels themselves, and a large collection of papers of a shipbuilding company in Bath active throughout the 19th century.

ME —BOWDOIN COLLEGE, Library, Brunswick, 04011. Dianne M Gutscher, Cur

of Special Collections
Holdings: Mss Pix
Notes: The Oliver Otis Howard Papers consist of more than 150,000 pieces of correspondence, articles, lectures, and ephemera for the period 1843-1908, covering his services as a Civil War officer, as founder of the Freedmen's Bureau, as president of Howard University, and as superintendent of the US Military Academy at West Point.

ME —MAINE HISTORICAL SOCIETY, Library, 485 Congress St, Portland, 04101.
Holdings: Vols (60,000) Cat Mss Maps Pix
Notes: The Society's holdings cover all of Maine in its scope, with special emphasis on the Portland region.

MD —US NAVAL ACADEMY, Nimitz Library, Annapolis, 21402. Alice S Creighton, Assistant Librn for Special Collections
Holdings: Vols (22,000) Cat Mss Pix
Notes: Books and periodicals, with emphasis on seapower. Incl rare and historically significant works, naval and general history. US Naval Academy materials (histories, class albums, Lucky Bags, student publications, etc), and copies of transcripts of the Naval Institute's oral history interviews with US naval officers. Manuscripts incl 205 volumes of ships' logs, letterbooks, order books, and watch, station and quarter bills, 1796-1938; papers of various naval officers, incl. Vice Admiral Wilson Brown, Commander George M Bache, Admiral Harry S Knapp, Lieutenant Edwin J DeHaven, and others; family correspondence of Admiral David Dixon Porter; and several thousand World War II naval action reports. Approximately 15,000 pictures incl portraits of naval officers, pictures of US and some foreign ships, World War II naval news photos and USNA photographs.

MD —MARYLAND HISTORICAL SOCIETY, Library, 201 W Monument St, Baltimore, 21201. William B Keller, Head Librn
Holdings: Vols (65,000) Cat Maps Pix Slides
Budget: ($8000)
Notes: Also 2 million ms pieces, 300 maps, 700 slides; 10,000 musical scores. Large collection of Maryland State Colonization Papers; Maryland and Baltimore business records; Baltimore & Ohio Railroad Papers; Baltimore Theater records and programs (late 18th, early 19th century); Maryland lottery tickets; Benjamin H Latrobe (architectural) Papers; Maryland maps, plats, prints, newspapers; Baltimore history, large collection (30,000 items Maryland local history and genealogy, 100,000 mss); iron industry papers; Maryland currency; sheet music (8000 pieces, largely Baltimore publishers); Lester S Levy "Star-Spangled Banner" collection (probably the largest in the world--over 250 pieces).

MD —WALTERS ART GALLERY, Library & Manuscripts & Rare Book Collection, 600 N Charles St, Baltimore, 21201. Muriel L Toppan, Reference Libn; Lilian M C Randall, Cur of Mss & Rare Books
Holdings: Vols (80,000) Cat Mss
Budget: ($35,000)
Notes: The collection supports the gallery's collections of art objects which date from 4000 BC to the end of the 19th century. The collection of medieval and renaissance illuminated mss (782 in number), incunabula (about 1400) and rare books are considered art objects. There are card catalogs providing indexing to the collection. The mss are listed in De Ricci and the incunabula in Goff. Photocopying permitted for Reference Library materials only.

MD —NATIONAL LIBRARY OF MEDICINE, 8600 Rockville Pike, Bethesda, 20209. Harold M Schoolinan, Actg Dir
Holdings: Vols (3,150,000) Cat Mss Audiotapes Videotapes 16mm Films Filmstrips Microforms
Budget: ($46,400)
Notes: The world's largest medical library. Materials are collected exhaustively in some 40 biomedical areas and, to a lesser degree, in related subject areas such as general chemistry, physics, zoology, botany, and

instrumentation. Holdings include 82,000 monographic volumes, pre-1871; 438,000 monographic volumes, 1871-present; 714,000 bound serial volumes; 281,000 theses; 172,000 pamphlets; 1,207,000 manuscripts; 156,000 microforms; 12,000 audiovisuals; and 75,000 prints and photographs. Pre-1871 material is in a separate historical collection. Approximately 24,000 serial titles are currenlty received.

MD —UNIVERSITY OF MARYLAND, Library, Archives & Manuscripts Dept, College Park, 20742. Mary A Boccaccio, Head
Holdings: Mss Pix
Notes: University of Maryland publications and archives; collections of organizational papers (eg, Baltimore & Ohio Railroad; various organizations concerned with the Chesapeake Bay and environs; various labor unions, particularly those involving the tabacco industry), mostly associated with literary and public figures (eg, the late Sanator Millard Tydings); oral histories relating to the archival and mss collections; associated memorabilia; photographs, mainly associated with Maryland. A guide to collections of personal, family, and organizational papers relating to Maryland is being prepared.

MA —JONES LIBRARY, 43 Amity St, Amherst, 01002. Daniel J Lombardo, Cur of Special Collections
Holdings: Vols (2710) Cat Maps Pix
Notes: The Boltwood Collection. Several thousand documents, cataloged, 18th and 19th centuries. The scope is primarily local, then regional, Massachusetts, New England. Several thousand local pictures, chiefly post-1926.

MA —BEDFORD FREE PUBLIC LIBRARY, 613 Pleasant St, Bedford, 02740. Paul A Cyr, Cur of the Melville Room
Holdings: Vols 1020 Cat Mss Pix
Notes: One of the nation's most extensive collections (72,000 pieces) on American whaling. Incl all forms of documents used in the industry, over 40,000 mss. Library has a printed list of its logbooks and a seamen's card file of men who sailed from New Bedford Customs District contains 250,000 names. Library has published an addendum to "Starbuck" and "Whaling Masters," and "Birth of a Whaleship," 1964, both by Reginald B Hegarty.

MA —BOSTON PUBLIC LIBRARY, Rare Books and Manuscripts, Copley Square, Boston, 02117. Laura V Monti, Keeper of Rare Books
Notes: Significant material, in volume, is devoted to economic and political relationships between New England and the Maritime Provinces in the 18th Century; much on Abolitionists and the antisalvery movement. Described in Canadian Manuscripts in the Boston Public Library (Boston: G K Hall), 1 vol. Incl about 17,000 items.

MA —FRANCIS A COUNTWAY LIBRARY OF MEDICINE, Boston Medical Library/ Harvard Medical Library, 10 Shattuck St, Boston, 02115. C Robin LeSueur, Librn; Richard J Wolfe, Cur, Rare Books & Manuscripts
Holdings: Vols (500,000) Mss Maps Pix
Budget: ($1,160,000)
Notes: Second largest medical library in the nation. Combines the resources of the Harvard Medical School and the Boston Medical Library, as well as the medical collections of many regional libraries. Outstanding in all areas of medical science. Author-title catalog of imprints through 1959 published by G K Hall, 1973. Strong in serials and medical history in all fields of medicine. Especially strong in subject areas incl incunabula, medical Judaica, Osleriana, O W Holmes, William Rimmer, non-medical books by doctors, travel books by physicians, X-ray (Dr Lloyd E Hawes, Hon Curator), prints and medical satire (Dr Mark D Altschule, Hon Curator), phrenology, witchcraft, gynecology and obstetrics, medical illustrations, birth control and sex research, medical numismatics, European imprints before 1850 and American imprints

MANUSCRIPTS—COLLECTIONS (cont.)

before 1870, Chinese and Japanese medicine, medicaldissertations (500,000), anatomy, anesthesia, botany, biochemistry and chemistry, alchemy, dental medicine, legal medicine, physiology, dental medicine, legal medicine, physiology, psychiatry, plastic surgery, surgery, zoology, ms collections, which incl the Harvard Medical Archives, probably the strongest in America.

MA —HARVARD UNIVERSITY, Graduate School of Business Administration, Baker Library, Soldiers Field, Boston, 02163. Mary V Chatfield, Librn; Florence Bartoshesky, Cur of Manuscripts and Archives
Holdings: Vols (75,000) Cat Mss Pix
Notes: Baker Library strong in historical aspects of business and economics incl original company records, company histories, business biographies, histories of industries, etc; 16,000 pictures. Ms collection of more than 75,000 incl original records of business firms from 1400 (Medici Collection) to present; especially strong in 19th century. New England enterprises, textile firms, international trade, China trade, railroads, papers of several Northeast merchant families, 19th century small business. Also incl pictures, trade cards, clipper ship cards, money, trade catalogs, business cartoons, prices current and exhibit items. See Robert W Lovett and Eleanor C Bishop, compilers, *Business Manuscripts in Baker Library* (Boston: The Library, 1978), 382 pp. Mss are described in the *National Union Catalog of Manuscript Collections* and in Hamer's *A Guide to Archives and Manuscripts in the United States.* Restricted use: Manuscripts noncirculating. Downs: 1636, 2122, 2616, 2675, 2677, 2698, 2700, 2701, 2702, 2706, 2708, 2711, 2713-15, 2716, 2717-18, 2721-26, 2734, 2737, 2774, 2814, 4300, 5162: Supplement 964, 965, 968, 998.

†MA —JOHN F KENNEDY LIBRARY, Columbia Point, Boston, 02125. Dan H Fenn Jr, Dir
Holdings: Vols 20,000 Cat Mss Maps Pix Slides Phonorecords Audiotapes Videotapes 16mm Films Microforms
Notes: The major collection about JFK, his life, family and administration. It contains personal papers, audiovisual materials, books, oral history interviews. Collection is described in "Historical Materials in the John F Kennedy Library." "The Kennedy Collection," a subject guide to the book collection, is available for sale. Also, the papers of Ernest Hemingway. Incl mss for almost all his works, published and unpublished, and a large volume of correspondence, photographs, clippings, and scrapbooks. It covers his entire life. An incomplete catalog is available. No photocopying.

MA —JOHN F KENNEDY LIBRARY, Columbia Point, Boston, 02125. Henry J Gwiazda II, Cur
Notes: The Robert F Kennedy Papers cover the period from 1937-1968 and are divided into four subcollections: the Pre-Administration, Attorney General's, Senate, and 1968 Presidential Campaign Papers. In the Pre-Administration Papers, over 140 archives boxes or 70 percent of the materials are open to research. The Personal and Political Papers of this subcollection are almost entirely open. Most of the unprocessed mss are in the Working Files and involve investigative work on labor racketeering. Seventy five percent or 185 archives boxes of the Attorney General's Papers are open, incl the correspondence, the John F Kennedy Library File, the Speech and Trip Files for 1961-1964. For the Senate Papers, 200 boxes are open for the 1964 Senate Campaign, the Legislative Subject File, and the Speech and Trip Files for 1964-1968. The speeches and press releases(incl in the Senate subcollection Speech File) and "The Black Books" (16 boxes) on state and delegate information are open for the 1968 campaign. Each subcollection has its own finding aid. The Library also has available for research about

100 audiotapes of Robert F Kennedy's public addresses from 1962-1966 and some 50 oral history interviews on RFK and one (1000 pages) by RFK. There are also available the major documentaries on RFK and a number of films donated by the major networks for research use in the Library.

MA —MASSACHUSETTS HISTORICAL SOCIETY LIBRARY, 1154 Boylston St, Boston, 02215. John D Cushing, Librn
Holdings: Mss Maps Microforms
Notes: One of more than 5000 individual collections in the Library, this collection incl the Adams Family papers and materials relating to Massachusetts and New England. The Library's collection of mss has been cataloged and issued in nine folio vols by G K Hall & Co of Boston. It is widely distributed throughout the United States and Europe.

MA —SECRETARY OF THE COMMONWEALTH, Archives Division, State House, Boston, 02133.

MA —SOCIETY FOR THE PRESERVATION OF NEW ENGLAND ANTIQUITIES, Library, 141 Cambridge St, Boston, 02114. Ellie Reichlin, Librn & Cur of Photographic Collections
Holdings: Vols (3000) Cat Pix Microforms
Budget: ($75,000)
Notes: Incl two types of mss: (1) Family papers relating to historic properties administered by SPNEA. Ca 125 linear feet, incl the Codman family archive, 1700s-1960s, with associated family photograph collection. (2) Misc mss with emphasis on topics relating to building, interior designs, material culture (ca 3500 items, cataloged). For further information, an *Annotated Checklist to Special Collections of SPNEA* Library is available. See also entry in *Architectural Records in Boston: A Guide to Architectural Research* (1983, Garland Publishing Co, New York). Additional collections incl prints, original artwork (largely by NE artists, engravers) relating to architectural subjects; maps; architectural periodicals (19th century).

MA —HARVARD UNIVERSITY, Harvard College Library, Fine Arts Library, Fogg Museum, 32 Quincy St, Cambridge, 02138. Wolfgang M Freitag, Librn
Holdings: Vols (202,000) Cat Mss Pix Slides
Budget: ($176,500)
Notes: All areas of art history, with emphasis on Italian primitives, Italian Renaissance, master drawings, Romanesque sculpture, architectural history, ms materials (particulary American artists'), conservation and restoration of art objects. Incl the Berenson repertory of photographs from the Harvard Center for Italian Renaissance Studies in Florence, and the Decimal Index to the Art of the Low Countries. Separate card catalogs for books, photographs and lantern slides, registers for ms holdings which are not incl in *National Union Catalog of Manuscript Collections.* Slides total over 230,000; over 745,000 pictures. *Fine Arts Library Catalogue* (14 volumes) and *Catalogue of Auction Sales Catalogues* (1 volume) (Boston: G K Hall, 1972); *A Guide to the Fine Arts Library* (Cambridge, Mass: 1971); *Guide to the Harvard Libraries,* microfiche edition of holdingscataloged through 1981 published 1984 (Munich/New York: Saur).

MA —BOSTON COLLEGE LIBRARIES, Thomas P O'Neill Library, Chestnut Hill, 02167. Frank J Seegraber, Special Collections Librn
Holdings: Vols 1300 Cat Mss Pix Phonorecords Audiotapes Microforms
Notes: This, the most complete collection of Thompsoniana in existence, incl notebooks, mss, letters, and rare editions, and collateral material relating to poet, his times and his work. The notebooks are the chief source of clues to the identification of 300 of Thompson's unsigned contributions to periodicals. *An Account of the Books and Manuscripts of Francis Thompson,* ed by Rev Terence L Connolly (Boston College, 1937). Works of Wilfrid and Alice Meynell and their children, Viola, Sir Francis, and Everard, are incl in this collection. The items

give a well-rounded view of this remarkable family as poets, fiction writers, essayists, biographers, prefacers, and editors. This collection incl mss, poems, correspondence, articles, and book reviews by Coventry Patmore, an English poet, essayist, and critic, and a good friend of Francis Thompson. Among thecorrespondents are Robert Browning, Alfred Tennyson, Matthew Arnold, Ralph Waldo Emerson, Nathaniel Hawthorne, Thomas Carlyle, and William Makepeace Thackeray. For reference use only, by arrangement with librarian.

MA —HISTORIC DEERFIELD-POCUMTUCK VALLEY MEMORIAL ASSOCIATION, Libraries, Memorial St, Box 53, Deerfield, 01342. David R Proper, Librn
Holdings: Vols (17,000) Cat Mss Maps Pix Microforms
Notes: Local and regional history, especially western Massachusetts. Also, remnants of several collection of books available to early Deerfield and Greenfield residents. Strong ms collection dealing with the region's families, businesses, etc. These consist of sermons, diaries, town and church records, voluntary societies' archives, etc. Extensive collection of photographs of the people and buildings of Deerfield and its environs, and travels in Maine, California, and England (1880s to 1920s). Also, large collection of glassplate negatives. Houses the Connecticut Valley Bibliography, a comprehensive card file on the history and culture of the Connecticut Valley of Massachusetts.

MA —CHINA TRADE MUSEUM, Library, 215 Adams St, Milton, 02186. Lisa L Gwirtzman, Librn
Holdings: Uncat Mss Maps Pix
Notes: A museum collection, archive and library devoted to a history of the China Trade to Boston, (1784-1900). Incl 30,000 papers of Captain Robert Bennet Forbes; 75,000 other China Trade documents; and 3500 period photographs.

MA —MERRIMACK VALLEY TEXTILE MUSEUM, Library, 800 Massachusetts Ave, North Andover, 01845. Clare Sheridan, Librn; Laurence Gross, Cur
Holdings: Vols (35,000) Cat Mss Maps Pix Slides
Notes: *Checklist of Prints, Drawings and Painting in the Merrimack Valley Textile* Museum, Helena E Wright, 1972; *Checklist of Finished Textiles,* Katherine R Koob, 1980; *New City on the Merrimack: Prints of Lawrence 1845-1876,* Helena Wright, 1974; *Homespun to Factory Made: Woolen Textiles in America 1776-1876* (exhibit catalog) 1978; *Textile Technology Prints: A Checklist of Prints, Drawings and Paintings in the Merrimack Valley Textile Museum,* Helena E Wright, 1980; *All Sorts of Good Sufficient Cloth: Linen-making in New England, 1640-1860,* (exhibit catalogue) 1980; *The Merrimack Valley Textile Museum: A Guide to the Manuscript Collections* Helena E Wright, Garland Press 1983.

MA —OLD STURBRIDGE VILLAGE, Research Library, Sturbridge, 01566. Theresa Rini Percy, Librn
Holdings: Cat Mss Maps Pix Audiotapes Microforms
Notes: Rural life in New England, 1790-1850. Farmers, artisans, craftsmen, professional and businessmen. No maritime material.

MA —AMERICAN ANTIQUARIAN SOCIETY LIBRARY, 185 Salisbury St, Worcester, 01609. Marcus A McCorison, Dir & Librn
Holdings: Cat Mss
Notes: Over half a million documents. Incl papers of Isaiah Thomas; Craigie, Carwen, Bentley Families; French and Indian War; American Revolution; Worcester; William Paine; Pliny Merrick; Salisbury Papers; Larned Papers; Jennison Biographical Papers. See *Proceedings* volumes for inventories of descriptions. Collection was the basis for *American Manuscripts 1763-1815,* Cripe and Campbell (Wilmington, Del, 1977).

MANUSCRIPTS—COLLECTIONS (cont.)

†MA —CLARK UNIVERSITY, Robert
Hutchings Goddard Library, Worcester,
01610. Dorothy Mosa Kowski, Rare Books
Librn
Holdings: Vols Cat Mss
Notes: Rare books, first editions, mss,
incunabula (50), bindings, fore-edge
paintings.

MI —UNIVERSITY OF MICHIGAN, Bentley
Historical Library, Michigan Historical
Collections, 1150 Beal Ave, Ann Arbor,
48109. Francis X Blovin Jr, Dir
Holdings: Vols (45,000) Cat Mss Maps Pix
Phonorecords Audiotapes Videotapes 16mm
Films Microforms
Budget: ($302,000)
Notes: A modern ms archives collecting
original source material pertaining to
Michigan, its people, its institutions and the
University of Michigan. Emphasizes the
accumulations of personal papers of
historically important persons, incl files of
correspondence, diaries and journals as well
as the records of significant Michigan
institutions. At present the collections
contain 45,000 printed vols, 40,000,000 mss
items, 3500 maps and 500,000 photographs.
The library maintains its own catalog and
published in 1976 a revised, 2nd updated
*Guide to the Michigan Historical
Collections*. Special areas of interest to the
collections are Philippine Islands history, the
history of the temperance and prohibition
movement in the US. Immigration to
Michigan, business history, church history,
and US-China relations.

MI —UNIVERSITY OF MICHIGAN, Library,
Dept of Rare Books & Special Collections,
Ann Arbor, 48109. Robert J Starring, Head
Holdings: Vols 177
Notes: Includes manuscripts in most of the
languages of Western Europe, but chiefly
Greek and Latin. Almost one-third are
manuscripts of the Greek New Testament.
Almost all are listed in *Census of Medieval
and Renaissance Manuscripts in the United
States and Canada*, by Seymour de Ricci and
W J Wilson (New York: H W Wilson Co,
1937), and *Supplement*, 1962. Also, over
1200 mss, chiefly in Arabic, but also in
Persian; Turkish, Coptic, Syriac, Ethiopic,
Hebrew, and Armenian. Incl the McGregor
collection on mathematics and astronomy,
the Tiflis collection, and portions of the
Abdul Hamid and Yahuda collections.

MI —UNIVERSITY OF MICHIGAN, William
L Clements Library, Ann Arbor, 48109.
John C Dann, Dir

Notes: The William L. Clements Library of
Americana is a non-circulating rare book library of
original source material, printed and manuscript,
dealing with America, from the discovery period
into the late nineteenth century. The collection
includes approximately 55,000 books and
pamphlets, 550 linear feet of manuscripts, 4,100
volumes of newspapers, 36,000 maps, 40,000
pieces of sheet music, and 1,000 prints. The
collection is strongest for the period of the
American Revolution, and includes the papers of
Thomas Gage, Sir Henry Clinton, and the Earl
of Shelburne. Other areas of strength include
antislavery, cartography and geography, discovery
and exploration, American Indians, The Civil War,
tune-books, sermons and orations, and the War of
1812. There are selective research collections
dealing with Christopher Columbus, Thomas
Paine, Benjamin Franklin, George Washington,
Thomas Jefferson, and the Federalist Papers.
Publications describing the collections of the
library are: Author/Title catalog of Americana
1493-1860 in the William L. Clements Library...
7 volumes, Boston, G. K. Hall, 1970; Guide to the
manuscript collections of the William L. Clements
Library, by Arlene P. Shy 3d edition, Boston,

G. K. Hall, 1978; Guide to the manuscript maps in
the William L. Clements Library, compiled by
Christian Burn, Ann Arbor, U. of Michigan, 1959;
and Research catalog of maps of America, to 1860
in the William L. Clements Library...,edited by
Douglas W. Marshall, 4 volumes, Boston, G. K.
Hall, 1972.

MI —EDISON INSTITUTE, Greenfield
Village and Henry Ford Museum, Archives
& Research Library, PO Box 1970,
Dearborn, 48121. Steve Hamp, Dir; Joan W
Gartland, Librn
Holdings: Vols 400,000 Cat Mss Maps
Microforms
Notes: 400,000 vols incl pamphlets. The
Archives and research library supports the
program of Greenfield Village and the Henry
Ford Museum. Special collections incl:
automotive literature, ephemera, McGuffey
Readers, trade catalogs, photographs and
graphics.

MI —DETROIT PUBLIC LIBRARY, Burton
Historical Collection, 5201 Woodward Ave,
Detroit, 48202. Alice Dalligan, Chief
Notes: Original source materials for research
in the history of Detroit and the Great
Lakes area include family papers, business
records, organization files, church records,
and archives of Detroit, Wayne County, and
Michigan Territory. The French, British, and
American periods are well represented. A
catalog is located in the Reading Room.

MI —WESTERN MICHIGAN UNIVERSITY,
Dwight B Waldo Library, Institute of
Cistercian Studies Library, Kalamazoo,
49008. Beatrice H Beck, Librn
Notes: Collection contains mss and early
editions of Cistercian liturgy and authors,
especially Bernard of Clairvaux. Ms sources
of Cistercian documentary history, abbey
histories and charters.

MN —SAINT JOHN'S ABBEY &
UNIVERSITY, Hill Monastic Manuscript
Library, Collegeville, 56321. Julian G Plante,
Dir
Holdings: Vols (61,000) Microfilms
Notes: Films of 61,000 mss. The total
number of codices or bound handwritten mss
represents the holdings of several hundred
libraries in Europe, mostly Austria, Spain,
Ethiopia, West Germany, Portugal, and also
Italy, Hungary, Poland, Great Britain,
Belgium, Yugoslavia, France, Switzerland,
and the Netherlands.

MS —UNIVERSITY OF SOUTHERN
MISSISSIPPI, William David McCain
Graduate Library, Box 5148, Southern Sta,
Hattiesburg, 39406.
Holdings: Mss Pix Maps
Notes: More than 100 mss collections
relating to such topics as children's
literature; Mississippi history, politics,
commerce, organizations and people;
railroadsd; band and march music; the civil
war; chemistry and polymer science; tung
oil; education; booksellers; lumbering; and
editorial cartoons. See individual subject
entries.

MS —MISSISSIPPI STATE UNIVERSITY,
Mitchell Memorial Library, Box 5408,
Mississippi State, 39762. Frances N
Coleman, Head, Special Collections
Holdings: Vols (15,000) Cat Mss Maps Pix
Microforms
Notes: Social and political history of
Mississippi, incl University Archives (now
separate branch). Microfilms of Protestant
Church records. There are strong collections
on history of the Southern States, Mississippi
authors (especially Faulkner, Williams,
Carter, Welty, and Young); also the John C

Stennis Collection of over 2 million items,
his books, papers, photographs, etc. Incl 400
collections of mss; papers of US Rep David
R Bowen 1973-1983; papers of US Rep G V
Montgomery 1967-.

MO —UNIVERSITY OF MISSOURI-
COLUMBIA, Museum of Anthropology
Archives, 104 Swallow Hall, Columbia,
65201. Lawrence H Feldman, Museum Dir
Holdings: Vols (30) Cat Mss Maps Slides
Microforms
Notes: Copies of Latin American and
colonial mss. Many of the ms copies are of
census, or census-like, documents of late
colonial Verapaz; a few are from Sonsonate,
El Salvador or Chiapas, Mexico. Additional
material in the archives incl an original
Eskimo manuscript (ca 1930) and an original
Diegueno Yuman card vocabulary (ca 1964)
and the Museum archives (papers on old
accession systems, etc). Uncataloged
microfilm copies of colonial Otomi and other
vocabularies are also part of the collection.
A catalog of material in this collection will
appear in the Annual Report of the Museum
of Anthropology, beginning with the 1976-
77 volume.

†MO —UNIVERSITY OF MISSOURI-
COLUMBIA, Western Historical
Manuscripts Collection, Columbia, 65201.
Notes: Over 4000 mss collections.

MO —CONCEPTION ABBEY, Library,
Conception, 64433.
Holdings: Vols (2425) // Uncat Mss
Microforms
Budget: ($20,000)
Notes: Rare Roman Catholic theological
books and mss, mostly 16th-19th centuries.
A partial catalog of the collection exists.
Basically this is a donation received in the
last quarter of the 19th century from a 900-
year-old Swiss abbey, Engelberg Abbey.
Most of our mss are listed in De Ricci
census. The incunabula are for the most part
listed in Goff's census. No photocopying.

MO —UNIVERSITY OF MISSOURI-
KANSAS CITY, General Library, State
Historical Society of Missouri Manuscripts,
5100 Rockhill Road, Kansas City, 64110.
Kenneth J LaBudde, Dir; Gordon
Hendrickson, Assoc Dir
Holdings: Mss
Notes: Joint Collection Western Historical
Manuscript Collection and the State Historical of
Missouri Manuscripts, University of Missouri-
Kansas City General Library, 5100 Rockhill Road,
Kansas City, MO 64110. Ca 2,500 linear feet of
manuscripts, blueprints and oral history tapes.
Notes: The manuscript collection includes material
which documents the history, growth and
development of Missouri, especially the Greater
Kansas City area. The personal papers of business,
civic, cultural, political and community leaders;
local historians and other individuals of families
from the area are within the collection as are the
records of associations, organizations and
institutions which reflect the history of the area.
Prominent among the collections are the papers of
Charles B. Wheeler, Jr., Charles N. Kimball,
Arthur Mag, Oscar D. Nelson, Lou B. Holland,
J. C. Nichols, Perry Cookingham, Blevins Davis
and Daniel Macmorris and the records of the
Kansas City Board of Trade. Architectural designs
and plans for approximately 3,500 Kansas City
buildings and the records of the Hoit, Price and
Barnes architectural firm and the papers of Asa
Beebe Cross, early Kansas City architect as well as
a number of oral histories with Kansas City Jazz
figures are in the collection.

MO —MISSOURI BOTANICAL GARDEN
LIBRARY, PO Box 299, Saint Louis, 63166.
M R Crosby, Dir of Research

MANUSCRIPTS—COLLECTIONS (cont.)

MO —MISSOURI HISTORICAL SOCIETY, Library, Jefferson Memorial Bldg, Saint Louis, 63112. Stephanie Klein, Librn-Archivist; Peter Michel, Cur of Manuscripts
Holdings: Cat Mss Maps Pix
Notes: Extensive ms holdings relating to Missouri, US history, etc. Also ms collections of many noted persons (all but subsequent additions listed in Hamer, 1961). Library holdings described in Whitehall, Walter Muir, *Independent Historical Societies* (Boston, 1962).

MO —SAINT LOUIS UNIVERSITY, Pius XII Memorial Library, Vatican Film Library Collection, 3655 W Pine Blvd, Saint Louis, 63108. Charles J Ermatinger, Librn
Holdings: Mss Slides Microforms
Notes: Vatican Film Library has 75 percent of the Greek, Latin and western European vernacular holdings in the Vatican Library, plus all the Hebrew, Arabic and Ethiopic holdings on film. Covers 5th-19th centuries. Sizable collection of western European books. In addition, has largest collection on the work of the Jesuits in Latin America, the US and the Philippines, filmed from European Jesuit archives. Excellent catalogs and guides to all collections. Also, 50,608 slides of illuminated mss; 26,470 reels of microfilm.

MO —WASHINGTON UNIVERSITY, John M Olin Library, Campus Box 1061, St Louis, 63130.
Notes: The bulk of the ms and archival collections are 20th century personal and professional papers of American literary, political, business and academic figures; these are entered under personal name elsewhere in this volume.

NV —NEVADA STATE HISTORICAL SOCIETY, Library, 1650 N Virginia St, Reno, 89503. Eric N Moody, Cur of Manuscripts; Lee Mortensen, Librn
Holdings: Vols 15,000 Cat Mss Maps Pix Slides Microforms
Budget: ($156,994)
Notes: Incl 2800 mss, 1500 maps and 70,000 pictures.

NH —NEW HAMPSHIRE HISTORICAL SOCIETY, Manuscripts Library, 30 Park St, Concord, 03301. Thomas E Camden, Cur
Holdings: Vols (500,000) Cat Mss
Budget: ($12,500)
Notes: Photocopying of individual items only. Consultation of original mss materials strongly encouraged. Mss and books related to New Hampshire history. Especially strong in politics, particularly during the post-Civil War 19th century and the early 20th century. Highlights Mason Weare Tappan Papers, Austin Pike Papers, Charles Marseilles Papers, Jacob H Gallinger Papers, James O Lyford Papers and George H Moses Papers. Also papers of many other New Hampshire people, among them--John Badger Bachelder, Josiah Bartlett, Moody Bedel, Timothy Bedel, Mary Baker Eddy, Joseph A Gilmore, John Hatch George, Issac Hill, John Langdon, Jeramiah Mason, Charles Sanger Mellen, John Fabyan Parrott, Nathaniel Peabody, William Plumer, Lorenzo Sabine, Jean Joseph Marie Toscan, Robert W Upton, John Wentworth and Levi Woodbury. The records of the Dover (New Hampshire) ManufacturingCompany; 650 account books, most of which were kept by general merchants in New Hampshire during the 18th and 19th centuries; town records, mostly before 1825, for approx 230 New Hamphire town; and military records and orderly books relating to New Hampshire military units of the 18th and 19th centuries (French & Indian War through the Civil War). About 500,000 ms pieces, 4000 books, 1000 maps.

NH —PORTSMOUTH ATHENAEUM, 9 Market Sq, Box 848, Portsmouth, 03801.

Joseph P Copley, Cur
Holdings: Vols Cat Mss
Notes: Incl Larkin Papers, 1758-1798 (235 items); papers of Daniel and John Peirce, cat 1730-1800 (115 items); and papers of NH Fire and Marine Insurance Co, 1803-1823 (1800 items).

NJ —FAIRLEIGH DICKINSON UNIVERSITY, Friendship Library, 285 Madison Ave, Madison, 07940. James Fraser, Library Dir; Renee Weber, Cur
Holdings: Vols 1200 Cat Mss Pix Slides Phonorecords 16mm Films
Notes: Official depository for the Outdoor Advertising industry. Collection initiated in August 1972. About 100,000 items. It is the concern of the Outdoor Advertising Association of America that this collection become the definitive collection on the industry in this country. Incl 20,000 mss, 10, 000 pictures, 30,000 slides. 15 original billboards.

NJ —NEW JERSEY HISTORICAL SOCIETY, Library and Museum, 230 Broadway, Newark, 07104. Joan C Hull, Exec Dir; Barbara S Irwin, Library Dir; Alan R Fraser, Cur
Holdings: Vols (45,000) Cat Mss Maps Pix Microforms
Budget: ($100,000)
Notes: Incl 1200 mss groups. See also Shelly, Fred, *Guide to the Manuscript Collection of the New Jersey Historical Society*, 1957 (out of print). Also Morris & Skemer, *Guide to the Manuscript Collections of the New Jersey Historical Society*, 1979.

NJ —RUTGERS, THE STATE UNIVERSITY OF NEW JERSEY, Alexander Library, Special Collections and Archives, College Ave & Huntington St, New Brunswick, 08903. Ronald L Becker, Cur of Manuscripts and Rare Books
Holdings: Mss
Notes: Papers of the Morris family, 1677-1948, the Neilson family, ca 1680-1930, William Paterson (1745-1806), Anthony Walton White (1750-1803), Senator Joseph S Frelinghuysen (1869-1948), the Gibbons family, 1767-1897, Philip Freneau (1752-1832), Samuel Smith (1721-1776), George H Cook (1818-1889), Samuel B How (1790-1868), Senator Clifford P Case (1904-), Walt Whitman (1819-1892). Records of many corporate bodies, societies, municipalities, etc. Over 2,000,000 pieces.

NJ —PASSAIC COUNTY HISTORICAL SOCIETY, Lamhurt Castle, Valley Rd, Paterson, 07503. Helen D Hamilton, Dir
Holdings: Vols (5000) Cat Mss Maps Pix
Notes: Material on the Society for the Establishment of Useful Manufacturing (founded) by Alexander Hamilton, papers relating to John Holland, who developed the submarine, the industrial magnates of the area who were active in the manufacture of locomotives, Colt revolvers, and textiles, especially silk.

NJ —PRINCETON UNIVERSITY, Library, Manuscript Collection, Nassau St, Princeton, 08540. Jean F Preston, Cur
Holdings: Mss Pix
Notes: The collection of medieval and Renaissance manuscripts, totaling 350 book manuscripts, incl items collected by Robert Garrett and Grenville Kane. The collection is supplemented by several single leaves. See *Princeton University Library Chronicle*, v 3, pp 123-35; v 11, pp 37-44. Ricci, Seymour de. *Census of Medieval and Renaissance Manuscripts in the United States and Canada* (New York: H W Wilson Co, 1935-40); and *Supplement*, ed by W H Bond, 1962.

NJ —FAIRLEIGH DICKINSON UNIVERSITY, Messler Library, New Jersey Room, 207 Montross Ave, Rutherford, 07070. Catharine M Fogarty, Librn
Holdings: Vols (4782) Cat Mss Maps Microforms
Budget: $2000
Notes: Separate card catalog; also, Hackensack-Ridgewood Local History Service. Manuscript-Microfilm Project. *A Guide to Manuscripts on Microfilm from the Collections of Bergen County Historical*

Society, River Edge; Johnson Free Public Library, Hackensack; New Jersey Room, Fairleigh Dickinson University, Rutherford; Ridgewood Public Library, Rev Bicentennial ed (Hackensack, NJ: Johnson Free Public Library, 1976). Collection is a New Jersey state documents depository containing over 4000 documents; 965 documents of New Jersey local governments.

NY —NEW YORK STATE LIBRARY, Manuscripts and Special Collections, Albany, 12230. Peter R Christoph, Associate Librn
Holdings: Cat Mss Maps Pix Microforms
Notes: Strong collection, all aspects: social, political legislative, economic history of the State and its people, incl Indians. Particularly valuable and extensive collection of historical mss, Colonial and State.

NY —STATE UNIVERSITY OF NEW YORK, BINGHAMTON, Glenn G Bartle Library, Binghamton, 13901. Marion Hanscom, Special Collections Librn
Holdings: Cat
Budget: ($8000)
Notes: Max Reinhardt Archive. Library has extensive (approx 250,000 items) archival material relating to Max Reinhardt, as well as his personal library. This personal library is not a subject collection per se, but contains much information about German theater in the 20th century. The archival material contains letters, prompt books, photographs, playbills, etc.

NY —ADIRONDACK HISTORICAL ASSOCIATION, Museum Library, Blue Mountain Lake, 12812. Jerold Pepper, Librn
Holdings: Vols (7500) Cat Mss Maps Pix Phonorecords Audiotapes 16mm Films Microforms
Notes: Anything about the Adirondacks--history, people, economics, places, things. Strong in Adirondack art, outdoor recreation, logging, small boats. Resources incl more than 1000 maps, 40,000 pictures, 1600 microfilm reels, 576 linear ft of ms material, and 12 cabinets of VF ephemera, etc.

NY —NEW YORK BOTANICAL GARDEN LIBRARY, Bronx, 10458. Charles R Long, Asst Vice Pres & Dir
Notes: One of the largest botanical collections in the world. Over 900,000 items. Covers botany (150,000 vols), botanists (3000), horticulture (45,000) plant diseases (25,000), plant physiology (15,000), history of botany (1500), conservation of natural resources (15,000), gardening (13,000), paleobotany (7000), ecology (20,000), forestry (5000) medical botany (3000), agriculture (9000) and biology (20,000). Reference library; materials do not circulate, except for member circulating collection (1200) and standard inter-library loan. About 5000 vols uncataloged. Incl art, books, serials, pamphlets, archives and manuscripts, vertical files, microfiche and microfilm, nursery and seed catalogs, photographs, paintings, prints, drawings and engravings. Covers all areas of botanical sciences. This is an OCLC library with fullresource services incl photocopying and photography.

NY —BUFFALO & ERIE COUNTY PUBLIC LIBRARY, Rare Book Room, Lafayette Sq, Buffalo, 14203. William H Loos, Cur
Notes: Literary autographs, letters, and mss; 4000 items, incl the ms of *Huckleberry Finn.*

NY —STATE UNIVERSITY OF NEW YORK, COLLEGE AT BUFFALO, Poetry/ Rare Books Collection, 420 Capen Hall, Buffalo, 14260. Robert J Bertholf, Cur
Holdings: Vols (75,000) Cat Mss Pix Phonorecords Audiotapes Microforms
Notes: The Poetry Collection, founded in 1937 by the late Charles D Abbott, is devoted to 20th century poetry in English and in translation. It contains some 75,000 vols in first and variant editions, 600 phonorecords and 400 audiotapes presenting poets who read from their own work; more than 3500 sets of little magazines covering the last 80 years; a unique collection of mss, letters, notebooks, worksheets, and noted by contemporary poets, explaining their methods of composition; and a number of portraits, sculptures and photographs. "The

MANUSCRIPTS—COLLECTIONS (cont.)

Poetry Collection is internationally known for its importance in the field of James Joyce (qv), Dylan Thomas, William Carlos Williams, Robert Graves, Martin Seymour-Smith and Robert Kelley."

†NY —STATE UNIVERSITY OF NEW YORK, COLLEGE AT FREDONIA, Daniel A Reed Library, Fredonia, 14063. Notes: Nearly 6500 letters written to Stefan Zweig, 1901-1942, added to the Stefan Zweig Archives.

NY —CORNELL UNIVERSITY, New York State School of Industrial & Labor Relations, Martin P Catherwood Library, Ives Hall, Ithaca, 14853. Shirley F Harper, Dir
Holdings: Vols (150,000) Cat Mss Pix Phonorecords Microforms
Notes: Collection incl approx 1000 periodicals and union journals currently received, and ms collections of labor unions, arbitrators, and scholars. 6000 linear ft. *Library Catalog of the New York State School of Industrial and Labor Relations* (Boston: G K Hall, 1967), 12 volumes; *Cumulation of the Library Catalog Supplements of the New York State School of Industrial and Labor Relations* (Boston: G K Hall, 1976), 8 volumes.

NY —QUEENS BOROUGH PUBLIC LIBRARY, Long Island Div, 89-11 Merrick Blvd, Jamaica, 11432. Nicholas Falco, Head
Holdings: Vols (22,000) Cat Mss Maps Pix Microforms
Budget: ($13,000)
Notes: Files of Long Island community newspapers, with strong holdings for Queens Borough. Also, 550 glass negatives of Long Island scenes, 1895-1915; with 32,750 other pictures; 5300 maps; 36,000 ms pieces. Extensive name indexes of births, deaths and marriages mainly from 19th century Long Island books and newspapers. Many cemetery records, etc. 60 VF drawers of clippings; over 500 broadsides, 1795-date, relating to Long Island, with chronological and community name indexes; books published by Marion Press, a private press in Jamaica, NY.

NY —AMERICAN INSTITUTE OF PHYSICS, Center for the History of Physics, Niels Bohr Library, 335 E 45 St, New York, 10017. John Aubry, Librn
Holdings: Vols (16,000) Cat Mss Pix Slides Phonorecords Audiotapes 16mm Films Microforms
Notes: The Library contains an extensive collection of published works relating to the history of modern physics and astronomy. Its archives incl letter, notebooks and other papers of physicists, as well as the records of leading American physics societies and institutions. Its collections of ms autobiographies, oral history interviews, and other tape recordings, and pictorial materials (incl unpublished film footage) are unrivaled in the field of history of science. It maintains the International Catalog of Sources for History of Physics and and Astronomy.

NY —COLUMBIA UNIVERSITY LIBRARIES, Teachers College, Milbank Memorial Library, 525 W 120 St, New York, 10027. Jane P Franck, Dir
Notes: Ms materials that were not generated by Teachers College or its faculty and affiliates and are not part of the College Archives. National Council for the Social Studies Records--160 cu ft; National Kindergarten Association--15 cu ft.

NY —GENERAL THEOLOGICAL SEMINARY, Saint Marks Library, 175 Ninth Ave, New York, 10011. David Green, Dir
Holdings: Vols (200,000) Cat Mss Maps Pix Slides Microforms
Notes: Extensive collection.

NY —HEBREW UNION COLLEGE, Jewish Institute of Religion, Klau Library, 1 W 4th St, New York, 10012. Philip Miller, Librn
Holdings: Vols (115,000) Cat Mss Microforms
Notes: Hebrew literature--ancient, medieval and modern.

NY —HISPANIC SOCIETY OF AMERICA, Library, 613 W 155 St, New York, 10032.

Martha M de Narvaez, Cur of Mss; Irene S Frye, Asst Librn
Holdings: Vols (150,000) Cat Mss Maps Pix Slides Phonorecords Microforms
Notes: History, art, literature and general culture of the Hispanic countries (where Spanish or Portuguese is spoken). Incl (18,000) vols printed before 1701, incl (250) incunabula; over (100,000) later vols, plus thousands of periodicals. About (200,000) mss incl ms maps. Printed atlases are in the Book Collection. Some microfilms, chiefly of our early books. Engraved and printed separate maps; reference collection of over 100,000 photographs; slides: all in Department of Iconography, not in library.
Catalogs: *Catalogue of the Hispanic Society of America* (Boston: G K Hall, 1962), 10 vols; *First Supplement* (Boston, 1970), 4 vols. Early books: *Printed Books 1468-1700;* Mss: *Catalogo de los Manuscritos Poeticos Castellanos* (15th-17th centuries; 3 vols); *Medieval Manuscripts in the Library; Golden Age Drama Manuscripts* (the latter in press).

NY —NEW YORK PUBLIC LIBRARY, Performing Arts Research Center, Billy Rose Theatre Collection, 111 Amsterdam Ave, New York, 10023. Dorothy L Swerdlove, Cur
Holdings: Cat Pix
Notes: The

NY —NEW YORK PUBLIC LIBRARY, Performing Arts Research Center, Dance Collection, 111 Amsterdam Ave, New York, 10023. Genevieve Oswald, Cur
Notes: Over 200,000 mss and letters. Major collections documenting the history of American dance are those of Maria Bonfanti, Loie Fuller, Isadora Duncan and Edward Gordon Craig, Irma Duncan, Ruth St Denis, Ted Shawn, Charles Weidman, Doris Humphrey, Jose Limon, Pauline Lawrence Limon, Louis Horst, Helen Tamiris, Ruth Page, Agnes De Mille, Valerie Bettis, Angna Enters, dance historian Lillian Moore, dance publicist and writer Irving Deakin, dance critic Walter Terry, the American Ballet Theatre, Morton Baum (director of the Ballet Russe de Monte Carlo). Other important collections are the Gabriel Astruc Papers, 1904-1925, relating to early activities of Sergei Diaghilev; letters of Mary Wigman, the great German Expressionist and modern dancer; the Leonide Massine Papers, 1932-1968; and the Claire Holt Collection of written and photographic documentation on Indonesiandance in the 1920s and 1930s and ancient and modern Indonesian art and culture. Outstanding individual items include the *Black Exercise Book,* 1909-11, of Sergei Diaghilev; notebooks of Sergei Grigoriev, regisseur of the Diaghilev and De Basil Ballets Russes; a 15th century dance treatise by the Jewish dancing master Guglielmo Ebreo; and 77 ms vols on microfilm of 15-17th century Bunraku dance notations from the Library of the Japanese Imperial Household. Registers published in *Bulletin of The New York Public Library* for Craig Duncan Collection, Gabriel Astruc Papers, Doris Humphrey Collection, and the Ruth Page Collection.

NY —NEW YORK PUBLIC LIBRARY, Oriental Div, Fifth Ave & 42 St, New York, 10018. E Christian Filstrup, Chief
Holdings: Cat Mss Microforms
Budget: ($56,455)
Notes: Described in *Dictionary Catalog of the Oriental Collection,* The Research Libraries of the New York Public Library, 1960, 16 vols, and *First Supplement,* 1976, 8 vols (144,000 cards). This catalog incl 318,000 entries for works in about 100 languages of the East, and all works in Western languages on Oriental subjects. The Oriental Collection numbers about 120,000 vols; its Arabic and Indic holdings and those on ancient Egypt and the ancient Near East are among the largest in the US. There is also a collection of 30,000 vols of PL 480 material from Egypt, Pakistan, and India to which there is main entry access, but which is not incorporated into the dictionary catalog. Other outstanding features of the Oriental Collection incl extensive holdings of

Japanese technical and scientific periodicals; a unique collection of linguistic works, grammars, anddictionaries; and unusually good coverage of the field of Oriental religions and philosophies. The catalog contains numerous subject references to periodical articles in all languages. All entries are arranged alphabetically according to the Roman alphabet.

NY —NEW YORK PUBLIC LIBRARY, Rare Books and Manuscripts Div, Fifth Ave & 42 St, New York, 10018. William L Joyce, Asst Dir; Susan E Davis, Cur of Mss
Holdings: Cat Mss
Budget: ($7161)
Notes: The division holds over 12 million pieces, incl Medieval, Renaissance, and Oriental examples. Major emphasis on American, incl exploration, discovery, Spanish expansion, US history and historical persons; political, economic, and literary materials up to the 20th century, especially post-Civil War period; diaries of interest to social historians; theatrical history; science and engineering in 19th century America. Incl, among many others, the Maloney Irish Historical Collections; collections on Korean history, 1870-1948; Archives of the NY World's Fairs, 1939-1940 and 1964-1965. Autograph collections, and fraudulent signatures and documents. See *Dictionary of the Manuscript Division. The Research Libraries of the New York Public Library.* 1967. 2 vols.

NY —NEW YORK PUBLIC LIBRARY, Music Div, 111 Amsterdam Ave, New York, 10023. Frank C Campbell, Chief
Holdings: Vols (300,000) Cat Mss Pix Microforms
Notes: Described in *Dictionary Catalog of the Music Collection, The Research Libraries of the New York Public Library,* 33 vols (532,000 cards), 1964, $2190; Supplement 1, 1 vol (17,000 cards), 1966, $100. Also, *Bibliographic Guide to Music,* 2 vols, 1975-1976, $70 ea. Literature pertaining to virtually all musical subjects, and scores covering the broadest range of musical style and history are represented in this catalog. Special strengths of the collection incl folk songs, 18th and 19th-century librettos, full scores of operas, complete works, historical editions, Beethoven, Americana, American music, periodicals, vocal music, literature on the voice, programs, record catalogs, and mss in detail; sheet music, 355,414; sound recordings, 400,000; clippings and programs, 2 million; broadsides, 1821; songsters, 375; pictures, 51,002; ms, 29,877.

NY —NEW YORK PUBLIC LIBRARY, Spencer Collection, Fifth Ave & 42 St, New York, 10018. Joseph T Rankin, Cur
Holdings: Vols (8000) Cat Mss
Notes: Rare illustrated and illuminated mss and books, in fine bindings, in all languages, of all countries, and of all periods, constituting the development of book illustration and the book arts the world around. See *Dictionary Catalog and Shelf List of the Spencer Collection,* New York Public Library, 1970. 2 vols, $155.

NY —NEW YORK UNIVERSITY, Elmer Holmes Bobst Library, Div of Special Collections, Washington Sq S, New York, 10012. Frank Walker, Librn; Patrick McGuire, Asst Librn
Holdings: Vols (100,000) Cat Mss Pix
Notes: The Fales Collection of first (and other) editions of English and American novels from about 1750 to date (about 70,000 titles). Mss (30,000) pieces.

NY —PIERPONT MORGAN LIBRARY, 29 E 36 St, New York, 10016. Herbert Cahoon, Librn
Notes: One of the largest collections, with many rarities, unique works and mss.

NY —STATE UNIVERSITY OF NEW YORK, COLLEGE AT PLATTSBURGH, Feinberg Library, Special Collections, 153 Hawkins Hall, Plattsburgh, 12901. Joseph G Swinyer, Librn
Holdings: Cat Mss Maps Pix Phonorecords Microforms
Notes: 200 linear feet of mss.
See also entry under New York (State) - History

MANUSCRIPTS—COLLECTIONS (cont.)

NY —UNIVERSITY OF ROCHESTER, Rush Rhees Library, Department of Rare Books and Special Collections, Rochester, 14627. Peter Dzwonkoski, Librn

NY —CANAL MUSEUM, Research Library, 318 Erie Blvd E, Syracuse, 13202. Todd S Weseloh, Librn & Archivist
Holdings: Vols 7000 Mss Maps Pix
Notes: Engineering and construction records of New York State Canal System (1833-1930). Enlargements of Erie Canal, construction of lateral canals, maintenance of New York canals, construction of Barge Canal System. Maps and surveys of canals and property along canals. Plans of canal structures: bridges, aqueducts, locks, waste weirs, culverts, dams, reservoirs, feeders, and others. 954 linear feet mss; 7000 mss and printed maps and plans.

NY —SYRACUSE UNIVERSITY LIBRARIES, Ernest S Bird Library, George Arents Research Library for Special Collections, Syracuse, 13210. Carolyn A Davis, Manuscripts Librn; Amy S Doherty, University Archivist; Mark F Weimer, Rare Book Librn
Notes: Private library of Leopold von Ranke, father of modern historical scholarship, acquired in 1886. More than 17,000 volumes, 4000 pamphlets, and 430 mss, and private papers and letters. A complete catalogue of the ms collection published in 1983. Incl more than 100 dispatches (Relazioni) from Venetian ambassadors, 1500-1800, etc. Much unpublished primary source material.

NY —US MILITARY ACADEMY LIBRARY, West Point, 10996. Marie T Capps, Maps & Mss Librn
Holdings: Maps Pix
Notes: Emphasis on the history of the Academy and its graduates. 180 collections; 8500 items. Partially cataloged.

NC —UNIVERSITY OF NORTH CAROLINA, CHAPEL HILL, Wilson Library, Rare Book Collection, Chapel Hill, 27514. Paul S Koda, Cur of Rare Books
Holdings: Vols 1000 Cat Mss
Notes: The Hanes Collection of the History of the Book consists of Sumerian and Babylonian clay tablets, papyri in Egyptian and in Greek, stone inscriptions, 24 olas, manuscripts, and 600 items of 16th, 17th, and 18th century printing, incl many landmarks in the history of printing. It also contains many books about books, incl some rare bibliographies, histories of presses and technology, and books on collecting.

NC —UNIVERSITY OF NORTH CAROLINA, CHAPEL HILL, Louis Round Wilson Academic Affairs Library, Southern Historical Collection, Chapel Hill, 27514. Carolyn Wallace, Librn
Holdings: Mss
Notes: 6,200,000 items relating to history of the Southern United States, as described in *The Southern Historical Collection: Supplementary Guide to Manuscripts*, 1970-1975, and *Guide to Manuscripts* issued in 1970.

NC —DUKE UNIVERSITY, William R Perkins Library, Durham, 27706. Elvin E Strowd, University Librn
Notes: Books, serials and pamphlets (2,820,527); music scores (31,551); motion pictures (285); microforms (1,055,627); tapes, cassettes and phonorecords, the library is a depository for Radio Canada International recordings, (2289); and manuscripts, US Government publications, maps, and broadsides, additions in all formats are ongoing.

NC —DUKE UNIVERSITY, William R Perkins Library, Manuscript Dept, Durham, 27706. Ellen Gartrell, Cur of Mss
Holdings: Mss Pix Slides Phonorecords Audiotapes Videotapes
Notes: Incl 7,000,000 items and ca 25,000 mss vols. The Manuscript Department has its own card catalog which is not duplicated in the main public catalog. Holdings date from the sixteenth century. Broad subject range, but geographic emphasis is on the southeastern region of the US. Inportant holdings of ca 50,000 mss related to England and the British Empire. See 1980 *Guide to the Cataloged Collections of the Manuscript Department of the William R Perkins Library*.

NC —DUKE UNIVERSITY, William R Perkins Library, Rare Book Room, Durham, 27706. John L Sharpe, III, Cur
Notes: Berthold Louis Ullmann collection. Classical manuscripts - "17 substantial codices, two fragmentary manuscripts and 30 of only a few pages each, a total of 49 written between 9th and 16th centuries. Among them are four of the works of Cicero in the hand of noted 15th century scribes and two 9th century fragments of a French Sacramentary - and early Roman Catholic Service book for the Mass."

ND —UNIVERSITY OF NORTH DAKOTA, Chester Fritz Library, Dept of Special Collections, Grand Forks, 58202. Daniel F Rylance, Special Collections Coordr
Holdings: Vols (5500) Uncat Mss Maps Pix Microforms
Budget: ($2500)
Notes: Also the Orin G Libby Manuscript Collection (900 collections), and the Aandahl Collection of Western History on North Dakota and the Northern Great Plains. Emphasis on agriculture, politics, pioneering, Germans from Russia, etc. Guides to the collections available from the Coordinator of Special Collections.

OH —HEBREW UNION COLLEGE-JEWISH INSTITUTE OF RELIGION, Klau Library, 3101 Clifton Ave, Cincinnati, 45220. David J Gilner, Reference Librn
Holdings: Cat Mss
Notes: About 6000 mss in Hebrew characters representing various languages, such as Hebrew, Ladino, Yiddish, Spanish, Italian, German; also mss in Arabic, Ethiopian, Chinese and Persian alphabets. Incl literary, archival, sermonic and halakhic mss.

OH —PUBLIC LIBRARY OF CINCINNATI & HAMILTON COUNTY, Dept of Rare Books & Special Collections, 800 Vine St, Library Square, Cincinnati, 45202. Yeatman Anderson III, Cur
Holdings: Cat Mss Maps Pix Slides Microforms
Notes: Inland River Collection. Incl logbooks, account books, personal correspondence, diaries, etc. Also, a picture collection of 14,000 items (steamboats, towboats, river views, crews, construction, barges, etc.)

OH —CLEVELAND PUBLIC LIBRARY, Fine Arts and Special Collections Department, 325 Superior Ave, Cleveland, 44114. Alice N Loranth, Head
Holdings: Vols 1500 Cat
Notes: Special emphasis is on chess, and on British India from 1750 to 1859. More than 250 vols (19,000 pages) are incl in the East India Company ms collection. Important Arabic texts, illuminated Persian mss, Mosu pictographs, and some unpublished Latin medieval compilations of legends and romances deserve special attention. The collection of original mss is well supplemented by several hundred copies of chess mss and facsimile editions with emphasis on Medieval texts and Mexican and Maya codices. In addition to the bound vols, extensive archival holdings are incl in the chess and folklore collections.
See also entries under Chess; Folklore; Oriental Languages and Literatures; Rare Books.

OH —OHIO HISTORICAL SOCIETY, Archives Library Division, 1982 Velma Ave, Columbus, 43211. Dennis East, Division Chief
Holdings: Vols (96,000) Cat Mss Maps Pix Slides Microforms
Budget: ($18,000)
Notes: This library is the primary collection for Ohio. Most purchases are on the rare and out of print market. Collection area is early American history, esp relating to exploration into the Northwest Territory. Also, Ohio archaeology, natural history, and artifacts. Major media collections are books (96,000), newspapers (25,000 vols and 22,000 microfilm), pictures (50,000), maps (2500), manuscripts (1,500,000). Library is noncirculating except through interlibrary loan of microfilm.

OH —OHIO STATE UNIVERSITY, William Oxley Thompson Memorial Library, Hilander Room, 1858 Neil Ave Mall, Columbus, 43210. Predrag Matejic, Cur; G Koolemans Beynen, Slavic Bibliographer
Holdings: Vols (200,000) Cat Maps Microforms
Budget: ($45,000)
Notes: Area studies of Central, Southeastern and Eastern Europe. Emphasis on on Slavic literatures, languages and history. At present economics, sociology, law (Russian only) have been added. Within this framework the following priorities have been established: Material in Russian problems; then Medieval Slavic (Cyrillic); then Polish, then Serbo-Croatian, then Bulgarian, and now Romanian. Special attention is paid to serials, bibliographies, ms descriptions and dictionaries (incl biographical and encyclopedias). Apart from materials in native languages, materials in the following languages are acquired: Old Church Slavonic, Greek, English, French, German, Italian, a few in Scandinavian languages, incl Finnish, and a few in Baltic languages. The Hillandar Room holds approx 2000 Slavic mss, 1050 from Hilandar Monastery, Mount Athos, on microform and a related referencecollection.

OH —OHIO STATE UNIVERSITY, William Oxley Thompson Memorial Library, 1858 Neil Ave, Columbus, 43210. A Robert Thorson, Head, Circulation Dept
Holdings: Cat Mss Microforms

OH —RUTHERFORD B HAYES LIBRARY, 1337 Hayes Ave, Fremont, 43420. Watt P Marchman, Dir
Holdings: Cat Mss Maps Pix Microforms
Notes: In addition to the book collection, the Library has several individual ms collections containing diaries, letters and other ms materials pertaining to the Civil War. Also numerous items pertaining to Civil War prisons, particularly Johnson's Island. Index. Listed under subject in *Guide to Manuscripts at the Ohio Historical Society*. 1300 items.

OH —MASSILLON PUBLIC LIBRARY, 208 Lincoln Way E, Massillon, 44646. Camille Leslie, Dir
Holdings: // Mss Maps
Notes: 22 linear ft. Correspondence and business papers of Thomas Rotch and Arvine Wales who migrated in 1811 from New England to Ohio; and of Arvine C Wales, his son, lawyer and civic leader in Massillon, Ohio. Covers period ca 1780-1880; contains much Quaker and anti-slavery material, as well as material on early Ohio. Index in preparation.

OH —HEIDELBERG COLLEGE, Beeghly Library, Tiffin, 44883. Janice G Strickland, Dir
Holdings: Vols 6,577 Cat
Budget: $3000
Notes: BESSE collection encompasses published English and American letters, some quite rare.

OK —THOMAS GILCREASE INSTITUTE OF AMERICAN HISTORY & ART LIBRARY, 1400 North 25th West Ave, Tulsa, 74127. Sarah Hirsch, Librn
Notes: Trans-Mississippi West, US, Indian and Hispanic history. The Gilcrease Library contains a total of about 40,000 mss; 10,000 imprints; 5000 photographs; 600 maps and 50,000 vols.

OR —UNIVERSITY OF OREGON LIBRARY, Special Collections Div, Eugene, 97403. Kenneth W Duckett, Curator
Holdings: Cat Mss
Notes: Nearly 2 million items. Materials emphasize political, social, economic, and literary history of the US in the 20th century. Special strengths incl papers of

MANUSCRIPTS—COLLECTIONS (cont.)

authors and illustrators of children's literature, political conservatives and libertarians, authors of popular fiction (mainly Western Fiction), missionaries to the Far East, and Oregon political figures, architects, and business records. There are also photographs relating mainly to the Pacific Northwest, Alaska, and Appalachia, broadsides, and popular sheet music. Publication: Martin Schmitt, comp, *Catalogue of Manuscripts in the University of Oregon Library* (Eugene: University of Oregon Books, 1971).

PA —MUHLENBERG COLLEGE, Haas Library, 2400 Chew St, Allentown, 18104. Linda Bowers
Holdings: Mss
Notes: Original mss, letters, etc, with numerous letters signed by famous Americans of the 18th and 19th centuries.

PA —AMERICAN PHILOSOPHICAL SOCIETY, Library, 105 S Fifth St, Philadelphia, 19106. Edward C Carter II, Librn
Holdings: Cat Mss Maps
Notes: Collection (as it was in 1970) is incl in *Catalog of Books in the American Philosophical Society Library* (Westport, Conn: Greenwood Publishing Corp, 1970) and *Catalog of Manuscripts in the American Philosophical Society Library* (Westport, Conn: Greenwood Publishing Corp, 1970). Both of these are reproductions of APS Library catalog cards, incl author, subject, and titles entries.

PA —COLLEGE OF PHYSICIANS OF PHILADELPHIA, Library, 19 S 22 St, Philadelphia, 19103. Anthony Aguirre, Libr Dir
Holdings: Vols (316,223) Cat Mss Microforms
Budget: ($1,096,557)
Notes: Incl 13,515 pamphlets; 1435 mss; 326,367 reports, dissertations, and reprints. Strong historical and bibliographical collections, as well as current materials. Medical documentation service provides current alerting, incl abstracting, etc.

PA —FREE LIBRARY OF PHILADELPHIA, Rare Book Dept, Logan Sq, Philadelphia, 19103. Marie E Korey, Rare Book Librn
Holdings: Cat Mss
Notes: The John Frederick Lewis and Joseph E Widener Collections of European Manuscripts incl 2200 bound volumes and separate illuminated leaves and text leaves.

†PA —LIBRARY COMPANY OF PHILADELPHIA, 1314 Locust St, Philadelphia, 19107. Edwin Wolf II, Librn
Holdings: Vols (450,000)

†PA —TEMPLE UNIVERSITY LIBRARIES, Special Collections Dept, Urban Archives Center, Philadelphia, 19122. Thomas Whitehead, Cur of Mss
Holdings: Mss
Notes: Ms collection focusing on urban life and development and drawing on the Philadelphia metropolitan area since the Civil War. Incl the papers of several private organizations, such as the Philadelphia Housing Association (1909-1972); Delaware Valley Regional Planning Commission (1965-1972); Greater Philadelphia Movement (1949-1976); YWCA of Philadelphia (1870-1960); YMCA of Philadelphia (1854-1970); Health and Welfare Council of Philadelpia (1922-1969); United Fund of Philadelphia and Vicinity (1920-1971); Philadelphia Urban League (1935-1967); ACLU-Philadelphia Chapter (1948-1975); Legal Aid Society of Philadelphia (1933-1976); etc. Also, letters and documents (15,000 items) of the archives of the london publishers, Constable and Company. Correspondence with close to 400 authors, most of it with Otto Kyllmann and Michael Sadlier, directors. Archives of ThomasNelson & Sons (USA) and of various Philadelphia publishers.

PA —UNIVERSITY OF PENNSYLVANIA, Van Pelt Library, Rare Books Collection, 34 & Walnut Sts, Philadelphia, 19104. Daniel Traister, Special Collections Librn
Notes: 1300 Medieval and Renaissance

codices. See published catalog: *Catalogue of Manuscripts in the Libraries of the University of Pennsylvania to 1800* by Norman P Zacour & Rudolf Hirsch (Philadelphia: University of Pennsylvania Press, 1965). Supplements: *Library Chronicle* (University of Pennsylvania). Vol 35, nos 1 & 2, 1969. *Catalogue of Manuscripts... Supplement A (1)* (University of Pennsylvania) *Library Chronicle*, Vol 36, *1970 Catalogue...Supplement A (2) & A (3)* (University of Pennsylvania) *Library Chronicle*, Vol 37, no 1, 1971. *Catalogue...Supplement A (4).*

PA —UNIVERSITY OF PITTSBURGH, Darlington Memorial Library, Special Collections, 601 Cathedral of Learning, Pittsburgh, 15260. Dennis Lambert, Darlington Libr
Holdings: Vols (17,000) Cat Mss Maps Pix
Notes: The Darlington Collection is especially rich in American history of the colonial period, the French and Indian War, the Revolution, and the War of 1812 with geographical emphasis on Western Pennsylvania and Ohio Valley history to 1870 and on Pittsburgh history to 1900. Indian treaties, captivity accounts, US and Pennsylvania travel and description, and early American fiction and prose are represented. A partial guide to the Darlington Manuscript Collections is available by writing for *Darlington Memorial Library: A Descriptive Checklist of its Manuscript Collections*, University of Pittsburgh Bibliographic Series 5, 1969. Noncirculating.

PA —FRIENDS HISTORICAL LIBRARY OF SWARTHMORE COLLEGE, Swarthmore, 19081. J William Frost, Dir
Holdings: Mss Microforms
Notes: Library's collection contain information on the history and doctrine of the Society of Friends, Quaker contributions to literature, science, business, education, and government, plus their reform efforts in peace, Indian rights, women's rights, and abolition of slavery. As an official depository of the records of the records of Philadelphia and Baltimore Yearly Meetings, the library holds, either in the original manuscript or on microfilm, the largest collection in the world of Quaker meeting archives, incl some records of Ohio and Illinois Yearly Meetings (Hicksite), and microfilm copies of minutes and registers of many meetings in New England, New York, North Carolina, Indiana, and Great Britain. Among the more than 250 mss collections, described in *Guide to the Manuscript Collections of Friends Historical Library of Swarthmore College* (1982), are papersof individual Quaker leaders, families, and organizations.

PA —WASHINGTON AND JEFFERSON COLLEGE, Library, Washington, 15301. Robert E Connell, Librn
Holdings: Vols 2100 Cat Mss Maps Pix
Notes: A general subject and author card catalog has been prepared for the ms collection. Published description of the collection appears in: Pennsylvania, Historical and Museum Commission, *Historical Manuscript Depositories in Pennsylvania* (Harrisburg, 1965), compiled by Irwin Richman. Incl are materials concerning the "Westward movement"-- letters, land grants, etc. Much on the Revolutionary War, the "Whiskey Rebellion" of 1794. Many other small collections of mss, some containing American Indian and Western Pennsylvania history.

RI —US NAVAL WAR COLLEGE, Historical Collection & Museum, Newport, 02841. Anthony S Nicolosi, Dir; Evelyn Cherpak, Cur
Holdings: Mss
Notes: Collections incl over 200,000 separate pieces; chiefly papers of naval officers and records of organizations associated with the US Navy, the Naval War College, the college's major study areas, and the Navy in the Narragansett Bay region; oral history collection; Naval War College Archives, 1884-present; records of conferences held at the College; newspaper collections dealing with naval themes and military conflicts.

RI —BROWN UNIVERSITY, John Hay Library, 20 Prospect St, Providence, 02912. Mark N Brown, Cur Mss
Holdings: Mss Maps Pix Microforms
Notes: Collection interest incl the history and development of the state of Rhode Island; American literature, with special emphasis on poetry and drama (Harris Collection of Manuscripts); the whaling industry and early American maritime history; the history of science, medicine and engineering in America; and American diplomatic history. Inquiries welcome.

RI —BROWN UNIVERSITY, John Hay Library, Anne S K Brown Military Collection, 20 Prospect St, Providence, 02912. Richard B Harrington, Cur
Holdings: Vols (40,000) Cat Mss Pix
Notes: The Anne S K Brown Military Collection has been formed over the past forty or more years by Mrs John Nicholas Brown, now of Newport, and contains approximately 40,000 volumes and 60,000 prints, drawings and watercolors as well as a number of oil paintings and about 5000 miniature model soldiers. At its beginning (and still today) the emphasis or focus of this collection has been upon the history of, and the accurate contemporary illustration of, military and naval uniforms of all nations from the early XVII century to the present. In the course of time, however, the collection has come to incl also a vast and related amount of material on military and naval history, military and naval arts and tactics, wars, campaigns, ceremonies, biography, portraits and caricatures of this and earlier periods. It has been probably the largest private collection of such a nature inthe world, and it contains much ms and graphic documentation which is unique. It has been useful to numerous scholars and historians, editors, filmmakers and publishers for research and for illustrative material and has also contributed to many museum exhibitions. In 1982 the entire collection, with its complete card catalog and subject index, has been presented to Brown University, where it is located in the John Hay Library. Special requests are taken care of by phone, mail and appointments with the curator.

SD —SOUTH DAKOTA HISTORICAL RESOURCE CENTER, Library, Soldiers Memorial Bldg, Pierre, 57501. Rosemary Evetts, Librn
Holdings: Vols 1020 Cat Mss Maps Pix
Budget: $2000
Notes: South Dakota state and territorial materials. Picture collection has been cataloged and numbers approximately 20,000 items, of which we have negatives for about half. South Dakota materials include items on general state and territorial history, biographical, autobiographical, political, geological, economic and county and town materials.

TX —TEXAS STATE LIBRARY, Archives Div, 1201 Brazos, PO Box 12927, Capitol Sta, Austin, 78711. David B Gracy II, State Archivist
Holdings: Vols 30,000 Cat Mss Maps Pix Microforms
Notes: Collections are limited to Texas history, primarily archives of the Texas state government. Mss, 25,000 cubic ft; 3000 maps; 35,000 pictures; 5000 microforms.

TX —UNIVERSITY OF TEXAS LIBRARIES, Nettie Lee Benson Latin American Collection, Sid Richardson Hall 1.109, Austin, 78712. Laura Gutierrez-Witt, Head Librn
Holdings: Vols (450,000) Cat Mss Maps Pix Phonorecords Filmstrips Microforms
See also entries under Latin America and Texas-History.

†TX —UNIVERSITY OF TEXAS LIBRARIES, General Libraries, Humanities Research Center, PO Box 7219, Austin, 78712. John Chalmers, Librn

TX —DALLAS PUBLIC LIBRARY, Central Library, Humanities Division, 1515 Young St, Dallas, 75201. Richard L Waters, Acting Dir; Ron Boyd, Fiction Librn
Holdings: Vols Cat Microforms
Notes: Cited in Tymn, Marshall, Roger C

MANUSCRIPTS—COLLECTIONS (cont.)

Schlobin, and L W Currey. *A Research Guide to Science Fiction* New York: Garland, 1977. The science fiction collection now exceeds 8000 circulating vols. In addition, the Library purchased in 1983 the personal library and archives of Brian Aldiss (which will be for reference use only). This collection consists of 350 books by Aldiss, 1900 other books by other science fiction writers, 800 issues of science fiction and fantasy periodicals, 100 vols concerning astronautics and space travel, over 1000 typescript pages of mss(incl 6 corrected mss), several sound recordings (incl BBC tapes), and a considerable amount of correspondence.

TX —ROSENBERG LIBRARY, Fox Rare Book Room, 2310 Sealy Ave, Galveston, 77550. Fernando Basilza, Rare Book Librn
Holdings: Vols (2000) Cat Mss Pix
Notes: The Col Milo Pitcher Fox and Agnes Peel Fox Rare Book Room contains 2000 vols incunabula, first printings, and modern fine printing. Incl clay tablets, horn books, parchment material, illuminated books and mss, fine printing (principally 15th-18th centuries), fine binding, fore-edge paintings, etc.

TX —ROSENBERG LIBRARY, Galveston and Texas History Center, 2310 Sealy Ave, Galveston, 77550. Jane Kenamore, Archivist
Holdings: Vols 7368 Cat Mss Maps Pix Slides Microforms
Budget: $60,000
Notes: Includes 1000 maps and charts dating from the 16th century, 1500 linear shelf feet of manuscript dating from 1817, 18000 photographs dating from 1850 as well as 19th and 20th century architectural drawings. Contains labor, black and German and Italian Language newspapers from 1840, as well as 200 oral history, interviews and related material regarding early Texas and Galveston.

TX —RICE UNIVERSITY, Fondren Library, Woodson Research Center, 6100 S Main St, PO Box 1892, Houston, 77251. Nancy Parker, Dir Woodson Research Center
Holdings: Uncat Mss Maps Pix
Notes: Incl Texas family papers, letters, diaries, business records in several collections.

TX —STEPHEN F AUSTIN STATE UNIVERSITY, Ralph W Steen Library, Special Collections Dept, Box 13055, SFA Sta, Nacogdoches, 75962. Linda Cheves Nicklas, Special Collections Librn
Holdings: Mss Maps Pix
Budget: ($5000)
Notes: Incl personal and business papers, letters, diaries, and other records of East Texans and East Texas institutions and businesses. Major collections incl papers of Karl Wilson Baker, George L Crocket, Bennett Blake, McFarland-Russell family, Orton family, Samuel E Asbury; and records of Nacogdoches University, East Texas Historical Association, Kelly Plow Company and many local organizations; 60 Thomas J Rusk letters. Indexes, calendars and inventories are available. Description: SFASU, *A Guide to Special Collections*, 1980.

†UT —UNIVERSITY OF UTAH, Marriott Library, Salt Lake City, 84112.
Notes: Collection of Professor Aziz S Atiya, mostly in Arabic languages.

UT —UNIVERSITY OF UTAH, Marriott Library, Special Collections, Salt Lake City, 84112. Gregory C Thompson, Cur
Notes: 800 separate collections, mostly Utah and the West.

VT —UNIVERSITY OF VERMONT, Guy W Bailey/David W Howe Library, Burlington, 05405. John Buehler, Asst Dir for Special Collections

VA —UNIVERSITY OF VIRGINIA, Alderman Library, Manuscripts Dept, Charlottesville, 22901. Edmund Berkeley Jr,

Cur
Holdings: Cat Mss Pix Phonorecords Audiotapes 16mm Films Microforms
Notes: Twentieth

VA —MOUNT VERNON LADIES' ASSOCIATION OF THE UNION, Research & Reference Library, Mount Vernon, 22121. Ellen McCallister Clark, Librn; John Rhodehamel, Dir of Education
Holdings: Vols (12,000) Cat Mss Maps Pix Slides
Notes: The Washington family and Mount Vernon. The history of the Mount Vernon Ladies' Association and historic preservation.

VA —MARINERS MUSEUM, Library, Newport News, 23606. Ardie L Kelly, Librn
Holdings: Vols (60,000) Cat Mss Maps Pix Slides
Notes: Incl collections of over 150,000 photographs of merchant ships, naval vessels, sailing ships, lighthouses, portraits of naval men, harbors, canals, etc, and maps, ships' papers, and log books. Catalogs of various parts of the collection published by G K Hall, Boston.

VA —PORTSMOUTH PUBLIC LIBRARY, 601 Court St, Portsmouth, 23704. Dean Burgess, Library Dir
Holdings: Vols 1600 Cat
Notes: Although particularly interested in Tidewater and Lower Tidewater history, we buy most books we can locate on Virgina as well. In 1972 we were given the distinguished collection of Judge White of Lynnhaven.

VA —VIRGINIA STATE LIBRARY, 12 & Capitol Sts, Richmond, 23219.
Holdings: Mss Maps Pix Microforms
Notes: Incl archives of Virginia, mainly noncurrent public records, but incl other mss, relating to Virginia and the South. Contains 80,000 bound vols, 27,000,000 ms pieces and 85,000 maps. Partially cataloged.

†WA —WASHINGTON STATE UNIVERSITY, Library, Manuscripts, Archives & Special Collections, Pullman, 99164. John F Guido, Head
Holdings: Cat Mss Maps Pix
Notes: Three collections: (1) The ms collections incl business and financial records of banks, breweries, insurance, land, lumber and livestock companies, trade and commodity associations; as well as the personal and professional papers of authors, aviators, educators, engineers, farmers, historians, pioneers, politicians and scientists; especially rich in documents relating to the exploration, settlement and development of the Palouse Country, the Inland Empire, the Columbia Basin and the Pacific Northwest. Described in *Selected Manuscript Resources in the Washington State University Library* (Pullman, 1974); and other published and unpublished inventories and registers. (2) Papers, 1821-1873, covering Father De Smet's early sojourns at Whitemarsh and St Louis, his founding of the Rocky Mountain Missions, his long service as Procurator and Socius of the MissouriProvince, and his many travels. Correspondence with his family in Belgium, mss of his published journals, 2 small maps, sketches and engravings used to illustrate his books. Incl about 100 small pencil sketches by Father Nicholas Point depicting the 1841 journey from Westport to St Mary's Mission in the Bitterroot Valley. Described in *The Record*, 30 (1969) 6-40; and 32 (1971) 47-63. (3) Regla, Counts of: The papers of the Romero de Terreros family, to whom were granted the titles of Regla, San Cristoval, and San Francisco, include wills, deeds, titles, property maps, litigation over such things as sheep walks, water rights, and the titles themselves. Incl also is much detailed correspondence between hacienda administrators and the family concerning weather, crops, and commodity prices. Several large vols, bound in 1783, document thehistory of land acquisitions by the Jesuit Colegio Maximo de San Pedro y San Pablo of Mexico City, especially the hacienda of Santa Lucia, from 1576 to the time of the Expulsion. Other early papers deal with the holdings and genealogy of the Marquisates

of Salinas, Salvatierra, and Santiago. Described by J Horace Nunemaker in the *Hispanic American Historical Review* (August 1945) 25:409; and by Jacquelyn M Gaines in *Three Centuries of Mexican Documents; A Partial Calendar of the Regla Papers* (Pullman, Washington, 1963).

WA —UNIVERSITY OF WASHINGTON LIBRARIES, Suzzallo Library, Manuscripts Section, FM-25, Seattle, 98195. Karyl Winn, Librn
Holdings: Mss
Notes: Personal papers and organizational records with emphasis on Pacific Northwest history and recent focus on twentieth century Western Washington. Holdings pertain to urban problems and policies, labor history, women's history, natural resource development, environmental politics, race relations, ethnic history, oral hsitory, and the arts. Holdings are complemented by textual records in the University Archives (7045 linear feet) and by graphic and printed holdings in the Pacific Northwest Collection. Described in *Comprehensive Guide to the Manuscripts Collection and to Personal Papers in the University Archives*, 1980 and in *Historical Records of Washington State: Records and Papers Held at Repositories*, 1981 and in unpublished inventories to most accessions. 15,981 linear feet of manuscripts.

WA —UNIVERSITY OF WASHINGTON LIBRARIES, Suzzallo Library, Manuscripts Section, FM-25, Seattle, 98195. Karyl Winn, Librn
Holdings: Mss Audiotapes
Notes: Personal papers and organizational records of the Jewish population of the greater Seattle, Washington area and to a lesser extent, Washington state. Holdings includes synagogue records, philanthropic and educational organization records, papers of community leaders and families, and recorded interviews. Photographs administered by the Libraries' Pacific Northwest Collection. Many interviews have been transcribed. Inventories for all larger accessions. Includes 260 linear feet of manuscript and 250 audiotapes.

WV —WEST VIRGINIA UNIVERSITY, Library, West Virginia and Regional History Collection, Morgantown, 26506. George P Parkinson Jr, Cur
Holdings: Vols 30,000 Cat Mss Maps Pix Audiotapes 16mm Films Filmstrips Microforms
Budget: ($20,000)
Notes: The West Virginia Collection contains over 10,000 linear ft of mss, broadsides, pictures, photographs, and other items relating to West Virginia and the Appalachian region. There are published guides of the collections.

WI —STATE HISTORICAL SOCIETY OF WISCONSIN, Archives, 816 State St, Madison, 53706. Harold L Miller, Reference Archivist
Holdings: Cat Mss Microforms
Notes: About 22 million pieces. Major ms emphasis is American, with special collections in the history of agriculture, industry, labor, mass communications, and Wisconsin. There is a separate card catalog to mss. Collections are described in the *Guide to Manuscripts of the State Historical Society of Wisconsin* (3 vols, 1944, 1957, 1966), in current accession notes in the *Wisconsin Magazine of History,* and in other special Society publications. Major collections are also listed in Hamer, *Guide to Manuscripts and Archives in the United States* (1961) and in the *National Union Catalog of Manuscript Collections* (1959-date). Original mss are noncirculating. Collections available in microfilm form may be used through interlibrary loan.

WI —UNIVERSITY OF WISCONSIN, MADISON, Memorial Library, Rare Books Collection, 728 State St, Madison, 53706. Gretchen Lagana, Cur
Holdings: // Mss
Notes: The English Manor Rolls number 186 in all and cover a period of more than two hundred years (1302-1506). With the exception of four rolls, each of which is dated 1302, all the rolls are from Wilberton

MANUSCRIPTS—COLLECTIONS (cont.)

Manor in Cambridgeshire in the bishopric of Ely. The rolls, grouped according to the regnal years of the various kings, are especially complete for the reigns of Richard II, Henry IV, Henry VI, Edward IV, and Henry VII. Housed in the Dept of Rare Books and Special Collections. No photocopying.

WY —UNIVERSITY OF WYOMING, William Robertson Coe Library, Western History Research Center, Laramie, 82071. Gene M Gressley, Dir, Asst to Pres
Holdings: Vols (35,000) Cat Mss Maps Pix Microforms
Notes: The Western History Research Center of the University of Wyoming's William Robertson Coe Library has sizable ms collections in several areas pertaining to the history and development of the American West. Principal ms collection areas incl; cattle industry history, western literature, mining and petroleum history, transportation history, conservation history, water resources history, and related western history topics. The collections are supplemented by a fine Western Americana book collection cataloged by the main library but located at the Western History Research Center.

AB —ALPINE CLUB OF CANADA LIBRARY, Archives of the Canadian Rockies, Box 160, Banff, T0L 0C0, Can. E J Hart, Head Archivist
Holdings: Vols (2429) Cat Mss Maps Pix Slides Audiotapes
Budget: ($1000)
Notes: Covers the Canadian Rocky Mountains from international border in the south to the St Elias Range in the North; eastern slopes of the Rockies, incl foothills, to the western slopes of the interior ranges of British Columbia. Include physical, natural, and human history. The Archives of the Canadian Rockies is the custodian of the library and archival collection of The Alpine Club of Canada. The materials cover mountaineering all over the world. Subject areas incl history, personal records, mountain rescue and medicine, alpine flora and fauna, guide books, manuals and handbooks. A large part of the archival collection in concentrated on the Canadian Rocky Mountains, as the headquarters of The Alpine Club of Canada is in Banff, Alberta.

AB —GLENBOW-ALBERTA INSTITUTE, Historical Library & Archives, 130 9th Avenue SE, Calgary, T2G 0P3, Can. Leonard J Gottseleg, Chief Librn
Holdings: Vols (60,000) Cat Mss Maps Pix Microforms
Notes: Main emphasis is on Western Canadian history. Equally important emphasis is placed on the Canadian Arctic and Alaska, Northwest Coast explorations, Aboriginal peoples of the North and Canadian West, and the fur trade in the US Northwest.

AB —UNIVERSITY OF CALGARY, Libraries, Special Collections Div, 2500 University Dr, Calgary, T2N 1N4, Can.
Holdings: Vols (5000) Cat Mss
Notes: The Division has extensive collections of the papers of modern Canadian authors (qv individuals), incl Hugh MacLennan, Mordecai Richler, Brian Moore, W O Mitchell, Cliff Faulknor, Christie Harris, Robert Kroetsch, Rudy Wiebe, Claude Peloquin, George Ryga, Andre Langevin, Malcolm Ross, Bruce Hutchison, John Mellor, Grant MacEwan, James Gray, Ernest Watkins, Len Peterson, Michael Cook, and Joanna Glass. The papers of musician Morris Surdin contain hundreds of Canadian Broadcasting Corporation scripts, and constitute a valuable addition to the purely literary ms collections. The Division's holdings also incl collections of scores by Canadian musicians R Murray Schafer and Bruce Mather. In addition, the records of the following Canadian publishing houses are on deposit: E C W Press, Hancock House Publishers Ltd and Coach

House Press. The Division alsohouses small collections of letters and mss of Canadian poets such as Earle Birney and George Bowering as well as the archives of the literary periodicals *Tish, Imago, Ariel, Descant, Canadian Review Magazine,* and *Canadian Short Story Magazine.* The ms collections are complemented by a book collection of some 5000 vols.

MB —HUDSON'S BAY CO, Library, 77 Main St, Winnipeg, R3C 2R1, Can. Carol Preston, Librn Hudson's Bay House
Holdings: Vols (6000) Cat Mss Maps Pix Slides
Notes: Main purpose is to provide research materials for production of the historical quarterly *The Beaver,* and to answer inquiries about the Company's history. Incl 250,000 pictures and 7000 VF pieces. No published catalog, but Library maintains author/subject/title card catalog. Limited photocopying. Mss of HBC Archives held by the Manitoba Provincial Archives. Published descriptions: Dowdall, Judi, "Hudson's Bay Company Library," *Canadian Library Journal,* June 1974, p 179; Preston, Carol, "Hudson's Bay Company Library," *Manitoba Library Association Bulletin,* June 1976, pp 24-25.

ON —NATIONAL LIBRARY OF CANADA, 395 Wellington St, Ottawa, K1A 0N4, Can. Andre Preibish, Dir
Notes: *The Jacob M Lowy Collection* over 2000 works of very rare Hebraica and Judaica. Among outstanding items are 30 incunabula - the first printed edition of the Babylonian Talmud, many editions of Flavius Josephus, including first edition of 1470 Early Bibles in many languages. *The Saul Hayes Collection* of Hebraic Manuscripts and microforms. Manuscripts from North Africa and the Orient; 300 reels of manuscripts held by libraries in Poland, USSR and Hungary. This collection is held in the Jacob M Lowy Room.

ON —PUBLIC ARCHIVES OF CANADA, Library, 395 Wellington St, Ottawa, K1A 0N3, Can. Dawn E Monroe, Collections Development Officer
Holdings: Vols (80,000) Cat
Notes: Comprised of several collections: J D Barrett Collection (10,000 items), 19th century trade literature and catalogs. Barnett's handwritten index is retained with additional mss in the Manuscript Division. E A Collard Collection (249 pamphlets), Montreal journalist Edgar Andrew Collard spent thirty-four years writing a weekly historical column of the editorial page of the Montreal *Gazette.* The pamphlet collection reflects Collard's varied interests during these years and also incl various City of Montreal publications. The Library is in the process of cataloging the collection. Charles Mayer Collection (400 titles), retained in part by the Manuscript Division, provides excellent material on some forty years of Canadian sport. Charles Mayer (1902-1971) worked as a journalist in Montreal from the 1920s through the 1950s. The papers and books in the collectionreflect his interest in such sports as harness racing, golf, skiing, tennis, football, boxing, baseball and hockey. There is excellent coverage of American Hockey League and National Hockey League publications. Andrew Merrilees Collection (about 1800 items), incl documents relating to transportation. His personal wealth, knowledge, business contacts and determination enabled him to obtain material many sources. The core of the collection concerns railways, a personal interest since his Andrew Merrilees Company bought and sold railroad materials. The collection has some of the best examples of material on the technical aspect of the railway business. Most has some connection to the Canadian rail industry from its early beginning until 1930. Access to the collection is restricted. Also, the Milborne Masonic Collection, a small number of items on Masonic drama and music, novelsand poems. The papers, notes and photographs which were presented with the Milborne Library are retained in the Manuscript Division.

ON —METROPOLITAN TORONTO LIBRARY, Theatre Dept, 789 Yonge St, Toronto, M4W 2G8, Can. Heather McCallum, Head
Holdings: Vols (30,500) Mss Pix Slides Phonorecords Microforms
Notes: Special collections relating to the history of the performing arts in Canada incl the records of the Taverner Company which played Eastern Canada and the United States in the late 19th century, Toronto's Grand Opera House, the Marks Brothers touring company, film actor Ned Sparks, the Canadian-born actress Judith Evelyn, Toronto's Crest Theatre, dancer/teacher Boris Volkoff, The Dumbells, the Canadian all-soldier concert party which originated in France in 1917 and vaudeville performer Charles Manny.

ON —METROPOLITAN TORONTO LIBRARY, Canadian History Dept, Baldwin Room Section, 789 Yonge St, Toronto, M4W 2G8, Can. David B Kotin, Head
Holdings: Vols (52,000) Mss Pix
Notes: This collection consists of material on Canadian history, geography, travel, archaeology, genealogy, retrospective city and telephone directories, collective biographies, native peoples (excluding customs, rights and social conditions), Arctic regions, military history and theory. It is an extremely strong collection of both current and retrospective material. Particular strengths are national and local history (especially Ontario), Arctic regions, native peoples, travel (especially Ontario), and military history. Incl 78,000 historical pictures, 235 linear meters mss, 14,000 broadsides and 3800 bound newspapers.

PQ —MCGILL UNIVERSITY, McLennan Library, Rare Books and Special Collections Dept, 3459 McTavish St, Montreal, H3A 1Y1, Can.
Notes: Medieval mss (ca 200 items) incl illuminated leaves, Books of Hours, miniatures, and initials; Oriental mss (100 items) incl Arabic, Persian, illuminated mss and Pali palm leaf mss.

SK —SASKATCHEWAN ARCHIVES BOARD, University of Regina, Regina, S4S 0A2, Can. Ian E Wilson, Provincial Archivist
Holdings: Mss Maps Pix Audiotapes Videotapes 16mm Films Microforms
Budget: $900,000
Notes: The Saskatchewan Archives Board attempts to document the history of the area now the Province of Saskatchewan and its communities through all archival media. Collection incl 5800 meters of mss, 4800 maps, 250,000 pictures, 10,000 architectural drawings, 4400 audiotapes, 1648 16mm films and 9400 microfilm reels. Individual collections are listed in *The Union List of Manuscripts in Canadian Repositories* (Ottawa, 1975 & 1976). Detailed catalogs, indexes and inventories are available in two offices. (Second office is located at University of Saskatchewan, Saskatoon, Sask S7N 0W0 Canada.)

YT —YUKON ARCHIVES, Box 2703, Whitehorse, Y1A 3C6, Can. Miriam McTiernan, Territorial Archivist
Holdings: Vols (8000) Cat Mss Maps Pix Phonorecords Audiotapes Videotapes 16mm Films Microforms
Budget: $15,000
Notes: Yukon and regional history and development. Incl also 500 mss; 10,000 maps; 30,000 pictures; 1200 microfilm rolls; 1115 oral history tapes, etc; Yukon newspapers.

MANUSCRIPTS—CONSERVATION AND RESTORATION

IL —NEWBERRY LIBRARY, 60 W Walton St, Chicago, 60610. Bonnie Jo Cullison, Preservation Librn
Holdings: Vols 700 Cat Slides
Budget: $350
Notes: Book and ms conservation and restoration; also 1500 slides and 1300 reports.

†NY —COLUMBIA UNIVERSITY LIBRARIES, Butler Library, Rare Book and

MANUSCRIPTS—CONSERVATION AND RESTORATION (cont.)

Manuscript Library, 535 W 114 St, New York, 10027.
Notes: Files relating to the American Library Association's Special Committee to Aid Italian Libraries' assistance to Italian libraries to help restore books, mss and other library materials after the 1966 floods in Florence.

MANUSCRIPTS—FORGERIES see Forgery of Manuscripts

MANUSCRIPTS—RESTORATION see Manuscripts—Conservation and Restoration

MANUSCRIPTS, ABYSSINIAN see Manuscripts, Ethiopic

MANUSCRIPTS, ANGLO-SAXON

KS —UNIVERSITY OF KANSAS, Kenneth Spencer Research Library, Special Collections Dept, Lawrence, 66045. Alexandra Mason, Librn
Holdings: Vols 213 Cat Mss
Notes: Collection name: The Clubb Collection. Anglo-Saxon texts printed in the special typefaces designed for that language; largely 16th-18th centuries. Works of the septentrional antiquaries. Anglo-Saxon mss.

MANUSCRIPTS, ARABIC

CA —UNIVERSITY OF CALIFORNIA, LOS ANGELES, Research Library, Dept of Special Collections, 405 Hilgard Ave, Los Angeles, 90024. Edward Shreeves, Chairman, Bibliographers Group; David S Zeidberg, Head
Holdings: Mss
Notes: 18,000,000 items in 1300 collections, emphasizing humanities and social sciences; particular strength in British and American literature and California history, but incl 125 medieval mss, part of the Orsini family archive, and 10,000 Arabic, Armenian, and Persian mss in 6000 volumes, and 94 linear feet of Turkish mss, mostly uncataloged.
CT —YALE UNIVERSITY, Box 1603A, Yale Station, New Haven, 06520.
IL —ORIENTAL INSTITUTE, 1155 E 58th St, Chicago, 60637. John Larsen, Archivist
Notes: The Bernhard Moritz Collection. Fine examples of bindings as well as of Islamic calligraphy and writing materials--papyrus, parchment, papers, etc. Extensive collection is also in the Beatty Library in Dublin, Ireland; Victoria and Albert Museum in London; Libraries in East and West Germany.
IL —NORTHWESTERN UNIVERSITY, Melville J Herskovits Library of African Studies, Evanston, 60201. Hans E Panofsky, Cur
Notes: Collected in depth. Incl a complete set of the recordings by and on African authors assembled by the Transcription Centre, London. Also, about 3000 books and pamphlets on African languages.
MA —HARVARD UNIVERSITY LIBRARY, Cambridge, 02138.
Holdings: Cat Mss (PL 480)
MI —UNIVERSITY OF MICHIGAN, Library, Dept of Rare Books & Special Collections, Ann Arbor, 48109. Robert J Starring, Head
Holdings: Mss
Notes: Over 1200 mss chiefly in Arabic, but also in Persian, Turkish, Coptic, Syrian, Ethiopic, Hebrew, and Armenian. Incl the McGregor collection on mathematics and astronomy, the Tiflis collection, and portions of the Abdul Hamid and Uahuda collections.
MO —SAINT LOUIS UNIVERSITY, Pius XII Memorial Library, Vatican Film Library Collection, 3655 W Pine Blvd, Saint Louis, 63108. Charles J Ermatinger, Librn
Holdings: Mss Slides Microforms
Notes: Vatican Film Library has 75 percent of the Greek, Latin and western European vernacular holdings in the Vatican Library,

plus all the Hebrew, Arabic and Ethiopic holdings on film. Covers 5th-19th centuries. Sizable collection of western European books. In addition, has largest collection on the work of the Jesuits in Latin America, the US and the Philippines, filmed from European Jesuit archives. Excellent catalogs and guides to all collections. Also, 50,608 slides of illuminated mss; 26,470 reels of microfilm.
MO —SAINT LOUIS UNIVERSITY, Pius XII Memorial Library, 3655 W Pine Blvd, Saint Louis, 63108. William Cole, Dir
Holdings: Slides Microforms
Notes: Collection covers all areas of learning and European history from Classical Antiquity to early modern period. Researchers using collection receive assistance in paleography, bibliography and reference search. Approx 10,000 1000-foot reels of microfilm (not counting master negatives) reproducing Vatican Library's Latin, Greek, Hebrew, Arabic and Ethiopic mss. Some 8000 100-foot reels of microfilm (again not counting master negative) reproducing rare and out of print books relating to subject areas in the mss. Over 50,000 color slides of medieval and Renaissance mss illuminations. A reference collection of modern materials relating to ms research.
NJ —PRINCETON UNIVERSITY, Library, Near East Collections, Princeton, 08540. James Weinberger, Cur
Holdings: Vols (100,000) Cat Mss Maps Phonorecords Audiotapes Microforms
Budget: ($72,000)
Notes: Princeton has the largest collection of Arabic mss in the US. Collections are particularly rich in classical Arabic and Persian texts, encompassing all the traditional genres. Of special note are the collections in Arabic and Persian literature, language, history, philosophy and theology and the religious sciences of Islam, both in ms and printed formats. A separate, additional collection of Arabic mss (about 2000 items) is being cataloged. It is especially rich in theology and philosophy of the classical Islamic period. Two printed catalogs are available: *Descriptive Catalog of the Garrett Collection of Arabic Manuscripts*, Philip K Hitti et al (Princeton: Princeton Univ Press, 1977).
NY —NEW YORK PUBLIC LIBRARY, Oriental Div, Fifth Ave & 42 St, New York, 10018. E Christian Filstrup, Chief
Holdings: Cat Mss Microforms
Budget: ($56,455)
Notes: Described in *Dictionary Catalog of the Oriental Collection*, The Research Libraries of the New York Public Library, 1960, 16 vols, and *First Supplement*, 1976, 8 vols (144,000 cards). This catalog incl 318,000 entries for works in about 100 languages of the East, and all works in Western languages on Oriental subjects. The Oriental Collection numbers about 120,000 vols; its Arabic and Indic holdings and those on ancient Egypt and the ancient Near East are among the largest in the US. There is also a collection of 30,000 vols of PL 480 material from Egypt, Pakistan, and India to which there is main entry access, but which is not incorporated into the dictionary catalog. Other outstanding features of the Oriental Collection incl extensive holdings of Japanese technical and scientific periodicals; a unique collection of linguistic works, grammars, anddictionaries; and unusually good coverage of the field of Oriental religions and philosophies. The catalog contains numerous subject references to periodical articles in all languages. All entries are arranged alphabetically according to the Roman alphabet.
OH —HEBREW UNION COLLEGE-JEWISH INSTITUTE OF RELIGION, Klau Library, 3101 Clifton Ave, Cincinnati, 45220. David J Gilner, Reference Librn
Holdings: Cat Mss
Notes: About 6000 mss in Hebrew characters representing various languages, such as Hebrew, Ladino, Yiddish, Spanish, Italian, German; also mss in Arabic, Ethiopian, Chinese and Persian alphabets. Incl literary, archival, sermonic and halakhic mss.

OH —CLEVELAND PUBLIC LIBRARY, Fine Arts and Special Collections Department, 325 Superior Ave, Cleveland, 44114. Alice N Loranth, Head
Holdings: Vols (170) Cat Mss
Notes: Middle Eastern mss incl original mss mostly in Arabic, Persian and Turkish, and some in Syriac, Ethiopic and Hebrew. Notable are the 79 Persian examples of illuminated codices and the 54 Arabic treatises on chess, religion, mathematics, medicine, etc. The chiefly unpublished original mss are well supplemented by several hundred vols of facsimile editions of mss. The library holdings of Istanbul and Skutari are described in a unique collection of 45 vols. Separate author entry catalogs by languages. Arabic holdings are described in Albin, M W: "Handlist of the Arabic Manuscripts in the John G White Department, Cleveland Public Library," *Bibliotheca Orientalis*, XXXIII, No 516, Sept-Nov 1976, pp 294-304.
See also entries under Manuscripts - Catalogs; Manuscripts, Oriental; Oriental Languages and Literatures.
UT —UNIVERSITY OF UTAH, Middle East Library, Salt Lake City, 84112. Ragai N Makar, Librn
Holdings: Vols 3000 Cat Mss Pix Microforms
Budget: ($40,000)
Notes: Mt Sinai Arabic Manuscripts collection. This incl about 800 Arabic manuscripts on microfilm. This collection is incl in the catalogue *The Arabic Manuscripts of Mt Sinai* by Professor Aziz S Atiya. Baltimore, The Johns Hopkins Press, 1955. All the mss are on the history and theology of the Eastern Christian Church. The Greek Manuscripts on microfilm collection of the Patriarchal Library of Alexandria, Egypt. This incl about 1000 mss on microfilm about the history and theology of the Greek Orthodox Church. This collection described in Studies and Documents edited by Jacob Geerlings. Vol XXVI Catalog of MSS of the Patriarchal Library of Alexandria by T D Mosconas, Salt Lake City, University of Utah Press, 1965. The Catholic Microfilm Center Syriac and Arabic Manuscript Collection. This incl about 985 Syriac and Arabic mss on microfilm all of whichis about the history and theology of the Eastern Orthodox Church.
PQ —MCGILL UNIVERSITY, McLennan Library, Rare Books and Special Collections Dept, 3459 McTavish St, Montreal, H3A 1Y1, Can.
Notes: 100 items in Arabic, Persian, Indian illuminated manuscripts and Pali palm leaf manuscripts.

MANUSCRIPTS, ARMENIAN

CA —UNIVERSITY OF CALIFORNIA, LOS ANGELES, Research Library, Dept of Special Collections, 405 Hilgard Ave, Los Angeles, 90024. Edward Shreeves, Chairman, Bibliographers Group; David S Zeidberg, Head
Holdings: Mss
Notes: 18,000,000 items in 1300 collections, emphasizing humanities and social sciences; particular strength in British and American literature and California history, but incl 125 medieval mss, part of the Orsini family archive, and 10,000 Arabic, Armenian, and Persian mss in 6000 volumes, and 94 linear feet of Turkish mss, mostly uncataloged.

MANUSCRIPTS, BIBLICAL see Bible—Manuscripts

MANUSCRIPTS, BULGARIAN

OH —OHIO STATE UNIVERSITY, William Oxley Thompson Memorial Library, 1858 Neil Ave, Columbus, 43210. A Robert Thorson, Head, Circulation Dept
Holdings: Cat Mss Microforms
Notes: This collection presently contains films of 2000 mss from the Hilandar Monastery, Mt Athos. Expansion will add Byzantine, Bulgarian, Russian and Valachian mss on film.

MANUSCRIPTS, BYZANTINE

OH —OHIO STATE UNIVERSITY, William Oxley Thompson Memorial Library, 1858 Neil Ave, Columbus, 43210. A Robert Thorson, Head, Circulation Dept
Holdings: Cat Mss Microforms
Notes: This collection presently contains films of 2000 mss from the Hilandar Monastery, Mt Athos. Expansion will add Byzantine, Bulgarian, Russian and Valachian mss on film.

MANUSCRIPTS, CHINESE

NY —INSTITUTE FOR ADVANCED STUDIES OF WORLD RELIGIONS (IASWR), Melville Memorial Library, State University of New York, Stony Brook, 11794. C T Shen, Dir
Holdings: Microforms
Notes: Microforms: Chinese mss from Tun-huang in the British Museum and Bibliotheque Nationale. Collected works for sale in microfiche editions. Refer inquiries to L L Yang.

OH —HEBREW UNION COLLEGE-JEWISH INSTITUTE OF RELIGION, Klau Library, 3101 Clifton Ave, Cincinnati, 45220. David J Gilner, Reference Librn
Holdings: Cat Mss
Notes: About 6000 mss in Hebrew characters representing various lanugages, such as Hebrew, Ladino, Yiddish, Spanish, Italian, German; also mss in Arabic, Ethiopian, Chinese and Persian alphabets. Incl literary, archival, sermonic and halakhic mss.

OH —CLEVELAND PUBLIC LIBRARY, Fine Arts and Special Collections Department, 325 Superior Ave, Cleveland, 44114. Alice N Loranth, Head
Holdings: Vols (206) Cat Mss
Notes: Part of the Oriental Manuscripts Collection, which is a choice collection of important, mostly unpublished works in Arabic, Persian, Syriac, Ethiopic, Pali, Sanskrit, Hebrew and Chinese. Incl historical, literary and scientific texts.
See also entries under Manuscripts - Catalogs; Manuscripts, Oriental; Oriental Languages and Literatures.

MANUSCRIPTS, ETHIOPIC

MN —SAINT JOHN'S ABBEY & UNIVERSITY, Hill Monastic Manuscript Library, Collegeville, 56321. Julian G Plante, Dir
Holdings: Vols 7500 Uncat Mss Slides Microforms
Notes: Microforms of 7500 Amharic and Geez mss, mostly from Ethiopia. A systematic program of microfilming mss in the monasteries and churches of Ethiopia was established in 1973. To complement this body of primary source material, a larger collection of secondary source materials published in the field of Ethiopic studies is available and being added to.

MO —SAINT LOUIS UNIVERSITY, Pius XII Memorial Library, Vatican Film Library Collection, 3655 W Pine Blvd, Saint Louis, 63108. Charles J Ermatinger, Librn
Holdings: Mss Slides Microforms
Notes: Vatican Film Library has 75 percent of the Greek, Latin and western European vernacular holdings in the Vatican Library, plus all the Hebrew, Arabic and Ethiopic holdings on film. Covers 5th-19th centuries. Sizable collection of western European books. In addition, has largest collection on the work of the Jesuits in Latin America, the US and the Philippines, filmed from European Jesuit archives. Excellent catalogs and guides to all collections. Also, 50,608 slides of illuminated mss; 26,470 reels of microfilm.

MO —SAINT LOUIS UNIVERSITY, Pius XII Memorial Library, 3655 W Pine Blvd, Saint Louis, 63108. William Cole, Dir
Notes: Collection covers all areas of learning and European history from Classical Antiquity to early modern period. Researchers using collection receive

assistance in paleography, bibliography and reference search. Approx 10,000 1000-foot reels of microfilm (not countng master negatives) reproducing Vatican Library's Latin, Greek, Hebrew, Arabic and Ethiopic mss. Some 8000 100-foot reels of microfilm (again not counting master negative) reproducing rare and out of print books relating to subject areas in the mss. Over 50,000 color slides of medieval and Renaissance mss illuminations. A reference collection of modern materials relating to ms research.

OH —HEBREW UNION COLLEGE-JEWISH INSTITUTE OF RELIGION, Klau Library, 3101 Clifton Ave, Cincinnati, 45220. David J Gilner, Reference Librn
Holdings: Cat Mss
Notes: About 6000 mss in Hebrew characters represcnting various languages, such as Hebrew, Ladino, Yiddish, Spanish, Italian, German; also mss in Arabic, Ethiopian, Chinese and Persian alphabets. Incl literary, archival, sermonic and halakhic mss.

OH —CLEVELAND PUBLIC LIBRARY, Fine Arts and Special Collections Department, 325 Superior Ave, Cleveland, 44114. Alice N Loranth, Head
Holdings: Vols (170) Cat Mss
Notes: Middle Eastern mss incl original mss mostly in Arabic, Persian and Turkish, and some in Syriac, Ethiopic and Hebrew. Notable are the 79 Persian examples of illuminated codices and the 54 Arabic treatises on chess, religion, mathematics, medicine, etc. The chiefly unpublished original mss are well supplemented by several hundred vols of facsimile editions of mss. The library holdings of Istanbul and Skutari are described in a unique collection of 45 vols. Separate author entry catalogs by languages.
See also entries under Manuscripts - Catalogs; Manuscripts, Oriental; Oriental Languages and Literatures.

MANUSCRIPTS, FORGERY OF see Forgery of Manuscripts

MANUSCRIPTS, GREEK

CT —YALE UNIVERSITY, Box 1603A, Yale Station, New Haven, 06520.
Holdings: Cat
Notes: Incl the Jacob Ziskind Trust Collection of Greek Manuscripts. See the Yale University Library Gazette, October 1957.

MO —SAINT LOUIS UNIVERSITY, Pius XII Memorial Library, Vatican Film Library Collection, 3655 W Pine Blvd, Saint Louis, 63108. Charles J Ermatinger, Librn
Holdings: Mss Slides Microforms
Notes: Vatican Film Library has 75 percent of the Greek, Latin and western European vernacular holdings in the Vatican Library, plus all the Hebrew, Arabic and Ethiopic holdings on film. Covers 5th-19th centuries. Sizable collection of western European books. In addition, has largest collection on the work of the Jesuits in Latin America, the US and the Philippines, filmed from European Jesuit archives. Excellent catalogs and guides to all collections. Also, 50,608 slides of illuminated mss; 26,470 reels of microfilm.

MO —SAINT LOUIS UNIVERSITY, Pius XII Memorial Library, 3655 W Pine Blvd, Saint Louis, 63108. William Cole, Dir
Holdings: Slides Microforms
Notes: Collection covers all areas of learning and European history from Classical Antiquity to early modern period. Researchers using collection receive assistance in paleography, bibliography and reference search. Approx 10,000 1000-foot reels of microfilm (not counting master negatives) reproducing Vatican Library's Latin, Greek, Hebrew, Arabic and Ethiopic mss. Some 8000 100-foot reels of microfilm (again not counting master negative) reproducing rare and out of print books relating to subject areas in the mss. Over 50,000 color slides of medieval and Renaissance mss illuminations. A reference collection of modern materials relating to ms research.

NC —DUKE UNIVERSITY, William R Perkins Library, Rare Book Room, Durham, 27706. John L Sharpe, III, Cur
Notes: Berthold Louis Ullmann collection. Classical manuscripts - "17 substantial codices, two fragmentary manuscripts and 30 of only a few pages each, a total of 49 written between 9th and 16th centuries. Among them are four of the works of Cicero in the hand of noted 15th century scribes and two 9th century fragments of a French Sacramentary - and early Roman Catholic Service book for the Mass." Also incl Kenneth Willis Clark Collection of ca 85 items.

UT —UNIVERSITY OF UTAH, Middle East Library, Salt Lake City, 84112. Ragai N Makar, Librn
Budget: ($40,000)
Notes: Mt Sinai Arabic Manuscripts collection. This incl about 800 Arabic manuscripts on microfilm. This collection is incl in the catalogue The Arabic Manuscripts of Mt Sinai by Professor Aziz S Atiya. Baltimore, The Johns Hopkins Press, 1955. All the mss are on the history and theology of the Eastern Christian Church. The Greek Manuscripts on microfilm collection of the Patriarchal Library of Alexandria, Egypt. This incl about 1000 mss on microfilm about the history and theology of the Greek Orthodox Church. This collection described in Studies and Documents edited by Jacob Geerlings. Vol XXVI Catalog of MSS of the Patriarchal Library of Alexandria by T D Mosconas, Salt Lake City, University of Utah Press, 1965. The Catholic Microfilm Center Syriac and Arabic Manuscript Collection. This incl about 985 Syriac and Arabic mss on microfilm all of whichis about the history and theology of the Eastern Orthodox Church.

MANUSCRIPTS, HEBREW

CA —JUDAH L MAGNES MEMORIAL MUSEUM, Morris Goldstein Library, 2911 Russell St, Berkeley, 94705. Jane Levy, Archivist
Holdings: Vols 7000 Cat Mss Maps 16mm Films
Notes: Judaica, incl Hebrew manuscripts, Yiddish literature, and Jewish music and art.

MO —SAINT LOUIS UNIVERSITY, Pius XII Memorial Library, Vatican Film Library Collection, 3655 W Pine Blvd, Saint Louis, 63108. Charles J Ermatinger, Librn
Holdings: Mss Slides Microforms
Notes: Vatican Film Library has 75 percent of the Greek, Latin and western European vernacular holdings in the Vatican Library, plus all the Hebrew, Arabic and Ethiopic holdings on film. Covers 5th-19th centuries. Sizable collection of western European books. In addition, has largest collection on the work of the Jesuits in Latin America, the US and the Philippines, filmed from European Jesuit archives. Excellent catalogs and guides to all collections. Also, 50,608 slides of illuminated mss; 26,470 reels of microfilm.

MO —SAINT LOUIS UNIVERSITY, Pius XII Memorial Library, 3655 W Pine Blvd, Saint Louis, 63108. William Cole, Dir
Holdings: Slides Microforms
Notes: Collection covers all areas of learning and European history from Classical Antiquity to early modern period. Researchers using collection receive assistance in paleography, bibliography and reference search. Approx 10,000 1000-foot reels of microfilm (not counting master negatives) reproducing Vatican Library's Latin, Greek, Hebrew, Arabic and Ethiopic mss. Some 8000 100-foot reels of microfilm (again not counting master negative) reproducing rare and out of print books relating to subject areas in the mss. Over 50,000 color slides of medieval and Renaissance mss illuminations. A reference collection of modern materials relating to ms research.

OH —HEBREW UNION COLLEGE-JEWISH INSTITUTE OF RELIGION, Klau Library, 3101 Clifton Ave, Cincinnati, 45220. David J Gilner, Reference Librn
Holdings: Cat Mss
Notes: About 6000 mss in Hebrew

MANUSCRIPTS, HEBREW (cont.)

characters representing various languages, such as Hebrew, Ladino, Yiddish, Spanish, Italian, German; also mss in Arabic, Ethiopian, Chinese and Persian alphabets. Incl literary, archival, sermonic and halakhic mss.

OH —CLEVELAND PUBLIC LIBRARY, Fine Arts and Special Collections Department, 325 Superior Ave, Cleveland, 44114. Alice N Loranth, Head
Holdings: Vols (170) Cat Mss
Notes: Middle Eastern mss incl original mss mostly in Arabic, Persian and Turkish, and some in Syriac, Ethiopic and Hebrew. Notable are the 79 Persian examples of illuminated codices and the 54 Arabic treatises on chess, religion, mathematics, medicine, etc. The chiefly unpublished original mss are well supplemented by several hundred vols of facsimile editions of mss. The library holdings of Istanbul and Skutari are described in a unique collection of 45 vols. Separate author entry catalogs by languages.
See also entries under, Judaica; Manuscripts - Catalogs; Manuscripts, Oriental; Oriental Languages and Literatures.

ON —NATIONAL LIBRARY OF CANADA, 395 Wellington St, Ottawa, K1A 0N4, Can. Andre Preibish, Dir
Notes: The Jacob M Lowy Collection over 2000 works of very rare Hebraica and Judaica. Among outstanding items are 30 incunabula - the first printed edition of the Babylonian Talmud, many editions of Flavius Josephus, including first edition of 1470 Early Bibles in many languages. The Saul Hayes Collection of Hebraic Manuscripts and microforms. Manuscripts from North Africa and the Orient; 300 reels of manuscripts held by libraries in Poland, USSR and Hungary. This collection is held in the Jacob M Lowy Room.

MANUSCRIPTS, ILLUMINATED see Illuminated Books and Manuscripts

MANUSCRIPTS, INDIC

RI —BROWN UNIVERSITY, John Hay Library, 20 Prospect St, Providence, 02912. Mark N Brown, Cur Mss
Holdings: Vols (53) //
Notes: Indic Manuscripts Collection. Codices written in Burmese, Cambodian, Telugu, Skandhas, Bengali, and Sinhalese script on palm leaves, encased within wood covers, some lacquered. Subjects include: Buddhist canon, Pali grammar and lexicons, epics, dance drama, and a treatise on midwifery. Recorded in A Census of Indic Manuscripts in the United States and Canada compiled by Horace I Poleman (New Haven: American Oriental Society, 1938).

PQ —MCGILL UNIVERSITY, McLennan Library, Rare Books and Special Collections Dept, 3459 McTavish St, Montreal, H3A 1Y1, Can.
Notes: 100 items in Arabic, Persian, Indian illuminated manuscripts and Pali palm leaf manuscripts.

MANUSCRIPTS, IOWA

IA —STATE HISTORICAL SOCIETY OF IOWA LIBRARY, 402 Iowa Ave, Iowa City, 52240. Darold J Brown, Librn
Holdings: Cat
Notes: Thousands of individual items and smaller collections. Two hundred larger collections incl the papers of Cyrus C Carpenter, Jonathan P Dolliver, Gilbert Haugen, W W Waymack, Ephraim Adams, A C Dodge, Dorothy Houghton, Jesse Macy, Agnes Samuelson, Donald Johnson, Jack Miller, Ruth Sayre, Samuel Kirkwood, Thomas McKnight, Robert Lucas, Dwight McCarty, William Larrabee. Includes church, school, company and organization records, Civil War materials.

MANUSCRIPTS, ISLAMIC

IL —ORIENTAL INSTITUTE, 1155 E 58th St, Chicago, 60637. John Larsen, Archivist
Notes: The Bernhard Moritz Collection.

Fine examples of bindings as well as of Islamic calligraphy and writing materials-- papyrus, parchment, papers, etc. Extensive collection is also in the Beatty Library in Dublin, Ireland; Victoria and Albert Museum in London; Libraries in East and West Germany.

MANUSCRIPTS, ITALIAN

IL —NEWBERRY LIBRARY, 60 W Walton St, Chicago, 60610. Diana Haskell, Cur of Modern Mss
Notes: Incl also mss of the Strozzi and Parravincini Families of Italy.

†IL —UNIVERSITY OF ILLINOIS, URBANA/CHAMPAIGN, Library, Special Collections Div, Urbana, 61801.
Notes: Incl mss of the Cavagna Family in Italy.

NC —UNIVERSITY OF NORTH CAROLINA, CHAPEL HILL, Wilson Library, Rare Book Collection, Chapel Hill, 27514. Paul S Koda, Cur of Rare Books
Holdings: Vols 506 Cat Mss
Notes: Incl mss from the 12th to 16th century, primarily Italian and Latin. Chiefly documents, books of hours, and literary works. It is part of the Hanes Collection of the History of the Book. Several hundred uncatalogued, post-1600 mss are grouped with this material.

PA —TEMPLE UNIVERSITY LIBRARIES, Special Collections Dept, Rare Books & Mss Section, Philadelphia, 19122. Thomas M Whitehead, Cur
Holdings: Vols 200 Cat Mss
Notes: Extensive collection of printed books and mss, 900 AD-1900 AD; Cochran History of Business Collection. Original documents, ledgers, contracts, business letters, indentures, statutes, etc. Emphasis on Italy, 13th-17th centuries. Partial listings and descriptions published in the Temple University Library Bulletin, 1950-1963. Catalog in preparation.

PA —UNIVERSITY OF PENNSYLVANIA, Lea Library, 3420 Walnut St, Philadelphia, 19104. Daniel Traister, Special Collections Librn
Notes: Lea Collection of Medieval and Renaissance period incl statutes of the city-state and the Medici-Gondi account books. See (University of Pennsylvania) Library Chronicle, vol 36, no 2, Spring 1970. Hirsch, Rudolf. "Catalogue of Manuscripts in the Libraries of the University of Pennsylvania to 1800: Supplement A (3) Medici-Gondi Archive II." and Library Chronicle, vol 37, no 1, winter 1971. Catalogue...Supplement A (4). Norman P Zacour and Rudolf Hirsch Catalogue of Manuscripts in the Libraries of the University of Pennsylvania to 1800 (Philadelphia: University of Pennsylvania Press, 1965).

†TX —UNIVERSITY OF TEXAS LIBRARIES, Humanities Research Center, Austin, 78712.
Notes: Incl Mss of the Ranuzzi family of Italy.

MANUSCRIPTS, LATIN

MN —SAINT JOHN'S ABBEY & UNIVERSITY, Hill Monastic Manuscript Library, Collegeville, 56321. Julian G Plante, Dir
Holdings: Vols (61,000) Microfilms
Notes: Films of 61,000 mss. The total number of codices or bound handwritten mss represents the holdings of several hundred libraries in Europe, mostly Austria, Spain, Ethiopia, West Germany, Portugal, and also Italy, Hungary, Poland, Great Britain, Belgium, Yugoslavia, France, Switzerland, and the Netherlands.

MO —SAINT LOUIS UNIVERSITY, Pius XII Memorial Library, Vatican Film Library Collection, 3655 W Pine Blvd, Saint Louis, 63108. Charles J Ermatinger, Librn
Holdings: Mss Slides Microforms
Notes: Vatican Film Library has 75 percent of the Greek, Latin and western European vernacular holdings in the Vatican Library, plus all the Hebrew, Arabic and Ethiopic holdings on film. Covers 5th-19th centuries.

Sizable collection of western European books. In addition, has largest collection on the work of the Jesuits in Latin America, the US and the Philippines, filmed from European Jesuit archives. Excellent catalogs and guides to all collections. Also, 50,608 slides of illuminated mss; 26,470 reels of microfilm.

MO —SAINT LOUIS UNIVERSITY, Pius XII Memorial Library, 3655 W Pine Blvd, Saint Louis, 63108. William Cole, Dir
Holdings: Slides Microforms
Notes: Collection covers all areas of learning and European history from Classical Antiquity to early modern period. Researchers using collection receive assistance in paleography, bibliography and reference search. Approx 10,000 1000-foot reels of microfilm (not counting master negatives) reproducing Vatican Library's Latin, Greek, Hebrew, Arabic and Ethiopic mss. Some 8000 100-foot reels of microfilm (again not counting master negative) reproducing rare and out of print books relating to subject areas in the mss. Over 50,000 color slides of medieval and Renaissance mss illuminations. A reference collection of modern materials relating to ms research.

NC —UNIVERSITY OF NORTH CAROLINA, CHAPEL HILL, Wilson Library, Rare Book Collection, Chapel Hill, 27514. Paul S Koda, Cur of Rare Books
Holdings: Vols 506 Cat Mss
Notes: Incl mss from the 12th to 16th century, primarily Italian and Latin. Chiefly documents, books of hours, and literary works. It is part of the Hanes Collection of the History of the Book. Several hundred uncatalogued, post-1600 mss are grouped with this material.

NC —DUKE UNIVERSITY, William R Perkins Library, Rare Book Room, Durham, 27706. John L Sharpe, III, Cur
Notes: Berthold Louis Ullmann collection. Classical manuscripts - "17 substantial codices, two fragmentary manuscripts and 30 of only a few pages each, a total of 49 written between 9th and 16th centuries. Among them are four of the works of Cicero in the hand of noted 15th century scribes and two 9th century fragments of a French Sacramentary - and early Roman Catholic Service book for the Mass." In addition, Greek mss, 87 in number, dating from the 10th to the 12th centuries, incl 24 New Testament mss.

MANUSCRIPTS, MALTESE

MN —SAINT JOHN'S ABBEY & UNIVERSITY, Hill Monastic Manuscript Library, Collegeville, 56321. Julian G Plante, Dir
Notes: Films of 61,000 mss. The total number of codices or bound handwritten mss represents the holdings of several hundred libraries in Europe, mostly Austria, Spain, Ethiopia, West Germany, Portugal, and also Italy, Hungary, Poland, Great Britain, Belgium, Yugoslavia, France, Switzerland, and the Netherlands.

MANUSCRIPTS, MEDIEVAL

CT —YALE UNIVERSITY, Beinecke Rare Book & Manuscript Library, Osborn Collection, New Haven, 06520. Stephen R Parks, Cur
Holdings: Mss
DC —LIBRARY OF CONGRESS, Rare Book & Special Collections Div, Washington, 20540. William Matheson, Chief
Holdings: Vols (200) Uncat
Notes: The collection incl mss from the 13th to the 16th century in a variety of hands and texts. Some classical and medieval texts are represented, but a proportionately larger number are Bibles, lectionaries, psalters, and books of hours (often with illuminations, or illuminated initials or borders). One of the most noted of the mss is the famous Nekcsei-Lipocz Bible. Other mss items form part of collections such as the Special Collection (5 papyrus fragments) and the Rosenwald Collection (the Giant Bible of Mainz). An inventory of the items in the

MANUSCRIPTS, MEDIEVAL (cont.)

Medieval and Renaissance Collection appears in Seymour De Ricci's *Census of Medieval and Renaissance Manuscripts in the US and Canada*, vol 1 (New York: 1935), pp 180-241, and the supplement to De Ricci by William Bond (New York: 1962), pp 117-126.

†IL —UNIVERSITY OF CHICAGO LIBRARIES, Joseph Regenstein Library, Dept of Special Collections, 1100 E 57th St, Chicago, 60637.
Notes: A collection of photostats and microfilms of 383 medieval mss gathered by Prof S Harrison Thomson in the course of his research on Robert Grosseteste and John Wyclyf. Inventory index of the collection available.

MD —WALTERS ART GALLERY, Library & Manuscripts & Rare Book Collection, 600 N Charles St, Baltimore, 21201. Muriel L Toppan, Reference Librn; Lilian M C Randall, Cur of Mss & Rare Books
Holdings: Vols (80,000) Cat Mss
Budget: ($35,000)
Notes: The collection supports the gallery's collections of art objects which date from 4000 BC to the end to the 19th century. The collection of medieval and renaissance illuminated mss (782 in number), incunabula (about 1400) and rare books are considered art objects. There are card catalogs providing indexing to the collection. The mss are listed in De Ricci and the incunabula in Goff. Photocopying permitted for Reference Library materials only.

MI —WESTERN MICHIGAN UNIVERSITY, Dwight B Waldo Library, Institute of Cistercian Studies Library, Kalamazoo, 49008. Beatrice H Beck, Librn
Notes: The Abbot Obrecht Collection of mss, incunabula, and other books from the Cistercian Abbey of Gethsemane at Trappist, Kentucky. On indefinite loan (1976).

MN —SAINT JOHN'S ABBEY & UNIVERSITY, Hill Monastic Manuscript Library, Collegeville, 56321. Julian G Plante, Dir
Holdings: Vols (61,000) Microfilms
Notes: Films of 61,000 mss. The total number of codices or bound handwritten mss represents the holdings of several hundred libraries in Europe, mostly Austria, Spain, Ethiopia, West Germany, Portugal, and also Italy, Hungary, Poland, Great Britain, Belgium, Yugoslavia, France, Switzerland, and the Netherlands.

NJ —PRINCETON UNIVERSITY, Library, Manuscript Collection, Nassau St, Princeton, 08540. Jean F Preston, Cur
Holdings: Mss Pix
Notes: The collection of Medieval and Renaissance manuscripts, totaling 350 book manuscripts, incl items collected by Robert Garrett and Grenville Kane. The collection is supplemented by several single leaves. See *Princeton University Library Chronicle*, vol 3, pp 123-35; vol 11, pp 37-44. Ricci, Seymour de. *Census of Medieval and Renaissance Manuscripts in the United States and Canada* (New York: H W Wilson Co, 1935-40); and *Supplement*, ed by W H Bond, 1962.

NY —THE CLOISTERS, Metropolitan Museum of Art (Branch), Fort Tryon Park, New York, 10040. Suse C Childs, Librn
Holdings: Vols (5000) Cat Mss Pix Slides
Notes: A branch of the Metropolitan Museum of Art devoted solely to the literature of medieval art. Incl 16,000 slides and 5000 photographs with unique strengths in certain aspects of medieval art.

NC —UNIVERSITY OF NORTH CAROLINA, CHAPEL HILL, Wilson Library, Rare Book Collection, Chapel Hill, 27514. Paul S Koda, Cur of Rare Books
Holdings: Vols 506 Cat Mss
Notes: Incl mss from the 12th to 16th century, primarily Italian and Latin. Chiefly documents, books of hours, and literary works. It is part of the Hanes Collection of the History of the Book. Several hundred uncatalogued, post-1600 mss are grouped with this material.

NC —DUKE UNIVERSITY, William R Perkins Library, Rare Book Room, Durham, 27706. John L Sharpe, III, Cur
Notes: Berthold Louis Ullmann collection. Classical manuscripts - "17 substantial codices, two fragmentary manuscripts and 30 of only a few pages each, a total of 49 written between 9th and 16th centuries. Among them are four of the works of Cicero in the hand of noted 15th century scribes and two 9th century fragments of a French Sacramentary - and early Roman Catholic Service book for the Mass."

PA —FREE LIBRARY OF PHILADELPHIA, Rare Book Dept, Logan Sq, Philadelphia, 19103. Marie E Korey, Rare Book Librn
Holdings: Cat Mss
Notes: The John Frederick Lewis and Joseph E Widener Collections of European Manuscripts incl 2200 bound volumes and separate illuminated leaves and text leaves.

PA —UNIVERSITY OF PENNSYLVANIA, Van Pelt Library, Rare Books Collection, 34 & Walnut Sts, Philadelphia, 19104. Daniel Traister, Special Collections Librn

PQ —MCGILL UNIVERSITY, McLennan Library, Rare Books and Special Collections Dept, 3459 McTavish St, Montreal, H3A 1Y1, Can.
Notes: Incl ca 200 illuminated leaves, Books of Hours, miniatures, and initials.

MANUSCRIPTS, MEXICAN

DC —LIBRARY OF CONGRESS, Manuscript Division, Washington, 20540. John C Broderick, Chief
Holdings: Cat Mss Pix
Notes: Mss, papers, records, etc.

TX —UNIVERSITY OF TEXAS LIBRARIES, Nettie Lee Benson Latin American Collection, Sid Richardson Hall 1.109, Austin, 78712. Laura Gutierrez-Witt, Head Librn
Holdings: Vols (450,000) Cat Mss Microforms
Notes: The Juan E Hernandez y Davalos ms collection contains nearly 3000 documents, 1692-1865, with special concentration on the Mexican War of Independence, 1808-1821. Several noteworthy Mexican ms collections deal largely with northern Mexico and with areas now part of the southwestern US. Among them are the William B Stephens collection of the Spanish Southwest, 1488-1860 (20,000 pages); the Archives of the presidio of Janos in Chihuahua, 1706-1858; the Lazaro de la Garza papers, 1913-1936 (4000 items), documenting his work as financial agent for General Francisco "Pancho" Villa; and some 8000 pages of documents and notes, originals and copies assembled by American historian Justin H Smith while writing *The War with Mexico*. More recent coverage of Mexico, particularly politics, is provided in the John W F Dulles Mexico Papers, 1950-1059 (1600 items).
See also entries under Latin America and Texas-History.

MANUSCRIPTS, MIDDLE EASTERN
see Manuscripts, Arabic

MANUSCRIPTS, MUSICAL

†CA —STANFORD UNIVERSITY LIBRARIES, Stanford, 94305.
Notes: In collection of English and American Literature.

IL —NEWBERRY LIBRARY, 60 W Walton St, Chicago, 60610. Diana Haskell, Cur of Modern Mss
Holdings: Vols 600 Cat Mss
Notes: Ranging from 13th century liturgical works through 16th-18th century choirbooks, 18th-19th century tunebooks and song collections. Incl small collection of representative 18th and 19th century master composers. Also letters of Theodore Thomas, Frederick Stock, Joseph Joachim and Rudolph Ganz. Restricted use: noncirculating.

NY —PIERPONT MORGAN LIBRARY, 29 E 36 St, New York, 10016. J Rigbie Turner, Cur
Holdings: Cat Mss
Notes: Musical mss, mainly of composers of the 18th-20th centuries. Incl the Mary Flagler Cary Music Collection.

NC —UNIVERSITY OF NORTH CAROLINA, CHAPEL HILL, Music Library, Hill Hall, Chapel Hill, 27514.
Holdings: Vols (90,000) Cat Mss Pix Slides Phonorecords Audiotapes Microforms
Budget: ($60,000)
Notes: Extensive holdings of early theoretical treatises; complete editions. Microfilms of important European primary sources. Substantial collection of shape-note hymnals, 19th and 20th century.

†TX —UNIVERSITY OF TEXAS LIBRARIES, Austin, 78712.
Notes: Collection of 89 autographed music manuscripts by five french composers: Gabriel Faure, Maurice Ravel, Claude Debussy, Robert Roussel, Paul Dukas. About 60 percent of Roussel's entire repertory is included, as well as nearly one-half of Ravel's total musical output.

MANUSCRIPTS, NORTH AFRICAN

ON —NATIONAL LIBRARY OF CANADA, 395 Wellington St, Ottawa, K1A 0N4, Can. Andre Preibish, Dir
Notes: *The Jacob M Lowy Collection* over 2000 works of very rare Hebraica and Judaica. Among outstanding items are 30 incunabula - the first printed edition of the Babylonian Talmud, many editions of Flavius Josephus, including first edition of 1470 Early Bibles in many languages. *The Saul Hayes Collection* of Hebraic Manuscripts and microforms. Manuscripts from North Africa and the Orient; 300 reels of manuscripts held by libraries in Poland, USSR and Hungary. This collection is held in the Jacob M Lowy Room.

MANUSCRIPTS, ORIENTAL

CT —YALE UNIVERSITY, Box 1603A, Yale Station, New Haven, 06520.

IL —NEWBERRY LIBRARY, 60 W Walton St, Chicago, 60610. Diana Haskell, Cur of Modern Mss
Holdings: Vols 149// Cat Mss
Notes: A representative collection, including Arabic, Hebrew, Persian, Pali, and Sanskirt, with numerous others. Restricted use: noncirculating.

OH —CLEVELAND PUBLIC LIBRARY, Fine Arts and Special Collections Department, 325 Superior Ave, Cleveland, 44114. Alice N Loranth, Head
Holdings: Vols 200 Cat Mss Pix
Notes: A choice collection of practically all important, mostly unpublished works in Arabic, Persian, Syriac, Ethiopic, Pali and Chinese. Incl historical, literary and scientific texts. The Persian group is the most important, incl Moghul charters and tax documents in addition to numerous illuminated specimens of historic or literary merit.

PA —HAVERFORD COLLEGE, Magill Library, Quaker Collection, Haverford, 19041. Edwin B Bonner, Librn & Cur
Holdings: Vols 60 // Cat Mss
Notes: Hebrew, Latin, Arabic, Syriac and Ethiopian rolls and codices.

PA —FREE LIBRARY OF PHILADELPHIA, Rare Book Dept, Logan Sq, Philadelphia, 19103. Marie E Korey, Rare Book Librn
Holdings: Cat Mss Pix
Notes: The John Frederick Lewis Collection of Oriental Manuscripts incl 1350 bound volumes, miniatures, and separate illustrated leaves.

RI —BROWN UNIVERSITY, John Hay Library, 20 Prospect St, Providence, 02912. Mark N Brown, Cur Mss
Holdings: Vols (53) //
Notes: Indic Manuscripts Collection; codices written in Burmese, Cambodian, Telugu, Skandhas, Bengali, and Sinhalese script on palm leaves, encased within wood covers, some lacquered. Subjects include: Buddhist canon, Pali grammar and lexicons, epics, dance drama, and a treatise on midwifery.

MANUSCRIPTS, ORIENTAL (cont.)

Recorded in *A Census of Indic Manuscripts in the United States and Canada* compiled by Horace I Poleman (New Haven: American Oriental Society, 1938).

ON —NATIONAL LIBRARY OF CANADA, 395 Wellington St, Ottawa, K1A 0N4, Can. Andre Preibish, Dir
Notes: *The Jacob M Lowy Collection* over 2000 works of very rare Hebraica and Judaica. Among outstanding items are 30 incunabula - the first printed edition of the Babylonian Talmud, many editions of Flavius Josephus, including first edition of 1470 Early Bibles in many languages. *The Saul Hayes Collection* of Hebraic Manuscripts and microforms. Manuscripts from North Africa and the Orient; 300 reels of manuscripts held by libraries in Poland, USSR and Hungary. This collection is held in the Jacob M Lowy Room.

PQ —MCGILL UNIVERSITY, McLennan Library, Rare Books and Special Collections Dept, 3459 McTavish St, Montreal, H3A 1Y1, Can.
Notes: 100 items in Arabic, Persian, Indian illuminated manuscripts and Pali palm leaf manuscripts.

MANUSCRIPTS, PALI

OH —CLEVELAND PUBLIC LIBRARY, Fine Arts and Special Collections Department, 325 Superior Ave, Cleveland, 44114. Alice N Loranth, Head
Holdings: Vols (206) Cat Mss
Notes: Part of the Oriental Manuscripts Collection, which is a choice collection of important, mostly unpublished works in Arabic, Persian, Syriac, Ethiopic, Pali, Sanskrit, Hebrew and Chinese. Incl historical, literary and scientific texts. Facsimile reproductions of mss supplement the originals.
See also entries under Manuscripts - Catalogs; Manuscripts, Oriental; Oriental Languages and Literatures; Pali Language and Literature.

PQ —MCGILL UNIVERSITY, McLennan Library, Rare Books and Special Collections Dept, 3459 McTavish St, Montreal, H3A 1Y1, Can.
Notes: 100 items in Arabic, Persian, Indian illuminated manuscripts and Pali palm leaf manuscripts.

MANUSCRIPTS, PERSIAN

CA —UNIVERSITY OF CALIFORNIA, LOS ANGELES, Research Library, Dept of Special Collections, 405 Hilgard Ave, Los Angeles, 90024. Edward Shreeves, Chairman, Bibliographers Group; David S Zeidberg, Head
Holdings: Mss
Notes: 18,000,000 items in 1300 collections, emphasizing humanities and social sciences; particular strength in British and American literature and California history, but incl 125 medieval mss, part of the Orsini family archive, and 10,000 Arabic, Armenian, and Persian mss in 6000 volumes, and 94 linear feet of Turkish mss, mostly uncataloged.

CT —YALE UNIVERSITY, Box 1603A, Yale Station, New Haven, 06520.

IL —ORIENTAL INSTITUTE, 1155 E 58th St, Chicago, 60637. John Larsen, Archivist
Notes: The Bernhard Moritz Collection. Fine examples of bindings as well as of Islamic calligraphy and writing materials-- papyrus, parchment, papers, etc. Extensive collection is also in the Beatty Library in Dublin, Ireland; Victoria and Albert Museum in London; Libraries in East and West Germany.

NJ —PRINCETON UNIVERSITY, Library, Near East Collections, Princeton, 08540. James Weinberger, Cur
Holdings: Vols (100,000) Cat Mss Maps Phonorecords Audiotapes Microforms
Budget: ($72,000)
Notes: Princeton has the largest collection of Arabic mss in the US. Collections are particularly rich in classical Arabic and Persian texts, encompassing all the traditional genres. Of special note are the collections in Arabic and Persian literature, language, history, philosophy and theology and the religious sciences of Islam, both in ms and printed formats. A separate, additional collection of Arabic mss (about 2000 items) is being cataloged. It is especially rich in theology and philosophy of the classical Islamic period. Two printed catalogs are available: *Descriptive Catalog of the Garrett Collection of Arabic Manuscripts*, Philip K Hitte et al (Princeton: Princeton Univ Press, 1938); and *Catalogue of Arabic Manuscripts (Yahuda Section) in the Garrett Collection, Princeton University*, Rudolf Mach (Princeton: Princeton Univ Press, 1977).

NY —COLUMBIA UNIVERSITY LIBRARIES, Rare Book & Manuscript Library, 801 Butler Library, 535 W 114 St, New York, 10027. Kenneth A Lohf, Librn
Holdings: Mss
Notes: Incl 100 items. Restricted use.

OH —HEBREW UNION COLLEGE-JEWISH INSTITUTE OF RELIGION, Klau Library, 3101 Clifton Ave, Cincinnati, 45220. David J Gilner, Reference Librn
Holdings: Cat Mss
Notes: About 6000 mss in Hebrew characters representing various languages, such as Hebrew, Ladino, Yiddish, Spanish, Italian, German; also mss in Arabic, Ethiopian, Chinese and Persian alphabets. Incl literary, archival, sermonic and halakhic mss.

OH —CLEVELAND PUBLIC LIBRARY, Fine Arts and Special Collections Department, 325 Superior Ave, Cleveland, 44114. Alice N Loranth, Head
Holdings: Vols (170) Cat Mss
Notes: Middle Eastern mss incl original mss mostly in Arabic, Persian and Turkish, and some in Syriac, Ethiopic and Hebrew. Notable are the 79 Persian examples of illuminated codices and the 54 Arabic treatises on chess, religion, mathematics, medicine, etc. The chiefly unpublished original mss are well supplemented by several hundred vols of facsimile editions of mss. Separate author entry catalogs by languages.
See also entries under Manuscripts - Catalogs; Manuscripts, Oriental; Oriental Languages and Literatures; Persian Language and Literature.

PQ —MCGILL UNIVERSITY, McLennan Library, Rare Books and Special Collections Dept, 3459 McTavish St, Montreal, H3A 1Y1, Can.
Notes: 100 items in Arabic, Persian, Indian illuminated manuscripts and Pali palm leaf manuscripts.

MANUSCRIPTS, PERUVIAN

DC —LIBRARY OF CONGRESS, Manuscript Division, Washington, 20540. John C Broderick, Chief
Holdings: Cat Mss Pix
Notes: Mss, papers, records, etc.

MANUSCRIPTS, RENAISSANCE

DC —LIBRARY OF CONGRESS, Rare Book & Special Collections Div, Washington, 20540. William Matheson, Chief
Notes: The Medieval and Renaissance Manuscripts Collection. See entry under Manuscripts, Medieval for extended description.

IL —NEWBERRY LIBRARY, 60 W Walton St, Chicago, 60610. Diana Haskell, Cur of Modern Mss
Holdings: Cat Mss
Notes: Incl Parravicini, Strozzi, and Barga family papers. Restricted use: noncirculating.

MD —WALTERS ART GALLERY, Library & Manuscripts & Rare Book Collection, 600 N Charles St, Baltimore, 21201. Muriel L Toppan, Reference Librn; Lilian M C Randall, Cur of Mss & Rare Books
Holdings: Vols (80,000) Cat Mss
Budget: ($35,000)
Notes: The collection supports the gallery's collections of art objects which date from 4000 BC to the end of the 19th century. The collection of medieval and renaissance illuminated mss (782 in number), incunabula (about 1400) and rare books are considered art objects. There are card catalogs providing indexing to the collection. The mss are listed in De Ricci and the incunabula in Goff. Photocopying permitted for Reference Library materials only.

MN —SAINT JOHN'S ABBEY & UNIVERSITY, Hill Monastic Manuscript Library, Collegeville, 56321. Julian G Plante, Dir
Holdings: Vols (61,000) Microfilms
Notes: Films of 61,000 mss. The total number of codices or bound handwritten mss represents the holdings of several hundred libraries in Europe, mostly Austria, Spain, Ethiopia, West Germany, Portugal, and also Italy, Hungary, Poland, Great Britain, Belgium, Yugoslavia, France, Switzerland, and the Netherlands.

MO —SAINT LOUIS UNIVERSITY, Pius XII Memorial Library, Vatican Film Library Collection, 3655 W Pine Blvd, Saint Louis, 63108. Charles J Ermatinger, Librn
Holdings: Mss Slides Microforms
Notes: Vatican Film Library has 75 percent of the Greek, Latin and western European vernacular holdings in the Vatican Library, plus all the Hebrew, Arabic and Ethiopic holdings on film. Covers 5th-19th centuries. Sizable collection of western European books. In addition, has largest collection on the work of the Jesuits in Latin America, the US and the Philippines, filmed from European Jesuit archives. Excellent catalogs and guides to all collections. Also, 50,608 slides of illuminated mss; 26,470 reels of microfilm.

NJ —PRINCETON UNIVERSITY, Library, Manuscript Collection, Nassau St, Princeton, 08540. Jean F Preston, Cur
Holdings: Mss Pix
Notes: The collection of Medieval and Renaissance manuscripts, totaling 350 book manuscripts, incl items collected by Robert Garrett and Grenville Kane. The collection is supplemented by several single leaves. See *Princeton University Library Chronicle*, vol 3, pp 123-35; vol 11, pp 37-44. Ricci, Seymour de. *Census of Medieval and Renaissance Manuscripts in the United States and Canada* (New York: H W Wilson Co, 1935-40); and *Supplement*, ed by W H Bond, 1962.

NC —UNIVERSITY OF NORTH CAROLINA, CHAPEL HILL, Wilson Library, Rare Book Collection, Chapel Hill, 27514. Paul S Koda, Cur of Rare Books
Holdings: Vols 506 Cat Mss
Notes: Incl mss from the 12th to 16th century, primarily Italian and Latin. Chiefly documents, books of hours, and literary works. It is part of the Hanes Collection of the History of the Book. Several hundred uncataloged, post-1600 mss are grouped with this material.

PA —UNIVERSITY OF PENNSYLVANIA, Lea Library, 3420 Walnut St, Philadelphia, 19104. Daniel Traister, Special Collections Librn
Notes: Lea Collection of Medieval and Renaissance period incl statutes of the city-state and the Medici-Gondi account books. See (*University of Pennsylvania*) *Library Chronicle*, vol 36, no 2, Spring 1970. Hirsch, Rudolf. "Catalogue of Manuscripts in the Libraries of the University of Pennsylvania to 1800: Supplement A (3) Medici-Gondi Archive II." and *Library Chronicle*, vol 37, no 1, winter 1971. *Catalogue...Supplement A (4)*. Norman P Zacour and Rudolf Hirsch *Catalogue of Manuscripts in the Libraries of the University of Pennsylvania to 1800* (Philadelphia: University of Pennsylvania Press, 1965).

MANUSCRIPTS, RUSSIAN

OH —OHIO STATE UNIVERSITY, William Oxley Thompson Memorial Library, 1858 Neil Ave, Columbus, 43210. A Robert Thorson, Head, Circulation Dept
Holdings: Cat Mss Microforms
Notes: This collection presently contains

MANUSCRIPTS, RUSSIAN (cont.)

films of 2000 mss from the Hilandar Monastery, Mt Athos. Expansion will add Byzantine, Bulgarian, Russian and Valachian mss on film.

MANUSCRIPTS, SERBIAN

OH —OHIO STATE UNIVERSITY, William Oxley Thompson Memorial Library, 1858 Neil Ave, Columbus, 43210. A Robert Thorson, Head, Circulation Dept
Holdings: Cat Mss Microforms
Notes: This collection presently contains films of 2000 mss from the Hilandar Monastery, Mt Athos. Expansion will add Byzantine, Bulgarian, Russian and Valachian mss on film.

MANUSCRIPTS, SLAVIC (CYRILLIC)

OH —OHIO STATE UNIVERSITY, William Oxley Thompson Memorial Library, Hilander Room, 1858 Neil Ave Mall, Columbus, 43210. Predrag Matejic, Cur; G Koolemans Beynen, Slavic Bibliographer
Holdings: Vols (200,000) Cat Maps Microforms
Budget: ($45,000)
Notes: Area studies of Central, Southeastern and Eastern Europe. Emphasis on on Slavic literatures, languages and history. At present economics, sociology, law (Russian only) have been added. Within this framework the following priorities have been established: Material in Russian Russian problems; then Medieval Slavic (Cyrillic); then Polish, then Serbo-Croatian, then Bulgarian and now Romanian. Special attention is paid to serials, bibliographies, ms descriptions and dictionaries (incl biographical and encyclopedias). Apart from materials in native languages, materials in the following languages are acquired: Old Church Slavonic, Greek, English, French, German, Italian, a few in Scandinavian languages, incl Finnish, and a few in Baltic languages. The Hillandar Room holds approx 2000 Slavic mss, 1050 from Hilandar Monastery, Mount Athos, on microform and a related referencecollection.

MANUSCRIPTS, SYRIAC

CT —YALE UNIVERSITY, American Oriental Society Library, 120 High St, New Haven, 06520. Rutherford B Rogers, Librarian
Notes: 6 mss.
MA —HARVARD UNIVERSITY, Harvard Divinity School, Andover-Harvard Theological Library, 45 Francis Ave, Cambridge, 02138. Maria Grossmann, Librn
Holdings: Vols (370,000) Cat
OH —CLEVELAND PUBLIC LIBRARY, Fine Arts and Special Collections Department, 325 Superior Ave, Cleveland, 44114. Alice N Loranth, Head
Holdings: Vols (170) Cat Mss
Notes: Middle Eastern mss incl original mss mostly in Arabic, Persian and Turkish, and some in Syriac, Ethiopic and Hebrew. Notable are the 79 Persian examples of illuminated codices and the 54 Arabic treatises on chess, religion, mathematics, medicine, etc. The chiefly unpublished original mss are well supplemented by several hundred vols of facsimile editions of mss. Separate author entry catalogs by languages.
See also entries under Manuscripts - Catalogs; Manuscripts, Oriental; Oriental Languages and Literatures.
UT —UNIVERSITY OF UTAH, Middle East Library, Salt Lake City, 84112. Ragai N Makar, Librn
Budget: ($40,000)
Notes: Mt Sinai Arabic Manuscripts collection. This incl about 800 Arabic manuscripts on microfilm. This collection is incl in the catalogue The Arabic Manuscripts of Mt Sinai by Professor Aziz S Atiya. Baltimore, The Johns Hopkins Press, 1955. All the mss are on the history and theology of the Eastern Christian Church. The Greek

Manuscripts on microfilm collection of the Patriarchal Library of Alexandria, Egypt. This incl about 1000 mss on microfilm about the history and theology of the Greek Orthodox Church. This collection described in Studies and Documents edited by Jacob Geerlings. Vol XXVI Catalog of MSS of the Patriarchal Library of Alexandria by T D Mosconas, Salt Lake City, University of Utah Press, 1965. The Catholic Microfilm Center Syriac and Arabic Manuscript Collection. This incl about 985 Syriac and Arabic mss on microfilm all of whichis about the history and theology of the Eastern Orthodox Church.

MANUSCRIPTS, TURKISH

CA —UNIVERSITY OF CALIFORNIA, LOS ANGELES, Research Library, Dept of Special Collections, 405 Hilgard Ave, Los Angeles, 90024. Edward Shreeves, Chairman, Bibliographers Group; David S Zeidberg, Head
Notes: 94 linear feet of unprocessed Turkish mss.
CT —YALE UNIVERSITY, Box 1603A, Yale Station, New Haven, 06520.
NJ —PRINCETON UNIVERSITY, Library, Near East Collections, Princeton, 08540. James Weinberger, Cur
Holdings: Vols (100,000) Cat Mss Maps Phonorecords Audiotapes Microforms
Budget: ($72,000)
Notes: Princeton has the largest collection of Arabic mss in the US. Collections are particularly rich in classical Arabic and Persian texts, encompassing all the traditional genres. Of special note are the collections in Arabic and Persian literature, language, history, philosophy and theology and the religious sciences of Islam, both in mss and printed formats. A separate, additional collection of Arabic mss (about 2000 items) is being cataloged. It is especially rich in theology and philosophy of the classical Islamic period. Two printed catalogs are available: Descriptive Catalog of the Garrett Collection of Arabic Manuscripts, Philip K Hitte et al (Princeton: Princeton Univ Press, 1938); and Catalogue of Arabic Manuscripts (Yahuda Section) in the Garrett Collection, Princeton University, Rudolf Mach (Princeton: Princeton Univ Press, 1977).
OH —CLEVELAND PUBLIC LIBRARY, Fine Arts and Special Collections Department, 325 Superior Ave, Cleveland, 44114. Alice N Loranth, Head
Holdings: Vols 27 Cat Mss
Notes: Middle Eastern mss incl original mss mostly in Arabic, Persian and Turkish, and some in Syriac, Ethiopic and Hebrew. Notable are the 79 Persian examples of illuminated codices and the 54 Arabic treatises on chess, religion, mathematics, medicine, etc. The chiefly unpublished original mss are well supplemented by several hundred vols of facsimile editions of mss. The library holdings of Istanbul and Skutari are described in a unique collection of 45 vols. Separate author entry catalogs by languages.
See also entries under Manuscripts - Catalogs; Manuscripts, Oriental; Oriental Languages and Literatures.

MANUSCRIPTS, VALACHIAN

OH —OHIO STATE UNIVERSITY, William Oxley Thompson Memorial Library, 1858 Neil Ave, Columbus, 43210. A Robert Thorson, Head, Circulation Dept
Holdings: Cat Mss Microforms
Notes: This collection presently contains films of 2000 mss from the Hilandar Monastery, Mt Athos. Expansion will add Byzantine, Bulgarian, Russian and Valachian mss of film.

MANUSCRIPTS, VIRGINIA

VA —VIRGINIA STATE LIBRARY, 12 & Capitol Sts, Richmond, 23219.
Holdings: Mss Maps Pix Microforms
Notes: Incl archives of Virginia, mainly

noncurrent public records, but incl other mss, relating to Virginia and the South. Contains 80,000 bound vols, 27,000,000 ms pieces and 85,000 maps. Partially cataloged.

MANUTIUS, ALDUS

CA —UNIVERSITY OF CALIFORNIA, LOS ANGELES, Research Library, Dept of Special Collections, 405 Hilgard Ave, Los Angeles, 90024. Edward Shreeves, Chairman, Bibliographers Group; David S Zeidberg, Head
Notes: 500 books printed by Aldus Manutius, his father-in-law, his son, and his grandson, incl 21 printed before 1501.

MANVELL, ROGER

KY —UNIVERSITY OF LOUISVILLE, Ekstrom Library, Rare Books & Special Collections, 2301 S Third St, Louisville, 40208. George T McWhorter, Cur; Delinda Stephens Buie, Asst Cur
Holdings: Vols 100 Uncat Mss Pix
Budget: ($1500)
Notes: Roger Manvell's work on the history of theatre and film and on the Third Reich. Incl his publications, 40 linear feet of mss, and 1500 international film stills from the silent era to the present day.

MANVILLE, WILLIAM

MA —BOSTON UNIVERSITY, Mugar Memorial Library, Special Collections Dept, 771 Commonwealth Ave, Boston, 02215. Howard B Gotlieb, Dir
Holdings: Mss

MANX LANGUAGE

IL —NEWBERRY LIBRARY, 60 W Walton St, Chicago, 60610. Diana Haskell, Cur of Modern Mss
Holdings: Cat Maps
Notes: The bulk of the collection (about 15, 000 vols) is in the Prince Lucien Bonaparte group, which deals with western European linguistics. In this group the major rare categories are Etruscan and Basque linguistic studies, although the bulk of the group treats the major European languages and their dialects, ie French, German, English, Spanish, Italian and Russian. There is also strong representation in Gaelic linguistics, particularly Irish, Cornish, Welsh and Manx. In other collections of the library, there are major groups of books and mss dealing with American Indian languages and Philippine languages (about 4500 books and mss).

MAORIS

CA —UNIVERSITY OF CALIFORNIA, LOS ANGELES, Research Library, Indo/Pacific Collection, 405 Hilgard Ave, Los Angeles, 90024. Edward Shreeves, Chairman, Bibliographers Group; Charlotte Spence, Indo/Pacific Bibliographer
Holdings: Vols Cat Mss Maps Pix Microforms
Notes: The Pacific area collection has been developed on a combination of the research and teaching levels. It focuses on the cultural, economic, political and social history of Australia, New Zealand and the various island groups. The accounts of the early European voyagers are well represented, with the highlight being the Captain Cook collection. An effort has also been made to collect the novels, poetry, drama, etc, of Australian and New Zealand authors.
CA —UNIVERSITY OF CALIFORNIA, SANTA CRUZ, University Library, Special Collections, Santa Cruz, 95064. Rita Bottoms, Special Collections Librn; Margaret Felts, South Pacific Collection Bibliographer
Holdings: Vols (10,000) Cat
Notes: South Pacific Collection. Monographs, rare books, serials, documents and atlases which treat of the Pacific areas of Polynesia, Melanesia, Micronesia, Australia and New Zealand, but excluding western New Guinea (Irian Jaya), the Philippines

MAORIS (cont.)

and Southeast Asia. Approximately 10 percent of the titles are multi-volume documents such as parliamentary papers, legislative journals, official yearbooks, statistical sourcebooks, laws and statutes. The collection includes an exhaustive selection of current journals and monographic series from and about the Pacific: early serials, South Pacific Commission publications, US Government and US Trust Territory publications, serials from museums, universities and scholarly societies. Chief emphasis has been placed on acquisition of the literature of history, description and travel, ethnology andanthropology, literature and literary criticism, political and constitutional histories. Other extensive holdings are in the fields of geography and maps, voyages, mission histories, mythology and folklore, art, linguistics, and science fields of natural history, environmental studies, biology, zoology, botany, geology and astronomy. Printed catalog is available. This is an on-going, growing collection.

NY —AMERICAN MUSEUM OF NATURAL HISTORY, Library Services Dept, Central Park W & 79th St, New York, 10024. Nina J Root, Chairwoman; Mary Genett, Asst Librn for Reference Services

NY —AUSTRALIAN CONSULATE-GENERAL, Australian Information Service, Reference Library, 636 Fifth Ave, New York, 10111. Jill Hutchison, Librn; Frank Long, Officer; Lynnette Shaw, Photo Librn & Press Asst
Notes: Books, pamphlets, bound periodical volumes, 1300 vertical files, 260 film titles, 2000 black and white photographs and 500 col slides; incl Australian federal government legislation, statistics, ministerial press releases and publications, Australian press clippings, newspapers, and magazines. Collection incl Australian history, law, politics and government, economics, flora and fauna, geography, social conditions, arts, science, literature, and the Aboriginals.

NY —NEW YORK PUBLIC LIBRARY, Research Libraries, General Research Division, Fifth Ave & 42 St, New York, 10018. Rodney Phillips, Chief
Holdings: Vols (2,225,000) Cat Maps Pix Microforms
Budget: ($775,718)

ON —UNIVERSITY OF TORONTO, Thomas Fisher Rare Book Library, 120 Saint George St, Toronto, M5S 1A5, Can. Richard G Landon, Head
Notes: Sheldon Collection of Australiana, named for collector William Sheldon. Especially rich in 19th century accounts of the exploration of the South Pacific and the interior of the Australian continent. Includes narratives of exiled Canadians who took part in the Rebellion of 1837 in Canada. Includes works on colonization and settlement, the gold-rush of the mid 19th century, and on the life of the indigenous peoples. Includes literature written by Australians or about Australia.

MAP LIBRARIANSHIP

PA —FREE LIBRARY OF PHILADELPHIA, Social Science and History Dept, Map Collection, Logan Sq, Philadelphia, 19103.
Holdings: Vols (30,000) Cat Mss Maps
Notes: Map collection incl atlases, maps, pamphlets, and aerial views. Incl a representative collection of early atlases (1534-1827). The collection emphasizes the Philadelphia, Pennsylvania and Delaware Valley areas in particular and the eastern seaboard in general. Low altitude oblique aerial photographs have been transferred to the Print and Picture Dept; high altitude vertical aerial photographs have been retained; some volumes and pamphlets reassigned within the Social Science and History Dept.

MAP READING see Maps, Military; Maps and Atlases—Collections

MAPS—HISTORY see Cartography—History

MAPS—OCEANS see Ocean—Maps

MAPS—VEGETATION

GA —UNIVERSITY OF GEORGIA, Libraries, Map Collection, Athens, 30602.

John Sutherland, Cur of Maps
Notes: Collection contains 291,165 cataloged maps and 192,068 aerial photographs, specializing in Georgia, Southeast US, Central and South America, and Europe. Major subject specializations are topography, geology, soils and vegetation. Special cartographic collection of Sanborn Fire Insurance Maps (7000 sheets).

MAPS, AERONAUTICAL see Aeronautics—Maps

MAPS, ARGRICULTURAL see Agriculture—Maps

MAPS, CAVE see Cave Maps

MAPS, FIRE INSURANCE see Insurance, Fire—Maps and Surveys

MAPS, INSURANCE

DC —LIBRARY OF CONGRESS, Geography and Map Division, Washington, 20540. John A Wolter, Chief
Notes: Sanborn Fire Insurance Map collection of insurance maps of US cities, late 19th and 20th centuries.

DC —LIBRARY OF CONGRESS, Washington, 20540.

ON —METROPOLITAN TORONTO LIBRARY, History Dept, 789 Yonge St, Toronto, M4W 2G8, Can. Michael Pearson, Head
Holdings: Maps
Notes: The collection comprises 40,000 maps: current topographic and thematic maps; depository for the Canadian National Topographic series; extensive historical collection specializing in Toronto and Ontario, incl insurance plans. 700 atlases: major world atlases, national and regional atlases; facsimiles of important early atlases, some originals. 400 current and retrospective gazetteers.

MAPS, MILITARY

CA —UNIVERSITY OF CALIFORNIA, BERKELEY, University Library, East Asiatic Library, Room 208, Durant Hall, Berkeley, 94720. Donald Shively, Head
Holdings: Vols 215,000 Cat Mss Maps Pix Microforms
Notes: The largest collection of Japanese-language materials at any American university. Subject coverage is universal in scope, but works in the humanities and the social sciences predominate. All historical periods are represented. The East Asiatic Library (like the Library of Congress) serves as a full depository for Japanese Government publications. The Library maintains a distinguished rare book collection, comprising, for instance, ancient woodblock color maps, manuscripts, early Buddhist Sutras, and rare and early editions. Outstanding resources include: the Murakami Collection of Meiji Literature; the Mitsui Library; and the Japanese Military Map Collection. Western-language materials in related fields are located in the Main Library. A G K Hall catalog of East Asiatic Library holdings has been published.

NJ —PRINCETON UNIVERSITY, Library, Manuscript Collection, Nassau St, Princeton, 08540. Jean F Preston, Cur
Holdings: Vols 24 Cat Mss Maps
Notes: About 100 of the French cartographer Louis Alexandre Berthier's maps and associated papers involving French campaigns in the Revolutionary War form the manuscript section of the collection. See *Princeton University Library Chronicle*, vol 1, no 1, pp 3-8. An unpublished guide (25 p) of the manuscripts and map section of the collection is available for consultation. See *The American Campaigns of Rochambeau's Army*, ed by Howard C Rice, Jr and Anne S K Brown (Princeton, 1972).

OK —US ARMY FIELD ARTILLERY SCHOOL LIBRARY, Morris Swett Library, Snow Hall, Fort Sill, 73503. Lester L Miller Jr, Chief Librn
Notes: Field artillery; artillery; ordnance;

military history; military science; weapons and weapons systems; ammunition; ballistics; missiles; Field Artillery unit histories; military periodicals analytical index file (VF). Incl US and foreign artillery; survey data; photographs on army subjects.

†VA —GEORGE C MARSHALL RESEARCH FOUNDATION AND LIBRARY, Drawer 920, Lexington, 24450. Royster Lyle Jr, Cur Collections
Holdings: Cat Maps
Notes: The William F. Friedman Collection. Separate catalog. Incl. papers and correspondence relating to William and Elizabeth S. Friedman's personal interests and U.S. government assignments: books, pamphlets, technical papers, periodicals, microfilm, slides and newspaper clippings dealing with cryptology. Items on secret writing and signaling, radar, telephony and telegraphy, and the study of the Shakespeare-Bacon authorship controversy, Vols. of fiction relating to spies and codes, cryptographic game books for children, Civil War code items. Examples of ancient writings of Europe, Crete, and Easter Island, and material on the Aztecs, Incas, and particularly the Mayans. Also a copy of the Voynich mss., an undeciphered work, and other rare vols. on the subject dating from the 17th century. The library also has a separate collection of diaries kept by Gilbert Sandford Vernam, cryptographer and inventor. The diary is an almost day-by-day record, 1918-1926, of Vernam's inventions and development of his outstanding contributions to cryptography including techniques widely adopted by the armed forces for enciphering and deciphering coded messages. There is a typed index to this collection. No photocopying.

VA —COLLEGE OF WILLIAM AND MARY, Earl Gregg Swem Library, Williamsburg, 23185. Margaret C Cook, Cur of Manuscripts & Rare Books
Holdings: Vols 100// Cat Maps
Notes: The John Womack Wright Collection incl 17th and 18th century books on fortifications and contemporary books on the campaigns of the Napoleonic wars. Also, 89 maps of theatre of war area of Napoleonic campaigns.

MAPS, PANORAMIC

DC —LIBRARY OF CONGRESS, Geography and Map Division, Washington, 20540. John A Wolter, Chief
Notes: The Thaddeus M Fowler Collection of panoramic maps of American cities, late 19th and early 20th centuries. Also, the Albert Ruger Collection of panoramic maps of US cities, late 19th century.

MAPS, PICTORIAL

DC —LIBRARY OF CONGRESS, Geography and Map Division, Washington, 20540. John A Wolter, Chief
Notes: The Ethel M Fair Collection contains 879 illustrated maps published in the 20th century.

MAPS, TOPOGRAPHIC see Topographic Maps

MAPS AND ATLASES—COLLECTIONS

†AL —AUBURN UNIVERSITY LIBRARY, Special Collections Dept, Auburn, 36830.
Holdings: Vols (45,000)
Notes: Incl Alabama and environs; historical maps of Alabama; aerial photographs.

MAPS AND ATLASES—COLLECTIONS
(cont.)

AL —BIRMINGHAM PUBLIC LIBRARY,
2020 Seventh Ave N, Birmingham, 35203.
Virginia K Scott, Librn
Holdings: Vols (2000) Cat Maps Pix
Notes: History and development of
cartography. 19th-century US atlases. Maps
of eastern US with most emphasis on
southeastern US. The Rucker Agee Map
Collection incl over 2000 maps. See *The
Rucker Agee Collection of the Birmingham
Public Library*, Birmingham Public Library,
1964; *Atlas Maior, Sive Cosmographia
Blaviana, Qva Solvm, Salvm, Coelvm,
Accvratissime Describvntvr*, Birmingham
Public Library, nd; 1570-1970. *An Exhibit in
Commemoration of the 400th Anniversary
of Publication by Abraham Ortelius of
Theatrum Orbis Terrarum; the World's First
Atlas*, Birmingham Public Library, 1970;
George Ray Stewart, *The Special Collections
in the Birmingham Public Library*, MA
thesis, Emory University, 1971; and *A List
of Nineteenth Century Maps of the State of
Alabama*, Birmingham Public Library, 1973.

AL —SAMFORD UNIVERSITY, Special
Collections Library, 800 Lakeshore Dr,
Birmingham, 35229. Annie Ford Wheeler,
Acting Head Librn
Holdings: Cat Maps
Notes: Emphases: early maps of Alabama
and the Southeast; local maps of Ireland
which support Irish history and genealogy
collection; some early atlases and
bibliographies; basic works on cartography
and map bibliography. Incl about 3000 maps.
Published catalog of the collection.

AL —UNITED STATES AIR FORCE, Air
University Library, Cartographic Information
Division, Maxwell Air Force Base, 36112.
Donald Flournoy, Cartographer
Notes: Approx 500,000 maps.

†AL —MOBILE PUBLIC LIBRARY, Gallalee
Cartographic Collection, 704 Government
St, Mobile, 36602.
Notes: A collection of maps of the Mobile
Bay and Gulf Coast area of Alabama, 80
percent of which are pre-1900.

AL —UNIVERSITY OF ALABAMA, W S
Hoole Special Collections Library, Amelia
Gayle Goorgas Library, PO Box S,
University, 35486. Joyce H Lamont, Cur
Holdings: Cat Maps
Notes: 3500 maps, primarily early maps of
Alabama and the Southeast, but also rare
16th and 17th century maps of Europe. Also
6000 Sanborn Fire Insurance Maps for every
Alabama county (1888-1925).

AK —UNIVERSITY OF ALASKA, Elmer E
Rasmuson Library, Fairbanks, 99701. Robert
H Geiman, Dir
Notes: The Alaska Collection is strong in all
disciplines concerning Alaska. Main
strengths are exploration and travel, pioneer
memoirs, and materials on Alaska natives.
Bulk of collection is in English with
significant holdings in Russian, Native
American, and European languages. Archival
holdings incl 6000 cu ft of mss, 110,000
historic photographs, 2319 tape recordings,
727 films and videotapes, 200 rare maps and
1273 microfilms. Ms collection strongest in
political and economic areas. There is a
guide published by the University of Alaska
to these collections and is available in hard
copy and microfiche.

AZ —NORTHERN ARIZONA
UNIVERSITY, Special Collection Library,
CU Box 6022, Flagstaff, 86011. Peter M
Whiteley, Coordr/Archivist; William
Mullane, Librn
Holdings: Maps
Notes: Early Travel and Exploration of the
West collection incl *Wheeler Atlas* of Israel
C Russell, 1870's. One of the most
comprehensive collections of Wheeler
Survey Maps in existence. Also, *Clarence
King Survey of the 40th Parallel*, 1877.

AZ —NORTHERN ARIZONA
UNIVERSITY, Special Collection Library,
CU Box 6022, Flagstaff, 86011. Peter M
Whiteley, Coordr/Archivist; William
Mullane, Librn
Notes: Approx 400 published and

unpublished maps in the Northern Arizona
Pioneer's Historical Society and NAU
Collections, primarily relating to Northern
Arizona. For exact holdings, see the
"Arizona Index" in Special Collections.

AZ —PHOENIX PUBLIC LIBRARY, Arizona
Room, 12 E McDowell, Phoenix, 85004.
Jeannette Brush, Librn
Holdings: Vols (30,000) Cat Maps Pix
Budget: ($12,000)
See also entry under Arizona - History.

AZ —ARIZONA STATE UNIVERSITY,
University Library, Map Service, Tempe,
85281.
Holdings: Maps
Notes: 150,000 maps which cover the world,
some concentration on Arizona and
Southwest. Also some historical maps.

AZ —ARIZONA HISTORICAL SOCIETY,
Research Library, Maps Section, 949 E
Second St, Tucson, 85710.
Holdings: Maps
Notes: Historical maps of Arizona and the
southwest. Ninety percent of collection is
pre-1900. 1500 maps in the collection.

AZ —UNIVERSITY OF ARIZONA, Library,
Map Collection, Tucson, 85721. Mary L
Blakely, Map Librn
Holdings: Maps
Notes: 180,000 for world special
concentration of Arizona and Southwest
maps.

†AR —UNIVERSITY OF ARKANSAS,
Mullins Library, Reference Dept and Special
Collections, Fayetteville, 72701.

CA —KERN COUNTY LIBRARY SYSTEM,
1315 Truxtun Ave, Bakersfield, 93301. Mary
Haas, Geology, Mining, Petroleum Librn
Holdings: Vols (28,256) Cat Maps
Microforms
Notes: Deals with California and western
states primarily. Incl 5000 maps.

†CA —UNIVERSITY OF CALIFORNIA,
BERKELEY, General Library, Map Room,
Berkeley, 94720.
Notes: Emphasis on US, particularly
California and the West.

CA —CALIFORNIA STATE UNIVERSITY,
CHICO, Library, Government Publications
and Maps, Chico, 95929. William Stuve,
Librn
Holdings: Vols (64,600)

CA —CLAREMONT COLLEGES, Honnold
Library, Ninth & Dartmouth, Claremont,
91711. Tania Rizzo, Special Collections
Dept Head
Holdings: Vols 561 // Uncat Mss Maps
Notes: Henry Raup Wagner Collection:
cartography of the West Coast, voyages,
related history and geography, 15th century
and later. Most maps are photostats from
European and American archives and
libraries. Bound typescripts of sources
Wagner used in preparing his *Evolution of
Maps of the Northwest Coast*, some
facsimiles of mss, with transliteration or
translation. Original copy (bound) of
typescript of his "The Cartography of the
Northwest Coast of America to the Year
1800" with pencilled and typed corrections
and notes. Downs 2725. Mario C Schnitzler,
"Annotated Bibliography of the Henry Raup
Wagner Collection of Early Hispanic-
American History and Geography" (thesis,
1955). Also the William Smith Mason
Collection of Western Americana, incl 16th-
18th century voyages and travels, Ptolemy,
Ortelius, Mercator, and Blaeu atlases; sheet
maps. Restricted use. See*Special Collections:
An Annotated Guide to the Holdings of the
Manuscript Division and the University
Archives and Research Collection.*

CA —UNIVERSITY OF CALIFORNIA,
DAVIS, Physical Sciences Library, Davis,
95616. Scott Kennedy, Head
Holdings: Vols (13,434) Cat Maps
Budget: ($10,000)
Notes: Complete files of US Geological
Survey and California State geology series.
Strong collection of western US geologic
guide books. Excellent paleontology
collection represented by catalogs of
foraminifera, ostracoda and radialaria. About
4000 geologic maps including western US
and basic collection of worldwide maps.
Access to online reference service.

†CA —CALIFORNIA STATE UNIVERSITY,
FRESNO, Library, Reference Dept, Fresno,
93740.

CA —CALIFORNIA STATE UNIVERSITY,
FULLERTON, Library, Box 4150,
Fullerton, 92634. Linda Herman, Special
Collections Librn
Holdings: Vols 4200 Cat Maps
Notes: Collection documents history of map-
making including 1500 rare maps pre-1901.

CA —CALIFORNIA STATE UNIVERSITY,
FULLERTON, Library, Box 4150,
Fullerton, 92634. Linda Herman, Special
Collections Librn
Holdings: Vols (1300) Cat Maps
Notes: The Collection for the History of
Cartography incl 1087 pre-1900 maps and
related books. Also 6 display catalogs from
annual rare map exhibits. No photocopying.
Noncirculating.

CA —UNIVERSITY OF CALIFORNIA, SAN
DIEGO, Central University Library,
Mandeville Dept of Special Collections, La
Jolla, 92093. Lynda Corey Claassen, Head
Notes: The Hill Collection of Pacific
Voyages, including reports and
commentaries of important voyages in the
Pacific, from those of Magellan and Sir
Francis Drake to explorations through the
first half of the 18th century. Includes many
rare overland accounts to the Pacific across
North America, Mexico, and Panama.
Bibliography: Silveira de Braganza, Ronald,
The Hill Collection of Pacific Voyages (La
Jolla: Calif, 1974).

CA —UNIVERSITY OF CALIFORNIA, SAN
DIEGO, Scripps Institution of
Oceanography Library, Mail Code C075C,
La Jolla, 92093. William J Goff, Librn;
Deborarh Day, Archivist
Holdings: Vols (178,000) Cat Maps
Microforms
Budget: ($308,200)
Notes: See *Catalogs of the Scripps
Institution of Oceanography Library* (Boston:
G K Hall, 1970-1980), 21 vols. Incl 44,000
maps, 17,000 microforms cat, 21,000
reprints, and 800 linear feet of archives.

CA —CALIFORNIA STATE UNIVERSITY,
LONG BEACH, Reference Center, 1250
Bellflower Blvd, Long Beach, 90840.
Holdings: Cat Maps
Budget: $2000
Notes: Incl 22,544 maps and 550 atlases.
The map collection is especially strong in
California topographical maps.

CA —LOS ANGELES PUBLIC LIBRARY,
Science & Technology Dept, 630 W Fifth St,
Los Angeles, 90071. Billie M Connor, Dept
Head
Holdings: Vols (18,000) Maps Microfiche
Notes: Extensive holdings of state geology
department publications and maps of the
Western states including Alaska and Hawaii,
US Geological Survey, US Bureau of Mines,
and the geology departments of major
universities. Complete sets of publications
and indexes of major geological societies
including the Geological Society of
American and the American Association of
Petroleum Geologists. Partially cataloged.

CA —LOS ANGELES PUBLIC LIBRARY,
History Dept, 630 W Fifth St, Los Angeles,
90071. Dorothy Mewshaw, Librn, Map Rm
Holdings: Vols (3000) Cat Maps
Budget: ($85,000)
Notes: The Mary Helen Peterson Collection
of Maps and Atlases. World wide coverage,
including topographic, political and special
purpose maps. Depository for US Geologic
Survey topographical maps, Defense
Mapping Agency, and National Ocean
Survey. Maps of Los Angeles City and
County.

CA —UNIVERSITY OF CALIFORNIA, LOS
ANGELES, Research Library, Dept of
Special Collections, 405 Hilgard Ave, Los
Angeles, 90024. Edward Shreeves,
Chairman, Bibliographers Group; David S
Zeidberg, Head
Holdings: Cat Maps
Notes: Various collections, incl the Baron
Charles Stuart de Rothesay Collection of
530 continental maps, 1715-1840; the
Richard C Rudolph Collection of 200
Japanese woodblock and ms maps, 1614-

MAPS AND ATLASES—COLLECTIONS (cont.)

1896; 1500 maps and atlases emphasizing the southwest US and Pacific voyages and travels; and 15 linear feet of pamphlet maps.

CA —UNIVERSITY OF CALIFORNIA, LOS ANGELES, Map Library, Los Angeles, 90024. Carlos B Hagen, Head
Holdings: Vols (5566) Cat Maps Pix
Notes: The Library is a depository for the publications of many world-wide mapping agencies. The collection incl 507,097 maps of all areas of the world (subject and topographic maps, nautical and aeronautical charts, historical maps, and city plans), gazetteers, atlases, aerial photographs, periodicals and other basic cartographic reference tools. Incl 2550 atlases; 10,424 aerial maps; 1035 technical reports; and 311 (titles) serials subscriptions.

CA —UNIVERSITY OF SOUTHERN CALIFORNIA, Allan Hancock Foundation, Hancock Library of Biology and Oceanography, Los Angeles, 90007. Kimberly Douglas, Librn
Holdings: Vols (16,000) Cat Maps
Notes: Mostly marine, but incl some land expeditions. Covers all geographical areas. Also incl serial collection of 80,000 vols.

CA —US GEOLOGICAL SURVEY LIBRARY, 345 Middlefield Rd, Menlo Park, 94025.
Holdings: Vols (200,000)

†CA —CALIFORNIA STATE UNIVERSITY, NORTHRIDGE, Map Library, Northridge, 91324.

CA —OAKLAND PUBLIC LIBRARY, Art, Music and Recreation Section, 125 14 St, Oakland, 94612. Richard Colvig, Senior Librn
Holdings: Pix
Budget: ($500)
Notes: About 350,000 mounted pictures, posters, pictorial maps, postal cards, art reproductions, framed and unframed.

CA —POMONA PUBLIC LIBRARY, Special Collections, 625 S Garey Ave, PO Box 2271, Pomona, 91766. David Streeter, Librn
Holdings: Cat Mss Maps
Notes: Some 4000 maps. Strong for Pomona Valley area: tract maps, water company maps; depository for USGS California topographic maps; California earthquake fault maps.

CA —A K SMILEY PUBLIC LIBRARY, 125 W Vine St, Redlands, 92373. Larry E Burgess, Archivist
Holdings: Vols (3500) Mss Maps Pix Phonorecords Microforms
Budget: ($45,000)
Notes: Emphasis on San Bernadino County and the Redlands area. Especially prized is *The Citrograph*, 1887-1908 (bound vols and microfilm) edited by Scipio Craig, prominent in state, national, and newspaper circles. The ms collection (250,000 pieces) incl the Smiley Family papers, much on water development, and on the citrus industry. The photograph collection (over 5000) covers the history of the area; there are many stereographs and glass slides. The collection on Indians of California and the Southwest was begun from a special gift by Andrew Carnegie honoring his friend, Albert K Smiley.

CA —CALIFORNIA STATE ARCHIVES, 1020 O St, Room 130, Sacramento, 95814. John F Burns, Chief of Archives; Joseph Samora, Head of Reference
Holdings: Vols (19)
Notes: A special collection of Spanish and Mexican land grants, ca 1784-1846.

CA —CALIFORNIA STATE LIBRARY, Library & Courts Bldg, 914 Capitol Mall, Sacramento, 95809. Gary Kurutz, Head of Special Collections
Notes: 150,000 photographs; 600 cu ft of mss; 4000 maps; 70,000 reels on microfilm; 8000 bound vols California newspapers; 500 prints of lithographs on California newpapers; 1000 posters; and vertical file materials.

†CA —SAN DIEGO STATE UNIVERSITY, Geography Dept, Map Library, San Diego, 92182.

†CA —CALIFORNIA ACADEMY OF SCIENCES LIBRARY, Golden State Park, San Francisco, 94118.

†CA —STANDARD OIL COMPANY OF CALIFORNIA, 225 Bush St, San Francisco, 92104.
Holdings: Maps
Notes: 8000 maps and charts.

CA —UNIVERSITY OF CALIFORNIA, SANTA BARBARA, Map and Imagery Laboratory, Santa Barbara, 93106. Larry Carver, Dept Head
Notes: Worldwide coverage of Landsat imagery donated by US Dept of Agriculture Aerial Photography Field Office. Consists of 153,000 scenes, covering most of the earth's surface between the years 1975 and 1980. Incl 300,000 maps, 1800 atlases, 9 globes, 300 relief models, 1,500,000 satellite imagery and aerial photographs, 700 reference books and gazetteers, 25 serials (titles received), and 21,000 microforms.

CA —UNIVERSITY OF CALIFORNIA, SANTA CRUZ, University Library, Special Collections, Santa Cruz, 95064. Rita Bottoms, Special Collections Librn; Margaret Felts, South Pacific Collection Bibliographer
Holdings: Vols (10,000) Cat
Notes: South Pacific Collection. Monographs, rare books, serials, documents and atlases which treat of the Pacific areas of Polynesia, Melanesia, Micronesia, Australia and New Zealand, but excluding western New Guinea (Irian Jaya), the Philippines and Southeast Asia. Approximately 10 percent of the titles are multi-volume documents such as parliamentary papers, legislative journals, official yearbooks, statistical sourcebooks, laws and statutes. The collection includes an exhaustive selection of current journals and monographic series from and about the Pacific: early serials, South Pacific Commission publications, US Government and US Trust Territory publications, serials from museums, universities and scholarly societies. Chief emphasis has been placed on acquisition of the literature of history, description and travel, ethnology andanthropology, literature and literary criticism, political and constitutional histories. Other extensive holdings are in the fields of geography and maps, voyages, mission histories, mythology and folklore, art, linguistics, and science fields of natural history, environmental studies, biology, zoology, botany, geology and astronomy. Printed catalog is available. This is an on-going, growing collection.

CA —HOOVER INSTITUTION ON WAR, REVOLUTION & PEACE, Stanford University, Stanford, 94305. Peter Duignan, Cur; Karen Fung, Deputy Cur
Holdings: Vols (60,000) Cat Mss Maps Pix Slides Microforms
Notes: Politics, economics, and history from 1870 to the present. About 500 current periodical titles, about 70 current newspaper titles. Legislative debates, political ephemera. Have microfilm of Portuguese African nationalist material, confidential prints of Great Britain's foreign and colonial offices 1870 through 1922, Nigerian pamphlets (market literature, political and historical tracts), collection of the correspondence, pamphlets and ephemera of Alfred B Xuma, collections on Zaire (1955-1963), South African nationalist publications on microfilm. Descriptions of the Collection: *African and Middle East Collections* pub by Hoover Institution, *Handbook of American Resources for African Studies* pub by Hoover. Holdings of the Collection in *Hoover Institution on War, Revolution, and Peace Library Catalog* pub by G K Hall,*Emerging Nationalism in Portuguese Africa: A Bibliography* pub by Hoover, *German Africa* pub by Hoover, *The Treason Trial in South Africa: A Guide to the Microfilm Record of the Trial* pub by Hoover.

CA —STANFORD UNIVERSITY, School of Earth Sciences, Branner Earth Sciences Library, Stanford, 94305. Charlotte Derksen, Head Librn
Holdings: Vols (70,000) Cat Maps
Notes: Incl 80,000 maps. Formerly the Branner Geological Library.

CA —WHITTIER COLLEGE, Wardman Library, Whittier, 90608. Christine Erdmann, Special Collections Librn
Holdings: // Cat Pix
Notes: Aerial photographs of California, 1927-1963. 100,000 aerial photo negatives (40,000 nitrate-base), 300,000 aerial photo prints, 1000 photomosaics, 750 orthophoto maps. Concentration in California, particularly in the Los Angeles region, and elsewhere in metropolitan areas. Many flights are among the earliest available and cover areas since developed. Sequential photos often allow documentation of the history of development or of natural effects. Prints may be borrowed for 2-week periods. Purchase of prints only through Teledyne-Geotronics, Long Beach, California. An inventory list of flights can be purchased through the Dept of Geology.

CO —DENVER PUBLIC LIBRARY, Western History Department, 1357 Broadway, Denver, 80203. Eleanor M Gehres, Head
Holdings: Vols (50,000) Cat Mss Maps Pix Audiotapes Microforms
Notes: Western US History. The department has a separate catalog, published in 1970 in 7 vols by G K Hall Co. First supplement published in 1975 in 1 vol. There is a subject index of some 3 million entries to newspapers and magazines of the Rocky Mountain region, added to daily. The Western Newspaper Microfilm Center contains approx 7000 reels of Western US newspapers. Collection has ca 275,000 negatives and prints of Western life; and ca 2500 maps, cataloged and classified.

†CO —COLORADO STATE UNIVERSITY LIBRARY, Fort Collins, 80523.

CO —COLORADO SCHOOL OF MINES, Arthur Lakes Library, 14 & Illinois Sts, Golden, 80401. Hartley K Phinney, Jr, Head Librn

CO —US GEOLOGICAL SURVEY LIBRARY, Denver Library, MS 914 Box 25046, Denver Federal Center, Lakewood, 80225. Robert A Bier, Jr, Librn; Majorie E Dalechek, Photographic Librn; Deborah Rowen, Field Records Librn
Notes: Main Geological Survey Library is in Reston, Virginia. US Geological Library in Denver has 74,000 maps and mss field notes in addition to its other holdings. The Photographic Library has 250,000 slides and photos. The Field Records Library has 15,000 notebooks, 2,000 folders, 2,400 maps groups and 60,000 aerial photos which are cataloged.

CT —CONNECTICUT HISTORICAL SOCIETY, One Elizabeth St, Hartford, 06105. Christopher Bickford, Dir
Notes: Over 70,000 books and periodicals, 3500 bound vols of newspapers, and thousands of broadsides, maps, prints, and photographs pertaining to Connecticut. Also, more than 1 1/2 million historical mss; incl personal correspondence, diaries, account books, business records, and town materials dating from the earliest settlement. Extensive New England town and county histories.

CT —CONNECTICUT STATE LIBRARY, 231 Capitol Ave, Hartford, 06106. Mark H Jones, Archivist; T O Wohlsen, Jr, Head Archives, Hist & Genealogy Unit; Ann Barry, Ref Librn
Notes: Books, maps, mss, archives pertaining to Connecticut state and local history and to the history of New England, etc. Archival collections incl state and local government records and papers of institutions and organizations in Connecticut. There are separate catalogs for archives maps, and genealogical works.

CT —HARTFORD PUBLIC LIBRARY, Reference & General Reading Dept, 500 Main St, Hartford, 06103. Beverly A Loughlin, Admin Asst

†CT —WESLEYAN UNIVERSITY, Science Library, Middletown, 06457.

CT —NEW HAVEN COLONY HISTORICAL SOCIETY, Whitney Library, 114 Whitney Ave, New Haven, 06510. M Ottilia Koel, Librn & Cur of Mss
Holdings: Vols 25,000 Cat Mss Maps Pix Microforms
Notes: 25,000 printed books and pamphlets;

MAPS AND ATLASES—COLLECTIONS (cont.)

ca 15,000 linear feet of manuscript material including historic manuscripts, records of education, maritime and harbor industry, private papers, business and family records; 40,000 photographic images; maps and microforms relating to the early settlement and subsequent history of New Haven and vicinity.

CT —YALE UNIVERSITY, Box 1603A, Yale Station, New Haven, 06520.
Holdings: Mss Maps
Notes: 80,000 items. Incl atlases.

CT —UKRAINIAN MUSEUM AND LIBRARY, 161 Glenbrook Rd, Stamford, 06902. Wasyl Lencyk, Dir
Holdings: Vols (20,000)

CT —UNIVERSITY OF CONNECTICUT, University Library, Map Room, Storrs, 06268. Thornton P McGalmery, Librn
Holdings: Vols (903) Cat Maps Pix
Budget: ($5000)
Notes: The Map Room is the largest publicly supported map library in any Connecticut institution of higher education. It is a depository library for the US Geological Survey, the Defense Mapping Agency, and the Metropolitan District (Hartford, Conn). Incl over 100,000 maps and 8523 aerial photographs. Of particular interest is the *Petersen Collection*, a group of photostats of old town maps of New England.

DE —HISTORICAL SOCIETY OF DELAWARE, Library, 505 Market St Mall, Wilmington, 19801. Barbara E Benson, Library Dir
Holdings: Cat Mss Maps Pix Slides
Notes: Collection incl papers and other mss materials.

DC —DISTRICT OF COLUMBIA PUBLIC LIBRARY, Martin Luther King Memorial Library, Washingtoniana Div and Washington Star Collection, 901 G St NW, Washington, 20001. Roxanna Deane, Chief
Notes: Covering the period from 1612-date. Plat maps are available from 1887 to 1977.

DC —LIBRARY OF CONGRESS, Geography and Map Division, Washington, 20540. John A Wolter, Chief
Holdings: Cat Mss Maps Pix Slides Microforms
Notes: *Cartographic Materials.* One of the largest cartographic collections in the world, all-inclusive in coverage. Early original manuscript maps, navigation charts by Italian, Portuguese, and Spanish 15th, 16th, and 17th-century cartographers; the Hummel & Warner Collections of rare manuscript and printed maps and atlases of China and Korea from the 17th, 18th, and 19th centuries; manuscript and printed maps of colonial America, the Revolutionary War, the War of 1812, the Civil War, and wars of the 20th century; individual sheets of large and medium-scale set maps and charts published in the 19th and 20th centuries, including official topographic, geologic, soil, mineral, and resource maps, and nautical and aeronautical charts for most countries of the world; special subject maps of the world and its various political entities; maps of the United States and the separateStates; county maps and plans of cities and towns, and the Sanborn Fire Insurance Maps, dating back to 1866 for some 13,000 cities in the United States. Atlases include earliest printed editions of Ptolemy's Geography (1482), and representative volumes of leading atlas publishers of the last five centuries covering individual continents, countries, states, counties, cities, and the world. Total: 3,800,000 maps, 49,000 atlases, 400 globes and 2000 relief models. See *The Geography and Map Division: A Guide to Its Collections and Services*, rev ed, 1975 (LC 5.2:SE6/975).

DC —METROPOLITAN WASHINGTON COUNCIL OF GOVERNMENTS, Map Library, 1875 Eye St NW, Suite 200, Washington, 20006. Susan Kalish, Librn
Holdings: Cat Maps
Notes: 3000 current and retrospective maps covering metropoliatan Washington region,

incl the District of Columbia; Montgomeray and Prince George's counties in Maryland; and Arlington, Fairfax, Prince William and Loudoun counties and the City of Alexandria in Virginia. Maps cover land use, community facilities, transportation, topography, statistical units, and socioeconomic information. Record of holdings on computer printout.

DC —NATIONAL GEOGRAPHIC SOCIETY, Library, 1146 16th St NW, Washington, 20036. Susan Fifer Canby, Dir
Holdings: Vols (63,000) Cat Mss Maps Pix
Notes: Material concerning land, sea, and space exploration--past and present. All fields of anthropology, natural history, geography, etc.

FL —UNIVERSITY OF MIAMI, Otto G Richter Library, PO Box 248214, Coral Gables, 33124. Frank Rodgers, Dir of Libraries
Holdings: Vols Microforms
Notes: The Rosenstiel School of Marine and Atmospheric Sciences Library is one of the major marine science collections in the United States and is especially strong in the literature of tropical oceanography. Special collections in the library incl 200 oceanographic atlases and more than 50 sets of the world's major expedition reports. The library also maintains a nautical chart collection. 3000 microforms; 1000 current subscriptions.

FL —UNIVERSITY OF FLORIDA, Coastal Engineering Archives, 433 Weil Hall, Gainesville, 32611. Lucile Lehmann, Librn
Holdings: Cat Maps Pix Slides
Budget: ($4000)
Notes: 7000 technical reports, in addition to maps, pictures, aerial photographs, 400 hydrographic surveys, etc. The Archives is not part of the University library system but is a special collection of the Coastal and Oceanographic Engineering Dept.

FL —FLORIDA STATE UNIVERSITY, Robert Manning Strozier Library, Maps Dept, Tallahassee, 32306. Marianne Donnell, Map Librn
Holdings: Vols (3314) Cat Maps Microforms
Notes: Emphasis on Florida and Florida history. Also a depository for USGS topographic maps of the entire US, National Ocean Survey nautical charts of all American waters, Defense Mapping Agency maps, and various special sets issued by National Ocean Survey. Incl 1140 vols of books, bibliographies, and periodicals; 2070 atlases; 136,000 sheet maps; 104 microfilm reels.

GA —UNIVERSITY OF GEORGIA, Libraries, Map Collection, Athens, 30602. John Sutherland, Cur of Maps
Holdings: Cat Maps
Budget: ($20,000)
Notes: Sheet maps, 285,000; aerial photographs, 186,000; three-dimensional maps, 40; atlases, 800 (note: the Libraries contain other atlases; these are part of the map collection as such). The collection contains maps from all countries and in all languages, although the area of specialization is the US, with particular emphasis on the southeastern sector. The collection is a depository for maps from the US Geological Survey, DMATC, NOAA, and Georgia's Dept of Transportation. Collection has 7100 sheets of Sanborn maps for Georgia. Bibliographies available for atlases, Sanborn sheets, and air photo holdings.

GA —UNIVERSITY OF GEORGIA, Libraries, Special Collections Division, Athens, 30602. Vesta Lee Gordon, Asst Dir for Special Collections
Holdings: Vols (75,000) Cat Mss Maps Pix
Notes: Materials on Georgia history, incl approx 3,000,000 items in 2000 collections of mss; 1200 maps; 6000 pictures and over 200 pieces of sheet music.

HI —BERNICE P BISHOP MUSEUM, Library, PO Box 19000-A, Honolulu, 96819. Cynthia Timberlake, Librn
Holdings: Vols (90,000) Cat Mss Maps Pix Slides Microforms
Budget: ($30,000)
Notes: Only American library devoted exclusively to the Pacific region. Collection

reflects historical and contemporary research emphases of Bishop Museum; ie the natural and cultural history of the Pacific. Areas of concentration incl archaeology, ethnology, linguistics, voyages and explorations, history, vertebrate and invertebrate zoology, botany and museology. Strong special collections incl photographs, mss and archives, maps and art. Publications: Quarterly "Additions to the Catalog," *Dictionary Catalog of the Library* (9 vols and 2 suppl; Boston: G K Hall, 1964-69).

HI —INTERNATIONAL TSUNAMI INFORMATION CENTER, PO Box 50027, Honolulu, 96850. Bonnie Dong, Librn
Notes: Large collection on tsunamis, their causes, oceanographic organization and mareographic records, forecasting, mapping, etc.

HI —PACIFIC SCIENTIFIC INFORMATION CENTER, Bernice P Bishop Library, Geography and Map Division, PO Box 19000A, Honolulu, 96819. Lee S Motteler, Geographer; Valerie T Higa, Asst Geographer
Holdings: Vols (2000) Cat Mss Maps Pix
Notes: Incl 20,000 maps and 70,000 aerial photos of Hawaii and the Pacific.

ID —IDAHO STATE UNIVERSITY, Library, Pocatello, 83209. Gary Domitz, Social Science Librn
Holdings: Uncat Maps
Notes: Depository for USGS, 11 western states; depository for Defense Mapping Agency Topographic Center; Idaho county maps.

IL —SOUTHERN ILLINOIS UNIVERSITY, CARBONDALE, Morris Library, Carbondale, 62901. Jean M Ray, Map Librn
Holdings: Cat Maps Pix
Budget: ($1070)
Notes: Emphasis of map collection is Southern Illinois and Mississippi Valley. Incl 158,000 maps; 47,000 aerial photographs of Southern Illinois; 2000 atlases, reference books, etc; 4000 issues of weather map series (historical, daily, monthly); and 360 Illinois county platbooks. Includes Sang Collection-- 60 early maps of North America, especially Mississippi Valley, 1584-1840.

IL —ILLINOIS STATE GEOLOGICAL SURVEY, Library, 615 E Peabody, Champaign, 61820. Mary Krick, Geological Librn

IL —CHICAGO HISTORICAL SOCIETY, Library, Clark St at North Ave, Chicago, 60614. Robert L Brubaker, Librn
Notes: About 10,000 maps and 640 atlases. Especially strong for Chicago, Illinois, and the Midwest. Also substantial holdings of general maps of the Americas from the 16th century to 1850, general maps of the US for the period to 1900, US transportation, and the Civil War. Incl most county altases for Illinois.

IL —ENCYCLOPAEDIA BRITANNICA, Editorial Library, 310 S Michigan Ave, Chicago, 60604. Terry Miller, Editorial Librn
Holdings: Vols (25,000) Cat Maps Microforms
Budget: ($80,000)
Notes: This collection is not open to the general public, but photocopies of materials will be made. Collection contains all major and most minor encyclopedias and dictionaries. A large collection of atlases and statistical data on all foreign countries is maintained.

IL —NEWBERRY LIBRARY, 60 W Walton St, Chicago, 60610. Robert W Karrow, Jr, Cur of Maps
Holdings: Cat Mss Maps Slides Microforms
Notes: Incl 1600 atlases; 13,000 separate maps (in 1984). A historical map collection, with a cut-off date of about 1900. Especially rich in classical geography (represented by almost all the printed editions of Ptolemy), in Renaissance cartography (incl an outstanding collection of Italian engraved maps), in nautical cartography (incl some exceptional portolan charts), in world atlases of the 16th-18th centuries, and in regional maps and atlases of North America from the 17th through the 19th centuries. The only

MAPS AND ATLASES—COLLECTIONS (cont.)

published catalog devoted exclusively to maps is Clara A Smith's *List of Manuscript Maps in the Edward E Ayer Collection* (Chicago, 1927). 1000 printed maps and 400 atlases are included in the *Dictionary Catalog of the Edward E Ayer Collection of Americana and American Indians,* 16 vols (Boston: G K Hall & Co, 1961) and in a 3-vol supplement (1970). An *Index to Maps in the Everett D Graff Collection of Western Americana* was published in 1972 (Chicago: H D Smith Center for the History of Cartography).

IL —NORTHWESTERN UNIVERSITY, Library, Map Collection, Evanston, 60201. Mary Fortney, Librn
Holdings: Vols 2085 Cat Maps Pix
Notes: Incl 170,104 maps, cataloged; 1540 aerial photographs, cataloged.

IL —ILLINOIS STATE HISTORICAL SOCIETY, Library, Old State Capitol, Springfield, 62706. Roger D Bridges, Head Librn
Holdings: Vols (146,000) Cat Mss Maps Pix Microforms
Budget: ($40,000)
Notes: Incl 4.6 million mss, nearly 2000 maps, 100,000 pictures and 52,000 microfilm reels. Downs 2546, 2606, 2612, 187, 188. See also *Guide to the Microfilm Edition of the Pierre Menard Collection in the Illinois State Historical Library.* Separate catalogs (card) for printed material, mss, broadsides.

IL —UNIVERSITY OF ILLINOIS, URBANA/CHAMPAIGN, Library, Illinois Historical Survey Library, 1408 W Gregory Dr, 1A Library, Urbana, 61801.
Holdings: Vols (6500) Cat Mss Maps Pix Microforms
Notes: Important ms collections incl: Randolph County Records, 1720-1853, 91 items, 59 reels of microfilm; St Clair County Records, 1722-1809, 6 items, 5 reels of microfilm; George Morgan, papers, 1766-1826, 280 items, 5 reels of microfilm. Pierre Menard, papers, 1780, 1802-1859, 155 items, 27 volumes, 29 reels of microfilm; Illinois Surveyors' field notes and plat maps, 1805-1850, 56 reels microfilm. Numerous county and local histories and plat books. 1733 maps, and thousands of Illinois pictures. Guide to the collections published in 1976.

IL —UNIVERSITY OF ILLINOIS, URBANA/CHAMPAIGN, Library, Map & Geography Library, 418 Main Library, Urbana, 61801. David Cobb, Librn
Holdings: Vols (14,500) Cat Maps Pix Microforms
Notes: Maps (over 325,000) of almost all types, incl topographic, soil, transportation, economic, hydrographic, weather, city, pictorial, and historical maps, are collected. Coverage is excellent for Illinois and for most parts of the United States and Canada. Good maps are available for Europe, Central America and the ocean areas. The early map collection is rich in maps of Illnois, Italy, and the western hemisphere. A large number of publishers' catalogs, particularly of foreign map publishings are kept on file. The collection of aerial photographs provides complete and sequential coverage of the State of Illinois from the late 1930s to the present. Much of the coverage is stereoscopic. Other map resources on the campus include about 50,000 geologic and topographic maps and aerial photographs in the Geology Library, a wall map collection in the Geography Department, several hundred early maps and atlases of the Illinois area in the Illinois Historical Survey, and geologic and topographic maps and aerial photographs in the Civil Engineering Department. Publication: *Biblio* (bi-monthly acquisitions list).

IL —UNIVERSITY OF ILLINOIS, URBANA/CHAMPAIGN, Library, Geology Library, 223 Natural History Bldg, Urbana, 61801. Dederick Ward, Librn
Holdings: Vols (105,186) Cat Maps Microforms
Notes: Incl complete sets of outstanding geological surveys of the US states, Canada and most foreign countries; espec strong for India and Latin America; the same is true for geological journals, incl Russia--a special strength since 1960. Extensive collection of early geological literature and rare books, perhaps the most extensive. Library houses the University's collection of 21,000 cataloged geological maps, incl many rarities. Special collection of aerial photographs.

IN —INDIANA UNIVERSITY, Lilly Library, Seventh St, Bloomington, 47405. William R Cagle, Librn
Holdings: Cat Maps
Notes: British maps (late 18th, 19th centuries); US maps (late 18th, 19th centuries); and extensive atlas collection, strong in Ptolemy, Pomponius Mela, and Ortelius. See "The Cartographic Treasures of the Lilly Library," *The Map Collector* No 22 (March 1983).

IN —INDIANA UNIVERSITY, Dept of Geology & Indiana Geological Survey, Geology Library, 100 S E 10th St, Bloomington, 47405. Lois Heiser, Librn
Holdings: Vols (70,000) Cat Maps Microforms
Notes: All aspects of geology; incl over 250,000 maps and 8000 microforms. Dictionary catalog for book and map materials. Technical report number index to microforms.

IN —INDIANA HISTORICAL SOCIETY, Library, 315 W Ohio St, Indianapolis, 46202. Robert K O'Neill, Dir
Notes: Incl rare books, mss, pictures, maps, and ephemera relating to the history of Indiana and the Old Northwest. Mss dealing with the Old Northwest, incl a large collection of William Henry Harrison materials; papers of leading nineteenth-century Indiana figures; letters of Civil War soldiers; records of twentieth-century social welfare organizations. Rare books collection incl *Relations,* early travel accounts, and early Indiana imprints. Pictures incl Indiana small-town life; Monon Railroad Colleciton; Callis Steamboat Collection, dealing with Terre Haute. Maps of Indiana; Sanborn real estate atlases for Indianapolis. Special collections in Indiana black, ethnic, and architectural history.

IN —PURDUE UNIVERSITY LIBRARIES, Engineering Library, A A Potter Engineering Center, West Lafayette, 47907. Edwin D Posey, Engineering Librn
Holdings: Vols (225,178) Cat Maps Audiotapes Microforms
Budget: ($300,000)

IA —STATE HISTORICAL SOCIETY OF IOWA LIBRARY, 402 Iowa Ave, Iowa City, 52240. Darold J Brown, Librn
Holdings: Vols 300 Cat Mss Maps
Notes: Iowa plat atlases cataloged. Approx 100 atlases of Iowa counties pre-1900 and approx 300 Iowa county atlases for the 20th century. Incl approx 1200 maps.

KS —UNIVERSITY OF KANSAS, Science Library, 6040 Malott Hall, Lawrence, 66045. Sharon R Cook, Asst Science Librn
Holdings: Vols Cat Maps Microforms
Notes: Incl US Geological Survey topographical maps.

KS —UNIVERSITY OF KANSAS, Kenneth Spencer Research Library, Kansas Collection, Lawrence, 66045. Sheryl K Williams, Cur
Notes: Incl 8000 maps of early Kansas.

KS —UNIVERSITY OF KANSAS, Kenneth Spencer Research Library, Map Collection, Lawrence, 66045. Richard L Embers, Map Cur
Holdings: Cat
Budget: ($3000)
Notes: (234,000 maps; 2500 books, atlases and gazetteers). A very strong collection for post-1900 maps in over 40 basic subjects. Depository for USGS and DMA. Maps are available for every country in the world with particular strength in North American, European, and East Asian maps. Excellent holdings for Kansas and the Mid-west. Library also has a large collection of books and serials dealing with cartography. Guide for readers available upon request.

KS —POTTAWATOMIE-WABAUNSEE REGIONAL LIBRARY, 605 W Bertrand St, Saint Marys, 66536. Judith A Muck, Dir
Holdings: Cat Mss Maps Pix
Notes: Most of the collection is of maps bound in elephant volumes. While the whole state is covered, emphasis is on Pottawatomie and Wabaunsee counties. County atlases from 1868 to 1935 comprise the largest part of the collection.

KS —WICHITA STATE UNIVERSITY, Ablah Library, Box 68, Wichita, 67208. Michael T Kelly, Cur of Special Collections
Holdings: Cat Maps Atlases
Notes: Incl the Robert W Baughman Collection of Kansas Maps.

KY —WESTERN KENTUCKY UNIVERSITY, Kentucky Library, Bowling Green, 42101. Riley Handy, Head, Special Collections; Connie Mills, Maps & Music Librn; Nancy Baird, Photographs Librn; Nancy Solley, Conservation Librn
Holdings: Vols (25,000) Cat Mss Maps Pix Microforms
Notes: Besides Kentucky history, other strengths are Mammoth Cave, South Union Shakers, Kentucky religion; and steamboat photos (3300 cataloged pictures); 8000 Kentucky postal cards, etc.

KY —UNIVERSITY OF KENTUCKY, Margaret I King Library, Dept of Special Collections, Lexington, 40506. William Marshall, Head
Holdings: Cat Maps
Notes: Emphasis is on early Kentucky maps to 1900 and basic maps of America to 1800.

KY —UNIVERSITY OF KENTUCKY, Geology Library, 100 Bowman Hall, Lexington, 40506. Vivian S Hall, Librn
Holdings: Vols (40,000) Cat Maps Microforms
Budget: ($30,000)
Notes: Incl comprehensive collection of maps on Kentucky; 98,900 maps in all. Also, 170 journal titles, 5000 microfiche titles.

KY —UNIVERSITY OF KENTUCKY, Margaret I King Library, Map Collection, Lexington, 40506. Gwen Curtis, Head
Holdings: Vols Maps
Notes: Depository for Defense Mapping Agency since 1940's. Post-1870, general collection excluding geology and hydrology, depository for Kentucky Geological Survey topographic. Collection of Sanborn Insurance maps of Kentucky cities, 99 percent complete.

LA —NEW ORLEANS PUBLIC LIBRARY, Louisiana Div & City Archives Dept, Louisiana History Collection, 219 Loyola Ave, New Orleans, 70140. Collin B Hamer Jr, Head
Holdings: Mss Maps Pix
Notes: Maps incl 3000 mss and printed maps, mostly for Greater New Orleans area. Also 16,700 aerial photographs.

LA —TULANE UNIVERSITY, Howard-Tilton Memorial Library, Special Collections Div, 7001 Freret St, New Orleans, 70118. Wilbur E Meneray, Librn
Holdings: Maps
Notes: Louisiana Collection incl about 1000 maps about equally divided between Louisiana (Territory and State) and New Orleans. Louisiana maps date from about 1600 to the present; New Orleans maps date from about 1740 to the present.

LA —R W NORTON ART GALLERY, Library, 4747 Creswell Ave, Shreveport, 71106. Jerry M Bloomer, Librn
Holdings: // Cat
Notes: Incl primarily rare atlases such as Ptolemy (1490 ed), Blau, Ortelius, Mercator, etc.

ME —MAINE HISTORICAL SOCIETY, Library, 485 Congress St, Portland, 04101.
Holdings: Vols (60,000) Cat Mss Maps Pix
Notes: The Society's holdings cover all of Maine in its scope, with special emphasis on the Portland region.

MD —JOHNS HOPKINS UNIVERSITY, Milton S Eisenhower Library, Charles & 34 Sts, Baltimore, 21218. Ann S Gwyn, Assistant Dir for Special Collections
Holdings: Cat Maps
Notes: 182,500 maps, US and foreign. Depository for USGS maps. Depository for Geological Survey of Canada. Also atlases and up-to-date road maps.

MAPS AND ATLASES—COLLECTIONS (cont.)

MD —MARYLAND HISTORICAL SOCIETY, Library, 201 W Monument St, Baltimore, 21201. William B Keller, Head Librn
Holdings: Cat Maps
Notes: Maryland maps, plats, prints, newspapers.

MD —UNIVERSITY OF BALTIMORE, Langsdale Library, 1420 Maryland Ave, Baltimore, 21201. Gerry Watkins, Head of Special Collections Dept
Holdings: Vols Maps
Notes: Incl misc maps and statistical charts (4 cubic feet).

MA —UNIVERSITY OF MASSACHUSETTS AT AMHERST, Library, Amherst, 01003. Siegfried Feller, Assoc Dir for Collection Development
Holdings: Maps
Notes: Special emphases: Defense Mapping Agency and US Geological Survey (topographic) depository; 700 sheets of Massachusetts cities and towns partially cataloged. US Geological Survey (geological) are cataloged and housed separately. In addition, Federal Land Bank Collection: state, county, and a few city, atlases for each New England state, New York, and New Jersey, mostly 19th century.
See also entry under Geology

MA —STATE LIBRARY OF MASSACHUSETTS, 341 State House, Boston, 02133. Gaspar Caso, State Librn
Holdings: Cat Maps
Notes: Incl 5000 roll maps, sheet maps, and atlases.

MA —HARVARD UNIVERSITY, Harvard College Library, Map Collection, Cambridge, 02138. Frank E Trout, Cur
Holdings: Cat Mss Maps
Notes: Harvard Map Collection is comprehensive in global coverage and historical depth. Incl books on history and science of cartography, gazetteers, topographic maps, urban plans, and thematic atlases.

MA —HARVARD UNIVERSITY LIBRARY, Geological Sciences Library, 24 Oxford St, Cambridge, 02138. Constance Wick, Librn
Holdings: Vols (51,000) Cat Mss Maps Pix 16mm Films Microforms
Notes: 15,000 geologic maps; special emphasis on New England states.

MA —OLD STURBRIDGE VILLAGE, Research Library, Sturbridge, 01566. Theresa Rini Percy, Librn
Holdings: Cat
Notes: New England to 1900.

†MA —CLARK UNIVERSITY, Robert Hutchings Goddard Library, Worcester, 01610. Dorothy Mosa Kowski, Rare Books Librn
Holdings: Vols Cat Maps
Notes: Incl 55,000 maps.

MI —UNIVERSITY OF MICHIGAN, Harlan Hatcher Graduate Library, Map Room, Ann Arbor, 48109. James O Minton, Map Librn
Notes: The collection consists of approx 300,000 sheet maps incl maps and charts received on deposit from the US Geological Survey, Defense Mapping Agency, and the National Ocean Service. The collection also incl approx 5000 reference volumes related to cartography, surveying, and mapping, with emphasis on place-name literature (gazetteers, dictionaries), books on how to use and interpret maps, carto-bibliographies, and state (provincial, etc), regional, national, and international atlases. The collection is strongest geographically in materials of Michigan, Midwest, Anglo-America, and Europe; chronologically, 1850-date; and thematically, in topographic and geologic maps, although all subjects are collected. The collection maintains a separate catalog of holdings. Reference volumes are fully cataloged and classified.

MI —UNIVERSITY OF MICHIGAN, Bentley Historical Library, Michigan Historical Collections, 1150 Beal Ave, Ann Arbor, 48109. Francis X Blovin Jr, Dir
Holdings: Vols (45,000) Cat Mss Maps
Budget: ($302,000)
Notes: A modern ms archives collecting original source material pertaining to Michigan, its people, its institutions and the University of Michigan. Emphasizes the accumulations of personal papers of historically important persons, incl files of correspondence, diaries and journals as well as the records of significant Michigan institutions. At present the collections contain 45,000 printed vols, 40,000,000 mss items, 3500 maps and 500,000 photographs. The library maintains its own catalog and published in 1976 a revised, 2nd updated *Guide to the Michigan Historical Collections.* Special areas of interest to the collections are Philippine Islands history, the history of the temperance and prohibition movement in the US. Immigration to Michigan, business history, church history, and US-China relations.

MI —UNIVERSITY OF MICHIGAN, William L Clements Library, Ann Arbor, 48109. John C Dann, Dir
Notes: The William L. Clements Library of Americana is a non-circulating rare book library of original source material, printed and manuscript, dealing with America, from the discovery period into the late nineteenth century. The collection includes approximately 55,000 books and pamphlets, 550 linear feet of manuscripts, 4,100 volumes of newspapers, 36,000 maps, 40,000 pieces of sheet music, and 1,000 prints. The collection is strongest for the period of the American Revolution, and includes the papers of Thomas Gage, Sir Henry Clinton, and the Earl of Shelburne. Other areas of strength include antislavery, cartography and geography, discovery and exploration, American Indians, The Civil War, tune-books, sermons and orations, and the War of 1812. There are selective research collections dealing with Christopher Columbus, Thomas Paine, Benjamin Franklin, George Washington, Thomas Jefferson, and the Federalist Papers. Publications describing the collections of the library are: Author/Title catalog of Americana 1493-1860 in the William L. Clements Library... 7 volumes, Boston, G. K. Hall, 1970; Guide to the manuscript collections of the William L. Clements Library, by Arlene P. Shy 3d edition, Boston, G. K. Hall, 1978; Guide to the manuscript maps in the William L. Clements Library, compiled by Christian Burn, Ann Arbor, U. of Michigan, 1959; and Research catalog of maps of America, to 1860 in the William L. Clements Library..., edited by Douglas W. Marshall, 4 volumes, Boston, G. K. Hall, 1972.

MI —DETROIT PUBLIC LIBRARY, Burton Historical Collection, 5201 Woodward Ave, Detroit, 48202. Alice Dalligan, Chief
Notes: Emphasis is placed on maps and atlases of the Great Lakes area and the St Lawrence river and valley. There are historical and rare maps of the eastern portion of the United States, manuscript maps, and atlases from 1645 to the present.

MN —MANKATO STATE UNIVERSITY, Memorial Library, Maywood & Ellis, Mankato, 56001. Russell K Amling, Map Librn
Holdings: Cat Maps
Budget: ($2000)
Notes: 74,736 maps and 685 atlases (mostly topographic and thematic) of the US, especially Minnesota (3000 maps). 16,369 aerial photos (incl Minnesota). Separate catalog.

MN —US DEPT OF AGRICULTURE, FOREST SERVICE, North Central Forest Experiment Station, Library, 1992 Fowell Ave, Saint Paul, 55108. Floyd L Henderson, Librn
Holdings: Vols (5000) Maps 16mm Films
Budget: ($14,000)
Notes: Forests of the North Central states. Incl some 6000 maps.

MO —MISSOURI BOTANICAL GARDEN LIBRARY, PO Box 299, Saint Louis, 63166. M R Crosby, Dir of Research

MO —SAINT LOUIS PUBLIC LIBRARY, History & Genealogy Dept, 1301 Olive Blvd, Saint Louis, 63103. Noel C Holobeck, Librn
Holdings: Cat Maps
Notes: Depository for US Army Maps and US Geological Survey maps. Collection of historic Missouri and Saint Louis atlases and maps, country atlases. Index to maps and atlases (card file). Vertical file of maps and travel brochures. 106,678 maps in collection.

MO —WASHINGTON UNIVERSITY, Earth and Planetary Sciences Library, Forsyth & Skinker Blvds, Saint Louis, 63130. Deborah Hartwig, Librn
Holdings: Cat Maps Pix Microforms
Notes: 76,716 maps, aerial, topographic, etc.

NE —NEBRASKA STATE HISTORICAL SOCIETY, Library, 1500 R St, Box 82554, Lincoln, 68501. M Ann Reinert, Library Dept Head
Holdings: Vols (100,000) Cat Maps Pix Microforms
Budget: ($200,000)
Notes: Extensive
See also entry under Great Plains

NV —NEVADA STATE HISTORICAL SOCIETY, Library, 1650 N Virginia St, Reno, 89503. Eric N Moody, Cur of Manuscripts; Lee Mortensen, Librn
Holdings: Vols 15,000 Cat Mss Maps Pix Slides Microforms
Budget: ($156,994)
Notes: Incl 2800 mss, 1500 maps and 70,000 pictures.

NV —UNIVERSITY OF NEVADA, RENO, University Library, Special Collections Dept, Reno, 89557. Robert E Blesse, Head
Holdings: Vols (3500) Cat Mss Pix Maps
Notes: Includes 2100 cu ft manuscripts, 25,000 photographs, maps, vertical file, microforms and oral histories.

NH —DARTMOUTH COLLEGE, Baker Memorial Library, Hanover, 03755.
Holdings: Cat Mss Maps
Notes: 1200 atlases and 90,000 maps. Areas of special interest: historical cartography, polar regions, USSR.

NJ —HAMMOND, Editorial Department Library, 515 Valley St, Maplewood, 07040. Ernest J Dupuy, Librn
Holdings: Vols (10,000) Cat Maps Pix
Notes: Also about 15,000 maps; 50 vertical file drawers of administrative, census, national parks, highway, and related materials. No photocopying.

NJ —RUTGERS, THE STATE UNIVERSITY OF NEW JERSEY, Alexander Library, Special Collections and Archives, College Ave & Huntington St, New Brunswick, 08903. Ronald L Becker, Cur of Manuscripts and Rare Books
Holdings: Maps
Notes: More than half (over 5000) of the collection of maps in printed, flat ms and roll form, represents New Jersey, although there are maps depicting all parts of the world. Some pieces date from the 16th century. Incl are topographic, road, railroad, county, ward geological and historical maps. There are over 100 19th and early 20th century lithographic city views. Of special interest and quality are 16 framed maps dating between 1507 and 1777 which are the gift of the late I Robert Kriendler. All pieces in the map collection are accessible through department checklists.

NJ —PRINCETON UNIVERSITY, Library, Rare Books Dept, Princeton, 08544. Stephen Ferguson, Cur
Holdings: Cat Maps
Notes: A collection of rare maps, incl early

MAPS AND ATLASES—COLLECTIONS
(cont.)

European woodcuts, representing works mainly of the 16th and 17th centuries, incl works by Ortelius, Speed and Joan Blaeu.

NM —US GEOLOGICAL SURVEY, Water Resources Division Library, Western Bank, 505 Marquette, Rm 714, Albuquerque, 87102. Janie S Jones, Librn
Holdings: Vols (38,000) Mss Maps
Notes: Primarily hydrology and geology of New Mexico. Incl 20,000 maps.

NY —NEW YORK STATE LIBRARY, State Education Bldg Annex, Washington Ave, Albany, 12224.
Holdings: Cat Maps
Notes: 500 atlases, 100,000 maps. All government-produced maps received on deposit: geological survey, meteorological, US Army, topographic, etc. An especially strong collection of historical and geographical maps featuring New York State (1600-present), the history and development of the Eastern United States (1600-1850), exploration and history of North America (1600-1800); maps of specific events, military maps of battle sites, newsmaps; transportation (NY State Dept of Transportation depository); New York State county maps.

NY —ADIRONDACK HISTORICAL ASSOCIATION, Museum Library, Blue Mountain Lake, 12812. Jerold Pepper, Librn
Holdings: Vols (7500) Cat Mss Maps Pix Phonorecords Audiotapes 16mm Films Microforms
Notes: Anything about the Adirondacks-- history, people, economics, places, things. Strong in Adirondack art, outdoor recreation, logging, small boats. Resources incl more than 1000 maps, 40,000 pictures, 1600 microfilm reels, 576 linear ft of ms material, and 12 cabinets of VF ephemera, etc.

NY —BROOKLYN PUBLIC LIBRARY, History Div Map Collection, Grand Army Plaza, Brooklyn, 11238. Tsugio Yoshinaga, Map Librn
Holdings: Cat Maps
Notes: 80,000 maps and 900 atlases for general reference. Depository for US Geological Survey and Defense Mapping Agency.

NY —LONG ISLAND HISTORICAL SOCIETY, 128 Pierrepont St, at Clinton St, Brooklyn, 11201.
Notes: Books and pamphlets relating to the history of Brooklyn. Over 350 newspapers and periodical resources, incl The Long Island Star (1809-1863) and Williamsburgh Gazette (1835-1853). 10,000 photographs. Paintings, prints, and broadsides. More than 1400 mss collections relating primarily to Brooklyn, dating from 1650 to 1980s. 750 maps and atlases, artifacts, archives, and Decorative Arts collections. Two published guides to Manuscripts: Calendar of Manuscripts: 1783-1783, LIHS by Karin N Mango. 1980. Also, A Guide to Brooklyn Manuscripts in the Long Island Historical Society. Prepared by Brooklyn Rediscovery, a program of the Brooklyn Educational and Cultural Alliance. 1980. Also, guide to Museum Exhibit, Brooklyn Before the Bridge - American paintings from the Long Island Historical Society. Published by Brooklyn Museum. 1982.

NY —BUFFALO & ERIE COUNTY PUBLIC LIBRARY, History, Travel & Government Dept, Lafayette Sq, Buffalo, 14203. Ruth Willet, Head
Holdings: Cat
Notes: Depository for US Geological Survey Topographic and Geological Quadrangle Maps; US Army Service Maps; other uncataloged maps and charts.

NY —QUEENS BOROUGH PUBLIC LIBRARY, Long Island Div, 89-11 Merrick Blvd, Jamaica, 11432. Nicholas Falco, Head
Holdings: Vols (22,000) Cat Mss Maps Pix Microforms
Budget: ($13,000)
Notes: Files of Long Island community newspapers, with strong holdings for Queens Borough. Also, 550 glass negatives of Long Island scenes, 1895-1915; with 32,750 other pictures; 5300 maps; 36,000 ms pieces. Extensive name indexes of births, deaths and marriages mainly from 19th century Long Island books and newspapers. Many cemetery records, etc. 60 VF drawers of clippings; over 500 broadsides, 1795-date, relating to Long Island, with chronological and community name indexes; books published by Marion Press, a private press in Jamaica, NY.

NY —AMERICAN MUSEUM OF NATURAL HISTORY, Library Services Dept, Central Park W & 79th St, New York, 10024. Nina J Root, Chairwoman; Mary Genett, Asst Librn for Reference Services
Holdings: Vols (385,000) Cat Mss Maps Pix Slides Microforms
Notes: Nearly all collections are outstanding for depth of coverage and international range. Early and historic works, rare books, colored illustrations, and relevant serial publications supplement the modern scientific publications necesary to the researches of the scientific staff and the work of the educational division. Open to the public.

NY —EXPLORERS CLUB, James B Ford Memorial Library, 46 E 70 St, New York, 10021. Janet Baldwin, Librn
Holdings: Vols (24,000) Cat Maps
Notes: Additions to the collection depend upon gifts. Access by appointment only.

NY —HISPANIC SOCIETY OF AMERICA, Library, 613 W 155 St, New York, 10032. Martha M de Narvaez, Cur of Mss; Irene S Frye, Asst Librn
Holdings: Vols (150,000) Cat Mss Maps Pix Slides Phonorecords Microforms
Notes: History, art, literature and general culture of the Hispanic countries (where Spanish or Portuguese is spoken). Incl (18,000) vols printed before 1701, incl (250) incunabula; over (100,000) later vols, plus thousands of periodicals. About (200,000) mss incl ms maps. Printed atlases are in the Book Collection. Some microfilms, chiefly of our early books. Engraved and printed separate maps; reference collection of over 100,000 photographs; slides: all in Department of Iconography, not in library.
Catalogs: Catalogue of the Hispanic Society of America (Boston: G K Hall, 1962), 10 vols; First Supplement (Boston, 1970), 4 vols. Early books: Printed Books 1468-1700; Mss: Catalogo de los Manuscritos Poeticos Castellanos (15th-17th centuries; 3 vols); Medieval Manuscripts in the Library; Golden Age Drama Manuscripts (the latter in press).
See also entry under Spain

NY —NEW YORK PUBLIC LIBRARY, Map Division, Fifth Ave & 42 St, New York, 10018. Alice Judson, Librn
Holdings: Vols (33,000) Cat Mss Maps Microforms
Notes: Incl 11,000 atlases and 354,000 maps. European maps from 1600. American from 1800 are in the Map Div; earlier maps are in the Rare Book Div. This collection incl topographical surveys, detailed plans of American cities; large-scale maps of all foreign countries; up-to-date road maps. There are atlases, gazetteers, and postal guides, and an index to periodical articles about maps. The collection of the history of cartography, the techniques of map making, and of county atlases of the US is exceptionally strong. See Dictionary Catalog of the Map Division, The Research Libraries of the New York Public Library, 10X14, est 175,000 cards, 10 vols, $730.

NY —UNITED NATIONS, Dag Hammarskjold Library, Rm L382, New York, 10017. Vladimir Orlov, Librn
Notes: Incl 70,000 maps.

NY —STATE UNIVERSITY OF NEW YORK, COLLEGE AT PLATTSBURGH, Feinberg Library, Special Collections, 153 Hawkins Hall, Plattsburgh, 12901. Joseph G Swinyer, Librn
Holdings: Vols (200) Cat Mss Maps Pix
See also entry under New York (State) - History

NY —UNIVERSITY OF ROCHESTER, Rush Rhees Library, Department of Rare Books and Special Collections, Rochester, 14627. Peter Dzwonkoski, Librn
Holdings: Vols 45 Cat Maps
Notes: Printed and manuscript maps and atlases of Western New York state. Cited in Creek, Maps of the Genesee Valley and Finger Lakes Region, 1776-1950. Rochester, NY, 1977.

NY —HISTORICAL SOCIETY OF THE TARRYTOWNS, Library, One Grove St, Tarrytown, 10591. Lucille O Hutchinson, Map Consultant
Holdings: Vols 675 Cat Maps
Notes: Emphasis on the Tarrytowns, Pocantico Hills, the Hudson River, and Westchester County, NY from the late 1700s to the present. Also incl 38 atlases.

NY —US MILITARY ACADEMY LIBRARY, West Point, 10996. Marie T Capps, Maps & Mss Librn
Holdings: Vols (2000) // Mss Maps
Notes: One descriptive catalog of a portion of this collection is: Marie T Capps and Theodore G Stroup, US Militarty Academy Library Map Collection: The Period of the American Revolution 1753-1800 (West Point, NY: US Military Academy, 1971), 82 pp.

NC —UNIVERSITY OF NORTH CAROLINA, CHAPEL HILL, Geology Library, Mitchell Hall 029A, Chapel Hill, 27514. Miriam L Sheaves, Librn
Holdings: Vols (41,000) Maps
Notes: Earth sciences, paleontology, oceanography, geology, geophysics. Incl theses and dissertations; 103,000 map sheets.

NC —UNIVERSITY OF NORTH CAROLINA, CHAPEL HILL, Wilson Library, Maps Collection, Chapel Hill, 27514. Celia D Poe, Map Librn
Holdings: Vols 2100 Cat Maps
Notes: Incl 92,000 maps of all areas of the world with an emphasis on the Southeastern US, Latin America, Eastern Europe, East Asia, and Eastern Africa. Among the subjects covered are topographic, administrative, historical, highway, city, vegetation, demographic, national parks, and economic. The Maps Collection is a depository for the US Geological Survey, the Defense Mapping Agency and the National Ocean Survey, and collects maps of the US Lake Survey. Volumes in the collection incl atlases (general, national, regional, city, historical, and other topical), gazetteers, bibliographies, catalogs of map collections and map publishers, and various cartographical reference volumes.

NC —DUKE UNIVERSITY, William R Perkins Library, Durham, 27706. Elvin E Strowd, University Librn
Notes: Books, serials and pamphlets (2,820,527); music scores (31,551); motion pictures (285); microforms (1,055,627); tapes, cassettes and phonorecords, the library is a depository for Radio Canada International recordings, (2289); and manuscripts, US Government publications, maps, and broadsides, additions in all formats are ongoing.

NC —DUKE UNIVERSITY, William R Perkins Library, Public Documents and Maps Department, Durham, 27706. Jaia Barrett, Head
Holdings: Vols Maps Pamphlets Microforms
Notes: A selective depository for US Government publications since 1890, the Department currently holds well over 500,000 items, plus publications of the European Community (a depository collection), the League of Nations, the UN and UN-affiliated agencies. Other international organizations, publications are acquired also, as are state government publications, especially from the Southeast, California, New York and Illinois. The Documents Department holds services the major map collections of Perkins Library. These collections include topographic, geologic, and special subject maps which are worldwide in coverage. The department is a depository for the US Defense Mapping Agency and the US Geological Survey. In addition, there are many other maps of general and specific interest, including US and foreign road maps. As appropriate, maps

MAPS AND ATLASES—COLLECTIONS (cont.)

are also held in the Perkins Library's Rare BookRoom and Manuscript Department. Atlases are shelved in the Reference Department and in the bookstacks of Perkins Library.

OH —HEBREW UNION COLLEGE-JEWISH INSTITUTE OF RELIGION, Klau Library, 3101 Clifton Ave, Cincinnati, 45220. David J Gilner, Reference Librn
Holdings: Uncat Maps
Notes: About 200 pre-1900 maps, some as old as early 16th century. About 400 post-1900, most in color. Primarily of Israel/Palestine.

OH —PUBLIC LIBRARY OF CINCINNATI & HAMILTON COUNTY, Map Collection, History Dept, 800 Vine St, Cincinnati, 45202. Carl G Marquette Jr, Librn
Holdings: Vols (1775) Cat Maps
Budget: ($4000)
Notes: The collection consists of 137,951 maps (uncataloged); 1250 atlases, with emphasis on Ohio county atlases, national atlases and facsimiles of important cartographic works; 125 bibliographies of maps or collections of maps and atlases; 400 gazetteers and other works, monographs series and journals (partially cataloged) relating to cartography and maps. The library is a depository for USGS and Defense Mapping Agency. Concentration of maps is Ohio, Hamilton County and Cincinnati. No catalog for flat maps.

OH —UNIVERSITY OF CINCINNATI, Geology-Geography Library, 103 Old Tech Bldg ML 13, Cincinnati, 45221. Richard Spohn, Sr Library Assoc
Holdings: Maps
Notes: Library is the depository for the US Geological Survey. Incl 80,000 maps partially cataloged.

OH —CLEVELAND PUBLIC LIBRARY, General Reference Dept, 325 Superior Ave, Cleveland, 44114. Donald Tipka, Head
Holdings: Cat Maps
Notes: Incl extensive collection of Cleveland and Cuyahoga County maps. Depository for Army Map Service and US Geological Survey topographic maps. Large collection of historical reproductions, national and international. Great Lakes navigation charts. Some aeronautical navigation charts.

OH —OHIO HISTORICAL SOCIETY, Archives Library Division, 1982 Velma Ave, Columbus, 43211. Dennis East, Division Chief
Holdings: Vols (96,000) Cat Mss Maps Pix Slides Microforms
Budget: ($18,000)
Notes: This library is the primary collection for Ohio. Most purchases are on the rare and out of print market. Collection area is early American history, esp relating to exploration into the Northwest Territory. Also, Ohio archaeology, natural history, and artifacts. Major media collections are books (96,000), newspapers (25,000 vols and 22,000 microfilm), pictures (50,000), maps (2500), manuscripts (1,500,000). Library is noncirculating except through interlibrary loan of microfilm.

OH —HIRAM COLLEGE, Teachout-Price Memorial Library, Hiram, 44234. Joanne M Sawyer, Archivist; Marjorie M Adams, Music Librn
Holdings: Vols 12 Maps
Notes: The Fox Collection of Antique, Regional Maps concentrates on Ohio's Western Reserve, Ohio, Upper Midwest, eastern Canada; earliest maps are of the New World; does not circulate; restricted hours: call or write in advance. Incl 66 maps.

OH —KENT STATE UNIVERSITY, Map Library, Kent, 44242. Julia Canan, Library Supvr
Notes: Incl gazetteers, 200,000 maps, 75 relief models, 368 folios, 974 books and 20 VF. Library temporarily closed; will be open in autumn of 1985.

OK —CENTRAL STATE UNIVERSITY, Library, 100 N University Dr, Edmond, 73034. Andrew Peters, Reference Librn
Holdings: Cat Maps Audiotapes Microforms
Notes: Microforms Research Center for

newspapers and periodicals, incl ERIC, LAC, LEL, HRAF, and annual reports, etc. Vols on microfilm reels, microfiche; microcards; academic and music audiotapes; and maps.

OK —UNIVERSITY OF OKLAHOMA, Geology Library, 830 Van Vleet Oval Rm 102, Norman, 73019. Claren Kidd, Geology Librn
Holdings: Cat Maps
Notes: Most are received as the result of Oklahoma Geological Survey exchanges or a depository status. 90,000 maps.

OK —OKLAHOMA STATE UNIVERSITY, Library, Stillwater, 74708. Roscoe Rouse, Dir
Holdings: Maps Uncat
Notes: Depository for USGS (full); Depository for Defense Mapping Agency; Oklahoma. 160,000 maps.

OK —SOCIETY FOR THE NORTH AMERICAN CULTURAL SURVEY, Dept of Geography, Oklahoma State University, Stillwater, 74078. John Rooney, Dir; Todd Zdorkowski, Asst
Notes: Has produced a cultural atlas of North America, 309 pages of maps and text gathered from the major geographical, historical, and cultural source-literatures.

OK —THOMAS GILCREASE INSTITUTE OF AMERICAN HISTORY & ART LIBRARY, 1400 North 25th West Ave, Tulsa, 74127. Sarah Hirsch, Librn
Holdings: Maps 600 Atlases
Notes: Trans-Mississippi West, US, Indian and Hispanic history. The Gilcrease Library contains a total of about 40,000 mss; 10,000 imprints; 5000 photographs; 600 maps and 50,000 vols.

OK —TULSA CITY-COUNTY LIBRARY, Business & Technology Dept, 400 Civic Center, Tulsa, 74103. Craig Buthod, Head
Holdings: Vols (18,000) Uncat
Notes: Original General Land Office survey maps for the states of Arizona, Arkansas, Colorado, Illinois, Indiana, Idaho, Kansas, Michigan, Missouri, Montana, Nebraska, Nevada, New Mexico, North Dakota, Ohio, Oklahoma, South Dakota, Utah and Wyoming. Imcomplete coverage of each state.

OR —OREGON STATE UNIVERSITY, Library, Corvallis, 97331. Melvin George, Dir
Holdings: Vols (980,000) Cat
Notes: Incl 155,000 maps.

OR —UNIVERSITY OF OREGON, Map Library, Eugene, 97403. Peter L Stark, Map Librarian
Holdings: Cat Maps
Budget: ($4000)
Notes: 2500 atlases, 247,000 maps, 330,000 aerial photos. Specializations for maps are Pacific Northwest, Latin America and West Africa. Incl topographic maps. Specialization for aerial photos is Oregon. Separate catalog and index. Atlases are fully cataloged; maps are classified with shelf list cards; aerial photographs are fully indexed.

PA —GETTYSBURG COLLEGE, Musselman Library, Gettysburg, 17325. Willis M Hubbard, College Librn
Holdings: // Maps
Notes: These maps from the J H W Stuckenberg Collection are largely 18th century European maps, although some of America, Africa and the Orient are included. A small number also date from the 16th century. No photocopying.

PA —PENNSYLVANIA GEOLOGICAL SOCIETY, Library, 916 Executive House, Second & Chestnut Sts, Harrisburg, 17120. Sandra Blust, Librn
Holdings: Vols (7600) Cat Mss Maps Microforms
Notes: Incl 200,000 aerial photographs and 250,000 maps.

PA —FREE LIBRARY OF PHILADELPHIA, Social Science and History Dept, Map Collection, Logan Sq, Philadelphia, 19103.
Holdings: Vols (30,000) Cat Mss Maps
Notes: Map collection incl atlases, maps, pamphlets, and aerial views. Incl a representative collection of early atlases (1534-1827). The collection emphasizes the Philadelphia, Pennsylvania and Delaware

Valley areas in particular and the eastern seaboard in general. Low altitude oblique aerial photographs have been transferred to the Print and Picture Dept; high altitude vertical aerial photographs have been retained; some volumes and pamphlets reassigned within the Social Science and History Dept.

PA —CARNEGIE LIBRARY OF PITTSBURGH, Science & Technology Dept, 4400 Forbes Ave, Pittsburgh, 15213. Catherine M Brosky, Dept Head
Holdings: Vols (380,000) Cat Maps Microforms
Budget: ($240,000)
Notes: Geologic, topographic, land use.

PA —UNIVERSITY OF PITTSBURGH, Darlington Memorial Library, Special Collections, 601 Cathedral of Learning, Pittsburgh, 15260. Dennis Lambert, Darlington Librn
Holdings: Vols (17,000) Cat Mss Maps Pix
Notes: The Darlington Collection is especially rich in American history of the colonial period, the French and Indian War, the Revolution, and the War of 1812 with geographical emphasis on Western Pennsylvania and Ohio Valley history to 1870 and on Pittsburgh history to 1900. Indian treaties, captivity accounts, US and Pennsylvania travel and description, and early American fiction and prose are represented. A partial guide to the Darlington Manuscript Collections is available by writing for *Darlington Memorial Library: A Descriptive Checklist of its Manuscript Collections*, University of Pittsburgh Bibliographic Series 5, 1969. Noncirculating.

PA —UNIVERSITY OF PITTSBURGH, Hillman Library, Pittsburgh, 15260. Jean Aiken, Information Librn
Holdings: Uncat Mss Maps
Notes: Depository for US Geological Survey Topographic Maps, Defense Mapping Agency Topographic Maps, Operational Navigation Charts and Nautical Charts, National Ocean Survey Nautical Charts and Aeronautical Charts, Incl US Geological Survey Land Use and Land Cover Maps, Defense Mapping Agency Jet Navigation Charts, National Ocean Survey Bathymetric Maps. Approx 75,000 maps.

PA —PENNSYLVANIA STATE UNIVERSITY, Fred Lewis Pattee Library, Maps Section, University Park, 16802. Karl Proehl, Head
Holdings: Vols (274,000) Cat Maps
Budget: ($3000)
Notes: Depositories for US Geological Survey topographic maps; Defense mapping agency topographic maps and nautical charts; National Ocean Survey nautical and aeronautical charts; Canadian topographic maps. Sanborn Fire Insurance maps for Pennsylvania villages and towns. 1970 and 1980 census maps for Pennsylvania counties, townships, and cities. General coverage for foreign countries-topographic and thematic maps. Map catalog by area and subdivided by subject; atlas catalog by author-title and area-subject; shelf list catalogs for maps and atlases. See *Pennsylvania Maps and Atlases in The Pennsylvania State University Libraries*, by Ruby M Miller (Pennsylvania State University Libraries, 1971. 682 pp).

RI —BROWN UNIVERSITY, John Carter Brown Library, Providence, 02912. Norman Fiering, Librn; Everett C Wilkie Jr, Bibliographer; Susan Danforth, Cur Maps & Prints
Holdings: Vols (40,000) Cat Mss Maps Pix
Notes: History of the Americans during the Colonial Period. See also *The John Carter Brown Library Catalogues; Opportunities for Research in the John Carter Brown Library; Reprint of the John Carter Brown Library Annual Reports and Index 1901-1966*.

RI —PROVIDENCE PUBLIC LIBRARY, Rhode Island Collection, 150 Empire St, Providence, 02903. Jeanne L Richardson, Librn
Holdings: Vols (7400) Cat Maps Pix Microforms
Budget: ($1500)
Notes: Rhode Island Collection is divided

MAPS AND ATLASES—COLLECTIONS (cont.)

into five categories: books; maps; pictures and pamphlets; plus the Rhode Island Index: 4 catalog cases (total of 185 drawers) containing index to material on Rhode Island. This is primarily a subject index. Author cards made only for books and articles by Rhode Island authors; title cards for periodicals in collection. *Providence Journal* and *Evening Bulletin* are indexed daily for all pertinent articles about the state and its people. Incl are cards for pertinent articles in books and periodicals in other parts of the library.

SC —SOUTH CAROLINA HISTORICAL SOCIETY LIBRARY, Fireproof Bldg, 100 Meeting St, Charleston, 29401. Gene Widdell, Dir
Holdings: Vols (50,000) Cat Mss Maps Pix Slides Microforms
Notes: No photocopying. Pamphlets; 2.5 million pages of mss.

SC —UNIVERSITY OF SOUTH CAROLINA, Thomas Cooper Library, Columbia, 29208. Kenneth E Toombs, Dir of Libraries; Roger Mortimer, Rare Book Librn
Holdings: Maps 177,000
Notes: Housed in Map Library, James F Byrnes Center. One of the largest collections of 20th century maps in the Southeastern US.

†SD —SOUTH DAKOTA SCHOOL OF MINES & TECHNOLOGY, Devereaux Library, Rapid City, 57701.
Holdings: Vols (166,200) Cat Maps Audiotapes Filmstrips Microforms
Budget: ($70,000)
Notes: Supportive collection incl an almost complete set of US Geological Survey materials (incl early Territorial Surveys); a microfilm copy (complete set) of the US Bureau of Mines "Mine Map Depository (Denver)" material; periodicals and technical reports (NASA, ACRL, JPL, etc) in engineering and geology; extensive goverment document materials (NBS, Bureau of Mines, etc).

TX —UNIVERSITY OF TEXAS, ARLINGTON, Library, PO Box 19497, Arlington, 76019. Chas Colley, Dir Special Collections
Holdings: Uncat Maps Slides
Notes: The Cartographic History Library, a center for the study of the history of five centuries of exploration and mapping of the New World. Library contains thousands of rare maps and atlases which feature the works of the great cartographers such as Ptolemy, Cornelli, DeLisle, Moll and Arrowsmith, as well as materials relating to trans-continental migration, transportation surveys and oil exploration. A wide variety of journals and reference materials pertaining to the collection is also available.

TX —UNIVERSITY OF TEXAS LIBRARIES, General Libraries, PO Box P, Austin, 78713. Carolyn Bucknell, Asst Dir for Collection Development
Holdings: Cat Maps

TX —TEXAS A&M UNIVERSITY, Sterling C Evans Library, College Station, 77843. Judith Rieke, Map Librn; Irene B Hoadley, Dir of Libraries
Holdings: Cat
Budget: ($10,000)
Notes: Maps of all areas of the world with geographic emphasis on the US and Texas. Subject emphasis on geology, petroleum, soils, highways and streets. Depository for NOS coastal and bathymetric charts, DMA maps, and USGS topographic and geologic maps. An extensive file of publisher's catalogs is available to the public. Collection incls aerial photographs (1100), atlases and gazetteers (1500), maps (82,600).

TX —DALLAS PUBLIC LIBRARY, Texas/ Dallas History and Archives Division, 1515 Young St, Dallas, 75201. Richard L Waters, Acting Dir; Wayne Gray, Manager
Holdings: Vols (30,000) Cat Maps Pix Slides Microforms
Budget: ($8450)
Notes: Dallas and Texas history.

TX —SOUTHERN METHODIST UNIVERSITY, Fondren Library, Dallas, 75275. Curt Holleman, Librn for Collection Development

TX —NORTH TEXAS STATE UNIVERSITY, Government Documents Dept, NT Station Box 5188, Denton, 76203. Melody Kelley, Librn
Holdings: Vols Cat Maps
Notes: 9000 maps, mostly Texas topographic maps.

TX —FORT WORTH PUBLIC LIBRARY, 300 Taylor St, Fort Worth, 76102. John R McCracken, Manager
Holdings: Cat Maps
Budget: ($21,000)
Notes: Topographic and geologic maps (16,000).

TX —ROSENBERG LIBRARY, Galveston and Texas History Center, 2310 Sealy Ave, Galveston, 77550. Jane Kenamore, Archivist
Holdings: Cat Maps
Notes: Galveston and Texas maps incl many rarities. USGS depository.

TX —UNIVERSITY OF TEXAS, Marine Science Institute Library, Port Aransas, 78373. Ruth Grundy, Librn
Holdings: Vols (45,000) Cat Maps Pix
Budget: ($70,000)
Notes: Current researches in marine science, especially concerning the Gulf of Mexico, the Texas Coastal Zone, and the Continental Shelf. Incl journals.

TX —BAYLOR UNIVERSITY, Moody Memorial Library, Texas History Collection, Waco, 76706. Kent Keeth, Librn
Holdings: Vols (80,000) Cat Mss Maps Pix Slides Phonorecords Audiotapes Microforms
Notes: The Texas Collection gathers materials which relate to life in Texas in all its aspects, from earliest days to present. Incl Baylor University Archives.

UT —UTAH STATE UNIVERSITY, Merrill Library, Department of Special Collections & Archives, Logan, 84322. A J Simmonds, Curator; Jeanie F Simmonds, Archivist; Bradford R Cole, Mss Librn
Holdings: Vols 1300 Maps
Notes: Collection tries to include eveything on Utah: its history, government education, agriculture, etc 300 ft of mss. Ephemeral materials and publications (incl 10,000 pamphlets), cataloged or registered. 800 microfilm rolls; 400 maps. Utah State Documents depository. Considerable overlap with the Library's Mormon History Collection (qv).

UT —UNIVERSITY OF UTAH, Marriott Library, Special Collections, Salt Lake City, 84112. Gregory C Thompson, Cur
Notes: Approx 1000 historical maps of Utah, including Sanborn Maps.

VA —GEORGE MASON UNIVERSITY, Fenwick Library, Special Collections Dept, 4400 University Drive, Fairfax, 22030. Ruth Kerns, Public Services Librn
Notes: C Harrison Mann Collection: 18 atlases and 76 single maps primarily from the late 1500s to the late 1800s, incl rare atlases and maps of early Virginia and Maryland, and several foreign regions of the world.

†VA —GEORGE C MARSHALL RESEARCH FOUNDATION AND LIBRARY, Drawer 920, Lexington, 24450. Royster Lyle Jr, Cur Collections
Holdings: Cat Maps
Notes: The William F. Friedman Collection. Separate catalog. Incl. papers and correspondence relating to William and Elizabeth S. Friedman's personal interests and U.S. government assignments: books, pamphlets, technical papers, periodicals, microfilm, slides and newspaper clippings dealing with cryptology. Items on secret writing and signaling, radar, telephony and telegraphy, and the study of the Shakespeare-Bacon authorship controversy, Vols. of fiction relating to spies and codes, cryptographic game books for children, Civil War code items. Examples of ancient writings of Europe, Crete, and Easter Island, and material on the Aztecs, Incas, and particularly the Mayans. Also a copy of the Voynich mss., an undeciphered work, and other rare vols. on the subject dating from the 17th century. The library also has a separate collection

of diaries kept by Gilbert Sandford Vernam, cryptographer and inventor. The diary is an almost day-by-day record, 1918-1926, of Vernam's inventions and development of his outstanding contributions to cryptography including techniques widely adopted by the armed forces for enciphering and deciphering coded messages. There is a typed index to this collection. No photocopying.

VA —LYNCHBURG COLLEGE, Knight-Capron Library, Lynchburg, 24501. Mary C Scudder, Dir
Holdings: Vols (847) Cat Maps
Notes: North America, 17th-19th century. Part of the Capron Collection. Incl over 200 maps.

VA —VIRGINIA STATE LIBRARY, 12 & Capitol Sts, Richmond, 23219.
Holdings: Cat Mss Maps
Notes: Incl 250 atlases, 85,000 maps, chiefly of Virginia, but incl Army map service and US Geological Survey maps.

VA —COLONIAL WILLIAMSBURG FOUNDATION, Research Center Library, PO Drawer C, Williamsburg, 23187. John E Ingram, Research Archivist
Holdings: Vols (30,000) Cat Mss Maps Pix Microforms
Budget: ($20,000)
Notes: Virginia and the Chesapeake in the 17th-18th centuries. Particular strengths include social, economic, agricultural and architectural history. The collection encompasses over 6000 rare books, 18th Century music scores and 12,000 manuscripts, as well as a complete set of Virginia Colonial Records Project microfilm (1000 reels).

WA —UNIVERSITY OF WASHINGTON LIBRARIES, Suzzallo Library, Map Section, FM-25, Seattle, 98195. Steve Hiller, Head
Holdings: Vols 1406 Cat Maps Microforms
Budget: ($8953)
Notes: Includes 217,012 uncataloged maps and 2116 sheets of microfiche.

WI —STATE HISTORICAL SOCIETY OF WISCONSIN, Archives, 816 State St, Madison, 53706. Harold L Miller, Reference Archivist
Holdings: Vols 2500 Cat Maps
Notes: Incl 25,000 sheet maps and 2500 atlases. Collection specializes in maps of Wisconsin, its counties, and its cities, but also is strong in coverage of adjacent states of Middle West and North America as a whole. We also have a collection of European atlases from the 16th through 18th centuries, and many maps of North American areas prior to 1800. There is a separate card catalog of the map collection, and a descriptive brochure is available upon request. Maps and atlases are noncirculating.

WI —UNIVERSITY OF WISCONSIN, MADISON, Geophysical & Polar Research Center Library, Weeks Hall, 1215 W Dayton St, Madison, 53706. Alison N Mares, Librn
Holdings: Vols (1000) Cat Mss Maps Microforms
Notes: Collection incl large bibliography of Arctic and Antarctic subjects available. Library has some 1500 pamphlets; 500 maps, mostly bathymetric and geological; reprint collection from Cold Regions Research & Engineering Lab (CRREL); collection of Russian materials, dealing mainly with the Antarctic.

WI —UNIVERSITY OF WISCONSIN, MADISON, Geography Library, 280 Science Hall, Madison, 53706. Miriam E

MAPS AND ATLASES—COLLECTIONS (cont.)

Kerndt, Librn
Holdings: Vols (40,000) Cat Microforms
Budget: ($35,000)
Notes: Geography Library collects books,
journals, and atlases in all fields of regional
and systematic geography to support
research and university teaching. Popular
works, travel accounts, and tourist literature
are not collected. Maps are collected in a
separate Map and Air Photo Library in the
same building.
WI —UNIVERSITY OF WISCONSIN,
MADISON, Arthur H Robinson Map
Library, 310 Science Hall, 550 N Park St,
Madison, 53706. Mary Galneder, Map Librn
Holdings: Cat Maps Pix
Notes: Incl mostly topographic and thematic
maps and Wisconsin air photos. 207,200
maps; 133,500 air photos.
WI —MILWAUKEE PUBLIC LIBRARY, 814
W Wisconsin Ave, Milwaukee, 53233.
Donald J Sager, City Librn
Holdings: Maps
Notes: Comprehensive collection of every
type map of Milwaukee metropolitan area
(2500). Incl fire insurance atlases, street car
and bus maps and other specialized maps.
Historical and contemporary. Goverment
and commerical publishers and unpublished
maps. Listed in library's main card catalog.
WI —UNIVERSITY OF WISCONSIN,
MILWAUKEE, American Geographical
Society Collection, 2311 E Hartford Ave,
PO Box 399, Milwaukee, 53201. Roman
Drazniowsky, Cur
Holdings: Vols (196,800)
Budget: ($270,000)
Notes: The largest special collection in the
field of geography, cartography, and related
fields in the Western Hemisphere. Incl 6469
atlases; 385,610 maps; 72 globes; 33,700
pamphlets; 79,000 photographs; 99,000
Landsat Images. Catalog published by G K
Hall, Boston.
WY —WYOMING STATE ARCHIVES
MUSEUMS, AND HISTORICAL
DEPARTMENT, Barrett Bldg, Cheyenne,
82002. Philip J Roberts, Documents Supvr;
Jean F Brainerd, Research Asst
Holdings: Vols (520) Cat Maps
Budget: ($430,000)
Notes: Extensive mss, map, pamphlet, and
picture collection relative to Wyoming,
regional, and western history. Publish *Annals
of Wyoming*.
AB —ALPINE CLUB OF CANADA
LIBRARY, Archives of the Canadian
Rockies, Box 160, Banff, T0L 0C0, Can. E J
Hart, Head Archivist
Holdings: Vols (2429) Cat Mss Maps Pix
Slides Audiotapes
Budget: ($1000)
Notes: The Archives of the Canadian
Rockies is the custodian of the library and
archival collection of the Alpine Club of
Canada. The materials cover mountaineering
technique and attempts worldwide, incl the
Alps, Rockies, Himalayas, Andes, etc.
Subject areas incl history, personal records,
mountain rescue and medicine, alpine flora
and fauna, guide books, manuals and
handbooks. A large part of the archival
collection is concentrated on the Canadian
Rocky Mountains, as the headquarters of
The Alpine Club of Canada is in Banff,
Alberta.
AB —PETER WHYTE FOUNDATION,
Archives of the Canadian Rockies, Box 160,
Banff, T0L 0C0, Can. Mary Andrews, ACR
Librn
Holdings: Vols (4247) Cat Mss Maps Pix
Slides Phonorecords Audiotapes Videotapes
16mm Films Filmstrips Microforms
Budget: ($1500)
Notes: Collect all available material which
touches on the Rocky Mountains of Canada
(from the US border to the Peace River in
the north; from west of Calgary on the east
to the town of Revelstoke, BC on the west).
This material incl history (the early
explorers, Indians, construction of the
railroads, mountaineering and development

of the national parks), natural history
(geology, botany, wildlife) and poetry and
fiction with the Rockies as a setting. Collect
maps of the area, photographs, tape
recordings of the pioneers. We also house on
our premises the Alpine Club of Canada's
library, which is one of the most
comprehensive collections on the subject of
mountaineering worldwide. Noncirculating.
BC —SIMON FRASER UNIVERSITY,
Library, Burnaby, V5A 1S6, Can. Percilla
Groves, Special Collections Librn
Holdings: Vols (9000) Cat Maps Microforms
Budget: ($11,000)
Notes: Emphasis on history and goverment
documents. Over 3000 maps; 1250
microforms.
NS —DALHOUSIE UNIVERSITY LIBRARY,
Halifax, B3H 4H8, Can.
Holdings: Cat Maps Pix
Notes: Approx 2000 lithographs, steel
engravings, fine prints and illustrated
historical maps from the 18th and 19th
centuries are in the collection. Subject
coverage is primarily of Nova Scotia, New
Brunswick, Prince Edward Island, and
Newfoundland scenery, street scenes, and
portrayals of prominent people, buildings
and events. Generally rich in illustrations of
the working and social life of the period.
Artists represented incl: J E Woolford, J F
W Desbarres, William Eagar, William
Bartlett and Richard Short. Historical maps
incl some of the earliest visual depictions of
the Atlantic coast. Material available for
editorial reproduction. Print fee charged. No
loans.
ON —QUEEN'S UNIVERSITY, Map and Air
Photo Library, Mackintosh-Corry Hall,
Kingston, K7L 5C4, Can. M B McBurney,
Chief Librn; Kathryn Harding, Senior
Technician
Holdings: Cat Maps
Notes: Major interest in Canadian maps.
Contains about 80,000 maps, 800 atlases and
30,000 air photos.
ON —AGRICULTURE CANADA, Research
Branch, Neatby Library, Rm 3032, K W
Neatby Bldg, CEF, Ottawa, K1A 0C6, Can.
Marcel Charette, Library Technician
Holdings: Vols 2100 Cat Maps
Notes: Soil Surveys. Soil science collection.
ON —ENERGY, MINES AND RESOURCES
CANADA, Map Resource Centre, 615
Booth St, Ottawa, K1A 0E9, Can.
Holdings: Maps
Notes: 250,000 maps; 1000 atlases; 600
gazetteers.
ON —GEOLOGICAL SURVEY OF
CANADA, Library, Dept of Energy, Mines,
& Resouces, 601 Booth St, Ottawa, K1A
0E8, Can. Annette E Bourgeois, Librn
Holdings: Vols (300,000) Cat Mss Maps
Microforms
Notes: All aspects of Geology are collected
and an attempt is made to collect all
Canadian geology information. The library is
a national resource collection in the
geosciences. Incl 40,000 book titles
(monographs), 4000 personals, 35,000
microfiche, 300,000 maps, 2000 translations
of reports, 20 verrtical files, 300,000 vols of
bound periodicals.
ON —PUBLIC ARCHIVES OF CANADA,
Library, 395 Wellington St, Ottawa, K1A
0N3, Can. Dawn E Monroe, Collections
Development Officer
Holdings: Vols (800)
Notes: Dr Alexander E MacDonald
collection of maps was the largest and most
significant known private collecton of pre-
1900 Canadian maps. The books collected by
Dr MacDonald to supplement this collection
either provide the text to accompany the
maps or describe the areas surrounding the
Great Lakes. The imprints span several
centuries, from 1500 to the twentieth
century. Vols providing early descriptions of
travels and voyages were collected along
with the popular nineteenth century guide
books to various areas such as "Romantic
Niagara." The collection was purchased from
the A E MacDonald estate in 1981. The
1981. The Library is in the process of
cataloging the collection.
ON —METROPOLITAN TORONTO
LIBRARY, History Dept, 789 Yonge St,

Toronto, M4W 2G8, Can. Michael Pearson,
Head
Holdings: Maps
Notes: The collection comprises 40,000
maps: current topographic and thematic
maps; depository for the Canadian National
Topographic series; extensive historical
collection specializing in Toronto and
Ontario, incl insurance plans. 700 atlases:
major world atlases, national and regional
atlases; facsimiles of important early atlases,
some originals. 400 current and retrospective
gazetteers.
ON —ONTARIO MINISTRY OF NATURAL
RESOURCES, Mines Library, 77 Grenville
St, Rm 812, Toronto, M5S 1B3, Can. Nancy
Thurston, Librn
Holdings: Vols (40,000) Cat Maps
Microforms
Budget: ($30,000)
Notes: Geology of Ontario. Incl 20,000
maps. Depository for US and Canadian
federal publications in geology and mining.
ON —UNIVERSITY OF TORONTO, Library,
Map Library, 130 St George St, Toronto,
M5S 1A5, Can. Joan Winearls, Map Librn
Holdings: Vols (10,376) Cat Maps
Notes: A collection of 183,000 current
topographic and thematic maps for all parts
of the world; strong in Canada, Ontario,
Toronto, Europe, US, parts of Latin America
and Africa, Near East and Far East. Good
atlas and cartography collection; 205,283
aerial photos, 1977-date, for Toronto, 1952-
date for southern Ontario and parts of
northern Ontario; files maintained of the
following: publishers catalogs; maps clipped
from newspapers and reports; articles on
cartography, particularly the history of
cartography; and base maps. In-house
bibliographies on Toronto maps, climate and
map interpretation. Map catalog is separate
and housed only in the Map Library.
Equipment, facilities for use of materials.
PQ —MCGILL UNIVERSITY, McLennan
Library, Rare Books and Special Collections
Dept, 3459 McTavish St, Montreal, H3A
1Y1, Can.
Notes: 5524 sheet maps, 370 atlases, 571
folded maps, 629 guide books, 248 reference
books. The coverage is worldwide,
specializing in North America, Canada,
Quebec, Montreal. Includes a collection of
guide books from the 1800s to the present
day, as well as a reference collection; there is
also a large collection of modern
topographical literature with worldwide
coverage, and an important collection of
postcards particularly of Montreal and the
Province of Quebec. A finding list is
available for 19th century guide books on
Canada: A Preliminary Guide to Nineteenth
Century Canadian Guide Books: a Survey of
the Holdings of the McLennan Library with
an Historical Introduction. Montreal, 1982.
PQ —TROIS-RIVIERES COLLEGE
LIBRARY, CEGEP de Trois-Rivieres-
Bibliotheque, 3500 de Courval, Trois-
Rivieres, G9A 5E6, Can. Denis Simard,
Librn
Holdings: Maps
Notes: A large collection of Canadian and
Artic Region maps.

MAPS AND MAP MAKING see Cartography

MARATHI LANGUAGE AND LITERATURE

DC —LIBRARY OF CONGRESS, African and
Middle Eastern Division, Washington,
20540.
Holdings: Cat Mss Microforms
Notes: Southern Asian: over 137,000 vols of
literature of the area from Pakistan to the
Philippines.
HI —UNIVERSITY OF HAWAII, Library,
2550 The Mall, Honolulu, 96822. Joyce
Wright, Head, Asia Collection; Masato
Matsu, Head, East Asia Vernacular
Collection
Holdings: Vols 75,215 Cat Microforms
Notes: The Asia Collection holds material
from and relating to Bangladesh, India,

MARATHI LANGUAGE AND LITERATURE (cont.)

Nepal, Pakistan, and Sri Lanka in western and Asian languages. South Asian languages currently acquired: Bengali, Hindi, Marathi, Nepali, Pali, Prakrit, Sanskrit, Tamil. Period emphasis is post-World War II. Subject emphases; social sciences and the humanities (literature, economics, history, religion/ philosophy). Holdings are supplemented by a large uncataloged backlog, much of it accessible through the Library of Congress Accessions Lists for the area and by over 7000 cataloged titles in the main library collection. *South Asian Library Resources in North America: A Survey Prepared for the Boston Conference, 1974*, ed by M L P Patterson (Zug, Switzerland: Tutes Documentation Company, 1975). (Bibliotheca Asiatica 12-), "University of Hawaii," pp 103-114.

MI —UNIVERSITY OF MICHIGAN, Graduate Library, South Asian Dept, Ann Arbor, 48109. Om P Sharma, Librn
Holdings: Vols (365,000) Cat Maps Slides Microforms
Notes: The major emphasis is on social sciences and humanities. Besides materials in classical languages, South Asian vernaculars being retained are Hindi, Bengali, Urdu, Marathi and Tami; strong in classical languages, especially Sanskrit, Pali, and Prakrit.

MI —MICHIGAN STATE UNIVERSITY, International Library, South and Southeast Asia Collection, East Lansing, 48824. Clinton Lockert, Bibliographer
Holdings: Vols 55,700 // Cat Mss Maps Audiotapes Microforms
Notes: Serials and monographs of South Asia received on PL 480 for India, Pakistan, Sri Lanka, and Nepal since 1968. Emphasis is upon social sciences, humanities, and science. Areas of strength are anthropology and rural development. This subject has been de-emphasized, additions are not being made.

NY —NEW YORK PUBLIC LIBRARY, Oriental Div, Fifth Ave & 42 St, New York, 10018. E Christian Filstrup, Chief
Holdings: Cat Mss Microforms
Budget: ($56,455)
Notes: Published catalog of holdings.

NY —NEW YORK PUBLIC LIBRARY, Donnell Foreign Language Library, 20 W 53 St, New York, 10019. Bosiljka Stevanovic, Supvr Librn
Holdings: Vols 101 Cat
Notes: Marathi collection incl Marathi authors of Marathi expression. No separate catalog.

NY —UNIVERSITY OF ROCHESTER, Rush Rhees Library, Rochester, 14627. Datta S Kharbas, Head
Holdings: Vols 100,000 Cat Maps Microforms
Notes: Area studies collection on East Asia and South Asia. Major emphasis is on social sciences and humanities. Over 57,000 volumes on East Asia, out of which 29,000 volumes are in Chinese and 15,000 in Japanese. Extensive holdings on Chinese and Japanese histories. Catalog of East Asian collection consisting of Chinese and Japanese language holdings published in 1968, with two subsequent supplements. Over 33,000 volumes on South Asia. Considerable depth in social sciences, history, politics and anthropology. Extensive holdings in Sanskrit, Hindi, and Marathi.

MARCHAND, JOHN B.

RI —US NAVAL WAR COLLEGE, Historical Collection & Museum, Newport, 02841. Anthony S Nicolosi, Dir; Evelyn Cherpak, Cur
Holdings: Mss
Notes: A collection of journals of cruises to the Mediterranean, South America, Far East and US; Civil War journals of blockade duty off Charleston, SC, Mobile, Ala and Galveston, Tex; copy book of official letters and naval signal books. Marchand was a Commander in the US Navy.

MARCHES

LA —TULANE UNIVERSITY, Howard-Tilton Memorial Library, Special Collections Div, William Ransom Hogan Jazz Archive, 7001 Freret, New Orleans, 70118. Richard B Allen, Acting Cur; Alma D Williams, Assistant to the Cur
Holdings: Vols (100,000) Cat Mss Pix Slides Phohorecords Audiotapes Videotapes 16mm Films Microforms
Budget: ($90,000)
Notes: Jazz music and musicians. Outstanding collection, incl books, music scores, serials, catalogs and other archival material. Music, history, etc.
See also entry under Jazz

MS —UNIVERSITY OF SOUTHERN MISSISSIPPI, William David McCain Graduate Library, Box 5148, Southern Sta, Hattiesburg, 39406.
Holdings: Mss
Notes: The Paul Yoder Collection (1940-1980; 30 cubic feet) contains original musical scores and published copies of band music which Yoder composed or arranged. Some of the band music was written for foreign bands, especially Japanese. Catalog in progress.

NC —DUKE UNIVERSITY, William R Perkins Library, Rare Book Room, Durham, 27706. John L Sharpe, III, Cur
Notes: Collection of more than 3500 titles of Confederate imprints. Possibly the largest such collection in the country, it includes broadsides, maps, music, newspapers, Union and Confederate regimental histories, and sheet music.

SC —COLLEGE OF CHARLESTON LIBRARY, Special Collections Dept, Charleston, 29401.
Notes: The Kenneth Hanson Archives of Sound Recordings chronicling the growth of the recording industry through the 1940s. Over 400 cylinder records of marches, popular songs, vaudeville acts, and speeches.

MARCUS, FRANK

MA —BOSTON UNIVERSITY, Mugar Memorial Library, Special Collections Dept, 771 Commonwealth Ave, Boston, 02215. Howard B Gotlieb, Dir
Holdings: Cat Mss Pix
Notes: Mss correspondence, etc collected in depth; incl publications by or about.

MARCUS AURELIUS

CT —YALE UNIVERSITY, Box 1603A, Yale Station, New Haven, 06520.

MARDI GRAS see New Orleans—Carnival

MAREK, GEORGE

MA —BOSTON UNIVERSITY, Mugar Memorial Library, Special Collections Dept, 771 Commonwealth Ave, Boston, 02215. Howard B Gotlieb, Dir
Holdings: Cat Mss Pix
Notes: Mss correspondence, etc collected in depth; incl publications by or about.

MAREK, KURT (C. W. CERAM)

MA —BOSTON UNIVERSITY, Mugar Memorial Library, Special Collections Dept, 771 Commonwealth Ave, Boston, 02215. Howard B Gotlieb, Dir
Holdings: // Cat Mss Pix
Notes: Mss correspondence, etc collected in depth; incl publications by or about.

MARGARET, HELEN

NY —NEW YORK PUBLIC LIBRARY, Fifth Ave & 42 St, New York, 10018.
Holdings: Cat Mss

MARGO JONES THEATER

TX —SOUTHERN METHODIST UNIVERSITY, Fondren Library, McCord

Theater Collection, Room 301, Dallas, 75275. Edyth Renshaw, Cur; Linda Sellers, Pub Serv
Holdings: Vols (2000) Uncat Mss Pix Slides Phonorecords
Notes: See *Theatre Collections in Libraries and Museums*, Gilder and Freedley (Theatre Arts, 1936). The McCord Theatre Collection encompasses the entire spectrum of the performing arts. The central purpose is to gather records of our regional theater before such ephemeral material is lost. Records of over two hundred early Texas theaters, some fragmentary and some relatively complete, are in the files. These records incl photographs of buildings, stagehands, orchestras, and performers. Local theatre history incl the once famous Dallas Little Theatre and the Margo Jones Theatre. The national theatre, opera, ballet, and circus archives incl pictures (some autographed), programs, posters, throw-aways, tear sheets, clippings, and letters. Our international archives are small, but we have some excellent material, eg, artifacts from Max Reinhardt's production of"The Miracle" which happened to go bankrupt in Dallas. After a few years the items were given to us. There are posters, tear sheets, souvenir programs, and other colorful items from Morris Gest and the Artef Collection. We have about 200 19th century English playbills and a few from the 18th century. There is a collection of modern English, French, and other European programs, many of them illustrated souvenir programs. Also, magazines on theater, cinema, and television (1800). Scrapbooks covering both southwest and Dallas theater, 1890s-1950s. Special Collections: artifacts and documents on puppets; masks; costume design; circus; and ballet and dance. The Harriet Bacon MacDonald Collection of over 200 photographs of musicians appearing in Dallas during the first three decades of the 20th century. Many autographed. Affiliated with Meadow Theatre of the Arts.

MARGOLIUS, SIDNEY

NJ —RUTGERS, THE STATE UNIVERSITY OF NEW JERSEY, Alexander Library, Special Collections and Archives, College Ave & Huntington St, New Brunswick, 08903. Ronald L Becker, Cur of Manuscripts and Rare Books
Notes: Papers of the Consumers League of New Jersey, Consumer Research Inc, and consumer advocate Sidney Margolius.

MARIA THERESIA, EMPRESS

CA —STANFORD UNIVERSITY LIBRARIES, Cecil H Green Library, Stanford, 94305. Peter R Frank, Cur, CDP-Germanic Collection
Notes: Extensive holdings, covering Austrian history of the Habsburg Empire to the present. Especially strong for the period of Maria Theresia and Joseph II, 19th & 20th century. Extremely rich in the Josephinic pamphlets (Broschuren-Literatur), broadsheets of the Napoleonic Wars and of the Revolution 1848/1849, rare periodicals. This and other rare material in the Stanford Collection of German, Austrian and Swiss Culture, Special Collections. Over 4,000 vols entered in RLIN. Description: "Narrative on a Good Meal: A Collection of Austriaca at Stanford University Libraries" by Peter R Frank.

MARIA Y CAMPOS, ARMANDO DE

†CA —UNIVERSITY OF CALIFORNIA, DAVIS, Davis, 95616.
Notes: General collection of materials dealing with the history of Mexico. Majority of the significant titles in the collection were obtained from the library of Armando de Maria y Campos, a mexican journalist.

MARIANA ISLANDS

DC —GEORGETOWN UNIVERSITY, Library, Special Collections Div, 37 & O Sts

MARIANA ISLANDS (cont.)

NW, Washington, 20057. George M Barringer, Special Collections Librn; Nicholas B Sheetz, Mss Librn
Holdings: Cat
Notes: Papers of Chauncey Brewster Chapman, Jr (1919-1980), attorney, from his early legal career in private practice and his years in the Department of Interior where he served as solicitor for territories from 1967-1979. The bulk of the papers concerns judicial and legal matters in regard to territories outside the United States, as well as internal departmental affairs. Of particular interest is material concerning Samoa from 1969-1980.

DC —LIBRARY OF CONGRESS, Manuscript Division, Washington, 20540. John C Broderick, Chief
Holdings: Cat Mss
Notes: Microfilm of records of the Spanish Colonial Government in the Mariana Islands, 1678-1899. Originals (5.5 linear ft) of these varied materials are in the Manuscript Division. See *LC Information Bulletin*, 18 July 1968.

PI —NIEVES M FLORES MEMORIAL LIBRARY, PO Box 652, Agana, Guam, 96910. Magdalena S Taitano, Territorial Librn
Holdings: Vols 3975 Cat Slides Microforms
Budget: $1000
Notes: Guam Micronesian collection. Incl 500 slides, 15,000 images and 249 microforms. Photocopying available.

MARIE, QUEEN, OF ROMANIA

OH —KENT STATE UNIVERSITY, Libraries, Dept of Special Collections, Kent, 44242. Dean H Keller, Cur
Holdings: Vols 175 Cat Mss Pix
Notes: The collection relates espec to Queen Marie.

MARII LANGUAGE see Cheremissian Language and Literature

MARIJUANA

CA —FITZ HUGH LUDLOW MEMORIAL LIBRARY, PO Box 99346, San Francisco, 94109. Michael R Aldrich, Exec Cur
Holdings: Vols (500)
Notes: Collection stored. Important mail inquiries only. No interlibrary lending or telephone queries. Emphasizes historical, literary aspects of cannabis use, as well as sociology, chemistry, pharmacology, botany, legal aspects. Incl complete archives of the California Marijuana Initiative, 1972-74, and many documents from the international marijuana law reform movement. Also incl a sizeable collection of phonograph records, artwork, rolling papers, smoking paraphernalia and research artifacts related to cannabis.

MARIJUANA TRADE see Drug Trade

MARIMBA

MD —TOWSON STATE UNIVERSITY, Fine Arts Bldg, Room 457, Towson, 21204. Edwin L Gerhardt, Curator
Notes: The Gerhardt Marimba Xylophone Collection is a unique and comprehensive accumulation of marimba and xylophone lore. It incl literature, phonograph and tape recordings, catalogs, music, methods, pictures, correspondence, personal reminiscences and miscellaneous information. It is *not* a collection of instruments. A detailed outline is available upon request. Direct all correspondence to the curator, Edwin L Gerhardt, 4926 Leeds Ave, Baltimore, MD 21227, (301) 242-0328.

MARINE ACCIDENTS

IL —CHICAGO HISTORICAL SOCIETY, Library, Clark St at North Ave, Chicago, 60614. Robert L Brubaker, Librn
Holdings: Cat
Notes: The J Norman Jensen Collection of Lake and River Disasters, 1679-1947. 8500 card entries.

MD —STEAMSHIP HISTORICAL SOCIETY OF AMERICA (SSHSA), University of Baltimore Library, 1420 Maryland Ave, Baltimore, 21201.
Holdings: Vols (3500) Cat Maps Pix Slides 16mm Films
Budget: ($15,000)
Notes: Powered Maritime Transportation Collection. Photo bank of over 15,000 negatives and 25,000 prints, arranged alphabetically by vessel name. Extensive blueprint and tracing collection. Collection documents history of steam navigation from the early 19th century to the present. Emphasis upon East Coast American vessels of late 19th and early 20th centuries and upon transatlantic vessels. Some coverage of Great Lakes and inland river steamboats. Very little about sailing vessels. No published catalog. Books listed in OCLC. Collection located at University of Baltimore. Address for Society is 414 Pelton Ave, Staten Island, NY 10310, attention: Alice S Wilson, Secretary and SSHSA Librn.

WI —MILWAUKEE PUBLIC LIBRARY, 814 W Wisconsin Ave, Milwaukee, 53233. Donald J Sager, City Librn
See also entry under Marine History.

MARINE AIDS see Aids to Navigation

MARINE ARCHAEOLOGY

MD —CALVERT MARINE MUSEUM, Library, PO Box 97, Solomons, 20688.
Holdings: Uncat Mss Maps
Notes: Result of an ongoing project with the Nautical Archeological Associates to obtain information on naval history of Patuxent River during the War of 1812.

MARINE ARCHITECTURE see Naval Architecture; Shipbuilding

MARINE BIOLOGY

CA —UNIVERSITY OF CALIFORNIA, SAN DIEGO, Scripps Institution of Oceanography Library, Mail Code C075C, La Jolla, 92093. William J Goff, Librn; Deborarh Day, Archivist
Holdings: Vols (178,000) Cat Maps Microforms
Budget: ($308,200)
Notes: See *Catalogs of the Scripps Institution of Oceanography Library* (Boston: G K Hall, 1970-1980), 21 vols. Incl 44,000 maps, 17,000 microforms cat, 21,000 reprints, and 800 linear feet of archives.

CA —STANFORD UNIVERSITY, Hopkins Marine Station Library, Cabrillo Point, Pacific Grove, 93950. Alan Baldridge, Librn
Holdings: Vols 22,000 Cat Mss Maps Pix Slides Microforms

CA —CALIFORNIA ACADEMY OF SCIENCES, J W Mailliard Jr Library, Golden Gate Park, San Francisco, 94118. Ray Brian, Librn
Notes: Downs No 2160.

CT —LEE ASH, (personal collection), 66 Humiston Dr, Bethany, 06525.

FL —UNIVERSITY OF MIAMI, Otto G Richter Library, PO Box 248214, Coral Gables, 33124. Frank Rodgers, Dir of Libraries
Holdings: Vols Microforms
Notes: The Rosenstiel School of Marine and Atmospheric Sciences Library is one of the major marine science collections in the United States and is especially strong in the literature of tropical oceanography. Special collections in the library incl 200 oceanographic atlases and more than 50 sets of the world's major expedition reports. The library also maintains a nautical chart collection. 3000 microforms; 1000 current subscriptions.

FL —INTERNATIONAL OCEANOGRAPHIC FOUNDATION/ PLANET OCEAN, Library, 3979 Rickenbacker Causeway, Virginia Key, Miami, 33149.
Notes: Noncirculating.

FL —FLORIDA DEPT OF NATURAL RESOURCES BUREAU OF MARINE RESEARCH, Library, 100 Eighth Ave SE, Saint Petersburg, 33701. Keir Gray, Archivist
Holdings: Vols (3400) Cat Maps Pix Slides 16mm Films Microforms
Budget: ($59,000)
Notes: The library supports the research of approx 50 biologists and technicians, with emphasis on the marine resources of Florida and nearby areas. An archives section houses original research data, reports, publications,, etc, developed by the scientific staff. Marine biological literature is received on exchange from laboratories and libraries throughout the world. There are approx 1400 journal titles in the collection. Current titles received number approx 600. The 33,000 reprints are cataloged by author and subject. Current laboratory activities incl marine studies in aquaculture, descriptive biology, ecological studies, fisheries biology, and oceanography.

ME —BIGELOW LABORATORY FOR OCEAN SCIENCES & MAINE DEPT OF MARINE RESOURCES, Library, McKown Point, West Boothbay Harbor, 04575. Pamela Shephard-Lupo, Librn
Holdings: Vols Cat Periodicals Maps
Budget: ($55,000)
Notes: This library presently serves two institutions. The Maine Dept of Marine Resources has maintained the library since 1957 and thus the majority of our holdings are geared to their needs, ie fish biology and stock assessment on a local, national and international level. In 1973 Bigelow Laboratory for Ocean Sciences came to West Boothbay Harbor and began to contribute to the library with a very specialized collection on the Gulf of Maine marine chemistry, phytoplankton and nutrient cycles.

†MD —SMITHSONIAN INSTITUTION LIBRARIES, Smithsonian Environmental Research Center, Branch Library, PO Box 28, Edgewater, 21037.
Holdings: Vols (1100)

MD —CALVERT MARINE MUSEUM, Library, PO Box 97, Solomons, 20688.
Holdings: Vols (2000) Cat Maps Pix Slides Audiotapes 16mm Films
Notes: Local maritime history, estuarine biology, and paleontolgy of southern Maryland. Large picture collection (1800), blueprints (385) and slides (1100).

MS —GULF COAST RESEARCH LABORATORY, Gordon Gunter Library, E Beach Rd, Ocean Springs, 39564. Malcolm Ware, Sr, Librn
Holdings: Vols (9000) Uncat Mss Pix Microforms
Notes: Also have reprint collection of 30,000 cataloged reprints, indexed by card catalog, on all aspects of marine biology.

NY —COLUMBIA UNIVERSITY LIBRARIES, Geoscience Library, Lamont-Doherty Geological Observatory, Palisades, 10964. Susan Klimley, Librn
Holdings: Vols (20,000) Cat
Notes: Geosciences, incl seismology, paleoclimatology and lunar studies.

NC —DUKE UNIVERSITY, Marine Laboratory, Beaufort, 28516. Jean Williams, Librn
Holdings: Vols 15,556

NC —NATIONAL MARINE FISHERIES SERVICE, SOUTHEAST FISHERIES CENTER, Beaufort Laboratory, Library, Beaufort, 28516. Ann Bowman Hall, Librn
Holdings: Vols (15,000) Cat

PA —CARNEGIE LIBRARY OF PITTSBURGH, Science & Technology Dept, 4400 Forbes Ave, Pittsburgh, 15213. Catherine M Brosky, Dept Head
Notes: Of secondary interest in acquisitions because of the department's role in cooperating with Pittsburgh institutions and others across the Commonwealth in sharing resources, the cooperative acquisition of materials, and the provision of services and information. However, some aspects of the subject are emphasized. There are separate entries for each of these specialties in this vol.

RI —UNIVERSITY OF RHODE ISLAND, Graduate School of Oceanography, Pell

MARINE BIOLOGY (cont.)

Library Bldg, Narragansett, 02882. Kenneth T Morse, Chief Librn
Notes: Incl 10,016 vols and monographs; 13, 578 bound vols periodicals; 1326 serial publications.

TX —TEXAS A&M UNIVERSITY AT GALVESTON, MOODY COLLEGE, Library, PO Box 1675, Galveston, 77553. Natalie W Shipman, Librn
Holdings: Vols (13,000) Cat
Budget: ($300,000)

TX —UNIVERSITY OF TEXAS, Marine Science Institute Library, Port Aransas, 78373. Ruth Grundy, Librn
Holdings: Vols (45,000) Cat Maps Pix
Budget: ($70,000)
Notes: Current researches in marine science, especially concerning the Gulf of Mexico, the Texas Coastal Zone, and the Continental Shelf. Incl journals.

†PR —UNIVERSITY OF PUERTO RICO, Mayaguez Campus Library, Marine Sciences Collection, Mayaguez, 00708. Sheila Dunstan, Head Librn; Alejandro Ayala, Asst Librn
Holdings: Vols 1169 Cat
Notes: Also, 3761 vols periodicals, 6248 documents, 130 theses, 885 microforms, 10, 016 microfilm. Subjects include fish biology; aquaculture; marine invertebrates; marine botany; marine ecology; chemical, physical, geological and biological oceanography.

PQ —MCGILL UNIVERSITY, Institute of Oceanography, Oceanography Library, 3620 University St, Montreal, H3A 2B2, Can. Yvonne Mahocks, Librn
Holdings: Vols (10,848) Cat Mss Maps Pix Microforms
Budget: ($1200)
Notes: Extensive periodical collection. 12, 332 government documents, . 322 microtech, 321 microfiche, 25,000 reprints.

PQ —MCGILL UNIVERSITY, Blacker-Wood Library of Zoology & Ornithology, 3459 McTavish St, Montreal, H3A 1Y1, Can. Eleanor MacLean, Librn
Holdings: Vols (77,600) // Cat Mss
Notes: Special features of collection incl: Robert Gurney Collection of reprints on Crustaceana; 3000 folders of letters from naturalists; over 9000 original paintings of wildlife; a small collection of falconry equipment; the archives of the Montreal Natural History Society; the archives of the North American Falconry Association; 156 17th-century feather pictures of birds and people. Does not incl entomology collection.

MARINE CHEMISTRY see Chemistry, Marine

MARINE DISASTERS see Shipwrecks

MARINE ECOLOGY

CA —CALIFORNIA STATE UNIVERSITY, FULLERTON, Library, Box 4150, Fullerton, 92634. Linda Herman, Special Collections Librn
Holdings: Cat
Notes: Dr Leonard B Schultz Ichtyology Collection of 13,000 pieces incl books, pamphlets, articles and ephemera. It is supplemented by the Ecology of Bay and Estuarine Fishes Collections.

FL —UNIVERSITY OF MIAMI, Otto G Richter Library, PO Box 248214, Coral Gables, 33124. Frank Rodgers, Dir of Libraries
Holdings: Vols Microforms
Notes: The Rosenstiel School of Marine and Atmospheric Sciences Library is one of the major marine science collections in the United States and is especially strong in the literature of tropical oceanography. Special collections in the library incl 200 oceanographic atlases and more than 50 sets of the world's major expedition reports. The library also maintains a nautical chart collection. 3000 microforms; 1000 current subscriptions.

NC —DUKE UNIVERSITY, Marine Laboratory, Beaufort, 28516. Jean Williams, Librn
Holdings: Vols 15,556

OR —OREGON STATE UNIVERSITY, Marine Science Center, Library, Newport, 97365. Marilyn Guin, Librn
Holdings: Vols (8000) Cat Maps Microforms
Budget: ($15,000)
Notes: Collection emphasizes marine ecology, invertebrate zoology and marine ecology, invertebrate zoology and marine algae. The portion of the collection concerned with fisheries emphasizes aquaculture. Collection is divided between the Marine Science Library and the Main OSU Library.

MARINE ENGINEERING

HI —PACIFIC SUBMARINE MUSEUM, Library, Naval Submarine Base, Pearl Harbor, 96860. Ray W de Yarmin, Cur
Holdings: Vols (1500) Cat Mss Maps Pix Slides Phonorecords 16mm Films
Budget: ($600)
Notes: Incl 3000 pictures. Extensive missile and torpedo collection; submarine models; salvage/deep-sea diver exhibit; Arctic exploration by submarines Worl War II submarine components. Research program for students, authors, lecturers, etc.

MA —MASSACHUSETTS INSTITUTE OF TECHNOLOGY MUSEUM, Hart Nautical Collections, 77 Massachusetts Ave, Rm 5-329, Cambridge, 02139. John W Waterhouse, Cur
Notes: Ships and marine engineering development Museum is under jurisdiction of MIT'S Dept of Ocean Engineering. Collection incl various collections of prints and photographs of ships and yachts; working drawings from the Herreshoff Manufacturing Co, 1870-1945, and of the George Lawley and Son Corp; working drawings and models from the Munro, Owen, and Paine Collections.

MI —UNIVERSITY OF MICHIGAN, Engineering-Transportation Library, 312 Undergraduate Library, Ann Arbor, 48109. Maurita Holland, Librn
Holdings: Vols (400,000) Cat Microforms
Budget: ($225,000)

NY —STATE UNIVERSITY OF NEW YORK, Maritime College, Stephen B Luce Library, Fort Schuyler, Bronx, 10465. Richard H Corson, Librn
Holdings: Vols (68,000) Cat Slides Videotapes 16mm Films Filmstrips Microforms
Budget: ($90,000)
Notes: Incl extensive holdings in periodical literature with long and complete runs of many titles. Approximately 3500 recent research reports in paper and microfiche format. Mainly English language.

NY —WEBB INSTITUTE OF NAVAL ARCHITECTURE, Livingston Library, Crescent Beach Rd, Glen Cove, 11542. Fred H Forrest, Librn
Holdings: Vols 550 Cat
Notes: Access by appointment only.

NY —ENGINEERING SOCIETIES LIBRARY, 345 E 47 St, New York, 10017. S Kirk Cabeen, Dir
Holdings: Vols 250,000 Cat Maps 16mm Films Microforms
Notes: One of the largest, most comprehensive engineering libraries in the world. Covers all engineering disciplines; particularly strong in electrical and electronic, mechanical, mining and metallurgical, petroleum, chemical, industrial, air conditioning and refrigeration engineering. Incl Wheeler Collection of early materials on magnetisn and electricity. 125, 000 bound periodical volumes; 10,000 maps; 5000 serial subscriptions (many foreign-language). Virtually all materials abstracted in *Engineering Index* (1884-date) are incl in Library. Noncirculating, except to members of professional engineering societies which support the Library. See *Engineering Societies Library, New York, Classed Subject Catalog and Index* (Boston: G K Hall, 1963); and *Supplements*, 1-10, 1964-1973.

NY —SEAMEN'S CHURCH INSTITUTE OF NEW YORK, Joseph Conrad Library, 15

State St, New York, 10004. Bonnie Golightly, Librn
Holdings: Vols (23,500) Cat Pix
Budget: ($8500)
Notes: Merchant seaman, merchant ships, voyages, navigation, marine engineering, shipbuilding. Large collection of ship registers: *Lloyd's Register of Shipping*, a partial coverage of the years 1764-1865 in reprints, complete coverage for the years 1877 to date; *American Bureau of Shipping*, 1916 to date; *Merchant Vessels of the US*, 1891 to date. *Society of Naval Architects and Marine Engineers Transactions*, vol 1, 1893 to date. The picture file consists mostly of photographs of merchant ships. This is supplemented by scrapbooks. The index to the pictures, scrapbooks, books and vertical file are in one subject catalog. We subscribe to and keep for several years numerous maritime periodicals. The maritime history collection incl sailing ships as well as steamships. In addition, the Bollman Collection, 3500 books devoted to maritime subjects, andpresented to The Joseph Conrad Library from the American Merchant Marine Library Association.

NC —DUKE UNIVERSITY, Marine Laboratory, Beaufort, 28516. Jean Williams, Librn
Holdings: Vols 15,556

OH —PREFORMED LINE PRODUCTS CO, Research & Engineering Library, 660 Beta Drive, Mayfield Village, (Mailing add: PO Box 91129, Cleveland, 44101). Edwina T Barron, Librn
Holdings: Vols (11,500) Cat Mss Microfiche Pix VF
Budget: ($30,500)
Notes: Library covering research and engineering fields emphasizing this subject. Aerodynamic characteristics and electrical characteristics of power cables, communication cables (including fiber optics), cable support systems, as well as associated fittings and hardware; in service behavior of manufactured products and materials as it relates to its static and dynamic forces and environmental conditions; oceanographic cable fittings and terminations.

PA —FRANKLIN INSTITUTE LIBRARY, 20 & The Parkway, Philadelphia, 19103. Miriam Padusis, Dir; Charles Wilt, Readers Servs Librn
Holdings: Vols (300,000) Cat Maps Pix Microforms

PA —US NAVY, Philadelphia Naval Shipyard Technical Library, Philadelphia Naval Shipyard, Philadelphia, 19112. Alice R Murray, Dir
Holdings: Vols (12,500) Cat Pix
Notes: The Library also has (70,000) technical manuals, (3500) research and development reports. Over (400) current periodicals.

ON —NATIONAL RESEARCH COUNCIL OF CANADA, Aeronautical/Mechanical Engineering Branch Library, Montreal Rd, Ottawa, K1A 0R6, Can. Louise Fletcher, Head
Notes: This branch library of the Canada Institute for Scientific and Technical Information (CISTI) of the National Research Council of Canada, Ottawa, has a collection strong in aeronautical engineering, automatic control, CAD/CAM, robotics, ocean, wind, and solar energy power, hydraulic and coastal engineering, icing, low temperature research, naval engineering, metals and metallurgy, incl composites, tribology, and air, railroad, marine transportation. Library supported the Council contribution to the development of the remote manipular Canadarm for NASA's Space Shuttle Orbiters and more recently, the Canadian Astronaut Program which will contribute payload specialists to NASA's Space Shuttle Program in 1984. 35, 000 monographs, 1200 serials. Report collection: over 500,000 items.

MARINE FAUNA

AK —NATIONAL OCEANIC AND ATMOSPHERIC ADMINISTRATION,

MARINE FAUNA (cont.)

National Marine Fisheries Service, Fisheries Laboratory Research Library, PO Box 155, Auke Bay, 99821. Paula Johnson, Librn
Holdings: Vols (2100) Cat Mss Maps Slides Microforms
Budget: ($20,000)
Notes: Much on the outer continental shelf, marine flora and fauna, fisheries.

CA —STANFORD UNIVERSITY, Hopkins Marine Station Library, Cabrillo Point, Pacific Grove, 93950. Alan Baldridge, Librn
Holdings: Vols 22,000 Cat Mss Maps Pix Slides Microforms

CA —CALIFORNIA ACADEMY OF SCIENCES, J W Mailliard Jr Library, Golden Gate Park, San Francisco, 94118.
Ray Brian, Librn
Notes: Downs No 2160.

DC —NATIONAL GEOGRAPHIC SOCIETY, Library, 1146 16th St NW, Washington, 20036. Susan Fifer Canby, Dir
Holdings: Vols (63,000) Cat Mss Maps Pix
Notes: Material concerning land, sea, and space exploration--past and present. All fields of anthropology, natural history, geography, etc.

DC —SMITHSONIAN INSTITUTION LIBRARIES, Natural History Branch, Washington, 20560. Sylvia Churgin, Chief Librn
Holdings: Vols (75,550) Cat Mss Maps Pix Slides Microforms
Notes: Incl vertebrate and invertebrate paleontology; vertebrate zoology: systematics and taxonomy.

FL —UNIVERSITY OF MIAMI, Otto G Richter Library, PO Box 248214, Coral Gables, 33124. Frank Rodgers, Dir of Libraries
Holdings: Vols Microforms
Notes: The Rosenstiel School of Marine and Atmospheric Sciences Library is one of the major marine science collections in the United States and is especially strong in the literature of tropical oceanography. Special collections in the library incl 200 oceanographic atlases and more than 50 sets of the world's major expedition reports. The library also maintains a nautical chart collection. 3000 microforms; 1000 current subscriptions.

FL —INTERNATIONAL OCEANOGRAPHIC FOUNDATION/ PLANET OCEAN, Library, 3979 Rickenbacker Causeway, Virginia Key, Miami, 33149.
Notes: Noncirculating.

IL —ILLINOIS NATURAL HISTORY SURVEY LIBRARY, 196 Natural Resources Bldg, Champaign, 61820. Carla G Heister, Librn
Holdings: Vols (36,000) Cat Microforms
Budget: ($25,500)
Notes: A Research and Science Branch of the State of Illinois, the Natural History Survey maintains a library of books, journals and reports on various aspects of natural history. Material is collected in all major languages. The library maintains its own exchange arrangements with some 600 worldwide institutions and organizations. Interlibrary loans and photocopy services are available through the University of Illinois Library. Publications issued regularly by the Survey incl *Biological Notes, The Bulletin, and Circulars.*

OR —OREGON STATE UNIVERSITY, Marine Science Center, Library, Newport, 97365. Marilyn Guin, Librn
Holdings: Vols (8000) Cat Maps Microforms
Budget: ($15,000)
Notes: Collection emphasizes marine ecology, invertebrate zoology and marine algae. The portion of the collection concerned with fisheries emphasizes aquaculture. Collection is divided between the Marine Science Library and the Main OSU Library.

RI —UNIVERSITY OF RHODE ISLAND, Graduate School of Oceanography, Pell Library Bldg, Narragansett, 02882. Kenneth T Morse, Chief Librn
Notes: Incl 10,016 vols and monographs; 13, 578 bound vols periodicals; 1326 serial publications.

TX —UNIVERSITY OF TEXAS, Marine Science Institute Library, Port Aransas, 78373. Ruth Grundy, Librn
Holdings: Vols (45,000) Cat Maps Pix
Budget: ($70,000)
Notes: Current researches in marine science, especially concerning the Gulf of Mexico, the Texas Coastal Zone, and the Continental Shelf. Incl journals.

PQ —MCGILL UNIVERSITY, Institute of Oceanography, Oceanography Library, 3620 University St, Montreal, H3A 2B2, Can. Yvonne Mahocks, Librn
Holdings: Vols (10,848) Cat Mss Maps Pix Microforms
Budget: ($1200)
Notes: Extensive periodical collection. 12, 332 government documents, , 322 microtech, 321 microfiche, 25,000 reprints.

MARINE FITTINGS

OH —PREFORMED LINE PRODUCTS CO, Research & Engineering Library, 660 Beta Drive, Mayfield Village, (Mailing add: PO Box 91129, Cleveland, 44101). Edwina T Barron, Librn
Holdings: Vols (11,500) Cat Mss Microfiche Pix VF
Budget: ($30,500)
Notes: Library covering research and engineering fields emphasizing this subject. Aerodynamic characteristics and electrical characteristics of power cables, communication cables (including fiber optics), cable support systems, as well as associated fittings and hardware; in service behavior of manufactured products and materials as it relates to its static and dynamic forces and environmental conditions; oceanographic cable fittings and terminations.

MARINE FLORA

AK —NATIONAL OCEANIC AND ATMOSPHERIC ADMINISTRATION, National Marine Fisheries Service, Fisheries Laboratory Research Library, PO Box 155, Auke Bay, 99821. Paula Johnson, Librn
Holdings: Vols (21,000) Cat Mss Maps Slides Microforms
Budget: ($20,000)
Notes: Much on the outer continental shelf, marine flora and fauna, fisheies.

CA —R MITCHEL BEAUCHAMP BOTANICAL LIBRARY, 1843 E 16th St, National City, 92050.
Notes: Native flora. Survey and exploration reports. American seed and bulb and bulb catalogs.

CA —STANFORD UNIVERSITY, Hopkins Marine Station Library, Cabrillo Point, Pacific Grove, 93950. Alan Baldridge, Librn
Holdings: Vols 22,000 Cat Mss Maps Pix Slides Microforms

CA —CALIFORNIA ACADEMY OF SCIENCES, J W Mailliard Jr Library, Golden Gate Park, San Francisco, 94118.
Ray Brian, Librn
Notes: Down No 2160.

DC —NATIONAL GEOGRAPHIC SOCIETY, Library, 1146 16th St NW, Washington, 20036. Susan Fifer Canby, Dir
Holdings: Vols (63,000) Cat Mss Maps Pix
Notes: Material concerning land, sea, and space exploration--past and present. All fields of anthropology, natural history, geography, etc.

DC —SMITHSONIAN INSTITUTION LIBRARIES, Natural History Branch, Washington, 20560. Sylvia Churgin, Chief Librn
Holdings: Vols (75,000) Cat Mss Maps Pix Slides Microforms
Notes: Incl vertebrate and invertebrate paleontology; vertebrate zoology: systematics and taxonomy.

FL —UNIVERSITY OF MIAMI, Otto G Richter Library, PO Box 248214, Coral Gables, 33124. Frank Rodgers, Dir of Libraries
Holdings: Vols Microforms
Notes: The Rosenstiel School of Marine and Atmospheric Sciences Library is one of the major marine science collections in the United States and is especially strong in the literature of tropical oceanography. Special collections in the library incl 200 oceanographic atlases and more than 50 sets of the world's major expedition reports. The library also maintains a nautical chart collection. 3000 microforms; 1000 current subscriptions.

FL —INTERNATIONAL OCEANOGRAPHIC FOUNDATION/ PLANET OCEAN, Library, 3979 Rickenbacker Causeway, Virginia Key, Miami, 33149.
Notes: Noncirculating.

ME —BIGELOW LABORATORY FOR OCEAN SCIENCES & MAINE DEPT OF MARINE RESOURCES, Library, McKown Point, West Boothbay Harbor, 04575. Pamela Shephard-Lupo, Librn
Holdings: Vols Cat Periodicals
Budget: ($55,000)
Notes: This library presently serves two institutions. The Maine Dept of Marine Resources has maintained the library since 1957 and thus the majority of our holdings are geared to their needs, ie fish biology and stock assessment on a local, national and international level. In 1973 Bigelow Laboratory for Ocean Sciences came to West Boothbay Harbor and began to contribute to the library with a very specialized collection on the Gulf of Maine marine chemistry, phytoplankton and nutrient cycles.

OR —OREGON STATE UNIVERSITY, Marine Science Center, Library, Newport, 97365. Marilyn Guin, Librn
Holdings: Vols (8000) Cat Maps Microforms
Budget: ($15,000)
Notes: Collection emphasizes marine ecology, invertebrate zoology and marine algae. The portion of the collection concerned with fisheries emphasizes aquaculture. Collection is divided between the Marine Science Library and the Main OSU Library.

RI —UNIVERSITY OF RHODE ISLAND, Graduate School of Oceanography, Pell Library Bldg, Narragansett, 02882. Kenneth T Morse, Chief Librn
Notes: Incl 10,016 vols and monographs; 13, 578 bound vols periodicals; 1326 serial publications.

TX —UNIVERSITY OF TEXAS, Marine Science Institute Library, Port Aransas, 78373. Ruth Grundy, Librn
Holdings: Vols (45,000) Cat Maps Pix
Budget: ($70,000)
Notes: Current researches in marine science, especially concerning the Gulf of Mexico, the Texas Coastal Zone, and the Continental Shelf. Incl journals.

PQ —MCGILL UNIVERSITY, Institute of Oceanography, Oceanography Library, 3620 University St, Montreal, H3A 2B2, Can. Yvonne Mahocks, Librn
Holdings: Vols (10,484) Cat Mss Maps Pix Microforms
Budget: ($1200)
Notes: Extensive periodical collection. 12, 332 government documents, , 322 microtech, 321 microfiche, 25,000 reprints.

MARINE GEOLOGY see Submarine Geology

MARINE LABORATORIES

TX —UNIVERSITY OF TEXAS, Marine Science Institute Library, Port Aransas, 78373. Ruth Grundy, Librn
Holdings: Vols (45,000) Cat Maps Pix
Budget: ($70,000)
Notes: Current researches in marine science, especially concerning the Gulf of Mexico, the Texas Coastal Zone, and the Continental Shelf. Incl journals.

MARINE PERIODICALS see Periodicals, Marine

MARINE RADIOECOLOGY

NC —NATIONAL MARINE FISHERIES SERVICE, SOUTHEAST FISHERIES

MARINE RADIOECOLOGY (cont.)

CENTER, Beaufort Laboratory, Library, Beaufort, 28516. Ann Bowman Hall, Librn
Holdings: Vols (15,000) Cat

MARINE RESOURCES

CA —UNIVERSITY OF CALIFORNIA, BERKELEY, Giannini Foundation of Agricultural Economics, Library, 248 Giannini Hall, Berkeley, 94720. Grace Dote, Librn
Holdings: Vols (18,000) Cat Mss Maps Microforms
Notes: Noncirculating collection. No interlibrary loans. Also about 124,000 unbound vols. Open to graduate students and faculties of universities and colleges, research workers and interested public. Mostly English language materials, primarily 1900 to date. Card catalog published by G K Hall Co. *Dictionary Catalog of the Giannini Foundation of Agricultural Economics Library, Univ of California,* 12 vols (Holdings thru 7/71).

FL —INTERNATIONAL OCEANOGRAPHIC FOUNDATION/ PLANET OCEAN, Library, 3979 Rickenbacker Causeway, Virginia Key, Miami, 33149.
Notes: Noncirculating.

MARINE SCIENCES

FL —UNIVERSITY OF MIAMI, Otto G Richter Library, PO Box 248214, Coral Gables, 33124. Frank Rodgers, Dir of Libraries
Holdings: Vols 38,000 Microforms
Notes: The Rosenstiel School of Marine and Atmospheric Sciences Library is one of the major marine science collections in the United States and is especially strong in the literature of tropical oceanography. Special collections in the library incl 200 oceanographic atlases and more than 50 sets of the world's major expedition reports. The library also maintains a nautical chart collection. 3000 microforms; 1000 current subscriptions.

FL —INTERNATIONAL OCEANOGRAPHIC FOUNDATION/ PLANET OCEAN, Library, 3979 Rickenbacker Causeway, Virginia Key, Miami, 33149.
Notes: Noncirculating.

OR —OREGON STATE UNIVERSITY, Marine Science Center, Library, Newport, 97365. Marilyn Guin, Librn
Holdings: Vols (8000) Cat Maps Microforms
Budget: ($15,000)
Notes: Collection emphasizes marine ecology, invertebrate zoology and marine algae. The portion of the collection concerned with fisheries emphasizes aquaculture. Collection is divided between the Marine Science Library and the Main OSU Library.

†TX —UNIVERSITY OF TEXAS LIBRARIES, General Libraries, Humanities Research Center, PO Box 7219, Austin, 78712. John Chalmers, Librn
Holdings: Mss
Notes: Papers of Maurice Ewing, geophysicist.

†PR —UNIVERSITY OF PUERTO RICO, Mayaguez Campus Library, Marine Sciences Collection, Mayaguez, 00708. Sheila Dunstan, Head Librn; Alejandro Ayala, Asst Librn
Holdings: Vols 1169 Cat
Notes: Also, 3761 vols periodicals, 6248 documents, 130 theses, 885 microforms, 10, 016 reprints. Subjects include fish biology; aquaculture; marine invertebrates; marine botany; marine ecology; chemical, physical, geological and biological oceanography.

NS —BEDFORD INSTITUTE OF OCEANOGRAPHY, Library, PO Box 1006, Dartmouth, B2Y 4A2, Can. J Elizabeth Sutherland, Librn Services
Holdings: Vols (15,000) Cat Microforms
Budget: ($90,000)
Notes: Incl 15,000 monographs, 1450 serial

titles and 20,000 microfiche, technical reports, 25,000 Maps.

MARINE SIGNALS see Aids to Navigation

MARINE TRANSPORTATION see Shipping

MARINE VIEWS

MA —SOCIETY FOR THE PRESERVATION OF NEW ENGLAND ANTIQUITIES, Library, 141 Cambridge St, Boston, 02114. Ellie Reichlin, Librn & Cur of Photographic Collections
Notes: Photograph collections, all media (incl daguerreotypes, ambrotypes, etc, stereographic views, carte de visite) depicting New England buildings; interiors; street and town views; occupations; pastimes; transport and personalities. Covers 1840s-1930s, with some more recent additons. Amateur and professional photographers represented. Cataloged in part, otherwise arranged by localities, subject, personal name. Special collections incl: marine photographs by N L Stebbins and Henry Peabody (1880s-1920s); Boston and Albany railroad photographic archive, early 1900s; Quabbin Valley views; historic American Buildings Survey photographs (17th to early 19th century architecture) by Arthur Haskell; Baldwin Coolidge collection, and many others. Size: 500,000 prints, ca 75,000 negatives (glass plates and copy negs). These are cataloged. Some special indexes incllandscape design (arbors, conservatories, flower beds, bandstands etc); photographers represented; architects represented (partial), and pending, interiors (specific features of); occupations.

MARINE ZOOLOGY see Marine Fauna

MARINER'S COMPASS see Compass

MARINETTI, F. T.

CT —YALE UNIVERSITY, Beinecke Rare Book & Manuscript Library, Osborn Collection, New Haven, 06520. Stephen R Parks, Cur
Holdings: Mss

IL —NORTHWESTERN UNIVERSITY, Library, Special Collections Dept, 1937 Sheridan Rd, Evanston, 60201. R Russell Maylone, Cur
Holdings: Vols 600 Cat Mss Pix
Notes: Futurism in art and literature, especially Italian. Books, periodicals, pamphlets, catalogs, ephemera. Incl correspondence of F T Marinetti.

MARION, IRA

NY —CITY UNIVERSITY OF NEW YORK, City College, Morris R Cohen Library, North Academic Center, Convent Ave & 137th St, New York, 10031. Barbara J Dunlap, Archivist
Holdings: // Mss Pix Phonorecords
Notes: Ira Marion (Ira Silberstein), a 1930 graduate of City College, was a voluminous writer of radio scripts for WJZ, The Blue Network, and ABC. The Collection consists of over 2000 scripts for such programs as "Milton Cross Presents," "Crime Doesn't Pay," "The Black Museum," etc. There is also some personal correspondence and correspondence with the networks. Collection is partially inventoried.

MARIONETTES see Puppets and Puppet Plays

MARITAIN, JACQUES

DC —GEORGETOWN UNIVERSITY, Library, Special Collections Div, 37 & O Sts NW, Washington, 20057. George M Barringer, Special Collections Librn; Nicholas B Sheetz, Mss Librn
Holdings: Mss Pix
Notes: Papers of Julia K Kernan, editor,

translator, and author of *Our Friend, Jacques Maritain - A Personal Memoir.* Miss Karnan was instrumental in establishing the French Book Club and later served on the editorial staff of Longmans, Green and Company and P J Kennedy and Sons. Among the papers are letters from Paul Claudel, Marie Belloc, and Francois Mauriac, as well as extensive correspondence from Jacques Maritain. Also incl are numerous photographs of such celebrities as Colette, Leon Bloy, Charles Peguy, Sigrid Undset and Marie Belloc Lowndes, in addition to photographs of Jacques Maritain used in *Our Friend.*

MARITIME DISASTERS

IL —CHICAGO HISTORICAL SOCIETY, Library, Clark St at North Ave, Chicago, 60614. Robert L Brubaker, Librn
Holdings: Cat
Notes: The J Norman Jensen Collection of Lake and River Disasters, 1679-1947. 8500 card entries.

NY —STATE UNIVERSITY OF NEW YORK, COLLEGE AT OSWEGO, Penfield Library, Oswego, 13126. Anne Commerton, Dir
Holdings: Cat Mss
Notes: Collection of data and newspapers, notes and correspondence for writing a book on shipwrecks on Lake Ontario and in particular, Oswego Harbor, by Richard F Palmer, Syracuse Newspapers reporter. Photographs accompanied this material but were removed to be added to our local history photograph collection. Eight inches of material.

MARITIME DISCOVERIES see Discovery and Exploration

MARITIME HISTORY

AK —ALASKA STATE LIBRARY, Alaska Historical Library Collection, Pouch G, Juneau, 99811. Phyllis Demuth, Readers Services Librn
Holdings: Vols (24,000) Cat Mss Maps Pix Slides Phonorecords Audiotapes Videotapes 16mm Films Microforms

CA —NATIONAL MARITIME MUSEUM, SAN FRANCISCO, J Porter Shaw Library, Golden Gate National Recreation Area, Fort Mason, San Francisco, 94123. David A Hull, Librn; Herbert Beckwith, Catalog Librn; Irene Stachura, Ref Librn; John Maounis, Photo Librn
Holdings: Vols (12,000) Mss Maps Pix Slides Microforms VF
Budget: ($4000)
Notes: Pacific Coast maritime history. The photo collection of 160,000 is partly cataloged and classified. The library has complete runs of *Merchant Vessels of US* and *Lloyd's Register of Shipping* to 1970. The collection is particularly strong on Pacific Coast and San Francisco maritime history. About 250 log books; scrapbooks. Ca 250 oral history interviews. 60 percent of books cataloged.

CT —TRINITY COLLEGE LIBRARY, Watkinson Library, 300 Summit St, Hartford, 06106. Jeffrey Kaimowitz, Cur
Holdings: Cat
Notes: Incl the Karl Vogel Collection.

CT —MYSTIC SEAPORT, MUSEUM, G W Blunt White Library, Greenmanville Ave, Mystic, 06355. Gerald E Morris, Librn
Holdings: Vols (40,000) Imprints Microforms
Budget: ($100,000)
Notes: American maritime history. The library is also a government depository for maritime materials with a subscription to 184 line items. Incl 400,000 mss, 4000 maps and charts, 30,000 ships' plans. Open to the public.

CT —YALE UNIVERSITY, Box 1603A, Yale Station, New Haven, 06520.

ME —MAINE MARITIME MUSEUM, Library and Archives, 963 Washington St, Bath, 04530. Nathan R Lipfert, Asst Cur
Holdings: Vols (5000) Cat Maps Pix Slides
Notes: The collection is limited primarily to

MARITIME HISTORY (cont.)

shipbuilding in Bath, Maine, and to a lesser extent Maine as a whole. The unique aspects of the collection of photographs of wooden shipbuilding and related trades, photographs of the vessels themselves, and a large collection of papers of a shipbuilding company in Bath active through the 19th century.

ME —ANTIQUE BOAT SOCIETY, Archives & Library, Learning Place, Manset, 04656. Admiral E R Welles, Cur
Holdings: Vols (200) Uncat Maps Pix
Notes: Data relative to mariner items that have aged 25 years or more, designs of boats and accessories, charts, pictures, books and sometimes original items themselves. This is a research library with no lending. Researchers should telephone (204) 244-5015 to make arrangements.

ME —WILLIAM A FARNSWORTH LIBRARY & ART MUSEUM, 19 Elm St, Rockland, 04841. Marius B Peladeau, Dir
Holdings: Vols (4000) Cat Pix Microfilms
Notes: Emphasis on American and European fine and decorative arts of all periods (largely modern). Other areas include marine history and Maine history (local); illustrated books and rare books also a part of our collection, which has its own catalog. Also, Louise Nevelsen, N C Wyeth Archives.

ME —PENOBSCOT MARINE MUSEUM, Library, Church St, Searsport, 04974. Charles Howard, Librn
Holdings: Vols (4000) Cat Mss Maps Pix
Budget: ($5000)
Notes: Maine maritime history, log books, journals, diaries, marine charts, ships registers, photographs, archives & mss, and books relating to world navigation. The greatest emphasis is placed on the Penobscot Bay region.

MD —STEAMSHIP HISTORICAL SOCIETY OF AMERICA (SSHSA), University of Baltimore Library, 1420 Maryland Ave, Baltimore, 21201.
Holdings: Vols (3500) Cat Maps Pix Slides 16mm Films
Budget: ($15,000)
Notes: Powered Maritime Transportation Collection. Photo bank of over 15,000 negatives and 25,000 prints, arranged alphabetically by vessel name. Extensive blueprint and tracing collection. Collection documents history of steam navigation from the early 19th century to the present. Emphasis upon East Coast American vessels of late 19th and early 20th centuries and upon transatlantic vessels. Some coverage of Great Lakes and inland river steamboats. Very little about sailing vessels. No published catalog. Books listed in OCLC. Collection located at University of Baltimore. Address for Society is 414 Pelton Ave, Staten Island, NY 10310, attention: Alice S Wilson, Secretary and SSHSA Librn.

MD —WASHINGTON COLLEGE, Clifton M Miller Library, Chestertown, 21620.
Notes: Archive-library of source material, incl primary sources in microform, on the Chesapeake Bay during the American Revolutinary period.

MD —SEAFARER'S HARRY LUNDEBERG SCHOOL OF SEAMANSHIP, Paul Hall Library and Maritime Museum, Piney Point, 20674. Janice McAteer Smolek, Librn
Holdings: Vols Cat Mss Pix Slides Audiotapes Videotapes 16mm Films Filmstrips Microforms
Notes: Special collection on maritime studies incl books, mss, periodicals, audiovisuals, and archival materials pertaining to maritime history and maritime labor union history and vocational skills required by the maritime industry. Incl some rare books.

MD —CALVERT MARINE MUSEUM, Library, PO Box 97, Solomons, 20688.
Holdings: Vols (2000) Uncat Mss Maps Pix Slides Audiotapes
Notes: Local maritime history, vessel lists of boats built in county; lists of vessels owned in Calvert County, ships papers, half models, building plans and blueprints, artifacts, shipyard papers (correspondence, material lists, etc) and contracts.
See also entries under Shipwreck and US - History - War of 1812.

MA —AUBURN PUBLIC LIBRARY, Court & Spring Sts, Auburn, 04210. Nann Blaine Hilyard, Dir; Lois C Wagner, Ref Librn
Holdings: Vols 100 Cat
Notes: Edgar J Wessen Collection, incl rare materials.

MA —STURGIS LIBRARY, Rte 6A, Barnstable, 02630. Susan R Klein, Chief Librn
Holdings: Vols (1000) Mss Pix Periodicals
Budget: ($500)
Notes: Massachusetts maritime history. The Henry Crocker Kittredge Maritime History Collection contains vols, mss, documents and photographs, many of great rarity, related to the history of maritime life of Barnstable County incl its shipmasters, shipbuilding and fishing industries. Major emphasis of materials is on 18th, 19th and early 20th centuries. The core of the collection was provided through an estate gift of Henry Crocker Kittredge, Harvard scholar and maritime historian (1890-1967).

MA —BEDFORD FREE PUBLIC LIBRARY, 613 Pleasant St, Bedford, 02740. Paul A Cyr, Cur of the Melville Room
Holdings: Vols 1020 Cat Mss Pix
Notes: One of the nation's most extensive collections (72,000 pieces) on American whaling. Incl all forms of documents used in the industry, over 40,000 mss. Library has a printed list of its logbooks and a seamen's card file of men who sailed from New Bedford Customs District contains 250,000 names. Library has published an addendum to "Starbuck" and "Whaling Masters," and "Birth of a Whaleship," 1964, both by Reginald B Hegarty.

MA —MASSACHUSETTS INSTITUTE OF TECHNOLOGY MUSEUM, Hart Nautical Collections, 77 Massachusetts Ave, Rm 5-329, Cambridge, 02139. John W Waterhouse, Cur
Holdings: Vols (800) Cat Maps Pix
Notes: Ship and marine engineering development. Museum is under jurisdiction of MIT's Dept of Ocean Engineering. Collection incl various collections of prints and photographs of ships and yachts; working drawings from the Herreshoff Manufacturing Co, 1870-1945, and of the George Lawley and Son Corp; working drawings and models from the Munro, Owen, and Paine Collections.

MA —MARINE MUSEUM AT FALL RIVER, INC, Library, PO Box 1147, Battleship Cove, Fall River, 02722.
Holdings: Vols 1250 Uncat Maps Pix Slides Microforms
Notes: No photocopying.

MA —ESSEX INSTITUTE, James Duncan Phillips Library, 132-34 Essex St, Salem, 01970. Prudence K Backman, Manuscript Librn
Holdings: Mss
Notes: Correspondence, business papers, account books and logbooks documenting Essex County commercial activity from late 18th and 19th centuries. Collection incl records of Elias Hasket Derby, George Crowninshield & Sons, Stone Silsbee & Pickman, Nathaniel L Rogers & Brothers, Nathaniel Silsbee and family, Ropes Emmerton & Co, Benjamin Pickman and Philip English.

MA —PEABODY MUSEUM OF SALEM, Phillips Library, E India Sq, Salem, 01970. Gregor Trinkaus-Randall, Librn
Holdings: Vols (100,000) Cat Mss Maps Pix
Notes: Maritime history of New England. No published indexes; listed in Hamer's Guide to Archives...

NH —STRAWBERY BANKE, Thayer Cumings Historical Reference Library, Portsmouth, 03801. Nicole R Osborn, Librn
Holdings: Vols (2850) Cat Mss Maps Pix Microforms
Budget: ($1900)
Notes: The Library is a small, highly specialized library with holdings in American art, architecture and decorative arts. The collection is especially strong in the American decorative arts, with additional concentration in European decorative arts. In addition, the collection contains books on American painting, American architecture, archaeology, technology, maritime history and boatbuilding, landscape gardening and design, as well as books on local and regional history and social and material culture of the 17th-19th centuries. Collection of mss microfilm and documents is related to important properties and personages of Portsmouth and the surrounding area.

NY —STATE UNIVERSITY OF NEW YORK, Maritime College, Stephen B Luce Library, Fort Schuyler, Bronx, 10465. Richard H Corson, Librn
Holdings: Vols (68,000) Cat Maps Pix Slides Phonorecords Audiotapes Videotapes 16 mm Films Filmstrips
Budget: ($90,000)
Notes: Incl history of ships with special emphasis on US sailing ships of the 19th century. Extensive holdings in periodical literature wih long and complete runs of many titles.

NY —WHALING MUSEUM SOCIETY, Cold Spring Harbor Whaling Museum, Main St, Cold Spring Harbor, 11724. Robert D Farwell, Dir
Holdings: Cat Mss Maps Pix
Notes: Library of bound and printed books covers Cold Spring Harbor whaling industry, in general, and maritime affairs. Archives contain thousands of original documents concerning whaling activities, the Cold Spring Harbor Whaling Company, and the extensive maritime coastal trade conducted out of Cold Spring Harbor after the whaling era (latter 1800s). Considerable material deals with the Jones and Hewlett families, important in both local commerce and Long Island and New York affairs.

NY —WEBB INSTITUTE OF NAVAL ARCHITECTURE, Livingston Library, Crescent Beach Rd, Glen Cove, 11542. Fred H Forrest, Librn
Holdings: Vols 625 Cat
Notes: Marine history, emphasizing ship history. Collection of ship plans. Access by appointment only.

NY —US MERCHANT MARINE ACADEMY, Schuyler Otis Bland Memorial Library, Steamboat Rd, Kings Point, 11024. Stephen R Wiist, Acting Chief Librn
Holdings: Vols (130,000) Cat Mss Maps Pix Slides Phonorecords Microforms
Budget: ($75,000)
Notes: All aspects of maritime affairs.

NY —NEW YORK HISTORICAL SOCIETY, Library, 170 Central Park W, New York, 10024. James Gregory, Librn
Holdings: Mss
Notes: Incl original mss, illustrative materials, etc.

NY —NEW YORK PUBLIC LIBRARY, Research Libraries, General Research Division, Fifth Ave & 42 St, New York, 10018. Rodney Phillips, Chief
Holdings: Vols (2,225,000) Cat Maps Pix Microforms
Budget: ($775,718)

NY —SEAMEN'S CHURCH INSTITUTE OF NEW YORK, Joseph Conrad Library, 15 State St, New York, 10004. Bonnie Golightly, Librn
Holdings: Vols (23,500) Cat Pix
Budget: ($8500)
Notes: Merchant seaman, merchant ships, voyages, navigation, marine engineering, shipbuilding. Large collection of ship registers: Lloyd's Register of Shipping, a partial coverage of the years 1764-1865 in reprints, complete coverage for the years 1877 to date; American Bureau of Shipping, 1916 to date; Merchant Vessels of the US, 1891 to date. Society of Naval Architects and Marine Engineers Transactions, vol 1, 1893 to date. The picture file consists mostly of photographs of merchant ships. This is supplemented by scrapbooks. The index to the pictures, scrapbooks, books and vertical file are in one subject catalog. We subscribe to and keep for several years numerous maritime periodicals. The maritime history collection incl sailing ships as well as steamships.

OH —RUTHERFORD B HAYES LIBRARY, 1337 Hayes Ave, Fremont, 43420. Watt P

MARITIME HISTORY (cont.)

Marchman, Dir
Holdings: Vols 500 Cat Mss Maps Pix Slides
Notes: The Great Lakes Marine Collection, incl the Capt Frank E Hamilton Collection; Great Lakes boats and shipping. Incl 300 charts; over 20,000 pictures (with 2500 negatives, 30 glass plates). Index and findings aids with the collection.

PA —PHILADELPHIA MARITIME MUSEUM, Library, 321 Chestnut St, Philadelphia, 19106. Dorothy H Mueller, Librn
Holdings: Vols (8000) Cat Mss Maps Pix Slides 16mm Films
Notes: Maritime history of Bay and River Delaware and of the port of Philadelphia. Includes shipbuilding and shipbuilders on the Delaware River, mercantile activity, recreational activity, maritime-related organizations, institutions and people, development of Philadelphia as a port, vessel register 1878-1970s. Also, artifacts and prints.

RI —US NAVAL WAR COLLEGE, Historical Collection & Museum, Newport, 02841. Anthony S Nicolosi, Dir; Evelyn Cherpak, Cur
Holdings: Mss
Notes: Collections incl over 200,000 separate pieces; chiefly papers of naval officers and records of organizations associated with the US Navy, the Naval War College, the college's major study areas, and the Navy in the Narragansett Bay region; oral history collection; Naval War College Archives, 1884-present; records of conferences held at the College; newspaper collections dealing with naval themes and military conflicts.

RI —BROWN UNIVERSITY, John Carter Brown Library, Providence, 02912. Norman Fiering, Librn; Everett C Wilkie Jr, Bibliographer; Susan Danforth, Cur Maps & Prints
Notes: Extensive collection, incl works on navigation, shipbuilding, mariners' health, and explorations accomplished by ship.

RI —PROVIDENCE PUBLIC LIBRARY, 150 Empire St, Providence, 02903. Lance J Bauer, Special Collections Librn
Holdings: Vols 225 // Uncat Pix
Notes: A fine collection of books, technical drawings, photographs, pamphlets and other ephemera concerned with naval architecture from the library of Alfred S Brownell. An important highlight of this collection are 11 ship models of Atlantic fishing craft, 9 of which were built by Brownell; these models are permanently on display. Incl 550 technical drawings, photographs, indexed.

TX —ROSENBERG LIBRARY, 2310 Sealy Ave, Galveston, 77550.
Holdings: Vols 1850
Notes: Focuses largely on the Gulf of Mexico. Incl rare books and maritime maps. Non-circulating.

VA —MARINERS MUSEUM, Library, Newport News, 23606. Ardie L Kelly, Librn
Holdings: Vols (60,000) Cat Mss Maps Pix Slides
Notes: Incl collections of over 150,000 photographs of merchant ships, naval vessels, sailing ships, lighthouses, portraits of naval men, harbors, canals, etc, and maps, ships' papers, and log books. Catalogs of various parts of the collection published by G K Hall, Boston.

WI —MILWAUKEE PUBLIC LIBRARY, 814 W Wisconsin Ave, Milwaukee, 53233. Donald J Sager, City Librn
Holdings: Vols 1500 Cat Mss Maps Pix Slides
Notes: The Great Lakes Marine Collection consists of Runge Marine Collection, Wilson Marine Collection, and other collections on Great Lakes Marine History. Has data on about 85,000 ships and more than 20,000 pictures of Great Lake vessels. Complete runs of reference material such as US List of merchant vessels, Greens, etc. Extensive collection of Great Lake charts.

BC —MARITIME MUSEUM OF BRITISH COLUMBIA, 28 Bastion Sq, Victoria, V8W

1H9, Can. C H Shaw, Dir
Holdings: Vols (2500) Cat Mss Maps Pix Slides Microforms
Budget: ($110,000)
Notes: Also 4000 registration cards; 6000 pictures.

NS —NOVA SCOTIA MUSEUM, Library, 1747 Summer St, Halifax, B3H 3A6, Can. M S Whiteside, Librn
Notes: Emphasis is on social history.

MARITIME LABOR see Merchant Seamen

MARITIME NEWSPAPERS see Newspapers, Maritime

MARITIME TRADES

NY —WHALING MUSEUM SOCIETY, Cold Spring Harbor Whaling Museum, Main St, Cold Spring Harbor, 11724. Robert D Farwell, Dir
Holdings: Cat Mss Maps Pix
Notes: Library of bound and printed books covers Cold Spring Harbor whaling industry, in general, and maritime affairs. Archives contain thousands of original documents concerning whaling activities, the Cold Spring Harbor Whaling Company, and the extensive maritime coastal trade conducted out of Cold Spring Harbor after the whaling era (latter 1800s). Considerable material deals with the Jones and Hewlett families, important in both local commerce and Long Island and New York affairs.

NY —SEAMEN'S CHURCH INSTITUTE OF NEW YORK, Joseph Conrad Library, 15 State St, New York, 10004. Bonnie Golightly, Librn
Holdings: Vols (23,500) Cat Pix
Budget: ($8500)
Notes: Merchant seaman, merchant ships, voyages, navigation, marine engineering, shipbuilding. Large collection of ship registers: *Lloyd's Register of Shipping*, a partial coverage of the years 1764-1865 in reprints, complete coverage for the years 1877 to date; *American Bureau of Shipping*, 1916 to date; *Merchant Vessels of the US*, 1891 to date. *Society of Naval Architects and Marine Engineers Transactions*, vol 1, 1893 to date. The picture file consists mostly of photographs of merchant ships. This is supplemented by scrapbooks. The index to the pictures, scrapbooks, books and vertical file are in one subject catalog. We subscribe to and keep for several years numerous maritime periodicals. The maritime history collection incl sailing ships as well as steamships.

MARKAM, WOLFE, 1892-1980

NY —CORNELL UNIVERSITY LIBRARIES, Collection of Regional History, Dept of Manuscripts and Univ Archives, Ithaca, 14853.
Notes: Architect. Papers, 1911-1975; 11 ft.

MARKETING

AL —UNIVERSITY OF ALABAMA, Business Library, Box 2937, University, 35486. Dorothy Eady Brown, Librn; Linda Suttle Harris, Ref Librn and Data Base Searcher
Holdings: Vols (105,000) Cat Microforms
Budget: ($60,000)
Notes: Incl 90,000 corporation reports and 38,500 microforms.

CA —UNIVERSITY OF CALIFORNIA, BERKELEY, Giannini Foundation of Agricultural Economics, Library, 248 Giannini Hall, Berkeley, 94720. Grace Dote, Librn
Holdings: Vols (18,000) Cat Mss Maps Microforms
Notes: Noncirculating collection. No interlibrary loans. Also about 124,000 unbound vols. Open to graduate students and faculties of universities and colleges, research workers and interested public. Mostly English language materials, primarily 1900 to date. Card catalog published by G K Hall Co. *Dictionary Catalog of the Giannini*

Foundation of Agricultural Economics Library, Univ of California, 12 vols (Holdings thru 7/71).

CA —UNIVERSITY OF CALIFORNIA, LOS ANGELES, Graduate School of Management Library, UCLA Campus, Los Angeles, 90024. Robert Bellanti, Head Librn
Holdings: Vols (128,000) Cat Mss Microforms
Notes: The

CA —UNIVERSITY OF SOUTHERN CALIFORNIA, Crocker Business Library, Hoffman Hall, University Park, Los Angeles, 90007. Judith A Truelson, Head Librn
Holdings: Vols (100,000) Cat Microforms
Notes: The Roy P Crocker Library of Business Administration, located in Hoffman Hall, houses more than 100,000 volumes and regularly receives approximately 1500 trade, financial, economics, labor, and general business periodicals and newspapers. The areas of subject concentration include business economics, finance and investments, general management/management theory, international business, finance and management, marketing/food marketing, and quantitative business analysis.

CA —ALAMEDA COUNTY LIBRARY SYSTEM, Business & Government Library, 2201 Broadway, Oakland, 94612. David Lewallen, Manager
Holdings: Vols (10,000) Cat Maps Microforms
Budget: ($50,000)

CO —STONE & WEBSTER ENGINEERING CORP, Technical Information Center, PO Box 5406, Denver, 80217. Sue Newhams, Librn
Holdings: Vols (5000) Cat Microforms
Notes: The subject emphasis of this collection is centered around the power industry and energy resources.

CT —LIFE INSURANCE MARKETING & RESEARCH ASSOCIATION, Library, 170 Sigourney St, PO Box 208, Hartford, 06141. William J Mortimer, Mgr, Library and Reference Services
Holdings: Vols 5000 Cat Audiotapes
Budget: ($10,000)
Notes: Incl 150-drawer vertical file on life insurance marketing and 250 audiotapes.

DC —EDISON ELECTRIC INSTITUTE, Library-8th Floor, 1111 19th St NW, Washington, 20036. Ethel Tiberg, Mgr, Library Services
Holdings: Vols (13,321) Cat Maps Pix Microforms

IL —AMERICAN MARKETING ASSOCIATION, Information Center, 250 S Wacker Drive, Suite 200, Chicago, 60606. Lorraine Caliendo, Librn
Holdings: Vols (3000) Cat
Budget: ($7000)
Notes: Incl marketing research, marketing management, advertising and salesmanship as they relate to the marketing process. Complete collection of AMA publications: *Journal of Marketing, Journal of Marketing Research, Marketing News*, proceedings of annual conferences, bibliographies and monographs on marketing subjects.

IL —J WALTER THOMPSON CO, Information Center, 875 N Michigan Ave, Chicago, 60611. Edward G Strable, Dir
Holdings: Vols 700 Cat Microforms
Notes: Importance of collection is in data file of fugitive materials-reports, clippings, releases, articles, studies-of appprox 50 drawers covering marketing information on most consumer products and services. Emphasis on currentness, not history. Indexing and organization make for rapid access.

IL —ARCHER DANIELS MIDLAND CO, Library, 4666 Faries Parkway, Decatur, 62525. Richard E Wallace, Manager, Information Services; Karen E Perman, Librn
Holdings: Vols 8000 Cat Maps Slides 16mm Films Microforms
Notes: Incl all aspects of foods--processing, economics, nutrition, science, technology, statistics, research, marketing, etc. Special interest in foods derived from plant materials. Incl 100 maps, 1200 slides, 105 films, over 2000 microforms, patents, and research reports.

MARKETING (cont.)

IN —MILES LABORATORIES, Library
Resources and Services, 1127 Myrtle St, PO
Box 40, Elkhart, 46515. Allam Hagopian,
Mgr
Holdings: Vols (16,500) Cat Audiotapes
Microforms
Notes: Incl files of pharmaceutical product
advertising pieces, extensive literature files
on company related drugs; domestic and
international marketing files. 32,000 bound
periodicals.

IN —PURDUE UNIVERSITY LIBRARIES,
Graduate School of Management, Krannert
Library, West Lafayette, 47907. Gordon
Law, Librn
Holdings: Vols (142,727) Cat Microforms
Budget: ($69,700)
Notes: An extensive marketing collection
with both current and historical materials.

MA —HARVARD UNIVERSITY, Graduate
School of Business Administration, Baker
Library, Soldiers Field, Boston, 02163. Mary
V Chatfield, Librn; Florence Bartoshesky,
Cur of Manuscripts and Archives

MA —STATE STREET BANK & TRUST CO,
Library, 225 Franklin St, Boston, 02110.
Debra Wahl, Librn
Holdings: Uncat

MA —BOSTON COLLEGE LIBRARIES,
Thomas P O'Neill Library, Chestnut Hill,
02167. John D J Slinn, Librn of the Central
Library
Holdings: Vols 62,000 Cat Maps Audiotapes
Filmstrips Microforms
Budget: ($120,000)

MI —OAKLAND COMMUNITY COLLEGE,
Auburn Hills Campus, Learning Resources
Center, 2900 Featherstone Rd, Auburn Hills,
48057. Eugene F Larson, Dept Chairman
Holdings: Vols 300 Cat Slides Phonorecords
Audiotapes 16mm Films Filmstrips

MI —D'ARCY, MACMANUS, MASIUS,
Library Information Center, 1725 N
Woodward, PO Box 811, Bloomfield Hills,
48303. Lois W Collet, Dir, Library
Information Services; Harriet Siden, Art
Librn
Holdings: Vols 3000 Cat Mss Pix
Microforms

NE —NORTHERN NATURAL GAS CO,
2223 Dodge St, Omaha, 68102. Marvin E
Lauver, Librn
Holdings: Vols 750 Cat

NY —BERNARD M BARUCH COLLEGE
(CUNY), Library, 156 E 25 St, New York,
10010. Alan Weiner, Head of Reference

NY —CONFERENCE BOARD, Information
Service Library, 845 Third Ave, New York,
10022. Tamsen M Hernandez, Dir
Holdings: Vols 25,000 Cat Microforms
Notes: Heavily directed to collection of
government materials and corporate data.

NY —INTERNATIONAL PAPER CO,
Corporate Information Center, 77 W 45 St,
New York, 10036. Elizabeth Skerritt,
Corporate Librn
Holdings: Vols 110 Cat Maps Pix Slides
Microforms
Notes: Extensive statistics and VF on paper
industry.

NY —DIRECT MAIL/MARKETING
ASSOCIATION, Information Central, 6 E
43 St, New York, 10017. Glenda Sasho, Dir
of Information Central & Research
Holdings: Vols (350) Cat Slides Audiotapes
Notes: Slide/tape presentations of award-
winning advertising direct marketing
advertising campaigns. Incl 3000 award
portfolios of direct marketing campaigns.
Restricted use.

NY —NEW YORK PUBLIC LIBRARY,
Research Libraries, Economic & Public
Affairs Div, Fifth Ave & 42 St, New York,
10018. Edward DiRoma, Chief
Holdings: Vols (1,500,000) Cat Microforms

NY —SALES & MARKETING EXECUTIVES
INTERNATIONAL, Marketing Information
Center, 330 W 42nd St, New York, 10036.
Alayne J Ambrogio, Dir
Holdings: Vols (600) Cat
Budget: ($1500)
Notes: Extensive collection incl many
textbooks. For members only.

NY —SALES & MARKETING
MANAGEMENT, Library, 633 Third Ave,
New York, 10017. John D Roberts, Librn
Holdings: Vols (500) Uncat

†NY —TECHNICAL CAREER INSTITUTE
LIBRARY, 320 W 31st Street, New York,
10001. Michael Brent, Librn
Holdings: Vols (3500)

NC —GREENSBORO PUBLIC LIBRARY,
Business Library, 201 Greene St, Drawer
X-4, Greensboro, 27402. Lebby B Lamb,
Business Librn
Holdings: Vols (6000) Cat Microforms
Budget: ($12,000)

NC —R J REYNOLDS TOBACCO CO,
Marketing Intelligence Div, 203 Reynolds
Bldg, Winston-Salem, 27102. Anita Scism,
Sr Information Center Adminr
Holdings: Vols 1900 Cat Maps Slides
Audiotapes Videotapes Microforms
Notes: Emphasis on tobacco and marketing.

OH —CLEVELAND PUBLIC LIBRARY,
Business, Economics and Labor Department,
325 Superior Ave, Cleveland, 44114. Joan
Sorger, Head
Holdings: Cat
Notes: Worldwide statistical data incl
Statistical Reference Index and *Index to
International Statistics* microfiches.
Extensive circulating collection of marketing
texts. Well developed export/import
collection incl relevant services. Business
International and OECD publications
complete.

RI —BRYANT COLLEGE, Edith M Hodgson
Memorial Library, Rte 7, Douglas Pike,
Smithfield, 02917. John P Hannon, Dir
Holdings: Vols (103,000) Cat Phonorecords
Audiotapes Videotapes 16mm Films
Filmstrips Microforms
Budget: ($175,000)
Notes: Incl 6000 bound periodical vols, 250
phonorecords, 220 audiotapes, 120
videotapes, 30 16mm films, 150 filmstrips
and 7500 microforms.

WY —US AIR FORCE INSTITUTE OF
TECHNOLOGY, Library, Dept 9 Bldg 831,
FE, Warren AFB, 82001. Patricia A
Johnson, Librn
Holdings: Vols (7000) Cat Microforms
Budget: ($9000)
Notes: The Library supports graduate
programs for students (Air Force Missile-
Combat Crewmen) seeking a Master of
Business Administration Degree. Civilian
students and other military personnel are
also admitted.

MB —UNIVERSITY OF MANITOBA,
Faculty of Administrative Studies,
Administrative Studies Library, Winnipeg,
R3T 2N2, Can. Judith Head, Librn
Holdings: Vols (15,000) Cat Microfiche
Notes: Incl 11,000 microfiche, cataloged;
annual reports of 800 companies.

MARKETING RESEARCH

IL —J WALTER THOMPSON CO,
Information Center, 875 N Michigan Ave,
Chicago, 60611. Edward G Strable, Dir
Holdings: Vols 100 Cat Microforms
Notes: Importance of collection is in data
file of fugitive materials-reports, clippings,
releases, articles, studies-of appprox 50
drawers covering marketing information on
most consumer products and services.
Emphasis on currentness, not history.
Indexing and organization make for rapid
access.

NY —ADVERTISING RESEARCH
FOUNDATION, Information Center, 3 E
54 St, New York, 10022. Elizabeth R
Proudfit, Mgr
Holdings: Vols (3000) Cat

MARKHAM, DEAN

†MA —JOHN F KENNEDY LIBRARY,
Columbia Point, Boston, 02125. Dan H Fenn
Jr, Dir
Holdings: // Cat Mss
Notes: The White House staff files of Dean
Markham, Executive Director, President's
Advisory Commission on Narcotic and Drug
Abuse, 1962-1965. 20 linear ft of mss.
Holdings are described in "Historical

Materials in the John F Kennedy Library."
Copies may be obtained by writing the
Research Archivist.

MARKS, GRAUMAN

LA —NEW ORLEANS PUBLIC LIBRARY,
Louisiana Div, 219 Loyola Ave, New
Orleans, 70140. Collin B Hamer Jr, Head;
Brenda M Osbey, Library Associate
Holdings: Cat Maps Pix
Notes: Louisiana and New Orleans Picture
File Collection ranges from the late 19th
century-date and incl the following separate
collections: Alexander Allison (ca 1898-
1951, 337 pieces); Charles Franck (ca 1920-
50, 170 pieces); Leda Plauche (ca 1935-53,
220 pieces); C Milo Williams (ca 1910, 85
pieces); Wilson S Howell (ca 1890, 49
pieces); Grauman Marks (ca 1960, 268
pieces); Robert Tallant (ca 1940-50, 70
pieces); Robert E Tracy (1959, 87 pieces);
Anthony J Flaherty (ca 1970-84, 83 pieces);
George F Mugnier (1880-1920, 186 pieces);
Color Slides (ca 1945-date, 500 pieces); 30,
000 photographs incl 500 color slides and
104 negatives. Use of the material is
restricted to on-site research. Publication
must be accompanied by credit cut line.

MARKS, PRINTERS' see Printers' Marks

MARKS, ROBERT WALTER

SC —COLLEGE OF CHARLESTON
LIBRARY, Special Collections Dept,
Charleston, 29401.
Notes: Papers, 1890-1980. Correspondence,
mss, published material, notes, and
photographs reflects Marks' multifarious
career in Charleston, New York, and Europe
as journalist covering a wide variety of fields,
professor of philosophy at the New School
for Social Research, author of numerous
books on mathematics and technological
developments, and writer of fiction. Among
the important correspondents are Ruth
Benedict, Laura Brogg, Alexander Calder,
Olin Downes, James Harold Easterby,
Buckminster Fuller, Barry Goldwater, Mark
Harris, Lewis Hine, J Edgar Hoover, Horace
Kallen, Deborah Kerr, Sophia Loren, Gypsy
Rose Lee, Jane Mansfield, Elsa Maxwell,
Kim Novak, Harrison Randolph, Pierre
Salinger, Edward Steichen, Alfred Stieglitz,
Thomas Tobias and Norbert Weiner.

MARKS BROTHERS

ON —METROPOLITAN TORONTO
LIBRARY, Theatre Dept, 789 Yonge St,
Toronto, M4W 2G8, Can. Heather
McCallum, Head
Notes: Special collections relating to the
history of the performing arts in Canada incl
the records of the Taverner Company which
played Eastern Canada and the United
States in the late 19th century, Toronto's
Grand Opera House, the Marks Brothers
touring company, film actor Ned Sparks, the
Canadian-born actress Judith Evelyn, Crest
Theatre (Toronto), the Canadian Players,
Montreal Repertory Theatre, dancer/teacher
Boris Volkoff, The Dumbells, the Canadian
all-soldier concert party which originated in
France in 1917, and vaudeville performer
Charles Manny.

MARKS IN PAPER see Watermarks
(Paper)

MARKSMANSHIP see Shooting

MARLATT, ABBY LILLIAN

KS —KANSAS STATE UNIVERSITY,
Library, Special Collections & University
Archives, Manhattan, 66506. Antonia Q
Pigno, Coordr; John J Vander Velde, Librn;
Anthony R Crawford, Univ Archivist
Holdings: Vols 4500 Cat Mss
Budget: ($10,000)
Notes: Cookbooks and related items on
home economics, nutrition and domestic
economy. Nucleus of the collection is from

MARLATT, ABBY LILLIAN (cont.)

the Abby Lillian Marlatt collection augmented by a sizable bequest from the estate of Clementine Paddleford. Includes about 600 volumes of rare cookbooks from the 16th, 17th, and 18th centuries as well as unprocessed papers (scrapbooks, recipe files and correspondence of Clementine Paddleford). A chronological bibliography is available for the pre-1900 portion of the collection: *The Kansas State University Receipt Book and Household Manual* (1968) by G A Rudolph.

MARLBOROUGH, JOHN CHURCHILL, DUKE OF

KS —UNIVERSITY OF KANSAS, Kenneth Spencer Research Library, Special Collections Dept, Lawrence, 66045. Alexandra Mason, Librn
Holdings: Vols 300 Cat Mss
Notes: In addition to Marlborough holdings throughout the 18th century collections, the department has particular strength in satire and panegyric on John Churchill, Duke of Marlborough, in the Robert Horn Collection (over 150 vols). See Hyde, Ann, *The Queen's General: John Churchill, First Duke of Marlborough, 1650-1722, an exhibition... in the Kenneth Spencer Research Library* (Lawrence: Univsersity of Kansas Libraries) 1972. Noncirculating.

MARLOWE, JULIA

CA —UNIVERSITY OF CALIFORNIA, DAVIS, Shields Library, Dept of Special Collections, Davis, 95616. Donald Kunitz, Head; C Danial Elliott, Asst Head
Holdings: Uncat Mss Pix
Notes: Photographs, clippings, and correspondence of personalities of American and British theatre in the 19th and 20th centuries, such as Edwin Booth, Joseph Jefferson, Julia Marlowe, E H Sothern, Ellen Terry, Henry Irving, McKee Rankin, Fanny Davenport, and Zero Mostel.

MARNEY, CARLYLE

NC —DUKE UNIVERSITY, William R Perkins Library, Manuscript Dept, Durham, 27706. Ellen Gartrell, Cur of Mss
Holdings: Cat Mss
Notes: Methodist Church Papers (records of local and regional units) also many personal and professional papers of clergy, missionaries and laymen, 19th-20th centuries, eg Methodist John Lakin Brasher (holiness movement leader), Carlyle Marney (Southern Baptist minister), Methodist Bishop James Cannon, missionary Martha Foster Crawford.

MARONITES

†NJ —ANTIOCHIAN ORTHODOX CHRISTIAN ARCHDIOCESE OF NORTH AMERICA, Library, 358 Mountain Rd, Englewood, 07631.
Notes: History of Arab Orthodox Christians in North America.
†OH —SAINT EPHREM EDUCATIONAL CENTER LIBRARY, 1555 South Meridian Rd, Youngstown, 44511.
Notes: History of Maronite Catholics in America.

MAROONS

PA —LIBRARY COMPANY OF PHILADELPHIA, 1314 Locust St, Philadelphia, 19107. Edwin Wolf II, Librn; Kenneth Finkel, Cur of Prints
Holdings: Cat

MARQUAND-SEDGWICK FAMILY

CT —YALE UNIVERSITY, Box 1603A, Yale Station, New Haven, 06520.
Holdings: Cat Mss
MA —BOSTON UNIVERSITY, Mugar Memorial Library, Special Collections Dept, 771 Commonwealth Ave, Boston, 02215. Howard B Gotlieb, Dir
Holdings: Cat Mss Pix
Notes: Mss, correspondence, etc collected in depth; incl publications by or about. Primarily Marquand-Sedgwick Family Papers 1911-1960.
MA —HARVARD UNIVERSITY LIBRARY, Cambridge, 02138.
Holdings: Cat Mss
NV —UNIVERSITY OF NEVADA, RENO, University Library, Special Collections Dept, Reno, 89557. Robert E Blesse, Head
Holdings: // Vols (50) Cat Other appearances 100 Cat
Notes: Includes individual works by author in all editions including translations; also prefaces, introductions, published correspondence, appearances in anthologies, periodicals, etc. Bibliographical research collection, part of Modern Authors Collection.

MARQUIS, DON

†NY —COLUMBIA UNIVERSITY LIBRARIES, Butler Library, Rare Book and Manuscript Library, 535 W 114 St, New York, 10027.
Notes: Books, letters, papers, mss, memorabilia, etc.

MARRIAGE

NY —YWCA NATIONAL BOARD, Library, 726-730 Broadway, New York, 10012. Elizabeth Norris, Librn
Holdings: Vols (3000) Cat Mss
Budget: ($2400)
Notes: Women and their contemporary interests.
OH —CLEVELAND PUBLIC LIBRARY, Social Sciences Department, 325 Superior Ave, Cleveland, 44114. Thelma Morris, Head
Notes: Incl books and periodicals on personal relationships, the family, and sex relations.
OH —OHIO STATE UNIVERSITY, Social Work Library, 1947 N College Rd, Columbus, 43210. Toyo S Kawakami, Librn
Holdings: Vols (46,410) Cat
Budget: ($11,960)
Notes: VF incl approx 4500 pamphlets, arranged by LC subject headings. 278 serial titles on social work, social and public service, crime and delinquency, corrections, criminal justice, marriage and the family, probation, and related topics, are received.
WI —UNIVERSITY OF WISCONSIN-STOUT, Library Learning Center, Menomonie, 54751. Philip Sawin Jr, Coll Develop Librn
Notes: One of eleven graduate programs in Marriage and Family Therapy in the United States. The program was begun in 1975. This special collection also includes video tapes of outstanding therapists and a specialized 16mm film collection.
ON —NATIONAL LIBRARY OF CANADA, 395 Wellington St, Ottawa, K1A 0N4, Can. Andre Preibish, Dir
Holdings: Vols 10,000
Notes: Includes 130 serial titles, theses, pamphlets, government publications relating to family and marriage. The following disciplines covered: anthropology, psychology and psychiatry, law, economics, religion, sociology, demography, education, political science and biology. Earliest title 1630.

MARRIAGE REGISTERS see Registers of Births, Etc.

MARRIAGE STATISTICS see Vital Statistics

MARRYAT, FREDERICK, 1792-1848

CA —UNIVERSITY OF CALIFORNIA, LOS ANGELES, Research Library, Dept of Special Collections, 405 Hilgard Ave, Los Angeles, 90024. Edward Shreeves, Chairman, Bibliographers Group; David S Zeidberg, Head
Holdings: Vols 250
Notes: 250 first and other editions of his books; 100 letters, documents, etc.

MARS (PLANET)

DC —SMITHSONIAN INSTITUTION LIBRARIES, National Air & Space Museum Branch, NASM Bldg, Sixth & Independence Ave SW, Washington, 20560. Frank A Pietropaoli, Branch Chief
Holdings: Vols (39,000) Cat Mss Maps Pix Slides Microforms
Notes: History of flight and aerospace development, incl biographical material on aviation pioneers, balloons and ballooning. Extensive photographic collection (600,000 pictures). Incl the Sherman Fairchild Collection of aeronautical photographs (transferred from the American Institute of Aeronautics and Astronautics). Also incl the Bella Landauer Aeronautical Sheet Music Collection (1500 pieces). 2000 films; 800,000 microforms; 9000 volumes bound.

MARSH, GEORGE E.

AZ —NORTHERN ARIZONA UNIVERSITY, Special Collection Library, CU Box 6022, Flagstaff, 86011. Peter M Whiteley, Coordr/Archivist; William Mullane, Librn
Notes: Charles Vogt Collection; papers of George E Marsh, who worked for the railroad in Arizona, and his family, incl deeds and mortgages for property in Phoenix, Ariz, 1891-1920.

MARSH, GEORGE PERKINS

VT —UNIVERSITY OF VERMONT, Guy W Bailey/David W Howe Library, Burlington, 05405. John Buehler, Asst Dir for Special Collections

MARSH, NGAIO

MA —BOSTON UNIVERSITY, Mugar Memorial Library, Special Collections Dept, 771 Commonwealth Ave, Boston, 02215. Howard B Gotlieb, Dir
Holdings: Cat Mss
Notes: Incl publications by or about.

MARSH, REGINALD

NY —NEW YORK PUBLIC LIBRARY, Fifth Ave & 42 St, New York, 10018.
Notes: Nearly 1000 drawings by the artist and book illustrator. An almost complete collection of original prints by the artist.

MARSH, W. WARD

OH —CLEVELAND PUBLIC LIBRARY, Literature Dept, 325 Superior Ave, Cleveland, 44114. Evelyn Ward, Head
Holdings: Cat Mss Pix
Notes: Personal library and other collections of W Ward Marsh, former film critic of the Cleveland *Plain Dealer*. The major categories of the bequest are: production stills which begin with the films of the Thirties and concentrate on those of the Forties and Fifties; an actor/actress file of folders for individual personalities containing studio and agent biographies, clippings and publicity photos; "pressbooks"--kits of advertising materials used for promoting a specific movie; a review file numbering over 20,000 critiques clipped from *Boxoffice, Variety*, and miscellaneous trade journals, incl Marsh's own reviews; and his correspondence. Also incl are a specially bound copy of the shooting script (accompanied by color transparencies) for Cecil B deMille's remake of *The Ten Commandments*; and a collection of more than 70046g X 56g glass slides--dating from the silent era--which were used by theatre owners to promote their upcoming attractions.

MARSHALL, BURKE

†MA —JOHN F KENNEDY LIBRARY, Columbia Point, Boston, 02125. Dan H Fenn

MARSHALL, BURKE (cont.)

Jr, Dir
Holdings: // Cat
Notes: Justice Department papers and some earlier and later files of Burke Marshall, Assistant Attorney General for Civil Rights, 1958-1965. Much on civil rights. 16 linear ft of mss. Holdings are described in "Historical Materials in the John F Kennedy Library." Copies may be obtained by writing the Research Archivist.
MA —JOHN F KENNEDY LIBRARY, Columbia Point, Boston, 02125. Henry J Gwiazda II, Cur
Notes: The Burke Marshall papers, 50 archives boxes re civil rights, 1961-1964 and the Bedford-Stuyvesant Development and Restoration Corporations; the Joseph Dolan papers, 1 box; the Thomas Johnston papers, 3 boxes; the James Mc Shane papers, 2 boxes; the Frank Mankiewicz papers, 15 boxes; and the Scott Rafferty papers, 4 boxes.

MARSHALL, CHARLES C.

DC —LIBRARY OF CONGRESS, Washington, 20540.
Holdings: Mss
Notes: His papers.

MARSHALL, EDISON, 1894-1967

MA —BOSTON UNIVERSITY, Mugar Memorial Library, Special Collections Dept, 771 Commonwealth Ave, Boston, 02215. Howard B Gotlieb, Dir
Holdings: // Cat Mss
Notes: Incl publications by.

MARSHALL, GEN. GEORGE CATLETT, 1880-1959

CA —HOOVER INSTITUTION ON WAR, REVOLUTION & PEACE, Stanford University, Stanford, 94305. Milorad M Drachkovitch, Archivist
Holdings: Maps Pix
Notes: Papers of Ambassador Philip D Sprouse, incl printed matter, news clippings, maps, invitations, programs of various events, diplomatic list, and photographs relating to the George C Marshall Mission to China, 1945-1946, activities of Philip D Sprouse as US Ambassador to Cambodia, 1962-1964, cultural and political aspects of recent Cambodian history. 2 ms boxes.
†VA —GEORGE C MARSHALL RESEARCH FOUNDATION AND LIBRARY, Drawer 920, Lexington, 24450. Royster Lyle Jr, Cur Collections
Holdings: Vols Cat Mss Maps Pix Microforms
Notes: The library was established as a research center for the study of 20th century military and diplomatic history, and international economic and political affairs. The collection focuses on the life and public service of Gen Marshall, with emphasis on the world wars, evolution of the national military establishment, post-war military occupation, and European recovery (Marshall Plan). Inventories, catalogs, and subject indexes are available.

MARSHALL, JOHN, 1776-1879

VA —COLLEGE OF WILLIAM AND MARY, Earl Gregg Swem Library, Williamsburg, 23185. Margaret C Cook, Cur of Manuscripts & Rare Books
Holdings: // Cat Mss
Notes: Collection incl letters to and from Marshall during his life (1775-1835), and his law notes compiled while he was a student of George Wythe at the College of William and Mary. 282 items.

MARSHALL, LENORE G., 1897-1971

MA —BOSTON UNIVERSITY, Mugar Memorial Library, Special Collections Dept, 771 Commonwealth Ave, Boston, 02215. Howard B Gotlieb, Dir
Holdings: // Cat Mss
Notes: Incl publications by.

MARSHALL, ORASMUS H.

NY —STATE UNIVERSITY OF NEW YORK, COLLEGE AT OSWEGO, Penfield Library, Oswego, 13126. Anne Commerton, Dir
Holdings: Cat Mss Pix
Notes: Correspondence, legal and business records and writings of members of the Sidney Shepard family, primarily reflecting business and personal relations with the family of Orasmus H Marshall, to which Shepard family was related by marriage. The papers cover the years 1838-1936. Incl records of Sidney Shepard Co and catalog of Shepard family library. Unpublished guide.

MARSHALL, SAMUEL L. A.

NY —SAINT BONAVENTURE UNIVERSITY, Friedsam Memorial Library, Saint Bonaventure, 14778. John Capozzi, OFM, Art Cur
Holdings: Mss
Notes: S L A Marshall Collection of 11 file cases of original mss, typescripts, and 9 books written by him.
TX —UNIVERSITY OF TEXAS, EL PASO, Special Collections Dept, The S L A Marshall Military History Collection, El Paso, 79968. Thomas Burdett, Cur
Holdings: Vols 7000 Cat Mss
Budget: $2000
Notes: The collection contains all of General Samuel Lyman Atwood Marshall's published works, his personal library and his personal papers. General Marshall was a prolific military historian and journalist. The collection's strengths are in its coverage of the wars of the twentieth century, specifically the two world wars, the Korean conflict and the war in Vietnam. The Marshall Room where the collection is housed is opened to the public.

MARSHALL AND FOX, ARCHITECTS

NY —CORNELL UNIVERSITY LIBRARIES, Collection of Regional History, Dept of Manuscripts and Univ Archives, Ithaca, 14853.
Notes: Incl records, 1925-26; details of a residence and of a stained glass window.

MARSHALL FAMILY

NY —STATE UNIVERSITY OF NEW YORK, COLLEGE AT OSWEGO, Penfield Library, Oswego, 13126. Anne Commerton, Dir
Holdings: Cat Mss Pix
Notes: About 20,000 items incl family correspondence, legal papers, historical notes and writings of three generations of a Buffalo, NY family. Persons represented include John E Marshall (1785-1838), physician; Ruth Holmes Marshall (1791-1872); O H Marshall (1813-1884), lawyer; Millient De Angelis Marshall (1813-1887); John E Marshall, Jr (1839-1900), manufacturer; Charles D Marshall (1841-1908), lawyer; Elizabeth E Marshall (1847-1894); and members of the Holmes and De Angelis families. Papers cover period 1820-1905. "Guide to the Marshall Family Papers," Donald W Barden and Charles W Brownson, eds (np, 1975).

MARSHALL PLAN

†VA —GEORGE C MARSHALL RESEARCH FOUNDATION AND LIBRARY, Drawer 920, Lexington, 24450. Royster Lyle Jr, Cur Collections
Holdings: Vols Cat Mss Pix Videotapes Films Filmstrips
Notes: The Harry B Price Collection contains over 650 typed pages of interviews with European and American officials concerning the Marshall Plan. This was in preparation for his book, *The Marshall Plan and its Meaning*. These interviews incl such people as Averell Harriman, George Kenna, and Marshall himself. 15 countries, OEEC (Organization for European Economic Cooperation), and USRO (US Special Representative in Europe) are represented in these interviews. Also in the collection are papers and materials that Cecilia "Jackie" Martin collected as picture editor for the Marshall Plan Information Service in Europe, 1950-54.

MARSTELLER, PHILIP

KS —SAINT MARY COLLEGE, Library, Leavenworth, 66048. Therese Deplazes, Special Collections Librn
Notes: Holographs of American personalities, mostly of Colonial, Revolutionary, Confederacy periods, and 19th Century. Incl ms letters, deeds, petitions, wills, slave papers. Holographs of Col Philip Marsteller (one of George Washington's pall bearers), family papers of Richard, Mary and Edward Cutts; love letters to Mary "Polly" Carter, Frank Ellery (grandson of William Ellery, signer of the Declaration of Independence), letters of Connie Mack and Babe Ruth, of some American authors.

MARSTON, STEPHEN, 1954-

CT —LEE ASH, (personal collection), 66 Humiston Dr, Bethany, 06525.
Holdings: Mss Pix
Notes: Letters and pictures of the Sharon, Conn. writer.

MARTI, JOSE

MO —WASHINGTON UNIVERSITY, John M Olin Library, Campus Box 1061, St Louis, 63130.
Holdings: Vols (50,000) Cat
Notes: Strong collection. Much unusual material.

MARTIAL ARTS

OH —OHIO UNIVERSITY, Vernon R Alden Library, Athens, 45701. Kent Mulliner, Africana Specialist
Notes: A collection of 634 vols of Chinese books covering a wide range of subjects incl art, culture, economics, geography, history, language, literature, martial arts, medical science, philosophy, and technology.

MARTIN, ERIC CHARLES FITZGERALD, 1905-1973

BC —UNIVERSITY OF VICTORIA, McPherson Library, Victoria, V8W 3H5, Can.
Notes: Brtish Columbia Minister of Health. Tapes and transcripts of interviews with R H Roy. Restrictions: use by permission only until 1985.

MARTIN, HAROLD H.

GA —EMORY UNIVERSITY, Robert W Woodruff Library, Special Collections Dept, Atlanta, 30322. Linda M Matthews, Head Special Collections; Virginia J H Cain, Processing Archivist; Richard H F Lindemann, Reference Archivist
Holdings: Cat Mss Pix Audiotapes
Notes: Extensive collections of papers of Henry W Grady, Corra Harris, Joel Chandler Harris, Julian LaRose Harris, Julia Collier Harris, Clark Howell, Ralph E McGill, Harold H Martin, Mildred Seydell, and Claude Sitton, among others, most associated with the Atlanta *Constitution*. Descriptions and index are availalbe in repository.

MARTIN, JOSEPH W., JR., 1884-1968

MA —STONEHILL COLLEGE, Cushing-Martin Library, Washington St, North Easton, 02356. James J Kenneally, Cur
Holdings: Cat Mss Pix
Notes: About 12,000 letters, speeches and photographs; 104 scrapbooks, plus other memorabilia of Representative Martin, of Massachusetts, 1925-1965; Speaker of the House, 1947-1949, 1953-1955.

MARTIN, RALPH

MA —BOSTON UNIVERSITY, Mugar
Memorial Library, Special Collections Dept,
771 Commonwealth Ave, Boston, 02215.
Howard B Gotlieb, Dir
Holdings: Mss Pix
Notes: Mss, correspondence, etc collected in
depth; incl publications by or about.

MARTIN, THOMAS E.

DC —GEORGETOWN UNIVERSITY,
Library, Special Collections Div, 37 & O Sts
NW, Washington, 20057. George M
Barringer, Special Collections Librn;
Nicholas B Sheetz, Mss Librn
Holdings: Cat Mss Pix
Notes: Panama Canal, and papers of Tomas
Herran, Earl Harding, Thomas E Martin,
William McCan, Clark Thompson, Leonor K
Sullivan, and Capt Miles Duval.

MARTIN FAMILY

NJ —PRINCETON UNIVERSITY, Library,
Manuscript Collection, Nassau St, Princeton,
08540. Jean F Preston, Cur
Holdings: // Mss Pix
Notes: The collection, which fills 11 ms
boxes, also includes some material on the
Martin family. An unpublished typescript
guide (111p) is available in the Library.

MARTIN-HARVEY, SIR JOHN

CA —UNIVERSITY OF CALIFORNIA,
DAVIS, Shields Library, Dept of Special
Collections, Davis, 95616. Donald Kunitz,
Head; C Danial Elliott, Asst Head
Holdings: Vols (112,000) Cat Mss Pix
Notes: Programs, playbills, posters, designs,
and scripts from 19th and 20th century
American and British theatre. American
materials incl the eastern United States
(NYC) and California. Production groupings
center in Sir Henry Irving, McKee Rankin,
Sir John Martin-Harvey, E L Davenport.
Clippings, photographs, and correspondence
of theatre personalities; records of the Bread
and Puppet Theatre, San Francisco Mime
Troupe, Living Theatre, Firehouse Theatre,
Squat Theatre, papers of Toby Cole.
Described in Sarlos, Robert K, "The Theatre
Collection at Davis," *American Society for
Theatre Research Newsletter,* vol 3, no 1,
fall 1974, pp 2-3, 9-10.

MARTINEAU, HARRIET

CA —UNIVERSITY OF CALIFORNIA, LOS
ANGELES, Research Library, Dept of
Special Collections, 405 Hilgard Ave, Los
Angeles, 90024. Edward Shreeves,
Chairman, Bibliographers Group; David S
Zeidberg, Head
Holdings: Vols 50
Notes: 50 first and other editions of her
books; 29 letters.

MARTINIQUE

CT —YALE UNIVERSITY, Sterling Memorial
Library, Latin American Collections, New
Haven, 06520. Lee H Williams Jr, Cur
Holdings: Vols (300,000) Cat Maps Pix
Slides Phonorecords 16mm Films Filmstrips
See also entry under Latin America

MARX, ARTHUR

MA —BOSTON UNIVERSITY, Mugar
Memorial Library, Special Collections Dept,
771 Commonwealth Ave, Boston, 02215.
Howard B Gotlieb, Dir
Holdings: Cat Mss

MARX, ERICA

MO —WASHINGTON UNIVERSITY,
Libraries, Special Collections Dept, Campus
Box 1061, St Louis, 63130.
Notes: A major collection, incl mss,
correspondence, literary papers, photographs,
etc. Described in *Special Collections: an*

Annotated Guide to the Holdings of the
Manuscript Division and the University
Archives and Research Collection.

MARXISM see Communism and Anticommunism; Socialism

MARXIST ECONOMICS

CA —SOUTHERN CALIFORNIA LIBRARY
FOR SOCIAL STUDIES & RESEARCH,
6120 S Vermont Ave, Los Angeles, 90044.
Sarah Cooper, Dir
Holdings: Vols (15,000) Mss Maps Pix Slides
Phonorecords Audiotapes 16mm Films
Budget: ($30,000)
Notes: Marxist, non-Marxist and anti-
Marxist approaches to social change. Other
important functions of the library: to make
available source materials to those engaged
in the Marxist vs no-Marxist dialog; to aid
historians, economists, sociologists, writers,
students and labor organizations researching
the history of grassroots social movements;
and to preserve primary and secondary
sources on labor, minorities, women and
radicalism. Collection incl 50 mss, 75 maps,
500 pictures, 1000 slides, 100 phonorecords,
2000 audiotapes, 50 16mm films and 150,
000 newspaper clippings.

MARY MCDOWELL SETTLEMENT

IL —CHICAGO HISTORICAL SOCIETY,
Library, Clark St at North Ave, Chicago,
60614. Archie Motley, Manuscript Librn
Notes: Papers of these Chicago setlement
houses: Association House; Chicago
Commons; Christopher House; Emerson
House; Erie Neighborhood House;
Fellowship House; Gads Hill Center;
Marillac House; Mary McDownell
Settlement (formerly the University of
Chicago Settlement); Olivet Community
Center; Parkway Community Center.

MARY, QUEEN OF SCOTS

MA —HARVARD UNIVERSITY LIBRARY,
Widener Library, Cambridge, 02138.
Holdings: Cat
NY —COLUMBIA UNIVERSITY
LIBRARIES, Rare Book & Manuscript
Library, 801 Butler Library, 535 W 114 St,
New York, 10027. Kenneth A Lohf, Librn
Holdings: Vols 500 Cat
Notes: 500 vols about Mary Queen of Scots
from the 16th to the 20th centuries.

MARY, VIRGIN

MO —SAINT LOUIS UNIVERSITY, Pius XII
Memorial Library, Saint Louis Room
Collection, 3655 W Pine Blvd, Saint Louis,
63108. Catherine E Weidle, Rare Books
Librn
Holdings: Vols Cat
Notes: Books on Jesuitica; also collections
on the Spiritual Exercises of St Ignatius
Loyola and on the Sodality of Our Lady.
OH —UNIVERSITY OF DAYTON, Marian
Library, 300 College Park Ave, Dayton,
45469. Rev Theodore Koehler, SM, Dir/Cur
Holdings: Vols (65,000) Cat Mss Pix Slides
Phonorecords Audiotapes Filmstrips
Microforms
Budget: ($12,000)
Notes: Largest and most comprehensive
collections of literature on Virgin Mary in
the world. Covers all five centuries of
printing. Some 50 languages represented.
Incl doctrinal, polemical, popular works,
children's books. Catholic and non-Catholic.
Especially strong in publications on French
shrines (Clugnet collection), on the
Immaculate Conception, and materials after
1950. Has Vloberg collection of pictures, ms
notes and offprints on Marian iconography.
Complete files of major journals in
Mariology and partial runs or more than 100
others. Files of 48,000 clippings from
domestic and foreign periodicals. 10,000
holy cards from 19th and 20th centuries.
2600 postcard views of shrines. 3000
postcards of Marian art. Philatelic collection

of 1000 stamps and 200 first-day cover.
1000 photographs. 300 medals. General
reference collection strong inpastristic
sources, biblical literature, religious
inconography (especially of Eastern
Churches), general bibliography, and
bibliography of religious orders. Union
catalog of Marian holdings in American and
others libraries. Library publishes *Marian
Library Studies* and *Marian Library*
Newsletter. Has had scholors in residence
since 1972. Since 1975 recognized as a
Pontifical Institute in affiliation with the
Marianum in Rome empowered to prepare
candidates for pontifical degree with
specialization in Marian studies. In 1976
began summer schools in Mariology. History
of the Library and description of its holdings
in Fackovec, William, S M, "The Marian
Library of the University of Dayton," in
Marian Library Studies (New Series) vol 1
(1969), pp 9-76.

MARYLAND

MD —JOHNS HOPKINS UNIVERSITY,
Milton S Eisenhower Library, Charles & 34
Sts, Baltimore, 21218. Ann S Gwyn,
Assistant Dir for Special Collections
MD —MARYLAND DEPT OF STATE
PLANNING, Library, 301 W Preston St
Rm 1101, Baltimore, 21201. Helene W Jeng,
Librn; John Somers, Asst Librn
Holdings: Vols (11,100) Cat
Notes: Includes depository of plans relating
to Maryland.
†MD —UNIVERSITY OF MARYLAND,
Library, Marylandia Dept, College Park,
20742. Nancy K Walton, Head
Holdings: Vols 40,000 Cat Maps Audiotapes
Microforms
Notes: Books, periodicals, maps, microforms,
etc, on the history of the State and the
University; works by Maryland authors;
state, county, and municipal documents;
University of Maryland theses and
dissertations. State, county, and municipal
documents are cataloged by subject. For a
description of archival and manuscript
materials in the Library, see entry under
Maryland - Description and Travel - Views.
MD —SALISBURY STATE COLLEGE,
Blackwell Library, Salisbury, 21801. James R
Thrash, Dir
Holdings: Vols 3000 Cat Maps Pix Slides
Filmstrips Microforms
MD —MARYLAND-NATIONAL CAPITAL
PARK & PLANNING COMMISSION,
Montgomery County Planning Department
Library, 8787 Georgia Ave, Silver Spring,
20907. Janice C Holt, Librn
Holdings: Vols (5000) Cat Slides
Notes: Specific subject areas include:
community facilities, conservation,
economics, flood control, highways, housing,
human and natural resources. landscape
architecture, open space, parks, pollution,
population, recreation, transportation, urban
renewal, and zoning. Commission's
publications are maintained by Records
Management (not Library).
MD —CALVERT MARINE MUSEUM,
Library, PO Box 97, Solomons, 20688.
Holdings: Vols (2000) Cat Mss Maps Pix
Slides Audiotapes 16mm Films
Notes: Local maritime history, history of
southern Maryland, estuarine biology, and
paleontology of southern Maryland. Large
picture collection (1800), blueprints (368)
and slides (1100).
MD —TAKOMA PARK MARYLAND
LIBRARY, 101 Philadelphia Ave, Takoma
Park, 20012. Ellen Spottswood, Dir
Holdings: Vols (665) Cat Maps Pix
Microforms
Notes: Collection is general but especially
strong in Maryland history and government;
also that of Montgomery County and
Takoma Park. Maryland- Hooker collection
consists of early colonial records, military
rosters, census lists, old Geological Survey
records, and Archives of State of Maryland.
Latter comprises old Court Proceedings and
Proceedings of Maryland General Assembly.
Newspaper microfilms are available of
Takoma Journal, 1923-1955.

MARYLAND—CITIES AND TOWNS—PLANNING

MD —HOWARD COUNTY LIBRARY, 10375 Little Patuxent Parkway, Columbia, 21044. Joyce Demmitt, Adult Services Coordr
Holdings: Vols (435) Cat Mss Maps Pix
Notes: New Towns, with emphasis on Columbia, Maryland.

MARYLAND—DESCRIPTION AND TRAVEL

MD —UNIVERSITY OF MARYLAND, BALTIMORE COUNTY, Albin O Kuhn Library and Gallery, 5401 Wilkens Ave, Baltimore, 21228. Ann Copeland, Special Collections Librn
Holdings: Vols (1500) Uncat Maps
Notes: The Edward G Howard Collection includes many 18th and 19th century first editions of foreign visitors' accounts of their travels through Baltimore and Maryland. These accounts provide excellent descriptions of Maryland history and culture. In addition to local histories and magazines, the collection also includes Francis Scott Key's personal copy of *Maryland in Liberia* and a strong section on the War of 1812. The collection is also strong in 20th century material.

MARYLAND—DESCRIPTION AND TRAVEL—VIEWS

MD —UNIVERSITY OF MARYLAND, Library, Archives & Manuscripts Dept, College Park, 20742. Mary A Boccaccio, Head
Holdings: Mss Pix
Notes: University of Maryland publications and archives; collections of organizational papers (eg, Baltimore and Ohio Railroad; various organizations concerned with the Chesapeake Bay and environs; various labor unions, particularly those involving the tobacco industry), mostly associated with Maryland; collections of papers and mss associated with literary and public figures (eg, the late Senator Millard Tydings); oral histories relating to the archival and mss collections; associated memorabilia; photographs, mainly associated with Maryland. A guide to collections of personal, family, and organizational papers relating to Maryland is being prepared.

MARYLAND—GENEALOGY

FL —ORLANDO PUBLIC LIBRARY, Local History & Genealogy Dept, 100 Block of Central Ave, Orlando, 32806. Eileen B Willis, Librn
Holdings: Vols 11,000 Cat Maps Microforms
Budget: $8000
Notes: Genealogy collection on Md, Del, W Va, NC, SC, Ala, Miss, La, Texas, Ark, Ky, Ohio, Ill, Ind, and Mich are well represented. Most other states are covered by smaller collections.
See also entry under Genealogy - Collections.
MD —MARYLAND STATE LAW LIBRARY, Courts of Appeal Bldg, 361 Rowe Blvd, Annapolis, 21401. Michael S Miller, Dir; Shirley A Rittenhouse, Librn
Holdings: Vols (180,000) Cat Microforms
Budget: ($114,750)
Notes: Comprehensive collection of published, secondary sources of Maryland genealogical research, incl Maryland census schedules, 1790-1910, original set *Maryland Gazette*, 1745-1838, *Baltimore Sun*, 1837-date.
MD —MARYLAND HISTORICAL SOCIETY, Library, 201 W Monument St, Baltimore, 21201. William B Keller, Head Librn
Holdings: Vols (65,000) Cat Maps Pix Slides
Budget: ($8000)
Notes: Baltimore history, large collection (30,000 Maryland local history and genealogy, 100,000 mss).

MD —CHARLES COUNTY COMMUNITY COLLEGE, Learning Resource Center, PO Box 910, La Plata, 20646. J Elaine Ryan, Dean
Holdings: Vols 200 Cat Microforms
Notes: Papers of Harry Wright Newman (100 cubic feet). Also incl complete census microfilm for Charles, Calvert and St Mary's Counties through 1910, and many 18th century mss. Additional points of coverage incl an index of marriages and an ongoing newspaper index of births, deaths, marriages and baptisms.
See also entry under Maryland - History
TN —CHATTANOOGA-HAMILTON COUNTY, Bicentennial Library, Local History and Genealogy Dept, 1001 Broad St, Chattanooga, 37402. Clara W Swann, Librn
Holdings: Vols (24,561) Cat Mss Maps Pix Microforms
Budget: ($7000)
Notes: Emphasis on southern states, and eastern Tennessee counties, with considerable material on New England, Pennsylvania, and Maryland genealogy and history. Census records on microfilm. Special indexes and clipping files. Noncirculating.

MARYLAND—GOVERNMENT PUBLICATIONS

MD —MARYLAND STATE LAW LIBRARY, Courts of Appeal Bldg, 361 Rowe Blvd, Annapolis, 21401. Michael S Miller, Dir; Shirley A Rittenhouse, Librn
Holdings: Vols (180,000) Cat Microforms
Budget: ($114,750)
Notes: The library has been a depository for state agency publications since 1840.
†MD —UNIVERSITY OF MARYLAND, Library, Marylandia Dept, College Park, 20742. Nancy K Walton, Head
Holdings: Vols 40,000 Cat Maps Audiotapes Microforms
Notes: Books, periodicals, maps, microforms, etc, on the history of the State and the University; works by Maryland authors; state, county, and municipal documents; University of Maryland theses and dissertations. State, county, and municipal documents are cataloged by subject. For a description of archival and manuscript materials in the Library, see entry under Maryland - Description and Travel - Views.

MARYLAND—HISTORY

AL —BIRMINGHAM PUBLIC LIBRARY, Southern History Dept, 2020 Seventh Ave N, Birmingham, 35203. Virginia K Scott, Head
Holdings: Vols (50,000) Cat Microforms
Notes: History and social conditions of the southeastern US. Significant holdings on border areas such as Texas, Pennsylvania, Maryland. Strong genealogical collection with emphasis on the southeastern area of the US. Very strong Civil War Collection and early southern travel accounts. See George Ray Stewart, *The Special Collections in the Birmingham Public Library*. MA Thesis, Emory University, 1971.
DC —DISTRICT OF COLUMBIA PUBLIC LIBRARY, Martin Luther King Memorial Library, Washingtoniana Div and Washington Star Collection, 901 G St NW, Washington, 20001. Roxanna Deane, Chief
Holdings: Vols (20,000) Cat Maps Pix Slides
Budget: ($5500)
Notes: *Washington Star* Collection was the working morgue and photo library of the *Washington Star* newspaper. There are an estimated one million photos dating from about 1930 to 1981. These are arranged by subject and personal name and cover international, national and local news. There are approx 13 million news clippings arranged by subject and personal name for the same period. Each *Star* article was clipped and placed in as many different files as was necessary to cover all topics or personal names mentioned in the article. Reproductions from the photo collection may be purchased.
DC —GEORGETOWN UNIVERSITY, Library, Special Collections Div, 37 & O Sts

NW, Washington, 20057. George M Barringer, Special Collections Librn; Nicholas B Sheetz, Mss Librn
Holdings: Cat Mss
Notes: Property leases, deeds, legal briefs, warrants, land surveys, and genealogical records pertaining to the Plowden family of Maryland, dating primarily from the 17th and 18th centuries. Correspondence among merchants in Maryland, the largest portion between two factors, Robert Ferguson and Alexander Hamilton. Ferguson (d 1813) was sent to Maryland as a factor for the John Glassford Company of Scotland. He left the colonies during the Revolution and returned to his native Scotland. In 1784 he came back to Maryland with power of attorney to collect debts and dispose of the company's property. He spent the remaining years of his life in America, working as a factor for numerous companies. Alexander Hamilton (d 1799), also a factor for the Glassford Company and a native of Scotland, chose to remain in this country until his death. The correspondence betweenthese two men concerns difficulties encountered in collecting debts after the Revolution.
MD —MARYLAND STATE LAW LIBRARY, Courts of Appeal Bldg, 361 Rowe Blvd, Annapolis, 21401. Michael S Miller, Dir; Shirley A Rittenhouse, Librn
Holdings: Vols (180,000) Cat Microforms
Budget: ($114,750)
Notes: Comprehensive collection of published histories of Maryland and each county in the state.
MD —BALTIMORE STREETCAR MUSEUM, Transit Research Center, 1901 Falls Rd, PO Box 7184, Baltimore, 21218. George F Nixon, Cur
Holdings: Cat Mss Pix Slides 16mm Films
Notes: Transit Research Center is devoted to the collection of memorabilia, photos, drawings, printed matter, etc, pertinent to public rail transportation in Baltimore and Maryland. Incl streetcar systems, interurban lines, and main line railroads in the area. Also incl bus history. Incl materials donated by The Baltimore Transit Co, United Railways and Electric Co, as well as private collections.

MD —ENOCH PRATT FREE LIBRARY, Humanities Dept, 400 Cathedral St, Baltimore, 21201. Neil R Jordahl, Librn
Holdings: Vols 4200 Cat Mss Pix
Notes: The definitive Mencken Collection; also incl over 2000 pamphlets. Mencken gave most of his books and papers to the library. Collection incl family papers, memorabilia, research notes, etc. Numerous presentation books given to Mencken, mostly inscribed.
MD —JOHNS HOPKINS UNIVERSITY, Milton S Eisenhower Library, Charles & 34 Sts, Baltimore, 21218. Ann S Gwyn, Assistant Dir for Special Collections
MD —JOHNS HOPKINS UNIVERSITY, Milton S Eisenhower Library, Special Collections, John Work Garrett Library, 4545 N Charles St, Baltimore, 21210. Jane Katz, Garrett Librn
MD —MARYLAND HISTORICAL SOCIETY, Library, 201 W Monument St, Baltimore, 21201. William B Keller, Head Librn
Holdings: Vols (65,000) Cat Maps Pix Slides
Budget: ($8000)
Notes: Also 2 million ms pieces, 300 maps, 700 slides; 10,000 musical scores. Large collection of Maryland State Colonization Papers; Maryland and Baltimore business records; Baltimore & Ohio Railroad Papers; Baltimore Theater records and programs (late 18th, early 19th century); Maryland lottery tickets; Benjamin H Latrobe (architectural) Papers; Maryland maps, plats, prints, newspapers; Baltimore history, large collection (30,000 items Maryland local history and genealogy, 100,000 mss); iron industry papers; Maryland currency; sheet music (8000 pieces, largely Baltimore publishers); Lester S Levy "Star-Spangled Banner" collection (probably the largest in the world--over 250 pieces).
MD —MEDICAL & CHIRURGICAL FACULTY OF THE STATE OF

MARYLAND—HISTORY (cont.)

MARYLAND, Library, 1211 Cathedral St, Baltimore, 21201. Joseph E Jensen, Librn
Holdings: Vols (10,000) // Cat Mss Maps Pix
See also entry under Medicine - History and Historic

MD —PEALE MUSEUM, Municipal Museum of Baltimore, 225 Holiday St, Baltimore, 21202. Nancy Brennan, Dir; Richard Flint, Cur Prints and Photos
Holdings: Cat Maps
Notes: Pictorial history of Baltimore. Collection of 100,00 items incl: T E Hambleton Collection of Historical Prints; A Aubrey Bodine Photographic Collection; John Dubas Collection of Photographs. Many original photographic negatives.

MD —SAINT MARY'S SEMINARY & UNIVERSITY, School of Theology Library, 5400 Roland Ave, Baltimore, 21210. David Siemen, Dir
Holdings: Vols (170,000) Cat Mss Maps Pix Audiotapes Videotapes Microforms

MD —UNIVERSITY OF MARYLAND, BALTIMORE COUNTY, Albin O Kuhn Library and Gallery, 5401 Wilkens Ave, Baltimore, 21228. Ann Copeland, Special Collections Librn
Holdings: Vols (1500) Uncat Maps
Notes: The Edward G Howard Collection includes many 18th and 19th century first editions of foreign vistors' accounts of their travels through Baltimore and Maryland. These accounts provide excellent descriptions of Maryland history and culture. In addition to local histories and magazines, the collection also includes Francis Scott Key's personal copy of *Maryland in Liberia* and a strong section on the War of 1812. The collection is also strong in 20th century material.

MD —WASHINGTON COLLEGE, Clifton M Miller Library, Chestertown, 21620.
Notes: Archive-library of source material, incl primary sources in microform, on the Chesapeake Bay during the American Revolutinary period.

†MD —UNIVERSITY OF MARYLAND, Library, Marylandia Dept, College Park, 20742. Nancy K Walton, Head
Holdings: Vols 40,000 Cat Maps Audiotapes Microforms
Notes: Books, periodicals, maps, microforms, etc, on the history of the State and the University; works by Maryland authors; state, county, and municipal documents; University of Maryland theses and dissertations. State, county, and municipal documents are cataloged by subject. For a description of archival and manuscript materials in the Library, see entry under Maryland - Description and Travel - Views.

MD —HOWARD COUNTY LIBRARY, 10375 Little Patuxemt Parkway, Columbia, 21044. Joyce Demmitt, Adult Services Coordr
Holdings: Vols (600) Cat Mss Maps VF
Notes: Columbia, Maryland.

MD —TALBOT COUNTY FREE LIBRARY, Maryland Room, 100 W Dover St, Easton, 21601. Marguerite W Harvey, Cur
Holdings: Vols 3900 Cat Mss Maps Pix Slides Phonorecords Audiotapes Videotapes
Notes: The Maryland Room of the Talbot County Free Library is probably the finest in the State outside of Baltimore. Incl history, description, Maryland authors, etc. Separate catalog. Collection described in *Guardian of Our Maryland Heritage: The Maryland Room, Talbot County Free Library* (Easton: The Library, 1968).

MD —MOUNT SAINT MARY'S COLLEGE, Hugh J Phillips Library, Emmitsburg, 21727. Stephen Rockwood, Librn
Holdings: Vols (140,000) Cat Mss Maps Pix
Notes: Early Catholic Americana, especially for western Maryland.

MD —WASHINGTON COUNTY FREE LIBRARY, 100 S Potomac St, Hagerstown, 21740. John Frye, Special Collections Librn
Holdings: Vols 3707 Cat mss Maps Pix Audiotapes Videotapes VF
Notes: Emphasis on Hagerstown, Washington County, and western Maryland. Also coverage of adjacent portions of Penn, Va, and WVa.

MD —PRINCE GEORGE'S COUNTY MEMORIAL LIBRARY SYSTEM, Hyattsville Branch Library, Maryland Room, 6530 Adelphi Rd, Hyattsville, 20782. John Krivak, Librn
Holdings: Vols (7000) Cat Mss Maps Pix Slides Audiotapes Microforms
Notes: Maryland, especially Prince George's County. Also 30 tapes; 30 file drawers of pamphlets and clippings; 62 microfilms of early Prince George's County court records. Maryland and US census 1790-1910.

MD —CHARLES COUNTY COMMUNITY COLLEGE, Learning Resource Center, PO Box 910, La Plata, 20646. J Elaine Ryan, Dean
Holdings: Vols (2000) Cat Mss Maps Pix Slides Audiotapes Videotapes Microforms
Notes: Southern Maryland incl Charles, Calvert, and St Mary's counties, as well as southern Prince Georges County (before the Civil War). Numerous original photographs, documents, etc. Also incl oral history, genealogy (100 cubic feet of mss).
See also entries under Maryland-Genealogy; Genealogy-Collections

MD —CALVERT MARINE MUSEUM, Library, PO Box 97, Solomons, 20688.
Holdings: Vols (2000) Uncat Mss Maps Pix Slides Audiotapes
Notes: Southern Maryland history, vessel lists of boats built in the county; lists of vessels owned in Calvert County, ships papers, half models, building plans and blueprints, artifacts, shipyard papers (correspondence, material lists, etc) and contracts.
See also entries under Shipwrecks; US - History - War of 1812.

MD —TAKOMA PARK MARYLAND LIBRARY, 101 Philadelphia Ave, Takoma Park, 20012. Ellen Spottswood, Dir
Holdings: Vols (665) Cat Maps Pix Microforms
Notes: Collection is general but especially strong in Maryland history and government; also that of Montgomery County and Takoma Park. Maryland- Hooker collection consists of early colonial records, military rosters, census lists, old Geological Survey records, and Archives of State of Maryland. Latter comprises old Court Proceedings and Proceedings of Maryland General Assembly. Newspaper microfilms are available of *Takoma Journal*, 1923-1955.

PA —FRIENDS HISTORICAL LIBRARY OF SWARTHMORE COLLEGE, Swarthmore, 19081. J William Frost, Dir
Holdings: Vols (35,000) Cat Mss Pix Microforms
Notes: Library's collections contain information on the history and doctrine of the Society of Friends, Quaker contributions to literature, science, business, education, and government, plus their reform efforts in peace, Indian rights, women's rights, and abolition of slavery. As an official depository of the records of the Philadelphia and Baltimore Yearly Meetings, the library holds, either in the original manuscript or on microfilm, records of Friends meetings in Maryland. Among the over 250 mss collections are several which concern Maryland Quaker leaders and Quaker families.

TN —CHATTANOOGA-HAMILTON COUNTY, Bicentennial Library, Local History and Genealogy Dept, 1001 Broad St, Chattanooga, 37402. Clara W Swann, Librn
Holdings: Vols (24,561) Cat Mss Maps Pix Microforms
Budget: ($7000)
Notes: Emphasis on southern states, and eastern Tennessee counties, with considerable material on New England, Pennsylvania, and Maryland genealogy and history. Census records on microfilm. Special indexes and clipping files. Noncirculating.

MARYLAND—IMPRINTS

MD —JOHNS HOPKINS UNIVERSITY, Milton S Eisenhower Library, Special Collections, John Work Garrett Library, 4545 N Charles St, Baltimore, 21210. Jane Katz, Garrett Librn
Holdings: Vols 105 Cat
Notes: Espec pre-1800 Maryland imprints.

MD —MARYLAND HISTORICAL SOCIETY, Library, 201 W Monument St, Baltimore, 21201. William B Keller, Head Librn
Holdings: Vols (65,000) Cat Mss Maps Pix Slides
Budget: $8000
Notes: Large collection of Maryland State Colonization Papers; Maryland and Baltimore business records; Baltimore & Ohio Railroad Papers; Baltimore Theatre records and programs (late 18th, early 19th century); Maryland lottery tickets; Benjamin H Latrobe (architectural) Papers; Maryland maps, plats, prints, newspapers; Baltimore history large collection (30,000 items Maryland local history and genealogy, 100, 000 mss); iron industry papers; Maryland currency; sheet music (8000 pieces, largely Baltimore publishers); Lester S Levy "Star-Spangled Banner" collection (probably the largest in the world-over 250 pieces).

MARYLAND—MAPS

DC —METROPOLITAN WASHINGTON COUNCIL OF GOVERNMENTS, Map Library, 1875 Eye St NW, Suite 200, Washington, 20006. Susan Kalish, Librn
Holdings: Cat Maps
Notes: 3000 current and retrospective maps covering metropolitan Washington region, incl the District of Columbia; Montgomery and Prince George's counties in Maryland; and Arlington, Fairfax, Prince William and Loudoun counties and the City of Alexandria in Virginia. Maps cover land use, community facilities, transportation, topography, statistical units, and socioeconomic information. Record of holdings on computer printout.

MD —JOHNS HOPKINS UNIVERSITY, Milton S Eisenhower Library, Special Collections, John Work Garrett Library, 4545 N Charles St, Baltimore, 21210. Jane Katz, Garrett Librn

MD —MARYLAND HISTORICAL SOCIETY, Library, 201 W Monument St, Baltimore, 21201. William B Keller, Head Librn
Notes: Maryland maps, plats, prints, newspapers.

VA —GEORGE MASON UNIVERSITY, Fenwick Library, Special Collections Dept, 4400 University Drive, Fairfax, 22030. Ruth Kerns, Public Services Librn
Notes: C Harrison Mann Collection: 18 atlases and 76 single maps primarily from the late 1500s to the late 1800s, incl rare atlases and maps of early Virginia and Maryland, and several foreign regions of the world.

MARYLAND—SOCIAL LIFE AND CUSTOMS

MD —UNIVERSITY OF MARYLAND, Maryland Folklore Archive, College Park, 20742. Barry Pearson, Lecturer in English
Holdings: Cat Mss
Notes: Maryland folk songs and folklore. 60 file drawers of mss, held in trust for the Maryland Arts Council. Subject index in preparation.

MARYLAND AUTHORS see Authors, Maryland

MARYLAND NATIONAL PARK AND PLANNING COMMISSION

DC —METROPOLITAN WASHINGTON COUNCIL OF GOVERNMENTS, Research Library, 1875 Eye St NW, Suite 200, Washington, 20006. Suan Kalish, Librn
Holdings: Vols (3000) Cat Microforms
Notes: Contains (on 75 reels of microfilm) archives of Maryland National Park and Planning Commission, archives of the Council of Governments, and audits and

MARYLAND NATIONAL PARK AND PLANNING COMMISSION (cont.)

financial reports of local governments (1950-date). Also incl annual reports, planning reports and budgets from each jurisdiction (1973-date).

MASARYK, THOMAS AND JAN

CA —UNIVERSITY OF CALIFORNIA, BERKELEY, University Library, Slavic Collections, Berkeley, 94720. Edward Kasinec, Librn
Holdings: Vols 1917 Cat Pix
Notes: The Masaryk-Benes Library is rich resource for the study of Czechoslovak and European history, especially for the period 1918-1939. It contains Masaryk's own works in original and later editions, as well as in translation (231 volumes), and books about Tomas and Jan Masaryk and family (573). Benes is represented by his own writings (100) and items about him and his family (69). Miscellaneous titles (335) on Slavic problems, and on the history of · Czechoslovakia, complete the monograph collection. The balance consists of periodical articles, reprints, and newspaper clippings. Publication dates range from 1883 to 1945, with the bulk of the material published during 1920-1940.

DC —GEORGETOWN UNIVERSITY, Library, Special Collections Div, 37 & O Sts NW, Washington, 20057. George M Barringer, Special Collections Librn; Nicholas B Sheetz, Mss Librn
Holdings: Mss Cat Pix
Notes: The personal papers of Richard T Crane (1882-1938), private secretary to Robert Lansing, 1915-1919; first American ambassador to Czechoslovakia, 1919-1921; and owner of the Westover Plantation in Virginia, 1921-1938. The papers - divided into three series, State Department, Prague and Westover - contain correspondence, memoranda, reports, diaries, documents, mss, printed material, and newspaper clippings. Correspondence incl letters from Robert Lansing, Charles Crane, Woodrow Wilson, Franklin Roosevelt, T G Masaryk, Jan Masaryk, Eduard Benes, Edward House, Herbert Hoover, Hugh Gibson, Joseph C Grew, Allan Dulles, and John Foster Dulles, among others.

IL —CHICAGO PUBLIC LIBRARY, Special Collections Div, Cultural Center, 78 E Washington St, Chicago, 60602. Laura Linard, Cur
Holdings: Vols 400 Cat Mss Pix
Notes: Works by, biographies and critical studies of, T G Masaryk, first President of Czechoslovakia. Contains works on Czechoslovakia, 1918-38. See *Collection Masaryk: A Catalog of the Books by and about Thomas Garrigue Masaryk, Presented by the Honorable John Toman to John Toman Branch of The Chicago Public Library*, 1939. This collection was permanently transferred from the Toman Branch to the Special Collections Division in 1975.

IL —UNIVERSITY OF ILLINOIS, URBANA/CHAMPAIGN, Slavic and East European Library, Urbana, 61801. Marianna Tax Choldin, Head
Holdings: Vols (35,000) Cat
Notes: Extensive coverage.

MA —HARVARD UNIVERSITY LIBRARY, Widener Library, Slavic Collections, Cambridge, 02138. Hugh M Olmsted, Slavic Dept Head
Holdings: Cat
Notes: A strong collection.

NE —UNIVERSITY OF NEBRASKA-LINCOLN, Don L Love Library, Czech Heritage Collection, Lincoln, 68588. Joseph G Svoboda, University Archivist
Holdings: Vols (3000) Cat Mss Pix Audiotapes Microforms
Notes: The Czech Heritage Collection.

†PA —UNIVERSITY OF PITTSBURGH, Hillman Library, Pittsburgh, 15260.
Notes: Unpublished drafts of letters, memoranda, and messages in either English

of Czech from Thomas Garrigue Masaryk to American and European Statesmen during the final phase of WWI and in the early period of Czechoslovakia's independence.

UT —UTAH STATE UNIVERSITY, Merrill Library, Department of Special Collections & Archives, Logan, 84322. A J Simmonds, Curator; Jeanie F Simmonds, Archivist; Bradford R Cole, Mss Librn
Holdings: Vols 1000 Uncat
Notes: Books and pamphlets on Thomas G. Masaryk and the Czechoslovak Republic, 1890-1949. Languages represented: Chech, Slovak, German, French, Russian, English.

MASARYK FAMILY

CA —UNIVERSITY OF CALIFORNIA, BERKELEY, University Library, Slavic Collections, Berkeley, 94720. Edward Kasinec, Librn
Holdings: Vols 1917 Cat Pix
Notes: The Masaryk-Benes Library is rich resource for the study of Czechoslovak and European history, especially for the period 1918-1939. It contains Masaryk's own works in original and later editions, as well as in translation (231 volumes), and books about Tomas and Jan Masaryk and family (573). Benes is represented by his own writings (100) and items about him and his family (69). Miscellaneous titles (335) on Slavic problems, and on the history of Czechoslovakia, complete the monograph collection. The balance consists of periodical articles, reprints, and newspaper clippings. Publication dates range from 1883 to 1945, with the bulk of the material published during 1920-1940.

MASEFIELD, CONSTANCE

†NY —COLUMBIA UNIVERSITY LIBRARIES, Butler Library, Rare Book and Manuscript Library, 535 W 114 St, New York, 10027.
Notes: The John Masefield Collection.

MASEFIELD, JOHN, 1878-1967

AL —SAMFORD UNIVERSITY, Special Collections Library, 800 Lakeshore Dr, Birmingham, 35229. Annie Ford Wheeler, Acting Head Librn
Holdings: Vols 400 Cat
Notes: Nucleus is the Clyde T Warren Collection.

CT —TRINITY COLLEGE LIBRARY, Watkinson Library, 300 Summit St, Hartford, 06106. Jeffrey Kaimowitz, Cur
Holdings: Cat
Notes: First editions, etc.

CT —YALE UNIVERSITY, Box 1603A, Yale Station, New Haven, 06520.
Holdings: Mss

CT —CONNECTICUT COLLEGE, Library, Mohegan Ave, New London, 06320. Brian Rogers, College Librn
Holdings: Vols 210 Uncat Mss Pix
Notes: The Charles H Simmons Collection.

IL —ILLINOIS STATE UNIVERSITY, Milner Library, Dept of Special Collections, Normal, 61761. Robert Sokan, Librn
Holdings: Vols 250 Cat Mss Pix Audiotapes
Notes: Letters and documents concerning an exhibition held in the Times Bookshop to celebrate the poet's 80th birthday, the letters being addressed to the manager. Incl a tape recording which Masefield made at his home in Abingdon shortly before the opening of the exhibition. This speech incl an unpublished poem, "On Coming Towards Eighty." Also letters and documents concerning an exhibition in memory of John Drinkwater which Masefield was invited to open. The taped speech was recorded at the actual private view, Masefield item. Also a revised and corrected ms of his long poem "Tristan and Isolt."

MA —HARVARD UNIVERSITY LIBRARY, Houghton Library, Cambridge, 02138. Rodney G Dennis, Cur of Manuscripts
Holdings: Cat Mss

MN —UNIVERSITY OF MINNESOTA, O Meredith Wilson Library, 309 19 Ave S, Minneapolis, 55455. Austin J McLean,

Chief, Special Collections
Holdings: Vols 149 Cat
Notes: First and special editions.

NY —ALFRED UNIVERSITY, Herrick Memorial Library, Alfred, 14802. June E Brown, Head Librn
Notes: The Evelyn Tennyson Openhym Collection of modern British literature and social history. Papers, incl correspondence of authors concerned with the business aspects of authorship. Gift of Evelyn Tennyson Openhym of Wellsville, NY. Also, 5300 volumes of British literature.

NY —COLGATE UNIVERSITY, Everett Needham Case Library, Hamilton, 13346. Bruce M Brown, Collections Librn
Holdings: Vols 312 Uncat Mss
Notes: Strong collection. Incl some mss.

NY —HOFSTRA UNIVERSITY, Library, 1000 Fulton Ave, Hempstead, 11550. Charles R Andrews, Dean of Library Services

NY —COLUMBIA UNIVERSITY LIBRARIES, Rare Book & Manuscript Library, 801 Butler Library, 535 W 114 St, New York, 10027. Kenneth A Lohf, Librn
Holdings: Mss
Notes: Mss, letters, etc, many containing critical commentaries on Housman, Frost, Hardy, Benet, etc. Also writings about him. 700 items. Restricted use.

NY —UNIVERSITY OF ROCHESTER, Rush Rhees Library, Department of Rare Books and Special Collections, Rochester, 14627. Peter Dzwonkoski, Librn
Holdings: Vols 170 Cat Mss Pix
Notes: Incl 66 letters from the Poet Laureate to Helen Rochester Rogers, and others; correspondence more than 20 mss of individual poems; extensive book collection.

†NC —WAKE FOREST UNIVERSITY, Z Smith Reynolds Library, Box 7777, Reynold Sta, Winston-Salem, 27109. Richard J Murdoch, Rare Book Librn
Holdings: Vols 90 Cat

PA —BRYN MAWR COLLEGE, Canaday Library, Bryn Mawr, 19010. James Tanis, Dir
Holdings: Mss
Notes: The Wilson W Mills Collection of books and mss. Also, rare books in the Adelman Collection.

VT —UNIVERSITY OF VERMONT, Guy W Bailey/David W Howe Library, Burlington, 05405. John Buehler, Asst Dir for Special Collections
Holdings: Vols 483 Cat Mss Phonorecords
Notes: Incl books and pamphlets by Masefield in both US and English first editions and first, limited, autographed editions. 3 document boxes of Masefield mss and correspondence.

ON —QUEEN'S UNIVERSITY, Douglas Library, Kingston, K7L 5C4, Can. William F E Morley, Cur, Special Collections
Holdings: Vols 175 Cat Mss Pix
Notes: Subject strength of the collections.

MASEREEL, FRANS, 1889-1971

CA —UNIVERSITY OF CALIFORNIA, LOS ANGELES, Research Library, Dept of Special Collections, 405 Hilgard Ave, Los Angeles, 90024. Edward Shreeves, Chairman, Bibliographers Group; David S Zeidberg, Head
Holdings: Vols 125 Pix
Notes: 125 first and other editions of his books; 12 letters; 50 watercolors; 333 ink drawings.

MO —WASHINGTON UNIVERSITY, Libraries, Campus Box 1061, Saint Louis, 63130.
Holdings: 4500 Vols
Notes: The private library of the late Gert von Gontard. Incl works on art, literature (especially German), music, and theater. Contains 1200 vols Goetheana, with first editions, autographed letters and original drawings by Goethe. Also material on the Austrian writer Karl Kraus and the Belgian artist Frans Masereel.

MASKOKI INDIANS see Creek Indians

MASKS

TX —SOUTHERN METHODIST UNIVERSITY, Fondren Library, McCord

MASKS (cont.)

Theater Collection, Room 301, Dallas, 75275. Edyth Renshaw, Cur; Linda Sellers, Pub Serv
Holdings: Vols (2000) Uncat Mss Pix Slides Phonrecords
Notes: See *Theatre Collections in Libraries and Museums*, Gilder and Freedley (Theatre Arts, 1936). The McCord Theatre Collection encompasses the entire spectrum of the performing arts. The central purpose is to gather records of our regional theater before such ephemeral material is lost. Records of over two hundred early Texas theaters, some fragmentary and some relatively complete, are in the files. These records incl photographs of buildings, stagehands, orchestras, and performers. Local theatre history incl the once famous Dallas Little Theatre and the Margo Jones Theatre. The national theatre, opera, ballet, and circus archives incl pictures (some autographed), programs, posters, throw-aways, tear sheets, clippings, and letters. Our international archives are small, but we have some excellent material, eg, artifacts from Max Reinhardt's production of"The Miracle" which happened to go bankrupt in Dallas. After a few years the items were given to us. There are posters, tear sheets, souvenir programs, and other colorful items from Morris Gest and the Artef Collection. We have about 200 19th century English playbills and a few from the 18th century. There is a collection of modern English, French, and other European programs, many of them illustrated souvenir programs. Also, magazines on theater, cinema, and television (1800). Scrapbooks covering both southwest and Dallas theater, 1890s-1950s. Special Collections: artifacts and documents on puppets; masks; costume design; circus; and ballet and dance. The Harriet Bacon MacDonald Collection of over 200 photographs of musicians appearing in Dallas during the first three decades of the 20th century. Many autographed. Affiliated with Meadow Theatre of the Arts.

MASOCHISM

CA —UNIVERSITY OF CALIFORNIA, LOS ANGELES, Research Library, Dept of Special Collections, 405 Hilgard Ave, Los Angeles, 90024. Edward Shreeves, Chairman, Bibliographers Group; David S Zeidberg, Head
Notes: 27 linear feet of books, photographs, clippings, and notebooks relating to sado-masochism.

IN —INDIANA UNIVERSITY, Institute for Sex Research Library, 416 Morrison Hall, Bloomington, 47401. Douglas Freeman, Collections and Services Librn; Joan Brewer, Information Services Librn
Holdings: Vols (62,000) Cat Mss Pix Microforms
See also entry under Sex.

MASON, F. VAN WYCK

MA —BOSTON UNIVERSITY, Mugar Memorial Library, Special Collections Dept, 771 Commonwealth Ave, Boston, 02215. Howard B Gotlieb, Dir
Holdings: Cat Mss Pix
Notes: Mss, correspondence, etc collected in depth; incl publications by or about.

MASON, KARL

TN —VANDERBILT UNIVERSITY, Medical Center Library, Nashville, 37232. Mary H Teloh, Special Collections Librn
Holdings: Uncat Mss Pix Videotapes
Notes: The nucleus of the developing nutrition collection at Vanderbilt is the papers of medical researcher Joseph Goldberger, MD, and his associate W Henry Sebrell, Jr, MD. The collection consists of first editions and translations of classic books on pellagra, and the letters, mss, and notebooks compiled by Dr Goldberger and Dr Sebrell during their years of research on

pellagra. See *Nutrition Reviews*, 33(10):310-312, Oct 1975. 10 linear ft of mss. Library also has the archives of the American Institute of Nutrition and manuscripts representing the work of Karl Mason, PhD, Helen S Mitchell, PhD, Lydia J Roberts, PhD, and John B Youmans, MD.

MASON, LOWELL AND LUTHER WHITING

CT —YALE UNIVERSITY, Music Library, 98 Wall St, New Haven, 06520. Harold E Samuel, Librn
Holdings: Vols 10,300 // Cat Mss Microforms
Notes: Over 10,000 books and mss from the library of Lowell Mason; also his correspondence and related historical documents. See Eva J O'Meara, "The Lowell Mason Library of Music," *Yale University Library Gazette*, vol XL (1965), pp 57-74; and "The Lowell Mason Library," *Music Library Association Notes*, vol 28 (1971), pp 197-208.

†MD —UNIVERSITY OF MARYLAND, Library, Music Educators National Conference Historical Center, College Park, 20742. Bruce Wilson, Cur
Holdings: Cat Mss Pix Audiotapes
Notes: The official archive of the Music Educators' National Conference (MENC), and a repository for the documentation of music education. Incl the papers of the MENC, state units, and associated organizations and committees; personal papers and association items (notably, relating to Frances Elliott Clark, Lowell Mason, and Luther Whiting Mason); published proceedings of MENC and other groups; oral histories, numerous school music textbooks, and the archive of the Contemporary Music Project.

†NY —STATE UNIVERSITY OF NEW YORK, COLLEGE AT FREDONIA, Daniel A Reed Library, Fredonia, 14063.
Holdings: Vols (8000) Cat Phonorecords Audiotapes
Budget: ($12,500)
Notes: The Music Library supports the curricular needs of a large department of music which now has programs in both music education and performance. Separate card catalogs are maintained for 26,000 scores and more than 12,000 recordings and tape cassettes. The library has a small collection of 19th century American tunebooks, some Lowell Mason materials and a collection of sheet music and dance band arrangements numbering more than 3200 pieces and covering the period from 1850 through the big band era.

MASON, LUCY RANDOLPH

NC —DUKE UNIVERSITY, William R Perkins Library, Manuscript Dept, Durham, 27706. Ellen Gartrell, Cur of Mss
Holdings: Cat Mss
Notes: Emphasis on US South, especially CIO Organizing Committee papers, 1946-53 (ca 143,00 items). Large percentage have been commercially microfilmed under title "Operation Dixie." Also papers of Lucy Randolph Mason, Frank deVyver, Frank Morrison.

MASONRY

PA —CARNEGIE LIBRARY OF PITTSBURGH, Science & Technology Dept, 4400 Forbes Ave, Pittsburgh, 15213. Catherine M Brosky, Dept Head
Notes: Collection incl material on general construction, carpentry, masonry, plumbing, heating, air conditioning, corrosion and painting and numerous other building trades. Sweets Architectural File complete except for a few years. *Car Builders Encyclopedia of American Practice*, most editions since 1879.

MASONS (SECRET ORDER) see Freemasons and Freemasonry

MASS CASUALTIES—TREATMENT see Emergency Medical Services

MASS COMMUNICATIONS see Communications; Telecommunications

MASS MEDIA see Communications; Telecommunications

MASS PSYCHOLOGY see Social Psychology

MASS TRANSFER

KY —UNIVERSITY OF KENTUCKY, Robert E Shaver Library of Engineering, 355

Anderson Hall, Lexington, 40506. Russell H Powell, Engineering Librn
Holdings: Vols (48,000) Cat Microforms

MASSACHUSETTS

MA —UNIVERSITY OF MASSACHUSETTS AT AMHERST, Library, Amherst, 01003. Siegfried Feller, Assoc Dir for Collection Development
Holdings: Cat
Notes: Incl some 1000 pamphlets by or about Massachusetts persons, or about Massachusetts places, societies, etc, 1729-1902. Indexed calendar.

MA —CAPE COD NATIONAL SEASHORE, Reference Library, Park Headquarters S, Wellfleet, 02663. Virginia Osborn, Librn
Holdings: Vols (3000) Cat Mss Maps Pix Slides Phonorecords 16mm Films
Budget: ($2000)
Notes: Cape Cod natural and human history.

MASSACHUSETTS—GENEALOGY

FL —ORLANDO PUBLIC LIBRARY, Local History & Genealogy Dept, 100 Block of Central Ave, Orlando, 32806. Eileen B Willis, Librn
Holdings: Vols 11,000 Cat Maps Microforms
Budget: $8000
Notes: Strong collection in local genealogy materials on Mass, NY, Va, Ga, and Florida. Contains exceptional holdings on all New England States, Penn, and NJ.
See also entry under Genealogy - Collections.

MA —STURGIS LIBRARY, Rte 6A, Barnstable, 02630. Susan R Klein, Chief Librn
Holdings: Vols (1500) Cat Mss Maps Microforms
Budget: ($1000)
Notes: Lothrop Room Collection of genealogy and history is considered to be the finest on Cape Cod. No printed vital records for the County of Barnstable, but 37 books of handwritten *Genealogical Notes of Cape Cod Families* (1620-1850), also on microfilm. Also incl is the Stanely W Smith Collection of books, pamphlets and manuscript materials (mostly original land deeds, all Cape Cod oriented, some of them Indian and dating from the early 1700s). The Percy F Rex Collection represents a unique library of Cape Cod literature. Many rarities, incl early sermons preached on the Cape and pamphlets on Cape Cod canal, etc.

MA —FREE PUBLIC LIBRARY, Genealogy Room, 613 Pleasant St, Bedford, 02740. Paul A Cyr, Librn
Holdings: Vols (10,000) Cat Mss Maps Pix Microforms
Budget: ($1000)
Notes: Extensive collection on the history and genealogy of New England, with a strong emphasis on southeastern Massachusetts. Materials incl books, periodicals, mss, microfilms, and pictures of New England life. Unique features of the collection incl the *Leonard Papers*, mss of vital records of early Bristol County, *Repertoires des Mariages* of Province Quebec, Canada, and a collection on the Society of Friends, or Quakers.

MA —NEW ENGLAND HISTORIC GENEALOGICAL SOCIETY, Library, 101 Newbury St, Boston, 02116. Ralph J Crandell, Dir
Holdings: Vols (250,000) Mss Maps Microforms Pix
Notes: New England genealogy. Especially strong Massachusetts, Maine, and New Hampshire, although all states are well represented, as are the relevancies of each subject listed in this volume with regard to British antecedent and contemporary history. Special strengths in local history and biography, obituaries, etc, incl parish registers, censuses, British and American. 3125 linear ft of mss.

MA —BRIDGEWATER PUBLIC LIBRARY, 15 South St, Bridgewater, 02324. Maryellen Remmert, Dir
Holdings: Cat Mss Maps Pix
Notes: Incl some genealogical material of

MASSACHUSETTS—GENEALOGY (cont.)

considerable interest since Bridgewater was the first inland colony of the Plymouth (Pilgrim) Colony, being known as the Duxbury Plantation.

MA —CONCORD FREE PUBLIC LIBRARY, 129 Main St, Concord, 01742. Rose Marie Mitten, Dir
Holdings: Vols 2000 Cat Mss Maps Pix
Notes: Also town, church and cemetery records.

MA —HISTORIC DEERFIELD-POCUMTUCK VALLEY MEMORIAL ASSOCIATION, Libraries, Memorial St, Box 53, Deerfield, 01342. David R Proper, Librn
Holdings: Vols (17,000) Cat Mss Maps Pix Microforms
Notes: Local and regional history, especially western Massachusetts. Also, remnants of several collection of books available to early Deerfield and Greenfield residents. Strong ms collection dealing with the region's families, businesses, etc. These consist of sermons, diaries, town and church records, voluntary societies' archives, etc. Extensive collection of photographs of the people and buildings of Deerfield and its environs, and travels in Maine, California, and England (1880s to 1920s). Also, large collection of glassplate negatives. Houses the Connecticut Valley Bibliography, a comprehensive card file on the history and culture of the Connecticut Valley of Massachusetts.

MA —DUKES COUNTY HISTORICAL SOCIETY, School & Cooke Sts, Edgartown, 02539. Thomas E Norton, Dir
Holdings: Cat Mss Maps Pix Audiotapes Microforms
Notes: History and genealogy of Massachusetts, especially Martha's Vineyard. Also, materials on whaling and Indians of the region.

MA —BERKSHIRE ATHENAEUM, 1 Wendell Ave, Pittsfield, 01201. Ruth T Degenhardt, Head Local History & Literature
Holdings: Vols (9000) Cat Mss Maps Pix Microforms
Budget: ($2000)
Notes: Cooke collection: typescript and manuscript copies of church and cemetery records for all towns in Berkshire County, and surrounding towns in Vermont and New York. Family History File incl abstracts of research by genealogists on families throughout New England. Browne Collection: personal notes and research material of noted genealogist concerned with all facets of Northern Berkshire genealogy. Surname index available. Shepard Collection: extensive collection of research notes and vital records of families throughout Western Massachusetts and bordering areas of New York and Vermont.

MA —PLYMOUTH PUBLIC LIBRARY, North St, Plymouth, 02360. Anne Clark, Reference Librn
Holdings: Vols 600 Cat Mss Maps Pix
Notes: Most of the collection deals with pre-1800 early journals, diaries, laws, records of Plymouth Colony and town.

MA —STOCKBRIDGE LIBRARY ASSOCIATION, Main St, Box H, Stockbridge, 01262. Rosemary Schmeyer, Librn
Holdings: Vols (1200) Cat Mss Maps Pix
Notes: The Historical Room contains approximately 1200 vols of genealogical reference, ie, Massachusetts Soldiers and Sailors of the Revolution, Vital Statistics for towns in Massachusetts, local history, Indian history, books by and about Stockbridge residents, and a large collection of family papers of the Sedgwick and Field families among many others. These are being cataloged with the help of a special grant.

MASSACHUSETTS—GOVERNMENT PUBLICATIONS

MA —UNIVERSITY OF MASSACHUSETTS AT AMHERST, Library, Amherst, 01003.

William R Thompson, Head, Documents Collection
Holdings: Vols 11,800
Notes: The Massachusetts State Documents collection contains Massachusetts Legislative Documents, 1850-date, the Massachusetts Public Documents series 1850-date, Massachusetts town reports, and current state agency publications. The major part of this collection is in hard copy; however, some of the more recent legislative and agency publications are on microfilm. A subject card catalog provides access to the agency publications and the Public Documents series.

MA —BOSTON PUBLIC LIBRARY, Government Documents Department, Boston, 02117. V Lloyd Jameson, Cur
Holdings: Maps Microforms
Notes: Massachusetts state documents. Maintain subject index to selected Massachusetts documents published since the 1960s. Depository.

MASSACHUSETTS—HISTORY

MA —UNIVERSITY OF MASSACHUSETTS AT AMHERST, Library, Amherst, 01003. Siegfried Feller, Assoc Dir for Collection Development
Holdings: Cat Microforms
Notes: The collections in Massachusetts history incl works on the history of the Commonwealth and of its subdivisions. Source materials incl letterpress editions of most important colony and town records, extensive holdings of published vital records, and a special collection of ca 1000 pamphlets by or about Massachusetts persons, or about Massachusetts places, societies, etc 1729-1902. Incl extensive microform holdings of: Massachusetts Archives (Felt Collection); original manuscripts census schedules for Massachusetts (1st-12th censuses), Suffolk County deeds (1629-1886); Suffolk County probate records (1628-1899); Hampshire County probate records (1660-1820); "Court Files Suffolk" (records of courts throughout the colony, province, state, and commonwealth, 1629-1797); Massachusetts city directories through 1860; Massachusetts newspapers in microform; and the microform publications of the Massachusetts Historical Society.

MA —STURGIS LIBRARY, Rte 6A, Barnstable, 02630. Susan R Klein, Chief Librn
Holdings: Vols (1500) Cat Mss Maps Microforms
Budget: ($1000)
Notes: Lothrop Room Collection of genealogy and history is considered to be the finest on Cape Cod. No printed vital records for the County of Barnstable, but 37 books of handwritten *Genealogical Notes of Cape Cod Families* (1620-1850), also on microfilm. Also incl is the Stanley W Smith Collection of books, pamphlets and manuscript materials (mostly original land deeds, all Cape Cod oriented, some of them Indian and dating from the early 1700s). The Percy F Rex Collection represents a unique library of Cape Cod literature. Many rarities, incl early sermons preached on the Cape and pamphlets on Cape Cod canal, etc.

MA —FREE PUBLIC LIBRARY, Genealogy Room, 613 Pleasant St, Bedford, 02740. Paul A Cyr, Librn
Holdings: Vols (10,000) Cat Mss Maps Pix Microforms
Budget: ($1000)
Notes: Extensive collection on the history and genealogy of New England, with a strong emphasis on southeastern Massachusetts. Materials incl books, periodicals, mss, microfilms, and pictures of New England life. Unique features of the collection incl the *Leonard Papers* ms of vital records of early Bristol County, *Repertoires des Mariages* of Province Quebec, Canada, and a collection on the Society of Friends, or Quakers.

MA —MASSACHUSETTS HISTORICAL SOCIETY LIBRARY, 1154 Boylston St, Boston, 02215. John D Cushing, Librn
Holdings: Mss Maps Microforms
Notes: One of more than 5000 individual

collections in the Library, this collection incl the Adams Family papers and materials relating to Massachusetts and New England. The Library's collection of mss has been cataloged and issued in nine folio vols by G K Hall & Co of Boston. It is widely distributed throughout the United States and Europe.

MA —NEW ENGLAND HISTORIC GENEALOGICAL SOCIETY, Library, 101 Newbury St, Boston, 02116. Ralph J Crandell, Dir
Holdings: Vols (250,000) Mss Maps Microforms Pix
Notes: New England genealogy. Especially strong Massachusetts, Maine, and New Hampshire, although all states are well represented, as are the relevancies of each subject listed in this volume with regard to British antecedent and contemporary history. Special strengths in local history and biography, obituaries, etc, incl parish registers, censuses, British and American. 3125 linear ft of mss.

MA —STATE LIBRARY OF MASSACHUSETTS, 341 State House, Boston, 02133. Gaspar Caso, State Librn
Holdings: Vols 10,000 Cat Maps Pix Microforms

MA —BRIDGEWATER PUBLIC LIBRARY, 15 South St, Bridgewater, 02324. Maryellen Remmert, Dir
Holdings: Cat Mss Maps Pix
Notes: Incl some genealogical material of considerable interest since Bridgewater was the first inland colony of the Plymouth (Pilgrim) Colony, being known as the Duxbury Plantation.

MA —PEABODY INSTITUTE LIBRARY, Danvers Archival Center, 15 Sylvan St, Danvers, 01923. Richard B Trask, Archivist, Rare Books & Special Collections
Holdings: Vols 5000 Cat Mss
Notes: The Ellerton J Brehaut Collection on New England witchcraft, especially Salem witchcraft. (Danvers, where the library is located, was part of Salem at the time of the witchcraft trials.) 17th and 18th century English and American books on witchcraft; transcripts of all known trial records. Manuscript records of the First Church of Salem Village. Special catalog to collection. Danvers History Collection consists of 5000 volumes, 250,000 mss, numerous photos, newspaper clippings, maps, audiotapes, and visual tapes.

MA —HISTORIC DEERFIELD-POCUMTUCK VALLEY MEMORIAL ASSOCIATION, Libraries, Memorial St, Box 53, Deerfield, 01342. David R Proper, Librn
Holdings: Vols (17,000) Cat Mss Maps Pix Microforms
Notes: Local and regional history, especially western Massachusetts. Also, remnants of several collection of books available to early Deerfield and Greenfield residents. Strong ms collection dealing with the region's families, businesses, etc. These consist of sermons, diaries, town and church records, voluntary societies' archives, etc. Extensive collection of photographs of the people and buildings of Deerfield and its environs, and travels in Maine, California, and England (1880s to 1920s). Also, large collection of glassplate negatives. Houses the Connecticut Valley Bibliography, a comprehensive card file on the history and culture of the Connecticut Valley of Massachusetts.

MA —DUKES COUNTY HISTORICAL SOCIETY, School & Cooke Sts, Edgartown, 02539. Thomas E Norton, Dir
Holdings: Cat Mss Maps Pix Audiotapes Microforms
Notes: History and genealogy of Massachusetts, especially Martha's Vineyard. Also, materials on whaling and Indians of the region.

MA —GREENFIELD COMMUNITY COLLEGE, Pioneer Valley Resource Center, One College Drive, Greenfield, 01301. Margaret E C Howland, Dir; Carol Letson, Librn
Holdings: Vols 2000 Cat Mss Pix Phonorecords Videotapes 16mm Film Microforms
Notes: A special collection of primary and

MASSACHUSETTS—HISTORY (cont.)

secondary material on the area surrounding the Connecticut River in Western Massachusetts. Covers every aspect of the Pioneer Valley, past and present, including art and artists, authors, census data, environment, ethnicity, geology, history, industry and commerce, literature, politics and government, etc. Separately housed. Open 20 hours a week.

MA —GROTON PUBLIC LIBRARY, Main St, Groton, 01450. Helen J Maynard, Librn
Holdings: Vols 100 // Cat Microforms
Notes: Town history of Groton, Mass.

MA —HINGHAM PUBLIC LIBRARY, 66 Leavitt St, Hingham, 02043. Walter T Dziura, Dir
Holdings: Cat mss Maps Pix Slides Microforms
Notes: A collection of about 2000 items relating to the history of the town from the 1600's to the present. Incl correspondence, legal documents, diaries and day books, account books, broadsides, pictures. Contains a large portion of four major collections; those of historian George Lincoln, historian Solomon Lincoln, historian Mason Foley and Hinghamiana collector Norman A Hersey. Items of special importance incl papers of town clerk Daniel Cushing, from the 1600's; Revolutionary War troop muster rolls; early land grant maps of the town; papers of artists Frank Vining Smith and Isaac Sprague; correspondence of Massachusetts governor John D Long; steamship history. An unpublished catalog of the collection is available through interlibrary loan. Most of the collection is on microfilm and may be borrowed through interlibrary loan.

MA —LENOX LIBRARY ASSOCIATION, Main St, Lenox, 01240. Denis J Lesieur, Dir
Holdings: Vols 800 Mss Maps Pix VF
Notes: Material covering Massachusetts and surrounding states with emphasis on Berkshire County, ca 1760-. Incl genealogy. 124 linear feet of documents.

MA —POLLARD MEMORIAL LIBRARY, 401 Merrimack St, Lowell, 01852. Walter V Hickey, Libr Asst
Holdings: Vols (3000) Cat Pix
Notes: Lowell History Collection. Most books were published in the late 1800s when Lowell was particularly prosperous. Holdings incl Lowell history, vital records, works by Lowell authors and biographies of former Lowell residents. Microfilm of Lowell newspapers from 1837 to the present, as well as City Directories from 1832. Also a full collection of Jack Kerouac's work. Also Town and County histories and published Genealogies, mostly from the late 1800's.

MA —UNIVERSITY OF LOWELL, Library, One University Ave, Lowell, 01854. Martha Mayo, Special Collections Librn
Holdings: Vols (25,000) Cat Mss Maps Pix Slides Microforms Videotapes
Notes: Special collections is the historical depository for several organizations involved with collecting all aspects of Lowell's history incl the Lowell Historical Society, the Lowell Museum, the Boston & Maine Historical Society, and the Middlesex Canal Association.

MA —NEEDHAM FREE PUBLIC LIBRARY, 1139 Highland Ave, Needham Heights, 02194. Vivian D McIver, Dir
Holdings: Vols 56 Cat Mss Maps Pix Slides Phonorecords Audiotapes Microforms
Notes: Local history of Needham, Mass. Partially cataloged.

MA —PETERSHAM HISTORICAL SOCIETY, Library, N Main St, Petersham, 01366. Delight G Haines, Librn
Holdings: Vols (900) Cat Mss Maps Pix
Notes: The Petersham area. Genealogical files on Petersham Families.

MA —BERKSHIRE ATHENAEUM, 1 Wendell Ave, Pittsfield, 01201. Ruth T Degenhardt, Head Local History & Literature
Holdings: Vols (9000) Cat Mss Maps Pix Microforms
Budget: ($2000)
Notes: Primary focus is on the development

of Berkshire, Massachusetts, regional history and culture, with particular emphasis on the industrial development of Berkshire County and the Colonial and Revolutionary periods in the Berkshires. Entire collection spans all New England states and New York State, on all topics. Special strength is in published local histories. No separate catalog. There is a reference index.

MA —BERKSHIRE COUNTY HISTORICAL SOCIETY, Margaret H Hall Library, 780 Holmes Rd, Pittsfield, 01201. Janet Low, Librn
Holdings: Vols 1200 Cat Mss Maps Pix
Budget: $300
Notes: History of Berkshire County and Herman Melville.

MA —PLYMOUTH PUBLIC LIBRARY, North St, Plymouth, 02360. Anne Clark, Reference Librn
Holdings: Vols 600 Cat Mss Maps Pix
Notes: Most of the collection deals with pre-1800 Plymouth. Includes facsimiles and/or printed editions of early journals, diaries, laws, records of Plymouth Colony and town.

MA —ESSEX INSTITUTE, James Duncan Phillips Library, 132-34 Essex St, Salem, 01970. Prudence K Backman, Manuscript Librn
Holdings: Vols Mss Pamphlets Broadsides Maps Newspapers Periodicals Pix
Notes: Over 300,000 printed items and 4000 cubic ft of mss all related to the history and culture of Essex County and New England. Incl writings of local authors, Nathaniel Hawthorne, Anne Bradstreet, Lucy Larcom, Jones Very, John Greenleaf Whittier, J P Marquand, Harriet Prescott Spofford, Mary Abigail Dodge and John Updike. Mss incl letters, business papers, diaries, and account books of Essex County residents from the 17th to 20th centuries.
See also entries under Maritime History; Hawthorne, Nathaniel; Larcom, Lucy; Witchcraft.

MA —SPRINGFIELD CITY LIBRARY, Genealogy and Local History Dept, 220 State St, Springfield, 01103. Joseph Carvalho III, Supervisor
Holdings: Vols (18,000) Cat Mss Maps Pix Microforms VF
Budget: ($8000)
Notes: New England, Massachusetts, local history (Springfield), and genealogy collections. collections. 18,000 pictures, 3200 microforms, ca 15,000 clippings, pamphlets, etc (280 ft of vertical files).

MA —STOCKBRIDGE LIBRARY ASSOCIATION, Main St, Box H, Stockbridge, 01262. Rosemary Schmeyer, Librn
Holdings: Vols (1200) Cat Mss Maps Pix
Notes: The Historical Room contains approximately 1200 vols of genealogical reference, ie, Massachusetts Soldiers and Sailors of the Revolution, Vital Statistics for towns in Massachusetts, local history, Indian history, books by and about Stockbridge residents, and a large collection of family papers of the Sedgwick and Field families among many others. These are being cataloged with the help of a special grant.

†MA —OLD STURBRIDGE VILLAGE, Research Library, Sturbridge, 01566.
Notes: Danvers history and Salem village history. Incl mss, pictures and material on Salem witchcraft trials.

MA —VINEYARD HAVEN PUBLIC LIBRARY, Main St, Vineyard Haven, 02563. Mary D Fullos, Librn
Holdings: Vols (200) Mss Maps Pix
Notes: History of Martha's Vineyard. Partially cataloged. Vineyard Gazette microfilmed.

MA —WENHAM HISTORICAL ASSOCIATION AND MUSEUM, Timothy Pickering Library, 132 Main St, Wenham, 01984. Eleanor E Thompson, Dir
Holdings: Vols (1000) Cat Mss Pix
Notes: Incl books and broadsides on agriculture from 1800s.

MA —WESTWOOD PUBLIC LIBRARY, Ernest J Baker Historical Collection, 668 High St, Westwood, 02090. Thomas Diti, Dir
Holdings: Vols 200 Cat Mss Maps Pix Slides

Audiotapes Microfilm
Notes: Separate catalog and printed list of most of materials cataloged. Special emphasis on Westwood history (incl Dedham, of which Westwood was a part until 1897). Albums containing photos of the older homes and the history of the various landmarks and town departments.

MA —WILMINGTON MEMORIAL LIBRARY, Middlesex Ave, Wilmington, 01887. Philip W Meriam, Dir
Holdings: Vols 528 Cat Maps Pix Microforms
Notes: Especially the Wilmington area and Middlesex County.

†MA —CLARK UNIVERSITY, Robert Hutchings Goddard Library, Worcester, 01610. Dorothy Mosa Kowski, Rare Books Librn
Holdings: Uncat
Notes: Ester Forbes' papers, 1906-1967; ca 250 items, ms of an unpublished novel entitled The Sons of Ugo; some hundreds of pages of notes concerning the early history of Massachusetts; carbon copy of typescript of the novel Paradise (1937); set of uncorrected printer's proofs of the novel The Running of the Tide (1948); and several hundred compositions, themes, essays, and stories, written by Miss Forbes both as school assignments and on her own, from childhood through high school and college. Gift from the family of Esther Forbes.

MASSACHUSETTS—IMPRINTS

MA —AMHERST COLLEGE, Library, Amherst, 01002. John Lancaster, Special Collections Librn
Holdings: Vols 550 Cat
Notes: Amherst imprints.

MA —STATE LIBRARY OF MASSACHUSETTS, 341 State House, Boston, 02133. Gaspar Caso, State Librn
Holdings: Vols 5000 Cat Maps

MASSACHUSETTS—MAPS

MA —UNIVERSITY OF MASSACHUSETTS AT AMHERST, Library, Amherst, 01003. Siegfried Feller, Assoc Dir for Collection Development
Notes: Special emphases: Defense Mapping Agency and US Geological Survey (topographic) depository; 700 sheets of Massachusetts cities and towns partially cataloged. US Geological Survey (geological) are cataloged and housed separately.

MASSACHUSETTS—PICTURES, ILLUSTRATIONS, ETC.

MA —LENOX LIBRARY ASSOCIATION, Main St, Lenox, 01240. Denis J Lesieur, Dir
Holdings: Pix
Notes: Edwin Hale Lincoln, (1848-1938), Pittsfield photographer. Collection contains glass plate negatives and platinum prints concentrating on Lenox estates, ca 1883-1933. Publication: A Pride of Places; Lenox Summer Cottages 1883-1933, Donald T Oakes, ed (Lenox Library Association, 1981).

MASSACHUSETTS—POLITICS AND GOVERNMENT

CA —WHITTIER COLLEGE, Wardman Library, Whittier, 90608. Christine Erdmann, Special Collections Librn
Notes: The Frederick M Meek Collection of 7000 items by and about John Greenleaf Whittier, incl copies of limited editions and association copies, virtually all of his published works in all states, issues and editions, runs of newspapers to which Whittier contributed, magazine articles, broadsides, handbills, pamphlets, and correspondence, incl much with Mass Gov Claflin on contemporary politics.

MA —STATE LIBRARY OF MASSACHUSETTS, 341 State House, Boston, 02133. Gaspar Caso, State Librn
Holdings: Vols 100,000 Cat Maps Pix Microforms
Notes: Legal repository for all state, county and town publications.

MASSACHUSETTS—POLITICS AND GOVERNMENT (cont.)

MA —BOSTON COLLEGE LIBRARIES, Chestnut Hill, 02167.
Notes: Papers of Congressman the Rev Robert Drinan.

MA —GREENFIELD COMMUNITY COLLEGE, Pioneer Valley Resource Center, One College Drive, Greenfield, 01301. Margaret E C Howland, Dir; Carol Letson, Librn
Holdings: Vols 2000 Cat Mss Pix Phonorecords Videotapes 16mm Film Microforms
Notes: A special collection of primary and secondary material on the area surrounding the Connecticut River in Western Massachusetts. Covers every aspect of the Pioneer Valley, past and present, including art and artists, authors, census data, environment, ethnicity, geology, history, industry and commerce, literature, politics and government, etc. Separately housed. Open 20 hours a week.

MA —STONEHILL COLLEGE, Cushing-Martin Library, Washington St, North Easton, 02356. James J Kenneally, Cur
Holdings: Cat Mss Pix
Notes: About 12,000 letters, speeches and photographs; 104 scrapbooks, plus other memorabilia of Representative Martin, of Massachusetts, 1925-1965; Speaker of the House, 1947-1949, 1953-1955.

MASSACHUSETTS—PROBATE COURT RECORDS

†MA —BOSTON PUBLIC LIBRARY, Copley Sq, Boston, 02117.
Holdings: Cat Microforms
Notes: Microform Publications: Suffolk County Probate Court Records, 1636- 1852; Middlesex County Probate Court Records, 1648-1871; Hampshire County Probate Court Records, 1660-1820.

MASSACHUSETTS AUTHORS see Authors, Massachusetts

MASSACHUSETTS FIRST CORPS OF CADETS

MA —BOSTON UNIVERSITY, Mugar Memorial Library, Special Collections Dept, 771 Commonwealth Ave, Boston, 02215. Howard B Gotlieb, Dir
Holdings: Vols 4000 Cat Mss Pix
Notes: Correspondence 1741-1960.

MASSACHUSETTS INSTITUTE OF TECHNOLOGY (MIT)

CA —CALIFORNIA INSTITUTE OF TECHNOLOGY, Robert A Millikan Memorial Library, Archives, 1201 E California Blvd, Pasadena, 91125. Judith R Goodstein, Archivist
Notes: The Lee A DuBridge papers, incl 228 boxes of correspondence, documents, reports, and memorabilia reflecting his tenure as head of MIT Radiation Laboratory, 1940-1946; as president of Caltech, 1946-1969; and his participation in professional and governmental organizations.

MA —MASSACHUSETTS INSTITUTE OF TECHNOLOGY, Institute Archives, Special Collections, Cambridge, 02139.
Notes: Institute Archives incl material documenting the evolution of modern science and engineering and its impact on society; the papers of Norbert Wiener, the Magnetic Core Memory (Whirlwind) Project, and the Recombinant DNA History Collection are rich resources in this area. Emphasis has also been placed on the role of scientists and engineers in the formation of science policy. Diverse contributions are illustrated by the papers of Karl T Compton, Vannevar Bush, James R Killian Jr, Jerome B Wiesner, Carroll Wilson, Bernard T Feld, and many other faculty members who have served in the government or taken public stands on science issues. The activities of private organizations are represented by such collections as the records of the Union of Concerned Scientists and the Citizens League Against the Sonic Boom.The research materials in the Archives are complemented by photographs, instruments, biographical files, and museum holding.

MASSACHUSETTS LAW see Law, Massachusetts

MASSACHUSETTS SOCIETY FOR PROMOTING AGRICULTURE

MA —WENHAM HISTORICAL ASSOCIATION AND MUSEUM, Timothy Pickering Library, 132 Main St, Wenham, 01984. Eleanor E Thompson, Dir
Holdings: Vols (1000) Cat Mss Pix
Notes: Incl books and broadsides on agriculture from 1800s.

MASSACHUSETTS SOCIETY FOR THE UNIVERSITY EDUCATION OF WOMEN

MA —BOSTON UNIVERSITY, Mugar Memorial Library, Special Collections Dept, 771 Commonwealth Ave, Boston, 02215. Howard B Gotlieb, Dir
Holdings: Cat Mss

MASSASOIT (INDIAN CHIEF)

RI —BROWN UNIVERSITY, John Hay Library, 20 Prospect St, Providence, 02912. Mark N Brown, Cur Mss
Holdings: // Mss
Notes: 8 mss in the hand of Roger Williams incl his copy of Chief Ousamaquin's (Massasoit's) deed of land (1646), letters to the Plymouth Colony, a copy of Proceedings of the General Assembly (1655), and his proposals to resolve the Pawtuxet-Providence boundary dispute.

MASSAWOMEKE INDIANS see Iroquois Indians

MASSEE, MAY

KS —EMPORIA STATE UNIVERSITY, William Allen White Library, Emporia, 66801. Mary E Bogan, Special Collections Librn
Holdings: Cat Mss Pix
Notes: The May Massee Collection of children's books edited by Miss Massee over a period of 40 years. Incl manuscripts, proofs, galleys, original art work, dummies, research notes, correspondence, research notes, reminiscences, ephemera, memorabilia, and audiovisual materials based on books published by her. A book catalog of the collection was published in 1979. Copies of this publication may be purchased from the William Allen White Library. The May Massee Collection: Creative Publishing for Children, 1923-1963, a Checklist, Dr George V Hodowanec, editor. William Allen White Library, Emporia State University, 1979. (2320 pieces of art work, 18 linear feet of other materials included in the library holdings.)
See also entry under Children's Literature

MASSENET, JULES

IL —NORTHWESTERN UNIVERSITY, Music Library, 1937 Sheridan Rd, Evanston, 60201. Don L Roberts, Head Music Librn
Holdings: Uncat Mss
Notes: Part of the materials are in the Moldenhauer Archive. Most of these materials are uncataloged at this time. 110 letters; music mss.

WA —UNIVERSITY OF WASHINGTON LIBRARIES, Music Library, DN-10, Seattle, 98195. David A Wood, Music Librn
Holdings: Vols (35,000) Cat Mss Microforms
Budget: ($11,700)
Notes: Special areas of strength incl the Hazel G Kinscella collection of colonial and early 19th-century Americana; a collection early opera scores (17th-19th centuries).

MASSIE, WILLIAM

TX —UNIVERSITY OF TEXAS LIBRARIES, General Libraries, Barker Texas History Center, PO Box P, Austin, 78712. Don Carleton, Dir

MASSINE, LEONIDE

KS —WICHITA PUBLIC LIBRARY, Art & Music Division, 223 S Main, Wichita, 67202. Leonard Messineo, Jr, Head, Art & Music Division; Deborah Hamilton, Special Collections Librn
Holdings: Uncat Audiotapes Videotape Pix
Notes: Alice Bauman Dance Symposia Collection. Contains 300 hours of audio tapes, 1 hour-long video tape, several hundred photographs, and fugitive material of the American Dance Symposia held in Wichita from 1968-1972. The symposia covered all dance idioms-ballet, modern, jazz, folk, ethnic, dance education and therapy-and featured such notable figures such as Leonide Massine, Martha Hill, William Christensen, Alfonso Cimber, Toni Intravaia, James Clouser, Eleo Pomare, Juana de Laban, and many others. Characterized by the Kansas City Star as the "most distinguished faculties of fine artists ever assembled in the contemporary world of dance."

NY —NEW YORK PUBLIC LIBRARY, Performing Arts Research Center, Dance Collection, 111 Amsterdam Ave, New York, 10023. Genevieve Oswald, Cur
Notes: Extensive biographical and visual material. Includes photographs, programs, clippings, scrapbooks, tape-recorded interviews, and films. The Leonide Massine Collection of over 300 ballet films documents much of Massine's choreographic work by various ballet companies from 1930 through the 1960s, with special emphasis on the Ballet Russe de Monte Carlo.

MASSINGHAM, HAROLD J.

IL —ILLINOIS STATE UNIVERSITY, Milner Library, Dept of Special Collections, Normal, 61761. Robert Sokan, Librn
Notes: First editions, limited editions, ephemera, etc.

MASTODON

IL —WHEATON COLLEGE, Buswell Memorial Library, Wheaton, 60187. Paul Snezek, Library Dir
Holdings: Mss Pix Cat
Notes: Comprehensive collection of material concerning the recovery and restoration of a Mastodod in DuPage County, IL.

MASTERS, EDGAR LEE

DC —GEORGETOWN UNIVERSITY, Library, Special Collections Div, 37 & O Sts NW, Washington, 20057. George M Barringer, Special Collections Librn; Nicholas B Sheetz, Mss Librn
Holdings: Vols (200) Uncat Mss Pix
Notes: Papers of Kimball Flaccus, American poet, relating to his unpublished biography of Masters; including correspondence from Masters, run of books by and about Masters.

IL —NEWBERRY LIBRARY, 60 W Walton St, Chicago, 60610. Diana Haskell, Cur of Modern Mss
Holdings: Vols 150 Cat Mss
Notes: Restricted use: noncirculting.

IN —INDIANA UNIVERSITY, Lilly Library, Seventh St, Bloomington, 47405. William R Cagle, Librn
Notes: Writings by author Edgar Lee Masters.

MO —SAINT LOUIS PUBLIC LIBRARY, Gardner Rare Book Room, 1301 Olive St, Saint Louis, 63103. Julanne M Good, Supervisor; Martha Riley, Rare Books Librn
Holdings: Vols (2300) Cat
Budget: ($5573)
Notes: First editions of authors having some association with William Marion Reedy and Reedy's Mirror, such as Sara Teasdale, Zoe

MASTERS, EDGAR LEE (cont.)

Akins, Fannie Hurst, Edgar Lee Masters, Babette Deutsch, Richard LeGallienne, etc. Also first editions of selected St Louis and/or Missouri authors such as T S Eliot, Samuel L Clemens, Theodore Dreiser and Tennessee Williams. Noncirculating.

RI —BROWN UNIVERSITY, John Hay Library, 20 Prospect St, Providence, 02912. Mark N Brown, Cur Mss
Holdings: // Mss
Notes: About 300 items for the period 1928 to 1942 consisting chiefly of letters to his son, Hilary T Masters, with ms poems, short stories, sketches, and two letters from H L Mencken to Hilary Masters. Restricted.

VA —UNIVERSITY OF VIRGINIA, Alderman Library, Clifton Waller Barrett Collection, Charlottesville, 22901. Joan St C Crane, Cur of American Literature Collections
Notes: Papers.

MASTERS, JOHN

MA —BOSTON UNIVERSITY, Mugar Memorial Library, Special Collections Dept, 771 Commonwealth Ave, Boston, 02215. Howard B Gotlieb, Dir
Holdings: //Cat Mss Correspondence

MASTURBATION

IN —INDIANA UNIVERSITY, Institute for Sex Research Library, 416 Morrison Hall, Bloomington, 47401. Douglas Freeman, Collections and Services Librn; Joan Brewer, Information Services Librn
Holdings: Vols (62,000) Cat Mss Pix Microforms
See also entry under Sex.

MATADOR LAND AND CATTLE COMPANY

TX —TEXAS TECH UNIVERSITY, Library, Lubbock, 79409. David J Murrah, Assoc Dir for Special Collections

MATAS, RUDOLPH

LA —TULANE UNIVERSITY, Howard-Tilton Memorial Library, Special Collections Div, 7001 Freret St, New Orleans, 70118. Wilbur E Meneray, Librn
Holdings: Vols (700) Cat Mss Pix
Notes: Publications of 19th and 20th century New Orleans and Louisiana medical associations and physicians. Correspondence and diaries of Louisiana physicians from the 18th century to the present including those of Charles Cassidy Bass, Stanford Emerson Chaille, Joseph Jones, Edmund Kells, Rudolph Matas, Joseph Montegut, John Leonard Riddell and Edmond Souchon.

MATCHBOOK COVERS see Matchcovers

MATCHCOVERS

OH —BOWLING GREEN STATE UNIVERSITY, Library, Popular Culture Library, Bowling Green, 43403.
Notes: Extensive holdings of Big-Little books, comic books, matchbook covers, picture postcards, personal scrapbooks, trading cards, posters, magazines, film pressbooks, juvenile series novels and popular literature.

MATCHETT, DAVID F.

IL —CHICAGO HISTORICAL SOCIETY, Library, Clark St at North Ave, Chicago, 60614. Archie Motley, Manuscript Librn
Notes: Papers of: Emmet Dedmon, newspaper editor; Richard J Finnegan, newspaper editor; Rev Andres M Greeley, sociologist and author; attorney and civil liberties activist Pearl Hart; Robert J Havighurst, educator; social activist John Kearney; Kenesaw Mountain Landis, Federal Judge and first Commissioner of Baseball; Judge David F Matchett; Ivan Molek,

Slovenian language publisher in Chicago; Max R Naiman, Communist Party activist; Ralph G Newman, book and autograph dealer and manuscript appraiser; Otto L Schmidt, physician and President of the Chicago and Illinois State Historical Societites; and Dempsey Travis, black mortgage banker.

MATERIA MEDICA

IN —ELI LILLY AND COMPANY, Scientific Library, 307 E McCarty St, Indianapolis, 46285. Adele Hoskin, Chief Librn
Holdings: Vols (35,000) Cat Microforms
Notes: Drug product information (1.7 million cards); drug encyclopedias, foreign and domestic; foreign pharmacopoeias. Restricted use: company employees and approved outsiders.

MD —MEDICAL & CHIRURGICAL FACULTY OF THE STATE OF MARYLAND, Library, 1211 Cathedral St, Baltimore, 21201. Joseph E Jensen, Librn
Holdings: Vols (10,000) // Cat Mss Maps Pix
See also entry under Medicine - History and Historic

NJ —PRINCETON UNIVERSITY, Library, Gest Oriental Library & East Asian Collections, 317 Palmer Hall, Princeton, 08544. D E Perushek, Cur
Holdings: Vols (1700) Cat Mss Pix
Notes: All in Chinese. Collection emphasis is on pre-20th century works on traditional medicine in all areas. Contemporary works on acupuncture and materia medica are also required.

†NY —MEDICAL RESEARCH LIBRARY OF BROOKLYN, Academy of Medicine of Brooklyn & The State University of New York Downstate Medical Center, 450 Clarkson St, Brooklyn, 11203. Kenneth E Moody, Dir
Notes: Extensive collection of 18th-19th century material.
See also entry under Medicine.

OH —LLOYD LIBRARY & MUSEUM, 917 Plum St, Cincinnati, 45202. John B Griggs, Librn
Notes: Extensive holdings in general pharmaceutical and vegetable materia medica.

MATERIA MEDICA, ARABIC see Medicine, Arabic

MATERIALS

CA —UNIVERSITY OF CALIFORNIA, LIVERMORE, Lawrence Livermore National Laboratory, Library, PO Box 5500, Livermore, 94550. John B Verity, Library Mgr
Holdings: Vols (160,000) Cat 16mm Films Microforms
Budget: ($2,323,000)
Notes: The LLL library system includes a central collection in physics, chemistry, engineering, geology, mathematics, and computer science; and branch holdings in bio-medicine, environmental science, nuclear chemistry, energy research, theoretical physics, materials science, and nuclear weapons. Collections include 160,000 books, 145,000 technical reports, 530,000 reports on microfiche, and 3000 periodical subscriptions. LLL libraries are not open to the public. Unclassified materials may be borrowed on interlibrary loan.

CA —UNIVERSITY OF CALIFORNIA, LOS ANGELES, Engineering & Mathematical Sciences Library, 405 Hilgard, Los Angeles, 90024. Rosalee I Wright, Librn
Holdings: Vols (180,000) Cat Microforms
See also entry under Engineering.

CA —CALIFORNIA DEPT OF TRANSPORTATION, Transportation Library, 5900 Folsom Blvd, PO Box 19128, Sacramento, 95819. Eva Caro, Librn
Holdings: Vols (10,000) Cat Mss Maps Pix Slides Phonorecords Audiotapes Videotapes 16mm Films Filmstrips Microforms

CA —INTERNATIONAL BUSINESS MACHINES RESEARCH LIBRARY, 5600

Cottle Rd, San Jose, 95193. Phil Grincewich, Mgr Technical Information
Holdings: Vols (13,500) Cat
Notes: Incl 21,000 vols of 770 journals. On-line search facility. Vols are divided into three libraries, Technical Research, Technical Information, and Programing. Not open to public.

CT —ROGERS CORP, Lurie Library, One Technology Drive, Rogers, 06263. Myrna D Riquier, Librn; Nini S Davis, Librn
Holdings: Vols (650) Cat
Notes: Emphasis on materials science, plastics, polymers, resins.

IL —ARGONNE NATIONAL LABORATORY, Library, Technical Information Services Dept, 9700 Cass Ave, Argonne, 60439. Hillis L Griffin, Dir
Notes: The ANL library system consists of eight branch libraries with centralized processing services. The entire collection numbers 70,000 monographic titles, 3700 journal titles, and over 1 million scientific and technical reports. Materials may be used by the public in the library by prior arrangement. Photocopies may be supplied for interlibrary loan, for which a processing and handling charge is made. The branch libraries are: Biological and Medical Research; Chemical Engineering; Chemistry; Mathematics/Physics/Computer Science; Reactor Science/Engineering; Materials Science; Solid State Physics; High-Energy Physics/Environmental Sciences.

IL —ARGONNE NATIONAL LABORATORY, Materials Sciences Branch Library, 9700 S Cass Ave, Argonne, 60439. Veronica E Johnson, Librn
Notes: Phase diagrams, ferrous metallurgy, physical metallurgy and properties of alloys. Incl 8000 vols monographs, 130 current journals, some scientific and technical reports. Materials may be used by the public in the library by prior arrangement. Photocopies may be supplied for interlibrary loan, for which a processing and handling charge is made.

IN —UNION CARBIDE CORP, Coatings Service Dept, Technical Library, 1500 Polco St, PO Box 24166, Indianapolis, 46224. Mary Ann Brady, Librn
Holdings: Vols 6000 Cat
Notes: Advanced materials incl those for use in extreme temperatures, materials with superior wear and anti-corrosion properties, and composites.

IN —PURDUE UNIVERSITY LIBRARIES, Engineering Library, A A Potter Engineering Center, West Lafayette, 47907. Edwin D Posey, Engineering Librn
Holdings: Vols (225,178) Cat Maps Audiotapes Microforms
Budget: ($300,000)

MA —RAYTHEON CO, Research Div, Library, 131 Spring St, Lerington, 02193. Martha C Adamson, Head Librn
Holdings: Vols 1000 Cat

MI —UNIVERSITY OF MICHIGAN, Engineering-Transportation Library, 312 Undergraduate Library, Ann Arbor, 48109. Maurita Holland, Librn
Holdings: Vols (400,000) Cat Microforms
Budget: ($225,000)

NJ —AT&T BELL LABORATORIES, Libraries and Information Systems Center, 600 Mountain Ave, Murray Hill, 07974. W D Penniman, Dir
Holdings: Vols (346,000) Cat Microforms
Notes: Restricted use to AT&T employees. Catalogs/Indexes: Bell Laboratories Library Network and Book Serial Catalogs; Bell Laboratories Translations. Bell Laboratories Library Network with New Jersey libraries located in Holmdel, Murray Hill, Piscataway, Whippany, Princeton, Short Hills, Summit, West Long Branch, Crawford Hill; libraries also in Allentown, Pennsylvania; Reading, Pennsylvania; New York, New York; Atlanta, Georgia; Columbus, Ohio; Naperville, Illinois; Indianapolis, Indiana; North Andover, Massachusetts.

NM —UNIVERSITY OF CALIFORNIA, Los Alamos National Laboratory, Libraries, PO Box 1663, MSP 362, Los Alamos, 87545. J Arthur Freed, Head Librn
Holdings: Vols (800,000) Cat Films

MATERIALS (cont.)

Microforms
Budget: ($700,000)
Notes: Incl 500,000 classified and
unclassified reports. There are 25 branch
libraries and a central collection. The
Medical Library contains about 40,000 vols
in the areas of biomedical research.

NY —ENGINEERING SOCIETIES
LIBRARY, 345 E 47 St, New York, 10017.
S Kirk Cabeen, Dir
Holdings: Vols 250,000 Cat Maps 16mm
Films Microforms
Notes: One of the largest, most
comprehensive engineering libraries in the
world. Covers all engineering disciplines;
particularly strong in electrical and
electronic, mechanical, mining and
metallurgical, petroleum, chemical,
industrial, air conditioning and refrigeration
engineering. Incl Wheeler Collection of early
materials on magnetism and electricity. 125,
000 bound periodical volumes; 10,000 maps;
5000 serial subscriptions (many foreign-
language). Virtually all materials abstracted
in *Engineering Index* (1884-date) are incl in
Library. Noncirculating, except to members
of professional engineering societies which
support the Library. See *Engineering
Societies Library, New York, Classed
Subject Catalog and Index* (Boston: G K
Hall, 1963); and *Supplements*, 1-10, 1964-
1973.

NC —DUKE UNIVERSITY, School of
Engineering, Library, Durham, 27706. Eric J
Smith, Librn
Holdings: Vols (72,000) Cat Microforms
Budget: ($110,000)

OH —UNIVERSITY OF CINCINNATI,
Engineering Library, 880 Baldwin Hall,
Cincinnati, 45221. Dorothy Furber Byers,
Head
Holdings: Vols (50,000) Cat Videotapes
Microforms
Budget: ($100,000)
Notes: Have NASA and DOE microfiche
collections.

PA —UNITED STATES STEEL CORP,
Research Laboratory, Technical Information
Center, MS 88, Monroeville, 15146. Angela
R Pollis, Staff Supvr of Technical
Information Services
Holdings: Vols (30,000) Cat Mss Microforms

PA —FRANKLIN INSTITUTE LIBRARY, 20
& The Parkway, Philadelphia, 19103.
Miriam Padusis, Dir; Charles Wilt, Readers
Servs Librn
Holdings: Vols (300,000) Cat Maps Pix
Microforms

PA —UNIVERSITY OF PENNSYLVANIA,
Towne Scientific Library, 220 S 33 St,
Philadelphia, 19104. Charles Meyers, Librn
Holdings: Vols (65,000) Cat

PA —ROCKWELL INTERNATIONAL,
General Industries Operations, Technical
Information Center, 400 N Lexington Ave,
Pittsburgh, 15208. Kathleen H Witkowski,
Library Coordr
Holdings: Vols Cat Microforms Mss
Documents Periodicals VF
Budget: ($5100)

TN —COMBUSTION ENGINEERING,
Metallurgical Materials Library, 911 W
Main St, Chattanooga, 37402. Nell T
Holder, Tech Librn
Holdings: Vols (10,000) Cat Microforms
Notes: Metallurgical research and
development.

TX —GENERAL DYNAMICS/FORT
WORTH DIV, Technical Library &
Information Services, PO Box 748, Mail
Zone 2246, Fort Worth, 76101. P Rogers de
Tonnancour, Dir
Holdings: Vols 36,000 Cat Maps Slides
Microforms
Budget: $100,000
Notes: Incl 500,000 microforms. Catalogs for
books and documents are separate.
Collection is strong in mathematics, nuclear
physics, materials and aerodynamics.
Emphasis on the mission of the division--the
development and production of manned
aircraft. Division also involved in electronic
manufacturing (avionic components), so

collection strength in this area is growing
very rapidly.

MATERIALS—DYNAMIC TESTING

OH —PREFORMED LINE PRODUCTS CO,
Research & Engineering Library, 660 Beta
Drive, Mayfield Village, (Mailing add: PO
Box 91129, Cleveland, 44101). Edwina T
Barron, Librn
Holdings: Vols (11,500) Cat Mss Microfiche
Pix VF
Budget: ($30,500)
Notes: Library covering research and
engineering fields emphasizing this subject.
Aerodynamic characteristics and electrical
characteristics of power cables,
communication cables (including fiber
optics), cable support systems, as well as
associated fittings and hardware; in service
behavior of manufactured products and
materials as it relates to its static and
dynamic forces and environmental
conditions; oceanographic cable fittings and
terminations.

MATERIALS—FATIGUE

MN —MTS SYSTEMS CORP, Information
Services, PO Box 24012, Minneapolis,
55424. Kathleen Werner, Technical Librn
Holdings: Cat Mss Pix Slides Phonorecords
Audiotapes Videotapes 16mm Films
Microforms
Notes: Material testing machines. Incl 2000
ms reports, 10,000 pictures, 6000 slides.

OH —PREFORMED LINE PRODUCTS CO,
Research & Engineering Library, 660 Beta
Drive, Mayfield Village, (Mailing add: PO
Box 91129, Cleveland, 44101). Edwina T
Barron, Librn
Holdings: Vols (11,500) Cat Mss Microfiche
Pix VF
Budget: ($30,500)
Notes: Library covering research and
engineering fields emphasizing this subject.
Aerodynamic characteristics and electrical
characteristics of power cables,
communication cables (including fiber
optics), cable support systems, as well as
associated fittings and hardware; in service
behavior of manufactured products and
materials as it relates to its static and
dynamic forces and environmental
conditions; oceanographic cable fittings and
terminations.

MATERIALS—TESTING

CA —CALIFORNIA DEPT OF
TRANSPORTATION, Transportation
Library, 5900 Folsom Blvd, PO Box 19128,
Sacramento, 95819. Eva Caro, Librn
Holdings: Vols (10,000) Cat Mss Maps Pix
Slides Phonorecords Audiotapes Videotapes
16mm Films Filmstrips Microforms

MN —MTS SYSTEMS CORP, Information
Services, PO Box 24012, Minneapolis,
55424. Kathleen Werner, Technical Librn
Holdings: Cat Mss Pix Slides Phonorecords
Audiotapes Videotapes 16mm Films
Microforms
Notes: Material testing machines. Incl 2000
ms reports, 10,000 pictures, 6000 slides.

MATERIALS, ADVANCED

IN —UNION CARBIDE CORP, Coatings
Service Dept, Technical Library, 1500 Polco
St, PO Box 24166, Indianapolis, 46224.
Mary Ann Brady, Librn
Holdings: Vols (6000) Cat
Notes: Incl materials for use in extreme
temperatures, materials with superior wear
and anticorrosion properties.

MA —RAYTHEON CO, Research Div,
Library, 131 Spring St, Lerington, 02193.
Martha C Adamson, Head Librn
Holdings: Vols (5000) Cat
Notes: 6000 technical reports, 125 journal
subscriptions.

MATERIALS, STRENGTH OF see
Strength of Materials

MATERIALS AT HIGH
TEMPERATURES

IN —UNION CARBIDE CORP, Coatings
Service Dept, Technical Library, 1500 Polco

St, PO Box 24166, Indianapolis, 46224.
Mary Ann Brady, Librn
Holdings: Vols 6000 Cat
Notes: Advanced materials incl those for use
in extreme temperatures, materials with
superior wear and anti-corrosion properties,
and composites.

MATERIALS AT LOW
TEMPERATURES

CA —UNIVERSITY OF CALIFORNIA,
BERKELEY, Bancroft Library, Manuscripts
Division, Berkeley, 94720. James D Hart,
Dir
Notes: Extensive collections of papers and
archives relative to the history of modern
chemistry.

IN —UNION CARBIDE CORP, Coatings
Service Dept, Technical Library, 1500 Polco
St, PO Box 24166, Indianapolis, 46224.
Mary Ann Brady, Librn
Holdings: Vols (6000) Cat

MATERIALS SCIENCE

IL —UNIVERSITY OF ILLINOIS,
URBANA/CHAMPAIGN, Library, 221
Engineering Hall, Urbana, 61801. William
Mischo, Librn
Holdings: Vols (175,000) Cat Slides
Notes: Material science. Incl 3500
periodicals. Collection designed to serve
teaching and research programs. Supports
instructional faculty research. Also 470
microfilm reels and 6000 microfiche sheets.

TX —UNIVERSITY OF TEXAS LIBRARIES,
Richard W McKinney Engineering Library,
1.3 ECJ, Austin, 78712. Susan B Ardis,
Librn
Holdings: Vols (83,548) Cat Microforms

MATERNAL AND INFANT WELFARE

MI —UNIVERSITY OF MICHIGAN, Public
Health Library, Ann Arbor, 48109. Mary
Townsend, Head
Holdings: Vols (55,000) Cat Maps Pix
Budget: ($24,000)

MATERNAL HEALTH SERVICES

WA —CHILDREN'S ORTHOPEDIC
HOSPITAL & MEDICAL CENTER,
Medical Library, 4800 Sand Point Way NE,
Seattle, 98105. Tamara A Turner, Librn
Holdings: Vols (10,000)
Notes: Specialize in pediatric texts and
journals, with an emphasis on neonatology,
perinatology and childhood cancer.

MATERNITY WELFARE see Maternal
and Infant Welfare

MATHEMATICAL DRAWING see
Mechanical Drawing

MATHEMATICAL PHYSICS

CA —CALIFORNIA INSTITUTE OF
TECHNOLOGY, Robert A Millikan
Memorial Library, Archives, 1201 E
California Blvd, Pasadena, 91125. Judith R
Goodstein, Archivist
Holdings: Vols (3000) Cat Mss Maps Pix
Slides Phonorecords Audiotapes Videotapes
16mm Films Microforms
Notes: Ms sources for the history of
astrophysics, cosmology, mathematical
physics, experimental physics, radio
astronomy, geophysics and biophysics.
Collections incl the papers of: George Ellery
Hale, Jesse Greenstein, H P Robertson,
Richard Feynman, Paul Epstein, Max
Delbruck, and Beno Gutenberg. Candid
photos of physicists at meetings; etchings
and photographs of Einstein; scientific
medals; selected pieces of scientific
apparatus (including the oil-drop machine
constructed by Millikan at Caltech in the
early 1920s); the reprint collection of Paul
Epstein; over 3000 landmark books in the
history of 20th century physics and
mathematics. Printed publications include:
Daniel Kevles, *Guide to the Microfilm*

MATHEMATICAL PHYSICS (cont.)

Edition of the George Ellery Hale Papers (Pasadena, Carnegie Institute of Washington and Caltech), 1968; Judith R Goodstein, *The Robert Andrews Millikan Collection at the California Institute of Technology: Guide to a Microfilm Edition* (Pasadena, Caltech), 1977; Judith R Goodstein and Carolyn Kopp, *The Theodore von Karman Collections at the California Institute of Technology* (Pasadena, Archives), 1981.

MO —WASHINGTON UNIVERSITY, Physics Dept Library, 6600 Millbrook Blvd, Saint Louis, 63130. Betty Eickhoff, Librn

NY —UNIVERSITY OF ROCHESTER, Physics-Optics-Astronomy Library, Bausch & Lomb Bldg, River Campus, Rochester, 14627. Loretta Caren, Librn
Holdings: Vols (20,000) Cat
Notes: Strong research level collection in the field and related areas.

TN —UNIVERSITY OF TENNESSEE, Space Institute Library, Tullahoma, 37388. Helen B Mason, Librn
Holdings: Vols (14,000) Cat Microforms
Budget: ($50,000)
Notes: Incl NASA and other series of technical reports.

MATHEMATICAL RECREATIONS

RI —BROWN UNIVERSITY, John Hay Library, 20 Prospect St, Providence, 02912. Mark N Brown, Cur Mss
Notes: The Royal Vale Heath Collection of about 200 of his designs, drawings, models, ocular, and verbal descriptions of simultaneous solutions to linear Diophantine equations in such examples as magic squares, Platonic solids, etc. These curious designs often were devised as talismans in ancient India and were first developed as mathematical problems by the Chinese.

MATHEMATICAL STATISTICS

CA —UNIVERSITY OF CALIFORNIA, BERKELEY, Science Libraries, Astronomy-Mathematics-Statistics-Computer Science Library, 100 Evans Hall, Berkeley, 94720. Kimiyo Hom, Head
Holdings: Vols (53,000) Cat Maps Microforms
Budget: ($117,301)
Notes: A research collection in the fields of astronomy, mathematics, statistics and computer science. In the field of astronomy, emphasis is given to star charts, atlases and catalogs. In mathematics, the collection's strengths are in pure mathematics, mathematical statistics and probability theory. The computer science holdings emphasize the mathematics and theory of the field. The Library's serial holdings are particularly rich in foreign-language materials. Some 1300 serial titles are currently being received; over 4000 pamphlets. (Holdings in the AMSCS Library are complemented by approx 15,000 additional vols in the Main Library, as well as rare book materials in The Bancroft Library.)

MA —UNIVERSITY OF MASSACHUSETTS AT AMHERST, Physical Sciences Library, Amherst, 01003. Siegfried Feller, Assoc Dir for Collection Development
Holdings: Cat
Notes: Extensive journal holdings, incl mathematical statistics.

NY —CORNELL UNIVERSITY LIBRARIES, Mathematics Library, White Hall, Ithaca, 14853. Steven W Rockey, Librn
Holdings: Vols 28,000 Cat Microforms

NY —UNIVERSITY OF ROCHESTER, Carlson Library, Hutchison Hall, River Campus, Rochester, 14627. Michael W Poulin, Librn
Holdings: Vols (48,720) Cat Microforms
Notes: Strong collection in the field and related areas.

MATHEMATICIANS

RI —BROWN UNIVERSITY, John Hay Library, 20 Prospect St, Providence, 02912.

Mark N Brown, Cur Mss
Holdings: // Mss Microforms
Notes: Correspondence

MATHEMATICS

AR —UNIVERSITY OF ARKANSAS, Technology Campus Library, 1201 McAlmont St, PO Box 3017, Little Rock, 72203. Brent Nelson, Librn
Holdings: Vols (20,849) Cat Slides Microforms
Budget: ($35,000)

CA —UNIVERSITY OF CALIFORNIA, BERKELEY, Science Libraries, Astronomy-Mathematics-Statistics-Computer Science Library, 100 Evans Hall, Berkeley, 94720. Kimiyo Hom, Head
Holdings: Vols (53,000) Cat Maps Microforms
Budget: ($117,301)
Notes: A research collection in the fields of astronomy, mathematics, statistics and computer science. In the field of astronomy, emphasis is given to star charts, atlases and catalogs. In mathematics, the collections's strengths are in pure mathematics, mathematical statistics and probability theory. The computer science holdings emphasize the mathematics and theory of the field. The Library serial holdings are particularly rich in foreign-language materials. Some 1300 serial titles are currently being received; over 4000 pamphlets. (Holdings in the AMSCS Library are complemented by approx 15,000 additional vols in the Main Library, as well as rare book materials in The Bancroft Library.)

CA —UNIVERSITY OF CALIFORNIA, DAVIS, Physical Sciences Library, Davis, 95616. Scott Kennedy, Head
Holdings: Vols 27,000 Cat
Notes: Theory of mathematics and computer sciences materials well represented. Teaching collection located in Shields Library. Good strength in journal runs.

CA —CALIFORNIA STATE UNIVERSITY, FULLERTON, Library, Box 4150, Fullerton, 92634. Linda Herman, Special Collections Librn
Holdings: Vols 14,730 Cat
Budget: $18,000
Notes: Incl large number of foreign journals--Russian, German, French, Rumanina, Hebrew and Armenian. Some pre-1920 journals.

CA —UNIVERSITY OF CALIFORNIA, LIVERMORE, Lawrence Livermore National Laboratory, Library, PO Box 5500, Livermore, 94550. John B Verity, Library Mgr
Holdings: Vols (160,000) Cat 16mm Films Microforms
Budget: ($2,323,000)
Notes: The LLL library system includes a central collection in physics, chemistry, engineering, geology, mathematics, and computer science; and branch holdings in bio-medicine, environmental science, nuclear chemistry, energy research, theoretical physics, materials science, and nuclear weapons. Collections include 160,000 books, 145,000 technical reports, 530,000 reports on microfiche, and 3000 periodical subscriptions. LLL libraries are not open to the public. Unclassified materials may be borrowed on interlibrary loan.

CA —UNIVERSITY OF CALIFORNIA, LOS ANGELES, Engineering & Mathematical Sciences Library, 405 Hilgard, Los Angeles, 90024. Rosalee I Wright, Librn
Holdings: Vols (180,000) Cat Microforms
Notes: Both pure and applied mathematics are represented; The teaching of mathematics is excluded. The mathematics journals include the principal foreign titles. Selected lecture note series.

CA —UNIVERSITY OF SOUTHERN CALIFORNIA, Seaver Science Library, University Park, Los Angeles, 90089. A Albert Baker, Head
Holdings: Vols (200,000) Microforms
Budget: ($700,000)
Notes: Includes technical reports (12,000), serial and periodical titles (3600).

CA —CUBIC CORP, Technical Library, 9333 Balboa Ave, PO Box 85587, San Diego, 92138. Maxine Moser, Mgr Tech Librn; Ann Viera, Librn
Holdings: Vols (2500) Cat Maps Microforms
Budget: ($60,000)
Notes: Incl about 20,000 microforms and 1000 bound periodicals, technical reports, technical memoranda. On-line search service for employees, including DIALOG, BRS, SDC, DTIC/DROLS, NASA/RECON, RLIN, DMS.

CA —STANFORD UNIVERSITY LIBRARIES, Mathematical & Computer Sciences Library, Stanford, 94305. Harry Llull, Branch Librn
Holdings: Vols (42,000) Cat

CO —UNIVERSITY OF COLORADO, Duane Physical Laboratories G140, Mathematics-Physics Library, Boulder, 80309. Allen Wynne, Head Librn
Holdings: Vols Cat Microforms
Notes: All areas of mathematics and physics with special emphasis on astrophysics, astrogeophysics, theoretical high energy physics and theoretical computer science. Also basic astronomy. The most comprehensive general mathematics and physics collection in the Rocky Mountain area, although not having sufficient depth to allow doctoral research in some specific areas. Excellent bibliographic control for current and retrospective searching as complete runs of most major subject indexing and abstracting services are present. ILL for businesses through the Colorado Technical Reference Center in main library building.

CT —YALE UNIVERSITY, Observatory Library, 260 Whitney Ave, Box 6666, New Haven, 06511.
Holdings: Vols (15,000) Cat Maps Pix
Budget: ($15,000)
Notes: Also an extensive collection of domestic and foreign observatory publications.

CT —YALE UNIVERSITY, Mathematics Library, 12 Hillhouse Ave, Box 2155, Yale Sta, New Haven, 06520. Paul Lukasiewicz, Librn
Holdings: Vols 24,000 Cat
Budget: $43,000

DC —US NAVAL OBSERVATORY LIBRARY, 30th & Massachusetts Ave, NW, Washington, 20016. Brenda G Corbin, Librn
Holdings: Vols (75,000) Cat Mss Maps Pix Slides Microforms
Notes: Incl 1000 journals, with monograph and serial publications in the fields of celestial mechanics, fundamental astronomy, time determination, photographic astrometry and astrophysics, data processing, mathematics.

GA —UNIVERSITY OF GEORGIA, Libraries, Athens, 30602. Arlene E Luchsinger, Asst Dir Branch Libraries
Holdings: Vols 19,500 Cat
Notes: The collection incl the bulk of the collection originally held by the American Mathematical Society, and purchased by the University of Georgia from Columbia University several years ago. It is strong in foreign dissertations in mathematics.

GA —GEORGIA INSTITUTE OF TECHNOLOGY, Price Gilbert Memorial Library, 225 North Ave, Atlanta, 30332. Edward Graham Roberts, Dir
Holdings: Vols (1,661,559) Cat Maps Slides Microforms
Budget: ($1,383,302)
Notes: Incl (4,307,996) patents and (568, 490) government documents.

IL —ARGONNE NATIONAL LABORATORY, Library, Technical Information Services Dept, 9700 Cass Ave, Argonne, 60439. Hillis L Griffin, Dir
Notes: The ANL library system consists of eight branch libraries with centralized processing services. The entire collection numbers 70,000 monographic titles, 3700 journal titles, and over 1 million scientific and technical reports. Materials may be used by the public in the library by prior arrangement. Photocopies may be supplied for interlibrary loan, for which a processing and handling charge is made. The branch

MATHEMATICS (cont.)

libraries are: Biological and Medical Research; Chemical Engineering; Chemistry; Mathematics/Physics/Computer Science; Reactor Science/Engineering; Materials Science; Solid State Physics; High-Energy Physics/Environmental Sciences.

IL —ARGONNE NATIONAL LABORATORY, Mathematics/Physics/ Computer Science Branch Library, 9700 S Cass Ave, Argonne, 60439.
Notes: Strong in pure mathematics and older classical mathematics. Incl 30,000 vols monographs, 190 current journals. Materials may be used by the public in the library prior arrangement. Photocopies may be supplied for interlibrary loan, for which a processing and handling charge is made.

IL —NORTHWESTERN UNIVERSITY, Mathematics Library, 2033 Sheridan Rd, Evanston, 60201. Zita Hayward, Library Asst
Holdings: Vols (25,000) Cat
Notes: Collection emphasizes pure mathematics on the graduate and research level.

IL —UNIVERSITY OF ILLINOIS, URBANA/CHAMPAIGN, Library, Mathematics Library, 216 Altgeld Hall, Urbana, 61801. Nancy D Anderson, Librn
Holdings: Vols 63,000 Cat Microforms
Budget: ($56,600)
Notes: The Mathematics Library is a comprehensive research collection. Subscribe to 450 periodical titles and 500 continuation titles. We collect essentially all monographs reviewed in Mathematical Reviews. Other strong areas are the collected works of the major mathematicians, arithmetics published prior to 1900, lecture notes, the publications of the major mathematical and scientific socieites, 1890 to date, and Eastern European mathematical works. Library has not collected as extensively in applied mathematics, statistics, mathematics of computation, and the teaching of mathematics.

IN —PURDUE UNIVERSITY LIBRARIES, Mathematical Sciences Library, West Lafayette, 47907. Richard Funkhouser, Librn
Holdings: Vols (44,005) Cat Microforms
Budget: ($67,985)

IA —IOWA STATE UNIVERSITY, Library, Ames, 50011. Warren B Kuhn, Dean of Library Services
Holdings: Cat
Notes: Extensive serial holdings.

LA —ETHYL CORP, Information & Library Services, Gulf States Rd, PO Box 2246, Baton Rouge, 70821. Lois M Skinner, Chemist-Librn
Holdings: Vols (15,000) Cat

LA —TULANE UNIVERSITY, Mathematics Research Library, New Orleans, 70118. Susan Bretz, Librn
Holdings: Vols 18,620 Cat
Budget: $35,719
Notes: Theoretical and applied mathematics.

MD —JOHNS HOPKINS UNIVERSITY, Milton S Eisenhower Library, Charles & 34 Sts, Baltimore, 21218. Ann S Gwyn, Assistant Dir for Special Collections
Notes: Foreign and American doctoral dissertations and reprints to 1964. Largest number in history of science, 85,000. Also biology, chemistry, geology, meteorology, psychology, physics and mathematics. Johns Hopkins not included. Incl 100,000 Western European doctoral dissertations, espec French and German; some Scandinavian. Collection is located in Gillman Storage Area accessible through Special Collection Division.

MD —JOHNS HOPKINS UNIVERSITY, Milton S Eisenhower Library, Charles & 34 Sts, Baltimore, 21218. Ann S Gwyn, Assistant Dir for Special Collections
Holdings: Vols 30,500 Cat Microforms
Notes: Strong in pure mathematics; less strong in applied mathematics.

MA —UNIVERSITY OF MASSACHUSETTS AT AMHERST, Physical Sciences Library, Amherst, 01003. Siegfried Feller, Assoc Dir for Collection Development
Holdings: Cat
Notes: Extensive journal holdings, incl mathematical statistics.

MA —HARVARD UNIVERSITY LIBRARY, Gordon McKay Library, Division of Applied Sciences, Pierce Hall, Oxford St, Cambridge, 02138. Julie Sandall Barlas, Librn
Holdings: Vols (100,000)

MA —HARVARD UNIVERSITY LIBRARY, George David Birkhoff Mathematical Library, Science Center, One Oxford St, Cambridge, 02138. Nancy Miller, Librn
Holdings: Vols 8000 Cat
Notes: Major research collection for mathematics is in general collection of the Science Center.

MA —SMITHSONIAN INSTITUTION LIBRARIES, Astrophysical Observatory Branch, 60 Garden St, Cambridge, 02138. Joyce Rey, Librn
Holdings: Vols (10,000) Cat Maps Pix Microforms

MA —BOSTON COLLEGE LIBRARIES, Science Library, Devlin Hall, Chestnut Hill, 02167. F Clifford McElroy, Science Librn
Holdings: Vols (54,508) Cat Maps Microforms
Budget: ($94,270)
Notes: Library is being absorbed into the general collection.

MA —TUFTS UNIVERSITY, Mathematics-Physics Library, Medford, 02155. Pauline Boucher, Librn
Holdings: Vols (2000) Periodicals
Notes: Incl 200 subscriptions.

MA —NORTON COMPANY, Library, 1 New Bond St, Worcester, 01606. Joan K Chaffey, Librn
Holdings: // Cat
Notes: Abrasive industry collection.

MI —UNIVERSITY OF MICHIGAN, Library, Dept of Rare Books & Special Collections, Ann Arbor, 48109. Robert J Starring, Head
Holdings: Mss
Notes: Over 1200 mss chiefly in Arabic, but also in Persian, Turkish, Coptic, Syriac, Ethiopic, Hebrew, and Armenian. Incl the McGregor collection on mathamatics and astronomy, the Tiflis collection, and portions of the Abdul Hamid and Yahuda collections.

NJ —AT&T BELL LABORATORIES, Libraries and Information Systems Center, 600 Mountain Ave, Murray Hill, 07974. W D Penniman, Dir
Holdings: Vols (346,000) Cat Microforms
Notes: Restricted use to AT&T employees. Catalogs/Indexes: Bell Laboratories Library Network and Book Serial Catalogs; Bell Laboratories Translations. Bell Laboratories Library Network with New Jersey libraries located in Holmdel, Murray Hill, Piscataway, Whippany, Princeton, Short Hills, Summit, West Long Branch, Crawford Hill; libraries also in Allentown, Pennsylvania; Reading, Pennsylvania; New York, New York; Atlanta, Georgia; Columbus, Ohio; Naperville, Illinois; Indianapolis, Indiana; North Andover, Massachusetts.

NJ —PRINCETON UNIVERSITY, Fine Hall Library of Mathematics, Physics & Statistics, Princeton, 08540. Peter Cziffra, Librn
Holdings: Vols (82,000) Cat Microforms
Budget: ($155,000)
Notes: All aspects of pure mathematics; applied mathematics, numerical methods, linear programming, etc are collected selectively. Emphasis on pure, as opposed to applied, physics; few acquisitions in plasma physics. Also, mathematical statistics. Separate catalog; most titles also in main catalog of Firestone Library.

NM —UNIVERSITY OF CALIFORNIA, Los Alamos National Laboratory, Libraries, PO Box 1663, MSP 362, Los Alamos, 87545. J Arthur Freed, Head Librn
Holdings: Vols (800,000) Cat Films Microforms
Budget: ($700,000)
Notes: Incl 500,000 classified and unclassified reports. There are 25 branch libraries and a central collection. The Medical Library contains about 40,000 vols in the areas of biomedical research.

NY —POLYTECHNIC INSTITUTE OF NEW YORK, Long Island Center Library, Route 110, Farmingdale, 11735. Lorraine Schein, Branch Librn
Holdings: Vols 4300 Cat

NY —CORNELL UNIVERSITY LIBRARIES, Mathematics Library, White Hall, Ithaca, 14853. Steven W Rockey, Librn
Holdings: Vols 28,000 Cat Microforms

NY —COLUMBIA UNIVERSITY LIBRARIES, Mathematics Library, 303 Mathematics, New York, 10027. Suzanne Fedunok, Librn
Holdings: Vols 26,000
Notes: Mathematical statistics and advanced mathematics.

NY —NEW YORK PUBLIC LIBRARY, Research Libraries, Science and Technology Research Center, Fifth Ave & 42 St, New York, 10018.
Holdings: Vols (1,100,000) Cat Microforms
Budget: ($647,259)

NY —NEW YORK PUBLIC LIBRARY, Oriental Div, Fifth Ave & 42 St, New York, 10018. E Christian Fllstrup, Chief
Holdings: Cat Mss Microforms
Budget: ($56,455)
Notes: Published catalog of holdings.

NY —NEW YORK PUBLIC LIBRARY, Mid-Manhattan Library, Science & Business Dept, 455 Fifth Ave, New York, 10016. Frederick E Dusold, Sr Principal Librn
Holdings: Vols (110,000) Cat Microforms
Budget: ($134,000)
Notes: With rare exceptions all works in English. Current material; policy precludes archival collecting. Collection geared toward the undergraduate college student, with consideration given to the professional, the lay reader and the beginning graduate student. A collection of monographs, texts, treatises, standard reference works and periodicals in the philosophy, history and theory of science. Special strength in mathematics and life sciences. Circulating books are available in addition to an extensive reference collection.

NY —NEW YORK UNIVERSITY, Courant Institute of Mathematical Sciences Library, 251 Mercer St, New York, 10012. Nancy Gubman, Librn
Holdings: Vols (52,000) Cat Audiotapes Microforms
Notes: Collection covers all aspects of mathematics, theoretical computer science, and mathematical physics on the level of graduate research. Catalog is located in Courant Institute Library.

†NY —TECHNICAL CAREER INSTITUTE LIBRARY, 320 W 31st Street, New York, 10001. Michael Brent, Librn
Holdings: Vols (3500)

NY —EASTMAN KODAK COMPANY, Research Library, Research Laboratories, Bldg 83, Rochester, 14650. E W Kraus, Head
Holdings: Vols 7700 Cat Microforms

NY —UNIVERSITY OF ROCHESTER, Carlson Library, Hutchison Hall, River Campus, Rochester, 14627. Michael W Poulin, Librn
Holdings: Vols (48,720) Cat Microforms
Notes: Strong collection in the field and related areas.

NC —DUKE UNIVERSITY, William R Perkins Library, Durham, 27706. Elvin E Strowd, University Librn
Notes: The James Ray Newman collection of several thousand books and more than 8000 manuscripts is broad in scope and particularly strong in mathematics, philosophy, logic and history and philosophy of science.

NC —DUKE UNIVERSITY, Mathematics-Physics Library, Durham, 27706. Mary Ann Southern, Librn
Holdings: Vols 69,171
Notes: A special collection is the Microwave Catalog from the University of Ulm, a bibliography of microwave literature divided into molecule types, ie radicals, linear, diatomic, symmetric tops, asymmetric tops, and hindered rotation; it is regularly updated by supplements.

NC —NORTH CAROLINA STATE UNIVERSITY, D H Hill Library, Box 7111, Raleigh, 27695. I T Littleton, Dir
Holdings: Vols 22,300 Cat
Budget: $15,000
Notes: Emphasis on applied mathematics. Incl monographs.

MATHEMATICS (cont.)

OH —FIRESTONE TIRE & RUBBER CO,
1200 Firestone Pkwy, Akron, 44317. S Koo,
Librn
Holdings: Vols (6000) Cat
Notes: Collection centered on engineering,
mathematics, physics, and manufacturing
(metal processing); no rubber or tires. Incl
several hundred government reports. No
index.

OK —OKLAHOMA STATE UNIVERSITY,
Library, Stillwater, 74708. Roscoe Rouse,
Dir
Holdings: Vols 19,840 Cat

OR —OREGON STATE UNIVERSITY,
Library, Corvallis, 97331. Melvin George,
Dir
Holdings: Vols 24,000 Cat

PA —FRANKLIN INSTITUTE LIBRARY, 20
& The Parkway, Philadelphia, 19103.
Miriam Padusis, Dir; Charles Wilt, Readers
Servs Librn
Holdings: Vols (300,000) Cat Maps Pix
Microforms

PA —UNIVERSITY OF PENNSYLVANIA,
Mathematics-Physics-Astronomy Library, 33
& Walnut Sts, Philadelphia, 19104. Marion
A Kreiter, Librn
Holdings: Cat

PA —US NAVY, Philadelphia Naval Shipyard
Technical Library, Philadelphia Naval
Shipyard, Philadelphia, 19112. Alice R
Murray, Dir
Holdings: Vols (12,500) Cat Pix
Notes: The Library also has (70,000)
technical manuals, (3500) research and
development reports. Over (400) current
periodicals.

PA —ROCKWELL INTERNATIONAL,
General Industries Operations, Technical
Information Center, 400 N Lexington Ave,
Pittsburgh, 15208. Kathleen H Witkowski,
Library Coordr
Holdings: Vols Cat Microforms Mss
Documents Periodicals VF
Budget: ($5100)

**PA —PENNSYLVANIA STATE
UNIVERSITY,** Mathematics Library, 109
McAllister Bldg, University Park, 16802.
Miriam D Pierce, Librn
Holdings: Vols (29,101) Cat
Budget: ($35,000)

RI —BROWN UNIVERSITY, John Hay
Library, 20 Prospect St, Providence, 02912.
Mark N Brown, Cur Mss
Notes: The Royal Vale Heath Collection of
about 200 of his designs, drawings, models,
ocular, and verbal descriptions of
simultaneous solutions to linear Diophantine
equations in such examples as magic squares,
Platonic solids, etc. These curious designs
often were devised as talismans in ancient
India and were first developed as
mathematical problems by the Chinese.

SC —WOFFORD COLLEGE, Sandor Teszler
Library, N Church St, Spartanburg, 29301.
Frank J Anderson, Librn
Holdings: Vols 400 Uncat
Notes: Mostly textbooks; from the 17th
century to date.

TN —UNIVERSITY OF TENNESSEE, Space
Institute Library, Tullahoma, 37388. Helen B
Mason, Librn
Holdings: Vols (14,000) Cat Microforms
Budget: ($50,000)
Notes: Incl NASA and other series of
technical reports.

TX —UNIVERSITY OF TEXAS LIBRARIES,
Physics-Mathematics-Astronomy Library,
PO Box P, Austin, 78712. John Fandey,
Librn
Holdings: Vols (55,000) Cat Microforms

**TX —SOUTHERN METHODIST
UNIVERSITY,** Fondren Library, Dallas,
75275. Curt Holleman, Librn for Collection
Development

**TX —GENERAL DYNAMICS/FORT
WORTH DIV,** Technical Library &
Information Services, PO Box 748, Mail
Zone 2246, Fort Worth, 76101. P Rogers de
Tonnancour, Dir
Holdings: Vols 36,000 Cat Maps Slides
Microforms
Budget: $100,000
Notes: Incl 500,000 microforms. Catalogs for

books and documents are separate.
Collection is strong in mathematics, nuclear
physics, materials and aerodynamics.
Emphasis on the mission of the division--the
development and production of manned
aircraft. Division also involved in electronic
manufacturing (avionic components), so
collection strength in this area is growing
very rapidly.

TX —RICE UNIVERSITY, Fondren Library,
6100 S Main St, PO Box 1892, Houston,
77251. Dr Samuel M Carrington, Jr,
University Librn
Holdings: Vols 12,375 Cat
Budget: $46,500
Notes: Each serial title counted once; incl
some computer science.

TX —TEXAS TECH UNIVERSITY, Library,
Lubbock, 79409. David J Murrah, Assoc Dir
for Special Collections

TX —SAINT MARY'S UNIVERSITY,
Library, 2700 Cincinnati Ave, San Antonio,
78284. Anita C Saxine, Special Collections
Librn

**WA —WASHINGTON STATE
UNIVERSITY,** Owen Science &
Engineering Library, Pullman, 99164.
Elizabeth P Roberts, Head
Holdings: Vols 14,900 Cat Microforms

**WA —BATTELLE-PACIFIC NORTHWEST
LABORTORIES,** Technical Library, PO
Box 999, Richland, 99352. Wayne Snyder,
Librn
Holdings: Vols (50,000) Cat Microforms
Budget: ($500,000)
Notes: Holdings: 50,000 books; 35,000
bound periodical volumes; 200,000 technical
reports; 200,000 technical reports in
microform. Subscriptions: 1800 journals and
other serials. Services: interlibrary loans;
literature searching; translation; library open
to public with restrictions.

**WA —UNIVERSITY OF WASHINGTON
LIBRARIES,** Mathematics Research
Library, GN-50, Seattle, 98195. Martha
Tucker Murdoch, Head
Holdings: Vols (25,388) Cat
Budget: ($68,364)
Notes: Broad collection of pure and
theoretical mathematics.
See also entry under Statistics.

**WY —US AIR FORCE INSTITUTE OF
TECHNOLOGY,** Library, Dept 9 Bldg 831,
FE, Warren AFB, 82001. Patricia A
Johnson, Librn
Holdings: Vols (7000) Cat Microforms
Budget: ($9000)
Notes: The Library supports graduate
programs for students (Air Force Missile-
Combat Crewmen) seeking a Master of
Business Administration Degree. Civilian
students and other military personnel are
also admitted.

MB —UNIVERSITY OF MANITOBA,
Science Library, Machray Hall, Winnipeg,
R3T 2N2, Can. V Simosko, Head
Holdings: Vols (90,000) Cat Microforms

**ON —ATOMIC ENERGY OF CANADA
LIMITED,** Main Library, Technical
Information Branch, Chalk River Nuclear
Laboratories, Chalk River, K0J 1J0, Can.
Harry Greenshields, Chief Librn
Holdings: Vols (128,700) Microforms
Budget: ($662,400)
Notes: The Main Library, Atomic Energy of
Canada Limited, is the Canadian repository
for the literature of nuclear science and
technology. Its collections reflect both
fundamental and nuclear aspects of biology,
chemistry, electronics, engineering,
mathematics, computers, metallurgy, physics
and other specific areas of science involving
nuclear technology with special emphasis on
heavy water reactor systems. 512,000
research reports are available in paper copy
and microfiche form. Incl US DOE, INIS
and other offshore nuclear research reports.
386,000 microforms.

**ON —ENERGY, MINES & RESOURCES
CANADA,** Earth Physics Branch Library,
Ottawa, K1A 0Y3, Can. W M Tsang, Chief
Librn
Holdings: Vols 4500 Cat Microforms

**ON —INSTITUTE OF CHARTERED
ACCOUNTANTS OF ONTARIO,** The
Merrilees Library, 69 Bloor St E, Toronto,

M4W 1B3, Can. Theresa Wolak, Librn
Holdings: Vols 21 Cat

MATHEMATICS—EARLY WORKS TO 1800

MA —BRANDEIS UNIVERSITY, Goldfarb
Library, 415 South St, Waltham, 02154.
Bessie Hahn, Dir
Notes: Vito Volterra Collection on the
History of Science and Mathematics. A
collection of more than 5000 vols containing
the major works in Volterra. Inclusive dates
are the 16th through the 20th century. The
collection also contains over 16,000 offprints
and pamphlets, most of which are dedication
copies from the author to Volterra. No
catalog of the books extant, but an author-
title finding list for the 16,000 offprints and
pamphlets is available in Special Collections.

MATHEMATICS—HISTORY

**CA —UNIVERSITY OF CALIFORNIA,
BERKELEY,** Bancroft Library, Manuscripts
Division, Berkeley, 94720. James D Hart,
Dir
Holdings: Vols Cat Mss
Notes: The personal papers and
correspondence (2000 pieces) of Rudjer
Josip Boskovic, an important Yugoslav,
18th-century Jesuit mathematician and
natural philosopher. Of particular importance
are 180 textual mss dealing with subjects in
the field of mechanics. A register of the
collection has been prepared. Also printed
books.

CA —CLAREMONT COLLEGES, Norman F
Sprague Memorial Library, 12 & Dartmouth,
Claremont, 91711. David Kuhner, Librn
Holdings: Vols (1000) Cat Mss Pix VF
Notes: President Herbert Hoover's personal
collection of rare technical books of the
15th-19th centuries. *Bibliotheca De Re
Metallica: The Herbert Clark Hoover
Collection of Mining and Metallurgy*
(Claremont, 1980). Restricted use.

**CA —CALIFORNIA INSTITUTE OF
TECHNOLOGY,** Robert A Millikan
Memorial Library, Archives, 1201 E
California Blvd, Pasadena, 91125. Judith R
Goodstein, Archivist
Holdings: Vols (3000) Cat Mss Maps Pix
Slides Phonorecords Audiotapes Videotapes
16mm Films Microforms
Notes: Ms sources for the history of
astrophysics, cosmology, mathematical
physics, experimental physics, radio
astronomy, geophysics and biophysics.
Collections incl the papers of: George Ellery
Hale, Jesse Greenstein, H P Robertson,
Richard Feynman, Paul Epstein, Max
Delbruck, and Beno Gutenberg. Candid
photos of physicists at meetings; etchings
and photographs of Einstein; scientific
medals; selected pieces of scientific
apparatus (including the oil-drop machine
constructed by Millikan at Caltech in the
early 1920s); the reprint collection of Paul
Epstein; over 3000 landmark books in the
history of 20th century physics and
mathematics. Printed publications include:
Daniel Kevles, *Guide to the Microfilm
Edition of the George Ellery Hale Papers*
(Pasadena, Carnegie Institute of Washington
and Caltech), 1968; Judith R Goodstein, *The
Robert Andrews Millikan Collection at the
California Institute of Technology: Guide to
a Microfilm Edition* (Pasadena, Caltech),
1977; Judith R Goodstein and Carolyn
Kopp, *The Theodore von Karman
Collections at the California Institute of
Technology* (Pasadena, Archives), 1981.

DC —AMERICAN UNIVERSITY LIBRARY,
Bender Library, 4400 Massachusetts Ave
NW, Washington, 20016.
Holdings: Vols 10,000 Cat
Notes: The Artemus Martin Library donated
to the University Library is an outstanding
collection of early and rare books published
in the field of mathematics. Separate shelflist
(incomplete) is available at the American
University Library.

GA —UNIVERSITY OF GEORGIA,
Libraries, Athens, 30602. Arlene E

MATHEMATICS—HISTORY (cont.)

Luchsinger, Asst Dir Branch Libraries
Holdings: Vols 19,500 Cat
Notes: The collection incl the bulk of the collection originally held by the American Mathematical Society, and purchased by the University of George from Columbia University several years ago. It is strong in foreign dissertations in mathematics.

IN —PURDUE UNIVERSITY LIBRARIES, Graduate School of Management, Krannert Library, West Lafayette, 47907. Gordon Law, Librn
Notes: Accounting history. The collection consist of books, journals and pamphlets dating from the early 16th to late 19th century, covering to a large degree early literature in economic thought and business practices both here and abroad. No photocopying.

KS —UNIVERSITY OF KANSAS, Kenneth Spencer Research Library, Special Collections Dept, Lawrence, 66045. Alexandra Mason, Librn
Holdings: Cat Mss Maps Pix
Notes: Ellis Collection of Ornithology, natural history and voyages and travels; botanical literature from Fitzpatrick collection (especially medical botany, early American botanists, renaissance herbals, Matthioli): some early chemistry and mathematics; scientific voyages and travels; De Beer collection of offprints in embryology, endocrinology, and systematic zoology; D'Arcy Wentworth Thompson collection of separates in natural history and classics; Herrick, Coghill and Roofe collections in neurology. Noncirculating.

KY —UNIVERSITY OF LOUISVILLE, Ekstrom Library, Rare Books & Special Collections, 2301 S Third St, Louisville, 40208. George T McWhorter, Cur; Delinda Stephens Buie, Asst Cur
Holdings: Vols 250 Uncat
Budget: ($1500)
Notes: The William Marshall Bullitt Collection of rare mathematics and astronomy books, incl first editions of Euclid, Copernicus, Euler, Gauss and others. Typed, annotated bibliography available.

MA —MASSACHUSETTS INSTITUTE OF TECHNOLOGY, Institute Archives, Special Collections, Cambridge, 02139.
Notes: Papers of Norbert Wiener, renowned mathematician, was instrumental in the development of communication and control theories. He coined the word "cybernetics" to describe this new science. Professional papers document the development of this theory, his development as a mathematician, and his effective collaboration with students and colleagues including Vannevar Bush and John von Neumann. Unpublished finding aid with correspondent index is available in the Institute Archives.

MA —BRANDEIS UNIVERSITY, Goldfarb Library, 415 South St, Waltham, 02154. Bessie Hahn, Dir
Notes: Vito Volterra Collection on the History of Science and Mathematics. A collection of more than 5000 vols containing the major works in Volterra. Inclusive dates are the 16th through the 20th century. The collection also contains over 16,000 offprints and pamphlets, most of which are dedication copies from the author to Volterra. No catalog of the books extant, but an author-title finding list for the 16,000 offprints and pamphlets is available in Special Collections.

MI —UNIVERSITY OF MICHIGAN, Library, Dept of Rare Books & Special Collections, Ann Arbor, 48109. Robert J Starring, Head
Notes: Pre-1800 editions, incl Euclid.

NY —CORNELL UNIVERSITY LIBRARIES, John M Olin Library, History of Science Collections, Ithaca, 14853. Lillian A Clark, Administrative Supervisor; David W Corson, History of Science Librn
Holdings: Vols (33,000) Cat
Notes: Extensive collection of history, biography, and bibliography. Incl archives of Baldassare Boncompagni-Ludovisi (1821-94) relating to his research in the history of mathematics. Noncirculating.
See also entries under Boncompagni-Ludovisi; Science - History

NY —COLUMBIA UNIVERSITY LIBRARIES, Rare Book & Manuscript Library, 801 Butler Library, 535 W 114 St, New York, 10027. Kenneth A Lohf, Librn
Holdings: Vols (13,000) Cat Mss
Notes: History of mathematics and astronomy from the 15th to the 20th centuries. Autograph letters, mss, 275 mathematical instruments and 1200 portraits of mathematicians. Collection formed by David Eugene Smith. Restricted use.

PA —LIBRARY COMPANY OF PHILADELPHIA, 1314 Locust St, Philadelphia, 19107. Edwin Wolf II, Librn; Kenneth Finkel, Cur of Prints
Holdings: Vols (400,000) Cat Maps Pix
Budget: ($25,000)
Notes: American science and industry before 1860. Books, pamphlets, etc on science incl math, pysics, astronomy, and industry, incl business and engineering. Incl many 18th century books printed in England and France but used by American colonials in their study and research. Impossible to estimate the exact size of collection since it is not separated from general collection.

PA —UNIVERSITY OF PITTSBURGH, Hillman Library, Pittsburgh, 15260.
Notes: Economic and philosophical papers of the English scholar Frank Plumpton Ramsey (1903-1930), incl mss of published and unpublished writings, reading notes, etc. Significant because of his work in modern mathematics, logic, probability, and economics. Complementary to the Library's holdings of the papers of the logical empiricists, Rudolf Carnap and Hans Reichenback.

RI —BROWN UNIVERSITY, John Hay Library, 20 Prospect St, Providence, 02912. Mark N Brown, Cur Mss
Notes: Papers of Augustus William Smith, 1802-1866, and James Joseph Sylvester, 1814-1897, English mathematician and professor at Oxford and Johns Hopkins. The Royal Vale Heath Collection of about 200 of his designs, drawings, models, ocular, and verbal descriptions of simultaneous solutions to linear Diophantine equations in such examples as magic squares, Platonic solids, etc. these curious designs often were devised as talismans in ancient India and were first developed as mathematical problems by the Chinese.

†TX —UNIVERSITY OF TEXAS LIBRARIES, General Libraries, Humanities Research Center, PO Box 7219, Austin, 78712. John Chalmers, Librn
Notes: Some of Albert Einstein's mathematical-physics topics, 230 pages, written by Albert Einstein during the period 1950-1955. These complement 250 pages of similar manuscripts notes from the same period already in the Einstein collection.

ON —UNIVERSITY OF TORONTO, Thomas Fisher Rare Book Library, 120 Saint George St, Toronto, M5S 1A5, Can. Richard G Landon, Head
Holdings: Vols 4000
Notes: The Science Collection is especially rich in works on Renaissance astronomy, physics and mechanics and has noteworthy holdings of works of English experimental scientists in the 17th and 18th centuries with excellent collections of the works of Robert Boyle, Robert Hooke, and Sir Isaac Newton. Includes virtually all important early editions of Euclid; alchemical works of the 16th and 17th centuries together with the works of 18th century chemists like Lavoisier and Priestly; works on agriculture with special emphasis on British agriculture in the 18th century; and a variety of other works important in the history of science in all its branches. In addition the Fisher Library has many other specialized scientific collections which are listed separately.

MATHEMATICS—LABORATORIES see
Computation Laboratories

MATHEMATICS—PROBLEMS, EXERCISES, ETC.

NY —CORNELL UNIVERSITY LIBRARIES, Mathematics Library, White Hall, Ithaca,

14853. Steven W Rockey, Librn
Notes: Incl applied math.

RI —BROWN UNIVERSITY, John Hay Library, 20 Prospect St, Providence, 02912. Mark N Brown, Cur Mss
Notes: The Royal Vale Heath Collection of about 200 of his designs, drawings, models, ocular, and verbal descriptions of simultaneous solutions to linear Diophantine equations in such examples as magic squares, Platonic solids, etc. These curious designs often were devised as talismans in ancient India and were first developed as mathematical problems by the Chinese.

MATHEMATICS—STUDY AND TEACHING

CA —UNIVERSITY OF CALIFORNIA, BERKELEY, Science Education Library, Lawrence Hall of Science, Berkeley, 94720. Ann M Jensen, Librn
Holdings: Vols (6000)
Notes: Emphasis on innovative materials in the field of science, mathematics, and environmental education.

NY —CORNELL UNIVERSITY LIBRARIES, Mathematics Library, White Hall, Ithaca, 14853. Steven W Rockey, Librn
Notes: Incl applied math.

RI —PROVIDENCE PUBLIC LIBRARY, 150 Empire St, Providence, 02903. Lance J Bauer, Special Collections Librn
Notes: Lippitt Hill Tutorial Shelf (Rochambeau Branch). A resource library for tutors and parents, centrally located and open after school; established in 1973. LHT is a non-profit school volunteer agency which provides in-school tutoring services, contributes money for the acquisition of new books for the LHT Shelf, and the Providence Public Library maintains the collection. A collection of educational materials, wich an emphasis on math and reading, for the information and use of the general public, parents, teachers, and especially, tutors. It is located near the front door of the Rochambeau Branch.

WA —PACIFIC SCIENCE CENTER FOUNDATION, Library, 200 Second Ave N, Seattle, 98109. Sally Luttrel-Monten, Mgr
Holdings: Vols (3000) Cat
Notes: A resource center for science teachers and museum education staff. It is not a technical or research science library. Materials in general science, science education, and math education.

MATHEMATICS PERIODICALS see
Periodicals, Mathematics

MATHEMATICS, CHINESE

RI —BROWN UNIVERSITY, John Hay Library, 20 Prospect St, Providence, 02912. Mark N Brown, Cur Mss
Notes: The Royal Vale Heath Collection of about 200 of his designs, drawings, models, ocular, and verbal descriptions of simultaneous solutions to linear Diophantine equations in such examples as magic squares, Platonic solids, etc. These curious designs often were devised as talismans in ancient India and were first developed as mathematical problems by the Chinese.

MATHER, BRUCE, 1939-

AB —UNIVERSITY OF CALGARY, Libraries, Special Collections Div, 2500 University Dr, Calgary, T2N 1N4, Can.
Holdings: Mss
Notes: Mss (50 cm) incl worksheet sketches, pencil and ink music scores, 1949-80.
See also entry under Musicians, Canadian.

MATHER, COTTON

MI —NORTHERN MICHIGAN UNIVERSITY, Lydia M Olson Library, Elizabeth L Harden Drive, Marquette, 49855. Stephen H Peters, Cataloger
Notes: A section of the personal library of Moses Coit Tyler, incl works by Thomas

MATHER, COTTON (cont.)

Hooker, John Cotton, Cotton Mather, and Jonathan Edwards.

MATHER, MELISSA

MA —BOSTON UNIVERSITY, Mugar Memorial Library, Special Collections Dept, 771 Commonwealth Ave, Boston, 02215. Howard B Gotlieb, Dir
Holdings: Cat Mss Correspondence

MATHER FAMILY

MA —AMERICAN CONGREGATIONAL ASSOCIATION, Congregational Library, 14 Beacon St, Boston, 02108. Harold F Worthley, Librn
Notes: "One of the outstanding collections in the country," incl Richard, Increase, Cotton, and other Mathers.
†MA —BOSTON PUBLIC LIBRARY, Copley Sq, Boston, 02117.
Holdings: Vols 277 Cat
Notes: The Prince, Lewis, and Barlow Collections. About half of the titles are represented by two or more copies. Incl 17th-18th century correspondence, from the Prince Collection.
MA —SECRETARY OF THE COMMONWEALTH, Archives Division, State House, Boston, 02133.
Holdings: Mss
Notes: Cotton, Increase, and Samuel Mather mss.
MA —HARVARD UNIVERSITY LIBRARY, Widener Library, Cambridge, 02138.
Holdings: Cat
Notes: See Downs 4071-4076 for lists showing Harvard holdings.
MA —AMERICAN ANTIQUARIAN SOCIETY LIBRARY, 185 Salisbury St, Worcester, 01609. Marcus A McCorison, Dir & Librn
Holdings: Mss
Notes: Incl holdings from the library collections of Increase, Samuel, and Cotton Mather, purchased in 1814.
OH —OHIO STATE UNIVERSITY, William Oxley Thompson Memorial Library, 1858 Neil Ave Mall, Columbus, 43210. Robert A Tibbetts, Cur of Special Collections
Holdings: Cat Mss
Notes: The papers of Thomas J Holmes.
VA —UNIVERSITY OF VIRGINIA, Alderman Library, Tracy W McGregor Collection, Charlottesville, 22901. William H Runge, Cur
Holdings: Vols 2500 Cat Mss
Notes: This collection was gathered by William Gwinn Mather, a direct descendant of the New England Mathers. It is one of the 3 important Mather collections in the world. Excellent collection on magic and witchcraft in America. Collection incl 20th century imprints. Thomas J Holmes used this collection as a basis for his monumental biographies of Increase Mather, Cotton Mather and the minor Mathers. See Holmes' "The Mather Collection [formerly] at Cleveland," and his published bibliographies.

MATHEWS, MITFORD

IN —INDIANA STATE UNIVERSITY, Cunningham Memorial Library, Dept of Rare Books & Special Collections, Terre Haute, 47809. Lawrence J McCrank, Head
Holdings: Mss
Notes: Papers of Milford Mathews. Supplements the Cordell Collection of rare dictionaries.

MATRICULATION RECORDS

SK —UNIVERSITY OF SASKATCHEWAN, Library, Saskatoon, S7N 0W0, Can. S Perkins, Librn
Notes: Extensive collection (in book form; some reprints) of matriculation records of English, Scottish, French, German, Italian, and other universities, dating from the Middle Ages and Renaissance.

MATRIMONY see Marriage

MATSON, HAROLD, LITERARY AGENCY

NY —COLUMBIA UNIVERSITY LIBRARIES, Rare Book & Manuscript Library, 801 Butler Library, 535 W 114 St, New York, 10027. Kenneth A Lohf, Librn
Holdings: Mss
Notes: Forty years of literary correspondence between the Harold Matson Literary Agency. Some 75,000 pieces written between 1937 and 1980. Restricted use.

MATTHES, GERARD HENDRIK, 1874-1959

NY —CORNELL UNIVERSITY LIBRARIES, Collection of Regional History, Dept of Manuscripts and Univ Archives, Ithaca, 14853.
Notes: Hydraulic and hydroelectric power engineer. Papers, ca 1928-55; 53 ft.

MATTHEWS, BRANDER

NY —COLUMBIA UNIVERSITY LIBRARIES, Rare Book & Manuscript Library, 801 Butler Library, 535 W 114 St, New York, 10027. Kenneth A Lohf, Librn
Holdings: Vols 5000 Cat Mss
Notes: First editions of plays, autograph letters and mss, most of which relate to Brander Matthews. Restricted use.

MATHEWS, J. B.

NC —DUKE UNIVERSITY, William R Perkins Library, Manuscript Dept, Durham, 27706. Ellen Gartrell, Cur of Mss
Holdings: Cat Mss
Notes: J B Mathews' extensive files on liberals and radicals, 1930s-60s.

MATTHEWS, KATE

KY —UNIVERSITY OF LOUISVILLE, Ekstrom Library, Photographic Archives, Louisville, 40292. J C Anderson, Cur; David G Horvath, Asst Cur
Holdings: Vols (750,000) Cat Pix Slides Budget: ($60,000)
Notes: Photographs, incl prototypes for "Little Colonel" series.

MATTHEWS, STANLEY

OH —RUTHERFORD B HAYES LIBRARY, 1337 Hayes Ave, Fremont, 43420. Watt P Marchman, Dir
Holdings: Cat Mss Pix Microforms
Notes: Papers of the Justice of the U S Supreme Court (3 linear feet). Cf *Guide to Manuscripts of the Ohio Historical Society*, 331. Index in collections.

MATTHEWS, WILLIAM, 1905-1975

CA —UNIVERSITY OF CALIFORNIA, LOS ANGELES, Research Library, Dept of Special Collections, 405 Hilgard Ave, Los Angeles, 90024. Edward Shreeves, Chairman, Bibliographers Group; David S Zeidberg, Head
Holdings: Mss
Notes: 6.5 linear feet of the UCLA English professor's papers, mss, etc.

MATTICK, HANS W.

IL —CHICAGO HISTORICAL SOCIETY, Library, Clark St at North Ave, Chicago, 60614. Archie Motley, Manuscript Librn
Notes: Papers.
See also entry under Public Welfare-History.

MATTHISON, EDITH WYNNE

CA —UNIVERSITY OF CALIFORNIA, LOS ANGELES, Research Library, Dept of Special Collections, 405 Hilgard Ave, Los Angeles, 90024. Edward Shreeves, Chairman, Bibliographers Group; David S Zeidberg, Head
Holdings: Vols 75 Mss
Notes: 75 books; 31 linear feet of clippings, mss, and carbons of correspondence, 1887-1947.

MATTIOLI, PIETRO ANDREA

KS —UNIVERSITY OF KANSAS, Kenneth Spencer Research Library, Special Collections Dept, Lawrence, 66045. Alexandra Mason, Librn
Holdings: Cat Mss Maps Pix
Notes: Elllis Collection of Ornithology, natural history and voyages and travels; botanical literature from Fitzpatrick collection (especially medical botany, early American botanists, renaissance herbals, Matthioli); some early chemistry and mathematics; scientific voyages and travels; De Beer collection of offprints in embryology, endocrinology, and systematic zoology; D'Arcy Wentworth Thompson collection of separates in natural history and classics; Herrick, Coghill and Roofe collections in neurology. Noncirculating.

MATUTE, ANA MARIA

MA —BOSTON UNIVERSITY, Mugar Memorial Library, Special Collections Dept, 771 Commonwealth Ave, Boston, 02215. Howard B Gotlieb, Dir
Holdings: Cat Mss Pix
Notes: Mss, correspondence, etc collected in depth; incl publications by or about.

MATZKIN, JACK

CA —UNIVERSITY OF CALIFORNIA, LOS ANGELES, Theater Arts Library, Los Angeles, 90024. Edward Shreeves, Chairman, Bibliographers Group; Audree Malkin, Head, Theater Arts Library
Notes: Jack Matzkin Collection: television variety and comedy shows, 1950-1970, incl scripts cast lists, rehearsal schedules, prop and wardrobe lists, set designs, and sheet music.

MAUER, JOAN AND NORMAN

CA —UNIVERSITY OF CALIFORNIA, LOS ANGELES, Theater Arts Library, Los Angeles, 90024. Edward Shreeves, Chairman, Bibliographers Group; Audree Malkin, Head, Theater Arts Library
Notes: Collection of animators Joan and Norman Mauer: scripts, outlines, and storyboards for such animated television shows as *Thundarr the Barbarian, Plastic Man, Richie Rich, Goldie Gold, Marmaduke, Laverne and Shirley, Happy Days Gang, Suprefriends, Scooby Doo, Dynomutt Dog Wonder,* and *Mork and Mindy.*

MAUGHAM, ROBIN

MA —BOSTON UNIVERSITY, Mugar Memorial Library, Special Collections Dept, 771 Commonwealth Ave, Boston, 02215. Howard B Gotlieb, Dir
Holdings: Mss

MAUGHAM, WILLIAM SOMERSET

CA —SAN DIEGO STATE UNIVERSITY, Malcolm A Love Library, 5300 Campanile Dr, San Diego, 92182. D Dickinson, Univ Librn; Don L Bosseau, Dir
Notes: Collected works in first edition of certain prominent authors, as H G Wells, Somerset Maugham, William Dean Howells, Gertrude Atherton, Tom Stoppard, James Clavell, G A Henty, Henry Raup Wagner.
CA —UNIVERSITY OF CALIFORNIA, SANTA BARBARA, Library, Dept of Special Collections, Santa Barbara, 93106. Christian F Brun, Head
Notes: Most comprehensive Maugham collection on the west coast. Assembled and donated by Raymond Toole Stott, Maugham's official bibliographer and friend. Incl nearly all early rare books, first editions, unusual variants, and a series of letters from Maugham to Stott.
CA —STANFORD UNIVERSITY LIBRARIES, Cecil H Green Library, Stanford, 94305. Michael T Ryan, Cur
Holdings: Vols Cat
Notes: Also incl correspondence and literary mss.
IN —INDIANA UNIVERSITY, Lilly Library, Seventh St, Bloomington, 47405. William R Cagle, Librn
Holdings: // Cat Mss
Notes: A collection of contracts and

MAUGHAM, WILLIAM SOMERSET (cont.)

correspondence about those contracts for production or publication of sixty Maugham works, 1904-1973. 1696 items. A collection of correspondence and writings by and about Maugham collected by Grenville Cook of Watford, Herts, England. Incl are letters of Maugham to Fred Bason as well as articles, etc by Bason about WSM; also Robin Maugham's ms for *Somerset and All the Maughams.* Cover 1899-1970. 304 items. Incl first editions of Maugham's works. No photocopying.

†NC —WAKE FOREST UNIVERSITY, Z Smith Reynolds Library, Box 7777, Reynold Sta, Winston-Salem, 27109. Richard J Murdoch, Rare Book Librn
Holdings: Vols 225 Cat
Notes: A significant collection.

OH —OHIO UNIVERSITY, Vernon R Alden Library, Department of Archives and Special Collections, Athens, 45701. Gary A Hunt, Head
Holdings: Vols 90 Cat
Notes: Mostly first editions, both English and American.

MAULDIN, BILL

KS —UNIVERSITY OF KANSAS, Kenneth Spencer Research Library, Kansas Collection, Lawrence, 66045. Sheryl K Williams, Cur
Holdings: Cat
Notes: The Albert T Reid Cartoon Collection. Nucleus of collection was Reid's personal collection of political and comic cartoons. Later cartoonists presented samples of their work. Bill Mauldin, Rollin Kirby, Daniel B Dowling, Thomas Nast, and other political cartoonists represented. Comic strips from the late 1920s and 1930s. The collection of cartoons is cataloged and represented in the Kansas Collection card catalog. A separate book catalog is maintained also. For description see: *Albert T Reid Cartoon Collection.* Lawrence, Kan, Published for the Journalistic Historical Center, University of Kansas by the William Allen White Foundation, University of Kansas, ca 1957. Originally maintained by the Journalistic Historical Center, William Allen White School of Journalism, the collection was transferred to the Kansas Collection, Kenneth Spencer Library in 1969.

MAULE, JANE, 1866-1939

NY —CORNELL UNIVERSITY LIBRARIES, John M Olin Library, Dept of Rare Books, Ithaca, 14853. Donald D Eddy, Librn
Holdings: Cat Mss

PA —HAVERFORD COLLEGE, Magill Library, Quaker Collection, Haverford, 19041. Edwin B Bonner, Librn & Cur
Notes: Journal of Jane Maule, 1866-1939.

MAUREPAS, JEAN FREDERIC PHELYPEAUX, COMTE DE, 1701-1781

NY —CORNELL UNIVERSITY LIBRARIES, John M Olin Library, Dept of Rare Books, Ithaca, 14853. Donald D Eddy, Librn
Holdings: Cat Mss
Notes: The ministerial papers of the naval minister of Louis XV. See Maurice Filion, *Maurepas, Minister of the Navy, 1723-1740: A New Portrait,* The Cornell Library Journal, Spring 1967.

NY —UNIVERSITY OF ROCHESTER, Rush Rhees Library, Department of Rare Books and Special Collections, Rochester, 14627. Peter Dzwonkoski, Librn
Holdings: // Cat Mss
Notes: Jean Frederic Phelypeaux, Comte de Maurepas. Manuscripts relating to the French in Canada and Louisiana in the mid-18th century.

MAURIN, JOAQUIN, 1896-

CA —HOOVER INSTITUTION ON WAR, REVOLUTION & PEACE, Stanford University, Stanford, 94305. Milorad M Drachkovitch, Archivist
Holdings: Mss Pix
Notes: Papers of Joaquin Maurin, Spanish political activist, journalist, and author, incl correspondence, writings, newspaper and magazine clippings, photographs, printed matter, and other material, 1920-1973, relating to his political and literary careers, communism and socialism in Spain, the Spanish Civil War, and the American Literary Agency. 23 ms boxes, 1 oversize box.

MAURITANIA

CA —HOOVER INSTITUTION ON WAR, REVOLUTION & PEACE, Stanford University, Stanford, 94305. Peter Duignan, Cur; Karen Fung, Deputy Cur
Holdings: Vols (100,000)
Notes: For full description of collection, see Hoover Institution entry under Near East.

MI —MICHIGAN STATE UNIVERSITY, International Library, Sahel Documentation Center, East Lansing, 48824. Eugene deBenko, Librn; Learthen Dorsey, Librn
Holdings: Vols (5100) Cat Mss Maps Pix Slides Phonorecords Audiotapes Videotapes Microforms
Budget: ($8000)
Notes: See description under The Sahel.

MAURITIUS

CA —UNIVERSITY OF CALIFORNIA, SANTA BARBARA, Library, Dept of Special Collections, Santa Barbara, 93106. Christian F Brun, Head
Holdings: Vols 316 Uncat
Notes: History and literature.

MAUZY, OSCAR

TX —NORTH TEXAS STATE UNIVERSITY, Archives, NT Station Box 5188, Denton, 76203. Robert LaForte, University Archivist
Notes: Part of Oral History Collection. Interviews with Texas legislator.

MAW, HERBERT

UT —UNIVERSITY OF UTAH, Marriott Library, Special Collections, Salt Lake City, 84112. Gregory C Thompson, Cur
Holdings: Cat Mss Microfilm Film Oral History
Notes: Papers of the Utah Governor.

MAWSON, THOMAS HAYTON, 1861-1933

AB —UNIVERSITY OF CALGARY, Libraries, Special Collections Div, 2500 University Dr, Calgary, T2N 1N4, Can.
Holdings: Cat // Pix
Notes: This collection consists of eighteen large drawings representing maps, building elevations and sections, and one bird's eye view of the *Calgary Plan,* 1914, by English landscape architect and town planner Thomas Hayton Mawson. The beginning of World War I prevented the execution of this ambitious scheme. Inventory at hand.

MAXIMILIAN AND CARLOTTA

AZ —UNIVERSITY OF ARIZONA, Library, Tucson, 85721. W David Laird, Librn
Notes: Strong collection on Maximilian and Carlotta and the French intervention in Mexico, some official publications.

CA —STANFORD UNIVERSITY LIBRARIES, Cecil H Green Library, Stanford, 94305. Michael T Ryan, Cur
Notes: Research collection.

IN —INDIANA UNIVERSITY, Lilly Library, Seventh St, Bloomington, 47405. William R Cagle, Cur
Holdings: Vols 10,000 // Cat Mss
Notes: Begins with the conquest of Mexico by Cortes and his letters to Charles V, in first and subsequent editions and translations, through the Revolution of 1910. Incl. the most important reforms of the Enlightenment concerning the economy, commerce, mining, science, and the expulsion of the Jesuits. The period of independence, the best represented aspects of which are the effect of the Napoleonic invasion of Spain in 1808, the constitutional crisis in Spain and the colonies provoked by the capture of the Spanish royal family by Napoleon, the policy of Ferdinand VII and the most important decisions by all the viceroys, bishops and archbishops. From the revolutionary side, the historical pronouncements and documents by the leaders of the movement of independence, such as Hidalgo, Morelos, Guerrero, and Iturbide, and the legal and political documents that gave structure to the Revolution. The empire with Iturbide and the period of political instability and strife that followed the independence, the reforms of Juarez, Maximillian's Empire, and its corollary, the dictatorial regime of Porfirio Diaz through the Revolution of 1910, are also well documented.

TX —RICE UNIVERSITY, Fondren Library, Woodson Research Center, 6100 S Main St, PO Box 1892, Houston, 77251. Nancy Parker, Dir Woodson Research Center
Holdings: // Mss Pix Microforms
Notes: Letters, broadsides, clippings, photographs, memorabilia, and microfilm, relating to the Maximilian era in Mexico. Incl letters from Carlotta as a young girl to members of her family.

WI —UNIVERSITY OF WISCONSIN, MADISON, Memorial Library, Ibero-American Studies Collection, 728 State St, Madison, 53706. Suzanne Hodgman, Bibliographer
Holdings: // Uncat
Notes: Maximilian Collection. Over 600 pamphlets on 19th century Mexico. The earliest is dated 1791 and the latest 1906, but the majority relate to the Reform and European Intervention, hence the popular title "Maximilian Collection." There are a few books, but most of the books contained in the original purchase are intergrated into the general library collection. A typescript listing of the collection is available. Pamphlets are housed in the Rare Book Department.

MAXIMS see Aphorisms, Apothegms, Epigrams, Maxims, and Proverbs

MAXON, WILLIAM RALPH

DC —SMITHSONIAN INSTITUTION, Archives Div, Washington, 20560. William W Moss, Archivist
Holdings: Cat Mss Pix
Notes: The Archives holds the records of the National Museum of Natural History's Division of Plants and the Department of Botany, 1870-1970, as well as correspondence of botanists incl Joseph Nelson Rose and William Ralph Maxon.

MAXSON, DARWIN E.

†WI —SEVENTH DAY BAPTIST HISTORICAL SOCIETY, Library, 3120 Kennedy St, PO Box 1678, Janesville, 53547.
Holdings: Vols 30 // Cat Mss
Notes: Darwin E Maxson, 1822-1895, was a member of the faculty of Alfred University, Alfred, NY, a chaplain with the Union Army during the Civil War, and pastor of several churches. Incl books, mss, etc.

MAXWELL, GAVIN

CT —LEE ASH, (personal collection), 66
Humiston Dr, Bethany, 06525.
Holdings: Cat Mss Pix
Notes: Incl books, letters, ephemera, etc.

MAXWELL, MARY ELIZABETH (BRADDON), 1837-1915

CA —UNIVERSITY OF CALIFORNIA, LOS
ANGELES, Research Library, Dept of
Special Collections, 405 Hilgard Ave, Los
Angeles, 90024. Edward Shreeves,
Chairman, Bibliographers Group; David S
Zeidberg, Head
Holdings: Vols 150
Notes: 150 first and other editions of her
books; 17 letters.
NJ —PRINCETON UNIVERSITY, Library,
Morris L Parrish Collection, Princeton,
08540. Alexander D Wainwright, Cur
Holdings: Vols 28
Notes: The collection contains over 6500
vols, as well as many theatre programs,
playbills, photographs, clippings and other
miscellanea. Parrish's goal was to assemble
in both the English and the American first
editions, in the original condition as issued,
everything that a given author published. He
was also interested in a high standard of
condition for his books. Many additions
have been acquired since the Parrish
collection came to the Library as a bequest
in 1944. The collection is an assemblage of
author collections, consisting of books by:
William Harrison Ainsworth, James
Matthew Barrie, William Black, The Brontes,
William Wilkie Collins, Dinah Mulock
Craik, Marie de la Ramee ("Ouida"),
Benjamin Disraeli, Charles Dickens, Charles
Dodgson, George du Maurier, George Eliot
(ie Mary Ann Evans), Elizabeth Gaskell,
Thomas Hardy, Thomas Hughes,Charles
Kingsley, Charles Lever, Edward George
Earle Bulwer-Lytton, Mary Maxwell, George
Meredith, Charles Reade, Walter Scott,
Robert Louis Stevenson, William Makepeace
Thackeray, Trollope Family, Ellen Wood,
and Charlotte Yonge.

MAXWELL, WILLIAM

OH —GREENE COUNTY DISTRICT
LIBRARY, 76 E Market St, PO Box 520,
Xenia, 45385. Julie M Overton, Local
History Coordr
Holdings: // Uncat
Notes: Galloway Collection of Ohio history
is housed in a five-drawer filing cabinet, incl
letters, some at the time of the Gold Rush;
family letters of the Galloways, Lyons,
Worthingtons and others; material about
William Maxwell, editor and publisher of the
first newspaper in the Northwest Territory,
also legal papers concerning him; papers,
some legal, concerning Galloways, incl "The
Galloway Lands in 1812," and papers about
the Worthingtons and Lyons; indentures;
Civil War diary of Clark Galloway, MD, a
surgeon in the war; pictures of families,
covered bridges, mills etc; material about
Tecumseh and some other Indians and their
traditions; galley sheets and correspondence
concerning the publishing of the New
Testament in the Shawnee language; material
about the railroad, OVCH (formerly OS&OS
Home) Antioch College, Wilberforce
University and other items about
Ohiohistory; many notes, papers and
correspondence acquired when William
Galloway was preparing to write the book
"Old Chillicothe," published posthumously in
1934.

MAY, CATHERINE

†WA —WASHINGTON STATE
UNIVERSITY, Library, Manuscripts,
Archives & Special Collections, Pullman,
99164. John F Guido, Head
Holdings: Vols Cat Mss Maps Pix
Microforms
Notes: Ms resources in the Washington State
University Library for the study of Pacific
Northwest history incl the personal papers of
Frank A Banks, William Compton Brown,
Enoch Albert Bryan, Ernest Otto Holland,
William Lon Johnson, Catherine May,
Lucullus Virgil McWhorter, Austin Mires,
Carl Parcher Russell, Pierre Jean de Smet,
Henry Harmon Spalding, Elkanah Walker,
John McAdam Webster, Marcus Whitman,
as well as many business records of banks,
insurance firms and agencies, breweries,
lumber mills, merchants, entrepreneurs and
farmers. All ms collections are described in a
catalog, a published register or an
unpublished finding aid.

MAY, ROBERT

PA —FREE LIBRARY OF PHILADELPHIA,
Rare Book Dept, Logan Sq, Philadelphia,
19103. Marie E Korey, Rare Book Librn
Holdings: Uncat Mss Phonorecords
Notes: The Colonel Richard Gimble
Collection of Robert L May's "Rudolph, the
Red-Nosed Reindeer": 200 books and
periodicals, manuscripts, musical scores,
newspaper clippings, and records.

MAYA LITERATURE

OH —CLEVELAND PUBLIC LIBRARY, Fine
Arts and Special Collections Department,
325 Superior Ave, Cleveland, 44114. Alice
N Loranth, Head
Holdings: Vols (1500) Cat
Notes: Several hundred facsimile editions of
Mexican and Maya codices.
See also entries under Manuscripts -
Collections.

MAYAN LANGUAGES

PA —UNIVERSITY OF PENNSYLVANIA,
University Museum Library, 33 & Spruce
Sts, Philadelphia, 19104. Jean S Adelman,
Librn
Holdings: Vols (80,000) Cat Mss Microforms
Notes: Incl the Daniel Garrison Brinton
collection of about 2000 vols, on aboriginal
American linguistics and ethnology. Espec
strong in Maya language materials.

MAYAS

†AL —UNIVERSITY OF ALABAMA, Amelia
Gayle Gorgas Library, PO Box S,
University, 35486.
Notes: This collection consists of 119 reels
of microfilm. Separately published
bibliography: A Catalog of the Yucatan
Collection on Microfilm in the University of
Alabama Libraries (University: University of
Alabama Press), 1872.
LA —TULANE UNIVERSITY, Howard-Tilton
Memorial Library, Latin American Library,
New Orleans, 70118. Thomas Niehaus, Dir
Holdings: Vols (150,000) Cat Mss Maps Pix
Microforms VF
Budget: ($67,000)
Notes: Catalog of the Latin American
Library (Boston: G K Hall, 1970, suppl.
1973,1975,1978); Downs 5338-41; suppl
(1961), 2727, 2737. The Latin American
Library is a general collection, but
specializes in Central American, Mexican,
and Brazilian materials. The disciplines
which are most strongly represented are
history, anthropology, and archaeology. The
Viceregal Ecclesiastical Mexican Collection
contains manuscripts from the colonial
period. The France V Scholes Collection
contains a large number of photoprints and
microfilm of colonial documents from the
archives of Spain and Mexico. The Merle
Greene Robertson Rubbings Collection
contains nearly five hundred rubbings of
relief sculpture from Mayan archaeological
sites in Mexico and Guatemala. The
Photographic Collection contains photos of
archaeological sites inMeso-America, of pre-
Columbian Peruvian architecture, and a
general group of historic photos from Latin
America.
TX —UNIVERSITY OF TEXAS LIBRARIES,
Nettie Lee Benson Latin American
Collection, Sid Richardson Hall 1.109,
Austin, 78712. Laura Gutierrez-Witt, Head
Librn
Holdings: Vols (450,000) Cat Mss Maps Pix
Phonorecords Filmstrips Microforms
See also entry under Latin America
TX —EL PASO PUBLIC LIBRARY, Mexican
American Collection, 501 N Oregon, El
Paso, 79901. Iris Espino, Librn
Notes: History and culture of Mexico from
pre-Columbian times to the present.
†VA —GEORGE C MARSHALL
RESEARCH FOUNDATION AND
LIBRARY, Drawer 920, Lexington, 24450.
Royster Lyle Jr, Cur Collections
Holdings: Vols Uncat Mss
Notes: Examples of ancient writings of
Europe, Crete, and Easter Island, and
material on the Aztecs, Incas, and
particularly the Mayans.

MAYER, MARIA GOEPPERT

CA —UNIVERSITY OF CALIFORNIA, SAN
DIEGO, Central University Library,
Mandeville Dept of Special Collections, La
Jolla, 92093. Lynda Corey Claassen, Head
Notes: Manuscript collection incl papers of
Nobel scientists Harold Urey and Maria
Goeppert Mayer. Papers of physicist Leo
Szilard are located in the department; special
arrangements are required for use.

MAYFIELD, EARLE BRADFORD, 1881-1964

DC —GEORGETOWN UNIVERSITY,
Library, Special Collections Div, 37 & O Sts
NW, Washington, 20057. George M
Barringer, Special Collections Librn;
Nicholas B Sheetz, Mss Librn
Holdings: Mss Cat Pix Phonorecords
Notes: Papers of the Honorable Earle
Bradford Mayfield (1881-1964), concerning
his business, legal and political careers. The
papers are particularly useful in the study of
Texas politics on the state and national
levels. Mayfield served in the Texas State
Senate from 1906-1912 and in the United
States Senate from 1923-1929. Also incl are
the papers of his wife Ora Limpkin Mayfield.

MAYHEW, ROBERT WELLINGTON, 1880-1971

BC —UNIVERSITY OF VICTORIA,
McPherson Library, Victoria, V8W 3H5,
Can.
Notes: Cabinet minister and diplomat.
Correspondence, diaries (several by Mrs
Grace G Mayhew), personal records,
photographs, clipping files.

MAYHEW FAMILY

MA —BOSTON UNIVERSITY, Mugar
Memorial Library, Special Collections Dept,
771 Commonwealth Ave, Boston, 02215.
Howard B Gotlieb, Dir
Holdings: // Cat
Notes: Correspondence and other papers
1648-1774.

MAYNARD, THEODORE

DC —GEORGETOWN UNIVERSITY,
Library, Special Collections Div, 37 & O Sts
NW, Washington, 20057. George M
Barringer, Special Collections Librn;
Nicholas B Sheetz, Mss Librn
Holdings: Vols (400) Uncat Mss Pix
Notes: Papers of Theodore Maynard; also,
his library including his own copies of his
works. Substantial correspondence between
Brooks and Theodore Maynard; virtually
complete run of Brooks' publications,
presented to Maynard.

MAYO, CHARLES HORACE AND WILLIAM JAMES

MN —MAYO HISTORICAL UNIT, Mayo
Clinic/Mayo Foundation, Rochester, 55905.
Clark W Nelson, Mayo History
Development Specialist
Holdings: Mss Pix Phonorecords Audiotapes

MAYO, CHARLES HORACE AND WILLIAM JAMES (cont.)

Videotapes 16mm Films
Notes: The collection generally relates to the history of the Mayo institutions--Mayo Clinic, Mayo Foundation, Mayo Medical School, and Mayo Graduate School. Its scope covers roughly the years 1860 to present. It features the papers and correspondence of Drs Charles Horace Mayo (1865-1939) and William James Mayo (1861-1939), founders of the Mayo institutions. Many items are also incl from other physicians and administrators who have been prominent in Mayo's development. Limited access collection. Inquiries subject to review. Application must be made in advance.

MAYO CLINIC

MN —MAYO MEDICAL LIBRARY, History of Medicine Collection, Rochester, 55905. Nancy R Hensel, Librn
Holdings: Pix
Notes: The Dr Howard F Polley Cartoon Collection; over 70 cartoons featured in newspapers nationally that relate to the Mayo Clinic and Rochester.

MAYORS

AL —BIRMINGHAM PUBLIC LIBRARY, Dept of Archives & Mss, 2020 Seventh Ave N, Birmingham, 35203. Marvin Y Whiting, Archivist & Cur
Holdings: Cat Docs Mss //
Notes: Collected papers, 1963-1967 for Albert Boutwell, first mayor of Birmingham, Alabama under the mayor-council form of government. His administration was dominated by several concerns: the Civil Rights Movement, the growth of police surveillance powers within the community, the effort to revitalize the inner city, and stimulate economic growth. Correspondence, memoranda, reports, and other documents are organized by subject categories. Collection of correspondence, reports, memoranda, scrapbooks, other documents, and photographs of Cooper Green, Mayor, Birmingham, Alabama from 1940 to 1953. The papers reflect changes in the city during World War II, post war business expansion, and concern over growing civil rights efforts by blacks.
DC —NATIONAL LEAGUE OF CITIES, Municipal Reference Service, 1301 Pennsylvania Ave NW, Washington, 20004. Olivia Kredel, Mgr
Holdings: Vols (20,000)
Notes: City reports and plans, financial reports, budgets, commission reports, plans, etc. Federal legislation on urban affairs, etc.

MAYTORENA, JOSE MARIA, 1867-1948

CA —CLAREMONT COLLEGES, Honnold Library, Ninth & Dartmouth, Claremont, 91711. Tania Rizzo, Special Collections Dept Head
Holdings: Cat Mss Pix Scrapbooks
Notes: Correspondence, mss, documents, clippings, photographs, and ephemera, 2200 pieces, some in carbon copies, of Jose Maytorena, from 1882-1947. Important correspondents incl Venustiano Carranza, Francisco Madero, and Alvaro Obregon, among many others. Guy T McCreary, *A Primary Study of the Revolutionary, Governor, General, Jose maria Maytorena and the Mexican Revolution* 1910-1916 (thesis, 1967) based on this collection. Restricted use.

MAZARINADES

CA —UNIVERSITY OF CALIFORNIA, LOS ANGELES, Research Library, Dept of Special Collections, 405 Hilgard Ave, Los Angeles, 90024. Edward Shreeves, Chairman, Bibliographers Group; David S Zeidberg, Head
Notes: 6 linear feet.

CA —STANFORD UNIVERSITY LIBRARIES, Cecil H Green Library, Stanford, 94305. Michael T Ryan, Cur
Holdings: Vols Cat
Notes: An emphasis in the Rare Book Collection.
CT —YALE UNIVERSITY, Box 1603A, Yale Station, New Haven, 06520.
IL —NEWBERRY LIBRARY, 60 W Walton St, Chicago, 60610. Diana Haskell, Cur of Modern Mss
Holdings: Cat
IL —NORTHWESTERN UNIVERSITY, Library, Special Collections Dept, 1937 Sheridan Rd, Evanston, 60201. R Russell Maylone, Cur
Holdings: Vols 1560
MD —UNIVERSITY OF MARYLAND, Library, Rare Book Collection, College Park, 20742. Donald Farren, Assoc Dir for Special Collections
Holdings: Vols (10,000) Cat
Notes: Ranging from the incunabula to modern first editions, the Rare Book Collection is particularly strong in materials relating to the history of France and in *exempla* of interest to students of bibliography. Related collections include sizable groups of books and other items relating to the Savoy, to *Expressionismus*, and to Pompeii. Pamphlet collections include many Mazarinades, many pamphlets relating to slavery and abolition, numerous French plays, and press books.
MA —HARVARD UNIVERSITY LIBRARY, Houghton Library, Cambridge, 02138. F Thomas Noonan, Cur, Reading Room; Lawrence Dowler, Associate Librn
Holdings: Vols 3900 Cat
Notes: See *Mazarinades; A Catalogue of the Collection of 17th-Century French Civil War Tracts in the Houghton Library,* ed by James E Walsh (Boston: G K Hall, 1976).
MN —UNIVERSITY OF MINNESOTA, O Meredith Wilson Library, 309 19 Ave S, Minneapolis, 55455. Austin J McLean, Chief, Special Collections
Holdings: Vols 2090 // Cat
Notes: Collection includes 22 items not listed by Moreau.
NY —STATE UNIVERSITY OF NEW YORK, COLLEGE AT BUFFALO, Poetry/Rare Books Collection, 420 Capen Hall, Buffalo, 14260. Robert J Bertholf, Cur
Holdings: Vols 444
Notes: Contemporary political pamphlets of the period of the Fronde, 1648-1653. 43 items not listed by Moreau. Checklisted in University Libraries Publication.
NY —NEW YORK PUBLIC LIBRARY, Research Libraries, General Research Division, Fifth Ave & 42 St, New York, 10018. Rodney Phillips, Chief
Holdings: Vols (2,225,000) Cat Maps Pix Microforms
Budget: ($775,718)
NC —UNIVERSITY OF NORTH CAROLINA, CHAPEL HILL, Wilson Library, Rare Book Collection, Chapel Hill, 27514. Paul S Koda, Cur of Rare Books
Holdings: Vols 800 // Uncat
Notes: Over 800 Mazarinades, incl works by Scarron, Cyrano de Bergerac, the Cardinal de Retz, and the Prince de Conti. Incl reference works: *La Mazarinade* and Moreau's *Bibliographie des Mazarinades.*
OH —CLEVELAND PUBLIC LIBRARY, History and Geography Department, 325 Superior Ave, Cleveland, 44114. JoAnn Petrello, Head
Holdings: Cat
Notes: Incl contemporary political pamphlets (2000) of the period of the Fronde, 1648-1653. Restricted use: reference only.
WI —UNIVERSITY OF WISCONSIN, MADISON, Memorial Library, Rare Books Collection, 728 State St, Madison, 53706. Gretchen Lagana, Cur
Holdings: // Cat
Notes: A collection of literary, political, and satirical pamphlets covering all aspects of French life and civilization during 1547-1648. Included in Robert O Lindsay and John Neu, *French Political Pamphlets 1547-1648* (Madison,1969). Housed in the Dept of Rare Books and Special Collections.

MAZDAISM see Zoroastrianism

MBOCHI LANGUAGE see Congo Languages and Literature

MBOMA LANGUAGE see Congo Languages and Literature

MEAD, MARGARET

DC —LIBRARY OF CONGRESS, Manuscript Division, Washington, 20540. John C Broderick, Chief
Notes: Papers of Margaret Mead (1901-1978). Approx 370,000 items, incl general correspondence files, correspondence with organizations, and correspondence about attendance at and participation in meetings and conferences. Also, items reflecting teaching and lecturing activities, and an extensive subject file. Drafts, galley proofs, research materials, notes, memoranda and correspondence representing her publication of books and articles, in addition to a comprehensive file of the published versions of her works. Other materials at American Museum of Natural History, New York, NY, and Columbia University Departments of Anthropology.
MA —AMHERST COLLEGE, Library, Amherst, 01002. John Lancaster, Special Collections Librn
Notes: Personal "working library" of Margaret Mead, donated by Mary Catherine Bateson, Dr Mead's daughter. Other collections of Margaret Mead's papers, books, mss, etc are at the Library of Congress, the American Museum of Natural History, etc. Dr Bateson has also given her mother's film collection to the Five College collection housed at Hampshire College.

MEAD, SHEPHERD

MO —WASHINGTON UNIVERSITY, Libraries, Special Collections Dept, Campus Box 1061, St Louis, 63130.
Notes: A major collection, incl books, mss, correspondence, literary papers, photographs, etc. Described in *Special Collections: an Annotated Guide to the Holdings of the Manuscript Division and the University Archives and Research Collection.*

MEAD JOHNSON AND COMPANY

IN —INDIANA STATE UNIVERSITY, EVANSVILLE, Library, 8600 University Blvd, Evansville, 47712. Gina R Walker, Acting Archivist
Holdings: Cat Mss Pix Slides Phonorecords 16mm Films Filmstrips
Notes: Historical documents, 1895 to the present, related to the growth and development of the Mead Johnson Company (a pharmaceutical company engaged in manufacture and research in Evansville, Indiana); papers concerning Company administration and organizations; industrial and public relations; marketing and merchandising; product histories of Mead products, both past and present; research and development; Johnson family pictures; product samples and memorabilia. Unpublished guide.

MEADE, GEN. GEORGE GORDON

PA —HISTORICAL SOCIETY OF PENNSYLVANIA, Library, 1300 Locust St, Philadelphia, 19107. David Fraser, Librn
Holdings: Vols (230,000) Mss Maps Pix Microforms
Notes: Incl over 14,000,000 ms pieces. The Library Company of Philadelphia mss are on deposit with the Historical Society of Pennsylvania. Many of the Society's rare books are on deposit with the Library Company. The Society maintains the collections of the Genealogical Society of Pennsylvania, incl some 20,000 printed genealogies, original mss, family, church, and civil records.

MEADE, JULIAN RUTHERFOORD

VA —UNIVERSITY OF VIRGINIA, Alderman Library, Manuscripts Dept,

MEADE, JULIAN RUTHERFOORD (cont.)

Charlottesville, 22901. Edmund Berkeley Jr, Cur
Notes: Letters of many other Virginia authors, such as Sherwood Anderson, Hawthorne Daniel, Murrell Edmunds, George Cary Eggleston, John Fox, John Pendleton Kennedy, Katie Letcher Lyle, Julian Rutherfoord Meade, Thomas Nelson Page, Virginius Dabney, Clifford Dowdey, Jane McClary, Peter Taylor, and others.

MEADOWS FAMILY

AZ —NORTHERN ARIZONA UNIVERSITY, Special Collection Library, CU Box 6022, Flagstaff, 86011. Peter M Whiteley, Coordr/Archivist; William Mullane, Librn
Notes: Lee Fitzhugh Collection; family history of the Meadows, who were involved in the Tonto Basin Massacre, near Payson, Ariz. One member of the family, "Arizona Charley," organized a Wild West Show.

MEALS FOR MILLIONS FOUNDATION

CA —UNIVERSITY OF CALIFORNIA, LOS ANGELES, Research Library, Dept of Special Collections, 405 Hilgard Ave, Los Angeles, 90024. Edward Shreeves, Chairman, Bibliographers Group; David S Zeidberg, Head
Notes: 23 linear feet of office and personal files of the Foundation and its executive secretary, Florence Rose.

MEARS, WALTER R.

IA —DRAKE UNIVERSITY, Cowles Library, 28 St & University Ave, Des Moines, 50311.
Holdings: Cat Mss Pix
Notes: Working papers and notes of Walter R Mears, Asst Bureau Chief for the Associated Press, concerning the 1964 Presidential Campaign of Senator Barry Goldwater.

MEASUREMENT, MENTAL see Mental Tests; Psychometrics

MEASUREMENT, PSYCHOLOGICAL see Psychometrics

MEASUREMENT OF STARS see Stars—Photographic Measurements

MEASURING see Mensuration

MEAT INDUSTRY

TX —AMARILLO PUBLIC LIBRARY, 413 E Fourth, Amarillo, 79101. Mary Kay Snell, Librn
Holdings: Vols 1210 Cat Maps Filmstrips VF
Notes: The Meat Industry Collection contains documents, periodicals, pamphlets, AV materials on the production of processing and marketing of cattle, swine, sheep, poultry and rabbits. Most of the collection circulates except for the magazines.
WI —UNIVERSITY OF WISCONSIN, MADISON, College of Agricultural & Life Sciences, Steenbock Memorial Library, 550 Babcock Dr, Madison, 53706. Jan Kennedy, Dir
Holdings: Vols (186,312) Cat Microforms
Notes: Extensive general agricultural collection supporting the College of Agricultural and Life Sciences in agronomy, dairy science, agricultural engineering, entomology, botany, natural resources, nutrition, forestry, genetics, veterinary science, meat and animal science, poultry science, soils. Collection incl USDA, USDI, experiment station and state documents.

MECHANIC ARTS see Industrial Arts

MECHANICAL ARITHMETIC see Calculating Machines

MECHANICAL BRAINS see Computers, Electronic; Cybernetics

MECHANICAL DRAWING

DC —LIBRARY OF CONGRESS, Prints & Photographs Div, Washington, 20540.
Notes: The Historic American Engineering Record contains measured drawings, photographs, and data sheets documenting works of American engineering.
NH —NEW HAMPSHIRE VOCATIONAL-TECHNICAL COLLEGE, Library, Prescott Hill, Laconia, 03246. Patty Miller, Librn
Holdings: Vols 440 Cat Filmstrips Microforms
Budget: $435
Notes: Incl industrial drafting information.
NY —COLUMBIA UNIVERSITY LIBRARIES, Avery Architectural and Fine Arts Library, 201 Avery Hall, New York, 10027. Angela Giral, Librn
SC —HORRY GEORGETOWN TECHNICAL COLLEGE, Library, Hwy 501, Box 1966, Conway, 29526. Barbara Brittain, Librn
Holdings: Vols (20,000) Cat Maps Slides Microforms

MECHANICAL ENGINEERING

AL —TUSKEGEE INSTITUTE, School of Engineering Library, Tuskegee Institute, 36088. Frances F Davis, Librn
Holdings: Vols 377 Cat
Budget: $3000
CA —UNIVERSITY OF CALIFORNIA, DAVIS, Physical Sciences Library, Davis, 95616. Scott Kennedy, Head
Notes: Collection covers aeronautical, agricultural, chemical, civil electrical, mechanical, water science, hydrology, nuclear reactor, extensive cold regions collection in vertical file drawers, and computer science engineering academic programs. Good strength in journal runs.
CA —UNIVERSITY OF CALIFORNIA, LOS ANGELES, Engineering & Mathematical Sciences Library, 405 Hilgard, Los Angeles, 90024. Rosalee I Wright, Librn
Holdings: Vols (180,000) Cat Microforms
See also entry under Engineering
CA —RAYMOND KAISER ENGINEERS INC, Engineering Library, 300 Lakeside Dr, PO Box 23210, Oakland, 94623. Elaine Zacher, Librn
Holdings: Vols 1000 Cat
CA —CALIFORNIA STATE POLYTECHNIC UNIVERSITY, POMONA, University Library, 3801 W Temple Ave, Pomona, 91768. Harold Schleiser, Actg Dir
Notes: General reference materials on aerospace, chemical, civil, electrical, electronics, industrial, mechanical and manufacturing engineering.
CA —COGSWELL COLLEGE, Library, 600 Stockton St, San Francisco, 94108. Judith Carson-Croes, Dir
Holdings: Vols (12,000) Cat
CA —HEALD COLLEGE TECHNICAL DIVISION, Learning Resource Center Library, 150 4th Street, San Francisco, 94103. Tom Casas, Dir
Holdings: Vols (1000) Cat
Budget: $680
FL —FLORIDA INSTITUTE OF TECHNOLOGY, Library, 150 W University Blvd, PO Box 1150, Melbourne, 32901. L L Henson, Dir of Libraries
Holdings: Vols (5000) Cat Microforms
GA —GEORGIA INSTITUTE OF TECHNOLOGY, Price Gilbert Memorial Library, 225 North Ave, Atlanta, 30332. Edward Graham Roberts, Dir
Holdings: Vols (1,661,559) Cat Maps Slides Microforms
Budget: ($1,383,302)
Notes: Incl (4,307,996) patents and (568,490) government documents.
IL —UNIVERSITY OF ILLINOIS, URBANA/CHAMPAIGN, Library, 221 Engineering Hall, Urbana, 61801. William Mischo, Librn
Holdings: Vols (175,000) Cat Slides Microforms
Notes: Incl 3500 periodicals. Collection designed to serve teaching and research programs. Supports instructional faculty research. Also, 470 microfilm reels and 6000 microfiche sheets.
IN —CUMMINS ENGINE CO, Information Center, 1000 Fifth St, Columbus, 47201. W E Poor, Tech Librn
Holdings: Vols 1000 Cat Mss

IN —PURDUE UNIVERSITY LIBRARIES, Engineering Library, A A Potter Engineering Center, West Lafayette, 47907. Edwin D Posey, Engineering Librn
Holdings: Vols (25,178) Cat Maps Audiotapes Microforms
Budget: ($300,000)
IA —IOWA STATE UNIVERSITY, Library, Ames, 50011. Warren B Kuhn, Dean of Library Services
Holdings: Cat Microforms
Notes: Extensive serial holdings.
KY —UNIVERSITY OF KENTUCKY, Robert E Shaver Library of Engineering, 355 Anderson Hall, Lexington, 40506. Russell H Powell, Engineering Librn
Holdings: Vols (48,000) Cat Microforms
MA —STONE & WEBSTER ENGINEERING CORP, Technical Information Center, Library, 245 Summer St, PO Box 2325, Boston, 02107. Nancy M Pellini, Mgr
Holdings: Vols (10,000) Cat Pix Microforms
Notes: Also over 1200 periodicals. Extensive vertical file collection, and 5 on-line system for search.
MI —UNIVERSITY OF MICHIGAN, Engineering-Transportation Library, 312 Undergraduate Library, Ann Arbor, 48109. Maurita Holland, Librn
Holdings: Vols (400,000) Cat Microforms
Budget: ($225,000)
NH —NEW HAMPSHIRE TECHNICAL INSTITUTE, Paul E Farnum Library, 5 Fan Rd, Concord, 03301. Wm John Hare, Librn
Holdings: Vols 1400 Cat
Budget: $1000
Notes: Incl mechanical engineering technology.
NY —COLUMBIA UNIVERSITY LIBRARIES, Engineering Library, 422 Mudd Bldg, New York, 10027.
Holdings: Vols (177,000) Cat
Notes: All aspects of engineering--aeronautical, industrial mining, civil, chemical, mechanical, electrical, nuclear. Incl applied mathematics and applied physical sciences. Over (1,000,000) technical reports.
NY —ENGINEERING SOCIETIES LIBRARY, 345 E 47 St, New York, 10017. S Kirk Cabeen, Dir
Holdings: Vols 250,000 Cat Maps 16mm Films Microforms
Notes: One of the largest, most comprehensive engineering libraries in the world. Covers all engineering disciplines; particularly strong in electrical and electronic, mechanical, mining and metallurgical, petroleum, chemical, industrial, air conditioning and refrigeration engineering. Incl Wheeler Collection of early materials on magnetism and electricity. 125,000 bound periodical volumes; 10,000 maps; 5000 serial subscriptions (many foreign-language). Virtually all materials abstracted in Engineering Index (1884-date) are incl in Library. Noncirculating, except to members of professional engineering societies which support the Library. See Engineering Societies, New York, Classed Subject Catalog and Index (Boston: G K Hall, 1963); and Supplements, 1-10, 1964-1973.
NY —NEW YORK PUBLIC LIBRARY, Research Libraries, Science and Technology Research Center, Fifth Ave & 42 St, New York, 10018.
Holdings: Vols (1,100,000) Cat Microforms
Budget: ($647,259)
NY —EASTMAN KODAK COMPANY, Kodak Park Div, Engineering Library, Bldg 23, Rochester, 14650. Raymond Curtin, Librn
Holdings: Vols (14,000) Uncat Microforms
Notes: The library is not open to the public. Use of the library for reference purposes may be requested and appointments may be obtained through the librarian.
NY —UNIVERSITY OF ROCHESTER, Engineering Library, Gavett Hall, River Campus, Rochester, 14627. Isabel Kaplan, Librn
Holdings: Vols (25,000)
Notes: Strong collection in the field and related areas.
NY —GENERAL ELECTRIC CO, Main Library, One River Rd, Schenectady, 12345. Julia Hewitt, Mgr
Holdings: Vols (56,000) Cat

MECHANICAL ENGINEERING (cont.)

NC —DUKE UNIVERSITY, School of
Engineering, Library, Durham, 27706. Eric J
Smith, Librn
Holdings: Vols (72,000) Cat Microforms
Budget: ($110,000)

OH —PUBLIC LIBRARY OF CINCINNATI
& HAMILTON COUNTY, Science &
Technology Dept, 800 Vine St, Cincinnati,
45202. Rosemary Gaiser, Head
Holdings: Vols (250,000) Cat
Notes: Pure and applied science. Incl over
1600 periodicals and serial titles and more
than 100 abstracting and indexing services in
major fields of science and technology.

OH —UNIVERSITY OF CINCINNATI,
Engineering Library, 880 Baldwin Hall,
Cincinnati, 45221. Dorothy Furber Byers,
Head
Holdings: Vols (50,000) Cat Videotapes
Microforms
Budget: ($100,000)
Notes: Have NASA and DOE microfiche
collections.

OH —OHIO STATE UNIVERSITY,
Engineering Library, 2024 Neil Ave,
Columbus, 43210. Mary Jo V Arnold, Librn
Holdings: Vols (132,000) Cat Microforms
Budget: ($110,000)

PA —FRANKLIN INSTITUTE LIBRARY, 20
& The Parkway, Philadelphia, 19103.
Miriam Padusis, Dir; Charles Wilt, Readers
Servs Librn
Holdings: Vols (300,000) Cat Maps Pix
Microforms

PA —UNIVERSITY OF PENNSYLVANIA,
Towne Scientific Library, 220 S 33 St,
Philadelphia, 19104. Charles Meyers, Librn
Holdings: Vols (65,000) Cat

PA —CARNEGIE LIBRARY OF
PITTSBURGH, Science & Technology Dept,
4400 Forbes Ave, Pittsburgh, 15213.
Catherine M Brosky, Dept Head
Holdings: Vols (380,000) Cat Maps
Microforms
Budget: ($240,000)
See also entry under Engineering.

PA —ROCKWELL INTERNATIONAL,
General Industries Operations, Technical
Information Center, 400 N Lexington Ave,
Pittsburgh, 15208. Kathleen H Witkowski,
Library Coordr
Holdings: Vols Cat Microforms Mss
Documents Periodicals VF

PA —PENNSYLVANIA STATE
UNIVERSITY, Engineering Library, 325
Hammond St, University Park, 16802. Tom
Conkling, Librn
Holdings: Vols (60,000) Microforms
Notes: This collection includes substantial
microform holdings and extensive runs of
periodicals.

†SD —SOUTH DAKOTA SCHOOL OF
MINES & TECHNOLOGY, Devereaux
Library, Rapid City, 57701.
Holdings: Vols (166,200) Cat Maps
Audiotapes Filmstrips Microforms
Budget: ($70,000)
Notes: Supportive collection incl an almost
complete set of U S Geological Survey
materials (incl early Territorial Surveys); a
microfilm copy (complete set) of the U S
Bureau of Mines "Mine Map Depository
(Denver)" material; periodicals and technical
reports (NASA, ACRL JPL, etc) in
engineering and geology; extensive
government document materials (NBS,
Bureau of Mines, etc).

TN —TENNESSEE VALLEY AUTHORITY
(TVA), Technical Library, 400 W Summit
Hill Dr, E2 B7, Knoxville, 37902. Jesse C
Mills, Chief Librn
Holdings: Vols (106,900) Cat Mss Maps Pix
Audiotapes Microforms
Budget: ($2,025,000)
Notes: The Technical Library Headquarters
Staff (order, cataloging, information, and
administration) is located in Knoxville,
Tenn. In addition there are branch libraries
in Knoxville, Norris, and Chattanooga,
Tennessee, and Muscle Shoals, Alabama.

TX —UNIVERSITY OF TEXAS LIBRARIES,
Richard W McKinney Engineering Library,
1.3 ECJ, Austin, 78712. Susan B Ardis,

Librn
Holdings: Vols (83,548) Cat Microforms
Notes: Strong collection of industrial
standards including federal and military
standards and specifications.

TX —RICE UNIVERSITY, Fondren Library,
6100 S Main St, PO Box 1892, Houston,
77251. Dr Samuel M Carrington, Jr,
University Librn
Holdings: Vols (4151) Cat
Budget: ($45,700)
Notes: Each serial title counted once.

VT —VERMONT TECHNICAL COLLEGE,
Hartness Library, Randolph Center, 05061.
Dewey Patterson, Library Dir
Holdings: Vols 5550 Cat

WI —MILWAUKEE SCHOOL OF
ENGINEERING, Library, 500 E Kilbourn
Ave, PO Box 644, Milwaukee, 53201. Mary
Ann Schmidt, Head Librn
Holdings: Vols (34,500) Cat
Budget: ($215,800)

AB —SOUTHERN ALBERTA INSTITUTE
OF TECHNOLOGY, Learning Resources
Centre, 1301 16 Ave NW, Calgary, T2M
0L4, Can. Tom Skinner, Historian
Holdings: Vols (26,000) Cat Maps Pix Slides
Films Videotapes Microforms
Budget: ($50,000)
Notes: Wide range of current technical
information about electronics and
engineering (mechanical, electrical,
chemical); emphasis on vocational-technical
material. Incl (50,000) slides, (300)
videotapes, and (500) films.

MB —UNIVERSITY OF MANITOBA,
Engineering Library, Winnipeg, R3T 2N2,
Can. Y Cho, Head
Holdings: Vols (28,000) Cat Videotapes
Microforms
Notes: The Engineering Library serves four
academic departments: Agricultural, Civil,
Electrical and Mechanical Engineering.

ON —NATIONAL RESEARCH COUNCIL
OF CANADA, Aeronautical/Mechanical
Engineering Branch Library, Montreal Rd,
Ottawa, K1A 0R6, Can. Louise Fletcher,
Head
Holdings: Microforms
Notes: This branch library of the Canada
Institute for Scientific and Technical
Information (CISTI) of the National
Research Council of Canada, Ottawa, has a
collection strong in aeronautical engineering,
automatic control, CAD/CAM, robotics,
ocean, wind, and solar energy power,
hydraulic and coastal engineering, icing, low
temperature research, naval engineering,
metals and metallurgy, incl composites,
tribology, and air, railroad, marine
transportation. Library supported the
Council contribution to the development of
the remote manipular Canadarm for
NASA's Space Shuttle Orbiters and more
recently, the Canadian Astronaut Program
which will contribute payload specialists to
NASA's Space Shuttle Program in 1984. 35,
000 monographs, 1200 serials. Report
collection: over 500,000 items.

MECHANICS

GA —GEORGIA INSTITUTE OF
TECHNOLOGY, Price Gilbert Memorial
Library, 225 North Ave, Atlanta, 30332.
Edward Graham Roberts, Dir
Holdings: Vols (1,661,559) Cat Maps Slides
Microforms
Budget: ($1,383,302)
Notes: Incl (4,307,996) patents and (568,
490) government documents.

NY —YONKERS PUBLIC LIBRARY,
Information Services, 7 Main St, Yonkers,
10701. Martita Schwarz, Dept Head
Holdings: Vols (21,500) Cat Maps
Microforms
Budget: ($30,000)

OH —CLEVELAND PUBLIC LIBRARY,
Science & Technology Dept, 325 Superior
Ave, Cleveland, 44114. Jean Z Piety, Head
Holdings: Cat
Notes: Collection contains much on history
and many early and rare volumes.

PA —FRANKLIN INSTITUTE LIBRARY, 20
& The Parkway, Philadelphia, 19103.
Miriam Padusis, Dir; Charles Wilt, Readers

Servs Librn
Holdings: Vols (300,000) Cat Maps Pix
Microforms

PA —UNIVERSITY OF PENNSYLVANIA,
Towne Scientific Library, 220 S 33 St,
Philadelphia, 19104. Charles Meyers, Librn
Holdings: Vols (65,000) Cat

PA —PENNSYLVANIA STATE
UNIVERSITY, Engineering Library, 325
Hammond St, University Park, 16802. Tom
Conkling, Librn
Notes: 59,500 items.

TX —UNIVERSITY OF TEXAS LIBRARIES,
Richard W McKinney Engineering Library,
1.3 ECJ, Austin, 78712. Susan B Ardis,
Librn
Holdings: Vols (103,000) Cat Microforms
Notes: Incl 400,000 uncataloged microfiche.

MECHANICS—EARLY WORKS TO 1800

CA —UNIVERSITY OF CALIFORNIA,
BERKELEY, Bancroft Library, Manuscripts
Division, Berkeley, 94720. James D Hart,
Dir
Holdings: Vols Cat Mss
Notes: The personal papers and
correspondence (2000 pieces) of Rudjer
Josip Boskovic, an important Yugoslav,
18th-century Jesuit mathematician and
natural philosopher. Of particular importance
are 180 textual mss dealing with subjects in
the field of mechanics. A register of the
collection has been prepared. Also printed
books.

ON —UNIVERSITY OF TORONTO, Thomas
Fisher Rare Book Library, 120 Saint George
St, Toronto, M5S 1A5, Can. Richard G
Landon, Head
Holdings: Vols 4000
Notes: The Science Collection is especially
rich in works on Renaissance astronomy,
physics and mechanics and has noteworthy
holdings of works of English experimental
scientists in the 17th and 18th centuries with
excellent collections of the works of Robert
Boyle, Robert Hooke, and Sir Isaac Newton.
Includes virtually all important early editions
of Euclid; alchemical works of the 16th and
17th centuries together with the works of
18th century chemists like Lavoisier and
Priestly; works on agriculture with special
emphasis on British agriculture in the 18th
century; and a variety of other works
important in the history of science in all its
branches. In addition the Fisher Library has
many other specialized scientific collections
which are listed separately.

MECHANICS, APPLIED

IL —UNIVERSITY OF ILLINOIS,
URBANA/CHAMPAIGN, Library, 221
Engineering Hall, Urbana, 61801. William
Mischo, Librn
Holdings: Vols (175,000) Cat Slides
Microforms
Notes: Incl 3500 periodicals. Collection
designed to serve teaching and research
programs. Supports instructional faculty
research. Also, 470 microfilm reels and 6000
microfiche sheets.

KY —UNIVERSITY OF KENTUCKY, Robert
E Shaver Library of Engineering, 355
Anderson Hall, Lexington, 40506. Russell H
Powell, Engineering Librn
Holdings: Vols (48,000) Cat Microforms

NY —QUEENSBOROUGH COMMUNITY
COLLEGE, Library, Springfield Blvd & L I
Expressway, Bayside, 11364. Carol Singer,
Chief Librn
Holdings: Cat
Notes: Films (nearly 300) on electrical and
mechanical technology. Incl 16mm films.

NY —ENGINEERING SOCIETIES
LIBRARY, 345 E 47 St, New York, 10017.
S Kirk Cabeen, Dir
Holdings: Vols 250,000 Cat Maps 16mm
Films Microforms
Notes: One of the largest, most
comprehensive engineering libraries in the
world. Covers all engineering disciplines;
particularly strong in electrical and
electronic, mechanical, mining and

MECHANICS, APPLIED (cont.)

metallurgical, petroleum, chemical, industrial, air conditioning and refrigeration engineering. Incl Wheeler Collection of early materials on magnetism and electricity. 125,000 bound periodical volumes; 10,000 maps; 5000 serial subscriptions (many foreign-language). Virtually all materials abstracted in *Engineering Index* (1884-date) are incl in Library. Noncirculating, except to members of professional engineering societies which support the Library. See *Engineering Societies Library, New York, Classed Subject Catalog and Index* (Boston: G K Hall, 1963); and *Supplements,* 1-10, 1964-1973.

OH —UNIVERSITY OF CINCINNATI, Engineering Library, 880 Baldwin Hall, Cincinnati, 45221. Dorothy Furber Byers, Head
Holdings: Vols (50,000) Cat Videotapes Microforms
Budget: ($100,000)
Notes: Have NASA and DOE microfiche collections.

MECHANICS, CELESTIAL

CT —YALE UNIVERSITY, Observatory Library, 260 Whitney Ave, Box 6666, New Haven, 06511.
Holdings: Vols (15,000) Cat Maps Pix
Budget: ($15,000)
Notes: Also an extensive collection of domestic and foreign observatory publications.

DC —US NAVAL OBSERVATORY LIBRARY, 30th & Massachusetts Ave, NW, Washington, 20016. Brenda G Corbin, Librn
Holdings: Vols (75,000) Cat Mss Maps Pix Slides Microforms
Notes: Incl 1000 journals, with monograph and serial publications in the fields of celestial mechanics, fundamental astronomy, time determination, photographic astrometry and astrophysics, data processing, mathematics.

MECKLENBURG DECLARATION OF INDEPENDENCE, 1775

NC —DAVIDSON COLLEGE, E H Little Library, Davidson, 28036. Leland M Park, Dir; Chalmers G Davidson, Dir
Holdings: Cat Mss Pix

MEDALLIONS see Medals

MEDALS

CO —AMERICAN NUMISMATIC ASSOCIATION LIBRARY, 818 N Cascade Ave, Colorado Springs, 80903. Nancy W Green, Librn
Holdings: Vols (20,000) Cat Slides
Budget: ($2000)
Notes: One of the largest numismatic libraries, the collection incl books, periodicals and auction catalogs on coins and coin collecting, medals, tokens, military orders and decorations, paper money, primitive money, banks and banking, seals and scarabs. ANA publishes a classified subject catalog of its collection and is open to the public for research and reference services. Only members may check books out.

IA —UNIVERSITY OF IOWA, University Libraries, Iowa City, 52242. Frank Paluka, Head, Special Collections Dept
Holdings: // Uncat
Notes: Collection of 842 Medals, described in Alan B Spitzer, "The Mabbott Collection of Medals of the French Revolution of 1848," *Books at Iowa,* no 24 (April 1976), pp 32-33, 38-39.

MO —SAINT LOUIS UNIVERSITY, Pius XII Memorial Library, 3655 W Pine Blvd, Saint Louis, 63108. William Cole, Dir
Holdings: Vols 246 // Uncat
Notes: The Haren Medal collection contains 246 medals of popes, etc. Not available to public.

NE —OMAHA PUBLIC LIBRARY, Omaha, 68102. Michael Phipps, Dir
Holdings: Vols 500 Cat
Notes: Incl the Byron Reed Library, approx 250 titles. Books in this collection have special cards in the main catalog. Important items in the collection incl 19th century vols of the *American Journal of Numismatics, Coin Collectors' Journal,* and *Numismatic Chronicle.* Also significant are early auction catalogs and medallic histories.

NY —AMERICAN NUMISMATIC SOCIETY LIBRARY, Broadway between 155 & 156 Sts, New York, 10032. Francis D Campbell Jr, Chief Librn
Holdings: Vols (50,000) Cat Mss Maps Pix Slides 16mm Films Microforms
Budget: ($6000)
Notes: Incl materials devoted to coins, medals, decorations, orders, tokens, paper money, seals, heraldry. Aids materials incl history, economic history, art history, archaeology, inscriptions and a number of encyclopedias and biographical dictionaries. Dictionary card catalog provides access to the materials: *Dictionary Catalogue of the Library of the American Numismatic Society.* (Boston: G K Hall, 1962). 6 vols and vol listing the auction catalogs in our collection; *First Supplement: 1962-1967; Second Supplement: 1968-1972; Third Supplement: 1973-1977* (Boston: G K Hall, 1967, 1973, 1978). Noncirculating.

RI —BROWN UNIVERSITY, John Hay Library, 20 Prospect St, Providence, 02912. Mark N Brown, Cur Mss
Holdings: Vols (130) Cat Mss Pix
Budget: ($250)
Notes: William Henry Hoffman Napoleon Collection of finely-bound books on the Napoleonic period plus over 3000 prints of Napoleonic interest and 200 art objects incl 120 miniature portraits on ivory, one being by Jean Baptiste Isabey, commemorative medals, and a portrait of Napoleon by Horace Vernet.
See also entry under Lincoln, Abraham.

RI —BROWN UNIVERSITY, John Hay Library, McLellan Lincoln Collection, 20 Prospect St, Providence, 02912. Jennifer B Lee, Special Collections Librn
Holdings: Vols (15,000) Cat Mss Pix Phonorecords
Notes: Museum objects incl over 550 medals, mourning and campaign badges, coins, postage stamps and other miscellany.

MEDALS, MEDICAL

CT —YALE UNIVERSITY, Medical Historical Library, 333 Cedar St, New Haven, 06510. Ferenc A Gyorgyey, Librn
Holdings: Uncat
Notes: 200 items.

FL —UNIVERSITY OF MIAMI, School of Medicine, Louis Calder Memorial Library, PO Box 520875, Miami, 33152. Henry L Lemkau, Jr, Dir
Holdings: Vols (127,843) Cat Mss Maps Pix Slides Phonorecords Audiotapes Videotapes 16mm Films Filmstrips Microforms
Budget: ($915,000)
Notes: Ophthalmology Branch Library of 6969 vols incl in total count; University of Miami School of Medicine dissertations; 209 medical medallions; physicians' bookplates; postage stamps with medical themes.

MEDALS, MILITARY AND NAVAL

CO —AMERICAN NUMISMATIC ASSOCIATION LIBRARY, 818 N Cascade Ave, Colorado Springs, 80903. Nancy W Green, Librn
Holdings: Vols (20,000) Cat Slides
Notes: One of the largest numismatic libraries, the collection incl books, periodicals and auction catalogs on coins and coin collecting, medals, tokens, military orders and decorations, paper money, primitive money, banks and banking, seals and scarabs. ANA publishes a classified subject catalog of its collection and is open to the public for research and reference services. Only members may check books out.

MEDARIS, MAJ. GEN. JOHN BRUCE

FL —FLORIDA INSTITUTE OF TECHNOLOGY, Library, 150 W University Blvd, PO Box 1150, Melbourne, 32901. L L Henson, Dir of Libraries
Holdings: Cat Mss Maps Pix
Notes: Mss, scrapbooks, photograph albums, military decorations, souvenirs, etc.

MEDICAL ART see Art, Medical

MEDICAL ASSISTANTS see Physicians' Assistants

MEDICAL BOTANY see Botany, Medical

MEDICAL CARE

CA —WESTERN MEDICAL CENTER, Medical Library, 1025 S Anaheim Blvd, Anaheim, 92805. Evelyn Simpson, Dir
Holdings: Vols 400 Cat Audiotapes Videotapes
Notes: Incl 400 audiotapes, 200 bound journals. Photocopying.

CA —UNIVERSITY OF CALIFORNIA, BERKELEY, Life Sciences Libraries, Public Health Library, 42 Earl Warren Hall, Berkeley, 94720. Thomas J Alexander, Librn
Holdings: Vols (75,000) Cat Microforms
Notes: Research collection covering all aspects of public health. Health Department annual reports from all 50 states are acquired, as well as such reports from all California health units and from major U S cities. Serial publications issued by Health Departments in the 13 western states are being received.

CA —KAISER FOUNDATION HOSPITAL, Management Effectiveness Library, 4747 Sunset Blvd, Los Angeles, 90027. Marilyn Crawford, Librn
Holdings: Vols (1000) Cat Maps Slides Audiotapes
Notes: Small, selective management, business, and health care collection, with many US and state health-related reports and a few health newsletters. Internal index to printed materials and audiotapes.

CA —BLUE CROSS OF SOUTHERN CALIFORNIA, Library, PO Box 70,000, Van Nuys, 91470. Frances Linke, Head Librn
Holdings: Vols (9500) Cat Mss Slides Audiotapes Videotapes 16mm Films Filmstrips Microforms
Budget: ($19,000)
Notes: Strong law collection.

CT —YALE UNIVERSITY, Box 1603A, Yale Station, New Haven, 06520.
Holdings: Mss Pix
Notes: The Contemporary Medical Care and Health Policy Collection. Letters, memos, records, photographs, etc of the principal strategists of the social medical movement in the U S.

CT —YALE UNIVERSITY, Medical Historical Library, 333 Cedar St, New Haven, 06510. Ferenc A Gyorgyey, Librn
Notes: Records of the Milbank Memorial Fund for the years 1922-1977. A part of the Contemporary Medical Care and Health Policy Collection.

DC —CENTER FOR BIOETHICS, Library, Kennedy Institute, Georgetown University, 3520 Prospect St NW, Washington, 20057. Doris Goldstein, Dir; Judith Mistichelli, Senior Librn
Holdings: Vols 8200
Notes: Largest library of its kind. Incl 31,000 journal articles. Collects in the following subject areas: applied ethics; medical ethics; philosophy of medicine; science, technology and society; sociology of medicine; patient-physician care; sexuality; contraception; abortion; population policy; reproductive technologies; in vitro fertilization; genetic counseling and screening; genetic engineering; mental organ transplantation; death and dying; "baby doe" issues; euthanasia; suicide; use of chemical and biological weapons. Produces computer database *Bioethicsline,* available through MEDLARS; and the printed annual *Bibliography of Bioethics.* Other library publications are: *New Titles in Bioethics* (monthly); *Scope Notes* series on current topics.

MEDICAL CARE (cont.)

HI —UNIVERSITY OF HAWAII, School of Public Health Reference Collection, 1960 East-West Rd, D-207, Honolulu, 96822. Carol W Arnold, Librn
Holdings: Vols (15,000) Cat Microforms
Budget: ($8,500)
Notes: Public health; also a microfiche collection of 25,000 items on medical care delivery and health administration.

IL —LIBRARY OF THE AMERICAN HOSPITAL ASSOCIATION, Asa S Bacon Memorial, 840 N Lake Shore Dr, Chicago, 60611. Eloise C Foster, Dir
Holdings: Vols (39,000) Cat
Budget: ($95,000)
Notes: Literature on non-clinical aspects of health care administration, planning and financing of hospitals and related health care institutions; administrative aspects of the medical, paramedical, and prepayment fields. Special Collection: Ray E Brown Management Collection. *Hospital Literature* Index prepared by the Library of the American Hospital Association in cooperation with the National Library of Medicine; *Catalog of the Library of the American Hospital Association,* published by G K Hall, Boston.

MD —US SOCIAL SECURITY ADMINISTRATION, Library, Library Information & Graphics Services Branch, Altmeyer Bldg Rm 571, 6401 Security Blvd, Baltimore, 21235. Rowena S Sadler, Chief
Holdings: Vols Cat
Notes: All phases of social insurance incl OASI pensions, welfare health insurance and medical economics.

MA —FRANCIS A COUNTWAY LIBRARY OF MEDICINE, Boston Medical Library/ Harvard Medical Library, 10 Shattuck St, Boston, 02115. C Robin LeSueur, Librn; Richard J Wolfe, Cur, Rare Books & Manuscripts
Holdings: Vols (500,000) Cat Mss Maps Pix Microforms
Notes: Combines resources of the Harvard Medical School and the Boston Medical Library. Strong in serials and medical history in all fields of medicine, incl incunabula, non-medical books by doctors, travel books by doctors. 500,000 medical dissertations and theses. Special strength in all medical subjects listed in this volume.

MA —HARVARD MEDICAL SCHOOL, Schering Foundation Library of Health Care, 643 Huntington Ave, Boston, 02115. Anne Alach, Librn
Holdings: Cat
Budget: ($3000)
Notes: Socioeconomic aspects of health care.

MA —US VETERANS ADMINISTRATION MEDICAL CENTER, Medical Library, 150 S Huntington Ave, Jamaica Plain, Boston, 02130. Patricia J McGrath, Chief Librn
Holdings: Vols (5702) Cat
Notes: Incl health care, surgery, neurology. 400 journal subscriptions, 5000 bound volumes.

MI —UNIVERSITY OF MICHIGAN, Public Health Library, Ann Arbor, 48109. Mary Townsend, Head
Holdings: Vols (55,000) Cat Maps Pix
Budget: ($24,000)

MO —WASHINGTON UNIVERSITY, School of Medicine, Archives, 660 S Euclid Ave, Saint Louis, 63110. Paul G Anderson, Archivist
Holdings: Mss Pix Audiotapes
Budget: ($38,000)
Notes: Institutional records and papers of faculty of Washington University School of Medicine and its predecessors and associated hospitals. Contains records of St Louis Medical College, Missouri Medical Barnard Free Skin and Cancer Hospital, Barnes Hospital, St Louis Children's Hospital and Jewish Hospital of St Louis. Incl papers of William Beaumont, Joseph Erlanger, Leo Loeb, Evarts Graham, Edmund V Cowdry, Helen Graham, Carl V Moore, Margaret Smith and others. Oral history program. See also: Anderson, Paul G and Hoolihan, Christopher, eds. *Special Collections* (St

Louis: Washington University School of Medicine, 1981). 960 linear feet.

†NM —UNIVERSITY OF NEW MEXICO, Medical Center Library, Albuquerque, 87131. Beatrice Kovacs, Chief, Collections and Resource Development
Notes: Concern is health care and health services in New Mexico; medicine and medicine men of Indian tribes of the Southwest; and history of medicine and health in the Southwest.

NY —NEW YORK ACADEMY OF MEDICINE, Library, 2 E 103 St, New York, 10029. Brett A Kirkpatrick, Librn
Holdings: Cat VF //
Notes: The Papers of Michael Davis, one of the most extensive files of correspondence, surveys, government reports, news clippings, ephemera, etc concerning the development of medical care programs in the United States and other countries. 14 vertical file cabinets.

PA —UNIVERSITY OF PENNSYLVANIA, Bio-Medical Library, Johnson Pavilion/G2, Philadelphia, 19104. Eleanor Goodchild, Librn
Holdings: Vols (139,000) Cat Slides Audiotapes Videotapes

WI —UNIVERSITY OF WISCONSIN, MADISON, W S Middleton Health Sciences Library, 1305 Linden Dr, Madison, 53706. Virginia Holtz, Dir
Holdings: Vols (200,000) Cat Pix Slides Audiotapes Videotapes Microforms

†ON —METROPOLITAN TORONTO LIBRARY, Social Sciences Dept, 789 Yonge St, Toronto, M4W 2G8, Can. Abdus Salam, Head
Holdings: Vols Cat Maps Phonorecords Audiotapes 16mm Films Microforms
Notes: Historical and contemporary Canadian material covering federal and provincial policies and programs in the fields of health care, geriatrics, child welfare, corrections, and care and rehabilitation of the physically and mentally handicapped.

MEDICAL CARE, PREPAID

CA —STANFORD UNIVERSITY LIBRARIES, Lane Medical Library, Stanford University, Medical Center, Stanford, 94305. Peter Stangl, Librn
Notes: Phillip King Brown's papers on health insurance and socialized medicine.

CO —MEDICAL GROUP MANAGEMENT ASSOCIATION, Information Service, 1355 S Colorado Blvd, Suite 900, Denver, 80222. Barbara V Hamilton, Dir; Linda S Elinoff, Asst Dir
Holdings: Vols (3000) Cat
Budget: ($7825)
Notes: Administration of medical group practice and health maintenance organization. Also, the professional papers of the Fellows of the American College of Medical Group Administrators.

CT —YALE UNIVERSITY, Medical Historical Library, 333 Cedar St, New Haven, 06510. Ferenc A Gyorgyey, Librn
Notes: Records of the Milbank Memorial Fund for the years 1922-1977. A part of the Contemporary Medical Care and Health Policy Collection.

NY —NEW YORK ACADEMY OF MEDICINE, Library, 2 E 103 St, New York, 10029. Brett A Kirkpatrick, Librn
Holdings: Cat VF //
Notes: The Papers of Michael Davis, one of the most extensive files of correspondence, surveys, government reports, news clippings, ephemera, etc concerning the development of medical care programs in the United States and other countries. 14 vertical file cabinets.

MEDICAL CHEMISTRY see Chemistry, Medical and Pharmaceutical

MEDICAL COLLEGES

CA —STANFORD UNIVERSITY LIBRARIES, Lane Medical Library, Stanford University, Medical Center, Stanford, 94305. Peter Stangl, Librn
Notes: Cooper Medical College and Clinics,

records; Stanford University School of Medicine, records, Levi Cooper Lane, mss; Ray Lyman Wilbur, mss on Commission on Medical Education.
See also entry under Medicine - History and Historic

CO —WESTERN INTERSTATE COMMISSION FOR HIGHER EDUCATION, Wiche Library, PO Drawer P, Boulder, 80302. Karon M Kelly, Dir Library Services
Holdings: Vols (10,000) Cat Microforms
Notes: Incl medical and nursing education, student exchange programs, minority involvement in education, management systems in higher education.

MO —WASHINGTON UNIVERSITY, School of Medicine, Archives, 660 S Euclid Ave, Saint Louis, 63110. Paul G Anderson, Archivist
Holdings: Mss Pix Audiotapes
Budget: ($38,000)
Notes: Institutional records and papers of faculty of Washington University School of Medicine and its predecessors and associated hospitals. Contains records of St Louis Medical College, Missouri Medical Barnard Free Skin and Cancer Hospital, Barnes Hospital, St Louis Children's Hospital and Jewish Hospital of St Louis. Incl papers of William Beaumont, Joseph Erlanger, Leo Loeb, Evarts Graham, Edmund V Cowdry, Helen Graham, Carl V Moore, Margaret Smith and others. Oral history program. See also: Anderson, Paul G and Hoolihan, Christopher, eds. *Special Collections* (St Louis: Washington University School of Medicine, 1981). 960 linear feet.

†NY —COLUMBIA UNIVERSITY LIBRARIES, Butler Library, Rare Book and Manuscript Library, 535 W 114 St, New York, 10027.
Notes: Papers of the American Bureau for Medical Aid to China, incl correspondence, memoranda, reports, minutes, membership and financial records, photographs, posters and printed material. Approx 45,000 pieces. Also, some 6000 photographs of Chinese medical colleges, hospitals, laboratories, and personnel.

PA —MEDICAL COLLEGE OF PENNSYLVANIA, Florence A Moore Library of Medicine, Archives & Special Collections on Women in Medicine, 3300 Henry Ave, Philadelphia, 19129. Sandra L Chaff, Archivist
Holdings: Vols 700 Cat Mss Pix Slides Phonorecords Audiotapes 16mm Films Filmstrips
Notes: "One of the most comprehensive US collections of historical material on women physicians." Incl personal papers of women physicians; audiotapes and transcripts of interviews conducted by the Oral History Project on Women Physicians; the American Medical Women's Association historical collection; the American Women's Hospitals Service collection; the Kate Campbell Hurd-Mead collection; a file of 10,000 photos relating to women physicians; and 5100 reprints of which 4000 citations appear in *Women in Medicine: A Bibliography of the Literature on Women Physicians,* by Sandra L Chaff et al. (Metuchen, NJ: Scarecrow Press, 1977).

MEDICAL COOPERATION

NY —MONTEFIORE HOSPITAL & MEDICAL CENTER, Karl Cherkasky Social Medicine Library, 111 E 210 St, Bronx, 10467. Victor Sidel, Dir
Holdings: Vols (500) Cat
Budget: ($1000)

MEDICAL DISCLOSURE see Informed Consent (Medical Law)

MEDICAL ECONOMICS

CA —KAISER FOUNDATION HOSPITAL, Management Effectiveness Library, 4747 Sunset Blvd, Los Angeles, 90027. Marilyn Crawford, Librn
Holdings: Vols (1000) Cat Maps Slides

MEDICAL ECONOMICS (cont.)

Audiotapes
Notes: Small, selective management, business, and health care collection, with many US and state health-related reports and a few health newsletters. Internal index to printed materials and audiotapes.

CA —STANFORD UNIVERSITY LIBRARIES, Lane Medical Library, Stanford University, Medical Center, Stanford, 94305. Peter Stangl, Librn
Holdings: Mss Cat
Notes: Ray Lyman Wilbur's Mss including work on Committee on Costs of Medical Care, 50 boxes. Phillip King Brown's Mss on health insurance and socialized medicine.

CA —BLUE CROSS OF SOUTHERN CALIFORNIA, Library, PO Box 70,000, Van Nuys, 91470. Frances Linke, Head Librn
Holdings: Vols (9500) Cat Mss Slides Audiotapes Videotapes 16mm Films Filmstrips Microforms
Budget: ($19,000)
Notes: Strong law collection.

CO —MEDICAL GROUP MANAGEMENT ASSOCIATION, Information Service, 1355 S Colorado Blvd, Suite 900, Denver, 80222. Barbara V Hamilton, Dir; Linda S Elinoff, Asst Dir
Holdings: Vols (3000) Cat
Budget: ($7825)
Notes: Administration of medical group practice and health maintenance organization. Also, the professional papers of the Fellows of the American College of Medical Group Administrators.

CT —YALE MEDICAL LIBRARY, 333 Cedar St, New Haven, 06510.
Notes: A special subject emphasis.

IL —BLUE CROSS AND BLUE SHIELD ASSOCIATION, Library, 804 N Lake Shore Dr, Chicago, 60611. Mary T Drazba, Librn
Holdings: Vols (15,000) Cat Microforms
Notes: Health care financing.

MD —US SOCIAL SECURITY ADMINISTRATION, Library, Library Information & Graphics Services Branch, Altmeyer Bldg Rm 571, 6401 Security Blvd, Baltimore, 21235. Rowena S Sadler, Chief
Holdings: Vols Cat
Notes: All phases of social insurance incl OASI pensions, welfare health insurance and medical economics.

MA —FRANCIS A COUNTWAY LIBRARY OF MEDICINE, Boston Medical Library/ Harvard Medical Library, 10 Shattuck St, Boston, 02115. C Robin LeSueur, Librn; Richard J Wolfe, Cur, Rare Books & Manuscripts
Holdings: Vols (500,000) Cat Mss Maps Pix Microforms
Notes: Combines resources of the Harvard Medical School and the Boston Medical Library. Strong in serials and medical history in all fields of medicine, incl incunabula, non-medical books by doctors, travel books by doctors. 500,000 medical dissertations and theses. Special strength in all medical subjects listed in this volume.

MA —HARVARD MEDICAL SCHOOL, Schering Foundation Library of Health Care, 643 Huntington Ave, Boston, 02115. Anne Alach, Librn
Holdings: Cat
Budget: ($3000)
Notes: Socioeconomic aspects of health care.

NY —NEW YORK ACADEMY OF MEDICINE, Library, 2 E 103 St, New York, 10029. Brett A Kirkpatrick, Librn
Holdings: Cat VF //
Notes: The Papers of Michael Davis, one of the most extensive files of correspondence, surveys, government reports, news clippings, ephemera, etc concerning the development of medical care programs in the United States and other countries. 14 vertical file cabinets.

MEDICAL EDUCATION see Medical Colleges; Medicine—Study and Teaching

MEDICAL ELECTRICITY see Electricity in Medicine

MEDICAL ELECTRONICS

MA —RAYTHEON CO, Research Div, Library, 131 Spring St, Lerington, 02193.

Martha C Adamson, Head Librn
Holdings: Vols (250) Cat

MA —INSTRUMENTATION LABORATORY, Library, 113 Hartwell Ave, Lexington, 02173. Jacqueline R Kates, Librn
Holdings: Vols (6000) Cat Microforms

MN —BAKKEN LIBRARY OF ELECTRICITY IN LIFE, 3537 Zenith Ave S, Minneapolis, 55416. John Edward Senior, Dir
Notes: Books (including periodicals, manuscripts, and archival materials) and instrument collection. 1500 instruments (focus-18th and 19th centuries). Relating to the history of electricity.

MEDICAL ENGINEERING see Biomedical Engineering

MEDICAL ETHICS

CA —UNIVERSITY OF CALIFORNIA, LOS ANGELES, Biomedical Library, Center for Health Sciences, Los Angeles, 90024. Louise Darling, Biomedical Librn

DC —CENTER FOR BIOETHICS, Library, Kennedy Institute, Georgetown University, 3520 Prospect St NW, Washington, 20057. Doris Goldstein, Dir; Judith Mistichelli, Senior Librn
Holdings: Vols (8200)
Notes: Largest library of its kind. Incl 31,000 journal articles on applied ethics. Produces computer database Bioethicsline, available through MEDLARS; and the printed annual Bibliography of Bioethics. Other library publications are: New Titles in Bioethics (monthly); Scope Notes series on current topics.

NY —STATE UNIVERSITY OF NEW YORK, State College of Optometry, Harold Kohn Vision Science Library, 100 E 24 St, New York, 10010. Margaret S Lewis, Librn
Holdings: Vols (23,000) Cat Audiotapes Microforms
Notes: All subjects related to visual disabilities; much on vision disorders among children.

ND —UNIVERSITY OF NORTH DAKOTA, Harley E French Medical Library, Grand Forks, 58202. David W Boilard, Dir; Lila Pedersen, Asst Dir
Holdings: Vols (56,000) Cat
Budget: ($206,000)
Notes: 1075 current periodical subscriptions.

MEDICAL ILLUSTRATION

CA —UNIVERSITY OF CALIFORNIA, SAN FRANCISCO, Library, Special Collections, San Francisco, 94143. Nancy Witten Zinn, Librn
Holdings: Uncat Pix
Notes: The Ralph Sweet Collection of Medical Illustrations.

CT —YALE UNIVERSITY, Medical Historical Library, 333 Cedar St, New Haven, 06510. Ferenc A Gyorgyey, Librn
Holdings: Cat Pix
Notes: The Clements C Fry Collection of Medical Prints and Drawings. About 2000 items. Also, about 3000 bookplates of physicians, many of medical interest.

GA —MEDICAL COLLEGE OF GEORGIA, Library, Laney Walker Blvd, Augusta, 30902. Dorothy H Mims, Librn for Special Collections
Holdings: Vols (2500) // Cat
Notes: Special collection of late 18th and early 19th century medical works, incl classic texts and atlases in anatomy. A number of hand-colored atlases from France.

IL —UNIVERSITY OF CHICAGO LIBRARY, Dept of Special Collections, 1100 E 57 St, Chicago, 60637.
Notes: Frank Collection of Anatomical Illustrations.

MD —NATIONAL LIBRARY OF MEDICINE, 8600 Rockville Pike, Bethesda, 20209. Harold M Schoolinam, Actg Dir
Holdings: Vols (3,150,000) Cat Mss Audiotapes Videotapes 16mm Films Filmstrips Microforms
Budget: ($46,400)
Notes: The world's largest medical library.

Materials are collected exhaustively in some 40 biomedical areas and, to a lesser degree, in related subject areas such as general chemistry, physics, zoology, botany, and instrumentation. Holdings include 82,000 monographic volumes, pre-1871; 438,000 monographic volumes, 1871-present; 714,000 bound serial volumes; 281,000 theses; 172,000 pamphlets; 1,207,000 manuscripts; 156,000 microforms; 12,000 audiovisuals; and 75,000 prints and photographs. Pre-1871 material is in a separate historical collection. Approximately 24,000 serial titles are currenlty received.

MA —FRANCIS A COUNTWAY LIBRARY OF MEDICINE, Boston Medical Library/ Harvard Medical Library, 10 Shattuck St, Boston, 02115. C Robin LeSueur, Librn; Richard J Wolfe, Cur, Rare Books & Manuscripts
Holdings: Vols (500,000) Cat Mss Maps Pix Microforms
Notes: Combines resources of the Harvard Medical School and the Boston Medical Library. Strong in serials and medical history in all fields of medicine, incl incunabula, non-medical books by doctors, travel books by doctors. 500,000 medical dissertations and theses. Special strength in all medical subjects listed in this volume.

PA —PHILADELPHIA MUSEUM OF ART, Ars Medica Center, Parkway at Fairmount, Box 7646, Philadelphia, 19101. Ellen Jacobowutz; Ann Percy
Holdings: Cat Mss Maps Pix Slides
Notes: An international medical arts center of prints, drawings and photographs, related illustrative medical material, and a research reference center.

MEDICAL INSTRUMENTS AND APPARATUS

CA —STANFORD UNIVERSITY LIBRARIES, Lane Medical Library, Stanford University, Medical Center, Stanford, 94305. Peter Stangl, Librn
Holdings: Slides Pix
Notes: Instruments from the last three centuries, representing all fields of medicine except anesthesia.

CT —YALE UNIVERSITY, Medical Historical Library, 333 Cedar St, New Haven, 06510. Ferenc A Gyorgyey, Librn
Holdings: Uncat

MD —NATIONAL LIBRARY OF MEDICINE, 8600 Rockville Pike, Bethesda, 20209. Harold M Schoolinam, Actg Dir
Holdings: Vols (3,150,000) Cat Mss Audiotapes Videotapes 16mm Films Filmstrips Microforms
Budget: ($46,400)
Notes: The world's largest medical library. Materials are collected exhaustively in some 40 biomedical areas and, to a lesser degree, in related subject areas such as general chemistry, physics, zoology, botany, and instrumentation. Holdings include 82,000 monographic volumes, pre-1871; 438,000 monographic volumes, 1871-present; 714,000 bound serial volumes; 281,000 theses; 172,000 pamphlets; 1,207,000 manuscripts; 156,000 microforms; 12,000 audiovisuals; and 75,000 prints and photographs. Pre-1871 material is in a separate historical collection. Approximately 24,000 serial titles are currently received.

MN —BAKKEN LIBRARY OF ELECTRICITY IN LIFE, 3537 Zenith Ave S, Minneapolis, 55416. John Edward Senior, Dir
Notes: Books (including periodicals, manuscripts, and archival materials) and instrument collection. 1500 instruments (focus-18th and 19th centuries). Relating to the historical medical instruments and apparatus.

PA —ENSANIAN PHYSICOCHEMICAL INSTITUTE, Electrotopography Library, PO Box 98, Eldred, 16731. Elisabeth Anahid Ensanian, Chief Librn
Holdings: Cat Maps Slides
Budget: ($45,000)
Notes: Electrotopography is a new science (the Institute has pioneered the field and has

MEDICAL INSTRUMENTS AND APPARATUS (cont.)

coined the terms "electrotopograph" and "electrotopography") concerned with the mapping of electrical fields associated with metals, alloys, semiconductors, and living organisms. These fields may be natural and/or induced, and are converted into mappings which exhibit certain systems characteristics for both normal and stress states.

MEDICAL INTENSIVE CARE see Intensive Care, Medical

MEDICAL JURISPRUDENCE

CA —UNIVERSITY OF CALIFORNIA, LOS ANGELES, Research Library, Dept of Special Collections, 405 Hilgard Ave, Los Angeles, 90024. Edward Shreeves, Chairman, Bibliographers Group; David S Zeidberg, Head
Notes: Marcus E Crahan's medical files relating to Los Angeles County court cases. Closed to access until 2004 AD.

CA —BLUE CROSS OF SOUTHERN CALIFORNIA, Library, PO Box 70,000, Van Nuys, 91470. Frances Linke, Head Librn
Holdings: Vols (9500) Cat Mss Slides Audiotapes Videotapes 16mm Films Filmstrips Microforms
Budget: ($19,000)
Notes: Strong law collection.

MA —HARVARD UNIVERSITY LIBRARY, Law School Library, Langdell Hall, Cambridge, 02138. Harry S Martin III, Librn
Holdings: Cat Mss Maps Pix Slides
Notes: Downs 1687, 1763, 1774, 1776-1779, 1782-1784, 1790-1793, 1809, 1764, 1768, 1796; Downs Supplement 789.
Comprehensive collection of English common law, American law (historical and current), foreign law, comparative law, international law, Roman law and Canon law. Over a million vols.

MI —MICHIGAN STATE UNIVERSITY, Libraries, Special Collections Div, East Lansing, 48824. Jannette Fiore, Librn
Holdings: Cat

NY —MILTON HELPERN LIBRARY OF LEGAL MEDICINE, 520 First Ave, New York, 10016. Barry W Seaver, Librn
Holdings: Vols (2480) Cat Pix Slides Microforms
Notes: Forensic (legal) medicine (incl forensic pathology, serology, toxicology and criminalistics).

MEDICAL LABORATORIES

MO —SAINT JOSEPH STATE HOSPITAL, Professional Library, 3400 Frederick Ave, Box 263, Saint Joseph, 64502. Martha Goodding, Librn
Holdings: Vols (3000) Cat Slides Phonorecords Audiotapes 16mm Films Filmstrips Videotapes

†NY —COLUMBIA UNIVERSITY LIBRARIES, Butler Library, Rare Book and Manuscript Library, 535 W 114 St, New York, 10027.
Notes: Papers of the American Bureau for Medical Aid to China, incl correspondence, memoranda, reports, minutes, membership and financial records, photographs, posters and printed material. Approx 45,000 pieces. Also, some 6000 photographs of Chinese medical colleges, hospitals, laboratories, and personnel.

ON —ONTARIO MINISTRY OF HEALTH, Laboratory Services Branch, Library, Box 9000, Terminal A, Toronto, M5W 1R5, Can. Doris A Standing, Librn
Holdings: Vols (4000) Cat
Budget: ($50,000)
Notes: Medical laboratory technology and related subjects: microbiology; environmental bacteriology (limited to testing of milk, food and water for bacterial quality, etc); biological chemistry (clinical); mycology; parasitology; virology; immunology; serology; automated laboratory techniques; biohazard control.

MEDICAL LIBRARIES

NY —UNITED HOSPITAL FUND OF NEW YORK, Library, 3 E 54th St, New York, 10022. Christine Bahr, Librn
Holdings: Vols (4000) Cat Mss Maps Pix
Notes: Also (525) current serials, and (85) vertical files.

MEDICAL MEDALS see Medals, Medical

MEDICAL PERIODICALS see Periodicals, Medical

MEDICAL PHYSICS

IL —UNIVERSITY OF ILLINOIS, URBANA/CHAMPAIGN, Library, Physics/Astronomy Library, 204 Loomis Laboratory, 1110 West Green St, Urbana, 61801. Bernice Lord Hulsizer, Librn
Holdings: Vols (34,000) Cat
Budget: ($130,000)
Notes: A new field in which we collect those titles which emphasize the physics of the area. At present, a small collection as we have access to the comprehensive collection in the Biology Library.

MEDICAL POLICY

AZ —NORTHERN ARIZONA UNIVERSITY, Special Collection Library, CU Box 6022, Flagstaff, 86011. Peter M Whiteley, Coordr/Archivist; William Mullane, Librn
Notes: Medicaid in Arizona Collection; materials and information about legislation concerning Medicaid in Arizona, 1973-1975.

CT —YALE MEDICAL LIBRARY, 333 Cedar St, New Haven, 06510.
Notes: A special subject emphasis.

NY —NEW YORK ACADEMY OF MEDICINE, Library, 2 E 103 St, New York, 10029. Brett A Kirkpatrick, Librn
Holdings: Cat VF //
Notes: The Papers of Michael Davis, one of the most extensive files of correspondence, surveys, government reports, news clippings, ephemera, etc concerning the development of medical care programs in the US and other countries. 14 vertical file cabinets.

NY —NEW YORK ACADEMY OF MEDICINE, Library, 2 E 103 St, New York, 10029. Brett A Kirkpatrick, Librn
Holdings: Uncat Mss Pix
Notes: Collection of personal papers of Frank George Boudreau, incl correspondence, from his birth to his early years as health officer in Ohio, through his international experience at the League of Nations, and as President of the Milbank Memorial Fund. Much on epidemiology, public health, and public medicine. Collection described in Lee Ash's "Frank George Boudreau, 18 July 1886-14 February 1970," *The Academy Bookman*, (New York Academy of Medicine, Friends of the Rare Room), Vol 26, No 1, 1973, pp 6-7.

MEDICAL PROFESSION see Medicine

MEDICAL RADIOLOGY see Radiology

MEDICAL RESEARCH

CA —PALO ALTO MEDICAL FOUNDATION, Barnett-Hall Library, 860 Bryant St, Palo Alto, 94301. Eileen Cassidy, Chief Librn
Holdings: Vols (11,872)

CT —YALE UNIVERSITY, School of Medicine, Dept of Obstetrics & Gynecology Library, Farnam Memorial Bldg, New Haven, 06510.
Holdings: Cat Mss Pix Slides
Notes: X-ray plates, 10,000 slides of monkey and human tissue and about 1000 slides of gynecological and obstetrical pathology, used as teaching and research materials. Other large collections of X-rays and radiotherapy photographs are in the Hunter Radiation Therapy Center.

MA —MASSACHUSETTS INSTITUTE OF TECHNOLOGY, Institute Archives, Special Collections, Cambridge, 02139.
Notes: Correspondence, newsletters, factsheets, newspaper and magazine articles, books and reports of the Citizens' League Against the Sonic Boom, established in 1967 by William Shurcliff to oppose the sonic boom, stop commercial supersonic transport production, and influence public opinion and policy decisions on the SST. Major correspondents incl Bo Lundberg, Richard Wiggs, several US congressmen, and CLASB members.

MN —MAYO MEDICAL LIBRARY, Rochester, 55905. Jack D Key, Dir
Holdings: Vols (244,000) Cat Maps Pix Slides Microforms
Notes: Research library for biomedical sciences, with broadly based complete serial holdings.

MEDICAL ROENTGENOGRAPHY see Tomography

MEDICAL SCHOOLS see Medical Colleges

MEDICAL SECRETARIES

OH —KETTERING COLLEGE OF MEDICAL ARTS, Learning Resources Center, 3737 Southern Blvd, Kettering, 45429. Edward Collins, Librn
Holdings: Vols 17 Cat Audiotapes Videotapes 16mm Films

MEDICAL SERVICE see Medical Care

MEDICAL SERVICE, PREPAID see Medical Care, Prepaid

MEDICAL SOCIAL WORK

CT —YALE UNIVERSITY, Medical Historical Library, 333 Cedar St, New Haven, 06510. Ferenc A Gyorgyey, Librn
Notes: Records of the Milbank Memorial Fund for the years 1922-1977. A part of the Contemporary Medical Care and Health Policy Collection.

NY —UNITED HOSPITAL FUND OF NEW YORK, Library, 3 E 54th St, New York, 10022. Christine Bahr, Librn
Holdings: Vols (4000) Cat Mss Maps Pix
Notes: Incl 100 journal titles.

MEDICAL SOCIETY OF THE STATE OF NEW YORK

NY —CORNELL UNIVERSITY LIBRARIES, Collection of Regional History, Dept of Manuscripts and Univ Archives, Ithaca, 14853.
Notes: Records, ca 1938-73; 220 ft.

MEDICAL SOCIOLOGY see Social Medicine

MEDICAL TECHNOLOGY

CA —LOS ANGELES PUBLIC LIBRARY, Science & Technology Dept, 630 W Fifth St, Los Angeles, 90071. Billie M Connor, Dept Head
Holdings: Vols (7500)
Notes: A well-rounded collection of materials related to consumer health, medicine and drugs as well as materials for the allied health and medical professions. Includes a sound representative selection of basic texts covering various aspects of medical treatment, drugs, diseases and syndromes. Indexes are collected as well as a basic collection of journals. The directories collection is strong. The broadest possible collection of books oriented toward consumer health, medicine, diets and nutrition is maintained, both traditional and alternative. Texts and examination study books are collected for nurses, laboratory technicians, physcial therapists, speech therapists, paramedics and other allied health professions.

NY —STATE UNIVERSITY OF NEW YORK, COLLEGE AT BUFFALO, Health

MEDICAL TECHNOLOGY (cont.)

Sciences Library, Stockton Kimball Tower, Buffalo, 14214. C K Huang, Dir
Holdings: Vols (222,108) Cat
Budget: ($493,931)

NY —ELIZABETH SETON COLLEGE LIBRARY, Yonkers, 10701. Sr Margaret Sullivan, Librn

ND —UNIVERSITY OF NORTH DAKOTA, Harley E French Medical Library, Grand Forks, 58202. David W Boilard, Dir; Lila Pedersen, Asst Dir
Holdings: Vols (56,000) Cat
Budget: ($206,000)
Notes: 1075 current periodical subscriptions.

OK —UNIVERSITY OF OKLAHOMA, Health Sciences Center, Library, 1000 Stanton L Young Blvd, PO Box 26901, Oklahoma City, 73190. C M Thompson, Jr, Dir
Holdings: Vols (155,434) Cat Slides Audiotapes Videotapes 16mm Films
Budget: ($374,960)
Notes: Incl physical therapy, occupational therapy, radiologic technology, clinical dietetic.

SC —BAPTIST MEDICAL CENTER, Amelia White Pitts Memorial Library, Taylor at Marion Sts, Columbia, 29220. Lois W Smith, Medical Librn
Holdings: Vols (3000) Cat

WI —MARQUETTE UNIVERSITY, Memorial Library, 1415 W Wisconsin Ave, Milwaukee, 53233. Jay Kirk, Health Sciences Librn
Notes: Supports curriculum and research.

MEDICI FAMILY

†CA —CLAREMONT COLLEGES, Honnold Library, Claremont, 91711.
Notes: Florentine Renaissance, particularly 1450-1500. Angelo Poliziano (1454-1494), the humanist scholars and writers of the Medici circle, and the Platonic Academy.

MA —HARVARD UNIVERSITY, Baker Library of the Graduate School of Business Administration, Kress Library of Business and Economics, Soldiers Field, Boston, 02163. Ruth E Rogers, Cur
Holdings: Cat Mss
Notes: Account books of the Medicis; see Gertrude R Richards, *Florentine Merchants* (Harvard University Press, 1932).

MEDICI-GONDI ACCOUNT BOOKS

PA —UNIVERSITY OF PENNSYLVANIA, Lea Library, 3420 Walnut St, Philadelphia, 19104. Daniel Traister, Special Collections Librn
Notes: Lea Collection of Medieval and Renaissance period incl statutes of the city-state and the Medici-Gondi account books. See (*University of Pennsylvania*) *Library Chronicle*, vol 36, no 2, Spring 1970. Hirsch, Rudolf. "Catalogue of Manuscripts in the Libraries of the University of Pennsylvania to 1800: Supplement A (3) Medici-Gondi Archive II." and *Library Chronicle*, vol 37, no 1, winter 1971. *Catalogue...Supplement A (4).* Norman P Zacour and Rudolf Hirsch *Catalogue of Manuscripts in the Libraries of the University of Pennsylvania to 1800* (Philadelphia: University of Pennsylvania Press, 1965).

MEDICINAL PLANTS see Botany, Medical

MEDICINE

AL —UNIVERSITY OF ALABAMA, BIRMINGHAM, Lister Hill Library of the Health Sciences, University Sta, Birmingham, 35294. Richard B Fredericksen, Dir
Holdings: Vols 167,000 Cat Mss Maps Pix Slides Phonorecords Audiotapes Videotapes 16mm Films Filmstrips Microforms
Budget: $405,000
Notes: Maintains research collection for all areas of medicine. Particularly strong in anatomy, physiology, cardiology, radiology, cancer, pediatrics. Resource library for Southeastern Atlantic Regional Medical Library Program. Holdings also incl medical school catalogs, theses and dissertations of UAB faculty and students, and medical museum pieces.

AL —DRUID CITY HOSPITAL, Library, Educational Tower, PO Box 6331, University, 35486. Lisa Raine, Dir
Holdings: Vols 9000 Cat
Notes: Serves the teaching faculty. 475 journal subscriptions, monograms.

AK —ALASKA HEALTH SCIENCES LIBRARY, 3211 Providence Dr, Anchorage, 99508. Stanley Truelson, Dir
Budget: ($56,000)
Notes: A unit of the Division of State Libraries and Museums, State of Alaska, but located in the University of Alaska, Anchorage Library, whose collection it shares.

AZ —SAINT MARY'S HOSPITAL, Ralph Fuller Medical Library, PO Box 5614, Tucson, 85703. Jeffrey St Clair, Librn
Holdings: Vols 1000 Cat

AZ —TUCSON MEDICAL CENTER, Medical Library, PO Box 6067, Tucson, 85733. Christee King, Mgr Library Services
Holdings: Vols 3500 Cat Slides Audiotapes Videotapes Filmstrips

CA —ALTA BATES HOSPITAL, Stuart Memorial Library, One Colby Plaza, Berkeley, 94705. Kathryn Kammerer, Librn
Holdings: Vols 1000 Cat
Budget: $5000

CA —UNIVERSITY OF CALIFORNIA, DAVIS, Health Sciences Library, Davis, 95616. Marjan Merala, Health Sciences Librn
Holdings: Vols (164,000) Cat Microforms
Budget: ($509,737)
Notes: Human medicine: ca 82,000 vols; veterinary medicine: ca 19,700 vols; allied sciences (biochemistry, physiology, etc); reference works: ca 62,300 vols.

CA —MEMORIAL MEDICAL CENTER, Medical Library, 2801 Atlantic Ave, PO Box 1428, Long Beach, 90801. Frances Lyon, Dir, Library Services
Holdings: Vols 45,597 Cat Slides Phonorecords Audiotapes Videotapes 16mm Films Filmstrips
Budget: $66,665
Notes: Also incl 41 records, 690 audiotapes, 661 videotapes.

CA —CEDARS-SINAI MEDICAL CENTER, Health Sciences Information Center, 8700 Beverly Blvd, Los Angeles, 90048. Ellen W Green, Dir
Holdings: Vols 10,000 Cat Pix Slides Microforms

CA —HOLLYWOOD PRESBYTERIAN MEDICAL CENTER, Health Sciences Library, 1300 N Vermont Ave, Los Angeles, 90027. Erika M Hansen, Chief Medical Librn
Notes: Medicine, nursing and allied health personnel, hospital adminstration. Incl audiovisual material.

CA —LOS ANGELES COUNTY MEDICAL ASSOCIATION, Library, 634 S Westlake Ave, Los Angeles, 90057. Elizabeth S Crahan, Chief Librn
Holdings: Cat Pix

CA —LOS ANGELES PUBLIC LIBRARY, Science & Technology Dept, 630 W Fifth St, Los Angeles, 90071. Billie M Connor, Dept Head
Holdings: Vols (7500)
Notes: A well-rounded collection of materials related to consumer health, medicine and drugs as well as materials for the allied health and medical professions. Includes a sound representative selection of basic texts covering various aspects of medical treatment, drugs, diseases and syndromes. Indexes are collected as well as a basic collection of journals. The directories collection is strong. The broadest possible collection of books oriented toward consumer health, medicine, diets and nutrition is maintained, both traditional and alternative. Texts and examination study books are collected for nurses, laboratory technicians, physcial therapists, speech therapists, paramedics and other allied health professions.

CA —UNIVERSITY OF CALIFORNIA, LOS ANGELES, Biomedical Library, Center for the Health Sciences, Los Angeles, 90024. Alison Bunting, Acting Biomedical Librn; Victoria Steele, Head, History & Special Collections Div
Holdings: Vols (400,000) Cat Slides Phonorecords Audiotapes Videotapes 16mm Films Microforms
Notes: The UCLA Biomedical Library serves primarily the Schools of Medicine, Dentistry, Nursing, and Public Health, the UCLA Medical Center, the Departments of Microbiology and Biology in the College of Letters and Science, and related institutes in biomedicine. The collections of the Library are broad in scope, designed not only to support the teaching and research needs of its many users, but also to function as a resource for the health sciences-biological field as a whole. The outstanding feature of the collection is the strength of its periodical holdings, both current and retrospective. The Library also has an excellent reference collection, a comprehensive historical section, and gives special emphasis to the fields of neuroscience, psychiatry, ophthalmology, radiation biology, molecular biology, and vertebrate zoology. Increased emphasis is being given to the acquisition of audiovisual materials.

†CA —UNIVERSITY OF CALIFORNIA LOS ANGELES, Center for the Study of Comparative Folklore and Mythology, Los Angeles, 90024.
Notes: Archive, consisting of nearly 500,000 entries and cross-references, developed by Prof Wayland D Hand over the past 40 years as part of his monumental *Dictionary of American Popular Beliefs and Superstitions.* Entries have been drawn from both field collections and from printed and published sources. Analytical data stress both the historical component and the comparative approach. Of special interest is the emphasis on magical medicine, although natural and botanical medicine are also well represented.

CA —PALO ALTO MEDICAL FOUNDATION, Barnett-Hall Library, 860 Bryant St, Palo Alto, 94301. Eileen Cassidy, Chief Librn
Holdings: Vols (11,872)

CA —KAISER PERMANENTE MEDICAL CENTER, Health Science Library, 13652 Cantara St, Panorama City, 91402. Winnie Yu, Librn; Susan Dagoberg, Librn
Holdings: Vols (2000) Cat Audiotapes Videotapes Filmstrips
Budget: $143,000

CA —HUNTINGTON MEMORIAL HOSPITAL, Health Science Library, 100 Congress St, Pasadena, 91105. Samir Maurice Zeind, Librn
Holdings: Vols 18,000 Cat Slides Audiotapes Microforms
Budget: $31,500
Notes: Library open to non-staff for research. Computer system.

CA —PATTON STATE HOSPITAL, Medical Library, 26802 E Highland Ave, Patton, 92369. Mary Stumberg, Sr Librn
Holdings: Vols (6000) Cat

CA —ROSEVILLE COMMUNITY HOSPITAL, Medical Library, 333 Sunrise Ave, Roseville, 95678. Helen R Asher, Librn
Holdings: Vols 1654 Cat Slides Audiotapes Videotapes Microforms
Budget: $3500
Notes: Incl 407 slides and 302 audiotapes.

CA —REES-STEALY MEDICAL CLINIC LIBRARY, 2001 Fourth Ave, San Diego, 92101. Margaret O'Rourke, Librn
Holdings: Vols 6600 Cat Tapes

MEDICINE (cont.)

CA —UNIVERSITY OF CALIFORNIA, SAN DIEGO, Medical Center Library, 225 W Dickinson St, San Diego, 92103. Sue Ann Johnson, Head Librn
Holdings: Vols 20,000 Cat Slides Audiotapes
Notes: 6008 slides, 1600 audiocassettes.

CA —CALIFORNIA COLLEGE OF PODIATRIC MEDICINE, Schmidt Medical Library, 1210 Scott St, San Francisco, 94115. Leonard P Shapiro, Library Dir
Holdings: Vols (20,000) Cat Mss Slides Phonorecords Audiotapes Videotapes File Materials VF Reprint File Archives
Budget: $99,762
Notes: General medical library with special emphasis on the foot and podiatry (500 vols). Also orthopedics, lower extremity materials, sports medicine.

CA —RALPH K DAVIES MEDICAL CENTER, Franklin Hospital Medical Library, Castro & Duboce, San Francisco, 94114. Anne L Shew, Librn
Holdings: Vols 1200 Cat Videotapes
Budget: $18,000
Notes: Incl 120 videotapes.

CA —SAN FRANCISCO GENERAL HOSPITAL, Barnett-Briggs Library, 1001 Potrero Ave, San Francisco, 94941. Miriam Hirsch, Librn
Holdings: Vols 10,000 Cat

CA —UNIVERSITY OF CALIFORNIA, SAN FRANCISCO, Library, San Francisco, 94143. David Bishop, University Librn
Holdings: Vols (502,261) Cat
Budget: ($602,604)

CA —COTTAGE HOSPITAL, David L Reeves Medical Library, Pueblo at Bath St, PO Box 689, Santa Barbara, 93102. Evelyn Fay, Librn
Holdings: Vols 10,000 Audiotapes
Budget: $131,000
Notes: Incl 400 audiotapes.

CA —STANFORD UNIVERSITY LIBRARIES, Lane Medical Library, Stanford University, Medical Center, Stanford, 94305. Peter Stangl, Librn
Holdings: Vols 272,000 Mss Pix
Budget: $368,535
Notes: Lane Library serves the schools of medicine and related basic sciences and the research, patient care and physician training activities of the Stanford University Medical Center. The collections cover clinical medicine and its specialties, the preclinical and basic sciences, public health, nursing and related fields. In addition to its current holdings Lane has a strong retrospective collection in both books and serials with long journals runs from the 18th and early 19th century. Separate collection are the Barkan Library of Ophthalmology and Otolaryngology and the Barkan History of Medicine library.
See also entry under Medicine - History and Historic

CA —LOS ANGELES COUNTY HARBOR-UCLA MEDICAL CENTER, A F Parlow Library of the Health Sciences, 1000 W Carson St, Torrance, 90509. Mary Ann Berliner, Dir of Library Services
Holdings: Vols 33,359
Notes: Special collection with emphasis on patient and consumer health education through Chips program. Medical collections support hospital staff and students of the health professions. Incl 753 journal titles, 3509 audiovisual materials, cataloged.

CO —DENVER MEDICAL LIBRARY, 1601 E 19 Ave, Denver, 80218. Mary De Mund, Librn
Holdings: Vols 40,000
Budget: $130,000
Notes: Incl book and journal volumes (cat). Private medical library. Part of Presbyterian/Sanit Luke's Medical Center's Library System.

†CO —NATIONAL JEWISH HOSPITAL AND RESEARCH CENTER-NATIONAL ATHSMA CENTER, Gerald Tucker Memorial Medical Library, 3800 Colfax Ave, Denver, 80206. Helen-Ann Brown, Librn
Holdings: Vols (8500)
Notes: Allergy, asthma, immunology, research in molecular and cellular biology, medicine, tuberculosis and diseases of the chest.

CO —UNIVERSITY OF COLORADO, Health Sciences Center, Charles Denison Memorial Library, 4200 E Ninth Ave, Denver, 80262. Margaret Butkovich, Interim Dir
Holdings: Vols 179,128 Cat

CO —SWEDISH MEDICAL CENTER LIBRARY, 501 E Hampden Ave, Englewood, 80110. Sandra Parker, Dir
Holdings: Vols (6000) Cat
Budget: ($40,000)

CT —SAINT VINCENT'S MEDICAL CENTER, Health Science Library, 2800 Mian St, Bridgeport, 06606. Janet Goerig, Dir of Library Services
Holdings: Vols (8000) Cat Slides

CT —UNIVERSITY OF CONNECTICUT HEALTH CENTER, Lyman Maynard Stowe Library, Farmington, 06032. Ralph D Arcari, Dir of Libraries
Holdings: Vols 99,250 Cat Slides Audiotapes Microforms
Budget: $330,700
Notes: Incl basic sciences supporting biomedical collection, biomedical research and clinical medicine. Separate catalog for AV materials. Library produces book catalogs of serial and audiovisuals titles.

CT —CONNECTICUT VALLEY HOSPITAL, Hallock Medical Library, Silver St, Middletown, 06457. Mildred Asbell, Medical Librn
Holdings: Vols (3400) Cat

CT —MIDDLESEX MEMORIAL HOSPITAL, Health Sciences Library, 28 Crescent St, Middletown, 06457. Evelyn M Breck, Dir
Holdings: Vols (2000) Cat
Budget: ($20,000)
Notes: 125 journals are kept for 10-year runs.

CT —YALE MEDICAL LIBRARY, 333 Cedar St, New Haven, 06510.
Holdings: Vols (334,215) Cat Mss Pix Slides Microforms
Budget: ($361,650)
Notes: Incl films, audiotapes, artifacts, etc.

CT —NORWALK HOSPITAL, Wiggins Library, 24 Stevens St, Norwalk, 06856. Joan Sjostrom, Dir
Holdings: Vols 1100 Cat

CT —SHARON HOSPITAL, Medical Library, Sharon, 06069. Jean Moore, Librn; Lucy Collins, Librn
Holdings: Vols 400 Uncat Audiotapes
Notes: Partially cataloged. Incl 360 audiotapes.

DE —SAINT FRANCIS HOSPITAL MEDICAL LIBRARY, Seventh & Clayton Sts, Wilmington, 19805. Sister Joan Ignatius McCleary, Librn
Holdings: Vols (3000) Cat Audiotapes

DE —US VETERANS ADMINISTRATION CENTER, Medical Library, Wilmington, 19805. Mrs Donald Passidoma, Chief Librn
Holdings: Vols (5000) Cat
Notes: Staff only.

†DC —CATHOLIC UNIVERSITY OFF AMERICA, Nursing & Biology Library, Washington, 20064. N L Powell, Head
Holdings: Vols (30,000)

DC —CENTER FOR BIOETHICS, Library, Kennedy Institute, Georgetown University, 3520 Prospect St NW, Washington, 20057. Doris Goldstein, Dir; Judith Mistichelli, Senior Librn
Holdings: Vols (8200)
Notes: Largest library of its kind. Incl 31,000 journal articles on applied ethics. Produces computer database Bioethicsline, available through MEDLARS; and the printed annual Bibliography of Bioethics. Other library publications are: New Titles in Bioethics (monthly); Scope Notes series on current topics.

DC —MALCOLM GROW USAF MEDICAL CENTER, Medical Library, Box 3097, Andrews AFB, Washington, 20331. Eunice M Lyon, Librn
Holdings: Vols (10,000) Maps Pix Slides Audiotapes Microforms
Budget: ($31,000)

DC —PAN AMERICAN HEALTH ORGANIZATION, Library, 525 23 St NW, Washington, 20037. Dr Carlos Gamboa, Chief of Library and Reference Services
Holdings: Vols 50,000 Cat Maps Slides Filmstrips

DC —WASHINGTON HOSPITAL CENTER MEDICAL LIBRARY, 110 Irving St NW, Washington, 20010. Marilyn Cook, Dir
Holdings: Vols 30,000 Cat Slides Audiotapes Videotapes 16mm Films Filmstrips Microforms

FL —HALIFAX HOSPITAL MEDICAL CENTER, Library, Clyde Morris Blvd, Daytona Beach, 32014. Ken Mead, Dir
Holdings: Vols 6695 Cat Maps Pix Slides Tapes
Budget: $9150

FL —FLORIDA INSTITUTE OF TECHNOLOGY, Medical Research Institute, Library, 7725 W New Haven Ave, Melbourne, 32901. Barbara Bratton, Librn
Holdings: Cat

FL —UNIVERSITY OF MIAMI, School of Medicine, Louis Calder Memorial Library, PO Box 520875, Miami, 33152. Henry L Lemkau, Jr, Dir
Holdings: Vols (127,843) Cat Mss Maps Pix Slides Phonorecords Audiotapes Videotapes 16mm Films Filmstrips Microforms
Budget: ($915,000)
Notes: Ophthalmology Branch Library of 5231 vols incl in total count; University of Miami School of Medicine dissertations; 209 medical medallions; physicians' bookplates; postage stamps with medical themes.

FL —US VETERANS ADMINISTRATION HOSPITAL, Medical Library, 1201 NW 16 St, Miami, 33125. Raissa Maurin, Chief Librn
Holdings: Vols 2700 Cat Cassettes
Notes: Also over 12,000 vols of journals.

FL —SAINT MARY'S HOSPITAL INC, Health Services Library, 901 45th St W, Palm Beach, 33407. Jennie Glock, Librn
Holdings: Vols (7000) Cat Slides Audiotapes

FL —UNIVERSITY OF SOUTH FLORIDA, Medical Center Library, 12901 N 30 St, Tampa, 33612. Maxyne Grimes, Dir
Holdings: Vols (75,383) Cat
Budget: ($325,000)

GA —CRAWFORD W LONG MEMORIAL HOSPITAL, Medical Library, 35 Linden Ave NE, Atlanta, 30365. Girija Vijay, Dir
Holdings: Vols Cat
Budget: ($119,200)
Notes: Collection contains materials for medical, nursing and allied health fields. Strong nursing collection. Collection incl 3956 (cat) books, 6571 vols bound periodicals and 2773 vols (cat) audiovisuals.

GA —CENTRAL STATE HOSPITAL, Medical Library, Medical/Surgical Center, Milledgeville, 31062. Aurelia S Spence, Librn
Holdings: Vols (2000) Cat Audiotapes Videotapes
Budget: ($6000)

HI —HAWAII MEDICAL LIBRARY, 1221 Punchbowl St, Honolulu, 96813. John A Breinich, Dir
Holdings: Vols (50,000) Cat Pix Audiotapes Videotapes
Budget: ($121,000)
Notes: Medline service available.

†HI —PACIFIC BIO-MEDICAL RESEARCH CENTER, 41 Ahui St, Honolulu, 96813.

HI —STRAUB CLINIC, Arnold Library, 888 S King St, Honolulu, 96822. Fran Smith, Librn
Notes: On-line search services; Medline, Dialog.

HI —HAWAII STATE HOSPITAL, Medical Library, 45-710 Keaahala Rd, Kaneohe, 96744. Diana Stephens, Medical Librn
Holdings: Vols 6000
Budget: $15,200

IL —ARGONNE NATIONAL LABORATORY, Library, Technical Information Services Dept, 9700 Cass Ave, Argonne, 60439. Hillis L Griffin, Dir
Notes: The ANL library system consists of eight branch libraries with centralized processing services. The entire collection numbers 70,000 monographic titles, 3700 journal titles, and over 1 million scientific and technical reports. Materials may be used by the public in the library by prior arrangement. Photocopies may be supplied

MEDICINE (cont.)

for interlibrary loan, for which a processing and handling charge is made.

IL —ARLINGTON HEIGHTS MEMORIAL LIBRARY, 500 N Dunton Ave, Arlington Heights, 60004. Caryl Mobley, Reference Librn
Holdings: Vols (5000) Cat
Budget: ($8000)
Notes: Medical sciences, nursing, and patient eduction.

IL —AMERICAN MEDICAL ASSOCIATION, Div of Library & Archival Services, 535 N Dearborn St, Chicago, 60610. Arthur W Hafner, Dir
Holdings: Vols (130,000) Cat Mss Pix Microforms
Notes: "One of world's most comprehensive collections in sociology and economics of medicine," some 150,000 items, 1964 to date. Archival collection of materials relating to history of AMA and its constituent societies. Incl historical biographical resource file on American physicians, incl obituary data and genealogy.

IL —CENTER FOR RESEARCH LIBRARIES, 6050 S Kenwood Ave, Chicago, 60637. Donald B Simpson, Dir; Esther Smith, Collection Development Librn
Notes: Large collection of publications in clinical medicine and related sciences, mostly older publications. Several hundred current serial subscriptions to infrequently held foreign titles. Foreign doctoral dissertations in medicine.

IL —JOHN CRERAR LIBRARY, 35 W 33 St, Chicago, 60616. William S Budington, Executive Dir & Librn

†IL —NORTHWESTERN UNIVERSITY, Medical School, Archibald Church Library, 303 E Chicago Ave, Chicago, 60611. Cecile E Kramer, Librn
Holdings: Cat Mss Pix Slides
Notes: Incl about 3000 vols, 5100 pictures and 1200 slides concerning the history of medicine.

IL —NORWEGIAN-AMERICAN HOSPITAL, Seufert Memorial Library, 1044 N Francisco Ave, Chicago, 60622. Estrella P de la Cruz, Librn
Holdings: Vols 800 Cat Slides Phonorecords Audiotapes

IL —ROSELAND COMMUNITY HOSPITAL, Health Science Library, 45 W 111 St, Chicago, 60628. Mary T Hanlon, Librn
Holdings: Vols (800) Cat
Budget: $3200

IL —UNIVERSITY OF CHICAGO LIBRARIES, John Crerar Library Collections, 1100 E 57th St, Chicago, 60637. Robert Rosenthal, Special Collections Librn
Notes: The John Crerar Library's extensive science, medicine, and engineering collections have been transferred in trust to the University of Chicago Libraries. Incl rare books and special collections as listed here.

IL —GOOD SAMARITAN HOSPITAL, Medical Library, 3815 Highland Ave, Downers Grove, 60695. Karen Ambrose, Librn
Holdings: Vols 500 Cat Audiotapes

IL —GLENVIEW PUBLIC LIBRARY, 1930 Glenview Rd, Glenview, 60025. Peter Bury, Librn
Holdings: Vols (3500) Cat Filmstrips
Notes: Maintained as health and domestic science subject center. Incl 1840 cookbooks.

IL —COMMUNITY MEMORIAL GENERAL HOSPITAL, Medical Library, 5101 Willow Springs Rd, La Grange, 60525. Patricia Grundke, Librn
Holdings: Vols 1500 Cat

IL —CHRIST HOSPITAL, Health Sciences Library, 4440 W 95 St, Oak Lawn, 60453. Gerald Dujsik, Library Mgr
Holdings: Vols 3700 Cat Audiotapes Videotapes
Budget: $33,000

IL —LUTHERAN GENERAL HOSPITAL LIBRARY, 1775 Dempster St, Park Ridge, 60068. Joanne Crispen, Dir of Library Services
Holdings: Vols (21,298) Cat Slides

Audiotapes Videotapes 16mm Films Filmstrips
Budget: ($52,600)

IL —UNIVERSITY OF ILLINOIS, Rockford School of Medicine, Woodruff L Crawford Branch, Library of the Health Sciences, 1601 Parkview Ave, Rockford, 61101. Stewart Kolner, Branch Librn
Holdings: Vols 30,000 Cat Slides Audiotapes Microforms
Budget: $75,000
Notes: Incl 7300 slides, 1000 audiotapes and 500 microforms.

IN —MILES LABORATORIES, Library Resources and Services, 1127 Myrtle St, PO Box 40, Elkhart, 46515. Allam Hagopian, Mgr
Holdings: Vols (16,500) Cat Audiotapes Microforms
Notes: Incl files of pharmaceutical product advertising pieces, extensive literature files on company related drugs; domestic and international marketing files. 32,000 bound periodicals.

IN —BRISTOL-MYERS PHARMACEUTICAL R&D DIVISION, Scientific Information Dept, 2404 W Pennsylvania St, Evansville, 47721. Alice Weisling, Mgr
Holdings: Vols 33,000 Cat Microforms

IN —SAINT MARGARET HOSPITAL, Sallie M Tyrrell MD Memorial Library, 5454 Hohman Ave, Hammond, 46320. Laurie Broadus, Library Coordr

IN —ELI LILLY AND COMPANY, Scientific Library, 307 E McCarty St, Indianapolis, 46285. Adele Hoskin, Chief Librn
Holdings: Vols (35,000) Cat Microforms
Notes: Drug product information (1.7 million cards); drug encyclopedias, foreign and domestic; foreign pharmacopoeias. Restricted use: company employees and approved outsiders.

IN —SAINT VINCENT HOSPITAL & HEALTH CARE CENTER, Garceau Library, 20001 W 86 St, Indianapolis, 46260. Virginia Durkin, Librn
Holdings: Vols (7500) Cat Pix Slides Phonorecords Audiotapes Videotapes 16mm Films Filmstrips Microforms
Notes: Building a collection on the history of the hospital.

IN —WISHARD MEMORIAL HOSPITAL, Professional Library, 1001 W Tenth St, Indianapolis, 46202. Fran Bischoff, Library Dir; Kirsten Quam, Librn
Holdings: Vols 3850 Cat
Notes: Clinically oriented collections.

IN —LOGANSPORT STATE HOSPITAL, Staff Library, Logansport, 46947. Terra Newton, Librn
Holdings: Vols (3000) Cat

IN —UNION HOSPITAL, Medical Library, 1606 N Seventh St, Terre Haute, 47804. Cassandra Brooks, Librn
Holdings: Vols 1500 Cat
Budget: ($8000)
Notes: Library serves the Family Practice Residency program and staff doctors and nurses and administrative staff.

IN —PURDUE UNIVERSITY LIBRARIES, Veterinary Medical Library, C J Lynn Hall of Veterinary Medicine, West Lafayette, 47907. Gretchen Stephens, Librn
Holdings: Vols (31,022) Cat
Budget: ($106,281)
Notes: The collection contains the outstanding books and serials in English that are germane to comparative and veterinary medicine. Foreign language materials are added selectively. Subjects of particular strength are laboratory animal medicine, pathology, comparative anatomy, animal behavior and clinical veterinary medicine.

IA —SAINT LUKE'S METHODIST HOSPITAL, Health Science Library, 1026 "A" Ave NE, Cedar Rapids, 52402. Sally Harms, Librn
Holdings: Vols 4000 Cat
Notes: Also 4000 bound periodical vols and AV materials.

IA —IOWA LUTHERAN HOSPITAL, Department of Educational Media, University at Penn, Des Moines, 50316. Wayne Pedersen, Dir of Educational Media
Holdings: Vols 2695 Cat Audiotapes

Videotapes Slides 16mm Films
Budget: ($15,000)
Notes: The department consists of 3 libraries: Levitt Health Sciences, Nursing Administrative. The Audio-Visual Division is also part of the department. Holdings incl 524 audiocassettes (cat); 177 videotapes (cat); 13 slide-tape kits (cat); 2 16mm films (cat).

IA —US VETERANS ADMINISTRATION MEDICAL CENTER, Medical Library, Iowa City, 52240. M J Kraus, Librn
Holdings: Vols 4878 Cat Slides Phonorecords Audiotapes Videotapes Microforms
Budget: $25,000

IA —US VETERANS ADMINISTRATION HOSPITAL, Medical Library, Knoxville, 50138. Roger B Sayers, Chief, Library Service
Holdings: Vols (3000)
Budget: ($2000)

KS —UNIVERSITY OF KANSAS MEDICAL CENTER, College of Health Sciences & Hospital, Dykes Library of Health Sciences, Rainbow Blvd at 39th, Kansas City, 66103. Earl Farley, Dir
Holdings: Vols 119,117 Cat

KS —KANSAS STATE UNIVERSITY, College of Veterinary Medicine, Veterinary Medical Library, Veterinary Medical Teaching Bldg, Rm 400, Manhattan, 66506. E Guy Coffee, Librn
Holdings: Vols (20,297) Cat Slides Audiotapes Videotapes Microforms
Notes: Veterinary medicine and comparative medicine.

KS —STORMONT-VAIL HOSPITAL, School of Nursing Library, 845 Washburn, Topeka, 66606. Shirley Borglund, Librn
Holdings: Vols (6000) Cat

KS —ST JOSEPH MEDICAL CENTER, Medical Library, 3600 E Harry St, Wichita, 67218. Carol Matulka, Librn
Holdings: Vols 4500 Cat
Budget: $38,000

KS —WESLEY MEDICAL CENTER, McKibbin Health Science Library, 550 N Hillside, Wichita, 67214. Jan Braden, Dir, Library Services
Holdings: Vols (29,000) Cat Slides Phonorecords Audiotapes Videotapes 16mm Films Filmstrips
Budget: ($200,000)

KY —NKC HOSPITALS, Medical Library, PO Box 35070, Louisville, 40232. Holly Shipp Buchanan, Dir
Holdings: Vols (4500) Cat Audiotapes Videotapes 16mm Films
Budget: $200,000
Notes: The Library has a special historical collection, corporate archives in honor of Dr Morris Flexner.

LA —US PUBLIC HEALTH SERVICE, National Hansen's Disease Center, Medical Library and Archives of Leprosy, Carville, 70721. Anna Belle Steinbach, Librn (Medical and Biological Sciences)
Holdings: Vols (8000) Cat
Notes: Only institution in the continental US devoted entirely to the treatment of leprosy and to worldwide education about this disease. Unique collection of over 5000 reprints collected from earliest times to the present. There are books, historical documents, newspaper clippings, scrapbooks and bibliographies in all languages; as well as current books, journals and research materials.

LA —NORTHEAST LOUISIANA UNIVERSITY, Library, 700 University Ave, Monroe, 71201. Clarrissa Pickett, Librn
Holdings: Vols 6500 Cat Microforms

LA —LOUISIANA STATE UNIVERSITY, Medical Center Library, 1542 Tulane Ave, New Orleans, 70112. John P Ische, Dir, Div of Libraries
Holdings: Vols 300 Cat
Notes: Incl the Yellow Fever Collection.

ME —MAINE MEDICAL CENTER, Library, 22 Bramhall St, Portland, 04102. Robin M Rand, Dir of Library Services
Holdings: Vols (5300)
Budget: ($274,185)
Notes: Incl 10,250 bound journals and 617 subscriptions. Also incl a collection of about

MEDICINE (cont.)

300 historical medical books, as well as a small collection of antique instruments and photographs.

MD —BALTIMORE CITY HOSPITALS, Harold E Harrison Library, 4940 Eastern Ave, Baltimore, 21224. Rebecca A Charton, Librn
Holdings: Vols 15,175 Cat
Budget: $45,000

MD —JOHNS HOPKINS UNIVERSITY, William H Welch Medical Library, 1900 E Monument St, Baltimore, 21205. Richard A Polacsek, Dir & Librn
Holdings: Vols (270,000) Cat Pix Slides Phonorecords Audiotapes Videotapes 16mm Films Filmstrips Microforms
Budget: ($497,000)

MD —MARYLAND GENERAL HOSPITAL, Medical Staff Library, 827 Linden Ave, Baltimore, 21201. Monica Yang, Coordinator of Library Services
Holdings: Vols 2000 Cat Slides Audiotapes
Notes: Incl 2800 slides, 400 audiotapes, also videot disk programs, film loop programs. No photocopying.

MD —MEDICAL & CHIRURGICAL FACULTY OF THE STATE OF MARYLAND, Library, 1211 Cathedral St, Baltimore, 21201. Joseph E Jensen, Librn
Holdings: Vols (110,000) Cat Mss Maps Pix Slides Audiotapes Videotapes Microforms
Budget: ($250,000)
Notes: Library for the state medical society. Open to the public, but circulation is restricted to members. The current acquisitions policy emphasizes English language monographs and periodicals on all aspects of clinical medicine, and on the social, economic, legal and administrative aspects of medical practice in the United States. The library subscribes to all state medical society journals in the United States. Holdings include a very fine history of medicine and rare medical book collection, and a strong collection of medical monographs and serials prior to 1900.

MD —SINAI HOSPITAL OF BALTIMORE, Medical & Nursing Libraries, Belvedere & Greenspring, Baltimore, 21215. Rita Matcher, Chief Librn
Holdings: Vols (6000) Cat

MD —UNION MEMORIAL HOSPITAL, Library Services, 201 E University Pkwy, Baltimore, 21218. Rena M Snyder, Dir
Holdings: Vols (5000) Cat Slides Audiotapes Videotapes
Budget: ($70,000)
Notes: Incl 1400 vols on clinical medicine.

MD —UNIVERSITY OF MARYLAND, BALTIMORE, Health Sciences Library, 111 S Greene St, Baltimore, 21201. Cyril C H Feng, Dir
Holdings: Vols 32,099

MD —NATIONAL LIBRARY OF MEDICINE, 8600 Rockville Pike, Bethesda, 20209. Harold M Schoolinam, Actg Dir
Holdings: Vols (3,150,000) Cat Mss Audiotapes Videotapes 16mm Films Filmstrips Microforms
Budget: ($46,400)
Notes: The world's largest medical library. Materials are collected exhaustively in some 40 biomedical areas and, to a lesser degree, in related subject areas such as general chemistry, physics, zoology, botany, and instrumentation. Holdings include 82,000 monographic volumes, pre-1871; 438,000 monographic volumes, 1871-present; 714,000 bound serial volumes; 281,000 theses; 172,000 pamphlets; 1,207,000 manuscripts; 156,000 microforms; 12,000 audiovisuals; and 75,000 prints and photographs. Pre-1871 material is in a separate historical collection. Approximately 24,000 serial titles are currently received.

MD —SPRING GROVE HOSPITAL CENTER, Sulzbacher Memorial Library, Catonsville, 21228. Charles H Johnson, Dir
Holdings: Vols (3800) Cat Slides Phonorecords Audiotapes

MD —FREDERICK MEMORIAL HOSPITAL, Walter F Prior Medical Library, W Seventh St, Frederick, 21701. Linda A Collenberg, Librn
Holdings: Vols 900 Cat

MD —WROTH MEMORIAL LIBRARY, Washington County Hospital Association, 251 E Antietam St, Hagerstown, 21740. Myra Binau, Dir & Librn
Holdings: Vols 5000 Cat
Budget: ($30,000)
Notes: Over 150 periodical titles.

MA —BOSTON CITY HOSPITAL, Dept of Health & Hospitals, Medical Library, 818 Harrison Ave, Boston, 02118. Margi Dempsey, Dir
Holdings: Vols (13,431)
Budget: ($32,000)
Notes: Medical Library serves as a reference medical library for the entire Department of Health and Hospitals for Boston. A special collection (Anthony Michelidakis Memorial Library, History of Medicine) is part of the Medical Library holdings. This special history of medicine collection covers medicine in early Boston and other books on the history of medicine in general. Collection contains some 131 vols.

MA —BOSTON UNIVERSITY, Medical Center, Alumni Medical Library, 80 E Concord St, Boston, 02118. Irene Christopher, Chief Librn
Holdings: Vols 89,448

MA —FRANCIS A COUNTWAY LIBRARY OF MEDICINE, Boston Medical Library/ Harvard Medical Library, 10 Shattuck St, Boston, 02115. C Robin LeSueur, Librn; Richard J Wolfe, Cur, Rare Books & Manuscripts
Holdings: Vols (500,000) Mss Maps Pix
Notes: Second largest medical library in the nation. Combines the resources of the Harvard Medical School and the Boston Medical Library, as well as the medical collections of many regional libraries. Outstanding in all areas of medical science. Author-title catalog of imprints through 1959 published by G K Hall, 1973. Strong in serials and medical history in all fields of medicine. Especially strong in subject areas incl incunabula, medical Judaica, Osleriana, O W Holmes, William Rimmer, non-medical books by doctors, travel books by physicians, X-ray (Dr Lloyd E Hawes, Hon Curator), prints and medical satire (Dr Mark D Altschule, Hon Curator), phrenology, witchcraft, gynecology and obstetrics, medical illustrations, birth control and sex research, medical numismatics, European imprints before 1850 and American imprints before 1870, Chinese and Japanese medicine, medicaldissertations (500,000), anatomy, anesthesia, botany, biochemistry and chemistry, alchemy, dental medicine, legal medicine, physiology, dental medicine, legal medicine, physiology, psychiatry, plastic surgery, surgery, zoology, ms collections, which incl the Harvard Medical Archives, probably the strongest in America.

MA —HARVARD MEDICAL SCHOOL, Schering Foundation Library of Health Care, 643 Huntington Ave, Boston, 02115. Anne Alach, Librn
Holdings: Vols 2926 Cat
Budget: $60,000

MA —NEW ENGLAND BAPTIST HOSPITAL, Medical Staff Library, 91 Parker Hill Ave, Boston, 02120. Paul E Woodard, Librn
Holdings: Cat
Budget: ($17,487)
Notes: No photocopying.

MA —TUFTS UNIVERSITY, Health Sciences Library, 136 Harrison Ave, Boston, 02111. Elizabeth K Eaton, Dir
Holdings: Vols (91,252) Cat Slides Phonorecords Audiotapes Videotapes Microforms
Budget: ($220,055)
Notes: Incl 219 titles, 4 journal titles, 653 videotapes, 3104 microfilms, 7027 microcards, and 1051 serials.

MA —US VETERANS ADMINISTRATION MEDICAL CENTER, Medical Library, 150 S Huntington Ave, Jamaica Plain, Boston, 02130. Patricia J McGrath, Chief Librn
Holdings: Vols (5702) Cat
Notes: Incl health care, surgery, neurology. 400 journal subscriptions, 5000 bound volumes.

MA —MOUNT AUBURN HOSPITAL, Health Sciences Library, 330 Mount Auburn St, Cambridge, 02138. Cherie Haitz, Librn
Holdings: Vols (3000) Cat Audiotapes Videotapes
Notes: Incl 300 periodical subscriptions.

MA —SAINT ANNE'S HOSPITAL, Saint Anne's Medical Library, 795 Middle St, Fall River, 02722. Elaine Crites, Librn
Holdings: Vols 1000 Cat
Budget: $6500

MA —LAWRENCE GENERAL HOSPITAL, Health Sciences Library, One General St, Lawrence, 01842. Carmel Gran, Librn
Holdings: Vols 1500 Cat Slides Audiotapes Videotapes 16mm Films Filmstrips
Budget: $18,000

MA —INSTRUMENTATION LABORATORY, Library, 113 Hartwell Ave, Lexington, 02173. Jacqueline R Kates, Librn
Holdings: Vols (6000) Cat Microforms

MA —BERKSHIRE MEDICAL CENTER, Medical Library, 725 North St, Pittsfield, 01201. Jutta Luhde, Medical Librn
Holdings: Vols (15,000) Cat
Notes: Medicine and allied health sciences.

MA —US DEPT OF HEALTH, EDUCATION & WELFARE, Public Health Service, FDA Winchester Engineering Analytical Center, 109 Holton St, Winchester, 01890. Lisa Leone, Librn
Holdings: Vols (3000) Mss Maps Audiotapes

MI —CATHERINE MCAULEY HEALTH CENTER, Riecker Memorial Library, 5301 E Huron River Drive, Ann Arbor, 48106. Metta T Lansdale, Jr, Librn
Holdings: Vols 4000 Cat

MI —WARNER-LAMBERT/PARKE-DAVIS, Research Library, 2800 Plymouth Rd, Ann Arbor, 48106. Katherine C Owen, Mgr, Library Services
Holdings: Vols (27,977) Cat

MI —UNIVERSITY OF MICHIGAN, Alfred Taubman Medical Library, 1135 E Catherine St, Ann Arbor, 48109. L Yvonne Wulff, Head
Holdings: Vols (260,300) Cat
Budget: ($438,000)

MI —HARPER-GRACE HOSPITALS, Grace Hospital Div, Oscar Leseure Professional Library, 18700 Myers Rd, Detroit, 48235. Frances Phillips, Chief Librn; Mary A Dery, Asst Librn
Holdings: Vols 8000 Cat Slides Microforms

MI —METROPOLITAN HOSPITAL, Medical Library, 1800 Tuxedo, Detroit, 48206. Carole M Gilbert, Dir
Holdings: Vols 5000 Cat Slides Audiotapes Microforms

MI —SAINT JOHN HOSPITAL, Medical Library, 22101 Moross Rd, Detroit, 48236. Marie K Bolanos, Dir
Holdings: Vols 5700 Cat Slides Videotapes Audiotapes

MI —WAYNE STATE UNIVERSITY, Vera Parshall Shiffman Medical Library, 4325 Brush St, Detroit, 48201. Faith Van Toll, Acting Head Librn
Holdings: Vols (158,612)
Budget: ($381,153)
Notes: Resource Library in Greater Midwest Regional Medical Library Network Program.

MI —SAINT MARY'S HOSPITAL, Library, 200 Jefferson SE, Grand Rapids, 49503. Mary A Hanson, Librn
Holdings: Vols (10,789) Cat
Budget: ($56,000)

MI —THE UPJOHN COMPANY, Corporate Technical Library, 301 Henrietta St, Kalamazoo, 49001. Lorraine Schulte, Manager
Holdings: Cat Microform Audiotapes Videotapes Books Journals

MI —EDWARD W SPARROW HOSPITAL, Medical Library, 1215 E Michigan Ave, PO Box 30480, Lansing, 48909. Doris H Asher, Medical Librn
Holdings: Vols (1800) Cat Audiotapes Videotapes
Budget: ($10,000)
Notes: Hospital employees and health sciences professional only.

MI —MOUNT CLEMENS GENERAL HOSPITAL, Byron H Stuck Medical Library, 1000 Harrington Blvd, Mount Clemens, 48043. Lynne L Coles, Librn; Kaye Roels, LTA
Holdings: Vols 2500 Cat Slides Audiotapes

MEDICINE (cont.)

Videotapes Journals
Budget: $58,000
Notes: Emphasis on clinical medicine.

MN —GOLDEN VALLEY HEALTH
CENTER, Medical Library, 4101 Golden
Valley Rd, Golden Valley, 55422. Carol
Nordky, Librn
Holdings: Vols 700 Cat Audiotapes
Budget: $1000
Notes: Incl 200 audiotapes.

MN —HENNEPIN COUNTY MEDICAL
CENTER, Health Sciences Library, 701
Park Ave, Minneapolis, 55416. Judith
Stanke, Medical Librn
Holdings: Vols (27,000) Cat Slides
Audiotapes Videotapes
Budget: ($150,000)

MN —UNIVERSITY OF MINNESOTA, Bio-
Medical Library, Diehl Hall, Minneapolis,
55455. Gertrude Foreman, Acting Dir
Holdings: Vols (263,361)
Budget: ($500,000)

MN —MAYO MEDICAL LIBRARY,
Rochester, 55905. Jack D Key, Dir
Holdings: Vols (244,000) Cat Maps Pix
Slides Microforms
Notes: Research library for biomedical
sciences, with broadly based complete serial
holdings.

MN —BETHESDA LUTHERAN MEDICAL
CENTER, Medical-Nursing Library, 570
Capitol Blvd, Saint Paul, 55101. Eileen M
Erlandson, Librn
Holdings: Vols (4383) Cat Slides Audiotapes
Filmstrips
Budget: ($8630)
Notes: Incl 800 slides, 106 audiotapes and
30 filmstrips.

MN —3M COMPANY, 3M Center, Riker
Laboratories, Saint Paul, 55101.
Holdings: Vols (6100) Cat
Budget: ($13,000)
Notes: Covers medical and pharmaceutical
chemistry and medical botany. Incl 2600
books (175 drug directories) and 3500 bound
journal vols.

MO —TRINITY LUTHERAN HOSPITAL,
Florence L Nelson Memorial Library, 3030
Baltimore, Kansas City, 64108. Cami L
Loucks, Dir
Holdings: Vols 7000 Cat Slides
Phonorecords Audiotapes Videotapes 16mm
Films Filmstrips Microforms
Notes: Incl 400 slides on nursing. Separate
AV catalog. Subscriber MEDLINE.

MO —UNIVERSITY OF MISSOURI-
KANSAS CITY, Health Sciences Library,
2411 Holmes St, Kansas City, 64108.
Marilyn Sullivan, Chief Medical Librn
Holdings: Vols (60,000) Cat Journals Slides
Audiotapes Videotapes
Budget: ($111,939)

MO —SAINT JOSEPH PUBLIC LIBRARY,
Tenth & Felix Sts, Saint Joseph, 64501.
Dorothy Sanborn Elliott, Dir
Holdings: Vols 3000 Cat
Budget: $3000
Notes: Medicine and health.

MO —SAINT JOSEPH STATE HOSPITAL,
Professional Library, 3400 Frederick Ave,
Box 263, Saint Joseph, 64502. Martha
Goodding, Librn
Holdings: Vols (3000) Cat Slides
Phonorecords Audiotapes 16mmo Films
Filmstrips Videotapes

MO —SAINT JOHN'S SCHOOL OF
NURSING LIBRARY, 1930 S National
Ave, Springfield, 65804. Marty Osredker,
Librn
Holdings: Vols 5200 Cat Audiotapes
Microforms
Budget: $5000
Notes: Nursing library with emphasis on
nursing, medicine and allied health.

NE —UNIVERSITY OF NEBRASKA-
LINCOLN, C Y Thompson Library, East
Campus, Lincoln, 68583. Lyle Schreiner,
Librn
Holdings: Vols (220,000) Cat
Notes: Agriculture, with major strength in
entomology, agronomy, and animal science;
medicine; veterinary medicine; and home
economics.

NE —US VETERANS ADMINISTRATION
HOSPITAL, Library, 600 S 70 St, Lincoln,
68510.
Holdings: Vols 1859 Cat Slides Audiotapes
Videotapes 16mm Films Microforms
Budget: $20,000
Notes: Incl 3277 periodical vols, 622 vols on
microfilm. Medline service.

NE —UNIVERSITY OF NEBRASKA
MEDICAL CENTER, Library, 42 & Dewey
Ave, Omaha, 68105. Robert M Braude, Dir
Holdings: Vols (196,313)
Budget: ($320,000)
Notes: Serves the Colleges of Medicine,
Nursing, Pharmacy, and the School of Allied
Health Professions; the Hospital and Clinics;
and several research institutes with a
collection that is broad in scope and both
current and retrospective.

NH —DARTMOUTH COLLEGE, Dartmouth-
Hitchcock Medical Center, Dana Biomedical
Library, Hanover, 03756. Shirley J Grainger,
Librn
Holdings: Vols (143,611) Cat Mss Pix Slides
Phonorecords Audiotapes Videotapes 16mm
Films Filmstrips Microforms
Budget: ($280,000)
Notes: Medicine and allied subjects; AV
collection of about 12,000 items. Separate
serials catalog available on microfilm or as
computer printout.

NJ —EAST ORANGE GENERAL
HOSPITAL, Library, 300 Central Ave, East
Orange, 07019. Joann Mehalick, Dir of
Library Services
Holdings: Vols (1500) Cat Videotapes

NJ —MOUNTAINSIDE HOSPITAL, Frank A
Assmann Memorial Library, Bay & Highland
Aves, Montclair, 07042. Patricia Regenberg,
Dir, Medical Library
Holdings: Vols 4200 Cat Slides Audiotapes
Videotapes
Budget: $22,000

NJ —NEWARK BETH ISRAEL, Medical
Center, Dr V Parsonnet Memorial Library,
201 Lyons Ave, Newark, 07112. Lillian
Bernstein, Librn
Holdings: Slides Audiotapes
Budget: $25,000
Notes: Collection incl surgery, pediatrics,
research, radiology, and anesthesiology.

NJ —SAINT MICHAEL'S MEDICAL
CENTER, Aquinas Medical Library, 268
High St, Newark, 07102. Betty L Garrison,
Dir; Valerie Manuel, Library Asst
Holdings: Vols (4500) Cat
Notes: Primarily bound journals, 1958-date.

NJ —UNIVERSITY OF MEDICINE AND
DENTISTRY OF NEW JERSEY, George F
Smith Library of the Health Sciences, 100
Bergen St, Newark, 07103. Philip
Rosenstein, Dir of Libraries
Holdings: Vols (110,000) Cat Slides
Audiotapes Videotapes 8mm Films
Filmstrips Microforms
Budget: ($380,880)
Notes: There is a separate a/v catalog
available, arranged by main entry and incl a
tracings index. Incl 70,648 slides, 19,298
microforms, 395 8mm films, 2150
audiotapes.

NJ —BERGEN PINES COUNTY HOSPITAL,
Medical Library, E Ridgewood Ave,
Paramus, 07652. Victoria Gonzalez, Medical
Librn
Holdings: Vols 1200 Cat Audiotapes
Notes: Library not open to public.

NJ —RUTGERS, THE STATE UNIVERSITY
OF NEW JERSEY, Library of Science &
Medicine, PO Box 1029, Piscataway, 08854.
Frank Polach, Dir
Holdings: Vols (275,000) Cat Maps

NJ —BECTON, DICKINSON & CO,
Corporate Library/Information Center,
Rutherford, 07070. Lynda M Wiseman,
Corporate Librn
Holdings: Vols (3500) Cat Microforms
Notes: Open to the public by appointment
and ILL.

NJ —NEW JERSEY DEPT OF HEALTH,
Library, CN 360, Trenton, 08625. Cathy A
Stout, Librn
Holdings: Vols (7000) // Cat Per
Microforms
Budget: $22,000

NM —UNIVERSITY OF NEW MEXICO,
Medical Center Library, North Campus,
Albuquerque, 87131. Erika Love, Dir
Notes: Health sciences collection, principally
medicine, but incl nursing, pharmacy, and
allied health sciences, in book, journal, and
multimedia formats. Library holdings include
33,427 book titles; 37,266 vols; 2,260
periodical subscriptions; 71,303 bound vols.

†NM —UNIVERSITY OF NEW MEXICO,
Medical Center Library, Albuquerque,
87131. Beatrice Kovacs, Chief, Collections
and Resource Development
Notes: Concern is health care and health
services in New Mexico; medicine and
medicine men of Indian tribes of the
Southwest; and history of medicine and
health in the Southwest.

NM —NEW MEXICO STATE HOSPITAL,
Ella P Kief Memorial Library, Hot Spring
Blvd, PO Box 1388, Las Vegas, 87701.
Hazel Hurley, Librn
Holdings: Vols (5000) Cat
Budget: ($2500)
Notes: Partially cataloged.

NM —UNIVERSITY OF CALIFORNIA, Los
Alamos National Laboratory, Libraries, PO
Box 1663, MSP 362, Los Alamos, 87545. J
Arthur Freed, Head Librn
Holdings: Vols (800,000) Cat Films
Microforms
Budget: ($700,000)
Notes: Incl 500,000 classified and
unclassified reports. There are 25 branch
libraries and a central collection. The
Medical Library contains about 40,000 vols
in the areas of biomedical research.

NY —NEW YORK STATE LIBRARY,
Medical Library, Albany, 12224. Christina
Bain, Librn
Notes: 71,000 titles in health sciences.

NY —US VETERANS ADMINISTRATION
HOSPITAL, Medical Library, 113 Holland
Ave, Albany, 12208. John Connors, Librn
Holdings: Vols 2600 Cat Slides Audiotapes
Videotapes Microforms

NY —ALBERT EINSTEIN COLLEGE OF
MEDICINE, D Samuel Gottesman Library,
1300 Morris Park Ave, Bronx, 10461.
Charlotte K Lindner, Dir

NY —US VETERANS ADMINISTRATION
HOSPITAL, Medical Library, 130 W
Kingsbridge Rd, Bronx, 10468. Margaret M
Kinney, Chief Librn
Holdings: Vols (23,000) Cat
Notes: No photocopying.

NY —BAPTIST MEDICAL CENTER OF
NEW YORK, Alyn M Steinhardt Library,
2749 Linden Blvd, Brooklyn, 11208. Ana
McBean, Librn
Holdings: Vols (150) Cat Slides
Phonorecords Audiotapes 16mm Films
Filmstrips

†NY —MEDICAL RESEARCH LIBRARY
OF BROOKLYN, Academy of Medicine of
Brooklyn & The State University of New
York Downstate Medical Center, 450
Clarkson St, Brooklyn, 11203. Kenneth E
Moody, Dir
Holdings: Vols Cat Microforms
Notes: Described in Draper, Wesley:
"Merger in Brooklyn: The Academy of
Medicine and the Downstate Medical Center
Libraries. History of the Academy of
Medicine of Brooklyn Library," *Bulletin of
the Medical Library Association,* 51:158-175
(April) 1963; and, Kovacs, Helen: "Merger
in Brooklyn: The Academy of Medicine and
the Downstate Medical Center Libraries.
Present and Future Plans," *Bulletin of the
Medical Library Association* 51:176-180
(April) 1963. Contains 241,548 volumes and
1660 current periodicals. One of the largest
medical school libraries in the US.

NY —BUFFALO GENERAL HOSPITAL, A
H Aaron Medical Library, 100 High St,
Buffalo, 14203. Wentsing Liu, Medical Librn
Holdings: Vols 3000 Cat Slides Audiotapes
Videotapes Videodiscs
Budget: $30,000

NY —ERIE COUNTY MEDICAL CENTER,
Medical Library, 462 Grider St, Buffalo,
14215. Anthony Ciko, Sr Medical Librn
Holdings: Vols (13,000) Cat Slides
Audiotapes Videotapes
Budget: ($42,000)

NY —STATE UNIVERSITY OF NEW
YORK, COLLEGE AT BUFFALO, Health

MEDICINE (cont.)

Sciences Library, Stockton Kimball Tower, Buffalo, 14214. C K Huang, Dir
Holdings: Vols (222,108) Cat
Budget: ($493,931)

NY —MARY IMOGENE BASSETT HOSPITAL, Medical Library, Copperstown, 13326. Wendy Rice, Librn
Holdings: Vols (30,000) Cat

NY —STATE UNIVERSITY OF NEW YORK, STONY BROOK, Health Sciences Library, PO Box 66, East Setauket, 11733.
Holdings: Uncat

NY —BOOTH MEMORIAL MEDICAL CENTER, Health Education Library, Main St at Booth Memorial Ave, Flushing, 11355. Rita Maier, Library Dir
Holdings: Vols (3000) Cat Audiotapes
Notes: Incl 7000 bound journals; software slide tape programs.

NY —FLUSHING HOSPITAL & MEDICAL CENTER, Medical Library, Parsons Blvd & 45 Ave, Flushing, 11355. Maria Czechowicz, Dir
Holdings: Vols (5741) Cat Audiotapes
Budget: ($11,000)

NY —NASSAU ACADEMY OF MEDICINE, John N Shell Medical Library, 1200 Stewart Ave, Garden City, 11530. Mary L Westermann, Librn
Holdings: Vols 40,000 Cat Audiotapes
Budget: $100,000
Notes: Approx 95 percent journals. Also incl 1250 audiotapes.

NY —SUFFOLK ACADEMY OF MEDICINE, Health Sciences Library, 850 Veterans Memorial Highway, Hauppauge, 11788. Isabel V Hathorn, Dir
Holdings: Vols (13,000) Cat Videotapes Microforms

NY —NASSAU COUNTY DEPARTMENT OF HEALTH, Division of Laboratories & Research, 209 Main St, Hempstead, 11550. Madeline Burston, Librn; Beatrice R Sewald, Asst Librn
Holdings: Vols (4076) Cat Mss Slides Microforms

NY —CORNELL UNIVERSITY, New York State College of Veterinary Medicine, Flower Veterinary Library, Ithaca, 14853. Susanne Whitaker, Librn
Holdings: Vols (74,000) Cat
Notes: Veterinary college library; incl biomedical publications as well as purely veterinary titles.

NY —NORTHERN WESTCHESTER HOSPITAL CENTER, Health Sciences Library, Mount Kisco, 10549. Nona C Willoughby, Librn
Notes: Core Collection: Over 1500 medical and nursing monographs and texts, primarily published within last five years. Subscribe to over 120 journals, bound journal vols kept for 10 years. MEDLARS online service. Audiodigests cassettes, six specialties, kept 5 years.

NY —MEDICAL LETTER, Library, 56 Harrison St, New Rochelle, 10801. Donna Goodstein, Librn
Holdings: Vols (1000) Cat
Budget: $5000
Notes: No separate catalog or index. Main holdings are in medical journals. Book collection consists of standard texts in medicine, pharmacology and therapeutics, plus many on specific drugs and adverse effects and interactions of drugs. Library is maintained primarily for in-house use.

NY —CABRINI MEDICAL CENTER, Bazzini Memorial Library, 227 E 19 St, New York, 10003. Jeanne Becker, Medical Librn
Holdings: Vols 8000 Cat Slides Audiotapes Videotapes 16mm Films Filmstrips
Budget: ($80,000)

NY —COLUMBIA UNIVERSITY LIBRARIES, Health Sciences Library, 701 W 168 St, New York, 10032. Rachael K Goldstein, Librn
Holdings: Vols 380,000 Cat
Notes: Restricted. 3300 current subscriptions, 3100 audiovisuals.

NY —CORNELL UNIVERSITY MEDICAL COLLEGE, Samuel J Wood Library, 1300 York Ave, New York, 10021. Erich

Meyerhoff, Dir
Holdings: Vols (9000) Cat Films
Notes: All aspects of muscle diseases.

NY —MUSCULAR DYSTROPHY ASSOCIATION, 810 Seventh Ave, New York, 10019. Marianthe Pappas, Librn
Holdings: Vols 8770 Cat
Budget: $55,000
Notes: All phases of muscular diseases. Incl some films.

NY —NEW YORK ACADEMY OF MEDICINE, Library, 2 E 103 St, New York, 10029. Brett A Kirkpatrick, Librn
Holdings: Vols 182,000 Cat
Notes: One of the strongest collections of clinical medical literature, the history of medicine, medical education, public health, and all paramedical subjects. Incl 482,000 pamphlets and 4000 serials currently received.

NY —NEW YORK UNIVERSITY, MEDICAL CENTER, Medical Library, 550 First Ave, New York, 10016. Gilbert J Clausman, Librn
Holdings: Vols (143,000) Cat Microforms
Budget: ($929,000)
Notes: Also over 11,000 microforms.

NY —SOUTH NASSAU COMMUNITIES HOSPITAL, Jules Redish Memorial Medical Library, 2445 Oceanside Rd, Oceanside, 11572. Claire Joseph, Dir
Holdings: Vols (750) Cat
Budget:
Notes: Incl (6500) bound journals.

NY —GENESEE HOSPITAL, Stabins Health Sciences Library, 224 Alexander St, Rochester, 14607. Sally M Gerling, Librn
Holdings: Vols 4000 Cat

NY —UNIVERSITY OF ROCHESTER, School of Medicine and Dentistry, Edward G Miner Library, 601 Elmwood Ave, Rochester, 14642. Lucretia McClure, Medical Librn; Janet Brady Berk, History of Medicine Librn
Holdings: Vols (185,000) Cat
Notes: The Edward G Miner Library serves the School of Medicine & Dentistry, the School of Nursing, and Strong Memorial Hospital. The collection encompasses all the biomedical fields, nursing and dental research, and is designed to serve the teaching, patient care and research needs of persons in the Medical Center. The Library subscribes to more than 2900 current journals and serials, has an excellent reference collection and an extensive collection of rare and historical works in medicine and nursing.
See also entry under Nurses and Nursing - History

NY —MERCY HOSPITAL, Medical Library, 1000 N Village Ave, Rockville Centre, 11570. Carol Reid, Librn
Holdings: Vols (2150) Cat
Budget: ($18,580)
Notes: Incl 1300 audiotapes.

NY —STATE UNIVERSITY OR NEW YORK, UPSTATE MEDICAL CENTER, Library, 766 Irving Ave, Syracuse, 13210. Evelyn L Hoey, Library Dir
Holdings: Vols (138,000) Cat Monographs Ser Pamphlets Mss Slides Phonorecords Audiotapes Videotapes 16mm Films Microforms
Budget: ($266,900)
Notes: Comprehensive collection of basic, experimental and clinical medical science books and journals. Incl medical museum pieces. Collection incl 46,219 vols, 92 monographs, 741 serials, 1115 pamphlets, 127 mss, 12,955 microform pieces, 601 audiocassettes, 87 mixed media packages, 70 motion pictures, 96 phono discs, 41,500 slides, 7 video discs, and 405 videotapes.

NY —REVLON HEALTH CARE GROUP, Information Services, One Scarsdale Ave, Tuckahoe, 10707. Rena Radovich, Manager
Holdings: Cat
Notes: Book vols & periodicals.

NY —WESTCHESTER COUNTY MEDICAL CENTER, Health Sciences Library, Valhalla, 10595. Charlene Sikorski, Medical Librn
Holdings: Vols (12,000) Cat

NY —WILLARD PSYCHIATRIC CENTER, Medical Library, Willard, 14588. Helen Bunting, Chief Library Services
Holdings: Vols (2078) Cat Audiotapes

NC —UNIVERSITY OF NORTH CAROLINA, CHAPEL HILL, Health Sciences Library, 223 H, Chapel Hill, 27514. Samuel Hitt, Dir
Holdings: Vols (200,000) Cat Slides Journals Audiotapes Videotapes Microforms
Budget: ($560,000)

NC —MERCY SCHOOL OF NURSING, Library, 1921 Vail Ave, Charlotte, 28207. Barbara Duval, Librn
Holdings: Vols (4600) Cat Audiotapes
Budget: $3500
Notes: Incl cassettes, charts, filmstrips, models; also, motion pictures, transparencies, x-ray sets (122 titles, 60 periodicals currently received). On-site use only to users not affiliated with Mercy School of Nursing, or Mercy Hospital, both in Charlotte, North Carolina.

NC —NORTH CAROLINA DEPT OF HUMAN RESOURCES, Div of Health Services, Public Health Library, PO Box 2091, Raleigh, 27602. Elnora H Turner, Librn
Holdings: Vols (15,000) Cat

NC —R J REYNOLDS TOBACCO CO, Scientific Information Services Library, Bowman Gray Technical Center, BGTC 611-12/205, Winston-Salem, 27102. Nellie W Sizemore, Librn
Holdings: Vols 2000 Cat

ND —SAINT LUKE'S HOSPITAL, Medical Library, Fifth St at Mills Ave, Fargo, 58122. Marcia Stephens, Dir
Holdings: Vols (3300) Cat Slides Audiotapes Videotapes 16mm Films Filmstrips

ND —US VETERANS ADMINISTRATION CENTER, Medical Library, 21 Ave N & Elm St, Fargo, 58102. Glenn Hasse, Chief Librn
Holdings: Vols 1910 Cat Slides Audiotapes Videotapes
Notes: Incl 1350 bound periodical vols. Plus microfilm.

ND —UNIVERSITY OF NORTH DAKOTA, Harley E French Medical Library, Grand Forks, 58202. David W Boilard, Dir; Lila Pedersen, Asst Dir
Holdings: Vols (56,000) Cat
Budget: ($206,000)
Notes: 1075 current periodical subscriptions.

OH —AULTMAN HOSPITAL SCHOOL OF NURSING, Library, 2614 Sixth St SW, Canton, 44710. Violet Russell, Librn
Holdings: Vols 1220 Cat
Budget: ($2800)

OH —CHRIST HOSPITAL INSTITUTE OF MEDICAL RESEARCH, Research Library, 2141 Auburn Ave, Cincinnati, 45219. Lisa L McCormick, Research Librn
Holdings: Vols 16,000
Budget: $36,000

OH —JEWISH HOSPITAL, Medical Library, 3200 Burnet Ave, Cincinnati, 45229. Barbara Lucas, Librn
Holdings: Vols 9034 Cat

OH —SAINT THOMAS INSTITUTE, Library, 1842 Madison Rd, Cincinnati, 45206. Sister M Virgil Ghering, O P Librn
Holdings: Vols 5800 Cat
Budget: ($39,878)

OH —UNIVERSITY OF CINCINNATI MEDICAL CENTER LIBRARIES, Health Sciences Library, 231 Bethesda Ave, Cincinnati, 45267. Nancy M Lorenzi, Dir
Holdings: Vols 113,050 Cat
Notes: In 1974, the Libraries of the College of Medicine and the Cincinnati General Hospital merged to form the Health Sciences Library. The Collections cover the medical sciences in the broadest sense: medicine, pharmacy, health care administration, and all clinical-medical specialties. The Media Resources Center is housed on the G Level of the Health Sciences Library and contains 2790 titles in various media (audiocassettes, filmstrips, slides, videocassettes, etc). Collection incl 43,920 monographs and 69, 130 journals.

OH —CLEVELAND MEDICAL LIBRARY ASSOCIATION/CASE WESTERN RESERVE UNIVERSITY, Cleveland Health Sciences Library, Historical Division, Allen Memorial Medical Library, 11000 Euclid Ave, Cleveland, 44106. Glen Jenkins, Rare Book Librarian & Archivist
Holdings: Vols 22,000 Cat Mss Maps Pix
Notes: Incl 15,000 historical vols, 6000 in

MEDICINE (cont.)

the supporting collection. Incl about 100 16th-18th century titles. Strength of collection: diseases epidemiology, anatomy, surgery, medicine, obstetrics, gynecology, pediatrics and yellow fever. Incl also medical Americana, listed in Robert B Austin *Early American Medical Imprints,* (1668-1820 Washington, DC, HEW Public Health Service, 1961) and ca 7000 19th century works. Total Americana collection also incl journals (not counted), mss and archives (900 linear ft) and 5000 pictures, especially of the Western Reserve. Anatomical works discussed in I Ebner and G Jenkins *Skeletons in Our Closet,* (Cleveland, Cleveland Health Sciences Library, 1983).

OH —MOUNT SINAI MEDICAL CENTER, George H Hays Library, University Circle, Cleveland, 44106. Pamela Alderman, Librn
Holdings: Vols (6000) Cat Mss Slides Phonorecords Filmstrips Audiotapes
Notes: Bound journals 4000; incl on line reference service with Dialog database.

OH —OHIO COLLEGE OF PODIATRIC MEDICINE LIBRARY, 10515 Carnegie Ave, Cleveland, 44106. Judy Cowell, Librn
Holdings: Vols 1000 Slides Audiotapes Videotapes
Notes: Incl podiatric medicine.

OH —MIAMI VALLEY HOSPITAL, Memorial Medical Library, 1 Wyoming St, Dayton, 45409. Margaret C Hardy, Dir
Holdings: Vols 40,000 Cat Pix Slides Audiotapes Videotapes
Budget: ($200,000)

OH —SAINT ELIZABETH MEDICAL CENTER, Health Sciences Library, 601 Miami Blvd W, Dayton, 45408. Ann Lewis, Librn
Holdings: Vols (13,000) Cat Slides Audiotapes Filmstrips

OK —SAMUEL ROBERTS NOBLE FOUNDATION, Biomedical Div Library, PO Box 2180, Ardmore, 73401. Loretta Cook, Librn
Holdings: Vols (11,000) Cat Microforms
Budget: ($32,600)
Notes: Biomedical literature.

OK —UNIVERSITY OF OKLAHOMA, Health Sciences Center, Library, 1000 Stanton L Young Blvd, PO Box 26901, Oklahoma City, 73190. C M Thompson, Jr, Dir
Holdings: Vols (155,434) Cat Slides Audiotapes Videotapes 16mm Films Microforms
Budget: ($374,690)
Notes: Incl (750) vols on the health and well-being of the American Indian, historically and currently.

OK —UNIVERSITY OF OKLAHOMA, Tulsa Medical College, Library, 2808 S Sheridan, Tulsa, 74129. Janet Minnerath, Dir

OR —EMANUEL HOSPITAL, Library, 2801 N Gantebein Ave, Portland, 97227. Katherin Rouzie, Librn
Holdings: Vols 4000 Cat Audiotapes
Notes: The library serves a 525-bed acute care hospital. Its main emphasis is medicine, with accompanying collections of nursing and other allied health subject areas. It includes 150 journal subscriptions and 3 audio-digest subscriptions.

OR —GOOD SAMARITAN HOSPITAL & MEDICAL CENTER, Health Sciences Library, 1015 NW 22 Ave, Portland, 97210. Melvina W Stell, Dir of Libraries
Holdings: Vols 7000 Cat Videotapes Audiotapes
Budget: ($90,000)

OR —OREGON HEALTH SCIENCES, University Libraries, PO Box 573, Portland, 97207. James E Morgan, Dir
Holdings: Vols (178,373) Cat Mss Pix Slides Audiotapes Videotapes Microforms
Notes: Libraries incl a medical/nursing library and a separate dental library. Medical history collection of books and artifacts emphasizes the Pacific Northwest.

PA —ALTOONA HOSPITAL, Glover Memorial Library, Howard Ave & Seventh St, Altoona, 16603. Caryn J Carr, Dir of Library; Bonnie K Lantz, Librn
Holdings: Vols (7475) Cat Pix Slides

Phonorecords Audiotapes Videotapes 16mm Films Filmstrips Microforms
Budget: ($14,000)
Notes: Incl 141 pictures, 1274 slides,, 94 records, 1193 audiotapes, films, 116 filmstrips, 28 microforms, 78 filmloops, and 269 journals.

PA —BRYN MAWR HOSPITAL, Medical Library, Bryn Mawr, 19010. LD Gundry, Medical Librn
Holdings: Vols (8000) Cat
Budget: $30,000
Notes: 234 current journals.

PA —LANCASTER GENERAL HOSPITAL, Mueller Health Sciences Library, 555 N Duke St, Lancaster, 17604. Claudette Strohm, Librn
Holdings: Vols (4431) Cat Audiotapes Microforms

PA —SAINT JOSEPH HOSPITAL, Hospital Library, 250 College Ave, PO Box 3509, Lancaster, 17604. Eileen B Doudna, Librn
Holdings: Vols (3000) Cat Journals Videocassettes Filmstrips Slides

PA —OHIO VALLEY GENERAL HOSPITAL, Health Library, McKees Rocks, 15136. Mary G Evans, Librn
Holdings: Vols (1900) Cat Slides
Budget: ($3300)

PA —JAMESON MEMORIAL HOSPITAL, Library, W Garfield Ave, New Castle, 16105. Joan T Whitman, Librn
Holdings: Vols 253 Cat
Budget: $2500

PA —COLLEGE OF PHYSICIANS OF PHILADELPHIA, Library, 19 S 22 St, Philadelphia, 19103. Anthony Aguirre, Libr Dir
Holdings: Vols (316,223) Cat Mss Microforms
Budget: ($1,096,557)
Notes: Incl 13,515 pamphlets; 1435 mss; 326,367 reports, dissertations, and reprints. Strong historical and bibliographical collections, as well as current materials. Medical documentation service provides current alerting, incl abstracting, etc.

PA —FRANKLIN INSTITUTE LIBRARY, 20 & The Parkway, Philadelphia, 19103. Miriam Padusis, Dir; Charles Wilt, Readers Servs Librn
Holdings: Vols (300,000) Cat Maps Pix Microforms

PA —PENNSYLVANIA COLLEGE OF PODIATRIC MEDICINE, Charles E Krausz Library, Race at Eighth St, Philadelphia, 19107. John C Harris, Librn; Frances E Peters, Librn; Lisabeth M Holloway, Archivist
Holdings: Vols (15,000) Cat
Budget: $125,000
Notes: Emphasis on podiatry and chiropody. Numerous rare books in collection.

PA —PENNSYLVANIA HOSPITAL MEDICAL AND NURSING LIBRARIES, Eighth and Spruce Sts, Philadelphia, 19107. Caroline Morris, Librn
Holdings: Vols (9300)
Budget: ($15,000)
Notes: 20th century journals and current medical books. Strong collection of nursing journals. Some historical nursing textbooks and a good collection on the history of nursing.

PA —PHILADELPHIA COLLEGE OF OSTEOPATHIC MEDICINE, O J Snyder Memorial Library, Evans Hall, 4150 City Ave, Philadelphia, 19131. Shanker H Vyas, Dir of Libraries
Holdings: Vols (50,000) Cat Audiotapes Videotapes 16mm Films Microforms
Notes: Osteopathy and all medical fields. Osteopathy collection incl 387 books, 98 theses, 66 pamphlets and periodicals, 1103 audiotapes and 946 videotapes.

PA —TEMPLE UNIVERSITY, Health Sciences Center Library, Broad & Tioga Sts, Philadelphia, 19140. Ruth Diamond, Dir
Holdings: Vols (87,480) Cat Slides Microforms
Budget: ($340,950)

PA —UNIVERSITY OF PENNSYLVANIA, Van Pelt Library, Rare Books Collection, 34 & Walnut Sts, Philadelphia, 19104. Daniel Traister, Special Collections Librn
Holdings: Vols 600 Cat Mss
Notes: Incl 400 Elzevier Press Leyden disserations.

PA —UNIVERSITY OF PENNSYLVANIA, Bio-Medical Library, Johnson Pavilion/G2, Philadelphia, 19104. Eleanor Goodchild, Librn
Holdings: Vols (139,000) Cat Slides Audiotapes Videotapes

PA —ALLEGHENY GENERAL HOSPITAL, Health Sciences Library, 320 E North Ave, Pittsburgh, 15212. Jennifer Angier, Dir
Holdings: Vols 3000 Cat Audiotapes
Notes: Incl 8000 journal vols and 400 audiotapes and media items.

PA —EYE & EAR HOSPITAL OF PITTSBURGH, Blair-Lippincott Library, 230 Lothrop St, Pittsburgh, 15213. Bruce A Johnston, Medical Librn
Holdings: Vols (6000) Cat
Notes: Special emphasis on ophthalmology, otorhinolaryngology, audiology, and speech pathology.

PA —FORBES METROPOLITAN HEALTH CENTER, Library, 225 Penn Ave, Pittsburgh, 15221. Sue Reber, Librn
Holdings: Vols 6065 Cat Tapes
Budget: $10,552

PA —SAINT MARGARET MEMORIAL HOSPITAL, School of Nursing Library, 4631 Davison St, Pittsburgh, 15201. Dorothy D Schiff, Librn
Holdings: Vols 2300 Cat Slides Phonorecords Audiotapes Videotapes 16mm Films Filmstrips
Notes: Strong effort to buy everything in nursing. Developing archives and rare books (in nursing only).

PA —UNIVERSITY OF PITTSBURGH, Falk Library of the Health Professions, History of Medicine Collection, Scaife Hall, Pittsburgh, 15261. Jonathon Erlen, Cur
Holdings: Vols (13,500) Cat Pix
Budget: ($425,269)
Notes: Medicine, dentistry, nursing, pharmacy, public health, psychiatry materials, incl some rare books and 300 pamphlets on anesthesia.

PA —READING HOSPITAL & MEDICAL CENTER, Medical Library, Sixth & Spruce St, Reading, 19603. Melinda Robinson Paquette, Librn
Holdings: Vols (1500) Cat Slides Audiotapes Videotapes
Notes: Staff use only; open to public only by appointment. No photocopying. Incl 180 periodical subscriptions; 10,000 bound periodicals.

PA —MERCK SHARP & DOHME, Research Laboratories, Literature Resource Center, West Point, 19486. Evelyn W Armstrong, Dir, Literature Resource Centers
Holdings: Cat Microforms
Notes: Monographs (3000) and journals (15, 000 vols).

RI —NEWPORT HOSPITAL, Ina Mosher Health Sciences Library, Friendship St, Newport, 02840. Tosca N Carpenter, Librn
Holdings: Vols 4278 Cat Slides Phonorecords Audiotapes Filmstrips

RI —RHODE ISLAND MEDICAL SOCIETY, Library, 106 Francis St, Providence, 02903. Marion N Sabella, Librn
Holdings: Vols 50,000 Per Monographs
Notes: Also Davenport Collection (2111 vols) of extra-professional writings of physicians, books about physicians and medicine; Charles F Gormley Collection of medicolegal books; Charles Value Chapin Collection of scrapbooks (1883-1939), medals, portraits, etc; Collection of state medical society journals.

SC —BAPTIST MEDICAL CENTER, Amelia White Pitts Memorial Library, Taylor at Marion Sts, Columbia, 29220. Lois W Smith, Medical Librn
Holdings: Vols (3000) Cat

SC —SOUTH CAROLINA DEPT OF HEALTH & ENVIRONMENTAL CONTROL, Educational Resource Center, 2600 Bull St, Columbia, 29201. Michael Kronenfeld, Librn
Holdings: Vols 2000

SD —US VETERANS ADMINISTRATION CENTER, Medical Library, 2501 W 22, Sioux Falls, 57101. Lori Klein, Librn
Holdings: Vols 14,750 Cat Slides Audiotapes Videotapes 16mm Films Microforms
Budget: $47,000

MEDICINE (cont.)

†TN —SAINT THOMAS HOSPITAL, Health Sciences Library, Box 380, Nashville, 37202. Dee Platt, Dir
Holdings: Vols (2600) Cat Slides

TX —TEXAS MEDICAL ASSOCIATION, Memorial Library, 1801 N Lamar, Austin, 78701. Betty Afflerbach, Dir
Holdings: Vols 54,000 Cat Slides Audiotapes 16mm Films
Notes: Incl 256 films, bound vols, journals and books, 1300 audio cassettes, 230 slide cassettes, 185 video cassettes.

TX —SAINT PAUL HOSPITAL, C B Sacher Library, 5909 Harry Hines Blvd, Dallas, 75235. Barbara J Miller, Medical Librn; Michael Zimmerman, Library Asst
Holdings: Cat Audiotapes
Budget: $3000

TX —SANTA ROSA MEDICAL CENTER, Health Science Library, PO Box 7330 Sta A, San Antonio, 78285. Marjorie McFarland, Librn
Holdings: Vols (6500) Cat
Budget: ($5000)
Notes: Special emphasis on pediatrics and orthopedics. Incl 947 audiotapes. Access to Medline.

TX —SCOTT AND WHITE MEMORIAL HOSPITAL, Medical Library, 2401 S 31 St, Temple, 76501. Mary H Spoede, Librn
Holdings: Vols (29,697) Cat Maps Pix Audiotapes
Budget: ($69,590)

†UT —LDS HOSPITAL MEDICAL LIBRARY, 325 Eighth Ave, Salt Lake City, 84143. Terry L Heyer, Librn
Holdings: Vols (2200) Cat Slides Phonorecords Audiotapes Videotapes

VT —PUTNAM MEMORIAL HOSPITAL, Medical Library, 100 Hospital Dr, Bennington, 05201. Lynn Crandall, Library Coordinator
Holdings: Vols (1000) Cat Audiotapes
Notes: Incl 10,000 journals (earliest 1975) and 8 titles in audiotapes.

VT —UNIVERSITY OF VERMONT, Charles A Dana Medical Library, Given Bldg, Burlington, 05405. Ellen Nagle, Medical Librn
Holdings: Vols 72,610 Cat Slides Audiotapes Videotapes 16mm Films Filmstrips Microforms Videodiscs
Budget: $258,248
Notes: Resource Library in the Greater Northeastern Regional Medical Library Program.

†VA —VIRGINIA COMMONWEALTH UNIVERSITY/MEDICAL COLLEGE OF VIRGINIA, Tompkins-McCaw Library, Box 667, MCV Sta, Richmond, 23298. J Craig McLean, Asst Dir of University Libraries
Holdings: Vols (155,000) Cat Mss Microforms
Budget: ($281,200)
Notes: Graduate sciences (biomedical emphasis). All newly cataloged books and journals are reported in the *Abridged Book Catalog*. Citations are limited to main entry and two subject entries. The catalog is cumulated monthly in 42x microfiche format. A cumulated Union Catalog covering 6 years and parts of 5 library collections is in preparation.

VA —RICHMOND MEMORIAL HOSPITAL, Medical Library, 1300 Westwood Ave, Richmond, 23227. Lynn Turman, Librn
Holdings: Vols (7000) Cat Slides Phonorecords Audiotapes Videotapes 16mm Films Filmstrips
Budget: $14,000

WA —WASHINGTON STATE UNIVERSITY, Veterinary Medical & Pharmacy Library, 701 Wegner Hall, Pullman, 99164. Vicki F Croft, Head
Holdings: Vols (42,000) Cat Mss Microforms
Budget: ($146,667)

WA —CHILDREN'S ORTHOPEDIC HOSPITAL & MEDICAL CENTER, Medical Library, 4800 Sand Point Way NE, Seattle, 98105. Tamara A Turner, Librn
Notes: Specialize in pediatric texts and journals.

WA —SWEDISH HOSPITAL MEDICAL CENTER, Medical Library, 747 Summit Ave, Seattle, 98104.
Holdings: Vols (2072) Cat

WA —UNIVERSITY OF WASHINGTON LIBRARIES, Health Sciences Library, SB-55, Seattle, 98195. Gerald J Oppenheimer, Dir
Holdings: Vols (232,000) Cat Slides Audiotapes Microforms
Budget: ($550,000)

WA —CENTRAL WASHINGTON HOSPITAL, Rose A Heminger Health Sciences Library, PO Box 1887, Wenatchee, 98801. Jane Belt, Librn & Coordr of Continuing Education
Holdings: Cat Slides Phonorecords Audiotapes Videotapes 16mm Films Filmstrips
Budget: ($5000)
Notes: Incl 100 slide sets, 500 audiotapes, 100 videotapes, and 50 filmstrip programs.

WV —US VETERANS ADMINISTRATION HOSPITAL, Library, Clarksburg, 26301. Edward H Poletti, Librn
Holdings: Vols (1336)

WV —US VETERANS ADMINISTRATION HOSPITAL, Library, 1540 Spring Valley Dr, Huntington, 25704. Evelyn J Schaffer, Librn
Holdings: Vols (3700) Cat Slides Phonorecords Audiotapes Videotapes 16mm Films Filmstrips Microforms

WV —HERBERT J THOMAS MEMORIAL HOSPITAL, Medical Library, 4605 MacCorkle Ave SW, South Charleston, 25309. Glenna F Wolfe, Art/Medical Secretary
Holdings: Vols 540 Cat

WI —SACRED HEART HOSPITAL, Medical Library, 900 W Clairemont Ave, Eau Claire, 54701. Bruno Warner, Librn
Holdings: Vols (2006) Cat Slides Phonorecords Audiotapes Videotapes
Notes: Incl 212 audiotapes and 93 videotapes.

WI —MERCY HOSPITAL, Medical Library, 1000 Mineral Point, Janesville, 53545. Lois Zuehlke, Librn
Holdings: Vols (769) Cat Slides Phonorecords Audiotapes Videotapes 16mm Films Filmstrips
Budget: $1000

WI —KENOSHA MEMORIAL HOSPITAL, Health Sciences Library, 6308 Eighth Ave, Kenosha, 53140. Esther L Puhek, Librn
Holdings: Vols (1825) Cat Slides Audiotapes Videotapes
Notes: Incl 300 videotapes.

WI —MADISON GENERAL HOSPITAL, Memorial Medical Library, 202 S Park St, Madison, 53715. Dona Bowman, Librn; Glen Salter, Librn
Holdings: Vols 4000 Cat Slides Audiotapes Videotapes
Budget: $30,000

WI —UNIVERSITY OF WISCONSIN, MADISON, Wisconsin Regional Primate Research Center, Primate Center Library, 1223 Capitol Court, Madison, 53715. Lawrence Jacobsen, Librn
Holdings: Vols (15,000) Cat Pix
Notes: Research in reproductive physiology, neurosciences, and behavior. Extensive subject orientated primate reprint file, audiovisual collection on primates. Current research uses approximately 25 species of nonhuman primates. Publications: *Primate Library Report*: print and non-print editions, biomonthly.

WI —UNIVERSITY OF WISCONSIN, MADISON, W S Middleton Health Sciences Library, 1305 Linden Dr, Madison, 53706. Virginia Holtz, Dir
Holdings: Vols (200,000) Cat Pix Slides Audiotapes Videotapes Microforms

WI —UNIVERSITY OF WISCONSIN, MADISON, School of Pharmacy, F B Power Pharmaceutical Library, 425 N Charter St, Madison, 53706. Dolores Nemec, Librn
Holdings: Vols 33,290 Cat Microforms
Notes: Library incl and administers the unique national historical pharmaceutical collection known as the Kremers Reference Files, and various special historical collections—historical drug catalogs; historical college catalogs (pharmacy); the Kremers manuscript encyclopedia of historical pharmacy; pharmaceutical corporation reports; representative prescription booksof pharmacies; and the pharmaco-literary collection. These collections are regularly supplemented with new materials, but are not incl in the library's holdings statement. The special collections contain about 800 volumes in book form; the Kremers Reference Files presently consist of 360 legal-size file drawers; and the Kremers manuscript encyclopedia comprises 145 file boxes. The Kremers Reference Files--which contain materials from 1850 to date in the form of letters, laboratoryrecords, minute books of organizations, biographical sketches, prescriptions, pictures, pamphlets, circulars, reprints, broadsides, and other printed matter--provide detailed historical information mainly relating to pharmaceutical subjects. Published catalog: *Catalog of the F B Power Pharmaceutical Library, School of Pharmacy, University of Wisconsin, Madison, Wisconsin* (Boston: GK Hall, 1976), 4 vols.

WI —MARQUETTE UNIVERSITY, Memorial Library, 1415 W Wisconsin Ave, Milwaukee, 53233. Jay Kirk, Health Sciences Librn
Notes: Supports curriculum and research.

WI —SAINT MARY'S HOSPITAL, Memorial Library, 2323 N Lake Dr, Box 503, Milwaukee, 53201. Carolyn Barloga, Health Sciences Librn
Holdings: Vols (4474) Cat Slides Audiotapes Videotapes Filmstrips
Budget: ($25,000)

WI —UNIVERSITY OF WISCONSIN, MILWAUKEE, Library, Box 604, Milwaukee, 53201. William C Roselle, Dir
Holdings: Cat Microforms
Notes: Wisconsin Legislative Reference Bureau Clippings File. Special strength in a collection mostly of Wisconsin emphasis. 440 reels of 16mm micorfilm. A subject-chronological arrangement (approximately 1200 subjects covering the years from the 1890s through 1970) of pamphlets and a variety of fugitive materials and of clippings from national and Wisconsin newspapers, popular magazines and scholarly journals, and federal, state, and local government documents.

WI —WAUKESHA MEMORIAL HOSPITAL, Medical Staff Library, 725 American Ave, Waukesha, 53186. Linda A Oddon, Medical Librn
Holdings: Vols (3336) Cat Pix Audiotapes Videotapes
Budget: ($4919)

BC —UNIVERSITY OF BRITISH COLUMBIA, Vancouver General Hospital, Biomedical Branch Library, 700 West 10th Ave, Vancouver, V5Z 1L5, Can. George C Freeman, Head
Holdings: Vols (25,300) Cat
Budget: ($82,400)
Notes: Clinical medicine.

MB —UNIVERSITY OF MANITOBA, Medical Library, 770 Bannatyne Ave, Winnipeg, R3E 0W3, Can. Audrey M Kerr, Professor & Head Librn
Holdings: Vols 86,500 Cat Pix Audiotapes
Notes: Incl a section on the history of medicine and a small but valuable collection of rare books in the Ross Mitchell Room. 3600 audiotapes; 1500 serials.

ON —CANADA INSTITUTE FOR SCIENTIFIC & TECHNICAL INFORMATION, Mcntreal Rd, Ottawa, K1A 0S2, Can. Elmer V Smith, Dir
Holdings: Vols Microforms
Budget: ($17,000,000)
Notes: National collection for science in Canada. Excellent collection of serials and technical reports. Journals do not circulate. 14 Branch Libraries maintain subject collections in aeronautical engineering, astromy, biotechnology, building and construction, biology, chemistry, electrical engineering, energy, industrial materials, physics, marine biology, ocean engineering. Access to these collections is available via the central library. 2,300,000 reports, books, serials and conference proceedings; 1,600,000 of these are on microfiche.

ON —CANADIAN MEDICAL ASSOCIATION, Library, PO Box 8650, Ottawa, K1G 0G8, Can. Kathleen Beaudoin,

MEDICINE (cont.)

Librn
Holdings: Vols 4000 Uncat
Notes: Mainly medical journals.

ON —UNIVERSITY OF OTTAWA, Health
Sciences Library, 451 Smyth Road, Ottawa,
K1H 8L5, Can. Myra Owen, Librn
Holdings: Vols (70,000) Slides Audiotapes
Films Filmstrips
Budget: ($325,000)
Notes: This collection is made up of works
in support of clinical and research studies in
all branches of medicine, nursing and
kinanthropology. Incl 1500 periodicals.

ON —METROPOLITAN TORONTO
LIBRARY, Science & Technology Dept, 789
Yonge St, Toronto, M4W 2G8, Can.
Margaret Walshe, Head
Holdings: Vols (120,000) Cat VF
Notes: Most aspects of the science and
technology for the specialist, student and
particularly, the general public.

ON —SAINT MICHAEL'S HOSPITAL,
Health Science Library, 30 Bond St,
Toronto, M5B 1W8, Can. Anita Wong, Dir
Holdings: Vols (5100) Cat
Budget: ($80,000)

ON —SUNNYBROOK HOSPITAL, Health
Sciences Library, 2075 Bayview Ave,
Toronto, M4N 3M5, Can. Linda McFarlane,
Librn
Holdings: Vols (12,000) Cat Audiotapes
Videotapes
Budget: ($40,000)
Notes: Emphasis on clinical medicine; also
have nursing and hospital administration.

PQ —MCGILL UNIVERSITY, Medical
Library, 3655 Drummond St, Montreal,
H3G 1Y6, Can. Frances Groen, Librn
Holdings: Vols (176,000) Cat Slides
Audiotapes Videotapes
Notes: General medicine collection, covering
all phases of medicine; emphasis on
ophthalmology.

PQ —MCGILL UNIVERSITY, Osler Library,
3655 Drummond St, Montreal, H3G 1Y6,
Can. Philip M Teigen, Librn
Holdings: Vols (35,000) Cat Mss Pix Slides
Microforms
Notes: The Osler Library is a research
library in the history of medicine and allied
sciences. Its scope incl the history of medical
practice, medical sciences (eg anatomy,
pathology), medical specialities (eg
psycholoy, genetics, biochemistry), and
medical statistics, historical demography,
and medical institutions. Partial listing in
Bibliotheca Osleriana, 1929, reprinted 1969;
Library publishes *Osler Library Newsletter,*
free on request.

PQ —MCGILL UNIVERSITY, Nursing/Social
Work Library, 3506 University St, Montreal,
H3A 1Y1, Can. Wendy Patrick, Librn
Holdings: Vols (35,000) Cat

PQ —CENTRE HOSPITALIER, HOSPITAL
SAINT FRANCOIS D'ASSISSE, Medical
and Administrative Library, SFA 10, Rue de
l'Espinay, Quebec, G1L 3L5, Can. Ulric
Lefebvre, Bibliotechnicienne
Holdings: Vols 7219 Cat Slides Audiotapes
16mm Films Filmstrips

PQ —CENTRE HOSPITALIER SAINT
VINCENT DE PAUL, Bibliotheque
Medicale, 300 E rue King, Sherbrooke, J1G
1B1, Can. Gilberte Poirier, Bibliographer
Holdings: Vols 3842 Cat
Notes: 114 titles of periodicals.

SK —VICTORIA UNION HOSPITAL
MEDICAL LIBRARY, 1200 24 St W,
Prince Albert, S6V 5T4, Can. Joan I Ryan,
Dir of Medical Records
Holdings: Vols 448 Uncat
Budget: $1000

MEDICINE—APPARATUS see Medical Instruments and Apparatus

MEDICINE—BIOGRAPHY

AL —UNIVERSITY OF ALABAMA,
BIRMINGHAM, Lister Hill Library of the
Health Sciences, University Sta,
Birmingham, 35294. Richard B Fredericksen,
Dir

DE —UNIVERSITY OF DELAWARE, Hugh
M Morris Library, S College Ave, Newark,
19711. T Stuart Dick, Special Collections
Holdings: Cat Ms
Notes: The Unidel History of Chemistry
Collection. 60 percent of the collection deals
with chemistry prior to 1780. Particularly
strong in alchemical works incl some 6
alchemical mss. Also works on mining,
medicine and pharamcy. Notable chemical
pioneers of the 1780-1860 period are well
represented by such men as Lavoisier,
Avogardo, Chaptal, Davy, Faraday,
Fourcroy, Liebig and Volta. Majority of the
collection in French and Italian.

IL —AMERICAN MEDICAL
ASSOCIATION, Div of Library & Archival
Services, 535 N Dearborn St, Chicago,
60610. Arthur W Hafner, Dir
Holdings: Vols (130,000) Cat Mss Pix
Microforms
Notes: "One of world's most comprehensive
collections in sociology and economics of
medicine," some 150,000 items, 1964 to
date. Archival collection of materials relating
to history of AMA and its constituent
societies. Incl historical biographical resource
file on American physicians, incl obituary
data and genealogy.

IN —INDIANA UNIVERSITY, Lilly Library,
Seventh St, Bloomington, 47405. William R
Cagle, Librn
Holdings: Cat
Notes: First appearances in print of great
medical discoveries.

KY —UNIVERSITY OF LOUISVILLE,
Kornhauser Health Sciences Library, 520 S
Preston St, PO Box 35260, Louisville,
40292. Leonard M Eddy, Dir; Sherrill R
McConnell, Archivist
Holdings: Cat Mss Pix
Notes: Kentucky physicians and medical
hitory (pictures and mss). Over 10,000 pages
of source material compiled under WPA for
history of medicine in Kentucky, plus
collection of photographs of Kentucky
physicians. WPA material being microfilmed.
Partly cataloged.

MA —FRANCIS A COUNTWAY LIBRARY
OF MEDICINE, Boston Medical Library/
Harvard Medical Library, 10 Shattuck St,
Boston, 02115. C Robin LeSueur, Librn;
Richard J Wolfe, Cur, Rare Books &
Manuscripts
Holdings: Vols (500,000) Cat Mss Maps Pix
Microforms
Notes: Combines resources of the Harvard
Medical School and the Boston Medical
Library. Strong in serials and medical history
in all fields of medicine, incl incunabula,
non-medical books by doctors, travel books
by doctors. 500,000 medical dissertations
and theses. Special strength in all medical
subjects listed in this volume.

MN —UNIVERSITY OF MINNESOTA,
Owen H Wangensteen Historical Library of
Biology & Medicine, Diehl Hall,
Minneapolis, 55455. Judith Overmier, Cur
Holdings: Vols (35,000) Cat
Budget: ($80,000)
Notes: Pre-1900 only.

MN —MAYO MEDICAL LIBRARY, History
of Medicine Collection, Rochester, 55905.
Nancy R Hensel, Librn
Holdings: Vols (18,000) Cat Mss Maps Pix
Slides
Notes: The collection consists of over 18,000
vols, 6500 of which are considered source
material (rare or reprint editions of classics).
4308 items from Garrison-Morton are
available in the collection. Appropriate
bibliographies, biographies and histories of
medicine are a part of the collection. Fields
of collecting interest are anesthesiology,
dermatology, cardiology, neurology,
immunology and radiology. Eight medical
incunabula.

NH —DARTMOUTH COLLEGE, Dartmouth-
Hitchcock Medical Center, Dana Biomedical
Library, Hanover, 03756. Shirley J Grainger,
Librn
Holdings: Vols (6000) Cat Mss
Notes: Collection incl the Connor Collection
of Medical Classics, history of medicine, etc.
No photocopying.

OH —CLEVELAND MEDICAL LIBRARY
ASSOCIATION/CASE WESTERN

RESERVE UNIVERSITY, Cleveland Health
Sciences Library, Historical Division, Allen
Memorial Medical Library, 11000 Euclid
Ave, Cleveland, 44106. Glen Jenkins, Rare
Book Librarian & Archivist
Holdings: Vols 1200 Cat Mss Pix
Notes: Incl health science professionals,
Sigmund Freud, and naturalists.

OH —RUTHERFORD B HAYES LIBRARY,
1337 Hayes Ave, Fremont, 43420. Watt P
Marchman, Dir
Holdings: Vols 425 Cat
Notes: A 19th century medical library.

PA —LIBRARY COMPANY OF
PHILADELPHIA, 1314 Locust St,
Philadelphia, 19107. Edwin Wolf II, Librn;
Kenneth Finkel, Cur of Prints
Holdings: Vols 1000 Cat Mss Maps
Budget: ($25,000)
Notes: Early American books, pamphlets
and broadsides concerning popular and
professional medicine, to 1820. Of major
importance are books owned by Benjamin
Rush, Revolutionary-era doctor. Many of his
mss, though housed in the Historical Society
of Pennsylvania, remain the property of the
Library Company.

MEDICINE—EARLY WORKS TO 1800

AL —UNIVERSITY OF ALABAMA,
BIRMINGHAM, Reynolds Historical
Library, University Sta, Birmingham, 35294.
Mary Claire Britt, Cur
Holdings: Vols 9300 Cat Mss Maps Pix
Slides
Notes: Incl 9 ivory anatomical manikins.
One of the outstanding collections in the US
Bibliography: *Rare Books and Collection of
the Reynolds Historical Library* (University
of Alabama Press, 1968).

CA —UNIVERSITY OF CALIFORNIA, LOS
ANGELES, Biomedical Library, Center for
the Health Sciences, Los Angeles, 90024.
Alison Bunting, Acting Biomedical Librn;
Victoria Steele, Head, History & Special
Collections Div
Holdings: Vols (21,000) Cat Mss Pix Slides
Microforms
Notes: The History and Special Collections
Division owns close to 13,000 rare books
comprising landmarks in biomedical history,
15th through 19th centuries. Approx 23,000
supporting monographs and serial volumes
related to the history of medicine, denistry,
nursing, public health and other life sciences.
Special historical collections in urology,
ophthalmology, neurology, ornithology,
mammalogy, Oriental medicine, Nicholas
Culpeper, Silas Weir Mitchell, Florence
Nightingale, Juan de Valverde (qv), and 19th
century German and Austrian medical works
(Franklin E Murphy Fund). Rare books are
for reference use only.

CA —UNIVERSITY OF CALIFORNIA, SAN
FRANCISCO, Library, Special Collections,
San Francisco, 94143. Nancy Witten Zinn,
Librn
Holdings: Vols (23,000) Cat Mss Audiotapes
Slides Microforms

CA —STANFORD UNIVERSITY
LIBRARIES, Lane Medical Library,
Stanford University, Medical Center,
Stanford, 94305. Peter Stangl, Librn
Holdings: Vols 10,000 Cat
Budget: ($2785)
Notes: Barkan collection of rare medical
books, including the Ernst Seidel collection
of Arabic and near Eastern medicine.

CT —YALE UNIVERSITY, Medical Historical
Library, Klebs Collection, 333 Cedar St,
New Haven, 06520. Ferenc A Gyorgyey,
Librn
Notes: Incl the collection of Harvey
Cushing, John Fulton and Arnold C Klebs,
and historical collections of the Yale
Medical Library.

DC —SMITHSONIAN INSTITUTION
LIBRARIES, National Museum of American
History Branch, Washington, 20560. Rhoda
S Ratner, Branch Librn
Holdings: Vols 2400 Cat Maps Pix

GA —MEDICAL COLLEGE OF GEORGIA,
Library, Laney Walker Blvd, Augusta,
30902. Dorothy H Mims, Librn for Special
Collections
Holdings: Vols (2500) // Cat
Notes: Special collection of about 2500

MEDICINE—EARLY WORKS TO 1800 (cont.)

medical books and periodicals, chiefly from the late 18th and early 19th century, which were part of the early library of the Medical College of Georgia. Incl some 17th and early 18th century works and a number of classics listed in Garrison-Morton, as well as typical texts of the period. Unusually strong in French medical works, as the core collection was purchased in France in 1834. No photocopying.

†IL —NORTHWESTERN UNIVERSITY, Medical School, Archibald Church Library, 303 E Chicago Ave, Chicago, 60611. Cecile E Kramer, Librn
Holdings: Cat Mss Pix Slides
Notes: Incl about 3000 vols, 5100 pictures and 1200 slides concerning the history of medicine.

IA —STATE LIBRARY COMMISSION OF IOWA, Iowa State Medical Library, Historical Bldg E 12 & Grand, Des Moines, 50319. Claudya Muller, State Librn
Holdings: Vols 1800 Cat Mss
Notes: General medical history, history of Iowa medicine, histories of medical institutions, biographies and diaries. No separate catalog.

MEDICINE—HISTORY AND HISTORIC

CA —LOMA LINDA UNIVERSITY, Dell E Webb Memorial Library, Loma Linda, 92350. H Maynard Lowrey, Librn
Holdings: Vols Cat
Notes: Incl works on hydrotherapy and works by William Beaumont and Daniel Drake.

CA —LOS ANGELES COUNTY MEDICAL ASSOCIATION, Library, 634 S Westlake Ave, Los Angeles, 90057. Elizabeth S Crahan, Chief Librn
Holdings: Vols 600 Cat Pix
Budget: $1000
Notes: History of medicine in California. Plus 250 journals.

†CA —UNIVERSITY OF CALIFORNIA LOS ANGELES, Center for the Study of Comparative Folklore and Mythology, Los Angeles, 90024.
Notes: Archive, consisting of nearly 500,000 entries and cross-references, developed by Prof Wayland D Hand over the past 40 years as part of his monumental *Dictionary of American Popular Beliefs and* Superstitions. Entries have been drawn from both field collections and from printed and published sources. Analytical data stress both the historical component and the comparative approach. Of special interest is the emphasis on magical medicine, although natural and botanical medicine are also well represented.

CA —UNIVERSITY OF SOUTHERN CALIFORNIA, School of Medicine, Norris Medical Library, 2025 Zonal Ave, Los Angeles, 90033. Nelson J Gilman, Librn
Notes: The Collection of American Indian Ethnopharmacology.

CA —WHITE MEMORIAL MEDICAL CENTER, Courville-Abbott Memorial Library, 1720 Brooklyn Ave, Los Angeles, 90033. Joyce Marson, Librn

CA —UNIVERSITY OF CALIFORNIA, SAN FRANCISCO, Library, Special Collections, San Francisco, 94143. Nancy Witten Zinn, Librn
Holdings: Vols (502,261) Cat
Budget: ($602,604)

CA —STANFORD UNIVERSITY LIBRARIES, Lane Medical Library, Stanford University, Medical Center, Stanford, 94305. Peter Stangl, Librn
Holdings: Vols 18,000 Mss Pix Cat Instruments
Budget: $2785
Notes: Barkan collection of the history of medicine including 9900 volumes of books published before 1850. Included in this is the Ernst Seidel collection on medicine of the near East and rare books and manuscripts. Approximately 2000 medical instruments and 250 linear feet of Mss. These latter include the records of Cooper Medical College and Clinics (the forerunner of the

Stanford University School of Medicine); papers of Levi Cooper Lane, founder of Cooper Medical College; Phillip King Brown's papers on health insurance and socialized medicine; Adelaide Brown - sanitation and prenatal care; William Stroebel Hunter - human locomotion; Russel V Lee - group medical practice, gerontology, Agency for International Development; Leo L Stanley - prison medicine; Ray Lyman Wilbur - medical economics, including his work on the Committee on the Cost of Medical Care and the Commission on Medical Education; Hospitals - California - History.

CA —UNIVERSITY OF THE PACIFIC, Holt-Atherton Pacific Center for Western Studies, Stockton, 95211. Hiram L Davis, Dir of Libraries
Holdings: // Uncat Mss Pix Slides
Notes: The Bolt family papers comprise primarily the diaries of Beatrice Rebecca (French) Bolt, and the papers of her husband, Dr Richard Auther Bolt (1880-1959), a noted US child health authority. 19 linear ft (42 document boxes).

CT —LEE ASH, (personal collection), 66 Humiston Dr, Bethany, 06525.
Holdings: Mss Maps Pix
Notes: First editions, mss, ephemera, memorabilia.

CT —INSTITUTE OF LIVING, Medical Library, 400 Washington St, Hartford, 06106. Helen Lansberg, Librn
Holdings: Vols (30,000) Cat Mss Maps Pix
Notes: Three special collections in psychiatry, neurology and related subjects. *See also* entry under Psychiatry

CO —PENROSE HOSPITAL, Webb Memorial Library, 2215 N Cascade Ave, Colorado Springs, 80907. Elana Heiberger, Librn
Holdings: Vols 150
Notes: Open to staff only.

CT —YALE UNIVERSITY, Box 1603A, Yale Station, New Haven, 06520.
Holdings: Vols Cat Mss Pix

DC —LIBRARY OF CONGRESS, Rare Book & Special Collections Div, Washington, 20540. William Matheson, Chief
Notes: The Joseph Meredith Toner Collection of American Medicine of the 18th and 19th centuries. Also, Toner's personal papers, correspondence, etc.

FL —FLORIDA INSTITUTE OF TECHNOLOGY, Medical Research Institute, Library, 7725 W New Haven Ave, Melbourne, 32901. Barbara Bratton, Librn
Holdings: Cat

FL —SAINT MARY'S HOSPITAL INC, Health Services Library, 901 45th St W, Palm Beach, 33407. Jennie Glock, Librn
Holdings: Vols (7000) Cat Slides Audiotapes

FL —UNIVERSITY OF MIAMI, School of Medicine, Louis Calder Memorial Library, PO Box 520875, Miami, 33152. Henry L Lemkau, Jr, Dir
Holdings: Vols (127,843) Cat Mss Maps Pix Slides Phonorecords Audiotapes Videotapes 16mm Films Filmstrips Microforms
Budget: ($915,000)
Notes: Ophthalmology Branch Library of 6969 vols incl in total count; University of Miami School of Medicine dissertations; 209 medical medallions; physicians' bookplates; postage stamps with medical themes.

IL —AMERICAN MEDICAL ASSOCIATION, Div of Library & Archival Services, 535 N Dearborn St, Chicago, 60610. Arthur W Hafner, Dir
Holdings: Vols (130,000) Cat Mss Pix Microforms
Budget: $1,250,000
Notes: "One of world's most comprehensive collections in sociology and economics of medicine," some 150,000 items, 1964 to date. Archival collection of materials relating to history of AMA and its constituent societies. Incl historical biographical resource file on American physicians, incl obituary data and genealogy.

†IL —NORTHWESTERN UNIVERSITY, Medical School, Archibald Church Library, 303 E Chicago Ave, Chicago, 60611. Cecile E Kramer, Librn
Holdings: Cat Mss Pix Slides
Notes: Incl about 3000 vols, 5100 pictures and 1200 slides concerning the history of medicine.

IL —RUSH-PRESBYTERIAN-ST. LUKE'S MEDICAL CENTER, Library of Rush University, 600 S Paulina St, Chicago, 60612. Doris Bolef, Dir
Holdings: Vols 3000
Notes: Rare books in medicine, medical Americana, local and regional imprints, books by faculty of Rush Medical College in the previous century.

IL —UKRAINIAN MEDICAL ASSOCIATION OF NORTH AMERICA, 2320 W Chicago Ave, Chicago, 60622. Dr Paul Pundy, Librn
Holdings: Vols (1000) Pix
Notes: History of Ukrainian medicine, and contributions of Ukrainian medical practitioners in the US and Canada. Library located in Ukrainian National Museum.

IL —UNIVERSITY OF CHICAGO LIBRARIES, John Crerar Library Collections, 1100 E 57th St, Chicago, 60637. Robert Rosenthal, Special Collections Librn
Notes: The John Crerar Library's extensive science, medicine, and engineering collections have been transferred in trust to the University of Chicago Libraries. Incl rare books and special collections as listed here.

IL —UNIVERSITY OF ILLINOIS AT CHICAGO, Library of the Health Sciences, 1750 W Polk St, PO Box 7509, Chicago, 60612. Robert J Adelsperger, Cur, Special Collections
Holdings: Vols 6000 Cat Mss Maps Pix Slides Microforms
Notes: The Special Collections Department holds materials on the history of medicine, dentistry, urology, neurology and psychiatry. Incl collection of pharmacopeias, dispensatories, formularies, and American and foreign herbals. A collection on books, monographs, and periodicals on medicine published in Chicago prior to 1871 is of special interest. Library holds the Medical Library Associaton Archives. Collections are described in *A Catalog of Prefire Chicago Imprints (1884-1871)*; *Pharmacopeias, Formularies, Dispensatories*; *A Catalog of the Percival Bailey Collection of Neurology and Psychiatry*; and *A Catalog of the Dental Literature Collection of the Library of the Health Sciences*; *The Joseph H Kiefer Catalog of History of Urology and Medicine*.

IN —INDIANA UNIVERSITY, Lilly Library, Seventh St, Bloomington, 47405. William R Cagle, Librn
Holdings: Cat Mss
Notes: First appearances in print of great medical discoveries. Mss incl papers of various 19th century midwestern physicians.

IN —INDIANA MEDICAL HISTORY MUSEUM, Old Pathology Bldg, 3000 W Washington St, Indianapolis, 46222. Katherine Mandusic McDonell, Cur
Budget: ($24,000)
Notes: Over 1000 volumes of mid-to-late 19th century medical works; bound volumes of the proceedings of Indiana State Medical Society (1857-1907); 100 volumes pertaining to the history of medicine; 50 volumes pertaining to museum studies; approximately 200 prints, paintings, and photographs relating to history of medicine in Indiana; early medical school diplomas; vertical files on history of medicine; materials (printed and manuscripts) pertaining to state's first mental hosptial-Central State Hospital.

IA —STATE LIBRARY COMMISSION OF IOWA, Iowa State Medical Library, Historical Bldg E 12 & Grand, Des Moines, 50319. Claudya Muller, State Librn
Holdings: Vols 1800 Cat Mss
Notes: General medical history, history of Iowa medicine, histories of medical institutions, biographies and diaries. No separate catalog.

IA —UNIVERSITY OF IOWA, Health Sciences Library, John Martin Rare Book Room, Iowa City, 52242. Richard Eimas, Librn
Holdings: Vols (2200) Cat Slides
Notes: Catalog: Iowa, University, Health Sciences Library. *Heirs of Hippocrates* (Iowa City, IA, Friends of the University of Iowa Libraries, 1980). Collection is particularly strong in areas of anatomy and surgery. It also contains 300 books and reprints by and

MEDICINE—HISTORY AND HISTORIC (cont.)

about Sir William Osler as well as over 80 letters written by Osler.

KS —UNIVERSITY OF KANSAS MEDICAL CENTER, College of Health Sciences & Hospital, Clendening History of Medicine Library, Rainbow Blvd at 39th, Kansas City, 66103. Robert P Hudson, Chmn/Cur
Holdings: Vols (15,725) Cat Mss
Notes: Strong in all fields of medical history. Incl incunabula and serials. Mss incl Jakob Henle, 1809-1885, papers (ca 4050 items); Howard Atwook Kelly, 1858-1943, correspondence (ca 90 items); Joseph Lister, 1827-1912, letters (7); Florence Nightingals, 1820-1910, letters (20); and Samuel Jay Crumbine, 1862-1954, papers (ca 2365 items).

KY —UNIVERSITY OF KENTUCKY, Margaret I King Library, Dept of Special Collections, Lexington, 40506. William Marshall, Head
Holdings: Vols 310// Cat Mss Pix
Notes: Collection assembled by Dr Emmet Field Horine to document the work and writings of Daniel Drake in medicine and history and education; includes Drake's own publications. (Daniel Drake is important to Ohio and Kentucky history in particular.) Incl oil portrait and bust.

KY —NKC HOSPITALS, Medical Library, PO Box 35070, Louisville, 40232. Holly Shipp Buchanan, Dir
Holdings: Vols (4500) Cat Audiotapes Videotapes 16mm Films
Budget: $200,000
Notes: The Library has a special historical collection, corporate archives in honor of Dr Morris Flexner.

KY —UNIVERSITY OF LOUISVILLE, Kornhauser Health Sciences Library, 520 S Preston St, PO Box 35260, Louisville, 40292. Leonard M Eddy, Dir; Sherrill R McConnell, Archivist
Holdings: Vols 7500 Cat Mss Audiotapes Videotapes
Notes: Incl 3500 vols purchased by faculty between 1837-1846; have 2 copies of printed catalog of 1847.

LA —LOUISIANA STATE UNIVERSITY, Medical Center Library, 1542 Tulane Ave, New Orleans, 70112. John P Ische, Dir, Div of Libraries
Holdings: Vols 300 Cat
Notes: Incl the Yellow Fever Collection.

LA —TULANE UNIVERSITY, Howard-Tilton Memorial Library, Special Collections Div, 7001 Freret St, New Orleans, 70118. Wilbur E Meneray, Librn
Holdings: Vols (700) Cat Mss Pix
Notes: Publications of 19th and 20th century New Orleans and Louisiana medical associations and physicians from the 18th century to the present including those of Charles Cassidy Bass, Standord Emerson Chaille, Joseph Jones, Edmund Kells, Rudloph Matas, Joseph Montegut, John Leonard Riddell and Edmond Souchon.

LA —TULANE UNIVERSITY, Rudolph Matas Medical Library, 1430 Tulane Ave, New Orleans, 70112. W D Postell Jr, Librn
Holdings: Cat Mss Pix
Notes: Incl the Elizabeth Bass Collection of personalized material on women doctors (3640 vols).

ME —MAINE MEDICAL CENTER, Library, 22 Bramhall St, Portland, 04102. Robin M Rand, Dir of Library Services
Holdings: Vols (5300)
Budget: ($274,185)
Notes: Incl 10,250 bound journals and 617 subscriptions. Also incl a collection of about 300 historical medical books, as well as a small collection of antique instruments and photographs.

MD —JOHNS HOPKINS UNIVERSITY, Institute of the History of Medicine, 1900 E Monument St, Baltimore, 21205. Doris Thibodeau, Librn
Holdings: Vols 50,000 Cat
Notes: One of the strongest history of medicine collections in the US.

MD —MEDICAL & CHIRURGICAL FACULTY OF THE STATE OF

MARYLAND, Library, 1211 Cathedral St, Baltimore, 21201. Joseph E Jensen, Librn
Holdings: Vols (10,000) // Cat Mss Maps Pix
Notes: The history of medicine and rare medical book collection incl early literature (some medical incunabula), texts, and periodicals (strong in Garrison & Morton items), histories, bibliographies, reprints, lecture notes, health department reports, hospital and physician records, medical society transactions, etc. Materials generally span the 16th through the 19th centuries. Very strong in Early American imprints relating to medicine (Austin items), European medical classics, and 18th and 19th century medical periodicals. Also incl the archives of the Medical and Chirugical Faculty of the State of Maryland, biographical information about Maryland physicians, and much material on the history of Maryland as it relates to medicine. Many items were donations from the collections of Osler, Steiner, Ruhrah, Chatard, Thayer, Welch, etc.

MD —UNIVERSITY OF MARYLAND, BALTIMORE, Health Sciences Library, 111 S Greene St, Baltimore, 21201. Cyril C H Feng, Dir
Holdings: Vols (3500) Cat Mss Pix VF
Notes: Eugene F Cordell Medical Historical Collection includes University of Maryland theses, 1817-1887; early history of medicine imprints including some landmarks; and excellent anatomy early imprint collection, and a bookplate collection. In addition, the John Crawford Collection (400 vols cataloged) includes works dating from 1565 to 1811 on the history of medicine, pharmacy, dentistry and nursing. This nucleus of books comprised the first library of the University of Maryland.

MD —BETHESDA NAVY HOSPITAL, Edward Rhodes Stitt Library, Bethesda, 20814. Jerry Meyer, Librn
Holdings: Vols 2000 Cat
Notes: Open only to Navy Medical clinicians. Interlibrary loan service offered.

MD —NATIONAL LIBRARY OF MEDICINE, 8600 Rockville Pike, Bethesda, 20209. Harold M Schoolinam, Actg Dir
Holdings: Vols (3,150,000) Cat Mss Audiotapes Videotapes 16mm Films Filmstrips Microforms
Budget: ($46,400)
Notes: The world's largest medical library. Materials are collected exhaustively in some 40 biomedical areas and, to a lesser degree, in related subject areas such as general chemistry, physics, zoology, botany, and instrumentation. Holdings include 82,000 monographic volumes, pre-1871; 438,000 monographic volumes, 1871-present; 714,000 bound serial volumes; 281,000 theses; 172,000 pamphlets; 1,207,000 manuscripts; 156,000 microforms; 12,000 audiovisuals; and 75,000 prints and photographs. Pre-1871 material is in a separate historical collection. Approximately 24,000 serial titles are currenlty received.

MA —BOSTON CITY HOSPITAL, Dept of Health & Hospitals, Medical Library, 818 Harrison Ave, Boston, 02118. Margi Dempsey, Dir
Holdings: Vols (13,431) Cat
Budget: ($32,000)
Notes: Medical Library serves as a reference medical library for the entire Department of Health and Hospitals for Boston. A special collection (Anthony Michelidakis Memorial Library, History of Medicine) is part of the Medical Library holdings. This special history of medicine collection covers medicine in early Boston and other books on the history of medicine in general. Collection contains some 131 vols.

MA —FRANCIS A COUNTWAY LIBRARY OF MEDICINE, Boston Medical Library/ Harvard Medical Library, 10 Shattuck St, Boston, 02115. C Robin LeSueur, Librn; Richard J Wolfe, Cur, Rare Books & Manuscripts
Holdings: Vols (500,000) Mss Maps Pix
Budget: ($1,160,000)
Notes: Second largest medical library in the nation. Combines the resources of the

Harvard Medical School and the Boston Medical Library, as well as the medical collections of many regional libraries. Outstanding in all areas of medical science. Author-title catalog of imprints through 1959 published by G K Hall, 1973. Strong in serials and medical history in all fields of medicine. Especially strong in subject areas incl incunabula, medical Judaica, Osleriana, O W Holmes, William Rimmer, non-medical books by doctors, travel books by physicians, X-ray (Dr Lloyd E Hawes, Hon Curator), prints and medical satire (Dr Mark D Altschule, Hon Curator), phrenology, witchcraft, gynecology and obstetrics, medical illustrations, birth control and sex research, medical numismatics, European imprints before 1850 and American imprints before 1870, Chinese and Japanese medicine, medicaldissertations (500,000), anatomy, anesthesia, botany, biochemistry and chemistry, alchemy, dental medicine, legal medicine, physiology, dental medicine, legal medicine, physiology, psychiatry, plastic surgery, surgery, zoology, ms collections, which incl the Harvard Medical Archives, probably the strongest in America.

MA —NEW ENGLAND BAPTIST HOSPITAL, Medical Staff Library, 91 Parker Hill Ave, Boston, 02120. Paul E Woodard, Librn
Holdings: Cat
Budget: ($17,487)
Notes: No photocopying.

MA —SPRINGFIELD ACADEMY OF MEDICINE, Medical Library, 1400 State St, Springfield, 01109. Margaret Stoler, Dir
Holdings: Vols (10,448) Cat
Notes: Extensive historical collection; some first editions.

MA —WORCESTER HAHNEMANN HOSPITAL, Medical Library, 281 Lincoln St, Worcester, 01605. Roger Manahan, Librn
Holdings: Vols 30 Uncat Pix
Notes: Collection of medical history, incl books written by and about Dr Samuel Hahnemann from 1829.

MI —UNIVERSITY OF MICHIGAN, Library, Dept of Rare Books & Special Collections, Ann Arbor, 48109. Robert J Starring, Head
Holdings: Cat Mss Pix
Notes: Chiefly pre-1800 imprints.

MI —UNIVERSITY OF MICHIGAN, Alfred Taubman Medical Library, 1135 E Catherine St, Ann Arbor, 48109. L Yvonne Wulff, Head
Holdings: Vols (260,300) Cat
Budget: ($438,000)

MI —SINAI HOSPITAL OF DETROIT, Samuel Frank Medical Library, 6767 W Outer Dr, Detroit, 48235. Barbara Finn, Dir
Holdings: Vols 800 Cat
Notes: Strength in anatomy, surgery, French medicine, and herbals.

MN —UNIVERSITY OF MINNESOTA, Owen H Wangensteen Historical Library of Biology & Medicine, Diehl Hall, Minneapolis, 55455. Judith Overmier, Cur
Holdings: Vols (35,000) Cat Mss
Budget: ($80,000)
Notes: Strength in anatomy, surgery, French medicine, pathology and herbals.

MN —MAYO HISTORICAL UNIT, Mayo Clinic/Mayo Foundation, Rochester, 55905. Clark W Nelson, Mayo History Development Specialist
Holdings: Mss Pix Phonorecords Audiotapes Videotapes 16mm Films
Notes: The collection generally relates to the history of the Mayo institutions--Mayo Clinic, Mayo Foundation, Mayo Medical School, and Mayo Graduate School. Its scope covers roughly the years 1860 to present. It features the papers and correspondence of Drs Charles Horace Mayo (1865-1939) and William James Mayo (1861-1939), founders of the Mayo institutions. Many items are also incl from other physicians and administrators who have been prominent in Mayo's development. Limited access collection. Inquiries subject to reviewal. Application must be made in advance.

MN —MAYO MEDICAL LIBRARY, History of Medicine Collection, Rochester, 55905. Nancy R Hensel, Librn
Holdings: Vols (18,000) Cat Mss Maps Pix

MEDICINE—HISTORY AND HISTORIC (cont.)

Slides
Notes: The collection consists of over 18,000 vols, 6500 of which are considered source material (rare or reprint editions of classics). 4308 items from Garrison-Morton are available in the collection. Appropriate bibliographies, biographies and histories of medicine are a part of the collection. Fields of collecting interest are anesthesiology, dermatology, cardiology, neurology, immunology and radiology. Eight medical incunabula.

MO —SAINT LOUIS UNIVERSITY, Pius XII Memorial Library, 3655 W Pine Blvd, Saint Louis, 63108. William Cole, Dir
Holdings: Slides Microforms
Notes: Collection covers all areas of learning and European history from Classical Antiquity to early modern period. Researchers using collection receive assistance in paleography, bibliography and reference search. Approx 10,000 1000-foot reels of microfilm (not counting master negatives) reproducing Vatican Library's Latin, Greek, Hebrew, Arabic and Ethiopic mss. Some 8000 100-foot reels of microfilm (again not counting master negative) reproducing rare and out of print books relating to subject areas in the mss. Over 50,000 color slides of medieval and Renaissance mss illuminations. A reference collection of modern materials relating to ms research.

MO —WASHINGTON UNIVERSITY, School of Medicine, Archives, 660 S Euclid Ave, Saint Louis, 63110. Paul G Anderson, Archivist
Holdings: Mss Pix Audiotapes
Budget: ($38,000)
Notes: Institutional records and papers of faculty of Washington University School of Medicine and its predecessors and associated hospitals. Contains records of St Louis Medical College, Missouri Medical Barnard Free Skin and Cancer Hospital, Barnes Hospital, St Louis Children's Hospital and Jewish Hospital of St Louis. Incl papers of William Beaumont, Joseph Erlanger, Leo Loeb, Evarts Graham, Edmund V Cowdry, Helen Graham, Carl V Moore, Margaret Smith and others. Oral history program. See also: Anderson, Paul G and Hoolihan, Christopher, eds. Special Collections (St Louis: Washington University School of Medicine, 1981). 960 linear feet.

MO —WASHINGTON UNIVERSITY, School of Medicine, Library, 660 South Euclid Ave, Saint Louis, 63110. Christopher Hoolihan, Rare Book Librn
Holdings: Vols 12,000 Cat
Budget: ($40,000)
Notes: Incl the Bernard Becker, MD Collection in Ophthalmology, the CID-Max A Goldstein Collection in Speech & Hearing, the General Rare Books Collection (pre-1821 imprints), and the Monuments of Medicine Collection (19th & 20th century imprints). The latter two collections incl works of historical importance in all the medical specialties, with special emphasis on midwifery and obstetrics, brain function localization, and the physiology of digestion. See also entries under Midwifery - History, Obstetrics - History, and Brain.

NE —UNIVERSITY OF NEBRASKA MEDICAL CENTER, Library, 42 & Dewey Ave, Omaha, 68105. Robert M Braude, Dir
Holdings: Vols (196,313)
Budget: ($320,000)
Notes: Selected collection of materials representative of major advances, schools, discoveries, and other historical events in the history of medicine. The collection reflects greater depth in the areas of obstetrics, gynecology, pediatrics, anatomy, embryology, and orthopedic surgery. The collection incl the H Winnett Orr Collection of the American College of Surgeons.

NH —DARTMOUTH COLLEGE, Dartmouth-Hitchcock Medical Center, Dana Biomedical Library, Hanover, 03756. Shirley J Grainger, Librn
Holdings: Vols (6000) Cat Mss
Notes: Collection incl the Conner Collection

of Medical Classics, history of medicine, etc. Also the Henry Schroeder Collection of Papers on Trace Elements and the Henry Kumm Index to Papers on Poliomyelitis and Tropical Medicine. No photocopying.

NJ —UNIVERSITY OF MEDICINE AND DENTISTRY OF NEW JERSEY, George F Smith Library of the Health Sciences, 100 Bergen St, Newark, 07103. Philip Rosenstein, Dir of Libraries
Holdings: Vols (528)
Notes: The Morris H Saffron Collection of Books on Historical Medicine contains 528 rare medical works published before 1900, 212 of which antedate 1800. The earliest is a 1517 printing of Savonarola's Practica de febribus and the major medical authors are well represented.

†NM —UNIVERSITY OF NEW MEXICO, Medical Center Library, Albuquerque, 87131. Beatrice Kovacs, Chief, Collections and Resource Development
Notes: Concern is health care and health services in New Mexico; medicine and medicine men of Indian tribes of the Southwest; and history of medicine and health in the Southwest.

†NY —MEDICAL RESEARCH LIBRARY OF BROOKLYN, Academy of Medicine of Brooklyn & The State University of New York Downstate Medical Center, 450 Clarkson St, Brooklyn, 11203. Kenneth E Moody, Dir
Holdings: Vols 5000 Cat
Notes: History of medicine, historic medicine, and about 4000 medical classics. See also entry under Medicine.

NY —STATE UNIVERSITY OF NEW YORK, STONY BROOK, Health Sciences Library, PO Box 66, East Setauket, 11733.
Notes: Slide Collection of Historical Medical Photographs is an archive of 3000 slides pertaining to the history of medical care in America--Medical and public health activities from the 1850s to the 1950s. An illustrated catalogue, published by Greenwood Press, is scheduled for 1984.

NY —CORNELL UNIVERSITY LIBRARIES, John M Olin Library, History of Science Collections, Ithaca, 14853. Lillian A Clark, Administrative Supervisor; David W Corson, History of Science Librn
Holdings: Vols (33,000) Cat
Notes: Early printed source materials in medicine and related sciences, 16th through 18th centuries. Emphasis is on basic sciences rather than clinical medicine and surgery. Incl Adelmann Collection in history of embryology and anatomy and extensive collection of early medical dissertations. Noncirculating. See also entries under Dissertations and Theses, Medical; Sciences - History

NY —COLUMBIA UNIVERSITY LIBRARIES, Health Sciences Library, 701 W 168 St, New York, 10032. Rachael K Goldstein, Librn
Holdings: Vols 15,000
Notes: Restricted. Incl mss, portraits, museum objects, archives. See also entry under Surgery, Plastic - History; Anatomy - History

NY —NEW YORK ACADEMY OF MEDICINE, Library, 2 E 103 St, New York, 10029. Brett A Kirkpatrick, Librn
Holdings: Vols 31,000
Notes: One of the strongest collections of medical literature, the history of medicine, medical classics, medical education, public health, and all paramedical subjects ranging in date from 1800 BC to 1799. Incl Samuel W Lambert, Jr Collection on anatomy, surgery, and history of medicine. Also incl the Edwin Smith papyrus on surgery (ca 1800 BC).

NY —NEW YORK ACADEMY OF MEDICINE, Library, 2 E 103 St, New York, 10029. Brett A Kirkpatrick, Librn
Holdings: Uncat Mss Pix
Notes: Collection of personal papers of Frank George Boudreau, incl correspondnece, from his birth to his early years as health officer in Ohio, through his international experience at the League of Nations, and as President of the Milbank Memorial Fund. Much on epidemiology,

public health, and public medicine. Collections described in Lee Ash's "Frank Geroge Boudreau, 18 July 1886-14 February 1970," The Academy Bookman (New York Academy of Medicine, Friends of the Rare Book Room), Vol 26, No 1, 1973, pp 6-7.

NY —NEW YORK UNIVERSITY, MEDICAL CENTER, Medical Library, 550 First Ave, New York, 10016. Gilbert J Clausman, Librn
Holdings: Vols (143,000) Cat Microforms
Budget: ($929,000)
Notes: Also over 11,000 microforms.

NY —UNIVERSITY OF ROCHESTER, School of Medicine and Dentistry, Edward G Miner Library, 601 Elmwood Ave, Rochester, 14642. Lucretia McClure, Medical Librn; Janet Brady Berk, History of Medicine Librn
Holdings: Vols (185,000) Cat
Notes: The Edward G Miner Library serves the School of Medicine & Dentistry, the School of Nursing, and Strong Memorial Hospital. The collection encompasses all the biomedical fields, nursing and dental research, and is designed to serve the teaching, patient care and research needs of persons in the Medical Center. The Library subscribes to more than 2900 current journals and serials, has an excellent reference collection and an extensive collection of rare and historical works in medicine and nursing. Strong in yellow fever, cholera, orthopedics, anatomy and original historic medical photographs.

†NY —UNIVERSITY OF ROCHESTER, Rush Rhees Library, History of Medicine Section, Rochester, 14627.
Notes: A collection of some 400 items, mostly letters and mss, relating to the Bartlett family of Rhode Island. Incl items concerning the medical career of Elisha Bartlett from 1832-1855; also correspondence with contemporary physicians and surgeons.

NY —STATE UNIVERSITY OR NEW YORK, UPSTATE MEDICAL CENTER, Library, 766 Irving Ave, Syracuse, 13210. Evelyn L Hoey, Library Dir
Notes: Strong in history in all fields of medicine, especially Blackwelliana, Medical Americana, and biographies. Incl medical museum pieces.

NY —UTICA-MARCY PSYCHIATRIC CENTER, UTICA CAMPUS, Library Services-Medical, 1213 Court St, Utica, 13502. Toms E Smith, Sr Librn
Holdings: Vols 400 Uncat Pix
Notes: Contains a number of books from Dr Amariah Brigham's personal library Dr Brigham was first director of Utica State Hospital, then New York State Lunatic Asylum, and was founder of American Journal of Insanity and its first editor. This journal was the first psychiatric journal in America and became the American Journal of Psychiatry. Also contains volumes on early aspects of psychiatric care, and some general books on medicine. Available to health care professionals and students.

NC —UNIVERSITY OF NORTH CAROLINA, CHAPEL HILL, Health Sciences Library, 223 H, Chapel Hill, 27514. Samuel Hitt, Dir
Holdings: Vols (200,000) Cat Slides Journals Audiotapes Videotapes Microforms
Budget: ($18,500)

NC —DUKE UNIVERSITY, Medical Center Library, Trent Collection, Durham, 27710. G S T Cavanagh, Cur
Holdings: Vols 20,000 Cat Mss Pix Slides Microforms
Notes: Incl museum objects.

ND —UNIVERSITY OF NORTH DAKOTA, Harley E French Medical Library, Grand Forks, 58202. David W Boilard, Dir; Lila Pedersen, Asst Dir
Holdings: Vols (56,000) Cat
Budget: ($206,000)
Notes: 1075 current periodical subscriptions.

OH —OHIO UNIVERSITY, Vernon R Alden Library, Department of Archives and Special Collections, Athens, 45701. Gary A Hunt, Head
Holdings: Vols 90 Cat Mss
Notes: History of Osteopathic Medicine,

MEDICINE—HISTORY AND HISTORIC (cont.)

concentrating on books published prior to 1940. Incl records of the Ohio Osteopathic Association and its predecessor, the Ohio Osteopathic Society, 1890-1970.

OH —AULTMAN HOSPITAL SCHOOL OF NURSING, Library, 2614 Sixth St SW, Canton, 44710. Violet Russell, Librn
Holdings: Vols 45 Cat
Budget: ($2800)

OH —JEWISH HOSPITAL, Medical Library, 3200 Burnet Ave, Cincinnati, 45229. Barbara Lucas, Librn
Notes: Special emphasis on local history of medicine (Cincinnati and Southwest Ohio).

OH —UNIVERSITY OF CINCINNATI MEDICAL CENTER LIBRARIES, History of Health Sciences Library & Museum, 231 Bethesda Ave ML 574, Cincinnati, 45267. Billie Broaddus, Dir
Holdings: Vols 30,000 Uncat Mss Pix Slides
Notes: The History of Health Sciences Library and Museum was established in 1977 and contains 30,000 old and rare medical books published between 1500 and 1920. These volumes are on all areas of the health professions and are in Latin, French, German, and English. The collection is particularly strong on European and American medicine in the 19th century and on medicine in Cincinnati. The collection incl Daniel Drake manuscripts and first editions, Cincinnati General Hospital Archives dating from 1837, photographs, and early medical instruments. The book collection is made up of David A Tucker, Jr Library, of which a bibliography has been published; Joan Titley, *David A Tucker, Jr Library of the History of Medicine: A Bibliography* (Cincinnati: Medical College, University of Cincinnati, 1959); the Mussey Collection, a library collected by Reuben D Mussey, the fourth president of the American Medical Association, who died in 1866; the Hospital Archival and Boston Collections, which are the combined old and rare book collections of the Medical School Library and the Cincinnati General Hospital Library, which merged in 1974; and the National Library of Medicine Collection, named for its classification scheme. These works are a collection of secondary and reference works related to the history of medicine. Also incls 3550 journals.

OH —CLEVELAND MEDICAL LIBRARY ASSOCIATION/CASE WESTERN RESERVE UNIVERSITY, Cleveland Health Sciences Library, Historical Division, Allen Memorial Medical Library, 11000 Euclid Ave, Cleveland, 44106. Glen Jenkins, Rare Book Librarian & Archivist
Holdings: Vols 25,000 Cat Mss Maps Pix
Notes: Incl 15,000 historical vols, 6000 in the supporting collection. Incl about 100 16th-18th century titles. Strength of collection: diseases epidemiology, anatomy, surgery, medicine, obstetrics, gynecology, pediatrics and yellow fever. Incl also medical Americana, listed in Robert B Austin *Early American Medical Imprints*, (1668-1820 Washington, DC, HEW Public Health Service, 1961) and ca 7000 19th century works. Total Americana collection also incl journals (not counted), mss and archives (900 linear ft) and 5000 pictures, especially of the Western Reserve. Anatomical works discussed in I Ebner and G Jenkins *Skeletons in Our Closet*, (Cleveland, Cleveland Health Sciences Library, 1983).

OH —OHIO STATE UNIVERSITY, Library, 1858 Neil Mall, Columbus, 43210. Dona Straley, Islamica Librn

OH —RUTHERFORD B HAYES LIBRARY, 1337 Hayes Ave, Fremont, 43420. Watt P Marchman, Dir
Holdings: Vols 500 Cat Mss Maps Pix
Notes: Drs John B and Robert H Rice of Fremont, Ohio. Incl 300 linear ft of mss, 25 boxes of pictures. Index in collection. Listed in *Guide to Manuscripts of the Ohio Historical Society*, 401.

OH —KETTERING COLLEGE OF MEDICAL ARTS, Learning Resources Center, 3737 Southern Blvd, Kettering, 45429. Edward Collins, Librn
Holdings: Vols 215 Cat Audiotapes
Budget: $120

OH —MIAMI UNIVERSITY, King Library, Walter Havighurst Special Collections Library, Oxford, 45056. Helen Ball, Cur of Special Collections
Holdings: Vols 150
Notes: American 19th century botanical medicine. Incl pamphlets, periodicals and ephemera.

OR —OREGON HEALTH SCIENCES, University Libraries, PO Box 573, Portland, 97207. James E Morgan, Dir
Holdings: Vols (178,373) Cat Mss Pix Slides Audiotapes Videotapes Microforms
Notes: Libraries incl a medical/nursing library and a separate dental library. Medical history collection of books and artifacts emphasizes the Pacific Northwest.

PA —COLLEGE OF PHYSICIANS OF PHILADELPHIA, Library, 19 S 22 St, Philadelphia, 19103. Anthony Aguirre, Libr Dir
Holdings: Vols (316,223) Cat Mss Microforms
Budget: ($1,096,557)
Notes: Incl 13,515 pamphlets; 1435 mss; 326,367 reports, dissertations, and reprints. Strong historical and bibliographical collections, as well as current materials. Medical documentation service provides current alerting, incl abstracting, etc.

PA —LIBRARY COMPANY OF PHILADELPHIA, 1314 Locust St, Philadelphia, 19107. Edwin Wolf II, Librn; Kenneth Finkel, Cur of Prints
Holdings: Vols 1000 Cat Mss Maps
Budget: ($25,000)
Notes: Early American books, pamphlets and broadsides concerning popular and professional medicine, to 1820. Of major importance are books owned by Benjamin Rush, Revolutionary-era doctor. Many of his mss, though housed in the Historical Society of Pennsylvania, remain the property of the Library Company.

PA —MEDICAL COLLEGE OF PENNSYLVANIA, Florence A Moore Library of Medicine, Archives & Special Collections on Women in Medicine, 3300 Henry Ave, Philadelphia, 19129. Sandra L Chaff, Archivist
Holdings: Vols 700 Cat Mss Pix Slides Phonorecords Audiotapes 16mm Films
Notes: "One of the most comprehensive US collections of historical material on women physicians." Incl personal papers of women physicians; audiotapes and transcripts of interviews conducted by the Oral History Project on Women Physicians; the American Medical Women's Association historical collection; the American Women's Hospitals Service collection; the Kate Campbell Hurd-Mead collection; a file of 10,000 photos relating to women physicians; and 5100 reprints of which 4000 citations appear in *Women in Medicine: A Bibliography of the Literature on Women Physicians*, by Sandra L Chaff et al. (Metuchen, NJ: Scarecrow Press, 1977).

PA —PENNSYLVANIA HOSPITAL HISTORICAL LIBRARY, Eighth & Spruce Sts, Philadelphia, 19107. Caroline Morris, Librn
Holdings: Vols (12,,963)// Cat Mss
Notes: First medical library in US. Rich in runs of 19th century medical libraries. Some early botany books. Some incunabula. Printed catalog was made in 1876. This collection is important because it reflects the history of medicine by the nature of the materials that were acquired. *However, no attempt is made to keep a current history of medicine library.*

PA —PHILADELPHIA COLLEGE OF OSTEOPATHIC MEDICINE, O J Snyder Memorial Library, Evans Hall, 4150 City Ave, Philadelphia, 19131. Shanker H Vyas, Dir of Libraries
Holdings: Vols (50,000) Cat Audiotapes Videotapes 16mm Films Microforms
Notes: Osteopathy and all medical fields. Osteopathy collection incl 387 books, 98 theses, 66 pamphlets and periodicals, 1103 audiotapes and 946 videotapes.

PA —PHILADELPHIA MUSEUM OF ART, Ars Medica Center, Parkway at Fairmount, Box 7646, Philadelphia, 19101. Ellen Jacobowutz; Ann Percy
Holdings: Cat Mss Maps Pix Slides
Notes: An international medical arts center of prints, drawings and photographs, related illustrative medical material and a research reference center.

PA —UNIVERSITY OF PITTSBURGH, Falk Library of the Health Professions, History of Medicine Collection, Scaife Hall, Pittsburgh, 15261. Jonathon Erlen, Cur
Holdings: Vols (13,500) Cat Pix
Budget: ($425,269)
Notes: Medicine, dentistry, nursing, pharmacy, public health, psychiatry materials, incl some rare books and 300 pamphlets on anesthesia.

RI —BROWN UNIVERSITY, John Hay Library, 20 Prospect St, Providence, 02912. Mark N Brown, Cur Mss
Holdings: Mss
Notes: See entry under Charles V Chapin; Solomon Drowne; William Keen; and Usher Parsons.

RI —BROWN UNIVERSITY, John Carter Brown Library, Providence, 02912. Norman Fiering, Librn; Everett C Wilkie Jr, Bibliographer; Susan Danforth, Cur Maps & Prints
Notes: Holdings reflect writings of doctors in the Americas, particularly the West Indies, and European reactions to new drugs and diseases that came from the New World.

RI —RHODE ISLAND MEDICAL SOCIETY, Library, 106 Francis St, Providence, 02903. Marion N Sabella, Librn
Holdings: Vols 50,000 Per Monographs
Notes: Also Davenport Collection (2111 vols) of extra-professional writings of physicians, books about physicians and medicine; Charles F Gormley Collection of medicolegal books; Charles Value Chapin Collection of scrapbooks (1883-1939), medals, portraits, etc; Collection of state medical society journals.

SC —COLLEGE OF CHARLESTON LIBRARY, Special Collections Dept, Charleston, 29401.
Notes: Journal kept by an unidentified physician (I.F.R.) as a medical student at the University of Pennsylvania and at the University of Louisiana in New Orleans, as a ship's surgeon for two years in the Caribbean, and as a private practitioner. Incl notes of lectures by Dr Samuel Jackson of the University of Pennsylvania.

SC —MEDICAL UNIVERSITY OF SOUTH CAROLINA, Waring Historical Library, 171 Ashley Ave, Charleston, 29425. W Curtis Worthington, Jr, Dir; Anne K Donato, Cur
Holdings: Vols 6000 Cat Mss Pix Slides Microforms
Budget: ($3000)
Notes: The nucleus of our collections are the rare medical books that belonged to the Library of the Medical Society of South Caroline (a Charleston society founded in 1789, which started our college of medicine in 1824). Our special interest is the collection of South Carolina medical material and anything connected with the Medical University of South Carolina. We have old medical instruments and equipment, also.

TN —VANDERBILT UNIVERSITY, Medical Center Library, Nashville, 37232. Mary H Teloh, Special Collections Librn
Holdings: Vols 3000 Cat Mss Pix Slides
Notes: The rare books collection incl works by Auenbrugger, Beaumont, Elyot, Jenner, Laennec, Vesalius, and Vigo. The working collection for the history of medicine is particularly strong in American imprints of the late 18th and 19th century. These emphases are supported in the general collection by some notable runs of the 18th and 19th century European and American medical journals. Strong subject collections include: military medicine, nutrition, surgery and urology. There is also under development a collection of the scientific writings of medical educators connected with Vanderbilt.

TX —UNIVERSITY OF TEXAS LIBRARIES, General Libraries, Barker Texas History

MEDICINE—HISTORY AND HISTORIC (cont.)

Center, PO Box P, Austin, 78712. Don Carleton, Dir
Notes: Papers of Dr Joseph Henry Barnard (1804-1861), surgeon in the 1836 Texas Revolution. Incl names and statistics relative to the Battle of Coleto, 19 March 1836; also other professional and financial papers.

TX —UNIVERSITY OF TEXAS, DALLAS, Health Science Center, Reference Dept & History of Health Sciences Dept, 5323 Harry Hines Blvd, Dallas, 75235. Helen Mayo, Head
Holdings: Vols (10,000) Cat Pix Slides Audiotapes Microforms
Notes: History of Medicine collection contains ca 10,000 vols. This total is comprised of pre-1900 journals, primary materials in the History of Medicine and the History of Science, and secondary studies in these two areas. The major strengths of this collection are in the areas of epidemics and plagues, military medicine, and collected works of famous medical pioneers. Incl in this collection are the medical journals published by the county medical societies in Texas, local publications by Dallas County medical organizations, and ephemeral material in a similar vein. The university archives contain all theses and dissertations form UTHSCD and miscellaneous institutional documents circulated by the school's administration.

TX —HOUSTON ACADEMY OF MEDICINE-TEXAS MEDICAL CENTER, Library, Jesse H Jones Library Bldg, Houston, 77030. Elizabeth Borst White, Special Collections Librn
Holdings: Uncat Mss Pix Videotapes
Notes: This collection documents the history of medical practice, education and research in Houston and Harris County, Texas. The archives concern institutions or hospitals within the Texas Medical Center and the careers of local physicians, nurses and biomedical researchers. 450 linear ft of mss, 6000 photographs.

TX —UNIVERSITY OF TEXAS HEALTH SCIENCE CENTER, SAN ANTONIO, 7703 Floyd Curl Dr, San Antonio, 78284. Joyce M Ray, Archivist/Special Collections Librn; JoAnn Glisson, Library Asst
Holdings: Vols 4000 Cat Mss Maps Pix
Notes: All catalog information on computer tape for bibliographic retrieval. Special listings can be produced on demand. Collection incl local medical history.

UT —UNIVERSITY OF UTAH, Middle East Library, Salt Lake City, 84112. Ragai N Makar, Librn
Holdings: Vols 3000 Cat Mss Pix Microforms
Budget: ($40,000)
Notes: The Martin Levey Collection, one of the finest on Arabic sciences and medicine in the country. Incl books and mss on all the sciences and medicine through the 14th century: 3000 books; 5000 offprints; 1000 microfilmed mss in German, Arabic, and French.

WA —UNIVERSITY OF WASHINGTON LIBRARIES, Health Sciences Library, SB-55, Seattle, 98195. Gerald J Oppenheimer, Dir

WI —UNIVERSITY OF WISCONSIN, MADISON, William S Middleton Health Sciences Library, Historical Collection, 1305 Linden Dr, Madison, 53706. Dorothy V Whitcomb, Librn
Holdings: Vols 25,000 Cat Microforms Cat Pamphlets
Budget: ($16,000)
Notes: Strength in anatomy, physiology, pathology, internal medicine, neurological sciences, immunology and anatomical-pathological illustration. Holdings partially listed in J Neu, Chemical Medical and Pharmaceutical Books Printed before 1800, Madison, 1965. Items cataloged since 1976 on OCLC.

WI —UNIVERSITY OF WISCONSIN, MADISON, William S Middleton Health Sciences Library, Historical Collection, 1305 Linden Dr, Madison, 53706. Dorothy V Whitcomb, Librn
Notes: Incl publications of persons known as the French Clinical School of the early 19th century; Goldschmid Collection, 250 early printed works in pathological anatomy housed in the new Medical Library; Mesmerism Collection, a small collection of pamphlets published about 1784 dealing with Franz Anton Mesmer and his cures; William Snow Miller Collection, the backbone of the historical collection in the Medical Library contains over 2000 vols with particular emphasis on anatomy; Richardson Collection, about 300 vols on medical subjects, particularly anatomy; Robinson-Waite Collection, private collections of two pioneer Wisconsin doctors, about 800 vols were donated to the Medical Library in the early 1900s; Tank Collection, ca 4800 vols and 374 pamphlets in theology, history, travels and science; and approx 160 vols published during the 18th and 19th centuries.

MB —UNIVERSITY OF MANITOBA, Elizabeth Dafoe Library, Archives and Special Collections Dept, Winnipeg, R3T 2N2, Can. Richard E Bennett, Dept Head; Corrado A Santoro, Reference Archivist
Notes: Correspondence, reports and various papers of Dr Bruce H Chown. Haemolitic diseases of the newborn, especially erthroblastosis fetalis and the maternal Rh-factor. Incl correspondence with Dr Louis Diamond of Boston. Also incl are human anthropological blood group studies of Eskimo, Indian and Canadian-Japanese communities.

MB —UNIVERSITY OF MANITOBA, Medical Library, 770 Bannatyne Ave, Winnipeg, R3E 0W3, Can. Audrey M Kerr, Professor & Head Librn
Holdings: Vols (86,500) Cat Pix Audiotapes
Notes: Incl a section on the history of medicine and a small but valuable collection of rare books in the Ross Mitchell Room. 3600 audiotapes; 1500 serials.

NF —WATERFORD HOSPITAL, Health Sciences Library, Waterford Bridge Rd, Saint John's, A1E 4J8, Can. Maisie Young, Librn
Holdings: Vols (2000) Cat Pix Phonorecords Audiotapes Videotapes 16mm Films Filmstrips
Notes: Material incl aspects of psychiatry related to medicine, nursing, phychology, social work, etc. Also incl manuscript work on a history of the hospital, which closely parallels a history of psychiatry in Newfoundland. Journals are only kept for ten years.

ON —QUEEN'S UNIVERSITY, Douglas Library, Kingston, K7L 5C4, Can. William F E Morley, Cur, Special Collections
Holdings: Vols 6980 Cat Mss Pix
Notes: Subject strength of the collections.

ON —UNIVERSITY OF TORONTO, Thomas Fisher Rare Book Library, 120 Saint George St, Toronto, M5S 1A5, Can. Richard G Landon, Head
Holdings: Vols (6000) Cat
Notes: Hannah Collection named in honour of Jason A Hannah, the founder of the Hannah Institute for the History of Medical and Related Sciences at the University of Toronto. Collection comprises a wide range of works in medicine, surgery, anatomy, physiology and other related sciences published in the major European countries and Great Britain from 1500 to 1900. Areas of special strength are psychology, gynecology and obstetrics. Highlights of collection described in two exhibition catalogues published by the Thomas Fisher Rare Book Library: The Early History of Medicine; An Exhibition of Books Selected from the Jason A Hannah Collection in the History of Medical and Related Sciences (March, 1974) and The Byrth of Mankynd (1981).

PQ —MCGILL UNIVERSITY, Osler Library, 3655 Drummond St, Montreal, H3G 1Y6, Can. Philip M Teigen, Librn
Holdings: Vols (35,000) Cat ;Mss Pix Slides Microforms
Notes: The Osler Library is a research library in the history of medicine and allied sciences. Its scope incl the history of medical practice, medical sciences (eg anatomy, pathology), medical specialities (eg psycholoy, genetics, biochemistry), and medical statistics, historical demography, and medical institutions. Partial listing in Bibliotheca Osleriana, 1929, reprinted 1969; Library publishes Osler Library Newsletter, free on request.

MEDICINE—HISTORY AND HISTORIC—CALIFORNIA

CA —UNIVERSITY OF CALIFORNIA, SAN FRANCISCO, Library, Special Collections, San Francisco, 94143. Nancy Witten Zinn, Librn
Holdings: Vols (23,000) Cat Mss Pix Microforms

MEDICINE—HISTORY AND HISTORIC—KENTUCKY

KY —UNIVERSITY OF LOUISVILLE, Kornhauser Health Sciences Library, 520 S Preston St, PO Box 35260, Louisville, 40292. Leonard M Eddy, Dir; Sherrill R McConnell, Archivist
Holdings: Cat Mss Pix
Notes: Kentucky physicians and medical hitory (pictures and mss). Over 10,000 pages of source material compiled under WPA for history of medicine in Kentucky, plus collection of photographs of Kentucky physicians. WPA material being microfilmed. Partly cataloged.

MEDICINE—INSTRUMENTS see Medical Instruments and Apparatus

MEDICINE—JEWS see Medicine, Jewish—History and Historic

MEDICINE—PICTURES, ILLUSTRATIONS, ETC.

KY —UNIVERSITY OF LOUISVILLE, Kornhauser Health Sciences Library, 520 S Preston St, PO Box 35260, Louisville, 40292. Leonard M Eddy, Dir; Sherrill R McConnell, Archivist
Holdings: Cat Mss Pix
Notes: Kentucky physicians and medical hitory (pictures and mss). Over 10,000 pages of source material compiled under WPA for history of medicine in Kentucky, plus collection of photographs of Kentucky physicians. WPA material being microfilmed. Partly cataloged.

LA —TULANE UNIVERSITY, Rudolph Matas Medical Library, 1430 Tulane Ave, New Orleans, 70112. W D Postell Jr, Librn
Holdings: Cat
Notes: Pictures of doctors-3400; Medical art-700.

NY —UNIVERSITY OF ROCHESTER, School of Medicine and Dentistry, Edward G Miner Library, 601 Elmwood Ave, Rochester, 14642. Lucretia McClure, Medical Librn; Janet Brady Berk, History of Medicine Librn
Notes: Strong in yellow fever, cholera, orthopaedics, anatomy and original historic medical photographs.

MEDICINE—RESEARCH see Medical Research

MEDICINE—SOCIAL ASPECTS see Social Medicine

MEDICINE—STUDY AND TEACHING

CA —STANFORD UNIVERSITY LIBRARIES, Lane Medical Library, Stanford University, Medical Center, Stanford, 94305. Peter Stangl, Librn
Holdings: Mss Pix Cat
Notes: Cooper Medical College and Clinics, records; Stanford University School of Medicine, records, Levi Cooper Lane, mss; Ray Lyman Wilbur, mss on Commission on Medical Education.

CO —WESTERN INTERSTATE COMMISSION FOR HIGHER

MEDICINE—STUDY AND TEACHING (cont.)

EDUCATION, Wiche Library, PO Drawer P, Boulder, 80302. Karon M Kelly, Dir Library Services
Holdings: Vols (10,000) Cat Microforms
Notes: Incl medical and nursing education, student exchange programs, minority involvement in education, management systems in higher education.

MD —JOHNS HOPKINS UNIVERSITY, William H Welch Medical Library, 1900 E Monument St, Baltimore, 21205. Richard A Polacsek, Dir & Librn
Holdings: Vols (275,000) Cat Pix Slides Phonorecords Audiotapes Videotapes 16mm Films Filmstrips Microforms
Budget: ($497,000)

MA —FRANCIS A COUNTWAY LIBRARY OF MEDICINE, Boston Medical Library/ Harvard Medical Library, 10 Shattuck St, Boston, 02115. C Robin LeSueur, Librn; Richard J Wolfe, Cur, Rare Books & Manuscripts
Holdings: Vols (500,000) Cat Mss Maps Pix Microforms
Notes: Combines resources of the Harvard Medical School and the Boston Medical Library. Strong in serials and medical history in all fields of medicine, incl incunabula, non-medical books by doctors, travel books by doctors. 500,000 medical dissertations and theses. Special strength in all medical subjects listed in this volume.

MEDICINE, AEROSPACE see Aerospace Medicine

MEDICINE, ARABIC

CA —STANFORD UNIVERSITY LIBRARIES, Lane Medical Library, Stanford University, Medical Center, Stanford, 94305. Peter Stangl, Librn
Notes: Barkan collection of rare medical books, including the Ernst Seidel collection of Arabic and near Eastern medicine.

UT —UNIVERSITY OF UTAH, Middle East Library, Salt Lake City, 84112. Ragai N Makar, Librn
Holdings: Vols 3000 Cat Mss Pix Microforms
Budget: ($40,000)
Notes: The Martin Levey Collection, one of the finest on Arabic sciences and medicine in the country. Incl books and mss on all the sciences and medicine through the 14th century: 3000 books; 5000 offprints; 1000 microfilmed mss in German, Arabic, and French.

MEDICINE, ATOMIC see Atomic Medicine

MEDICINE, AVIATION see Aerospace Medicine

MEDICINE, BOTANIC

†CA —UNIVERSITY OF CALIFORNIA LOS ANGELES, Center for the Study of Comparative Folklore and Mythology, Los Angeles, 90024.
Notes: Archive, consisting of nearly 500,000 entries and cross-references, developed by Prof Wayland D Hand over the past 40 years as part of his monumental *Dictionary of American Popular Beliefs and Superstitions.* Entries have been drawn from both field collections and from printed and published sources. Analytical data stress both the historical component and the comparative approach. Of special interest is the emphasis on magical medicine, although natural and botanical medicine are also well represented.

DE —UNIVERSITY OF DELAWARE, Hugh M Morris Library, S College Ave, Newark, 19711. T Stuart Dick, Special Collections
Holdings: Cat Mss Pix
Notes: Unidel History of Horticulture and Landscape Architecture Collection. Focus is on the origins of horticulture and landscape architecture in America. Particularly strong in early American, English and continental works. Landscape architecture is represented by of the great English and American works as well as the French and Italian ones. There is a small but important group of American works on botanic medicine. Some of the great herbals are also present as well as a number of early American periodicals.

OH —LLOYD LIBRARY & MUSEUM, 917 Plum St, Cincinnati, 45202. John B Griggs, Librn
Notes: Extensive holdings on drug plants, plant drugs, pharmacognosy, and plant chemistry.

MEDICINE, CHINESE

CA —UNIVERSITY OF CALIFORNIA, SAN FRANCISCO, Library, San Francisco, 94143. Atsumi Minami, Librn
Holdings: Vols (11,990) Cat Mss
Notes: Collection consists of titles in Chinese, Japanese and other languages from 12th century mss to contemporary publications, and items such as artifacts and prints on the subject.

CT —YALE UNIVERSITY, Medical Historical Library, 333 Cedar St, New Haven, 06510. Ferenc A Gyorgyey, Librn
Holdings: Pix
Notes: Pictures of 86 patients with pronounced pathological conditions, painted in China by Lam-Qua in the 19th century, commissioned by Dr Peter Parker, a medical missionary.

MD —JOHNS HOPKINS UNIVERSITY, Institute of the History of Medicine, 1900 E Monument St, Baltimore, 21205. Doris Thibodeau, Librn
Holdings: Vols 380
Notes: In Chinese.

MD —NATIONAL LIBRARY OF MEDICINE, 8600 Rockville Pike, Bethesda, 20209. Harold M Schoolinam, Actg Dir
Budget: ($46,400)

MA —FRANCIS A COUNTWAY LIBRARY OF MEDICINE, Boston Medical Library/ Harvard Medical Library, 10 Shattuck St, Boston, 02115. C Robin LeSueur, Librn; Richard J Wolfe, Cur, Rare Books & Manuscripts
Holdings: Vols (500,000) Cat Mss Maps Pix Microforms
Notes: Combines resources of the Harvard Medical School and the Boston Medical Library. Strong in serials and medical history in all fields of medicine, incl incunabula, non-medical books by doctors, travel books by doctors. 500,000 medical dissertations and theses. Special strength in all medical subjects listed in this volume.

NJ —PRINCETON UNIVERSITY, Library, Gest Oriental Library & East Asian Collections, 317 Palmer Hall, Princeton, 08544. D E Perushek, Cur
Holdings: Vols (1700) Cat Mss Pix
Notes: All in Chinese. Collection emphasis is on pre-20th century works on traditional medicine in all areas. Contemporary works on acupuncture and materia medica are also required.

†NY —COLUMBIA UNIVERSITY LIBRARIES, Butler Library, Rare Book and Manuscript Library, 535 W 114 St, New York, 10027.
Notes: Papers of the American Bureau for Medical Aid to China, incl correspondence, memoranda, reports, minutes, membership and financial records, photographs, posters and printed material. Approx 45,000 pieces. Also, some 6000 photographs of Chinese medical colleges, hospitals, laboratories, and personnel.

OH —OHIO UNIVERSITY, Vernon R Alden Library, Athens, 45701. Kent Mulliner, Africana Specialist
Notes: A collection of 634 vols of Chinese books covering a wide range of subjects incl art, culture, economics, geography, history, language, literature, martial arts, medical science, philosophy, and technology.

MEDICINE, CHINESE—HISTORY AND HISTORIC

CA —UNIVERSITY OF CALIFORNIA, SAN FRANCISCO, Library, San Francisco, 94143. Atsumi Minami, Librn
Holdings: Vols (11,990) Cat Mss
Notes: Collection consists of titles in Chinese, Japanese and other languages from 12th century mss to contemporary publications, and items such as artifacts and prints on the subject.

MEDICINE, CLINICAL

CA —BURBANK COMMUNITY HOSPITAL, Medical Library, 466 E Olive Ave, Burbank, 91501. Narciso Merioles Garganta, Medical Librn
Holdings: Vols 1000 Cat Audiotapes Videotapes

CA —LONG BEACH COMMUNITY HOSPITAL, Medical Library, 1720 Termino Ave, PO Box 2587, Long Beach, 90801. Lois O Clark, Librn
Holdings: Vols (3800) Cat Audiotapes Videotapes 16mm Films Filmstrips
Budget: ($3000)
Notes: Incl 2800 audiotapes and 280 videotapes.

CA —PALO ALTO MEDICAL FOUNDATION, Barnett-Hall Library, 860 Bryant St, Palo Alto, 94301. Eileen Cassidy, Chief Librn
Holdings: Vols (11,872)

DE —US VETERANS ADMINISTRATION CENTER, Medical Library, Wilmington, 19805. Mrs Donald Passidoma, Chief Librn
Holdings: Vols (5000) Cat
Notes: Staff only

IL —CENTER FOR RESEARCH LIBRARIES, 6050 S Kenwood Ave, Chicago, 60637. Donald B Simpson, Dir; Esther Smith, Collection Development Librn
Notes: Large collection of publications in clinical medicine and related sciences, mostly older publication. Several hundred current serial subscriptions to infrequently held foreign titles. Foreign doctoral dissertations in medicine.

IN —US VETERANS ADMINISTRATION HOSPITAL, Library, 1600 Randalia Dr, Fort Wayne, 46805. M Woytassek, Dir
Holdings: Vols 500 Cat Tapes

LA —LAFAYETTE CHARITY HOSPITAL, Health Science Library, 311 W St Mary, Lafayette, 70501. Denise Goetting, Librn
Holdings: Vols 2500 Cat Slides Audiotapes

LA —TOURO INFIRMARY, Hospital Library, 1401 Foucher, New Orleans, 70115. Patricia J Greenfield, Head
Holdings: Vols (3000) Cat Audiotapes Videotapes
Budget: $80,752
Notes: Clinical medicine and nursing. Photocopying.

MD —JOHNS HOPKINS UNIVERSITY, William H Welch Medical Library, 1900 E Monument St, Baltimore, 21205. Richard A Polacsek, Dir & Librn
Holdings: Vols (270,000) Cat Pix Slides Phonorecords Audiotapes Videotapes 16mm Films Filmstrips Microforms
Budget: ($497,000)

MD —PROVIDENT HOSPITAL, Health Sciences Library, 2600 Liberty Heights Ave, Baltimore, 21215. Bertha G Wilson, Librn
Holdings: Vols (5077) Cat Slides Audiotapes Microforms
Notes: Incl 1000 slides, 300 audiotapes and 104 microforms.

MD —UNION MEMORIAL HOSPITAL, Library Services, 201 E University Pkwy, Baltimore, 21218. Rena M Snyder, Dir
Holdings: Vols (5000) Cat Slides Audiotapes Videotapes
Budget: ($70,000)
Notes: Incl 1400 vols on clinical medicine.

MD —BETHESDA NAVY HOSPITAL, Edward Rhodes Stitt Library, Bethesda, 20814. Jerry Meyer, Librn
Holdings: Vols (60,000) Cat Slides Videotapes
Notes: Open only to Navy Medical clinicians. Interlibrary loan service offered.

MA —FRANCIS A COUNTWAY LIBRARY OF MEDICINE, Boston Medical Library/ Harvard Medical Library, 10 Shattuck St, Boston, 02115. C Robin LeSueur, Librn; Richard J Wolfe, Cur, Rare Books & Manuscripts
Holdings: Vols (500,000) Cat Mss Maps Pix

MEDICINE, CLINICAL (cont.)

Microforms
Notes: Combines resources of the Harvard
Medical School and the Boston Medical
Library. Strong in serials and medical history
in all fields of medicine, incl incunabula,
non-medical books by doctors, travel books
by doctors, 500,000 medical dissertations
and theses. Special strength in all medical
subjects listed in this volume.

NY —MISERICORDIA HOSPITAL, Medical
Library, 600 E 233 St, Bronx, 10466. Jeanne
Atkinson, Librn
Holdings: Vols 7000 Cat Audiotapes

NY —NORTHERN WESTCHESTER
HOSPITAL CENTER, Health Sciences
Library, Mount Kisco, 10549. Nona C
Willoughby, Librn
Notes: Core Collection: Over 1500 medical
and nursing monographs and texts, primarily
published within last five years. Subscribe to
over 120 journals, bound journal vols kept
for 10 years. MEDLARS online service.
Audiodigests cassettes, six specialties, kept 5
years.

NY —SAINT CLARE'S HOSPITAL &
HEALTH CENTER, Medical Library, 415
W 51 St, New York, 10019. James H Kirk,
Librn
Holdings: Vols (1500) Cat Slides Audiotapes
Microforms
Budget: ($17,000)
Notes: Clinical medicine and surgery. Also
5600 bound journals and 650 audiotapes.
Shelf list; separate catalog in progress.

NY —STATE UNIVERSITY OR NEW
YORK, UPSTATE MEDICAL CENTER,
Library, 766 Irving Ave, Syracuse, 13210.
Evelyn L Hoey, Library Dir
Holdings: Vols (138,000) Cat Monographs
Ser Mss Pamphlets Slides Phonorecords
Audiotapes Videotapes 16mm Films
Microforms
Budget: ($266,900)
Notes: Comprehensive collection of basic,
experimental and clinical medical science
books and journals. Incl medical museum
pieces. Collection incl 46,219 vols, 92
monographs, 741 serials, 1115 pamphlets,
127 mss, 12,955 microform pieces, 601
audiocassettes, 87 mixed media packages, 70
motion pictures, 96 phono discs, 41,500
slides, 7 video discs, and 405 videotapes.

OH —GOOD SAMARITAN HOSPITAL &
HEALTH CENTER, Shank Memorial
Library, 2222 Philadelphia Dr, Dayton,
45406. Elizabeth A Robinson, Librn
Holdings: Vols 15,500 Cat Slides Audiotapes
Videotapes Microforms
Budget: $33,000
Notes: Incl 1000 slides, 800 audiotapes, 25
videotapes, and 15 microforms.

PA —ENSANIAN PHYSICOCHEMICAL
INSTITUTE, Electrotopography Library, PO
Box 98, Eldred, 16731. Elisabeth Anahid
Ensanian, Chief Librn
Holdings: Cat Maps Slides
Budget: ($45,000)
Notes: Electrotopography is a new science
(the Institute has pioneered the field and has
coined the terms "electrotopograph" and
"electrotopography") concerned with the
mapping of electrical fields associated with
metals, alloys, semiconductors, and living
organisms. These fields may be natural and/
or induced, and are converted into mappings
which exhibit certain systems characteristics
for both normal and stress states.

PA —COLLEGE OF PHYSICIANS OF
PHILADELPHIA, Library, 19 S 22 St,
Philadelphia, 19103. Anthony Aguirre, Libr
Dir
Holdings: Vols (316,223) Cat Mss
Microforms
Budget: ($1,096,557)
Notes: Incl 13,515 pamphlets; 1435 mss;
326,367 reports, dissertations, and reprints.
Strong historical and bibliographical
collections, as well as current materials.
Medical documentation service provides
current alerting, incl abstracting, etc.

RI —MIRIAM HOSPITAL MEDICAL
LIBRARY, 164 Summit Ave, Providence,
02906. Ann LeClaire, Dir of Library

Services
Holdings: Cat Cassettes
Notes: Special collection on the renal system
with emphasis on kidney transplantation and
dialysis.

WI —HOLY FAMILY HOSPITAL, Health
Sciences Library, 21 & Western Ave,
Manitowoc, 54220. Dan Eckert, Librn
Holdings: Vols 1500 Cat Audiotapes
Videotapes
Budget: $5500

BC —UNIVERSITY OF BRITISH
COLUMBIA, Vancouver General Hospital,
Biomedical Branch Library, 700 West 10th
Ave, Vancouver, V5Z 1L5, Can. George C
Freeman, Head
Holdings: Vols (25,300) Cat
Budget: ($83,400)
Notes: Clinical medicine.

ON —SUNNYBROOK HOSPITAL, Health
Sciences Library, 2075 Bayview Ave,
Toronto, M4N 3M5, Can. Linda McFarlane,
Librn
Holdings: Vols (12,000) Cat Audiotapes
Videotapes
Budget: ($40,000)
Notes: Emphasis on clinical medicine; also
have nursing and hospital administration.

MEDICINE, COMPARATIVE

IN —PURDUE UNIVERSITY LIBRARIES,
Veterinary Medical Library, C J Lynn Hall
of Veterinary Medicine, West Lafayette,
47907. Gretchen Stephens, Librn
Holdings: Vols (31,022) Cat
Budget: ($106,281)
Notes: The collection contains the
outstanding books and serials in English that
are germane to comparative and veterinary
medicine. Foreign language materials are
added selectively. Subjects of particular
strength are laboratory animal medicine,
pathology, comparative anatomy, animal
behavior and clinical veterinary medicine.

WA —WASHINGTON STATE
UNIVERSITY, Veterinary Medical &
Pharmacy Library, 701 Wegner Hall,
Pullman, 99164. Vicki F Croft, Head
Holdings: Vols (42,000) Cat Mss Microforms
Budget: ($146,667)

MEDICINE, DENTAL see
Teeth—Diseases

MEDICINE, ECLECTIC

†CA —UNIVERSITY OF CALIFORNIA LOS
ANGELES, Center for the Study of
Comparative Folklore and Mythology, Los
Angeles, 90024.
Notes: Archive, consisting of nearly 500,000
entries and cross-references, developed by
Prof Wayland D Hand over the past 40
years as part of his monumental *Dictionary
of American Popular Beliefs and
Superstitions*. Entries have been drawn from
both field collections and from printed and
published sources. Analytical data stress
both the historical component and the
comparative approach. Of special interest is
the emphasis on magical medicine, although
natural and botanical medicine are also well
represented.

OH —LLOYD LIBRARY & MUSEUM, 917
Plum St, Cincinnati, 45202. John B Griggs,
Librn
Notes: Said to be the world's largest
collection on eclectic medicine.

MEDICINE, ENVIRONMENTAL see
Environmental Medicine

MEDICINE, EXPERIMENTAL

CT —YALE MEDICAL LIBRARY, 333 Cedar
St, New Haven, 06510.
Holdings: Vols (334,215) Cat Mss Pix Slides
Microforms
Budget: ($361,650)
Notes: Incl films, audiotapes, artifacts, etc.

CT —YALE UNIVERSITY, School of
Medicine, Dept of Obstetrics & Gynecology
Library, Farnam Memorial Bldg, New
Haven, 06510.
Holdings: Cat Mss Pix Slides
Notes: X-ray plates, 10,000 slides of monkey

and human tissue and about 1000 slides of
gynecological and obstetrical pathology, used
as teaching and research materials. Other
large collections of X-ray and radiotherapy
photographs are in the Hunter Radiation
Therapy Center.

NY —STATE UNIVERSITY OR NEW
YORK, UPSTATE MEDICAL CENTER,
Library, 766 Irving Ave, Syracuse, 13210.
Evelyn L Hoey, Library Dir
Holdings: Vols (138,000) Cat Monographs
Ser Pamphlets Mss Slides Phonorecords
Audiotapes Videotapes 16mm Films
Microforms
Budget: ($266,900)
Notes: Comprehensive collection of basic,
experimental and clinical medical science
books and journals. Incl medical museum
pieces. Collection incl 46,219 vols, 92
monographs, 741 serials, 1115 pamphlets,
127 mss, 12,955 microform pieces, 601
audiocassettes, 87 mixed media packages, 70
motion pictures, 96 phono discs, 41,500
slides, 7 video discs, and 405 videotapes.

MEDICINE, FOLK see Folk Medicine

MEDICINE, FORENSIC see Medical
Jurisprudence

MEDICINE, FRENCH

MD —MEDICAL & CHIRURGICAL
FACULTY OF THE STATE OF
MARYLAND, Library, 1211 Cathedral St,
Baltimore, 21201. Joseph E Jensen, Librn
Holdings: Vols (10,000)// Cat Mss Maps Pix
Notes: Part of the history of medicine and
rare medical book collection. Includes early
literature (some medical incunabula), texts
and periodicals (strong in Garrison and
Morton items), histories, bibliographies,
reprints, lecture notes, health department
reports, hospital and physician records,
medical society transactions, etc. Materials
generally span the 16th through the 19th
centuries. European medical classics, and
18th and 19th century medical periodicals.

MEDICINE, FRENCH—HISTORY AND
HISTORIC

GA —MEDICAL COLLEGE OF GEORGIA,
Library, Laney Walker Blvd, Augusta,
30902. Dorothy H Mims, Librn for Special
Collections
Holdings: Vols (2500) // Cat
Notes: Special collection of about 2500
medical books and periodicals, chiefly from
the late 18th and early 19th century, which
were part of the early library of the Medical
College of Georgia. Incl some 17th and early
18th century works and a number of classics
listed in Garrison-Morton, as well as typical
texts of the period. Unusually strong in
French medical works, as the core collection
was purchased in France in 1834. No
photocopying.

MN —UNIVERSITY OF MINNESOTA,
Owen H Wangensteen Historical Library of
Biology & Medicine, Diehl Hall,
Minneapolis, 55455. Judith Overmier, Cur
Holdings: Vols (35,000) Cat Mss
Budget: ($80,000)

MEDICINE, GERMAN

MD —MEDICAL & CHIRURGICAL
FACULTY OF THE STATE OF
MARYLAND, Library, 1211 Cathedral St,
Baltimore, 21201. Joseph E Jensen, Librn
Holdings: Vols (10,000) // Cat Mss Maps
Pix
Notes: Part of the history of medicine and
rare medical book collection. Includes early
literature (some medical incunabula), texts
and periodicals (strong in Garrison and
Morton items), histories, bibliographies,
reprints, lecture notes, health department
reports, hospital and physician records,
medical society transactions, etc. Materials
generally span the 16th through the 19th
centuries. European medical classics, and
18th and 19th century medical periodicals.

MEDICINE, INDUSTRIAL

DE —E I DUPONT DE NEMOURS & CO,
Haskell Laboratory for Toxicology &

MEDICINE, INDUSTRIAL (cont.)

Industrial Medicine, Library, Elkton Rd, Newark, 19711. Nancy S Selzer, Librn
Holdings: Vols (19,000) Cat Microforms

MEDICINE, INTERNAL

CT —YALE MEDICAL LIBRARY, 333 Cedar St, New Haven, 06510.
Holdings: Vols (334,215) Cat Mss Pix Slides Microforms
Budget: ($361,650)
Notes: Incl films, audiotapes, artifacts, etc.

NJ —BERLEX LABORATORIES, Research & Development Library, 110 E Hanover Ave, Cedar Knolls, 07927. Lorene Lingelbach, Librn
Holdings: Vols (10,000) Cat Microforms
Notes: The library was established in 1972 by consolidating the collections of companies which merged with Berlex Laboratories. 425 periodical titles are received currently.

MEDICINE, JAPANESE

CA —UNIVERSITY OF CALIFORNIA, SAN FRANCISCO, Library, San Francisco, 94143. Atsumi Minami, Librn
Holdings: Vols (11,990) Cat Mss
Notes: Collection consists of titles in Chinese, Japanese and other languages from 12th century mss to contemporary publications, and items such as artifacts and prints on the subject.

MA —FRANCIS A COUNTWAY LIBRARY OF MEDICINE, Boston Medical Library/ Harvard Medical Library, 10 Shattuck St, Boston, 02115. C Robin LeSueur, Librn; Richard J Wolfe, Cur, Rare Books & Manuscripts
Holdings: Vols (500,000) Cat Mss Maps Pix Microforms
Notes: Combines resources of the Harvard Medical School and the Boston Medical Library. Strong in serials and medical history in all fields of medicine, incl incunabula, non-medical books by doctors, travel books by doctors. 500,000 medical dissertations and theses. Special strength in all medical subjects listed in this volume.

MEDICINE, JAPANESE—HISTORY AND HISTORIC

CA —UNIVERSITY OF CALIFORNIA, SAN FRANCISCO, Library, San Francisco, 94143. Atsumi Minami, Librn
Holdings: Vols (11,990) Cat Mss
Notes: Collection consists of titles in Chinese, Japanese and other languages from 12th century mss to contemporary publications, and items such as artifacts and prints on the subject.

MEDICINE, JEWISH—HISTORY AND HISTORIC

MA —FRANCIS A COUNTWAY LIBRARY OF MEDICINE, Boston Medical Library/ Harvard Medical Library, 10 Shattuck St, Boston, 02115. C Robin LeSueur, Librn; Richard J Wolfe, Cur, Rare Books & Manuscripts
Holdings: Vols 500

MA —HEBREW COLLEGE, Jacob & Rose Grossman Library and Lawrence Jay & Anne Cable Rubenstein Library, 43 Hawes St, Brookline, 02146. Maurice Tuchman, Librn
Holdings: Vols 700 Cat Mss
Notes: Harry A and Beatrice C Savitz Medical Library History Collection. Collection of material on Jewish medical history.

MEDICINE, LASERS IN see Lasers in Medicine

MEDICINE, LEGAL see Medical Jurisprudence

MEDICINE, MILITARY

MD —MEDICAL & CHIRURGICAL FACULTY OF THE STATE OF

MARYLAND, Library, 1211 Cathedral St, Baltimore, 21201. Joseph E Jensen, Librn
Holdings: Vols (10,000) // Cat Mss Maps Pix
See also entry under Medicine - History and Historic

MD —BETHESDA NAVY HOSPITAL, Edward Rhodes Stitt Library, Bethesda, 20814. Jerry Meyer, Librn
Holdings: Vols 500 Cat
Notes: Open only to Navy Medical clinicians. Interlibrary loan service offered.

TN —VANDERBILT UNIVERSITY, Medical Center Library, Nashville, 37232. Mary H Teloh, Special Collections Librn
Holdings: Vols 3000 Cat
Notes: The rare books collection incl works by Auenbrugger, Beaumont, Elyot, Jenner, Laennec, Vesalius, and Vigo. The working collection for the history of medicine is particularly strong in American imprints of the late 18th and 19th century. These emphases are supported in the general collection by some notable runs of the 18th and 19th century European and American medical journals. Strong subject collections include: military medicine, nutrition, surgery and urology. There is also under development a collection of the scientific writings of medical educators connected with Vanderbilt.

TX —US AIR FORCE, School of Aerospace Medicine, Strughold Aeromedical Library, Brooks AFB, 78235. Fred W Todd, Chief Librn
Holdings: Vols (119,188) Cat Mss Maps Pix Microforms
Budget: ($499,000)
Notes: Aviation and space medicine and physiology, including the physiological effects of altitude and decompression. Biomedical and and human engineering. Military medicine, including chemical and biological warfare. Emergency medicine in both professional and technical areas. Radiobiology, including atomic medicine, nuclear medicine, and space radiation. Material not oriented to the School of Aerospace Medicine are excluded. Incl also 45,787 microforms and 142,371 technical documents.

TX —UNIVERSITY OF TEXAS, DALLAS, Health Science Center, Reference Dept & History of Health Sciences Dept, 5323 Harry Hines Blvd, Dallas, 75235. Helen Mayo, Head
Holdings: Vols (10,000) Cat Pix Slides Audiotapes Videotapes Microforms
Notes: History of Medicine collection contains ca 16,000 volumes. This total is comprised of pre-1900 journals, primary materials in the History of Medicine and the History of Science, and secondary studies in these two areas. The major strengths of this collection are in the areas of epidemics and plagues, military medicine, and collected works of famous medical pioneers. Southwestern Collection contains items focusing on medicine and history of the Southwest, particularly Texas. Included in this collection are the medical journals published by the county medical societies in Texas, local publications by Dallas County medical organizations, and ephemeral material in a similar vein. The university archives contain all theses and dissertations from UTHSCD, books by members of the school's faculty, and all materials circulated by the school's administration.

MEDICINE, NUCLEAR see Nuclear Medicine

MEDICINE, ORIENTAL

CA —UNIVERSITY OF CALIFORNIA, LOS ANGELES, Biomedical Library, Center for the Health Sciences, Los Angeles, 90024. Alison Bunting, Acting Biomedical Librn; Victoria Steele, Head, History & Special Collections Div
Holdings: Vols 380// Cat Pix
Notes: Medicine, surgery, and physiology, 17th-19th centuries; books and prints.

CA —UNIVERSITY OF CALIFORNIA, SAN FRANCISCO, Library, San Francisco,

94143. Atsumi Minami, Librn
Holdings: Vols (11,990) Cat Mss
Notes: Collection consists of titles in Chinese, Japanese and other languages from 12th century mss to contemporary publications, and items such as artifacts and prints on the subject.

CA —STANFORD UNIVERSITY LIBRARIES, Lane Medical Library, Stanford University, Medical Center, Stanford, 94305. Peter Stangl, Librn
Holdings: Vols 1000 Cat
Budget: ($2785)
Notes: Ernst Seidel collection of Arabic medicine and Barkan collection of rare books.

CT —YALE UNIVERSITY, Medical Historical Library, 333 Cedar St, New Haven, 06510. Ferenc A Gyorgyey, Librn
Holdings: Pix
Notes: Pictures of 86 patients with pronounced pathological conditions, painted in China by Lam-Qua in the 19th century, commissioned by Dr Peter Parker, a medical missionary.

MA —FRANCIS A COUNTWAY LIBRARY OF MEDICINE, Boston Medical Library/ Harvard Medical Library, 10 Shattuck St, Boston, 02115. C Robin LeSueur, Librn; Richard J Wolfe, Cur, Rare Books & Manuscripts
Holdings: Vols (500,000) Cat Mss Maps Pix Microforms
Notes: Combines resources of the Harvard Medical School and the Boston Medical Library. Strong in serials and medical history in all fields of medicine, incl incunabula, non-medical dissertations and theses. Special strength in all medical subjects listed in this volume.

NY —INSTITUTE FOR ADVANCED STUDIES OF WORLD RELIGIONS (IASWR), Melville Memorial Library, State University of New York, Stony Brook, 11794. C T Shen, Dir
Holdings: Vols 70 Cat
Notes: Works on traditional Asian systems of medicine in Sanskrit, Chinese, Tibetan and an few English translations. Refer inquiries to H G Robinson and L L Yang.

MEDICINE, PORTUGUESE—HISTORY AND HISTORIC

MA —FRANCIS A COUNTWAY LIBRARY OF MEDICINE, Boston Medical Library/ Harvard Medical Library, 10 Shattuck St, Boston, 02115. C Robin LeSueur, Librn; Richard J Wolfe, Cur, Rare Books & Manuscripts
Holdings: Cat Mss Microforms
Notes: Early Portuguese medicine and the role of Portugal in disseminating knowledge of Western Medicine and science in Africa, Asia, and America.

MEDICINE, PREVENTIVE

IN —WISHARD MEMORIAL HOSPITAL, Professional Library, 1001 W Tenth St, Indianapolis, 46202. Fran Bischoff, Library Dir; Kirsten Quam, Librn
Holdings: Vols 50 Cat

PQ —UNIVERSITY OF MONTREAL, Bibliotheque Para-medicale, 2375 Chemin de la Cote Ste Catherine, Montreal, H3C 3J7, Can. Johanne Hopper, Head Librn
Holdings: Vols 1700 Cat
Budget: $4000
Notes: Social medicine, preventive medicine, epidemiology, industrial health and hygiene, and environmental factors (pollution) as related to health Depository for World Health Organization publications.

MEDICINE, PSYCHIC

IL —INSTITUTE FOR PSYCHOANALYSIS, McLean Library, 180 N Michigan Ave, Chicago, 60601. Glenn Miller, Librn
Holdings: Vols (10,000) Cat Mss Pix Audiotapes Videotapes 16mm Films Microforms
Budget: ($87,000)
Notes: The collection is the data base for the

MEDICINE, PSYCHIC (cont.)

Chicago Psychoanalytic Literature Index, a computer-generated quarterly subject guide to books, monographs, journals, symposia, tapes, films, and unpublished material indexed to a depth determined by the quality of the data. The *Index* is published by the Institute in Chicago; a sample is available on request.

NY —PARAPSYCHOLOGY SOURCES OF INFORMATION CENTER, 2 Plane Tree Lane, Dix Hills, 11746. Rhea A White, Dir
Holdings: Vols (4000)
Notes: The PSI Center includes 4000 books, 100 periodical titles, cassette tapes, and unpublished mss dealing with parapsychology and the transformation of consciousness, also 12,000 articles, reprints, etc. There is a charge for reference service and bibliographies.

VA —ASSOCIATION FOR RESEARCH & ENLIGHTENMENT, Library, 67 & Atlantic Avenue, PO Box 595, Virginia Beach, 23451. Stephen Jordan, Library Mgr
Holdings: Vols (250) Cat Audiotapes
Notes: Book collection plus Edgar Cayce Collection of Readings-384 looseleaf binders with typescripts of 14,250 discourses and answers given by him in response to questions while in a trance state. Readings cover period 1903 to September 1944. Subjects range from "Attitudes and Emotions" through "World Affairs" and "Yoga." Medical files cover common ailments from "Acne" and "Arthritis" through "Whooping Cough."

MEDICINE, PSYCHOSOMATIC

IL —INSTITUTE FOR PSYCHOANALYSIS, McLean Library, 180 N Michigan Ave, Chicago, 60601. Glenn Miller, Librn
Holdings: Vols (10,000) Cat Mss Pix Audiotapes Videotapes 16mm Films Microforms
Budget: ($87,000)
Notes: The collection is the data base for the *Chicago Psychoanalytic Literature Index*, a computer-generated quarterly subject guide to books, monographs, journals, symposia, tapes, films, and unpublished material indexed to a depth determined by the quality of the data. The *Index* is published by the Institute in Chicago; a sample is available on request.

MEDICINE, RUSSIAN

NY —NEW YORK ACADEMY OF MEDICINE, Library, 2 E 103 St, New York, 10029. Brett A Kirkpatrick, Librn
Holdings: Uncat
Notes: Over 1000 monographs, pamphlets, journals, correspondence and personal files donated by Dr Joseph Wortis. Represents nearly the entire volume of literature on Russian psychiatry published between 1950 and 1965 in the Russian, German, and English languages.

MEDICINE, SOCIAL see Social Medicine

MEDICINE, SOCIALIZED see Medical Care, Prepaid

MEDICINE, SPACE see Aerospace Medicine

MEDICINE, STATE see Medical Policy

MEDICINE, TROPICAL see Tropical Medicine

MEDICINE, UKRAINIAN

IL —UKRAINIAN MEDICAL ASSOCIATION OF NORTH AMERICA, 2320 W Chicago Ave, Chicago, 60622. Dr Paul Pundy, Librn
Holdings: Vols (1000) Pix
Notes: History of Ukrainian medicine, and contributions of Ukrainian medical practitioners in the US and Canada. Library located in Ukrainian National Museum.

MEDICINE, VETERINARY see Veterinary Medicine

MEDICINE, WOMEN IN see Women in Medicine; Women Physicians

MEDICINE, WORLD

NY —NEW YORK ACADEMY OF MEDICINE, Library, 2 E 103 St, New York, 10029. Brett A Kirkpatrick, Librn
Holdings: Uncat Mss Pix
Notes: Collection of personal papers of Frank George Boudreau, incl correspondence, from his birth to his early years as health officer in Ohio, through his international experience at the League of Nations, and as President of the Milbank Memorial Fund. Much on epidemiology, public health, and public medicine. Collection described in Lee Ash's "Frank Geroge Boudreau, 18 July 1886-14 February 1970," *The Academy Bookman*, (New York Academy of Medicine, Friends of the Rare Book Room), Vol 26, No 1, 1973, pp 6-7.

MEDICINE AND SPORTS see Sports Medicine

MEDICINE AND STATE see Medical Policy

MEDICINES, PATENT, PROPRIETARY, ETC.

†MA —UNIVERSITY OF LOWELL, Library, Lowell, 01854.
Notes: Some materials on manufacturing companies which made Lowell, Massachusetts, the first industrial city in the US.

MEDICINES, PHYSIOLOGICAL EFFECT OF see Pharmacology

MEDICOLEGAL HEMATOLOGY see Forensic Hematology

MEDIEVAL ARCHITECTURE see Architecture, Medieval

MEDIEVAL ART see Art, Medieval

MEDIEVAL CIVILIZATION see Civilization, Medieval

MEDIEVAL HISTORY see Middle Ages—History

MEDIEVAL LAW see Law, Medieval

MEDIEVAL LITERATURE see Literature, Medieval

MEDIEVAL MANUSCRIPTS see Manuscripts, Medieval

MEDIEVAL MUSIC see Music, Medieval

MEDIEVAL PHILOSOPHY see Philosophy, Medieval

MEDINA, JOSE TORIBIO

CT —UNIVERSITY OF CONNECTICUT, Library, Storrs, 06268. R H Schimmelpfeng, Dir of Special Collections
Holdings: Vols 310 Cat
Notes: Comprehensive collection of the first editions and reprints of the bibliographical and historical writings of the Chilean bibliographer.

FL —UNIVERSITY OF FLORIDA, Libraries, Special Collections, W University Ave, Gainesville, 32611. Sidney Ives, Librn & Rare Books
Holdings: Vols (8000) Cat Mss

TX —UNIVERSITY OF TEXAS LIBRARIES, Nettie Lee Benson Latin American Collection, Sid Richardson Hall 1.109, Austin, 78712. Laura Gutierrez-Witt, Head Librn
Holdings: Vols (450,000) Cat Maps Microforms
Notes: Private collection of Diego Munoz relating to Chile, Bolivia, Peru and Ecuador. Incl extensive coverage of the laws of Chile and of the Congress of Chile during the 19th century; also, 200 volumes of works of Jose Toribio Medina.

MEDITATION

TX —OBLATE SCHOOL OF THEOLOGY, Library, 285 Oblate Dr, San Antonio, 78216. James Maney, Libr Dir
Holdings: Vols (22,000) Cat
Budget: ($15,500)

VA —ASSOCIATION FOR RESEARCH & ENLIGHTENMENT, Library, 67 & Atlantic Avenue, PO Box 595, Virginia Beach, 23451. Stephen Jordan, Library Mgr
Holdings: Vols (3000) Cat
Notes: Emphasis on Christian, Buddhist, Hindu religions, mysticism, comparative religion, psychological approach to biofeedback, autogenics, etc.

MEDITATION (BON)

†NY —INSTITUTE FOR ADVANCED STUDIES OF WORLD RELIGIONS (IASWR), Library, State University of New York at Stony Brook, Stony Brook, 11794. C T Shen, Librn
Holdings: Vols 4400 Mss Microforms

MEDITATION (BUDDHISM)

NY —INSTITUTE FOR ADVANCED STUDIES OF WORLD RELIGIONS (IASWR), Melville Memorial Library, State University of New York, Stony Brook, 11794. C T Shen, Dir
Holdings: Vols 25,000 Cat Mss Microforms
Notes: Collection rich in works in English and other European languages and about 25 Asian languages. Incl specific instruction manuals as well as works on the religious, psychological, philosophical, ethical, and artistic aspects of Buddhist meditation. *See also* entries under Buddha and Buddhism; Tantrism, Buddhist; Tibetan Buddhism

MEDITERRANEAN FLORA see Botany—Mediterranean Region

MEDIUM ENERGY PHYSICS

NM —UNIVERSITY OF CALIFORNIA, Los Alamos National Laboratory, Libraries, PO Box 1663, MSP 362, Los Alamos, 87545. J Arthur Freed, Head Librn
Holdings: Vols (800,000) Cat Films Microforms
Budget: ($700,000)
Notes: Incl 500,000 classified and unclassified reports. There are 25 branch libraries and a central collection. The Medical Library contains about 40,000 vols in the areas of biomedical research.

MEDIUMISTIC TRANCE see Trance

MEDIUMS

NY —AMERICAN SOCIETY FOR PSYCHICAL RESEARCH LIBRARY, 5 W 73 St, New York, 10023. Rhea A White, Consultant to the Library
Holdings: Vols (7000) Cat Mss Pix
Budget: ($1500)
Notes: Incl books on spiritualism, as well as works in psychology, religion, philosophy, physics, anthropology, etc which have a possible bearing on parapsychology. An attempt is made to obtain all serious books on parapsychology in English.

RI —BROWN UNIVERSITY, John Hay Library, 20 Prospect St, Providence, 02912. Mark N Brown, Cur Mss
Holdings: Vols (900) // Mss
Notes: John William Graham Collection of Literature of Psychic Science; 350 predominantly late 19th and early 20th

MEDIUMS (cont.)

century books dealing with alchemy, black magic, dreams, demonology, church history, mysticism, mediumship, physical and somatic types of psychic experience. Collection described in *Index to Psychic Science* compiled by S R Morgan (Swarthmore, 1950). Also, the Damon Collection of Occult and Visionary Literature; 550 vols devoted to the development of western mysticism with particular emphasis on American and British thought, incl texts on alchemy, black magic, esoteric church history, dream interpretations, mysticism, witchcraft, the Kabbalah, and visionary testaments and manifestations of all types printed during the 16th to 20th centuries; and the Samuel Wyllys Papers; 125 mss, transcripts, and photocopies of legal and government papers relating to Indian affairs, colonial wars, civil and criminal cases, and the witchcraft trials of 1692-1693. Partially cataloged.

MEEDS, LLOYD

WA —UNIVERSITY OF WASHINGTON LIBRARIES, Suzzallo Library, Manuscripts Section, FM-25, Seattle, 98195. Karyl Winn, Librn
Notes: Incl 371 linear feet, circa 1965-1978.

MEEHAN, ELIZABETH, 1905-

CA —UNIVERSITY OF CALIFORNIA, LOS ANGELES, Research Library, Dept of Special Collections, 405 Hilgard Ave, Los Angeles, 90024. Edward Shreeves, Chairman, Bibliographers Group; David S Zeidberg, Head
Notes: 23 television scripts, screenplays, and treatments.

MEEHAN, THOMAS F., 1854-1943

DC —GEORGETOWN UNIVERSITY, Library, Special Collections Div, 37 & O Sts NW, Washington, 20057. George M Barringer, Special Collections Librn; Nicholas B Sheetz, Mss Librn
Holdings: Mss Cat Pix
Notes: Correspondence addressed to Thomas F Meehan (1854-1943), historian, journalist and editor who served on the editorial staff of numerous publications, incl *Irish-American*, *America*, and the *Catholic Encyclopedia*. Correspondence contains letters from prominent Irish-American Catholic politicians, journalists, and Church prelates, Patrick Andrew Collins, Martin Griffin, and John Boyle O'Reilly, are among the correspondents.

MEEKS, BERNARD

†VA —UNIVERSITY OF VIRGINIA, Library, Charlottesville, 22901.
Notes: Bernard Meeks original cartoons and drawings collection, 326 items incl some original comic strip art. Fred O Seibel collection of ca 6000 original drawings, and cartoonists' working papers and files. Additional collection of editorial cartoons by Oscar Cesare, Jeff MacNelly, Art Wood, etc. Examples of almost all political and many comic artists working in he mid-20th century.

MEEM, JOHN GAW

NM —UNIVERSITY OF NEW MEXICO, Zimmerman Library, Albuquerque, 87131.
Holdings: Mss Pix
Notes: Entire professional library and archives of John Gaw Meem, architect of the Southwest. Incl pictures of many buildings taken by noted photographers.

MEET THE PRESS

DC —LIBRARY OF CONGRESS, Motion Pictures, Broadcasting and Recorded Sound Div, Washington, 20540.
Notes: Recordings, videotapes, and films of

Meet the Press, papers of its producer Lawrence E Spivak, and related pictorial material.

MEGGERS, WILLIAM

NY —AMERICAN INSTITUTE OF PHYSICS, Center for the History of Physics, Niels Bohr Library, 335 E 45 St, New York, 10017. John Aubry, Librn
Notes: Papers and records.

MEIGS, RETURN J.

OH —RUTHERFORD B HAYES LIBRARY, 1337 Hayes Ave, Fremont, 43420. Watt P Marchman, Dir
Notes: 19th century.

MEISSNER, GEORGE N.

MO —WASHINGTON UNIVERSITY, Libraries, Special Collections Dept, Campus Box 1061, St Louis, 63130.
Notes: Family and business correspondence.

MELANCHTHON, PHILIP

CA —STANFORD UNIVERSITY LIBRARIES, Cecil H Green Library, Stanford, 94305. Peter R Frank, Cur, CDP-Germanic Collection
Notes: Extensive holdings in the field of Reformation and Counter-Reformation. First and early editions by Luther, Melanchthon, Bugenhagen, Cochleus, Eck, Hutten, Reuchlin, and minor figures in Special Collections.
CT —YALE UNIVERSITY, Box 1603A, Yale Station, New Haven, 06520.
NC —DUKE UNIVERSITY, William R Perkins Library, Rare Book Room, Durham, 27706. John L Sharpe, III, Cur
Holdings: Vols 300
Notes: Sixteenth century books and pamphlets reflecting both sides of the Reformation, including extensive Luther and Melancthon holdings.
PA —LUTHERAN THEOLOGICAL SEMINARY, Krauth Memorial Library, 7301 Germantown Ave, Philadelphia, 19119. Rev David J Wartluft, Dir Libr
Holdings: Vols (7500) Cat Maps Pix
Notes: Materials by and about the reformers and the history of Reformation. Incl approximately 2000 16th century imprints. Also the critical editions of all major and many minor reformation figures.
See also entry under Numismatics

MELANESIA see Islands of the Pacific

MELCHER, FREDERIC G.

NY —R R BOWKER CO, Frederick G Melcher Library, 205 E 42nd St, New York, 10036. Nancy Dvorin, Librn
Holdings: Vols (15,000) Cat
Notes: Also have an 80-drawer vertical file. No photocopying.

MEL'GUNOV, SERGEI P.

CA —HOOVER INSTITUTION ON WAR, REVOLUTION & PEACE, Stanford University, Stanford, 94305. Milorad M Drachkovitch, Archivist
Holdings: // Mss
Notes: Correspondence, reminiscences, memoranda of political prisoners, and newspaper clippings relating to the activities of the Cheka, the secret police of the RSFSR, and the Russian Red Terror, 1918-1937. 9 ft.

MELLOR, JOHN

AB —UNIVERSITY OF CALGARY, Libraries, Special Collections Div, 2500 University Dr, Calgary, T2N 1N4, Can.
Notes: Papers, mss, etc. The ms collections are complemented by a book collection of some 5000 vols.

MELTZER, DAVID

IN —INDIANA UNIVERSITY, Lilly Library, Seventh St, Bloomington, 47405. William R

Cagle, Librn
Holdings: Cat Mss Pix
Notes: Correspondence and writings of poet David Meltzer, 1954-76. Incl texts and galleys for *Tree* and writings by several other authors appearing in *Tree* or published by Tree Books, 3041 items. Incl first editions of Meltzer's publications.
MO —WASHINGTON UNIVERSITY, Libraries, Campus Box 1061, Saint Louis, 63130.
Holdings: Mss
Notes: Correspondence and literary mss of the San Francisco poet described in *Special Collections: An Annotated Guide to the Holdings of the Manuscript Division and the University Archives and Research Collection.*

MELVILLE, HERMAN, 1819-1891

CA —CLAREMONT COLLEGES, Ella Strong Denison Library, Scripps College, Claremont, 91711. Judy Harvey Sahak, Librn
Holdings: Vols 175 Cat
Notes: The William S Ament Collection.
IL —NEWBERRY LIBRARY, 60 W Walton St, Chicago, 60610. Diana Haskell, Cur of Modern Mss
Holdings: Cat Mss Pix
Notes: Almost all editions. Used as a working collection for the Northwestern/Newberry edition of Melville's *Writings*, Harrison Hayford, General Editor.
IL —ILLINOIS STATE UNIVERSITY, Milner Library, Dept of Special Collections, Normal, 61761. Robert Sokan, Librn
Holdings: Vols 180 Cat
Notes: First editions and books about Melville.
MA —HARVARD UNIVERSITY LIBRARY, Houghton Library, Cambridge, 02138. Rodney G Dennis, Cur of Manuscripts
Holdings: Cat Mss
Notes: For manuscripts see *Harvard Library Notes*, III (1938), 172-173.
MA —BERKSHIRE ATHENAEUM, 1 Wendell Ave, Pittsfield, 01201. Ruth T Degenhardt, Head Local History & Literature
Holdings: Vols 450 Cat Mss Pix Slides Microforms
Budget: ($2000)
Notes: Largest collection of Melville memorabilia. Incl first editions of published Melville works; family correspondence; published biographies and literary criticism and analysis of Melville and his writings; annotated volumes from Melville's personal library. Also contains the Willis Milham Scrimshaw Collection: over two hundred pieces of scrimshaw. Published guide to collection: Leyda, Jay, ed, *The Melville Log* (NY: Gordian Press, 1969).
MA —BERKSHIRE COUNTY HISTORICAL SOCIETY, Margaret H Hall Library, 780 Holmes Rd, Pittsfield, 01201. Janet Low, Librn
MA —ESSEX INSTITUTE, James Duncan Phillips Library, 132-34 Essex St, Salem, 01970. Prudence K Backman, Manuscript Librn
Notes: The Frazer Clark Collection of over 8000 Hawthorne pieces, incl over 300 editions of *The Scarlet Letter*. The Institute is now said to have the world's most comprehensive collection of Hawthorne, with much correspondence from Melville, Thoreau, etc.
NY —NEW YORK PUBLIC LIBRARY, Rare Books and Manuscripts Div, Fifth Ave & 42 St, New York, 10018. William L Joyce, Asst Dir; Susan E Davis, Cur of Mss
Holdings: Mss
Budget: ($7161)
Notes: Incl personal and literary mss, papers, etc.
RI —BROWN UNIVERSITY, John Hay Library, 20 Prospect St, Providence, 02912. Mark N Brown, Cur Mss
Holdings: Vols (1200) Cat Mss Pix
Notes: Morse Whaling Collection incl books, monographs, pamphlets, mss, log books, photographs, printed laws and statutes, blue prints of whaling vessels, and serial

MELVILLE, HERMAN, 1819-1891 (cont.)

publications. Emphasis is on American works of 19th and 20th centuries with some works in Dutch, French, German and Japanese dating from the 18th century. Collection is strong in classics of whaling literature, personal narratives, whaling town histories, ships' registers, account books, and photographs of whaling vessels and processes; incl extensive files of the *Whaleman's Shipping List* (New Bedford), the *Merchant's Transcript* (New Bedford), and the *Friend* (Honolulu).

VA —UNIVERSITY OF VIRGINIA, Alderman Library, Clifton Waller Barrett Collection, Charlottesville, 22901. Joan St C Crane, Cur of American Literature Collections
Holdings: Vols 180 Cat Mss
Notes: Collection includes proofs corrected by Melville; letters; first editions; critical works; etc.

WA —UNIVERSITY OF WASHINGTON LIBRARIES, Suzzallo Library, Special Collections Division, Rare Book Collection, FM-25, Seattle, 98195. Gary Menges, Coordinator for Special Collections
Notes: Printing history, including early printed books and modern fine printing; book arts, including papermaking, decorated papers, bookbinding, book design, and artist's books; American literature, 19th century includes: Stephen Crane, Ralph Waldo Emerson, Nathaniel Hawthorne, Henry James, Henry Wadsworth Longfellow, Herman Melville, Frank Norris, Harriet Beecher Stowe and Walt Whitman and 20th century includes: Theodore Roethke; illustrated books, including emblem books, historical children's illustration, books illustrated with prints, and artist's books; costume history; voyages and travels; preservation of library materials.

MEMMINGER, CHARLES, 1803-1888

SC —COLLEGE OF CHARLESTON LIBRARY, Special Collections Dept, Charleston, 29401.
Notes: Papers, 1864.

MEMOIRS see Biography—Collections

MEMORIA TECHNICA see Mnemonics

MEMORY

NY —MORRIS N & CHESLEY V YOUNG LIBRARY OF MNEMONICS, 270 Riverside Dr, New York, 10025. Morris N Young, Cur
Holdings: Cat Mss Maps Pix Phonorecords Audiotapes 16mm Films Microforms
Notes: Collection of 5000 books, pamphlets, pictures, memorabilia, etc incl medieval art of memory; psychology of memory, forgetting and reading; medical aspects of memory, amnesia, dyslexia; biomedical aspects of learning and memory; information storage, retrieval and cybernetics; memory prodigies, lightning calculators, calendars; remembrance cups and memory mementos. All languages. Memorabilia incl engravings, posters, programs, advertisements, birthday cards, teaching cards, ASLs, and Mark Twain's Memory Builder game and other games. Items range from 1410 to 1980s.

MEMORY DEVICES see Magnetic Memory (Electronic Computers)

MEMORY TRAINING see Mnemonics

MEMPHIS, TENNESSEE—HISTORY

TN —MEMPHIS STATE UNIVERSITY, John Willard Brister Library, Memphis, 38152. John Terreo, Special Collections Librn
Notes: 1968 Memphis Sanitation Workers Strike. A collection of audiotape interviews with Memphis governmental officals and administrators, strikers, union leaders, religious leaders, and other significant persons involved in the strike, during which civil rights leader Dr Martin Luther King, Jr was assassinated. Also incl are photographic prints and negatives and the news outakes from the news departments of the three Memphis television stations as well as clippings from newspapers and periodicals. Published finding aid can be found in the Mississippi Valley Collection.

TN —MEMPHIS/SHELBY COUNTY PUBLIC LIBRARY & INFORMATION CENTER, History & Travel Dept, 1850 Peabody Ave, Memphis, 38104. James R Johnson, Head
Holdings: (5100) Cat Microforms
Budget:
Notes: Covers Memphis and Shelby County, all subject areas. Features special materials and mss, groups of Memphis persons. Incl newspaper clipping file, 1930-date, of local subjects. Various indexes incl photo, biography, occupation, first facts (incl genealogy). Pratial index to early Memphis newspapers in progress.

MEMPHIS POWER AND LIGHT COMPANY

TN —MEMPHIS STATE UNIVERSITY, John Willard Brister Library, Memphis, 38152. John Terreo, Special Collections Librn
Notes: Memphis Power and Light Company Records, 1897-1950.

MENAGERIES see Zoological Gardens

MENANGKABU LANGUAGE

NY —NEW YORK PUBLIC LIBRARY, Oriental Div, Fifth Ave & 42 St, New York, 10018. E Christian Filstrup, Chief
Holdings: // Cat Mss Microforms
Budget: ($56,455)
Notes: Published catalog of holdings.

MENARD, PIERRE

IL —UNIVERSITY OF ILLINOIS, URBANA/CHAMPAIGN, Library, Illinois Historical Survey Library, 1408 W Gregory Dr, 1A Library, Urbana, 61801.
Holdings: Vols (6500) Cat Mss Maps Pix Microforms
Notes: Important ms collections incl: Randolph County Records, 1720-1853, 91 items, 59 reels of microfilm; St Clair County Records, 1722-1809, 6 items, 5 reels of microfilm; George Morgan, papers, 1766-1826, 280 items, 5 reels of microfilm; William Morrison, papers, 1805-1855, 7 reels of microfilm; Pierre Menard, papers, 1780, 1802-1859, 155 items, 27 volumes, 29 reels microfilm; Illinois Surveyors' field notes and plat maps, 1805-1850, 56 reels microfilm. Numerous county and local histories and plat books. 1733 maps, and thousands of Illinois pictures. Guide to the collections published in 1976.

MENARD FAMILY

IL —CHICAGO HISTORICAL SOCIETY, Library, Clark St at North Ave, Chicago, 60614. Archie Motley, Manuscript Librn
Notes: Papers of the Menard Family, fur traders and merchants.

MENCKEN, HELEN

NY —NEW YORK PUBLIC LIBRARY, Performing Arts Research Center, Billy Rose Theatre Collection, 111 Amsterdam Ave, New York, 10023. Dorothy L Swerdlove, Cur
Holdings: Cat Mss Pix
Notes: Papers, scrapbooks, mss, photographs, memorabilia, etc.

MENCKEN, HENRY LOUIS

CA —AZUSA PACIFIC COLLEGE, Marshburn Memorial Library, Citrus & Alosta, Azusa, 91702. Edward Peterman, Librn
Holdings: Vols (150) Uncat
Notes: The Odo B Stade Collection of Literary First Editions. No photocopying.

CA —SAN DIEGO STATE UNIVERSITY, Malcolm A Love Library, 5300 Campanile Dr, San Diego, 92182. D Dickinson, Univ Librn; Don L Bosseau, Dir
Notes: H L Mecken Collection. Includes books by and about him, mostly first edition, autographed; letters, clippings, pamphlets, etc. 200 items.

CT —YALE UNIVERSITY, Box 1603A, Yale Station, New Haven, 06520.
Holdings: Cat Mss

DC —GEORGETOWN UNIVERSITY, Library, Special Collections, 37 & O Sts NW, Washington, 20057. George M Barringer, Special Collections Librn; Nicholas B Sheetz, Mss Librn
Holdings: Mss Cat
Notes: Correspondence between the author and poet Sister Miriam Gallagher; and numerous authors such as Theodore Maynard, Robert Tristram Coffin, and John Hall Wheelock, among others. Of particular interest are long runs of correspondence from H L Mencken (1937-1943, 64 TLS) and Odell Shepard (1933-1945, 47 TLS and ALS). Also, correspondence in the Fulton Oursler Collection.

IL —SOUTHERN ILLINOIS UNIVERSITY, CARBONDALE, Delyte W Morris Library, Special Collections Dept, Carbondale, 62901. David V Koch, Cur of Special Collections; Louisa Bowen, Cur of Manuscripts
Holdings: Cat Mss
Notes: Papers and correspondence of Theodore A Schroeder, constitutional lawyer and founder, with Lincoln Steffens, of the Free Speech League, a forerunner of the American Civil Liberties Union. Contains extensive correspondence with Comstock, Gompers, Debs, H Ellis, Sanger, Sinclair, John Dewey, Darrow, Mencken, A G Hays, Emma Goldman, W E B Dubois, etc. Incl several thousand letters; notes and mss, records of legal cases and extensive files relating to the early history of psychiatry.

KS —UNIVERSITY OF KANSAS, Kenneth Spencer Research Library, Special Collections Dept, Lawrence, 66045. Alexandra Mason, Librn
Holdings: Cat Mss Pix
Notes: The Elizabeth Morrison Snyder Collection: books by and about Mencken, periodicals, clippings, pictures, and mss. Being donated over a period of years. Noncirculating.

KY —UNIVERSITY OF LOUISVILLE, Ekstrom Library, Rare Books & Special Collections, 2301 S Third St, Louisville, 40208. George T McWhorter, Cur; Delinda Stephens Buie, Asst Cur
Holdings: Vols 500 Cat Mss Pix
Budget: ($1500)
Notes: The Victor T Reno Collection. Signed first editions, periodical publications, correspondence between Mencken and Reno, and memorabilia.

MD —ENOCH PRATT FREE LIBRARY, Humanities Dept, 400 Cathedral St, Baltimore, 21201. Neil R Jordahl, Librn
Holdings: Vols 4200 Cat Mss Pix
Notes: The definitive Mencken Collection; also incl over 2000 pamphlets. Mencken gave most of his books and papers to the library. Collection incl family papers, memorabilia, research notes, etc. Numerous presentation books given to Mencken, mostly inscribed.

NH —DARTMOUTH COLLEGE, Baker Memorial Library, Hanover, 03755.
Holdings: Cat Mss Pix
Notes: First editions, mss, etc. Noncirculating.

NY —NEW YORK PUBLIC LIBRARY, Rare Books and Manuscripts Div, Fifth Ave & 42 St, New York, 10018. William L Joyce, Asst Dir; Susan E Davis, Cur of Mss
Holdings: Mss
Budget: ($7161)
Notes: Incl personal and literary mss, papers, etc. One of the world's largest collections of H L Mencken's correspondence, some 30,000 letters to and from the American writer and editor.

PA —GETTYSBURG COLLEGE, Musselman Library, Gettysburg, 17325. Willis M Hubbard, College Librn
Holdings: Vols 150 Cat Mss Pix

MENCKEN, HENRY LOUIS (cont.)

Phonorecords 16mm Films
Notes: The Wilton C Dinges collection of all books by and about Mencken. Includes the film "Mencken's America"; the LC recording of his voice; 640 photostats of his editorials in the *Baltimore Sun*, clippings, manuscripts and letters. Noncirculating. This collection also includes the complete files of *The Smart Set* and *American Mercury* during Mencken's connection with those journals.
PA —UNIVERSITY OF PENNSYLVANIA, Van Pelt Library, Rare Books Collection, 34 & Walnut Sts, Philadelphia, 19104. Daniel Traister, Special Collections Librn
Holdings: Vols 100 Cat
Notes: The Collection incl 1260 letters. No mss.
TX —UNIVERSITY OF TEXAS, EL PASO, Library, El Paso, 79968. Fred W Hanes, Dir
VA —UNIVERSITY OF VIRGINIA, Alderman Library, Clifton Waller Barrett Collection, Charlottesville, 22901. Joan St C Crane, Cur of American Literature Collections
Notes: Papers.

MENDENHALL, THOMAS CORWIN

NY —AMERICAN INSTITUTE OF PHYSICS, Center for the History of Physics, Niels Bohr Library, 335 E 45 St, New York, 10017. John Aubry, Librn
Notes: Papers and records.

MENEN, AUBREY

MA —BOSTON UNIVERSITY, Mugar Memorial Library, Special Collections Dept, 771 Commonwealth Ave, Boston, 02215. Howard B Gotlieb, Dir
Holdings: Cat Mss Pix
Notes: Mss, correspondence, etc collected in depth; incl publications by or about.

MENGWE INDIANS see Iroquois Indians

MENKE, ERIC F., 1901-1980

DC —GEORGETOWN UNIVERSITY, Library, Special Collections Div, 37 & O Sts NW, Washington, 20057. George M Barringer, Special Collections Librn; Nicholas B Sheetz, Mss Librn
Holdings: Mss Cat Maps Pix
Notes: The Eric F Menke Collection. Incl the papers of the landscape architect Eric F Menke (1901-1980), and a large collection of mms, documents, and photographs pertaining to the history of Washington, DC.

MENNEVEE COLLECTION

CA —UNIVERSITY OF CALIFORNIA, LOS ANGELES, Research Library, Western European Collection, Los Angeles, 90024. Edward Shreeves, Chairman, Bibliographers Group; Mary E Greco, Western European Bibliographer
Holdings: Mss Maps Pix Microforms
Budget: ($5000)
Notes: Early modern and modern France. Special strengths in intellectual and religious history of the seventeenth and eighteenth centuries, Jansenism in particular, and popular culture of the nineteenth and twentieth centuries. Good coverage.

MENNINGER CLINIC

KS —MENNINGER FOUNDATION, Archives, 5600 W Sixth St, Box 829, Topeka, 66601. Alice Brand, Librn; Mark West, Archivist
Notes: The material in the Institutional Archives dates from the opening of the Menninger Clinic in 1925-date. Incl records from nearly every facet of the Foundation, incl the C F Menninger Memorial Hospital, the Children's Division, the Karl Menninger School of Psychiatry, Research Department, the Department of Neurology, Neurosurgery, the Topeka Institute for Psychoanalysis, and the Will Menninger

Center for Applied Behavioral Sciences. Patient reocrds and personnel files are not incl in the Institutional Archives.

MENNINGER FAMILY

KS —MENNINGER FOUNDATION, Archives, 5600 W Sixth St, Box 829, Topeka, 66601. Alice Brand, Librn; Mark West, Archivist
Notes: The Menninger Family Archives. Incl papers of founders of the Menninger Foundation: Dr Charles F Menninger, Dr Karl A Menninger and Dr William C Menninger. Also incl in the Archives is material relating to other family members.

MENNONITES

AZ —NORTHERN ARIZONA UNIVERSITY, Special Collection Library, CU Box 6022, Flagstaff, 86011. Peter M Whiteley, Coordr/Archivist; William Mullane, Librn
Notes: Mennonite Library and Archives Collection, incl in P David Seaman Collection; incl photocopy of H R Voth mss, "Hopi-English Vocabulary," 1902, and "Hopi Field Notes," 1890's.
CA —CENTER FOR MENNONITE BRETHREN STUDIES, Pacific College, Hiebert Library, 1717 S Chestnut, Fresno, 93702. Rachel Hiebert, Archivist
Holdings: Vols 6000 Mss Maps Slides Phonorecords Audiotapes Microfilms
Budget: $60,000
Notes: Integral part of the Mennonite Brethren Biblical Seminary. Founded 1974. Official depository for all General Conference records of the Mennonite Brethren. Sponsored by the Conference Historical Commission. Dr Paul Toews, director; Rachel Hiebert, archivist. Holdings incl all minutes and reports of the Mennonite Brethren General Conference Boards as well as materials which relate to the history, theology and development of the Mennonite Brethren. Partially cataloged.
†IN —GOSHEN COLLEGE, Archives of the Mennonite Church, Goshen, 46526.
Notes: Official records of the Mennonite Church, its boards, committees, agencies and institutions, peace collections, archives collection of the Mennonite Central Committee, private papers of 500 church leaders.
KS —CENTER FOR MENNONITE BRETHREN STUDIES, Tabor College Library, 401 S Jefferson, Hillsboro, 67063. Wesley J Prieb, Dir
Holdings: Uncat Mss Maps Pix Slides Phonorecords Audiotapes 16mm Films Filmstrips Microforms
Budget: ($25,000)
Notes: Historical materials relating to Mennonite Brethern Conference of churches and its activities. Focus on US Conference of Mennonites, incl minutes and correspondence. Keeps all data for districts, except the Pacific. Collects all data on birth of Mennonites incl local church histories, family records, and genealogy. Anabaptists classics and picture collection. Periodicals and papers incl; collection partly cataloged.
†KS —BETHEL COLLEGE, Mennonite Library and Archives, North Newton, 67117.
Notes: Anabaptists, Mennonites in Europe, America, Latin America and Asia.
OH —BLUFFTON COLLEGE, Mennonite Historical Library, Bluffton, 45817. Delbert Gratz, Librn
Holdings: Vols (15,000) Cat Mss Maps Pix Slides Phonorecords 16mm Films Microforms
Budget: $1500
Notes: Collection incl all materials available relating to Mennonites, Anabaptists, Amish, Hutterian Brethren and related religious bodies, as well as the topic of peace. The library has a special collection and index of Mennonite and Amish family histories and genealogies; also a special index to periodical articles in non-Mennonite periodicals that relate to Mennonites, Amish, and Anabaptists. Library is a depository for the

Central District of the General Conference Mennonite Church and the Africa Inter-Mennonite Mission. Incl archives of the Africa Inter-Mennonite Mission.
PA —LANCASTER MENNONITE CONFERENCE HISTORICAL SOCIETY LIBRARY, 2215 Millstream Rd, Lancaster, 17602. Lloyd Zeager, Librn; David J Smucker, Genealogist
Holdings: Vols (55,000) Cat Mss Maps Pix Slides Phonorecords Microforms
Budget: ($3186)
Notes: Depository for the Lancaster Mennonite Conference. Large collection of Mennonite and Amish history books, current Mennonite titles, Mennonite periodicals and newspapers, and archival collection. Publish quarterly journal *Pennsylvania Mennonite Heritage*. Membership organization of 1700.
†PA —EASTERN PENNSYLVANIA MENNONITE LIBRARY, 1000 Forty Foot Rd, Lansdale, 19446.
Notes: Church history.
VA —EASTERN MENNONITE COLLEGE, Menno Simons Historical Library & Archives, Harrisonburg, 22801. Grace Showalter, Librn
Holdings: Vols (15,318) Cat Mss Maps Pix Slides Audiotapes Microforms VF
Budget: ($30,500)
Notes: Anabaptist, Mennonite, and local history and genealogy.
MB —MANITOBA MENNONITE HISTORICAL SOCIETY, Reimer Historical Library, Box 1136, Steinbach, R0A 2A0, Can. Peter Goertzen, Manager
Holdings: Vols (2500) Cat Mss Maps Pix Phonorecords
Notes: Mennonite history and teachings. Also incl material on pioneer settlers in Manitoba. Incl 1000 mss and 600 pictures.

MENOMINEE INDIANS

WI —SHAWANO CITY-COUNTY LIBRARY, 128 S Sawyer St, Shawano, 54166. Michael Hille, Dir
Holdings: Vols 400 Cat Mss Slides
Notes: This collection is known by the general name of Indians of North America. However, the library specializes in materials of all sorts on the Menominee Indians. Some general books on the topic are paperback and uncataloged--perhaps 75 titles.

MEN'S MUSICAL CLUB OF WINNIPEG

MB —UNIVERSITY OF MANITOBA, Elizabeth Dafoe Library, Archives and Special Collections Dept, Winnipeg, R3T 2N2, Can. Richard E Bennett, Dept Head; Corrado A Santoro, Reference Archivist
Notes: Papers include a history of the club, membership records, etc. 7 boxes of materials.

MENSURATION

BC —CANADIAN FORESTRY SERVICE, Pacific Forest Research Centre, Library, 506 West Burnside Rd, Victoria, V8Z 1M5, Can. Alice Solyma, Librn
Holdings: Vols (60,500) Cat Microforms
Notes: Incl forest and plant pathology, entomology, silviculture, meteorology, mensuration, fire research, hydrology, environmental science and ecology, biometrics, land use and classification, soil science, and forest economics. 400 microforms; 40,000 documents and reports.

MENTAL CHRONOMETRY see Time Perception

MENTAL DISORDERS see Mental Illness; Mentally Handicapped

MENTAL HEALING

AZ —WORLD UNIVERSITY, Library, 711 E Blacklidge Dr, Tucson, 85719. Howard John Zitko, Cur
Holdings: Vols (15,000) Cat Mss Maps Audiotapes
Notes: Collection concerns the "frontier sciences". No interlibrary loan.

MENTAL HEALING (cont.)

VA —ASSOCIATION FOR RESEARCH &
ENLIGHTENMENT, Library, 67 &
Atlantic Avenue, PO Box 595, Virginia
Beach, 23451. Stephen Jordan, Library Mgr
Holdings: Vols (1800) Cat
Notes: A R E Library Booklist incl 6000
items in 24 subject categories. This special
collection is especially strong in the
following subjects: astrology, spiritualism,
reincarnation, healing arts, Theosophy,
Atlantis, parapsychology and transpersonal
psychology.

MENTAL HEALTH see Mental Hygiene

MENTAL HEALTH SERVICES, COMMUNITY see Community Mental Health Services

MENTAL HYGIENE

CA —UNIVERSITY OF CALIFORNIA,
BERKELEY, Life Sciences Libraries, Public
Health Library, 42 Earl Warren Hall,
Berkeley, 94720. Thomas J Alexander, Librn
Holdings: Vols (75,000) Cat Microforms
Notes: Research collection covering all
aspects of public health. Health Department
annual reports from all 50 states are
acquired, as well as such reports from all
California health units and from major US
cities. Serial publications issued by Health
Department in the 13 western states are
being received.

CA —WOMEN'S HISTORY RESEARCH
CENTER, Microfilm Library, 2325 Oak St,
Berkeley, 94708. Laura X, Librn
Holdings: Mss Pix Microforms
Notes: Incl material (150 subject files) on
physical and mental health and illnesses; sex
roles; biology; women and the life cycle;
birth/population control; sex and sexuality;
black and Third World women. Collection at
University of Wyoming. Archive of
Contemporary History, PO Box 3334,
Laramie, Wyoming 82701, c/o David
Crosson. Research inquiries accepted.
Microfilm of collection (14 reels and reel
guides) available at many universities and
through Women's History Research Center,
2325 Oak St, Berkeley, CA 94708. No
collections housed at this address.

CA —REISS-DAVIS CHILD STUDY
CENTER, Research Library, 3200 Motor
Ave, Los Angeles, 90034. Lee Freehling,
Librn
Holdings: Vols (12,000) Cat
Notes: Child study, child psychiatry,
psychoanalysis, clinical psychology,
psychiatric social work. Incl 500 audiotapes;
25 16mm Films.

CA —LANGLEY PORTER PSYCHIATRIC
INSTITUTE LIBRARY, University of
California, 401 Parnassus Ave Box 13-B, San
Francisco, 94143. Lisa M Dunkel, Librn
Holdings: Vols (11,700) Cat
Notes: Attempt to cover, selectively,
literature in psychiatry, psychoanalysis,
clinical psychology, and allied fields for an
institute which is involved in clinical work,
training and research.

CO —WESTERN INTERSTATE
COMMISSION FOR HIGHER
EDUCATION, Wiche Library, PO Drawer
P, Boulder, 80302. Karon M Kelly, Dir
Library Services
Holdings: Vols (10,000) Cat Microforms
Notes: Incl medical and nursing education,
student exchange programs, minority
involvement in education, management
systems in higher education.

CT —YALE MEDICAL LIBRARY, 333 Cedar
St, New Haven, 06510.
Notes: A special subject emphasis.

FL —FLORIDA STATE HOSPITAL, Patient/
Staff Library, Chattahoochee, 32324. Linda
Brown, Librn
Holdings: Vols 12,000 Cat Slides
Phonorecords Filmstrips

GA —CENTRAL STATE HOSPITAL, Mental
Health Library, Milledgeville, 31062.
Katherine J Ridley, Librn
Holdings: Vols (2100) Cat Audiotapes
Budget: ($5000)

IL —INSTITUTE FOR PSYCHOANALYSIS,
Gitelson Film Library, 180 N Michigan Ave,
Chicago, 60601. Glenn Miller, Librn
Holdings: Vols 150 Cat Videotapes 16mm
Films
Notes: The library contains a "living history"
series entitled "Portraits in Psychoanalysis,"
a group of videotaped interviews with some
notable present and past staff members of
the Institute. The Film Library is available to
other mental health facilities on a rental
basis. A catalog of the films is available on
request.

IL —ILLINOIS DEPT OF MENTAL
HEALTH & DEVELOPMENTAL
DISABILITIES, Adolf Meyer Mental
Health Center, Professional Library, 2310 E
Mound Rd, Decatur, 62526.
Holdings: Vols (1000) Cat Audiotapes
Videotapes Microforms
Budget: ($4500)
Notes: Mental health, in general, incl
personal mental health and community
mental health, the behavioral sciences
(biomedical, psychological, and social), and
treatment modalities of mental illness, with
primary emphasis on community mental
health and treatment modalities of mental
health.

IN —SOUTHWEST INDIANA MENTAL
HEALTH CENTER, Library, 415 Mulberry,
Evansville, 47714. Donna Yuschak, Librn
Holdings: Vols 850 Cat Slides Audiotapes
16mm Films
Budget: $4000
Notes: Also about 500 pamphlets on
psychotherapy, social work, and therapeutic
recreation.

IN —LARUE D CARTER MEMORIAL
HOSPITAL, Medical Library, 1315 W
Tenth St, Indianapolis, 46202. Philip I Enz,
Librn
Holdings: Vols (14,600) Audiotapes
Budget: ($15,500)
Notes: Incl 100 audiotapes and 219 journal
subscriptions.

KS —JOHNSON COUNTY MENTAL
HEALTH CENTER, John R Keach
Memorial Library, 6000 Lamar Ave,
Mission, 66202. Krista Hilton-Ross, Librn
Holdings: Vols (1000) Cat Mss

KS —TOPEKA STATE HOSPITAL STAFF
LIBRARY, 2700 W Sixth St, Topeka,
66606. Laura Schafer, Librn
Holdings: Vols (10,000) Cat

LA —CENTRAL LOUISIANA STATE
HOSPITAL, Medical & Professional Library,
PO Box 31, Pineville, 71360. B Carol
McGee, Librn
Holdings: Vols 9400 Cat Audiotapes 16mm
Films
Budget: $25,000

MA —MCLEAN HOSPITAL MEDICAL
LIBRARY, 115 Mill St, Belmont, 02178.
Hector Bossange, Dir
Holdings: Vols 25,611 Cat
Notes: Extensive collection.

MA —MASSACHUSETTS
REHABILITATION COMMISSION,
Library, 20 Park Plaza, Boston, 02116. June
C Holt, Librn
Holdings: Vols (15,000) Cat Audiotapes
16mm Films Microforms
Budget: ($18,000)
Notes: For staff and community interested in
rehabilitation literature, defined as
publications which deal with impairments
resulting in disabling conditions; mental and
behavioral disorders; employment of the
handicapped; counseling techniques with
handicapped populations; sheltered
workshops, rehabilitation facilities; halfway
houses and independent living arrangements;
psychological aspects of disability; attitudes
toward the handicapped; and other material
on services for the handicapped. Library
subscribes to 70 journals relating to disability
and rehabilitation.

MI —MICHIGAN DEPARTMENT OF
MENTAL HEALTH LIBRARY, Lewis
Case Bldg, 6th Floor, Lansing, 48926.
Thomas DeLoch, Librn
Holdings: Vols (950) Uncat 16mm Films
Notes: Collection is being cataloged.
Annotated film catalog available.

NE —HASTINGS REGIONAL CENTER,
Medical Library, Hastings, 68901. Ruth
Swingle, Dir
Holdings: Vols 3500 Cat

NV —NEVADA MENTAL HEALTH
INSTITUTE, Library, 480 Galletti Way,
Reno, 89512. Robert D Armstrong, Librn
Holdings: Vols (2500) Cat Audiotapes

NH —NEW HAMPSHIRE TECHNICAL
INSTITUTE, Paul E Farnum Library, 5 Fan
Rd, Concord, 03301. Wm John Hare, Librn
Holdings: Vols 1000
Budget: $300
Notes: Collection incl mental health,
alcoholism, counseling.

NJ —RUTGERS, THE STATE UNIVERSITY
OF NEW JERSEY, Center of Alcohol
Studies Library, Smithers Hall, New
Brunswick, 08903. Penny Page, Librn
Holdings: Vols (8075) Cat Mss Microforms
Budget: ($110,000)
See also entry under Alcoholism

NY —MONTEFIORE HOSPITAL &
MEDICAL CENTER, Karl Cherkasky
Social Medicine Library, 111 E 210 St,
Bronx, 10467. Victor Sidel, Dir
Holdings: Vols (500) Cat
Budget: ($1000)

NY —COLUMBIA UNIVERSITY
LIBRARIES, Whitney M Young Jr
Memorial Library of Social Work, 420 W
118 St, New York, 10027. Tyrone Cannon,
Librn
Holdings: Vols (118,646) Cat
Notes: The collection covers the history and
philosophy of social work, social work
methodology, and all aspects of social
welfare services, especially child welfare,
mental hygiene, correction, the aging, social
security and medical care, rehabilitation,
aspects and problems of civil rights and
automation. There is also a substantial
representation of literature in psychiatry and
the behavioral and social sciences. The
reference section includes more than 419
periodicals, publications issued by voluntary
agencies, government publications, doctoral
dissertations and masters' essays in the field
and standard reference works. Reference
service is available.

NY —ASTOR HOME FOR CHILDREN,
Professional Library, 36 Mills St, Rhinebeck,
12572. William J Nichols, Librn
Holdings: Vols (2850) Cat Mss Audiotapes
Notes: Child psychiatry with emphasis on
child mental health, encompassing child
psychology, residential treatment centers,
social work and related areas.

NY —UNIVERSITY OF ROCHESTER, Rush
Rhees Library, Department of Rare Books
and Special Collections, Rochester, 14627.
Peter Dzwonkoski, Librn
Holdings: Cat Mss
Notes: Correspondence, reports, articles
written by Wile on birth control (including
many letters from Margaret Sanger), left and
right handedness, sex education, child
development, and mental hygiene.

NY —WILLARD PSYCHIATRIC CENTER,
Medical Library, Willard, 14588. Helen
Bunting, Chief Library Services
Holdings: Vols (2078) Cat Audiotapes

OH —ATHENS MENTAL HEALTH &
MENTAL RETARDATION CENTER,
Staff Library, Richland Ave, Athens, 45701.
Judy McGinn, Librn
Holdings: Vols (3000) Cat Audiotapes

PA —HAVERFORD STATE HOSPITAL,
Medical Library, 3500 Darby Rd, Haverford,
19041. Don Halberstadt, Librn
Holdings: Vols 4500 Cat Audiotapes
Budget: $6000
Notes: Incl 5000 journal vols.

TN —WESTERN MENTAL HEALTH
INSTITUTE, Edwin M Levy Professional
Library, Bolivar, 38074. Lee Oda Chambers,
Librn
Holdings: Vols 1500

TX —TEXAS DEPT OF MENTAL HEALTH
& MENTAL RETARDATION, Central
Office Library, 909 W 45, Box 12668,
Austin, 78711. Becky Renfro, Librn
Holdings: Vols (4600) Cat

WA —WESTERN STATE HOSPITAL,
Library, Fort Steilacoom, 98494. Neal Van
Der Voorn, Librn
Holdings: Vols (5900) Cat Audiotapes
Notes: Collection incl 5500 journal vols,
1800 pamphlets and 420 audiotapes.

WI —MENDOTA MENTAL HEALTH
INSTITUTE, Library-Media Center, 301

MENTAL HYGIENE (cont.)

Troy Dr, Madison, 53704. Margaret Tiekle
Grinnell, Librn
Holdings: Vols 14,800 Cat Slides
Phonorecords Audiotapes Videotapes 16mm
Films Filmstrips

WI —UNIVERSITY OF WISCONSIN,
MADISON, W S Middleton Health
Sciences Library, 1305 Linden Dr, Madison,
53706. Virginia Holtz, Dir
Holdings: Vols (200,000) Cat Pix Slides
Audiotapes Videotapes Microforms

WI —MILWAUKEE COUNTY MENTAL
HEALTH COMPLEX, Michael Kasak
Library, 9455 Watertown Plank Rd,
Milwaukee, 53226. Anna M Green, Librn
Holdings: Vols (12,000) Cat Audiotapes
Videotapes 16mm Films Filmstrips
Microforms
Budget: $34,000
Notes: Incl 500 audiotapes and 150
videotapes.

†ON —METROPOLITAN TORONTO
LIBRARY, Social Sciences Dept, 789 Yonge
St, Toronto, M4W 2G8, Can. Abdus Salam,
Head
Holdings: Vols Cat Maps Phonorecords
Audiotapes 16mm Films Microforms
Notes: Includes books on general psychology
and its history. Also, a strong collection of
the works of individual psychologists and
critical works about them. The following
specialized areas of psychology are also well
covered: child psychology, psychology and
mental health, and parapsychology.

ON —ONTARIO MINISTRY OF
COMMUNITY & SOCIAL SERVICES,
Library, 880 Bay St, Rm 663, Toronto, M7A
1E9, Can. Sandra Walsh, Chief Librn
Holdings: Vols (30,000) Cat Slides
Videotapes 16mm Films Microforms

MENTAL ILLNESS

CA —LANGLEY PORTER PSYCHIATRIC
INSTITUTE LIBRARY, University of
California, 401 Parnassus Ave Box 13-B, San
Francisco, 94143. Lisa M Dunkel, Librn
Holdings: Vols (11,700) Cat
Notes: Attempt to cover, selectively,
literature in psychiatry, psychoanalysis,
clinical psychology, and allied fields for an
institute which is involved in clinical work,
training and research.

CT —INSTITUTE OF LIVING, Medical
Library, 400 Washington St, Hartford,
06106. Helen Lansberg, Librn
Holdings: Vols (30,000) Cat Mss Maps Pix
Notes: Three special collections in
psychiatry, neurology and related subjects.
See also entry under Psychiatry

IN —CENTRAL STATE HOSPITAL, Medical
Library, 3000 W Washington St,
Indianapolis, 46222. Aurella S Baker, Librn
Holdings: Vols (10,400) Cat Audiotapes
Budget: ($41,000)

LA —CENTRAL LOUISIANA STATE
HOSPITAL, Medical & Professional Library,
PO Box 31, Pineville, 71360. B Carol
McGee, Librn
Holdings: Vols 9400 Cat Audiotapes 16mm
Films
Budget: $25,000

MA —MASSACHUSETTS
REHABILITATION COMMISSION,
Library, 20 Park Plaza, Boston, 02116. June
C Holt, Librn
Notes: For staff and community interested in
rehabilitation literature, defined as
publications which deal with impairments
resulting in disabling conditions; mental and
behavioral disorders; employment of the
handicapped; counseling techniques with
handicapped populations; sheltered
workshops, rehabilitation facilities; halfway
houses and independent living arrangements;
psychological aspects of disability; attitudes
toward the handicapped; and other material
on services for the handicapped. Library
subscribes to 70 journals relating to disability
and rehabilitation.

MI —LAFAYETTE CLINIC LIBRARY, 951
E Lafayette, Detroit, 48207. Nancy E Ward,
Librn
Holdings: Vols (7000) Cat
Notes: Special emphasis on the biological

aspects, causes and treatment of mental
illness. Also geriatrics.

NE —HASTINGS REGIONAL CENTER,
Medical Library, Hastings, 68901. Ruth
Swingle, Dir
Holdings: Vols 3500 Cat

NJ —RUTGERS, THE STATE UNIVERSITY
OF NEW JERSEY, Center of Alcohol
Studies Library, Smithers Hall, New
Brunswick, 08903. Penny Page, Librn
Holdings: Vols (8075) Cat Mss Microforms
Budget: ($110,000)
See also entry under Alcoholism

NY —ALBERT EINSTEIN COLLEGE OF
MEDICINE, D Samuel Gottesman Library,
1300 Morris Park Ave, Bronx, 10461.
Charlotte K Lindner, Dir

TX —TEXAS DEPT OF MENTAL HEALTH
& MENTAL RETARDATION, Central
Office Library, 909 W 45, Box 12668,
Austin, 78711. Becky Renfro, Librn
Holdings: Vols (4600) Cat

VA —CENTRAL STATE HOSPITAL,
Medical Library, PO Box 4030, Petersburg,
23803. P D Upadyaya, Medical Librn
Holdings: Vols (9000) Cat
Budget: ($6000)

VA —COLLEGE OF WILLIAM AND
MARY, Earl Gregg Swem Library,
Williamsburg, 23185. Margaret C Cook, Cur
of Manuscripts & Rare Books
Holdings: Vols 80// Cat
Notes: Galt Collection of 19th century
European vols on psychiatry and mental
illness.

WA —WESTERN STATE HOSPITAL,
Library, Fort Steilacoom, 98494. Neal Van
Der Voorn, Librn
Holdings: Vols (5900) Cat Audiotapes
Notes: Collection incl 5500 journal vols,
1800 pamphlets and 420 audiotapes.

WI —MENDOTA MENTAL HEALTH
INSTITUTE, Library-Media Center, 301
Troy Dr, Madison, 53704. Margaret Tiekle
Grinnell, Librn
Holdings: Vols 14,800 Cat Slides
Phonorecords Audiotapes Videotapes 16mm
Films Filmstrips

ON —ONTARIO MINISTRY OF
COMMUNITY & SOCIAL SERVICES,
Library, 880 Bay St, Rm 663, Toronto, M7A
1E9, Can. Sandra Walsh, Chief Librn
Holdings: Vols (30,000) Cat Slides
Videotapes 16mm Films Microforms

MENTAL PHILOSOPHY see Philosophy; Psychology

MENTAL PHYSIOLOGY AND HYGIENE see Mental Hygiene

MENTAL PRAYER see Meditation

MENTAL SUGGESTION

CA —GRADUATE THEOLOGICAL UNION
LIBRARY, New Religious Movements
Research Collection, Public Services and
Special Collections Dept, 2400 Ridge Road,
Berkeley, 94709. Diane Choquette, Dept
Head
Holdings: Vols (3000) Mss Pix
Notes: Begun in 1977, the collection focuses
on religious movements new to America
since 1960, and unorthodox religious
movements resurgent since 1960. American
forms of Hinduism, Buddhism, Sikhism, and
Sufism are included along with occultism,
Neo-Paganism, esoteric and alternative
forms of Christianity, feminist spirituality,
and human potential movements having a
spiritual aspect. Legal issues, such as
deprogramming, and the question of church/
state relations are an important part of the
collection. The Library is a depository for
publications of the Unification Church in
America, the Church of Scientology, and the
International Society for Krishna
Consciousness (America). The responses of
mainstream religions and concerned citizens
groups are also included. Besides 3000
monographs, the library has 400 periodical
titles, 200 posters from the San
FranciscoBay Area, 1965-77, 300 research
papers, and 31 linear feet of ephemera.

MENTAL TESTS

CT —YALE UNIVERSITY, Medical Historical
Library, 333 Cedar St, New Haven, 06510.
Ferenc A Gyorgyey, Librn

IL —UNIVERSITY OF ILLINOIS,
URBANA/CHAMPAIGN, Library,
University Archives, 19 Library, 1408 W
Gregory Drive, Urbana, 61801. Maynard
Brichford, University Archivist
Holdings: Vols (6000) Cat
Budget: $1500
Notes: The Odell Test Collection contains
3150 items comprising intelligence,
achievement, subject, and character and
personality tests. Almost every educational
and psychological test of consequence prior
to the early 1950s is included. The collection
is located in the Education and Social
Science Library and is integrated into a
comprehensive collection of current and
recent standardized tests. The indexing of
the collection follows the scheme created
and used by Oscar K Buros in his Mental
Measurement Yearbooks and in the
predecessors to the Yearbooks which
appeared in the Rutgers Studies in Education
series. The collection was a gift in 1960 of
Charles Watters Odell, Professor Emeritus of
Education. No photocopying.

NJ —EDUCATIONAL TESTING SERVICE,
Carl Campbell Brigham Library, Princeton,
08540. Janet Williams, Librn
Holdings: Vols 15,000 Cat Microforms
Budget: ($35,000)
Notes: Literature related to tests and
measurements.

OH —UNIVERSITY OF AKRON, Archives of
the History of American Psychology, Akron,
44325. John A Popplestone, Dir
Holdings: Cat Mss Pix Slides Films
Notes: Nearly 1200 ft of psychologists'
personal papers and documents, as well as
organizational records, and over 600 items of
historic laboratory apparatus. Also,
photographs, films, intelligence and aptitude
tests, etc, from the 19th century to date.

MENTALLY HANDICAPPED

CA —STOCKTON STATE HOSPITAL,
Professional Library, 510 Magnolia,
Stockton, 95202. Walter L Greening, Senior
Librn
Holdings: Vols (7000) Cat Microforms
Audiotapes
Budget: ($6000)
Notes: Incl both historical and current
materials on care and treatment of the
mentally retarded: residential care; nursing
and medical care; rehabilitation; recreational
and occupational therapy; teaching; social
services; psychological services. Current
emphasis on the care and treatment of the
multiply handicapped.

IL —JACKSONVILLE STATE HOSPITAL,
Training & Research Library, 1201 S Main
St, Jacksonville, 62650. Lois E Wells, Librn
Holdings: Vols (10,000) Cat
Notes: Concerned particularly with
developmental disabilities.

KS —KANSAS NEUROLOGICAL
INSTITUTE, Menninger Professional
Library, 3107 W 21 St, Topeka, 66604.
Richard Gray, Librn
Holdings: Vols 1244 Cat
Notes: Incl development disabilities; special
education; nursing care for the handicapped;
programs for the mentally retarded;
behavioral psychology; supervision in mental
health/mental retardation; staff training in
mental health/mental retardation.

ME —PINELAND CENTER, Al Rosen
Memorial Library, Box C, Pownal, 04069.
Pat Foley, Acting Librn
Holdings: Vols 200 Cat Audiotapes
Budget: $2500
Notes: Developmental disabilties. Vols
cataloged 1970-date.

MA —MASSACHUSETTS
REHABILITATION COMMISSION,
Library, 20 Park Plaza, Boston, 02116. June
C Holt, Librn
Notes: For staff and community interested in
rehabilitation literature, defined as

MENTALLY HANDICAPPED (cont.)

publications which deal with impairments resulting in disabling conditions; mental and behavioral disorders; employment of the handicapped; counseling techniques with handicapped populations; sheltered workshops, rehabilitation facilities; halfway houses and independent living arrangements; psychological aspects of disability; attitudes toward the handicapped; and other material on services for the handicapped. Library subscribes to 70 journals relating to disability and rehabilitation.

MI —MICHIGAN DEPARTMENT OF MENTAL HEALTH LIBRARY, Lewis Case Bldg, 6th Floor, Lansing, 48926. Thomas DeLoch, Librn
Holdings: Vols (950) Uncat 16mm Films
Notes: Collection is being cataloged. Annotated film catalog available.

MN —CAMBRIDGE STATE HOSPITAL, Staff Library, Cambridge, 55008. Jean Peterson, Librn
Holdings: Vols 625 Cat
Budget: $2650

NJ —NORTH PRINCETON DEVELOPMENT CENTER, Medical Library, PO Box 1000, Princeton, 08540. Donald W Biggs, Librn
Holdings: Vols 1000 Microforms
Budget: ($7000)
Notes: Incl 70 periodicals and 500 microforms.

OH —ATHENS MENTAL HEALTH & MENTAL RETARDATION CENTER, Staff Library, Richland Ave, Athens, 45701. Judy McGinn, Librn
Holdings: Vols (3000) Cat Audiotapes

SC —SOUTH CAROLINA STATE DEPT OF MENTAL RETARDATION, Whitten Center Library, PO Box 239, Clinton, 29325. H Y Keng, Head Librn
Holdings: Vols (20,000) Cat Phonorecords Audiotapes Videotapes 16mm Films Filmstrips Microforms
Notes: Mental retardation, mental deficiency; mentally handicapped education. Materials for the mentally handicapped, incl toys and games. Incl 15,000 microforms.

VA —CENTRAL VIRGINIA TRAINING CENTER, Professional Library, PO Box 1098, Lynchburg, 24505. Helen Hester, Librn
Holdings: Vols 5095 Cat Slides Audiotapes
Budget: $10,000
Notes: Our collection will be focusing on all aspects of the severely and profoundly mentally retarded--education, medical care, research, behavior modification, recreation and social needs, therapy and basic self-help skill training. Extensive periodical collection for professionals.

VA —CENTRAL STATE HOSPITAL, Medical Library, PO Box 4030, Petersburg, 23803. P D Upadyaya, Medical Librn
Holdings: Vols (10,000) Cat

MENTALLY HANDICAPPED—BIOGRAPHY

MN —MAYO MEDICAL LIBRARY, History of Medicine Collection, Rochester, 55905. Nancy R Hensel, Librn
Holdings: Vols 800 Cat
Notes: The Walter C Alvarez Collection of autobiographies of the physically and mentally handicapped. Collection described in *Mayo Clin Proc*, 47:125-127, Feb 1972.

MENTALLY HANDICAPPED CHILDREN

PQ —HOPITAL SAINTE-JUSTINE POUR LES ENFANTS, Centre d'Information sur la Sante de l'Enfant, 3175 Cote Sainte-Catherine, Montreal, H3T 1C5, Can. Louis LucLecompte, Librn
Holdings: Vols (7000) Cat Audiotapes Videotapes 16mm Films Microforms
Budget: ($11,000)
Notes: 40 percent of collection in French.

MENTALLY RETARDED CHILDREN see Mentally Handicapped Children

MENUS—COLLECTIONS

CA —UNIVERSITY OF CALIFORNIA, DAVIS, Shields Library, Dept of Special Collections, Davis, 95616. Donald Kunitz, Head; C Danial Elliott, Asst Head
Holdings: Uncat
Notes: Menus from the Bohemian Club, the Confrerie des Chevaliers du Tastevin, and the Wine and Food Society, among others. About 400 items.

CA —UNIVERSITY OF CALIFORNIA, LOS ANGELES, Research Library, Dept of Special Collections, 405 Hilgard Ave, Los Angeles, 90024. Edward Shreeves, Chairman, Bibliographers Group; David S Zeidberg, Head
Notes: 8 linear feet of menus, chiefly from restaurants in California and the greater Los Angeles area. Some US and foreign ones are included.

CA —CITY COLLEGE OF SAN FRANCISCO, Alice Statler Library, Hotel & Restaurant Dept, 50 Phelan Ave, San Francisco, 94112. Mary B Smyth, Librn
Holdings: Vols (7300) Cat Slides 16mm Films Filmstrips Microforms
Budget: ($5000)
Notes: The collection covers all aspects of the public hospitality industry. In addition to the book collection, it has 6000 cataloged pamphlets, 1500 menus. It also has bound hotel and restaurant magazines dating back to the 19th century. Receives 85 current periodicals in hospitality industry.

IN —WILLARD LIBRARY, 21 First Ave, Evansville, 47710. Joan Elliott, Special Collections Librn
Holdings: Vols (525) Cat
Notes: Menus from 1920-1950s, foreign and domestic, with emphasis on menus from famous trains and ships.

IN —INDIANAPOLIS-MARION COUNTY PUBLIC LIBRARY, Business, Science & Technology Div, 40 E Saint Clair St, Indianapolis, 46204. Mark Leggett, Head
Holdings: Vols 400 Cat
Notes: The Wright Marble Collection of Cookbooks and Menus. Menus uncataloged. Restricted use. No photocopying.

MA —AMERICAN ANTIQUARIAN SOCIETY LIBRARY, 185 Salisbury St, Worcester, 01609. Marcus A McCorison, Dir & Librn
Notes: About 2000 items from 1770 on.

NJ —RUTGERS, THE STATE UNIVERSITY OF NEW JERSEY, Alexander Library, Special Collections and Archives, College Ave & Huntington St, New Brunswick, 08903. Ronald L Becker, Cur of Manuscripts and Rare Books
Holdings: Uncat
Notes: Several thousand items, 19th-20th century.

NY —NEW YORK CITY TECHNICAL COLLEGE, Library, 300 Jay St, Brooklyn, 11201. Catherine T Brody, Chief Librn
Holdings: Vols 1500 Cat Pix Microforms
Notes: Incl menus representing restaurants of the US and many other countries. One bibliography available: *Guide to Hotel and Restaurant Management Resources in the Namm Hall Library*.

NY —NEW YORK PUBLIC LIBRARY, Research Libraries, General Research Division, Fifth Ave & 42 St, New York, 10018. Rodney Phillips, Chief
Holdings: Vols (2,225,000) Cat Maps Pix Microforms
Budget: ($775,718)
Notes: Extensive collection (The Buttolph Collection).

OH —PUBLIC LIBRARY OF CINCINNATI & HAMILTON COUNTY, Science & Technology Dept, 800 Vine St, Cincinnati, 45202. Rosemary Gaiser, Head
Holdings: Vols 8000 Cat
Notes: American and foreign cookbooks; specialty cooking; menus.

TX —TEXAS WOMAN'S UNIVERSITY, Bralley Memorial Library, Box 23715, TWU Sta, Denton, 76204. Metta Nicewarner, Spec Collections Libn
Holdings: Vols 790 Cat
Notes: Foreign menus; banquets and special dinner menus; United States (23 envelopes); Texas (6 envelopes). Many signed and dated by restaurant personnel.

MERCER, CHARLES

MA —BOSTON UNIVERSITY, Mugar Memorial Library, Special Collections Dept, 771 Commonwealth Ave, Boston, 02215. Howard B Gotlieb, Dir
Holdings: Cat Mss

MERCIER, LOUIS J. A., 1880-1953

DC —GEORGETOWN UNIVERSITY, Library, Special Collections Div, 37 & O Sts NW, Washington, 20057. George M Barringer, Special Collections Librn; Nicholas B Sheetz, Mss Librn
Holdings: Mss
Notes: A portion of the papers of the philosopher and educator, Dr Louis J A Mercier (1880-1953), containing manuscripts, correspondence, and published articles.

MERCER, JOHNNY

GA   GEORGIA STATE UNIVERSITY, William R Pullen Library, Atlanta, 30303. Leslie S Hough, Dir
Notes: Large collection of the papers of songwriter, singer, composer, and publisher Johnny Mercer. Incl correspondence, music scores, an unpublished autobiography, phono discs, water colors, etc.

MERCHANDISE, DISPLAY OF see Display of Merchandise

MERCHANT, LIVINGSTON T., 1903-1976

NJ —PRINCETON UNIVERSITY, Seeley G Mudd Manuscript Library, Public Affairs Papers Collection, Princeton, 08544. Nancy Bressler, Cur
Notes: Incl 26 boxes; 3 cartons. The papers cover the period 1953-61. An unpublished 18p guide is available in the Library.

MERCHANT MARINE

MD —SEAFARER'S HARRY LUNDEBERG SCHOOL OF SEAMANSHIP, Paul Hall Library and Maritime Museum, Piney Point, 20674. Janice McAteer Smolek, Librn
Holdings: Mss Pix Slides Audiotapes Videotapes 16mm Films Filmstrips Microforms
Notes: Special collection on maritime studies incl books, mss, periodicals, audiovisuals, and archival materials pertaining to maritime history and maritime labor union history and vocational skills required by the maritime industry. Incl some rare books.

MA —OLD DARTMOUTH HISTORICAL SOCIETY, 18 Johnny Cake Hill, New Bedford, 02740. Richard C Kugler, Dir
Holdings: Vols (15,000) Cat Mss Maps Pix Slides Phonorecords Audiotapes 16mm Films Microforms
Budget: ($5000)
Notes: Whaling Museum Library contains one of the most comprehensive collections of printed and manuscript material ever assembled on the history of the whaling industry. Although primary emphasis is on American participation in this industry, foreign works are well-represented. Particularly noteworthy are the 5000 rare books and pamphlets assembled by the distinguished whaling scholar, Charles F Batchelder. Also, material on merchant ships and the natural history of whales. Incl 750 ft mss, 1070 log books, 650 maps, 25,000 pix, and 1800 microforms.

NY —STATE UNIVERSITY OF NEW YORK, Maritime College, Stephen B Luce Library, Fort Schuyler, Bronx, 10465. Richard H Corson, Librn
Holdings: Vols (68,000) Cat Maps Pix Slides Phonorecords Audiotapes Videotapes 16mm Films Filmstrips Microforms
Budget: ($90,000)
Notes: Focuses on all aspects of the maritime industry; marine engineering, marine transportation, maritime labor, maritime law, naval architecture, navigation, ports and harbors, shipbuilding, shipping, and ships. Extensive holdings in periodical literature with long and complete runs of many titles. Approximately 3500 recent

MERCHANT MARINE (cont.)

research reports in paper and microfiche formats. Mainly English language.

NY —US MERCHANT MARINE ACADEMY, Schuyler Otis Bland Memorial Library, Steamboat Rd, Kings Point, 11024. Stephen R Wiist, Acting Chief Librn
Holdings: Vols (130,000) Cat Mss Maps Pix Slides Phonorecords Microforms
Budget: ($75,000)
Notes: All aspects of maritime affairs.

NY —SEAMEN'S CHURCH INSTITUTE OF NEW YORK, Joseph Conrad Library, 15 State St, New York, 10004. Bonnie Golightly, Librn
Holdings: Vols (23,500) Cat Pix
Budget: ($8500)
Notes: Merchant seamen, merchant ships, voyages, navigation, marine engineering, shipbuilding. Large collection of ship registers: *Lloyd's Register of Shipping*, a partial coverage of the years 1764-1865 in reprints, complete coverage for the years 1877 to date; *American Bureau of Shipping*, 1916 to date; *Merchant Vessels of the US*, 1891 to date. *Society of Naval Architects an Marine Engineers Transactions*, vol 1, 1893 to date. The picture file consists mostly of photographs of merchant ships. This is supplemented by scrapbooks. The index to the pictures, scrapbooks, books and vertical file are in one subject catalog. We subscribe to and keep for several years numerous maritime periodicals. The maritime history collection incl sailing ships as well as steamships.

TX —TEXAS A&M UNIVERSITY AT GALVESTON, MOODY COLLEGE, Library, PO Box 1675, Galveston, 77553. Natalie W Shipman, Librn
Holdings: Vols (13,000) Cat
Budget: ($300,000)

MERCHANT MARINE—LISTS OF VESSELS see Ship Registers

MERCHANT MARINE—PERSONNEL see Merchant Seamen

MERCHANT MARKS see Trademarks

MERCHANT SEAMEN see Sailors, Merchant

MERCHANT SHIPS

MA —OLD DARTMOUTH HISTORICAL SOCIETY, 18 Johnny Cake Hill, New Bedford, 02740. Richard C Kugler, Dir
Holdings: Vols (15,000) Cat Mss Maps Pix Slides Phonorecords Audiotapes 16mm Films Microforms
Budget: ($5000)
Notes: Whaling Museum Library contains one of the most comprehensive collections of printed and manuscript material ever assembled on the history of the whaling industry. Although primary emphasis is on American participation in this industry, foreign works are well-represented. Particularly noteworthy are the 5000 rare books and pamphlets assembled by the distinguished whaling scholar, Charles F Batchelder. Also, material on merchant ships and the natural history of whales. Incl 750 ft mss, 1070 log books, 650 maps, 25,000 pix, and 1800 microforms.

MA —PEABODY MUSEUM OF SALEM, Phillips Library, E India Sq, Salem, 01970. Gregor Trinkaus-Randall, Librn
Holdings: Vols (100,000) Cat Mss Maps Pix
Notes: Maritime history of New England. No published indexes; listed in Hamer's *Guide to Archives...*

NY —US MERCHANT MARINE ACADEMY, Schuyler Otis Bland Memorial Library, Steamboat Rd, Kings Point, 11024. Stephen R Wiist, Acting Chief Librn
Holdings: Vols (130,000) Cat Mss Maps Pix Slides Phonorecords Microforms
Budget: ($75,000)
Notes: All aspects of maritime affairs.

NY —SEAMEN'S CHURCH INSTITUTE OF NEW YORK, Joseph Conrad Library, 15 State St, New York, 10004. Bonnie Golightly, Librn
Holdings: Vols (23,500)
Budget: ($8500)
Notes: Merchant seamen, merchant ships, voyages, navigation, marine engineering, shipbuilding. Large collection of ship registers: *Lloyd's Register of Shipping*, a partial coverage of the years 1764-1865 in reprints, complete coverage for the years 1877 to date; *American Bureau of Shipping*, 1916 to date; *Merchant Vessels of the US*, 1891 to date. *Society of Naval Architects and Marine Engineers Transactions*, vol 1, 1893 to date. The picture file consists mostly of photographs of merchant ships. This is supplemented by scrapbooks. The index to the pictures, scrapbooks, books and vertical file are in one subject catalog. We subscribe to and keep for several years numerous maritime periodicals. The maritime history collection incl sailing ships as well as steamships.

MERCHANT SHIPS—REGISTERS see Ship Registers

MERCHANT SHIPS—REGISTRATION see Ships—Registration and Transfer

MERCHANTMEN see Merchant Ships

MERCURY

CA —STANFORD UNIVERSITY LIBRARIES, Cecil H Green Library, Stanford, 94305. Michael T Ryan, Cur
Notes: Research collection.

MERCURY THEATRE

IN —INDIANA UNIVERSITY, Lilly Library, Seventh St, Bloomington, 47405. William R Cagle, Librn
Holdings: Mss Pix
Notes: Correspondence, papers, and memorabilia, 1930-1959, of actor, producer, writer, and director Orson Welles. Includes material on the Federal Theater Project, Mercury Theatre, radio programming, film-making, RKO studios, etc. Radio scripts, screen plays, movie stills, and tape recordings of the radio shows done by Welles are all present. 19,875 items.

MEREDITH, EDWIN THOMAS

IA —UNIVERSITY OF IOWA, University Libraries, Iowa City, 52242. Robert A McCown, Mss Librn
Holdings: Mss Pix
Notes: Correspondence, speeches, articles, scrapbooks, pamphlets, clippings, photos, and other materials dealing with politics, publishing, farm relief, and land development of a former US Secretary of Agriculture and founder of the Meredith Publishing Company, Des Moines, Iowa. Unpublished index in the library. Described in *Books at Iowa*, no 7 (Nov 1967), pp 32-40, "Some Research Opportunities in the Papers of Edwin T Meredith, 1876-1928," by Peter L Petersen, 38 ft of mss.

MEREDITH, GEORGE

CT —YALE UNIVERSITY, Beinecke Rare Book & Manuscript Library, Osborn Collection, New Haven, 06520. Stephen R Parks, Cur
Holdings: Mss

NJ —PRINCETON UNIVERSITY, Library, Morris L Parrish Collection, Princeton, 08540. Alexander D Wainwright, Cur
Holdings: Vols 150
Notes: The collection contains over 6500 vols, as well as many theatre programs, playbills, photographs, clippings and other miscellanea. Parrish's goal was to assemble in both the English and the American first editions, in the original condition as issued, everything that a given author published. He was also interested in a high standard of condition for his books. Many additions have been acquired since the Parrish collection came to the Library as a bequest in 1944. The collection is an assemblage of author collections, consisting of books by: William Harrison Ainsworth, James Matthew Barrie, William Black, The Brontes, William Wilkie Collins, Dinah Mulock Craik, Marie de la Ramee ("Ouida"), Benjamin Disraeli, Charles Dickens, Charles Dodgson, George du Maurier, George Eliot (ie Mary Ann Evans), Elizabeth Gaskell, Thomas Hardy, Thomas Hughes, Charles Kingsley, Charles Lever, Edward George Earle Bulwer-Lytton, Mary Maxwell, George Meredith, Charles Reade, Walter Scott, Robert Louis Stevenson, William Makepeace Thackeray, Trollope Family, Ellen Wood, and Charlotte Yonge.

VA —SWEET BRIAR COLLEGE, Library, Sweet Briar, 24595. John Jaffe, Librn
Holdings: Vols 475 Cat Mss
Budget: $500
Notes: Incl 33 manuscripts, letters. We have a bronze medallion of Meredith's profile--the work of Theodore Spicer-Simpson, whose autograph it carries. Only 3 medallions were struck from the matrix. The other two are in England.

MEREDITH, SAMUEL

DE —UNIVERSITY OF DELAWARE, Hugh M Morris Library, S College Ave, Newark, 19711. T Stuart Dick, Special Collections
Holdings: // Mss
Notes: Incl Samuel Meredith's household, farming and business receipts, representing quite fully the day-to-day expenses of a wealthy Philadelphian of the 1780s and 1790s. Meredith was a member of the Continental Congress, 1787-1788 and first Treasurer of the United States, 1789-1801. The papers cover the years 1764-1814.

MERICI, ANGELA

NY —COLLEGE OF NEW ROCHELLE, Gill Library, Castle Place, New Rochelle, 10801. Gloria T Greco, Librn
Holdings: Vols 242 Cat Mss Microforms
Notes: Ursuline Collection: mss and early editions of works pertaining to the history of the Order of St Ursula, founded by Angela Merici in 1535. Separate shelflist.

MERINO SHEEP

NY —NEW YORK STATE OFFICE OF PARKS & RECREATION, TACONIC REGION, Clermont State Historic Park, Library, RR 1, Box 215, Germantown, 12526. Bruce E Naramore, Historic Site Manager
Holdings: Vols (5000) Cat Mss Maps
Notes: Period editions of pre- and post-American Revolutionary War agricultural technology. Many belonged to the Chancellor Robert R Livingston (1746-1813). Incl land drainage, hybrids, fertilizers, and the introduction of Merino sheep.

MERLIN (MAGAZINE)

MO —WASHINGTON UNIVERSITY, Libraries, Special Collections Dept, Campus Box 1061, St Louis, 63130.
Notes: The Archives of this English literary magazine and press.

MERRIAM, HENRY CLAY

ME —COLBY COLLEGE, Miller Library, Alfred King Chapman Room, Waterville, 04901.
Holdings: Mss
Notes: Papers, etc.

MERRIAM, JOHN CAMPBELL

CA —UNIVERSITY OF CALIFORNIA, BERKELEY, Bancroft Library, Manuscripts Division, Berkeley, 94720. James D Hart, Dir
Holdings: Cat Mss Maps Pix Microforms
Notes: Papers, correspondence, etc.

MERRILL, JAMES

MO —WASHINGTON UNIVERSITY, John M Olin Library, Campus Box 1061, St Louis,

MERRILL, JAMES (cont.)

63130.
Notes: A major collection, incl books, mss, correspondence, literary papers, photographs, etc. Described in *Special Collections: an Annotated Guide to the Holdings of the Manuscript Division and the University Archives and Research Collection.*

MERRIMACK (SHIP)

VA —PORTSMOUTH PUBLIC LIBRARY, 601 Court St, Portsmouth, 23704. Dean Burgess, Library Dir
Holdings: Vols 500 Cat Mss Maps Pix Slides Microforms
Notes: Portsmouth was founded in 1752 and was the headquarters for the British army throughout the Revolution. It has the oldest and now the largest American Navy Shipyard dating to before the Revolution and called the Norfolk Naval Shipyard. It also was the site of the building of the Merimac (which battled the Monitor off Portsmouth's waterfront). Several pre-revolutionary houses remain in the historic downtown area although most are from the Federal period 1800-1830. Portsmouth is often neglected in American history books perhaps because it was a Tory town.

MERRIMACK RIVER

MA —UNIVERSITY OF LOWELL, Library, One University Ave, Lowell, 01854. Martha Mayo, Special Collections Librn
Holdings: Vols 3000 Cat Mss Maps Pix
Notes: The Locks and Canals Collection consist of the 19th century engineering library of the Proprietors of the Locks and Canals on Merrimack River 1793-present. This collection also contains 5000 photographs and 8000 architectural and engineering drawings.

MERRIMACK VALLEY REGION

MA —MERRIMACK VALLEY TEXTILE MUSEUM, Library, 800 Massachusetts Ave, North Andover, 01845. Clare Sheridan, Librn; Laurence Gross, Cur
Notes: *Checklist of Prints, Drawings and Painting in the Merrimack Valley Textile Museum,* Helena E Wright, 1972; *Checklist of Finished Textiles,* Katherine K Koob, 1980; *New City on the Merrimack: Prints of Lawrence 1845-1876,* Helena Wright, 1974; *Homespun to Factory Made: Wollen Textiles in America 1776-1876* (exhibit catalog) 1978; *Textile Technology Prints: A Checklist of Prints, Drawings and Paintings in the Merrimack Valley Textile Museum,* Helena E Wright, 1980; *All Sorts of Good Sufficient Cloth: Linen-making in New England, 1640-1860,* (exhibit catalogue) 1980; *The Merrimack Valley Textile Museum: A Guide to the Manuscript Collections* Helena E Wright, Garland Press 1983.

MERRIMAN, HENRY SETON (SCOTT, HUGH SEWELL), 1862-1903

CA —UNIVERSITY OF CALIFORNIA, LOS ANGELES, Research Library, Dept of Special Collections, 405 Hilgard Ave, Los Angeles, 90024. Edward Shreeves, Chairman, Bibliographers Group; David S Zeidberg, Head
Holdings: Vols 25
Notes: 25 first and other editions of his books; 43 letters.

MERRITT, ERNEST GEORGE, 1865-1948

NY —CORNELL UNIVERSITY LIBRARIES, Collection of Regional History, Dept of Manuscripts and Univ Archives, Ithaca, 14853.
Notes: Professor of physics. Incl papers, ca 1898-1911; 4 volumes of notes taken at Merritt's lectures; resolutions, reports, minutes, and statements of various committees of the Graduate Faculty of Cornell University, NY.

MERRIWELL, FRANK

CT —YALE UNIVERSITY, Box 1603A, Yale Station, New Haven, 06520.
Notes: The Merriwell Series, by Burt L Standish.

MERTLE, JOSEPH S.

MN —3M COMPANY, Mertle Library, 3M Center, Bldg 235-1D, Saint Paul, 55101.
Holdings: Vols (4000) Cat Mss Pix
Notes: The collection of Joseph S Mertle, includes patents, portraits, a clipping file, and other historical graphic arts books and periodicals.

MERTON, THOMAS

KY —UNIVERSITY OF KENTUCKY, Margaret I King Library, Dept of Special Collections, Lexington, 40506. William Marshall, Head
Holdings: Cat Mss Pix
Notes: Merton correspondence, misc papers, etc; printed publications are comprehensive (incl translations, offprints, articles, poems excerpted); mimeographed articles and poems. Use restricted by Merton Trust. No photocopying.
KY —BELLARMINE COLLEGE, Thomas Merton Studies Center, 2001 Newburg Rd, Louisville, 40205. Robert E Daggy, Cur
Holdings: Vols 1000 Cat Mss Maps Pix Slides Phonorecords Audiotapes Videotapes Microforms
Budget: $3000
Notes: The Thomas Merton Collection contains some 15,000 items of published editions, incl translations, books with marginalia, mss, galley proofs, journals, notebooks, diaries, theses, clippings, calligraphies and drawings, photographs, films, audiotapes, videotapes, letters, and memorabilia by and about Merton. Material on various Merton seminars, symposia and retreats is also maintained. Collection is cataloged and/or indexed. Use of collection and photocopying are restricted. The Center issues an occasional newsletter and supplies bibliographies upon request. All materials have been moved to the Center from the Abbey of Gethsemani, which maintains no Merton Collection for public use.
MA —BOSTON COLLEGE LIBRARIES, Thomas P O'Neill Library, Chestnut Hill, 02167. John D J Slinn, Librn of the Central Library
Holdings: Cat Mss Pix
NY —COLUMBIA UNIVERSITY LIBRARIES, Rare Book & Manuscript Library, 801 Butler Library, 535 W 114 St, New York, 10027. Kenneth A Lohf, Librn
Holdings: Mss
Notes: Incl Thomas Merton papers and Mark Van Doren papers. Restricted use.
NY —SAINT BONAVENTURE UNIVERSITY, Friedsam Memorial Library, Saint Bonaventure, 14778. John Capozzi, OFM, Art Cur
Notes: Collection consists of nine large file cases containing correspondence, original mss, articles by and about him and his works, as well as a representative number of his works in English and foreign languages. Incl several thousand letters, notes, etc.

MERWIN, W.S.

†MD —UNIVERSITY OF MARYLAND, Library, College Park, 20742. Donald Farren, Assoc Dir for Special Collections
Holdings: Cat
Notes: First appearances in book form, in anthologies, and in periodicals; subsequent editions, with differences in text, etc; works edited or translated; association items, especially with marginalia. Secondary works are generally excluded.
MO —WASHINGTON UNIVERSITY, Libraries, Campus Box 1061, Saint Louis, 63130.
Notes: A collection of primary material.

NV —UNIVERSITY OF NEVADA, RENO, University Library, Special Collections Dept, Reno, 89557. Robert E Blesse, Head
Holdings: Vols (58) Cat Other appearances 1500 Cat
Notes: Includes individual works by author in all editions including translations; also prefaces, introductions, published correspondence, appearances in anthologies, periodicals, etc. Bibliographical research collection, part of Modern Authors Collection.

MESCAL (CACTUS) see Peyote

MESCAL AND MESCALINE

CA —FITZ HUGH LUDLOW MEMORIAL LIBRARY, PO Box 99346, San Francisco, 94109. Michael R Aldrich, Exec Cur
Holdings: Vols (1000) Cat Mss Maps Pix Slides Phonorecords Audiotapes Videotapes
Notes: Collection stored. Important mail inquiries only. No interlibrary lending or telephone inquiries. Hallucinogens as used in historical and contemporary cultures. Nearly complete collection of books and articles by or about Timothy Leary, incl manuscripts; also nearly complete collection of the writings of Aldous Huxley concerning drugs. Much autographed or inscribed material, mostly popular music from the 1960s but also incl ethnographic music. Emphasis on psychoactive drugs relative to religion, literature, art. Also an excellent collection of research papers (chemistry, pharmacology, epidemiology, sociology, ethnobotany) in this field, as well as artifacts and artwork relating to the field.

MESKWAKI INDIANS see Fox Indians

MESMERISM see Hypnotism

MESOPOTAMIA

CA —CALIFORNIA STATE COLLEGE, STANISLAUS, Library, 801 W Monte Vista Ave, Turlock, 95380. J Carlyle Parker, Actg Library Dir
Holdings: Vols 100 // Uncat
Notes: The Sayad Collection of Assyriana consists of books in the Syriac dialect of the modern Assyrians, often called Nestorians, who are natives of northwestern Iran. Other books in English relating to the modern Assyrians are also in the collection. Also books on Mesopotamia civilizations.
CT —YALE UNIVERSITY, Sterling Memorial Library, Babylonian Collection, 120 High St, New Haven, 06520. William W Hallo, Cur
Holdings: Vols (12,000) Cat Mss Pix
Budget: $2500
Notes: 30,000 mss in form of Babylonian tablets; 6000 seals and other art objects from Mesopotamia and the rest of the Ancient Near East.

MESSER, ASA, 1769-1836

RI —BROWN UNIVERSITY, John Hay Library, 20 Prospect St, Providence, 02912. Mark N Brown, Cur Mss
Holdings: // Mss
Notes: Papers of Asa Messer, Baptist clergyman and President of Brown University. 100 letters, mss, documents, etc, for the period 1791 to 1832 concerning Brown University, the Baptist clergy in England and America, personal affairs, religion, politics, patents for Messer's inventions, and 72 notebooks of essays and sermons. Register available.

MESSERSMITH, GEORGE S.

DE —UNIVERSITY OF DELAWARE, Hugh M Morris Library, S College Ave, Newark, 19711. T Stuart Dick, Special Collections
Holdings: Cat Mss Pix
Notes: Incl letters and confidential diplomatic dispatches written while George Messersmith was American Consul in Berlin, 1930-34; Ambassador to Cuba; Ambassador to Austria, 1934; Ambassador to Mexico, 1941-42; Ambassador to Argentina, 1942-46;

MESSERSMITH, GEORGE S. (cont.)

Business correspondence as President of the Mexican Light and Power Co, 1947-60. Calendar and index available.

MESSIAEN, OLIVIER

DC —LIBRARY OF CONGRESS, Music Division, Washington, 20540.
Notes: Mss in Koussevitzky Archives.

MESSNER, ELMER

NY —UNIVERSITY OF ROCHESTER, Rush Rhees Library, Department of Rare Books and Special Collections, Rochester, 14627. Peter Dzwonkoski, Librn
Notes: Original drawings by Thomas Nast; also World War II political cartoons by Elmer Messher, cartoonist for Rochester, New York newspaper.

METAL CASTINGS

IL —AMERICAN FOUNDRYMEN'S SOCIETY, Technical Information Center, Golf & Wolf Rds, Des Plaines, 60016. Ann V Duggan, Mgr Library Services
Holdings: Vols (3000) 16mm Films
Notes: Incl current awareness service.
TN —COMBUSTION ENGINEERING, Metallurgical Materials Library, 911 W Main St, Chattanooga, 37402. Nell T Holder, Tech Librn
Holdings: Vols (10,000) Cat
Notes: Metallurgical research and development. 350 serials and periodicals, 800 translations of foreign articles. 250,000 US Government Reports. MF Collection C-E Technical reports ASME.

METAL CHELATE COMPOUNDS see Organometallic Compounds

METAL CUTTING

MI —GENERAL ELECTRIC COMPANY, Carboloy Systems Department, Library, Box 237, GPO, Detroit, 48232.
Holdings: Vols (4500) Cat Maps Slides 16mm Films Filmstrips Microforms
Budget: ($5000)
Notes: Collection covers cemented carbide cutting tools, powder metallurgy, metal cutting, metalworking, machining, and related subjects. Also numerical control, statistics (related to the cutting tool industry) and general management. Incl 500 maps, 4000 slides, 61 films, 261 filmstrips, 700 microfiche, 7000 patents, and 300 periodical titles.

METAL FINISHING see Metals—Finishing

METAL INDUSTRIES see Metal Trade; Metalwork; Mineral Industries

METAL TRADE

MI —OMI INTERNATIONAL CORP, Udylite Div, Research Library, 21441 Hoover Rd, Warren, 48089. Lynn PeFley, Librn
Holdings: Vols (1600) Cat
Notes: Metal finishing literature (chemical, physical properties, structure).
PA —CARNEGIE LIBRARY OF PITTSBURGH, Science & Technology Dept, 4400 Forbes Ave, Pittsburgh, 15213. Catherine M Brosky, Dept Head
Holdings: Vols (380,000) Cat Maps Microforms
Budget: ($240,000)
Notes: General information acquired in various subject areas especially those relating to iron and steel and other metals. Manufacturers directories, including old editions, standards and specifications, trade catalogs, basic periodicals, indexes, and bibliographies.
See also entry under Technology.

METAL WORK

CA —CALIFORNIA COLLEGE OF ARTS & CRAFTS, Meyer Library, Broadway at

College, Oakland, 94618. Robert L Harper, Head Librn
Holdings: Vols (29,000) Cat Pix
Budget: ($10,000)
Notes: All fields of arts and crafts, incl art metal work.
MA —OLD STURBRIDGE VILLAGE, Research Library, Sturbridge, 01566. Theresa Rini Percy, Librn
Holdings: Cat Mss Pix
Notes: Iron, tin, copper, brass, pewter, silver in New England, to 1850.
MI —GENERAL ELECTRIC COMPANY, Carboloy Systems Department, Library, Box 237, GPO, Detroit, 48232.
Holdings: Vols (4500) Cat Maps Slides 16mm Films Filmstrips Microforms
Budget: ($5000)
Notes: Collection covers cemented carbide cutting tools, powder metallurgy, metal cutting, metalworking, machining, and related subjects. Also numerical control, statistics (related to the cutting tool industry) and general management. Incl 500 maps, 4000 slides, 61 films, 261 filmstrips, 700 microfiche, 7000 patents, and 300 periodical titles.
MI —OMI INTERNATIONAL CORP, Udylite Div, Research Library, 21441 Hoover Rd, Warren, 48089. Lynn PeFley, Librn
Holdings: Vols (1600) Cat
Notes: Metal finishing literature (chemical, physical properties, structure).
NY —COLUMBIA UNIVERSITY LIBRARIES, Avery Architectural and Fine Arts Library, 201 Avery Hall, New York, 10027. Angela Giral, Librn
Holdings: Vols (6000) Cat
Notes: Emphasis on decorative art. Restricted use: noncirculating.
OH —CLEVELAND PUBLIC LIBRARY, Science & Technology Dept, 325 Superior Ave, Cleveland, 44114. Jean Z Piety, Head
Holdings: Cat
Notes: Part of the Handicrafts Collection, which incl crafts of many ethnic groups in Cleveland.
PA —FRANKLIN INSTITUTE LIBRARY, 20 & The Parkway, Philadelphia, 19103. Miriam Padusis, Dir; Charles Wilt, Readers Servs Librn
Holdings: Vols (300,000) Cat Maps Pix Microforms
PA —CARNEGIE LIBRARY OF PITTSBURGH, Science & Technology Dept, 4400 Forbes Ave, Pittsburgh, 15213. Catherine M Brosky, Dept Head
Holdings: Vols (380,000) Cat Maps Microforms
Budget: ($240,000)
Notes: Incl much of the material in *Index to Handicrafts*. Books for the home owner, repairman and craftsman and the general builder and mechanics are emphasized. Information on the use of tools and materials especially for woodworking and metal crafts; also optical instruments, clocks, guns, and other mechanic trades. Maintains supplement to *Index to Handicrafts*.

METALLIC ALLOYS see Alloys

METALLIC CERAMICS see Ceramic Metals

METALLOGRAPHY

OH —TIMKEN CO, Timken Research Library, 1835 Dueber Ave SW, Canton, 44706. Joellen A Hadbavny, Librn
Holdings: Vols (20,000) Cat Mss Slides
Notes: Incl (7500) translations, reports, etc.
PA —FRANKLIN INSTITUTE LIBRARY, 20 & The Parkway, Philadelphia, 19103. Miriam Padusis, Dir; Charles Wilt, Readers Servs Librn
Holdings: Vols (300,000) Cat Maps Pix Microforms
TN —COMBUSTION ENGINEERING, Metallurgical Materials Library, 911 W Main St, Chattanooga, 37402. Nell T Holder, Tech Librn
Holdings: Vols (10,000) Cat
Notes: Metallurgical research and

development. 350 serials and periodicals, 800 translations of foreign articles. 250,000 US Government Reports. MF Collection C-E Technical reports ASME.

METALLOGRAPHY, X-RAY see X-Ray Metallography

METALLO-ORGANIC COMPOUNDS see Organometallic Compounds

METALLURGICAL ENGINEERING

KY —UNIVERSITY OF KENTUCKY, Robert E Shaver Library of Engineering, 355 Anderson Hall, Lexington, 40506. Russell H Powell, Engineering Librn
Holdings: Vols (48,000) Cat Microforms
†SD —SOUTH DAKOTA SCHOOL OF MINES & TECHNOLOGY, Devereaux Library, Rapid City, 57701.
Holdings: Vols (166,200) Cat Maps Audiotapes Filmstrips Microforms
Budget: ($70,000)
Notes: Supportive collection incl an almost complete set of US Geological Survey materials (incl early Territorial Surveys); a microfilm copy (complete set) of the US Bureau of Mines "Mine Map Depository (Denver)" material; periodicals and technical reports (NASA, ACRL, JPL, etc) in engineering and geology; extensive government document materials (NBS, Bureau of Mines, etc).

METALLURGY

AL —UNITED STATES PIPE & FOUNDRY CO, Technical Services Library, PO Box 10406, Birmingham, 35202. Phil McGrath, Mgr
Holdings: Vols (3100) Cat
Notes: Books and periodicals on ferrous metallurgy and allied subjects. Restricted use: company personnel and interlibrary loan only.
CA —STANFORD UNIVERSITY, School of Earth Sciences, Branner Earth Sciences Library, Stanford, 94305. Charlotte Derksen, Head Librn
Holdings: Vols (70,000) Cat Maps
CO —COLORADO SCHOOL OF MINES, Arthur Lakes Library, 14 & Illinois Sts, Golden, 80401. Hartley K Phinney, Jr, Head Librn
Holdings: Vols (270,557) Cat Maps Microforms
ID —EG&G, INEL Technical Library, 1776 Science Center, Idaho Falls, 83401. Brent Jacobsen, Head Librn; Heather Redding, Ref Librn
Holdings: Vols (33,000) Cat Microforms
Notes: Energy research and development included in libraries collection. Incl over 500,000 AEC, ERDA, NRC, and foreign reports. Unclassified materials may be used by the public in the library by appointment or borrowed by interlibrary loan. Incl 12,000 bound documents, 520,000 microfiche, 400 periodical subscriptions.
IL —ARGONNE NATIONAL LABORATORY, Materials Sciences Branch Library, 9700 S Cass Ave, Argonne, 60439. Veronica E Johnson, Librn
Notes: Phase diagrams, ferrous metallurgy, physical metallurgy and properties of alloys. Incl 8000 vols monographs, 130 current journals, some scientific and technical reports. Materials may be used by the public in the library by prior arrangement. Photocopies may be supplied for interlibrary loan, for which a processing and handling charge is made.
IL —CHICAGO BRIDGE & IRON CO, Technical Library, 800 Jorie Blvd, Oak Brook, 60521. Susan Beatty, Librn
Holdings: Vols (7500) Cat
Budget: ($39,500)
IL —UNIVERSITY OF ILLINOIS, URBANA/CHAMPAIGN, Library, 221 Engineering Hall, Urbana, 61801. William Mischo, Librn
Holdings: Vols (175,000) Cat Slides Microforms
Notes: Incl 3500 periodicals. Collection

METALLURGY (cont.)

designed to serve teaching and research
programs. Supports instructional faculty
research. Also, 470 microfilm reels and 6000
microfiche sheets.

IN —INLAND STEEL RESEARCH
LABORATORIES, Research Library, 3001
E Columbus Dr, East Chicago, 46312.
Barbara Minne Banek, Librn
Holdings: Vols (4500) Cat 16mm Films
Filmstrips Microforms
Notes: Emphasis on metallurgy and steel.
Also 7000 bound periodical vols; 3500
government publications, 47 vertical file
drawers of translations, 15 vertical file
drawers of patents.

IN —CABOT CORP, Stellite Div, Technical
Library, 1020 W Park Ave, Kokomo, 46901.
Betty Hollis, Librn
Holdings: Vols (10,000) Cat Slides
Microforms
Notes: Emphasis on metallurgy. Incl 12,000
internal technical reports, 4 Lektriever units.

IN —PURDUE UNIVERSITY LIBRARIES,
Engineering Library, A A Potter
Engineering Center, West Lafayette, 47907.
Edwin D Posey, Engineering Librn
Holdings: Vols (225,178) Cat Maps
Audiotapes Microforms
Budget: ($300,000)

IA —IOWA STATE UNIVERSITY, Library,
Ames, 50011. Warren B Kuhn, Dean of
Library Services
Holdings: Cat
Notes: Specific strength: rare-earth metals
and alloys.

MD —US BUREAU OF MINES, Avondale
Metallurgy Research Center, Library, 4900
La Salle Rd, Avondale, 20782. Paul F
Moran, Librn
Holdings: Vols (11,000) CAt
Budget: ($35,000)

MI —GENERAL ELECTRIC COMPANY,
Carboloy Systems Department, Library, Box
237, GPO, Detroit, 48232.
Holdings: Vols (4500) Cat Maps Slides
16mm Films Filmstrips Microforms
Budget: ($5000)
Notes: Collection covers cemented carbide
cutting tools, powder metallurgy, metal
cutting, metalworking, machining, and
related subjects. Also numerical control,
statistics (related to the cutting tool
industry) and general management. Incl 500
maps, 4000 slides, 61 films, 261 filmstrips,
700 microfiche, 7000 patents, and 300
periodical titles.

MI —OMI INTERNATIONAL CORP,
Udylite Div, Research Library, 21441
Hoover Rd, Warren, 48089. Lynn PeFley,
Librn
Holdings: Vols (1600) Cat
Notes: Metal finishing literature (chemical,
physical properties, structure).

NY —ENGINEERING SOCIETIES
LIBRARY, 345 E 47 St, New York, 10017.
S Kirk Cabeen, Dir
Holdings: Vols 250,000 Cat Maps 16mm
Films Microforms
Notes: One of the largest, most
comprehensive engineering libraries in the
world. Covers all engineering disciplines;
particularly strong in electrical and
electronic, mechanical, mining and
metallurgical, petroleum, chemical,
industrial, air conditioning and refrigeration
engineering. Incl Wheeler Collection of early
materials on magnetism and electricity. 125,
000 bound periodical volumes; 10,000 maps;
5000 serial subscriptions (many foreign-
language). Virtually all materials abstracted
in *Engineering Index* (1884-date) are incl in
Library. Noncirculating, except to members
of professional engineering societies which
support the Library. See *Engineering
Societies Library, New York, Classed
Subject Catalog and Index* (Boston: G K
Hall, 1963); and *Supplements*, 1-10, 1964-
1973.

NY —GENERAL ELECTRIC CO, Main
Library, One River Rd, Schenectady, 12345.
Julia Hewitt, Mgr
Holdings: Vols (56,000) Cat

OH —TIMKEN CO, Timken Research Library,
1835 Dueber Ave SW, Canton, 44706.

Joellen A Hadbavny, Librn
Holdings: Vols (20,000) Cat Mss Slides
Notes: Incl (7500) translations, reports, etc.

OH —PUBLIC LIBRARY OF CINCINNATI
& HAMILTON COUNTY, Science &
Technology Dept, 800 Vine St, Cincinnati,
45202. Rosemary Gaiser, Head
Holdings: Vols (250,000) Cat
Notes: Pure and applied science. Incl over
1600 periodicals and serial titles and more
than 100 abstracting and indexing services in
major fields of science and technology.

OH —UNIVERSITY OF CINCINNATI,
Engineering Library, 880 Baldwin Hall,
Cincinnati, 45221. Dorothy Furber Byers,
Head
Holdings: Vols (50,000) Cat Videotapes
Microforms
Budget: ($100,000)
Notes: Have NASA and DOE microfiche
collections.

OH —OHIO STATE UNIVERSITY, Materials
Engineering Library, Watts Hall, 2041 N
College Road, Columbus, 43210. Mary Jo V
Arnold, Librn
Holdings: Vols (15,000) Cat Microforms
Budget: ($30,000)

†OH —GENERAL MOTORS CORP, Inland
Manufacturing Div, Engineering Library, PO
Box 1224, Dayton, 45401.

OR —OREGON STATE UNIVERSITY,
Library, Corvallis, 97331. Melvin George,
Dir
Holdings: Vols (980,000) Cat

PA —UNITED STATES STEEL CORP,
Research Laboratory, Technical Information
Center, MS 88, Monroeville, 15146. Angela
R Pollis, Staff Supvr of Technical
Information Services
Holdings: Vols 30,000 Cat Mss Microforms
Notes: Ferrous metallurgy.

PA —FRANKLIN INSTITUTE LIBRARY, 20
& The Parkway, Philadelphia, 19103.
Miriam Padusis, Dir; Charles Wilt, Readers
Servs Librn
Holdings: Vols (300,000) Cat Maps Pix
Microforms

PA —UNIVERSITY OF PENNSYLVANIA,
Towne Scientific Library, 220 S 33 St,
Philadelphia, 19104. Charles Meyers, Librn
Holdings: Vols (65,000) Cat

PA —CARNEGIE LIBRARY OF
PITTSBURGH, Science & Technology Dept,
4400 Forbes Ave, Pittsburgh, 15213.
Catherine M Brosky, Dept Head
Holdings: Vols (380,000) Cat Maps
Microforms
Budget: ($240,000)

PA —COLT INDUSTRIES, Crucible Research
Center Library, Box 88, Pittsburgh, 15230.
Patricia J Aducci, Technical Librn

PA —PENNSYLVANIA STATE
UNIVERSITY, Earth & Mineral Sciences
Library, 105 Deike Bldg, University Park,
16802. Emilie McWilliams, Head Librn
Holdings: Vols (58,000) Cat Maps
Microforms
Budget: ($49,750)
Notes: Incl holdings on material science and
engineering, mineral economy and
engineering, geomechanics, mineral genergy
management, processing, conservation and
constitution.

†SD —SOUTH DAKOTA SCHOOL OF
MINES & TECHNOLOGY, Devereaux
Library, Rapid City, 57701.
Holdings: Vols (166,200) Cat Maps
Audiotapes Filmstrips Microforms
Budget: ($70,000)
Notes: Supportive collection incl an almost
complete set of US Geological Survey
materials (incl early Territorial Surveys); a
microfilm copy (complete set) of the US
Bureau of Mines "Mine Map Depository
(Denver)" material; periodicals and technical
reports (NASA, ACRL, JPL, etc) in
engineering and geology; extensive
government document materials (NBS,
Bureau of Mines, etc).

TN —COMBUSTION ENGINEERING,
Metallurgical Materials Library, 911 W
Main St, Chattanooga, 37402. Nell T
Holder, Tech Librn
Holdings: Vols (10,000) Cat Microforms
Notes: Metallurgical research and
development.

TN —UNIVERSITY OF TENNESSEE, Space
Institute Library, Tullahoma, 37388. Helen B
Mason, Librn
Holdings: Vols (14,000) Cat Microforms
Budget: ($50,000)
Notes: Incl NASA and other series of
technical reports.

TX —AUSTIN PUBLIC LIBRARY, Austin
History Center, 810 Guadalupe Street, PO
Box 2287, Austin, 78768. Audray Bateman,
Cur
Holdings: Vols 2000 Cat Maps Microforms

TX —RICE UNIVERSITY, Fondren Library,
6100 S Main St, PO Box 1892, Houston,
77251. Dr Samuel M Carrington, Jr,
University Librn
Holdings: Vols (4151) Cat
Budget: ($45,700)
Notes: Each serial title counted once.

TX —ECTOR COUNTY LIBRARY,
Department of Business and Technology,
321 W 5th St, Odessa, 79760. Pat Jones,
Dept Head
Holdings: Vols 250 Cat

WA —PUGET SOUND NAVAL SHIPYARD,
Engineering Library, Code 202.5, Bremerton,
98314. Carol J Swanson, Engineering Librn
Holdings: Vols Cat Maps

WA —BATTELLE-PACIFIC NORTHWEST
LABORTORIES, Technical Library, PO
Box 999, Richland, 99352. Wayne Snyder,
Librn
Holdings: Vols (50,000) Cat Microforms
Budget: ($500,000)
Notes: Holdings: 50,000 books; 35,000
bound periodical volumes; 200,000 technical
reports; 200,000 technical reports in
microform. Subscriptions: 1800 journals and
other serials. Services: interlibrary loans;
literature searching; translation; library open
to public with restrictions.

AB —SHERRITT RESEARCH CENTRE,
Library, Sherritt Gordon Mines Ltd, Fort
Saskatchewan, T8L 2P2, Can. D Sim, Librn
Holdings: Vols (7000)
Budget: $20,000

ON —ATOMIC ENERGY OF CANADA
LIMITED, Main Library, Technical
Information Branch, Chalk River Nuclear
Laboratories, Chalk River, K0J 1J0, Can.
Harry Greenshields, Chief Librn
Holdings: Vols (128,700) Microforms
Budget: ($662,400)
Notes: The Main Library, Atomic Energy of
Canada Limited, is the Canadian repository
for the literature of nuclear science and
technology. Its collections reflect both
fundamental and nuclear aspects of biology,
chemistry, electronics, engineering,
mathematics, computers, metallurgy, physics
and other specific areas of science involving
nuclear technology with special emphasis on
heavy water reactor systems. 512,000
research reports are available in paper copy
and microfiche form. Incl US DOE, INIS
and other offshore nuclear research reports.
386,000 microforms.

ON —ONTARIO RESEARCH
FOUNDATION, Library, Sheridan Park,
Mississauga, L5K 1B3, Can. Carl K Wei,
Librn
Holdings: Vols (13,000) Cat
Budget: ($14,000)

ON —NATIONAL RESEARCH COUNCIL
OF CANADA, Aeronautical/Mechanical
Engineering Branch Library, Montreal Rd,
Ottawa, K1A 0R6, Can. Louise Fletcher,
Head
Notes: This branch library of the Canada
Institute for Scientific and Technical
Information (CISTI) of the National
Research Council of Canada, Ottawa, has a
collection strong in aeronautical engineering,
automatic control, CAD/CAM, robotics,
ocean, wind, and solar energy power,
hydraulic and coastal engineering, icing, low
temperature research, naval engineering,
metals and metallurgy, incl composites,
tribology, and air, railroad, marine
transportation. Library supported the
Council contribution to the development of
the remote manipular Canadarm for
NASA's Space Shuttle Orbiters and more
recently, the Canadian Astronaut Program
which will contribute payload specialists to
NASA's Space Shuttle Program in 1984. 35,

METALLURGY (cont.)

000 monographs, 1200 serials. Report collection: over 500,000 items.

PQ —NORANDA RESEARCH CENTRE, Library, 240 Hymus Blvd, Pointe-Claire, H9R 1G5, Can. Shirley Courtis, Librn
Holdings: Vols (7000)

PQ —SERVICE DE LA DOCUMENTATION ET DES RENSEIGNEMENTS MINISTERE DE L'ENERGIE ET DES RESSOURCES, 2000B, chemin Sainte-Foy, 7th floor, Quebec, G1R 4X7, Can. Normand Guerette, Dir
Holdings: Vols (114,800) Slides Videotapes
Notes: In 1979, the Bibliotheque du ministere des Richesses naturelles du Quebec merged with the Bibliotheque du ministere des Terres et Forets. The result of this merger was the creation of the service de la Documentation et des Renseignements du ministere de l'Energie et des Ressources. Publications: Info-Biblio Terres et Forets; Mines; Energy.

METALLURGY—HISTORY

CA —CLAREMONT COLLEGES, Norman F Sprague Memorial Library, 12 & Dartmouth, Claremont, 91711. David Kuhner, Librn
Holdings: Vols 1000 Cat Mss Maps Pix
Notes: The reference library collected by Herbert Clark Hoover and Lou Henry Hoover in the preparation of their 1912 translation of *De re metallica*. Incl 24 incunabula, 6 mss, titles of 16th to 19th centuries, with emphasis on mining, metallurgy, early science, and travel. Hoover's correspondence (approx 600 pieces) with British & European booksellers, period 1907-1914. Printed catalog, "Bibliotheca de Re Metallica," published in 1980. Restricted use.

CO —UNIVERSITY OF COLORADO, Libraries, Special Collections, Boulder, 80309. Nora J Quinlan, Head
Holdings: Vols 200 Cat
Notes: The Sam Tour Library.

DE —HAGLEY MUSEUM AND LIBRARY, Eleutherian Mills-Hagley Foundation Inc, PO Box 3630, Greenville, 19807. Richmond D Williams, Dir; Heddy A Richter, Imprints Librn
Holdings: Vols 14,000
Notes: Our collection documents the history of American technology, especially the period in which mass production replaced the American system. Our holdings are strong in chemical technology, transportation, explosives, pyrotechnics, metallurgy and engineering.

METALLURGY, POWDER see Powder Metallurgy

METALORGANIC COMPOUNDS see Organometallic Compounds

METALS

CA —UNIVERSITY OF CALIFORNIA, LOS ANGELES, Engineering & Mathematical Sciences Library, 405 Hilgard, Los Angeles, 90024. Rosalee I Wright, Librn
Holdings: Vols (180,000) Cat
Notes: Subject emphasis for materials are metals, composite materials, and ceramics. Standards and technical publications of ASM (inclusive), ASTM (inclusive); SAE Aerospace Standards.
See also entry under Engineering

CA —CONTRA COSTA COUNTY LIBRARY, 1750 Oak Park Blvd, Pleasant Hill, 94523. Barbara Potter, Librn
Holdings: Vols (18,000)

IL —CHICAGO BRIDGE & IRON CO, Technical Library, 800 Jorie Blvd, Oak Brook, 60521. Susan Beatty, Librn
Holdings: Vols (7500) Cat
Budget: ($39,500)

IA —IOWA STATE UNIVERSITY, Library, Ames, 50011. Warren B Kuhn, Dean of Library Services
Holdings: Cat
Notes: Specific strength: rare-earth metals and alloys.

KY —UNIVERSITY OF KENTUCKY, Robert E Shaver Library of Engineering, 355 Anderson Hall, Lexington, 40506. Russell H Powell, Engineering Librn
Holdings: Vols (29,660) Cat Microforms

MI —MICHIGAN STATE UNIVERSITY, Science Library, East Lansing, 48824. Carole S Armstrong, Head
Holdings: Vols 200 Cat
Notes: Both books and journals include titles in English, French, German and Russian, with a few in other languages. The scope includes general toxicology, industrial toxicology, veterinary toxicology, the toxicology of metals and insecticides, and poisons as studied in experimental pharmacology.

NY —ENGINEERING SOCIETIES LIBRARY, 345 E 47 St, New York, 10017. S Kirk Cabeen, Dir
Holdings: Vols 250,000 Cat Maps 16mm Films Microforms
Notes: One of the largest, most comprehensive engineering libraries in the world. Covers all engineering disciplines; particularly strong in electrical and electronic, mechanical, mining and metallurgical, petroleum, chemical, industrial, air conditioning and refrigeration engineering. Incl Wheeler Collection of early materials on magnetism and electricity. 125,000 bound periodical volumes; 10,000 maps; 5000 serial subscriptions (many foreign-language). Virtually all materials abstracted in *Engineering Index* (1884-date) are incl in Library. Noncirculating, except to members of professional engineering societies which support the Library. See *Engineering Societies Library, New York, Classed Subject Catalog and Index* (Boston: G K Hall, 1963); and *Supplements*, 1-10, 1964-1973.

NY —NEW YORK PUBLIC LIBRARY, Research Libraries, Science and Technology Research Center, Fifth Ave & 42 St, New York, 10018.
Holdings: Vols (1,100,000) Cat Microforms
Budget: ($647,259)

OH —FIRESTONE TIRE & RUBBER CO, 1200 Firestone Pkwy, Akron, 44317. S Koo, Librn
Holdings: Vols (6000) Cat
Notes: Collection centered on engineering, mathematics, physics, and manufacturing (metal processing); no rubber or tires. Incl several hundred government reports. No index.

OH —BRUSH WELLMAN, Technical Library, 17876 Saint Clair Ave, Cleveland, 44110. Nancie Skonezny, Tech Librn
Holdings: Vols 1000 Cat
Notes: Beryllium technology--its metals, alloys and ceramics. Incl approx 5000 uncat government documents and international technical reports.

†OH —GENERAL MOTORS CORP, Inland Manufacturing Div, Engineering Library, PO Box 1224, Dayton, 45401.

OH —HOBART BROTHERS TECHNICAL CENTER, John H Blankenbuehler Memorial Library, Trade Sq E, Plant WS1PL, Troy, 45373. Martha Baker, Librn
Holdings: Vols 2000 Cat
Notes: Reference collection on welding and allied subjects, incl handbooks and standards of US and foreign technical and engineering societies, eg, American Welding Society, American Society for Metals, The Welding Institute of Engineering; and about 125 journal titles.

PA —ENSANIAN PHYSICOCHEMICAL INSTITUTE, Electrotopography Library, PO Box 98, Eldred, 16731. Elisabeth Anahid Ensanian, Chief Librn
Holdings: Cat Maps Slides
Budget: ($45,000)
Notes: Electrotopography is a new science (the Institute has pioneered the field and has coined the terms "electrotopograph" and "electrotopography") concerned with the mapping of electrical fields associated with metals, alloys, semiconductors, and living organisms. These fields may be natural and/or induced, and are converted into mappings which exhibit certain systems characteristics for both normal and stress states.

PA —FRANKLIN INSTITUTE LIBRARY, 20 & The Parkway, Philadelphia, 19103. Miriam Padusis, Dir; Charles Wilt, Readers Servs Librn
Holdings: Vols (300,000) Cat Maps Pix Microforms

PA —CABOT CORPORATION, Reading Technology Library, PO Box 1296, Reading, 19603. Pamela L Hehr, Librn
Holdings: Vols (3800) Cat Mss Slides Microforms
Notes: Copper-beryllium and special metals and alloys. Incl 2100 patents, 9000 reports and articles.

METALS—CORROSION see Corrosion and Anticorrosives

METALS—MICROSCOPIC STRUCTURE see Metallography

METALS—TOXICOLOGY

MD —NATIONAL LIBRARY OF MEDICINE, 8600 Rockville Pike, Bethesda, 20209. Harold M Schoolinam, Actg Dir
Budget: ($46,400)

METALS, HEAVY see Heavy Metals

METALS, TRANSMUTATION OF see Alchemy

METAPHYSICS

AZ —WORLD UNIVERSITY, Library, 711 E Blacklidge Dr, Tucson, 85719. Howard John Zitko, Cur
Holdings: Vols (15,000) Cat Mss Maps Audiotapes
Notes: Collection concerns the "frontier sciences." No interlibrary loan.

CA —LOS ANGELES PUBLIC LIBRARY, Philosophy & Religion Dept, 630 W Fifth St, Los Angeles, 90071. Marilyn C Wherley, Librn
Holdings: Vols 700 Cat
Budget: ($60,000)
Notes: Comprehensive coverage of popular and scholarly works on all aspects of the occult including black magic, witchcraft, demonology, paranormal occurances, psychical research and metaphysics. Includes many serials, periodicals and special indexes.

MO —UNITY LIBRARY, Unity School of Christianity, Unity Village, 64065. Alfreda Williams, Library Dir
Holdings: Vols (50,000) Cat Mss Maps Pix Slides Microforms
Notes: Incl Archives and Historical collections of the Unity School of Christianity, as well as the archives of the International New Thought Alliance.

PA —UNIVERSITY OF PITTSBURGH, Hillman Library, Pittsburgh, 15260. Glenora E Rossell, Head
Holdings: Vols (6100) Cat Microforms
Notes: This History and Philosophy of Science collection is rapidly growing to support research interests in a very new synoptic approach in the integration of history of science, philosophy of science, and history of philosophy, and the intensive new program of instruction. The trend of collection is to include works in philosophical foundations of contemporary physics and cosmology, the philosophical problems of the social sciences, science and theology in the 17th century, the relation between science and epistemology in the 18th and 19th centuries; problems of microphysics, history of molecular biology, theories of scientific explanation, and relation between science and metaphysics.

WA —UNIVERSITY OF WASHINGTON LIBRARIES, Philosophy Library, 331 Savery, DK-50, Seattle, 98195. Carolyn Mateer, Acting Selector
Holdings: Vols (18,302) Cat
Budget: ($27,516)
Notes: Collection includes materials in philosophy of language, law, mind, ethics, logic, mataphysics, religion, science, epistemology, social and political philosophy and the history of philosophy.

METAPSYCHOLOGY see Spiritualism

METCALF, JOHN, 1938-

AB —UNIVERSITY OF CALGARY,
Libraries, Special Collections Div, 2500
University Dr, Calgary, T2N 1N4, Can.
Holdings: Mss
Notes: Correspondence, scrapbooks,
photographs, research notes, mss (3 meters)
and reviews for fiction and nonfictiono,
1964-80.

METCALF, KEYES D.

CO —UNIVERSITY OF DENVER, Center for
the Study of Library Architecture, Graduate
School of Librarianship and Information
Management, University Park, Denver,
80208
Notes: The personal papers of Keyes D
Metcalf, former Harvard University
Librarian. The collection represents the most
extensive collection on Library buildings in
the US and twelve foreign countries built
during the 20th century. Incl plans for the
IBM Research Center, Stanford University
Library, the US Air Force Academy Library,
the National Library of Medicine, and the
National Library of Australia. Incl 5000
slides.

METEORITES

DC —SMITHSONIAN INSTITUTION
LIBRARIES, Natural History Branch,
Washington, 20560. Sylvia Churgin, Chief
Librn
Holdings: Vols (2350) Cat Maps Pix
IL —FIELD MUSEUM OF NATURAL
HISTORY, Library, Roosevelt Rd & Lake
Shore Dr, Chicago, 60605. W Peyton
Fawcett, Librn; Benjamin W Williams, Assoc
Librn
Holdings: Vols (210,000) Cat
Budget: ($100,000)
Notes: Extensive collections--publications of
learned societies and institutions and
monographic works--in all fields of natural
history, with emphasis on taxonomy and
evolutionary biology; and on museum
publications, American and foreign:
anthropology, especially archaeology and
ethnology of the Americas, Africa, East
Asia, and Oceania; botany, particularly
strong for the Americas; geology, chiefly
paleontology and meteoritic studies; and
zoology, worldwide (birds, fishes, insects,
mammals, mollusks, reptiles and
amphibians).

METEORITIC HYPOTHESIS

DC —SMITHSONIAN INSTITUTION
LIBRARIES, Natural History Branch,
Washington, 20560. Sylvia Churgin, Chief
Librn
Holdings: Vols (2350) Cat Maps Pix

METEOROLOGY

CA —UNIVERSITY OF CALIFORNIA, LOS
ANGELES, Engineering & Mathematical
Sciences Library, 405 Hilgard, Los Angeles,
90024. Rosalee I Wright, Librn
Holdings: Vols (180,000) Cat Microforms
Notes: Collection includes WMO
publications (comprehensive); IGY data
series on surface observations, radiosonde
and rawinsonde observations, upper wind
observations, and radiation data (mostly in
microform); selected government report or
data series, eg from NOAA, NCC and AF
Geophysics Laboratory.
CT —YALE UNIVERSITY, Geology Library,
210 Whitney Ave, PO Box 6666, New
Haven, 06511. Harry Scammell, Librn
Holdings: Vols (100,000) Cat Maps Pix
Microforms
Budget: ($115,100)
Notes: The O C Marsh Collection
(vertebrate paleontology) is also here.
DC —SMITHSONIAN INSTITUTION
LIBRARIES, Natural History Branch,
Washington, 20560. Sylvia Churgin, Chief
Librn
Holdings: Vols (2350) Cat Maps Pix

IL —UNIVERSITY OF ILLINOIS,
URBANA/CHAMPAIGN, Library,
Geology Library, 223 Natural History Bldg,
Urbana, 61801. Dederick Ward, Librn
Holdings: Vols (105,186) Cat Maps
Microforms
IN —PURDUE UNIVERSITY LIBRARIES,
Geosciences Library, West Lafayette, 47907.
Carolyn Lassoon, Librn
Holdings: Vols (15,000) Cat
Notes: Geosciences.
IA —IOWA STATE UNIVERSITY, Library,
Ames, 50011. Warren B Kuhn, Dean of
Library Services
Holdings: Cat
Notes: Incl agricultural climatology,
meteorology. Extensive serial holdings.
KS —UNIVERSITY OF KANSAS, Science
Library, 6040 Malott Hall, Lawrence, 66045.
Sharon R Cook, Asst Science Librn
Holdings: Vols Cat Maps Microforms
Notes: Incl US Geological Survey
topographical maps.
MD —JOHNS HOPKINS UNIVERSITY,
Milton S Eisenhower Library, Charles & 34
Sts, Baltimore, 21218. Ann S Gwyn,
Assistant Dir for Special Collections
Holdings: Vols (225,000) Cat
Notes: Foreign and American doctoral
dissertations and reprints to 1964. Largest
number in history of science, 85,000. Also
biology, chemistry, geology, meteorology,
psychology, physics and mathematics. Johns
Hopkins not included. Incl 100,000 Western
European doctoral dissertations, espec
French and German; some Scandinavian.
Collection is located in Gillman Storage
Area accessible through Special Collection
Division.
MD —NATIONAL OCEANIC &
ATMOSPHERIC ADMINISTRATION,
Library & Information Sciences Division,
Central Library & Information Sciences
Bldg, 6009 Executive Blvd, Rockville,
20852. Elizabeth J Yeates, Chief
Holdings: Vols (175,000) Cat Maps
Microforms
MA —HARVARD UNIVERSITY LIBRARY,
Gordon McKay Library, Division of Applied
Sciences, Pierce Hall, Oxford St, Cambridge,
02138. Julie Sandall Barlas, Librn
Holdings: Vols (100,000) Cat Microforms
MA —BOSTON COLLEGE LIBRARIES,
Catherine B O'Connor Geophysics Library,
Weston Observatory, Weston, 02193. F
Clifford McElroy, Science Librn
Holdings: Vols (10,231) Cat Maps
Microforms
Budget: ($10,000)
Notes: This collection is being absorbed into
the general collection.
NV —UNIVERSITY OF NEVADA, RENO,
Desert Research Institute, PO Box 60220,
Reno, 89557. Roberta Kiefer Orcutt, Librn
Holdings: Vols (10,480) Cat Maps
Microforms
Notes: Incl materials in atmospheric physics,
meteorology, climatology, weather
modification, antarctic studies and related
materials in basic sciences. Over 3000
microforms; also 1300 technical reports and
18,000 government publications.
NY —AMERICAN MUSEUM-HAYDEN
PLANETARIUM, Richard S Perkin Library,
81 St & Central Park W, New York, 10024.
Sandra Kitt, Librn
Holdings: Vols (15,000) Cat Maps Pix Slides
Budget: ($8000)
Notes: Considered one of the strongest and
most complete astronomy libraries on the
east coast. Contains the Bliss Collection of
Ancient Astronomical Instruments; also the
Mt Wilson/Bloman Sky Survey to the 45
degree declination; the Lick Observatory
Survey; *American Ephemeris and Nautical
Almanac*, 1855-date.
NY —AMERICAN MUSEUM OF
NATURAL HISTORY, Library Services
Dept, Central Park W & 79th St, New York,
10024. Nina J Root, Chairwoman; Mary
Genett, Asst Librn for Reference Services
Holdings: Vols (385,000) Cat Mss Maps Pix
Slides Microforms
Notes: Nearly all collections are outstanding
for depth of coverage and international
range. Early and historic works, rare books,

colored illustrations, and relevant serial
publications supplement the modern
scientific publications necessary to the
researches of the scientific staff and the
work of the educational division. Open to
the public.
NY —ENGINEERING SOCIETIES
LIBRARY, 345 E 47 St, New York, 10017.
S Kirk Cabeen, Dir
Holdings: Vols 250,000 Cat Maps 16mm
Films Microforms
Notes: One of the largest, most
comprehensive engineering libraries in the
world. Covers all engineering disciplines;
particularly strong in electrical and
electronic, mechanical, mining and
metallurgical, petroleum, chemical,
industrial, air conditioning and refrigeration
engineering. Incl Wheeler Collection of early
materials on magnetisn and electricity. 125,
000 bound periodical volumes; 10,000 maps;
5000 serial subscriptions (many foreign-
language). Virtually all materials abstracted
in *Engineering Index* (1884-date) are incl in
Library. Noncirculating, except to members
of professional engineering societies which
support the Library. See *Engineering
Societies Library, New York, Classed
Subject Catalog and Index* (Boston: G K
Hall, 1963); and *Supplements*, 1-10, 1964-
1973.
NY —NEW YORK PUBLIC LIBRARY,
Research Libraries, Science and Technology
Research Center, Fifth Ave & 42 St, New
York, 10018.
Holdings: Vols (1,100,000) Cat Microforms
Budget: ($647,259)
NY —COLUMBIA UNIVERSITY
LIBRARIES, Geoscience Library, Lamont-
Doherty Geological Observatory, Palisades,
10964. Susan Klimley, Librn
Holdings: Vols (20,000) Cat
Notes: Geosciences, incl geochemistry,
marine geology, seismology and
paleoclimatology.
PA —UNIVERSITY OF PITTSBURGH,
Hillman Library, Pittsburgh, 15260.
Holdings: Vols (6000) Cat Maps Pix Slides
Microforms
Notes: The Geography collection is
strengthened by US Geological Survey
depository collection; US Army Map Service
depository collection; US government
publications depository collection; Canadian
government publications; and UN depository
(partial) collection.
PA —PENNSYLVANIA STATE
UNIVERSITY, Earth & Mineral Sciences
Library, 105 Deike Bldg, University Park,
16802. Emilie McWilliams, Head Librn
Holdings: Vols (58,000) Cat Maps
Microforms
Budget: ($49,750)
Notes: This collection includes substantial
numbers of geological maps, and strong
periodical holdings including microform.
†SD —SOUTH DAKOTA SCHOOL OF
MINES & TECHNOLOGY, Devereaux
Library, Rapid City, 57701.
Holdings: Vols (166,200) Cat Maps
Audiotapes Filmstrips Microforms
Notes: Supportive collection incl periodicals
and technical reports (NASA, ACRL, JPL,
etc); and extensive government document
materials (NBS, Dept of Commerce, HEW,
etc).
UT —NORTH AMERICAN WEATHER
CONSULTANTS, Technical Library, 1141
E 3900 South, Suite A130, Salt Lake City,
84124. Eleanor Furnival, Librn
Holdings: Vols (7000) Cat Maps 16mm
Films Microforms
Budget: ($5000)
Notes: Incl 500 maps and 3000 microforms.
BC —CANADIAN FORESTRY SERVICE,
Pacific Forest Research Centre, Library, 506
West Burnside Rd, Victoria, V8Z 1M5, Can.
Alice Solyma, Librn
Holdings: Vols (60,500) Cat Microforms
Notes: Incl forest meteorology and also a
general meteorology collection.
NS —ENVIRONMENT CANADA, Dept of
Environment Regional Library, 1497
Bedford Hwy, Bedford, E4A 1E5, Can.
Fraizer Macniel, Special Collections Librn
Holdings: Vols 500 Maps Microforms
Notes: Reference collection for a regional

METEOROLOGY (cont.)

weather analysis and forecasting center and to a small staff of professionals involved in consultation and applications. Principal meteorological and related journals are purchased. Library also houses regional climatological data base. Partially cataloged.

PQ —SERVICE DE LA DOCUMENTATION ET DES RENSEIGNEMENTS MINISTERE DE L'ENERGIE ET DES RESSOURCES, 2000B, chemin Sainte-Foy, 7th floor, Quebec, G1R 4X7, Can. Normand Guerette, Dir
Holdings: Vols (114,800) Slides Videotapes
Notes: In 1979, the Bibliotheque du ministere des Richesses naturelles du Quebec merged with the Bibliotheque du ministere des Terres et Forets. The result of this merger was the creation of the service de la Documentation et des Renseignements du ministere de l'Energie et des Ressources. Publications: Info-Biblio Terres et Forets; Mines; Energy.

METEOROLOGY, AGRICULTURAL

MD —US DEPT OF AGRICULTURE, National Agricultural Library, 10301 Baltimore Blvd, Beltsville, 20705. Joseph H Howard, Director
Holdings: Vols (2,000,000) Cat Mss Maps Pix Slides Microforms
Notes: Crop ecology, agro-climatic analogs; air pollution effects. Agronomy: agriculture and tropical and desert agriculture. For use by the staff of the Institute. Incl 5000 pamphlet items. Former collection of American Institute of Crop Ecology.

ON —AGRICULTURE CANADA, Research Branch, Neatby Library, K W Neatby Bldg, Rm 3032, Ottawa, K1A 0C6, Can. Marcel Charette, Clerk-in-Charge
Holdings: Vols 1800 Cat
Budget: $2300

METEORS

DC —SMITHSONIAN INSTITUTION LIBRARIES, Natural History Branch, Washington, 20560. Sylvia Churgin, Chief Librn
Holdings: Vols (2350) Cat Maps Pix

NY —AMERICAN MUSEUM-HAYDEN PLANETARIUM, Richard S Perkin Library, 81 St & Central Park W, New York, 10024. Sandra Kitt, Librn
Holdings: Vols (15,000) Cat Maps Pix Slides
Budget: ($8000)
Notes: Considered one of the strongest and most complete astronomy libraries on the east coast. Contains the Bliss Collection of Ancient Astronomical Instruments; also the Mt Wilson/Bloman Sky Survey to the 45 degree declination; the Lick Observatory Survey; American Ephemeris and Nautical Almanac, 1855-date.

NY —AMERICAN MUSEUM OF NATURAL HISTORY, Library Services Dept, Central Park W & 79th St, New York, 10024. Nina J Root, Chairwoman; Mary Genett, Asst Librn for Reference Services
Holdings: Vols (385,000) Cat Mss Maps Pix Slides Microforms
Notes: Nearly all collections are outstanding for depth of coverage and international range. Early and historic works, rare books, colored illustrations, and relevant serial publications supplement the modern scientific publications necessary to the researches of the scientific staff and the work of the educational division. Open to the public.

METERED MAIL see Postage Meters

METHANOL

MI —US ENVIRONMENTAL PROTECTION AGENCY, Motor Vehicle Emission Laboratory Library, 2565 Plymouth Rd, Ann Arbor, 48105. Debra Talsma, Librn
Holdings: // Uncat Microforms
Notes: No separate catalog. Collection

described in: US EPA, Library System Branch, Guide to EPA Libraries, July, 1977. Collection includes 9500 technical reports on air pollution from mobile sources (especially automobiles); air pollution legislation (350 vols); fuel economy and conservation (800 technical reports); automobile engineering (300 vols); emission control technology for mobile source (8000 reports and papers); use of methanol and other alternative fuels in motor vehicles (600 technical reports).

NY —CARY ARBORETUM OF THE NEW YORK BOTANICAL GARDEN, Library, Box AB, Millbrook, 12545. Fred Strum, Librn
Notes: This collection of alternative energy sources consists of publications concerned with solar energy, wind power, biofuel, methanol, small hydorelectric projects, and wood power.

METHODISM AND METHODIST CHURCH

AL —BIRMINGHAM-SOUTHERN COLLEGE, Charles Andrew Rush Learning Center, N Ala Conference, Birmingham, 35204. Keener Barnes, Exec Secy
Holdings: Vols (100,000) Cat Microforms
Budget: $500
Notes: Collection is almost completely concerned with Alabama Methodism. Incl an almost complete collection of United Methodist Christian Advocate, to incl the Alabama Christian Advocate from the first issue May 1881 - 1983 (micro), and the Nashville Christian Advocates 1910 - 1917 & 1922 - 1927 (bd). Also incl Alabama-West Florida Journals (bd) from 1886 - present.

†AL —HUNTINGDON COLLEGE, Houghton Memorial Library, 1500 E Fairview Ave, Montgomery, 36106. Bob Chapel, Dir
Notes: Archives and history of United Methodist Chruch, Alabama-West Florida Conference.

CA —AZUSA PACIFIC COLLEGE, Marshburn Memorial Library, Citrus & Alosta, Azusa, 91702. Edward Peterman, Librn
Holdings: Vols 275 Cat
Notes: Historical collection of the early days of the Free Methodist Church--incl conference minutes down to current issues. Completely cataloged and incl, with special designation, in regular library catalog.

CA —CLAREMONT COLLEGES, Honnold Library, Ninth & Dartmouth, Claremont, 91711. Tania Rizzo, Special Collections Dept Head
Holdings: Vols 3500 Cat Mss Phonorecords
Notes: Card index by Mr and Mrs Robert Guy McCutchan, donors. Mainly American, 17th century to present. Most complete for Methodist hymnbooks. Donor was editor of 1935 edition of Methodist Hymnal. Scrapbooks of McCutchan's life, accomplishments, and tributes, compiled by his widow.

CA —POINT LOMA NAZARENE COLLEGE, Ryan Library, 3900 Lomaland Dr, San Diego, 92106. Esther Schandorff, Librn
Holdings: Vols 1600 Cat Mss Pix
Notes: Arminian-Wesleyan Theological Collection. Historical material from the period of the Wesleyan revival to the present day.

CA —UNIVERSITY OF THE PACIFIC, Holt-Atherton Pacific Center for Western Studies, Stockton, 95211. Hiram L Davis, Dir of Libraries
Holdings: Uncat Mss Maps Pix
Notes: The Fry Library collection contains records, publications and ephemera of the California-Nevada Conference of the Methodist Episcopal Church. Included are parish records, Methodist periodicals, reminiscences, church and congregational histories. 500 linear ft of mss.

DC —WESLEY THEOLOGICAL SEMINARY, 4400 Massachusetts Ave NW, Washington, 20016. Roland E Kircher, Librn
Holdings: Vols (106,000) Cat Mss Pix
Notes: Wesleyana. Extensive collection of the historical records and publications of the former Methodist Protestant Church.

FL —FLORIDA SOUTHERN COLLEGE, Roux Library, Johnson at McDonald, Lakeland, 33802. Larry Stallings, Special Collections Librn
Holdings: Vols (5100) Cat Mss
Notes: Incl Florida church histories and minutes of District Conventions. Methodist-related books and hymnals, and many old Bibles, are included. Separate indexes.

GA —EMORY UNIVERSITY, Robert W Woodruff Library, Special Collections Dept, Atlanta, 30322. Linda M Matthews, Head Special Collections; Virginia J H Cain, Processing Archivist; Richard H F Lindemann, Reference Archivist
Holdings: Vols (16,000) Cat Mss Maps Pix Microforms
Notes: Letters and other writings of John Wesley, Charles Wesley and other members of the Wesley family. Description and index available in repository.

GA —EMORY UNIVERSITY, Candler School of Theology, Pitts Theology Library, Atlanta, 30322. Channing Jeschke, Librn; Anita K Delaries, Curator
Holdings: Cat Mss
Notes: Incl records (85 vols) of the Methodist Church in Georgia; 1614 mss and ms volumes dating from 1830.

GA —AGNES SCOTT COLLEGE, McCain Library, E College Ave, Decatur, 30030. Judith Bourgeois Jensen, Librn
Holdings: Vols (945) Uncat
Budget: $300
Notes: The Frontier Religion Collection, which was given by Prof Walter Brownlow Posey, traces the effects of slavery on religion in the Old South Frontier prior to 1860. A catalog file (by author entry only) accompanies the collection at present. Noncirculating.

IL —ILLINOIS STATE HISTORICAL SOCIETY, Library, Old State Capitol, Springfield, 62706. Roger D Bridges, Head Librn
Notes: Papers, 55 items, 1827-1857. Methodist pioneer circuit-rider.

IN —INDIANA CENTRAL UNIVERSITY, Krannert Memorial Library, 1400 E Hanna Ave, Indianapolis, 46227. Florabelle Wilson, Librn
Holdings: Vols 561 Cat
Notes: Collection of books and pamphlets which have been written by members of the United Brethren (UB), Evangelical United Bretheren (EUB) and United Methodist (UM) Church. The collection has conference yearbooks, proceedings, and annuals, as well as biographies and historical information about the origin and development of these faiths.

IN —MARION COLLEGE LIBRARY, 4201 S Washington St, Marion, 46952. Harold W Boyce, Dir of Library Services
Holdings: Vols 850 Cat
Notes: Wesleyan history.

IN —FREE METHODIST CHURCH OF NORTH AMERICA, Marston Memorial Historical Center Library, 901 College Ave, Winona Lake, 46590. Evelyn L Mottweiler, Librn
Holdings: Vols (6000) Cat Mss
Budget: ($16,000)
Notes: Denominational headquarters of the Free Methodist Church in North America. Collection includes Wesleyan Movement in 18th Century England, beginnings of Methodism in England and America. Movement of Methodism across America. Biographies, periodicals (incl Methodist Quarterly Review) doctrinal works, Disciplines. Methodist holdings (4500 vols) of the Library are included in the Methodist Union Catalog: Pre-1976 Imprints, ed by Kenneth E Rowe.
See also entry under Wesley, John.

KS —UNITED METHODIST HISTORICAL COLLECTION AND LIBRARY, Baker University Library, Lower Floor, Eighth St, Baldwin City, 66006. Maxine Kreutziger, Secy; John Forbes, Supvr
Holdings: Cat Mss Maps Pix Microforms
Budget: ($2000)
Notes: United Methodist Church history, espec in Kansas. Persons desiring to visit the collection are advised to make an

METHODISM AND METHODIST CHURCH (cont.)

appointment or phone ahead to Baker University (913-594-6451 ext 380 or 414) to assure that collection is open.

KY —ASBURY THEOLOGICAL SEMINARY, B L Fisher Library, Wilmore, 40390. D William Faupel, Dir of Library Services
Holdings: Vols 6000 Cat Pix Microforms
Budget: ($40,000)

LA —CENTENARY COLLEGE OF LOUISIANA, Magale Library, Shreveport, 71104. Carolyn Garison, Archivist
Holdings: Vols (2000) Cat Mss Pix Microforms
Budget: ($750)
Notes: Depository for the records of the Louisiana Conference and materials relating to all the antecedent bodies of United Methodism in Louisiana. Also, collections of personal and family papers relating to Louisiana Methodist history and church histories. We are trying to locate church records for microfilming. Further emphasis on Northern Louisiana and Shreveport history. Catalogs and inventories for all manuscript and archival materials are housed with the collection in the Cline Room. Citations on part of this material will be found in NUCMC MS65-1830 and Hamer's *Guide to Archives and Manuscripts in the United States.*

MD —JOHNS HOPKINS UNIVERSITY, Milton S Eisenhower Library, George Peabody Collection, 17 E Mt Vernon Place, Baltimore, 21201. Lyn Hart, Peabody Librn
Notes: Emphasis on materials published before 1950. Strength is a good collection through the 19th century.

MD —LOVELY LANE MUSEUM, Library, 2200 St Paul St, Baltimore, 21218. Edwin Schell, Exec Secy & Librn
Holdings: Vols 3560 Cat Mss Maps Pix Slides
Notes: Richest in Methodist history of Maryland, Pennsylvania, Washington, DC, Virginia, and West Virginia.

MA —UNITED METHODIST CHURCH, SOUTHERN NEW ENGLAND CONFERENCE, Commission on Archives & History, New England Methodist Historical Society Library, 745 Commonwealth Ave, Boston, 02215. William E Zimpfer, Librn
Holdings: Vols 13,750 Cat Mss
Budget: $800
Notes: Mainly records of New England Methodist churches and of Methodist conferences and institutions in New England. It is the official repository of the Southern New England Conference of the United Methodist Church.

MI —ADRIAN COLLEGE, Shipman Library, Adrian, 49221. Ronald A Brunger, Cur
Holdings: Vols (1500) Cat Mss
Budget: ($400)
Notes: United Methodist Church, Detroit Conference, Archives. Incl materials on John Wesley; the Rise of Methodism in Britain, Canada and America; the Bishops; Biographies of leaders and Writings of leaders. Incl materials on Methodist Episcopal, Evangelical United Brethren, Methodist Protestant and United Methodist Churches. Incl Minutes of Annual and General Conferences; Methodist Protestant 1838-86, the True Wesleyan 1844-49, Zion's Watchman 1838-41, New York Watchman 1842, Juvenile Wesleyan 1843-44.

MS —MILLSAPS COLLEGE, Millsaps-Wilson Library, Jackson, 39210. Kathy Holden, College Archivist
Holdings: Vols 500 Mss Microforms
Notes: Mississippi Methodist Historical Archives Collection housed in the J B Cain Archives of Mississippi Methodism, in addition to Millsaps College Archives.

MO —CENTRAL METHODIST COLLEGE, George M Smiley Memorial Library, Fayette, 65248. C E Hix, Dir
Holdings: Vols (1300) Cat Mss
Notes: Archives of the Missouri West Conference of the United Methodist Church. Incl journals and books.

MT —ROCKY MOUNTAIN COLLEGE, Paul M Adams Memorial Library, 1511 Poly Dr, Billings, 59102. Sue Walker, Dir
Holdings: Cat Maps
Notes: Large collection on geology. Also, deposit of the Billings Archaeological Society, the Mountain Methodist Historical Library (incl papers of Brother Van Oursdale, pioneer circuit rider) and the Montana Congregational Archives.

NE —NEBRASKA WESLEYAN UNIVERSITY, Cochrane-Woods Library, 50 & St Paul, Lincoln, 68504. Lois W Collings, Dir
Holdings: Vols 15,000 Cat Mss Maps Pix Slides Microforms
Notes: Nebraska history of the United Methodist Church.

NJ —DREW UNIVERSITY, Library, Madison, 07940. Caroline Coughlin, Assoc Dir
Notes: Large historical collection covering the worldwide history of Methodism.

NJ —UNITED METHODIST CHURCH, Commission on Archives and History, 36 Madison Ave, PO Box 127, Madison, 07940. Charles Yrigoyen, Jr, General Secy
Holdings: Vols 40,000 Cat Mss Maps Pix Slides Microforms
Budget: $110,000
Notes: The United Methodist Church Collection includes these churches and dates: The United Evangelical Church, 1891-1922; The Evangelical Association, 1800-1922; The Evangelical Church, 1922-1946; The United Brethren in Christ, 1800-1946; The Evangelical United Brethren Church, 1946-1968; The Methodist Episcopal Church, 1773-1939; The Methodist Episcopal Church, South, 1844-1939; The Methodist Church, 1939-1968; The United Methodist Church, 1968-date. There is no published catalog. The Depository is a specialized collection pertaining to manuscript and published material dealing with the United Methodist Church and its antecedent bodies. It is the official church depository for preservation of records-over 2 million items.

NY —HOUGHTON COLLEGE, Willard J Houghton Library, Houghton, 14744. Joyce Moore, Librn
Holdings: Vols 1200 Cat
Notes: Methodism and the Wesleys; books related to Wesleyan Methodism comprise the greatest part of the collection. To be incl in the Methodist Union Catalog being prepared under the editorial supervision of Dr Kenneth E Rowe of Drew University.

NY —ROBERTS WESLEYAN COLLEGE, Kenneth B Keating Library, 2301 Westside Dr, Rochester, 14624. Charles H Canon
Holdings: Vols (500) Cat Mss Pix
Notes: This is not a large or comprehensive collection, but it does contain unique mss and pictorial material, particularly material pertaining to the Roberts family. Benjamin Titus Roberts, the founder of this institution, was a principal founder of the Free Methodist Church.

NY —SYRACUSE UNIVERSITY LIBRARIES, Ernest S Bird Library, George Arents Research Library for Special Collections, Syracuse, 13210. Carolyn A Davis, Manuscripts Librn; Amy S Doherty, University Archivist; Mark F Weimer, Rare Book Librn
Holdings: Vols 2000 Uncat

NC —DUKE UNIVERSITY, William R Perkins Library, Manuscript Dept, Durham, 27706. Ellen Gartrell, Cur of Mss
Holdings: Cat Mss
Notes: Records of Methodist congregations, circuits, districts, and conferences, primarily in North Carolina. Papers of Bishop James Cannon and other clergy; Frank Baker Collection of Wesleyana and British Methodism.

NC —DUKE UNIVERSITY, William R Perkins Library, Manuscript Dept, Durham, 27706. Ellen Gartrell, Cur of Mss
Holdings: Cat Mss
Notes: Methodist Church Papers (records of local and regional units) also many personal and professional papers of clergy, missionaries and laymen, 19th-20th centuries, eg Methodist John Lakin Brasher (holiness movement leader), Carlyle Marney (Southern Baptist minister), Methodist Bishop James Cannon, missionary Martha Foster Crawford.

NC —DUKE UNIVERSITY, Divinity School Library, Durham, 27706. Donn Michael Farris, Librn
Holdings: Vols (225,000)
Notes: Special collections and subject emphases in this library include: Archaeology, Egyptian; Archaeology, Middle Eastern; Art, Jewish; Bible; Bible-New Testament; Bible-Symbolism; Church Architecture; Egyptology; Fathers of the Church; Society of Friends; Great Britain-Religion-Methodism and Methodist Church; Hymns and Hymnals; Jansenists and Jansenism; Judaica; Mediaeval Christian Mysticism; Methodism and Methodist Church; Methodist Episcopal Church; Methodist Episcopal Church, South; Reformation; Religion-US-History; Rural Church; Theology-Great Britain-17th Century; Theology-Great Britain-18th Century; United Methodist Church; US-Church History; John Wesley.

OH —CINCINNATI HISTORICAL SOCIETY, Library, (formerly Historical & Philosophical Society of Ohio), Eden Park, Cincinnati, 45202. Laura L Chace, Librn
Holdings: Cat Mss Pix
Notes: Entire collection of papers, printed materials, photographs, etc, of the German Methodist Episcopal Church in the US, 1835-1942 (when it merged with the United Methodist Church). Incl diaries of ministers, organizational records, church and institutional archives, etc.

SC —WOFFORD COLLEGE, Sandor Teszler Library, N Church St, Spartanburg, 29301. Frank J Anderson, Librn
Holdings: Vols 1247 Cat
Notes: Mainly 19th century, incl biographies of 19th century Methodist preachers. Listed in: *Biography*, compiled by Elizabeth Sabin and edited by Frank J Anderson (Wofford College Library. Special Collections Checklist no 4), Spartanburg, SC; Wofford Library Press, 1970; 31 pp, mimeo. Also, Methodist hymnals from the early 1800s to date. Also Haynes-Brown Hymnal Collection consists of many denominations of rare items and colonial imprints, incl Saur and Isaiah Thomas imprints. Collection is being augmented by Pierce Gault of Washington, DC.

TN —TENNESSEE WESLEYAN COLLEGE, Merner-Pfeiffer Library, PO Box 40, Athens, 37303. Louise I Harms, Librn
Holdings: Vols 1436 Cat Mss Pix
Notes: Emphasis on the Methodist Episcopal Church, North; some material on Methodist Episcopal Church, South. Many old or rare items, some from 1750. No separate catalog.

WV —WEST VIRGINIA WESLEYAN COLLEGE, Annie Merner Pfeiffer Library, Buckhannon, 26201. Ben Crutchfield, Jr, Dir
Holdings: Vols 5000 Cat Mss Pix
Notes: Depository for the Methodist Historical Collection of the United Methodist Church of West Virginia.

WI —UNIVERSITY OF WISCONSIN, MADISON, Memorial Library, Western European Humanities Collection, 728 State St, Madison, 53706. Charles Szabo, Bibliographer
Notes: Tank collection. The core of this extensive collection is its works on theology, the largest portion of which deals with Calvinism. Practically all the printed sermons of the major Calvinist preachers of the 18th century are represented. Includes many 16th and 17th century sermons. About a third of the collection deals with Church history; not only are Calvinist histories represented but also 18th century histories of Methodists, Quakers, and Moravians. Supplements the Montauban Collection (French Protestantism) and the Chwalibog Collection (theology).

ON —TORONTO SCHOOL OF THEOLOGY, Consortium of Libraries, University of Toronto, Toronto, M5S 1A5, Can. R Grane Bracewell, Library Coordr
Holdings: Cat
Notes: A consortium of 7 theological college and faculty libraries at the University of Toronto.

METHODISM AND METHODIST CHURCH (cont.)

ON —VICTORIA UNIVERSITY, Library, 71 Queen's Park Crescent, Toronto, M5S 1K7, Can. Robert C Brandeis, Chief Librn
Holdings: Vols (1300) Cat Mss
Notes: Wesleyana and Green Collections: works of John, Charles and Samuel Wesley incl the collection of Dr Richard Green upon which his *The Works of John and Charles Wesley: A Bibliography* (London, 1906, 2nd rev ed) was based. Likely the strongest collection of the Wesleys' publications in North America.

METHODIST EPISCOPAL CHURCH

CA —UNIVERSITY OF THE PACIFIC, Holt-Atherton Pacific Center for Western Studies, Stockton, 95211. Hiram L Davis, Dir of Libraries
Holdings: Uncat Mss Maps Pix
Notes: The Fry Library collection contains records, publications and ephemera of the California-Nevada Conference of the Methodist Episcopal Church. Included are parish records, Methodist periodicals, reminiscences, church and congregational histories. 500 linear ft of mss.

MI —ADRIAN COLLEGE, Shipman Library, Adrian, 49221. Ronald A Brunger, Cur
Holdings: Vols (4500) Cat Mss
Budget: ($4600)
Notes: United Methodist Church, Detroit Conference, Archives. Incl Minutes of the annual Conferences since 1773; Journals of General Conferences; Biographies of Asbury, Coke and other Bishops, as well as of Circuit Riders; histories and books on the Church. Incl materials on Methodism, Evangelical United Brethren, Methodist Protestant and United Methodist Churches.

NJ —UNITED METHODIST CHURCH, Commission on Archives and History, 36 Madison Ave, PO Box 127, Madison, 07940. Charles Yrigoyen, Jr, General Secy
Holdings: Vols 40,000 Cat Mss Maps Pix Slides Microforms
Budget: $110,000
Notes: The United Methodist Church Collection includes these churches and dates: The United Evangelical Church, 1891-1922; The Evangelical Association, 1800-1922; The Evangelical Church, 1922-1946; The United Brethren in Christ, 1800-1946; The Evangelical United Brethren Church, 1946-1968; The Methodist Episcopal Church, 1773-1939; The Methodist Episcopal Church, South, 1844-1939; The Methodist Church, 1939-1968; The United Methodist Church, 1968-date. There is no published catalog. The Depository is a specialized collection pertaining to manuscript and published material dealing with the United Methodist Church and its antecedent bodies. It is the official church depository for preservation of records-over 2 million items.

NY —CORNELL UNIVERSITY LIBRARIES, Collection of Regional History, Dept of Manuscripts and Univ Archives, Ithaca, 14853.
Notes: Records, ca 1870-1904, of First Methodist Epsiscopal Church, Auburn, NY; 8 vols.

NC —DUKE UNIVERSITY, Divinity School Library, Durham, 27706. Donn Michael Farris, Librn
Holdings: Vols (225,000)
Notes: Special collections and subject emphases in this library include: Archaeology, Egyptian; Archaeology, Middle Eastern; Art, Jewish; Bible; Bible-New Testament; Bible-Symbolism; Church Architecture; Egyptology; Fathers of the Church; Society of Friends; Great Britain-Religion-Methodism and Methodist Church; Hymns and Hymnals; Jansenists and Jansenism; Judaica; Mediaeval Christian Mysticism; Methodism and Methodist Church; Methodist Episcopal Church; Methodist Episcopal Church, South; Reformation; Religion-US-History; Rural Church; Theology-Great Britain-17th Century; Theology-Great Britain-18th Century; United Methodist Church; US-Church History; John Wesley.

TN —TENNESSEE WESLEYAN COLLEGE, Merner-Pfeiffer Library, PO Box 40, Athens, 37303. Louise I Harms, Librn
Holdings: Vols 1436 Cat Mss Pix
Notes: Emphasis on the Methodist Episcopal Church, North; some material on Methodist Episcopal Church, South. Many old or rare items, some from 1750. No separate catalog.

METHODIST EPISCOPAL CHURCH, SOUTH

NJ —UNITED METHODIST CHURCH, Commission on Archives and History, 36 Madison Ave, PO Box 127, Madison, 07940. Charles Yrigoyen, Jr, General Secy
Holdings: Vols 40,000 Cat Mss Maps Pix Slides Microforms
Budget: $110,000
Notes: The United Methodist Church Collection includes these churches and dates: The United Evangelical Church, 1891-1922; The Evangelical Association, 1800-1922; The Evangelical Church, 1922-1946; The United Brethren in Christ, 1800-1946; The Evangelical United Brethren Church, 1946-1968; The Methodist Episcopal Church, 1773-1939; The Methodist Episcopal Church, South, 1844-1939; The Methodist Church, 1939-1968; The United Methodist Church, 1968-date. There is no published catalog. The Depository is a specialized collection pertaining to manuscript and published material dealing with the United Methodist Church and its antecedent bodies. It is the official church depository for preservation of records-over 2 million items.

NC —DUKE UNIVERSITY, Divinity School Library, Durham, 27706. Donn Michael Farris, Librn
Holdings: Vols 225,000
Notes: Special collections and subject emphases in this library include: Archaeology, Egyptian; Archaeology, Middle Eastern; Art, Jewish; Bible; Bible-New Testament; Bible-Symbolism; Church Architecture; Egyptology; Fathers of the Church; Society of Friends; Great Britain-Religion-Methodism and Methodist Church; Hymns and Hymnals; Jansenists and Jansenism; Judaica; Mediaeval Christian Mysticism; Methodism and Methodist Church; Methodist Episcopal Church; Methodist Episcopal Church, South; Reformation; Religion-US-History; Rural Church; Theology-Great Britain-17th Century; Theology-Great Britain-18th Century; United Methodist Church; US-Church History; John Wesley.

METHODIUS, ST.

PA —SLOVAK EASTERN CATHOLIC SYNOD OF AMERICA, 515 W Main, Monongahela, 15063.
Holdings: 1500 Vols
Notes: Promotes use of the Byzantine Rite among Slovak-Americans. Special interest in Sts Cyril and Methodius.

METHODS ENGINEERING see Industrial Engineering

METRO-GOLDWYN-MAYER

CA —ACADEMY OF MOTION PICTURE ARTS & SCIENCES, Margaret Herrick Library, 8949 Wilshire Blvd, Beverly Hills, 90211. Linda Harris Mehr, Library Administrator
Notes: Stills archive.
See also entry under Moving Pictures.

CA —UNIVERSITY OF CALIFORNIA, LOS ANGELES, Theater Arts Library, Los Angeles, 90024. Edward Shreeves, Chairman, Bibliographers Group; Audree Malkin, Head, Theater Arts Library
Holdings: Cat Mss Pix
Notes: Script Collection, Screenplays: a collection of more than 32,636 unpublished scripts for American, British and some foreign language films. An important part of the collection is the Metro-Goldwyn-Mayer Screenplay Collection which covers the period 1924-1947. Incl are the *Andy Hardy, Dr Kildare,* and *Maisie* film series which are virtually complete, and a number of short features, such as *Robert Benchley Series, Pete Smith Specialties,* and *Our Gang* Comedies. Walt Disney Collection: A small, but rare collection of cartoon continuities and shooting scripts dated 1937-1939.

CA —UNIVERSITY OF SOUTHERN CALIFORNIA, Edward L Doheny Memorial Library, Archives of Performing Arts, University Park, Los Angeles, 90089. Robert Knutson, Librn
Holdings: Mss
Notes: Metro-Goldwyn-Mayer Collecton incl screeplays from 1919-1958.

NY —NEW YORK PUBLIC LIBRARY, Performing Arts Research Center, Billy Rose Theatre Collection, 111 Amsterdam Ave, New York, 10023. Dorothy L Swerdlove, Cur
Holdings: Cat
See also entry under Moving Picture Industry

METROLOGY see Mensuration

METROPOLITAN GOVERNMENT

CA —ASSOCIATION OF BAY AREA GOVERNMENTS, MTC/ABAG Library, 101 Eighth St, Oakland, 94607. Diane Gillman, Information Coord
Notes: Concentrates heavily on the nine-county Bay Area region. About 10,000 monographs and serials. Title catalog, OCLC/ATS. Central collection of documents for six transit properties in Bay Area.

DC —METROPOLITAN WASHINGTON COUNCIL OF GOVERNMENTS, Research Library, 1875 Eye St NW, Suite 200, Washington, 20006. Suan Kalish, Librn
Holdings: Vols (3000) Cat Microforms
Notes: Contains (on 75 reels of microfilm) archives of Maryland-National Park and Planning Commission, archives of the Council of Governments, and audits and financial reports of local governments (1950-date). Also incl annual reports, planning reports and budgets from each jurisdiction (1973-date).

FL —MIAMI-DADE PUBLIC LIBRARY SYSTEM, Urban Affairs Library, 1 Biscayne Blvd, Miami, 33132. Richard G Frow, Librn
Holdings: Vols 3078 Cat
Notes: Local government administration and planning. Incl materials concerning local government administration and planning exclusive of Florida, chosen primarily to suit needs of local governmental officials, although use by local college students, land developers and the general public is considered. Incl 8627 pamphlets cat and 98 periodicals. Library has access to LOGIN and DIALOG databases.

METROPOLITAN OPERA

NY —NEW YORK PUBLIC LIBRARY, Performing Arts Research Center, Rodgers & Hammerstein Archives of Recorded Sound, 111 Amsterdam Ave, New York, 10023.
Holdings: Audiotapes
Notes: Established with the co-sponsorship of the Metropolitan Opera Association, the Metropolitan Opera Archive is a collection on tape of all the existing broadcasts of Met performances since 1931.

MEXICAN-AMERICAN BORDER see Border Studies

MEXICAN AMERICAN NEWSPAPERS see Newspapers, Mexican American

MEXICAN AMERICANS

†CA —ANAHEIM PUBLIC LIBRARY, 500 W Broadway, Anaheim, 92805.

CA —CALIFORNIA STATE UNIVERSITY, FULLERTON, Library, Box 4150, Fullerton, 92634. Alfredo H Zuniga, Coord
Notes: Some materials on Mexican

MEXICAN AMERICANS (cont.)

Americans. Not maintained as a separate collection.

CA —UNIVERSITY OF CALIFORNIA, LOS ANGELES, Research Library, Dept of Special Collections, 405 Hilgard Ave, Los Angeles, 90024. Edward Shreeves, Chairman, Bibliographers Group; David S Zeidberg, Head
Holdings: // Uncat Mss
Notes: The Carey McWilliams Collection of personal papers, clippings and reports. Incl material on the problems of the Mexican American, 1930-1940, and on the Zoot-Suit Riots.

CA —STANFORD UNIVERSITY LIBRARIES, Cecil H Green Library, Stanford, 94305. Michael T Ryan, Cur
Notes: Papers of Ernesto Galarza, Bert Corona, Manuel Ruiz, Jr, Eduardo Queredo, Edward Valenzuela.

KS —UNIVERSITY OF KANSAS, Kenneth Spencer Research Library, Kansas Collection, Lawrence, 66045. Sheryl K Williams, Cur
Holdings: Vols (92,000) Mss Pix Audiotapes
Notes: Collection includes photographs and transcripts of interviews with Mexican-Americans in Kansas.

MN —MINNESOTA HISTORICAL SOCIETY LIBRARY, 690 Cedar St, Saint Paul, 55101. Patricia C Harpole, Chief of Reference Library; Bonnie G Wilson, Head of Special Libraries
Notes: Oral History Collection contains tapes of representatives of ethnic groups in Minnesota interviewed as a part of special projects incl Blacks, Mexican-Americans, Finns in northern Minnesota, and Jews in Minneapolis.

TX —UNIVERSITY OF TEXAS LIBRARIES, Nettie Lee Benson Latin American Collection, Sid Richardson Hall 1.109, Austin, 78712. Laura Gutierrez-Witt, Head Librn
Holdings: Vols (450,000) Cat Slides 16mm Films Microforms
Notes: The Mexican American Library Project has, since 1974, collected materials relating to all aspects of Spanish-speaking people in the US, with emphasis on Mexican Americans.
See also entry under Latin America

TX —EL PASO PUBLIC LIBRARY, Mexican American Collection, 501 N Oregon, El Paso, 79901. Iris Espino, Librn
Holdings: Vols 3000 Cat
Notes: Current and historical information about Mexican-Americans throughout the US. Incl current social and economic writings about Mexican-Americans, Chicano literature, history and culture of Mexico from pre-Columbian times to the present, translations of Mexican authors, and Mexicans in current society.

TX —OBLATE SCHOOL OF THEOLOGY, Library, 285 Oblate Dr, San Antonio, 78216. James Maney, Libr Dir
Holdings: Vols (22,000) Cat
Budget: ($15,500)

MEXICAN ART see Art, Mexican

MEXICAN AUTHORS see Authors, Mexican

MEXICAN DRAMA

IL —NORTHWESTERN UNIVERSITY, Library, Special Collections Dept, 1937 Sheridan Rd, Evanston, 60201. R Russell Maylone, Cur
Holdings: Vols (15,000) Cat
Notes: Spanish drama from the 18th to 20th centuries, incl Castilian, Catalan, Valencian, and Mexican. Additional material in general collection.

MEXICAN LITERATURE

AZ —UNIVERSITY OF ARIZONA, Library, Tucson, 85721. W David Laird, Librn

CA —UNIVERSITY OF CALIFORNIA, SAN DIEGO, Central University Library, Mandeville Dept of Special Collections, La Jolla, 92093. Lynda Corey Claassen, Head
Notes: Hispanic Collection: Approx 6000 vols describe cultures of Spain, Portugal, Mexico, Latin America, and South America. Works of literature, history, philosophy and art date from the 15th to the mid-19th century. Highlights of the collection include rare 18th century Spanish provincial dramas and works on the history of Seville and Andalusia.

IL —SOUTHERN ILLINOIS UNIVERSITY, CARBONDALE, Delyte W Morris Library, Carbondale, 62901.
Holdings: Vols (19,000) Cat
Notes: Especially strong in Ecuadorean and Mexican literature; complete or almost complete files of many important literary journals published in Spanish America. Described in Woodbridge, Hensley C, "Faculty and library collaboration in developing the Latin American collection for area studies programs at Southern Illinois University," Twelfth Seminar on the Acquisition of Latin American Library Materials, Final Report and Working Papers, vol 2, pp 99-108 (1967).

NJ —RUTGERS, THE STATE UNIVERSITY OF NEW JERSEY, Alexander Library, Special Collections and Archives, College Ave & Huntington St, New Brunswick, 08903. Ronald L Becker, Cur of Manuscripts and Rare Books
Holdings: Cat
Notes: Incl the 600 vol collection on modern Mexican literature of Dr Elias Nandino.

NM —NEW MEXICO STATE UNIVERSITY, Library, Box 3475, Las Cruces, 88003. James Dyke, Dir
Holdings: Vols 4200// Cat
Notes: Personal library of Prof Ignacio Medina Alvarado of the Universidad de Mexico which includes an extensive collection of Mexicn literature and poetry. Many volumes are autographed.

MEXICAN MANUSCRIPTS see Manuscripts, Mexican

MEXICAN NEWSPAPERS see Newspapers, Mexican

MEXICAN PLAYERS

CA —POMONA PUBLIC LIBRARY, Special Collections, 625 S Garey Ave, PO Box 2271, Pomona, 91766. David Streeter, Librn
Holdings: Uncat Mss
Notes: 14 linear feet of theater archives incl original play scripts, original music compositions, tape recordings of play performances, theater advertising, photographs of players, play bills, etc. Theatrical group was also known as The Mexican Players. Period covered: 1930's-1960's.

MEXICAN POETRY

NM —NEW MEXICO STATE UNIVERSITY, Library, Box 3475, Las Cruces, 88003. James Dyke, Dir
Holdings: Vols 4200// Cat
Notes: Personal library of Prof Ignacio Medina Alvarado of the Universidad de Mexico which includes an extensive collection of Mexican literature and poetry. Many volumes are autographed.

MEXICAN WAR, 1845-1848 see U.S. —History—War with Mexico, 1845-1848

MEXICAN WEST COAST DEVELOPMENT COMPANY

CA —CALIFORNIA STATE UNIVERSITY, FRESNO, Henry Madden Library, Dept of Special Collections, Fresno, 93740. Ronald J Mahoney, Head
Holdings: // Uncat Mss
Notes: Unsuccessful American venture to exploit the agricultural and mineral resources of western Mexico, ca 1920. 65 ms pieces.

MEXICANS

TX —UNIVERSITY OF TEXAS, EL PASO, Library, Special Collections Dept, El Paso, 79968. Cesar Caballero, Dept Head
Notes: Oral History Collection. A product of the Oral History Institute at U T El Paso, this collection consists of tapes and transcripts of interviews with prominent and not so prominent persons of the community of El Paso, Juarez and other parts of the Border region.

MEXICANS IN THE U.S.

CA —LOS ANGELES PUBLIC LIBRARY, Social Sciences Dept, 630 W Fifth St, Los Angeles, 90071. Marilyn C Wherley, Principal Librn
Holdings: Vols 10,000 Microforms
Budget: ($150,000)
Notes: Emphasis on minorities; immigration policies, background and social problems of ethnic minorities in the US and the Southwest in particular. Incl periodicals, government publications and documents, popular and scholarly works on Blacks, Hispanics and Asians predominantly.

CA —STANFORD UNIVERSITY LIBRARIES, Cecil H Green Library, Stanford, 94305. Michael T Ryan, Cur
Notes: Correspondence, papers, and material on farm labor and migrant workers of recent years. Incl papers of Ernesto Galarza and the National Agricultural Workers Union (NAWU), Fr Victor Salandini and Fr James L Vizzard.
See also entry under Chicano Studies

PA —BALCH INSTITUTE FOR ETHNIC STUDIES, Library, 18 S Seventh St, Philadelphia, 19106. R Joseph Anderson, Library Dir
Holdings: Vols 250 Cat Microforms

TX —FORT WORTH PUBLIC LIBRARY, North Branch, 601 Park St, Fort Worth, 76106. Betty M Hennington, Branch Head
Holdings: Vols 1000 Cat Phonorecords Audiotapes Filmstrips
Notes: Collection is entirely non-fiction. Although an effort is made to have novels by Mexican-American authors, these are not included in this collection. The criteria for the collection is anything written about Mexican Americans or books in which a large portion is devoted to the Mexican American. The history of Mexico until 1920 is included, but there are no books dealing with the history of Mexico since that time. Travel books are not included. An effort is made to obtain all current materials and to acquire retrospective materials when available, especially in the field of education and teaching.

MEXICO

AZ —YUMA CITY-COUNTY LIBRARY, 350 Third Ave, Yuma, 85364. Nancy R Cummings, Library Dir
Holdings: Vols 2500 Cat Microforms
Notes: The Southwest Collection incl Yuma, Arizona, surrounding states and Northern Mexico.

CA —UNIVERSITY OF CALIFORNIA, BERKELEY, University Library, Hispanic Collections, Berkeley, 94720. Gaston Somoshegyi-Szokol, Librn
Holdings: Vols (45,000)
Notes: Outstanding collection of classic and standard works (writings of the pioneers and of major contributors of the field) and of studies published on colonial Mexico. An immense collection of manuscripts, original documents, and microfilmed materials from the Spanish and Mexican national archives, as well as an abundance of smaller archival and document collections.

CA —UNIVERSITY OF CALIFORNIA, SAN DIEGO, Central University Library, Mandeville Dept of Special Collections, La Jolla, 92093. Lynda Corey Claassen, Head
Notes: Hispanic Collection: Approx 6000 vols describe cultures of Spain, Portugal, Mexico, Latin America, and South America. Works of literature, history, philosophy and art date from the 15th to the mid-19th century. Highlights of the collection include rare 18th century Spanish provincial dramas and works on the history of Seville and Andalusia.

MEXICO (cont.)

CT —YALE UNIVERSITY, Box 1603A, Yale
Station, New Haven, 06520.

CT —YALE UNIVERSITY, Sterling Memorial
Library, Latin American Collections, New
Haven, 06520. Lee H Williams Jr, Cur
Holdings: Vols (300,000) Cat Maps Pix
Slides Phonorecords 16mm Films Filmstrips
Notes: Unusual strength in 19th century
Mexico. Recently cataloged collection of
about 10,000 Mexican 19th century
pamphlets.
See also entry under Latin America

CT —YALE UNIVERSITY, Beincke Rare
Book & Manuscript Library, Western
Americana Collection, Wall & High St, New
Haven, 06520. George Miles, Cur
Holdings: Cat Mss Maps Pix
Notes: Incl much historical ephemeral
material.

FL —UNIVERSITY OF MIAMI, Otto G
Richter Library, PO Box 248214, Coral
Gables, 33124. Frank Rodgers, Dir of
Libraries
Notes: Special collections on Cuba, Jamaica,
Colombia, Brazil, Panama, and Mexico are
supported by a general collection pertaining
to the history and culture of Latin America.
The collection incl the Agencia
Latinoamericana papers. Emphasis is on
Cuba and the Caribbean area.

KY —UNIVERSITY OF KENTUCKY,
Margaret I King Library, Dept of Special
Collections, Lexington, 40506. William
Marshall, Head
Holdings: Vols 79 Cat
Notes: Incl 1 map; period covered: 1601-
1978.

PA —UNIVERSITY OF PITTSBURGH,
Hillman Library, Pittsburgh, 15260. Glenora
E Rossell, Head
Holdings: Vols (172,000) Cat Microforms
Notes: The Latin American collection,
although it contains good coverage of all
countries and subjects related to those
countries, has been developed giving special
emphasis to materials related to Cuba,
Ecuador, Guatemala, Mexico, Bolivia, and
Peru. The collection is outstanding for
research on Bolivia and contemporary Cuba.
It incl 1500 periodical titles, 400 of which
are currently being received. Especially
strong on revolutionary and radical
movements, and social change. Incl the John
M Malone Collection (300 vols) and the
Casasola collection of photographs of 20th
century Mexico; virtually all the works of
the Mexican philosopher Jose Vasconcelos.

TX —TRINITY UNIVERSITY, Elizabeth
Coates Maddux Library, 715 Stadium Dr,
San Antonio, 78284. Richard Hume
Werking, Library Dir; Craig Likness, Head
Bibliographer
Holdings: Microfilm Reels
Notes: Municipal and Parochial Archives of
the States of Nuevo Leon and Coahuila,
Mexico. Incl 4375 microfilm reels.

MEXICO—ANTIQUITIES

AZ —FULTON-HAYDEN MEMORIAL
LIBRARY, Dragoon, 85609. Mario Nick
Klimiades, Librn
Holdings: Vols 17,000 Cat Mss Maps Pix
Microforms
Budget: $3500
Notes: The Fulton-Hayden Memorial
Library is a special collection of books about
archaeology and ethnology specifically as
they pertain to the western hemisphere and
particularly to Mexico and the greater
American Southwest.

MEXICO—CIVILIZATION

CA —UNIVERSITY OF CALIFORNIA, SAN
DIEGO, Central University Library,
Mandeville Dept of Special Collections, La
Jolla, 92093. Lynda Corey Claassen, Head
Notes: Hispanic Collection: Approx 6000
vols describe cultures of Spain, Portugal,
Mexico, Latin America, and South America.
Works of literature, history, philosophy and
art date from the 15th to the mid-19th

century. Highlights of the collection include
rare 18th century Spanish provincial dramas
and works on the history of Seville and
Andalusia.

KY —UNIVERSITY OF KENTUCKY,
Margaret I King Library, Dept of Special
Collections, Lexington, 40506. William
Marshall, Head
Holdings: Vols 79 Cat
Notes: Incl 1 map; period covered: 1601-
1978.

MA —HARVARD UNIVERSITY LIBRARY,
Botanical Museum Library, Cambridge,
02138.
Holdings: Vols (2400) Mss Pix
Notes: The Tina and Gordon Wisson
Ethnomycological Collection, one of the
most important modern collections, acquired
as an adjunct to the Museum's Economic
Botany Library of Oakes Ames. From 15th
to 20th century, it deals with hallucinogenic
mushrooms in art, religion, and folklore;
chemistry, pharmacology, linguistics,
archaeological artifacts of Mexico,
Guatemala, India, Japan, China, etc.
Personal papers, etc.

MEXICO—DESCRIPTION AND TRAVEL

CA —LOS ANGELES PUBLIC LIBRARY,
History Dept, 630 W Fifth St, Los Angeles,
90071. Mary Pratt, Principal Librn
Holdings: Vols 3000 Cat Maps
Notes: Books, pamphlets and serials on
Mexico from the Aztecs to the present day.
The collection includes a significant number
of 17th century imprints and 19th century
travel books.

MEXICO—HISTORY

†AL —UNIVERSITY OF ALABAMA, Amelia
Gayle Gorgas Library, PO Box S,
University, 35486.
Notes: This collection consists of 119 reels
of microfilm. Separately published
bibliography: *A Catalog of the Yucatan
Collection on Microfilm in the University of
Alabama Libraries* (University: University of
Alabama Press), 1972.

AZ —UNIVERSITY OF ARIZONA, Library,
Tucson, 85721. W David Laird, Librn
Notes: Latin

CA —UNIVERSITY OF CALIFORNIA,
BERKELEY, Bancroft Library, Manuscripts
Division, Berkeley, 94720. James D Hart,
Dir
Holdings: Vols Cat Mss Maps Pix Slides
Microforms
Notes: Primary emphasis on Mexico, with a
lesser emphasis on the Central American
Republics. In general, The Bancroft Library
seeks to acquire historical and biographical
works and primary source materials,
documenting: the development of a
geographic area or political unit; man and his
activities and his impact on the land and on
his institutions. Methodological and
theoretical works, and texts in the physical
and biological sciences, are not collected, as
a rule; exceptions here are publications
essential to the study of an area's historical
development, and those providing general
background information. The Bancroft
Library's collections are noncirculating. A G
K Hall catalog has been published.

CA —UNIVERSITY OF CALIFORNIA,
BERKELEY, University Library, Hispanic
Collections, Berkeley, 94720. Gaston
Somoshegyi-Szokol, Librn
Holdings: Vols (45,000)
Notes: Outstanding collection of classic and
standard works (writings of the pioneers and
of major contributors of the field) and of
studies published on colonial Mexico. An
immense collection of manuscripts, original
documents, and microfilmed materials from
the Spanish and Mexican national archives,
as well as an abundance of smaller archival
and document collections.

CA —CLAREMONT COLLEGES, Honnold
Library, Ninth & Dartmouth, Claremont,
91711. Tania Rizzo, Special Collections
Dept Head
Holdings: Vols 328 Cat
Notes: Restricted use. Incl 98 newspaper

titles representing, 19th and early 20th
centuries. In addition William Smith Mason
Collection of Western Americana (7182
vols) includes early histories of Mexico.

†CA —UNIVERSITY OF CALIFORNIA,
DAVIS, Davis, 95616.
Notes: General collection of materials
dealing with the history of Mexico. Majority
of the significant titles in the collection were
obtained from the library of Armando de
Maria y Campos, a mexican journalist.

CA —CALIFORNIA STATE UNIVERSITY,
FRESNO, Henry Madden Library, Dept of
Special Collections, Fresno, 93740. Ronald J
Mahoney, Head
Holdings: Vols 130 Cat Mss Maps Pix
Notes: Archives of Albert Kinsey Owen,
founder of the utopian colony at
Topolobampo, Sinaloa, Mexico. Over 10,000
letters, maps, documents, pictures,
newspapers, pamphlets, and plans, relating to
the colony and the Credit Foncier Company
already represented in the Library by the
Viola Gabriel Collection of about 800 similar
items and nearly 400 photographs. See *Cat's
Paw Utopia*, by Ray Reynolds (El Cajon,
Calif, 1971). Incl 20 linear feet of ms
material. Partially cataloged. Also, 65 ms
pieces on the Mexican West Coast
Development Company, an unsuccessful
American venture to exploit the agricultural
and mineral resources of western Mexico, ca
1920.

CA —CALIFORNIA STATE UNIVERSITY,
FULLERTON, Library, Box 4150,
Fullerton, 92634. Alfredo H Zuniga, Coord
Notes: Some materials on the subject; not
maintained as a separate collection.

CA —UNIVERSITY OF CALIFORNIA, SAN
DIEGO, Central University Library,
Mandeville Dept of Special Collections, La
Jolla, 92093. Lynda Corey Claassen, Head
Holdings: Vols (2400) Cat Mss Maps
Notes: The Hill Collection of Pacific
Voyages, including reports and
commentaries of important voyages in the
Pacific, from those of Magellan and Sir
Francis Drake to exploration through the
first half of the 19th century. Includes many
rare overland accounts to the Pacific across
North America, Mexico, and Panama.
Bibliography: Silveira de Braganza, Ronald,
The Hill Collection of Pacific Voyages (La
Jolla: Calif, 1974-1983).

CA —UNIVERSITY OF CALIFORNIA, SAN
DIEGO, Central University Library,
Mandeville Dept of Special Collections, La
Jolla, 92093. Lynda Corey Claassen, Head
Holdings: Vols (5000) Cat Maps Pix
Notes: The Jose and Maria Teresa
Fernandez de Miranda Collection of about
5000 vols, incl history of Mexico, Spain, and
Latin America. Also archaeology,
anthropology, and linguistics of
Mesoamerica.

CA —LOS ANGELES PUBLIC LIBRARY,
History Dept, 630 W Fifth St, Los Angeles,
90071. Mary Pratt, Principal Librn
Holdings: Vols 3000 Cat Maps
Notes: Books, pamphlets and serials on
Mexico from the Aztecs to the present day.
The collection includes a significant number
of 17th century imprints and 19th century
travel books.

CA —OCCIDENTAL COLLEGE, Library,
1600 Campus Rd, Los Angeles, 90041.
Michael C Sutherland, Special Collections
Librn
Holdings: Vols 2000 Cat
Notes: Cleland Library of Hispanic
American History relating to Mexican and
Latin American History, given in honor of
Dr Robert Glass Cleland. Additions to the
collection are being made from time to time
by Occidental alumnus Arthur H Clark, Jr.

CA —UNIVERSITY OF CALIFORNIA, LOS
ANGELES, Research Library, Dept of
Special Collections, 405 Hilgard Ave, Los
Angeles, 90024. Edward Shreeves,
Chairman, Bibliographers Group; David S
Zeidberg, Head
Holdings: Cat
Notes: Political broadsides (Californian,
Mexican, student protest of the 60s). Incl in
the Broadsides Collection. Also, the
Frederick Starr Collection: 4 linear feet of

MEXICO—HISTORY (cont.)

materials relating to Mexican history and popular culture.

CA —UNIVERSITY OF CALIFORNIA, LOS ANGELES, William Andrews Clark Memorial Library, 2520 Cimarron St, Los Angeles, 90018.
Holdings: // Cat Mss
Notes: 18th and early 19th century mss, incl reports and correspondence on missions, Indians, New Mexico, Alta and Baja California.

CA —UNIVERSITY OF CALIFORNIA, RIVERSIDE, University Library, 4045 Canyon Crest Dr, Box 5900, Riverside, 92517.
Holdings: Vols 75
Notes: Collection of printed contemporary and modern sources relating especially to William Walker, Nicaragua and the Filibusters of 1855-60, as well as to American Filibusters in Mexico.

CA —UNIVERSITY OF SAN FRANCISCO, Richard A Gleeson Library, The Countess Bernardine Murphy Donohue Rare Book Room, San Francisco, 94117. D Steven Corey, Special Collections Librn
Holdings: Vols 3 Mss
Notes: Birth, marriage and death records for Mission Santa Rosalia de Mulege, 1718-1853.

CA —STANFORD UNIVERSITY LIBRARIES, Cecil H Green Library, Stanford, 94305. Michael T Ryan, Cur
Notes: Research collection.

CT —YALE UNIVERSITY, Sterling Memorial Library, Latin American Collections, New Haven, 06520. Lee H Williams Jr, Cur
Holdings: Vols (300,000) Cat Maps Pix Slides Phonorecords 16mm Films Filmstrips
See also entry under Latin America

CT —UNIVERSITY OF CONNECTICUT, Library, Storrs, 06268. R H Schimmelpfeng, Dir of Special Collections
Notes: Collection of newspapers and periodicals formerly belonging to the Duque de T'Serclaes. Ranging from the 17th century through the 20th, the bulk of titles are from 1800-1840, covering the Napoleonic period and the Latin American wars of independence.

DC —GEORGETOWN UNIVERSITY, Library, Special Collections Div, 37 & O Sts NW, Washington, 20057. George M Barringer, Special Collections Librn; Nicholas B Sheetz, Mss Librn
Holdings: Vols (100) Cat Mss Pix
Notes: Includes papers of Mexican Emperor Iturbide; President and General Santa Anna; and of Revs Richard Tierney, SJ, Edmund A Walsh, SJ, and Wilfrid Parsons, SJ.

DC —LIBRARY OF CONGRESS, Manuscript Division, Washington, 20540. John C Broderick, Chief
Notes: The Harkness Collection contains documents relating to the first 200 years of Spanish rule in Mexico and Peru.

IL —CENTER FOR RESEARCH LIBRARIES, 6050 S Kenwood Ave, Chicago, 60637. Donald B Simpson, Dir; Esther Smith, Collection Development Librn
Holdings: Microforms
Budget: $4000
Notes: Microfilm of British Foreign Office records relating to Mexico. Microfilm of Mexican parliamentary debates, 1876-1914.

IN —INDIANA UNIVERSITY, Lilly Library, Seventh St, Bloomington, 47405. William R Cagle, Librn
Holdings: Vols 10,000 // Cat Mss

Notes: Begins with the conquest of Mexico by Cortes and his letters to Charles V, in first and subsequent editions and translations, through the Revolution of 1910. Incl. the most important reforms of the Enlightenment concerning the economy, commerce, mining, science, and the expulsion of the Jesuits. The period of independence, the best represented aspects of which are the effect of the Napoleonic invasion of Spain in 1808, the constitutional crisis in Spain and the colonies provoked by the capture of the Spanish royal family by Napoleon, the policy of Ferdinand VII and the most important decisions

by all the viceroys, bishops and archbishops. From the revolutionary side, the historical pronouncements and documents by the leaders of the movement of independence, such as Hidalgo, Morelos, Guerrero, and Iturbide, and the legal and political documents that gave structure to the Revolution. The empire with Iturbide and the period of political instability and strife that followed the independence, the reforms of Juarez, Maximillian's Empire, and its corollary, the dictatorial regime of Porfirio Diaz through the Revolution of 1910, are also well documented.

LA —TULANE UNIVERSITY, Howard-Tilton Memorial Library, Latin American Library, New Orleans, 70118. Thomas Niehaus, Dir
Holdings: Vols (150,000) Cat Mss Maps Pix Microforms VF
Budget: ($67,000)
Notes: Catalog of the Latin American Library (Boston: G K Hall, 1970, suppl. 1973,1975,1978); Downs 5338-41; suppl (1961), 2727, 2737. The Latin American Library is a general collection, but specializes in Central American, Mexican, and Brazilian materials. The disciplines which are most strongly represented are history, anthropology, and archaeology. The Viceregal Ecclesiastical Mexican Collection contains manuscripts from the colonial period. The France V Scholes Collection contains a large number of photoprints and microfilm of colonial documents from the archives of Spain and Mexico. The Merle Greene Robertson Rubbings Collection contains nearly five hundred rubbings of relief sculpture from Mayan archaeological sites in Mexico and Guatemala. The Photographic Collection contains photos of archaeological sites in Meso-America, of pre-Columbian Peruvian architecture, and a general group of historic photos from Latin America.

NE —AMERICAN HISTORICAL SOCIETY OF GERMANS FROM RUSSIA (AHSGR), 615 Twelfth St, Lincoln, 68502. Mary Lynn Tuck, Librn
Holdings: Vols (1900) Mss Maps Pix Phonorecords Videotapes Audiotapes Microforms VF
Notes: History of German people from Russia and history of people of German-Russian ancestry. Including times in Russia, Germany, US, Canada, Mexico, Argentina, Brazil, Paraguay, Korea, and Japan. This Society has fifty-six chapters in the United States. 1900 volumes, 100 maps; 500 mss; 1200 vertical files; 2000 pictures; 40,000 obituary files, 40,000 family group charts, 50 phonorecords, 20 videotapes, 50 audiotapes, 15 reel-to-reel tapes, 150 periodicals, 250 microforms, 250 family histories-published and unpublished.

NM —NEW MEXICO STATE UNIVERSITY, Library, Box 3475, Las Cruces, 88003. James Dyke, Dir
Holdings: Vols 685 Cat
Notes: Comprehensive collection of materials on political history and the Revolution of Mexico.

NM —NEW MEXICO HIGHLANDS UNIVERSITY, Donnelly Library, National Ave, Las Vegas, 87701. Karen Jaggers, Assoc Librn
Holdings: Vols (5000) Cat Mss Maps Pix Microforms
Notes: The outstanding collection is the Arrott Collection on Fort Union, New Mexico. 1851-1891. Other collections incl Spanish Archives, Mexican Archives, Archdiocese of Santa Fe, Archivo del Parral; New Mexico Land Grants.

NM —ROSWELL PUBLIC LIBRARY, 301 N Pennsylvania Ave, Roswell, 88201. Sarah Beth Galloway, Library Dir
Holdings: Vols (2000) Cat Maps
Budget: $1000

Notes: Covers literature (fiction and nonfiction), history, biography, geography, law, architecture of Oklahoma, Texas, Colorado, New Mexico, Arizona and Northern Mexico.

NY —COLUMBIA UNIVERSITY LIBRARIES, Rare Book & Manuscript Library, 801 Butler Library, 535 W 114 St, New York, 10027. Kenneth A Lohf, Librn
Holdings: Mss
Notes: The papers of Professor Frank Tannenbaum, approx 28,000 items of correspondence and mss relating to Latin American and Mexican history. Professor Tannenbaum also bequeathed his research library of more than 3000 vols on all phases of Latin American history and literature to Columbia. Restricted use.

NY —NEW YORK PUBLIC LIBRARY, Research Libraries, American History Div, Fifth Ave & 42 St, New York, 10018.
Holdings: Vols (20,000) Cat Maps Microforms
Notes: Encompasses all countries of Latin America. Outstanding collection of materials on Mexico and material on boundary disputes among countries of the Western Hemisphere. Local history materials for Latin America are incl. See Dictionary Catalog of the History of Americas Collection (Boston: G K Hall, 1961), 28 vols.

PA —UNIVERSITY OF PITTSBURGH, Hillman Library, Pittsburgh, 15260. Glenora E Rossell, Head
Holdings: Vols (172,000) Cat Microforms
Notes: A research collection on the Mexican revolution, with special emphasis on publications of the immediate postrevolutionary period.

TX —HARDIN-SIMMONS UNIVERSITY, Richardson Library, Abilene, 79601. Joe F Dahlstrom, Dir
Holdings: Vols (10,000) Cat Mss Maps Pix Microforms
Notes: Special collection name is Richardson Research Center, named in honor of Dr Rupert N Richardson. Collect in the areas of his own research interests, especially that portion of the US that was once a part of Mexico. Emphases on the history of ranching, railroads, discovery and exploration, Texas county histories, etc. Incl 350 items printed and/or designed by El Paso printer Carl Hertzog; the Judge R C Crane collection of Texana and a similiar collection of Louise Kelley's; and the Research Publication's Western Americana collection (microfilm).

TX —UNIVERSITY OF TEXAS, ARLINGTON, Library, PO Box 19497, Arlington, 76019. Chas Colley, Dir Special Collections
Holdings: // Uncat Microforms
Notes: The Yucatan Archives. The University of Texas at Arlington Library has microfilmed the pre-1900 holdings of the Archivo Notarial de Yucatan, a small part of the Archivo General del Estado (the Documentos Coloniales and Sesiones del Congreso, 1823-1933), about half of the Archivo del Arzobispado (Archivo de la Secretaria del Arzobispado), and most of the newspapers held by the Hemeroteca del Estado de Yucatan. The collection contains 1052 rolls of 35mm microfilm copies. A preliminary guide is available upon request.

TX —UNIVERSITY OF TEXAS LIBRARIES, Nettie Lee Benson Latin American Collection, Sid Richardson Hall 1.109, Austin, 78712. Laura Gutierrez-Witt, Head Librn
Holdings: Vols (450,000) Cat Mss Maps Pix Phonorecords Filmstrips Microforms
See also entry under Latin America

TX —SOUTHERN METHODIST UNIVERSITY, DeGolyer Library, Box 396, SMU, Dallas, 75275. Clifton H Jones, Dir
Holdings: Vols 50,000 Cat Mss Maps Pix
Notes: History of the trans-Mississippi West

MEXICO—HISTORY (cont.)

and Mexico, from discovery to present. Original editions of most of the important early collections of travels.

TX —EL PASO PUBLIC LIBRARY, Mexican American Collection, 501 N Oregon, El Paso, 79901. Iris Espino, Librn
Holdings: Vols 3000 Cat
Notes: Current and historical information about Mexican-Americans throughout the US. Incl current social and economic writings about Mexican-Americans, Chicano literature, history and culture of Mexico from pre-Columbian times to the present, translations of Mexican authors, and Mexicans in current society.

TX —UNIVERSITY OF TEXAS, EL PASO, Special Collections, Mexican Archives, El Paso, 79968. Cesar Caballero, Special Collections Librn; Bud Newman, Special Collections Librn
Budget: $5000
Notes: Incl 24 archival collections on over 2000 microform reels. Made up of church and civil archives in several cities of Texas, New Mexico, Chihuahua and Durango, the collection covers both the Spanish and Mexican epochs of the region. A holdings list and guide to the collection is available for purchase.

TX —UNIVERSITY OF TEXAS, EL PASO, Library, Special Collections Dept, El Paso, 79968. Cesar Caballero, Dept Head
Holdings: Vols 2000 Cat
Budget: ($5000)
Notes: Southwest and Border Studies Collection. Encyclopedic sets, some profusely illustrated, are among the many volumes on Mexican history in this collection. The revolutionary period of 1910-1929 is very well covered and includes many fine books on Zapata, Madero, Villa and other prominent Mexican revolutionaries.

TX —RICE UNIVERSITY, Fondren Library, Woodson Research Center, 6100 S Main St, PO Box 1892, Houston, 77251. Nancy Parker, Dir Woodson Research Center
Holdings: // Mss Pix Microforms
Notes: Letters, broadsides, clippings, photographs, memorabilia, and microfilm, relating to the Maximilian era in Mexico. Incl letters from Carlotta as a young girl to members of her family.

TX —STEPHEN F AUSTIN STATE UNIVERSITY, Ralph W Steen Library, Special Collections Dept, Box 13055, SFA Sta, Nacogdoches, 75962. Linda Cheves Nicklas, Special Collections Librn
Holdings: Vols (93)// Cat
Notes: The Robert Bruce Blake Collection. Volumes contain the official and private documents and proceedings of the 18th and 19th century Spanish and Mexican governments in Texas, translations of the Bexar and Nacogdoches Archives, biographies of East Texas families, general historical essays on Texas topics and other materials relating to Texas and East Texas. A description of contents and a partial name index are available. Description: SFASU, *A Guide to Special Collections*, 1980.

TX —SAINT MARY'S UNIVERSITY, Library, 2700 Cincinnati Ave, San Antonio, 78284. Anita C Saxine, Special Collections Librn
Notes: Spanish Colonial History of the Texas Borderlands incl the Spanish archives of Laredo, 1749-1850. Two bibliographical guides to materials in Special Collections were compiled by Anita C Saxine in 1983: *Reference Sources in Spanish Colonial History of Texas* (Academic Library Guide, no 12, 27 pp); *Penisular War, 1807-1814 by Contemporary Observers* (Academic Library Guide, no 13, 18 pp).

†WA —WASHINGTON STATE UNIVERSITY, Library, Manuscripts, Archives & Special Collections, Pullman, 99164. John F Guido, Head
Holdings: // Cat Mss Maps
Notes: Regla, Counts of: The papers of the Romero de Terreros family, to whom were granted the titles of Regla, San Cristoval, and San Francisco, include wills, deeds,

titles, property maps, litigation over such things as sheep walks, water rights, and the titles themselves. Incl also is much detailed correspondence between hacienda administrators and the family concerning weather, crops, and commodity prices. Several large vols, bound in 1783, document the history of land acquisitions by the Jesuit Colegio Maximo de San Pedro y San Pablo of Mexico City, especially the hacienda of Santa Lucia, from 1576 to the time of the Expulsion. Other early papers deal with the holdings and genealogy of the Marquisates of Salinas, Salvatierra, and Santiago. Described by J Horace Nunemaker in the *Hispanic American Historical Review* (August 1945) 25:409; and by Jacquelyn M Gaines in *Three Centuries of Mexican Documents: A Partial Calendar of the Regla Papers* (Pullman, Washington, 1963).

WI —UNIVERSITY OF WISCONSIN, MADISON, Memorial Library, Ibero-American Studies Collection, 728 State St, Madison, 53706. Suzanne Hodgman, Bibliographer
Holdings: // Uncat
Notes: Maximilian Collection. Over 600 pamphlets on 19th century Mexico. The earliest is dated 1791 and the latest 1906, but the majority relate to the Reform and European Intervention, hence the popular title "Maximilian Collection." There are a few books, but most of the books contained in the original purchase are intergrated into the general library collection. A typescript listing of the collection is available. Pamphlets are housed in the Rare Book Department.

MEXICO—HISTORY—WARS OF INDEPENDENCE, 1810-1821

CT —YALE UNIVERSITY, Box 1603A, Yale Station, New Haven, 06520.
Notes: Rare imprints from local Mexican presses.

CT —UNIVERSITY OF CONNECTICUT, Library, Storrs, 06268. R H Schimmelpfeng, Dir of Special Collections
Holdings: Cat
Notes: Collection of newspapers and periodical formerly belonging to the Duque de T'Serclaes. Ranging from the 17th century through the 20th, the bulk of titles are from 1800-1840, covering the Napoleonic period and the Latin American wars of independence.

IN —INDIANA UNIVERSITY, Lilly Library, Seventh St, Bloomington, 47405. William R Cagle, Librn
Holdings: Vols 10,000 // Cat Mss
Notes: Begins with the conquest of Mexico by Cortes and his letters to Charles V, in first and subsequent editions and translations, through the Revolution of 1910. Incl. the most important reforms of the Enlightenment concerning the economy, commerce, mining, science, and the expulsion of the Jesuits. The period of independence, the best represented aspects of which are the effect of the Napoleonic invasion of Spain in 1808, the constitutional crisis in Spain and the colonies provoked by the capture of the Spanish royal family by Napoleon, the policy of Ferdinand VII and the most important decisions by all the viceroys, bishops and archbishops. From the revolutionary side, the historical pronouncements and documents by the leaders of the movement of independence, such as Hidalgo, Morelos, Guerrero, and Iturbide, and the legal and political documents that gave structure to the Revolution. The empire with Iturbide and the period of political instability and strife that followed the independence, the reforms of Juarez, Maximillian's Empire, and its corollary, the dictatorial regime of Porfirio Diaz through the Revolution of 1910, are also well documented.

TX —UNIVERSITY OF TEXAS LIBRARIES, Nettie Lee Benson Latin American Collection, Sid Richardson Hall 1.109, Austin, 78712. Laura Gutierrez-Witt, Head Librn
Holdings: Vols (450,000) Cat Microforms
Notes: The Juan E Hernandez y Davalos ms collection of 3000 documents, 1692-1865, with special concentration on the Mexican War of Independence, 1808-1821.
See also entry under Latin America

MEXICO—HISTORY—WAR WITH THE U.S., 1845-1848 see U.s.—History_War with Mexico, 1845-1848

MEXICO—HISTORY—REVOLUTION OF 1910

CA —CLAREMONT COLLEGES, Honnold Library, Ninth & Dartmouth, Claremont, 91711. Tania Rizzo, Special Collections Dept Head
Holdings: Cat Mss Pix Scrapbooks
Notes: Correspondence, mss, documents, clippings, photographs, and ephemera, 2200 pieces, some in carbon copies, of Jose Maytorena, from 1882-1947. Important correspondents incl Venustiano Carranza, Francisco Madero, and Alvaro Obregon, among many others. Guy T McCreary, *A Primary Study of the Revolutionary, Governor, General, Jose maria Maytorena and the Mexican Revolution 1910-1916* (thesis, 1967) based on this collection. Restricted use.

IL —SOUTHERN ILLINOIS UNIVERSITY, CARBONDALE, Delyte W Morris Library, Special Collections Dept, Carbondale, 62901. David V Koch, Cur of Special Collections; Louisa Bowen, Cur of Manuscripts
Holdings: Cat Mss
Notes: Personal papers of Francisco Vazquez Gomez, 1906-1939, 27 linear feet. Collection relates almost entirely to the Mexican revolution of 1910. Inventory available at library.

IN —INDIANA UNIVERSITY, Lilly Library, Seventh St, Bloomington, 47405. William R Cagle, Librn
Holdings: Vols 10,000 // Cat Mss
Notes: Begins with the conquest of Mexico by Cortes and his letters to Charles V, in first and subsequent editions and translations, through the Revolution of 1910. Incl. the most important reforms of the Enlightenment concerning the economy, commerce, mining, science, and the expulsion of the Jesuits. The period of independence, the best represented aspects of which are the effect of the Napoleonic invasion of Spain in 1808, the constitutional crisis in Spain and the colonies provoked by the capture of the Spanish royal family by Napoleon, the policy of Ferdinand VII and the most important decisions by all the viceroys, bishops and archbishops. From the revolutionary side, the historical pronouncements and documents by the leaders of the movement of independence, such as Hidalgo, Morelos, Guerrero, and Iturbide, and the legal and political documents that gave structure to the Revolution. The empire with Iturbide and the period of political instability and strife that followed the independence, the reforms of Juarez, Maximillian's Empire, and its corollary, the dictatorial regime of Porfirio Diaz through the Revolution of 1910, are also well documented.

MEXICO—HISTORY—REVOLUTION OF 1910 (cont.)

NM —NEW MEXICO STATE UNIVERSITY,
Library, Box 3475, Las Cruces, 88003.
James Dyke, Dir
Holdings: Vols 685 Cat
Notes: Comprehensive collection of
materials on political history and the
Revolution of Mexico.

PA —UNIVERSITY OF PITTSBURGH,
Hillman Library, Pittsburgh, 15260. Glenora
E Rossell, Head
Holdings: Vols (172,000) Cat Maps Pix
Notes: Incl the John M Malone Collection
(300 vols), and the Casasola collection of
photographs of 20th century Mexico;
virtually all the works of the Mexican
philosopher Jose Vasconcelos.

TX —EL PASO PUBLIC LIBRARY,
Southwest Collection, 501 N Oregon, El
Paso, 79901. Mary A Sarber, Head
Holdings: Vols (12,000) Cat Mss Maps Pix
Budget: ($11,000)
Notes: Research collection includes rare
books and mss journals, vertical files, index
to El Paso newspapers, microfilmed
newspapers, photographs, and architectural
plans. Separate catalog. Limited to materials
on Texas, New Mexico, Arizona and
Mexico. Special collections of material by
and about Tom Lea Jr, and Carl Hertzog.
Aultman Collection of photographs includes
3500 on El Paso Southwest and 2500 on
Mexican Revolution. Cited in Lovelace,
Lisa, "The Southwest Collection of the El
Paso Public Library". *Great Plains Journal*,
vol 2, no 2, pp 161-166; Aultman, Otis A
*Photographs from the Border: The Otis A
Aultman Collection*, El Paso Public Library
Association, 1977.

MEXICO—IMPRINTS

CT —YALE UNIVERSITY, Box 1603A, Yale
Station, New Haven, 06520.
Notes: Largely pamphlets and broadsides,
many relating to the US war with Mexico,
1845-1848.

IN —INDIANA UNIVERSITY, Lilly Library,
Seventh St, Bloomington, 47405. William R
Cagle, Librn
Holdings: Vols 6000 // Cat
Notes: Research and rare book collection
(Bernardo Mendel) of first or only editions, mostly
printed in Latin America, from the discovery of
the New World through 1830. Special strength in
discoveries and exploration, history (mainly period
of independence), Inquisition, missionary works
by the Augustinians, Dominicans, Franciscans,
and the Jesuits, and the history of the Catholic
Church in these countries. Major geographic
concentration is on the three great viceroyalties
of Mexico (ca. 10,000 titles, plus over 10,000
official Mexican broadsides), Peru (2000 titles),
and Argentina (4000 titles), incl. in Argentina
a substantial amount of printings from the
Imprenta de Ninos Expositos, and the Coleccion
Santamarina. A special Bolivian Collection (2500
titles), mostly history, from the establishment
of the press there, ca. 1826, through the beginning
of the 20th century. Part of the Mendel Collection
is the select Bibliotheca Boxeriana from Charles
R. Boxer (1000 titles) on European expansion into
Asia, and into the New World, mainly Brazil,
during the 16th-18th centuries. The collection
is supplemented by substantial material from
the private collection of Josiah K. Lilly. See also
entries under Spain-History, Portugal-History,
and Mexico-History.

TX —UNIVERSITY OF TEXAS LIBRARIES,
Nettie Lee Benson Latin American
Collection, Sid Richardson Hall 1.109,
Austin, 78712. Laura Gutierrez-Witt, Head
Librn
Holdings: Vols (450,000) Cat Microforms
Notes: Private collection of Joaquin Garcia
Icazbalceta, scholar, bibliophile and authority
on 16th century Mexico. Collection is rich in
early Mexican imprints, incl 45 from the
16th century.

MEXICO—INDUSTRIES

CA —CALIFORNIA STATE UNIVERSITY,
FRESNO, Henry Madden Library, Dept of
Special Collections, Fresno, 93740. Ronald J
Mahoney, Head
Holdings: // Uncat Mss
Notes: Unsuccessful American venture to
exploit the agricultural and mineral resources
of western Mexico, ca 1920. 65 ms pieces.

PA —TEMPLE UNIVERSITY LIBRARIES,
Special Collections Dept, Rare Books & Mss
Section, Philadelphia, 19122. Thomas M
Whitehead, Cur
Budget: ($25,000)
Notes: The lithography collection
emphasizes the technical process rather than
the artistic medium and stresses the years
1800-1835. Significant are the early manuals,
the Kubilius Louis Prang Collection and the
documentation of early Mexican lithography.
Some holdings are listed in the 1972
publication: *Aloys Senefelder 1771-1834: A
Catalogue of Early Technical Literature and
Selected Lithographs....*A register of the
Mexican documents is available.

MEXICO—SINALOA

CA —CALIFORNIA STATE UNIVERSITY,
FRESNO, Henry Madden Library, Dept of
Special Collections, Fresno, 93740. Ronald J
Mahoney, Head
Holdings: Vols 130 Cat Mss Maps Pix
Notes: Archives of Albert Kimsey Owen,
founder of the utopian colony at
Topolobampo, Sinaloa, Mexico. Over 10,000
letters, maps, documents, pictures,
newspapers, pamphlets, and plans, relating
the the colony and the Credit Foncier
Company already represented in the Library
by the Viola Gabriel Collection of about 800
similar items and nearly 400 photographs.
See *Cat's Paw Utopia*, by Ray Reynolds (El
Cajon, Calif, 1971). Incl 20 linear feet of ms
material. Partially cataloged.

MEXICO—SOCIAL LIFE AND CUSTOMS

**CA —UNIVERSITY OF CALIFORNIA, LOS
ANGELES,** Research Library, Dept of
Special Collections, 405 Hilgard Ave, Los
Angeles, 90024. Edward Shreeves,
Chairman, Bibliographers Group; David S
Zeidberg, Head
Notes: The Frederick Starr Collection: 4
linear feet of materials relating to Mexican
history and popular culture.

**IL —UNIVERSITY OF ILLINOIS,
URBANA/CHAMPAIGN,** Library,
University Archives, 1408 W Gregory Drive,
Urbana, 61801. Maynard Brichford, Univ
Archivist
Holdings: Cat Mss Pix
Notes: Original mss and 91 tapes of
interviews for anthropological work, the gift
of Oscar Lewis, largely concerning his
studies of the culture of poverty.

KY —UNIVERSITY OF KENTUCKY,
Margaret I King Library, Dept of Special
Collections, Lexington, 40506. William
Marshall, Head
Holdings: Vols 79 Cat
Notes: Incl 1 map; period covered: 1601-
1978.

MEYER, CONRAD FERDINAND

MD —JOHNS HOPKINS UNIVERSITY,
Milton S Eisenhower Library, Charles & 34
Sts, Baltimore, 21218. Ann S Gwyn,
Assistant Dir for Special Collections
Holdings: Vols 255 Cat Mss
Notes: Very complete collection incl a few
letters and 1 ms.

MEYER, EDITH PATTERSON

MA —BOSTON UNIVERSITY, Mugar
Memorial Library, Special Collections Dept,
771 Commonwealth Ave, Boston, 02215.
Howard B Gotlieb, Dir
Holdings: Cat Mss

MEYERS, BEN

IL —CHICAGO HISTORICAL SOCIETY,
Library, Clark St at North Ave, Chicago,
60614. Archie Motley, Manuscript Librn
Notes: Papers of labor union counsel.
See also entry under Labor-History.

MEYERS, IRVING

IL —CHICAGO HISTORICAL SOCIETY,
Library, Clark St at North Ave, Chicago,
60614. Archie Motley, Manuscript Librn
Notes: Papers of Irving Meyers and David
Rothstein, law partners.

MEYERS, WILLIAM STARR, 1877-1956

NJ —PRINCETON UNIVERSITY, Library,
Manuscript Collection, Nassau St, Princeton,
08540. Jean F Preston, Cur
Holdings: // Mss Pix
Notes: Incl 24 boxes; 8 cartons of papers.

MEYNELL, SIR FRANCIS

DC —GEORGETOWN UNIVERSITY,
Library, Special Collections Div, 37 & O Sts
NW, Washington, 20057. George M
Barringer, Special Collections Librn;
Nicholas B Sheetz, Mss Librn
Holdings: Mss Cat
Notes: The literary papers of author and art
curator, James Laver (1899-1975), and those
of his wife, the actress Veronica Turleigh;
consisting of letters, with a considerable
number written by Lady Cnythia Asquith;
Clifford Box; Enid Bagnold; Nicholas
Bentley; Violet Clifton; Desmond
MacCarthy; Sir Edward Marsh; Sir Francis
Meynell; Kate O'Brien; Dorothy L Sayers;
Andre Simon; Enid Starkie; A J A Symons;
Angela Thirkell; and Alec Waugh.

MEYNELL, LAURENCE

MA —BOSTON UNIVERSITY, Mugar
Memorial Library, Special Collections Dept,
771 Commonwealth Ave, Boston, 02215.
Howard B Gotlieb, Dir
Holdings: Cat Mss
Notes: Incl publications by.

MEYNELL, SIR WILFRID

DC —GEORGETOWN UNIVERSITY,
Library, Special Collections Div, 37 & O Sts
NW, Washington, 20057. George M
Barringer, Special Collections Librn;
Nicholas B Sheetz, Mss Librn
Holdings: Mss Cat Pix
Notes: The papers of the Irish man-of-letters
Sir Shane Leslie (1885-1971) containing
letters, mss, diaries, notebooks, clippings,
and photographs. Extensive correspondence
by Margot Asquith, countess of Oxford and
Asquith; Lady Violet Bonham-Carter; Burke
Cochran; Lord Alfred Douglas; Moreton
Frewen; Cardinal Gasquet; Vyvyan Holland;
Lady Leonie Leslie; Sir Wilfrid Meynell; Sir

MEYNELL, SIR WILFRID (cont.)

Horace Plunkett; John Quinn; Frederick Rolfe (Baron Corvo); and Elizabeth Russell, among others. Also incl are research files on Sir Winston Churchill (Leslie's first cousin); Leonard Jerome; Maria Anne Fitzherbet (wife of King George IV); Ghosts and Ghost stories; and Eton College.

MEYNELL FAMILY

MA —BOSTON COLLEGE LIBRARIES, Thomas P O'Neill Library, Chestnut Hill, 02167. Frank J Seegraber, Special Collections Librn
Holdings: Vols 1300 Cat Mss Pix Phonorecords Audiotapes Microforms
Notes: This, the most complete collection of Thompsoniana in existence, incl notebooks, manuscripts, letters, and rare editions, and collateral material relating to the poet, his times, and his work. The notebooks are the chief source of clues of the identification of 300 of Thompson's unsigned contributions to periodicals. *An Account of the Books and Manuscripts of Francis Thompson*, ed by Rev Terence L Connolly (Boston College [1937]). Works of Wilfrid and Alice Meynell and their children--Viola, Sir Francis, and Everard--are incl in this collection. The items give a well-rounded view of this remarkable family as poets, fiction writers, essayists, biographers, prefacers, and editors. This collection incl manuscripts poems, correspondence, articles, and book reviews by Coventry Patmore, an English poet, essayist, and critic, and a good friend of Francis Thompson. Among thecorrespondents are Robert Browning, Alfred Tennyson, Matthew Arnold, Ralph Waldo Emerson, Nathaniel Hawthorne, Thomas Carlyle, and William Makepeace Thackeray. For reference use only, by arrangement with librarian.

MHD see Magnetohydrodynamics (Mhd)

MHD GENERATORS see Magnetohydrodynamic (Mhd) Generators

MICE

ME —JACKSON LABORATORY, Research Laboratory, Bar Harbor, 04609.
Notes: "Subject: *Strain Bibliography* of inbred strains of mice, transplantable tumors, and named genes in mice ..." *Mouse News* Letter. Database discontinued 1984, and has become an archival record.

MICHAELS, BARBARA

MA —BOSTON UNIVERSITY, Mugar Memorial Library, Special Collections Dept, 771 Commonwealth Ave, Boston, 02215. Howard B Gotlieb, Dir
Holdings: Cat Mss
Notes: Mss, correspondence, etc collected in depth; incl publications by or about.

MICHEELS, WILLIAM JORDAN

WI —UNIVERSITY OF WISCONSIN-STOUT, Library Learning Center, Menomonie, 54751. Philip Sawin Jr, Coll Develop Librn
Notes: A very strong collection of his papers, including his personal correspondence, speeches, materials from work as a consultant, course materials, copies of books and journal articles, and miscellaneous materials. The collection contains eight archival boxes.

MICHELSON, ALBERT ABRAHAM, 1852-1931

MD —US NAVAL ACADEMY, Nimitz Library, Annapolis, 21402. Alice S Creighton, Assistant Librn for Special Collections
Holdings: Mss Pix 16mm Films
Notes: The Michelson Collection contains approximately 55 feet of publications and related materials by and about Michelson, including scientific papers, patents, journal reprints, biographical sketches, evaluations, manuscripts and laboratory notebooks. Also includes photographs, medals and awards, and instruments and associated hardware.

MICHELSON, HERMAN

MA —BOSTON UNIVERSITY, Mugar Memorial Library, Special Collections Dept, 771 Commonwealth Ave, Boston, 02215. Howard B Gotlieb, Dir
Holdings: Mss Pix
Notes: Mss, correspondence, etc collected in depth; incl publications by or about.

MICHIE, ALLAN A.

MA —BOSTON UNIVERSITY, Mugar Memorial Library, Special Collections Dept, 771 Commonwealth Ave, Boston, 02215. Howard B Gotlieb, Dir
Holdings: Cat Mss Pix
Notes: Mss, correspondence, etc collected in depth; incl publications by or about.

MICHIGAN

MI —R E OLDS MUSEUM LIBRARY, 240 Museum Drive, Lansing, 48933.
Notes: Emphasizes the contributions that Lansing has made to transportation history; materials on Oldsmobile, Reo, Star, Durant, and Bates cars. Incl books, manuals, magazines, advertisements, photographs, films, slides, audiotapes, videotapes, VF, and art reproductions.

MI —MONROE COUNTY LIBRARY SYSTEM, Ellis Reference and Information Center, 3700 S Custer Rd, Monroe, 48161. Marie D Chulski, Head of Reference Services
Holdings: Vols 60,000 // Cat Maps Pix Mss Slides 16mm Films Microforms
Budget: $25,000
Notes: Incl individual county histories, atlases, biographies, etc. The Monroe County history collection contains veteran records, plat books, oral history tapes, family histories, church records, cemetery index, atlases and census records. Genealogy emphasis is not only Monroe County but incl surrounding counties and the states with large migration to the area, such as Ohio, Kentucky, Tennessee and the New England states.

MICHIGAN—AERIAL PHOTOGRAPHS

MI —UNIVERSITY OF MICHIGAN, Harlan Hatcher Graduate Library, Map Room, Ann Arbor, 48109. James O Minton, Map Librn
Notes: The collection consists of approx 300,000 sheet maps incl maps and charts received on deposit from the US Geological Survey, Defense Mapping Agency, and the National Ocean Service. The collection also incl approx 5000 reference volumes related to cartography, surveying, and mapping, with emphasis on place-name literature (gazetteers, dictionaries), books on how to use and interpret maps, carto-bibliographies, and state (provincial, etc) regional, national, and international atlases. The collection is strongest geographically in materials of Michigan, Midwest, Anglo-America, and Europe; chronologically, 1850-date; and thematically, in topographic and geologic maps, although all subjects are collected. The collection maintains a separate catalog of holdings. Reference volumes are fully cataloged and classified.

MICHIGAN—GENEALOGY

FL —ORLANDO PUBLIC LIBRARY, Local History & Genealogy Dept, 100 Block of Central Ave, Orlando, 32806. Eileen B Willis, Librn
Holdings: Vols 11,000 Cat Maps Microforms
Budget: $8000
Notes: Genealogy collection on Md, Del, W Va, NC, SC, Ala, Miss, La, Texas, Ark, Ky, Ohio, Ill, Ind, and Mich are well represented. Most other states are covered by smaller collections.
See also entry under Genealogy - Collections.

MI —VAN BUREN COUNTY LIBRARY, Webster Memorial Library Bldg, 200 Phelps St, Decatur, 49045. David Fate, Dir
Holdings: Vols 3000 Cat Maps Microforms
Notes: Concentrating on local history, especially family histories of area families. Vital records of the county, cemetery records, births, deaths, marriages. Other area information as funds permit. Census records for Van Buren County from 1790 to 1910.

MI —MITCHELL PUBLIC LIBRARY, 22 N Manning St, Hillsdale, 49242. Arlene Elliott, Head Librn
Holdings: Vols 500 Cat Maps Pix Microforms
Notes: Emphasis on Hillsdale and surrounding counties. Incl local newspaper on both microfilm and in bound volumes; city and county directories; county plat books; local and family histories; and works of local authors. Newspapers being put on microfilm.

MI —MONROE COUNTY LIBRARY SYSTEM, Ellis Reference and Information Center, 3700 S Custer Rd, Monroe, 48161. Marie D Chulski, Head of Reference Services
Notes: Historic Monroe County, tracing its beginnings to 1780, is a definite part of Michigan's history. Many events of the area and citizens are part of Michigan's heritage. The Michigan collection besides general works contains individual county histories, atlases, biographies, etc. The Monroe County history collection contains veteran records, plat books, oral history tapes, family histories, church records, cemetery index, atlases and census records. Genealogy emphasis is not only Monroe County but includes surrounding counties and the states with large migration to the area, such as Ohio, Kentucky, Tennessee and the New England states.

MI —SAINT CLAIR COUNTY LIBRARY, 210 McMorran Blvd, Port Huron, 48060. Frances A Marshall, Local History Librn
Holdings: Vols 5116 Cat Mss Maps Pix Microforms
Notes: The

MICHIGAN—HISTORY

MI —UNIVERSITY OF MICHIGAN, Bentley Historical Library, Michigan Historical Collections, 1150 Beal Ave, Ann Arbor, 48109. Francis X Blovin Jr, Dir
Holdings: Vols (45,000) Cat Mss Maps Pix Phonorecords Audiotapes Videotapes 16mm Films Microforms
Budget: ($302,000)
Notes: A modern ms archives collecting original source material pertaining to Michigan, its people, its institutions and the University of Michigan. Emphasizes the accumulations of personal papers of historically important persons, incl files of correspondence, diaries and journals as well as the records of significant Michigan institutions. At present the collections contain 45,000 printed vols, 40,000,000 mss items, 3500 maps and 500,000 photographs. The library maintains its own catalog and published in 1976 a revised, 2nd updated *Guide to the Michigan Historical Collections*. Special areas of interest to the collections are Philippine Islands history, the history of the temperance and prohibition movement in the US. Immigration to Michigan, business history, church history, and US-China relations.

MI —MUSEUM OF THE GREAT LAKES, Bay County Historical Society, Library, 1700 Center Ave, Bay City, 48706. Eurdine Ringwelski, Librn
Holdings: Vols (800) Cat Mss Maps Pix Slides 16mm Films
Notes: Focuses on the Bay County region in an historical perspective. Incl books, mss, photos, maps, vertical files, and scrapbooks on the history of Bay County and the Saginaw Valley, Michigan.

MI —FERRIS STATE COLLEGE ARCHIVES, 901 S State St, Big Rapids,

MICHIGAN—HISTORY (cont.)

49307. R Lawrence Martin, Coordr
Holdings: Mss Pix
Notes: Collecting program embraces the northwestern quarter of the lower peninsula of the state, but most of the collection at present deals with Big Rapids and Mecosta County. Includes Big rapids city directories. Mecosta County cemetery records, printed histories of the area and the assessment rolls for Grant Township, Mecosta County, 1890-1971.

MI —CASS COUNTY LIBRARY, 319 M-62, N, Cassopolis, 49031. Donna Kowalewski, Librn
Holdings: Vols 150 Cat Mss Maps Microforms
Notes: Cass County history emphasis. Have Cassopolis *Vigilant* on microfilm. Edwardsburg *Argus*, Marcellus News. Also, Black local history.

MI —DETROIT PUBLIC LIBRARY, Burton Historical Collection, 5201 Woodward Ave, Detroit, 48202. Alice Dalligan, Chief
Holdings: Vols 250,000 Cat Mss Maps Slides Microforms
Notes: History of Detroit, Michigan, and the Old Northwest. Incl the Clarence Monroe Burton Collection with materials illustrating the history of Detroit.

MI —UNIVERSITY OF MICHIGAN, FLINT, Library, Genesee Historical Center, 1321 E Court St, Flint, 48503. Darwin Matthews, Archivist
Holdings: Vols 100
Notes: History of Genesee County.

MI —MITCHELL PUBLIC LIBRARY, 22 N Manning St, Hillsdale, 49242. Arlene Elliott, Head Librn
Holdings: Vols 500 Cat Maps Pix Microforms
Notes: Emphasis on Hillsdale and surrounding counties. Incl local newspaper on both microfilm and in bound volumes; city and county directories; county plat books; local and family histories; and works of local authors. Newspapers being put on microfilm.

MI —MICHIGAN TECHNOLOGICAL UNIVERSITY, Archives, Copper County Historical Collections, Houghton, 49931. Theresa Sanderson Spence, University Archivist
Holdings: Vols (1500) Cat Mss Maps Pix Slides Microforms
Notes: Michigan-Copper Country. Description of collection in *Michigan Chronicle*, 1st quarter, 1973. Accession lists are available for some of the collections. The collecting program embraces the university and all areas of the economic, cultural and social life of the people and institutions of the Copper Country (Baraga, Houghton, Keweenaw, and Ontonogan Counties), incl wide variety of material on fishing, lumbering and marine activities. Special interest in Great Lakes shipping. Special strength is in the mining history and mining company reports. Personal and business records, maps and photographs, broadsides, family histories, newspapers, publicaions, and oral materials as well as slides and film have been collected. Extensive holdings in area newspapers. As a regional depository for the state archives, provides access to a variety of research materials. Also,Keweenaw Historical Society Collection, see *Michigan History Magazine*, vol 1 (1917), 129-155.

MI —LANSING PUBLIC LIBRARY, Local History Room, 401 S Capitol Ave, Lansing, 48914. Jane McClary, Local History Librn
Holdings: Vols (6000) Cat Mss Maps Pix Microforms VF
Notes: Separate catalog.

MI —MACKINAC ISLAND STATE PARK COMMISSION, Library, Bos 30028, Lansing, 48909. Keith R Widder, Cur
Holdings: Vols (1000) Cat Mss Maps Pix Slides Audiotapes
Budget: ($2500)
Notes: Mackinac area history-research collection: archaeology, historic preservation, etc. Great Lakes ships and shipping.

MI —MASON COUNTY HISTORICAL SOCIETY, Rose Hawley Museum Library,

305 E Filer St, Ludington, 49431. Thomas A Hawley, Exec Dir
Holdings: Vols 3000 Cat Maps Pix Slides
Notes: History of Mason County, Michigan. Incl oral histories.

MI —MONROE COUNTY HISTORICAL COMMISSION ARCHIVES, Library, 126 S Monroe St, Monroe, 48161. Christine L Kull, Archivist
Holdings: Cat Mss Maps Pix Audiotapes
Notes: Monroe County, Michigan history, 1782-date. Incl personal papers and business, organization and government records. Separate catalog for photo collection.

MI —MONROE COUNTY LIBRARY SYSTEM, Ellis Reference and Information Center, 3700 S Custer Rd, Monroe, 48161. Marie D Chulski, Head of Reference Services
Notes: Incl individual county histories, atlases, biographies, etc. The Monroe County history collection contains veteran records, plat books, oral history tapes, family histories, church records, cemetery index, atlases and census records. Genealogy emphasis is not only Monroe County but incl surrounding counties and the states with large migration to the area, such as Ohio, Kentucky, Tennessee and the New England states.

MI —CENTRAL MICHIGAN UNIVERSITY, Clarke Historical Library, Mount Pleasant, 48859. William H Mulligan, Jr, Dir; William Miles, Biography Collections Librn
Holdings: Vols 60,000 Mss Maps Pix
Notes: Emphasis on history and culture of Michigan and Great Lakes states. See also Children's Literature, Custer, George Armstrong; Biography - Collections; Africana.

MI —HACKLEY PUBLIC LIBRARY, 316 W Webster Ave, Muskegon, 49440. Dale H Pretzer, Dir
Holdings: Cat
Notes: Muskegon history.

MI —SAINT CLAIR COUNTY LIBRARY, 210 McMorran Blvd, Port Huron, 48060. Frances A Marshall, Local History Librn
Holdings: Vols 5116 Cat Mss Maps Pix Microforms
Notes: The

MI —LAKE SUPERIOR STATE COLLEGE, Library, College Dr, Sault Sainte Marie, 49783. Frederick A Michels, Dir
Holdings: Vols (400) Cat Maps Pix Slides
Notes: Michigan history with emphasis on Sault Ste Marie, eastern end of of Upper Peninsula, and area Indians (Chippewa or Ojibway).

MN —UNIVERSITY OF MINNESOTA, DULUTH, Library & Learning Resources Service, Duluth, 55812. James V. Litha, Archivist
Holdings: Vols (1700) Cat Mss Maps Pix
Notes: The Voyageur Collection incl the Grace Lee Nute Papers. Books and materials relating to the Voyageur period (1650-1850) and the area of Northeastern Minnesota, Michigan, Wisconsin, Southern Canada. Emphasis on all subjects listed in this volume.

MICHIGAN—MAPS

MI —UNIVERSITY OF MICHIGAN, Harlan Hatcher Graduate Library, Map Room, Ann Arbor, 48109. James O Minton, Map Librn
Notes: The collection consists of approx 300,000 sheet maps incl maps and charts received on deposit from the US Geological Survey, Defense Mapping Agency, and the National Ocean Service. The collection also incl approx 5000 reference volumes related to cartography, surveying, and mapping, with emphasis on place-name literature (gazetteers, dictionaries), books on how to use and interpret maps, carto-bibliographies, and state (provincial, etc), regional, national, and international atlases. The collection is strongest geographically in materials of Michigan, Midwest, Anglo-America, and Europe; chronologically, 1850-date; and thematically, in topographic and geologic maps, although all subjects are collected. The collection maintains a separate catalog of holdings. Reference volumes are fully cataloged and classified.

OK —TULSA CITY-COUNTY LIBRARY, Business & Technology Dept, 400 Civic Center, Tulsa, 74103. Craig Buthod, Head
Notes: Original General Land Office survey maps for the states of Arizona, Arkansas, Colorado, Illinois, Indiana, Idaho, Kansas, Michigan, Missouri, Montana, Nebraska, Nevada, New Mexico, North Dakota, Ohio, Oklahoma, South Dakota, Utah and Wyoming. Incomplete coverage of each state.

MICHIGAN—NATURAL RESOURCES

MI —UNIVERSITY OF MICHIGAN, Biological Station Library, Pellston, 49769. Patricia B Devlin, Librn
Holdings: Vols (10,000) Cat Mss Maps Pix Microforms
Notes: Library is intended primarily for the needs of teaching and research at the Biological Station--the world's largest inland field station for instruction and investigation in biological science. Collection contains considerable information on the natural science aspects of the Douglas Lake area, Cheboygan County, Michigan.

MICHIGAN—POLITICS AND GOVERNMENT

MI —FERRIS STATE COLLEGE ARCHIVES, 901 S State St, Big Rapids, 49307. R Lawrence Martin, Coordr
Holdings: Vols 11,500 Cat Mss Pix Audiotapes
Notes: Incl 36 volumes of letters written by W N Ferris as well as numerous ms letters; also Ferris State College history. Ferris was founder of the college, Governor of Michigan (1913-1916), and a US Senator (1923-1928).

MICHIGAN—SOCIAL LIFE AND CUSTOMS

MI —MICHIGAN STATE UNIVERSITY, Libraries, Special Collections Div, East Lansing, 48824. Jannette Fiore, Librn
Notes: Ku Klux Klan pamphlets, magazines, and ephemera dating from the late 1920s and early 1930s. Incl issues of the *Kourier*, the official monthly magazine of the Klan; a Klan newspaper published in Alma, Mich; position pamphlets and leaflets; advertisements for Klan merchandise; and Michigan Klan ephemera.

MICHIGAN AUTHORS see Authors, Michigan

MICHIGAN MUSIC see Music, Michigan

MICHIGAN NEWSPAPERS see Newspapers, Michigan

MICROBES see Bacteriology; Virology

MICROBIOLOGY

CA —SUNKIST GROWERS, Research Library, 760 E Sunkist St, Ontario, 91761. Martha C Nemeth, Librn
Holdings: Vols (1500) Cat
Budget: ($10,000)
Notes: Technology of citrus fruit and citrus fruit products, primarily Californian. Strong in organic and food chemistry, with additional coverage of food technology, essential oils, microbiology and environmental protection.

CA —CALIFORNIA STATE POLYTECHNIC UNIVERSITY, POMONA, University Library, 3801 W Temple Ave, Pomona, 91768. Harold Schleiser, Actg Dir
Holdings: Vols (25,000)
Budget: ($20,000)
Notes: Biological Sciences Collection.

CT —YALE MEDICAL LIBRARY, 333 Cedar St, New Haven, 06510.
Holdings: Vols (334,215) Cat Mss Pix Slides Microforms
Budget: ($361,650)
Notes: Incl films, audiotapes, artifacts, etc.

DC —AMERICAN SOCIETY FOR MICROBIOLOGY, Archives, 1913 I Street

MICROBIOLOGY (cont.)

NW, Washington, 20006. Donald Shay, Archivist
Notes: Collection of American and foreign books (texts, monographs, laboratory manuals, etc) on microbiology. 10,000 reprints are mostly old or connected to a past officer or award recipient. 150 theses incl American and foreign. Reprint collection incl Pratt collection on antibiotics, and C W Dodge collection on medical mycology. Ownership of all titles resides with the Society; Special Collections of University of Maryland Baltimore County serves as repository. The Society address is in Washington.

IL —UNIVERSITY OF ILLINOIS, URBANA/CHAMPAIGN, Library, Biology Library, 101 Burrill Hall, 407 S Goodwin, Urbana, 61801. Elisabeth B Davis, Librn
Holdings: Vols (115,000) Cat Microforms
Budget: ($200,000)
Notes: The Biology Library incl books, periodicals, and reference works that cover the fields of anatomy, biophysics, botany, ecology, entomology, genetics, immunology, microbiology, physiology and zoology. About three-quarters of the total collection is made up of journals and other serials representing 2000 distinctive titles. The serial list is comprehensive for the biological sciences, contains most of the major international titles and consists of complete runs for almost all titles. Additional materials (approx 90,000 vols) in the biological sciences are available in the Natural History Survey Library and the bookstacks at the Main Library on the Urbana campus. Professional assistance is available for reference service, online searching, and library instruction. Interlibrary loan service is provided. Photocopying.

IN —INDIANA UNIVERSITY, Biology Library, Jordan Hall, Bloomington, 47405. Steven Sowell, Head
Holdings: Vols (105,461) Cat

IN —MILES LABORATORIES, Library Resources and Services, 1127 Myrtle St, PO Box 40, Elkhart, 46515. Allam Hagopian, Mgr
Holdings: Vols (16,500) Cat Audiotapes Microforms
Notes: Incl files of pharmaceutical product advertising pieces, extensive literature files on company related drugs; domestic and international marketing files. 32,000 bound periodicals.

IN —ELI LILLY AND COMPANY, Scientific Library, 307 E McCarty St, Indianapolis, 46285. Adele Hoskin, Chief Librn
Holdings: Vols (35,000) Cat Microforms
Notes: Drug product information (1.7 million cards); drug encyclopedias, foreign and domestic; foreign pharmacopoeias. Restricted use: company employees and approved outsiders.

IA —IOWA STATE UNIVERSITY, Library, Ames, 50011. Warren B Kuhn, Dean of Library Services
Holdings: Cat
Notes: Extensive serial holdings.

IA —ARCHER DANIELS MIDLAND, Research Library, PO Box 340, Clinton, 52732. Carol L Kolk, Research Librn
Holdings: Vols 2200 Cat Microforms
Notes: Card index to patent file. Keydex index to Research Experiment Reports.

MD —UNIVERSITY OF MARYLAND, BALTIMORE COUNTY, Albin O Kuhn Library and Gallery, 5401 Wilkens Ave, Baltimore, 21228. Ann Copeland, Special Collections Librn
Holdings: Vols (3000) Cat
Notes: The Archives of the American Society for Microbiology (ASM) are strong in 20th century English-language immunological and bacteriological works, incl nearly every edition of every major microbiological title published in England and the US. The reprint collection is also excellent, incl significant material published in non-bacteriological journals. The theses are largely European, pre-1900 inaugural dissertations. The collection also incl mss, proceedings, memorabilia and correspondence of the Society.

MD —UNIVERSITY OF MARYLAND, White Memorial Library, College Park, 20742. Elizabeth W McElroy, Head
Holdings: Vols (48,000) Cat Microforms
Budget: ($193,000)
Notes: Current periodicals. Have own card catalog, which is included also in the total university catalog.

MA —UNIVERSITY OF MASSACHUSETTS AT AMHERST, Library, Amherst, 01003. Siegfried Feller, Assoc Dir for Collection Development
Holdings: Cat
Notes: Microbiology, incl bacteriology, immunology, virology, and pathology.

MA —HARVARD MEDICAL SCHOOL, New England Primate Research Center Library, 1 Pine Hill Dr, Southborough, 01772. Sydney Fingold, Librn
Holdings: Vols (4000)

MI —WARNER-LAMBERT/PARKE-DAVIS, Research Library, 2800 Plymouth Rd, Ann Arbor, 48106. Katherine C Owen, Mgr, Library Services
Holdings: Vols (27,977) Cat

MI —THE UPJOHN COMPANY, Corporate Technical Library, 301 Henrietta St, Kalamazoo, 49001. Lorraine Schulte, Manager
Holdings: Cat Microforms Books Journals

MS —GULF COAST RESEARCH LABORATORY, Gordon Gunter Library, E Beach Rd, Ocean Springs, 39564. Malcolm Ware, Sr, Librn
Holdings: Vols (9000) Uncat Mss Pix Microforms
Notes: Also have reprint collection of 30,000 cataloged reprints, indexed by card catalog, on all aspects of marine biology.

NJ —RUTGERS, THE STATE UNIVERSITY OF NEW JERSEY, Waksman Institute of Microbiology, Library, PO Box 759, Piscataway, 08854. Helen Hoffman, Librn
Holdings: Vols (17,000) Cat
Budget: ($40,000)
Notes: Primarily concerned with basic research and applied microbiology. Little emphasis on clinical microbiology.

NY —COLD SPRING HARBOR LABORATORY, Library, PO Box 100, Cold Spring Harbor, 11724. Susan Gensel, Library Dir; Genemary Falvey, Librn
Holdings: Vols (30,000)
Budget: ($103,500)
Notes: The highly technical collection is comprised of 20,000 serial vols and 10,000 monographs. The library receives 500 current serial titles. Subjects covered incl molecular and cellular biology, virology, biochemistry, microbiology, oncology, neurobiology, biological risk assessment and genetic engineering/biotechnology. Special collections in eugenics and genetics are primarily historical dealing with the development of genetics in the US which had its beginnings here.

NY —NASSAU COUNTY DEPARTMENT OF HEALTH, Division of Laboratories & Research, 209 Main St, Hempstead, 11550. Madeline Burston, Librn; Beatrice R Sewald, Asst Librn
Holdings: Vols (4076) Cat Mss Slides Microforms

NY —UNIVERSITY OF ROCHESTER, Carlson Library, Hutchison Hall, River Campus, Rochester, 14627. Michael W Poulin, Librn
Holdings: Vols (48,720) Cat Microforms
Notes: Strong collection in the field and related areas.

ND —UNIVERSITY OF NORTH DAKOTA, Harley E French Medical Library, Grand Forks, 58202. David W Boilard, Dir; Lila Pedersen, Asst Dir
Holdings: Vols (56,000) Cat
Budget: ($206,000)
Notes: 1075 current periodical subscriptions.

OH —OHIO STATE UNIVERSITY, Biological Sciences Library, 1735 Neil Ave, Columbus, 43210. Victoria Welborn, Librn
Holdings: Vols (85,000) Cat Mss Maps Microforms

PA —UNIVERSITY OF PITTSBURGH, Langley Library, A-217 Langley Hall, Pittsburgh, 15260. D L Johnston, Librn
Holdings: Vols (14,000) Cat
Budget: ($30,000)

PA —PENNSYLVANIA STATE UNIVERSITY, Fred Lewis Pattee Library, Life Sciences Library, University Park, 16802. Keith Roe, Head
Notes: This collection is strong in periodical runs, particularly European learned societies and agriculture. It contains extensive collections of Experiment Station publications and has developed specialties in Mycology and Fusaria. There is also a special collection of 1105 glass slides on early Pennsylvania lumbering.

TX —UNIVERSITY OF TEXAS LIBRARIES, Science Library, PO Box P, Austin, 78712. Betty White, Librn
Holdings: Vols (103,000) Cat Microforms

TX —UNIVERSITY OF TEXAS, Marine Science Institute Library, Port Aransas, 78373. Ruth Grundy, Librn
Holdings: Vols (45,000) Cat Maps Pix
Budget: ($70,000)
Notes: Current researches in marine science, especially concerning the Gulf of Mexico, the Texas Coastal Zone, and the Continental Shelf. Incl journals.

BC —CANADIAN FORESTRY SERVICE, Pacific Forest Research Centre, Library, 506 West Burnside Rd, Victoria, V8Z 1M5, Can. Alice Solyma, Librn
Holdings: Vols (60,500) Cat Microforms
Notes: Incl soil biology, soil microbiology, soil ecology, fauna, fertility, moisture.

MB —UNIVERSITY OF MANITOBA, Science Library, Machray Hall, Winnipeg, R3T 2N2, Can. V Simosko, Head
Holdings: Vols (90,000) Cat Microforms

ON —AGRICULTURE CANADA, Research Branch, Neatby Library, Rm 3032, K W Neatby Bldg, CEF, Ottawa, K1A 0C6, Can. Marcel Charette, Library Technician
Holdings: Vols 1400 Cat

ON —ONTARIO MINISTRY OF HEALTH, Laboratory Services Branch, Library, Box 9000, Terminal A, Toronto, M5W 1R5, Can. Doris A Standing, Librn
Holdings: Vols (4000) Cat
Budget: ($50,000)
Notes: Medical laboratory technology and related subjects: microbiology; environmental bacteriology (limited to testing of milk, food and water for bacterial quality, etc); biological chemistry (clinical); mycology; parasitology; virology; immunology; serology; automated laboratory techniques; biohazard control.

MICROBIOLOGY, AMERICAN SOCIETY FOR see American Society for Microbiology

MICROCIRCUIT TECHNOLOGY

MN —CONTROL DATA CORP, Corporate Library, 8100-34th Ave So, Box O, HQW O6Z, Minneapolis, 55440. Gloria T Andrew, Mgr

MICROELECTRONICS

CA —HUGHES AIRCRAFT CO, Solid State Products Library, 500 Superior Ave, Newport Beach, 92663. Barbara Squyres, Librn
Holdings: Vols (5310) Cat Microforms
Notes: Incl 55 microform rolls, 375 microfiches.

MICROELEMENTS see Trace Elements

MICROGRAPHIC ANALYSIS see Metallography; Microscopes and Microscopy

MICROGRAPHICS

CA —UPDATA PUBLICATIONS INC, Library, 1756 Westwood Blvd, Los Angeles, 90024. Sara Ferguson, Dir; Judith Harrington, Librn
Holdings: Vols (300) Uncat Maps Microforms
Notes: Incl 800,000 microforms, 35 periodicals.

MICROGRAPHICS (cont.)

IN —CUMMINS ENGINE CO, Information Center, 1000 Fifth St, Columbus, 47201. W E Poor, Tech Librn

MD —ARCHIVE OF MICROGRAPHICS, 1100 Wayne St, Suite 1100, Silver Spring, 20910. Nila Zynjuk, Archivist
Holdings: Vols 7000 Uncat Pix Microforms
Notes: Micrographics: microfilm, microprint, microfiche; etc. Collection is in organizational stages and not open to the public at present except by appointment. Database available. No photocopying. Also, a collection of early equipment, photographs, and memorabilia.

NY —XEROX CORP, Technical Information Center, PO Box 305, Webster, 14580. Michael D Majcher, Mgr
Holdings: Vols (30,000) Cat Microfilms

MICRONESIA see Islands of the Pacific

MICRONUTRIENTS see Trace Elements

MICROPALEONTOLOGY

IL —UNIVERSITY OF ILLINOIS, URBANA/CHAMPAIGN, Library, Geology Library, 223 Natural History Bldg, Urbana, 61801. Dederick Ward, Librn
Holdings: Vols (105,186) Cat Maps Microforms

LA —LOUISIANA STATE UNIVERSITY, Troy H Middleton Library, Louisiana Room, Baton Rouge, 70803. Evangeline Mills Lynch, Head Librn; Ruth Murray, Associate Librn
Holdings: Vols (33,500) Cat Maps VF
Notes: Louisiana Collection of history, description and travel, biography, agriculture, literature, politics and government, folklore, anthropology, geography, geology, education, language, music and natural history. Especially large subject collections may be found on Louisiana, the history of the lower Mississippi Valley, Abraham Lincoln, Romance languages and literatures, sugar culture and technology, Southern history, petroleum engineering, plant pathology, micropaleontology, ornithology, and various aspects of crawfish life, biology and culture. Complete depository of Louisiana State Documents; extensive newspapers clipping files; separate card catalog; items listed in Louisiana Union Catalog; restricted use (research and reference). Incl both materials about Louisiana and by Louisianians without regard to subject. LSU Press Collection(preservation copy of each title kept for exhibit purposes only). LSU theses and dissertations from 1900-date. LSU Faculty Collection. Also, 1300 maps, 104 VF drawers, 250 boxes of uncataloged pamphlets.

NY —AMERICAN MUSEUM OF NATURAL HISTORY, Library Services Dept, Central Park W & 79th St, New York, 10024. Nina J Root, Chairwoman; Mary Genett, Asst Librn for Reference Services
Holdings: Vols (385,000) Cat Mss Maps Pix Slides Microforms
Notes: Nearly all collections are outstanding for depth of coverage and international range. Early and historic works, rare books, colored illustrations, and relevant serial publications supplement the modern scientific publications necessary to the researches of the scientific staff and the work of the educational division. Open to the public.

MICROPHYSICS

PA —UNIVERSITY OF PITTSBURGH, Hillman Library, Pittsburgh, 15260. Glenora E Rossell, Head
Holdings: Vols (6100) Cat Microforms
Notes: The History and Philosophy of Science collection is rapidly growing to support research interests in a very new synoptic approach in the integration of history of science, philosophy of science, and history of philosophy, and the intensive new program of instruction. The trend of collection is to include works in philosophical foundations of contemporary physics and cosmologyk, the philosophical problems of the social sciences, science and theology in the 17th century, the relation between science and epistermology in the 18th and 19th centuries; problems of microphysics, history of molecular biology, theories of scientific explanation, and relation between science and metaphysics

MICROPROCESSORS

TX —TEXAS INSTRUMENTS INC, Library, PO Box 1443, Houston, 77001. Helen Manning, Librn
Holdings: Vols (800) Cat Microforms
Notes: Systems, design, and marketing of microprocessors and electronic semiconductors. Not open to the public.

MICROSCOPES AND MICROSCOPY

†DC —CATHOLIC UNIVERSITY OFF AMERICA, Nursing & Biology Library, Washington, 20064. N L Powell, Head
Holdings: Vols (17,000) Cat Microforms

KY —UNIVERSITY OF KENTUCKY, Margaret I King Library, Dept of Special Collections, Lexington, 40506. William Marshall, Head
Holdings: Uncat
Notes: A small collection of "landmark" publications, 17th to early 19th century (45 titles); 2 original drawings and ms notes by G Adams, instrument maker; also drawing by Luccatelli.

MD —MEDICAL & CHIRURGICAL FACULTY OF THE STATE OF MARYLAND, Library, 1211 Cathedral St, Baltimore, 21201. Joseph E Jensen, Librn
Holdings: Vols (10,000) // Cat Mss Maps Pix
See also entry under Medicine - History and Historic

MA —SMITH COLLEGE, Library, Northampton, 01063. Ruth Mortimer, Cur of Rare Books
Holdings: Vols 145 // Cat
Notes: Thornton Collection of 15th-19th century herbals, early microscopy, Linneaus, biography.

†NY —MEDICAL RESEARCH LIBRARY OF BROOKLYN, Academy of Medicine of Brooklyn & The State University of New York Downstate Medical Center, 450 Clarkson St, Brooklyn, 11203. Kenneth E Moody, Dir
Holdings: Vols 5000 Cat
Notes: History of medicine, historic medicine, and about 4000 medical classics. See also entry under Medicine.

NY —UNION COLLEGE, Schaffer Library, Schenectady, 12308. Ann Seemann, Librn; Ellen Fladger, Archivist
Holdings: Vols 500 Cat
Notes: The Ellis Kellert Collection of monographs and journals on microscopes and microscopy.

PA —CARNEGIE LIBRARY OF PITTSBURGH, Science & Technology Dept, 4400 Forbes Ave, Pittsburgh, 15213. Catherine M Brosky, Dept Head
Notes: Of secondary interest in acquisitions because of the department's role in cooperating with Pittsburgh institutions and others across the Commonwealth in sharing resources, the cooperative acquisition of materials, and the provision of services and information. However, some aspects of the subject are emphasized.

MICROSCOPIC ANALYSIS see Metallography; Microscopes and Microscopy

MICROSCOPIC ANATOMY see Histology

MICROSCOPIC BOOKS see Bibliography—Microscopic and Miniature Editions

MICROWAVES

CA —UNIVERSITY OF CALIFORNIA, BERKELEY, Bancroft Library, Manuscripts Division, Berkeley, 94720. James D Hart, Dir
Holdings: Mss
Notes: Papers of Samuel Silver, specialist on applied electromagnetic, microwave, and radio astronomical problems. Much on the International Union of Radio Science. 48 linear ft.

KY —UNIVERSITY OF KENTUCKY, Robert E Shaver Library of Engineering, 355 Anderson Hall, Lexington, 40506. Russell H Powell, Engineering Librn
Holdings: Vols (48,000) Cat Microforms

NC —DUKE UNIVERSITY, Mathematics-Physics Library, Durham, 27706. Mary Ann Southern, Librn
Holdings: Vols 69,171
Notes: A special collection is the Microwave Catalog from the University of Ulm, a bibliography of microwave literature divided into molecule types, ie radicals, linear, diatomic, symmetric tops, asymmetric tops, and hindered rotation; it is regularly updated by supplements.

MIDDLE AGES—HISTORY

CT —YALE UNIVERSITY, Law Library, 127 Wall St, New Haven, 06520. Morris L Cohen, Librn
Holdings: Cat Mss

DC —CATHOLIC UNIVERSITY OF AMERICA, Mullen Library, 620 Michigan Ave NE, Washington, 20064. B Gutekunst, Humanities Librn
Holdings: Vols (20,000) Cat

DC —HARVARD UNIVERSITY, Dumbarton Oaks, Research Library, 1703 32nd St NW, Washington, 20007. Irene Vaslef, Librn

IL —QUINCY COLLEGE LIBRARY, Quincy, 62301. Victor Kingery, OFM, Librn
Holdings: Vols 2000 Cat
Budget: $500

KS —UNIVERSITY OF KANSAS, Kenneth Spencer Research Library, Special Collections Dept, Lawrence, 66045. Alexandra Mason, Librn
Holdings: Cat Mss
Notes: Summerfield Collection of Renaissance and Early Modern Printed Books contains many mediaeval texts. Ms collection incl over 650 mss and documents written before 1500. Noncirculating.

MD —JOHNS HOPKINS UNIVERSITY, Milton S Eisenhower Library, George Peabody Collection, 17 E Mt Vernon Place, Baltimore, 21201. Lyn Hart, Peabody Librn
Notes: Noncirculating.

MN —SAINT JOHN'S ABBEY & UNIVERSITY, Hill Monastic Manuscript Library, Collegeville, 56321. Julian G Plante, Dir
Holdings: Vols (61,000) Microfilms
Notes: Films of 61,000 mss. The total number of codices or bound handwritten mss represents the holdings of several hundred libraries in Europe, mostly Austria, Spain, Ethiopia, West Germany, Portugal, and also Italy, Hungary, Poland, Great Britain, Belgium, Yugoslavia, France, Switzerland, and the Netherlands.

MO —SAINT LOUIS UNIVERSITY, Pius XII Memorial Library, 3655 W Pine Blvd, Saint Louis, 63108. William Cole, Dir
Holdings: Slides Microforms
Notes: Collection covers all areas of learning and European history from Classical Antiquity to early modern period. Researchers using collection receive assistance in paleography, bibliography and reference search. Approx 10,000 1000-foot reels of microfilm (not counting master negatives) reproducing Vatican Library's Latin, Greek, Hebrew, Arabic and Ethiopic mss. Some 8000 100-foot reels of microfilm (again not counting master negative) reproducing rare and out of print books relating to subject areas in the mss. Over 50,000 color slides of medieval and Renaissance mss illuminations. A reference collection of modern materials relating to ms research.

NJ —PRINCETON UNIVERSITY, Library, Manuscript Collection, Nassau St, Princeton, 08540. Jean F Preston, Cur
Holdings: Mss Pix
Notes: The collection of Medieval and

MIDDLE AGES—HISTORY (cont.)

Renaissance manuscripts, totaling 350 book manuscripts, incl items collected by Robert Garrett and Grenville Kane. The collection is supplemented by several single leaves. See *Princeton University Library Chronicle*, v 3, p 123-35; v 11, p 37-44. Ricci, Seymour de. *Census of Medieval and Renaissance Manuscripts in the United States and Canada* (New York: H W Wilson Co 1935-40); and *Supplement*, ed by W H Bond 1962.

NY —THE CLOISTERS, Metropolitan Museum of Art (Branch), Fort Tryon Park, New York, 10040. Suse C Childs, Librn
Holdings: Vols (5000) Cat Mss Pix Slides
Notes: A branch of the Metropolitan Museum of Art devoted solely to the literature of medieval art. Incl 16,000 slides and 5000 photographs with unique strengths in certain aspects of medieval art.

NC —DUKE UNIVERSITY, Divinity School Library, Durham, 27706. Donn Michael Farris, Librn
Holdings: Vols (225,000)
Notes: Special collections and subject emphases in this library include: Archaeology, Egyptian; Archaeology, Middle Eastern; Art, Jewish; Bible; Bible-New Testament; Bible-Symbolism; Church Architecture; Egyptology; Fathers of the Church; Society of Friends; Great Britain-Religion-Methodism and Methodist Church; Hymns and Hymnals; Jansenists and Jansenism; Judaica; Mediaeval Christian Mysticism; Methodism and Methodist Church; Methodist Episcopal Church; Methodist Episcopal Church, South; Reformation; Religion-US-History; Rural Church; Theology-Great Britain-17th Century; Theology-Great Britain-18th Century; United Methodist Church; US-Church History; John Wesley.

PA —UNIVERSITY OF PENNSYLVANIA, Lea Library, 3420 Walnut St, Philadelphia, 19104. Daniel Traister, Special Collections Librn
Holdings: Vols (20,000) Cat Mss
Notes: Collection incl works on Church history, the history of jurisprudence, political theory, Byzantine history, the Crusades and medieval urban history. See Downs, 4241, 4234.

PA —DUQUESNE UNIVERSITY, Library, Pittsburgh, 15282. Dena F Jacobson, Music and Reference Librn
Holdings: Vols 3000 Cat
Notes: Main emphasis of collection is on history of Jewish philosophy in the Missle Ages and relationship between Jewish and Christian scholars; collection incl works by 14th century writer Nicolas de Lyra and general Judaica, history of the Jews, theology, Bible texts and commentaries, literature, grammatical works and dictionaries, etc.

PA —ROSEMONT COLLEGE, Gertrude Kistier Memorial Library, Rosemont, 19010. Sister Mary Dennis Lynch, SHCJ, Dir of Library Services
Holdings: Cat Maps Microforms

WI —UNIVERSITY OF WISCONSIN, MADISON, Seminary of Medieval Spanish Studies, 1130 Van Hise Hall, Madison, 53706. Lloyd A Kasten, Emeritus Prof of Spanish
Holdings: Vols (7500) // Cat Mss Pix Slides Microforms
Notes: Medieval materials and subjects. 100 reels of microfilm, 2500 pamphlets and reprints. Incl a 300-volume collection on 13th century Spanish law. Other emphases: language studies (incl 616,247 vocabulary cards), dictionaries, bibliographies, periodicals. The nucleus of the collection is photostats of the mss of unpublished works of Alfonso X. Restricted circulation.

ON —TORONTO SCHOOL OF THEOLOGY, Consortium of Libraries, University of Toronto, Toronto, M5S 1A5, Can. R Grane Bracewell, Library Coordr
Holdings: Cat
Notes: A consortium of 7 theological college and faculty libraries at the University of Toronto.

SK —UNIVERSITY OF REGINA, Campion College, Library, Regina, S4S 0A2, Can. Myfanwy Truscott, Librn
Notes: Religious studies.

SK —UNIVERSITY OF SASKATCHEWAN, Library, Saskatoon, S7N 0W0, Can. S Perkins, Librn
Notes: Extensive collection (in book form; some reprints) of matriculation records of English, Scottish, French, German, Italian, and other universities, dating from the Middle Ages and Renaissance.

MIDDLE EAST see Near East

MIDDLE ENGLISH see English Language—Middle English (1100-1500)

MIDDLE HIGH GERMAN LANGUAGE AND LITERATURE see German Language and Literature—Middle High German

MIDDLE WEST

DC —LIBRARY OF CONGRESS, Prints & Photographs Div, Washington, 20540.
Notes: The Joseph S Allen Collection of architectural photographs. Covering the period 1945 to 1967, the collection consists of photographs of churches, colleges, government buildings, residential structures, and historic monuments in 27 eastern and mid-western states. Incl 11,427 items in the collection.

IL —MCLEAN COUNTY HISTORICAL SOCIETY LIBRARY & MUSEUM, 201 E Grove, Bloomington, 61701. Barbara Dunbar, Dir; Greg Koos, Archivist
Holdings: Vols (3000) Cat Mss Maps Pix
Notes: Collection also strong in social history, educational history (one room schools and rural education), womens history.

IL —CHICAGO HISTORICAL SOCIETY, Library, Clark St at North Ave, Chicago, 60614. Robert L Brubaker, Librn
Holdings: Vols (150,000) Cat Mss Maps Pix Slides Microforms
Notes: Subjects: United States history (specialties: Chicago, Midwest, Lincoln, Civil War). Special collections: Chicago directories, trade catalogs, advertising cards (6000), theatre programs (5000), and sheet music (4600); personal papers and records of Chicago leaders and organizations; negatives and prints from Chicago leaders and organizations; negatives and prints from Chicago newspaper morgues, 1900-1965 (250,000); Meserve Americana, 27 vols, mostly of period of Civil War (8000 portraits); American city prints (historic); J Norman Jensen Collection of Lake and River Disasters, 1679-1947(8500 cards). Jensen Collection of Lake and River Disasters, 1679-1947 (8500 cards). Holdings: 422,000 books and pamphlets; 16,000 bound periodical vols; 7300 vols of newspapers; 14,000 broadsides and posters; 10,000 maps; 640 atlases; 50,000 clippings; 2500 vols of CHS archives; 35,000miscellaneous printed pieces; 8600 reels of microfilm; 4000 linear feet of mss; 500,000 prints and photographs (black-and-white photographs, daguerreotypes, ambrotypes, stereographs, negatives, engravings, and lithographs).

IL —NORTHERN ILLINOIS REGIONAL HISTORY CENTER, Sven Parson Hall, Northern Illinois University, De Kalb, 60115. Glen Gildemeister, Dir
Holdings: Cat Mss Maps Pix Slides Phonorecords Audiotapes 16mm Films Microfilms
Notes: "A research center for advanced research in the humanities. This northern area of Illinois (excluding Cook County) has been virtually untouched by collecting agencies and we hope to fill that void. We will be strong in agribusiness, agricultural implement business, and hybrid farming mechanics....Will be primarily a ms repository, but [have] already taken responsibility for many artifacts and books, some rare."

IL —AUGUSTANA COLLEGE, Library, Rock Island, 61201. Marjorie M Miller, Special

Collections Librn
Holdings: Vols 2000 Cat Mss
Notes: The John Hauberg Upper Mississippi Valley Collection. Incl strong collection of immigrant guide books for the Midwestern states. Fine collection relative to the Sauk and Fox tribes and Black Hawk in particular.

IA —DRAKE UNIVERSITY, Cowles Library, 28 St & University Ave, Des Moines, 50311.
Notes: Nearly 3000 musical works used by orchestras and musicians to accompany silent films, donated by Dorman Hundling who had played in orchestras in theatres owned by his family in South Dakota and Iowa.

MN —ENVIRONMENTAL CONSERVATION LIBRARY OF MINNESOTA (ECOL), 300 Nicollet Mall, Minneapolis, 55401. Linda R Fritschel, Librn
Holdings: Vols 17,000 Cat Microforms Audiotapes
Budget: $18,000
Notes: Special focus on environment of Upper Midwest and impact of man upon it. Collection incl documents from state and local agencies as well as federal documents. Materials circulate, and are available to anyone in Minnesota without charge. Publication: *Minnesota Environmental Organizations: A Directory*, (Minneapolis Public Library, 1982), 301 pp; available from the Minneapolis Public Library for $5.00 plus $1.00 postage from the above address.

MN —US DEPT OF AGRICULTURE, FOREST SERVICE, North Central Forest Experiment Station, Library, 1992 Fowell Ave, Saint Paul, 55108. Floyd L Henderson, Librn
Holdings: Vols (5000) Maps 16mm Films
Budget: ($14,000)
Notes: Forests of the North Central states.

MO —CULVER-STOCKTON COLLEGE, Carl Johann Memorial Library, Canton, 63435. Robert Lin, Librn
Holdings: Vols 1500 Cat
Budget: $1000
Notes: The Johann Collection covers all aspects of Midwest Americana, with special emphasis on Missouri and Mark Twain.

NE —DANA COLLEGE, C A Dana-Life Library, Blair, 68008. Ronald D Johnson, Head Librn
Holdings: Vols)10,000) Cat Audiotapes
Notes: Strong emphasis on Danish literature although we include other Scandinavian countries. Have an oral history tape collection with recordings of Danish emigrants to the midwest. Our book collection is strongest in the literature area with history a close second.

SD —AUGUSTANA COLLEGE, Mikkelsen Library & Learning Resource Center, Center for Western Studies, Sioux Falls, 57197. Ronelle Thompson, Dir Library
Holdings: Vols (40,000) Cat Mss Maps Pix Slides Microforms
Budget: ($130,000)
Notes: The Center for Western Studies, located in the Mikkelsen Library, is an archival and research agency of Augustana College. Dedicated to the history and culture of the Great Plains and the Trans-Mississippi West, the Center collects and preserves materials relating to Plains Indians, immigrant settlers, Norwegiana, Western Americana, Herbert Krause, Frederick Manfred, Donald Parker, Richard F Pettigrew, Augustana College, the Episcopal Diocese of South Dakota, the South Dakota District of the American Lutheran Church, the South Dakota Penitentiary and Minnehaha County.

MIDDLE WEST—DESCRIPTION AND TRAVEL

IL —AUGUSTANA COLLEGE, Library, Rock Island, 61201. Marjorie M Miller, Special Collections Librn
Holdings: Vols (2000) Cat Mss
Notes: The John Hauberg Upper Mississippi Valley Collection. Strong collection of immigrant guide books for the Midwestern states. Fine collection relative to the Sauk and Fox tribes and Black Hawk in particular.

MIDDLE WEST—DESCRIPTION AND TRAVEL (cont.)

IL —UNIVERSITY OF ILLINOIS, URBANA/CHAMPAIGN, Library, Illinois Historical Survey Library, 1408 W Gregory Dr, 1A Library, Urbana, 61801.
Holdings: Vols 150 Cat Mss Maps
Notes: Travel and description in the Midwest, particularly Illinois. The majority of these items were published in the 19th century. Guide to the collections published in 1976.

MIDDLE WEST—GENEALOGY

IL —NEWBERRY LIBRARY, 60 W Walton St, Chicago, 60610. Diana Haskell, Cur of Modern Mss
Holdings: Cat Mss
Notes: Very strong collection.

NE —OMAHA PUBLIC LIBRARY, Omaha, 68102. Michael Phipps, Dir
Holdings: Vols 3133 Cat
Budget: $2200
Notes: The collection chiefly covers the US east of the Missouri River, plus Nebraska. Census indexes.

MIDDLE WEST—HISTORY

IL —UNIVERSITY OF ILLINOIS, URBANA/CHAMPAIGN, Library, Illinois Historical Survey Library, 1408 W Gregory Dr, 1A Library, Urbana, 61801.
Holdings: Vols 150 Cat Mss Maps
Notes: Travel and description in the Midwest, particularly Illinois. The majority of these items were published in the 19th century. Guide to the collections published in 1976.

MIDDLE WEST—PICTURES, ILLUSTRATIONS, ETC.

IL —CHICAGO HISTORICAL SOCIETY, Library, Graphics Collection, Clark St at North Ave, Chicago, 60614. Larry A Viskochil, Cur
Notes: About 50,000 pieces. Emphasis on Chicago, Illinois, and the Midwest, but includes many views of other cities and localities and substantial holdings concerning important leaders and events in the history of the US.

MIDDLE WEST UTILITIES COMPANY

IL —LOYOLA UNIVERSITY OF CHICAGO, E M Cudahy Memorial Library, 6525 N Sheridan Rd, Chicago, 60626.
Holdings: Mss Clippings
Notes: General correspondence and personal papers. Collection also incl papers of the Middle West Utilities Company 1913-1933, and misc materials from other Samuel Insull controlled enterprises. Transcript of United States vs Insull and his memoirs are also available. To be used under the direct supervision of the archivist at all times.

MIDDLEMAS, KEITH

CA —HOOVER INSTITUTION ON WAR, REVOLUTION & PEACE, Stanford University, Stanford, 94305. Milorad M Drachkovitch, Archivist
Notes: Collection of sound recordings of interviews with British, Portuguese and South African diplomats, politicans, economic advisors, journalists, and businessmen, 1970-76, relating to political events in Portugal and Southern Africa, collected by Keith Middlemas, Professor at the University of Sussex, England. Also incl are documents and correspondence pertaining to British, Portuguese and South African relations and various political events, 1966-1973. 7 ms boxes.

MIDDLESEX CANAL

MA —UNIVERSITY OF LOWELL, Library, One University Ave, Lowell, 01854. Martha Mayo, Special Collections Librn
Holdings: Vols 200 Cat Mss Maps Pix Microforms
Notes: The Middlesex Canal Collection originates from two sources: the Middlesex Canal Association and the Middlesex Canal Company Records. This collection documents the history of the Middlesex Canal 1797-1851 which ran between Lowell and Charlestown, Massachusetts.

MIDDLETON, GEORGE

DC —LIBRARY OF CONGRESS, Manuscript Division, Washington, 20540. John C Broderick, Chief
Holdings: Cat Mss Pix
Notes: Incl correspondence, literary mss, reports, notes, scrapbooks, photographs, etc. About 10,000 items.

MIDDLETON, NATHANIEL RUSSELL

SC —COLLEGE OF CHARLESTON LIBRARY, Special Collections Dept, Charleston, 29401.
Notes: Contains essays, addresses, papers, sermons and correspondence.

MIDDLETON, GEN. TROY H.

LA —LOUISIANA STATE UNIVERSITY, Troy H Middleton Library, Baton Rouge, 70803. Lance E Dickson, Acting Dir
Holdings: Vols (1000) Cat Mss Maps Pix Audiotapes
Notes: The Troy H Middleton Collection. Contains vols on military history and tactics. Letters, documents, photographs, and mementos belonging to Troy H Middleton, former President of LSU and distinguished military leader. Also, tape recordings by some of Gen Middleton's associates in the Army, incl Gen Eisenhower, and on civilian life and reminiscences by Gen Middleton. The Library has other materials on military history also.

MIDDLETON FAMILY

SC —COLLEGE OF CHARLESTON LIBRARY, Special Collections Dept, Charleston, 29401.
Notes: Papers, 1809-1867 incl 34 architectural sketches and plans of Thomas Walker (1809), John Izard Middleton (1811), and William Middleton (1864); a color wheel and two maps, one of New England and the other of the Middle Atlantic States, drawn by Henry Middleton, Jr (1867).

MIDDLETOWN U.S.A.

DC —LIBRARY OF CONGRESS, Manuscript Division, Washington, 20540. John C Broderick, Chief
Notes: Papers of Robert and Helen Lynd.

IN —BALL STATE UNIVERSITY, University Libraries, Special Collections Dept, University Ave, Muncie, 47306. David C Tambo, Head of Special Collections
Holdings: Vols Mss Maps Pix Audiotapes Videotapes
Notes: Incl one half million feet of film. Center for Middletown Studies holdings include materials by Robert and Helen Lynd, Middletown III Project and Peter Davis' Middletown Film Project.

MIDRASH—FOLKLORE see Folklore, Jewish

MIDWEST see Middle West

MIDWESTERN STATES see Middle West

MIDWIFERY see Obstetrics

MIELZINER, JO

MA —BOSTON UNIVERSITY, Mugar Memorial Library, Special Collections Dept, 771 Commonwealth Ave, Boston, 02215. Howard B Gotlieb, Dir
Holdings: Cat Mss Pix
Notes: Mss, correspondence, scripts for which he did set designs, etc collected in depth; incl publications by or about.

NY —NEW YORK PUBLIC LIBRARY, Performing Arts Research Center, Billy Rose Theatre Collection, 111 Amsterdam Ave, New York, 10023. Dorothy L Swerdlove, Cur
Holdings: Mss Pix
Notes: Incl correspondence as well as original designs, working plans, architectural renderings, and elevations of all the works of Mielziner's professional career. Although uncataloged as yet, the material may be used by researchers by special arrangement.

MIGRANT LABOR

CA —CALIFORNIA STATE UNIVERSITY, NORTHRIDGE, Delmar T Oviatt & South Libraries, 1811 Nordhoff St, Northridge, 91330. Donald L Read, Special Collections Dept
Notes: Three newspaper boxes. Some runs incomplete. Between 1935 and 1939, the US Government maintained camps to assist the migrant farm laborers of the Great Depression. This small collection records the activities of those camps.

CA —STANFORD UNIVERSITY LIBRARIES, Cecil H Green Library, Stanford, 94305. Michael T Ryan, Cur
Notes: Correspondence, papers, and material on farm labor and migrant workers of recent years. Incl papers of Ernesto Galarza and the National Agricultural Workers Union (NAWU), Fr Victor Salandini and Fr James L Vizzard.
See also entry under Chicano Studies

DC —LIBRARY OF CONGRESS, American Folklife Center, Archive of Folk Culture, Washington, 20540.
Notes: The Charles Todd and Robert Sonkin Collection of field recordings made in California migratory labor camps, 1940-41.

MIGRATORY WORKERS see Migrant Labor

MIGUEIS, JOSE RODRIGUES, 1901-1979

RI —BROWN UNIVERSITY, John Hay Library, 20 Prospect St, Providence, 02912. Mark N Brown, Cur Mss
Notes: The Jose Rodrigues Migueis Collection of his works, personal library, correspondence, some manuscripts, diaries, drawings, notebooks, photographs, etc. Incl reprints, and thousands of newspaper clippings relating to him, Portugal's most important 20th century writer. Much of the correspondence is with Portuguese and other writers, academics, and political figures. Migueis was very active in modern Portuguese politics and Portuguese American studies.

MIKHAILOVICH, GEORGII, GRAND DUKE, ?-1919

CA —HOOVER INSTITUTION ON WAR, REVOLUTION & PEACE, Stanford University, Stanford, 94305. Milorad M Drachkovitch, Archivist
Holdings: Mss
Notes: Letters (handwritten in Russian), 1914-18, of Grand Duke Georgii Mikhailovich, son of Grand Duke Mikhail Nikolaevich (son of Tsar Nicholas I, nephew of Tsar Alexander II), and special representatives of Tsar Nicholas II at various fronts during World War I, to his daughter Princess Ksenia dealing with his official functions; events before, during and after the Revolution; and family matters. 2 ms boxes.

MILBANK MEMORIAL FUND

CT —YALE UNIVERSITY, Medical Historical Library, 333 Cedar St, New Haven, 06510. Ferenc A Gyorgyey, Librn
Notes: Records of the Milbank Memorial Fund for the years 1922-1977. A part of the Contemporary Medical Care and Health Policy Collection.

MILBANK MEMORIAL FUND (cont.)

NY —NEW YORK ACADEMY OF
MEDICINE, Library, 2 E 103 St, New
York, 10029. Brett A Kirkpatrick, Librn
Holdings: Uncat Mss Pix
Notes: Collection of personal papers of
Frank George Boudreau, incl
correspondence, from his birth to his early
years as health officer in Ohio, through his
international experience at the League of
Nations Nations, and as President of the
Milbank Memorial Fund. Much on
epidemology, public health, and public
medicine. Collection described in Lee Ash's
"Frank George Boudreau, 18 July 1886-14
February 1970." *The Academy Bookman*,
(New York Academy of Medicine, Friends
of the Rare Book Room). Vol 26, No 1,
1973, pp 6-7.

MILES, JAMES WARLEY, 1818-1875

SC —COLLEGE OF CHARLESTON
LIBRARY, Special Collections Dept,
Charleston, 29401.
Notes: Papers, 1850-1875 incl
correspondence addresses and sermons.

MILES, JOSEPHINE

MO —WASHINGTON UNIVERSITY,
Libraries, Special Collections Dept, Campus
Box 1061, St Louis, 63130.
Notes: A small but significant collection
described in *Special Collections: an
Annotated Guide to the Holdings of the
Manuscript Division and the University
Archives and Research Collection.*
NV —UNIVERSITY OF NEVADA, RENO,
University Library, Special Collections Dept,
Reno, 89557. Robert E Blesse, Head
Holdings: Vols (25) Cat Other appearances
400 Cat
Notes: Includes individual works by author
in all editions including translations; also
prefaces, introductions, published
correspondence, appearances in anthologies,
periodicals, etc. Bibliographical research
collection, part of Modern Authors
Collection.

MILESTONE, LEWIS

CA —ACADEMY OF MOTION PICTURE
ARTS & SCIENCES, Margaret Herrick
Library, 8949 Wilshire Blvd, Beverly Hills,
90211. Linda Harris Mehr, Library
Administrator
Notes: Papers.
See also entry under Moving Pictures.

MILHAUD, DARIUS

DC —LIBRARY OF CONGRESS, Music
Division, Washington, 20540.
Notes: Mss in Koussevitzky Archives.

MILITARY AERONAUTICS see
Aeronautics, Military

MILITARY ART AND SCIENCE

CA —HUMAN RESOURCES RESEARCH
ORGANIZATION (HUMRRO), Western
Div Library, 27857 Berwick Dr, Carmel,
93923. Dianalee Stickler, Librn
Notes: Citations for HumRRO reports
appear in *HumRRO Bibliography of
Publications, 1971* and *HumRRO
Bibliography of Publications and
Presentations During FY, 1972-77.* Library
is inactive.
CA —R & D ASSOCIATES, Technical
Information Center, 4640 Admiralty Way,
PO Box 9695, Marina del Rey, 90291.
Margaret R Anderson, Mgr
Holdings: Vols (10,000) Cat Mss Maps
Microforms
Notes: Military arts and sciences, tactical
and strategic, studies, and defense systems.
Incl 45,000 government contractor and
technical reports; and briefing charts
(transparencies).
CA —GTE COMMUNICATIONS PRODUCT
CORP, Sylvania Systems Group, Western

Division Library, MC-2201, PO Box 7188,
Mountain View, 94039. J B Fierro,
Supervisor Library Services
Holdings: Vols (10,000) Cat
Notes: Interlibrary loan.
CA —LOGICON INC, Strategic & Information
Systems Division, Information Center, 255
W Fifth St, Box 471, San Pedro, 90731.
Constance B Davenport, Supervisor
Holdings: Vols (3000) Cat Mss Microforms
Notes: Incl about 3000 books, 250 periodial
titles, 5000 technical reports, 10,000
microfiche, 750 standards and specifications.
Catalog is computerized. Interactive search
capability with Dialog, Orbit, DMS on-line,
NASA Recon. Material on computer
programming, systems analysis, military
systems and operations research.
CO —US AIR FORCE ACADEMY, Library,
USAF Academy, Colorado Springs, 80840.
Reiner H Schaeffer, Dir
Holdings: Vols 3800 Cat
CO —COLORADO STATE UNIVERSITY,
Libraries, Fort Collins, 80523. John
Newman, Special Collections Librn
Holdings: Vols (900) Cat
Budget: ($7000)
Notes: The Imaginary Wars Collection incl
fictional accounts of future wars, imaginary
wars in the past and the greatly altered
outcomes of real wars. Stories must depict
known societies on Earth or close parallels
to known societies. At present, the collection
consists primarily of monographs. Future
plans call for the identification of appropriate
short stories. For an annotated bibliography
of American imprints in the collection see
John Newman, "America at War: Horror
Stories for a Society," *Extrapolation*, XVI,
No 1 and 2 (December 1974 and May
1975).
DC —DEFENSE INTELLIGENCE
AGENCY, Library, RTS-2A, Washington,
20301. H Holzbauer, Librn
Holdings: Vols (250,000) Cat Mss Maps Pix
Slides Microforms

Notes: Not open to the General Public.
DC —US ARMS CONTROL &
DISARMAMENT AGENCY, Library,
George Washington Univ Special
Collections, Washington, 21 St & Virginia
Ave, NW, Rm 5851, Washington, 20451.
Diane Ferguson, Librn
Holdings: Vols 4500 // Cat
Notes: Arms control, disarmament and
related topics.
GA —US ARMY INFANTRY CENTER,
National Infantry Museum, Fort Benning,
31905. Dick D Grube, Dir; Z Frank Hanner,
Cur; Carol Sims, Librn
Holdings: Vols (6000) Cat Mss Maps Pix
Slides
Notes: Published and unpublished works
dealing with infantry history, equipment, and
units, for research on the Museum's
collections of artifacts. Items cannot be
checked out except under unusual and
compelling circumstances. The collection
traces the two centuries of history of the US
Infantry. Of special interest are: unpublished
reports of tests conducted on US Army
Infantry equipment; photographs showing
the history of Fort Benning; books and
periodical articles dealing with Infantry small
arms, both American and foreign, especially
Japanese, Soviet, Chinese, and British; US
Army manuals, incl many from the early
20th and late 19th centuries; WWII
battlefield maps; WWI and WWII posters;
histories of WWI; US Army insignia and
medals; WWII era German uniforms and
insignia. Also, over 2500 weapons.
GA —US ARMY INFANTRY SCHOOL
LIBRARY, Fort Benning, 31905. Vivian S
Dodson, Chief Librn
Holdings: Vols 165,000 Microforms
Budget: $47,000
Notes: Each Army service school and
branch school has an academic library. Incl
books, classified and unclassified documents,
periodicals (cat).
LA —LOUISIANA STATE UNIVERSITY,
Troy H Middleton Library, Baton Rouge,
70803. Lance E Dickson, Acting Dir
Holdings: Vols (1000) Cat Mss Maps Pix

Audiotapes
Notes: The Troy H Middleton Collection.
Contains vols on military history and tactics.
Letters, documents, photographs, and
mementos belonging to Troy H Middleton,
former President of LSU and distinguished
military leader. Also, tape recordings by
some of Gen Middleton's associates in the
Army, incl Gen Eisenhower, and on civilian
life and reminiscences by Gen Middleton.
The Library has other materials on military
history also.
NY —CORNELL UNIVERSITY LIBRARIES,
Collection of Regional History, Dept of
Manuscripts and Univ Archives, Ithaca,
14853.
Notes: Records of the US Army Reserve
Officer Training Corps basic and advanced
training at Cornell University, NY.
Restricted.
NY —NEW YORK PUBLIC LIBRARY,
Research Libraries, General Research
Division, Fifth Ave & 42 St, New York,
10018. Rodney Phillips, Chief
Holdings: Vols (2,225,000) Cat Maps Pix
Microforms
Budget: ($775,718)
NY —NEW YORK PUBLIC LIBRARY,
Research Libraries, Science and Technology
Research Center, Fifth Ave & 42 St, New
York, 10018.
Holdings: Vols (1,100,000) Cat Microforms
Budget: ($647,259)
NY —US MILITARY ACADEMY LIBRARY,
West Point, 10996. Alan C Aimone, Military
History Librn
Holdings: Vols 100,000 Cat Mss Maps Pix
Slides Phonorecords Audiotapes Videotapes
Films Filmstrips Microforms
Notes: Military Art including unit histories
and bound periodicals. Also, 10,000 vols of
periodicals. Egon A Weiss and J Thomas
Russell, *Subject Catalog of the Military Art
and Science Collection in the Library of the
United States Military Academy,* with
selected author and added entries incl a
preliminary guide to the ms collection.
Westport, Connecticut: Greenwood
Publishing Co, 1969, 4 vols. See also Alan C
Aimone, *Military History Bibliography,* 4th
ed (USMA Bulletin 14B). West Point, 1982.
NC —US ARMY SPECIAL WARFARE
CENTER, Marquat Library, Fort Bragg,
28307. Frank Lundgren, Librn
Holdings: Vols (45,000) Cat Microforms
Notes: Guerilla warfare, unconventional
warfare, strategy, etc. International aspect in
political science. 425 periodicals, serial
subject collections; newspapers, HRAF
microfiche subscription.
OK —US ARMY FIELD ARTILLERY
SCHOOL LIBRARY, Morris Swett Library,
Snow Hall, Fort Sill, 73503. Lester L Miller
Jr, Chief Librn
Holdings: Vols 265,958 Documents Pix
Maps Slides Microforms
Notes: Field artillery; artillery; ordnance;
military history; military science; weapons
and weapons systems; ammunition; ballistics;
missiles; Field Artillery unit histories;
military periodicals analytical index file
(VF). Incl US and foreign artillery; survey
data; historical material on the army in
Indian Territory and settlement of the
southwest; photographs on army subjects,
Indian Territory, Oklahoma history, Indians
of the southwest.
PA —US ARMY WAR COLLEGE LIBRARY,
Carlisle Barracks, 17013. Barbara E Stevens,
Dir
Holdings: Vols (125,000) Cat Maps
Microforms Audiotapes
Budget: ($251,000)
Notes: Physical access to the collection is
limited. Individual items available on
interlibrary loan. Older historical material is
in the US Army Military History Institute,
Carlisle Barracks, Pennsylvania, 17013.
RI —PROVIDENCE PUBLIC LIBRARY, 150
Empire St, Providence, 02903. Lance J
Bauer, Special Collections Librn
Notes: The Daniel Berkeley Updike
Autograph Collection of 800 ms letters and
historical documents, primarily New
England, from late 17th to mid-19th century
with emphasis on Rhode Island politics;

MILITARY ART AND SCIENCE (cont.)

American Revolution; French military figures; naval heroes of the Revolution, Tripolitan War and War of 1812; Civil War figures and US presidents. Illustrious personages represented incl: Henry David Thoreau, Daniel Webster, John Hay, Marquis de Lafayette, Henry Wadsworth Longfellow, and other notables. Material must be used in-house. Limited photocopying for educational purposes only.

RI —PROVIDENCE PUBLIC LIBRARY, 150 Empire St, Providence, 02903. Lance J Bauer, Special Collections Libren
Holdings: Vols 5000
Notes: The Harris Collection on the American Civil War and Slavery. Incl 18th and 19th century books, rare pamphlets, and periodicals concerning slavery and the slave trade, and origins, progress and results of the Civil Civil War; also regimental histories; military and naval tactics; personal narratives; women's accounts of the Civil War; works on abolition; sheet music; Union and Confederate broadside ballads; Confederate imprints; *The Liberator* from 1843 through the Civil War; and over 85 editions of *Uncle Tom's Cabin* in 14 languages. Excellent primary and secondary sources for the study of the Civil War and slavery. Material must be used in-house. Photocopying when condition of material allows.

VA —US NATIONAL PARK SERVICE, Harpers Ferry Center, Library, Harpers Ferry, 25425. David Nathanson, Chief Libren
Holdings: Vols 3000 Mss Maps Pix Microforms

VA —ARMED FORCES STAFF COLLEGE LIBRARY, 7800 Hampton Blvd, Norfolk, 23511. Margaret J Martin, Libren
Holdings: Vols (135,000) Cat Microforms
Budget: $64,000
Notes: Collection incl about 45,000 documents. Not open to the public. Interlibrary loan with government and educational institution libraries.

ON —NATIONAL DEFENCE COLLEGE & CANADIAN LAND FORCES COMMAND & STAFF COLLEGE, Fort Frontenac Library and Staff College Library, Fort Frontenac, Kingston, K7K 2X8, Can. S K Kamra, Chief Libren
Holdings: Vols 70,000 Cat Maps
Budget: $50,000

ON —NATIONAL MUSEUMS OF CANADA, Library Services Directorate, Ottawa, K1A 0M8, Can. Valerie Monkhouse, Director
Holdings: Vols 12,000 Cat
Budget: ($60,000)
Notes: Collection includes; arms and armour, military aeronautics, military and naval arts and sciences, military and naval equipment, general military and naval history, military and naval history of Canada. Research collection, interlibrary loans available, public may use on the premises.

MILITARY ART AND SCIENCE—HISTORY

CA —RAND CORP, Library, 1700 Main St, Santa Monica, 90406. Vivian J Arterbery, Library Mgr
Holdings: Vols 1800 Cat
Notes: Military history of World War II and subsequent time.

†DC —US MARINE CORPS HISTORICAL CENTER, Library, Code HDS-5 Bldg 58, Washington Navy Yard, Washington, 20374. Evelyn Englander, Libren

IL —CHICAGO PUBLIC LIBRARY, Special Collections Div, Cultural Center, 78 E Washington St, Chicago, 60602. Laura Linard, Cur
Holdings: Vols (7000) Cat Mss Maps Pix
Notes: The Civil War and American History Research Collection at the Chicago Public Library is our largest collection. It spans the pre-war sectional crisis as well as Reconstruction. Scarce slavery pamphlets; large collection of regimental histories; manuscripts of US Grant, Sherman,

Breckinridge; letters and diaries of soldiers and other officers; original photographs of individuals and field shots; Confederate Battle Plan for the Battle of Shiloh (original); swords, rifles, uniforms, flags and other military accessories. A substantial part of this collection has been cataloged. The museum objects are inventoried (Grand Army Hall and Memorial Association of Illinois Collection).See *Treasures of The Chicago Public Library*, comp by Thomas A Oriando and Marie Gecik, 1977, pp 36-79.

IL —NEWBERRY LIBRARY, 60 W Walton St, Chicago, 60610. Diana Haskell, Cur of Modern Mss
Holdings: Cat Pix
Notes: Art of war before 1900.

MD —JOHNS HOPKINS UNIVERSITY, Milton S Eisenhower Library, Charles & 34 Sts, Baltimore, 21218. Ann S Gwyn, Assistant Dir for Special Collections
Holdings: Vols (20,500) Cat Mss
Notes: Several individuals' libraries combine to make a strong collection of German literature: Leonard L Mackall's German literature, Hermann Coblitz German linguistics, and the largest, William Kurreimeyer's collection including incunabula and mss, and 16-18th century works on the art of warfare. Literary journals, reference works, and most important editions of all major 18th and 19th century writers.

MA —BOSTON UNIVERSITY, Mugar Memorial Library, Special Collections Dept, 771 Commonwealth Ave, Boston, 02215. Howard B Gotlieb, Dir
Holdings: Vols 7500 Cat Mss Pix
See also entries under Massachusetts First Corps of Cadets; Military Historical Society of Massachusetts

MI —UNIVERSITY OF MICHIGAN, Library, Dept of Rare Books & Special Collections, Ann Arbor, 48109. Robert J Starring, Head
Holdings: Cat Mss Maps Pix
Notes: Chiefly in the Stephen Spaulding Collection which concerns every aspect of the art and science of war. Rich in early works, incl incunabula. Non-rare works are in the Graduate Library. Partially listed in *Early Military Books in the University of Michigan Libraries*, by Thomas M Spaulding and Louis C Karpinski, Ann Arbor: The Univ Michigan Press, 1941 (University of Michigan General Library Publications, no 5).

MN —UNIVERSITY OF MINNESOTA, O Meredith Wilson Library, 309 19 Ave S, Minneapolis, 55455. Austin J McLean, Chief, Special Collections
Holdings: Vols (410) Cat
Notes: Fortification from the Renaissance to 1800. Related materials on attack and defense and accounts of famous sieges.

NY —US MILITARY ACADEMY LIBRARY, West Point, 10996. Egon A Weiss, Libren
Holdings: Vols (100,000) Cat Mss Maps Pix Slides Phonorecords Videotapes 16mm Films Filmstrips Microforms
Notes: Described in *Subject Catalog of the Military Art and Science Collection in the Library of the US Military Academy* (Greenwood Publishing Corp, 1969).

PA —US ARMY MILITARY HISTORY INSTITUTE, Carlisle Barracks, 17013. Richard J Sommers, Chief Archivist-Historian
Notes: Books 350,000; bound periodicals 30,000; military publications 700,000; periodical subscriptions 110; microform 12,000 incl fiche 6000, reels 6000; reports and studies 150,000; military unit histories 5000. The World War I survey: Personal correspondence, diaries, and memoirs of American officers and enlisted men of Regular, National Guard, and National Army units (also sailors, Marines, and Coast Guardsmen) serving in the United States, England, France, Italy, Germany, the Ottoman Empire, and Russia during and immediately after the First World War. This is the largest collection anywhere of personal papers of US forces in the Great War. (6500 folders and 100 boxes mss.) The World War II collection: Personal letters, daily logs, reminiscences, speeches, and official papers

of American officers and soldiersserving in the European, Mediterranean, Middle Eastern, China-Burma-India, Southwest Pacific, and Central Pacific Theaters and in the Zone of the Interior during the Second World War. Most of these collections are mss of General officers, incl Omar Bradley, Stephen Chamberlin, Lewis Hershey, John Lucas, William Simpson, and Brehon Somervell. The Korean War collection: Personal correspondence, daily logs, recollections, and official papers of US officers and soldiers serving in the Korean War, incl Generals Edward Almond, George Barth, Bruce Clarke, Matthewe Ridgway, and Arthur Trudeau. The Viet Nam War collection: Personal letters, daily logs, memoirs, speeches, and official paeprs of American officers and soldiers serving in Viet Nam or elsewhere in the world during the era. Almost all these paeprs are from Generals, incl William DePuy, Harold K Johnson, Bruce Palmer,Jonathan Seaman, and William Westmoreland. (2000 boxes mss.)

RI —BROWN UNIVERSITY, John Hay Library, Anne S K Brown Military Collection, 20 Prospect St, Providence, 02912. Richard B Harrington, Cur
Notes: The Anne S K Brown Military Collection has been formed over the past forty or more years by Mrs John Nicholas Brown, now of Newport, and contains approximately 40,000 volumes and 60,000 prints, drawings and watercolors as well as a number of oil paintings and about 5000 miniature model soldiers. At its beginning (and still today) the emphasis or focus of this collection has been upon the history of, and the accurate contemporary illustration of, military and naval uniforms of all nations from the early XVII century to the present. In the course of time, however, the collection has come to incl also a vast and related amount of material on military and naval history, military and naval arts and tactics, wars, campaigns, ceremonies, biography, portraits and caricatures of this and earlier periods. It has been probably the largest private collection of such a nature inthe world, and it contains much ms and graphic documentation which is unique. It has been useful to numerous scholars and historians, editors, filmmakers and publishers for research and for illustrative material and has also contributed to many museum exhibitions. In 1982 the entire collection, with its complete card catalog and subject index, has been presented to Brown University, where it is located in the John Hay Library. Special requests are taken care of by phone, mail and appointments with the curator.

†VA —GEORGE C MARSHALL RESEARCH FOUNDATION AND LIBRARY, Drawer 920, Lexington, 24450. Royster Lyle Jr, Cur Collections
Holdings: Vols Uncat Mss
See also entry under Cryptography

†WY —UNIVERSITY OF WYOMING, William Robertson Coe Library, Archives of Contemporary History, 13th & Ivinson, Laramie, 82071.
Notes: The papers of Victor Gondos. Incl journals and books, several hundred folders on military and archival history, his diaries from 1920-1974, and more than 1500 letters on historical research and architecture.

BC —ROYAL ROADS MILITARY COLLEGE, Coronel Memorial Library, Victoria, V0S 1B0, Can. Susan Day, Libren
Holdings: Vols (7500) Cat
Budget: ($3000)
Notes: A collection of world military history in the English language with a particular emphasis on British military history in World WarII and Canadian military history of the two world wars.

MILITARY AUTOMOBILES see Automobiles, Military

MILITARY AVIATION see Aeronautics, Military

MILITARY BALLOONS see Balloons and Balloonists

MILITARY COSTUME see Uniforms, Military and Naval

MILITARY DECORATIONS see Medals, Military and Naval

MILITARY ENGINEERING

CA —R & D ASSOCIATES, Technical Information Center, 4640 Admiralty Way,

MILITARY ENGINEERING (cont.)

PO Box 9695, Marina del Rey, 90291.
Margaret R Anderson, Mgr
Holdings: Vols (10,000) Cat Mss Maps
Microforms
Notes: Military arts and sciences, tactical
and strategic studies, and defense systems.
Incl 45,000 government contractor and
technical reports; and briefing charts
(transparencies).

NY —NEW YORK STATE LIBRARY, State
Education Bldg Annex, Washington Ave,
Albany, 12224.
Notes: Select collection, contemporary
materials on fortification and allied subjects.
Primarily European and American and
before 1900. Restricted use: Most items
exclusive of manuscripts, local histories and
genealogies are available for loan.

NY —IBM CORP, Information Retrieval and
Library Services, Owego, 13827. Richard
Duffy, Librn
Holdings: Vols 12,000 Cat Pix Microforms
Notes: Computer technology for military and
space use. Also 45,000 reports, 7500 bound
period vols.

NY —US MILITARY ACADEMY LIBRARY,
West Point, 10996. Robert E Schnare, Asst
Librn, Special Collections
Holdings: Cat
Notes: Early British and American imprints
from the 16th to early 20th century, incl
Schley Collection of Military Engineering
and the West Point Thayer collection.

PA —SWARTHMORE COLLEGE, Library,
Swarthmore, 19081. Michael J Durkan,
Librn
Holdings: Vols 959 Cat Mss
Notes: This was the collection belonging to
Greville Bathe. It is comprised of books on
machines and steam engines published from
the 16th-20 century. Also works on military
engineering.

MILITARY GOVERNMENT

NY —US MILITARY ACADEMY LIBRARY,
West Point, 10996. Egon A Weiss, Librn
Holdings: Vols (65,000) Cat Mss Maps Pix
Slides Phonorecords Videotapes 16mm Films
Filmstrips Microforms
Notes: Described in Subject Catalog of the
Military Art and Science Collection in the
Library of the US Military Academy
(Greenwood Publishing Corp, 1969).

†VA —GEORGE C MARSHALL
RESEARCH FOUNDATION AND
LIBRARY, Drawer 920, Lexington, 24450.
Royster Lyle Jr, Cur Collections
Holdings: Cat Mss Maps Pix
Notes: The Collas Harris papers incl 1000
pages of SCAP Civil Information and
Education Series; miscellaneous papers
concerning SCAP and the occupation of
Japan, 1945-1947. The Francis P Miller
papers incl intelligence papers from OSS and
Operation Sussex, SHAEF (incl Battle of the
Bulge), Germany's occupation; and the US
Senate's investigation of military
government in occupied Europe.

MILITARY HISTORICAL SOCIETY OF MASSACHUSETTS

MA —BOSTON UNIVERSITY, Mugar
Memorial Library, Special Collections Dept,
771 Commonwealth Ave, Boston, 02215.
Howard B Gotlieb, Dir
Holdings: Cat Mss Maps Pix
Notes: Incl the library and archives of the
Military Historical Society of Massachusetts.

MILITARY HISTORY

AZ —FORT HUACHUCA HISTORICAL
ASSOCIATION, Fort Huachuca, 85705.
James P Finley, Dir
Holdings: Cat Mss Maps Pix Slides
Microforms
Notes: Voluminous collection of documents
concerning Fort Huachuca, southeastern
Arizona, Indians, pioneer settlements, and
military history. About 50,000 manuscript
pieces and documents.

AZ —ARIZONA HERITAGE CENTER,
Library, 949 E Second St, Tucson, 85719.
Michael Weber, Dir
Notes: Espec with reference to Arizona, the
West, and the Southwest.

CA —LOS ANGELES PUBLIC LIBRARY,
History Dept, 630 W Fifth St, Los Angeles,
90071. Frank Louch, Sr Librn
Holdings: Vols 28,500 Cat Maps
Budget: ($85,000)
Notes: A well-rounded collection with
emphasis on unit histories of American
Wars, especially World War II.

CA —LOGICON INC, Strategic & Information
Systems Division, Information Center, 255
W Fifth St, Box 471, San Pedro, 90731.
Constance B Davenport, Supervisor
Holdings: Vols (3000) Cat Mss Micorforms
Notes: Incl about 3000 books, 250 periocial
titles, 5000 technical reports, 10,000
microfiche, 750 standards and specifications.
Catalog is computerized. Interactive search
capability with Dialog, Orbit, DMS on-line,
NASA Recon. Material on computer
programming, systems analysis, military
systems and operations research.

CA —HOOVER INSTITUTION ON WAR,
REVOLUTION & PEACE, Stanford
University, Stanford, 94305. Milorad M
Drachkovitch, Archivist
Notes: Several important military collections
incl the papers of Adm Charles M Cooke,
Major Gen Robert T Frederick, Gen Robert
C Richardson, Colonel M Preston
Goodfellow, Vice Adm Milton E Miles,
Colonel Lee V Harris, Brigadier, Gen L R
Boyd.

CO —US AIR FORCE ACADEMY, Library,
USAF Academy, Colorado Springs, 80840.
Reiner H Schaeffer, Dir
Holdings: Vols 6500 Cat Microforms

CT —UNIVERSITY OF CONNECTICUT,
Library, Storrs, 06268. R H Schimmelpfeng,
Dir of Special Collections
Holdings: // Uncat Mss
Notes: Manuscript material relating to
activities in the Phillippines and Spain of
Valenano Weyler y Nicolau, Duque de Rubi
("Butcher Weyler").

DC —SMITHSONIAN INSTITUTION
LIBRARIES, National Museum of American
History Branch, Washington, 20560. Rhoda
S Ratner, Branch Librn
Holdings: Vols 1800 Cat Maps Pix

†DC —US MARINE CORPS HISTORICAL
CENTER, Library, Code HDS-5 Bldg 58,
Washington Navy Yard, Washington, 20374.
Evelyn Englander, Librn

GA —US ARMY INFANTRY SCHOOL
LIBRARY, Fort Benning, 31905. Vivian S
Dodson, Chief Librn
Holdings: Vols 165,000 Microforms
Budget: $47,000
Notes: Military art and science, with
emphasis on infantry. Each Army service
school and branch school has an academic
library. Incl books, classified and unclassified
documents, periodicals (cat).

IL —MCLEAN COUNTY HISTORICAL
SOCIETY LIBRARY & MUSEUM, 201 E
Grove, Bloomington, 61701. Barbara
Dunbar, Dir; Greg Koos, Archivist
Holdings: Vols (3000) Cat Mss Maps Pix
Notes: Illinois history, emphasis on McLean
County. Strong in military heritage of
Illinois, particularly the 33rd and 94th
regiments (III Vol Inf) in the Civil War. Incl
150 LF archives and 1000 pictures.
Photocopying.

IL —CHICAGO HISTORICAL SOCIETY,
Library, Clark St at North Ave, Chicago,
60614. Archie Motley, Manuscript Librn
Notes: Materials on American wars: The
American Revolution, War of 1812; Black
Hawk War, 1832; War with Mexico;
political, military, and social history of the
Civil War, incl many Confederate States of
America materials; Spanish-American War;
World War I; World War II.

IL —CHICAGO PUBLIC LIBRARY, Special
Collections Div, Cultural Center, 78 E
Washington St, Chicago, 60602. Laura
Linard, Cur
Holdings: Vols (7000) Cat Mss Maps Pix
Notes: The Civil War and American History
Research Collection at the Chicago Public
Library is our largest collection. It spans the
pre-war sectional crisis as well as
Reconstruction. Scarce slavery pamphlets;
large collection of regimental histories;
manuscripts of US Grant, Sherman,
Breckinridge; letters and diaries of soldiers
and other officers; original photographs of
individuals and field shots; Confederate
Battle Plan for the Battle of Shiloh (original);
swords, rifles, uniforms, flags and other
military accessories. A substantial part of
this collection has been cataloged. The
museum objects are inventoried (Grand
Army Hall and Memorial Association of
Illinois Collection).See Treasures of The
Chicago Public Library, comp by Thomas A
Oriando and Marie Gecik, 1977, pp 36-79.

LA —LOUISIANA STATE UNIVERSITY,
Troy H Middleton Library, Baton Rouge,
70803. Lance E Dickson, Acting Dir
Holdings: Vols (1000) Cat Mss Maps Pix
Audiotapes
Notes: The Troy H Middleton Collection.
Contains vols on military history and tactics.
Letters, documents, photographs, and
mementos belonging to Troy H Middleton,
former President of LSU and distinguished
military leader. Also, tape recordings by
some of Gen Middleton's associates in the
Army, incl Gen Eisenhower, and on civilian
life and reminiscences by Gen Middleton.
The Library has other materials on military
history also.

†MA —BOSTON PUBLIC LIBRARY, Copley
Sq, Boston, 02117.
Holdings: Vols 2800 Cat Mss Maps Pix
Notes: Collection formed by John Quincy
Adams and General Sylvanus Thayer,
supplemented by material in the Civil War
Collection, and purchases of early European
works.

MA —BOSTON UNIVERSITY, Mugar
Memorial Library, Special Collections Dept,
771 Commonwealth Ave, Boston, 02215.
Howard B Gotlieb, Dir
Holdings: Cat Mss Maps Pix
Notes: Incl the library and archives of the
Military Historical Society of Massachusetts;
also of the First Corps of Cadets
(Massachusetts).

NM —NEW MEXICO HIGHLANDS
UNIVERSITY, Donnelly Library, National
Ave, Las Vegas, 87701. Karen Jaggers,
Assoc Librn
Holdings: // Mss Maps Microforms
Notes: The outstanding collection is the
Arrott Collection on Fort Union, New
Mexico, 1851-1891. Other collection incl
Spanish Archives, Mexican Archives,
Archdiocese of Santa Fe, Archivo del Parral;
New Mexico Land Grants.

NY —BUFFALO & ERIE COUNTY
HISTORICAL SOCIETY, 25 Nottingham
Court, Buffalo, 14216. Herman Sass, Librn
Notes: Collection strong on War of 1812,
Civil War and the two World Wars. Material
on all phases of military history. In various
resource departments. No separate catalog.

NY —NEW YORK PUBLIC LIBRARY,
Research Libraries, General Research
Division, Fifth Ave & 42 St, New York,
10018. Rodney Phillips, Chief
Holdings: Vols (2,225,000) Cat Pix Maps
Microforms
Budget: ($775,718)
Notes: The Strong Collection of regimental
unit history; US, Great Britain, and
European countries.

NY —NEW YORK PUBLIC LIBRARY,
Slavonic Div, Fifth Ave & 42 St, New York,
10018. Edward Kasinec, Chief
Holdings: Vols 122,000 Cat Microforms
Notes: Russian language materials form the
main body (ca 70 percent) of the extensive
Slavic and Baltic collections of the Slavonic
Division. The strength of the collection is in
humanities and social sciences, incl military
history and government documents.
Periodicals and publications of learned

MILITARY HISTORY (cont.)

societies form an important part of the collection. Holdings of rare books are considerable. Polish history, and especially military history, are well represented. See New York Public Library, *Dictionary Catalog of the Slavonic Collection* (Boston: G K Hall, 1974), 44 vols.

NY —SUFFOLK COUNTY HISTORICAL SOCIETY, Library, 300 W Main St, Riverhead, 11901. Betty Carpenter, Librn
Holdings: Vols (15,000) Cat Mss Maps Pix

NY —SAINT BONAVENTURE UNIVERSITY, Friedsam Memorial Library, Saint Bonaventure, 14778. John Capozzi, OFM, Art Cur
Holdings: Mss
Notes: S L A Marshall Collection of 11 file cases of original mss, typescripts, and 9 books written by him.

NY —US MILITARY ACADEMY LIBRARY, West Point, 10996. Alan C Aimone, Military History Librn
Holdings: Vols 100,000 Cat Mss Maps Pix Slides Phonorecords Audiotapes Videotapes Films Filmstrips Microforms
Notes: Military Art including unit histories and bound periodicals. Also, 10,000 vols of periodicals. Egon A Weiss and J Thomas Russell, *Subject Catalog of the Military Art and Science Collection in the Library of the United States Military Academy,* with selected author and added entries incl a preliminary guide to the ms collection. Westport, Connecticut: Greenwood Publishing Co, 1969, 4 vols. See also Alan C Aimone, *Military History Bibliography,* 4th ed (USMA Bulletin 14B). West Point, 1982.

NC —DUKE UNIVERSITY, William R Perkins Library, Durham, 27706. Elvin E Strowd, University Librn

ND —UNIVERSITY OF NORTH DAKOTA, Chester Fritz Library, Dept of Special Collections, Grand Forks, 58202. Daniel F Rylance, Special Collections Coordr
Holdings: Vols (5500) Uncat Mss Maps Pix Microforms
Budget: ($2500)
Notes: Also the Orin G Libby Manuscript Collection (900 collections), and the Aandahl Collection of Western History on North Dakota and the Northern Great Plains. Emphasis on agriculture, politics, pioneering, Germans from Russia, etc. Guides to the collections available from the Coordinator of Special Collections.

OH —OHIO HISTORICAL SOCIETY, Archives Library Division, 1982 Velma Ave, Columbus, 43211. Dennis East, Division Chief
Holdings: Vols (96,000) Cat Mss Maps Pix Slides Microforms
Budget: ($18,000)
Notes: This library is the primary collection for Ohio. Most purchases are on the rare and out of print market. Collection area is early American history, esp relating to exploration into the Northwest Territory. Also, Ohio archaeology, natural history, and artifacts. Major media collections are books (96,000), newspapers (25,000 vols and 22,000 microfilm), pictures (50,000), maps (2500), manuscripts (1,500,000). Library is noncirculating except through interlibrary loan of microfilm.

OH —RUTHERFORD B HAYES LIBRARY, 1337 Hayes Ave, Fremont, 43420. Watt P Marchman, Dir
Holdings: Cat Mss Pix
Notes: Papers of Gen H W Benham, largely business and American military. Index with the collection. Listed in *Guide to Manuscripts of the Ohio Historical Society,* 32 (1 linear foot).

OK —US ARMY FIELD ARTILLERY SCHOOL LIBRARY, Morris Swett Library, Snow Hall, Fort Sill, 73503. Lester L Miller Jr, Chief Librn
Holdings: Vols 265,958 Documents Pix Maps Slides Microforms
Notes: Field artillery; artillery; ordnance; military history; military science; weapons and weapons systems; ammunition; ballistics; missiles; Field Artillery unit histories;

military periodicals analytical index file (VF). Incl US and foreign artillery; survey data; historical material on the army in Indian Territory and settlement of the southwest; photographs on army subjects, Indian Territory, Oklahoma history, Indians of the southwest.

PA —US ARMY MILITARY HISTORY INSTITUTE, Carlisle Barracks, 17013. Richard J Sommers, Chief Archivist-Historian
Notes: Books 350,000; bound periodicals 30,000; military publications 700,000; periodical subscriptions 110; microform 12,000 incl fiche 6000, reels 6000; reports and studies 150,000; military unit histories 5000. The World War I survey: Personal correspondence, diaries, and memoirs of American officers and enlisted men of Regular, National Guard, and National Army units (also sailors, Marines, and Coast Guardsmen) serving in the United States, England, France, Italy, Germany, the Ottoman Empire, and Russia during and immediately after the First World War. This is the largest collection anywhere of personal papers of US forces in the Great War. (6500 folders and 100 boxes mss.) The World War II collection: Personal letters, daily logs, reminiscences, speeches, and official papers of American officers and soldiers serving in the European, Mediterranean, Middle Eastern, China-Burma-India, Southwest Pacific, and Central Pacific Theaters and in the Zone of the Interior during the Second World War. Most of these collections are mss of General officers, incl Omar Bradley, Stephen Chamberlin, Lewis Hershey, John Lucas, William Simpson, and Brehon Somervell. The Korean War collection: Personal correspondence, daily logs, recollections, and official papers of US officers and soldiers serving in the Korean War, incl Generals Edward Almond, George Barth, Bruce Clarke, Matthewe Ridgway, and Arthur Trudeau. The Viet Nam War collection: Personal letters, daily logs, memoirs, speeches, and official paeprs of American officers and soldiers serving in Viet Nam or elsewhere in the world during the era. Almost all these paeprs are from Generals, incl William DePuy, Harold K Johnson, Bruce Palmer,Jonathan Seaman, and William Westmoreland. (2000 boxes mss.)

PA —UNIVERSITY OF PITTSBURGH, Hillman Library, Pittsburgh, 15260.
Holdings: Vols (10,000)
Notes: The entire contents of the oldest used book ship in Pittsburgh, the John C Daub Book Store. The collection deals mainly in the areas of military history; works dealing with the Civil War, the World Wars and other military topics; and local history: county histories, city, state or regional histories. Also incl are military works containing colored plates; a large group of Americana; and many framed, colored prints of military subjects.

RI —BROWN UNIVERSITY, John Hay Library, Anne S K Brown Military Collection, 20 Prospect St, Providence, 02912. Richard B Harrington, Cur
Holdings: Vols (40,000) Cat Mss Pix
Notes: The Anne S K Brown Military Collection has been formed over the past forty or more years by Mrs John Nicholas Brown, now of Newport, and contains approximately 40,000 volumes and 60,000 prints, drawings and watercolors as well as a number of oil paintings and about 5000 miniature model soldiers. At its beginning (and still today) the emphasis or focus of this collection has been upon the history of, and the accurate contemporary illustration of, military and naval uniforms of all nations from the early XVII century to the present. In the course of time, however, the collection has come to incl also a vast and related amount of material on military and naval history, military and naval arts and tactics, wars, campaigns, ceremonies, biography, portraits and caricatures of this and earlier periods. It has been probably the largest private collection of such a nature inthe world, and it contains much ms and

graphic documentation which is unique. It has been useful to numerous scholars and historians, editors, filmmakers and publishers for research and for illustrative material and has also contributed to many museum exhibitions. In 1982 the entire collection, with its complete card catalog and subject index, has been presented to Brown University, where it is located in the John Hay Library. Special requests are taken care of by phone, mail and appointments with the curator.

TX —UNIVERSITY OF TEXAS, EL PASO, Special Collections Dept, The S L A Marshall Military History Collection, El Paso, 79968. Thomas Burdett, Cur
Holdings: Vols 7000 Cat Periodicals Mss
Budget: $2000
Notes: The collection contains all of General Samuel Lyman Atwood Marshall's published works, his personal library and his personal papers. General Marshall was a prolific military historian and journalist. The collection's strengths are in its coverage of the wars of the twentieth century, specifically the two world wars, the Korean conflict and the war in Vietnam. The Marshall Room where the collection is housed is opened to the public.

TX —SAINT MARY'S UNIVERSITY, Library, 2700 Cincinnati Ave, San Antonio, 78284. Anita C Saxine, Special Collections Librn

UT —UNIVERSITY OF UTAH, Marriott Library, Special Collections, Salt Lake City, 84112. Gregory C Thompson, Cur
Notes: Utah and the West.

VA —COLLEGE OF WILLIAM AND MARY, Earl Gregg Swem Library, Williamsburg, 23185. Margaret C Cook, Cur of Manuscripts & Rare Books
Holdings: Vols 100 // Cat Maps
Notes: The John Womack Wright Collection incl 17th and 18th century books on fortifications and contemporary books on the campaigns of the Napoleonic wars. Also, 89 maps of theatre of war area of Napoleonic campaigns.

ON —FORT MALDEN NATIONAL HISTORIC PARK, Library, 100 Laird Ave, Box 38, Amherstburg, N9V 2Z2, Can. Sally E Snyder, Librn
Holdings: Vols (400) Cat Mss Pix Slides
Notes: British and Canadian military life, weaponry, uniforms, from about 1760 to 1860.

ON —MCMASTER UNIVERSITY, Mills Memorial Library, Div of Archives & Research Collections, Hamilton, L8S 4L6, Can. G R Hill, Univ Librn
Holdings: // Mss Maps Pix
Notes: Colonel Steer-Webster played a leading part in the invention, design, and development of the "Mulberry" artifical harbor installations used for the invasion of Europe in WW II. The collection comprises memoranda, drawings, photographs, and maps.

ON —METROPOLITAN TORONTO LIBRARY, History Dept, 789 Yonge St, Toronto, M4W 2G8, Can. Michael Pearson, Head
Holdings: Vols (11,000) Cat Phonorecords Audiotapes Microforms
Notes: Includes British army and navy lists and Prussian and French army lists from 18th century on; British regimental histories; works on military uniforms and insignia, especially European; Napoleonic and First and Second World Wars well represented.

ON —ROYAL CANADIAN MILITARY INSTITUTE, Library, 426 University Ave, Toronto, M5G 1S9, Can. W G Heard, Cur
Holdings: Vols 12,000 Cat Mss Maps Pix
Budget: $50,000
Notes: Military history, incl 20 handwritten diaries; 50 mss, 200 bound periodicals; maps; charts; photographs; antique papers; 100 journal and 12 newspaper subscriptions; Army, Navy, Air Force lists, 1749-date. Special catalogs of regimental histories of British and Canadian armies, navies and air forces. Restricted use: by appointment only.

MILITARY HISTORY—PICTURES, ILLUSTRATIONS, ETC.

DC —LIBRARY OF CONGRESS, Prints & Photographs Div, Washington, 20540.
Holdings: Cat Pix
Notes: Civil War Photograph Collection incl

MILITARY HISTORY—PICTURES, ILLUSTRATIONS, ETC. (cont.)

photographs commissioned by Mathew Brady and others. Brady employed 20 photographers at the height of his operations. His staff incl Alexander and James Gardner, James F Gibson, and Thomas C Roche.

OK —US ARMY FIELD ARTILLERY SCHOOL LIBRARY, Morris Swett Library, Snow Hall, Fort Sill, 73503. Lester L Miller Jr, Chief Librn
Notes: Incl data on Fort Sill, Indian Territory, settlement of Kiowa, Apache and Commanche tribes, imprisonment of Geronimo, Oklahoma territory, settlement of Lawton. Unit histories, incl 10th Cavalry (Buffalo Soldiers, a black unit that built Fort Sill); working papers of Sheridan, Grierson and other commanders; Field Artillery School. Photographs on army subjects, Fort Sill, Indians, Indian Territory, settlement of Southwest Oklahoma.

RI —BROWN UNIVERSITY, John Hay Library, Anne S K Brown Military Collection, 20 Prospect St, Providence, 02912. Richard B Harrington, Cur
Notes: The Anne S K Brown Military Collection has been formed over the past forty or more years by Mrs John Nicholas Brown, now of Newport, and contains approximately 40,000 volumes and 60,000 prints, drawings and watercolors as well as a number of oil paintings and about 5000 miniature model soldiers. At its beginning (and still today) the emphasis or focus of this collection has been upon the history of, and the accurate contemporary illustration of, military and naval uniforms of all nations from the early XVII century to the present. In the course of time, however, the collection has come to incl also a vast and related amount of material on military and naval history, military and naval arts and tactics, wars, campaigns, ceremonies, biography, portraits and caricatures of this and earlier periods. It has been probably the largest private collection of such a nature inthe world, and it contains much ms and graphic documentation which is unique. It has been useful to numerous scholars and historians, editors, filmmakers and publishers for research and for illustrative material and has also contributed to many museum exhibitions. In 1982 the entire collection, with its complete card catalog and subject index, has been presented to Brown University, where it is located in the John Hay Library. Special requests are taken care of by phone, mail and appointments with the curator.

MILITARY HISTORY, BRITISH

ON —FORT MALDEN NATIONAL HISTORIC PARK, Library, 100 Laird Ave, Box 38, Amherstburg, N9V 2Z2, Can. Sally E Snyder, Librn
Holdings: Vols (400) Cat Mss Pix Slides
Notes: British and Canadian military life, weaponry, uniforms, from about 1760 to 1860.

MILITARY HISTORY, CANADIAN

ON —FORT MALDEN NATIONAL HISTORIC PARK, Library, 100 Laird Ave, Box 38, Amherstburg, N9V 2Z2, Can. Sally E Snyder, Librn
Holdings: Vols (400) Cat Mss Pix Slides
Notes: British and Canadian military life, weaponry, uniforms from about 1760 to 1860.

ON —NATIONAL DEFENCE HEADQUARTERS, Directorate of History, Ottawa, K1A 0K2, Can. Peter Greig, Collections Dept
Holdings: Vols (5000) Cat Mss Maps Pix Microforms
Notes: History of the Canadian Armed Forces. The document collection dates from the Second World War and later periods, WW II papers are being transferred to the Public Archives of Canada where earlier

ones have already gone. The holdings of regulations for the RCN, Canadian Army and the RCAF (before 1964) and those for the Canadian Armed Forces (since that date) are comprehensive. Admiralty Fleet Orders, 1910-1964, are held. These are listed in *Union List of Manuscripts in Canadian Repositories.*

ON —NATIONAL MUSEUMS OF CANADA, Library Services Directorate, Ottawa, K1A 0M8, Can. Valerie Monkhouse, Director
Holdings: Vols 12,000 Cat
Budget: ($60,000)
Notes: Collection includes; arms and armour, military aeronautics, military and naval arts and sciences, military and naval equipment, general military and naval history, military and naval history of Canada. Research collection, interlibrary loans available, public may use on the premises.

ON —METROPOLITAN TORONTO LIBRARY, Canadian History Dept, Baldwin Room Section, 789 Yonge St, Toronto, M4W 2G8, Can. David B Kotin, Head
Holdings: Vols (52,000) Mss Pix
Notes: This collection consists of material on Canadian history, geography, travel, archaeology, genealogy, retrospective city and telephone directories, collective biographies, native peoples (excluding customs, rights and social conditions), Arctic regions, military history and theory. It is an extremely strong collection of both current and retrospective material. Particular strengths are national and local history (especially Ontario), Arctic regions, native peoples, travel (especially Ontario), and military history. Incl 78,000 historical pictures, 235 linear meters mss, 14,000 broadsides and 3800 bound newspapers.

ON —ROYAL CANADIAN MILITARY INSTITUTE, Library, 426 University Ave, Toronto, M5G 1S9, Can. W G Heard, Cur
Holdings: Vols 12,000 Cat Mss Maps Pix
Budget: $50,000
Notes: Military history, incl 20 handwritten diaries; 50 mss, 200 bound periodicals; maps; charts; photographs; antique papers; 100 journal and 12 newspaper subscriptions; Army, Navy, Air Force lists, 1749-date. Special catalogs of regimental histories of British and Canadian armies, navies and air forces. Restricted use: by appointment only.

MILITARY HISTORY, ITALIAN

†NY —LIBRARY OF THE ITALIAN RISORGIMENTO, Garibaldi and Meucci Memorial Museum, John Jay Homestead, Box AH, Katonah, 10536.
Notes: History of the Italian Unification Wars and mementos of Garibaldi.

MILITARY INTELLIGENCE

CA —HUMAN RESOURCES RESEARCH ORGANIZATION (HUMRRO), Western Div Library, 27857 Berwick Dr, Carmel, 93923. Dianalee Stickler, Librn
Notes: Citations for HumRRO reports appear in *HumRRO Bibliography of Publications,* 1971 and *HumRRO Bibliography of Publications and Presentations During FY,* 1972-77. Library is inactive.

CA —HARVEY G WOLFE LIBRARY, PO Box 3514, Grand Central Sta, Glendale, 91201. Douglas L Evans, Librn
Holdings: Vols (6580) Mss Maps Pix
Budget: ($4500)
Notes: Main emphasis on espionage, military intelligence, and sabotage.

CA —HOOVER INSTITUTION ON WAR, REVOLUTION & PEACE, Stanford University, Stanford, 94305. Milorad M Drachkovitch, Archivist
Notes: Papers of Yves Godard, officer, French Army, (1932-1961); director of police in Algeria, (1958-1960); and organizer of the Organisation de l'Armee Secrete (OAS,) 1961-62; incl correspondence, messages, reports dossiers, maps, photos, news clippings, speeches and writings, and other material, 1929-74, related to military and resistance operations during Indochinese

War; and to military, police and terrorist activities during the Algerian independence struggle. Incl records of the Armee Secrete de Haute-Savoie (Secret Army of Resistance Fighters of Haute-Savoie). 13 ms boxes; 1 oversize volume; 1 envelope.

CA —HOOVER INSTITUTION ON WAR, REVOLUTION & PEACE, Stanford University, Stanford, 94305. Milorad M Drachkovitch, Archivist
Holdings: Mss Pix
Notes: Ms diaries, 1914-1924, microfilms, photographs and photostats of documents from the *Personlicher Stab Reichsfuhrer SS,* Schriffgutverwaltung dealing with the life and career of Himmler as Reichsfuhrer SS and Chief der Deufschen Polizei, 1934-1945, 6 notebooks (plus 25 loose pages), 5 microfilm reels, 2 photo albums, 14 ms boxes. Incl 24 tapes of Himmler speeches, 1940-44.

CA —HOOVER INSTITUTION ON WAR, REVOLUTION & PEACE, Stanford University, Stanford, 94305. Milorad M Drachkovitch, Archivist
Notes: Papers of Ivan D Yeaton, Colonel, US Army; Military Attache in Moscow, 1939-41; Commanding Officer of the Yenan Observer Group in China, 1945-1946; incl drafts and final copy of his memoirs, reports, memoranda, correspondence, orders and citations, charts, photographs, and other material, 1919-76; relating to Soviet military strength in 1941; US-Soviet relations, 1941-49; organization of US military intelligence during World War II; lend-lease operations; US relations with the Chinese communists, 1944-46; and the inspection of US Army procurement contracts, 1952-53. 2 ms boxes, 7 envelopes.

DC —DEFENSE INTELLIGENCE AGENCY, Library, RTS-2A, Washington, 20301. H Holzbauer, Librn
Holdings: Vols (250,000) Cat Mss Maps Pix Slides Microforms
Budget: ($95,000)
Notes: Not open to the General Public.

DC —GEORGETOWN UNIVERSITY, Library, Special Collections Div, 37 & O Sts NW, Washington, 20057. George M Barringer, Special Collections Librn; Nicholas B Sheetz, Mss Librn
Holdings: Cat
Notes: The Russell J Bowen Collection on Intelligence, Security, and Covert Activities. The collection extends over several hundred years, and incl early wars and conflicts in Europe, the American Revolutionary era, the Civil War in the United States, the World Wars, and other events. Intelligence and espionage activities during World War II, the Cold War, and recent events are extensively documented. See *Scholar's Guide to Intelligence Literature: Bibliography of the Russell J Bowen Collection* (1983).

†VA —GEORGE C MARSHALL RESEARCH FOUNDATION AND LIBRARY, Drawer 920, Lexington, 24450. Royster Lyle Jr, Cur Collections
Holdings: Vols Uncat Mss Slides Microforms
Notes: The William F. Friedman Collection. Separate catalog. Incl. papers and correspondence relating to William and Elizabeth S. Friedman's personal interests and U.S. government assignments: books, pamphlets, technical papers, periodicals, microfilm, slides and newspaper clippings dealing with cryptology. Items on secret writing and signaling, radar, telephony and telegraphy, and the study of the Shakespeare-Bacon authorship controversy, Vols. of fiction relating to spies and codes, cryptographic game books for children, Civil War code items. Examples of ancient writings of Europe, Crete, and Easter Island, and material on the Aztecs, Incas, and particularly the Mayans. Also a copy of the Voynich mss., an undeciphered work, and other rare vols. on the subject dating from the 17th century. The library also has a separate collection of diaries kept by Gilbert Sandford Vernam, cryptographer and inventor. The diary is an almost day-by-day record, 1918-1926, of Vernam's inventions and development of his outstanding contributions to cryptography including techniques widely adopted by the armed forces for enciphering and deciphering coded messages.

MILITARY INTELLIGENCE (cont.)

There is a typed index to this collection. No photocopying.

VA —MACARTHUR MEMORIAL, Library & Archives, MacArthur Sq, Norfolk, 23510. Ellen E Folkama, Asst Archivist
Holdings: Vols (4000) Cat Maps Pix Slides Phonorecords Audiotapes 16mm Films Microforms
Notes: Everything relating to the life and related activities of MacArthur. The Archives of the collection consist of 600 shelf-feet of documents from Gen MacArthur's official headquarters files over the period 1941-1951. These papers pertain to all matters with which his various commands were involved: military, naval and air matters; international relations; political science; Japanese occupation, peace treaty and Constitution, etc. Each Record Group is indexed. The indexes are retained here since they are being expanded. They are available for researchers.

MILITARY MAPS see Maps, Military

MILITARY MEDICINE see Medicine, Military

MILITARY MINIATURES

RI —BROWN UNIVERSITY, John Hay Library, Anne S K Brown Military Collection, 20 Prospect St, Providence, 02912. Richard B Harrington, Cur
Notes: The Anne S K Brown Military Collection has been formed over the past forty or more years by Mrs John Nicholas Brown, now of Newport, and contains approximately 40,000 volumes and 60,000 prints, drawings and watercolors as well as a number of oil paintings and about 5000 miniature model soldiers. At its beginning (and still today) the emphasis or focus of this collection has been upon the history of, and the accurate contemporary illustration of, military and naval uniforms of all nations from the early XVII century to the present. In the course of time, however, the collection has come to incl also a vast and related amount of material on military and naval history, military and naval arts and tactics, wars, campaigns, ceremonies, biography, portraits and caricatures of this and earlier periods. It has been probably the largest private collection of such a nature in the world, and it contains much ms and graphic documentation which is unique. It has been useful to numerous scholars and historians, editors, filmmakers and publishers for research and for illustrative material and has also contributed to many museum exhibitions. In 1982 the entire collection, with its complete card catalog and subject index, has been presented to Brown University, where it is located in the John Hay Library. Special requests are taken care of by phone, mail and appointments with the curator.

MILITARY MINES see Mines, Military and Submarine

MILITARY MODELS see Military Miniatures

MILITARY MUSIC

IL —UNIVERSITY OF ILLINOIS, URBANA/CHAMPAIGN, Library, Bands & Busch Instrument Collection, 1103 S Sixth St, Champaign, 61820. John Cranford, Librn
Holdings: Vols (8600) Cat Mss
Notes: Printed music, about 8400; plus the Sousa Library, 1900 vols, printed music about 1500; also the Clarke Library, 400 vols, printed music, approximately 375. No photocopying.

IN —INDIANA UNIVERSITY, Lilly Library, Seventh St, Bloomington, 47405. William R Cagle, Librn
Holdings: // Uncat
Notes: 19th and 20th century sheet music in the Starr Collection.

MD —TOWSON STATE UNIVERSITY, Fine Arts Bldg, Room 457, Towson, 21204. Edwin L Gerhardt, Curator
Notes: The Gerhardt Library of Musical Information is a segregated representative collection of music literature, phonograph and tape recordings, pictures and artifacts. It incl special sections on Thomas Alva Edison and the phonograph, John Philip Sousa and bands, old popular songs and percussion. Most of the material is out of print and hard to find. It is *not* a collection of scores or manuscripts. A detailed outline is available upon request. Direct all correspondence to the curator, Edwin L Gerhardt, 4926 Leeds Ave, Baltimore, MD 21227, (301) 242-0328. *See also* entry under Sousa, John Philip

NC —DUKE UNIVERSITY, William R Perkins Library, Rare Book Room, Durham, 27706. John L Sharpe, III, Cur
Notes: Collection of more than 3500 titles of Confederate imprints. Possibly the largest such collection in the country, it includes broadsides, maps, music, newspapers, Union and Confederate regimental histories, and sheet music.

WI —UNIVERSITY OF WISCONSIN, MADISON, Memorial Library, Rare Books Collection, 728 State St, Madison, 53706. Gretchen Lagana, Cur
Holdings: Vols (12)// Mss Pix
Notes: Mss, part books, and photographs of the Brodhead Wisconsin Silver Cornet Band which during the latter parts of the Civil War, formed the band of the 1st Brigade, 3rd Division, 15th Army Corp, which marched across Georgia with General Sherman. Housed in the Dept of Rare Books and Special Collections.

MILITARY OCCUPATION

†DC —US MARINE CORPS HISTORICAL CENTER, Library, Code HDS-5 Bldg 58, Washington Navy Yard, Washington, 20374. Evelyn Englander, Librn

†VA —GEORGE C MARSHALL RESEARCH FOUNDATION AND LIBRARY, Drawer 920, Lexington, 24450. Royster Lyle Jr, Cur Collections
Holdings: Cat Mss Maps Pix
Notes: The Collas Harris papers incl 1000 pages of SCAP Civil Information and Education Series; miscellaneous papers concerning SCAP and the occupation of Japan, 1945-1947. The Francis P Miller papers incl intelligence papers from OSS and Operation Sussex, SHAEF (incl Battle of the Bulge), Germany's occupation; and the US Senate's investigation of military government in occupied Europe.

MILITARY ORDERS AND DECORATIONS

CO —AMERICAN NUMISMATIC ASSOCIATION LIBRARY, 818 N Cascade Ave, Colorado Springs, 80903. Nancy W Green, Librn
Notes: One of the largest numismatic libraries, the collection incl books, periodicals and auction catalogs on coins and coin collecting, medals, tokens, military orders and decorations, paper money, primitive money, banks and banking, seals and scarabs. ANA publishes a classified subject catalog of its collection and is open to the public for research and reference services. Only members may check books out.

MILITARY POSTS—PICTURES, ILLUSTRATIONS, ETC.

NM —MUSEUM OF NEW MEXICO, Photo Archives, Box 2087, Santa Fe, 87503. Arthur L Olivas, Cur; Richard Rudisill, Photo Historian
Holdings: Cat Pix Slides
Budget: ($9000)
Notes: Archives incl 200,000 photographs, cataloged, and 40,000 slides. Primary function of the archives is to preserve significant historical material, and these pictures are mainly for research rather than general browsing. Photographs may be ordered as research copies for set fees. Reproduction or publication requires written permission plus additional required fees. Subject matter covered is extensive, incl Southwest town views, Southwest Indians, military subjects, missions, pioneer life, recreation (indoor and outdoor, toys, games, gambling, camping, etc), disasters, exhibits and expositions, portraits (those identified filed by last name), tools and equipment (agricultural, mechanical, housekeeping, etc), and transportation (railroad, stagecoaches, carriages, wagons, etc).

OK —US ARMY FIELD ARTILLERY SCHOOL LIBRARY, Morris Swett Library, Snow Hall, Fort Sill, 73503. Lester L Miller Jr, Chief Librn
Notes: Incl data on Fort Sill, Indian Territory, settlement of Kiowa, Apache and Commanche tribes, imprisonment of Geronimo, Oklahoma territory, settlement of Lawton. Unit histories, incl 10th Cavalry (Buffalo Soldiers, a black unit that built Fort Sill); working papers of Sheridan, Grierson and other commanders; Field Artillery School. Photographs on army subjects, Fort Sill, Indians, Indian Territory, settlement of Southwest Oklahoma.

MILITARY POWER see Military Art and Science

MILITARY RELIGIOUS ORDERS

CO —AMERICAN NUMISMATIC ASSOCIATION LIBRARY, 818 N Cascade Ave, Colorado Springs, 80903. Nancy W Green, Librn
Holdings: Vols (20,000) Cat Slides
Notes: One of the largest numismatic libraries, the collection incl books, periodicals and auction catalogs on coins and coin collecting, medals, tokens, military orders and decorations, paper money, primitive money, banks and banking, seals and scarabs. ANA publishes a classified subject catalog of its collection and is open to the public for research and reference services. Only members may check books out.

NY —AMERICAN NUMISMATIC SOCIETY LIBRARY, Broadway between 155 & 156 Sts, New York, 10032. Francis D Campbell Jr, Chief Librn
Holdings: Vols (50,000) Cat Mss Maps Pix Slides 16mm Films Microforms
Budget: ($6000)
Notes: Incl materials devoted to coins, medals, decorations, orders, tokens, paper money, seals, heraldry. Aids materials incl history, economic history, art history, archaeology, inscriptions and a number of encyclopedias and biographical dictionaries. Dictionary card catalog provides access to the materials: *Dictionary Catalogue of the Library of the American Numismatic Society.* (Boston: G K Hall, 1962). 6 vols and vol listing the auction catalogs in our collection; *First Supplement: 1962-1967; Second Supplement: 1968-1972; Third Supplement: 1973-1977* (Boston: G K Hall, 1967, 1973, 1978). Noncirculating.

MILITARY SCIENCE see Military Art and Science

MILITARY SERVICE, COMPULSORY

PA —SWARTHMORE COLLEGE, Peace Collection, Swarthmore, 19081. Jean R Soderlund, Cur of Peace Collection
Notes: The history of pacifism has been one of the major subject emphases of the Peace Collection since its inception in 1930. In addition to books, pamphlets, and current

MILITARY SERVICE, COMPULSORY (cont.)

materials of all kinds on the subject, the Peace Collection is the official depository for many 20th century pacifist organizations and papers of individual peace leaders. These incl Women's International League for Peace and Freedom; War Resisters League; Fellowship of Reconciliation; SANE, A Committee for a Sane Nuclear Policy; Friends Committee on National Legislation; CCCO1 An Agency for Military and Draft Counseling; National Interreligious Service Board for Conscientious Objectors; A J Muste (1885-1967); and Devere Allen (1891-1955). Other materials collected incl records and memorabilia of 19th and early 20th century peace leaders and organizations, such as the American Peace Society and itsbranches, Jane Addams (1860-1935), the Wisbech Local Peace Association (England), Emily Greene Balch (1867-1961), English and American Friends' Peace Societies, the Universal Peace Union, William Ladd (1778-1841), Elihu Burritt (1810-1879), and Benjamin F Trueblood (1847-1916). The Peace Collection has been described in Downs 972, 978, 4633, and in Downs 1950-1961 Supplement 507 and 916. For descriptions of major document groups, see the *Guide to the Swarthmore College Peace Collection*, 2nd ed (1981).

MILITARY STRATEGY see Strategy (Military)

MILITARY SUPPLIES

MN —HONEYWELL, Defense Systems Div, Engineering Library, 600 Second St N, Hopkins, 55343. Lawrence Werner, Librn
Holdings: Vols (4000)
Budget: ($30,000)
Notes: Incl 100,000 microforms.

MILITARY TRAINING CAMPS ASSOCIATION

IL —CHICAGO HISTORICAL SOCIETY, Library, Clark St at North Ave, Chicago, 60614. Archie Motley, Manuscript Librn
Notes: Papers.

MILITARY TRANSPORTATION see Transportation, Military

MILITARY TRUCKS see Vehicles, Military

MILITARY UNIFORMS see Uniforms, Military and Naval

MILITARY VEHICLES see Vehicles, Military

MILITENSA see Knights of Malta

MILK AND MILK PRODUCTS see Dairy Products

MILK HYGIENE—HISTORY

MD —US DEPT OF AGRICULTURE, National Agricultural Library, 10301 Baltimore Blvd, Beltsville, 20705. Joseph H Howard, Director
Notes: Papers of Charles E North, bacteriologist and milk hygienist.

MILL, JOHN STUART

IL —NORTHWESTERN UNIVERSITY, Library, Special Collections Dept, 1937 Sheridan Rd, Evanston, 60201. R Russell Maylone, Cur
Holdings: Mss
Notes: 44 rough drafts and final copies of letters to Herbert Spencer from J S Mill.
MD —JOHNS HOPKINS UNIVERSITY, Milton S Eisenhower Library, Charles & 34 Sts, Baltimore, 21218. Ann S Gwyn, Assistant Dir for Special Collections
Holdings: Vols Cat Mss
Notes: Chiefly original sources of English

economic thought and history since Adam Smith, Chartism, trades unions, the Factory Acts, Luddites, Poor Law, Owensim, early socialism, Nauvoo Colony. Most items are rarities. J S Mill mss letters and correspondence, and original papers on the inception of the Industrial Revolution. 56 titles from library of Adam Smith. Important editions of *The Wealth of Nations*. Also many pamphlets from 16th century, and the Mercantilists. No published catalog. Cards in main catalog. Collection housed separately in Abram Hutzler Reading Room.

MILL GIRLS

MA —UNIVERSITY OF LOWELL, Library, One University Ave, Lowell, 01854. Martha Mayo, Special Collections Librn
Holdings: Vols 30 Cat Mss Pix
Notes: Lowell History Collection contains photographs, lithographs, post cards, stereoviews, and lanternslides pertaining to the history of the area with special focus on the textile industry and the men and women who worked in the mills from New England Yankee farm girls to the Irish, French-Canadian, and Greek immigrants. The Locks and Canals Collection contains photographs taken from 1875-1947 showing the day to day operations of the company.

MILL WORKERS UNION see International Union of Mine, Mill, and Smelter Workers

MILL YARD, LONDON

WI —SEVENTH DAY BAPTIST HISTORICAL SOCIETY, Library, 3120 Kennedy Rd, PO Box 1678, Janesville, 53547. D Scott Smith, Historian
Holdings: Vols 200 Uncat Mss Pix
Notes: English Seventh Day Baptists Collection. These materials have to do with early and middle years of Baptist movement (1662-1920) in England, incl work of John James, Joseph Stennett, Peter Chamberlen, et al, Sabbatarians or Seventh Day Baptists. About 300 items incl record books, tracts, correspondence.

MILLAY, EDNA ST. VINCENT

CT —TRINITY COLLEGE LIBRARY, Watkinson Library, 300 Summit St, Hartford, 06106. Jeffrey Kaimowitz, Cur
Holdings: Cat
Notes: The H Bacon Collamore Collection, incl first editions, association items.
DC —LIBRARY OF CONGRESS, Manuscript Division, Washington, 20540. John C Broderick, Chief
Holdings: Cat Mss Pix
Notes: Mss, papers, records, etc.
ME —WESTBROOK COLLEGE, Library, 716 Stevens Ave, Portland, 04103. Dorothy M Healy, Special Collections Librn
Holdings: Vols (3000) Cat Mss Pix
Notes: Collection incl work of Maine women writers. Many mss and scrapbooks are incl. Memorabilia of Mrs Robert E Peary, Mary Ellen Chase, Florence B Jacobs, Celia Thaxter, and Edna St Vincent Millay are notable items. Some rare books, ie Madame Wood novels, are part of the collection.
NV —UNIVERSITY OF NEVADA, RENO, University Library, Special Collections Dept, Reno, 89557. Robert E Blesse, Head
Holdings: // Vols 64 Cat Other appearances 490 Cat
Notes: Includes individual works by author in all editions including translations; also prefaces, introductions, published correspondence, appearances in anthologies, periodicals, etc. Bibliographical research collection, part of Modern Authors Collection.
†NY —NEW YORK ACADEMY OF MEDICINE, Library, 2 E 103 ST, New York, 10029.
Notes: Papers of Walter Timme, MD (1874-1956). Timme was a pioneer endocrinologist; described pluriglandular disease, "Timme's Syndrome." Incl correspondence from

Harvey Cushing, Paul Dudley White, Charles A Elsberg, Louis I Dublin, Ely Smith Jelliffe, John F Fulton, Edna St Vincent Millay, Eva Le Gallienne, and Irving Ramsey Wiles.
NC —UNIVERSITY OF NORTH CAROLINA, CHAPEL HILL, Wilson Library, Rare Book Collection, Chapel Hill, 27514. Paul S Koda, Cur of Rare Books
Holdings: Cat
Notes: Fully representative collection.
RI —UNIVERSITY OF RHODE ISLAND, Library, Special Collections, Kingston, 02881. David Maslyn, Head
Notes: Extensive Collection.
VA —UNIVERSITY OF VIRGINIA, Alderman Library, Clifton Waller Barrett Collection, Charlottesville, 22901. Joan St C Crane, Cur of American Literature Collections
Holdings: Vols 123 Cat Mss
Notes: First editions, etc. Over 500 mss.

MILLBROOK HUNT

NY —MERCY COLLEGE LIBRARY, Dobbs Ferry, 10522. Larry Earle Bone, Dir
Holdings: Vols (406) Cat Pix
Notes: General collection of American and British books and periodicals on horses, hounds and hunting, with special emphasis on the Millbrook Hunt. 15 percent of the collection is rare books and periodicals. Rare photographs and paintings also incl. Many of the books are from the private libraries of members of the Millbrook Hunt. Collection formerly at Bennett College, Millbrook, New York.

MILLER, ADOLPH C., 1866-1953

DC —LIBRARY OF CONGRESS, Manuscript Division, Washington, 20540. John C Broderick, Chief
Notes: Papers of Adolph C Miller (1866-1953), economist and original appointee and member of the Federal Reserve Board of Governors (1914-36). Approx 10,000 items, incl personal and professional files.

MILLER, CINCINNATUS HINER (JOAQUIN), 1839-1913

CA —CLAREMONT COLLEGES, Honnold Library, Ninth & Dartmouth, Claremont, 91711. Tania Rizzo, Special Collections Dept Head
Holdings: Vols 200 // Cat Mss Pix
Notes: Incl 50 first and limited editions of Cincinnatus Hiner ("Joaquin") Miller, many inscribed, many with ALsS laid in; ms diary, 1855-1857; 500 periodical and newspaper clippings of Miller's stories, articles and poems; 400 biographical articles, reviews, and notices; correspondence (106 pieces) and 3 notebooks of the collector, Willard Samuel Morse; 170 pictures. Restricted use.
CA —OAKLAND PUBLIC LIBRARY, Oakland History Room, 125 14th St, Oakland, 94612. William W Sturm, Librn
Holdings: Cat Mss
Notes: Manuscript pages and letters.

MILLER, EVGENII KARLOVICH

CA —HOOVER INSTITUTION ON WAR, REVOLUTION & PEACE, Stanford University, Stanford, 94305. Milorad M Drachkovitch, Archivist
Holdings: // Mss
Notes: Papers, 1917-1924, of Evgenii Karlovich Miller, chief military representative in Paris of Gen Peter Wrangel, commander-in-chief of the White Russian forces. Documents relating to the activities of the White Russian forces, consisting chiefly of correspondence of Gen Miller with Wrangel's military representatives in various countries.

MILLER, FLOURNOY

†MD —MARYLAND HISTORICAL SOCIETY, Library, 201 W Monument St, Baltimore, 21201.
Notes: Eubie Blake's personal and

MILLER, FLOURNOY (cont.)

professional archive. Incl the Baltimore-born pianist, composer, and songwriter's collection of songs and instrumental pieces in mss, extensive documentation of his collaboration with Noble Sissle, Flournog Miller, Milton Reddie, and others. The Broadway musical comedy, Shuffle Along, is represented in box office records, programs, scores and parts, photographs, and sheet music. Blake's involvement with other productions is similarly documented.

MILLER, FLOYD

MA —BOSTON UNIVERSITY, Mugar Memorial Library, Special Collections Dept, 771 Commonwealth Ave, Boston, 02215. Howard B Gotlieb, Dir
Holdings: Cat Mss Correspondence

MILLER, COL. FRANCIS P.

VA —UNIVERSITY OF VIRGINIA, Alderman Library, Manuscripts Dept, Charlottesville, 22901. Edmund Berkeley Jr, Cur
Holdings: Cat Mss Pix Phonorecords
Notes: Papers of the liberal Democrat who challenged the Byrd "organization" in the years after World War II and Presbyterian lay leader active in the World Student Christian Federation and the World Council of Churches (60 linear feet).

†VA —GEORGE C MARSHALL RESEARCH FOUNDATION AND LIBRARY, Drawer 920, Lexington, 24450. Royster Lyle Jr, Cur Collections
Holdings: Cat Mss Maps Pix
Notes: The Collas Harris papers incl 1000 pages of SCAP Civil Information and Education Series; miscellaneous papers concerning SCAP and the occupation of Japan, 1945-1947. The Francis P Miller papers incl intelligence papers from OSS and Operation Sussex, SHAEF (incl Battle of the Bulge), Germany's occupation; and the US Senate's investigation of military government in occupied Europe.

MILLER, HENRY, 1891-1980

CA —FRANCIS BACON LIBRARY, 655 N Dartmouth Ave, Claremont, 91711. Elizabeth S Wrigley, Dir
Holdings: Mss Pix
Notes: Arensberg's miscellaneous correspondence with American literary figures (1920's-50's) including Bruce Bliven, Catherine Drinker Bowen, Kay Boyle, Witter Bynner, Edwin Corle, Helen A Keller, Lysander Kemp, Kenneth Macgowan, John Macy, Henry Miller, Lewis Mumford, Clifford Odets, Kenneth Patchen, Irving Stone, and William Carlos Williams.

CA —UNIVERSITY OF CALIFORNIA, LOS ANGELES, Research Library, Dept of Special Collections, 405 Hilgard Ave, Los Angeles, 90024. Edward Shreeves, Chairman, Bibliographers Group; David S Zeidberg, Head
Holdings: Vols 700 Mss
Notes: 700 first and other editions of his books; 75 linear feet of papers, incl correspondence, mss, etc. Permission of Mr Miller's heirs is required to consult this material.

CA —UNIVERSITY OF CALIFORNIA, SANTA BARBARA, Library, Dept of Special Collections, Santa Barbara, 93106. Christian F Brun, Head

IL —SOUTHERN ILLINOIS UNIVERSITY, CARBONDALE, Delyte W Morris Library, Special Collections Dept, Carbondale, 62901. David V Koch, Cur of Special Collections; Louisa Bowen, Cur of Manuscripts
Holdings: Vols 64 Mss Pix
Notes: Collection of personal papers from his bibliographer, family, and friends. 5 linear feet.

IL —NORTHWESTERN UNIVERSITY, Library, Special Collections Dept, 1937 Sheridan Rd, Evanston, 60201. R Russell Maylone, Cur
Holdings: Vols 165 Cat Mss
Notes: Henry Miller: first editions, letters,

ephemera. Incl all mss, correspondence, and production files from the Loujon Press.

MN —UNIVERSITY OF MINNESOTA, O Meredith Wilson Library, 309 19 Ave S, Minneapolis, 55455. Austin J McLean, Chief, Special Collections
Holdings: Vols (576) Uncat Pix Slides Phonorecords
Notes: Published writings of Henry Miller in all languages are contained in this collection, along with information about him, his work, and censorship as it relates to his career. A complete listing is available in the Division.

NV —UNIVERSITY OF NEVADA, RENO, University Library, Special Collections Dept, Reno, 89557. Robert E Blesse, Head
Holdings: // Vols 307 Cat
Notes: Includes individual works by author in all editions including translations; also prefaces, introductions, published correspondence, appearances in anthologies, periodicals, etc. Bibliographical research collection, part of Modern Authors Collection.

NY —NEW YORK UNIVERSITY, Elmer Holmes Bobst Library, Div of Special Collections, Washington Sq S, New York, 10012. Frank Walker, Librn; Patrick McGuire, Asst Librn
Holdings: Vols (100,000) Cat Mss Pix
Notes: The Fales Collection of first (and other) editions of English and American novels from about 1750 to date (about 70, 000 titles). Mss (30,000) pieces.

VA —RANDOLPH-MACON COLLEGE, Walter Hines Page Library, Ashland, 23005. Flavia Reed Owen, Librn
Holdings: Vols 200 Cat Pix Phonorecords
Notes: Published description of collection in Collector's Quest: The Correspondence of Henry Miller and J Rives Childs, 1947-1965 (University Press of Virginia, 1968, for Randolph-Macon College).

BC —UNIVERSITY OF VICTORIA, McPherson Library, Victoria, V8W 3H5, Can.
Notes: Letters and postcards to Alfred Perles, Graham Ackroyd, Father Brocard Sewell; miscellaneous letters to and from publishers and others; mss, watercolors, sketches, and photographs.

MILLER, HERBERT ADOLPHUS

PA —TEMPLE UNIVERSITY LIBRARIES, Special Collections Dept, Conwellana-Templana Collection, 13 & Berks St, Philadelphia, 19122. Miriam I Crawford, Cur
Holdings: Vols 3 // Cat Mss Maps Pix Newsclippings
Budget: ($30,000)
Notes: Correspondence, manuscripts, published writings, and newspaper clippings of Herbert Adolphus Miller, from 1918 to 1951, sociologist, college teacher, active protagonist of the early Czechoslovak nation, and in the fight against racism. 25 letters, 10 manuscripts and about 50 news items, journal articles and pamphlets. Incl draft of a book by Miller on Czechoslovakia.

MILLER, HOWARD F., 1920-1982

NY —STATE UNIVERSITY OF NEW YORK AT ALBANY, Library, Special Collections Dept, 1400 Washington Ave, Albany, 12222. Marion P Munzer, Coordr
Notes: Howard F Miller's correspondence, lecture outlines, reports, relating to academic and administrative career in public budgeting (8.6 linear feet).
See also entries under Budgeting; Finance, Public

MILLER, JACK

IA —STATE HISTORICAL SOCIETY OF IOWA LIBRARY, 402 Iowa Ave, Iowa City, 52240. Darold J Brown, Librn
Holdings: Cat
Notes: Thousands of individual items and smaller collections. Two hundred larger collections incl the papers of Cyrus C Carpenter, Jonathan P Dolliver, Gilbert Haugen, W W Waymack, Ephraim Adams, A C Dodge, Dorothy Houghton, Jesse

Macy, Agnes Samuelson, Donald Johnson, Jack Miller, Ruth Sayre, Samuel Kirkwood, Thomas McKnight, Robert Lucas, Dwight McCarty, William Larrabee. Includes church, school, company and organization records, Civil War materials.

MILLER, JOAQUIN see Miller, Cincinnatus Hiner (Joaquin), 1839-1913

MILLER, LOYE HOLMES

CA —UNIVERSITY OF CALIFORNIA, BERKELEY, Bancroft Library, Manuscripts Division, Berkeley, 94720. James D Hart, Dir
Holdings: Cat Mss Maps Pix Microforms
Notes: Papers, correspondence, etc.

MILLER, MARY OWINGS

MD —UNIVERSITY OF BALTIMORE, Langsdale Library, 1420 Maryland Ave, Baltimore, 21201. Gerry Watkins, Head of Special Collections Dept
Holdings: Vols Mss
Notes: Poetry, poetry books, correspondence, financial records of Mary Owings Miller (1918-); 3.5 cubic feet.

MILLER, MERLE

MA —BOSTON UNIVERSITY, Mugar Memorial Library, Special Collections Dept, 771 Commonwealth Ave, Boston, 02215. Howard B Gotlieb, Dir
Holdings: Cat Mss Pix
Notes: Mss, correspondence, etc collected in depth; incl publications by or about.

MILLER, PAUL

†OK —OKLAHOMA STATE UNIVERSITY, Library, Stillwater, 74074.
Notes: Papers of Paul Miller, chairman emeritus of the Gannett Company. Incl personal papers reflecting his career in journalism and as president of the Associated Press.

MILLER, SAMUEL, 1769-1850

NJ —PRINCETON UNIVERSITY, Library, Manuscript Collection, Nassau St, Princeton, 08540. Jean F Preston, Cur
Holdings: Mss
Notes: The collection totals 1550 pieces. See Princeton University Library Chronicle, v 4, p 68-75.

MILLER, WILLIAM, 1958-

CT —LEE ASH, (personal collection), 66 Humiston Dr, Bethany, 06525.
Holdings: Mss Pix
Notes: Letters and pictures of the Sharon, Conn, writer and librarian.

MILLER, WILLIAM, 1782-1849, AND THE MILLERITE MOVEMENT

IL —AURORA COLLEGE, Library, 347 Gladstone Ave, Aurora, 60506. Mary M Howrey, Library Dir
Holdings: Vols 2260 Cat Mss Pix Microforms
Notes: The Orrin Roe Jenks Memorial Collection of Adventual Materials. The Millerite Movement is incl in the cataloged materials of the Jenks Memorial Collection of Adventual Materials. The papers of William Miller, 1782-1849, correspondence, sermon notes, date books, personal affidavits are housed as a unit. Also, Dr Jenks assembled a collection of writings relating to the history and theology of the Adventist Christian Church. There is a separate card catalog for the books; some archival materials, reports, and minutes of organizations are in files. Also have Prophetic Charts.

MILLER, WILLIAM EDWARD, 1914-

NY —CORNELL UNIVERSITY LIBRARIES, Collection of Regional History, Dept of

**MILLER, WILLIAM EDWARD, 1914-
(cont.)**

Manuscripts and Univ Archives, Ithaca,
14853.
Notes: US Congressman, attorney,
Republican candidate for Vice-President of
the US, 1964. Incl papers, ca 1949-64;
correspondence, newspaper clippings, press
releases, speeches, bills he introduced,
campaign speeches, and photos. Unpublished
guide available. Restricted.

MILLIKAN, ROBERT ANDREWS

CA —CALIFORNIA INSTITUTE OF
TECHNOLOGY, Robert A Millikan
Memorial Library, Archives, 1201 E
California Blvd, Pasadena, 91125. Judith R
Goodstein, Archivist
Holdings: Vols (3000) Cat Mss Maps Pix
Slides Phonorecords Audiotapes Videotapes
16mm Films Microforms
Notes: Ms sources for the history of
astrophysics, cosmology, mathematical
physics, experimental physics, radio
astronomy, geophysics and biophysics.
Collections incl the papers of: George Ellery
Hale, Jesse Greenstein, H P Robertson,
Richard Feynman, Paul Epstein, Max
Delbruck, and Beno Gutenberg. Candid
photos of physicists at meetings; etchings
and photographs of Einstein; scientific
medals; selected pieces of scientific
apparatus (including the oil-drop machine
constructed by Millikan at Caltech in the
early 1920s); the reprint collection of Paul
Epstein; over 3000 landmark books in the
history of 20th century physics and
mathematics. Printed publications include:
Daniel Kevles, *Guide to the Microfilm
Edition of the George Ellery Hale Papers*
(Pasadena, Carnegie Institute of Washington
and Caltech), 1968; Judith R Goodstein,*The
Robert Andrews Millikan Collection at the
California Institute of Technology: Guide to
a Microfilm Edition* (Pasadena, Caltech),
1977; Judith R Goodstein and Carolyn
Kopp, *The Theodore von Karman
Collections at the California Institute of
Technology* (Pasadena, Archives), 1981.
IA —HERBERT HOOVER PRESIDENTIAL
LIBRARY, West Branch, 52358. Dale C
Mayer, Archivist
Notes: Papers of Lewis L Strauss, former
Chairman of the Atomic Energy
Commission. These papers are being
processed and opened for research as rapidly
as possible, but certain sections remain
closed for research. Correspondence with
and about a large number of physicists and
atomic scientists is contained in the
collection.

**MILLING TRADE see Flour and Feed
Trade**

MILLS, OGDEN

DC —LIBRARY OF CONGRESS, Manuscript
Division, Washington, 20540. John C
Broderick, Chief
Holdings: Cat Mss Pix
Notes: Mss, papers, records, etc.

MILLS, ROBERT, 1781-1855

DC —GEORGETOWN UNIVERSITY,
Library, Special Collections Div, 37 & O Sts
NW, Washington, 20057. George M
Barringer, Special Collections Librn;
Nicholas B Sheetz, Mss Librn
Holdings: Mss Cat
Notes: The Richard X Evans Collection. The
family archives of Richard X Evans, incl the
papers of General John Smith (1750-1836), a
member of Congress; Robert Mills (1781-
1855); architect; and Alexander Dimitry
(1805-1883), educator and diplomat.

MILLS, TEXTILE see Textile Mills

MILLS, WATER see Water Mills

MILLS AND MILLWORK

MA —OLD STURBRIDGE VILLAGE,
Research Library, Sturbridge, 01566.

Theresa Rini Percy, Librn
Holdings: Cat Mss Pix
Notes: New England, 1790-1850

MILLSTONE POWER PLANTS

CT —WATERFORD PUBLIC LIBRARY,
Millstone Power Plants Local Documents
Room, 49 Rope Ferry Rd, Waterford, 06385.
Vincent Juliano, Library Dir; Carolyn
Greene, Millstone File Coordinator
Holdings: Uncat Mss
Notes: Collection is part of Nuclear
Regulatory Commission's Local Public
Document Room project and all materials
are arranged by system developed by NRC/
LPDR. No subject index is available.
Additional materials on microfilm.

MILTON, JOHN, 1608-1674

CA —CLAREMONT COLLEGES, Honnold
Library, Ninth & Dartmouth, Claremont,
91711. Tania Rizzo, Special Collections
Dept Head
Holdings: Vols 77 //
Notes: The William W Clary Collection.
First, limited, and special editions of books,
pamphlets, offprints by or about him.
CA —UNIVERSITY OF CALIFORNIA,
DAVIS, Shields Library, Dept of Special
Collections, Davis, 95616. Donald Kunitz,
Head; C Danial Elliott, Asst Head
Holdings: Cat Mss
Notes: Relatively strong holdings.
CA —UNIVERSITY OF CALIFORNIA, LOS
ANGELES, William Andrews Clark
Memorial Library, 2520 Cimarron St, Los
Angeles, 90018.
Holdings: Cat
Notes: Extensive collection, first editions,
etc.
CT —YALE UNIVERSITY, Beinecke Rare
Book & Manuscript Library, Osborn
Collection, New Haven, 06520. Stephen R
Parks, Cur
Holdings: Mss
IL —UNIVERSITY OF ILLINOIS,
URBANA/CHAMPAIGN, Library, Rare
Book Room, 346 Library, Urbana, 61801.
Norman B Brown, Asst Dir for Special
Collections; N Frederick Nash, Librn
Holdings: Cat Mss Maps Pix Slides
Microforms
Notes: Extensive collection, described in:
Catalog of the Rare Book Room, (Boston: G
K Hall, 1972). Supplement (1978).
IN —INDIANA UNIVERSITY, Lilly Library,
Seventh St, Bloomington, 47405. William R
Cagle, Librn
Holdings: Vols 300 Cat
Notes: First editions through 19th century
printings, by and about Milton.
KY —UNIVERSITY OF KENTUCKY,
Margaret I King Library, Dept of Special
Collections, Lexington, 40506. William
Marshall, Head
Holdings: Vols 600 Cat
Notes: Some first editions of Milton's works,
other early editions, and books and articles
about him and his work.
MD —JOHNS HOPKINS UNIVERSITY,
Milton S Eisenhower Library, Charles & 34
Sts, Baltimore, 21218. Ann S Gwyn,
Assistant Dir for Special Collections
Holdings: Vols Cat Mss Microforms
Notes: The Osler Collection (Tudor and
Stuart Club) contains original editions of
Shelley, Milton, Keats, Donne, Defoe,
Thomas Fuller, Golden Book of Marcus
Aurelius (1559). A collection of his articles
made by Walt Whitman. 17th and 18th
century commonplace books in English and
French, in ms. Most English translations of
Jakob Boehme. Cards in main catalog. Also,
not included in the above figure, Pollard and
Redgrave's, and Wing's Early English Books
on microfilm.
MA —HARVARD UNIVERSITY LIBRARY,
Widener Library, Cambridge, 02138.
Holdings: Cat
MI —UNIVERSITY OF MICHIGAN, Library,
Dept of Rare Books & Special Collections,
Ann Arbor, 48109. Robert J Starring, Head
Holdings: Cat Mss
NY —NEW YORK PUBLIC LIBRARY,
Research Libraries, General Research

Division, Fifth Ave & 42 St, New York,
10018. Rodney Phillips, Chief
Holdings: Vols (2,225,000) Cat Maps Pix
Microforms
Budget: ($775,718)
NY —NEW YORK PUBLIC LIBRARY, Rare
Books and Manuscripts Div, Fifth Ave & 42
St, New York, 10018. William L Joyce, Asst
Dir; Francis O Mattson, Curator
Holdings: Cat
Budget: ($7161)
Notes: Literary first editions. Incl notable
collections of Shakespeare, Milton, Walton,
Bunyan and Whitman (The Oscar Lion
Collection).
TX —UNIVERSITY OF TEXAS LIBRARIES,
General Libraries, PO Box P, Austin, 78713.
Carolyn Bucknell, Asst Dir for Collection
Development
Holdings: Cat Microforms

MILWAUKEE, WISCONSIN

WI —LEGISLATIVE REFERENCE BUREAU
LIBRARY, City of Milwaukee, City Hall
Rm 404, 200 E Wells St, Milwaukee, 53202.
Ronald Leonhardt, Dir
Holdings: Vols (50,000) Cat Maps Pix
Microforms
Notes: Official depository for City of
Milwaukee documents.
WI —MILWAUKEE PUBLIC LIBRARY, 814
W Wisconsin Ave, Milwaukee, 53233.
Donald J Sager, City Librn
Holdings: Cat Mss Maps Pix
Notes: Incl books, newspapers, pictures
(photo and litho), mss, maps, pamphlets,
City of Milwaukee Archives, documents,
periodicals. Incl index to the *Milwaukee
Sentinel*, 1837-1890. Also 2500 maps of all
types of the city and county.

**MIME TROUPE, SAN FRANCISCO see
San Francisco Mime Troupe**

MIMES AND MIMING

CA —UNIVERSITY OF CALIFORNIA,
DAVIS, Shields Library, Dept of Special
Collections, Davis, 95616. Donald Kunitz,
Head; C Danial Elliott, Asst Head
Holdings: Cat Mss Pix
Notes: 21,000 items. Records incl scripts,
scenarios, clippings, business clippings,
business correspondence, etc.
See also entry under San Francisco Mime
Troupe
CA —UNIVERSITY OF CALIFORNIA, LOS
ANGELES, Research Library, Dept of
Special Collections, 405 Hilgard Ave, Los
Angeles, 90024. Edward Shreeves,
Chairman, Bibliographers Group; David S
Zeidberg, Head
Holdings: Cat
Notes: 50 British and American turn-ups or
Harlequinades.
KY —HOPKINSVILLE COMMUNITY
COLLEGE, Library, North Dr,
Hopkinsville, 42240. Marjanna J Frising,
Librn
Holdings: Vols (500) Cat Phonorecords
Audiotapes Filmstrips
Notes: Incl most notable Broadway plays,
both musical and non-musical, with sound-
tracks available for most. Also a large
collection of children's and one-act plays,
incl comedy and mystery plays.
MA —HARVARD UNIVERSITY LIBRARY,
Theatre Collection, Cambridge, 02138.
Jeanne T Newlin, Cur
Holdings: Cat Mss Pix Slides Microforms
Notes: One of the largest existing collections
of playbills, programs, prints, photographs,
promptbooks, and other materials relating to
the performing arts, the scope is worldwide;
resources on the English-speaking stage of
the 18th and 19th centuries are unequalled.
Incl materials on ballet and modern dance,
the circus, magic, minstrel shows, cinema,
and pantomime. For description, see
Harvard Library Bulletin, VI (1925): pp 281-
301.
†NY —NEIGHBORHOOD PLAYHOUSE
SCHOOL OF THE THEATRE, Irene
Lewisohn Library, 340 E 54 St, New York,
10022. Alice G Owen, Librn
Holdings: Vols 360

MIMES AND MIMING (cont.)

NY —NEW YORK PUBLIC LIBRARY,
Performing Arts Research Center, Billy Rose
Theatre Collection, 111 Amsterdam Ave,
New York, 10023. Dorothy L Swerdlove,
Cur
Holdings: Cat
Notes: The collection incl the Townsend
Walsh Collection, a rare assembling of 19th
and early 20th century circus material--route
books, programs, posters--mostly on the
circus in the US and Great Britain, but with
extensive material on European circus--19th-
20th centuries. Also, American Mime
Theatre. Incl photographs, programs, etc.

BC —UNIVERSITY OF VICTORIA,
McPherson Library, Victoria, V8W 3H5,
Can.
Notes: The II C Sage Collection of English
Juvenile Drama. Representative material on
pantomime figures, etc, by the early 20th-
century publisher, George Conetta.

ON —METROPOLITAN TORONTO
LIBRARY, Theatre Dept, 789 Yonge St,
Toronto, M4W 2G8, Can. Heather
McCallum, Head
Holdings: Vols (30,500) Mss Pix Slides
Phonorecords Microforms
Notes: Book and nonbook materials in all
areas of the performing arts except music:
theatre and drama, moving pictures, dance,
television and radio programming, and
varieties of popular entertainment such as
circus, music hall, vaudeville, puppetry and
pantomime. Special collections relating to
the history of the performing arts in Canada.
Access to the book and periodical collection
is provided through a divided dictionary
COM catalog on microfiche. In addition,
extensive card indexes are available.
Published descriptions of the collection:
Heather McCallum. Research Collections in
Canadian Libraries, Part II. Special Studies
no I. *Theatre resources in Canadian
collections* (Ottawa: National Library of
Canada, 1973); Heather McCallum. "The
Theatre Department of the Metropolitan
Toronto Library" in *Special Collections,* vol
1 (1), fall 1981.

MIMIC THEATRE see Toy Theatres

MINANGKABU LANGUAGE see
Menangkabu Language

MIND see Intellect; Psychology

MIND AND BODY

AZ —WORLD UNIVERSITY, Library, 711 E
Blacklidge Dr, Tucson, 85719. Howard John
Zitko, Cur
Holdings: Vols (15,000) Cat Mss Maps
Audiotapes
Notes: Collection concerns the "frontier
sciences." No interlibrary loan.

MIND CURE see Christian Science;
Mental Healing; Mind and Body

MINE PLANTING see Mines, Military
and Submarine

MINE WORKERS, UNITED see United
Mine Workers

MINE WORKERS UNION see
International Union of Mine, Mill, and
Smelter Workers

MINER, EARL ROY

CA —UNIVERSITY OF CALIFORNIA, LOS
ANGELES, Research Library, Dept of
Special Collections, 405 Hilgard Ave, Los
Angeles, 90024. Edward Shreeves,
Chairman, Bibliographers Group; David S
Zeidberg, Head
Notes: 18 linear feet of papers.

MINERAL DRESSING

PQ —NORANDA RESEARCH CENTRE,
Library, 240 Hymus Blvd, Pointe-Claire,

H9R 1G5, Can. Shirley Courtis, Librn
Holdings: Vols (7000)

MINERAL INDUSTRIES

CO —COLORADO SCHOOL OF MINES,
Arthur Lakes Library, 14 & Illinois Sts,
Golden, 80401. Hartley K Phinney, Jr, Head
Librn
Holdings: Vols (270,557) Cat Mss Maps
Microforms

MI —MICHIGAN TECHNOLOGICAL
UNIVERSITY, Archives, Copper County
Historical Collections, Houghton, 49931.
Theresa Sanderson Spence, University
Archivist
Notes: A collection of late 19th and early
20th century materials relating to mining,
incl documents, drawings, and other
artifacts. More than 100,000 items from
UOP, Inc, Des Plaines, Ill.

ON —ENERGY, MINES & RESOUCES
CANADA, Headquarters, 580 Booth St,
Ottawa, K1A 0E4, Can. F B Scollie, Chief
Librn
Holdings: Vols (65,000) Cat Microforms
Budget: ($200,000)
Notes: EMR Libraries Network includes the
Headquarters, Conservation and Non-
Petroleum Branch, and Petroleum Incentives
Branch. Topics incl energy and mineral
economics, especially Canadian.

PQ —NORANDA RESEARCH CENTRE,
Library, 240 Hymus Blvd, Pointe-Claire,
H9R 1G5, Can. Shirley Courtis, Librn
Holdings: Vols (7000) Cat Microforms

MINERAL LANDS see Mines and
Mineral Resources

MINERAL OILS—LAW AND
LEGISLATION see Petroleum Law and
Legislation

MINERAL RESOURCES see Mines and
Mineral Resources

MINERAL WATERS

†CT —YALE UNIVERSITY, Medical Library,
333 Cedar St, New Haven, 06520.
Notes: Incl large world-wide pamphlet
collection, arranged geographically, of
resorts, etc, favorable to good health.

IN —HURTY-PECK LIBRARY OF
BEVERAGE LITERATURE, 5650 W
Raymond Street, PO Box 41167,
Indianapolis, 46208. Ben Wilson, Librn
Holdings: Vols (6000) Cat //
Notes: The most comprehensive collection,
in English, in the world on beverages of all
types. History, manufacture, formulae,
customs. Books on beer and brewing; cocoa
and chocolate; coffee; liquors and spirits; soft
drinks; tea; and wine.

MINER, DWIGHT CARROLL

†NY —COLUMBIA UNIVERSITY
LIBRARIES, Butler Library, Rare Book and
Manuscript Library, 535 W 114 St, New
York, 10027.
Notes: The papers of Dwight Carroll Miner,
comprising the extensive files of
correspondence, mss, notes, and printed
materials relating to the history of Columbia
University. Incl the papers of University
Librarian and historian Roger Howson.

MINERALOGY

CA —STANFORD UNIVERSITY, School of
Earth Sciences, Branner Earth Sciences
Library, Stanford, 94305. Charlotte Derksen,
Head Librn
Holdings: Vols (70,000) Cat Maps
Notes: Incl 80,000 maps. Formerly the
Branner Geological Library.

CO —COLORADO SCHOOL OF MINES,
Arthur Lakes Library, 14 & Illinois Sts,
Golden, 80401. Hartley K Phinney, Jr, Head
Librn
Holdings: Vols (270,557) Cat Mss Maps
Microforms

DC —NATIONAL GEOGRAPHIC
SOCIETY, Library, 1146 16th St NW,

Washington, 20036. Susan Fifer Canby, Dir
Holdings: Vols (63,000) Cat Mss Maps Pix
Notes: Material concerning land, sea, and
space exploration--past and present. All
fields of anthropology, natural history,
geography, etc.

DC —SMITHSONIAN INSTITUTION
LIBRARIES, Natural History Branch,
Washington, 20560. Sylvia Churgin, Chief
Librn
Holdings: Vols (2350) Cat Maps Pix

IL —UNIVERSITY OF ILLINOIS,
URBANA/CHAMPAIGN, Library,
Geology Library, 223 Natural History Bldg,
Urbana, 61801. Dederick Ward, Librn
Holdings: Vols (105,186) Cat Maps
Microforms

IN —PURDUE UNIVERSITY LIBRARIES,
Geosciences Library, West Lafayette, 47907.
Carolyn Lassoon, Librn
Holdings: Vols (15,000) Cat
Notes: Geosciences.

ME —BOWDOIN COLLEGE, Library,
Brunswick, 04011. Dianne M Gutscher, Cur
of Special Collections
Holdings: Cat Mss
Notes: The Parker Cleaveland Papers cover
the period 1795-1858 and number about
1600 items. They are principally concerned
with his tenure as professor of chemistry,
mineralogy, and natural philosophy at
Bowdoin. They incl personal
correspondence, lecture notes, and writings
on scientific subjects, incl his mss of the first
American work on mineralogy and geology.

MD —US BUREAU OF MINES, Avondale
Metallurgy Research Center, Library, 4900
La Salle Rd, Avondale, 20782. Paul F
Moran, Librn
Holdings: Vols (11,000) Cat
Budget: ($35,000)
Notes: Incl corrosion, flotation, particulate
mineralogy.

MA —HARVARD UNIVERSITY LIBRARY,
Geological Sciences Library, 24 Oxford St,
Cambridge, 02138. Constance Wick, Librn
Holdings: Vols (51,000) Cat Mss Maps Pix
16mm Films Microforms
Notes: The Geological Sciences Library
supports the research efforts of faculty,
graduate students, and upper-level
undergraduate and graduate instruction in
the geological sciences. Subjects collected
deal with the earth sciences in general,
mineralogy, petrology, geochemistry,
geophysics, crystallography, structural
geology, regional geology, economic geology,
some geomorphology, and some gemology.
The collection incl 850 serial publications
and 15,000 maps.

NM —ROSWELL PUBLIC LIBRARY, 301 N
Pennsylvania Ave, Roswell, 88201. Sarah
Beth Galloway, Library Dir
Holdings: Vols Uncat Maps
Notes: Great majority of collection consists
of bound copies of professional journals.
Many items on petroleum and minerals, with
emphasis on Southwestern US.

NY —AMERICAN MUSEUM OF
NATURAL HISTORY, Library Services
Dept, Central Park W & 79th St, New York,
10024. Nina J Root, Chairwoman; Mary
Genett, Asst Librn for Reference Services
Holdings: Vols (385,000) Cat Mss Maps Pix
Slides Microforms
Notes: Nearly all collections are outstanding
for depth of coverage and international
range. Early and historic works, rare books,
colored illustrations, and relevant serial
publications supplement the modern
scientific publications necessary to the
researches of the scientific staff and the
work of the educational division. Open to
the public.

NY —ENGINEERING SOCIETIES
LIBRARY, 345 E 47 St, New York, 10017.
S Kirk Cabeen, Dir
Holdings: Vols 250,000 Cat Maps 16mm
Films Microforms
Notes: One of the largest, most
comprehensive engineering libraries in the
world. Covers all engineering disciplines;
particularly strong in electrical and
electronic, mechanical, mining and
metallurgical, petroleum, chemical,
industrial, air conditioning and refrigeration

MINERALOGY (cont.)

engineering. Incl Wheeler Collection of early materials on magnetism and electricity. 125,000 bound periodical volumes; 10,000 maps; 5000 serial subscriptions (many foreign-language). Virtually all materials abstracted in *Engineering Index* (1884-date) are incl in Library. Noncirculating, except to members of professional engineering societies which support the Library. See *Engineering Societies Library, New York, Classed Subject Catalog and Index* (Boston: G K Hall, 1963) and *Supplements*, 1-10, 1964-1973.

NY —NEW YORK PUBLIC LIBRARY, Research Libraries, Science and Technology Research Center, Fifth Ave & 42 St, New York, 10018.
Holdings: Vols (1,100,000) Cat Microforms
Budget: ($647,259)

NY —UNIVERSITY OF ROCHESTER, Rush Rhees Library, Geology/Map Library, Rochester, 14627. Arleen N Somerville, Librn
Holdings: Vols (12,424) Cat Maps
Notes: Strong collection in the field and related areas.

PA —CARNEGIE LIBRARY OF PITTSBURGH, Science & Technology Dept, 4400 Forbes Ave, Pittsburgh, 15213. Catherine M Brosky, Dept Head
Holdings: Vols (380,000) Cat Maps Microforms
Budget: ($240,000)
Notes: Subject area well developed with emphasis on North American geology; other continents of secondary interest. Long runs of journals, reports of geological surveys and society publications. Incl abstracts, indexes, bibliographies, literature guides, dictionaries, handbooks, manuals, compilations of data, maps, history and biography. Complete sets of US topographic maps and geologic folios, climatological data, water supply papers and soil surveys.

PA —PENNSYLVANIA STATE UNIVERSITY, Earth & Mineral Sciences Library, 105 Deike Bldg, University Park, 16802. Emilie McWilliams, Head Librn
Holdings: Vols (58,000) Cat Maps Microforms
Budget: ($49,750)
Notes: Incl holdings on material science and engineering, mineral economy and engineering, geomechanics, mineral genergy management, processing, conservation and constitution.

†SD —SOUTH DAKOTA SCHOOL OF MINES & TECHNOLOGY, Devereaux Library, Rapid City, 57701.
Holdings: Vols 6635 Cat Maps Microforms
Notes: This is an updating of information; in flood of 9-10 June 1972, the entire periodical collection was lost. Almost complete set of US Geological Survey (incl early territorial surveys) and Bureau of Mines materials. Also have a supporting collection of periodicals in the areas of geology, mineralogy, mining and metallurgical engineering. Microfilm copy (complete set) of the US Bureau of Mines "Mine Map Depository (Denver)" material.

WI —MILWAUKEE PUBLIC MUSEUM, Reference Library, 800 W Wells St, Milwaukee, 53233. Judith Campbell Turner, Museum Librn
Holdings: Vols (90,000) Cat Maps Microforms

WI —UNIVERSITY OF WISCONSIN, MILWAUKEE, Greene Memorial Museum, 3367 N Downer Ave, PO Box 413, Milwaukee, 53201. Robert E Gernand, Acting Cur
Holdings: Vols (250) Uncat
Notes: Noncirculating collection of books used by Thomas A Greene in his study of minerals and fossils, 1860-1894. Incl 150,000 specimens.

AB —ALBERTA OIL SANDS INFORMATION CENTRE, 6th Floor, Highfield Place, 10010-106 St, Edmonton, T5J 3L8, Can. Helga Radvanyi, Mgr
Notes: "Major activity of the Centre has been preparation of the Alberta Oil Sands

Index. However...scope has broadened to include the Heavy Oil/Enhanced Recovery Index," and other informative literature.

ON —NATIONAL MUSEUMS OF CANADA, Library Services Directorate, Ottawa, K1A 0M8, Can. Valerie Monkhouse, Director
Holdings: Vols (90,000) Cat Mss Microforms
Budget: ($81,000)
Notes: Emphasis on Canadian and circumpolar natural history. Collection incl botany, herpetology, ichthyology, invertebrate zoology, malacology, mammology, mineralogy, ornithology, paleobiology, zooarchaeology. Exceptional collections in lichenology, bryology, malacology, ornithology. Research collection, interlibrary loans available, public may use on the premises.

ON —ROYAL ONTARIO MUSEUM, Main Library and Archives, 100 Queen's Park, Toronto, M5S 2C6, Can. Julia Matthews, Head Librn
Holdings: Vols (85,000) Cat
Notes: Since January 1977, acquisitions have been entered in UTLAS.

MINERALS see Mineralogy; Mines and Mineral Resources

MINERS

CO —UNIVERSITY OF COLORADO, Libraries, Western Historical Collections, Boulder, 80309.
Holdings: Mss Pix
Notes: The Western Federation of Miners was a radical hard-rock miners' union that began in Montana and spead to Idaho, Washington, Utah, Colorado, Arizona, New Mexico, Nevada, and California. Its successor, Mine-Mill, resurged during the New Deal years. It merged with the United Steelworkers in 1967. This collection consists of 700 boxes of files, correspondence, and publications; 500 bound vols of minutes, ledgers, magazines, and court proceedings; the library of the Research Department, consisting of approx 360 linear feet of books, pamphlets, and periodicals; a number of artifacts and curios incl union banners and seals, convention delegates' ribbons, photographs and membership cards. Most of the materials are for the period 1936-1967. Finding aides are available.

IN —INDIANA UNIVERSITY, Lilly Library, Seventh St, Bloomington, 47405. William R Cagle, Librn
Holdings: Cat Mss
Notes: 1000 issues of California gold rush newspapers. Mss include some overland diaries and correspondence of miners.

MINERS—FOLKLORE see Folklore of Mines

MINES, LOST see Lost Mines

MINES, MILITARY AND SUBMARINE

FL —US NAVAL COASTAL SYSTEMS CENTER, Technical Information Service Branch, Panama City, 32407. Myrtle J Rhodes, Librn
Holdings: Vols (30,000) Cat
Notes: Coastal and ocean technology, inshore undersea warfare, mine countermeasures, torpedo defense, underwater sound.

PA —PENNSYLVANIA STATE UNIVERSITY, Earth & Mineral Sciences Library, 105 Deike Bldg, University Park, 16802. Emilie McWilliams, Head Librn
Holdings: Vols (58,000) Cat Maps Microforms
Budget: ($49,750)
Notes: This collection includes substantial numbers of geological maps, and strong periodical holdings including microform.

MINES AND MINERAL RESOURCES

CA —UPDATA PUBLICATIONS INC, Library, 1756 Westwood Blvd, Los Angeles,

90024. Sara Ferguson, Dir; Judith Harrington, Librn
Holdings: Vols (300) Uncat Maps Microforms
Notes: Earth resources. Incl 800,000 microforms, 35 periodicals.

CO —COLORADO GEOLOGICAL SURVEY, Library, 1313 Sherman St Rm 715, Denver, 80203. Louise Slade, Librn
Holdings: Vols (3000) Uncat Mss Maps Pix Microforms
Notes: Mineral resources of Colorado.

NM —ROSWELL PUBLIC LIBRARY, 301 N Pennsylvania Ave, Roswell, 88201. Sarah Beth Galloway, Library Dir
Holdings: Vols 600 Cat Maps
Notes: Great majority of collection consists of bound copies of professional journals. Many items on petroleum and minerals, with emphasis on Southwestern US.

NY —NEW YORK PUBLIC LIBRARY, Research Libraries, Science and Technology Research Center, Fifth Ave & 42 St, New York, 10018.
Holdings: Vols (1,100,000) Cat Microforms
Budget: ($647,259)

PA —FRANKLIN INSTITUTE LIBRARY, 20 & The Parkway, Philadelphia, 19103. Miriam Padusis, Dir; Charles Wilt, Readers Servs Librn
Holdings: Vols (300,000) Cat Maps Pix Microforms

AB —ALBERTA OIL SANDS INFORMATION CENTRE, 6th Floor, Highfield Place, 10010-106 St, Edmonton, T5J 3L8, Can. Helga Radvanyi, Mgr
Notes: "Major activity of the Centre has been preparation of the Alberta Oil Sands Index. However...scope has broadened to include the Heavy Oil/Enhanced Recovery Index," and other informative literature.

ON —ENERGY, MINES & RESOUCES CANADA, Headquarters, 580 Booth St, Ottawa, K1A 0E4, Can. F B Scollie, Chief Librn
Holdings: Vols (65,000) Cat Microforms
Budget: ($200,000)
Notes: EMR Libraries Network includes the Headquarters, Conservation and Non-Petroleum Branch, and Petroleum Incentives Branch. Topics incl energy and mineral economics, especially Canadian.

ON —ONTARIO MINISTRY OF NATURAL RESOURCES, Mines Library, 77 Grenville St, Rm 812, Toronto, M5S 1B3, Can. Nancy Thurston, Librn
Holdings: Vols (40,000) Cat Maps Microforms
Budget: ($30,000)
Notes: Geology of Ontario. Incl 20,000 maps. Depository for US and Canadian federal publications in geology and mining.

MINES AND MINERAL RESOURCES—FOLKLORE see Folklore of Mines

MINES AND MINERAL RESOURCES—HISTORY

AZ —NORTHERN ARIZONA UNIVERSITY, Special Collection Library, CU Box 6022, Flagstaff, 86011. Peter M Whiteley, Coordr/Archivist; William Mullane, Librn
Holdings: Uncat Mss
Notes: (1) Report by G W Crane, a mining geologist, entitled *Allison Mine, Pima County, Arizona*, containing information on the mine's history, geology, production, and prospective development, 1940. (2) Charles Dunning Collection: Detailed notes of Arizona mining history used in preparation for his book, *Rocks to Riches; The Story of American Mining, Past, Present, and Future, as Reflected in the Colorful History of Mining in Arizona* (Phoenix: Southwest Publishing Company, 1959). (3) Mining Reports Collection: reports on various mines mostly located in southern Arizona, ie, Banner Mining District, Gold Bullion Mine, and Baboquivari Mining District, 1929, 1936, 1939, and 1951. (4) Daniel M Phillips Collection: four stock certificates of the Mexican Mine Developing Company in the

MINES AND MINERAL RESOURCES—HISTORY (cont.)

Arizona Territory, bought by Daniel M Phillips, 1904. (5) Louis Reber Collection: Reber, first paid geologist of the United Verde Copper Company, developed the concept of aerial photography for ore identification. Incl correspondence and records of mining activities in Arizona and the US, 1912-1950's and mining activities in South Africa and Rhodesia, 1920's.
See also entries under Copper Mines and Mining; Mines and Mining

CA —UNIVERSITY OF CALIFORNIA, DAVIS, Shields Library, Dept of Special Collections, Davis, 95616. Donald Kunitz, Head; C Danial Elliott, Asst Head
Holdings: Uncat Mss Maps Pix
Notes: Business records and ms materials related to the growth of mining in the California gold fields incl account books, stock records, bullion books of mining companies such as the Empire Mine, Pioneer Reduction Company, Granite Hill Mining Company; personal correspondence, accounts, and memorabilia of pioneers; photographs of mining towns and mines in operation; related printed material. Collection covers 1849-1920. 2800 items.

MI —MICHIGAN TECHNOLOGICAL UNIVERSITY, Archives, Copper County Historical Collections, Houghton, 49931. Theresa Sanderson Spence, University Archivist
Holdings: Vols (1500) Cat Mss Maps Pix Slides Microforms
Notes: Michigan-Copper Country. Description of collection in *Michigan Chronicle*, 1st quarter, 1973. Accession lists are available for some of the collections. The collecting program embraces the university and all areas of the economic, cultural and social life of the people and institutions of the Copper Country (Baraga, Houghton, Keweenaw, and Ontonogan Counties). Special strength is in the mining history and mining company reports. Personal and business records, maps and photographs, broadsides, family histories, newspapers and oral materials as well as slides and film have been collected. Extensive holdings in area newspapers. As a regional depository for the state archives, provides access to a variety of research materials. Also, Keweenaw Historical Society Collection, see *Michigan History Magazine*, vols 1 (1917), 129-155.

WY —UNIVERSITY OF WYOMING, William Robertson Coe Library, Western History Research Center, Laramie, 82071. Gene M Gressley, Dir, Asst to Pres
Holdings: Mss
Notes: One of the collecting areas at the Western History Research Center is "Mining History," featuring the papers and memorabilia of approximately 105 outstanding mining engineers active in the 20th-century American West, and papers of some individuals active prior to the turn of the century.

MINES AND MINERAL RESOURCES—MAPS

†CA —UNIVERSITY OF CALIFORNIA, DAVIS, Peter J Shields Memorial Library, Map Collection, Davis, 95616.

DC —LIBRARY OF CONGRESS, Geography and Map Division, Washington, 20540. John A Wolter, Chief
Holdings: Cat Mss Maps Pix Slides Microforms
See also entry under Maps and Atlases - Collections

MINES AND MINING

AL —US DEPT OF AGRICULTURE, SCIENCE & EDUCATION ADMINISTRATION, National Tillage Machinery Laboratory, Library, PO Box 792, Auburn, 36830. William A Gill, Collaborator
Holdings: Vols (39,000) Cat Mss Maps Pix Slides 16mm Films Microforms
Budget: ($20,000)
Notes: The National Tillage Machinery

Laboratory (NTML) has a special technical library comprised of highly selective engineering and physical science materials pertinent to soil-machine relations, such as tillage, earthmoving, mining, soil trafficability, and vehicle mobility. A high percentage of the library material comes from sources outside the US and outside agriculture. Particularly strong in Russian-language literature.

AZ —PHOENIX PUBLIC LIBRARY, Arizona Room, 12 E McDowell, Phoenix, 85004. Jeannette Brush, Librn
Holdings: Vols (30,000) Cat Maps Pix
Budget: ($12,000)
See also entry under Arizona - History.

AZ —ARIZONA STATE UNIVERSITY, Library, Arizona Collection, Tempe, 85281. Edward C Oetting, Head
Holdings: Cat Mss
Notes: Papers of 50 individuals associated with Arizona politics, business, mines, and cattle ranching.

CA —KERN COUNTY LIBRARY SYSTEM, 1315 Truxtun Ave, Bakersfield, 93301. Mary Haas, Geology, Mining, Petroleum Librn
Holdings: Vols (28,256) Cat Maps Microforms
Budget: (28,256) Cat Maps Microforms
Notes: Deals with California and western states primarily. Incl 5000 maps.

CA —CLAREMONT COLLEGES, Norman F Sprague Memorial Library, 12 & Dartmouth, Claremont, 91711. David Kuhner, Librn
Holdings: Vols 1000 Cat Mss Maps Pix
Notes: The reference library collected by Herbert Clark Hoover and Lou Henry Hoover in the preparation of their 1912 translation of *De re metallica*. Incl 24 incunabula, 6 mss, titles of 16th to 19th centuries, with emphasis on mining, metallurgy, early science, and travel. Hoover's correspondence (approx 600 pieces) with British & European booksellers, period 1907-1914. Printed catalog, "Bibliotheca de Re Metallica," published in 1980. Restricted use.

CA —LOS ANGELES PUBLIC LIBRARY, Science & Technology Dept, 630 W Fifth St, Los Angeles, 90071. Billie M Connor, Dept Head
Holdings: Vols 18,000 Maps Microforms
Notes: Extensive holdings of state geology department publications and maps of the Western states including Alaska and Hawaii, US Geological Survey, US Bureau of Mines, and the geology departments of major universities. Complete sets of publications and indexes of major geological societies including the Geological Society of American and the American Association of Petroleum Geologists. Partially cataloged.

CA —UNIVERSITY OF CALIFORNIA, LOS ANGELES, Research Library, Dept of Special Collections, 405 Hilgard Ave, Los Angeles, 90024. Edward Shreeves, Chairman, Bibliographers Group; David S Zeidberg, Head
Notes: Photographs of the Mother Lode country by Louis J Stellman.

CA —CALIFORNIA DIVISION OF MINES AND GEOLOGY LIBRARY, Ferry Bldg, Rm 2022, San Francisco, 94111. Angela Brunton, Librn
Holdings: Vols (28,500) Cat Mss Maps Pix Microforms
Budget: ($5650)
Notes: Incl theses on California geology; publications of USGS and USBM, state governments (other than California) concerning mining and geology; publications of foreign governments concerning geology and mining; history of mining in California.

CA —STANFORD UNIVERSITY LIBRARIES, Cecil H Green Library, Stanford, 94305. Michael T Ryan, Cur
Notes: Research collection.

CO —UNIVERSITY OF COLORADO, Libraries, Western Historical Collections, Boulder, 80309.
Holdings: Mss Pix
Notes: The Western Federation of Miners was a radical hard-rock miners' union that began in Montana and spead to Idaho, Washington, Utah, Colorado, Arizona, New Mexico, Nevada, and California. Its

successor, Mine-Mill, resurged during the New Deal years. It merged with the United Steelworkers in 1967. This collection consists of 700 boxes of files, correspondence, and publications; 500 bound vols of minutes, ledgers, magazines, and court proceedings; the library of the Research Department, consisting of approx 360 linear feet of books, pamphlets, and periodicals; a number of artifacts and curios incl union banners and seals, convention delegates' ribbons, photographs and membership cards. Most of the materials are for the period 1936-1967. Finding aides are available.

CO —COLORADO HISTORICAL SOCIETY, Research Collections, 1300 Broadway, Denver, 80203. Catherine Kane, Head Public Service and Access
Holdings: Cat Pix Slides
Notes: 250,000 photographs of western and Colorado subjects incl gold rush, mining, Indians, natural features, transportation, cities and towns, portraits. William Henry Jackson photographs of area west of Mississippi.

CO —DENVER PUBLIC LIBRARY, Western History Department, 1357 Broadway, Denver, 80203. Eleanor M Gehres, Head
Holdings: Vols (50,000) Cat Mss Maps Pix Audiotapes Microforms
Notes: Western US History. The department has a separate catalog, published in 1970 in 7 vols by G K Hall Co. First supplement published in 1975 in 1 vol. There is a subject index of some 3 million entries to newspapers and magazines of the Rocky Mountain region, added to daily. The Western Newspaper Microfilm Center contains approx 7000 reels of Western US newspapers. Collection has ca 275,000 negatives and prints of Western life; and ca 2500 maps, cataloged and classified.

CO —FORT LEWIS COLLEGE, Library, Southwest Collection, College Heights, Durango, 81301. Daniel W Lester, Dir
Holdings: Vols (7000) Cat Mss Maps Pix Slides Microforms
Budget: ($3800)
Notes: Also have separate catalog of the special collections concerning the Southwest, Indians, mine records, railroad records, etc.

CO —COLORADO SCHOOL OF MINES, Arthur Lakes Library, 14 & Illinois Sts, Golden, 80401. Hartley K Phinney, Jr, Head Librn
Holdings: Vols (270,557) Cat Mss Maps Microforms

MD —US BUREAU OF MINES, Avondale Metallurgy Research Center, Library, 4900 La Salle Rd, Avondale, 20782. Paul F Moran, Librn
Holdings: Vols (11,000) Cat
Budget: ($35,000)
Notes: Incl corrosion, flotation, particulate mineralogy.

MI —MICHIGAN TECHNOLOGICAL UNIVERSITY, Archives, Copper County Historical Collections, Houghton, 49931. Theresa Sanderson Spence, University Archivist
Notes: A collection of late 19th and early 20th century materials relating to mining, incl documents, drawings, and other artifacts. More than 100,000 items from UOP, Inc, Des Plaines, Ill.

MN —NORTHEAST MINNESOTA HISTORICAL CENTER, University of Minnesota, Duluth, Library 375, Duluth, 55812. Patricia Maus, Administrator
Notes: The Northeast Minnesota Historical Center is jointly maintained by the University of Minnesota, Duluth, and the St Louis County Historical Society. Local and regional history collections with emphasis on transportation, lumbering, mining. Photograph collection. Photocopy service available.

MO —WASHINGTON UNIVERSITY, Earth and Planetary Sciences Library, Forsythe & Skinker Blvds, Saint Louis, 63130. Deborah Hartwig, Librn
Holdings: Vols (25,335) Cat Maps Pix Microforms

MT —MONTANA STATE UNIVERSITY, Library, Bozeman, 59717. Minnie Ellen

MINES AND MINING (cont.)

Paugh, Special Collections Librn
Holdings: Vols (7000)// Mss Maps Pix
Notes: Leggat-Donahoe Collection.
Collection of Alexander Leggat of Butte,
whose father was active in opening the
mines. Mr Leggat's interests were mining,
exploration, and the fur trade. There are
excellent Indian materials in the collection.

NV —UNIVERSITY OF NEVADA, RENO,
Mines Library, Reno, 89557. Mary B Ansari,
Mines Librn; Linda P Newman, Asst Mines
and Map Librn
Holdings: Vols (32,000) Cat Maps
Microforms
Budget: ($52,000)
Notes: Mines Library attempts to collect all
PhD and Masters theses on Nevada geology.
Only those originating at the University of
Nevada, Reno, are available for ILL.
Maintains an index of references to the
literature on Nevada geology and mining.

NJ —SUSSEX COUNTY LIBRARY, Franklin
Area Branch, 103 Main St, Franklin, 07416.
Holdings: // Uncat Mss Maps Pix
Notes: The gift of Franklin native Fred J
Stephens, the History of Mining in Northern
New Jersey Collection will be housed at the
Franklin Area Branch of the Sussex County
Library. Extensive manuscript collection incl
reports, photos, maps, books, pamphlets,
periodicals, and correspondence amassed
during years of research.

NM —MUSEUM OF NEW MEXICO, Photo
Archives, Box 2087, Santa Fe, 87503.
Arthur L Olivas, Cur; Richard Rudisill,
Photo Historian
Holdings: Cat Pix Slides
Budget: ($9000)
Notes: Archives incl 200,000 photographs,
cataloged, and 40,000 slides. Primary
function of the archives is to preserve
significant historical material, and these
pictures are mainly for research rather than
general browsing. Photographs may be
ordered as research copies for set fees.
Reproduction or publication requires written
permission plus additional required fees.
Subject matter covered is extensive, incl
Southwest town views, Southwest Indians,
military subjects, missions, pioneer life,
recreation (indoor and outdoor, toys, games,
gambling, camping, etc), disasters, exhibits
and expositions, portraits (those identified
filed by last name), tools and equipment
(agricultural, mechanical, housekeeping, etc),
and transportation (railroad, stagecoaches,
carriages, wagons, etc).

NY —COLUMBIA UNIVERSITY
LIBRARIES, Rare Book & Manuscript
Library, 801 Butler Library, 535 W 114 St,
New York, 10027. Kenneth A Lohf, Librn
Notes: More than 32,000 items documenting
the rise of William Russell Grace's shipping
business and other materials relating to his
career as mayor of New York. Incl records
and correspondence relating to all aspects of
the shipping business in New York and
South America, mining interest in Peru and
Chile, and transportation in Costa Rica and
Nicaragua. Family memorabilia and
photographs, materials concerning New
York Politics, banking and insurance, real
estate interests and Catholic charities, and
letters from Chester A Arthur, John Jacob
Astor, Andrew Carnegie, Grover Cleveland,
Hamilton Fish, John Hay and J Pierpont
Morgan. Restricted use.

OR —BAKER COUNTY PUBLIC LIBRARY,
2400 Resort St, Baker, 97814. Paul C
Crouthamal, Librn
Holdings: Vols (1700) Cat Mss Maps Pix
Microforms
Budget: ($2000)
Notes: Baker County, Oregon materials,
historical and current, emphasizing
genealogy, mining, agriculture and the
people. Incl any fiction with Oregon as the
locale. Local newspapers on microfilm, 1870-
date, but incomplete for early years. 50 files
on local plants, 1953-date. with separate
catalog. Incl 300 maps.

PA —PENNSYLVANIA DEPT OF
ENVIRONMENTAL RESOURCES, Office
of Environmental Protection, Technical
Reference Library, Fulton Bldg, 17th Floor,
Box 2063, Harrisburg, 17120. Wanda R Bell,
Librn
Holdings: Vols (2000) Cat Slides Microfilm
Microfiche
Budget: 5
Notes: 10,000 technical reports; water and
wastewater feasibility plans; PA Bulletin,
1970-Present; water pollution; solid waste;
mining and reclamation; air quality; acid
mine drainage.

PA —PENNSYLVANIA STATE
UNIVERSITY, Earth & Mineral Sciences
Library, 105 Deike Bldg, University Park,
16802. Emilie McWilliams, Head Librn
Holdings: Vols (58,000) Cat Maps
Microforms
Budget: ($49,750)
Notes: Incl holdings on material science and
engineering, mineral economy and
engineering, geomechanics, mineral energy
management, processing, conservation and
constitution.

RI —BROWN UNIVERSITY, John Hay
Library, 20 Prospect St, Providence, 02912.
Mark N Brown, Cur Mss
Holdings: Vols (3500) // Cat Mss Maps
Notes: George Earl Church Collection,
formed by a civil engineer, explorer and
Fellow of the Royal Geographic Society,
who specialized in railroad construction.
Although part of the collection is devoted to
American Revolutionary and Civil War
history, the majority, over 2000 volumes,
pertains to Central and South America. The
imprints, which are predominantly 18th
century, include Lima, Madrid, Rome,
Mexico City, Seville, Barcelona, Lisbon, and
Cadiz as well as *Nova orbis regionum as
insularum veteribus incognitarum* (Basle:
1537). Major subject areas are: anthropology,
commerce, economics, engineering,
ethnology, geography, history, law, mineral
resources, railroad surveys, voyages of
exploration and dictionaries of the South
American Indian languages. The most
significant ms is historical account of the
Bolivian mining town of Potosi from p1545-
1737.

†SD —SOUTH DAKOTA SCHOOL OF
MINES & TECHNOLOGY, Devereaux
Library, Rapid City, 57701.
Holdings: Vols (166,200) Cat Maps
Audiotapes Filmstrips Microforms
Budget: ($70,000)
Notes: Supportive collection incl an almost
complete set of US Geological Survey
materials (incl early Territorial Surveys); a
micrifilm copy (complete set) of the US
Bureau of Mines "Mine Map Depository
(Denver)" material; periodicals and technical
reports (NASA, ACRL, JPL, etc) in
engineering and geology; extensive
government document materials (NBS,
Bureau of Mines, etc).

WA —WESTERN WASHINGTON
UNIVERSITY, Center for Pacific Northwest
Studies, High St, Bellingham, 98225. James
W Scott, Dir
Holdings: // Mss Maps
Notes: The Trinity Development Company
was involved in North Cascades mining
operations from the 1920s and into the
1930s. These remaining records were
recovered from an abandoned mine near
Lake Chelan. Incl are numerous maps and
blueprints in various stages of deterioration,
and a variety of operational financial
records. Partially cataloged.

†WA —WASHINGTON STATE
UNIVERSITY, Library, Manuscripts,
Archives & Special Collections, Pullman,
99164. John F Guido, Head
Holdings: Cat Mss Maps Pix
Notes: The Carl Parcher Russell papers, a
vast resource (24,916 items; 45 linear feet)
on American Indian and Western pioneer
activities and artifacts. Much on the fur
trade; pioneer life; mountain men and
trapping; wildlife; primitive life in detail.
Also the National Park Service, parks,
monuments, etc. Described in *Carl Parcher
Russell: An Indexed Register of His
Scholarly and Professional Papers, 1920-
1967, in the Washington State University
Library* (Pullman, 1970), 149 pp.

WY —UNIVERSITY OF WYOMING,
William Robertson Coe Library, Western
History Research Center, Laramie, 82071.
Gene M Gressley, Dir, Asst to Pres
Holdings: Mss
Notes: One of the collecting areas at the
Western History Research Center is "Mining
History," featuring the papers and
memorabilia of approximately 105
outstanding mining engineers active in the
20th-century American West, and papers of
some individuals active prior to the turn of
the century.

AB —ALBERTA OIL SANDS
INFORMATION CENTRE, 6th Floor,
Highfield Place, 10010-106 St, Edmonton,
T5J 3L8, Can. Helga Radvanyi, Mgr
Notes: "Major activity of the Centre has
been preparation of the Alberta Oil Sands
Index. However...scope has broadened to
include the Heavy Oil/Enhanced Recovery
Index," and other informative literature.

AB —SHERRITT RESEARCH CENTRE,
Library, Sherritt Gordon Mines Ltd, Fort
Saskatchewan, T8L 2P2, Can. D Sim, Librn
Holdings: Vols (7000)
Budget: $20,000

PQ —SERVICE DE LA DOCUMENTATION
ET DES RENSEIGNEMENTS
MINISTERE DE L'ENERGIE ET DES
RESSOURCES, 2000B, chemin Sainte-Foy,
7th floor, Quebec, G1R 4X7, Can. Normand
Guerette, Dir
Holdings: Vols (114,800) Slides Videotapes
Notes: In 1979, the Bibliotheque du
ministere des Richesses naturelles du Quebec
merged with the Bibliotheque du ministere
des Terres et Forets. The result of this
merger was the creation of the service de la
Documentation et des Renseignements du
ministere de l'Energie et des Ressources.
Publications: Info-Biblio Terres et Forets;
Mines; Energy.

MINES AND MINING—CHILE

†NY —COLUMBIA UNIVERSITY
LIBRARIES, Butler Library, Rare Book and
Manuscript Library, 535 W 114 St, New
York, 10027.
Notes: The papers of William Russell Grace,
founder of W R Grace & Co and mayor of
New York City, 1880-82 and 1885-86.
Documents the rise of the Grace shipping
business, mining interests in Peru and Chile,
and transportation in Costa Rica and
Nicaragua. Also materials concerning New
York politics, banking and insurance, real
estate interests and Catholic charities.

MINES AND MINING—FOLKLORE see Folklore of Mines

MINES AND MINING—HISTORY

AZ —NORTHERN ARIZONA
UNIVERSITY, Special Collection Library,
CU Box 6022, Flagstaff, 86011. Peter M
Whiteley, Coordr/Archivist; William
Mullane, Librn
Notes: Various collections, incl (1) letter
written by J C Brown about some mineral
claims near the Gap Trading Post (located
some 110 miles north of Flagstaff, Ariz),
1937. (2) Report by Guy W Crane, a mining
geologist, entitled "Allison Mine, Pima
County, Arizona," containing information on
the mine's history, geology, production, and
prospective development, 1940. (3) Charles
Dunning Collection: detailed notes of
Arizona mining history used in preparation
for his book, *Rocks to Riches; The Story of
American Mining, Past, Present, and Future,
as Reflected in the Colorful History of
Mining in Arizona*, Phoenix: Southwest
Publishing Company, 1959. (4) Hotel
Sullivan, Jerome, Ariz, Collection: financial
records, 1917-1931, 1943. Hotel register,
1916-1917. Also incl some records of the
Yavapai Drug Store of Jerome, 1927-1932.
(5) Joe Larson Collection: correspondence
and files concerning mining in Jerome, Ariz,
1897-1950's. Incl the files on the Calumet
and Jerome Copper Companies and the
United Verde Extension Copper Company.

MINES AND MINING—HISTORY (cont.)

Correspondents incl Lewis and Jerome Douglas. (6) Reese Ling Collection: Correspondence, 1912-1916. Incl files on the Arizona Securities and Investment Company, Navajo and Apache County Bank and Trust Company, Bullwacker Gold and Copper Company, McCabe Extension Mining Company of Arizona, Arizona Democratic Party, and Maricopa County Democratic Central Committee. Ling was a lawyer in Arizona. (7) Perry Ling Collection: correspondence and files relating to Jerome and the Verde Valley, 1917-1940's. Incl records of the "Town of Jerome," Verde Valley Game Protection Association, Shea CopperCompany, and United Verde Extension Mining Company. (8) Mascot Copper Company Collection: record books and engineering notebooks of the company in Dos Cabezos, Ariz, 1912-1922. (9) Mining Reports Collection: reports on various mines mostly located in southern Ariz, ie, Banner Mining District, Gold Bullion Mine, and Baboquivari Mining District, 1929, 1936, 1939, 1951. (10) Daniel M Phillips Collection: 4 stock certificates of the Mexican Mine Developing Company in the Arizona Territory bought by Daniel M Phillips, 1904. (11) Jean Provence Collection: financial and mining records, 1908-1911. Gold Star Mining Company, Polaris-Kofa, Yuma County, Ariz. Inventory available. (12) C H Scott Collection: correspondence to his daughter, C F Eastman, Syracuse, NY, 1913-1920, regarding activitiesand life of a solitary miner, Mohave County, Ariz. (13) Jacob Weinberger Collection: Globe Western Copper Company, records, 1906. Delegate to the Arizona Constitutional Convention, 1910. Resident of Globe, Ariz.
See also entries under Copper Mines and Mining; Mines and Mineral Resources-History

CA —CLAREMONT COLLEGES, Norman F Sprague Memorial Library, 12 & Dartmouth, Claremont, 91711. David Kuhner, Librn
Holdings: Vols Cat
Notes: Incl President Herbert Hoover's personal collection of rare technical books (about 1000 vols of the 15th-17th centuries).

NY —STATE UNIVERSITY OF NEW YORK, BINGHAMTON, Glenn G Bartle Library, Binghamton, 13901. Marion Hanscom, Special Collections Librn
Notes: Papers, correspondence, etc of the former aide to the Rockefeller enterprises. Incl much on the Colorado mine strikes.

UT —UNIVERSITY OF UTAH, Marriott Library, Special Collections, Salt Lake City, 84112. Gregory C Thompson, Cur

BC —UNIVERSITY OF BRITISH COLUMBIA, Library, Special Collections Div, 1956 Main Mall, Vancouver, V6T 1Y3, Can. Anne Yandle, Librn
Notes: Records of the Cariboo Gold Quartz Mining Co, Ltd, 1933-1967, Wells, BC.

MINES AND MINING—NEVADA

NV —UNIVERSITY OF NEVADA, RENO, University Library, Special Collections Dept, Reno, 89557. Robert E Blesse, Head
Holdings: Vols (400) Cat Pix Mss
Notes: An extensive collection of books, photographs (2000), and manuscripts (100 cu ft), published reports, government publications dealing with mining in Nevada from the mid 19th century to the present. Primary emphasis is on the Comstock Lode, Virginia City, Nevada but material is available on mining in all geographic areas of the state. The 105 manuscript collections include business papers and records of mining companies, and papers of firms which provided materials and equipment to the mining industry.

MINES AND MINING—PERU

†NY —COLUMBIA UNIVERSITY LIBRARIES, Butler Library, Rare Book and Manuscript Library, 535 W 114 St, New York, 10027.
Notes: The papers of William Russell Grace, founder of W R Grace & Co and mayor of New York City, 1880-82 and 1885-86. Documents the rise of the Grace shipping business, mining interests in Peru and Chile, and transportation in Costa Rica and Nicaragua. Also materials concerning New York politics, banking and insurance, real estate interests and Catholic charities.

MINHAGIM see Jews—Rites and Ceremonies

MINIATURE BOOKS see Bibliography—Microscopic and Miniature Editions

MINIATURE PAINTINGS

MN —SAINT JOHN'S ABBEY & UNIVERSITY, Hill Monastic Manuscript Library, Collegeville, 56321. Julian G Plante, Dir
Holdings: Vols Cat Mss Slides Microforms
Notes: Wherever miniatures and illuminations appear in a ms these are microfilmed in color. In addition to the usual ms catalogs of the collections, a partial iconographic card catalog is available. Reasonable requests will be honored. Incl 70,000 exposures.

MO —THE NELSON-ATKINS MUSEUM OF ART, Kenneth & Helen Spencer Art Reference Library, 4525 Oak St, Kansas City, 64111. Stanley W Hess, Librn

MINIATURE SCORES (MUSIC)

CA —BERKELEY PUBLIC LIBRARY, Art and Music Div, 2090 Kittredge St, Berkeley, 97404. Diane Davenport, Reference
Holdings: Vols (20,000) Cat Pix Slides Audiotapes

CA —OAKLAND PUBLIC LIBRARY, Art, Music and Recreation Section, 125 14 St, Oakland, 94612. Richard Colvig, Senior Librn
Holdings: Vols (5000) Cat Phonorecords Audiotapes
Budget: ($6700)
Notes: 10,000 scores, incl chamber music, instrumental music (piano and organ collections especially strong), miniature scores, opera scores, songs and song collections; 30,000 octavos (anthems and choral music of all kinds); 5000 books about music; 8000 phonorecords; and audiocassettes.

CA —SAN DIEGO PUBLIC LIBRARY, Art, Music & Recreation Sect, 820 E St, San Diego, 92101. Barbara A Tuhill, Supvr
Holdings: Cat
Notes: Score collection of 17,000 pieces covers all types of music incl religious works, opera scores, musical plays, 2200 miniature scores. Complete works of Bach, Berlioz, Beethoven, Mozart, and others are added as published in German reprint. Also, thematic indexes, and study and instructions for playing various musical instruments. General circulation.

OH —CLEVELAND PUBLIC LIBRARY, Fine Arts and Special Collections Department, 325 Superior Ave, Cleveland, 44114. Alice N Loranth, Head
Holdings: Cat
Notes: Incl 2500 miniature and study scores.

PA —WEST CHESTER UNIVERSITY, Music Library, Swope Hall, University Ave, West Chester, 19383. Ruth I Weidner, Music Librn
Budget: ($26,000)
Notes: Large basic music collection (scores, sheet music, and 21,000 phonorecords) which is especially strong in collected works, historical editions, opera, keyboard music, and miniature scores. Incl 24,000 music scores. All music is fully cataloged. Scope of collection is broad and excludes only music education and curriculum materials. Collection does not include books about music or periodicals but does have about 500 reference books. For the most part collection is music published during or availalbe within the past twenty years.

MINIATURES (PORTRAITS) see Miniature Paintings

MINIATURES, MILITARY see Military Miniatures

MINIATURISTS see Miniature Paintings

MINIMAL ART see Art, Minimal

MINIMAL SCULPTURE see Sculpture, Minimal

MINING see Mineral Industries; Mines and Mining; Mining Engineering

MINING ENGINEERING

CA —RAYMOND KAISER ENGINEERS INC, Engineering Library, 300 Lakeside Dr, PO Box 23210, Oakland, 94623. Elaine Zacher, Librn
Holdings: Vols 1000 Cat

KY —UNIVERSITY OF KENTUCKY, Robert E Shaver Library of Engineering, 355 Anderson Hall, Lexington, 40506. Russell H Powell, Engineering Librn
Holdings: Vols (48,000) Cat Microforms

MI —MICHIGAN TECHNOLOGICAL UNIVERSITY, Archives, Copper County Historical Collections, Houghton, 49931. Theresa Sanderson Spence, University Archivist
Notes: A collection of late 19th and early 20th century materials relating to mining, incl documents, drawings, and other artifacts. More than 100,000 items from UOP, Inc, Des Plaines, Ill.

NY —COLUMBIA UNIVERSITY LIBRARIES, Engineering Library, 422 Mudd Bldg, New York, 10027.
Holdings: Vols (177,000) Cat
Notes: All aspects of engineering-- aeronautical, industrial mining, civil, chemical, mechanical, electrical, nuclear. Incl applied mathematics and applied physical sciences. Over (1,000,000) technical reports.

NY —ENGINEERING SOCIETIES LIBRARY, 345 E 47 St, New York, 10017. S Kirk Cabeen, Dir
Holdings: Vols 250,000 Cat Maps 16mm Films Microforms
Notes: One of the largest, most comprehensive engineering libraries in the world. Covers all engineering disciplines; particularly strong in electrical and electronic, mechanical, mining and metallurgical, petroleum, chemical, industrial, air conditioning and refrigeration engineering. Incl Wheeler Collection of early materials on magnetisn and electricity. 125,000 bound periodical volumes; 10,000 maps; 5000 serial subscriptions (many foreign- language). Virtually all materials abstracted in *Engineering Index* (1884-date) are incl in Library. Noncirculating, except to members of professional engineering societies which support the Library. See *Engineering Societies Library, New York, Classed Subject Catalog and Index* (Boston: G K Hall, 1963); and *Supplements*, 1-10, 1964-1973.

NY —NEW YORK PUBLIC LIBRARY, Research Libraries, Science and Technology Research Center, Fifth Ave & 42 St, New York, 10018.
Holdings: Vols (1,100,000) Cat Microforms
Budget: ($647,259)

PA —PENNSYLVANIA DEPT OF ENVIRONMENTAL RESOURCES, Office of Environmental Protection, Technical Reference Library, Fulton Bldg, 17th Floor, Box 2063, Harrisburg, 17120. Wanda R Bell, Librn
Holdings: Vols (2000) Cat Slides Microfilm Microfiche
Budget: 5
Notes: 10,000 technical reports; water and wastewater feasibility plans; PA Bulletin, 1970-Present; water pollution; solid waste; mining and reclamation; air quality; acid mine drainage.

MINING ENGINEERING (cont.)

PA —FRANKLIN INSTITUTE LIBRARY, 20
& The Parkway, Philadelphia, 19103.
Miriam Padusis, Dir; Charles Wilt, Readers
Servs Librn
Holdings: Vols (300,000) Cat Maps Pix
Microforms

†SD —SOUTH DAKOTA SCHOOL OF
MINES & TECHNOLOGY, Devereaux
Library, Rapid City, 57701.
Holdings: Vols (166,200) Cat Maps
Audiotapes Fimstrips Microforms
Budget: ($70,000)
Notes: Supportive collection incl an almost
complete set of US Geological Survey
materials (incl early Territorial Surveys); a
microfilm copy (complete set) of the US
Bureau of Mines "Mine Map Depository
(Denver)" material; periodicals and technical
reports (NASA, ACRL, JPL,etc) in
engineering and geology; extensive
government document materials (NBS,
Bureau of Mines, etc). Emphasis on White
River Badlands.

TX —UNIVERSITY OF TEXAS, EL PASO,
Library, El Paso, 79968. Fred W Hanes, Dir
Holdings: Vols (433,245) Cat
Budget: ($550,667)
Notes: Selective depository of US and Texas
state documents. Complete publications of
USGS and Bureau of Mines. Journal
holdings incl complete backfiles of many
English and US titles in fields of mining and
metallurgical engineering and geology.

ON —RIO ALGOM LIMITED, Library, 120
Adelaide St W, Toronto, M5H 1W5, Can.
Penny Lipman, Librn
Holdings: Vols (1500) Cat
Budget: ($7000)
Notes: Espec mining of uranium and copper;
geology; mining methods; nuclear energy.

PQ —NORANDA RESEARCH CENTRE,
Library, 240 Hymus Blvd, Pointe-Claire,
H9R 1G5, Can. Shirley Courtis, Librn
Holdings: Vols (7000)

MINING ENGINEERING—HISTORY

CA —CLAREMONT COLLEGES, Norman F
Sprague Memorial Library, 12 & Dartmouth,
Claremont, 91711. David Kuhner, Librn
Notes: President Herbert Hoover's personal
collection of rare mining books-about 1000
vols of the 15th-17th centuries.

DE —UNIVERSITY OF DELAWARE, Hugh
M Morris Library, S College Ave, Newark,
19711. T Stuart Dick, Special Collections
Holdings: Cat Mss
Notes: The Unidel History of Chemistry
Collection. 60 percent of the collection deals
with chemistry prior to 1780. Particularly
strong in alchemical works incl some 6
alchemical mss. Also works on mining,
medicine and pharmacy. Notable chemical
pioneers of the 1780-1860 period are well
represented by such men as Lavoisier,
Avogardo, Chaptal, Davy, Faraday,
Fourcroy, Liebig and Volta. Majority of the
collection in French and Italian.

WY —UNIVERSITY OF WYOMING,
William Robertson Coe Library, Performing
Arts Collections, Laramie, 82071. Gene M
Gressley, Dir
Holdings: Mss
Notes: One of the collecting areas at the
Western History Research Center is "Mining
History," featuring the papers and
memorabilia of approximately 75 outstanding
mining engineers active in the 20th-century
American West, and papers of some
individuals active prior to the turn of the
century.

MINISTERS, WOMEN see Women Ministers

MINISTRY see Pastoral Theology

MINKOWSKI, RUDOLPH L., 1895-1976

CA —UNIVERSITY OF CALIFORNIA,
BERKELEY, Bancroft Library, Manuscripts
Division, Berkeley, 94720. James D Hart,
Dir
Notes: Papers.

MINNEAPOLIS, MINNESOTA

MN —MINNEAPOLIS PUBLIC LIBRARY &
INFORMATION CENTER, Minneapolis
History Collection, 300 Nicollet Mall,
Minneapolis, 55401. Dorothy M Burke,
Librn
Holdings: Vols (20,000) Cat Mss Maps Pix
Slides Phonorecords Audiotapes
Budget: ($850)
Notes: Collection contains print and film
materials pertaining to Minneapolis, includes
some Minnesota history. Also have 29 five-
drawer legal files of clips and ephemeral
materials, and direct access to the 119-file
morgue of the old *Minneapolis Times*, a
newspaper which ceased publishing in 1948.
This is especially useful for items covering
the 20s, 30s and 40s. Special card indexes to
plates in architectural serials (local), houses,
buildings, streets, parks, etc; also indexes to
10-20 local newspapers and magazines.
Collection of about 60 neighborhood
newspapers (current and retrospective) and
about 1000 maps and atlases; nearly 250,000
pictures; early (1859-1920) city directories.

MN —MINNEAPOLIS PUBLIC LIBRARY &
INFORMATION CENTER, Municipal
Information Library & Archives, 302 City
Hall, Minneapolis, 55401. Nancy Corcoran,
Librn
Holdings: Vols (55,000) Cat Mss Slides
Notes: Urban affairs, with emphasis on
Minneapolis and Minnesota documents.
Publications: *A Directory of City/County
Information and Service Resources*, and
Minneapolis Communities: A Bibliography.

MINNESOTA

MN —MINNEAPOLIS PUBLIC LIBRARY &
INFORMATION CENTER, Municipal
Information Library & Archives, 302 City
Hall, Minneapolis, 55401. Nancy Corcoran,
Librn
Holdings: Vols 55,000 Cat Mss Slides
Budget: ($6264)
Notes: Urban affairs, with emphasis on
Minneapolis and Minnesota documents.
Publications: *A Directory of City/County
Information and Service Resources*, and
Minneapolis Communities: A Bibliography.

MN —UNIVERSITY OF MINNESOTA,
Libraries, Children's Literature Research
Collections, 109 Walter Library,
Minneapolis, 55455. Karen Nelson Hoyle,
Cur
Holdings: Vols (200) Cat Mss Pix
Notes: Incl first editions, mss, and
illustrations for children's books. Newbery
and Caldecott award books and honor books
and their translations; Mildred L Batchelder
Award nominees in original and US editions;
Minnesota; Dakota and Ojibway Indian
tribes; languages other than English;
correspondence between authors and
illustrators and Dr Irvin Kerlan, Kerlan
Collection.

MINNESOTA—GENEALOGY

MN —BROWN COUNTY HISTORICAL
SOCIETY, Museum and Archives, Center St
and Broadway, Box 116, New Ulm, 56073.
Paul Klammer, Dir
Holdings: Vols (250) Mss Maps Pix Slides
Phonorecords Audiotapes Videotapes 16mm
Films Filmstrips Microforms
Notes: History of Brown County, Minn.
Also have *Historical Files*, about 500 pieces
in vertical files incl newspaper clippings,
advertising, letterheads, etc, pertaining to
Brown County businesses, industry, schools,
governmental units, etc. *Family Files*, about
2500 pioneer families. Files incl obituaries,
pictures, documents, letters, etc. Also
collection on Siouan Uprising of 1862-
clippings, copies of treaties, letters, etc (65
vols, 10 mss, 25 maps, 40 pix, 50 slides).

MN —MINNESOTA HISTORICAL
SOCIETY LIBRARY, 690 Cedar St, Saint
Paul, 55101. Patricia C Harpole, Chief of
Reference Library; Bonnie G Wilson, Head
of Special Libraries

MINNESOTA—HISTORY

CA —HOOVER INSTITUTION ON WAR,
REVOLUTION & PEACE, Stanford

University, Stanford, 94305. Milorad M
Drachkovitch, Archivist
Holdings: // mss
Notes: Papers, 1914-1947, of Ernest
Lundeen, state legislator and US
Representative and Senator from Minnesota.
Correspondence, subject files, documents
and other papers, relating to Lundeen's
political career. 335 boxes. Unpublished
preliminary inventory in the repository.

MN —NORTHEAST MINNESOTA
HISTORICAL CENTER, University of
Minnesota, Duluth, Library 375, Duluth,
55812. Patricia Maus, Administrator
Notes: The Northeast Minnesota Historical
Center is jointly maintained by the
University of Minnesota, Duluth, and the St
Louis County Historical Society. Local and
regional history collections with emphasis on
transportation, lumbering, mining.
Photograph collection. Photocopy service
available.

MN —UNIVERSITY OF MINNESOTA,
DULUTH, Library & Learning Resources
Service, Duluth, 55812. James V. Litha,
Archivist
Holdings: Vols (1700) Cat Mss Maps Pix
Notes: The Voyageur Collection incl the
Grace Lee Nute Papers. Books and materials
relating to the Voyageur period (1650-1850)
and the area of Northeastern Minnesota,
Michigan, Wisconsin, Southern Canada.
Emphasis on all subjects listed in this
volume.

MN —MANKATO STATE UNIVERSITY,
Memorial Library, Center for Minnesota
Studies, Maywood & Ellis, Mankato, 56001.
Marilyn J Lass, Librn
Holdings: Vols 5000 Cat Mss Maps Pix
Microforms
Notes: The Center for Minnesota Studies
collection is housed in Memorial Library.
Materials in all subject areas are collected;
history is the strongest single area, incl a
comprehensive collection of Minnesota
county histories. The library is an official
repository for Minnesota state documents;
approximately 5000 are held in the Center.
Mss are collected under the direction and
supervision of the Minnesota Historical
Society, cataloged and retained in the Center
for Minnesota Studies. Ms collections listed
in Guide to the Holdings of the Minnesota
Regional Research Centers (St Paul;
Minnesota Historical Society).

MN —MINNEAPOLIS PUBLIC LIBRARY &
INFORMATION CENTER, Minneapolis
History Collection, 300 Nicollet Mall,
Minneapolis, 55401. Dorothy M Burke,
Librn
Holdings: Vols (20,000) Cat Mss Maps Pix
Slides Phonorecords Audiotapes
Budget: ($850)
Notes: Collection contains print and film
materials pertaining to Minneapolis, includes
some Minnesota history. Also have 29 five-
drawer legal files of clips and ephemeral
materials, and direct access to the 119-file
morgue of the old *Minneapolis Times*, a
newspaper which ceased publishing in 1948.
This is especially useful for items covering
the 20s, 30s and 40s. Special card indexes to
plates in architectural serials (local), houses,
buildings, streets, parks, etc; also indexes to
10-20 local newspapers and magazines.
Collection of about 60 neighborhood
newspapers (current and retrospective) and
about 1000 maps and atlases; nearly 250,000
pictures; early (1859-1920) city directories.

MN —BROWN COUNTY HISTORICAL
SOCIETY, Museum and Archives, Center St
and Broadway, Box 116, New Ulm, 56073.
Paul Klammer, Dir
Holdings: Vols (250) Mss Maps Pix Slides
Phonorecords Audiotapes Videotapes 16mm
Films Filmstrips Microforms
Notes: History of Brown County, Minn.
Also have *Historical Files*, about 500 pieces
in vertical files incl newspaper clippings,
advertising, letterheads, etc, pertaining to
Brown County businesses, industry, schools,
governmental units, etc. *Family Files*, about
2500 pioneer families. Files incl obituaries,
pictures, documents, letters, etc. Also
collection on Siouan Uprising of 1862-
clippings, copies of treaties, letters, etc (65
vols, 10 mss, 25 maps, 40 pix, 50 slides).

MINNESOTA—HISTORY (cont.)

MN —MINNESOTA HISTORICAL
SOCIETY LIBRARY, 690 Cedar St, Saint
Paul, 55101. Patricia C Harpole, Chief of
Reference Library; Bonnie G Wilson, Head
of Special Libraries
Notes: The Minnesota Historical Society
conducts its own oral history program,
sponsors special projects, and collects
materials of other sponsoring groups and
individuals. The collection of oral history
tapes contains, amoung others, the following
notable series: (1) Interviews with every
governor (except Floyd B Olson) from J A
O Preus (1921-25) to Harold LeVander
(1967-71). (2) Representatives of ethnic
groups in Minnesota interviewed as a part of
special projects include Blacks, Mexican-
Americans, Finns in Northern Minnesota,
and Jews in Minneapolis. (3) Leaders of both
state houses have been interviewed during
each legislative session from 1969 to 1976.
State politics in the 1930's and 1940's is a
recurring subject. Interviews with
Minnesotans in government, including
congressman, United States ambassadors,
state officers, and others, are also part of
thisseries. (4) Industries in Minnesota which
have been documented in interviews include
lumbering, commercial fishing on the North
Shore of Lake Superior, and printing and
graphics in the Twin Cities. (5) Activities of
such groups as the Women's International
League for Peace and Freedom, labor
organizations, and the Izaak Walton League
are discussed in interviews. (6) Interviews
with Minnesota's educational leaders,
expecially in the area of higher education,
are in this series. (7) Interviews with the
early builders of Minnesota touch on a wide
range of subjects.
SD —AUGUSTANA COLLEGE, Mikkelsen
Library & Learning Resource Center, Center
for Western Studies, Sioux Falls, 57197.
Ronelle Thompson, Dir Library
Notes: The Center for Western Studies,
located in the Mikkelsen Library, is an
archival and research agency of Augustana
College. Dedicated to the history and culture
of the Great Plains and the Trans-Mississippi
West, the Center collects and preserves
materials relating to Plains Indians,
immigrant settlers, Norwegiana, Western
Americana, Herbert Krause, Frederick
Manfred, Donald Parker, Richard F
Pettigrew, Augustana College, the Episcopal
Diocese of South Dakota, the South Dakota
District of the American Lutheran Church,
the South Dakota Penitentiary and
Minnehaha County.

MINNESOTA—MAPS

MN —MANKATO STATE UNIVERSITY,
Memorial Library, Maywood & Ellis,
Mankato, 56001. Russell K Amling, Map
Librn
Notes: 74,736 maps and 685 atlases (mostly
topographic and thematic) of the US,
especially Minnesota (3000 maps). 16,369
aerial photos (incl Minnesota). Separate
catalog.

MINNESOTA—POLITICS AND
GOVERNMENT

MN —MINNESOTA HISTORICAL
SOCIETY LIBRARY, 690 Cedar St, Saint
Paul, 55101. Patricia C Harpole, Chief of
Reference Library; Bonnie G Wilson, Head
of Special Libraries
Notes: Interviews with every governor
(except Floyd B Olson) from J A O Preus
(1921-25) to Harold LeVander (1967-71).
Leaders of both state houses have been
interviewed during each legislative session
from 1969 to 1976. State politics in the
1930's and 1940's is a recurring subject.
Interviews with Minnesotans in government,
including congressman, United States
ambassadors, state officers, and other, are
also a part of this series. The Public Affairs
Center of the Minnesota Historical Society
has thousands of tape recordings containing

speeches, radio and television interviews,
press conferences, and political campaign
materials by such well-known figures as
Hubert H. Humphrey, Eugene J. McCarthy,
Orville L Freeman, Maurice H. Stans,
Donald M Fraser, Albert H Quie, Clark
MacGregor and John A Blatnik. A list of
theseholdings is on file in the Audio-Visual
Library, the tapes are housed in the MHS
Research Center, 1500 Mississippi Street, St
Paul, Minn.

MINNESOTA ARCHITECTURE see
Architecture, Minnesota

MINNESOTA AUTHORS see Authors,
Minnesota

MINOR, FRED H.

TX —NORTH TEXAS STATE UNIVERSITY,
Archives, NT Station Box 5188, Denton,
76203. Robert LaForte, University Archivist
Notes: 72 linear feet. Texas political
manuscript collections housed in the NTSU
Archives incl the Fred H Minor Collection
(former Texas Speaker of the House), the
Alvin M Owsley Collection (former US
diplomat from Texas), and the Bullock
Hyder Collection (former representative to
Texas House from Lewisville). The
collections cover Texas politics from the
1920's to the 1970's. Published Description:
Fred H Minor Collection, *The National
Union Catalog of Manuscript Collections:
Catalog 1979* Washington: Library of
Congress, 1980. Alvin M Owsley Collection,
Ibid, Hermine Tobolowsky Equal Legal
Rights Collection, Ibid.

MINOR, WILSON F.

MS —MISSISSIPPI STATE UNIVERSITY,
Mitchell Memorial Library, Box 5408,
Mississippi State, 39762. Frances N
Coleman, Head, Special Collections
Holdings: Mss
Notes: Papers of Wilson F Minor, journalist
and editor of the Jackson, Mississippi
Capitol Reporter.

MINOR PLANETS see Asteroids

MINORITIES

CA —UNIVERSITY OF CALIFORNIA,
BERKELEY, Institute of Governmental
Studies Library, 109 Moses Hall, Berkeley,
94720. Jack Leister, Head Librn
Holdings: Vols (350,000) Cat Mss Maps
Microforms
Budget: ($160,000)
Notes: The library collects primarily
pamphlets. Incl in the library's holdings are
documents from all levels of government, as
well as publications issued by professional
associations and special interest groups. A G
K Hall catalog covering the Institute's
Library holdings is available. Since 1937,
Library has been depository for all California
local documents (city, county & special
district). Formerly: Bureau of Public
Administration.
CA —CRAFT AND FOLK ART MUSEUM,
Library, 5814 Wilshire Blvd, Los Angeles,
90036. Joan M Benedetti, Museum Librn
Holdings: Vols (2000) Slides VF
Notes: Incl 2000 books; 70 journal
subscriptions; artists' biographical files: 6 file
drawers; clipping files: 8 file drawers; 20,000
slides. Representation of the material culture
of all people, traditional and contemporary
expressions. Incl visual and printed
information on ethnic, traditional, popular,
decorative, idiosyncratic, and contemporary
crafts as well as vernacular architecture,
handmade houses, and design. Information
about and for professional artists on health
hazards, conservation, and career
management. Anthropological and art
historical works; exhibition catalogues; slides,
photographs, audiocassettes; clipping and
pamphlet files. Contemporary Slide Registry
of Craftspeople and extensive biographical
files of contemporary craft artists.

Information and referral files of craft related
galleries, shops, festivals, organizations, etc.
CA —LOS ANGELES PUBLIC LIBRARY,
Social Sciences Dept, 630 W Fifth St, Los
Angeles, 90071. Marilyn C Wherley,
Principal Librn
Holdings: Vols 4000 Microforms
Budget: ($150,000)
Notes: Emphasis on minorities; immigration
policies, background and social problems of
ethnic minorities in the US and the
Southwest in particular. Incl periodicals,
government publications and documents,
popular and scholarly works on Blacks,
Hispanics and Asians predominantly.
CA —UNIVERSITY OF CALIFORNIA, LOS
ANGELES, Research Library, Dept of
Special Collections, 405 Hilgard Ave, Los
Angeles, 90024. Edward Shreeves,
Chairman, Bibliographers Group; David S
Zeidberg, Head
Holdings: Cat Mss Pix
Notes: (1) 1277 linear feet of legal,
organizational, and education files relating to
the work of the American Civil Liberties
Union of Southern California. Incl
correspondence, scrapbooks, and ephemera.
Additional material in the papers of Ed
Cray, Stanley Fleishman, Nathan L
Schoichet, etc. (2) The Carey McWilliams
Collection of papers, clippings and reports
relating to migrant farm labor and the
problems of the Mexican American, 1930-
1940, incl material on the Zoot-Suit Riots.
(3) 50 linear feet of mss, correspondence,
research notes, etc, relating to the career of
T Scott Miyakawa, first director of the
Japanese American Research Center at
UCLA (1962-1965).
CO —WESTERN INTERSTATE
COMMISSION FOR HIGHER
EDUCATION, Wiche Library, PO Drawer
P, Boulder, 80302. Karon M Kelly, Dir
Library Services
Holdings: Vols (10,000) Cat Microforms
Notes: Incl; medical and nursing education,
student exchange programs, minority
involvement in education, management
systems in higher education.
DC —US COMMISSION ON CIVIL
RIGHTS, National Clearinghouse Library,
1121 Vermont Ave NW, Washington,
20005. Lenora McMillan, Chief Librn
Holdings: Vols (10,200) Cat Slides
Microforms
Notes: The National Clearinghouse Library
has a special collection of the US
Commission on Civil Rights publications
from its inception (1957) to present date.
IL —ILLINOIS STATE UNIVERSITY, Milner
Library, Dept of Special Collections,
Normal, 61761. Robert Sokan, Librn
Holdings: Vols 2100 // Uncat
Notes: Sigmund Livingston Collection on
Intergroup Relations, 1944 to the present.
The material is divided into subject headings
which contain pamphlets, newsletters and
commission reports.
LA —AMISTAD RESEARCH CENTER, 400
Esplanade Ave, New Orleans, 70116. Clifton
H Johnson, Exec Dir; Florence E Borders,
Senior Archivist
Holdings: Vols (10,000) Cat Mss Pix
Audiotapes Microforms
Budget: ($315,000)
Notes: In addition, 8,000,000 ms pieces, 10,
000 pictures, 3500 microforms, and 500
audiotapes. Amistad Research Center is an
historical research library devoted to the
collection and use of primary source
materials on the history of America's ethnic
minorities, with particular emphasis on Afro-
Americans, American Indians, and
immigrant groups. Among the larger
institutional collections held are the archives
and records of the American Missionary
Association, the American Home Missionary
Society, the Race Relations Dept of the
Anti-Defamation League, the Catholic
Committee of the South, and the National
Association of Human Rights Workers,
(formerly NAIRO, National Association of
Intergroup Related Officials). Also, private
papers of the Harlem Renaissance poet,
Countee Cullen; educator and civil rights
leader, Mary McLeod Bethune;20th century

MINORITIES (cont.)

civil rights lawyer, Alexander P Tureaud;
19th century Black attorney and judge,
George Ruffin; founder and director of
Operation Crossroads Africa, Dr James H
Robinson; and over 70 others.

†MA —JOHN F KENNEDY LIBRARY,
Columbia Point, Boston, 02125. Dan H Fenn
Jr, Dir
Holdings: Cat Mss
Notes: Papers of JFK and White House
aides Lee White and Harris Wofford and
RFK and Justice Department aide Burke
Marshall, dealing with civil rights, 1961-
1964. 42 linear ft of mss. Holdings are
described in "Historical Materials in the
John F Kennedy Library." Copies may be
obtained by writing the Research Archivist.

MA —HARVARD UNIVERSITY LIBRARY,
Law School Library, Langdell Hall,
Cambridge, 02138. Harry S Martin III, Librn
Notes: Personal and legal papers of William
Henry Hastic, Governor of the Virgin
Islands, Judge of the US Court of Appeals,
Third Circuit, who died in April 1976. Much
on his involvement in civic and
antidiscrimination cases.

MI —WAYNE STATE UNIVERSITY, Kresge
Library (Education), Detroit, 48202.
Theodore Manheim, Librn
Holdings: Vols (65,000) Cat Mss Microforms
Budget: ($2000)
Notes: The Eloise Ramsey Collection (10,
000 vols). See, *The Eloise Ramsey
Collection of Literature for Young People: A
Catalogue;* compiled by Joan Cusenza
(Detroit: Wayne State University Libraries,
1967). Besides the Ramsey Collection, which
is housed separately and does not circulate,
the Education Library has approx 55,000
volumes of children's and young adults'
literature, with a very large picture-book
collection, a large poetry collection; all with
special emphasis on urban and ethnic
materials.

NY —HOFSTRA UNIVERSITY, Library,
1000 Fulton Ave, Hempstead, 11550.
Charles R Andrews, Dean of Library
Services
Notes: The personal library of Paul Radin.
See description of the American
Philosophical Society Library's collection of
his anthropological papers under this entry
(Pa).

NY —LESBIAN HERSTORY
EDUCATIONAL FOUNDATION INC,
Lesbian Herstory Archives, PO Box 1258,
New York, 10116. Deborah Edel, Treasurer
Notes: Lesbian, feminist, and Gay books and
periodicals on all aspects of Lesbian culture,
photographs and slides of Lesbians and
Lesbian art, records, tapes, graphics and
crafts. Also, unpublished materials such as
first drafts, term papers from Lesbian and
Gay studies courses, diaries, letters, poetry,
and conference notes.

NY —NEW YORK PUBLIC LIBRARY,
Research Libraries, American History Div,
Fifth Ave & 42 St, New York, 10018.
Notes: The collection of histories of ethnic
groups in the US should be viewed in
context of holdings of other units of The
Research Libraries, including microforms
and separately cataloged pamphlets.
Outstanding collection of materials on Black
history, which is now being collected for The
Research Libraries by the Schomburg Center
for Research in Black Culture.

NY —NEW YORK STATE DIVISION OF
HUMAN RIGHTS, Reference Library, Two
World Trade Center, Rm 5356, New York,
10047. Rosalind Spriggs, Librn
Holdings: Vols 2000 Cat
Notes: Human rights and intergroup
relations. This special collection covers the
materials on civil rights and civil liberties.
Intergroup relations and ethnic
organizations. Minority and religious groups.
Discriminations in education, employment
and housing, especially, after the year 1971.
*Bibliography on Human Rights and
Intergroup Relations,* Special Collection no
4, 1977. This special collection contains
about 2000 items: books, studies, journals,

pamphlets, reprints, research data and
reports of state and city commissions against
discrimination.

NY —YWCA NATIONAL BOARD, Library,
726-730 Broadway, New York, 10012.
Elizabeth Norris, Librn
Holdings: Vols (3000) Cat Mss
Budget: ($2400)
Notes: Women and their contemporary
interests.

PA —HAVERFORD COLLEGE, Magill
Library, Quaker Collection, Haverford,
19041. Edwin B Bonner, Librn & Cur
Holdings: Vols (32,000) Cat Mss Maps Pix
Phonorecords Audiotapes Microforms
Notes: Incl material about Society of Friends
from inception in England, 1650, to the
present. Formats incl periodicals, diaries,
documents of individual Friends, families,
Quaker Meetings and institutions, incl
archives of Haverford College. Emphases on
American Indians, antislavery, women,
minorities, the Rufus M Jones Mysticism
collection, Quaker fiction, and Delaware
Valley, Pennsylvania.

PA —AMERICAN PHILOSOPHICAL
SOCIETY, Library, 105 S Fifth St,
Philadelphia, 19106. Edward C Carter II,
Librn
Notes: The anthropological papers of Paul
Radin in fields of ethnology, social
organization, primitive religion, linguistics,
and mythology. He worked mostly among
the Winnebago, Ojibwa, Fox, Zapotec,
Wappo, Wintun, and Huave Indian tribes;
also Italian and other ethnic minorities of
San Francisco.

PA —BALCH INSTITUTE FOR ETHNIC
STUDIES, Library, 18 S Seventh St,
Philadelphia, 19106. R Joseph Anderson,
Library Dir
Holdings: Vols 30,000 Cat Mss Pix
Microforms

PA —TEMPLE UNIVERSITY LIBRARIES,
Special Collections Dept, Contemporary
Culture Collection, Philadelphia, 19122.
Patricia J Case, Cur
Notes: The Contemporary Culture
Collection. See full entry under US-Social
Life and Customs.

BC —SELKIRK COLLEGE, Library, PO Box
1200, Castlegar, V1N 3J1, Can. John
Mansbridge, Dir
Holdings: Vols 1000 Cat Mss Pix
Microforms
Notes: The West Kootenay History
Collection is particularly rich in works on
the Doukhobor people. The West Kootenay
area of BC is bounded on the south by the
US border, on the north by the Trans-
Canada Highway, on the east by Kootenay
Lake, and on the west by the Okanagan
Valley.

†ON —METROPOLITAN TORONTO
LIBRARY, Social Sciences Dept, 789 Yonge
St, Toronto, M4W 2G8, Can. Abdus Salam,
Head
Holdings: Vols Cat Maps Phonorecords
Audiotapes 16mm Films Microforms
Notes: Collection is both current and
historical. Strong in immigrants' guides,
government reports and statistics, analyses,
histories and studies of ethnic groups. Strong
on the Underground Railroad.

MINORITY GROUPS see Minorities

MINSTRELS AND MINSTREL SHOWS

IN —INDIANA UNIVERSITY, Lilly Library,
Seventh St, Bloomington, 47405. William R
Cagle, Librn
Holdings: // Uncat
Notes: In the Starr Collection of American
Sheet Music.

MA —HARVARD UNIVERSITY LIBRARY,
Theatre Collection, Cambridge, 02138.
Jeanne T Newlin, Cur
Holdings: Cat Mss Pix Slides Microforms
Notes: One of the largest existing collections
of playbills, programs, prints, photographs,
promptbooks, and other materials relating to
the performing arts, the scope is worldwide;
resources on the English-speaking stage of
the 18th and 19th centuries are unequalled.
Incl materials on ballet and modern dance,

the circus, magic, minstrel shows, cinema,
and pantomime. For description, see
Harvard Library Bulletin, VI (1925): pp 281-
301.

NY —BUFFALO & ERIE COUNTY PUBLIC
LIBRARY, Rare Book Room, Lafayette Sq,
Buffalo, 14203. William H Loos, Cur
Holdings: Vols 90 Cat
Notes: The collection has been microfilmed
and the film is available for interlibrary loan.

NY —BARNARD A & MORRIS N YOUNG
LIBRARY OF EARLY AMERICAN
POPULAR MUSIC, 270 Riverside Dr, New
York, 10025. Morris N Young, Cur
Holdings: Cat Mss Pix Phonorecords
Audiotapes Microforms
Notes: 48,000 items of American popular
music, mostly 1790-1910. Incl books, serials,
sheet music, broadsides, anthologies, air
checks, broadcasting and music business
memorabilia, and correspondence.

NY —NEW YORK PUBLIC LIBRARY,
Performing Arts Research Center, Billy Rose
Theatre Collection, 111 Amsterdam Ave,
New York, 10023. Dorothy L Swerdlove,
Cur
Holdings: Cat
See also entry under Theatre - History.

PA —BALCH INSTITUTE FOR ETHNIC
STUDIES, Library, 18 S Seventh St,
Philadelphia, 19106. R Joseph Anderson,
Library Dir

PA —FREE LIBRARY OF PHILADELPHIA,
Theatre Collection, Logan Sq, Philadelphia,
19103. Geraldine Duclow, Librn-in-Charge
Holdings: Vols (1,250,000) Uncat Pix
Notes: The Theatre Collection contains
books, magazines, playbills, broadsides,
posters, photographs, and other memorabilia
covering theatre, motion pictures, minstrels,
vaudeville, circus, radio and television. The
Library's Philadelphia Theatre Index lists
the major productions here since 1855, and
partially indexes the collection of local
playbills which date back to 1803. There are
also programs from many other cities, incl
New York; some from London date back to
1800. Early film companies as well as the
present movie industry are represented by
advertising materials and over 30,000 film
stills. The Lubin Film Co (1910-1916)
Archive has been established with over 600
photographs and related items. Circus
programs and route books date back to 1900.
There are minstrel programs as early as
1865. Most significant are the mss from
Philadelphia's Dumont Minstrels.
Variousfiles contain autographs, photographs,
newspaper articles and reviews in all
pertinent subject areas. Noncirculating.

RI —BROWN UNIVERSITY, John Hay
Library, Harris Collection, Prospect St,
Providence, 02912. Rosemary L Cullen, Cur
Holdings: Vols (200,000) Cat Mss
Phonorecords Microforms
Budget: ($15,000)
Notes: The Harris Collection of American
Poetry and Plays is principally composed of
American and Canadian poetry and plays,
17th century-date. Collections incl 200,000
vols, 30,000 broadsides, 55,000 mss, 170,000
pieces of sheet music, 450 phonorecords, and
375 microfilm reels. Incl an extensive
collection of sheet music by and relating to
Afro-Americans, from the 19th and 20th
centuries. See *Dictionary Catalog of the
Harris Collection of American Poetry,*
(Boston: G K Hall, 1972), 13 vols.
Supplement, (1977), 3 vols. See also:
*American Poetry, A Collection of Microfilm,
Segment I* (1609-1820), *Segment II* (1821-
1850); *Segment III* (1851-1870)
(Woodbridge, Conn: Research Publications).
Separate catlog.

TX —DALLAS PUBLIC LIBRARY, Fine Arts
Div, 1515 Young St, Dallas, 75201. Richard
L Waters, Acting Dir; Jane Holahan,
Manager
Notes: 18th-20th century.

MIRES, AUSTIN

†WA —WASHINGTON STATE
UNIVERSITY, Library, Manuscripts,
Archives & Special Collections, Pullman,
99164. John F Guido, Head
Holdings: Vols Cat Mss Maps Pix

MIRES, AUSTIN (cont.)

Microforms
Notes: Ms resources in the Washington State
University Library for the study of Pacific
Northwest history incl the personal papers of
Frank A Bands, William Compton Brown,
Enoch Albert Bryan, Ernest Otto Holland,
William Lon Johnson, Catherine May,
Lucullus Virgil McWhorter, Austin Mires,
Carl Parcher Russell, Pierre Jean de Smet,
Henry Harmon Spaulding. Elkanah Walker,
John McAdam Webster, Marcus Whitman,
as well as many business records of banks,
insurance firms and agencies, breweries,
lumber mills, merchants, entrepreneurs and
farmers. All ms collections are described in a
catalog, a published register or an
unpublished finding aid.

MIRISCH PRODUCTIONS, INC.

CA —UNIVERSITY OF CALIFORNIA, LOS
ANGELES, Research Library, Dept of
Special Collections, 405 Hilgard Ave, Los
Angeles, 90024. Edward Shreeves,
Chairman, Bibliographers Group; David S
Zeidberg, Head
Notes: 20 linear feet of correspondence,
contracts, and scripts. Permission is required
to consult the material.

MISCARRIAGE see Abortion

MISCEGENATION

DC —HOWARD UNIVERSITY, Moorland-
Spingarn Research Center, 500 Howard
Place NW, Washington, 20059. Clifford L
Muse, Jr, Acting Dir
Holdings: Vols (106,086) Mss Maps Pix
Microforms
Budget: ($854,753)
See also entry under Blacks
PA —BALCH INSTITUTE FOR ETHNIC
STUDIES, Library, 18 S Seventh St,
Philadelphia, 19106. R Joseph Anderson,
Library Dir

MISDEMEANORS (LAW) see Criminal Law

MISHIMA, YUKIO

FL —UNIVERSITY OF FLORIDA, Libraries,
Gainesville, 32611. Ray Jones, Research
Librn; Max Willocks, Librn
Holdings: Vols (2000)
Notes: An extensive collection of modern
and premodern Japanese prose fiction in
English translation and Japanese. Incl
complete works of a number of important
modern Japanese authors such as Yasunari
Kawabata, Naoya Shiga, Junichiro Tanizaki,
and Yukio Mishima.

MISKIN, LIONEL

MA —BOSTON UNIVERSITY, Mugar
Memorial Library, Special Collections Dept,
771 Commonwealth Ave, Boston, 02215.
Howard B Gotlieb, Dir
Holdings: Cat Mss

MISSILES, GUIDED see Guided Missiles

MISSION INDIANS OF CALIFORNIA
see Indians of North America and
Mexico—California

MISSIONARIES

CA —AZUSA PACIFIC COLLEGE,
Marshburn Memorial Library, Citrus &
Alosta, Azusa, 91702. Edward Peterman,
Librn
Holdings: Vols 175 Cat Mss
Notes: The Clifford M Drury Collection on
the Protestant Missionary in the Far West.
No photocopying.
IL —WHEATON COLLEGE, Buswell
Memorial Library, Wheaton, 60187. Paul
Snezek, Library Dir
Holdings: Vols 200
Notes: A wide rings of topic relating to

missionary work. Most of the publications
are from the late 19th and early 20th
centuries.
IN —INDIANA UNIVERSITY, Lilly Library,
Seventh St, Bloomington, 47405. William R
Cagle, Librn
Holdings: Vols (2000) // Cat Mss
Notes: The core of the collection is the
specialized library of Charles R Boxer (1000
titles) dealing with the history of the Iberians
in the East, 16th-18th century. Mainly incl
works on China, Japan and the Philippines
during the period of their early intercourse
with the West through 1800, as well as
materials on the English and Dutch East
India Companies, and the 17th century
Anglo-Dutch naval wars. Special mention
should be made of the valuable letters from
missions by the Jesuits, and the works in this
area by the Augustinians, Franciscans, and
Dominicans, from the time of the arrival of
the Iberians in Asia. The collection is a
valuable source of information for the study
of the European expansion into the area,
including Southeast Asia.
ME —BOWDOIN COLLEGE, Library,
Brunswick, 04011. Dianne M Gutscher, Cur
of Special Collections
Holdings: Mss
Notes: A small collection of Cyrus Hamlin
material is supplemented by about 500
letters in the Abbott Memorial Collection
from and to this missionary, founder of
Robert College in Bebek, Turkey, and
president of Middlebury College (Vermont).
MN —UNIVERSITY OF MINNESOTA,
DULUTH, Library & Learning Resources
Service, Duluth, 55812. James V. Litha,
Archivist
Holdings: Vols (1700) Cat Mss Maps Pix
Notes: The Voyageur Collection incl the
Grace Lee Nute Papers. Books and materials
relating to the Voyageur period (1650-1850)
and the area of Northeastern Minnesota,
Michigan, Wisconsin, Southern Canada.
Emphasis on all subjects listed in this
volume.
NY —STATE UNIVERSITY OF NEW YORK
AT ALBANY, Library, Special Collections
Dept, 1400 Washington Ave, Albany, 12222.
Marion P Munzer, Coordr
Notes: Fred R Brown's correspondence,
mss, photographs, and maps. He was as
Methodist missionary to China from 1910-31
(6 linear feet). Part of the Library's German
Exile Collection.
See also entries under Missions - China;
China - History; Fred R Brown
NC —DUKE UNIVERSITY, William R
Perkins Library, Manuscript Dept, Durham,
27706. Ellen Gartrell, Cur of Mss
Holdings: Cat Mss
Notes: Especially US South, eg Methodist
Church Papers (records of local and regional
units) also many personal and professional
papers of clergy, missionaries and laymen,
19th-20th centuries, eg Methodist John
Lakin Brasher (holiness movement leader),
Carlyle Marney (Southern Baptist minister),
Methodist Bishop James Cannon, missionary
Martha Foster Crawford.
NC —SOUTHEASTERN BAPTIST
THEOLOGICAL SEMINARY LIBRARY,
PO Box 752, Wake Forest, 27587. H Eugene
McLeod, Librn
Holdings: Cat Slides Audiotapes Videotapes
Films Microforms
OH —KENT STATE UNIVERSITY,
University Archives, Kent, 44242. Stephen C
Morton, University Archivist
Holdings: Uncat Mss
Notes: The ms material contained in 6 boxes
(5 1/2 cubic feet). The collection comprises
correspondence, journals, account books,
sermons and miscellaneous material. From
1811 to 1834 Rev Cowles' journals provide
an almost unbroken account of his activities
as minister and missionary in the Western
Reserve region of Ohio. There is also a
sizable collection of material on the Fuller
Family of Austinburg, Ohio (qv).
OR —UNIVERSITY OF OREGON
LIBRARY, Special Collections Div, Eugene,
97403. Kenneth W Duckett, Curator
Holdings: Cat Mss
Notes: Ca 50 mss collections of

correspondence, journals, mss and artifacts
created and collected by missionaries to the
Far East, mostly China. Publication: Martin
Schmitt, comp, Catalogue of Manuscripts in
the University of Oregon Library (Eugene:
University of Oregon Books, 1971). The
general library has a significant collection of
books written by missionaries and the
publications of societies and associations incl
serials.
WI —SEVENTH DAY BAPTIST
HISTORICAL SOCIETY, Library, 3120
Kennedy Rd, PO Box 1678, Janesville,
53547. D Scott Smith, Historian
Holdings: Vols (600) Cat Mss Maps Pix
Notes: US Seventh Day Baptists Collection,
incl records, letters. Established at Newport,
Rhode Island, in 1671, this denomination is
a part of the Free-Church evangelical
movement in America. The General
Conference was organized in 1801. The
national and international headquarters of
the Seventh Day Baptist denomination is
located at Janesville, Wisconsin. Also have
records, publications, etc of the
denomination's mission in Shanghai, 1846-
1950; further, materials (6 boxes) on the
Church's work in Nyasaland (Malawi),
1895-1914, and then at a later period.
BC —TERRACE PUBLIC LIBRARY, 4610
Park Ave, Terrace, V8G 1V6, Can. Ed
Curell, Librn; Gillian Campbell, Librn,
Terrace Collection
Holdings: Vols (270) Cat
Budget: ($250)
Notes: The collection is limited to books and
pamphlets relating to Terrace, Skeena, and
Nass River District history and geography.
Emphasis on art and sociology of the Niska
and Tsimshian and lives of early
missionaries.
ON —VICTORIA UNIVERSITY, Library, 71
Queen's Park Crescent, Toronto, M5S 1K7,
Can. Robert C Brandeis, Chief Librn
Holdings: Vols (1000)// Cat Mss Maps Pix
Notes: Collection consists of books,
pamphlets, and government reports mainl
dealing with North American Indians and
western explorations and missionary
enterprises among the Indian tribes in
Canada. Incl Indian Bibles and hymnbooks,
and mss and vols by Peter Jones (an Indian
missionary) and James Evans (inventor of
the Cree syllabic alphabet).

MISSIONARY ASSOCIATION, AMERICAN see American Missionary Association

MISSIONARY SOCIETY, AMERICAN HOME see American Home Missionary Society

MISSIONS

CA —AZUSA PACIFIC COLLEGE,
Marshburn Memorial Library, Citrus &
Alosta, Azusa, 91702. Edward Peterman,
Librn
Holdings: Vols 175 Cat Mss
Notes: The Clifford M Drury Collection on
the Protestant Missionary in the Far West.
No photocopying.
CA —BIOLA UNIVERSITY, Rose Memorial
Library, 13800 Biola Ave, La Mirada,
90639. A Lawrence Marshburn
Holdings: Vols (178,000) Cat Maps Pix
Microforms
Budget: ($430,000)
Notes: Biblical and evangelical materials.
CA —UNIVERSITY OF CALIFORNIA, LOS
ANGELES, Research Library, African
Studies Collection, 405 Hilgard Ave, Los
Angeles, 90024. Edward Shreeves,
Chairman, Bibliographers Group; Joseph J
Lauer, African Studies Bibliographer
Holdings: Maps Pix Slides Phonorecords
Audiotapes Microforms
Notes: General collection mainly in the
humanities and social sciences, covering
prehistoric times to the present. Particular
strengths include: early travel and
exploration, mission field, literature,
vernacular languages and literatures,
Portuguese Africa, slavery (have the British

MISSIONS (cont.)

Foreign Office's *General Correspondence.
Slave Trade* on microfilm). Extensive
holdings of journals, newspapers and
government publications. The collection was
described in the *Handbook of American
Resources for African Studies* (1967).

CT —YALE UNIVERSITY, Box 1603A, Yale
Station, New Haven, 06520.
Holdings: Vols Cat Mss

DC —DOMINICAN HOUSE OF STUDIES,
Dominican College Library, 487 Michigan
Ave NE, Washington, 20017. J Raymond
Vandegrift, OP, Librn
Holdings: Vols (5000) Cat
Budget: ($1350)
Notes: The Dominican Order (its history,
spirituality, government, liturgy), its
members (directories, biographies,
bibliographies, lives of saints) and works
written by Dominicans: incunabula, rare
books, dissertations, periodicals (2300 vols),
monographs. Incl periodicals either about the
Order or edited by Dominicans. Does not
incl titles about the congregations of
Dominican Sisters. The Library's catalog
contains analytics for Dominican
contributors to monographs.

IL —LOYOLA UNIVERSITY OF CHICAGO,
E M Cudahy Memorial Library, 6525 N
Sheridan Rd, Chicago, 60626.
Holdings: Mss
Notes: Correspondence and other papers of
the Catholic Church Extension Society
covering the years 1905-1962. The Society
was established in 1905 and has played an
important role in domestic missionary work,
particularly in the subsidization of church
construction and Newman Center projects.
To be used under the direct supervision of
the archivist at all times. Incl 10,000 photos.

IL —NEWBERRY LIBRARY, 60 W Walton
St, Chicago, 60610. Diana Haskell, Cur of
Modern Mss
Holdings: Vols 1500 Cat
Notes: Work among Indians. Missions of all
sects in the US and Canada. The Edward E
Ayer Collection.

IL —WHEATON COLLEGE, Billy Graham
Center Library and Archives, Wheaton,
60187. Ferne Lauraine Weimer, Dir of
Library; Robert Shuster, Dir of Archives
Notes: Archives of the Center.

†IL —WHEATON COLLEGE, Billy Graham
Center, Wheaton, 60187.
Notes: Papers of the Woman's Union
Missionary Society, an evangelical group
founded in New York in 1861. Records
document their missionary work in India,
China, Japan, Burma, Pakistan, Greece, and
Cyprus.

LA —AMISTAD RESEARCH CENTER, 400
Esplanade Ave, New Orleans, 70116. Clifton
H Johnson, Exec Dir; Florence E Borders,
Senior Archivist
Holdings: Vols (10,000) Cat Mss Pix
Audiotapes Microforms
Budget: ($315,000)
Notes: In addition, 8,000,000 ms pieces, 10,
000 pictures, 3500 microforms, and 500
audiotapes. Amistad Research Center is an
historical research library devoted to the
collection and use of primary source
materials on the history of America's ethnic
minorities, with particular emphasis on Afro-
Americans, American Indians, and
immigrant groups. Among the larger
institutional collections held are the archives
and records of the American Missionary
Association, the American Home Missionary
Society, the Race Relations Dept of the
Anti-Defamation League, the Catholic
Committee of the South, and the National
Association of Human Rights Workers,
(formerly NAIRO, National Association of
Intergroup Related Officials). Also, private
papers of the Harlem Renaissance poet,
Countee Cullen; educator and civil rights
leader, Mary McLeod Bethune;20th century
civil rights lawyer, Alexander P Tureaud;
19th century Black attorney and judge,
George Ruffin; founder and director of
Operation Crossroads Africa, Dr James H
Robinson; and over 70 others.

ME —BOWDOIN COLLEGE, Library,
Brunswick, 04011. Dianne M Gutscher, Cur
of Special Collections
Holdings: Mss
Notes: The Charles Henry Howard Papers
contain more than 400 pieces of
correspondence, articles, and addresses,
1852-1907, of this Civil War officer and
Secretary of the American Missionary
Association. The papers complement those
of his brother, Oliver Otis Howard.

MD —JOHNS HOPKINS UNIVERSITY,
Milton S Eisenhower Library, George
Peabody Collection, 17 E Mt Vernon Place,
Baltimore, 21201. Lyn Hart, Peabody Librn
Notes: Emphasis on materials published
before 1950. Strength is a good collection
through the 19th century.

NY —GENERAL THEOLOGICAL
SEMINARY, Saint Marks Library, 175
Ninth Ave, New York, 10011. David Green,
Dir
Holdings: Vols (200,000) Cat
Notes: Extensive collection.

NC —SOUTHEASTERN BAPTIST
THEOLOGICAL SEMINARY LIBRARY,
PO Box 752, Wake Forest, 27587. H Eugene
McLeod, Librn
Holdings: Cat Slides Audiotapes Videotapes
Films Microforms

†NC —MORAVIAN CHURCH IN
AMERICA-SOUTHERN PROVINCE,
Drawer M, Salem Station, Winston-Salem,
27108.
Notes: Moravian church history, Moravian
missions, North Carolina.

OK —MIDWEST CHRISTIAN COLLEGE,
Library, 6600 N Kelley Ave, Oklahoma
City, 73111. Jean Cavett, Dir
Holdings: Vols (7000) Cat Pix Phonorecords
Audiotapes Filmstrips Microforms
Notes: The Restoration Movement
(Independent Christian Church) to restore
the Church to its New Testament form. Incl
churches called "Christian Churches,"
"Churches of Christ," "Disciples of Christ,"
and a few called just "Christ's Church."

OR —MULTNOMAH SCHOOL OF THE
BIBLE, Library, 8435 NE Gilsan St,
Portland, 97220. James F Scott, Dir of
Library; Susan Johnson, Asst Librn
Holdings: Vols (40,686) Cat Slides
Phonorecords Audiotapes Filmstrips
Budget: ($33,950)
Notes: Multnomah School of the Bible is an
evangelical school that educates students
through a program of instruction having the
Bible as its center. It supports this
centralized Bible major with several
ancillary, pertinent supporting minors, ie,
Christian education, pastoral, missions and
New Testament Greek.

RI —BROWN UNIVERSITY, John Hay
Library, 20 Prospect St, Providence, 02912.
Mark N Brown, Cur Mss
Holdings: Vols (2000) Cat Mss
Notes: Several collections of religious history
strong in material on Baptist,
Congregational, and Unitarian Churches in
the 19th century, incl the ms records some
Rhode Island congregations plus the papers
of Isaac Backus, Brown University presidents
and faculty, Jones Very, Mary Ann Atwood,
Thomas Ustick, and Charles King Newcomb;
incl numerous ephemeral and pamphlet
publications that relate to Baptist Church
history, creed, biography, Sunday School
literature and missions.

RI —BROWN UNIVERSITY, John Hay
Library, 20 Prospect St, Providence, 02912.
Mark N Brown, Cur Mss
Holdings: // Mss
Notes: Eli H Canfield mss reflect issues of
the day and incl the subjects of missions,
religious education, temperance, Prohibition,
and Reconstruction. There are also 300
letters from Canfield to his son and
grandchildren; letters from Europe and the
South during and after the Civil War; and
papers relating to Christ Church, Brooklyn.
Register available. See "The Rev Eli Canfield
(1817-1898): Low-church Yankee
Episcopalian," ed by Willian G McLoughlin,
Jr, in *Books at Brown*, vol XXIII (1969), pp
135-68.

TN —COVENANT COLLEGE, Anna Emma
Kresge Memorial Library, Lookout

Mountain, 37350. Gary B Huisman, Librn
Notes: Soltau Coll.

MISSIONS—CALIFORNIA

AZ —ARIZONA STATE MUSEUM, Library,
University of Arizona, Tucson, 85721. Hans
R Bart, Museum Librn
Holdings: Vols 300 Cat Mss
Notes: Books on Spanish missions in
Arizona, New Mexico, Texas, California and
particularly northern Mexico (Sonora). A
private collection given to the library; it is
not kept separate.

CA —CLAREMONT COLLEGES, Honnold
Library, Ninth & Dartmouth, Claremont,
91711. Tania Rizzo, Special Collections
Dept Head
Holdings: 300 // Cat Mss
Notes: McPherson Collection of San Gabriel
Mission matrimonial investigations, letters
and documents, 1773-1872. 330 pieces.
Restricted use.

MISSIONS—CHINA

CT —YALE UNIVERSITY, Beinecke Rare
Book & Manuscript Library, Osborn
Collection, New Haven, 06520. Stephen R
Parks, Cur
Holdings: Mss

IL —CENTER FOR RESEARCH
LIBRARIES, 6050 S Kenwood Ave,
Chicago, 60637. Donald B Simpson, Dir;
Esther Smith, Collection Development Librn
Holdings: Vols Cat Microforms
Notes: Mainland China newspapers,
periodicals and clippings, early western
language newspapers in China, Hong Kong
newspapers in English, British Foreign
Office and US State Dept records relating to
China, Dunhuang manuscripts, missionary
periodicals. Microfilm and reprints of
newspapers, serials and monographs from
Center for Chinese Research Materials.
Hunter collection of Chinese communist
propaganda (ca 1000 vols). Microfilm and
originals of Maritime Customs publications.
Microfilm of press summaries prepared by
US Consulate, Hong Kong, archives of
missionary organizations, Chinese folk
literature, etc. Descriptive pamphlet
available.

†IL —WHEATON COLLEGE, Billy Graham
Center, Wheaton, 60187.
Notes: Papers of the Woman's Union
Missionary Society, an evangelical group
founded in New York in 1861. Records
document their missionary work in India,
China, Japan, Burma, Pakistan, Greece, and
Cyprus.

NY —STATE UNIVERSITY OF NEW YORK
AT ALBANY, Library, Special Collections
Dept, 1400 Washington Ave, Albany, 12222.
Marion P Munzer, Coordr
Notes: Fred R Brown's correspondence,
mss, photographs, and maps. He was a
Methodist missionary to China from 1910-31
(6 linear feet). Part of the Library's German
Exile Collection.
See also entries under Missionaries; China -
History; Fred R Brown.

OH —RUTHERFORD B HAYES LIBRARY,
1337 Hayes Ave, Fremont, 43420. Watt P
Marchman, Dir
Holdings: Uncat Pix Microforms
Notes: The Frank Ohlinger Family
Collection: American religion; Chinese
missionary; education. (9 linear feet). Index
in collections.

VA —UNIVERSITY OF VIRGINIA,
Alderman Library, Manuscripts Dept,
Charlottesville, 22901. Edmund Berkeley Jr,
Cur
Holdings: Cat Mss
Notes: Papers, 1906-1951, of Harry Baylor
Taylor. Episcopal Medical Missionary in
Anking.

MISSIONS—HAWAII

HI —HAWAIIAN MISSION CHILDREN'S
SOCIETY LIBRARY, 553 S King St,
Honolulu, 96813. Mary Jane Knight, Librn
Holdings: Vols 15,000 Cat Mss Pix
Notes: Missionary period of Hawaiian

MISSIONS—HAWAII (cont.)

history, 1819-1880, incl a general collection of Hawaiian history and travel, an outstanding collection of early voyages to the Pacific, and an almost complete collection of early Hawaiian imprints, ie, publications in the Hawaiian language during the 19th century. Ms material incl letters, journals and reports of the Protestant missionaries who came to Hawaii (the Sandwich Islands) under the auspices of the American Board of Commissioners for Foreign Missions. The material is for research only; the stacks are closed. Unpublished papers may be examined by qualified researchers on application to the librarian. Published material is cataloged. Hawaiian imprints arc cataloged, except for the Dewey classification 300's which are mainly governmentdocuments. Ms collections are cataloged or in the process of being completely arranged and cataloged.

MISSIONS—INDIA

†IL —WHEATON COLLEGE, Billy Graham Center, Wheaton, 60187.
Notes: Papers of the Woman's Union Missionary Society, an evangelical group founded in New York in 1861. Records document their missionary work in India, China, Japan, Burma, Pakistan, Greece, and Cyprus.

VA —UNIVERSITY OF VIRGINIA, Alderman Library, Manuscripts Dept, Charlottesville, 22901. Edmund Berkeley Jr, Cur
Holdings: Cat Mss
Notes: Papers of Samuel Higginbottom and his family; missionary to India. (30 linear feet).

MISSIONS—JEWS

CA —BIOLA UNIVERSITY, Rose Memorial Library, 13800 Biola Ave, La Mirada, 90639. A Lawrence Marshburn
Holdings: Vols (178,000) Cat Maps Pix Microforms
Budget: ($430,000)
Notes: Biblical and evangelical materials.

MISSIONS—MEXICO

AZ —ARIZONA STATE MUSEUM, Library, University of Arizona, Tucson, 85721. Hans R Bart, Museum Librn
Holdings: Vols 250 Cat Mss
Notes: Books on Spanish missions in Arizona, New Mexico, Texas, California and particularly northern Mexico (Sonora). A private collection given to the library; it is not kept separate.

CA —UNIVERSITY OF CALIFORNIA, LOS ANGELES, William Andrews Clark Memorial Library, 2520 Cimarron St, Los Angeles, 90018.
Holdings: // Cat Mss
Notes: 18th and early 19th century mss, incl reports and correspondence on missions, Indians, New Mexico, Alta and Baja California.

MISSIONS—NORTHWEST, PACIFIC

†WA —WASHINGTON STATE UNIVERSITY, Library, Manuscripts, Archives & Special Collections, Pullman, 99164. John F Guido, Head
Holdings: Vols Cat Mss Maps Pix
Notes: Ms resources incl the papers of missionaries Henry Harmon Spalding, Elkanah Walker and Marcus Whitman; as well as the papers of their historian Clifford Merrill Drury. Unpublished container lists to these collections are in the library. Also, papers, 1821-1873, covering Father DeSmet's early sojourns at Whitemarsh and St Louis, his founding of the Rocky Mountain Missions, his long service as Procurator and Socius of the Missouri Province, and his many travels. Correspondence with his family in Belgium, mss of his published journals, 2 small maps,

sketches and engravings used to illustrate his books. Inc about 100 small pencil sketches by Father Nicholas Point depicting the 1841 journey from Westport to St Mary's Mission in the Bitterroot Valley. Described in *The Record,* 30 (1971) 47-63.

MISSIONS—SOUTHWEST

AZ —ARIZONA STATE MUSEUM, Library, University of Arizona, Tucson, 85721. Hans R Bart, Museum Librn
Holdings: Vols 100 Cat Mss
Notes: Books on Spanish missions in Arizona, New Mexico, Texas, California and particularly northern Mexico (Sonora). A private collection given to the library; it is not kept separate.

TX —AMARILLO PUBLIC LIBRARY, 413 E Fourth, Amarillo, 79101. Mary Kay Snell, Librn
Holdings: Vols Cat Mss Maps Pix
Notes: The southwest collections incl materials on the history of Texas, Louisiana, New Mexico, Arkansas, Missouri and Kansas. General subjects covered incl overland journeys, early narratives, early biographies, Indian captivities, outlaws, US government reports, Mississippi and Ohio Rivers, the Mexican War, reports of Catholic missionaries, Niles Register, early publications, fur trade, western trails, Texas Rangers, sheriffs and Texas as a sovereign state, buffalo hunting, Indian wars, cowboys, the arrival of farmers, fences, and towns. Over 1600 items which incl books, documents, maps, mss, pamphlets, unpublished theses, interviews and photographs. The three major collections are the William Henry Bush Collection, the Laurence J Fitzsimon Collection and the Calendar of John L McCarty.

TX —UNIVERSITY OF TEXAS LIBRARIES, Nettie Lee Benson Latin American Collection, Sid Richardson Hall 1.109, Austin, 78712. Laura Gutierrez-Witt, Head Librn
Holdings: Vols (450,000) Cat Mss Maps Pix Phonorecords Filmstrips Microforms
See also entries under Latin America; Texas-History

MISSIONS—SOUTHWEST—PICTURES, ILLUSTRATIONS, ETC.

NM —MUSEUM OF NEW MEXICO, Photo Archives, Box 2087, Santa Fe, 87503. Arthur L Olivas, Cur; Richard Rudisill, Photo Historian
Holdings: Cat Pix Slides
Budget: ($9000)
Notes: Archives incl 200,000 photographs, cataloged, and 40,000 slides. Primary function of the archives is to preserve significant historical material, and these pictures are mainly for research rather than general browsing. Photographs may be ordered as research copies for set fees. Reproduction or publication requires written permission plus additional required fees. Subject matter covered is extensive, incl Southwest town views, Southwest Indians, military subjects, missions, pioneer life, recreation (indoor and outdoor, toys, games, gambling, camping, etc), disasters, exhibits and expositions, portraits (those identified filed by last name), tools and equipment (agricultural, mechanical, housekeeping, etc), and transportation (railroad, stagecoaches, carriages, wagons, etc).

MISSIONS, FOREIGN

CA —UNIVERSITY OF CALIFORNIA, SANTA CRUZ, University Library, Special Collections, Santa Cruz, 95064. Rita Bottoms, Special Collections Librn; Margaret Felts, South Pacific Collection Bibliographer
Budget: ($2000)
Notes: Monographs, rare books, serials, documents and atlases which treat of the Pacific areas of Polynesia, Melanesia, Micronesia, Australia and New Zealand, but excluding western New Guinea (Irian Jaya), the Phillippines and Southeast Asia.

Approximately 10 per cent of the titles are multi-volume documents such as parliamentary papers, legislative journals, official yearbooks, statistical sourcebooks, laws and statutes. The collection includes an exhaustive selection of current journals and monographic series from and about the Pacific: early serials, South Pacific Commission publications. US Government and US Trust Territory publications, serials from museums, universities and scholarly societies. Chief emphasis has been placed on acquisition of the literature of history, description and travel, ethnology and anthropology, literature and literary criticism,political and constitutional histories. Other extensive holdings are in the fields of geography and maps, voyages, mission histories, mythology and folklore, art, linguistics, and science fields of natural history, environmental studies, biology, zoology, botany, geology and astronomy.

CT —YALE UNIVERSITY, Box 1603A, Yale Station, New Haven, 06520.

CT —YALE UNIVERSITY, Divinity School Library, 409 Prospect St, New Haven, 06520. John Bollier, Librarian
Holdings: Vols (340,000)
Notes: Collection incl 340,000 vols, 1452 periodical subscriptions, 8500 microforms and 3500 films.

HI —HAWAIIAN MISSION CHILDREN'S SOCIETY LIBRARY, 553 S King St, Honolulu, 96813. Mary Jane Knight, Librn
Holdings: Vols 15,000 Cat Mss Pix
Notes: Missionary period of Hawaiian history, 1819-1880, incl a general collection of Hawaiian history and travel, an outstanding collection of early voyages to the Pacific, and an almost complete collection of early Hawaiian imprints, ie, publications in the Hawaiian language during the 19th century. Ms material incl letters, journals and reports of the Protestant missionaries who came to Hawaii (the Sandwich Islands) under the auspices of the American Board of Commissioners for Foreign Missions. The material is for research only; the stacks are closed. Unpublished papers may be examined by qualified researchers on application to the librarian. Published material is cataloged. Hawaiian imprints are cataloged, except for the Dewey classification 300's which are mainly governmentdocuments. Ms collections are cataloged or in the process of being completely arranged and cataloged.

MD —JOHNS HOPKINS UNIVERSITY, Milton S Eisenhower Library, George Peabody Collection, 17 E Mt Vernon Place, Baltimore, 21201. Lyn Hart, Peabody Librn
Notes: Emphasis on materials published before 1950. Strength is a good collection through the 19th century.

MA —HARVARD UNIVERSITY LIBRARY, Houghton Library, Cambridge, 02138. Rodney G Dennis, Cur of Manuscripts
Holdings: Cat Mss
Notes: Incl Archives of American Board of Commissioners for Foreign Missions: see *Harvard Library Bulletin,* VI (1952), 52-68.

MA —BOSTON COLLEGE LIBRARIES, Thomas P O'Neill Library, Chestnut Hill, 02167. Frank J Seegraber, Special Collections Librn
Holdings: Vols (1500) Cat
Notes: Jesuitana Collection of early and rare works by and about Jesuits, 1540-1773. Incl annual letters from Jesuit missionaries in the Far East, Jesuit missionary activities in the New World, anti-Jesuit materials. Complete set of *Jesuit Relations.* For reference use only, by arrangement with librarian.

NY —UNION THEOLOGICAL SEMINARY, Library, 3041 Broadway at Reinhold Niebuhr Place, New York, 10027. Richard D Spoor, Dir
Holdings: Cat Mss Microforms
Notes: Missionary Research Library Collection (100,000 items). One of the strongest subject collections.

OR —UNIVERSITY OF OREGON LIBRARY, Special Collections Div, Eugene, 97403. Kenneth W Duckett, Curator
Holdings: Cat Mss
Notes: Ca 50 mss collections of

MISSIONS, FOREIGN (cont.)

correspondence, journals, mss and artifacts created and collected by missionaries to the Far East, mostly China. Publication: Martin Schmitt, comp, *Catalogue of Manuscripts in the University of Oregon Library* (Eugene: University of Oregon Books, 1971). The general library has a significant collection of books written by missionaries and the publications of societies and associations incl serials.

VA —UNIVERSITY OF VIRGINIA, Alderman Library, Manuscripts Dept, Charlottesville, 22901. Edmund Berkeley Jr, Cur
Holdings: Cat Mss
Notes: Papers of Samuel Higginbottom and his family; missionary to India. (30 linear feet).
See also entry under Mission - China.

WI —SEVENTH DAY BAPTIST HISTORICAL SOCIETY, Library, 3120 Kennedy Rd, PO Box 1678, Janesville, 53547. D Scott Smith, Historian
Holdings: Vols (150) Cat Mss Maps Pix
Notes: US Seventh Day Baptists Collection, incl records, letters. Established at Newport, Rhode Island, in 1671, this denomination is a part of the Free-Church evangelical movement in America. The General Conference was organized in 1801. The national and international headquarters of the Seventh Day Baptist denomination is located at Janesville, Wisconsin. Also have records, publications, etc of the denomination's mission in Shanghai, 1846-1950; further, materials (6 boxes) on the Church's work in Nyasaland (Malawi), 1895-1914, and then at a later period.

MISSIONS, INDIAN see
Indians—Missions

MISSIONS, MEDICAL

MA —BRANDEIS UNIVERSITY, Goldfarb Library, 415 South St, Waltham, 02154. Bessie Hahn, Dir
Notes: Albert Schweitzer Collection. This collection consists of 255 letters of correspondence to and from Dr Albert Schweitzer and other staff members of the Lambarene Hospital, Gabon, Africa. Also included in the collection are some artifacts, memorabilia and two commemorative Albert Schweitzer volumes. A guide to the collection was published in *Guide to Albert Schweitzer Collections in the United States.* New York, 1981.

MISSISSIPPI

LA —LOUISIANA STATE UNIVERSITY, Middleton Library, Dept of Archives & Manuscripts, Room 202, Baton Rouge, 70803. M Stone Miller Jr, Head
Holdings: Cat Mss Maps Pix Microforms
Notes: History of Louisiana and lower Mississippi Valley, colonial through 20th century. Scope: political, social and literary history; economic history, incl forestry, banking, agriculture, transportation and trade; national, regional, and Louisiana history; military history. About 4,500,000 items.

MS —UNIVERSITY OF SOUTHERN MISSISSIPPI, William David McCain Graduate Library, Box 5148, Southern Sta, Hattiesburg, 39406.
Holdings: Vols 12,000 Cat Mss Maps Pix Microforms
Notes: Mississippiana Collection. Includes government publications and newspapers of the state, works on geography, literature, politics, and travel.

MS —MISSISSIPPI LIBRARY COMMISSION, 1221 Ellis Ave, Box 10700, Jackson, 39209. Gerald Buchanan, Asst Dir
Holdings: Vols 10,000 Cat
Notes: Circulating collection of books and other materials by or about Mississippians and Mississippi. Archival and circulating collections of indexed but uncataloged Mississippi state government publications since 1965.

MISSISSIPPI—GENEALOGY

FL —ORLANDO PUBLIC LIBRARY, Local History & Genealogy Dept, 100 Block of Central Ave, Orlando, 32806. Eileen B Willis, Librn
Holdings: Vols 11,000 Cat Maps Microforms
Budget: $8000
Notes: Genealogy collection on Md, Del, W Va, NC, SC, Ala, Miss, La, Texas, Ark, Ky, Ohio, Ill, Ind, and Mich are well represented. Most other states are covered by smaller collections.
See also entry under Genealogy - Collections.

MS —UNIVERSITY OF SOUTHERN MISSISSIPPI, William David McCain Graduate Library, Box 5148, Southern Sta, Hattiesburg, 39406.
Holdings: Vols 1200 Cat Maps Mss Microforms
Notes: Mississippi will; marriages, estates, tax records; 1820-1900 censuses; military records; family histories; cemetary records.

MISSISSIPPI—HISTORY

LA —LOUISIANA STATE UNIVERSITY, Middleton Library, Dept of Archives & Manuscripts, Room 202, Baton Rouge, 70803. M Stone Miller Jr, Head
Holdings: Cat Mss Maps Pix Microforms
Notes: History of Louisiana and lower Mississippi Valley, colonial through 20th century. Scope: political, social and literary history; economic history, incl forestry, banking, agriculture, transportation and trade; national, regional, and Louisiana history; military history. About 4,500,000 items.

LA —TULANE UNIVERSITY, Howard-Tilton Memorial Library, Special Collections Div, 7001 Freret St, New Orleans, 70118. Wilbur E Meneray, Librn
Holdings: Cat Mss Pix Slides Audiotapes Videotapes 16mm Films Microforms
Notes: The majority of the 2000 plus collections relate to 18th, 19th and 20th century New Orleans, South Louisana and South Mississippi. See *Brief Guide to the Manuscripts Section of the Special Collections Division Tulane University Library* (New Orleans 1977).

MS —MISSISSIPPI BAPTIST HISTORICAL COMMISSION, Leland Speed Library, Mississippi College, PO Box 51, Clinton, 39056. Alice G Cox, Librn; Jack W Gunn, Exec Secretary
Holdings: Vols (956) Cat Mss Maps Pix Slides Audiotapes Microforms VF
Notes: Principal objective is to collect and preserve primary historical materials about churches and other institutions affiliated with the Mississippi Baptist Convention. Incl 489 volumes of church minutes. 4000 folders of materials about various churches, individuals, etc. Card index to the (Mississippi) *Baptist Record* (in progress). Incl 165 slides, 153 audiotapes, 578 microforms. Available to researchers but materials do not circulate.

MS —UNIVERSITY OF SOUTHERN MISSISSIPPI, William David McCain Graduate Library, Box 5148, Southern Sta, Hattiesburg, 39406.
Holdings: Vols (12,000) Cat Mss Maps Pix Microforms
Notes: Mississippiana Collection, 1699-date. Incl the papers of Theodore G Bilbo and William M Colmer, Paul B Johnson, Jr, and other ms collections. Also incl state government publications, the University of Southern Mississippi Archives, an oral history, and fiction. Mississippi newspapers on microfilm.

MS —FIRST REGIONAL LIBRARY, 59 Commerce St NW, Hernando, 38632. Jo Ann Wilroy, Asst Dir
Holdings: Vols 525 Cat Maps Pix
Notes: Materials about Mississippi or written by Mississippi authors.

MS —JACKSON METROPOLITAN LIBRARY SYSTEM, Information, Reference & Referral Div, 301 N State St, Jackson, 39201. Kathy Smith, Senior Ref Librn
Holdings: Vols 4500 Cat
Notes: Mississippi history, with emphasis on the city of Jackson. Also, files of Mississippi periodicals; Mississippi authors.

MS —MILLSAPS COLLEGE, Millsaps-Wilson Library, Jackson, 39210. Kathy Holden, College Archivist
Holdings: Vols 500 Mss Microforms
Notes: Mississippi Methodist Historical Archives Collection housed in the J B Cain Archives of Mississippi Methodism, in addition to Millsaps College Archives.

MS —MISSISSIPPI DEPARTMENT OF ARCHIVES AND HISTORY, Archives and Library Division, PO Box 571, Jackson, 39205. Madel J Morgan, Dir, Archives and Library Div
Holdings: Vols 38,000 Cat Mss Maps Pix Slides Phonorecords Audiotapes Videotapes Filmstrips Microforms
Budget: $38,000
Notes: Archives and secondary materials from 1678 to date: military records, private papers, mss, maps, church records, county records, genealogical materials, architectural drawings, etc. Newsfilm (video). VF.

MS —MISSISSIPPI LIBRARY COMMISSION, 1221 Ellis Ave, Box 10700, Jackson, 39209. Gerald Buchanan, Asst Dir
Holdings: Vols 3000 Cat

MS —MISSISSIPPI STATE UNIVERSITY, Mitchell Memorial Library, Box 5408, Mississippi State, 39762. Frances N Coleman, Head, Special Collections
Holdings: Vols (15,000) Cat Mss Maps Pix Microforms
Notes: Social and political history of Mississippi, incl University Archives (now separate branch). Microfilms of Protestant Church records. There are strong collections on history of the Southern States, Mississippi authors (especially Faulkner, Williams, Carter, Welty, and Young); also the John C Stennis Collection of over 2 million items, his books, papers, photographs, etc. Incl 400 collections of mss; papers of US Rep David R Bowen 1973-1983; papers of US Rep G V Montgomery 1967-; papers of Hodding Carter II, the editor/publisher of the Greenville, Mississsippi *Delta Democrat-Times.*

MS —JUDGE GEORGE W ARMSTRONG LIBRARY, Box 1406, Natchez, 39120. Eleanora Gralow, Dir
Holdings: Vols (1600) Cat Mss Maps Pix Microforms
Notes: Incl Natchez Newspaper and county newspapers on microforms. Extensive Natchez and Wilkinson County materials. Card index for material not containing its own index.

MS —TOUGALOO COLLEGE, L Zenobia Coleman Library, Tougaloo, 39174. Virgia Brocks-Shedd, Acting Dir
Holdings: Uncat Mss Maps Pix
Notes: Civil rights cases and legal papers; lawsuits; Mississippi, 1960-1968. Local attorneys have donated papers of cases they have handled, espec attorneys of two government-funded legal services offices. Incl VF holdings of articles from 1930 and on.

RI —BROWN UNIVERSITY, John Hay Library, 20 Prospect St, Providence, 02912. Mark N Brown, Cur Mss
Holdings: // Mss
Notes: Some papers of Thomas Rodney, farmer, Revolutionary War officer, member of the Continental Congress, Judge of the Delaware Supreme Court, and US Judge for the Mississippi Territory. 73 letters, essays, poems, documents, notes on court cases in Mississippi and Delaware for the period 1791-1810, and a journal for 1792-1800 about personal matters and Delaware politics. Register available.

TN —MEMPHIS STATE UNIVERSITY, John Willard Brister Library, Memphis, 38152. John Terreo, Special Collections Librn
Notes: Jefferson Davis-Joel Addison Family papers, 1864-1889. President of the Confederacy. Personal and business correspondence, receipts, notes, cancelled checks, and other papers, of Davis, following the Civil War (primarily 1877-1889) and his

MISSISSIPPI—HISTORY (cont.)

son-in-law, Joel Addison Hayes (1848-1919), banker of Memphis, TN, relating chiefly to management of Davis' plantation, Brierfield, near Vicksburg, MS, stocks and mining investments, and land sales. Incl correspondence between Davis' wife Varina (Howell) Davis and her daughter Margaret Howell (Davis) (1848-1908), and between Addison Hayes and members of his family.

MISSISSIPPI—POLITICS AND GOVERNMENT

MS —MISSISSIPPI STATE UNIVERSITY, Mitchell Memorial Library, Box 5408, Mississippi State, 39762. Frances N Coleman, Head, Special Collections
Holdings: Mss
Notes: Papers of US Rep David R Bowen 1973-1983.

MISSISSIPPI ASSOCIATION OF EDUCATORS

MS —UNIVERSITY OF SOUTHERN MISSISSIPPI, William David McCain Graduate Library, Box 5148, Southern Sta, Hattiesburg, 39406.
Holdings: Uncat Mss
Notes: Records (1967-1975; 2 cubic feet) of the Mississippi Association of Educators concerning the merger of the predominantly Black, Mississippi Teachers Association and the predominantly White, Mississippi Education Association. The collection incl correspondence, minutes of meetings, conference hearings, resolutions, proposals and constitutions from various state education associations.

MISSISSIPPI AUTHORS see Authors, Mississippi

MISSISSIPPI CENTRAL RAILROAD

MS —UNIVERSITY OF SOUTHERN MISSISSIPPI, William David McCain Graduate Library, Box 5148, Southern Sta, Hattiesburg, 39406.
Holdings: Cat Mss
Notes: These records (1898-1967; 245 cubic feet) incl correspondence, financial records, statistical records, statistical reports, and solicitation records of the Mississippi Central Railroad (1904-1967) and it predecessors. This railroad connected Natchez and Hattiesburg, Mississippi. It was taken over by the Illinois Central Railroad in 1967. A guide to the records is available for loan.

MISSISSIPPI RIVER

LA —LOUISIANA STATE UNIVERSITY, SHREVEPORT, Library-Archives, 8515 Youree Dr, Shreveport, 71129. Patricia L Meador, Archivist & Asst Librn
Notes: See Louisiana - History entry for LSU Archives.
WI —UNIVERSITY OF WISCONSIN, LA CROSSE, Murphy Library, 1631 Pine St, La Crosse, 54601. Edwin L Hill, Special Collections Librn
Holdings: Vols 50 Cat Pix
Budget: $9000
Notes: The steamboat project undertakes to collect photographs, sketches, and basic information on upper Mississippi River steamboats. Collection now incl about 20,000 photographs and sketches, with data file. Most photos are copy prints; some are protected by copyright and may not be used for commercial purposes. Most photos are unpublished. Collecting and data searching actively pursued. Boats from tributary rivers included. Collection is supplemented by primary and secondary sources and active field research. Overall arrangement is alphabetical by boat name, with notation of special categories of boats.

MISSISSIPPI VALLEY

IL —SOUTHERN ILLINOIS UNIVERSITY, CARBONDALE, Morris Library,

Carbondale, 62901. Jean M Ray, Map Librn
Holdings: Cat Maps Pix
Budget: ($1070)
Notes: Emphasis of map collection is Southern Illinois and Mississippi Valley. Incl 158,000 maps; 47,000 aerial photographs of Southern Illinois; 2000 atlases, reference books, etc; 4000 issues of weather map series (historical, daily, monthly); and 360 Illinois county platbooks. Includes Sang Collection-- 60 early maps of North America, especially Mississippi Valley, 1584-1840.
IL —UNIVERSITY OF CHICAGO LIBRARY, Dept of Special Collections, 1100 E 57 St, Chicago, 60637.
Notes: Source material regarding first contact of White men and Indians in Mississippi Valley. Part of Ethno-History Collection.
IL —AUGUSTANA COLLEGE, Library, Rock Island, 61201. Marjorie M Miller, Special Collections Librn
Holdings: Vols 2000 Cat Mss
Notes: The John Hauberg Upper Mississippi Valley Collection. Incl strong collection of immigrant guide books for the Midwestern states. Fine collection relative to the Sauk and Fox tribes and Black Hawk in particular.
IL —UNIVERSITY OF ILLINOIS, URBANA/CHAMPAIGN, Library, Urbana, 61801.
LA —TULANE UNIVERSITY, Howard-Tilton Memorial Library, Special Collections Div, 7001 Freret St, New Orleans, 70118. Wilbur E Meneray, Librn
Notes: Louisiana Collection incl manuscripts, books, photographs, newspapers, prints and maps pertaining to the history and development of Louisiana and the Mississippi Valley from colonial times to the present.
MI —DETROIT PUBLIC LIBRARY, Burton Historical Collection, 5201 Woodward Ave, Detroit, 48202. Alice Dalligan, Chief
MO —WASHINGTON UNIVERSITY, John M Olin Library, Campus Box 1061, St Louis, 63130.
Holdings: Vols (1800) Cat Mss
Notes: Incl material from the Arthur C Hoskins, Richard S Hawes, Ernst C Krohn, George N Meissner, Stratford Lee Morton, and Edgar M Queeny collections; strong in early travel literature of the US and Latin America; accounts of exploration in the Mississippi Valley and Trans-Mississippi West; miscellaneous accounts of history, pioneer life, and travel in the Ohio Valley, Old Southwest, and California; material on the American Indian; 18th century American music; early American imprints.
TN —MEMPHIS STATE UNIVERSITY, John Willard Brister Library, Memphis, 38152. John Terreo, Special Collections Librn
Holdings: Vols (25,000) Cat Mss Maps Pix Slides Microforms
Notes: The history, literature, culture, and geography of the lower Mississippi Valley. Unpublished finding aids for cataloged manuscript collections and a few of the audio-video collections exist in the MVC. All books amd pamphlets are cataloged and cards pertaining to them can be found in the MVC. Cataloging of materials is in progress, but as of yet no comprehensive listing to the MVC's total holdings exists. Manuscript collections of significance include: Dyer Marion "Ichabod" Reynolds Circus Collection, 1878-1980; Theatre Collection, 1789-1972; 1968 Memphis Sanitation Workers Strike (during this strike civil rights activist Dr Martin Luther King, Jr was assassinated); Jefferson Davis-Joel Addison Hayes, Jr Family Papers, 1864-1889.

MISSISSIPPI VALLEY—HISTORY

AR —UNIVERSITY OF CENTRAL ARKANSAS, Torreyson Library, Conway, 72032. Douglas A Green, Library Dir
Holdings: Vols 181 Cat Maps Microforms
Notes: Colonial history of the lower Mississippi River Valley. Incl 260 maps.
TN —MEMPHIS STATE UNIVERSITY, John Willard Brister Library, Memphis, 38152. John Terreo, Special Collections Librn
Holdings: Vols (25,000) Cat Mss Maps Pix

Slides Microforms
Notes: The history, literature, culture, and geography of the lower Mississippi Valley. Unpublished finding aids for cataloged manuscript collections and a few of the audio-video collections exist in the MVC. All books amd pamphlets are cataloged and cards pertaining to them can be found in the MVC. Cataloging of materials is in progress, but as of yet no comprehensive listing to the MVC's total holdings exists. Manuscript collections of significance include: Dyer Marion "Ichabod" Reynolds Circus Collection, 1878-1980; Theatre Collection, 1789-1972; 1968 Memphis Sanatation Workers Strike (during this strike civil rights activist Dr Martin Luther King, Jr was assassinated); Jefferson Davis-Joel Addison Hayes, Jr Family Papers, 1864-1889.
PQ —BIBLIOTHEQUE DES ARCHIVES NATIONALES DU QUEBEC, CP 10450, Sainte-Foy, G1V 4N1, Can. Collete Barry, Dir
Holdings: Vols (50,000) Cat Mss Maps Pix Microforms
Budget: ($25,000)
Notes: Dictionary catalog on cards (unpublished). Official Quebec documents published before 1867.

MISSISSIPPI VALLEY, LOWER

AR —PUBLIC LIBRARY OF PINE BLUFF AND JEFFERSON COUNTY, Library System, 200 E Eighth Ave, Pine Bluff, 71601. Cora M Dorsett, Dir
Holdings: Vols 131 Cat Microforms Maps
Notes: Incl microforms (19), maps (280).
LA —LOUISIANA STATE UNIVERSITY, Troy H Middleton Library, Louisiana Room, Baton Rouge, 70803. Evangeline Mills Lynch, Head Librn; Ruth Murray, Associate Librn
Holdings: Vols (33,500) Cat Maps VF
Notes: Louisiana Collection of history, description and travel, biography, agriculture, literature, politics and government, folklore, anthropology, geography, geology, education, language, music and natural history. Especially large subject collections may be found on Louisiana, the history of the lower Mississippi Valley, Abraham Lincoln, Romance languages and literatures, sugar culture and technology, Southern history, petroleum engineering, plant pathology, micropaleontology, ornithology, and various aspects of crawfish life, biology and culture. Complete depository of Louisiana State Documents; extensive newspapers clipping files; separate card catalog; items listed in Louisiana Union Catalog; restricted use (research and reference). Incl both materials about Louisiana and by Louisianians without regard to subject. LSU Press Collection(preservation copy of each title kept for exhibit purposes only). LSU theses and dissertations from 1900-date. LSU Faculty Collection. Also, 1300 maps, 104 VF drawers, 250 boxes of uncataloged pamphlets.
TN —MEMPHIS STATE UNIVERSITY, John Willard Brister Library, Memphis, 38152. John Terreo, Special Collections Librn
Holdings: Vols (25,000) Cat Mss Maps Pix Slides Microforms
Notes: The history, literature, culture, and geography of the lower Mississippi Valley. Unpublished finding aids for cataloged manuscript collections and a few of the audio-video collections exist in the MVC. All books amd pamphlets are cataloged and cards pertaining to them can be found in the MVC. Cataloging of materials is in progress, but as of yet no comprehensive listing to the MVC's total holdings exists. Manuscript collections of significance include: Dyer Marion "Ichabod" Reynolds Circus Collection, 1878-1980; Theatre Collection, 1789-1972; 1968 Memphis Sanitation Workers Strike (during this strike civil rights activist Dr Martin Luther King, Jr was assassinated); Jefferson Davis-Joel Addison Hayes, Jr Family Papers, 1864-1889.

MISSISSIPPI VALLEY INDUSTRIAL ARTS CONFERENCE

IL —UNIVERSITY OF ILLINOIS, URBANA/CHAMPAIGN, Library,

MISSISSIPPI VALLEY INDUSTRIAL ARTS CONFERENCE (cont.)

University Archives, 19 Library, 1408 W Gregory Drive, Urbana, 61801. Maynard Brichford, University Archivist
Holdings: Cat Mss Maps Pix Slides Microforms
Notes: Papers, archival records, etc.

MISSOURI

MO —NORTHEAST MISSOURI STATE UNIVERSITY, Pickler Memorial Library, Kirksville, 63501. George N Hartje, Librn
Holdings: Vols 5300 Cat Mss Maps Pix
Budget: $500
MO —MISSOURI WESTERN STATE COLLEGE, Hearnes Learning Resources Center, 4525 Downs Dr, Saint Joseph, 64507. Susan Bushhammer, Librn
Holdings: Vols (1200) Cat Maps
Notes: Became a state document depository in 1976.
MO —SPRINGFIELD-GREENE COUNTY PUBLIC LIBRARY, 397 E Central, PO Box 737, Springfield, 65801. Jewell Smith, Administrative Librn
Holdings: Vols 7100 Cat Maps Pix Microforms
Notes: Missouri and Ozarks collection. Incl uncataloged pamphlets. Special indexes have been prepared.

MISSOURI—GENEALOGY

MO —SAINT JOSEPH PUBLIC LIBRARY, Tenth & Felix Sts, Saint Joseph, 64501. Dorothy Sanborn Elliott, Dir
Holdings: Vols 550 Cat
MO —MISSOURI HISTORICAL SOCIETY, Library, Jefferson Memorial Bldg, Saint Louis, 63112. Stephanie Klein, Librn-Archivist; Peter Michel, Cur of Manuscripts
Holdings: Cat Mss Maps Pix
Notes: Extensive ms holdings relating to Missouri, US history, etc. Also ms collections of many noted persons (all but subsequent additions listed in Hamer, 1961). Library holdings described in Whitehall, Walter Muir, *Independent Historical Societies* (Boston, 1962).

MISSOURI—GOVERNMENT PUBLICATIONS

MO —SAINT LOUIS PUBLIC LIBRARY, Documents Dept, 1301 Olive St, Saint Louis, 63103. Anne Watts, Librn
Holdings: Vols 750,000 Uncat Maps Microforms
Notes: St Louis Public Library is a depository for Missouri and US Documents.

MISSOURI—HISTORY

MD —JOHNS HOPKINS UNIVERSITY, Milton S Eisenhower Library, Charles & 34 Sts, Baltimore, 21218. Ann S Gwyn, Assistant Dir for Special Collections
MO —CULVER-STOCKTON COLLEGE, Carl Johann Memorial Library, Canton, 63435. Robert Lin, Librn
Holdings: Vols 1500 Cat
Budget: $1000
Notes: The Johann Collection covers all aspects of Midwest Americana, with special emphasis on Missouri and Mark Twain.
MO —MISSOURI STATE LIBRARY, 308 E High St, Jefferson City, 65101. Charles O'Halloran, State Librn
Holdings: Vols 500 Cat
Notes: Collection of reference sources relating to contemporary Missouri government and its operation. Special emphasis on 1960's, 70's and 80's. Newspaper items on state government issues.
MO —UNIVERSITY OF MISSOURI-KANSAS CITY, General Library, Snyder Collection of Americana, 5100 Rockhill Road, Kansas City, 64110. Kenneth J LaBudde, Dir; Robert Paustian, Asst Dir
Holdings: Vols 25,000 Cat
Notes: Nucleus was Robert M Snyder, Jr Americana Collection of some 14,000 items.

Contains printed materials on 19th-century American history, especially the Trans-Mississippi West. Strengths include the history of Kansas City and Jackson County, Missouri, Kansas and Missouri county and state histories, American frontier religion (esp the Mormons and Alexander Campbell's Disciples of Christ), the history of railroads and transportation, the cattle trade, 19th-Century biography and autobiography, North American Indians and early Kansas and Missouri imprints.

MO —UNIVERSITY OF MISSOURI-KANSAS CITY, General Library, State Historical Society of Missouri Manuscripts, 5100 Rockhill Road, Kansas City, 64110. Kenneth J LaBudde, Dir; Gordon Hendrickson, Assoc Dir
Holdings: Mss
Notes: Joint Collection Western Historical Manuscript Collection and the State Historical of Missouri Manuscripts, University of Missouri-Kansas City General Library, 5100 Rockhill Road, Kansas City, MO 64110. Ca 2,500 linear feet of manuscripts, blueprints and oral history tapes.
Notes: The manuscript collection includes material which documents the history, growth and development of Missouri, especially the Greater Kansas City area. The personal papers of business, civic, cultural, political and community leaders; local historians and other individuals of families from the area are within the collection as are the records of associations, organizations and institutions which reflect the history of the area. Prominent among the collections are the papers of Charles B. Wheeler, Jr., Charles N. Kimball, Arthur Mag, Oscar D. Nelson, Lou B. Holland, J. C. Nichols, Perry Cookingham, Blevins Davis and Daniel Macmorris and the records of the Kansas City Board of Trade. Architectural designs and plans for approximately 3,500 Kansas City buildings and the records of the Hoit, Price and Barnes architectural firm and the papers of Asa Beebe Cross, early Kansas City architect as well as a number of oral histories with Kansas City Jazz figures are in the collection.

MO —NORTHEAST MISSOURI STATE UNIVERSITY, Pickler Memorial Library, Kirksville, 63501. George N Hartje, Librn
Holdings: Vols 5300 Cat Mss Maps Pix
Budget: $500

MO —NORTHWEST MISSOURI STATE UNIVERSITY, B D Owens Library, Maryville, 64468. Charles W Koch, Dir of Learning Resources
Holdings: Vols 2118 Cat Mss Maps Pix Microforms

MO —SAINT JOSEPH PUBLIC LIBRARY, Tenth & Felix Sts, Saint Joseph, 64501. Dorothy Sanborn Elliott, Dir
Holdings: Vols 300 Cat
Notes: Incl local newspapers, 1850s-date.

MO —MISSOURI HISTORICAL SOCIETY, Library, Jefferson Memorial Bldg, Saint Louis, 63112. Stephanie Klein, Librn-Archivist; Peter Michel, Cur of Manuscripts
Holdings: Cat Mss Maps Pix
Notes: Extensive ms holdings relating to Missouri, US history, etc. Also ms collections of many noted persons (all but subsequent additions listed in Hamer, 1961). Library holdings described in Whitehall, Walter Muir, *Independent Historical Societies* (Boston, 1962).

MO —SAINT LOUIS PUBLIC LIBRARY, Gardner Rare Book Room, 1301 Olive St,

Saint Louis, 63103. Julanne M Good, Supervisor; Martha Riley, Rare Books Librn
Holdings: Vols 100 Cat Maps
Budget: ($5573)
Notes: Small growing collection of travels incl St Louis or Missouri, largely transferred from the general stacks, although an occasional purchase in made. Incl early business directories of St Louis, river pilots' handbooks and maps. Noncirculating.
MO —SAINT LOUIS PUBLIC LIBRARY, History & Genealogy Dept, 1301 Olive Blvd, Saint Louis, 63103. Noel C Holobeck, Librn
Holdings: Cat Maps Microforms
Notes: Extensive collection. See also *Genealogical Materials and Local Histories in the St Louis Public Library*, by Georgia Gambrill, 1966; first supplement, 1971. Local history index (card file). Vertical file material.
MO —UNIVERSITY OF MISSOURI-SAINT LOUIS, Thomas Jefferson Library, Manuscript and Historical Society Collection, 8001 Natural Bridge Rd, Saint Louis, 63121.
Holdings: Mss Pix Tapes
Notes: ca
MO —WASHINGTON UNIVERSITY, John M Olin Library, Campus Box 1061, St Louis, 63130.
Holdings: Cat
Notes: Source materials and early Missouri imprints (atlases, gazetteers, illustrated books and travel accounts).
MO —WASHINGTON UNIVERSITY, Libraries, Special Collections Dept, Campus Box 1061, St Louis, 63130.
Notes: Terminal Railroad Association Records (1889-date), of more than 450 original tracings of the Eads Bridge (1874-date). Drawings show in fine and complete detail all the design features of this internationally known St Louis landmark; the Spanish Archive of St Louis Collection; St Louis Mayoral Papers Collection, incl papers of Aloys P Kaufmann, 1944-49, Raymond R Tucker, 1953-65, Alphonso J Cervantes, 1965-73, John H Poelker, 1973-77, James F Conway, 1977-81; papers of the prominent Link Family of 1809-1921.
TX —AMARILLO PUBLIC LIBRARY, 413 E Fourth, Amarillo, 79101. Mary Kay Snell, Librn
Holdings: Vols Cat Mss Maps Pix
Notes: The southwest collections incl materials on the history of Texas, Louisiana, New Mexico, Arkansas, Missouri and Kansas. General subjects covered incl overland journeys, early narratives, early biographies, Indian captivities, outlaws, US government reports, Mississippi and Ohio Rivers, the Mexican War, reports of Catholic missionaries, Niles Register, early publications, fur trade, western trails, Texas Rangers, sheriffs and Texas as a sovereign state, buffalo hunting, Indian wars, cowboys, the arrival of farmers, fences, and towns. Over 1600 items which incl books, documents, maps, mss, pamphlets, unpublished theses, interviews and photographs. The three major collections are the William Henry Bush Collection, the Laurence J Fitzsimon Collection and the Calendar of John L McCarty.

MISSOURI—MAPS

MO —SAINT LOUIS PUBLIC LIBRARY, History & Genealogy Dept, 1301 Olive Blvd, Saint Louis, 63103. Noel C Holobeck, Librn
Notes: Depository for US Army Maps and US Geological Survey maps. Collection of historic Missouri and Saint Louis atlases and maps, country atlases. Index to maps and atlases (card file). Vertical file of maps and travel brochures. 106,678 maps in collection.
OK —TULSA CITY-COUNTY LIBRARY, Business & Technology Dept, 400 Civic Center, Tulsa, 74103. Craig Buthod, Head
Notes: Original General Land Office survey maps for the states of Arizona, Arkansas, Colorado, Illinois, Indiana, Idaho, Kansas, Michigan, Missouri, Montana, Nebraska, Nevada, New Mexico, North Dakota, Ohio,

MISSOURI—MAPS (cont.)

Oklahoma, South Dakota, Utah and Wyoming. Incomplete coverage of each state.

MISSOURI—POLITICS AND GOVERNMENT

MO —MISSOURI STATE LIBRARY, 308 E High St, Jefferson City, 65101. Charles O'Halloran, State Librn
Holdings: Vols 500 Cat
Notes: Collection of reference sources relating to contemporary Missouri government and its operation. Special emphasis on 1960s, 70s and 80s. Newspaper items on state government issues.

MO —UNIVERSITY OF MISSOURI-SAINT LOUIS, Thomas Jefferson Library, Manuscript and Historical Society Collection, 8001 Natural Bridge Rd, Saint Louis, 63121.
Holdings: Mss Pix Tapes
Notes: ca

MO —WASHINGTON UNIVERSITY, Libraries, Special Collections Dept, Campus Box 1061, St Louis, 63130.
Notes: St Louis Mayoral Papers Collection: Papers of Aloys P Kaufmann, 1944-49; Raymond R Tucker, 1953-65; Alphonso J Cervantes, 1965-73; John H Poelker, 1973-77; James F Conway, 1977-81.

MISSOURI BOTANICAL GARDEN, ST. LOUIS

MO —MISSOURI BOTANICAL GARDEN LIBRARY, PO Box 299, Saint Louis, 63166. M R Crosby, Dir of Research
Holdings: Uncat Mss Maps Pix
Notes: Papers of Henry Shaw relating to St Louis business and economy history and founding of the Missouri Botanical Garden. About 40 vols and 60 boxes of files containing 40,000 ms pieces.

MISSOURI RIVER

IA —SIOUX CITY PUBLIC LIBRARY, 705 Sixth St, Sioux City, 51105. Betsy Thompson, Head Librn
Holdings: Vols 3700 Cat Mss Maps Pix Microforms
Notes: Emphasis on Sioux City and Iowa history, the Missouri River region. Microfilm copies of early newspapers, etc.

MISTRAL, FREDERIC

MA —HARVARD UNIVERSITY LIBRARY, Houghton Library, Cambridge, 02138. Rodney G Dennis, Cur of Manuscripts
Holdings: Mss

MISTRAL, GABRIELA

NY —BARNARD COLLEGE LIBRARY, Broadway & 117 St, New York, 10027. Patricia K Ballou, Archivist and Tech Services Librn
Holdings: Vols 990 Cat
Notes: Volumes from the personal library of Gabriela Mistral (Lucila Godoy Alcayaga), significant for her ms annotations, the author's inscription, or other special characteristics. Published catalog available. No photocopying.

MITANI LANGUAGE see Mittanian Language

MITCHELL, ARTHUR W.

IL —CHICAGO HISTORICAL SOCIETY, Library, Clark St at North Ave, Chicago, 60614. Robert L Brubaker, Librn
Holdings: Papers

MITCHELL, DONALD GRANT

CT —YALE UNIVERSITY, Box 1603A, Yale Station, New Haven, 06520.
Holdings: Cat Mss
Notes: Incl mss and books from his library.

MITCHELL, EVERETT

IL —WHEATON COLLEGE, Buswell Memorial Library, Wheaton, 60187. Paul Snezek, Library Dir
Holdings: Mss
Notes: 5 linear feet of mss material and a collection of cassette tapes of Mitchell. *Related Topics:* Radio.

MITCHELL, HELEN S.

TN —VANDERBILT UNIVERSITY, Medical Center Library, Nashville, 37232. Mary H Teloh, Special Collections Librn
Holdings: Uncat Mss Pix Videotapes
Notes: The nucleus of the developing nutrition collection at Vanderbilt is the papers of medical researcher Joseph Goldberger, MD, and his associate W Henry Sebrell, Jr, MD. The collection consists of first editions and translations of classic books on pellagra, and the letters, mss, and notebooks compiled by Dr Goldberger and Dr Sebrell during their years of research on pellagra. See *Nutrition Reviews*, 33(10):310-312, Oct 1975. 10 linear ft of mss. Library also has the archives of the American Institute of Nutrition and manuscripts representing the work of Karl Mason, PhD, Helen S Mitchell, PhD, Lydia J Roberts, PhD, and John B Youmans, MD.

MITCHELL, HUGH B.

WA —UNIVERSITY OF WASHINGTON LIBRARIES, Suzzallo Library, Manuscripts Section, FM-25, Seattle, 98195. Karyl Winn, Librn
Notes: Incl 59 linear ft, circa 1944-46 and 1948-52.

MITCHELL, JOHN M.

MI —MICHIGAN STATE UNIVERSITY, Labor and Industrial Relations Library, East Lansing, 48824. Martha Jane Soltow, Librn
Holdings: Cat Microforms
Notes: This material is composed primarily of special collection of papers on microfilm or microfiche.

MITCHELL, MARGARET

GA —AGNES SCOTT COLLEGE, McCain Library, E College Ave, Decatur, 30030. Judith Bourgeois Jensen, Librn
Holdings: Vols 104// Uncat
Notes: The collection was given by Miss Margaret E Baugh. It contains 50 editions of *Gone With the Wind*; 43 of these editions are translations from 19 countries.

MA —BOSTON UNIVERSITY, Mugar Memorial Library, Special Collections Dept, 771 Commonwealth Ave, Boston, 02215. Howard B Gotlieb, Dir
Holdings: // Cat
Notes: Correspondence, incl publications by.

MA —HARVARD UNIVERSITY LIBRARY, Cambridge, 02138.

MITCHELL, MARIA

NY —VASSAR COLLEGE, Library, Rare Books & Manuscripts Collection, Box 20, Poughkeepsie, 12601. Lisa Browar, Cur
Holdings: Mss Pix
Notes: Emphasis is on women in the US, women's rights, suffrage and Equal Rights Amendment. Manuscript collections incl papers of Elizabeth Cady Stanton, Paulina Wright Davis, Maria Mitchell and Alma Lutz.

MITCHELL, SILAS WEIR, 1829-1914

CA —UNIVERSITY OF CALIFORNIA, LOS ANGELES, Biomedical Library, Center for the Health Sciences, Los Angeles, 90024. Alison Bunting, Acting Biomedical Librn; Victoria Steele, Head, History & Special Collections Div
Holdings: Vols 92// Cat Mss
Notes: Presented by Dr and Mrs Elmer Belt. Books, memorabilia and mss.

CT —YALE UNIVERSITY, Medical Historical Library, 333 Cedar St, New Haven, 06510. Ferenc A Gyorgyey, Librn
Holdings: Vols 200 Cat Mss

KS —MENNINGER FOUNDATION, Archives, 5600 W Sixth St, Box 829, Topeka, 66601. Alice Brand, Librn; Mark West, Archivist
Notes: 1 box, 1876-1911. Incl correspondence and miscellaneous materials.

MA —HARVARD UNIVERSITY LIBRARY, Cambridge, 02138.
Holdings: Cat Mss

PA —COLLEGE OF PHYSICIANS OF PHILADELPHIA, Library, 19 S 22 St, Philadelphia, 19103. Christine Ruggere, Cur, Historical Collections
Holdings: Vols (316,223) Cat Mss
Budget: ($1,096,557)
Notes: Very strong collection.
See also entry under Medicine

PA —UNIVERSITY OF PENNSYLVANIA, Van Pelt Library, Rare Books Collection, 34 & Walnut Sts, Philadelphia, 19104. Daniel Traister, Special Collections Librn
Holdings: Vols 80 Cat Mss
Notes: Collection incl 19 vols of bound mss.

MITCHELL, W.O., 1914-

AB —UNIVERSITY OF CALGARY, Libraries, Special Collections Div, 2500 University Dr, Calgary, T2N 1N4, Can.
Holdings: Cat Mss
Notes: The Mitchell papers consists of manuscripts of "Jake and the Kid," Canadian Broadcasting Corporation scripts, personal and business correspondence, drafts and page proofs of novels, plays, and short stories, scrapbooks, photographs, and other memorabilia.

MITCHELL, WILLIAM (BILLY)

DC —LIBRARY OF CONGRESS, Manuscript Division, Washington, 20540. John C Broderick, Chief
Holdings: Cat Mss Pix
Notes: Mss, papers, records, etc.

MITES

HI —BERNICE P BISHOP MUSEUM, Library, PO Box 19000-A, Honolulu, 96819. Cynthia Timberlake, Librn
Holdings: Vols (90,000) Cat Mss Maps Pix Slides Microforms
Budget: ($30,000)
Notes: Only American library devoted exclusively to the Pacific region. Collection reflects historical and contemporary research emphases of Bishop Museum; ie the natural and cultural history of the Pacific. Areas of concentration incl archaeology, ethnology, linguistics, voyages and explorations, history, vertebrate and invertebrate zoology, botany and museology. Strong special collections incl photographs, mss and archives, maps and art. Publications: Quarterly "Additions to the Catalog," *Dictionary Catalog of the Library* (9 vols and 2 suppl; Boston: G K Hall, 1964-69).

MITFORD, MARY RUSSELL, 1787-1855

CA —UNIVERSITY OF CALIFORNIA, LOS ANGELES, Research Library, Dept of Special Collections, 405 Hilgard Ave, Los Angeles, 90024. Edward Shreeves, Chairman, Bibliographers Group; David S Zeidberg, Head
Holdings: Vols 25
Notes: 25 first and other editions of her books; 20 letters.

MITFORD, NANCY

DC —GEORGETOWN UNIVERSITY, Library, Special Collections Div, 37 & O Sts NW, Washington, 20057. George M Barringer, Special Collections Librn; Nicholas B Sheetz, Mss Librn
Holdings: Mss Pix
Notes: The papers of Christopher Sykes, biographer, journalist, and novelist; containing mss, letters, photographs, and

MITFORD, NANCY (cont.)

drawings. With extensive correspondence from Harold Acton; Angela, Countess of Antrim; Sir John Betjeman; Ivy Compton-Burnett; Alick Dru; T S Eliot; Max Beerbohm; Graham Greene; John Hayward; Lord Patrick Kinross; Compton Mackenzie; Nancy Mitford; Anthony Powell; Dame Flora Robson; Cecil Roth; Sir John Russell; Osbert Sitwell; John Sparrow; Freya Stark; James Stern; and Evelyn Waugh, among others. Also, considerable research material about Evelyn Waugh, Adam von Trott, Robert Byron, Lady Nancy Astor; and the foundation of the state of Israel.

MITTANIAN LANGUAGE

NY —NEW YORK PUBLIC LIBRARY, Oriental Div, Fifth Ave & 42 St, New York, 10018. E Christian Filstrup, Chief
Holdings: Cat Mss Microforms
Budget: ($56,455)
Notes: Published catalog of holdings.

MIXED LANGUAGES see Languages, Mixed

MIYAKAWA, T. SCOTT

CA —UNIVERSITY OF CALIFORNIA, LOS ANGELES, Research Library, Dept of Special Collections, 405 Hilgard Ave, Los Angeles, 90024. Edward Shreeves, Chairman, Bibliographers Group; David S Zeidberg, Head
Notes: 50 linear feet of mss, correspondence, research notes, etc, relating to Tetsuo Scott Miyakawa's career and involvement in documenting the Japanese American experience. He was the first director of the Japanese-American Research Center at UCLA (1962-1965).

MIZENER, ARTHUR

DE —UNIVERSITY OF DELAWARE, Hugh M Morris Library, S College Ave, Newark, 19711. T Stuart Dick, Special Collections
Holdings: Cat Mss Pix
Notes: Early typescript draft of biography of F Scott Fitzgerald incl critical comment and correspondence from Edmund Wilson.

MNEMONICS

CT —YALE UNIVERSITY, Beinecke Rare Book & Manuscripts Library, Wall & High St, New Haven, 06520. Louis A Martz, Dir
Holdings: Cat
See also entry under Zufall, Bernard
MD —JOHNS HOPKINS UNIVERSITY, Milton S Eisenhower Library, George Peabody Collection, 17 E Mt Vernon Place, Baltimore, 21201. Lyn Hart, Peabody Librn
Notes: Noncirculating.
NY —MORRIS N & CHESLEY V YOUNG LIBRARY OF MNEMONICS, 270 Riverside Dr, New York, 10025. Morris N Young, Cur
Holdings: Cat Mss Maps Pix Phonorecords Audiotapes 16mm Films Microforms
Notes: Collection of 5000 books, pamphlets, pictures, memorabilia, etc incl medieval art of memory; psychology of memory, forgetting and reading; medical aspects of memory, amnesia, dyslexia; biomedical aspects of learning and memory; information storage, retrieval and cybernetics; memory prodigies, lightning calculators, calendars; remembrance cups and memory mementos. All languages. Memorabilia incl engravings, posters, programs, advertisements, birthday cards, teaching cards, ASLs, and Mark Twain's Memory Builder game and other games. Items range from 1410 to 1980s.

MOATS, ALICE-LEONE

MA —BOSTON UNIVERSITY, Mugar Memorial Library, Special Collections Dept, 771 Commonwealth Ave, Boston, 02215. Howard B Gotlieb, Dir
Holdings: Cat Mss Pix
Notes: Mss, correspondence, etc. collected in depth; incl publications by or about.

MOBILE, ALABAMA—HISTORY

AL —MOBILE PUBLIC LIBRARY, Special Collections Div, 701 Government St, Mobile, 36602.
Notes: The Mobile area; incl papers of the Forbes Trading Co, 1795-1840; Bank of Mobile papers, 1820-.
†AL —MUSEUMS OF THE CITY OF MOBILE, Reference Library, 355 Government St, Mobile, 36602. Caldwell Delaney, Adminr
Notes: Collections incl: History of Mobile from 1702; City of Mobile Coll; Siege of Mobile (1861-1865) Coll.
AL —SPRING HILL COLLEGE, Thomas Byrne Memorial Library, Mobile, 36608. Benjamin F Shearer, Librn
Holdings: Vols (1350) Cat Mss Maps Pix
Budget: ($225,000)
Notes: Mobiliana, Incl pamphlets.

MOBILIZATION FOR YOUTH, NEW YORK

†NY —COLUMBIA UNIVERSITY LIBRARIES, Butler Library, Rare Book and Manuscript Library, 535 W 114 St, New York, 10027.
Notes: Papers of Mobilization for Youth, a New York City social service agency. Incl correspondence, minutes, memoranda, reports, project proposals, financial records, and related printed material.

MODERN, FRED

CA —CALIFORNIA STATE UNIVERSITY, LONG BEACH, Library, Dept of Special Collections & Archives, 1250 Bellflower Blvd, Long Beach, 90840. John Ahouse, Special Collections Librn
Holdings: Vols 600
Notes: Libraries of Dr Fred Modern and photojournalist Richard Cross, and incl signed books and photographs of photographer Ansel Adams.

MODEL SOLDIERS AND SAILORS see Military Miniatures

MODELL, MERRIAM

MA —BOSTON UNIVERSITY, Mugar Memorial Library, Special Collections Dept, 771 Commonwealth Ave, Boston, 02215. Howard B Gotlieb, Dir
Holdings: Cat Mss

MODELS, MILITARY see Military Miniatures

MODERN ART see Art, Modern—20th Century

MODERN AUTHORS see Authors, Modern

MODERN COMMUNES see Collective Settlements

MODERN DANCE

CA —MILLS COLLEGE LIBRARY, Oakland, 94613. Steven P Pandolfo, Librn
Holdings: Vols (500) Cat Pix
Notes: Jane Bourne Parton Collection of Books on the Dance. History of the dance with emphasis on Western ballet and modern dance. Incl works from 16th-20th centuries.
KS —WICHITA PUBLIC LIBRARY, Art & Music Division, 223 S Main, Wichita, 67202. Leonard Messineo, Jr, Head, Art & Music Division; Deborah Hamilton, Special Collections Librn
Holdings: Uncat Audiotapes Videotape Pix
Notes: Alice Bauman Dance Symposia Collection. Contains 300 hours of audio tapes, 1 hour-long video tape, several hundred photographs, and fugitive material of the American Dance Symposia held in Wichita from 1968-1972. The symposia covered all dance idioms-ballet, modern,

jazz, folk, ethnic, dance education and therapy-and featured such notable figures such as Leonide Massine, Martha Hill, William Christensen, Alfonso Cimber, Toni Intravaia, James Clouser, Eleo Pomare, Juana de Laban, and many others. Characterized by the Kansas City Star as the "most distinguished faculties of fine artists ever assembled in the contemporary world of dance."
NY —NEW YORK PUBLIC LIBRARY, Performing Arts Research Center, Dance Collection, 111 Amsterdam Ave, New York, 10023. Genevieve Oswald, Cur
Holdings: Vols (40,000) Cat Mss Pix Audiotapes Videotapes 16mm Films Microforms
Budget: ($9,280)
Notes: Multi-media collection. Comprehensive documentation of all aspects of modern dance, especially in the United States. Extensive material on American dancers Ted Shawn, Ruth St Denis, Doris Humphrey, Isadora Duncan, Charles Weidman, Helen Tamiris, Jose Limon, Loie Fuller Limon, Hanya Holm, and Martha Graham, as well as on more recent avant-garde artists. Includes manuscripts and letters, photographs, drawings, stage designs, clippings, programs and posters, scrapbooks, tape-recorded interviews, moving picture films, and videotapes. Holdings listed in Dictionary Catalog of the Dance Collection, Boston, G K Hall, 1974, 10 vols. Annual supplements: Bibliographic Guide to Dance, also published by G K Hall, 1975-.

MODERN LANGUAGE ASSOCIATION

†ON —UNIVERSITY OF WESTERN ONTARIO, School of Library and Information Science, Special Collections Room, London, N6A 5B9, Can.
Notes: Archive of lexicographical materials of the Committee on Lexicography of the Modern Language Association. Incl lexicographical slips for The United States Air Force Dictionary and The Second Aerospace Glossary, by Woodford Heflin. 13 cartons of slips.

MODERN LITERATURE see Literature, Modern

MODERN MOVEMENT BOOKS

NM —NEW MEXICO STATE UNIVERSITY, Library, Box 3475, Las Cruces, 88003. James Dyke, Dir
Holdings: Cat
Notes: The collection contains 38,630 items--a vast quantity of little magazines and Anglo-American Modernism published between 1900-1975. Little poetry magazines are an exceptionally strong part of this collection.

MODERN MUSIC (JOURNAL)

DC —LIBRARY OF CONGRESS, Music Division, Washington, 20540.
Notes: Archives of Modern Music, 1924-46.

MODERN MUSIC—20TH CENTURY see Music, Modern—20th Century

MODERN PAINTING—20TH CENTURY see Painting, Modern—20th Century

MODERN PHILOSOPHY see Philosophy, Modern

MODERN POETRY see Poetry, Modern

MODERN THEATRE—20TH CENTURY see Theatre, Modern—20th Century

MODERNISM (CATHOLIC CHURCH)

CA —UNIVERSITY OF SAN FRANCISCO, Richard A Gleeson Library, The Countess Bernardine Murphy Donohue Rare Book Room, San Francisco, 94117. D Steven

MODERNISM (CATHOLIC CHURCH) (cont.)

Corey, Special Collections Librn
Holdings: Vols 1200 Mss Pix
Notes: Modernism Controversy, 1890-1910.
Incl extensive holdings concerning George
Tyrrell, Alfred Loisy, and Baron Friedrich
von Hugel.

MODJESKA, HELENA

MA —HARVARD UNIVERSITY LIBRARY,
Cambridge, 02138.
Holdings: Cat Mss

MOESSBAUER EFFECT

†DC —CATHOLIC UNIVERSITY OFF
AMERICA, Nursing & Biology Library,
Washington, 20064. N L Powell, Head
Holdings: Vols (16,000) Cat
Notes: Espec strong in organometallic,
Moessbauer and physical chemistry.
NY —UNIVERSITY OF ROCHESTER,
Carlson Library, Hutchison Hall, River
Campus, Rochester, 14627. Michael W
Poulin, Librn
Holdings: Vols (48,720) Cat Microforms
Notes: Strong collection in the field and
related areas.

MOFFETT, GEORGE C.

TX —NORTH TEXAS STATE UNIVERSITY,
Archives, NT Station Box 5188, Denton,
76203. Robert LaForte, University Archivist
Notes: Part of Oral History Collection.
Interviews with Moffett, member of Texas
legislature.
TX —MIDWESTERN STATE UNIVERSITY,
Moffett Library, 3400 Taft St, Wichita Falls,
76308.
Holdings: // Uncat Mss
Notes: Papers and correspondence of State
Senator George Moffett (Texas) from 1931-
1964. No separate catalog or index to the
collection.

MOFFETT, GUY

VA —UNIVERSITY OF VIRGINIA,
Alderman Library, Manuscripts Dept,
Charlottesville, 22901. Edmund Berkeley Jr,
Cur
Holdings: Cat Mss
Notes: Papers of Guy Moffett, Executive of
the Spelman Fund, and active with the Civil
Service Commission, the International Bank
and the Fair Employment Board; about 1500
items, 1920-63.

MOFFETT, ADM. WILLIAM ADGER, 1869-1933

MD —US NAVAL ACADEMY, Nimitz
Library, Annapolis, 21402. Alice S
Creighton, Assistant Librn for Special
Collections
Holdings: Mss
Notes: The William Adger Moffett Papers
are a collection of official and personal
letters, speeches, news releases,
communications, memoranda, notes, news
clippings, etc, by and about Rear Admiral
William Adger Moffett, first Chief of the
Bureau of Aeronautics, US Navy. The
collection is a primary source for any
research regarding the early history of naval
aviation. Papers relate to numerous topics,
including the London Naval Treaty and its
ramifications, military airships, United Air
Service controversy, coastal defense, carriers,
etc. Index available in Special Collections
Department.

MOHAMMEDAN CIVILIZATION see Civilization, Islamic

MOHAMMEDAN PHILOSOPHY see Philosophy, Islamic

MOHAVE INDIANS

AZ —COLORADO RIVER INDIAN TRIBES
MUSEUM/LIBRARY, Rte One, Box 23-B,
Parker, 85344. Priscilla Johnson, Librn
Holdings: Cat Mss Maps Pix Slides
Audiotapes Microforms
Budget: es Microp
Notes: Library deals with the four tribes of
the Colorado River Indian Reservation:
Mojave, Chemehuevi, Navajo, and Hopi.
Emphasis is also given to the prehistoric
cultures of this area; Patayan and Hohokam.
Library collections include original
manuscripts and other documents,
photographs, oral history tape recordings,
cultural items and artifacts. Copies of many
documents relating to the reservation are in
bound volumes, microfilm, and photocopies.
Photos relative to the reservation from
various other collections are copied in our
collection. Of particular interest is the
museum basket collection which incl about
1000 Chemehuevi baskets--the largest
Chemehuevi basket collection. Other
artifacts give special emphasis to the Mojave
culture.
CA —UNIVERSITY OF CALIFORNIA, LOS
ANGELES, Research Library, Dept of
Special Collections, 405 Hilgard Ave, Los
Angeles, 90024. Edward Shreeves,
Chairman, Bibliographers Group; David S
Zeidberg, Head
Holdings: Mss Pix
Notes: Mss, correspondence, photographs,
and other material collected and used by
Lorraine Miller Sherer in her research of
Mojave Indian history and culture.

MOISTURE CONTROL IN BUILDINGS see Dampness in Buildings

MOISTURE OF SOILS see Forests and Forestry-Moisture; Soil Moisture

MOJAVE INDIANS see Mohave Indians

MOKI INDIANS see Hopi Indians

MOLD (BOTANY) see Molds (Botany)

MOLD, VEGETABLE see Soils

MOLDS (BOTANY)

NY —ROCKEFELLER UNIVERSITY,
Rockefeller Archive Center, Hillcrest,
Pocantico Hills, North Tarrytown, 10591.
Joseph W Ernst, Dir; J William Hess, Assoc
Dir
Notes: Papers of Edward L Tatum,
Rockefeller University professor. Conducted
research in the genetics and metabolism of
bacteria, yeasts, and molds. In 1958, he was
joint recipient, with Joshua Lederberg and
George Beadle, of the Nobel Prize in
medicine and physiology.

MOLECULAR BIOLOGY

CA —UNIVERSITY OF CALIFORNIA, LOS
ANGELES, Biomedical Library, Center for
the Health Sciences, Los Angeles, 90024.
Alison Bunting, Acting Biomedical Librn;
Victoria Steele, Head, History & Special
Collections Div
Holdings: Vols (400,000) Cat Slides
Phonorecords Audiotapes Videotapes 16mm
Films Microforms
Notes: The UCLA Biomedical Library serves
primarily the Schools of Medicine, Dentistry,
Nursing, and Public Health, the UCLA Medical
Center, the Departments of Microbiology and
Biology in the College of Letters and Science, and
related institutes in biomedicine. The collections of
the Library are broad in scope, designed not only
to support the teaching and research needs of its
many users, but also to function as a resource for
the health sciences-biological field as a whole. The
outstanding feature of the collection is the strength
of its periodical holdings, both current and
retrospective. The Library also has an excellent
reference collection, a comprehensive historical
section, and gives special emphasis to the fields of
neuroscience, psychiatry, ophthalmology, radiation
biology, molecular biology, and vertebrate
zoology. Increased emphasis is being given to the
acquisition of audiovisual materials.

†CO —NATIONAL JEWISH HOSPITAL
AND RESEARCH CENTER-NATIONAL
ATHSMA CENTER, Gerald Tucker
Memorial Medical Library, 3800 Colfax
Ave, Denver, 80206. Helen-Ann Brown,
Librn
Holdings: Vols (8500)
Notes: Allergy, asthma, immunology,
research in molecular and cellular biology,
medicine, tuberculosis and diseases of the
chest.

CT —YALE MEDICAL LIBRARY, 333 Cedar
St, New Haven, 06510.
Notes: A special subject emphasis.

MA —MASSACHUSETTS INSTITUTE OF
TECHNOLOGY, Institute Archives, Special
Collections, Cambridge, 02139.
Notes: Collection incl over 100 oral history
interviews with scientists, legislators,
lobbyists, environmentalists, journalists,
university administration, and citizen review
board members concerned with recombinant
DNA technology. Also incl are audiotapes,
videotapes, and printed material collected in
preparations for oral history interviews.

NM —UNIVERSITY OF CALIFORNIA, Los
Alamos National Laboratory, Libraries, PO
Box 1663, MSP 362, Los Alamos, 87545. J
Arthur Freed, Head Librn
Holdings: Vols (800,000) Cat Films
Microforms
Budget: ($700,000)
Notes: Incl 500,000 classified and
unclassified reports. There are 25 branch
libraries and a central collection. The
Medical Library contains about 40,000 vols
in the areas of biomedical research.

NY —ALBERT EINSTEIN COLLEGE OF
MEDICINE, D Samuel Gottesman Library,
1300 Morris Park Ave, Bronx, 10461.
Charlotte K Lindner, Dir
NY —US DEPT OF AGRICULTURE,
Agriculture Research Service, Plum Island
Animal Disease Laboratory, PO Box 848,
Greenport, 11944. Stephen Perlman, Librn
Holdings: Vols (15,000) Cat Pix Slides
Microforms
Budget: ($37,000)
NY —COLUMBIA UNIVERSITY
LIBRARIES, Biological Sciences Library,
601 Fairchild, New York, 10027. Barbara A
List, Reference/Collection Development
Librn
Holdings: Vols 38,000 Cat
Notes: Incl biochemistry and molecular
biology.
NY —UNIVERSITY OF ROCHESTER,
Carlson Library, Hutchison Hall, River
Campus, Rochester, 14627. Michael W
Poulin, Librn
Holdings: Vols (48,720) Cat Microforms
Notes: Strong collection in the field and
related areas.
PA —CARNEGIE-MELLON UNIVERSITY,
Mellon Institute Library, 4400 Fifth Ave,
Pittsburgh, 15213. Mary J Volk, Librn
Holdings: Vols (60,000) Cat
Notes: Emphasis is on chemistry and
biological sciences, with material at the
graduate and research level.
PQ —MCGILL UNIVERSITY, Botany-
Genetics Library, 1205 McGregor Ave,
Montreal, H3A 1B1, Can. Eleanor MacLean,
Librn
Holdings: Vols (20,000) Cat

MOLECULAR BIOLOGY—HISTORY

CA —CALIFORNIA INSTITUTE OF
TECHNOLOGY, Robert A Millikan
Memorial Library, Archives, 1201 E

MOLECULAR BIOLOGY—HISTORY (cont.)

California Blvd, Pasadena, 91125. Judith R Goodstein, Archivist
Holdings: Vols (3000) Uncat Mss Maps Pix Slides Phonorecords Audiotapes Videotapes 16mm Films Microforms
Notes: Over 70 collections (1830s-present) relating to history of 19th-20th centuries science and technology and the history of the Institute. Included are personal and professional papers of Caltech scientists and administrative officers; divisional records and faculty committees; over 5000 photographs of American and European scientists. Mss collections documents more than a century of American political, social, and intellectual history; the development of the physical sciences, aeronautics, molecular biology, and seismology in the US and abroad; and social and political conditions in Europe between the two World Wars. There are also family letters relating to 19th century American life before and during the Civil War (the Morley and A G Throop papers); to 19th century social conditions in Russia and Hungary (the Paul Epstein papers and Theodore von Karman papers); andto the development of 20th century Italian mathematics.

PA —UNIVERSITY OF PITTSBURGH, Hillman Library, Pittsburgh, 15260. Glenora E Rossell, Head
Holdings: Vols (6100) Cat Microforms
Notes: This History and Philosophy of Science collection is rapidly growing to support research interests in a very new synoptic approach in the integration of history of science, philosophy of science, and history of philosophy, and the intensive new program of instruction. The trend of collection is to include works in philosophical foundations of contempory physics and cosmology, the philosophical problems of the social sciences, science and theology in the 17th century, the relation between science and epistemology in the 18th and 19th centuries; problems of microphysics, history of molecular biology, theories of scientific explanation, and relation between science and metaphysics.

MOLECULAR PHYSICS

CA —INTERNATIONAL BUSINESS MACHINES RESEARCH LIBRARY, 5600 Cottle Rd, San Jose, 95193. Phil Grincewich, Mgr Technical Information
Holdings: Vols (13,500) Cat
Notes: Collection includes emphasis on laser spectroscopy, organic photomaterial and chemical dynamics. Incl 21,000 vols of 770 journals. On-line search facility. Vols are divided into three libraries, Technical Research, Technical Information, and Programing. Not open to public.

NY —ENGINEERING SOCIETIES LIBRARY, 345 E 47 St, New York, 10017. S Kirk Cabeen, Dir
Holdings: Vols 250,000 Cat Maps 16mm Films Microforms
Notes: One of the largest, most comprehensive engineering libraries in the world. Covers all engineering disciplines; particularly strong in electrical and electronic, mechanical, mining and metallurgical, petroleum, chemical, industrial, air conditioning and refrigeration engineering. Incl Wheeler Collection of early materials on magnetism and electricity. 125,000 bound periodical volumes; 10,000 maps; 5000 serial subscriptions (many foreign-language). Virtually all materials abstracted in *Engineering Index* (1884-date) are incl in Library. Noncirculating, except to members of professional engineering societies which support the Library. See *Engineering Societies Library, New York, Classed Subject Catalog and Index* (Boston: G K Hall, 1963); and *Supplements*, 1-10 1964-1973.

MOLECULAR PHYSIOLOGY see Biological Physics

MOLECULAR SPECTRA

CA —INTERNATIONAL BUSINESS MACHINES RESEARCH LIBRARY, 5600 Cottle Rd, San Jose, 95193. Phil Grincewich, Mgr Technical Information
Holdings: Vols (13,500) Cat
Notes: Collection includes emphasis on laser spectroscopy, organic photomaterial and chemical dynamics. Incl 21,000 vols of 770 journals. On-line search facility. Vols are divided into three libraries, Technical Research, Technical Information, and Programing. Not open to public.

MOLECULAR THEORY

CA —INTERNATIONAL BUSINESS MACHINES RESEARCH LIBRARY, 5600 Cottle Rd, San Jose, 95193. Phil Grincewich, Mgr Technical Information
Holdings: Vols (13,500) Cat
Notes: Incl 21,000 vols of 770 journals. On-line search facility. Vols are divided into three libraries, Technical Research, Technical Information, and Programing. Not open to public.

MOLEK, IVAN

IL —CHICAGO HISTORICAL SOCIETY, Library, Clark St at North Ave, Chicago, 60614. Archie Motley, Manuscript Librn
Notes: Papers of: Emmet Dedmon, newspaper editor; Richard J Finnegan, newspaper editor; Rev Andres M Greeley, sociologist and author; attorney and civil liberties activist Pearl Hart; Robert J Havighurst, educator; social activist John Kearney; Kenesaw Mountain Landis, Federal Judge and first Commissioner of Baseball; Judge David F Matchett; Ivan Molek, Slovenian language publisher in Chicago; Max R Naiman, Communist Party activist; Ralph G Newman, book and autograph dealer and manuscript appraiser; Otto L Schmidt, physician and President of the Chicago and Illinois State Historical Societites; and Dempsey Travis, black mortgage banker.

MOLESWORTH, NIGEL

CT —MOLESWORTH INSTITUTE, Memorial Library, 143 Hanks Hill Rd, Storrs, 06268. Norman D Stevens, Dir, Cur, and Librn
Holdings: Vols (1000) Uncat Mss
Notes: Incl material relating to the Molesworth Family, books by and about any person named Molesworth as well as original materials upon which the legendary Molesworth Institute was founded. In addition the collections now contain over 20,000 library postcards and approx 375 library commemoratives acquired as part of the Institute's research work.

IL —HILLIS L GRIFFIN, (personal collection), 5800 Carpenter Ave, Downers Grove, 60515.
Notes: Definitive collection of the elusive Nigel Molesworth and the Molesworth Institute.
See also entry under Literary Forgeries and Mystifications.

MOLEY, RAYMOND

CA —HOOVER INSTITUTION ON WAR, REVOLUTION & PEACE, Stanford University, Stanford, 94305. Milorad M Drachkovitch, Archivist
Holdings: Mss
Notes: Papers, 1900-1967, of Raymond Moley, political adviser to Franklin D Roosevelt and political columnist. Correspondence, reports, memoranda, speeches and writings, notes, and printed matter. The most prominent part of the collection consists of ms drafts of 81 Roosevelt speeches with annotations by both Moley and Roosevelt. 220 ms boxes. Unpublished register is available in repository.

MOLIERE, JEAN B. P.

CA —UNIVERSITY OF CALIFORNIA, LOS ANGELES, William Andrews Clark Memorial Library, 2520 Cimarron St, Los Angeles, 90018.
Holdings: Cat
Notes: Original editions.

CT —YALE UNIVERSITY, Box 1603A, Yale Station, New Haven, 06520.

MA —HARVARD UNIVERSITY LIBRARY, Widener Library, Cambridge, 02138. Assunta S Pisani, Specialist in Book Selection
Holdings: Cat
Notes: For catalog see Harvard University Library, *Bibliographical Contributions*, 57 (1906); see also *Harvard Library Notes*, II (1925), 9-11.

MOLINARO, URSULE

MA —BOSTON UNIVERSITY, Mugar Memorial Library, Special Collections Dept, 771 Commonwealth Ave, Boston, 02215. Howard B Gotlieb, Dir
Holdings: Cat Mss Pix
Notes: Mss, correspondence, etc collected in depth; incl publications by or about.

MOLLUSKS

CA —STANFORD UNIVERSITY, Hopkins Marine Station Library, Cabrillo Point, Pacific Grove, 93950. Alan Baldridge, Librn
Holdings: // Cat
Notes: The Opisthobranchiata Molluscan Library of Frank Mace MacFarland; 800 items.

DC —SMITHSONIAN INSTITUTION, Archives Div, Washington, 20560. William W Moss, Archivist
Holdings: Cat Mss Maps Pix Slides
Notes: The Archives holds the records of the National Museum of Natural History's Dept of Invertebrate Zoology, Division of Echinoderms, Division of Marine Invertebrates, and Division of Mollusks, ca 1853-1975, as well as the personal papers of William H Dall, Paul Bartsch, Austin H Clark, and Waldo LaSalle Schmitt.

DC —SMITHSONIAN INSTITUTION LIBRARIES, Natural History Branch, Washington, 20560. Sylvia Churgin, Chief Librn
Holdings: Vols 4400 Cat Maps Pix Slides

FL —ROLLINS COLLEGE, Mills Memorial Library, Winter Park, 32789. Patricia J Delks, Dir of Libraries
Notes: Special shell museum collection. Restricted use.

HI —BERNICE P BISHOP MUSEUM, Library, PO Box 19000-A, Honolulu, 96819. Cynthia Timberlake, Librn
Holdings: Vols (90,000) Cat Mss Maps Pix Slides
Budget: ($30,000)
Notes: Only American library devoted exclusively to the Pacific region. Collection reflects historical and contemporary research emphases of Bishop Museum; ie the natural and cultural history of the Pacific. Areas of concentration incl archaeology, ethnology, linguistics, voyages and explorations, history, vertebrate and invertebrate zoology, botany and museology. Strong special collections incl photographs, mss and archives, maps and art. Publications: Quarterly "Additions to the Catalog," *Dictionary Catalog of the Library* (9 vols and 2 suppl; Boston: G K Hall, 1964-69).

IL —FIELD MUSEUM OF NATURAL HISTORY, Library, Roosevelt Rd & Lake Shore Dr, Chicago, 60605. W Peyton Fawcett, Librn; Benjamin W Williams, Assoc Librn
Holdings: Vols (210,000) Cat
Budget: ($100,000)
Notes: Extensive collections--publications of learned societies and institutions and monographic works--in all fields of natural history, with emphasis on taxonomy and evolutionary biology; and on museum publications, American and foreign: anthropology, especially archaeology and ethnology of the Americas, Africa, East Asia, and Oceania; botany, particularly strong for the Americas; geology, chiefly paleontology and meteoritic studies; and zoology, worldwide (birds, fishes, insects, mammals, mollusks, reptiles and amphibians).

MI —UNIVERSITY OF MICHIGAN, Museums Library, Ann Arbor, 48109. Patricia B Yocum, Librn
Holdings: Vols 6000 Cat

MOLLUSKS (cont.)

NY —PALEONTOLOGICAL INSTITUTION,
Library, 1259 Trumansburg Rd, Ithaca,
14850. Peter Hoover, Dir
Holdings: Vols (60,000) Maps Pix

NY —AMERICAN MUSEUM OF
NATURAL HISTORY, Library Services
Dept, Central Park W & 79th St, New York,
10024. Nina J Root, Chairwoman; Mary
Genett, Asst Librn for Reference Services

PA —ACADEMY OF NATURAL SCIENCES
LIBRARY, 19 Benjamin Franklin Parkway,
Philadelphia, 19103.
Holdings: Vols (180,000) Cat Mss Pix Slides
Microforms
Notes: Incl (250,000) mss. Described in
*Academy of Natural Sciences of
Philadelphia: Catalog* (Boston: G K Hall,
1972); *Guide to the Manuscript Collections
in the Academy of Natural Sciences of
Philadelphia*, by Venia T Phillips
(Philadelphia: Academy of Natural Sciences,
1963).

PA —CARNEGIE LIBRARY OF
PITTSBURGH, Science & Technology Dept,
4400 Forbes Ave, Pittsburgh, 15213.
Catherine M Brosky, Dept Head
Notes: Subject of secondary interest with
emphasis on North America. Covers
paleobotany, vertebrates and invertebrates,
foraminifera, mollusks, fish, reptiles,
mammals, Abstracts, indexes, catalogs,
bibliographies, journals, continuations,
federal, state and society publications
available.

ON —NATIONAL MUSEUMS OF
CANADA, Library Services Directorate,
Ottawa, K1A 0M8, Can. Valerie
Monkhouse, Director
Holdings: Vols (90,000) Cat Mss Microforms
Budget: ($81,000)
Notes: Emphasis on Canadian and
circumpolar natural history. Collection incl
botany, herpetology, ichthyology,
invertebrate zoology, malacology,
mammology, mineralogy, ornithology,
paleobiology, zooarchaeology. Exceptional
collections in lichenology, bryology,
malacology, ornithology. Research
collection, interlibrary loans available, public
may use on the premises.

MOLLUSKS—NOMENCLATURE
(POPULAR) see Shells

MOLLUSKS—PICTORIAL WORKS see
Shells

MOLNAR, FERENC

NY —NEW YORK PUBLIC LIBRARY,
Performing Arts Research Center, Billy Rose
Theatre Collection, 111 Amsterdam Ave,
New York, 10023. Dorothy L Swerdlove,
Cur
Holdings: Cat Mss Pix
Notes: Papers, scrapbooks, mss, photographs,
memorabilia, etc.

MOLOKAN FOLK MUSIC see Folk
Music, Molokan

MOLOKANS

DC —LIBRARY OF CONGRESS, American
Folklife Center, Archive of Folk Culture,
Washington, 20540.
Notes: The Sidney Robertson Cowell
Collection of her folk music recordings, 1937
to 1957. Incl very unusual contributions by
the Molokan community in the Potrero Hill
neighborhood of San Francisco, a breakaway
sect from the Russian Orthodox Church.

MOLTEN METALS see Liquid Metals

MOLUCCAS see Indonesia

MOLYBDENUM

MI —ACHESON COLLOIDS, Library, 511
Port St, Port Huron, 48060. Myles T
Musgrave, Librn
Holdings: Vols (5000) Cat Mss Microforms
Notes: Solid lubricants: graphite,
molybdenum disulfide and related organic
and inorganic compounds used as solid
lubricants (in films, liquids, greases, etc) for
industrial applications. Incl extensive patent
collection (US and foreign).

MONACHISM see Monasticism and
Religious Orders

MONARCHY, FRENCH

MI —MICHIGAN STATE UNIVERSITY,
Libraries, Special Collections Div, East
Lansing, 48824. Jannette Fiore, Librn
Holdings: Vols 10,000 Uncat
Notes: A collection of monographs and
pamphlets 16th through 19th centuries, all
bearing to some degree on the French
monarchy.

MONASTERIES AND MONASTICISM
see Monasticism and Religious Orders

MONASTIC ORDERS see Monasticism
and Religious Orders

MONASTICISM AND RELIGIOUS
ORDERS

DC —DOMINICAN HOUSE OF STUDIES,
Dominican College Library, 487 Michigan
Ave NE, Washington, 20017. J Raymond
Vandegrift, OP, Librn
Holdings: Vols (5000) Cat
Budget: ($1350)
Notes: The Dominican Order (its history,
spirituality, government, liturgy), its
members (directories, biographies,
bibliographies, lives of saints) and works
written by Dominicans: incunabula, rare
books, dissertations, periodicals (2300 vols),
monographs. Incl periodicals either about the
Order or edited by Dominicans. Does not
incl titles about the congregations of
Dominican Sisters. The Library's catalog
contains analytics for Dominican
contributors to monographs.

IN —INDIANA UNIVERSITY, Lilly Library,
Seventh St, Bloomington, 47405. William R
Cagle, Librn
Holdings: Vols 6000 // Cat
Notes: This

MD —JOHNS HOPKINS UNIVERSITY,
Milton S Eisenhower Library, George
Peabody Collection, 17 E Mt Vernon Place,
Baltimore, 21201. Lyn Hart, Peabody Librn
Notes: Emphasis on materials published
before 1950. Strength is a good collection
through the 19th century.

MD —SOVEREIGN HOSPITALLER ORDER
OF SAINT JOHN, Villa Anneslie, 529
Dunkirk Road, Baltimore, 21212.
Notes: The Sovereign Hospitaller Order of
Saint John is an ecumenical Christian
religious Order founded in the 11th century;
successor Order to the Knights of Rhodes
and the Knights of Malta.

MN —SAINT JOHN'S ABBEY &
UNIVERSITY, Hill Monastic Manuscript
Library, Collegeville, 56321. Julian G Plante,
Dir
Holdings: Vols (61,000) Cat Mss Pix Slides
Microforms
Notes: Films of 61,000 mss. The total
number of codices or bound handwritten mss
represents the holdings of several hundred
libraries in Europe, mostly Austria, Spain,
Ethiopia, West Germany, Portugal, and also
Italy, Hungary, Poland, Great Britain,
Belgium, Yugoslavia, France, Switzerland,
and the Netherlands.

MN —SAINT JOHN'S UNIVERSITY, Alcuin
Library, Collegeville, 56321. Michael
Kathman, Dir
Holdings: Vols (300,000) Cat Maps Slides
Phonorecords Audiotapes Videotapes
Filmstrips Microforms
Budget: ($176,000)
Notes: St John's University is operated by St
John's Abbey. The library includes a large
collection of materials on monasticism and
religious orders.

NY —FORDHAM UNIVERSITY LIBRARY,
Bronx, 10458. Joseph A LoSchiavo,
Reference Librn
Holdings: Vols 600 Cat Mss Pix
Notes: The Zema Memorial Collection.

NC —BELMONT ABBEY COLLEGE, Abbot
Vincent Taylor Library, Belmont, 28012.
Marjorie McDermott, Dir
Holdings: Vols 3500 Cat Pix
Notes: The Benedictine Collection contains
books and periodicals written and published
by Benedictine monks and nuns, and books
which deal with the Benedictine monastic
life. Incl are many rare volumes published in
the last 200 years, and several journals
published by European abbeys, some of
which are difficult to locate elsewhere. The
collection is limited exclusively to
Benedictine monasticism. As far as we know,
it is the only collection of its type in the
entire South. It is housed in a special room
in the library. Access to the collection is
through the main card catalog.

OH —UNIVERSITY OF DAYTON, Marian
Library, 300 College Park Ave, Dayton,
45469. Rev Theodore Koehler, SM, Dir/Cur
Holdings: Vols (65,000) Cat Mss Pix Slides
Phonorecords Audiotapes Filmstrips
Microforms
Budget: ($12,000)
Notes: Largest and most comprehensive
collections of literature on Virgin Mary in
the world. Covers all five centuries of
printing. Some 50 languages represented.
Incl doctrinal, polemical, popular works,
children's books. Catholic and non-Catholic.
Especially strong in publications on French
shrines (Clugnet collection), on the
Immaculate Conception, and materials after
1950. Has Vloberg collection of pictures, ms
notes and offprints on Marian iconography.
Complete files of major journals in
Mariology and partial runs or more than 100
others. Files of 48,000 clippings from
domestic and foreign periodicals. 10,000
holy cards from 19th and 20th centuries.
2600 postcard views of shrines. 3000
postcards of Marian art. Philatelic collection
of 1000 stamps and 200 first-day cover.
1000 photographs. 300 medals. General
reference collection strong inpastristic
sources, biblical literature, religious
inconography (especially of Eastern
Churches), general bibliography, and
bibliography of religious orders. Union
catalog of Marian holdings in American and
others libraries. Library publishes *Marian
Library Studies* and *Marian Library*
Newsletter. Has had scholors in residence
since 1972. Since 1975 recognized as a
Pontifical Institute in affiliation with the
Marianum in Rome empowered to prepare
candidates for pontifical degree with
specialization in Marian studies. In 1976
began summer schools in Mariology. History
of the Library and description of its holdings
in Fackovec, William, S M, "The Marian
Library of the University of Dayton," in
Marian Library Studies (New Series) vol 1
(1969), pp 9-76.

MONDELL, FRANK W.

WY —ANNA MILLER MUSEUM LIBRARY,
PO Box 698, Newcastle, 82701. Mabel E
Brown, Museum Dir
Holdings: Vols (1000) Cat
Notes: The Frank W Mondell Collection
(Wyoming Congressman 1892-1922) incl
congressional and senate records and
reports, reports of government agencies,
bound periodicals, law, special subject vols.
Supporting materials, local history collection
contains materials on Newcastle phase of
Mondell career.

MONETARY AFFAIRS,
INTERNATIONAL see International
Monetary Affairs

MONETARY MANAGEMENT see
Monetary Policy

MONETARY POLICY

NJ —PRINCETON UNIVERSITY, Library,
Manuscript Collection, Nassau St, Princeton,
08540. Jean F Preston, Cur
Holdings: Cat Mss
Notes: Incl 43 file drawers; 19 boxes; 15

MONETARY POLICY (cont.)

cartons. The Economists' National Committee on Monetary Policy archives cover the period 1933-52.

MONETARY QUESTION see Money

MONEY

CO —UNIVERSITY OF COLORADO, Libraries, Special Collections, Boulder, 80309. Nora J Quinlan, Head
Holdings: Vols Cat
Notes: Dickson H Leavens Collection. Over 750 vols and 500 binders of material (incl clippings and pamphlets) related to the history of silver money. An extensive and all-encompassing collection on the subject.

CO —AMERICAN NUMISMATIC ASSOCIATION LIBRARY, 818 N Cascade Ave, Colorado Springs, 80903. Nancy W Green, Librn
Holdings: Vols (20,000) Cat Slides
Notes: One of the largest numismatic libraries, the collection incl books, periodicals and auction catalogs on coins and coin collecting, medals, tokens, military orders and decorations, paper money, primitive money, banks and banking, seals and scarabs. ANA publishes a classified subject catalog of its collection and is open to the public for research and reference services. Only members may check books out.

DC —INTERNATIONAL MONETARY FUND AND WORLD BANK, Joint Bank-Fund Library, Washington, 20431. Maureen M Moore, Librn
Holdings: Vols Cat Films Microforms
Notes: Incl foreign trade and statistical bulletins and yearbooks, central bank reports and bulletins, budget papers, security yearbooks, economic development plans and reports on economic conditions from the 132 member countries. An index of periodical material compiled by the Library staff has been published as: *Economics and Finance; Index to Periodical Articles, 1947-1971;* First Supplement, 1972, 1973, 1974 (Second Supplement, 1975, 1976, 1977, in preparation), 5 vols. (Boston: G K Hall, 1972, 1975). Also, The Developing Areas: *A Classed Bibliography of the Joint Bank-Fund Library,* Vol 1: *Latin America and the Caribbean;* Vol 2: *Africa and the Middle East;* Vol 3: *Asia and Oceania* (Boston: G K Hall, 1976).

MA —HARVARD UNIVERSITY, Baker Library of the Graduate School of Business Administration, Kress Library of Business and Economics, Soldiers Field, Boston, 02163. Ruth E Rogers, Cur
Holdings: Cat
Notes: Covers the progress of economic thought and the evolution of economic institutions and business life, with special strength in agriculture, banking, commerce, finance, industry, money, railroads, socialism, tariff. Restricted use: noncirculating. Collection available on microfilm: *Goldsmiths'-Kress Library of Economic Literature,* published by Research Publications, Inc. Downs 1477, 2704, 2712, 2719, 2727, Supplement 962, 963.

MA —AMERICAN ANTIQUARIAN SOCIETY LIBRARY, 185 Salisbury St, Worcester, 01609. Marcus A McCorison, Dir & Librn
Notes: Colonial American currency; also Confederate money, and State Bank notes.

MI —UNIVERSITY OF MICHIGAN, Dept of Rare Books & Special Collections, Ann Arbor, 48109. Edward C Weber, Head, Labadie Collection
Notes: Protest against the US monetary system, with many plans for substitute schemes, including bi-metallism and paper currency.

NY —NEW YORK PUBLIC LIBRARY, Research Libraries, Economic & Public Affairs Div, Fifth Ave & 42 St, New York, 10018. Edward DiRoma, Chief
Holdings: Vols (1,500,000) Cat Microforms

NC —DUKE UNIVERSITY, William R Perkins Library, Durham, 27706. Elvin E

Strowd, University Librn
Notes: The Flowers Collection of Southern Americana currently consists of 4,300,500 items. Additions are ongoing. Included in this collection are several types of materials, which are housed in appropriate sections of the library. The various types of materials are: manuscripts, books, pamphlets, maps, music, broadsides, newspapers, photographs, engravings, prints and memorabilia.

NC —DUKE UNIVERSITY, William R Perkins Library, Manuscript Dept, Durham, 27706. Ellen Gartrell, Cur of Mss
Holdings: Cat Mss
Notes: Currency collection of 4900 paper items, 1746-1982, incl Colonial, Revolutionary and Civil War money (especially Confederate); some foreign.

MONEY, STAGE see Stage Money

MONEY RAISING see Fund Raising

MONTGOLFIER, JOSEPH AND JACQUES

DC —LIBRARY OF CONGRESS, Manuscript Division, Washington, 20540. John C Broderick, Chief
Notes: Documents the history of aeronautics from the Montgolfier brothers to General William "Billy" Mitchell, General Henry H "Hap" Arnold and the development of the modern air force.

MONGOLIA

IL —FIELD MUSEUM OF NATURAL HISTORY, The Berthold Laufer Library, Roosevelt Rd & Lake Shore Dr, Chicago, 60605. W Peyton Fawcett, Librn
Holdings: Vols (12,000)// Cat Mss Maps
Notes: The part of the museum's collection of Berthold Laufer (1874-1934), Curator of Anthropology, dealing with the peoples of the pre-19th century Chinese Empire (incl Manchuria, Mongolia, Sinkiang and Tibet); their anthropology, art and religion; influences upon their cultures by those of India, Siberia, Japan, Indonesia, and Oceania--and vice versa. Incl about 500 books in Tibetan. About 2/3 of the collection is cataloged.

MONGOLIAN LANGUAGE AND LITERATURE

MD —JOHNS HOPKINS UNIVERSITY, Milton S Eisenhower Library, Charles & 34 Sts, Baltimore, 21218. Ann S Gwyn, Assistant Dir for Special Collections
Holdings: Vols 1000// Cat Mss
Notes: Hauer Collection incl numerous rare texts and unusual pamphlets. History, philosophy, geography, politics. Chiefly in German; also French and English.

MA —HARVARD UNIVERSITY LIBRARY, Harvard-Yenching Library, 2 Divinity Ave, Cambridge, 02138. Eugene W Wu, Librn
Notes: Incl the "red copy" of the Mongolian Kanjur printed in 1724.

NJ —PRINCETON UNIVERSITY, Library, Gest Oriental Library & East Asian Collections, 317 Palmer Hall, Princeton, 08544. D E Perushek, Cur
Holdings: Cat Mss
See also entry under China.

NY —COLUMBIA UNIVERSITY LIBRARIES, C V Starr East Asian Library, 300 Kent Hall, New York, 10027. James Reardon-Anderson, Librn
Holdings: Vols 115 // Cat
Notes: Publications in Mongolian: chiefly Mongolian translations of Chinese literature, the Bible, and language aids, published in the Ch'ing dynasty (1644-1911).

NY —NEW YORK PUBLIC LIBRARY, Oriental Div, Fifth Ave & 42 St, New York, 10018. E Christian Filstrup, Chief
Holdings: Cat Mss Microforms
Budget: ($56,455)
Notes: Published catalog of holdings.

MONHEGAN ISLAND, MAINE

CT —LEE ASH, (personal collection), 66 Humiston Dr, Bethany, 06525.
Holdings: Cat Mss Maps Pix Slides

Microforms
Notes: Especially history, biography, bibliography (and citations), illus material, association items, ephemera, etc.

NY —LOUIS A RACHOW, (personal collection), 528 W 114 St, New York, 10025.
Holdings: Cat Maps Pix

MONITOR (U.S. IRONCLAD)

NJ —STEVENS INSTITUTE OF TECHNOLOGY, Samuel C Williams Library, Castle Point Sta, Hoboken, 07030. Jane G Hartye, Special Collections Librn
Holdings: // Cat Mss Pix
Notes: Known as the US Ironclad Monitor, it was designed by Capt John Ericsson and launched January 30, 1862. The "Monitor" participated in the historic battle with the "Merrimack" on March 9, 1862. It sank off Cape Hatteras on December 31, 1862. Our collection includes original design drawings of the "Monitor," 38 of which were drawn by Capt Ericsson and 34 by C W McCord. The copies of these drawings are now in the National Archives. No photocopying.

MONKEYS

OR —OREGON REGIONAL PRIMATE RESEARCH CENTER, Library, 505 NW 185 Ave, Beaverton, 97006. Isabel McDonald, Librn
Holdings: Vols (765) Cat Audiotapes 16mm Films Microforms
Notes: Incl small collection of dissertations and theses.

WI —UNIVERSITY OF WISCONSIN, MADISON, Wisconsin Regional Primate Research Center, Primate Center Library, 1223 Capitol Court, Madison, 53715. Lawrence Jacobsen, Librn
Holdings: Vols (15,000) Cat Pix
Notes: Research in reproductive physiology, neurosciences, and behavior. Extensive subject orientated primate reprint file, audiovisual collection on primates. Current research uses approximately 25 species of nonhuman primates. Publications: *Primate Library Report:* print and non-print editions, biomonthly.

MONKEYS AS LABORATORY ANIMALS

CT —YALE UNIVERSITY, School of Medicine, Dept of Obstetrics & Gynecology Library, Farnam Memorial Bldg, New Haven, 06510.
Holdings: Cat Mss Pix Slides
Notes: X-ray plates, 10,000 slides of monkey and human tissue and about 1000 slides of gynecological and obstetrical pathology, used as teaching and research materials. Other large collections of X-rays and radiotherapy photographs are in the Hunter Radiation Therapy Center.

MA —HARVARD MEDICAL SCHOOL, New England Primate Research Center Library, 1 Pine Hill Dr, Southborough, 01772. Sydney Fingold, Librn
Holdings: Vols (4000)

MONKS see Monasticism and Religious Orders

MONMOUTH, BATTLE OF, 1778

NJ —MONMOUTH COUNTY HISTORICAL ASSOCIATION, Library, 70 Court St, Freehold, 07728. Loretta M Zwolak, Archivist & Librn
Holdings: Vols (6500) Cat Mss Maps Pix Slides Microforms
Budget: ($15,800)
Notes: Especially Monmouth County area. See *Monmouth County Historical Association Bulletin,* vol 1, no 2 July 1948, p 23-48. Allaire Papers (Howell Works); Battle of Monmouth; Mott Family Papers; North American Phalanx; Philip Freneau; Steamship Coll.

MONOGRAPHIC SERIES

CA —UNIVERSITY OF CALIFORNIA, LOS ANGELES, Research Library, Dept of

MONOGRAPHIC SERIES (cont.)

Special Collections, 405 Hilgard Ave, Los Angeles, 90024. Edward Shreeves, Chairman, Bibliographers Group; David S Zeidberg, Head
Holdings: Vols 1000
Notes: American Paperback Fiction Collection: 3500 turn-of-the-century American paperback novels and 1000 boys' books published in series.

†IA —UNIVERSITY OF IOWA LIBRARIES, Dept of Special Collections, Iowa City, 52240. Robert A McCown, Librn
Notes: Extensive series books.

†KS —UNIVERSITY OF KANSAS, Spencer Research Library, Dept of Special Collections, Lawrence, 66045. Alexandra Mason, Librn
Notes: Extensive science fiction, 6 ft of fanzines, 500 Big-Little Books, extensive series books, James E Gunn and Lloyd Biggle special collections in the Dept of Special Collections.

†MI —MICHIGAN STATE UNIVERSITY, Libraries, East Lansing, 48824. Jannette Flore, Librn
Notes: About 3000 vols each of series books, westerns, gothic, and romance, science fiction, and mystery.

†MN —UNIVERSITY OF MINNESOTA, Walter Library, Room 109, Minneapolis, 55455.
Notes: 10,000 vols of series books.

MONON RAILROAD

IN —INDIANA HISTORICAL SOCIETY, Library, 315 W Ohio St, Indianapolis, 46202. Robert K O'Neill, Dir
Notes: Incl rare books, mss, pictures, maps, and ephemera relating to the history of Indiana and the Old Northwest. Mss dealing with the Old Northwest, incl a large collection of William Henry Harrison materials; papers of leading nineteenth-century Indiana figures; letters of Civil War soldiers; records of twentieth-century social welfare organizations. Rare books collection incl Jesuit *Relations*, early travel accounts, and early Indiana imprints. Pictures incl Indiana small-town life; Monon Railroad Collection; Callis Steamboat Collection, dealing with Terre Haute. Maps of Indiana; Sanborn real estate atlases for Indianapolis. Special collections in Indiana black, ethnic, and architectural history.

MONORAIL RAILROADS

NY —ELECTRIC RAILROADERS ASSOCIATION, Frank J Sprague Memorial Library, 89 E 42nd St, New York, 10018. Hugh A Dunne, First VP
Notes: Private library. Incl all forms of railroads operated by electricity. Forms of electric railroads included: street railways, subways & elevated lines, high-speed interurbans, suburban commuter lines, electrified trunk lines, monorails, mountain climbing inclines, etc. Also railroad timetables.

MONRO, HAROLD, 1879-1932

CA —UNIVERSITY OF CALIFORNIA, LOS ANGELES, Research Library, Dept of Special Collections, 405 Hilgard Ave, Los Angeles, 90024. Edward Shreeves, Chairman, Bibliographers Group; David S Zeidberg, Head
Holdings: Vols 100 Mss
Notes: 100 books written or published by him; 1500 items incl letters (mostly relating to the Poetry Bookshop) and mss.

MA —AMHERST COLLEGE, Library, Amherst, 01002. John Lancaster, Special Collections Librn
Holdings: Vols (500) Uncat Mss
Notes: Concentration on the Georgian poets Lascelles Abercrombie, Edward Blunden, W H Davies, John Drinkwater, Wilfrid Gibson, Harold Monro, Edward Thomas.

MONROE, EASON

†CA —UNIVERSITY OF CALIFORNIA, Library, Los Angeles, 90024.

MONROE, HARRIET

IL —UNIVERSITY OF CHICAGO LIBRARY, Dept of Special Collections, 1100 E 57 St, Chicago, 60637.
Notes: A magazine of verse incl personal papers of Harriet Monroe.

MA —HARVARD UNIVERSITY LIBRARY, Cambridge, 02138.
Holdings: Cat Mss

MONROE, JAMES, 1783-1831

DC —LIBRARY OF CONGRESS, Manuscript Division, Washington, 20540. John C Broderick, Chief
Notes: The Presidential Papers collection incl the papers, etc, of numerous Presidents.

NY —NEW YORK PUBLIC LIBRARY, Rare Books and Manuscripts Div, Fifth Ave & 42 St, New York, 10018. William L Joyce, Asst Dir; Susan E Davis, Cur of Mss
Holdings: Mss
Budget: ($7161)
Notes: Incl personal and literary mss, papers, etc.

VA —UNIVERSITY OF VIRGINIA, Alderman Library, Manuscripts Dept, Charlottesville, 22901. Edmund Berkeley Jr, Cur
Holdings: Cat Mss
Notes: Papers, Curtis W Garrison, ed, *Guide to the Microfilm Edition of James Monroe Papers in Virginia Repositories* (University of Virginia: Microfilm Publications, 1969).

VA —COLLEGE OF WILLIAM AND MARY, Earl Gregg Swem Library, Williamsburg, 23185. Margaret C Cook, Cur of Manuscripts & Rare Books
Holdings: // Cat Mss
Notes: James Monroe Papers, 1783-1831, incl letters to and from Monroe. Correspondents incl John Q Adams, John Marshall, Thomas Jefferson, and John C Calhoun. 167 items.

MONROE, VAUGHN

MA —BOSTON UNIVERSITY, Mugar Memorial Library, Special Collections Dept, 771 Commonwealth Ave, Boston, 02215. Howard B Gotlieb, Dir
Holdings: Cat Mss Pix
Notes: Mss, correspondence, etc collected in depth; incl publications by or about.

MONRONEY, A. S. MIKE

OK —UNIVERSITY OF OKLAHOMA, Bizzell Memorial Library, Western History Collections, 401 W Brooks, Norman, 73069. John Ezell, Cur
Holdings: Mss Pix Maps Audiotapes
Notes: US Senator. His papers. Guide available.

MONSEY, DEREK

MA —BOSTON UNIVERSITY, Mugar Memorial Library, Special Collections Dept, 771 Commonwealth Ave, Boston, 02215. Howard B Gotlieb, Dir
Holdings: Cat Mss Pix Audiotapes
Notes: Mss, correspondence, etc collected in depth; incl publications by or about.

MONSTERS

†NY —MEDICAL RESEARCH LIBRARY OF BROOKLYN, Academy of Medicine of Brooklyn & The State University of New York Downstate Medical Center, 450 Clarkson St, Brooklyn, 11203. Kenneth E Moody, Dir
Notes: Extensive collection of 18th-19th century material.
See also entry under Medicine

MONTAIGNE, MICHEL DE

MA —HARVARD UNIVERSITY LIBRARY, Widener Library, Cambridge, 02138. Assunta S Pisani, Specialist in Book Selection
Holdings: Cat
Notes: See *Harvard Library Notes*, II (1925), 9-11.

NJ —PRINCETON UNIVERSITY, Library, Rare Books Dept, Princeton, 08544. Stephen Ferguson, Cur
Holdings: Cat
Notes: For particulars refer to: Imbrie Buffum, "Special Collections at Princeton; II. The Le Brun Collection of Montaigne" in the *Princeton University Library Chronicle* I, (February, 1940) pp 11-16.

MONTANA

UT —UNIVERSITY OF UTAH, Marriott Library, Special Collections, Salt Lake City, 84112. Gregory C Thompson, Cur

WA —WASHINGTON STATE LIBRARY, Washington/Northwest Rm, State Library Bldg, Olympia, 98504. Nancy B Pryor, Research Consultant
Holdings: Vols 8000 Cat Mss Maps Pix Microforms
Notes: Mss, photographs and microfilm largely limited to Washington territorial and state materials as is the file of pamphlets and newspaper clippings, which inlcudes both historical and current material. The book collection incl works on the four Pacific Northwest States, Alaska, and British Columbia, and books by Wahington authors.

WA —UNIVERSITY OF WASHINGTON LIBRARIES, Pacific Northwest Collection, Seattle, 98195. Andrew F Johnson, Librn
Holdings: Vols (50,000) Cat Maps Pix
Budget: ($12,000)
Notes: The Pacific Northwest Collection contains printed materials documenting the historic and contemporary life and culture of the region in a broad range of subject areas. The Pacific Northwest is defined as the geographic region including Washington, Oregon, Idaho, Montana, British Columbia, Yukon Territory, and Alaska. Printed materials including books, periodicals, government documents, maps, weekly and local regional newspapers, theses and dissertations, as well as photographs and architectural drawings are included in the Pacific Northwest Collection. Photographic works of over 200 photographers active in the Pacific Northwest, Alaska, and the Yukon Territory (Canada) during the period 1860-1930, including Asahel and Edward S Curtis, Eric Hegg, and Clark Kinsey, are represented in a print collection of more than 300,000 images. The architecturaldrawings collection includes over 19,000 original plans, drawings, sketches, renderings and blue prints pertaining to the history of architecture and urban planning and landscape gardening in the Pacific Northwest ca 1880-1940. Areas of particular strength are the holdings of over 1100 published journals of Pacific Northwest exploration expeditions, photographs of Northwest Coast Native Americans and of historic Seattle, newspapers issued within the Japanese-American relocation camps, 1942-1945, materials relating to the 1980 eruption of Mt St Helens, and Sanborne fire insurance maps for Washington. A unique feature of the Collection is the subject index to regional periodicals and local newspapers maintained by the PNW Collection staff; over 100 titles are currently indexed. G K Hall Company published a books catalog of the Pacific Northwest Collectionin 1973.

MONTANA—ANTIQUITIES

MT —ROCKY MOUNTAIN COLLEGE, Paul M Adams Memorial Library, 1511 Poly Dr, Billings, 59102. Sue Walker, Dir
Holdings: Cat Maps
Notes: Large collection on geology. Also, deposit of the Billings Archaeological Society, the Montana Methodist Historical Library (incl papers of Brother Van Oursdale, pioneer circuit rider) and the Montana Congregational Archives.

MONTANA—HISTORY

CA —UNIVERSITY OF CALIFORNIA, LOS ANGELES, William Andrews Clark Memorial Library, 2520 Cimarron St, Los

MONTANA—HISTORY (cont.)

Angeles, 90018.
Holdings: Vols 2000 // Cat Mss Maps Pix Slides
Notes: The Charles Kessler Collection, incl also about 4000 pamphlets, documents, etc, with more than 60 volumes of the *Book of Mormon* in English and foreign languages.
MT —EASTERN MONTANA COLLEGE, Library, 1500 N 30 St, Billings, 59101. Edward Neroda, Dir
Holdings: Vols 2186 Cat Maps Pix
Notes: The Dora White Collection of Western History; emphasis on Pacific Northwest and Montana.
MT —ROCKY MOUNTAIN COLLEGE, Paul M Adams Memorial Library, 1511 Poly Dr, Billings, 59102. Sue Walker, Dir
Holdings: Cat Maps
Notes: Large collection on geology. Also, deposit of the Billings Archaeological Society, the Montana Methodist Historical Library (incl papers of Brother Van Oursdale, pioneer circuit rider) and the Montana Congregational Archives.
MT —MONTANA STATE UNIVERSITY, Library, Bozeman, 59717. Minnie Ellen Paugh, Special Collections Librn
Holdings: Vols 3000 Cat Mss Maps Pix Slides Audiotapes Microforms
Budget: $1000
MT —GREAT FALLS PUBLIC LIBRARY, Second Ave N & Third St, Great Falls, 59401. Frank H Mackaman, Exec Dir
Holdings: Vols 5500 Cat Mss Maps Pix
Notes: Extensive collections of newspaper clippings and pamphlets, separately indexed.
MT —MONTANA HISTORICAL SOCIETY LIBRARY, 225 N Roberts St, Helena, 59601. Robert M Clark, Librn; Brian Cockhill, State Archivist
Holdings: Cat Mss Maps Pix Slides Microforms
Notes: Incl state publications and state agency archives.
MT —UNIVERSITY OF MONTANA, Library, Missoula, 59801. Katherine Schaefer, Special Collections Librn
Holdings: Vols 6300 Cat Mss Maps Pix Slides Microforms
Notes: About 200 ms collections, measuring 5000 feet, with emphasis on Montana business and political history (papers of Senators Joseph M Dixon, James E Murray, and US Ambassador James W Gerard). Also first editions and mss of Montana authors.
NE —UNIVERSITY OF NEBRASKA-LINCOLN, Don L Love Library, University Archives and Special Collections, Lincoln, 68588. Joseph G Svoboda, University Archivist
Holdings: Pix Slides
Notes: R D Warden Collection of Charles Marion Russell, "Largest private collection of literature on Russell, 'The Cowboy Artist,'" 7000 items, incl first editions of every book and pamphlet by Russell and over 1000 periodical appearances of his art; 900 color prints; 142 drawings; color slides; scrapbooks about Russell and his family, from 1889.

MONTANA—MAPS

OK —TULSA CITY-COUNTY LIBRARY, Business & Technology Dept, 400 Civic Center, Tulsa, 74103. Craig Buthod, Head
Notes: Original General Land Office survey maps for the states of Arizona, Arkansas, Colorado, Illinois, Indiana, Idaho, Kansas, Michigan, Missouri, Montana, Nebraska, Nevada, New Mexico, North Dakota, Ohio, Oklahoma, South Dakota, Utah and Wyoming. Incomplete coverage of each state.

MONTANA AUTHORS see Authors, Montana

MONTEZUMA, CARLOS

AZ —NORTHERN ARIZONA UNIVERSITY, Special Collection Library, CU Box 6022, Flagstaff, 86011. Peter M Whiteley, Coordr/Archivist; William

Mullane, Librn
Notes: Papers, 1892-1937. Microfilm collection. Originals located at the State Historical Society of Wisconsin. C Montezuma was a Mohave-Apache physician (10 reels microfilm).

MONTGOMERY, G. V.

MS —MISSISSIPPI STATE UNIVERSITY, Mitchell Memorial Library, Box 5408, Mississippi State, 39762. Frances N Coleman, Head, Special Collections
Holdings: Mss
Notes: Papers of US Rep G V Montgomery, 1967-.

MONTGOMERY, LUCY MUD

ON —UNIVERSITY OF GUELPH, Library, Guelph, N1G 2W1, Can. Margaret Beckman, Chief Librn; Ellen Pearson, Ref Librn
Notes: Her diaries and papers.

MONTGOMERY, JOHN DICKEY, 1920-

CA —HOOVER INSTITUTION ON WAR, REVOLUTION & PEACE, Stanford University, Stanford, 94305. Milorad M Drachkovitch, Archivist
Holdings: Mss
Notes: Papers of John D Montgomery, political scientist and author, incl mss of writings, reports, notes, interview summaries, and printed matter, 1946-1959, relating to US aid to South Vietnam and other southeast Asian countries, Japanese and German public opinion regarding the purge of wartime leaders after World War II, and political, socialism and economic effects of the purge on Japan and Germany. 15ms boxes.

MONTHERLANT, HENRY MILON DE

IN —INDIANA UNIVERSITY, Lilly Library, Seventh St, Bloomington, 47405. William R Cagle, Librn
Notes: Letters of Henry Mildon de Montherlant, 1895-1972 (111 items).

MONTREAL, QUEBEC

PQ —MCGILL UNIVERSITY, McLennan Library, Rare Books and Special Collections Dept, 3459 McTavish St, Montreal, H3A 1Y1, Can.
Notes: 5524 sheet maps, 370 atlases, 571 folded maps, 629 guide books, 248 reference books. The coverage is worldwide, specializing in North America, Canada, Quebec, Montreal. Includes a collection of guide books from the 1800s to the present day, as well as a reference collection; there is also a large collection of modern topographical literature with worldwide coverage, and an important collection of postcards particularly of Montreal and the Province of Quebec. A finding list is available for 19th century guide books on Canada: A Preliminary Guide to Nineteenth Century Canadian Guide Books: a Survey of the Holdings of the McLennan Library with an Historical Introduction. Montreal, 1982.

MONTREAL—HISTORY

PQ —MCGILL UNIVERSITY, McLennan Library, Rare Books and Special Collections Dept, 3459 McTavish St, Montreal, H3A 1Y1, Can.
Notes: Significant collection of primary source and secondary material on Montreal, to be found throughout the collections, consisting of much non-book materials, eg, prints, maps, manuscripts, printed ephemera, postcards, etc.

MONTREAL AMATEUR ATHLETIC ASSOCIATION

†ON —PUBLIC ARCHIVES OF CANADA, Library, 395 Wellington St, Ottawa, K1A 0N3, Can.
Notes: The historical papers of the Montreal

Amateur Athletic Association. Incl minute books, annual reports, correspondence, posters, and souvenir programs from 1861 to 1934.

MONTREAL REPERTORY THEATRE

ON —METROPOLITAN TORONTO LIBRARY, Theatre Dept, 789 Yonge St, Toronto, M4W 2G8, Can. Heather McCallum, Head
Notes: Special collections relating to the history of the performing arts in Canada incl the records of the Taverner Company which played Eastern Canada and the United States in the late 19th century, Toronto's Grand Opera House, the Marks Brothers touring company, film actor Ned Sparks, the Canadian-born actress Judith Evelyn, Crest Theatre (Toronto), the Canadian Players, Montreal Repertory Theatre, dancer/teacher Boris Volkoff, The Dumbells, the Canadian all-soldier concert party which originated in France in 1917, and vaudeville performer Charles Manny.

MONUMENTAL BRASSES see Brasses

MONUMENTAL THEOLOGY see Bible—Antiquities; Christian Antiquities

MONUMENTS AND STATUES

OH —OBERLIN COLLEGE LIBRARY, Clarence Ward Art Library, Allen Art Bldg, Oberlin, 44074. Jeffrey Weidman, Librn
Holdings: Vols (62,000) Cat Microforms
Notes: Strong in medieval European architecture and American architecture. Incl the Jefferson Collection, an almost complete duplication of the architectural books in Thomas Jefferson's library. Also incl Frederick B Artz Collection of books on architecture and gardening dating from the 16th through the 19th centuries. Significant holdings in early serials (see *ARLO Union List of Serials*).

MOODY, DAN

TX —NORTH TEXAS STATE UNIVERSITY, Archives, NT Station Box 5188, Denton, 76203. Robert LaForte, University Archivist
Notes: Part of Oral History Collection. Interviews with Mrs Dan Moody, wife of former Texas governor. Some restrictions.

MOODY, R. BRUCE

MA —BOSTON UNIVERSITY, Mugar Memorial Library, Special Collections Dept, 771 Commonwealth Ave, Boston, 02215. Howard B Gotlieb, Dir
Holdings: Cat Mss Pix Correspondence

MOODY, WILLIAM VAUGHN

IL —UNIVERSITY OF CHICAGO LIBRARY, Dept of Special Collections, 1100 E 57 St, Chicago, 60637.
Notes: Papers.
MA —HARVARD UNIVERSITY LIBRARY, Cambridge, 02138.

MOON

DC —SMITHSONIAN INSTITUTION LIBRARIES, National Air & Space Museum Branch, NASM Bldg, Sixth & Independence Ave SW, Washington, 20560. Frank A Pietropaoli, Branch Chief
Holdings: Vols (39,000) Cat Mss Maps Pix Slides Microforms
Notes: History of flight and aerospace development, incl biographical material on aviation pioneers, balloons and ballooning. Extensive photographic collection (600,000 pictures). Incl the Sherman Fairchild Collection of aeronautical photographs (transferred from the American Institute of Aeronautics and Astronautics). Also incl the Bella Landauer Aeronautical Sheet Music Collection (1500 pieces). 2000 films; 800,000 microforms; 9000 volumes bound.
IL —UNIVERSITY OF ILLINOIS, URBANA/CHAMPAIGN, Library,

MOON (cont.)

Geology Library, 223 Natural History Bldg,
Urbana, 61801. Dederick Ward, Librn
Holdings: Vols (105,186) Cat Maps
Microforms
NY —COLUMBIA UNIVERSITY
LIBRARIES, Geoscience Library, Lamont-
Doherty Geological Observatory, Palisades,
10964. Susan Klimley, Librn
Holdings: Vols (20,000) Cat
Notes: Geosciences, incl geochemistry,
marine geology, seismology and
paleoclimatology.
TX —LUNAR & PLANETARY INSTITUTE,
Library/Information Center, 3303 Nasa Rd
One, Houston, 77058. Frances B Waranius,
Library/Information Center Mgr
Holdings: Cat Mss Maps Pix Slides
Microforms
Notes: Development of collection begun in
1972 to incl lunar studies from approx 1950
forward. Planets, meteorites, asteroids and
comets added 1978. Seek to become as
inclusive as possible.

MOON—GEOLOGY see Lunar Geology

MOON—RESEARCH see Lunar Studies

MOON, JAMES

NY —SAINT LAWRENCE UNIVERSITY,
Owen D Young Library, Canton, 13617.
Mahlon Peterson, Librn
Holdings: Mss
Notes: Records of the land business of James
Moon of Middleton, Pa, who owned part of
Macomb's Purchase in northern New York.
He sold this land to settlers through his
relatives and agents, Daniel and Moses
Child. The collection, incl maps, deeds,
accounts and correspondence, covers the
years 1818-1855 and numbers approx 100
items.

MOON, REV. SUN MYUNG

CA —GRADUATE THEOLOGICAL UNION
LIBRARY, New Religious Movements
Research Collection, Public Services and
Special Collections Dept, 2400 Ridge Road,
Berkeley, 94709. Diane Choquette, Dept
Head
Holdings: Vols (3000) Mss Pix
Notes: Begun in 1977, the collection focuses
on religious movements new to America
since 1960, and unorthodox religious
movements resurgent since 1960. American
forms of Hinduism, Buddhism, Sikhism, and
Sufism are included along with occultism,
New-Paganism, esoteric and alternative
forms of Christianity, feminist spirituality,
and human potential movements having a
spiritual aspect. Legal issues, such as
deprogramming, and the question of church/
state relations are an important part of the
collection. The Library is a depository for
publications of the Unification Church in
America, the Church of Scientology, and the
International Society for Krishna
Consciousness (America). The responses of
mainstream religions and concerned citizens
groups are also included. Besides 3000
monographs, the library has 350 periodical
titles, 200 posters from the San
FranciscoBay Area, 1965-77, 300 research
papers, and 24 linear feet of ephemera.

MOON'S TYPE FOR THE BLIND see
Blind—Printing and Writing Systems

MOORE, A.

TX —SAN ANTONIO COLLEGE, Library,
1001 Howard St, San Antonio, 78284. James
O Wallace, Dir
Holdings: Vols 2500 Cat Microforms
Notes: The Morrison Collection of
Eighteenth Century British Literature.
Partially described in: Hennington, Betty M
"Lois G Morrison Collection of Eighteenth
Century English Literature: a Checklist"
(unpublished MLS thesis) Texas Woman's
University, 1968, also see "The Morrison

Collection." Scriblerian, vol 1, pp 32-33
(spring 1969). Especially strong in material
relating to Eustace Budgell; A Moore, W
Webb and Edmund Curll imprints. A
separate catalog is maintained for the
collection with entries for author, title,
personal subjects, printers and booksellers,
date of publication, engravers and
association copies.

MOORE, BRIAN, 1921-

AB —UNIVERSITY OF CALGARY,
Libraries, Special Collections Div, 2500
University Dr, Calgary, T2N 1N4, Can.
Holdings: Cat Mss
Notes: Manuscripts, page proofs, galley
proofs for all Brian Moore's novels, and
correspondence with publishers, admirers
and friends.

MOORE, CARL V.

MO —WASHINGTON UNIVERSITY, School
of Medicine, Archives, 660 S Euclid Ave,
Saint Louis, 63110. Paul G Anderson,
Archivist
Holdings: Mss Pix Audiotapes
Budget: ($38,000)
Notes: Institutional records and papers of
faculty of Washington University School of
Medicine and its predecessors and associated
hospitals. Contains records of St Louis
Medical College, Missouri Medical Barnard
Free Skin and Cancer Hospital, Barnes
Hospital, St Louis Children's Hospital and
Jewish Hospital of St Louis. Incl papers of
William Beaumont, Joseph Erlanger, Leo
Loeb, Evarts Graham, Edmund V Cowdry,
Helen Graham, Carl V Moore, Margaret
Smith and others. Oral history program. See
also: Anderson, Paul G and Hoolihan,
Christopher, eds. Special Collections (St
Louis: Washington University School of
Medicine, 1981). 960 linear feet.

MOORE, CLEMENT CLARKE

FL —FLORIDA STATE UNIVERSITY,
Robert Manning Strozier Library, Special
Collections Dept, Tallahassee, 32306. Opal
M Free, Head, Special Collections
Holdings: Vols 257 Uncat
Notes: Editions of Clement Moore's The
Night Before Christmas. No photocopying.
IN —INDIANA UNIVERSITY, Lilly Library,
Seventh St, Bloomington, 47405. William R
Cagle, Librn
Holdings: Vols 100 // Cat
Notes: Early and later printings of The
Night Before Christmas.
MA —HARVARD UNIVERSITY LIBRARY,
Cambridge, 02138.
Holdings: Cat Mss
NY —GENERAL THEOLOGICAL
SEMINARY, Saint Marks Library, 175
Ninth Ave, New York, 10011. David Green,
Dir
Holdings: Vols (200,000) Cat
RI —BROWN UNIVERSITY, John Hay
Library, Harris Collection, Prospect St,
Providence, 02912. Rosemary L Cullen, Cur
Holdings: Vols (200,000) Cat Mss Pix
Phonorecords Microforms
Budget: ($15,000)
Notes: Numerous editions of Moore's The
Night Before Christmas. See Dictionary
Catalog of the Harris Collection of American
Poetry and Plays (Boston: G K Hall, 1972),
13 vols; Supplement (1977), 3 vols. See also,
American Poetry, 1609-1900, A Collection
on Microfilm, Segment I (1609-1820);
Segment II (1821-1850); Segment III
(1851-1870) (Woodbridge, Conn: Research
Publications). Separate catalog.

MOORE, DOUGLAS STUART

DC —LIBRARY OF CONGRESS, Music
Division, Washington, 20540.
Notes: Mss in Koussevitzky Archives.
†NY —COLUMBIA UNIVERSITY
LIBRARIES, Butler Library, Rare Book and
Manuscript Library, 535 W 114 St, New
York, 10027.
Notes: Mss of three symphonic works by
Douglas Stuart Moore.

MOORE, EDWARD, 1712-1757

OH —OHIO UNIVERSITY, Vernon R Alden
Library, Department of Archives and Special
Collections, Athens, 45701. Gary A Hunt,
Head
Holdings: Vols 125 Cat
Notes: The J Homer Caskey Collection. Incl
works by Arthur Murphy and Edward
Moore, in various editions, plus related
items, mostly 18th century drama.

MOORE, EDWARD MOTT

NY —UNIVERSITY OF ROCHESTER, Rush
Rhees Library, Department of Rare Books
and Special Collections, Rochester, 14627.
Peter Dzwonkoski, Librn
Holdings: Mss
Notes: Papers, correspondence, mss
ephemera, etc. Concerning Moore's medical
career and other subjects; includes a number
of letters written by his young children in
the 1860's.

MOORE, G. E.

†IL —SOUTHERN ILLINOIS UNIVERSITY,
CARBONDALE, Library, Special
Collections Dept, Carbondale, 62901.
Notes: Archives of the Library of Living
Philosophers, a publishing project founded
by Paul Arthur Schilpp in 1938 to provide a
forum for contemporary philosophers to
reply to their critics. Incl correspondence
from John Dewey, George Santayana, Alfred
North Whitehead, G E Moore, and Albert
Einstein.

MOORE, GEORGE, 1853-1933

AZ —ARIZONA STATE UNIVERSITY,
Library, Tempe, 85287. Marilyn
Wurzburger, Special Collections Librn
Holdings: Vols 514 Cat Mss
Notes: 45 letters. This collection served as
the primary source for Edwin Gilcher in
preparing his Bibliography of George Moore,
1970. Catalog: Books and Other Printed
Items by George Moore in the Library of
Edwin Gilcher (Cherry Plain, NY, 1974).
CA —UNIVERSITY OF SAN FRANCISCO,
Richard A Gleeson Library, The Countess
Bernardine Murphy Donohue Rare Book
Room, San Francisco, 94117. D Steven
Corey, Special Collections Librn
Holdings: Vols 113 Mss
Notes: Comprehensive collection of first
editions.
IL —ILLINOIS STATE UNIVERSITY, Milner
Library, Dept of Special Collections,
Normal, 61761. Robert Sokan, Librn
Notes: First editions, limited editions,
ephemera, etc.
MO —DRURY COLLEGE, Library,
Springfield, 65802. Judith Armstrong, Dir
Holdings: Vols 75 Cat
Notes: First editions, corrected galley proofs,
with many letters to publishers, etc.
NY —CORNELL UNIVERSITY LIBRARIES,
John M Olin Library, Dept of Rare Books,
Ithaca, 14853. Donald D Eddy, Librn
Holdings: Vols 200 Cat Mss
OH —OHIO UNIVERSITY, Vernon R Alden
Library, Department of Archives and Special
Collections, Athens, 45701. Gary A Hunt,
Head
Holdings: Vols 155 Cat Mss
Notes: A comprehensive collection of
Moore's published works. All editions of all
titles are collected. A few of Moore's letters
are also in the library, along with corrected
proofs of several works.
PA —BUCKNELL UNIVERSITY, Ellen
Clarke Bertrand Library, Lewisburg, 17837.
Ann de Klerk, Librn
Holdings: Cat Mss
BC —UNIVERSITY OF VICTORIA,
McPherson Library, Victoria, V8W 3H5,
Can.
Notes: Papers.

MOORE, HUGH, 1887-1972

NJ —PRINCETON UNIVERSITY, Seeley G
Mudd Manuscript Library, Public Affairs

MOORE, HUGH, 1887-1972 (cont.)

Papers Collection, Princeton, 08544. Nancy Bressler, Cur
Notes: Incl 17 boxes. The papers cover the period 1939-72. An unpublished 6p checklist is available in the Library.

MOORE, JAMES E.

PA —US ARMY MILITARY HISTORY INSTITUTE, Carlisle Barracks, 17013. Richard J Sommers, Chief Archivist-Historian
Holdings: Mss
Notes: The James E Moore papers as Chief of Staff of the 9th Army, 1944-1945.
See also entry under World War, 1939-1945

MOORE, LILLIAN, 1911-1967

NY —NEW YORK PUBLIC LIBRARY, Performing Arts Research Center, Dance Collection, 111 Amsterdam Ave, New York, 10023. Genevieve Oswald, Cur
Notes: The Lillian Moore Correspondence, ca 1936-67, and papers, comprise 20 drawers of holographs, typescripts, notebooks, and miscellaneous printed materials, reflecting the extent and scope of research done by Miss Moore for her numerous scholarly writings on the dance. The Lillian Moore Collection also contains books, photographs, prints, films, and memorabilia. Special emphasis on 19th century ballet, early American dance, and Danish ballet. Numerous rare and unique items.

MOORE, MARIANNE

CT —TRINITY COLLEGE LIBRARY, Watkinson Library, 300 Summit St, Hartford, 06106. Jeffrey Kaimowitz, Cur
Holdings: Cat
Notes: The H Bacon Collamore Collection.
†MD —UNIVERSITY OF MARYLAND, Library, College Park, 20742. Donald Farren, Assoc Dir for Special Collections
Holdings: Cat
Notes: First appearances in book form, in anthologies, and in periodicals; subsequent editions, with differences in text, etc; works edited or translated; association items, especially with marginalia. Secondary works are generally excluded.
MA —HARVARD UNIVERSITY LIBRARY, Cambridge, 02138.
Holdings: Cat Mss
MO —WASHINGTON UNIVERSITY, Libraries, Campus Box 1061, Saint Louis, 63130.
Notes: A collection of primary material.
NV —UNIVERSITY OF NEVADA, RENO, University Library, Special Collections Dept, Reno, 89557. Robert E Blesse, Head
Holdings: // Vols (60) Cat Other appearances 750 Cat
Notes: Includes individual works by author in all editions including translations; also prefaces, introductions, published correspondence, appearances in anthologies, periodicals, etc. Bibliographical research collection, part of Modern Authors Collection.
PA —BRYN MAWR COLLEGE, Canaday Library, Bryn Mawr, 19010. James Tanis, Dir
Notes: Rare books and manuscripts.
PA —PHILIP H & A S W ROSENBACH FOUNDATION LIBRARY, 2010 DeLancey Pl, Philadelphia, 19103. Clive E Driver, Dir
Holdings: Vols Mss Pix
Notes: Marianne Moore's personal collections, including letters and books written by notable Modernist writers such as T S Eliot, Ezra Pound and William Carlos Williams. Collection has 200,000 items. Also watercolors and personal possessions.

MOORE, MARY CARR

CA —UNIVERSITY OF CALIFORNIA, LOS ANGELES, Music Library, Schonberg Hall, Los Angeles, 90024. Stephen M Fry, Music Librn
Notes: Mss.

MOORE, MERRILL

MA —HARVARD UNIVERSITY LIBRARY, Cambridge, 02138.
Holdings: Cat Mss
Notes: (Many medical history collections incl selections of Merrill Moore's works or complete sets--LA)
TN —VANDERBILT UNIVERSITY, Library, Nashville, 37240. Marice Wolfe, Special Collections Librn
Holdings: Vols 1000 Cat Mss Pix
Notes: Collection relating to the Fugitive poets of the 1920s, the Agrarian writers of the 1930s and their subsequent careers, as a complement to extensive mss collections in this field. Chief figures incl Allen Tate, John Crowe Ransom, Robert Penn Warren, Andrew Lytle, Donald Davidson, Merrill Moore, Laura Riding, et al.

MOORE, RAYLYN

MA —BOSTON UNIVERSITY, Mugar Memorial Library, Special Collections Dept, 771 Commonwealth Ave, Boston, 02215. Howard B Gotlieb, Dir
Holdings: Mss Correspondence

MOORE, RUTH

MA —BOSTON UNIVERSITY, Mugar Memorial Library, Special Collections Dept, 771 Commonwealth Ave, Boston, 02215. Howard B Gotlieb, Dir
Holdings: Cat Mss Pix
Notes: Mss, correspondence, etc collected in depth; incl publications by or about.

MOORE, THOMAS, 1779-1852

NC —DUKE UNIVERSITY, William R Perkins Library, Durham, 27706. Elvin E Strowd, University Librn
Notes: The Shelley-Goodwin Collection of Lord Abinger is a microfilm copy of the Shelley and Godwin collection. Lord Abinger's entire manuscript collection, representing the last portion of the papers of Sir Percy Florence Shelley which is still in private hands, has been reproduced on 16 reels of film. The Bodleian Library is the only other location for this film.
TX —RICE UNIVERSITY, Fondren Library, Woodson Research Center, 6100 S Main St, PO Box 1892, Houston, 77251. Nancy Parker, Dir Woodson Research Center
Holdings: Mss Pix Microforms
Notes: Incl several hundred letters and other ms pieces, music, photos, 5 reels of microfilm and some items of memorabilia.

MOORE, THOMAS STURGE

NY —HOFSTRA UNIVERSITY, Library, 1000 Fulton Ave, Hempstead, 11550. Charles R Andrews, Dean of Library Services
Notes: Strong collection. Incl some mss.

MOORE, VARDINE R.

IN —INDIANA STATE UNIVERSITY, EVANSVILLE, Library, 8600 University Blvd, Evansville, 47712. Gina R Walker, Acting Archivist
Holdings: Cat Mss
Notes: Typescripts and galleys (with author's corrections) of Mrs Moore's books and stories for children. Restricted use: noncirculating.

MOORE, VICTOR

NY —NEW YORK PUBLIC LIBRARY, Performing Arts Research Center, Billy Rose Theatre Collection, 111 Amsterdam Ave, New York, 10023. Dorothy L Swerdlove, Cur
Holdings: Cat Mss Pix
Notes: Papers, scrapbooks, mss, photographs, memorabilia, etc.

MOOREHOUSE, LEE

OR —UMATILLA COUNTY LIBRARY, 214 N Main St, Pendleton, 97801. Barbara L

Bishop, Dir
Holdings: Vols (675) Cat Mss Pix Audiotapes 16mm Films Microforms
Notes: Oregon history, especially Umatilla County. Photos (glass negatives)--1004 negatives, use restricted to professional photographers, copies may be made on premises only. Also 3 rolls of microfilm of Moorehouse photos.

MOORES, CHARLES WASHINGTON, 1862-1923

IN —BUTLER UNIVERSITY, Irwin Library, Hugh Thomas Miller Rare Book Room, 4600 Sunset Ave, Indianapolis, 46208. Gisela Terrell, Rare Books Librn
Holdings: Vols Cat Mss Newspapers
Notes: Lincoln Collection. Assembled for the greater part by Charles W Moores, 1862-1923; accepted by Butler U 1925; sorted and catalogued 1981-82. The newspapers, clippings, other memorabilia. Books and pamphlets include materials related to the Civil War in general. An annotated bibliography of the booklets, pamphlets and most mss was printed in 1983; it is available for $10. A related collection of materials about Lincoln statues and their sculptors remains to be sorted.

MOORES, DICK

OH —OHIO STATE UNIVERSITY, Library for Communication and Graphic Arts, 242 W 18th St, Columbus, 43210. Lucy S Caswell, Curator
Notes: Original cartoons by Winsor McCay, John T McCutcheon, Dick Moores, Ned White, Walter Berndt, Jim Larrick, Carl Rose and Bill Crawford.

MOORISH LANGUAGE (INDIA) see Urdu Language and Literature

MOQUI INDIANS see Hopi Indians

MORAL PHILOSOPHY see Ethics

MORAL RE-ARMAMENT

DC —LIBRARY OF CONGRESS, Manuscript Division, Washington, 20540. John C Broderick, Chief
Notes: The records of Moral Re-Armament, incl the personal papers of its founder, Frank N D Buchman (357,000 items).

MORAL THEOLOGY see Christian Ethics

MORALITY see Ethics

MORAN, HUGH ANDERSON

CA —HOOVER INSTITUTION ON WAR, REVOLUTION & PEACE, Stanford University, Stanford, 94305. Milorad M Drachkovitch, Archivist
Holdings: // Mss
Notes: Papers, 1916-1932, of Hugh Anderson Moran, clergyman. Correspondence, photos, memoranda, ms articles and other papers relating to Moran's work as director of prisoner-of-war relief in Siberia, 1916-1917, as special aid to the Elihu Root diplomatic mission to Russia, 1917, and as secretary to the Young Men's Christian Association in Manchuria, 1918, and to his later interests in Russian affairs. 2 ft.
NY —CORNELL UNIVERSITY LIBRARIES, Collection of Regional History, Dept of Manuscripts and Univ Archives, Ithaca, 14853.
Notes: Presbyterian clergyman. Incl papers, 1919-47; religious plays, essays, worship services, notes, religious poetry, correspondence, his autobiography to 1919, and other items.

MORAN, JAMES

MO —WASHINGTON UNIVERSITY, Libraries, Campus Box 1061, Saint Louis, 63130.
Notes: Correspondence and ms material.

MORANT, MATILDA, 1925-

OK —NINETY-NINES, Library, PO Box 59964, Will Rogers World Airport, Oklahoma City, 73159. Lorretta Craig, Librn
Holdings: Vols 350 Cat Pix
Notes: 10,000 books, periodicals, catalogs on history of aviation. Women's aviation resource center. Collection from the first women aviatrix, Harriet Quinley, 1905-, Matilda Morant, 1925-. 7000 bound periodicals from 1929, 10 issues a year, from the magazine first called "Airwomen" to the "Ninety-Nines". Members of the "Ninety-Nines" incl 7 women astronauts (Betty Smith).

MORAVIAN CHURCH AND MORAVIANS

NE —UNIVERSITY OF NEBRASKA-LINCOLN, Don L Love Library, Czech Heritage Collection, Lincoln, 68588. Joseph G Svoboda, University Archivist
Holdings: Vols (3000) Cat Mss Pix Audiotapes Microforms
Notes: The Czech Heritage Collection.

NY —NEW YORK STATE LIBRARY, State Education Bldg Annex, Washington Ave, Albany, 12224.
Notes: The papers of William Beauchamp (ca 1860-1930), consisting mainly of his notebooks and scrapbooks concerning the history of the Iroquois Indians. Incl 13 boxes material on Indian language, folklore, and place names, the Moravians, and New York State archeology.

†NC —MORAVIAN CHURCH IN AMERICA-SOUTHERN PROVINCE, Drawer M, Salem Station, Winston-Salem, 27108.
Notes: Moravian church history, Moravian missions, North Carolina.

NC —MORAVIAN MUSIC FOUNDATION, Peter Memorial Library, 20 Cascade Ave, Winston-Salem, 27107. James Boeringer, Dir
Holdings: Vols (6000) Cat Phonorecords
Budget: ($2500)
Notes: Emphasis on 18th and 19th century music, incl hymns, Moravian music, etc.

†NC —OLD SALEM, INC, Library, Drawer F, Salem Station, Winston-Salem, 27108.
Notes: Moravians in North Carolina.

†PA —MORAVIAN CHURCH IN AMERICA-NORTHERN PROVINCE, Moravian Archives, 41 West Locust St, Bethlehem, 18018.
Notes: Moravian church history, general and American.

WI —UNIVERSITY OF WISCONSIN, MADISON, Memorial Library, Western European Humanities Collection, 728 State St, Madison, 53706. Charles Szabo, Bibliographer
Notes: Tank Collection. The core of this extensive collection is its works on theology, the largest portion of which deals with Calvinism. Practically all the printed sermons of the major Calvinist preachers of the 18th century are represented. Includes many 16th and 17th century sermons. About a third of the collection deals with Church history; not only are Calvinist histories represented but also 18th century histories of Methodists, Quakers, and Moravians. Supplements the Montauban Collection (French Protestantism) and the Chwalibog Collection (theology).

MORAY, ANN

MA —BOSTON UNIVERSITY, Mugar Memorial Library, Special Collections Dept, 771 Commonwealth Ave, Boston, 02215. Howard B Gotlieb, Dir
Holdings: Cat Mss

MORDEN, WILLIAM J.

NY —AMERICAN MUSEUM OF NATURAL HISTORY, Library Services Dept, Central Park W & 79th St, New York, 10024. Nina J Root, Chairwoman; Mary Genett, Asst Librn for Reference Services
Holdings: Cat Mss Maps Pix Slides 16mm Films
Notes: Manuscripts, diaries, correspondence, artifacts, some art work, and collected materials. Not all cataloged as of 1983.

MORDVINIAN LANGUAGE AND LITERATURE

NY —NEW YORK PUBLIC LIBRARY, Slavonic Div, Fifth Ave & 42 St, New York, 10018. Edward Kasinec, Chief
Holdings: Cat Microforms
Notes: See New York Public Library, *Dictionary Catalog of the Slavonic Collection* (Boston: G K Hall, 1974), 44 vols.

MORE, PAUL ELMER, 1864-1937

MA —HARVARD UNIVERSITY LIBRARY, Cambridge, 02138.
Holdings: Cat Mss

NJ —PRINCETON UNIVERSITY, Library, Manuscript Collection, Nassau St, Princeton, 08540. Jean F Preston, Cur
Holdings: Mss
Notes: The manuscripts fill 36 ms boxes. See *Princeton University Library Chronicle*, v 22, 163-68. An unpublished typescript guide (21p) is available in the Library.

MORE, ST. THOMAS, 1478-1535

CA —UNIVERSITY OF SAN FRANCISCO, Richard A Gleeson Library, The Countess Bernardine Murphy Donohue Rare Book Room, San Francisco, 94117. D Steven Corey, Special Collections Librn
Holdings: Vols 750
Notes: One of the most complete collections of works by or about St Thomas More. There are also related collections of Erasmus and English Rescusant Literature (1558-1640).

CT —YALE UNIVERSITY, Box 1603A, Yale Station, New Haven, 06520.
Notes: Editorial center for "Works of St Thomas More" project.

IL —LOYOLA UNIVERSITY OF CHICAGO, E M Cudahy Memorial Library, 6525 N Sheridan Rd, Chicago, 60626.
Notes: Thomas Cranmer's working library and papers, incl ms of a critical edition of Thomas Cranmer's *Censurae* that Fr Surtz was working on at the time of his death.

IL —NEWBERRY LIBRARY, 60 W Walton St, Chicago, 60610. Diana Haskell, Cur of Modern Mss
Holdings: Cat
Notes: A strong collection.

†KY —THOMAS MORE COLLEGE, Library, Fort Mitchell, 41017.

MA —HARVARD UNIVERSITY LIBRARY, Widener Library, Cambridge, 02138.
Holdings: Cat

NY —COLLEGE OF NEW ROCHELLE, Gill Library, Castle Place, New Rochelle, 10801. Gloria T Greco, Librn
Holdings: Vols 120 Cat Microforms
Notes: The Thomas More Collection: early works pertaining to the life and times and writings of More. Collection described in *Moreana*, vol 51, 1976, pp 77-78.

MORELOS, JOSE MARIA

IN —INDIANA UNIVERSITY, Lilly Library, Seventh St, Bloomington, 47405. William R Cagle, Librn
Holdings: Vols (10,000) // Cat Mss
Notes: Historical pronouncements and documents by the leaders of the movement of Mexican independence. Partially cataloged.
See also entry under Mexico - History.

MORGAN, ARTHUR E.

OH —ANTIOCH COLLEGE, Olive Kettering Library, Livermore St, Yellow Springs, 45387. Nina Myatt, Cur
Holdings: Cat Mss Pix
Notes: Personal papers and correspondence (1920-1975) of Arthur E Morgan former President of Antioch (1920-1936), first director of Ohio's Miami Valley Conservancy District, and first Chairman of the Tennessee Valley Authority (TVA). Mss, film, out-takes, much on the engineering of over 50 water-control projects in this country, Africa, and India. Materials on Edward Bellamy (Morgan wrote biography of Bellamy). Incl family papers. About 175 file boxes.

MORGAN, DICK THOMPSON

OK —UNIVERSITY OF OKLAHOMA, Bizzell Memorial Library, Western History Collections, 401 W Brooks, Norman, 73069. John Ezell, Cur
Holdings: Mss Documents Maps Pix
Notes: US Representative. His papers. Guide available.

MORGAN, EDMUND MORRIS, 1878-1966

MA —HARVARD UNIVERSITY LIBRARY, Law School Library, Langdell Hall, Cambridge, 02138. Erika S Chadbourn, Cur of Mss
Holdings: Cat Mss
Notes: Professional papers; legal documents. Typed inventory in repository. Inclusive dates: 1925-1949.

MORGAN, EDWIN D.

NY —NEW YORK STATE LIBRARY, State Education Bldg Annex, Washington Ave, Albany, 12224.
Holdings: Cat Mss
Notes: His papers.

MORGAN, GEORGE

IL —UNIVERSITY OF ILLINOIS, URBANA/CHAMPAIGN, Library, Illinois Historical Survey Library, 1408 W Gregory Dr, 1A Library, Urbana, 61801.
Holdings: Vols 500 Cat Mss Maps Microforms
Notes: Colonial and Revolutionary Period--Midwest, particularly Illinois. Important ms collections (75 cubic feet) under this subject incl: Baynton, Wharton and Morgan, papers, 1757-1799, 6 reels of microfilm; British Archives, 1547-1858, 7000 items, 40 reels of microfilm; Cunningham Collection, 1600-1836, 40 cubic feet (typed copies from Archives in Spain and South America); French Archives, 1671-1796, 3500 items; Gage, Thomas, papers, 1759-1773, 1300 items; Morgan, George, papers, 1766-1826, 280 items, 5 reels of microfilm; Randolph County Records, 1720-1853, 91 items, 59 reels of microfilm; St Clair County Records, 1722-1809, 6 items, 5 reels of microfilm. Guide to the collections published: Maynard J Brichford, Robert M Sutton, Dennis F Walle, *Manuscripts Guide to Collections at the University of Illinois at Urbana-Champaign* (Urbana, Chicago, London: University of Illinois Press, 1976).

MORGAN, J. PIERPONT

NY —COLUMBIA UNIVERSITY LIBRARIES, Rare Book & Manuscript Library, 801 Butler Library, 535 W 114 St, New York, 10027. Kenneth A Lohf, Librn
Notes: More than 32,000 items documenting the rise of William Russell Grace's shipping business and other materials relating to his career as mayor of New York. Incl records and correspondence relating to all aspects of the shipping business in New York and South America, mining interest in Peru and Chile, and transportation in Costa Rica and Nicaragua. Family memorabilia and photographs, materials concerning New York Politics, banking and insurance, real estate interests and Catholic charities, and letters from Chester A Arthur, John Jacob Astor, Andrew Carnegie, Grover Cleveland, Hamilton Fish, John Hay and J Pierpont Morgan. Restricted use.

MORGAN, JAMES

TX —ROSENBERG LIBRARY, Galveston and Texas History Center, 2310 Sealy Ave,

MORGAN, JAMES (cont.)

Galveston, 77550. Jane Kenamore, Archivist
Holdings: Cat Mss
Notes: Papers of Colonel James Morgan who was in command of the port of Galveston during part of the Texas revolution. Incl military papers, orders from Presidents Burnet and Houston, family papers and correspondence with Samuel Swartout of New York on land speculation in Texas.

MORGAN, JULIA

CA —CALIFORNIA POLYTECHNIC STATE UNIVERSITY LIBRARY, Special Collections and University Archives, San Luis Obispo, 93407. Nancy E Loe, Head Librn
Holdings: Vols (100) Cat Mss
Notes: Herpersonal papers covering her architectural career of forty years, which incl several Hearst estates as well as private residences in the California Arts and Crafts style. Incl Hearst/Morgan correspondence and telegrams; business correspondence, travel accounts, sketchbooks, awards, photographs and several hundred architectural drawings. Hearst Castle Collection incl 8500 architectural drawings for Hearst's residences at San Simeon, Jolon, Wyntoon, and Santa Monica and approx 100 vols of secondary source material. The Asilomar Collection contains 145 architectural drawings for the Morgan-designed YWCA facility near Monterey, California. Incl blueprints, diplomas, personal papers. Finding aid in progress. Incl 10,000 pieces of ms material, 10,000 architectural drawings and blueprints.

MORGAN, LEWIS HENRY, 1818-1881

NY —CITY UNIVERSITY OF NEW YORK, City College, Morris R Cohen Library, North Academic Center, Convent Ave & 137th St, New York, 10031. Barbara J Dunlap, Archivist
Holdings: Vols 40 Uncat Mss
Notes: Aaron Orange Collection of the Works of Lewis Henry Morgan. This is a small collection of books by the noted anthropologist, Lewis Henry Morgan. It also contains articles by him and a box of related materials.
NY —UNIVERSITY OF ROCHESTER, Rush Rhees Library, Department of Rare Books and Special Collections, Rochester, 14627. Peter Dzwonkoski, Librn
Holdings: Vols 100 Cat Mss
Notes: The printed material includes editions of Lewis Henry Morgan's works, and material about him. Also have his papers (approximately 12 feet of manuscript material) and a collection of several hundred pamphlets which were owned by him. Each letter in the collection has been indexed by the name of the letter writer. Unpublished register is available in the repository.

MORGAN, THOMAS

MA —BOSTON UNIVERSITY, Mugar Memorial Library, Special Collections Dept, 771 Commonwealth Ave, Boston, 02215. Howard B Gotlieb, Dir
Holdings: Cat Mss Pix
Notes: Mss, correspondence, etc collected in depth; incl publications by or about.

MORGAN, THOMAS J.

IL —UNIVERSITY OF ILLINOIS, URBANA/CHAMPAIGN, Library, Illinois Historical Survey Library, 1408 W Gregory Dr, 1A Library, Urbana, 61801.
Holdings: Vols 50 Cat Mss Pix Microforms
Notes: Important ms collections on the labor movement and radicalism incl: Adolph Germer, papers, 1918, 1928, 1930-31, 44 folders; Thomas J Morgan, 1880-1910, 64 folders, 19 volumes; John H Walker, papers, 1910-1955, 66 boxes. Guide to the collections published in 1976.

MORICE, ANNE

MA —BOSTON UNIVERSITY, Mugar Memorial Library, Special Collections Dept,
771 Commonwealth Ave, Boston, 02215. Howard B Gotlieb, Dir
Holdings: Cat Mss
Notes: Mss, correspondence, etc collected in depth; incl publications by or about.

MORICE, CHARLES

PA —TEMPLE UNIVERSITY LIBRARIES, Special Collections Dept, Rare Books & Mss Section, Philadelphia, 19122. Thomas M Whitehead, Cur
Holdings: Vols 100 Uncat Mss Pix
Notes: Collection of French symbolist poets based on the personal papers of Charles Morice, French poet and critic; first editions and inscribed copies of Morice, Verlaine, Mallarme et al; supportative titles: *La Plume,* etc. Incl correspondence.

MORISON, STANLEY

†DC —LIBRARY OF CONGRESS, Manuscript Division, Washington, 20540.
Notes: The papers, etc, of Stanley Morison.
MO —WASHINGTON UNIVERSITY, Libraries, Campus Box 1061, Saint Louis, 63130.
Notes: Correspondence and ms material.

MORIYAMA, RAYMOND, ARCHITECTS AND PLANNERS

AB —UNIVERSITY OF CALGARY, Libraries, Special Collections Div, 2500 University Dr, Calgary, T2N 1N4, Can.
Holdings: Cat Mss Pix
Notes: Collection consists of 6791 architectural drawings, office files, records, correspondence, etc for projects from 1959 onwards, of the architectural firm of Raymond Moriyama. Included is almost every type of building, public and private, and numerous designs for competitions. A project list is on hand. 16 meters documents.

MORLEY, CHRISTOPHER

CA —UNIVERSITY OF CALIFORNIA, RIVERSIDE, University Library, 4045 Canyon Crest Dr, Box 5900, Riverside, 92517.
Holdings: Vols 170 Cat
Notes: First editions, limited editions, ephemera.
IL —ILLINOIS STATE UNIVERSITY, Milner Library, Dept of Special Collections, Normal, 61761. Robert Sokan, Librn
Notes: First editions, limited editions, ephemera, etc.
NY —ADELPHI UNIVERSITY, Library, Garden City, 11530. Jerome Yavarkovsky, Dean of Libraries
Holdings: Vols 190 Cat Mss Pix
NY —UNIVERSITY OF ROCHESTER, Rush Rhees Library, Department of Rare Books and Special Collections, Rochester, 14627. Peter Dzwonkoski, Librn
Holdings: Vols Cat Mss
Notes: A large collection including numerous ephemeral publications. Described in exhibition catalogue, "The Manuel Berlove Collection of Christopher Morley," University of Rochester Library, 20 September-20 November, 1981.
OH —MIAMI UNIVERSITY, King Library, Walter Havighurst Special Collections Library, Oxford, 45056. Helen Ball, Cur of Special Collections
Holdings: Vols 250 Uncat
PA —HAVERFORD COLLEGE, Magill Library, Quaker Collection, Haverford, 19041. Edwin B Bonner, Librn & Cur
Holdings: Vols 420 Mss Pix
Notes: Books by and about Christopher Morley. More than 1000 letters, memorabilia.
PA —FREE LIBRARY OF PHILADELPHIA, Rare Book Dept, Logan Sq, Philadelphia, 19103. Marie E Korey, Rare Book Librn
Holdings: Vols 60 Cat
Notes: A collection of first editions incl the gifts of W Atlee Burpee.
PA —EASTERN COLLEGE, Frank Warner Memorial Library, Saint Davids, 19087.

James L Sauer, Librn
Holdings: Uncat Mss Pix
Notes: The Harry C Goebel Collection. Incl Bruce Rogers printings (over 460); press books (about 350); oriental art (over 250); bookplates (with a separate collection of an almost complete set of bookplates designed by Edwin Davis French); Christmas Books; art and graphic arts (incl the French Graphic Arts Collection of Adolph DeMilly); first editions of Christopher Morley; Print Collection (1315 prints); Oriental art realia and artifacts.
†TX —UNIVERSITY OF TEXAS LIBRARIES, General Libraries, Humanities Research Center, PO Box 7219, Austin, 78712. John Chalmers, Librn

MORLEY, EDWARD WILLIAMS, AND FAMILY

CA —CALIFORNIA INSTITUTE OF TECHNOLOGY, Robert A Millikan Memorial Library, Archives, 1201 E California Blvd, Pasadena, 91125. Judith R Goodstein, Archivist
Notes: 10 boxes. Letters to Edward Williams Morley (1838-1923), chemist and physicist, from his father, Sardis Brewster Morley (1804-1889), Congregational clergyman in Massachusetts and Connecticut, his mother, Anna Clarissa (Treat) Morley, brothers John Henry Morley, Congregational clergyman in the Midwest, and Frank Gibson Morley (d 1875), and sister Lizzie Morley; together with correspondence between the other members of the family; letters to Sardis Brewster Morley from classmates at Williams college, many relating to theological questions; other family papers; and reprints of Edward Williams Morley's scientific writings, incl those relating to the Michelson-Morley experiment. Incl Civil War letters of Sardis Brewster Morley (a chaplain), John Henry Morley, and Frank Gibson Morley; letters by Lizzie Morley written from Mount Holyoke Female Seminaryand Dio Lewis' school for young ladies at Lexington, Mass; letters from John Henry Morley in Magnolia and Sioux City, Iowa, and while superintendent of Congregational Home Missionary Society in Minneapolis, Minn; family chronology (1864-1885) kept by Anna Clarissa (Treat) Morley; and Treat family papers. Unpublished finding aid in the repository.

MORLEY, SYLVANUS G.

PA —AMERICAN PHILOSOPHICAL SOCIETY, Library, 105 S Fifth St, Philadelphia, 19106. Edward C Carter II, Librn
Notes: Papers, incl American Indian anthropological studies.

MORLEY FAMILY

CA —CALIFORNIA INSTITUTE OF TECHNOLOGY, Robert A Millikan Memorial Library, Archives, 1201 E California Blvd, Pasadena, 91125. Judith R Goodstein, Archivist
Holdings: Vols (3000) Uncat Mss Maps Pix Slides Phonorecords Audiotapes Videotapes 16mm Films Microforms
Notes: Over 70 collections (1830s-present) relating to history of 19th-20th centuries science and technology and the history of the Institute. Included are personal and professional papers of Caltech scientists and administrative officers; divisional records and faculty committees; over 5000 photographs of American and European scientists. Mss collections documents more than a century of American political, social, and intellectual history; the development of the physical sciences, aeronautics, molecular biology, and seismology in the US and abroad; and social and political conditions in Europe between the two World Wars. There are also family letters relating to 19th century American life before and during the Civil War (the Morley and A G Throop papers); to 19th century social conditions in Russia and Hungary (the

MORLEY FAMILY (cont.)

Paul Epstein papers and Theodore von Karman papers); andto the development of 20th century Italian mathematics.

MORMONS AND MORMONISM

AZ —NORTHERN ARIZONA UNIVERSITY, Special Collection Library, CU Box 6022, Flagstaff, 86011. Peter M Whiteley, Coordr/Archivist; William Mullane, Librn
Holdings: Cat Mss
Notes: Various collections, incl (1) Henry William Bigler Collection. He was a Mormon pioneer with the Mormon Battalion, and was present at the Sutter gold discovery in Calif; incl journal, 1846-1853 (original in the Henry E Huntington Library). (2) Frihoff Godfrey Nielson Collection (Joseph City, Ariz, Mormon pioneer). Incl journal, autobiography, and notes. (3) George S Tanner Collection; records of the Mormon settlement of Northern Arizona. Incl copies of numerous diaries, journals, correspondence, church records, pioneer reminiscences, and other research data. The bulk of the collection incl documents from 1876 through the early 1900's, with continuous materials through the 1970's. See *Register of the Records of the Mormon Settlement in Arizona*, Register 8, Salt Lake City, Special Collections, University of Utah Library, 1974. Also incl drafts ofGeorge S Tanner's book, *Colonization on the Little Colorado: The Joseph City Region*. (4) James S Brown (Mormon pioneer and missionary) Collection; diary, 1875-1877. (5) John Bushman Collection; diaries and journals, 1871-1923, Joseph City, Ariz. Mormon history.

CA —AZUSA PACIFIC COLLEGE, Marshburn Memorial Library, Citrus & Alosta, Azusa, 91702. Edward Peterman, Librn
Holdings: Vols (6000) Uncat
Budget: ($30,000)
Notes: Significant holdings in the George E Fullerton Library of Californiana and Western Americana.

CA —SAN BERNARDINO COUNTY LIBRARY, 104 W Fourth St, San Bernardino, 92415.
Holdings: Cat Mss Maps Pix
Budget: ($3000)

CT —YALE UNIVERSITY, Box 1603A, Yale Station, New Haven, 06520.
Holdings: Vols Cat

HI —BRIGHAM YOUNG UNIVERSITY, HAWAII CAMPUS, Joseph F Smith Library, 55-220 Kulanui St, Laie, 96762. E Curtis Fawson, Dir
Holdings: Vols 3500 Cat Mss Maps Pix Phonorecords Audiotapes Videotapes 16mm Films Filmstrips Microforms

IL —CHICAGO HISTORICAL SOCIETY, Library, Clark St at North Ave, Chicago, 60614. Robert L Brubaker, Dir
Holdings: Vols (150,000) Cat Mss Pix
Notes: Primarily in Illinois and Missouri.

IL —NEWBERRY LIBRARY, 60 W Walton St, Chicago, 60610. Diana Haskell, Cur of Modern Mss
Holdings: Cat
Notes: Historical aspects; much primary material.

IL —WHEATON COLLEGE, Buswell Memorial Library, Wheaton, 60187. Paul Snezek, Library Dir
Holdings: Vols 350 Cat
Notes: Material includes pamphlets and books from the 19th century.

IA —GRACELAND COLLEGE, Frederick Madison Smith Library, Lamoni, 50140. Volante H Russell, Cur
Holdings: Vols 3000 Cat Mss Microforms
Notes: Mormonism and RLDS Church history. No photocopying.

LA —TULANE UNIVERSITY, Howard-Tilton Memorial Library, Special Collections Div, 7001 Freret St, New Orleans, 70118. Wilbur E Meneray, Librn
Holdings: Cat Mss
Notes: Official, personal and family correspondence of Albert Sidney Johnston incl letter and order books. Incl the Mexican War, the Utah Campaign and the Civil War. Indexed.

MA —HARVARD UNIVERSITY LIBRARY, Widener Library, Cambridge, 02138.
Holdings: Cat
Notes: See *Arizona and the West*, X (1968), 211-224.

MO —UNIVERSITY OF MISSOURI-KANSAS CITY, General Library, Snyder Collection of Americana, 5100 Rockhill Road, Kansas City, 64110. Kenneth J LaBudde, Dir; Robert Paustian, Asst Dir
Holdings: Vols 25,000 Cat
Notes: Nucleus was Robert M Snyder, Jr Americana Collection of some 14,000 items. Contains printed materials on 19th-century American history, especially the Trans-Mississippi West. Strengths include the history of Kansas City and Jackson County, Missouri, Kansas and Missouri county and state histories, American frontier religion (esp the Mormons and Alexander Campbell's Disciples of Christ), the history of railroads and transportation, the cattle trade, 19th-Century biography and autobiography, North American Indians and early Kansas and Missouri imprints.

NJ —PRINCETON UNIVERSITY, Library, Princeton, 08540. Alfred Bush, Cur
Holdings: Cat

NY —NEW YORK PUBLIC LIBRARY, Research Libraries, General Research Division, Fifth Ave & 42 St, New York, 10018. Rodney Phillips, Chief
Holdings: Vols (2,225,000) Cat Maps Pix Microforms
Budget: ($775,718)

TX —ABILENE CHRISTIAN UNIVERSITY, Margaret & Herman Brown Library, ACU Sta, Abilene, 79601. Callie Faye Milliken, Assoc Dir
Holdings: Vols 3000 // Cat
Notes: Lambert Collection on Catholicism and Mormonism.

TX —UNIVERSITY OF TEXAS LIBRARIES, General Libraries, Barker Texas History Center, PO Box P, Austin, 78712. Don Carleton, Dir
Holdings: Vols (132,000) Cat Mss Maps Pix Slides Phonorecords Audiotapes Microforms
Notes: See description of collection under Texas-History.

UT —UTAH STATE UNIVERSITY, Merrill Library, Department of Special Collections & Archives, Logan, 84322. A J Simmonds, Curator; Jeanie F Simmonds, Archivist; Bradford R Cole, Mss Librn
Holdings: Vols 7600 Cat Mss Maps Microforms
Notes: Incl all LDS Churches, though major emphasis is on the Salt Lake based Church of Jesus Christ of Latter-Day Saints and on the Mormon fundamentalists (polygamists). Additional material in the Library's Utah Collection. 800 rolls microform, 1000 linear feet Mss.

UT —BRIGHAM YOUNG UNIVERSITY, Harold B Lee Library, Unversity Hill, Provo, 84602. Sterling Albrecht, Dir
Holdings: Vols 64,000 Cat Mss Maps Pix Microforms

UT —PROVO CITY PUBLIC LIBRARY, 13 N 100 E, Provo, 84601. Larry Hortin, Dir
Holdings: Vols (600) Cat
Notes: Western states history with emphasis on Utah State and Utah County.

UT —CHURCH OF JESUS CHRIST OF LATTER-DAY SAINTS, Genealogical Dept Library, 50 E N Temple, Salt Lake City, 84150. David M Mayfield, Dir
Holdings: Vols Cat Mss Maps Audiotapes Microforms
Notes: Genealogical research materials on Mormons incl history, family history, biographies, original records or copies of original records. Copies of the catalog are available at branches of the main library.

UT —UNIVERSITY OF UTAH, Marriott Library, Special Collections, Salt Lake City, 84112. Gregory C Thompson, Cur
Notes: Extensive collection, catalogs, manuscripts, pamphlets, rare books, oral history.

UT —UNIVERSITY OF UTAH, Marriott Library, Special Collections, Salt Lake City, 84112. Gregory C Thompson, Cur
Notes: Collections incl papers, correspondence, and manuscripts, of Sonia Johnson, excommunicated Mormon feminist. Part of the collection has a time seal on it.

UT —UTAH STATE HISTORICAL SOCIETY, Library, 300 Rio Grande, Salt Lake City, 84101. Jay M Haymond, Coordr, Collections & Research Services
Holdings: Vols (20,000) Cat Mss Maps Pix Slides Phonorecords Audiotapes 16mm Films Filmstrips Microforms
Budget: $37,000

MORNING-GLORIES

CA —FITZ HUGH LUDLOW MEMORIAL LIBRARY, PO Box 99346, San Francisco, 94109. Michael R Aldrich, Exec Cur
Holdings: Cat Mss Maps Pix Slides Phonorecords Audiotapes Videotapes
Notes: Collection stored. Important mail inquiries only. No interlibrary lending or telephone inquiries. Hallucinogens as used in historical and contemporary cultures. Nearly complete collection of books and articles by or about Timothy Leary, incl manuscripts; also nearly complete collection of the writings of Aldous Huxley concerning drugs. Much autographed or inscribed material, mostly popular music from the 1960s but also incl ethnographic music. Emphasis on psychoactive drugs relative to religion, literature, art. Also an excellent collection of research papers (chemistry, pharmacology, epidemiology, sociology, ethnobotany) in this field, as well as artifacts and artwork relating to the field.

MOROCCO

CA —HOOVER INSTITUTION ON WAR, REVOLUTION & PEACE, Stanford University, Stanford, 94305. Peter Duignan, Cur; Karen Fung, Deputy Cur
Holdings: Vols (100,000)
Notes: For full description of collection, see Hoover Institution entry under Near East.

DC —HOWARD UNIVERSITY, Moorland-Spingarn Research Center, 500 Howard Place NW, Washington, 20059. Clifford L Muse, Jr, Acting Dir

MA —HARVARD UNIVERSITY LIBRARY, Cambridge, 02138.
Holdings: Cat

VA —UNIVERSITY OF VIRGINIA, Alderman Library, Manuscripts Dept, Charlottesville, 22901. Edmund Berkeley Jr, Cur
Holdings: Cat Mss Pix
Notes: Papers of J Rives Childs, foreign sevice officer in Saudi Arabia, Yemen, Ethiopia, and Morocco, and Casanova scholar.

MORONS see Mentally Handicapped

MORRIS, EDITA

MA —BOSTON UNIVERSITY, Mugar Memorial Library, Special Collections Dept, 771 Commonwealth Ave, Boston, 02215. Howard B Gotlieb, Dir
Holdings: Cat Mss
Notes: Mss, correspondence, etc collected in depth; incl publications by or about.

MORRIS, FRANKLIN

NY —SYRACUSE UNIVERSITY LIBRARIES, Ernest S Bird Library, George Arents Research Library for Special Collections, Syracuse, 13210. Carolyn A Davis, Manuscripts Librn; Amy S Doherty, University Archivist; Mark F Weimer, Rare Book Librn
Notes: American Music Collection. Papers of Ernst Bacon, Louis Krasner, Franklin Morris, William Henry Berwald, Earl George, and Arthur Polster.

MORRIS, GEORGE POPE

MA —HARVARD UNIVERSITY LIBRARY, Cambridge, 02138.
Holdings: Cat Mss

MORRIS, IVAN

†NY —COLUMBIA UNIVERSITY
LIBRARIES, Butler Library, Rare Book and
Manuscript Library, 535 W 114 St, New
York, 10027.
Notes: Papers of Dr Ivan Morris, American
Section chairman of Amnesty International,
his researches into Japanese literature and
culture, and his books on puzzles.

MORRIS, JOHN

MO —WASHINGTON UNIVERSITY,
Libraries, Special Collections Dept, Campus
Box 1061, St Louis, 63130.
Notes: A small but significant collection.

MORRIS, NELL

TX —TEXAS WOMAN'S UNIVERSITY,
Bralley Memorial Library, Box 23715, TWU
Sta, Denton, 76204. Metta Nicewarner, Spec
Collections Libn
Holdings: Uncat Mss Pix
Notes: Nell Morris concerns the Texas
dietian, educator, poet, home economist for
Frito-Lay, 1950-1971. Includes professional
documents and correspondence, menus,
recipes, cookbooks, scrapbooks, personal
memorabilia.

MORRIS, RICHARD B.

NY —COLUMBIA UNIVERSITY
LIBRARIES, Rare Book & Manuscript
Library, 801 Butler Library, 535 W 114 St,
New York, 10027. Kenneth A Lohf, Librn
Holdings: Cat Mss
Notes: Papers, incl mss, letters, reviews, etc.
Restricted use.

MORRIS, ROBERT

MD —JOHNS HOPKINS UNIVERSITY,
Milton S Eisenhower Library, Charles & 34
Sts, Baltimore, 21218. Ann S Gwyn,
Assistant Dir for Special Collections
NY —NEW YORK PUBLIC LIBRARY, Rare
Books and Manuscripts Div, Fifth Ave & 42
St, New York, 10018. William L Joyce, Asst
Dir; Susan E Davis, Cur of Mss
Holdings: Mss
Budget: ($7161)
Notes: Incl personal and literary mss, papers,
etc.

MORRIS, TOBY

OK —UNIVERSITY OF OKLAHOMA,
Bizzell Memorial Library, Western History
Collections, 401 W Brooks, Norman, 73069.
John Ezell, Cur
Holdings: Mss Documents Maps
Notes: US Representative. His papers.

MORRIS, WILLIAM

CA —UNIVERSITY OF THE PACIFIC,
Library, Stockton, 95211. Hiram L Davis,
Dir of Libraries
Holdings: Vols (350) Uncat Pix
Notes: A general collection of Victorian
literature and life given to the University by
James M Perrin in 1968-1970. The primary
specialization is material by and about
William Morris and the Kelmscott Press, but
the collection also is rich in Victorian first
editions, Pre-Raphaelites and Pre-
Raphaelitism, and early colored illustrations
and chromolithography.
IN —INDIANA UNIVERSITY, Lilly Library,
Seventh St, Bloomington, 47405. William R
Cagle, Librn
Holdings: // Cat
Notes: Complete collection of items printed
at the Kelmscott Press.
NC —DUKE UNIVERSITY, William R
Perkins Library, Durham, 27706. Elvin E
Strowd, University Librn
Notes: The Bath Collection of F Darlington
Wardle contains more than 800 books, and
additions are ongoing. One third of the
collection relates to Bath and Somersetshire.
There are first editions of William Morris,

Robert Louis Stevenson and Rudyard
Kipling; Dicken's *Barnaby Rudge* in parts;
and the Nuremberg Bible of 1478. Among
the manuscripts are 92 William Morris
letters, and an autograph book containing
signatures of such literary men and women
as Samuel Clemens, Elizabeth Browning, G
K Chesterton, Rudyard Kipling and Arnold
Bennett.
NC —DUKE UNIVERSITY, William R
Perkins Library, Manuscript Dept, Durham,
27706. Ellen Gartrell, Cur of Mss
Holdings: Cat Mss
Notes: Papers of various southern textile
mills, especially North Carolina, 19th-20th
century, incl material on unions and strikes;
Sir Thomas Wardle Papers (93 letters of
William Morris).
PA —BRYN MAWR COLLEGE, Canaday
Library, Bryn Mawr, 19010. James Tanis,
Dir
Notes: Rare books in the Adelman
Collection.

MORRIS, WILLIAM, THEATRICAL AGENCY

NY —NEW YORK PUBLIC LIBRARY,
Performing Arts Research Center, Billy Rose
Theatre Collection, 111 Amsterdam Ave,
New York, 10023. Dorothy L Swerdlove,
Cur
Holdings: Cat Microforms
Notes: Incl several scrapbooks on microfilm.

MORRIS, WRIGHT

NE —UNIVERSITY OF NEBRASKA-
LINCOLN, Don L Love Library, University
Archives and Special Collections, Lincoln,
68588. Joseph G Svoboda, University
Archivist
Notes: Virginia Faulkner was recognized as
one of Nebraska's most distinguished writers
and scholars. The Virginia Faulkner
Collection, containing over 2000 titles, is
housed in the Special Collections
Department of Love Library. It is especially
strong in twentieth century writers and in
University of Nebraska Press publications.
Of especial value to scholars are her
extensive holdings of Willa Cather, Wright
Morris, and John Neihardt. Her
correspondence with S N Behrman, E B
White, Edward Wagenknecht, Donald
Sutherland, Wright Morris, Louise Pound,
Mari Sandoz, Hazel Barnes, Alfred A and
Blanche Knopf, and others provide insight
into the literary development of these
figures, as well as chronicle the intellectual
thought of the period. Amassed in a separate
file, these letters are available to interested
scholars.
NE —UNIVERSITY OF NEBRASKA,
OMAHA, Library, 60 & Dodge Sts, Omaha,
68132. Mel Bohn, Librn
Holdings: Vols 59 Cat
NV —UNIVERSITY OF NEVADA, RENO,
University Library, Special Collections Dept,
Reno, 89557. Robert E Blesse, Head
Holdings: Vols (78) Cat Other appearances
100 Cat
Notes: Includes individual works by author
in all editions including translations; also
prefaces, introductions, published
correspondence, appearances in anthologies,
periodicals, etc. Bibliographical research
collection, part of Modern Authors
Collection.

MORRIS FAMILY, 1677-1948

NJ —RUTGERS, THE STATE UNIVERSITY
OF NEW JERSEY, Alexander Library,
Special Collections and Archives, College
Ave & Huntington St, New Brunswick,
08903. Ronald L Becker, Cur of Manuscripts
and Rare Books
Holdings: // Mss
Notes: Papers, etc (15 linear feet).

MORRISON, DELESSEPS STORY

LA —TULANE UNIVERSITY, Howard-Tilton
Memorial Library, Special Collections Div,

7001 Freret St, New Orleans, 70118. Wilbur
E Meneray, Librn
Holdings: Cat Mss Pix Audiotapes
Videotapes
Notes: Papers of Louisiana politicians,
including Thomas Hale Boggs, Felix Edward
Hebert, Sam Houston Jones and deLesseps
Story Morrison.

MORRISON, FRANK

NC —DUKE UNIVERSITY, William R
Perkins Library, Manuscript Dept, Durham,
27706. Ellen Gartrell, Cur of Mss
Holdings: Cat Mss
Notes: Emphasis on US South, especially
CIO Organizing Committee papers, 1946-53
(ca 143,00 items). Large percentage have
been commercially microfilmed under title
"Operation Dixie." Also papers of Lucy
Randolph Mason, Frank deVyver, Frank
Morrison.

MORRISON, WILLIAM

IL —UNIVERSITY OF ILLINOIS,
URBANA/CHAMPAIGN, Library, Illinois
Historical Survey Library, 1408 W Gregory
Dr, 1A Library, Urbana, 61801.
Holdings: Vols (6500) Cat Mss Maps Pix
Microforms
Notes: Important ms collections incl:
Randolph County Records, 1720-1853, 91
items, 59 reels of microfilm; St Clair County
Records, 1722-1809, 6 items, 5 reels of
microfilm; George Morgan, papers, 1766-
1826, 280 items, 5 reels of microfilm;
William Morrison, papers, 1805-1855, 7 reels
of microfilm. Pierre Menard, papers, 1780,
1802-1859, 155 items, 27 volumes, 29 reels
microfilm; Illinois Surveyors' field notes and
plat maps, 1805-1850, 56 reels microfilm.
Numerous county and local histories and
plat books. 1733 maps, and thousands of
Illinois pictures. Guide to the collections
published in 1976.

MORRISON MILLING COMPANY

TX —NORTH TEXAS STATE UNIVERSITY,
Archives, NT Station Box 5188, Denton,
76203. Robert LaForte, University Archivist
Notes: Morrison Milling Company
Collection (14 linear feet), Tom Harpool
Seed Company Collection (17 linear feet).
The development of agriculture and
businesses dependent on agriculture in the
North Texas area is a collecting strength at
the NTSU Archives. The Morrison Milling
Company Collection and the Tom Harpool
Seed Company Collection focus on
agricultural businesses in the city of Denton
from the 1930s to the early 1980s.

MORRISON, PEGGY (MARCH COST)

MA —BOSTON UNIVERSITY, Mugar
Memorial Library, Special Collections Dept,
771 Commonwealth Ave, Boston, 02215.
Howard B Gotlieb, Dir
Holdings: Cat Mss Correspondence

MORROW, DWIGHT

MA —AMHERST COLLEGE, Library,
Amherst, 01002. John Lancaster, Special
Collections Librn
Holdings: // Cat Mss Pix
Notes: Ambassador to Mexico; father-in-law
of Charles A Lindbergh. 35 file drawers of
papers, etc. Amherst College holds
publication rights to unpublished Morrow
material.

MORROW, E. FREDERIC

MA —BOSTON UNIVERSITY, Mugar
Memorial Library, Special Collections Dept,
771 Commonwealth Ave, Boston, 02215.
Howard B Gotlieb, Dir
Holdings: Cat Mss
Notes: Mss, correspondence, etc collected in
depth; incl publications by or about.

MORROW, STANLEY J.

FL —FLORIDA DEPT OF STATE, Florida
State Archives, Florida Photographic

MORROW, STANLEY J. (cont.)

Collection, R A Gray Bldg, Tallahassee, 32301. Mrs Allen Morris, Archives Supervisor
Holdings: Maps Pix Slides Films Audiotapes
Notes: Mr Morrow learned his craft under Mathew B Brady. He worked in Florida from 1882-1887. Collection has several hundred of his glass negatives that document a period of southward expansion in Florida.

MORSE, DAVID A., 1907-

NJ —PRINCETON UNIVERSITY, Seeley G Mudd Manuscript Library, Public Affairs Papers Collection, Princeton, 08544. Nancy Bressler, Cur
Notes: Incl 144 boxes. The papers cover the period 1930-81. An unpublished 119p guide is available in the Library.

MORSE, F. BRADFORD

MA —BOSTON UNIVERSITY, Mugar Memorial Library, Special Collections Dept, 771 Commonwealth Ave, Boston, 02215. Howard B Gotlieb, Dir
Holdings: Mss Pix
Notes: Mss, correspondence, etc collected in depth; incl publications by or about.

MORSE, JEBEDIAH

CT —YALE UNIVERSITY, Box 1603A, Yale Station, New Haven, 06520.
Holdings: Cat Mss

MORSE, SAMUEL FINLEY BREESE

CT —YALE UNIVERSITY, Box 1603A, Yale Station, New Haven, 06520.
Holdings: Cat Mss
DC —LIBRARY OF CONGRESS, Manuscript Division, Washington, 20540. John C Broderick, Chief
Holdings: Cat Mss Pix
Notes: Mss, papers, records, etc.
NY —UNIVERSITY OF ROCHESTER, Rush Rhees Library, Department of Rare Books and Special Collections, Rochester, 14627. Peter Dzwonkoski, Librn
Holdings: Mss
Notes: Eleven letters to his cousin Margaret Breese.

MORSE, WAYNE L.

OR —UNIVERSITY OF OREGON LIBRARY, Eugene, 97403.
Notes: His papers.

MORSE FAMILY

CT —YALE UNIVERSITY, Box 1603A, Yale Station, New Haven, 06520.
Notes: Incl mss.
MA —NEW ENGLAND HISTORIC GENEALOGICAL SOCIETY, Library, 101 Newbury St, Boston, 02116. Ralph J Crandell, Dir
Notes: Family papers, likely to incl personal correspondence, diaries, business records, etc.

MORSON, HUGH

NC —NORTH CAROLINA DIV OF ARCHIVES & HISTORY, 109 E Jones St, Raleigh, 27611.
Notes: Papers, 1877-1931; 348 items.

MORTALITY

TX —HOUSTON ACADEMY OF MEDICINE-TEXAS MEDICAL CENTER, Library, Jesse H Jones Library Bldg, Houston, 77030. Elizabeth Borst White, Special Collections Librn
Holdings: Vols (900) Cat
Notes: Mading Collection on Public Health. English-language materials dealing with American public health conditions before 1925. Emphasis is on epidemiology and infectious diseases (excluding venereal disease), incl material on sanitation and climatology. Federal, state or municipal reports on health, mortality and sanitation are included. Also 500 pamphlets.

MORTGAGES

ON —CANADIAN HOUSING INFORMATION CENTER, Canada Mortgage and Housing Corp, CMHC Annex Bldg Ground Floor, Montreal Rd, Ottawa, K1A 0P7, Can. Leslie Jones, Mgr
Holdings: Cat

MORTIMER, JOHN

MA —BOSTON UNIVERSITY, Mugar Memorial Library, Special Collections Dept, 771 Commonwealth Ave, Boston, 02215. Howard B Gotlieb, Dir
Holdings: Cat Mss

MORTIMER, WYNDHAM

†CA —UNIVERSITY OF CALIFORNIA, Library, Los Angeles, 90024.

MORTON, CHARLES

MA —BOSTON UNIVERSITY, Mugar Memorial Library, Special Collections Dept, 771 Commonwealth Ave, Boston, 02215. Howard B Gotlieb, Dir
Holdings: Mss Pix
Notes: Mss, correspondence, etc collected in depth; incl publications by or about.

MORTON, FERDINAND 'JELLY ROLL'

DC —LIBRARY OF CONGRESS, American Folklife Center, Archive of Folk Culture, Washington, 20540.
Notes: Recordings of jazz musician Jelly Roll Morton, 1938.

MORTON, STERLING

IL —CHICAGO HISTORICAL SOCIETY, Library, Clark St at North Ave, Chicago, 60614. Archie Motley, Manuscript Librn
Notes: Papers of industrialist, chairman of board of Morton Salt Co.

MORTON, STRATFORD LEE

MO —WASHINGTON UNIVERSITY, Libraries, Special Collections Dept, Campus Box 1061, St Louis, 63130.
Notes: Family and business correspondence.

MORTON, SEN. THRUSTON BALLARD

KY —UNIVERSITY OF KENTUCKY, Margaret I King Library, Dept of Special Collections, Lexington, 40506. William Marshall, Head
Holdings: Cat Mss Pix Audiotapes Films
Notes: Public career of Sen Morton. Contains 296,352 pieces, chiefly letters. Unpublished inventory.

MORTON FAMILY

IL —CHICAGO HISTORICAL SOCIETY, Library, Clark St at North Ave, Chicago, 60614. Archie Motley, Manuscript Librn
Notes: Papers of Sterling Morton, Joy Morton and other Morton family men and women.

MORTUARY STATISTICS see Mortality

MOSAIC LAW see Jewish Law

MOSBY, JOHN S.

VA —UNIVERSITY OF VIRGINIA, Alderman Library, Manuscripts Dept, Charlottesville, 22901. Edmund Berkeley Jr, Cur
Holdings: Cat Mss Maps Pix
Notes: About 1500 collections have material pertaining to the Civil War and particularly to the Army of Northern Virginia and campaigns and battles in Virginia. There are letters, diaries, reminiscences, maps, and pictorial material of Confederate soldiers and civilians, as well as papers of Robert E Lee, J E B Stuart, Thomas L Rosser, Jubal A Early, John Daniel Imboden, William "Extra Billy" Smith, Henry Alexander Wise, Eppa Hunton, and John S Mosby.

MOSES, MONTROSE JONAS

NC —DUKE UNIVERSITY, William R Perkins Library, Durham, 27706. Elvin E Strowd, University Librn
Holdings: Cat Mss Pix
Notes: Montrose J Moses' collection of books, mss, and papers, mostly concerned with men and women of the theatre, and creative writers of the first third of the century. 3000 books; 22,000 mss.

MOSHER, THOMAS BIRD

AZ —ARIZONA STATE UNIVERSITY, Library, Tempe, 85287. Marilyn Wurzburger, Special Collections Librn
Holdings: Vols 1286
Notes: This collection, according to the Hatch *Check-list* is complete except for 54 items. It also contains the post-1923 Mosher imprints as well as personal and business memorabilia and papers.
ME —MAINE STATE LIBRARY, Special Collections Dept, Cultural Bldg, Station 64, Augusta, 04333. Shirley Thayer, Librn
Holdings: Vols 600 //
Budget: ($2,500,000)
Notes: A collection of imprints by the Mosher Press, Portland, Maine.
†ON —UNIVERSITY OF WESTERN ONTARIO, School of Library and Information Science, Special Collections Room, London, N6A 5B9, Can.
Notes: Small collection of examples of Mosher's printing.

MOSIER, CHARLES A.

FL —FLORIDA DEPT OF STATE, Florida State Archives, Florida Photographic Collection, R A Gray Bldg, Tallahassee, 32301. Mrs Allen Morris, Archives Supervisor
Notes: Charles A Mosier, Charles Torrey Simpson and J K Small, 500 photographs of Florida flora, made by these famous naturalists, mostly in South Dade county. Added March, 1983, 2200 glass and nitrate negatives by J K Small.

MOSKOWITZ, BELLE I., 1877-1933

CT —CONNECTICUT COLLEGE, Library, Mohegan Ave, New London, 06320. Brian Rogers, College Librn
Holdings: // Uncat Mss
Notes: A collection of the papers of Belle Moskowitz, a prominent figure in New York politics and government with Alfred E Smith.

MOSLEM ARCHITECTURE see Architecture, Islamic

MOSLEM ART see Art, Islamic

MOSLEMS see Civilization, Islamic; Islam

MOSQUITO KINGDOM

CT —YALE UNIVERSITY, Box 1603A, Yale Station, New Haven, 06520.
Holdings: Cat Mss
Notes: Incl the ms minutes of the Council of State of the Mosquito Kingdom, September 1846-1847, the British protectorate on the coast of Nicaragua.

MOSQUITOES

IA —IOWA STATE UNIVERSITY, Library, Ames, 50011. Warren B Kuhn, Dean of Library Services
Holdings: Cat
Notes: Specific strengths: flies, mosquitoes and ticks.

MOSQUITOES (cont.)

NY —AMERICAN MUSEUM OF
NATURAL HISTORY, Library Services
Dept, Central Park W & 79th St, New York,
10024. Nina J Root, Chairwoman; Mary
Genett, Asst Librn for Reference Services
Notes: A major literature collection
supplements the museum's entomology
collections; perhaps the largest in the world.

MOSS, SEN. FRANK

UT —UNIVERSITY OF UTAH, Marriott
Library, Special Collections, Salt Lake City,
84112. Gregory C Thompson, Cur
Holdings: Cat Mss Microfilm Film Oral
History
Notes: Papers.

MOSSBAUER EFFECT see Moessbauer Effect

MOSSES

MA —HARVARD UNIVERSITY LIBRARY,
Farlow Reference Library, 20 Divinity Ave,
Cambridge, 02138. Geraldine C Kaye, Librn
Holdings: Vols (60,000) Cat Mss Serials Pix
Microforms
Notes: The Farlow Reference Library
provides complete coverage of the
systematic literature on algae, bryophytes,
fungi, and lichens. Established by bequest of
Professor William G Farlow, it is one of the
most extensive cryptogamic botany libraries
in the US. Books do not circulate.
MO —MISSOURI BOTANICAL GARDEN
LIBRARY, PO Box 299, Saint Louis, 63166.
M R Crosby, Dir of Research
Notes: The William Campbell Steere
Collection of over 1000 volumes and 5000
pamphlets on bryology. Especially strong in
the 19th century literature and from 1750 to
the present.
ON —NATIONAL MUSEUMS OF
CANADA, Library Services Directorate,
Ottawa, K1A 0M8, Can. Valerie
Monkhouse, Director
Holdings: Vols (90,000) Cat Mss Microforms
Budget: ($81,000)
Notes: Emphasis on Canadian and
circumpolar natural history. Collection incl
botany, herpetology, ichthyology,
invertebrate zoology, malacology,
mammology, mineralogy, ornithology,
paleobiology, zooarchaeology. Exceptional
collections in lichenology, bryology,
malacology, ornithology. Research
collection, interlibrary loans available, public
may use on the premises.
ON —LAURENTIAN UNIVERSITY
LIBRARY, Ramsey Lake Rd, Sudbury, P3E
2C6, Can. Suzanne Brunette, Special
Collection Librn; Sue Vongpeisal, Head
Librn
Notes: Materials on northern Canada, incl
2200 books and pamphlets, 60,000 press
clippings on northern topics 75 series of
periodicals and over 1500 maps, plus
photographs and thousands of samples of
arctic and subarctic plants incl mosses,
lichens, algae and wood sections. Much of
the material is in French.

MOSSIKER, FRANCES

MA —BOSTON UNIVERSITY, Mugar
Memorial Library, Special Collections Dept,
771 Commonwealth Ave, Boston, 02215.
Howard B Gotlieb, Dir
Holdings: Cat Mss Pix
Notes: Mss, correspondence, etc collected in
depth; incl publications by or about.

MOSTEL, ZERO

CA —UNIVERSITY OF CALIFORNIA,
DAVIS, Shields Library, Dept of Special
Collections, Davis, 95616. Donald Kunitz,
Head; C Danial Elliott, Asst Head
Notes: Photographs, clippings, and
correspondence of personalities of American
and British theatre in the 19th and 20th
centuries, such as Edwin Booth, Joseph

Jefferson, Julia Marlowe, E H Sothern, Ellen
Terry, Henry Irving, McKee Rankin, Fanny
Davenport, and Zero Mostel.

MOTELS see Tourist Camps, Hotels, Etc.

MOTHER GOOSE

CA —LOS ANGELES PUBLIC LIBRARY,
Children's Literature Dept, 630 W 5th St,
Los Angeles, 90071. Serenna Day, Sr Librn
Holdings: Vols (2120) Cat Phonorecords
Filmstrips
Notes: Also includes reference collection,
covering some 50 years of published folklore
and modern fairy tales. Includes extensive
Mother Goose collection, examples of the
work of such outstanding illustrators as
Edmund Dulac and Arthur Rackham. Many
volumes out of print. Index to titles of
stories in collections.
MI —AQUINAS COLLEGE, Learning
Resource Center, 1607 Robinson Rd SE,
Grand Rapids, 49506. Larry Zysk, Dir
Holdings: Vols (55)// Cat
Notes: Mother Goose in all languages. Built
on a collection begun as a gift from a former
Grand Rapids teacher, Miss Coye.
RI —BROWN UNIVERSITY, John Hay
Library, Harris Collection, Prospect St,
Providence, 02912. Rosemary L Cullen, Cur
Holdings: Vols (200,000) Cat Mss Pix
Phonorecords Microforms
Budget: ($15,000)
Notes: The Harris Collection of American
Poetry and Plays is principally composed of
American and Canadian poetry and plays
from the 17th century to the present.
Extensive holdings in juvenile poetry (incl
Mother Goose and The Night Before
Christmas in many editions). See Dictionary
Catalog of The Harris Collection of
American Poetry and Plays (Boston: G K
Hall, 1972), 13 vols; Supplement (1977), 3
vols. See also, American Poetry, 1609-1900,
A Collection on Microfilm, Segment I
(1609-1820); Segment II (1821-1850);
Segment III (1851-1870) (Woodbridge,
Conn: Research Publications). Separate
catalog.
TX —DALLAS PUBLIC LIBRARY, Central
Library, Humanities Division, 1515 Young
St, Dallas, 75201. Richard L Waters, Acting
Dir; Muriel W Brown, Children's Literature
Specialist; Rosemarie Dunlap, Assistant to
Children's Literature Specialist
Holdings: Vols (56,000) Cat Mss Pix
Microforms
Notes: Incl Mother Goose Books,
autographed Newberry and Caldecott
winners, books important in the history of
children's literature, foreign language books,
and Texas books in addition to a general
collection.
WI —UNIVERSITY OF WISCONSIN,
MADISON, Cooperative Children's Book
Center, Helen C White Hall, Rm 4290, 600
N Park St, Madison, 53706. Ginny Moore
Kruse, Dir
Holdings: Vols (25,000) Cat
Notes: Cooperative Children's Book Center
collections incl most US trade books
published for children in last 24 months; first
editions of recommended US children's
trade books published since 1965; over 400
alternative press books published for children
in US and Canada since 1970; children's
books about Wisconsin and by Wisconsin
authors and illustrators; representative 19th
and early 20th century American children's
books; 19th century children's periodicals;
first and significant editions of Newbury and
Caldecott Medal books; historical and
contemporary toybooks; 75 vols of Mother
Goose published since 1828; 160 vols of
Thorton Burgess books, many first editions;
ms and original artwork for Ellen Raskin's
The Westing Game and The Mysterious
Disappearance of Leon (I Mean Noel);
juvenile mass market and traderomance
fiction.

MOTHERS—HEALTH

CA —UNIVERSITY OF CALIFORNIA,
BERKELEY, Life Sciences Libraries, Public

Health Library, 42 Earl Warren Hall,
Berkeley, 94720. Thomas J Alexander, Librn
Holdings: Vols (75,000) Cat Microforms
Notes: Research collection covering all
aspects of public health. Health Department
annual reports from all 50 states are
acquired, as well as such reports from all
California health units and from major US
cities. Serial publications issued by Health
Departments in the 13 western states are
being received.
GA —MEDICAL COLLEGE OF GEORGIA,
Library, Laney Walker Blvd, Augusta,
30902. Dorothy H Mims, Librn for Special
Collections
Holdings: Vols (2500)// Cat
Notes: Special collection of late 18th and
early 19th century medical books, incl
classics on diseases of children and advice to
mothers on care of children.

MOTHS see Butterflies and Moths

MOTION, PHYSIOLOGICAL

†CT —YALE UNIVERSITY, Medical Library,
333 Cedar St, New Haven, 06520.

MOTION PICTURE RESEARCH COUNCIL

CA —HOOVER INSTITUTION ON WAR,
REVOLUTION & PEACE, Stanford
University, 94305. Milorad M
Drachkovitch, Archivist
Holdings: Mss
Notes: Correspondence, by-laws, minutes,
administrative reports, records, and research
and reference materials, 1927-1941, of the
Motion Picture Research Council, an
organization which carried out research on
the film industry. 78 ms boxes and 8
volumes.

MOTION PICTURES see Moving Pictures

MOTION STUDIES

IN —PURDUE UNIVERSITY LIBRARIES,
Special Collections Dept, West Lafayette,
47907. Keith Dowden, Asst Dir, Special
Collections
Holdings: Vols (500) // Cat Mss Pix Slides
Notes: The Gilbreth Collection. Incl motion
study equipment and personal working
papers and photographs of Frank B and
Lillian Gilbreth's work in the development
of the field of industrial management. Also,
correspondence, certificates, diplomas,
memorabilia, published and nonprint
material.
NJ —STEVENS INSTITUTE OF
TECHNOLOGY, Samuel C Williams
Library, Castle Point Sta, Hoboken, 07030.
Jane G Hartye, Special Collections Librn
Holdings: Vols (180) Cat Pix Slides
Budget: ($1500)
Notes: Frederick Winslow Taylor is known
as the "father of scientific management," and
we have in our collection volumes of
correspondence relating to the introduction
of this system into industry, government, the
army and navy, etc. This collection also
includes many personal items belonging to
and used by Mr Taylor. Our collection is the
most complete one on the subject of
scientific management.

MOTIVATION RESEARCH (MARKETING)

IL —J WALTER THOMPSON CO,
Information Center, 875 N Michigan Ave,
Chicago, 60611. Edward G Strable, Dir
Holdings: Vols 50 Cat Microforms
Notes: Importance of collection is in data
file of fugitive materials-reports, clippings,
releases, articles, studies-of appprox 50
drawers covering marketing information on
most consumer products and services.
Emphasis on currentness, not history.
Indexing and organization make for rapid
access.

MOTLEY, JOHN L.

MA —HARVARD UNIVERSITY LIBRARY,
Houghton Library, Cambridge, 02138.

MOTLEY, JOHN L. (cont.)

Rodney G Dennis, Cur of Manuscripts
Holdings: Cat Mss

MOTLEY DESIGNERS

IL —UNIVERSITY OF ILLINOIS,
URBANA/CHAMPAIGN, Library, 1408 W
Gregory Drive, Urbana, 61801. Norman B
Brown, Asst Dir for Special Collections
Notes: More than 3000 costume sketches
from Motley, designers, of New York and
London, a firm whose influence covered 50
years of the London and New York stages,
particularly Shakespeare productions. Incl
story boards and fabric swatches from 160
productions. Part of the Rare Book Room.

MOTOR ABILITY

CT —YALE UNIVERSITY, Box 1603A, Yale
Station, New Haven, 06520.
IL —UNIVERSITY OF ILLINOIS,
URBANA/CHAMPAIGN, Library, Applied
Life Studies Library, 1408 W Gregory Dr,
Urbana, 61801.
Holdings: Vols (38,000) Cat Microforms
See also entry under Physical Education and
Training.
ON —UNIVERSITY OF WINDSOR, Leddy
Library, Windsor, N9B 3P4, Can. P Jerome
Malone, Librn
Notes: Human kinetics, with emphasis on
the history, psychology, sociology,
philosophy, and administration of sports and
their organization. Also hold archival
records, etc of numerous Canadian sports
organizations: Canadian Intercollegiate
Athletic Union (CIAU), Ontario-Quebec
AA, Ontario Universities AA, etc. Local and
Regional history. 40 feet of materials.
PQ —UNIVERSITY OF MONTREAL,
Physical Education Library, Montreal, H3C
3J7, Can. Lisa Mayrand, Dir

MOTOR BUS LINES

IL —CHICAGO TRANSIT AUTHORITY,
Anthon Memorial Library, Merchandise
Mart Plaza, PO Box 3555, Chicago, 60654.
Joseph Benson, Dir
Holdings: Vols (10,000) Cat Maps Slides
Microforms
Budget: ($27,200)
Notes: Urban transportation. Use of
collection by appointment with Librarian.
NJ —NEW JERSEY DEPT OF
TRANSPORTATION, Library, 1035
Parkway Ave, Trenton, 08625. Margaret L
Webb, Librn
Holdings: Vols 2000 Cat Mss Maps
Microforms
Notes: Emphasis is on highway, bus, rail,
and air transportation. There is a finding-list-
index to the department archives, over 1800
items.

MOTOR BUSES

MD —BALTIMORE STREETCAR
MUSEUM, Transit Research Center, 1901
Falls Rd, PO Box 7184, Baltimore, 21218.
George F Nixon, Cur
Holdings: Cat Mss Pix Slides 16mm Films
Notes: Transit Research Center is devoted to
the collection of memorabilia, photos,
drawings, printed matter, etc, pertinent to
public rail transportation in Baltimore and
Maryland. Incl streetcar systems, interurban
lines, and main line railroads in the area.
Also incl bus history. Existing collection
moved to larger facilities (Feb 1978). Incl
materials donated by The Baltimore Transit
Co, United Railways and Electric Co, as well
as private collections.

MOTOR CARS see Automobiles

MOTOR COURTS see Tourist Camps, Hotels, Etc.

MOTOR DEXTERITY see Motor Ability

MOTOR SKILL see Motor Ability

MOTOR TRUCKS see Trucks

MOTOR VEHICLE DRIVERS see Automobile Drivers

MOTOR VEHICLES—EMISSION CONTROL DEVICES see Motor Vehicles—Pollution Control Devices

MOTOR VEHICLES—MAINTENANCE AND REPAIR

KS —WICHITA PUBLIC LIBRARY, 223 S
Main, Wichita, 67202. Larry DePiesse,
Head, Business & Technology Dept; Jayne F
Young, Business & Technology Dept
Holdings: Vols 2452 Uncat
Budget: $1300
Notes: Unusual collection which dates back
many years on every make of car for which
repair manuals can be purchased. Lend only
on money deposit. No interlibrary loans.
WI —MADISON AREA TECHNICAL
COLLEGE, Technical Center Library, 2125
Commercial Ave, Madison, 53704. J B
Jeffcott, Librn
Holdings: Vols 1200 Cat Slides
Phonorecords Audiotapes Videotapes 16mm
Films Filmstrips Microforms
Notes: Automotive technology.

MOTOR VEHICLES—POLLUTION CONTROL DEVICES

MI —US ENVIRONMENTAL
PROTECTION AGENCY, Motor Vehicle
Emission Laboratory Library, 2565
Plymouth Rd, Ann Arbor, 48105. Debra
Talsma, Librn
Holdings: // Uncat Microforms
Notes: No separate catalog. Collection
described in: US EPA, Library System
Branch, Guide to EPA Libraries, July, 1977.
Collection includes 9500 technical reports on
air pollution from mobile sources (especially
automobiles); air pollution legislation (350
vols); fuel economy and conservation (800
technical reports); automobile engineering
(300 vols); emission control technology for
mobile source (8000 reports and papers); use
of methanol and other alternative fuels in
motor vehicles (600 technical reports).

MOTOR VEHICLES—SERVICING AND REPAIR see Motor Vehicles—Maintenance and Repair

MOTOR VEHICLES, AMPHIBIOUS

VA —US ARMY TRANSPORTATION
MUSEUM, Library, Bldg 300, Fort Eustis,
23604. Dennis P Mroczkowski, Museum Cur
Holdings: Vols (1254) Uncat Maps Pix
16mm Films
Budget: ($150)
Notes: Mainly US Army transportation from
WW II on.

MOTOR VEHICLES IN WAR see Automobiles, Military; Tanks (Military Science); Transportation, Military

MOTORCYCLES

PA —FREE LIBRARY OF PHILADELPHIA,
Automobile Reference Collection, Logan Sq,
Philadelphia, 19103. Louis G Helverson, Jr,
Librn in Charge
Holdings: Vols (14,000) Cat Pix Slides
Notes: Collection is concerned with all
aspects of automotive industry and its
history. Includes shop manuals, instruction
books, parts books, and periodicals dealing
with all types of bicycles, tricyles and motor
vehicles. Industry statistics, corporate annual
reports, environmental problems, safety. Incl
18,000 pictures, 1700 slides, 648 microfilm
reels, 23,000 sales catalogs, 500 pieces of
ephemera.

MOTORLESS FLIGHT see Gliding and Soaring

MOTT, LEWIS F.

NY —CITY UNIVERSITY OF NEW YORK,
City College, Morris R Cohen Library,
North Academic Center, Convent Ave &
137th St, New York, 10031. Barbara J
Dunlap, Archivist
Holdings: Cat Mss Pix
Notes: Incl personal papers.

MOTT, LUCRETIA COFFIN, 1793-1880

DC —LIBRARY OF CONGRESS, Manuscript
Division, Washington, 20540. John C
Broderick, Chief
Notes: Susan B Anthony's papers in the
Manuscript Division incl scrapbooks,
correspondence, speeches, and related
material. Diaries from the years 1865-1906
contain brief comments regarding her lecture
tours on behalf of woman suffrage and
referrences to such associates as Amelia
Bloomer, Lucretia Mott, and Lucy Stone.
PA —FRIENDS HISTORICAL LIBRARY OF
SWARTHMORE COLLEGE, Swarthmore,
19081. J William Frost, Dir
Holdings: Vols (35,000) Cat Mss Pix
Notes: Works by and about this Quaker
antislavery worker who was also interested
in women's rights, education and peace.
About 400 mss, mostly letters.

MOTT FAMILY PAPERS

CT —YALE UNIVERSITY, Beinecke Rare
Book & Manuscript Library, Osborn
Collection, New Haven, 06520. Stephen R
Parks, Cur
Holdings: Mss
NJ —MONMOUTH COUNTY HISTORICAL
ASSOCIATION, Library, 70 Court St,
Freehold, 07728. Loretta M Zwolak,
Archivist & Librn
Holdings: Vols (6500) Cat Mss Maps Pix
Slides Microforms
Budget: ($15,800)
Notes: Especially Monmouth County area.
See Monmouth County Historical
Association Bulletin, vol 1, no 2 July 1948, p
23-48. Allaire Papers (Howell Works); Battle
of Monmouth; Mott Family Papers; North
American Phalanx; Philip Freneau;
Steamship Coll.

MOTTRAM, RALPH HALE

IL —ILLINOIS STATE UNIVERSITY, Milner
Library, Dept of Special Collections,
Normal, 61761. Robert Sokan, Librn
Notes: First editions, limited editions,
ephemera, etc.

MOULD (BOTANY) see Molds (Botany)

MOULD, VEGETABLE see Soils

MOULTON, LOUISE CHANDLER

DC —LIBRARY OF CONGRESS, Manuscript
Division, Washington, 20540. John C
Broderick, Chief
Holdings: Cat Mss Pix
Notes: Mss, papers, records, etc.

MOUNT ATHOS MANUSCRIPTS

DC —LIBRARY OF CONGRESS, General
Reading Rooms Division, Microform
Reading Room, Washington, 20540.
Holdings: Cat Mss Maps Pix Microforms
Notes: Microform materials only in this LC
Division. Works of individual authors;
holdings of collections; archival records, etc,
press releases and translations, etc.
OH —OHIO STATE UNIVERSITY, William
Oxley Thompson Memorial Library,
Hilander Room, 1858 Neil Ave Mall,
Columbus, 43210. Predrag Matejic, Cur; G
Koolemans Beynen, Slavic Bibliographer
Holdings: Vols (200,000) Cat Maps
Microforms
Budget: ($45,000)
Notes: Area studies of Central, Southeastern
and Eastern Europe. Emphasis on on Slavic
literatures, languages and history. At present
economics, sociology, law (Russian only)
have been added. Within this framework the
following priorities have been established:
Material in Russian problems; then Medieval
Slavic (Cyrillic); then Polish, then Serbo-
Croatian, then Bulgarian, and now
Romanian. Special attention is paid to
serials, bibliographies, ms descriptions and
dictionaries (incl biographical and
encyclopedias). Apart from materials in
native languages, materials in the following
languages are acquired: Old Church
Slavonic, Greek, English, French, German,
Italian, a few in Scandinavian languages, incl
Finnish, and a few in Baltic languages. The
Hillandar Room holds approx 2000 Slavic
mss, 1050 from Hilandar Monastery, Mount

MOUNT ATHOS MANUSCRIPTS (cont.)

Athos, on microform and a related referencecollection.

MOUNT SINAI MANUSCRIPTS

DC —LIBRARY OF CONGRESS, General Reading Rooms Division, Microform Reading Room, Washington, 20540.
Holdings: Cat Mss Maps Pix Microforms
Notes: Microform materials only in this LC Division. Works of individual authors; holdings of collections; archival records, etc, press releases and translations, etc.

MOUNTAIN CLIMBING see Mountaineering

MOUNTAIN MEN

†WA —WASHINGTON STATE UNIVERSITY, Library, Manuscripts, Archives & Special Collections, Pullman, 99164. John F Guido, Head
Holdings: Cat Mss Maps Pix
Notes: The Carl Parcher Russell papers, a vast resource (24,916 items; 45 linear feet) on American Indian and Western pioneer activities and artifacts. Much on the fur trade; pioneer life; mountain men and trapping; wildlife; primitive life in detail. Also the National Park Service, parks, monuments, etc. Described in *Carl Parcher Russell: An Indexed Register of His Scholarly and Professional Papers, 1920-1967, in the Washington State University Library* (Pullman, 1970), 149 pp.

MOUNTAIN RAILROADS

NY —ELECTRIC RAILROADERS ASSOCIATION, Frank J Sprague Memorial Library, 89 E 42nd St, New York, 10018. Hugh A Dunne, First VP
Notes: Private library. Incl all forms of railroads operated by electricity. Forms of electric railroads included: street railways, subways & elevated lines, high-speed interurbans, suburban commuter lines, electrified trunk lines, monorails, mountain climbing inclines, etc. Also railroad timetables.

MOUNTAINEERING

CA —UNIVERSITY OF CALIFORNIA, LOS ANGELES, Research Library, Dept of Special Collections, 405 Hilgard Ave, Los Angeles, 90024. Edward Shreeves, Chairman, Bibliographers Group; David S Zeidberg, Head
Holdings: Vols 2000 Cat
Notes: 2000 books in the Francis P Farquhar Collection of Mountaineering Literature.
CO —UNIVERSITY OF COLORADO, Libraries, Special Collections, Boulder, 80309. Nora J Quinlan, Head
Holdings: Vols Cat
Notes: Over 2500 vols on the history of mountaineering covering everything from the Golden Age of mountaineering in the nineteenth century to accounts of expeditions undertaken today. In addition runs of such journals as the Rock and Fell Club, the Ladies' Alpine Club Journal, etc. Subjects covered incl history, technique, medicine, biographies, illustrations, etc. In addition, approx 15 1/2 feet of ms material.
CO —VAIL PUBLIC LIBRARY, 292 W Meadow Dr, Vail, 81657. Charlyn M C Canada, Librn
Holdings: Vols (500) Cat Maps
Budget: ($5300)
Notes: The alpine environment.
CT —YALE UNIVERSITY, Box 1603A, Yale Station, New Haven, 06520.
MA —APPALACHIAN MOUNTAIN CLUB, 5 Joy St, Boston, 02108. Fran Belcher, Librn
Holdings: Vols (6500) Cat Maps Pix Slides
Budget: ($3000)
Notes: Mountaineering, espec the White Mountains. Bound editions of other countries, mountaineering journals.
NH —DARTMOUTH COLLEGE, Baker Memorial Library, Hanover, 03755.
Holdings: Cat

NJ —PRINCETON UNIVERSITY, Library, Rare Books Dept, Princeton, 08544. Stephen Ferguson, Cur
Holdings: Mss
Notes: A premier collection of mountaineering literature. The papers and personal library of James Ramsey Ullman, incl his correspondence, diaries, memorabilia and mss of all his works (his published writings, scripts for his plays, his magazine articles and travel journals).
NY —ADIRONDACK HISTORICAL ASSOCIATION, Museum Library, Blue Mountain Lake, 12812. Jerold Pepper, Librn
Holdings: Vols (7500) Cat Mss Maps Pix Phonorecords Audiotapes 16mm Films Microforms
Notes: Anything about the Adirondacks-- history, people, economics, places, things. Strong in Adirondack art, outdoor recreation, logging, small boats. Resources incl more than 1000 maps, 40,000 pictures, 1600 microfilm reels, 576 linear ft of ms material, and 12 cabinets of VF ephemera, etc.
NY —NEW YORK PUBLIC LIBRARY, Research Libraries, General Research Division, Fifth Ave & 42 St, New York, 10018. Rodney Phillips, Chief
Holdings: Vols (2,225,000) Cat Maps Pix Microforms
Budget: ($775,718)
NY —RACQUET & TENNIS CLUB, Library, 370 Park Ave, New York, 10022. Gerald Belliveau, Jr, Librn
Holdings: Vols (17,500) Cat
Budget: ($6000)
Notes: Specializes in court tennis, lawn tennis, early American sport. See *Dictionary Catalogue of the Library of Sports in the Racquet and Tennis Club* (Boston: G K Hall, 1971). Also, Robert W Henderson, *Early American Sport*, 3rd ed. (Cranbury, NJ: Fairleigh Dickinson University Press, 1977).
WA —MOUNTAINEERS INC, Library, 300 3rd Ave West, Seattle, 98119. Verna M Ness, Library Cur
Holdings: Vols (3000) Cat
Notes: Collection incl some 19th century vols of Alpine information, incl the first issue of *The Alpine Journal* (1863). Bound serials of many important American climbing publications. Small sub-collections for American Alpine Club members and for The Mountaineer Foundation, the latter on conservation and ecology. In the main collection backpacking, skiing and natural history are also represented.
AB —ALPINE CLUB OF CANADA LIBRARY, Archives of the Canadian Rockies, Box 160, Banff, T0L 0C0, Can. E J Hart, Head Archivist
Holdings: Vols (2429) Cat Mss Maps Pix Slides Audiotapes
Budget: ($1000)
Notes: The Archives of the Canadian Rockies is the custodian of the library and archival collection of the Alpine Club of Canada. The materials cover mountaineering technique and attempts worldwide, incl the Alps, Rockies, Himalayas, Andes, etc. Subject areas incl history, personal records, mountain rescue and medicine, alpine flora and fauna, guide books, manuals and handbooks. A large part of the archival collection is concentrated on the Canadian Rocky Mountains, as the headquarters of The Alpine Club of Canada is in Banff, Alberta.
AB —PETER WHYTE FOUNDATION, Archives of the Canadian Rockies, Box 160, Banff, T0L 0C0, Can. Mary Andrews, ACR Librn
Holdings: Vols (4247) Cat Mss Maps Pix Slides Phonorecords Audiotapes Videotapes 16mm Films Filmstrips Microforms
Budget: ($1500)
Notes: Collect all available material which touches the Rocky Mountains of Canada (from the US border to the Peace River in the north; from the west of Calgary on the east to the town of Revelstoke, BC on the west). This material incl history (the early explorers, Indians, construction of the railroads, mountaineering, and development of the national parks), natural history

(geology, botany, wildlife) and poetry and fiction with the Rockies as a setting. Collect maps of the area, photographs, tape recordings of the pioneers. We also house on our premises the Alpine Club of Canada's library, which is one of the most comprehensive collections on the subject of mountaineering worldwide. Noncirculating.
BC —UNIVERSITY OF BRITISH COLUMBIA, Library, 1956 Main Mall, Vancouver, V6T 1Y3, Can. Anne Yandle, Special Collections Librn
Notes: British Columbia Mountaineering Club photograph collection covering many years of activities. Incl 420 negatives, 2 albums (photos), 1 book.

MOUNTAINS

CA —UNIVERSITY OF CALIFORNIA, LOS ANGELES, Research Library, Dept of Special Collections, 405 Hilgard Ave, Los Angeles, 90024. Edward Shreeves, Chairman, Bibliographers Group; David S Zeidberg, Head
Notes: 2000 books in the Francis P Farquhar Collection of Mountaineering Literature.
CO —WORLD DATA CENTER A: GLACIOLOGY (SNOW AND ICE), CIRES, University of Colorado, Boulder, 80309. Ann M Brennan, Librn
Holdings: Vols 10,000 Maps Pix Microforms
Budget: $2000
Notes: Glaciology, all forms of snow and ice. Bibliographic information will be contained in a data file which will be fully searchable. Partially cataloged (UDC).
CO —VAIL PUBLIC LIBRARY, 292 W Meadow Dr, Vail, 81657. Charlyn M C Canada, Librn
Holdings: Vols (500) Cat Maps
Budget: ($5300)
Notes: The alpine environment.
NV —FORESTA INSTITUTE FOR OCEAN AND MOUNTAIN STUDIES, Library, 6205 Franktown Rd, Carson City, 89701. Shannon Porter, Librn
Holdings: Vols (3000) Cat Mss Maps Pix Slides
Notes: Material on plant, animal, and human ecology with special emphasis on far western US and Nevada ecology and environmental problems. Also hold about 2000 reprints, pamphlets, reports, etc.

MOUSE see Mice

MOUTH

PA —UNIVERSITY OF PENNSYLVANIA, School of Dental Medicine, Leon Levy Library, 4001 Spruce St, Philadelphia, 19104. John M Whittock Jr, Librn
Holdings: Vols (45,000) Cat Pix Slides
Notes: Collection is comprised of 15,250 monographs, 25,250 bound periodical vols. Library currently receives about 700 dental and medical journals. Houses S S White Dental Manufacture Co collection of Ú S dental patents, 1797-1966, and U S and foreign dental catalogs. 1000 rare books on dentistry and oral biology. 3000 pictures and 1000 slides.

MOVE GAMES see Board Games

MOVEMENT, ECUMENICAL see Ecumenical Movement

MOVEMENT, NOTATION OF see Dance Notation

MOVING PICTURE CARTOONS

CA —SAN FRANCISCO ACADEMY OF COMIC ART, Library, 2850 Ulloa, San Francisco, 94116.
Notes: Incl largest collection of pulp magazines in US. Paper copies of all major American newspapers, emphasis on Hearst papers. Extensive collection of Sherlockiana and a member of the National Sherlockiana Society. Also extensive collection of early motion picture tapes, books, magazines and posters. 19th and early 20th century

MOVING PICTURE CARTOONS (cont.)

children's books also in the holdings.
Collection incl 1,000,000 comic strips, 22,
000 comic books, 12,500 hard cover mystery
books, 8000 hard cover science fiction books
and copies of all science fiction pulp
magazines.

CA —CALIFORNIA INSTITUTE OF THE
ARTS, Library, 24700 McBean Pkwy,
Valencia, 91355. James Elrod, Dir
Holdings: Vols (61,000) Cat Videotapes
16mm Films
Budget: ($7500)
Notes: Incl 320 videotapes and 776 16mm
films.

IN —INDIANA UNIVERSITY, Lilly Library,
Seventh St, Bloomington, 47405. William R
Cagle, Librn
Holdings: Cat Mss
Notes: 1500 issues of Marvel Comics. Mss
incl illustrations for Toonerville Trolley and
Brenda Starr; also a growing collection of
individual pieces representative of comic
strip art and animation.

NY —NEW YORK STATE ARCHIVES, 9049
Cultural Education Center, Albany, 12230.
Richard Andress, Archivist
Notes: Scripts read by the Motion Picture
Division of the NYS Education Departments
for the purposes of rating and approval, with
orders by Department for deletions or
changes in dialogue. Between 1910-1966 all
moving pictures shown in New York were
reviewed by this Board. Incl animated
cartoon films. 54,000 items.

NY —MUSEUM OF CARTOON ART
LIBRARY, Comly Avenue, Rye Brook,
10573.
Notes: Original comics and cartoon art, 60,
000 pieces. 800 animated cartoons. Disney
collection extensive. Samples of Big-Little
Books, foreign comics, fanzines, cartoon
related games, posters, pulps, undergrounds.
Hal Foster, Walt Kelly, Gene Byrns, Tad
Dorgan, Chester Gould extensive original art
collections.

MOVING PICTURE CIRCULATION see
Moving Pictures—Distribution

MOVING PICTURE DISTRIBUTION see
Moving Pictures—Distribution

MOVING PICTURE EQUIPMENT

NY —NEW YORK PUBLIC LIBRARY,
Performing Arts Research Center, Billy Rose
Theatre Collection, 111 Amsterdam Ave,
New York, 10023. Dorothy L Swerdlove,
Cur
Holdings: Cat
See also entry under Moving Picture
Industry

MOVING PICTURE FESTIVALS

CA —AMERICAN FILM INSTITUTE, Louis
B Mayer Library, 2021 N Western Ave, PO
Box 27999, Los Angeles, 90027. Anne G
Schlosser, Dir
Holdings: Vols (3500) Cat
Notes: Film Festival Files contain entry
forms, programs/brochures, awards, and
other information of US and foreign
festivals.

NY —EDUCATIONAL FILM LIBRARY
ASSOCIATION, Film Reference Library, 45
John St, New York, 10038. Nadine Covert,
Exec Dir
Holdings: Vols (2600) Cat Pix 16mm Films
Filmstrips
Budget: ($1500)
Notes: Primarily a print collection
emphasizing the documentary and
educational film areas, but also film as art,
animation and independent film in general.
Maintain film title file of over 60,000 cards
(primarily educational film titles), incl credit
information, running time, release date,
summary, and distributor. File is a mixture
of EFLA evaluations, LC cards, etc. Subject
file also separates film flyers by subject or
topic. Maintain festivals file (film festivals,
educational film festivals, etc); a film library

administration file; a filmmakers file (with
bio, credits, clippings, program notes); and a
vertical file (incl information on grants,
distribution, showcases, film activities in the
metropolitan area and in major film centers
around the country). Membership
organization providing telephone, mail and
in-person reference. Open to the
general public. Do not publish a catalog, but
publish annual Film Library Administration
bibliography of current or noteworthy
reference books for $2.00.

MOVING PICTURE INDUSTRY

CA —ACADEMY OF MOTION PICTURE
ARTS & SCIENCES, Margaret Herrick
Library, 8949 Wilshire Blvd, Beverly Hills,
90211. Linda Harris Mehr, Library
Administrator
Holdings: Vols (16,000) Cat Mss Pix Slides
Budget: ($250,000)
Notes: Also posters, scrapbooks, clippings
and press books. Collection emphases are the
moving picture industry, moving picture
history, biographical material on actors,
actresses and industry personnel. Files on
specific films, reviews, cast and credits,
production data, etc, on more than 65,000
moving pictures. (Over 5000 films, incl early
28mm films in Film Archive). Over 5 million
pictures. Special collections: papers of Mary
Pickford, Mack Sennett, Adolph Zukor,
Lewis Milestone, George Stevens, George
Cukor, John Huston, Edith Head;
Paramount scripts and stills archive, MGM
stills archive, RKO stills archive, Thomas H
Ince stills collection, Cecil B DeMille stills
collection.

CA —UNIVERSITY OF CALIFORNIA, LOS
ANGELES, Theater Arts Library, Los
Angeles, 90024. Edward Shreeves,
Chairman, Bibliographers Group; Audree
Malkin, Head, Theater Arts Library
Holdings: Cat Mss Pix Slides
Notes: An extensive collection of articles,
pamphlets, clippings, program notes, reviews,
and other ephemera about personalities,
films, and subjects relating to all aspects of
film, radio and television. *Harold Leonard
Collection*: A large collection of clippings
and photographs related to the film industry
for the period 1930-1960. *Film Posters and
Programs*: A diverse collection of rare and
early film posters, programs, and advertising
campaign books for American films dating
from 1915. Posters and programs for Polish
and Czechoslovakian productions are also
represented. The following related
collections are housed in the Department of
Special Collections: *George Johnson
Collection*, about Blacks in the motion
picture industry; *Walter Beyer Papers*;
Republic Studios Collection.

CA —HOOVER INSTITUTION ON WAR,
REVOLUTION & PEACE, Stanford
University, Stanford, 94305. Milorad M
Drachkovitch, Archivist
Holdings: Mss
Notes: Correspondence, by-laws, minutes,
administrative reports, records, and research
and reference materials, 1927-1941, of the
Motion Picture Research Council, an
organization which carried out research on
the film industry. 78 ms boxes and 8
volumes.

DC —GEORGETOWN UNIVERSITY,
Library, Special Collections Div, 37 & O Sts
NW, Washington, 20057. George M
Barringer, Special Collections Librn;
Nicholas B Sheetz, Mss Librn
Holdings: Vols 500 Cat Pix
Notes: Incorporates the picture "morgue" of
the Quigley Publishing Company and
archival runs of its publications. Over 50,000
pictures. The library has additional picture
resources of over 100,000 photographs.

DC —LIBRARY OF CONGRESS, Motion
Pictures, Broadcasting and Recorded Sound
Div, Washington, 20540.
Notes: Incl correspondence, literary mss,
reports, notes, scrapbooks, photographs, etc.
About 10,000 items.

NY —NEW YORK PUBLIC LIBRARY,
Performing Arts Research Center, Billy Rose
Theatre Collection, 111 Amsterdam Ave,

New York, 10023. Dorothy L Swerdlove,
Cur
Holdings: Cat Pix

Notes: As early as 1941 the American Television
Society appointed the Theatre Collection the
official repository of their archives and urged its
members to deposit materials in the Collection.
The Collection maintains clipping files on radio
and television programs, and on the personnel of
these programs. It collects photographs of these
individuals, of television and radio studios,
equipment, etc. There is a collection of television
production scripts, with most of the "Hallmark
Hall of Fame" specials and "Studio One" scripts,
1948-1952. The collection of radio scripts incl
material regarding the Radio Writers Guild of
America and also runs of several serials written by
Elaine Carrington. The book material incl the
standard works on the history of broadcasting and
telecasting, vols. on the techniques of the industry.

NY —STATE UNIVERSITY OF NEW
YORK, COLLEGE AT PURCHASE,
Library, Lincoln Ave, Purchase, 10577.
Robert W Evans, Dir
Holdings: Vols (1400) Mss Pix Slides
Notes: The Gerald D McDonald Collection.
Over 1400 books on moving pictures and all
aspects of the industry: production,
directing, acting. Thousands of pictures of
actors and actresses, directors, etc. Also
about 2000 slides picturing movie
personalities, etc; stereopticon pictures,
buttons, bottle caps, playing cards, etc.

WY —UNIVERSITY OF WYOMING,
William Robertson Coe Library, Performing
Arts Collections, Laramie, 82071. Gene M
Gressley, Dir
Holdings: Mss
Notes: Collections in the Performing Arts
area incl some 300 collections of outstanding
music composers, arrangers, film industry
directors, writers, performers, and
individuals prominent in all aspects of music,
theatre, radio, television and film industry.

MOVING PICTURE MUSIC

CA —UNIVERSITY OF CALIFORNIA, LOS
ANGELES, Music Library, Schonberg Hall,
Los Angeles, 90024. Stephen M Fry, Music
Librn
Holdings: Mss
Notes: Special and archival collections:
George Antheil, Hugo Davise, Walter Lantz,
Harry Lubin, Henry Mancini, Alex North,
Eugene Zador, Edward Powell, Andre
Previn, Edward Ward, and Mortimer
Wilson. Ca 35,000 mss. Also, the Harry
Roth Library of American Theater Music,
the Meredith Wilson Library of Popular
Sheet Music, and the Library of American
Motion Picture Music.

CA —SAN DIEGO STATE UNIVERSITY,
Malcolm A Love Library, 5300 Campanile
Dr, San Diego, 92182. D Dickinson, Univ
Librn; Don L Bosseau, Dir
Notes: Sheet Music Collection. Original
pieces of sheet music dating from 1817 to
the present. Includes the Leta Knox Ehmcke
Collection of Silent Film Music. (4000
items)

CA —UNIVERSITY OF CALIFORNIA,
SANTA BARBARA, Arts Library, Music
Section, Santa Barbara, 93106. Susan Sonnet
Bower, Asst Music Librn
Holdings: Mss
Notes: Collection of holograph music
manuscripts of the late American composer,
Bernard Herrmann, 1911-1975. Collection

MOVING PICTURE MUSIC (cont.)

contains 53 manuscript scores of both music written for the films and non-film music. Incl the film scores for "Vertigo," "Pschyo," "North by Northwest," "Marnie," "Magnificent Ambersons," "Devil and Daniel Webster (All That Money Can Buy)" Academy Award, 1941. Non-film Music: Symphony (1941) Moby Dick (Dramatic Cantata), Wuthering Heights (Opera in 4 Acts, 1950) with text by Lucille Fletcher, first performed by Portland Opera Association, Nov 6, 1982.

IN —INDIANA UNIVERSITY, Lilly Library, Seventh St, Bloomington, 47405. William R Cagle, Librn
Holdings: // Uncat
Notes: American sheet music from the Starr Collection.

IA —DRAKE UNIVERSITY, Cowles Library, 28 St & University Ave, Des Moines, 50311.
Notes: Nearly 3000 musical works used by orchestras and musicians to accompany silent films, donated by Dorman Hundling who had played in orchestras in theatres owned by his family in South Dakota and Iowa.

NY —MUSEUM OF MODERN ART, Dept of Film, 11 W 53 St, New York, 10019. Eileen Bowser, Cur
Holdings: Mss
Notes: Special collections: D W Griffith: personal papers and scrapbooks (cataloged); Carl Lerner Collection: notebooks, scripts, letters (cataloged); Harry McWilliams Collection: promotional and advertising material; Merritt Crawford Collection: documents and letters on early film history (cataloged). Also, special material relating to Robert Flaherty, Helen Van Dongen, Thomas Ince, Paul Terry, G W Pabst, film censorship. Extensive clipping files and scripts on motion pictures. Partially cataloged.

MOVING PICTURE NEWSPAPERS see Newspapers, Moving Picture

MOVING PICTURE PERIODICALS see Periodicals, Moving Picture

MOVING PICTURE PLAYS—PRODUCTION AND DIRECTION see Moving Pictures—Production and Direction

MOVING PICTURE PRODUCTION see Moving Pictures—Production and Direction

MOVING PICTURES

CA —ACADEMY OF MOTION PICTURE ARTS & SCIENCES, Margaret Herrick Library, 8949 Wilshire Blvd, Beverly Hills, 90211. Linda Harris Mehr, Library Administrator
Holdings: Vols (16,000) Cat Mss Pix Slides
Budget: ($250,000)
Notes: Also posters, scrapbooks, clippings and press books. Collection emphases are the moving picture industry, moving picture history, biographical material on actors, actresses and industry personnel. Files on specific films, reviews, cast and credits, production data, etc, on more than 65,000 moving pictures. (Over 5000 films, incl early 28mm films in Film Archive. Over 5 million pictures. Special collections: papers of Mary Pickford, Mack Sennett, Adolph Zukor, Lewis Milestone, George Stevens, George Cukor, John Huston, Edith Head; Paramount scripts and stills archive, MGM stills archive, RKO stills archive, Thomas H Ince stills collection, Cecil B DeMille stills collection.

CA —WESTERN COSTUME COMPANY, Research Library, 5335 Melrose Ave, Hollywood, 90038. Nancy S Kinney, Dir of Research
Holdings: Vols 6000
Notes: Incl 70 vertical file drawers of

photographs, 200 bound periodicals, 80 mail order catalogs (Sears, etc). Wardrobe stills. 5 periodical subscriptions. Collection can be used only by the customers of Western Costume Company. All other use is on a fee basis. Collection is non-circulating. Photocopying available.

CA —AMERICAN FILM INSTITUTE, Louis B Mayer Library, 2021 N Western Ave, PO Box 27999, Los Angeles, 90027. Anne G Schlosser, Dir
Holdings: Vols (3500) Cat
Notes: Collection contains 2500 American film scripts and 1000 television scripts; oral histories conducted in the American Film Institute Louis B Mayer Oral History Program; the MGM Script Collection of 400 MGM scripts from the silent period up to the mid-1950's; Columbia Stills Collection covering the period 1930-1950; special mss collections of Henry Hathaway (director), Harry Horner, Buster Keaton, George Byron Sage and Stewart Stern (writer). Also clipping files on motion pictures, personalities, television shows, production organizations and technical topics; film festival file of all US and foreign festivals. Rare periodical holdings incl *Film Daily* newspaper (1923-1969); *Radio-TV Daily* newspaper (1939-1964); *RKO Radio Flash,* house organ of RKO (1932-1955); *TV Guide* (1948 to date).

CA —UNIVERSITY OF CALIFORNIA, LOS ANGELES, Theater Arts Library, Los Angeles, 90024. Edward Shreeves, Chairman, Bibliographers Group; Audree Malkin, Head, Theater Arts Library
Holdings: Vols (12,500) Mss
Notes: Major research collections covering the historical, critical, aesthetic, biographical and technical aspects of film, television and radio, and the non-book and primary source material in these fields. Also 166,000 pamphlets, photographs, microforms and sound recordings. Incl over 4,000,000 moving picture stills, over 32,636 screenplays, and scripts from American and British Films. Incl 1740 radio scripts and a collection of 3000 television scripts. Also incl film festival programs, motion picture programs, lobby cards, original sketches and production materials; the personal and business papers, records and correspondence of actors, directors, producers, art directors and screen and television writers. Incl 100,000 mss. Extensive poster collection (over 7000, 1915 to date), many forPolish and Czech productions. Limited photocopying.

CA —UNIVERSITY OF CALIFORNIA, LOS ANGELES, Theater Arts Library, Los Angeles, 90024. Edward Shreeves, Chairman, Bibliographers Group; Audree Malkin, Head, Theater Arts Library
Holdings: Cat Mss Pix Slides
Notes: An extensive collection of articles, pamphlets, clippings, program notes, reviews, and other ephemera about personalities, films, and subjects relating to all aspects of film, radio and television. *Harold Leonard* Collection: A large collection of clippings and photographs related to the film industry for the period 1930-1960. *Film Posters and* Programs: A diverse collection of rare and early film posters, programs, and advertising campaign books for American films dating from 1915. Posters and programs for Polish and Czechoslovakian productions are also represented. The following related collections are housed in the Department of Special Collections: *George Johnson* Collection, about Blacks in the motion picture industry; Walter Beyer Papers; Republic Studios Collection.

CA —UNIVERSITY OF CALIFORNIA, RIVERSIDE, University Library, 4045 Canyon Crest Dr, Box 5900, Riverside, 92517.
Holdings: Vols (30,000)
Notes: The Eaton Collection of science fiction and fantasy materials, incl 5,600 pulp magazines; also horror, supernatural, and Gothic mystery fiction; boys' books; utopian and dystopian fiction, imaginary voyages, future war and lost race fiction; large holdings in French language science fiction

and fantasy; critical and scholarly works pertaining to these genres; videotapes of science fiction/fantasy films and shooting scripts. Collection covers science fiction/ fantasy literature from the 16th-17th centuries to the present. Strong individual author collections of Jules Verne, H Rider Haggard, H G Wells, Edgar Rice Burroughs, and Philip K Dick. For a complete description of the collection see: George Slusser, "The J Lloyd Eaton Collection," *Special Collections*, II, 1/2, 25-38 (1983), and*Dictionary Catalog of the J Lloyd Eaton Collection of Science Fiction and Fantasy Literature* (Boston: G K Hall) 1982.

CA —SAN FRANCISCO ART INSTITUTE, Anne Bremer Memorial Library, 800 Chestnut St, San Francisco, 94133. Jeff Gunderson, Librn
Holdings: Vols (23,144) Cat Pix Slides Audiotapes 16mm Films Microforms
Budget: ($15,000)

CA —CALIFORNIA INSTITUTE OF THE ARTS, Library, 24700 McBean Pkwy, Valencia, 91355. James Elrod, Dir
Holdings: Vols (61,000) Cat Videotapes 16mm Films
Budget: ($7500)
Notes: Incl 320 videotapes and 776 16mm films.

CT —GREENWICH LIBRARY, 101 W Putnam Ave, Greenwich, 06830. Wayne T Campbell Jr, Film Services Coordr
Holdings: Vols 874 Cat Videotapes Films
Notes: Collection is very broad. Supplemented by books on film making in both this collection and the photographic collection. Also supplemented by 16mm film collection and videocassettes.

CT —YALE UNIVERSITY, Drama Library, 222 York St, Box 1903A, Yale Station, New Haven, 06520. Pamela C Jordan, Librn
Holdings: Vols (24,000) Cat Pix Slides Audiotapes
Budget: ($6000)
Notes: Book collection covers all phases of the dramatic arts: theatre, film, opera, dance, etc, with an emphasis on 20th century theatre. Incl audiotapes of Yale Drama School and Repertory Theatre productions, other plays and dramatic readings, and dialect tapes. Incl 1200 slides on costume design and 2000 slides on architecture, interiors, and furniture. Also incl more than 80,000 pictures on set and costume design.

DC —LIBRARY OF CONGRESS, Motion Pictures, Broadcasting and Recorded Sound Div, Washington, 20540.
Notes: The Motion Picture, Broadcasting, and Recorded Sound Division has custody of the largest and most varied collection of sound recordings, motion picture and television films, and videotapes in the US. The division also houses a small collection of reference books, film stills, and descriptive material for motion pictures registered for copyright after 1912.

GA —UNIVERSITY OF GEORGIA, Libraries, Special Collections Division, Athens, 30602. Vesta Lee Gordon, Asst Dir for Special Collections
Notes: The Arbitron Collection of television and radio program ratings, 1949-date (except past year). In-depth, statistical analyses of the listening public by age, sex, county, some ethnic groups, farm population, listening preferences, etc. 26,302 bound vols. 2 reports, 1949-81. To be added to annually.

IN —INDIANA STATE UNIVERSITY, EVANSVILLE, Library, 8600 University Blvd, Evansville, 47712. Gina R Walker, Acting Archivist
Holdings: Vols 20 Cat Pix
Notes: Over 800 movie press kits sent to local film critics; 1955-present, plus some photos of entertainers from the early 1920s. Photos of film, opera and television entertainers.

IA —UNIVERSITY OF IOWA, University Libraries, Iowa City, 52242. Robert A McCown, Mss Librn
Holdings: Mss Pix

MOVING PICTURES (cont.)

Notes: Five collections: Robert Blees collection of motion picture and television material, 1925-65, inc, including stories, still production photos, and motion picture and television scripts of a motion picture and television script writer; David Swift collection of motion picture and television material, 1951-65, including scripts, posters, photos, drawings, and blueprints for final set construction of a motion picture and television producer and writer; the Albert Jay Cohen collection of motion picture and television production material, 1948-58, including correspondence, film scripts, stories, photos, financial and production papers, and censorship records; the Arthur A. Ross collection of motion picture and television material, 1943-65, including correspondence, scripts, photos, production records, and artists' sketches of a motion picture and television script writer; and the Norman Felton Papers, 1937-1978, including correspondence, notes, notebooks, subject files, budgets, other financial records, photographs, and scripts relating to such television series as The Eleventh Hour, The Lieutenant, The Man From U.N.C.L.E., Jericho, The Strange Report, The Psychiatrist, Hawkins, and Dr. Kildare, produced by Felton, 124 ft. of mss.

MA —BRANDEIS UNIVERSITY, Goldfarb Library, 415 South St, Waltham, 02154. Bessie Hahn, Dir
Notes: 3 linear ft of motion picture stills dating from the 1950s and 1960s. This collection is unprocessed, spring 1984. George Froeschel Collection: 27 linear ft of books and 30 linear ft of material, correspondence, photographs and memorabilia of this novelist and former Hollywood screen writer. The collection is unprocessed, spring 1984.

MI —DETROIT PUBLIC LIBRARY, Music & Performing Arts Dept, 5201 Woodward, Detroit, 48202. Jean Currie Church, Cur
Holdings: Vols (1375) Cat Mss Pix
Notes: The E Azalia Hackley Collections document achievements of Blacks in the fields of music, dance, theatre, motion pictures, and broadcasting. World-wide in scope. Extensive clipping files arranged by personal names, titles and subjects. Incl musical scores (1500), recordings, and plays. No taping or other copying of recordings permitted.

MI —MICHIGAN STATE UNIVERSITY, Libraries, Special Collections Div, East Lansing, 48824. Jannette Fiore, Librn
Notes: The Russel B Nye Popular Culture Collection in the Michigan State Univ Libraries incl over (45,000) items. Most of the collection is organized into 4 categories: comic art, popular fiction, popular information materials and materials relating to the popular performing arts. Materials relating to popular theatre, music, television, radio, and film. Theatre is best represented. A significant collection of primary materials relating to the tent show incl photographs, financial and other records of the Henderson Stock Company, correspondence, leaflets, handbills and other ephemera from many of the companies playing in the upper midwest in the 1920s and 1930s, and photocopies of 250 tent show scripts.

MN —MINNEAPOLIS COLLEGE OF ART & DESIGN, Library, 200 E 25 St, Minneapolis, 55404. Richard Kronstedt, Head Librn
Holdings: Vols 700 Cat Slides

MO —SAINT LOUIS PUBLIC LIBRARY, Film Library, 1301 Olive St, Saint Louis, 63103. Rita Broughton, Film Librn
Holdings: Vols 2300 16mm Films

NJ —ENGLEWOOD LIBRARY, 31 Engle St, Englewood, 07631. N E Rhoades, Reference Librn
Holdings: Vols (8200) Cat

NY —NEW YORK STATE ARCHIVES, 9049 Cultural Education Center, Albany, 12230. Richard Andress, Archivist
Notes: Records of the New York State Education Department's former Motion Picture Division 1921 to 1965, which exercised censorship control over all films offered for public viewing in New York State. Incl large collection of film scripts. 54,000 items.

†NY —NEIGHBORHOOD PLAYHOUSE SCHOOL OF THE THEATRE, Irene Lewisohn Library, 340 E 54 St, New York, 10022. Alice G Owen, Librn
Holdings: Vols (4952) Cat Mss Pix
See also entry under Theatre - History.

NY —NEW YORK PUBLIC LIBRARY, Performing Arts Research Center, Billy Rose Theatre Collection, 111 Amsterdam Ave, New York, 10023. Dorothy L Swerdlove, Cur
Holdings: Cat
See also entry under Moving Pictures - History.

NY —STATE UNIVERSITY OF NEW YORK, COLLEGE AT PURCHASE, Library, Lincoln Ave, Purchase, 10577. Robert W Evans, Dir
Holdings: Vols (1400) Mss Pix Slides
Notes: The Gerald D McDonald Collection. Over 1400 books on moving pictures and all aspects of the industry: production, directing, acting. Thousands of pictures of actors and actresses, directors, etc. Also about 2000 slides picturing movie personalities, etc; stereopticon pictures, buttons, bottle caps, playing cards, etc.

NC —DUKE UNIVERSITY, William R Perkins Library, Durham, 27706. Elvin E Strowd, University Librn
Notes: Books, serials and pamphlets (2,820,527); music scores (31,551); motion pictures (285); microforms (1,055,627); tapes, cassettes and phonorecords, the library is a depository for Radio Canada International recordings, (2289); and manuscripts, US Government publications, maps, and broadsides, additions in all formats are ongoing.

OH —OHIO UNIVERSITY, Vernon R Alden Library, Fine Arts Library, Athens, 45701. Anne Braxton, Fine Arts Librn
Holdings: Vols (40,000) Cat Pix Slides Microforms
Notes: Strong collection in history of film and photography; general art collection incl some 2000 exhibition catalogs.

OH —PUBLIC LIBRARY OF CINCINNATI & HAMILTON COUNTY, Art & Music Dept, 800 Vine St, Cincinnati, 45202. R Jayne Craven, Head
Holdings: Vols (122,185) Cat Pix
Budget: ($56,100)
Notes: Special collections: Eda Kuhn Loeb, "Artist and the Book, 1875-Date" (now shelved in Rare Book Room); music librettos (2345); exhibition catalogs (5474); large prints and posters (5051); Cincinnati artists vertical files; picture collection (673,906 clippings).

OH —CLEVELAND PUBLIC LIBRARY, Literature Dept, 325 Superior Ave, Cleveland, 44114. Evelyn Ward, Head
Holdings: Vols Cat Pix Phonorecords Microforms VF
Notes: Working collection of books on the motion picture. File of Film Daily reviews from the late 1920s and other clippings from 1961. Large collection of stills and photographs from cinema and television. Variety on microfilm 1905-date.

PA —FREE LIBRARY OF PHILADELPHIA, Theatre Collection, Logan Sq, Philadelphia, 19103. Geraldine Duclow, Librn-in-Charge
Holdings: Vols (1,250,000) Uncat Pix
Notes: The Theatre Collection contains books, magazines, playbills, broadsides, posters, photographs, and other memorabilia

covering theatre, motion pictures, minstrels, vaudeville, circus, radio and television. The Library's Philadelphia Theatre Index lists the major productions here since 1855, and partially indexes the collection of local playbills which date back to 1803. There are also programs from many other cities, incl New York; some from London date back to 1800. Early film companies as well as the present movie industry are represented by advertising materials and over 30,000 film stills. The Lubin Film Co (1910-1916) Archive has been established with over 600 photographs and related items. Circus programs and route books date back to 1900. There are minstrel programs as early as 1865. Most significant are the mss from Philadelphia's Dumont Minstrels. Variousfiles contain autographs, photographs, newspaper articles and reviews in all pertinent subject areas. Noncirculating.

TX —SOUTHERN METHODIST UNIVERSITY, Fondren Library, McCord Theater Collection, Room 301, Dallas, 75275. Edyth Renshaw, Cur; Linda Sellers, Pub Serv
Holdings: Vols (2000) Uncat Mss Pix Slides Phonorecords
Notes: See Theatre Collections in Libraries and Museums, Gilder and Freedley (Theatre Arts, 1936). The McCord Theatre Collection encompasses the entire spectrum of the performing arts. The central purpose is to gather records of our regional theater before such ephemeral material is lost. Records of over two hundred early Texas theaters, some fragmentary and some relatively complete, are in the files. These records incl photographs of buildings, stagehands, orchestras, and performers. Local theatre history incl the once famous Dallas Little Theatre and the Margo Jones Theatre. The national theatre, opera, ballet, and circus archives incl pictures (some autographed), programs, posters, throw-aways, tear sheets, clippings, and letters. Our international archives are small, but we have some excellent material, eg, artifacts from Max Reinhardt's production of"The Miracle" which happened to go bankrupt in Dallas. After a few years the items were given to us. There are posters, tear sheets, souvenir programs, and other colorful items from Morris Gest and the Artef Collection. We have about 200 19th century English playbills and a few from the 18th century. There is a collection of modern English, French, and other European programs, many of them illustrated souvenir programs. Also, magazines on theater, cinema, and television (1800). Scrapbooks covering both southwest and Dallas theater, 1890s-1950s. Special Collections: artifacts and documents on puppets; masks; costume design; circus; and ballet and dance. The Harriet Bacon MacDonald Collection of over 200 photographs of musicians appearing in Dallas during the first three decades of the 20th century. Many autographed. Affiliated with Meadow Theatre of the Arts.

†WI —STATE HISTORICAL SOCIETY OF WISCONSIN, Library, 816 State St, Madison, 53706.
Notes: Scripts, notes, correspondence and other items concerning the collaboration of Howard Lindsay and Russel Crouse for the theater, motion pictures and television, as well as the work of each with other collaborators and individually.

BC —VANCOUVER PUBLIC LIBRARY, Art Div, 750 Burrard St, Vancouver, V6Z 1X5, Can.
Holdings: Cat Pix
Notes: Book and pamphlet collection. Also, (1) Newspaper Clippings File: 31 drawers of relevant clippings from major newspapers, incl the Sun, Province, Toronto Globe and Mail, Christian Science Monitor, New York Times, etc on arts, music, architecture; incl biographical material (16 drawers). (2) Picture File about 500,000 pictures in 150 cabinet drawers, strong in architecture, costume, interior decoration, painting, sculpture, also portraits. (3) Exhibition Catalogs File: British Columbia and elsewhere. (4) Association and Organization

MOVING PICTURES (cont.)

File: organizations in the Lower Mainland in arts, music, city planning, etc, begun in 1940s; (5) Canadian Artists Index: begun in 1964, alphabetically by artist, with about 300,000 citationsto reproductions of work and biographical material on Canadian artist from the division's books and other sources; (6) Miscellaneous Index: material not covered in other special or published indexes, primarily of Canadian and local cultural events, hard-to-find informations, etc. Local newspapers, special Canadian publications and British film journals are the most regularly indexed items. (7) Song Index started in the 1930s. (8) Title Index to song collections and sheet music in the VPL collection, approx 100,000 entries.

ON —NATIONAL FILM, TELEVISION AND SOUND ARCHIVES, Documentation & Public Service, 395 Wellington St, Ottawa, K1A 0N3, Can. Jana Vosikovska, Chief; Gloria Grant, Librn; Sylvie Robitaille, Stills and Posters Librn
Holdings: Vols (7000) Pix
Budget: ($35,000)
Notes: Several collections supporting the documentation on film, television and recorded sound: 1060 periodical titles (450 current), some on microfilm. Picture-stills, 265,000; moving picture posters, 6000; cataloged microfiche, 33,000 (vertical file material put on microfilm, then into a fiche format). Index cards (periodical references, credits): 334,000 cards (Film Title Index: 250,000 cards; Personalities Index: 84,000 cards).

ON —METROPOLITAN TORONTO LIBRARY, Theatre Dept, 789 Yonge St, Toronto, M4W 2G8, Can. Heather McCallum, Head
Holdings: Vols (30,500) Mss Pix Microforms
Notes: There is a strong collection of books on the film, incl many foreign language titles, incl addition to full runs of numerous standard film periodicals. A large collection of film stills, photographs of personalities and files of film reviews complete the collection.

PQ —NATIONAL FILM BOARD OF CANADA, Reference Library, PO Box 6100, Station A, Montreal, H3C 3H5, Can. Rose-Aimee Todd, Librn; Bernard Lutz, Librn
Holdings: Vols 2250 Cat VF
Notes: Incl French and English "Challenge for Change Collection." Incl 350 pamphlets 30 VF drawers and 100 periodical titles.

MOVING PICTURES—AESTHETICS

NY —ANTHOLOGY FILM ARCHIVES, 491 Broadway, New York, 10012. Jonas Mekas, Dir; Nadia Shtendara, Librn
Holdings: Vols Cat Periodicals Mss Pix
Notes: Documents and associated items relating to film and video as art, with special emphasis on critical material on experimental and avant-garde films. Published bibliography of the collection: *The Essential Cinema*, vol 1, ed by P Adams Sitney (New York: Anthology Film Archives & New York Univ Press, 1975).

NY —NEW YORK PUBLIC LIBRARY, Performing Arts Research Center, Billy Rose Theatre Collection, 111 Amsterdam Ave, New York, 10023. Dorothy L Swerdlove, Cur
Holdings: Cat
See also entry under Moving Picture Industry

MOVING PICTURES—ANIMATION see Animation (Cinematography)

MOVING PICTURES—CATALOGS

NY —EDUCATIONAL FILM LIBRARY ASSOCIATION, Film Reference Library, 45 John St, New York, 10038. Nadine Covert, Exec Dir
Holdings: Vols (2600) Cat Pix 16mm Films Filmstrips
Budget: ($1500)
Notes: Primarily a print collection

emphasizing the documentary and educational film areas, but also film as art, animation and independent film in general. Maintain film title file of over 60,000 cards (primarily educational film titles), incl credit information, running time, release date, summary, and distributor. File is a mixture of EFLA evaluations, LC cards, etc. Subject file also separates film flyers by subject or topic. Maintain festivals file (film festivals, educational film festivals, etc); a film library administration file; a filmmakers file (with bio, credits, clippings, program notes); and a vertical file (incl information on grants, distribution, showcases, film activities in the metropolitan area and in major film centers around the country). Membership organization providing telephone, mail and in-person reference. Open to the generalpublic. Do not publish a catalog, but publish annual Film Library Administration bibliography of current or noteworthy reference books for $2.00.

NY —NEW YORK PUBLIC LIBRARY, Performing Arts Research Center, Billy Rose Theatre Collection, 111 Amsterdam Ave, New York, 10023. Dorothy L Swerdlove, Cur
Holdings: Cat
See also entry under Moving Pictures - History

PA —UNIVERSITY OF PENNSYLVANIA, Annenberg School of Communications Library, 3620 Walnut St, Philadelphia, 19104. Sandra B Grilikhes, Head
Holdings: Vols 20,000 Cat Microforms
Notes: Theory and research in communication, incl visual communication, via social psychology, anthropology, ethnography, and sociology. All aspects of mass media with emphasis on methodology in research. Utilizes content analysis and computer operations. Special collections: film catalogs; collection of Annenberg Faculty Publications.

MOVING PICTURES—CENSORSHIP

NY —NEW YORK STATE ARCHIVES, 9049 Cultural Education Center, Albany, 12230. Richard Andress, Archivist
Notes: Records of the New York State Education Department's former Motion Picture Division 1921 to 1965, which exercised censorship control over all films offered for public viewing in New York State. Incl large collection of film scripts. 54,000 items.

MOVING PICTURES—CIRCULATION see Moving Pictures—Distribution

MOVING PICTURES—COLLECTIONS

CA —LOS ANGELES PUBLIC LIBRARY, Art, Music & Recreation Dept, 630 W Fifth St, Los Angeles, 90071. Melvin H Rosenberg, Mgr & Principal Librn
Notes: Large collections.

CA —LOS ANGELES PUBLIC LIBRARY, Central Library, Audio Visual Dept, 630 W Fifth St, Los Angeles, 90071. Richard V Partlow, Principal Librn
Budget: ($71,989)
Notes: Includes 16mm film (4300), VHS video (300), audio recordings (20,000), audio cassettes (5500), picture file (220,000 estimated clippings), filmstrips (60), periodicals (65). Material on all subject areas are included.

CA —LOS ANGELES PUBLIC LIBRARY, Frances Howard Goldwyn Hollywood Regional Library, 1623 Ivar Ave, Los Angeles, 90028. Sally Dumaux, Librn
Holdings: Vols (100,000) Cat Mss Pix VF
Budget: ($60,000)
Notes: A general and a research collection covering motion pictures, radio broadcasting, and television. Over 2000 motion picture and television scripts. Biographical information on actors and actresses. Casts, credits, and other production information on over 1500 motion pictures from the 1920s to the present. Collections also include posters, lobby cards, souvenir programs, scrapbooks,

vertical files, and over 3000 publicity stills. Including the following Special Collections: Fred Archer Collection, photographs, including the Hunchback of Notre Dame (1923), and personalities of the stage and screen, 1907-1930; Gilbert A Adrian, designer, sketches and photographs; Hazel Flynn, publicist, correspondence and photographs.

CA —UNIVERSITY OF CALIFORNIA, LOS ANGELES, Theater Arts Library, Los Angeles, 90024. Edward Shreeves, Chairman, Bibliographers Group; Audree Malkin, Head, Theater Arts Library
Holdings: Vols (12,500)
Notes: Major research collections covering the historical, critical, aesthetic, biographical and technical aspects of film, television and radio, and the non-book and primary source material in these fields. Also 166,000 pamphlets, photographs, microforms and sound recordings. Incl over 4,000,000 moving picture stills, over 32,636 screenplays, and scripts from American and British Films. Incl 1740 radio scripts and a collection of 3000 television scripts. Also incl portraits, clippings files, film festival programs, motion picture programs, lobby cards, original sketches and production materials; the personal and business papers, records and correspondence of actors, directors, producers, art directors and screen and television writers. Incl 100,000 mss. Extensive poster collection (over 7000, 1915 to date), many forPolish and Czech productions. Limited photocopying.

CA —UNIVERSITY OF CALIFORNIA, LOS ANGELES, Music Library, Schonberg Hall, Los Angeles, 90024. Stephen M Fry, Music Librn
Notes: The Philip Kahgan Collection of music films, letters, programs, and photographs important to the Southern California classical music scene. Incl 16mm "home movies" of more than thirty renowned conductors and performers during Hollywood Bowl rehearsals in the late 1930s. Incl Kahgan correspondence, memorabilia, 35 scrapbooks, etc.

CA —UNIVERSITY OF SOUTHERN CALIFORNIA, Edward L Doheny Memorial Library, Archives of Performing Arts, University Park, Los Angeles, 90089. Robert Knutson, Librn
Holdings: Vols (15,000) Mss Videotapes Audiotapes Pix
Notes: Approx 15,000 vols of books and serials about film, incl a large collection of foreign language books and periodicals. Current subscriptions to over 200 serials. Large collection of clippings about motion pictures and television. Warner Brothers Films Collection (1920-1968) incl 700,000 stills and negatives; 3,000 titles of feature, short subject and television screenplays, script materials, set designs, engineering drawings, production records, patent records, music and legal files. Over 1000 bound vols describing the inventory and 100 bound vols of index to the inventory. Universal Pictures Corporation Collection incl 600 boxes of production and publicity department records, incl 1,500 screenplays. Metro-Goldwyn-Mayer Collection incl screenplays from 1919-1958. Twentieth Century-Fox Collection incl screenplays and story department notes from 1919-1967.Hal Roach Studio Collection contains studio records from 1916-mid fifties. More than 150 personal collections from actors, directors, producers, writers, etc. Also have 2,000 additional screenplays; 1,000 posters, 110,000 photographs; 750 recorded soundtracks; 1,500 interview tapes; 400 David Wolper videotapes. A collection of feature films on videotape is being created. There is also a historical collection of motion picture cameras, projectors and other equipment from the earliest times to present.

CA —SAN DIEGO STATE UNIVERSITY, Malcolm A Love Library, 5300 Campanile Dr, San Diego, 92182. D Dickinson, Univ Librn; Don L Bosseau, Dir
Notes: Theatre and Film Programs Collection. Includes programs from theatrical performances and film showings; theatre

MOVING PICTURES—COLLECTIONS
(cont.)

programs date from 1850 to the present; the film programs date from the beginning of silent films to the present (2500 items).

CA —HOOVER INSTITUTION ON WAR, REVOLUTION & PEACE, Stanford University, Stanford, 94305. Milorad M Drachkovitch, Archivist
Notes: The Herman Axelbank Film Collection on Russian history. Much footage dating from about 1901-1921. Subjects incl Royal Family, Moscow and St Petersburg scenes, the Revolution and Civil War, espec good coverage of Leon Trotsky's role, Siberia, and the Far East. The first 28 of 266 reels have been received (April 1983).

DC —LIBRARY OF CONGRESS, Washington, 20540.
Notes: The Charles Eames Collection of original negatives and prints of each of the 106 films he created, business correspondence from 1944 to 1978, approximately 400,000 color slides, 31,000 black-and-white photographs, production materials for exhibits, and drawings for all the major furniture designs. Acquired on a grant of $500,000 from IBM.

DC —LIBRARY OF CONGRESS, Motion Pictures, Broadcasting and Recorded Sound Div, Washington, 20540.
Holdings: Cat Mss Pix
Notes: Motion Picture Film. Early film dating from 1894; paper print collection of early film (1897-1915) deposited for copyright, converted to projectable film. George Kleine Collection (1900-1920); Edison Laboratories Collection; Theodore Roosevelt Memorial Association Collection; American Film Institute Collection (theatrical films from 1897 to 1956 and theatrical shorts from all periods); German, Japanese, and Italian collections received through transfer from other Government agencies and by exchange with foreign governments; American Copyright Collection of films (incl television shows) selected from those registered for copyright from 1942 to the present. Collection of stills; poster collection; script and continuity collection. Holdings: motion pictures, 50,000 titles; 300,000 stills; 8000 posters; 137,000 scripts and continuities.

FL —MIAMI-DADE PUBLIC LIBRARY SYSTEM, One Biscayne Blvd, Miami, 33132. Don Chauncey, AV Librn; Barbara Young, Art & Music Dept Librn
Holdings: Cat Films Filmstrips
Budget: $106,000
Notes: 4402 16mm films; 100 8mm films; 540 filmstrips.

KY —LOUISVILLE FREE PUBLIC LIBRARY, Fourth & York Sts, Louisville, 40203. Barbara L Pickett, Mgr Reference & Adult Servs
Holdings: Cat 16mm Films Filmstrips Slides Videotapes
Budget: $20,000
Notes: 2,644 16mm films, 393 videocassettes, 1,483 filmstrips, and slide sets on a variety of subjects for adults and children. Circulating, no interlibrary loan, no copying.

MD —NATIONAL LIBRARY OF MEDICINE, 8600 Rockville Pike, Bethesda, 20209. Harold M Schoolinam, Actg Dir
Holdings: Vols (3,150,000) Cat Mss Audiotapes Videotapes 16mm Films Filmstrips Microforms
Budget: ($46,400)
Notes: The world's largest medical library. Materials are collected exhaustively in some 40 biomedical areas and, to a lesser degree, in related subject areas such as general chemistry, physics, zoology, botany, and instrumentation. Holdings include 12,000 audiovisuals. Pre-1871 material is in a separate historical collection.

MA —AMHERST COLLEGE, Library, Amherst, 01002. John Lancaster, Special Collections Librn
Notes: Personal "working library" of Margaret Mead, donated by Mary Catherine Bateson, Dr Mead's daughter. Other collections of Margaret Mead's papers, books, mss, etc are at the Library of Congress, the American Museum of Natural History, etc. Dr Bateson has also given her mother's film collection to the Five College collection housed at Hampshire College.

MO —SAINT LOUIS PUBLIC LIBRARY, Film Dept, 1624 Locust St, Saint Louis, 63103. Rita Broughton, Librn
Holdings: Cat
Budget: $36,000
Notes: Incl 2500 16mm sound educational films. See also *Joint Film Catalog, Saint Louis County Library,* Saint Louis Public Library, 1984.

NY —QUEENSBOROUGH COMMUNITY COLLEGE, Library, Springfield Blvd & L I Expressway, Bayside, 11364. Carol Singer, Chief Librn
Holdings: Cat
Notes: Films (nearly 300) on electrical and mechanical technology. Incl 16mm films.

NY —MUSEUM OF MODERN ART, Dept of Film, 11 W 53 St, New York, 10019. Eileen Bowser, Cur
Holdings: Mss
Notes: Special collections: D W Griffith: personal papers and scrapbooks (cataloged); Carl Lerner Collection: notebooks, scripts, letters (cataloged); Harry McWilliams Collection: promotional and advertising material; Merritt Crawford Collection: documents and letters on early film history (cataloged); Thomas J Brandon Collection: documents and letters on the US labor movement and independent filmmaking, scripts, unpublished mss and research material (partially cataloged). Also, special material relating to Robert Flaherty, Helen Van Dongen, Thomas Ince, Paul Terry, G W Pabst, film censorship. Extensive clipping files and scripts on motion pictures. Partially cataloged.

NY —NEW YORK PUBLIC LIBRARY, Performing Arts Research Center, Dance Collection, 111 Amsterdam Ave, New York, 10023. Genevieve Oswald, Cur
Holdings: Videotapes Films
Budget: ($9280)

Notes: The Jerome Robbins Film Archives include over 2.6 million feet of motion picture film representing 2230 individual film titles, and 1650 videotape titles. Every type of dance is included: ballet, modern dance, ethnic, rituals, social, and folk, with the major emphasis on ballet and modern dance. All aspects of dance are documented: performance, rehearsal, training, and therapy. Original filming includes a project to record masterworks of major American choreographers and companies, a Bicentennial project to record representative American regional professional companies outside of New York, and an Asian Dance Project. Special collections include: Ted Shawn and Jacob's Pillow collections, Leonide Massine Collection, Martha Hill Collection from the Juilliard School, Chapman Collection of ballet films, 1937-47, Victor Jessen Collection, Laird Goldsborough Collection, American Telephone and Telegraph Company's gift of dance programs from the Bell Telephone Hour, Ruth Page Collection of Ballet Russe films. Also represented are: rare film footage of Anna Pavlova and Loie Fuller, the Kirov Ballet School training films, the complete PBS Dance in America series, the CBS Camera Three Television series, 197 films of Asian dance and works of such choreographers as Jerome Robbins, George Balanchine, Martha Graham, Agnes De Mille, Doris Humphrey, Jose Limon, Charles Weidman, Ted Shawn, Ruth St Denis, Twyla Tharp, Anthony Tudor, Eliot Feld, Frederick Ashton, Glen Tetley, Robert Joffrey, viewing facilities available, on a first-come, first-serve basis. No loans or copying permitted, Cataloged films and videotapes listed in published catalog: Dictionary Catalog of the Dance Collection, Boston G K Hall 1974, 10 vols. Annual supplements: Bibliographic Guide to Dance, also published by G K Hall, 1975.

NY —YIVO INSTITUTE FOR JEWISH RESEARCH, Library & Archives, 1048 Fifth Ave, New York, 10028. Dina Abramowicz, Librn; Marek Web, Archivist
Holdings: Cat Mss Pix Slides
Notes: Yiddish drama in the original and in English translation from its 19th-century beginnings to the present; the Yiddish theatre in the Soviet Union and the theatrical activities in the ghettos during the Nazi regime; special collections of Sholem Perelmuter, Mendl Elkin, Maurice Schwartz, Abraham Goldfaden, Jacob Gordin, and Mark Schweid; records of the Union of Jewish Actors in Poland between the two world wars; the Vilna YIVO Collection of posters, playbills, and photographs; recordings.

OH —PUBLIC LIBRARY OF CINCINNATI & HAMILTON COUNTY, Films and Recordings Center, 800 Vine St, Cincinnati, 45202. Robert Hudzik, Head
Holdings: Vols 2475 Cat
Notes: This circulating collection includes 3231 reels of 16mm films on subjects ranging from history of the motion picture, documentaries and animated shorts to psychology, business, and social issues. There is a card catalog index and printed subject index. The Film Center has just initiated a circulating video cassette collection (105 titles).

OH —CLEVELAND PUBLIC LIBRARY, Films Department, 325 Superior Ave, Cleveland, 44114. Arnold McClain, Head
Holdings: Cat Films Videotapes Slides
Notes: Circulating collection incl 4,127 titles (5,163 reels) 16mm films; 119 titles (1,263 reels) 8mm films; 300 videotape titles, 100 slides. Restricted to Cuyahoga County residents. No photocopying.

RI —RHODE ISLAND HISTORICAL SOCIETY, Library, 121 Hope St, Providence, 02906. Paul R Campbell, Library Dir
Notes: Rhode Island Film Archive. 3,000,000 feet of documentary and television newsfilm.

†TX —UNIVERSITY OF TEXAS LIBRARIES, General Libraries, Humanities Research Center, PO Box 7219, Austin, 78712. John Chalmers, Librn

ON —NATIONAL FILM, TELEVISION AND SOUND ARCHIVES, Documentation & Public Service, 395 Wellington St, Ottawa, K1A 0N3, Can. Jana Vosikovska, Chief; Gloria Grant, Librn; Sylvie Robitaille, Stills and Posters Librn
Holdings: Vols (7000) Pix
Budget: ($35,000)
Notes: Several collections supporting the documentation on film, television and recorded sound: 1060 periodical titles (450 current), some on microfilm. Picture-stills, 265,000; moving picture posters, 6000; cataloged microfiche, 33,000 (vertical file material put on microfilm, then into a fiche format). Index cards (periodical references, credits): 334,000 cards (Film Title Index: 250,000 cards; Personalities Index: 84,000 cards).

MOVING PICTURES—COSTUME see Costume

MOVING PICTURES—DIRECTION see Moving Pictures—Production and Direction

MOVING PICTURES—DISTRIBUTION

NY —EDUCATIONAL FILM LIBRARY ASSOCIATION, Film Reference Library, 45

MOVING PICTURES—DISTRIBUTION (cont.)

John St, New York, 10038. Nadine Covert, Exec Dir
Holdings: Vols (2600) Cat Pix 16mm Films Filmstrips
Budget: ($1500)
Notes: Primarily a print collection emphasizing the documentary and educational film areas, but also film as art, animation and independent film in general. Maintain film title file of over 60,000 cards (primarily educational film titles), incl credit information, running time, release date, summary, and distributor. File is a mixture of EFLA evaluations, LC cards, etc. Subject file also separates film flyers by subject or topic. Maintain festivals file (film festivals, educational film festivals, etc); a film library administration file; a filmmakers file (with bio, credits, clippings, program notes); and a vertical file (incl information on grants, distribution, showcases, film activities in the metropolitan area and in major film centers around the country). Membership organization providing telephone, mail and in-person reference. Open to the generalpublic. Do not publish a catalog, but publish annual Film Library Administration bibliography of current or noteworthy reference books for $2.00.

MOVING PICTURES—EQUIPMENT see Moving Picture Equipment

MOVING PICTURES—FESTIVALS see Moving Picture Festivals

MOVING PICTURES—HISTORY

AZ —NORTHERN ARIZONA UNIVERSITY, Special Collection Library, CU Box 6022, Flagstaff, 86011. Peter M Whiteley, Coordr/Archivist; William Mullane, Librn
Holdings: Cat Mss Pix
Notes: More than 15,000 photographs of the Grand Canyon taken by the Kolb Brothers, 1902-1970.
See also entry under Kolb, Emery

AZ —ARIZONA STATE UNIVERSITY, Library, Tempe, 85287. Marilyn Wurzburger, Special Collections Librn
Notes: The Jimmy Starr Film History Collection contains the personal library and working materials of Jimmy Starr, Hollywood movie columnist from the 1920s-1960s. In addition to working as a press agent, Mr Starr was a columnist for the now defunct *Los Angeles Record* and the *Los Angeles Herald & Express*, and his columnswere widely syndicated; he also wrote silent comedies for Mack Sennett, scripts for the talkies, as well as several mystery novels. The collection incl over 2100 biographical files of entertainers containing well over 20,000 contemporary newspaper and periodical clippings; over 3000 stills; reviews, premiere invitations and other ephemera for over 6000 films; and other writers. Also, there are reference books, selected film periodicals and scrapbooks which round out the collection. The material is partially cataloged; finding guides are available.

CA —ACADEMY OF MOTION PICTURE ARTS & SCIENCES, Margaret Herrick Library, 8949 Wilshire Blvd, Beverly Hills, 90211. Linda Harris Mehr, Library Administrator
Holdings: Vols (16,000) Cat Mss Pix Slides
Budget: ($250,000)
Notes: Also posters, scrapbooks, clippings and press books. Collection emphases are the moving picture industry, moving picture history, biographical material on actors, actresses and industry personnel. Files on specific films, reviews, cast and credits, production data, etc, on more than 65,000 moving pictures. (Over 5000 films, incl early 28mm films in Film Archive). Over 5 million pictures. Special collections: papers of Mary Pickford, Mack Sennett, Adolph Zukor, Lewis Milestone, George Stevens, George

Cukor, John Huston, Edith Head; Paramount scripts and stills archive, MGM stills archive, RKO stills archive, Thomas H Ince stills collection, Cecil B DeMille stills collection. In addition, the Black American Film History Collection, the first permanent collection of material related to Blacks in American motion pictures.

CA —AMERICAN FILM INSTITUTE, Louis B Mayer Library, 2021 N Western Ave, PO Box 27999, Los Angeles, 90027. Anne G Schlosser, Dir
Holdings: Vols (3500) Cat
Notes: Collection contains 2500 American film scripts and 1000 television scripts; oral histories conducted in the American Film Institute Louis B Mayer Oral History Program; the MGM Script Collection of 400 MGM scripts from the silent period up to the mid-1950's; Columbia Stills Collection covering the period 1930-1950; special mss collections of Henry Hathaway (director), Harry Horner, Buster Keaton, George Byron Sage and Stewart Stern (writer). Also clipping files on motion pictures, personalities, television shows, production organizations and technical topics; film festival file of all US and foreign festivals. Rare periodical holdings incl *Film Daily* newspaper (1923-1969); *Radio-TV Daily* newspaper (1939-1964); *RKO Radio Flash*, house organ of RKO (1932-1955); *TV Guide* (1948 to date).

CA —INSTITUTE OF THE AMERICAN MUSICAL, Library, 121 N Detroit St, Los Angeles, 90036. Miles Kreuger, Cur
Holdings: Cat Mss Maps Pix Slides Phonorecords
Notes: Reference materials on the American musical theatre and motion pictures incl 40,000 phonograph records, sound tapes, and cylinders dating back to the 1890s; record catalogs to 1900; thousands of theatre and film programs, periodicals, sheet music and vocal scores as early as 1830; thousands of motion picture press books and over 200,000 stills from 1914 to the present; every musical comedy script published in America and dozens in ms form, original or photocopy materials from the archives of movie palaces, films and record companies, incl discographies of many major Broadway and Hollywood stars; and thousands of books on theatre, film, broadcasting, world's fairs and other allied areas of showmanship.

CA —LOS ANGELES PUBLIC LIBRARY, Frances Howard Goldwyn Hollywood Regional Library, 1623 Ivar Ave, Los Angeles, 90028. Sally Dumaux, Librn
Holdings: Vols (100,000) Cat Mss VF
Budget: ($60,000)
Notes: A general and a research collection covering motion pictures, radio broadcasting, and television. Over 2000 motion picture and television scripts. Biographical information on actors and actresses. Casts, credits, and other production information on over 1500 motion pictures from the 1920s to the present. Collections also include posters, lobby cards, souvenir programs, scrapbooks, vertical files, and over 3000 publicity stills. Including the following Special Collections: Fred Archer Collection, photographs, including the Hunchback of Notre Dame (1923), and personalities of the stage and screen, 1907-1930; Gilbert A Adrian, designer, sketches and photographs; Hazel Flynn, publicist, correspondence and photographs.

CA —UNIVERSITY OF CALIFORNIA, LOS ANGELES, Research Library, Dept of Special Collections, 405 Hilgard Ave, Los Angeles, 90024. Edward Shreeves, Chairman, Bibliographers Group; David S Zeidberg, Head
Notes: In various collections, incl the Russell Birdwell, George P Johnson Negro Film, and Victor Mansfield Shapiro collections.

CA —UNIVERSITY OF CALIFORNIA, LOS ANGELES, Theater Arts Library, Los Angeles, 90024. Edward Shreeves, Chairman, Bibliographers Group; Audree Malkin, Head, Theater Arts Library
Notes: The Charlton Heston Archives, incl correspondence, scripts, movie posters, still photographs, scrapbooks, interviews, awards,

etc, covering his forty-year acting career in fifty-four films. He served six terms as President of the Screen Actors Guild, longer than anyone else.

CA —UNIVERSITY OF CALIFORNIA, LOS ANGELES, Theater Arts Library, Los Angeles, 90024. Edward Shreeves, Chairman, Bibliographers Group; Audree Malkin, Head, Theater Arts Library
Holdings: Vols (12,500)
Notes: Major research collections covering the historical, critical, aesthetic, biographical and technical aspects of film, television and radio, and the non-book and primary source material in these fields. Also 166,000 pamphlets, photographs, microforms and sound recordings. Incl over 4,000,000 moving picture stills, over 32,636 screenplays, and scripts from American and British Films. Incl 1740 radio scripts and a collection of 3000 television scripts. Also incl portraits, clippings files, film festival programs, motion picture programs, lobby cards, original sketches and production materials; the personal and business papers, records and correspondence of actors, directors, producers, art directors and screen and television writers. Incl 100,000 mss. Extensive poster collection (over 7000, 1915 to date), many forPolish and Czech productions. Limited photocopying.

†CA —UNIVERSITY OF CALIFORNIA, RIVERSIDE, Library, PO Box 5900, Riverside, 92507. George Slusser, Librn
Notes: ca 100 videotapes of SF/fantasy films and a large archive of books, clippings and articles pertaining to the history of film.

CA —SAN FRANCISCO ART INSTITUTE, Anne Bremer Memorial Library, 800 Chestnut St, San Francisco, 94133. Jeff Gunderson, Librn
Holdings: Vols (23,144) Cat Pix Slides Audiotapes 16mm Films Microforms
Budget: ($15,000)

DC —LIBRARY OF CONGRESS, Motion Pictures, Broadcasting and Recorded Sound Div, Washington, 20540.
Holdings: Cat Mss Pix
Notes: Motion Picture Film. Early film dating from 1894; paper print collection of early film (1897-1915) deposited for copyright, converted to projectable film. George Kleine Collection (1900-1920); Edison Laboratories Collection; Theodore Roosevelt Memorial Association Collection; American Film Institute Collection (theatrical films from 1897 to 1956 and theatrical shorts from all periods); German, Japanese, and Italian collections received through transfer from other Government agencies and by exchange with foreign governments; American Copyright Collection of films (incl television shows) selected from those registered for copyright from 1942 to the present. Collection of stills; poster collection; script and continuity collection. Holdings: motion pictures, 50,000 titles; 300,000 stills; 8000 posters; 137,000 scripts and continuities.

IN —INDIANA UNIVERSITY, Lilly Library, Seventh St, Bloomington, 47405. William R Cagle, Librn
Holdings: // Uncat Mss
Notes: 2300 positive photographs and 800 negatives, largely stills for Eisenstein's film "Thunder over Mexico." Ms includes the papers of director John Ford and actor Orson Welles.

IA —DRAKE UNIVERSITY, Cowles Library, 28 St & University Ave, Des Moines, 50311.
Notes: Nearly 3000 musical works used by orchestras and musicians to accompany silent films, donated by Dorman Hundling who had played in orchestras in theatres owned by his family in South Dakota and Iowa.

NJ —FORT LEE PUBLIC LIBRARY, 320 Main St, Fort Lee, 07024. Nancy V Gallo, Dir
Holdings: Vols (575) Cat Pix Slides Videotapes 16mm Films
Notes: Specializes in the history of film, particularly in Fort Lee, NJ. Also, books on film generally. The picture collection consists of pictures of Fort Lee film productions, both stills and production shots

MOVING PICTURES—HISTORY (cont.)

and some portraits. Some of these are duplicated in 35mm slide form. The videotapes are interviews with people who participated in the making of movies in Fort Lee. The project is still in progress. Also, 35 original movies made in Fort Lee and a documentary about the motion picture industry here.

NJ —PRINCETON UNIVERSITY, Library, William Seymour Theatre Collection, Princeton, 08544. Mary Ann Jensen, Cur
Notes: Orchestral parts and conductor's scores for several thousand popular songs and special musical effects used in movie houses to the end of the silent picture era.

NY —SAINT LAWRENCE UNIVERSITY, Owen D Young Library, Canton, 13617. Mahlon Peterson, Librn
Holdings: Cat Mss Pix
Notes: Collection consists of letters sent to Edith O'Dell Black and Pomeroy Burton of the New York *World* from 1903 to 1944. Also incl are works by Alexander Black, a novelist, and manuscripts which he wrote for "picture plays," the forerunners of the modern moving pictures. Approx 350 items.

NY —ANTHOLOGY FILM ARCHIVES, 491 Broadway, New York, 10012. Jonas Mekas, Dir; Nadia Shtendara, Librn
Holdings: Videotapes 16mm Films
Budget: ($400,000)
Notes: An extensive library of information on avant-garde cinema, incl program notes, biographies and photographs. Also publish books (6) and *Film Culture* magazine.

NY —MUSEUM OF MODERN ART, Dept of Film, 11 W 53 St, New York, 10019. Eileen Bowser, Cur
Holdings: Mss
Notes: Special collections: D W Griffith: personal papers and scrapbooks (cataloged); Carl Lerner Collection: notebooks, scripts, letters (cataloged); Harry McWilliams Collection: promotional and advertising material; Merritt Crawford Collection: documents and letters on early film history (cataloged); Thomas J Brandon Collection: documents and letters on the US labor movement and independent filmmaking, scripts, unpublished mss and research material (partially cataloged). Also, special material relating to Robert Flaherty, Helen Van Dongen, Thomas Ince, Paul Terry, G W Pabst, film censorship. Extensive clipping files and scripts on motion pictures. Partially cataloged.

NY —NEW YORK PUBLIC LIBRARY, Performing Arts Research Center, Billy Rose Theatre Collection, 111 Amsterdam Ave, New York, 10023. Dorothy L Swerdlove, Cur
Holdings: Cat Pix

Notes: As early as 1941 the American Television Society appointed the Theatre Collection the official repository of their archives and urged its members to deposit materials in the Collection. The Collection maintains clipping files on radio and television programs, and on the personnel of these programs. It collects photographs of these individuals, of television and radio studios, equipment, etc. There is a collection of television production scripts, with most of the "Hallmark Hall of Fame" specials and "Studio One" scripts, 1948-1952. The collection of radio scripts incl. material regarding the Radio Writers Guild of America and also runs of several serials written by Elaine Carrington. The book material incl. the standard works on the history of broadcasting and telecasting, vols. on the techniques of the industry.

NY —STATE UNIVERSITY OF NEW YORK, COLLEGE AT PURCHASE, Library, Lincoln Ave, Purchase, 10577. Robert W Evans, Dir
Holdings: Vols (1400) Mss Pix Slides
Notes: The Gerald D McDonald Collection. Over 1400 books on moving pictures and all aspects of the industry: production, directing, acting. Thousands of pictures of actors and actresses, directors, etc. Also about 2000 slides picturing movie personalities, etc; stereopticon pictures, buttons, bottle caps, playing cards, etc.

NY —INTERNATIONAL MUSEUM OF PHOTOGRAPHY AT GEORGE EASTMAN HOUSE, Archives, 900 East Ave, Rochester, 14607. Rachel Stuhlman, Head Librn
Holdings: Vols (30,000) Cat Mss Microforms
Budget: ($104,000)
Notes: History, aesthetics and technology of photography and cinematography, incl the Gabriel Cromer, Josef Maria Eder, Alden Scott Boyer, Louis Walton Sipley/3M Collections, and the James Card Collection from 1893. Covers photographic, especially cinematographic history; also hundreds of negatives of Edward Muybridge as well as his notebooks. Incl 450,000 pictures and slides. Also the Lewis Hine Collection of social documentary photography.

OH —CLEVELAND PUBLIC LIBRARY, Literature Dept, 325 Superior Ave, Cleveland, 44114. Evelyn Ward, Head
Holdings: Cat Mss Pix
Notes: Personal library and other collections of W Ward Marsh, former film critic of the Cleveland *Plain Dealer*. The major categories of the bequest are: production stills which begin with the films of the Thirties and concentrate on those of the Forties and Fifties; an actor/actress file of folders for individual personalities containing studio and agent biographies, clippings and publicity photos; "pressbooks"--kits of advertising materials used for promoting a specific movie; a review file numbering over 20,000 critiques clipped from *Boxoffice*, *Variety*, and miscellaneous trade journals, incl Marsh's own reviews; and his correspondence. Also incl are a specially bound copy of the shooting script (accompanied by color transparencies) for Cecil B deMille's remake of *The Ten Commandments*; and a collection of more than 70046g X 56g glass slides--dating from the silent era--which were used by theatre owners to promote their upcoming attractions.

OH —OHIO STATE UNIVERSITY, Library for Communication and Graphic Arts, 242 W 18th St, Columbus, 43210. Lucy S Caswell, Curator
Notes: Library will receive collection of materials on this subject at a future date.

†TX —UNIVERSITY OF TEXAS LIBRARIES, Hoblitzelle Theatre Arts Library, Austin, 78712.
Notes: A 100,000-item collection of correspondence and documents related to the career and personal life of Gloria Swanson, one of the largest archives from 1913 to 1983. Correspondence with Mary Pickford, William Faulkner, and the Kennedy Family, the latter to remain sealed until the year 2000.

UT —BRIGHAM YOUNG UNIVERSITY, Harold B Lee Library, Unversity Hill, Provo, 84602. Sterling Albrecht, Dir
Holdings: Vols (162,000) Mss
Notes: Archives of Cecile B De Mille. 400 cubic ft.

WI —STATE HISTORICAL SOCIETY OF WISCONSIN, Archives, 816 State St, Madison, 53706. Harold L Miller, Reference Archivist
Holdings: Mss Pix Microforms
Notes: Holdings incl records and papers of prominent organizations and individuals in the theater and motion picture industry, motion picture and television films, scripts, and still photographs, incl the archives of the United Artists Corporation. Collections are described in *Sources for Mass Communications, Film and Theater Research: A Guide*, (1982) and in current accession notes in the *Wisconsin Magazine of History*. Major collections are also in Hamer, *Guide to Manuscripts and Archives in the United States*, (1961) and in the *National Union Catalog of Manuscripts Collections*, (1959-date).

WI —UNIVERSITY OF WISCONSIN, MADISON, Memorial Library, 728 State St, Madison, 53706. Erwin K Welsch, Social Studies Bibliographer
Notes: A collection of 750 vols, pamphlets and periodicals on moving pictures and related subjects.

WY —UNIVERSITY OF WYOMING, William Robertson Coe Library, Performing Arts Collections, Laramie, 82071. Gene M Gressley, Dir
Holdings: Mss
Notes: Collections in the Performing Arts area incl some 300 collections of outstanding music composers, arrangers, film industry directors, writers, performers, and individuals prominent in all aspects of music, theatre, radio, television and film industry.

ON —NATIONAL FILM, TELEVISION AND SOUND ARCHIVES, Documentation & Public Service, 395 Wellington St, Ottawa, K1A 0N3, Can. Jana Vosikovska, Chief; Gloria Grant, Librn; Sylvie Robitaille, Stills and Posters Librn
Holdings: Vols (7000) Pix
Budget: ($35,000)
Notes: Several collections supporting the documentation on film, television and recorded sound: 1060 periodical titles (450 current), some on microfilm. Picture-stills, 265,000; moving picture posters, 6000; cataloged microfiche, 33,000 (vertical file material put on microfilm, then into a fiche format). Index cards (periodical references, credits): 334,000 cards (Film Title Index: 250,000 cards; Personalities Index: 84,000 cards).

MOVING PICTURES—MUSICAL ACCOMPANIMENT see Moving Picture Music

MOVING PICTURES—NEWSREELS

CA —HOOVER INSTITUTION ON WAR, REVOLUTION & PEACE, Stanford University, Stanford, 94305. Milorad M Drachkovitch, Archivist
Holdings: Mss
Notes: Newsreels, 1939-1942, produced by Universum-Aktiengesllschaft (UFA), a German motion picture company, and distributed in Spain, relating to military campaigns and conditions in Germany during World War II. Incl a few photographs. In German and Spanish. Ca 460 reels.

†SC —UNIVERSITY OF SOUTH CAROLINA, Libraries, Columbia, 29208.
Notes: Newsreels made from 1919-63 by Twentieth Century Fox.

MOVING PICTURES—PRODUCTION AND DIRECTION

CA —BURBANK PUBLIC LIBRARY, 110 N Glenoaks Blvd, Burbank, 91502. Mary Ann Grasso, Coordr; Barbara Stones, Coordr, Media Project
Holdings: Vols (32,000) Cat Clippings Pix VF

Notes: The Warner Research Collection is a full service research division designed to serve the production needs of the motion picture, television, theatrical, and creative arts communities. This is a see-based service available by appointment only. Subject specialties include costumes, U.S. military, crime and criminals, transportation, license plates, and Sears catalogues.

CA —AMERICAN FILM INSTITUTE, Louis B Mayer Library, 2021 N Western Ave, PO

MOVING PICTURES—PRODUCTION AND DIRECTION (cont.)

Box 27999, Los Angeles, 90027. Anne G Schlosser, Dir
Notes: The AFI/Louis B Mayer Oral History Program Collection includes over 40 interviews with pioneers of the film industry. Also included in the collection are transcripts of seminars (1969-1981) and tapes (1981-) containing interviews with professionals from the film and television industry on how films and TV shows are produced. Include directors, writers, cinimatographers, editors, art directors, agents, lawyers, producers, etc. A film production and file index provides original documentation on nearly all US films from 1930-1969; tracks a film from first trade announcement regarding film production to final release.

CA —UNIVERSITY OF CALIFORNIA, LOS ANGELES, Research Library, Dept of Special Collections, 405 Hilgard Ave, Los Angeles, 90024. Edward Shreeves, Chairman, Bibliographers Group; David S Zeidberg, Head
Notes: In various collections, incl Hans Dreier, Anton Grot, John Houseman, George P Johnson, Stanley Kramer, Mirisch Productions, Paul Rotha, Preston Sturges, and King Vidor collections.

CA —UNIVERSITY OF CALIFORNIA, LOS ANGELES, Theater Arts Library, Los Angeles, 90024. Edward Shreeves, Chairman, Bibliographers Group; Audree Malkin, Head, Theater Arts Library
Notes: The George Jenkins Collection is comprised of his archive of art direction materials for more than 30 films and television specials. Incl scripts, set lists, 1/4" ground plans, budget records, research photographs and notes, original set sketches, storyboards, blueprints, construction and prop stills, and other production materials.

CA —UNIVERSITY OF CALIFORNIA, LOS ANGELES, Theater Arts Library, Los Angeles, 90024. Edward Shreeves, Chairman, Bibliographers Group; Audree Malkin, Head, Theater Arts Library
Holdings: Vols (12,500)
Notes: Major research collections covering the historical, critical, aesthetic, biographical and technical aspects of film, television and radio, and the non-book and primary source material in these fields. Also 166,000 pamphlets, photographs, microforms and sound recordings. Incl over 4,000,000 moving picture stills, over 32,636 screenplays, and scripts from American and British Films. Incl 1740 radio scripts and a collection of 3000 television scripts. Also incl portraits, clippings files, film festival programs, motion picture programs, lobby cards, original sketches and production materials; the personal and business papers, records and correspondence of actors, directors, producers, art directors and screen and television writers. Incl 100,000 mss. Extensive poster collection (over 7000, 1915 to date), many forPolish and Czech productions. Limited photocopying.

CA —SAN DIEGO STATE UNIVERSITY, Malcolm A Love Library, 5300 Campanile Dr, San Diego, 92182. D Dickinson, Univ Librn; Don L Bosseau, Dir
Notes: Desi Arnaz Collection of Film and Television Production Material. Includes films, television tapes, out-takes, scripts, correspondence, publicity material. (350 linear ft.)

CT —GREENWICH LIBRARY, 101 W Putnam Ave, Greenwich, 06830. Wayne T Campbell Jr, Film Services Coordr
Holdings: Vols 874 Cat Videotapes Films
Notes: Collection is very broad. Supplemented by books on film making in both this collection and the photographic collection. Also supplemented by 16mm film collection and videocassettes.

NY —NEW YORK PUBLIC LIBRARY, Performing Arts Research Center, Billy Rose Theatre Collection, 111 Amsterdam Ave, New York, 10023. Dorothy L Swerdlove, Cur
Holdings: Cat
See also entry under Moving Pictures - History.

†TX —UNIVERSITY OF TEXAS LIBRARIES, Humanities Research Center, Harry Ransom Center, PO Box 7219, Austin, 78712.
Notes: The David O Selznick archives, incl 1961 file boxes of correspondence and 38 four-drawer file cases of manuscript materials, drawings, and paintings.

MOVING PICTURES—SCRIPTS

CA —ACADEMY OF MOTION PICTURE ARTS & SCIENCES, Margaret Herrick Library, 8949 Wilshire Blvd, Beverly Hills, 90211. Linda Harris Mehr, Library Administrator
Holdings: Vols (16,000) Cat Mss Pix Slides
Budget: ($250,000)
Notes: Also posters, scrapbooks, clippings and press books. Collection emphasis are the moving picture industry, moving picture history, biographical material on actors, actresses and industry personnel. Files on specific films, reviews, cast and credits, production data, etc, on more than 65,000 moving pictures. (Over 5000 films, incl early 28mm films in Film Archive). Over 5 million pictures. Special collections: papers of Mary Pickford, Mack Sennett, Adolph Zukor, Lewis Milestone, George Stevens, George Cukor, John Huston, Edith Head; Paramount scripts and stills archive, MGM stills archive, RKO stills archive, Thomas H Ince stills collection, Cecil B DeMille stills collection.

CA —BURBANK PUBLIC LIBRARY, 110 N Glenoaks Blvd, Burbank, 91502. Mary Ann Grasso, Coordr; Barbara Stones, Coordr, Media Project
Holdings: Vols (500) Manuals Videocassettes Audiocassettes
Notes: This collection (including technical manuals, production directories, scripts, production lectures, seminars, and university classes), is a free public clearinghouse of industry trends, job skills information, technical advances and management practices required for film and video production. Information covers such technical categories as cinematography, editing, sound recording, lighting, and special effects. Craft areas include directing, scriptwriting, art direction and costume design. Management information covers producing, programming, financing, budgets and distribution for theatrical, broadcast, and non-broadcast markets. Bulk of collection circulates. Reference texts and some other restricted material available for in-library study only. List of holdings available on request.
See also entries under Moving Pictures - Production and Direction; Television

CA —AMERICAN FILM INSTITUTE, Louis B Mayer Library, 2021 N Western Ave, PO Box 27999, Los Angeles, 90027. Anne G Schlosser, Dir
Notes: Script Collection includes 2500 motion picture scripts, 1000 television scripts. Film scripts include annotated working scripts for directors, writers, editors, and script supervisors. Television collection includes series and TV movies. Also MGM Script Collection of 400 scripts from the silent period up to the mid-1950's.

CA —LOS ANGELES PUBLIC LIBRARY, Frances Howard Goldwyn Hollywood Regional Library, 1623 Ivar Ave, Los Angeles, 90028. Sally Dumaux, Librn
Holdings: Vols (100,000) Cat Mss Pix VF
Budget: ($60,000)
Notes: A general and a research collection covering motion pictures, radio broadcasting, and television. Over 2000 motion picture and television scripts. Biographical information on actors and actresses. Casts, credits, and other production information on over 1500 motion pictures from the 1920s to the present. Collections also include posters, lobby cards, souvenir programs, scrapbooks, vertical files, and over 3000 publicity stills. Including the following Special Collections: Fred Archer Collection, photographs, including the Hunchback of Notre Dame (1923), and personalities of the stage and screen, 1907-1930; Gilbert A Adrian,

designer, sketches and photographs; Hazel Flynn, publicist, correspondence and photographs.

CA —UNIVERSITY OF CALIFORNIA, LOS ANGELES, Research Library, Dept of Special Collections, 405 Hilgard Ave, Los Angeles, 90024. Edward Shreeves, Chairman, Bibliographers Group; David S Zeidberg, Head
Notes: In various collections, incl the Stanley Chase, Tony Curtis, Ken Englund, Mort Fine, Elizabeth Meehan, Dudley Nichols, John Paxton, Republic Pictures Corporation, Preston Sturges, Lawrence Turman, and King Vidor collections. No photocopying.

CA —UNIVERSITY OF CALIFORNIA, LOS ANGELES, Theater Arts Library, Los Angeles, 90024. Edward Shreeves, Chairman, Bibliographers Group; Audree Malkin, Head, Theater Arts Library
Holdings: Vols (12,500)
Notes: Major research collections covering the historical, critical, aesthetic, biographical and technical aspects of film, television and radio, and the non-book and primary source material in these fields. Also 166,000 pamphlets, photographs, microforms and sound recordings. Incl over 4,000,000 moving picture stills, over 32,636 screenplays, and scripts from American and British Films. Incl 1740 radio scripts and a collection of 3000 television scripts. Also incl portraits, clippings files, film festival programs, motion picture programs, lobby cards, original sketches and production materials; the personal and business papers, records and correspondence of actors, directors, producers, art directors and screen and television writers. Incl 100,000 mss. Extensive poster collection (over 7000, 1915 to date), many forPolish and Czech productions. Limited photocopying.

CA —UNIVERSITY OF CALIFORNIA, LOS ANGELES, Theater Arts Library, Los Angeles, 90024. Edward Shreeves, Chairman, Bibliographers Group; Audree Malkin, Head, Theater Arts Library
Holdings: Cat Mss Pix
Notes: An important part of the collection is the Metro-Goldwyn-Mayer Screenplay Collection which covers the period 1924-1947. Incl the Andy Hardy, Dr Kildare, and Maisie film series which are virtually complete, and a number of short features, such as Robert Benchley Series, Pete Smith Specialties, and Our Gang Comedies. Walt Disney Collection: A small but rare collection of cartoon continuities and shooting scripts dated 1937-1939. Television Scripts: approximately 3500 scripts incl such television series as Mission Impossible, all episodes for the years 1966-1970; The Real McCoys, 78 episodes, 1959-1961; My Friend Irma, 1965-1966; The George Burns Show, 232 episodes, 1958-1959; My Mother the Car, 30 episodes, 1965-1966. Radio Scripts: A collection of more than 1000 scripts which include the complete Amos 'n Andy radio series, 354 episodes dating from1943-1953; Our Miss Brooks, 222 scripts from 1948-1954; The Bob Hope Show, 29 scripts, 1949-1950; Philco Radio Time, starring Bing Crosby, 7 scripts and 6 comedy sketches, 1946-1947.

CA —UNIVERSITY OF CALIFORNIA, RIVERSIDE, University Library, 4045 Canyon Crest Dr, Box 5900, Riverside, 92517.
Holdings: Vols (30,000)
Notes: The Eaton Collection of science fiction and fantasy materials, incl 5,600 pulp magazines; also horror, supernatural, and Gothic mystery fiction; boys' books; utopian and dystopian fiction, imaginary voyages, future war and lost race fiction; large holdings in French language science fiction and fantasy; critical and scholarly works pertaining to these genres; videotapes of science fiction/fantasy films and shooting scripts. Collection covers science fiction/ fantasy literature from the 16th-17th centuries to the present. Strong individual author collections of Jules Verne, H Rider Haggard, H G Wells, Edgar Rice Burroughs, and Philip K Dick. For a complete

MOVING PICTURES—SCRIPTS (cont.)

description of the collection see: George Slusser, "The J Lloyd Eaton Collection," *Special Collections*, II, 1/2, 25-38 (1983), and *Dictionary Catalog of the J Lloyd Eaton Collection of Science Fiction and Fantasy Literature* (Boston: G K Hall) 1982.

DC —LIBRARY OF CONGRESS, Motion Pictures, Broadcasting and Recorded Sound Div, Washington, 20540.
Holdings: Cat Mss Pix
Notes: Motion Picture Film. Early film dating from 1894; paper print collection of early film (1897-1915) deposited for copyright, converted to projectable film. George Kleine Collection (1900-1920); Edison Laboratories Collection; Theodore Roosevelt Memorial Association Collection; American Film Institute Collection (theatrical films from 1897 to 1956 and theatrical shorts from all periods); German, Japanese, and Italian collections received through transfer from other Government agencies and by exchange with foreign governments; American Copyright Collection of films (incl television shows) selected from those registered for copyright from 1942 to the present. Collection of stills; poster collection; script and continuity collection. Holdings: motion pictures, 50,000 titles; 300,000 stills; 8000 posters; 137,000 scripts and continuities.

†IL —UNIVERSITY OF ILLINOIS, URBANA/CHAMPAIGN, Library, Wright St, 230 Library UIUC, Urbana, 61801.

IN —INDIANA UNIVERSITY, Lilly Library, Seventh St, Bloomington, 47405. William R Cagle, Librn
Holdings: Vols 950 Cat Mss
Notes: Includes scripts from movie serials and film shorts. Ms collections include filmscripts in the John Ford, John McGreevey, and Orson Welles papers.

IA —UNIVERSITY OF NORTHERN IOWA, Library, Cedar Falls, 50613. Gerald L Peterson, Special Collections Librn
Holdings: Vols (3500) Audiotapes
Budget: ($2000)
Notes: This is a collection of work done by American novelists who began their work after 1960. First editions only. We add as these novelists continue to publish. Include galley and page proofs when possible--also movie scripts and typescripts. Cataloged.

IA —UNIVERSITY OF IOWA, University Libraries, Iowa City, 52242. Robert A McCown, Mss Librn
Holdings: Mss Pix

Notes: Five collections: Robert Blees collection of motion picture and television material, 1925-65, inc, including stories, still production photos, and motion picture and television scripts of a motion picture and television script writer; David Swift collection of motion picture and television material, 1951-65, including scripts, posters, photos, drawings, and blueprints for final set construction of a motion picture and television producer and writer; the Albert Jay Cohen collection of motion picture and television production material, 1948-58, including correspondence, film scripts, stories, photos, financial and production papers, and censorship records; the Arthur A. Ross collection of motion picture and television material, 1943-65, including correspondence, scripts, photos, production records, and artists' sketches of a motion picture and television script writer; and the Norman Felton Papers, 1937-1978, including correspondence, notes, notebooks, subject files, budgets, other financial records, photographs, and scripts relating to such television series as The Eleventh Hour, The Lieutenant, The Man From U.N.C.L.E., Jericho, The Strange Report, The Psychiatrist, Hawkins, and Dr. Kildare, produced by Felton, 124 ft. of mss.

†MA —BOSTON UNIVERSITY, Mugar Memorial Library, Special Collections Dept, 771 Commonwealth Avenue, Boston, 02215. Howard B Gotlieb, Dir
Notes: Extensive papers of mystery and science fiction writers, and film, radio and TV writers, performers, etc. 14 years of original Little Orphan Annie art. Collections built around papers of individuals are supplemented by their printed works.

NH —DARTMOUTH COLLEGE, Baker Memorial Library, Hanover, 03755.
Holdings: Vols 2700 Cat
Notes: The Irving Thalberg Collection. Largely 1930-1940s. Noncirculating, no reproduction. No photocopying.

NY —NEW YORK STATE ARCHIVES, 9049 Cultural Education Center, Albany, 12230. Richard Andress, Archivist
Notes: Scripts read by the Motion Picture Division of the NYS Education Departments for the purposes of rating and approval, with orders by Department for deletions or changes in dialogue. Between 1910-1966 all moving pictures shown in New York were reviewed by this Board. Incl animated cartoon films. 54,000 items.

NY —NEW YORK PUBLIC LIBRARY, Performing Arts Research Center, Billy Rose Theatre Collection, 111 Amsterdam Ave, New York, 10023. Dorothy L Swerdlove, Cur
Holdings: Cat
See also entry under Moving Pictures - History

NY —NEW YORK PUBLIC LIBRARY, General Library of the Performing Arts, 111 Amsterdam Ave, New York, 10023. Larry Cioppa, Drama Specialist
Holdings: Vols (40,000) Cat Phonorecords
Notes: Drama material on all aspects of the theater. Film, radio, television and related performing arts. Incl 5000 drama recordings.

OH —OHIO STATE UNIVERSITY, William Oxley Thompson Memorial Library, 1858 Neil Ave Mall, Columbus, 43210. Robert A Tibbetts, Cur of Special Collections
Holdings: Vols (475) Cat Mss

PA —FRANKLIN & MARSHALL COLLEGE, Library, Lancaster, 17604. Kathleen J Moretto, Library Dir
Holdings: Mss Pix
Notes: The Franklin J Schaffner Film Library consists of shooting scripts in various drafts, still photos, posters and other memorabilia of all the motion picture films directed by Mr Schaffner. Actual prints of all the films incl, but not circulated.

†VA —GEORGE C MARSHALL RESEARCH FOUNDATION AND LIBRARY, Drawer 920, Lexington, 24450. Royster Lyle Jr, Cur Collections
Holdings: Vols Cat Mss Pix
Notes: The making of the film *Patton*, from its incipient idea to screening. Incl Academy Award ceremonies, over 400 photographs, the majority of which are of the General himself; files compiled over a 10-year period of scripts and treatments; correspondence dealing with production, screenings, and congratulations. Should be of interest to Patton students and military researchers as the massive amount of historical research done for the film forms the nucleus of this collection given us by the film's producer Frank McCarthy. Typed index to the collection available. General Patton's papers are in the Library of Congress.

MOVING PICTURES, AVANT-GARDE

NY —ANTHOLOGY FILM ARCHIVES, 491 Broadway, New York, 10012. Jonas Mekas, Dir; Nadia Shtendara, Librn
Holdings: Vols Cat Periodicals Mss Pix
Notes: Documents and associated items relating to film and video as art, with special emphasis on critical material on experimental and avant-garde films. Published bibliography of the collection: *The Essential Cinema*, vol 1, ed by P Adams Sitney (New York: Anthology Film Archives & New York Univ Press, 1975).

NY —NEW YORK PUBLIC LIBRARY, Performing Arts Research Center, Billy Rose Theatre Collection, 111 Amsterdam Ave, New York, 10023. Dorothy L Swerdlove, Cur
Holdings: Cat
See also entry under Moving Pictures - History.

MOVING PICTURES, CANADIAN

PQ —NATIONAL FILM BOARD OF CANADA, Reference Library, PO Box 6100, Station A, Montreal, H3C 3H5, Can. Rose-Aimee Todd, Librn; Bernard Lutz, Librn
Holdings: Vols (2250) Cat VF
Notes: Incl French and English "Challenge for Change Collection." Incl 350 pamphlets 30 VF drawers and 100 periodical titles.

MOVING PICTURES, DOCUMENTARY

DC —LIBRARY OF CONGRESS, Motion Pictures, Broadcasting and Recorded Sound Div, Washington, 20540.
Notes: German films, 1930s and 1940s, incl silent and sound features, newsreels, and educational, entertainment, documentary, and propaganda shorts. 500 documentary, newsreel, feature, educational, and propaganda films produced in Italy between 1930 and 1943.

IA —IOWA STATE UNIVERSITY, Library, Dept of Special Collections, Ames, 50011. Stanley M Yates, Head
Holdings: Mss Audiotapes 16mm Films Filmstrips
Notes: Contains over 7000 films and papers and records of individuals and organizations active in the field of the nontheatrical film. This is the first serious attempt by a major institution to collect materials relating to the factual film in the US and abroad.

NY —EDUCATIONAL FILM LIBRARY ASSOCIATION, Film Reference Library, 45 John St, New York, 10038. Nadine Covert, Exec Dir
Holdings: Vols (2600) Cat Pix 16mm Films Filmstrips
Budget: ($1500)
Notes: Primarily a print collection emphasizing the documentary and educational film areas, but also film as art, animation and independent film in general. Maintain film title file of over 60,000 cards (primarily educational film titles), incl credit information, running time, release date, summary, and distributor. File is a mixture of EFLA evaluations, LC cards, etc. Subject file also separates film flyers by subject or topic. Maintain festivals file (film festivals, educational film festivals, etc); a film library administration file; a filmmakers file (with bio, credits, clippings, program notes); and a vertical file (incl information on grants, distribution, showcases, film activities in the metropolitan area and in major film centers around the country). Membership organization providing telephone, mail and in-person reference. Open to the general public. Do not publish a catalog, but publish annual Film Library Administration bibliography of current or noteworthy reference books for $2.00.

MOVING PICTURES, EXPERIMENTAL

CA —CALIFORNIA INSTITUTE OF THE ARTS, Library, 24700 McBean Pkwy, Valencia, 91355. James Elrod, Dir
Holdings: Vols (61,000) Cat Videotapes 16mm Films
Budget: ($7500)
Notes: Incl 320 videotapes and 776 16mm films.

NY —ANTHOLOGY FILM ARCHIVES, 491 Broadway, New York, 10012. Jonas Mekas, Dir; Nadia Shtendara, Librn
Holdings: Vols Cat Periodicals Mss Pix
Notes: Documents and associated items

MOVING PICTURES, EXPERIMENTAL (cont.)

relating to film and video as art, with special emphasis on critical material on experimental and avant-garde films. Published bibliography of the collection: *The Essential Cinema,* vol 1, ed by P Adams Sitney (New York: Anthology Film Archives & New York Univ Press, 1975).
NY —NEW YORK PUBLIC LIBRARY, Performing Arts Research Center, Billy Rose Theatre Collection, 111 Amsterdam Ave, New York, 10023. Dorothy L Swerdlove, Cur
Holdings: Cat
See also entry under Moving Pictures - History.

MOVING PICTURES, FOREIGN

CA —UNIVERSITY OF CALIFORNIA, LOS ANGELES, Theater Arts Library, Los Angeles, 90024. Edward Shreeves, Chairman, Bibliographers Group; Audree Malkin, Head, Theater Arts Library
Holdings: Vols (12,500) Cat Mss Films
Notes: Major research collections covering the historical, critical, aesthetic, biographical and technical aspects of film, television and radio, and the non-book and primary source material in these fields. Also 166,000 pamphlets, photographs, microforms and sound recordings. Incl over 4,000,000 moving picture stills, over 32,000 screenplays, and scripts from American and British Films. Incl 1740 radio scripts and a collection of 3000 television scripts. Also incl portraits, clippings files, film festival programs, motion picture programs, lobby cards, original sketches and production materials; the personal and business papers, records and correspondence of actors, directors, producers, art directors and screen and television writers. Incl 100,000 mss. Extensive poster collection (over 7000, 1915 to date), many forPolish and Czech productions. Limited photocopying.
CA —UNIVERSITY OF CALIFORNIA, LOS ANGELES, Theater Arts Library, Los Angeles, 90024. Edward Shreeves, Chairman, Bibliographers Group; Audree Malkin, Head, Theater Arts Library
Notes: Mexican Motion Picture Production Stills: approx 35,000 stills from motion pictures made by Mexican production companies, 1950-1960.
NY —NEW YORK PUBLIC LIBRARY, Performing Arts Research Center, Billy Rose Theatre Collection, 111 Amsterdam Ave, New York, 10023. Dorothy L Swerdlove, Cur
Holdings: Cat
See also entry under Moving Pictures - History.

MOVING PICTURES, GERMAN

DC —LIBRARY OF CONGRESS, Motion Pictures, Broadcasting and Recorded Sound Div, Washington, 20540.
Notes: German films, 1930s and 1940s, incl silent and sound features, newsreels, and educational, entertainment, documentary, and propaganda shorts.
NY —NEW YORK PUBLIC LIBRARY, Performing Arts Research Center, Billy Rose Theatre Collection, 111 Amsterdam Ave, New York, 10023. Dorothy L Swerdlove, Cur
Holdings: Cat

NY —VISUAL STUDIES WORKSHOP, Research Center, 31 Prince St, Rochester, 14607. Linn Underhill, Coordr; Robert Bretz, Librn
Holdings: Vols (8000) Cat Pix Slides Audiotapes Videotapes
Notes: Strong emphasis on photography (over 1,000,000 pictures) and the photographic arts in many subject areas incl in this volume. Heavy emphasis on early photographic processes and collections of examples of them. Also collections of individual photographers' works.

MOVING PICTURES, ITALIAN

DC —LIBRARY OF CONGRESS, Motion Pictures, Broadcasting and Recorded Sound Div, Washington, 20540.
Notes: 500 documentary, newsreel, feature, educational, and propaganda films produced in Italy between 1930 and 1943.

MOVING PICTURES, JAPANESE

DC —LIBRARY OF CONGRESS, Motion Pictures, Broadcasting and Recorded Sound Div, Washington, 20540.
Holdings: Vols 1300
Notes: Japanese feature films, newsreels, documentaries and short subjects from 1930s and early 1940s.

MOVING PICTURES, POLISH

CA —THE POLISH ARTS AND CULTURE FOUNDATION, 1290 Sutter St, San Francisco, 94109. Wanda Tomczykowska, President
Notes: Mostly on art and culture of Poland, documentary history.

MOVING PICTURES, TALKING

CA —CALIFORNIA INSTITUTE OF THE ARTS, Library, 24700 McBean Pkwy, Valencia, 91355. James Elrod, Dir
Holdings: Vols (61,000) Cat Videotapes 16mm Films
Budget: ($7500)
Notes: Incl 320 videotapes and 776 16mm films.
IL —UNIVERSITY OF ILLINOIS, URBANA/CHAMPAIGN, Library, 1408 W Gregory Drive, Urbana, 61801. Norman B Brown, Asst Dir for Special Collections
Holdings: Cat Mss Pix Tapes
Notes: The papers of Joseph T Tykociner (a pioneer in the field of wireless, electronics, sound movies and zetetics). Incl correspondence, notes, books, articles and reprints, photographs and negatives, biographical materials and sound tapes.
NY —NEW YORK PUBLIC LIBRARY, Performing Arts Research Center, Billy Rose Theatre Collection, 111 Amsterdam Ave, New York, 10023. Dorothy L Swerdlove, Cur
Holdings: Cat

MOVING PICTURES, WIDE SCREEN see Wide Screen Processes (Cinematography)

MOVING PICTURES AS COMMUNICATION

IL —UNIVERSITY OF ILLINOIS, URBANA/CHAMPAIGN, Library, Communications Library, 122 Gregory Hall, Urbana, 61801. Nancy Allen, Librn
Holdings: Vols (18,000) Cat
Budget: ($27,000)
Notes: Motion picture history, theory and effects.

MOVING PICTURES IN EDUCATION

NY —EDUCATIONAL FILM LIBRARY ASSOCIATION, Film Reference Library, 45 John St, New York, 10038. Nadine Covert, Exec Dir
Holdings: Vols (2600) Cat Pix 16mm Films Filmstrips
Budget: ($1500)
Notes: Primarily a print collection emphasizing the documentary and educational film areas, but also film as art, animation and independent film in general. Maintain film title file of over 60,000 cards (primarily educational film titles), incl credit information, running time, release date, summary, and distributor. File is a mixture of EFLA evaluations, LC cards, etc. Subject file also separates film flyers by subject or topic. Maintain festivals file (film festivals, educational film festivals, etc); a film library administration file; a filmmakers file (with bio, credits, clippings, program notes); and a vertical file (incl information on grants, distribution, showcases, film activities in the metropolitan area and in major film centers around the country). Membership organization providing telephone, mail and in-person reference. Open to the generalpublic. Do not publish a catalog, but publish annual Film Library Administration bibliography of current or noteworthy reference books for $2.00.

MOWAT, FARLEY, 1921-

ON —MCMASTER UNIVERSITY, Mills Memorial Library, Div of Archives & Research Collections, Hamilton, L8S 4L6, Can. G R Hill, Univ Librn
Holdings: Mss
Notes: Original mss and research files for all published books, incl *The People of the Deer, Tundra, Never Cry Wolf,* etc. Also correspondence. Collection partially described in *McMaster University Library Research News,* vol 2, no 6, September 1974.

MOWRER, PAUL SCOTT

IL —NEWBERRY LIBRARY, 60 W Walton St, Chicago, 60610. Diana Haskell, Cur of Modern Mss
Holdings: Cat Mss
Notes: Incl nearly 700 pieces. Restricted use: noncirculating.

MOYER, BURTON J., 1912-1973

CA —UNIVERSITY OF CALIFORNIA, BERKELEY, Bancroft Library, Manuscripts Division, Berkeley, 94720. James D Hart, Dir
Notes: Papers.

MOZAMBIQUE

CA —HOOVER INSTITUTION ON WAR, REVOLUTION & PEACE, Stanford University, Stanford, 94305. Milorad M Drachkovitch, Archivist
Notes: Collection of leaflets, newsletters, pamphlets, and other ephemera of various political action groups and other organizations, 1969-1974, relating to political and economic developments in southern African countries, incl Angola, Mozambique, Rhodesia (Zimbabwe), Union of South Africa, and South West Africa (Namibia). 5 ms boxes.

MOZART, WOLFGANG AMADEUS

CA —UNIVERSITY OF CALIFORNIA, BERKELEY, Humanities-Social Sciences Libraries, Music Library, 24 Morrison Hall, Berkeley, 94720. Michael A Keller, Head Librn
Holdings: Vols 3000 Cat Mss
Notes: The Alfred Einstein *Nachlass* comprises a scholar's working library in music history (ca 2000 vols), plus a special collection of research materials devoted to Mozart, and to Einsteins's studies of the Italian madrigal. The collection also incl a file of music criticism by Einstein and selected correspondence; *Cum Notis Variorum, the Newsletter of the Music Library of the University of California* (Published 10 times annually since April 1976).
IL —NEWBERRY LIBRARY, 60 W Walton St, Chicago, 60610. Diana Haskell, Cur of Modern Mss
Holdings: Vols 800 Cat
Notes: Books about Mozart. Also six autograph scores.
NY —NEW YORK PUBLIC LIBRARY, Music Div, 111 Amsterdam Ave, New York, 10023. Frank C Campbell, Chief
WA —UNIVERSITY OF WASHINGTON LIBRARIES, Music Library, DN-10, Seattle, 98195. David A Wood, Music Librn
Budget: ($7373)
Notes: The Eric Offenbacher Collection of

MOZART, WOLFGANG AMADEUS (cont.)

pre-LP recordings of the vocal music of Mozart, 1,200 items.

MS (MAGAZINE)

MA —RADCLIFFE COLLEGE, Arthur & Elizabeth Schlesinger Library on the History of Women in America, 3 James St, Cambridge, 02138. Patricia Miller King, Dir; Eva Moseley, Cur of Mss
Notes: Over a decade's worth of letters to the editor from *MS* readers whose lives have been touched by the women's movement; most, except ERA letters are restricted.

MU-YU-SHU FOLK LITERATURE

WA —UNIVERSITY OF WASHINGTON LIBRARIES, East Asia Library, DO-27, Seattle, 98195. Karl Lo, Head
Holdings: Vols (300,000) Cat Microforms Budget: ($200,000)
Notes: Southwest China: Joseph Rock Collection, ca 2000 vols; modern Chinese poetry, 1919 to date: ca 700 titles; Asian art, esp Japanese painting: 4097 vols; Tiao-yu-t'ai movement in the US: ca 400 items of periodicals and pamphlets; modern Korean poetry, ancient and modern: ca 1000 titles; Mu-yo-shu folk literature: ca 1000 items.

MUGGERIDGE, MALCOLM

IL —WHEATON COLLEGE, Buswell Memorial Library, Wheaton, 60187. Paul Snezek, Library Dir
Holdings: Vols 80 Cat Mss
Notes: The collection includes books videos, cassettes, articles and manuscripts, by and about Muggeridge.

MUGGLETON, LODOWICKE

SC —UNIVERSITY OF SOUTH CAROLINA, Thomas Cooper Library, Columbia, 29208. Kenneth E Toombs, Dir of Libraries; Roger Mortimer, Rare Book Librn
Holdings: Vols 45 Cat
Notes: One of the few very strong collections of Muggletonian theology.

MUGNIER, GEORGE F.

LA —NEW ORLEANS PUBLIC LIBRARY, Louisiana Div, 219 Loyola Ave, New Orleans, 70140. Collin B Hamer Jr, Head; Brenda M Osbey, Library Associate
Holdings: Cat Maps Pix
Notes: Louisiana and New Orleans Picture File Collection ranges from the late 19th century-date and incl the following separate collections: Alexander Allison (ca 1898-1951, 337 pieces); Charles Franck (ca 1920-50, 170 pieces); Leda Plauche (ca 1935-53, 220 pieces); C Milo Williams (ca 1910, 85 pieces); Wilson S Howell (ca 1890, 49 pieces); Grauman Marks (ca 1960, 268 pieces); Robert Tallant (ca 1940-50, 70 pieces); Robert E Tracy (1959, 87 pieces); Anthony J Flaherty (ca 1970-84, 83 pieces); George F Mugnier (1880-1920, 186 pieces); Color Slides (ca 1945-date, 500 pieces); 30,000 photographs incl 500 color slides and 104 negatives. Use of the material is restricted to on-site research. Publication must be accompanied by credit cut line.

MUHAMMADAN CIVILIZATION see Civilization, Islamic

MUHAMMADAN PHILOSOPHY see Philosophy, Islamic

MUHLENBERG, HENRY MELCHIOR, AND FAMILY

CT —TRINITY COLLEGE LIBRARY, 300 Summit St, Hartford, 06106. Peter J Knapp, Archivist
Holdings: Uncat // Mss Pix
Notes: Late 18th and 19th century mss, letter, diaries, etc of the Curtis Family of Connecticut and New York, with emphasis on: William Edmond (1755-1838), US Congressman from Conn; Holbrook Curtis (1787-1858); William Edmond Curtis (1823-1880), Chief Justice of Superior Court of New York; Mary Ann Scovill Curtis (1831-1908); and William Edmond Curtis Jr, (1855-1923), US Asst Secy of the Treasury. Incl on basis of relation through marriage are late 18th and 19th century mss, letters and diaries of the Hiester, McLanahan and Muhlenberg Families of Pennsylvania, with emphasis on Joseph Hiester (1752-1832), US Congressman and Governor of Pennsylvania; and Andrew Gregg (1755-1835), US Congressman and Senator from Pennsylvania. 12 linear feet.

PA —MUHLENBERG COLLEGE, Haas Library, 2400 Chew St, Allentown, 18104. Linda Bowers
Holdings: Mss
Notes: Original mss, letters, etc, with numerous letters signed by famous Americans of the 18th and 19th centuries.

PA —LUTHERAN THEOLOGICAL SEMINARY, Krauth Memorial Library, 7301 Germantown Ave, Philadelphia, 19119. Rev David J Wartluft, Dir Libr
Holdings: Vols (3500) Cat Mss Microforms
Notes: Incl published minutes of United Lutheran Church in America, Lutheran Church in America, General Council and General Synod affiliated churches. Archives of General Council housed in library, also New Jersey Synod, Northeastern Pennsylvania Synod, Southeastern Pennsylvania Synod, Upper New York Synod and Slovak Zion Synod. Also incl papers of early Lutheran leaders: Muhlenbergs, Henkels, etc.

MUIR, EDWIN

IL —NEWBERRY LIBRARY, 60 W Walton St, Chicago, 60610. Diana Haskell, Cur of Modern Mss
Holdings: Cat
Notes: Good collection of several hundred first and subsequent editions, criticism of Muir's work, etc.

NV —UNIVERSITY OF NEVADA, RENO, University Library, Special Collections Dept, Reno, 89557. Robert E Blesse, Head
Holdings: // Vols (72) Cat Other appearances 410 Cat
Notes: Includes individual works by author in all editions including translations; also prefaces, introductions, published correspondence, appearances in anthologies, periodicals, etc. Bibliographical research collection, part of Modern Authors Collection.

MUIR, JOHN

CA —AZUSA PACIFIC COLLEGE, Marshburn Memorial Library, Citrus & Alosta, Azusa, 91702. Edward Peterman, Librn
Holdings: Vols (150) Uncat
Notes: The Odo B Stade Collection of Literary First Editions. No photocopying.

CA —UNIVERSITY OF THE PACIFIC, Library, Stockton, 95211. Hiram L Davis, Dir of Libraries
Holdings: Cat Mss Maps Pix
Notes: 80 document boxes, organized in seven series: correspondence from 1854-1914, incl letters received and letters sent; journals from 1854-1913; mss and published works, 1860-1914; related articles and scraps, 1873-1967; related papers, 1850-1966; pictorial works, and a collection of books and other miscellaneous documents which were originally part of John Muir's library. The entire collection is on indefinite loan to the university from the grandchildren of John Muir.

VA —UNIVERSITY OF VIRGINIA, Alderman Library, Clifton Waller Barrett Collection, Charlottesville, 22901. Joan St C Crane, Cur of American Literature Collections
Notes: Papers.

MUKDEN INCIDENT, 1931

CA —HOOVER INSTITUTION ON WAR, REVOLUTION & PEACE, Stanford University, Stanford, 94305. Milorad M Drachkovitch, Archivist
Holdings: Mss Maps Pix
Notes: Papers of Vladimir D Pastuhov, 1927-1938, incl correspondence, memoranda, reports, interviews, maps, photographs, and printed matter, relating to the investigation of the Manchurian incident of 1931 by the Lytton Commission of the League of Nations, of which V D Pastuhov was Secretary. Most of the material is in English; some is in French, Russian and Chinese. 58 ms boxes and 3 oversize packages. 13 photograph albums.

MULLAN, JOHN, 1859-1940

DC —GEORGETOWN UNIVERSITY, Library, Special Collections Div, 37 & O Sts NW, Washington, 20057. George M Barringer, Special Collections Librn; Nicholas B Sheetz, Mss Librn
Holdings: Mss Cat
Notes: The papers of the explorer John Mullan (1859-1940), containing correspondence, letter books, legal documents, photographs, and clippings; for the most part pertaining to Mullan's activities as claims agent for Washington Territory; the states of California, Oregon, Nevada, and Colorado; and a few individuals. Of interest for the study of mandamus and estoppel in contract law in the Progressive Era, as well as in the study of claims activities, and anti-lawyer sentiment in the West during the same period. There is also present a small amount of material on the Military Road from Fort Walla Walla to Fort Benton.

MULKS FAMILY

NY —CORNELL UNIVERSITY LIBRARIES, Collection of Regional History, Dept of Manuscripts and Univ Archives, Ithaca, 14853.
Notes: Incl 27 pieces; papers, 1799-1877; deeds, mortgages and other legal documents concerning the acquisition of land by the Mulks family

MULLER, HERMANN, 1890-1967

IN —INDIANA UNIVERSITY, Lilly Library, Seventh St, Bloomington, 47405. William R Cagle, Librn
Holdings: // Mss Pix
Notes: Collections incl papers of geneticists and biologists, most notably those of Nobel Prize winner Hermann Joseph Muller, 1890-1967, and Tracy Morton Sonneborn, 1905-1981. Also papers of plant geneticist Ralph Erskine Cleland, 1892-1971, and Paul Weatherwax, 1888-1976.

MULTIPLE PERSONALITY

NC —DUKE UNIVERSITY, William R Perkins Library, Manuscript Dept, Durham, 27706. Ellen Gartrell, Cur of Mss
Notes: The personal papers of Chris Costner Sizemore, who is widely known as the subject of the book and movie, "The Three Faces of Eve." Incl poems and other writings, diaries, drawings, photographs, tapes of interviews, and some printed material.

MULVIHILL, WILLIAM

MA —BOSTON UNIVERSITY, Mugar Memorial Library, Special Collections Dept, 771 Commonwealth Ave, Boston, 02215. Howard B Gotlieb, Dir
Holdings: Cat Mss

MUMFORD, BENJAMIN MAVERICK

NY —NEW YORK HISTORICAL SOCIETY, Library, 170 Central Park W, New York, 10024. James Gregory, Librn
Notes: The papers of historian and judge William W Campbell; business papers of Benjamin Maverick Mumford, insurance broker and ship owner. About 2300 items.

MUMFORD, LEWIS

CA —FRANCIS BACON LIBRARY, 655 N Dartmouth Ave, Claremont, 91711.

MUMFORD, LEWIS (cont.)

Elizabeth S Wrigley, Dir
Holdings: Mss Pix
Notes: Arensberg's miscellaneous
correspondence with American literary
figures (1920's-50's) including Bruce Bliven,
Catherine Drinker Bowen, Kay Boyle, Witter
Bynner, Edwin Corle, Helen A Keller,
Lysander Kemp, Kenneth Macgowan, John
Macy, Henry Miller, Lewis Mumford,
Clifford Odets, Kenneth Patchen, Irving
Stone, and William Carlos Williams.

MUNDELL, ELMORE H.

GA —UNIVERSITY OF GEORGIA,
Libraries, Special Collections Division,
Athens, 30602. Vesta Lee Gordon, Asst Dir
for Special Collections
Holdings: Vols (8000)
Notes: One of the larger collections of
private press books, pamphlets, and
ephemera. The Elmore H Mundell
Collection of materials from over 1200
different private printers.

MUNGO, RAYMOND

MA —BOSTON UNIVERSITY, Mugar
Memorial Library, Special Collections Dept,
771 Commonwealth Ave, Boston, 02215.
Howard B Gotlieb, Dir
Holdings: Cat Mss

MUNI, PAUL

NY —NEW YORK PUBLIC LIBRARY,
Performing Arts Research Center, Billy Rose
Theatre Collection, 111 Amsterdam Ave,
New York, 10023. Dorothy L Swerdlove,
Cur
Holdings: Cat Mss Pix
Notes: Papers, scrapbooks, mss, photographs,
memorabilia, etc.

MUNICIPAL ADMINISTRATION see
Municipal Government

MUNICIPAL BUDGETS

DC —METROPOLITAN WASHINGTON
COUNCIL OF GOVERNMENTS,
Research Library, 1875 Eye St NW, Suite
200, Washington, 20006. Suan Kalish, Librn
Holdings: Vols (3000) Cat Microforms
Notes: Contains (on 75 reels of microfilm)
archives of Maryland-National Park and
Planning Commission, archives of the
Council of Governments, and audits and
financial reports of local governments (1950-
date). Also incl annual reports, planning
reports and budgets from each jurisdiction
(1973-date).

MUNICIPAL CODES

DC —NATIONAL LEAGUE OF CITIES,
Municipal Reference Service, 1301
Pennsylvania Ave NW, Washington, 20004.
Olivia Kredel, Mgr
Holdings: Vols (20,000)
Notes: City reports and plans, financial
reports, budgets, commission reports, plans,
etc. Federal legislation on urban affairs, etc.

MUNICIPAL DOCUMENTS

CA —LOS ANGELES PUBLIC LIBRARY,
Municipal Reference Library, Rm 530, City
Hall E, 200 N Main St, Los Angeles, 90012.
C Grimsley, Senior Librn
Holdings: Vols (86,000) Cat
Budget: ($33,000)
Notes: Emphasis on cities over 500,000 with
special collection of municipal documents
from large cities. Biographical material on
local government officials.
CA —UNIVERSITY OF CALIFORNIA, LOS
ANGELES, Research Library, Public Affairs
Service, 405 Hilgard Ave, Los Angeles,
90024. Edward Shreeves, Chairman,
Bibliographers Group; Eugenia Eaton, Head,
Public Affairs Service
Holdings: Microforms
Notes: Depository for the official

publications of California cities and counties,
the state of California, the United States
government, the United Nations and some of
its specialized agencies (including the Food
and Agricultural Organization and
UNESCO), and such regional organizations
as the European Communities and
Organization of American States. Selected
publications of other American cities and
counties, of the other states and possessions
of the United States, of interstate
organizations, and of foreign governments
(with emphasis on major world powers,
Africa, Latin America and the Near and
Middle East) and intergovernmental
organizations.
DC —LIBRARY OF CONGRESS, Serial and
Government Publications Division,
Washington, 20540.
Notes: Serials. One of the largest and most
extensive collections in the world, incl
periodicals; scientific and learned journals in
all languages and in all fields except
agriculture and medicine; US Government
serials (Federal, State, County, and
Municipal); national foreign government
serials from all countries; provincial serials
from provinces possessing autonomy;
municipal serials from principal cities;
newspapers (850,000 unbound issues, 75,000
bound vols, 270,000 microfilm reels), 12,000
microprint cards of early American
newspapers, 1704-1820, incl 1500 titles
currently received, 500 of these being
representative titles from all States of the
Union and 1000 from all foreign countries.
DC —US BUREAU OF THE CENSUS,
Library, Federal Office Bldg 3, Rm 2451,
Washington, 20233. Betty Baxtresser, Chief,
ASD Library Branch
Holdings: Vols (64,000) Cat
Notes: Periodic reports from the
governments of the states, counties, cities
with populations of over 10,000 and selected
special districts of the US. Emphasis is on
the financial aspects of governments.
Reports are listed in a computer print-out
comprising a volume of the printed *Catalogs
of the Bureau of the Census Library*.

MUNICIPAL GOVERNMENT

AZ —TUCSON PUBLIC LIBRARY,
Governmental Reference Library, PO Box
27210, City Hall, Tucson, 85726. Ann
Strickland, Librn
Holdings: Vols (4000) Cat Maps Audiotapes
Microforms
Notes: Special emphasis on public
administration, including public finance,
public personnel management, social
services, urban planning, public
transportation, public works, water
management, solid waste management,
public recreation and government of growing
southwestern US cities in 200,000 to 500,
000 population range.
CA —LOS ANGELES PUBLIC LIBRARY,
Municipal Reference Library, Rm 530, City
Hall E, 200 N Main St, Los Angeles, 90012.
C Grimsley, Senior Librn
Holdings: Vols 37,500 Cat
Budget: $14,500
Notes: Emphasis on cities over 500,000 with
special collection of municipal documents
from large cities. Biographical material on
local government officials.
CA —ALAMEDA COUNTY LIBRARY
SYSTEM, Business & Government Library,
2201 Broadway, Oakland, 94612. David
Lewallen, Manager
Holdings: Vols (10,000) Cat Maps
Microforms
Budget: ($50,000)
CA —SACRAMENTO PUBLIC LIBRARY,
828 I St, Sacramento, 95814. Dorothy
Harvey, Librn, Special Collections
Holdings: Vols (4000) Cat
Notes: Incl books on public administration
and police science, local government (city
and county). Have over 4000 Sacramento
city and county documents.
FL —MIAMI-DADE PUBLIC LIBRARY
SYSTEM, Urban Affairs Library, 1 Biscayne
Blvd, Miami, 33132. Richard G Frow, Librn
Holdings: Vols 3078 Cat
Notes: Local government administration and

planning. Incl materials concerning local
government administration and planning
exclusive of Florida, chosen primarily to suit
needs of local governmental officials,
although use by local college students, land
developers and the general public is
considered. Incl 8627 pamphlets cat and 98
periodicals. Library has access to LOGIN
and DIALOG databases.
IL —MUNICIPAL REFERENCE LIBRARY,
City Hall, Rm 1004, Chicago, 60602. Joyce
Malden, Librn
Holdings: Vols (68,000) Cat Maps
Microforms
Budget: ($60,000)
MO —WASHINGTON UNIVERSITY, John
M Olin Library, Lindell & Skinker Blvd,
Saint Louis, 63130. Beryl H Manne,
Archivist
Holdings: Mss Pix Audiotapes 16mm Films
Filmstrips Microforms
Notes: The University Archives and
Research Collection at the John M Olin
Library of Washington University is a
growing ms archives collecting original
source material pertaining to 20th century
political, business, and social welfare history
of the St Louis metropolitan area. Incl the
personal papers of prominent St Louis
politicians, businessmen, engineers,
educators, scientists, architects. Holdings
especially strong in municipal and county
governmental affairs.
NY —NEW YORK STATE DEPT OF
STATE, Community Affairs Library, 162
Washington Ave, Albany, 12231. M L
Johnson, Librn
Holdings: Vols (14,640) Cat
Notes: Local government. Serves as research
arm for official activities. 16,000 items in
vertical files; 150 periodicals. Unique
Community File collection of about 1600
local governments arranged by counties in
the state.
NY —STATE UNIVERSITY OF NEW YORK
AT ALBANY, Library, Special Collections
Dept, 1400 Washington Ave, Albany, 12222.
Marion P Munzer, Coordr
Notes: Personal and family records of
Howard Palfrey Jones (12 linear feet);
correspondence, articles, and texts of
speeches relating to municipal reform;
proposals on tax reforms.
See also entries under Jones, Howard
Palfrey; Taxation
NC —GREENSBORO PUBLIC LIBRARY,
Oral History Program Library, Drawer X-4,
Greensboro, 27402. Eugene Edwin Pfaff, Jr,
Librn
Holdings: Videotapes Audiotapes
Notes: Oral history on the cultural, social,
and economic development of Greensboro
and Guilford County; the program is
expanding to incl prominent North
Carolinians throughout the State. Collection
consists of 42 videotapes and 93 audiotapes
which are uncataloged.
OH —PUBLIC LIBRARY OF CINCINNATI
& HAMILTON COUNTY, Government
and Business Dept, 800 Vine St, Cincinnati,
45202. Paul T Hudson, Head
Holdings: Vols 2000 Cat
Notes: The Murray Seasongood Collection
of Government, Law and Public
Administration contains works on local
government, city management, public
finance and municipal law. The collection
also houses the collected works of Murray
Seasongood.
PA —UNIVERSITY OF PITTSBURGH,
Library, Graduate School of Public and
International Affairs, Forbes Quadrangle, 1st
floor West, Pittsburgh, 15260. Nicholas C
Caruso, Librn
Holdings: Vols (80,000) Cat
Budget: ($150,000)
Notes: The library attempts to collect as
many national economic and social
development plans as possible from the
developing countries of the world. It also
holds city, regional and state plans for
Pennsylvania, particularly, the 9
southwestern counties of Pennsylvania.
TX —DALLAS PUBLIC LIBRARY, Urban
Information Center, 1515 Young St, Dallas,
75201. Mary Todd, Mgr
Holdings: Vols 1550 Cat Microforms
Notes: Collection is being developed to meet

MUNICIPAL GOVERNMENT (cont.)

the information needs of local government and to serve as a depository for municipal publications. At the present time, a separate catalog does not exist.

WA —SEATTLE PUBLIC LIBRARY, Governmental Research Assistance Library, 307 Municipal Bldg, Seattle, 98104. Barbara J Guptill, Librn
Holdings: Vols (18,000) Cat Mss Maps
Budget: ($16,700)
Notes: Includes pamphlets and clippings on municipal affairs, especially Seattle. Emphasis on urban planning, criminal investigation, policy analysis, finance. Also, materials of aid to city employees (7500 vols).

WI —LEGISLATIVE REFERENCE BUREAU LIBRARY, City of Milwaukee, City Hall Rm 404, 200 E Wells St, Milwaukee, 53202. Ronald Leonhardt, Dir
Holdings: Vols (50,000) Cat Mss Maps Pix Microforms
Budget: ($8000)
Notes: Housing, public finance.

PR —UNIVERSITY OF PUERTO RICO, Graduate School of Public Administration, Library, Graduate Social Sciences Bldg, Rio Piedras, 00931. Perfecto Camacho, Library Dir
Holdings: Vols (15,000) Cat
Budget: $22,000
Notes: Public administration, economics, and elections. Especially materials related to or about the separate municipalities of Puerto Rico and the Commonwealth of Puerto Rico. Documents collection.

ON —METROPOLITAN TORONTO LIBRARY, Municipal Reference Library, City Hall, Toronto, M5H 2N1, Can. Margot Hewings, Head
Holdings: Vols (60,000) Cat Maps Pix Microforms Slides VF
Budget: ($112,600)
Notes: Community development; municipal finance; local municipal government; housing; urban pollution; urban transportation; urban affairs; urban geography.

ON —ONTARIO MINISTRY OF TREASURY & ECONOMICS, Library Services, Frost Bldg N, Queen's Park, Toronto, M7A 1Y8, Can. Barbara Weatherhead, Head Librn
Holdings: Vols (100,000) Cat Microforms
Budget: ($76,500)
Notes: Index to Ontario regulations.

MUNICIPAL LEAGUES

DC —NATIONAL LEAGUE OF CITIES, Municipal Reference Service, 1301 Pennsylvania Ave NW, Washington, 20004. Olivia Kredel, Mgr
Holdings: Vols (20,000)
Notes: Collection of publications of state municipal leagues. Archives of National League of Cities.

MUNICIPAL TRANSIT see Local Transit

MUNICIPAL UTILITIES see Public Utilities

MUNICIPALITIES see Cities and Towns

MUNRO, H. H.

NY —ALFRED UNIVERSITY, Herrick Memorial Library, Alfred, 14802. June E Brown, Head Librn
Notes: The Evelyn Tennyson Openhym Collection of modern British literature and social history. Papers, incl correspondence of authors concerned with the business aspects of authorship. Gift of Evelyn Tennyson Openhym of Wellsville, NY. Also, 5300 volumes of British literature.

MUNRO, SIR THOMAS, 1761-1827

WI —UNIVERSITY OF WISCONSIN, MADISON, Memorial Library, South Asian Collection, 728 State St, Madison, 53706.

Jack C Wells, Bibliographer
Notes: Public and private papers as Governor of Madras, India.

MUNZ, PHILIP

†CA —RANCHO SANTA ANA BOTANIC GARDEN LIBRARY, 1500 N College Ave, Claremont, 91711. Beatrice M Beck, Librn
Holdings: Vols (20,000)
Notes: California flora nd gardening, world floras, taxonomic literature, evolutionary biology, and the papers and collections of Marcus Jones and Philip Munz.

MURAL PAINTING AND DECORATION

OH —OHIO STATE UNIVERSITY, Fine Arts Library, 1813 N High St, Columbus, 43210. Susan Wyngaard, Head, Fine Arts Library
Notes: Receive Slavic titles, many on Byzantine frescoes.

MURATHEE LANGUAGE see Marathi Language and Literature

MURCHIE, GUY

MA —BOSTON UNIVERSITY, Mugar Memorial Library, Special Collections Dept, 771 Commonwealth Ave, Boston, 02215. Howard B Gotlieb, Dir
Holdings: Cat Mss Pix
Notes: Mss, correspondence, etc collected in depth; incl publications by or about.

MURDER

NY —NEW YORK STATE HISTORICAL ASSOCIATION, Library, Lake Rd, Cooperstown, 13326. Amy Barnum, Librn
Holdings: Vols 400 Cat
Notes: At the present time a marked copy of T M McDade's *Annals of Murder* (1961), with additions, serves as a finding aide. Essentially collection consists of 18th-19th century American murder pamphlets. Noncirculating.

NY —NEW YORK HISTORICAL SOCIETY, Library, 170 Central Park W, New York, 10024. James Gregory, Librn
Notes: Books and pamphlets devoted to homicide and murder.

PA —TEMPLE UNIVERSITY LIBRARIES, Special Collections Dept, Conwellana-Templana Collection, 13 & Berks St, Philadelphia, 19122. Miriam I Crawford, Cur
Holdings: Vols (22)// Cat Mss Pix
Notes: Personal papers of Negley K Teeters. The published writings, manuscripts, correspondence, and research materials of Teeters, criminologist and faculty member of Temple University, covering the years 1927-1971. Contains extended correspondence with his co-author, Harry Elmer Barnes, from 1940 to 1968, and materials dealing with their investigation of the murder trial of Caryl Chessman, which failed to halt his execution in California in 1960. *Descriptive Inventory of the Personal Papers of Negley K Teeters* (1896-1971) (Conwellana-Templana Collection, Temple University, 1971, addenda 1972 and 1974. 6 leaves. Unpublished typescript).

MURDOCH, IRIS

IA —UNIVERSITY OF IOWA, University Libraries, Iowa City, 52242. Robert A McCown, Mss Librn
Holdings: Vols 170 Cat Mss
Notes: Collection includes drafts of 16 novels and other manuscripts. See William M Murray, "A Note on the Iris Murdoch Manuscripts in the University of Iowa Libraries," *Modern Fiction Studies* 15 (Autumn, 1969), pp 445-448; and Frank Baldanza, "The Murdoch Manuscripts at the University of Iowa: An Addendum," *Modern Fiction Studies* 16 (Summer, 1970), pp 201-202.

NV —UNIVERSITY OF NEVADA, RENO, University Library, Special Collections Dept, Reno, 89557. Robert E Blesse, Head
Holdings: Vols (93) Cat Other appearances

75 Cat
Notes: Includes individual works by author in all editions including translations; also prefaces, introductions, published correspondence, appearances in anthologies, periodicals, etc. Bibliographical research collection, part of Modern Authors Collection.

MURPHY, ARTHUR, 1727-1805

OH —OHIO UNIVERSITY, Vernon R Alden Library, Department of Archives and Special Collections, Athens, 45701. Gary A Hunt, Head
Holdings: Vols 125 Cat
Notes: The J Homer Caskey Collection. Incl works by Arthur Murphy and Edward Moore, in various editions, plus related items, mostly 18th century drama.

MURPHY, GARDNER

KS —MENNINGER FOUNDATION, Archives, 5600 W Sixth St, Box 829, Topeka, 66601. Alice Brand, Librn; Mark West, Archivist
Notes: 75 boxes, 1952-69. Incl reports, correspondence, and memoranda. Most of his papers relate to his work at the Foundation.

MURPHY, HERBERT H., 1881-1964

BC —UNIVERSITY OF VICTORIA, McPherson Library, Victoria, V8W 3H5, Can.
Notes: Medical Administrator. Personal diary of Dr Murphy when he was setting up the original Victoria Cancer Clinic.

MURPHY, JOHN

MA —BOSTON UNIVERSITY, Mugar Memorial Library, Special Collections Dept, 771 Commonwealth Ave, Boston, 02215. Howard B Gotlieb, Dir
Holdings: Cat Mss
Notes: Mss, correspondence, etc collected in depth; incl publications by or about.

MURPHY, LOIS B., 1902-

KS —MENNINGER FOUNDATION, Archives, 5600 W Sixth St, Box 829, Topeka, 66601. Alice Brand, Librn; Mark West, Archivist
Notes: 70 boxes, 1937-69. Consists of research material, correspondence and mss.

MURPHY, ROBERT WILLIAM, 1902-1971

MA —BOSTON UNIVERSITY, Mugar Memorial Library, Special Collections Dept, 771 Commonwealth Ave, Boston, 02215. Howard B Gotlieb, Dir
Holdings: Cat Mss Pix
Notes: Mss, correspondence, etc collected in depth; incl publications by or about.

MURPHY, WILLIAM CAMERON, 1905-1961

BC —UNIVERSITY OF VICTORIA, McPherson Library, Victoria, V8W 3H5, Can.
Notes: Incl 3 cm, 1945; Collins Royal Diary 1945 with holograph entries from Sunday, February 18, 1945; carbon transcripts.

MURRAY, JAMES E.

MT —UNIVERSITY OF MONTANA, Library, Missoula, 59801. Katherine Schaefer, Special Collections Librn
Holdings: Vols 6300 Cat Mss Maps Pix Slides Microforms
Notes: About 200 ms collections, measuring 5000 feet, with emphasis on Montana business and political history (papers of Senators Joseph M Dixon, James E Murray, and US Ambassador James W Gerard). Also first editions and mss of Montana authors.

MURRAY, REV. JOHN COURTNEY, S.J.

DC —GEORGETOWN UNIVERSITY, Library, Special Collections Div, 37 & O Sts

MURRAY, REV. JOHN COURTNEY, S.J. (cont.)

NW, Washington, 20057. George M
Barringer, Special Collections Librn;
Nicholas B Sheetz, Mss Librn
Holdings: Cat Mss
Notes: His papers, etc.

MURRAY, JOHN MIDDLETON

IL —NORTHWESTERN UNIVERSITY,
Library, Special Collections Dept, 1937
Sheridan Rd, Evanston, 60201. R Russell
Maylone, Cur
Holdings: Vols 450 Cat Mss
Notes: Incl 137 letters from T S Eliot to
Stephen Spender, and 70 letters from Eliot
to John Middleton Murray.
BC —UNIVERSITY OF VICTORIA,
McPherson Library, Victoria, V8W 3H5,
Can.

MURRAY, WILLIAM HENRY

OK —UNIVERSITY OF OKLAHOMA,
Bizzell Memorial Library, Western History
Collections, 401 W Brooks, Norman, 73069.
John Ezell, Cur
Holdings: Vols Mss Maps Documents Pix
Notes: Governor of Oklahoma; US
Representative. His papers.

MURROW, EDWARD R.

MA —TUFTS UNIVERSITY, Fletcher School
of Law & Diplomacy, Murrow Center of
Public Diplomacy, Medford, 02155. Natalie
Schatz, Cur of Special Collections
Holdings: Vols (1500)// Cat Mss Pix
Phonorecords Audiotapes 16mm Films
Notes: Professional correspondence, reports,
speeches, scripts and interviews relating to
Murrow's career in broadcasting; reports,
hearings and speeches from his years as
Director of USIA, as well as personal
correspondence, memorabilia, books, some
films and audio tapes. 43,300 pieces.

MUSCLES

NY —UNIVERSITY OF ROCHESTER,
School of Medicine and Dentistry, Edward
G Miner Library, 601 Elmwood Ave,
Rochester, 14642. Lucretia McClure,
Medical Librn; Janet Brady Berk, History of
Medicine Librn
Holdings: Slides
Notes: Very rare historical collection of
some 300 glass slides, most of which relate
to human gait, the foot, footwear, and
myodynamics.

MUSCLES—DISEASES

CT —NEWINGTON CHILDREN'S
HOSPITAL, Professional Library, 181 E
Cedar St, Newington, 06111. Jean Long,
Librn
Holdings: Vols (3500) Cat
Budget: ($6500)
NY —CORNELL UNIVERSITY MEDICAL
COLLEGE, Samuel J Wood Library, 1300
York Ave, New York, 10021. Erich
Meyerhoff, Dir
Holdings: Vols (9000) Cat Films
Notes: All aspects of muscle diseases.
NY —MUSCULAR DYSTROPHY
ASSOCIATION, 810 Seventh Ave, New
York, 10019. Marianthe Pappas, Librn
Holdings: Vols 8770 Cat
Budget: $55,000
Notes: All phases of muscular diseases. Incl
some films.

MUSCOGEE INDIANS see Creek Indians

MUSCOLOGY see Bryology

MUSCULAR ATROPHY see Atrophy, Muscular

MUSCULAR COORDINATION see Motor Ability

MUSCULAR DISEASES see Muscles—Diseases

MUSCULAR DYSTROPHY

NY —CORNELL UNIVERSITY MEDICAL
COLLEGE, Samuel J Wood Library, 1300

York Ave, New York, 10021. Erich
Meyerhoff, Dir
Holdings: Vols (9000) Cat Films
Notes: All aspects of muscle diseases.
NY —MUSCULAR DYSTROPHY
ASSOCIATION, 810 Seventh Ave, New
York, 10019. Marianthe Pappas, Librn
Holdings: Vols 8770 Cat
Budget: $55,000
Notes: All phases of muscular diseases. Incl
some films.

MUSCULAR PHYSIOLOGY

†CT —YALE UNIVERSITY, Medical Library,
333 Cedar St, New Haven, 06520.

MUSEUM CONSERVATION (MATERIALS CONSERVATION) see Conservation, Museum (Materials Conservation)

MUSEUM PERIODICALS see Periodicals, Museum

MUSEUMS—PUBLICATIONS

IL —FIELD MUSEUM OF NATURAL
HISTORY, Library, Roosevelt Rd & Lake
Shore Dr, Chicago, 60605. W Peyton
Fawcett, Librn; Benjamin W Williams, Assoc
Librn
Holdings: Vols (210,000) Cat
Budget: ($100,000)
Notes: Extensive collections--publications of
learned societies and institutions and
monographic works--in all fields of natural
history, with emphasis on taxonomy and
evolutionary biology; and on museum
publications, American and foreign:
anthropology, especially archaeology and
ethnology of the Americas, Africa, East
Asia, and Oceania; botany, particularly
strong for the Americas; geology, chiefly
paleontology and meteoritic studies; and
zoology, worldwide (birds, fishes, insects,
mammals, mollusks, reptiles and
amphibians).
ON —NATIONAL MUSEUMS OF
CANADA, Library Services Directorate,
Ottawa, K1A 0M8, Can. Valerie
Monkhouse, Director
Holdings: Vols 40,000 Cat
Budget: $43,000
Notes: Chiefly publications issued by
museums (throughout the world), many
acquired through publications exchange
programs, and also general works on
museology, conservation of museum objects,
architecture, display and other related
subjects.

MUSEUMS, CHILDREN'S see Children's Museums

MUSEUMS, MUSIC see Music Museums

MUSEUMS AND MUSEOLOGY

CA —FIRST INTERSTATE BANK, Athletic
Foundation, 2141 W Adams, Los Angeles,
90018. W R Schroeder, Managing Dir
Notes: One of the most extensive library and
museum collections relating to sports, the
Olympic Games, etc. Bound vols of sports
sections from several newspapers. Large
collection of college and university annuals
and yearbooks; souvenir publications from
amateur, college, and professional sporting
events. Also, large museum collection of
sports memorabilia, ledger of halls of fame
with thousands of names of outstanding
athletes in all sports. Repository for the
Association of Sports Museums and Halls of
Fame. Noncirculating.
CT —LEE ASH, (personal collection), 66
Humiston Dr, Bethany, 06525.
Holdings: Cat Mss Pix
Notes: Incl books, letters, ephemera, etc.
DC —HOWARD UNIVERSITY, Moorland-
Spingarn Research Center, 500 Howard
Place NW, Washington, 20059. Clifford L
Muse, Jr, Acting Dir
Holdings: Vols (106,086) Mss Maps Pix

Slides Phonorecords Audiotapes 16mm
Films Filmstrips Microforms
Budget: ($854,753)
See also entry under Blacks
DC —NATIONAL ENDOWMENT FOR
THE ARTS, Library, 1100 Pen Ave NW,
Rm 213, Washington, 20506. Christine
Morrison, Arts Librn
Holdings: Vols (6000) Cat
Notes: Incl arts and education and public
policy in the arts.
DC —SMITHSONIAN INSTITUTION,
Archives Div, Washington, 20560. William
W Moss, Archivist
Holdings: Cat Mss Pix
Notes: The Archives holds the records of the
old United States National Museum and of
the current Smithsonian Museums that have
superseded it.
DC —SMITHSONIAN INSTITUTION
LIBRARIES, General Library, Washington,
20560. Mary Claire Grey, Chief Cent Ref &
Loan Servs
Holdings: Vols (79,000) Cat Mss Maps Pix
Slides Microforms
Notes: Incl publications of foreign and
domestic museums, and all phases of
museum work.
HI —BERNICE P BISHOP MUSEUM,
Library, PO Box 19000-A, Honolulu, 96819.
Cynthia Timberlake, Librn
Holdings: Vols (90,000) Cat Mss Maps Pix
Slides Microforms
Budget: ($30,000)
Notes: Only American library devoted
exclusively to the Pacific region. Collection
reflects historical and contemporary research
emphases of Bishop Museum; ie the natural
and cultural history of the Pacific. Areas of
concentration incl archaeology, ethnology,
linguistics, voyages and explorations, history,
vertebrate and invertebrate zoology, botany
and museology. Strong special collections
incl photographs, mss and archives, maps
and art. Publications: Quarterly "Additions
to the Catalog," Dictionary Catalog of the
Library (9 vols and 2 suppl; Boston: G K
Hall, 1964-69).
IL —MUSEUM OF SCIENCE AND
INDUSTRY, Library, 57th St and Lake
Shore Dr, Chicago, 60637. Carla Hayden,
Coordinator
Holdings: Vols Cat Maps Pix Slides
Notes: Occupying the site of the Fine Arts
Building of Chicago's Columbian Exposition
of 1893, the Museum Library has been the
recipient of numerous gifts in this field, not
only of materials from Chicago's Columbian
Expositons, Century of Progress and
Railroad Fairs but also from the New York
World's Fair, St Louis, Paris Exposition
Universelle, San Francisco's Panama-Pacific
etc. Incl blueprints of some buildings and
areas. No separate catalog or index to this
extensive collection.
KY —WESTERN KENTUCKY
UNIVERSITY, The Kentucky Museum and
Library, Bowling Green, 42101. Diane L
Alpert, Cur of the Museum
Holdings: Vols 60 Uncat Pix Slides
Audiotapes
Notes: Also individual and general research
files on 150,000 museum objects and
regional museum collections. No
photocopying.
MA —CHILDREN'S MUSEUM, Resource
Center, Museum Wharf, 300 Congress St,
Boston, 02210. Marie Ariel, Librn; Maria
Russell, Resource Services Mgr
Holdings: Vols (1300) Cat Mss Slides
Audiotapes
Notes: All aspects of the museum profession;
extensive collection of current museum
brochures and serials; exhibit and program
documentation.
MA —HARVARD UNIVERSITY, Harvard
College Library, Fine Arts Library, Fogg
Museum, 32 Quincy St, Cambridge, 02138.
Wolfgang M Freitag, Librn
Holdings: Vols (202,000) Cat Mss Pix Slides
Budget: ($176,500)
Notes: All areas of art history, with
emphasis on Italian primitives, Italian
Renaissánce, master drawings, Romanesque
sculpture, architectural history, ms materials
(particulary American artists'), conservation

MUSEUMS AND MUSEOLOGY (cont.)

and restoration of art objects. Incl the Berenson repertory of photographs from the Harvard Center for Italian Renaissance Studies in Florence, and the Decimal Index to the Art of the Low Countries. Separate card catalogs for books, photographs and lantern slides, registers for ms holdings which are not incl in *National Union Catalog of Manuscript Collections*. Slides total over 230,000; over 745,000 pictures. *Fine Arts Library Catalogue* (14 volumes) and *Catalogue of Auction Sales Catalogues* (1 volume) (Boston: G K Hall, 1972); *A Guide to the Fine Arts Library* (Cambridge, Mass: 1971); *Guide to the Harvard Libraries*, microfiche edition of holdings cataloged through 1981 published 1984 (Munich/New York: Saur).

MA —OLD STURBRIDGE VILLAGE, Research Library, Sturbridge, 01566. Theresa Rini Percy, Librn
Holdings: Cat Pix
Notes: Basic books and periodicals on management of museums, conservation techniques, etc.

MI —UNIVERSITY OF MICHIGAN, Museums Library, Ann Arbor, 48109. Patricia B Yocum, Librn
Holdings: Vols (100,000) Cat Maps Microforms

MO —SAINT LOUIS ART MUSEUM, Richardson Memorial Library, Saint Louis, 63110. Ann B Abid, Librn
Holdings: Vols (30,000) Cat Pix Slides Microforms
Notes: Art history, incl decorative arts, catalogs, exhibitions, etc.

NY —NEW YORK STATE HISTORICAL ASSOCIATION, Library, Lake Rd, Cooperstown, 13326. Amy Barnum, Librn
Holdings: Vols (55,000) Cat Mss Pix Slides
Notes: Noncirculating.

NY —AMERICAN MUSEUM OF NATURAL HISTORY, Library Services Dept, Central Park W & 79th St, New York, 10024. Nina J Root, Chairwoman; Mary Genett, Asst Librn for Reference Services
Holdings: Vols (385,000) Cat Mss Maps Pix Slides Microforms
Notes: Nearly all collections are outstanding for depth of coverage and international range. Early and historic works, rare books, colored illustrations, and relevant serial publications supplement the modern scientific publications necessary to the researches of the scientific staff and the work of the educational division. Open to the public.

NY —COLUMBIA UNIVERSITY LIBRARIES, Rare Book & Manuscript Library, 801 Butler Library, 535 W 114 St, New York, 10027. Kenneth A Lohf, Librn
Holdings: Mss
Notes: The Calvin S Hathaway Collection on the protection and salvaging of artisic and historic documents and art objects during and after two world wars. 6500 items. Restricted use.

NY —METROPOLITAN MUSEUM OF ART, Thomas J Watson Library, Fifth Ave & 82 St, New York, 10028. William B Walker, Chief Librn
Holdings: Vols (250,000) Cat Mss Microforms
Notes: All fields of art: 1400 periodicals, incl bulletins and annual reports, catalogs, etc of American and foreign art societies, museums, etc; incl sales catalogs, exhibition catalogs, clipping file on individual artists and subjects, autograph letters. See *Library Catalog of the Metropolitan Museum of Art, New York*, second ed, rev and enl (Boston, G K Hall, 1980, 48 v and first supplement, 1982). Since 1980, holdings have been cataloged in RLIN.

NY —MARGARET WOODBURY STRONG MUSEUM, 1 Manhattan Square, Rochester, 14607.
Holdings: Vols (20,000) Cat
Notes: The Margaret Woodbury Strong Museum Library contains a collection of approx 20,000 books, periodicals and ephemera of and concerning the 19th and early 20th centuries. A large part of the library's holdings reflect the interests of Margaret Strong and her family: domestic life and literature of the 19th century and world travel, with particular emphasis on the Orient. The library's resources are available to all visitors for research. Book stacks and rare book storage are not open for browsing and do not circulate, but facilities are provided in reading room for study.

OH —CLEVELAND PUBLIC LIBRARY, Fine Arts and Special Collections Department, 325 Superior Ave, Cleveland, 44114. Alice N Loranth, Head
Holdings: Vols (12,000) Cat Pix
Notes: Part of the Art Collection, which covers all periods and fields of art with special emphasis on contemporary and American art. 200 periodicals, incl bulletins of American museums.

OH —DAYTON ART INSTITUTE LIBRARY, 405 W Riverview Ave, PO Box 941, Dayton, 45401. Helen L Pinkney, Librn and Assoc Cur
Holdings: Vols (23,220) Cat Mss Pix Slides Microforms VF
Budget: ($7000)
Notes: Incl museum catalogs and bulletins and collection of slides of stained glass.

OR —SOUTHERN OREGON HISTORICAL SOCIETY, Jacksonville Museum Library, 206 N Fifth St, PO Box 480, Jacksonville, 97530. Richard H Engeman, Librn
Holdings: Vols 300 Cat
Budget: ($5200)

SD —SIOUXLAND HERITAGE MUSEUMS, Pettigrew Museum Library, 131 N Duluth Ave, Sioux Falls, 57104. Ms Lee N McLaird, Cur of Collections
Holdings: Vols (7500) Cat Mss Maps Pix
Budget: ($900)
Notes: Pettigrew Museum Library is a support service of the Siouxland Heritage Museums. US Senator R F Pettigrew established the core collection in 1926, covering natural history (incl North American Indian anthropology) and state-local history (concentrating on exploration and settlement to about 1900). The collection also incl the Senator's private papers (ca 1870-1926). Additions to the collection since 1926 have emphasized Plains Indian anthropology, state-local history, baseball and museology, supporting the work of the Museum staff. The collection is mostly cataloged and is inter-indexed with Augustana College, Sioux Falls College, and Sioux Falls Public Libraries (as well as having its own catalog). The photograph collection includes prints by D F Barry as well as other photographers' work with native peoples.

†WA —WASHINGTON STATE UNIVERSITY, Library, Manuscripts, Archives & Special Collections, Pullman, 99164. John F Guido, Head
Holdings: Cat Mss Maps Pix
Notes: The Carl Parcher Russell papers, a vast resource (24,916 items; 45 linear feet) on American Indian and Western pioneer activities and artifacts. Much on the fur trade; pioneer life; mountain men and trapping; wildlife; primitive life in detail. Also the National Park Service, parks, monuments, etc. Described in *Carl Parcher Russell: An Indexed Register of His Scholarly and Professional Papers, 1920-1967, in the Washington State University Library* (Pullman, 1970), 149 pp.

WI —MILWAUKEE PUBLIC MUSEUM, Reference Library, 800 W Wells St, Milwaukee, 53233. Judith Campbell Turner, Museum Librn
Holdings: Vols (90,000) Cat Maps Microforms

MB —MANITOBA MUSEUM OF MAN & NATURE, Library, 190 Rupert Ave, Winnipeg, R3B 0N2, Can. V Hatten, Librn
Holdings: Vols (20,000) Cat

NS —NOVA SCOTIA MUSEUM, Library, 1747 Summer St, Halifax, B3H 3A6, Can. M S Whiteside, Librn
Holdings: Vols 2000

ON —CANADIAN MUSEUMS ASSOCIATION, Resource Centre, 280 Metcalfe Suite 202, Ottawa, K2P 0G5, Can. Denis Roussel, Library Tech
Holdings: Vols (700) Cat Mss Slides Audiotapes
Budget: ($4000)
Notes: Emphasis on museology and administration of art galleries, museum techniques, etc. An extensive bibliography has been published containing articles and books contained in the library. The bibliography is supplemented as new titles are acquired. It is arranged alphabetically under relevant subject headings.

ON —NATIONAL MUSEUMS OF CANADA, Library Services Directorate, Ottawa, K1A 0M8, Can. Valerie Monkhouse, Director
Holdings: Vols 40,000 Cat
Budget: $43,000
Notes: Chiefly publications issued by museums (throughout the world), many acquired through publications exchange programs, and also general works on museology, conservation of museum objects, architecture, display and other related subjects.

ON —ROYAL ONTARIO MUSEUM, Main Library and Archives, 100 Queen's Park, Toronto, M5S 2C6, Can. Julia Matthews, Head Librn
Holdings: Vols (85,000) Cat
Notes: Since January 1977, acquisitions have been entered in UTLAS.

MUSEUMS AND MUSEOLOGY—CATALOGS

NY —COLUMBIA UNIVERSITY LIBRARIES, Avery Architectural and Fine Arts Library, 201 Avery Hall, New York, 10027. Angela Giral, Librn
Holdings: Vols 1000 Cat
Notes: Restricted use: noncirculating.

MUSEUMS FOR CHILDREN see Children's Museums

MUSGRAVE, SUSAN, 1951-

ON —MCMASTER UNIVERSITY, Mills Memorial Library, Div of Archives & Research Collections, Hamilton, L8S 4L6, Can. G R Hill, Univ Librn
Holdings: Mss
Notes: Original mss of published and unpublished poetry and prose, and correspondence.

MUSHROOMS

CA —FITZ HUGH LUDLOW MEMORIAL LIBRARY, PO Box 99346, San Francisco, 94109. Michael R Aldrich, Exec Cur
Holdings: Cat Mss Maps Pix Slides Phonorecords Audiotapes Videotapes
Notes: Collection stored. Important mail inquiries only. No interlibrary lending or telephone inquiries. Hallucinogens as used in historical and contemporary cultures. Nearly complete collection of books and articles by or about Timothy Leary, incl manuscripts; also nearly complete collection of the writings of Aldous Huxley concerning drugs. Much autographed or inscribed material, mostly popular music from the 1960s but also incl ethnographic music. Emphasis on psychoactive drugs relative to religion, literature, art. Also an excellent collection of research papers (chemistry, pharmacology, epidemiology, sociology, ethnobotany) in this field, as well as artifacts and artwork relating to the field.

†IL —NORTHWESTERN UNIVERSITY, Robert E Machol Library, Leverone Hall, Evanson, 60201.
Notes: Espec 18th-19th century illustrated works. Early works on mushrooms, and popular texts in 30 languages.

MA —HARVARD UNIVERSITY LIBRARY, Farlow Reference Library, 20 Divinity Ave, Cambridge, 02138. Geraldine C Kaye, Librn
Holdings: Vols (60,000) Cat Mss Serials Pix Microforms
Notes: The Farlow Reference Library provides complete coverage of the systematic literature on algae, bryophytes,

MUSHROOMS (cont.)

fungi, and lichens. Established by bequest of Professor William G Farlow, it is one of the most extensive cryptogamic botany libraries in the US. Books do not circulate.

MA —HARVARD UNIVERSITY LIBRARY, Botanical Museum Library, Cambridge, 02138.
Holdings: Vols (2400) Mss Pix
Notes: The Tina and Gordon Wisson Ethnomycological Collection, one of the most important modern collections, acquired as an adjunct to the Museum's Economic Botany Library of Oakes Ames. From 15th to 20th century, it deals with hallucinogenic mushrooms in art, religion, and folklore; chemistry, pharmacology, linguistics, archaeological artifacts of Mexico, Guatemala, India, Japan, China, etc. Personal papers, etc.

†NC —UNIVERSITY OF NORTH CAROLINA, CHAPEL HILL, Department of Botany Library, 301 Coker Hall 010-A, Chapel Hill, 27514. William R Burk, Botany Librn
Notes: The mycology collection incl some 6000 pamphlets. It contains papers of the following scientists: William C Coker, John N Couch, Lindsay F Olive, mycologists; also, Victor A Greulach, plant pathologist. The mycology catalog is in preparation (1983), and will provide author, title, and subject access.

ON —AGRICULTURE CANADA, Library Division, Plant Research Library, 49 Central Experimental Farm Bldg, Ottawa, K1A 0C6, Can. Eva Gavora, Plant Research Librn
Holdings: (15,000) Items
Notes: Emphasis on flora of North America.

MUSIC

CA —BERKELEY PUBLIC LIBRARY, Art and Music Div, 2090 Kittredge St, Berkeley, 97404. Diane Davenport, Reference
Holdings: Vols (20,000) Cat Pix Slides Audiotapes

CA —UNIVERSITY OF CALIFORNIA, BERKELEY, Humanities-Social Sciences Libraries, Music Library, 24 Morrison Hall, Berkeley, 94720. Michael A Keller, Head Librn
Holdings: Vols 115,000 Cat Mss Slides Microforms
Notes: The Library maintains an outstanding music reference collection. It is rich in primary source materials for research, particularly in the areas of opera, 18th-century instrumental music, music theory. Incl 30,000 sound recordings. See the following: Vincent Dukles and Minnie Elmer, *Thematic Catalogue of a Collection of 18th-Century Italian Instrumental Music in the Music Library of the University of California, Berkeley* (Univ of California Press, 1963); Alan Curtis, Musique classique francaise a Berkeley, in *Revue de Musicologie*, 56 (1970) pp 123-164. Minnie Elmer, *Autograph Manuscripts of Ernest Bloch at the University of California; Cum Notis Variorum, the Newsletter of the Music Library of the University of California* (Published 10 times annually since April 1976).

CA —CALIFORNIA STATE UNIVERSITY, LONG BEACH, Library, Dept of Special Collections & Archives, 1250 Bellflower Blvd, Long Beach, 90840. John Ahouse, Special Collections Librn
Notes: Almost all of the papers, recordings, etc, published and unpublished, of Gerald V Strang.

CA —LOS ANGELES PUBLIC LIBRARY, Art, Music & Recreation Dept, 630 W Fifth St, Los Angeles, 90071. Melvin H Rosenberg, Mgr & Principal Librn
Holdings: Vols (68,000) Cat Mss
Budget: ($102,244)
Notes: Incl 44,000 music scores, 3000 mss, 100,000 song sheets, and newspaper clippings.

CA —UNIVERSITY OF CALIFORNIA, LOS ANGELES, Music Library, Schonberg Hall, Los Angeles, 90024. Stephen M Fry, Music Librn
Holdings: Vols (95,000) Cat Mss Microforms
Notes: Broad scholarly scope with emphasis on musicology, incl books on music; musical scores (scholarly and practical editions) incl instrumental, vocal, chamber music with parts; periodicals; 35,000 musical recordings (disc and tape); microforms; mss. Special and archival collections. Manuscripts: Henry Mancini, Alex North, Eugene Zodor, Rudolf Friml, George Antheil, Fannie Charles Dillon, Walter Lantz, Harry Lubin, Clarence Mader, Colin McPhee, Mary Carr Moore, Alfred Newman, Edward B Powell, Andre Previn, Joseph Rumshinsky, Lester Spencer, Henry Temianka, Ernst Toch, John Vincent, Edward Ward, Mortimer Wilson, and Eric Zeisl. Collections: guitar music, 17th-18th century Dutch song and psalm books, 17th-18th century Venetian opera librettos, 18th-19thcentury opera scores, 18th-early 19th century French and German opera librettos, folk songs and dances of the British Isles, (popular American sheet music, ca 1830-present, about 750,000 items), Alfred Newman Collection of film score recordings; 40,000 other musical scores. Published descriptions of collections: Walter H Rubsamen, Unusual music holdings of libraries on the West Coast, *MLA Notes, X*, no 4 (September 1953), pp 546-554; Malcolm Cole, A Pleyel Collection at UCLA, *MLA Notes, XXIX*, no 2 (December 1972), pp 215-223. "The Music Library" *UCLA Librarian, XXXIV* no 3-4 (March-April 1978) pp 12-14.

CA —OAKLAND PUBLIC LIBRARY, Art, Music and Recreation Section, 125 14 St, Oakland, 94612. Richard Colvig, Senior Librn
Holdings: Vols (5000) Cat Phonorecords Audiotapes
Budget: ($6700)
Notes: 10,000 scores, incl chamber music, instrumental music (piano and organ collections especialy strong), miniature scores, opera scores, songs and song collections; 30,000 octavos (anthems and choral music of all kinds); 5000 books about music; 8000 phonorecords; and audiocassettes.

CA —PALO ALTO CITY LIBRARY, 1213 Newell Rd, Palo Alto, 94303. Mary Jo Levy, Dir
Holdings: Vols (1550) Cat

CA —PASADENA PUBLIC LIBRARY, Alice Coleman Batchelder Music Library, Reference Services, 285 E Walnut, Pasadena, 91101. Anne Cain, Principal Librn
Holdings: Vols (8012) Cat Pix
Notes: Separate record catalog of over 10,000 phonorecords; over 4400 music scores. Special index of songs in collection. Over 150,000 pictures.

CA —UNIVERSITY OF CALIFORNIA, RIVERSIDE, University Library, 4045 Canyon Crest Dr, Box 5900, Riverside, 92517.
Notes: The Oswald Jonas Memorial Collection holds the musicological mss, letters, biographical materials, and notebooks of Heinrich Schenker and also the papers of the late Oswald Jonas, musicologist and leading authority on the life and work of Schenker. Incl Schenker's diary; correspondence with Anthony van Hoboken, Reinhard Oppel, Moriz Violin, Eugen d'Albert, and Oswald Jonas; the proofs and mss of his published works; printed editions from his library with notes, marginalia, and critical annotations; *Urlinie* tables; and miscellanea. A guide to the collection will be published by the library.

CA —SACRAMENTO PUBLIC LIBRARY, 828 I St, Sacramento, 95814. Dorothy Harvey, Librn, Special Collections
Holdings: Vols (26,000) Cat Phonorecords
Notes: Incl scores, sheet music, card indexes.

CA —SANTA CRUZ PUBLIC LIBRARY, Art, Music, Film Dept, 224 Church St, Santa Cruz, 95060. Alma Westberg, Librn
Holdings: Vols (1500) Cat Mss
Budget: ($750)
Notes: The music collection is in a catalog separate from the general one. It consists of approx 1700 cataloged books about music; 2100 bound, cataloged books of music incl opera and musical comedy scores; 2700 pieces of sheet music which incl sacred, art and popular songs, and instrumental solos. Good collection of chamber music from baroque to contemporary composers. Also a special collection of 10,000 pieces of American popular sheet music of the period from the 1860s to 1970s incl songs of California. The record collection, primarily classical, consists of about 5500 records.

CA —UNIVERSITY OF CALIFORNIA, SANTA CRUZ, University Library, Special Collections, Santa Cruz, 95064. Rita Bottoms, Special Collections Librn; Margaret Felts, South Pacific Collection Bibliographer

CA —STANFORD UNIVERSITY LIBRARIES, Cecil H Green Library, Stanford, 94305. Michael T Ryan, Cur
Holdings: Vols (1500) Cat Mss
Notes: The Memorial Library of Music. Mss, letters, and first editions of printed scores. A catalog of the Library, compiled by Nathan Van Patten, was published in 1950.

CA —CALIFORNIA INSTITUTE OF THE ARTS, Library, 24700 McBean Pkwy, Valencia, 91355. James Elrod, Dir
Holdings: Vols (61,000) Cat Phonorecords Audiotapes
Budget: ($8500)
Notes: Incl 11,656 audiotapes and 16,000 music scores. Cataloged.

CA —MARISKA ALDRICH MEMORIAL FOUNDATION, Library of Rare Music, PO Box 369, 8451-8491 Swarthout Canyon Rd, Wrightwood, 92397. Anna Mary Anderson, Pres
Holdings: Vols (6000) Uncat Pix Slides Phonorecords Audiotapes
Notes: Collection incl 35,000 recordings, 52,000 editions, 11,000 LPRS, 2000 Piano Rolls (for Amtico, Dew Art, Art Echo), 22,000 tapes scores and sheet music. All dating back to 1900, all in mint condition. Starting a new collection of videotapes. Reference use only.

CT —YALE UNIVERSITY, Sterling Memorial Library, Yale Collection of Historical Sound Recordings, 120 High St, New Haven, 06520. Richard Warren Jr, Cur
Holdings: Vols Mss Pix Phonorecords Audiotapes
Notes: Incl classical music (concert music) of all types from Western culture, jazz, the American Musical Theatre, spoken material (literary, dramatic, documentary). The aim of the Collection is to document performance practice in the fields collected. See the article by Karol Berger in the *Journal of the Association of Recorded Sound Collections*, vol VI, no 1, pp 13-25. Partially cataloged.

CT —YALE UNIVERSITY, Music Library, 98 Wall St, New Haven, 06520. Harold E Samuel, Librn
Holdings: Vols (118,000) Cat Mss Pix Phonorecords Audiotapes Microforms
Notes: General reference and research materials. Performing editions. Strong in theoretical literature, opera, 17-18th century music (incl mss), J S Bach and sons in early editions and mss, Russian liturgical music (Tkaczenko Collection), hymnology, American music. Also collection of musical pictures and portraits.

CT —CONNECTICUT COLLEGE, Greer Music Library, New London, 06320. Philip Youngholm, Music Librn
Holdings: Vols 6000 Cat Mss Phonorecords Audiotapes Microforms
Budget: ($12,000)
Notes: Incl 9000 music scores, 11,000 phonodiscs, 100 audiotapes and 40 microforms.

CT —UNIVERSITY OF CONNECTICUT, University Library, Music Library, U-Box 12, Storrs, 06268. Dorothy Bognar, Librn
Notes: A comparatively small branch (35,000 pieces) of a university library, with separate facilities located in the University Fine Arts Center. All materials relate to the field of music (scores, books, periodicals, microfilm, phonodiscs, tapes). Materials include 10,000 scores and 15,000 sound recordings. Maintain catalogs for books,

MUSIC (cont.)

scores, and recordings, and have listening facilities within the Music Library. The Music Department also maintains separate collections of performance parts for choral, orchestral, and band music. No photocopying.

CT —UNIVERSITY OF HARTFORD, Hartt School of Music, Allen Memorial Library, 200 Bloomfield Ave, West Hartford, 06117. Ethel Bacon, Music Librn
Holdings: Vols (56,806) Cat Slides Phonorecords Audiotapes Filmstrips Microforms
Budget: ($14,500)
Notes: Cataloged materials incl 12,000 books on music, 66 slides, 17,000 phonorecords, 1000 audiotapes, 57 filmstrips, 683 microforms, and 26,000 music scores. Also, the Kalmen Opperman Collection: 350 vols of clarinet music, solo through ensemble. Also, the Robert E Smith Collections of 34,000 phonorecords, 150 audiotapes with 80 vols of transcripts from his two radio programs: Your Box At The Opera; Theater of Melody (uncataloged).

†DC —CATHOLIC UNIVERSITY OF AMERICA, Music Library, Washington, 20064. Betty Libbey, Head Music Library
Holdings: Cat Microforms
Notes: A large collection to support advanced degree study. Emphasis on church music, musicology, history and criticism, instrumental and vocal music, solo music for all voices, instruments, and musical forms.

DC —LIBRARY OF CONGRESS, Music Division, Washington, 20540.
Holdings: Cat Mss Maps Pix Slides Microforms
Notes: Probably the largest collection (more than 3,500,000 items) of music and music literature in the world. Incl autograph mss and letters of Bach, Haydn, Mozart, Beethoven, Weber, Schubert, Mendelssohn, Schumann, Liszt, Brahms, Wagner, Delibes, Schoenberg, Bartok, Hindemith, Stravinsky, MacDowell and others.

DC —NATIONAL ENDOWMENT FOR THE ARTS, Library, 1100 Pen Ave NW, Rm 213, Washington, 20506. Christine Morrison, Arts Librn
Holdings: Vols (6000) Cat
Notes: Incl arts and education and public policy in the arts.

FL —UNIVERSITY OF MIAMI, Music Library, PO Box 248165, Coral Gables, 33124. Nancy Kobialke, Librn
Holdings: Vols Cat Phonorecords
Budget: ($25,000)
Notes: Emphasis on research editions and performing editions with parts for 2-8 players. Nearly 24,000 musical scores. Recordings are mostly classical, but incl 1200 jazz LPs and 1200 ethnic LPs from all parts of world. *Inter-American Music Archive* is special catalog of Latin American holdings. Collection incl 15,500 cataloged phonorecords.

FL —MIAMI-DADE PUBLIC LIBRARY SYSTEM, One Biscayne Blvd, Miami, 33132. Don Chauncey, AV Librn; Barbara Young, Art & Music Dept Librn
Holdings: Vols 3000 Cat Phonorecords
Notes: Incl 8250 pieces of popular sheet music; 1500 classical scores; 200 musical shows; separate index to songs in collections; 29,000 musical recordings.

FL —FLORIDA STATE UNIVERSITY, Warren D Allen Music Library, Tallahassee, 32306. Dale L Hudson, Music Librn
Holdings: Cat Phonorecords Audiotapes Microforms
Notes: General music collection serving the School of Music. Incl 40,000 music scores, 19,000 phonorecords, 1500 audiotapes and 2000 microforms.

IL —CHICAGO PUBLIC LIBRARY, Music Section, Fine Arts Division, 78 E Washington St, Chicago, 60602. Rosalinda I Hack, Fine Arts Division Chief; Richard C Schwegel, Head, Music Section
Holdings: Vols (130,000) Cat Microforms Phonorecords Videocassettes
Notes: Collection of books, scores,

recordings, periodicals, clippings programs, video, in all areas of music. Special emphasis on popular music, rock, jazz, blues, discography, therapy, music business. 17,000 cataloged pieces of sheet music and 20,000 cataloged bound volumes of music including chamber music parts and small but growing collection of orchestral music parts. Indexed collection of over 7000 popular sheet music titles dating from mid-19th century. Sets of complete and collected works of 50 major composers. Cataloged record collection (50,000) covering all areas with developed collection of local artists, rock and new wave. Periodical collection (600 titles) and many programs of US orchestras including Chicago Symphony. Book collection includes dissertations in areas of jazz, blues, and popular music. Special collections include Balaban & Katz Orchestralcollection, 15,000 titles of arranged classical and dance band music from 1920-50's used at Chicago Theatre (primarily in storage), Chicago Blues Archive (video and recordings), New Music Chicago Archive (tapes, scores, etc of local composers and performers). Services: Listening center and practice rooms with pianos. Monthly exhibits relating to music; weekly concerts sponsored by Chicago Council on Fine Arts and the library.

IL —NEWBERRY LIBRARY, 60 W Walton St, Chicago, 60610. Diana Haskell, Cur of Modern Mss
Holdings: Cat Mss
Notes: Collection primarily musicological, not performance. 55,000 scores; 100,000 pieces of sheet music. Primary and secondary materials for the study of Western European music from the Middle Ages through the 19th century, and of American music from its beginnings. Strongest holdings are: early theory, music literature and scores of the Renaissance and Baroque periods, opera scores (3600), and libretti, early American psalmody and religious music, music periodicals, monumental editions and monographs, popular sheet music and music mss. See article by Donald W Krummel, "The Newberry Library, Chicago" in *Fontes artis musicae*, 1969/3. Restricted use: noncirculating.

IL —ROOSEVELT UNIVERSITY, Murray-Green Library, 430 S Michigan Ave, Chicago, 60605. Donald Draganski, Music Librn
Holdings: Vols (28,000) Uncat Mss Pix Microforms
Notes: Subscribe to over 92 music periodicals; record collection of more than 10,000 albums; 8000 pieces of sheet music; pamphlet file; music theses on microfilm; complete file of music publishers catalogs; scores; tapes of old 78 recordings; music education; and electronic music.

IL —NORTHWESTERN UNIVERSITY, Music Library, 1937 Sheridan Rd, Evanston, 60201. Don L Roberts, Head Music Librn
Holdings: Vols (140,000) Cat Mss Phonorecords Audiotapes Microforms
Notes: Main emphasis is on the documentation (incl 2000 ms pieces) of 20th century music. Broad acquisitions of mss, books, music and recordings relating to 20th century music. Library contains a portion of the Moldenhauer Archive and the John Cage "Notations Collection".

IL —UNIVERSITY OF ILLINOIS, URBANA/CHAMPAIGN, Library, Music Library, Urbana, 61801. William M McClellan, Librn
Holdings: Vols (200,000) Cat Mss Slides Sound Recordings Microforms Books Scores
Budget: ($65,000)
Notes: Introductory, instructive, research and reference materials to support work at graduate level in ethnomusicology,, musicology, music education, performance areas. Special areas incl about 2500 pre-1800 music mss and editions of music on microfilm, 2400 graduate music theses on microfilm, a special collection of 30,000 titles of American vocal sheet music covering the period 1790-1970, the Rafael Joseffy Collection of about 2000 pieces of 19th century piano music (incl performer markings), the Joseph Szigeti Collection (700

items: published music, mss, recordings), mainly violin and piano music by various commposers. Also incl a special collection of 45,000 78 rpm sound recordings (uncat) of classical music and jazz; a collection of 2900 titles from Chicago radio station WGN. Incl orchestrations, a collection of 500,000 items (uncat) from stock of Hunleth Music Store, St Louis, Missouri, mainly early 20th century imprints of songs, wind music, string music, piano, sets of theatre orchestra parts, dance band orchestrations. A separate collection of choral octavos and instrumental parts is maintained, incl 135,000 pieces of choral music, 30,500 orchestral parts, and 5500 wind ensemble parts. Also, music publishers' catalogues (mainly European and American), ca 126 cubic feet, 1860s-1950s.

IN —INDIANA UNIVERSITY, Music Library, Bloomington, 47401. David E Fenske, Head
Holdings: Cat Slides Phonorecords Audiotapes Videotapes Filmstrips Microforms
Budget:
Notes: 120,000 books and scores; 185,583 choral and orchestral parts; 33,000 phonorecords; 37,000 audiotapes.

IN —BUTLER UNIVERSITY, Jordan College of Music, Library, 4600 Sunset, Indianapolis, 46208. Phyllis J Schoonover, Librn
Holdings: Vols (5383) Cat Phonorecords Audiotapes
Budget: ($16,500)
Notes: There is a separate card catalog for 3800 scores, 4673 phonorecords, and books.

IN —BALL STATE UNIVERSITY, Alexander M Bracken Library, Muncie, 47306. Nyal Williams, Music Librn
Holdings: Vols (30,000) Cat Mss
Budget: ($20,000)
Notes: Incl archives of International Horn Society, Tubists Universal Brotherhood Association Library, Cecil Leeson Archival Saxophone Collection, and Archives of Buescher Music Instrument Manufacturing Company.

IA —PUBLIC LIBRARY OF DES MOINES, 100 Locust, Des Moines, 50309. Stephen R Brogden, Head, Fine Arts Dept; Martha Gerstenberger, Music Librn
Holdings: Vols (8300) Cat Phonorecords
Budget: ($5000)
Notes: Incl compositions about Iowa, clippings, and biographical data. Incl 25,000 scores and sheet music.

IA —UNIVERSITY OF IOWA, School of Music, Rita Benton Music Library, Iowa City, 52242.
Holdings: Vols 55,000 Cat Mss Pix Phonorecords Audiotapes Microforms
Budget: $30,000
Notes: Incl large collection of music periodicals. Holdings of rare books listed in: *An Annotated Catalog of Rare Musical Items in the Libraries of the University of Iowa*, by Frederick K Gable (Iowa City: Univ of Iowa Libraries, 1963), 130 pp; *and...Additions, 1963-1972*, comp by Gordon S Rowley (Iowa City: Univ of Iowa Libraries, 1973), 121 pp General description of music collection in The Music Library of the University of Iowa, by Rita Benton, *Fontes Artis Musicae*, vol 16 (1969), pp 124-129.

KS —KANSAS STATE UNIVERSITY, Library, Special Collections & University Archives, Manhattan, 66506. Antonia Q Pigno, Coordr; John J Vander Velde, Librn; Anthony R Crawford, Univ Archivist
Holdings: Vols 1000 Cat
Notes: Eclectic collection of scores and books from the library of Professor Charles Stratton. Sound recordings and additional scores from this collection are located in the library's Audio Visual Department.

KY —UNIVERSITY OF KENTUCKY, Music Library, 116 Fine Arts Bldg, Lexington, 40506. Cathy S Hunt, Music Librn
Holdings: Vols 18,000 Cat Microforms Scores Recordings
Notes: Collection incl books (14,000), includes music history, theory, music eduction, jazz, etc cat. Music Scores (18,000) cat. Serials (3200 vols) cat. Microforms (6300) cat. Recordings (9100) cat. Collected

MUSIC (cont.)

Editions (complete Works of composers, large sets, etc) (7100) cat. The Alfred Cortot Collection (about 300 vols of rare, early music theory books) is housed in the Rare Books Room of the Main Library.

KY —UNIVERSITY OF LOUISVILLE, School of Music, Dwight Anderson Memorial Music Library, 2301 S Third St, Louisville, 40292. Marion Korda, Librn
Holdings: Vols 50,000 Cat Mss Pix Phonorecords Audiotapes Microforms
Budget: $25,000
Notes: Plus 20,000 uncataloged pieces. 296 serial publications on monthly computer print-out. Participating member of Metroversity library system, as well as state-wide University Referral Center, serves research and study needs at preparatory, undergraduate and graduate levels of the University.

LA —LOUISIANA STATE UNIVERSITY, Troy H Middleton Library, Louisiana Room, Baton Rouge, 70803. Evangeline Mills Lynch, Head Librn; Ruth Murray, Associate Librn
Holdings: Vols (33,500) Cat Maps VF
Notes: Louisiana Collection of history, description and travel, biography, agriculture, literature, politics and government, folklore, anthropology, geography, geology, education, language, music and natural history. Especially large subject collections may be found on Louisiana, the history of the lower Mississippi Valley, Abraham Lincoln, Romance languages and literatures, sugar culture and technology, Southern history, petroleum engineering, plant pathology, micropaleontology, ornithology, and various aspects of crawfish life, biology and culture. Complete depository of Louisiana State Documents; extensive newspapers clipping files; separate card catalog; items listed in Louisiana Union Catalog; restricted use (research and reference). Incl both materials about Louisiana and by Louisianians without regard to subject. LSU Press Collection(preservation copy of each title kept for exhibit purposes only). LSU theses and dissertations from 1900-date. LSU Faculty Collection. Also, 1300 maps, 104 VF drawers, 250 boxes of uncataloged pamphlets.

LA —NEW ORLEANS PUBLIC LIBRARY, Art & Music Div, 219 Loyola Ave, New Orleans, 70140. Marilyn Wilkins, Head
Holdings: Vols 24,100 Cat Pix Phonorecords
Budget: $23,500
Notes: Working collection of scores, books and phonorecords; incl music for performance, literature about music and reference works. Incl 24,100 vols of books, 700 pieces of early New Orleans sheet music, early southern sheet music, and 25,000 phonorecords. Catalogs.

LA —LOUISIANA STATE UNIVERSITY, SHREVEPORT, Library-Archives, 8515 Youree Dr, Shreveport, 71129. Patricia L Meador, Archivist & Asst Librn
Notes: Theatre and music is documented in the John Wray and Margaret Mary Young Theatre Collection, (5 linear ft), (1929-1981), the Joe Gifford Papers (1946-1960) (3 linear ft), the Shreveport Little Theatre Records (6 linear ft), the Nathaniel S Allen Papers (1860-1930), the records of the Shreveport Symphony (1948-1978) and oral history interviews on the topics. The archives collection also incl 60 linear ft of records (1949-1981) of Holiday-In-Dixie, Shreveport-Bossier's spring-time festival.

ME —PORTLAND PUBLIC LIBRARY, 5 Monument Sq, Portland, 04101. Edward V Chenevert, Library Dir
Holdings: Vols (16,108) Audiotapes Phonorecords
Budget: $11,300
Notes: Collection incl 5000 phonorecords, 400 cassettes. Other collections within the department include sheet music, songbooks, picture file, periodicals, and choral music.

MD —JOHNS HOPKINS UNIVERSITY, Milton S Eisenhower Library, Charles & 34

Sts, Baltimore, 21218. Ann S Gwyn, Assistant Dir for Special Collections
Holdings: Vols 8500 Cat Phonorecords
Notes: The best American and foreign music recordings are added each year. Rose and Morris Light Record Collection, and the Salmieri Jazz Record Collection.

MD —PEABODY CONSERVATORY LIBRARY, 21 E Mt Vernon Place, Baltimore, 21202. Edwin A Quist, Librn
Holdings: Vols 70,000 Cat Mss Pix Phonorecords Audiotapes Videotapes Microforms
Budget: $30,000
Notes: The Peabody Conservatory Library, formerly a part of the Peabody Institute Library (now the George Peabody Library of the Johns Hopkins University) supplies the library needs of the faculty and student body of the Peabody Conservatory of Music. While the collection has numerous research capabilities, it is basically a collection of musical scores. The entire history of Western music is represented through collected editions, monumental anthologies, study scores, performing editions and a large collection of books and music periodicals. This collection is supplemented by a listening facility containing 14,000 discs and an ensembles library containing scores and parts of orchestral, band and chorus works.

MA —BOSTON PUBLIC LIBRARY, Music Division, 666 Boylston St, Box 286, Boston, 02117. Ruth Bleecker, Cur of Music
Holdings: Vols 100,000 Cat Mss Pix Microforms
Notes: The Allen A Brown Music Library is the nucleus of the collection. There is a *Dictionary Catalog of the Music Collection* (Boston: G K Hall, 1976; 24 vols). Incl music scores. The Handel and Haydn Society Collection, and the Walter Piston Collection are housed in the Rare Books and Manuscripts Department. The Karl Geiringer Collection (1000 glass slides) of musical instruments and musicians are housed in the Print Department.

MA —BOSTON UNIVERSITY, Mugar Memorial Library, Special Collections Dept, 771 Commonwealth Ave, Boston, 02215. Howard B Gotlieb, Dir
Notes: Personal collection of Arthur Fiedler, incl 6000 scores and sound recordings, manuscripts, photographs, memorabilia, library, and test pressings of Fiedler's performances. In addition, archives of the Paris Conservatoire de Musique of individual musicians, composers.

MA —NEW ENGLAND CONSERVATORY OF MUSIC, Harriet M Spaulding Library, 33 Gainsborough St, Boston, 02115.
Notes: Incl 55,000 books and music scores of New England composers; the Preston Collection of Musicians' Letters; Firestone Hour Collection of Music; and Vaughn Monroe Collection of Camel Caravan.

MA —HARVARD UNIVERSITY LIBRARY, Eda Kuhn Loeb Music Library, Harvard University Music Library Bldg, Cambridge, 02138. Michael Ochs, Librn
Holdings: Vols Microforms
Notes: See *Harvard Library Bulletin*, XII (1958), 410-417; and, for Isham collection of early instrumental music, VI (1952), 376-380. Contains 32,500 titles.

MA —HARVARD UNIVERSITY LIBRARY, Hilles Library, Susan A E Morse Music Collection, 59 Shepard St, Cambridge, 02138. Cathy Balshone-Becze, Music Librn
Holdings: Cat Phonorecords
Notes: Incl more than 9000 phonograph records and 6500 scores.

MA —MASSACHUSETTS INSTITUTE OF TECHNOLOGY, Music Library, 14E-109, Cambridge, 02139. Linda I Solow, Librn
Holdings: Vols (47,000) Cat Phonorecords Audiotapes Scores
Notes: Described in *Directory of Music Libraries and Collections in New England*, 6th ed (Music Library Assn, New England Chapter, 1981); Bradley, Carol J, *Music collections in American libraries: a chronology* (Detroit, Information Coordinators, 1981); *Music Industry Directory* 7th ed (Chicago Marquis Who's Who, 1983). Borrowing of circulating

collection limited to MIT community; limited room access to outside users. Reference service weekdays.

MA —MELROSE PUBLIC LIBRARY, 69 W Emerson St, Melrose, 02176. Diane E Shaw, Art Librn
Holdings: Vols (8500) Cat Pix Slides Phonorecords
Budget: ($6900)
Notes: Framed and unframed art reproductions (110), slides (2773), periodicals, clippings, sound recordings (3000). Incl the Mary Livermore Collection of Sacred Art, the Odlin Collection, and the Pierre Gendrot Collection of Fine Art.

MA —SMITH COLLEGE, Werner Josten Library for the Performing Arts, Northampton, 01063. Marlene M Wong, Librn
Notes: Special collection: Einstein Collection of Music of the 16th-18th centuries copied in score by Alfred Einstein; also 29,000 music scores, 36,000 phonorecords, 1400 slides, 150 microforms. No photocopying.

MA —SPRINGFIELD CITY LIBRARY, Art & Music Dept, 220 State St, Springfield, 01103. Karen A Dorval, Supvr & Art Librn; Sylvia A Saint Amand, Music Librn
Holdings: Vols (22,500) Cat Pix Phonorecords Audiotapes Microforms
Budget: ($183,000)
Notes: Art: books (17,500), pamphlets (8000), pictures (120,000); music: books (5000), music scores (10,000), phonorecords (18,000), Audiocassettes (288 titles). Also microfilm (75 reels). Separate catalogs for art, music, and phonorecords and audiocassettes.

MA —OLD STURBRIDGE VILLAGE, Research Library, Sturbridge, 01566. Theresa Rini Percy, Librn
Holdings: Cat Mss Microforms
Notes: Incl church, folk and popular music of New England, 1790-1850.

MA —WELLESLEY COLLEGE, Music Library, Wellesley, 02181. Mary Wallace Davidson, Music Librn
Holdings: Vols 19,000 Cat
Budget: ($18,500)
Notes: Incl 12,500 bound vols of music scores and 12,000 phonorecords and tapes.

MI —UNIVERSITY OF MICHIGAN, School of Music, Music Library, Moore Bldg, Ann Arbor, 48109. Peggy Daub, Head
Holdings: Vols (90,000) Cat Mss Microforms
Notes: The collection covers music history and music education in depth, supporting a curriculum from the undergraduate to the doctoral level. Rare book material strong in early editions of works by the sons of J S Bach and 18th-19th century opera scores. Incl 1200 microforms of important European and American primary sources.

MI —DETROIT PUBLIC LIBRARY, Music & Performing Arts Dept, 5201 Woodward, Detroit, 48202. Agatha Pfeiffer Kalkanis, Chief
Holdings: Vols 19,000 Cat Mss Pix Microforms
Notes: Also incl (77,000) scores. General collection intended for practical use in performance and for scholarly research. Good working collection of bibliographies, thematic catalogs, dictionaries and encyclopedias, periodical indexes. Many sets of collected works, monumental editions, historical anthologies. Good representation of opera and operetta, art song and folk song, solo instrumental literature and chamber music in practical editions. 2575 titles of choral music, chiefly sacred, for use by choirs. 17,000 titles of popular sheet music, uncataloged but thoroughly indexed. Considerable recent holdings of books and periodicals in foreign languages. Special collections of black and local materials. 25,000 recordings and extensive discographical literature. Collection of publishers' trade catalogs.

MI —MICHIGAN STATE UNIVERSITY, Libraries, Special Collections Div, East Lansing, 48824. Jannette Fiore, Librn
Notes: The Russel B Nye Popular Culture Collection in the Michigan State Univ Libraries incl over (45,000) items. Most of the collection is organized into 4 categories:

MUSIC (cont.)

comic art, popular fiction, popular information materials and materials relating to the popular performing arts. Materials relating to popular theatre, music, television, radio, and film. Theatre is best represented. A significant collection of primary materials relating to the tent show incl photographs, financial and other records of the Henderson Stock Company, correspondence, leaflets, handbills and other ephemera from many of the companies playing in the upper midwest in the 1920s and 1930s, and photocopies of 250 tent show scripts.

MI —MICHIGAN STATE UNIVERSITY, Music Library, East Lansing, 48824. Roseann Hammill, Librn
Holdings: Cat
Notes: 17,987 scores; 5,851 recordings.

MI —WESTERN MICHIGAN UNIVERSITY, Harper C Maybee Music and Dance Library, Dalton Center, Kalamazoo, 49008. Gregory Fitzgerald, Librn
Holdings: Vols 10,000 Cat
Notes: Incl 12,000 music scores; 10,000 sound recordings. Collection has separate catalog.

MN —MINNEAPOLIS PUBLIC LIBRARY & INFORMATION CENTER, Art, Music & Films Dept, 300 Nicollet Mall, Minneapolis, 55401. Mary Alice Walker, Music Specialist
Holdings: Vols (94,200) Cat Phonorecords Audiotapes
Budget: ($111,642)
Notes: Collection incl phonorecords (15,000 78 rpm's; 31,732 LP's); audiotapes (1450); and sheet music (60,540).

MN —SAINT PAUL PUBLIC LIBRARY, Arts & Audiovisual Services, 90 W Fourth St, Saint Paul, 55102. Delores Sundbye, Supervising Librn
Holdings: Cat Pix Slides Phonorecords Audiotapes
Budget: ($20,000)
Notes: The Art and Music Dept incl 10,000 books on art and architecture, 4000 books on music and 10,000 cataloged music scores. Collection of 650 color reproduction, 10,000 mounted pictures and 500 exhibit catalogs. Complete set of first edition of Arundel Prints (color lithographic copies of Renaissance paintings, published by the Arundel Society, 1849-1897).

MO —UNIVERSITY OF MISSOURI-COLUMBIA, Ellis Library, Art, Archaeology and Music Dept, Columbia, 65201. Bonnie MacEwan, Librn
Holdings: Vols Cat
Notes: Russian editions of complete works of Glinka, Tchaikowsky and Rimsky-Korsakov. Also microforms of 15th and 16th century music.

MO —UNIVERSITY OF MISSOURI-KANSAS CITY, General Library, Conservatory of Music Library, 5100 Rockhill Road, Kansas City, 64110. Kenneth J LaBudde, Dir; Richard Belanger, Librn
Holdings: Vols 46,337 Cat
Notes: 276 current serial subscriptions, 7462 microforms, 16,702 sound recordings, some 70,000 other items with specialists in American Music, Virgil Thomson and hymnology.

MO —SAINT LOUIS PUBLIC LIBRARY, Popular Library, 1301 Olive Blvd, Saint Louis, 63103. Mary Lou Allen, Librn
Holdings: Vols (54,255) Cat
Budget: ($10,253)
Notes: Incl music books (7,000); scores (24,000); recordings (discs & tapes, 23,200); music periodicals (55).

MO —WASHINGTON UNIVERSITY, Gaylord Music Library, Saint Louis, 63130. Suzanne Bell, Music Librn
Holdings: Cat Microforms
Notes: Music books, bound periodicals (65,294); recordings (discs and and tapes, 16,114); sheet music, (50,000); choral music (8000). 345 microfilm; 390 microcards.

NJ —ELIZABETH PUBLIC LIBRARY, Art & Music Dept, 11 S Broad St, Elizabeth, 07202. Roman Sawycky, Head
Holdings: Vols (20,000) Cat Pix

Phonorecords 16mm Films Filmstrips
Budget: ($10,000)
Notes: Incl 200,000 pictures, 12,000 phonorecords and 700 films and filmstrips.

NJ —NEWARK PUBLIC LIBRARY, Art & Music Dept, 5 Washington St, Newark, 07101. William J Dane, Supv
Holdings: Vols (25,000) Cat Mss Audiotapes Microforms VF
Notes: Music literature, scores, librettos, extensive vertical file, song sheets, special indexes, music periodicals. John Tasker Howard collection of notes and letters. Some special material on New Jersey and Newark music.

NJ —RUTGERS, THE STATE UNIVERSITY OF NEW JERSEY, Institute of Jazz Studies, 135 Bradley Hall, Newark, 07102. Dan Morgenstern, Dir; Edward Berger, Cur; Maxie Griffin, Librn
Holdings: Vols 3000 Cat Pix Phonorecords Audiotapes Films Microforms VF
Notes: Incl jazz records, books, periodicals etc as well as some roots and peripheral material--African music, gospel music, rhythm and blues, rock etc (both written and recorded). Incl 60,000 records.

NJ —PRINCETON UNIVERSITY, Library, Rare Books Dept, Princeton, 08544. Stephen Ferguson, Cur
Holdings: Vols Mss Microforms
Notes: Incl serials and scores.

NJ —WESTMINSTER CHOIR COLLEGE, Talbott Library, Hamilton Ave at Walnut Lane, Princeton, 08540. Sherry L Vellucci, Acting Dir
Holdings: Vols (43,500) Cat Scores Periodicals Phonorecords Audiotapes Videotapes Microforms
Budget: ($30,000)
Notes: Talbott Library supports the curriculum of a music college which grants undergraduate and graduate degrees in church music, music education and music performance (voice, piano, organ and choral conducting), with an emphasis on choral music. Incl 7000 phonorecords, 3500 titles in quantity of choral music, 30,000 single copies of choral music.

NM —UNIVERSITY OF NEW MEXICO, Fine Arts Library, Fine Art Bldg, Albuquerque, 87131. James B Wright, Librn
Notes: Incl the archives of the New Mexico Symphony Orchestra. 6 linear ft.

NY —NEW YORK STATE LIBRARY, State Education Bldg Annex, Washington Ave, Albany, 12224.
Notes: American sheet music, late 18th to early 20th century. Mainly popular music, some New York State emphasis. 20,000 titles. Not completely organized; not centralized in one library section. General music collection of about 5000 vols.

NY —STATE UNIVERSITY OF NEW YORK, BUFFALO, Baird Music Library, Baird Hall, Amherst, 14260. James B Coover, Dir
Holdings: Vols (104,000) Cat Mss Pix Slides Phonorecords Microforms
Notes: Nearly complete collections of *Denkmaeler and Gesamtausgaben* and other historical sets. Strong collection of dictionaries, bibliographies, biographies, facsimiles, works on the "new" music, organology and ethnomusicology. Special emphasis on operas, scores of the avant-garde, jazz and urban popular music, discography and music librarianship. Good collection of medieval and Renaissance anthologies, contemporary and avant-garde recordings. Houses Archives of the Center of the Creative and Performing Arts. Collections incl 2100 slides, 22,000 phonorecords, 46,000 scores and parts, 29,000 books and 4900 microforms. Computerized record catalog in process.

NY —STATE UNIVERSITY OF NEW YORK, COLLEGE AT FREDONIA, Daniel A Reed Library, Fredonia, 14063. John P Saulitis, Dir of Library Services; Joanne L Schweik, Supv of Special Collections; Joseph Chouinard, Music Librn
Holdings: Vols 10,600 Cat Phonorecords Audiotapes VF
Budget: $16,000
Notes: The Music Library supports the

curricular needs of a large department of music which now has programs in applied music (performance), music education, music theory and composition, musical theatre (with the Theatre Department), music therapy, and sound recording technology (Tonmeister). The Library has a collection of 19th century American tunebooks, some Lowell Mason materials, and a collection of sheet music and dance band arrangements numbering more than 3200 pieces and covering the period from 1850 through the big band era. The entire music collection is supportive of both instruction and advanced research needs in the programs offered.

NY —CORNELL UNIVERSITY LIBRARIES, Collection of Regional History, Dept of Manuscripts and Univ Archives, Ithaca, 14853.
Notes: Incl papers (1884-1954) of the Cornell University Department of Music; programs for concerts, organ recitals and music festivals; musical scores, documents and historical sketches.

NY —CORNELL UNIVERSITY LIBRARIES, Music Library, 225 Lincoln Hall, Ithaca, 14853. Lenore Coral, Music Librn
Holdings: Vols (106,022) Cat Phonorecords Microforms
Budget: ($64,000)
Notes: Music Library is especially strong in good editions of music, in music history sources, bibliography, periodicals, and historical/scientific editions of music. There is little on music education. Collection is particularly strong in the areas of opera and Russian music. Good collection of Oriental music and books about music at Cornell. Developing 18th century materials, particularly Haydn and Mozart source materials. Repository for Alessandro Scarlatti sources. Good collection of LP phonorecords (26,000). Significant additions to collection of libretti and chamber music collection. This is primarily a collection in support of programs in music history and theory.

NY —QUEENS BOROUGH PUBLIC LIBRARY, Art & Music Div, 89-11 Merrick Blvd, Jamaica, 11432. Dorothea Wu, Head
Holdings: Vols (85,000) Cat Maps Pix Phonorecords Audiotapes Microforms
Budget: ($44,000)
Notes: The Picture Collection, covering all subjects, consists of approximately 1,500,000 pictures, mainly reproductions and clippings from books and magazines, photographs, and postcards on all subjects; The Framed Picture Collection, approx 180 framed pictures, mostly reproductions of paintings from various periods; and The Phonorecord and Cassette Collection consists of approx 3500 reference phonorecords and 6500 circulating records as well as 1000 reference cassettes and 1500 circulating cassettes.

NY —NEW ROCHELLE PUBLIC LIBRARY, Fine Arts Dept, Library Plaza, New Rochelle, 10801. Eugene L Mittelgluck, Library Dir
Holdings: Vols (13,000) Cat Pix Slides
Budget: ($10,000)
Notes: Incl (430,000) pictures and (6300) slides.
See also entries under Art; Ballet and the Dance; Costume.

NY —COLUMBIA UNIVERSITY LIBRARIES, Music Library, 701 Dodge, Broadway & 116 St, New York, 10027. M Haefliger, Librn
Holdings: Vols (55,020) Cat Phonorecords Audiotapes Microforms
Notes: Strong collections in Medieval and Renaissance music studies, all aspects of music theory, early music treatises and journals, historical musicology and ethnomusicology, early 20th century imprints, early pre-electric vocal 78 rpm recordings, and music scores.

NY —NEW YORK PUBLIC LIBRARY, Music Div, 111 Amsterdam Ave, New York, 10023. Frank C Campbell, Chief
Holdings: Vols (300,000) Cat Mss Pix Microforms
Notes: Described in *Dictionary Catalog of the Music Collection, The Research Libraries of the New York Public Library,*

MUSIC (cont.)

33 vols (532,000 cards), 1964, $2190; Supplement 1, 1 vol (17,000 cards), 1966, $100. Literature pertaining to virtually all musical subjects, and scores covering the broadest range of musical style and history are represented in this catalog. Special strengths of the collection incl folk songs, 18th and 19th-century librettos, full scores of operas, complete works, historical editions, Beethoven, Americana, American music, periodicals, vocal music, literature on the voice, programs, record catalogs, and mss in detail: sheet music, 355,414; sound recordings, 400,000; clippings and programs, 2 million; broadsides, 1821; songsters, 375; pictures, 51,002; mss, 29,877.

NY —NEW YORK PUBLIC LIBRARY, General Library and Museum of the Performing Arts, 111 Amsterdam Ave, New York, 10023. George Louis Mayer, Coordinator; Kris Shuman, Music Specialist
Holdings: Vols 35,000 Cat
Budget: ($17,000)

NY —NEW YORK PUBLIC LIBRARY, Performing Arts Research Center, Music Div, Lincoln Center, New York, 10018.
Notes: New York Pro Musica Archives, and personal papers of Noah Greenberg, founder.

NY —VASSAR COLLEGE, George Sherman Dickinson Music Library, Skinner Hall, Poughkeepsie, 12601. Sabrina L Weiss, Music Librn
Holdings: Vols (50,000) Cat Mss Phonorecords Audiotapes Microforms
Budget: ($25,000)
Notes: Areas of strength incl *Collected Works and Historical Monuments* (Denkmaeler), facsimile editions, periodicals, reference works (dictionaries, library catalogs), contemporary music, biography, and a balanced collection of musicological works. Incl 30,000 scores, 20,000 books and 25,000 phonorecords. Partly described in: G S Dickinson, "The Living Library," *MLA Notes III* (June 1946), 247-55; J B Coover, "...A College Music Library," *Papers & Addresses of the College Music Association, 9th Annual Meeting* (1955), pp 5-16; Carol June Bradley & James B Coover, "Vassar's Music Library," *MLA Notes* (June 1979), pp 819-46; *Grove's Dictionary of Music & Musicians* (5th ed, 1954; 6th ed, 1975); and *New Grove Dictionary of Music and Musicians* (1980).

NY —EASTMAN SCHOOL OF MUSIC, Sibley Music Library, 44 Swan St, Rochester, 14604. Ruth Watanabe, Librn
Holdings: Vols (360,000) Cat Mss Pix Phonorecords Microforms Music Scores
Notes: Research material for music theory, history, and performance. Incl an additional uncataloged collection of 300,000 pieces. The Sibley Music Library is a full-service branch of the University of Rochester Library System. Bibliographical lists of journals prepared twice annually. Historical items described in *University of Rochester Library Bulletin*. List of new reference work compiled quarterly.

NY —SYRACUSE UNIVERSITY LIBRARIES, Music Collection, 222 Waverly Ave, Syracuse, 13210. Donald Seibert, Librn
Holdings: // Cat Microforms
Notes: Nearly 1000 compositions survive in this collection of 17th century music deriving from the reign of Karl Liechtenstein-Castelcorn as Prince-Bishop of Olomouc. The music is preserved on microfilm in the George Arents Research Library at Syracuse University. Contents range from complete settings of masses, vesperae and litaniae to ensemble sonatas and balletti. The collection contains works by over 100 identified composers, including many who were associated with the Imperial court of Leopold I in Vienna, as well as numerous anonymous compositions. A large portion of the music remains unpublished. A catalog of the collection has been published by the Syracuse University Libraries, viz: Otto, Craig A, comp, *Seventeenth Century Music from Kromeriz, Czechoslovakia: A Catalog of the Liechtenstein Music*

Collection on Microfilm at Syracuse University(duplicated typescript; 209 pp).

NY —YONKERS PUBLIC LIBRARY, Grinton I Will Library, 1500 Central Park Ave, Yonkers, 10701. Joan W Stevenson, Head of Fine Arts Dept
Holdings: Vols (12,000) Cat
Budget: ($36,000)
Notes: Incl periodicals, 70 titles (ca 15 yr back issues); 27 vertical file drawers (18 on artists & musicians); 1230 slides; 2200 music scores; cat; sheet music, ca 1200 titles; 140 libretti; 13,000 phonograph albums; cat; 1000 cassettes. Books, scores, phonograph albums, cassettes are cataloged. Rare collection of 57 test pressings of Geraldine Farrar, some of which have never been issued.

NC —APPALACHIAN STATE UNIVERSITY, Music Library, Broyhill Music Center, Boone, 28608. Joan O Falconer, Librn
Holdings: Vols 1800 Phonorecords
Budget: ($9500)
Notes: A collection of music scores, chamber music, and 7000 recordings, supported by basic reference books. Former emphasis on music education materials now being expanded to include extensive performance materials and titles appropriate to a liberal arts curriculum through the master's degree level. The University Library (Belk Library) houses the main collection of book materials in music. Incl 12,000 music scores and parts and 7000 phonorecords.

NC —UNIVERSITY OF NORTH CAROLINA, CHAPEL HILL, Music Library, Hill Hall, Chapel Hill, 27514.
Holdings: Vols (90,000) Cat Mss Pix Slides Phonorecords Audiotapes Microforms
Budget: ($60,000)
Notes: Extensive holdings of early theoretical treatises; complete editions; performing scores; music periodicals; reference works. Special interests reflected in holdings of sonatas; oratorios; requiems; operas; microfilms of Vatican Library holdings of mss containing hymns; microfilms from the Deutsches Musikgeschichtliches Archiv; microfilms of important European primary sources; contemporary chamber music. Approx 5000 pieces of early American sheet music, primarily antebellum. Substantial collection of shape-note hymnals, 19th and 20th century. Dictionary catalog of books, scores, microforms and recordings. Separate card catalog of early American music and song anthologies held by Music Library. Partial book catalog of libretto collection.

NC —MARS HILL COLLEGE, Music Dept, Music Library, Mars Hill, 28754. Pat McManus, Music Librn
Holdings: Vols 8000 Cat
Budget: $3500

NC —NORTH CAROLINA STATE UNIVERSITY, D H Hill Library, Box 7111, Raleigh, 27695. I T Littleton, Dir
Holdings: Vols (2000) Cat Phonorecords Audiotapes
Budget: $1000
Notes: Winston Music Collection. Serves the sophisticated listener rather than the musicologist. Incl monographs.

NC —NORTH CAROLINA SCHOOL OF THE ARTS, Semans Library, PO Box 12189, Winston-Salem, 27107. William D VanHoven, Head Librn
Holdings: Vols (98,000) Cat Microforms Phonorecords Films
Budget: ($105,000)
Notes: Incl clippings, pictures and programs.

OH —PUBLIC LIBRARY OF CINCINNATI & HAMILTON COUNTY, Art & Music Dept, 800 Vine St, Cincinnati, 45202. R Jayne Craven, Head
Holdings: Vols (122,185) Cat Pix
Budget: ($56,100)
Notes: Special collections: Eda Kuhn Loeb, "Artist and the Book, 1875-Date" (now shelved in Rare Book Room); music librettos (2345); exhibition catalogs (5474); large prints and posters (5051); Cincinnati artists vertical files; picture collection (673,906 clippings).

OH —CASE WESTERN RESERVE UNIVERSITY, Kulas Music Library, 11118

Bellflower Rd, Cleveland, 44106. Timothy Robson, Music Librn
Notes: Containing deposit of a collection of some 800 records of music and the spoken word in French, English, and Spanish presented by Radio Canada International in Montreal.

OH —CLEVELAND PUBLIC LIBRARY, Fine Arts and Special Collections Department, 325 Superior Ave, Cleveland, 44114. Alice N Loranth, Head
Holdings: Vols 72,050 Cat Mss Phonorecords
Notes: Incl 11,000 phonorecords and bound vols of music and books about music; study scores of orchestral and chamber music. Large sets of complete works, dance band music orchestrations, sheet music. Programs of leading Cleveland and other national musical organizations appearing in Cleveland, phonograph records, pamphlets and clippings on music and musicians. Subscriptions to about 60 music periodicals. Incl the Johann H Beck Collection and the Charles V Rychlik Collection of manuscripts. Extensive VF of music clippings and ephemera.

OH —HIRAM COLLEGE, Teachout-Price Memorial Library, Hiram, 44234. Joanne M Sawyer, Archivist; Marjorie M Adams, Music Librn
Holdings: Phonorecords
Notes: The Geidlinger Listening Center of the Music Dept has stereo equipment and listening resources of 4914 recordings and 2107 musical scores.

OH —KENT STATE UNIVERSITY, Music Library, Kent, 44242. Judith B McCarron, Library Coord
Holdings: Vols (15,000) Uncat Phonorecords Audiotapes Microforms
Notes: Recordings 23,000, incl records, discs, cassettes; microfilm 506, periodicals 110.

OH —OBERLIN COLLEGE, Oberlin Conservatory of Music, Mary M Vial Library, Oberlin, 44074. John E Druesedow Jr, Dir
Holdings: Vols (75,000) Cat Phonorecords Audiotapes Filmstrips Microforms
Budget: ($60,000)
Notes: Special emphases; history and literature of the organ; music before 1700; music since 1950; music education; opera; American music; chamber and solistic music. Published catalog: *Mr and Mrs C W Best Collection of Autographs in the Mary M Vial Music Library of the Oberlin College Conservatory of Music* (Oberlin, Ohio: Oberlin College, 1967).

OH —WITTENBERG UNIVERSITY, Thomas Library, Springfield, 45501. Betty Beatty, Dir
Holdings: Cat Mss
Notes: No photocopying.

OR —UNIVERSITY OF OREGON LIBRARY, Music Dept, Eugene, 97403. Leslie K Greer, Music Librn
Holdings: Vols Cat Scores Phonorecords Audiotapes
Budget: $21,000
Notes: In addition to books, there is a collection of over 25,500 sound recordings and 15,000 scores.

OR —LIBRARY ASSOCIATION OF PORTLAND, Art & Music Dept, 801 S W Tenth Ave, Portland, 97205. Barbara K Padden, Librn
Holdings: Vols Cat Pix Slides Phonorecords
Notes: Art book titles: 21,325; music book titles (incl dance books): 10,800; sheet music titles: 19,550; slides on art subjects: about 12,000; phonorecord albums: 27,000; picture clippings: about 2 million; color reproductions of old and modern masters: about 640.

PA —BALA CYNWYD LIBRARY, Old Lancaster Rd & N Highland Ave, Bala Cynwyd, 19004. Rosalind Leighton, Reference Librn
Holdings: Phonorecords Audiotapes
Notes: 1,235 records and 522 cassettes. Incl opera, musicals, symphonies, concertos, chamber music, folk, pop, choral, etc.

PA —CARNEGIE LIBRARY OF PITTSBURGH, Music and Art Dept, 4400

MUSIC (cont.)

Forbes Ave, Pittsburgh, 15213. Ida Reed, Dept Head
Holdings: Vols 96,000 Cat Mss Pix Phonorecords
Notes: Emphasis in lending collection on practical editions of music since 1600. Reference collection incl early and first editions, monumental sets, historical anthologies, bibliographies. Thematic catalogs, dictionaries, encyclopedias, etc. Files of periodicals begin with year 1722 and incl notable collection of 19th century American music journals. Also, 30,000 phonorecords. Library compiles indexes of orchestral performances, piano, song, organ, and violin materials.

PA —UNIVERSITY OF PITTSBURGH, Music Library, B-31 Music Bldg, Pittsburgh, 15260. Norris L Stephens, Music Librn
Holdings: Vols 35,000 Cat Mss Maps Pix Slides Microforms
Notes: Collection contains over 1000 titles of music and music literature printed before 1801. A Union Catalogue of Music and Books on Music Printed before 1801 in Pittsburgh Libraries by Theodore M Finney, 1963 is currently being corrected and updated. Also 21,000 pieces of choral music 20,000 phonorecords.

PA —PENNSYLVANIA STATE UNIVERSITY, Arts Library, 405 E Pattee Library, University Park, 16802. Daniel Zager, Music Librn
Holdings: Vols 14,000 Cat Phonorecords
Notes: The music collection supports a School of Music curriculum which is comprehensive at the undergraduate and masters degree levels. The collection includes scores (collected works and performance editions), books (13,000), periodicals, and recordings. The Special Collections area of the library includes the following music collections: the manuscripts, published scores, personal papers, and some recordings of the American composer Charles Wakefield Cadman; 18th and 19th century American tunebooks and 18th and 19th century Pennsylvania German hymnbooks and songbooks; and the Doyle Guntharp collection of field recordings of fiddlers' performances and interviews from Central Pennsylvania.

RI —BROWN UNIVERSITY, John Hay Library, 20 Prospect St, Providence, 02912. Mark N Brown, Cur Mss
Holdings: Mss
Notes: Papers of William O Fuller (1828-1910), music teacher of Providence, comprising letters 1848 from Europe, incl a letter from Franz Liszt; papers of Johann Christian Gottlieb Graupner (1767-1836) and John Rowe Parker (fl 1820s) collected by Horace Mason Reynolds, relating to the music-publishing business in Boston, 1802-1838; papers of the American folklorist Mellinger Edward Henry (1873-1946) relating to his research and publications on American folk-songs 1910-1942; papers, 1912-1948, of Providence composer Hugh Frederick MacColl (1885-1953); papers of Frances Herriot Sargent, stage manager for "Porgy" and "Porgy and Bess", relating to productions of these, 1928-1942.

SC —CONVERSE COLLEGE, Gwathmey Library, Spartanburg, 29301. Darlene E Fawver, Music Librn
Holdings: Cat Mss Pix Microforms Phonorecords
Budget: ($17,000)
Notes: Incl 7,000 music book titles, 10,000 scores and 10,000 phonorecords; Lily Strickland Collection (manuscripts, printed music, memorabilia); Radiana Pazmor Collection (personal correspondence with Aaron Copland, Charles Ives, Darius Milhaud, Maurice Ravel, Virgil Thomson and others); autographed books, scores, manuscripts, and facsimiles of former Deans of the School of Music (R H Peters, Ernst Bacon, Edwin Gerschefski) and such notables as Henry Cowell and Carlisle Floyd.

TN —UNIVERSITY OF TENNESSEE, KNOXVILLE, Music Library, Knoxville,

37996. Pauline S Bayne, Music Librn
Holdings: Vols 34,070 Cat Microforms
Budget: $25,000
Notes: Separate catalog; holdings also listed in comprehensive public catalog in Main Library. Holdings incl books, scores, and sound recordings. Galston Music Collection and Galston-Busoni Archive, housed in Hoskins Library, Special Collections Department, incl mss, scores and memorabilia.

TN —VANDERBILT UNIVERSITY, Music Library, 419 21st Ave South, Nashville, 37203. Shirley Marie Watts, Librn
Holdings: Vols (23,000) Phonorecords Audiotapes Microforms
Budget: ($10,600)
Notes: Tapes of lectures, master classes and recitals incl in Seminars in Piano Teaching held at George Peabody College for Teachers, 1970-76. Also, Francis Robinson Collection of Sound Recordings. 23,000 books and musical scores, 10,000 phonorecords, 350 audiotapes, 1650 microforms. All materials cataloged.

†TX —UNIVERSITY OF TEXAS LIBRARIES, General Libraries, Humanities Research Center, PO Box 7219, Austin, 78712. John Chalmers, Librn

TX —UNIVERSITY OF TEXAS LIBRARIES, Music Library, PO Box P, Austin, 78712. Olga Buth, Librn
Holdings: Vols (21,862) Cat Phonorecords Audiotapes Microforms
Notes: Collection incl 36,462 scores, 3505 bound periodicals, 4506 microforms, 289 periodical subscriptions, 312 serials and monographs, 13,706 phonodiscs, and 922 phonotapes.

TX —DALLAS PUBLIC LIBRARY, Fine Arts Div, 1515 Young St, Dallas, 75201. Richard L Waters, Acting Dir; Jane Holahan, Manager
Notes: Papers of John Rosenfield, eminent Dallas critic for 41 years.

TX —NORTH TEXAS STATE UNIVERSITY, Audio Center, Box 5188, NT Station, Denton, 76203. Morris Martin, Music Librn
Notes: Supports wide range of music curricula and research with over 100,000 volumes incl music books, periodicals, scores, sheet music of all kinds, chamber music, recordings; special collections incl the libraries of musicologists Lloyd Hibberd and Helen Hewitt, bandleader Stan Kenton, composer Don Gillis, radio stations WFAA and WBAP; archives of Source magaine, mss of Arnold Schoenberg, recording collections (Arturo Toscanini, Don Gillis, Duke Ellington and other jazz musicians).

TX —TEXAS CHRISTIAN UNIVERSITY, Mary Couts Burnett Library, Music Dept, Fort Worth, 76129. Sheila Madden, Librn
Holdings: Vols 23,000 Cat Phonorecords Audiotapes Microforms
Budget: $12,125
Notes: Incl 1200 phonorecords and 1600 audiotapes.

VA —UNIVERSITY OF VIRGINIA, Alderman Library, Music Collection, Charlottesville, 22901. Evan Bonds, Music Librn
Holdings: Vols (38,000) Cat Mss Microforms
Budget: ($50,000)
Notes: Sizeable amount of rare book material: extensive ms collections, principally of traditional music; extensive collection of miscellaneous imprints of performing editions; valuable collection of 18th-century imprints incl rare tutors, etc in the Alexander MacKay-Smith Collection; the Monticello Music Collection; printed and ms collection of the music of John Powell; extensive collections, ms and typescript, and discs of traditional music; some Randall Thompson mss; 250 tapes; 9000 phonorecords.

VA —SWEET BRIAR COLLEGE, Library, Sweet Briar, 24595. John Jaffe, Librn
Holdings: Vols 175 // Cat Phonorecords
Notes: Sigred Onegin Collection. Incl 18th and 19th century opera scores; 4000 songs; and phonorecords.

†WA —SEATTLE PUBLIC LIBRARY, Music Dept, Fourth & Madison, Seattle, 98104. Carolyn Holmquist, Head
Holdings: Vols 34,803
Notes: 30,362 phonorecords.

WA —UNIVERSITY OF WASHINGTON LIBRARIES, Music Library, DN-10, Seattle, 98195. David A Wood, Music Librn
Holdings: Vols 46,212 Cat Mss Phonorecords Audiotapes Microforms
Budget: $44,522
Notes: Incl the Hazel G Kinscella Collection of colonial and early 19th-century musical Americana. Also have 28,874 phonorecords and 7,823 audiotapes, collection of 17th-19th century opera scores.

WI —MILWAUKEE PUBLIC LIBRARY, 814 W Wisconsin Ave, Milwaukee, 53233. Donald J Sager, City Librn
Holdings: Vols Cat
Budget: $9866
Notes: An extensive general music literature collection incl classical, contemporary, jazz, and musical biographies, as well as the most significant reference works in music. Also incl 46,708 sound recordings, 73,150 historical recorded sound collection, 20,000 historic popular song collection, and WPA copied music. Local area music materials incl concert programs and newspaper clippings.

WY —UNIVERSITY OF WYOMING, William Robertson Coe Library, Archives - American Heritage Center, PO Box 3412, Laramie, 82071.
Notes: Music manuscripts of Carl W Stalling, writer of music for such cartoons as "Mickey Mouse," "Silly Symphonies," "Three Little Pigs," "Bugs Bunny," "Looney Tunes," and other productions of Walt Disney and Warner Brothers. Incl 1300 complete original scores, more than 2000 sheets of other music, and many other materials.

PR —UNIVERSITY OF PUERTO RICO, Jose M Lazaro Memorial Library, Music Room, Box C, University of Puerto Rico Sta, Rio Piedras, 00931. Ramon Arollo, Librn
Holdings: Vols 42,550 Cat Mss Slides Phonorecords Audiotapes Microforms
Notes: Incl over 9142 scores, 19,000 phonorecords, 7488 music books, 5191 newspapers, and 134 audiotapes.

BC —VANCOUVER PUBLIC LIBRARY, Art Div, 750 Burrard St, Vancouver, V6Z 1X5, Can.
Holdings: Cat Pix
Notes: Book and pamphlet collection. Also, (1) Newspaper Clippings File: 31 drawers of relevant clippings from major newspapers, incl the Sun, Province, Toronto Globe and Mail, Christian Science Monitor, New York Times, etc on arts, music, architecture; incl biographical material (16 drawers). (2) Picture File about 500,000 pictures in 150 cabinet drawers, strong in architecture, costume, interior decoration, painting, sculpture, also portraits. (3) Exhibition Catalogs File: British Columbia and elsewhere. (4) Association and Organization File: organizations in the Lower Mainland in arts, music, city planning, etc, begun in 1940s; (5) Canadian Artists Index: begun in 1964, alphabetically by artist, with about 300,000 citationsto reproductions of work and biographical material on Canadian artist from the division's books and other sources; (6) Miscellaneous Index: material not covered in other special or published indexes, primarily of Canadian and local cultural events, hard-to-find informations, etc. Local newspapers, special Canadian publications and British film journals are the most regularly indexed items. (7) Song Index started in the 1930s. (8) Title Index to song collections and sheet music in the VPL collection, approx 100,000 entries.

MB —UNIVERSITY OF MANITOBA, Music Library, 223 Music Bldg, Winnipeg, R3T 2N2, Can. Vladimir Simosko, Head
Holdings: Vols 15,000 Cat
Notes: Incl performance music (27,750 items); 4200 phonorecords.

NB —MOUNT ALLISON UNIVERSITY, Alfred Whitehead Memorial Music Library, Sackville, E0A 3C0, Can. Bert Meerveld, Music Librn
Holdings: Vols (16,411) Cat Slides Phonorecords Audiotapes Filmstrips Microforms
Notes: Large collection of Canadian music. Described in Canadian Music Scores and

MUSIC (cont.)

Recordings: A Classified Catalogue of the Holdings of Mount Allison University Libraries, comp by Gwendolyn Creelman, Esther Cooke and Geraldine King, 1976. Collection incl 5057 phonorecords; 38 tapes; 99 cassettes; 16,411 monographs, scores and bound periodicals; 101 reels of microfilm; and 3287 sheets of microfiche. Cataloged.

ON —UNIVERSITY OF OTTAWA, Morisset Library, 65 Hastey St, Ottawa, K1N 9A5, Can. Yvon Richer, University Chief Librn
Holdings: Vols (12,000)
Notes: Incl 100 periodicals, 16,000 scores and 5150 sound recordings. Scores and recordings are housed in the music department and monographs and periodicals in the Morisset Library. The collection is particularly strong in sixteenth to nineteenth century continental European music and musicology.

ON —METROPOLITAN TORONTO LIBRARY, Music Dept, 789 Yonge St, Toronto, M4W 2G8, Can. Isabel Rose, Head
Holdings: Cat
Budget: ($54,000)
Notes: 14,800 books, 40,000 scores; 1900 pieces of retrospective Canadian sheet music; 500 pieces of American and British sheet music, pre-1980; 17,000 phonorecords; 180 current periodical titles; 2800 bound peiodicals; 340 reels of microfilmed periodicals; 16,000 concert programs, chiefly Toronto city; 8850 newspaper clipping files; music picture files integrated with Fine Art Dept picture collection.

ON —UNIVERSITY OF TORONTO, Edward Johnson Music Library, Toronto, M5S 1A1, Can. Kathleen McMorow, Librn; James Creighton, Sound Archivist
Holdings: Vols 100,000 Cat Phonorecords Audiotapes Microforms
Notes: Reference and research collection in music of the western "classical" tradition and music of other traditions as investigated by western scholarship. Emphasis on historical editions (eg, Denkmaeler, Monumenta) and collected works of individual composers, scores and parts to represent the basic repertoire, reference works, back files of musicological journals, and historical and biographical monographs in all European languages. Collection incl 3000 audiotapes and 125,000 phonorecords, of which 61,000 are 78 rpm.

†PQ —UNIVERSITE DU QUEBEC A MONTREAL, Bibliotheque de Musique, BP 8889, Succursale A, Montreal, H3C 3P3, Can.

PQ —UNIVERSITY OF MONTREAL, Bibliotheque de Musique, 200 Vincent d'Indy, bp 6128, succursale "A", Montreal, H3C 3J7, Can. Claude Soulard, Librn
Holdings: Vols 9900 Phonorecords Audiotapes Microforms
Budget: $62,000
Notes: Special emphasis on the classical period and contemporary music. Incl 11,895 music scores, 11,857 records and tapes and 6250 microforms.

MUSIC—BIBLIOGRAPHY

NY —NEW YORK PUBLIC LIBRARY, Music Div, 111 Amsterdam Ave, New York, 10023. Frank C Campbell, Chief
NC —UNIVERSITY OF NORTH CAROLINA, CHAPEL HILL, Music Library, Hill Hall, Chapel Hill, 27514.
Holdings: Vols (90,000) Cat Mss Pix Slides Phonorecords Audiotapes Microforms
Budget: ($60,000)
Notes: Extensive holdings.
TX —NORTH TEXAS STATE UNIVERSITY, Audio Center, Box 5188, NT Station, Denton, 76203. Morris Martin, Music Librn

MUSIC—BIOGRAPHY see Composers; Musicians; Singers; Conductors (Music); Musical Instruments—Makers

MUSIC—BLACKS

DC —HOWARD UNIVERSITY, Moorland-Spingarn Research Center, 500 Howard Place NW, Washington, 20059. Clifford L Muse, Jr, Acting Dir
Holdings: Vols (106,086) Cat Mss Maps Pix Slides Phonorecords Audiotapes 16mm Films Filmstrips Microforms
Budget: ($854,753)
Notes: The Glenn Carrington Collection: A Guide to the Books, Manuscripts, Music and Recordings (DC MSRC, 1977). Dictionary Catalog of the Jesse E Moorland Collection of Negro Life and History, 9 vols and Supplement, 3 vols (Boston: G K Hall, 1970, 1977). Dictionary Catalog of the Arthur Spingarn Collection of Negro Authors, 2 vols (Boston: G K Hall, 1970). Guide to Processed Collections in the Manuscript Division of the Moorland-Spingarn Research Center (DC, MSRC, 1983). The Moorland-Spingran Research Center is recognized as one of the largest and most comprehensive repositories in the world for the collection, preservation and dissemination of historical materials documenting from antiquity to the present the history and culture of Black people in Africa, Europe, the Caribbean and the US. Since 1973, the Research Center has greatly expanded its facilitiesand resources and currently provides research services in all aspects of library and archival research, including manuscripts, oral history, music, prints and photographs and general library materials. The Research Center also maintains professional zerographic, micrographic, photographic and similar reproduction laboratories.

IN —INDIANA UNIVERSITY, Lilly Library, Seventh St, Bloomington, 47405. William R Cagle, Librn
Holdings: // Uncat
Notes: In the Starr Collection of American Sheet Music.

LA —TULANE UNIVERSITY, Howard-Tilton Memorial Library, Special Collections Div, William Ransom Hogan Jazz Archive, 7001 Freret, New Orleans, 70118. Richard B Allen, Acting Cur; Alma D Williams, Assistant to the Cur
Holdings: Vols (100,000) Cat Mss Pix Slides Phonorecords Audiotapes Videotapes 16mm Films Microforms
Budget: ($90,000)
Notes: Jazz music and musicians. Outstanding collection, incl books, music scores, serials, catalogs and other archival material. Music, history, etc.
See also entry under Jazz

NY —STATE UNIVERSITY OF NEW YORK, BUFFALO, Baird Music Library, Baird Hall, Amherst, 14260. James B Coover, Dir
Holdings: Vols (104,000) Cat Mss Pix Slides Phonorecords Microforms
Notes: Nearly complete collections of Denkmaeler and Gesamtausgaben and other historical sets. Strong collection of dictionaries, bibliographies, biographies, facsimiles, works on the "new" music, organology and ethnomusicology. Special emphasis on operas, scores of the avant-garde, jazz and urban popular music, discography and music librarianship. Good collection of medieval and Renaissance anthologies, contemporary and avant-garde recordings. Houses Archives of the Center of the Creative and Performing Arts. Collections incl 2100 slides, 22,000 phonorecords, 46,000 scores and parts, 29,000 books, 4900 microforms. Computerized record catalog in process.

NY —BARNARD A & MORRIS N YOUNG LIBRARY OF EARLY AMERICAN POPULAR MUSIC, 270 Riverside Dr, New York, 10025. Morris N Young, Cur
Holdings: Cat Mss Pix Phonorecords Audiotapes Microforms
Notes: 48,000 items of American popular music, mostly 1790-1910. Incl books, serials, sheet music, broadsides, anthologies, air checks, broadcasting and music business memorabilia, and correspondence.

PA —ERIE COUNTY HISTORICAL SOCIETY LIBRARY, 417 State St, Erie, 16501. Helen Andrews, Librn
Notes: Original research materials in 16 legal size drawers, including Pennsylvania Population Company papers, Old Erie Academy papers, Erie Street railway papers, Harry Burleigh (black singer & composer) transcripts and research papers; also four letter size drawers with old account books.

PA —UNIVERSITY OF PITTSBURGH, Stephen Foster Memorial, Foster Hall Collection, Pittsburgh, 15260. Deane L Root, Cur
Holdings: Vols (1000) Cat Mss Pix Phonorecords VF //
Budget: ($50,000)
Notes: Collection comprises more than 10,000 separate American items; original mss and letters; first editions, and early modern editions of Foster's music; personal possessions of the composer; books; magazine and newspaper articles; pictures and portraits; phonograph records; broadsides; and other material.

TN —COUNTRY MUSIC FOUNDATION, Library & Media Center, 4 Music Sq E, Nashville, 37203. Charlie Seemann, Dir
Holdings: Vols (6000) Mss Pix Slides Phonorecords Audiotapes Videotapes 16mm Films Microforms
Notes: The largest collection in the world dealing with American country music. Related subject areas are also included-- Anglo-American folksong, popular music in general (soul, jazz, rock and roll, rhythm and blues, etc), recorded sound technology, music law.

MUSIC—CHICAGO

IL —NEWBERRY LIBRARY, 60 W Walton St, Chicago, 60610. Diana Haskell, Cur of Modern Mss
Holdings: Cat Mss
Notes: Papers of Theodore Thomas, Frederick Stock, Frederick Grant Gleason, Bernhard Ziehn, Felix Borowski, Rudolph Ganz and others. Some 900 titles of printed music catalogued.

MUSIC—COMPOSITION see Composition (Music)

MUSIC—CRITICISM see Music—History and Criticism

MUSIC—DETROIT

MI —DETROIT PUBLIC LIBRARY, Music & Performing Arts Dept, 5201 Woodward, Detroit, 48202. Agatha Pfeiffer Kalkanis, Chief
Holdings: Cat
Notes: Collection of 5000 song collections of all types, as well as individual sacred and secular songs and folk songs. Incl all collections in standard indexes (Sears, DeCharms & Breed, Leigh, etc). Printed indexes supplemented by song index on cards in department, which incorporates title entries for more than 17,000 titles of 19th and 20th century popular sheet music, otherwise uncataloged. Popular music collection rich in show tunes, added on current basis, and in songs by Detroit writers and printed by publishing houses once active in Detroit (Remich, Whitney, etc). Much on Blacks' music and songs.

MUSIC—ECONOMIC ASPECTS see Music Industry

MUSIC—FACSIMILES

NY —STATE UNIVERSITY OF NEW YORK, BUFFALO, Baird Music Library, Baird Hall, Amherst, 14260. James B Coover, Dir
Holdings: Vols (104,000) Cat Mss Pix Slides Phonorecords Microforms
Notes: Nearly complete collections of Denkmaeler and Gesamtausgaben and other historical sets. Strong collection of dictionaries, bibliographies, biographies, facsimiles, works on the "new" music, organology and ethnomusicology. Special emphasis on operas, scores of the avant-garde, jazz and urban popular music, discography and music librarianship. Good collection of medieval and Renaissance

MUSIC—FACSIMILES (cont.)

anthologies, contemporary and avant-garde recordings. Houses Archives of the Center of the Creative and Performing Arts. Collections incl 2100 slides, 22,000 phonorecords, 46,000 scores and parts, 29, 000 books, 4900 microforms. Computerized record catalog in process.

MUSIC—HISTORIOGRAPHY

CA —UNIVERSITY OF CALIFORNIA, BERKELEY, Humanities-Social Sciences Libraries, Music Library, 24 Morrison Hall, Berkeley, 94720. Michael A Keller, Head Librn
Holdings: Vols 115,000 Cat Mss Slides Microforms
Notes: The Library maintains an outstanding music reference collection. It is rich in primary source materials for research, particularly in the areas of opera, 18th-century instrumental music, music theory. Incl 20,000 sound recordings. See the following: Vincent Duckles and Minnie Elmer, *Thematic Catalogue of a Collection of 18th-Century Italian Instrumental Music in the Music Library of the University of Califonia, Berkeley* (Univ of California Press, 1963); Alan Curtis, "Musique classique francaise a Berkeley," in *Revue de Musicologie,* 56 (1970) pp 123-164. Minnie Elmer, *Autograph Manuscripts of Ernest Bloch at the University of California; Cum Notis Variorum, the Newsletter of the Music Library of the University of California* (Published 10 times annually since April 1976).

IL —NEWBERRY LIBRARY, 60 W Walton St, Chicago, 60610. Diana Haskell, Cur of Modern Mss
Holdings: Vols (200,000) Cat Mss
Notes: Incl 45,000 vols 55,000 scores; 100, 000 pieces of sheet music. Primary and secondary materials for the study of Western European music from the Middle Ages through the 19th century and of American music from it beginnings. Strong periodical holdings and monumental editions. Restricted use: noncirculating.

KY —UNIVERSITY OF KENTUCKY, Margaret I King Library, Dept of Special Collections, Lexington, 40506. William Marshall, Head
Holdings: Vols 292
Notes: Alfred Cortot History of Music Collection, covers years 1491-1818.

MUSIC—HISTORY AND CRITICISM

CA —UNIVERSITY OF CALIFORNIA, BERKELEY, Humanities-Social Sciences Libraries, Music Library, 24 Morrison Hall, Be keley, 94720. Michael A Keller, Head Li rn
Holdings: Vols 3000 Cat Mss
Notes: The Alfred Einstein *Nachlass* comprises a scholar's working library in music history (ca 2000 vols), plus a special collection of research materials devoted to Mozart, and to Einstein's studies of the Italian madrigal. The collection also incl a file of music criticism by Einstein and selected correspondence.

CA —MUSIC CENTER OPERATING CO, Music Center Archives, 135 N Grand Ave, Los Angeles, 90012. Fran Morris Rosman, Librn
Holdings: Uncat Mss Pix Slides Videotapes Filmstrips
Notes: History of music and the dance as developed and performed here. Extensive collection. Incl also the history of the performing arts.

CA —SAN FRANCISCO STATE UNIVERSITY, Frank V de Bellis Collection, 1630 Holloway Ave, San Francisco, 94132. Serena de Bellis, Cur
Holdings: Uncat Mss Phonorecords Audiotapes Microforms
Notes: Rare and current materials. Music by Italian composers, medieval through contemporary (10,000 scores). Phonorecords, cylinders, tapes, etc (20,000);

primarily vocal--all nationalities--and music by Italian composers.

CT —YALE UNIVERSITY, Music Library, 98 Wall St, New Haven, 06520. Harold E Samuel, Librn
Holdings: Vols (118,000) Cat Mss Pix Phonorecords Audiotapes Microforms
Notes: General reference and research materials. Performing editions. Strong in theoretical literature, opera, 17-18th century music (incl mss), J S Bach and sons in early editions and mss, Russian liturgical music (Tkaczenko Collection), hymnology, American music. Also collection of musical pictures and portraits.

†DC —CATHOLIC UNIVERSITY OF AMERICA, Music Library, Washington, 20064. Betty Libbey, Head Music Library
Holdings: Cat Microforms
Notes: A large collection to support advanced degree study. Emphasis on church music, musicology, history and criticism, intrumental and vocal music, solo music for all voices, instruments, and musical forms.

DC —HARVARD UNIVERSITY, Dumbarton Oaks, Research Library, 1703 32nd St NW, Washington, 20007. Irene Vaslef, Librn
Holdings: Vols (91,000) Cat Maps Pix Slides Microforms
Budget: ($219,000)
Notes: Byzantine civilization (including art, archaeology, literature, history, religion, law, music, etc). Extensive supplemental material on Classical, Hellenistic, Medieval, Islamic, Medieval Slavic cultures. 62,000 b/w photographs, 25,000 slides and transparencies, 1000 microfilms of books and manuscripts. Printed description of collection in *Harvard Library Bulletin,* vol 19, no 1 (Jan 1971), pp 25-35 and vol 19, no 2 (April 1971), pp 204-214, pp 25-35 and vol 19, no 2 (April 1971), pp 204-214.

DC —LIBRARY OF CONGRESS, Music Division, Washington, 20540.
Notes: Literature on virtually every aspect of the history and performance of Western music from earliest times to the present. Its greatest strengths are collections relating to the music of the US, opera, the work of the so-called second Viennese school, and early music printing.

FL —UNIVERSITY OF MIAMI, Music Library, PO Box 248165, Coral Gables, 33124. Nancy Kobialke, Librn
Holdings: Vols Cat Phonorecords
Budget: ($25,000)
Notes: Emphasis on research editions and performing editions with parts for 2-8 players. Nearly 24,000 musical scores. Recordings are mostly classical, but incl 1200 jazz LPs and 1200 ethnic LPs from all parts of world. *Inter-American Music Archive* is special catalog of Latin American holdings. Collection incl 15,500 cataloged phonorecords.

IL —UNIVERSITY OF ILLINOIS, URBANA/CHAMPAIGN, Library, Bands & Busch Instrument Collection, 1103 S Sixth St, Champaign, 61820. John Cranford, Librn
Notes: This collection of 212 old and unusual wind and percussion instruments comes from two sources: The Carl Busch collection, and instruments collected by the late Director of University Bands Emeritus, Dr A A Harding. The museum is open from 8 to 5 Monday through Friday, by appointment only.

IL —NEWBERRY LIBRARY, 60 W Walton St, Chicago, 60610. Diana Haskell, Cur of Modern Mss
Holdings: Vols (200,000) Cat Mss
Notes: Incl 45,000 vols; 55,000 scores; 100, 000 pieces of sheet music. Primary and secondary materials for the study of Western European music from the Middle Ages through the 19th century and of American music from its beginnings. Strong periodical holdings and monumental editions. Restricted use: noncirculating.

IL —NORTHWESTERN UNIVERSITY, Music Library, 1937 Sheridan Rd, Evanston, 60201. Don L Roberts, Head Music Librn
Holdings: Vols (140,000) Cat Mss Phonorecords Audiotapes Microforms
Notes: Main emphasis is on the documentation (incl 2000 ms pieces) of 20th

century music. Broad acquisitions of mss, books, music and recordings relating to 20th century music. Library contains a portion of the Moldenhauer Archive and the John Cage "Notations Collection".

IN —BUTLER UNIVERSITY, Irwin Library, Hugh Thomas Miller Rare Book Room, 4600 Sunset Ave, Indianapolis, 46208. Gisela Terrell, Rare Books Librn
Holdings: Cat
Notes: Sibelius Collection. It contains mostly the lesser-known compositions, and includes scores in print, hectograph, and manuscript, many of them unpublished and unknown in the US. Also rare secondary sources, mostly Finnish and Swedish imprints. Also a collection of mostly historical recordings, probably complete up to 1972. Placed in trust in the Rare Book Room by Dr Harold E Johnson, Sibelius scholar, 1982-1983. A preliminary checklist is available. The recordings include many pieces by lesser-known Finnish composers.

KY —UNIVERSITY OF KENTUCKY, Music Library, 116 Fine Arts Bldg, Lexington, 40506. Cathy S Hunt, Music Librn
Holdings: Vols 18,000 Cat Microforms Scores Recordings
Notes: Collection incl books (14,000), includes music history, theory, music eduction, jazz, etc cat. Music Scores (18, 000) cat. Serials (3200 vols) cat. Microforms (6300) cat. Recordings (9100) cat. Collected Editions (complete Works of composers, large sets, etc) (7100) cat. The Alfred Cortot Collection (about 300 vols of rare, early music theory books) is housed in the Rare Books Room of the Main Library.

KY —UNIVERSITY OF LOUISVILLE, School of Music, Dwight Anderson Memorial Music Library, 2301 S Third St, Louisville, 40292. Marion Korda, Librn
Holdings: Vols 35,000 Cat Mss Pix Phonorecords Audiotapes Microforms
Budget: $15,000
Notes: Plus 20,000 uncataloged pieces. 296 serial publications on monthly computer print-out. Participating member of Metroversity library system, as well as state-wide University Referral Center, serves research and study needs at preparatory, undergraduate and graduate levels of the University. Music History materials in general library available through union list. No photocopying.

LA —LOUISIANA STATE MUSEUM, Louisiana Historical Center, 400 Esplanade Ave, (Mailing add: 751 Chartres St, New Orleans, 70116). Edward F Haas, Chief Cur
Holdings: Vols 2000 Cat Pix Slides Phonorecords Audiotapes
Notes: New Orleans Jazz Museum and Archives Collection. Donated to the Louisiana State Museum by the New Orleans Jazz Club in 1977. If was formerly a private museum sponsored by the Jazz Club and housed at 833 Conti St, New Orleans, La 70130. Emphasis is New Orleans jazz, incl 8000 pieces of sheet music; 12,000 phonorecords; 15,000 pictures; 1000 slides; and 1000 audiotapes. A guide to the collection is in preparation.

LA —TULANE UNIVERSITY, Howard-Tilton Memorial Library, Special Collections Div, William Ransom Hogan Jazz Archive, 7001 Freret, New Orleans, 70118. Richard B Allen, Acting Cur; Alma D Williams, Assistant to the Cur
Holdings: Vols (100,000) Cat Mss Pix Slides Phonorecords Audiotapes Videotapes 16mm Films Microforms
Budget: ($90,000)
Notes: Jazz music and musicians. Outstanding collection, incl books, music scores, serials, catalogs and other archival material. Music, history, etc. *See also* entry under Jazz

MD —PEABODY CONSERVATORY LIBRARY, 21 E Mt Vernon Place, Baltimore, 21202. Edwin A Quist, Librn
Holdings: Vols 70,000 Cat Mss Pix Phonorecords Audiotapes Videotapes Microforms
Budget: $30,000
Notes: The Peabody Conservatory Library, formerly a part of the Peabody Institute

MUSIC—HISTORY AND CRITICISM (cont.)

Library (now the George Peabody Library of the Johns Hopkins University) supplies the library needs of the faculty and student body of the Peabody Conservatory of Music. While the collection has numerous research capabilities, it is basically a collection of musical scores. The entire history of Western music is represented through collected editions, monumental anthologies, study scores, performing editions and a large collection of books and music periodicals. This collection is supplemented by a listening facility containing 14,000 discs and an ensembles library containing scores and parts of orchestral, band and chorus works.

MD —TOWSON STATE UNIVERSITY, Fine Arts Bldg, Room 457, Towson, 21204. Edwin L Gerhardt, Curator
Notes: The Gerhardt Library of Musical Information is a segregated representative collection of music literature, phonograph and tape recordings, pictures and artifacts. It incl special sections on Thomas Alva Edison and the phonograph, John Philip Sousa and bands, old popular songs and percussion. Most of the material is out of print and hard to find. It is *not* a collection of scores or manuscripts. A detailed outline is available upon request. Direct all correspondence to the curator, Edwin L Gerhardt, 4926 Leeds Ave, Baltimore, MD 21227, (301) 242-0328.

MA —MASSACHUSETTS INSTITUTE OF TECHNOLOGY, Music Library, 14E-109, Cambridge, 02139. Linda I Solow, Librn
Holdings: Vols (47,000) Cat Phonorecords Audiotapes Scores
Notes: Described in *Directory of Music Libraries and Collections in New England,* 6th ed (Music Library Assn, New England Chapter, 1981); Bradley, Carol J, *Music collections in American libraries: a chronology* (Detroit, Information Coordinators, 1981); *Music Industry Directory* 7th ed (Chicago Marquis Who's Who, 1983). Borrowing of circulating collection limited to MIT community; limited room access to outside users. Reference service weekdays.

MI —UNIVERSITY OF MICHIGAN, School of Music, Music Library, Moore Bldg, Ann Arbor, 48109. Peggy Daub, Head
Holdings: Vols (90,000) Cat Mss Microforms
Notes: Reference and research materials, as well as performing editions. Rare materials (including the Stellfeld Collection) are strong in early editions of works by the sons of J S Bach and 18th-19th century opera scores, particularly French. Includes 1200 microfilms of important European and American primary sources. See L Cuyler, H David & G Sutherland: "The University of Michigan's Purchase of the Stellfeld Music Library," *MLA Notes* 12 (1954-5), 3-19.
See also entries under Women Composers; Jacob M Coopersmith.

MO —SAINT LOUIS UNIVERSITY, Pius XII Memorial Library, 3655 W Pine Blvd, Saint Louis, 63108. William Cole, Dir
Holdings: Slides Microforms
Notes: Collection covers all areas of learning and European history from Classical Antiquity to early modern period. Researchers using collection receive assistance in paleography, bibliography and reference search. Approx 10,000 1000-foot reels of microfilm (not counting master negatives) reproducing Vatican Library's Latin, Greek, Hebrew, Arabic and Ethiopic mss. Some 8000 100-foot reels of microfilm (again not counting master negative) reproducing rare and out of print books relating to subject areas in the mss. Over 50,000 color slides of medieval and Renaissance mss illuminations. A reference collection of modern materials relating to ms research.

MO —WASHINGTON UNIVERSITY, Libraries, Campus Box 1061, Saint Louis, 63130.
Holdings: 4500 Vols
Notes: The private library of the late Gert von Gontard. Incl works on art, literature (especially German), music, and theater.

Contains 1200 vols Goetheana, with first editions, autographed letters and original drawings by Goethe. Also material on the Austrian writer Karl Kraus and the Belgian artist Frans Masereel.

NJ —FAIRLEIGH DICKINSON UNIVERSITY, Friendship Library, 285 Madison Ave, Madison, 07940. James Fraser, Library Dir; Renee Weber, Cur
Notes: Incl 5000 phonorecords (all 78 rpm); cylinders; 1500 pieces of sheet music; publishers catalogs; victrolas. The George H Moss Collection traces the history of music and theatre from 1890-1950 through publisher's catalogs, sheet music, cylinders and phonorecordings. A published list of the sheet music is available.

NJ —PRINCETON UNIVERSITY, Library, Rare Books Dept, Princeton, 08544. Stephen Ferguson, Cur
Notes: The James S Hall Collection (from Walmer, England). One of the major collections.
See also entry under Handel, George Frederick

NM —NEW MEXICO STATE UNIVERSITY, Library, Box 3475, Las Cruces, 88003. James Dyke, Dir
Holdings: Vols 4000 // Cat
Notes: Jazz, Blues, and music history. Collection of music periodical and monographs of the 1930s, 1940s and 1950s.

NY —STATE UNIVERSITY OF NEW YORK, BUFFALO, Baird Music Library, Baird Hall, Amherst, 14260. James B Coover, Dir
Holdings: Vols (104,000) Cat Mss Pix Slides Phonorecords Microforms
Notes: Music: history and criticism. Nearly complete collections of *Denkmaeler and Gesamtausgaben* and other historical sets. Strong collection of dictionaries, bibliographies, biographies, facsimiles, works on the "new" music, organology and ethnomusicology. Special emphasis on operas, scores of the avant-garde, jazz and urban popular music, discography and music librarianship. Good collection of medieval and Renaissance anthologies, contemporary and avant-garde recordings. Houses Archives of the Center of the Creative and Performing Arts. Collections incl 2100 slides, 22,000 phonorecords, 46,000 scores and parts, 29,000 books, 4900 microforms. Computerized record catalog in process.

NY —BROOKLYN PUBLIC LIBRARY, Art & Music Div, Grand Army Plaza, Brooklyn, 11238. Sue H Sharma, Chief
Holdings: Vols (4500) Cat Mss
Notes: Over 50,000 items, most of which circulate to the public. The collection contains some reference materials, incl the complete works of many composers; over 3500 popular song folios with our own in-house index for locating individual songs; some rare editions and mss of local composers; and a small collection of rare sheet music beginning with the 18th century. The circulating collection incl standard vocal scores, methods, piano music, etc, and is one of the largest public library collections in the country.

NY —BUFFALO & ERIE COUNTY PUBLIC LIBRARY, Music Dept, Lafayette Sq, Buffalo, 14203. Norma Jean Lamb, Head
Holdings: Cat
Notes: 76,400 bound vols of music and music literature. Complete works of the great composers, and historical editions. Orchestral scores and parts.

NY —BARNARD A & MORRIS N YOUNG LIBRARY OF EARLY AMERICAN POPULAR MUSIC, 270 Riverside Dr, New York, 10025. Morris N Young, Cur
Holdings: Cat Mss Pix Phonorecords Audiotapes Microforms
Notes: 48,000 items of American popular music, mostly 1790-1910. Incl books, serials, sheet music, broadsides, anthologies, air checks, broadcasting and music business memorabilia, and correpondence.

NY —COLUMBIA UNIVERSITY LIBRARIES, Music Library, 701 Dodge, Broadway & 116 St, New York, 10027. M Haefliger, Librn
Holdings: Vols (55,020) Cat Phonorecords

Audiotapes Microforms
Notes: Strong collections in Medieval and Renaissance music studies, all aspects of music theory, early music treatises and journals, historical musicology and ethnomusicology, early 20th century imprints, early pre-electric vocal 78 rpm recordings, and music scores.

NY —NEW YORK PUBLIC LIBRARY, Music Div, 111 Amsterdam Ave, New York, 10023. Frank C Campbell, Chief
Holdings: Vols (300,000) Cat Mss Pix Microforms
Notes: Described in *Dictionary Catalog of the Music Collection, The Research Libraries of the New York Public Library,* 33 vols (532,000 cards), 1964, $2190; Supplement 1, 1 vol (17,000 cards), 1966, $100. Also, *Bibliographic Guide to Music,* 2 vols, 1975-1976, $70 ea. Literature pertaining to virtually all musical subjects, and scores covering the broadest range of musical style and history are represented in this catalog. Special strengths of the collection incl folk songs, 18th and 19th-century librettos, full scores of operas, complete works, historical editions, Beethoven, Americana, American music, periodicals, vocal music, literature on the voice, programs, record catalogs, and mss in detail; sheet music, 355,414; sound recordings, 400,000; clippings and programs, 2 million; broadsides, 1821; songsters, 375; pictures, 51,002; ms, 29,877.

NY —EASTMAN SCHOOL OF MUSIC, Sibley Music Library, 44 Swan St, Rochester, 14604. Ruth Watanabe, Librn
Holdings: Vols (360,000) Cat Mss Pix Phonorecords Microforms
Notes: Research material for music theory, history, and performance. Incl an additional uncataloged collection of 300,000 pieces. The Sibley Music Library is a full-service branch of the University of Rochester Library System. Bibliographical lists of journals prepared twice annually. Historical items described in *University of Rochester Library Bulletin.* List of new reference work compiled quarterly.

NC —UNIVERSITY OF NORTH CAROLINA, CHAPEL HILL, Music Library, Hill Hall, Chapel Hill, 27514.
Holdings: Vols (90,000) Cat Mss Pix Slides Phonorecords Audiotapes Microforms
Budget: ($60,000)
Notes: Extensive holdings of early theoretical treatises; complete editions; performing scores; music periodicals; reference works. Special interests reflected in holdings of sonatas; oratorios; requiems; operas; microfilms of Vatican Library holdings of mss containing hymns; microfilms from the Deutsches Musikgeschichtliches Archiv; microfilms of important European primary sources; contemporary chamber music. Approx 5000 pieces of early American sheet music, primarily antebellum. Substantial collection of shape-note hymnals, 19th and 20th century. Dictionary catalog of books, scores, microforms and recordings. Separate card catalog of early American music and song anthologies held by Music Library. Partial book catalog of libretto collection.

OH —TOLEDO MUSEUM OF ART, Reference Library, PO Box 1013, Toledo, 43697. Anne O Reese, Head Librn
Holdings: Vols 1925 Cat

PA —UNIVERSITY OF PENNSYLVANIA, Van Pelt Library, Rare Books Collection, 34 & Walnut Sts, Philadelphia, 19104. Daniel Traister, Special Collections Librn
Holdings: Cat Mss
Notes: "Note on the Alma Mahler Werfel Collection," by Adolf Klarmann and Rudolf Hirsch, (University of Pennsylvania) *Library Chronicle,* vol 35, no 1 and 2, 1969. Also 24 holograph mss of Werfel's works, some in two versions.

PA —UNIVERSITY OF PITTSBURGH, Hillman Library, Pittsburgh, 15260.
Holdings: DELETE
Notes: Incl the William Steinberg Collection of 800 musical scores, many signed by composers, and 1400 vols of English, French, German, Japanese, and Chinese literature.

MUSIC—HISTORY AND CRITICISM (cont.)

PA —PENNSYLVANIA STATE
UNIVERSITY, Arts Library, 405 E Pattee
Library, University Park, 16802. Daniel
Zager, Music Librn
Holdings: Vols 14,000 Cat Scores
Phonorecords
Notes: The music collection supports a
School of Music curriculum which is
comprehensive at the undergraduate and
masters degree levels. The collection
includes scores (collected works and
performance editions), books, (13,000),
periodicals, and recordings. The Special
Collections area of the library includes the
following music collections: the manuscripts,
published scores, personal papers, and some
recordings of the American composer
Charles Wakefield Cadman; 18th and 19th
century American tunebooks and 18th and
19th century Pennsylvania German
hymnbooks and songbooks; and the Doyle
Guntharp collection of field recordings of
fiddler's performances and interviews from
Central Pennsylvania.

RI —BROWN UNIVERSITY, John Hay
Library, 20 Prospect St, Providence, 02912.
Mark N Brown, Cur Mss
Holdings: Mss
Notes: Various ms collections relating to
music. See also entry under Music Scores-
Collections.

SC —CONVERSE COLLEGE, Gwathmey
Library, Spartanburg, 29301. Darlene E
Fawver, Music Librn
Holdings: Vols (3250) Cat Mss Pix
Phonorecords Microforms
Budget: ($8000)

SD —UNIVERSITY OF SOUTH DAKOTA,
Shrine to Music Museum, USD Box 194,
Vermillion, 57069. Andre P Larson, Dir
Holdings: Vols Cat
Budget: ($205,036)
Notes: The Shrine to Music Museum is one
of America's major collections of musical
resource materials, incl more than 4000
antique musical instruments from all over
the world, plus an extensive supporting
library of several thousand books, music,
periodicals, recordings, photographs, and
related musical memorabilia. The collection
of 19th and early 20th-century sheet music
and music for wind instruments is probably
the most extensive in the country. Inquiries
and visits are welcomed.

TX —DALLAS PUBLIC LIBRARY, Fine Arts
Div, 1515 Young St, Dallas, 75201. Richard
L Waters, Acting Dir; Jane Holahan,
Manager
Holdings: Uncat Mss Pix
Notes: The Dallas Symphony Orchestra;
printed programs beginning with first concert
in 1900 are bound. Subscription series
indexed by composition performed and guest
artists. Scrapbooks assembled by Symphony
PR office and Symphony League kept on file
in Division. Reviews of performances filed.
Photographs of all conductors on file. Photos
of Symphony on stage. Dallas Civic Opera;
printed programs as well as reviews and
other related newspaper articles; also a
collection of 200 artists' renderings of set
designs, costumes, etc. The John Rosenfield
Papers: Mr Rosenfield, Amusements Editor
for the Dallas Morning News for over 40
years, had collected letters received from
persons in the Performing Arts, mostly
music, over the years. There are also
photographs of many of the stars who
performed in Dallas and whom he met in
both New York and Hollywood. The
Manuscript ArchivesCommittee of the Texas
Federation of Music Clubs works with the
Fine Arts Division in collecting holograph
mss of those Texas composers whom the
Committee feels are doing the best music
composition in the state. At present there
are about 50 composers represented in the
Archives. Holograph mss of 3 works
commissioned by the Division--the
composers of which are Darius Milhaud,
Gunther Schuller, and Alberto Ginastera.
Also mss of the two books by John Ardoin,

Callas: the Art and the Life; and The Callas
Legacy, are in the collection.

TX —RICE UNIVERSITY, Fondren Library,
Woodson Research Center, 6100 S Main St,
PO Box 1892, Houston, 77251. Nancy
Parker, Dir Woodson Research Center
Holdings: Vols 600 // Cat
Notes: The Bartlett Beethoven Collection of
books about the life and works of Beethoven,
incl musicology, biography, studies of the
composer by his contemporaries, and
detailed studies of his compositions.

TX —BAYLOR UNIVERSITY, Moody
Memorial Library, Crouch Music Library,
1312 S Third St, PO Box 6307, Waco,
76706. Avery T Sharp, Librn
Holdings: Vols (75,000) Cat Phonorecords
Audiotapes Microforms
Budget: ($48,000)
Notes: Areas of strength: The Frances G
Spencer Collection of American Printed
Music, 30,000 items of popular sheet music
of the 19th and 20th centuries, completely
cataloged; complete collection of Denkmaler,
Gesamtausgeben and other historical sets,
periodicals, dictionaries, library catalogs,
thematic indexes, etc; 55,000 volumes of
music scores and music literature; 20,000
phonorecords, tapes and microfilm; 400 early
American hymn books. Collection has
separate catalog.

ON —UNIVERSITY OF TORONTO, Edward
Johnson Music Library, Toronto, M5S 1A1,
Can. Kathleen McMorow, Librn; James
Creighton, Sound Archivist
Holdings: Vols 100,000 Cat Phonorecords
Audiotapes Microforms
Notes: Reference and research collection in
music of the western "classical" tradition and
music of other traditions as investigated by
western scholarship. Emphasis on historical
editions (eg, Denkmaeler, Monumenta) and
collected works of individual composers,
scores and parts to represent the basic
repertoire, reference works, back files of
musicological journals, and historical and
biographical monographs in all European
languages. Collection incl 3000 audiotapes
and 125,000 phonorecords, of which 61,000
are 78 rpm.

MUSIC—ICONOGRAPHY

NY —STATE UNIVERSITY OF NEW
YORK, BUFFALO, Baird Music Library,
Baird Hall, Amherst, 14260. James B
Coover, Dir
Holdings: Vols (104,000) Cat Mss Pix Slides
Phonorecords Microforms
Notes: Nearly complete collections of
Denkmaeler and Gesamtausgaben and other
historical sets. Strong collection of
dictionaries, bibliographies, biographies,
facsimiles, works on the "new" music,
organology and ethnomusicology. Special
emphasis on operas, scores of the avant-
garde, jazz and urban popular music,
discography and music librarianship. Good
collection of medieval and Renaissance
anthologies, contemporary and avant-garde
recordings. Houses Archives of the Center of
the Creative and Performing Arts.
Collections incl 2100 slides, 22,000
phonorecords, 46,000 scores and parts, 29,
000 books, 4900 microforms. Computerized
record catalog in process.

MUSIC—INSTRUCTION AND STUDY

†DC —CATHOLIC UNIVERSITY OF
AMERICA, Music Library, Washington,
20064. Betty Libbey, Head Music Library
Holdings: Cat Microforms
Notes: A large collection to support
advanced degree study. Emphasis on church
music, musicology, history and criticism,
instrumental and vocal music, solo music for
all voices, instruments, and musical forms.

IL —ROOSEVELT UNIVERSITY, Murray-
Green Library, 430 S Michigan Ave,
Chicago, 60605. Donald Draganski, Music
Librn
Holdings: Vols (28,000) Uncat Mss Pix
Microforms
Notes: Subscribe to over 92 music
periodicals; record collection of more than

10,000 albums; 8000 pieces of sheet music;
pamphlet file; music theses on microfilm;
complete file of music publishers catalogs;
scores; tapes of old 78 recordings; music
education; and electronic music.

KY —UNIVERSITY OF KENTUCKY, Music
Library, 116 Fine Arts Bldg, Lexington,
40506. Cathy S Hunt, Music Librn
Holdings: Vols 18,000 Cat Microforms
Scores Recordings
Notes: Collection incl books (14,000),
includes music history, theory, music
eduction, jazz, etc cat. Music Scores (18,
000) cat. Serials (3200 vols) cat. Microforms
(6300) cat. Recordings (9100) cat. Collected
Editions (complete Works of composers,
large sets, etc) (7100) cat. The Alfred Cortot
Collection (about 300 vols of rare, early
music theory books) is housed in the Rare
Books Room of the Main Library.

†MD —UNIVERSITY OF MARYLAND,
Library, Music Educators National
Conference Historical Center, College Park,
20742. Bruce Wilson, Cur
Holdings: Cat Mss Pix Audiotapes
Notes: The official archive of the Music
Educators' National Conference (MENC),
and a repository for the documentation of
music education. Incl the papers of the
MENC, state units, and associated
organizations and committees; personal
papers and association items (notably,
relating to Frances Elliott Clark, Lowell
Mason, and Luther Whiting Mason);
published proceedings of MENC and other
groups; oral histories, numerous school
music textbooks, and the archive of the
Contemporary Music Project.

MI —UNIVERSITY OF MICHIGAN, School
of Music, Music Library, Moore Bldg, Ann
Arbor, 48109. Peggy Daub, Head
Notes: The collection supports the study of
classical music from the undergraduate to
the doctoral level. It is especially strong in
collected works and historical editions. Rare
scores include early editions of works by the
sons of J S Bach and many 18th-19th
century operas, particularly French.

NJ —WESTMINSTER CHOIR COLLEGE,
Talbott Library, Hamilton Ave at Walnut
Lane, Princeton, 08540. Sherry L Vellucci,
Acting Dir
Holdings: Vols (43,500) Cat Scores
Periodicals Phonorecords Audiotapes
Videotapes Microforms
Budget: ($30,000)
Notes: Talbott Library supports the
curriculum of a music college which grants
undergraduate and graduate degrees in
church music, music education and music
performance (voice, piano, organ and choral
conducting), with an emphasis on choral
music. Incl 7000 phonorecords, 3500 titles in
quantity of choral music, 30,000 single
copies of choral music.

†NY —STATE UNIVERSITY OF NEW
YORK, COLLEGE AT FREDONIA,
Daniel A Reed Library, Fredonia, 14063.
Holdings: Vols (8000) Cat Phonorecords
Audiotapes
Budget: ($12,500)
Notes: The Music Library supports the
curricular needs of a large department of
music which now has programs in both
music education and performance. Separate
card catalogs are maintained for 26,000
scores and more than 12,000 recordings and
tape cassettes. The library has a small
collection of 19th century American
tunebooks, some Lowell Mason materials
and a collection of sheet music and dance
band arrangements numbering more than
3200 pieces and covering the period from
1850 through the big band era.

NC —APPALACHIAN STATE
UNIVERSITY, Music Library, Broyhill
Music Center, Boone, 28608. Joan O
Falconer, Librn
Holdings: Vols 1800 Phonorecords
Budget: ($9500)
Notes: A collection of music scores, chamber
music, and 7000 recordings, supported by
basic reference books. Former emphasis on
music education materials now being
expanded to include extensive performance
materials and titles appropriate to a liberal

MUSIC—INSTRUCTION AND STUDY (cont.)

arts curriculum through the master's degree level. The University Library (Belk Library) houses the main collection of book materials in music. Incl 12,000 music scores and parts and 7000 phonorecords.

OH —OBERLIN COLLEGE, Oberlin Conservatory of Music, Mary M Vial Library, Oberlin, 44074. John E Druesedow Jr, Dir
Holdings: Vols (75,000) Cat Phonorecords Audiotapes Filmstrips Microforms
Budget: ($60,000)
Notes: Special emphases; history and literature of the organ; music before 1700; music since 1950; music education; opera; American music; chamber and solistic music. Published catalog: *Mr and Mrs C W Best Collection of Autographs in the Mary M Vial Music Library of the Oberlin College Conservatory of Music* (Oberlin, Ohio: Oberlin College, 1967).

MUSIC—MUSEUMS see Music Museums

MUSIC—PERFORMANCE

MD —PEABODY CONSERVATORY LIBRARY, 21 E Mt Vernon Place, Baltimore, 21202. Edwin A Quist, Librn
Holdings: Vols 70,000 Cat Mss Pix Phonorecords Audiotapes Videotapes Microforms
Budget: $30,000
Notes: The Peabody Conservatory Library, formerly a part of the Peabody Institute Library (now the George Peabody Library of the Johns Hopkins University) supplies the library needs of the faculty and student body of the Peabody Conservatory of Music. While the collection has numerous research capabilities, it is basically a collection of musical scores. The entire history of Western music is represented through collected editions, monumental anthologies, study scores, performing editions and a large collection of books and music periodicals. This collection is supplemented by a listening facility containing 14,000 discs and an ensembles library containing scores and parts of orchestral, band and chorus works.

NJ —WESTMINSTER CHOIR COLLEGE, Talbott Library, Hamilton Ave at Walnut Lane, Princeton, 08540. Sherry L Vellucci, Acting Dir
Holdings: Vols (43,500) Cat Scores Periodicals Phonorecords Audiotapes Videotapes Microforms
Budget: ($30,000)
Notes: Talbott Library supports the curriculum of a music college which grants undergraduate and graduate degrees in church music, music education and music performance (voice, piano, organ and choral conducting), with an emphasis on choral music. Incl 7000 phonorecords, 3500 titles in quantity of choral music, 30,000 single copies of choral music.

NY —STATE UNIVERSITY OF NEW YORK, BUFFALO, Baird Music Library, Baird Hall, Amherst, 14260. James B Coover, Dir
Holdings: Vols (104,000) Cat Mss Pix Slides Phonorecords Microforms
Notes: Nearly complete collections of *Denkmaeler and Gesamtausgaben* and other historical sets. Strong collection of dictionaries, bibliographies, biographies, facsimiles, works on the "new" music, organology and ethnomusicology. Special emphasis on operas, scores of the avant-garde, jazz and urban popular music, discography and music librarianship. Good collection of medieval and Renaissance anthologies, contemporary and avant-garde recordings. Houses Archives of the Center of the Creative and Performing Arts. Collections incl 2100 slides, 22,000 phonorecords, 46,000 scores and parts, 29,000 books, 4900 microforms. Computerized record catalog in process.

NY —EASTMAN SCHOOL OF MUSIC, Sibley Music Library, 44 Swan St, Rochester, 14604. Ruth Watanabe, Librn
Holdings: Vols (360,000) Cat Mss Pix Phonorecords Microforms Music Scores
Notes: Research material for music theory, history, and performance. Incl an additional uncataloged collection of 300,000 pieces. The Sibley Music Library is a full-service branch of the University of Rochester Library System. Bibliographical lists of journals prepared twice annually. Historical items described in *University of Rochester Library Bulletin.* List of new reference work compiled quarterly.

MUSIC—PROGRAMS see Programs, Music

MUSIC—STUDY AND TEACHING see Music—Instruction and Study

MUSIC—THEORY

CT —YALE UNIVERSITY, Music Library, 98 Wall St, New Haven, 06520. Harold E Samuel, Librn
Holdings: Vols (118,000) Cat Mss Pix Phonorecords Audiotapes Microforms
Notes: General reference and research materials. Performing editions. Strong in theoretical literature, opera, 17-18th century music (incl mss), J S Bach and sons in early editions and mss, Russian liturgical music (Tkaczenko Collection), hymnology, American music. Also collection of musical pictures and portraits.

†DC —CATHOLIC UNIVERSITY OF AMERICA, Music Library, Washington, 20064. Betty Libbey, Head Music Library
Holdings: Cat Microforms
Notes: A large collection to support advanced degree study. Emphasis on church music, musicology, history and criticism, instrumental and vocal music, solo music for all voices, instruments, and musical forms.

IL —NEWBERRY LIBRARY, 60 W Walton St, Chicago, 60610. Diana Haskell, Cur of Modern Mss
Holdings: Vols (200,000) Cat Mss
Notes: Incl 45,000 vols; 55,000 scores; 100,000 pieces of sheet music. Primary and secondary materials for the study of Western European music from the Middle Ages through the 19th century and of American music from its beginnings. Strong periodical holdings and monumental editions. Restricted use: noncirculating.

KY —UNIVERSITY OF KENTUCKY, Music Library, 116 Fine Arts Bldg, Lexington, 40506. Cathy S Hunt, Music Librn
Holdings: Vols 18,000 Cat Microforms Scores Recordings
Notes: Collection incl books (14,000), includes music history, theory, music eduction, jazz, etc cat. Music Scores (18,000) cat. Serials (3200 vols) cat. Microforms (6300) cat. Recordings (9100) cat. Collected Editions (complete Works of composers, large sets, etc) (7100) cat. The Alfred Cortot Collection (about 300 vols of rare, early music theory books) is housed in the Rare Books Room of the Main Library.

NY —STATE UNIVERSITY OF NEW YORK, BUFFALO, Baird Music Library, Baird Hall, Amherst, 14260. James B Coover, Dir
Holdings: Vols (104,000) Cat Mss Pix Slides Phonorecords Microforms
Notes: Nearly complete collections of *Denkmaeler and Gesamtausgaben* and other historical sets. Strong collection of dictionaries, bibliographies, biographies, facsimiles, works on the "new" music, organology and ethnomusicology. Special emphasis on operas, scores of the avant-garde, jazz and urban popular music, discography and music librarianship. Good collection of medieval and Renaissance anthologies, contemporary and avant-garde recordings. Houses Archives of the Center of the Creative and Performing Arts. Collections incl 2100 slides, 22,000 phonorecords, 46,000 scores and parts, 29,000 books, 4900 microforms. Computerized record catalog in process.

NY —COLUMBIA UNIVERSITY LIBRARIES, Music Library, 701 Dodge, Broadway & 116 St, New York, 10027. M Haefliger, Librn
Holdings: Vols (55,020) Cat Phonorecords Audiotapes Microforms
Notes: Incl strong collection in all aspects of the theory of music (except theory teaching textbooks).

NY —NEW YORK PUBLIC LIBRARY, Music Div, 111 Amsterdam Ave, New York, 10023. Frank C Campbell, Chief

NY —EASTMAN SCHOOL OF MUSIC, Sibley Music Library, 44 Swan St, Rochester, 14604. Ruth Watanabe, Librn
Holdings: Vols (360,000) Cat Mss Pix Phonorecords Microforms Music Scores
Notes: Research material for music theory, history, and performance. Incl an additional uncataloged collection of 300,000 pieces. The Sibley Music Library is a full-service branch of the University of Rochester Library System. Bibliographical lists of journals prepared twice annually. Historical items described in *University of Rochester Library Bulletin.* List of new reference work compiled quarterly.

NC —UNIVERSITY OF NORTH CAROLINA, CHAPEL HILL, Music Library, Hill Hall, Chapel Hill, 27514.
Holdings: Vols (90,000) Cat Mss Pix Slides Phonorecords Audiotapes Microforms
Budget: ($60,000)
Notes: Extensive holdings of early theoretical treatises; complete editions; performing scores; music periodicals; reference works.

MUSIC—THERAPEUTIC USE see Music Therapy

MUSIC, ADVENT see Advent Music

MUSIC, AFRICAN

DC —HOWARD UNIVERSITY, Moorland-Spingarn Research Center, 500 Howard Place NW, Washington, 20059. Clifford L Muse, Jr, Acting Dir

NJ —RUTGERS, THE STATE UNIVERSITY OF NEW JERSEY, Institute of Jazz Studies, 135 Bradley Hall, Newark, 07102. Dan Morgenstern, Dir; Edward Berger, Cur; Maxie Griffin, Librn
Holdings: Vols 3000 Cat Pix Phonorecords Audiotapes Films Microforms VF
Notes: Incl jazz records, books, periodicals etc as well as some roots and peripheral material--African music, gospel music, rhythm and blues, rock etc (both written and recorded). Incl 60,000 records.

NY —COLUMBIA UNIVERSITY LIBRARIES, Center for Studies in Ethnomusicology Library, Music Dept, 417 Dodge, New York, 10027. Dieter Christensen, Cur
Holdings: Cat
Notes: A particularly strong collection of recorded ethnic music.

MUSIC, AFRO-AMERICAN

IN —INDIANA UNIVERSITY, Lilly Library, Seventh St, Bloomington, 47405. William R Cagle, Librn
Holdings: // Uncat
Notes: In the Starr Collection of American Sheet Music.

IN —INDIANA UNIVERSITY, Music Library, Bloomington, 47401. David E Fenske, Head
Holdings: Vols (4000) Cat Mss Microforms
Budget:
Notes: Incl scores, books and 1000 phonorecords (discs and tapes, commerical and instantaneous--incl music and interviews).

LA —TULANE UNIVERSITY, Howard-Tilton Memorial Library, Special Collections Div, William Ransom Hogan Jazz Archive, 7001 Freret, New Orleans, 70118. Richard B Allen, Acting Cur; Alma D Williams, Assistant to the Cur
Holdings: Vols (100,000) Cat Mss Pix Slides Phonorecords Audiotapes Videotapes 16mm Films Microforms
Notes: Jazz music and musicians.

MUSIC, AFRO-AMERICAN (cont.)

Outstanding collection, incl books, music scores, serials, catalogs and other archival material. Music, history, etc.
See also entry under Jazz

NY —STATE UNIVERSITY OF NEW YORK, BUFFALO, Baird Music Library, Baird Hall, Amherst, 14260. James B Coover, Dir
Holdings: Vols (104,000) Cat Mss Pix Slides Phonorecords Microforms
Notes: Nearly complete collections of *Denkmaeler and Gesamtausgaben* and other historical sets. Strong collection of dictionaries, bibliographies, biographies, facsimiles, works on the "new" music, organology and ethnomusicology. Special emphasis on operas, scores of the avant-garde, jazz and urban popular music, discography and music librarianship. Good collection of medieval and Renaissance anthologies, contemporary and avant-garde recordings. Houses Archives of the Center of the Creative and Performing Arts. Collections incl 2100 slides, 22,000 phonorecords, 46,000 scores and parts, 29,000 books, 4900 microforms. Computerized record catalog in process.

NY —BARNARD A & MORRIS N YOUNG LIBRARY OF EARLY AMERICAN POPULAR MUSIC, 270 Riverside Dr, New York, 10025. Morris N Young, Cur
Holdings: Cat Mss Pix Phonorecords Audiotapes Microforms
Notes: 48,000 items of American popular music, mostly 1790-1910. Incl books, serials, sheet music, broadsides, anthologies, air checks, broadcasting and music business memorabilia, and correspondence.

MUSIC, ALEATORY see Chance Composition (Music)

MUSIC, AMERICAN

CA —LONG BEACH PUBLIC LIBRARY, Art, Music & Philosophy Dept, Art, Music & Philosophy Dept, 101 Pacific Ave, Long Beach, 90802. Barbara Davis, Librn
Holdings: Vols 15,000 Cat
Notes: Popular sheet music, 1790 to date. Indexed.

CA —UNIVERSITY OF CALIFORNIA, LOS ANGELES, Music Library, Schonberg Hall, Los Angeles, 90024. Stephen M Fry, Music Librn
Notes: Incl the Harry Roth Library of American Theater Music, the Meredith Wilson Library of Popular Sheet Music, and the library of American Motion Picture Music.

CT —TRINITY COLLEGE LIBRARY, Watkinson Library, 300 Summit St, Hartford, 06106. Jeffrey Kaimowitz, Cur
Holdings: // Cat Mss
Notes: Incl 18th and 19th century sheet music.

CT —YALE UNIVERSITY, Music Library, 98 Wall St, New Haven, 06520. Harold E Samuel, Librn
Holdings: Vols (118,000) Cat Mss Pix Phonorecords Audiotapes
Notes: Manuscript and archive collection comprising over 500 individual musical mss as well as the personal papers and musical mss of such American musicians and composers as Charles Ives, Carl Ruggles, Haratio Parker, Quincy Porter, Richard Donovan and David Stanley Smith, Leo Ornstein, Armin Loos, Duane Davidson, Alonzo Elliott, John Rosamund Johnson, Hope Leroy Baumgartner, Gustave Stoeckel, Hershy Kay, Virgil Thomson, Kurt Weill, Lotte Lenya, Lowell Mason, Parker Bailey, Henry Gilbert, Seymour Shifrin, Lehman Engel, Ernest Trow Carter, and Alec Templeton. Extensive Paul Hindemith Collection. Also ca 35,000 pieces of American sheet music, both instrumental and vocal as well as extensive holdings of 17th & 18th century American hymn books.

IL —NEWBERRY LIBRARY, 60 W Walton St, Chicago, 60610. Diana Haskell, Cur of Modern Mss
Holdings: Cat Mss
Notes: Entry also at Newberry Library.
See also entry under Music

IN —INDIANA UNIVERSITY, Lilly Library, Seventh St, Bloomington, 47405. William R Cagle, Librn
Holdings: // Uncat Mss
Notes: Starr Collection of American Sheet Music 100,000 sheets.

KY —UNIVERSITY OF LOUISVILLE, School of Music, Dwight Anderson Memorial Music Library, 2301 S Third St, Louisville, 40292. Marion Korda, Librn
Holdings: Uncat
Notes: Early American sheet music; emphasis on Louisville imprints. A collection of songs and piano music. 192 vols of early music, plus 1000 single items; 82 vols of Louisville music programs; information file; additional 85 vols of songsters. Incl "Traipsin Women" (Jean Thomas) Collection; archives. No photocopying.

LA —TULANE UNIVERSITY, Howard-Tilton Memorial Library, Special Collections Div, William Ransom Hogan Jazz Archive, 7001 Freret, New Orleans, 70118. Richard B Allen, Acting Cur; Alma D Williams, Assistant to the Cur
Holdings: Vols (100,000) Cat Mss Pix Slides Phonorecords Audiotapes Videotapes 16mm Films Microforms
Budget: ($90,000)
Notes: Jazz music and musicians. Outstanding collection, incl books, music scores, serials, catalogs and other archival material. Music, history, etc.
See also entry under Jazz

MD —JOHNS HOPKINS UNIVERSITY, Milton S Eisenhower Library, Special Collections, John Work Garrett Library, 4545 N Charles St, Baltimore, 21210. Jane Katz, Garrett Librn
Holdings: // Cat Mss
Notes: Music related to the works of Poe. Cataloged in *Music and Edgar Allen Poe: A Bibliographical Study*, by May Garrettson Evans (Baltimore: John Hopkins Univ Press, 1939).

MD —UNIVERSITY OF MARYLAND, BALTIMORE COUNTY, Albin O Kuhn Library and Gallery, 5401 Wilkens Ave, Baltimore, 21228. Ann Copeland, Special Collections Librn
Holdings: 1000 Cat Phonorecords Audiotapes
Notes: American regional musical traditions: Appalachian, Cajun, Southwest. Stylistic sub-genres: blues, rhythm and blues, string band, gospel, Western Swing, honky-tonk, rockabilly, bluegrass, Tex-Mex. Commercial country music, 1920 to the present.

MA —BRANDEIS UNIVERSITY, Goldfarb Library, 415 South St, Waltham, 02154. Bessie Hahn, Dir
Notes: Early American Sheet Music Collection. Consists of 30 linear ft of early American song sheets of the 20th century. This collection is unprocessed, spring 1984.

MI —UNIVERSITY OF MICHIGAN, William L Clements Library, Ann Arbor, 48109. John C Dann, Dir

Notes: The William L. Clements Library of Americana is a non-circulating rare book library of original source material, printed and manuscript, dealing with America, from the discovery period into the late nineteenth century. The collection includes approximately 60,000 books and pamphlets, 550 linear feet of manuscripts, 4,100 volumes of newspapers, 36,000 maps, 40,000 pieces of sheet music, and 1,000 prints. The collection is strongest for the period of the American Revolution, and includes the papers of Thomas Gage, Sir Henry Clinton, and the Earl of Shelburne. Other areas of strength include antislavery, cartography and geography, discovery and exploration, American Indians, The Civil War, tune-books, sermons and orations, and the War of 1812. There are selective research collections dealing with Christopher Columbus, Thomas Paine, Benjamin Franklin, George Washington, Thomas Jefferson, and the Federalist Papers. Publications describing the collections of the library are: Author/Title catalog of Americana 1493-1860 in the William L. Clements Library... 7 volumes, Boston, G. K. Hall, 1970; Guide to the manuscript collections of the William L. Clements Library, by Arlene P. Shy 3d edition, Boston, G. K. Hall, 1978; Guide to the manuscript maps in the William L. Clements Library, compiled by Christian Burn, Ann Arbor, U. of Michigan, 1959; and Research catalog of maps of America, to 1860 in the William L. Clements Library...,edited by Douglas W. Marshall, 4 volumes, Boston, G. K. Hall, 1972.

MO —UNIVERSITY OF MISSOURI-KANSAS CITY, General Library, Conservatory of Music Library, 5100 Rockhill Road, Kansas City, 64110. Kenneth J LaBudde, Dir; Richard Belanger, Librn
Holdings: Vols 46,337 Cat
Notes: 276 current serial subscriptions, 7462 microforms, 16,702 sound recordings, some 70,000 other items with specialists in American Music, Virgil Thomson and hymnology.

MO —MISSOURI HISTORICAL SOCIETY, Library, Jefferson Memorial Bldg, Saint Louis, 63112. Stephanie Klein, Librn-Archivist; Peter Michel, Cur of Manuscripts
Holdings: Vols (500) Cat
Notes: Five hundred volumes of sheet music. In additions, over 5000 pieces of individual sheet music. Most of this music was published in St Louis, and many have St Louis themes. Collection will remain in storage until 1986.

MO —WASHINGTON UNIVERSITY, John M Olin Library, Campus Box 1061, St Louis, 63130.
Holdings: Vols (1800) Cat Mss
Notes: Incl material from the Authur C Hoskins, Richard S Hawes, Ernst C Krohn, George N Meissner, Stratford Lee Morton,, and Edgar M Queeny collections; strong in early travel literature of the US and Latin America; accounts of exploration in the Mississippi Valley and Trans-Mississippi West; miscellaneous accounts of history, pioneer life, and travel in the Ohio Valley, Old Southwest, and California; material on the American Indian; 18th century American music; early American imprints.

NJ —NEWARK PUBLIC LIBRARY, Art & Music Dept, 5 Washington St, Newark, 07101. William J Dane, Supv
Holdings: Vols (25,000) Cat Mss Audiotapes Microforms VF
Notes: Music, literature, scores, librettos, extensive vertical file, song sheets, special indexes, music periodicals. John Tasker Howard collection of notes and letters. Some special material on New Jersey and Newark music.

NM —NEW MEXICO STATE UNIVERSITY, Library, Box 3475, Las Cruces, 88003. James Dyke, Dir
Holdings: Vols 4000 // Cat
Notes: Jazz, Blues, and music history. Collection of music periodicals and monographs of the 1930s, 1940s and 1950s.

NY —BUFFALO & ERIE COUNTY PUBLIC LIBRARY, Music Dept, Lafayette Sq, Buffalo, 14203. Norma Jean Lamb, Head
Notes: 103,000 song sheets (80,000 loose; 23,000 in bound volumes). Unique items of 18th century American music publications. Large collection of 19th century broadsides and songsters. Some mss of contemporary American composers.

NY —BARNARD A & MORRIS N YOUNG LIBRARY OF EARLY AMERICAN

MUSIC, AMERICAN (cont.)

POPULAR MUSIC, 270 Riverside Dr, New York, 10025. Morris N Young, Cur
Holdings: Cat Mss Pix Phonorecords Audiotapes Microforms
Notes: 48,000 items of American popular music, mostly 1790-1910. Incl books, serials, sheet music, broadsides, anthologies, air checks, broadcasting and music business memorabilia, and correspondence.

NY —NEW YORK PUBLIC LIBRARY, Music Div, 111 Amsterdam Ave, New York, 10023. Frank C Campbell, Chief
Holdings: Cat Mss Pix Microforms
Notes: Books, scores, autograph mss letters, pictures. Covers classical and popular music and jazz.

NY —SYRACUSE UNIVERSITY LIBRARIES, Ernest S Bird Library, George Arents Research Library for Special Collections, Syracuse, 13210. Carolyn A Davis, Manuscripts Librn; Amy S Doherty, University Archivist; Mark F Weimer, Rare Book Librn
Notes: American Music Collection. Papers of Ernst Bacon, Louis Krasner, Franklin Morris, William Henry Berwald, Earl George, and Arthur Polster.

NC —UNIVERSITY OF NORTH CAROLINA, CHAPEL HILL, Music Library, Hill Hall, Chapel Hill, 27514.
Holdings: Vols (90,000) Cat Mss Pix Slides Phonoreocrds Audiotapes Microforms
Budget: ($60,000)
Notes: Extensive holdings of early theoretical treatises; complete editions; performing scores; music periodicals; reference works. Special interests reflected in holdings of sonatas, oratorios, requiems; operas; microfilms of Vatican Library holdings of mss containing hymns; microfilms from the Deutsches Musikgeschichtliches Archiv; microfilms of important European primary sources; contemporary chamber music. Approx 5000 pieces of early American sheet music, primarily antebellum. Substantial collection of shape-note hymnals, 19th and 20th century. Dictionary catalog of books, scores, microforms and recordings. Separate card catalog of early American music and song anthologies held by Music Library. Partial book catalog of libretto collection.

OH —CASE WESTERN RESERVE UNIVERSITY LIBRARIES, Cleveland, 44106. Susie Hanson, Special Collections Librn
Notes: Manuscripts of compositions and other archival materials by the American composer Donald Erb. Contains sketches and pencil scores covering the period of Erb's 30 year career, programs, reviews, newspaper clippings, and correspondence.

OH —OHIO STATE UNIVERSITY, William Oxley Thompson Memorial Library, 1858 Neil Ave Mall, Columbus, 43210. Robert A Tibbetts, Cur of Special Collections
Holdings: Vols 7000 Cat
Notes: American popular music, mostly c 1880-1935; about 7000 pieces of sheet music.

OH —OBERLIN COLLEGE, Oberlin Conservatory of Music, Mary M Vial Library, Oberlin, 44074. John E Druesedow Jr, Dir
Holdings: Vols (75,000) Cat Phonorecords Audiotapes Filmstrips Microforms
Budget: ($60,000)
Notes: Special emphases; history and literature of the organ; music before 1700; music since 1950; music education; opera; American music; chamber and solistic music. Published catalog: *Mr and Mrs C W Best Collection of Autographs in the Mary M Vial Music Library of the Oberlin College Conservatory of Music* (Oberlin, Ohio: Oberlin College, 1967).

OR —UNIVERSITY OF OREGON LIBRARY, Special Collections Div, Eugene, 97403. Kenneth W Duckett, Curator
Holdings: Cat
Notes: Over 20,000 pieces of sheet music of popular songs arranged for voice and piano, 1852-1976 (bulk dates: 1890-1939).
See also entry under Composers

OR —UNIVERSITY OF OREGON LIBRARY, Music Dept, Eugene, 97403. Leslie K Greer, Music Librn
Holdings: Cat
Notes: Also over 50,000 pieces of American popular sheet music.

PA —FREE LIBRARY OF PHILADELPHIA, Sheet Music Collection, Logan Sq, Philadelphia, 19103. Connie Jessum, Librn
Budget: ($2000)
Notes: Covers entire span of American popular expression in song and instrumental music (piano) from colonial times to the present. Incl Newland-Zeuner and Edward I Keffer Collections on loan from the Musical Fund Society. Items printed before 1825 indexed in Sonneck-Upton and Wolfe. Checklists for cover illustrations, musical shows or films and special subjects. Songs are filed by title; piano music by composer. Examples of special materials not filed in regular collection incl early Philadelphia composers and publications, national (centennial and state), patriotic ("Star-Spangled Banner"), political (Presidents), and war (1861; 1914; 1939) songs. Most of the ms materials are anonymous. Collection contains 138,360 pieces of sheet music.

PA —UNIVERSITY OF PITTSBURGH, Stephen Foster Memorial, Foster Hall Collection, Pittsburgh, 15260. Deane L Root, Cur
Holdings: Vols (1000) Cat Mss Pix Phonorecords VF //
Budget: ($50,000)
Notes: Collection comprises more than 10,000 separate American items: original mss and letters; first editions, and early modern editions of Foster's music; personal possessions of the composer; books; magazine and newspaper articles; pictures and portraits; phonograph records; broadsides; and other material.

PA —PENNSYLVANIA STATE UNIVERSITY, Arts Library, 405 E Pattee Library, University Park, 16802. Daniel Zager, Music Librn
Notes: The Special Collections area of the library includes the following collections related to American music: the manuscripts, published scores, personal papers, and some recordings of the American composer Charles Wakefield Cadman; 18th and 19th century American tunebooks and 18th and 19th century Pennsylvania German hymnbooks and songbooks; and the Doyle Gunthorp collection of field recordings of fiddler's performances and interviews from Central Pennsylvania.
See also entry under Music.

RI —BROWN UNIVERSITY, John Hay Library, 20 Prospect St, Providence, 02912. Mark N Brown, Cur Mss
Holdings: Uncat
Notes: The Sheet Music Collection concentrates on music of American imprint, incl 170,000 vocal pieces filed by title, plus 80,000 instrumental pieces filed by composer. Major strengths are in 19th century music, especially prior to 1830; Civil War music, both Union and Confederate; lithographic covers; World War I songs; political campaign music; and band music. An additional 100,000 pieces of American and European imprint remain unprocessed.
See also entry under Foster, Stephen Collins; US - History - Civil War

TN —TENNESSEE STATE LIBRARY & ARCHIVES, 403 Seventh Ave N, Nashville, 37219. Olivia K Young, State Librn & Archivist
Holdings: Cat
Notes: Collection of popular American sheet music, of interest as social rather than musicical history. About 10,000 titles and editions.

TX —BAYLOR UNIVERSITY, Moody Memorial Library, Crouch Music Library, 1312 S Third St, PO Box 6307, Waco, 76706. Avery T Sharp, Librn
Holdings: Vols (75,000) Cat Phonorecords Audiotapes Microforms
Budget: ($48,000)
Notes: Areas of strength: The Frances G Spencer Collection of American Printed Music, 30,000 items of popular sheet music

of the 19th and 20th centuries, completely cataloged; complete collection of Denkmaler, Gesamtausgeben and other historical sets, periodicals, dictionaries, library catalogs, thematic indexes, etc; 55,000 volumes of music scores and music literature; 20,000 phonorecords, tapes and microfilm; 400 early American hymn books. Collection has separate catalog.

VA —UNIVERSITY OF VIRGINIA, Alderman Library, Music Collection, Charlottesville, 22901. Evan Bonds, Music Librn
Holdings: Cat
Notes: McRae, Lynn T *Computer Catalog of 19th-Century American-Imprint Sheet Music* (Charlottesville, Univ of Va, 1977).

†WA —WASHINGTON STATE UNIVERSITY, Library, Manuscripts, Archives & Special Collections, Pullman, 99164. John F Guido, Head
Holdings: // Cat Mss Pix
Notes: The Robert Cushman Butler Collection of Theatrical Illustrations contains: approx 1600 illustrations, sheet music covers, programs and playbills; approx 100 ms of actors, actresses and playwrights; and approx 200 volumes of theatrical history and reminiscences, several extra-illustrated, concentrating on 18th-19th century British and American drama. A guide to the collection is in preparation.

WA —UNIVERSITY OF WASHINGTON LIBRARIES, Music Library, DN-10, Seattle, 98195. David A Wood, Music Librn
Holdings: Vols (46,212) Cat
Budget: ($44,522)
Notes: Incl the Hazel G Kinscella Collection of colonial and early 19th-century musical Americana.

WI —UNIVERSITY OF WISCONSIN, MADISON, Mills Music Library, 728 State St, Madison, 53706. Arne Arneson, Music Librn
Holdings: // Uncat Mss
Notes: Tams-Witmark Collection formed part of the rental collection of the firm bearing that name. Includes piano-conductor scores (some in mss); ca 65 sets of orchestral parts of operas; 70 vocal scores of works by American composers including Herbert, Sousa, Edwards and De Koven; ca 100 sets of orchestral parts of comic operas; ca 4000 vocal scores of European operas. Restricted use.

MUSIC, AMERICAN PATRIOTIC see Patriotic Music, American

MUSIC, ASIAN

NY —NEW YORK PUBLIC LIBRARY, Performing Arts Research Center, Rodgers & Hammerstein Archives of Recorded Sound, 111 Amsterdam Ave, New York, 10023.
Holdings: // Phonorecords Audiotapes
Notes: Some 160 audiotapes were given by the Asia Society through Dr Willard Rhodes, and comprise field recordings, lectures, and related materials covering a variety of regions, including Indonesia, Korea, the various regions of India, Thailand, Laos, Viet Nam, Malaysia, Japan, China, Iran, Afghanistan, Pakistan, the Philippines.

MUSIC, BAND see Band Music

MUSIC, BAROQUE

IL —NEWBERRY LIBRARY, 60 W Walton St, Chicago, 60610. Diana Haskell, Cur of Modern Mss
Holdings: Cat Mss
Notes: Entry also under Newberry Library.
See also entry under Music

NY —STATE UNIVERSITY OF NEW YORK, COLLEGE AT PURCHASE, Library, Purchase, 10577. Mark E Smith, Music Librn
Holdings: Vols (6500) // Cat Microforms
Notes: Noah Greenberg Collection of monographs, journals, scholarly editions of medieval, Renaissance, and early Baroque music and performance materials, and

MUSIC, BAROQUE (cont.)

microfilms of music manuscripts. Collection was acquired from the defunct New York Pro Musica Antiqua.

MUSIC, BLACK see Music—Blacks

MUSIC, BLUES see Blues (Songs, Etc.)

MUSIC, BYELORUSSIAN

NJ —BYELORUSSIAN INSTITUTE OF ARTS AND SCIENCES, INC, 230 Springfield Ave, Rutherford, 07070.
Holdings: Vols 2000 Mss
Notes: Incl Byelorussian art, pictures, and music on types.

MUSIC, BYZANTINE

†MA —HELLENIC COLLEGE AND HOLY CROSS GREEK ORTHODOX SCHOOL OF THEOLOGY, Cotsidas-Tonna Library, 50 Goddard Ave, Brookline, 02146.
Notes: Modern Greek literature, Greek Orthodox theology, Byzantine history, music and culture, patristic literature, Orthodox liturgics.

MUSIC, CALIFORNIA

CA —CALIFORNIA STATE UNIVERSITY, LONG BEACH, Library, Dept of Special Collections & Archives, 1250 Bellflower Blvd, Long Beach, 90840. John Ahouse, Special Collections Librn
Holdings: Cat Mss Pix Audiotapes
Notes: Manuscripts, programs, ALS, articles, clippings and recordings pertaining to the musical careers of Wesley Kuhnle, Gerald Strang, Dane Rudhyar, Richard Buhlig, Morris Ruger and other artists active in Southern California, 1930-1960. Partially cataloged.
CA —UNIVERSITY OF CALIFORNIA, LOS ANGELES, Music Library, Schonberg Hall, Los Angeles, 90024. Stephen M Fry, Music Librn
Notes: The Philip Kahgan Collection of music films, letters, programs, and photographs important to the Southern California classical music scene. Incl 16mm "home movies" of more than thirty renowned conductors and performers during Hollywood Bowl rehearsals in the late 1930s. Incl Kahgan correspondence, memorabilia, 35 scrapbooks, etc.
CA —SOCIETY OF CALIFORNIA PIONEERS, Library, 456 McAllister St, San Francisco, 94102. Grace E Baker, Librn
Holdings: Vols (12,000) Cat Mss Maps Pix Microforms
Notes: California history, especially the gold rush and the San Francisco earthquake, Sherman collection of early California music, business letterheads of early California firms, San Francisco City Directories 1850-1944, records of California Battalion 1846-47, ms material on overland diaries, ships' logs and passenger lists. Also, large photograph collection.
CA —SANTA CRUZ PUBLIC LIBRARY, Art, Music, Film Dept, 224 Church St, Santa Cruz, 95060. Alma Westberg, Librn
Holdings: Vols (1500) Cat Mss
Budget: ($750)
Notes: The music collection is in a catalog separate from the general one. It consists of approx 1700 cataloged books about music; 2100 bound, cataloged books of music incl opera and musical comedy scores; 2700 pieces of sheet music which incl sacred, art and popular songs, and instrumental solos. Good collection of chamber music from baroque to contemporary composers. Also a special collection of 10,000 pieces of American popular sheet music of the period from the 1860s to 1970s incl songs of California. The record collection, primarily classical, consists of about 5500 records.
DC —LIBRARY OF CONGRESS, American Folklife Center, Archive of Folk Culture, Washington, 20540.
Notes: The Charles Todd and Robert Sonkin

Collection of field recordings made in California migratory labor camps, 1940-41.

MUSIC, CANADIAN

MI —UNIVERSITY OF MICHIGAN, School of Music, Music Library, Moore Bldg, Ann Arbor, 48109. Peggy Daub, Head
Holdings: Vols (19,000) Cat Phonorecords
Notes: A collection of current recordings intended primarily to support curricular needs. Also includes 1500 volumes deposited by Radio Canada International.
OH —CASE WESTERN RESERVE UNIVERSITY, Kulas Music Library, 11118 Bellflower Rd, Cleveland, 44106. Timothy Robson, Music Librn
Notes: Selected as a full depository for recordings of Radio Canada International. Includes some 800 recordings of music and the spoken word in French, English, and Spanish. Literary, cultural, and political materials are included.
MB —UNIVERSITY OF MANITOBA, Elizabeth Dafoe Library, Archives and Special Collections Dept, Winnipeg, R3T 2N2, Can. Richard E Bennett, Dept Head; Corrado A Santoro, Reference Archivist
Notes: Papers incl a history of the Mens Musical Club of Winnipeg, membership reocrds, constitutions and by-laws, minutes-of-meetings, programs, publicity and correspondence.
NB —MOUNT ALLISON UNIVERSITY, Alfred Whitehead Memorial Music Library, Sackville, E0A 3C0, Can. Bert Meerveld, Music Librn
Holdings: Vols (16,411) Cat Slides Phonorecords Audiotapes Filmstrips Microforms
Notes: Large collection of Canadian music. Described in *Canadian Music Scores and Recordings: A Classified Catalogue of the Holdings of Mount Allison University Libraries*, comp by Gwendolyn Creelman, Esther Cooke and Geraldine King, 1976. Collection incl 5057 phonorecords; 38 tapes; 99 cassettes; 16,411 monographs, scores and bound periodicals; 101 reels of microfilm; and 3287 sheets of microfiche. Cataloged.
ON —NATIONAL LIBRARY OF CANADA, 395 Wellington St, Ottawa, K1A 0N4, Can. Andre Preibish, Dir
Holdings: Vols 35,000
Notes: Books, papers, and artifacts from Percival Price, renowned authority on campanology and first Dominion carilloneur (1927-39). Incl designs of bells and bell towers around the world, sound recordings, programs, etc. Some bells. About a third of the collection refers to Canadian carillons and carilloneurs.
See also entry under Sound Recordings and Reproductions - Collections.
ON —METROPOLITAN TORONTO LIBRARY, Music Dept, 789 Yonge St, Toronto, M4W 2G8, Can. Isabel Rose, Head
Holdings: Cat
Budget: ($54,000)
Notes: 14,800 books, 40,000 scores; 1900 pieces of retrospective Canadian sheet music; 500 pieces of American and British sheet music, pre-1980; 17,000 phonorecords; 180 current periodical titles; 2800 bound peiodicals; 340 reels of microfilmed periodicals; 16,000 concert programs, chiefly Toronto city; 8850 newspaper clipping files; music picture files integrated with Fine Art Dept picture collection.

MUSIC, CARTOON see Caricatures and Cartoons—Music

MUSIC, CHANCE see Chance Composition (Music)

MUSIC, CHINESE

CA —UNIVERSITY OF CALIFORNIA, BERKELEY, University Library, East Asiatic Library, Room 208, Durant Hall, Berkeley, 94720. Donald Shively, Head
Holdings: Vols 245,000 Cat Mss Maps Pix Microforms
Notes: Research

CA —UNIVERSITY OF CALIFORNIA, LOS ANGELES, Music Dept, Ethnomusicology Archive, 405 Hilgard Ave, Los Angeles, 90024. Ann Briegleb, Ethnomusicology Librn
Notes: Minimal collection of recordings, uncataloged.

MUSIC, CHORAL see Choral Music

MUSIC, CIVIL WAR see U.S. —History – Civil War – Music

MUSIC, CLASSICAL

†NY —SYRACUSE UNIVERSITY LIBRARIES, Ernest S Bird Library, Syracuse, 13210.
Notes: Louis Krasner Collection, with original scores by classic composers.
PA —JANKOLA LIBRARY AND SLOVAK ARCHIVES, Danville, 17821.
Holdings: Vols 800
Notes: Folk instruments and dances.

MUSIC, COMPUTER see Electronic Music

MUSIC, CONCRETE see Concrete Music

MUSIC, COUNTRY

KY —WESTERN KENTUCKY UNIVERSITY, Kentucky Building, Folklore, Folklife & Oral History Archives, Bowling Green, 42101. Patricia M Hodges, Archivist
Holdings: Cat Mss Audiotapes Videotapes
Notes: Archive contains manuscripts of field collection projects done by students and faculty. There is a large folk song collection in manuscript and tapes of local performers of traditional songs and music. Materials generally relate to Kentucky and surrounding areas; or to country music and traditional music. 3500 tapes; 135 linear ft of manuscripts.
TN —COUNTRY MUSIC FOUNDATION, Library & Media Center, 4 Music Sq E, Nashville, 37203. Charlie Seemann, Dir
Holdings: Vols (6000) Mss Pix Slides Phonorecords Audiotapes Videotapes 16mm Films Microforms.
Notes: The largest collection in the world dealing with American country music. Related subject areas are also included-- Anglo-American folksong, popular music in general (soul, jazz, rock and roll, rhythm and blues, etc), recorded sound technology, music law.

MUSIC, COWBOY

NM —UNIVERSITY OF NEW MEXICO, Fine Arts Library, Fine Art Bldg, Albuquerque, 87131. James B Wright, Librn
Notes: The John Donald Robb Archives of Southwestern Music, incl 22,000 titles on Native American music, Hispanic music and cowboy music.

MUSIC, DANCE see Dance Music

MUSIC, DANCE ORCHESTRA see Dance Orchestra Music

MUSIC, DRAMATIC see Music, Incidental; Music in Theatres; Opera

MUSIC, DUTCH

CA —UNIVERSITY OF CALIFORNIA, LOS ANGELES, Music Library, Schonberg Hall, Los Angeles, 90024. Stephen M Fry, Music Librn
Notes: 17th-18th century Dutch song and psalm books.

MUSIC, EARLY

CT —YALE UNIVERSITY, Music Library, 98 Wall St, New Haven, 06520. Harold E Samuel, Librn
Holdings: Vols (118,000) Cat Mss Pix Phonorecords Audiotapes Microforms
Notes: General reference and research

MUSIC, EARLY (cont.)

materials. Performing editions. Strong in theoretical literature, opera, 17-18th century music (incl mss), J S Bach and sons in early editions and mss, Russian liturgical music (Tkaczenko Collection), hymnology, American music. Also collection of musical pictures and portraits.

IL —NEWBERRY LIBRARY, 60 W Walton St, Chicago, 60610. Diana Haskell, Cur of Modern Mss
Holdings: Cat Mss
Notes: About 18,000 books and 22,000 scores. The library of Count Pio Resse and a portion of the library of Alfred Cortot. Especially rich in Italian Renaissance sources. Restricted use: reference only.

NY —SYRACUSE UNIVERSITY LIBRARIES, Music Collection, 222 Waverly Ave, Syracuse, 13210. Donald Seibert, Librn
Holdings: // Cat Microforms
Notes: Nearly 1000 compositions survive in this collection of 17th century music deriving from the reign of Karl Liechtenstein-Castelcorn as Prince-Bishop of Olomouc. The music is preserved on microfilm in the George Arents Research Library at Syracuse University. Contents range from complete settings of masses, vesperae and litaniae to ensemble sonatas and balletti. The collection contains works by over 100 identified composers, including many who were associated with the Imperial court of Leopold I in Vienna, as well as numerous anonymous compositions. A large portion of the music remains unpublished. A catalog of the collection has been published by the Syracuse University Libraries, viz: Otto, Craig A, comp, *Seventeenth Century Music from Kromeriz, Czechoslovakia: A Catalog of the Liechtenstein Music Collection on Microfilm at Syracuse University*(duplicated typescript; 209 pp).

ON —UNIVERSITY OF OTTAWA, Morisset Library, 65 Hastey St, Ottawa, K1N 9A5, Can. Yvon Richer, University Chief Librn
Holdings: Vols (12,000)
Notes: Incl 100 periodicals, 16,000 scores and 5150 sound recordings. Scores and recordings are housed in the music department and monographs and periodicals in the Morisset Library. The collection is particularly strong in sixteenth to nineteenth century continental European music and musicology.

MUSIC, EFFECT OF see Music Therapy

MUSIC, ELECTRONIC see Electronic Music

MUSIC, ENGLISH

CA —UNIVERSITY OF CALIFORNIA, LOS ANGELES, William Andrews Clark Memorial Library, 2520 Cimarron St, Los Angeles, 90018.
Holdings: Cat Mss
Notes: Extensive collection, first editions, etc, almost all 17th-18th century.

CT —YALE UNIVERSITY, Music Library, 98 Wall St, New Haven, 06520. Harold E Samuel, Librn
Holdings: Vols (118,000) Cat Mss Pix Phonorecords Audiotapes Microforms
Notes: General reference and research materials. Performing editions. Strong in theoretical literature, opera, 17-18th century music (incl mss), J S Bach and sons in early editions and mss, Russian liturgical music (Tkaczenko Collection), hymnology, American music. Also collection of musical pictures and portraits.

MA —BOSTON PUBLIC LIBRARY, Music Division, 666 Boylston St, Box 286, Boston, 02117. Ruth Bleecker, Cur of Music
Holdings: Vols 32 Cat Mss
Notes: Thomas Warren's working collection of 32 ms vols of catches, canon, and glees, 1763-1794, incl 2277 compositions, probably half unpublished.

MUSIC, ETHNIC

DC —LIBRARY OF CONGRESS, American Folklife Center, Archive of Folk Culture,

Washington, 20540.
Notes: The Sidney Robertson Cowell Collection of her folk music recordings, 1937 to 1957. Incl very unusual contributions by the Molokan community in the Potrero Hill neighborhood of San Francisco, a breakaway sect from the Russian Orthodox Church.

FL —UNIVERSITY OF MIAMI, Music Library, PO Box 248165, Coral Gables, 33124. Nancy Kobialke, Librn
Holdings: Vols Cat Phonorecords
Budget: ($25,000)
Notes: Emphasis on research editions and performing editions with parts for 2-8 players. Nearly 24,000 musical scores. Recordings are mostly classical, but incl 1200 jazz LPs and 1200 ethnic LPs from all parts of world. *Inter-American Music Archive* is special catalog of Latin American holdings. Collection incl 15,500 cataloged phonorecords.

MUSIC, EUROPEAN

ON —UNIVERSITY OF OTTAWA, Morisset Library, 65 Hastey St, Ottawa, K1N 9A5, Can. Yvon Richer, University Chief Librn
Holdings: Vols (12,000)
Notes: Incl 100 periodicals, 16,000 scores and 5150 sound recordings. Scores and recordings are housed in the music department and monographs and periodicals in the Morisset Library. The collection is particularly strong in sixteenth to nineteenth century continental European music and musicology.

MUSIC, FOLK see Folk Music

MUSIC, FRENCH

CA —STANFORD UNIVERSITY LIBRARIES, Cecil H Green Library, Stanford, 94305. Michael T Ryan, Cur
Notes: Large archive. To be incl in the Stanford University international Lully Archive of microfilm of primary Lully sources. The first of 64 vols (Sacred Music) scheduled for 1984 publication.

MUSIC, FUNERAL see Funeral Music

MUSIC, GERMAN

ON —UNIVERSITY OF OTTAWA, Morisset Library, 65 Hastey St, Ottawa, K1N 9A5, Can. Yvon Richer, University Chief Librn
Holdings: Vols (12,000)
Notes: Incl 100 periodicals, 16,000 scores and 5150 sound recordings. Scores and recordings are housed in the music department and monographs and periodicals in the Morisset Library. The collection is particularly strong in sixteenth to nineteenth century continental European music and musicology.

MUSIC, GOSPEL

NJ —RUTGERS, THE STATE UNIVERSITY OF NEW JERSEY, Institute of Jazz Studies, 135 Bradley Hall, Newark, 07102. Dan Morgenstern, Dir; Edward Berger, Cur; Maxie Griffin, Librn
Holdings: Vols 3000 Cat Pix Phonorecords Audiotapes Films Microforms VF
Notes: Incl jazz records, books, periodicals etc as well as some roots and peripheral material--African music, gospel music, rhythm and blues, rock etc (both written and recorded). Incl 60,000 records.

MUSIC, GREEK

†MA —HELLENIC COLLEGE AND HOLY CROSS GREEK ORTHODOX SCHOOL OF THEOLOGY, Cotsidas-Tonna Library, 50 Goddard Ave, Brookline, 02146.
Notes: Modern Greek literature, Greek Orthodox theology, Byzantine history, music and culture, patristic literature, Orthodox liturgics.

MA —HARVARD UNIVERSITY LIBRARY, Widener Library, Modern Greek Collection, Cambridge, 02138. Evangelie Flessas, Librn
Holdings: Vols (80,000) Cat Mss Microforms

MUSIC, HEBREW see Music, Jewish

MUSIC, HISPANIC

NM —UNIVERSITY OF NEW MEXICO, Fine Arts Library, Fine Art Bldg, Albuquerque, 87131. James B Wright, Librn
Notes: The John Donald Robb Archives of Southwestern Music, incl 22,000 titles on Native American music, Hispanic music and cowboy music.

MUSIC, HUNGARIAN

FL —FLORIDA STATE UNIVERSITY, Warren D Allen Music Library, Tallahassee, 32306. Dale L Hudson, Music Librn
Holdings: // Uncat
Notes: The Carl Helwig Hungarian-Slavic-Americana Recorded Sound Collection is in accessible storage, with 6000 discs and 1400 tapes arranged as nearly as possible according to Helwig's plan. Tapes dated, but not yet shelved in any visible order. Special equipment would be required to do any transcription; hence study of the contents needs to be made before attempt to rerecord. Some materials are deteriorating. Mr Helwig made radio transcriptions, recorded speeches and celebrations, choral concerts and many other perhaps unique performances. Some commercial recordings, but the great bulk of collection produced by Mr Helwig himself. Also some correspondence, espec concerning recording contracts.

MUSIC, ICELANDIC

MB —UNIVERSITY OF MANITOBA, Elizabeth Dafoe Library, Icelandic Collection, Winnipeg, R3T 2N2, Can. Sigrid Johnson, Librn
Holdings: Vols (22,500) Cat Mss Maps Pix Audiotapes Microforms
Budget: ($4200)
Notes: Material mostly in Icelandic, some in other Scandinavian languages. All subject areas incl with primary emphasis placed on language, literature and history of Icelanders in Canada, especially Manitoba (incl mss); early publications of sagas and religious literature; numerous periodicals and newspapers, incl Islandske Maanedstidender, 1773, the first Icelandic periodical, and Framfari, 1877, the first Icelandic newspaper in North America; collections of Icelandic music, such as S K Hall Collection (published and mss); Guttormur J Guttormsson and Stephan G Stephansson Memorial Collections; Vilhjalmur Stefansson publications. Cited in, Saunderson, H H, *The Chair of Icelandic Language and Literature at the University of Manitoba*. Winnipeg: University of Manitoba, 1961.

MUSIC, INCIDENTAL

IL —UNIVERSITY OF ILLINOIS, URBANA/CHAMPAIGN, Library, Music Library, Urbana, 61801. William M McClellan, Librn
Holdings: Vols (200,000) Cat Mss Slides Sound Recordings Microforms Books Scores
Budget: ($65,000)
Notes: Introductory, instructive, research and reference materials to support work at graduate level in ethnomusicology,, musicology, music education, performance areas. Special areas incl about 2500 pre-1800 music mss and editions of music on microfilm, 2400 graduate music theses on microfilm, a special collection of 30,000 titles of American vocal sheet music covering the period 1790-1970, the Rafael Joseffy Collection of about 2000 pieces of 19th century piano music (incl performer markings), the Joseph Szigeti Collection (700 items: published music, mss, recordings), mainly violin and piano music by various commposers. Also incl a special collection of 45,000 78 rpm sound recordings (uncat) of classical music and jazz; a collection of 2900 titles from Chicago radio station WGN. Incl orchestrations, a collection of 500,000 items (uncat) from stock of Hunleth Music Store,

MUSIC, INCIDENTAL (cont.)

St Louis, Missouri, mainly early 20th century imprints of songs, wind music, string music, piano, sets of theatre orchestra parts, dance band orchestrations. A separate collection of choral octavos and instrumental parts is maintained, incl 135,000 pieces of choral music, 30,500 orchestral parts, and 5500 wind ensemble parts. Also, music publishers' catalogues (mainly European and American), ca 126 cubic feet, 1860s-1950s.

IN —INDIANA UNIVERSITY, Lilly Library, Seventh St, Bloomington, 47405. William R Cagle, Librn
Holdings: // Uncat
Notes: Theatre music in the Starr Collection of American Sheet Music.

IN —INDIANA UNIVERSITY, SOUTH BEND, Library, 1700 Mishawaka Ave, South Bend, 46615. James L Mullins, Dir
Holdings: Vols (1490) Cat Mss Maps Pix Phonorecords
Notes: Incl design materials, scripts, theatre music, rare editions, theatre programs, playbills, clippings and periodicals from the 1850s to the 1940s.

NJ —PRINCETON UNIVERSITY, Library, Rare Books Dept, Princeton, 08544. Stephen Ferguson, Cur
Notes: The Valva Collection (gift of the Worcester, Massachusetts Public Library). Orchestral parts and conductors' scores for several thousand popular songs and musical effects used in movie houses and vaudeville from the turn of the century to the end of the silent movie era.

OH —CLEVELAND PUBLIC LIBRARY, Fine Arts and Special Collections Department, 325 Superior Ave, Cleveland, 44114. Alice N Loranth, Head
Holdings: Vols 1750
Notes: Part of the Orchestral Music Collection, which incl scores and parts ranging in size from theatre to symphony orchestra. Incl symphonies, concertos, incidental music and light classical. Indexed. Available for circulation in Cuyahoga County area.

MUSIC, INDIAN (NATIVE AMERICAN)

AZ —NAVAJO COMMUNITY COLLEGE, Naaltsoos Ba' Hoogan, Library, Tsaile, 86556. Marvin E Pollard Jr, Dir, Library Services
Holdings: Vols (10,000) Cat Mss Maps Pix Slides Phonorecords Audiotapes Videotapes 16mm Films Filmstrips Microforms
Budget: ($15,000)
Notes: The Moses/Donner Collection emphasizes Navajos and other tribes of the Southwest; also, all Indians of North America and Mexico. All aspects of the geology, geography, sociology, archaeology, anthropology, etc, of the Four Corners region. The Collection includes a comprehensive collection of Doctoral dissertations dealing with Indians of North America and Mexico.

NM —UNIVERSITY OF NEW MEXICO, Fine Arts Library, Fine Art Bldg, Albuquerque, 87131. James B Wright, Librn
Notes: The John Donald Robb Archives of Southwestern Music, incl 22,000 titles on Native American music, Hispanic music and cowboy music.

MUSIC, INSTRUMENTAL see Instrumental Music

MUSIC, IRISH

†IL —IRISH-AMERICAN CULTURAL ASSOCIATION LIBRARY, 10415 South Western, Chicago, 60643.
Notes: Irish literature, history, biography, art, music.

MUSIC, ITALIAN

CA —UNIVERSITY OF CALIFORNIA, BERKELEY, Humanities-Social Sciences Libraries, Music Library, 24 Morrison Hall, Berkeley, 94720. Michael A Keller, Head Librn
Holdings: // Cat Mss Microforms
Notes: A special collection of about 1000 mss originating in Padua during the 2nd half of the 18th century, devoted to the music of Tartini and his school. A catalog has been published: Duckles, Vincent and Minnie Elmer, Thematic Catalog of a Manuscript Collection of 18th-century Italain Instrumental Music in the University of Calif, Berkeley, Music Library (Berkeley and Los Angeles: Univ of Calif Press, 1963).

CA —SAN FRANCISCO STATE UNIVERSITY, Frank V de Bellis Collection, 1630 Holloway Ave, San Francisco, 94132. Serena de Bellis, Cur
Holdings: Uncat Mss Phonorecords Audiotapes Microforms
Notes: Rare and current materials. Music by Italian composers, medieval through contemporary (10,000 scores). Phonorecords, cylinders, tapes, scores, etc (20,000).

IL —NEWBERRY LIBRARY, 60 W Walton St, Chicago, 60610. Diana Haskell, Cur of Modern Mss
Holdings: Cat Mss
Notes: About 18,000 books and 22,000 scores. The library of Count Pio Resse and a portion of the library of Alfred Cortot. Especially rich in Italian Renaissance sources. Restricted use: reference only.

ON —UNIVERSITY OF OTTAWA, Morisset Library, 65 Hastey St, Ottawa, K1N 9A5, Can. Yvon Richer, University Chief Librn
Holdings: Vols (12,000)
Notes: Incl 100 periodicals, 16,000 scores and 5150 sound recordings. Scores and recordings are housed in the music department and monographs and periodicals in the Morisset Library. The collection is particularly strong in sixteenth to nineteenth century continental European music and musicology.

MUSIC, JAPANESE

MS —UNIVERSITY OF SOUTHERN MISSISSIPPI, William David McCain Graduate Library, Box 5148, Southern Sta, Hattiesburg, 39406.
Holdings: Cat Mss
Notes: The Paul Yoder Collection (1940-1980; 30 cubic feet) contains original musical scores and published copies of band music which Yoder composed or arranged. Some of the band music was written for foreign bands, especially Japanese. Catalog in progress.

MUSIC, JEWISH

DC —LIBRARY OF CONGRESS, Motion Pictures, Broadcasting and Recorded Sound Div, Washington, 20540.
Notes: The Benedict Stambler Archive of Recorded Jewish Music. Nearly 1400 commercial phonographic discs.

NY —NEW YORK PUBLIC LIBRARY, Performing Arts Research Center, Rodgers & Hammerstein Archives of Recorded Sound, 111 Amsterdam Ave, New York, 10023.
Holdings: Phonorecords
Notes: Collection given by Helen Stambler Latner in memory of her husband, Benedict Stambler, comprises some 4000 phonodiscs, LPs and 78s covering the entire range of Jewish music represented on commercial sound recordings, 1900-1970. Basic areas are cantorial (synagogue music), Yiddish Theatre, folk and popular music, Israeli material, religious instructional material. Virtually all major cantors and theatrical persons who made commercial recordings are represented, with much of the material being rare European original discs. Catalog access presently limited to inventory list with performer index. Large collection of broadcast tapes from Israeli Broadcasting Service.

NY —YIVO INSTITUTE FOR JEWISH RESEARCH, Library & Archives, 1048 Fifth Ave, New York, 10028. Dina Abramowicz, Librn; Marek Web, Archivist
Holdings: Cat Mss Slides
Notes: Collections of Jewish music organizations in pre-World War I Russia, and collections of individual musicians and composers, among them the Bernstein collection from Vilna and Leo Low collection from New York. Secular, liturgical, folk music, theatrical songs in the form of sheet music is represented. Partially cataloged.

OH —HEBREW UNION COLLEGE-JEWISH INSTITUTE OF RELIGION, Klau Library, 3101 Clifton Ave, Cincinnati, 45220. David J Gilner, Reference Librn
Holdings: Vols 5000 Cat Mss
Notes: Incl the Birnbaum Jewish Music Collection of 3000 mss; Jewish song index of recordings in the Hebrew Union College collection.

RI —BROWN UNIVERSITY, John Hay Library, Harris Collection, Prospect St, Providence, 02912. Rosemary L Cullen, Cur
Holdings: Vols (200,000) Cat Mss Pix Phonorecords Microforms
Budget: ($15,000)
Notes: The Harris Collection of American Poetry and Plays is principally composed of American and Canadian poetry and plays, 17th century-date. Extensive holdings in songsters, gift books and annuals, hymnals, pageants, broadside verse, carriers' addresses, women poets, juvenile poetry, (incl Mother Goose and The Night Before Christmas), sheet music with lyrics, small press publications, fine printing, black poets, "little magazines," Yiddish-American literature. All movements or schools of American poetry are represented. Incl first editions of most American poets and playwrights, notably Whitman, Poe, Wallace Stevens, Eugene O'Neill, Edward Albee, Ezra Pound, T S Eliot, William Carlos Williams, Amy Lowell, Phyllis Wheatley, Robert Frost, Allen Ginsberg, Bliss Carman, and Stephen Foster sheet music. Also incl the Saunders Walt Whitman Collection (1300 vols); the LangdonCollection of Pageants (250 vols); the Asa Cushman Collection of plays in ms and prompt copies; the MacDougall Collection of Psalters and Hymnals; 4000 plays issued by Walter H Baker Co, Boston (1890-1957); the Vaxer Collection of Yiddish Poetry, Plays and Music (1700 vols). Collections incl 200,000 vols, 30,000 broadsides, 55,000 mss, 170,000 pieces of sheet music, 450 phonorecords, and 375 microfilm reels. See Dictionary Catalog of the Harris Collection of American Poetry and Plays (Boston: G K Hall, 1972), 13 vols; Supplement (1977), 3 vols. See also, American Poetry, 1609-1900, A Collection on Microfilm, Segment I (1609-1820); Segment II (1821-1850); Segment III (1851-1870) (Woodbridge, Conn: Research Publications). Separate catalog.

MUSIC, KEYBOARD see Keyboard Music

MUSIC, LATIN AMERICAN

FL —UNIVERSITY OF MIAMI, Music Library, PO Box 248165, Coral Gables, 33124. Nancy Kobialke, Librn
Holdings: Vols Cat Phonorecords
Budget: ($25,000)
Notes: Emphasis on research editions and performing editions with parts for 2-8 players. Nearly 24,000 musical scores. Recordings are mostly classical, but incl 1200 jazz LPs and 1200 ethnic LPs from all parts of world. Inter-American Music Archive is special catalog of Latin American holdings. Collection incl 15,500 cataloged phonorecords.

IN —INDIANA UNIVERSITY, Music Library, Bloomington, 47401. David E Fenske, Head
Holdings: Vols (4000) Cat Microforms
Budget:
Notes: This collection of Latin American music was funded by the Rockefeller Foundation as part of the activities of the Latin-American Music Center. Interlibrary loan encouraged. Incl 1000 phonorecords. See Juan Orrego-Salas, Music from Latin America available at Indiana University: scores, tapes, and records (Bloomington: Latin-American Music Center, 1971), 412 pp.

MUSIC, MAINE

ME —MAINE STATE LIBRARY, Special
Collections Dept, Cultural Bldg, Station 64,
Augusta, 04333. Shirley Thayer, Librn
Holdings: Mss
Budget: ($2,500,000)
Notes: Over 1000 items in collection; incl
sheet music by over 200 Maine composers.

ME —PORTLAND PUBLIC LIBRARY, 5
Monument Sq, Portland, 04101. Edward V
Chenevert, Library Dir
Holdings: Cat Mss
Notes: The Maine Music Collection. (In
cooperation with the Maine Federation of
Music Clubs). Music written by Maine
composers predominantly 19th and 20th
centuries. Various forms. Indexed. Other
materials on Maine composers and music
also available. 1723 pieces of sheet music;
849 titles.

MUSIC, MARCH see Marches

MUSIC, MEDIEVAL

NY —STATE UNIVERSITY OF NEW
YORK, BUFFALO, Baird Music Library,
Baird Hall, Amherst, 14260. James B
Coover, Dir
Holdings: Vols (104,000) Cat Mss Pix Slides
Phonoreforms Microforms
Notes: Music: history and criticism. Nearly
complete collections of Denkmaeler and
Gesamtausgaben and other historical sets.
Strong collection of dictionaries,
bibliographies, biographies, facsimiles, works
on the "new" music, organology and
ethnomusicology. Special emphasis on
operas, scores of the avant-garde, jazz and
urban popular music, discography and music
librarianship. Good collection of medieval
and Renaissance anthologies, contemporary
and avant-garde recordings. Houses Archives
of the Center of the Creative and Performing
Arts. Collections incl 2100 slides, 22,000
phonorecords, 46,000 scores and parts, 29,
000 books, 4900 microforms. Computerized
record catalog in process.

NY —COLUMBIA UNIVERSITY
LIBRARIES, Music Library, 701 Dodge,
Broadway & 116 St, New York, 10027. M
Haefliger, Librn
Holdings: Vols (55,020) Cat Phonorecords
Audiotapes Microforms
Notes: Strong collection of Medieval and
Renaissance music studies.

NY —NEW YORK PUBLIC LIBRARY,
Performing Arts Research Center, Music
Div, Lincoln Center, New York, 10018.
Notes: New York Pro Musica Archives, and
personal papers of Noah Greenberg, founder.

NY —STATE UNIVERSITY OF NEW
YORK, COLLEGE AT PURCHASE,
Library, Purchase, 10577. Mark E Smith,
Music Librn
Holdings: Vols (6500) // Cat Microforms
Notes: Noah Greenberg Collection of
monographs, journals, scholarly editions of
medieval, Renaissance, and early Baroque
music and performance materials, and
microfilms of music manuscripts. Collection
was acquired from the defunct New York
Pro Musica Antiqua.

MUSIC, MICHIGAN

MI —DETROIT PUBLIC LIBRARY, Music &
Performing Arts Dept, 5201 Woodward,
Detroit, 48202. Jean Currie Church, Cur
Holdings: Cat Mss Pix Phonorecords
Notes: Michigan Collection designed to
reflect performing arts activity in Michigan,
primarily music. Over 4000 cataloged and
indexed titles of music by Michigan
composers and Michigan publishers.
Extensive clipping files documenting Detroit
area concerts and local performers
supplemented by card index. Also incl 150
recordings.

MUSIC, MILITARY see Military Music

MUSIC, MODERN—20TH CENTURY

CA —CALIFORNIA INSTITUTE OF THE
ARTS, Library, 24700 McBean Pkwy,

Valencia, 91355. James Elrod, Dir
Holdings: Vols (61,000) Cat Phonorecords
Audiotapes
Budget: ($8500)
Notes: Incl 11,656 audiotapes. Cataloged.

DC —LIBRARY OF CONGRESS, Music
Division, Washington, 20540.
Holdings: Mss Pix
Notes: Archives of Modern Music magazine,
1924-1946. Incl photographs, documents,
etc.

NY —NEW YORK PUBLIC LIBRARY,
Performing Arts Research Center, Rodgers
& Hammerstein Archives of Recorded
Sound, 111 Amsterdam Ave, New York,
10023.
Holdings: // Cat Audiotapes
Notes: The Serge Koussevitzky Music
Foundation at the Library of Congress
established in 1958 a tape recording project
devoted to documenting for limited library
distribution the current or near-current
output of contemporary composers,
American and European. By the time the
last tapes from the project were received in
1971, close to 300 composers were
represented. Together with the Library of
Congress and a small group of similar
institutions, the Rodgers and Hammerstein
Archives was one of the recipients of this
series.

TX —NORTH TEXAS STATE UNIVERSITY,
Audio Center, Box 5188, NT Station,
Denton, 76203. Morris Martin, Music Librn
Notes: Emphasis on Contemporary and
Avant Garde music. More than 450 musical
compositions (mostly manuscript, many
multi-media). This is an archive of materials
published in, or submitted for publication to,
the contemporary music magazine Source,
the Music of the Avant Garde which
appeared from 1967-1977 (although bearing
dates only through 1973). Composers
represented are the editors (Larry Austin
and Stanley Lunetta), John Cage, Steve
Reich, Pauline Oliveros, Harry Partch,
Morton Feldman, Lukas Foss, Barney
Childs, David Cope, Peter Garland, Philip
Glass, Ben Johnston, Alcides Lanza, Alvin
Lucier, David Rosenboom, Dane Rudhyar,
and Nicolas Slonimsky.

MUSIC, NEW JERSEY

NJ —NEWARK PUBLIC LIBRARY, Art &
Music Dept, 5 Washington St, Newark,
07101. William J Dane, Supv
Holdings: Vols (25,000) Cat Mss Audiotapes
Microforms VF
Notes: Music literature, scores, librettos,
extensive vertical file, song sheets, special
indexes, music periodicals. John Tasker
Howard collection of notes and letters. Some
special material on New Jersey and Newark
music.

MUSIC, NEW ORLEANS

LA —TULANE UNIVERSITY, Howard-Tilton
Memorial Library, Special Collections Div,
William Ransom Hogan Jazz Archive, 7001
Freret, New Orleans, 70118. Richard B
Allen, Acting Cur; Alma D Williams,
Assistant to the Cur
Holdings: Vols (100,000) Cat Mss Pix Slides
Phonorecords Audiotapes Videotapes 16mm
Films Microforms
Budget: ($90,000)
Notes: Jazz music and musicians.
Outstanding collection, incl books, music
scores, serials, catalogs and other archival
material. Music, history, etc.
See also entry under Jazz

MUSIC, ORGAN see Organ Music

MUSIC, PARADE see Marches

MUSIC, PATRIOTIC see Patriotic Music, American

MUSIC, PERCUSSION see Percussion Instruments and Music

MUSIC, PHYSICAL EFFECT OF see Music Therapy

MUSIC, PIANO see Piano Music

MUSIC, POLISH

CA —THE POLISH ARTS AND CULTURE
FOUNDATION, 1290 Sutter St, San

Francisco, 94109. Wanda Tomczykowska,
President
Holdings: Phonorecords Audiotapes
Notes: Covers Polish music from the earliest
times to current. Incl several hundred tapes,
records, books, and programs.

NY —POLISH SINGERS ALLIANCE OF
AMERICA, 180 2nd Ave, New York,
10003.
Notes: About 2000 pieces of music.
Cataloged.

PA —ALLIANCE COLLEGE, Washington
Hall Library, Fullerton Ave, Cambridge
Springs, 16403. Stanley J Kozaczka, Head
Librn
Holdings: 23,000 Vols
Notes: Polish cultural history, art, music,
and literature collection. Much on Poles in
the US. Polish newspapers and literary
periodicals of 19th century in microform.

PA —POLISH NATIONAL UNION OF
AMERICA, 1004 Pittston Ave, Scranton,
18505.

MUSIC, POPULAR

AZ —ARIZONA STATE UNIVERSITY,
Music Library, Tempe, 85281. Arlys L
McDonald, Music Librn
Holdings: Vols 5446 // Uncat Phonorecords
16mm Films
Notes: The Wayne King Collection of
popular music titles arranged for and used by
the Wayne King Orchestra from the 1930s-
1960s. It includes full score arrangements
with parts, charts, recordings and 16mm
films of his television shows originating from
Chicago, 1949-1952. The collection is
indexed by title. No photocopying.

CA —CALIFORNIA STATE UNIVERSITY,
HAYWARD, Library, Hayward, 94542.
Melissa Rose, Dir
Holdings: Vols (15,986) Cat Phonorecords
Budget: ($21,000)
Notes: The score collection covers the entire
range of instrumental and vocal concert
music, incl collected works of various
composers, and representative collections of
hymnals, folk music, musical comedy, and
some popular music. Sound recordings range
from ethnomusicological collections to
electronic music. Emphasis is on concert
music, but there is a large collection of jazz
and a selective collection of popular music.
Separate catalog.

CA —LOS ANGELES PUBLIC LIBRARY,
Art, Music & Recreation Dept, 630 W Fifth
St, Los Angeles, 90071. Melvin H
Rosenberg, Mgr & Principal Librn
Holdings: Vols (68,000) Cat Mss
Budget: ($102,244)
Notes: Incl 44,000 music scores, 3000 mss,
100,000 song sheets, and newspaper
clippings. Index to the song collection on
cards.

CA —UNIVERSITY OF CALIFORNIA, LOS
ANGELES, Music Library, Schonberg Hall,
Los Angeles, 90024. Stephen M Fry, Music
Librn
Notes: Incl the Harry Roth Library of
American Theater Music, the Meredith
Wilson Library of Popular Sheet Music, and
the library of American Motion Picture
Music.

CA —SAN DIEGO PUBLIC LIBRARY, Art,
Music & Recreation Sect, 820 E St, San
Diego, 92101. Barbara A Tuhill, Supvr
Holdings: Vols 132 Cat
Notes: A collection of gift sheet music has
been organized into bound vols by date of
copyright covering popular songs form the
1800s through the 1950s. Each volume is
arranged with a table of contents by title,
and is also indexed in a special Song Title
Index. Special vols also cover the hits of
World War I, ballads, religious songs and
other subjects. Reference use only.

CT —YALE UNIVERSITY, Sterling Memorial
Library, Yale Collection of Historical Sound
Recordings, 120 High St, New Haven,
06520. Richard Warren Jr, Cur
Holdings: Mss Pix Phonorecords Audiotapes
Notes: Incl "classical music" ("concert
music") of all types from Western culture,
jazz, the American Musical Theatre, spoken
material (literary, dramatic, documentary).

MUSIC, POPULAR (cont.)

The aim of the Collection is to document performance practice in the fields collected. See the article by Karol Berger in the *Journal of the Association for Recorded Sound Collections*, vol VI, no 1, pp 13-25. Partially cataloged.

FL —ORLANDO PUBLIC LIBRARY, 100 Block of Central Ave, Orlando, 32806. Helen M Struthers, AV Librn
Holdings: Cat Phonorecords Audiotapes
Budget: ($5500)
Notes: 7155 LP recordings with emphasis on classical music; also jazz, country-western, easy-listening, spoken arts, foreign language study, dictation. Young Adult Dept has additional 850 contemporary and rock records. Library serves as subregional talking book library for the blind and physically handicapped, maintaining 7858. Also 681 audiotapes.

IL —CHICAGO PUBLIC LIBRARY, Music Section, Fine Arts Division, 78 E Washington St, Chicago, 60602. Rosalinda I Hack, Fine Arts Division Chief; Richard C Schwegel, Head, Music Section
Notes: Extensive collection in books, dissertations, periodicals, scores, and recordings. Collect local artists and magazines. Major US periodicals and several foreign publications. Strong collection of discography. In house Lyric File consists of several thousand song lyrics on cards.

IL —CHICAGO PUBLIC LIBRARY, Music Section, Fine Arts Division, 78 E Washington St, Chicago, 60602. Rosalinda I Hack, Fine Arts Division Chief; Richard C Schwegel, Head, Music Section
Holdings: // Uncat
Notes: The Chicago Public Library received the Sheet Music Archive (1700 cu ft) of the Plitt Theatre Corporation, Chicago, in 1975. This vast, unprossed collection contains thousands of pieces of music played during intermissions in the Plitt Theatre palaces in Chicago during the 1920-40s. An inventory; of the collection is available, organized by composer and form (eg "Fox Trots"); titles are not yet compiled. The collection is presently in storage at the Record Center Corporation, The Chicago Public Library's storage facility for little-used materials.

IL —NEWBERRY LIBRARY, 60 W Walton St, Chicago, 60610. Diana Haskell, Cur of Modern Mss
Holdings: Vols 100,000
Notes: Emphasis on 18th and 19th century American titles. 6300 items cataloged. Incl J Francis Driscoll Collection. Noncirculating.

IL —UNIVERSITY OF ILLINOIS, URBANA/CHAMPAIGN, Library, Music Library, Urbana, 61801. William M McClellan, Librn
Holdings: Vols (200,000) Cat Mss Slides Sound Recordings Microforms Books Scores
Budget: ($65,000)
Notes: Introductory, instructive, research and reference materials to support work at graduate level in ethnomusicology,, musicology, music education, performance areas. Special areas incl about 2500 pre-1800 music mss and editions of music on microfilm, 2400 graduate music theses on microfilm, a special collection of 30,000 titles of American vocal sheet music covering the period 1790-1970, the Rafael Joseffy Collection of about 2000 pieces of 19th century piano music (incl performer markings), the Joseph Szigeti Collection (700 items: published music, mss, recordings), mainly violin and piano music by various commposers. Also incl a special collection of 45,000 78 rpm sound recordings (uncat) of classical music and jazz; a collection of 2900 titles from Chicago radio station WGN. Incl orchestrations, a collection of 500,000 items (uncat) from stock of Hunleth Music Store, St Louis, Missouri, mainly early 20th century imprints of songs, wind music, string music, piano, sets of theatre orchestra parts, dance band orchestrations. A separate collection of choral octavos and instrumental parts is maintained, incl 135,000 pieces of choral music, 30,500 orchestral parts, and

5500 wind ensemble parts. Also, music publishers' catalogues (mainly European and American), ca 126 cubic feet, 1860s-1950s.

IN —INDIANA UNIVERSITY, Lilly Library, Seventh St, Bloomington, 47405. William R Cagle, Librn
Holdings: // Uncat
Notes: In the Starr Collection of American Sheet Music.

IN —MORRISSON-REEVES LIBRARY, 80 N Sixth St, Richmond, 47374. Harriet E Bard, Librn
Holdings: Cat
Notes: Singin' Sam (Harry Frankel) Collection: popular and semipopular sheet music (4340 //). Also, audiotapes (142 //) of Singin' Sam's radio programs from the 1930s and 1940s. Sheet music noncirculating; photocopying available.

KY —HOPKINSVILLE COMMUNITY COLLEGE, Library, North Dr, Hopkinsville, 42240. Marjanna J Frising, Librn
Holdings: Vols (500) Cat Phonorecords Audiotapes Filmstrips
Notes: Incl most notable Broadway plays, both musical and non-musical, with soundtracks available for most. Also a large collection of children's and one-act plays as well as non-musical but best known 3-act plays, incl comedy and mystery plays.

LA —TULANE UNIVERSITY, Howard-Tilton Memorial Library, Special Collections Div, William Ransom Hogan Jazz Archive, 7001 Freret, New Orleans, 70118. Richard B Allen, Acting Cur; Alma D Williams, Assistant to the Cur
Holdings: Vols (100,000) Cat Mss Pix Slides Phonorecords Audiotapes Videotapes 16mm Films Microforms
Budget: ($90,000)
Notes: Jazz music and musicians. Outstanding collection, incl books, music scores, serials, catalogs and other archival material. Music, history, etc.
See also entry under Jazz

MD —TOWSON STATE UNIVERSITY, Fine Arts Bldg, Room 457, Towson, 21204. Edwin L Gerhardt, Curator
Notes: The Gerhardt Library of Musical Information is a segregated representative collection of music literature, phonograph and tape recordings, pictures and artifacts. It incl special sections on Thomas Alva Edison and the phonograph, John Philip Sousa and bands, old popular songs and percussion. Most of the material is out of print and hard to find. It is *not* a collection of scores or manuscripts. A detailed outline is available upon request. Direct all correspondence to the curator, Edwin L Gerhardt, 4926 Leeds Ave, Baltimore, MD 21227, (301) 242-0328.

MA —NORTHEASTERN UNIVERSITY LIBRARIES, Special Collections, 360 Huntington Ave, Boston, 02115. Nieves F Farin, Head Collection Development Librn
Notes: Glen Gray and the Casa Loma Orchestra. 2000 items: sheet music, programs, pictures, clippings on swing music in the 1930s.

MA —BRANDEIS UNIVERSITY, Goldfarb Library, 415 South St, Waltham, 02154. Bessie Hahn, Dir
Notes: 39 linear ft of musical mss, phonodiscs and memorabilia. A finding list to the collection is located in Special Collections. Early American Sheet Music: 30 linear ft of early American song sheets of the 20th century. This collection is unprocessed, spring 1984.

MI —DETROIT PUBLIC LIBRARY, Music & Performing Arts Dept, 5201 Woodward, Detroit, 48202. Agatha Pfeiffer Kalkanis, Chief
Holdings: Cat
Notes: Over 5000 song collections of all types. Incl all collections in standard indexes (Sears, DeCharms & Breed, Leigh, etc). Printed indexes supplemented by extensive song index on cards in department. Also incl about 1000 commercial recordings of folk music. See entry under Songs.

MN —SAINT PAUL PUBLIC LIBRARY, Arts & Audiovisual Services, 90 W Fourth St, Saint Paul, 55102. Delores Sundbye, Supervising Librn
Holdings: Vols (30,000)
Notes: The Field Collection of 15,000 pieces

of sheet music of 19th and 20th century popular songs. Indexed but not cataloged.

NJ —NEWARK PUBLIC LIBRARY, Art & Music Dept, 5 Washington St, Newark, 07101. William J Dane, Supv
Holdings: Vols Uncat
Notes: 2500 song sheets of popular music, with emphasis on late 19th and 20th century titles. General collection of art songs, sacred songs, folk songs, Tune Dex and standard song collections incl all of Sears. Special song indexes supplement printed indexes.

NJ —PRINCETON UNIVERSITY, Library, Rare Books Dept, Princeton, 08544. Stephen Ferguson, Cur
Notes: The Valva Collection (gift of the Worcester, Massachusetts Public Library). Orchestral parts and conductors' scores for several thousand popular songs and musical effects used in movie houses and vaudeville from the turn of the century to the end of the silent movie era.

NM —NEW MEXICO STATE UNIVERSITY, Library, Box 3475, Las Cruces, 88003. James Dyke, Dir
Holdings: Vols 4000 // Cat
Notes: Jazz, Blues, and music history. Collection of music periodicals and monographs of the 1930s, 1940s and 1950s.

NY —STATE UNIVERSITY OF NEW YORK, BUFFALO, Baird Music Library, Baird Hall, Amherst, 14260. James B Coover, Dir
Holdings: Vols (104,000) Cat Mss Pix Slides Phonorecords Microforms
Notes: Nearly complete collections of *Denkmaeler and Gesamtausgaben* and other historical sets. Strong collection of dictionaries, bibliographies, biographies, facsimiles, works on the "new" music, organology and ethnomusicology. Special emphasis on operas, scores of the avant-garde, jazz and urban popular music, discography and music librarianship. Good collection of medieval and Renaissance anthologies, contemporary and avant-garde recordings. Houses Archives of the Center of the Creative and Performing Arts. Collections incl 2100 slides, 22,000 phonorecords, 46,000 scores and parts, 29, 000 books, 4900 microforms. Computerized record catalog in process.

NY —BROOKLYN PUBLIC LIBRARY, Art & Music Div, Grand Army Plaza, Brooklyn, 11238. Sue H Sharma, Chief
Holdings: Vols (4500) Cat Mss
Notes: Over 50,000 items, most of which circulate to the public. The collection contains some reference materials, incl the complete works of many composers; over 3500 popular song folios with our own in-house index for locating individual songs; some rare editions and mss of local composers; and a small collection of rare sheet music beginning with the 18th century. The circulating collection incl standard vocal scores, methods, piano music, etc, and is one of the largest public library collections in the country.

NY —STATE UNIVERSITY OF NEW YORK, COLLEGE AT BUFFALO, E H Butler Library, 1300 Elmwood Ave, Buffalo, 14222. Sister Martin Joseph Jones, Assoc Librn
Holdings: Uncat Phonorecords
Notes: The William H Tallmadge Collection of jazz, pop, and country music (691 phonorecords) incl 46 Hill and Dale records with standing record player.

NY —BARNARD A & MORRIS N YOUNG LIBRARY OF EARLY AMERICAN POPULAR MUSIC, 270 Riverside Dr, New York, 10025. Morris N Young, Cur
Holdings: Cat Mss Pix Phonorecords Audiotapes Microforms
Notes: 48,000 items of American popular music, mostly 1790-1910. Incl books, serials, sheet music, broadsides, anthologies, air checks, broadcasting and music business memorabilia, and correspondence.

NY —NEW YORK PUBLIC LIBRARY, Performing Arts Research Center, Rodgers & Hammerstein Archives of Recorded Sound, 111 Amsterdam Ave, New York, 10023. Holdings: Cat Phonorecords Audiotapes
Notes: 400,000 sound recordings on disc,

MUSIC, POPULAR (cont.)

tape, wire, and cylinder; classical and popular music, jazz, speech, etc. Printed materials related to the subject. Major collection of manufacturers' catalogs.

NY —NEW YORK PUBLIC LIBRARY, Music Div, 111 Amsterdam Ave, New York, 10023. Frank C Campbell, Chief
Holdings: Cat Mss Pix Microforms
Notes: Books, scores, autographs, mss letter, pictures. Cover classical and popular music and jazz.

NC —CAMPBELL COLLEGE, Carrie Rich Memorial Library, Box 98, Buies Creek, 27506. Helen Sistrunk, Asst to Dir
Budget: $710
Notes: Late nineteenth and twentieth century popular music.

NC —CUMBERLAND COUNTY PUBLIC LIBRARY, North Carolina Foreign Language Center, 328 Gillespie St, Fayetteville, 28301. Patrick M Valentine, Coordinator
Holdings: Phonorecords
Budget: $500
Notes: Popular music from around the world, in foreign languages, incl 300 cataloged records.

OH —CLEVELAND PUBLIC LIBRARY, Fine Arts and Special Collections Department, 325 Superior Ave, Cleveland, 44114. Alice N Loranth, Head
Holdings: Vols (72,050) Cat Phonorecords
Notes: Part of the Music Collection which incl books, scores and 15,300 recordings on classical, modern, jazz and popular music.

OR —UNIVERSITY OF OREGON LIBRARY, Special Collections Div, Eugene, 97403. Kenneth W Duckett, Curator
Holdings: Cat
Notes: Over 20,000 pieces of sheet music of popular songs arranged for voice and piano, 1852-1976 (bulk dates: 1890-1939).
See also entry under Composers

PA —FREE LIBRARY OF PHILADELPHIA, Sheet Music Collection, Logan Sq, Philadelphia, 19103. Connie Jessum, Librn
Budget: ($2000)
Notes: Covers entire span of American popular music in song and instrumental music (piano) from colonial times to the present. Incl Newland-Zeuner and Edward I Keffer Collections on loan from the Musical Fund Society. Items printed before 1825 indexed in Sonneck-Upton and Wolfe. Checklists for cover illustrations, musical shows or films and special subjects. Songs are filed by title; piano music by composer. Examples of special materials not filed in regular collection incl early Philadelphia composers and publications, national (centennial and state), patriotic ("Star-Spangled Banner"), political (Presidents), and war (1861; 1914; 1939) songs. Most of the ms materials are anonymous. Collection contains 138,360 pieces of sheet music.

RI —BROWN UNIVERSITY, John Hay Library, 20 Prospect St, Providence, 02912. Mark N Brown, Cur Mss
Notes: The Sheet Music Collection concentrates on music of American imprint, incl 170,000 vocal pieces filed by title, plus 80,000 instrumental pieces filed by composer. Major strengths are in 19th century music, especially prior to 1830; Civil War music, both Union and Confederate; lithographic covers; World War I songs; political campaign music; and band music. An additional 100,000 pieces of American and European imprint remain unprocessed.

TN —COUNTRY MUSIC FOUNDATION, Library & Media Center, 4 Music Sq E, Nashville, 37203. Charlie Seemann, Dir
Holdings: Vols (6000) Mss Pix Slides Phonorecords Audiotapes Videotapes 16mm Films Microforms
Notes: The largest collection in the world dealing with American country music. Related subject areas are also included-- Anglo-American folksong, popular music in general (soul, jazz, rock and roll, rhythm and blues, etc), recorded sound technology, music law.

TX —FORT WORTH PUBLIC LIBRARY, Arts Division, 300 Taylor St, Fort Worth,

76102. Heather Gobel, Head
Holdings: Vols (21,500) Cat Mss Phonorecords
Budget: ($26,700)
Notes: Emphasis is on older popular music and musical comedies, folk songs, operas, music composed by Fort Worth and Texas composers, and music about Texas. Sheet music has a separate index.

WI —MILWAUKEE PUBLIC LIBRARY, 814 W Wisconsin Ave, Milwaukee, 53233. Donald J Sager, City Librn
Holdings: Vols Cat
Notes: An extensive general music literature collection incl classical, contemporary, jazz, and musical biographies, as well as the most significant reference works in music. Also incl 46,708 sound recordings, 73,150 historical recorded sound collection, 20,000 historic popular song collection, and WPA copied music. Local area music materials incl concert programs and newspaper clippings.

MUSIC, POPULAR—WRITING AND PUBLISHING

†MD —MARYLAND HISTORICAL SOCIETY, Library, 201 W Monument St, Baltimore, 21201.
Notes: Eubie Blake's personal and professional archive. Incl the Baltimore-born pianist, composer, and songwriter's collection of songs and instrumental pieces in mss, extensive documentation of his collaboration with Noble Sissle, Flournog Miller, Milton Reddie, and others. The Broadway musical comedy, Shuffle Along, is represented in box office records, programs, scores and parts, photographs, and sheet music. Blake's involvement with other productions is similarly documented.

MUSIC, PRIMITIVE

CA —UNIVERSITY OF CALIFORNIA, LOS ANGELES, Music Dept, Ethnomusicology Archive, 405 Hilgard Ave, Los Angeles, 90024. Ann Briegleb, Ethnomusicology Librn
Holdings: Cat Mss Maps Pix Slides Audiotapes Phonorecords
Notes: Ethnomusicology of the non-Western world. Incl 7769 tapes and 8957 phonodisc recordings.

NY —COLUMBIA UNIVERSITY LIBRARIES, Center for Studies in Ethnomusicology Library, Music Dept, 417 Dodge, New York, 10027. Dieter Christensen, Cur
Notes: A particularly strong collection of recorded ethnic music.

MUSIC, RELIGIOUS see Church Music

MUSIC, RENAISSANCE

IL —NEWBERRY LIBRARY, 60 W Walton St, Chicago, 60610. Diana Haskell, Cur of Modern Mss
Holdings: Cat Mss Microforms
Notes: Incl the library of Count Pio Resse and a portion of Alfred Cortot library. Particularly strong in Italian theoretical treatises, vocal music and music for fretted instruments. Restricted use: noncirculating.

NY —STATE UNIVERSITY OF NEW YORK, BUFFALO, Baird Music Library, Baird Hall, Amherst, 14260. James B Coover, Dir
Notes: Good collection of medieval and Renaissance anthologies, contemporary and avant-garde recordings.

NY —COLUMBIA UNIVERSITY LIBRARIES, Music Library, 701 Dodge, Broadway & 116 St, New York, 10027. M Haefliger, Librn
Holdings: Vols (55,020) Cat Phonorecords Audiotapes Microforms
Notes: Strong collection of Medieval and Renaissance music studies.

NY —NEW YORK PUBLIC LIBRARY, Performing Arts Research Center, Music Div, Lincoln Center, New York, 10018.
Notes: New York Pro Musica Archives, and personal papers of Noah Greenberg, founder.

NY —STATE UNIVERSITY OF NEW YORK, COLLEGE AT PURCHASE, Library, Purchase, 10577. Mark E Smith, Music Librn
Holdings: Vols (6500) // Cat Microforms
Notes: Noah Greenberg Collection of monographs, journals, scholarly editions of medieval, Renaissance, and early Baroque music and performance materials, and microfilms of music manuscripts. Collection was acquired from the defunct New York Pro Musica Antiqua.

ON —UNIVERSITY OF OTTAWA, Morisset Library, 65 Hastey St, Ottawa, K1N 9A5, Can. Yvon Richer, University Chief Librn
Notes: Incl 100 periodicals, 16,000 scores and 5150 sound recordings. Scores and recordings are housed in the music department and monographs and periodicals in the Morisset Library. The collection is particularly strong in sixteenth to nineteenth century continental European music and musicology.

MUSIC, ROCK

CA —FITZ HUGH LUDLOW MEMORIAL LIBRARY, PO Box 99346, San Francisco, 94109. Michael R Aldrich, Exec Cur
Holdings: Vols Cat Mss Pix Phonorecords Audiotapes
Notes: Collection stored. Important mail inquiries. No interlibrary lending or telephone inquiries. Collection emphasizes books, songbooks, discographies, and phonograph records relative to psychoctive drug-using musicians and their art. Incl many pictures, sheet music, and some autographed or inscribed materials, mostly from the 20th century of works by or about Milton "Mezz" Mezzrow, Billie Holiday, the Beatles, Bob Dylan, and recent drug-related rock music. About 600 record albums.

FL —ORLANDO PUBLIC LIBRARY, 100 Block of Central Ave, Orlando, 32806. Helen M Struthers, AV Librn
Holdings: Cat Phonorecords Audiotapes
Budget: ($5500)
Notes: 7155 LP recordings with emphasis on classical music; also jazz, country-western, easy listening, spoken arts, foreign language study, dictation. Young Adult Dept has additional 850 contemporary and rock records. Library serves as subregional talking book library for the blind and physically handicapped, maintaining 7858 titles. Also, 681 audiotapes on all subjects. All materials circulate for 3 weeks.

IL —CHICAGO PUBLIC LIBRARY, Music Section, Fine Arts Division, 78 E Washington St, Chicago, 60602. Rosalinda I Hack, Fine Arts Division Chief; Richard C Schwegel, Head, Music Section
Notes: Extensive collection in books, disserations, periodicals, scores and recordings. Many foreign publications. Major US magazines (complete Billboard) and many specialty titles. Strong collection of discography. Record collection strong in current popular, new wave, and local artists; some retrospective.

MI —DETROIT PUBLIC LIBRARY, Music & Performing Arts Dept, 5201 Woodward, Detroit, 48202. Agatha Pfeiffer Kalkanis, Chief
Holdings: Vols 19,000 Cat Mss Pix Microforms
Notes: Also incl (77,000) scores. General collection intended for practical use in performance and for scholarly research. Good working collection of bibliographies, thematic catalogs, dictionaries and encyclopedias, periodical indexes. Many sets of collected works, monumental editions, historical anthologies. Good representation of opera and operetta, art song and folk song, solo instrumental literature and chamber music in practical editions. 2575 titles of choral music, chiefly sacred, for use by choirs. 17,000 titles of popular sheet music, uncataloged but thoroughly indexed. Considerable recent holdings of books and periodicals in foreign languages. Special collections of black and local materials. 25, 000 recordings and extensive discographical literature. Collection of publishers' trade catalogs.

MUSIC, ROCK (cont.)

NJ —RUTGERS, THE STATE UNIVERSITY
OF NEW JERSEY, Institute of Jazz Studies,
135 Bradley Hall, Newark, 07102. Dan
Morgenstern, Dir; Edward Berger, Cur;
Maxie Griffin, Librn
Holdings: Vols 3500 Cat Pix Phonorecords
Audiotapes Films Microforms VF
Notes: Incl jazz records, books, periodicals
etc as well as some roots and peripheral
material--African music, gospel music,
rhythm and blues, rock etc (both written and
recorded). Incl 60,000 records.

TN —COUNTRY MUSIC FOUNDATION,
Library & Media Center, 4 Music Sq E,
Nashville, 37203. Charlie Seemann, Dir
Holdings: Vols (6000) Mss Pix Slides
Phonorecords Audiotapes Videotapes 16mm
Films Microforms
Notes: The largest collection in the world
dealing with American country music.
Related subject areas are also included--
Anglo-American folksong, popular music in
general (soul, jazz, rock and roll, rhythm and
blues, etc), recorded sound technology,
music law.

MUSIC, RUSSIAN

CT —YALE UNIVERSITY, Music Library, 98
Wall St, New Haven, 06520. Harold E
Samuel, Librn
Notes: General reference and reseach
materials. Performing editions. Strong in
theoretical literature, opera, 17-18th century
music (incl mss), J S Bach and sons in early
editions and mss, Russian liturgical music
(Tkaczenko Collection), hymnology,
American music. Also collection of musical
pictures and portraits.

MA —HARVARD UNIVERSITY LIBRARY,
Houghton Library, Cambridge, 02138.
Rodney G Dennis, Cur of Manuscripts
Holdings: Mss
Notes: See *Music Library Association Notes*,
2nd series, XVII (1959/60), 539-558.

NY —CORNELL UNIVERSITY LIBRARIES,
Music Library, 225 Lincoln Hall, Ithaca,
14853. Lenore Coral, Music Librn
Holdings: Vols (106,022) Cat
Notes: See entry under Music.

VA —UNIVERSITY OF VIRGINIA,
Alderman Library, Music Collection,
Charlottesville, 22901. Evan Bonds, Music
Librn
Holdings: // Cat Mss Pix
Notes: Scores, books, correspondence of the
Russian music historian Alfred J Swan,
related to his study of Soviet music
(particularly Russian church music and folk
songs) and musicians. Published description:
Vilimirovic, Milos, "Swan Music Collection,"
Chapter & Verse (journal of the Associates
of the Univ of Va Library), Nov 1977, pp
20-21.

MUSIC, SACRED see Church Music

MUSIC, SLAVIC

FL —FLORIDA STATE UNIVERSITY,
Warren D Allen Music Library, Tallahassee,
32306. Dale L Hudson, Music Librn
Holdings: // Uncat
Notes: The Carl Helwig Hungarian-Slavic-
Americana Recorded Sound Collection is in
accessible storage, with 6000 discs and 1400
tapes arranged as nearly as possible
according to Helwig's plan. Tapes dated, but
not yet shelved in any visible order. Special
equipment would be required to do any
transcription; hence study of the contents
needs to be made before attempt to rerecord.
Some materials are deteriorating. Mr Helwig
made radio transcriptions, recorded speeches
and celebrations, choral concerts and many
other perhaps unique performances. Some
commercial recordings, but the great bulk of
collection produced by Mr Helwig himself.
Also some correspondence, espec concerning
recording contracts.

MUSIC, SLOVAK

OH —SLOVAK INSTITUTE, Saint Andrew's
Abbey, 2900 King Dr, Cleveland, 44104.

Rev Andrew Pier, Dir
Holdings: Vols (10,000)
Notes: Promotes cultural interests, especially
work of Slovak authors, artists, and
musicians through its Slovak Writers and
Artists Association. Private library.
Permission required.

MUSIC, SOUL

TN —COUNTRY MUSIC FOUNDATION,
Library & Media Center, 4 Music Sq E,
Nashville, 37203. Charlie Seemann, Dir
Holdings: Vols (6000) Mss Pix Slides
Phonorecords Audiotapes Videotapes 16mm
Films Microforms
Notes: The largest collection in the world
dealing with American country music.
Related subject areas are also included--
Anglo-American folksong, popular music in
general (soul, jazz, rock and roll, rhythm and
blues, etc), recorded sound technology,
music law.

MUSIC, SOUTHERN

LA —NEW ORLEANS PUBLIC LIBRARY,
Art & Music Div, 219 Loyola Ave, New
Orleans, 70140. Marilyn Wilkins, Head
Holdings: Cat
Notes: About 700 pieces of early New
Orleans sheet music; early southern sheet
music, and New Orleans imprints. Catalog.

NC —DUKE UNIVERSITY, William R
Perkins Library, Durham, 27706. Elvin E
Strowd, University Librn

MUSIC, TEXAS

TX —DALLAS PUBLIC LIBRARY, Fine Arts
Div, 1515 Young St, Dallas, 75201. Richard
L Waters, Acting Dir; Jane Holahan,
Manager
Holdings: Uncat Mss Pix
Notes: *The Dallas Symphony Orchestra;*
printed programs beginning with first concert
in 1900 are bound. Subscription series
indexed by composition performed and guest
artists. Scrapbooks assembled by Symphony
PR office and Symphony League kept on file
in Division. Reviews of performances filed.
Photographs of all conductors on file. Photos
of Symphony on stage. *Dallas Civic Opera;*
printed programs as well as reviews and
other related newspaper articles; also a
collection of 200 artists' renderings of set
designs, costumes, etc. *The John Rosenfield*
Papers: Mr Rosenfield, Amusements Editor
for the *Dallas Morning News* for over 40
years, had collected letters received from
persons in the Performing Arts, mostly
music, over the years. There are also
photographs of many of the stars who
performed in Dallas and whom he met in
both New York and Hollywood. The
Manuscript ArchivesCommittee of the Texas
Federation of Music Clubs works with the
Fine Arts Division in collecting holograph
mss of those Texas composers whom the
Committee feels are doing the best music
composition in the state. At present there
are about 50 composers represented in the
Archives. Holograph mss of 3 works
commissioned by the Division--the
composers of which are Darius Milhaud,
Gunther Schuller, and Alberto Ginastera.
Also mss of the two books by John Ardoin,
Callas: the Art and the Life; and *The Callas
Legacy,* are in the collection.

TX —FORT WORTH PUBLIC LIBRARY,
Arts Division, 300 Taylor St, Fort Worth,
76102. Heather Gobel, Head
Holdings: Vols (21,500) Cat Mss
Phonorecords
Budget: ($26,700)
Notes: Emphasis is on older popular music
and musical comedies, folk songs, operas,
music composed by Fort Worth and Texas
composers, and music about Texas. Sheet
music has a separate index.

MUSIC, THEATRE see Music in Theatres

MUSIC, THEATRICAL see Music, Incidental; Music in Theatres; Opera

MUSIC, UKRAINIAN

PA —MANOR JUNIOR COLLEGE, Basileiad
Library, Fox Chase Manor, Jenkintown,

19046. Sister M Anne, OSBM, Cur
Holdings: Vols 2500 Cat 200 Uncat Maps
Slides Phonorecords

MUSIC, VOCAL see Vocal Music

MUSIC, YIDDISH see Music, Jewish

MUSIC AND DRUGS

CA —FITZ HUGH LUDLOW MEMORIAL
LIBRARY, PO Box 99346, San Francisco,
94109. Michael R Aldrich, Exec Cur
Holdings: Vols (200) Cat Mss Pix
Phonorecords Audiotapes
Notes: Collection stored. Important mail
inquiries. No interlibrary lending or
telephone inquiries. Collection emphasizes
books, songbooks, discographies, and
phonograph records relative to psychoctive
drug-using musicians and their art. Incl
many pictures, sheet music, and some
autographed or inscribed materials, mostly
from the 20th century of works by or about
Milton "Mezz" Mezzrow, Billie Holiday, the
Beatles, Bob Dylan, and recent drug-related
rock music. About 600 record albums.

MUSIC BOXES

NY —MUSICAL MUSEUM AND LIBRARY,
Deansboro, 13328. Arthur H Sanders, Cur
Holdings: Vols 1000 Uncat Mss Pix Slides
Notes: Antique musical instruments and
music boxes.

MUSIC COMPOSERS see Composers, Music

MUSIC CONDUCTORS see Conductors (Music)

MUSIC EDUCATORS' NATIONAL CONFERENCE

†MD —UNIVERSITY OF MARYLAND,
Library, Music Educators National
Conference Historical Center, College Park,
20742. Bruce Wilson, Cur
Holdings: Cat Mss Pix Audiotapes
Notes: The offical archive of the Music
Educators' National Conference (MENC)
and a repository for the documentation of
music education. Incl the papers of the
MENC, state units, and associated
organizations and committees; personal
papers and association items (notably,
relating to Frances Elliott Clark, Lowell
Mason, and Luther Whiting Mason);
published proceedings of MENC and other
groups; oral histories, numerous school
music textbooks, and the archive of the
Contemporary Music Project.

MUSIC FESTIVALS

MA —LENOX LIBRARY ASSOCIATION,
Main St, Lenox, 01240. Denis J Lesieur, Dir
Holdings: Pix Docs
Notes: Repository for the official records of
the Berkshire Music Festival, located in
Lenox, Mass, ca 1934- (11 linear feet).

MUSIC FOR THE BLIND see Blind, Music for the

MUSIC HALLS (VARIETY THEATRES, CABARETS, NIGHT CLUBS, ETC.)

IL —ILLINOIS STATE UNIVERSITY, Milner
Library, Dept of Special Collections,
Normal, 61761. Robert Sokan, Librn
Holdings: Vols (6200) Cat Mss Pix Slides
Notes: Circus and related arts collection
consists of approx 6200 book items and
approx 250,000 nonbook items. The books
date from the 16th century to the present,
and incl vols specifically concerned with the
circus past and present, vaudeville, music
halls and variety theaters, theatrical and
animal history, biographies, autobiographies
and memoirs, novels, poetry, drama,
juvenalia and other subjects relating to the
circus. Many of the books are limited

MUSIC HALLS (VARIETY THEATRES, CABARETS, NIGHT CLUBS, ETC.) (cont.)

editions, presentation copies or autographed copies. Incl archives of the Dobritch International Circus (20,000 items).

LA —TULANE UNIVERSITY, Howard-Tilton Memorial Library, Special Collections Div, William Ransom Hogan Jazz Archive, 7001 Freret, New Orleans, 70118. Richard B Allen, Acting Cur; Alma D Williams, Assistant to the Cur
Holdings: Vols (100,000) Cat Mss Pix Slides Phonorecords Audiotapes Videotapes 16mm Films Microforms
Budget: ($90,000)
Notes: Jazz music and musicians. Outstanding collection, incl books, music scores, serials, catalogs and other archival material. Music, history, etc.
See also entry under Jazz

NY —NEW YORK PUBLIC LIBRARY, Performing Arts Research Center, Billy Rose Theatre Collection, 111 Amsterdam Ave, New York, 10023. Dorothy L Swerdlove, Cur
Holdings: Cat Pix
Notes: Clippings photographs, reviews of acts, etc, periodicals devoted to news of activity in the field.

ON —METROPOLITAN TORONTO LIBRARY, Theatre Dept, 789 Yonge St, Toronto, M4W 2G8, Can. Heather McCallum, Head
Holdings: Vols (30,500) Mss Pix Slides Phonorecords Microforms

Notes: The Theatre Department is one of eleven subject departments of the Metropolitan Toronto Library, which is generally acknowledged to be the most comprehensive of Canadian public library collections. The department balances book and non book materials in all areas of the performing arts except music: theatre and drama, moving pictures, dance, television and radio programming, and varieties of popular entertainment such as circus, music hall, vaudeville, puppetry and pantomime. The department's substantial holdings of rare books include over 75 court festival books. The collection is international in scope and is particularly strong in materials relating to Canadian theatre history and drama. Non-book holdings include extensive files of newspaper clippings, playbills, programs, production and publicity photographs, posters, and original stage designs, all of which document for the most part the history of Canadian theatre and dance companies, a large collection of British and American theatre portrait engravings, and a representative selection of 19th century, Japanese woodblock prints. Special collections relating to the history of the performing arts in Canada include the records of the Taverner Company which played Eastern Canada and the United States in the late 19th century, Toronto's Grand Opera House, the Marks Brothers touring company, film actor Ned Sparks, the Canadian-born actress Judith Evelyn, Toronto's Crest Theatre, the Canadian Players, Montreal Repertory Theatre, dancer/teacher Boris Volkoff, the Dumbells, the Canadian all-soldier concert party which originated in France in 1917, and vaudeville performer Charles Manny.

MUSIC IN MEDICINE

BC —CAPILANO COLLEGE, Media Centre, 2055 Purcell Way N, Vancouver, V7J 3H5, Can. Pat Biggins, Reference Librn
Holdings: Vols 3000 Cat Phonorecords Audiotapes Periodicals

MUSIC IN THEATRES

CA —UNIVERSITY OF CALIFORNIA, LOS ANGELES, Music Library, Schonberg Hall, Los Angeles, 90024. Stephen M Fry, Music Librn
Notes: Incl the Harry Roth Library of American Theater Music, the Meredith Wilson Library of Popular Sheet Music, and the library of American Motion Picture Music.

CT —YALE UNIVERSITY, Sterling Memorial Library, Yale Collection of Historical Sound Recordings, 120 High St, New Haven, 06520. Richard Warren Jr, Cur
Holdings: Mss Pix Phonorecords Audiotapes
Notes: Incl "classical music" ("concert music") of all types from Western culture, jazz, the American Musical Theatre, spoken material (literary, dramatic, documentary). The aim of the Collection is to document performance practice in the fields collected. See the article by Karol Berger in the *Journal of the Association for Recorded Sound Collections*, vol VI, no 1, pp 13-25. Partially cataloged.

IL —CHICAGO PUBLIC LIBRARY, Music Section, Fine Arts Division, 78 E Washington St, Chicago, 60602. Rosalinda I Hack, Fine Arts Division Chief; Richard C Schwegel, Head, Music Section
Holdings: // Uncat
Notes: The Chicago Public Library received the Sheet Music Archive (1700 cu ft) of the Plitt Theatre Corporation, Chicago, in 1975. This vast, unprocessed collection contains thousands of pieces of music played during intermissions in the Plitt Theatre palaces in Chicago during the 1920-40s. An inventory of the collection is available, organized by composer and form (eg "Fox Trots"); titles are not yet compiled. The collection is presently in storage at the Record Center Corporation, The Chicago Public Library's storage facility for little-used materials.

IL —UNIVERSITY OF ILLINOIS, URBANA/CHAMPAIGN, Library, Music Library, Urbana, 61801. William M McClellan, Librn
Holdings: Vols (200,000) Cat Mss Slides Sound Recordings Microforms Books Scores
Budget: ($65,000)
Notes: Introductory, instructive, research and reference materials to support work at graduate level in ethnomusicology,, musicology, music education, performance areas. Special areas incl about 2500 pre-1800 music mss and editions of music on microfilm, 2400 graduate music theses on microfilm, a special collection of 30,000 titles of American vocal sheet music covering the period 1790-1970, the Rafael Joseffy Collection of about 2000 pieces of 19th century piano music (incl performer markings), the Joseph Szigeti Collection (700 items: published music, mss, recordings), mainly violin and piano music by various commposers. Also incl a special collection of 45,000 78 rpm sound recordings (uncat) of classical music and jazz; a collection of 2900 titles from Chicago radio station WGN. Incl orchestrations, a collection of 500,000 items (uncat) from stock of Hunleth Music Store, St Louis, Missouri, mainly early 20th century imprints of songs, wind music, string music, piano, sets of theatre orchestra parts, dance band orchestrations. A separate collection of choral octavos and instrumental parts is maintained, incl 135,000 pieces of choral music, 30,500 orchestral parts, and 5500 wind ensemble parts. Also, music publishers' catalogues (mainly European and American), ca 126 cubic feet, 1860s-1950s.

IN —INDIANA UNIVERSITY, Lilly Library, Seventh St, Bloomington, 47405. William R Cagle, Librn
Holdings: // Uncat
Notes: Theatre music in the Starr Collection of American Sheet Music.

IN —INDIANA UNIVERSITY, SOUTH BEND, Library, 1700 Mishawaka Ave, South Bend, 46615. James L Mullins, Dir
Holdings: Vols (1490) Cat Mss Maps Pix Phonorecords
Notes: Incl design materials, scripts, theatre music, rare editions, theatre programs, playbills, clippings and periodical from the 1850s to the 1940s.

IA —DRAKE UNIVERSITY, Cowles Library, 28 St & University Ave, Des Moines, 50311.
Notes: Nearly 3000 musical works used by orchestras and musicians to accompany silent films, donated by Dorman Hundling who had played in orchestras in theatres owned by his family in South Dakota and Iowa.

KY —HOPKINSVILLE COMMUNITY COLLEGE, Library, North Dr, Hopkinsville, 42240. Marjanna J Frising, Librn
Holdings: Vols (500) Cat Phonorecords Audiotapes Filmstrips
Notes: Incl most notable Broadway plays, both musical and non-musical, with sound-tracks available for most. Also a large collection of children's and one-act plays, incl comedy and mystery plays.

NJ —PRINCETON UNIVERSITY, Library, Rare Books Dept, Princeton, 08544. Stephen Ferguson, Cur
Notes: The Valva Collection (gift of the Worcester, Massachusetts Public Library). Orchestral parts and conductors' scores for several thousand popular songs and musical effects used in movie houses and vaudeville from the turn of the century to the end of the silent movie era.

VA —GEORGE MASON UNIVERSITY, Fenwick Library, Special Collections Dept, 4400 University Drive, Fairfax, 22030. Ruth Kerns, Public Services Librn
Notes: Some 275,000 items (incl administrative, play service and research, library and production records) pertaining to the WPA Federal Theatre Project, on permanent loan from the Library of Congress.

MUSIC INDUSTRY

IL —CHICAGO PUBLIC LIBRARY, Music Section, Fine Arts Division, 78 E Washington St, Chicago, 60602. Rosalinda I Hack, Fine Arts Division Chief; Richard C Schwegel, Head, Music Section
Notes: Strong collection of books and dissertations on music and record business, careers, song writing, unions, etc. Some cassettes. Periodical collection includes major titles *Billboard* and *Variety* (complete runs), *Cashbox*, *Music Report* and numerous others.

NY —BARNARD A & MORRIS N YOUNG LIBRARY OF EARLY AMERICAN POPULAR MUSIC, 270 Riverside Dr, New York, 10025. Morris N Young, Cur
Holdings: Cat Mss Pix Phonorecords Audiotapes Microforms
Notes: 48,000 items of American popular music, mostly 1790-1910. Incl books, serials, sheet music, broadsides, anthologies, air checks, broadcasting and music business memorabilia, and correspondence.

MUSIC LIBRARIANSHIP

NY —STATE UNIVERSITY OF NEW YORK, BUFFALO, Baird Music Library, Baird Hall, Amherst, 14260. James B Coover, Dir
Holdings: Vols (104,000) Cat Mss Pix Slides Phonorecords Microforms
Notes: Nearly complete collections of *Denkmaeler and Gesamtausgaben* and other historical sets. Strong collection of dictionaries, bibliographies, biographies, facsimiles, works on organology and ethnomusicology. Special emphasis on operas, scores of the avant-garde and urban

MUSIC LIBRARIANSHIP (cont.)

popular music and music librarianship. Good collection of medieval and Renaissance anthologies, contemporary and avant-garde recordings. Houses Archives of the Center of the Creative and Performing Arts. Collections incl 1000 slides, 14,000 phonorecords, and 33,000 scores and parts. Computerized record catalog in process.

MUSIC LIBRARIES

NY —STATE UNIVERSITY OF NEW YORK, BUFFALO, Baird Music Library, Baird Hall, Amherst, 14260. James B Coover, Dir
Holdings: Vols (104,000) Cat Mss Pix Slides Phonorecords Microforms
Notes: Nearly complete collections of *Denkmaeler and Gesamtausgaben* and other historical sets. Strong collection of dictionaries, bibliographies, biographies, facsimiles, works on the "new" music, organology and ethnomusicology. Special emphasis on operas, scores of the avant-garde, jazz and urban popular music, discography and music librarianship. Good collection of medieval and Renaissance anthologies, contemporary and avant-garde recordings. Houses Archives of the Center of the Creative and Performing Arts. Collections incl 2100 slides, 22,000 phonorecords, 46,000 scores and parts, 29,000 books, 4900 microforms. Computerized record catalog in process.

MUSIC MUSEUMS

SD —UNIVERSITY OF SOUTH DAKOTA, Shrine to Music Museum, USD Box 194, Vermillion, 57069. Andre P Larson, Dir
Holdings: Vols Cat Mss Documents Pix Phonorecords Slides
Budget: ($205,036)
Notes: The Shrine to Music Museum is one of America's major collections of musical resource materials, incl more than 4000 antique musical instruments from all over the world, plus an extensive supporting library of several thousand books, music, periodicals, recordings, photographs, and related musical memorabilia. The collection of 19th and early 20th-century sheet music and music for wind instruments is probably the most extensive in the country. Inquiries and visits are welcomed.

MUSIC PERIODICALS see Periodicals, Music

MUSIC PRINTING

†IL —NEWBERRY LIBRARY, Chicago, 60610.
Notes: Charles Bradlee was a music publisher in Boston and used Graupner and Ashton plates. His music, from the J Francis Driscoll Collection.
IL —ROOSEVELT UNIVERSITY, Murray-Green Library, 430 S Michigan Ave, Chicago, 60605. Donald Draganski, Music Librn
Holdings: Vols (28,000) Uncat Mss Pix Microforms
Notes: Subscribe to over 92 music periodicals; record collection of more than 10,000 albums; 8000 pieces of sheet music; pamphlet file; music theses on microfilm; complete file of music publishers catalogs; scores; tapes of old 78 recordings; music education; and electronic music.

MUSIC PUBLISHERS see Music Printing; Publishers and Publishing

MUSIC RECORDING see Sound Recordings and Reproductions—Collections

MUSIC SCORES—COLLECTIONS

AZ —ARIZONA STATE UNIVERSITY, Music Library, Tempe, 85281. Arlys L McDonald, Music Librn
Notes: Incl the Wayne King Collection.

AR —CENTRAL ARKANSAS LIBRARY SYSTEM, Little Rock Public Library, 700 Louisiana, Little Rock, 72201. Roberta A Muelling, Librn
Holdings: Vols 400 Cat //
Notes: Collection of sheet music, primarily from 1910 to 1930, contains approximately 30 bound anthologies (vocal and instrumental), 30 piano pieces, 200 solo vocal (primarily popular), and 100 choral vocal pieces (ranging up to four voices). A gift of the Little Rock Musical Coterie. A separate title, composer and first-line catalog is available.
CA —BERKELEY PUBLIC LIBRARY, Art and Music Div, 2090 Kittredge St, Berkeley, 97404. Diane Davenport, Reference
Holdings: Vols (20,000) Cat Pix Slides Audiotapes
CA —CLAREMONT COLLEGES, Honnold Library, Ninth & Dartmouth, Claremont, 91711. Tania Rizzo, Special Collections Dept Head
Holdings: Vols 500 // Uncat Mss Pix Slides
Notes: Joseph W Clokey Collection. 250 ms items, scores, opaques, transparencies and transcriptions of church choral music, often with orchestral and organ accompaniments; 195 printed copies of published works; 15 folders of correspondence with his publishers, miscellaneous notes and typescripts. Restricted use. No photocopies permitted. On deposit.
CA —CALIFORNIA STATE UNIVERSITY, HAYWARD, Library, Hayward, 94542. Melissa Rose, Dir
Holdings: Vols (15,986) Cat Phonorecords
Budget: ($21,000)
Notes: The score collection covers the entire range of instrumental and vocal concert music, incl collected works of various composers, and representative collections of hymnals, folk music, musical comedy, and some popular music. Sound recordings range from ethnomusicological collections to electronic music. Emphasis is on concert music, but there is a large collection of jazz and a selective collection of popular music. Separate catalog.
CA —LONG BEACH PUBLIC LIBRARY, Art, Music & Philosophy Dept, Art, Music & Philosophy Dept, 101 Pacific Ave, Long Beach, 90802. Barbara Davis, Librn
Holdings: Vols 15,000 Cat
Notes: Popular sheet music, 1790 to date. Indexed.
CA —INSTITUTE OF THE AMERICAN MUSICAL, Library, 121 N Detroit St, Los Angeles, 90036. Miles Kreuger, Cur
Holdings: Cat Mss Maps Pix Slides Phonorecords
Notes: Reference materials on the American musical theatre and motion pictures incl 40,000 phonograph records, sound tapes, and cylinders dating back to the 1890s; record catalogs to 1900; thousands of theatre and film programs, periodicals, sheet music and vocal scores as early as 1830; thousands of motion picture press books and over 200,000 stills from 1914 to the present; every musical comedy script published in America and dozens in ms form, original or photocopy materials from the archives of movie palaces, films and record companies, incl discographies of many major Broadway and Hollywood stars; and thousands of books on theatre, film, broadcasting, world's fairs and other allied areas of showmanship.
CA —LOS ANGELES PUBLIC LIBRARY, Art, Music & Recreation Dept, 630 W Fifth St, Los Angeles, 90071. Melvin R Rosenberg, Mgr & Principal Librn
Holdings: Vols (68,000) Cat Mss
Budget: ($102,244)
Notes: Incl 44,000 music scores, 3000 ms, 100,000 song sheets, and newspaper clippings.
CA —UNIVERSITY OF CALIFORNIA, LOS ANGELES, Music Library, Schonberg Hall, Los Angeles, 90024. Stephen M Fry, Music Librn
Holdings: Vols Cat Mss Microforms
Notes: Approx 6000 scores for European and American operas, ca 1700-present. Published descriptions of collection: University of California Music Libraries,

Berkeley, Los Angeles, *Catalog of the Opera Collections*, (Boston: G K Hall, 1983).
CA —UNIVERSITY OF CALIFORNIA, LOS ANGELES, Music Library, Schonberg Hall, Los Angeles, 90024. Stephen M Fry, Music Librn
Notes: Incl the Harry Roth Library of American Theater Music, the Meredith Wilson Library of Popular Sheet Music, and the library of American Motion Picture Music.
CA —UNIVERSITY OF CALIFORNIA, LOS ANGELES, William Andrews Clark Memorial Library, 2520 Cimarron St, Los Angeles, 90018.
Holdings: Cat Mss Pix
Notes: Predominantly 17th-18th century English chamber music.
CA —PASADENA PUBLIC LIBRARY, Alice Coleman Batchelder Music Library, Reference Services, 285 E Walnut, Pasadena, 91101. Anne Cain, Principal Librn
Holdings: Vols (8012) Cat Pix
Notes: Separate record catalog of over 10,000 phonorecords; over 4400 music scores. Special index of songs in collection. Over 150,000 pictures.
CA —UNIVERSITY OF CALIFORNIA, RIVERSIDE, University Library, 4045 Canyon Crest Dr, Box 5900, Riverside, 92517.
Notes: In circulating music collection.
CA —SACRAMENTO PUBLIC LIBRARY, 828 I St, Sacramento, 95814. Dorothy Harvey, Librn, Special Collections
Holdings: Vols 26,000 Cat
Notes: Scores, sheet music, phonorecords and card indexes.
CA —SAN DIEGO PUBLIC LIBRARY, Art, Music & Recreation Sect, 820 E St, San Diego, 92101. Barbara A Tuhill, Supvr
Holdings: Cat
Notes: Score collection of 17,000 pieces covers all types of music incl religious works, opera scores, musical plays, miniature scores. Complete works of Bach, Berlioz, Beethoven, Mozart, and others are added as published in German reprint. Also, thematic indexes, and study and instructions for playing various musical instruments. General circulation.
CA —SAN DIEGO STATE UNIVERSITY, Malcolm A Love Library, 5300 Campanile Dr, San Diego, 92182. D Dickinson, Univ Librn; Don L Bosseau, Dir
Notes: Sheet Music Collection. Original pieces of sheet music dating from 1817 to the present. Includes the Leta Knox Ehmcke Collection of Silent Film Music. (4000 items)
CA —UNIVERSITY OF CALIFORNIA, SANTA BARBARA, Arts Library, Music Section, Santa Barbara, 93106. Susan Sonnet Bower, Asst Music Librn
Holdings: Mss
Notes: Collection of holograph music manuscripts of the late American composer, Bernard Herrmann, 1911-1975. Collection contains 53 manuscript scores of both music written for the films and non-film music. Incl the film scores for "Vertigo," "Pschyo," "North by Northwest," "Marnie," "Magnificent Ambersons," "Devil and Daniel Webster (All That Money Can Buy)" Academy Award, 1941. Non-film Music: Symphony (1941) Moby Dick (Dramatic Cantata), Wuthering Heights (Opera in 4 Acts, 1950) with text by Lucille Fletcher, first performed by Portland Opera Association, Nov 6, 1982.
CA —UNIVERSITY OF SANTA CLARA, Michel Orradre Library, Santa Clara, 95053. Alice Whistler, Ref Librn
Holdings: Vols 121 Cat Phonorecords Pix
Notes: Of the 121 musical scores, seven received Academy Award nominations. All were directed, between 1947 and 1967, by Lionel Newman, the Musical Director of the 20th Century Fox. Also incl in this collection are twelve albums with the original motion picture soundtrack for such productions as "The Gift of Love," "Sing Boy Sing," "Say One for Me," and "Marilyn." Also in the collection are over 60 pictures of actors and actresses who participated in some of the motion pictures.

MUSIC SCORES—COLLECTIONS
(cont.)

CA —SANTA CRUZ PUBLIC LIBRARY, Art, Music, Film Dept, 224 Church St, Santa Cruz, 95060. Alma Westberg, Librn
Holdings: Vols (1500) Cat Mss
Budget: ($750)
Notes: The music collection is in a catalog separate from the general one. It consists of approx 1700 cataloged books about music; 2100 bound, cataloged books of music incl opera and musical comedy scores; 2700 pieces of sheet music which incl sacred, art and popular songs, and instrumental solos. Good collection of chamber music from baroque to contemporary composers. Also a special collection of 10,000 pieces of American popular sheet music of the period from the 1860s to 1970s incl songs of California. The record collection, primarily classical, consists of about 5500 records.

CA —STANFORD UNIVERSITY LIBRARIES, Cecil H Green Library, Stanford, 94305. Michael T Ryan, Cur
Holdings: Vols (1500) Cat Mss
Notes: The Memorial Library of Music. Mss, letters, and first editions of printed scores. A catalog of the Library, compiled by Nathan Van Patten, was published in 1950.

CA —CALIFORNIA INSTITUTE OF THE ARTS, Library, 24700 McBean Pkwy, Valencia, 91355. James Elrod, Dir
Holdings: Vols (61,000) Cat Phonorecords Audiotapes
Notes: Incl 10,797 music scores.

CT —TRINITY COLLEGE LIBRARY, Watkinson Library, 300 Summit St, Hartford, 06106. Jeffrey Kaimowitz, Cur
Holdings: // Cat Mss
Notes: Incl 25,000 pieces of 18th and 19th century sheet music.

CT —CONNECTICUT COLLEGE, Greer Music Library, New London, 06320. Philip Youngholm, Music Librn
Holdings: Vols 9000 Cat
Budget: ($12,000)
Notes: Incl 9000 music scores, 11,000 phonodiscs, 100 audiotapes and 40 microforms.

CT —UNIVERSITY OF CONNECTICUT, University Library, Music Library, U-Box 12, Storrs, 06268. Dorothy Bognar, Librn
Notes: A comparatively small branch (35,000 pieces) of a university library, with separate facilities located in the University Fine Arts Center. All materials relate to the field of music (scores, books, periodicals, microfilm, phonodiscs, tapes). Materials include 10,000 scores and 15,000 sound recordings. Maintain catalogs for books, scores, and recordings, and have listening facilities within the Music Library. The Music Department also maintains separate collections of performance parts for choral, orchestral, and band music. No photocopying.

CT —UNIVERSITY OF HARTFORD, Hartt School of Music, Allen Memorial Library, 200 Bloomfield Ave, West Hartford, 06117. Ethel Bacon, Music Librn
Holdings: Vols (56,806) Cat Slides Phonorecords Audiotapes Filmstrips Microforms
Budget: ($14,500)
Notes: Cataloged materials incl 12,000 books on music, 66 slides, 17,000 phonorecords, 1000 audiotapes, 57 filmstrips, 683 microforms, and 26,000 music scores. Also, the Kalmen Opperman Collection: 350 vols of clarinet music, solo through ensemble. Also, the Robert E Smith Collections of 34,000 phonorecords, 150 audiotapes with 80 vols of transcripts from his two radio programs: Your Box At The Opera; Theater of Melody (uncataloged).

†DC —CATHOLIC UNIVERSITY OF AMERICA, Music Library, Washington, 20064. Betty Libbey, Head Music Library
Holdings: Cat Microforms
Notes: A large collection to support advanced degree study. Emphasis on church music, musicology, history and criticism, instrumental and vocal music, solo music for all voices, instruments, and musical forms.

DC —HOWARD UNIVERSITY, Moorland-Spingarn Research Center, 500 Howard Place NW, Washington, 20059. Clifford L Muse, Jr, Acting Dir
Holdings: Vols (106,086) Mss Maps Pix Slides Phonorecords Audiotapes 16mm Films Filmstrips Microforms
Budget: ($854,753)
See also entry under Blacks

DC —SMITHSONIAN INSTITUTION LIBRARIES, National Air & Space Museum Branch, NASM Bldg, Sixth & Independence Ave SW, Washington, 20560. Frank A Pietropaoli, Branch Chief
Holdings: Vols (39,000) Cat Mss Maps Pix Slides Microforms
Notes: History of flight and aerospace development, incl biographical material on aviation pioneers, balloons and ballooning. Extensive photographic collection (600,000 pictures). Incl the Sherman Fairchild Collection of aeronautical photographs (transferred from the American Institute of Aeronautics and Astronautics). Also incl the Bella Landauer Aeronautical Sheet Music Collection (1500 pieces). 2000 films; 800,000 microforms; 9000 volumes bound.

FL —MIAMI-DADE PUBLIC LIBRARY SYSTEM, One Biscayne Blvd, Miami, 33132. Don Chauncey, AV Librn; Barbara Young, Art & Music Dept Librn
Holdings: Vols 9750 Cat Phonorecords
Notes: Incl 8250 pieces of sheet music; 1500 classical scores; 200 musical shows; separate song index to reference music collection.

FL —FLORIDA STATE UNIVERSITY, Warren D Allen Music Library, Tallahassee, 32306. Dale L Hudson, Music Librn
Holdings: Cat Phonorecords Audiotapes Microforms
Notes: General music collection serving the School of Music. Incl 40,000 music scores, 19,000 phonorecords, 1500 audiotapes and 2000 microforms.

GA —UNIVERSITY OF GEORGIA, Libraries, Special Collections Division, Athens, 30602. Vesta Lee Gordon, Asst Dir for Special Collections
Holdings: Vols (75,000) Cat Mss Maps Pix
Notes: Materials on Georgia history, incl approx 3,000,000 items in 2000 collections of mss; 1200 maps; 6000 pictures and over 200 pieces of sheet music.

IL —AURORA PUBLIC LIBRARY, 1 Benton St, Aurora, 60506. Mary E Clark, Head Librn
Holdings: Vols (23,000) Cat
Notes: Plus 1000 pieces of early popular sheet music (uncataloged). Collection espec strong in vocal and piano music and in chamber music.

IL —UNIVERSITY OF ILLINOIS, URBANA/CHAMPAIGN, Library, Bands & Busch Instrument Collection, 1103 S Sixth St, Champaign, 61820. John Cranford, Librn
Holdings: Vols (8600) Cat Mss
Notes: Printed music, about 8400; plus the Sousa Library, 1900 vols, printed music about 1500; also the Clarke Library, 400 vols, printed music, approximatelly 375. No photocopying.

IL —CHICAGO PUBLIC LIBRARY, Music Section, Fine Arts Division, 78 E Washington St, Chicago, 60602. Rosalinda I Hack, Fine Arts Division Chief; Richard C Schwegel, Head, Music Section
Holdings: Vols 44,000 Cat
Notes: 17,000 cataloged pieces of sheet music 20,000 cataloged bound volumes of music including chamber music parts and a growing collection of orchestral sets. Indexed collection of over 7000 popular sheet music titles dating from mid-19th century. Sets of complete and collected works of 50 major composers. Extensive holdings in popular music and musical comedy scores. Also, depository (1984) for New Music Chicago of works and recordings by local composers and musicians.

IL —CHICAGO PUBLIC LIBRARY, Music Section, Fine Arts Division, 78 E Washington St, Chicago, 60602. Rosalinda I Hack, Fine Arts Division Chief; Richard C Schwegel, Head, Music Section
Notes: The Chicago Public Library received the Sheet Music Archive (1700 cu ft) of the Pitt Theatre Corporation, Chicago, in 1975. This vast, unprocessed collection contains thousands of pieces of music played during intermissions in the Pitt Theatre palaces in Chicago during the 1920-40s. An inventory of the collectionis available, organized by composer and form (eg "Fox Trots"); titles are not yet compiled. The collectionis presently in storage at the Record Center Corporation. The Chicgao Public Library's storage facility for little-used materials.

IL —NEWBERRY LIBRARY, 60 W Walton St, Chicago, 60610. Diana Haskell, Cur of Modern Mss
Holdings: Cat Mss
Notes: Collection primarily musicological, not performance. 55,000 scores; 100,000 pieces of sheet music. Primary and secondary materials for the study of Western European music from the Middle Ages through the 19th century, and of American music from its beginnings. Strongest holdings are: early theory, music literature and scores of the Renaissance and Baroque periods, opera scores (3600), and libretti, early American psalmody and religious music, music periodicals, monumental editions and monographs, popular sheet music and music mss. See article by Donald W Krummel, "The Newberry Library, Chicago" in *Fontes artis musicae*, 1969/3. Restricted use: noncirculating.

IL —ROOSEVELT UNIVERSITY, Murray-Green Library, 430 S Michigan Ave, Chicago, 60605. Donald Draganski, Music Librn
Holdings: Vols (28,000) Uncat Mss Pix Microforms
Notes: Subscribe to over 92 music periodicals; record collection of more than 10,000 albums; 8000 pieces of sheet music; pamphlet file; music theses on microfilm; complete file of music publishers catalogs; scores; tapes of old 78 recordings; music education; and electronic music.

IL —UNIVERSITY OF ILLINOIS, URBANA/CHAMPAIGN, Library, Music Library, Urbana, 61801. William M McClellan, Librn
Holdings: Vols (200,000) Cat Mss Slides Sound Recordings Microforms Books Scores
Budget: ($65,000)
Notes: Introductory, instructive, research and reference materials to support work at graduate level in ethnomusicology,, musicology, music education, performance areas. Special areas incl about 2500 pre-1800 music mss and editions of music on microfilm, 2400 graduate music theses on microfilm, a special collection of 30,000 titles of American vocal sheet music covering the period 1790-1970, the Rafael Joseffy Collection of about 2000 pieces of 19th century piano music (incl performer markings), the Joseph Szigeti Collection (700 items: published music, mss, recordings), mainly violin and piano music by various commposers. Also incl a special collection of 45,000 78 rpm sound recordings (uncat) of classical music and jazz; a collection of 2900 titles from Chicago radio station WGN. Incl orchestrations, a collection of 500,000 items (uncat) from stock of Hunleth Music Store, St Louis, Missouri, mainly early 20th century imprints of songs, wind music, string music, piano, sets of theatre orchestra parts, dance band orchestrations. A separate collection of choral octavos and instrumental parts is maintained, incl 135,000 pieces of choral music, 30,500 orchestral parts, and 5500 wind ensemble parts. Also, music publishers' catalogues (mainly European and American), ca 126 cubic feet, 1860s-1950s.

IN —INDIANA UNIVERSITY, Lilly Library, Seventh St, Bloomington, 47405. William R Cagle, Librn
Notes: Extensive holdings of American sheet music; first editions of works by great composers (operas, symphonies, chamber music, etc); scores annotated for performances conducted by Fritz Busch.

IN —INDIANA UNIVERSITY, Music Library, Bloomington, 47401. David E Fenske, Head
Holdings: Cat Slides Phonorecords Audiotapes Videotapes Filmstrips

MUSIC SCORES—COLLECTIONS
(cont.)

Microforms
Budget:
Notes: 120,000 books and scores; 185,583 choral and orchestral parts; 33,000 phonorecords; 37,000 audiotapes.

IN —BUTLER UNIVERSITY, Jordan College of Music, Library, 4600 Sunset, Indianapolis, 46208. Phyllis J Schoonover, Librn
Holdings: Vols (5383) Cat Phonorecords Audiotapes
Budget: ($16,500)
Notes: There is a separate card catalog for 3800 scores, 4673 phonorecords, and books.

IN —MORRISSON-REEVES LIBRARY, 80 N Sixth St, Richmond, 47374. Harriet E Bard, Librn
Holdings: Vols 4340 // Sheet Music Cat
Notes: Restricted use, noncirculating. Singin' Sam Collection: popular and semipopular sheet music for the years 1895-1940.

IA —DRAKE UNIVERSITY, Cowles Library, 28 St & University Ave, Des Moines, 50311.
Notes: Nearly 3000 musical works used by orchestras and musicians to accompany silent films, donated by Dorman Hundling who had played in orchestras in theatres owned by his family in South Dakota and Iowa.

IA —PUBLIC LIBRARY OF DES MOINES, 100 Locust, Des Moines, 50309. Stephen R Brogden, Head, Fine Arts Dept; Martha Gerstenberger, Music Librn
Holdings: Vols (8300) Cat Phonorecords
Budget: ($5000)
Notes: Incl compositions about Iowa, clippings, and biographical data. Incl 25,000 scores and sheet music.

KS —SAINT MARY COLLEGE, Library, Leavenworth, 66048. Therese Deplazes, Special Collections Librn
Holdings: Cat Phonorecords

KS —KANSAS STATE UNIVERSITY, Library, Special Collections & University Archives, Manhattan, 66506. Antonia Q Pigno, Coordr; John J Vander Velde, Librn; Anthony R Crawford, Univ Archivist
Holdings: Vols 1000 Cat
Notes: Eclectic collection of scores and books from thelibrary of Prof Charles Stratton. Sound recordings and additional scores from this collection are located in the library's Audio Visual Department.

KY —WESTERN KENTUCKY UNIVERSITY, Kentucky Library, Bowling Green, 42101. Riley Handy, Head, Special Collections; Connie Mills, Maps & Music Librn; Nancy Baird, Photographs Librn; Nancy Solley, Conservation Librn
Holdings: Vols (25,000) Cat Mss Maps Pix Microforms
Notes: Besides Kentucky history, other strengths are Mammoth Cave, South Union Shakers, Kentucky religion; and steamboat photos (3300 cataloged pictures); 8000 Kentucky postal cards, etc.

KY —HOPKINSVILLE COMMUNITY COLLEGE, Library, North Dr, Hopkinsville, 42240. Marjanna J Frising, Librn
Holdings: Vols (500) Cat Phonorecords Audiotapes Filmstrips
Notes: Incl most notable Broadway plays, both musical and non-musical, with soundtracks available for most. Also a large collection of children's and one-act plays as well as non-musical but best known 3-act plays, incl comedy and mystery plays.

KY —UNIVERSITY OF KENTUCKY, Margaret I King Library, Dept of Special Collections, Lexington, 40506. William Marshall, Head
Holdings: Cat Mss Pix Films Videotapes Audiotapes Phonorecords
Notes: Incl 2100 pieces, emphasis on Kentucky imprints and 19th century. Also, collection documenting career of John Jacob Niles, as as composer, artist and collector of ballads; period covered: 1887, 1905-1982. Unpublished inventory, correspondence. 95 boxes, musical instruments.

KY —UNIVERSITY OF KENTUCKY, Music Library, 116 Fine Arts Bldg, Lexington,

40506. Cathy S Hunt, Music Librn
Holdings: Vols 18,000 Cat Microforms Scores Recordings
Notes: Collection incl books (14,000), includes music history, theory, music eduction, jazz, etc cat. Music Scores (18,000) cat. Serials (3200 vols) cat. Microforms (6300) cat. Recordings (9100) cat. Collected Editions (complete Works of composers, large sets, etc) (7100) cat. The Alfred Cortot Collection (about 300 vols of rare, early music theory books) is housed in the Rare Books Room of the Main Library.

KY —UNIVERSITY OF LOUISVILLE, School of Music, Dwight Anderson Memorial Music Library, 2301 S Third St, Louisville, 40292. Marion Korda, Librn
Holdings: Uncat Mss
Notes: Early American sheet music; emphasis on Louisville imprints. Basically a collection of songs, with some piano music. 184 vols of early Louisville music programs, plus 325 single items; 42 vols of current Louisville music programs; information file; additional 31 vols of songsters. Incl "Traipsin' Woman" (Jean Thomas) Collection; archives. No photocopying.

LA —LOUISIANA STATE MUSEUM, Louisiana Historical Center, 400 Esplanade Ave, (Mailing add: 751 Chartres St, New Orleans, 70116). Edward F Haas, Chief Cur
Holdings: Vols 2000 Cat Pix Slides Phonorecords Audiotapes
Notes: New Orleans Jazz Museum and Archives Collection. Donated to the Louisiana State Museum by the New Orleans Jazz Club in 1977. It was formerly a private museum sponsored by the Jazz Club and housed at 833 Conti St, New Orleans, La 70130. Emphasis is New Orleans jazz, incl 8000 pictures of sheet music; 12,000 phonorecords; 15,000 pictures; 1000 slides; and 1000 audiotapes. A guide to the collection is in preparation.

LA —NEW ORLEANS BAPTIST THEOLOGICAL SEMINARY, Martin Music Library, 4110 Seminary Place, New Orleans, 70126. Douglas G Broomoe, Music Librn
Holdings: Vols 38,000 Cat Mss Microforms
Budget: ($10,000)
Notes: Martin Music Library serves the Division of Church Music Ministries of the New Orleans Baptist Theological Seminary. As such, its holdings lean toward church music: books (7500); scores (11,000); anthems (15,000); records (4500). Martin Music Library is maintained as a separate division of the Seminary's library and is housed in the main library. Separate catalog.

LA —NEW ORLEANS PUBLIC LIBRARY, Art & Music Div, 219 Loyola Ave, New Orleans, 70140. Marilyn Wilkins, Head
Holdings: Cat
Notes: About 700 pieces of early New Orleans sheet music; early southern sheet music, and New Orleans imprints. Catalog.

LA —TULANE UNIVERSITY, Howard-Tilton Memorial Library, Special Collections Div, William Ransom Hogan Jazz Archive, 7001 Freret, New Orleans, 70118. Richard B Allen, Acting Cur; Alma D Williams, Assistant to the Cur
Notes: Jazz music and musicians. Outstanding collection, incl books, music scores (16,205), serials, catalogs and other archival material. Music, history, etc. Some of these scores may be searched through OCLC. See Richard B Allen's article on the John Robichaux collection in Footnote, Vol VII No 4 (April/May 1977).

ME —BOWDOIN COLLEGE, Library, Brunswick, 04011. Dianne M Gutscher, Cur of Special Collections
Notes: The Henry Wadsworth Longfellow Collection, incl about 665 pieces of music.

ME —PORTLAND PUBLIC LIBRARY, 5 Monument Sq, Portland, 04101. Edward V Chenevert, Library Dir
Holdings: Cat Mss
Notes: The Maine Music Collection. (In cooperation with the Maine Federation of Music Clubs.) Music written by Maine composers predominantly 19th and 20th centuries. Various forms. Indexed. Other materials on Maine composers and music

also available. 1723 pieces of sheet music; 849 titles.

MD —MARYLAND HISTORICAL SOCIETY, Library, 201 W Monument St, Baltimore, 21201. William B Keller, Head Librn
Holdings: Vols (65,000) Cat Maps Pix Slides
Budget: ($8000)
Notes: Also 2 million ms pieces, 300 maps, 700 slides; 10,000 musical scores. Large collection of Maryland State Colonization Papers; Maryland and Baltimore business records; Baltimore & Ohio Railroad Papers; Baltimore Theater records and programs (late 18th, early 19th century); Maryland lottery tickets; Benjamin H Latrobe (architectural) Papers; Maryland maps, plates, prints, newspapers; Baltimore history, large collection (30,000 Maryland local history and genealogy, 100,000 mss); iron industry papers; Maryland currency; sheet music (8000 pieces, largely Baltimore publishers); Lester S Levy Star-Spangled Banner collection--the largest in the world-- over 250 pieces.

MD —PEABODY CONSERVATORY LIBRARY, 21 E Mt Vernon Place, Baltimore, 21202. Edwin A Quist, Librn
Holdings: Vols 70,000 Cat Mss Pix Phonorecords Audiotapes Videotapes Microforms
Budget: $30,000
Notes: The Peabody Conservatory Library, formerly a part of the Peabody Institute Library (now the George Peabody Library of the Johns Hopkins University) supplies the library needs of the faculty and student body of the Peabody Conservatory of Music. While the collection has numerous research capabilities, it is basically a collection of musical scores. The entire history of Western music is represented through collected editions, monumental anthologies, study scores, performing editions and a large collection of books and music periodicals. This collection is supplemented by a listening facility containing 14,000 discs and an ensembles library containing scores and parts of orchestral, band and chorus works.

MD —UNIVERSITY OF MARYLAND, BALTIMORE COUNTY, Albin O Kuhn Library and Gallery, 5401 Wilkens Ave, Baltimore, 21228. Larry Wilt, Collection Management Librn
Holdings: Vols (2764) Cat
Notes: Collection incl musical monuments, collected editions, full scores, performing editions and study scores. Particularly strong in performing editions of chamber music (classical and romantic periods). Coverage of modern period incl Igor Stravinski, John Cage, Charles Ives, Karlheinz Stockhausen, Kenneth Gabino, Mauricio Kagel, Stuart Smith, Herbert Brun. Recent collecting has emphasized graphic notation in music.

†MD —UNIVERSITY OF MARYLAND, Library, The National Association of College Wind & Percussion Instructors Library, College Park, 20742. Pearl Z Tubiash, Supvr
Holdings: Cat
Notes: Primarily scores, along with some organizational papers and publications.

MA —BOSTON PUBLIC LIBRARY, Print Collection, Dartmouth St at Copley Sq, Boston, 02117. Sinclair H Hitchings, Keeper of Prints
Holdings: Cat
Notes: There are especially large number of French and American lithographs, incl a large collection of proofs of the Prang Company, Boston, from 1858 to 1900; also, 300 mid-19th century American illustrated music sheets; and vast collections of early Parisian lithography (several hundred items); and of the lithographs of Daumier, Gavarni, Charlet and others. In addition there are turn-of-the-century posters, 400 American and 100 European. Most lithographs are cataloged by artist or by country.

MA —BOSTON PUBLIC LIBRARY, Music Division, 666 Boylston St, Box 286, Boston, 02117. Ruth Bleecker, Cur of Music
Holdings: Vols (100,000) Cat Mss Pix Microforms
Notes: The Allen A Brown Music Library is the nucleus of the collection. There is a

MUSIC SCORES—COLLECTIONS (cont.)

Dictionary Catalog of the Music Collection (Boston: G K Hall, 1976; 24 vols). Incl music scores.

MA —BOSTON UNIVERSITY, Mugar Memorial Library, Special Collections Dept, 771 Commonwealth Ave, Boston, 02215. Howard B Gotlieb, Dir
Notes: Personal collection of Arthur Fiedler, incl 6000 scores and sound recordings, manuscripts, photographs, memorabilia, library, and test pressings of Fiedler's performances.
See also entries under Boston Symphony Orchestra; Liszt, Franz; Calloway, Cab; Spalding, Albert; Shaw, Artie

MA —NEW ENGLAND CONSERVATORY OF MUSIC, Harriet M Spaulding Library, 33 Gainsborough St, Boston, 02115.
Notes: Incl 55,000 books and music scores of New England composers; the Preston Collection of Musicians' Letters; Firestone Hour Collection of Music; and Vaughn Monroe Collection of Camel Caravan.

MA —HARVARD UNIVERSITY LIBRARY, Eda Kuhn Loeb Music Library, Harvard University Music Library Bldg, Cambridge, 02138. Michael Ochs, Librn
Holdings: Vols Microforms
Notes: See *Harvard Library Bulletin*, XII (1958), 410-417; and, for Isham collection of early instrumental music, VI (1952), 376-380. Contains 56,250 titles.

MA —HARVARD UNIVERSITY LIBRARY, Hilles Library, Susan A E Morse Music Collection, 59 Shepard St, Cambridge, 02138. Cathy Balshone-Becze, Music Librn
Holdings: Cat Phonorecords
Notes: Incl more than 9000 phonograph records and 6500 scores.

MA —MASSACHUSETTS INSTITUTE OF TECHNOLOGY, Music Library, 14E-109, Cambridge, 02139. Linda I Solow, Librn
Holdings: Vols (47,000) Cat Phonorecords Audiotapes Scores
Notes: Described in *Directory of Music Libraries and Collections in New England*, 6th ed (Music Library Assn, New England Chapter, 1981); Bradley, Carol J, *Music collections in American libraries: a chronology* (Detroit, Information Coordinators, 1981); *Music Industry Directory* 7th ed (Chicago Marquis Who's Who, 1983). Borrowing of circulating collection limited to MIT community; limited room access to outside users. Reference service weekdays.

MA —SMITH COLLEGE, Werner Josten Library for the Performing Arts, Northampton, 01063. Marlene M Wong, Librn
Notes: Special collection: Einstein Collection of Music of the 16th-18th centuries copied in score by Alfred Einstein; 25,982 books, also 34,131 music scores, 42,405 phonorecords, 150 microforms. No photocopying.

MA —SPRINGFIELD CITY LIBRARY, Art & Music Dept, 220 State St, Springfield, 01103. Karen A Dorval, Supvr & Art Librn; Sylvia A Saint Amand, Music Librn
Holdings: Vols (22,500) Cat Pix Phonorecords Audiotapes Microforms
Budget: ($183,000)
Notes: Art: books (17,500), pamphlets (8000), pictures (120,000); music: books (5000), music scores (10,000), phonorecords (18,000), Audiocassettes (288 titles). Also microfilm (75 reels). Separate catalogs for art, music, and phonorecords and audiocassettes.

MA —AMERICAN JEWISH HISTORICAL SOCIETY, Library, 2 Thornton Rd, Waltham, 02154. Nathan M Kaganoff, Librn-Editor
Holdings: Vols 78,000 Cat Mss Pix Microforms
Budget: ($9000)
Notes: American Jewish history; incl paintings (100), theatre posters (500), sheet music (3500), mss (4 million). Calendar to individual collection published (2 vols).

MA —BRANDEIS UNIVERSITY, Goldfarb Library, 415 South St, Waltham, 02154.

Bessie Hahn, Dir
Notes: Early American Sheet Music Collection. Consists of 30 linear ft of early American song sheets of the 20th century. This collection is unprocessed, spring 1984.

MA —WELLESLEY COLLEGE, Music Library, Wellesley, 02181. Mary Wallace Davidson, Music Librn
Holdings: Vols 12,500 Cat
Budget: ($18,500)
Notes: Incl 12,500 bound vols of music scores and 12,000 phonorecords and tapes. Beginning to collect music by women composers.

MA —AMERICAN ANTIQUARIAN SOCIETY LIBRARY, 185 Salisbury St, Worcester, 01609. Marcus A McCorison, Dir & Librn
Holdings: Cat Pix
Notes: Secular songs (2000 pieces); American sheet music collection (about 60,000 pieces) is the largest to 1800 and the third largest to 1825. Also the most extensive collection of American psalmody (over 5000 vols before 1880).

MI —UNIVERSITY OF MICHIGAN, School of Music, Music Library, Moore Bldg, Ann Arbor, 48109. Peggy Daub, Head
Holdings: Vols 30,000 Cat Mss Microforms
Notes: The collection supports the study of classical music from the undergraduate to the doctoral level. Is is especially strong in collected works and historical editions. Rare scores include early editions of works by the sons of J S Bach and many 18th-19th century operas, particularly French.

MI —UNIVERSITY OF MICHIGAN, William L Clements Library, Ann Arbor, 48109. John C Dann, Dir

Notes: The William L. Clements Library of Americana is a non-circulating rare book library of original source material, printed and manuscript, dealing with America, from the discovery period into the late nineteenth century. The collection includes approximately 55,000 books and pamphlets, 550 linear feet of manuscripts, 4,100 volumes of newspapers, 36,000 maps, 40,000 pieces of sheet music, and 1,000 prints. The collection is strongest for the period of the American Revolution, and includes the papers of Thomas Gage, Sir Henry Clinton, and the Earl of Shelburne. Other areas of strength include antislavery, cartography and geography, discovery and exploration, American Indians, The Civil War, tune-books, sermons and orations, and the War of 1812. There are selective research collections dealing with Christopher Columbus, Thomas Paine, Benjamin Franklin, George Washington, Thomas Jefferson, and the Federalist Papers. Publications describing the collections of the library are: Author/Title catalog of Americana 1493-1860 in the William L. Clements Library . . . 7 volumes, Boston, G. K. Hall, 1970; Guide to the manuscript collections of the William L. Clements Library, by Arlene P. Shy 3d edition, Boston, G. K. Hall, 1978; Guide to the manuscript maps in the William L. Clements Library, compiled by Christian Burn, Ann Arbor, U. of Michigan, 1959; and Research catalog of maps of America, to 1860 in the William L. Clements Library . . . ,edited by Douglas W. Marshall, 4 volumes, Boston, G. K. Hall, 1972.

MI —DETROIT PUBLIC LIBRARY, Music & Performing Arts Dept, Detroit, 48202. Agatha Pfeiffer Kalkanis, Chief
Holdings: Vols 19,000 Cat Mss Pix Microforms
Notes: Also incl (77,000) scores. General collection intended for practical use in performance and for scholarly research. Good working collection of bibliographies, thematic catalogs, dictionaries and encyclopedias, periodical indexes. Many sets of collected works, monumental editions, historical anthologies. Good representation of opera and operetta, art song and folk song, solo instrumental literature and chamber music in practical editions. 2575 titles of choral music, chiefly sacred, for use by choirs. 17,000 titles of popular sheet music, uncataloged but thoroughly indexed. Considerable recent holdings of books and periodicals in foreign languages. Special collections of black and local materials. 25,000 recordings and extensive discographical literature. Collection of publishers' trade catalogs.

MI —MICHIGAN STATE UNIVERSITY, Music Library, East Lansing, 48824. Roseann Hammill, Librn
Holdings: Cat
Notes: 17,987 scores; 5,851 recordings.

MI —WESTERN MICHIGAN UNIVERSITY, Harper C Maybee Music and Dance Library, Dalton Center, Kalamazoo, 49008. Gregory Fitzgerald, Librn
Holdings: Vols 12,200 Cat Music Scores
Notes: Incl 12,000 books on music; 10,000 sound recordings. Collection has separate catalog.

MN —MINNEAPOLIS PUBLIC LIBRARY & INFORMATION CENTER, Art, Music & Films Dept, 300 Nicollet Mall, Minneapolis, 55401. Mary Alice Walker, Music Specialist
Holdings: Vols 94,200 Cat Phonorecords Audiotapes
Budget: ($111,642)
Notes: Collection incl phonorecords (15,000 78 rpm's; 31,732 LP's); audiotapes (1450); and sheet music (60,540).

MN —SAINT PAUL PUBLIC LIBRARY, Arts & Audiovisual Services, 90 W Fourth St, Saint Paul, 55102. Delores Sundbye, Supervising Librn
Holdings: Vols
Budget: ($20,000)
Notes: The Field Collection of 15,000 pieces of sheet music of 19th and 20th century popular songs. Indexed but not cataloged.

MS —UNIVERSITY OF SOUTHERN MISSISSIPPI, William David McCain Graduate Library, Box 5148, Southern Sta, Hattiesburg, 39406.
Holdings: Mss
Notes: The Paul Yoder Collection (1940-1980; 30 cubic feet) contains original musical scores and published copies of band music which Yoder composed or arranged. Some of the band music was written for foreign bands, especially Japanese. Catalog in progress.

MO —MISSOURI HISTORICAL SOCIETY, Library, Jefferson Memorial Bldg, Saint Louis, 63112. Stephanie Klein, Librn-Archivist; Peter Michel, Cur of Manuscripts
Holdings: Vols (500) Cat
Notes: Five hundred volumes of sheet music. In additions, over 5000 pieces of individual sheet music. Most of this music was published in St Louis, and many have St Louis themes. Collection will remain in storage until 1986.

MO —SAINT LOUIS PUBLIC LIBRARY, Popular Library, 1301 Olive Blvd, Saint Louis, 63103. Mary Lou Allen, Librn
Holdings: Vols (54,255) Cat
Budget: ($10,253)
Notes: Incl music books (7,000); scores (24,000); recordings (discs & tapes, 23,200); music periodicals (55).

MO —WASHINGTON UNIVERSITY, Gaylord Music Library, Saint Louis, 63130. Suzanne Bell, Music Librn
Holdings: Vols Cat Mss Microforms
Notes: Music books, scores, bound periodicals (65,294); recordings (discs and and tapes, 16,114); sheet music, (50,000);

MUSIC SCORES—COLLECTIONS (cont.)

choral music (8000). 345 microfilm; 390 microcards.

NJ —ELIZABETH PUBLIC LIBRARY, Art & Music Dept, 11 S Broad St, Elizabeth, 07202. Roman Sawycky, Head
Holdings: Vols (20,000) Cat Pix Phonorecords 16mm Films Filmstrips
Budget: ($10,000)
Notes: Incl 200,000 pictures, 12,000 phonorecords and 700 films and filmstrips.

NJ —FAIRLEIGH DICKINSON UNIVERSITY, Friendship Library, 285 Madison Ave, Madison, 07940. James Fraser, Library Dir; Renee Weber, Cur
Notes: Incl 5000 phonorecords; cylinders; 1500 pieces of sheet music; publishers catalogs; victrolas. The George H Moss Collection traces the history of music and theatre from 1890-1950 through publisher's catalogs; sheet music; cylinders and phonorecords. A published list of the sheet music is available.

NJ —NEWARK PUBLIC LIBRARY, Art & Music Dept, 5 Washington St, Newark, 07101. William J Dane, Supv
Holdings: Vols (25,000) Cat Mss Audiotapes Microforms VF
Notes: Music literature, scores, librettos, extensive vertical file, song sheets, special indexes, music peiodicals. John Tasker Howard collection of notes and letters. Some special material on New Jersey and Newark music.

NJ —PRINCETON UNIVERSITY, Library, William Seymour Theatre Collection, Princeton, 08544. Mary Ann Jensen, Cur
Notes: Orchestral parts and conductor's scores for several thousand popular songs and special musical effects used in movie houses to the end of the silent picture era.

NM —UNIVERSITY OF NEW MEXICO, Fine Arts Library, Fine Art Bldg, Albuquerque, 87131. James B Wright, Librn
Notes: The Charles Gigante Collection of orchestral scores with string bowing.

NY —NEW YORK STATE LIBRARY, State Education Bldg Annex, Washington Ave, Albany, 12224.
Notes: American sheet music, late 18th to early 20th century. Mainly popular music, some New York State emphasis, 20,000 titles. Not completely organized; not centralized in one library section. General music collection of about 5000 vols.

NY —STATE UNIVERSITY OF NEW YORK, BUFFALO, Baird Music Library, Baird Hall, Amherst, 14260. James B Coover, Dir
Holdings: Vols (104,000) Cat Mss Pix Slides Phonorecords Microforms
Notes: Nearly complete collections of *Denkmaeler and Gesamtausgaben* and other historical sets. Strong collection of dictionaries, bibliographies, biographies, facsimiles, works on organology and ethnomusicology. Special emphasis on operas, scores of the avant-garde and urban popular music and music librarianship. Good collection of medieval and Renaissance anthologies, contemporary and avant-garde recordings. Houses Archives of the Center of the Creative and Performing Arts. Collections incl 1000 slides, 14,000 phonorecords, and 33,000 scores and parts. Computerized record catalog in process.

NY —BROOKLYN PUBLIC LIBRARY, Art & Music Div, Grand Army Plaza, Brooklyn, 11238. Sue H Sharma, Chief
Notes: Over 50,000 items, most of which circulate to the public. The collection contains some reference materials, incl the complete works of many composers; over 3500 popular song folios with our own in-house index for locating individual songs; some rare editions and mss of local composers; and a small collection of rare sheet music beginning with the 18th century. The circulating collection incl standard vocal scores, methods, piano music, etc, and is one of the largest public library collections in the country.

NY —BUFFALO & ERIE COUNTY PUBLIC LIBRARY, Music Dept, Lafayette Sq,

Buffalo, 14203. Norma Jean Lamb, Head
Notes: 76,400 bound vols of music and music literature. Complete works of the great composers, and historical editions. Orchestral scores and parts.

NY —NATIONAL BASEBALL HALL OF FAME AND MUSEUM, National Baseball Library, Cooperstown, 13326. Thomas R Heitz, Librn
Notes: A representative collection of sheet music with a baseball theme or connection.

†NY —STATE UNIVERSITY OF NEW YORK, COLLEGE AT FREDONIA, Daniel A Reed Library, Fredonia, 14063.
Holdings: Vols (8000) Cat Phonorecords Audiotapes
Budget: ($12,500)
Notes: The Music Library supports the curricular needs of a large department of music which now has programs in both music education and performance. Separate card catalogs are maintained for 26,000 scores and more than 12,000 recordings and tape cassettes. The library has a small collection of 19th century American tunebooks, some Lowell Mason materials and a collection of sheet music and dance band arrangements numbering more than 3200 pieces and covering the period from 1850 through the big band era.

NY —QUEENS BOROUGH PUBLIC LIBRARY, Art & Music Div, 89-11 Merrick Blvd, Jamaica, 11432. Dorothea Wu, Head
Holdings: Vols (85,000) Cat Maps Pix Phonorecords Audiotapes Microforms
Budget: ($44,000)
Notes: The Picture Collection, covering all subjects, consists of approximately 1,500,000 pictures, mainly reproductions and clippings from books and magazines, photographs, and postcards on all subjects; The Framed Picture Collection, approx 180 framed pictures, mostly reproductions of paintings from various periods; and The Phonorecord and Cassette Collection consists of approx 3500 reference phonorecords and 6500 circulating records as well as 1000 reference cassettes and 1500 circulating cassettes.

NY —BARNARD A & MORRIS N YOUNG LIBRARY OF EARLY AMERICAN POPULAR MUSIC, 270 Riverside Dr, New York, 10025. Morris N Young, Cur
Holdings: Cat Mss Pix Phonorecords Audiotapes Microforms
Notes: 48,000 items of American popular music, mostly 1790-1910. Incl books, serials, sheet music, broadsides, anthologies, air checks, broadcasting and music business memorabilia, and correspondence.

NY —COLUMBIA UNIVERSITY LIBRARIES, Music Library, 701 Dodge, Broadway & 116 St, New York, 10027. M Haefliger, Librn
Holdings: Vols (55,020) Cat Phonorecords Audiotapes Microforms
Notes: Score collection places acquisition emphasis on study scores of music pieces, and avoids collecting performance parts for ensemble music.

†NY —COLUMBIA UNIVERSITY LIBRARIES, Butler Library, Rare Book and Manuscript Library, 535 W 114 St, New York, 10027.
Notes: Mss of three symphonic works by Douglas Stuart Moore.

†NY —NEIGHBORHOOD PLAYHOUSE SCHOOL OF THE THEATRE, Irene Lewisohn Library, 340 E 54 St, New York, 10022. Alice G Owen, Librn
Notes: Books and 1137 music scores.

NY —NEW YORK PUBLIC LIBRARY, Music Div, 111 Amsterdam Ave, New York, 10023. Frank C Campbell, Chief
Holdings: Vols (300,000) Cat Mss Pix Microforms
Notes: Incl the Thomas Sherman Collection, the CBS Music Library Collection and the Opera Collection among 33,925 orchestral sets. Described in *Dictionary Catalog of the Music Collection, The Research Libraries of the New York Public Library*, 33 vols (532,000 cards), 1964, $2190; Supplement 1, 1 vol (17,000 cards), 1966, $100. Also, *Bibliographic Guide to Music*, 2 vols, 1975-1976, $70 ea. Literature pertaining to virtually all musical subjects, and scores

covering the broadest range of musical style and history are represented in this catalog. Special strengths of the collection incl folk songs, 18th and 19th-century librettos, full scores of operas, complete works, historical editions, Beethoven, Americana, American music, periodicals, vocal music, literature on the voice, programs, record catalogs, and mss in detail; sheet music, 355,414; sound recordings,400,000; clippings and programs, 2 million; broadsides, 1821; songsters, 375; pictures, 51,002; ms, 29,877.

NY —NEW YORK PUBLIC LIBRARY, Library & Museum of the Performing Arts, 111 Amsterdam Ave, New York, 10023. Elsie L Peck, Dance Specialist
Holdings: Vols (11,400) Cat Phonorecords Audiotapes
Budget: ($8670)
Notes: Circulating collection of books, scores, records and cassettes covering all areas of dance and related fields. Incl 8670 books and 1652 scores.

NY —NEW YORK PUBLIC LIBRARY, General Library and Museum of the Performing Arts, 111 Amsterdam Ave, New York, 10023. George Louis Mayer, Coordinator; Kris Shuman, Music Specialist
Holdings: Vols 78,000 Cat
Budget: ($28,000)
Notes: Circulating collections incl 78,000 scores.

†NY —SHUBERT ARCHIVE, Lyceum Theatre, 149 W 45th St, New York, 10036. Brigitte Kueppers, Archivist
Notes: The vast Shubert Archive, mostly unexplored is the largest collection in the world representative of the "business" of the theatre. It includes almost all of the Shubert empire's correspondence from the turn of the century to the 1950s, road company records, thousands of playscripts (American and European), set and costume designs, music scores for Shubert productions, business, financial, and legal records, actors' contracts, etc.

NY —YIVO INSTITUTE FOR JEWISH RESEARCH, Library & Archives, 1048 Fifth Ave, New York, 10028. Dina Abramowicz, Librn; Marek Web, Archivist
Holdings: Cat Mss Slides
Notes: Collections of Jewish music organizations in pre-World War I Russia, and collections of individual musicians and composers, among them the Bernstein collection from Vilna and Leo Low collection from New York. Secular, liturgical, folk music, theatrical songs in the form of sheet music is represented. Partially cataloged.

NY —VASSAR COLLEGE, George Sherman Dickinson Music Library, Skinner Hall, Poughkeepsie, 12601. Sabrina L Weiss, Music Librn
Holdings: Vols (50,000) Cat Mss Phonorecords Audiotapes Microforms
Budget: ($25,000)
Notes: Areas of strength incl *Collected Works and Historical Monuments* (Denkmaeler), facsimile editions, periodicals, reference works (dictionaries, library catalogs), contemporary music, biography, and a balanced collection of musicological works. Incl 30,000 scores, 20,000 books and 25,000 phonorecords. Partly described in: G S Dickinson, "The Living Library," *MLA Notes III* (June 1946), 247-55; J B Coover, "...A College Music Library," *Papers & Addresses of the College Music Association, 9th Annual Meeting* (1955), pp 5-16; Carol June Bradley & James B Coover, "Vassar's Music Library," *MLA Notes* (June 1979), pp 819-46; *Grove's Dictionary of Music & Musicians* (5th ed, 1954; 6th ed, 1975); and *New Grove Dictionary of Music and Musicians* (1980).
See also entry under Libraries

NY —STATE UNIVERSITY OF NEW YORK, COLLEGE AT PURCHASE, Library, Purchase, 10577. Mark E Smith, Music Librn
Holdings: Vols (6500) // Cat Microforms
Notes: Noah Greenberg Collection of monographs, journals, scholarly editions of medieval, Renaissance, and early Baroque music and performance materials, and

MUSIC SCORES—COLLECTIONS
(cont.)

microfilms of music manuscripts. Collection was acquired from the defunct New York Pro Musica Antiqua.

NY —YONKERS PUBLIC LIBRARY, Grinton I Will Library, 1500 Central Park Ave, Yonkers, 10701. Joan W Stevenson, Head of Fine Arts Dept
Holdings: Vols (12,000) Cat
Budget: ($36,000)
Notes: Incl periodicals, 70 titles (ca 15 yr back issues); 27 vertical file drawers (18 on artists & musicians); 1230 slides; 2200 music scores; cat; sheet music, ca 1200 titles; 140 libretti; 13,000 phonograph albums; cat; 1000 cassettes. Books, scores, phonograph albums, cassettes are cataloged. Rare collection of 57 test pressings of Geraldine Farrar, some of which have never been issued.

NC —APPALACHIAN STATE UNIVERSITY, Music Library, Broyhill Music Center, Boone, 28608. Joan O Falconer, Librn
Holdings: Vols 1800 Phonorecords
Budget: ($9500)
Notes: A collection of music scores, chamber music, and 7000 recordings, supported by basic reference books. Former emphasis on music education materials now being expanded to include extensive performance materials and titles appropriate to a liberal arts curriculum through the master's degree level. The University Library (Belk Library) houses the main collection of book materials in music. Incl 12,000 music scores and parts and 7000 phonorecords.

NC —UNIVERSITY OF NORTH CAROLINA, CHAPEL HILL, Music Library, Hill Hall, Chapel Hill, 27514.
Holdings: Vols (90,000) Cat Mss Pix Slides Phonorecords Audiotapes Microforms
Budget: ($60,000)
Notes: Extensive holdings of early theoretical treatises; complete editions; performing scores; music periodicals; reference works. Special interests reflected in holdings of sonatas; oratorios; requiems; operas; microfilms of Vatican Library holdings of mss containing hymns; microfilms from the Deutsches Musikgeschichtliches Archiv; microfilms of important European primary sources; contemporary chamber music. Approx 5000 pieces of early American sheet music, primarily antebellum. Substantial collection of shape-note hymnals, 19th and 20th century. Dictionary catalog of books, scores, microforms and recordings. Separate card catalog of early American music and song anthologies held by Music Library. Partial book catalog of libretto collection.

NC —DUKE UNIVERSITY, William R Perkins Library, Durham, 27706. Elvin E Strowd, University Librn
Notes: Books, serials and pamphlets (2,820,527); music scores (31,551); motion pictures (285); microforms (1,055,627); tapes, cassettes and phonorecords, the library is a depository for Radio Canada International recordings, (2289); and manuscripts, US Government publications, maps, and broadsides, additions in all formats are ongoing.

NC —DUKE UNIVERSITY, William R Perkins Library, Rare Book Room, Durham, 27706. John L Sharpe, III, Cur
Notes: Sheet music collection consisting of 6000 items. Primarily 19th century American imprints.

NC —MORAVIAN MUSIC FOUNDATION, Peter Memorial Library, 20 Cascade Ave, Winston-Salem, 27107. James Boeringer, Dir
Holdings: Vols (6000) Cat Phonorecords
Budget: ($2500)
Notes: Emphasis on 18th and 19th century music, incl hymns, Moravian music, etc.

OH —AKRON-SUMMIT COUNTY PUBLIC LIBRARY, 55 S Main St, Akron, 44326. Steven Hawk, Dir
Holdings: Cat Pix Phonorecords
Budget: ($9600)
Notes: General music and fine arts

collection, incl 16,515 phonorecords, 2951 music scores, 3000 pieces of sheet music and 55,472 pictures.

OH —HEBREW UNION COLLEGE-JEWISH INSTITUTE OF RELIGION, Klau Library, 3101 Clifton Ave, Cincinnati, 45220. David J Gilner, Reference Librn
Holdings: Vols 5000 Cat Mss
Notes: Incl the Birnbaum Jewish Music Collection of 3000 mss; Jewish song index of recordings in the Hebrew Union College collection.

OH —PUBLIC LIBRARY OF CINCINNATI & HAMILTON COUNTY, Art & Music Dept, 800 Vine St, Cincinnati, 45202. R Jayne Craven, Head
Holdings: Vols (122,185) Cat Pix
Budget: ($56,100)
Notes: Special collections: Eda Kuhn Loeb, "Artist and the Book, 1875-Date" (now shelved in Rare Book Room); music librettos (2345); exhibition catalogs (5474); large prints and posters (5051); Cincinnati artists vertical files; picture collection (673,906 clippings).

OH —CLEVELAND PUBLIC LIBRARY, Fine Arts and Special Collections Department, 325 Superior Ave, Cleveland, 44114. Alice N Loranth, Head
Holdings: Cat
Notes: Incl 37,850 scores, 20,430 pieces of sheet music. Every type of score from opera, piano orchestral, instrumental, etc. Large editions and anthologies. Primarily classical in scope, scores are also available for musical comedies with a sampling of popular music incl, particularly in older sheet music. Incl are 2500 miniature and study scores. Misc collections (songs, hymns, piano, violin and organ) are indexed for contents.

OH —OHIO STATE UNIVERSITY, William Oxley Thompson Memorial Library, 1858 Neil Ave Mall, Columbus, 43210. Robert A Tibbetts, Cur of Special Collections
Holdings: Vols 7000 Cat
Notes: American popular music, mostly ca 1880-1935; about 7000 pieces of sheet music.

OH —KENT STATE UNIVERSITY, Music Library, Kent, 44242. Judith B McCarron, Library Coord
Holdings: Vols (15,000) Microforms
Notes: 20,000 music scores.

OR —UNIVERSITY OF OREGON LIBRARY, Music Dept, Eugene, 97403. Leslie K Greer, Music Librn
Holdings: Vols 15,000 Cat
Budget: ($13,000)
Notes: 20,000 pieces of American popular sheet music in Special Collections section.

OR —JACKSON COUNTY LIBRARY SYSTEM, 413 W Main, Medford, 97501. Hardin E Smith, Librn
Holdings: Cat
Notes: Werner Collection of sheet music, 1880-1945; 3000 pieces.

OR —LIBRARY ASSOCIATION OF PORTLAND, Art & Music Dept, 801 S W Tenth Ave, Portland, 97205. Barbara K Padden, Librn
Holdings: Vols Cat Pix Slides Phonorecords
Notes: Art book titles: 21,325; music book titles (incl dance books): 10,800; sheet music titles: 19,550; slides on art subjects: about 12,000; phonorecord albums: 27,000; picture clippings: about 2 million; color reproductions of old and modern masters: about 640.

PA —BALA CYNWYD LIBRARY, Old Lancaster Rd & N Highland Ave, Bala Cynwyd, 19004. Rosalind Leighton, Reference Librn
Holdings: Vols (813) Cat
Notes: Including librettos, piano-vocal scores of operas and musicals, chamber music, solo works for various instruments, etc.

PA —FREE LIBRARY OF PHILADELPHIA, Sheet Music Collection, Logan Sq, Philadelphia, 19103. Connie Jessum, Librn
Budget: ($2000)
Notes: Covers entire span of American popular expression in song and instrumental music (piano) from colonial times to the present. Incl Newland-Zeuner and Edward I Keffer Collections on loan from the Musical Fund Society. Items printed before 1825

indexed in Sonneck-Upton and Wolfe. Checklists for cover illustrations, musical shows or films and special subjects. Songs are filed by title; piano music by composer. Examples of special materials not filed in regular collection incl early Philadelphia composers and publications; national (centennial and state), patriotic ("Star-Spangled Banner"), political (Presidents), and war (1861; 1914; 1939) songs. Most of the ms materials are anonymous. Collection contains 138,360 pieces of sheet music.

PA —UNIVERSITY OF PITTSBURGH, Music Library, B-31 Music Bldg, Pittsburgh, 15260. Norris L Stephens, Music Librn
Holdings: Vols 8000 Cat
Notes: Incl the private collections of Theodore M Finney and William Steinberg.

PA —PENNSYLVANIA STATE UNIVERSITY, Arts Library, 405 E Pattee Library, University Park, 16802. Daniel Zager, Music Librn
Holdings: Vols (14,000) Cat
Notes: The collection includes both collected works and performance editions.
See also entry under Music.

PA —WARREN LIBRARY ASSOCIATION, 205 Market St, Warren, 16365. Ann Lesser, Dir
Holdings: // Cat
Notes: Popular American sheet music, 1834-1955 (3578 pieces).

PA —WEST CHESTER UNIVERSITY, Music Library, Swope Hall, University Ave, West Chester, 19383. Ruth I Weidner, Music Librn
Budget: ($26,000)
Notes: Large basic music collection (scores, sheet music, and 21,000 phonorecords) which is especially strong in collected works, historical editions, opera, keyboard music, and miniature scores. Incl 24,000 music scores. All music is fully cataloged. Scope of collection is broad and excludes only music education and curriculum materials. Collection does not include books about music or periodicals but does have about 500 reference books. For the most part collection is music published during or available within the past twenty years.

RI —BROWN UNIVERSITY, John Hay Library, 20 Prospect St, Providence, 02912. Mark N Brown, Cur Mss
Notes: The Sheet Music Collection concentrates on music of American imprint, incl 170,000 vocal pieces filed by title, plus 80,000 instrumental pieces filed by composer. Major strengths are in 19th century music, especially prior to 1830; Civil War music, both Union and Confederate; lithographic covers; World War I songs; political campaign music; and band music. An additional 100,000 pieces of American and European imprint remain unprocessed. Also the Sackett Collection of 750 scores of orchestral and chamber music works, primarily late 18th to early 20th centuries.
See also entry under Song Books - Collections.

RI —BROWN UNIVERSITY, John Hay Library, Harris Collection, Prospect St, Providence, 02912. Rosemary L Cullen, Cur
Holdings: Vols (200,000) Cat Mss Phonorecords Microforms
Budget: ($15,000)
Notes: The Harris Collection of American Poetry and Plays is principally composed of American and Canadian poetry and plays, 17th century-date. Extensive holdings in songsters, gift books and annuals, hymnals, pageants, broadside verse, carriers' addresses, women poets, juvenile poetry (incl Mother Goose and *The Night before Christmas*), sheet music with lyrics, small press publications, fine printing, black poets, "little magazines", Yiddish-American literature. Incl Stephen Foster sheet music; the MacDougall Collection of Psalters and Hymnals; the Vaxer Collection of Yiddish Poetry, Plays and Music (1700 vols). Collections incl 200,000 vols, 30,000 broadsides, 55,000 mss, 170,000 pieces of sheet music, 450 phonorecords, and 375 microfilm reels. See *Dictionary Catalog of the Harris Collection of American Poetry and Plays* (Boston: G K Hall, 1972), 13 vols;

MUSIC SCORES—COLLECTIONS (cont.)

Supplement(1977), 3 vols. See also, *American Poetry, 1609-1900, A Collection on Microfilm, Segment I (1609-1820); Segment II (1821-1850); Segment III (1851-1870)* (Woodbridge, Conn: Research Publications). Separate catalog.

RI —BROWN UNIVERSITY, John Hay Library, McLellan Lincoln Collection, 20 Prospect St, Providence, 02912. Jennifer B Lee, Special Collections Librn
Holdings: Vols (15,000) Cat Mss Pix Phonorecords
Notes: Sheet music collection has almost every piece of Lincoln sheet music known to exist from minstrel songs to funeral marches, memorial songs and campaign songs. Statuary is well represented and incl two Rogers groups, an original Truman Bartlett plaster statuette of Lincoln, and replicas of Leonard Volk's work.

RI —PROVIDENCE PUBLIC LIBRARY, 150 Empire St, Providence, 02903. Lance J Bauer, Special Collections Librn
Holdings: Vols (5000) Cat Mss Pix
Notes: The musical compositions of David Wallis Reeves, director of the Rhode Island American Band from 1866-1900, are preserved in this collection of approx 150 mss of band, orchestral and conductor's scores, many in Reeves' hand. Memorabilia incl photographs, letters, and the Band's Minute Book, 1859-1906. There are also very large holdings of 19th century sheet music, some of it unpublished. Complete inventory of all mss and sheet music. Photocopying on a restricted basis only for educational purposes when condition of this frequently fragile material allows.
See also entry under Broadsides - Collections

SC —CHARLESTON MUSEUM LIBRARY, 360 Meeting St, Charleston, 29403. K Sharon Bennett, Librn
Holdings: Vols (500)// Cat
Notes: The Governor William Aiken Collection. Housed at the Aiken House on Elizabeth Street, includes 400-500 volumes as well as numerous magazines and over 5000 pieces of sheet music, 1820-1880. Its value lies in its reflection of the habits and tastes of the upper class during this time.

SC —CONVERSE COLLEGE, Gwathmey Library, Spartanburg, 29301. Darlene E Fawver, Music Librn
Budget: ($17,000)
Notes: Incl 10,000 scores.

SD —UNIVERSITY OF SOUTH DAKOTA, Shrine to Music Museum, USD Box 194, Vermillion, 57069. Andre P Larson, Dir
Holdings: Uncat Mss
Budget: ($205,036)
Notes: The Shrine to Music Museum is one of America's major collections of musical resource materials, incl more than 4000 antique musical instruments from all over the world, plus an extensive supporting library of several thousand books, music, periodicals, recordings, photographs, and related musical memorabilia. The collection of 19th and early 20th-century sheet music and music for wind instruments is probably the most extensive in the country. Inquiries and visits are welcomed.

TN —COUNTRY MUSIC FOUNDATION, Library & Media Center, 4 Music Sq E, Nashville, 37203. Charlie Seemann, Dir
Holdings: Vols (6000) Mss Pix Slides Phonorecords Audiotapes Videotapes 16mm Films Microforms
Notes: The largest collection in the world dealing with American country music. Related subject areas are also included-- Anglo-American folksong, popular music in general (soul, jazz, rock and roll, rhythm and blues, etc), recorded sound technology, music law.

TN —TENNESSEE STATE LIBRARY & ARCHIVES, 403 Seventh Ave N, Nashville, 37219. Olivia K Young, State Librn & Archivist
Holdings: Cat
Notes: Collection of popular American sheet

music, of interest as social rather than musical history. About 10,000 titles and editions.

TX —UNIVERSITY OF TEXAS LIBRARIES, Music Library, PO Box P, Austin, 78712. Olga Buth, Librn
Holdings: Vols (21,862) Cat Phonorecords Audiotapes Microforms
Notes: Collection incl 36,462 scores, 3505 bound periodicals, 4506 microforms, 289 periodical subscriptions, 312 serials and monographs, 13,706 phonodiscs, and 922 phonotapes.

TX —NORTH TEXAS STATE UNIVERSITY, Audio Center, Box 5188, NT Station, Denton, 76203. Morris Martin, Music Librn
Notes: Supports wide range of music curricula and research with over 100,000 volumes incl music books, periodicals, scores, sheet music of all kinds, chamber music, recordings; special collections incl the libraries of musicologists Lloyd Hibberd and Helen Hewitt, bandleader Stan Kenton, composer Don Gillis, radio stations WFAA and WBAP; archives of *Source* magaine, mss of Arnold Schoenberg, recording collections (Arturo Toscanini, Don Gillis, Duke Ellington and other jazz musicians).

TX —FORT WORTH PUBLIC LIBRARY, Arts Division, 300 Taylor St, Fort Worth, 76102. Heather Gobel, Head
Holdings: Vols (21,500) Cat Mss Phonorecords
Budget: ($26,700)
Notes: Emphasis is on older popular music and musical comedies, folk songs, operas, music composed by Fort Worth and Texas composers, and music about Texas. Sheet music has a separate index.

TX —SOUTHWESTERN BAPTIST THEOLOGICAL SEMINARY, Music Library, Fort Worth, 76122. Phillip W Sims, Librn
Holdings: Vols (19,000) Cat
Budget: ($30,000)
Notes: Incl in the Treasure Section are approx 250 tune books, plus many very old hymnals and other antiquarian items. Incl 97,000 pieces of sheet music, 24,000 scores, 7500 phonograph records and 3500 audiocassettes. The entire collection is cataloged except the periodicals and about one fourth of the sheet music.

TX —BAYLOR UNIVERSITY, Moody Memorial Library, Crouch Music Library, 1312 S Third St, PO Box 6307, Waco, 76706. Avery T Sharp, Librn
Holdings: Vols (75,000) Cat Phonorecords Audiotapes Microforms
Budget: ($48,000)
Notes: Areas of strength: The Frances G Spencer Collection of American Printed Music, 30,000 items of popular sheet music of the 19th and 20th centuries, completely cataloged; complete collection of Denkmaler, Gesamtausgeben and other historical sets, periodicals, dictionaries, library catalogs, thematic indexes, etc; 55,000 volumes of music scores and music literature; 20,000 phonorecords, tapes and microfilm; 400 early American hymn books. Collection has separate catalog.

VT —MIDDLEBURY COLLEGE, Starr Library, Flanders Ballad Collection, Middlebury, 05753. Jennifer Post Quinn, Cur
Notes: Begun as Helen Hartness Flanders' private collection in 1930, given to Middlebury College, 1941. Incl over 9000 New England items recorded or transcribed since 1930: ballads and folk songs of British, American, French-Canadian, and Russian origin; religious songs; fiddle tunes; dance music. Inclusive research collection of folklore and folksong monographs, scores, tunebooks, journals. Reference: Quinn, Jennifer Post. *An Index to the Field Recordings in the Flanders Ballad Collection at Middlebury College, Middlebury, Vermont* Middlebury, VT, Middlebury College, 1983.

VA —UNIVERSITY OF VIRGINIA, Alderman Library, Music Collection, Charlottesville, 22901. Evan Bonds, Music Librn
Holdings: Cat
Notes: McRae, Lynn T *Computer Catalog of*

19th-Century American-Imprint Sheet Music (Charlottesville, Univ of Va, 1977).

VA —GEORGE MASON UNIVERSITY, Fenwick Library, Special Collections Dept, 4400 University Drive, Fairfax, 22030. Ruth Kerns, Public Services Librn
Notes: The Federal Theatre Project Collection includes 5000 playscripts, 2500 radio scripts, 25,000 photographs, 40 blueprints, 1000 posters, over 1600 costume designs, 350 scene designs, 750 production notebooks, 1700 programs and heralds, 26 musical scores and 18 cubic feet of research materials and play readers reports.

VA —CBN UNIVERSITY, Virginia Beach, 23463. Jack L Ralston, Fine Arts Librn
Holdings: Vols 9000
Notes: The Keith C Clark Collection of hymnology; hymnals, psazlters, oblong tune-books, hymnody, church music, composers, early sermons on church music, and journals. See Clark's *Selective Bibliography for the Study of Hymns* (1980).

VA —COLONIAL WILLIAMSBURG FOUNDATION, Research Center Library, PO Drawer C, Williamsburg, 23187. John E Ingram, Research Archivist
Holdings: Vols (30,000) Cat Mss Maps Pix Microforms
Budget: ($20,000)
Notes: Virginia and the Chesapeake in the 17th-18th centuries. Particular strengths include social, economic, agricultural and architectural history. The collection encompasses over 6000 rare books, 18th Century music scores and 12,000 manuscripts, as well as a complete set of Virginia Colonial Records Project microfilm (1000 reels).

†WA —SEATTLE PUBLIC LIBRARY, Music Dept, Fourth & Madison, Seattle, 98104. Carolyn Holmquist, Head
Holdings: Vols 22,300 Cat
Notes: Books 11,000, music 10,000, dance 1300 vols, 14,000 phonorecords, 28,000 pieces of sheet music. Special indexes: symphony orchestra program notes. World, National and local premiere dates. Song titles in collections, 60,000 cards. Music literature, printed music and sheet music, and phonograph record collections all have separate catalogs.

WI —UNIVERSITY OF WISCONSIN, MADISON, Mills Music Library, 728 State St, Madison, 53706. Arne Arneson, Music Librn
Holdings: Cat
Notes: Sheet music (vocal and instrumental) and hymnals bearing US imprints. Includes part of the library of J P Webster. Also, the Tams-Witmark Collection, which formed part of the rental collection of the firm bearing that name. Includes piano-conductor scores (some in mss); ca 65 sets of orchestral parts for operas; 70 vocal scores of works by American composers including Herbert, Sousa, Edwards and De Koven; ca 100 sets of orchestral parts of comic operas; ca 4000 vocal scores of European operas. Uncataloged. Restricted use.

WI —MILWAUKEE PUBLIC LIBRARY, 814 W Wisconsin Ave, Milwaukee, 53233. Donald J Sager, City Librn
Holdings: Vols Cat
Notes: Good collection of folios of American popular songs, mainly of the 50s and 60s, separately indexed. Also sheet music of American popular songs from 1890-1950.

WY —UNIVERSITY OF WYOMING, William Robertson Coe Library, Archives - American Heritage Center, PO Box 3412, Laramie, 82071.
Notes: Music mss and papers of Carl W Stallings. Incl 1300 complete original scores and more than 2000 sheets of other music.

PR —UNIVERSITY OF PUERTO RICO, Jose M Lazaro Memorial Library, Music Room, Box C, University of Puerto Rico Sta, Rio Piedras, 00931. Ramon Arollo, Librn
Holdings: Vols 42,550 Cat Mss Slides Phonorecords Audiotapes Microforms
Notes: Incl over 9142 scores, 19,000 phonorecords, 7488 music books, 5191 newspapers, and 134 audiotapes.

MB —UNIVERSITY OF MANITOBA, Music Library, 223 Music Bldg, Winnipeg, R3T

MUSIC SCORES—COLLECTIONS (cont.)

2N2, Can. Vladimir Simosko, Head
Holdings: Vols 15,000
Notes: Incl performance music (27,750 items); 4200 phonorecords.

NB —MOUNT ALLISON UNIVERSITY, Alfred Whitehead Memorial Music Library, Sackville, E0A 3C0, Can. Bert Meerveld, Music Librn
Holdings: Vols (16,411) Cat Slides Phonorecords Audiotapes Filmstrips Microforms
Notes: Large collection of Canadian music. Described in *Canadian Music Scores and Recordings: A Classified Catalogue of the Holdings of Mount Allison University Libraries*, comp by Gwendolyn Creelman, Esther Cooke and Geraldine King, 1976. Collection incl 5057 phonorecords; 38 tapes; 99 cassettes; 16,411 monographs, scores and bound periodicals; 101 reels of microfilm; and 3287 sheets of microfiche. Cataloged.

ON —QUEEN'S UNIVERSITY, Douglas Library, Kingston, K7L 5C4, Can. William F E Morley, Cur, Special Collections
Holdings: Cat
Notes: Canadian sheet music; over 1000 pieces.

ON —NATIONAL LIBRARY OF CANADA, 395 Wellington St, Ottawa, K1A 0N4, Can. Andre Preibish, Dir
Notes: Includes 2000 pieces of Canadian sheet music (mostly 19th century imprints), 40,000 cylinders, discs, tapes; over 600 serials titles devoted to music; 200 archival collections of composers, musicians and conductors, eg papers of Healy Willan, eminent composer; Glen Gould, well-known pianist; Sir Ernest MacMillan, conductor, director and composer. Since 1950 the Canadian imprints have been received on legal deposit. Intensive purchases aim at a comprehensive collection of Canadian music.

ON —UNIVERSITY OF OTTAWA, Morisset Library, 65 Hastey St, Ottawa, K1N 9A5, Can. Yvon Richer, University Chief Librn
Holdings: Vols (12,000)
Notes: Incl 100 periodicals, 16,000 scores and 5150 sound recordings. Scores and recordings are housed in the music department and monographs and periodicals in the Morisset Library. The collection is particularly strong in sixteenth to nineteenth century continental European music and musicology.

ON —METROPOLITAN TORONTO LIBRARY, Music Dept, 789 Yonge St, Toronto, M4W 2G8, Can. Isabel Rose, Head
Holdings: Cat
Budget: ($54,000)
Notes: 14,800 books, 40,000 scores; 1900 pieces of retrospective Canadian sheet music; 500 pieces of American and British sheet music, pre-1980; 17,000 phonorecords; 180 current periodical titles; 2800 bound peiodicals; 340 reels of microfilmed periodicals; 16,000 concert programs, chiefly Toronto city; 8850 newspaper clipping files; music picture files integrated with Fine Art Dept picture collection.

PQ —UNIVERSITY OF MONTREAL, Bibliotheque de Musique, 200 Vincent d'Indy, bp 6128, succursale "A", Montreal, H3C 3J7, Can. Claude Soulard, Librn
Notes: Special emphasis on the classical period and contemporary music. Incl 11,895 music scores, 11,857 records and tapes and 6250 microforms.

MUSIC THEORY see Music—Theory

MUSIC THERAPY

BC —CAPILANO COLLEGE, Media Centre, 2055 Purcell Way N, Vancouver, V7J 3H5, Can. Pat Biggins, Reference Librn
Holdings: Phonorecords Audiotapes
Notes: 3000 items.

MUSIC TRADE see Music Industry

MUSICAL BOXES see Music Boxes

MUSICAL COMEDIES see Musical Revues, Comedies, Etc.

MUSICAL COMPOSITION see Composition (Music)

MUSICAL CRITICISM

CA —UNIVERSITY OF CALIFORNIA, BERKELEY, Humanities-Social Sciences

Libraries, Music Library, 24 Morrison Hall, Berkeley, 94720. Michael A Keller, Head Librn
Holdings: Vols 115,000 Cat Mss Slides Microforms
Notes: The Library maintains an outstanding music reference collection. It is rich in primary source materials for research, particularly in the areas of opera, 18th-century instrumental music, music theory. Incl 20,000 sound recordings. See the following: Vincent Duckles and Minnie Elmer, *Thematic Catalogue of a Collection of 18th-Century Italian Instrumental Music in the Music Library of the University of Califonia, Berkeley* (Univ of California Press, 1963); Alan Curtis, "Musique classique francaise a Berkeley," in *Revue de Musicologie*, 56 (1970) pp 123-164. Minnie Elmer, *Autograph Manuscripts of Ernest Bloch at the University of California*; *Cum Notis Variorum, the Newsletter of the Music Library of the University of California* (Published 10 times annually since April 1976).

MUSICAL EDUCATION see Music—Instruction and Study

MUSICAL EFFECTS

IL —CHICAGO PUBLIC LIBRARY, Music Section, Fine Arts Division, 78 E Washington St, Chicago, 60602. Rosalinda I Hack, Fine Arts Division Chief; Richard C Schwegel, Head, Music Section
Holdings: // Uncat
Notes: The Chicago Public Library received the Sheet Music Archive (1700 cu ft) of the Plitt Theatre Corporation, Chicago, in 1975. This vast, unprocessed collection contains thousands of pieces of music played during intermissions in the Plitt Theatre palaces in Chicago during the 1920-40s. An inventory of the collection is available, organized by composer and form (eg "Fox Trots"); titles are not yet compiled. The collection is presently in storage at the Record Center Corporation, The Chicago Public Library's storage facility for little-used materials.

NJ —PRINCETON UNIVERSITY, Library, William Seymour Theatre Collection, Princeton, 08544. Mary Ann Jensen, Cur
Notes: Orchestral parts and conductor's scores for several thousand popular songs and special musical effects used in movie houses to the end of the silent picture era.

MUSICAL FESTIVALS see Music Festivals

MUSICAL FUND SOCIETY

PA —FREE LIBRARY OF PHILADELPHIA, Music Dept, Logan Sq, Philadelphia, 19103. Frederick James Kent, Head
Notes: The American Hymnody Collection incl early psalters, hymn books and anthologies of sacred music published in the 18th and 19th centuries. Examples of holdings are Lyon's *Urania* (1761), Billings' *Singing Master's Assistant* (1778), and Wyeth's *Repository of Sacred Music*. Arrangements to use the collection should be made in advance.

PA —FREE LIBRARY OF PHILADELPHIA, Sheet Music Collection, Logan Sq, Philadelphia, 19103. Connie Jessum, Librn
Budget: ($2000)
Notes: Covers entire span of American popular expression in song and instrumental music (piano) from colonial times to the present. Incl Newland-Zeuner and Edward I Keffer Collections on loan from the Musical Fund Society. Items printed before 1825 indexed in Sonneck-Upton and Wolfe. Checklists for cover illustrations, musical shows or films and special subjects. Songs are filed by title; piano music by composer. Examples of special materials not filed in regular collection incl early Philadelphia composers and publications, national (centennial and state), patriotic ("Star-Spangled Banner"), political (Presidents), and war (1861; 1914; 1939) songs. Most of the

ms materials are anonymous. Collection contains 138,360 pieces of sheet music.

MUSICAL INSTRUCTION see Music—Instruction and Study

MUSICAL-INSTRUMENT MAKERS see Musical Instruments—Makers

MUSICAL INSTRUMENTS

CT —YALE UNIVERSITY, Box 1603A, Yale Station, New Haven, 06520.

†DC —CATHOLIC UNIVERSITY OF AMERICA, Music Library, Washington, 20064. Betty Libbey, Head Music Library
Holdings: Cat Microforms
Notes: A large collection to support advanced degree study. Emphasis on church music, musicology, history and criticism, instrumental and vocal music, solo music for all voices, instruments, and musical forms.

DC —SMITHSONIAN INSTITUTION LIBRARIES, National Museum of American History Branch, Washington, 20560. Rhoda S Ratner, Branch Librn
Holdings: Vols 1155 Cat Pix Slides

IL —UNIVERSITY OF ILLINOIS, URBANA/CHAMPAIGN, Library, Bands & Busch Instrument Collection, 1103 S Sixth St, Champaign, 61820. John Cranford, Librn
Notes: This collection of 212 old and unusual wind and percussion instruments comes from two sources: The Carl Busch collection, and instruments collected by the late Director of University Bands Emeritus, Dr A A Harding. The museum is open from 8 to 5 Monday through Friday, by appointment only.

IN —BALL STATE UNIVERSITY, Alexander M Bracken Library, Muncie, 47306. Nyal Williams, Music Librn
Holdings: Vols (30,000) Cat Mss
Budget: ($20,000)
Notes: Incl archives of International Horn Society, Tubists Universal Brotherhood Association Library, Cecil Leeson Archival Saxophone Collection, and Archives of Buescher Music Instrument Manufacturing Company.

KY —UNIVERSITY OF KENTUCKY, Margaret I King Library, Dept of Special Collections, Lexington, 40506. William Marshall, Head
Holdings: Cat Mss Pix Films Videotapes Audiotapes Phonorecords
Notes: Incl 95 boxes, musical instruments. Collection documents the career of John Jacob Niles as composer, artist and collector of ballads; period covered: 1887, 1905-1982. Unpublished inventory, correspondence.

MD —TOWSON STATE UNIVERSITY, Fine Arts Bldg, Room 457, Towson, 21204. Edwin L Gerhardt, Curator
Notes: The Gerhardt Marimba Xylophone Collection is a unique and comprehensive accumulation of marimba and xylophone lore. It incl literature, phonograph and tape recordings, catalogs, music, methods, pictures, correspondence, personal reminiscences and miscellaneous information. It is *not* a collection of instruments. A detailed outline is available upon request. Direct all correspondence to the curator, Edwin L Gerhardt, 4926 Leeds Ave, Baltimore, MD 21227, (301) 242-0328.

MA —BOSTON PUBLIC LIBRARY, Print Collection, Dartmouth St at Copley Sq, Boston, 02117. Sinclair H Hitchings, Keeper of Prints
Notes: Approx 1000 glass slides which were the basis of Prof Geiringer's book, *Musical Instruments*, and were used in his teaching. The slides represent musical instruments, portraits and caricatures of musicians, and facsimiles of musical compositions and correspondence.

MI —UNIVERSITY OF MICHIGAN, School of Music, Stearns Collection of Musical Instruments, Ann Arbor, 48109. William P Malm, Dir; James M Borders, Assoc Dir
Holdings: Vols 80 Uncat Pix
Notes: Collection of 2000 musical instruments, 80 books and pamphlets, and 1000 photographs. Photography is permitted.

MUSICAL INSTRUMENTS (cont.)

Professional photography is available at cost plus materials. Stanley, Albert A. *Catalogue of The Stearns Collection of Musical Instruments,* Ann Arbor, University of Michigan, 1918; 1921 (out of print). Warner, Robert Austin. *The Stearns Collection of Musical Instruments-1965.* Ann Arbor: The School of Music, University of Michigan, 1965 (out of print); Borders, James M *Historical Wind Instruments in the Stearns Collection, University of Michigan,* (forthcoming, 1984).

NY —NEW YORK PUBLIC LIBRARY, Performing Arts Research Center, Music Div, Lincoln Center, New York, 10018.
Notes: New York Pro Musica Archives, and personal papers of Noah Greenberg, founder.

MUSICAL INSTRUMENTS—MAKERS

NY —NEW YORK PUBLIC LIBRARY, Performing Arts Research Center, Music Div, Lincoln Center, New York, 10018.
Notes: New York Pro Musica Archives, and personal papers of Noah Greenberg, founder.

MUSICAL INSTRUMENTS (MECHANICAL)

NY —MUSICAL MUSEUM AND LIBRARY, Deansboro, 13328. Arthur H Sanders, Cur
Holdings: Vols 1000 Uncat Mss Pix Slides
Notes: Antique musical instruments and music boxes.

MUSICAL INSTRUMENTS—CATALOGS AND COLLECTIONS

NY —MUSICAL MUSEUM AND LIBRARY, Deansboro, 13328. Arthur H Sanders, Cur
Holdings: Vols 1000 Uncat Mss Pix Slides
Notes: Antique musical instruments and music boxes.

SD —UNIVERSITY OF SOUTH DAKOTA, Shrine to Music Museum, USD Box 194, Vermillion, 57069. Andre P Larson, Dir
Holdings: Vols Cat
Budget: ($205,036)
Notes: The Shrine to Music Museum is one of America's major collections of musical resource materials, incl more than 4000 antique musical instruments from all over the world, plus an extensive supporting library of several thousand books, music, periodicals, recordings, photographs, and related musical memorabilia. The collection of 19th and early 20th-century sheet music and music for wind instruments is probably the most extensive in the country. Inquiries and visits are welcomed.

MUSICAL INSTRUMENTS—INDUSTRY AND TRADE see Music Trade

MUSICAL INSTRUMENTS—INSTRUCTION AND STUDY see Instrumental Music—Instruction and Study

MUSICAL INSTRUMENTS, FOLK

DC —LIBRARY OF CONGRESS, American Folklife Center, Archive of Folk Culture, Washington, 20540.
Notes: The Sidney Robertson Cowell Collection of her folk music recordings, 1937 to 1957. Incl very unusual contributions by the Molokan community in the Potrero Hill neighborhood of San Francisco, a breakaway sect from the Russian Orthodox Church.

PA —JANKOLA LIBRARY AND SLOVAK ARCHIVES, Danville, 17821.
Holdings: Vols 800
Notes: Folk instruments and dances.

MUSICAL INSTRUMENTS, PRIMITIVE

IL —UNIVERSITY OF ILLINOIS, URBANA/CHAMPAIGN, Library, Bands & Busch Instrument Collection, 1103 S Sixth St, Champaign, 61820. John Cranford, Librn
Notes: This collection of 212 old and unusual wind and percussion instruments comes from two sources: The Carl Busch collection, and instruments collected by the late Director of University Bands Emeritus, Dr A A Harding. The museum is open from 8 to 5 Monday through Friday, by appointment only.

SD —UNIVERSITY OF SOUTH DAKOTA, Shrine to Music Museum, USD Box 194, Vermillion, 57069. Andre P Larson, Dir
Holdings: Vols Slides Phonorecords Cat
Budget: ($205,036)
Notes: The Shrine to Music Museum is one of America's major collections of musical resource materials, incl more than 4000 antique musical instruments from all over the world, plus an extensive supporting library of several thousand books, music, periodicals, recordings, photographs, and related musical memorabilia. The collection of 19th and early 20th-century sheet music and music for wind instruments is probably the most extensive in the country. Inquiries and visits are welcomed.

MUSICAL INSTRUMENT MAKERS see Musical Instruments—Makers

MUSICAL MANUSCRIPTS see Manuscripts, Musical

MUSICAL RESEARCH see Musicology

MUSICAL REVUES, COMEDIES, ETC.

CA —CALIFORNIA STATE UNIVERSITY, HAYWARD, Library, Hayward, 94542. Melissa Rose, Dir
Holdings: Vols (15,986) Cat Phonorecords
Budget: ($21,000)
Notes: The score collection covers the entire range of instrumental and vocal concert music, incl collected works of various composers, and representative collections of hymnals, folk music, musical comedy, and some popular music. Sound recordings range from ethnomusicological collections to electronic music. Emphasis is on concert music, but there is a large collection of jazz and a selective collection of popular music. Separate catalog.

CA —INSTITUTE OF THE AMERICAN MUSICAL, Library, 121 N Detroit St, Los Angeles, 90036. Miles Kreuger, Cur
Holdings: Cat Mss Maps Pix Slides Phonorecords
Notes: Reference materials on the American musical theatre and motion pictures incl 40,000 phonograph records, sound tapes, and cylinders dating back to the 1890s; record catalogs to 1900; thousands of theatre and film programs, periodicals, sheet music and vocal scores as early as 1830; thousands of motion picture press books and over 200,000 stills from 1914 to the present; every musical comedy script published in America and dozens in ms form, original or photocopy materials from the archives of movie palaces, films and record companies, incl discographies of many major Broadway and Hollywood stars; and thousands of books on theatre, film, broadcasting, world's fairs and other allied areas of showmanship.

CA —SAN DIEGO PUBLIC LIBRARY, Art, Music & Recreation Sect, 820 E St, San Diego, 92101. Barbara A Tuhill, Supvr
Holdings: Cat
Notes: Score collection of 17,000 pieces covers all types of music incl religious works, opera scores, musical plays, miniature scores. Complete works of Bach, Berlioz, Beethoven, Mozart, and others are added as published in German reprint. Also, thematic indexes, and study and instructions for playing various musical instruments. General circulation.

CA —SANTA CRUZ PUBLIC LIBRARY, Art, Music, Film Dept, 224 Church St, Santa Cruz, 95060. Alma Westberg, Librn
Holdings: Vols (1500) Cat Mss
Budget: ($750)
Notes: The music collection is in a catalog separate from the general one. It consists of approx 1700 cataloged books about music; 2100 bound, cataloged books of music incl opera and musical comedy scores; 2700 pieces of sheet music which incl sacred, art and popular songs, and instrumental solos. Good collection of chamber music from baroque to contemporary composers. Also a special collection of 10,000 pieces of American popular sheet music of the period from the 1860s to 1970s incl songs of California. The record collection, primarily classical, consists of about 5500 records.

CT —YALE UNIVERSITY, Box 1603A, Yale Station, New Haven, 06520.
Holdings: Cat Mss Pix
Notes: Incl American Musical theatre and complete archives of the Theatre Guild; also memorabilia.

FL —MIAMI-DADE PUBLIC LIBRARY SYSTEM, One Biscayne Blvd, Miami, 33132. Don Chauncey, AV Librn; Barbara Young, Art & Music Dept Librn
Holdings: Vols 200 Cat Phonorecords
Notes: Incl 200 musical show scores; 200 recordings of musical shows.

IN —INDIANA UNIVERSITY, Lilly Library, Seventh St, Bloomington, 47405. William R Cagle, Librn
Holdings: // Uncat
Notes: In the Starr Collection of American Sheet Music.

MI —DETROIT PUBLIC LIBRARY, Music & Performing Arts Dept, 5201 Woodward, Detroit, 48202. Agatha Pfeiffer Kalkanis, Chief
Holdings: Cat
Notes: Collection of 5000 song collections of all types, as well as individual sacred and secular songs and folk songs. Incl all collections in standard indexes (Sears, DeCharms & Breed, Leigh, etc). Printed indexes supplemented by song index on cards in department, which incorporates title entries for more than 17,000 titles of 19th and 20th century popular sheet music, otherwise uncataloged. Popular music collection rich in show tunes, added on current basis, and in songs by Detroit writers and printed by publishing houses once active in Detroit (Remick, Whitney, etc). Much on Blacks' music and songs.

NY —NEW YORK PUBLIC LIBRARY, Performing Arts Research Center, Billy Rose Theatre Collection, 111 Amsterdam Ave, New York, 10023. Dorothy L Swerdlove, Cur
Holdings: Cat Videotapes 16mm Films
Notes: See entries under Theatre--History, Rudolf Friml, and Gilbert and Sullivan.

NY —NEW YORK PUBLIC LIBRARY, Performing Arts Research Center, Rodgers & Hammerstein Archives of Recorded Sound, 111 Amsterdam Ave, New York, 10023.
Holdings: Cat Phonorecords Audiotapes
Notes: Comprehensive collection of commercial recordings of American musicals. Part of this collection consists of aircheck recordings from the broadcast *Railroad Hour* series produced by Jerome Lawrence and Robert E Lee between 1948 and 1954, comprising in abridged form productions of American operetta and musical comedy from the Victor Herbert era to the post-World War II period, and featuring leading stars in the lead roles. Virtually the entire history of the American musical theatre from the turn of the century is covered. Many of the productions represented have never appeared on commercial discs. Important collection of early vaudeville and music hall performers on tape.

OH —CLEVELAND PUBLIC LIBRARY, Fine Arts and Special Collections Department, 325 Superior Ave, Cleveland, 44114. Alice N Loranth, Head
Holdings: Vols 72,070 Cat
Notes: Part of the Music Collection, which incl 37,850 scores and 20,430 pieces of sheet music incl some musical comedy scores and a sampling of popular collections, particularly older sheet music.

PA —FREE LIBRARY OF PHILADELPHIA, Sheet Music Collection, Logan Sq,

MUSICAL REVUES, COMEDIES, ETC. (cont.)

Philadelphia, 19103. Connie Jessum, Librn
Budget: ($2000)
Notes: Covers entire span of American popular expression in song and instrumental music (piano) from colonial times to the present. Incl Newland-Zeuner and Edward I Keffer Collections on loan from the Musical Fund Society. Items printed before 1825 indexed in Sonneck-Upton and Wolfe. Checklists for cover illustrations, musical shows or films and special subjects. Songs are filed by title; piano music by composer. Examples of special materials not filed in regular collection incl early Philadelphia composers and publications, national (centennial and state), patriotic ("Star-Spangled Banner"), political (Presidents), and war (1861; 1914; 1939) songs. Most of the ms materials are anonymous. Collection contains 138,360 pieces of sheet music.

PA —UNIVERSITY OF PITTSBURGH, Special Collections Dept, Curtis Theatre Collection, 363 Hillman Library, Pittsburgh, 15260. Jeanette Blanco, Cur
Holdings: Vols (4000) Cat Mss Documents Microforms Pix Slides VF
Notes: The legitimate theatre of plays, musicals and vaudeville, chiefly of New York City and Pittsburgh, from 1865, and other US, community, summer, college and foreign theatre. Incl 500,000 programs, 12,000 pictures, 300 posters, the Oliver P Merriman Scrapbooks and 300 other scrapbooks, clippings and other ephemera. Vols incl over 3000 acting editions and playscripts. Separate collections: Ralph G Allen Burlesque Skits Collection; Michael Ellis Papers; William P Halstead Theatre Collection; Kenyon Family Papers; Philip Dunning Playscripts Collection; Pittsburgh Playhouse Records; Pittsburgh Savoyards Records. Noncirculating.

TX —FORT WORTH PUBLIC LIBRARY, Arts Division, 300 Taylor St, Fort Worth, 76102. Heather Gobel, Head
Holdings: Vols (21,500) Cat Mss Phonorecords
Budget: ($26,700)
Notes: Emphasis is on older popular music and musical comedies, folk songs, operas, music composed by Fort Worth and Texas composers, and music about Texas. Sheet music has a separate index.

WI —UNIVERSITY OF WISCONSIN, MADISON, Mills Music Library, 728 State St, Madison, 53706. Arne Arneson, Music Librn
Holdings: // Uncat Mss
Notes: Tams-Witmark Collection formed part of the rental collection of the firm bearing that name. Includes piano-conductor scores (some in mss); ca 65 sets of orchestral parts for operas; 70 vocal scores of works by American composers including Herbert, Sousa, Edwards and De Koven; ca 100 sets of orchestral parts of comic operas; ca 4000 vocal scores of European operas. Restricted use.

MUSICAL THERAPY see Music Therapy

MUSICIANS

CA —CALIFORNIA STATE UNIVERSITY, LONG BEACH, Library, Dept of Special Collections & Archives, 1250 Bellflower Blvd, Long Beach, 90840. John Ahouse, Special Collections Librn
Holdings: Cat Mss Pix Phonorecords Audiotapes
Notes: Manuscripts, programs, ALS, articles, clippings and recordings pertaining to the musical careers of Wesley Kuhnle, Gerald Strang, Dane Rudhyar, Richard Buhlig, Morris Ruger and other artists active in Southern California, 1930-1960. Partially cataloged.

CA —UNIVERSITY OF CALIFORNIA, LOS ANGELES, Music Library, Schonberg Hall, Los Angeles, 90024. Stephen M Fry, Music Librn
Notes: The Philip Kahgan Collection of music films, letters, programs, and photographs important to the Southern California classical music scene. Incl 16mm "home movies" of more than thirty renowned conductors and performers during Hollywood Bowl rehearsals in the late 1930s. Incl Kahgan correspondence, memorabilia, 35 scrapbooks, etc. Also the papers of Sol Babitz (1911-1982), Los Angeles violinist and music scholar.

CA —HOOVER INSTITUTION ON WAR, REVOLUTION & PEACE, Stanford University, Stanford, 94305. Milorad M Drachkovitch, Archivist
Holdings: Mss
Notes: Papers of I J Paderewski, Polish statesman and pianist, incl correspondence, speeches, clippings, printed matter, and photographs, 1894-1941, relating to his political and musical careers. 6 1/2 ms boxes.

CT —YALE UNIVERSITY, Music Library, 98 Wall St, New Haven, 06520. Harold E Samuel, Librn
Holdings: Vols (118,000) Cat Mss Pix Phonorecords Audiotapes
Notes: Manuscript and archive collection comprising over 500 individual musical mss as well as the personal papers and musical mss of such American musicians and composers as Charles Ives, Carl Ruggles, Haratio Parker, Quincy Porter, Richard Donovan and David Stanley Smith, Leo Ornstein, Armin Loos, Duane Davidson, Alonzo Elliott, John Rosamund Johnson, Hope Leroy Baumgartner, Gustave Stoeckel, Hershy Kay, Virgil Thomson, Kurt Weill, Lotte Lenya, Lowell Mason, Parker Bailey, Henry Gilbert, Seymour Shifrin, Lehman Engel, Ernest Trow Carter, and Alec Templeton. Extensive Paul Hindemith Collection. Also ca 35,000 pieces of American sheet music, both instrumental and vocal as well as extensive holdings of 17th & 18th century American hymn books.

GA —GEORGIA STATE UNIVERSITY, William R Pullen Library, Atlanta, 30303. Leslie S Hough, Dir
Notes: Papers, etc, of Johnny Mercer, song writer, singer, composer, and publisher.

IL —NEWBERRY LIBRARY, 60 W Walton St, Chicago, 60610. Diana Haskell, Cur of Modern Mss
Holdings: Vols 800
Notes: The Bernard E Wilson Collection of books about Mozart. Incl autographs of contemporary musicians, etc.

IN —BALL STATE UNIVERSITY, Alexander M Bracken Library, Muncie, 47306. Nyal Williams, Music Librn
Holdings: Vols (30,000) Cat Mss
Budget: ($20,000)
Notes: Incl archives of International Horn Society, Tubists Universal Brotherhood Association Library, Cecil Leeson Archival Saxophone Collection, and Archives of Buescher Music Instrument Manufacturing Company.

LA —TULANE UNIVERSITY, Howard-Tilton Memorial Library, Special Collections Div, William Ransom Hogan Jazz Archive, 7001 Freret, New Orleans, 70118. Richard B Allen, Acting Cur; Alma D Williams, Assistant to the Cur
Holdings: Vols (100,000) Cat Mss Pix Slides Phonorecords Audiotapes Videotapes 16mm Films Microforms
Budget: ($90,000)
Notes: Jazz music and musicians. Outstanding collection, incl books, music scores, serials, catalogs and other archival material. Music, history, etc.
See also entry under Jazz

†MD —MARYLAND HISTORICAL SOCIETY, Library, 201 W Monument St, Baltimore, 21201.
Notes: Eubie Blake's personal and professional archive. Incl the Baltimore-born pianist, composer, and songwriter's collection of songs and instrumental pieces in mss, extensive documentation of his collaboration with Noble Sissle, Flournoy Miller, Milton Reddie, and others. The Broadway musical comedy, Shuffle Along, is represented in box office records, programs, scores and parts, photographs, and sheet music. Blake's involvement with other productions is similarly documented.

MA —BOSTON UNIVERSITY, Mugar Memorial Library, Special Collections Dept, 771 Commonwealth Ave, Boston, 02215. Howard B Gotlieb, Dir
Holdings: Cat Mss Pix
Notes: Incl personal papers and literary productions of numerous modern actors, actresses, musicians (composers and performers) of all kinds. A complete list is available.

MI —DETROIT PUBLIC LIBRARY, Music & Performing Arts Dept, 5201 Woodward, Detroit, 48202. Jean Currie Church, Cur
Holdings: Vols (1375) Cat Mss Pix
Notes: The E Azalia Hackley Collections document achievements of Blacks in the fields of music, dance, theatre, motion pictures, and broadcasting. World-wide in scope. Extensive clipping files arranged by personal names, titles and subjects. Incl musical scores (1500), recordings, and plays. No taping or other copying of recordings permitted.

MO —UNIVERSITY OF MISSOURI-COLUMBIA, Ellis Library, Language and Literature Dept, Columbia, 65201. Jeaneice Brewer, Librn
Notes: Papers, mss, music, etc of Virgil Thomson, noted music critic and musician.

NY —STATE UNIVERSITY OF NEW YORK AT ALBANY, Library, Special Collections Dept, 1400 Washington Ave, Albany, 12222. Marion P Munzer, Coordr
Notes: Music scores; recordings; reviews of Yella Pessl's music performances (1.2 linear feet; 30 volumes from her personal library). Part of the Library's German Exile Collection.
See also entry under Pessl, Yella

NY —NEW YORK PUBLIC LIBRARY, Performing Arts Research Center, Music Div, Lincoln Center, New York, 10018.
Notes: New York Pro Musica Archives, and personal papers of Noah Greenberg, founder.

NY —YONKERS PUBLIC LIBRARY, Grinton I Will Library, 1500 Central Park Ave, Yonkers, 10701. Joan W Stevenson, Head of Fine Arts Dept
Holdings: Vols (12,000) Cat
Budget: ($36,000)
Notes: Incl periodicals, 70 titles (ca 15 yr back issues); 27 vertical file drawers (18 on artists & musicians); 1230 slides; 2200 music scores; cat; sheet music, ca 1200 titles; 140 libretti; 13,000 phonograph albums; cat; 1000 cassettes. Books, scores, phonograph albums, cassettes are cataloged. Rare collection of 57 test pressings of Geraldine Farrar, some of which have never been issued.

NC —UNIVERSITY OF NORTH CAROLINA, GREENSBORO, Walter Clinton Jackson Library, Special Collections Dept, 1000 Spring Garden St, Greensboro, 27412. Emilie W Mills, Cur
Holdings: Vols (2000) Cat Mss Pix Phonorecords Microforms
Notes: The original collection of over 2000 books, mss, music scores, published and unpublished cello compositions, notes, programs, photographs and related items came from the library of Luigi Silva, cellist, teacher, and musicologist. Special strength is in recital pieces for the cello. The cello music dates from the 18th century and incl Silva's own transcriptions and arrangements for his projected edition of all the Boccherini sonatas, left incomplete at the time of his death in 1961. Silva's own history of cello techniques, also unfinished, is in the collection. Several 18th century cello sonatas were added to the collection by Silva's long-time friend and eminent cellist, Janos Scholz. A published catalog is available.

TX —SOUTHERN METHODIST UNIVERSITY, Fondren Library, McCord Theater Collection, Room 301, Dallas, 75275. Edyth Renshaw, Cur; Linda Sellers, Pub Serv
Holdings: Vols (2000) Uncat Mss Pix Slides Phonrecords
Notes: See Theatre Collections in Libraries and Museums, Gilder and Freedley (Theatre Arts, 1936). The McCord Theatre Collection

MUSICIANS (cont.)

encompasses the entire spectrum of the performing arts. The central purpose is to gather records of our regional theater before such ephemeral material is lost. Records of over two hundred early Texas theaters, some fragmentary and some relatively complete, are in the files. These records incl photographs of buildings, stagehands, orchestras, and performers. Local theatre history incl the once famous Dallas Little Theatre and the Margo Jones Theatre. The national theatre, opera, ballet, and circus archives incl pictures (some autographed), programs, posters, throw-aways, tear sheets, clippings, and letters. Our international archives are small, but we have some excellent material, eg, artifacts from Max Reinhardt's production of"The Miracle" which happened to go bankrupt in Dallas. After a few years the items were given to us. There are posters, tear sheets, souvenir programs, and other colorful items from Morris Gest and the Artef Collection. We have about 200 19th century English playbills and a few from the 18th century. There is a collection of modern English, French, and other European programs, many of them illustrated souvenir programs. Also, magazines on theater, cinema, and television (1800). Scrapbooks covering both southwest and Dallas theater, 1890s-1950s. Special Collections: artifacts and documents on puppets; masks; costume design; circus; and ballet and dance. The Harriet Bacon MacDonald Collection of over 200 photographs of musicians appearing in Dallas during the first three decades of the 20th century. Many autographed. Affiliated with Meadow Theatre of the Arts.

TX —FORT WORTH PUBLIC LIBRARY, Arts Division, 300 Taylor St, Fort Worth, 76102. Heather Gobel, Head
Notes: Photographs of concert artists appearing on Fort Worth stages (many are autographed). Nucleus collection from the estate of the late Mrs John F Lyons. Additions are made as performing artists make their appearances in this area.

AB —UNIVERSITY OF CALGARY, Libraries, Special Collections Div, 2500 University Dr, Calgary, T2N 1N4, Can. Holdings: Vols (5000) Cat Mss
Notes: The Division has extensive collections of the papers of modern Canadian authors (qv individuals), incl Hugh MacLennan, Mordecai Richler, Brian Moore, W O Mitchell, Cliff Faulknor, Christie Harris, Robert Kroetsch, Rudy Wiebe, Claude Peloquin, George Ryga, Andre Langevin, Malcolm Ross, Bruce Hutchison, John Mellor, Grant MacEwan, James Gray, Ernest Watkins, Len Peterson, Michael Cook, & Joanna Glass. The papers of musician Morris Surdin contain hundreds of Canadian Broadcasting Corporation scripts, and constitute a valuable addition to the purely literary ms collections. The Division's holdings also incl collections of scores by Canadian musicians R Murray Schafer and Bruce Mather. In addition, the records of the following Canadian publishing houses are on deposit: E C W Press, Hancock House Publishers Ltd and Coach House Press. The Division alsohouses small collections of letters and mss of Canadian poets such as Earle Birney and George Bowering as well as the archives of the literary periodicals *Tish, Imago, Ariel, Descant, Canadian Review Magazine,* and *Canadian Short Story Magazine.* The ms collections are complemented by a book collection of some 5000 vols.

ON —NATIONAL LIBRARY OF CANADA, 395 Wellington St, Ottawa, K1A 0N4, Can. Andre Preibish, Dir
Holdings: Vols 35,000
Notes: Includes 2000 pieces of Canadian sheet music (mostly 19th century imprints), 40,000 cylinders, discs, tapes; over 600 serials titles devoted to music; 200 archival collections of composers, musicians and conductors, eg papers of Healy Willan, eminent composer; Glen Gould, well-known

pianist; Sir Ernest MacMillan, conductor, director and composer. Since 1950 the Canadian imprints have been received on legal deposit. Intensive purchases aim at a comprehensive collection of Canadian music.

ON —UNIVERSITY OF OTTAWA, Morisset Library, 65 Hastey St, Ottawa, K1N 9A5, Can. Yvon Richer, University Chief Librn
Holdings: Vols (12,000)
Notes: Incl 100 periodicals, 16,000 scores and 5150 sound recordings. Scores and recordings are housed in the music department and monographs and periodicals in the Morisset Library. The collection is particularly strong in sixteenth to nineteenth century continental European music and musicology.

MUSICIANS, CANADIAN

AB —UNIVERSITY OF CALGARY, Libraries, Special Collections Div, 2500 University Dr, Calgary, T2N 1N4, Can. Holdings: Mss
Notes: The Division has extensive collections of the papers of modern Canadian authors (qv individuals), incl Hugh MacLennan, Mordecai Richler, Brian Moore, W O Mitchell, Cliff Faulknor, Christie Harris, Robert Kroetsch, Rudy Wiebe, Claude Peloquin, George Ryga, Andre Langevin, Malcolm Ross, Bruce Hutchison, John Mellor, Grant MacEwan, James Gray, Ernest Watkins, Len Peterson, Michael Cook, & Joanna Glass. The papers of musician Morris Surdin contain hundreds of Canadian Broadcasting Corporation scripts, and constitute a valuable addition to the purely literary ms collections. The Division's holdings also incl collections of scores by Canadian musicians R Murray Schafer and Bruce Mather. In addition, the records of the following Canadian publishing houses are on deposit: E C W Press, Hancock House Publishers Ltd and Coach House Press. The Division alsohouses small collections of letters and mss of Canadian poets such as Earle Birney and George Bowering as well as the archives of the literary periodicals *Tish, Imago, Ariel, Descant, Canadian Review Magazine,* and *Canadian Short Story Magazine.* The ms collections are complemented by a book collection of some 5000 vols.

ON —NATIONAL LIBRARY OF CANADA, 395 Wellington St, Ottawa, K1A 0N4, Can. Andre Preibish, Dir
Holdings: Vols 35,000
Notes: Includes 2000 pieces of Canadian sheet music (mostly 19th century imprints), 40,000 cylinders, discs, tapes; over 600 serials titles devoted to music; 200 archival collection of composers, musicians and conductors, eg papers of Healy Willan - eminent composer; Glen Gould - well known pianist; Sir Ernest MacMillan - conductor, director and composer. Since 1950 the Canadian imprints have been received on legal deposit. Intensive purchases aim at a comprehensive collection of Canadian music.

MUSICIANS AND DRUGS

CA —FITZ HUGH LUDLOW MEMORIAL LIBRARY, PO Box 99346, San Francisco, 94109. Michael R Aldrich, Exec Cur
Holdings: Vols (200) Cat Mss Pix Phonorecords Audiotapes
Notes: Collection stored. Important mail inquiries. No interlibrary lending or telephone inquiries. Collection emphasizes books, songbooks, discographies, and phonograph records relative to psychoctive drug-using musicians and their art. Incl many pictures, sheet music, and some autographed or inscribed materials, mostly from the 20th century of works by or about Milton "Mezz" Mezzrow, Billie Holiday, the Beatles, Bob Dylan, and recent drug-related rock music. About 600 record albums.

MUSICOLOGY

CA —UNIVERSITY OF CALIFORNIA, BERKELEY, Humanities-Social Sciences Libraries, Music Library, 24 Morrison Hall,

Berkeley, 94720. Michael A Keller, Head Librn
Holdings: Vols 115,000 Cat Mss Slides Microforms
Notes: The Library maintains an outstanding music reference collection. It is rich in primary source materials for research, particularly in the areas of opera, 18th-century instrumental music, music theory. Incl 30,000 sound recordings. See the following: Vincent Dukles and Minnie Elmer, *Thematic Catalogue of a Collection of 18th-Century Italian Instrumental Music in the Music Library of the University of California, Berkeley* (Univ of California Press, 1963); Alan Curtis, Musique classique francaise a Berkeley, in *Revue de Musicologie,* 56 (1970) pp 123-164. Minnie Elmer, *Autograph Manuscripts of Ernest Bloch at the University of California; Cum Notis Variorum, the Newsletter of the Music Library of the University of California* (Published 10 times annually since April 1976).

CA —CALIFORNIA STATE UNIVERSITY, HAYWARD, Library, Hayward, 94542. Melissa Rose, Dir
Holdings: Vols (15,986) Cat Phonorecords Budget: ($21,000)
Notes: The score collection covers the entire range of instrumental and vocal concert music, incl collected works of various composers, and representative collections of hymnals, folk music, musical comedy, and some popular music. Sound recordings range from ethnomusicological collections to electronic music. Emphasis is on concert music, but there is a large collection of jazz and a selective collection of popular music. Separate catalog.

CA —UNIVERSITY OF CALIFORNIA, SAN DIEGO, Central University Library, Mandeville Dept of Special Collections, La Jolla, 92093. Lynda Corey Claassen, Head
Notes: Manuscript Collection incl the correspondence and writings of composer Ernst Krenek and musicologist Peter Yates.

CA —UNIVERSITY OF CALIFORNIA, LOS ANGELES, Music Library, Schonberg Hall, Los Angeles, 90024. Stephen M Fry, Music Librn
Holdings: Vols Cat Mss Microforms
Notes: Broad scholarly scope with emphasis on musicology, incl books on music; musical scores (scholarly and practical editions) incl instrumental, vocal, chamber music with parts; periodicals; 30,000 musical recordings (disc and tape); microforms; mss. Special and archival collections.

CA —UNIVERSITY OF CALIFORNIA, RIVERSIDE, University Library, 4045 Canyon Crest Dr, Box 5900, Riverside, 92517.
Notes: The Oswald Jonas Memorial Collection holds the musicological mss, letters, biographical materials, and notebooks of Heinrich Schenker and also the papers of the late Oswald Jonas, musicologist and leading authority on the life and work of Schenker. Incl Schenker's diary; correspondence with Anthony van Hoboken, Reinhard Oppel, Moriz Violin, Eugen d'Albert, and Oswald Jonas; the proofs and mss of his published works; printed editions from his library with notes, marginalia, and critical annotations; *Urlinie* tables; and miscellanea. A guide to the collection will be published by the library.

CT —YALE UNIVERSITY, Music Library, 98 Wall St, New Haven, 06520. Harold E Samuel, Librn
Holdings: Vols (118,000) Cat Mss Pix Phonorecords Audiotapes Microforms
Notes: General reference and research materials. Performing editions. Strong in theoretical literature, opera, 17-18th century music (incl mss), J S Bach and sons in early editions and mss, Russian liturgical music (Tkaczenko Collection), hymnology, American music. Also collection of musical pictures and portraits.

†DC —CATHOLIC UNIVERSITY OF AMERICA, Music Library, Washington, 20064. Betty Libbey, Head Music Library
Holdings: Cat Microforms
Notes: A large collection to support

MUSICOLOGY (cont.)

advanced degree study. Emphasis on church music, musicology, history and criticism, instrumental and vocal music, solo music for all voices, instruments, and musical forms.

DC —LIBRARY OF CONGRESS, Music Division, Washington, 20540.
Notes: The collections of Oscar George Theodore Sonneck, first chief of the Music Division, Library of Congress.

IL —NEWBERRY LIBRARY, 60 W Walton St, Chicago, 60610. Diana Haskell, Cur of Modern Mss
Holdings: Cat Mss Microforms
Notes: 45,000 books; 55,000 scores; 100,000 pieces of sheet music. Historical musicology. Restricted use: noncirculating.

MI —UNIVERSITY OF MICHIGAN, School of Music, Music Library, Moore Bldg, Ann Arbor, 48109. Peggy Daub, Head
Holdings: Vols (90,000) Cat Mss Microforms
Notes: Reference and research materials, as well as performing editions. Rare materials (including the Stellfeld Collection) are strong in early editions of works by the sons of J S Bach and 18th-19th century opera scores, particularly French. Includes 1200 microfilms of important European and American primary sources. See L Cuyler, H David & G Sutherland: "The University of Michigan's Purchase of the Stellfeld Music Library," *MLA Notes* 12 (1954-5), 3-19. *See also* entries under Women Composers; Jacob M Coopersmith.

NY —STATE UNIVERSITY OF NEW YORK AT ALBANY, Library, Special Collections Dept, 1400 Washington Ave, Albany, 12222. Marion P Munzer, Coordr
Notes: Papers of Erwin Bodky, 1896-1958.

NY —COLUMBIA UNIVERSITY LIBRARIES, Music Library, 701 Dodge, Broadway & 116 St, New York, 10027. M Haefliger, Librn
Holdings: Vols (55,020) Cat Phonorecords Audiotapes Microforms
Notes: Strong collection of historical musicology of all periods.

NY —EASTMAN SCHOOL OF MUSIC, Sibley Music Library, 44 Swan St, Rochester, 14604. Ruth Watanabe, Librn
Holdings: Vols (360,000) Cat Mss Pix Phonorecords Microforms Music Scores
Notes: Research material for music theory, history, and performance. Incl an additional uncataloged collection of 300,000 pieces. The Sibley Music Library is a full-service branch of the University of Rochester Library System. Bibliographical lists of journals prepared twice annually. Historical items described in *University of Rochester Library Bulletin*. List of new reference work compiled quarterly.

TX —NORTH TEXAS STATE UNIVERSITY, Audio Center, Box 5188, NT Station, Denton, 76203. Morris Martin, Music Librn
Notes: Supports wide range of music curricula and research with over 100,000 volumes incl music books, periodicals, scores, sheet music of all kinds, chamber music, recordings; special collections incl the libraries of musicologists Lloyd Hibberd and Helen Hewitt, bandleader Stan Kenton, composer Don Gillis, radio stations WFAA and WBAP; archives of *Source* magaine, mss of Arnold Schoenberg, recording collections (Arturo Toscanini, Don Gillis, Duke Ellington and other jazz musicians).

VA —US NATIONAL PARK SERVICE, Harpers Ferry Center, Library, Harpers Ferry, 25425. David Nathanson, Chief Librn
Holdings: Vols 1000 Mss Microforms Pix Slides

ON —UNIVERSITY OF OTTAWA, Morisset Library, 65 Hastey St, Ottawa, K1N 9A5, Can. Yvon Richer, University Chief Librn
Holdings: Vols (12,000)
Notes: Incl 100 periodicals, 16,000 scores and 5150 sound recordings. Scores and recordings are housed in the music department and monographs and periodicals in the Morisset Library. The collection is particularly strong in sixteenth to nineteenth century continental European music and musicology.

MUSIL, ROSEMARY

AZ —ARIZONA STATE UNIVERSITY, Library, Tempe, 85287. Marilyn Wurzburger, Special Collections Librn
Holdings: Vols (108) Pix
Notes: Collection covers various aspects of Children's Theatre from 1944 through the present. Areas of emphasis incl International and National Child Drama Associations, award-winning theatres, educational programs, regional groups and prominent figures in Children's Theatre incl: Irene Vickers Baker, Isabel Burger, Virginia Lee Comer, Rita Criste, Moses Goldberg, Kenneth Graham, Aurand Harris, Paul Kozelka, George Latshaw, Rosemary Musil, Sara Spencer, Winifred Ward, Susan Zeder and Lin Wright. Publications incl newsletters, research papers, bibliographies and records of the proceedings of the Children's Theatre Association of America. 80 linear feet of scripts, documents, publications, films, tapes (oral history) programs, correspondence, photographs, working papers and clippings. Partially indexed; finding guides available.

MUSKETS see Rifles

MUSKOGEE INDIANS see Creek Indians

MUSKOKI INDIANS see Creek Indians

MUSKWAKI INDIANS see Fox Indians

MUSLIM ARCHITECTURE see Architecture, Islamic

MUSLIM ART see Art, Islamic

MUSLIMS see Civilization, Islamic; Islam

MUSQUAKIE INDIANS see Fox Indians

MUSSOLINI, BENITO

DC —GEORGETOWN UNIVERSITY, Library, Special Collections Div, 37 & O Sts NW, Washington, 20057. George M Barringer, Special Collections Librn; Nicholas B Sheetz, Mss Librn
Holdings: Cat
Notes: A microfilm of the papers of Dino Grandi (1895-), Conte di Mordano and former Italian minister of foreign affairs and of justice; and ambassador to Great Britain. Grandi played an important role in the Mussolini government and, as president of the Grand Council, presented the resolution removing Mussolini from power in July, 1943.

MUTAGENESIS

AR —NATIONAL CENTER FOR TOXICOLOGICAL RESEARCH, Library, Jefferson, 72079. Susan Laney-Sheehan, Supvr Librn
Holdings: Vols (15,000) Cat Mss Slides Audiotapes 16mm Films Microforms
Notes: Incl (860) journal titles, (230) current subscriptions.

NC —NATIONAL INSTITUTE OF ENVIRONMENTAL HEALTH SCIENCES, Library, PO Box 12233, Research Triangle Park, 27709. W Davenport Robertson, Head Librn
Holdings: Vols (9000) Cat Mss Audiotapes Microforms
Notes: The subject, "environmental health," incl toxicology, carcinogenesis, pharmacology, genetics, biophysics, and biochemistry. Special emphasis is placed on cell biology. The collection does not incl works on pollution control or law. In addition to the collection there are some 2500 vols in the laboratories. The library has an automated catalog.

MUTATION (BIOLOGY) see Evolution; Mutagenesis

MUTEFERRIKA, IBRAHIM

IN —INDIANA UNIVERSITY, Lilly Library, Seventh St, Bloomington, 47405. William R Cagle, Librn
Holdings: Vols 28 // Cat
Notes: One example of each of 28 books printed by Ibrahim Müteferrika, the first Turkish printer.

MUTUAL INSURANCE see Insurance

MUYBRIDGE, EADWEARD

MD —UNIVERSITY OF MARYLAND, BALTIMORE COUNTY, Library and Gallery, Edward L Bafford Photography Collection, 5401 Wilkens Ave, Baltimore, 21228. Tom Beck, Cur
Holdings: Pix
Notes: The Edward L Bafford Photography Collection contains more than 200,000 images, negatives, cameras and books representing the entire history and aesthetics of photography. Incl are photographs by Eadweard Muybridge.
See also entry under Photographs - Collections.

NY —INTERNATIONAL MUSEUM OF PHOTOGRAPHY AT GEORGE EASTMAN HOUSE, Archives, 900 East Ave, Rochester, 14607. Rachel Stuhlman, Head Librn
Holdings: Vols (30,000) Cat Mss Microforms
Budget: ($104,000)
Notes: History, aesthetics and technology of photography and cinematography, incl the Gabriel Cromer, Josef Maria Eder, Alden Scott Boyer, Louis Walton Sipley/3M Collections, and the James Card Collection from 1893. Covers photographic, especially cinematographic history; also hundreds of negatives of Edward Muybridge as well as his notebooks. Incl 450,000 pictures and slides. Also the Lewis Hine Collection of social documentary photography.

MYASTHENIA GRAVIS

NY —CORNELL UNIVERSITY MEDICAL COLLEGE, Samuel J Wood Library, 1300 York Ave, New York, 10021. Erich Meyerhoff, Dir
Holdings: Vols (9000) Cat Films
Notes: All aspects of muscle diseases.

NY —MUSCULAR DYSTROPHY ASSOCIATION, 810 Seventh Ave, New York, 10019. Marianthe Pappas, Librn
Holdings: Vols 8770 Cat
Budget: $55,000
Notes: All phases of muscular diseases. Incl some films.

MYCOLOGY

†IL —NORTHWESTERN UNIVERSITY, Robert E Machol Library, Leverone Hall, Evanson, 60201.
Notes: Espec 18th-19th century illustrated works. Early works on mushrooms, and popular texts in 30 languages.

IA —IOWA STATE UNIVERSITY, Library, Ames, 50011. Warren B Kuhn, Dean of Library Services
Holdings: Cat Mss
Notes: Specific strengths: botanical taxonomy, ferns, mycology and plant pathology. Extensive serial holdings.

MA —UNIVERSITY OF MASSACHUSETTS AT AMHERST, Library, Amherst, 01003. Siegfried Feller, Assoc Dir for Collection Development
Holdings: Cat
Notes: Botanical taxonomy, physiology, pathology and mycology.

MA —HARVARD UNIVERSITY LIBRARY, Botanical Museum Library, Cambridge, 02138.
Holdings: Vols (2400) Mss Pix
Notes: The Tina and Gordon Wisson Ethnomycological Collection, one of the most important modern collections, acquired as an adjunct to the Museum's Economic Botany Library of Oakes Ames. From 15th to 20th century, it deals with hallucinogenic mushrooms in art, religion, and folklore; chemistry, pharmacology, linguistics, archaeological artifacts of Mexico, Guatemala, India, Japan, China, etc. Personal papers, etc.

MYCOLOGY (cont.)

MI —UNIVERSITY OF MICHIGAN, Herbarium Library, University Herbarium, 2003 N University Bldg, Ann Arbor, 48109. Robert L Shaffer, Dir, Herbarium
Holdings: Vols (22,000) Cat Mss Maps Microforms
Notes: Systematic Botany including floristics, revisions and monographs in all groups of plants. Collection incl maps, mss (fieldbooks, correspondence, etc), photographs, microfiches, and approx 100,000 reprints that are not officially part of the University Library. These are indexed and are available to qualified scholars. Incl botanical libraries of Parke, Davis & Co, Harley H Bartlett, Bruce Fink (lichens), Howard A Kelly (mycology).

†NH —UNIVERSITY OF NEW HAMPSHIRE, Biological Science Library, Kendall Hall, Durham, 03824. Lloyd Heldgard, Librn
Holdings: Vols (45,000)

†NC —UNIVERSITY OF NORTH CAROLINA, CHAPEL HILL, Department of Botany Library, 301 Coker Hall 010-A, Chapel Hill, 27514. William R Burk, Botany Librn
Notes: The mycology collection incl some 6000 pamphlets. It contains papers of the following scientists: William C Coker, John N Couch, Lindsay F Olive, mycologists; also, Victor A Greulach, plant pathologist. The mycology catalog is in preparation (1983), and will provide author, title, and subject access.

OH —LLOYD LIBRARY & MUSEUM, 917 Plum St, Cincinnati, 45202. John B Griggs, Librn
Notes: Large collection of books, journals and research reports on mycology. Incl all of Curtis Gates Lloyd's writings.

PA —PENNSYLVANIA STATE UNIVERSITY, Fred Lewis Pattee Library, Life Sciences Library, University Park, 16802. Keith Roe, Head
Notes: This collection is strong in periodical runs, particularly European learned societies and agriculture. In contains extensive collections of Experiment Station publications and has developed specialties in Mycology and Fusaria. There is also a special collection of 1105 glass slides on early Pennsylvania lumbering.

WA —WASHINGTON STATE UNIVERSITY, Owen Science & Engineering Library, Pullman, 99164. Elizabeth P Roberts, Head
Holdings: Vols 8900 Cat Microforms
Notes: Collection of books and journals on mycology, plant pathology, and related subjects. In addition, there are 63,800 reprints of articles accessible through author and title.

WI —US FOREST SERVICE, Forest Products Laboratory Library, Box 5130, Madison, 53705. Roger Schurmer, Librn; Dr Regis Miller, Librn; Dr Harold H Burdsall, Jr, Librn
Notes: 30,000 specimens wood-decay fungi; 15,000 cultures wood-decay fungi.

ON —AGRICULTURE CANADA, Plant Research Library, Research Branch, Central Experimental Farm 49, Ottawa, K1A 0C6, Can. Mrs E Gavora, Librn
Holdings: Vols (10,500) Cat Maps Microforms
Notes: One of the most extensive botanical collections in Canada, especially in the taxonomy of higher plants and fungi. Contains many of the basic works from the starting point of botany in 1753 to date. Major botanical works of Linnaeus and others, covering flora of land areas of most parts of the world.

ON —AGRICULTURE CANADA, Library Division, Plant Research Library, 49 Central Experimental Farm Bldg, Ottawa, K1A 0C6, Can. Eva Gavora, Plant Research Librn
Holdings: (15,000) Items
Notes: Emphasis on flora of North America.

ON —ONTARIO MINISTRY OF HEALTH, Laboratory Services Branch, Library, Box 9000, Terminal A, Toronto, M5W 1R5, Can.

Doris A Standing, Librn
Holdings: Vols (4000) Cat
Budget: ($50,000)
Notes: Medical laboratory technology and related subjects: microbiology; environmental bacteriology (limited to testing of milk, food and water for bacterial quality, etc); biological chemistry (clinical); mycology; parasitology; virology; immunology; serology; automated laboratory techniques; biohazard control.

MYCOPLASMA

OH —OHIO AGRICULTURAL RESEARCH & DEVELOPMENT CENTER, Dept of Plant Pathology, Madison Ave, Wooster, 44691. Richard M Ritter
Holdings: Vols 2000 Papers Journal Reprints
Notes: Maize viruses and corn stunt. The Maize Virus Information Service (Mavis) was started in 1971 and aims to become the world center for this literature. The collection aims to be exhaustive for all true virus diseases affecting the maize plant (corn) and for corn stunt, which is caused by a mycoplasma, but was once thought to be caused by a virus. A preliminary list (500 refs) was published in 1971, with yearly supplements.

MYERS, JEROME

DE —DELAWARE ART MUSEUM, Library, 2301 Kentmere Pkwy, Wilmington, 19806. Anne Hoslam, Librn
Holdings: Vols (25,000) Cat Mss
Notes: The collection is rich in the following subjects: Howard Pyle and his pupils; John Sloan and the eight; history of the book and printing; and English and American illustrated books. There is also a section on contemporary photography. Archival material on Albert Mumford Lindsay, Jerome Myers, Everett Shinn, Gayle Porter Hoskins, Frank Schoonover

MYODYNAMICS

NY —UNIVERSITY OF ROCHESTER, School of Medicine and Dentistry, Edward G Miner Library, 601 Elmwood Ave, Rochester, 14642. Lucretia McClure, Medical Librn; Janet Brady Berk, History of Medicine Librn
Holdings: Slides
Notes: Very rare historical collection of some 300 glass slides, most of which relate to human gait, the foot, footwear, and myodynamics.

MYOSITIS see Muscles—Diseases

MYOTONIA

NY —CORNELL UNIVERSITY MEDICAL COLLEGE, Samuel J Wood Library, 1300 York Ave, New York, 10021. Erich Meyerhoff, Dir
Holdings: Vols (9000) Cat Films
Notes: All aspects of muscle diseases.

NY —MUSCULAR DYSTROPHY ASSOCIATION, 810 Seventh Ave, New York, 10019. Marianthe Pappas, Librn
Holdings: Vols 8770 Cat
Budget: $55,000
Notes: All phases of muscular diseases. Incl some films.

MYRER, ANTON

MA —BOSTON UNIVERSITY, Mugar Memorial Library, Special Collections Dept, 771 Commonwealth Ave, Boston, 02215. Howard B Gotlieb, Dir
Holdings: Cat Mss

MYSTERY STORIES see Adventure and Adventurers; Detective and Mystery Stories

MYSTICAL THEOLOGY see Mysticism

MYSTICISM

CA —ROSICRUCIAN ORDER, AMORC, Research Library, Rosicrucian Park, San

Jose, 95191. Clara Campbell, Librn
Holdings: Cat
Notes: Collection incl materials on Rosicrucians, ancient Egyptian history, parapsychology and mysticism. No interlibrary loans.

CT —YALE UNIVERSITY, Box 1603A, Yale Station, New Haven, 06520.

IL —UNIVERSITY OF ILLINOIS, URBANA/CHAMPAIGN, Library, University Archives, 19 Library, 1408 W Gregory Drive, Urbana, 61801. Maynard Brichford, University Archivist
Holdings: Vols (5000) Cat
Budget: ($7000)
Notes: The Mandeville Collection in Parapsychology and Occult Sciences. Titles in the Merten J Mandeville Collection are purchased by funds from an endowment provided specifically for the collection on its establishment in 1966 by Merten J Mandeville, Professor Emeritus of Management, who donated 400 vols from his personal library as the nucleus of the collection. There are currently about 5000 titles in the collection, supplemented by related materials in the general collection. Topics include astrology, extrasensory perception, yoga, magic, satanism, faith healing, hypnosis, Eastern religions, witchcraft, fortune telling, reincarnation, flying saucers, ghosts, dreams, numerology, graphology, and mysticism. Biographies and reference books as a part of the collection as are journals devoted to the scientific study of parapsychology.

IA —GRAND LODGE OF IOWA, AF & AM Iowa Masonic Library, 813 First Ave SE, Cedar Rapids, 52406. Tom Eggleston, Librn
Holdings: Vols 135 // Cat
Notes: The Arthur E Waite Collection of Mysticism, Freemasonry, Alchemy. No photocopying.

MI —WESTERN MICHIGAN UNIVERSITY, Dwight B Waldo Library, Institute of Cistercian Studies Library, Kalamazoo, 49008. Beatrice H Beck, Librn
Notes: The Abbott Obrecht Collection of mss, incunabula, and other books from the Cistercian Abbey of Gethsemane at Trappist, Kentucky. On indefinite loan (1976).

NY —PARAPSYCHOLOGY FOUNDATION, Eileen J Garrett Library, 228 E 71st St, New York, 10021. Wayne Norman, Librn
Holdings: Vols (9300) Cat
Notes: One of the largest libraries on parapsychology. Main emphasis is on the literature of contemporary parapsychology; also a strong collection on the history of parapsychology (early spiritualism, mysticism, relevant philosophical works, etc). Rare book collection incl early rare books and periodicals on psychical research and psychical phenomena. Receives about 100 titles of periodicals and binds the more significant titles. The library maintains its own periodicals index to parapsychological literature, dating from 1966. Main emphasis literature is on experimental parapsychology, or those publications that approach the subject with an objective and/or analytic point of view.

NC —DUKE UNIVERSITY, Divinity School Library, Durham, 27706. Donn Michael Farris, Librn
Holdings: Vols (225,000)
Notes: Special collections and subject emphases in this library include: Archaeology, Egyptian; Archaeology, Middle Eastern; Art, Jewish; Bible; Bible-New Testament; Bible-Symbolism; Church Architecture; Egyptology; Fathers of the Church; Society of Friends; Great Britain-Religion-Methodism and Methodist Church; Hymns and Hymnals; Jansenists and Jansenism; Judaica; Mediaeval Christian Mysticism; Methodism and Methodist Church; Methodist Episcopal Church; Methodist Episcopal Church, South; Reformation; Religion-US-History; Rural Church; Theology-Great Britain-17th Century; Theology-Great Britain-18th Century; United Methodist Church; US-Church History; John Wesley.

PA —HAVERFORD COLLEGE, Magill Library, Quaker Collection, Haverford,

MYSTICISM (cont.)

19041. Edwin B Bonner, Librn & Cur
Holdings: Vols (32,000) Cat Mss Maps Pix Phonorecords Audiotapes Microforms
Notes: Incl material about Society of Friends from inception in England, 1650, to the present. Formats incl periodicals, diaries, documents of individual Friends, families, Quaker Meetings and institutions, incl archives of Haverford College. Emphases on American Indians, antislavery, women, minorities, the Rufus M Jones Mysticism collection, Quaker fiction, and Delaware Valley, Pennsylvania.

RI —BROWN UNIVERSITY, John Hay Library, 20 Prospect St, Providence, 02912. Mark N Brown, Cur Mss
Holdings: Vols (900) // Mss
Notes: John William Graham Collection of Literature of Psychic Science; 350 predominantly late 19th and early 20th century books dealing with alchemy, black magic, dreams, demonology, church history, mysticism, mediumship, physical and somatic types of psychic experience. Collection described in *Index to Psychic Science* compiled by S R Morgan (Swarthmore, 1950). Also, the Damon Collection of Occult and Visionary Literature; 550 vols devoted to the development of western mysticism with particular emphasis on American and British thought, incl texts on alchemy, black magic, esoteric church history, dream interpretations, mysticism, witchcraft, the Kabbalah, and visionary testaments and manifestations of all types printed during the 16th to 20th centuries; and the Samuel Wyllys Papers; 125 mss, transcripts, and photocopies of legal and government papers relating to Indianaffairs, colonial wars, civil and criminal cases, and the witchcraft trials of 1692-1693. Partially cataloged.

TX —OBLATE SCHOOL OF THEOLOGY, Library, 285 Oblate Dr, San Antonio, 78216. James Maney, Libr Dir
Holdings: Vols (22,000) Cat
Budget: ($15,500)

VA —ASSOCIATION FOR RESEARCH & ENLIGHTENMENT, Library, 67 & Atlantic Avenue, PO Box 595, Virginia Beach, 23451. Stephen Jordan, Library Mgr
Holdings: Vols (3000) Cat
Notes: Emphasis on Christian, Buddhist, Hindu religions, mysticism, comparative religion, psychological approach to biofeedback, autogenics, etc.

MYTHOLOGY

CA —LOS ANGELES PUBLIC LIBRARY, Philosophy & Religion Dept, 630 W Fifth St, Los Angeles, 90071. Marilyn C Wherley, Librn
Holdings: Vols 500 Cat
Budget: ($60,000)
Notes: Comprehensive coverage of popular and scholarly works on myths, legends, superstitions and primitive religions.

†CA —UNIVERSITY OF CALIFORNIA LOS ANGELES, Center for the Study of Comparative Folklore and Mythology, Los Angeles, 90024.
Notes: Archive, consisting of nearly 500,000 entries and cross-references, developed by Prof Wayland D Hand over the past 40 years as part of his monumental *Dictionary of American Popular Beliefs and Superstitions*. Entries have been drawn from both field collections and from printed and published sources. Analytical data stress both the historical component and the comparative approach. Of special interest is the emphasis on magical medicine, although natural and botanical medicine are also well represented.

CA —FITZ HUGH LUDLOW MEMORIAL LIBRARY, PO Box 99346, San Francisco, 94109. Michael R Aldrich, Exec Cur
Holdings: Vols Cat Mss Maps Pix Slides Phonorecords Audiotapes Videotapes
Notes: Collection stored. Important mail inquiries only. No interlibrary lending or telephone queries. Index to hundreds of drug-related illustrations, filed in several binders by topic (Cannabis, Hallucinogens, Cocaine, Music, etc). We have photostats of about 500 of the best illustrations available to researchers and writers as a graphics archive; copyright and reproduction permission must however be obtained by the user of publisher, in addition to a nominal fee (per illustration) paid to the Library. We also collect original art works, artifacts, paraphernalia, comic books, newspaper illustrations, and drug advertisements relating to psychoactive drug use and abuse. In addition we have available many illustrations pertinent to mythology (ancient and modern) peripherally related to drug history and folklore.

IL —UNIVERSITY OF ILLINOIS, URBANA/CHAMPAIGN, Library, University Archives, 19 Library, 1408 W Gregory Drive, Urbana, 61801. Maynard Brichford, University Archivist
Holdings: Vols 30,000 Cat
Notes: The School Collection consists of fiction and nonfiction for children and young adults. Included are children's classics, easy readers, picture books, folk literature and mythology. In addition to the Newbery and Caldecott winners, national award-winning books which encompass the areas of literature, science and the social sciences are collected. Current representative children's magazines are also part of the collection. A reference collection relevant to the study of children's literature is maintained. An exellent representation of historical children's literature dating back to 1800 is part of the School Collection. Special reprint collections are *Classics of Children's Literature 1621-1932* and the *Osborne Collection of Early Children's Books*. Children's materials from 1600-1800 are in the Rare Book Room.

NY —UNITED LODGE OF THEOSOPHISTS LIBRARY, 347 E 72 St, New York, 10021.
Notes: Ancient and modern philosophy and psychology; comparative religion and mythology; parapsychology; reincarnation research in science and religion.

MYTHOLOGY, GERMANIC

NY —CORNELL UNIVERSITY LIBRARIES, John M Olin Library, Fiske Icelandic Collection, Ithaca, 14853. Louis A Pitschmann, Librn
Holdings: Vols (34,000) Cat Mss Maps Pix Microforms
Budget: ($3000)
Notes: Collection aims at comprehensive coverage of Iceland in all aspects with major emphasis on the literature and language (both old and modern). Such subjects as runology, Scandinavian and Germanic mythology, early Norwegian history and history of the Viking period and of the Norse explorations of Greenland and North America are also well represented. For printed catalogs of the Collection's holdings see Downs 3608, 3609. Records for approximately 40 percent of the collection have been entered into OCLC and RLIN.

MYTHOLOGY, GREEK

DC —HARVARD UNIVERSITY, Center for Hellenic Studies Library, 3100 Whitehaven St NW, Washington, 20008. Jeno Platthy, Librn
Holdings: Vols (42,000) Cat Maps
Budget: ($76,824)
Notes: In addition to a large collection of editions of ancient Greek authors, the library is well equipped to cover every aspect of ancient Greek civilization from prehistoric times to about AD 200. The subject fields covered include epigraphy, paleography, papyrology, history, literature, philosophy, religion, mythology, archaeology and art. A small collection of works on Patristics as well as all important Latin authors complete the Center's holdings.

MYTHOLOGY, NORSE

NY —CORNELL UNIVERSITY LIBRARIES, John M Olin Library, Fiske Icelandic Collection, Ithaca, 14853. Louis A Pitschmann, Librn
Holdings: Vols (34,000) Cat Mss Maps Pix Microforms
Budget: ($3000)
Notes: Collection aims at comprehensive coverage of Iceland in all aspects with major emphasis on the literature and language (both old and modern). Such subjects as runology, Scandinavian and Germanic mythology, early Norwegian history and history of the Viking period and of the Norse explorations of Greenland and North America are also well represented. For printed catalogs of the Collection's holdings see Downs 3608, 3609. Records for approximately 40 percent of the collection have been entered into OCLC and RLIN.

MYTHS see Mythology

MYTINGER, DEWITT

AZ —NORTHERN ARIZONA UNIVERSITY, Special Collection Library, CU Box 6022, Flagstaff, 86011. Peter M Whiteley, Coordr/Archivist; William Mullane, Librn
Notes: Dewitt Mytinger Collection; incl instrumental sheet music for all band instruments used by Mytinger when he was a US Army band leader. Contains good examples of 20th century popular music styles.

N

NABOKOV, VLADIMIR

MO —WASHINGTON UNIVERSITY, John
M Olin Library, Campus Box 1061, St Louis,
63130.
Notes: Extensive collection of printed
material.

NV —UNIVERSITY OF NEVADA, RENO,
University Library, Special Collections Dept,
Reno, 89557. Robert E Blesse, Head
Holdings: Vols (221) Cat Other appearances
380 Cat
Notes: Includes individual works by author
in all editions including translations; also
prefaces, introductions, published
correspondence, appearances in anthologies,
periodicals, etc. Bibliographical research
collection, part of Modern Authors
Collection.

†TX —UNIVERSITY OF TEXAS
LIBRARIES, General Libraries, Humanities
Research Center, PO Box 7219, Austin,
78712. John Chalmers, Librn
Notes: A collection of the works of Vladimir
Nabokov. Contains almost 500 items, incl
his English and Russian language books,
translations, periodicals and publications
about him. Also incl some of his
entomological writings. Nabokov was an
authority on certain species of butterflies.

NACHMANSOHN, DAVID

†CT —YALE UNIVERSITY, Medical Library,
333 Cedar St, New Haven, 06520.
Notes: Strong neurochemistry collection, incl
the David Nachmansohn collection of seven
volumes of collected reprints of various
authors, many Nachmansohn's own.

NACHOD, HANS

TX —NORTH TEXAS STATE UNIVERSITY,
Audio Center, Box 5188, NT Station,
Denton, 76203. Morris Martin, Music Librn
Notes: Arnold Schoenberg manuscripts
(compositions, sketches, exercises,
arrangements) and correspondence with
Hans Nachod covering almost 50 years. See
Newlin Dika, "The Schoenberg-Nachod
Collection: a Preliminary Report," in *Musical
Quarterly*, vol 54 (1968), pp. 31-46;
Kimmey, John A, Jr *The Arnold
Schoenberg-Hans Nachod Collection*
(Detroit Studies in Music Bibliography, No.
41) Detroit: Information Coordinators, 1979.

NADOWESSIOUX INDIANS see Dakota Indians

NAGASAKI, JAPAN

OH —WILMINGTON COLLEGE, Peace
Resource Center, Hiroshima/Nagasaki
Memorial Collection, Pyle Center Box 1183,
Wilmington, 45177. Helen Redding, Librn
Notes: The Hiroshima/Nagasaki Memorial
Collection is nationally known and respected
as a major source of information, films, slides
and audiotapes about the atomic bombings of
Hiroshima and Nagasaki. An especially
signifciant part of the Collection is a
continually growing library in Japanese
currently numbering more than 500 vols.
Here are recorded eyewitness account of the
atomic bombings, as well as details of what
life has been like in the intervening years for
the thousands of survivors (*hibakusha*). Also
incl are books of poetry, photo books,
juvenile literature, and books dealing with
medical information, peace research, peace
education, nuclear power, etc. All books in
the Hiroshima/Nagasaki Memorial
Collection are available for interlibrary loan.
An *Annotated Bibliography of Japanese A-
Bomb Literature* may be purchased or
borrowed from the PRC. In it are
briefsummaries in English of each book in
the Collection.

NAGEL, ERNEST

†NY —COLUMBIA UNIVERSITY
LIBRARIES, Butler Library, Rare Book and
Manuscript Library, 535 W 114 St, New
York, 10027.
Notes: Papers, mss, etc.

NAGRIN, DANIEL, 1917-

CA —UNIVERSITY OF CALIFORNIA, LOS
ANGELES, Research Library, Dept of
Special Collections, 405 Hilgard Ave, Los
Angeles, 90024. Edward Shreeves,
Chairman, Bibliographers Group; David S
Zeidberg, Head
Notes: 1 linear foot of ephemera
documenting his career as a dancer and
choreographer.

NAHUATL LANGUAGE see Aztec Language

NAIMAN, MAX R.

IL —CHICAGO HISTORICAL SOCIETY,
Library, Clark St at North Ave, Chicago,
60614. Archie Motley, Manuscript Librn
Notes: Papers of: Emmet Dedmon,
newspaper editor; Richard J Finnegan,
newspaper editor; Rev Andres M Greeley,
sociologist and author; attorney and civil
liberties activist Pearl Hart; Robert J
Havighurst, educator; social activist John
Kearney; Kenesaw Mountain Landis, Federal
Judge and first Commissioner of Baseball;
Judge David F Matchett; Ivan Molek,
Slovenian language publisher in Chicago;
Max R Naiman, Communist Party activist;
Ralph G Newman, book and autograph
dealer and manuscript appraiser; Otto L
Schmidt, physician and President of the
Chicago and Illinois State Historical
Societites; and Dempsey Travis, black
mortgage banker.

NAIPALI LANGUAGE see Nepali Language and Literature

NAISMITH, JAMES

MA —NAISMITH MEMORIAL
BASKETBALL HALL OF FAME, Edward
J & Gena G Hickox Library, 460 Alden St,
Box 175, Springfield, 01109. June Harrison
Steitz, Librn
Holdings: Vols 2476 Cat Mss Pix
Phonorecords 16mm Films
Budget: $2000
Notes: Incl 48 VF drawers of reports,
documents, programs, pressbooks, etc; 20 VF
drawers of pictures and photographs;
complete sets of basketball rule books, NBA
and ABA guides, Converse Basketball
Yearbooks; minutes of NABC conventions;
and complete basketball library of William G
Mokray.

MA —SPRINGFIELD COLLEGE LIBRARY,
Babson Library, Springfield, 01109. Henry
Dutcher, Reference Librn
Holdings: Vols (130,000) Cat
Budget: ($65,000)

NAIVE PAINTING see Painting, Naive

NAMES, BUSINESS OR TRADE see Business Names

NAMES, CHRISTIAN see Names, Personal

NAMES, GEOGRAPHICAL

IL —NEWBERRY LIBRARY, 60 W Walton
St, Chicago, 60610. Diana Haskell, Cur of
Modern Mss
Holdings: Cat
Notes: Gazetteers and place name literature,
Western Europe and the Americas.

IL —RAND MCNALLY LIBRARY, Box
7600, Chicago, 60680. Philip L Forstall,
Librn
Holdings: Cat Maps
Notes: Place names (toponomy).

MI —UNIVERSITY OF MICHIGAN, Harlan
Hatcher Graduate Library, Map Room, Ann
Arbor, 48109. James O Minton, Map Librn
Notes: The collection consists of approx 300,
000 sheet maps incl maps and charts
received on deposit from the US Geological
Survey, Defense Mapping Agency, and the
National Ocean Service. The collection also
incl approx 5000 reference volumes related
to cartography, surveying, and mapping, with
emphasis on place-name literature
(gazetteers, dictionaries), books on how to
use and interpret maps, carto-bibliographies,
and state (provincial, etc), regional, national,
and international atlases. The collection is
strongest geographically in materials of
Michigan, Midwest, Anglo-America, and
Europe; chronologically, 1850-date; and
thematically, in topographic and geologic
maps, although all subjects are collected. The
collection maintains a separate catalog of
holdings. Reference volumes are fully
cataloged and classified.

NE NEBRASKA STATE HISTORICAL
SOCIETY, Archives, 1500 R St, Box 82554,
Lincoln, 68501. James E Potter, State
Archivist
Holdings: Cat Mss Maps Pix Slides
Microforms
Notes: Incl the ms material of John T Link
on research into Nebraska place-names.

PA —FREE LIBRARY OF PHILADELPHIA,
Social Science and History Dept, Map
Collection, Logan Sq, Philadelphia, 19103.
Holdings: Vols (30,000) Cat Mss Maps
Notes: Map collection incl atlases, maps,
pamphlets, and aerial views. Incl a
representative collection of early atlases
(1534-1827). The collection emphasizes the
Philadelphia, Pennsylvania and Delaware
Valley areas in particular and the eastern
seaboard in general. Low altitude oblique
aerial photographs have been transferred to
the Print and Picture Dept; high altitude
vertical aerial photographs have been
retained; some vols and pamphlets
reassigned within the Social Science and
History Dept.

TX —EAST TEXAS STATE UNIVERSITY,
James G Gee Library, Special Collections
Dept, East Texas Station, Commerce, 75428.
James Conrad, Dept Head
Holdings: Vols (3500) Cat Mss Pix Slides
Notes: The books on Black Literature (with
the exception of those on Texas folklore)
and Slavery in the US have been transferred
to the general stack area of the library;
however, our collection of county histories
of Texas, which is still housed in the Special
Collections, continues to grow. In addition,
we have acquired sizable collections of books
on Texas, folklore and Texas placenames;
and World War II posters. Another new area
is printing arts in Texas. There is a separate
dictionary card catalog for the book
collection in the Special Collections
Department.

NAMES, PERSONAL

CA —LOS ANGELES PUBLIC LIBRARY,
Genealogy & Local History Dept, 630 W
5th St, Los Angeles, 90071. Lucile Lipman,
Sr Librn
Holdings: Vols (55,000) Cat Mss Maps Pix
Microforms
Budget: ($16,000)
Notes: Extensive onomastics collection with
emphasis on North American and Western
European names.

DE —HISTORICAL SOCIETY OF
DELAWARE, Library, 505 Market St Mall,
Wilmington, 19801. Barbara E Benson,
Library Dir
Holdings: Vols 600 Cat Mss Microforms
Notes: Printed works fully cataloged.
Emphasis on Delaware families, but
supporting material from adjacent states.
Delaware census material on microfilm; 8
linear feet of manuscript genealogical notes
and charts; extensive surname file (10,000
entries); good run of *New England Historical
and Genealogical Register*.

DC —LIBRARY OF CONGRESS,
Washington, 20540.
Holdings: Vols (25,000) Cat
Notes: Local History and Genealogy Room
has reference collection of 5000 vols (1800
on genealogy). General collections contain
25,000 vols on US and European genealogy.
Additional large collection of American

NAMES, PERSONAL (cont.)

telephone and city directories. Card files in LH&G Room include: Family Name index; Analytical Surname Index; US Biographical Index; Key to Rider's American Genealogical-Biographical Index; Author Catalog of Genealogy, Heraldry, and Local History. Family Name Index was published in two vols in 1972 by Magna Carta Book Company as *Genealogies in the Library of Congress, A Bibliography*; 1977 supplement covers 3000 additional titles through July 1976.

FL —ORLANDO PUBLIC LIBRARY, Local History & Genealogy Dept, 100 Block of Central Ave, Orlando, 32806. Eileen B Willis, Librn
Holdings: Vols 11,000 Cat Maps Microforms
Budget: $8000
Notes: The

NY —NEW YORK PUBLIC LIBRARY, Local History and Genealogy Div, Fifth Ave & 42 St, New York, 10018. Gunther E Pohl, Chief
Holdings: Vols (160,000) Cat
Budget: ($38,548)
Notes: Origin and meaning of forenames and surnames. Library has published a bibliography of its holdings: Elsdon C Smith, *Personal Names: An Annotated Bibliography*, 1952.

NAMIBIA

CA —HOOVER INSTITUTION ON WAR, REVOLUTION & PEACE, Stanford University, Stanford, 94305. Milorad M Drachkovitch, Archivist
Notes: Collection of leaflets, newsletters, pamphlets, and other ephemera of various political action groups and other organizations, 1969-1974, relating to political and economic developments in southern African countries, incl Angola, Mozambique, Rhodesia (Zimbabwe), Union of South Africa, and South West Africa (Namibia). 5 ms boxes.

DC —HOWARD UNIVERSITY, Moorland-Spingarn Research Center, 500 Howard Place NW, Washington, 20059. Clifford L Muse, Jr, Acting Dir

NANAI DIALECT see Goldian Dialect

NAPIER, SIR ROBERT

CA —UNIVERSITY OF CALIFORNIA, LOS ANGELES, Research Library, Dept of Special Collections, 405 Hilgard Ave, Los Angeles, 90024. Edward Shreeves, Chairman, Bibliographers Group; David S Zeidberg, Head
Holdings: Pix
Notes: 73 photographs of the British Expeditionary Force in Abyssinia, 1867-1868, under General Sir Robert Napier.

NAPOLEON AND NAPOLEONIC PERIOD

CA —UNIVERSITY OF CALIFORNIA, LOS ANGELES, Research Library, Dept of Special Collections, 405 Hilgard Ave, Los Angeles, 90024. Edward Shreeves, Chairman, Bibliographers Group; David S Zeidberg, Head
Notes: 8.5 linear feet of Italian broadsides, ca 1676-1821, primarily from the period of Napoleonic domination of Italy. Texts incl edicts, decrees, proclamations, etc, of church, military, and local governments.

CT —YALE UNIVERSITY, Box 1603A, Yale Station, New Haven, 06520.

CT —UNIVERSITY OF CONNECTICUT, Library, Storrs, 06268. R H Schimmelpfeng, Dir of Special Collections
Holdings: Cat
Notes: Collection of newspapers and periodicals formerly belonging to the Duque de T'Serclaes. Ranging from the 17th century through the 20th, the bulk of titles are from 1800-1840, covering the Napoleonic period and the Latin American wars of independence.

DE —HAGLEY MUSEUM AND LIBRARY, Eleutherian Mills-Hagley Foundation Inc,

PO Box 3630, Greenville, 19807. Richmond D Williams, Dir; Heddy A Richter, Imprints Librn
Holdings: Vols 6000 Pamphlets
Notes: The French history collection is especially good in pamphlets of the Revolutionary and Napoleonic periods; French 18th Century economic theory, especially Physiocracy; and the works of or concerning P S du Pont de Nemours.

FL —FLORIDA STATE UNIVERSITY, Robert Manning Strozier Library, Special Collections Dept, Tallahassee, 32306. Opal M Free, Head, Special Collections
Holdings: Vols (12,616) Cat Mss Maps Pix Microforms
Notes: One of the most extensive collections in this period in the US. Several hundred volumes are held in the US only in this collection. See Donald D Horward, *The French Revolution and Napoleonic Collection at Florida State University: A Bibliographical Guide* (Tallahassee: Friends of Florida State Univ, 1973). (A second vol is expected early in 1984.) No photocopying.

IL —DE PAUL UNIVERSITY, Library, 2323 N Seminary, Chicago, 60614. Kathryn De Graff, Special Collections Librn
Holdings: Vols (4000) Cat Maps Pix
Budget: $1500
Notes: The Lemke Napoleon Collection of approx 4000 vols. Rich in contemporary literary works, pamphlets, broadsides, illustrations, military maps and atlases. A catalog was prepared by Mrs Virginia Goult and published in 1941, with an addendum in 1978.

IL —NEWBERRY LIBRARY, Spencer Collection of Napoleonica, 60 W Walton St, Chicago, 60618. Diana Haskell, Cur of Modern Mss
Notes: Incl letters, documents, portraits, and lithographs.

IN —INDIANA UNIVERSITY, Lilly Library, Seventh St, Bloomington, 47405. William R Cagle, Librn
Holdings: // Cat Mss
Notes: Collection focuses on the effect of the Napoleonic invasion of Spain in 1808, the constitutional crisis in Spain and the colonies provoked by the capture of the Spanish royal family by Napoleon, the policy of Ferdinand VII and the most important decisions by all the viceroys, bishops and archbishops.

MA —HARVARD UNIVERSITY LIBRARY, Widener Library, Cambridge, 02138.
Holdings: Cat Mss Microforms
Notes: For 131 invasion broadsides of 1803, see *Harvard Library Bulletin*, VIII (1954), 14-40.

NY —CORNELL UNIVERSITY LIBRARIES, Manuscript and Archives Division, Ithaca, 14853. H Thomas Hickerson, Special Collections Librn

NY —UNIVERSITY CLUB, Library, One W 54 St, New York, 10019. Guy St Clair, Library Dir
Holdings: Vols (100,000) Cat Mss Maps Pix
Notes: A private library for the members of the University Club, their guests, and serious scholars upon written application to the Library Director.

NY —US MILITARY ACADEMY LIBRARY, West Point, 10996. Alan C Aimone, Military History Librn
Holdings: Vols Cat Mss Maps Pix
Notes: Egon A Weiss and J Thomas Russell, *Subject Catalog of the Military Art and Science Collection in the Library of the United States Military Academy with Selected Author and Added Entries, Including a Preliminary Guide to the Ms Collectin*. Westport, Conn: Greenwood Publishing Co, 1969 4 vols.

NC —UNIVERSITY OF NORTH CAROLINA, CHAPEL HILL, Wilson Library, Rare Book Collection, Chapel Hill, 27514. Paul S Koda, Cur of Rare Books
Holdings: Vols 6000 Cat Mss Pix
Notes: The William Henry Hoyt Collection of French History contains over 6000 vols primarily concerned with the French Revolution and the Napoleonic era. There is also personal correspondence of Napoleon, as well as 27 boxes of pamphlets, 1650-1779.

OH —WESTERN RESERVE HISTORICAL SOCIETY, History Library, William P

Palmer Civil War Collection, 10825 East Blvd, Cleveland, 44106. Kermit J Pike, Dir
Holdings: Mss
Notes: The David Z Norton Napoleonic collection, one of the largest Napoleonic collections in the US. Incl pamphlets, prints, and cartoons.

OH —KENT STATE UNIVERSITY, SALEM CAMPUS, Library, 2491 Star Rte, Salem, 44460. Barbara Spahlinger, Librn
Holdings: Vols 100 // Uncat

RI —BROWN UNIVERSITY, John Hay Library, 20 Prospect St, Providence, 02912. Mark N Brown, Cur Mss
Holdings: Vols (130) Cat Mss Pix
Notes: William Henry Hoffman Napoleon Collection of finely-bound books on the Napoleonic period plus over 3000 prints of Napoleonic interest and 200 art objects incl 120 miniature portraits on ivory, one being by Jean Baptiste Isabey, commemorative medals, and a portrait of Napoleon by Horace Vernet. The mss include 140 of Napoleonic interest and 40 assorted letters and documents signed by famous personages such as: Alexander I of Russia, Louis II, Prince de Conde, Charles James Fox, Frederick the Great, George III, Marquis de Lafayette, Louis XIV, Louis Phillipe, Ludwig I of Bavaria, Napoleon III, Madame Recamier, Cardinal Richelieu, and Wilhelm I of Germany; also the Paul Revere Bullard Collection of 185 19th century caricatures (uncat) by English, French, German, Russian, and Spanish cartoonists who lampooned throughout his career, plus 220 similar caricatures from otherNapoleon sources. The major English artists represented are: James Gillray, George and Isaac Cruikshank, Thomas Rowlandson, and George Woodard. Some items also part of Anne S K Brown Military Collection at Brown University.

TX —SAINT MARY'S UNIVERSITY, Library, 2700 Cincinnati Ave, San Antonio, 78284. Anita C Saxine, Special Collections Librn

VA —COLLEGE OF WILLIAM AND MARY, Earl Gregg Swem Library, Williamsburg, 23185. Margaret C Cook, Cur of Manuscripts & Rare Books
Holdings: Vols 100 // Cat Maps
Notes: The John Womack Wright Collection incl 17th and 18th century books on fortifications and contemporary books on the campaigns of the Napoleonic wars. Also, 89 maps of theatre of war area of Napoleonic cmapaigns.

WA —WHITMAN COLLEGE, Penrose Memorial Library, 345 Boyer, Walla Walla, 99362. Lawrence L Dodd, Cur
Holdings: Vols 400 // Cat
Notes: The Elbridge H Stuart Napoleonic Collection. Majority of the materials are 18th and 19th century works.

ON —METROPOLITAN TORONTO LIBRARY, History Dept, 789 Yonge St, Toronto, M4W 2G8, Can. Michael Pearson, Head
Holdings: Vols (11,000) Cat Phonorecords Audiotapes Microforms
Notes: Includes British army and navy lists and Prussian and French army lists from 18th century on; British regimental histories; works on military uniforms and insignia, especially European; Napoleonic and First and Second World Wars well represented.

PQ —MCGILL UNIVERSITY, McLennan Library, Rare Books and Special Collections Dept, 3459 McTavish St, Montreal, H3A 1Y1, Can.
Notes: 3521 prints contemporary with Napoleon incl portraits of Napoleon and his contemporaries and scenes from his life, domestic and military.

NAPOLEON AND NAPOLEONIC PERIOD—AUTOGRAPHS

IL —NEWBERRY LIBRARY, 60 W Walton St, Chicago, 60610. Diana Haskell, Cur of Modern Mss
Holdings: Mss Cat
Notes: Correspondence and documents of Napoleon and his circle.

NAPOLEON AND NAPOLEONIC PERIOD—AUTOGRAPHS (cont.)

MI —UNIVERSITY OF MICHIGAN, Library, Dept of Rare Books & Special Collections, Ann Arbor, 48109. Robert J Starring, Head
Holdings: // Cat Mss Pix
Notes: A collection of 60 documents and letters, largely official, of Napoleon I, his marshals and cabinet ministers, brought together by the donor, Orla B Taylor. Each is accompanied by a letterpress copy and translation into English. There are also 130 portraits.

NAPOLEON AND NAPOLEONIC PERIOD—PORTRAITS, CARICATURES

RI —BROWN UNIVERSITY, John Hay Library, 20 Prospect St, Providence, 02912. Mark N Brown, Cur Mss
Holdings: Vols (130) Cat Mss Pix
Notes: William Henry Hoffman Napoleon Collection of finely-bound books on the Napoleonic period plus over 3000 prints of Napoleonic interest and 200 art objects incl 120 miniature portraits on ivory, one being by Jean Baptiste Isabey, commemorative medals, and a portrait of Napoleon by Horace Vernet. The mss include 140 of Napoleonic interest and 40 assorted letters and documents signed by famous personages such as: Alexander I of Russia, Louis II, Prince de Conde, Charles James Fox, Frederick the Great, George III, Marquis de Lafayette, Louis XIV, Louis Phillipe, Ludwig I of Bavaria, Napoleon III, Madame Recamier, Cardinal Richelieu, and Wilhelm I of Germany; also the Paul Revere Bullard Collection of 185 19th century caricatures (uncat) by English, French, German, Russian, and Spanish cartoonists who lampooned throughout his career, plus 220 similar caricatures from other Napoleon sources. The major English artists represented are: James Gillray, George and Isaac Cruikshank, Thomas Rowlandson, and George Woodard. Some items also part of Anne S K Brown Military Collection at Brown University.

NAPOLEONIC WARS see France—History—Revolution, 1789-1799

NARAYAN, R. K.

MA —BOSTON UNIVERSITY, Mugar Memorial Library, Special Collections Dept, 771 Commonwealth Ave, Boston, 02215. Howard B Gotlieb, Dir
Holdings: Cat Mss Correspondence

NARCOTIC HABIT see Drug Habit

NARCOTIC LAWS see Drugs—Laws and Legislation

NARCOTIC TRADE AND TRAFFIC see Drug Trade

NARCOTICS see Drugs

NARCOTICS—LAWS AND LEGISLATION see Drugs—Laws and Legislation

NARCOTICS, CONTROL OF see Dangerous Drugs, Control of

NARCOTICS IN LITERATURE see Drugs in Literature

NAROPA INSTITUTE

MO —WASHINGTON UNIVERSITY, Libraries, Special Collections Dept, Campus Box 1061, St Louis, 63130.
Notes: A small but significant collection.

NARRAGANSETT BAY

RI —US NAVAL WAR COLLEGE, Historical Collection & Museum, Newport, 02841.

Anthony S Nicolosi, Dir; Evelyn Cherpak, Cur
Holdings: Mss
Notes: Collections incl over 200,000 separate pieces; chiefly papers of naval officers and records of organizations associated with the US Navy, the Naval War College, the college's major study areas, and the Navy in the Narragansett Bay region; oral history collection; Naval War College Archives, 1884-present; records of conferences held at the College; newspaper collections treating with naval themes and military conflicts.

NASA see U.S. National Aeronautics and Space Administration

NASBY, PETROLEUM V.

OH —RUTHERFORD B HAYES LIBRARY, 1337 Hayes Ave, Fremont, 43420. Watt P Marchman, Dir
Holdings: Cat Mss Pix
Notes: Papers, correspondence and literary mss (approx 6 linear ft) pertaining to "Petroleum V Nasby" and his son, Robinson Locke, both of Toledo *Blade*. Index in the collection. Cf *Guide to Manuscripts of the Ohio Historical Society*, 304.

NASH, HARRY H.

AZ —NORTHERN ARIZONA UNIVERSITY, Special Collection Library, CU Box 6022, Flagstaff, 86011. Peter M Whiteley, Coordr/Archivist; William Mullane, Librn
Notes: Collection of Frank Gold, lawyer. File on Martin F Schwab/Harry H Nash sensational murder trial, Flagstaff, 1920-1921. Also incl photographs of biographical material on Gold.

NASH, OGDEN

NV —UNIVERSITY OF NEVADA, RENO, University Library, Special Collections Dept, Reno, 89557. Robert E Blesse, Head
Holdings: Vols (65) Cat
Notes: Includes individual works by author in all editions including translations; also prefaces, introductions, published correspondence, appearances in anthologies, periodicals, etc. Bibliographical research collection, part of Modern Authors Collection. Other appearances 735 cataloged.

NAST, THOMAS, 1857-1902

DC —LIBRARY OF CONGRESS, Prints & Photographs Div, Washington, 20540.
Notes: Swann Collection is strong in the work of contemporary cartoonists. Among the 400 artists represented are Peter Arno, Bil Canfield, Al Capp, Miguel Covarrubias, Louis Dalrymple, Whitney Darrow, Rube Goldberg, Thomas Nast, Jose Guadalupe Posada, Edward Sorel, and John Tenniel.

IN —INDIANA UNIVERSITY, Lilly Library, Seventh St, Bloomington, 47405. William R Cagle, Librn
Notes: Contemporary with and depicting Lincoln; the War of 1812 and other periods. Incl significant mss of the modern cartoonists and caricaturists Ardizzone, Beerbohm, Fontane Fox, Kin Hubbard, Charles Bacon Jackson, McCutcheon, Messick, Nast, Rothenstein, Sendak, and many miscellaneous items.

KS —UNIVERSITY OF KANSAS, Kenneth Spencer Research Library, Kansas Collection, Lawrence, 66045. Sheryl K Williams, Cur
Holdings: Cat
Notes: The Albert T Reid Cartoon Collection. Nucleus of collection was Reid's personal collection of political and comic cartoons. Later cartoonists presented samples of their work. Bill Mauldin, Rollin Kirby, Daniel B Dowling, Thomas Nast, and other political cartoonists are represented. Comic strips from the late 1920s and 1930s also. The collection of cartoons is catloged and represented in the Kansas Collection

card catalog. A separate book catalog is maintained also. For description see: *Albert T Reid Cartoon Collection*. Lawrence, Kan. Published for the Journalistic Historical Center, University of Kansas by the William Allen White Foundation, University of Kansas, ca 1957. Originally maintained by the Journalistic Historical Center, William Allen White School of Journalism, the collection was transferred to the Kansas Collection, Kenneth Spencer Library in 1969.

MA —BOSTON PUBLIC LIBRARY, Print Collection, Dartmouth St at Copley Sq, Boston, 02117. Sinclair H Hitchings, Keeper of Prints
Holdings: Cat
Notes: The caricature collection incl 300 American prints (colonial period to 1900), 65 of these are by Thomas Nast; 400 English prints (mostly 18th century) many by Thomas Rowlandson and James Gillray; and several thousand 19th century French items, large numbers of them by Daumier. Items are cataloged by artist when known; or else by publisher or country. In addition, the American caricatures are arranged chronologically.

NJ —MACCULLOCH HALL HISTORICAL MUSEUM, Morristown, 07960. Alice A Caulkins, Curator
Notes: The W Parsons Todd Collection.

NY —UNIVERSITY OF ROCHESTER, Rush Rhees Library, Department of Rare Books and Special Collections, Rochester, 14627. Peter Dzwonkoski, Librn
Notes: Original drawings by Thomas Nast; also World War II political cartoons by Elmer Messher, cartoonist for Rochester, New York newspaper.

OH —RUTHERFORD B HAYES LIBRARY, 1337 Hayes Ave, Fremont, 43420. Watt P Marchman, Dir
Holdings: Cat Mss Pix
Notes: Correspondence, diary (1860-61), literary mss, account book, scrapbooks, sketches, caricatures, clippings, designs and misc printed matter of Thomas Nast.

NATHAN, GEORGE JEAN

NY —CORNELL UNIVERSITY LIBRARIES, John M Olin Library, Dept of Rare Books, Ithaca, 14853. Donald D Eddy, Librn
Holdings: Vols 1153 Cat Mss Pix

NATHAN, ROBERT

MO —WASHINGTON UNIVERSITY, Libraries, Campus Box 1061, Saint Louis, 63130.
Notes: A collection of primary material.

NATHAN, ROBERT GRUNTAL

CT —YALE UNIVERSITY, Box 1603A, Yale Station, New Haven, 06520.
Holdings: Cat Mss

NATION, CARRY

MO —MISSOURI HISTORICAL SOCIETY, Library, Jefferson Memorial Bldg, Saint Louis, 63112. Stephanie Klein, Librn-Archivist; Peter Michel, Cur of Manuscripts
Notes: A collection of material on 119 women who lived or worked in St Louis and Missouri as educators, artists, and homemakers, or played significant roles in US politics and social reform. Incl Sacajawea, Susan B Anthony, Fannie Hurst, Carry Nation, Patience Worth, etc.

NATIONAL ABORTION RIGHTS ACTION LEAGUE

MA —RADCLIFFE COLLEGE, Arthur & Elizabeth Schlesinger Library on the History of Women in America, 3 James St, Cambridge, 02138. Patricia Miller King, Dir; Eva Moseley, Cur of Mss
Holdings: Vols (23,000) Cat Mss Pix Microforms
Budget: ($300,000)
Notes: Ms collection incl Blackwell family,

NATIONAL ABORTION RIGHTS ACTION LEAGUE (cont.)

Beecher-Stowe family, Betty Friedan, Charlotte Perkins Gilman, Emma Goldman, Dr Alice Hamilton and the Hamilton family, the National Abortion Rights Action League, the National Organization for Women, Leonora O'Reilly, and the Women's Equity Action League.

NATIONAL ACADEMY OF TELEVISION ARTS AND SCIENCES

CA —UNIVERSITY OF CALIFORNIA, LOS ANGELES, Theater Arts Library, Los Angeles, 90024. Edward Shreeves, Chairman, Bibliographers Group; Audree Malkin, Head, Theater Arts Library
Notes: National Academy of Television Arts and Sciences Collection incl programs, clippings, publicity releases, biographical material, correspondence, financial records, and miscellaneous memorabilia relating to NATAS and to the Emmy Awards, 1948-1954. Also, the Syd Cassyd Collection. He was the first president of the National Academy of Television Arts and Sciences. Collection contains material relating to his career, 1935-1977; incl screenplay, television and radio scripts; treatments; pre-production and production material; production stills, portraits, souvenir motion picture programs; awards programs; clippings; personal notes.

NATIONAL ADVISORY COMMITTEE FOR AERONAUTICS see U.S. National Advisory Committee for Aeronautics

NATIONAL AERONAUTICS AND SPACE ADMINISTRATION see U.S. National Aeronautics and Space Administration

NATIONAL AMERICAN WOMAN SUFFRAGE ASSOCIATION

DC —LIBRARY OF CONGRESS, Rare Book & Special Collections Div, Washington, 20540. William Matheson, Chief
Notes: A collection of books on the women's movement and kindred subjects presented to the library by the National American Woman Suffrage Association and its president, Mrs Carrie Chapman Catt. It consists of the feminist library of Mrs Catt, collected since 1890, and various older books contributed from the libraries of Elizabeth Cady Stanton, Susan B Anthony (qv), Lucy Stone, Alice Stone Blackwell, Julia Ward Howe, Mary A Livermore and others, together with bound sets of periodicals relating to woman suffrage.
DC —LIBRARY OF CONGRESS, Manuscript Division, Washington, 20540. John C Broderick, Chief
Holdings: Cat Mss Pix
Notes: Mss, papers, records, etc.

NATIONAL ASSOCIATION FOR THE ADVANCEMENT OF COLORED PEOPLE (NAACP)

CA —UNIVERSITY OF CALIFORNIA, BERKELEY, University Library, Afro-American Studies, Berkeley, 94720. Phyllis Bischof, Librn
Notes: Extensive holdings of books, manuscripts, newspapers, serials, dissertations, documents, oral histories, music, recordings, microforms. Research level collection, with Afro-American materials collected by more than twenty campus libraries. Mss collections incl the papers of the NAACP Western Regional Office, 1944-1980, the records of the Brotherhood of Sleepinng Car Porters, and some mss and letters of Langston Hughes. The Afro-American Writers Collection of The Bancroft Library incl first editions, correspondence, and mss of black writers, particularly those working or living in the western United States.

DC —LIBRARY OF CONGRESS, Manuscript Division, Washington, 20540. John C Broderick, Chief
Notes: The papers of Roy Wilkins, former Executive Director, NAACP. Noncurrent records and photographs of the NAACP. Archives (1945-70) of the NAACP Legal Defense and Educational Fund.
MA —UNIVERSITY OF MASSACHUSETTS AT AMHERST, Library, Archives and Manuscripts, Amherst, 01003. Siegfried Feller, Assoc Dir for Collection Development
Holdings: Mss Pix
Notes: Papers of the NAACP's *The Crisis* during W E B Du Bois' editorship, 1910-34. Incl W E B Du Bois papers.
SC —COLLEGE OF CHARLESTON LIBRARY, Special Collections Dept, Charleston, 29401.
Notes: Septima Poinsette Clark Collection contains personal papers, recorded interviews and discussions, numerous writings for speeches and/or publication, various honorary degrees and awards, and materials reflecting Septima Poinsette Clark's activities as educator and civil rights activist, among them papers from the National Association for the Advancement of Colored People and the Southern Christian Leadership Conference.

NATIONAL ASSOCIATION FOR WOMEN DEANS, COUNSELORS AND ADMINISTRATORS (NAWDAC)

OH —BOWLING GREEN STATE UNIVERSITY, Jerome Library, Center for Archival Collections, Bowling Green, 43403. Paul D Yon, Dir; Elaine R Ezell, Reference Archivist; Nancy Steen, Rare Books Librn
Notes: Incl pamphlets. The archives of four national professional associations have been donated to the CAC, creating a special collecting area concerning student affairs in higher education. The National Association for Women Deans, Counselors and Administrators (NAWDAC), the National Association of Student Personnel Administrators (NASPA), the American College Personnel Association (ACPA), and the Association of Fraternity Advisors (AFA), to date, have designated the CAC as the repository for their archives. These collections document the issues, professional education and activities of those employed within the student affairs area in colleges and universities in the US.

NATIONAL ASSOCIATION OF COLLEGE WIND AND PERCUSSION INSTRUMENTS

†MD —UNIVERSITY OF MARYLAND, Library, The National Association of College Wind & Percussion Instructors Library, College Park, 20742. Pearl Z Tubiash, Supvr
Holdings: Cat
Notes: Primarily scores, along with some organizational papers and publications.

NATIONAL ASSOCIATION OF HUMAN RIGHTS WORKERS

LA —AMISTAD RESEARCH CENTER, 400 Esplanade Ave, New Orleans, 70116. Clifton H Johnson, Exec Dir; Florence E Borders, Senior Archivist
Holdings: Vols (10,000) Cat Mss Pix Audiotapes Microforms
Budget: ($315,000)
Notes: In addition, 8,000,000 ms pieces, 10,000 pictures, 3500 microforms, and 500 audiotapes. Amistad Research Center is an historical research library devoted to the collection and use of primary source materials on the history of America's ethnic minorities, with particular emphasis on Afro-Americans, American Indians, and immigrant groups. Among the larger institutional collections held are the archives and records of the American Missionary Association, the American Home Missionary Society, the Race Relations Dept of the Anti-Defamation League, the Catholic Committee of the South, and the National Association of Human Rights Workers, (formerly NAIRO, National Association of Intergroup Relations Officials). Also, private papers of the Harlem Renaissance poet, Countee Cullen; educator and civil rights leader, Mary McLeod Bethune;20th century civil rights lawyer, Alexander P Tureaud; 19th century Black attorney and judge, George Ruffin; founder and director of Operation Crossroads Africa, Dr James H Robinson; and over 70 others.

NATIONAL ASSOCIATION OF MANUFACTURERS (NAM)

DE —HAGLEY MUSEUM AND LIBRARY, Eleutherian Mills-Hagley Foundation Inc, PO Box 3630, Greenville, 19807. Richmond D Williams, Dir; Heddy A Richter, Imprints Librn
Notes: National Association of Manufacturers Records (1910-1975; 1000 cubic feet) incl minutes of adminstrative committees, reports, correspondence, and printed material.

NATIONAL ASSOCIATION OF PHYSICAL EDUCATION IN HIGHER EDUCATION

NC —UNIVERSITY OF NORTH CAROLINA, GREENSBORO, Walter Clinton Jackson Library, Special Collections Dept, 1000 Spring Garden St, Greensboro, 27412. Emilie W Mills, Librn
Notes: The archive of the NAPEHE incl all business correspondence, memoranda, bulletins, photographs, proceedings and reports from 1897 to the present. NAPEHE was formed by the merger in 1978 of the National Association of Physical Education for College Men and the National Association of Physical Education for College Women.

NATIONAL ASSOCIATION OF PUBLIC SCHOOL ADULT EDUCATORS

NY —SYRACUSE UNIVERSITY LIBRARIES, Ernest S Bird Library, George Arents Research Library for Special Collections, Syracuse, 13210. Carolyn A Davis, Manuscripts Librn; Amy S Doherty, University Archivist; Mark F Weimer, Rare Book Librn
Notes: Records of the National Association of Public School Adult Educators. Papers 1934-64 (3 linear feet).

NATIONAL ASSOCIATION OF STUDENT PERSONNEL ADMINISTRATORS (NASPA)

OH —BOWLING GREEN STATE UNIVERSITY, Jerome Library, Center for Archival Collections, Bowling Green, 43403. Paul D Yon, Dir; Elaine R Ezell, Reference Archivist; Nancy Steen, Rare Books Librn
Notes: Incl pamphlets. The archives of four national professional associations have been donated to the CAC, creating a special collecting area concerning student affairs in higher education. The National Association for Women Deans, Counselors and Administrators (NAWDAC), the National Association of Student Personnel Administrators (NASPA), the American College Personnel Association (ACPA), and the Association of Fraternity Advisors (AFA), to date, have designated the CAC as the repository for their archives. These collections document the issues, professional education and activities of those employed within the student affairs area in colleges and universities in the US.

NATIONAL BALLET

DC —DISTRICT OF COLUMBIA PUBLIC LIBRARY, Martin Luther King Memorial Library, Washingtoniana Div and Washington Star Collection, 901 G St NW,

NATIONAL BALLET (cont.)

Washington, 20001. Roxanna Deane, Chief
Notes: Archival collections from various
organizations such as the National Ballet and
the League of Women Voters.

NATIONAL BIBLIOGRAPHY see
Bibliography, National

NATIONAL BOARD OF HEALTH

MD —NATIONAL LIBRARY OF
MEDICINE, 8600 Rockville Pike, Bethesda,
20209. Harold M Schoolinam, Actg Dir
Budget: ($46,400)
Notes: Correspondence of George E Waring,
pioneering American sanitary engineer of the
19th century.

NATIONAL BROADCASTING COMPANY (NBC)

DC —LIBRARY OF CONGRESS, Motion
Pictures, Broadcasting and Recorded Sound
Div, Washington, 20540.
Notes: The entire radio archive of the
National Broadcasting Company. Incl 175,
000 recordings of radio programs and events
broadcast from 1933-70. Duplicated at the
Museum of Broadcasting in New York City.
NY —MUSEUM OF BROADCASTING,
Library, 1 E 53rd St, New York, 10022.
Douglas Gibbons, Dir
Notes: The entire radio archive of the
National Broadcasting Company. Incl 175,
000 recordings of radio programs and events
broadcast from 1933-1970. Duplicated at the
Library of Congress.

NATIONAL CHILD LABOR COMMITTEE

DC —LIBRARY OF CONGRESS, Manuscript
Division, Washington, 20540. John C
Broderick, Chief
Notes: Records and photographs of the
National Child Labor Committee, 1904-53.

NATIONAL CIVIC FOUNDATION

NY —ROCKEFELLER UNIVERSITY,
Rockefeller Archive Center, Hillcrest,
Pocantico Hills, North Tarrytown, 10591.
Joseph W Ernst, Dir; J William Hess, Assoc
Dir
Notes: Papers relative to the Rockefeller
Family, Foundations, University, and other
specific enterprises and contributions to
particular areas of social, physical,
educational, and historic reform,
preservation, conservation, or development.
Extensive records of administrative,
financial, physical, or intellectual
relationships.

NATIONAL CIVIL SERVICE LEAGUE

DC —US OFFICE OF PERSONNEL
MANAGEMENT, Library, 1900 E St NW,
Washington, 20415. Betty B Guerin, Supv
Librn
Holdings: Vols 10,000 Cat Mss Pix
Microforms
Notes: US Civil Service Commission
terminated by Act of Congress, 10/78. US
Office of Personnel Management created
and effective 1/79. Library houses a
comprehensive collection of civil service
documents, newspaper clippings, legislative
histories of all major legislation relating to
civil service incl microfilms of dissertations,
mss, rare items and a complete collection of
agency issuances.

NATIONAL COTTON COUNCIL OF AMERICA

MS —UNIVERSITY OF SOUTHERN
MISSISSIPPI, William David McCain
Graduate Library, Box 5148, Southern Sta,
Hattiesburg, 39406.
Holdings: Vols 35 Cat
Notes: Oral history interviews with 35

individuals associated with the National
Cotton Council of America (ca 1940-1980).
Subject matter deals with the history of the
Council and all aspects of the cotton
industry, incl producers, ginners,
warehouses, seed crushers, merchants,
cooperatives and spinners.

NATIONAL COUNCIL OF CATHOLIC WOMEN

DC —GEORGETOWN UNIVERSITY,
Library, Special Collections Div, 37 & O Sts
NW, Washington, 20057. George M
Barringer, Special Collections Librn;
Nicholas B Sheetz, Mss Librn
Holdings: Mss
Notes: Transcripts and other material
concerning the National Council of Catholic
Women. Incl are transcripts from the
"Catholic Hour," a program sponsored by the
Council from 1960-1968; published
proceedings of the NCCW conventions from
1932-1962; and printed material on the
"Parish Program," a service offered by the
Council.

NATIONAL CUSTOMS

MI —APPLE TREE PRESS, Library, Box
1012, Flint, 48501. W D Chase, Editor/
Librn
Holdings: Vols (1200) Uncat Mss Maps Pix
Microforms

NATIONAL DANCES see Folk Dancing

NATIONAL DEFENSE SYSTEMS see
Weapons Systems

NATIONAL FARMERS PROCESS TAX RECOVERY ASSOCIATION

IA —IOWA STATE UNIVERSITY, Library,
Dept of Special Collections, Ames, 50011.
Stanley M Yates, Head
Holdings: // Mss
Notes: Formed in 1936, the Association
wanted to recover the process tax levied by
the Agricultural Adjustment Act which was
later declared unconstitutional. 17 linear ft,
finding aid available.

NATIONAL FARMERS UNION

CO —UNIVERSITY OF COLORADO,
Libraries, Western Historical Collections,
Boulder, 80309.
Holdings: Cat Mss
Notes: The Farmers Union was founded in
Texas in 1902. After its early strength in the
South waned it became the strongest farners'
organization in the high plains,
headquartered in Denver, Colorado. The
collection contains financial records,
congressional testimony, convention
proceedings, and national and state farmers
union newspapers (1902-1966). 80 boxes. A
typescript inventory is available.

NATIONAL FEDERATION OF BUSINESS AND PROFESSIONAL WOMEN

DC —BUSINESS & PROFESSIONAL
WOMEN'S FOUNDATION, Marguerite
Rawalt Resource Center, 2012
Massachusetts Ave NW, Washington, 20036.
Cheryl A Sloan, Librn
Holdings: Vols (20,000) Cat Microforms VF
Budget: ($10,000)
Notes: Now Business and Professional
Women's Foundation. VF, containing about
13,000 items (studies, periodical articles,
newspaper clippings, documents) current. All
items are filed by subject and indexed in our
card catalog by author, title and subject. 200
tape recordings in Oral History Collection.
The Resource Center is currently being
automated starting with thesaurus
construction, then data base design, and
finally the implementaion phase which incl
cataloging, abstracting, and indexing each
item. Microfilms are mainly of doctoral

theses. Our emphasis is on the working
woman and encompasses economic issues of
concern to women such as education for
women, working mothers, sex roles, women
executives, counseling for women, and work
force entry by mature women. Most of the
material is about women in the United
States. Collection incl 500 microfilms.Publish
a bimonthly selected acquisitions list.

NATIONAL FEDERATION OF GRAIN COOPERATIVES

NY —CORNELL UNIVERSITY LIBRARIES,
Collection of Regional History, Dept of
Manuscripts and Univ Archives, Ithaca,
14853.
Notes: Records, ca 1946-1968; 39 ft.

NATIONAL FILM BOARD, CANADA

ON —NATIONAL FILM BOARD,
CANADA, Tunney's Pasture Area, Ottawa,
K1A 0M9, Can.
Notes: Photo library of 225,000 Canadian
images, incl 33,000 slides.
PQ —NATIONAL FILM BOARD OF
CANADA, Reference Library, PO Box
6100, Station A, Montreal, H3C 3H5, Can.
Rose-Aimee Todd, Librn; Bernard Lutz,
Librn
Holdings: VF
Notes: Incl French and English "Challenge
for Change Collection." Incl 350 pamphlets
30 VF drawers and 100 periodical titles.

NATIONAL FOREST PRODUCTS ASSOCIATION

CA —FOREST HISTORY SOCIETY INC,
Library, 109 Coral St, Santa Cruz, 95060.
Mary E Johnson, Librn
Notes: Incl archives of the Society of
American Foresters, the American Forestry
Association, the National Lumber
Manufacturers Association, National Forest
Product Association, and the American
Forest Institute.

NATIONAL GRANGE

NY —CORNELL UNIVERSITY LIBRARIES,
Collection of Regional History, Dept of
Manuscripts and Univ Archives, Ithaca,
14853.
Notes: The noncurrent records, letters,
records of meetings and other historic data
dating back to Dec 4, 1867, the date of
organization of the National Grange. Also
the papers of Louis I Taber, National Master
of the Grange from 1923 to 1941.

NATIONAL GREENBACK PARTY

NE —NEBRASKA STATE HISTORICAL
SOCIETY, Archives, 1500 R St, Box 82554,
Lincoln, 68501. James E Potter, State
Archivist
Holdings: Uncat Mss
Notes: Silver and the money question; also
material on the Greenback Party. Printed
speeches and tracts relating to the money
question, 1890-1895. Many written by
prominent political figures of the day. Also,
pamphlets which relate to income tax, tariffs,
free trade, soldiers' pensions, railroads,
election laws and public lands. Collection of
John Davis, Congressman from Kansas,
1891-1895.

NATIONAL HOLIDAYS see Holidays

NATIONAL HOTEL, WASHINGTON, D.C.

DC —GEORGETOWN UNIVERSITY,
Library, Special Collections Div, 37 & O Sts
NW, Washington, 20057. George M
Barringer, Special Collections Librn;
Nicholas B Sheetz, Mss Librn
Holdings: Mss Cat
Notes: Series of register books from the
National Hotel in Washington, DC. The
hotel, built in 1827 at the corner of
Pennsylvania Avenue and 6th Street, was the

NATIONAL HOTEL, WASHINGTON, D.C. (cont.)

first hotel in Washington approximating the dimensions of a modern hotel.

NATIONAL HUGUENOT SOCIETY

PA —BALCH INSTITUTE FOR ETHNIC STUDIES, Library, 18 S Seventh St, Philadelphia, 19106. R Joseph Anderson, Library Dir

NATIONAL JAPANESE AMERICAN STUDENT RELOCATION COUNCIL

CA —HOOVER INSTITUTION ON WAR, REVOLUTION & PEACE, Stanford University, Stanford, 94305. Milorad M Drachkovitch, Archivist
Holdings: Mss
Notes: Correspondence, questionaires, student education records, and other miscellaneous items pertaining to the National Japanese American Student Relocation Council, 1942-1946. 101 cartons and 17 drawers of index cards.

NATIONAL LEAGUE FOR NURSING

MD —NATIONAL LIBRARY OF MEDICINE, History of Medicine Division, 8600 Rockville Pike, Bethesda, 20014.
Notes: Books and journals related to nursing and the nursing profession, both early and current items. A manuscripts collection incl the archives of the American College of Nurse Midwives (1946-1976) and the National League for Nursing (1894-1952). Photographs in the Prints and Photographs Collection document the history of nursing from the Middle Ages to the 1960s.

NATIONAL LEAGUE OF CITIES

DC —NATIONAL LEAGUE OF CITIES, Municipal Reference Service, 1301 Pennsylvania Ave NW, Washington, 20004. Olivia Kredel, Mgr
Holdings: Vols (20,000)
Notes: Archives of National League of Cities.

NATIONAL LUMBER MANUFACTURERS ASSOCIATION

CA —FOREST HISTORY SOCIETY INC, Library, 109 Coral St, Santa Cruz, 95060. Mary E Johnson, Librn
Notes: Incl archives of the Society of American Foresters, the American Forestry Association, the National Lumber Manufacturers Association, National Forest Products Association, and the American Forest Institute.

NATIONAL MILITARY PARKS see National Parks and Reserves

NATIONAL NOISE ABATEMENT COUNCIL

NY —AMERICAN INSTITUTE OF PHYSICS, Center for the History of Physics, Niels Bohr Library, 335 E 45 St, New York, 10017. John Aubry, Librn
Notes: Papers and records.

NATIONAL OCEAN SURVEY

MI —UNIVERSITY OF MICHIGAN, Harlan Hatcher Graduate Library, Map Room, Ann Arbor, 48109. James O Minton, Map Librn
Notes: The collection consists of approx 300,000 sheet maps incl maps and charts received on deposit from the US Geological Survey, Defense Mapping Agency, and the National Ocean Service. The collection also incl approx 5000 reference volumes related to cartography, surveying, and mapping, with emphasis on place-name literature (gazetteers, dictionaries), books on how to use and interpret maps, CARTo-bibliographies, and state (provincial, etc),

regional, national, and international atlases. The collection is strongest geographically in materials of Michigan, Midwest, Anglo-America, and Europe; chronologically, 1850-date; and thematically, in topographic and geologic maps, although all subjects are collected. The collection maintains a separate catalog of holdings. Reference volumes are fully cataloged and classified.

NATIONAL ORGANIZATION FOR PUBLIC HEALTH NURSING

MA —SIMMONS COLLEGE ARCHIVES, 300 The Fenway, Boston, 02115. Megan Sniffin-Marinoff, College Archivist
Notes: Archives of the Simmons College School of Public Health Nursing (later reorganized into the School of Nursing) cover the years 1902-1970. Important correspondents in the collection incl M Adelaide Nutting, Mary Beard, Isabel Stewart, and Anne Hervey Strong, etc. Incl Strong's records of activity with regard to nursing education in the National Organization for Public Health Nursing, 1918-22. 1000 linear feet in institution, incl special collections nursing and photographs, nursing.

NATIONAL ORGANIZATION FOR WOMEN (NOW)

MA —RADCLIFFE COLLEGE, Arthur & Elizabeth Schlesinger Library on the History of Women in America, 3 James St, Cambridge, 02138. Patricia Miller King, Dir; Eva Moseley, Cur of Mss
Notes: Library collects only the records of the National Office, task forces, and the Massachusetts chapter of NOW.
NY —CORNELL UNIVERSITY LIBRARIES, Collection of Regional History, Dept of Manuscripts and Univ Archives, Ithaca, 14853.
Notes: Ithaca Chapter. Education Committee questionnaires, 1968-69; .6 ft.

NATIONAL PARKS AND RESERVES

CA —UNIVERSITY OF CALIFORNIA, LOS ANGELES, Research Library, Dept of Special Collections, 405 Hilgard Ave, Los Angeles, 90024. Edward Shreeves, Chairman, Bibliographers Group; David S Zeidberg, Head
Notes: Correspondence and ephemera of Horace M Albright recording his activity as a conservationist and his directorship of the National Park Service.
CA —UNIVERSITY OF CALIFORNIA, SANTA BARBARA, Library, Dept of Special Collections, Santa Barbara, 93106. Christian F Brun, Head
Holdings: Vols (95,980) Cat Mss
Notes: The Pearl Chase Collections of Community Development and Conservation. Papers of outstanding California leaders in conservation, community planning, Indian affairs, national parks.
CA —UNIVERSITY OF THE PACIFIC, Library, Stockton, 95211. Hiram L Davis, Dir of Libraries
Notes: The John Muir papers. Muir was the founder of the Sierra Club, a prime mover in the development of the national park systems, and a major force in the preservationist branch of the conservation movement.
NJ —HAMMOND, Editorial Department Library, 515 Valley St, Maplewood, 07040. Ernest J Dupuy, Librn
Holdings: Vols (10,000) Cat Maps Pix
Notes: Also about 15,000 maps; 50 vertical file drawers of administrative, census, national parks, highway, and related materials. No photocopying.
NY —ROCKEFELLER UNIVERSITY, Rockefeller Archive Center, Hillcrest, Pocantico Hills, North Tarrytown, 10591. Joseph W Ernst, Dir; J William Hess, Assoc Dir
Notes: The Rockefeller Archive Center, a division of The Rockefeller University, preserves and makes available to scholars the

records of the University, the Rockefeller Foundation, the Rockefeller Brothers Fund, members of the family, and those of other individuals and organizations associated with their endeavors. Collections at the Center document a century of philanthropy by legions of associated social and scientific pioneers, providing a unique window into the past.
VA —US NATIONAL PARK SERVICE, Harpers Ferry Center, Library, Harpers Ferry, 25425. David Nathanson, Chief Librn
Holdings: Vols (8000) Cat Mss Maps Pix Slides Phonorecords Audiotapes 16mm Films Microforms VF
Budget: ($105,000)
†WA —WASHINGTON STATE UNIVERSITY, Library, Manuscripts, Archives & Special Collections, Pullman, 99164. John F Guido, Head
Holdings: Cat Mss Maps Pix
Notes: The Carl Parcher Russell papers, a vast resource (24,916 items; 45 linear feet) on American Indian and Western pioneer activities and artifacts. Much on the fur trade; pioneer life; mountain men and trapping; wildlife; primitive life in detail. Also the National Park Service, parks, monuments, etc. Described in *Carl Parcher Russell: An Indexed Register of His Scholarly and Professional Papers, 1920-1967, in the Washington State University Library* (Pullman, 1970), 149 pp.
AB —PETER WHYTE FOUNDATION, Archives of the Canadian Rockies, Box 160, Banff, T0L 0C0, Can. Mary Andrews, ACR Librn
Holdings: Vols (4247) Cat Mss Maps Pix Slides Phonorecords Audiotapes Videotapes 16mm Films Filmstrips Microforms
Budget: ($1500)
Notes: Collect all available material which touches on the Rocky Mountains of Canada (from the US border to the Peace River in the north; from west of Calgary on the east to the town of Revelstoke, BC on the west). This material incl history (the early explorers, Indians, construction of the railroads, mountaineering, and development of the national parks), natural history (geology, botany, wildlife) and poetry and fiction with the Rockies as a setting. Collect maps of the area, photographs, tape recordings of the pioneers. We also house on our premises the Alpine Club of Canada's library, which is one of the most comprehensive collection on the subject of mountaineering worldwide. Noncirculating.

NATIONAL PLANNING see Economic Policy

NATIONAL PRESS CLUB, WASHINGTON, D.C.

DC —LIBRARY OF CONGRESS, Motion Pictures, Broadcasting and Recorded Sound Div, Washington, 20540.
Notes: Recordings of speeches given at the National Press Club, Washington, D.C., 1952-present.

NATIONAL PRISON ASSOCIATION

OH —RUTHERFORD B HAYES LIBRARY, 1337 Hayes Ave, Fremont, 43420. Watt P Marchman, Dir
Holdings: Vols 10,000 Cat Mss Maps Pix
Budget: $15,000
Notes: The Rutherford B Hayes personal library collection (10,000 vols) incl the Robert Clarke Collection of Americana which Hayes purchased in 1874, and also part of the library of James Hall. Also have about 1800 vols from the personal libraries of the Hayes children. Further correspondence, letterbooks, diaries, speeches, account books, financial and real estate records, law cases, memorabilia and ephemera of or relating to President Hayes. Much on US political activities of friends and opponenets of the period (search individual names).

NATIONAL PUBLIC RADIO

DC —LIBRARY OF CONGRESS, Motion Pictures, Broadcasting and Recorded Sound

NATIONAL PUBLIC RADIO (cont.)

Div, Washington, 20540.
Notes: Broadcast recordings of National
Public Radio's cultural programs.

NATIONAL REPUBLIC (MAGAZINE)

CA —HOOVER INSTITUTION ON WAR,
REVOLUTION & PEACE, Stanford
University, Stanford, 94305. Milorad M
Drachkovitch, Archivist
Holdings: Mss Pix
Notes: Records of *National Republic*
magazine, incl newspaper clippings, printed
matter, pamphlets, reports, indices, notes,
bulletins, lettergrams, weekly letters, and
photographs, 1905-1960, relating to pacifist,
communist, fascist, and other radical
movements as well as political developments
in the US and Soviet Russia. 826 ms boxes.

NATIONAL RESOURCES see Natural Resources

NATIONAL SEA GRANT DEPOSITORY

RI —UNIVERSITY OF RHODE ISLAND,
Graduate School of Oceanography, Pell
Library Bldg, Narragansett, 02882. Kenneth
T Morse, Chief Librn
Notes: Incl 10,016 vols and monographs; 13,
578 bound vols periodicals; 1326 serial
publications.

NATIONAL SLOVAK SOCIETY

PA —BALCH INSTITUTE FOR ETHNIC
STUDIES, Library, 18 S Seventh St,
Philadelphia, 19106. R Joseph Anderson,
Library Dir

NATIONAL SOCIALISM

CA —UNIVERSITY OF CALIFORNIA, LOS
ANGELES, Research Library, Dept of
Special Collections, 405 Hilgard Ave, Los
Angeles, 90024. Edward Shreeves,
Chairman, Bibliographers Group; David S
Zeidberg, Head
Holdings: Cat
Notes: Captured Nazi records filmed at the
Berlin Document Center of the US
Department of State. As of the summer of
1970, UCLA holdings constitute 254 reels of
microfilm. The Nazi Ephemera and Artifacts
Collection contains 10 linear feet of German
and US pictures, books, ephemera, and
objects.
CA —UNIVERSITY OF CALIFORNIA,
RIVERSIDE, University Library, 4045
Canyon Crest Dr, Box 5900, Riverside,
92517.
Holdings: Vols 5,000 Cat
Notes: Printed works on Nazism, German
history and politics 1918-1945, supported by
two closely related collections of
contemporary publications on 19th-century
European socialism and labor movements;
incl many NSDAP publications.
CA —HOOVER INSTITUTION ON WAR,
REVOLUTION & PEACE, Stanford
University, Stanford, 94305. Milorad M
Drachkovitch, Archivist
Holdings: Mss Pix
Notes: Ms diaries, 1914-1924, microfilms,
photographs and photostats of documents
from the *Personlicher Stab Reichsfuhrer SS,*
Schriftgutverwaltung dealing wiht the life
and career of Himmler as Reichsfuhrer SS
and Chef der Deutschen Polizei, 1934-1945.
6 notebooks (plus 25 loose pages), 5
microfilm reels, 2 photo albums, 14 ms
boxes. Incl 24 tapes of Himmler speeches,
1940-44.
CT —YALE UNIVERSITY, Box 1603A, Yale
Station, New Haven, 06520.
Holdings: Pix
Notes: Incl a collection of 116 photographs
of leaders of the Nazi Party, 1941-1944.
DC —LIBRARY OF CONGRESS, Rare Book
& Special Collections Div, Washington,
20540. William Matheson, Chief
Holdings: Vols 1019 Cat
Notes: The Third Reich Collection

comprises books and miscellaneous materials
that originally belonged to the Reichskanzlei
in Berlin or were in the Berghof, Hitler's
mountain retreat. It contains some books
specially printed or designed for Adolf
Hitler, but principally regular trade books;
periodicals; and books owned by or bearing
autographs of Hitler's associates. Incl
materials from the libraries of Hermann
Goering, Heinrich Himmler, and Franz
Xaver Schwarz.
DC —LIBRARY OF CONGRESS, Prints &
Photographs Div, Washington, 20540.
Notes: Personal photo albums of Hermann
Goring provide detailed coverage of his
activities during World War I and the years
1933-42. Biographical photographs of
Hermann Goring incl pictures by Helmuth
Kurth and Eitel Lange.
IL —CHICAGO PUBLIC LIBRARY, Special
Collections Div, Cultural Center, 78 E
Washington St, Chicago, 60602. Laura
Linard, Cur
Holdings: Vols 400 // Cat
Notes: This small collection of Naziana is
significant in that most of it was collected by
Wallace Deuel, a Chicago newspaper
correspondent in Berlin during the 1930s.
The books, in English and German, were for
the most part purchased in Europe at the
time and are annotated throughout by Deuel.
The collection also contains titles on Italian
fascism and the Soviet Union, 1917-37.
IL —NORTHERN ILLINOIS UNIVERSITY,
Founders Memorial Library, Rare Books and
Special Collections Dept, De Kalb, 60115.
William R DuBois, Dept Head
Holdings: Vols (1350) // Cat
Notes: American, British and Soviet
pamphlet publications, ca 1860-1955 by or
about the radical labor movement, socialists,
communists and the radical right. Some
Nazi/anti-Nazi material. Collection is
computer-indexed by author, title, series,
publisher and date.
IL —NORTHWESTERN UNIVERSITY,
Library, Special Collections Dept, 1937
Sheridan Rd, Evanston, 60201. R Russell
Maylone, Cur
Holdings: Vols 550 Cat
Notes: World War II underground
publications. Additional 400 monographs
and serials from Denmark; 65 vols from
Norway; 80 vols from misc other European
countries under Nazi occupation.
IL —LAKE FOREST COLLEGE, Donnelley
Library, Lake Forest, 60045. Arthur H
Miller Jr, College Librn
Holdings: Vols (700) Microform
Notes: Pese Collection of books, pamphlets,
and journals on Hitler, Hitler's foreign
policy, and Nazi era Germany.
IN —BALL STATE UNIVERSITY, University
Libraries, Special Collections Dept,
University Ave, Muncie, 47306. David C
Tambo, Head of Special Collections
Holdings: Vols 251 // Cat
Notes: Nazi Collection, primarily in German
with some titles in English or French.
IA —UNIVERSITY OF IOWA, University
Libraries, Iowa City, 52242.
Holdings: Vols 1850 Mss
Notes: The Leo W Schwarz Collection, a
valuable and rare group of books dealing
with Hasidic literature, a portion on Old
Testament studies and works on Jewish
history, philosophy and culture, the Jews in
Nazi Germany, Jewish folklore and the
history of the Jews in the US. Incl about 850
books in Hebrew and 1000 in other
languages, mss of several of Schwarz's books
and articles, correspondence, notes, and
background research relating to his
publications.
MA —HARVARD UNIVERSITY LIBRARY,
Cambridge, 02138.
Holdings: Cat
Notes: Nazi publications, incl "Sturm und
Drang" materials.
MA —BRANDEIS UNIVERSITY, Goldfarb
Library, 415 South St, Waltham, 02154.
Bessie Hahn, Dir
Notes: Theresienstadt Concentration Camp
Documents. Consists of over 200 "daily
order" bulletins issued by the German
command. Many of them contain lists of

arrival and departure of internees. A finding
list to the documents is located in Special
Collections. No photocopying of the
documents is permitted. Hall-Hoag Archives
on Extremism in the US. Approx 5000
pieces of Extremist literature, both Right and
Left, dealing with various social, religious
and political aspects of the US from the
1960s, 1970s and 1980s. A finding list is in
Special Collections. Material is arranged by
the name of the sponsoring organization in
alphabetical order.
MA —BRANDEIS UNIVERSITY, Goldfarb
Library, 415 South St, Waltham, 02154.
Bessie Hahn, Dir
Notes: Nazi Documents Collection: 3 linear
ft of documents and letters of major Nazi
officials prior to and during World War II. A
finding list to the documents is in Special
Collections. Hall-Hoag Archives on
Extremism in the US. Approx 5000 pieces of
Extremist literature, both Right and Left,
dealing with various social, religious and
political aspects of the US from the 1960s,
1970s and 1980s. A finding list is in Special
Collections. Material is arranged by the
name of the sponsoring organization in
alphabetical order.
MI —UNIVERSITY OF MICHIGAN, Library,
Dept of Rare Books & Special Collections,
Ann Arbor, 48109. Robert J Starring, Head
Holdings: Uncat Mss Pix
Notes: Especially the period 1920-1945. The
Myers Collection contains over 3,000
German pamphlets, brochures, serials, and
circulars of the Weimar and Nazi period.
Partially listed in H P Rothfeder, *Checklist
of Selected German Pamphlets...of the
Weimar and Nazi Period in the University of
Michigan Library* (Ann Arbor, 1961). The
German Archival Papers include the official
papers, chiefly correspondence, 1931-1944,
of Hermann Kohler, District leader of the
Nationalsozialistische Deutsche Arbeiter-
Partei, Eisenach District, consisting of 3300
items plus 3 feet, and 7 photograph albums.
Described in G L Weinberg, *German
Archival Material In the Rare Book Room,
the University of Michigan Library* (Ann
Arbor, nd).
MI —UNIVERSITY OF MICHIGAN, Library,
Dept of Rare Books & Special Collections,
Ann Arbor, 48109. Robert J Starring, Head
Holdings: Cat Mss Microforms
Notes: Espec strong in literature of the Nazi
period. These have been partially described
in *Checklist of Selected German Pamphlets
and Booklets of the Wiemar and Nazi Period
in the University of Michigan Library,* by
Herbert P Rothfeder, and *German Archival
Material in the Rare Book Room, University
of Michigan Library* by Professor Gerhard
Weinberg. Also on microfilm selected
German naval records issued between 1870
and 1944, German Foreign Ministry
Archives covering the period 1867-1920, and
selected records from military, ministerial,
and party archives covering the years 1933-
1945.
NY —ALFRED UNIVERSITY, Herrick
Memorial Library, Alfred, 14802. June E
Brown, Head Librn
Holdings: Vols (700) // Uncat Pix
Notes: The Waid Collection. Incl a number
of rare titles from the Nazi period. Books in
the collection, not on the "verboten list," incl
the writings of Stegmann, Ganghofer, Brandi
and Sealsfield.
†NY —COLUMBIA UNIVERSITY
LIBRARIES, Butler Library, Rare Book and
Manuscript Library, 535 W 114 St, New
York, 10027.
Notes: Papers relating to Prof Walter Lewis
Dorn's work as special advisor to Gen
Lucius D Clay on denazification of
Germany.
NY —YIVO INSTITUTE FOR JEWISH
RESEARCH, Library & Archives, 1048
Fifth Ave, New York, 10028. Dina
Abramowicz, Librn; Marek Web, Archivist
Holdings: Cat Mss Pix Slides
Notes: Special collection of books and
periodicals, incl government publications,
which appeared in Germany between the
years 1933-1945. Extensive library and
archives collections on history of Jews under

NATIONAL SOCIALISM (cont.)

Nazi rule in Europe, 1933-1945, in all languages. Hundreds of memorial vols for towns destroyed by Nazis.

NY —STATE UNIVERSITY OF NEW YORK, STONY BROOK, Melville Library, Stony Brook, 11794. John B Smith, Dir
Holdings: Cat
Notes: Modern German history. Part of the Library's general research collections.

NC —DUKE UNIVERSITY, William R Perkins Library, Durham, 27706. Elvin E Strowd, University Librn
Notes: The (Quasi)-Nazi collection consists of approximately 7000 items, primarily pamphlets published in the United States by and about Nazi sympathizers Gerald K Smith, Father Coughlin, etc and organizations with Nazi leanings.

TX —ABILENE CHRISTIAN UNIVERSITY, Margaret & Herman Brown Library, ACU Sta, Abilene, 79601. Callie Faye Milliken, Assoc Dir
Holdings: Vols 5000 // Cat
Notes: Donner Library of Americanism. Books, pamphlets, documents, and periodical materials dealing with American politics of the far right collected by Robert Donner during and after World War II. Also incl materials on Jews and Freemasonry.

WI —UNIVERSITY OF WISCONSIN, MADISON, Memorial Library, 728 State St, Madison, 53706. Erwin K Welsch, Social Studies Bibliographer
Holdings: Vols (15,000) Cat Mss Microforms
Notes: A collection of pamphlets, books, and periodicals relating to the rise and dominance of National Socialism in Germany. There is particular strength in the periodicals collection with many titles unusually complete. Among the manuscripts are those of a soldier on the eastern front and of a Nazi school for girls.

NATIONAL SONGS

NY —BARNARD A & MORRIS N YOUNG LIBRARY OF EARLY AMERICAN POPULAR MUSIC, 270 Riverside Dr, New York, 10025. Morris N Young, Cur
Holdings: Cat Mss Pix Phonorecords Audiotapes Microforms
Notes: 48,000 items of American popular music, mostly 1790-1910. Incl books, serials, sheet music, broadsides, anthologies, air checks, broadcasting and music business memorabilia, and correspondence.

NATIONAL STUDENT ASSOCIATION
see U.S. National Student Association

NATIONAL THEATRE CONFERENCE

IN —INDIANA UNIVERSITY, Lilly Library, Seventh St, Bloomington, 47405. William R Cagle, Librn
Holdings: // Mss Pix
Notes: Files of the National Theatre Conference, 1932-1965. Incl the papers of past presidents, executive secretary, and treasurer of the NTC (17,596 items). Also mss of individual plays, eg, Synge's *Playboy of the Western World*, Pinter's *The Caretaker*, Barrie's *Peter Pan*, John Whiting's *The Gates of Summer*, Archibald MacLeish's *JB*, LeRoi Jones' *The Baptism* and *Dutchman*, etc.

NY —NEW YORK PUBLIC LIBRARY, Performing Arts Research Center, Billy Rose Theatre Collection, 111 Amsterdam Ave, New York, 10023. Dorothy L Swerdlove, Cur
Holdings: Cat
Notes: Incl reports, correspondence, minutes of meetings, etc.

NATIONAL TRADE AND PROFESSIONAL SCHOOL FOR WOMEN AND GIRLS, INC.

DC —LIBRARY OF CONGRESS, Manuscript Division, Washington, 20540. John C Broderick, Chief
Holdings: 135,200 Items
Notes: Correspondence, reports, student and financial records, subject files, scrapbooks, clippings, photographs, printed matter, and other memorabilia of Nannie Helen Burroughs (1878-1961).

NATIONAL TRAINING SCHOOL FOR WOMEN AND GIRLS

DC —LIBRARY OF CONGRESS, Manuscript Division, Washington, 20540. John C Broderick, Chief
Holdings: 135,200 Items
Notes: Correspondence, reports, student and financial records, subject files, scrapbooks, clippings, photographs, printed matter, and other memorabilia of Nannie Helen Burroughs (1878-1961).

NATIONAL URBAN LEAGUE

DC —LIBRARY OF CONGRESS, Manuscript Division, Washington, 20540. John C Broderick, Chief
Notes: Records; additions, 1977- .

NATIONAL VOLLEYBALL ASSOCIATION

TX —UNIVERSITY OF TEXAS LIBRARIES, General Libraries, PO Box P, Austin, 78713. Carolyn Bucknell, Asst Dir for Collection Development
Holdings: Cat
Notes: Official archives of the National Volleyball Association.

NATIONAL WAR LABOR BOARD

IL —CENTER FOR RESEARCH LIBRARIES, 6050 S Kenwood Ave, Chicago, 60637. Donald B Simpson, Dir; Esther Smith, Collection Development Librn

NATIONAL WELFARE RIGHTS ORGANIZATION

DC —HOWARD UNIVERSITY, Moorland-Spingarn Research Center, 500 Howard Place NW, Washington, 20059. Clifford L Muse, Jr, Acting Dir
Holdings: Vols (106,086) Mss Maps Pix Slides Phonorecords Audiotapes 16mm Films Filmstrips Microforms
Budget: ($854,753)
See also entry under Blacks

NATIONAL WOMAN'S PARTY

DC —LIBRARY OF CONGRESS, Manuscript Division, Washington, 20540. John C Broderick, Chief
Notes: Records; additions, 1977- .

NATIONAL WOMEN'S TRADE UNION LEAGUE OF AMERICA

DC —LIBRARY OF CONGRESS, Manuscript Division, Washington, 20540. John C Broderick, Chief
Notes: Papers.

NATIONALISM—AFRICA

CA —HOOVER INSTITUTION ON WAR, REVOLUTION & PEACE, Stanford University, Stanford, 94305. Peter Duignan, Cur; Karen Fung, Deputy Cur
Holdings: Vols (60,000) Cat Mss Maps Pix Slides Microforms
Notes: Politics, economics, and history from 1870 to the present. About 500 current periodicals titles, about 90 current newspaper titles. Legislative debates, political ephemera. Have microfilm of Portuguese African nationalist material, confidential prints of Great Britian's foreign and colonial offices 1870 through 1922. Nigerian pamphlets (market literature, political and historical tracts), collection of the correspondence pamphlets and ephemera of Alfred B Xuma, collections on Zaire (1955-1963), South African nationalist publications on microfilm. Descriptions of the Collection: *African and Middle East Collections* pub by Hoover Institute, *Handbook of American Resources for African Studies* pub by Hoover. Holdings of the Collection in *Hoover Institute on War, Revolution, and Peace Library Catalog* pub by G K Hall, *Emerging Nationalism in Portuguese Africa: A Bibliography* pub by Hoover, *German Africa* pub by Hoover. *The Treason Trail in South Africa: A Guide to the Microfilm Record of the Trial* pub by Hoover. *History of the Library and Archives of the Hoover Institution on War, Revolution and Peace*, edited by Peter Duignan (Hoover Institution Press), *Guide to Non-federal Archives and Manuscripts in the United States Relating to Africa*, compiled Aloha P Smith (East Ardsley, Eng, Microform Ltd).

DC —HOWARD UNIVERSITY, Moorland-Spingarn Research Center, 500 Howard Place NW, Washington, 20059. Clifford L Muse, Jr, Acting Dir

NATIONALISM—INDIA

DC —GEORGETOWN UNIVERSITY, Library, Special Collections Div, 37 & O Sts NW, Washington, 20057. George M Barringer, Special Collections Librn; Nicholas B Sheetz, Mss Librn
Holdings: Mss Cat
Notes: The papers of Taraknath Das containing correspondence, mss, and newspaper clippings. The correspondence concerns the publication of Das' *Indien in der Weltpolitik* (Munchen, 1932). Incl are acknowledgement letters from Adolf Hitler (1 TLS, 1932) and from von Hindenburg (1 TLS, 1932). Also inc in the papers are numerous mss of articles written by Das, chiefly on Indian nationalism. Das joined the nationalist movement in India in 1903. Restricted.

NATIONALISM, BLACK see Black Nationalism

NATIONS, LAW OF see International Law

NATIVE AMERICAN NEWSPAPERS see Newspapers, Native American

NATIVE RACES

NY —NEW YORK PUBLIC LIBRARY, Research Libraries, General Research Division, Fifth Ave & 42 St, New York, 10018. Rodney Phillips, Chief
Holdings: Vols (2,225,000) Cat Maps Pix Microforms
Budget: ($775,718)

MB —HUDSON'S BAY CO, Library, 77 Main St, Winnipeg, R3C 2R1, Can. Carol Preston, Librn Hudson's Bay House
Holdings: Vols (6000) Cat Mss Maps Pix Slides
Notes: Main purpose is to provide research materials for production of the historical quarterly *The Beaver,* and to answer inquiries about the Company's history. Incl 250,000 pictures and 7000 VF pieces. No published catalog, but Library maintains author/subject/title card catalog. Limited photocopying. Mss of HBC Archives held by the Manitoba Provincial Archives. Published descriptions: Dowdall, Judi, "Hudson's Bay Company Library," *Canadian Library Journal*, June 1974, p 179; Preston, Carol, "Hudson's Bay Company Library," *Manitoba Library Association Bulletin*, June 1976, pp 24-25.

NATIVISM

PA —BALCH INSTITUTE FOR ETHNIC STUDIES, Library, 18 S Seventh St, Philadelphia, 19106. R Joseph Anderson, Library Dir
Holdings: Vols 200 Cat
Notes: Especially in the US and Canada.

NATONEK, HANS, 1892-1963

NY —STATE UNIVERSITY OF NEW YORK AT ALBANY, Library, Special Collections Dept, 1400 Washington Ave, Albany, 12222.

NATONEK, HANS, 1892-1963 (cont.)

Marion P Munzer, Coordr
Notes: Mss and publications by and about
Hans Natonek (15 linear feet). Part of the
Library's German Exile Collection.
See also entry under Authors

NATURAL BOUNDARIES see
Boundaries

NATURAL HISTORY

AK —ALASKA STATE LIBRARY, Alaska
Historical Library Collection, Pouch G,
Juneau, 99811. Phyllis Demuth, Readers
Services Librn
Holdings: Vols (24,000) Cat Mss Maps Pix
Slides Phonorecords Audiotapes Videotapes
16mm Films Microforms

AZ —ARIZONA-SONORA DESERT
MUSEUM, Library, Rte 9, Box 900, Tucson,
85743. Janice Hunter, Librn
Holdings: Vols (3000) Cat Pix Slides
Videotapes 16mm Films
Notes: Ecology and natural history of the
Southwest. Carr Collection on beavers. Incl
200 pictures, 5000 slides, 40 videotapes, and
6 films. Separate index of slides.

CA —UNIVERSITY OF CALIFORNIA,
BERKELEY, Museum of Vertebrate
Zoology, Grinnell-Miller Library, Berkeley,
94720.
Holdings: Vols (2000) Cat
Notes: Vertebrate zoology, with emphasis on
birds and mammals of the Pacific States.

CA —DEATH VALLEY NATIONAL
MONUMENT, Library, Death Valley,
92328. Shirley Harding, Cur/Librn
Holdings: Vols 3000 Cat Mss Maps Pix
Slides
Notes: Death Valley (History, Archeology,
Geology, Natural History, etc). Reference
Library only.

CA —UNIVERSITY OF CALIFORNIA, LOS
ANGELES, Biomedical Library, Center for
the Health Sciences, Los Angeles, 90024.
Alison Bunting, Acting Biomedical Librn;
Victoria Steele, Head, History & Special
Collections Div
Notes: Particularly strong in English and
French landmark titles, eg Darwin (first ed.)
and Buffon.

CA —UNIVERSITY OF SOUTHERN
CALIFORNIA, Allan Hancock Foundation,
Hancock Library of Biology and
Oceanography, Los Angeles, 90007.
Kimberly Douglas, Librn
Holdings: Vols (16,000) Cat Maps
Notes: Mostly marine, but incl some land
expeditions. Covers all geographical areas.
Also incl serial collection of 80,000 vols.

†CA —ZOOLOGICAL SOCIETY OF SAN
DIEGO, Ernst Schwarz Library, San Diego
Zoo, Box 551, San Diego, 92112.

CA —CALIFORNIA ACADEMY OF
SCIENCES, J W Mailliard Jr Library,
Golden Gate Park, San Francisco, 94118.
Ray Brian, Librn
Notes: Downs No 2160.

†CA —HUNTINGTON BOTANICAL
GARDENS LIBRARY, 1151 Oxford Rd,
San Marino, 91108. Ann Ravenscroft,
Secretary
Holdings: Vols (8000)
Notes: Emphases on history of botanical
science; papers and notes of American
botanists and naturalists of The West;
botanical illustration, etc. Subtropical
horticulture, incl cacti and succulents of
Australia, South Africa, and Mexico.

CA —UNIVERSITY OF CALIFORNIA,
SANTA BARBARA, Library, Dept of
Special Collections, Santa Barbara, 93106.
Christian F Brun, Head
Holdings: Cat Mss Pix
Notes: Letters and mss of American
naturalist and author Donald Culross Peattie;
15,343 items.

CA —UNIVERSITY OF CALIFORNIA,
SANTA CRUZ, University Library, Special
Collections, Santa Cruz, 95064. Rita
Bottoms, Special Collections Librn; Margaret
Felts, South Pacific Collection Bibliographer
Holdings: Vols (10,000) Cat
Notes: South Pacific Collection.

Monographs, rare books, serials, documents
and atlases which treat of the Pacific areas of
Polynesia, Melanesia, Micronesia, Australia
and New Zealand, but excluding western
New Guinea (Irian Jaya), the Philippines
and Southeast Asia. Approximately 10
percent of the titles are multi-volume
documents such as parliamentary papers,
legislative journals, official yearbooks,
statistical sourcebooks, laws and statutes.
The collection includes an exhaustive
selection of current journals and
monographic series from and about the
Pacific: early serials, South Pacific
Commission publications, US Government
and US Trust Territory publications, serials
from museums, universities and scholarly
societies. Chief emphasis has been placed on
acquisition of the literature of history,
description and travel, ethnology
andanthropology, literature and literary
criticism, political and constitutional
histories. Other extensive holdings are in the
fields of geography and maps, voyages,
mission histories, mythology and folklore,
art, linguistics, and science fields of natural
history, environmental studies, biology,
zoology, botany, geology and astronomy.
Printed catalog is available. This is an ongoing, growing collection.

CA —UNIVERSITY OF THE PACIFIC,
Library, Stockton, 95211. Hiram L Davis,
Dir of Libraries
Holdings: Cat Mss Pix
Notes: Papers of John Muir. Incl are
correspondence, mss, clippings, pamphlets,
drawings and photgraphs.

CO —COLORADO STATE UNIVERSITY,
Libraries, Fort Collins, 80523. Curtis L
Gifford, Forestry & Agricultural Sciences
Librn
Holdings: Vols 18,944 Cat Maps
Budget: $9000
Notes: Colorado State University Libraries
are particularly strong in genetics.

CO —VAIL PUBLIC LIBRARY, 292 W
Meadow Dr, Vail, 81657. Charlyn M C
Canada, Librn
Holdings: Vols (500) Cat Maps
Budget: ($5300)
Notes: The alpine environment.

CT —LEE ASH, (personal collection), 66
Humiston Dr, Bethany, 06525.
Holdings: Mss Maps Pix
Notes: First editions, mss, ephemera,
memorabilia; especially bibliography of
natural history.

CT —WHITE MEMORIAL
CONSERVATION CENTER, Route 202
PO Box 368, Litchfield, 06759. Gene F
Marra, Exec Dir
Holdings: Vols (3300) Cat Phonorecords VF
Budget: ($1000)
Notes: Library is housed in museum located
on grounds of a private 4000 acre nature
preserve managed for use by the public.

CT —YALE UNIVERSITY, Beinecke Rare
Book & Manuscript Library, Osborn
Collection, New Haven, 06520. Stephen R
Parks, Cur
Holdings: Mss

CT —UNIVERSITY OF CONNECTICUT,
Museum of Natural History, Storrs, 06268.

†CT —UNIVERSITY OF CONNECTICUT
LIBRARY, Special Collections Dept, Storrs,
06268. Richard H Schimmelpfeng, Dir of
Special Collections
Notes: Papers, incl mss, etc. of the naturalist
Edwin Way Teale.

DC —LIBRARY OF CONGRESS, Rare Book
& Special Collections Div, Washington,
20540. William Matheson, Chief
Notes: President Theodore Roosevelt's
library of late 19th and early 20th century
works on hunting, exploration, and natural
history, with a few earlier classics in these
fields.

DC —NATIONAL GEOGRAPHIC
SOCIETY, Library, 1146 16th St NW,
Washington, 20036. Susan Fifer Canby, Dir
Holdings: Vols (63,000) Cat Mss Maps Pix
Notes: Material concerning land, sea, and
space exploration--past and present. All
fields of anthropology, natural history,
geography, etc.

DC —SMITHSONIAN INSTITUTION,
Archives Div, Washington, 20560. William

W Moss, Archivist
Holdings: Mss Maps Pix
Notes: The Archives holds the records of the
National Museum of Natural History, as
well as the papers of many naturalists and
the records of professional societies relating
to natural history.

DC —SMITHSONIAN INSTITUTION,
Smithsonian Tropical Research Institute,
Washington, 20560. Carol Jopling, Chief
Librn
Holdings: Vols (22,000) Cat Mss Maps Pix
Slides 16mm Films Microforms
Budget: ($70,000)
Notes: Smithsonian Institution, Smithsonian
Tropical Research Institute is located in
Balboa, Panama.

DC —SMITHSONIAN INSTITUTION
LIBRARIES, Natural History Branch,
Washington, 20560. Sylvia Churgin, Chief
Librn
Holdings: Vols (75,550) Cat Mss Maps Pix
Slides Microforms
Notes: Incl vertebrate and invertebrate
paleontology; vertebrate zoology: systematics
and taxonomy.

FL —UNIVERSITY OF MIAMI, Otto G
Richter Library, PO Box 248214, Coral
Gables, 33124. Frank Rodgers, Dir of
Libraries
Holdings: Vols Microforms
Notes: The Rosenstiel School of Marine and
Atmospheric Sciences Library is one of the
major marine science collections in the
United States and is especially strong in the
literature of tropical oceanography. Special
collections in the library incl 200
oceanographic atlases and more than 50 sets
of the world's major expedition reports. The
library also maintains a nautical chart
collection. 3000 microforms; 1000 current
subscriptions.

FL —ARCHBOLD BIOLOGICAL STATION,
Library, Rt 2, Box 180, Lake Placid, 33852.
Fred E Lohrer, Librn
Holdings: Vols (2000) Cat Periodicals

HI —BERNICE P BISHOP MUSEUM,
Library, PO Box 19000-A, Honolulu, 96819.
Cynthia Timberlake, Librn

IL —ILLINOIS NATURAL HISTORY
SURVEY LIBRARY, 196 Natural Resources
Bldg, Champaign, 61820. Carla G Heister,
Librn
Holdings: Vols (36,000) Cat Microforms
Budget: ($25,500)
Notes: A Research and Science Branch of
the State of Illinois, the Natural History
Survey maintains a library of books, journals
and reports on various aspects of natural
history. Material is collected in all major
languages. The library maintains its own
exchange arrangements with some 600
worldwide institutions and organizations.
Interlibrary loans and photocopy services are
available through the University of Illinois
Library. Publications issued regularly by the
Survey incl *Biological Notes, The Bulletin,
and Circulars.*

IL —FIELD MUSEUM OF NATURAL
HISTORY, Library, Roosevelt Rd & Lake
Shore Dr, Chicago, 60605. W Peyton
Fawcett, Librn; Benjamin W Williams, Assoc
Librn
Holdings: Vols (210,000) Cat
Budget: ($100,000)
Notes: Extensive collections--publications of
learned societies and institutions and
monographic works--in all fields of natural
history, with emphasis on taxonomy and
evolutionary biology; and on museum
publications, American and foreign:
anthropology, especially archaeology and
ethnology of the Americas, Africa, East
Asia, and Oceania; botany, particularly
strong for the Americas; geology, chiefly
paleontology and meteoritic studies; and
zoology, worldwide (birds, fishes, insects,
mammals, mollusks, reptiles and
amphibians).

IL —CHICAGO BOTANIC GARDEN
LIBRARY, PO Box 400, Glencoe, 60022.
Virginia Henrichs, Librn
Holdings: Vols 6000

IL —UNIVERSITY OF ILLINOIS,
URBANA/CHAMPAIGN, Library, Biology
Library, 101 Burrill Hall, 407 S Goodwin,

NATURAL HISTORY (cont.)

Urbana, 61801. Elisabeth B Davis, Librn
Holdings: Vols (115,000) Cat Microforms
Budget: ($200,000)
Notes: The Biology Library incl books, periodicals, and reference works that cover the fields of anatomy, biophysics, botany, ecology, entomology, genetics, immunology, microbiology, physiology and zoology. About three-quarters of the total collection is made up of journals and other serials representing 2000 distinctive titles. The serial list is comprehensive for the biological sciences, contains most of the major international titles and consists of complete runs for almost all titles. Additional materials (approx 90,000 vols) in the biological sciences are available in the Natural History Survey Library and the bookstacks at the Main Library on the Urbana campus. Professional assistance is available for reference service, online searching, and library instruction. Interlibrary loan service is provided. Photocopying.

IL —UNIVERSITY OF ILLINOIS, URBANA/CHAMPAIGN, Slavic and East European Library, Urbana, 61801. Marianna Tax Choldin, Head
Holdings: Vols (420,000) Cat Microforms
Notes: One of the largest Slavic and East European collections. Strong in Russian and Soviet materials-humanities, sciences, and social sciences; languages and literatures; periodicals, newspapers, and microforms. Ca 260,000 volumes in languages of the Soviet Union plus 20,000 Russian and Ukrainian titles on microform. Extensive coverage of Czechoslovakia (35,000 vols); Yugoslavia (31,000 vols); Bulgaria (9200 vols); Poland (34,600 vols); Romania (13,000 vols); and Hungary (18,000 vols) and the languages, literatures, and history of these countries.

IA —IOWA STATE UNIVERSITY, Library, Ames, 50011. Warren B Kuhn, Dean of Library Services
Holdings: Cat
Notes: Monographs, rare books, extensive serial holdings. Strong in all biological fields.

KS —UNIVERSITY OF KANSAS, Kenneth Spencer Research Library, Special Collections Dept, Lawrence, 66045. Alexandra Mason, Librn
Holdings: Cat Mss Pix
Notes: Ellis Collection of Ornithology, Natural History and Voyages and Travels. Medical botany and herbals. Linnaeus Collection. Noncirculating.

KS —KANSAS STATE UNIVERSITY, Library, Special Collections & University Archives, Manhattan, 66506. Antonia Q Pigno, Coordr; John J Vander Velde, Librn; Anthony R Crawford, Univ Archivist
Holdings: Vols 1280 Cat Microforms
Budget: ($10,000)
Notes: Catalog: Rudolph, G A and Williams, Evan. Linneana. Manhattan, Kansas: Kansas State University Library, 1970.

KS —TOPEKA ZOOLOGICAL PARK, Topeka Zoo Library, 635 Gage Blvd, Topeka, 66606. Ron Kaufman, Education Coordinator
Holdings: Vols (800) Cat Mss Maps Pix Slides Audiotapes 16mm Films Filmstrips Microforms
Budget: ($500)

LA —LOUISIANA STATE UNIVERSITY, Troy H Middleton Library, Baton Rouge, 70803. Lance E Dickson, Acting Dir
Holdings: Vols (3500) Cat Maps Pix
Notes: Noncirculating collection.

LA —LOUISIANA STATE UNIVERSITY, Troy H Middleton Library, Louisiana Room, Baton Rouge, 70803. Evangeline Mills Lynch, Head Librn; Ruth Murray, Associate Librn
Holdings: Vols (33,500) Cat Maps VF
Notes: Louisiana Collection of history, description and travel, biography, agriculture, literature, politics and government, folklore, anthropology, geography, geology, education, language, music and natural history. Especially large subject collections may be found on

Louisiana, the history of the lower Mississippi Valley, Abraham Lincoln, Romance languages and literatures, sugar culture and technology, Southern history, petroleum engineering, plant pathology, micropaleontology, ornithology, and various aspects of crawfish life, biology and culture. Complete depository of Louisiana State Documents; extensive newspapers clipping files; separate card catalog; items listed in Louisiana Union Catalog; restricted use (research and reference). Incl both materials about Louisiana and by Louisianians without regard to subject. LSU Press Collection(preservation copy of each title kept for exhibit purposes only). LSU theses and dissertations from 1900-date. LSU Faculty Collection. Also, 1300 maps, 104 VF drawers, 250 boxes of uncataloged pamphlets.

ME —COLLEGE OF THE ATLANTIC, Thorndike Library, Bar Harbor, 04609. Marcie L Dworak, Libr Dir
Notes: A rebuilding, fire-destroyed library (1983).

ME —BOWDOIN COLLEGE, Library, Brunswick, 04011. Dianne M Gutscher, Cur of Special Collections
Holdings: Vols Cat Mss
Notes: (1) A collection of the works of Henry Beston, naturalist and author. (2) The Kate Furbish Collection of the "Flora of Maine" consists of her watercolor sketches of specimens collected between 1870 and 1908. (3) A miscellaneous collection of ten logs and journals kept by members of the Bowdoin expeditions to Labrador in 1860 and 1891; as well as 29 letters, a log book, and about 100 newsclippings from the John C Parker Papers, concerning the Labrador expedition of 1891; and about 200 nitrate negatives and 200 mounted prints of those negatives done by Alfred O Gross, professor of biology at Bowdoin, when he accompanied Donald B MacMillan on an expedition to Labrador in 1934. Most of the pictures are of native birds and nesting sites.

ME —BATES COLLEGE, George & Helen Ladd Library, Special Collections, Bardwell St, Lewiston, 04240. Mary Riley, Special Collections Librn
Holdings: Vols 602// Cat
Notes: Ornithological and natural history books from the collections of Bates Professor Jonathan Young Stanton, 1834-1918.

ME —UNIVERSITY OF MAINE AT PRESQUE ISLE LIBRARY, 181 Main St, Presque Isle, 04769. Anna McGrath, Technical Services Librn
Holdings: Vols 1100
Budget: $500
Notes: Aroostook County, Maine. Vertical file material, photographs, artifacts, tapes (oral history), maps, scrapbooks, diaries, journals.

MD —JOHNS HOPKINS UNIVERSITY, Milton S Eisenhower Library, Charles & 34 Sts, Baltimore, 21218. Ann S Gwyn, Assistant Dir for Special Collections
Holdings: Vols (46,500) Cat
Notes: Very strong in all the biological fields except taxonomy. Strongest in molecular biology, cell physiology and premedical areas. Strong in journals, espec in biochemistry. Many long runs of rare journals. Natural science not as strong as biochemistry. Contemporary monographs better than earlier ones.

MD —JOHNS HOPKINS UNIVERSITY, Milton S Eisenhower Library, Special Collections, John Work Garrett Library, 4545 N Charles St, Baltimore, 21210. Jane Katz, Garrett Librn
Holdings: Vols Cat Mss Maps
Notes: The John Work Garrett Library incl 100 maps; 1500 autograph letters; early voyages and travels; Americana; early Maryland imprints and Marylandia; Bible collection; 17th century English Literature (4 Shakespeare folios, 2 quartos); ornithology and natural history (complete set of Gould's Birds); early illustrated books; 19th and 20th century adult and children's illustrated books; typography (Kent Currie), limited editions, incl Bruce Rogers proof sheets; Fowler Architectural Collection (has own

book catalog); Sidney Lanier Personal Library, books he wrote and his ms music collection. Downs (1961-70) 444.

MD —MARYLAND ACADEMY OF SCIENCES, Maryland Science Center, 601 Light Street, Baltimore, 21230.
Notes: Planetarium and exhibits.

MD —NATIONAL AQUARIUM IN BALTIMORE, Pier 3, 501 East Pratt St, Baltimore, 21202. Lee Campbell, Librn
Notes: Staff members only.

MA —HABITAT INSTITUTE FOR THE ENVIRONMENT, Library, 10 Juniper Rd, Belmont, 02178. Barbara Herzstein, Librn
Holdings: Vols 3000 // Cat

MA —APPALACHIAN MOUNTAIN CLUB, 5 Joy St, Boston, 02108. Fran Belcher, Librn
Holdings: Vols (6500) Cat Maps Pix Slides
Budget: ($3000)
Notes: Mountaineering, espec the White Mountains. Bound editions of other countries, mountaineering journals.

MA —CHILDREN'S MUSEUM, Resource Center, Museum Wharf, 300 Congress St, Boston, 02210. Marie Ariel, Librn; Maria Russell, Resource Services Mgr
Holdings: Vols 400 Cat Mss Filmstrips
Notes: Curriculum materials and materials for children and adults. Available for reference use by the public; borrowing privileges for Museum members; activity and curriculum kits available to public, schools and community groups for rental fee. Subject-related programs and services offered by Museum staff.

MA —MUSEUM OF SCIENCE, Library, Science Park, Boston, 02114. Edward D Pearce, Librn
Holdings: Vols 15,000 Cat Mss Pix
Notes: 18th, 19th, 20th century American. Almost all in English language. Downs 2298. Incl archives of the Boston Society of Natural History.

MA —CAPE COD MUSEUM OF NATURAL HISTORY, Clarence L Hay Library, Rte 6A, Brewster, 02631. Eileen R Bush, Librn
Holdings: Vols (4000) Cat Maps Pix Slides Phonorecords
Budget: ($1900)
Notes: No photocopying.

MA —HARVARD UNIVERSITY LIBRARY, Gray Herbarium Library, 22 Divinity Ave, Cambridge, 02138. Barbara A Callahan, Librn
Notes: Arnold Arboretum and Gray Herbarium Libraries hold one of the nation's largest collections (149,000 items).

MA —NEW ENGLAND WILD FLOWER SOCIETY, INC, Lawrence Newcomb Library, Hemenway Rd, Framingham, 01701. Mary M Walker, Librn
Holdings: Vols (2500)
Budget: ($1000)
Notes: Incl 15,000 slides (35mm) and 4 vertical files.

MA —MASSACHUSETTS AUDUBON SOCIETY, Hathaway Environmental Education Institute, Lincoln, 01773. Louise C Maglione, Librn
Holdings: Cat Maps Pix Slides Phonorecords Audiotapes 16mm Films Filmstrips
Notes: Largest and most comprehensive collection in the field of environmental education; especially good in the curriculum area. Extensive sections on animal, behavioral and environmental issues, and quality of environment.

MA —OLD DARTMOUTH HISTORICAL SOCIETY, 18 Johnny Cake Hill, New Bedford, 02740. Richard C Kugler, Dir
Holdings: Vols (15,000) Mss Maps Pix Microforms
Notes: Whaling Museum Library contains one of the most comprehensive collections of printed and manuscript material ever assembled on the history of the whaling industry. Although primary emphasis is on American participation in this industry, foreign works are well-represented. Particularly noteworthy are the 5000 rare books and pamphlets assembled by the distinguished whaling scholar, Charles F Batchelder. Also, material on merchant ships and the natural history of whales. Incl 750 ft mss, 1070 log books, 650 maps, 25,000 pix and 25,000 photographs, and 1800 microforms.

NATURAL HISTORY (cont.)

MA —PEABODY MUSEUM OF SALEM,
Phillips Library, E India Sq, Salem, 01970.
Gregor Trinkaus-Randall, Librn
Holdings: Vols (100,000) Cat
Notes: Majority of books published before
1900. No published indexes.

MA —CAPE COD NATIONAL SEASHORE,
Reference Library, Park Headquarters S,
Wellfleet, 02663. Virginia Osborn, Librn
Holdings: Vols (3000) Cat Mss Maps Pix
Slides Phonorecords 16mm Films
Budget: ($2000)
Notes: Cape Cod natural and human history.

MI —UNIVERSITY OF MICHIGAN,
Museums Library, Ann Arbor, 48109.
Patricia B Yocum, Librn
Holdings: Vols (100,000) Cat Maps
Microforms

MI —DETROIT PUBLIC LIBRARY, Rare
Books Department, 5201 Woodward Ave,
Detroit, 48202.
Holdings: Cat Maps Pix

MN —MINNESOTA ZOOLOGICAL
GARDEN, Apple Valley, 55124. Angela
Norell, Librn
Notes: Classified card catalog; Journal
reprints are fairly comprehensive for the
animals in the collection, which are primarily
Southeast Asian, Northern-dwelling, and
native Minnesotan. Collection includes 2000
books, 60 periodical subscriptions and 3000
reprints of journal articles.

MN —UNIVERSITY OF MINNESOTA,
Landscape Arboretum, Andersen
Horticultural Library, 3675 Arboretum
Drive, Box 39, Chanhassen, 55317. June
Rogier, Head
Holdings: Vols (8000)

MN —MINNEAPOLIS PUBLIC LIBRARY &
INFORMATION CENTER, 300 Nicollet
Mall, Minneapolis, 55401. Richard J
Hofstad, Athenaeum Librn
Holdings: Vols 700 Cat Pix
Notes: Incl rare books in natural history.
Emphasis on botany and ornithology.

MN —MAYO MEDICAL LIBRARY, History
of Medicine Collection, Rochester, 55905.
Nancy R Hensel, Librn
Holdings: Vols 50 Cat
Notes: The C Wilbur Rucker "Pliny"
Collection, incl 43 14th, 15th and 16th
editions of the more than 200 editions of
Historica naturalis by C Plinius Secundus.

MO —MISSOURI BOTANICAL GARDEN
LIBRARY, PO Box 299, Saint Louis, 63166.
M R Crosby, Dir of Research
Holdings: Cat
Notes: Sturtevant Collection of pre-Linnean
(pre-1753) books and Linnean collection.
Also George Engelmann's correspondence
with famous botanists and 6000 letters
discussing botanical species. Also 60 vols of
his notes and beautifully drawn sketches
from his extensive studies on Cactaceae,
Coniferae, Yucca, Agave, Isoetes, etc.

MO —SAINT LOUIS PUBLIC LIBRARY,
Gardner Rare Book Room, 1301 Olive St,
Saint Louis, 63103. Julanne M Good,
Supervisor; Martha Riley, Rare Books Librn
Holdings: Vols 600 Cat
Notes: Collection of natural history from the
library of Benjamin Franklin Shumard,
nineteenth century paleontologist and
conchologist, and selected material pre-
dating 1870 transferred from St Louis Public
Library's general stack area. Noncirculating.

NJ —NEWARK MUSEUM LIBRARY, 49
Washington St, PO Box 540, Newark,
07101. Margaret DiSalvi, Librn
Holdings: Vols 1650 Cat

NJ —PRINCETON UNIVERSITY, Library,
Manuscript Collection, Nassau St, Princeton,
08540. Jean F Preston, Cur
Holdings: Vols 166 Cat Mss Pix
Notes: Mss incl 3 prose works, 25 notes for
animals in the *Quadrupeds*, over fifty letters,
and several watercolors and oils. See
Princeton University Library Chronicle, v
21, p 9-88. An unpublished typescript
catalog of the mss is available for
consultation.

NY —ADIRONDACK HISTORICAL
ASSOCIATION, Museum Library, Blue
Mountain Lake, 12812. Jerold Pepper, Librn
Holdings: Vols (7500) Cat Mss Maps Pix
Phonorecords Audiotapes 16mm Films
Microforms
Notes: Anything about the Adirondacks--
history, people, economics, places, things.
Strong in Adirondack art, outdoor
recreation, logging, small boats. Resources
incl more than 1000 maps, 40,000 pictures,
1600 microfilm reels, 576 linear ft of ms
material, and 12 cabinets of VF ephemera,
etc.

NY —NEW YORK ZOOLOGICAL SOCIETY
LIBRARY, Bronx Zoo, Bronx, 10460.
Steven P Johnson, Archivist and Librn
Holdings: Vols (6000) Cat Mss
Budget: ($50,000)
Notes: Collection consists primarily of
journals in captive management of animals,
vertebrate zoology, and veterinary medicine.
Primarily intended for the scientific staff, the
collection is open to the public on a
noncirculating basis, by appointment, (212)
220-6874.

NY —BUFFALO MUSEUM OF SCIENCE,
Buffalo Society of Natural Sciences,
Research Library, Humboldt Park, Buffalo,
14211. Marcia T Morrison, Chief Librn
Holdings: Vols 37,000 Cat Mss Pix
Notes: Natural sciences, anthropology,
archaeology.

NY —CORNELL UNIVERSITY LIBRARIES,
John M Olin Library, History of Science
Collections, Ithaca, 14853. Lillian A Clark,
Administrative Supervisor; David W Corson,
History of Science Librn
Notes: Very extensive collection of history,
biography and bibliography.
See also entry under Science - History

NY —AMERICAN MUSEUM OF
NATURAL HISTORY, Library Services
Dept, Central Park W & 79th St, New York,
10024. Nina J Root, Chairwoman; Mary
Genett, Asst Librn for Reference Services
Holdings: Vols (385,000) Cat Mss Maps Pix
Slides Microforms
Notes: Nearly all collections are outstanding
for depth of coverage and international
range. Early and historic works, rare books,
colored illustrations, and relevant serial
publications supplement the modern
scientific publications necessary to the
researches of the scientific staff and the
work of the educational division. Open to
the public. Also, The Ernest Thompson
Seton diaries. Thousands of pages of an
unpublished 67-year diary record of one of
the world's most famous naturalists, the gift
of Joseph F Cullman II, a Trustee of the
Museum. Preserved in 35 protective cases,
the gift incl unpublished diaries, notebooks,
and some other writings.

NY —EXPLORERS CLUB, James B Ford
Memorial Library, 46 E 70 St, New York,
10021. Janet Baldwin, Librn
Holdings: Vols (24,000) Cat Maps
Notes: Additions to the collection depend
upon gifts. Access by appointment only.

NY —NEW YORK HISTORICAL SOCIETY,
Library, 170 Central Park W, New York,
10024. James Gregory, Librn
Holdings: Mss
Notes: Incl original mss, illustrative
materials, etc.

NY —NEW YORK PUBLIC LIBRARY,
Research Libraries, General Research
Division, Fifth Ave & 42 St, New York,
10018. Rodney Phillips, Chief
Holdings: Vols (2,225,000) Cat Maps Pix
Microforms
Budget: ($775,718)

NY —SCHOELKOPF GEOLOGICAL
MUSEUM, Library, Prospect Park, Niagara
Falls, 14303. Robert Kesil, Librn
Holdings: Vols 200 Uncat
Notes: Natural history of Niagara Falls.

NY —VASSAR COLLEGE, Library, Rare
Books & Manuscripts Collection, Box 20,
Poughkeepsie, 12601. Lisa Browar, Cur
Notes: John Burroughs' 53 notebooks
comprising his manuscript journals, 1876 to
1921. Devoted principally to his
observations of nature, with many comments
of literary and political observations.

NC —SCHIELE MUSEUM OF NATURAL
HISTORY, Library, 1500 E Garrison Blvd,
Gastonia, 28052. Dot Gray, Librn; Margaret
Summerill, Librn
Holdings: Vols (3800) Cat Maps Pix Slides
Phonorecords Audiotapes 16mm Films
Filmstrips Microforms
Budget: ($2800)
Notes: Listed on RECON computer with
Library of Congress as Reference Center in
Southeast in subject areas of natural
sciences, aerospace and plantetarium
technology and anthropology.

ND —THEODORE ROOSEVELT
NATIONAL PARK, Library, PO Box 7,
Medora, 58645. Susan Snow, Librn; Miki
Hellickson, Chief Naturalist
Holdings: Vols (1500) Cat Mss Maps Pix
Slides Audiotapes 16mm Films
Budget: ($5000)
Notes: Theodore Roosevelt, cattle country
history, natural history. Also 2400 pictures
and 2200 slides.

OH —PUBLIC LIBRARY OF CINCINNATI
& HAMILTON COUNTY, Science &
Technology Dept, 800 Vine St, Cincinnati,
45202. Rosemary Gaiser, Head
Holdings: Vols (250,000) Cat
Notes: Pure and applied science. Incl over
1600 periodicals and serial titles and more
than 100 abstracting and indexing services in
major fields of science and technology.

OH —CLEVELAND MUSEUM OF
NATURAL HISTORY, Harold T Clark
Library, Wade Oval, University Circle,
Cleveland, 44106. Mary Baum, Librn
Holdings: Vols 30,000 Cat
Budget: $16,000

OH —CLEVELAND PUBLIC LIBRARY,
Science & Technology Dept, 325 Superior
Ave, Cleveland, 44114. Jean Z Piety, Head
Holdings: Cat Pix
Notes: Special collection covers the
environmental sciences concerned with the
Great Lakes-St Lawrence drainage basins.
Emphasis is on limnology, ecology,
meteorology, hydraulics, biology, pollution
of air and water, natural history and general
research. Most of the material indexed has
been donated by numerous agencies around
the Great Lakes.

OH —OHIO HISTORICAL SOCIETY,
Archives Library Division, 1982 Velma Ave,
Columbus, 43211. Dennis East, Division
Chief
Holdings: Vols (96,000) Cat Mss Maps Pix
Slides Microforms
Budget: ($18,000)
Notes: This library is the primary collection
for Ohio. Most purchases are on the rare
and op market. Collecting area is early
American history, esp relating to exploration
into the Northwest Territory. Major subject
areas are Ohio politics and government (8
presidents) military history (good collection
of regimental histories and Ohio narratives
of the Civil War), economic and social
history, local history, esp county histories &
atlases and city directories. Also, Ohio
archaeology, natural history, artifacts. Major
media collections are books (96,000),
newspapers (25,000 vols and 22,000
microfilm), pictures (50,000), maps (2500),
manuscripts (1,500,000). Library is
noncirculating except through interlibrary
loan of microfilm.

OH —HOLDEN ARBORETUM, Warren H
Corning Library, 9500 Sperry Rd, Mentor,
44060. Paul C Spector, Dir of Education
Holdings: Vols (5500) Cat
Notes: Extensive collection of horticultural
classics, floras, herbals and monographs prior
to 1850. Primarily European works.

OH —WARREN H CORNING LIBRARY,
9500 Sperry Rd, Mentor, 44060. Paul C
Spector, Dir of Education
Holdings: Vols (5400) Cat VF
Notes: 1500 vols of Warren H Corning
Horticulture Classics. Also 80 periodicals
and 10 vertical files.

PA —ACADEMY OF NATURAL SCIENCES
LIBRARY, 19 Benjamin Franklin Parkway,
Philadelphia, 19103.
Holdings: Vols (180,000) Cat Mss Maps Pix
Slides Microforms
Notes: Incl (250,000) mss. Described in
*Academy of Natural Sciences of
Philadelphia: Catalog* (Boston: G K Hall,

NATURAL HISTORY (cont.)

1972); *Guide to the Manuscript Collections in the Academy of Natural Sciences of Philadelphia*, by Venia T Phillips (Philadelphia: Academy of Natural Sciences, 1963).

PA —LIBRARY COMPANY OF PHILADELPHIA, 1314 Locust St, Philadelphia, 19107. Edwin Wolf II, Librn; Kenneth Finkel, Cur of Prints
Holdings: Vols (450,000) Cat
Notes: Significant collection of works on natural history of the Americas to 1860.

PA —ZOOLOGICAL SOCIETY OF PHILADELPHIA, Library, 34 & Girard Ave, Philadelphia, 19104. Alyssa N Scheuermann, Librn
Holdings: Vols (500) Cat
Notes: Photocopying with permission.

PA —CARNEGIE LIBRARY OF PITTSBURGH, Science & Technology Dept, 4400 Forbes Ave, Pittsburgh, 15213. Catherine M Brosky, Dept Head
Holdings: Vols (380,000) Cat Maps Microforms
Budget: ($240,000)
Notes: Incl both modern and classic works. Abstracts, indexes, bibliographies, taxonomic manuals and standard reference books. Many journals and society publications complete from the beginning.

PA —READING PUBLIC MUSEUM & ART GALLERY, Museum Library, 19611 Museum Rd, Reading, 19611. Bruce Dietrich, Dir
Holdings: Vols 8000 Cat

RI —UNIVERSITY OF RHODE ISLAND, Library, Special Collections, Kingston, 02881. David Maslyn, Head
Notes: Extensive collections.

RI —PROVIDENCE ATHENAEUM, 251 Benefit St, Providence, 02903. Sally Duplaix, Dir
Holdings: Vols 2,600 Cat
Notes: Incl many rare books in natural history.

SC —CHARLESTON MUSEUM LIBRARY, 360 Meeting St, Charleston, 29403. John Brumgardt, Museum Dir
Holdings: Vols 30,000 Cat Mss Maps Pix
Notes: Worldwide scope, emphasis on South Carolina.

SC —UNIVERSITY OF SOUTH CAROLINA, Thomas Cooper Library, Columbia, 29208. Kenneth E Toombs, Dir of Libraries; Roger Mortimer, Rare Book Librn
Holdings: Vols 1000 Cat
Notes: Especially for 1750-1850.

SD —SOUTH DAKOTA HISTORICAL RESOURCE CENTER, Library, Soldiers Memorial Bldg, Pierre, 57501. Rosemary Evetts, Librn
Holdings: Vols 1020 Cat Mss Maps Pix
Budget: $2000
Notes: South Dakota state and territorial materials. Picture collection has been cataloged and numbers approx 20,000 items, of which we have negatives for about half. South Dakota materials include items on general state and territorial history, biographical, autobiographical, political, geological, economic and county and town materials.

SD —SIOUXLAND HERITAGE MUSEUMS, Pettigrew Museum Library, 131 N Duluth Ave, Sioux Falls, 57104. Ms Lee N McLaird, Cur of Collections
Holdings: Vols (7500) Cat Mss Maps Pix
Budget: ($900)
Notes: Pettigrew Museum Library is a support service of the Siouxland Heritage Museums. US Senator R F Pettigrew established the core collection in 1926, covering natural history (incl North American Indian anthropology) and state-local history (concentrating on exploration and settlement to about 1900). The collection also incl the Senator's private papers (ca 1870-1926). Additions to the collection since 1926 have emphasized Plains Indian anthropology, state-local history, baseball and museology, supporting the work of the Museum staff. The collection is mostly cataloged and is inter-indexed with

Augustana College, Sioux Falls College, and Sioux Falls Public Libraries (as well as having its own catalog). The photograph collection includes prints by D F Barry as well as other photographers' work with native peoples.

TX —UNIVERSITY OF TEXAS, Marine Science Institute Library, Port Aransas, 78373. Ruth Grundy, Librn
Holdings: Vols (45,000) Cat Maps Pix
Budget: ($70,000)
Notes: Current researches in marine science, especially concerning the Gulf of Mexico, the Texas Coastal Zone, and the Continental Shelf. Incl journals.

UT —ZION NATIONAL PARK, Library, Springdale, 84767. Roy Given, Asst Chief Park Naturalist; Marion Hilkey, Librn
Holdings: Vols (2700) Cat Mss Maps Pix Audiotapes
Budget: ($1000)
Notes: Emphasis on history and natural history of Zion National Park and vicinity and other information bearing on the management and operation of the Park. ILL permitted upon prior approval of the Park Superintendent.

†WA —WASHINGTON STATE UNIVERSITY, Library, Manuscripts, Archives & Special Collections, Pullman, 99164. John F Guido, Head
Holdings: // Mss Maps Pix
Notes: Papers, 1821-1873, covering Father De Smet's early sojourns at Whitemarsh and St Louis, his founding of the Rocky Mountain Missions, his long service as Procurator and Socius of the Missouri Province, and his many travels. Correspondence with his family in Belgium, mss of his published journals, 2 small maps, sketches and engravings used to illustrate his books. Incl about 100 small pencil sketches by Father Nicholas Point depicting the 1841 journey from Westport to St Mary's Mission in the Bitteroot Valley. Described in *The Record*, 30 (1969) 6-40; and 32 (1971) 47-63.

WA —MOUNTAINEERS INC, Library, 300 3rd Ave West, Seattle, 98119. Verna M Ness, Library Cur
Holdings: Vols (3000) Cat
Notes: Collection incl some 19th century vols of Alpine information, incl the first issue of *The Alpine Journal* (1863). Bound serials of many important American climbing publications. Small sub-collections for American Alpine Club members and for The Mountaineer Foundation, the latter on conservation and ecology. In the main collection backpacking, skiing and natural history are also represented.

WI —MILWAUKEE PUBLIC MUSEUM, Reference Library, 800 W Wells St, Milwaukee, 53233. Judith Campbell Turner, Museum Librn
Holdings: Vols (90,000) Cat Maps Microforms

WY —UNIVERSITY OF WYOMING, William Robertson Coe Library, Western History Research Center, Laramie, 82071. Gene M Gressley, Dir, Asst to Pres
Holdings: Mss
Notes: One of the collecting areas of the Western History Research Center is "Conservation History", a relatively new program featuring the collection of papers and memorabilia of individuals who have played a significant role in the history and development of the American Conservation Movement.

AB —ALPINE CLUB OF CANADA LIBRARY, Archives of the Canadian Rockies, Box 160, Banff, T0L 0C0, Can. E J Hart, Head Archivist
Holdings: Vols (2429) Cat Mss Maps Pix Slides Audiotapes
Budget: ($1000)
Notes: The Archives of the Canadian Rockies is the custodian of the library and archival collection of the Alpine Club of Canada. The materials cover mountaineering technique and attempts worldwide, incl the Alps, Rockies, Himalayas, Andes, etc. Subject areas incl history, personal records, mountain rescue and medicine, alpine flora and fauna, guide books, manuals and

handbooks. A large part of the archival collection is concentrated on the Canadian Rocky Mountains, as the headquarters of The Alpine Club of Canada is in Banff, Alberta.

AB —PETER WHYTE FOUNDATION, Archives of the Canadian Rockies, Box 160, Banff, T0L 0C0, Can. Mary Andrews, ACR Librn
Holdings: Vols (4247) Cat Mss Maps Pix Slides Phonorecords Audiotapes Videotapes 16mm Films Filmstrips Microforms
Budget: ($1500)
Notes: Collect all available material which touches on the Rocky Mountains of Canada (from the US border to the Peace River in the north; from west of Calgary on the east to the town of Revelstoke, BC on the west). This material incl history (the early explorers, Indians, construction of the railroads, mountaineering, and development of the national parks), natural history (geology, botany, wildlife) and poetry and fiction with the Rockies as a setting. Collect maps of the area, photographs, tape recordings of the pioneers. We also house on our premises the Alpine Club of Canada's library, which is one of the most comprehensive collections on the subject of mountaineering worldwide. Subject areas incl history, personal records, mountain rescue and medicine, alpine flora and fauna, guide books, manuals and handbooks. A large part of the archival collection is concentrated on the Canadian Rocky Mountains, as the headquarters of The Alpine Club of Canada is in Banff, Alberta. Noncirculating.

MB —MANITOBA MUSEUM OF MAN & NATURE, Library, 190 Rupert Ave, Winnipeg, R3B 0N2, Can. V Hatten, Librn
Holdings: Vols (20,000) Cat Maps Slides Audiotapes Videotapes Microforms
Notes: Human and natural history of Manitoba.

NS —NOVA SCOTIA MUSEUM, Library, 1747 Summer St, Halifax, B3H 3A6, Can. M S Whiteside, Librn
Holdings: Vols 4000 Cat
Notes: Emphasis on Nova Scotia natural history.

ON —CHATHAM PUBLIC LIBRARY, 120 Queen St, Chatham, N7M 2G6, Can. Arlene Mason, Head of Reference
Holdings: Mss Maps Pix Slides Microforms
Notes: Collection incl books on Black history, especially the Underground Railroad pertaining to the Chatham and Windsor area; many articles, and a few pictures of these subjects; also Indians of Kent County. Kent County and Southern Ontario History is also a subject of this collection, especially United Empire Loyalists in Southern Ontario. There are a number of books on Natural History of Ontario.

ON —ROYAL BOTANICAL GARDENS, Library, Box 399, Hamilton, L8N 3H8, Can. Ina Vrugtman, Librn
Holdings: Vols (5000) Cat
Budget: ($13,000)
Notes: Botany and ornamental horticulture. Incl 10,000 slides. Periodicals are not yet union listed. Collection of nursery and seed trade catalogs; *Gray Herbarium Index;* Centre for Canadian Historical Horitcultural Studies. The library is located in the headquarters building of the Royal Botanical Gradens, 680 Plains Road West (Highway No 2) Burlington, Ontario. Phone: (416) 527-1158. Road West (Highway No 2) Burlington, Ontario. Phone: (416) 527-1158.

ON —METROPOLITAN TORONTO LIBRARY, Science & Technology Dept, 789 Yonge St, Toronto, M4W 2G8, Can. Margaret Walshe, Head
Holdings: Vols (120,000) Cat Maps
Notes: Some aspects of science for the specialist, the student, and the general public. The department gives high priority to Canadian materials.

ON —UNIVERSITY OF TORONTO, Thomas Fisher Rare Book Library, 120 Saint George St, Toronto, M5S 1A5, Can. Richard G Landon, Head
Holdings: Vols 1700 Uncat
Notes: Popular scientific books on English natural history written in the 19th century

NATURAL HISTORY (cont.)

for the amateur observer and collector. Particularly notable for holdings of Philip Henry Gosse.

PQ —MCGILL UNIVERSITY, Blacker-Wood Library of Zoology & Ornithology, 3459 McTavish St, Montreal, H3A 1Y1, Can. Eleanor MacLean, Librn
Holdings: Vols (77,600) Cat Mss
Notes: Special features of collection incl: Robert Gurney Collection of reprints on Crustaceana (//); 3000 folders of letters from naturalists (//); over 9000 original paintings of wildlife; a small collection of falconry equipment (//); the archives of the Montreal Natural History Society (//); the archives of the North American Falconry Association; 156 17th-century feather pictures of birds and people (//). Does not incl entomology collection.

NATURAL PHILOSOPHY see Physics

NATURAL RESOURCES

AK —ALASKA STATE LIBRARY, Alaska Historical Library Collection, Pouch G, Juneau, 99811. Phyllis Demuth, Readers Services Librn
Holdings: Vols (24,000) Cat Mss Maps Pix Slides Phonorecords Audiotapes Videotapes 16mm Films Microforms

CA —UNIVERSITY OF CALIFORNIA, BERKELEY, Giannini Foundation of Agricultural Economics, Library, 248 Giannini Hall, Berkeley, 94720. Grace Dote, Librn
Holdings: Vols (16,000) Cat Mss Maps Microforms
Notes: Noncirculating collection. No interlibrary loans. Also about 124,000 unbound vols. Open to graduate students and faculties of universities and college research workers and interested public. Mostly English language materials, primarily 1900 to date. Card catalog published by G K Hall Co *Dictionary Catalog of the Giannini Foundation of Agricultural Economics Library, Univ of California*, 12 vols. Holdings through 7/71.

CA —UNIVERSITY OF CALIFORNIA, BERKELEY, Life Sciences Libraries, Forestry Library, 260 Mulford Hall, Berkeley, 94720. Esther Johnson, Librn; Pete Evans, Ref Librn
Holdings: Vols (28,000) Cat Microforms
Budget: ($15,800)
Notes: Areas of particular strength are forestry, conservation, and wildlife management. The collection is rich in pamphlet material and serials, especially foreign publications. Although holdings are world-wide in scope, coverage of the western USA is given the highest priority. Dissertation and theses collection also. Forestry Library holdings are complemented by a 8000-vol specialized collection at the Forest Products Laboratory in Richmond, California.

CA —CALIFORNIA STATE UNIVERSITY, FULLERTON, Library, Box 4150, Fullerton, 92634. Linda Herman, Special Collections Librn
Holdings: Vols (3530) Cat Mss
Notes: Capt P Markham Kerridge Angling Collection incl materials on angling, entomology, ichthyology, conservation, travel, recreation, and related areas. A computer author printout with title, imprint, and various codes is updated annually. Books and pamphlets are supplemented by 2750 periodical issues, and extensive ephemera. No photocopying.

CA —LAKE COUNTY LIBRARY, 200 Park St, Lakeport, 95453. Kathleen Jansen, Librn
Holdings: Cat Maps Pix
Notes: Large collection of books, articles, and reports on geothermal resources, especially in California. Partially cataloged.

CA —UNIVERSITY OF CALIFORNIA, LOS ANGELES, Research Library, Dept of Special Collections, 405 Hilgard Ave, Los Angeles, 90024. Edward Shreeves, Chairman, Bibliographers Group; David S

Zeidberg, Head
Notes: Horace M Albright's correspondence and ephemera recording his activity as a conservationist and his directorship of the National Park Service.

CA —UNIVERSITY OF CALIFORNIA, SANTA BARBARA, Map and Imagery Laboratory, Santa Barbara, 93106. Larry Carver, Dept Head
Notes: Worldwide coverage of Landsat imagery donated by US Dept of Agriculture Aerial Photography Field Office. Consists of 153,000 scenes, covering most of the earth's surface between the years 1975 and 1980. Incl 300,000 maps, 1800 atlases, 9 globes, 300 relief models, 1,500,000 satellite imagery and aerial photographs, 700 reference books and gazetteers, 25 serials (titles received), and 21,000 microforms.

CA —FOREST HISTORY SOCIETY INC, Library, 109 Coral St, Santa Cruz, 95060. Mary E Johnson, Librn
Holdings: Vols (4000) Cat Mss Maps Pix Slides Audiotapes Microforms Films Serials
Budget: ($2000)
Notes: Incl archives of the Society of American Foresters, the American Forestry Association, the National Lumber Manufacturers Association, National Forest Products Association, and the American Forest Institute.

CA —UNIVERSITY OF THE PACIFIC, Library, Stockton, 95211. Hiram L Davis, Dir of Libraries
Holdings: Cat Mss Pix
Notes: Papers of John Muir. Incl are correspondence, mss, clippings, pamphlets, drawings and photographs.

CO —COLORADO GEOLOGICAL SURVEY, Library, 1313 Sherman St Rm 715, Denver, 80203. Louise Slade, Librn
Holdings: Vols (3000) Uncat Mss Maps Pix Microforms
Notes: Mineral resources of Colorado.

CO —DENVER PUBLIC LIBRARY, Conservation Library Center, 1357 Broadway, Denver, 80203.
Holdings: Vols (10,330) Cat
Notes: Historical, sociological, and economic aspects, but not scientific, except for Colorado research reports. Also, fish and wildlife reports of all states.

CO —VAIL PUBLIC LIBRARY, 292 W Meadow Dr, Vail, 81657. Charlyn M C Canada, Librn
Holdings: Vols (500) Cat Maps
Budget: ($5300)
Notes: The alpine environment.

CT —YALE UNIVERSITY, Forestry Library, 205 Prospect St, New Haven, 06511. Joseph A Miller, Librn
Holdings: Vols (115,000) Cat Microforms
Notes: The Forestry Library is a unit of the Yale University Library, housed in and serving primarily the School of Forestry and Environmental Studies. Founded in 1900, it has become one of the largest forestry libraries in the world. Forestry is construed broadly to incl underlying or closely related social, physical, and biological sciences. The literature of North American forestry and forest products is most completely covered, though other countries and foreign languages are well represented. Environmental studies and allied fields of natural resources management have been emphasized during the past 10 years. See *Dictionary Catalog of the Yale Forestry Library*, 12 vols (Boston: G K Hall, 1962).

DC —CONSERVATION FOUNDATION, Library, 1717 Massachusetts Ave NW, Washington, 20036. Barbara K Rodes, Librn
Holdings: Vols (8000) Cat Maps
Notes: Collection incl natural resources, ecology, city and regional planning, land use, recreation, energy conservation, environmental economics, pollution control, water resources.

DC —NATIONAL FOREST PRODUCTS ASSOCIATION, Bemis Information Center, 1619 Massachusetts Ave NW, Washington, 20036. Barbara A Beall, Mgr
Holdings: Vols (5000) Cat Maps Pix
Notes: Plus 25,000 pamphlets.

DC —US ENVIRONMENTAL PROTECTION AGENCY, 401 M St SW,

Washington, 20460. Sarah T Kadec, Dir Information Management & Services Division
Holdings: Vols (480,000) Cat Maps Pix Microforms

FL —MAITLAND LIBRARY, Florida Audubon Society, 501 S Maitland Ave, Maitland, 32751. Mary Kinney, Librn
Holdings: Cat Maps Pix Slides 16mm Films Microforms
Notes: General and technical literature on many aspects of conservation and environmental topics, indexed by subject and source. Coverage is local, statewide and national. Most materials on microfilm and microfiche.

FL —FLORIDA DEPT OF NATURAL RESOURCES BUREAU OF MARINE RESEARCH, Library, 100 Eighth Ave SE, Saint Petersburg, 33701. Keir Gray, Archivist
Holdings: Vols (3400) Cat Maps Pix Slides 16mm Films Microforms
Budget: ($27,500)
Notes: The library supports the research of approx 50 biologists and technicians, with emphasis on the marine resources of Florida and nearby areas. An archives section houses original research data, reports, publications, etc, developed by the scientific staff. Marine biological literature is received on exchange from laboratories and libraries throughout the world. There are approx 1400 journal titles in the collection. Current titles received number approx 600. The 33,000 reprints are cataloged by author and subject. Current laboratory activities incl marine studies in aquaculture, descriptive biology, ecological studies, fisheries biology, and oceanography.

HI —BERNICE P BISHOP MUSEUM, Library, PO Box 19000-A, Honolulu, 96819. Cynthia Timberlake, Librn
Holdings: Vols (90,000) Cat Mss Maps Pix Slides Microforms
Budget: ($30,000)
Notes: Only American library devoted exclusively to the Pacific region. Collection reflects historical and contemporary research emphases of Bishop Museum; ie the natural and cultural history of the Pacific. Areas of concentration incl archaeology, ethnology, linguistics, voyages and explorations, history, vertebrate and invertebrate zoology, botany and museology. Strong special collections incl photographs, mss and archives, maps and art. Publications: Quarterly "Additions to the Catalog," *Dictionary Catalog of the Library* (9 vols and 2 suppl; Boston: G K Hall, 1964-69).

IL —CHICAGO PUBLIC LIBRARY, Business/Science/Technology Div, Science/Technology Information Center, 425 North Michigan Ave, Chicago, 60611. Lynda Sanford, Head; John R Moore, Environment Collection Coordinator & Engineering Librn
Holdings: Vols 240 Cat Maps Films Slides Phonorecords Audiotapes Microforms
Budget: $900
Notes: Incl Aaron Montgomery Ward Collection.

IA —IOWA STATE UNIVERSITY, Library, Dept of Special Collections, Ames, 50011. Stanley M Yates, Head
Notes: Louis H Pammel (1862-1931) was professor of botany (1889-1931) and head of department of botany. Collection incl correspondence, collected works, speeches, interviews and articles. Collection is 39 linear feet. Important in conservation movement; founder of Iowa State Park System; teacher and friend of George Washington Carver. Also have one box of mss on the American School of Wildlife Protection.

KS —UNIVERSITY OF KANSAS, Kenneth Spencer Research Library, Kansas Collection, Lawrence, 66045. Sheryl K Williams, Cur
Holdings: Vols (92,000) Cat Mss
Notes: Personal papers of conservationists, newsletter and other publications of conservation organizations. Concentrates generally on northern Great Plains region. 1930s-.

MD —MARYLAND-NATIONAL CAPITAL PARK & PLANNING COMMISSION,

NATURAL RESOURCES (cont.)

Montgomery County Planning Department Library, 8787 Georgia Ave, Silver Spring, 20907. Janice C Holt, Librn
Holdings: Vols (5000) Cat
Notes: Specific subject areas include: community facilities, conservation, economics, flood control, highways, housing, human and natural resources, landscape architecture, open space, parks, pollution, population, recreation, transportation, urban renewal, and zoning. Commission's publications are maintained by Records Management (not Library).

MI —GREAT LAKES COMMISSION, Institute of Science and Technology Bldg, 2200 Bonisteel Blvd, Ann Arbor, 48109. Michael J Donahue, Natural Resources Specialist
Holdings: Vols (4000)
Notes: Incl directories, reports and related documents covering Great Lakes-related natural resources management, transportation and economic development issues. The library is available for limited public use upon appointment.

MI —UNIVERSITY OF MICHIGAN, Biological Station Library, Pellston, 49769. Patricia B Devlin, Librn
Holdings: Vols (10,000) Cat Mss Maps Pix Microforms
Notes: Library is intended primarily for the needs of teaching and research at the Biological Station--the world's largest inland field station for instruction and investigation in biological science. Collection contains considerable information on the natural science aspects of the Douglas Lake area, Cheboygan County, Michigan.

NY —STATE UNIVERSITY OF NEW YORK AT ALBANY, Library, Special Collections Dept, 1400 Washington Ave, Albany, 12222. Marion P Munzer, Coordr
Notes: Correspondence, lecture notes, speeches, mss, clippings dealing with work by Robert Rienow and his wife, Leona Train, on wildlife conservation, anti-nuclear movement, and population control (15 linear feet).
See also entries under Rienow, Robert; Population; Wildlife Conservation

NY —NEW YORK BOTANICAL GARDEN LIBRARY, Bronx, 10458. Charles R Long, Asst Vice Pres & Dir
Holdings: Vols (385,000) Cat Mss Pix Slides Microforms VF
Budget: ($356,000)
Notes: One of the largest botanical collections in the world. Covers botany (150, 000 vols), botanists (3000), horticulture (45, 000), plant diseases (25,000), plant physiology (15,000), history of botany (1500), conservation of natural resources (15,000), gardening (13,000), paleobotany (7000), ecology (20,000), forestry (5000), medical botany (3000), agriculture (9000) and biology (20,000). Reference library; materials do not circulate, except via standard inter-library loan. About 5000 vols uncataloged. Incl archives, art and vertical files. An OCLC library.

NY —AMERICAN MUSEUM OF NATURAL HISTORY, Library Services Dept, Central Park W & 79th St, New York, 10024. Nina J Root, Chairwoman; Mary Genett, Asst Librn for Reference Services
Holdings: Vols (385,000) Cat Mss Maps Pix Slides Microforms
Notes: Nearly all collections are outstanding for depth of coverage and international range. Early and historic works, rare books, colored illustrations, and relevant serial publications supplement the modern scientific publications necessary to the researches of the scientific staff and the work of the educational division. Open to the public.

NY —STATE UNIVERSITY OF NEW YORK, COLLEGE OF ENVIRONMENTAL SCIENCE AND FORESTRY, F Franklin Moon Library, Syracuse, 13210. Donald F Webster, Librn
Holdings: Vols (86,430) Cat
Budget: ($120,000)

NC —NORTH CAROLINA STATE UNIVERSITY, Forest Resources Library, 4012 Biltmore Hall, Raleigh, 27650. Pamela E Puryear, Head
Holdings: Vols (9000) Cat Microforms
Notes: Forestry, wood and paper sciences; recreation; remote sensing; FAO and forest service and forest products labs. Publications and audiovisual materials.

OR —UNIVERSITY OF OREGON, Library, Eugene, 97403. Kenneth W Duckett, Curator
Notes: Incl the Ralph W Chaney Collection of books and about 12,000 letters; mss, of books and articles.

OR —PORTLAND STATE UNIVERSITY LIBRARY, 934 SW Harrison, PO Box 1151, 97207, Portland, 97201. Kenneth W Butler, Asst Dir
Holdings: Vols (669,592) Uncat Mss Maps Pix Microforms
Budget: ($1,321,288)
Notes: Northwest natural resources and electrical power development. Incl the Ivan Bloch Collection.

OR —US DEPT OF ENERGY, Bonneville Power Administration Library, 1002 NE Holladay St, PO Box 3621, Portland, 97232. Karen Hadman, Chief of Library Branch
Notes: Emphasis is on Federal and Pacific Northwest law and in subject areas of interest to the Departments of Energy and Interior.

†PA —LIBRARY COMPANY OF PHILADELPHIA, 1314 Locust St, Philadelphia, 19107. Edwin Wolf II, Librn
Holdings: Vols (450,000)

PA —UNIVERSITY OF PITTSBURGH, Economics/Center for Regional Economics Studies Library, 4956 Forbes Quad, Pittsburgh, 15260. Patricia Suozzi-Crehan, Librn
Holdings: Vols 20,000
Budget: ($25,724)
Notes: Card catalog for collection. Cards for Economics Collection are in Hillman Library catalog. Collections are working collections reflecting the research and teaching interests of the Dept of Economics faculty and graduate students. The collection covers all aspects of the field of economics and demography.

TN —TENNESSEE VALLEY AUTHORITY (TVA), Technical Library, 400 W Summit Hill Dr, E2 B7, Knoxville, 37902. Jesse C Mills, Chief Librn
Holdings: Vols (106,900) Cat Mss Maps Pix Audiotapes Microforms
Budget: ($2,025,000)
Notes: The Technical Library Headquarters Staff (order, cataloging, information, and administration) is located in Knoxville, Tenn. In addition there are branch libraries in Knoxville, Norris, and Chattanooga, Tennessee, and Muscle Schoals, Alabama.

TN —TENNESSEE VALLEY AUTHORITY (TVA), Norris Branch Library, Norris, 37828. Debra D Mills, Librn
Holdings: Vols (8000) Cat Microforms
Budget: ($35,000)

†TX —UNIVERSITY OF TEXAS, EL PASO, Library, El Paso, 79968.
Notes: Significant collections of water resources information about Texas and California.

UT —UNIVERSITY OF UTAH, Marriott Library, Special Collections, Salt Lake City, 84112. Gregory C Thompson, Cur

WA —MOUNTAINEERS INC, Library, 300 3rd Ave West, Seattle, 98119. Verna M Ness, Library Cur
Holdings: Vols (3000) Cat
Notes: Collection incl some 19th century vols of Alpine information, incl the first issue of The Alpine Journal (1863). Bound serials of many important American climbing publications. Small sub-collections for American Alpine Club members and for The Mountaineer Foundation, the latter on conservation and ecology. In the main collection backpacking, skiing and natural history are also represented.

WA —UNIVERSITY OF WASHINGTON LIBRARIES, Suzzallo Library, Manuscripts Section, FM-25, Seattle, 98195. Karyl Winn, Librn
Holdings: Mss
Notes: Personal papers and organizational records with emphasis on Pacific Northwest history and recent focus on twentieth century Western Washington. Holdings pertain to urban problems and policies, labor history, women's history, natural resource development, environmental politics, race relations, ethnic history, oral hsitory, and the arts. Holdings are complemented by textual records in the University Archives (7045 linear feet) and by graphic and printed holdings in the Pacific Northwest Collection. Described in Comprehensive Guide to the Manuscripts Collection and to Personal Papers in the University Archives, 1980 and in Historical Records of Washington State: Records and Papers Held at Repositories, 1981 and in unpublished inventories to most accessions. 15,981 linear feet of manuscripts.

WI —UNIVERSITY OF WISCONSIN, MADISON, College of Agricultural & Life Sciences, Steenbock Memorial Library, 550 Babcock Dr, Madison, 53706. Jan Kennedy, Dir
Holdings: Vols (186,312) Cat Docs Maps Microforms
Notes: Supports programs relating to soil and water conservation, wildlife ecology, recreation, biomass conversion and pollution.

AB —ALBERTA DEPT OF THE ENVIRONMENT, Library, Oxbridge Place, 9820 106th St, Edmonton, T5K 2J6, Can. Marilyn Corbett, Head, Library Services Branch
Holdings: Vols (20,000) Cat Microforms

BC —KAMLOOPS MUSEUM & ARCHIVES, Reference Library, 207 Seymour St, Kamloops, V2C 2E7, Can. Kem Favrholdt, Curator
Holdings: Vols (900) Cat Mss Maps Pix Slides Audiotapes Microforms
Budget: ($500)
Notes: British Columbia in general, but concentrating on the Thompson Valley drainage basin. Incl history of the Kamloops District up to 1914, of Kamloops, 1914-1945.

MB —UNIVERSITY OF MANITOBA, Elizabeth Dafoe Library, Government Publications Section, Winnipeg, R3T 2N2, Can. June Dutka, Head
Holdings: Uncat Maps Pix Microforms
Notes: The Canadian National Energy Board's Polar Gas Project documentation provides an extremely useful source of information describing the proposed construction of the pipeline route which would generally pass from the Arctic Islands through the Northwest Territories, northern Manitoba and into Ontario, Canada.

ON —ONTARIO MINISTRY OF NATURAL RESOURCES, Natural Resources Library, Whitney Block 4540, Toronto, M5S 1B3, Can. Sandra Louet, Librn
Holdings: Cat

PQ —SERVICE DE LA DOCUMENTATION ET DES RENSEIGNEMENTS MINISTERE DE L'ENERGIE ET DES RESSOURCES, 2000B, chemin Sainte-Foy, 7th floor, Quebec, G1R 4X7, Can. Normand Guerette, Dir
Holdings: Vols 60,000 Cat Mss Maps Pix
Budget: $90,000
Notes: Natural resources of Quebec. Printed catalog. Incl a selection of documents with subject index. Incl 500 periodical titles.

NATURAL RESOURCES—AFRICA

OH —ANTIOCH COLLEGE, Olive Kettering Library, Livermore St, Yellow Springs, 45387. Nina Myatt, Cur
Notes: Personal papers and correspondence (1920-1975) of Arthur E Morgan former President of Antioch (1920-1936), first director of Ohio's Miami Valley Conservancy District, and first Chairman of the Tennessee Valley Authority (TVA). Mss, film, out-takes, much on the engineering of over 50 water-control projects in this country, Africa, and India. Materials on Edward Bellamy (Morgan wrote biography of Bellamy). Incl family papers. About 175 file boxes.

NATURAL RESOURCES—CANADA

AB —ALBERTA OIL SANDS INFORMATION CENTRE, 6th Floor,

NATURAL RESOURCES—CANADA
(cont.)

Highfield Place, 10010-106 St, Edmonton, T5J 3L8, Can. Helga Radvanyi, Mgr
Notes: "Major activity of the Centre has been preparation of the Alberta Oil Sands Index. However...scope has broadened to include the Heavy Oil/Enhanced Recovery Index," and other informative literature.

NATURAL RESOURCES—INDIA

OH —ANTIOCH COLLEGE, Olive Kettering Library, Livermore St, Yellow Springs, 45387. Nina Myatt, Cur
Notes: Personal papers and correspondence (1920-1975) of Arthur E Morgan former President of Antioch (1920-1936), first director of Ohio's Miami Valley Conservancy District, and first Chairman of the Tennessee Valley Authority (TVA). Mss, film, out-takes, much on the engineering of over 50 water-control projects in this country, Africa, and India. Materials on Edward Bellamy (Morgan wrote biography of Bellamy). Incl family papers. About 175 file boxes.

NATURAL RESOURCES—CONSERVATION see Natural Resources

NATURAL RESOURCES—LAW AND LEGISLATION

DC —US ENVIRONMENTAL PROTECTION AGENCY, 401 M St SW, Washington, 20460. Sarah T Kadec, Dir Information Management & Services Division
Holdings: Vols (480,000) Cat Maps Pix Microforms

NATURAL RESOURCES—MAPS

DC —LIBRARY OF CONGRESS, Geography and Map Division, Washington, 20540. John A Wolter, Chief
Holdings: Cat Mss Maps Pix Slides Microforms
See also entry under Maps and Atlases - Collections

NATURAL SCENERY see Pictures—Collections; Postal Cards—Collections; Views

NATURAL SCIENCE see Biology; Chemistry; Natural History; Physics; Science

NATURAL SELECTION

ON —UNIVERSITY OF TORONTO, Thomas Fisher Rare Book Library, 120 Saint George St, Toronto, M5S 1A5, Can. Richard G Landon, Head
Holdings: Vols 2000 Uncat
Notes: Darwin Collection is a comprehensive collection of editions of works by Charles Darwin, including separate issues of editions published in his lifetime which show revisions of text; works by predecessors and contemporaries on concepts of evolution and natural selection. Collection described in Landon, R G Species of Origin (Toronto, 1971). Holdings listed in Freeman, R B, Charles Darwin: A Bibliographical Handlist, 2nd ed (London, 1977).

NATURALISTS

†CA —HUNTINGTON BOTANICAL GARDENS LIBRARY, 1151 Oxford Rd, San Marino, 91108. Ann Ravenscroft, Secretary
Holdings: Vols (8000)
Notes: Emphases on history of botanical science; papers and notes of American botanists and naturalists of The West; botanical illustration, etc. Subtropical

horticulture, incl cacti and succulents of Australia, South Africa, and Mexico.
†CT —UNIVERSITY OF CONNECTICUT LIBRARY, Special Collections Dept, Storrs, 06268. Richard H Schimmelpfeng, Dir of Special Collections
Notes: Papers, incl mss, etc. of the naturalist Edwin Way Teale.
DC —LIBRARY OF CONGRESS, Manuscript Division, Washington, 20540. John C Broderick, Chief
Notes: Papers of William T Hornaday, Naturalist.
ME —BOWDOIN COLLEGE, Library, Brunswick, 04011. Dianne M Gutscher, Cur of Special Collections
Holdings: Vols Cat Mss
Notes: A collection of the works of Henry Beston, naturalist and author.
NY —VASSAR COLLEGE, Library, Rare Books & Manuscripts Collection, Box 20, Poughkeepsie, 12601. Lisa Browar, Cur
Notes: John Burroughs' 53 notebooks comprising his manuscript journals, 1876 to 1921. Devoted principally to his observations of nature, with many comments of literary and political observations.
NY —UNIVERSITY OF ROCHESTER, Rush Rhees Library, Department of Rare Books and Special Collections, Rochester, 14627. Peter Dzwonkoski, Librn
Notes: Incl correspondence, reports, diaries related to Henry Augustus Ward's work as a naturalist and founder of Ward's Natural Science Establishment.
OH —CLEVELAND MEDICAL LIBRARY ASSOCIATION/CASE WESTERN RESERVE UNIVERSITY, Cleveland Health Sciences Library, Historical Division, Allen Memorial Medical Library, 11000 Euclid Ave, Cleveland, 44106. Glen Jenkins, Rare Book Librarian & Archivist
Holdings: Cat
Notes: Biographies of health science professionals, Sigmund Frued, and naturalists.

NATURE see Natural History

NATURE CONSERVATION

CA —UNIVERSITY OF CALIFORNIA, BERKELEY, Life Sciences Libraries, Forestry Library, 260 Mulford Hall, Berkeley, 94720. Esther Johnson, Librn; Pete Evans, Ref Librn
Notes: Areas of particular strength are forestry, conservation, and wildlife management. The collection is rich in pamphlet material and serials, especially foreign publications. Although holdings are world-wide in scope, coverage of the western USA is given the highest priority. Dissertation and thesis collection also. Forestry Library holdings are complemented by a 6000-vol specialized collection at the Forest Products Laboratory in Richmond, California.
CA —CALIFORNIA STATE UNIVERSITY, FULLERTON, Library, Box 4150, Fullerton, 92634. Linda Herman, Special Collections Librn
Notes: Capt P Markham Kerridge Angling Collection incl materials on angling, entomology, ichthyology, conservation, travel, recreation, and related areas. A computer author printout with title, imprint, and various codes is updated annually. Books and pamphlets are supplemented by 2750 periodical issues, and extensive ephemera. No photocopying.
CA —UNIVERSITY OF THE PACIFIC, Library, Stockton, 95211. Hiram L Davis, Dir of Libraries
Notes: Papers of John Muir. Incl are corresspondence, mss, clippings, pamphlets, drawings and photographs.
FL —MAITLAND LIBRARY, Florida Audubon Society, 501 S Maitland Ave, Maitland, 32751. Mary Kinney, Librn
Notes: General and technical literature on many aspects of conservation and environmental topics, indexed by subject and source. Coverage is local, statewide and national. Most materials on microfilm and microfiche.

IA —IOWA STATE UNIVERSITY, Library, Dept of Special Collections, Ames, 50011. Stanley M Yates, Head
Notes: Louis H Pammel (1862-1931) was professor of botany (1889-1931) and head of department of botany. Collection incl correspondence, collected works, speeches, interviews and articles. Collection is 39 linear feet. Important in conservation movement; founder of Iowa State Park System; teacher and friend of George Washington Carver. Also have one box of mss on the American School of Wildlife Protection.
MD —MARYLAND-NATIONAL CAPITAL PARK & PLANNING COMMISSION, Montgomery County Planning Department Library, 8787 Georgia Ave, Silver Spring, 20907. Janice C Holt, Librn
Notes: Specific subject areas include: community facilities, conservation, economics, flood control, highways, housing, human and natural resources. landscape architecture, open space, parks, pollution, population, recreation, transportation, urban renewal, and zoning. Commission's publications are maintained by Records Management (not Library).
NY —STATE UNIVERSITY OF NEW YORK AT ALBANY, Library, Special Collections Dept, 1400 Washington Ave, Albany, 12222. Marion P Munzer, Coordr
Notes: Correspondence, lecture notes, speeches, mss, clippings dealing with work by Robert Rienow and his wife, Leona Train, on wildlife conservation, anti-nuclear movement, and population control (15 linear feet).
PA —ZOOLOGICAL SOCIETY OF PHILADELPHIA, Library, 34 & Girard Ave, Philadelphia, 19104. Alyssa N Scheuermann, Librn
Holdings: Vols (500) Cat
Notes: Photocopying with permission.
WA —MOUNTAINEERS INC, Library, 300 3rd Ave West, Seattle, 98119. Verna M Ness, Library Cur
Notes: Collection incl some 19th century vols of Alpine information, incl the first issue of The Alpine Journal (1863). Bound serials of many important American climbing publications. Small sub-collections for American Alpine Club members and for The Mountaineer Foundation, the latter on conservation and ecology. In the main collection, backpacking, skiing and natural history are also represented.

NATURE PROTECTION see Nature Conservation

NATUROPATHY

AZ —WORLD UNIVERSITY, Library, 711 E Blacklidge Dr, Tucson, 85719. Howard John Zitko, Cur
Holdings: Vols (15,000) Cat Mss Maps Audiotapes
Notes: Collection concerns the "frontier sciences". No interlibrary loan.

NAUDOWESSIE INDIANS see Dakota Indians

NAUTICAL CHARTS

CA —UNIVERSITY OF CALIFORNIA, LOS ANGELES, Map Library, Los Angeles, 90024. Carlos B Hagen, Head
Holdings: Vols (5566) Cat Maps Pix
Notes: The Library is a depository for the publications of many world-wide mapping agencies. The collection incl 507,097 maps of all areas of the world (subject and topographic maps, nautical and aeronautical charts, historical maps, and city plans), gazetteers, atlases, aerial photographs, periodicals and other basic cartographic reference tools. Incl 2550 atlases; 10,424 aerial maps; 1035 technical reports; and 311 (titles) serials subscriptions.
CT —MYSTIC SEAPORT, MUSEUM, G W Blunt White Library, Greenmanville Ave, Mystic, 06355. Gerald E Morris, Librn
Holdings: Vols (40,000) Imprints

NAUTICAL CHARTS (cont.)

Microforms
Budget: ($100,000)
Notes: American maritime history. The library is also a government depository for maritime materials with a subscription to 184 line items. Incl 400,000 mss, 4000 maps and charts, 30,000 ships' plans. Open to the public.

CT —YALE UNIVERSITY, Box 1603A, Yale Station, New Haven, 06520.
Holdings: Cat Maps
Notes: "The best collection of printed rutters in America is that of Henry C Taylor at Yale University Library," S E Morison, *The European Discovery of America*, 1971, p 150.

DC —LIBRARY OF CONGRESS, Geography and Map Division, Washington, 20540. John A Wolter, Chief
Holdings: Cat Mss Maps Pix Slides Microforms
Notes: Incl rare nautical charts on Vellum. *See also* entry under Maps and Atlases - Collections

FL —UNIVERSITY OF MIAMI, Otto G Richter Library, PO Box 248214, Coral Gables, 33124. Frank Rodgers, Dir of Libraries
Holdings: Vols Microforms
Notes: The Rosenstiel School of Marine and Atmospheric Sciences Library is one of the major marine science collections in the United States and is especially strong in the literature of tropical oceanography. Special collections in the library incl 200 oceanographic atlases and more than 50 sets of the world's major expedition reports. The library also maintains a nautical chart collection. 3000 microforms; 1000 current subscriptions.

FL —FLORIDA STATE UNIVERSITY, Robert Manning Strozier Library, Maps Dept, Tallahassee, 32306. Marianne Donnell, Map Librn
Holdings: Vols (3314) Cat Maps Microforms
Notes: Emphasis on Florida and Florida history. Also a depository for USGS topographic maps of the entire US, National Ocean Survey nautical charts of all American waters, Defense Mapping Agency maps, and various special sets issued by National Ocean Survey. Incl 1140 vols of books, bibliographies, and periodicals; 2070 atlases; 136,000 sheet maps; 104 microfilm reels.

IL —NEWBERRY LIBRARY, 60 W Walton St, Chicago, 60610. Robert W Karrow, Jr, Cur of Maps
Holdings: Cat Maps
Notes: Historical map collection, with cut-off date of about 1900, incl 1600 atlases and 13,000 separate maps (in 1984). Rich in nautical cartography, incl some exceptional portolan charts.
See also entry under Maps and Atlases - Collections.

ME —PENOBSCOT MARINE MUSEUM, Library, Church St, Searsport, 04974. Charles Howard, Librn
Holdings: Vols (4000) Cat Mss Maps Pix
Budget: ($5000)
Notes: Marine maritime history, log books, journals, diaries, marine charts, ships registers, photographs, archives & mss, and books relating to world navigation. The greatest emphasis is placed on the Penobscot Bay region.

MD —MARYLAND HISTORICAL SOCIETY, Library, 201 W Monument St, Baltimore, 21201. William B Keller, Head Librn
Holdings: Maps Pix Films
Notes: Ships and shipping, description and travel, yachts and yachting, sailing, marine transport, Baltimore, and the Port of Maryland. Incl books, periodicals, maps, charts, pictures, ship plans, log books, films, etc.

OH —RUTHERFORD B HAYES LIBRARY, 1337 Hayes Ave, Fremont, 43420. Watt P Marchman, Dir
Holdings: Vols 500 Cat Mss Maps Pix Slides
Notes: The Great Lakes Marine Collection,

incl the Capt Frank E Hamilton Collection; Great Lakes boats and shipping. Incl 300 charts; over 20,000 pictures (with 2500 negatives, 30 glass plates). Index and findings aids with the collection.

PA —PENN SHIP BUILDING CO, Library, Morton Ave, Chester, 19013. John Del Razo, Librn
Holdings: Vols 16,269 Cat Maps
Notes: Shipbuilding. Incl nautical charts.

TX —TEXAS A&M UNIVERSITY, Sterling C Evans Library, College Station, 77843. Judith Rieke, Map Librn; Irene B Hoadley, Dir of Libraries
Holdings: Cat
Budget: ($10,000)
Notes: Maps of all areas of the world with geographic emphasis on the US and Texas. Subject emphasis on geology, petroleum, soils, highways and streets. Depository for NOS coastal and bathymetric charts, DMA maps, and USGS topographic and geologic maps. Bathymetric maps of US coastal areas, general world ocean maps, and 60 atlases covering ocean depths, temperature, salinity, etc.

WI —UNIVERSITY OF WISCONSIN, MADISON, Memorial Library, 728 State St, Madison, 53706. Erwin K Welsch, Social Studies Bibliographer
Notes: Approx 125 vols of official and other reports on hydrography in the Netherlands in the late 18th and 19th centuries.

WI —MILWAUKEE PUBLIC LIBRARY, 814 W Wisconsin Ave, Milwaukee, 53233. Donald J Sager, City Librn
Holdings: Vols 1500 Cat Mss Maps Pix Slides
Notes: The Great Lakes Marine Collection consists of Runge Marine Collection, Wilson Marine Collection, and other collections on Great Lakes Marine History. Has data on about 85,000 ships and more than 20,000 pictures of Great Lake vessels. Complete runs of reference material such as US List of merchant vessels, Greens, etc. Extensive collection of Great Lake charts.

NAUTICAL SCIENCES

VA —CHRISTOPHER NEWPORT COLLEGE, Captain John Smith Library, 50 Shoe Lane, PO Box 6070, Newport News, 23606.
Holdings: Vols 1200 Cat
Notes: Alexander C Brown Nautical Collection, the gift of Alexander Crosby Brown, a noted author and nautical book reviewer who continues to add to the collection. A large number of the books in the collection incl newspaper reviews.

NAVAJO INDIANS

AZ —NORTHERN ARIZONA UNIVERSITY, Special Collection Library, CU Box 6022, Flagstaff, 86011. Peter M Whiteley, Coordr/Archivist; William Mullane, Librn
Holdings: Vols 100 Mss Pix
Notes: (1) Florence Barker Collection. She was a missionary nurse on the Navajo, Havasupai, Acoma and Laguna Indian Reservations. Incl diaries, 1922-1927 (Immanuel Mission, Navajo Reservation), also some copied textual material of interest concerning the Immanuel Mission during the 1920's. (2) James Biglin Collection; computer printout data for his publication: *Cultural Values in Indian Education: A Study of Parental Attitudes and Values Toward Education on the Navajo and and Hopi Reservations*, Flagstaff: Southwest Behavioral Institute, 1971-1972. (3) Day Family Collection. They were Anglo traders on the eastern Navajo reservation. Correspondence, files of trading and other activities of Sam, Anna, Charles, and Sam Day, Jr, 1880's-1930's.Incl unpublished mss on Navajo ceremonies and correspondence relating to the looting of Canyon del Muerto. (4) Navajo Burial Collection contains original and some handwritten field notes of interviews with funeral directors on the Navajo Reservation and border towns. One copy of *Navajo Burials, Anglo-Style,*

MNA Research Paper Number 18, 1980, and *American Indian Quarterly*, vol 4, number 4, 1978.

AZ —HUBBELL TRADING POST NATIONAL HISTORIC SITE, Library, PO Box 150, Ganado, 86505. L Edward Gastellum, Supt
Holdings: Vols (500) Cat Mss Maps Pix Slides Audiotapes
Notes: Incl copies of the Hubbell Trading Post manuscripts and archives. Much on Navajo Indian life.

AZ —COLORADO RIVER INDIAN TRIBES MUSEUM/LIBRARY, Rte One, Box 23-B, Parker, 85344. Priscilla Johnson, Librn
Holdings: Cat Mss Maps Pix Slides Audiotapes Microforms
Notes: Library deals with the four tribes of the Colorado River Indian Reservation: Mojave, Chemehuevi, Navajo, and Hopi. Emphasis is also given to the prehistoric cultures of this area; Patayan and Hohokam. Library collections include original manuscripts and other documents, photographs, oral history tape recordings, cultural items and artifacts. Copies of many documents relating to the reservation are in bound volumes, microfilm, and photocopies. Photos relative to the reservation are copied from various other collections are copied in our collection. Of particular interest is the museum basket collection which incl about 1000 Chemehuevi baskets--the largest Chemehuevi basket collection. Other artifacts give special emphasis to the Mojave culture.

AZ —NAVAJO COMMUNITY COLLEGE, Naaltsoos Ba' Hoogan, Library, Tsaile, 86556. Marvin E Pollard Jr, Dir, Library Services
Holdings: Vols (10,000) Cat Mss Maps Pix Slides Phonorecords Audiotapes Videotapes 16mm Films Filmstrips Microforms
Budget: ($15,000)
Notes: The Moses/Donner Collection emphasizes Navajos and other tribes of the Southwest; also, all Indians of North America and Mexico. All aspects of the geology, geography, sociology, archaeology, anthropology, etc, of the Four Corners region. The Collection includes a comprehensive collection of Doctoral dissertations dealing with Indians of North America and Mexico.

AZ —UNIVERSITY OF ARIZONA, Center for Creative Photography, 843 E University Blvd, Tucson, 85721. James Enyeart, Dir; Terence Pitts, Cur and Librn
Holdings: Pix
Notes: The Marion Palfi Photo Archive. Famous portrayals of, espec, poverty-stricken and victimized persons in the US, 1940 through 1970s, incl Hopi, Navajo, and Papago Indians on reservations, in urban relocation, and acculturation centers. Over 1500 master prints, 10,000 work prints, hundreds of glass plate and film negatives, manuscripts, etc.

AZ —NAVAJO TRIBAL MUSEUM, Navajo Historical Library, Window Rock, 86515. Russell P Hartman, Cur
Notes: Navajo history, art, social life and customs.

CO —FORT LEWIS COLLEGE, Library, Southwest Collection, College Heights, Durango, 81301. Daniel W Lester, Dir
Holdings: Vols (7000) Cat Mss Maps Pix Slides Microforms
Budget: ($3800)
Notes: Also have separate catalog of the special collections concerning the Southwest, Indians, mine records, railroad records, etc.

NM —ALBUQUERQUE PUBLIC LIBRARY, 501 Copper Ave NW, Albuquerque, 87102. Alan B Clark, Dir
Holdings: Vols (4000) Cat Microforms Records Maps VF
Notes: Large collection of materials on all aspects of New Mexico history and cultures. In-house index accesses VF materials and local and regional periodicals. Special emphasis on Indians of New Mexico and northeastern Arizona, particularly the Navajo, Hopi, Pueblos and Apache. Reference copies of many works are housed at the Special Collections Library, 423 Central Ave NE, Albuquerque, NM 87102.

NAVAJO INDIANS (cont.)

NM —GALLUP PUBLIC LIBRARY, 115 W
Hill Ave, Gallup, 87301. Octavia Fellin, Dir
Holdings: Vols (8000) Cat Maps Pix

NAVAJO RESERVATION

AZ —NORTHERN ARIZONA
UNIVERSITY, Special Collection Library,
CU Box 6022, Flagstaff, 86011. Peter M
Whiteley, Coordr/Archivist; William
Mullane, Librn
Notes: Navajo Burial Collection contains
original and some handwritten field notes of
interviews with funeral directors on the
Navajo Reservation and border towns. One
copy of *Navajo Burials, Anglo-Style, MNA
Research Paper Number 18,* 1980, and
American Indian Quarterly, vol 4, number 4,
1978.

NAVAL ACADEMY, U.S. see U.S. Naval Academy at Annapolis

NAVAL ADMINISTRATION see Naval Art and Science

NAVAL AERONAUTICS see Aeronautics, Military

NAVAL ARCHITECTURE

DC —LIBRARY OF CONGRESS, Manuscript
Division, Washington, 20540. John C
Broderick, Chief
Notes: The Naval Historical Foundation
Collection contains personal papers relating
to American naval history.
MI —UNIVERSITY OF MICHIGAN,
Engineering-Transportation Library, 312
Undergraduate Library, Ann Arbor, 48109.
Sharon A Balius, Assoc Librn
Holdings: Mss Pix
Notes: The collection contains 475 items
covering the construction of the Panama
Canal, incl 24 vols of photographs compiled
by John G Clayburn, a superintendent of the
Dredging Division.
NY —STATE UNIVERSITY OF NEW
YORK, Maritime College, Stephen B Luce
Library, Fort Schuyler, Bronx, 10465.
Richard H Corson, Librn
Holdings: Vols (68,000) Cat Pix Slides
Videotapes 16mm Films Filmstrips
Microforms
Budget: ($90,000)
Notes: Incl extensive holdings in periodical
literature with long and complete runs of
many titles containing diagrams and plans,
many of which are fold-outs. Approx 3500
research reports in paper and microfiche
format. Mainly English language.
NY —WEBB INSTITUTE OF NAVAL
ARCHITECTURE, Livingston Library,
Crescent Beach Rd, Glen Cove, 11542. Fred
H Forrest, Librn
Holdings: Vols 1850 Cat
Notes: Access by appointment only.
NY —US MERCHANT MARINE
ACADEMY, Schuyler Otis Bland Memorial
Library, Steamboat Rd, Kings Point, 11024.
Stephen R Wiist, Acting Chief Librn
Holdings: Vols (130,000) Cat Mss Maps Pix
Slides Phonorecords Microforms
Budget: ($75,000)
Notes: All aspects of maritime affairs.
PA —FRANKLIN INSTITUTE LIBRARY, 20
& The Parkway, Philadelphia, 19103.
Miriam Padusis, Dir; Charles Wilt, Readers
Servs Librn
Holdings: Vols (300,000) Cat Maps Pix
Microforms
PA —US NAVY, Philadelphia Naval Shipyard
Technical Library, Philadelphia Naval
Shipyard, Philadelphia, 19112. Alice R
Murray, Dir
Holdings: Vols (12,500) Cat Pix
Notes: The Library also has (70,000)
technical manuals, (3500) research and
development reports. Over (400) current
periodicals.
RI —PROVIDENCE PUBLIC LIBRARY, 150
Empire St, Providence, 02903. Lance J
Bauer, Special Collections Librn
Holdings: Vols 225 // Uncat Pix
Notes: A fine collection of books, technical
drawings, photographs, pamphlets and other
ephemera concerned with naval architecture
from the library of Alfred S Brownell. An
important highlight of this collection are 11
ship models of Atlantic fishing craft, 9 of
which were built by Brownell; these models
are permanently on display. Incl 550
technical drawings, photographs, indexed.
WA —PUGET SOUND NAVAL SHIPYARD,
Engineering Library, Code 202.5, Bremerton,
98314. Carol J Swanson, Engineering Librn
Holdings: Vols 2000 Cat

NAVAL ARCHITECTURE—DESIGNS AND PLANS

CT —MYSTIC SEAPORT, MUSEUM, G W
Blunt White Library, Greenmanville Ave,
Mystic, 06355. Gerald E Morris, Librn
Holdings: Vols (40,000) Imprints
Microforms
Budget: ($100,000)
Notes: American maritime history. The
library is also a government depository for
maritime materials with a subscription to
184 line items. Incl 400,000 mss, 4000 maps
and charts, 30,000 ships' plans. Open to the
public.
NJ —STEVENS INSTITUTE OF
TECHNOLOGY, Samuel C Williams
Library, Castle Point Sta, Hoboken, 07030.
Jane G Hartye, Special Collections Librn
Holdings: // Cat Mss Pix
Notes: Known as the US Ironclad Monitor,
it was designed by Capt John Ericsson and
launched January 30, 1862. The "Monitor"
participated in the historic battle with the
"Merrimac" on March 9, 1862. It sank off
Cape Hatteras on December 31, 1862. Our
collection includes original design drawings
of the "Monitor", 38 of which were drawn by
Capt Ericsson and 34 by C W McCord. The
copies of these drawings are now in the
National Archives. No photocopying.

NAVAL ARCHITECTURE—HISTORY

MI —UNIVERSITY OF MICHIGAN,
Engineering-Transportation Library, 312
Undergraduate Library, Ann Arbor, 48109.
Sharon A Balius, Assoc Librn
Holdings: Pix
Budget:
Notes: The collection contains 475 items
covering the construction of the Panama
Canal, incl 24 vols of photographs compiled
by John G Clayburn, a superintendent of the
Dredging Division.

NAVAL ART AND SCIENCE

CO —COLORADO STATE UNIVERSITY,
Libraries, Fort Collins, 80523. John
Newman, Special Collections Librn
Holdings: Vols (900) Cat
Budget: ($7000)
Notes: The Imaginary Wars Collection incl
fictional accounts of future wars, imaginary
wars in the past and the greatly altered
outcomes of real wars. Stories must depict
known societies on Earth or close parallels
to known societies. At present, the collection
consists primarily of monographs. Future
plans coll for the identification of
appropriate short stories. For an annotated
bibliography of American imprints in the
collection see John Newman, "America at
War: Horror Stories for a Society,"
Extrapolation, XVI, No 1 and 2 (December
1974 and May 1975).
HI —PACIFIC SUBMARINE MUSEUM,
Library, Naval Submarine Base, Pearl
Harbor, 96860. Ray W de Yarmin, Cur
Holdings: Vols (1500) Cat Mss Maps Pix
Slides Phonorecords 16mm Films
Budget: ($600)
Notes: Incl 3000 pictures. Extensive missile
and torpedo collection; submarine models;
salvage/deep-sea diver exhibit; Arctic
exploration by submarines Worl War II
submarine components. Research program
for students, authors, lecturers, etc.
KY —NAVAL ORDNANCE SYSTEMS
COMMAND, Technical Library, Code
50122, Louisville, 40214. Libby Miles, Librn
Holdings: Vols 5500 Cat Maps Microforms
Notes: Excel in Government specifications,
ordnance pamphlets, and all types of other
Government documents. Large service in
Industry Standard on film, some volumes.
MD —US NAVAL ACADEMY, Nimitz
Library, Annapolis, 21402. Alice S
Creighton, Assistant Librn for Special
Collections
Holdings: Vols (22,000) Cat Mss Pix
Notes: Books and periodicals, with emphasis
on seapower. Incl rare and historically
significant works, naval and general history.
US Naval Academy materials (histories,
class albums, Lucky Bags, student
publications, etc), and copies of transcripts
of the Naval Institute's oral history
interviews with US naval officers.
Manuscripts incl 205 volumes of ships' logs,
letterbooks, order books, and watch, station
and quarter bills, 1796-1938; papers of
various naval officers, incl. Vice Admiral
Wilson Brown, Commander George M
Bache, Admiral Harry S Knapp, Lieutenant
Edwin J DeHaven, and others; family
correspondence of Admiral David Dixon
Porter; and several thousand World War II
naval action reports. Approximately 15,000
pictures incl portraits of naval officers,
pictures of US and some foreign ships,
World War II naval news photos and USNA
photographs.
NY —NEW YORK PUBLIC LIBRARY,
Research Libraries, Science and Technology
Research Center, Fifth Ave & 42 St, New
York, 10018.
Holdings: Vols (1,100,.000) Cat Microforms
Budget: ($647,259)
RI —US NAVAL WAR COLLEGE, Historical
Collection & Museum, Newport, 02841.
Anthony S Nicolosi, Dir; Evelyn Cherpak,
Cur
Holdings: Mss
Notes: Collections incl over 200,000
separate pieces; chiefly papers of naval
officers and records of organizations
associated with the US Navy, the Naval War
College, the college's major study areas, and
the Navy in the Narragansett Bay region;
oral history collection; Naval War College
Archives, 1884-present; records of
conferences held at the College; newspaper
collections dealing with naval themes and
military conflicts.
RI —PROVIDENCE PUBLIC LIBRARY, 150
Empire St, Providence, 02903. Lance J
Bauer, Special Collections Librn
Holdings: Vols 5000
Notes: The Harris Collection on the
American Civil War and Slavery. Incl 18th
and 19th century books, rare pamphlets, and
periodicals concerning slavery and the slave
trade, and origins, progress and results of the
Civil Civil War; also regimental histories;
military and naval tactics; personal
narratives; women's accounts of the Civil
War; works on abolition; sheet music; Union
and Confederate broadside ballads;
Confederate imprints; *The Liberator* from
1843 through the Civil War; and over 85
editions of *Uncle Tom's Cabin* in 14
languages. Excellent primary and secondary
sources for the study of the Civil War and
slavery. Material must be used in-house.
Photocopying when condition of material
allows.
VA —CHRISTOPHER NEWPORT
COLLEGE, Captain John Smith Library, 50
Shoe Lane, PO Box 6070, Newport News,
23606.
Holdings: Vols 1200 Cat
Notes: Alexander C Brown Nautical
Collection, the gift of Alexande Crosby
Brown, a noted author and nautical book
reviewer who continues to add to the
collection. A large number of the books in
the collection incl newspaper reviews.
ON —NATIONAL MUSEUMS OF
CANADA, Library Services Directorate,
Ottawa, K1A 0M8, Can. Valerie
Monkhouse, Director
Holdings: Vols 12,000 Cat
Budget: ($60,000)
Notes: Collection includes; arms and armour,
military aeronautics, military and naval arts
and sciences, military and naval equipment,

NAVAL ART AND SCIENCE (cont.)

general military and naval history, military and naval history of Canada. Research collection, interlibrary loans available, public may use on the premises.

NAVAL ART AND SCIENCE—HISTORY

RI —BROWN UNIVERSITY, John Hay Library, Anne S K Brown Military Collection, 20 Prospect St, Providence, 02912. Richard B Harrington, Cur
Notes: The Anne S K Brown Military Collection has been formed over the past forty or more years by Mrs John Nicholas Brown, now of Newport, and contains approximately 40,000 volumes and 60,000 prints, drawings and watercolors as well as a number of oil paintings and about 5000 miniature model soldiers. At its beginning (and still today) the emphasis or focus of this collection has been upon the history of, and the accurate contemporary illustration of, military and naval uniforms of all nations from the early XVII century to the present. In the course of time, however, the collection has come to incl also a vast and related amount of material on military and naval history, military and naval arts and tactics, wars, campaigns, ceremonies, biography, portraits and caricatures of this and earlier periods. It has been probably the largest private collection of such a nature inthe world, and it contains much ms and graphic documentation which is unique. It has been useful to numerous scholars and historians, editors, filmmakers and publishers for research and for illustrative material and has also contributed to many museum exhibitions. In 1982 the entire collection, with its complete card catalog and subject index, has been presented to Brown University, where it is located in the John Hay Library. Special requests are taken care of by phone, mail and appointments with the curator.

NAVAL AVIATION see Aeronautics, Military

NAVAL CONSTRUCTION see Naval Architecture; Shipbuilding

NAVAL ENGINEERING see Marine Engineering

NAVAL HISTORY

†AL —MUSEUMS OF THE CITY OF MOBILE, Reference Library, 355 Government St, Mobile, 36602. Caldwell Delaney, Adminr
CA —NAVAL POSTGRADUATE SCHOOL, Dudley Knox Library, Monterey, 93940. Paul Spinks, Prof of Library Science & Librn
Holdings: Vols 8000 Cat
Notes: This is a collection of books devoted mainly to naval history and the sea. It resulted from a gift collection received many years ago from a private donor. Since it is not within our curricular areas, no attempt has been made to continue acquisitions for it except from private donors.
CA —SAN DIEGO PUBLIC LIBRARY, Social Sciences Section, 820 E St, San Diego, 92101. Margaret E Queen, Supvr
Budget: ($36,000)
Notes: Books on the history of commercial and naval ships. Almost complete file of Jane's Fighting Ships, 1898 to the present; Lloyd's Register of Ships, 1764-1900 and 1950 to the present.
CA —HOOVER INSTITUTION ON WAR, REVOLUTION & PEACE, Stanford University, Stanford, 94305. Milorad M Drachkovitch, Archivist
Holdings: Mss Pix
Notes: Two collections: (1) Several important military collections incl the papers of Adm Charles M Cooke, Major Gen Robert T Frederick, Gen Robert C Richardson, Colonel M Preston Goodfellow,

Vice Adm Milton E Miles, Colonel Lee V Harris, Brigadier Gen L R Boyd. (2) Papers of Lloyd M Bucher, Commander, US Navy, and Commander of the USS Pueblo, incl correspondence, newspaper clippings, reports, copies of court inquiries, photographs, plaques, memorabilia, and other materials, 1970-75, relating to the Pueblo incident and its aftermath. Incl is a typewritten manuscript of his memoirs, entitled "Bucher, My Story". 68 ms boxes, 1 oversize package.
CT —YALE UNIVERSITY, Beinecke Rare Book & Manuscript Library, Osborn Collection, New Haven, 06520. Stephen R Parks, Cur
Holdings: Mss
DE —HAGLEY MUSEUM AND LIBRARY, Eleutherian Mills-Hagley Foundation Inc, PO Box 3630, Greenville, 19807. Richmond D Williams, Dir; Heddy A Richter, Imprints Librn
Holdings: Mss
Notes: 1500 cubic feet of mss. The library holds the books and papers of Pierre Samuel du Pont de Nemours (173-1817), physiocrat and economic theorist; the papers of E I du Pont (1771-1834), powder company founder; and his brother Victor (1767-1827). The Admiral Samuel Francis du Pont (1803-1865) papers contain some 49,000 items documenting in detail his naval career and the papers of General Henry du Pont (1812-1889) illuminate Delaware's history during the Civil war. Also held are the papers of Colonel Henry A du Pont (1838-1926).
DC —GEORGETOWN UNIVERSITY, Library, Special Collections Div, 37 & O Sts NW, Washington, 20057. George M Barringer, Special Collections Librn; Nicholas B Sheetz, Mss Librn
Holdings: Mss Cat
Notes: Correspondence, mss, and documents from the naval career of Rear-Admiral Thomas Tingey Craven (1808-1887). The papers principally concern Craven's command of the US Frigate "Congress" in the Mediterranean squadron, 1856-58, as well as his duties as commander of the US practice ship "Plymouth" at Annapolis from 1860-61. Craven's long naval career incl participation in the Wilkes Expedition (1838-39), assisting Commodore Perry in the suppression of slave trade (1843), command of the "Brooklyn" in Farragut's squadron (1861-62), and the capture of the Confederate steamer "Georgia" (1864).
DC —LIBRARY OF CONGRESS, Manuscript Division, Washington, 20540. John C Broderick, Chief
Notes: The Naval Historical Foundation Collection contains personal papers relating to American naval history.
IN —INDIANA UNIVERSITY, Lilly Library, Seventh St, Bloomington, 47405. William R Cagle, Librn
Holdings: Vols (2000) // Cat
Notes: The core of the collection is the specialized library of Charles R Boxer (1000) dealing with the history of the Iberians in the East, 16th-18th century. Mainly incl works on China, Japan and the Philippines during the period of their early intercourse with the West through 1800, as well as materials on the English and Dutch East India Companies, and the 17th century Anglo-Dutch naval wars. Special mention should be made of the valuable letters from missions by the Jesuits, and the works in this area by the Augustinians, Franciscans, and Dominicans, from the time of the arrival of the Iberians in Asia. The collection is a valuable source of information for the study of the European expansion into the area, including Southeast Asia.
MD —US NAVAL ACADEMY, Nimitz Library, Annapolis, 21402. Alice S Creighton, Assistant Librn for Special Collections
Holdings: Vols (22,000) Cat Mss Pix
Notes: Books and periodicals, with emphasis on seapower. Incl rare and historically significant works, naval and general history. US Naval Academy materials (histories, class albums, Lucky Bags, student publications, etc), and copies of transcripts

of the Naval Institute's oral history interviews with US naval officers. Manuscripts incl 205 volumes of ships' logs, letterbooks, order books, and watch, station and quarter bills, 1796-1938; papers of various naval officers, incl. Vice Admiral Wilson Brown, Commander George M Bache, Admiral Harry S Knapp, Lieutenant Edwin J DeHaven, and others; family correspondence of Admiral David Dixon Porter; and several thousand World War II naval action reports. Approximately 15,000 pictures incl portraits of naval officers, pictures of US and some foreign ships, World War II naval news photos and USNA photographs.
MA —HARVARD UNIVERSITY LIBRARY, Cambridge, 02138.
Holdings: Cat
NJ —STEVENS INSTITUTE OF TECHNOLOGY, Samuel C Williams Library, Castle Point Sta, Hoboken, 07030. Jane G Hartye, Special Collections Librn
Holdings: // Cat Mss Pix
Notes: Known as the US Ironclad Monitor, it was designed by Capt John Ericsson and launched January 30, 1862. The "Monitor" participated in the historic battle with the "Merrimac" on March 9, 1862. It sank off Cape Hatteras on December 31, 1862. Our collection includes original design drawings of the "Monitor", 38 of which were drawn by Capt Ericsson and 34 by C W McCord. The copies of these drawings are now in the National Archives. No photocopying.
NJ —PRINCETON UNIVERSITY, Library, Manuscript Collection, Nassau St, Princeton, 08540. Jean F Preston, Cur
Holdings: Mss Pix
Notes: The Blair-Lee Families Collection, which deals in large part with American political and naval history of the period 1733 to 1916, fills over 300 ms boxes. It incl the papers of Francis Preston Blair, Sr, Samuel Phillips Lee, Elizabeth Blair Lee, and Blair Lee. An unpublished partial typescript guide (75 p) is available in the Library.
NY —WEBB INSTITUTE OF NAVAL ARCHITECTURE, Livingston Library, Crescent Beach Rd, Glen Cove, 11542. Fred H Forrest, Librn
Holdings: Vols 400 Cat
Notes: Access by appointment only.
NY —C W POST CENTER OF LONG ISLAND UNIVERSITY, B Davis Schwartz Memorial Library, Greenvale, 11548. Jean Goldberg, Special Collections Librn
Notes: Theodore Roosevelt Collection. Primarily naval and US history. Incl almost all his writings.
NY —NEW YORK HISTORICAL SOCIETY, Library, 170 Central Park W, New York, 10024. James Gregory, Librn
NY —NEW YORK PUBLIC LIBRARY, Research Libraries, General Research Division, Fifth Ave & 42 St, New York, 10018. Rodney Phillips, Chief
Holdings: Vols (2,225,000) Cat Maps Pix Microforms
Budget: ($775,718)
PA —UNIVERSITY OF PITTSBURGH, Hillman Library, Pittsburgh, 15260.
Holdings: Vols (10,000)
Notes: The entire contents of the oldest used book shop in Pittsburgh, the John C Daub Book Store. The collection deals mainly in the areas of military history; works dealing with the Civil War, the World Wars and other military topics; and local history: county histories, city, state or regional histories. Also incl are military works containing colored plates; a large group of Americana; and many framed, colored prints on military subjects.
RI —BROWN UNIVERSITY, John Hay Library, Anne S K Brown Military Collection, 20 Prospect St, Providence, 02912. Richard B Harrington, Cur
Holdings: Vols (40,000) Cat Mss Pix
Notes: The Anne S K Brown Military Collection has been formed over the past forty or more years by Mrs John Nicholas Brown, now of Newport, and contains approximately 40,000 volumes and 60,000 prints, drawings and watercolors as well as a number of oil paintings and about 5000

NAVAL HISTORY (cont.)

miniature model soldiers. At its beginning (and still today) the emphasis or focus of this collection has been upon the history of, and the accurate contemporary illustration of, military and naval uniforms of all nations from the early XVII century to the present. In the course of time, however, the collection has come to incl also a vast and related amount of material on military and naval history, military and naval arts and tactics, wars, campaigns, ceremonies, biography, portraits and caricatures of this and earlier periods. It has been probably the largest private collection of such a nature inthe world, and it contains much ms and graphic documentation which is unique. It has been useful to numerous scholars and historians, editors, filmmakers and publishers for research and for illustrative material and has also contributed to many museum exhibitions. In 1982 the entire collection, with its complete card catalog and subject index, has been presented to Brown University, where it is located in the John Hay Library. Special requests are taken care of by phone, mail and appointments with the curator.

TN —PT BOATS MUSEUM & LIBRARY, PO Box 109, Memphis, 38101. J M "Boats" Newberry, Librn
Holdings: Vols (2000) Uncat Maps Pix Slides Phonorecords Audiotapes 16mm Films Microforms Videotapes Biographies
Budget: ($25,000)
Notes: PT Boats, Inc is an 8000 man organization of PT boat veterans, families, modelers and history buffs who have donated a sizable collection of artifacts and records pertaining to their PT boat service. The collection also contains an 80-foot Elco PT boat and a 78-foot Higgins PT boat, both restored. National headquarters and archives are in Memphis, and the display collection is located on board the USS Massachusetts at Battleship Cove, Fall River, Mass, 02721. To use the library, write PT Boat Coordinator, William C Hindle and/or Don Rhoads, Chief Administrative Officer in Memphis. Memphis headquarters has some 10,000 photos and line drawings with specifications.

VA —UNIVERSITY OF VIRGINIA, Alderman Library, Manuscripts Dept, Charlottesville, 22901. Edmund Berkeley Jr, Cur
Holdings: Cat Mss Maps Pix
Notes: Personal and official papers of Sir Andrew Snape Hamond and Graham Eden Hamond concern British naval operations during the American Revolution and in the Mediterranean during the Napoleonic Wars. Paul P Hoffman (ed) *Guide to the Naval Papers of Sir Andrew Snape Hamond . . . and Sir Graham Eden Hamond . . .* (Charlottesville, Va: Microfilm Publications, University of Virginia, 1966). Papers of US and Confederate naval officer Samuel Barron; US fleet surgeon and Brooklyn Navy Yard surgeon Gustavus R B Horner; US naval surgeon John S Whittle on a scientific expedition to the Pacific, 1838-1841; and US naval officer William Conway Whittle on West Indies and Mediterranean cruises, 1823-1831.

VA —PORTSMOUTH PUBLIC LIBRARY, 601 Court St, Portsmouth, 23704. Dean Burgess, Library Dir
Holdings: Vols 1300 Cat
Notes: Although particularly interested in Tidewater and Lower Tidewater history, we buy most books we can locate on Virginia as well. In 1972 we were given the distinguished collection of Judge White of Lynnhaven.

BC —MARITIME MUSEUM OF BRITISH COLUMBIA, 28 Bastion Sq, Victoria, V8W 1H9, Can. C H Shaw, Dir
Holdings: Vols (2500) Cat Mss Maps Pix Slides Microforms
Budget: ($110,000)
Notes: Also 4000 registration cards; 6000 pictures.

ON —NATIONAL MUSEUMS OF CANADA, Library Services Directorate,

Ottawa, K1A 0M8, Can. Valerie Monkhouse, Director
Holdings: Vols 12,000 Cat
Budget: ($60,000)
Notes: Collection includes; arms and armour, military aeronautics, military and naval arts and sciences, military and naval equipment, general military and naval history, military and naval history of Canada. Research collection, interlibrary loans available, public may use on the premises.

NAVAL HISTORY—PICTURES, ILLUSTRATIONS, ETC.

DC —LIBRARY OF CONGRESS, Prints & Photographs Div, Washington, 20540.
Holdings: Cat Pix

RI —BROWN UNIVERSITY, John Hay Library, Anne S K Brown Military Collection, 20 Prospect St, Providence, 02912. Richard B Harrington, Cur
Notes: The Anne S K Brown Military Collection has been formed over the past forty or more years by Mrs John Nicholas Brown, now of Newport, and contains approximately 40,000 volumes and 60,000 prints, drawings and watercolors as well as a number of oil paintings and about 5000 miniature model soldiers. At its beginning (and still today) the emphasis or focus of this collection has been upon the history of, and the accurate contemporary illustration of, military and naval uniforms of all nations from the early XVII century to the present. In the course of time, however, the collection has come to incl also a vast and related amount of material on military and naval history, military and naval arts and tactics, wars, campaigns, ceremonies, biography, portraits and caricatures of this and earlier periods. It has been probably the largest private collection of such a nature inthe world, and it contains much ms and graphic documentation which is unique. It has been useful to numerous scholars and historians, editors, filmmakers and publishers for research and for illustrative material and has also contributed to many museum exhibitions. In 1982 the entire collection, with its complete card catalog and subject index, has been presented to Brown University, where it is located in the John Hay Library. Special requests are taken care of by phone, mail and appointments with the curator.

NAVAL ORDNANCE see Ordnance, Naval

NAVAL POWER see Sea Power

NAVAL SCIENCE see Naval Art and Science

NAVAL SHIPS see Warships

NAVAL STORES

GA —EMORY UNIVERSITY, Robert W Woodruff Library, Special Collections Dept, Atlanta, 30322. Linda M Matthews, Head Special Collections; Virginia J H Cain, Processing Archivist; Richard H F Lindemann, Reference Archivist
Notes: Correspondence and other materials of Charles Holmes Herty (1867-1937), who was known for his work in applying chemistry to the improvement of industry and who served as president of the American Chemical Association; items reflect Herty's naval stores and other forestry products. 300,000 items.

NAVAL STRATEGY see Strategy (Military)

NAVAL UNIFORMS see Uniforms, Military and Naval

NAVAL WAR COLLEGE see U.S. Naval War College

NAVAL WARFARE see Naval Art and Science

NAVIGATION

DC —US NAVAL OBSERVATORY LIBRARY, 30th & Massachusetts Ave, NW,

Washington, 20016. Brenda G Corbin, Librn
Holdings: Vols (75,000) Cat Mss Maps Pix Slides Microforms
Notes: Incl 1000 journals, with monograph and serial publications in the fields of celestial mechanics, fundamental astronomy, time determination, photographic astrometry and astrophysics, data processing, mathematics.

FL —MARTIN COUNTY PUBLIC LIBRARY, 701 E Ocean Blvd, Stuart, 33494. LeRoy Hennings Jr, Dir
Holdings: Vols 173 Cat
Notes: Selim Walker McArthur collection on sailing. The heart of the collection deals with the building of sailing ship models and dates from the 1920s. This material is unique.

ME —PENOBSCOT MARINE MUSEUM, Library, Church St, Searsport, 04974. Charles Howard, Librn
Holdings: Vols (4000) Cat Mss Maps Pix
Budget: ($5000)
Notes: Marine maritime history, log books, journals, diaries, marine charts, ships registers, photographs, archives & mss, and books relating to world navigation. The greatest emphasis is placed on the Penobscot Bay region.

MA —MASSACHUSETTS INSTITUTE OF TECHNOLOGY, Institute Archives, Special Collections, Cambridge, 02139.
Notes: Bryant, Clark, and Forbes collections on early navigation and shipbuilding.

NY —STATE UNIVERSITY OF NEW YORK, Maritime College, Stephen B Luce Library, Fort Schuyler, Bronx, 10465. Richard H Corson, Librn
Holdings: Vols (68,000) Cat Maps Slides Videotapes 16mm Films
Budget: ($90,000)
Notes: Incl extensive holdings in periodical literature with long and complete runs of many titles. Approx 3500 recent research reports in paper and microfiche format. Mainly English language.

NY —US MERCHANT MARINE ACADEMY, Schuyler Otis Bland Memorial Library, Steamboat Rd, Kings Point, 11024. Stephen R Wiist, Acting Chief Librn
Holdings: Vols (130,000) Cat Mss Maps Pix Slides Phonorecords Microforms
Budget: ($75,000)
Notes: All aspects of maritime affairs.

NY —AMERICAN MUSEUM-HAYDEN PLANETARIUM, Richard S Perkin Library, 81 St & Central Park W, New York, 10024. Sandra Kitt, Librn
Holdings: Vols (15,000) Cat Maps Pix Slides
Budget: ($8000)
Notes: Considered one of the strongest and most complete astronomy libraries on the east coast. Contains the Bliss Collection of Ancient Astronomical Instruments; also the Mt Wilson/Bloman Sky Survey to the 45 degree declination; the Lick Observatory Survey; *American Ephemeris and Nautical Almanac*, 1855-date.

NY —NEW YORK PUBLIC LIBRARY, Research Libraries, Science and Technology Research Center, Fifth Ave & 42 St, New York, 10018.
Holdings: Vols (1,100,000) Cat Microforms
Budget: ($647,259)

NY —SEAMEN'S CHURCH INSTITUTE OF NEW YORK, Joseph Conrad Library, 15 State St, New York, 10004. Bonnie Golightly, Librn
Holdings: Vols (23,500) Cat Pix
Budget: ($8500)
Notes: Merchant seamen, merchant ships, voyages, navigation, marine engineering, shipbuilding. Large collection of ship registers: *Lloyd's Register of Shipping*, a partial coverage of the years 1764-1865 in reprints, coverage for the years 1877 to date; *American Bureau of Shipping*, 1916 to date; *Merchant Vessels of the US*, 1891 to date. *Society of Naval Architects and Marine Engineers Transactions*, vol 1, 1893 to date. The picture file consists of mostly of photographs of merchant ships. This is supplemented by scrapbooks. The index to the pictures, scrapbooks, books and vertical file are in one subject catalog. We subscribe to and keep for several years numerous maritime periodicals. The maritime history

NAVIGATION (cont.)

collection incl sailing ships as well as
steamships.

PA —US NAVY, Philadelphia Naval Shipyard
Technical Library, Philadelphia Naval
Shipyard, Philadelphia, 19112. Alice R
Murray, Dir
Holdings: Vols (12,500) Cat Pix
Notes: The Library also has (70,000)
technical manuals, (3500) research and
development reports. Over (400) current
periodicals.

TN —TENNESSEE VALLEY AUTHORITY
(TVA), Technical Library, 400 W Summit
Hill Dr, E2 B7, Knoxville, 37902. Jesse C
Mills, Chief Librn
Holdings: Vols (106,900) Cat Mss Maps Pix
Audiotapes Microforms
Budget: ($2,025,000)
Notes: The Technical Library Headquarters
Staff (order, cataloging, information, and
administration) is located in Knoxville,
Tenn. In addition there are branch libraries
in Knoxville, Norris, and Chattanooga,
Tennessee, and Muscle Shoals, Alabama.

NS —CANADIAN COAST GUARD
COLLEGE, Library, PO Box 4500, Sydney,
B1P 6L1, Can. David MacSween, Librn
Holdings: Vols 4000 Cat 16mm Films

NAVIGATION—HISTORY

CT —YALE UNIVERSITY, Beinecke Rare
Book & Manuscript Library, Henry C Taylor
Collection, New Haven, 06520.
Holdings: Vols 396 Cat Mss
Notes: Early navigation and Americana. See
Kebabian, John S, *The Henry C Taylor
Collection* (New Haven: Yale University
Library, 1971).

IL —ADLER PLANETARIUM, History of
Astronomy Collection, 1300 S Lake Shore
Dr, Chicago, 60605. Roderick Webster, Cur;
Marjorie Webster, Cur; Sara Schechner
Genuth, Asst Cur
Holdings: Vols (430) Uncat Mss Maps Pix
Notes: Historical navigational instruments.
Price Photographic Archives (2800)
containing prints of instruments. Incl
scientific instruments (1000). Noncirculating.
See also entries under Astronomy - History;
Surveying - History; Horology.

PA —PENNSYLVANIA STATE
UNIVERSITY, Fred Lewis Pattee Library,
University Park, 16802. Stuart Forth, Dean
of Libraries
Holdings: Vols Cat Maps
Notes: Based primarily on an interest in
Australia and the Pacific Ocean, the
Pennsylvania State University Libraries have
developed a strong collection of voyages,
including many 17th and 18th century
editions of specific voyages, eg, Cook, La
Perouse, Vancouver, collected editions both
French and English, together with related
publications, eg, De Broses, Dalrymple. The
collections include both exploration and
scientific voyages in original editions and
reprints.

RI —BROWN UNIVERSITY, John Carter
Brown Library, Providence, 02912. Norman
Fiering, Librn; Everett C Wilkie Jr,
Bibliographer; Susan Danforth, Cur Maps &
Prints
Notes: Extensive collection, incl works on
navigation, shipbuilding, mariners' health,
and explorations accomplished by ship.

NAVIGATION, ELECTRONICS IN see
Electronics in Navigation

NAVIGATION, INERTIAL
(ASTRONAUTICS) see Inertial Navigation
Systems

NAVIGATION, INLAND see Inland
Navigation

NAVIGATION CHARTS see Nautical
Charts

NAVIGATORS see Discovery and
Exploration; Explorers

NAVY see Naval Art and Science

NAVY CLEARANCE DIVING TEAMS
see Underwater Demolition Teams

NAWDOWISSNEE INDIANS see Dakota
Indians

NAZARENES see Church of the Nazarene

NAZIS see National Socialism; Neo-Nazis

NEAL, HARRY EDWARD

VA —UNIVERSITY OF VIRGINIA,
Alderman Library, Manuscripts Dept,
Charlottesville, 22901. Edmund Berkeley Jr,
Cur
Holdings: Cat Mss Pix
Notes: Extensive collection of mss and
printed materials.

NEAR EAST

CA —UNIVERSITY OF CALIFORNIA, LOS
ANGELES, Research Library, Near Eastern
Collection, Los Angeles, 90024. Edward
Shreeves, Chairman, Bibliographers Group;
Dunning Wilson, Near Eastern Bibliographer
Holdings: Vols (200,000) Cat Mss Maps
Microforms
Notes: Incl ancient cultures and history.

CA —HOOVER INSTITUTION ON WAR,
REVOLUTION & PEACE, Stanford
University, Stanford, 94305. Peter Duignan,
Cur; Karen Fung, Deputy Cur
Holdings: Vols (100,000)
Notes: Materials in Arabic, Turkish, and
Persian and western languages concerning
political, economic, and social developments
of the Middle East and North Africa in the
19th and 20th centuries. Countries covered
incl Turkey, Iran, Afghanistan, Israel,
Cyprus, Greece, the 18 states of the Arab
League, and Mauritania. Incl books,
periodicals, newspapers, government
documents. Current publications received
under P L 480 assignment from Cairo until
1978. The published catalog of the Arabic
collection and the published catalog of the
Turkish and Persian collections are listed in
Downs, Supplement 1961-1970, no 181. The
Middle East collection is described in
*African and Middle East Collections: A
Survey of Holdings at the Hoover Institution
on War, Revolution and Peace*.

CT —YALE UNIVERSITY, American Oriental
Society Library, 120 High St, New Haven,
06520. Rutherford B Rogers, Librarian
Holdings: Vols 22,000 Cat Mss
Notes: On deposit.

DC —GEORGETOWN UNIVERSITY,
Library, Special Collections Div, 37 & O Sts
NW, Washington, 20057. George M
Barringer, Special Collections Librn;
Nicholas B Sheetz, Mss Librn
Holdings: Vols 2500 Cat
Notes: In large measure the former library of
the American Friends of the Middle East.
Incl large collection of cataloged articles and
pamphlet publications, especially modern
Near East.

DC —LIBRARY OF CONGRESS, African and
Middle Eastern Division, Washington,
20540.
Holdings: Cat Mss Microforms
Notes: Near East: Over 75,000 vols, Arabic,
Armenian, Turkish, Persian, and related
languages. Special subject strengths incl
Islamic philosophy, history, and literature.

MA —HARVARD UNIVERSITY, Center for
Middle Eastern Studies, Library, Coolidge
Hall, 1737 Cambridge St, Cambridge, 02138.
Barbara Mitchell, Librn
Holdings: Vols (5000) Periodicals
Notes: Some history of countries of the
Middle East; increasingly emphasizes culture
and politics of the current Middle Eastern
area. Special collection of Energy Economics
Research. Library currently receives 15
periodical titles.

MA —HARVARD UNIVERSITY LIBRARY,
Widener Library, Middle Eastern Dept,
Cambridge, 02138. David H Partington,
Librn
Holdings: Vols (70,000) Cat
Budget: ($55,000)
Notes: The Middle Eastern Collections
consist of separately housed and cataloged
books in Arabic, Turkish, Persian, Kurdish,
and Urdu. Approx 4000 titles are added per
year in the principal subject fields of
language, literature, Islamic studies, and the
modern social science disciplines. The
Armenian collection is especially strong in
classical and medieval texts. The Library's
published *Catalogue of Arabic, Persian, and
Ottoman Turkish Books* (1968) lists some
40,000 vols in the languages named; these
are supplemented by many thousands in
western languages. See *Harvard Library
Bulletin*, XVI (1968), 313-325. Egyptian

publications are received under P L 480. The
1983 six-volume catalog of the Arabic
Collection covers North African imprints as
well as Near Eastern.

MI —UNIVERSITY OF MICHIGAN,
Graduate Library, Near East Dept, Ann
Arbor, 48109. John A Eilts, Bibliographer
Holdings: Vols (150,000) Cat Mss Maps
Microforms
Notes: Excludes Islam in the Far East,
Judaism in general, though it does incl
specifically Near Eastern Judaism. Incl
Bahaism and Arab philosophy, fields of
study connected with Islamic or Arabic
studies, Turkish language and literature.

NJ —PRINCETON UNIVERSITY, Library,
Near East Collections, Princeton, 08540.
James Weinberger, Cur
Holdings: Vols (100,000) Cat Mss Maps
Phonorecords Audiotapes Microforms
Budget: ($72,000)
Notes: Princeton has the largest collection of
Arabic mss in the US. Collections are
particularly rich in classical Arabic and
Persian texts, encompassing all the
traditional genres. Of special note are the
collections in Arabic and Persian literature,
language, history, philosophy and theology
and the religious sciences of Islam, both in
ms and printed formats. A separate,
additional collection of Arabic mss (about
2000 items) is being cataloged. It is
especially rich in theology and philosophy of
the classical Islamic period. Two printed
catalogs are available: *Descriptive Catalog of
the Garrett Collection of Arabic
Manuscripts*, Philip K Hitti et al (Princeton:
Princeton Univ Press, 1938); and *Catalogue
of Arabic Manuscripts (Yahuda Section) in
the Garrett Collection, Princeton University*,
Rudolf Mach (Princeton: Princeton Unvi
Press, 1977).

NY —STATE UNIVERSITY OF NEW
YORK, COLLEGE AT NEW PALTZ,
Sojourner Truth Library, World Study
Center, New Paltz, 12561. Corinne Nyquist,
Librn
Holdings: Vols (36,294) Cat Maps Pix
Notes: 36,294 volumes on Africa, Asia and
the Near East, not incl reference books or
pamphlets which have been integrated into
the general collection.

NY —NEW YORK PUBLIC LIBRARY,
Oriental Div, Fifth Ave & 42 St, New York,
10018. E Christian Filstrup, Chief
Holdings: Cat Mss Microforms
Budget: ($56,455)
Notes: Described in *Dictionary Catalog of
the Oriental Collection*, The Research
Libraries of the New York Public Library,
1960, 16 vols, and *First Supplement*, 1976, 8
vols (144,000 cards). This catalog incl 318,
000 entries for works in about 100 languages
of the East, and all works in Western
languages on Oriental subjects. The Oriental
Collection numbers about 120,000 vols; its
Arabic and Indic holdings and those on
ancient Egypt and the ancient Near East are
among the largest in the US. There is also a
collection of 30,000 vols of PL 480 material
from Egypt, Pakistan, and India to which
there is main entry access, but which is not
incorporated into the dictionary catalog.
Other outstanding features of the Oriental
Collection incl extensive holdings of
Japanese technical and scientific periodicals;
a unique collection of linguistic works,
grammars, anddictionaries; and unusually
good coverage of the field of Oriental
religions and philosophies. The catalog
contains numerous subject references to
periodical articles in all languages. All
entries are arranged alphabetically according
to the Roman alphabet.

OH —CLEVELAND PUBLIC LIBRARY, Fine
Arts and Special Collections Department,
325 Superior Ave, Cleveland, 44114. Alice
N Loranth, Head
Holdings: Vols (54,400) Cat Mss
Notes: Part of the research and reference
collection on Orientalia. Contains scholarly
books, periodicals, and serials in Western
and in the vernacular language. Incl all
aspects of Near Eastern civilizations:
archaeology (7000 vols), history, language,
literature, philology, philosophy and religion

NEAR EAST (cont.)

prior to the impact of Western inlfuence.
Strong holdings in scholarly editions of
classic texts, their versions and translations.
Holdings in vernacular languages incl: 2640
vols in Arabic, 1000 vols in Persian, 500 vols
in Hebrew, 130 vols in Armenian, in
addition to materials in Urdu, Pushto,
Ethiopic, Syriac, etc. Some museum objects.
See also entries under Folklore; Manuscripts,
Arabic; Oriental Languages and Literatures.
OR —PORTLAND STATE UNIVERSITY
LIBRARY, 934 SW Harrison, PO Box 1151,
97207, Portland, 97201. Kenneth W Butler,
Asst Dir
Holdings: Vols (30,968) Cat Maps Pix
Microforms
Notes: Incl PL 480 holdings.
PA —SCRANTON PUBLIC LIBRARY, Vine
& N Washington Sts, Scranton, 18503.
Thomas McHale, Dir
Holdings: Vols (192) Cat
Budget: ($7000)
Notes: Foreign trade information service.
TX —UNIVERSITY OF TEXAS LIBRARIES,
Middle East Collection, PO Box P, Austin,
78712. Abazar Sepehri, Librn
Holdings: Vols (45,000) Cat Microforms
Notes: Arabic, Persian and Turkish materials
in the humanities and social sciences. Incl
350 periodical and 45 newspaper titles from
most of the countries of the Arab League,
Turkey, Iran and Afghanistan.
UT —UNIVERSITY OF UTAH, Middle East
Library, Salt Lake City, 84112. Ragai N
Makar, Librn
Holdings: Vols 50,000
Budget: ($40,000)
UT —UNIVERSITY OF UTAH, Marriott
Library, Special Collections, Salt Lake City,
84112. Gregory C Thompson, Cur
Holdings: Vols 100,000
Notes: Incl all Near East languages,
microfilm, mss rare books.
†WA —UNIVERSITY OF WASHINGTON
LIBRARIES, Seattle, 98195.

NEAR EAST—ANTIQUITIES

CT —YALE UNIVERSITY, Sterling Memorial
Library, Babylonian Collection, 120 High St,
New Haven, 06520. William W Hallo, Cur
Holdings: Vols (12,000) Cat Mss Pix
Budget: $2500
Notes: 30,000 mss in form of Babylonian
tablets; 6000 seals and other art objects from
Mesopotamia and the rest of the Ancient
Near East.
DC —FREER GALLERY OF ART, Library,
12th & Jefferson Dr SW, Washington,
20560. Ellen A Nollman, Librn
NY —NEW YORK PUBLIC LIBRARY,
Oriental Div, Fifth Ave & 42 St, New York,
10018. E Christian Filstrup, Chief
Holdings: Cat Mss Microforms
Budget: ($56,455)
Notes: Described in *Dictionary Catalog of
the Oriental Collection,* The Research
Libraries of the New York Public Library,
1960, 16 vols, and *First Supplement,* 1976, 8
vols (144,000 cards). This catalog incl 318,
000 entries for works in about 100 languages
of the East, and all works in Western
languages on Oriental subjects. The Oriental
Collection numbers about 120,000 vols; its
Arabic and Indic holdings and those on
ancient Egypt and the ancient Near East are
among the largest in the US. There is also a
collection of 30,000 vols of PL 480 material
from Egypt, Pakistan, and India to which
there is main entry access, but which is not
incorporated into the dictionary catalog.
Other outstanding features of the Oriental
Collection incl extensive holdings of
Japanese technical and scientific periodicals;
a unique collection of linguistic works,
grammars, anddictionaries; and unusually
good coverage of the field of Oriental
religions and philosophies. The catalog
contains numerous subject references to
periodical articles in all languages. All
entries are arranged alphabetically according
to the Roman alphabet.
NC —DUKE UNIVERSITY, Divinity School
Library, Durham, 27706. Donn Michael
Farris, Librn

NC —SOUTHEASTERN BAPTIST
THEOLOGICAL SEMINARY LIBRARY,
PO Box 752, Wake Forest, 27587. H Eugene
McLeod, Librn
Holdings: Cat Maps Slides
Notes: Near Eastern archaeology related to
biblical studies.
PA —BRYN MAWR COLLEGE, Canaday
Library, Bryn Mawr, 19010. James Tanis,
Dir
Notes: Classical and Near Eastern
archaeology, Greek architecture and
sculpture; Anatolian and Aegean
Archaeology. In Art and Archaeology
Library.

NEAR EAST—DESCRIPTION AND TRAVEL

DC —CATHOLIC UNIVERSITY OF
AMERICA, Mullen Library, ICOR/Semitics
Library, Room 20, Washington, 20064.
Monica J Blanchard, Librn
Notes: The bulk of the ICOR/Semitics
Library collection belongs to the Institute of
Christian Oriental Research which supports
the work of the Corpus Scriptorum
Christianorum Orientalium. The holdings are
chiefly concerned with Christian Egypt and
the Coptic Church, Syriac and Syrian
patristic studies, and the Syriac and Arabic
speaking eastern churches. There are less
extensive holdings of Ethiopic, Armenian
and Georgian material. ICOR titles are
cataloged by the ICOR/Semitic Library, and
ICOR holdings do not appear in the general
catalogue of the University Library.
OH —OHIO STATE UNIVERSITY, Library,
1858 Neil Mall, Columbus, 43210. Dona
Straley, Islamica Librn
Holdings: Vols (25,000) Cat Maps
Microforms
Budget: ($30,000)
Notes: The bulk of the Arabic language
collection is in the field of language and
literature, with large and medium collections
in the fields of Islamica and Middle East
history. There are also approx 2000 Persian
language vols and approx 3000 vols in
Turkish. Scholarly translations of Arabic,
Persian and Turkish materials are acquired
as available. Also a substantial supporting
collection of materials on Arabic language
and literature, Islamica, and Middle East
history in all of the major European
languages. PL 480 recipient since 1975. No
ms holdings.

NEAR EAST—DESCRIPTION AND TRAVEL—VIEWS

NM —MUSEUM OF NEW MEXICO, Photo
Archives, Box 2087, Santa Fe, 87503.
Arthur L Olivas, Cur; Richard Rudisill,
Photo Historian
Holdings: Cat Pix Slides
Notes: Extensive picture collections of
Australia, New Zealand, China, India and
the East taken in the 19th century. The
Photo Archives contain approx 250,000
items, of which 200,000 are cataloged. The
primary function of the archives is
preserving significant historical material, and
these pictures are mainly for research rather
than for general browsing.

NEAR EAST—ECONOMIC CONDITIONS

MA —HARVARD UNIVERSITY, Center for
Middle Eastern Studies, Library, Coolidge
Hall, 1737 Cambridge St, Cambridge, 02138.
Barbara Mitchell, Librn
Holdings: Vols (5000) Periodicals
Notes: Some history of countries of the
Middle East; increasingly emphasizes culture
and politics of the current Middle Eastern
area. Special collection of Energy Economics
Research. Library currently receives 15
periodical titles.

NEAR EAST—GOVERNMENT PUBLICATIONS

CA —UNIVERSITY OF CALIFORNIA, LOS
ANGELES, Research Library, Public Affairs

Service, 405 Hilgard Ave, Los Angeles,
90024. Edward Shreeves, Chairman,
Bibliographers Group; Eugenia Eaton, Head,
Public Affairs Service
Holdings: Microforms
Notes: Depository for the official
publications of California cities and counties,
the state of California, the United States
government, the United Nations and some of
its specialized agencies (including the Food
and Agricultural Organization and
UNESCO), and such regional organizations
as the European Communities and
Organization of American States. Selected
publications of other American cities and
counties, of the other states and possessions
of the United States, of interstate
organizations, and of foreign governments
(with emphasis on major world powers,
Africa, Latin America and the Near and
Middle East) and intergovernmental
organizations.

NEAR EAST—HISTORY

CA —UNIVERSITY OF CALIFORNIA, LOS
ANGELES, Research Library, Near Eastern
Collection, Los Angeles, 90024. Edward
Shreeves, Chairman, Bibliographers Group;
Dunning Wilson, Near Eastern Bibliographer
Holdings: Vols (200,000) Cat Mss Maps
Microforms
Notes: Incl ancient cultures and history.
OH —OHIO STATE UNIVERSITY, Library,
1858 Neil Mall, Columbus, 43210. Dona
Straley, Islamica Librn
Holdings: Vols (25,000) Cat Maps
Microforms
Budget: ($30,000)
Notes: The bulk of the Arabic language
collection is in the field of language and
literature, with large and medium collections
in the fields of Islamica and Middle East
history. There are also approx 2000 Persian
language vols and approx 3000 vols in
Turkish. Scholarly translations of Arabic,
Persian and Turkish materials are acquired
as available. Also a substantial supporting
collection of materials on Arabic language
and literature, Islamica, and Middle East
history in all the major European languages.
PL 480 recipient since 1975. No ms
holdings.
UT —UNIVERSITY OF UTAH, Middle East
Library, Salt Lake City, 84112. Ragai N
Makar, Librn
Budget: ($40,000)
WA —UNIVERSITY OF WASHINGTON
LIBRARIES, Suzzallo Library, Near East
Section, FM-25, Seattle, 98195. Fawzi W
Khoury, Head
Holdings: Vols (81,359) Cat Mss Maps
Slides Phonorecords 16mm Films filmstrips
Microforms
Budget: ($52,752)

NEAR EAST—PICTURES, ILLUSTRATIONS

DC —LIBRARY OF CONGRESS, Prints &
Photographs Div, Washington, 20540.
Notes: The Matson Photo Service Collection
contains photographs of the Middle East,
1896-1946.

NEAR EAST—POLITICS AND GOVERNMENT

MA —HARVARD UNIVERSITY, Center for
Middle Eastern Studies, Library, Coolidge
Hall, 1737 Cambridge St, Cambridge, 02138.
Barbara Mitchell, Librn
Holdings: Vols (5000) Periodicals
Notes: Some history of countries of the
Middle East; increasingly emphasizes culture
and politics of the current Middle Eastern
area. Special collection of Energy Economics
Research. Library currently receives 15
periodical titles.

NEAR EAST RELIEF—ORGANIZATION

CA —UNIVERSITY OF CALIFORNIA, LOS
ANGELES, Research Library, Dept of

NEAR EAST RELIEF—ORGANIZATION (cont.)

Special Collections, 405 Hilgard Ave, Los Angeles, 90024. Edward Shreeves, Chairman, Bibliographers Group; David S Zeidberg, Head
Notes: 11 linear feet of maps, photographs, memorabilia, and ephemera relating to the Near Eastern Relief Fund, of which he was the Los Angeles Director.

NEBRASKA

NE —NEBRASKA LIBRARY COMMISSION, Publications Clearinghouse, 1420 P St, Lincoln, 68508. Patricia Sloan, Federal Documents Librn; Vern Buis, State Documents Librn
Holdings: Vols 36,500
Notes: Depository for all Nebraska state government publications since July 1972. State publications are indexed in *Nebraska State Publications Checklist,* published by the Publications Clearinghouse and issued biomonthly in microfiche format.

NEBRASKA—GENEALOGY

NE —KEENE MEMORIAL LIBRARY, 1030 N Broad St, Fremont, 68025. William S McDermott, Dir
Holdings: Vols (10) Cat
Notes: Cemetery indexes compiled from gravestones, etc, for all cemeteries in Dodge and Washington counties. The project will incl surrounding counties in the future. These indexes are also available at the Nebraska State Historical Society, Lincoln.
NE —NEBRASKA STATE HISTORICAL SOCIETY, Archives, 1500 R St, Box 82554, Lincoln, 68501. James E Potter, State Archivist
Holdings: Cat Mss Microforms
Budget: ($290,000)
Notes: Collection

NEBRASKA—HISTORY

KS —UNIVERSITY OF KANSAS, Kenneth Spencer Research Library, Kansas Collection, Lawrence, 66045. Sheryl K Williams, Cur
Holdings: Vols (90,000) Cat Mss Maps Pix
Notes: All aspects of the American West and trans-Mississippi history, especially northern and central regions. Overland diaries, cartographic history, Indians, emigration and immigration, printing history, cattle industry, agriculture and farm life, conservation are some special interests, in addition to the usual political, economic, military and social interests.
NE —NEBRASKA STATE HISTORICAL SOCIETY, Fort Robinson Museum, Box 304, Crawford, 69339. Vance Nelson, Cur
Holdings: Vols (1500) Cat Mss Maps Pix Slides Phonorecords Audiotapes 16mm Films Microforms
Notes: Materials related to the history of Fort Robinson, and incl the Post Medical library, reference books on state government, etc, Western Americana: books on ranching, homesteaders, Indian wars, etc; microfilm records for Fort Robinson records, Red Cloud and Spotted Tail Agency records, Crawford and Chadron, Nebraska newspapers, diaries and interviews. Library incl the E Kopac Collection of books dealing with Western Americana; particularly Indian wars, transportation, guns and railroads.
NE —ADAMS COUNTY HISTORICAL SOCIETY, Library, 1330 N Burlington Ave, Hastings, 68901. Corinne Cody, Secretary
Holdings: Vols (200) Cat Mss Maps Pix Slides Phonorecords Audiotapes Videotapes 16mm Films Microforms
Budget: ($5000)
Notes: The most noteworthy portions of the Adams County Collection are the church and school records from the county, useful for case studies on many aspects of life on the Great Plains. The photographic collection is intensively indexed. A catalog and a guide to Adams County material available locally are in progress.

NE —KEARNEY STATE COLLEGE, Calvin T Ryan Library, Kearney, 68847. John Mayeski, Dir; Anita Norman, Reference Librn
Holdings: Vols (1700) Cat Mss Maps Pix Slides Microforms
Notes: Collection attempts to cover total historical development of Nebraska. Special strengths incl overland journeys, pony express, sod houses, and the Union Pacific. Special consideration has been given to Indians of Nebraska and the cattle industry. The collection is well supported by the library's general strength of Western Americana.

NE —LINCOLN CITY LIBRARIES, Bennett Martin Public Library, 14 & N Sts, Lincoln, 68508. Carol J Connor, Dir
Holdings: Vols (4750) Cat Mss Maps Pix Slides Phonorecords Audiotapes Videotapes 16mm Films Filmstrips
Notes: Incl works by authors born in the state, resident in the state for a significant period of life, or resident in the state while producing a significant work. Also incl critical and biographical works about Nebraska authors; city, county, and state histories and documents; and other notebook materials. Incl first and other rare editions and a number of mss. Collection is noncirculating.

NE —NEBRASKA STATE HISTORICAL SOCIETY, Archives, 1500 R St, Box 82554, Lincoln, 68501. James E Potter, State Archivist
Holdings: Cat Mss Microforms
Budget: ($290,000)
Notes: Collection

NE —UNIVERSITY OF NEBRASKA-LINCOLN, Don L Love Library, University Archives and Special Collections, Lincoln, 68588. Joseph G Svoboda, University Archivist
Holdings: Vols (1000) // Cat Mss Maps Pix Audiotapes 16mm Films

Notes: The Mari Sandoz Collection consists of four basic parts. The first contains correspondence files, 25,000 letters in all, including letters received from 1925 on and carbon copies of letters sent. The correspondence files are a rich source of information about the author's life and career, creative writing, and Plains Indian and western American history. The second portion of the collection is the author's personal library of books and periodicals, many annotated. Part three contains the author's published works, including most of the editions, foreign and domestic and some unpublished manuscripts as well. Many of the early drafts of books, copy-edited manuscripts, and galley and proofs are also contained in this portion of the collection. The final part of the collections consists of the author's resource files, research and reading notes, clippings, and related materials. These materials fill over fifty standard letter boxes. In addition, the prepared 45,000 index cards refering to information contained both in and out of the collection.

NE —UNIVERSITY OF NEBRASKA-LINCOLN, Don L Love Library, Czech Heritage Collection, Lincoln, 68588. Joseph G Svoboda, University Archivist
Holdings: Vols (3000) Cat Mss Pix Audiotapes Microforms
Notes: The Czech Heritage Collection.

NE —JOSLYN ART REFERENCE LIBRARY, Joslyn Art Museum, 2200 Dodge St, Omaha, 68102. Ann Birney, Librn; Marie Sedlacek, Cataloger-Slide Librn
Holdings: Vols (17,000) Cat Slides
Notes: Incl catalogs of exhibitions and western US materials, especially early Omaha and Nebraska. Large collections of vertical files on subjects and artists; also mounted prints, reproductions, slides. filmstrips.

NE —OMAHA PUBLIC LIBRAY, Omaha, 68102. Michael Phipps, Dir
Holdings: Vols 2000 Cat Mss Maps Pix Microforms
Notes: Incl city, county and state histories and documents. Local scrapbooks and portfolios of pictures available. Census materials and local newspapers on microfilm. First editions and/or mss of Nebraska authors. Rare state and local serial titles in collection.

NE —UNIVERSITY OF NEBRASKA, OMAHA, Library, 60 & Dodge Sts, Omaha, 68132. Mel Bohn, Librn
Holdings: Vols 75 Cat
Notes: Omaha history. 30 linear ft of WPA manuscripts and news clippings.

NE —YORK COLLEGE, Levitt Library, York, 67467. Charles Van Baucom, Dir
Holdings: Vols 80 Cat Mss Pix Audiotapes
Notes: Yorkana Collection incl titles on the college, the city and the county. There is also an active oral history program that has produced 51 tapes. It is to be cataloged and continued.

NEBRASKA—MAPS

NE —NEBRASKA STATE HISTORICAL SOCIETY, Library, 1500 R St, Box 82554, Lincoln, 68501. M Ann Reinert, Library Dept Head
Holdings: Vols (100,000) Cat Maps Pix Microforms
Budget: ($200,000)
Notes: Collection of 400 atlases and 3000 separate maps 1854-present.
See also entry under Great Plains

OK —TULSA CITY-COUNTY LIBRARY, Business & Technology Dept, 400 Civic Center, Tulsa, 74103. Craig Buthod, Head
Notes: Original General Land Office survey maps for the states of Arizona, Arkansas, Colorado, Illinois, Indiana, Idaho, Kansas, Michigan, Missouri, Montana, Nebraska, Nevada, New Mexico, North Dakota, Ohio, Oklahoma, South Dakota, Utah and Wyoming. Incomplete coverage of each state.

NEBRASKA—POLITICS AND GOVERNMENT

NE —NEBRASKA STATE HISTORICAL SOCIETY, Archives, 1500 R St, Box 82554, Lincoln, 68501. James E Potter, State Archivist
Holdings: Cat Mss Microforms
Budget: ($290,000)

Notes: Collection estimated 4,000 cu. ft. of personal papers, business records, church records, and organizational records relating to the history of Nebraska and the Great Plains, ca. 1854-present with a particularly strong emphasis in the subject areas of Indians of North America, agriculture, railroad history, 19th century agrarian political movements, irrigation, and settlement of the Great Plains. Public records holdings of an estimated 10,000 cu. ft. of Nebraska state, county and some municipal government agencies include the official files of Nebraska governors, the Nebraska Legislature, and many territorial and state agencies 1854-present; and numerous tax records, court records, marriage records, naturalization records, and school census records for Nebraska counties. Newspaper collection of 20,000 rolls of microfilm, non-circulating but available for purchase, cataloged according to place published so specific titles must be requested. See A GUIDE TO THE NEWSPAPER COLLECTION OF THE STATE ARCHIVES (Lincoln: Nebraska State Historical Society, 1977), A GUIDE TO THE

NEBRASKA—POLITICS AND GOVERNMENT (cont.)

MANUSCRIPT DIVISION OF THE STATE ARCHIVES (Lincoln: Nebraska State Historical Society, 1974), and A GUIDE TO THE MANUSCRIPT DIVISION OF THE STATE ARCHIVES, a supplement (Lincoln: Nebraska State Historical Society, 1983). Microform holdings of manuscript and public records can also be purchased.

NEBRASKA AUTHORS see Authors, Nebraska

NECROMANCY see Magic and Magicians

NEEDLEWORK

IN —ALLEN COUNTY PUBLIC LIBRARY, 900 Webster St, Fort Wayne, 46802. Paul Deane, Reader Services Dept Head; Kay Lynn Isca, Art Music & AV Dept Head
Holdings: Vols 1257 Cat Pix

MA —HISTORIC DEERFIELD-POCUMTUCK VALLEY MEMORIAL ASSOCIATION, Libraries, Memorial St, Box 53, Deerfield, 01342. David R Proper, Librn
Holdings: Vols (6500) Cat Mss Maps Pix Slides Microforms
Notes: American decorative arts, from colonial times to date. Also, a substantial collection of sketches, patterns, mss, printed material, and color swatches relating to needlework, embroidery and related arts.

OH —CLEVELAND PUBLIC LIBRARY, Science & Technology Dept, 325 Superior Ave, Cleveland, 44114. Jean Z Piety, Head
Holdings: Cat
Notes: Part of the handicrafts collection, which incl crafts of many ethnic groups in Cleveland.

VT —SHELBURNE MUSEUM, Library, Shelburne, 05482. Barbara Reenstierna, Librn
Holdings: Vols (275) Cat Slides

NEEDLEWORK—PATTERNS

CA —CARLSBAD CITY LIBRARY, 1250 Elm Ave, Carlsbad, 92008. Clifford E Lange, Library Dir
Holdings: Vols (2297) Cat
Notes: Collection of sewing patterns. Catalogs of the patterns have been made up with complete information on size, etc, and have been divided into subject areas, such as gift ideas, toys, dolls, women's clothes, men's clothes, children's clothes, etc. Also patterns for knitted and crocheted wearing apparel. Incl patterns for children's costumes, historical fashions and antique dolls.

NEELY, RICHARD

MA —BOSTON UNIVERSITY, Mugar Memorial Library, Special Collections Dept, 771 Commonwealth Ave, Boston, 02215. Howard B Gotlieb, Dir
Holdings: Cat Mss

NEERGAARD, CHARLES F.

†CT —YALE UNIVERSITY, Medical Library, 333 Cedar St, New Haven, 06520.
Notes: Extensive collection of books, illustrations, pamphlets, etc, incl three vols of Charles F Neergaard's "Occasional Papers on Hospital Adminstration."

NEGRI, POLA

TX —TRINITY UNIVERSITY, Elizabeth Coates Maddux Library, 715 Stadium Dr, San Antonio, 78284. Richard Hume Werking, Library Dir; Craig Likness, Head Bibliographer
Holdings: Vols 573
Notes: Private library of Pola Negri. No personal papers. World literature and theatre dominate the collection.

NEGROES see Blacks

NEIGHBORHOOD CENTERS see Social Settlements

NEIGHBORHOOD PLAYHOUSE

†NY —NEIGHBORHOOD PLAYHOUSE SCHOOL OF THE THEATRE, Irene Lewisohn Library, 340 E 54 St, New York, 10022. Alice G Owen, Librn
Holdings: Vols Cat Mss Pix
Notes: Theatre and drama are the primary emphases, but incl books on costume, dance, film, poetry, and general literature. Collection supports the school program and class work. 9 VF drawers of scenes, Neighborhood Playhouse-iana, pictures, music scores, sheet music, etc. A few rare vols are cataloged. Scenes are indexed; music scores are cataloged.

NEIGHBORHOOD STUDIES

IL —CHICAGO PUBLIC LIBRARY, Special Collections Div, Cultural Center, 78 E Washington St, Chicago, 60602. Laura Linard, Cur
Holdings: Mss Maps Pix Slides Microforms
Notes: A vast amount of material on Chicago neighborhood history is housed at several locations in The Chicago Public Library system. A centralized program for organizing, storing and accessing this material was begun by the Special Collections Division in 1977. Major neighborhood collections which have been organized and are now accessible to researchers include: The Papers of the Calumet Pioneer Historical Society, The Calumet Region Community Collection. The Lawndale-Crawford Community Collection, The Papers of the Lawndale-Crawford Historical Association, and the Historic Pullman Collection (all of these collections are housed in the Special Collections Division). Also, the Ravenswood-Lake View Community Collection and the Papers of the Ravenswood-Lake View Historical Association are located at the Hild Regional Library and are open foruse by appointment. Several other neighborhood collections are still housed at branch libraries and are currently being organized. Principal contact person for these neighborhood collections is Robert Marshall, Archivist.

†PA —TEMPLE UNIVERSITY LIBRARIES, Special Collections Dept, Urban Archives Center, Philadelphia, 19122. Thomas Whitehead, Cur of Mss
Holdings: Cat
Notes: Incl the records of several separate collections which are deposited in the Urban Archives Center. Many collections contain photographs, maps and pamphlets, in addition to manuscripts. All collections in the Urban Archives are separately cataloged.

NEIGHBORS, DARRELL

CA —CALIFORNIA STATE UNIVERSITY, LONG BEACH, Library, Dept of Special Collections & Archives, 1250 Bellflower Blvd, Long Beach, 90840. John Ahouse, Special Collections Librn
Holdings: Mss Maps Pix
Notes: Earth Subsidence Collection incl the personal files of Darrell Neighbors and Jan Law.

NEIHARDT, JOHN G.

MO —UNIVERSITY OF MISSOURI-COLUMBIA, Ellis Library, Language and Literature Dept, Columbia, 65201. Jeaneice Brewer, Librn
Holdings: Vols (3500) Cat
Notes: Consists of the personal library of John G Neihardt, 1881-1973, poet, literary critic, and lecturer. Lived among Omaha Indians and Ogalala Sioux Indians to study their character and history. Poet laureate of Nebraska. Literary editor of St Louis Post-Dispatch, 1926-38. Poet in residence and lecturer in English, U of Missouri, 1949-66. Manuscripts are housed separately in Western Historical Manuscripts Collection of Ellis Library.

NE —NEIHARDT STUDY CENTER, Library, Bancroft, 68004. John Lindahl, Cur; Ann Reinert, Librn
Notes: The Center will preserve the published works and papers of John G Neihardt, State Poet Laureate and authority on Plains Indians.

NE —UNIVERSITY OF NEBRASKA-LINCOLN, Don L Love Library, University Archives and Special Collections, Lincoln, 68588. Joseph G Svoboda, University Archivist
Notes: Virginia Faulkner was recognized as one of Nebraska's most distinguished writers and scholars. The Virginia Faulkner Collection, containing over 2000 titles, is housed in the Special Collections Department of Love Library. It is especially strong in twentieth century writers and in University of Nebraska Press publications. Of especial value to scholars are her extensive holdings of Willa Cather, Wright Morris, and John Neihardt. Her correspondence with S N Behrman, E B White, Edward Wagenknecht, Donald Sutherland, Wright Morris, Louise Pound, Mari Sandoz, Hazel Barnes, Alfred A and Blanche Knopf, and others provide insight into the literary development of these figures, as well as chronicle the intellectual thought of the period. Amassed in a separate file, these letters are available to interested scholars.

NIEHAUS, LENNIE

TX —NORTH TEXAS STATE UNIVERSITY, Audio Center, Box 5188, NT Station, Denton, 76203. Morris Martin, Music Librn
Notes: More than 1600 manuscript jazz compositions, (incl scores and parts, alternate versions, expanded arrangements) by Stan Kenton, Johnny Richards, Joe Coccia, Lennie Niehaus, Pete Rugolo, Willie Maiden, Bob Curnow, Ken Hanna, Gene Rowland, Bob Graettinger and others, used by the Stan Kenton Band and given to North Texas State University in 1962 and at Kenton's death in 1979. Unpublished catalog: Breeden, Leon, Stan Kenton Music in the NTSU Jazz Studies Library and the NTSU Music Library, Denton, 1983 (99 pages).

NEILSON, HARRY B., 1861-1941

CA —UNIVERSITY OF CALIFORNIA, LOS ANGELES, Research Library, Dept of Special Collections, 405 Hilgard Ave, Los Angeles, 90024. Edward Shreeves, Chairman, Bibliographers Group; David S Zeidberg, Head
Notes: 2 linear feet of original drawings and watercolors, mss, and proofs.

NEILSON FAMILY, 1680-1930

NJ —RUTGERS, THE STATE UNIVERSITY OF NEW JERSEY, Alexander Library, Special Collections and Archives, College Ave & Huntington St, New Brunswick, 08903. Ronald L Becker, Cur of Manuscripts and Rare Books
Holdings: // Mss
Notes: Papers, etc (120 linear feet).

NEISSER, HANS PHILIP

NY —STATE UNIVERSITY OF NEW YORK AT ALBANY, Library, Special Collections

NEISSER, HANS PHILIP (cont.)

Dept, 1400 Washington Ave, Albany, 12222.
Marion P Munzer, Coordr
Notes: Papers (2.5 linear feet) of Hans Philip
Neisser, German economist who came to the
United States in 1933. Correspondence,
lecture notes, mss, and publications. Part of
the library's German Exile Collection.

NELL, WILLIAM C.

NY —UNIVERSITY OF ROCHESTER, Rush
Rhees Library, Department of Rare Books
and Special Collections, Rochester, 14627.
Peter Dzwonkoski, Librn
Holdings: Cat Mss
Notes: Autograph letters of Frederick
Douglass, William C Nell, Gerritt Smith,
and other mss incl in the Isaac and Amy
Post family papers, and the William Henry
Seward Papers.

NELLIGAN, REP. JAMES L.

PA —KING'S COLLEGE, D Leonard Corgan
Library, 14 W Jackson St, Wilkes-Barre,
18711. Judith Tierney, Special Collections
Librn
Notes: Papers of James L Nelligan,
Representative of the 11th Congressional
District of Pennsylvania to the US Congress.
60 linear ft (1981-82).

NELSON, HORATIO

MA —HARVARD UNIVERSITY LIBRARY,
Houghton Library, Cambridge, 02138.
Rodney G Dennis, Cur of Manuscripts
Holdings: Cat Mss
Notes: Manuscripts described in *Harvard
Library Notes*, II (1929), 213-220.

NELSON, OSCAR D.

MO —UNIVERSITY OF MISSOURI-
KANSAS CITY, General Library, State
Historical Society of Missouri Manuscripts,
5100 Rockhill Road, Kansas City, 64110.
Kenneth J LaBudde, Dir; Gordon
Hendrickson, Assoc Dir
Holdings: Mss
Notes: Western Historical Manuscript
Collection incl papers of Charles B Wheeler,
Jr, Charles N Kimball, Arthur Mag, Oscar D
Nelson, Lou B Holland, J C Nichols, Perry
Cookingham, Blevins Davis, Daniel
MacMorris, and the records of the Kansas
City Board of Trade.

NELSON, RALPH, 1916-

CA —UNIVERSITY OF CALIFORNIA, LOS
ANGELES, Research Library, Dept of
Special Collections, 405 Hilgard Ave, Los
Angeles, 90024. Edward Shreeves,
Chairman, Bibliographers Group; David S
Zeidberg, Head
Holdings: Mss Pix
Notes: 35 linear feet of correspondence,
television scripts, and memorabilia.

NELSON, THOMAS, AND SONS

PA —TEMPLE UNIVERSITY LIBRARIES,
Special Collections Dept, Rare Books & Mss
Section, Philadelphia, 19122. Thomas M
Whitehead, Cur
Holdings: Cat Mss
Budget: M
Notes: Letters and documents (15,000 items)
of the archives of the London publishers,
Constable and Company. Correspondence
with close to 400 authors, most of it with
Otto Kyllmann and Michael Sadlier,
directors. Archives of Thomas Nelson &
Sons (USA) and of various Philadelphia
publishers.

**NEMATODA—RESEARCH see
Nematology**

NEMATOLOGY

CA —UNIVERSITY OF CALIFORNIA,
DAVIS, General Library, Davis, 95616.

Bernard Kreissman, University Librn; C
Danial Elliott, Asst Head, Dept Special
Collections
Notes: Relatively strong in materials
published from 1920 to date. Areas of
entomology that are emphasized incl bees
(apiculture), nematology, parasitology and
the control of insect publications. The slides
and specimens in the collection are housed
in the research collection of the Department
of Entomology.
CA —UNIVERSITY OF CALIFORNIA,
RIVERSIDE, University Library, Bio-
Agricultural Library, Batchelor Hall,
Riverside, 92521. Barbara Montanary, Head
Holdings: Vols (130,000) Cat Mss Maps Pix
Microforms
Notes: The Bio-Agricultural Library
(formerly the Library of Citrus Experiment
Station of the University of California) is
well known for its complete collections in
the fields of the agriculture sciences. It is
especially known for its emphasis on
entomology, incl bio-control; botany,
citriculture, plant sciences, nematology and
plant pathology; arid and semi-arid lands
research and subtropical agriculture. Specific
areas of interest are avocados, dates, desert
flora, jojoba, guayule and carob.
FL —FLORIDA DEPARTMENT OF
AGRICULTURE & CONSUMER
SERVICES, Div of Plant Industry, Library,
PO Box 1269, Gainesville, 32602. June B
Jacobson, Librn; Alice Richards, Asst Librn
Holdings: Vols (11,455) Cat Mss Microforms
Budget: ($23,798)
Notes: Collection is primarily taxonomic.
464 periodical, current and antiquariat titles.
PE —AGRICULTURE CANADA, Research
Station Library, PO Box 1210,
Charlottetown, C1A 7M8, Can. Barrie
Stanfield, Librn
Holdings: Vols (2300) Cat
Budget: ($5000)

NEMATOSPORA see Yeast

NEMEROV, HOWARD

MO —WASHINGTON UNIVERSITY, John
M Olin Library, Campus Box 1061, St Louis,
63130.
Notes: A major collection, incl mss,
correspondence, literary papers, drafts of
individual poems and collections of poems,
some of his essays and addresses,
photographs, etc. Described in *Special
Collections: an Annotated Guide to the
Holdings of the Manuscripts Division and
the University Archives and Research
Collection*.
NV —UNIVERSITY OF NEVADA, RENO,
University Library, Special Collections Dept,
Reno, 89557. Robert E Blesse, Head
Holdings: Vols (36) Cat Other appearances
560 Cat
Notes: Includes individual works by author
in all editions including translations; also
prefaces, introductions, published
correspondence, appearances in anthologies,
periodicals, etc. Bibliographical research
collection, part of Modern Authors
Collection.

NEO-FASCISM see Fascism

**NEO-GREEK LITERATURE see Greek
Language and Literature, Modern**

**NEO-LATIN LANGUAGES see Romance
Languages and Literatures**

NEONATALOGY see Pediatrics

NEO-NAZIS

†NY —COLUMBIA UNIVERSITY
LIBRARIES, Butler Library, Rare Book and
Manuscript Library, 535 W 114 St, New
York, 10027.
Notes: Papers relating to Prof Walter Lewis
Dorn's work as special advisor to Gen
Lucius D Clay on denazification of
Germany.
NC —DUKE UNIVERSITY, William R
Perkins Library, Durham, 27706. Elvin E

Strowd, University Librn
Notes: The (Quasi)-Nazi collection consists
of approximately 7000 items, primarily
pamphlets published in the United States by
and about Nazi sympathizers Gerald K
Smith, Father Coughlin, etc and
organizations with Nazi leanings.
PA —TEMPLE UNIVERSITY LIBRARIES,
Special Collections Dept, Contemporary
Culture Collection, Philadelphia, 19122.
Patricia J Case, Cur
Notes: The Contemporary Culture
Collection. See full entry under US-Social
Life and Customs.

NEO-PAGANISM

CA —GRADUATE THEOLOGICAL UNION
LIBRARY, New Religious Movements
Research Collection, Public Services and
Special Collections Dept, 2400 Ridge Road,
Berkeley, 94709. Diane Choquette, Dept
Head
Holdings: Vols (3000) Mss Pix
Notes: Begun in 1977, the collection focuses
on religious movements new to America
since 1960, and unorthodox religious
movements resurgent since 1960. American
forms of Hinduism, Buddhism, Sikhism, and
Sufism are included along with occultism,
Neo-Paganism, esoteric and alternative
forms of Christianity, feminist spirituality,
and human potential movements having a
spiritual aspect. Legal issues, such as
deprogramming, and the question of church/
state relations are an important part of the
collection. The Library is a depository for
publications of the Unification Church in
America, the Church of Scientology, and the
International Society for Krishna
Consciousness (America). The responses of
mainstream religions and concerned citizens
groups are also included. Besides 3000
monographs, the library has 400 periodical
titles, 200 posters from the San
FranciscoBay Area, 1965-77, 300 research
papers, and 31 linear feet of ephemera.

NEOPLASMS see Tumors

NEOPLATONISM

MO —UNIVERSITY OF MISSOURI-
COLUMBIA, Ellis Library, Special
Collections Dept, Ninth & Lowry, Columbia,
65201. Margaret A Howell, Head, Special
Collections
Holdings: Vols 1700 // Cat
Notes: The Thomas Moore Johnson
Collection. There is a printed catalog.

NEOPRENE see Rubber, Artificial

NEPAL

CA —UNIVERSITY OF CALIFORNIA,
BERKELEY, University Library, 438 Main
Library, Berkeley, 94720. Kenneth R Logan,
South Asia Librn
Notes: South Asia collection (India,
Pakistan, Bangladesh, Nepal, Sri Lanka)
contain 150,000-200,000 titles. Covers at
research level the social sciences and
humanities in western languages and 20
South Asian languages. Subject areas:
history, political science, lanuage and
literature (especially strong in Hindi, Urdu,
Tamil, Sanskrit and Nepali), art and art
history, sociology, education, music,
environmental design, philosophy and
religion, anthropology, geography, national
and local government publications. Formats:
monographs, periodicals, newspapers,
microforms, maps, sound recordings, videotapes, pamphlets. Special strengths: modern
Hindi literature; history of South Asian
countries; government publications of India,
late 19th and 20th centuries. Member of
South Asia Microform Project; Participant in
Library of Congress AcquisitionsPrograms
for India, Pakistan, Nepal, and Bangladesh.
HI —UNIVERSITY OF HAWAII, Library,
2550 The Mall, Honolulu, 96822. Joyce
Wright, Head, Asia Collection; Masato
Matsu, Head, East Asia Vernacular
Collection
Holdings: Vols 75,215 Cat Microforms
Notes: The Asia Collection holds material

NEPAL (cont.)

from and relating to Bangladesh, India, Nepal, Pakistan, and Sri Lanka in western and Asian languages. South Asian languages currently acquired: Bengali, Hindi, Marathi, Nepali, Pali, Prakrit, Sanskrit, Tamil. Period emphasis is post-World War II. Subject emphases: social sciences and the humanities (literature, economics, history, religion/ philosophy). Holdings are supplemented by a large uncataloged backlog, much of it accessible through the Library of Congress Accessions Lists for the area and by over 7000 cataloged titles in the main library collection. *South Asian Resources in North America: A Survey Prepared for the Boston Conference, 1974,* ed by M L P Patterson (Zug, Switzerland: Tutes Documentation Company, 1975). (Bibliotheca Asiatica 12-), "University of Hawaii," pp 103-114.

IL —CENTER FOR RESEARCH LIBRARIES, 6050 S Kenwood Ave, Chicago, 60637. Donald B Simpson, Dir; Esther Smith, Collection Development Librn
Notes: Monographs, serials and government documents from 1969, received on PL 480. 4 newspapers on microfilm.

MI —UNIVERSITY OF MICHIGAN, Graduate Library, South Asian Dept, Ann Arbor, 48109. Om P Sharma, Librn
Holdings: Vols (365,000) Cat Maps Slides Microforms
Notes: The major emphasis is on social sciences and the humanities. Besides materials in classical languages, South Asian vernaculars being retained are Hindi, Bengali, Urdu, Marathi and Tamil; strong in classical languages, especially Sanskrit, Pali, and Prakrit.

MO —UNIVERSITY OF MISSOURI-COLUMBIA, Ellis Library, Ninth and Lowry, Columbia, 65201. Murari Lal Nagar, Librn
Holdings: Vols 100,000 Maps Microforms
Notes: The South Asia Studies Program at the University of Missouri-Columbia, is an interdepartmental, multi-disciplinary area studies program on India, Pakistan, Bangladesh, Sri Lanka and Nepal. Depository for the PL480 Program of the Library of Congress in many languages from South Asia. There are library resources in Sanskskrit, Hindi, Bengali, Panjabi, and Malayalam. The library is particularly strong in Baroda, Bengal and the Punjab.

NEPALESE LANGUAGE see Nepali Language and Literature

NEPALI LANGUAGE AND LITERATURE

CA —UNIVERSITY OF CALIFORNIA, BERKELEY, University Library, 438 Main Library, Berkeley, 94720. Kenneth R Logan, South Asia Librn
Notes: South Asia collection (India, Pakistan, Bangladesh, Nepal, Sri Lanka) contain 150,000-200,000 titles. Covers at research level the social sciences and humanities in western languages and 20 South Asian languages. Subject areas: history, political science, lanugage and literature (especially strong in Hindi, Urdu, Tamil, Sanskrit and Nepali), art and art history, sociology, education, music, environmental design, philosophy and religion, anthropology, geography, national and local government publications. Formats: monographs, periodicals, newspapers, microforms, maps, sound recordings, video-tapes, pamphlets. Special strengths: modern Hindi literature; history of South Asian countries; government publications of India, late 19th and 20th centuries. Member of South Asia Microform Project; Participant in Library of Congress AcquisitionsPrograms for India, Pakistan, Nepal, and Bangladesh.

DC —LIBRARY OF CONGRESS, African and Middle Eastern Division, Washington, 20540.
Holdings: Cat Mss Microforms
Notes: Southern Asian: over 137,000 vols of literature of the area from Pakistan to the Philippines.

HI —UNIVERSITY OF HAWAII, Library, 2550 The Mall, Honolulu, 96822. Joyce Wright, Head, Asia Collection; Masato Matsu, Head, East Asia Vernacular Collection
Holdings: Vols 75,215 Cat Microforms
Notes: The Asia Collection holds materials from and about Southeast Asia: Brunei, Burma, Cambodia (Kampuchea), Indonesia, Laos, Malaysia, Philippines, Singapore, Thailand. Large contemporary Indonesian language collection. Several thousand vols in Thai and in Vietnamese. Minimal holdings in Burmese, Khmer, Lao languages. Social sciences and humanities emphasis for the post-World War II period. Western language coverage supplemented by retrospective holdings in the main library collection.

NERBER, JOHN

CT —LEE ASH, (personal collection), 66 Humiston Dr, Bethany, 06525.
Holdings: Mss Pix
Notes: Mss, published writings, letters, etc, by this poet or his family.

NERUDA, PABLO, 1904-1973

NY —STATE UNIVERSITY OF NEW YORK, STONY BROOK, Melville Library, Dept of Special Collections, Stony Brook, 11794. Evert Volkersz, Head
Holdings: Vols 175 Cat Mss

NERVOUS SYSTEM—DISEASES see Neuropathology

NERVOUS SYSTEM—SURGERY

CA —WHITE MEMORIAL MEDICAL CENTER, Courville-Abbott Memorial Library, 1720 Brooklyn Ave, Los Angeles, 90033. Joyce Marson, Librn
CT —YALE MEDICAL LIBRARY, 333 Cedar St, New Haven, 06510.
Notes: A special subject emphasis.
ND —NEUROPSYCHIATRIC INSTITUTE, Medical Library, 700 First Ave S, Fargo, 58103. Diane Nordeng, Librn
Holdings: Vols (1000) Cat
Budget: ($8000)
PQ —MONTREAL NEUROLOGICAL INSTITUTE AND HOSPITAL LIBRARY, 3801 University St, Montreal, H3A 2B4, Can. Marina M Boski, Librn
Holdings: Vols (5800) Cat
Notes: Neurosciences collection serving as a tool in the training of neurologists and neurosurgeons, and in current research. About 500 vols comprise the historical section--original works of early neurologists and neurosurgeons published between 1850 and 1945. 50 percent of the total number of vols are bound periodicals.

NESBITT, ESTA

AZ —UNIVERSITY OF ARIZONA, Center for Creative Photography, 843 E University Blvd, Tucson, 85721. James Enyeart, Dir; Terence Pitts, Cur and Librn
Notes: Center has significant collections consisting of more than 25 photographs plus other archival material such as negatives, contact sheets, work prints, correspondence, financial records, diaries, project files, etc. Inventories of the collections are available to researchers. Published guides available for some collections.

NESTOR, AGNES

IL —CHICAGO HISTORICAL SOCIETY, Library, Clark St at North Ave, Chicago, 60614. Archie Motley, Manuscript Librn
Notes: Papers of labor leaders.
See also entry under Labor-History.

NESTORIANS

CA —CALIFORNIA STATE COLLEGE, STANISLAUS, Library, 801 W Monte Vista Ave, Turlock, 95380. J Carlyle Parker, Actg Library Dir
Holdings: Vols 100 // Uncat
Notes: The Sayad Collection of Assyriana

consists of books in the Syriac dialect of the modern Assyrians, often called Nestorians, who are natives of northwestern Iran. Other books in English relating to the modern Assyrians are also in the collection. Also books on Mesopotamian civilizations.

NESTS OF BIRDS see Birds—Eggs and Nests

NETHERLANDS—HISTORY

IL —NORTHWESTERN UNIVERSITY, Library, Special Collections Dept, 1937 Sheridan Rd, Evanston, 60201. R Russell Maylone, Cur
Notes: Incl 2500 pamphlets dealing with the Brabant Revolution. Additional 14,000 pamphlets, legal documents, and periodical issues published in France 1787-1800. Also, World War II underground publications (550 vols). Additional 400 monographs and serials from Denmark; 65 vols from Norway; 80 vols from misc other European countries under Nazi occupation.

MA —HARVARD UNIVERSITY LIBRARY, Widener Library, Cambridge, 02138.
Holdings: Cat
Notes: See *Distributable Union Catalog* (Harvard).

MI —UNIVERSITY OF MICHIGAN, Library, Dept of Rare Books & Special Collections, Ann Arbor, 48109. Robert J Starring, Head
Holdings: Cat
Notes: Incl a collection of some 400 Dutch and Belgian historical tracts for the 16th and 17th centuries.

MN —UNIVERSITY OF MINNESOTA, O Meredith Wilson Library, 309 19 Ave S, Minneapolis, 55455. Austin J McLean, Chief, Special Collections
Holdings: Vols 1690 Cat
Notes: Books and pamphlets relating to Dutch history covering the period 1574-1782, but chiefly 17th century.

NY —NEW YORK PUBLIC LIBRARY, Research Libraries, General Research Division, Fifth Ave & 42 St, New York, 10018. Rodney Phillips, Chief
Holdings: Vols (2,225,000) Cat Maps Pix Microforms
Budget: ($775,718)

WI —UNIVERSITY OF WISCONSIN, MADISON, Memorial Library, 728 State St, Madison, 53706. Erwin K Welsch, Social Studies Bibliographer
Notes: Incl a collection of about 200 pamphlets: lampoons, libels and broadsides in prose as well as verse, covering the second half of the 80 years' war with Spain (1568-1648), the 12 years' truce (1609-1621), and the wars with England and France, with special emphasis on the year of disasters, 1672. Also, the Remonstrant Collection: materials on the theological struggle within the Dutch Reformed Church during the early part of the 17th century.

MB —UNIVERSITY OF MANITOBA, Elizabeth Dafoe Library, Archives and Special Collections Dept, Winnipeg, R3T 2N2, Can. Richard E Bennett, Dept Head; Corrado A Santoro, Reference Archivist
Holdings: Pix
Notes: Postcards and photographs showing details of Nazi Germany's bombings and occupation of Holland in 1940. 37 items.

NETHERLANDS ANTILLES see Curacao

NETHERLANDS EAST INDIES see Indonesia

NETHERLANDS WEST INDIES see West Indies

NETWORK OF PATRIOTIC LETTER WRITERS

CA —UNIVERSITY OF CALIFORNIA, LOS ANGELES, Research Library, Dept of Special Collections, 405 Hilgard Ave, Los Angeles, 90024. Edward Shreeves, Chairman, Bibliographers Group; David S Zeidberg, Head
Holdings: Cat Mss Pix
Notes: 11 cartons of materials, recordings,

NETWORK OF PATRIOTIC LETTER WRITERS (cont.)

etc, relating to the John Birch Society, incl runs of many relevant periodicals, government documents, etc.

NETWORKING see Computers

NEUGASS, FRITZ, 1899-1979

NY —STATE UNIVERSITY OF NEW YORK AT ALBANY, Library, Special Collections Dept, 1400 Washington Ave, Albany, 12222. Marion P Munzer, Coordr
Notes: Mss, publications, photographs relating to the work of Fritz Neugass as art correspondent for foreign newspapers and periodicals, specializing in the American art market (53 linear feet, 25 feet of auction catalogs). Part of the Library's German Exile Collection.
See also entries under Journalists; Art Auctions; Photographers

NEUMANN, JOHN VON

MA —MASSACHUSETTS INSTITUTE OF TECHNOLOGY, Institute Archives, Special Collections, Cambridge, 02139.
Notes: Papers of Norbert Wiener, renowned mathematician, was instrumental in the development of communication and control theories. He coined the word "cybernetics" to describe this new science. Professional papers document the development of this theory, his development as a mathematician, and his effective collaboration with students and colleagues including Vannevar Bush and John von Neumann. Unpublished finding aid with correspondent index is available in the Institute Archives.

NEUROANATOMY

IN —PURDUE UNIVERSITY LIBRARIES, Veterinary Medical Library, C J Lynn Hall of Veterinary Medicine, West Lafayette, 47907. Gretchen Stephens, Librn
Notes: Veterinary medicine, comparative anatomy, and veterinary pathology.
WI —UNIVERSITY OF WISCONSIN, MADISON, Wisconsin Regional Primate Research Center, Primate Center Library, 1223 Capitol Court, Madison, 53715. Lawrence Jacobsen, Librn
Holdings: Vols (15,000) Cat Pix
Notes: Research in reproductive physiology, neurosciences, and behavior. Extensive subject orientated primate reprint file, audiovisual collection on primates. Current research uses approximately 25 species of nonhuman primates. Publications: *Primate Library Report*: print and non-print editions, biomonthly.

NEUROBIOLOGY

CA —STANFORD UNIVERSITY, Hopkins Marine Station Library, Cabrillo Point, Pacific Grove, 93950. Alan Baldridge, Librn
NY —COLD SPRING HARBOR LABORATORY, Library, PO Box 100, Cold Spring Harbor, 11724. Susan Gensel, Library Dir; Genemary Falvey, Librn
Holdings: Vols (30,000)
Budget: ($103,500)
Notes: The highly technical collection is comprised of 20,000 serial vols and 10,000 monographs. The library receives 500 current serial titles. Subjects covered incl molecular and cellular biology, virology, biochemistry, microbiology, oncology, neurobiology, biological risk assessment and genetic engineering/biotechnology. Special collections in eugenics and genetics are primarily historical dealing with the development of genetics in the US which had its beginnings here.

NEUROCHEMISTRY

†CT —YALE UNIVERSITY, Medical Library, 333 Cedar St, New Haven, 06520.
Notes: Strong neurochemistry collection, incl

the David Nachmansohn collection of seven volumes of collected reprints of various authors, many Nachmansohn's own.

NEUROLOGICAL DISEASES see Neuropathology

NEUROLOGY

CA —WHITE MEMORIAL MEDICAL CENTER, Courville-Abbott Memorial Library, 1720 Brooklyn Ave, Los Angeles, 90033. Joyce Marson, Librn
CT —INSTITUTE OF LIVING, Medical Library, 400 Washington St, Hartford, 06106. Helen Lansberg, Librn
Holdings: Vols (30,000) Cat Mss Maps Pix
Notes: Psychiatry, neurology and related subjects. There are 3 special collections in the Library in addition to the regular collection, which contains about 19,500 books and journals and a quanity of historical material incl letters and papers of Dr Eli Todd. The following collections are complete: (1) The Smith Ely Jelliffe Collection. Slighty over 10,000 books and journals on psychoanalysis, psychiatry, neurology and related subjects, almost all published before 1940, and some of great historical interest. (2) The Gregory Zilboorg Collection. About 300 books from the 16th, 17th, 18th and 19th centuries, most of them landmarks in the history of psychiatry, especially psychiatric theory. (3) The Hubert J Norman Collection. About 300 books from the 18th, 19th and 20th centuries, relating to or illustrating mental illness. Incl many pamphlets, pictures, etc.Emphasis is on legal psychiatry, the development of hospitals, and the experience of the patient. No photocopying.
CT —YALE MEDICAL LIBRARY, 333 Cedar St, New Haven, 06510.
Holdings: Vols (334,215) Cat Mss Pix Slides Microforms
Budget: ($361,650)
Notes: Incl films, audiotapes, artifacts, etc.
IN —INDIANA UNIVERSITY, Optometry Branch Library, Bloomington, 47405. Roger Deckman, Head; Elizabeth Egan, Branch Librn
Holdings: Vols (11,000) Cat Slides Microforms
Budget:
Notes: Incl all aspects of vision: anatomy, physiology, pathology of the eye, neurophysiology, perception, colorimetry, illumination, safety, etc. Interlibrary loans through Main Library, Indiana University, Bloomington.
KS —UNIVERSITY OF KANSAS, Kenneth Spencer Research Library, Special Collections Dept, Lawrence, 66045. Alexandra Mason, Librn
Holdings: Cat Mss Maps Pix
Notes: Ellis Collection of Ornithology, natural history and voyages and travels; botanical literature from Fitzpatrick collection (especially medical botany, early American botanists, renaissance herbals, Matthioli); some early chemistry and mathematics; scientific voyages and travels; De Beer collection of offprints in embryology, endocrinology, and systematic zoology; natural history and classics; Herrick, Coghill and Roofe collections in neurology. Noncirculating.
KS —KANSAS NEUROLOGICAL INSTITUTE, Menninger Professional Library, 3107 W 21 St, Topeka, 66604. Richard Gray, Librn
Holdings: Vols 244 Cat
Notes: Incl development disabilities; special education; nursing care for the handicapped; programs for the mentally retarded; behavioral psychology; supervision in mental health/mental retardation; staff training in mental health/mental retardation.
MD —MEDICAL & CHIRURGICAL FACULTY OF THE STATE OF MARYLAND, Library, 1211 Cathedral St, Baltimore, 21201. Joseph E Jensen, Librn
Holdings: Vols (110,000) Cat Mss Maps Pix Slides Audiotapes Videotapes Microforms
Budget: ($250,000)
Notes: Library for the state medical society.

Open to the public, but circulation is restricted to members. The current acquisitions policy emphasizes English language monographs and periodicals on all aspects of clinical medicine, and on the social, economic, legal and administrative aspects of medical practice in the United States. The library subscribes to all state medical society journals in the United States. Holdings include a very fine history of medicine and rare medical book collection, and a strong collection of medical monographs and serials prior to 1900.
MD —UNIVERSITY OF MARYLAND, White Memorial Library, College Park, 20742. Elizabeth W McElroy, Head
Holdings: Vols (48,000) Cat Microforms
Budget: ($193,000)
Notes: Current periodicals. Have own card catalog, which is included also in the total university catalog.
MA —MCLEAN HOSPITAL MEDICAL LIBRARY, 115 Mill St, Belmont, 02178. Hector Bossange, Dir
Holdings: Vols 25,611 Cat
Notes: Extensive collection.
MA —US VETERANS ADMINISTRATION MEDICAL CENTER, Medical Library, 150 S Huntington Ave, Jamaica Plain, Boston, 02130. Patricia J McGrath, Chief Librn
Holdings: Vols (5702) Cat
Notes: Incl health care, surgery, neurology. 400 journal subscriptions, 5000 bound volumes.
MA —MASSACHUSETTS INSTITUTE OF TECHNOLOGY, Institute Archives, Special Collections, Cambridge, 02139.
Holdings: Vols 5000 Cat Mss
Notes: Neurosciences (brain sciences); incl reprints and reports. Also incl are records of Neurosciences Research Program and papers of Frances O Schmitt, the Program's founder.
MI —LAFAYETTE CLINIC LIBRARY, 951 E Lafayette, Detroit, 48207. Nancy E Ward, Librn
Holdings: Vols (7000) Cat
Notes: Special emphasis on epilepsy, movement disorders, Parkinson's Disease and the biological aspects, causes and treatment of mental illness.
MO —MISSOURI INSTITUTE OF PSYCHIATRY LIBRARY, 5400 Arsenal St, Saint Louis, 63139. Connie Wolf, Librn
Holdings: Vols (18,000) Cat
Notes: Subscribe to 430 journals.
NY —ALBERT EINSTEIN COLLEGE OF MEDICINE, D Samuel Gottesman Library, 1300 Morris Park Ave, Bronx, 10461. Charlotte K Lindner, Dir
NY —COLUMBIA UNIVERSITY LIBRARIES, Neurological Institute Library, 710 W 168 St, New York, 10032.
Holdings: Vols 3800 Cat
Notes: Not open to the public.
NY —CREEDMOOR PSYCHIATRIC CENTER, Health Sciences Library, Bldg 51, 80-45 Winchester Blvd, Queens Village, 11427. Susan Taubman, Dir of Library; Pushpa Bhati, Sr Librn
Holdings: Vols (12,000) Cat Slides Phonorecords Audiotapes Filmstrips Microfiche
Budget: ($50,000)
Notes: Particularly strong in the areas of neurology, pharmacology, psychoanalysis, and psychopharmacology.
NY —UTICA-MARCY PSYCHIATRIC CENTER, MARCY CAMPUS, Professional Library, 1213 Court St, Utica, 13502. Janina Strife, Librn
Holdings: Vols (3000) Cat
Budget: ($6000)
ND —NEUROPSYCHIATRIC INSTITUTE, Medical Library, 700 First Ave S, Fargo, 58103. Diane Nordeng, Librn
Holdings: Vols (1000) Cat
Budget: ($8000)
PA —WESTERN PSYCHIATRIC INSTITUTE & CLINIC, Library, 3811 O'Hara St, Pittsburgh, 15261. Lucile Stark, Dir
Holdings: Vols 50,000 Cat Mss Pix Films Microforms Audiotapes
Budget: ($180,000)
Notes: Also incl the archives of the Institute and other ms material relating to the

NEUROLOGY (cont.)

development of psychiatry in Western Pennsylvania, specifically in Pittsburgh. Incl 12,000 pamphlets on all aspects of psychiatry, etc. Rich in bibliographies and reference materials. Incl 750 journal titles.

RI —MIRIAM HOSPITAL MEDICAL LIBRARY, 164 Summit Ave, Providence, 02906. Ann LeClaire, Dir of Library Services
Holdings: Cat Cassettes
Notes: Special collection on the renal system with emphasis on kidney transplantation and dialysis.

WI —UNIVERSITY OF WISCONSIN, MADISON, Wisconsin Regional Primate Research Center, Primate Center Library, 1223 Capitol Court, Madison, 53715. Lawrence Jacobsen, Librn
Holdings: Vols (15,000) Cat Pix
Notes: Research in reproductive physiology, neurosciences, and behavior. Extensive subject orientated primate reprint file, audiovisual collection on primates. Current research uses approximately 25 species of nonhuman primates. Publications: *Primate Library Report*: print and non-print editions, biomonthly.

PQ —MONTREAL NEUROLOGICAL INSTITUTE AND HOSPITAL LIBRARY, 3801 University St, Montreal, H3A 2B4, Can. Marina M Boski, Librn
Holdings: Vols (5800) Cat
Notes: Neurosciences collection serving as a tool in the training of neurologists and neurosurgeons, and in current research. About 500 vols comprise the historical section--original works of early neurologists and neurosurgeons published between 1850 and 1945. 50 percent of the total number of vols are bound periodicals.

NEUROLOGY—HISTORY

CA —UNIVERSITY OF CALIFORNIA, LOS ANGELES, Biomedical Library, Center for the Health Sciences, Los Angeles, 90024. Alison Bunting, Acting Biomedical Librn; Victoria Steele, Head, History & Special Collections Div
Holdings: // Uncat Mss Pix
Notes: The Webb Haymaker Archive of Neurology. Consists of 5 file drawers of largely biographical material compiled in connection with Haymaker's *Founders of Neurology*, (Springfield, IL: Thomas), 1953 and 1970.

CA —WHITE MEMORIAL MEDICAL CENTER, Courville-Abbott Memorial Library, 1720 Brooklyn Ave, Los Angeles, 90033. Joyce Marson, Librn

IL —UNIVERSITY OF ILLINOIS AT CHICAGO, Library of the Health Sciences, 1750 W Polk St, PO Box 7509, Chicago, 60612. Robert J Adelsperger, Cur, Special Collections
Holdings: Vols 750 // Cat
Notes: The Percival Bailey Collection on Neurology and Psychiatry is closed. Printed catalog: A Catalog of the Percival Bailey Collection of Neurology and Psychiatry (Chicago, 1973).

MN —MAYO MEDICAL LIBRARY, History of Medicine Collection, Rochester, 55905. Nancy R Hensel, Librn
Holdings: Vols (18,000) Cat Mss Maps Pix Slides
Notes: The collection consists of over 18,000 vols, 6500 of which are considered source material (rare or reprint editions of classics). 4308 items from Garrison-Morton are available in the collection. Appropriate bibliographies, biographies and histories of medicine are a part of the collection. Fields of collecting interest are anesthesiology, dermatology, cardiology, neurology, immunology and radiology. Eight medical incunabula.

PQ —MONTREAL NEUROLOGICAL INSTITUTE AND HOSPITAL LIBRARY, 3801 University St, Montreal, H3A 2B4, Can. Marina M Boski, Librn
Holdings: Vols (5800) Cat
Notes: Neurosciences collection serving as a tool in the training of neurologists and neurosurgeons, and in current research. About 500 vols comprise the historical section--original works of early neurologists and neurosurgeons published between 1850 and 1945. 50 percent of the total number of vols are bound periodicals.

NEUROPATHOLOGY

CT —YALE UNIVERSITY, School of Medicine, Section of Neuropathology Library, Brain Tumor Registry, New Haven, 06520. Dr Elias Manuelidis, Cur
Holdings: Cat Slides
Notes: The Ernest Sachs Collection of about 8000 microscopic slides of brain tumors. Also the Harvey Cushing Collection of 800 jars of brain tissue in Formalin, and about 2500 microscopic slides. Another collection, belonging to the Pathology Department, consists of brain sections from about 100 monkeys, with 30 slides from each brain. Not cataloged, in boxes and inaccessible.

CT —NEWINGTON CHILDREN'S HOSPITAL, Professional Library, 181 E Cedar St, Newington, 06111. Jean Long, Librn
Holdings: Vols (3500) Cat
Budget: ($6500)

ND —NEUROPSYCHIATRIC INSTITUTE, Medical Library, 700 First Ave S, Fargo, 58103. Diane Nordeng, Librn
Holdings: Vols (1000) Cat
Budget: ($8000)

WI —UNIVERSITY OF WISCONSIN, MADISON, Wisconsin Regional Primate Research Center, Primate Center Library, 1223 Capitol Court, Madison, 53715. Lawrence Jacobsen, Librn
Holdings: Vols (15,000) Cat Pix
Notes: Research in reproductive physiology, neurosciences, and behavior. Extensive subject orientated primate reprint file, audiovisual collection on primates. Current research uses approximately 25 species of nonhuman primates. Publications: *Primate Library Report*: print and non-print editions, biomonthly.

NEUROPHYSIOLOGY

CA —UNIVERSITY OF CALIFORNIA, LOS ANGELES, Biomedical Library, Center for the Health Sciences, Los Angeles, 90024. Alison Bunting, Acting Biomedical Librn; Victoria Steele, Head, History & Special Collections Div
Holdings: Vols (400,000) Cat Slides Phonorecords Audiotapes Videotapes 16mm Films Microforms

Notes: The UCLA Biomedical Library serves primarily the Schools of Medicine, Dentistry, Nursing, and Public Health, the UCLA Medical Center, the Departments of Microbiology and Biology in the College of Letters and Science, and related institutes in biomedicine. The collections of the Library are broad in scope, designed not only to support the teaching and research needs of its many users, but also to function as a resource for the health sciences-biological field as a whole. The outstanding feature of the collection is the strength of its periodical holdings, both current and retrospective. The Library also has an excellent reference collection, a comprehensive historical section, and gives special emphasis to the fields of neuroscience, psychiatry, ophthalmology, radiation biology, molecular biology, and vertebrate zoology. Increased emphasis is being given to the acquisition of audiovisual materials.

CT —YALE MEDICAL LIBRARY, 333 Cedar St, New Haven, 06510.
Notes: A special subject emphasis.

IL —UNIVERSITY OF ILLINOIS, URBANA/CHAMPAIGN, Library, Biology Library, 101 Burrill Hall, 407 S Goodwin, Urbana, 61801. Elisabeth B Davis, Librn
Holdings: Vols (115,000) Cat Microforms
Budget: ($200,000)
Notes: The Biology Library incl books, periodicals, and reference works that cover the fields of anatomy, biophysics, botany, ecology, entomology, genetics, immunology, microbiology, physiology and zoology. About three-quarters of the total collection is made up of journals and other serials representing 2000 distinctive titles. The serial list is comprehensive for the biological sciences, contains most of the major international titles and consists of complete runs for almost all titles. Additional materials (approx 90,000 vols) in the biological sciences are available in the Natural History Survey Library and the bookstacks at the Main Library on the Urbana campus. Professional assistance is available for reference service, online searching, and library instruction. Interlibrary loan service is provided. Photocopying.

MD —UNIVERSITY OF MARYLAND, White Memorial Library, College Park, 20742. Elizabeth W McElroy, Head
Holdings: Vols (48,000) Cat Microforms
Budget: ($193,000)
Notes: Current periodicals. Have own card catalog, which is included also in the total university catalog.

MA —MASSACHUSETTS INSTITUTE OF TECHNOLOGY, Research Laboratory of Electronics, Document Room 36-412, Cambridge, 02139. J E Woore, Head
Holdings: Vols (15,000)
Notes: Incl World War II technical reports on radar. Current electromagnetism and electronic engineering, radar, etc.

NY —COLUMBIA UNIVERSITY LIBRARIES, Biological Sciences Library, 601 Fairchild, New York, 10027. Barbara A List, Reference/Collection Development Librn
Holdings: Vols 38,000 Cat
Notes: Incl biochemistry and molecular biology.

NEUROPSYCHIATRY

ND —NEUROPSYCHIATRIC INSTITUTE, Medical Library, 700 First Ave S, Fargo, 58103. Diane Nordeng, Librn
Holdings: Vols (1000) Cat
Budget: ($8000)

NEUROSURGERY see Nervous System—Surgery

NEUTRA, RICHARD J., 1892-1970

CA —UNIVERSITY OF CALIFORNIA, LOS ANGELES, Research Library, Dept of Special Collections, 405 Hilgard Ave, Los Angeles, 90024. Edward Shreeves, Chairman, Bibliographers Group; David S Zeidberg, Head
Holdings: Vols 2
Notes: Incl 4 linear feet of travel sketches; 100 linear feet of drawings, blueprints, and correspondence.

NEUXVILLE, JOHN

SC —COLLEGE OF CHARLESTON LIBRARY, Special Collections Dept, Charleston, 29401.
Notes: Papers, 1787.

NEVADA

NV —FORESTA INSTITUTE FOR OCEAN AND MOUNTAIN STUDIES, Library, 6205 Franktown Rd, Carson City, 89701. Shannon Porter, Librn
Holdings: Vols (3000) Cat Mss Maps Pix Slides
Notes: Material on plant, animal, and human

NEVADA (cont.)

ecology with special emphasis on far western US and Nevada ecology and environmental problems. Also hold about 2000 reprints, pamphlets, reports, etc.

NV —UNIVERSITY OF NEVADA SYSTEM, Elko Community College, Learning Resources Center, Elko, 89801. Juanita R Karr, Dir
Holdings: Vols 300 Cat Maps
Budget: $300

NV —CLARK COUNTY LIBRARY DISTRICT, Las Vegas Library, 1726 E Charleston, Las Vegas, 89104. Jack Gardner, Librn Administrator
Holdings: Vols (2000) Cat Maps Pix Microforms
Notes: Separate catalog and index to collection. Incl fiction, nonfiction, juvenile. The Library indexes the *Las Vegas Review-Journal* and the *Las Vegas Sun* (June 1972-date) by personal name and subject, excl national, international and sports news. The newspapers are held on microfilm. The index is produced on microfiche and cumulated monthly.

NV —UNIVERSITY OF NEVADA, RENO, Mines Library, Reno, 89557. Mary B Ansari, Mines Librn; Linda P Newman, Asst Mines and Map Librn
Holdings: Vols (32,000) Cat Maps Microforms
Budget: ($52,000)
Notes: Mines Library attempts to collect all PhD and Masters theses on Nevada geology. Only those originating at the University of Nevada, Reno, are available for ILL. Maintains an index of references to the literature on Nevada geology and mining.

UT —UNIVERSITY OF UTAH, Marriott Library, Special Collections, Salt Lake City, 84112. Gregory C Thompson, Cur

NEVADA—DESCRIPTION AND TRAVEL—VIEWS

CA —POMONA PUBLIC LIBRARY, Special Collections, 625 S Garey Ave, PO Box 2271, Pomona, 91766. David Streeter, Librn
Holdings: Uncat Slides
Notes: Contains 550 lantern slides (mostly of California) and 4200 color 35mm transparencies of world travel, 1960s. Also, the Burton Frasher Postal Card Collection of 60,000 negatives and prints of California, Arizona, Colorado, New Mexico, Nevada, and Utah; 30,000 world views; 8000 California views. There are also world views in nearly 1000 stereophotographs.

NEVADA—GOVERNMENT PUBLICATIONS

NV —NEVADA STATE LIBRARY, Capitol Complex, Carson City, 89710. Joyce C Lee, Dir, Public Services Div
Notes: Most comprehensive collection of documents issued by state agencies available. Both historical and current materials. Available for interlibrary loan.

NEVADA—HISTORY

NV —NEVADA STATE LIBRARY, Capitol Complex, Carson City, 89710. Joyce C Lee, Dir, Public Services Div
Holdings: Vols 2800 Cat Maps Microforms
Budget: $2500
Notes: State Library maintains collection of Nevada history in cooperation with the University of Nevada and the State Historical Society. The State Library also operates the State Publications Distribution Center (1971-date), which acquires, organizes and distributes Nevada government publications to depositories, and maintains a comprehensive collection of these materials, 1863-date.

NV —NORTHEASTERN NEVADA MUSEUM, Library, 1515 Idaho St, PO Box 2550, Elko, 89801. Howard Hickson, Museum Dir
Holdings: Vols 2000 Cat Mss Maps Pix Slides Audiotapes
Budget: $8000
Notes: Emphasis on northeastern Nevada

and Elko County. Incl 140 mss, 65 maps, 1500 pictures, 2000 slides, and 35 audiotapes.

NV —CLARK COUNTY LIBRARY DISTRICT, Las Vegas Library, 1726 E Charleston, Las Vegas, 89104. Jack Gardner, Librn Administrator
Holdings: Vols (2000) Cat Maps Pix Microforms
Notes: Separate catalog and index to collection. Incl fiction, nonfiction, juvenile. The Library indexes the *Las Vegas Review-Journal* and the *Las Vegas Sun* (June 1972-date) by personal name and subject, excl national, international and sports news. The newspapers are held on microfilm. The index is produced on microfiche and cumulated monthly.

NV —NEVADA STATE HISTORICAL SOCIETY, Library, 1650 N Virginia St, Reno, 89503. Eric N Moody, Cur of Manuscripts; Lee Mortensen, Librn
Holdings: Vols 15,000 Cat Mss Maps Pix Slides Microforms
Budget: ($156,994)
Notes: Incl 2800 mss, 1500 maps and 70,000 pictures.

NV —UNIVERSITY OF NEVADA, RENO, University Library, Special Collections Dept, Reno, 89557. Robert E Blesse, Head
Holdings: Vols (3500) Cat Mss Maps Photogs
Notes: Includes 2100 cu ft manuscripts, 25,000 photographs, maps, vertical file, microforms and oral histories. Both primary and secondary materials are collected which document the history and development of Nevada and the Great Basin region from its beginnings too the present day. Areas of strength include mining, politics, water resources, railroads, biography, land use, anthropology, architecture, Lake Tahoe, lumbering, and early Nevada imprints. Major emphasis is on the prehistory and history of Nevada with lesser emphasis on bordering states and the Great Basin region. Specialized catalogs and indexes are available in the department.

NEVADA—IMPRINTS

NV —UNIVERSITY OF NEVADA, RENO, University Library, Special Collections Dept, Reno, 89557. Robert E Blesse, Head
Holdings: Vols (3500) Cat Mss Pix Maps
Notes: Includes 2100 cu ft manuscripts, 25,000 photographs, maps, vertical file, microforms and oral histories. Both primary and secondary materials are collected which document the history and development of Nevada and the Great Basin region from its beginnings too the present day. Areas of strength include mining, politics, water resources, railroads, biography, land use, anthropology, architecture, Lake Tahoe, lumbering, and early Nevada imprints. Major emphasis is on the prehistory and history of Nevada with lesser emphasis on bordering states and the Great Basin region. Specialized catalogs and indexes are available in the department.

NEVADA—MAPS

NV —UNIVERSITY OF NEVADA, RENO, University Library, Special Collections Dept, Reno, 89557. Robert E Blesse, Head
Holdings: Vols (3500) Cat Mss Pix Maps
Notes: Includes 2100 cu ft manuscripts, 25,000 photographs, maps, vertical file, microforms and oral histories.

OK —TULSA CITY-COUNTY LIBRARY, Business & Technology Dept, 400 Civic Center, Tulsa, 74103. Craig Buthod, Head
Notes: Original General Land Office survey maps for the states of Arizona, Arkansas, Colorado, Illinois, Indiana, Idaho, Kansas, Michigan, Missouri, Montana, Nebraska, Nevada, New Mexico, North Dakota, Ohio, Oklahoma, South Dakota, Utah and Wyoming. Incomplete coverage of each state.

NEVADA—POLITICS AND GOVERNMENT

NV —UNIVERSITY OF NEVADA, RENO, University Library, Special Collections Dept,

Reno, 89557. Robert E Blesse, Head
Holdings: Vols (3500) Cat Mss Pix Maps
Notes: Includes 2100 cu ft manuscripts, 25,000 photographs, maps, vertical file, microforms and oral histories. Both primary and secondary materials are collected which document the history and development of Nevada and the Great Basin region from its beginnings too the present day. Areas of strength include mining, politics, water resources, railroads, biography, land use, anthropology, architecture, Lake Tahoe, lumbering, and early Nevada imprints. Major emphasis is on the prehistory and history of Nevada with lesser emphasis on bordering states and the Great Basin region. Specialized catalogs and indexes are available in the department.

NEVADA COPPER BELT RAILROAD

NV —UNIVERSITY OF NEVADA, RENO, University Library, Special Collections Dept, Reno, 89557. Robert E Blesse, Head
Holdings: Vols (150) Cat Mss Pix Maps
Notes: Includes 370 cu ft manuscripts, 2000 photographs. Major collection include papers of Nevada railroad companies Virginia and Truckee, Carson and Colorado, Eureka and Palisade, and Nevada Copper Belt. Materials are collected which deal with the history and development of railroads within Nevada and those which have run through the state.

NEVE, FREDERICK W.

VA —UNIVERSITY OF VIRGINIA, Alderman Library, Manuscripts Dept, Charlottesville, 22901. Edmund Berkeley Jr, Cur
Notes: The collection incl church records and clergymen's papers from several denominations particularly those of Frederick W Neve, archdeacon of the Blue Ridge, an Episcopal mission organizer.

NEVILLE, ALISON

MA —BOSTON UNIVERSITY, Mugar Memorial Library, Special Collections Dept, 771 Commonwealth Ave, Boston, 02215. Howard B Gotlieb, Dir
Holdings: Cat Mss
Notes: Mss, correspondence, etc collected in depth; incl publications by or about.

NEVIN, ETHELBERT

PA —UNIVERSITY OF PITTSBURGH, Music Library, B-31 Music Bldg, Pittsburgh, 15260. Norris L Stephens, Music Librn
Holdings: Uncat Mss
Notes: Mss, printed music, etc. A catalog is in preparation. The University of Pittsburgh has in its possession many artifacts from the Nevin estate, incl his piano and other furniture from his studio. No photocopying.

NEW AMERICAN LIBRARY

WY —UNIVERSITY OF WYOMING, William Robertson Coe Library, 13 & Ivinson, Laramie, 82071.
Notes: Archives of publishers Penguin Books and New American Library.

NEW BRUNSWICK, CANADA

NB —LEGISLATIVE LIBRARY, Legislative Bldg, Queen St, PO Box 6000, Fredericton, E3B 5H1, Can. Jocelyne LeBel, Dir
Holdings: Cat Pix Microforms
Notes: Incl also over 2000 items written by New Brunswickers on or about New Brunswick; with a full analytical catalog of New Brunswickiana. Largest collection of New Brunswick government documents.

NEW BRUNSWICK, CANADA—HISTORY

NB —KINGS LANDING CORP, Library, PO Box 522, Fredericton, E3B 5A6, Can.
Holdings: Vols 1700 Cat
Notes: In addition, 850 books used to reflect

NEW BRUNSWICK, CANADA—HISTORY (cont.)

the tone of each family of the period in the rooms of our restoration.
NB —SAINT JOHN REGIONAL LIBRARY,
1 Market Square, Saint John, E2L 4Z6, Can.
Barbara A Malcolm, Reference Librn
Holdings: Vols 300 // Cat Microforms
Notes: Scrapbooks of New Brunswick history, 1870-1920. Partially indexed to complete this project. The period covered in these holdings is 85652 1870-1920.

NEW CANADIAN LIBRARY SERIES

AB —UNIVERSITY OF CALGARY,
Libraries, Special Collections Div, 2500 University Dr, Calgary, T2N 1N4, Can.
Holdings: Cat Mss
Notes: The Malcolm Ross papers include correspondence about Ross's academic career from 1934 to the present and his correspondence with other scholars. There is an important collection of correspondence with Canadian writers and poets. The major part of the papers consists of Malcolm Ross's editorial correspondence about the New Canadian Library reprint series from 1962-1976.

NEW CASTLE AND FRENCHTOWN RAILROAD

DE —HISTORICAL SOCIETY OF DELAWARE, Library, 505 Market St Mall, Wilmington, 19801. Barbara E Benson, Library Dir
Holdings: Cat Mss Maps
Notes: Collection incl papers and other mss materials.

NEW CHURCH see New Jerusalem Church

NEW DEAL (U.S.)

KS —KANSAS STATE UNIVERSITY,
Library, Special Collections & University Archives, Manhattan, 66506. Antonia Q Pigno, Coordr; John J Vander Velde, Librn; Anthony R Crawford, Univ Archivist
Holdings: Vols 25 // Cat Mss
Notes: Dan Casement, 1868-1953, was a wealthy Manhattan rancher. He graduated from Princeton in 1890. During the years 1897-1901 he helped his father, Jack, build a railroad across Costa Rica. Jack had built the Union Pacific across the US. Dan Casement opposed the New Deal, incl the Agricultural Adjustment Act; he wrote articles and made radio speeches against them. Most of the 2500 letters congratulate him on his stand.
†MA —JOHN F KENNEDY LIBRARY,
Columbia Point, Boston, 02125. Dan H Fenn Jr, Dir
Holdings: // Cat
Notes: Louis Brownlow's papers relating to government reorganization during the Roosevelt administration and James P Warburg's personal papers and general files relating to the New Deal and his role as advisor to FDR. 23 linear ft of mss.
Holdings are described in "Historical Materials in the John F Kennedy Library". Copies may be obtained by writing the Reserach Archivist.
RI —BROWN UNIVERSITY, John Hay Library, 20 Prospect St, Providence, 02912.
Mark N Brown, Cur Mss
Holdings: Mss
Notes: The Isabel Harris Metcalf Peaceana Collection, 1918-1942, consists of mounted and loose newspaper clippings (in 57 vols and numerous boxed envelopes) attempting to document the peace issue in the world and the world and the New Deal in the US. The clippings are classified by country, topic, and date. Also incl related correspondence, pamphlets, and broadsides.
TX —NORTH TEXAS STATE UNIVERSITY, Archives, NT Station Box 5188, Denton, 76203. Robert LaForte, University Archivist
Notes: The NTSU Archives houses the patron's copy of oral history interviews that are part of the Oral History Collection, an independent project not part of the Archives. This collection of interviews covers, in part, the following subject areas: World War II Pearl Harbor survivors, World War II prisoners of war, Texas legislators, ex-governors of Texas, Texans employed by the administrations of FDR, Texas businessmen and businesswomen, development of the Coastal Bend area of south Texas, and Mexican-American social action activities. Cataloged. Transcriptions available. See *Oral History Collection*, North Texas State University Bulletin, April 1981.

NEW ENGLAND

CT —YALE UNIVERSITY, Box 1603A, Yale Station, New Haven, 06520.
Holdings: Vols Cat Mss
VT —MIDDLEBURY COLLEGE, Starr Library, Flanders Ballad Collection, Middlebury, 05753. Jennifer Post Quinn, Cur
Notes: Begun as Helen Hartness Flanders' private collection in 1930, given to Middlebury College, 1941. Incl over 9000 New England items recorded or transcribed since 1930: ballads and folk songs of British, American, French-Canadian, and Russian origin; religious songs; fiddle tunes; dance music. Incl research collection of folklore and folksong monographs, scores, tunebooks, journals. Reference: Quinn, Jennifer Post. *An Index to the Field Recordings in the Flanders Ballad Collection at Middlebury College, Middlebury, Vermont* Middlebury, VT, Middlebury College, 1983.

NEW ENGLAND—ANTIQUITIES

CT —CONNECTICUT HISTORICAL SOCIETY, One Elizabeth St, Hartford, 06105. Christopher Bickford, Dir
Notes: Over 70,000 books and periodicals, 3500 bound vols of newspapers, and thousands of broadsides, maps, prints, and photographs pertaining to Connecticut. Also, more than 1 1/2 million historical mss; incl personal correspondence, diaries, account books, business records, and town materials dating from the earliest settlement. Extensive genealogical holdings, incl nearly 4000 printed genealogies and New England town and county histories.
MA —SOCIETY FOR THE PRESERVATION OF NEW ENGLAND ANTIQUITIES, Library, 141 Cambridge St, Boston, 02114.
Ellie Reichlin, Librn & Cur of Photographic Collections
Holdings: Vols (3000) Cat Pix Microforms
Budget: ($75,000)
Notes: Photograph collections, all media (incl daguerreotypes, ambrotypes, etc, stereographic views, carte de visite) depicting New England buildings; interiors; street and town views; occupations; pastimes; transport and personalities. Covers 1840s-1930s, with some more recent additons. Amateur and professional photographers represented. Cataloged in part, otherwise arranged by localities, subject, personal name. Special collections incl: marine photographs by N L Stebbins and Henry Peabody (1880s-1920s); Boston and Albany railroad photographic archive, early 1900s; Quabbin Valley views; historic American Buildings Survey photographs (17th to early 19th century architecture) by Arthur Haskell; Baldwin Coolidge collection, and many others. Size: 500,000 prints, ca 75,000 negatives (glass plates and copy negs). These are cataloged. Some special indexes incllandscape design (arbors, conservatories, flower beds, bandstands etc); photographers represented; architects represented (partial), and pending, interiors (specific features of); occupations.
NY —NASSAU COUNTY MUSEUM, Sands Pt Preserve, Middleneck Rd, Sand Points, 11050.
Holdings: Vols (2500)
Notes: Collection contains almost every published reference on Long Island archaeology, ethnology, and geology, and incl most of those pertaining to the coastal New York area. Open by appointment. No photocopying.

NEW ENGLAND—CENSUSES

†MA —BOSTON PUBLIC LIBRARY, Copley Sq, Boston, 02117.
Holdings: Cat Microforms
Notes: Microform Publication by National Archives. US Census-Federal Population Schedules, 1790-1890; New England states only.

NEW ENGLAND—DESCRIPTION AND TRAVEL—VIEWS

MA —UNIVERSITY OF MASSACHUSETTS AT AMHERST, Library, Amherst, 01003.
Siegfried Feller, Assoc Dir for Collection Development
Holdings: Vols Cat Maps
Notes: Transportation, tourist travel accounts and guides, resort literature, for New England and adjacent areas.
See also entry under Maps and Atlases - Collections.

NEW ENGLAND—GENEALOGY

CT —CONNECTICUT HISTORICAL SOCIETY, One Elizabeth St, Hartford, 06105. Christopher Bickford, Dir
Notes: Over 70,000 books and periodicals, 3500 bound vols of newspapers, and thousands of broadsides, maps, prints, and photographs pertaining to Connecticut. Also, more than 1 1/2 million historical mss; incl personal correspondence, diaries, account books, business records, and town materials dating from the earliest settlement. Extensive genealogical holdings, incl nearly 4000 printed genealogies and New England town and county histories.
CT —NEW HAVEN COLONY HISTORICAL SOCIETY, Whitney Library, 114 Whitney Ave, New Haven, 06510. M Ottilia Koel, Librn & Cur of Mss
Notes: 25,000 printed books and pamphlets; ca 1500 linear ft of manuscript material including historic manuscripts, records of education, maritime and harbour industry, private papers, business and family records; 40,000 photographic images; maps and microforms relating to the early settlement and subsequent history of New Haven and vicinity.
CT —STAMFORD'S PUBLIC LIBRARY, Ferguson Library, Adult Services Dept, 96 Broad St, Stamford, 06901. Ernest A DiMattia Jr, Dir; Doris Goodlett, Head Adult Servs
Holdings: Vols 4200 Cat Pix Microforms
Notes: Collection specializes in the genealogy of New England states and incl a comprehensive collection of local history. Also subscribes to many periodicals through the Stamford Genealogical Society. The Barbour Collection (Vital Record of Connecticut) is on microfilm and indexed by towns and by families. Library owns vols 1-165 of the DAR lineage books.
CT —SILAS BRONSON LIBRARY, 267 Grand St, Waterbury, 06702. Patricia L Joy, Reference Dept Head
Holdings: Vols 1500 Cat
Budget: $200
Notes: Incl are genealogies of families particularly from Connecticut and the other New England states.
FL —ORLANDO PUBLIC LIBRARY, Local History & Genealogy Dept, 100 Block of Central Ave, Orlando, 32806. Eileen B Willis, Librn
Holdings: Vols 11,000 Cat Maps Microforms
Budget: $8000
Notes: Strong collection in local genealogy materials on Mass, NY, Va, Ga, and Florida. Contains exceptional holdings on all New England States, Penn, and NJ.
See also entry under Genealogy - Collections.
IL —NEWBERRY LIBRARY, 60 W Walton St, Chicago, 60610. Diana Haskell, Cur of Modern Mss
Holdings: Cat
Notes: Very strong collection.

NEW ENGLAND—GENEALOGY
(cont.)

ME —MAINE STATE LIBRARY, Special Collections Dept, Cultural Bldg, Station 64, Augusta, 04333. Shirley Thayer, Librn
Holdings: Cat
Budget: ($2,500,000)
Notes: An extensive collection of Maine genealogy with a good representation of all of New England. Non-circulating. 5000 books and microfiche.

MA —JONES LIBRARY, 43 Amity St, Amherst, 01002. Daniel J Lombardo, Cur of Special Collections
Holdings: Vols (2710) Cat Maps Pix
Notes: The Boltwood Collection. Several thousand documents, cataloged, 18th and 19th centuries. The scope is primarily local, then regional, Massachusetts, New England. Several thousand local pictures, chiefly post-1926.

MA —FREE PUBLIC LIBRARY, Genealogy Room, 613 Pleasant St, Bedford, 02740. Paul A Cyr, Librn
Holdings: Vols (10,000) Cat Mss Maps Pix Microforms
Budget: ($1000)
Notes: Extensive collection on the history and genealogy of New England, with a strong emphasis on southeastern Massachusetts. Materials incl books, periodicals, mss, microfilms, and pictures of New England life. Unique features of the collection incl the *Leonard Papers* ms of vital records of early Bristol County, *Repertoires des Mariages* of Province Quebec, Canada, and a collection on the Society of Friends, or Quakers.

MA —BOSTON UNIVERSITY, Mugar Memorial Library, Special Collections Dept, 771 Commonwealth Ave, Boston, 02215. Howard B Gotlieb, Dir
Holdings: // Mss

MA —NEW ENGLAND HISTORIC GENEALOGICAL SOCIETY, Library, 101 Newbury St, Boston, 02116. Ralph J Crandell, Dir
Holdings: Vols (250,000) Mss Maps Microforms Pix
Notes: New England genealogy. Especially strong Massachusetts, Maine, and New Hampshire, although all states are well represented, as are the relevancies of each subject listed in this volume with regard to British antecedent and contemporary history. Special strengths in local history and biography, obituaries, etc, incl parish registers, censuses, British and American. 3125 linear ft of mss.

MA —BERKSHIRE ATHENAEUM, 1 Wendell Ave, Pittsfield, 01201. Ruth T Degenhardt, Head Local History & Literature
Holdings: Vols (9000) Cat Mss Maps Pix Microforms
Budget: ($2000)
Notes: Cooke collection: typescript and manuscript copies of church and cemetery records for all towns in Berkshire County, and surrounding towns in Vermont and New York. Family History File incl abstracts of research by genealogists on families throughout New England. Browne Collection: personal notes and research material of noted genealogist concerned with all facets of Northern Berkshire genealogy. Surname index available. Shepard Collection: extensive collection of research notes and vital records of families throughout Western Massachusetts and bordering areas of New York and Vermont.

MA —SPRINGFIELD CITY LIBRARY, Genealogy and Local History Dept, 220 State St, Springfield, 01103. Joseph Carvalho III, Supervisor
Holdings: Vols (17,000) Cat Mss Maps Pix Microforms VF
Budget: ($8000)
Notes: New England, Massachusetts, local history, and genealogy collections. 18,000 pictures, 3200 microforms, ca 15,000 clippings, pamphlets, etc (280 ft of vertical files).

MA —AMERICAN ANTIQUARIAN SOCIETY LIBRARY, 185 Salisbury St,

Worcester, 01609. Marcus A McCorison, Dir & Librn
Holdings: Vols 14,000 Cat
Notes: Incl heraldry, biography, etc. Numerous special indexes and clipping files supplement the book collection.

MI —MONROE COUNTY LIBRARY SYSTEM, Ellis Reference and Information Center, 3700 S Custer Rd, Monroe, 48161. Marie D Chulski, Head of Reference Services
Notes: Incl individual county histories, atlases, biographies, etc. The Monroe County history collection contains veteran records, plat books, oral history tapes, family histories, church records, cemetery index, atlases and census records. Genealogy emphasis is not only Monroe County but incl surrounding counties and the states with large migration to the area, such as Ohio, Kentucky, Tennessee and the New England states.

NH —NEW HAMPSHIRE HISTORICAL SOCIETY, Library, 30 Park St, Concord, 03301. William Copeley, Assoc Librn
Holdings: Vols 10,000 Cat Mss
Budget: ($9000)
Notes: New Hampshire and New England genealogy. All genealogical material is cataloged. Separate genealogy card index lists the material in the collection alphabetically by family name.

NJ —PLAINFIELD PUBLIC LIBRARY, Eighth St at Park Ave, Plainfield, 07060. Thomas H Ballard, Dir

NY —NEW YORK STATE LIBRARY, State Education Bldg Annex, Washington Ave, Albany, 12224.
Holdings: Cat Mss Maps Pix Microforms
Notes: Extensive collection on American local history incl books and pamphlets on American genealogy. Major strength northeastern United States. Maintain unique card index to regional historical and genealogical materials in periodicals not indexed elsewhere, pamphlets, and comprehensive works; about 1912-date.

NY —NEW YORK GENEALOGICAL & BIOGRAPHICAL SOCIETY, Library, 122 E 58 St, New York, 10022. James P Gregory, Librn
Holdings: Vols 63,500 Cat Mss Maps Microforms
Notes: The Society has copied and has in its ms collections a great many church records from all parts of New York State and several from adjacent states; and many very valuable ms genealogies and family Bible records which have never been published. The Society library is noncirculating and one of the principal genealogical reference libraries in the country. It has accumulated in its collections approximately 63 thousand vols on genealogy, local history and biography. In addition it has a rapidly expanding microfilm division which presently numbers over 2000 reels and keeps four microfilm readers in continuous use.

NY —ONONDAGA COUNTY PUBLIC LIBARY, Local History and Genealogy Dept, 335 Montgomery St, Syracuse, 13202. Gerald James Parsons, Head
Holdings: Vols (30,000) Cat Mss Maps Pix Microforms
Budget: ($12,000)
Notes: Collection of local history and genealogy covers primarily Syracuse, Onondaga County, New York State and the northeast, ie, New England, New Jersey and Pennsylvania.

RI —RHODE ISLAND HISTORICAL SOCIETY, Library, 121 Hope St, Providence, 02906. Paul R Campbell, Library Dir
Holdings: Vols (150,000) Cat Mss Maps Pix Films Microforms
Notes: Books do not circulate. No interlibrary loan.

TN —CHATTANOOGA-HAMILTON COUNTY, Bicentennial Library, Local History and Genealogy Dept, 1001 Broad St, Chattanooga, 37402. Clara W Swann, Librn
Holdings: Vols (24,561) Cat Mss Maps Pix Microforms
Budget: ($7000)
Notes: Emphasis on southern states, and

eastern Tennessee counties, with considerable material on New England, Pennsylvania, and Maryland genealogy and history. Census records on microfilm. Special indexes and clipping files. Noncirculating.

VT —BENNINGTON MUSEUM, Genealogical Library, W Main St, Bennington, 05201. Charles G Bennett, Librn
Holdings: Vols 1400 Uncat Maps Pix
Notes: Vermont regional history and genealogy emphasis.

NEW ENGLAND—HISTORY

CT —CONNECTICUT HISTORICAL SOCIETY, One Elizabeth St, Hartford, 06105. Christopher Bickford, Dir
Notes: Over 70,000 books and periodicals, 3500 bound vols of newspapers, and thousands of broadsides, maps, prints, and photographs pertaining to Connecticut. Also, more than 1 1/2 million historical mss; incl personal correspondence, diaries, account books, business records, and town materials dating from the earliest settlement. Extensive genealogical holdings, incl nearly 4000 printed genealogies and New England town and county histories.

CT —CONNECTICUT STATE LIBRARY, 231 Capitol Ave, Hartford, 06106. Mark H Jones, Archivist; T O Wohlsen, Jr, Head Archives, Hist & Genealogy Unit; Ann Barry, Ref Librn
Holdings: Cat Mss Maps
Notes: Books, maps, mss, archives pertaining to Connecticut state and local history and to the history of New England, etc. Archival collections incl state and local government records and papers of institutions and organizations in Connecticut. There are separate catalogs for archives maps, and genealogical works.

CT —YALE UNIVERSITY, Box 1603A, Yale Station, New Haven, 06520.

CT —STAMFORD'S PUBLIC LIBRARY, Ferguson Library, Adult Services Dept, 96 Broad St, Stamford, 06901. Ernest A DiMattia Jr, Dir; Doris Goodlett, Head Adult Servs
Holdings: Vols 4200 Cat Pix Microforms
Notes: Collection specializes in the genealogy of New England states and incl a comprehensive collection of local history. Also subscribes to many periodicals through the Stamford Genealogical Society. The Barbour Collection (Vital Record of Connecticut) is on microfilm and indexed by towns and by families. Library owns vols 1-165 of the DAR lineage books.

CT —SILAS BRONSON LIBRARY, 267 Grand St, Waterbury, 06702. Patricia L Joy, Reference Dept Head
Holdings: Vols 1300 Cat
Budget: $200
Notes: Many individual town histories.

FL —FLORIDA STATE UNIVERSITY, Robert Manning Strozier Library, Special Collections Dept, Tallahassee, 32306. Opal M Free, Head, Special Collections
Holdings: Vols (12,254) Cat
Notes: The Venila Lovina Shores Bequest.

ME —BOWDOIN COLLEGE, Library, Brunswick, 04011. Dianne M Gutscher, Cur of Special Collections
Holdings: Mss
Notes: The Mellen Papers contain approx 5000 printed and mss items relating to New England history from the 18th to the 20th centuries. Of primary importance are the Henry Sewall papers, which incl his Revolutionary War correspondence, addresses, genealogical notes, and other documents. The archive also incl papers from the Mellen, Hawkins, Manley, Harward, and other New England families.

MA —JONES LIBRARY, 43 Amity St, Amherst, 01002. Daniel J Lombardo, Cur of Special Collections
Holdings: Vols (2710) Cat Maps Pix
Notes: The Boltwood Collection. Several thousand documents, cataloged, 18th and 19th centuries. The scope is primarily local, then regional, Massachusetts, New England. Several thousand local pictures, chiefly post-1926.

NEW ENGLAND—HISTORY (cont.)

MA —UNIVERSITY OF MASSACHUSETTS
AT AMHERST, Library, Amherst, 01003.
Siegfried Feller, Assoc Dir for Collection
Development
Notes: The collections in Massachusetts
history incl works on the history of the
Commonwealth and of its subdivisions.
Source materials incl letterpress editions of
most important colony and town records,
extensive holdings of published vital records,
and a special collection of ca 1000
pamphlets by or about Massachusetts
persons, or about Massachusetts places,
societies, etc 1729-1902. Incl extensive
microform holdings of: Massachusetts
Archives (Felt Collection); original
manuscripts census schedules for
Massachusetts (1st-12th censuses), Suffolk
County deeds (1629-1886); Suffolk County
probate records (1628-1899); Hampshire
County probate records (1660-1820); "Court
Files Suffolk" (records of courts throughout
the colony, province, state, and
commonwealth, 1629-1797); Massachusetts
city directories through 1860; Massachusetts
newspapers in microform; andthe microform
publications of the Massachusetts Historical
Society.

MA —STURGIS LIBRARY, Rte 6A,
Barnstable, 02630. Susan R Klein, Chief
Librn
Holdings: Vols (1500) Cat Mss Maps
Microforms
Budget: ($1000)
Notes: Lothrop Room Collection of
genealogy and history is considered to be the
finest on Cape Cod. No printed vital records
for the County of Barnstable, but 37 books
of handwritten Genealogical Notes of Cape
Cod Families (1620-1850), also on
microfilm. Also incl is the Stanley W Smith
Collection of books, pamphlets and
manuscript materials (mostly original land
deeds, all Cape Cod oriented, some of them
Indian and dating from the early 1700s). The
Percy F Rex Collection represents a unique
library of Cape Cod literature. Many
rareties, incl early sermons preached on the
Cape and pamphlets on Cape Cod canal, etc.

MA —FREE PUBLIC LIBRARY, Genealogy
Room, 613 Pleasant St, Bedford, 02740. Paul
A Cyr, Librn
Holdings: Vols (10,000) Cat Mss Maps Pix
Microforms
Budget: ($1000)
Notes: Extensive collection of the history
and genealogy of New England, with a
strong emphasis on southeastern
Massachusetts. Materials incl books,
periodicals, mss, microfilms, and pictures of
New England life. Unique features of the
collection incl the Leonard Papers ms of
vital records of early Bristol County,
Repertoires des Mariages of Province
Quebec, Canada, and a collection on the
Society of Friends, or Quakers.

MA —MASSACHUSETTS HISTORICAL
SOCIETY LIBRARY, 1154 Boylston St,
Boston, 02215. John D Cushing, Librn
Holdings: Mss Maps Microforms
Notes: One of more than 5000 individual
collections in the Library, this collection incl
the Adams Family papers and materials
relating to Massachusetts and New England.
The Library's collection of mss has been
cataloged and issued in nine folio vols by G
K Hall & Co of Boston. It is widely
distributed throughout the United States and
Europe.

MA —NEW ENGLAND HISTORIC
GENEALOGICAL SOCIETY, Library, 101
Newbury St, Boston, 02116. Ralph J
Crandell, Dir
Holdings: Vols (250,000) Mss Maps
Microforms Pix
Notes: New England genealogy. Especially
strong Massachusetts, Maine, and New
Hampshire, although all states are well
represented, as are the relevancies of each
subject listed in this volume with regard to
British antecedent and contemporary history.
Special strengths in local history and
biography, obituaries, etc, incl parish

registers, censuses, British and American.
3125 linear ft of mss.

MA —SOCIETY FOR THE PRESERVATION
OF NEW ENGLAND ANTIQUITIES,
Library, 141 Cambridge St, Boston, 02114.
Ellie Reichlin, Librn & Cur of Photographic
Collections
Holdings: Vols (3000) Cat Pix Microforms
Budget: ($75,000)
Notes: Photograph collections, all media
(incl daguerreotypes, ambrotypes, etc,
stereographic views, carte de visite)
depicting New England buildings; interiors;
street and town views; occupations; pastimes;
transport and personalities. Covers 1840s-
1930s, with some more recent additons.
Amateur and professional photographers
represented. Cataloged in part, otherwise
arranged by localities, subject, personal
name. Special collections incl: marine
photographs by N L Stebbins and Henry
Peabody (1880s-1920s); Boston and Albany
railroad photographic archive, early 1900s;
Quabbin Valley views; historic American
Buildings Survey photographs (17th to early
19th century architecture) by Arthur
Haskell; Baldwin Coolidge collection, and
many others. Size: 500,000 prints, ca 75,000
negatives (glass plates and copy negs). These
are cataloged. Some special indexes
incllandscape design (arbors, conservatories,
flower beds, bandstands etc); photographers
represented; architects represented (partial),
and pending, interiors (specific features of);
occupations.

MA —HISTORIC DEERFIELD-
POCUMTUCK VALLEY MEMORIAL
ASSOCIATION, Libraries, Memorial St,
Box 53, Deerfield, 01342. David R Proper,
Librn
Holdings: Vols (17,000) Cat Mss Maps Pix
Microforms
Notes: Local and regional history, especially
western Massachusetts. Also, remnants of
several collection of books available to early
Deerfield and Greenfield residents. Strong
ms collection dealing with the region's
families, businesses, etc. These consist of
sermons, diaries, town and church records,
voluntary societies' archives, etc. Extensive
collection of photographs of the people and
buildings of Deerfield and its environs, and
travels in Maine, California, and England
(1880s to 1920s). Also, large collection of
glassplate negatives. Houses the Connecticut
Valley Bibliography, a comprehensive card
file on the history and culture of the
Connecticut Valley of Massachusetts.

MA —STONEHILL COLLEGE, Donahue
Hall, Washington St, North Easton, 02356.
Louise M Kenneally, Archivist & Special
Collections Librn
Holdings: Mss
Notes: The Arnold B Tofias Industrial
Archives; 2000 linear feet of records and
correspondence of the Ames Shovel
Company of North Easton, Mass. About 800
shovels and other artifacts. Covers the
period 1774-1956.

MA —BERKSHIRE ATHENAEUM, 1
Wendell Ave, Pittsfield, 01201. Ruth T
Degenhardt, Head Local History &
Literature
Holdings: Vols (9000) Cat Mss Maps Pix
Microforms
Budget: ($2000)
Notes: Primary focus is on the development
of Berkshire, Massachusetts, regional history
and culture, with particular emphasis on the
industrial development of Berkshire County
and the Colonial and Revolutionary periods
in the Berkshires. Entire collection spans all
New England states and New York State, on
all topics. Special strength is in published
local histories. No separate catalog. There is
a reference index.

MA —PEABODY MUSEUM OF SALEM,
Phillips Library, E India Sq, Salem, 01970.
Gregor Trinkaus-Randall, Librn
Holdings: Vols (100,000) Cat Mss Maps Pix
Notes: Maritime history of New England.
No published indexes; listed in Hamer's
Guide to Archives...

MA —OLD STURBRIDGE VILLAGE,
Research Library, Sturbridge, 01566.
Theresa Rini Percy, Librn
Holdings: Cat Mss Maps Microforms
Notes: Mainly 1790-1850, incl town
histories, directories, official records, etc.

NH —NEW HAMPSHIRE HISTORICAL
SOCIETY, Library, 30 Park St, Concord,
03301. William Copeley, Assoc Librn
Holdings: Vols 30,000 Cat Mss Maps Pix
Budget: ($9000)
Notes: New England and New Hampshire
state, county, and local history and
biography.

NY —MARGARET WOODBURY STRONG
MUSEUM, 1 Manhattan Square, Rochester,
14607.
Holdings: Vols (1500)
Notes: Social and cultural development of
Northeastern America in the 1820-1830
period.

NY —ONONDAGA COUNTY PUBLIC
LIBARY, Local History and Genealogy
Dept, 335 Montgomery St, Syracuse, 13202.
Gerald James Parsons, Head
Holdings: Vols (30,000) Cat Mss Maps Pix
Microforms
Budget: ($12,000)
Notes: Collection of local history and
genealogy covers primarily Syracuse,
Onondaga County, New York State and the
northeast, ie, New England, New Jersey and
Pennsylvania.

RI —BROWN UNIVERSITY, John Hay
Library, 20 Prospect St, Providence, 02912.
Mark N Brown, Cur Mss
Holdings: Vols (15,000) // Cat Mss Maps
Pix
Notes: Sidney S Rider Collection of 5000
books, 10,000 pamphlets and 8000 mss
formed in the 19th century by a Providence
antiquarian bookseller. The primary focus is
on all aspects of Rhode Island: social,
political, and economic history from the
17th to the mid-19th century, with some
attention given to general New England
history. The most significant group of
primary materials within the collection
relates to Thomas Wilson Dorr and the
political movements in Rhode Island ca
1840-1850, especially the Dorr Rebellion
over the issue of suffrage.

RI —PROVIDENCE PUBLIC LIBRARY, 150
Empire St, Providence, 02903. Lance J
Bauer, Special Collections Librn
Notes: The Daniel Berkeley Updike
Autograph Collection of 800 ms letters and
historical documents, primarily New
England, from late 17th to mid-19th century
with emphasis on Rhode Island politics;
American Revolution; French military
figures; naval heroes of the Revolution,
Tripolitan War and War of 1812; Civil War
figures and US presidents. Illustrious
personages represented incl: Henry David
Thoreau, Daniel Webster, John Hay,
Marquis de Lafayette, Henry Wadsworth
Longfellow, and other notables. Material
must be used in-house. Limited
photocopying for educational purposes only.

TN —CHATTANOOGA-HAMILTON
COUNTY, Bicentennial Library, Local
History and Genealogy Dept, 1001 Broad St,
Chattanooga, 37402. Clara W Swann, Librn
Holdings: Vols (24,561) Cat Mss Maps Pix
Microforms
Budget: ($7000)
Notes: Emphasis on southern states, and
eastern Tennessee counties, with
considerable material on New England,
Pennsylvania, and Maryland genealogy and
history. Census records on microfilm. Special
indexes and clipping files. Noncirculating.

VT —BENNINGTON MUSEUM,
Genealogical Library, W Main St,
Bennington, 05201. Charles G Bennett,
Librn
Holdings: Vols 1400 Uncat Maps Pix
Notes: Vermont regional history and
genealogy emphasis.

VT —MIDDLEBURY COLLEGE, Egbert
Starr Library, Middlebury, 05753. Hans
Raum, Cur
Holdings: Vols 2500
Budget: $2000
Notes: New England historical and literary
materials, incl Vermontiana and Vermont
estate documents.

VA —UNIVERSITY OF VIRGINIA,
Alderman Library, Tracy W McGregor
Collection, Charlottesville, 22901. William H
Runge, Cur
Holdings: Vols 2500 Cat Mss
Notes: This collection was gathered by

NEW ENGLAND—HISTORY (cont.)

William Gwinn Mather, a direct descendant of the New England Mathers, It is one of the 3 important Mather collections in the world. Excellent collection on magic and witchcraft in America. Collection incl 20th century imprints. Thomas J Holmes used this collection as a basis for his monumental biographies of Increase Mather, Cotton Mather and the minor Mathers.

NEW ENGLAND—IMPRINTS

CT —YALE UNIVERSITY, Box 1603A, Yale Station, New Haven, 06520.

NEW ENGLAND—MAPS

CT —CONNECTICUT HISTORICAL SOCIETY, One Elizabeth St, Hartford, 06105. Christopher Bickford, Dir
Notes: Over 70,000 books and periodicals, 3500 bound vols of newspapers, and thousands of broadsides, maps, prints, and photographs pertaining to Connecticut. Also, more than 1 1/2 million historical mss; incl personal correspondence, diaries, account books, business records, and town materials dating from the earliest settlement. Extensive genealogical holdings, incl nearly 4000 printed genealogies and New England town and county histories.
CT —CONNECTICUT STATE LIBRARY, 231 Capitol Ave, Hartford, 06106. Mark H Jones, Archivist; T O Wohlsen, Jr, Head Archives, Hist & Genealogy Unit; Ann Barry, Ref Librn
Notes: Books, maps, mss, archives pertaining to Connecticut state and local history and to the history of New England, etc. Archival collections incl state and local government records and papers of institutions and organizations in Connecticut. There are separate catalogs for archives maps, and genealogical works.
CT —YALE UNIVERSITY, Box 1603A, Yale Station, New Haven, 06520.
Notes: Maps and atlas collection.
CT —UNIVERSITY OF CONNECTICUT, University Library, Map Room, Storrs, 06268. Thornton P McGalmery, Librn
Holdings: Vols (903) Cat Maps Pix
Budget: ($5000)
Notes: The Map Room is the largest publicly supported map library in any Connecticut institution of higher education. It is a depository library for the US Geological Survey, the Defense Mapping Agency, and the Metropolitan District (Hartford, Conn). Incl over 100,000 maps and 8523 aerial photographs. Of particular interest is the *Petersen Collection*, a group of photostats of old town maps of New England.
ME —UNIVERSITY OF MAINE AT PRESQUE ISLE LIBRARY, 181 Main St, Presque Isle, 04769. Anna McGrath, Technical Services Librn
Holdings: Vols 1100
Budget: $500
Notes: Aroostook County, Maine. Vertical file material, photographs, artifacts, tapes (oral history), maps, scrapbooks, diaries, journals.

NEW ENGLAND—PICTURES, ILLUSTRATIONS, ETC.

MA —JONES LIBRARY, 43 Amity St, Amherst, 01002. Daniel J Lombardo, Cur of Special Collections
Holdings: Vols (2710) Cat Maps Pix
Notes: The Boltwood Collection. Several thousand documents, cataloged, 18th and 19th centuries. The scope is primarily local, then regional, Massachusetts, New England. Several thousand local pictures, chiefly post-1926.
MA —SOCIETY FOR THE PRESERVATION OF NEW ENGLAND ANTIQUITIES, Library, 141 Cambridge St, Boston, 02114. Ellie Reichlin, Librn & Cur of Photographic Collections
Holdings: Vols (3000) Pix Microforms
Budget: ($75,000)
Notes: Photograph collections, all media

(incl daguerreotypes, ambrotypes, etc, stereographic views, carte de visite) depicting New England buildings; interiors; street and town views; occupations; pastimes; transport and personalities. Covers 1840s-1930s, with some more recent additons. Amateur and professional photographers represented. Cataloged in part, otherwise arranged by localities, subject, personal name. Special collections incl: marine photographs by N L Stebbins and Henry Peabody (1880s-1920s); Boston and Albany railroad photographic archive, early 1900s; Quabbin Valley views; historic American Buildings Survey photographs (17th to early 19th century architecture) by Arthur Haskell; Baldwin Coolidge collection, and many others. Size: 500,000 prints, ca 75,000 negatives (glass plates and copy negs). These are cataloged. Some special indexes incllandscape design (arbors, conservatories, flower beds, bandstands etc); photographers represented; architects represented (partial), and pending, interiors (specific features of); occupations.
MA —SPRINGFIELD CITY LIBRARY, Genealogy and Local History Dept, 220 State St, Springfield, 01103. Joseph Carvalho III, Supervisor
Holdings: Vols (17,000) Cat Mss Maps Pix Microforms
Budget: ($8000)
Notes: New England, Massachusetts, local history, and genealogy collections. 18,000 pictures, 3200 microforms, ca 15,000 clippings, pamphlets, etc (280 ft of vertical files).

NEW ENGLAND ARCHITECTURE see Architecture, New England

NEW ENGLAND ARTISTS see Artists, New England

NEW ENGLAND EMIGRANT AID COMPANY

RI —BROWN UNIVERSITY, John Hay Library, 20 Prospect St, Providence, 02912. Mark N Brown, Cur Mss
Notes: Papers of Eli Thayer, eduator, US Congressman from Massachusetts, and organizer of the New England Emigrant Aid Company. Brown class of 1845. About 1000 letters, speeches, and articles on political subjects for the period 1841-1898; also Thayer's journal from 1853-1857.

NEW ENGLAND HOSPITAL FOR WOMEN AND CHILDREN

MA —BOSTON UNIVERSITY, Mugar Memorial Library, Special Collections Dept, 771 Commonwealth Ave, Boston, 02215. Howard B Gotlieb, Dir
Holdings: // Mss Pix
Notes: Correspondence.

NEW ENGLAND LAW see Law, New England

NEW ENGLAND NEWS COMPANY

MA —SOCIETY FOR THE PRESERVATION OF NEW ENGLAND ANTIQUITIES, Library, 141 Cambridge St, Boston, 02114. Ellie Reichlin, Librn & Cur of Photographic Collections
Notes: Views of vernacular housing, business districts, public buildings and manufacturing plants in southern and eastern Massachusetts, New Hampshire, and Maine prepared for eventual use as postcards; publicizes small towns which might have otherwise remained obscure. Some copy negatives. Ca 3500 pieces.

NEW FRANCE

DC —GEORGETOWN UNIVERSITY, Library, Special Collections Div, 37 & O Sts NW, Washington, 20057. George M Barringer, Special Collections Librn; Nicholas B Sheetz, Mss Librn
Holdings: Cat Mss Maps
Notes: New France, to 1763.

MI —DETROIT PUBLIC LIBRARY, Burton Historical Collection, 5201 Woodward Ave, Detroit, 48202. Alice Dalligan, Chief
ON —PUBLIC ARCHIVES OF CANADA, Library, 395 Wellington St, Ottawa, K1A 0N3, Can. Dawn E Monroe, Collections Development Officer
Holdings: Vols (80,000) Cat
Notes: The official publications for the New France period (1608-1760) comprise mainly edicts, ordinances and judgments issued by the King of France or his colonial representatives. The Library has transcripts of these documents, most of them handwritten, as well as several published works, such as the *Recueil des declarations, edits, lettres patentes et arrests du Conseil d'Etat du Roi enregistres au parlement de Dijon...* (Dijon: Jean Ressayre, (1689-1786?), 18 vols).

NEW FRANCE—HISTORY

PQ —BIBLIOTHEQUE DES ARCHIVES NATIONALES DU QUEBEC, CP 10450, Sainte-Foy, G1V 4N1, Can. Collete Barry, Dir
Holdings: Vols (50,000) Cat Mss Maps Pix Microforms
Budget: ($25,000)
Notes: Dictionary catalog on cards (unpublished). Official Quebec documents published before 1867.

NEW GUINEA

NY —AMERICAN MUSEUM OF NATURAL HISTORY, Library Services Dept, Central Park W & 79th St, New York, 10024. Nina J Root, Chairwoman; Mary Genett, Asst Librn for Reference Services

NEW GUINEA, WEST see Indonesia

NEW HAMPSHIRE

NH —DARTMOUTH COLLEGE, Baker Memorial Library, Hanover, 03755.
Holdings: Cat Mss Maps Pix
NH —PLYMOUTH STATE COLLEGE, Lamson Library, Plymouth, 03264. Phillip Wei, Dir of Library Services
Holdings: Vols 1200 Cat Mss Maps Pix Microforms
Notes: Mostly government publications from earliest settlement. Depository for current New Hampshire state publications. Early mss and varia on town of Plymouth.

NEW HAMPSHIRE—GENEALOGY

MA —NEW ENGLAND HISTORIC GENEALOGICAL SOCIETY, Library, 101 Newbury St, Boston, 02116. Ralph J Crandell, Dir
Holdings: Vols (250,000) Mss Maps Microforms Pix
Notes: New England genealogy. Especially strong Massachusetts, Maine, and New Hampshire, although all states are well represented, as are the relevancies of each subject listed in this volume with regard to British antecedent and contemporary history. Special strengths in local history and biography obituaries, etc, incl parish registers, censuses, British and American. 3125 linear ft of mss.
NH —NEW HAMPSHIRE HISTORICAL SOCIETY, Library, 30 Park St, Concord, 03301. William Copeley, Assoc Librn
Holdings: Vols 5000 Cat Mss
Budget: ($9000)
Notes: New Hampshire genealogy. All genealogical material is cataloged. Separate genealogy card index lists the material in the collection alphabetically by family name.
NH —DOVER PUBLIC LIBRARY, 73 Locust St, Dover, 03820. Donald K Mullen, Librn
Holdings: Cat Mss Maps Pix Microforms
Notes: Collection contains a variety of New Hampshire records, clippings, town histories, genealogies, Quaker Meeting House records to the late 18th century. Local newspapers to early 19th century.
NH —DARTMOUTH COLLEGE, Baker Memorial Library, Hanover, 03755.
Holdings: Cat Mss Pix Microforms
Notes: Microfilm copy of Dr Gilman Frost's extensive records.

NEW HAMPSHIRE—GENEALOGY
(cont.)

NH —KEENE STATE COLLEGE, Wallace E
Mason Library, 229 Main St, Keene, 03431.
Edward A Scott, Librn; Clifford Mead,
Special Collections Librn
Holdings: Vols (2000) Cat Mss Maps Pix
Audiotapes Microforms
Budget: ($7500)
Notes: New Hampshire history, genealogy,
authors, imprints (especially Keene
imprints), Keene State College materials, and
newspapers (microfilm).

NH —MANCHESTER HISTORIC
ASSOCIATION, Library, 129 Amherst St,
Manchester, 03104. Elizabeth Lessard, Librn
Notes: Business and production records of
the Amoskeag Manufacturing Company
(1831-1936); incl real estate holdings;
personnel name index (70,000 pieces;
biographies of employees); insurance
surveys, etc. Photographs, glass negatives
(1414 pieces), cynotypes, reproductions of
glass negatives (3 volumes), prints (3
volumes and 500 items).

NEW HAMPSHIRE—HISTORY

MA —NEW ENGLAND HISTORIC
GENEALOGICAL SOCIETY, Library, 101
Newbury St, Boston, 02116. Ralph J
Crandell, Dir
Holdings: Vols (250,000) Mss Maps
Microforms Pix
Notes: New England genealogy. Especially
strong Massachusetts, Maine, and New
Hampshire, although all states are well
represented, as are the relevancies of each
subject listed in this volume with regard to
British antecedent and contemporary history.
Special strengths in local history and
biography, obituaries, etc, incl parish
registers, censuses, British and American.
3125 linear ft of mss.

MA —OLD STURBRIDGE VILLAGE,
Research Library, Sturbridge, 01566.
Theresa Rini Percy, Librn
Holdings: Cat Microforms
Notes: To 1900.

NH —NEW HAMPSHIRE HISTORICAL
SOCIETY, Manuscripts Library, 30 Park St,
Concord, 03301. Thomas E Camden, Cur
Budget: ($12,500)
Notes: Photocopying of individual items
only. Consultation of original mss materials
strongly encouraged. Mss and books related
to New Hampshire history. Especially strong
in politics, particularly during the post-Civil
War 19th century and the early 20th
century. Highlights: Mason Weare Tappan
Papers, Austin Pike Papers, Charles
Marseilles Papers, Jacob H Gallinger Papers,
James O Lyford Papers and George H
Moses Papers. Also papers of many other
New Hampshire people, among them--John
Badger Bachelder, Josiah Bartlett, Moody
Bedel, Timothy Bedel, Mary Baker Eddy,
Joseph A Gilmore, John Hatch George,
Isaac Hill, John Langdon, Jeremiah Mason,
Charles Sanger Mellen, John Fabyan Parrott,
Nathaniel Peabody, William Plumer,
Lorenzo Sabine, Jean Joseph Marie Toscan,
Robert W Upton, John Wentworth and Levi
Woodbury. The records of the Dover (New
Hampshire) Manufacturing Company;
650account books, most of which were kept
by general merchants in New Hampshire
during the 18th and 19th centuries; town
records, mostly before 1825, for approx 230
New Hampshire towns; and military records
and orderly books relating to New
Hampshire military units of the 18th and
19th centuries (French & Indian War
through the Civil War). About 500,000 ms
pieces, 4000 books, 1000 maps. Two million
items.

NH —NEW HAMPSHIRE STATE LIBRARY,
20 Park St, Concord, 03301. Shirley G
Adamovich, Librn
Holdings: Vols (683,015) Cat Mss Maps
Phonorecords 16mm Films Filmstrips
Microforms
Budget: ($124,119)
Notes: Microfilm holdings of early NH town

records, and legislative journals of colonial
and early state periods; laws of the US and
all states and territories from the time of
their settlement or organization; law library
collection of 72,000 volumes; NH state
documents, earliest to present; NH imprints.

NH —DOVER PUBLIC LIBRARY, 73 Locust
St, Dover, 03820. Donald K Mullen, Librn
Holdings: Cat Mss Maps Pix Microforms
Notes: Collection contains a variety of New
Hampshire records, clippings, town histories,
genealogies, Quaker Meeting House records
to the late 18th century. Local newspapers
to early 19th century.

NH —UNIVERSITY OF NEW HAMPSHIRE,
Dimond Library, Durham, 03824. Barbara A
White, Special Collections Librn
Holdings: Vols 20,000 Cat Mss Maps Pix
Slides Phonorecords
Budget: $1000

NH —KEENE STATE COLLEGE, Wallace E
Mason Library, 229 Main St, Keene, 03431.
Edward A Scott, Librn; Clifford Mead,
Special Collections Librn
Holdings: Vols (2000) Cat Mss Maps Pix
Audiotapes Microforms
Budget: ($7500)
Notes: New Hampshire history, genealogy,
authors, imprints (especially Keene
imprints), Keene State College materials, and
newspapers (microfilm).

NH —PORTSMOUTH ATHENAEUM, 9
Market Sq, Box 848, Portsmouth, 03801.
Joseph P Copley, Cur
Holdings: Vols Cat Mss
Notes: Incl Larkin Papers, 1758-1798 (235
items); papers of Daniel and John Peirce, ca
1730-1800 (115 items); and papers of NH
Fire and Marine Insurance Co, 1803-1823
(1800 items). Also contains information
relating to shipping, biography, government,
printed mss, and military (1690-present).

NH —STRAWBERY BANKE, Thayer
Cumings Historical Reference Library,
Portsmouth, 03801. Nicole R Osborn, Librn
Holdings: Vols (2850) Cat Mss Maps Pix
Microforms
Budget: ($1900)
Notes: The Library is a small, highly
specialized library with holdings in American
art, architecture and decorative arts. The
collection is especially strong in the
American decorative arts, with additional
concentration in European decorative arts.
In addition, the collection contains books on
American painting, American architecture,
archaeology, technology, maritime history
and boatbuilding, landscape gardening and
design, as well as books on local and
regional history and social and material
culture of the 17th-19th centuries. Collection
of mss microfilm and documents is related to
important properties and personages of
Portsmouth and the surrounding area. Incl
over 2000 photographs of Portsmouth in
early 1900's.

NEW HAMPSHIRE—IMPRINTS

NH —UNIVERSITY OF NEW HAMPSHIRE,
Dimond Library, Durham, 03824. Barbara A
White, Special Collections Librn
Holdings: 800 Vols
Notes: The Lewis M Stark, '29, Collection.
Stark was head of the Rare Book Division,
New York Public Library, 1947-1972.

NH —DARTMOUTH COLLEGE, Baker
Memorial Library, Hanover, 03755.
Holdings: Cat
Notes: Noncirculating.

NH —KEENE STATE COLLEGE, Wallace E
Mason Library, 229 Main St, Keene, 03431.
Edward A Scott, Librn; Clifford Mead,
Special Collections Librn
Holdings: Vols (2000) Cat Mss Maps Pix
Audiotapes Microforms
Budget: ($7500)
Notes: New Hampshire history, genealogy,
authors, imprints (especially Keene
imprints), Keene State College materials, and
newspapers (microfilm).

NEW HAMPSHIRE—PICTURES,
ILLUSTRATIONS, ETC.

NH —NEW HAMPSHIRE HISTORICAL
SOCIETY, Library, 30 Park St, Concord,

03301. William Copeley, Assoc Librn
Holdings: Uncat Pix
Budget: ($9000)
Notes: 20,000 pictures incl views of New
Hampshire towns, New Hampshire buildings
and photographs of New Hampshire
notables. Incl stereoscopic views and
postcards.

NH —STRAWBERY BANKE, Thayer
Cumings Historical Reference Library,
Portsmouth, 03801. Nicole R Osborn, Librn
Holdings: Vols (2850) Cat Mss Maps Pix
Microforms
Budget: ($1900)
Notes: The Library is a small, highly
specialized library with holdings in American
art, architecture and decorative arts. The
collection is especially strong in the
American decorative arts, with additional
concentration in European decorative arts.
In addition, the collection contains books on
American painting, American architecture,
archaeology, technology, maritime history
and boatbuilding, landscape gardening and
design, as well as books on local and
regional history and social and material
culture of the 17th-19th centuries. Collection
of mss microfilm and documents is related to
important properties and personages of
Portsmouth and the surrounding area. Incl
over 2000 photographs of Portsmouth in
early 1900's.

NEW HAMPSHIRE—POLITICS AND
GOVERNMENT

ME —MARGARET CHASE SMITH
LIBRARY CENTER, Skowhegan, 04976.
James C MacCampbell, Dir
Notes: Papers of Senator Margaret Chase
Smith; considerable on Senator Joseph
McCarthy.

NH —NEW HAMPSHIRE HISTORICAL
SOCIETY, Library, 30 Park St, Concord,
03301. William Copeley, Assoc Librn
Holdings: Cat Mss Pix Audiotapes 16mm
Films
Notes: Perkins Bass, lawyer, US
Representative and Republican politician of
NH. 60 linear feet of correspondence,
speeches, press releases, scrapbooks, photos,
memorabilia relating to public career 1935-
62. Register available.

NH —UNIVERSITY OF NEW HAMPSHIRE,
Dimond Library, Durham, 03824. Barbara A
White, Special Collections Librn
Notes: Senatorial papers, Thomas J
McIntyre, (D-NH, 1962-78), incl
correspondence, speeches, legislation, voting
records, campaign materials, reports to New
Hampshire, and other papers dealing with
the state.

NEW HAMPSHIRE AUTHORS see
Authors, New Hampshire

NEW HAMPSHIRE FIRE AND
MARINE INSURANCE COMPANY

NH —PORTSMOUTH ATHENAEUM, 9
Market Sq, Box 848, Portsmouth, 03801.
Joseph P Copley, Cur
Notes: Incl Larkin Papers, 1758-1798 (235
items); papers of Daniel and John Peirce, ca
1730-1800 (115 items); and papers of NH
Fire and Marine Insurance Co, 1803-1823
(1800 items).

NEW HAMPSHIRE NEWSPAPERS see
Newspapers, New Hampshire

NEW HARMONY, INDIANA

IL —UNIVERSITY OF ILLINOIS,
URBANA/CHAMPAIGN, Library, Illinois
Historical Survey Library, 1408 W Gregory
Dr, 1A Library, Urbana, 61801.
Holdings: Vols 50 Cat Mss Maps Pix
Microforms
Notes: Communitarianism in America. The
ms material, contained in 30 separate
collections (10 cubic feet), concentrates on
the period 1840-70. It incl correspondence,
records, minutes, ledgers and diaries.
Communal societies such as Bishop Hill,

NEW HARMONY, INDIANA (cont.)

Brook Farm, New Harmony, the North American Phalanx and the Sodus Bay Phalanx are represented. Among the correspondents are Albert Brisbane, Parke Godwin, Sarah Grimke, Richard Owen, Robert Owen, Robert Dale Owen, and George Ripley. Numerous pictures. Guide to the collections published in 1976.

IN —INDIANA STATE UNIVERSITY, EVANSVILLE, Library, 8600 University Blvd, Evansville, 47712. Gina R Walker, Acting Archivist
Holdings: Vols (120) Cat Mss
Notes: Communal societies, past and present. Secondary sources on historic communes; correspondence with, and brochures and newsletters concerning, contemporary communes.

IN —INDIANA HISTORICAL SOCIETY, Library, 315 W Ohio St, Indianapolis, 46202. Robert K O'Neill, Dir
Holdings: Cat Mss Maps Pix Slides Microforms

PA —PENNSYLVANIA DIV OF ARCHIVES & MANUSCRIPTS, State Archives, PO Box 1026, Harris, 17108. Roland M Baumann, Chief, History & Museums
Holdings: Vols (3000) // Uncat Mss Maps Pix
Budget: ($40,000)
Notes: The Harmony Society (1785-1905), a German communistic and spiritual community, which immigrated to the US in 1805 and established their community in Harmony, Pennsylvania, moved to New Harmony, Indiana, and returned to Pennsylvania to set up the town of Economy, 20 miles north of Pittsburgh on the Ohio River. The Harmonists had a vast impact on the economy of the areas in which they lived. They were involved in agriculture, manufacturing and investing. 300,000 cu ft.

NEW HAVEN, CONNECTICUT—HISTORY

CT —NEW HAVEN COLONY HISTORICAL SOCIETY, Whitney Library, 114 Whitney Ave, New Haven, 06510. M Ottilia Koel, Librn & Cur of Mss
Holdings: Vols 25,000 Cat Mss Maps Pix Microforms
Notes: 25,000 printed books and pamphlets; ca 15,000 linear feet of manuscript material including historic manuscripts, records of education, maritime and harbor industry, private papers, business and family records; 40,000 photographic images; maps and microforms relating to the early settlement and subsequent history of New Haven and vicinity.

CT —YALE UNIVERSITY, Box 1603A, Yale Station, New Haven, 06520.

NEW HUMANISTS

OH —SAINT GREGORY SEMINARY, ATHENAEUM OF OHIO, 6616 Beechmont Ave, Cincinnati, 45230. Sister Loretto Driscoll, Librn
Holdings: // Mss
Notes: Letters, literary mss, reviews, reprints, research notes of Robert Shafer, English scholar, author, professor; active in "New Humanism." His name is frequently found in literature among that group of men known as the "new humanists" in the late twenties and early thirties. He is best known as the author of *From Beowulf to Thomas Hardy,* one of the first English literature survey texts, used for many years in college courses. An unpublished biography and guide to the collection is available for users. (A similar collection of materials is owned by the Univeristy of Wyoming.)

NEW JERSEY

NJ —SOMERSET COUNTY LIBRARY, Northbridge & Vogt Dr, Box 6700, Bridgewater, 08807. Elizabeth Griesbach, Head Reference Librn
Holdings: Vols (2500) Cat Mss Maps Pix

Audiotapes
Notes: Historical and modern history; state (NJ) depository documents; juvenile collection; New Jersey periodicals; vertical files (26 drawers); and landmark survey on each county municipality. Separate catalog in New Jersey Room. Restricted use; noncirculating.

NJ —ENGLEWOOD LIBRARY, 31 Engle St, Englewood, 07631. N E Rhoades, Reference Librn
Holdings: Vols 1120 Cat Maps

NJ —LYNDHURST PUBLIC LIBRARY, Valley Brook Ave, Lyndhurst, 07071. Rhoda Portugal, Dir
Holdings: Vols 450 Cat Maps Pix Slides Audiotapes Videotapes Filmstrips Microforms

NJ —BURLINGTON COUNTY LIBRARY, W Woodlane Rd, Mount Holly, 08060. Donna H Sereduk, Librn
Holdings: Vols 2000 Cat Mss Maps Pix Slides Audiotapes Microforms
Notes: New Jersey Documents Depository Collection. Also incl postcards and newspapers.

NJ —SUSSEX COUNTY LIBRARY, Rd 3, Box 76, Newton, 07860. Judith Gessel, Reference Librn
Holdings: Cat Maps Slides 16mm Films Filmstrips
Notes: The Sussex County Area Reference Library is one of several locations which were named repositories for materials related to the restudy of the Tocks Island Lake Project. The items in the repository were distributed by the Delaware River Basin Commision. Collection incl study-related hearing transcripts, public notices, press clippings, correspondence, and reports of concern to the Delaware Water Gap National Recreation Area/Tocks Island Area. The Tocks Island Regional Advisory Council, when disbanded, presented its library to the Sussex County Library in 1974. The collection incl reports, surveys, maps, slides, and other materials collected or produced by TIRAC since 1965.

NJ —PLAINFIELD PUBLIC LIBRARY, Eighth St at Park Ave, Plainfield, 07060. Thomas H Ballard, Dir
Holdings: Vols (2000) Cat Mss Maps Pix Slides Audiotapes Microforms
Notes: A New Jersey State Document Depository Library. There is also a separate collection of approx 1500 New Jersey documents and periodicals. Approx 3000 vols on every aspect of New Jersey.

NJ —ROSELLE FREE PUBLIC LIBRARY, Fourth Ave & Chestnut St, Roselle, 07203. Evelyn N Olson, Dir
Notes: Incl 793 books and 679 pamphlets, pictures and mss.

NJ —TRENTON STATE COLLEGE, Roscoe L West Library, Pennington Rd, PO Box 940, Trenton, 08625. Paul A DuBois, Dir
Holdings: Vols 2500 Cat

NJ —WILLIAM PATERSON COLLEGE OF NEW JERSEY, Sarah Byrd Askew Library, 300 Pompton Rd, Wayne, 07470. Robert Lopresti, Librn
Holdings: Vols 1200 Cat Maps
Notes: Laws of New Jersey, 1703 to date. Selective bibliography of the collection: Glen Bencivengo and Amy Jobe, *From Point to Cape* (NJ Hist Commission 1982).

NJ —MONMOUTH COLLEGE, Murry & Leonie Guggenheim Memorial Library, New Jersey Collection, West Long Branch, 07764. Audrey K Wilson, Librn
Holdings: Vols (3025) Cat Maps Pix Microforms
Budget: ($1000)
Notes: Espec Monmouth County region. Incl periodicals, pamphlets, clippings. New Jersey Documents Depository. Picture collection, incl pictures of theatre personalities who came to this popular summer resort. Weather records kept by William Martin and his father at Long Branch, 1909-1963. Collection noncirculating.

NEW JERSEY—DESCRIPTION AND TRAVEL—VIEWS

NJ —RUTGERS, THE STATE UNIVERSITY OF NEW JERSEY, Alexander Library,

Special Collections and Archives, College Ave & Huntington St, New Brunswick, 08903. Ronald L Becker, Cur of Manuscripts and Rare Books
Notes: Over 18,000 postal cards, some from 1900; about 10,000 depict New Jersey scenes.

NEW JERSEY—GENEALOGY

FL —ORLANDO PUBLIC LIBRARY, Local History & Genealogy Dept, 100 Block of Central Ave, Orlando, 32806. Eileen B Willis, Librn
Notes: Strong collection in local genealogy materials on Mass, NY, Va, Ga, and Florida. Contains exceptional holdings on all New England States, Penn, and NJ.
See also entry under Genealogy - Collections.

NJ —ATLANTIC CITY FREE PUBLIC LIBRARY, Illinois & Pacific Aves, Atlantic City, 08401. Paul Nee, Adult Serv Librn
Holdings: Vols 2000 Cat
Notes: See *Colonial Genealogist,* April 1971, pp 256-57.

NJ —BURLINGTON COUNTY HISTORICAL SOCIETY, Delia Biddle Pugh Library, 457 High St, Burlington, 08016. Carol Lipinsky, Librn
Holdings: Vols (2000) Cat Mss Maps Pix
Notes: History of Burlington County, NJ; West Jersey, NJ, also genealogy-mostly Burlington County families. Books, pix and vertical files cataloged.

NJ —MONMOUTH COUNTY HISTORICAL ASSOCIATION, Library, 70 Court St, Freehold, 07728. Loretta M Zwolak, Archivist & Librn
Holdings: Vols (6500) Cat Mss Maps Pix Slides Microforms
Notes: Especially Monmouth County area. See *Monmouth County Historical Association Bulletin,* vol 1, no 2 July 1948, p 23-48. Allaire Papers (Howell Works); Battle of Monmouth; Mott Family Papers; North American Phalanx; Philip Freneau; Steamship Coll.

NJ —GLASSBORO STATE COLLEGE, Savitz Library, Stewart Room, Glassboro, 08028. Clara Kirner, Special Collection Librn
Holdings: Cat Mss
Notes: Emphasis on southern and central New Jersey. 5000 misc ms items, 500 deeds, 45 linear ft of bks and folders. Papers of Browning, Falkenburg, Haines, Hayes, Hosell, Inskeep, Ladd, Leaming, Lippincott, and Somers families. Journal of Elizabeth Haddon. Journals and ledgers of Samuel Mickle. Complete file of genealogical notes made on over 1000 families by Mrs Lois Satterthwaite.

NJ —HISTORICAL SOCIETY OF HADDONFIELD, 343 King's Highway, E, Haddonfield, 08033. Doug Rauschenberger, Librn
Holdings: Vols 6000 Cat Mss Maps Pix Slides Audiotapes Microforms
Notes: New Jersey, especially history of the Haddonfield area, incl special material on Quakers in Haddonfield. Local newspapers on microfilm from 1920. Property deeds; local genealogies.

NJ —BURLINGTON COUNTY LIBRARY, W Woodlane Rd, Mount Holly, 08060. Donna H Sereduk, Librn
Holdings: Vols 150 Mss
Notes: Incl Charts, church and cemetary records, and vital statistic records.

NJ —NEW JERSEY HISTORICAL SOCIETY, Library and Museum, 230 Broadway, Newark, 07104. Joan C Hull, Exec Dir; Barbara S Irwin, Library Dir; Alan R Fraser, Cur
Holdings: Vols 20,000 Cat Mss Maps Microforms
Budget: ($100,000)

NJ —PISCATAWAY TOWNSHIP LIBRARIES, John F Kennedy Library, 500 Hoes Lane, Piscataway, 08854. Fran Burke, Head of Adult Services
Holdings: Vols (75) Cat Mss Pix Audiotapes
Notes: History of Piscataway Area.

NJ —PLAINFIELD PUBLIC LIBRARY, Eighth St at Park Ave, Plainfield, 07060.

NEW JERSEY—GENEALOGY (cont.)

Thomas H Ballard, Dir
Notes: A New Jersey State Document
Depository Library. There is also a separate
collection of approx 1500 New Jersey
documents and periodicals. Approx 3000
vols on every aspect of New Jersey.

NJ —ATLANTIC COUNTY HISTORICAL
LIBRARY, 907 Shore Rd, Somers Point,
08244. Elaine Abrahamson, Dir
Holdings: Vols 1000 Cat Mss Maps Pix
Slides Microforms
Notes: Emphasis on local history.

NJ —GLOUCESTER COUNTY
HISTORICAL SOCIETY LIBRARY, 17
Hunter St, PO Box 409, Woodbury, 08096.
Edith E Hoelle, Librn
Holdings: Cat Mss
Notes: Nicholson Collection of Genealogical
records researched and accumulated by
Anne L Nicholson of St Davids,
Pennsylvania. Pertains to South Jersey-
Delaware Valley familes and is
predominantly concerned with research into
the 17th and 18th centuries (approx 15 cubic
feet).

NY —NEW YORK GENEALOGICAL &
BIOGRAPHICAL SOCIETY, Library, 122
E 58 St, New York, 10022. James P
Gregory, Librn
Holdings: Vols 63,500 Cat Mss Maps
Microforms
Notes: The Society has copied and has in its
ms collections a great many church records
from all parts of New York State and several
from adjacent states; and many very valuable
ms genealogies and family Bible records
which have never been published. The
Society library is noncirculating and one of
the principal genealogical reference libraries
in the country. It has accumulated in its
collections approximately 63 thousand vols
on genealogy, local history and biography. In
addition it has a rapidly expanding microfilm
division which presently numbers over 2000
reels and keeps four microfilm readers in
continuous use.

NY —ONONDAGA COUNTY PUBLIC
LIBRARY, Local History and Genealogy
Dept, 335 Montgomery St, Syracuse, 13202.
Gerald James Parsons, Head
Holdings: Vols (30,000) Cat Mss Maps Pix
Microforms
Budget: ($12,000)
Notes: Collection of local history and
genealogy covers primarily Syracuse,
Onondaga County, New York State and the
northeast, ie, New England, New Jersey and
Pennsylvania.

NEW JERSEY—HISTORY

NJ —ATLANTIC CITY FREE PUBLIC
LIBRARY, Illinois & Pacific Aves, Atlantic
City, 08401. Paul Nee, Adult Serv Librn
Holdings: Cat Maps
Notes: Incl 2000 postcards.

NJ —SOMERSET COUNTY LIBRARY,
Northbridge & Vogt Dr, Box 6700,
Bridgewater, 08807. Elizabeth Griesbach,
Head Reference Librn
Holdings: Vols (2500) Cat Mss Maps Pix
Audiotapes
Notes: Historical and modern history; state
(NJ) depository documents; juvenile
collection; New Jersey periodicals; vertical
files (26 drawers); and landmark survey on
each county municipality. Separate catalog
in New Jersey Room. Restricted use;
noncirculating.

NJ —BURLINGTON COUNTY
HISTORICAL SOCIETY, Delia Biddle
Pugh Library, 457 High St, Burlington,
08016. Carol Lipinsky, Librn
Holdings: Vols (2000) Cat Mss Maps Pix
Notes: History of Burlington County, NJ;
West Jersey, NJ, also genealogy-mostly
Burlington County families. Books, pix and
vertical files cataloged.

NJ —JAMES H JOHNSON MEMORIAL
LIBRARY, 670 Popular Ave, Deptford
Township, 08096. Lois B Greene, Library
Dir

NJ —SUSSEX COUNTY LIBRARY, Franklin
Area Branch, 103 Main St, Franklin, 07416.
Holdings: Uncat Mss Maps Pix
Notes: The gift of Franklin native Fred J

Stephens, the History of Mining in Northern
New Jersey Collection will be housed at the
Franklin Area Branch of the Sussex County
Library. Extensive manuscript collection incl
reports, photos, maps, books, pamphlets,
periodicals, and correspondence amassed
during years of research.

NJ —MONMOUTH COUNTY HISTORICAL
ASSOCIATION, Library, 70 Court St,
Freehold, 07728. Loretta M Zwolak,
Archivist & Librn
Holdings: Vols (6500) Cat Mss Maps Pix
Slides Microforms
Budget: ($15,800)
Notes: Especially Monmouth County area.
See Monmouth County Historical
Association Bulletin, vol 1, no 2 July 1948, p
23-48. Allaire Papers (Howell Works); Battle
of Monmouth; Mott Family Papers; North
American Phalanx; Philip Freneau;
Steamship Collection.

NJ —GLASSBORO STATE COLLEGE,
Savitz Library, Stewart Room, Glassboro,
08028. Clara Kirner, Special Collection
Librn
Holdings: Vols 3000 Cat Maps Pix
Notes: Incl county and local histories, major
New Jersey reference works. Periodicals,
rare imprints from the 1760s. Mss incl
Provincial legislative acts, 1740-1775 (39),
State Legislative Acts, 1776-1787 (134),
Diaries of S Mickle, etc. Predominantly
Colonial and and Revolutionary period.

NJ —HISTORICAL SOCIETY OF
HADDONFIELD, 343 King's Highway, E,
Haddonfield, 08033. Doug Rauschenberger,
Librn
Holdings: Microforms
Notes: New Jersey, especially history of the
Haddonfield area, incl special material on
Quakers in Haddonfield. Local newspapers
on microfilm from 1920. Property deeds;
local genealogies.

NJ —STEVENS INSTITUTE OF
TECHNOLOGY, Samuel C Williams
Library, Castle Point Sta, Hoboken, 07030.
Jane G Hartye, Special Collections Librn
Holdings: Vols (250) Cat Pix Microforms
Budget: ($1500)
Notes: Col John Stevens and his sons Robert
Livingston Stevens and Edwin Augustus
Stevens. They were responsible for the first
steam locomotives and railroad; they were
involved in shipbuilding, building the
"Juliana," the "Phoenix" and ferries. We have
a huge amount of uncataloged data on the
"Stevens Battery." The Stevens family played
an extremely important role in developing
the City of Hoboken; Edwin Augustus
Stevens established Stevens Institute of
Technology. Through the Stevens family, we
have much historical data on the City of
Hoboken and the State of New Jersey. Our
collection includes microfilm of the Stevens
Papers and of Hoboken.

NJ —NEW JERSEY HISTORICAL
SOCIETY, Library and Museum, 230
Broadway, Newark, 07104. Joan C Hull,
Exec Dir; Barbara S Irwin, Library Dir; Alan
R Fraser, Cur
Holdings: Vols (45,000) Cat Mss Maps Pix
Microforms
Budget: ($100,000)
Notes: Partially described in: Shelley, Fred,
Guide to the Manuscript Collection of the
New Jersey Historical Society, 1957 (out of
print). For mss materials, see Morris &
Skemer, Guide to the Manuscript
Collections of the New Jersey Historical
Society, 1979. Also printed and manuscript
collections incl church registries.

NJ —RUTGERS, THE STATE UNIVERSITY
OF NEW JERSEY, Alexander Library,
Special Collections and Archives, College
Ave & Huntington St, New Brunswick,
08903. Ronald L Becker, Cur of Manuscripts
and Rare Books
Holdings: Mss Maps Pix
Notes: Large, active collection in all
categories of research material, incl mss,
pictures, maps; many rare items.

NJ —PASSAIC COUNTY HISTORICAL
SOCIETY, Lamhurt Castle, Valley Rd,
Paterson, 07503. Helen D Hamilton, Dir
Holdings: Vols (5000) Cat Mss Maps Pix
Notes: Material on the Society for the

Establishment of Useful Manufacturing
(founded) by Alexander Hamilton, papers
relating to John Holland, who developed the
submarine, the industrial magnates of the
area who were active in the manufacture of
locomotives, Colt revolvers, and textiles,
especially silk.

NJ —PISCATAWAY TOWNSHIP
LIBRARIES, John F Kennedy Library, 500
Hoes Lane, Piscataway, 08854. Fran Burke,
Head of Adult Services
Holdings: Vols (75) Cat Mss Pix Audiotapes
Notes: History of Piscataway Area.

NJ —EMANUEL EINSTEIN PUBLIC
LIBRARY, 333 Wanaque Ave, Pompton
Lakes, 07442. John Donovan, Librn
Holdings: Vols 202 Cat Maps
Notes: The Van Orden Historical Collection
incl much of New Jersey archives, some
geological surveys, New Jersey museum
reports (early 20th century), histories of
New Jersey. Also histories of counties,
towns, churches, etc. Incl 18th-19th century
maps.

NJ —HISTORICAL SOCIETY OF
PRINCETON, NEW JERSEY, 158 Nassau
St, Princeton, 08542. Ann C Johanson, Librn
Holdings: Vols (2000) Cat Mss Maps Pix
Slides Audiotapes Microforms
Notes: History of Princeton, New Jersey.
Incl 80 linear ft of mss, 100 maps, 1000
pictures and 10,000 glass plate negatives.

NJ —FAIRLEIGH DICKINSON
UNIVERSITY, Messler Library, New Jersey
Room, 207 Montross Ave, Rutherford,
07070. Catharine M Fogarty, Librn
Holdings: Vols (5812) Cat Mss Maps
Microforms
Budget: $2000
Notes: Separate card catalog; also,
Hackensack-Ridgewood Local History
Service. Manuscript-Microfilm Project. A
Guide to Manuscripts on Microfilm from the
Collections of Bergen County Historical
Society, River Edge; Johnson Free Public
Library, Hackensack; New Jersey Room,
Fairleigh Dickinson University, Rutherford;
Ridgewood Public Library, Rev Bicentennial
ed (Hackensack, NJ: Johnson Free Public
Library, 1976). Collection is a New Jersey
state documents depository containing over
4000 documents; 965 documents of New
Jersey local governments.

NJ —ATLANTIC COUNTY HISTORICAL
LIBRARY, 907 Shore Rd, Somers Point,
08244. Elaine Abrahamson, Dir
Holdings: Vols 1000 Cat Mss Maps Pix
Slides Microforms
Notes: Emphasis on local history.

NJ —SETON HALL UNIVERSITY
MUSEUM, Archaeological Research Center,
S Orange Ave, South Orange, 07079.
Herbert C Craft, Dir
Holdings: Vols (750) Cat
Notes: Primarily books and periodicals
related to New Jersey and northeastern
states prehistory and archaeology.

NJ —TRENTON FREE PUBLIC LIBRARY,
120 Academy St, Trenton, 08608. Nan
Wright, Supervising Reference Librn
Holdings: Vols 3300 Cat Mss Maps Pix
Slides Microforms
Notes: Incl 4400 cataloged pamphlets of
Trentoniana. 169 New Jersey periodicals
currently received; 21 file drawers of
clippings and pamphlets; photographs and
slides. 250 mss; maps and prints.

NJ —WILLIAM PATERSON COLLEGE OF
NEW JERSEY, Sarah Byrd Askew Library,
300 Pompton Rd, Wayne, 07470. Robert
Lopresti, Librn
Notes: The professional papers of William
Paterson, 1745-1806, second governor of
New Jersey. Incl more than a thousand
letters, ledgers, and legal papers, most of
which were written in Paterson's own hand
during his political life and in his legal
practice. Bibliography of cataloged items
available.

NJ —GLOUCESTER COUNTY
HISTORICAL SOCIETY LIBRARY, 17
Hunter St, PO Box 409, Woodbury, 08096.
Edith E Hoelle, Librn
Holdings: Cat Microforms
Notes: New Jersey history, especially
Gloucester, Camden, and Atlantic counties,

NEW JERSEY—HISTORY (cont.)

1686-1900. Incl 1050 microfilm reels concerning deeds, mortgages, wills, etc, of Gloucester County, 1787-1900; bound county newspapers, 1819-1940; documents of the Revolutionary War and the Civil War; federal and state (New Jersey) census records, 1830-1905; New Jersey mortality schedules, 1850-1880; and Court records. Extensive program of publishing on Southern New Jersey. Some 75,000 documents pertaining to the court proceedings from 1686-1900. Incl slave records, Revolutionary War claims; Whiskey Rebellion enlistments of 1792, 1793; election returns, Civil War records, tavern licenses, town officers, road petitions and surveys; also affidavits, bonds, appeals, writs, indictments and railroad records, etc.

NY —HOLLAND SOCIETY OF NEW YORK, Library, 122 E 58 St, New York, 10022. Linda Rolufs, Librn
Notes: Specializes in New Netherland (New York, New Jersey, Delaware) history during the Dutch period, materials on the Dutch Reformed Church, and Dutch-American family genealogy.

NY —ONONDAGA COUNTY PUBLIC LIBRARY, Local History and Genealogy Dept, 335 Montgomery St, Syracuse, 13202. Gerald James Parsons, Head
Holdings: Vols (30,000) Cat Mss Maps Pix Microforms
Budget: ($12,000)
Notes: Collection of local history and genealogy covers primarily Syracuse, Onondaga County, New York State and the northeast, ie, New England, New Jersey and Pennsylvania.

PA —FRIENDS HISTORICAL LIBRARY OF SWARTHMORE COLLEGE, Swarthmore, 19081. J William Frost, Dir
Holdings: Vols (35,000) Cat Mss Pix Microforms
Notes: Library's collection contain information on the history and doctrine of the Society of Friends, Quaker contributions to literature, science, business, education, and government, plus their reform efforts in peace, Indian rights, women's rights, and abolition of slavery. Library is an official depository of the records of the Philadelphia Yearly Meeting and holds on microfilm records of most meetings affiliated with New York Yearly Meeting; thus the archives of Friends meetings in New Jersey are available either in the original manuscript or on microfilm. Among the more than 250 mss collections are several which concern New Jersey Quaker leaders and Quaker families.

NEW JERSEY—INDUSTRIES

NJ —RUTGERS, THE STATE UNIVERSITY OF NEW JERSEY, Institute of Management & Labor Relations, Ryders Lane & Clifton Ave, New Brunswick, 08903. Bernard F Downey, Librn
Holdings: Vols (18,530) Cat Slides Phonorecords 16mm Films Filmstrips
Budget: ($7300)
Notes: Separate card catalog for collection. Particular emphasis on dispute settlement. Strong collection on public sector labor relations, emphasizing New Jersey publications.

NEW JERSEY—MAPS

NJ —RUTGERS, THE STATE UNIVERSITY OF NEW JERSEY, Alexander Library, Special Collections and Archives, College Ave & Huntington St, New Brunswick, 08903. Ronald L Becker, Cur of Manuscripts and Rare Books
Holdings: Maps
Notes: More than half (over 5000) of the collection of maps in printed, flat ms and roll form, represents New Jersey, although there are maps depicting all parts of the world. Some pieces date from the 16th century. Incl are topographic, road, railroad, county, ward geological and historical maps. There are over 100 19th and early 20th century lithographic city views. Of special interest and quality are 16 framed maps dating between 1507 and 1777 which are the gift of the late I Robert Kriendler. All pieces in the map collection are accessible through department checklists (incl over 3000 maps).

NEW JERSEY—POLITICS AND GOVERNMENT

NJ —WILLIAM PATERSON COLLEGE OF NEW JERSEY, Sarah Byrd Askew Library, 300 Pompton Rd, Wayne, 07470. Robert Lopresti, Librn
Notes: The professional papers of William Paterson, 1745-1806, second governor of New Jersey. Incl more than a thousand letters, ledgers, and legal papers, most of which were written in Paterson's own hand during his political life and in his legal practice. Bibliography of cataloged items available.

NEW JERSEY MUSIC see Music, New Jersey

NEW JERSEY SEVENTH DAY BAPTISTS

†WI —SEVENTH DAY BAPTIST HISTORICAL SOCIETY, Library, 3120 Kennedy St, PO Box 1678, Janesville, 53547.
Holdings: Vols (600) Cat Mss Maps Pix
Notes: US Seventh Day Baptists Collection, incl records, letters. Established at Newport, Rhode Island, in 1971, this denomination is part of the Free-Church evangelical movement in America. The national and international headquarters of the Seventh Day Baptist denomination is located at Janesville, Wisconsin (formerly Plainfield, NJ). Also have records, publications, etc, of the denomination's mission in Shanghai, 1846-1950; further, materials (6 boxes) on the Church's work in Nyasaland (Malawi), 1895-1914, and then at a later period.

NEW JERUSALEM CHURCH

MD —JOHNS HOPKINS UNIVERSITY, Milton S Eisenhower Library, George Peabody Collection, 17 E Mt Vernon Place, Baltimore, 21201. Lyn Hart, Peabody Librn
Notes: Noncirculating.
MA —HARVARD UNIVERSITY LIBRARY, Widener Library, Cambridge, 02138.
Holdings: Cat

NEW LEFT

MI —MICHIGAN STATE UNIVERSITY, Libraries, Special Collections Div, East Lansing, 48824. Jannette Fiore, Librn
Holdings: Vols (10,500) Cat Mss
Notes: Published and unpublished material generated by (1) American left and right, 1900, (2) the New Left, 1969-1970, and (3) current left, right, and alternate life-style groups. (Supported by appropriate secondary material in the Research Library). Also have in microform radical pamphlet literature from the Tamiment Library (New York University), the Right Wing Collection of the University of Iowa, et al.
NC —UNIVERSITY OF NORTH CAROLINA, CHARLOTTE, J Murrey Atkins Library, UNCC Station, Charlotte, 28223. Robert F Brabham Jr, Special Collections Librn
Holdings: Cat Mss Pix
Notes: Incl pamphlets, newspapers, and ephemera published by various radical groups, 1960s and 1970s, based largely in the Midwest; also papers of T J Reddy, a member of the Charlotte 3, concerning civil rights, the Wilmington 10, and prison reforms.

NEW MEXICO

CA —UNIVERSITY OF CALIFORNIA, LOS ANGELES, William Andrews Clark Memorial Library, 2520 Cimarron St, Los Angeles, 90018.
Holdings: // Cat Mss
Notes: 18th and early 19th century mss, incl reports and correspondence on missions, Indians, New Mexico, Alta and Baja California.

NM —ALBUQUERQUE PUBLIC LIBRARY, 501 Copper Ave NW, Albuquerque, 87102. Alan B Clark, Dir
Holdings: Vols (4000) Cat Microforms Records Maps VF
Notes: Large collection of materials on all aspects of New Mexico history and cultures. In-house index accesses VF materials and local and regional periodicals. Special emphasis on Indians of New Mexico and northeastern Arizona, particularly the Navajo, Hopi, Pueblos and Apache. Reference copies of many works are housed at the Special Collections Library, 423 Central Ave NE, Albuquerque, NM 87102.

†NM —UNIVERSITY OF NEW MEXICO, Medical Center Library, Albuquerque, 87131. Beatrice Kovacs, Chief, Collections and Resource Development
Notes: Concern is health care and health services in New Mexico; medicine and medicine men of Indian tribes of the Southwest; and history of medicine and health in the Southwest.

UT —UNIVERSITY OF UTAH, Marriott Library, Special Collections, Salt Lake City, 84112. Gregory C Thompson, Cur

NEW MEXICO—DESCRIPTION AND TRAVEL—VIEWS

CA —POMONA PUBLIC LIBRARY, Special Collections, 625 S Garey Ave, PO Box 2271, Pomona, 91766. David Streeter, Librn
Holdings: Uncat Slides
Notes: Contains 550 lantern slides (mostly of California) and 4200 color 35mm transparencies of world travel, 1960s. Also, the Burton Frasher Postal Card Collection of 60,000 negatives and prints of California, Arizona, Colorado, New Mexico, Nevada, and Utah; 30,000 world views; 8000 California views. There are also world views in nearly 1000 stereophotographs.

NEW MEXICO—GENEALOGY

NM —ALBUQUERQUE PUBLIC LIBRARY, 423 Central Ave NE, Albuquerque, 87102. Laurel Drew, Librn
Holdings: Vols (5000) Cat Mss Maps Microforms Audiotapes
Notes: Collection of materials for genealogical research in the United States. Incl materials for New Mexico family research. Emphasis on New Mexico and on eastern US.

NEW MEXICO—HISTORY

CA —AZUSA PACIFIC COLLEGE, Marshburn Memorial Library, Citrus & Alosta, Azusa, 91702. Edward Peterman, Librn
Holdings: Vols (6000) Uncat
Budget: ($30,000)
Notes: Significant holdings in the George E Fullerton Library of Californiana and Western Americana.

MS —UNIVERSITY OF SOUTHERN MISSISSIPPI, William David McCain Graduate Library, Box 5148, Southern Sta, Hattiesburg, 39406.
Holdings: Cat Mss
Notes: Correspondence and records (1847-1892) relating to Alexander Melvorne Jackson's participation in the Mexican War, his service as Secretary of the State of the New Mexico Territory (1857-1861), and his participation in the Civil War on the side of the Confederacy. Among his correspondents were Albert Gallatin Brown, Reuben Davis, Miguel A Otero, Jacob Thompson, and John Ireland. Incl are photographs of Austin, Texas, ca 1890. 1.1 cubic feet holdings.

NM —ALBUQUERQUE PUBLIC LIBRARY, 423 Central Ave NE, Albuquerque, 87102. Laurel Drew, Librn
Holdings: Vols (6500) Cat Mss Maps Pix Audiotapes
Notes: All fields related to New Mexico. Special emphasis on Albuquerque and

NEW MEXICO—HISTORY (cont.)

vicinity. Additional holdings are at the Main Library, Albuquerque Public Library, 501 Copper Ave NW, Albuquerque, NM 87102.

NM —GALLUP PUBLIC LIBRARY, 115 W Hill Ave, Gallup, 87301. Octavia Fellin, Dir
Holdings: Vols 3000 Cat

NM —THOMAS BRANIGAN MEMORIAL LIBRARY, 200 E Picacho Ave, Las Cruces, 88001. Don Dresp, Dir
Notes: Helen P Caffey Collection (cat).

NM —NEW MEXICO HIGHLANDS UNIVERSITY, Donnelly Library, National Ave, Las Vegas, 87701. Karen Jaggers, Assoc Librn
Holdings: // Mss Maps Microforms
Notes: The outstanding collection is the Arrott Collection on Fort Union, New Mexico, 1851-1891. Other collections incl Spanish Archives, Mexican Archives, Archdiocese of Santa Fe, Archivo del Parral; New Mexico Land Grants.

NM —EASTERN NEW MEXICO UNIVERSITY, Golden Library, Special Collections, Portales, 88130. Mary Jo Walker, Special Collections Librn
Holdings: Cat Mss Pix Audiotapes
Notes: Incl 176 cataloged books by F Stanley (pseudonym of Catholic priest and historian Stanley Francis Louis Crocchiola), plus his collection of periodicals and books by other writers pertaining to southwestern history (particularly New Mexico and the Texas panhandle); 22.25 cubic ft of mss, correspondence files, photographs of F Stanley and others, and two oral history interviews with F Stanley. Unpublished register of collection available. Bio/ bibliography of F Stanley in preparation.

NM —ROSWELL PUBLIC LIBRARY, 301 N Pennsylvania Ave, Roswell, 88201. Sarah Beth Galloway, Library Dir
Holdings: Vols (2000) Cat Maps
Budget: $1500
Notes: Covers literature (fiction and nonfiction), history, biography, geography, of Oklahoma, Texas, Colorado, New Mexico and Arizona.

NM —MUSEUM OF NEW MEXICO, History Library, PO Box 2087, Santa Fe, 87503. Orlando Romero
Holdings: Vols 12,000 Cat Mss Maps Microforms
Budget: $64,000
Notes: History of the Southwest, emphasis on history of New Mexico, incl New Mexican newspapers. Restricted use; noncirculating. 2500 maps; 700 microforms.

TX —AMARILLO PUBLIC LIBRARY, 413 E Fourth, Amarillo, 79101. Mary Kay Snell, Librn
Holdings: Vols Cat Mss Maps Pix
Notes: The southwest collections incl materials on the history of Texas, Louisiana, New Mexico, Arkansas, Missouri and Kansas. General subjects covered incl overland journeys, early narratives, early biographies, Indian captivities, outlaws, US government reports, Mississippi and Ohio Rivers, the Mexican War, reports of Catholic missionaries, Niles Register, early publications, fur trade, western trails, Texas Rangers, sheriffs and Texas as a sovereign state, buffalo hunting, Indian wars, cowboys, the arrival of farmers, fences, and towns. Over 1600 items which incl books, documents, maps, mss, pamphlets, unpublished theses, interviews and photographs. The three major collections are the William Henry Bush Collection, the Laurence J Fitzsimon Collection and the Calendar of John L McCarty.

TX —UNIVERSITY OF TEXAS LIBRARIES, General Libraries, Barker Texas History Center, PO Box P, Austin, 78712. Don Carleton, Dir
Holdings: Vols (110,000) Cat Mss Maps Pix Slides Phonorecords Audiotapes Microforms
Notes: See description of collection under Texas--History.

TX —EL PASO PUBLIC LIBRARY, Southwest Collection, 501 N Oregon, El Paso, 79901. Mary A Sarber, Head
Holdings: Vols (12,000) Cat Mss Maps Pix
Budget: ($11,000)
Notes: Research collection includes rare

books and mss journals, vertical files, index to El Paso newspapers, microfilmed newspapers, photographs, and architectural plans. Separate catalog. Limited to materials on Texas, New Mexico, Arizona and Mexico. Special collections of material by and about Tom Lea Jr, and Carl Hertzog. Aultman Collection of photographs includes 3500 on El Paso Southwest and 2500 on Mexican Revolution. Cited in Lovelace, Lisa, "The Southwest Collection of the El Paso Public Library". *Great Plains Journal*, vol 2, no 2, pp 161-166; Aultman, Otis A *Photographs from the Border: The Otis A Aultman Collection,* El Paso Public Library Association, 1977.

TX —ECTOR COUNTY LIBRARY, Texas-Southwest History & Genealogy Dept, 321 W 5th St, Odessa, 79761. Jan Carter, Head
Holdings: Vols (8500) Cat Maps Pix
Budget: ($4000)
Notes: A card catalog of Texas-History; Southwest, New-History; Oklahoma-History is located in the Texas-Southwest History Dept. A card file by subject is a guide to vertical file materials and Texas, New Mexico, Oklahoma, Arizona periodicals. The Texas-History collection has reference, closed shelf, and circulating books.

UT —UTAH STATE UNIVERSITY, Merrill Library, Department of Special Collections & Archives, Logan, 84322. A J Simmonds, Curator; Jeanie F Simmonds, Archivist; Bradford R Cole, Mss Librn
Holdings: Vols 4000 Cat
Notes: Books pamphlets, manuscripts on the history of Arizona and New Mexico. Complete holding of the Wallace bibliography citations. All books Cat.

NEW MEXICO—MAPS

NM —US GEOLOGICAL SURVEY, Water Resources Division Library, Western Bank, 505 Marquette, Rm 714, Albuquerque, 87102. Janie S Jones, Librn
Notes: Primarily hydrology and geology of New Mexico. Incl 20,000 maps.

OK —TULSA CITY-COUNTY LIBRARY, Business & Technology Dept, 400 Civic Center, Tulsa, 74103. Craig Buthod, Head
Notes: Original General Land Office survey maps for the states of Arizona, Arkansas, Colorado, Illinois, Indiana, Idaho, Kansas, Michigan, Missouri, Montana, Nebraska, Nevada, New Mexico, North Dakota, Ohio, Oklahoma, South Dakota, Utah and Wyoming. Incomplete coverage of each state.

NEW MEXICO—PICTURES, ILLUSTRATIONS, ETC.

NM —MUSEUM OF NEW MEXICO, Photo Archives, Box 2087, Santa Fe, 87503. Arthur L Olivas, Cur; Richard Rudisill, Photo Historian
Holdings: Cat Pix Slides
Budget: ($9000)

Notes: 90,000 photographs, cataloged, and 1000 slides. Photographs may be ordered as research copies for set fees. Reproduction or publication requires written permission plus additional required fees. Incl. special groups of photographs, e.g. T. Harmon Parkhurst Collection-ca. 15,000 photos, 1915-1950, Southwest Indians, scenic views, town views; H. F. Robinson Collection-ca. 1000 items, ca. 1910-1920, Southwest Indians, esp. Hopi and Blackfoot; Ben Wittick Collection-ca. 1500 items, 1879-1903, Southwest Indians, military, town views. Many other of the important early photographers are represented, especially large collections of the work of G. C. Bennett, William H. Brown, Dana B. Chase, Edward S. Curtis, H. H. Dorman, Rev. J. C. Gullette, P. E. Harroun, William H. Jackson, Charles F. Lummis, Jesse L. Nussbaum, Henry A. Schmidt, and about a hundred others.

NEW MEXICO—POLITICS AND GOVERNMENT

AZ —NORTHERN ARIZONA UNIVERSITY, Special Collection Library, CU Box 6022, Flagstaff, 86011. Peter M Whiteley, Coordr/Archivist; William Mullane, Librn
Notes: Leonard Ritt Collection; county election data from Northern Arizona and New Mexico, collection for use in a study of Navajo voting patterns, 1950's-1970's.

NM —EASTERN NEW MEXICO UNIVERSITY, Golden Library, Special Collections, Portales, 88130. Mary Jo Walker, Special Collections Librn
Notes: Papers and files of the late Congressman Harold Runnels (D NMex).

NEW MEXICO NEWSPAPERS see Newspapers, New Mexico

NEW MEXICO SYMPHONY ORCHESTRA

NM —UNIVERSITY OF NEW MEXICO, Fine Arts Library, Fine Art Bldg, Albuquerque, 87131. James B Wright, Librn
Notes: Incl the archives of the New Mexico Symphony Orchestra. 6 linear ft.

NEW NETHERLANDS—HISTORY

NY —HOLLAND SOCIETY OF NEW YORK, Library, 122 E 58 St, New York, 10022. Linda Rolufs, Librn
Holdings: Vols (6000) Cat Mss
Notes: New York City history in the Dutch Period (New Netherlands); the Dutch Reformed Church; and Dutch-American family genealogy.

NY —NEW YORK HISTORICAL SOCIETY, Library, 170 Central Park W, New York, 10024. James Gregory, Librn
Holdings: Mss
Notes: Incl original mss, illustrative materials, etc.

NEW ORLEANS—CARNIVAL

LA —NEW ORLEANS PUBLIC LIBRARY, Louisiana Div & City Archives Dept, Louisiana History Collection, 219 Loyola Ave, New Orleans, 70140. Collin B Hamer Jr, Head
Holdings: Cat Mss Pix
Notes: The Carnival Collection incl 11,000 programs, costume designs and memorabilia relative to annual Mardi Gras festivities, 1852-date. Use is restricted to on-site research by adults.

LA —TULANE UNIVERSITY, Howard-Tilton Memorial Library, Special Collections Div, William Ransom Hogan Jazz Archive, 7001 Freret, New Orleans, 70118. Richard B Allen, Acting Cur; Alma D Williams, Assistant to the Cur
Holdings: Vols (100,000) Cat Mss Pix Slides Phonorecords Audiotapes Videotapes 16mm Films Microforms
Budget: ($90,000)
Notes: Jazz music and musicians. Outstanding collection. Music, history, etc. *See also* entry under Jazz

NEW ORLEANS—HISTORY

LA —HISTORIC NEW ORLEANS COLLECTION, 533 Royal St, New Orleans, 70130. Stanton M Frazar, Dir; Dode Platou, Chief Cur; Florence M Jumonville, Head Librn
Holdings: Vols (15,000) Cat Mss Maps Pix Microforms
Notes: Books, pamphlets, and vertical files covering all aspects of life pertaining to New Orleans, Louisiana, and the Lower Mississippi Valley. Our research facilities

NEW ORLEANS—HISTORY (cont.)

also include an archive and curatorial department. *A Guide to Research* is available.

LA —LOUISIANA STATE MUSEUM, Louisiana Historical Center, 400 Esplanade Ave, (Mailing add: 751 Chartres St, New Orleans, 70116). Edward F Haas, Chief Cur
Holdings: Vols 2000 Cat Pix Slides Phonorecords Audiotapes
Notes: New Orleans Jazz Museum and Archives Collection. Donated to the Louisiana State Museum by the New Orleans Jazz in 1977. It was formerly a private museum sponsored by the Jazz Club and housed at 833 Conti St, New Orleans, La 70130. Emphasis is New Orleans jazz, incl 8000 pieces of sheet music; 12,000 phonorecords; 15,000 pictures; 1000 slides; and 1000 audiotapes. A guide to the collection is in preparation.

LA —NEW ORLEANS PUBLIC LIBRARY, Louisiana Div, 219 Loyola Ave, New Orleans, 70140. Collin B Hamer Jr, Head; Jean M Jones, Doc Librn
Holdings: Vols 2000 Cat Pix Slides Phonorecords 16mm Films Microforms
Notes: City archives collection covers the period 1769 to date and incl 12,000 ms vols, 3848 rolls of microfilm, 5900 wire and phonodisc recordings, 387 16mm films, and printed reorts of municipal agencies. Library is a legally apointed depository for all noncurrent official records of historic value. Material is restricted to on-site use.

LA —TULANE UNIVERSITY, Howard-Tilton Memorial Library, Special Collections Div, 7001 Freret St, New Orleans, 70118. Wilbur E Meneray, Librn
Notes: Louisiana Collection incl manuscripts, books, photographs, newspapers, prints and maps pertaining to the history and development of Louisiana and the Mississippi Valley from colonial times to the present.

LA —TULANE UNIVERSITY, Howard-Tilton Memorial Library, Special Collections Div, William Ransom Hogan Jazz Archive, 7001 Freret, New Orleans, 70118. Richard B Allen, Acting Cur; Alma D Williams, Assistant to the Cur
Holdings: Vols (100,000) Cat Mss Pix Slides Phonorecords Audiotapes Videotapes 16mm Films Microforms
Budget: ($90,000)
Notes: Jazz music and musicians. Outstanding collection, incl books, music scores, serials, catalogs and other archival material. Music, history, etc. See entry under Jazz for complete description.

NEW ORLEANS—MAPS

LA —TULANE UNIVERSITY, Howard-Tilton Memorial Library, Special Collections Div, 7001 Freret St, New Orleans, 70118. Wilbur E Meneray, Librn
Holdings: Maps
Notes: Louisiana Collection incl about 1000 maps about equally divided between Louisiana (Territory and State) and New Orleans. Louisiana maps date from about 1600 to the present; New Orleans maps date from about 1740 to the present.

NEW ORLEANS ARCHITECTURE see Architecture, New Orleans

NEW ORLEANS MUSIC see Music, New Orleans

NEW RELIGIONS see Religions, New

NEW SCHOOL FOR SOCIAL RESEARCH

NY —STATE UNIVERSITY OF NEW YORK AT ALBANY, Library, Special Collections Dept, 1400 Washington Ave, Albany, 12222. Marion P Munzer, Coordr
Notes: Concentration of materials from 1940-1960, relative to the family of Hans Staudinger and his administrative positions at the New School for Social Research; to

his interests in the Deutsche Theatre; and to his work in aiding German exiles. Incl 31.5 linear feet of mss and teaching materials; personal library of books, periodicals, pamphlets. Part of the Library's German Exile Collection.
See also entries under Hans Staudinger; Exiles, Political; Sociologists; Economists.

NEW SOUTHWEST see Southwest—History

NEW THOUGHT

AZ —WORLD UNIVERSITY, Library, 711 E Blacklidge Dr, Tucson, 85719. Howard John Zitko, Cur
Holdings: Vols (15,000) Cat Mss Maps Audiotapes
Notes: Collection concern the "frontier sciences." No interlibrary loan.

NEW TOWNS

MD —HOWARD COUNTY LIBRARY, 10375 Little Patuxemt Parkway, Columbia, 21044. Joyce Demmitt, Adult Services Coordr
Holdings: Vols (435) Cat Mss Maps Pix
Notes: New Towns, with emphasis on Columbia, Maryland.

NEW WESTMINSTER, BRITISH COLUMBIA

BC —NEW WESTMINSTER PUBLIC LIBRARY, 716 Sixth Ave, New Westminster, V3M 2B3, Can. Alan Woodland, Dir
Holdings: Cat Ms Maps Pix Slides Microforms
Notes: Attempts to gather as much information as possible about the history of the city of New Westminster. Collection based on almost complete run of *Columbian* Newspaper (1861-date); *The Weekly Columbian Newspaper* (1902-1954), and other newspapers and documents. Indexing of the *Columbian Newspaper* is taking place slowly. Have 25 maps, 1800 pictures, 110 slides, microforms, newspaper. Copies of photographs and documents are made when these become available.

NEW YORK (CITY)—CHARITIES

†NY —COLUMBIA UNIVERSITY LIBRARIES, Butler Library, Rare Book and Manuscript Library, 535 W 114 St, New York, 10027.
Notes: Papers of Mobilization for Youth, a New York City social service agency. Incl correspondence, minutes, memoranda, reports, project proposals, financial records, and related printed material. Also, papers of the Community Service Society, a New York City social service agency. Incl correspondence, reports, memoranda, case records, photographs, and printed materials.

NEW YORK (CITY)—CHINATOWN

†NY —NEW YORK PUBLIC LIBRARY, Chatham Square Branch, 33 E Broadway, New York, 10002.
Notes: New York's Chinatown, Chinese in the US, local Chinese newspapers.

NEW YORK (CITY)—COMMERCE

NY —COLUMBIA UNIVERSITY LIBRARIES, Rare Book & Manuscript Library, 801 Butler Library, 535 W 114 St, New York, 10027. Kenneth A Lohf, Librn
Notes: More than 32,000 items documenting the rise of William Russell Grace's shipping business and other materials relating to his career as mayor of New York. Incl records and correspondence relating to all aspects of the shipping business in New York and South America, mining interest in Peru and Chile, and transportation in Costa Rica and Nicaragua. Family memorabilia and photographs, materials concerning New York Politics, banking and insurance, real

estate interests and Catholic charities, and letters from Chester A Arthur, John Jacob Astor, Andrew Carnegie, Grover Cleveland, Hamilton Fish, John Hay and J Pierpont Morgan. Restricted use.

NEW YORK (CITY)—DESCRIPTION—VIEWS

DC —LIBRARY OF CONGRESS, Prints & Photographs Div, Washington, 20540.
Holdings: Cat Pix

NY —MUSEUM OF THE CITY OF NEW YORK, Photo Archives, Fifth Ave & 103 St, New York, 10029. Esther Brumberg, Librn
Holdings: Mss Maps Pix
Notes: All aspects of New York City-- history, costume, social life and customs, etc. Also, Byron Collection--about 10,000 prints, 1880-1930, of views of New York, commercial interiors, interiors and exteriors of private residences, social events, shipping, immigration; Wurts Collection--15,000 glass negatives, 1890-1940, mostly architectural; 100,000 Wurts Architectural Photographs, to be cataloged. Underhill Collection--about 900 glass negatives, mostly architectural, 1896-1936; McKim, Mead & White Collection--1000 glass negatives of the work of the firm, 1880-1915; and Berenice Abbott Collection, Changing New York--about 350 negatives taken by Miss Abbott for the Federal Arts Project, 1930s. Other FAP photographs incl a series on Coney Island, one on Harlem, Sewing Project, and Sabbath Studies.

NY —NEW YORK HISTORICAL SOCIETY, Library, 170 Central Park W, New York, 10024. James Gregory, Librn
Holdings: Mss
Notes: Incl original mss, illustrative materials, etc.

NY —NEW YORK PUBLIC LIBRARY, Local History and Genealogy Div, Fifth Ave & 42 St, New York, 10018. Gunther E Pohl, Chief
Holdings: Vols (160,000) Cat Pix
Budget: ($38,548)
Notes: Extensive collection of county, city, town and village histories of the United States. All other local, state, and national histories are part of the General Research and Humanities Division. Collection includes over 60,000 mounted photographs of New York City views arranged by address and/or subject. 20,000 film and glass plate negatives depicting NYC tenement housing conditions (1902-1938). Also the Lloyd L Acker collection of 48,000 film negatives depicting NYC buildings, 1935-1975. Collection of Lewis W Hine photographic prints made by the photographer on immigration, child labor, women at work and men at work. Eugene Armbruster collection of Long Island views; D B Austin's photographs of Long Island and western Americana; scrapbooks, and postcards of NYC and other US localities (200,000). See*United States Local History Catalog* (Boston: GK Hall, 1974), 2 vols.

NEW YORK (CITY)—FICTION

NY —STATE UNIVERSITY OF NEW YORK, STONY BROOK, Melville Library, Dept of Special Collections, Stony Brook, 11794. Evert Volkersz, Head
Holdings: Vols Uncat
Notes: A growing collection of fiction and literature with Long Island, incl Queens and Brooklyn, as a fictional setting.

NEW YORK (CITY)—GENEALOGY

NY —HOLLAND SOCIETY OF NEW YORK, Library, 122 E 58 St, New York, 10022. Linda Rolufs, Librn
Holdings: Vols (6000) Cat Mss
Notes: New York City history in the Dutch Period (New Netherlands); the Dutch Reformed Church; and Dutch-American family genealogy.

NEW YORK (CITY)—HISTORY

DC —LIBRARY OF CONGRESS, Prints & Photographs Div, Washington, 20540.
Notes: The George Grantham Bain

NEW YORK (CITY)—HISTORY (cont.)

Collection documents New York City sports events, theater, celebrities, crime, disasters, political activities, conventions, and public celebrations of the early 20th century with approximately 120,000 glass plate negatives and 240,000 photoprints acquired from the Bain News Service.

MD —JOHNS HOPKINS UNIVERSITY, Milton S Eisenhower Library, Charles & 34 Sts, Baltimore, 21218. Ann S Gwyn, Assistant Dir for Special Collections

NY —BRONX COUNTY HISTORICAL SOCIETY, Bronx County Research Library, 3309 Bainbridge Ave, Bronx, 10467. Gary Hermalyn, Exec Dir
Holdings: Vols 1000 Cat Mss Maps Pix Phonorecords Audiotapes 16mm Films Filmstrips Microforms
Notes: Historical Bronx. Publishes *The Bronx County Historical Society Journal.*

NY —CITY UNIVERSITY OF NEW YORK, BROOKLYN COLLEGE, Library, Special Collections Div, Bedford Ave & Ave H, Brooklyn, 11210. Antoinette Ciolli, Chief
Holdings: Cat
Notes: The Brooklyniana Collection is composed of books, clippings, and maps on the history and culture of Brooklyn and its neighborhoods.

NY —SAINT FRANCIS COLLEGE, The James A Kelly Institute for Local Historical Studies, 180 Remsen St, Brooklyn, 11201.
Notes: 250 cubic feet of records of the six original towns of Brooklyn dating from 1643 to 1898. Incl original Dutch patents, minutes of town meetings, assessment and census rolls, court records, wills, property transactions, account books, and school and highway records. Also incl papers of prominent Brooklyn political figures, maps, photographs, vertical files, and theses on Brooklyn history.

NY —ADELPHI UNIVERSITY, Library, Garden City, 11530. Jerome Yavarkovsky, Dean of Libraries
Holdings: Vols 461 Cat Mss Maps Pix
Notes: New York City and Long Island Region.

NY —QUEENS BOROUGH PUBLIC LIBRARY, Social Sciences Div, 89-11 Merrick Blvd, Jamaica, 11432. Nathan Shoengold, Head; Renee Kaplan, Asst Div Head
Holdings: Vols (45,000) Cat Microforms
Notes: Extensive pamphlet collection, incl New York State and New York City curriculum bulletins. Also education periodicals, some in microform. A separate catalog to the social sciences contains the education collection.

NY —GENERAL THEOLOGICAL SEMINARY, Saint Marks Library, 175 Ninth Ave, New York, 10011. David Green, Dir
Holdings: Vols (200,000) Cat Mss Maps Pix Slides Microforms

NY —HOLLAND SOCIETY OF NEW YORK, Library, 122 E 58 St, New York, 10022. Linda Rolufs, Librn
Holdings: Vols (6000) Cat Mss
Notes: New York City history in the Dutch Period (New Netherlands); the Dutch Reformed Church; and Dutch-American family genealogy.

NY —MUSEUM OF THE CITY OF NEW YORK, Photo Archives, Fifth Ave & 103 St, New York, 10029. Esther Brumberg, Librn
Holdings: Mss Maps Pix
Notes: All aspects of New York City--history, costume, social life and customs, etc. Also, Byron Collection--about 10,000 prints, 1880-1930, of views of New York, commercial interiors, interiors and exteriors of private residences, social events, shipping, immigration; Wurts Collection--15,000 glass negatives, 1890-1940, mostly architectural; 100,000 Wurts Architectural Photographs, to be cataloged. Underhill Collection--about 900 glass negatives, mostly architectural, 1896-1936; McKim, Mead & White Collection--1000 glass negatives of the work of the firm, 1880-1915; and Berenice Abbott Collection, Changing New York--about 350

negatives taken by Miss Abbott for the Federal Arts Project, 1930s. Other FAP photographs incl a series on Coney Island, one on Harlem, Sewing Project, and Sabbath Studies.

NY —NEW YORK HISTORICAL SOCIETY, Library, 170 Central Park W, New York, 10024. James Gregory, Librn
Notes: An extensive collection of eighteenth and early nineteenth century American newspapers. Incl the most complete set of original colonial New York papers and the fourth largest collection of newspapers printed in the US prior to 1821.

NY —NEW YORK PUBLIC LIBRARY, Mid-Manhattan Library, History and Social Sciences Dept, 455 Fifth Ave, New York, 10016. Robert Sheehan, Sr Principal Librn
Holdings: Vols 3500 Cat
Budget: $2500
Notes: Incl many out of print books for reference use only. Material is incorporated into a general history and social sciences collection.

NY —NEW YORK PUBLIC LIBRARY, Local History and Genealogy Div, Fifth Ave & 42 St, New York, 10018. Gunther E Pohl, Chief
Holdings: Vols (160,000) Cat Pix
Budget: ($38,548)
Notes: Extensive collection of county, city, town and village histories of the United States. All other local, state, and national histories are part of the General Research and Humanities Division. Collection includes over 60,000 mounted photographs of New York City views arranged by address and/or subject. 20,000 film and glass plate negatives depicting NYC tenement housing conditions (1902-1938). Also the Lloyd L Acker collection of 48,000 film negatives depicting NYC buildings, 1935-1975. Collection of Lewis W Hine photographic prints made by the photographer on immigration, child labor, women at work and men at work. Eugene Armbruster Collection of Long Island views; D B Austin's photographs of Long Island and western Americana; scrapbooks, and postcards of NYC and other US localities (200,000). See *United States Local History Catalog* (Boston: GK Hall, 1974), 2 vols.

NY —UNIVERSITY CLUB, Library, One W 54 St, New York, 10019. Guy St Clair, Library Dir
Holdings: Vols (100,000) Cat Mss Maps Pix
Notes: A private library for the members of the University Club, their guests, and serious scholars upon written application to the Library Director.

NY —STATEN ISLAND HISTORICAL SOCIETY LIBRARY, Centre St, Staten Island, 10306. Stephen Barto, Librn
Holdings: Vols (9000) Uncat Periodicals Mss Maps Pix Microforms
Notes: Holdings incl 25 current periodical titles. Visitors by appointment only.

NEW YORK (CITY)—PICTURES, ILLUSTRATIONS, ETC.

DC —LIBRARY OF CONGRESS, Prints & Photographs Div, Washington, 20540.
Notes: The George Grantham Bain Collection documents New York City sports events, theater, celebrities, crime, disasters, political activities, conventions, and public celebrations of the early 20th century with approximately 120,000 glass plate negatives and 240,000 photoprints acquired from the Bain News Service. Incl the Angelo A Rizzuto Collection of photographs of New York City, 1950s and 1960s. Also, the *New York World-Telegram and Sun* Collection contains news photographs, 1920-1960s.

NY —COLUMBIA UNIVERSITY LIBRARIES, Rare Book & Manuscript Library, 801 Butler Library, 535 W 114 St, New York, 10027. Kenneth A Lohf, Librn
Holdings: Mss
Notes: Papers of the Community Service Society of New York. Incl files, books, photographs (1000) and bound volumes of periodicals and conference proceedings. Among the papers are central and district administrative records, committee

correspondence and minutes, and files of programs sponsored by the organization. Also more than 1000 photographs by Jessie Tarbox Beals and Lewis W Hine depicting conditions of the poor. 276,000 items. Restricted use.

NY —NEW YORK PUBLIC LIBRARY, Local History and Genealogy Div, Fifth Ave & 42 St, New York, 10018. Gunther E Pohl, Chief
Notes: Over 350,000 photographs and postcard views of New York City and other local areas of the US.

NY —NEW YORK PUBLIC LIBRARY, Print Collection, Fifth Ave & 42 St, New York, 10018. Robert Rainwater, Keeper
Notes: An extensive collection of drawings, watercolors, lithographs, and engravings.

NEW YORK (CITY)—POLITICS AND GOVERNMENT

CT —CONNECTICUT COLLEGE, Library, Mohegan Ave, New London, 06320. Brian Rogers, College Librn
Holdings: // Uncat Mss
Notes: A collection of the papers of Belle Moskowitz, a prominent figure in New York politics and government with Alfred E Smith.

DC —LIBRARY OF CONGRESS, Prints & Photographs Div, Washington, 20540.
Notes: The George Grantham Bain Collection documents New York City sports events, theater, celebrities, crime, disasters, political activities, conventions, and public celebrations of the early 20th century with approximately 120,000 glass plate negatives and 240,000 photoprints acquired from the Bain News Service.

NY —COLUMBIA UNIVERSITY LIBRARIES, Rare Book & Manuscript Library, 801 Butler Library, 535 W 114 St, New York, 10027. Kenneth A Lohf, Librn
Notes: More than 32,000 items documenting the rise of William Russell Grace's shipping business and other materials relating to his career as mayor of New York. Incl records and correspondence relating to all aspects of the shipping business in New York and South America, mining interest in Peru and Chile, and transportation in Costa Rica and Nicaragua. Family memorabilia and photographs, materials concerning New York Politics, banking and insurance, real estate interests and Catholic charities, and letters from Chester A Arthur, John Jacob Astor, Andrew Carnegie, Grover Cleveland, Hamilton Fish, John Hay and J Pierpont Morgan. Restricted use.

NEW YORK (CITY)—POOR

†NY —COLUMBIA UNIVERSITY LIBRARIES, Butler Library, Rare Book and Manuscript Library, 535 W 114 St, New York, 10027.
Notes: Papers of Mobilization for Youth, a New York City social service agency. Incl correspondence, minutes, memoranda, reports, project proposals, financial records, and related printed material. Also, papers of the Community Service Society, a New York City social service agency. Incl correspondence, reports, memoranda, case records, photographs, and printed materials.

NEW YORK (CITY)—SOCIAL LIFE AND CUSTOMS

DC —LIBRARY OF CONGRESS, Prints & Photographs Div, Washington, 20540.
Notes: The George Grantham Bain Collection documents New York City sports events, theater, celebrities, crime, disasters, political activities, conventions, and public celebrations of the early 20th century with approximately 120,000 glass plate negatives and 240,000 photoprints acquired from the Bain News Service.

NY —COLUMBIA UNIVERSITY LIBRARIES, Rare Book & Manuscript Library, 801 Butler Library, 535 W 114 St, New York, 10027. Kenneth A Lohf, Librn
Holdings: Mss
Notes: Papers of the Community Service

NEW YORK (CITY)—SOCIAL LIFE AND CUSTOMS (cont.)

Society of New York. Incl files, books, photographs (1000) and bound volumes of periodicals and conference proceedings. Among the papers are central and district administrative records, committee correspondence and minutes, and files of programs sponsored by the organization. Also more than 1000 photographs by Jessie Tarbox Beals and Lewis W Hine depicting conditions of the poor. 276,000 items. Restricted use.

NY —MUSEUM OF THE CITY OF NEW YORK, Photo Archives, Fifth Ave & 103 St, New York, 10029. Esther Brumberg, Librn
Holdings: Mss Maps Pix
Notes: All aspects of New York City-- history, costume, social life and customs, etc. Also, Byron Collection--about 10,000 prints, 1880-1930, of views of New York, commercial interiors, interiors and exteriors of private residences, social events, shipping, immigration; Wurt: ection--15,000 glass negatives, 1890-1940, mostly architectural; 100,000 Wurts Architectural Photographs, to be cataloged. Underhill Collection--about 900 glass negatives, mostly architectural, 1896-1936; McKim, Mead & White Collection--1000 glass negatives of the work of the firm, 1880-1915; and Berenice Abbott Collection, Changing New York--about 350 negatives taken by Miss Abbott for the Federal Arts Project, 1930s. Other FAP photographs incl a series on Coney Island, one on Harlem, Sewing Project, and Sabbath Studies.

NY —NEW YORK HISTORICAL SOCIETY, Library, 170 Central Park W, New York, 10024. James Gregory, Librn
Notes: An extensive collection of eighteenth and early nineteenth century American newspapers. Incl the most complete set of original colonial New York papers and the fourth largest collection of newspapers printed in the US prior to 1821.

NY —NEW YORK PUBLIC LIBRARY, Rare Books and Manuscripts Div, Fifth Ave & 42 St, New York, 10018. William L Joyce, Asst Dir; Susan E Davis, Cur of Mss
Notes: The papers of Jacob A Riis, incl diaries, ms, etc, and many other collections.

NY —NEW YORK UNIVERSITY, Elmer Holmes Bobst Library, Div of Special Collections, Washington Sq S, New York, 10012. Frank Walker, Librn; Patrick McGuire, Asst Librn
Notes: Extensive Geoffrey T Hellman collection of articles, letters and memorabilia; much material concerning Harold Ross; a great deal on New York City.

NEW YORK (CITY)—SPORTS

NY —COLUMBIA UNIVERSITY LIBRARIES, Rare Book & Manuscript Library, 801 Butler Library, 535 W 114 St, New York, 10027. Kenneth A Lohf, Librn
Notes: Restricted use. The Paul Magriel Boxing Collection on the history and literature of pugilism. The L S Alexander Gumby Collection, which incl 9 Joe Lewis scrapbooks, and much on Jack Johnson, Sugar Ray Robinson, Jackie Robinson. Much on Columbia sports and athletics. Good strengths in material on Columbia's sports figures, incl Lou Gehrig, Lou Little, etc.

NEW YORK (CITY)—WATER SUPPLY

NY —JERVIS PUBLIC LIBRARY, 613 N Washington St, Rome, 13440. William A Dillon, Dir
Holdings: Vols (1500) // Cat Mss Maps Slides
Notes: John Bloomfield Jervis Collection contains personal library (1500 vols) and papers (1300 items) of chief engineer of Croton aqueduct and other waterworks, canals, and railroads circa 1825-1860. Papers available from Jervis Public Library.

NEW YORK (CITY) NEWSPAPERS see Newspapers, New York (City)

NEW YORK (STATE)—ANTIQUITIES

NY —NEW YORK STATE LIBRARY, State Education Bldg Annex, Washington Ave, Albany, 12224.
Notes: The papers of William Beauchamp (ca 1860-1930), consisting mainly of his notebooks and scrapbooks concerning the history of the Iroquois Indians. Incl 13 boxes material on Indian language, folklore, and place names, the Moravians, and New York State archeology.

NY —NASSAU COUNTY MUSEUM, Sands Pt Preserve, Middleneck Rd, Sand Points, 11050.
Holdings: Vols (2500)
Notes: Collection contains almost every published reference on Long Island archaeology, ethnology, and geology, and incl most of those pertaining to the coastal New York area. Open by appointment. No photocopying.

NEW YORK (STATE)—DESCRIPTION AND TRAVEL

NY —NEW YORK HISTORICAL SOCIETY, Library, 170 Central Park W, New York, 10024. James Gregory, Librn
Holdings: Mss
Notes: Incl original mss, illustrative materils, etc.

†NY —UNION COLLEGE, Adirondack Research Center, Schenectady, 12308.
Notes: Books, periodicals, maps, and historical and political records of the Adirondack Park area.

NEW YORK (STATE)—FICTION

NY —STATE UNIVERSITY OF NEW YORK, STONY BROOK, Melville Library, Dept of Special Collections, Stony Brook, 11794. Evert Volkersz, Head
Holdings: Vols Uncat
Notes: A growing collection of fiction and literature with Long Island, incl Queens and Brooklyn, as a fictional setting.

NEW YORK (STATE)—GENEALOGY

FL —ORLANDO PUBLIC LIBRARY, Local History & Genealogy Dept, 100 Block of Central Ave, Orlando, 32806. Eileen B Willis, Librn
Holdings: Vols 11,000 Cat Maps Microforms
Budget: $8000
Notes: Strong collection in local genealogy materials on Mass, NY, Va, Ga, and Florida. Contains exceptional holdings on all New England States, Penn, and NJ.
See also entry under Genealogy - Collections.

NJ —PLAINFIELD PUBLIC LIBRARY, Eighth St at Park Ave, Plainfield, 07060. Thomas H Ballard, Dir

NY —NEW YORK STATE LIBRARY, State Education Bldg Annex, Washington Ave, Albany, 12224.
Holdings: Cat Mss Maps Pix Microforms
Notes: Extensive Collection on American local history incl books and pamphlets on American genealogy. Major strength northeastern United States. Maintain unique card index to regional historical and genealogical materials in periodicals not indexed elsewhere, pamphlets, and comprehensive works; about 1912-date.

NY —ST LAWRENCE COUNTY HISTORICAL LIBRARY & ARCHIVES ASSOCIATION, Library, 3 E Main St, PO Box 506, Canton, 13617. John Baule, County Librn
Holdings: Vols (600) Uncat Mss Pix Audiotapes Microforms
Notes: Genealogical Research Collection: Saint Lawrence County printed and manuscript records, military records, diaries, account books, burial, church, school records. Complete "Alms House" of county records (1825-1975). Many scrapbooks, census microfilm, court records, etc. Housed in the Silas Wright House and Museum.

NY —NEW YORK STATE HISTORICAL ASSOCIATION, Library, Lake Rd, Cooperstown, 13326. Amy Barnum, Librn
Holdings: Vols (55,000) Cat Mss Microforms
Notes: Emphasis on New York State, more espec. Otsego and contiguous countries. Noncirculating.

NY —CORTLAND COUNTY HISTORICAL SOCIETY, Library, 25 Homer Ave, Cortland, 13045. Shirely G Heppell, Librn
Holdings: Vols 2077 Cat Mss Maps Pix Slides Microforms
Notes: Emphasis on Cortland County area. Collection includes 620 cubic feet of mss; business & organizational records, personal papers, town & village records, school and church records, genealogies, etc. Also extensive collections of cemetery records, vital records, directories, censuses, handbills, and programs.

NY —STATE UNIVERSITY OF NEW YORK, COLLEGE OF ARTS & SCIENCE AT GENESEO, Milne Library, Geneseo, 14454. William T Lane, Head of Information Services & Archivist
Notes: Genesee Valley Historical Collection. County, town, village, family and church histories for the counties of Allegany, Genesee, Livingston, Monroe, Orleans and Wyoming. Materials on the Seneca Indians, Genesee Valley Canal, and the geology of western New York state. Also, the Wadsworth Family Papers (145 linear ft, uncataloged). Business and family correspondence, account books, maps, deeds, leases, and business records of the Wadsworth Family, early landowners in the Genesee region of western New York. Major family members represented in the collection incl Jeremiah Wadsworth (1743-1804), William Wadsworth (1761-1833), Daniel Wadsworth (1771-1848), James Wadsworth (1768-1844), James Samuel Wadsworth (1807-1864), William Wolcott Wadsworth (1810-1852), Emmeline Austin Wadsworth (1808-1885), JamesWolcott Wadsworth (1846-1926), William Austin Wadsworth (1847-1918), Herbert Wadsworth (1851-1930), Martha Blow Wadsworth (1864-1934), Craig W Wadsworth (1872-1960), Charles F Wadsworth (1835-1899), James Wolcott Wadsworth, Jr (1877-1952), James Jeremiah Wadsworth (1905-), and William P Wadsworth (1906-1982). Inventory in repository. Open to qualified investigators with permission of archivist. Gift of William P Wadsworth and the Hon James J Wadsworth, Geneseo, NY, 1976- , and Michael Moukhanoff, Ashantee, NY 1976. The Wadsworth Family papers cover the years from 1790 to the early 20th century.

NY —NEW YORK STATE OFFICE OF PARKS & RECREATION, TACONIC REGION, Clermont State Historic Park, Library, RR 1, Box 215, Germantown, 12526. Bruce E Naramore, Historic Site Manager
Holdings: Vols (5000) Cat Mss Maps Pix Slides Audiotapes
Notes: Family Bibles and many period editions of the Livingston family. Bibles go back to 1594. As family intermarried so many other prominent Hudson River Valley families, editions highlight a great deal of history and genealogy of other people's lives, as well as their own. No photocopying.

NY —HUNTINGTON HISTORICAL SOCIETY LIBRARY, New York Ave & High St, Huntington, 11743. Agnes K Packard, Librn
Holdings: Vols (3000) Mss Maps Pix Slides Audiotapes Microforms
Budget: ($60,000)
Notes: Huntington, NY, and Long Island history and genealogy.

NY —FENTON HISTORICAL SOCIETY, Library, 67 South Washington, Jamestown, 14701. Ellen Fessenden, Co-Dir; Candy Larson, Co-Dir
Holdings: Vols (3000) Mss Maps Pix Slides Microforms
Notes: Incl Chautauqua County family histories, genealogical charts, Bibles records, burial records of southern Chautauqua County cemeteries; deaths and marriages copied from newspapers Jamestown and Mayville, NE; directories; ms collection consists of locally made genealogical charts. Plus State and Federal Census records.

NY —JOHNSTOWN PUBLIC LIBRARY, 38 S Market St, Johnstown, 12095. Barbara Germain, Dir
Holdings: Vols (1200) Cat Maps Microfilm
Notes: State and local history and genealogy.

NEW YORK (STATE)—GENEALOGY
(cont.)

Incl VF, scrapbooks. Census collection for some counties.

NY —NEW YORK GENEALOGICAL & BIOGRAPHICAL SOCIETY, Library, 122 E 58 St, New York, 10022. James P Gregory, Librn
Holdings: Vols 63,500 Cat Mss Maps Microforms
Notes: The Society has copied and has in its ms collections a great many church records from all parts of New York State and several from adjacent states; and many very valuable ms genealogies and family Bible records which have never been published. The Society library is noncirculating and one of the principal genealogical reference libraries in the country. It has accumulated in its collections approximately 63 thousand vols on genealogy, local history and biography. In addition it has a rapidly expanding microfilm division which presently numbers over 2000 reels and keeps four microfilm readers in continuous use.

NY —NEW YORK HISTORICAL SOCIETY, Library, 170 Central Park W, New York, 10024. James Gregory, Librn
Holdings: Mss
Notes: Incl original mss, illustrative materials, etc.

NY —RYE HISTORICAL SOCIETY, Library, One Purchase St, Box 155, Rye, 10580. Susan A Morison, Dir
Holdings: Vols (1000) Mss Maps Pix Slides Audiotapes
Notes: History of Rye, NY. About 125 books on colonial arts and crafts. Partially cataloged.

NY —SMITHTOWN LIBRARY, Long Island Room, Hanley Collection, 1 N Country Rd, Smithtown, 11787. Vera Toman, Librn
Holdings: Vols (20,000) Cat Mss Maps Pix Microforms
Budget: ($3000)
Notes: Strong history collection for the colonial period through the Civil War for Suffolk County and Queens and Kings counties. Special emphasis on history of Smithtown, incl the Charles E Lawrence and Judge J Lawrence Smith mss collections. Also, genealogies of many early Long Island families and census records on microfilm, 1890-1910, for Naussau and Suffolk counties. Incl 20,000 mss, 350 maps and 700 pictures.

NY —STATEN ISLAND HISTORICAL SOCIETY LIBRARY, Centre St, Staten Island, 10306. Stephen Barto, Librn
Holdings: Vols (9000) Uncat Periodicals Mss Maps Pix Microforms VF
Notes: Holdings incl 4 drawers of vertical files. Visitors by appointment only.

NY —ONONDAGA COUNTY PUBLIC LIBARY, Local History and Genealogy Dept, 335 Montgomery St, Syracuse, 13202. Gerald James Parsons, Head
Holdings: Vols (30,000) Cat Mss Maps Pix Microforms
Budget: ($12,000)
Notes: Collection of local history and genealogy covers primarily Syracuse, Onondaga County, New York State and the northeast, ie, New England, New Jersey and Pennsylvania.

NY —ROSWELL P FLOWER MEMORIAL LIBRARY, 229 Washington St, Watertown, 13601. Anthony F Cozzie, Dir
Holdings: Vols (2112) Cat Maps Pix
Budget: ($475)
Notes: Emphasis on Jefferson County.

NEW YORK (STATE)—GOVERNMENT PUBLICATIONS

NY —NEW YORK STATE DEPT OF STATE, Community Affairs Library, 162 Washington Ave, Albany, 12231. M L Johnson, Librn
Holdings: Vols (14,640) Cat
Notes: Local government. Serves as research arm for official activities. 16,000 items in vertical files; 150 periodicals. Unique Community File collection of about 1600

local governments arranged by counties in the state.

NY —NEW YORK STATE LIBRARY, State Education Bldg Annex, Washington Ave, Albany, 12224.
Holdings: Cat
Notes: Offical depository of New York State publications. Card index supplementing Hasse (for NY) 1905-1939; since 1947 Library has published *Checklist* of official publications with author index, agency listing.

NY —HEMPSTEAD PUBLIC LIBRARY, 115 Nichols Court, Hempstead, 11550. Irene A Duszkiewicz, Dir
Holdings: Vols 1944 Uncat Pamphlets
Notes: Official full depository for New York State Documents.

NC —DUKE UNIVERSITY, William R Perkins Library, Public Documents and Maps Department, Durham, 27706. Jaia Barrett, Head
Holdings: Vols Maps Pamphlets Microforms
Notes: A selective depository for US Government publications since 1890, the Department currently holds well over 500, 000 items, plus publications of the European Community (a depository collection), the League of Nations, the UN and UN-affiliated agencies. Other international organizations, publications are acquired also, as are state government publications, especially from the Southeast, California, New York and Illinois. The Documents Department holds services the major map collections of Perkins Library. These collections include topographic, geologic, and special subject maps which are worldwide in coverage. The department is a depository for the US Defense Mapping Agency and the US Geological Survey. In addition, there are many other maps of general and specific interest, including US and foreign road maps. As appropriate, maps are also held in the Perkins Library's Rare BookRoom and Manuscript Department. Atlases are shelved in the Reference Department and in the bookstacks of Perkins Library.

NEW YORK (STATE)—HISTORY

MA —BERKSHIRE ATHENAEUM, 1 Wendell Ave, Pittsfield, 01201. Ruth T Degenhardt, Head Local History & Literature
Holdings: Vols (9000) Cat Maps Pix Microforms
Budget: ($2000)
Notes: Primary focus is on the development of Berkshire, Massachusetts, regional history and culture, with particular emphasis on the industrial development of Berkshires. Entire collection spans all New England states and New York State, on all topics. Special strength is in published local histories. No separate catalog. There is a reference index.

NY —ALBANY INSTITUTE OF HISTORY & ART, McKinney Library, 125 Washington Ave, Albany, 12210. Daryl Severson, Actg Librn; Suzanne Roberson, Photographic Librn
Holdings: Vols 5000 Cat Mss Maps Pix Slides
Notes: History of the Albany, New York area and the arts related to it. The Albany area incl the original Albany County before 1790; now incl the present counties of Albany, Rensselaer, Columbia, Greene, and Schenectady.

NY —NEW YORK STATE LIBRARY, Manuscripts and Special Collections, Albany, 12230. Peter R Christoph, Associate Librn
Holdings: Cat Mss Maps Pix Microforms
Notes: Strong collection, all aspects: social, political, legislative, economic history of the State and its people, incl Indians. Particularly valuable and extensive collection of historical mss, Colonial and State.

NY —BALLSTON SPA PUBLIC LIBRARY, 21 Milton Ave, Ballston Spa, 12020. Elsie Maddaus, Librn
Holdings: Vols 1000 Cat Pix Microfilm
Notes: All aspects of Saratoga County history, social and religious life. Incl Bruce

M Manzer Saratoga Collection consisting of books collected over 17 years. Ballston Journal (newspaper) from 1847-date on microfilm.

NY —ADIRONDACK HISTORICAL ASSOCIATION, Museum Library, Blue Mountain Lake, 12812. Jerold Pepper, Librn
Holdings: Vols (7500) Cat Mss Maps Pix Phonorecords
Notes: Anything about the Adirondacks--history, people, economics, places, things. Strong in Adirondack art, outdoor recreation, logging, small boats. Resources incl more than 1000 maps, 40,000 pictures, 1600 microfilm reels, 576 linear ft of ms material, and 12 cabinets of VF ephemera, etc.

NY —BUFFALO & ERIE COUNTY HISTORICAL SOCIETY, 25 Nottingham Court, Buffalo, 14216. Herman Sass, Librn
Notes: 70 indexes and catalog aids have been created pertaining to various aspects of this collection. There are special collections within this special collection. Niagara Frontier History is the major collection of the society, and its main purpose is to build this collection.

NY —BUFFALO & ERIE COUNTY PUBLIC LIBRARY, History, Travel & Government Dept, Lafayette Sq, Buffalo, 14203. Ruth Willet, Head
Holdings: Vols 4000 Cat
Notes: Emphasis on Buffalo and Erie County.

NY —SAINT LAWRENCE UNIVERSITY, Owen D Young Library, Canton, 13617. Mahlon Peterson, Librn
Holdings: Cat Mss Maps Pix
Notes: Northern New York and the Adirondacks (900 items). Also, the Parish-Rosseel Papers. The bulk of the material falls within the period 1807-1816 and consists of the correspondence of David Parish and Joseph Rosseel. Very valuable source of information on the settlement of the North Country and the War of 1812 as well as the general social and economic conditions of the time (1600 items). Also, the Child Collection which is conceived mainly with the development of the area around the town of LeRoy (100 items). Business and personal letters and documents dating from 1816-1847 written by Silas Wright, governor of New York, and incl some papers of family and friends (approx 100 items). Also records of land business of James Moon of Middleton, Pa, who owned part of Macomb's Purchase in northern New York. He sold this land to settlers throughhis relatives and agents, Daniel and Moses Child. The collection, incl maps, deeds, accounts and correspondence, covers the years 1818-1855 and numbers approx 100 items.

NY —ST LAWRENCE COUNTY HISTORICAL LIBRARY & ARCHIVES ASSOCIATION, Library, 3 E Main St, PO Box 506, Canton, 13617. John Baule, County Librn
Holdings: Vols (1900) Uncat Mss Maps Pix Slides Audiotapes Microforms
Notes: Genealogical Research Collection: Saint Lawrence County printed and manuscript records; military records, diaries, account books, burial, church, school records. Complete "Alms House" of county records (1825-1975). Many scrapbooks, census microfilm, court records, etc. Housed in the Silas Wright House and Museum.

NY —WHALING MUSEUM SOCIETY, Cold Spring Harbor Whaling Museum, Main St, Cold Spring Harbor, 11724. Robert D Farwell, Dir
Holdings: Cat Mss Maps Pix
Notes: Library of bound and printed books covers Cold Spring harbor whaling industry, in general, and maritime affairs. Archives contain thousands of original documents concerning whaling activities, the Cold Spring Harbor Whaling Company, and the extensive maritime coastal trade conducted out of Cold Spring Harbor after the whaling era (latter 1800s). Considerable material deals with the Jones and Hewlett families, important in both local commerce and Long Island and New York affairs.

NEW YORK (STATE)—HISTORY (cont.)

NY —NEW YORK STATE HISTORICAL
ASSOCIATION, Library, Lake Rd,
Cooperstown, 13326. Amy Barnum, Librn
Holdings: Vols (55,000) Cat Mss Maps Pix
Slides Tapes
Notes: Emphasis on Otsego County area.
Incl Smith-Telfer Collection of 60,000 glass
plate negatives, Otsego County, ca 1850-
1950; also, picture collection (14 file
drawers); also, postal cards Noncirculating.

NY —CORTLAND COUNTY HISTORICAL
SOCIETY, Library, 25 Homer Ave,
Cortland, 13045. Shirely G Heppell, Librn
Holdings: Vols 2077 Cat Mss Maps Pix
Slides Microforms
Notes: Emphasis on Cortland County area.
Collection includes 620 cubic feet of mss;
business & organizational records, personal
papers, town & village records, school and
church records, genealogies, etc. Also
extensive collections of cemetery records,
vital records, directories, censuses, handbills,
and programs.

NY —GREENE COUNTY HISTORICAL
SOCIETY, Vedder Memorial Library, RD,
Coxsackie, 12051. Raymond Beecher, Librn
Holdings: Vols (3500) Cat Mss Maps Pix
Slides
Budget: ($500)
Notes: Collection strong in Greene County,
the mid-Hudson region and the Catskill
Mountains. County newspapers, pictorial
county file, very large mss collection for
region, incl Greene County mss, 1800-1900.

NY —EASTCHESTER HISTORICAL
SOCIETY LIBRARY, Box 37, Eastchester,
10709. Madeline D Schaeffer, Librn
Holdings: Vols (6000) Cat Mss Maps Pix
Slides
Notes: New York State history with
emphasis on Westchester County and local
area. Also children's literature, 1750-1910,
and juvenile textbooks, 1790-1910. No
photocopying.

NY —NASSAU COUNTY MUSEUM,
Reference Library, Eisenhower Park, East
Meadow, 11554. Richard Winsche,
Historian; Monica Albala, Museum Cur
Holdings: Vols 1000 Cat Mss Maps Pix
Slides 16mm Films
Notes: Long Island history.

NY —GEORGE F JOHNSON MEMORIAL
LIBRARY, 1001 Park St, Endicott, 13760. S
Judson Locke, Dir
Holdings: Cat Maps Pix Microforms
Notes: Particularly Endicott and vicinity. Of
special interest are pictures and files of old
newspapers, some on microfilm.

NY —STATE UNIVERSITY OF NEW
YORK, COLLEGE AT FREDONIA,
Daniel A Reed Library, Fredonia, 14063.
John P Saulitis, Dir of Library Services;
Joanne L Schweik, Supv of Special
Collections; Joseph Chouinard, Music Librn
Holdings: Vols 1750 Cat Mss Maps Pix
Slides Audiotapes Videotapes Microforms
Budget: $1000
Notes: The Reed Library Local History
Collection includes materials pertaining to
Chautauqua and Cattaraugus Counties in
Western New York, and to some extent
materials of Allegany County. The collection
ranges from rare items (such as early County
histories, early survey maps and atlases, and
records from the establishment of the
College, the Fredonia Academy, in 1827,
which is now the State University College at
Fredonia) to current publications (County
Legislature Proceedings, Health Department
reports, directories, etc) Of special note are
diaries, a series of oral history tapes on rural
education; geological materials, incl aerial
photographs, and some Indian history of the
Seneca National.

NY —STATE UNIVERSITY OF NEW
YORK, COLLEGE OF ARTS & SCIENCE
AT GENESEO, Milne Library, Geneseo,
14454. William T Lane, Head of Information
Services & Archivist
Holdings: Vols (3700) Cat Mss Maps Pix
Slides Microforms
Budget: ($1000)
Notes: Genesee Valley Historical Collection.

County, town, village, family and church
histories for the counties of Allegany,
Genesee, Livingston, Monroe, Orleans and
Wyoming. Materials on the Seneca Indians,
Genesee Valley Canal, and the geology of
western New York state.

NY —GENEVA HISTORICAL SOCIETY,
James Luckett Memorial Archives, 543 S
Main St, Geneva, 14456. Eleanore Clise,
Librn
Holdings: Vols 2000 Uncat Maps Pix Slides
Audiotapes
Notes: History of Geneva and Ontario
County, New York. Incl 40 maps, 1000 glass
plate negatives, 3000 slides and 60
audiotapes. Cataloging in process.

NY —NEW YORK STATE OFFICE OF
PARKS & RECREATION, TACONIC
REGION, Clermont State Historic Park,
Library, RR 1, Box 215, Germantown,
12526. Bruce E Naramore, Historic Site
Manager
Holdings: Vols (5000) Cat Mss Slides
Audiotapes
Notes: This library may be considered
unique in that seven generations of the
Livingston family owned and added to it
throughout the years (1730-1962). Many of
these items belonged to the Chancellor
Robert R Livingston (1746-1813), prominent
early American statesman. Many volumes
concern Livingston family history, the
forming of the US, and early history of the
Hudson River Valley (pre - and post-
American Revolutionary War). Many first
editions. Also concerns agriculture,
technology, poetry, politics, etc. Additions to
the collection are being considered if it can
be ascertained that the volume belonged to
the family or the estate. No photocopying.

NY —GLOVERSVILLE FREE LIBRARY, 58
E Fulton St, Gloversville, 12078. Anne E
Simon, Library Dir; Alyce Lanphere, Asst
Dir & Local History Librn
Holdings: Vols 750 Cat Mss Maps Pix
Budget: $1000
Notes: Fulton County and environs;
Gloversville; Johnstown; Montgomery
County; Hamilton County; Saratoga County;
Albany County; Schenectady County;
Mohawk Valley; Delaware; Central
Pennsylvania; Westchester County;
Southeastern New York; New Jersey;
Indians of the Mohawk Valley; Capital
District (or Region). Incl scrapbooks and
pamphlets.

NY —HEMPSTEAD PUBLIC LIBRARY, 115
Nichols Court, Hempstead, 11550. Irene A
Duszkiewicz, Dir
Holdings: Vols (1000) Cat Mss Maps Pix
Microforms
Notes: Local Hempstead Village history,
Long Island genealogy. Also, New York
State History Collection.

NY —HOFSTRA UNIVERSITY, Library,
1000 Fulton Ave, Hempstead, 11550.
Charles R Andrews, Dean of Library
Services
See also entry under Long Island, New York
- History.

NY —HUNTINGTON HISTORICAL
SOCIETY LIBRARY, New York Ave &
High St, Huntington, 11743. Agnes K
Packard, Librn
Holdings: Vols (3000) Mss Maps Pix Slides
Audiotapes Microforms
Budget: ($60,000)
Notes: Huntington, NY, and Long Island
history and genealogy.

NY —QUEENS BOROUGH PUBLIC
LIBRARY, Social Sciences Div, 89-11
Merrick Blvd, Jamaica, 11432. Nathan
Shoengold, Head; Renee Kaplan, Asst Div
Head
Holdings: Vols (45,000) Cat Microforms
Notes: Extensive pamphlet collection, incl
New York State and New York City
curriculum bulletins. Also education
periodicals, some in microform. A separate
catalog to the social sciences contains the
education collection.

NY —FENTON HISTORICAL SOCIETY,
Library, 67 South Washington, Jamestown,
14701. Ellen Fessenden, Co-Dir; Candy
Larson, Co-Dir
Holdings: Vols 1000 Mss Maps Pix
Notes: Chautauqua County and Jamestown
history; much Civil War period material.

NY —JERICHO PUBLIC LIBRARY, Local
History Collection, One Merry Lane,
Jericho, 11753. R M Stern, Librn
Holdings: Vols 350 Cat Mss Maps Pix Slides
Phonorecords Audiotapes
Notes: There are separate catalogs for books
and pictures. The collection also incl a
pamphlet file and scrapbooks on the history
of Jericho and Long Island; local newpapers;
magazines and journals, pertaining to Long
Island; and paintings of Long Island houses.
Oral tapes are basically reminiscences with
long-time residents of Jericho and Long
Island. Added: Toledot, the journal of Jewish
Genealogy.

NY —JOHNSTOWN PUBLIC LIBRARY, 38
S Market St, Johnstown, 12095. Barbara
Germain, Dir
Holdings: Vols (1200) Cat Maps Microfilm
Notes: State and local history and genealogy.
Incl VF files, scrapbooks.

NY —KATONAH VILLAGE, Library,
Katonah, 10536. Elizabeth Beardsley, Dir
Holdings: Cat Mss Maps Pix
Notes: Especially the Katonah and
Westchester areas.

NY —ONONDAGA COUNTY DEPT OF
PARKS AND RECREATION, Office of
Museums and Historical Sites, PO Box 146,
Liverpool, 13088. Elaine Wisowaty, Asst
Cur; Dennis Connors, Cur
Holdings: Vols 200 Cat Mss Maps
Budget: ($3500)
Notes: Concentration in 17th century
French activity in upstate New York. Incl
100 maps; 3 linear feet mss. Also, history of
the NY State Salt Industry in Onondaga
County. 50 vols.

NY —WAYNE COUNTY HISTORICAL
SOCIETY, 21 Butternut St, Lyons, 14489.
Fred Rollins, Dir
Holdings: Vols 3000 Cat Mss Pix Slides
Phnorecords Microforms
Notes: History of Wayne County and Lyons,
New York.

NY —MANHASSET PUBLIC LIBRARY, 30
Onderdonk Ave, Manhasset, 11030. Sylvia
Levin, Dir
Holdings: Vols 450 Cat Maps

NY —MERRICK LIBRARY, 2279 Merrick
Ave, Merrick, 11566.
Holdings: Pix Microforms
Notes: Local history. Collection suported by
the Historical Society of the Merricks.
Newspapers from 1927-present.

NY —MOUNT SAINT MARY COLLEGE,
Curtin Memorial Library, Liberty St,
Newburgh, 12550. Estelle McKeever, Librn
Holdings: Vols (110) Cat
Notes: Monihan Collection of Hudson
Valley History. Emphasis on Orange County
and Newburgh.

NY —HOLLAND SOCIETY OF NEW
YORK, Library, 122 E 58 St, New York,
10022. Linda Rolufs, Librn
Notes: Specializes in New Netheland (New
York, New Jersey, Delaware) history during
the Dutch period, materials on the Dutch
Reformed Church, and Dutch-American
family genealogy.

NY —NEW YORK HISTORICAL SOCIETY,
Library, 170 Central Park W, New York,
10024. James Gregory, Librn
Holdings: Mss
Notes: Incl original mss, illustrative
materials, etc.

NY —UNIVERSITY CLUB, Library, One W
54 St, New York, 10019. Guy St Clair,
Library Dir
Holdings: Vols (100,000) Cat Mss Maps Pix
Notes: A private library for the members of
the University Club, their guests, and serious
scholars upon written application to the
Library Director.

NY —NIAGARA FALLS PUBLIC LIBRARY,
1425 Main St, Niagara Falls, 14305. Donald
E Loker, Local History Specialist
Holdings: Vols (10,000) Cat Mss Maps Pix
Slides Microforms
Notes: Incl prints, pamphlets and ephemera.
Local newspapers are indexed. Special
emphasis on Niagara Falls and River.

NY —STATE UNIVERSITY OF NEW
YORK, COLLEGE AT ONEONTA, James
M Milne Library, Oneonta, 13820. Richard
D Johnson, Librn
Holdings: Vols (427,646) Cat Mss Maps Pix

NEW YORK (STATE)—HISTORY (cont.)

Slides Phonorecords Audiotapes 16mm
Films Filmstrips Microfroms
Budget: ($338,299)
Notes: New York State Collection; 19th &
20th century popular fiction; New York
State Verse Collection; Early Textbook &
Early Educational Theory Collection.

NY —FORT ONTARIO HISTORIC SITE,
Oswego, 13126. Shelley B Weinreb, Historic
Site Mgr
Holdings: Vols (400) Cat Mss Maps Pix
Slides
Notes: Primary focus is upon military
activities at the mouth of the Oswego River
and the utilization of fortifications (Fort
Ontario, Fort Oswego, and Fort George) at
that point which served to control the outlet
of the traditional Mohawk-Oneida-Oswego
route to the Great Lakes. A limited number
of sources on fortification design, weapons,
uniforms, and military equipment are
included. Also incl 4000 slides and 400
pictures.

NY —STATE UNIVERSITY OF NEW
YORK, COLLEGE AT OSWEGO, Penfield
Library, Oswego, 13126. Anne Commerton,
Dir
Holdings: // Cat Mss Maps
Notes: Collection of Charles M Snyder,
professor of History at Oswego and
Collector of local and regional history.
Collection also incl Snyder's class notes and
materials; and notes aand mss of books
Snyder wrote or planned to write. 4 linear ft.
Also, the Bradley Benedict Burt papers, with
much on Oswego County.

NY —PLATTSBURGH PUBLIC LIBRARY,
Local History Collection, 15 Oak St, Box
570, Plattsburgh, 12901. Katherine S Cayea,
Librn
Holdings: Vols (2200) Cat Mss Maps Pix
Microforms
Budget: $500
Notes: Local Plattsburgh and Clinton
County, NY, history collection and some
300 genealogical items. Have city
directories, postcards, newspapers, cemetery
records, scrapbooks, etc. Listed in *Historical
Materials Relating to Northern New York:
A Union Catalog* (North Country Reference
and Research Resources Council, 1976).

NY —STATE UNIVERSITY OF NEW
YORK, COLLEGE AT PLATTSBURGH,
Feinberg Library, Special Collections, 153
Hawkins Hall, Plattsburgh, 12901. Joseph G
Swinyer, Librn
Holdings: Vols (5000) Cat Mss Maps Pix
Phonorecords Microforms
Notes: History of upstate New York and
Vermont; Canadiana; folklore of
Adirondacks and Champlain Valley, early
imprints maps, charts, plates and
architectural drawings; recent environmental,
industrial and demographic studies of the
region; University archives. Incl the Marjorie
Lansing Porter Folk Music Collection
(original discs and tapes); Kent-Delord
papers; Bailey-Moore Collection of North
Country Mss; Truesdell Print Collection;
Signor/Langlois Collection of architectural
drawings and maps. Collections incl 40,000
ms pieces, 4000 maps, 4000 pictures, 500
phonorecords, and 1750 microforms.

NY —POTSDAM PUBLIC LIBRARY, Civic
Center, Park St, Potsdam, 13676. Kathy Ann
Cassel, Dir
Holdings: Vols 350 Cat Maps Pix
Notes: Very modest collection; especially of
the Potsdam area.

NY —SUFFOLK COUNTY HISTORICAL
SOCIETY, Library, 300 W Main St,
Riverhead, 11901. Betty Carpenter, Librn
Holdings: Vols 4500 Cat Mss Maps Pix
Notes: Suffolk County history.

NY —LANDMARK SOCIETY OF
WESTERN NEW YORK, Wenrich
Memorial Library, 130 Spring Rd,
Rochester, 14608.
Holdings: Vols (2000) Cat Maps Pix Slides
Budget: ($500)
Notes: Paintings, slides, drawings, as well as
the Society's archives of local architecture
and information on presevation and

restoration techniques. Much on
preservation ordinances; legal, physical and
financial aspects of building preservation;
local and regional history, especially of
Rochester and Monroe County.

NY —UNIVERSITY OF ROCHESTER, Rush
Rhees Library, Department of Rare Books
and Special Collections, Rochester, 14627.
Peter Dzwonkoski, Librn
Holdings: Vols Cat Mss Pix Maps
Notes: Particularly strong for the area of
Central and Western New York State.

NY —RYE HISTORICAL SOCIETY, Library,
One Purchase St, Box 155, Rye, 10580.
Susan A Morison, Dir
Holdings: Vols (1000) Mss Maps Pix Slides
Audiotapes
Notes: History of Rye, NY. About 125
books on colonial arts and crafts. Partially
cataloged.

NY —SKIDMORE COLLEGE, Lucy Scribner
Library, Saratoga Springs, 12866. David
Eyman, Librn
Holdings: Cat Maps Pix
Budget: $1000
Notes: Anita Pohndoff Yates Collection of
Saratogiana. 2500 items, incl maps, pictures,
clippings, prints, music, etc.

NY —SMITHTOWN LIBRARY, Long Island
Room, Hanley Collection, 1 N Country Rd,
Smithtown, 11787. Vera Toman, Librn
Holdings: Vols (20,000) Cat Mss Maps Pix
Microforms
Budget: ($3000)
Notes: Strong history collection for the
colonial period through the Civil War for
Suffolk County and Queens and Kings
counties. Special emphasis on history of
Smithtown, incl the Charles E Lawrence and
Judge J Lawrence Smith mss collections.
Also, genealogies of many early Long Island
families and census records on microfilm,
1890-1910, for Naussau and Suffolk
counties. Incl 20,000 mss, 350 maps and 700
pictures.

NY —CANAL MUSEUM, Research Library,
318 Erie Blvd E, Syracuse, 13202. Todd S
Weseloh, Librn & Archivist
Holdings: Vols (6000) Uncat Mss Maps Pix
Slides
Notes: Collections on American Canals,
English Canals and Panama Canal. Main
focus on canals of New York State from
1793 to present. Engineering, finance,
maintenance, construction, canal life, canal
boats and impact of canals on New York.
Limited genealogical value. 954 linear feet
mss, 46,000 photos and slides, 7000 mss,
maps and plans.

NY —ONONDAGA COUNTY PUBLIC
LIBARY, Local History and Genealogy
Dept, 335 Montgomery St, Syracuse, 13202.
Gerald James Parsons, Head
Holdings: Vols (30,000) Cat Mss Maps Pix
Microforms
Budget: ($12,000)
Notes: Collection of local history and
genealogy covers primarily Syracuse.
Onondaga County, New York State and the
northeast, ie, New England, New Jersey and
Pennsylvania.

NY —HISTORICAL SOCIETY OF THE
TARRYTOWNS, Library, One Grove St,
Tarrytown, 10591. Ruth Neuendorffer, Librn
Holdings: Vols (3000) Cat Mss Maps Pix
Microforms
Notes: History of the Tarrytowns and
vicinity. Incl newspapers, 1875-1946, on
microfilm. Bound volumes of Tarrytown
Daily News, 1916-1937.

NY —ROSWELL P FLOWER MEMORIAL
LIBRARY, 229 Washington St, Watertown,
13601. Anthony F Cozzie, Dir
Holdings: Vols (4732) Cat Mss Maps Pix
Budget: ($1200)

NY —HISTORICAL SOCIETY OF THE
WESTBURIES, Westbury Memorial Public
Library, 454 Rockland St, Westbury, 11590.
Richard Gachot, Cur
Holdings: Vols 1200 Cat Mss Maps Pix
Audiotapes
Notes: History of Westbury and Old
Westbury, New York.

NY —YONKERS PUBLIC LIBRARY,
Information Services, 7 Main St, Yonkers,
10701. Martita Schwarz, Dept Head
Notes: Hudson River Museum branch has

closed. Materials on history of Yonkers, with
some materials on Hudson River history
have been distributed to several other
branches in the library system.

PA —FRIENDS HISTORICAL LIBRARY OF
SWARTHMORE COLLEGE, Swarthmore,
19081. J William Frost, Dir
Holdings: Vols (35,000) Cat Mss Pix
Microforms
Notes: Library's collection contain
information on the history and doctrine of
the Society of Friends, Quaker contributions
to literature, science, business, education,
and government, plus their reform efforts in
peace, Indian rights, women's rights, and
abolition of slavery. The library holds, either
in the original manuscript or on microfilm,
the largest collection in the world of Quaker
meeting archives, incl microfilm copies of
minutes and registers of many meetings in
New York. Among the over 250 mss
collections are several which concern New
York Quaker leaders, families, and
organizations.

NEW YORK (STATE)—IMPRINTS

NY —NEW YORK STATE LIBRARY, State
Education Bldg Annex, Washington Ave,
Albany, 12224.
Holdings: Microforms
Notes: Extensive collection; imprints before
1800; New York State Imprints to 1850. Not
indexed for complete retrieval. Also Readex
microprint edition of Early American
imprints, 1639-1800 (indexed by Evans) and
Second Series 1801-1819 (indexed by Shaw-
Shoemaker).

NY —STATE UNIVERSITY OF NEW
YORK, COLLEGE AT PLATTSBURGH,
Feinberg Library, Special Collections, 153
Hawkins Hall, Plattsburgh, 12901. Joseph G
Swinyer, Librn
Holdings: Vols (1000) Cat
See also entry under New York (State) -
History

NY —UNIVERSITY OF ROCHESTER, Rush
Rhees Library, Department of Rare Books
and Special Collections, Rochester, 14627.
Peter Dzwonkoski, Librn
Holdings: Vols 500 Cat
Notes: Incl Canadaigua, Ithaca, Buffalo, with
special strengths for Auburn and Rochester.
Period covered is through 1860. There is a
special card index for the collection
department.

NEW YORK (STATE)—LAWS AND LEGISLATION

NY —NEW YORK STATE DEPT OF
STATE, Community Affairs Library, 162
Washington Ave, Albany, 12231. M L
Johnson, Librn
Holdings: Vols (14,640) Cat
Notes: Local government. Serves as research
arm for official activities. 16,000 items in
vertical files; 150 periodicals. Unique
Community File collection of about 1600
local governments arranged by counties in
the state.

NEW YORK (STATE)—MAPS

DC —LIBRARY OF CONGRESS, Geography
and Map Division, Washington, 20540. John
A Wolter, Chief
Notes: The American Map Collection incl
167 works produced between 1750 and 1790
incl copies of *A Map of the Most Inhabited
Part of Virginia* by Joshua Fry and Peter
Jefferson (1755 and 1775 editions), John
Montresor's *A Map of the Province of New
York* (1777), William Gerard De Brahm's *A
Map of South Carolina and a Part of
Georgia* (1757), and *A Plan of the City of
Philadelphia* (1776) by Benjamin Easburn.

NY —NEW YORK STATE LIBRARY, State
Education Bldg Annex, Washington Ave,
Albany, 12224.
Notes: 500 atlases, 100,000 maps. All
government-produced maps received on
deposit: geological survey, meteorological,
US Army, topographic, etc. An especially
strong collection of historical and

NEW YORK (STATE)—MAPS (cont.)

geographical maps featuring New York State (1600-present), the history and development of the Eastern United States (1600-1850), exploration and history of North America (1600-1800); maps of specific events, military maps of battle sites, newsmaps; transportation (NY State Dept of Transportation depository); New York State county maps.

NY —UNIVERSITY OF ROCHESTER, Rush Rhees Library, Department of Rare Books and Special Collections, Rochester, 14627. Peter Dzwonkoski, Librn
Notes: Printed and manuscript maps and atlases of Western New York state. Cited in Creek, *Maps of the Genesee Valley and Finger Lakes Region, 1776-1950.* Rochester, NY, 1977.

NY —HISTORICAL SOCIETY OF THE TARRYTOWNS, Library, One Grove St, Tarrytown, 10591. Lucille O Hutchinson, Map Consultant
Notes: Emphasis on the Tarrytowns, Pocantico Hills, the Hudson River, and Westchester County, NY from the late 1700s to the present. Also incl 38 atlases.

NEW YORK (STATE)—POLITICS AND GOVERNMENT

CT —TRINITY COLLEGE LIBRARY, 300 Summit St, Hartford, 06106. Peter J Knapp, Archivist
Holdings: Uncat // Mss Pix
Notes: Late 18th and 19th century mss, letter, diaries, etc of the Curtis Family of Connecticut and New York, with emphasis on: William Edmond (1755-1838), US Congressman from Conn; Holbrook Curtis (1787-1858); William Edmond Curtis (1823-1880), Chief Justice of Superior Court of New York; Mary Ann Scovill Curtis (1831-1908); and William Edmond Curtis Jr, (1855-1923), US Asst Secy of the Treasury. Incl on basis of relation through marriage are late 18th and 19th century mss, letters and diaries of the Hiester, McLanahan and Muhlenberg Families of Pennsylvania, with emphasis on Joseph Hiester (1752-1832), US Congressman and Governor of Pennsylvania; and Andrew Gregg (1755-1835), US Congressman and Senator from Pennsylvania. 12 linear feet.

DC —LIBRARY OF CONGRESS, Manuscript Division, Washington, 20540. John C Broderick, Chief
Notes: Papers of Representative Emanuel Celler.

MA —RADCLIFFE COLLEGE, Arthur & Elizabeth Schlesinger Library on the History of Women in America, 3 James St, Cambridge, 02138. Patricia Miller King, Dir; Eva Moseley, Cur of Mss
Notes: Papers of New York's Democratic Representative Elizabeth Holtzman, graduate of Radcliffe. Most are restricted.

NY —NEW YORK STATE DEPT OF STATE, Community Affairs Library, 162 Washington Ave, Albany, 12231. M L Johnson, Librn
Holdings: Vols (14,640) Cat
Notes: Local government. Serves as research arm for official activities. 16,000 items in vertical files; 150 periodicals. Unique Community File collection of about 1600 local governments arranged by counties in the state.

NY —NEW YORK STATE LIBRARY, State Education Bldg Annex, Washington Ave, Albany, 12224.
Holdings: Cat Mss Maps Pix Microforms Archives
Notes: All aspects of New York State, history development and activity, past and present. Official depository of New York State documents including legislative documents. Bills 1830-date; bill jackets and veto jackets (archival record of legislative intent); 1905, 1921-1958. Legislative Reference, Law, Education, Medical, Manuscripts and History Libraries all with strong emphasis on New York State. Currently official repository for State

archival materials, principal collections incl constitutional conventions, papers of some governors, Executive Dept, State Comptroller, original laws and the colonial records.

NY —NEW YORK STATE LIBRARY, State Education Bldg Annex, Washington Ave, Albany, 12224.
Notes: The papers of former Senator Jacob Javits, covering his press releases, speeches, and campaign materials for the years 1957-1978. Incl 6 boxes materials.

†NY —COLUMBIA UNIVERSITY LIBRARIES, Butler Library, Rare Book and Manuscript Library, 535 W 114 St, New York, 10027.
Notes: Papers of Eugene H Nickerson. Approx 173 items of the Nassau County executive.

NY —STATE UNIVERSITY OF NEW YORK, COLLEGE AT OSWEGO, Penfield Library, Oswego, 13126. Anne Commerton, Dir
Holdings: // Cat Mss Maps Pix
Notes: Collection documents Edward F Crawford's public life and political career while serving as Republic Assemblyman from Oswego County, 1956-1973 and Supreme Court Judge, 1973-1975. Incl are correspondence, scrapbooks, photographs, official property surveys, and maps. 14 ft of mss.

NY —STATE UNIVERSITY OF NEW YORK, STONY BROOK, Melville Library, Dept of Special Collections, Stony Brook, 11794. Evert Volkersz, Head
Notes: The political papers of New York State Republican Jacob K Javits, who served in the US House of Representatives from 1948-54 and in the US Senate from 1956-81. The collection is expected to be open for research in 1985, when finding aids will be available.

NEW YORK (STATE) ART see Art, New York (State)

NEW YORK, ONTARIO AND WESTERN RAILWAY COMPANY

NY —CORNELL UNIVERSITY LIBRARIES, Collection of Regional History, Dept of Manuscripts and Univ Archives, Ithaca, 14853.
Notes: Incl papers, 1866-1960. These records selected for preservation from the company archives are alphabetized and arranged in general categories.

NEW YORK CITY BALLET

NY —NEW YORK PUBLIC LIBRARY, Performing Arts Research Center, Dance Collection, 111 Amsterdam Ave, New York, 10023. Genevieve Oswald, Cur
Holdings: Vols (40,000) Cat Mss Pix Audiotapes Videotapes 16mm Films
Budget: ($9280)
Notes: Multi-media collection with extensive material on this major American company and its predecessors Ballet Society, American Ballet Company, Ballet Caravan, and American Ballet Caravan. Extensive documentation on dancers, choreographers, designers and productions of the company as well as on its ballet masters George Balanchine and Jerome Robbins. Collection includes programs, souvenir booklets, clippings and reviews, photographs, stage and costume designs for various productions, tape-recorded interviews by and about company members, mss and letters, scrapbooks, motion pictures and videotapes of productions. Cataloged items appear in: *Dictionary Catalog of the Dance Collection,* published by G K Hall, Boston, 1974, 10 vols, and annual supplements: *Bibliographic Guide to Dance,* also published by G K Hall.

NEW YORK DRAMA CRITICS' CIRCLE

NY —NEW YORK PUBLIC LIBRARY, Performing Arts Research Center, Billy Rose Theatre Collection, 111 Amsterdam Ave,

New York, 10023. Dorothy L Swerdlove, Cur
Holdings: Cat
Notes: Considerable material on The Circle, incl minutes, correspondence, etc.

NEW YORK NEWS

IL —LAKE FOREST COLLEGE, Donnelley Library, Lake Forest, 60045. Arthur H Miller Jr, College Librn
Holdings: Vols (1000) Mss Pix
Notes: Working files (1919-1946) of Capt Joseph-Medill Patterson, founder of the New York *News.*

NEW YORK POINT BOOKS

NY —NEW YORK STATE LIBRARY, Library for the Blind and Visually Handicapped, Cultural Education Center, Empire State Plaza, Albany, 12230.
Holdings: Cat
Notes: Small collection of New York Point books retained to preserve specimens of now defunct print for blind readers.

NEW YORK PRO MUSICA

NY —NEW YORK PUBLIC LIBRARY, Performing Arts Research Center, Music Div, Lincoln Center, New York, 10018.
Notes: New York Pro Musica Archives, and personal papers of Noah Greenberg, founder.

NEW YORK STATE FEDERATION OF WOMEN'S CLUBS

NY —ELMIRA COLLEGE, Gannett-Tripp Learning Center, Elmira, 14901. James D Gray, Dir
Holdings: Cat Pix
Notes: Collection on the history and condition of women, to 1900. Also, archives of the New York State Federation of Women's Clubs.

NEW YORK TIMES (NEWSPAPER)

MA —RADCLIFFE COLLEGE, Arthur & Elizabeth Schlesinger Library on the History of Women in America, 3 James St, Cambridge, 02138. Patricia Miller King, Dir; Eva Moseley, Cur of Mss
Notes: The papers of the 1974 class action suit against *The New York Times* that charged the newspaper with "a pattern and practice of discrimination in employment on the basis of sex." The *Times* agreed to an Affirmative Action plan, and the suit was resolved in 1978.

NJ —PRINCETON UNIVERSITY, Seeley G Mudd Manuscript Library, Public Affairs Papers Collection, Princeton, 08544. Nancy Bressler, Cur
Holdings: Mss
Notes: Arthur Krock's personal papers, 1909-1974. Incl 93 boxes.

NY —ROCHESTER INSTITUTE OF TECHNOLOGY, Melbert B Cary Jr Graphic Arts Collection, School of Printing, One Lomb Memorial Drive, Rochester, 14623. David Pankow, Cur
Holdings: Vols (11,000) Cat Mss Pix
Notes: Incl the *New York Times Museum of the Printed Word.* Also incl specimens.

NEW YORK WORLD'S FAIRS

IL —MUSEUM OF SCIENCE AND INDUSTRY, Library, 57th St and Lake Shore Dr, Chicago, 60637. Carla Hayden, Coordinator
Holdings: Vols Cat Maps Pix Slides
Notes: Occupying the site of the Fine Arts Building of Chicago's Columbian Exposition of 1893, the Museum Library has been the recipient of numerous gifts in this field, not only of materials from Chicago's Columbian Expositons, Century of Progress and Railroad Fairs but also from the New York World's Fair, St Louis, Paris Exposition Universelle, San Francisco's Panama-Pacific etc. Incl blueprints of some buildings and areas. No separate catalog or index to this extensive collection.

NEW YORK WORLD'S FAIRS (cont.)

NY —NEW YORK PUBLIC LIBRARY, Rare
Books and Manuscripts Div, Fifth Ave & 42
St, New York, 10018. William L Joyce, Asst
Dir; Susan E Davis, Cur of Mss
Holdings: Cat Mss
Budget: ($7161)
Notes: Incl Archives of the NY World's
Fairs, 1939-40 and 1964-65.

NEW YORKER (MAGAZINE)

DC —LIBRARY OF CONGRESS, Prints &
Photographs Div, Washington, 20540.
Notes: *The New Yorker* Collection contains
original cartoons and cover illustrations from
the magazine, mid-20th century.
NY —NEW YORK PUBLIC LIBRARY,
Performing Arts Research Center, Billy Rose
Theatre Collection, 111 Amsterdam Ave,
New York, 10023. Dorothy L Swerdlove,
Cur
Holdings: Cat
Notes: A large collection of original
caricatures, many of which appeared in the
New Yorker magazine, 1925-1962. Published
description: Frueh, Alfred J, *Frueh on the
Theatre; Theatrical Caricatures, 1906-1962*,
(New York Public Library, 1972). See also
entry under Sardi's Restaurant.

NEW ZEALAND

CA —UNIVERSITY OF CALIFORNIA, LOS
ANGELES, Research Library, Indo/Pacific
Collection, 405 Hilgard Ave, Los Angeles,
90024. Edward Shreeves, Chairman,
Bibliographers Group; Charlotte Spence,
Indo/Pacific Bibliographer
Holdings: Vols Cat Mss Maps Pix
Microforms
Notes: The Pacific area collection has been
developed on a combination of the research
and teaching levels. It focuses on the
cultural, economic, political and social
history of Australia, New Zealand and the
various island groups. The accounts of the
early European voyagers are well
represented, with the highlight being the
Captain Cook collection. An effort has also
been made to collect the novels, poetry,
drama, etc, of Australian and New Zealand
authors.
CA —UNIVERSITY OF CALIFORNIA,
SANTA CRUZ, University Library, Special
Collections, Santa Cruz, 95064. Rita
Bottoms, Special Collections Librn; Margaret
Felts, South Pacific Collection Bibliographer
Holdings: Vols (10,000) Cat
Notes: Monographs, rare books, serials,
documents and atlases which treat of the
Pacific areas of Polynesia, Melanesia,
Micronesia, Australia and New Zealand, but
excluding western New Guinea (Irian Jaya),
the Phillipines and Southeast Asia.
Approximately 10 per cent of the titles are
multi-volume documents such as
parliamentary papers, legislative journals,
official yearbooks, statistical sourcebooks,
laws and statutes. The collection includes an
exhaustive selection of current journals and
monographic series from and about the
Pacific: early serials, South Pacific
Commission publications. US Government
and US Trust Territory publications, serials
from museums, universities and scholarly
societies. Chief emphasis has been placed on
acquisition of the literature of history,
description and travel, ethnology and
anthropology, literature and literary
criticism,political and constitutional histories.
Other extensive holdings are in the fields of
geography and maps, voyages, mission
histories, mythology and folklore, art,
linguistics, and science fields of natural
history, environmental studies, biology,
zoology, botany, geology and astronomy.
NY —AMERICAN MUSEUM OF
NATURAL HISTORY, Library Services
Dept, Central Park W & 79th St, New York,
10024. Nina J Root, Chairwoman; Mary
Genett, Asst Librn for Reference Services
NY —BOOKS-ACROSS-THE-SEA, The
English-Speaking Union, 16 E 69 St, New

York, 10021. Catherine Nolan, Librn
Holdings: Vols (6500) Cat
Budget: ($25,000)
Notes: Deals mainly with humanities and
social sciences of Great Britain, Australia,
New Zealand, and Canada; adult books.
Collection started in 1942; current titles
added through exchange.
NY —NEW YORK PUBLIC LIBRARY,
Research Libraries, General Research
Division, Fifth Ave & 42 St, New York,
10018. Rodney Phillips, Chief
Holdings: Vols (2,225,000) Cat Maps Pix
Microforms
Budget: ($775,718)
PA —PENNSYLVANIA STATE
UNIVERSITY, Fred Lewis Pattee Library,
University Park, 16802. Stuart Forth, Dean
of Libraries
Holdings: VOLS (8000) Cat Mss Maps Pix
Budget: ($1,400,000)
Notes: The Pennsylvania State University
has for several years had a strong interest in
the South Pacific, based on Australia but
extending to New Zealand and other island
groups, together with an interest in voyages
of exploration and scientific discovery. The
collection is particularly strong in literature
but extends to history, political science, the
arts and humanities generally. Holdings
housed in Special Collections include the
Moody gift of 90 prints and paintings, press
collections including the Wattle Grove press,
and Golden Cockerell Press publications
associated with Norman Lindsay. The
special collection of Australiana is dedicated
to Bruce Sutherland and was described in his
publication *Australiana in the PSU Libraries*
(Pennsylvania State University Libraries,
1969), 390 pp. A separate card file is
maintained.

NEW ZEALAND—DESCRIPTION AND TRAVEL—VIEWS

NM —MUSEUM OF NEW MEXICO, Photo
Archives, Box 2087, Santa Fe, 87503.
Arthur L Olivas, Cur; Richard Rudisill,
Photo Historian
Holdings: Cat Pix Slides
Notes: Extensive picture collections of
Australia, New Zealand, China, India and
the East taken in the 19th century. The
Photo Archives contain approx 250,000
items, of which 200,000 are cataloged. The
primary function of the archives is
preserving significant historical material, and
these pictures are mainly for research rather
than for general browsing.

NEW ZEALAND AUTHORS see Authors, New Zealand

NEW ZEALAND LITERATURE

CA —UNIVERSITY OF CALIFORNIA, LOS
ANGELES, Research Library, Indo/Pacific
Collection, 405 Hilgard Ave, Los Angeles,
90024. Edward Shreeves, Chairman,
Bibliographers Group; Charlotte Spence,
Indo/Pacific Bibliographer
Holdings: Vols Cat Mss Maps Pix
Microforms
Notes: The Pacific area collection has been
developed on a combination of the research
and teaching levels. It focuses on the
cultural, economic, political and social
history of Australia, New Zealand and the
various island groups. The accounts of the
early European voyagers are well
represented, with the highlight being the
Captain Cook collection. An effort has also
been made to collect the novels, poetry,
drama, etc, of Australian and New Zealand
authors.
PA —PENNSYLVANIA STATE
UNIVERSITY, Fred Lewis Pattee Library,
University Park, 16802. Stuart Forth, Dean
of Libraries
Holdings: Vols (3000) Cat Phonorecords
Microforms
Budget: ($1,400,000)
Notes: Strong in Australian Literature, lesser
holdings in Canadian, Caribbean, New
Zealand, Indian and West African. Special

collections of African Plays, Australian
Literature.

NEWBERRY, JOHN

IN —INDIANA UNIVERSITY, Lilly Library,
Seventh St, Bloomington, 47405. William R
Cagle, Librn
Holdings: Uncat Mss
Notes: The Elisabeth Ball Collection consists
of more than 7000 books and many
manuscripts from the late seventeenth to the
early twentieth centuries. Strengths incl
Newberry and other early imprints,
chapbooks, horn books, harlequinades, street
cries, and miniature books.

NEWBERY AWARD BOOKS

FL —FLORIDA STATE UNIVERSITY,
Robert Manning Strozier Library, Special
Collections Dept, Tallahassee, 32306. Opal
M Free, Head, Special Collections
Holdings: Vols 60 Uncat
Notes: Noncirculating.
MI —WAYNE STATE UNIVERSITY, Kresge
Library (Education), Detroit, 48202.
Theodore Manheim, Librn
Holdings: Vols (65,000) Cat Mss Microforms
Budget: ($2000)
Notes: The Eloise Ramsey Collection (10,
000 vols). See, *The Eloise Ramsey
Collection of Literature for Young People: A
Catalogue;* compiled by Joan Cusenza
(Detroit: Wayne State University Libraries,
1967). Besides the Ramsey Collection, which
is housed separately and does not circulate,
the Education Library has approx 55,000
volumes of children's and young adults'
literature, with a very large picture-book
collection, a large poetry collection; all with
special emphasis on urban and ethnic
materials.
MN —UNIVERSITY OF MINNESOTA,
Libraries, Children's Literature Research
Collections, 109 Walter Library,
Minneapolis, 55455. Karen Nelson Hoyle,
Cur
Holdings: Vols (500) Cat Mss Pix
Notes: Incl first editions, mss, and
illustrations for children's books. Newbery
and Caldecott award books and honor books
and their translations; Mildred L Batchelder
Award nominees in original and US editions;
Minnesota; Dakota and Ojibway Indian
tribes; languages other than English;
correspondence between authors and
illustrators and Dr Irvin Kerlan, Kerlan
Collection. 350 volumes in translation.
TX —DALLAS PUBLIC LIBRARY, Central
Library, Humanities Division, 1515 Young
St, Dallas, 75201. Richard L Waters, Acting
Dir; Muriel W Brown, Children's Literature
Specialist; Rosemarie Dunlap, Assistant to
Children's Literature Specialist
Holdings: Vols (56,000) Cat Mss Pix
Microforms
Notes: Incl Mother Goose Books,
autographed Newbery and Caldecott
winners, books important in the history of
children's literature, foreign language books,
and Texas books in addition to a general
collection.
WI —UNIVERSITY OF WISCONSIN,
MADISON, Cooperative Children's Book
Center, Helen C White Hall, Rm 4290, 600
N Park St, Madison, 53706. Ginny Moore
Kruse, Dir
Holdings: Vols (25,000) Cat
Notes: Cooperative Children's Book Center
collections incl most US trade books
published for children in last 24 months; first
editions of recommended US children's
trade books published since 1965; over 400
alternative press books published for children
in US and Canada since 1970; children's
books about Wisconsin and by Wisconsin
authors and illustrators; representative 19th
and early 20th century American children's
books; 19th century children's periodicals;
first and significant editions of Newbury and
Caldecott Medal books; historical and
contemporary toybooks; 75 vols of Mother
Goose published since 1828; 160 vols of
Thorton Burgess books, many first editions;
ms and original artwork for Ellen Raskin's

NEWBERY AWARD BOOKS (cont.)

The Westing Game and *The Mysterious Disappearance of Leon (I Mean Noel)*; juvenile mass market and traderomance fiction.

NEWCOMB, CHARLES KING, 1820-1894

RI —BROWN UNIVERSITY, John Hay Library, 20 Prospect St, Providence, 02912. Mark N Brown, Cur Mss
Holdings: // Mss
Notes: Charles King Newcomb, Rhode Islnd Transcendentalist, member of Brook Farm community, and Brown Class of 1837. Incl 2 ms boxes of letters for the period 1802 to 1849 written by Mrs Rhoda M Newcomb, incl letters to her son Charles King Newcomb while he was in tehological seminary from 1838 to 1840, and while he lived at Brook Farm from 1841 to 1846. Also 11 ms volumes of his Commonplace Book and 27 ms journals containing thoughts on principles of life, nature, Shakespeare, and scholarship. Members of the community at Brook Farm as well as the literati of Concord, Massachusetts, and those of Providence, especially Sarah Helen Whitman, Margaret Fuller, R W Emerson, and Bronson Alcott, are discussed.

NEWCOMB, RICHARD F.

MA —BOSTON UNIVERSITY, Mugar Memorial Library, Special Collections Dept, 771 Commonwealth Ave, Boston, 02215. Howard B Gotlieb, Dir
Holdings: Cat Mss Pix
Notes: Mss, correspondence, etc collected in depth; incl publications by or about.

NEWFOUNDLAND

NF —MEMORIAL UNIVERSITY OF NEWFOUNDLAND, University Library, Centre for Newfoundland Studies, Elizabeth Ave, Saint John's, A1C 5S7, Can. Anne Hart, Head
Holdings: Vols (48,000) Cat Maps Microforms
Budget: ($50,000)
Notes: Materials about Newfoundland, by Newfoundlanders, or published in Newfoundland, incl Labrador. Also, Saint Pierre and Miquelon. Bibliography of Newfoundland materials is being compiled (now over 7,000 items).

NEWKIRK, ELIZA see Rogers, Eliza Newkirk, 1877-1966

NEWLEY, ANTHONY

MA —BOSTON UNIVERSITY, Mugar Memorial Library, Special Collections Dept, 771 Commonwealth Ave, Boston, 02215. Howard B Gotlieb, Dir
Holdings: Cat Mss Pix
Notes: Mss, correspondence, etc collected in depth; incl publications by or about.

NEWMAN, ALFRED

CA —UNIVERSITY OF SOUTHERN CALIFORNIA, Edward L Doheny Memorial Library, Archives of Performing Arts, University Park, Los Angeles, 90089. Robert Knutson, Librn
Holdings: Mss Pix
Notes: Personal collection of papers, pictures, etc.

NEWMAN, JARED TREMAN, 1855-1937

NY —CORNELL UNIVERSITY LIBRARIES, Collection of Regional History, Dept of Manuscripts and Univ Archives, Ithaca, 14853.
Notes: Attorney and bank official. Incl papers, 1880-1936; one scrapbook, correspondence, blueprints, maps, clippings, and legal documents.

NEWMAN, JOHN HENRY CARDINAL, 1801-1890

CA —MOUNT SAINT MARY'S COLLEGE, Charles Willard Coe Memorial Library, 12001 Chalon Rd, Los Angeles, 90049. Erika M Condon, Head Librn
Holdings: Vols 276 Cat Mss Pix Microforms
Notes: Incl 9 letters of Cardinal Newman, microfilm of 90 letters (2 letters of Pusey's, 3 of Keble's). 13 first editions of Newman's writings.
CA —SAINT MARY'S COLLEGE, Library, Moraga, 94575. Brother Casimir Reichlin, Dir of the Library; Brother Richard Lemberg FSC, Asst Librn
Holdings: Vols 1746
Notes: Biographical information on Oxford Movement figures, esp John Henry Newman.
DC —GEORGETOWN UNIVERSITY, Library, Special Collections Div, 37 & O Sts NW, Washington, 20057. George M Barringer, Special Collections Librn; Nicholas B Sheetz, Mss Librn
Holdings: Vols 150 Cat Mss Pix
Notes: Mss incl over 375 letters, principally to Henry Wilberforce.
MA —NEWMAN PREPARATORY SCHOOL LIBRARY, 245 Marlborough St, Boston, 02116.
Holdings: Cat Mss Pix
Notes: Mss and books by him.
MA —COLLEGE OF THE HOLY CROSS, Dinand Library, College St, Worcester, 01610. James M Mahoney, Cur of Special Collection
Holdings: Cat Mss
Notes: Ms letters of Newman (45); first editions of his writings. The J J Reilly library is the core of this collection. Restricted use; noncirculating.

NEWMAN, PETER CHARLES, 1929-

ON —MCMASTER UNIVERSITY, Mills Memorial Library, Div of Archives & Research Collections, Hamilton, L8S 4L6, Can. G R Hill, Univ Librn
Holdings: Mss
Notes: Research files, correspondence and mss for his publications.

NEWMAN, RALPH G.

IL —CHICAGO HISTORICAL SOCIETY, Library, Clark St at North Ave, Chicago, 60614. Archie Motley, Manuscript Librn
Holdings: Ms
Notes: Papers of Ralph G Newman, relative to his Abraham Lincoln Book Shop and other business and public service ventures. Also, membership recrds of the South Shore Country Club and papers of other Chicago-area activities.

NEWMAN, ROBERT

MA —BOSTON UNIVERSITY, Mugar Memorial Library, Special Collections Dept, 771 Commonwealth Ave, Boston, 02215. Howard B Gotlieb, Dir
Holdings: Cat Mss
Notes: Mss correspondence, etc collected in depth; incl publications by or about.

NEWSFILM

WA —UNIVERSITY OF WASHINGTON LIBRARIES, Suzzallo Library, Manuscripts Section, FM-25, Seattle, 98195. Karyl Winn, Librn
Notes: Files of locally produced newsfilm from station KOMO-TV in Seattle, from 1954.

NEWSLETTERS

DC —LIBRARY OF CONGRESS, Manuscript Division, Washington, 20540. John C Broderick, Chief
MD —UNIVERSITY OF MARYLAND, Library, East Asia Collection, College Park, 20742. Frank Joseph Shulman, Curator and Head
Holdings: Vols
Budget: $300
Notes: Very extensive (600) vertical files of Western-language newsletters and association bulletins published since the early 1960s that relate in whole or in part to Asian Studies. Some titles have been listed in Frank Joseph Shulman's Newsletters and Association Bulletins on Asia: An Annotated Guide to Current Academic Resources, *Asian Studies Professional Review*, vols 4 (1974-75) and 5 (1975-76). All disciplines covered. Most newsletters and bulletins are academically or culturally oriented; newsletters of the business world and of foreign embassies and their information centers are generally excluded. These files are believed to constitute the single most comprehensive collection of their kind in the world. This collection is not a component part of the University of Maryland Libraries, but all communications should beaddressed to Frank Joseph Shulman, c/o the University's East Asia Collection.
ON —METROPOLITAN TORONTO LIBRARY, Science & Technology Dept, 789 Yonge St, Toronto, M4W 2G8, Can. Margaret Walshe, Head
Holdings: Vols (40,000) Cat Microforms
Notes: Department has over 1300 current subscriptions. Acquires most titles indexed in *Applied Science and Technology Index*. Some back files of periodicals from 1800s. Newsletters are also collected; emphasis is on Canadian content.

NEWSMEN see Newswriters

NEWSPAPER EDITORS

IL —NEWBERRY LIBRARY, 60 W Walton St, Chicago, 60610. Diana Haskell, Cur of Modern Mss
Holdings: Cat Mss Pix Slides Microforms
Notes: Working and personal papers of editors and feature writers for the *Chicago Daily News*, the *Chicago Tribune* and others. Housed in The Midwest Manuscripts Collections. Restricted use: noncirculating.
KS —BUTLER COUNTY HISTORICAL SOCIETY, 383 E Central, El Dorado, 67042.
Holdings: Vols 300
Notes: Books by and owned by William Allen White, Emporia newspaperman

NEWSPAPERS—COLLECTIONS

CA —HEMET PUBLIC LIBRARY, 510 E Florida Ave, Hemet, 92343. James P Boulton, Chief Librn
Holdings: Vols (3000) Cat Mss Maps Pix
Notes: Special emphasis on southern California and Indians of the Southwest. Local newspaper collection from 1907 to date.
CT —YALE UNIVERSITY, Box 1603A, Yale Station, New Haven, 06520.
Notes: Especially American Colonial, and English 18th and 19th centuries.
DE —HISTORICAL SOCIETY OF DELAWARE, Library, 505 Market St Mall, Wilmington, 19801. Barbara E Benson, Library Dir
Holdings: Cat Mss Microforms
Notes: Collection incl papers and other mss materials.
DC —LIBRARY OF CONGRESS, Serial and Government Publications Division, Washington, 20540.
Notes: Serials. One of the largest and most extensive collections in the world, incl periodicals; scientific and learned journals in all languages and in all fields except agriculture and medicine; US Government serials (Federal, State, County, and Muncipal); national foreign government serials from all countries; provincial serials from provinces possessing autonomy; municipal serials from principal cities; newpapers (850,000 unbound issues, 75,000 bound vols, 270,000 microfilm reels), 12,000 microprint cards of early American newspapers, 1704-1820, incl 1500 titles currently received, 500 of these being reprsentative titles from all States of the Union and 1000 from all foreign countries.
FL —MIAMI-DADE PUBLIC LIBRARY SYSTEM, 1 Biscayne Blvd, Miami, 33132.

NEWSPAPERS—COLLECTIONS (cont.)

Samuel J Boldrick, Librn
Holdings: Vols (4950) Cat Mss Maps Pix Audiotapes Microforms
Notes: Also incl 40,000 state and local documents; 700,000 newspaper clippings; and 195 reels of microfilmed newspaper clippings. Separate finding aids incl the *Miami Newspapers Index*, a computer generated index to six Miami newspapers which is on an in house on-line database.

ID —IDAHO STATE HISTORICAL SOCIETY, Library, 610 N Julia Davis Dr, Boise, 83706. Elizabeth Jacox, Librn
Holdings: Vols 2000 Cat Microforms
Notes: Idaho newspapers and documents with microfilm files.

IL —CHICAGO PUBLIC LIBRARY, Newspapers & General Periodicals Center, 425 N Michigan Ave, Chicago, 60611. Jerry Delaney, Head
Holdings: Microforms
Notes: Collection consists of current (one month) copies of daily papers from every state and over forty foreign countries. The permanent newspaper collection (on microfilm) incl many Chicago dailies, some as far back as 1833. It also incl indexed dailies from major cities, the Readex microprint "Early Americn Newspapers", and Bell and Howell's "Underground Newspaper Collection".

IL —FREEPORT PUBLIC LIBRARY, 314 W Stephenson St, Freeport, 61032. John Locascio, Head Librn
Holdings: Vols (400) Cat Microforms Clippings
Notes: Freeport, Illinois, and Stephenson County history. Incl 3 file cabinets of clippings. German language newspapers, 1854-1917; English language newspapers, 1847-date. 507 newspaper file microfilm reels.

KS —MENNINGER FOUNDATION, Archives, 5600 W Sixth St, Box 829, Topeka, 66601. Alice Brand, Librn; Mark West, Archivist
Notes: 5 boxes, 1800-1899. Consists of over 300 19th century newspapers containing articles about mental illness.

LA —LOUISIANA STATE UNIVERSITY, SHREVEPORT, Library-Archives, 8515 Youree Dr, Shreveport, 71129. Patricia L Meador, Archivist & Asst Librn
Notes: See Louisiana - History entry for LSU Archives.

†MA —BOSTON PUBLIC LIBRARY, Copley Sq, Boston, 02117.
Holdings: Cat Micrforms
Notes: Microform Publications: Early American Newspapers, 1704-1820, by Readex Microprint Corp: special emphasis on Boston newspapers, general, local and ethnic; selected newspapers from New England, US and Europe.

MA —AMERICAN ANTIQUARIAN SOCIETY LIBRARY, 185 Salisbury St, Worcester, 01609. Marcus A McCorison, Dir & Librn
Holdings: Vols 60,000 Cat
Notes: Sixty percent of the total of books and pamphlets known to have been printed in the United States before 1821. Source of Readex Microprint Corp project called *Early American Imprints, 1639-1800*, a Microprint edition of every extant book, pamphlet, and broadside printed in what is now the United States. Keyed to Evans *American Bibliography*, it reprints in full the texts of nearly 50,000 titles and includes all of Shipton's revision of Evans. A second series, keyed to Shaw and Shoemaker's *American Bibliography*, will bring these Microprint reproductions up to 1820. One of the great strengths of the collection is its broadsides and American newspapers, the best anywhere. From it emerged Clarence Brigham's monumental *History and Bibliography of American Newspapers, 1690-1820*, which located every surviving copy of every newspaper printed in the United States before 1821.
ReadexMicroprint Corp is also reproducing this collection. The Society's collections

extend beyond 1820, in special strengths, to the turn of the century. The collection incl unusual strengths in Amateur Newspapers (about 50,000 issues), and Bolivian, Chilean, and West Indian newspapers.

NE —NEBRASKA STATE HISTORICAL SOCIETY, Archives, 1500 R St, Box 82554, Lincoln, 68501. James E Potter, State Archivist
Holdings: Cat Mss Microforms
Budget: ($290,000)
Notes: Newspaper collection of 20,000 rolls of microfilm, non-circulating but available for purchase, cataloged according to place published so specific titles must be requested. See *A Guide to the Newspaper Collection of the State Archives*, (Lincoln: Nebraska State Historical Society, 1977).

NY —NEW YORK STATE LIBRARY, State Education Bldg Annex, Washington Ave, Albany, 12224.
Holdings: Uncat Microforms
Notes: Selected list of major American and a few foreign papers.
See also entry under Newspapers - US

NY —GANNETT NEWSPAPERS, Press & Sun Bulletin, Vestal Parkway E, Binghamton, 13902. Jorette Martin, Librn
Holdings: Cat Maps Pix Microfiche
Notes: Incl 100 filing cabinets of the Gannett newspapers morgue and files since 1904.

NY —NEW YORK HISTORICAL SOCIETY, Library, 170 Central Park W, New York, 10024. James Gregory, Librn
Notes: An extensive collection of eighteenth and early nineteenth century American newspapers. Incl the most complete set of original colonial New York papers and the fourth largest collection of newspapers printed in the US prior to 1821.

NY —NEW YORK PUBLIC LIBRARY, Annex Section, 521 W 43 St, New York, 10036. Richard L Hill, First Asst
Holdings: Vols 24,000 Cat Microforms
Notes: Comprehensive New York (City) coverage; selective coverage of other US and foreign countries. Incl 24,000 bound volumes; 86,000 microfilm reels.

OH —CLEVELAND PUBLIC LIBRARY, General Reference Dept, 325 Superior Ave, Cleveland, 44114. Donald Tipka, Head
Notes: Extensive Cleveland historical collection. Modern holdings with wide geographical US coverage plus selective foreign representation. Microfilm readers and reader printer available in room for use of materials in this format. Restricted use; noncirculating. Retrospective holdings in microformat.

OH —PLAIN DEALER LIBRARY, 1801 Superior Ave, Cleveland, 44114. Patti A Graziano, Library Dir
Holdings: Vols 3800 Cat
Notes: Ohio history, with emphasis on Cleveland. Incl 3 million newspaper clippings; 1 million pictures, 1858-date; 100 maps; and 6000 microforms.

OH —OHIO HISTORICAL SOCIETY, Archives Library Division, 1982 Velma Ave, Columbus, 43211. Dennis East, Division Chief
Holdings: Vols (96,000) Cat Mss Maps Pix Slides Microforms
Budget: ($18,000)
Notes: This library is the primary collection for Ohio. Most purchases are on the rare and out of print market. Collection area is early American history, esp relating to exploration into the Northwest Territory. Also, Ohio archaeology, natural history, and artifacts. Major media collections are books (96,000), newspapers (25,000 vols and 22, 000 microform), pictures (50,000), maps (2500), manuscripts (1,500,000). Library is noncirculating except through interlibrary loan of microfilm.

OK —CENTRAL STATE UNIVERSITY, Library, 100 N University Dr, Edmond, 73034. Andrew Peters, Reference Librn
Holdings: Cat Maps Audiotapes Microforms
Notes: Microforms Research Center for newspapers and periodicals, incl ERIC, LAC, LEL, HRAF, and annual reports, etc. Vols on microfilm reels, microfiche; microcards; academic and music audiotapes; and maps.

OR —UNIVERSITY OF OREGON LIBRARY, Microforms and Recordings Section, Eugene, 97403. Rory Funke, Head
Holdings: Cat Microforms
Notes: Most Oregon newspapers microfilmed on a current basis. Extensive collection of negative microfilm; 30,000 reels of microfilm. Publication: *Oregon Newspapers; Negative Held by University of Oregon Library*. (Eugene, Oregon: University of Oregon Library, 1970).

TX —UNIVERSITY OF TEXAS LIBRARIES, General Libraries, Barker Texas History Center, PO Box P, Austin, 78712. Don Carleton, Dir

WA —WASHINGTON STATE LIBRARY, Washington/Northwest Rm, State Library Bldg, Olympia, 98504. Nancy B Pryor, Research Consultant
Holdings: Uncat Microforms
Notes: The State Library is a depository for newspapers published in Washington State, presently receiving 186 current newspapers, incl about 12 out-of-state papers. Since 1951 the State Library has been engaged in a newsaper microfilming project in cooperation with the University of Washington, Washington State University and other libraries in the state. A great number of original files have been filmed, and the filming of the remainder is continuing as rapidly as possible (25,000 microfilm reels). We loan on interlibrary loan all of our positive newspaper microfilm. We will also, on request, provide prints of articles from the microfilm. Except for some territorial newspapers, we have disposed of the original files as they were microfilmed and will continue to do so. If possible we try to place each file in a library, historical society or museum inthe area in which it was published.

WA —UNIVERSITY OF WASHINGTON LIBRARIES, Microforms Newspaper Section, FM-25, Seattle, 98195. Glenda J Pearson, Microforms Reference Librn
Holdings: Microforms
Budget: ($86,000)
Notes: Current and historical files of selected newspapers, foreign and US, most on microfilm. "Early American Newspapers" set (incomplete), "Underground Newspapers Collection" set, comprehensive Seattle area and Washington State and Territory coverage, other regional titles including ethnic and special interest papers. Publication: *Pacific Northwest Newspapers on Microfilm at the University of Washington Libraries* (Seattle: University of Washington Libraries, 1983).

YT —YUKON ARCHIVES, Box 2703, Whitehorse, Y1A 3C6, Can. Miriam McTiernan, Territorial Archivist
Holdings: Vols (8000) Cat Mss Maps Pix Phonorecords Audiotapes Videotapes 16mm Films Microforms
Budget: $15,000
Notes: Yukon and regional history and development. Incl also 500 mss; 10,000 maps; 30,000 pictures; 1200 microfilm rolls; 1115 oral history tapes, etc; Yukon newspapers.

NEWSPAPERS—INDEXES

IL —UNIVERSITY OF ILLINOIS, URBANA/CHAMPAIGN, Library, Newspaper Library, 1408 W Gregory Drive, Urbana, 61801. Betty L Hildwein, Librn
Holdings: Vols 1200 Cat
Notes: A list of newspaper indexes (current and retrospective) held in newspaper library was prepared in 1982. The library contains over 2000 vols of reference guides, bibliographies and histories.

NEWSPAPERS, AFRICAN

CA —UNIVERSITY OF CALIFORNIA, LOS ANGELES, Research Library, African Studies Collection, 405 Hilgard Ave, Los Angeles, 90024. Edward Shreeves, Chairman, Bibliographers Group; Joseph J Lauer, African Studies Bibliographer
Holdings: Maps Pix Slides Phonorecords Audiotapes Microforms
Notes: General collection mainly in the

NEWSPAPERS, AFRICAN (cont.)

humanities and social sciences, covering prehistoric times to the present. Particular stengths include: early travel and exploration, mission field, literature, vernacular languages and literatures, Portuguese Africa, slavery (have the British Foreign Office's *General Correspondence. Slave Trade* on microfilm). Extensive holdings of journals, newspapers and government publications. The collection was described in the *Handbook of American Resources for African Studies* (1967).

CA —HOOVER INSTITUTION ON WAR, REVOLUTION & PEACE, Stanford University, Stanford, 94305. Peter Duignan, Cur; Karen Fung, Deputy Cur
Holdings: Vols (60,000) Cat Mss Maps Pix Slides Microforms
Notes: Politics, economics, and history from 1870 to the present. About 500 current periodicals titles, about 90 current newspaper titles. Legislative debates, political ephemera. Have microfilm of Portuguese African nationalist material, confidential prints of Great Britian's foreign and colonial offices 1870 through 1922. Nigerian pamphlets (market literature, political and historical tracts), collection of the correspondence pamphlets and ephemera of Alfred B Xuma, collections on Zaire (1955-1963), South African nationalist publications on microfilm. Descriptions of the Collection: *African and Middle East Collections* pub by Hoover Institute, *Handbook of American Resources for African Studies* pub by Hoover. Holdings of the Collection in *Hoover Institute on War, Revolution, and Peace Library Catalog* pub by G K Hall, *Emerging Nationalism in Portuguese Africa: A Bibliography* pub by Hoover, *German Africa* pub by Hoover. *The Treason Trail in South Africa: A Guide to the Microfilm Record of the Trial* pub by Hoover. *History of the Library and Archives of the Hoover Institution on War, Revolution and Peace*, edited by Peter Duignan (Hoover Institution Press), *Guide to Non-federal Archives and Manuscripts in the United States Relating to Africa*, compiled Aloha P Smith (East Ardsley, Eng, Microform Ltd).

DC —HOWARD UNIVERSITY, Moorland-Spingarn Research Center, 500 Howard Place NW, Washington, 20059. Clifford L Muse, Jr, Acting Dir

IL —NORTHWESTERN UNIVERSITY, Library, Newspaper-Microtext Dept, Evanston, 60201. Stephen Marek, Microtext Librn
Holdings: Vols 800 Cat Microforms
Notes: Incl 96 currently published titles as well as retrospective titles.

NEWSPAPERS, AGRICULTURAL

IL —NORTHERN ILLINOIS REGIONAL HISTORY CENTER, Sven Parson Hall, Northern Illinois University, De Kalb, 60115. Glen Gildemeister, Dir
Holdings: Cat Mss Maps Pix Slides Phonorecords Audiotapes 16mm Films Microforms
Notes: "A research center for advanced research in the humanities. This northern area of Illinois (excluding Cook County) has been virtually untouched by collecting agencies and we hope to fill that void. We will be strong in agribusiness, agricultural implement business, and hybrid farming mechanics....Will be primarily a ms repository, but [have] already taken responsibility for many artifacts and books, some rare."

IL —UNIVERSITY OF ILLINOIS, URBANA/CHAMPAIGN, Library, Newspaper Library, 1408 W Gregory Drive, Urbana, 61801. Betty L Hildwein, Librn

NEWSPAPERS, ALASKAN

WA —UNIVERSITY OF WASHINGTON LIBRARIES, Microforms Newspaper Section, FM-25, Seattle, 98195. Glenda J Pearson, Microforms Reference Librn
Holdings: Microforms
Budget: ($86,000)
Notes: Extensive historical newspaper collection of Alaskan newspapers pertaining to gold rush period (includes Yukon Territory newspapers) and early 20th century development. Negative bank.
Publications: *Pacific Northwest Newspapers on Microfilm at the University of Washington Libraries* (Seattle: University of Washington Libraries, 1983).

NEWSPAPERS, AMATEUR

MA —AMERICAN ANTIQUARIAN SOCIETY LIBRARY, 185 Salisbury St, Worcester, 01609. Marcus A McCorison, Dir & Librn
Holdings: Cat
Notes: A special strength.

OR —AMERICAN PRIVATE PRESS ASSOCIATION, 112 E Burnett St, Stayton, 97383. Martin M Horvat, Librn
Notes: The collection is divided into two primary segments: the first is the traditional one of Amateur Journalism, the second is science fiction and fantasy oriented. The collection was once at New York University Libraries but moved in 1981.

NEWSPAPERS, AMERICAN

AL —MOBILE PUBLIC LIBRARY, Special Collections Div, 701 Government St, Mobile, 36602.
Notes: The Mobile area; incl papers of the Forbes Trading Co, 1795-1840; Bank of Mobile papers, 1820-.

CO —DENVER PUBLIC LIBRARY, Western History Department, 1357 Broadway, Denver, 80203. Eleanor M Gehres, Head
Holdings: Vols (50,000) Cat Mss Maps Pix Audiotapes Microforms
Notes: Western US History. The department has a separate catalog, published in 1970 in 7 vols by G K Hall Co. First supplement published in 1975 in 1 vol. There is a subject index of some 3 million entries to newspapers and magazines of the Rocky Mountain region, added to daily. The Western Newspaper Microfilm Center contains approx 7000 reels of Western US newspapers. Collection has ca 275,000 negatives and prints of Western life; and ca 2500 maps, cataloged and classified.

CT —CONNECTICUT HISTORICAL SOCIETY, One Elizabeth St, Hartford, 06105. Christopher Bickford, Dir
Notes: Over 70,000 books and periodicals, 3500 bound vols of newspapers, and thousands of broadsides, maps, prints, and photographs pertaining to Connecticut. Also, more than 1 1/2 million historical mss; incl personal correspondence, diaries, account books, business records, and town materials dating from the earliest settlement. Extensive genealogical holdings, incl nearly 4000 printed genealogies and New England town and county histories.

DC —DISTRICT OF COLUMBIA PUBLIC LIBRARY, Martin Luther King Memorial Library, Washingtoniana Div and Washington Star Collection, 901 G St NW, Washington, 20001. Roxanna Deane, Chief
Notes: *Washington Star* Collection was the working morgue and photo library of the *Washington Star* newspaper. There are an estimated one million photos dating from about 1930 to 1981. These are arranged by subject and personal name and cover international, national and local news. There are approx 13 million news clippings arranged by subject and personal name for the same period. Each *Star* article was clipped and placed in as many different files as was necessary to cover all topics or personal names mentioned in the article. Reproductions from the photo collection may be purchased.

DC —LIBRARY OF CONGRESS, Manuscript Division, Washington, 20540. John C Broderick, Chief
Notes: Papers of Roy W Howard (1883-1964), past president and chairman of the board of Scripps-Howard Newspapers. Some 85,000 items for the years 1923-64, incl business and personal correspondence, maintained under state and city of origin, with separate files in each year for the various Scripps-Howard newspapers, especially for the *World Telegram* (New York City).

IL —CENTER FOR RESEARCH LIBRARIES, 6050 S Kenwood Ave, Chicago, 60637. Donald B Simpson, Dir; Esther Smith, Collection Development Librn
Holdings: Vols 8000 Cat Microforms
Budget: $40,000
Notes: About 8000 vols of older newspapers in original, and 66 current microfilm subscriptions, with microfilm backfiles of some titles. Use of microfilm restricted to members of the center.

IL —CHICAGO PUBLIC LIBRARY, Newspapers & General Periodicals Center, 425 N Michigan Ave, Chicago, 60611. Jerry Delaney, Head
Holdings: Microforms
Notes: Collection consists of current (one month) copies of daily papers from every state and over forty foreign countries. The permanent newspaper collection (on microfilm) incl many Chicago dailies, some as far back as 1833. It also incl indexed dailies from major cities, the Readex microprint "Early Americn Newspapers", and Bell and Howell's "Underground Newspaper Collection".

IL —UNIVERSITY OF ILLINOIS, URBANA/CHAMPAIGN, Library, Newspaper Library, 1408 W Gregory Drive, Urbana, 61801. Betty L Hildwein, Librn
Notes: Incl 40,000 microfilm reels. The Newspaper Library subscribes to 125 titles on newsprint and 100 titles on microfilm. The collection incl at least one daily from most major metropolitan areas and regions, particularly the Upper Mississippi Valley. Black newspapers, undergraduate college dailies, the "underground press", religious titles, US foreign language weeklies, business, agricultural, literary and political titles represent a wide spectrum of opinion. Extensive or complete back files exist for many prominent titles. Although the collection is concentrated in the last 30 years, some papers date from the early 1700s. The library contains over 2000 vols of reference guides, bibliographies and histories. In 1977 the library prepared a 23-page *Newspaper Library Microfilm Holdings List* and in 1982 prepared a 6-page update. A list of US newspapers currently received is also available.

MA —AMERICAN ANTIQUARIAN SOCIETY LIBRARY, 185 Salisbury St, Worcester, 01609. Marcus A McCorison, Dir & Librn
Holdings: Vols 60,000 Cat
Notes: Sixty percent of the total of books and pamphlets known to have been printed in the United States before 1821. Source of Readex Microprint Corp project called *Early American Imprints, 1639-1800*, a Microprint edition of every extant book, pamphlet, and broadside printed in what is now the United States. Keyed to Evans *American Bibliography*, it reprints in full the texts of nearly 50,000 titles and includes all of Shipton's revision of Evans. A second series, keyed to Shaw and Shoemaker's *American Bibliography*, will bring these Microprint reproductions up to 1820. One of the great strengths of the collection is its broadsides and American newspapers, the best anywhere. From it emerged Clarence Brigham's monumental *History and Bibliography of American Newspapers, 1690-1820*, which located every surviving copy of every newspaper printed in the United States before 1821. Readex Microprint Corp is also reproducing this collection. The Society's collections extend beyond 1820, in special strengths, to the turn of the century. The collection incl unusual strengths in Amateur Newspapers (about 50,000 issues), and Bolivian, Chilean, and West Indian newspapers.

MS —MISSISSIPPI STATE UNIVERSITY, Mitchell Memorial Library, Box 5408, Mississippi State, 39762. Frances N Coleman, Head, Special Collections
Holdings: Mss
Notes: Papers of Hodding Carter II and Betty Werlein Carter, editor/publisher of the

NEWSPAPERS, AMERICAN (cont.)

Greenville, Mississippi *Delta Democrat-Times*. Papers of Turner Catlede, editor of the *New York Times;* papers of Norman Bradley, editor of the *Chattanooga Post* and the *Chatanooga Times;* papers of Wilson F Minor, journalist and editor of the Jackson, Mississippi *Capitol Reporter.*

MO —UNIVERSITY OF MISSOURI-COLUMBIA, Ellis Library, Special Collections Dept, Ninth & Lowry, Columbia, 65201. Margaret A Howell, Head, Special Collections
Holdings: Microfilm Cat
Notes: Backfiles of over 400 US titles (most are complete runs) plus a collection of underground newspapers. It also includes current files of about two dozen metropolitan daily newspapers.

NH —NEW HAMPSHIRE HISTORICAL SOCIETY, Library, 30 Park St, Concord, 03301. William Copeley, Assoc Librn
Holdings: Vols 1000 Cat
Notes: Early New Hampshire newspapers, 1756-1900. 650 titles, mostly not microfilmed, Indexed by title and town.

NJ —RUTGERS, THE STATE UNIVERSITY OF NEW JERSEY, Alexander Library, Special Collections and Archives, College Ave & Huntington St, New Brunswick, 08903. Ronald L Becker, Cur of Manuscripts and Rare Books
Notes: The newspaper holdings heavily favor New Jersey, New York, and Philadelphia, late 18th and early 19th centuries. The general cut-off date for US and foreign newspapers is 1820; New Jersey titles are collected through 1865 and sometimes later. Smaller catagories incl historical, political, amateur, business, and special newspapers.

NY —NEW YORK STATE LIBRARY, State Education Bldg Annex, Washington Ave, Albany, 12224.
Holdings: Uncat Microforms
Notes: Extensive collection of both old or defunct and current newspapers, complete runs, partial runs, individual items. An attempt is made currently to receive newspapers from: major American cities, some major foreign cities, each county in New York (only Allegany, Seneca, Tioga are not represented). The historical collection is particularly strong in (but by no means confined to) New York State and Northeastern American papers. Extensive pre-Civil War holdings. Valuable or disintegrating records being microfilmed. Some major papers received in microfilm to preserve space. Significant early papers also being secured in microform.

NY —NEW YORK HISTORICAL SOCIETY, Library, 170 Central Park W, New York, 10024. James Gregory, Librn
Notes: An extensive collection of eighteenth and early nineteenth century American newspapers. Incl the most complete set of original colonial New York papers and the fourth largest collection of newspapers printed in the US prior to 1821.

NY —NEW YORK PUBLIC LIBRARY, Rare Books and Manuscripts Div, Fifth Ave & 42 St, New York, 10018. William L Joyce, Asst Dir; Francis O Mattson, Curator
Budget: ($7161)
Notes: A large collection of American newspapers through 1800. Holdings are well recorded in Clarence S Brigham's *History and Bibliography of American Newspapers,* 1690-1820. Newspapers are not listed in the Dictionary Catalog.

NC —DUKE UNIVERSITY, William R Perkins Library, Rare Book Room, Durham, 27706. John L Sharpe, III, Cur
Notes: Newspaper collection of more than 300 titles. A collection of 18th century British and 19th century American newspapers.

RI —WESTERLY PUBLIC LIBRARY, Broad St, Westerly, 02891. David J Panciera, Library Dir
Notes: Single issues of early 19th century newspapers from various towns in US. Broken runs of early 19th century newspapers of Rhode Island and Eastern

Connecticut towns. Complete run of local *Westerly Sun,* 1893-present. Complete run *Narragansett Weekly,* 1858-1899.

TX —AMON CARTER MUSEUM, Library, 3501 Camp Bowie Blvd, PO Box 2365, Fort Worth, 76101. Milan R Hughston, Microfilm Librn
Holdings: Cat
Notes: Earliest newspaper is from 1787 (Kentucky), and cut-off date is 1900. Trying to get a good coverage of the entire nation and Western Canada for the 19th century. The archivist has prepared a card index of selected stories from the entire runs of *Harper's Weekly and Leslie's Illustrated* Newspaper. This subject index fills 24 catalog drawers. The selections were made on the basis of current and potential research being done by the curatorial staff, with emphasis on the American and Canadian West, Indians, artists, railroads and pictorial matter. The index also incl subject entries for stories from other papers, such as the *Arkansas Gazette, Missouri Republican* and various Texas newspapers. These have not been read systematically, as were the above, but as they are found they are added to the index.

†VA —GEORGE C MARSHALL RESEARCH FOUNDATION AND LIBRARY, Drawer 920, Lexington, 24450. Royster Lyle Jr, Cur Collections
Holdings: Vols Cat Mss Pix
Notes: Papers of Forrest C Pogue, Army historian, Marshall biographer. Also over 300 German propaganda and military handbooks, and miscellaneous German pre-War books; French, German and American WW II newspapers (approx 300).

VA —VIRGINIA STATE LIBRARY, 12 & Capitol Sts, Richmond, 23219.
Holdings: Cat
Notes: Virginia newspapers. Incl 535 bound vols, 22,396 reels of microfilm. Most files after 1870 now on microfilm.

WI —STATE HISTORICAL SOCIETY OF WISCONSIN, Library, Newspaper and Periodicals Section, 816 State St, Madison, 53706. James P Danky, Librn
Holdings: Cat
Notes: Second largest collection of newspapers in the US incl titles published in every state and Canadian province plus many territories, in both bound volumes and micro-formats. Holdings described in Clarence Brigham's *History and Bibliography of American Newspapers,* 1690-1820; Winifred Gregory's *American Newspapers, 1821-1936; Newspapers* in Microform; and other specialized guides. 325 titles received currently. Only positive microfilm circulates on ILL.

NEWSPAPERS, AMERICAN FOREIGN LANGUAGE

IL —CENTER FOR RESEARCH LIBRARIES, 6050 S Kenwood Ave, Chicago, 60637. Donald B Simpson, Dir; Esther Smith, Collection Development Librn
Holdings: Vols 4000 Cat Microforms
Notes: American newspapers published in foreign languages or English for special ethnic groups. About 500 titles, 55 received currently. Part of collection now on microfilm.

IL —CHICAGO PUBLIC LIBRARY, Newspapers & General Periodicals Center, 425 N Michigan Ave, Chicago, 60611. Jerry Delaney, Head
Holdings: Microforms
Notes: Collection consists of current (one month) copies of 41 newspapers in twenty languages.

IL —UNIVERSITY OF ILLINOIS, URBANA/CHAMPAIGN, Library, Newspaper Library, 1408 W Gregory Drive, Urbana, 61801. Betty L Hildwein, Librn
Holdings: Cat Microforms

MA —BOSTON PUBLIC LIBRARY, South End Branch, Multilingual Library, 685 Tremont St, Boston, 02118. Laura H Reyes, Librn
Holdings: Cat

PA —BALCH INSTITUTE FOR ETHNIC STUDIES, Library, 18 S Seventh St,

Philadelphia, 19106. R Joseph Anderson, Library Dir
Holdings: Cat Microfrms

TX —UNIVERSITY OF TEXAS LIBRARIES, Middle East Collection, PO Box P, Austin, 78712. Abazar Sepehri, Librn
Holdings: Vols (45,000) Cat Microforms
Notes: Arabic, Persian and Turkish materials in the humanities and social sciences. Incl 350 periodical and 45 newspaper titles from most of the countries of the Arab League, Turkey, Iran and Afghanistan.

NEWSPAPERS, AMERICAN INDIAN

WI —STATE HISTORICAL SOCIETY OF WISCONSIN, Library, Newspaper and Periodicals Section, 816 State St, Madison, 53706. James P Danky, Librn
Notes: The largest collection of Native American periodicals and newspapers in the US. Holdings described in: *Native American Periodicals and Newspapers, 1828-1982, Bibliography, Publishing Record and Holdings.* Westport, Conn, Greenwood Press, 1983. Described over 1160 currently published and ceased titles, over 800 of which are in the Society's collection.

NEWSPAPERS, ARIZONA

AZ —NORTHERN ARIZONA UNIVERSITY, Special Collection Library, CU Box 6022, Flagstaff, 86011. Peter M Whiteley, Coordr/Archivist; William Mullane, Librn
Notes: Various collections: (1) *Arizona Champion-Coconino Sun* Newspaper Index Collection; index (typescript); 1883-1894, 20 volumes, 2000 pages. This index is available for sale to the public. Bound copies are located in Special Collections. Inc a comprehensive name and subject index for all Arizona related information. See *Flagstaff Cooperative Indexing Project Collection.* (2) *Arizona Daily Sun* Newspaper Index Collection; incomplete and unedited index of the *Arizona Daily Sun* (Flagstaff, Ariz) for 1977. Incl file on procedures. (3) William Lyon Collection; Articles of Incorporation of dissolved newspapers in Arizona, photocopies, 1887-1929.

AZ —ARIZONA STATE UNIVERSITY, Library, Arizona Collection, Tempe, 85281. Edward C Oetting, Head
See also entry under Arizona - History

NEWSPAPERS, ARMENIAN

CA —UNIVERSITY OF CALIFORNIA, LOS ANGELES, Research Library, Armenian Collection, 405 Hilgard Ave, Los Angeles, 90024. Edward Shreeves, Chairman, Bibliographers Group; Gia Aivazian, Armenian Bibliographer
Holdings: Mss
Notes: Incl one of the largest collections in the US of publications in Armenian and relating to Armenia. Approx 50 titles.

NEWSPAPERS, ARMENIAN AMERICAN

CA —UNIVERSITY OF CALIFORNIA, LOS ANGELES, Research Library, Armenian Collection, 405 Hilgard Ave, Los Angeles, 90024. Edward Shreeves, Chairman, Bibliographers Group; Gia Aivazian, Armenian Bibliographer
Holdings: Mss
Notes: Incl one of the largest collections in the US of publications in Armenian and relating to Armenia. Approx 15 titles.

PA —BALCH INSTITUTE FOR ETHNIC STUDIES, Library, 18 S Seventh St, Philadelphia, 19106. R Joseph Anderson, Library Dir

NEWSPAPERS, ASIAN

MD —UNIVERSITY OF MARYLAND, Library, East Asia Collection, College Park, 20742. Frank Joseph Shulman, Curator and Head
Holdings: Vols
Budget: $300
Notes: Very extensive (600) vertical files of

NEWSPAPERS, ASIAN (cont.)

Western-language newsletters and association bulletins published since the early 1960s that relate in whole or in part to Asian Studies. Some titles have been listed in Frank Joseph Shulman's Newsletters and Association Bulletins on Asia: An Annotated Guide to Current Academic Resources, *Asian Studies Professional Review*, vols 4 (1974-75) and 5 (1975-76). All disciplines covered. Most newsletters and bulletins are academically or culturally oriented; newsletters of the business world and of foreign embassies and their information centers are generally excluded. These files are believed to constitute the single most comprehensive collection of their kind in the world. This collection is not a component part of the University of Maryland Libraries, but all communications should be addressed to Frank Joseph Shulman, c/o the University's East Asia Collection.

NY —CORNELL UNIVERSITY LIBRARIES, John M Olin Library, John M Echols Collection on Southeast Asia, Ithaca, 14853. Giok Po Oey, Curator
See also entry under Asia, Southeast.

WA —UNIVERSITY OF WASHINGTON LIBRARIES, East Asia Library, DO-27, Seattle, 98195. Karl Lo, Head
Holdings: Vols (300,000) Cat Microforms
Budget: ($200,000)
Notes: Southwest China: Joseph Rock Collection, ca 2000 vols; modern Chinese poetry, 1919 to date: ca 700 titles; Asian art, esp Japanese painting: 4097 vols; Tiao-yu-t'ai movement in the US: ca 400 items of periodicals and pamphlets; modern Korean poetry, ancient and modern: ca 1000 titles; Mu-yu-shu folk literature: ca 1000 items.

WI —STATE HISTORICAL SOCIETY OF WISCONSIN, Library, Newspaper and Periodicals Section, 816 State St, Madison, 53706. James P Danky, Librn
Notes: One of the largest collections of Asian American periodicals and newspapers in the US. Holdings described in *Asian American Periodicals and Newspapers: A Union List....* Madison, The Society, 1979. (ERIC Report ED 220 102).

NEWSPAPERS, ASIAN AMERICAN

WI —STATE HISTORICAL SOCIETY OF WISCONSIN, Library, Newspaper and Periodicals Section, 816 State St, Madison, 53706. James P Danky, Librn
Notes: One of the largest collections of Asian American periodicals and newspapers in the US. Holdings described in *Asian American Periodicals and Newspapers: A Union List....* Madison, The Society, 1979. (ERIC Report ED 220 102).

NEWSPAPERS, AUSTRO-HUNGARIAN EMPIRE

TX —RICE UNIVERSITY, Fondren Library, 6100 S Main St, PO Box 1892, Houston, 77251. Dr Samuel M Carrington, Jr, University Librn
Holdings: Vols 21,500 // Cat Maps Pix
Notes: The Austro-Hungarian Empire of Franz Josef. Historical and literary materials. Incl newspapers. Downs 2706.

NEWSPAPERS, BASQUE

NV —UNIVERSITY OF NEVADA, RENO, Noble H Getchell Library, Reno, 89557. William A Douglass, Coordinator
Holdings: Vols (15,000)
Notes: American's largest collection of Basque materials, both retrospective and current. Semi-annual *Newsletter*.

NEWSPAPERS, BLACK

DC —HOWARD UNIVERSITY, Moorland-Spingarn Research Center, 500 Howard Place NW, Washington, 20059. Clifford L Muse, Jr, Acting Dir

DC —LIBRARY OF CONGRESS, General Reading Rooms Division, Microform Reading Room, Washington, 20540.
Holdings: Cat Mss Maps Pix Microforms
Notes: Microform materials only in this LC Division. Works of individual authors; holdings of collections; archival records, etc, press releases and translations, etc.

IL —UNIVERSITY OF ILLINOIS, URBANA/CHAMPAIGN, Library, Newspaper Library, 1408 W Gregory Drive, Urbana, 61801. Betty L Hildwein, Librn
Holdings: Cat Microforms
Notes: Includes 12 microfilm reels, microfilm series Negro newspapers for the American Council of Learned Societies and American newspapers.

PA —BALCH INSTITUTE FOR ETHNIC STUDIES, Library, 18 S Seventh St, Philadelphia, 19106. R Joseph Anderson, Library Dir

WI —STATE HISTORICAL SOCIETY OF WISCONSIN, Library, Newspaper and Periodicals Section, 816 State St, Madison, 53706. James P Danky, Librn
Notes: One of the largest collections of US and Canadian Black newspapers and periodicals in the US dating from the early 19th century to the present. Holdings described in *Black Periodicals: A Union List of Holdings in Libraries of the University of Wisconsin and the Library of the State Historical Society of Wisconsin* (Second Edition 1979). (ERIC Report ED 192800).

ON —CHATHAM PUBLIC LIBRARY, 120 Queen St, Chatham, N7M 2G6, Can. Arlene Mason, Head of Reference
Holdings: Microforms
Notes: Microfilms of *The Provinical Freeman*, vol 1, 1853, vol 4, 1857; and *The Voice of the Fugitive*, ed by Henry Bibb.

NEWSPAPERS, BOLIVIAN

MA —AMERICAN ANTIQUARIAN SOCIETY LIBRARY, 185 Salisbury St, Worcester, 01609. Marcus A McCorison, Dir & Librn
Holdings: Cat
Notes: A special strength.

NEWSPAPERS, BRITISH see
Newspapers, Great Britain

NEWSPAPERS, BROOKLYN

NY —BROOKLYN PUBLIC LIBRARY, Brooklyn Collection, Grand Army Plaza, Flatbush Ave and Eastern Parkway, Brooklyn, 11238.
Notes: More than 3000 books, pamphlets, and documents cover such topics as history, religion, literature, and politics. Microfilm copies of now defunct Brooklyn daily newspapers as well as recent issues of local Brooklyn papers. Incl the morgue of the *Brooklyn Daily Eagle* (1841-1955). Also, more than 25,000 photographs of Brooklyn people, places, and things dating from 1870 to the present, incl those by George Brainard and Daniel Berry Austin. Old town records, vertical files, maps, and institutional archives.

NY —LONG ISLAND HISTORICAL SOCIETY, 128 Pierrepont St, at Clinton St, Brooklyn, 11201.
Notes: Books and pamphlets relating to the history of Brooklyn. Over 350 newspapers and periodical resources, incl *The Long Island Star* (1809-1863) and *Williamsburgh Gazette* (1835-1853). 10,000 photographs. Paintings, prints, and broadsides. More than 1400 mss collections relating primarily to Brooklyn, dating from 1650 to 1980s. 750 maps and atlases, artifacts, archives, and Decorative Arts collections. Two published guides to Manuscripts: *Calendar of Manuscripts: 1783-1783*, LIHS by Karin N Mango, 1980. Also, *A Guide to Brooklyn Manuscripts in the Long Island Historical Society*. Prepared by Brooklyn Rediscovery, a program of the Brooklyn Educational and Cultural Alliance, 1980. Also, guide to Museum Exhibit, *Brooklyn Before the Bridge - American paintings from the Long Island Historical Society*. Published by Brooklyn Museum, 1982.

NEWSPAPERS, BUSINESS

IL —UNIVERSITY OF ILLINOIS, URBANA/CHAMPAIGN, Library, Newspaper Library, 1408 W Gregory Drive, Urbana, 61801. Betty L Hildwein, Librn

NEWSPAPERS, CALIFORNIA

CA —UNIVERSITY OF CALIFORNIA, LOS ANGELES, Research Library, Dept of Special Collections, 405 Hilgard Ave, Los Angeles, 90024. Edward Shreeves, Chairman, Bibliographers Group; David S Zeidberg, Head
Notes: (1) *Los Angeles Daily News* morgue contains clipping and research files; an index to the paper; 200,000 negatives, with an index; 20,000 prints, with an index. Collection also includes (2) 1.5 million negatives and 300,000 prints from the morgue of *Los Angeles Times*.

CA —CALIFORNIA STATE UNIVERSITY, NORTHRIDGE, Delmar T Oviatt & South Libraries, 1811 Nordhoff St, Northridge, 91330. Donald L Read, Special Collections Dept
Notes: Three newspaper boxes. Some runs incomplete. Between 1935 and 1939, the US Government maintained camps to assist the migrant farm laborers of the Great Depression. This small collection records the activities of those camps.

CA —A K SMILEY PUBLIC LIBRARY, 125 W Vine St, Redlands, 92373. Larry E Burgess, Archivist
Holdings: Vols (3500) Mss Maps Pix Phonorecords Microforms
Budget: ($45,000)
Notes: Emphasis on San Bernadino County and the Redlands area. Especially prized is *The Citrographic*, 1887-1908 (bound vols and microfilm) edited by Scipio Craig, prominent in state, national, and newspaper circles. The ms collection (250,000 pieces) incl the Smily Family papers, much on water development, and onthe citrus industry. The photograph collection (over 5000) covers the history of the area; there are many stereographs and glass slides. The collection on Indians of California and the Southwest was begun from a special gift by Andrew Carnegie honoring his friend, Albert K Smiley.

CA —SAN DIEGO PUBLIC LIBRARY, 820 E St, San Diego, 92101. Rhoda E Kruse, Sr Librn
Notes: Also 450 bound periodicals. Incl extensive local history; papers of Foss and Kelly families; some material on John D Spreckels; papers of Southern California Exposition, San Diego 200th Anniversary Committee; Census microfilms; registers of voters 1866-1909; *San Diego Union* Index, which also incl material on Baja Califorina; records of Little Landers Colony, a 1910 Utopian group founded in the Tia Juana River Valley.

CA —CALIFORNIA HISTORICAL SOCIETY, Schubert Hall Library, 2099 Pacific Ave, San Francisco, 94109. Bruce L Johnson, Library Dir
Holdings: Vols (50,000) Cat Mss Maps Pix
See also entry under California - History

CA —STOCKTON-SAN JOAQUIN COUNTY PUBLIC LIBRARY, California Reference Room, 605 N El Dorado St, Stockton, 95202.
Holdings: Vols (6300) Cat Maps Phonorecords Microforms
Budget: ($2000)
Notes: Emphasis on Stockton and San Joaquin County with lesser coverage of other Northern California cities and counties. Collection consists of books, periodicals, scrapbooks, and subject index of articles from about 60 books and periodicals dealing with California. Local history collection incl Stockton and San Joaquin County special reports and studies, vertical file materials by subject, an index to local newspapers, 1850-date (1899-1925 in progress), first editions of local authors, Harriet Chalmers Adams collection (qv).

IN —INDIANA UNIVERSITY, Lilly Library, Seventh St, Bloomington, 47405. William R

NEWSPAPERS, CALIFORNIA (cont.)

Cagle, Librn
Holdings: // Cat Mss
Notes: First editions and early accounts, including 1000 issues of California gold rush newspapers.

NY —NEW YORK HISTORICAL SOCIETY, Library, 170 Central Park W, New York, 10024. James Gregory, Librn
Notes: One of the largest collections in the East of California newspapers printed in the 1850s.

NEWSPAPERS, CANADIAN

TX —AMON CARTER MUSEUM, Library, 3501 Camp Bowie Blvd, PO Box 2365, Fort Worth, 76101. Milan R Hughston, Microfilm Librn
Holdings: Cat
Notes: Earliest newspaper is from 1787 (Kentucky), and cut-off date is 1900. Trying to get a good coverage of the entire nation and Western Canada for the 19th century. The archivist has prepared a card index of selected stories from the entire runs of Harper's Weekly and Leslie's Illustrated Newspaper. This subject index fills 24 catalog drawers. The selections were made on the basis of current and potential research being done by the curatorial staff, with emphasis on the American and Canadian West, Indians, artists, railroads and pictorial matter. The index also incl subject entries for stories from other papers, such as the Arkansas Gazette, Missouri Republican and various Texas newspapers. These have not been read systematically, as were the above, but as they are found they are added to the index.

WA —UNIVERSITY OF WASHINGTON LIBRARIES, Pacific Northwest Collection, Seattle, 98195. Andrew F Johnson, Librn
Holdings: Vols (50,000) Cat Mss Maps Pix
Budget: ($12,000)
Notes: The Pacific Northwest Collection contains printed materials documenting the historic and contemporary life and culture of the region in a broad range of subject areas. The Pacific Northwest is defined as the geographic region including Washington, Oregon, Idaho, Montana, British Columbia, Yukon Territory, and Alaska. Printed materials including books, periodicals, government documents, maps, weekly and local regional newspapers, theses and dissertations, as well as photographs and architectural drawings are included in the Pacific Northwest Collection. Photographic works of over 200 photographers active in the Pacific Northwest, Alaska, and the Yukon Territory (Canada) during the period 1860-1930, including Asahel and Edward S Curtis, Eric Hegg, and Clark Kinsey, are represented in a print collection of more than 300,000 images. The architecturaldrawings collection includes over 19,000 original plans, drawings, sketches, renderings and blue prints pertaining to the history of architecture and urban planning and landscape gardening in the Pacific Northwest ca 1880-1940. Areas of particular strength are the holdings of over 1100 published journals of Pacific Northwest exploration expeditions, photographs of Northwest Coast Native Americans and of historic Seattle, newspapers issued within the Japanese-American relocation camps, 1942-1945, materials relating to the 1980 eruption of Mt St Helens, and Sanborne fire insurance maps for Washington. A unique feature of the Collection is the subject index to regional periodicals and local newspapers maintained by the PNW Collection staff; over 100 titles are currently indexed. G K Hall Company published a books catalog of the Pacific Northwest Collectionin 1973.

WI —STATE HISTORICAL SOCIETY OF WISCONSIN, Library, Newspaper and Periodicals Section, 816 State St, Madison, 53706. James P Danky, Librn
Holdings: Cat
Notes: One of the largest collections of Canadian newspapers in the US incl titles published in all provinces and territories, in both bound volumes and micro-formats. Holdings described in Newspapers in Microform; and other specialized guides. One title received currently. Only positive microfilm circulates on ILL.

MB —UNIVERSITY OF MANITOBA, Elizabeth Dafoe Library, Archives and Special Collections Dept, Winnipeg, R3T 2N2, Can. Richard E Bennett, Dept Head; Corrado A Santoro, Reference Archivist
Holdings: Mss
Notes: Newsclippings from the Tribune dating from the mid-1920's to 1980. Index in Reading Room and also Unpublished Register.

†MB —UNIVERSITY OF MANITOBA, Library, Winnipeg, R3T 2N2, Can.
Notes: Complete research archive of ninety years of the Winnipeg Times, defunct in 1980. Millions of newspaper clippings, indexed and in chronological order; about one million photographs, identified and dated; 10,000 books, etc.

ON —LIBRARY OF PARLIAMENT, Parliament Bldgs, Ottawa, K1A 0A9, Can. Erik J Spicer, Parliamentary Librn
Holdings: Vols 711 Uncat
Notes: Some 20,000 microfilm reels of Canadian newspapers.

ON —NATIONAL LIBRARY OF CANADA, 395 Wellington St, Ottawa, K1A 0N4, Can. Andre Preibish, Dir
Holdings: Vols 16,000
Budget: $88,000
Notes: Over 50,000 reels of microfilm. The largest collection of Canadian newspapers in Canada; includes many ethnic newspapers. Microfilms circulate on interlibrary loan.

NEWSPAPERS, CARIBBEAN AREA

VI —VIRGIN ISLANDS BUREAU OF LIBRARIES, MUSEUMS & ARCHAEOLOGICAL SERVICES, Enid M Baa Library & Archives, Von Scholten Collection, PO Box 390, Saint Thomas, 00801. June A V Lindqvist, Cur
Holdings: Vols (13,000) Cat Mss Maps Pix Microforms
Notes: Caribbeana, with emphasis on the Virgin Islands. Library collects in all aspects of Virgin Islands life, incl natural and cultural history. Collection is especially strong in Danish West Indian and Virgin Islands newspapers and in dissertations on Caribbean subjects. Library is a full depository for USVI documents. Auxiliary collections are located in the Bureau's libraries in St Croix and St John.

NEWSPAPERS, CARPATHO-RUTHENIAN

PA —UNIVERSITY OF PITTSBURGH, Hillman Library, Pittsburgh, 15260.
Notes: 250 reels of microfilm containing approximately sixty titles of newspapers and serials of the Carpatho-Ruthenian Community in America.

NEWSPAPERS, CATHOLIC

DC —CATHOLIC UNIVERSITY OF AMERICA, Mullen Library, Washington, 20064. Harriet O Nelson, Coordinator, Reference Div
Holdings: Cat Microforms
Notes: A collection of microfilm copies of important Catholic diocesan and national newspapers, many dating back to the 19th century; incl complete runs of such major titles as Boston Pilot, Brooklyn Tablet, US Catholic Miscellaney. Also a few major foreign Catholic titles, complete run of Le Croix, L'Osservatore Romano. About 60 titles in the entire collection. Mimeo listing of titles available upon request. Available through intelibrary loan with some restrictions.

NEWSPAPERS, CHICAGO

IL —CHICAGO HISTORICAL SOCIETY, Library, Clark St at North Ave, Chicago, 60614. Robert L Brubaker, Librn
Holdings: Vols (150,000) Cat Mss Maps Pix Slides Microforms
Notes: Subjects: United States history (specialties: Chicago, Midwest, Lincoln, Civil War). Special collections: Chicago directories, trade catalogs, advertising cards (6000), theatre programs (5000), and sheet music (4600); personal papers and records of Chicago leaders and organizations; negatives and prints from Chicago newspaper morgues, 1900-1965 (250,000); Meserve Americana, 27 vols, mostly of period of Civil War (8000 portraits); American city prints (historic); J Norman Jensen Collection of Lake and River Disasters, 1679-1947 (8500 cards). Holdings: 422,000 books and pamphlets; 16,000 bound periodical vols; 7300 vols of newspapers; 14,000 broadsides and posters; 10,000 maps; 640 atlases; 50,000 clippings; 2500 vols of CHS archives; 35,000 miscellaneous printed pieces; 8600 reels of microfilm; 4000 linear feet of mss; 50,000 prints and photographs(black-and-white photographs, daguerreotypes ambrotypes, stereographs, negatives, engravings, and lithographs).

IL —LAKE FOREST COLLEGE, Donnelley Library, Lake Forest, 60045. Arthur H Miller Jr, College Librn
Holdings: Vols (1500) Mss Microforms
Notes: Book holdings (largely post-Fire) incl Chicago poetry, prose, historical writing, social topics, and World's Columbian Exposition. The Capt Joseph Medill Patterson Library and Archive (received 1983) incl working papers relating to the Chicago Tribune and general material on the Patterson family. Tribune complete on film.

NEWSPAPERS, CHILEAN

MA —AMERICAN ANTIQUARIAN SOCIETY LIBRARY, 185 Salisbury St, Worcester, 01609. Marcus A McCorison, Dir & Librn
Holdings: Cat
Notes: A special strength.

NY —STATE UNIVERSITY OF NEW YORK, STONY BROOK, Melville Library, Dept of Special Collections, Stony Brook, 11794. Evert Volkersz, Head
Holdings: // Cat
Notes: Primarily early 19th century Chilean newspapers and journals (41 titles) published in Santiago de Chile. A list of holdings is available. No photocopying.

NEWSPAPERS, CHINESE

IL —CENTER FOR RESEARCH LIBRARIES, 6050 S Kenwood Ave, Chicago, 60637. Donald B Simpson, Dir; Esther Smith, Collection Development Librn
Holdings: Microforms
Budget: ($3000)
Notes: 2000 reels of microfilm of mainland Chinese newspapers, periodicals and clippings. Microfilm of early newspapers published in China in western languages. Microfilm of files of Hong Kong newspapers in English c 1875-1965. Microfilm of newspapers from Center for Chinese research materials and other newspapers.

NJ —PRINCETON UNIVERSITY, Library, Gest Oriental Library & East Asian Collections, 317 Palmer Hall, Princeton, 08544. D E Perushek, Cur
Holdings: Vols (267,000) Cat Mss Maps Pix Microforms
Notes: Mostly in Chinese. Subject areas incl. Chinese civilization, language, literature, philosophy, religion, history, geography, traditional medicine and materia medica, history of books and printing, sociology, economics, politics, and other social sciences. With regard to Chinese art and archaeology, only works of a general or cultural nature and primary textual sources are collected. For works on Chinese population only the historical and economic aspects are acquired. Subject areas in science and technology, except those materials dealing with indigenous developments and historical aspects, are excluded. No historical period is excluded. The collection is particularly noted for its strength in pre-20th

NEWSPAPERS, CHINESE (cont.)

century works on traditional Chinese medicine in all areas, and in works on the Ming period. Some Western-language reference works as well as Western-language works on Chinese literature, language, and linguistics. Emphasis is on current publications. Separate card catalog. Publications on collection: Ch'u Wan-li, A Catalogue of the Chinese Rare Books in the Gest collection of the Princeton University Library (Taiperi: Yee Wen Publishing Co., 1974). (In Chinese): Gillis, I. V. & Pai Ping-ch'i, Title Index to the Catalogue of the Gest Oriental Library (Peking Kwei LI Press, 1941). (In Chinese): Hu, Shih, "The Gest Oriental Library at Princeton University," Princeton University Chronicle, vol. xv (Spring 1954), 113-141; Rice, Howard C., Jr., Shih-kang Tung & Frederick W. Mote, East and West, Europe's Discovery of China and China's Response to Europe, 1511-1839: A Check-list of the Exhibition in the Princeton University Library, February 15-April 30, 1957 (Princeton: Princeton University Library, 1957); and Tung, Shih-kang, Chinese Microfilms in Princeton University: A Checklist of the Gest Oriental Library (Washington, Center for Chinese Research Materials, Association of Research Libraries, 1969).

NY —NEW YORK PUBLIC LIBRARY, Oriental Div, Fifth Ave & 42 St, New York, 10018. E Christian Filstrup, Chief
Holdings: Cat Mss Microforms
Budget: ($56,455)
Notes: Described in Dictionary Catalog of the Oriental Collection, The Research Libraries of the New York Public Library, 1960, 16 vols, and First Supplement, 1976, 8 vols (144,000 cards). This catalog incl 318,000 entries for works in about 100 languages of the East, and all works in Western languages on Oriental subjects. The Oriental Collection numbers about 120,000 vols; its Arabic and Indic holdings and those on ancient Egypt and the ancient Near East are among the largest in the US. There is also a collection of 30,000 vols of PL 480 material from Egypt, Pakistan, and India to which there is main entry access, but which is not incorporated into the dictionary catalog. Other outstanding features of the Oriental Collection incl extensive holdings of Japanese technical and scientific periodicals; a unique collection of linguistic works, grammars, anddictionaries; and unusually good coverage of the field of Oriental religions and philosophies. The catalog contains numerous subject references to periodical articles in all languages. All entries are arranged alphabetically according to the Roman alphabet.

†NY —NEW YORK PUBLIC LIBRARY, Chatham Square Branch, 33 E Broadway, New York, 10002.
Notes: New York's Chinatown, Chinese in the US, local Chinese newspapers.

NC —DUKE UNIVERSITY, William R Perkins Library, Durham, 27706. Elvin E Strowd, University Librn
Notes: The Thomas collection relating to China and the Far East contains more than 1500 items. It is a comprehensive body of books, newspapers, prints and other materials dealing with many phases of the culture of the Orient. Additions are ongoing.
RI —BROWN UNIVERSITY, John Hay Library, 20 Prospect St, Providence, 02912. Mark N Brown, Cur Mss
Holdings: Vols (74,000) Cat Microforms
Budget: ($10,000)
Notes: East Asia Collection-the primary focus is on Chinese studies with a small segment of approx 700 vols devoted to Japanese studies. Major subject areas, in descending order of strength, are: literature, incl classics, history, geography, social sciences, philosophy and religion, fine arts, science and technology. This incl the personal collection (20,000 vols) formed by Harvard University Sinologist Dr Charles Sidney Gardner, which is especially rich in materials relating to the Ch'ing Dynasty (1644-1912). In addition to books, there are 500 reels of microfilm, plus runs of 8 Chinese newspapers and 26 current Chinese periodicals.
SK —UNIVERSITY OF SASKATCHEWAN, Library, Saskatoon, S7N 0W0, Can. S Perkins, Librn
Notes: Documents on Contemporary China, 1949-1975, 525 microfiches; material from a wide variety of sources. Much on Red Guard and the Cultural Revolution. The Library also holds the Survey of China Mainland Press.

NEWSPAPERS, CHINESE AMERICAN

†NY —NEW YORK PUBLIC LIBRARY, Chatham Square Branch, 33 E Broadway, New York, 10002.
Notes: New York's Chinatown, Chinese in the US, local Chinese newspapers.
PA —BALCH INSTITUTE FOR ETHNIC STUDIES, Library, 18 S Seventh St, Philadelphia, 19106. R Joseph Anderson, Library Dir

NEWSPAPERS, CINCINNATI

OH —PUBLIC LIBRARY OF CINCINNATI & HAMILTON COUNTY, History Dept, 800 Vine St, Cincinnati, 45202. J Richard Abell, Head
Holdings: Vols (5831) Microforms
Notes: Cincinnati Newspaper Collection incl 21 daily, 19 weekly and 3 biweekly English-language papers, 9 daily and 3 weekly German-language papers. Dates range from 1793 to date. Microfilm incl two present daily papers, Cincinnati Enquirer, June 1818-and the Cincinnati Post, July 1882- , as well as the Cincinnatier Freie Presses, Aug-1874-July 1964, Cincinnati Volkesfruend, 1831-1959, Cincinnati Commercial (name changes Com Gazette, Com Tribue) Jan 1858-Dec 1930. And 12 additional titles. Reader-printers, are available. Library maintains a selective index to current daily newspapers as well as the Cincinnati Times-Star and the Cincinnati Commercial Tribune. Only material relating to Cincinnati/Hamilton County is indexed. Index began 1912, discontinued 1919, resumed 1926. Some retrospective indexing is done. Partially cataloged.

NEWSPAPERS, COLORADO

CO —COLORADO HISTORICAL SOCIETY, Research Collections, 1300 Broadway, Denver, 80203. Catherine Kane, Head Public Service and Access
Holdings: Microforms
Budget:
Notes: The major collection of Colorado newspapers is located here. Of 2844 titles listed in Donald E Oehlerts, Guide to Colorado Newspapers, 1859-1963 (Denver: Bibliographical Center for Research, Rocky Mountain Region, Inc, 1964) the society has over 600 bound and/or microfilmed.

NEWSPAPERS, CONFEDERATE STATES

GA —UNIVERSITY OF GEORGIA, Libraries, Special Collections Division, Athens, 30602. Vesta Lee Gordon, Asst Dir for Special Collections
Holdings: Vols 7300 Maps
Notes: The Confederate Imprints Collection, arranged by Crandell numbers, also incl 500 sheets of music, approx 350 broadsides and approx 1600 newspapers.
NY —NEW YORK HISTORICAL SOCIETY, Library, 170 Central Park W, New York, 10024. James Gregory, Librn
Notes: A collection of newspapers published in all of the major Northern and Southern cities froم the 1850s through Reconstruction. Incl a selection of newspapers put out by various Civil War army and navy units.

NEWSPAPERS, CONNECTICUT

CT —CONNECTICUT HISTORICAL SOCIETY, One Elizabeth St, Hartford, 06105. Christopher Bickford, Dir
Notes: Over 70,000 books and periodicals, 3500 bound vols of newspapers, and thousands of broadsides, maps, prints, and photographs pertaining to Connecticut. Also, more than 1 1/2 million historical mss; incl personal correspondence, diaries, account books, business records, and town materials dating from the earliest settlement. Extensive genealogical holdings, incl nearly 4000 printed genealogies and New England town and county histories.
CT —CONNECTICUT STATE LIBRARY, Readers Service Div, 231 Capitol Ave, Hartford, 06106. Ablene Bielefield, Head
Holdings: Cat
Budget: ($600,000)
Notes: Contains material of Connecticut legislative and legal sources, incl legislative histories, Connecticut Supreme Court Records and Briefs, and other sources.
CT —CONNECTICUT STATE LIBRARY, 231 Capitol Ave, Hartford, 06115. Al Palko, Collections Librn
Holdings: Cat Microforms
Notes: The largest collection of Connecticut newspapers, from Colonial times to the present.

NEWSPAPERS, CUBAN AMERICAN

FL —UNIVERSITY OF MIAMI, Otto G Richter Library, PO Box 248214, Coral Gables, 33124. Frank Rodgers, Dir of Libraries
Notes: The Cuban exile periodicals incl 412 titles of which 381 have been published in Miami, Florida. The archival material incl 54 cubic feet of mss, invitations, programs, broadsides, posters, postcards, prints, reports, maps, etc. This collection incl personal and corporate papers of Cubans settled in the US or in other countries. The truth about Cuban Committee Papers: 40 cubic feet. Contains records and correspondence of intellectual and professional Cuban and American leaders in the US dedicated to the course of eliminating Communism from the Western Hemisphere.

NEWSPAPERS, CZECH AMERICAN

NE —UNIVERSITY OF NEBRASKA-LINCOLN, Don L Love Library, Czech Heritage Collection, Lincoln, 68588. Joseph G Svoboda, University Archivist
Holdings: Vols (3000) Cat Mss Pix Audiotapes Microforms
Notes: he Czech Heritage Collection.
PA —BALCH INSTITUTE FOR ETHNIC STUDIES, Library, 18 S Seventh St, Philadelphia, 19106. R Joseph Anderson, Library Dir

NEWSPAPERS, DANISH

NE —DANA COLLEGE, C A Dana-Life Library, Blair, 68008. Ronald D Johnson,

NEWSPAPERS, DANISH (cont.)

Head Librn
Holdings: Vols (10,000) Cat Audiotapes
Notes: Strong emphasis on Danish literature although we include other Scandinavian countries. Have an oral history tape collection with recordings of Danish emigrants to the midwest. Our book collection is strongest in the literature area with history a close second.

NEWSPAPERS, DELAWARE

DE —HISTORICAL SOCIETY OF DELAWARE, Library, 505 Market St Mall, Wilmington, 19801. Barbara E Benson, Library Dir
Notes: 1750 linear ft of Delaware and other newspapers.

NEWSPAPERS, DETROIT

MI —DETROIT PUBLIC LIBRARY, Burton Historical Collection, 5201 Woodward Ave, Detroit, 48202. Alice Dalligan, Chief

NEWSPAPERS, ENGLISH

CT —YALE UNIVERSITY, Box 1603A, Yale Station, New Haven, 06520.

NEWSPAPERS, FOREIGN

IL —CENTER FOR RESEARCH LIBRARIES, 6050 S Kenwood Ave, Chicago, 60637. Donald B Simpson, Dir; Esther Smith, Collection Development Librn
Holdings: Microforms
Budget: $63,000
Notes: About 114 current microfilm subscriptions. This is the Foreign Newspapers on Microfilm Project of the Association of Research Libraries. Items may be loaned only to subscribers to the project but copies may be sold to nonsubscribers. Files from 1956 only; in some cases from 1938. Besides this collection there are foreign newspapers that are not part of the ARL/FNMP. These are some 6000 vols, mostly European, 19th century and first half of 20th century; also all newspapers from PL 480 countries available on microfilm.

IL —CHICAGO PUBLIC LIBRARY, Newspapers & General Periodicals Center, 425 N Michigan Ave, Chicago, 60611. Jerry Delaney, Head
Holdings: Microforms
Notes: The collection consists of current (one month) copies of 72 papers from 46 countries. The permanent newspaper collection (on microform) incl the *London Times* from 1785 and the *Toronto Star* from 1977.

IL —UNIVERSITY OF ILLINOIS, URBANA/CHAMPAIGN, Slavic and East European Library, Urbana, 61801. Marianna Tax Choldin, Head
Holdings: Vols (420,000) Cat Microforms
Notes: One of the largest Slavic and East European collections. Strong in Russian and Soviet materials-humanities, sciences, and social sciences; languages and literatures; periodicals, newspapers, and microforms. Ca 260,000 volumes in languages of the Soviet Union plus 20,000 Russian and Ukrainian titles on microform. Extensive coverage of Czechoslovakia (35,000 vols); Yugoslavia (31,000 vols); Bulgaria (9200 vols); Poland (34,600 vols); Romania (13,000 vols); and Hungary (18,000 vols) and the languages, literatures, and history of these countries.

IL —UNIVERSITY OF ILLINOIS, URBANA/CHAMPAIGN, Library, Newspaper Library, 1408 W Gregory Drive, Urbana, 61801. Betty L Hildwein, Librn
Holdings: Vols 3500 Cat Microforms
Notes: Incl 17,000 microfilm reels. The Newspaper Library subscribes to 150 foreign titles on newsprint and 80 on microfilm. Although the collection incl current newspapers from all over the world, the great majority are from Eastern and Western Europe, the Soviet Union, India, the Middle East and Latin America. Titles dating from World War II represent about one half the collection, with the rest being primarily 19th and early 20th century British. French and German papers. The library incl Latin American and Soviet titles. Separate newspapers title, geographic and chronological catalogs describe the holdings. In 1977 the library prepared a 23-page newspaper library microfilm holdings list and in 1982 prepared a 6-page update. A list of Illinois papers currently received by county is also available.

MA —UNIVERSITY OF MASSACHUSETTS AT AMHERST, Library, Amherst, 01003.
Holdings: Cat Microforms
Notes: Latin American studies. Special strengths: Literature, history (especially Argentine history), anthropology. Newspapers on microfilm.

MA —HARVARD UNIVERSITY LIBRARY, Harvard-Yenching Library, 2 Divinity Ave, Cambridge, 02138. Eugene W Wu, Librn
Holdings: Vols 312
Notes: National and local newspapers from East Asia. Also leading English-language newspapers published in East Asia.

MA —HARVARD UNIVERSITY LIBRARY, Widener Library, Modern Greek Collection, Cambridge, 02138. Evangelie Flessas, Librn
Holdings: Vols (80,000) Cat Mss Microforms
Notes: In Greek language.

NJ —PRINCETON UNIVERSITY, Library, Gest Oriental Library & East Asian Collections, 317 Palmer Hall, Princeton, 08544. D E Perushek, Cur
Holdings: Vols (370,000) Cat Mss Maps Pix Microforms
Notes: Materials collected are mostly in East Asian languages: Chinese, Japanese and Korean. Subject emphasis is on East Asia, China, Japan and Korea, their civilization and societies, languages, literature, philosophy, religion, history, politics and sociology. No historical period is excluded. The Gest Library also acquires works on East Asian art and archaeology that are of a general or cultural nature and primary textual sources (extensive collections on East Asian art and archaeology are held and maintained at the University Art Library). Works on historical and economic aspects of East Asian population are also acquired (while population censuses and vital statistics are held at the University Population Research Library). Subject areas in sciences and technology, except those materials dealing with indigenous developments and historical aspects, are excluded. Withregard to the Korean collection in a holding position with a minimum budget allocation, Western-language reference works in all fields of East Asian studies and Western-language monographs of importance on East Asian literature, language, and linguistics are collected. Preference is given to works in English. Emphasis is on current publications. All other Western-language works on East Asia are located elsewhere in the University Library system. The existing collections also incl books and manuscripts in the Manchu, Mongolian, and Tibetan languages. However, acquisitions in these languages are now made on a highly selective basis. Separate card catalogs are maintained for Chinese, Japanese, Korean, and Western-language collections. See also Chen, Frances M & Maureen H Donovan: Periodicals on Asia; Serials in the Princeton University Library inWestern Languages (Princeton: Princeton University Library, 1975).

NY —COLUMBIA UNIVERSITY LIBRARIES, Lehman Library, Slavic and East Central European Collection, 420 W 118 St, New York, 10027. Nina Lencek, Bibliographer
Holdings: // Uncat Microforms
Notes: Collection consists of a total of 988 Russian and East European newspapers: of these 614 are Russian pre-1917 and post-Revolution newspapers and 16 Russian emigre titles published in Russian and in Western languages in Western Europe and America; 297 newspapers are in other East European languages published in Eastern Europe, and 61 East European emigre newspapers published in the West. In addition to these newspapers, Lehman Library holds a number of cataloged East European and Russian newspapers in microform. The collection is available for research to qualified scholars with special permission.

NY —NEW YORK PUBLIC LIBRARY, Annex Section, 521 W 43 St, New York, 10036. Richard L Hill, First Asst
Holdings: Vols 24,000 Cat Microforms
Notes: Comprehensive New York (City) coverage; selective coverage of other US and foreign countries. Incl 24,000 bound volumes; 86,000 microfilm reels.

PA —BALCH INSTITUTE FOR ETHNIC STUDIES, Library, 18 S Seventh St, Philadelphia, 19106. R Joseph Anderson, Library Dir

†VA —GEORGE C MARSHALL RESEARCH FOUNDATION AND LIBRARY, Drawer 920, Lexington, 24450. Royster Lyle Jr, Cur Collections
Holdings: Vols Cat Mss Pix
Notes: Papers of Forrest C Pogue, Army historian, Marshall biographer. Also over 300 German propaganda and military handbooks, and miscellaneous German pre-War books; French, German and American WW II newspapers (approx 300).

NEWSPAPERS, FOREIGN LANGUAGE

DC —LIBRARY OF CONGRESS, Serial and Government Publications Division, Washington, 20540.
Notes: Serials. One of the largest and most extensive collections in the world, incl periodicals; scientific and learned journals in all languages and in all fields except agriculture and medicine; US Government serials (Federal, State, County, and Muncipal): national foreign government serials from all countries; provincial serials from provinces possessing autonomy; municipal serials from principal cities; newspapers (850,000 unbound issues, 75,000 bound vols, 270,000 microfilm reels), 12,000 microprint cards of early American newspapers, 1704-1820, incl 1500 titles currently received, 500 of these being representative titles from all States of the Union and 1000 from all foreign countries.

MA —BOSTON PUBLIC LIBRARY, South End Branch, Multilingual Library, 685 Tremont St, Boston, 02118. Laura H Reyes, Librn
Holdings: Cat

†MA —BOSTON PUBLIC LIBRARY, Copley Sq, Boston, 02117.
Holdings: Cat Microforms
Notes: Microform Publications: Early American Newspapers, 1704-1820, by Readex Microprint Corp: special emphasis on Boston newspapers, general, local and ethnic; selected newspapers from New England, US, and Europe.

PA —BALCH INSTITUTE FOR ETHNIC STUDIES, Library, 18 S Seventh St, Philadelphia, 19106. R Joseph Anderson, Library Dir

ON —METROPOLITAN TORONTO LIBRARY, Languages Centre, 789 Yonge St, Toronto, M4W 2G8, Can. Barbara Gunther, Head
Holdings: Vols (90,000) Cat Phonorecords Audiotapes
Notes: Original literature in over 80 languages; books, records, cassettes, microfilm on language studies; newspapers and periodicals from 50 countries. Language study materials. Issue quarterly additions lists by language. Collect North American Indian and Eskimo language materials. Occasional bibliographies.

NEWSPAPERS, FRENCH

CA —UNIVERSITY OF CALIFORNIA, LOS ANGELES, Research Library, Western European Collection, Los Angeles, 90024. Edward Shreeves, Chairman, Bibliographers Group; Mary E Greco, Western European Bibliographer
Holdings: Microforms
Notes: Microfilm records (8 reels) of 51

NEWSPAPERS, FRENCH (cont.)

newspapers and periodicals of the French Resistance, from 1940 to 1944.

NH —ASSOCIATION CANADO-AMERICAIN (FRATERNAL LIFE INSURANCE SOCIETY), Institute Canado-Americain, 52 Concord St, Manchester, 03101. Robert A Beaudoin, Librn
Holdings: Vols (40,000) Cat Mss Pix Slides Phonorecords Audiotapes Microforms
Budget: ($2000)
Notes: Contains books, pamphlets, mss, university dissertations, newspapers, manuscripts, periodicals, and archives of various other societies (active of defunct). Subjects covered incl art, music, literature, folklore, religion, politics, sociology, history, etc of the French in France, Canada, and US (especially New England's Franco-Americans, Louisiana's Cajuns, and Quebec's French-Canadians). There is also an extensive collection of genealogical works dealing with Quebec Acadia, and New England Francophones. Articles dealing with the library are: "The Library of the Association Canado-Americaine" by Edward B Ham in *Modern Language Notes*, vol LII, no 7, November 1937 and a bilingual article "Appel d'un jeune aux jeunes en faveur de al Bibliotheque ACA" by Robert B Perreault in *Le Canado-Americain*, nouvelle serie, vol 1, no 5, julliet-aout-septembre 1975, pp 18-19.

NEWSPAPERS, FRENCH AMERICAN

†MA —BOSTON PUBLIC LIBRARY, Copley Sq, Boston, 02117.
Notes: Archives of Wilfred Beaulieu, founder and editor of the Franco-American newspaper *Le Travailleur*.

PA —BALCH INSTITUTE FOR ETHNIC STUDIES, Library, 18 S Seventh St, Philadelphia, 19106. R Joseph Anderson, Library Dir

NEWSPAPERS, GERMAN

CA —HOOVER INSTITUTION ON WAR, REVOLUTION & PEACE, Stanford University, Stanford, 94305. Milorad M Drachkovitch, Archivist
Holdings: (16,000) Cat Mss Pix Microforms
Notes: The German history collections extend from a set of Reichstag Debates, 1870-1918, the Revolution of 1918-1919, the Weimar Government, the National Socialists State, World War II, the period of Allied Occupation to the present, incl materials for both the Federal Republic of Germany and the Democratic Republic. Particularly noteworthy are holdings of newspapers, incl. *Vorwaerts, Voelkischer Beobachter*, and periodicals, incl. *Sueddeutsche Monatshefte, Einheit*. Of archival interest are the microfilms of the NSDAP Hauptarchiv (155 reels). Guides: *The Hoover Library Collections on Germany*, Hildegard R Boeninger (Stanford, 1955) and *Western Europe*, Agnes F Peterson (Stanford, 1970).

NY —STATE UNIVERSITY OF NEW YORK AT ALBANY, Library, Special Collections Dept, 1400 Washington Ave, Albany, 12222. Marion P Munzer, Coordr
Notes: Correspondence regarding Karl Otto Paetel and his German language newspaper, *Aufbau;* mss and letters concerning the German youth movement, Ernst Jünger, German resistance, and the refugee question (3.8 linear feet). Part of the Library's German Exile Collection.
See also entries under German Youth Movement; Paetel, Karl Otto; Jünger, Ernst

NC —DUKE UNIVERSITY, William R Perkins Library, Durham, 27706. Elvin E Strowd, University Librn

NEWSPAPERS, GERMAN AMERICAN

IN —WILLARD LIBRARY, 21 First Ave, Evansville, 47710. Joan Elliott, Special Collections Librn
Holdings: Vols (800) Cat Mss Maps Pix Microforms
Budget: ($4000)
Notes: General local history collection, incl

books, pamphlets, mss, and documents relating to the histories of Evansville and Vanderburgh and surrounding counties, with considerable material on Indiana as a whole. Incl extensive collection of German-language newspapers published in Evansville, 1850-1918.

OH —PUBLIC LIBRARY OF CINCINNATI & HAMILTON COUNTY, History Dept, 800 Vine St, Cincinnati, 45202. J Richard Abell, Head
Holdings: Vols (5831) Microforms
Notes: Cincinnati Newspaper Collection incl 21 daily, 19 weekly and 3 biweekly English-language papers, 9 daily and 3 weekly German-language papers. Dates range from 1793 to date. Microfilm incl two present daily papers, Cincinnati *Enquirer*, June 1818-and the Cincinnati *Post*, July 1882- , as well as the Cincinnatier Freie Presses, Aug-1874-July 1964, Cincinnati *Volkesfruend*, 1831-1959, Cincinnati Commercial (name changes Com Gazette, Com Tribue) Jan 1858-Dec 1930. And 12 additional titles. Reader-printers, are available. Library maintains a selective index to current daily newspapers as well as the Cincinnati *Times-Star* and the Cincinnati *Commercial Tribune*. Only material relating to Cincinnati/Hamilton County is indexed. Index began 1912, discontinued 1919, resumed 1926. Some retrospective indexing is done. Partially cataloged.

PA —BALCH INSTITUTE FOR ETHNIC STUDIES, Library, 18 S Seventh St, Philadelphia, 19106. R Joseph Anderson, Library Dir

NEWSPAPERS, GOLD RUSH

IN —INDIANA UNIVERSITY, Lilly Library, Seventh St, Bloomington, 47405. William R Cagle, Librn
Holdings: // Cat
Notes: First editions and early accounts, including 1000 issues of California gold rush newspapers.

NY —NEW YORK HISTORICAL SOCIETY, Library, 170 Central Park W, New York, 10024. James Gregory, Librn
Notes: One of the largest collections in the East of California newspapers printed in the 1850s.

†WA —UNIVERSITY OF WASHINGTON LIBRARIES, Seattle, 98195.

NEWSPAPERS, GREAT BRITAIN

KS —UNIVERSITY OF KANSAS, Kenneth Spencer Research Library, Special Collections Dept, Lawrence, 66045. Alexandra Mason, Librn
Holdings: Vols 1600 Cat
Notes: English newspapers and periodicals, 17th and 18th centuries. Noncirculating. Based on Richmond P and Marjorie N Bond Collection (which is being acquired over a period of years) with additional material. Described in: Bond, Richmond P, *The Tatler and the Spectator and the Development of the Early Periodic Press in England; a Checklist of the Collection of Richmond P Bond and Marjorie N Bond* (Chapel Hill, NC, 1965). *Books and Libraries at the University of Kansas*, v 7:1, Feb 1970.

NC —DUKE UNIVERSITY, William R Perkins Library, Rare Book Room, Durham, 27706. John L Sharpe, III, Cur
Notes: Newspaper collection of more than 300 titles. A collection of 18th century British and 19th century American newspapers.

NEWSPAPERS, GREEK AMERICAN

PA —BALCH INSTITUTE FOR ETHNIC STUDIES, Library, 18 S Seventh St, Philadelphia, 19106. R Joseph Anderson, Library Dir
Holdings: Mss Cat Pix
Notes: The records of the Greek-American newspaper *Atlantis* span its entire publishing history, 1894-1973. Although the prewar years and the final years are best documented, there are substantive records throughout. The records are of many types:

correspondence, legal files and memoranda, cablegrams, clipping and petition scrapbooks, press releases, book inventories, business records such as subscription and newsdealers reports, audits, tax returns, and accounting records incl ledgers, journals, and worksheets. There also are photographs and news library files. Some business records of the Vlasto family also have survived. Much of the material is in Greek. The proportion of Greek to English language in the subject, correspondence, and labor relations records varies. The legal files contain translations into English of all contested editorials, but the language of trhe legalcorrespondence varies. Foreign correspondents' cables are in Greek. Most financial records are in English.

NEWSPAPERS, GUATEMALAN

KS —UNIVERSITY OF KANSAS, Kenneth Spencer Research Library, Special Collections Dept, Lawrence, 66045. Alexandra Mason, Librn
Holdings: Vols 4400 Uncat Mss
Notes: William Griffith Collection on Central America, especially Guatemalan imprints, late 18th to mid-20th century, incl many newpapers and broadsides. Noncirculating.

NEWSPAPERS, HAWAIIAN

HI —BERNICE P BISHOP MUSEUM, Library, PO Box 19000-A, Honolulu, 96819. Cynthia Timberlake, Librn
Notes: Early voyages, natural and general history, archaeology, and ethnology of the Pacific area. Hawaiian materials incl mss, maps, 360,000 photographs dating from 1845, and Hawaiian language newspapers.

NEWSPAPERS, HEBREW

OH —HEBREW UNION COLLEGE-JEWISH INSTITUTE OF RELIGION, Klau Library, 3101 Clifton Ave, Cincinnati, 45220. David J Gilner, Reference Librn
Notes: American Jewish Periodical Center aims to microfilm every American Jewish newspaper and periodical up to 1925 and selectively since. See: American Jewish Periodical Center, *Jewish Newspapers and Periodicals on Microfilm Available at the AJPC* (Cincinnati, 1983).

NEWSPAPERS, HISPANIC AMERICAN

WI —STATE HISTORICAL SOCIETY OF WISCONSIN, Library, Newspaper and Periodicals Section, 816 State St, Madison, 53706. James P Danky, Librn
Notes: One of the largest collections of Hispanic American periodicals and newspapers in the US. Holdings described in *Hispanic Americans in the United States: A Union List....* Madison, The Society, 1979. (ERIC Report 220 110).

NEWSPAPERS, HONG KONG

IL —CENTER FOR RESEARCH LIBRARIES, 6050 S Kenwood Ave, Chicago, 60637. Donald B Simpson, Dir; Esther Smith, Collection Development Librn
Holdings: Microforms
Notes: Microfilm of files of Hond Kong newspapers in English 1875-1965.

NEWSPAPERS, HUNGARIAN AMERICAN

PA —BALCH INSTITUTE FOR ETHNIC STUDIES, Library, 18 S Seventh St, Philadelphia, 19106. R Joseph Anderson, Library Dir

NEWSPAPERS, ICELANDIC—CANADA

PA —BALCH INSTITUTE FOR ETHNIC STUDIES, Library, 18 S Seventh St, Philadelphia, 19106. R Joseph Anderson, Library Dir

MB —UNIVERSITY OF MANITOBA, Elizabeth Dafoe Library, Icelandic

NEWSPAPERS, ICELANDIC—CANADA (cont.)

Collection, Winnipeg, R3T 2N2, Can. Sigrid Johnson, Librn
Holdings: Vols (22,500) Cat Mss Maps Pix Audiotapes Microforms
Notes: Material mostly in Icelandic, some in other Scandinavian languages. All subject areas incl with primary emphasis placed on language, literature and history of Icelanders in Canada, especially Manitoba (incl mss); early publications of sagas and religious literature; numerous periodicals and newspapers, incl Islandske Maanedstidender, 1773, the first Icelandic periodical, and Framfari, 1877, the first Icelandic newspaper in North America; collections of Icelandic music, such as S K Hall Collection (published and mss); Guttormur J Guttormsson and Stephan G Stephansson Memorial Collections; Vilhjalmur Stefansson publications. Cited in, Saunderson, H H, *The Chair of Icelandic Language and Literature at the University of Manitoba.* Winnipeg: University of Manitoba, 1961.

NEWSPAPERS, ILLINOIS

IL —UNIVERSITY OF ILLINOIS, URBANA/CHAMPAIGN, Library, Newspaper Library, 1408 W Gregory Drive, Urbana, 61801. Betty L Hildwein, Librn
Holdings: Vols 1400 Cat Microforms
Notes: Incl 13,000 microfilm reels. The Newspaper Library subscribes to 175 Illinois titles on newsprint and 20 on microfilm which incl papers for major metropolitan areas and those regions of the state for which the University of Illinois at Urbana-Champaign assumes a major responsibility in coperation with other state research institutions. The collection dates from 1831 and contains complete or extensive back runs for 12 metropolitan Illinois papers including five Chicago, two Springfield, and many Urbana-Champaign titles. Separate newspaper title, geographic and chronological catalogs describe the holdings.

NEWSPAPERS, INDONESIAN

IL —CENTER FOR RESEARCH LIBRARIES, 6050 S Kenwood Ave, Chicago, 60637. Donald B Simpson, Dir; Esther Smith, Collection Development Librn
Holdings: Microforms
Notes: 14 newspapers on microfilm, mostly from 1966.

IL —NORTHERN ILLINOIS UNIVERSITY, Founders Memorial Library, Southeast Asia Collection, Normal Rd, De Kalb, 60115. Lee S Dutton Dr, Cur
Holdings: Vols (34,000) Cat Maps Microforms
Notes: An extensive collection of books, periodicals, newspapers, maps, and microforms from or about Southeast Asia. Areas of concentration incl Thailand, Malaysia, Indonesia, Singapore, Brunei, Philippines, Laos, and Burma. Holdings (except rare books, maps, and microforms) are housed in a separate area collection within the Founders Library. A departmental card catalog and specialized reference collection support reference services. A Thai collection of several thousand vols is the largest vernacular component. Extensive Malaysia, Indonesia, Singapore, and Brunei holdings have been acquired through the NPAC program. A collection of Filipino-American newspapers, and a growing collection of children's literature in common and uncommon Southeast Asian languages are available. Resources are accessible to borrowers through OCLC.

NEWSPAPERS, IOWA

IA —IOWA STATE HISTORICAL DEPT, Div of Museum & Archives, Newspaper Library, Historical Bldg, E 12 & Grand Ave, Des Moines, 50319. Jon Robison, Dept Head
Holdings: Vols 15,000 Cat
Budget: $28,000
Notes: 300 weekly and daily newspapers received; 20,000 microfilms; 15,000 bound vols 5000 rolls of Iowa courthouse microfilm. Work not complete. The collection will probably number fifteen thousand when filming is done. All Iowa state and federal census on 2300 rolls of microfilm.

IA —STATE HISTORICAL SOCIETY OF IOWA LIBRARY, 402 Iowa Ave, Iowa City, 52240. Darold J Brown, Librn
Holdings: Vols 13,000 Microforms
Notes: Iowa newspapers: 13,000 bound vols; 9000 microfilms.

NEWSPAPERS, IRISH AMERICAN

NY —AMERICAN IRISH HISTORICAL SOCIETY, Library, 991 Fifth Ave, New York, 10028. Lisa M Hottin, Cur; William D Griffin, Librn
Holdings: Vols (20,000) Cat Maps Pix Slides
Notes: Archives and Manuscripts: The documents and papers of Friends of Irish Freedom, The Land League, the Society of the Friendly Sons of St Patrick, the Catholic Club, and the Guild of Catholic Lawyers. The papers of New York State Supreme Court Justice Daniel F Cohalan. This is the largest and most complete collection of over 20,000 American Irish and Irish history, biography and literature in the United States. Incl American-Irish Newspaper collections dating from 1811, the most comprehensive in the US; 1000 rare books and special editions. Special collections incl regular exhibits of Irish or American Irish interest incl mss, letters, books, photographs and memorabilia. Permanent collection of representative works of Irish painters.

PA —BALCH INSTITUTE FOR ETHNIC STUDIES, Library, 18 S Seventh St, Philadelphia, 19106. R Joseph Anderson, Library Dir

NEWSPAPERS, ITALIAN

LA —LOUISIANA STATE UNIVERSITY, SHREVEPORT, Library-Archives, 8515 Youree Dr, Shreveport, 71129. Patricia L Meador, Archivist & Asst Librn
Notes: See Louisiana - History entry for LSU Archives.

MI —MICHIGAN STATE UNIVERSITY, Libraries, Special Collections Div, East Lansing, 48824. Jannette Fiore, Librn
Notes: The primary emphasis of this collection is on the central period of the Italian Risorgimento, 1845-1870. It includes account by eyewitnesses, works by significant polical figures, many scarce political pamphlets and complete runs of several key serial publications. The library is actively acquiring additional materials to support and expand this subject collection. 1500 pamphlets; 7000 issues of newspapers and periodicals.

NEWSPAPERS, ITALIAN AMERICAN

PA —BALCH INSTITUTE FOR ETHNIC STUDIES, Library, 18 S Seventh St, Philadelphia, 19106. R Joseph Anderson, Library Dir

NEWSPAPERS, JAPANESE

MD —UNIVERSITY OF MARYLAND, Library, East Asia Collection, College Park, 20742. Frank Joseph Shulman, Curator and Head
Holdings: Vols (90,000) // Mss
Notes: Japanese books, newspapers, periodicals, etc, of the Allied Occupation period (1945-1952), including files of censored publications. Books number 40,000; periodical titles, 13,000; newspaper titles, ca 16,500. The special collection relating to the Occupation period is supplemented by a growing collection (now ca 50,000 vols) of Chinese, Japanese, and Korean publications which form the basis of the University's general collection in East Asian language materials.

NEWSPAPERS, JAPANESE AMERICAN

†CA —LOS ANGELES COUNTY PUBLIC LIBRARY, Gardena Library, 1731 W Gardena Blvd, Gardena, 90247.
Notes: Japanese language materials, incl World War II period Japanese-American newspapers; Japanese-American monographs on microfilm; Japanese-American newspapers.

PA —BALCH INSTITUTE FOR ETHNIC STUDIES, Library, 18 S Seventh St, Philadelphia, 19106. R Joseph Anderson, Library Dir
Holdings: Cat Microforms

NEWSPAPERS, JEWISH AMERICAN

OH —HEBREW UNION COLLEGE-JEWISH INSTITUTE OF RELIGION, 3101 Clifton Ave, Cincinnati, 45220. David J Gilner, Reference Librn
Notes: American Jewish Periodical Center aims to microfilm every American Jewish newspaper and periodical up to 1925 and selectively since. See: American Jewish Periodical Center, *Jewish Newspapers and Periodicals on Microfilm Available at the AJPC* (Cincinnati, 1983).

NEWSPAPERS, KENTUCKY

KY —LOUISVILLE FREE PUBLIC LIBRARY, Fourth & York Sts, Louisville, 40203. Mark Harris, Head, Kentucky Division
Holdings: Vols 10,500 Cat Maps Microforms
Notes: The Kentucky Division incl a complete microfilm of *The Louisville Courier-Journal* newspaper which has been selectively card indexed for state and local items since 1918; also a complete microfilm file of *The Louisville Times.* Holdings of local newspapers on microfilm have been submitted to the Library of Congress' *Newspapers on Microfilm.* Noncirculating.

NEWSPAPERS, KOREAN AMERICAN

PA —BALCH INSTITUTE FOR ETHNIC STUDIES, Library, 18 S Seventh St, Philadelphia, 19106. R Joseph Anderson, Library Dir

NEWSPAPERS, LABOR

CA —UNIVERSITY OF CALIFORNIA, BERKELEY, University Library, Social Science Library, 30 Stephens Hall, Berkeley, 94720. Bette Erskine, Librn
Holdings: Vols 11,000 Cat Mss Microforms
Notes: The Labor Union Collection consists primarily of labor union journals, newspapers, proceedings and constitutions. Holdings are largely national in scope, with emphasis on Northern California. Approximately 850 current serials are being received. This collection is complemented by labor union materials in the Institute of Industrial Relations Library and in The Bancroft Library, and by holdings in Labor History in the Main Library. Incl 1683 microfilm reels.

IL —UNIVERSITY OF ILLINOIS, URBANA/CHAMPAIGN, Library, Newspaper Library, 1408 W Gregory Drive, Urbana, 61801. Betty L Hildwein, Librn
Holdings: Vols 3300 Cat Microforms
Notes: Incl 2000 microfilm reels. Among the 80 labor and business titles currently received, the Newspaper Library acquires the official organs of national and international labor unions and of Illinois labor organizations. The collection incl socialist, trade commerce, livestock and specialized classified titles which reflect a diverse range of views. Holdings span the entire 20th century, but are particularly strong since World War I. Unlike most other major newspaper groupings at Illinois, the labor collection is primarily on bound newsprint and is classified by subject call number. A title-subject catalog and separate shelf list describe the holdings. In 1980 the library prepared a list of newspapers classified by subject.

WI —STATE HISTORICAL SOCIETY OF WISCONSIN, Library, Newspaper and Periodicals Section, 816 State St, Madison, 53706. James P Danky, Librn
Notes: One of the largest collections of

NEWSPAPERS, LABOR (cont.)

Labor newspapers in the US. Holdings described in *Labor papers on Microfilm: A Combined List*, (Madison, The Society, 1965) and in Naas and Sakr's *American Labor Union Periodicals: A Guide to Their Location*. Only positive microfilm circulates on ILL.

NEWSPAPERS, LATIN AMERICAN

LA —TULANE UNIVERSITY, Howard-Tilton Memorial Library, Latin American Library, New Orleans, 70118. Thomas Niehaus, Dir
Holdings: Vols (150,000) Cat Mss Maps Pix Microforms VF
Budget: ($67,000)
Notes: *Catalog of the Latin American Library* (Boston: G K Hall, 1970, suppl. 1973,1975,1978); Downs 5338-41; suppl (1961), 2727, 2737. The Latin American Library is a general collection, but specializes in Central American, Mexican, and Brazilian materials. The disciplines which are most strongly represented are history, anthropology, and archaeology. The Viceregal Ecclesiastical Mexican Collection contains manuscripts from the colonial period. The France V Scholes Collection contains a large number of photoprints and microfilm of colonial documents from the archives of Spain and Mexico. The Merle Greene Robertson Rubbings Collection contains nearly five hundred rubbings of relief sculpture from Mayan archaeological sites in Mexico and Guatemala. The Photographic Collection contains photos of archaeological sites inMeso-America, of pre-Columbian Peruvian architecture, and a general group of historic photos from Latin America.

TX —UNIVERSITY OF TEXAS LIBRARIES, Nettie Lee Benson Latin American Collection, Sid Richardson Hall 1.109, Austin, 78712. Laura Gutierrez-Witt, Head Librn
Holdings: Vols (450,000) Cat Mss Maps Pix Phonorecords Filmstrips Microforms
See also entry under Latin America.

NEWSPAPERS, LATVIAN

NY —NEW YORK PUBLIC LIBRARY, Slavonic Div, Fifth Ave & 42 St, New York, 10018. Edward Kasinec, Chief
Holdings: Cat Microforms
Notes: See: New York Public Library, Slavonic Div, *Dictionary Catalog of the Slavonic Collection*, 2nd ed, rev and enl (Boston: G K Hall, 1974), 44 vols; and New York Public Library, *Dictionary Catalog of the Research Libraries* (New York, 1972-).

NEWSPAPERS, LITHUANIAN

MN —UNIVERSITY OF MINNESOTA, Immigration History Research Center, 826 Berry St, Saint Paul, 55114. Susan Griegs, Cur
Notes: 500 separate titles of Lithuanian immigrant publications; materials published in displaced persons' camps by Lithuanians during and after World War II.

NY —NEW YORK PUBLIC LIBRARY, Slavonic Div, Fifth Ave & 42 St, New York, 10018. Edward Kasinec, Chief
Holdings: Cat Microforms
Notes: See: New York Public Library, Slavonic Div, *Dictionary Catalog of the Slavonic Collection*, 2nd ed, rev and enl (Boston: G K Hall, 1974), 44 vols; and New York Public Library, *Dictionary Catalog of the Research Libraries* (New York, 1972-).

NEWSPAPERS, LITHUANIAN AMERICAN

PA —BALCH INSTITUTE FOR ETHNIC STUDIES, Library, 18 S Seventh St, Philadelphia, 19106. R Joseph Anderson, Library Dir

NEWSPAPERS, LOUISIANA

LA —LOUISIANA STATE UNIVERSITY, SHREVEPORT, Library-Archives, 8515 Youree Dr, Shreveport, 71129. Patricia L Meador, Archivist & Asst Librn
Notes: Archives incl catalogued manuscripts and records, 500 maps, more than 5000 photographs, 1000 architectural drawings, slides. The archives has on microfilm more than 200 letters (1827-1842) of Henry Miller Shreve, relating to the improvement of the Ohio, Mississippi and Red Rivers. Microfilm records also include those of the Shreveport City Council, Caddo and Bossier Parish Police Juries, Caddo Levee Board, the Shreveport Chamber of Commerce, and the Louisiana State Fair. Original and microfilm copies of the *Italia Moderna*, an Italian newspaper published by Frank Fulco in Shreveport, 1929-1946, are available for use in the archives. Other area newspapers are on microfilm and available for use.

NEWSPAPERS, MAINE

ME —MAINE STATE LIBRARY, Special Collections Dept, Cultural Bldg, Station 64, Augusta, 04333. Shirley Thayer, Librn
Holdings: Periodicals Microforms
Budget: ($2,500,000)
Notes: Maine newspapers. Major Maine newspapers on microfilm from 1803 to the present.

ME —PORTLAND PUBLIC LIBRARY, 5 Monument Sq, Portland, 04101. Edward V Chenevert, Library Dir
Holdings: Vols 1324 Cat Microforms
Notes: There is some duplication between 1324 bound vols and 2200 reels of microfilmed newspapers. Collection consists of Portland and Maine newspapers from 1785 to date. An *Index to Early Maine Newspapers* cites approx 27,700 Maine-related articles from 16 Maine newspapers covering the period 1784-1835. An incomplete continuation of this index contains approx 5500 citations covering the years 1835-1845. A current *Index of Maine Newspapers* covers Maine subjects for the years 1940 to date. It contains approx 160,000 entries.

NEWSPAPERS, MARITIME

NY —STATE UNIVERSITY OF NEW YORK, Maritime College, Stephen B Luce Library, Fort Schuyler, Bronx, 10465. Richard H Corson, Librn
Holdings: Vols (68,000)
Budget: ($90,000)
Notes: Incl full runs of newspapers of the major maritime unions on microfilm.

NEWSPAPERS, MASSACHUSETTS

†MA —UNIVERSITY OF MASSACHUSETTS AT AMHERST, Library, Amherst, 01003.
Notes: Microform collections of materials in other American libraries.

NEWSPAPERS, MEXICAN

CA —CLAREMONT COLLEGES, Honnold Library, Ninth & Dartmouth, Claremont, 91711. Tania Rizzo, Special Collections Dept Head
Holdings: Vols 328 // Cat
Notes: Restricted use. Incl 98 newspaper titles represented, 19th and early 20th centuries.

NEWSPAPERS, MEXICAN AMERICAN

PA —BALCH INSTITUTE FOR ETHNIC STUDIES, Library, 18 S Seventh St, Philadelphia, 19106. R Joseph Anderson, Library Dir

NEWSPAPERS, MIAMI (FLORIDA)

FL —MIAMI-DADE PUBLIC LIBRARY SYSTEM, 1 Biscayne Blvd, Miami, 33132. Alicia Godoy, Foreign Language Librn
Holdings: Vols 32,000 Cat Maps Microforms Phonorecords Audiotapes VF
Notes: Incl books in 17 languages, mainly Spanish; fiction, technical, biography, travel, history, mysteries, westerns, science-fiction and grammar; 200 language records, 100 language cassettes, 3 vertical files of clippings related to Latin America, Spain, Miami, etc; 35 magazines, 10 newspapers (daily local paper: Diario las Americas, El Miami Herald-El Mundo Puerto Rico); Sunday editions of Latin American newspapers from Argentina, Colombia, Chile, Mexico and Brazil; 1 Yiddish and 1 German newspaper.

FL —MIAMI-DADE PUBLIC LIBRARY SYSTEM, 1 Biscayne Blvd, Miami, 33132. Samuel J Boldrick, Librn
Holdings: Vols (4950) Cat Mss Maps Pix Audiotapes Microforms
Notes: Also incl 40,000 state and local documents; 700,000 newspaper clippings; and 195 reels of microfilmed newspaper clippings. Separate finding aids incl the *Miami Newspapers Index*, a computer generated index to six Miami newspapers which is on an in house on-line database.

NEWSPAPERS, MICHIGAN

MI —UNIVERSITY OF MICHIGAN, Bureau of Government Library, 100A Rackman Bldg, Ann Arbor, 48109. Barbara Landay, Technical Libr Assistant
Holdings: Vols (66,000) Cat
Budget: ($10,000)
Notes: Established in 1914 to serve faculty and students of Institute of Public Policy Studies. Particularly concerned with state and local documents, but incl some federal documents. Also has a pamphlet and newspaper clipping collection on Michigan. Some information on foreign governments.

MI —MICHIGAN TECHNOLOGICAL UNIVERSITY, Archives, Copper County Historical Collections, Houghton, 49931. Theresa Sanderson Spence, University Archivist
Holdings: Vols (1500) Cat Mss Maps Pix Slides Microforms
Notes: Michigan-Copper Country. Description of collection in *Michigan Chronicle*, 1st quarter, 1973. Accession lists are available for some of the collections. The collecting program embraces the university and all areas of the economic, cultural and social life of the people and institutions of the Copper Country (Baraga, Houghton, Keweenaw, and Ontonogan Counties). Special strength is in the mining history and mining company reports. Personal and business records, maps and photographs, broadsides, family histories, newspapers and oral materials as well as slides and film have been collected. Extensive holdings in area newspapers. As a regional depository for the state archives, provides access to a variety of research materials. Also, Keweenaw Historical Society Collection, see *Michigan History Magazine*,vols 1 (1917), 129-155.

NEWSPAPERS, MINNESOTA

MN —MINNESOTA HISTORICAL SOCIETY LIBRARY, 690 Cedar St, Saint Paul, 55101. Patricia C Harpole, Chief of Reference Library; Bonnie G Wilson, Head of Special Libraries
Notes: Minnesota Newpapers, 1849-to-date.

NEWSPAPERS, MISSISSIPPI

MS —UNIVERSITY OF SOUTHERN MISSISSIPPI, William David McCain Graduate Library, Box 5148, Southern Sta, Hattiesburg, 39406.
Holdings: 374 Titles
Notes: 1800-date. Incl early Mississippi Territory newspapers to date from all areas of the state. Greatest concentration of modern newspapers are from the southern third (23 counties) of the state.

NEWSPAPERS, MOVING PICTURE

CA —AMERICAN FILM INSTITUTE, Louis B Mayer Library, 2021 N Western Ave, PO Box 27999, Los Angeles, 90027. Anne G Schlosser, Dir
Notes: Rare periodical holdings: *Film Daily* newspaper (1923-1969); *Radio-TV Daily*

NEWSPAPERS, MOVING PICTURE (cont.)

newspaper (1939-1964); *RKO Radio Flash,*
house organ for RKO (1932-1955); *TV Guide* (1948 to date).

NY —NEW YORK PUBLIC LIBRARY,
Performing Arts Research Center, Billy Rose
Theatre Collection, 111 Amsterdam Ave,
New York, 10023. Dorothy L Swerdlove,
Cur
Holdings: Cat
See also entry under Moving Picture
Industry; Theatre.

NEWSPAPERS, NATIVE AMERICAN

WI —STATE HISTORICAL SOCIETY OF
WISCONSIN, Library, Newspaper and
Periodicals Section, 816 State St, Madison,
53706. James P Danky, Librn
Notes: The largest collection of Native
American periodicals and newspapers in the
US. Holdings described i: *Native American
Periodicals and Newspapers, 1828-1982.
Bibliography, Publishing Record and
Holdings.* Westport, Conn, Greenwood
Press, 1983. Describes over 1160 currently
published and ceased titles, over 800 of
which are in the Society's collection.

NEWSPAPERS, NEVADA

NV —NEVADA STATE LIBRARY, Capitol
Complex, Carson City, 89710. Joyce C Lee,
Dir, Public Services Div
Holdings: Uncat Microforms
Budget: $3500
Notes: Comprehensive, retrospective
collection of Nevada newspapers on
microfilm. Kept up-to-date by an ongoing
microfilming project of the Nevada State
Library, Nevada Historical Society,
University of Nevada (Las Vegas) Library,
and the University of Nevada (Reno)
Library. Incl 6000 reels of microfilm.

NV —UNIVERSITY OF NEVADA, RENO,
University Library, Special Collections Dept,
Reno, 89557. Robert E Blesse, Head
Holdings: Cat titles (800) Microfilm
Notes: Nevada newspapers 1859 to current.
Holdings include physical copies to 1950s,
microfilm copies as part of the Nevada
Newspaper Microfilming Project. Guide:
Lingenfelter and Gash. *Newspapers of
Nevada 1854-1979. A History and
Bibliography* (University of Nevada Press,
1984).

NEWSPAPERS, NEW HAMPSHIRE

NH —NEW HAMPSHIRE STATE LIBRARY,
20 Park St, Concord, 03301. Shirley G
Adamovich, Librn
Holdings: Vols (683,015) Cat Mss Maps
Phonorecords 16mm Films Filmstrips
Microforms
Budget: ($124,119)
Notes: Microfilm holdings of early NH town
records, daily and weekly NH newspapers,
8837; NH laws and legislative journals of
colonial and early state periods; laws of the
US and all states and territories from the
time of their settlement or organization; law
library collection of 72,000 volumes; NH
state documents, earliest to present; NH
imprints.

NH —KEENE STATE COLLEGE, Wallace E
Mason Library, 229 Main St, Keene, 03431.
Edward A Scott, Librn; Clifford Mead,
Special Collections Librn
Holdings: Vols (2000) Cat Maps Pix
Audiotapes Microforms
Budget: ($7500)
Notes: New Hampshire history, genealogy,
authors, imprints (especially Keene
imprints), Keene State College materials, and
newspapers (microfilm).

NEWSPAPERS, NEW JERSEY

NJ —RUTGERS, THE STATE UNIVERSITY
OF NEW JERSEY, Alexander Library,
Special Collections and Archives, College
Ave & Huntington St, New Brunswick,
08903. Ronald L Becker, Cur of Manuscripts
and Rare Books
Notes: The newspaper holdings heavily favor
New Jersey, New York, and Philadelphia,
late 18th and early 19th centuries. The
general cut-off date for US and foreign
newspapers is 1820; New Jersey titles are
collected through 1865 and sometimes later.
Smaller catagories incl historical, political,
amateur, business, and special newspapers.

NEWSPAPERS, NEW MEXICO

NM —MUSEUM OF NEW MEXICO, History
Library, PO Box 2087, Santa Fe, 87503.
Orlando Romero
Holdings: Vols 12,000 Cat Mss Maps
Microforms
Budget: $64,000
Notes: History of the Southwest, emphasis
on history of New Mexico, incl New
Mexican newspapers. Restricted use;
noncirculating. 2500 maps; 700 microforms.

NEWSPAPERS, NEW YORK (CITY)

IL —LAKE FOREST COLLEGE, Donnelley
Library, Lake Forest, 60045. Arthur H
Miller Jr, College Librn
Holdings: Vols (1000) Mss Pix
Notes: Working files (1919-1946) of Capt
Joseph-Medill Patterson, founder of the New
York *News.*

NJ —RUTGERS, THE STATE UNIVERSITY
OF NEW JERSEY, Alexander Library,
Special Collections and Archives, College
Ave & Huntington St, New Brunswick,
08903. Ronald L Becker, Cur of Manuscripts
and Rare Books
Notes: The newspaper holdings heavily favor
New Jersey, New York, and Philadelphia,
late 18th and early 19th centuries. The
general cut-off date for US and foreign
newspapers is 1820; New Jersey titles are
collected through 1865 and sometimes later.
Smaller catagories incl historical, political,
amateur, business, and special newspapers.

NY —NEW YORK HISTORICAL SOCIETY,
Library, 170 Central Park W, New York,
10024. James Gregory, Librn
Notes: An extensive collection of eighteenth
and early nineteenth century American
newspapers. Incl the most complete set of
original New York papers and the fourth
largest collection of newspapers printed in
the US prior to 1821.

NY —NEW YORK PUBLIC LIBRARY,
Annex Section, 521 W 43 St, New York,
10036. Richard L Hill, First Asst
Holdings: Vols 24,000 Cat Microforms
Notes: Comprehensive New York (City)
coverage; selective coverage of other US and
foreign countries. Incl 24,000 bound
volumes; 86,000 microfilm reels.

NEWSPAPERS, NORTHWEST (PACIFIC)

WA —UNIVERSITY OF WASHINGTON
LIBRARIES, Pacific Northwest Collection,
Seattle, 98195. Andrew F Johnson, Librn
Holdings: Vols (50,000) Cat Mss Maps Pix
Budget: ($12,000)
Notes: The Pacific Northwest Collection
contains printed materials documenting the
historic and contemporary life and culture of
the region in a broad range of subject areas.
The Pacific Northwest is defined as the
geographic region including Washington,
Oregon, Idaho, Montana, British Columbia,
Yukon Territory, and Alaska. Printed
materials including books, periodicals,
government documents, maps, weekly and
local regional newspapers, theses and
dissertations, as well as photographs and
architectural drawings are included in the
Pacific Northwest Collection. Photographic
works of over 200 photographers active in
the Pacific Northwest, Alaska, and the
Yukon Territory (Canada) during the period
1860-1930, including Asahel and Edward S
Curtis, Eric Hegg, and Clark Kinsey, are
represented in a print collection of more
than 300,000 images. The
architecturaldrawings collection includes
over 19,000 original plans, drawings,
sketches, renderings and blue prints
pertaining to the history of architecture and
urban planning and landscape gardening in
the Pacific Northwest ca 1880-1940. Areas
of particular strength are the holdings of
over 1100 published journals of Pacific
Northwest exploration expeditions,
photographs of Northwest Coast Native
Americans and of historic Seattle,
newspapers issued within the Japanese-
American relocation camps, 1942-1945,
materials relating to the 1980 eruption of Mt
St Helens, and Sanborne fire insurance maps
for Washington. A unique feature of the
Collection is the subject index to regional
periodicals and local newspapers maintained
by the PNW Collection staff; over 100 titles
are currently indexed. G K Hall Company
published a books catalog of the Pacific
Northwest Collectionin 1973.

WA —UNIVERSITY OF WASHINGTON
LIBRARIES, Microforms Newspaper
Section, FM-25, Seattle, 98195. Glenda J
Pearson, Microforms Reference Librn
Holdings: Microfilm
Budget: ($86,000)
Notes: 1200 regional newspaper titles on
microfilm, particularly Washington, historical
and current. Many local newspapers
microfilmed on a current basis. Extensive
negative bank. Publication: *Pacific
Northwest Newspapers on Microfilm at the
University of Washington Libraries* (Seattle:
University of Washington Libraries, 1983).

NEWSPAPERS, NORWEGIAN AMERICAN

MN —NORWEGIAN-AMERICAN
HISTORICAL ASSOCIATION, Rolvaag
Memorial Library, Saint Olaf College,
Northfield, 55057. Lloyd Hustvedt,
Archivist
Holdings: Vols (10,000) Cat Mss Pix Slides
Microforms
Notes: The purpose of the collection is to
collect and preserve the records of
Norwegian-Americans by maintaining
archives and publishing books, on history
literature, art, and culture. Books and
periodicals are cataloged for the Association
by the St Olaf College Library. The
manuscripts and other archival material are
kept in a separate collection where they are
inventoried, indexed and shelved.

PA —BALCH INSTITUTE FOR ETHNIC
STUDIES, Library, 18 S Seventh St,
Philadelphia, 19106. R Joseph Anderson,
Library Dir

NEWSPAPERS, OHIO

OH —OHIO UNIVERSITY, Vernon R Alden
Library, Department of Archives and Special
Collections, Athens, 45701. Gary A Hunt,
Head
Holdings: Vols 825 Cat Mss Maps Pix
Microforms, VF
Notes: The Ohio Historical Collections can
be divided into 4 major parts: Ohio
University Archives, containing institutional
records, dating from 1804, of the oldest
university West of the Alleghenies; Local
Government Records Collection, containing
birth, death, marriage, tax and other public
records from an 18-county region of
Southeastern Ohio; Ohioana Collection,
consisting of published books, periodicals,
newspapers, documents, directories and
other printed materials (incl imprints)
relating to this region; and the Manuscript
Collections, containing both personal papers
as well as family, business and organizational
records pertaining to Southeastern Ohio.

OH —PUBLIC LIBRARY OF CINCINNATI
& HAMILTON COUNTY, History Dept,
800 Vine St, Cincinnati, 45202. J Richard
Abell, Head
Holdings: Vols (5831) Microforms
Notes: Cincinnati Newspaper Collection incl
21 daily, 19 weekly and 3 bioweekly
English-language papers, 9 daily and 3
weekly German-language papers. Dates
range from 1793 to date. Microfilm incl two

NEWSPAPERS, OHIO (cont.)

present daily papers, Cincinnati *Enquirer,* June 1818- and the Cincinnati *Post,* July 1882- , as well as the Cincinnati *Volkesfruend,* 1853-1908, and 12 additional titles. Reader-printer is available. Library maintains a selective index to current daily newspapers as well as the Cincinnati *Times-Star* and the Cincinnati *Commercial Tribune.* Only material relating to Cincinnati/Hamilton County is indexed. Index began 1912, discontinued 1919, resumed 1926. Some retrospective indexing is done. Partially cataloged.

OH —OHIO HISTORICAL SOCIETY, Archives Library Division, 1982 Velma Ave, Columbus, 43211. Dennis East, Division Chief
Holdings: Vols 25,000 Cat Microforms
Notes: This collection is the primary one for Ohio newspapers, 1793, to date (25,000 volumes; 22,000 microfilm reels). Microfilming service is offered on cost basis for titles not filmed.

NEWSPAPERS, OKLAHOMA

OK —OKLAHOMA HISTORICAL SOCIETY, Library, Historical Bldg, Oklahoma City, 73105. Andrea Clark, Dir, Library Resources Division
Holdings: Microforms
Notes: This is an ongoing program of microfilming current and backfiles for Oklahoma newspapers. Not available for interlibrary loan; however, a specific article will be checked if the exact date and city are given.

NEWSPAPERS, OREGON

OR —BAKER COUNTY PUBLIC LIBRARY, 2400 Resort St, Baker, 97814. Paul C Crouhamal, Librn
Holdings: Vols (1700) Cat Mss Maps Pix Microforms
Budget: ($2000)
Notes: Baker County, Oregon materials, historical and current, emphasizing genealogy, mining, agriculture and the people. Incl any fiction with Oregon as the locale. Local newspapers on microfilm, 1870-date, but incomplete for early years. 50 files on local plants, 1953-date, with separate catalog. Incl 300 maps.

OR —UNIVERSITY OF OREGON LIBRARY, Microforms and Recordings Section, Eugene, 97403. Rory Funke, Head
Holdings: Cat Microforms
Notes: Most Oregon newspapers microfilmed on a current basis. Extensive collection of negative microfilm; 30,000 reels of microfilm. Publication: *Oregon Newspapers; Negative Held by University of Oregon Library.* (Eugene, Oregon: University of Oregon Library, 1970).

NEWSPAPERS, ORIENTAL

NC —DUKE UNIVERSITY, William R Perkins Library, Durham, 27706. Elvin E Strowd, University Librn
Notes: The Thomas collection relating to China and the Far East contains more than 1500 items. It is a comprehensive body of books, newspapers, prints and other materials dealing with many phases of the culture of the Orient. Additions are ongoing.

NEWSPAPERS, PENNSYLVANIA

PA —ERIE COUNTY HISTORICAL SOCIETY LIBRARY, 417 State St, Erie, 16501. Helen Andrews, Librn
Notes: Erie Newspapers, 36 titles.

PA —HISTORICAL SOCIETY OF PENNSYLVANIA, Library, 1300 Locust St, Philadelphia, 19107. David Fraser, Librn
Holdings: Vols (230,000) Mss Maps Pix Microforms
Notes: Incl over 14,000,000 ms pieces. The Library Company of Philadelphia mss are on deposit with the Historical Society of Pennsylvania. Many of the Society's rare books are on deposit with the Library Compny. The Society maintains the collections of the Genealogical Society of Pennsylvania, incl some 20,000 printed genealogies, original mss, family, church, and civil records.

NEWSPAPERS, PERSIAN

TX —UNIVERSITY OF TEXAS LIBRARIES, Middle East Collection, PO Box P, Austin, 78712. Abazar Sepehri, Librn
Holdings: Vols (45,000) Cat Microforms
Notes: Arabic, Persian and Turkish materials in the humanities and social sciences. Incl 350 periodical and 45 newspaper titles from most of the countries of the Arab League, Turkey, Iran and Afghanistan.

NEWSPAPERS, PHILADELPHIA

NJ —RUTGERS, THE STATE UNIVERSITY OF NEW JERSEY, Alexander Library, Special Collections and Archives, College Ave & Huntington St, New Brunswick, 08903. Ronald L Becker, Cur of Manuscripts and Rare Books
Notes: The newspaper holdings heavily favor New Jersey, New York, and Philadelphia, late 18th and early 19th centuries. The general cut-off date for US and foreign newspapers is 1820; New Jersey titles are collected through 1865 and sometimes later. Smaller categories incl historical, political, amateur, business, and special newspapers.

PA —TEMPLE UNIVERSITY LIBRARIES, Special Collections Dept, Rare Books & Mss Section, Philadelphia, 19122. Thomas M Whitehead, Cur
Holdings: 15,000 Images
Notes: "Photojournalism Collection". Curated by George Brightbill and Elaine Clever. News photography archives: News films from two Philadelphia television stations WPVI (nee WFIL) 1947-date, and KYW, 1950-1960's; 1937-1972 photoarchives of the Philadelphia Inquirer newspaper and the Index, clipping file, photo-archive and library of the Evening Bulletin newspaper. Archival set of the Bulletin, 1847-1982.

NEWSPAPERS, PHILIPPINO-AMERICAN

IL —NORTHERN ILLINOIS UNIVERSITY, Founders Memorial Library, Southeast Asia Collection, Normal Rd, De Kalb, 60115. Lee S Dutton Dr, Cur
Holdings: Vols (34,000) Cat Maps Microforms
Notes: An extensive collection of books, periodicals, newspapers, maps, and microforms from or about Southeast Asia. Areas of concentration incl Thailand, Malaysia, Indonesia, Singapore, Brunei, Philippines, Laos, and Burma. Holdings (except rare books, maps, and microforms) are housed in a separate area collection within the Founders Library. A departmental card catalog and specialized reference collection support reference services. A Thai collection of several thousand vols is the largest vernacular component. Extensive Malaysia, Indonesia, Singapore, and Brunei holdings have been acquired through the NPAC program. A collection of Filipino-American newspapers, and a growing collection of children's literature in common and uncommon Southeast Asian languages are available. Resources are accessible to borrowers through OCLC.

NE —UNIVERSITY OF NEBRASKA-LINCOLN, Don L Love Library, Lincoln, 68588. Joseph G Svoboda, University Archivist
Notes: World War II - Pacific Theater - Psychological Warfare Collection, 1944-45, ca 1000 item. Leaflets dropped from US airplanes, scrapbooks, Japanese propaganda materials, newspapers published by US armed forces in the Philippines. Collection assembled by J Robert Sandberg and Frank M Hallgren who served in Psychological Warfare Branch.

NEWSPAPERS, POLISH

IL —CENTER FOR RESEARCH LIBRARIES, 6050 S Kenwood Ave, Chicago, 60637. Donald B Simpson, Dir; Esther Smith, Collection Development Librn
Holdings: Cat Microforms
Notes: 26 current newspapers on microfilm.

IL —POLISH NATIONAL ALLIANCE OF THE UNITED STATES OF NORTH AMERICA (PNA), 6100 N Cicero Ave, Chicago, 60646. Josephine Rzewska, Librn
Holdings: Vols 18,000
Notes: This fraternal society also supports Alliance College, Cambridge Springs, PA. Also publish *Polish Daily Zgoda,* 1908- , Daily.

NY —NEW YORK PUBLIC LIBRARY, Slavonic Div, Fifth Ave & 42 St, New York, 10018. Edward Kasinec, Chief
Holdings: Cat Microforms
Notes: See: New York Public Library, Slavonic Div, *Dictionary Catalog of the Slavonic Collection,* 2nd ed, rev and encl (Boston G K Hall, 1974), 44 vols; and New York Public Library, *Dictionary Catalog of the Research Libraries* (New York, 1972-).

PA —ALLIANCE COLLEGE, Washington Hall Library, Fullerton Ave, Cambridge Springs, 16403. Stanley J Kozaczka, Head Librn
Notes: Microfilm: *Trybuna Polska* (Erie, PA), 1920-1939; *Zycie* (Warsaw), 1887-1890; *Tygodnik Illustrowany* (Warsaw), 1859-1939 with some gaps; *Kurier Warszawski* (Warsaw), 1821-1831.

PA —POLISH NATIONAL UNION OF AMERICA, 1004 Pittston Ave, Scranton, 18505.

NEWSPAPERS, POLISH AMERICAN

PA —BALCH INSTITUTE FOR ETHNIC STUDIES, Library, 18 S Seventh St, Philadelphia, 19106. R Joseph Anderson, Library Dir

NEWSPAPERS, PORTUGUESE

MA —SOUTHEASTERN MASSACHUSETTS UNIVERSITY, Library Communications Center, Old Westport Rd, North Dartmouth, 02747.

NEWSPAPERS, PUERTO RICAN

NY —HUNTER COLLEGE, Centro de Estudios Puertorriquenos, Library, 695 Park Ave, New York, 10021. Nelida Perez, Librn; Felix Rivera, Asst; Amilcar Tirado, Librn
Holdings: Vols 5000 Cat Microforms
Notes: Materials concerning the historical experience, culture, and present condition of Puerto Ricans. Incl numerous periodicals, pamphlets, reports, over 700 doctoral dissertations, and, on microfilm, government documents and 19th and 20th century newspapers.

NEWSPAPERS, REFUGEE

†NY —STATE UNIVERSITY OF NEW YORK, COLLEGE AT BUFFALO, Vietnamese Immigration Collection, Buffalo, 14260.
Notes: Oral history, interviews, orientation materials, and refugee camp newspapers.

NEWSPAPERS, RELIGIOUS

IL —UNIVERSITY OF ILLINOIS, URBANA/CHAMPAIGN, Library, Newspaper Library, 1408 W Gregory Drive, Urbana, 61801. Betty L Hildwein, Librn
Holdings: Cat Microforms

NEWSPAPERS, RHODE ISLAND

RI —WESTERLY PUBLIC LIBRARY, Broad St, Westerly, 02891. David J Panciera, Library Dir
Notes: Single issues of early 19th century newspapers from various towns in US. Broken runs of early 19th century newspapers of Rhode Island and Eastern

NEWSPAPERS, RHODE ISLAND (cont.)

Connecticut towns. Complete run of local *Westerly Sun*, 1893-present. Complete run *Narragansett Weekly*, 1858-1899.

NEWSPAPERS, RUSSIAN

CA —UNIVERSITY OF CALIFORNIA, LOS ANGELES, Library, Slavic Collection, 405 Hilgard Ave, Los Angeles, 90024. Edward Shreeves, Chairman, Bibliographers Group; Leon Ferder, Slavic Bibliographer
Holdings: Vols (250,000) Cat
Notes: The Slavic Collection at UCLA consists of materials from and relating to Russia and the Soviet Union, Poland, Czechoslovakia, Yugoslavia, Bulgaria, the Sorbians in East Germany, and works by Slavic emigres. The collection contains nearly 250,000 vols, and is particularly strong in linguistics, literature, history and social sciences, and reference materials. Slavic materials are collected in hard copy and microform, and incl monographs, serials (incl newspapers), reference works, proceedings of Slavistic congresses and symposia, and also *Festschriften* and dissertations.

IL —UNIVERSITY OF ILLINOIS, URBANA/CHAMPAIGN, Slavic and East European Library, Urbana, 61801. Marianna Tax Choldin, Head
Holdings: Vols (420,000) Cat Microforms
Notes: One of the largest Slavic and East European collections. Strong in Russian and Soviet materials-humanities, sciences, and social sciences; languages and literatures; periodicals, newspapers, and microforms. Ca 260,000 volumes in languages of the Soviet Union plus 20,000 Russian and Ukrainian titles on microform. Extensive coverage of Czechoslovakia (35,000 vols); Yugoslavia (31,000 vols); Bulgaria (9200 vols); Poland (34,600 vols); Romania (13,000 vols); and Hungary (18,000 vols) and the languages, literatures, and history of these countries.

NY —COLUMBIA UNIVERSITY LIBRARIES, Lehman Library, Slavic and East Central European Collection, 420 W 118 St, New York, 10027. Nina Lencek, Bibliographer
Holdings: // Uncat Microforms
Notes: Collection consists of a total of 988 Russian and East European newspapers: of these 614 are Russian pre-1917 and post-Revolution newspapers and 16 Russian emigre titles published in Russian and in Western languages in Western Europe and America; 297 newspapers are in other East European languages published in Eastern Europe, and 61 East European emigre newspapers published in the West. In addition to these newspapers, Lehman Library holds a number of cataloged East European and Russian newspapers in microform. The collection is available for research to qualified scholars with special permission.

†NY —US ARMY RUSSIAN INSTITUTE (USARI), APO, New York, 09053.
Holdings: Vols (24,841)
Notes: A research and language facility of the Army Foreign Affairs Officers Speciality (USSR), located in Garmisch, West Germany. 65 percent of the collection is in Russian; 35 percent in English and other languages. Contains most representative Soviet Newspapers and periodicals, as well as American and other English language publications.

WI —UNIVERSITY OF WISCONSIN, MADISON, Memorial Library, Slavic Studies Collection, 728 State St, Madison, 53706. Aleksander Rolich, Bibliographer for Slavic Studies; Robert P Gakovich, Slavic Cataloger; Valdis J Zeps, Baltic Studies Center
Notes: Russian Underground Collection. Materials in the Russian Underground Collection embrace the Russian Revolutionary Movement from 1825 to 1917, including a considerable number of Free Press publications. Among the 1500 titles are included about 100 journals, many

political tracts, leaflets, broadsides and brochures of various political groups, largely socialist, religious nonconformists (L Tolstoi) and a large number of the satirical journals that appeared between 1905-1907. Restricted use: Rare Book Department.

NEWSPAPERS, RUSSIAN AMERICAN

PA —BALCH INSTITUTE FOR ETHNIC STUDIES, Library, 18 S Seventh St, Philadelphia, 19106. R Joseph Anderson, Library Dir

NEWSPAPERS, SERBIAN

NY —NEW YORK PUBLIC LIBRARY, Slavonic Div, Fifth Ave & 42 St, New York, 10018. Edward Kasinec, Chief
Holdings: Cat Microforms
Notes: See: New York Public Library, Slavonic Div, *Dictionary Catalog of the Slavonic Collection*, 2nd ed, rev and enl (Boston: G K Hall, 1974), 44 vols; and New York Public Library, *Dictionary Catalog of the Research Libraries* (New York, 1972-).

NEWSPAPERS, SLAVIC

CA —UNIVERSITY OF CALIFORNIA, LOS ANGELES, Library, Slavic Collection, 405 Hilgard Ave, Los Angeles, 90024. Edward Shreeves, Chairman, Bibliographers Group; Leon Ferder, Slavic Bibliographer
Holdings: Vols (250,000)
Notes: The Slavic Collection at UCLA consists of materials from and relating to Russia and the Soviet Union, Poland, Czechoslovakia, Yugoslavia, Bulgaria, the Sorbians in East Germany, and works by Slavic emigres. The collection contains nearly 250,000 vols, and is particularly strong in linguistics, literature, history and social sciences, and reference materials. Slavic materials are collected in hard copy and microform, and incl monographs, serials (incl newspapers), reference works, proceedings of Slavistic congresses and symposia, and also *Festschriften* and dissertations.

NY —COLUMBIA UNIVERSITY LIBRARIES, Lehman Library, Slavic and East Central European Collection, 420 W 118 St, New York, 10027. Nina Lencek, Bibliographer
Holdings: // Uncat Microforms
Notes: Collection consists of a total of 988 Russian and East European newspapers: of these 614 are Russian pre-1917 and post-Revolution newspapers and 16 Russian emigre titles published in Russian and in Western languages in Western Europe and America; 297 newspapers are in other East European languages published in Eastern Europe, and 61 East European emigre newspapers published in the West. In addition to these newspapers, Lehman Library holds a number of cataloged East European and Russian newspapers in microform. The collection is available for research to qualified scholars with special permission.

NY —NEW YORK PUBLIC LIBRARY, Slavonic Div, Fifth Ave & 42 St, New York, 10018. Edward Kasinec, Chief
Holdings: Cat Microforms
Notes: Described in *Dictionary Catalog of the Slavonic Collection* (Boston: G K Hall, 1974), 44 vols.

PA —JANKOLA LIBRARY AND SLOVAK ARCHIVES, Danville, 17821.
Holdings: Vols (1500)
Notes: Slovak studies and representation of other Slavic groups.

PA —THE SLOVAK MUSEUM AND ARCHIVES AT JEDNOTA ESTATES, Rosedale & Jednota Sts, PO Box 150, Middletown, 17057. Edward A Tuleya, Cur & Archivist
Notes: Incl periodicals and newspapers.

NEWSPAPERS, SLOVENIAN AMERICAN

PA —BALCH INSTITUTE FOR ETHNIC STUDIES, Library, 18 S Seventh St,

Philadelphia, 19106. R Joseph Anderson, Library Dir

NEWSPAPERS, SOLDIERS'

NE —UNIVERSITY OF NEBRASKA-LINCOLN, Don L Love Library, Lincoln, 68588. Joseph G Svoboda, University Archivist
Notes: World War II - Pacific Theater - Psychological Warfare Collection, 1944-45, ca 1000 item. Leaflets dropped from US airplanes, scrapbooks, Japanese propaganda materials, newspapers published by US armed forces in the Philippines. Collection assembled by J Robert Sandberg and Frank M Hallgren who served in Psychological Warfare Branch.

PA —TEMPLE UNIVERSITY LIBRARIES, Special Collections Dept, Contemporary Culture Collection, Philadelphia, 19122. Patricia J Case, Cur
Notes: The Contemporary Culture Collection. See full entry under US-Social Life and Customs.

NEWSPAPERS, SOUTH ASIAN

†WA —UNIVERSITY OF WASHINGTON LIBRARIES, Seattle, 98195.

NEWSPAPERS, SOUTHERN STATES

NC —DUKE UNIVERSITY, William R Perkins Library, Durham, 27706. Elvin E Strowd, University Librn
Notes: The Flowers Collection of Southern Americana currently consists of 4,300,500 items. Additions are ongoing. Included in this collection are several types of materials, which are housed in appropriate sections of the library. The various types of materials are: manuscripts, books, pamphlets, maps, music, broadsides, newspapers, photographs, engravings, prints and memorabilia.

NEWSPAPERS, SPANISH

CT —UNIVERSITY OF CONNECTICUT, Library, Storrs, 06268. R H Schimmelpfeng, Dir of Special Collections
Holdings: Cat
Notes: Collection of newspapers and periodicals formerly belonging to the Duque de T'Serclaes. Ranging from the 17th century through the 20th the bulk of titles are from 1800-1840, covering the Napoleonic period and the Latin American wars of independence.

NEWSPAPERS, SPANISH AMERICAN

PA —BALCH INSTITUTE FOR ETHNIC STUDIES, Library, 18 S Seventh St, Philadelphia, 19106. R Joseph Anderson, Library Dir

NEWSPAPERS, STUDENT

CA —UNIVERSITY OF CALIFORNIA, LOS ANGELES, Research Library, Social Sciences Collection, 405 Hilgard Ave, Los Angeles, 90024. Edward Shreeves, Chairman, Bibliographers Group; Oscar L Sims, Social Sciences Bibliographer
Notes: A collection of over 200 underground newspapers on 26 reels of microfilm. Among the titles included are: *The Tribe, The Berkeley Barb, New York Roach, Rat*, and *Win*.

NEWSPAPERS, SWEDISH AMERICAN

PA —BALCH INSTITUTE FOR ETHNIC STUDIES, Library, 18 S Seventh St, Philadelphia, 19106. R Joseph Anderson, Library Dir

NEWSPAPERS, SYRIAN AMERICAN

PA —BALCH INSTITUTE FOR ETHNIC STUDIES, Library, 18 S Seventh St, Philadelphia, 19106. R Joseph Anderson, Library Dir

NEWSPAPERS, TENNESSEE

MS —MISSISSIPPI STATE UNIVERSITY, Mitchell Memorial Library, Box 5408,

NEWSPAPERS, TENNESSEE (cont.)

Mississippi State, 39762. Frances N
Coleman, Head, Special Collections
Holdings: Mss
Notes: Papers of Norman Bradley, editor of
The Chattanooga Post and *The Chattanooga
Times.*

NEWSPAPERS, TEXAS

TX —UNIVERSITY OF TEXAS LIBRARIES,
General Libraries, Barker Texas History
Center, PO Box P, Austin, 78712. Don
Carleton, Dir
Holdings: Vols (132,000) Cat Mss Maps Pix
Slides Phonorecords Audiotapes Microforms
Notes: Newspapers: 2011 individual titles.
Materials pertaining to the historical, social,
economic, scientific, humanistic and literary
development of Texas. Rich in early state
imprints, as well as the period of the
Republic. Texas archival and ms holdings
number over 18,000,000 items. Texas history
prior to the Republic is covered by the Bexar
Archives.

TX —EL PASO PUBLIC LIBRARY,
Southwest Collection, 501 N Oregon, El
Paso, 79901. Mary A Sarber, Head
Holdings: Vols (12,000) Cat Mss Maps Pix
Budget: ($11,000)
Notes: Research collection includes rare
books and mss journals, vertical files, index
to El Paso newspapers, microfilmed
newspapers, photographs, and architectural
plans. Separate catalog. Limited to materials
on Texas, New Mexico, Arizona and
Mexico. Special collections of material by
and about Tom Lea Jr, and Carl Hertzog.
Aultman Collection of photographs includes
3500 on El Paso Southwest and 2500 on
Mexican Revolution. Cited in Lovelace,
Lisa, "The Southwest Collection of the El
Paso Public Library". *Great Plains Journal,*
vol 2, no 2, pp 161-166; Aultman, Otis A
*Photographs from the Border: The Otis A
Aultman Collection,* El Paso Public Library
Association, 1977.

TX —BAYLOR UNIVERSITY, Moody
Memorial Library, Texas History Collection,
Waco, 76706. Kent Keeth, Librn
Holdings: Vols (80,000) Cat Mss Maps Pix
Slides Phonorecords Audiotapes Microforms
Notes: The Texas Collection gathers
materials which relate to life in Texas in all
its aspects, from earliest days to the present.
Incl Baylor University Archives.

NEWSPAPERS, THEATRE

NY —NEW YORK PUBLIC LIBRARY,
Performing Arts Research Center, Billy Rose
Theatre Collection, 111 Amsterdam Ave,
New York, 10023. Dorothy L Swerdlove,
Cur
Holdings: Cat
Notes: See entry under Theatre.

NEWSPAPERS, TORONTO

ON —METROPOLITAN TORONTO
LIBRARY, Canadian History Dept, Baldwin
Room Section, 789 Yonge St, Toronto,
M4W 2G8, Can. David B Kotin, Head
Holdings: Vols (52,000) Mss Pix
Notes: This collection consists of material on
Canadian history, geography, travel,
archaeology, genealogy, retrospective city
and telephone directories, collective
biographies, native peoples (excluding
customs, rights and social conditions), Arctic
regions, military history and theory. It is an
extremely strong collection of both current
and retrospective material. Particular
strengths are national and local history
(especially Ontario), Arctic regions, native
peoples, travel (especially Ontario), and
military history. Incl 78,000 historical
pictures, 235 linear meters mss, 14,000
broadsides and 3800 bound newspapers.

NEWSPAPERS, TURKISH

TX —UNIVERSITY OF TEXAS LIBRARIES,
Middle East Collection, PO Box P, Austin,

78712. Abazar Sepehri, Librn
Holdings: Vols (45,000) Cat Microforms
Notes: Arabic, Persian and Turkish materials
in the humanities and social sciences. Incl
350 periodical and 45 newspaper titles from
most of the countries of the Arab League,
Turkey, Iran and Afghanistan.

NEWSPAPERS, UKRAINIAN

NJ —UKRAINIAN NATIONAL
ASSOCIATION, 30 Montgomery St, Jersey
City, 07303.
Holdings: Vols 9000 Mss Pix
Notes: Newspapers are kept only from
previous year.

NY —NEW YORK PUBLIC LIBRARY,
Slavonic Div, Fifth Ave & 42 St, New York,
10018. Edward Kasinec, Chief
Holdings: Cat Microforms
Notes: See: New York Public Library,
Slavonic Div, *Dictionary Catalog of the
Slavonic Collection,* 2nd ed rev and enl
(Boston: GK Hall, 1974), 44 vols; and New
York Public Library, *Dictionary Catalog of
the Research Libraries* (New York, 1972-).

NEWSPAPERS, UKRAINIAN AMERICAN

PA —BALCH INSTITUTE FOR ETHNIC
STUDIES, Library, 18 S Seventh St,
Philadelphia, 19106. R Joseph Anderson,
Library Dir
Holdings: Cat Microforms
Notes: Newspapers on microform.
See also entry under Ethnic Newspapers -
North America.

NEWSPAPERS, UNDERGROUND

CA —UNIVERSITY OF CALIFORNIA, LOS
ANGELES, Research Library, Social
Sciences Collection, 405 Hilgard Ave, Los
Angeles, 90024. Edward Shreeves,
Chairman, Bibliographers Group; Oscar L
Sims, Social Sciences Bibliographer
Notes: A collection of over 200 underground
newspapers on 26 reels of microfilm. Among
the titles included are: *The Tribe, The
Berkeley Barb, New York Roach, Rat,* and
Win.

CA —FITZ HUGH LUDLOW MEMORIAL
LIBRARY, PO Box 99346, San Francisco,
94109. Michael R Aldrich, Exec Cur
Holdings: Mss Maps Pix Slides
Phonorecords Audiotapes Videotapes
Notes: Collection stored. Important mail
inquiries only. No interlibrary lending or
telephone queries. The heart of this special
collection of psychoactive drug literature is
about 400 vols of memoirs or lightly-
disguised fiction concerning psychoactive
drugs, plus about 600 vols related to Beat
writers of the 1950s-60s, plus about 300 vols
related to the "Hippie" movement of the
1960s, plus 600 vols (mostly paperback) of
drug-related pornography, and several
hundred vols related to drug slang, drugs
and music, drug art, drug cuisine, etc. In
addition we have many boxes of offprints,
files of newspaper clippings, complete runs
to underground newspapers, and many
artifacts related to this area. Much of the
1950s-60s-70s literature is autographed or
inscribed.

CA —HOOVER INSTITUTION ON WAR,
REVOLUTION & PEACE, Stanford
University, Stanford, 94305. Milorad M
Drachkovitch, Archivist
Notes: The New Left Politics Collection
consists of monographs and serials on the
New Left that are cataloged. In addition, the
collection subscribes to numerous
underground newspapers and has obtained
special subject collections such as the Free
Speech Movement at Berkeley 1964-1965,
SNCC and Mississippi Summer 1964, and
the insurrection at San Francisco State
College in 1968-1969. There is also a good
collection on the French student revolts of
1968. The collection is a supervised one and
not open to browsers. Interested students
and scholars are welcome. Only limited
photocopying is permitted.

CT —UNIVERSITY OF CONNECTICUT,
Library, Storrs, 06268. Ellen Embardo, Cur
Special Collections
Holdings: Cat
Notes: Alternative Press Collection.
Primarily periodicals and newspapers from
the 1960s to today of an alternative or
underground nature. Books and pamphlets
are incl, representing both the left and the
right-wing viewpoints. A catalog is available.
Also have archives of the First Casualty
Press, which was deeply involved with
Vietnam veterans' experiences in Vietnam.

DC —LIBRARY OF CONGRESS, Serial and
Government Publications Division,
Washington, 20540.
Notes: The Alternative Press Collection
contains American newspaper-format
publications issued outside the publishing
mainstream since the mid-1960s. Approx
350 titles from 26 states.

IL —CHICAGO PUBLIC LIBRARY,
Newspapers & General Periodicals Center,
425 N Michigan Ave, Chicago, 60611. Jerry
Delaney, Head
Holdings: Microforms
Notes: The collection consists of the
Underground Newspaper Microfilm
Collection, (1963-1981), published by Bell
and Howell.

IL —NORTHWESTERN UNIVERSITY,
Library, Special Collections Dept, 1937
Sheridan Rd, Evanston, 60201. R Russell
Maylone, Cur
Budget: Vols 100 Cat
Notes: Very large collection of original
journals from the 1960s and 1970s, mostly
American and Canadian, but also several
English and French. Also high school
papers. Subjects incl left-wing politics,
American Indian ecology, drug culture, anti-
war and environmental issues. Women's
collection of serial holdings largest in
country. All hard copy with exception of
some of the Women's collection.

IL —UNIVERSITY OF ILLINOIS,
URBANA/CHAMPAIGN, Library,
Newspaper Library, 1408 W Gregory Drive,
Urbana, 61801. Betty L Hildwein, Librn
Notes: Four cataloged volumes, 402
cataloged microforms, 4 portfolios of local
underground papers, 2 microfilm reels of
local underground papers, 400 microfilm
reels of Bell and Howell underground
newspaper collection.

MA —AMHERST COLLEGE, Library,
Amherst, 01002. John Lancaster, Special
Collections Librn
Notes: The files of the Liberation News
Service from the basis of the collection; ca
2000 titles uncat.

MI —OAKLAND UNIVERSITY, Kresge
Library, Rochester, 48063. Suzanne O
Frankie, Dean; Elizabeth Titus, Special
Collections Librn
Holdings: Uncat Microforms
Notes: Underground newspapers
predominantly of Michigan and the
Midwest; 750 titles. Some indexed in
Underground Newspaper Microfilm
Collection, by Bell and Howell or the
Alternative Press Index.

MO —UNIVERSITY OF MISSOURI-
COLUMBIA, Ellis Library, Special
Collections Dept, Ninth & Lowry, Columbia,
65201. Margaret A Howell, Head, Special
Collections
Holdings: Microfilm Cat
Notes: Backfiles of over 400 US titles (most
are complete runs) plus a collection of
underground newspapers. It also includes
current files of about two dozen
metropolitan daily newspapers.

NY —YIVO INSTITUTE FOR JEWISH
RESEARCH, Library & Archives, 1048
Fifth Ave, New York, 10028. Dina
Abramowicz, Librn; Marek Web, Archivist
Holdings: Cat Mss Pix Slides
Notes: Jewish life in Eastern Europe is one
of the areas of emphasis. The books and
periodicals include the literature of the
Jewish Enlightenment in Russia (first half of
the 19th century), first periodicals of Russian
Jewry in Yiddish, Hebrew and Russian, a
complete set of the main organ or Russian
Jewry in the last century: *Voskhod,*

NEWSPAPERS, UNDERGROUND (cont.)

underground publications of Jewish labor and radical groups in the Czarist Empire, extensive collection of the Soviet-Yiddish press and literature, publications of the refugee groups outside Russia in the Far East and the West and in present-day Israel. Jewish life in Poland of the interbellum period is presented by the press in Yiddish, Hebrew and Polish, by publications of numerous Jewish organizations and political parties in the fields of education, economy, medicine and the arts. Source materials on Jews in the Balticcountries and Rumania are also represented. Music, folklore and art of Jews in Eastern Europe is well-covered.

PA —TEMPLE UNIVERSITY LIBRARIES, Special Collections Dept, Contemporary Culture Collection, Philadelphia, 19122. Patricia J Case, Cur
Notes: The Contemporary Culture Collection. See full entry under US-Social Life and Customs.

WI —STATE HISTORICAL SOCIETY OF WISCONSIN, Library, Newspaper and Periodicals Section, 816 State St, Madison, 53706. James P Danky, Librn
Notes: Incl largest collection (over 4000) of US and Canadian underground or alternative publications in North America. Only postive microfilm circulates on ILL. Holdings described in James Danky's *Undergrounds: A Union List of Alternative Periodicals in Libraries of the United States and Canada* (1974).

WI —UNIVERSITY OF WISCONSIN, MADISON, Memorial Library, Slavic Studies Collection, 728 State St, Madison, 53706. Aleksander Rolich, Bibliographer for Slavic Studies; Robert P Gakovich, Slavic Cataloger; Valdis J Zeps, Baltic Studies Center
Notes: Russian Underground Collection. Materials in the Russian Underground Collection embrace the Russian Revolutionary Movement from 1825 to 1917, including a considerable number of Free Press publications. Among the 1500 titles are included about 100 journals, many political tracts, leaflets, broadsides and brochures of various political groups, largely socialist, religious nonconformists (L Tolstoi) and a large number of the satirical journals that appeared between 1905-1907. Restricted use: Rare Book Department.

NEWSPAPERS, UTAH

UT —UNIVERSITY OF UTAH, Marriott Library, Special Collections, Salt Lake City, 84112. Gregory C Thompson, Cur
Notes: Nearly complete collection of all newspapers produced in Utah.

NEWSPAPERS, VERMONT

VT —VERMONT DEPARTMENT OF LIBRARIES, Law & Documents Unit, 111 State St, Montpelier, 05602. Vivian Bryan, Librn
Holdings: Vols (42,000) Cat Maps Microforms
Budget: ($3000)
Notes: Vermontiana. Incl largest known collection of Vermont newspapers, authors and imprints. The library prepares an annual *Checklist of Available Vermont State Publications.*

NEWSPAPERS, VIETNAMESE AMERICAN

†NY —STATE UNIVERSITY OF NEW YORK, COLLEGE AT BUFFALO, Vietnamese Immigration Collection, Buffalo, 14260.
Notes: Oral history, interviews, orientation materials, and refugee camp newspapers.

NEWSPAPERS, VIRGINIA

VA —COLLEGE OF WILLIAM AND MARY, Earl Gregg Swem Library, Williamsburg, 23185. Margaret C Cook, Cur of Manuscripts & Rare Books
Holdings: Vols 2000 Cat Mss Maps
Notes: Virginia books and pamphlets through 1870. This collection incl files of 18th and 19th century Virginia newspapers.

NEWSPAPERS, WASHINGTON

WA —UNIVERSITY OF WASHINGTON LIBRARIES, Microforms Newspaper Section, FM-25, Seattle, 98195. Glenda J Pearson, Microforms Reference Librn
Holdings: Microforms
Budget: ($86,000)
Notes: 1010 Washington State and Territory newspapers on microfilm, historical and current. Many local newspapers microfilmed on a current basis. Extensive negative bank.
Publication: *Pacific Northwest Newspapers on Microfilm at the University of Washington Libraries* (Seattle: University of Washington Libraries, 1983).

NEWSPAPERS, WELSH AMERICAN

PA —BALCH INSTITUTE FOR ETHNIC STUDIES, Library, 18 S Seventh St, Philadelphia, 19106. R Joseph Anderson, Library Dir

NEWSPAPERS, WEST INDIAN

MA —AMERICAN ANTIQUARIAN SOCIETY LIBRARY, 185 Salisbury St, Worcester, 01609. Marcus A McCorison, Dir & Librn
Holdings: Cat
Notes: A special strength.

NEWSPAPERS, WHITE RUSSIAN

NY —COLUMBIA UNIVERSITY LIBRARIES, Lehman Library, Slavic and East Central European Collection, 420 W 118 St, New York, 10027. Nina Lencek, Bibliographer
Holdings: // Uncat Microforms
Notes: Collection consists of a total of 988 Russian and East European newspapers: of these 614 are Russian pre-1917 and post-Revolution newspapers and 16 Russian emigre titles published in Russian and in Western languages in Western Europe and America; 297 newspapers are in other East European languages published in Eastern Europe, and 61 East European emigre newspapers published in the West. In addition to these newspapers, Lehman Library holds a number of cataloged East European and Russian newspapers in microform. The collection is available for research to qualified scholars with special permission.

NY —NEW YORK PUBLIC LIBRARY, Slavonic Div, Fifth Ave & 42 St, New York, 10018. Edward Kasinec, Chief
Holdings: Vols 2200 Cat Microforms
Notes: Subjects strength is in literature, incl the literature of the early 20th century. Linguistics and folklore are also well represented. The collection of early White Russian newspapers in quite strong. See New York Public Library, *Dictionary Catalog of the Slavonic Collection* (Boston: GK Hall, 1974), 44 vols.

NEWSPAPERS, WISCONSIN

WI —STATE HISTORICAL SOCIETY OF WISCONSIN, Library, Newspaper and Periodicals Section, 816 State St, Madison, 53706. James P Danky, Librn
Holdings: Cat Microforms
Notes: Most complete file of Wisconsin newspapers dating from 1833. 282 titles received currently. Restricted use: only positive microfilm circulates. Donald E Oehlerts' *Guide to Wisconsin Newspapers*, 1883-1958 lists all newspapers published in Wisconsin together with a holdings directory.

NEWSPAPERS, WOMEN'S

WI —STATE HISTORICAL SOCIETY OF WISCONSIN, Library, Newspaper and Periodicals Section, 816 State St, Madison, 53706. James P Danky, Librn
Notes: The largest collection of women's periodicals and newspapers in the US. The library's resources as well as those in other areas of the Society are described in *Women's History: Resources at the State Historical Society of Wisconsin.* Madison, The Society. 4th edition, 1982. (ERIC Report ED 225922). Holdings described in: *Women's Periodicals and Newspapers from the 18th Century to 1981: A Union List...* Boston, G K Hall, 1982.

NEWSPAPERS, WYOMING

WY —WYOMING STATE ARCHIVES MUSEUMS, AND HISTORICAL DEPARTMENT, Barrett Bldg, Cheyenne, 82002. Philip J Roberts, Documents Supvr; Jean F Brainerd, Research Asst
Holdings: Vols (400)
Notes: Extensive mss, map, pamphlet, and picture collection relative to Wyoming, regional, and western history. Publish *Annals of Wyoming.*

NEWSPAPERS, YIDDISH AMERICAN

OH —HEBREW UNION COLLEGE-JEWISH INSTITUTE OF RELIGION, Klau Library, 3101 Clifton Ave, Cincinnati, 45220. David J Gilner, Reference Librn
Notes: American Jewish Periodical Center aims to microfilm every American Jewish newspaper and periodical up to 1925 and selectively since. See: American Jewish Periodical Center, *Jewish Newspapers and Periodicals on Microfilm Available at the AJPC* (Cincinnati, 1983).

PA —BALCH INSTITUTE FOR ETHNIC STUDIES, Library, 18 S Seventh St, Philadelphia, 19106. R Joseph Anderson, Library Dir

NEWSPAPERS, YUKON TERRITORY

†WA —UNIVERSITY OF WASHINGTON LIBRARIES, Seattle, 98195.

NEWSPAPERS, YUGOSLAVIAN

IL —CENTER FOR RESEARCH LIBRARIES, 6050 S Kenwood Ave, Chicago, 60637. Donald B Simpson, Dir; Esther Smith, Collection Development Librn

NEWSREELS see Moving Pictures—Newsreels

NEWSWRITERS

DC —LIBRARY OF CONGRESS, Manuscript Division, Washington, 20540. John C Broderick, Chief
Notes: His papers; 45,000 items.

NEWTON, ALFRED EDWARD

PA —FREE LIBRARY OF PHILADELPHIA, Rare Book Dept, Logan Sq, Philadelphia, 19103. Marie E Korey, Rare Book Librn
Holdings: Cat Mss Pix
Notes: The A Edward Newton Collection of his own writings and publications including 350 books, periodicals, proof sheets, manuscripts, autograph letters, association copies and memorabilia. The gift of Swift Newton.

RI —PROVIDENCE PUBLIC LIBRARY, 150 Empire St, Providence, 02903. Lance J Bauer, Special Collections Librn
Holdings: Vols (6300) Cat Mss Pix
Notes: The

NEWTON, SIR ISAAC

CA —UNIVERSITY OF CALIFORNIA, LOS ANGELES, William Andrews Clark Memorial Library, 2520 Cimarron St, Los Angeles, 90018.
Holdings: Cat Mss
Notes: Extensive collection, first editions, etc.

CA —STANFORD UNIVERSITY LIBRARIES, Cecil H Green Library,

NEWTON, SIR ISAAC (cont.)

Stanford, 94305. Michael T Ryan, Cur
Holdings: Vols 4000 Cat Mss Pix
Notes: The Frederick E Brasch Collection. History of science, with particular emphasis on Newton, his precursors, contemporaries, and successors.

MA —BABSON COLLEGE, Horn Library, Babson Park, 02157. Elizabeth E Di Bartolomeis, Special Collections Librn
Holdings: Vols 1100 Cat Mss Maps Pix Slides
Budget: $2500
Notes: All important editions of Newton's works, a large body of contemporary commentary and several books from his own library with annotations in his hand; memorabilia incl contemporary portraits and a reconstruction of the "fore-parlor" of his London house with original pine panelling and other woodwork; catalog 232 pp (1950), supplement, 90 pp (1955).

MN —UNIVERSITY OF MINNESOTA, O Meredith Wilson Library, 309 19 Ave S, Minneapolis, 55455. Austin J McLean, Chief, Special Collections
Holdings: Vols (103) // Cat Mss
Notes: Basically mathematical astronomy with emphasis on eclipses. Particular strengths are the works of such authors as Delambre, Euclid, Newton, Ptolemy, and Rhaticus. Important in this respect are 6 of the 10 known printed editions of the Alphonsine Astronomical Tables.

PA —AMERICAN PHILOSOPHICAL SOCIETY, Library, 105 S Fifth St, Philadelphia, 19106. Edward C Carter II, Librn
Holdings: Vols 150 Cat
Notes: Collection (as it was in 1970) is included in *Catalog of Books in the American Philosophical Society Library* (Westport, Conn: Greenwood Publishing Corp, 1970). The catalog reproduces the APS Library catalog cards, incl author, subject, and title entries.

ON —UNIVERSITY OF TORONTO, Thomas Fisher Rare Book Library, 120 Saint George St, Toronto, M5S 1A5, Can. Richard G Landon, Head
Holdings: Vols 4000
Notes: The Science Collection is especially rich in works on Renaissance astronomy, physics and mechanics and has noteworthy holdings of works of English experimental scientists in the 17th and 18th centuries with excellent collections of the works of Robert Boyle, Robert Hooke, and Sir Isaac Newton. Includes virtually all important early editions of Euclid; alchemical works of the 16th and 17th centuries together with the works of 18th century chemists like Lavoisier and Priestly; works on agriculture with special emphasis on British agriculture in the 18th century; and a variety of other works important in the history of science in all its branches. In addition the Fisher Library has many other specialized scientific collections which are listed separately.

NEY, MICHAEL, MARSHAL OF FRANCE

NC —DAVIDSON COLLEGE, E H Little Library, Davidson, 28036. Leland M Park, Dir; Chalmers G Davidson, Dir
Holdings: Vols 30 Cat Mss Pix
Notes: The collection primarily concerns the possible identification of Peter Stuart Ney, designer of the Davidson College seal, with Marshal Ney of France.

NEZ PERCE INDIANS

†WA —WASHINGTON STATE UNIVERSITY, Library, Manuscripts, Archives & Special Collections, Pullman, 99164. John F Guido, Head
Holdings: Cat Mss Maps Pix
Notes: The collection is especially rich in documents relating to the exploration, settlement and development of the Palouse Country, the Inland Empire, the Columbia Basin and the Pacific Northwest. Described in *Selected Manuscript Resources in the Washington State Univeristy Library* (Pullman, 1974); and other published and unpublished inventories and registers.

NGBAKA TRIBE

IL —WHEATON COLLEGE, Buswell Memorial Library, Wheaton, 60187. Paul Snezek, Library Dir
Holdings: Mss Cat
Notes: Material consists of word lists, a conversation manual, a dictionary and the translated New Testament. All of the material collected by Zaire Missionary pioneer, Theodore B Wallin. *Related Topics:* Radio.

NIAGARA FALLS

NY —BUFFALO & ERIE COUNTY HISTORICAL SOCIETY, 25 Nottingham Court, Buffalo, 14216. Herman Sass, Librn
Notes: Some books and pamphlets. Many prints, maps and pictures. In various resources departments. No separate catalog.

NY —BUFFALO & ERIE COUNTY PUBLIC LIBRARY, Rare Book Room, Lafayette Sq, Buffalo, 14203. William H Loos, Cur
Holdings: Uncat
Notes: 220 prints of various views of the falls.

NY —NIAGARA FALLS PUBLIC LIBRARY, 1425 Main St, Niagara Falls, 14305. Donald E Loker, Local History Specialist
Holdings: Vols 10,000 Cat Mss Maps Pix Slides Microforms
Notes: Incl prints, pamphlets and ephemera. Local newspapers are indexed. Special emphasis on Niagara Falls and River.

NY —SCHOELKOPF GEOLOGICAL MUSEUM, Library, Prospect Park, Niagara Falls, 14303. Robert Kesil, Librn
Holdings: Vols 200 Uncat
Notes: Natural history of Niagara Falls.

NIAGARA FRONTIER—HISTORY

NY —BUFFALO & ERIE COUNTY HISTORICAL SOCIETY, 25 Nottingham Court, Buffalo, 14216. Herman Sass, Librn
Notes: 70 indexes and catalog aids have been created pertaining to various aspects of this collection. There are special collections within this special collection. Niagara Frontier History is the major collection of of the society, and its main purpose is to build this collection.

NIBELUNGENLIED

OH —CLEVELAND PUBLIC LIBRARY, Fine Arts and Special Collections Department, 325 Superior Ave, Cleveland, 44114. Alice N Loranth, Head
Holdings: Vols (3000) Cat Mss
Notes: Part of the Romances Collection, which incl critical studies, and early printed editions. The Arthurian and Charlemagne cycles, the Nibelungenlied and other Germanic titles, Amadis de Gaula and his numerous progeny, Alexander the Great, Barlaam and Joasaph, and the Seven Wise Masters of Rome are some of the strengths of the collection. Material in the Dewey/Brett Collection is classified by related cycles and their versions in various languages.
See also entry under Romances.

NICARAGUA

CT —YALE UNIVERSITY, Sterling Memorial Library, Latin American Collections, New Haven, 06520. Lee H Williams Jr, Cur
Holdings: Vols (300,000) Cat Maps Pix Slides Phonorecords 16mm Films Filmstrips
Notes: See entry for Yale University under Latin America.

KS —UNIVERSITY OF KANSAS, Watson Library, Lawrence, 66045. George Jerkovich, Cur Slavic Collections
Notes: Over 6000 valuable Central American titles, of which fewer than half in a random sample are presently located in OCLC, and over half not incl in published holdings of the University of Texas or Tulane University. A special grant is supporting cataloging of the collection.

MA —PAN AMERICAN SOCIETY OF NEW ENGLAND, Shattuck Library, 152 North Street, Boston, 02109. Vivian Ingrao, Dir
Holdings: Vols (10,000) Cat Slides Phonorecords
Notes: Books on art, literature, history, and economy of Pan American countries.

NY —COLUMBIA UNIVERSITY LIBRARIES, Rare Book & Manuscript Library, 801 Butler Library, 535 W 114 St, New York, 10027. Kenneth A Lohf, Librn
Notes: More than 32,000 items documenting the rise of William Russell Grace's shipping business and other materials relating to his career as mayor of New York. Incl records and correspondence relating to all aspects of the shipping business in New York and South America, mining interest in Peru and Chile, and transportation in Costa Rica and Nicaragua. Family memorabilia and photographs, materials concerning New York Politics, banking and insurance, real estate interests and Catholic charities, and letters from Chester A Arthur, John Jacob Astor, Andrew Carnegie, Grover Cleveland, Hamilton Fish, John Hay and J Pierpont Morgan. Restricted use.

NICARAGUA—:IISTORY

CA —UNIVERSITY OF CALIFORNIA, RIVERSIDE, University Library, 4045 Canyon Crest Dr, Box 5900, Riverside, 92517.
Holdings: Vols 75
Notes: Collection of printed contemporary and modern sources relating especially to William Walker, Nicaragua and the Filibusters of 1855-60, as well as to American Filibusters in Mexico.

CT —YALE UNIVERSITY, Box 1603A, Yale Station, New Haven, 06520.
Holdings: Cat Mss
Notes: Incl the ms minutes of the Council of State of the Mosquito Kingdom, September 1846-1847, the British protectorate on the coast of Nicaragua.

DE —UNIVERSITY OF DELAWARE, Hugh M Morris Library, S College Ave, Newark, 19711. T Stuart Dick, Special Collections
Holdings: // Mss
Notes: Personal and business papers of the Potter Family, a Philadelphia merchant family prominent in the inport trade with Central America, particularly Nicaragua (1801-1943).

TX —UNIVERSITY OF TEXAS LIBRARIES, Nettie Lee Benson Latin American Collection, Sid Richardson Hall 1.109, Austin, 78712. Laura Gutierrez-Witt, Head Librn
Holdings: Vols (450,000) Cat Maps Microforms
Notes: Private library of Arturo Taracena Flores, providing extensive coverage of all Central American countries. Incl nearly all Guatemala imprints, 1800-1964; also incl broadsides.
See also entry under Latin America.

NICHOL, B. P.

BC —SIMON FRASER UNIVERSITY, Library, Burnaby, V5A 1S6, Can. Percilla Groves, Special Collections Librn
Holdings: Cat Mss
Notes: Mss for most published books, 1961-1982, plus various drafts, proofs and layouts for published work, plus unpublished mss and notebooks. Approx seven feet.

NICHOLAS, WILSON CARY

VA —UNIVERSITY OF VIRGINIA, Alderman Library, Manuscripts Dept, Charlottesville, 22901. Edmund Berkeley Jr, Cur
Holdings: Cat Mss
See also entry under Virginia - History

NICHOLS, DUDLEY, 1895-1960

CA —UNIVERSITY OF CALIFORNIA, LOS ANGELES, Research Library, Dept of

NICHOLS, DUDLEY, 1895-1960 (cont.)

Special Collections, 405 Hilgard Ave, Los Angeles, 90024. Edward Shreeves, Chairman, Bibliographers Group; David S Zeidberg, Head
Notes: 55 screenplays; a few articles and related ephemera.

NICHOLS, ERNEST FOX

NH —DARTMOUTH COLLEGE, Baker Memorial Library, Hanover, 03755.
Notes: Papers as President of Dartmouth.

NICHOLS, J. C.

MO —UNIVERSITY OF MISSOURI-KANSAS CITY, General Library, State Historical Society of Missouri Manuscripts, 5100 Rockhill Road, Kansas City, 64110. Kenneth J LaBudde, Dir; Gordon Hendrickson, Assoc Dir
Holdings: Mss
Notes: Western Historical Manuscript Collection incl papers of Charles B Wheeler, Jr, Charles N Kimball, Arthur Mag, Oscar D Nelson, Lou B Holland, J C Nichols, Perry Cookingham, Blevins Davis, Daniel MacMorris, and the records of the Kansas City Board of Trade.

OK —UNIVERSITY OF OKLAHOMA, Bizzell Memorial Library, Western History Collections, 401 W Brooks, Norman, 73069. John Ezell, Cur
Holdings: Mss Documents
Notes: US Representative. His papers. Guide available.

NICHOLS, ROBERT MALISE BOWYER

NY —HOFSTRA UNIVERSITY, Library, 1000 Fulton Ave, Hempstead, 11550. Charles R Andrews, Dean of Library Services
Notes: Strong collection. Incl some mss.

NICHOLS, RUTH, 1948-

ON —MCMASTER UNIVERSITY, Mills Memorial Library, Div of Archives & Research Collections, Hamilton, L8S 4L6, Can. G R Hill, Univ Librn
Holdings: Mss
Notes: Mss of published and unpublished novels.

NICKEL NOVELS see Dime Novels

NICKERSON, EUGENE H.

†NY —COLUMBIA UNIVERSITY LIBRARIES, Butler Library, Rare Book and Manuscript Library, 535 W 114 St, New York, 10027.
Notes: Papers of Eugene H Nickerson. Approx 173 items of the Nassau County executive.

NICKERSON FAMILY

MA —NEW ENGLAND HISTORIC GENEALOGICAL SOCIETY, Library, 101 Newbury St, Boston, 02116. Ralph J Crandell, Dir
Notes: Family papers, likely to incl personal correspondence, diaries, business records, etc.

NICOLAS DE LYRE

PA —DUQUESNE UNIVERSITY, Library, Pittsburgh, 15282. Dena F Jacobson, Music and Reference Librn
Holdings: Vols 3000 Cat
Notes: Main emphasis of collection is on history of Jewish philosophy in the Middle Ages and relationship between Jewish and Christian scholars; collection incl works by 14th century writer Nicolas de Lyra and general Judaica, history of the Jews, theology, Bible texts and commentaries, literature,, grammatical works and dictionaries, etc.

NICOLSON, SIR HAROLD, 1886-1968

IN —INDIANA UNIVERSITY, Lilly Library, Seventh St, Bloomington, 47405. William R Cagle, Librn
Notes: Letters of Sir Harold Nicolson, (1886-1968), and his wife, Lady Victoria Sackville-West (1892-1962). About 10,500 letters exchanged between 1910 and 1962.

NICOLSON, JOHN

AZ —NORTHERN ARIZONA UNIVERSITY, Special Collection Library, CU Box 6022, Flagstaff, 86011. Peter M Whiteley, Coordr/Archivist; William Mullane, Librn
Notes: Papers, incl newspaper and magazine articles, 1950's-1980's concerning the US, Europe, Middle East, USSR, etc. Oral history tapes, personal correspondence, and photographs (9 feet).

NICOTINE

MD —OFFICE ON SMOKING AND HEALTH, Park Bldg, Rm 116, 5600 Fishers Lane, Rockville, 20857. Donald R Shopland, Technical Information Officer
Notes: Smoking, tobacco and nicotine as related to health. Approx 40,000 reprints. The technical information center of the clearinghouse issues at irregular intervals (about 6 times per year) the *Smoking and Health Bulletin*. The *Bulletin* contains those items added to the collection from the world-wide literature on smoking. Bibliographic and reference services can be obtained by writing or calling the Clearinghouse. Over 10,000 records, 1970-present, are stored in an automated file and are capable of search and retrieval. Printout information corresponds to that found in the *Smoking and Health Bulletin*. The Clearinghouse has been named the "Collaborating Center for Smoking and Health" by the World Health Organization.

NC —NORTH CAROLINA STATE UNIVERSITY, Tobacco Literature Service, 2314 D H Hill Library, Box 7111, Raleigh, 27695. Carmen M Marin, Dir
Holdings: Vols 27 Cat
Notes: The D H Hill Library in cooperation with the Agricultural Research Service operates a Tobacco Literature service. The service publishes bimonthly *Tobacco Abstracts: Citations and Abstracts on World Literature on Nicotiana*. Collection incl 73, 000 abstracts.

NIDOLOGY see Birds—Eggs and Nests

NIEBUHR, REINHOLD

DC —LIBRARY OF CONGRESS, Manuscript Division, Washington, 20540. John C Broderick, Chief
Holdings: Cat Mss Pix
Notes: Mss, papers, records, etc.

NIEDECKER, LORINE

MA —BOSTON UNIVERSITY, Mugar Memorial Library, Special Collections Dept, 771 Commonwealth Ave, Boston, 02215. Howard B Gotlieb, Dir
Holdings: Cat Mss

NIEDERLAND, WILLIAM G.

DC —LIBRARY OF CONGRESS, Manuscript Division, Washington, 20540. John C Broderick, Chief
Notes: Papers of the psychiatrist, William G Niederland; 4000 items.

NIELSEN, HELEN

MA —BOSTON UNIVERSITY, Mugar Memorial Library, Special Collections Dept, 771 Commonwealth Ave, Boston, 02215. Howard B Gotlieb, Dir
Holdings: Cat Mss
Notes: Mss, correspondence, etc collected in depth incl publications by or about.

NIELSON, FRIHOFF GODFREY

AZ —NORTHERN ARIZONA UNIVERSITY, Special Collection Library, CU Box 6022, Flagstaff, 86011. Peter M Whiteley, Coordr/Archivist; William Mullane, Librn
Notes: Frihoff Godfrey Nielson Collection; (Joseph City, Ariz, Mormon pioneer). Incl journal, autobiography, and notes.

NIERIKER, MAY ALCOTT

MA —CONCORD FREE PUBLIC LIBRARY, 129 Main St, Concord, 01742. Rose Marie Mitten, Dir
Notes: Alcott Collection, primarily material on Amos Bronson Alcott and Louisa May Alcott, incl some representation of Abigail May Alcott and May Alcott Nieriker material (for example, May Alcott's *Concord Sketches*).

NIETZ, JOHN A.

PA —UNIVERSITY OF PITTSBURGH, Hillman Library, Special Collections Dept, John A Nietz Textbook Collection, 363 Hillman Library, Pittsburgh, 15260. Charles E Aston, Jr, Coordr
Holdings: Vols 13,480 Cat Vols 3000 Uncat Mss
Notes: The John A Nietz Textbook Collection of primarily American textbooks in 3 areas; primary school books to 1900, secondary texts to ca 1930 and pedagogical books (1000 vols on the history and theory of education incl writings of the key figures in the field of education). Books are cataloged via an inhouse computer printout, and are accessible via name, title, subject, place, publisher and date. Late 18th and all of the 19th century are well represented. Important titles in each subject are discussed in John A Nietz's *Old Textbooks* (Pittsburgh, 1961) and in his *The Evolution of American Secondary School Textbooks* (Rutland, Vt, 1966). Collection also incl the papers (noncirculating) of Prof John A Nietz.

NIGER

DC —HOWARD UNIVERSITY, Moorland-Spingarn Research Center, 500 Howard Place NW, Washington, 20059. Clifford L Muse, Jr, Acting Dir

MI —MICHIGAN STATE UNIVERSITY, International Library, Sahel Documentation Center, East Lansing, 48824. Eugene deBenko, Librn; Learthen Dorsey, Librn
Holdings: Vols (5100) Cat Mss Maps Pix Slides Phonorecords Audiotapes Videotapes Microforms
Budget: ($8000)
Notes: See description under The Sahel.

NIGERIA

CA —HOOVER INSTITUTION ON WAR, REVOLUTION & PEACE, Stanford University, Stanford, 94305. Peter Duignan, Cur; Karen Fung, Deputy Cur
Holdings: Vols (60,000) Cat Mss Maps Pix Slides Microforms
Notes: Politics, economics, and history from 1870 to the present. About 500 current periodicals titles, about 90 current newspaper titles. Legislative debates, political ephemera. Have microfilm of Portuguese African nationalist material, confidential prints of Great Britian's foreign and colonial offices 1870 through 1922. Nigerian pamphlets (market literature, political and historical tracts), collection of the correspondence pamphlets and ephemera of Alfred B Xuma, collections on Zaire (1955-1963), South African nationalist publications on microfilm. Descriptions of the Collection: *African and Middle East Collections* pub by Hoover Institute, *Handbook of American Resources for African Studies* pub by Hoover. Holdings of the Collection in *Hoover Institute on War, Revolution, and Peace Library Catalog* pub by G K Hall, *Emerging Nationalism in Portuguese Africa: A Bibliography* pub by Hoover, *German Africa* pub by Hoover. *The Treason Trail in South Africa: A Guide to the Microfilm Record of the Trial* pub by Hoover. *History of the Library and Archives*

NIGERIA (cont.)

of the Hoover Institution on War, Revolution and Peace, edited by Peter Duignan (Hoover Institution Press), *Guide to Non-federal Archives and Manuscripts in the United States Relating to Africa*, compiled Aloha P Smith (East Ardsley, Eng, Microform Ltd).

DC —HOWARD UNIVERSITY, Moorland-Spingarn Research Center, 500 Howard Place NW, Washington, 20059. Clifford L Muse, Jr, Acting Dir

MI —MICHIGAN STATE UNIVERSITY, International Library, Africana Collection, East Lansing, 48824. Eugene de Benko, Librn; Onuma Ezera, Bibliographer for Africana
Holdings: Vols (82,700) Cat Mss Maps Pix Slides Phonorecords Audiotapes Videotapes Filmstrips Microforms
Budget: ($78,000)
See also entry under Africa for full description.

OH —OHIO UNIVERSITY, Vernon R Alden Library, Athens, 45701. Kent Mulliner, Africana Specialist
Holdings: Vols (30,000) Cat Maps Microforms
Notes: Major emphasis on South Africa, East Africa, and Nigeria. Incl extensive collection of government reports and newspapers on microfilm.

NIGHT CLUBS see Music Halls (Variety Theatres, Cabarets, Night Clubs, Etc.)

NIGHTINGALE, FLORENCE, 1820-1910

CA —UNIVERSITY OF CALIFORNIA, LOS ANGELES, Biomedical Library, Center for the Health Sciences, Los Angeles, 90024. Alison Bunting, Acting Biomedical Librn; Victoria Steele, Head, History & Special Collections Div
Holdings: Vols 73// Cat
Notes: Presented by Dr and Mrs Elmer Belt. Books by and about Florence Nightingale.

KS —UNIVERSITY OF KANSAS MEDICAL CENTER, College of Health Sciences & Hospital, Clendening History of Medicine Library, Rainbow Blvd at 39th, Kansas City, 66103. Robert P Hudson, Chmn/Cur
Holdings: Vols (15,725) Cat Mss
Notes: Letters, 1856-93. 19 items. In part, photocopies of 2 letters to W Clark made from originals in Chldren's Hospital, Boston, Mass, and Cornell University School of Nursing, New York, NY. Nurse and reformer. Correspondents incl Mr Burton, schoolmaster and Alice Hepworth.

MD —UNIVERSITY OF MARYLAND, BALTIMORE, Health Sciences Library, 111 S Greene St, Baltimore, 21201. Cyril C H Feng, Dir
Holdings: Vols (25) Cat Mss Documents Art Reproductions VF
Notes: Consists chiefly of works by Florence Nightingale including her notebooks, nursing manuals, letters, etc.

MA —BOSTON UNIVERSITY, Mugar Memorial Library, Special Collections Dept, 771 Commonwealth Ave, Boston, 02215. Howard B Gotlieb, Dir
Holdings: Cat Pix
Notes: Correspondence, etc collected in depth; incl publications by or about.

NY —COLUMBIA UNIVERSITY LIBRARIES, Health Sciences Library, 701 W 168 St, New York, 10032. Rachael K Goldstein, Librn
Notes: Ca 300 Nightingale letters, 50 books by and about her, and ca 30 pieces of memorabilia. Restricted. Photocopying limited.

NIJINSKY, VASLAV, 1890-1950

NY —NEW YORK PUBLIC LIBRARY, Performing Arts Research Center, Dance Collection, 111 Amsterdam Ave, New York, 10023. Genevieve Oswald, Cur
Notes: Extensive biographical and visual material. Includes over 200 original photographs, as well as original drawings, newspaper clippings and reviews, programs, and posters.
See also entry under Ballets Russes de Diaghilev.

NIN, ANAIS, 1903-1977

CA —UNIVERSITY OF CALIFORNIA, LOS ANGELES, Research Library, Dept of Special Collections, 405 Hilgard Ave, Los Angeles, 90024. Edward Shreeves, Chairman, Bibliographers Group; David S Zeidberg, Head
Holdings: Mss
Notes: 5 linear feet of papers, incl her diaries. No photocopying.

IL —NORTHWESTERN UNIVERSITY, Library, Special Collections Dept, 1937 Sheridan Rd, Evanston, 60201. R Russell Maylone, Cur
Holdings: Vols 40 Cat Mss
Notes: First editons, letters. Literary mss of novels, short stories and essays, some unpublished and some variant versions of published material. Incl galley proofs and the ms of *The Winter of Artifice* with corrections, criticisms and handwritten comments by Henry Miller. Literature: Zee, *An Index to the Collection of Manuscripts, Proofs, Galleys, etc, of Anais Nin in the Special Collections Department of Northwestern University Library*, rev by Tina Howe (Evanston, 1973).

NISEI see Japanese Americans

NISKA INDIANS

BC —TERRACE PUBLIC LIBRARY, 4610 Park Ave, Terrace, V8G 1V6, Can. Ed Curell, Librn; Gillian Campbell, Librn, Terrace Collection
Holdings: Vols (270) Cat
Budget: ($250)
Notes: The collection is limited to books and pamphlets relating to Terrace, Skenna, and Nass River District history and geography. Emphasis on art and sociology of the Niska and Tsimshian and lives of early missionaries.

NITOBE, INAZO, 1862-1933

PA —FRIENDS HISTORICAL LIBRARY OF SWARTHMORE COLLEGE, Swarthmore, 19081. J William Frost, Dir
Holdings: Cat (35,000) Mss Microforms
Notes: Collection of mss of Inazo Nitobe, Japanese educator and diplomat, with many books written by him.

NIVKH LANGUAGE see Gilyak Language

NIXDORFF, SAMUEL P.

NY —UNION COLLEGE, Schaffer Library, Archives of Science and Technology, Schenectady, 12308. Ellen Fladger, Archivist
Notes: Papers etc.

NIXON, RICHARD MILHOUS

†CA —RICHARD M NIXON PRESIDENTIAL LIBRARY, San Clemente, 92672.
Notes: Library is planned (1984) to be built with private funds raised by the Richard M Nixon Archives Foundation. Not expected to open prior to 1987.

CA —WHITTIER COLLEGE, Wardman Library, Whittier, 90608. Christine Erdmann, Special Collections Librn
Holdings: Vols 384 Uncat Pix Audiotapes
Notes: Chiefly published materials.

†NY —COLUMBIA UNIVERSITY LIBRARIES, Butler Library, Rare Book and Manuscript Library, 535 W 114 St, New York, 10027.
Notes: The Papers of Dr David Abrahamsen, incl letters and mss. Contains letters from and interviews with family and friends of Richard M Nixon and 167 typed and handwritten letters sent by David Berkowitz to Dr Abrahamsen from Attica Prison during 1979-81.

NY —NEW YORK PUBLIC LIBRARY, Performing Arts Research Center, Rodgers & Hammerstein Archives of Recorded Sound, 111 Amsterdam Ave, New York, 10023.
Holdings: Cat Tapes
Notes: A collection of taped interviews, representing over 400 prominent figures. Incl are voices of Richard Nixon, Billy Graham, Maurice Chevalier, Sammy Davis, Jr, Dr Albert Sabin, etc.

OK —UNIVERSITY OF OKLAHOMA, Bizzell Memorial Library, Western History Collections, 401 W Brooks, Norman, 73069. John Ezell, Cur
Holdings: Mss Documents Newspapers Pix Maps
Notes: Stage actress, Helen Gahagan Douglas, US Representative. Her papers. Guide available.

†UT —UNIVERSITY OF UTAH, Marriott Library, Salt Lake City, 84112.
Notes: Manuscripts and papers of historian-biographer Fawn M Brodie (d 1981). Incl taped interviews with Richard Nixon, and notes, clippings, reviews, articles, and about 400 books used in her researches on Nixon, Thomas Jefferson, and Sir Richard Burton, in preparation of their biographies.

NOBEL PRIZE AND NOBELISTS

DC —LIBRARY OF CONGRESS, European Division, Washington, 20540.
Notes: The Library of Congress collection of "Solidarity" and other uncensored Polish materials incl books, periodicals, documents, bulletins, cartoons, and posters, most of which are photocopies of originals held by other libraries.

IN —INDIANA UNIVERSITY, Lilly Library, Seventh St, Bloomington, 47405. William R Cagle, Librn
Notes: Collections incl papers of geneticists and biologists, most notably those of Nobel Prize winner Hermann Joseph Muller, 1890-1967 and Tracy Morton Sonneborn, 1905-1981. Also papers of plant geneticists Ralph Cleland, 1892-1971, and Paul Weatherwax, 1888-1976.

IN —PURDUE UNIVERSITY LIBRARIES, Chemistry Library, West Lafayette, 47907. John Pinzelik, Librn
Holdings: Vols 49,900 Cat Microforms
Budget: $142,800
Notes: Archives of H C Brown, 1979 Nobel Laureate in Chemistry.

MS —UNIVERSITY OF SOUTHERN MISSISSIPPI, William David McCain Graduate Library, Box 5148, Southern Sta, Hattiesburg, 39406.
Holdings: Vols 23 Uncat Mss
Notes: Various editions of Maeterlinck's works (some signed), correspondence, literary mss (1 cubic foot), articles, essays and other publications (circa 1920-1950) by and about this Belgian born Nobel Prize winning author.

MO —WASHINGTON UNIVERSITY, School of Medicine, Archives, 660 S Euclid Ave, Saint Louis, 63110. Paul G Anderson, Archivist
Notes: Papers of Joseph Erlanger.

NY —AMERICAN INSTITUTE OF PHYSICS, Center for the History of Physics, Niels Bohr Library, 335 E 45 St, New York, 10017. John Aubry, Librn
Notes: Primarily professional correspondence from the 1920s to the 1970s of Prof John Hasbrouck Van Vleck, first American awarded a PhD in theoretical physics (1922). Won the Nobel Prize for his work in quantum physics theory and on solid state physics. Other of his papers are deposited in the Harvard University Archives.

NY —ROCKEFELLER UNIVERSITY, Rockefeller Archive Center, Hillcrest, Pocantico Hills, North Tarrytown, 10591. Joseph W Ernst, Dir; J William Hess, Assoc Dir
Notes: Papers of Edward L Tatum, Rockefeller University professor. Conducted research in the genetics and metabolism of bacteria, yeasts, and molds. In 1958, he was joint recipient, with Joshua Lederberg and

NOBEL PRIZE AND NOBELISTS (cont.)

George Beadle, of the Nobel Prize in medicine and physiology.

NO DRAMAS see Noh Dramas

NOBILE, PHILIP

MA —BOSTON UNIVERSITY, Mugar Memorial Library, Special Collections Dept, 771 Commonwealth Ave, Boston, 02215. Howard B Gotlieb, Dir
Holdings: Cat Mss Pix
Notes: Mss, correspondence, etc collected in depth; incl publications by or about.

NOBILITY, BRITISH see Great Britain—Nobility

NOBILITY, POLISH see Poland—Nobility

NOBILITY, RUSSIAN see Russian Nobility

NODIER, CHARLES

CT —TRINITY COLLEGE LIBRARY, Watkinson Library, 300 Summit St, Hartford, 06106. Jeffrey Kaimowitz, Cur
Holdings: // Cat
Notes: The Duncan B Macdonald Collection.

NOEL, FRANCES N.

CA —UNIVERSITY OF CALIFORNIA, LOS ANGELES, Research Library, Dept of Special Collections, 405 Hilgard Ave, Los Angeles, 90024. Edward Shreeves, Chairman, Bibliographers Group; David S Zeidberg, Head
Notes: 5.5 linear feet of correspondence, pamphlets, clippings, etc, relating to the labor and women's movements in Los Angeles.

NOEL, RODEN

MO —WASHINGTON UNIVERSITY, Libraries, Special Collections Dept, Campus Box 1061, St Louis, 63130.
Notes: Small but significant collection.

NOELS

ON —UNIVERSITY OF TORONTO, Thomas Fisher Rare Book Library, 120 Saint George St, Toronto, M5S 1A5, Can. Richard G Landon, Head
Holdings: Vols (300) Cat
Notes: Noels Collection of French carols and hymns in a variety of dialects, 18th and 19th centuries.

NOGAI LANGUAGE

NY —NEW YORK PUBLIC LIBRARY, Oriental Div, Fifth Ave & 42 St, New York, 10018. E Christian Filstrup, Chief
Holdings: Cat Mss Microforms
Budget: ($56,455)
Notes: Published catalog of holdings.

NOGAKU see Noh Dramas

NOGALES BEY, GEN. RAFAEL DE

CT —LEE ASH, (personal collection), 66 Humiston Dr, Bethany, 06525.
Holdings: Mss Pix
Notes: Books, ephemera, etc, by or about him.

NOH DANCE PRINTS

MA —HARVARD UNIVERSITY LIBRARY, Theatre Collection, Cambridge, 02138. Jeanne T Newlin, Cur
Holdings: Uncat
Notes: See *Harvard Library Notes*, III (1938), 158-159.

NOH DRAMAS

NY —NEW YORK PUBLIC LIBRARY, Performing Arts Research Center, Dance Collection, 111 Amsterdam Ave, New York, 10023. Genevieve Oswald, Cur
See also entry under Asian Dance

NOISE

NY —AMERICAN INSTITUTE OF PHYSICS, Center for the History of Physics, Niels Bohr Library, 335 E 45 St, New York, 10017. John Aubry, Librn
Notes: Papers and records.

NOISE POLLUTION AND CONTROL

CA —CALIFORNIA DEPT OF TRANSPORTATION, Transportation Library, 5900 Folsom Blvd, PO Box 19128, Sacramento, 95819. Eva Caro, Librn
Holdings: Vols (10,000) Cat Mss Maps Pix Slides Phonorecords Audiotapes Videotapes 16mm Films Filmstrips Microforms
MA —MASSACHUSETTS INSTITUTE OF TECHNOLOGY, Institute Archives, Special Collections, Cambridge, 02139.
Notes: Correspondence, newsletters, fact-sheets, newspaper and magazine articles, books and reports of the Citizens' League Against the Sonic Boom, established in 1967 by William Shurcliff to oppose the sonic boom, stop commercial supersonic transport production, and influence public opinion and policy decisions on the SST. Major correspondents incl Bo Lundberg, Richard Wiggs, several US congressmen, and CLASB members.

NOLI, FAN S.

†MA —ST GEORGE ALBANIAN ORTHODOX CATHEDRAL, Fan S Noli Library, South Boston, 02127.

NON-ARISTOTELIAN PHILOSOPHY see General Semantics

NONCONFORMISTS, RELIGIOUS see Dissenters, Religious

NONDESTRUCTIVE TESTING

IL —CHICAGO BRIDGE & IRON CO, Technical Library, 800 Jorie Blvd, Oak Brook, 60521. Susan Beatty, Librn
Holdings: Vols (7500) Cat
Budget: ($39,500)
Notes: Quality control and nondestructive testing.
TN —COMBUSTION ENGINEERING, Metallurgical Materials Library, 911 W Main St, Chattanooga, 37402. Nell T Holder, Tech Librn
Holdings: Vols (10,000) Cat
Notes: Metallurgical research and development. 350 serials and periodicals, 800 translations of foreign articles. 250,000 US Government Reports. MF Collection C-E Technical reports ASME.

NONPARTISAN LEAGUE

ND —NORTH DAKOTA STATE UNIVERSITY, Library, Fargo, 58105. John E Bye, Archivist
Holdings: Vols (2500) Cat Mss Maps Pix
Budget: ($14,000)
Notes: The Collection is administered by the North Dakota Institute for Regional Studies. It contains materials on North Dakota history, especially the Red River Valley, with emphasis on bonanza farming, pioneer life, agriculture, local history, literary figures, business, Fargo, ND, and some political collections, particularly of the Nonpartisan League. Also, there is an extensive photographic collection covering the pioneer to post-World War I period and includes the "Hultstrand 'History in Pictures' Collection" of sod houses, pioneer life and farming. For the small collections, there has been published, *Guide to the Small Collection Manuscripts of the North Dakota Institute for Regional Studies*, by John E Bye, 1977.

NONPRINT JOURNALISM see Journalism, Nonprint

NONVIOLENCE

PA —SWARTHMORE COLLEGE, Peace Collection, Swarthmore, 19081. Jean R Soderlund, Cur of Peace Collection
Holdings: Vols (10,000) Cat
Notes: Incl peace plays which date mostly from 1912-40, in print or mimeographed; about 1/4 are juvenile; most are American. Book and pamphlet collections incl drama, poetry, fiction and juvenile literature on the subjects of peace, nonviolence and biographies of peace leaders. The aims of current acquisitions incl collecting as much as possible in this area, in order to amplify the main body of the collection. The Peace Collection has been described in Downs 972, 978, 4633, and in Downs 1950-1961 Supplement 507 and 916.

NOOK FARM

CT —STOWE-DAY LIBRARY, 77 Forest St, Hartford, 06105. Diana J Royce, Librn
Holdings: Vols (15,000) Cat Mss Pix
Notes: 150,000 cataloged mss and publications concerning architecture, decorative arts, history and literature of the period 1840-1900, with emphasis on Nook Farm, Mark Twain, Harriet Beecher Stowe, Calvin E Stowe, Charles Dudley Warner, William Hooker Gillette, Isabella Beecher Hooker. Incl 5000 pictures.

NOON, REV. WILLIAM T., S.J.

NY —LE MOYNE COLLEGE, Library, Le Moyne Heights, Syracuse, 13214. James J Simonis, Dir; Annette M Monaco, Special Colelctions Librn
Holdings: Vols (1614) // Cat Mss Slides
Notes: Incl 614 monographs and 1000 pamphlets, reprint articles, and periodical issues. Represents the Irish Literature Collection, covering the modern Irish Literature period from 1880 to 1950, and the Rev William T Noon SJ Collection. Father Noon had James Joyce as his main interest. Manuscripts of Noon's books *Joyce and Aquinas* (Yale University, 1957) and *Poetry and Prayer* (Rutgers University, 1957) are incl. There are several hundred pieces of correspondence which incl authors who had similar interests. The collection also incl his class notes and cutouts from newspapers, pamphlets, periodical articles, many of which have notes written by him. Monographs are represented by an author file. Pamphlets and reprint articles are organized in boxes and numbered numerically.

NOOSPHERE

NY —AMERICAN TEILHARD ASSOCIATION FOR THE FUTURE OF MAN, Dept of Religious Studies, Manhattan College, Bronx, 10471. Donald P Gray, Librn
Holdings: Vols 450 Cat Slides
Notes: Material by and about Teilhard de Chardin, philosopher and paleontologist.

NORDIC COUNCIL

CA —CLAREMONT COLLEGES, Honnold Library, Ninth & Dartmouth, Claremont, 91711. Franklin D Scott, Cur, Nordic Collection; Penelope Garris, Librn
Holdings: Vols (25,000) Cat Maps Pix Slides Audiotapes Videotapes Periodicals
Notes: Eight vertical file drawers of news bulletins in English or vernaculars, 1941-. Complete publications of Nordic Council. See: Franklin D Scott, "The Westergaard-Bjork Collection at the Honnold Library, the Claremont Colleges," *Scandinavian Studies*, 41 (1969) 346-354.

NORDICA, LILLIAN

ME —NORIDICA MEMORIAL ASSOCIATION, Library, RFD 3, Farmington, 04938.

NORDLANDER, BIRGER W.

NY —UNION COLLEGE, Schaffer Library, Archives of Science and Technology, Schenectady, 12308. Ellen Fladger, Archivist
Notes: Papers etc.

NORFOLK (COUNTY), ENGLAND

BC —VANCOUVER PUBLIC LIBRARY,
History & Government Div, 750 Burrard St,
Vancouver, V6Z 1X5, Can.
Holdings: Vols 220 Cat Maps Pix
Notes: Antiquities, archaeology, biography,
history, description, travel, etc concerning
Norfolk and East Anglia in England. (Gift of
the Bulwer Family; additional parts of the
gift are at the Univeristy of British Columbia
Library.)

NORFOLK AND WESTERN RAILWAY

VA —VIRGINIA POLYTECHNIC
INSTITUTE AND STATE UNIVERSITY
LIBRARY, Blacksburg, 24061. Glenn L
McMullen, Special Collections Librn
Holdings: Vols (1000) Cat Mss Maps
Notes: Collection of ca 300 linear feet of
archival records (1830-1940) of the Norfolk
and Western Railway, its predecessors, and
subsidiaries, and of the defunct predecessors
of the Southern Railway. The collection incl
minutebooks, correspondence and subject
files, and other ms materials for ca 200
railroad companies operating in the
Southeast and Midwest, incl the Norfolk and
Western; Norfolk and Petersburg; Southside;
Atlantic, Mississippi, and Ohio; Virginia and
Tennessee; Richmond and Danville;
Memphis and Charleston; East Tennessee
and Virginia; and South Carolina Canal and
Railroad Company. The collection also incl
printed materials such as annual reports and
other documents for these companies.

NORLIN, GEORGE

CO —UNIVERSITY OF COLORADO,
Libraries, Western Historical Collections,
Boulder, 80309.
Holdings: // Cat Mss
Notes: Papers of George Nolin who was a
professor of Greek at the University of
Colorado from 1896 to 1919; in 1919 he
became president of the university, holding
this post until 1939. The collection consists
of correspondence, essays, speeches, personal
papers, and pamphlets, concerned with such
subjects as his stay in Germany during the
years just prior to World War II, also
Nazism, the Civil War, and the history of
the University of Colorado. 5 boxes. A
typescript inventory is available.

NORRIS, FRANK, 1870-1902

CA —UNIVERSITY OF CALIFORNIA,
BERKELEY, Bancroft Library, Manuscripts
Division, Berkeley, 94720. James D Hart,
Dir
Holdings: Cat Mss
Notes: The collection comprises 6 boxes and
3 cartons of mss and correspondence, as well
as presentation copies of Frank Norris'
works. A key to the arrangement of the
collection is available.
WA —UNIVERSITY OF WASHINGTON
LIBRARIES, Suzzallo Library, Special
Collections Division, Rare Book Collection,
FM-25, Seattle, 98195. Gary Menges,
Coordinator for Special Collections
Notes: Printing history, including early
printed books and modern fine printing;
book arts, including papermaking, decorated
papers, bookbinding, book design, and
artist's books; American literature, 19th
century includes: Stephen Crane, Ralph
Waldo Emerson, Nathaniel Hawthorne,
Henry James, Henry Wadsworth Longfellow,
Herman Melville, Frank Norris, Harriet
Beecher Stowe and Walt Whitman and 20th
century includes: Theodore Roethke;
illustrated books, including emblem books,
historical children's illustration, books
illustrated with prints, and artist's books;
costume history; voyages and travels;
preservation of library materials.

NORRIS, KATHLEEN

DC —GEORGETOWN UNIVERSITY,
Library, Special Collections Div, 37 & O Sts

NW, Washington, 20057. George M
Barringer, Special Collections Librn;
Nicholas B Sheetz, Mss Librn
Holdings: Mss
Notes: The Archives of the Gallery of Living
Catholic Authors was founded in 1932 by
Sister Mary Joseph of the Sisters of Loretto
to focus attention on modern Catholic
literature, and to provide a depository for
manuscripts, letters, photographs, and books
by contemporary Catholic writers. Contains
material by hundreds of writers, incl Hilaire
Belloc, Roy Campbell, Padraic Colum, Eric
Gill, Paul Horgan, Mary Lavin, Marie Belloc
Lowndes, Kathleen Norris, Alred Noyes,
Sheila Kaye-Smith, Sigrid Undset, and
Evelyn Waugh, to name only a few.

NORSE LANGUAGES AND
LITERATURE see Icelandic and Old
Norse Languages and Literature

NORSE MYTHOLOGY see Mythology,
Norse

NORTH, ALEX

CA —UNIVERSITY OF CALIFORNIA, LOS
ANGELES, Music Library, Schonberg Hall,
Los Angeles, 90024. Stephen M Fry, Music
Librn
Notes: Mss.

NORTH, CHARLES E.

MD —US DEPT OF AGRICULTURE,
National Agricultural Library, 10301
Baltimore Blvd, Beltsville, 20705. Joseph H
Howard, Director
Notes: Papers of Charles E North,
bacteriologist and milk hygienist.

NORTH, JOSEPH

MA —BOSTON UNIVERSITY, Mugar
Memorial Library, Special Collections Dept,
771 Commonwealth Ave, Boston, 02215.
Howard B Gotlieb, Dir
Holdings: // Cat Mss Pix
Notes: Mss, correspondence, etc collected in
depth; incl publications by or about.

NORTH, STERLING

MA —BOSTON UNIVERSITY, Mugar
Memorial Library, Special Collections Dept,
771 Commonwealth Ave, Boston, 02215.
Howard B Gotlieb, Dir
Holdings: // Cat Mss Pix
Notes: Mss, correspondence, etc collected in
depth; incl publications by or about.

NORTH AMERICA—DESCRIPTION
AND TRAVEL

MN —UNIVERSITY OF MINNESOTA,
James Ford Bell Library, 309 19th Ave S,
Minneapolis, 55455. John Parker, Cur
Holdings: Vols (11,000) Cat Mss Maps
Notes: The Library is a collection of original
materials relating to European expansion,
1400-1800.

NORTH AMERICA—DISCOVERY AND
EXPLORATION see America—Discovery
and Exploration

NORTH AMERICAN ASSOCIATION
OF DIRECTORY PUBLISHERS

IN —ALLEN COUNTY PUBLIC LIBRARY,
Fred J Reynolds Historical Genealogy
Collection, 900 Webster St, Fort Wayne,
46802. Rick J Ashton, Dir; Michael B Clegg,
Manager
Holdings: Vols 200,000 Cat Mss Maps Pix
Microforms
Notes: The depository for the North
American Association of Directory
Publishers since 1964.

NORTH AMERICAN INDIANS see
Indians of North America and Mexico

NORTH AMERICAN PHALANX

IL —UNIVERSITY OF ILLINOIS,
URBANA/CHAMPAIGN, Library, Illinois

Historical Survey Library, 1408 W Gregory
Dr, 1A Library, Urbana, 61801.
Holdings: Vols 50 Cat Mss Maps Pix
Microforms
Notes: Communitarianism in America. The
ms material, contained in 30 separate
collections (10 cubic feet), concentrates on
the period 1840-70. It incl correspondence,
records, minutes, ledgers and diaries.
Communal societies such as Bishop Hill,
Brook Farm, New Harmony, the North
American Phalanx and the Sodus Bay
Phalanx are represented. Among the
correspondents are Albert Brisbane, Parke
Godwin, Sarah Grimke, Richard Owen,
Robert Owen, Robert Dale Owen, and
George Ripley. Numerous pictures. Guide to
the collections published in 1976.
NJ —MONMOUTH COUNTY HISTORICAL
ASSOCIATION, Library, 70 Court St,
Freehold, 07728. Loretta M Zwolak,
Archivist & Librn
Holdings: Vols (6500) Cat Mss Maps Pix
Slides Microforms
Budget: ($15,800)
Notes: Especially Monmouth County area.
See *Monmouth County Historical
Association Bulletin*, vol 1, no 2 July 1948, p
23-48. Allaire Papers (Howell Works); Battle
of Monmouth; Mott Family Papers; North
American Phalanx; Philip Freneau;
Steamship Coll.

NORTH AMERICAN TREATY
ORGANIZATION (NATO)

DC —LIBRARY OF CONGRESS, Manuscript
Division, Washington, 20540. John C
Broderick, Chief
Notes: The papers of former Secretary of
State Alexander M Haig. Access to the
collection is restricted.

NORTH BENNETT STREET
INDUSTRIAL SCHOOL (BOSTON)

MA —SIMMONS COLLEGE ARCHIVES,
300 The Fenway, Boston, 02115. Megan
Sniffin-Marinoff, College Archivist
Notes: (I) Minutes of the Industrial
Committee of the Woman's Education
Association (1873-1929) from Feb 15, 1872
to Dec 5, 1882. Primarily concerned with
the Committee's development of the Boston
Cooking School. Figuring prominently in the
minutes are Maria Parloa (1843-1909), one
of the first instructors at the school, and
Mary Johnson Bailey Lincoln (1844-1921),
under whose leadership the Boston Cooking
School began to attain a national reputation.
For further information on these women, see
Notable American Women. The
Committee's relationship with the NY Diet
Kitchen, the North Bennett St Industrial
School (Boston), and the Massachusetts
Institute of Technology also are discussed in
the minutes. In addition to organizing a
school for cooking, the Committee
concerned itself with the education for
women in dressmaking, nursing,
phonography, andwoodcarving (based on the
Cincinnati carving school). (II) Account
books of the Household Aid Co (The
Domestic Economy Committee) of the
Woman's Education Association from
August, 1903 to May, 1905. Organized by
the Association of Collegiate Alumnae and
the Woman's Education Association, the
company was a cooperative residence for 20
servants with a training and placement
program and a mediation service to deal
with employers.

NORTH CAROLINA

NC —WESTERN CAROLINA UNIVERSITY,
Hunter Memorial Library, Cullowhee,
28723. James B Lloyd, Cur
Budget: $1000
Notes: Incl a regional ms collection
documenting the social and natural history
of Appalachia in general and western North
Carolina in particular. Subject emphasis incl
the Cherokee Indian, the establishment of
the Great Smoky Mountains National Park,

NORTH CAROLINA (cont.)

and the continuing use of Appalachian wilderness. 1000 feet holdings.

NC —DUKE UNIVERSITY, William R Perkins Library, Durham, 27706. Elvin E Strowd, University Librn
Notes: The Flowers Collection of Southern Americana currently consists of 4,300,500 items. Additions are ongoing. Included in this collection are several types of materials, which are housed in appropriate sections of the library. The various types of materials are: manuscripts, books, pamphlets, maps, music, broadsides, newspapers, photographs, engravings, prints and memorabilia.

NC —DUKE UNIVERSITY, William R Perkins Library, Public Documents and Maps Department, Durham, 27706. Jaia Barrett, Head
Holdings: Vols Maps Pamphlets Microforms
Notes: A selective depository for US Government publications since 1890, the Department currently holds well over 500,000 items, plus publications of the European Community (a depository collection), the League of Nations, the UN and UN-affiliated agencies. Other international organizations, publications are acquired also, as are state government publications, especially from the Southeast, California, New York and Illinois. The Documents Department holds services the major map collections of Perkins Library. These collections include topographic, geologic, and special subject maps which are worldwide in coverage. The department is a depository for the US Defense Mapping Agency and the US Geological Survey. In addition, there are many other maps of general and specific interest, including US and foreign road maps. As appropriate, maps are also held in the Perkins Library's Rare BookRoom and Manuscript Department. Atlases are shelved in the Reference Department and in the bookstacks of Perkins Library.

NC —GREENSBORO PUBLIC LIBRARY, 201 N Greene St, Drawer X-4, Greensboro, 27402. J Douglas Kerr, Caldwell Jones Librn
Holdings: Vols 8000 Cat Mss Maps Pix Microforms
Notes: Incl books by North Carolina authors and about North Carolina; a vertical file of pamphlets and newspaper clippings, microfilmed Federal Census of Population 1790-1910 for the state, some early maps of the state. There is a separate catalog to the collection.

NC —NEW BERN-CRAVEN COUNTY PUBLIC LIBRARY, 400 Johnson St, New Bern, 28560. Elinor D Hawkins, Dir
Holdings: Vols (3926) Cat Pix

†NC —WAKE FOREST UNIVERSITY, Z Smith Reynolds Library, Box 7777, Reynold Sta, Winston-Salem, 27109. Richard J Murdoch, Rare Book Librn
Holdings: Vols 9500 Cat

NORTH CAROLINA—GENEALOGY

FL —ORLANDO PUBLIC LIBRARY, Local History & Genealogy Dept, 100 Block of Central Ave, Orlando, 32806. Eileen B Willis, Librn
Holdings: Vols 11,000 Cat Maps Microforms
Budget: $8000
Notes: Genealogy collection on Md, Del, W Va, NC, SC, Ala, Miss, La, Texas, Ark, Ky, Ohio, Ill, Ind, and Mich are well represented. Most other states are covered by smaller collections.
See also entry under Genealogy - Collections.

NC —PACK MEMORIAL PUBLIC LIBRARY, North Carolina Collection, 67 Haywood St, Asheville, 28801. John Toms, Dept Head
Notes: Collection incl early ms accounts of western North Carolina; Civil War letters; letters, diary, and mss of Horace Kephart; mss of Thomas Dixon; Thomas Wolfe Collection; contemporary North Carolina authors; North Carolina censuses, 1790-1910; rare newspapers and runs of local

newspapers, and clippings from Asheville newspapers, from 1920s; early maps; information on Cherokee Indians; approx 400 vols of North Carolina genealogy and file of unpublished genealogies. Collection concentrates on western North Carolina, with some general Appalachian materials. Incl 4000 local and state photographs, separate catalog.

NC —PUBLIC LIBRARY OF CHARLOTTE & MECKLENBURG COUNTY, Local History and Genealogy Dept, 310 N Tryon St, Charlotte, 28202. Mary L Phillips, Librn
Holdings: Vols (2153) Cat Mss Microforms
Notes: Special interest in North Carolina, South Carolina, and Southern genealogy. Incl 5552 microforms.

NC —DUKE UNIVERSITY, William R Perkins Library, Durham, 27706. Elvin E Strowd, University Librn

NC —GREENSBORO PUBLIC LIBRARY, Oral History Program Library, Drawer X-4, Greensboro, 27402. Eugene Edwin Pfaff, Jr, Librn
Holdings: Videotapes Audiotapes
Notes: Oral history on the cultural, social, and economic development of Greensboro and Guilford County; the program is expanding to incl prominent North Carolinians throughout the State. Collection consists of 42 videotapes and 93 audiotapes which are uncataloged.

NC —ONSLOW COUNTY PUBLIC LIBRARY, 501 Doris Ave E, Jacksonville, 28540. Janet Haddow-Green, Community Information Specialist
Holdings: Vols 500 Cat
Notes: Onslow County history and genealogy. Incl index to local gravestone names.

NC —LENOIR COMMUNITY COLLEGE, Learning Resources Center, PO Box 188, Kinston, 28501. Mildred Boney Matthis, Dir
Holdings: Vols 175 Cat Maps Pix Slides Microforms
Notes: The collection incl the 17th and 18th century newspapers of importance for the eastern counties of North Carolina. The counties represented are Lenoir, Jones, Greene, Craven, Pitt, Beaufort and Wayne. Records incl deeds, wills, marriage record, census records and other pertinent county records for genealogical research up to approx 1900 (from the earliest preserved records for each county).

NC —NEW BERN-CRAVEN COUNTY PUBLIC LIBRARY, 400 Johnson St, New Bern, 28560. Elinor D Hawkins, Dir
Holdings: Vols (3926) Cat Pix

NC —ROWAN PUBLIC LIBRARY, History and Genealogy Dept, Salisbury, 28144. Philip Barton, Dir
Holdings: Vols (2800) Cat Mss Maps Microforms
Budget: ($1500)
Notes: Generally, the History and Genealogy Collection is composed of materials relating to local and North Carolina State history and materials for genealogical research. Primary emphasis is on genealogical research materials. The nucleus of the genealogical collection is the McCubbins Collection. The collection consists primarily of deed abstracts of Rowan County. Another collection representing part of the genealogical research collection is the Smith Collection, consisting of notes and correspondence collected over a wide span of years about Smiths of the US. A recent addition is the Archibald Henderson Collection of literary works of North Carolinians, Transylvania materials and materials dealing with North Carolina State history and political science.

NC —PUBLIC LIBRARY OF JOHNSTON COUNTY & SMITHFIELD, 305 Market St, Smithfield, 27577. Kenneth M Reading, Dir
Holdings: Vols 1000 Maps Pix Microforms
Budget: $800
Notes: Emphasis on Johnston County. Partially cataloged.

NC —IREDELL COUNTY LIBRARY, 135 E Water St, Statesville, 28677. Flint Norwood, Librn
Holdings: Vols 1400 Cat Mss Slides Audiotapes Videotapes 16mm Films

Filmstrips Microforms
Budget: $3000
Notes: Collection focuses on history of North Carolina and Iredell County. Incl backlog of local newspapers, census records, wills amd deeds, court of pleas and quarters, marriage records, land entries, probate minutes, minutes of superior court, etc, on microfilm.

NC —FORSYTH COUNTY PUBLIC LIBRARY, North Carolina Collection, 660 W Fifth St, Winston-Salem, 27101. Anne R Correll, Head, North Carolina Collection
Holdings: Vols 10,000 Cat Maps Microforms
Budget: $3200
Notes: Collection newly organized 1975. Incl genealogy materials with limited materials on the Southeast. Separate card catalog for this collection.

NC —WAKE FOREST UNIVERSITY, Z Smith Reynolds Library, North Carolina Baptist Collection, PO Box 7777 Reynolda Station, Winston-Salem, 27109. John R Woodard, Jr, Dir
Holdings: Vols (7000) Cat Mss Maps Pix Slides Microforms
Budget: ($20,000)
Notes: The Ethel Taylor Crittenden Collection in Baptist History includes special index files for biographical references. Collection emphasizes the Baptists of North Carolina in particular. Much, however, from other states, the Southern Baptist Convention and the American Baptist Convention. Also Negro, Primitive and Free-Will Baptist items. There is a general card file to all holdings, an alphabetical and chronological file (incl extinct churches), the NC church file, vital statistics.

NORTH CAROLINA—GOVERNMENT PUBLICATIONS

NC —DUKE UNIVERSITY, William R Perkins Library, Durham, 27706. Elvin E Strowd, University Librn
Notes: The Weldon N Edwards and Marmaduke Hawkins collection consists of 2500 volumes. It includes many rare North Carolina state documents and materials on history and agriculture.

NORTH CAROLINA—HISTORY

DC —LIBRARY OF CONGRESS, Manuscript Division, Washington, 20540. John C Broderick, Chief
Holdings: Cat Mss

NC —PACK MEMORIAL PUBLIC LIBRARY, North Carolina Collection, 67 Haywood St, Asheville, 28801. John Toms, Dept Head
Notes: Collection incl early ms accounts of western North Carolina; Civil War letters; letters, diary, and mss of Horace Kephart; mss of Thomas Dixon; Thomas Wolfe Collection; contemporary North Carolina authors; North Carolina censuses, 1790-1910; rare newspapers and runs of local newspapers, and clippings from Asheville newspapers, from 1920s; early maps; information on Cherokee Indians; approx 400 vols of North Carolina genealogy and file of unpublished genealogies. Collection concentrates on western North Carolina, with some general Appalachian materials. Incl 4000 local and state photographs, separate catalog.

NC —BELMONT ABBEY COLLEGE, Abbot Vincent Taylor Library, Belmont, 28012. Marjorie McDermott, Dir
Holdings: Vols (1000) Cat
Notes: Consists of books dealing with the history of North and South Carolina from colonial times to the present. Incl are several county histories, some early newspapers, and a strong section on the history of religion (especially the Roman Catholic Church) in the two states.

NC —UNIVERSITY OF NORTH CAROLINA, CHAPEL HILL, Louis Round Wilson Academic Affairs Library, Southern Historical Collection, Chapel Hill, 27514. Carolyn Wallace, Librn
Notes: The papers of Algernon Lee Butler,

NORTH CAROLINA—HISTORY (cont.)

former judge of the United States Court for the Eastern District of North Carolina (1959-1975).

NC —PUBLIC LIBRARY OF CHARLOTTE & MECKLENBURG COUNTY, Local History and Genealogy Dept, 310 N Tryon St, Charlotte, 28202. Mary L Phillips, Librn
Holdings: Vols 5223 Cat Mss Maps Pix Microforms
Notes: Pamphlets and clippings in 63 vertical file drawers. Microfilm materials incl the Federal Population Census, 1790-1880 for North and South Carolina as well as most states of the southeastern region.

NC —UNIVERSITY OF NORTH CAROLINA, CHARLOTTE, J Murrey Atkins Library, UNCC Station, Charlotte, 28223. Robert F Brabham Jr, Special Collections Librn
Holdings: Vols Cat Mss Pix Maps Microforms
Notes: Papers of individuals and organizations which document the history, culture, and civiliation of North and South Carolina. Emphasis is on the Metrolina region of the two states with particular attention on the social, political, and architectural history of Charlotte and Mecklenburg County, NC.

NC —DUKE UNIVERSITY, William R Perkins Library, Durham, 27706. Elvin E Strowd, University Librn
Notes: The Weldon N Edwards and Marmaduke Hawkins collection consists of 2500 volumes. It includes many rare North Carolina state documents and materials on history and agriculture.

NC —DUKE UNIVERSITY, William R Perkins Library, Manuscript Dept, Durham, 27706. Ellen Gartrell, Cur of Mss
Holdings: Cat Mss
Notes: Especially strong for North Carolina, South Carolina, Virginia, Georgia, and Alabama. 18th-20th centuries. See *Guide to the Cataloged Collections of the Manuscript Department of the William R Perkins Library* (1980, ed by Richard C Davis and Linda A Miller).

NC —GREENSBORO PUBLIC LIBRARY, Oral History Program Library, Drawer X-4, Greensboro, 27402. Eugene Edwin Pfaff, Jr, Librn
Holdings: Videotapes Audiotapes
Notes: Oral history on the cultural, social, and economic development of Greensboro and Guilford County; the program is expanding to incl prominent North Carolinians throughout the State. Collection consists of 42 videotapes and 93 audiotapes which are uncataloged.

NC —UNIVERSITY OF NORTH CAROLINA, GREENSBORO, Walter Clinton Jackson Library, Special Collections Dept, 1000 Spring Garden St, Greensboro, 27412. Emilie W Mills, Librn
Holdings: Vols (3500) Cat Mss Pixx
Notes: Incl books printed from 16th century to early 20th century. Major authors incl Mary Wollstonecraft, Aphra Behn, Mary Astell; North Carolina 19th century authors. The collection is primarily 19th and 20th century with emphasis on non-fiction. Subjects incl education, hygiene, physical education, household economy, women's rights. Organization and private papers of state/regional groups and eminent women incl Harriet Wisemen Elliot Papers, Ellen Black Winston Papers, North Carolina Council of Women's Organizations, Southern Association of Physical Education for College Women (see entries for more information about each collection). The University Archives houses 80 years of the history of the school, once the largest state-supported residential college for women in the US, whichbecame coeducational in 1963.

NC —ONSLOW COUNTY PUBLIC LIBRARY, 501 Doris Ave E, Jacksonville, 28540. Janet Haddow-Green, Community Information Specialist
Holdings: Vols 500 Cat
Notes: Onslow County history and genealogy. Incl index to local gravestone names.

NC —LENOIR COMMUNITY COLLEGE, Learning Resources Center, PO Box 188, Kinston, 28501. Mildred Boney Matthis, Dir
Holdings: Vols 175 Cat Maps Pix Slides Microforms
Notes: The collection incl the 17th and 18th century newspapers of importance for the eastern counties of North Carolina. The counties represented are Lenoir, Jones, Greene, Craven, Pitt, Beaufort and Wayne. Records incl deeds, wills, marriage record, census records and other pertinent county records for genealogical research up to approx 1900 (from the earliest preserved records for each county).

NC —NATIONAL PARK SERVICE, Cape Hatteras National Seashore, Reference Library, Rte 1, Box 675, Manteo, 27954.
Holdings: Cat Mss Maps Pix
Notes: US Lifesaving Service, records and annual reports.

NC —MOUNT OLIVE COLLEGE, Moye Library, Free Will Baptist Historical Collection, Mount Olive, 28365. Gary Fenton Barefoot, Librn
Holdings: Vols 800 Cat Mss Pix Audiotapes 8mm Films Microforms
Notes: Free Will Baptist history in general, with concentration in North Carolina and the South. The collection was begun in 1954 by joint action of the college and the Historical Commission of the North Carolina State Convention of Original Free Will Baptists. Collection is perhaps the best on the Free Will Baptists denomination in existence. Particular strength lies in the 225 vols of mss and printed minutes of associations, etc. Over 5000 clippings and pamphlets. The collection is housed and cataloged separately from the main library collection. Various special indexes (obituaries, church, etc) are also maintained. Quite a number of vols and materials of associational value related to the General Baptists, etc, are also a part of the collection. The cataloged vols are represented in the North Carolina Union Catalog and in Starr's Baptist Bibliography. Inthe case of Starr, however, holdings are only incl in the more recent vols.

NC —CRAVEN COMMUNITY COLLEGE, Godwin Memorial Library, S Glenburnie Rd, New Bern, 28560. Vance Harper Jones, Librn
Holdings: Vols 390 Cat Mss Maps Slides Audiotapes Microforms
Notes: Special emphasis on the New Bern area.

NC —TRYON PALACE RESTORATION, Library, 613 Pollock St, New Bern, 28560. Grace C Ipock, Registrar
Holdings: Vols 1400 Cat Maps Pix Slides
Notes: Governor Tryon's recreated library at Tryon Palace comprises 517 titles published before 1770. Other shelves at the historic houses in the complex incl vols published until ca 1820. Sixteen percent of Governor Tryon's inventoried library of 1770 is still sought. No photocopying.

NC —ROWAN PUBLIC LIBRARY, History and Genealogy Dept, Salisbury, 28144. Philip Barton, Dir
Holdings: Vols (2800) Cat Mss Maps Microforms
Budget: ($1500)
Notes: Generally, the History and Genealogy Collection is composed of materials relating to local and North Carolina State history and materials for genealogical research. Primary emphasis is on genealogical research materials. The nucleus of the genealogical collection is the McCubbins Collection. The Collection consists primarily of deed abstracts of Rowas County. Another collection representing part of the genealogical research collection is the Smith Collection, consisting of notes and correspondence collected over a wide span of years about Smiths of the US. A recent addition is the Archibald Henderson Collection of literary works of North Carolinians, Transylvania materials and materials dealing with North Carolina State history and political science.

NC —PUBLIC LIBRARY OF JOHNSTON COUNTY & SMITHFIELD, 305 Market St,

Smithfield, 27577. Kenneth M Reading, Dir
Holdings: Vols 1000 Maps Pix Microforms
Budget: $800
Notes: Emphasis on Johnson County. Partially cataloged.

NC —IREDELL COUNTY LIBRARY, 135 E Water St, Statesville, 28677. Flint Norwood, Librn
Holdings: Vols 1400 Cat Mss Slides Audiotapes Videotapes 16mm Films Filmstrips Microforms
Budget: $3000
Notes: Collection focuses on history of North Carolina and Iredell County. Incl backlog of local newspapers, census records, wills amd deeds, court of pleas and quarters, marriage records, land entries, probate minutes, minutes of superior court, etc, on microfilm.

NC —FORSYTH COUNTY PUBLIC LIBRARY, North Carolina Collection, 660 W Fifth St, Winston-Salem, 27101. Anne R Correll, Head, North Carolina Collection
Holdings: Vols 10,000 Cat Maps Microforms
Budget: $3200
Notes: Collection newly organized 1975. Incl genealogy materials with limited materials on the Southeast. Separate card catalog for this collection.

NC —WAKE FOREST UNIVERSITY, Z Smith Reynolds Library, North Carolina Baptist Collection, PO Box 7777 Reynolda Station, Winston-Salem, 27109. John R Woodard, Jr, Dir
Holdings: Vols (7000) Cat Mss Maps Pix Slides Microforms
Budget: ($20,000)
Notes: The Ethel Taylor Crittenden Collection in Baptist History, emphasizes the Baptists of North Carolina in particular. Much, however, from other states, the Southern Baptist Convention and the American Baptist Convention. Also Negro, Primitive and Free-Will Baptist items. There is a general card file to all holdings, an alphabetical and chronological file (incl extinct churches), and special index files for biographical references; the NC Church file; vital statistics.

VA —CHESAPEAKE PUBLIC LIBRARY, Jody C Treadway, William McGehee Wallace Memorial Collection, Civic Center, 300 Cedar Rd, Chesapeake, 23320.
Holdings: Vols (3400) Cat Mss Maps Pix Microforms
Notes: This collection is the property of the Norfolk County Historical Society. Partially cataloged.

NORTH CAROLINA—POLITICS AND GOVERNMENT

NC —WESTERN CAROLINA UNIVERSITY, Hunter Memorial Library, Cullowhee, 28723. James B Lloyd, Cur
Notes: The papers of former North Carolina state senators William E Breese, Jr (1875-1939), W Frank Forsyth (1913-70), and Carl Dan Killian, Sr (1903-76).

NC —DUKE UNIVERSITY, William R Perkins Library, Durham, 27706. Elvin E Strowd, University Librn

NORTH CAROLINA—SOCIAL LIFE AND CUSTOMS

DC —LIBRARY OF CONGRESS, Prints & Photographs Div, Washington, 20540.
Holdings: 93 Items
Notes: The William A Barnhill Collection is a photographic study of the inhabitants of western North Carolina (1914-17) performing such daily tasks as milling, weaving, preparing food, and making baskets, shingles, and pottery.

NC —DUKE UNIVERSITY, William R Perkins Library, Durham, 27706. Elvin E Strowd, University Librn

NC —NORTH CAROLINA DIV OF ARCHIVES & HISTORY, 109 E Jones St, Raleigh, 27611.
Holdings: Mss
Notes: The papers of Gertrude Weil, correspondence, material about her activities in various organizations, particularly for women's interests. 51 cubic ft of mss.

NORTH CAROLINA—SOCIAL LIFE AND CUSTOMS (cont.)

†NC —OLD SALEM, INC, Library, Drawer F, Salem Station, Winston-Salem, 27108.
Notes: Moravians in North Carolina.

NORTH CAROLINA AUTHORS see Authors, North Carolina

NORTH CAROLINA COUNCIL OF WOMEN'S ORGANIZATIONS

NC —UNIVERSITY OF NORTH CAROLINA, GREENSBORO, Walter Clinton Jackson Library, Special Collections Dept, 1000 Spring Garden St, Greensboro, 27412. Emilie W Mills, Librn
Holdings: Mss Pix
Notes: Papers of this state-wide clearing house for women's groups which was chartered in 1959. Activities extended to safety, continuing education and the implementation of the Status of Women Report. By 1970, incl 39 affiliated organizations with membership of over half a million women. Collection incl 1000 items.

NORTH CELESTIAL POLE see North Pole, Celestial

NORTH CENTRAL ASSOCIATION

IL —UNIVERSITY OF ILLINOIS, URBANA/CHAMPAIGN, Library, University Archives, 19 Library, 1408 W Gregory Drive, Urbana, 61801. Maynard Brichford, University Archivist
Holdings: Cat Mss Pix Slides Microforms
Notes: Papers, archival records, etc.

NORTH CENTRAL STATES see Middle West

NORTH DAKOTA

ND —NORTH DAKOTA STATE LIBRARY, Capitol Grounds, Bismarck, 58505. Darrell McNemere, State Librn
Holdings: Vols 13,000 Cat
Notes: Incl North Dakota State Documents, 1966-date. Published catalogs of books and documents.

ND —MINOT STATE COLLEGE, Memorial Library, Minot, 58701. Ronald J Rudser, Dir
Holdings: Vols 3000 Cat Maps Microforms

SD —AUGUSTANA COLLEGE, Mikkelsen Library & Learning Resource Center, Center for Western Studies, Sioux Falls, 57197. Ronelle Thompson, Dir Library
Holdings: Vols (40,000) Cat Mss Maps Pix Slides Microforms
Budget: ($150,000)
Notes: The Center for Western Studies, located in the Mikkelsen Library, is an archival and research agency of Augustana College. Dedicated to the history and culture of the Great Plains and the Trans-Mississippi West, the Center collects and preserves materials relating to Plains Indians, immigrant settlers, Norwegiana, Western Americana, Herbert Krause, Frederick Manfred, Donald Parker, Richard F Pettigrew, Augustana College, the Episcopal Diocese of South Dakota, the South Dakota District of the American Lutheran Church, the South Dakota Penitentiary and Minnehaha County.

NORTH DAKOTA—BIOGRAPHY

ND —NORTH DAKOTA STATE UNIVERSITY, Library, Fargo, 58105. John E Bye, Archivist
Notes: North Dakota Biography Index, which is a card index to published biographical sketches found in over 450 publications. It contains over 120,000 names. In addition, collection on Germans from Russia documents the migration of Germans to Russia, especially the Black Sea region, in the early 19th century and their later immigration to the United States.

NORTH DAKOTA—GENEALOGY

ND —NORTH DAKOTA STATE UNIVERSITY, Library, Fargo, 58105. John

E Bye, Archivist
Notes: The "Germans from Russia Heritage Collection" consists of over 300 volumes, newspapers, other printed materials and audio-visual records, both in English and German. The collection documents the migration of Germans in Russia, especially the Black Sea region, in the early 19th century and their later immigration to the United States. An annotated bibliography of the collection is now being prepared. to be available in mid-1984.

NORTH DAKOTA—GOVERNMENT PUBLICATIONS

ND —UNIVERSITY OF NORTH DAKOTA, Chester Fritz Library, Dept of Special Collections, Grand Forks, 58202. Daniel F Rylance, Special Collections Coordr
Holdings: Vols 15,000 Cat
Notes: An official state depository. This collection is retrospective to the beginning of the Dakota Territorial Government 1861.

NORTH DAKOTA—HISTORY

KS —UNIVERSITY OF KANSAS, Kenneth Spencer Research Library, Kansas Collection, Lawrence, 66045. Sheryl K Williams, Cur
Holdings: Vols (92,000) Cat Mss Maps Pix
Notes: All aspects of the American West and trans-Mississippi history, especially northern and central regions. Overland diaries, cartographic history, Indians, emigration and immigration, printing history, cattle industry, agriculture and farm life, conservation are some special interests, in addition to the usual political, economic, military and social interests.

ND —NORTH DAKOTA STATE UNIVERSITY, Library, Fargo, 58105. John E Bye, Archivist
Holdings: Vols (2500) Cat Mss Maps Pix
Budget: ($14,000)
Notes: The Collection is administered by the North Dakota Institute for Regional Studies. It contains materials on North Dakota history, especially the Red River Valley, with emphasis on bonanza farming, pioneer life, agriculture, local history, literary figures, business, Fargo, ND, and some political collections, particularly of the Nonpartisan League. Also, there is an extensive photographic collection covering the pioneer to post-World War I period and includes the "Hultstrand 'History in Pictures' Collection" of sod houses, pioneer life and farming. For the small collections, there has been published, *Guide to the Small Collection Manuscripts of the North Dakota Institute for Regional Studies*, by John E Bye, 1977.

ND —UNIVERSITY OF NORTH DAKOTA, Chester Fritz Library, Dept of Special Collections, Grand Forks, 58202. Daniel F Rylance, Special Collections Coordr
Holdings: Vols (5500) Uncat Mss Maps Pix Microforms
Budget: ($2500)
Notes: Also the Orin G Libby Manuscript Collection (900 collections), and the Aandahl Collection of Western History on North Dakota and the Northern Great Plains. Emphasis on agriculture, politics, pioneering, Germans from Russia, etc. Guides to the collections available from the Coordinator of Special Collections.

ND —THEODORE ROOSEVELT NATIONAL PARK, Library, PO Box 7, Medora, 58645. Susan Snow, Librn; Miki Hellickson, Chief Naturalist
Holdings: Vols (1500) Cat Mss Maps Pix Slides Audiotapes 16mm Films
Notes: Theodore Roosevelt, cattle country history, natural history. Also 2400 pictures and 2200 slides.

NORTH DAKOTA—MAPS

OK —TULSA CITY-COUNTY LIBRARY, Business & Technology Dept, 400 Civic Center, Tulsa, 74103. Craig Buthod, Head
Notes: Original General Land Office survey maps for the states of Arizona, Arkansas,

Colorado, Illinois, Indiana, Idaho, Kansas, Michigan, Missouri, Montana, Nebraska, Nevada, New Mexico, North Dakota, Ohio, Oklahoma, South Dakota, Utah and Wyoming. Incomplete coverage of each state.

NORTH DAKOTA AUTHORS see Authors, North Dakota

NORTH POLE

DC —NATIONAL GEOGRAPHIC SOCIETY, Library, 1146 16th St NW, Washington, 20036. Susan Fifer Canby, Dir
Holdings: Vols (63,000) Cat Mss Maps Pix
Notes: Material concerning land, sea, and space exploration--past and present. All fields of anthropology, natural history, geography, etc.

MI —OLIVET COLLEGE, Burrage Library, Olivet, 49076. Chris Miko, Dir
Holdings: Vols (2000) Cat
Notes: The collection consists primarily of early printed voyages of the artic and antartic from the earliest times to the mid-20th century.

NY —COLUMBIA UNIVERSITY LIBRARIES, Rare Book & Manuscript Library, 801 Butler Library, 535 W 114 St, New York, 10027. Kenneth A Lohf, Librn
Holdings: Vols 700 Cat
Notes: First editions, mss, letters and memorabilia relating to the exploration of the North and South Poles. 500 items. Restricted use.

NY —EXPLORERS CLUB, James B Ford Memorial Library, 46 E 70 St, New York, 10021. Janet Baldwin, Librn
Holdings: Vols (24,000) Cat Maps
Notes: Additions to the collection depend upon gifts. Access by appointment only.

NY —NEW YORK PUBLIC LIBRARY, Research Libraries, General Research Division, Fifth Ave & 42 St, New York, 10018. Rodney Phillips, Chief
Holdings: Vols (2,225,000) Cat Maps Pix Microforms
Budget: ($775,718)

VA —UNIVERSITY OF VIRGINIA, Alderman Library, Manuscripts Dept, Charlottesville, 22901. Edmund Berkeley Jr, Cur
Holdings: Cat Mss Pix
Notes: Papers of Edwin Swift Balch, author of *The North Pole* and *Bradley Land*, and *Antarctica*, and authority on the Cook-Peary controversy incl scrapbooks and correspondence.

NORTH POLE, CELESTIAL

CT —YALE UNIVERSITY, Dept of Astronomy Library, 260 Whitney Ave, Box 6666, New Haven, 06511.
Holdings: Cat Pix Slides
Notes: Over 3000 plates of asteroids, pictures taken with Yale telescopes in the Northern and Southern Hemispheres. Also about 65,000 stellar parallax plates and about 1000 (17 x 17 in) zone catalog plates recording some 200,000 star positions. There is also a collection of about 500 plates recording the location of the north celestial pole among the stars. Of this latter, only one other similar collection exists, at the Pulkova Observatory, near Leningrad.

NORTH WEST COMPANY

MN —GRAND PORTAGE NATIONAL MONUMENT, Library, Box 666, Grand Marais, 55604.
Holdings: Vols (1000) Cat Mss Pix
Notes: Deals primarily with the Canadian fur trade, especially the activities of the North West Co and the Hudson's Bay Co.

NORTHEAST BOUNDARY OF THE U.S.

ME —MAINE STATE LIBRARY, Special Collections Dept, Cultural Bldg, Station 64, Augusta, 04333. Shirley Thayer, Librn
Holdings: // Mss Maps
Budget: ($2,500,000)
Notes: Maine history, incl correspondence

NORTHEAST BOUNDARY OF THE U.S. (cont.)

and documents on the Northeastern boundary controversy.

ME —BOWDOIN COLLEGE, Library, Brunswick, 04011. Dianne M Gutscher, Cur of Special Collections
Holdings: Mss
Notes: The Charles S Daveis Papers consist of about 400 items of correspondence, addresses, and documents, 1808-1864, of this Portland, Maine, lawyer who was active in the settlement of the dispute with Great Britain over Maine's northeastern boundary.

ME —MAINE HISTORICAL SOCIETY, Library, 485 Congress St, Portland, 04101.
Holdings: Vols (60,000) Cat Mss Maps Pix
Notes: The Society's holdings cover all of Maine in its scope, with special emphasis on the Portland region.

NORTHEAST KINGDOM

VT —LYNDON STATE COLLEGE LIBRARY, Lyndonville, 05851. Suzanne Gallagher, Head Librn
Holdings: Vols (1200) Cat Mss Maps Pix Microforms
Notes: Collection incl any and all works on Vermont and Vermonters as well as reports from state and local government agencies. Particular attention is paid to Northeast Kingdom.

NORTHERN LEAGUE BASEBALL

SD —SIOUXLAND HERITAGE MUSEUMS, Pettigrew Museum Library, 131 N Duluth Ave, Sioux Falls, 57104. Ms Lee N McLaird, Cur of Collections
Notes: The collection includes the Records of Northern League Baseball.

NORTHERN PACIFIC RAILROAD

MN —MINNESOTA HISTORICAL SOCIETY LIBRARY, 690 Cedar St, Saint Paul, 55101. Patricia C Harpole, Chief of Reference Library; Bonnie G Wilson, Head of Special Libraries
Notes: Records.

NORTHWEST, CANADIAN see Northwest Coast of North America

NORTHWEST MOUNTED POLICE see Royal Canadian Northwest Mounted Police

NORTHWEST, OLD

DC —SOCIETY OF THE CINCINNATI, Library, 2118 Massachusetts Ave NW, Washington, 20008. John D Kilbourne, Dir of Museum & Library
Holdings: Vols (12,000) Cat Mss Maps Pix Slides Microforms
Budget: ($65,000)
Notes: Because of the French connections of the Society of the Cincinnati, a particular effort is made to incl information about the French contribution to the American Revolution. The collection is also rich in biographical materials concerning the officer personnel of the American and French armies of the American Revolution. There are two significant sub-sections of this collection: The George Rogers Clark Collection concerning the history of the Old Northwest (to 1820); and the Member-Author collection, writings of members of the Society of the Cincinnati in various fields. It is advisable to make an appointment for use of the collections.

IL —CHICAGO HISTORICAL SOCIETY, Library, Clark St at North Ave, Chicago, 60614. Robert L Brubaker, Librn
Holdings: Vols (150,000) Cat Mss Maps Pix
Notes: Extensive holdings of maps and accounts of travel and description from the 16th century to the present; files of many early newspapers and periodicals.

IL —KNOX COLLEGE, Henry M Seymour Library, Galesburg, 61401. Douglas L Wilson, Dir
Holdings: Vols 4780 Cat Mss Maps Pix
Notes: Special emphasis on the earliest

European contacts in the upper Mississippi, early settlement in Illinois.

IN —FRANKLIN COLLEGE OF INDIANA, Library, Special Collections Dept, Franklin, 46131. Mary Alice Medlicott, Cur
Holdings: Vols (12,000) Cat Mss Maps Pix
Budget: ($151,189)
Notes: David Demaree Banta Indiana Collection. Contains material relating to the area which became the Northwest Territory, the State of Indiana, its official publications; description, incl county and city histories, atlases and biographies; literary and scientific works of Hoosier authors. Printed catalog of collection available on request. Third edition of catalog is completed in manuscript.

IN —INDIANA HISTORICAL SOCIETY, Library, 315 W Ohio St, Indianapolis, 46202. Robert K O'Neill, Dir
Holdings: Vols Cat Mss Maps Pix
Notes: Papers of a number of individuals involved in the settlement of Indiana and the Old Northwest in the late 18th and early 19th centuries. Incl papers of William Henry Harrison.

MI —DETROIT PUBLIC LIBRARY, Burton Historical Collection, 5201 Woodward Ave, Detroit, 48202. Alice Dalligan, Chief
Holdings: Vols 250,000 Cat Mss Maps Pix Slides Microforms Microfilms Pamphlets Newspapers
Notes: History of Detroit, Michigan, and the Old Northwest.

OH —MIAMI UNIVERSITY, King Library, Walter Havighurst Special Collections Library, Oxford, 45056. Helen Ball, Cur of Special Collections
Holdings: Vols (6000) Cat Mss Maps
Notes: Regional history of the Old Northwest Territory and especially of the Ohio River Valley. Incl periodicals.

NORTHWEST, PACIFIC

CA —CLAREMONT COLLEGES, Honnold Library, Ninth & Dartmouth, Claremont, 91711. Tania Rizzo, Special Collections Dept Head
Holdings: Vols (561) // Cat Mss Maps
Notes: Henry Raup Wagner Collection: cartography of the West Coast, voyages, related history and geography, 15th century and later. Most maps are photostats from European and American archives and libraries. Bound typescripts of sources Wagner used in preparing his *Evolution of Maps of the Northwest Coast*, some facsimiles of mss, with transliteration or translation. Original copy (bound) of typescript of his "The Cartography of the Northwest Coast of America to the Year 1800" with pencilled and typed corrections and notes. Downs 2725. Mario C Schnitzler, "Annotated Bibliography of the Henry Raup Wagner Collection of Early Hispanic-American History and Geography" (thesis, 1955).

ID —UNIVERSITY OF IDAHO, Library, Dept of Special Collections & Archives, Moscow, 83843.
Holdings: Vols (11,000) Cat Mss Maps Pix Slides Microforms
Budget: ($4000)
Notes: Emphasis on Idaho and the Pacific Northwest. Incl 20,000 pictures and 700 slides. Charles A Webbert, *Check List of Western Americana in the Day-NW Collection, University of Idaho Library, July 1, 1969* (University of Idaho Publication No 8, June 1970).

ID —IDAHO STATE UNIVERSITY, Library, Pocatello, 83209. Gary Domitz, Social Science Librn
Holdings: Cat Mss Maps Pix
Notes: Extensive collection.

MT —EASTERN MONTANA COLLEGE, Library, 1500 N 30 St, Billings, 59101. Edward Neroda, Dir
Holdings: Vols 2186 Cat Maps Pix
Notes: The Dora White Collection of Western History; emphasis on Pacific Northwest and Montana.

MT —MONTANA STATE UNIVERSITY, Library, Bozeman, 59717. Minnie Ellen Paugh, Special Collections Librn
Holdings: Vols (7000) // Mss Maps Pix
Notes: Leggat-Donahoe Collection.

Collection of Alexander Leggat of Butte, whose father was active in opening the mines. Mr Leggat's interests where mining, exploration, and the fur trade. There are excellent Indian materials in the collection.

OR —UNIVERSITY OF OREGON, Map Library, Eugene, 97403. Peter L Stark, Map Librarian
Holdings: Cat Maps Aerial Photographs
Budget: ($4000)
Notes: Incl cartographic materials covering the states of Idaho, Montana, Oregon and Washington, and the Province of British Columbia.

OR —UNIVERSITY OF OREGON LIBRARY, Special Collections Div, Eugene, 97403. Kenneth W Duckett, Curator
Holdings: Vols (35,000) Cat Mss Pix
Notes: Extensive mss collections of diaries and correspondence relating primarily to Oregon history and politics, files and drawings of primarily Oregon architects, and business and organization records.
Publication: Martin Schmitt, *Catalogue of Manuscripts in the University of Oregon Library.* Eugene, Oregon: University of Oregon Books, 1971. The Oregon Collection contains ca 35,000 vols relating to Oregon history, life and letters, incl Oregon State documents.
See also entry under Architects

OR —WESTERN OREGON STATE COLLEGE, College Library, 345 N Monmouth St, Monmouth, 97361. Clarence Gorchels, Dir
Holdings: Vols 8500 Cat Mss Maps Pix Slides 16mm Films Filmstrips Microforms
Budget: $4000
Notes: The John C Higgins Memorial Collection on the history and culture of the Pacific Northwest.

†OR —LEWIS AND CLARK COLLEGE, Library, 615 SW Palatine Hill Rd, Portland, 97219.

OR —LIBRARY ASSOCIATION OF PORTLAND, 801 SW Tenth St, Portland, 97205. James Burghardt, Head Librn
Holdings: Vols 22,500 Cat Microforms
Notes: Official publications of the State of Oregon and other governmental bodies within the State; books and pamphlets relating to Oregon and the Oregon Territory; periodicals; maps.

OR —PORTLAND STATE UNIVERSITY LIBRARY, 934 SW Harrison, PO Box 1151, 97207, Portland, 97201. Kenneth W Butler, Asst Dir
Holdings: Vols (669,592) Uncat Mss Maps Pix Microforms
Budget: ($1,321,288)
Notes: Northwest natural resources and electrical power development. Incl the Ivan Bloch Collection.

OR —US DEPT OF ENERGY, Bonneville Power Administration Library, 1002 NE Holladay St, PO Box 3621, Portland, 97232. Karen Hadman, Chief of Library Branch
Holdings: Vols (10,000) Cat Microforms
Budget: ($185,000)
Notes: Emphasis is on Federal and Pacific Northwest law and in subject areas of interest to the Departments of Energy and Interior.

OR —WILLAMETTE UNIVERSITY, Library, 900 State St, Salem, 97301.
Holdings: Vols 500
Notes: Archival Collection.

WA —WESTERN WASHINGTON UNIVERSITY, Center for Pacific Northwest Studies, High St, Bellingham, 98225. James W Scott, Dir
Holdings: Cat Mss Maps Pix
Notes: The Percival R Jeffcott Collection of Local History is particularly rich in photographic materials, incl about 1800 negatives and about 1100 photographs, which deal with pioneer settlement and economic and cultural developments in Whatcom County, Washington, and a few adjacent areas, such as the Lower Mainland of British Columbia to the north and neighboring counties of Washington to the south and west. Incl also ms versions of Jeffcott's published works: *Nooksack Tales and Trails, Chechaco and Sourdough* and *Blankey Bill Jarman* and numerous

NORTHWEST, PACIFIC (cont.)

unpublished papers and workbooks. A small collection of Jeffcott materials is housed in the Washington State Historical Society, tacoma, and for this there is an unpublished inventory. An inventory of the present collection is being prepared for publication by the Center for Pacific Northwest Studies.

WA —WASHINGTON STATE LIBRARY, Washington/Northwest Rm, State Library Bldg, Olympia, 98504. Nancy B Pryor, Research Consultant
Holdings: Vols 8000 Cat Mss Maps Pix Microforms
Notes: Mss photographs and microfilm largely limited to Washington territorial and state materials as is the file of pamphlets and newspaper clippings, which includes both historical and current material. The book collection incl works on the four Pacific Northwest States, Alaska, and British Columbia, and books by Washington authors.

†WA —WASHINGTON STATE UNIVERSITY, Library, Manuscripts, Archives & Special Collections, Pullman, 99164. John F Guido, Head
Holdings: Cat Mss Maps Pix
Notes: The ms collection incl business and financial records of banks, breweries, insurance, land, lumber and livestock companies, trade and commodity associations; as well as the personal and professional papers of authors, aviators, educators, engineers, farmers, historians, pioneers, politicians and scientists; especially rich in documents relating to the exploration, settlement and development of the Palouse Country, the Inland Empire, the Columbia Basin and the Pacific Northwest. Described in *Selected Manuscript Resources in the Washington State University Library* (Pullman, 1974); and other published and unpublished inventories and registers. Also, papers, 1821-1873, covering Father De Smet's early sojourns at Whitemarsh and St Louis, his founding of the Rocky Mountain Missions, his long service as Procurator and Socius of the Missouri Province, and hismany travels. Correspondence with his family in Belgium, mss of his published journals, 2 small maps, sketches and engravings used to illustrate his books. Incl about 100 small pencil sketches by Father Nicholas Point depicting the 1841 journey from Westport to St Mary's Mission in the Bitterroot Valley. Described in *The Record*, 30 (1969) 6-40 and 32 (1971) 47-63.

WA —SEATTLE PUBLIC LIBRARY, 1000 Fourth Ave, Seattle, 98104. Ronald A Dubberly, City Librn
Holdings: Cat Mss Maps Pix Microforms

WA —UNIVERSITY OF WASHINGTON LIBRARIES, Pacific Northwest Collection, Seattle, 98195. Andrew F Johnson, Librn
Holdings: Vols (50,000) Cat Maps Pix
Budget: ($12,000)
Notes: The Pacific Northwest Collection contains printed materials documenting the historic and contemporary life and culture of the region in a broad range of subject areas. The Pacific Northwest is defined as the geographic region including Washington, Oregon, Idaho, Montana, British Columbia, Yukon Territory, and Alaska. Printed materials including books, periodicals, government documents, maps, weekly and local regional newspapers, theses and dissertations, as well as photographs and architectural drawings are included in the Pacific Northwest Collection. Photographic works of over 200 photographers active in the Pacific Northwest, Alaska, and the Yukon Territory (Canada) during the period 1860-1930, including Asahel and Edward S Curtis, Eric Hegg, and Clark Kinsey, are represented in a print collection of more than 300,000 images. The architecturaldrawings collection includes over 19,000 original plans, drawings, sketches, renderings and blue prints pertaining to the history of architecture and urban planning and landscape gardening in the Pacific Northwest ca 1880-1940. Areas

of particular strength are the holdings of over 1100 published journals of Pacific Northwest exploration expeditions, photographs of Northwest Coast Native Americans and of historic Seattle, newspapers issued within the Japanese-American relocation camps, 1942-1945, materials relating to the 1980 eruption of Mt St Helens, and Sanborne fire insurance maps for Washington. A unique feature of the Collection is the subject index to regional periodicals and local newspapers maintained by the PNW Collection staff; over 100 titles are currently indexed. G K Hall Company published a books catalog of the Pacific Northwest Collectionin 1973.

WA —UNIVERSITY OF WASHINGTON LIBRARIES, Suzzallo Library, Special Collections Division, Rare Book Collection, FM-25, Seattle, 98195. Gary Menges, Coordinator for Special Collections
Holdings: Pix
Notes: Broad selection of the work (200,000 pictures) of more than 200 photographers working in Pacific Northwest, Alaska and the Yukon Territory (of Canada) during the period 1860-1930. Only research oriented photographic collection in region. Work by individual photographers maintained intact. Incl important segments of the work of Asahel & Edward S Curtis, Eric A Hegg, Darius & Clark Kinsey, Wilhelm Hester, E H Latham, A H Barnes, Dr Kyo Koike and Lawrence Lindsley.

WA —UNIVERSITY OF WASHINGTON LIBRARIES, Forest Resources Library, AQ-15, Seattle, 98195. Barbara B Gordon, Head
Holdings: Vols 63,000 Cat Maps Microforms
Budget: $12,500
Notes: Modern imprints only. Mostly in English, some German, Slavic, and East Asian languages. No geographical limits but emphasis is on Pacific Northwest. Northern service center for Pacific Forestry Research Information Network (PACFORNET); southern center is at USFS Pacific Southwest Experiment Station, Bereley, California. Partially cataloged.

WA —UNIVERSITY OF WASHINGTON LIBRARIES, Suzzallo Library, Manuscripts Section, FM-25, Seattle, 98195. Karyl Winn, Librn
Notes: Files of locally produced newsfilm from station KOMO-TV in Seattle, from 1954.

WA —WASHINGTON STATE HISTORICAL SOCIETY LIBRARY, 315 N Stadium Way, Tacoma, 98403. Frank L Green, Librn
Holdings: Vols 15,000 Cat Mss Maps Pix Microforms
Notes: Scope is entire Pacific Northwest, with emphasis on Washington.

WA —FORT VANCOUVER NATIONAL HISTORIC SITE, E Evergreen Blvd, Vancouver, 98661. Kent Taylor, Supervisory Ranger
Holdings: Vols (600) Cat Maps Pix Slides Audiotapes Videotapes 16mm Films
Notes: Fur trade of the Northwest.

WA —WHITMAN COLLEGE, Penrose Memorial Library, 345 Boyer, Walla Walla, 99362. Lawrence L Dodd, Cur
Holdings: Vols 3800 Cat Mss Maps Pix Slides Microforms
Notes: The Eells Library of Northwest History.

WY —WYOMING STATE ARCHIVES MUSEUMS, AND HISTORICAL DEPARTMENT, Barrett Bldg, Cheyenne, 82002. Philip J Roberts, Documents Supvr; Jean F Brainerd, Research Asst
Holdings: Vols (12,000) Cat
Budget: ($430,000)
Notes: Extensive mss, map, pamphlet, and picture collection relative to Wyoming, regional, and western history. Publish *Annals of Wyoming*.

BC —LIBRARY SERVICES BRANCH, Peace River Associated Libraries, 1017 105th Ave, Dawson Creek, V1G 2L3, Can. Mary E Grant, Librn
Holdings: Vols (350) Cat Mss Pix
Notes: Incl relevant newspapers files.

BC —UNIVERSITY OF BRITISH COLUMBIA, Library, Special Collections Div, 1956 Main Mall, Vancouver, V6T 1Y3,

Can. Anne Yandle, Head
Holdings: Vols Cat Mss Maps Pix
Notes: Strongest in pre-1846 material.

BC —VANCOUVER PUBLIC LIBRARY, History & Government Div, 750 Burrard St, Vancouver, V6Z 1X5, Can.
Holdings: Vols 5000 Cat Microforms
Notes: Geographical limits of the collection are the present area of British Columbia, Oregon and Washington Territory to 1846, some Alberta material for approach to the mountain barrier and its exploration, pre-1898 Yukon Territory and the Klondike gold rush, Alaska pre-1867, Bering Sea fur seal arbitration issue. The chronological limit is 1950. Incl 500 maps, 25 atlases.

NORTHWEST, PACIFIC—DESCRIPTION AND TRAVEL—VIEWS

†OR —LEWIS AND CLARK COLLEGE, Library, 615 SW Palatine Hill Rd, Portland, 97219.

NORTHWEST, PACIFIC—GENEALOGY

WA —SEATTLE PUBLIC LIBRARY, 1000 Fourth Ave, Seattle, 98104. Ronald A Dubberly, City Librn
Holdings: Cat Mss Maps Microforms
Notes: Largest library of this type in Pacific Northwest. Supported by Seattle Genealogical Society, Northwest Lineage Researchers, Boone Family Association of Washington, and various patrotic societies.

NORTHWEST, PACIFIC—HISTORY

CA —AZUSA PACIFIC COLLEGE, Marshburn Memorial Library, Citrus & Alosta, Azusa, 91702. Edward Peterman, Librn
Holdings: Vols (6000) Uncat
Budget: ($30,000)
Notes: Significant holdings in the George E Fullerton Library of California and Western Americana.

CA —BURBANK PUBLIC LIBRARY, 110 N Glenoaks Blvd, Burbank, 91502. Mary Ann Grasso, Coordr; Barbara Stones, Coordr, Media Project
Holdings: Vols 4000 Cat
Notes: Incl material on all states of the Mississippi River. Many good runs of state historical journals and regional periodicals. About half the listings in J Frank Dobie's *Guide to Life and Literature of the Southwest*. See description in California Librarian, April 1965, "The Burbank Western History Collection", by Thomas F Parker.

IN —INDIANA UNIVERSITY, Lilly Library, Seventh St, Bloomington, 47405. William R Cagle, Librn
Holdings: Vols 400 // Cat Mss
Notes: Largely 19th and early 20th century printings.

OR —WESTERN OREGON STATE COLLEGE, College Library, 345 N Monmouth St, Monmouth, 97361. Clarence Gorchels, Dir
Holdings: Vols 8500 Cat Mss Maps Pix Slides 16mm Films Filmstrips Microforms
Budget: $4000
Notes: The John C Higgins Memorial Collection on the history and culture of the Pacific Northwest.

OR —GEORGIA-PACIFIC HISTORICAL MUSEUM, Library, 900 SW Fifth, Portland, 97204. Richard Thompson, Museum Dir
Holdings: Vols (300) Uncat Videotapes 16mm Films Pix
Notes: Use of collection is by written request for specific information or materials.

WA —WESTERN WASHINGTON UNIVERSITY, Center for Pacific Northwest Studies, High St, Bellingham, 98225. James W Scott, Dir
Holdings: Mss Pix Videotapes
Notes: The Galen A Biery Collection. One of the Pacific Northwest's best-known and most active local historians. Incl in the collection are the copy books of the Sehome

NORTHWEST, PACIFIC—HISTORY (cont.)

Coal Co which flourished in the 1870s and 1880s, and a variety of business records of the Pacific American Fisheries Co. See also entry for Archie W Shiels. Partially cataloged. Also, the Bellingham Bay Improvement Company Collection. The records of 6 companies formerly operative in NW Washington: Bellingham Bay Coal Co; Bellingham Bay Improvement Co; Bellingham Bay Lumber Co; Bellingham Terminals and Railroad Co; Bellingham Securities Syndicate. The records cover 1864-1942. Officers of the companies incl many important PNW businessmen incl PB Cornwall, Joshua Green, JJ Donavan and JH Bloedel. A published listing and description is available: *Informational Paper* 1 of the Center for PNW Studies. Partially cataloged.

WA —SKAGIT COUNTY HISTORICAL MUSUEM, Library, Po Box 818, La Conner, 98257. David J Van Meer, Cur & Librn
Holdings: Vols 240 Cat Mss Maps Pix Slides Audiotapes
Notes: History of Skagit County and the Pacific Northwest. Incl 179 mss, 109 maps, 8000 pictures, 100 slides and 235 audiotapes.

†WA —WASHINGTON STATE UNIVERSITY, Library, Manuscripts, Archives & Special Collections, Pullman, 99164. John F Guido, Head
Holdings: Cat Mss Maps Pix
Notes: The manuscript collection incl business and financial records of banks, breweries, fisheries, insurance, land, lumber and livestock companies, trade and commodity associations; as well as the personal and professional papers of authors, aviators, educators, engineers, farmers, historians, pioneers, politicains and scientists; especially rich in documents relating to the exploration, settlement and development of the Palouse Country, the Inland Empire, the Columbia Basin and the Pacific Northwest. Described in *Selected Manuscript Resources in the Washington State University Library* (Pullman, 1974); and other published and unpublished inventories and registers.

WA —HISTORICAL SOCIETY OF SEATTLE AND KING COUNTY, Sophie Frye Bass Library, 2161 E Hamlin, Seattle, 98112. Rick Caldwell, Librn
Holdings: Vols (20,000) Cat Mss Maps Pix Slides
Notes: Incl 15,000 pictures on Pacific Northwest.

WA —UNIVERSITY OF WASHINGTON LIBRARIES, Pacific Northwest Collection, Seattle, 98195. Andrew F Johnson, Librn
Holdings: Vols (50,000) Cat Mss Maps Pix
Budget: ($12,000)
Notes: The Pacific Northwest Collection contains printed materials documenting the historic and contemporary life and culture of the region in a broad range of subject areas. The Pacific Northwest is defined as the geographic region including Washington, Oregon, Idaho, Montana, British Columbia, Yukon Territory, and Alaska. Printed materials including books, periodicals, government documents, maps, weekly and local regional newspapers, theses and dissertations, as well as photographs and architectural drawings are included in the Pacific Northwest Collection. Photographic works of over 200 photographers active in the Pacific Northwest, Alaska, and the Yukon Territory (Canada) during the period 1860-1930, including Asahel and Edward S Curtis, Eric Hegg, and Clark Kinsey, are represented in a print collection of more than 300,000 images. The architectural drawings collection includes over 19,000 original plans, drawings, sketches, renderings and blue prints pertaining to the history of architecture and urban planning and landscape gardening in the Pacific Northwest ca 1880-1940. Areas of particular strength are the holdings of over 1100 published journals of Pacific Northwest exploration expeditions, photographs of Northwest Coast Native Americans and of historic Seattle,

newspapers issued within the Japanese-American relocation camps, 1942-1945, materials relating to the 1980 eruption of Mt St Helens, and Sanborne fire insurance maps for Washington. A unique feature of the Collection is the subject index to regional periodicals and local newspapers maintained by the PNW Collection staff; over 100 titles are currently indexed. G K Hall Company published a books catalog of the Pacific Northwest Collection in 1973.

WA —TACOMA PUBLIC LIBRARY, 1102 Tacoma Ave S, Tacoma, 98402. Kevin Hegarty, Dir
Holdings: Vols 10,000 Mss Maps Pix
Notes: Major emphasis on Pacific Northwest, incl mss, archives, 250 linear ft 175,000 photographic negatives from collections of Marvin D Boland and Chapin Bowen, etc 40 vertical file drawers of clippings (maintained since 1909) under 2600 subject headings. Genealogies, official records, etc. Picture collection also incl 20,000 mounted and 5000 unmounted items, with posters, postcards, matted reproductions, etc.

NORTHWEST COAST OF NORTH AMERICA

AK —ALASKA STATE LIBRARY, Alaska Historical Library Collection, Pouch G, Juneau, 99811. Phyllis Demuth, Readers Services Librn
Holdings: Vols (24,000) Cat Mss Maps Pix Slides Phonorecords Audiotapes Videotapes 16mm Films Microforms

CA —CLAREMONT COLLEGES, Honnold Library, Ninth & Dartmouth, Claremont, 91711. Tania Rizzo, Special Collections Dept Head
Holdings: Vols (561) // Cat Maps Mss
Notes: Henry Raup Wagner Collection: cartography of the West Coast, voyages, related history and geography, 15th century and later. Most maps are photostats from European and American archives and libraries. Bound typescripts of sources Wagner used in preparing his *Evolution of Maps of the Northwest Coast*, some facsimiles of mss, with transliteration or translation. Original copy (bound) of typescript of his "The Cartography of the Northwest Coast of America to the Year 1800" with pencilled and typed corrections and notes. Downs 2725. Mario C Schnitzler, "Annotated Bibliography of the Henry Raup Wagner Collection of Early Hispanic-American History and Geography" (thesis, 1955).

†OR —LEWIS AND CLARK COLLEGE, Library, 615 SW Palatine Hill Rd, Portland, 97219.
Holdings: Vols 30,000 Mss Maps Pix

AB —GLENBOW-ALBERTA INSTITUTE, Historical Library & Archives, 130 9th Avenue SE, Calgary, T2G 0P3, Can. Leonard J Gottseleg, Chief Librn
Holdings: Vols (60,000) Cat Mss Maps Pix Microforms
Notes: Main emphasis is on Western Canadian history. Equally important emphasis is placed on the Canadian Arctic and Alaska, Northwest Coast explorations, Aboriginal peoples of the North and Canadian West, and the fur trade in the US Northwest.

NORTHWEST INDIANS see Indians of North America and Mexico—Northwest, Pacific

NORTHWEST PASSAGE

ON —UNIVERSITY OF TORONTO, Thomas Fisher Rare Book Library, 120 Saint George St, Toronto, M5S 1A5, Can. Richard G Landon, Head
Holdings: Vols 30,000 Mss Maps Pix
Notes: Great variety of material relating to early exploration and settlement of Canada, including the search for the Northwest Passage and the subsequent exploration of the Arctic. Manuscript and printed material pertaining to the overland exploration of northwestern Canada and the Barren Lands.

Manuscript and printed material documenting early emigration schemes and colonization attempts, including Selkirk's Red River settlement.

NORTHWEST TERRITORIES, CANADA

MB —UNIVERSITY OF MANITOBA, Elizabeth Dafoe Library, Government Publications Section, Winnipeg, R3T 2N2, Can. June Dutka, Head
Holdings: Uncat Maps Pix Microforms
Notes: The Canadian National Energy Board's Polar Gas Project documentation provides an extremely useful source of information describing the proposed construction of the pipeline route which would generally pass from the Arctic Island through the Northwest Territories, northern Manitoba and into Ontario, Canada.

NT —NORTHWEST TERRITORIES PUBLIC LIBRARY SERVICES, Bos 1100, Hay River, X0E 0R0, Can.
Holdings: Vols (1235) Cat Maps Audiotapes
Notes: Originally intended to provide items of historical significance on the Northwest Territories. It contains a number of first editions, some of which have since become available in reprint form. Copies of material in relevant native languages and on learning languages.

NORTHWEST TERRITORY

MI —LANSING PUBLIC LIBRARY, Local History Room, 401 S Capitol Ave, Lansing, 48914. Jane McClary, Local History Librn
Holdings: Vols (6000) Cat Mss Maps Pix Microforms VF
Notes: Separate catalog.

OH —CINCINNATI HISTORICAL SOCIETY, Library, (formerly Historical & Philosophical Society of Ohio), Eden Park, Cincinnati, 45202. Laura L Chace, Librn
Holdings: Vols 60,000 Cat Mss Maps Pix Slides Microforms
Budget: ($8000)
Notes: Regional history relating to Cincinnati, the Northwest Territory and Ohio River Valley.

OH —OHIO HISTORICAL SOCIETY, Archives Library Division, 1982 Velma Ave, Columbus, 43211. Dennis East, Division Chief
Holdings: Vols (96,000) Cat Mss Maps Pix Slides Microforms
Budget: ($18,000)
Notes: This library is the primary collection for Ohio. Most purchases are on the rare and out of print market. Collection area is early American history, esp relating to exploration into the Northwest Territory. Also, Ohio archaeology, natural history, and artifacts. Major media collections are books (96,000), newspapers (25,000 vols and 22,000 microfilm), pictures (50,000), maps (2500), manuscripts (1,500,000). Library is noncirculating except through interlibrary loan of microfilm.

OH —GREENE COUNTY DISTRICT LIBRARY, 76 E Market St, PO Box 520, Xenia, 45385. Julie M Overton, Local History Coordr
Holdings: // Uncat
Notes: Galloway Collection of Ohio history is housed in a five-drawer filing cabinet, incl letters, some at the time of the Gold Rush; family letters of the Galloways, Lyons, Worthingtons and others; material about William Maxwell, editor and publisher of the first newspaper in the Northwest Territory, also legal papers concerning him; papers, some legal, concerning Galloways incl "The Galloway Lands in 1812," and papers about the Worthingtons and Lyons; indentures; Civil War diary of Clark Galloway, MD, a surgeon in the war; pictures of families, covered bridges, mills etc; material about Tecumseh and some other Indians and their traditions; galley sheets and correspondence concerning the publishing of the New Testament in the Shawnee language; material about the railroad, OVCH (formerly OS&OS Home) Antioch College, Wilberforce

NORTHWEST TERRITORY (cont.)

University and other items about Ohiohistory; many notes, papers and correspondence acquired when William Galloway was preparing to write the book "Old Chillicothe," published posthumously in 1934.

NORTON, ANDRE

CA —SAN DIEGO STATE UNIVERSITY, Malcolm A Love Library, 5300 Campanile Dr, San Diego, 92182. D Dickinson, Univ Librn; Don L Bosseau, Dir
Holdings: Mss Cassettes
Notes: Elizabeth Chater Collection in Science Fiction. Includes Tolkien Collection, fantasy, folklore, Gothic novels, mostly autographed first editions, some rare and scarce, includes manuscripts, graphics, cassette tapes. Examples: authors included, Isaac Asimov, Ray Bradbury, Joan Vinge, Greg Baer, Frederick Pohl, Andre Norton, etc. Examples of periodicals, Amazing Stories, Famous Fantastic Mysteries of the 1940s, The Black Cat, 1895. (3000 items)

NORTON, CAROLINE S.

CT —YALE UNIVERSITY, Box 1603A, Yale Station, New Haven, 06520.
Holdings: Cat Mss

NORTON, CHARLES ELIOT

MA —HARVARD UNIVERSITY LIBRARY, Houghton Library, Cambridge, 02138. Rodney G Dennis, Cur of Manuscripts
Holdings: Cat Mss

NORTON, MORGAN GLENN

CA —UNIVERSITY OF CALIFORNIA, LOS ANGELES, Research Library, Dept of Special Collections, 405 Hilgard Ave, Los Angeles, 90024. Edward Shreeves, Chairman, Bibliographers Group; David S Zeidberg, Head
Notes: 1.5 linear feet of correspondence, aircraft flight logs, handbooks, and manuals.

NORTON, ROBERT, 1896-1974

CA —HOOVER INSTITUTION ON WAR, REVOLUTION & PEACE, Stanford University, Stanford, 94305. Milorad M Drachkovitch, Archivist
Holdings: Mss Pix
Notes: Papers of Robert Norton, US attorney and journalist (editor of *China Today*), incl correspondence, speeches and writings, clippings, printed matter, photographs, and other materials, 1935-1948, relating to US relations with China and Japan, India's independence from Great Britain, Japanese military incursions into China, and United Nations assistance to China. 3 1/2 ms boxes.

NORTON, W. W., COMPANY

NY —COLUMBIA UNIVERSITY LIBRARIES, Rare Book & Manuscript Library, 801 Butler Library, 535 W 114 St, New York, 10027. Kenneth A Lohf, Librn
Holdings: Mss
Notes: Correspondence files of the W W Norton Co, 1923-1965. Subsequent files likely to be given to the library. Described in *Wilson Library Bulletin,* March 1968. 165, 000 items. Restricted use.

NORWAY—FOREIGN RELATIONS

RI —BROWN UNIVERSITY, John Hay Library, 20 Prospect St, Providence, 02912. Mark N Brown, Cur Mss
Holdings: // Mss
Notes: Papers of Jonathan Russell, merchant, diplomat, and Massachusetts Congressman. Brown Class of 1791. A collection of 7000 items containing a diary and a letterbook (1809-1813); records of US Commissioners at Ghent (1813-1814) and of the American Legation at Stockholm (1814-1816); correspondence and documents for the period 1795-1830; and notes, largely official, when Russell was Charge d Affaires at Paris (1810) and for 1814-1818 when he was Minister to Sweden and Norway and a member of the US Congress.

NORWAY—HISTORY

CA —CLAREMONT COLLEGES, Honnold Library, Ninth & Dartmouth, Claremont, 91711. Franklin D Scott, Cur, Nordic Collection; Penelope Garris, Librn
Holdings: Vols (25,000) Cat Maps Pix Slides Audiotapes Videotapes Periodicals
Notes: Nordic Collections are broadly inclusive, but emphasize history of Scandinavia, Baltic countries, and Hanseatic cities. Nucleus of collections from gifts and endowment of Waldemar Westergaard, supplemented with relevant collections of David Bjork, John H Wuorinen, Ingolf Olsen, Henry Steele Commager, Franklin Scott (incl Scandinavian migration to America), and other gifts and purchases. Eight vertical file drawers of news bulletins in English or vernaculars, 1941-. See: Franklin D Scott, "The Westergaard-Bjork Collection at the Honnold Library, the Claremont Colleges," *Scandinavian Studies,* 41 (1969), 346-354. Collection incl complete publications of Nordic Council.
IL —NORTHWESTERN UNIVERSITY, Library, Special Collections Dept, 1937 Sheridan Rd, Evanston, 60201. R Russell Maylone, Cur
Holdings: Vols 65 Cat
Notes: World War II underground publications. Additional 400 monographs and serials from Denmark; 550 vols from the Netherlands; 80 vols from miscellaneous other European countries under Nazi occupation.
MN —NORWEGIAN-AMERICAN HISTORICAL ASSOCIATION, Rolvaag Memorial Library, Saint Olaf College, Northfield, 55057. Lloyd Hustvedt, Archivist
Holdings: Vols (10,000) Cat Mss Pix Slides Microforms
Notes: The purpose of the collection is to collect and preserve the records of Norwegian-Americans by maintaining archives and publishing books on history, literature, art, and culture. Books and periodicals are cataloged for the Association by the St Olaf College Library. The manuscripts and other archival material are kept in a seperate collection where they are inventoried, indexed and shelved.
NY —CORNELL UNIVERSITY LIBRARIES, John M Olin Library, Fiske Icelandic Collection, Ithaca, 14853. Louis A Pitschmann, Librn
Holdings: Vols (34,000) Cat Mss Maps Pix Microforms
Budget: ($3000)
Notes: Collection aims at comprehensive coverage of Iceland in all aspects with major emphasis on the literature and language (both old and modern). Such subjects as runology, Scandinavian and Germanic mythology, early Norwegian history and history of the Viking period and of the Norse explorations of Greenland and North America are also well represented. For printed catalogs of the Collection's holdings see Downs 3608, 3609. Records for approximately 40 percent of the collection have been entered into OCLC and RLIN.
SD —AUGUSTANA COLLEGE, Mikkelsen Library & Learning Resource Center, Center for Western Studies, Sioux Falls, 57197. Ronelle Thompson, Dir Library
Holdings: Vols (40,000) Cat Mss Maps Pix Slides Microforms
Budget: ($130,000)
Notes: The Center for Western Studies, located in the Mikkelsen Library, is an archival and research agency of Augustana College. Dedicated to the history and culture of the Great Plains and the Trans-Mississippi West, the Center collects and preserves materials relating to Plains Indians, immigrant settlers, Norwegiana, Western Americana, Herbert Krause, Frederick Manfred, Donald Parker, Richard F Pettigrew, Augustana College, the Episcopal Diocese of South Dakota, the South Dakota District of the American Lutheran Church, the South Dakota Penitentiary and Minnehaha County.
WA —UNIVERSITY OF WASHINGTON LIBRARIES, Suzzallo Library, Scandinavian Collections, FM-25, Seattle, 98195. A Gerald Anderson, Librn
Holdings: Vols (50,000) Cat Mss Pix
Budget: ($15,546)
Notes: Research collections with emphasis on languages and literatures, and auxiliary strengths in history, political science, social science. Archival and other speical materials relating to Scandinavian-Americans in the Pacific Northwest are located in other appropriate collections.
WI —UNIVERSITY OF WISCONSIN, MADISON, Memorial Library, 728 State St, Madison, 53706. Sandra Pfahler, Librn
Holdings: Vols 2000 Cat
Notes: Norwegian local history and genealogy. Collection incl primary and secondary sources, as well as extensive runs of basic periodicals and serials. Excl are genealogies of individual families, in most cases, and local journals of a popular character or of very limited interest. Aside from these, the collection, which originated in the 19th century, attempts to be as comprehensive as possible.

NORWEGIAN AMERICAN NEWSPAPERS see Newspapers, Norwegian American

NORWEGIAN LANGUAGE AND LITERATURE

CA —LOS ANGELES PUBLIC LIBRARY, Foreign Languages Dept, 630 W Fifth St, Los Angeles, 90071. Sylva Manoogian, Principal Librn
Holdings: Vols 1442 Cat
Budget: ($41,500)
IL —NORTH PARK COLLEGE LIBRARY, 5125 N Spaulding Ave, Chicago, 60625. Dorothy-Ellen Gross, Dir
Holdings: Vols (4500) Cat
Notes: Scandinavian Collection, with materials mostly Swedish, but some titles in Norwegian, Danish, Finnish and Icelandic. Separate shelf list, but also incl in union catalog. General collection with emphasis on literature and history. Other Swedish books in the field of religion available through Mellander Library on same campus.
MN —NORWEGIAN-AMERICAN HISTORICAL ASSOCIATION, Rolvaag Memorial Library, Saint Olaf College, Northfield, 55057. Lloyd Hustvedt, Archivist
Holdings: Vols (10,000) Cat Mss Pix Slides Microforms
Notes: The purpose of the collection is to collect and preserve the records of Norwegian-Americans by maintaining archives and publishing books on history, literature, art, and culture. Books and periodicals are cataloged for the Association by the St Olaf College Library. The manuscripts and other archival material are kept in a separate collection where they are inventoried, indexed and shelved.
NY —NEW YORK PUBLIC LIBRARY, Donnell Foreign Language Library, 20 W 53 St, New York, 10019. Bosiljka Stevanovic, Supvr Librn
Holdings: Vols 282 Cat
Notes: Norwegian collection incl Norwegian authors of Norwegian expression. No separate catalog.
NC —DUKE UNIVERSITY, William R Perkins Library, Durham, 27706. Elvin E Strowd, University Librn
Notes: The Scandinavian collection of 3000 items is a collection of Scandinavian literature, primarily representing the latter half of the 18th century and early 19th century.
OH —CLEVELAND PUBLIC LIBRARY, Foreign Literature Dept, 325 Superior Ave,

NORWEGIAN LANGUAGE AND LITERATURE (cont.)

Cleveland, 44114. Natalia Bezugloff, Head
Holdings: Vols 2100 Cat
Notes: A popular circulating collection containing classics and the standard works with emphasis on belles lettres, history and biography. A variety of other subjects such as learning languages, how to do books, art, children's books, spoken phonodiscs and cassettes, periodicals, etc.
See also entry under Foreign Language Collections

SD —AUGUSTANA COLLEGE, Mikkelsen Library & Learning Resource Center, Center for Western Studies, Sioux Falls, 57197. Ronelle Thompson, Dir Library
Holdings: Vols (40,000) Cat Mss Maps Pix Slides
Budget: ($130,000)
Notes: The Center for Western Studies, located in the Mikkelsen Library, is an archival and research agency of Augustana College. Dedicated to the history and culture of the Great Plains and the Trans-Mississippi West, the Center collects and preserves materials relating to Plains Indians, immigrant settlers, Norwegiana, Western Americana, Herbert Krause, Frederick Manfred, Donald Parker, Richard F Pettigrew, Augustana College, the Episcopal Diocese of South Dakota, the South Dakota District of the American Lutheran Church, the South Dakota Penitentiary and Minnehaha County.

WA —UNIVERSITY OF WASHINGTON LIBRARIES, Suzzallo Library, Scandinavian Collections, FM-25, Seattle, 98195. A Gerald Anderson, Librn
Holdings: Vols (50,000) Cat Mss Pix
Budget: ($15,546)
Notes: Research collections with emphasis on languages and literatures, and auxiliary strengths in history, political science, social science. Archival and other special materials relating to Scandinavian-Americans in the Pacific Northwest are located in other appropriate collections.

WI —UNIVERSITY OF WISCONSIN, MADISON, Memorial Library, 728 State St, Madison, 53706. Erwin K Welsch, Social Studies Bibliographer
Holdings: Vols (17,000) Cat Mss
Notes: Strong

NORWEGIANS IN THE U.S.

†IA —LUTHER COLLEGE, Preus Library, Decorah, 52101.

MN —NORWEGIAN-AMERICAN HISTORICAL ASSOCIATION, Rolvaag Memorial Library, Saint Olaf College, Northfield, 55057. Lloyd Hustvedt, Archivist
Holdings: Vols (10,000) Cat Mss Pix Slides Microforms
Notes: The purpose of the collection is to collect and preserve the records Norwegian-Americans by maintaining archives and publishing books on history, literature, art, and culture. Books and periodicals are cataloged for the Association by the St Olaf College Library. The manuscripts and other archival material are kept in a seperate collection where they are inventories, indexed and shelved.

ND —UNIVERSITY OF NORTH DAKOTA, Chester Fritz Library, Dept of Special Collections, Grand Forks, 58202. Daniel F Rylance, Special Collections Coordr
Holdings: Vols (5500) Uncat Mss Maps Pix Microforms
Budget: ($2500)
Notes: Also the Orin G Libby Manuscript Collection (900 collections), and the Aandahl Collection of Western History on North Dakota and the Northern Great Plains. Emphasis on agriculture, politics, pioneering, Germans from Russia, etc. Guides to the collections available from the Coordinator of Special Collections.

PA —BALCH INSTITUTE FOR ETHNIC STUDIES, Library, 18 S Seventh St, Philadelphia, 19106. R Joseph Anderson, Library Dir
Holdings: Vols 500 Cat

SD —AUGUSTANA COLLEGE, Mikkelsen Library & Learning Resource Center, Center for Western Studies, Sioux Falls, 57197. Ronelle Thompson, Dir Library
Notes: The Center for Western Studies, located in the Mikkelsen Library, is an archival and research agency of Augustana College. Dedicated to the history and culture of the Great Plains and the Trans-Mississippi West, the Center collects and preserves materials relating to Plains Indians, immigrant settlers, Norwegiana, Western Americana, Herbert Krause, Frederick Manfred, Donald Parker, Richard F Pettigrew, Augustana College, the Episcopal Diocese of South Dakota, the South Dakota District of the American Lutheran Church, the South Dakota Penitentiary and Minnehaha County.

WA —UNIVERSITY OF WASHINGTON LIBRARIES, Suzzallo Library, Scandinavian Collections, FM-25, Seattle, 98195. A Gerald Anderson, Librn
Holdings: Vols (50,000) Cat Mss Pix
Budget: ($15,546)
Notes: Research collections with emphasis on languages and literatures, and auxiliary strengths in history, political science, social science. Archival and other special materials relating to Scandinavian-Americans in the Pacific Northwest are located in other apropriate collections.

NOSKOWIAK, SONYA

AZ —UNIVERSITY OF ARIZONA, Center for Creative Photography, 843 E University Blvd, Tucson, 85721. James Enyeart, Dir; Terence Pitts, Cur and Librn
Notes: Center has significant collections consisting of more than 25 photographs plus other archival material such as negatives, contact sheets, work prints, correspondence, financial records, diaries, project files, etc. Inventories of the collections are available to researchers. Published guides available for some collections.

NOTABLE PERSONS

MA —BRANDEIS UNIVERSITY, Goldfarb Library, 415 South St, Waltham, 02154. Bessie Hahn, Dir
Notes: Carl Van Vechten Photographic Collection. Consists of approx 8 linear ft of photographs of famous American personage taken by Carl Van Vechten. The collection is unprocessed.

NOTTINGHAM, WAYNE B., 1899-1964

MA —MASSACHUSETTS INSTITUTE OF TECHNOLOGY, Institute Archives, Special Collections, Cambridge, 02139.
Notes: Papers (1928-1962).

NOURSE, ALAN E.

MA —BOSTON UNIVERSITY, Mugar Memorial Library, Special Collections Dept, 771 Commonwealth Ave, Boston, 02215. Howard B Gotlieb, Dir
Holdings: Cat Mss Pix
Notes: Mss, correspondence, etc collected in depth; incl publications by or about.

NOURSE, EDWIN GRISWOLD, 1883-1974

MA —BOSTON UNIVERSITY, Mugar Memorial Library, Special Collections Dept, 771 Commonwealth Ave, Boston, 02215. Howard B Gotlieb, Dir
Holdings: Cat Mss

NY —CORNELL UNIVERSITY LIBRARIES, Collection of Regional History, Dept of Manuscripts and Univ Archives, Ithaca, 14853.
Notes: Economist. Papers, 1908-63; 2 ft, 4 reels microfilm, 1 vol.

NOVA SCOTIA—HISTORY

NS —DALHOUSIE UNIVERSITY LIBRARY, Halifax, B3H 4H8, Can.
See also entry under Haliburton, Thomas Chandler

NS —LEGISLATIVE LIBRARY OF NOVA SCOTIA, Province House, Halifax, B3J 2P8, Can. Ilga Leja, Librn
Holdings: Vols 11,000 Cat Mss Maps Pix Microforms
Notes: Part of the library's mandate is to collect all material relating to Nova Scotia and by Nova Scotia authors. This material is shelved separately from the rest of the collection (68,000 vols) and does not include Nova Scotia government documents, which are not cataloged under Dewey, as is the rest of the collection. The material is available through interlibrary loan whenever feasible.

NS —NOVA SCOTIA MUSEUM, Library, 1747 Summer St, Halifax, B3H 3A6, Can. M S Whiteside, Librn
Holdings: Vols 4000 Cat
Notes: Emphasis on Social History.

NS —THOMAS MCCULLOCH HISTORIC HOUSE, Library, PO Box 1210, Picton, B0K 1H0, Can. Gary Selig, Cur
Holdings: Mss
Notes: Books, mss, and genealogical materials by or about Picton County. Also incl the library of the Rev Thomas McColloch, brought from Scotland in 1803, mostly scientific and theological works. Microfilmed *Picton Advocate* from 1895 to 1950.

NOVA SCOTIA—SOCIAL CONDITIONS

NS —DALHOUSIE UNIVERSITY LIBRARY, Halifax, B3H 4H8, Can.
Holdings: Vols 2000
Notes: Nova Scotia history pamphlets. Compiled by a Nova Scotia newspaper editor, J J Stewart, the pamphlet collection provides a comprehensive view of Nova Scotia society in the 19th century, religious, political, educational, economic, and moral issues are all hotly debated in the collection's pamphlets. Many unique items are to be found in the collection.

NOVAK, MICHAEL

MA —STONEHILL COLLEGE, Donahue Hall, Washington St, North Easton, 02356. Louise M Kenneally, Archivist & Special Collections Librn
Holdings: Vols Mss
Notes: 110 linear feet of material deposited by Stonehill alumnus, Michael Novak, author, philosopher-theologian, currently resident scholar at the American Enterprise Institute for Public Policy Research in Washington, DC. Collection incl essays, speeches, correspondence, 1955-present.

NOVELS see Fiction

NOVELS, DIME AND NICKEL see Dime Novels

NOWLAN, ALDEN, 1933-1983

AB —UNIVERSITY OF CALGARY, Libraries, Special Collections Div, 2500 University Dr, Calgary, T2N 1N4, Can.
Holdings: Mss
Notes: Correspondence, scrapbooks, research and mss (10 meters) for fiction, nonfiction, poetry and drama, 1950-80.

NOYES, ALRED

DC —GEORGETOWN UNIVERSITY, Library, Special Collections Div, 37 & O Sts NW, Washington, 20057. George M Barringer, Special Collections Librn; Nicholas B Sheetz, Mss Librn
Holdings: Mss
Notes: The Archives of the Gallery of Living Catholic Authors was founded in 1932 by Sister Mary Joseph of the Sisters of Loretto to focus attention on modern Catholic literature, and to provide a depository for manuscripts, letters, photographs, and books by contemporary Catholic writers. Contains material by hundreds of writers, incl Hilaire Belloc, Roy Campbell, Padraic Colum, Eric Gill, Paul Horgan, Mary Lavin, Marie Belloc

NOYES, ALRED (cont.)

Lowndes, Kathleen Norris, Alred Noyes,
Sheila Kaye-Smith, Sigrid Undset, and
Evelyn Waugh, to name only a few.

NOYES, JOHN HUMPHREY

NY —NEW YORK STATE LIBRARY, State
Education Bldg Annex, Washington Ave,
Albany, 12224.
Holdings: Cat
Notes: Strong collection of Oneida
Community publications.
NY —SYRACUSE UNIVERSITY
LIBRARIES, Ernest S Bird Library, George
Arents Research Library for Special
Collections, Syracuse, 13210. Carolyn A
Davis, Manuscripts Librn; Amy S Doherty,
University Archivist; Mark F Weimer, Rare
Book Librn
Holdings: Vols 180 Cat Pix
Notes: Extensive collection on Oneida
Community and John Humphrey Noyes.
Library has published *The Oneida
Community Collection in the Syracuse
University Library*, 1961.

NOYES, WILLIAM

IL —UNIVERSITY OF ILLINOIS,
URBANA/CHAMPAIGN, Library,
University Archives, 19 Library, 1408 W
Gregory Drive, Urbana, 61801. Maynard
Brichford, University Archivist
Holdings: Cat Mss Maps Pix Slides
Microforms
Notes: Papers, archival records, etc.

NOZZLES

IA —DELEVAN DIVISION OF COLT
INDUSTRIES INC, Engineering Library,
811 Fourth St, PO Box 100, West Des
Moines, 50265. G A Hartman, Librn
Holdings: Vols 2000 Cat Mss Slides
Microforms
Budget: $400
Notes: Incl liquid atomization, droplet size
measurement and representation, fuel
nozzles for combustors, and spray nozzles
for industrial and agricultural applications.

NUBIOLOGY

NY —BROOKLYN MUSEUM, Wilbour
Library of Egyptology, Eastern Parkway,
Brooklyn, 11238. Diane Guzman, Librn
Holdings: Vols (30,000) Cat Maps
Notes: The Wilbour Library of Egyptology
ranks as one of the world's finest, most
complete collections of works on all aspects
of the culture of Ancient Egypt (down to the
Islamic conquest). A card catalog records
authors, subjects, series and titles of all
books, periodicals and and 12,000
pamphlets. A description of the collection, as
of 1924, may be found in: William Burt
Cook, Jr, *Catalogue of the Egyptological
Library and other Books from the Collection
of the Late Charles Edwin Wilbour*
(Brooklyn, NY: Brooklyn Museum, 1924).
Middle Eastern art formerly included, now
transferred to the Brooklyn Museum.

NUCLEAR CHEMISTRY

CA —UNIVERSITY OF CALIFORNIA,
BERKELEY, Bancroft Library, Manuscripts
Division, Berkeley, 94720. James D Hart,
Dir
Notes: Extensive collections of papers and
archives relative to the history of modern
nuclear science.
CA —UNIVERSITY OF CALIFORNIA,
LIVERMORE, Lawrence Livermore
National Laboratory, Library, PO Box 5500,
Livermore, 94550. John B Verity, Library
Mgr
Holdings: Vols (160,000) Cat 16mm Films
Microforms
Budget: ($2,323,000)
Notes: The LLL library system includes a
central collection in physics, chemistry,
engineering, geology, mathematics, and

computer science; and branch holdings in
bio-medicine, environmental science, nuclear
chemistry, energy research, theoretical
physics, materials science, and nuclear
weapons. Collections include 160,000 books,
145,000 technical reports, 530,000 reports
on microfiche, and 3000 periodical
subscriptions. LLL libraries are not open to
the public. Unclassified materials may be
borrowed on interlibrary loan.
IL —ARGONNE NATIONAL
LABORATORY, Chemistry Branch Library,
9700 S Cass Ave, Argonne, 60439. Betty
Guttman, Librn
Notes: Incl 20,000 vols monographs, 190
current journals. Materials may be used by
the public in the library by prior
arrangement. Photocopies may be supplied
for interlibrary loan, for which a processing
and handling charge is made.
MD —UNIVERSITY OF MARYLAND,
White Memorial Library, College Park,
20742. Elizabeth W McElroy, Head
Holdings: Vols (48,000) Cat Microforms
Budget: ($193,000)
Notes: Current periodicals. Have own card
catalog, which is included also in the total
university catalog.
NM —UNIVERSITY OF CALIFORNIA, Los
Alamos National Laboratory, Libraries, PO
Box 1663, MSP 362, Los Alamos, 87545. J
Arthur Freed, Head Librn
Holdings: Vols (800,000) Cat Films
Microforms
Budget: ($700,000)
Notes: Incl 500,000 classified and
unclassified reports. There are 25 branch
libraries and a central collection. The
Medical Library contains about 40,000 vols
in the areas of biomedical research.
NY —UNIVERSITY OF ROCHESTER,
Carlson Library, Hutchison Hall, River
Campus, Rochester, 14627. Michael W
Poulin, Librn
Holdings: Vols (48,720) Cat Microforms
ON —ATOMIC ENERGY OF CANADA
LIMITED, Main Library, Technical
Information Branch, Chalk River Nuclear
Laboratories, Chalk River, K0J 1J0, Can.
Harry Greenshields, Chief Librn
Holdings: Vols (128,700) Microforms
Budget: ($662,400)
Notes: The Main Library, Atomic Energy of
Canada Limited, is the Canadian repository
for the literature of nuclear science and
technology. Its collections reflect both
fundamental and nuclear aspects of biology,
chemistry, electronics, engineering,
mathematics, computers, metallurgy, physics
and other specific areas of science involving
nuclear technology with special emphasis on
heavy water reactor systems. 512,000
research reports are available in paper copy
and microfiche form. Incl US DOE, INIS
and other offshore nuclear research reports.
386,000 microforms.

NUCLEAR ENERGY see Atomic Energy

NUCLEAR ENGINEERING

AL —TUSKEGEE INSTITUTE, School of
Engineering Library, Tuskegee Institute,
36088. Frances F Davis, Librn
Holdings: Vols 308 // Cat
Budget: $2000
CA —UNIVERSITY OF CALIFORNIA,
DAVIS, Physical Sciences Library, Davis,
95616. Scott Kennedy, Head
Notes: Collection covers aeronautical,
agricultural, chemical, civil, electrical,
mechanical, water science, hydrology,
nuclear reactor, extensive cold regions
collection in vertical file drawers, and
computer science engineering academic
programs. Good strength in journal runs.
CA —UNIVERSITY OF CALIFORNIA,
LIVERMORE, Lawrence Livermore
National Laboratory, Library, PO Box 5500,
Livermore, 94550. John B Verity, Library
Mgr
Holdings: Vols (160,000) Cat 16mm Films
Microforms
Budget: ($2,323,000)
Notes: The LLL library system includes a
central collection in physics, chemistry,

engineering, geology, mathematics, and
computer science; and branch holdings in
bio-medicine, environmental science, nuclear
chemistry, energy research, theoretical
physics, materials science, and nuclear
weapons. Collections include 160,000 books,
145,000 technical reports, 530,000 reports
on microfiche, and 3000 periodical
subscriptions. LLL libraries are not open to
the public. Unclassified materials may be
borrowed on interlibrary loan.
CA —UNIVERSITY OF CALIFORNIA, LOS
ANGELES, Engineering & Mathematical
Sciences Library, 405 Hilgard, Los Angeles,
90024. Rosalee I Wright, Librn
Holdings: Vols (180,000) Cat Microforms
Notes: Complete depository of unclassified
technical reports from AEC, ERDA, and
DOE; selected IAEA publications, NRC
dockets.
CA —R & D ASSOCIATES, Technical
Information Center, 4640 Admiralty Way,
PO Box 9695, Marina del Rey, 90291.
Margaret R Anderson, Mgr
Holdings: Vols (10,000) Cat Mss Maps
Microforms
Notes: Military arts and sciences, tactical
and strategic studies, and defense systems.
Incl 45,000 government contractor and
technical reports; and briefing charts
(transparencies).
GA —GEORGIA INSTITUTE OF
TECHNOLOGY, Price Gilbert Memorial
Library, 225 North Ave, Atlanta, 30332.
Edward Graham Roberts, Dir
Holdings: Vols (1,661,559) Cat Maps Slides
Microforms
Budget: ($1,383,302)
Notes: Incl (4,307,996) patents and (568,
490) government documents.
ID —EG&G, INEL Technical Library, 1776
Science Center, Idaho Falls, 83401. Brent
Jacobsen, Head Librn; Heather Redding, Ref
Librn
Holdings: Vols (33,000) Cat Microforms
Notes: Incl over 500,000 AEC, ERDA,
NRC, and foreign reports. Unclassified
materials may be used by the public in the
library by appointment or borrowed by
interlibrary loan. Incl 12,000 bound
documents, 520,000 microfiche, 400
periodical subscriptions.
IL —ARGONNE NATIONAL
LABORATORY, Reactor Science/
Engineering Branch Library, 9700 S Cass
Ave, Argonne, 60439. Marion Benson, Librn
Notes: Incl 10,000 vols monographs, 200
current journals, a comprehensive collection
of AEC, ERDA, DOE, and NRC scientific
and technical reports. Materials may be used
by the public in the library by prior
arrangement. Photocopies may be supplied
for interlibrary loan, for which a processing
and handling charge is made.
IL —UNIVERSITY OF ILLINOIS,
URBANA/CHAMPAIGN, Library, 221
Engineering Hall, Urbana, 61801. William
Mischo, Librn
Holdings: Vols (175,000) Cat Slides
Microforms
Notes: Incl 3500 periodicals. Collection
designed to serve teaching and research
programs. Supports instructional faculty
research. Also, 470 microfilm reels and 6000
microfiche sheets.
IN —PURDUE UNIVERSITY LIBRARIES,
Engineering Library, A A Potter
Engineering Center, West Lafayette, 47907.
Edwin D Posey, Engineering Librn
Holdings: Vols (225,178) Cat Maps
Audiotapes Microforms
Budget: ($300,000)
IA —IOWA STATE UNIVERSITY, Library,
Ames, 50011. Warren B Kuhn, Dean of
Library Services
Holdings: Cat Microforms
Notes: Extensive serial holdings.
MA —STONE & WEBSTER ENGINEERING
CORP, Technical Information Center,
Library, 245 Summer St, PO Box 2325,
Boston, 02107. Nancy M Pellini, Mgr
Holdings: Vols (10,000) Cat Pix Microforms
Notes: Also over 1200 periodicals. Extensive
vertical file collection, and 5 on-line system
for search.
MI —UNIVERSITY OF MICHIGAN, North
Engineering Library, 1002 I St, Ann Arbor,

NUCLEAR ENGINEERING (cont.)

48109. Maurita Holland, Librn
Holdings: Vols (60,000) Cat Microforms
Budget: ($60,000)
Notes: Formerly a depository for US AEC technical reports, the library still acquires technical reports on microfiche (approx 12,000 sheets per year) from the US DOE. As of 6/30/83, the library held 60,000 vols and 500,000 microforms (fiche and cards). The technical report collection, both full-size and microform, is uncataloged. A local "document catalog" lists reports by report number only.

NY —COLUMBIA UNIVERSITY LIBRARIES, Engineering Library, 422 Mudd Bldg, New York, 10027.
Holdings: Vols (177,000) Cat
Notes: All aspects of engineering--aeronautical, industrial mining, civil, chemical, mechanical, electrical, nuclear. Incl applied mathematics and applied physical sciences. Over (1,000,000) technical reports.

NY —ENGINEERING SOCIETIES LIBRARY, 345 E 47 St, New York, 10017. S Kirk Cabeen, Dir
Holdings: Vols 250,000 Cat Maps 16mm Films Microforms
Notes: One of the largest, most comprehensive engineering libraries in the world. Covers all engineering disciplines; particularly strong in electrical and electronic, mechanical, mining and metallurgical, petroleum, chemical, industrial, air conditioning and refrigeration engineering. Incl Wheeler Collection of early materials on magnetisn and electricity. 125,000 bound periodical volumes; 10,000 maps; 5000 serial subscriptions (many foreign-language). Virtually all materials abstracted in *Engineering Index* (1884-date) are incl in Library. Noncirculating, except to members of professional engineering societies which support the Library. See *Engineering Societies Library, New York, Classed Subject Catalog and Index* (Boston: G K Hall, 1963); and *Supplements*, 1-10, 1964-1973.

NC —NORTH CAROLINA STATE UNIVERSITY, D H Hill Library, Box 7111, Raleigh, 27695. I T Littleton, Dir
Holdings: Vols 1310 Cat
Budget: $1500
Notes: An AEC depository; library. Vol count does not incl AEC reports.

OH —UNIVERSITY OF CINCINNATI, Engineering Library, 880 Baldwin Hall, Cincinnati, 45221. Dorothy Furber Byers, Head
Holdings: Vols (50,000) Cat Videotapes Microforms
Budget: ($100,000)
Notes: Have NASA and DOE microfiche collections.

PA —FRANKLIN INSTITUTE LIBRARY, 20 & The Parkway, Philadelphia, 19103. Miriam Padusis, Dir; Charles Wilt, Readers Servs Librn
Holdings: Vols (300,000) Cat Maps Pix Microforms

PA —PENNSYLVANIA STATE UNIVERSITY, Engineering Library, 325 Hammond St, University Park, 16802. Tom Conkling, Librn
Holdings: Vols (60,000) Microforms
Notes: This collection includes substantial microform holdings and extensive runs of periodicals.

TN —TENNESSEE VALLEY AUTHORITY (TVA), Technical Library, 400 W Summit Hill Dr, E2 B7, Knoxville, 37902. Jesse C Mills, Chief Librn
Holdings: Vols (106,900) Cat Mss Maps Pix Audiotapes Microforms
Budget: ($2,025,000)
Notes: The Technical Library Headquarters Staff (order, cataloging, information, and administration) is located in Knoxville, Tenn. In addition there are branch libraries in Knoxville, Norris, and Chattanooga, Tennessee, and Muscle Schoals, Alabama.

TN —US DEPT OF ENERGY, Technical Information Center, PO Box 62, Oak Ridge,

37831. Joseph G Coyne, Manager
Notes: TIC manages the technical information program of the DOE through which the DOE scientific research and development information is disseminated for offical and public use. TIC is also responsible for producing the DOE Energy Data Base and a number of abstracting and indexing journals which provide worldwide coverage of the energy literature. Cataloged holdings incl 500,000 reports, 94,000 engineering drawings and 10,000 books. 800 journal titles are received, with most not being retained.

WA —PUGET SOUND NAVAL SHIPYARD, Engineering Library, Code 202.5, Bremerton, 98314. Carol J Swanson, Engineering Librn
Holdings: Vols (500) Cat

WA —BATTELLE-PACIFIC NORTHWEST LABORTORIES, Technical Library, PO Box 999, Richland, 99352. Wayne Snyder, Librn
Holdings: Vols (50,000) Cat Microforms
Budget: ($500,000)
Notes: Holdings: 50,000 books; 35,000 bound periodical volumes; 200,000 technical reoports; 200,000 technical reports in microform. Subscriptions: 1800 journals and other serials. Services: interlibrary loans; literature searching; translation; library open to public with restrictions.

ON —ATOMIC ENERGY OF CANADA LIMITED, Main Library, Technical Information Branch, Chalk River Nuclear Laboratories, Chalk River, K0J 1J0, Can. Harry Greenshields, Chief Librn
Holdings: Vols (128,700) Microforms
Budget: ($662,400)
Notes: The Main Library, Atomic Energy of Canada Limited, is the Canadian repository for the literature of nuclear science and technology. Its collections reflect both fundamental and nuclear aspects of biology, chemistry, electronics, engineering, mathematics, computers, metallurgy, physics and other specific areas of science involving nuclear technology with special emphasis on heavy water reactor systems. 512,000 research reports are available in paper copy and microfiche form. Incl US DOE, INIS and other offshore nuclear research reports. 386,000 microforms.

NUCLEAR FUEL CYCLE

IL —ARGONNE NATIONAL LABORATORY, Chemical Engineering Branch Library, 9700 S Cass Ave, Argonne, 60439. John P Frazier III, Librn
Notes: Incl 9000 vols monographs, 115 current journals, substantial collection of scientific and technical reports. Materials may be used by the public in the library by prior arrangement. Photocopies may be supplied for interlibrary loan, for which a processing and handling charge is made.

NUCLEAR MEDICINE

CA —UNIVERSITY OF CALIFORNIA, LIVERMORE, Lawrence Livermore National Laboratory, Library, PO Box 5500, Livermore, 94550. John B Verity, Library Mgr
Holdings: Vols (160,000) Cat 16mm Films Microforms
Budget: ($2,323,000)
Notes: The LLL library system includes a central collection in physics, chemistry, engineering, geology, mathematics, and computer science; and branch holdings in bio-medicine, environmental science, nuclear chemistry, energy research, theoretical physics, materials science, and nuclear weapons. Collections include 160,000 books, 145,000 technical reports, 530,000 reports on microfiche, and 3000 periodical subscriptions. LLL libraries are not open to the public. Unclassified materials may be borrowed on interlibrary loan.

MD —US ARMED FORCES RADIOBIOLOGY RESEARCH INSTITUTE, Naval Medical Command, Bethesda, 20014. Nannette M Pope, Head, Library Division
Holdings: Vols (50,000)
Budget: ($150,000)
Notes: Collection consists of monographs,

technical reports, serials, and microfiche related to radiation effects on human and animal biology.

MA —MASSACHUSETTS INSTITUTE OF TECHNOLOGY, Institute Archives, Special Collections, Cambridge, 02139.
Holdings: Mss
Notes: The Robley Evans papers, etc.

NM —UNIVERSITY OF CALIFORNIA, Los Alamos National Laboratory, Libraries, PO Box 1663, MSP 362, Los Alamos, 87545. J Arthur Freed, Head Librn
Holdings: Vols (800,000) Cat Films Microforms
Budget: ($700,000)
Notes: Incl 500,000 classified and unclassified reports. There are 25 branch libraries and a central collection. The Medical Library contains about 40,000 vols in the areas of biomedical research.

RI —MIRIAM HOSPITAL MEDICAL LIBRARY, 164 Summit Ave, Providence, 02906. Ann LeClaire, Dir of Library Services
Holdings: Cat Cassettes
Notes: Special collection on the renal system with emphasis on kidney transplantation and dialysis.

TX —US AIR FORCE, School of Aerospace Medicine, Strughold Aeromedical Library, Brooks AFB, 78235. Fred W Todd, Chief Librn
Holdings: Vols (199,188) Cat Mss Maps Pix Microforms
Budget: ($499,000)
Notes: Aviation and space medicine and physiology, including the physiological effects of altitude and decompression. Biomedical and and human engineering. Military medicine, including chemical and biological warfare. Emergency medicine in both professional and technical areas. Radiobiology, including atomic medicine, nuclear medicine, and space radiation. Material not oriented to the School of Aerospace Medicine are excluded. Incl also 45,787 microforms and 142,371 technical documents.

TX —UNIVERSITY OF TEXAS, M D Anderson Hospital and Tumor Institute, Research Medical Library, Texas Medical Center, Houston, 77030. Marie Harvin, Research Medical Librn
Holdings: Vols (48,000) Cat
Notes: Library attempts to collect every publication in all languages related to clinical cancer (or oncology). Aim is an exhaustive collection in this field. Collect heavily (research level) in pathology, radiology, nuclear medicine, genetics and cell biology.

ON —ATOMIC ENERGY OF CANADA LIMITED, Main Library, Technical Information Branch, Chalk River Nuclear Laboratories, Chalk River, K0J 1J0, Can. Harry Greenshields, Chief Librn
Holdings: Vols (128,700) Microforms
Budget: ($662,400)
Notes: The Main Library, Atomic Energy of Canada Limited, is the Canadian repository for the literature of nuclear science and technology. Its collections reflect both fundamental and nuclear aspects of biology, chemistry, electronics, engineering, mathematics, computers, metallurgy, physics and other specific areas of science involving nuclear technology with special emphasis on heavy water reactor systems. 512,000 research reports are available in paper copy and microfiche form. Incl US DOE, INIS and other offshore nuclear research reports. 386,000 microforms.

NUCLEAR PARTICLES see Particles (Nuclear Physics)

NUCLEAR PHYSICS

CA —UNIVERSITY OF CALIFORNIA, BERKELEY, Bancroft Library, Manuscripts Division, Berkeley, 94720. James D Hart, Dir
Holdings: // Cat Mss
Notes: The papers and correspondence of EO Lawrence, the eminent nuclear physicist, who was a central figure in the founding of

NUCLEAR PHYSICS (cont.)

the Berkeley Radiation Laboratory and the creation of the cyclotron. Approximately 50 cartons of mss, complemented by oral histories with laboratory personnel.

CA —UNIVERSITY OF CALIFORNIA, DAVIS, Physical Sciences Library, Davis, 95616. Scott Kennedy, Head
Holdings: Vols (17,372) Cat Microforms
Notes: Strong in journal runs and reference materials. Nuclear physics represented by microcopy depository collection of US Dept of Energy (AEC and ERDA) technical reports (est 462,574). Selected NASA reports on microfiche since 1975. Access to online information bases.

CA —UNIVERSITY OF CALIFORNIA, LIVERMORE, Lawrence Livermore National Laboratory, Library, PO Box 5500, Livermore, 94550. John B Verity, Library Mgr
Holdings: Vols (160,000) Cat 16mm Films Microforms
Budget: ($2,323,000)
Notes: The LLL library system includes a central collection in physics, chemistry, engineering, geology, mathematics, and computer science; and branch holdings in bio-medicine, environmental science, nuclear chemistry, energy science, theoretical physics, materials science, and nuclear weapons. Collections include 160,000 books, 145,000 technical reports, 530,000 reports on microfiche, and 3000 periodical subscriptions. LLL libraries are not open to the public. Unclassified materials may be borrowed on interlibrary loan.

CA —UNIVERSITY OF CALIFORNIA, LOS ANGELES, Physics Library, 213 Kinsey Hall, Los Angeles, 90024. J Wally Pegram, Librn
Holdings: Vols (37,000) Cat
Notes: UCLA physics theses; current SLAC preprints in high-energy physics. (592) current serials subscriptions.

ID —EG&G, INEL Technical Library, 1776 Science Center, Idaho Falls, 83401. Brent Jacobsen, Head Librn; Heather Redding, Ref Librn
Holdings: Vols (33,000) Cat Microforms
Notes: Incl over 500,000 AEC, ERDA, NRC, and foreign reports. Unclassified materials may be used by the public in the library by appointment or borrowed by interlibrary loan. Incl 12,000 bound documents, 520,000 microfiche, 400 periodical subscriptions.

IL —UNIVERSITY OF ILLINOIS, URBANA/CHAMPAIGN, Chemistry Library, 255 Noyes Laboratory, Urbana, 61801. Lucille M Wert, Chemistry Librn; Susan Eilering, Asst Chemistry Librn
Holdings: Vols (150,000) Cat Microforms
Notes: Collection incl monographs, treatises and serials covering all the fields of chemistry.

IA —IOWA STATE UNIVERSITY, Library, Ames, 50011. Warren B Kuhn, Dean of Library Services
Holdings: Cat Microforms
Notes: Extensive serial holdings.

MA —MASSACHUSETTS INSTITUTE OF TECHNOLOGY, Institute Archives, Special Collections, Cambridge, 02139.
Holdings: Mss
Notes: The Robley Evans papers, etc.

NM —UNIVERSITY OF CALIFORNIA, Los Alamos National Laboratory, Libraries, PO Box 1663, MSP 362, Los Alamos, 87545. J Arthur Freed, Head Librn
Holdings: Vols (800,000) Cat Films Microforms
Budget: ($700,000)
Notes: Incl 500,000 classified and unclassified reports. There are 25 branch libraries and a central collection. The Medical Library contains about 40,000 vols in the areas of biomedical research.

NY —COLUMBIA UNIVERSITY LIBRARIES, Physics Library, 810 Pupin, 535 W 114 St, New York, 10027. Mary Kay, Librn
Holdings: Vols 26,000 Cat
Notes: Theoretical aspects of physics, particularly atomic and nuclear physics.

NY —ENGINEERING SOCIETIES LIBRARY, 345 E 47 St, New York, 10017. S Kirk Cabeen, Dir
Holdings: Vols 250,000 Cat Maps 16mm Films Microforms
Notes: One of the largest, most comprehensive engineering libraries in the world. Covers all engineering disciplines; particularly strong in electrical and electronic, mechanical, mining and metallurgical, petroleum, chemical, industrial, air conditioning and refrigeration engineering. Incl Wheeler Collection of early materials on magnetisn and electricity. 125,000 bound periodical volumes; 10,000 maps; 5000 serial subscriptions (many foreign-languag•). Virtually all materials abstracted in *Engineering Index* (1884-date) are incl in Library. Noncirculating, except to members of professional engineering societies which support the Library. See *Engineering Societies Library, New York, Classed Subject Catalog and Index* (Boston: G K Hall, 1963); and *Supplements*, 1-10, 1964-1973.

NY —UNIVERSITY OF ROCHESTER, Physics-Optics-Astronomy Library, Bausch & Lomb Bldg, River Campus, Rochester, 14627. Loretta Caren, Librn
Holdings: Vols (20,000) Cat
Notes: Strong research level collection in the field and related areas. Also, at Laser Laboratory, 1000 vols on nuclear fusion and applied laser technology.

PA —FRANKLIN INSTITUTE LIBRARY, Dept of Historical Programs, 20th St and Parkway, Philadelphia, 19103.
Notes: The atomic physics research records of the Bartol Foundation (1923-1940).

PA —UNIVERSITY OF PITTSBURGH, Physics Library, 208 Engineering Hall, Pittsburgh, 15260. Paul J Kobulnicky, Physical Sciences Librn
Holdings: Vols (25,000) Cat Microforms
Budget: ($100,000)
Notes: The Physics Library collection is both a graduate student research-level collection in basic experimental and theorecical physics with emphasis on solid-state, nuclear, upper-atmosphere, space, and crystallography, and also a collection in the earth and planetary sciences, serving both graduate and undergraduate students. The collection is cataloged in both the University of Pittsburgh, Hillman Library union catalog and in a seperate catalog in the Physics Library.

TN —US DEPT OF ENERGY, Technical Information Center, PO Box 62, Oak Ridge, 37831. Joseph G Coyne, Manager
Notes: TIC manages the technical information program of the DOE through which the DOE scientific research and development information is disseminated for offical and public use. TIC is also responsible for producing the DOE Energy Data Base and a number of abstracting and indexing journals which provide worldwide coverage of the energy literature. Cataloged holdings incl 500,000 reports, 94,000 engineering drawings and 10,000 books. 800 journal titles are received, with most not being retained.

WA —BATTELLE-PACIFIC NORTHWEST LABORTORIES, Technical Library, PO Box 999, Richland, 99352. Wayne Snyder, Librn
Holdings: Vols (50,000) Cat Microforms
Budget: ($500,000)
Notes: Holdings 50,000 books; 35,000 bound periodical volumes; 200,000 technical reports; 200,000 technical reports in microforms. Subscriptions; 1800 journals and other serials. Services: interlibrary loans; literature searching; translation; library open to public with restrictions.

ON —ATOMIC ENERGY OF CANADA LIMITED, Main Library, Technical Information Branch, Chalk River Nuclear Laboratories, Chalk River, K0J 1J0, Can. Harry Greenshields, Chief Librn
Holdings: Vols (128,700) Microforms
Budget: ($662,400)
Notes: The Main Library, Atomic Energy of Canada Limited, is the Canadian repository for the literature of nuclear science and

technology. Its collections reflect both fundamental and nuclear aspects of biology, chemistry, electronics, engineering, mathematics, computers, metallurgy, physics and other specific areas of science involving nuclear technology with special emphasis on heavy water reactor systems. 512,000 research reports are available in paper copy and microfiche form. Incl US DOE, INIS and other offshore nuclear research reports. 386,000 microforms.

NUCLEAR PHYSICS—RESEARCH see Nuclear Research

NUCLEAR RADIATION

MD —NATIONAL LIBRARY OF MEDICINE, 8600 Rockville Pike, Bethesda, 20209. Harold M Schoolinam, Actg Dir
Budget: ($46,400)

OH —WILMINGTON COLLEGE, Peace Resource Center, Hiroshima/Nagasaki Memorial Collection, Pyle Center Box 1183, Wilmington, 45177. Helen Redding, Librn
Holdings: Vols Pix Slides Audiotapes Videotapes Film VF
Notes: Extensive collection of materials on the Hiroshima and Nagasaki atomic bombings and on nuclear issues in general.

NUCLEAR REACTORS

ID —EG&G, INEL Technical Library, 1776 Science Center, Idaho Falls, 83401. Brent Jacobsen, Head Librn; Heather Redding, Ref Librn
Holdings: Vols (33,000) Cat Microforms
Notes: Incl over 500,000 AEC, ERDA, NRC, and foreign reports. Unclassified materials may be used by the public in the library by appointment or borrowed by interlibrary loan. Incl 12,000 bound documents, 520,000 microfiche, 400 periodical subscriptions.

IL —ARGONNE NATIONAL LABORATORY, Library, Technical Information Services Dept, 9700 Cass Ave, Argonne, 60439. Hillis L Griffin, Dir
Notes: The ANL library system consists of eight branch libraries with centralized processing services. The entire collection numbers 70,000 monographic titles, 3700 journal titles, and over 1 million scientific and technical reports. Materials may be used by the public in the library by prior arrangement. Photocopies may be supplied for interlibrary loan, for which a processing and handling charge is made. The branch libraries are: Biological and Medical Research; Chemical Engineering; Chemistry; Mathematics/Physics/Computer Science; Reactor Science/Engineering; Materials Science; Solid State Physics; High-Energy Physics/Environmental Sciences.

IL —ARGONNE NATIONAL LABORATORY, Reactor Science/ Engineering Branch Library, 9700 S Cass Ave, Argonne, 60439. Marion Benson, Librn
Notes: Incl 10,000 vols monographs, 200 current journals, a comprehensive collection of AEC, ERDA, DOE, and NRC scientific and technical reports. Materials may be used by the public in the library by prior arrangement. Photocopies may be supplied for interlibrary loan, for which a processing and handling charge is made.

KY —UNIVERSITY OF KENTUCKY, Robert E Shaver Library of Engineering, 355 Anderson Hall, Lexington, 40506. Russell H Powell, Engineering Librn
Holdings: Vols (48,000) Cat Microforms

NM —UNIVERSITY OF CALIFORNIA, Los Alamos National Laboratory, Libraries, PO Box 1663, MSP 362, Los Alamos, 87545. J Arthur Freed, Head Librn
Holdings: Vols (800,000) Cat Films Microforms
Budget: ($700,000)
Notes: Incl 500,000 classified and unclassified reports. There are 25 branch libraries and a central collection. The Medical Library contains about 40,000 vols in the areas of biomedical research.

†NY —COLUMBIA UNIVERSITY LIBRARIES, Butler Library, Rare Book and

NUCLEAR REACTORS (cont.)

Manuscript Library, 535 W 114 St, New York, 10027.
Notes: Papers of the Citizen's Committee for the Protection of the Environment, Ossining, NY, whose activities are centered on the environmental hazards of Consolidated Edison's Indian Point nuclear power plants.

TN —US DEPT OF ENERGY, Technical Information Center, PO Box 62, Oak Ridge, 37831. Joseph G Coyne, Manager
Notes: TIC manages the technical information program of the DOE through which the DOE scientific research and development information is disseminated for offical and public use. TIC is also responsible for producing the DOE Energy Data Base and a number of abstracting and indexing journals which provide worldwide coverage of the energy literature. Cataloged holdings incl 500,000 reports, 94,000 engineering drawings and 10,000 books. 800 journal titles are received, with most not being retained.

ON —ATOMIC ENERGY OF CANADA LIMITED, Main Library, Technical Information Branch, Chalk River Nuclear Laboratories, Chalk River, K0J 1J0, Can. Harry Greenshields, Chief Librn
Holdings: Vols (128,700) Microforms
Budget: ($662,400)
Notes: The Main Library, Atomic Energy of Canada Limited, is the Canadian repository for the literature of nuclear science and technology. Its collections reflect both fundamental and nuclear aspects of biology, chemistry, electronics, engineering, mathematics, computers, metallurgy, physics and other specific areas of science involving nuclear technology with special emphasis on heavy water reactor systems. 512,000 research reports are available in paper copy and microfiche form. Incl US DOE, INIS and other offshore nuclear research reports. 386,000 microforms.

NUCLEAR REACTORS—ACCIDENTS

DC —NATIONAL ARCHIVES AND RECORDS SERVICE, Civil Archives Division, Washington, 20408.
Notes: Records of the President's Commission on the Accident at Three Mile Island (May-December 1979).

NUCLEAR RESEARCH

CA —UNIVERSITY OF CALIFORNIA, LIVERMORE, Lawrence Livermore National Laboratory, Library, PO Box 5500, Livermore, 94550. John B Verity, Library Mgr
Holdings: Vols (160,000) Cat 16mm Films Microforms
Budget: ($2,323,000)
Notes: The LLL library system includes a central collection in physics, chemistry, engineering, geology, mathematics, and computer science; and branch holdings in bio-medicine, environmental science, nuclear chemistry, energy research, theoretical physics, materials science, and nuclear weapons. Collections include 160,000 books, 145,000 technical reports, 530,000 reports on microfiche, and 3000 periodical subscriptions. LLL libraries are not open to the public. Unclassified materials may be borrowed on interlibrary loan.

IL —ARGONNE NATIONAL LABORATORY, Library, Technical Information Services Dept, 9700 Cass Ave, Argonne, 60439. Hillis L Griffin, Dir
Notes: The ANL library system consists of eight branch libraries with centralized processing services. The entire collection numbers 70,000 monographic titles, 3700 journal titles, and over 1 million scientific and technical reports. Materials may be used by the public in the library by prior arrangement. Photocopies may be supplied for interlibrary loan, for which a processing and handling charge is made. The branch libraries are: Biological and Medical

Research; Chemical Engineering; Chemistry; Mathematics/Physics/Computer Science; Reactor Science/Engineering; Materials Science; Solid State Physics; High-Energy Physics/Environmental Sciences.

MO —UNIVERSITY OF MISSOURI-COLUMBIA, Research Park Library, 131 Dalton Research Center, Columbia, 65211. Janice Dysart, Librn
Holdings: Uncat Microforms
Notes: An almost complete collection of the AEC-ERDA-DOE research and development reports, as well as reports from foreign organizatons with which AEC-ERDA-DOE had/has agreements for technical cooperation, covering the years 1948 to date. The collection consists primarily of 750,000 microcards and microfiche, with some hard copies supplied from the UMC Library Government Documents collection. The collection is indexed in *Nuclear Science Abstracts, Energy Research Abstracts,* and *INIS Atomindex.*

NM —UNIVERSITY OF CALIFORNIA, Los Alamos National Laboratory, Libraries, PO Box 1663, MSP 362, Los Alamos, 87545. J Arthur Freed, Head Librn
Holdings: Vols (800,000) Cat Films Microforms
Budget: ($700,000)
Notes: Incl 500,000 classified and unclassified reports. There are 25 branch libraries and a central collection. The Medical Library contains about 40,000 vols in the areas of biomedical research.

PA —FRANKLIN INSTITUTE LIBRARY, Dept of Historical Programs, 20th St and Parkway, Philadelphia, 19103.
Notes: The atomic physics research records of the Bartol Foundation (1923-1940).

WA —BATTELLE-PACIFIC NORTHWEST LABORTORIES, Technical Library, PO Box 999, Richland, 99352. Wayne Snyder, Librn
Holdings: Vols (50,000) Cat Microforms
Budget: ($500,000)
Notes: Holdings: 50,000 books, 35,000 bound periodical volumes; 200,000 technical reports; 200,000 technical reports in microform. Subscriptions: 1800 journals and other serials. Services: interlibrary loans; literature searching; translation; library open to public with restrictions.

ON —ATOMIC ENERGY OF CANADA LIMITED, Main Library, Technical Information Branch, Chalk River Nuclear Laboratories, Chalk River, K0J 1J0, Can. Harry Greenshields, Chief Librn
Holdings: Vols (128,700) Microforms
Budget: ($662,400)
Notes: The Main Library, Atomic Energy of Canada Limited, is the Canadian repository for the literature of nuclear science and technology. Its collections reflect both fundamental and nuclear aspects of biology, chemistry, electronics, engineering, mathematics, computers, metallurgy, physics and other specific areas of science involving nuclear technology with special emphasis on heavy water reactor systems. 512,000 research reports are available in paper copy and microfiche form. Incl US DOE, INIS and other offshore nuclear research reports. 386,000 microforms.

NUCLEAR SCIENCE ADVISORY COMMITTEE

CA —CALIFORNIA INSTITUTE OF TECHNOLOGY, Robert A Millikan Memorial Library, Archives, 1201 E California Blvd, Pasadena, 91125. Judith R Goodstein, Archivist
Notes: Correspondence and printed matter of William A Fowler, Nuclear Science Advisory Committee, 1977-1980; the National Academy of Science's Astronomy Survey Committee, 1979-1980; the National Science Foundation's Astronomy Advisory Committee, 1978-1979; and proceedings of the Pugwash Conference for the years 1960, 1962-1963.

NUCLEAR TECHNOLOGY

CA —GENERAL ELECTRIC CO, ANTO, Library, PO Box 3508, Sunnyvale, 94088.

Dorothy A Hutson, Mgr Information Servs
Holdings: Vols 3000
Notes: Advanced nuclear technology, liquid metals, properties of materials, metallurgy. Incl 150 journal subscriptions, 30,000 reports.

ID —EG&G, INEL Technical Library, 1776 Science Center, Idaho Falls, 83401. Brent Jacobsen, Head Librn; Heather Redding, Ref Librn
Holdings: Vols (33,000) Cat Microforms
Notes: Energy research and development included in libraries collection. Incl over 500,000 AEC, ERDA, NRC, and foreign reports. Unclassified materials may be used by the public in the library by appointment or borrowed by interlibrary loan. Incl 12,000 bound documents, 520,000 microfiche, 400 periodical subscriptions.

IL —ARGONNE NATIONAL LABORATORY, Chemical Engineering Branch Library, 9700 S Cass Ave, Argonne, 60439. John P Frazier III, Librn
Notes: Nuclear fuel cycle. Incl 9000 vols monographs, 115 current journals, substantial collection of scientific and technical reports. Materials may be used by the public in the library by prior arrangement. Photocopies may be supplied for interlibrary loan, for which a processing and handling charge is made.

NUCLEAR WEAPONS see Atomic Weapons

NUCLEONS see Particles (Nuclear Physics)

NUCLEUS OF THE ATOM see Nuclear Physics

NUGENT, FRANK

MA —BOSTON UNIVERSITY, Mugar Memorial Library, Special Collections Dept, 771 Commonwealth Ave, Boston, 02215. Howard B Gotlieb, Dir
Holdings: Mss //
Notes: Mss, correspondence, etc collected in depth incl publications by or about.

NUMBER GAMES see Mathematical Recreations

NUMBER STUDY see Numbers, Theory of

NUMBER THEORY see Numbers, Theory of

NUMBERS, SACRED see Symbolism of Numbers

NUMBERS, THEORY OF

RI —BROWN UNIVERSITY, John Hay Library, 20 Prospect St, Providence, 02912. Mark N Brown, Cur Mss
Notes: The Royal Vale Heath Collection of about 200 of his designs, drawings, models, ocular, and verbal descriptions of simultaneous solutions to linear Diophantine equations in such examples as magic squares, Platonic solids, etc. These curious designs often were devised as talismans in ancient India and were first developed as mathematical problems by the Chinese.

NUMERICAL ANALYSIS LABORATORIES see Computation Laboratories

NUMERICAL CALCULATIONS

CA —STANFORD UNIVERSITY LIBRARIES, Mathematical & Computer Sciences Library, Stanford, 94305. Harry Llull, Branch Librn
Holdings: Vols (42,000) Cat Microforms
Notes: There is a computer-listed keyword index to technical reports (about 20,000 items).

NUMEROLOGY

IL —UNIVERSITY OF ILLINOIS, URBANA/CHAMPAIGN, Library,

NUMEROLOGY (cont.)

University Archives, 19 Library, 1408 W Gregory Drive, Urbana, 61801. Maynard Brichford, University Archivist
Holdings: Vols (5000) Cat
Budget: ($7000)
Notes: The Mandeville Collection in Parapsychology and Occult Sciences. Titles in the Merten J Mandeville Collection are purchased by funds from an endowment provided specifically for the collection on its establishment in 1966 by Merten J Mandeville, Professor Emeritus of Management, who donated 400 vols from his personal library as the nucleus of the collection. There are currently about 5000 titles in the collection, supplemented by related materials in the general collection. Topics include astrology, extrasensory perception, yoga, magic, satanism, faith healing, hypnosis, Eastern religions, witchcraft, fortune telling, reincarnation, flying saucers, ghosts, dreams, numerology, graphology, and mysticism. Biographies and reference books are a part of the collection as are journals devoted to the scientific study of parapsychology.

NUMISMATICS

CA —UNIVERSITY OF CALIFORNIA, LOS ANGELES, Research Library, Medieval and Renaissance Collection, 405 Hilgard Ave, Los Angeles, 90024. Edward Shreeves, Chairman, Bibliographers Group; Frances K Zeitlin, Medievan and Renaissance Bibliographer
Holdings: Vols 5000 Cat
Notes: Incl Edward Gans Numismatic Library. Emphasis on Western Europe from antiquity to 1600. Strong in periodicals and auction catalogs.

CA —LINCOLN MEMORIAL SHRINE, A K Smiley Public Library, 125 W Vine St, Redlands, 92373. Larry E Burgess, Archivist
Holdings: Vols (3000) Cat Mss Maps Pix Slides Phonorecords 16mm Films Microforms
Budget: ($18,000)
Notes: One of the larger collections on Lincoln and his times. Incl broadsides, letters, prints, campaign badges, stamps, coins, medals; bust, by George Grey Bernard. Endowment of Watchorn Lincoln Memorial Association. There is an additional pamphlet collection of more than 3000 pieces; an extensive philately collection incl first-day covers, commemorative and foreign issues, and Civil War envelopes.

CO —UNIVERSITY OF COLORADO, Libraries, Special Collections, Boulder, 80309. Nora J Quinlan, Head
Notes: Dickson H Leavens Collection. Over 750 vols and 500 binders of material (incl clippings and pamphlets) related to the history of silver money. An extensive and all-encompassing collection on the subject.

CO —AMERICAN NUMISMATIC ASSOCIATION LIBRARY, 818 N Cascade Ave, Colorado Springs, 80903. Nancy W Green, Librn
Holdings: Vols (20,000) Cat Slides
Notes: One of the largest numismatic libraries, the collection incl books, periodicals and auction catalogs on coins and coin collecting, medals, tokens, military orders and decorations, paper money, primitive money, banks and banking, seals and scarabs. ANA publishes a classified subject catalog of its collection and is open to the public for research and reference services. Only members may check books out.

CT —YALE UNIVERSITY, Box 1603A, Yale Station, New Haven, 06520.
Holdings: Vols Cat

DC —HARVARD UNIVERSITY, Dumbarton Oaks, Research Library, 1703 32nd St NW, Washington, 20007. Irene Vaslef, Librn
Notes: Roman and Byzantine.

DC —SMITHSONIAN INSTITUTION LIBRARIES, National Museum of American History Branch, Washington, 20560. Rhoda S Ratner, Branch Librn
Holdings: (7700) Cat Maps Pix

FL —UNIVERSITY OF MIAMI, School of Medicine, Louis Calder Memorial Library, PO Box 520875, Miami, 33152. Henry L Lemkau, Jr, Dir
Holdings: Vols (127,843) Cat Mss Maps Pix Slides Phonorecords Audiotapes Videotapes 16mm Films Filmstrips Microforms
Budget: ($915,000)
Notes: Ophthalmology Branch Library of 6969 vols incl in total count; University of Miami School of Medicine dissertations; 209 medical medallions; physicians' bookplates; postage stamps with medical themes.

IL —BALZEKAS MUSEUM OF LITHUANIAN CULTURE, Research Library, 4012 S Archer Ave, Chicago, 60632. Jurgis Kasakaitis, Head Librn
Holdings: Vols 15,000 Cat Maps Pix Slides Phonorecords
Notes: Incl folklore, art, social life and customs, history, literature, poetry, anthropology, numismatics, armor, etc. All books published in Lithuanian, some in English on Lithuanian subjects. Incl newspaper clippings.

IL —UNIVERSITY OF ILLINOIS, URBANA/CHAMPAIGN, Library, Classics Library, 419A Main Library, Urbana, 61801. Suzanne N Griffiths, Librn
Holdings: Vols (10,000) Cat
Notes: Ancient history section of Classics Library is strong in numismatics and in inscription materials; also incl ancient archaeology.

KY —KENTUCKY WESLEYAN COLLEGE LIBRARY, 3000 Frederica, Owensboro, 42301. Stuart Stiffler, Dir
Notes: The Dr and Mrs M David Orrahood Collection.

LA —R W NORTON ART GALLERY, Library, 4747 Creswell Ave, Shreveport, 71106. Jerry M Bloomer, Librn
Holdings: Vols 35 Cat

MD —JOHNS HOPKINS UNIVERSITY, Milton S Eisenhower Library, Special Collections, John Work Garrett Library, 4545 N Charles St, Baltimore, 21210. Jane Katz, Garrett Librn
Holdings: Vols 1600 Cat Coins
Notes: Very complete collection for identification of old coins.

MA —HARVARD UNIVERSITY LIBRARY, Cambridge, 02138.
Holdings: Cat

MO —WASHINGTON UNIVERSITY, Art & Architecture Library, Saint Louis, 63130. Imre Meszaros, Librn
Holdings: Vols 550 Cat
Notes: The Wulfing Collection. Separate catalog available. Incl books and coins.

NE —BOYS TOWN PHILAMATIC CENTER, Box One, Boys Town, 68010. Ivan E Sawyer, Asst Cur
Holdings: Vols 2000

NE —OMAHA PUBLIC LIBRARY, Omaha, 68102. Michael Phipps, Dir
Holdings: Vols 500 Cat
Notes: Incl the Byron Reed Library, approx 250 titles. Books in this collection have special cards in the main catalog. Important items in the collection incl 19th century vols of the *American Journal of Numismatics*, *Coin Collectors' Journal*, and *Numismatic Chronicle*. Also significant are early auction catalogs and medallic histories.

NJ —NEWARK MUSEUM LIBRARY, 49 Washington St, PO Box 540, Newark, 07101. Margaret DiSalvi, Librn
Holdings: Vols 250 Cat

NY —AMERICAN NUMISMATIC SOCIETY LIBRARY, Broadway between 155 & 156 Sts, New York, 10032. Francis D Campbell Jr, Chief Librn
Holdings: Vols (50,000) Cat Mss Maps Pix Slides 16mm Films Microforms
Budget: ($6000)
Notes: Incl materials devoted to coins, medals, decorations, orders, tokens, paper money, seals, heraldry. Aids materials incl history, economic history, art history, archaeology, inscriptions and a number of encyclopedias and biographical dictionaries. Dictionary card catalog provides access to the materials: *Dictionary Catalogue of the Library of the American Numismatic Society*. (Boston: G K Hall, 1962). 6 vols

and vol listing the auction catalogs in our collection; *First Supplement: 1962-1967; Second Supplement: 1968-1972; Third Supplement: 1973-1977* (Boston: G K Hall, 1967, 1973, 1978). Noncirculating.

NC —DUKE UNIVERSITY, William R Perkins Library, Durham, 27706. Elvin E Strowd, University Librn
Notes: The Flowers Collection of Southern Americana currently consists of 4,300,500 items. Additions are ongoing. Included in this collection are several types of materials, which are housed in appropriate sections of the library. The various types of materials are: manuscripts, books, pamphlets, maps, music, broadsides, newspapers, photographs, engravings, prints and memorabilia.

PA —LUTHERAN THEOLOGICAL SEMINARY, Krauth Memorial Library, 7301 Germantown Ave, Philadelphia, 19119. Rev David J Wartluft, Dir Librn
Holdings: Cat
Notes: The Otto Louis Schreiber Collection of Martin Luther and the Reformation in Numismatic Art. Also limited items in Melanchton, Johann Sebastian Bach, and Anti-papal medals. This is most complete collection on the subject in America--1000 items. A printed descriptive catalog is available.

WI —MILWAUKEE PUBLIC LIBRARY, 814 W Wisconsin Ave, Milwaukee, 53233. Donald J Sager, City Librn
Holdings: Vols 6240 Cat
Notes: Milwaukee Public Library is the major area resource in this field, with the exception of Graeco-Roman numismatics.

ON —METROPOLITAN TORONTO LIBRARY, Fine Arts Dept, 789 Yonge St, Toronto, M4W 2G8, Can. Alan Suddon, Head
Holdings: Vols (42,000) Cat Pix Microforms
Notes: Extensive collection.

NUNEZ ALONSO, ALEJANDRO

MA —BOSTON UNIVERSITY, Mugar Memorial Library, Special Collections Dept, 771 Commonwealth Ave, Boston, 02215. Howard B Gotlieb, Dir
Holdings: Cat Mss
Notes: Mss, correspondence, etc collected in depth; incl publications by or about.

NUREMBERG TRIALS see War Crime Trials

NURI LANGUAGE

NY —NEW YORK PUBLIC LIBRARY, Oriental Div, Fifth Ave & 42 St, New York, 10018. E Christian Filstrup, Chief
Holdings: Cat Mss Microforms
Budget: ($56,455)
Notes: Published catalog of holdings.

NURSERIES (HORTICULTURE)

CA —UNIVERSITY OF CALIFORNIA, DAVIS, Shields Library, Dept of Special Collections, Davis, 95616. Donald Kunitz, Head; C Danial Elliott, Asst Head
Holdings: Cat Mss Pix
Notes: The Nursery Catalog Collection, with 6500 catalogs from both foreign and domestic seed and plant dealers, spans the late 19th and 20th centuries. Records, photographs, seed posters, and scrapbooks of the Ferry-Morse Company document the success of this well-known nursery. 12,000 items.

IA —IOWA STATE UNIVERSITY, Library, Ames, 50011. Warren B Kuhn, Dean of Library Services
Holdings: Cat
Notes: Extensive serial holdings.

NURSERY CATALOGS see Catalogs, Nursery

NURSERY SCHOOLS

NY —BANK STREET COLLEGE OF EDUCATION LIBRARY, 610 W 112 St, New York, 10025. Eleanor Kule Seid,

NURSERY SCHOOLS (cont.)

Library Dir
Holdings: Vols (90,000) Cat Microforms
Notes: Education, guidance, psychology, educational subjects are integrated in one professional collection; in addition there are two separately cataloged and shelved collections: Children's and Elementary Curriculum Materials.

OH —OHIO STATE UNIVERSITY, Home Economics Library, Campbell Hall Rm 325, 1787 Neil Ave, Columbus, 43210. Neosha Mackey, Librn
Holdings: Vols (14,000) Cat Microforms
Notes: Separate catalog. Also, book catalog: *Catalog of the Home Economics Library* (Boston: G K Hall, 1976), 3 vols.

NURSES AND NURSING

AL —UNIVERSITY OF ALABAMA, BIRMINGHAM, Lister Hill Library of the Health Sciences, University Sta, Birmingham, 35294. Richard B Fredericksen, Dir

CA —LONG BEACH COMMUNITY HOSPITAL, Medical Library, 1720 Termino Ave, PO Box 2587, Long Beach, 90801. Lois O Clark, Librn
Holdings: Vols (3800) Cat Audiotapes Videotapes 16mm Films Filmstrips
Budget: ($3000)
Notes: Incl 2800 audiotapes and 280 videotapes.

CA —HOLLYWOOD PRESBYTERIAN MEDICAL CENTER, Health Sciences Library, 1300 N Vermont Ave, Los Angeles, 90027. Erika M Hansen, Chief Medical Librn
Notes: Medicine, nursing and allied health personnel, hosptial administration. Incl audiovisual material.

CA —LOS ANGELES PUBLIC LIBRARY, Science & Technology Dept, 630 W Fifth St, Los Angeles, 90071. Billie M Connor, Dept Head
Holdings: Vols (7500)
Notes: A well-rounded collection of materials related to consumer health, medicine and drugs as well as materials for the allied health and medical professions. Includes a sound representative selection of basic texts covering various aspects of medical treatment, drugs, diseases and syndromes. Indexes are collected as well as a basic collection of journals. The directories collection is strong. The broadest possible collection of books oriented toward consumer health, medicine, diets and nutrition is maintained, both traditional and alternative. Texts and examination study books are collected for nurses, laboratory technicians, physcial therapists, speech therapists, paramedics and other allied health professions.

CA —UNIVERSITY OF CALIFORNIA, LOS ANGELES, Biomedical Library, Center for the Health Sciences, Los Angeles, 90024. Alison Bunting, Acting Biomedical Librn; Victoria Steele, Head, History & Special Collections Div
Holdings: Vols (400,000) Cat Slides Phonorecords Audiotapes Videotapes 16mm Films Microforms

Notes: The UCLA Biomedical Library serves primarily the Schools of Medicine, Dentistry, Nursing, and Public Health, the UCLA Medical Center, the Departments of Microbiology and Biology in the College of Letters and Science, and related institutes in biomedicine. The collections of the Library are broad in scope, designed not only to support the teaching and research needs of its many users, but also to function as a resource for the health sciences-biological field as a whole. The outstanding feature of the collection is the strength of its periodical holdings, both current and retrospective. The Library also has an excellent reference collection, a comprehensive historical section, and gives special emphasis to the fields of neuroscience, psychiatry, ophthalmology, radiation biology, molecular biology, and vertebrate zoology. Increased emphasis is being given to the acquisition of audiovisual materials.

CA —UNIVERSITY OF CALIFORNIA, SAN DIEGO, Medical Center Library, 225 W Dickinson St, San Diego, 92103. Sue Ann Johnson, Head Librn
Holdings: Vols (20,000) Cat Slides Audiotapes

CA —UNIVERSITY OF CALIFORNIA, SAN FRANCISCO, Library, San Francisco, 94143. David Bishop, University Librn
Holdings: Vols (502,261) Cat
Budget: ($602,604)

CA —COLLEGE OF SAN MATEO, Library, 1700 W Hillsdale Blvd, San Mateo, 94402. Gregg T Atkins, Coordinator of Library Services
Holdings: Vols 3600 Cat
Notes: In addition, in the Media Center we have hundreds of tapes and media kits (not cataloged).

CA —STANFORD UNIVERSITY LIBRARIES, Lane Medical Library, Stanford University, Medical Center, Stanford, 94305. Peter Stangl, Librn
Notes: Mss Lane Hospital School of Nursing and Stanford University School of Nursing, experiences of nurses who were captured on Bataan, Phillipine Islands.

CO —WESTERN INTERSTATE COMMISSION FOR HIGHER EDUCATION, Wiche Library, PO Drawer P, Boulder, 80302. Karon M Kelly, Dir Library Services
Holdings: Vols (10,000) Cat Microforms
Notes: Incl medical and nursing education, student exchange programs, minority involvement in education, management systems in higher education.

CO —SWEDISH MEDICAL CENTER LIBRARY, 501 E Hampden Ave, Englewood, 80110. Sandra Parker, Dir
Holdings: Vols (6000) Cat
Budget: ($40,000)

CT —SAINT VINCENT'S MEDICAL CENTER, Health Science Library, 2800 Mian St, Bridgeport, 06606. Janet Goerig, Dir of Library Services
Holdings: Vols (8000)

CT —UNIVERSITY OF CONNECTICUT HEALTH CENTER, Lyman Maynard Stowe Library, Farmington, 06032. Ralph D Arcari, Dir of Libraries
Holdings: Vols 9650 Cat Slides Audiotapes Microforms Videocassettes
Budget: $32,150
Notes: Incl basic sciences supporting biomedical collection, biomedical research and clinical medicine, specializing in clinical and graduate level nursing. Separate catalog for AV materials. Library produces book catalogs of serial and audiovisuals titles.

CT —MIDDLESEX MEMORIAL HOSPITAL, Health Sciences Library, 28 Crescent St, Middletown, 06457. Evelyn M Breck, Dir
Holdings: Vols (2000) Cat
Budget: ($20,000)
Notes: 125 journals are kept for 10 year runs.

CT —YALE MEDICAL LIBRARY, 333 Cedar St, New Haven, 06510.
Holdings: Vols (334,215) Cat Mss Pix Slides Microforms
Budget: ($361,650)
Notes: Incl films, audiotapes, artifacts, etc.

DE —SAINT FRANCIS HOSPITAL MEDICAL LIBRARY, Seventh & Clayton Sts, Wilmington, 19805. Sister Joan Ignatius McCleary, Librn
Holdings: Vols (3000) Cat Audiotapes

DE —US VETERANS ADMINISTRATION CENTER, Medical Library, Wilmington,

19805. Mrs Donald Passidoma, Chief Librn
Holdings: Vols (5000) Cat
Notes: Staff only.

†DC —CATHOLIC UNIVERSITY OFF AMERICA, Nursing & Biology Library, Washington, 20064. N L Powell, Head
Holdings: Vols 30,000 Cat Slides Audiotapes Videotapes 16mm Films Filmstrips Microforms
Budget: $5000

DC —WASHINGTON HOSPITAL CENTER MEDICAL LIBRARY, 110 Irving St NW, Washington, 20010. Marilyn Cook, Dir
Holdings: Vols 30,000 Cat Slides Audiotapes Videotapes 16mm Films Filmstrips Microforms

FL —BREVARD COMMUNITY COLLEGE, Learning Resources Center, Cocoa Campus, Clearlake Rd, Cocoa, 32922. John S French, Ref Librn
Holdings: Vols 680 Cat
Notes: Our strongest subject collection. Contains extensive audio visual materials. Collection supports the college nursing program. Periodical indexes and titles strong in this subject area.

FL —SAINT MARY'S HOSPITAL INC, Health Services Library, 901 45th St W, Palm Beach, 33407. Jennie Glock, Librn
Holdings: Vols (7000) Cat Slides Audiotapes

FL —UNIVERSITY OF SOUTH FLORIDA, Medical Center Library, 12901 N 30 St, Tampa, 33612. Maxyne Grimes, Dir
Holdings: Vols (75,383)
Budget: ($325,000)

GA —CRAWFORD W LONG MEMORIAL HOSPITAL, Medical Library, 35 Linden Ave NE, Atlanta, 30365. Girija Vijay, Dir
Holdings: Vols Cat
Budget: ($119,200)
Notes: Collection contains materials for medical, nursing and allied health fields. Strong nursing collection. Collection incl 3956 (cat) books, 6571 vols bound periodicals and 2773 vols (cat) audiovisuals.

GA —CENTRAL STATE HOSPITAL, Mental Health Library, Milledgeville, 31062. Katherine J Ridley, Librn
Holdings: Vols 450 Cat Audiotapes Filmstrips
Budget: ($5000)

HI —HAWAII MEDICAL LIBRARY, 1221 Punchbowl St, Honolulu, 96813. John A Breinich, Dir
Holdings: Vols (50,000) Cat Pix Audiotapes Videotapes
Budget: ($121,000)
Notes: Medline service available.

IL —ARLINGTON HEIGHTS MEMORIAL LIBRARY, 500 N Dunton Ave, Arlington Heights, 60004. Caryl Mobley, Reference Librn
Holdings: Vols (5000) Cat
Budget: ($8000)
Notes: Medical sciences, nursing, and patient education.

IL —LIBRARY OF THE AMERICAN HOSPITAL ASSOCIATION, Asa S Bacon Memorial, 840 N Lake Shore Dr, Chicago, 60611. Eloise C Foster, Dir
Holdings: Vols (39,000) Cat
Budget: ($95,000)
Notes: Literature on non-clinical aspects of health care administration, planning and financing of hospitals and related health care institutions; administrative aspects of the medical, paramedical, and prepayment fields. Special Collection: Ray E Brown Management Collection. *Hospital Literature Index* prepared by the Library of the American Hospital Association in cooperation with the National Library of Medicine; *Catalog of the Library of the American Hospital Association*, published by G K Hall, Boston.

IL —ROSELAND COMMUNITY HOSPITAL, Health Science Library, 45 W 111 St, Chicago, 60628. Mary T Hanlon, Librn
Holdings: Vols (800) Cat
Budget: $3200

IL —EVANGELICAL SCHOOL OF NURSING, Wojniak Memorial Library, 9345 S Kilbourn, Oak Lawn, 60453. Gerald Dujsik, Library Mgr
Holdings: Vols 3100 Cat
Budget: $6000
Notes: Covers nursing, nursing education,

NURSES AND NURSING (cont.)

and administration. Nonprint materials in separate AV department.

IL —LUTHERAN GENERAL HOSPITAL LIBRARY, 1775 Dempster St, Park Ridge, 60068. Joanne Crispen, Dir of Library Services
Holdings: Vols (21,298) Cat Slides Audiotapes Videotapes 16mm Films Filmstrips
Budget: ($52,600)

IN —CENTRAL STATE HOSPITAL, Medical Library, 3000 W Washington St, Indianapolis, 46222. Aurella S Baker, Librn
Holdings: Vols (10,400) Cat Audiotapes
Budget: ($41,000)

IN —SAINT VINCENT HOSPITAL & HEALTH CARE CENTER, Garceau Library, 20001 W 86 St, Indianapolis, 46260. Virginia Durkin, Librn
Holdings: Vols (7500) Cat Pix Slides Phonorecords Audiotapes Videotapes 16mm Films Filmstrips Microforms
Notes: Building a collection on the history of the hospital.

IN —WISHARD MEMORIAL HOSPITAL, Professional Library, 1001 W Tenth St, Indianapolis, 46202. Fran Bischoff, Library Dir; Kirsten Quam, Librn
Holdings: Vols 3850 Cat
Notes: Clinically oriented collections.

IN —LOGANSPORT STATE HOSPITAL, Staff Library, Logansport, 46947. Terra Newton, Librn
Holdings: Vols (3000) Cat

IN —PURDUE UNIVERSITY LIBRARIES, Pharmacy, Nursing and Health Sciences Library, Pharmacy Bldg, West Lafayette, 47907. Theodora Andrews, Librn
Holdings: Vols (4000) Cat
Notes: There is a separate catalog to the collection. Contains research level materials as well as undergraduate.

IA —SAINT LUKE'S METHODIST HOSPITAL, Health Science Library, 1026 "A" Ave NE, Cedar Rapids, 52402. Sally Harms, Librn
Holdings: Vols 4000 Cat
Notes: Also 4000 bound periodicals vols and AV materials.

IA —IOWA LUTHERAN HOSPITAL, Department of Educational Media, University at Penn, Des Moines, 50316. Wayne Pedersen, Dir of Educational Media
Holdings: Vols 2695 Cat Audiocassettes Videotapes Slides 16mm Films
Budget: ($15,000)
Notes: The department consists of 3 libraries: Levitt Health Sciences, Nursing Administrative. The Audio-Visual Division is also part of the department. Holdings incl 524 audiocassettes (cat); 177 videotapes (cat); 13 slide-tape kits (cat); 2 16mm films (cat).

IA —IOWA METHODIST SCHOOL OF NURSING, Marjorie Gertrude Morrow Library, 1117 Pleasant St, Des Moines, 50309. Nancy O'Brien, Librn
Holdings: Vols 4000 Cat Slides Videotapes 16mm Films Filmstrips VF
Notes: Photocopying.

KS —KANSAS NEUROLOGICAL INSTITUTE, Menninger Professional Library, 3107 W 21 St, Topeka, 66604. Richard Gray, Librn
Holdings: Vols 161 Cat
Notes: Incl development disabilities; special education; nursing care for the handicapped; programs for the mentally retarded; behavioral psychology; supervision in mental health/mental retardation; staff training in mental health/mental retardation.

KS —STORMONT-VAIL HOSPITAL, School of Nursing Library, 845 Washburn, Topeka, 66606. Shirley Borglund, Librn
Holdings: Vols (6000) Cat

KS —WESLEY MEDICAL CENTER, McKibbin Health Science Library, 550 N Hillside, Wichita, 67214. Jan Braden, Dir, Library Services
Holdings: Vols (29,000) Cat Slides Phonorecords Audiotapes Videotapes 16mm Films Filmstrips
Budget: ($200,000)

KY —NKC HOSPITALS, Medical Library, PO Box 35070, Louisville, 40232. Holly Shipp Buchanan, Dir
Holdings: Vols (4500) Cat Audiotapes Videotapes 16mm Films
Budget: $200,000
Notes: The Library has a special historical collection, corporate archives in honor of Dr Morris Flexner.

LA —TOURO INFIRMARY, Hospital Library, 1401 Foucher, New Orleans, 70115. Patricia J Greenfield, Head
Holdings: Vols (3000) Cat Audiotapes
Budget: $80,752
Notes: Clinical medicine and nursing. Photocopying.

MD —HUMNER-MORGAN MEDICAL LIBRARY, Jessie Kendall Memorial Library, Nursing, 100 N Broadway, Baltimore, 21231. Dorothy Echols, Librn
Holdings: Vols 700 Cat Pix Slides Phonorecords Audiotapes 16mm Films Filmstrips Microforms
Notes: Church Hospital and Humner-Morgan Library have merged.

MD —JOHNS HOPKINS UNIVERSITY, William H Welch Medical Library, 1900 E Monument St, Baltimore, 21205. Richard A Polacsek, Dir & Librn
Holdings: Vols (270,000) Cat Pix Slides Phonorecords Audiotapes Videotapes 16mm Films Filmstrips Microforms
Budget: ($497,000)

MD —MERCY HOSPITAL, Nursing Library, 301 Saint Paul Place, Baltimore, 21202. Arlene Gillis, Librn
Holdings: Vols 6500 // Cat Maps Phonorecords Audiotapes 16mm Films Filmstrips
Notes: Incl 26 maps, 50 phonorecords, 15 audiotapes, 5 16mm films, and 65 filmstrips.

MD —PROVIDENT HOSPITAL, Health Sciences Library, 2600 Liberty Heights Ave, Baltimore, 21215. Bertha G Wilson, Librn
Holdings: Vols (5077) Cat Slides Audiotapes Microforms
Budget: ($14,000)
Notes: Incl 1000 slides, 300 audiotapes and 104 microforms.

MD —SAINT JOSEPH HOSPITAL, School of Nursing Library, 7620 York Rd, Baltimore, 21204. Mary Weihs, Librn
Holdings: Vols 2500 Cat Slides Phonorecords Audiotapes 16mm Films Filmstrips
Budget: $4600
Notes: No photocopying.

MD —SINAI HOSPITAL OF BALTIMORE, Medical & Nursing Libraries, Belvedere & Greenspring, Baltimore, 21215. Rita Matcher, Chief Librn
Holdings: Vols (6000) Cat

MD —UNION MEMORIAL HOSPITAL, Nursing Library, 3301 N Calvert St, Baltimore, 21218. Carolyn Daugherty, Librn
Holdings: Vols (4000) Cat Mss Pix

MD —UNIVERSITY OF MARYLAND, BALTIMORE, Health Sciences Library, 111 S Greene St, Baltimore, 21201. Cyril C H Feng, Dir
Holdings: Vols 2214

MD —NATIONAL LIBRARY OF MEDICINE, 8600 Rockville Pike, Bethesda, 20209. Harold M Schoolinam, Actg Dir
Budget: ($46,400)

MD —WROTH MEMORIAL LIBRARY, Washington County Hospital Association, 251 E Antietam St, Hagerstown, 21740. Myra Binau, Dir & Librn
Holdings: Vols 5000 Cat
Budget: ($30,000)
Notes: Over 150 periodical titles.

†MA —UNIVERSITY OF MASSACHUSETTS AT AMHERST, Library, Amherst, 01003.
Notes: Special emphases: medical-surgical, psychiatric and mental health, and community health.

MA —MASSACHUSETTS COLLEGE OF PHARMACY AND ALLIED HEALTH SCIENCES, Sheppard Library, 179 Longwood Ave, Boston, 02115. Barbara M Hill, Librn
Holdings: Vols (56,000) Cat

MA —MASSACHUSETTS GENERAL HOSPITAL, Health Sciences Library, Fruit St, Boston, 02114. Jacqueline Bastille, Librn
Holdings: Vols 12,849 Cat Pix Slides Phonorecords Audiotapes 16mm Films Filmstrips Microforms
Budget: $28,000
Notes: Health Sciences Library is the library for the Massachusetts General Hospital School of Nursing--the oldest existing diploma school of nursing in the US (100th anniversary--1973).

MA —MOUNT AUBURN HOSPITAL, Health Sciences Library, 330 Mount Auburn St, Cambridge, 02138. Cherie Haitz, Librn
Holdings: Vols (3000) Cat Audiotapes Videotapes
Notes: Incl 300 periodical subscriptions.

MA —BOSTON COLLEGE LIBRARIES, School of Nursing, Library, Cushing Hall, Chestnut Hill, 02167. Mary L Pekarski, Librn
Holdings: Vols 30,000 Cat Slides Audiotapes Videotapes Filmstrips Microforms
Budget: $24,650
Notes: This collection is being absorbed in the general collection.

MA —BERKSHIRE MEDICAL CENTER, Medical Library, 725 North St, Pittsfield, 01201. Jutta Luhde, Medical Librn

MA —WORCESTER CITY HOSPITAL SCHOOL OF NURSING, Library, 26 Queen St, Worcester, 01610. Jamie McAlister, Librn
Holdings: Vols (6100) Cat Slides Videotapes Filmstrips
Notes: Incl 100 videotapes, vertical files.

MI —UNIVERSITY OF MICHIGAN, Alfred Taubman Medical Library, 1135 E Catherine St, Ann Arbor, 48109. L Yvonne Wulff, Head
Holdings: Vols (260,300) Cat
Budget: ($438,000)

MI —HARPER-GRACE HOSPITALS, Grace Hospital Div, Oscar Leseure Professional Library, 18700 Myers Rd, Detroit, 48235. Frances Phillips, Chief Librn; Mary A Dery, Asst Librn

MI —MERCY COLLEGE OF DETROIT, Library, 8200 Wouter Dr, Detroit, 48129. Mary Jo Wylis, Librn
Holdings: Vols (850) Cat Mss Maps Pix Slides Phonorecords Audiotapes Videotapes 16mm Films Filmstrips

MI —SAINT MARY'S HOSPITAL, Library, 200 Jefferson SE, Grand Rapids, 49503. Mary A Hanson, Librn
Holdings: Vols (10,789) Cat
Budget: ($56,000)

MN —HENNEPIN COUNTY MEDICAL CENTER, Health Sciences Library, 701 Park Ave, Minneapolis, 55416. Judith Stanke, Medical Librn
Holdings: Vols (27,000) Cat Slides Audiotapes Videotapes
Budget: ($150,000)

MN —UNIVERSITY OF MINNESOTA, Bio-Medical Library, Diehl Hall, Minneapolis, 55455. Gertrude Foreman, Acting Dir
Holdings: Vols (263,361)
Budget: ($500,000)

MN —BETHESDA LUTHERAN MEDICAL CENTER, Medical-Nursing Library, 570 Capitol Blvd, Saint Paul, 55101. Eileen M Erlandson, Librn
Holdings: Vols (4383) Cat Slides Audiotapes Filmstrips
Budget: ($8360)
Notes: Incl 800 slides, 106 audiotapes and 30 filmstrips.

MO —TRINITY LUTHERAN HOSPITAL, Florence L Nelson Memorial Library, 3030 Baltimore, Kansas City, 64108. Cami L Loucks, Dir
Holdings: Vols 7000 Cat Slides Phonorecords Audiotapes Videotapes 16mm Films Filmstrips Microforms
Notes: Incl 400 slides on nursing. Separate AV catalog. Subscriber to MEDLINE, Mednet, Octanet, Dialog.

MO —UNIVERSITY OF MISSOURI-KANSAS CITY, Health Sciences Library, 2411 Holmes St, Kansas City, 64108. Marilyn Sullivan, Chief Medical Librn
Holdings: Vols (60,000) Cat Journals Slides Audiotapes Videotapes
Budget: ($111,939)

MO —SAINT JOSEPH STATE HOSPITAL, Professional Library, 3400 Frederick Ave,

NURSES AND NURSING (cont.)

Box 263, Saint Joseph, 64502. Martha Goodding, Librn
Holdings: Vols (3000) Cat Slides Phonorecords Audiotapes 16mm Films Filmstrips Videotapes

MO —SAINT JOHN'S SCHOOL OF NURSING LIBRARY, 1930 S National Ave, Springfield, 65804. Marty Osredker, Librn
Holdings: Vols 5200 Cat Audiotapes Microforms
Budget: $5000
Notes: Nursing library with emphasis on nursing, medicine and allied health.

NE —UNIVERSITY OF NEBRASKA MEDICAL CENTER, Library, 42 & Dewey Ave, Omaha, 68105. Robert M Braude, Dir
Holdings: Vols (196,313)
Budget: ($320,000)
Notes: Serves the Colleges of Medicine, Nursing, Pharmacy, and the School of Allied Health Professions; the Hospital and Clinics; and several research institutes with a collection that is broad in scope and both current and retrospective.

NH —NEW HAMPSHIRE TECHNICAL INSTITUTE, Paul E Farnum Library, 5 Fan Rd, Concord, 03301. Wm John Hare, Librn
Holdings: Vols 2825 Cat Slides Audiotapes Videotapes Filmstrips
Budget: $2200

NH —DARTMOUTH COLLEGE, Dartmouth-Hitchcock Medical Center, Dana Biomedical Library, Hanover, 03756. Shirley J Grainger, Librn
Holdings: Vols (146,611) Audiotapes Videotapes
Budget: ($280,000)

NH —NEW HAMPSHIRE VOCATIONAL TECHNICAL COLLEGE, Library, 277 R Portsmouth Ave, Stratham, 03885. Nancy L Dodge, Librn
Holdings: Vols 3000 Cat Microforms
Budget: ($9500)

NJ —EAST ORANGE GENERAL HOSPITAL, Library, 300 Central Ave, East Orange, 07019. Joann Mehalick, Dir of Library Services
Holdings: Vols (1500) Cat Videotapes

NM —UNIVERSITY OF NEW MEXICO, Medical Center Library, North Campus, Albuquerque, 87131. Erika Love, Dir
Notes: Health sciences collection, principally medicine, but incl nursing, pharmacy, and allied health sciences, in book, journal, and multimedia formats. Library holdings include 33,427 book titles; 37,266 vols; 2,260 periodical subscriptions; 71,303 bound vols.

NM —NEW MEXICO STATE HOSPITAL, Ella P Kief Memorial Library, Hot Spring Blvd, PO Box 1388, Las Vegas, 87701. Hazel Hurley, Librn
Holdings: Vols (5000) Cat
Budget: ($2500)
Notes: Partially cataloged.

†NY —MEDICAL RESEARCH LIBRARY OF BROOKLYN, Academy of Medicine of Brooklyn & The State University of New York Downstate Medical Center, 450 Clarkson St, Brooklyn, 11203. Kenneth E Moody, Dir
Holdings: Vols 3000 Cat
See also entry under Medicine.

NY —ERIE COUNTY MEDICAL CENTER, Medical Library, 462 Grider St, Buffalo, 14215. Anthony Ciko, Sr Medical Librn
Holdings: Vols (13,000) Cat Slides Audiotapes Videotapes
Budget: ($42,000)

NY —STATE UNIVERSITY OF NEW YORK, COLLEGE AT BUFFALO, Health Sciences Library, Stockton Kimball Tower, Buffalo, 14214. C K Huang, Dir
Holdings: Vols (222,108) Cat
Budget: ($493,931)

NY —BOOTH MEMORIAL MEDICAL CENTER, Health Education Library, Main St at Booth Memorial Ave, Flushing, 11355. Rita Maier, Library Dir
Holdings: Vols (3000) Cat Audiotapes
Notes: Incl 7000 bound journals; software slide tape programs.

NY —FLUSHING HOSPITAL & MEDICAL CENTER, Medical Library, Parsons Blvd &

45 Ave, Flushing, 11355. Maria Czechowicz, Dir
Holdings: Vols (5741) Cat Audiotapes
Budget: ($11,000)

NY —LONG ISLAND JEWISH-HILLSIDE MEDICAL CENTER, Hillside Div, Health Sciences Library, PO Box 38, Glen Oaks, 11004. Joan L Kauff, Librn
Holdings: Vols (9000) Cat

NY —SUFFOLK ACADEMY OF MEDICINE, Health Sciences Library, 850 Veterans Memorial Highway, Hauppauge, 11788. Isabel V Hathorn, Dir
Holdings: Vols (13,000) Cat Videotapes Microforms

NY —NORTHERN WESTCHESTER HOSPITAL CENTER, Health Sciences Library, Mount Kisco, 10549. Nona C Willoughby, Librn
Notes: Core Collection: Over 1500 medical and nursing monographs and texts, primarily published within last five years. Subscribe to over 120 journals, bound journal vols kept for 10 years. MEDLARS online service. Audiodigests cassettes, six specialties, kept 5 years.

NY —AMERICAN JOURNAL OF NURSING CO, Sophia F Palmer Library, 555 W 57th St, New York, 10019. Frederick W Pattison, Librn
Holdings: Cat Mss Pix
Notes: Collection described in *Catalog of the Sophia F Palmer Memorial Library, American Journal of Nursing Co, New York City* (Boston: G K Hall, 1973), 2 vols.

NY —COLUMBIA UNIVERSITY LIBRARIES, Health Sciences Library, 701 W 168 St, New York, 10032. Rachael K Goldstein, Librn
Notes: Restricted.
See also entry under Medicine

NY —SOUTH NASSAU COMMUNITIES HOSPITAL, Jules Redish Memorial Medical Library, 2445 Oceanside Rd, Oceanside, 11572. Claire Joseph, Dir
Holdings: Vols (750) Cat
Budget:
Notes: Incl (6500) bound journals.

NY —GENESEE HOSPITAL, Stabins Health Sciences Library, 224 Alexander St, Rochester, 14607. Sally M Gerling, Librn
Holdings: Vols 4000 Cat

NY —UNIVERSITY OF ROCHESTER, School of Medicine and Dentistry, Edward G Miner Library, 601 Elmwood Ave, Rochester, 14642. Lucretia McClure, Medical Librn; Janet Brady Berk, History of Medicine Librn
Holdings: Vols (185,000) Cat
Notes: The Edward G Miner Library serves the School of Medicine & Dentistry, the School of Nursing, and Strong Memorial Hospital. The collection encompasses all the biomedical fields, nursing and dental research, and is designed to serve the teaching, patient care and research needs of persons in the Medical Center. The Library subscribes to more than 2900 current journals and serials, has an excellent reference collection and an extensive collection of rare and historical works in medicine and nursing.

NY —CROUSE-IRVING MEMORIAL HOSPTIAL, School of Nursing, Library, 736 Irving Ave, Syracuse, 13210. Frances R Shelander, Head
Holdings: Vols 3900 Cat Slides Phonorecords Audiotapes Videotapes 16mm Films Filmstrips
Notes: Incl 185 journals; computer searching.

NY —SAINT JOSEPH'S SCHOOL OF NURSING AND MEDICAL LIBRARY, 206 Prospect Ave, Syracuse, 13203. V Juchimek, Head Librn
Holdings: Vols 10,000 Cat Pix Slides
Budget: ($12,000)
Notes: Incl 24 vertical file drawers.

NY —UTICA-MARCY PSYCHIATRIC CENTER, MARCY CAMPUS, Professional Library, 1213 Court St, Utica, 13502. Janina Strife, Librn
Holdings: Vols (3000) Cat
Budget: ($6000)

NY —WESTCHESTER COUNTY MEDICAL CENTER, Health Sciences Library, Valhalla,

10595. Charlene Sikorski, Medical Librn
Holdings: Vols (12,000) Cat

NY —ELIZABETH SETON COLLEGE LIBRARY, Yonkers, 10701. Sr Margaret Sullivan, Librn

NC —UNIVERSITY OF NORTH CAROLINA, CHAPEL HILL, Health Sciences Library, 223 H, Chapel Hill, 27514. Samuel Hitt, Dir
Holdings: Vols (200,000) Cat Slides Journals Audiotapes Videotapes Microforms
Budget: ($560,000)

NC —MERCY SCHOOL OF NURSING, Library, 1921 Vail Ave, Charlotte, 28207. Barbara Duval, Librn
Holdings: Vols (4600) Cat Audiotapes
Budget: $3500
Notes: Incl cassettes, charts, filmstrips, models; also, motion pictures, transparencies, x-ray sets (122 titles, 60 periodicals currently received). On-site use only to users not affiliated with Mercy School of Nursing, or Mercy Hospital, both in Charlotte, North Carolina.

NC —TECHNICAL INSTITUTE OF ALAMANCE, Learning Resources Center, Jimmy Kerr Rd, PO Box 623, Haw River, 27258. Ron Plummer, Coordr
Holdings: Vols (1605) Cat Pix Audiotapes 16mm Films Filmstrips Microforms
Notes: Practical nursing only.

NC —NORTH CAROLINA DEPT OF HUMAN RESOURCES, Div of Health Services, Public Health Library, PO Box 2091, Raleigh, 27602. Elnora H Turner, Librn
Holdings: Vols (15,000) Cat

ND —UNIVERSITY OF NORTH DAKOTA, Harley E French Medical Library, Grand Forks, 58202. David W Boilard, Dir; Lila Pedersen, Asst Dir
Holdings: Vols (56,000) Cat
Budget: ($206,000)
Notes: 1075 current periodical subscriptions.

OH —ATHENS MENTAL HEALTH & MENTAL RETARDATION CENTER, Staff Library, Richland Ave, Athens, 45701. Judy McGinn, Librn
Holdings: Vols (3000) Cat Audiotapes

OH —AULTMAN HOSPITAL SCHOOL OF NURSING, Library, 2614 Sixth St SW, Canton, 44710. Violet Russell, Librn
Holdings: Vols 3642 Cat
Budget: ($2800)

OH —ROLLMAN PSYCHIATRIC INSTITUTE, Clinical Library, 3009 Burnet Ave, Cincinnati, 45219. M Glassmann, Dir
Holdings: Vols (3000) Cat

OH —UNIVERSITY OF CINNCINNATI NURSING AND HEALTH LIBRARIES, Solomon Levi Memorial Library, Procter Hall, Cincinnati, 45219. Ava Fried, Librn
Holdings: Vols 9500 Cat

OH —MOUNT SINAI MEDICAL CENTER, George H Hays Library, University Circle, Cleveland, 44106. Pamela Alderman, Librn
Holdings: Vols (6000) Cat Mss Slides Phonorecords Filmstrips Audiotapes
Notes: Bound journals 4000; incl on line reference service with Dialog database.

OH —MIAMI VALLEY HOSPITAL, Memorial Medical Library, 1 Wyoming St, Dayton, 45409. Margaret C Hardy, Dir
Holdings: Vols 40,000 Cat Pix Slides Audiotapes Videotapes
Budget: ($200,000)

OH —KETTERING COLLEGE OF MEDICAL ARTS, Learning Resources Center, 3737 Southern Blvd, Kettering, 45429. Edward Collins, Librn
Holdings: Vols 995 Cat Audiotapes Videotapes 16mm Films
Budget: $1153

OK —UNIVERSITY OF OKLAHOMA, Health Sciences Center, Library, 1000 Stanton L Young Blvd, PO Box 26901, Oklahoma City, 73190. C M Thompson, Jr, Dir
Holdings: Vols (155,434) Cat Slides Audiotapes Videotapes 16mm Films Microforms
Budget: ($374,960)

OR —EMANUEL HOSPITAL, Library, 2801 N Gantebein Ave, Portland, 97227. Katherin Rouzie, Librn
Holdings: Vols 4000 Cat Audiotapes
Notes: The library serves a 525-bed acute

NURSES AND NURSING (cont.)

care hospital. Its main emphasis is medicine, with accompanying collections of nursing and other allied health subject areas. It includes 150 journal subscriptions and 3 audio-digest subscriptions.

OR —GOOD SAMARITAN HOSPITAL & MEDICAL CENTER, Health Sciences Library, 1015 NW 22 Ave, Portland, 97210. Melvina W Stell, Dir of Libraries
Holdings: Vols 7000 Cat Videotapes Audiotapes
Budget: ($90,000)

OR —OREGON HEALTH SCIENCES, University Libraries, PO Box 573, Portland, 97207. James E Morgan, Dir
Holdings: Vols (178,373) Cat Mss Pix Slides Audiotapes Videotapes Microforms
Notes: Libraries incl a medical/nursing library and a separate dental library. Medical history collection of books and artifacts emphasizes the Pacific Northwest.

PA —ALTOONA HOSPITAL, Glover Memorial Library, Howard Ave & Seventh St, Altoona, 16603. Caryn J Carr, Dir of Library; Bonnie K Lantz, Librn
Holdings: Vols (7475) Cat Pix Slides Phonorecords Audiotapes Videotapes 16mm Films Filmstrips Filmloops Microforms
Budget: ($14,000)
Notes: Incl 141 pictures, 1274 slides,, 94 records, 1193 audiotapes, films, 116 filmstrips, 28 microforms, 78 filmloops, and 269 journals.

PA —SAINT LUKE'S HOSPITAL, School of Nursing, Trexler Nurses' Library, Bishopthorpe & Ostrum, Bethlehem, 18015. Diane Frantz, Librn
Holdings: Vols (3600) Cat Slides Films Filmstrips Phonorecords Audiotapes Models
Budget: $3700

PA —BRYN MAWR HOSPITAL, Medical Library, Bryn Mawr, 19010. LD Gundry, Medical Librn
Holdings: Vols (8000) Cat
Budget: $30,000
Notes: 234 current journals.

PA —LANCASTER GENERAL HOSPITAL, Mueller Health Sciences Library, 555 N Duke St, Lancaster, 17604. Claudette Strohm, Librn
Holdings: Vols (4431) Cat Audiotapes Microforms

PA —SAINT JOSEPH HOSPITAL, Hospital Library, 250 College Ave, PO Box 3509, Lancaster, 17604. Eileen B Doudna, Librn
Holdings: Vols (3000) Cat Journals Videocassettes Filmstrips Slides
Budget:

PA —OHIO VALLEY GENERAL HOSPITAL, Health Library, McKees Rocks, 15136. Mary G Evans, Librn
Holdings: Vols (1900) Cat Slides
Budget: ($3300)

PA —COLLEGE OF PHYSICIANS OF PHILADELPHIA, Library, 19 S 22 St, Philadelphia, 19103. Anthony Aguirre, Libr Dir
Holdings: Vols (316,223) // Cat Mss Microforms
Budget: ($1,096,557)
Notes: Incl 13,515 pamphlets; 1435 mss; 326,367 reports, dissertations, and reprints. Strong historical and bibliographical collections, as well as current materials. Medical documentation service provides current alerting, incl abstracting, etc.

PA —LANKENAU HOSPITAL, School of Nursing Library, City Ave at 64 St, Philadelphia, 19151. Sister Alma Koder, Librn
Holdings: Vols 4000 Cat
Budget: $2000

PA —PENNSYLVANIA HOSPITAL HISTORICAL LIBRARY, Eighth & Spruce Sts, Philadelphia, 19107. Caroline Morris, Librn
Holdings: Vols (13,009)
Budget: ($15,000)
Notes: 20th century journals and current medical books. Strong collection of nursing journals. Some historical nursing textbooks and a good collection on the history of nursing.

PA —TEMPLE UNIVERSITY, Health Sciences Center Library, Broad & Tioga Sts, Philadelphia, 19140. Ruth Diamond, Dir
Holdings: Vols (87,480) Cat Slides Microforms
Budget: ($340,950)

PA —UNIVERSITY OF PENNSYLVANIA, Bio-Medical Library, Johnson Pavilion/G2, Philadelphia, 19104. Eleanor Goodchild, Librn
Holdings: Vols (139,000) Cat Slides Audiotapes Videotapes

PA —FORBES METROPOLITAN HEALTH CENTER, Library, 225 Penn Ave, Pittsburgh, 15221. Sue Reber, Librn
Holdings: Vols 6065 Cat Tapes
Budget: $10,552

PA —SAINT MARGARET MEMORIAL HOSPITAL, School of Nursing Library, 4631 Davison St, Pittsburgh, 15201. Dorothy D Schiff, Librn
Holdings: Vols 2300 Cat Slides Phonorecords Audiotapes Videotapes 16mm Films Filmstrips
Notes: Strong effort to buy everything in nursing. Developing archives and rare books (in nursing only).

PA —UNIVERSITY OF PITTSBURGH, Falk Library of the Health Professions, History of Medicine Collection, Scaife Hall, Pittsburgh, 15261. Jonathon Erlen, Cur
Holdings: Vols (13,500) Cat Pix
Budget: ($425,269)
Notes: Medicine, dentistry, nursing, pharmacy, public health, psychiatry materials, incl some rare books and 300 pamphlets on anesthesia.

PA —PENNSYLVANIA STATE UNIVERSITY, Fred Lewis Pattee Library, Life Sciences Library, University Park, 16802. Keith Roe, Head

RI —NEWPORT HOSPITAL, Ina Mosher Health Sciences Library, Friendship St, Newport, 02840. Tosca N Carpenter, Librn
Holdings: Vols 4278 Cat Slides Phonorecords Audiotapes Filmstrips

SC —BAPTIST MEDICAL CENTER, Amelia White Pitts Memorial Library, Taylor at Marion Sts, Columbia, 29220. Lois W Smith, Medical Librn
Holdings: Vols (3000) Cat

SC —SOUTH CAROLINA DEPT OF HEALTH & ENVIRONMENTAL CONTROL, Educational Resource Center, 2600 Bull St, Columbia, 29201. Michael Kronenfeld, Librn
Holdings: Vols 1500

TX —TEXAS TECH UNIVERSITY HEALTH SCIENCES CENTER, Amarillo Branch, Harrington Library of Health Sciences, 1400 Wallace Blvd, Amarillo, 79106. Carolyn Patrick, Assoc Dir
Holdings: Vols (12,000) Cat
Budget: ($6600)
Notes: Supports Diploma School of Nursing (Northwest Texas Hospital School of Nursing). Also incl 13,000 bound journals, 5100 audiovisual items.

TX —UNIVERSITY OF TEXAS LIBRARIES, General Libraries, PO Box P, Austin, 78713. Carolyn Bucknell, Asst Dir for Collection Development
Holdings: Cat Microforms

TX —SAINT PAUL HOSPITAL, C B Sacher Library, 5909 Harry Hines Blvd, Dallas, 75235. Barbara J Miller, Medical Librn; Michael Zimmerman, Library Asst
Holdings: Cat Audiotapes
Budget: $3000

TX —SCOTT AND WHITE MEMORIAL HOSPITAL, Medical Library, 2401 S 31 St, Temple, 76501. Mary H Spoede, Librn
Holdings: Vols (29,697) Cat Maps Pix Audiotapes
Budget: ($3700)

†UT —LDS HOSPITAL MEDICAL LIBRARY, 325 Eighth Ave, Salt Lake City, 84143. Terry L Heyer, Librn
Holdings: Vols (2200) Cat Slides Phonorecords Audiotapes Videotapes

VT —UNIVERSITY OF VERMONT, Charles A Dana Medical Library, Given Bldg, Burlington, 05405. Ellen Nagle, Medical Librn
Notes: Resource Library in the Greater Northeastern Regional Medical Library Program.

†VA —VIRGINIA COMMONWEALTH UNIVERSITY/MEDICAL COLLEGE OF VIRGINIA, Tompkins-McCaw Library, Box 667, MCV Sta, Richmond, 23298. J Craig McLean, Asst Dir of University Libraries
Holdings: Vols (155,000) Cat Mss Microforms
Budget: ($281,200)
Notes: Graduate sciences (biomedical emphasis). All newly cataloged books and journals are reported in the Abridged Book Catalog. Citations are limited to main entry and two subject entries. The catalog is cumulated monthly in 42x microfiche format. A cumulated Union Catalog covering 6 years and parts of 5 library collections is in preparation.

VA —RICHMOND MEMORIAL HOSPITAL, Medical Library, 1300 Westwood Ave, Richmond, 23227. Lynn Turman, Librn
Holdings: Vols (1800) Cat Slides Phonorecords Audiotapes Videotapes 16mm Films Filmstrips
Budget: $5000

WA —SWEDISH HOSPITAL MEDICAL CENTER, Medical Library, 747 Summit Ave, Seattle, 98104.
Holdings: Vols (2072) Cat

WA —UNIVERSITY OF WASHINGTON LIBRARIES, Health Sciences Library, SB-55, Seattle, 98195. Gerald J Oppenheimer, Dir

WA —CENTRAL WASHINGTON HOSPITAL, Rose A Heminger Health Sciences Library, PO Box 1887, Wenatchee, 98801. Jane Belt, Librn & Coordr of Continuing Education
Holdings: Cat Slides Audiotapes Videotapes 16mm Films Filmstrips
Budget: ($5000)
Notes: Incl 100 slide sets, 500 audiotapes, 100 videotapes, and 50 filmstrip programs.

WV —US VETERANS ADMINISTRATION HOSPITAL, Library, Clarksburg, 26301. Edward H Poletti, Librn
Holdings: Vols (1336)

WV —US VETERANS ADMINISTRATION HOSPITAL, Library, 1540 Spring Valley Dr, Huntington, 25704. Evelyn J Schaffer, Librn
Holdings: Vols (3700) Cat Slides Phonorecords Audiotapes Videotapes 16mm Films Filmstrips Microforms

WV —SALEM COLLEGE, Library, Salem, 26426. Myron J Smith, Jr, Librn

WI —SACRED HEART HOSPITAL, Medical Library, 900 W Clairemont Ave, Eau Claire, 54701. Bruno Warner, Librn
Holdings: Vols (2006) Cat Slides Phonorecords Audiotapes Videotapes
Notes: Incl 212 audiotapes and 93 videotapes.

WI —BLACKHAWK TECHNICAL INSTITUTE, PO Box 5009, 6004 Prairie Rd, Janesville, 53547. Grace M Sweeney, Libn
Holdings: Vols 6000 Cat
Budget: $2000

WI —MERCY HOSPITAL, Medical Library, 1000 Mineral Point, Janesville, 53545. Lois Zuehlke, Librn
Holdings: Vols (550) Cat Slides Phonorecords Audiotapes Videotapes 16mm Films Filmstrips
Budget: $1000

WI —KENOSHA MEMORIAL HOSPITAL, Health Sciences Library, 6308 Eighth Ave, Kenosha, 53140. Esther L Puhek, Librn
Holdings: Vols (1825) Cat Slides Audiotapes Videotapes
Notes: Incl 300 videotapes.

WI —UNIVERSITY OF WISCONSIN, MADISON, W S Middleton Health Sciences Library, 1305 Linden Dr, Madison, 53706. Virginia Holtz, Dir
Holdings: Vols (200,000) Cat Pix Slides Audiotapes Videotapes Microforms

WI —SAINT JOSEPH'S HOSPITAL, School of Nursing, Learning Resource Center, 611 St Joseph's Ave, Marshfield, 54449. Margaret A Allen, Librn
Holdings: Vols (3600) Cat Slides Phonorecords Audiotapes Videotapes 16mm Films Filmstrips
Budget: ($9,000)
Notes: Collection supports nursing education. Historical material incl nursing journals, 1914-date.

NURSES AND NURSING (cont.)

WI —MARQUETTE UNIVERSITY, Memorial Library, 1415 W Wisconsin Ave, Milwaukee, 53233. Jay Kirk, Health Sciences Librn
Notes: Supports curriculum and research.

WI —SAINT MARY'S HOSPITAL, Memorial Library, 2323 N Lake Dr, Box 503, Milwaukee, 53201. Carolyn Barloga, Health Sciences Librn
Holdings: Vols (4474) Cat Slides Audiotapes Videotapes Filmstrips
Budget: ($25,000)

WI —WAUKESHA MEMORIAL HOSPITAL, Medical Staff Library, 725 American Ave, Waukesha, 53186. Linda A Oddon, Medical Librn
Holdings: Vols (3336) Cat Pix Audiotapes Videotapes
Budget: ($4919)

AB —ALBERTA ASSOCIATION OF REGISTERED NURSES, Library, 10256 112th St, Edmonton, T5K 1M6, Can. Lloanne Walker, Librn
Holdings: Vols 2500 Cat

BC —VANCOUVER COMMUNITY COLLEGE, Langara Library, 100 W 49 Ave, Vancouver, V5Y 2Z6, Can. Mary Anne Epp, Librn
Holdings: Vols (70,000) Cat Maps Slides Audiotapes 16mm Films Microforms

NF —S A GRACE GENERAL HOSPITAL, School of Nursing, Library, Lemarchant Rd, Saint John's, A1E 1P9, Can. Catherine Ryan, Librn
Holdings: Vols 2500 Cat 35mm Filmstrips Tapes

NF —WATERFORD HOSPITAL, Health Sciences Library, Waterford Bridge Rd, Saint John's, A1E 4J8, Can. Maisie Young, Librn
Holdings: Vols (2000) Cat Pix Phonorecords Audiotapes Videotapes 16mm Films Filmstrips
Notes: Material incl aspects of psychiatry related to medicine, nursing, psychology, social work, etc. Also incl manuscript work on a history of the hospital, which closely parallels a history of psychiatry in Newfoundland. Journals are only kept for ten years.

ON —CANADIAN NURSES' ASSOCIATION, 50 The Driveway, Ottawa, K2P 1E2, Can. Linda Solomon Shiff, Librn Mgr
Holdings: Vols 14,000 Cat Pix Slides Film VF
Notes: National nursing library; repository of studies by Canadian nurses or about nursing in Canada. Incl 475 subscriptions to periodicals.

ON —UNIVERSITY OF OTTAWA, Health Sciences Library, 451 Smyth Road, Ottawa, K1H 8L5, Can. Myra Owen, Librn
Holdings: Vols (70,000) Slides Audiotapes Films Filmstrips
Budget: ($325,000)
Notes: This collection is made up of works in support of clinical and research studies in all branches of medicine, nursing and kinanthropology. Incl 1500 periodicals.

ON —METROPOLITAN TORONTO LIBRARY, Science & Technology Dept, 789 Yonge St, Toronto, M4W 2G8, Can. Margaret Walshe, Head
Holdings: Vols (120,000) Cat VF
Notes: All aspects of technology for the specialist, the student, and the general public. The department gives high priority to Canadian material.

ON —SUNNYBROOK HOSPITAL, Health Sciences Library, 2075 Bayview Ave, Toronto, M4N 3M5, Can. Linda McFarlane, Librn
Holdings: Vols (12,000) Cat Audiotapes Videotapes
Budget: ($40,000)
Notes: Emphasis on clinical medicine; also have nursing and hospital administration.

PQ —MCGILL UNIVERSITY, Nursing/Social Work Library, 3506 University St, Montreal, H3A 1Y1, Can. Wendy Patrick, Librn
Holdings: Vols (35,000) Cat

PQ —UNIVERSITY OF MONTREAL, Bibliotheque Para-medicale, 2375 Chemin de la Cote Ste Catherine, Montreal, H3C 3J7, Can. Johanne Hopper, Head Librn
Holdings: Vols 2500 Cat Slides Audiotapes Filmstrips Videotapes
Budget: $23,000
Notes: Collection exhaustive. 15 percent in French. Also have doctoral theses in nursing from 1978-, on microfiche.

NURSES AND NURSING—HISTORY

CA —UNIVERSITY OF CALIFORNIA, LOS ANGELES, Biomedical Library, Center for the Health Sciences, Los Angeles, 90024. Alison Bunting, Acting Biomedical Librn; Victoria Steele, Head, History & Special Collections Div
Holdings: Vols (36,000) Cat Mss Pix Slides Microforms
Notes: Early imprints (approx 13,000 volumes) comprising landmarks in biomedical history, 15th through 19th centuries. Approx 23,000 supporting monographs and serial volumes related to the history of medicine, dentistry, nursing, public health and other life sciences. Special historical collections in urology, ophthalmology, neurology, ornithology, mammalogy, Oriental medicine, Nicholas Culpeper, Silas Weir Mitchell, Florence Nightingale, Juan de Valverde (qv). Also, a collection of 19th century German and Austrian medical works (Franklin E Murphy Fund). Rare books for reference use only.

CA —UNIVERSITY OF CALIFORNIA, SAN FRANCISCO, Library, San Francisco, 94143. David Bishop, University Librn
Holdings: Vols (502,261) Cat
Budget: ($602,604)

CA —STANFORD UNIVERSITY LIBRARIES, Lane Medical Library, Stanford University, Medical Center, Stanford, 94305. Peter Stangl, Librn
Holdings: Vols (10,000) Mss Pix
Budget: ($2785)
Notes: Mss Lane Hospital School of Nursing and Stanford University School of Nursing, experiences of nurses who were captured on Bataan, Phillipine Islands.

MD —JOHNS HOPKINS UNIVERSITY, William H Welch Medical Library, 1900 E Monument St, Baltimore, 21205. Richard A Polacsek, Dir & Librn
Holdings: Vols 2000 // Cat Mss Pix
Notes: Nursing Historical Collection. Incl memorabilia. Use restricted to staff and alumni of Johns Hopkins University.

MD —UNIVERSITY OF MARYLAND, BALTIMORE, Health Sciences Library, 111 S Greene St, Baltimore, 21201. Cyril C H Feng, Dir
Holdings: Vols (25) Cat Mss Documents Art Reproductions VF
Notes: Consists chiefly of works by Florence Nightingale including her notebooks, nursing manuals, letters, etc.

MD —NATIONAL LIBRARY OF MEDICINE, History of Medicine Division, 8600 Rockville Pike, Bethesda, 20014.
Notes: Books and journals related to nursing and the nursing profession, both early and current items. A manuscripts collection incl the archives of the American College of Nurse Midwives (1946-1976) and the National League for Nursing (1894-1952). Photographs in the Prints and Photographs Collection document the history of nursing from the Middle Ages to the 1960s.

MA —BOSTON UNIVERSITY, Mugar Memorial Library, Special Collections Dept, 771 Commonwealth Ave, Boston, 02215. Howard B Gotlieb, Dir
Holdings: Cat Mss Pix
Notes: Ca 120 collections of organizations, institutions and individuals incl the Sophia F Plamer Historical Collection of the American Journal of Nursing Co and records of the American Nurses Association. See also names of person, organizations, institutions. Complete list available.

MA —FRANCIS A COUNTWAY LIBRARY OF MEDICINE, Boston Medical Library/ Harvard Medical Library, 10 Shattuck St, Boston, 02115. C Robin LeSueur, Librn; Richard J Wolfe, Cur, Rare Books & Manuscripts
Holdings: Vols (500,000) Cat Mss Maps Pix Microforms
Notes: Combines resources of the Harvard Medical School and the Boston Medical Library. Strong in serials and medical history in all fields of medicine, incl incunabula, non-medical books by doctors, travel books by doctors. 500,000 medical dissertations and theses. Special strength in all medical subjects listed in this volume.

MA —MASSACHUSETTS GENERAL HOSPITAL, Health Sciences Library, Fruit St, Boston, 02114. Jaqueline Bastille, Librn
Holdings: Vols 12,849 Cat Pix Slides Phonorecords Audiotapes 16mm Films Filmstrips Microforms
Notes: Health Sciences Library is the library for the Massachusetts General Hospital School of Nursing--the oldest existing diploma school of nursing in the US (100th anniversary--1973).

MA —SIMMONS COLLEGE ARCHIVES, 300 The Fenway, Boston, 02115. Megan Sniffin-Marinoff, College Archivist
Notes: Archives of the Simmons College School of Public Health Nursing (later reorganized into the School of Nursing) cover the years 1902-1970. Important correspondents in the collection incl M Adelaide Nutting, Mary Beard, Isabel Stewart, and Anne Hervey Strong, etc. Incl Strong's records of activity with regard to nursing education in the National Organization for Public Health Nursing, 1918-22. 1000 linear feet in institution, incl special collections nursing and photographs, nursing.

MA —BOSTON COLLEGE LIBRARIES, School of Nursing, Library, Cushing Hall, Chestnut Hill, 02167. Mary L Pekarski, Librn
Holdings: Vols 30,000 Cat Slides Audiotapes Videotapes Filmstrips Microrms
Budget: $24,650
Notes: This collection is being absorbed in the general collection.

NY —COLUMBIA UNIVERSITY LIBRARIES, Teachers College, Milbank Memorial Library, 525 W 120 St, New York, 10027. Jane P Franck, Dir
Holdings: Vols 1700 Cat Mss Pix Slides
Notes: The Adelaide Nutting Historical Nursing Collection. Strong in history of nursing and in 20th century texts. Downs 2403. Printed catalog to 1929. Also in microfiche, with printed index. University Microfilms International filming and cataloging entire collection currently.

NY —UNIVERSITY OF ROCHESTER, School of Medicine and Dentistry, Edward G Miner Library, 601 Elmwood Ave, Rochester, 14642. Lucretia McClure, Medical Librn; Janet Brady Berk, History of Medicine Librn
Holdings: Vols (185,000) Cat
Notes: The Edward G Miner Library serves the School of Medicine & Dentistry, the School of Nursing, and Strong Memorial Hospital. The collection encompasses all the biomedical fields, nursing and dental research, and is designed to serve the teaching, patient care and research needs of persons in the Medical Center. The Library subscribes to more than 2900 current journals and serials, has an excellent reference collection and an extensive collection of rare and historical works in medicine and nursing.

OH —AULTMAN HOSPITAL SCHOOL OF NURSING, Library, 2614 Sixth St SW, Canton, 44710. Violet Russell, Librn
Holdings: Vols 49 Cat
Budget: ($2800)

OH —UNIVERSITY OF CINNCINNATI NURSING AND HEALTH LIBRARIES, Solomon Levi Memorial Library, Procter Hall, Cincinnati, 45219. Ava Fried, Librn
Holdings: Vols 1000 // Cat Pix

PA —PENNSYLVANIA HOSPITAL HISTORICAL LIBRARY, Eighth & Spruce Sts, Philadelphia, 19107. Caroline Morris, Librn
Holdings: Vols (13,009)
Budget: ($15,000)
Notes: 20th century journals and current medical books. Strong collection of nursing journals. Some historical nursing textbooks and a good collection on the history of nursing.

NURSES AND NURSING—HISTORY (cont.)

TX —NORTH TEXAS STATE UNIVERSITY, Archives, NT Station Box 5188, Denton, 76203. Robert LaForte, University Archivist
Notes: Oral History Collection. Incl interviews with survivors of attack on Pearl Harbor, incl soldiers, sailors, nurses, civilians, family members present during the attack. Cataloged. Transcriptions available.

NURSES AND NURSING—PICTURES, ILLUSTRATIONS, ETC.

MD —NATIONAL LIBRARY OF MEDICINE, History of Medicine Division, 8600 Rockville Pike, Bethesda, 20014.
Notes: Books and journals related to nursing and the nursing profession, both early and current items. A manuscripts collection incl the archives of the American College of Nurse Midwives (1946-1976) and the National League for Nursing (1894-1952). Photographs in the Prints and Photographs Collection document the history of nursing from the Middle Ages to the 1960s.

NURSING, PRACTICAL see Practical Nursing

NURSING, PSYCHIATRIC see Psychiatric Nursing

NURSING HOMES

OR —UNIVERSITY OF OREGON LIBRARY, 1607 Agate St, Eugene, 97403. Ruth M Brewer, Resource Librn
Notes: Social and psychological aspects of aging.

NUSATENGGARA see Indonesia

NUSSBAUM, JESSE L.

NM —MUSEUM OF NEW MEXICO, Photo Archives, Box 2087, Santa Fe, 87503. Arthur L Olivas, Cur; Richard Rudisill, Photo Historian
Holdings: Cat Pix Slides
Notes: Extensive collection of his works.

NUTE, GRACE LEE

MN —UNIVERSITY OF MINNESOTA, DULUTH, Library & Learning Resources Service, Duluth, 55812. James V. Litha, Archivist
Holdings: Vols (1700) Cat Mss Maps Pix
Notes: The Voyageur Collection incl the Grace Lee Nute Papers. Books and materials relating to the Voyageur period (1650-1850) and the area of Northeastern Minnesota, Michigan, Wisconsin, Southern Canada. Emphasis on all subjects listed in this volume.

NUTRIENT CYCLES

ME —BIGELOW LABORATORY FOR OCEAN SCIENCES & MAINE DEPT OF MARINE RESOURCES, Library, McKown Point, West Boothbay Harbor, 04575. Pamela Shephard-Lupo, Librn
Holdings: Vols Cat Periodicals Mss
Budget: ($55,000)
Notes: This library presently serves two institutions. The Maine Dept of Marine Resources has maintained the library since 1957 and thus the majority of our holdings are geared to their needs, ie fish biology and stock assessment on a local, national and international level. In 1973 Bigelow Laboratory for Ocean Sciences came to West Boothbay Harbor and began to contribute to the library with a very specialized collection on the Gulf of Maine marine chemistry; phytoplankton and nutrient cycles.

NUTRITION

CA —LOS ANGELES PUBLIC LIBRARY, Science & Technology Dept, 630 W Fifth St, Los Angeles, 90071. Billie M Connor, Dept Head
Holdings: Vols (7500)
Notes: A well-rounded collection of materials related to consumer health, medicine and drugs as well as materials for the allied health and medical professions. Includes a sound representative selection of basic texts covering various aspects of medical treatment, drugs, diseases and syndromes. Indexes are collected as well as a basic collection of journals. The directories collection is strong. The broadest possible collection of books oriented toward consumer health, medicine, diets and nutrition is maintained, both traditional and alternative. Texts and examination study books are collected for nurses, laboratory technicians, physcial therapists, speech therapists, paramedics and other allied health professions.

CO —COLORADO STATE UNIVERSITY, Libraries, Fort Collins, 80523. Marjorie Rhoades, Engineering Sciences Librn
Holdings: Vols (6000) Cat
Budget: ($5000)
Notes: Water and Soil in Arid Regions (WASAR) is an index and guide to books, conference papers, journal articles, government documents and technical reports, mostly in English, within the appropriate subject areas and held by Colorado State University Libraries. The bibliographical citations are of selected items dealing with soils, water, arid lands, crops, foods and nutrition with certain economic, political, ecological and historical parameters also included. The information needs of developing countries and of those who serve them are the prime criteria for inclusion.

CT —YALE UNIVERSITY, Box 1603A, Yale Station, New Haven, 06520.

DC —LIBRARY OF CONGRESS, Rare Book & Special Collections Div, Washington, 20540. William Matheson, Chief
Holdings: Cat
Notes: The Katherine Golden Bitting Gastronomic Library. The collection comprises materials on the sources, preparation and consumption of foods from the earliest times to the present day, embracing the whole range of human interest in food. Incl an important 15th century Italian ms, a large number of early French, Italian, English and German works (incl incunabula) and a range of early American cookbooks and works on domestic science. Regional cookbooks and works on the chemistry, bacteriology and preservation of food are strongly represented among titles of more recent date. The majority of the volumes in the collection are described in Mrs Bitting's *Gastronomic Bibliography* (San Francisco, 1939). Also, personal library of Elizabeth Robins Pennell, magazine journalist and wife of artist Joseph Pennell, incl ca 430 cookbooks in English, French and German, 16th to 18th century, described in Mrs. Pennell's *My Cookery Books* (Boston, Houghton-Mifflin, 1903).

DC —LIBRARY OF CONGRESS, Manuscript Division, Washington, 20540. John C Broderick, Chief
Notes: Papers of Robert Ramapatnam Williams (1886-1965), a pioneer in the field of nutrition and public health who synthesized thiamin (vitamin B1), helped to effect the widespread enrichment of foodstuff grains, and developed the Williams-Waterman Fund to combat diseases caused by inadequate nutrition. 20,000 items, incl correspondence, reports, photographs, and glass spectographic plates, document research on and production of vitamin B1, enrichment of cereal products, and the Williams-Waterman Fund.

DC —SMITHSONIAN INSTITUTION LIBRARIES, National Zoological Park Branch, Washington, 20008. Kay Kenyon, Chief Librn
Holdings: Vols (5500) Cat
Notes: Collection incl animal nutrition, capture and care of animals in captivity, conservation and endangered species, pathology, veterinary medicine, zoology.

FL —UNIVERSITY OF FLORIDA, Institute of Food & Agricultural Sciences, Hume Library, Gainesville, 32611. Albert C Strickland, Librn
Holdings: Vols (135,000) Cat Mss Microforms
Notes: Including journals and monographs, this collection is a general agricultural one. The emphasis is on tropical agriculture, especially Latin America. Entomology is very strong. The library offers on-line information retrieval using Lockheed and SDC data bases.

IL —UNIVERSITY OF ILLINOIS, URBANA/CHAMPAIGN, Library, Home Economics Library, 314 Bevier Hall, Champaign, 61820. Barbara C Swain, Librn
Holdings: Vols Cat Microforms
Notes: Foods and Nutrition.
See also entry under Diet and Disease

IL —ARCHER DANIELS MIDLAND CO, Library, 4666 Faries Parkway, Decatur, 62525. Richard E Wallace, Manager, Information Services; Karen E Perman, Librn
Holdings: Vols 8000 Cat Maps Slides 16mm Films Microforms
Notes: Incl all aspects of foods--processing, economics, nutrition, science, technology, statistics, research, marketing, etc. Special interest in foods derived from plant materials. Incl 100 maps, 1200 slides, 105 films, over 2000 microforms, patents, and research reports.

IL —NATIONAL DAIRY COUNCIL, Library, 6300 N River Rd, Rosemont, 60018. Diana Culbertson, Librn
Holdings: Vols (7500) Cat Microforms
Budget: ($62,000)
Notes: Dairies and dairying, with emphasis on human nutrition in the US.

IN —BRISTOL-MYERS PHARMACEUTICAL R&D DIVISION, Scientific Information Dept, 2404 W Pennsylvania St, Evansville, 47721. Alice Weisling, Mgr
Holdings: Vols 33,000 Cat Microforms

IN —PURDUE UNIVERSITY LIBRARIES, Consumer & Family Sciences Library, Stone Hall W, West Lafayette, 47907. Emily Alward, Librn
Holdings: Vols (14,000) Cat

IA —IOWA STATE UNIVERSITY, Library, Ames, 50011. Warren B Kuhn, Dean of Library Services
Holdings: Cat
Notes: Incl animal nutrition, dietetics and food science, and research. Extensive serial holdings.

KS —KANSAS STATE UNIVERSITY, Library, Special Collections & University Archives, Manhattan, 66506. Antonia Q Pigno, Coordr; John J Vander Velde, Librn; Anthony R Crawford, Univ Archivist
Holdings: Vols 4500 Cat Mss
Budget: ($10,000)
Notes: Cookbooks and related items on home economics, nutrition and domestic economy. Nucleus of the collection is from the Abby Lillian Marlatt collection augmented by a sizable bequest from the estate of Clementine Paddleford. Includes about 600 volumes of rare cookbooks from the 16th, 17th, and 18th centuries as well as unprocessed papers (scrapbooks, recipe files and correspondence of Clementine Paddleford). A chronological bibliography is available for the pre-1900 portion of the collection: *The Kansas State University Receipt Book and Household Manual* (1968) by G A Rudolph.

KY —UNIVERSITY OF KENTUCKY, Agricultural Library, Agricultural Science Center North, Lexington, 40506. Antoinette Paris Powell, Librn
Holdings: Vols (90,000) Cat Microforms
Budget: ($110,385)

MD —US DEPT OF AGRICULTURE, National Agricultural Library, 10301 Baltimore Blvd, Beltsville, 20705. Joseph H Howard, Director
Notes: Worldwide coverage of all aspects of agriculture and related fields. Crop ecology, agro-climatic analogs; air pollution effects. Agronomy: agricultural and tropical and desert agriculture. For use by the staff of the USDA. Incl in the former collections of American Institute of Crop Ecology.

NUTRITION (cont.)

MA —UNIVERSITY OF MASSACHUSETTS
AT AMHERST, Library, Amherst, 01003.
Siegfried Feller, Assoc Dir for Collection
Development
Holdings: Cat
Notes: Veterinary medicine and animal
sciences. Special emphases: reproductive
physiology, poultry genetics, animal
nutrition.

MA —TUFTS UNIVERSITY, Health Sciences
Library, 136 Harrison Ave, Boston, 02111.
Elizabeth K Eaton, Dir
Holdings: Vols (91,252) Cat Slides
Phonorecords Audiotapes Videotapes
Microforms
Budget: ($220,055)
Notes: Incl 219 titles, 4 journal titles, 653
videotapes, 3104 microfilms, 7027
microcards, and 1051 serials.

MA —HARVARD MEDICAL SCHOOL, New
England Primate Research Center Library, 1
Pine Hill Dr, Southborough, 01772. Sydney
Fingold, Librn
Holdings: Vols (4000)

MI —UNIVERSITY OF MICHIGAN, Public
Health Library, Ann Arbor, 48109. Mary
Townsend, Head
Holdings: Vols (55,000) Cat Maps Pix
Budget: ($24,000)

MO —PET INCORPORATED, Information
Center, 400 S Fourth St, PO Box 392, Saint
Louis, 63166. L R Walton, Corporate Librn
Holdings: Vols (21,000) Cat Microforms

NJ —RUTGERS, THE STATE UNIVERSITY
OF NEW JERSEY, Center of Alcohol
Studies Library, Smithers Hall, New
Brunswick, 08903. Penny Page, Librn
Holdings: Vols (8075) Cat Mss Microforms
Budget: ($110,000)
See also entry under Alcoholism

NJ —CPC INTERNATIONAL, Best Food
Research & Engineering Center, Information
Center, 1120 Commerce Ave, Union, 07083.
Anne Troop, Mgr
Holdings: Vols (5000) Cat Slides Videotapes
16mm Films Microforms
Notes: Nutrition and toxicology.

NY —NEW YORK ZOOLOGICAL SOCIETY
LIBRARY, Bronx Zoo, Bronx, 10460.
Steven P Johnson, Archivist and Librn
Holdings: Vols (6000) Cat Mss
Budget: ($50,000)
Notes: Collection consists primarily of
journals in captive management of animals,
vertebrate zoology, and veterinary medicine.
Primarily intended for the scientific staff, the
collection is open to the public on a
noncirculating basis, by appointment, (212)
220-6874.

NY —US VETERANS ADMINISTRATION
HOSPITAL, Medical Library, 130 W
Kingsbridge Rd, Bronx, 10468. Margaret M
Kinney, Chief Librn
Holdings: Vols (23,000) Cat
Notes: No photocopying.

†NY —MEDICAL RESEARCH LIBRARY
OF BROOKLYN, Academy of Medicine of
Brooklyn & The State University of New
York Downstate Medical Center, 450
Clarkson St, Brooklyn, 11203. Kenneth E
Moody, Dir
Holdings: Vols 1500 Cat
See also entry under Medicine.

NY —ROCKEFELLER UNIVERSITY,
Rockefeller Archive Center, Hillcrest,
Pocantico Hills, North Tarrytown, 10591.
Joseph W Ernst, Dir; J William Hess, Assoc
Dir
Notes: Papers relative to the Rockefeller
Family, Foundations, University, and other
specific enterprises and contributions to
particular areas of social, physical,
educational, and historic reform,
preservation, conservation, or development.
Extensive records of administrative,
financial, physical, or intellectual
relationships.

NC —NORTH CAROLINA DEPT OF
HUMAN RESOURCES, Div of Health
Services, Public Health Library, PO Box
2091, Raleigh, 27602. Elnora H Turner,
Librn
Holdings: Vols (15,000) Cat

OH —OHIO STATE UNIVERSITY, Home
Economics Library, Campbell Hall Rm 325,
1787 Neil Ave, Columbus, 43210. Neosha
Mackey, Librn
Holdings: Vols (14,000) Cat Microforms
Notes: Separate catalog. Also, book catalog:
Catalog of the Home Economics Library
(Boston: G K Hall, 1976), 3 vols.

OH —MIAMI VALLEY HOSPITAL,
Memorial Medical Library, 1 Wyoming St,
Dayton, 45409. Margaret C Hardy, Dir
Holdings: Vols 40,000 Cat Pix Slides
Audiotapes Videotapes
Budget: ($200,000)

OR —OREGON STATE UNIVERSITY,
Library, Corvallis, 97331. Melvin George,
Dir
Holdings: Vols (980,000) Cat

PA —DREXEL UNIVERSITY LIBRARIES,
W W Hagerty Library, 32 & Chestnut Sts,
Philadelphia, 19104. R L Snyder, Dir
Holdings: Vols (5000) Cat
Budget: ($9000)
Notes: Food technology and management
with emphasis on nutrition. Also incl
collection of cookbooks which stress cultural
differences and the best in sound American
cooking.

TN —VANDERBILT UNIVERSITY, Medical
Center Library, Nashville, 37232. Mary H
Teloh, Special Collections Librn
Holdings: Uncat Mss Pix Videotapes
Notes: The nucleus of the developing
nutrition collection at Vanderbilt is the
papers of medical researcher Joseph
Goldberger, MD, and his associate W Henry
Sebrell, Jr, MD. The collection consists of
first editions and translations of classic books
on pellagra, and the letters, mss, and
notebooks compiled by Dr Goldberger and
Dr Sebrell during their years of research on
pellagra. See Nutrition Reviews, 33(10):310-
312, Oct 1975. 10 linear ft of mss. Library
also has the archives of the American
Institute of Nutrition and manuscripts
representing the work of Karl Mason, PhD,
Helen S Mitchell, PhD, Lydia J Roberts,
PhD, and John B Youmans, MD.

TX —UNIVERSITY OF TEXAS LIBRARIES,
John W Mallet Chemistry Library, Welch
Hall 2132, Austin, 78712. A E Skinner,
Chemistry Librn
Holdings: Vols (44,000) Cat Microforms
Notes: Described in The John W Mallet
Chemistry Library (The University of Texas
at Austin) (Austin: The General Libraries,
1975).

WA —UNIVERSITY OF WASHINGTON
LIBRARIES, Suzzallo Library, Natural
Sciences Library, FM-25, Seattle, 98195.
Nancy G Blase, Head
Holdings: Vols (192,353) //
Budget: ($219,809)

WI —UNIVERSITY OF WISCONSIN,
MADISON, College of Agricultural & Life
Sciences, Steenbock Memorial Library, 550
Babcock Dr, Madison, 53706. Jan Kennedy,
Dir
Holdings: Vols (186,312) Cat Docs
Computer software
Notes: Collection includes human and
animal nutrition; and food science,
toxicology and microbiology.

WI —UNIVERSITY OF WISCONSIN-
STOUT, Library Learning Center,
Menomonie, 54751. Philip Sawin Jr, Coll
Develop Librn
Notes: Supports graduate program in Foods
and Nutrition, which was begun in 1960.
Quite specific collection with emphasis on
the clinical aspects of nutrition.

ON —RYERSON POLYTECHNICAL
INSTITUTE LIBRARY, 50 Gould St,
Toronto, M5B 1E8, Can. J North, Dir
Holdings: Vols 100,000 Cat Mss

PQ —UNIVERSITY OF MONTREAL,
Bibliotheque Para-medicale, 2375 Chemin de
la Cote Ste Catherine, Montreal, H3C 3J7,
Can. Johanne Hopper, Head Librn
Holdings: Vols 3000 Cat
Budget: $6000

NUTTING, HELEN

IL —NORTHWESTERN UNIVERSITY,
Library, Special Collections Dept, 1937
Sheridan Rd, Evanston, 60201. R Russell
Maylone, Cur
Holdings: Mss
Notes: 500 ms pieces incl diaries,
correspondence and notes.

NUTTING, M. ADELAIDE

MA —SIMMONS COLLEGE ARCHIVES,
300 The Fenway, Boston, 02115. Megan
Sniffin-Marinoff, College Archivist
Notes: Archives of the Simmons College
School of Public Health Nursing (later
reorganized into the School of Nursing)
cover the years 1902-1970. Important
correspondents in the collection incl M
Adelaide Nutting, Mary Beard, Isabel
Stewart, and Anne Hervey Strong, etc. Incl
Strong's records of activity with regard to
nursing education in the National
Organization for Public Health Nursing,
1918-22. 1000 linear feet in institution, incl
special collections nursing and photographs,
nursing.

NYASALAND see Malawi

O

O. HENRY

NC —GREENSBORO PUBLIC LIBRARY, 201 N Greene St, Drawer X-4, Greensboro, 27402. J Douglas Kerr, Caldwell Jones Librn
Holdings: Mss Pix
Notes: In addition to his books and biographies, there are 3 vertical file drawers of material pertaining to him—newspapers articles, pamphlets, magazine articles, etc. Also, notes of his biographer Dr C A Smith; letters, mss and drawings by O Henry; other memorabilia.

VA —UNIVERSITY OF VIRGINIA, Alderman Library, Clifton Waller Barrett Collection, Charlottesville, 22901. Joan St C Crane, Cur of American Literature Collections
Notes: Papers.

WI —UNIVERSITY OF WISCONSIN, MADISON, Memorial Library, Rare Books Collection, 728 State St, Madison, 53706. Gretchen Lagana, Cur
Holdings: Vols 20 // Cat Mss
Notes: O Henry Collection. Donated by Norman Bassett, the collection contains almost every first edition of Porter in book form. It also includes several items of Porteriana and the original contract between Porter and McClure, Phillips and Company for the twenty-five stories which became the major portion of *The Four Million*. Supplements other O Henry library holdings. Restricted use: Rare Book Department.

OATES, JOYCE CAROL

AZ —UNIVERSITY OF ARIZONA, University Library, Special Collections, Tucson, 85721. Louis A Hieb, Head
Holdings: Vols (7000) Cat Mss Microforms
Budget: ($30,000)
Notes: In the 20th century, the major emphasis is Bukowski, Wakoski, Wilder, Reznikoff, Ginzberg, Ferlinghetti, Snyder, Whalen, Everson, Joyce Carol Oates, and Kurt Vonnegut.

NV —UNIVERSITY OF NEVADA, RENO, University Library, Special Collections Dept, Reno, 89557. Robert E Blesse, Head
Holdings: Vols (123) Cat
Notes: Includes individual works by author in all editions including translations; also prefaces, introductions, published correspondence, appearances in anthologies, periodicals, etc. Bibliographical research collection, part of Modern Authors Collection. Other appearances 380 cataloged.

OBERAMMERGAU PASSION PLAY

DC —GEORGETOWN UNIVERSITY, Library, Special Collections Div, 37 & O Sts NW, Washington, 20057. George M Barringer, Special Collections Librn; Nicholas B Sheetz, Mss Librn
Holdings: Mss
Notes: The papers of Miss Janet E Richards, lecturer and columnist, consisting of correspondence, family records, and photographs; incl material on women's suffrage and the Oberammergau Passion Play.

OBERHOLZER, EMIL, 1883-1958

KS —MENNINGER FOUNDATION, Archives, 5600 W Sixth St, Box 829, Topeka, 66601. Alice Brand, Librn; Mark West, Archivist
Notes: Incl in his papers are mss, correspondence, research notes, and miscellaneous materials. Most of the papers in the collection are written in German.

OBEY, ANDRE

ON —MCMASTER UNIVERSITY, Mills Memorial Library, Div of Archives & Research Collections, Hamilton, L8S 4L6, Can. G R Hill, Univ Librn
Holdings: // Mss
Notes: Correspondence between Jacques Copeau and Andre Obey concerning the French theatre, 1924-1945.

OBITUARIES—COLLECTIONS

MA —NEW ENGLAND HISTORIC GENEALOGICAL SOCIETY, Library, 101 Newbury St, Boston, 02116. Ralph J Crandell, Dir
Holdings: Vols (250,000) Mss Maps Microforms Pix
Notes: New England genealogy. Especially strong Massachusetts, Maine, and New Hampshire, although all states are well represented, as are the relevancies of each subject listed in this volume with regard to British antecedent and contemporary history. Special strengths in local history and biography, obituaries, etc, incl parish registers, censuses, British and American. 3125 linear ft of mss.

OH —CLEVELAND PUBLIC LIBRARY, General Reference Dept, 325 Superior Ave, Cleveland, 44114. Donald Tipka, Head
Notes: Approximately 800,000 entries. Microfilm and computer printout of death notices from Cleveland newspapers: 1833-1975, 1976-date, index by computer; also cemetery records to 1939 for Cuyahoga County cemeteries. Photocopying.

OBREGON, ALVARO

CA —CLAREMONT COLLEGES, Honnold Library, Ninth & Dartmouth, Claremont, 91711. Tania Rizzo, Special Collections Dept Head
Holdings: Cat Mss Pix Scrapbooks
Notes: Correspondence, mss, documents, clippings, photographs, and ephemera, 2200 pieces, some in carbon copies, of Jose Maytorena, from 1882-1947. Important correspondents incl Venustiano Carranza, Francisco Madero, and Alvaro Obregon, among many others. Guy T McCreary, *A Primary Study of the Revolutionary, Governor, General, Jose maria Maytorena and the Mexican Revolution* 1910-1916 (thesis, 1967) based on this collection. Restricted use.

O'BRIAN, HUGH

CA —UNIVERSITY OF CALIFORNIA, LOS ANGELES, Theater Arts Library, Los Angeles, 90024. Edward Shreeves, Chairman, Bibliographers Group; Audree Malkin, Head, Theater Arts Library
Notes: Hugh O'Brian (actor) Collection: screenplays, theater and television scripts, television series presentations, musical scores, and clippings from O'Brian's career.

O'BRIEN, KATE

DC —GEORGETOWN UNIVERSITY, Library, Special Collections Div, 37 & O Sts NW, Washington, 20057. George M Barringer, Special Collections Librn; Nicholas B Sheetz, Mss Librn
Holdings: Mss Cat
Notes: The literary papers of author and art curator, James Laver (1899-1975), and those of his wife, the actress Veronica Turleigh; consisting of letters, with a considerable number written by Lady Cnythia Asquith; Clifford Box; Enid Bagnold; Nicholas Bentley; Violet Clifton; Desmond MacCarthy; Sir Edward Marsh; Sir Francis Meynell; Kate O'Brien; Dorothy L Sayers; Andre Simon; Enid Starkie; A J A Symons; Angela Thirkell; and Alec Waugh.

IL —NORTHWESTERN UNIVERSITY, Library, Special Collections Dept, 1937 Sheridan Rd, Evanston, 60201. R Russell Maylone, Cur
Holdings: Cat Mss Paintings
Notes: First, limited, special editions, letters, ephemera of major 20th century Irish writers such as James Joyce and W B Yeats, as well as representative minor writers. Incl the Dublin Gate Theatre Archive, several paintings by Jack B Yeats and a large collection of Kate O'Brien mss. Literature: Tina Howe, *A Guide to the Books and Collection of Manuscripts of Novels, Plays, Short Stories, Articles, Talks, and Letters of Kate O'Brien in the Special Collections Department, Northwestern University Library* (January, 1975).

O'BRIEN, LAWRENCE

†MA —JOHN F KENNEDY LIBRARY, Columbia Point, Boston, 02125. Dan H Fenn Jr, Dir
Holdings: // Cat Mss
Notes: Lawrence O'Brien's papers relating to his position as Special Assistant to the President for Congressional Relations, 1961-1963. 13 linear ft of mss. Holdings are described in "Historical Materials in the John F Kennedy Library." Copies may be obtained by writing the Research Archivist.

O'BRYANT, JANE

KS —WICHITA PUBLIC LIBRARY, Art & Music Division, 223 S Main, Wichita, 67202. Leonard Messineo, Jr, Head, Art & Music Division; Deborah Hamilton, Special Collections Librn
Notes: Joan O'Bryant Kansas Folklore Collection. Contains approximately 200 hours of folkmusic and oral histories on tape; over 27,000 note cards covering topics such as anecdotes, beliefs, customs, games, jokes, medicines and cures, proverbs, recipes, rhymes, riddles, sayings, songs, speech and dialect, etc; 102 research papers covering family histories, town and area histories, biographies, tales, recipes, etc; and well over 70 mounted quilt blocks-covering the folk history of Kansas. This material was collected by Joan O'Bryant and her students from 1947-1964, the period in which she taught Folklore and English at Wichita State University.

OBSERVATORIES, ASTRONOMICAL
see Astronomical Observatories

OBSTETRICS

CT —YALE MEDICAL LIBRARY, 333 Cedar St, New Haven, 06510.
Holdings: Vols (334,215) Cat Mss Pix Slides Microforms
Budget: ($361,650)
Notes: Incl films, audiotapes, artifacts, etc.

CT —YALE UNIVERSITY, School of Medicine, Dept of Obstetrics & Gynecology Library, Farnam Memorial Bldg, New Haven, 06510.
Holdings: Cat Mss Pix Slides X-Rays
Notes: X-ray plates, 10,000 slides of monkey and human tissue and about 1000 slides of gynecological and obstetrical pathology, used as teaching and research materials. Other large collections of X-rays and radiotherapy photographs are in the Hunter Radiation Therapy Center.

IL —UNIVERSITY OF CHICAGO LIBRARY, Dept of Special Collections, 1100 E 57 St, Chicago, 60637.

MA —FRANCIS A COUNTWAY LIBRARY OF MEDICINE, Boston Medical Library/ Harvard Medical Library, 10 Shattuck St, Boston, 02115. C Robin LeSueur, Librn; Richard J Wolfe, Cur, Rare Books & Manuscripts
Holdings: Vols (500,000) Cat Mss Maps Pix Microforms
Notes: Combines resources of the Harvard Medical School and the Boston Medical Library. Strong in serials and medical history in all fields of medicine, incl incunabula, non-medical books by doctors, travel books by doctors. 500,000 medical dissertations and theses. Special strength in all medical subjects listed in this volume.

†NY —MEDICAL RESEARCH LIBRARY OF BROOKLYN, Academy of Medicine of Brooklyn & The State University of New York Downstate Medical Center, 450 Clarkson St, Brooklyn, 11203. Kenneth E Moody, Dir
See also entry under Medicine.

NY —FLUSHING HOSPITAL & MEDICAL CENTER, Medical Library, Parsons Blvd & 45 Ave, Flushing, 11355. Maria Czechowicz,

OBSTETRICS (cont.)

Dir
Holdings: Vols (5741) Cat Audiotapes
Budget: ($11,000)

OBSTETRICS—HISTORY

CA —UNIVERSITY OF CALIFORNIA, SAN
FRANCISCO, Library, Special Collections,
San Francisco, 94143. Nancy Witten Zinn,
Librn
Holdings: Vols (23,000) Cat Mss Pix
Budget: ($8500)

GA —MEDICAL COLLEGE OF GEORGIA,
Library, Laney Walker Blvd, Augusta,
30902. Dorothy H Mims, Librn for Special
Collections
Holdings: Vols (2500) Cat
Notes: Special collection of late 18th and
early 19th century medical works includes
both the typical and the classic books on
midwifery and diseases of women.

MD —MEDICAL & CHIRURGICAL
FACULTY OF THE STATE OF
MARYLAND, Library, 1211 Cathedral St,
Baltimore, 21201. Joseph E Jensen, Librn
Holdings: Vols (10,000) // Cat Mss Maps
Pix
See also entry under Medicine - History and
Historic

MO —WASHINGTON UNIVERSITY, School
of Medicine, Library, 660 South Euclid Ave,
Saint Louis, 63110. Christopher Hoolihan,
Rare Book Librn
Holdings: Vols (12,000) Cat
Budget: ($40,000)
Notes: A comprehensive collection of 16th
through 19th century works illustrating the
progress of obstetrical science in Europe and
North America.

NE —UNIVERSITY OF NEBRASKA
MEDICAL CENTER, Library, 42 & Dewey
Ave, Omaha, 68105. Robert M Braude, Dir
Holdings: Vols (196,313)
Budget: ($320,000)
Notes: History of Medicine Collection
particularly strong in obstetrics and
gynecology.

NY —NEW YORK UNIVERSITY,
MEDICAL CENTER, Medical Library, 550
First Ave, New York, 10016. Gilbert J
Clausman, Librn
Holdings: Vols (143,000) Cat Microforms
Budget: ($929,000)
Notes: Also over 11,000 microforms.

NY —UNIVERSITY OF ROCHESTER,
School of Medicine and Dentistry, Edward
G Miner Library, 601 Elmwood Ave,
Rochester, 14642. Lucretia McClure,
Medical Librn; Janet Brady Berk, History of
Medicine Librn
Notes: Strong in yellow fever, cholera,
orthopaedics, anatomy and original historic
medical photographs.

OH —CLEVELAND MEDICAL LIBRARY
ASSOCIATION/CASE WESTERN
RESERVE UNIVERSITY, Cleveland Health
Sciences Library, Historical Division, Allen
Memorial Medical Library, 11000 Euclid
Ave, Cleveland, 44106. Glen Jenkins, Rare
Book Librarian & Archivist
Notes: Incl 15,000 historical vols, 6000 in
the supporting collection. Incl about 1000
16th-18th century titles. Strength of
collection: diseases, epidemiology, anatomy,
surgery, medicine, obstetrics, gynecology,
pediatrics and yellow fever. Incl also medical
Americana, listed in Robert B Austin Early
American Medical Imprints, 1668-1820
(Washington, DC, HEW, Public Health
Service, 1961) and ca 7000 19th century
works. Our total medical Americana
collection also incl journals (not counted),
mss and archives (900 linear ft) and 5000
pictures, especially of the Western Reserve.
Anatomical works discussed in I Ebner and
G Jenkins Skeletons in Our Closet
(Cleveland, Cleveland Health Sciences
Library, 1983)

ON —UNIVERSITY OF TORONTO, Thomas
Fisher Rare Book Library, 120 Saint George
St, Toronto, M5S 1A5, Can. Richard G
Landon, Head
Holdings: Vols (6000) Cat
Notes: Hannah Collection named in honour
of Jason A Hannah, the founder of the
Hannah Institute for the History of Medical
and Related Sciences at the University of
Toronto. Collection comprises a wide range
of works in medicine, surgery, anatomy,
physiology and other related sciences
published in the major European countries
and Great Britain from 1500 to 1900. Areas
of special strength are psychology,
gynecology and obstetrics. Highlights of
collection described in two exhibition
catalogues published by the Thomas Fisher
Rare Book Library: The Early History of
Medicine; An Exhibition of Books Selected
from the Jason A Hannah Collection in the
History of Medical and Related Sciences
(March, 1974) and The Byrth of Mankynd
(1981).

O'CASEY, SEAN

NY —NEW YORK PUBLIC LIBRARY, Berg
Collection of English & American Literature,
Fifth Ave & 42 St, New York, 10018. Lola
L Szladits, Cur
Holdings: Cat Mss
Notes: Largest known assemblage of Sean
O'Casey's literary papers. Complements the
Lady Gregory archive and makes the library
a center for study of the Irish Literary
Revival.

OCCIDENT AND ORIENT see East and West

OCCITANE LANGUAGE see Provencal Language and Literature

OCCULT SCIENCES

AZ —WORLD UNIVERSITY, Library, 711 E
Blacklidge Dr, Tucson, 85719. Howard John
Zitko, Cur
Holdings: Vols (15,000) Cat Mss Maps
Audiotapes
Notes: Collection concerns the "frontier
sciences." No interlibrary loan.

CA —GRADUATE THEOLOGICAL UNION
LIBRARY, New Religious Movements
Research Collection, Public Services and
Special Collections Dept, 2400 Ridge Road,
Berkeley, 94709. Diane Choquette, Dept
Head
Holdings: Vols (3000) Mss Pix
Notes: Begun in 1977, the collection focuses
on religious movements new to America
since 1960, and unorthodox religious
movements resurgent since 1960. American
forms of Hinduism, Buddhism, Sikhism, and
Sufism are included along with occultism,
Neo-Paganism, esoteric and alternative
forms of Christianity, feminist spirituality,
and human potential movements having a
spiritual aspect. Legal issues, such as
deprogramming, and the question of church/
state relations are an important part of the
collection. The Library is a depository for
publications of the Unification Church in
America, the Church of Scientology, and the
International Society for Krishna
Consciousness (America). The responses of
mainstream religions and concerned citizens
groups are also included. Besides 3000
monographs, the library has 400 periodical
titles, 200 posters from the San
FranciscoBay Area, 1965-77, 300 research
papers, and 31 linear feet of ephemera.

CA —FRANCIS BACON LIBRARY, 655 N
Dartmouth Ave, Claremont, 91711.
Elizabeth S Wrigley, Dir
Notes: Collection includes witchcraft and
magic from early items to the 20th century.
Many 17th century volumes.

CA —LOS ANGELES PUBLIC LIBRARY,
Philosophy & Religion Dept, 630 W Fifth St,
Los Angeles, 90071. Marilyn C Wherley,
Librn
Holdings: Vols 700 Cat
Budget: ($60,000)
Notes: Comprehensive coverage of popular
and scholarly works on all aspects of the
occult including black magic, witchcraft,
demonology, paranormal occurances,
psychical research and metaphysics. Includes
many serials, periodicals and special indexes.

CA —UNIVERSITY OF CALIFORNIA, LOS
ANGELES, Research Library, Dept of
Special Collections, 405 Hilgard Ave, Los
Angeles, 90024. Edward Shreeves,
Chairman, Bibliographers Group; David S
Zeidberg, Head
Holdings: Mss Pix
Notes: 1200 linear feet of political,
economic, financial, press, diplomatic,
espionage, secret societies, occultism, and
contemporary bibliographical archives and
documents, 1910-1965, assembled by Roger
Mennevee, editor of Les documents
politiques, diplomatiques et financiers.

CA —SAN DIEGO PUBLIC LIBRARY,
Literature & Language Sect, 820 E St, San
Diego, 92101. Alyce Archuleta, Senior Librn
Holdings: Cat
Notes: Old and current reference and
circulating works on the subject. Incl
complete works by Blavatsky, much by
Rudolf Steiner, and C Zain. Strong in
astrology, witchcraft, parapsychology.

CT —YALE UNIVERSITY, Box 1603A, Yale
Station, New Haven, 06520.

DE —UNIVERSITY OF DELAWARE, Hugh
M Morris Library, S College Ave, Newark,
19711. T Stuart Dick, Special Collections
Holdings: Cat
Notes: Part of the Unidel Collection of the
History of Chemistry.

IL —UNIVERSITY OF ILLINOIS,
URBANA/CHAMPAIGN, Library,
University Archives, 19 Library, 1408 W
Gregory Drive, Urbana, 61801. Maynard
Brichford, University Archivist
Holdings: Vols (5000) Cat
Budget: ($7000)
Notes: The Mandeville Collection in
Parapsychology and Occult Sciences. Titles
in the Merten J Mandeville Collection are
purchased by funds from an endowment
provided specifically for the collection on its
establishment in 1966 by Merten J
Mandeville, Professor Emeritus of
Management, who donated 400 vols from his
personal library as the nucleus of the
collection. There are currently about 5000
titles in the collection, supplemented by
related materials in the general collection.
Topics include astrology, extrasensory
perception, yoga, magic, satanism, faith
healing, hypnosis, Eastern religions,
witchcraft, fortune telling, reincarnation,
flying saucers, ghosts, dreams, numerology,
graphology, and mysticism. Biographies and
reference books are a part of the collection
as are journals devoted to the scientific study
of parapsychology.

MA —HEBREW COLLEGE, Jacob & Rose
Grossman Library and Lawrence Jay &
Anne Cable Rubenstein Library, 43 Hawes
St, Brookline, 02146. Maurice Tuchman,
Librn
Holdings: Vols 600 Cat Mss
Notes: Hassidic and Cabalistic literature.

NJ —SOCIETY FOR THE INVESTIGATION
OF THE UNEXPLAINED, Library, PO
Box 265, Little Silver, 07739. Robert C
Warth, Pres
Holdings: Mss Maps Pix Slides Videotapes
Notes: Information file of original material,
map collection, and specialized library.

NY —PARAPSYCHOLOGY SOURCES OF
INFORMATION CENTER, 2 Plane Tree
Lane, Dix Hills, 11746. Rhea A White, Dir
Holdings: Vols (4000)
Notes: The PSI Center includes 4000 books,
100 periodical titles, cassette tapes, and
unpublished mss dealing with
parapsychology and the transformation of
consciousness, also 12,000 articles, reprints,
etc. There is a charge for reference service
and bibliographies.

NY —AMERICAN SOCIETY FOR
PSYCHICAL RESEARCH LIBRARY, 5 W
73 St, New York, 10023. Rhea A White,
Consultant to the Library
Holdings: Vols (7000) Cat Mss Pix
Budget: ($1500)
Notes: Incl books on spiritualism, as well as
works in psychology, religion, philosophy,
physics, anthropology, etc which have a
possible bearing on parapsychology,. An
attempt is made to obtain all serious books
on parapsychology in English.

OCCULT SCIENCES (cont.)

NY —NEW YORK PUBLIC LIBRARY, Research Libraries, General Research Division, Fifth Ave & 42 St, New York, 10018. Rodney Phillips, Chief
Notes: See *Bibliographic Guide to Psychology, 1976* (Boston: G K Hall, 1977). Incl publications cataloged during the year, with additional entries from MARC tapes.

OH —CLEVELAND PUBLIC LIBRARY, Fine Arts and Special Collections Department, 325 Superior Ave, Cleveland, 44114. Alice N Loranth, Head
Holdings: Vols 2500 Cat Mss
Notes: Emphasis is on historical treatises, folklore aspects and the classic texts pertaining to apparitions, ghosts, divinations, oracles, omens, witchcraft, magic, and sorcery in various civilizations. Astrology, palmistry, psychical research and contemporary manifestations are almost entirely omitted.
See also entries under Folklore; Witchcraft.

RI —BROWN UNIVERSITY, John Hay Library, 20 Prospect St, Providence, 02912. Mark N Brown, Cur Mss
Holdings: Vols (900) Mss
Notes: John William Graham Collection of Literature of Psychic Science; 350 predominantly late 19th and early 20th century books dealing with alchemy, black magic, dreams, demonology, church history, mysticism, mediumship, physical and somatic types of psychic experience. Collection described in *Index to Psychic Science* compiled by S R Morgan (Swarthmore, 1950). Also, the Damon Collection of Occult and Visionary Literature; 550 vols devoted to the development of western mysticism with particular emphasis on American and British thought, incl texts on alchemy, black magic, esoteric church history, dream interpretations, mysticism, witchcraft, the Kabbalah, and visionary testaments and manifestations of all types printed during the 16th to 20th centuries; and the Samuel Wyllys Papers; 125 mss, transcripts, and photocopies of legal and government papers relating to Indianaffairs, colonial wars, civil and criminal cases, and the witchcraft trials of 1692-1693. Partially cataloged.

VA —ASSOCIATION FOR RESEARCH & ENLIGHTENMENT, Library, 67 & Atlantic Avenue, PO Box 595, Virginia Beach, 23451. Stephen Jordan, Library Mgr
Holdings: Vols (1800) Cat
Notes: A R E Library Booklist incl 6000 items in 24 subject categories. This special collection is especially strong in the following subjects: astrology, spiritualism, reincarnation, healing arts, Theosophy, Atlantis, parapsychology and transpersonal psychology.

ON —QUEEN'S UNIVERSITY, Douglas Library, Kingston, K7L 5C4, Can. William F E Morley, Cur, Special Collections
Holdings: Vols 2050 Cat
Notes: The library has purchased the H P Lovecraft collection (225 vols) and has built up a most interesting collection in Gothic Fantasy and tales of the occult. Also, 6500 pulp magazines, uncat. (List available).

†PQ —MCGILL UNIVERSITY, Osler Library, 3655 Drummond St, Montreal, H3G 1Y6, Can.
Notes: The Osler Library is a research library in the history of medicine and allied sciences. Partial listing in *Bibliotheca Osleriana*, 1929, reprinted 1969.

OCCULTISM see Occult Sciences

OCCULTISM IN LITERATURE

OH —BOWLING GREEN STATE UNIVERSITY, Jerome Library, Center for Archival Collections, Bowling Green, 43403. Paul D Yon, Dir; Elaine R Ezell, Reference Archivist; Nancy Steen, Rare Books Librn
Holdings: Vols 1600 Cat Mss Letters Pix
Budget: ($3000)
Notes: The Robert Aickman Collection contains about 40 of Aickman's manuscripts

of both published and unpublished works as well as the late author's personal library which is strong in the areas of English literature and theatre of the 19th and 20th centuries and in the area of the supernatural.

ON —QUEEN'S UNIVERSITY, Douglas Library, Kingston, K7L 5C4, Can. William F E Morley, Cur, Special Collections
Holdings: Vols 2050 Cat
Notes: The library has purchased the H P Lovecraft collection (225 vols) and has built up a most interesting collection in Gothic Fantasy and tales of the occult. Also, 6500 pulp magazines, uncat. (List available).

OCCUPATION, CHOICE OF see Vocational Guidance

OCCUPATION, MILITARY see Military Occupation

OCCUPATIONAL DISEASES

DC —US DEPT OF LABOR, Library, 200 Constitution Ave NW, Washington, 20210. Sabina Jacobson, Dir
Holdings: Vols (550,000) Cat

IL —INSTITUTE ON THE CHURCH IN URBAN-INDUSTRIAL SOCIETY, Library, 5700 S Woodlawn, Chicago, 60637.
Holdings: Vols 1000 Cat Microforms
Notes: Urban-industrial involvement of the churches world-wide, international urban literature, corporate responsibility, human factors of urbanization and industrialization. Library holdings are dorment at present.

MI —UNIVERSITY OF MICHIGAN, Public Health Library, Ann Arbor, 48109. Mary Townsend, Head
Holdings: Vols (55,000) Cat Maps Pix
Budget: ($24,000)

NY —CENTER FOR LABOR STUDIES, SUNY, Empire State College, Labor College Library, 330 W 42nd St, New York, 10036. Jayne Adler, Librn
Holdings: Vols (3000) Cat Videotapes VF
Budget: ($4000)
Notes: Areas being emphasized in development of the library are: Women and Labor, Occupational Health and Safety, and Trade Union Leadership.

WV —NATIONAL INSTITUTE FOR OCCUPATIONAL SAFETY & HEALTH, NIOSH/ALOSH Library, 944 Chestnut Ridge Rd, Morgantown, 26505. Colleen M Herrington, Librn
Holdings: Vols (6000) Cat Microforms
Notes: Occupational safety and health. Main Library located at 4676 Columbia Pkwy, Cincinnati, Ohio. Incl 120,000 microforms.

ON —CANADA DEPT OF LABOUR, Library, Ottawa, K1A 0J2, Can. Monique Marchand, Chief Librn
Holdings: Vols (100,000) Cat Microforms

ON —ONTARIO MINISTRY OF LABOUR, Library, 400 University Ave, Toronto, M7A 1T7, Can. Jean Collins-Williams, Librn
Holdings: Vols (80,000) Microforms Films

PQ —NORANDA RESEARCH CENTRE, Library, 240 Hymus Blvd, Pointe-Claire, H9R 1G5, Can. Shirley Courtis, Librn
Holdings: Vols (7000)

OCCUPATIONAL HEALTH AND SAFETY see Industrial Hygiene; Industrial Safety

OCCUPATIONAL THERAPY

ND —UNIVERSITY OF NORTH DAKOTA, Harley E French Medical Library, Grand Forks, 58202. David W Boilard, Dir; Lila Pedersen, Asst Dir
Holdings: Vols (56,000)
Budget: ($206,000)
Notes: Some 1075 current periodical subscriptions.

OCCUPATIONS

CA —WESTERN COSTUME COMPANY, Research Library, 5335 Melrose Ave, Hollywood, 90038. Nancy S Kinney, Dir of Research
Holdings: Vols 1000
Notes: Incl 9 vertical file drawers of

photographs, 65 binders of current police uniforms incl sheriffs, state police, etc. 6 periodical subs on police profession. Card file index on selected uniform pictures from periodicals holdings. Collection can be used only by the customers of Western Costume Company. All other use is on a fee basis. Collection is non-circulating. Photocopying available.

DC —INTERNATIONAL LABOR ORGANIZATION, International Labor Office, Washington Branch Library, 1750 New York Ave NW, Rm 330, Washington, 20006. Karen J Mark, Librn
Holdings: Vols (13,500) Cat Pix 16mm Films Monographs
Notes: Wide range of titles dealing with worldwide labor and social matters. The library contains ILO publications and documentation only, dating back to 1919. Also, a collection of ILO films and photos. See *Subject Guide to Publications of the ILO, 1919-1964* and *ILO Catalogue of Publications in Print, 1982* (ILO).

MA —HARVARD UNIVERSITY, Graduate School of Business Administration, Baker Library, Soldiers Field, Boston, 02163. Mary V Chatfield, Librn; Florence Bartoshesky, Cur of Manuscripts and Archives

NY —CATALYST, Library, 14 E 60 St, New York, 10022. Gurley Turner, Dir of Information Services
Holdings: Vols (6000) Cat Mss VF
Notes: Working Women (current information); career and family issues plus career library.

NY —FEDERATION EMPLOYMENT & GUIDANCE SERVICE, Richard J Bernhard Memorial Library, 510 Sixth Ave, 4th Floor, New York, 10011. Otto Kanocz, Chief Librn
Holdings: Vols (4000) Cat Microforms Videotapes Audiotapes VF
Notes: Occupational information, guidance and counseling, vocational rehabilitation. Incl 30,000 pamphlets; 200 periodical titles. Also incl 50 vertical files and microfiche. Open to the public.

NC —FORSYTH COUNTY PUBLIC LIBRARY, Adult Continuing Education (ACE) Div, 660 W Fifth St, Winston-Salem, 27101. Ann R Gehlen, Librn
Holdings: Vols 3500 Phonorecords Audiotapes Videotapes 16mm Films Filmstrips Microforms
Budget: $6900
Notes: Special emphasis on high school equivalency preparation, adult new readers, improvement in language and math, secretarial skills, job-hunting techniques, college alternatives, test preparation, and support to independent study in popular subject areas. Extensive pamphlet files of up-to-date career information, indexed. Some 600 bound college catalogs plus national microfiche collection. Current local job openings on microfiche. Information and referral files maintained to relevant local resources (courses, etc). Partially cataloged.

OCCUPATIONS—DISEASES see Occupational Diseases

OCCUPATIONS—HYGIENIC ASPECTS see Industrial Hygiene

OCCUPIED TERRITORY see Military Occupation

OCEAN—MAPS

CA —UNIVERSITY OF CALIFORNIA, SAN DIEGO, Scripps Institution of Oceanography Library, Mail Code C075C, La Jolla, 92093. William J Goff, Librn; Deborarh Day, Archivist
Holdings: Vols (178,000) Cat Maps Microforms
Budget: ($308,200)
Notes: See *Catalogs of the Scripps Institution of Oceanography Library* (Boston: G K Hall, 1970-1980), 21 vols. Incl 44,000 maps, 17,000 microforms cat, 21,000 reprints, and 800 linear feet of archives.

OCEAN LIFE see Marine Biology

OCEAN SURVEY, NATIONAL see National Ocean Survey

OCEAN THERMAL ENERGY

TX —MCDERMOTT HUDSON ENGINEERING, Library, 5900 Hillcroft,

OCEAN THERMAL ENERGY (cont.)

Houston, 77036. Chris Ramirez, Librn
Holdings: Vols (750) Uncat Microforms
Notes: Emphasis is on all forms of
alternative energy sources and energy
conversion.

OCEAN TRANSPORTATION see Shipping

OCEANIA see Islands of the Pacific

OCEANIC ART see Art, Oceanic

OCEANOGRAPHIC ENGINEERING

MI —UNIVERSITY OF MICHIGAN,
Engineering-Transportation Library, 312
Undergraduate Library, Ann Arbor, 48109.
Maurita Holland, Librn
Holdings: Vols (400,000) Cat Microforms
Budget: ($225,000)
NY —ENGINEERING SOCIETIES
LIBRARY, 345 E 47 St, New York, 10017.
S Kirk Cabeen, Dir
Holdings: Vols 250,000 Cat Maps 16mm
Films Microforms
Notes: One of the largest, most
comprehensive engineering libraries in the
world. Covers all engineering disciplines;
particularly strong in electrical and
electronic, mechanical, mining and
metallurgical, petroleum, chemical,
industrial, air conditioning and refrigeration
engineering. Incl Wheeler Collection of early
materials on magnetism and electricity. 125,
000 bound periodical volumes; 10,000 maps;
5000 serial subscriptions (many foreign-
language). Virtually all materials abstracted
in *Engineering Index* (1884-date) are incl in
Library. Noncirculating, except to members
of professional engineering societies which
support the Library. See *Engineering
Societies Library, New York, Classed
Subject Catalog and Index* (Boston: G K
Hall, 1963); and *Supplements*, 1-10, 1964-
1973.
NC —DUKE UNIVERSITY, School of
Engineering, Library, Durham, 27706. Eric J
Smith, Librn
Holdings: Vols (72,000) Cat Microforms
Budget: ($110,000)
OH —PREFORMED LINE PRODUCTS CO,
Research & Engineering Library, 660 Beta
Drive, Mayfield Village, (Mailing add: PO
Box 91129, Cleveland, 44101). Edwina T
Barron, Librn
Holdings: Vols (11,500) Cat Mss Microfiche
Pix VF
Budget: ($30,500)
Notes: Library covering research and
engineering fields emphasizing this subject.
Aerodynamic characteristics and electrical
characteristics of power cables,
communication cables (including fiber
optics), cable support systems, as well as
associated fittings and hardware; in service
behavior of manufactured products and
materials as it relates to its static and
dynamic forces and environmental
conditions; oceanographic cable fittings and
terminations.
RI —UNIVERSITY OF RHODE ISLAND,
Graduate School of Oceanography, Pell
Library Bldg, Narragansett, 02882. Kenneth
T Morse, Chief Librn
Notes: Incl 10,016 vols and monographs; 13,
578 bound vols periodicals; 1326 serial
publications.

OCEANOGRAPHY

CA —UNIVERSITY OF CALIFORNIA, SAN
DIEGO, Scripps Institution of
Oceanography Library, Mail Code C075C,
La Jolla, 92093. William J Goff, Librn;
Deborarh Day, Archivist
Holdings: Vols (178,000) Cat Maps
Microforms
Budget: ($308,200)
Notes: See *Catalogs of the Scripps
Institution of Oceanography Library* (Boston:
G K Hall, 1970-1980), 21 vols. Incl 44,000
maps, 17,000 microforms cat, 21,000
reprints, and 800 linear feet of archives.

CA —UNIVERSITY OF SOUTHERN
CALIFORNIA, Allan Hancock Foundation,
Hancock Library of Biology and
Oceanography, Los Angeles, 90007.
Kimberly Douglas, Librn
Holdings: Vols (16,000) Cat Maps
Notes: Mostly marine, but incl some land
expeditions. Covers all geographical areas.
Also incl serial collection of 80,000 vols.
CA —STANFORD UNIVERSITY, Hopkins
Marine Station Library, Cabrillo Point,
Pacific Grove, 93950. Alan Baldrige, Librn
Holdings: Vols 22,000 Cat Mss Maps Pix
Slides Microforms
CA —SAN DIEGO PUBLIC LIBRARY,
Science & Industry Section, 820 E St, San
Diego, 92101. Joanne Anderson, Senior
Librn
Holdings: Vols 1000 Cat Microforms
Notes: Also, extensive periodical collection.
CT —LEE ASH, (personal collection), 66
Humiston Dr, Bethany, 06525.
CT —YALE UNIVERSITY, Kline Science
Library, Kline Biology Tower Rm C-8, PO
Box 6666, New Haven, 06511. Richard J
Dionne, Head
Holdings: Vols (175,480) Cat 16mm Films
Microforms
Budget: ($340,000)
Notes: Comprehensive collection on
biological sciences, physics, and chemistry.
Incl Evans Collection of Bryology and
Lichenology (with catalog cards in both
Kline Science Library and Sterling Memorial
Library). Also incl AEC reports (hardcopy
and microform) to 1970.
CT —YALE UNIVERSITY, Geology Library,
210 Whitney Ave, PO Box 6666, New
Haven, 06511. Harry Scammell, Librn
Holdings: Vols (100,000) Cat Maps Pix
Microforms
Budget: ($115,000)
Notes: The O C Marsh Collection
(vertebrate paleontology) is also here.
DC —NATIONAL GEOGRAPHIC
SOCIETY, Library, 1146 16th St NW,
Washington, 20036. Susan Fifer Canby, Dir
Holdings: Vols (63,000) Cat Mss Maps Pix
Notes: Material concerning land, sea, and
space exploration--past and present. All
fields of anthropology, natural history,
geography, etc.
DC —SMITHSONIAN INSTITUTION
LIBRARIES, Natural History Branch,
Washington, 20560. Sylvia Churgin, Chief
Librn
Holdings: Vols (75,550) Cat Mss Maps Pix
Slides Microforms
Notes: Incl vertebrate and invertebrate
paleontology; vertebrate zoology: systematics
and taxonomy.
FL —UNIVERSITY OF MIAMI, Otto G
Richter Library, PO Box 248214, Coral
Gables, 33124. Frank Rodgers, Dir of
Libraries
Holdings: Vols 38,000 Microforms
Notes: The Rosenstiel School of Marine and
Atmospheric Sciences Library is one of the
major marine science collections in the
United States and is especially strong in the
literature of tropical oceanography. Special
collections in the library incl 200
oceanographic atlases and more than 50 sets
of the world's major expedition reports. The
library also maintains a nautical chart
collection. 3000 microforms; 1000 current
subscriptions.
FL —FLORIDA INSTITUTE OF
TECHNOLOGY, Library, 150 W University
Blvd, PO Box 1150, Melbourne, 32901. L L
Henson, Dir of Libraries
Holdings: Vols 2000 Cat Maps Pix
FL —INTERNATIONAL
OCEANOGRAPHIC FOUNDATION/
PLANET OCEAN, Library, 3979
Rickenbacker Causeway, Virginia Key,
Miami, 33149.
Notes: Noncirculating.
FL —US NAVAL COASTAL SYSTEMS
CENTER, Technical Information Service
Branch, Panama City, 32407. Myrtle J
Rhodes, Librn
Holdings: Vols (30,000) Cat
Notes: Coastal and ocean technology,
inshore undersea warfare, mine
countermeasures, torpedo defense,
underwater sound.

FL —FLORIDA DEPT OF NATURAL
RESOURCES BUREAU OF MARINE
RESEARCH, Library, 100 Eighth Ave SE,
Saint Petersburg, 33701. Keir Gray,
Archivist
Holdings: Vols (3400) Cat Maps Pix Slides
16mm Films Microforms
Notes: The library supports the research of
approx 50 biologists and technicians, with
emphasis on the marine resources of Florida
and nearby areas. An archives section houses
original research data, reports, publications,,
etc, developed by the scientific staff. Marine
biological literature is received on exchange
from laboratories and libraries throughout
the world. There are approx 1400 journal
titles in the collection. Current titles
received number approx 600. The 33,000
reprints are cataloged by author and subject.
Current laboratory activities incl marine
studies in aquaculture, descriptive biology,
ecological studies, fisheries biology, and
oceanography.
HI —INTERNATIONAL TSUNAMI
INFORMATION CENTER, PO Box
50027, Honolulu, 96850. Bonnie Dong,
Librn
Notes: Large collection on tsunamis, their
causes, oceanographic organization and
mareographic records, forecasting, mapping,
etc.
IL —UNIVERSITY OF ILLINOIS,
URBANA/CHAMPAIGN, Library,
Geology Library, 223 Natural History Bldg,
Urbana, 61801. Dederick Ward, Librn
Holdings: Vols (105,186) Cat Maps
Microforms
IN —PURDUE UNIVERSITY LIBRARIES,
Geosciences Library, West Lafayette, 47907.
Carolyn Lassoon, Librn
Holdings: Vols (15,000) Cat
Notes: Geosciences.
ME —BIGELOW LABORATORY FOR
OCEAN SCIENCES & MAINE DEPT OF
MARINE RESOURCES, Library, McKown
Point, West Boothbay Harbor, 04575.
Pamela Shephard-Lupo, Librn
Holdings: Vols Cat Periodicals
Budget: ($55,000)
Notes: This library presently serves two
institutions. The Maine Dept of Marine
Resources has maintained the library since
1957 and thus the majority of our holdings
are geared to their needs, ie fish biology and
stock assessment on a local, national and
international level. In 1973 Bigelow
Laboratory for Ocean Sciences came to West
Boothbay Harbor and began to contribute to
the library with a very specialized collection
on the Gulf of Maine marine chemistry,
phytoplankton and nutrient cycles.
MD —NATIONAL OCEANIC &
ATMOSPHERIC ADMINISTRATION,
Library & Information Sciences Division,
Central Library & Information Sciences
Bldg, 6009 Executive Blvd, Rockville,
20852. Elizabeth J Yeates, Chief
Holdings: Vols (175,000) Cat Microforms
MA —HARVARD UNIVERSITY, Museum of
Comparative Zoology, Library, 26 Oxford St,
Cambridge, 02138. Eva S Jonas, Librn
Holdings: Cat Maps Pix
MA —HARVARD UNIVERSITY LIBRARY,
Gordon McKay Library, Division of Applied
Sciences, Pierce Hall, Oxford St, Cambridge,
02138. Julie Sandall Barlas, Librn
Holdings: Vols (100,000)
MA —BOSTON COLLEGE LIBRARIES,
Catherine B O'Connor Geophysics Library,
Weston Observatory, Weston, 02193. F
Clifford McElroy, Science Librn
Holdings: Vols (10,231) Cat Maps
Microforms
Budget: ($10,000)
Notes: This collection is being absorbed into
the general collection.
NV —FORESTA INSTITUTE FOR OCEAN
AND MOUNTAIN STUDIES, Library,
6205 Franktown Rd, Carson City, 89701.
Shannon Porter, Librn
Holdings: Vols (3000) Cat Mss Maps Pix
Slides
Notes: Material on plant, animal, and human
ecology with special emphasis on far western
US and Nevada ecology and environmental
problems. Also hold about 2000 reprints,
pamphlets, reports, etc.

OCEANOGRAPHY (cont.)

NY —AMERICAN MUSEUM OF
NATURAL HISTORY, Library Services
Dept, Central Park W & 79th St, New York,
10024. Nina J Root, Chairwoman; Mary
Genett, Asst Librn for Reference Services

NY —ENGINEERING SOCIETIES
LIBRARY, 345 E 47 St, New York, 10017.
S Kirk Cabeen, Dir
Holdings: Vols 250,000 Cat Maps 16mm
Films Microforms
Notes: One of the largest, most
comprehensive engineering libraries in the
world. Covers all engineering disciplines;
particularly strong in electrical and
electronic, mechanical, mining and
metallurgical, petroleum, chemical,
industrial, air conditioning and refrigeration
engineering. Incl Wheeler Collection of early
materials on magnetism and electricity. 125,
000 bound periodical volumes; 10,000 maps;
5000 serial subscriptions (many foreign-
language). Virtually all materials abstracted
in *Engineering Index* (1884-date) are incl in
Library. Noncirculating, except to members
of professional engineering societies which
support the Library. See *Engineering
Societies Library, New York, Classed
Subject Catalog and Index* (Boston: G K
Hall, 1963); and *Supplements*, 1-10, 1964-
1973.

NY —EXPLORERS CLUB, James B Ford
Memorial Library, 46 E 70 St, New York,
10021. Janet Baldwin, Librn
Holdings: Vols (24,000) Cat Maps
Notes: Additions to the collection depend
upon gifts. Access by appointment only.

NY —COLUMBIA UNIVERSITY
LIBRARIES, Geoscience Library, Lamont-
Doherty Geological Observatory, Palisades,
10964. Susan Klimley, Librn
Holdings: Vols (20,000) Cat
Notes: Geosciences, incl geochemistry,
marine geology, seismology and
paleoclimatology.

NC —NATIONAL MARINE FISHERIES
SERVICE, SOUTHEAST FISHERIES
CENTER, Beaufort Laboratory, Library,
Beaufort, 28516. Ann Bowman Hall, Librn
Holdings: Vols (15,000) Cat

NC —UNIVERSITY OF NORTH
CAROLINA, CHAPEL HILL, Geology
Library, Mitchell Hall 029A, Chapel Hill,
27514. Miriam L Sheaves, Librn
Holdings: Vols (41,000) Cat Maps
Notes: Earth sciences, paleontology,
oceanography, geology, geophysics. Incl
theses and dissertations; 103,000 map sheets.

OR —OREGON STATE UNIVERSITY,
Library, Corvallis, 97331. Melvin George,
Dir
Holdings: Vols 6000 Cat

OR —OREGON STATE UNIVERSITY,
Marine Science Center, Library, Newport,
97365. Marilyn Guin, Librn
Holdings: Vols (8000) Cat Maps Microforms
Budget: ($15,000)
Notes: Collection emphasizes marine
ecology, invertebrate zoology and marine
ecology, invertebrate zoology and marine
algae. The portion of the collection
concerned with fisheries emphasizes
aquaculture. Collection is divided between
the Marine Science Library and the Main
OSU Library.

PA —UNIVERSITY OF PITTSBURGH,
Langley Library, A-217 Langley Hall,
Pittsburgh, 15260. D L Johnston, Librn
Holdings: Vols (500) Cat
Budget: ($1000)

RI —UNIVERSITY OF RHODE ISLAND,
Graduate School of Oceanography, Pell
Library Bldg, Narragansett, 02882. Kenneth
T Morse, Chief Librn
Notes: Incl 10,016 vols and monographs; 13,
578 bound vols periodicals; 1326 serial
publications.

TX —TEXAS A&M UNIVERSITY, Sterling C
Evans Library, College Station, 77843.
Judith Rieke, Map Librn; Irene B Hoadley,
Dir of Libraries
Holdings: Cat
Budget: ($10,000)
Notes: Maps of all areas of the world with

geographic emphasis on the US and Texas.
Subject emphasis on geology, petroleum,
soils, highways and streets. Depository for
NOS coastal and bathymetric charts, DMA
maps, and USGS topographic and geologic
maps. An extensive file of publisher's
catalogs is available to the public. Collection
incls aerial photographs (1100), atlases and
gazetteers (1500), maps (82,600).
Bathymetric maps of US coastal areas,
general world ocean maps, and 60 atlases
covering ocean depths, temperature, salinity,
etc.

TX —TEXAS A&M UNIVERSITY, Sterling C
Evans Library, Documents Div, College
Station, 77843. Lisa Abbott, Technical
Reports Librn; Jan Swanbeck, Doc Librn
Holdings: Vols Cat Mss Microforms
Notes: Technical Reports Department incl
24,045 state and foreign government reports
on water, transportation, and oceanography,
as well as servicing the NTIS microfiche
collection of 600,000 films.

TX —UNIVERSITY OF TEXAS, Marine
Science Institute Library, Port Aransas,
78373. Ruth Grundy, Librn
Holdings: Vols (45,000) Cat Maps Pix
Budget: ($70,000)
Notes: Current researches in marine science,
especially concerning the Gulf of Mexico,
the Texas Coastal Zone, and the Continental
Shelf. Incl journals.

WA —UNIVERSITY OF WASHINGTON
LIBRARIES, Fisheries-Oceanography
Library, WB-30, Seattle, 98195. Thomas D
Moritz, Head Librn
Holdings: Vols (49,000)
Budget: ($83,000)
Notes: Chemical, physical, geological and
biological oceanography are incl as well as
applied aspects of oceanography.

†PR —UNIVERSITY OF PUERTO RICO,
Mayaguez Campus Library, Marine Sciences
Collection, Mayaguez, 00708. Sheila
Dunstan, Head Librn; Alejandro Ayala, Asst
Librn
Holdings: Vols 1169 Cat
Notes: Also, 3761 vols periodicals, 6248
documents, 130 theses, 885 microforms, 10,
016 reprints. Subjects include fish biology;
aquaculture; marine invertebrates; marine
botany; marine ecology; chemical, physical,
geological and biological oceanography.

NS —BEDFORD INSTITUTE OF
OCEANOGRAPHY, Library, PO Box 1006,
Dartmouth, B2Y 4A2, Can. J Elizabeth
Sutherland, Librn Services
Holdings: Vols (15,000) Cat Microforms
Budget: ($90,000)
Notes: Incl 15,000 monographs, 1450 serial
titles and 20,000 microfiche, technical
reports, 25,000 Maps.

ON —NATIONAL RESEARCH COUNCIL
OF CANADA, Aeronautical/Mechanical
Engineering Branch Library, Montreal Rd,
Ottawa, K1A 0R6, Can. Louise Fletcher,
Head
Notes: This branch library of the Canada
Institute for Scientific and Technical
Information (CISTI) of the National
Research Council of Canada, Ottawa, has a
collection strong in aeronautical engineering,
automatic control, CAD/CAM, robotics,
ocean, wind, and solar energy power,
hydraulic and coastal engineering, icing, low
temperature research, naval engineering,
metals and metallurgy, incl composites,
tribology, and air, railroad, marine
transportation. Library supported the
Council contribution to the development of
the remote manipular Canadarm for
NASA's Space Shuttle Orbiters and more
recently, the Canadian Astronaut Program
which will contribute payload specialists to
NASA's Space Shuttle Program in 1984. 35,
000 monographs, 1200 serials. Report
collection: over 500,000 items.

PQ —MCGILL UNIVERSITY, Institute of
Oceanography, Oceanography Library, 3620
University St, Montreal, H3A 2B2, Can.
Yvonne Mahocks, Librn
Holdings: Vols (10,848) Cat Mss Maps Pix
Microforms
Budget: ($1200)
Notes: Extensive periodical collection. 12,
332 government documents, , 322 microtech,
321 microfiche, 25,000 reprints.

OCEANOGRAPHY, BIOLOGICAL see
Marine Ecology

OCEANOLOGY see Oceanography

OCEANS

CA —LOS ANGELES PUBLIC LIBRARY,
History Dept, 630 W Fifth St, Los Angeles,
90071. Dorothy Mewshaw, Librn, Map Rm
Holdings: Vols (3000) Cat Maps
Budget: ($85,000)
Notes: The Mary Helen Peterson Collection
of Maps and Atlases. World wide coverage,
including topographic, political and special
purpose maps. Depository for US Geologic
Survey topographical maps, Defense
Mapping Agency, and National Ocean
Survey. Maps of Los Angeles City and
County.

CA —NAVAL POSTGRADUATE SCHOOL,
Dudley Knox Library, Monterey, 93940.
Paul Spinks, Prof of Library Science & Librn
Holdings: Vols 8000 Cat
Notes: This is a collection of books devoted
mainly to naval history and the sea. It
resulted from a gift collection received many
years ago from a private donor. Since it is
not within our curricular areas, no attempt
has been made to continue acquisitions for it
except from private donors.

FL —INTERNATIONAL
OCEANOGRAPHIC FOUNDATION/
PLANET OCEAN, Library, 3979
Rickenbacker Causeway, Virginia Key,
Miami, 33149.
Notes: Noncirculating.

FL —US NAVAL COASTAL SYSTEMS
CENTER, Technical Information Service
Branch, Panama City, 32407. Myrtle J
Rhodes, Librn
Holdings: Vols (30,000) Cat
Notes: Coastal and ocean technology,
inshore undersea warfare, mine
countermeasures, torpedo defense,
underwater sound.

MI —UNIVERSITY OF MICHIGAN, Harlan
Hatcher Graduate Library, Map Room, Ann
Arbor, 48109. James O Minton, Map Librn
Notes: The collection consists of approx 300,
000 sheet maps incl maps and charts
received on deposit from the US Geological
Survey, Defense Mapping Agency, and the
National Ocean Service. The collection also
incl approx 5000 reference volumes related
to cartography, surveying, and mapping, with
emphasis on place-name literature
(gazetteers, dictionaries), books on how to
use and interpret maps, carto-bibliographies,
and state (provincial, etc), regional, national,
and international atlases. The collection is
strongest geographically in materials of
Michigan, Midwest, Anglo-America, and
Europe; chronologically, 1850-date; and
thematically, in topographic and geologic
maps, although all subjects are collected. The
collection maintains a separate catalog of
holdings. Reference volumes are fully
cataloged and classified.

NV —FORESTA INSTITUTE FOR OCEAN
AND MOUNTAIN STUDIES, Library,
6205 Franktown Rd, Carson City, 89701.
Shannon Porter, Librn
Holdings: Vols (3000) Cat Mss Maps Pix
Slides
Notes: Material on plant, animal, and human
ecology with special emphasis on far western
US and Nevada ecology and environmental
problems. Also hold about 2000 reprints,
pamphlets, reports, etc.

ON —NATIONAL RESEARCH COUNCIL
OF CANADA, Aeronautical/Mechanical
Engineering Branch Library, Montreal Rd,
Ottawa, K1A 0R6, Can. Louise Fletcher,
Head
Notes: This branch library of the Canada
Institute for Scientific and Technical
Information (CISTI) of the National
Research Council of Canada, Ottawa, has a
collection strong in aeronautical engineering,
automatic control, CAD/CAM, robotics,
ocean, wind, and solar energy power,
hydraulic and coastal engineering, icing, low
temperature research, naval engineering,

OCEANS (cont.)

metals and metallurgy, incl composites, tribology, and air, railroad, marine transportation. Library supported the Council contribution to the development of the remote manipular Canadarm for NASA's Space Shuttle Orbiters and more recently, the Canadian Astronaut Program which will contribute payload specialists to NASA's Space Shuttle Program in 1984. 35,000 monographs, 1200 serials. Report collection: over 500,000 items.

OCEANS—ECONOMIC ASPECTS see Marine Resources; Shipping

OCHIPAWA INDIANS see Chippewa Indians

O'CONNOR, ELEANOR MANNING, 1884-1973

MA —MASSACHUSETTS INSTITUTE OF TECHNOLOGY, Institute Archives, Special Collections, Cambridge, 02139.
Notes: Papers of Howe, Manning and Almy, an architectural firm that started in 1913 as Lois Lilley Howe and Manning, was an unusual and successful partnership of women architects. The collection incl correspondence, financial data, reports, specifications, photographs, blueprints, drawings, and research material from the firm. Housing projects incl Mariemont, Ohio, as well as designs and renovations for New England especially in the Colonial Revival style.

O'CONNOR, FLANNERY

GA —GEORGIA COLLEGE, Ina Dillard Russell Library, Special Collections Dept, Milledgeville, 31061. Janice C Fennell, Dir of Libraries; Nancy Davis, Special Collections Assoc
Holdings: Films
Notes: Incl 328 folders of mss. Restricted use: graduate students and scholars by appointment only. No photocopying.
†MD —UNIVERSITY OF MARYLAND, Library, College Park, 20742. Donald Farren, Assoc Dir for Special Collections
Holdings: Cat
Notes: First appearances in book form, in anthologies, and in periodicals; subsequent editions, with differences in text, etc; works edited or translated; association items, especially with marginalia. Secondary works are generally excluded.
MO —WASHINGTON UNIVERSITY, Libraries, Special Collections Dept, Campus Box 1061, St Louis, 63130.
Notes: A small but significant collection.
NV —UNIVERSITY OF NEVADA, RENO, University Library, Special Collections Dept, Reno, 89557. Robert E Blesse, Head
Holdings: // Vols (29) Cat Other appearances 95 Cat
Notes: Includes individual works by author in all editions including translations; also prefaces, introductions, published correspondence, appearances in anthologies, periodicals, etc. Bibliographical research collection, part of Modern Authors Collection.

O'CONNOR, FRANK

MA —BOSTON UNIVERSITY, Mugar Memorial Library, Special Collections Dept, 771 Commonwealth Ave, Boston, 02215. Howard B Gotlieb, Dir
Holdings: // Cat Mss Pix
Notes: Mss, correspondence, etc collected in depth; incl publications by or about.
NV —UNIVERSITY OF NEVADA, RENO, University Library, Special Collections Dept, Reno, 89557. Robert E Blesse, Head
Holdings: Vols (55) Cat Other appearances 205 Cat
Notes: Includes individual works by author in all editions including translations; also prefaces, introductions, published correspondence, appearances in anthologies, periodicals, etc. Bibliographical research collection, part of Modern Authors Collection.

BC —UNIVERSITY OF VICTORIA, McPherson Library, Victoria, V8W 3H5, Can.
Notes: (Frank O'Connor) Incl Michael O'Donnovan, author, librn, director of Abbey Theatre, Dublin. Mss, "Scholar and Artist," "The Beauty," "Fish for Friday," "The Others," "The Weeping Children," "Modern Irish Literature," "The Lament for Art O'Leary," and "Oration at W B Yeats' Graveside" by Frank O'Connor.

O'CONNOR, HARVEY

MI —WAYNE STATE UNIVERSITY, Walter P Reuther Library, Archives of Labor & Urban Affairs, Detroit, 48202. Philip Mason, Dir
Notes: Papers, etc of Harvey O'Connor, editor and author associated with the Chicago and Pittsburgh Civil Liberties Commissions and the Emergency Civil Liberties Commission.
RI —BROWN UNIVERSITY, John Hay Library, 20 Prospect St, Providence, 02912. Mark N Brown, Cur Mss
Holdings: Vols Mss
Notes: Papers of Harvey O'Connor (1897-), writer, labor and civil rights activist. Consists principally of printed and mimeographed material relating to civil rights organizations.

O'CONNOR, JERIMIAH J.

DC —GEORGETOWN UNIVERSITY, Library, Special Collections Div, 37 & O Sts NW, Washington, 20057. George M Barringer, Special Collections Librn; Nicholas B Sheetz, Mss Librn
Holdings: Cat Mss Maps Pix
Notes: Collection assembled by Jerimiah J O'Connor consisting of a wide assortment of materials pertaining to railroads, principally in the United States. Incl are train schedules and time tables, printed promotional material, published manufacturer's brochures and catalogues, stock certificates, maps, photographs, and a variety of printed and other types of ephemera.

O'CONNOR, LEN

IL —CHICAGO HISTORICAL SOCIETY, Library, Clark St at North Ave, Chicago, 60614. Archie Motley, Manuscript Librn
Notes: Papers of newsman Len O'Connor.

O'CONNOR, TOM

MA —BRANDEIS UNIVERSITY, Goldfarb Library, 415 South St, Waltham, 02154. Bessie Hahn, Dir
Notes: Sacco and Vanzetti Case Collection. Consists of 23 linear ft of material collected by both Tom O'Connor and Francis Russell relating to this celebrated American trial. This collection is unprocessed, spring 1984.

O'CONNOR, ULICK

DE —UNIVERSITY OF DELAWARE, Hugh M Morris Library, S College Ave, Newark, 19711. T Stuart Dick, Special Collections
Holdings: Cat Mss Pix
Notes: Manuscripts, etc, incl literary correspondence.

O'CONNOR, WILLIAM DOUGLAS

DC —LIBRARY OF CONGRESS, Washington, 20540.

O'CONNOR SISTERS

ON —METROPOLITAN TORONTO LIBRARY, Theatre Dept, 789 Yonge St, Toronto, M4W 2G8, Can. Heather McCallum, Head
Notes: Collections of playbills, clippings and correspondence document the career of Charles Manny (1890-1962) in both England and the United States; interviews and reminiscences on tape are available for the

first all-sister act in vaudeville, the Canadian born O'Conner Sisters.
See also entry under Theatre - Canada.

O'DONNELL, GEORGE MARION

MO —WASHINGTON UNIVERSITY, Libraries, Special Collections Dept, Campus Box 1061, St Louis, 63130.
Notes: A major collection, incl mss, correspondence, literary papers, photographs, etc. Described in *Special Collections: an Annotated Guide to the Holdings of the Manuscript Division and the University Archives and Research Collection.*

O'DELL, EDITH

NY —SAINT LAWRENCE UNIVERSITY, Owen D Young Library, Canton, 13617. Mahlon Peterson, Librn
Holdings: Cat Mss Pix
Notes: Collection consists of letters sent to Edith O'Dell Black and Pomeroy Burton of the New York *World* from 1903 to 1944. Also incl are works by Alexander Black, a novelist, and manuscripts which he wrote for "picture plays," the forerunners of the modern moving pictures. Approx 350 items.

ODETS, CLIFFORD

CA —FRANCIS BACON LIBRARY, 655 N Dartmouth Ave, Claremont, 91711. Elizabeth S Wrigley, Dir
Holdings: Mss Pix
Notes: Arensberg's miscellaneous correspondence with American literary figures (1920's-50's) including Bruce Bliven, Catherine Drinker Bowen, Kay Boyle, Witter Bynner, Edwin Corle, Helen A Keller, Lysander Kemp, Kenneth Macgowan, John Macy, Henry Miller, Lewis Mumford, Clifford Odets, Kenneth Patchen, Irving Stone, and William Carlos Williams.

O'DONNELL, LILLIAN

MA —BOSTON UNIVERSITY, Mugar Memorial Library, Special Collections Dept, 771 Commonwealth Ave, Boston, 02215. Howard B Gotlieb, Dir
Holdings: Cat Mss
Notes: Mss, correspondence, etc collected in depth; incl publications by or about.

O'DONOVAN, MICHAEL see O'Connor, Frank

O'DWYER, PAUL

NY —SAINT JOHN'S UNIVERSITY, Special Collections Dept, Grand Central & Utopia Pkwys, Jamaica, 11439. Szilvia E Szmuk, Librn
Holdings: // Uncat Mss
Notes: O'Dwyer Collections: papers dealing with Northern Ireland, 1973-1977; American Friends of Irish Neutrality, World War II a) The Paul O'Dwyer Papers deal with conditions in Northern Ireland, incl correspondence, speeches, press releases, and periodical articles contained in 18 labeled manila envelopes and roughly indexed b) American Friends of Irish Neutrality collection consists of 109 letters, membership and donation cards, minutes, press clippings, post cards, speeches, pamphlets, in 6 manila evelopes. No photocopying.

OECOLOGY see Ecology

OENOLOGY see Enology

OENSLAGER, DONALD

NY —NEW YORK PUBLIC LIBRARY, Performing Arts Research Center, Billy Rose Theatre Collection, 111 Amsterdam Ave, New York, 10023. Dorothy L Swerdlove, Cur
Holdings: Cat
Notes: Incl correspondence, as well as original designs, working plans, architectural

OENSLAGER, DONALD (cont.)

renderings, and elevations made during most of his career.

O'FAOLAIN, SEAN

CA —UNIVERSITY OF CALIFORNIA, BERKELEY, Bancroft Library, Manuscripts Division, Berkeley, 94720. James D Hart, Dir
Holdings: Uncat Mss
Notes: Collection consists mainly of drafts and revisions of O'Faolain's short stores. Also incl are mss of his autobiography, *Vive Moi!* and of a novel, *The Land of Dreams.* 4 boxes incl printed books.

NV —UNIVERSITY OF NEVADA, RENO, University Library, Special Collections Dept, Reno, 89557. Robert F. Blesse, Head
Holdings: Vols (54) Cat Other appearances 205 Cat
Notes: Includes individual works by author in all editions including translations; also prefaces, introductions, published correspondence, appearances in anthologies, periodicals, etc. Bibliographical research collection, part of Modern Authors Collection.

OFF AND OFF-OFF BROADWAY THEATRE

MA —HARVARD UNIVERSITY LIBRARY, Theatre Collection, Cambridge, 02138. Jeanne T Newlin, Cur
Notes: One of the largest existing collections of playbills, programs, prints, photographs, promptbooks, and other materials relating to the performing arts, the scope is worldwide; resources on the English-speaking stage of the 18th and 19th centuries are unequalled. Incl materials on ballet and modern dance, the circus, magic, minstrel shows, cinema, and pantomime. For description, see *Harvard Library Bulletin,* VI (1925): pp 281-301. Also, papers of Robert E Sherwood (1896-1955), John Mason Bowers, George Pierce Baker, Edward Sheldon, Percy Mackaye; Angus McBean collection of photographs of the London Stage, 1937-1965; Alix Jeffry collection of photographs of the Off-Broadway Theatre; and others.

NY —HAMPDEN-BOOTH THEATRE LIBRARY AT THE PLAYERS, 16 Gramercy Park, New York, 10003. Louis A Rachow, Librn/Cur
Holdings: Mss
Notes: La Mama Experimental Theatre Club. The holdings include printed, typescript and manuscript material and relate chiefly to the period when La Mama, under the guidance of Ellen Stewart, was located at 122 Second Avenue--a symbol of the Off-Off Broadway movement of the 1960s. The collection if divided into three sections (1) Chronological records of productions containing approximately 140 manuscript and typescript leaves as well as some additional eighty pages of source material and worksheets, (2) Clippings and press coverage including 123 clippings from Scottish, English, German and American newspapers and periodicals, and (3) Playbills and programs consisting of 143 broadsides and handbills together with miscellaneous bills of productions and lectures by La Mama artists. Each section has its own calendar and the holdings as a whole are considered to be the mostcomplete in existence for the years 1965-68, since no systematic archives were maintained until after La Mama's move from Second Avenue in 1968. The collection has been designated the Paul F Cranefield Collection of the La Mama Experimental Theatre Club. Described in *Theatre & Performing Arts* Collections (New York: Haworth Press, 1981)

NY —NEW YORK PUBLIC LIBRARY, Performing Arts Research Center, Billy Rose Theatre Collection, 111 Amsterdam Ave, New York, 10023. Dorothy L Swerdlove, Cur
Holdings: Cat
Notes: Includes a large collection of off-off

Broadway scripts deposited in memory of the proprietor of the Caffe Cino.
See also entry under Theatre.

PA —UNIVERSITY OF PITTSBURGH, Special Collections Dept, Curtis Theatre Collection, 363 Hillman Library, Pittsburgh, 15260. Jeanette Blanco, Cur
Holdings: Vols (4000) Cat Mss Documents Microforms Pix Slides VF
Notes: The legitimate theatre of plays, musicals and vaudeville, chiefly of New York City and Pittsburgh, from 1865, and other US, community, summer, college and foreign theatre. Foundation of the collection is systematic file of theatre programs, supported by articles, reviews, journals and pictures. Incl 500,000 programs, posters, the Oliver P Merriman Scrapbooks and 300 other scrapbooks, clippings and other ephemera. Separate collections: Ralph G Allen Burlesque Skits Collection; Kenyon Family Papers; Philip Dunning Playscripts Collection; and the Pittsburgh Savoyards Records. Noncirculating.

OFFICE, TENURE OF see Civil Service

OFFICE OF WAR INFORMATION

DC —LIBRARY OF CONGRESS, Prints & Photographs Div, Washington, 20540.
Notes: Thousands of mounted and captioned photoprints, original negatives, and copy negatives that were assembled for use in OWI publications, exhibits, and filmstrips.

DC —LIBRARY OF CONGRESS, Motion Pictures, Broadcasting and Recorded Sound Div, Washington, 20540.
Notes: Nearly 50,000 acetate disc recordings of foreign and domestic radio broadcasts English-language programs, which were usually recorded live off the air, incl news, entertainment, and informational reports from 1942, 1944, and 1945. These, together with recordings in French and German, have been taped and listed chronologically in a descriptive file.

O'DONNELL, REV. CHARLES L., C.S.C.

DC —GEORGETOWN UNIVERSITY, Library, Special Collections Div, 37 & O Sts NW, Washington, 20057. George M Barringer, Special Collections Librn; Nicholas B Sheetz, Mss Librn
Holdings: Mss Cat
Notes: The papers of the Kilmer family incl letters and mss by the poet Joyce Kilmer and his wife, Aline Kilmer, also a poet and essayist. The papers incl correspondence by various authors, among them Rev James J Daly, SJ and Rev Charles L O'Donnell, CSC.

OFFICE PRACTICE

NH —NEW HAMPSHIRE VOCATIONAL-TECHNICAL COLLEGE, Library, Prescott Hill, Laconia, 03246. Patty Miller, Librn
Holdings: Vols 570 Cat Phonorecords Audiotapes Filmstrips Microforms
Budget: $475
Notes: Incl overhead transparencies. Information on Secretarial Science.

NC —GREENSBORO PUBLIC LIBRARY, Business Library, 201 Greene St, Drawer X-4, Greensboro, 27402. Lebby B Lamb, Business Librn
Holdings: Vols (6000) Cat Microforms
Budget: ($12,000)

NC —TECHNICAL INSTITUTE OF ALAMANCE, Learning Resources Center, Jimmy Kerr Rd, PO Box 623, Haw River, 27258. Ron Plummer, Coordr
Holdings: Vols 664 Cat Audiotapes Filmstrips Microforms
Notes: Executive, legal and medical secretary, general office technology.

WI —BLACKHAWK TECHNICAL INSTITUTE, PO Box 5009, 6004 Prairie Rd, Janesville, 53547. Grace M Sweeney, Libn
Notes: Secretarial and Marketing, and Computer training.

OFFICIAL GAZETTES see Gazettes

OFFICIAL PUBLICATIONS see Government Publications

OFFICIALS see Public Officers

O'FLAHERTY, LIAM

IL —ILLINOIS STATE UNIVERSITY, Milner Library, Dept of Special Collections, Normal, 61761. Robert Sokan, Librn
Notes: First editions, limited editions, ephemera, etc.

OGDEN, CHARLES KAY, 1889-1957

CA —UNIVERSITY OF CALIFORNIA, LOS ANGELES, Research Library, Dept of Special Collections, 405 Hilgard Ave, Los Angeles, 90024. Edward Shreeves, Chairman, Bibliographers Group; David S Zeidberg, Head
Holdings: Vols Mss
Notes: 6.5 linear feet of mss, correspondence, and other materials related to Basic English; books by various authors published in Basic English.

OGDEN, WILLIAM B.

IL —CHICAGO HISTORICAL SOCIETY, Library, Clark St at North Ave, Chicago, 60614. Archie Motley, Manuscript Librn
Notes: Papers of railroad executive, realtor, Mayor of Chicago.

OGG, OSCAR

VA —UNIVERSITY OF VIRGINIA, Alderman Library, Rare Book Dept, Charlottesville, 22901. Julius P Barclay, Cur
Holdings: Vols (6500) // Mss
Notes: The Oscar Ogg Collection of Book Arts covers calligraphy, letterforms, typography, printing, and graphic arts. Contains early writing books and printed works, as well as modern manuals and other works on printing, publishing, and promotion through graphic arts. The Dept also has the Edward L Stone Collection of Printing Specimens, 3000 items. Contains materials tracing the history of printing, inks, binding styles and materials, types. Also the Tompkins Collection (2000 vols), and the Stevens Watts collection (900 vols).

OGLETHORPE, JAMES EDWARD

GA —OGLETHORPE UNIVERSITY, Library, 4484 Peachtree RD, NE, Atlanta, 30319. Thomas W Chandler, Librn
Holdings: Vols 90 Cat Pix
Notes: Books and materials which deal exclusively or primarily with Oglethorpe. Incl paintings and clippings.

O'HARA, FRANK, 1926-1966

CT —UNIVERSITY OF CONNECTICUT, Library, Storrs, 06268. George F Butterick, Cur of Literary Archives
Holdings: Mss Pix
Notes: Collected in depth; incl publications by and about him.

BC —UNIVERSITY OF VICTORIA, McPherson Library, Victoria, V8W 3H5, Can.
Notes: Poet, playwright, art critic. Typescripts of "Love's Labor, Graphan Clogue;" "The General's Return from One Place to Another."

O'HARA, JOHN

NV —UNIVERSITY OF NEVADA, RENO, University Library, Special Collections Dept, Reno, 89557. Robert E Blesse, Head
Holdings: Vols (136) Cat Other appearances 290 Cat
Notes: Includes individual works by author in all editions including translations; also prefaces, introductions, published correspondence, appearances in anthologies,

O'HARA, JOHN (cont.)

periodicals, etc. Bibliographical research collection, part of Modern Authors Collection.

PA —PENNSYLVANIA STATE UNIVERSITY, Fred Lewis Pattee Library, University Park, 16802.
Holdings: Cat Mss Pix
Notes: Extensive ms additions, incl letters. Reconstruction of O'Hara's study, with his desk, etc.

O'HARA, JOHN MYERS

IL —NEWBERRY LIBRARY, 60 W Walton St, Chicago, 60610. Diana Haskell, Cur of Modern Mss
Holdings: Cat Mss Pix
Notes: Books, mss, correspondence, extra-illustrated works. Restricted use: noncirculating.

OHIO

OH —CLEVELAND PUBLIC LIBRARY, Social Sciences Department, 325 Superior Ave, Cleveland, 44114. Thelma Morris, Head
Holdings: Cat Maps Pix
Notes: Library collection in the subject departments incl: state and local history; city directories; business and industry; canals and waterworks; technology; local authors and artists; tourist and travel information (only advisory), vital statistics. Early Ohio pictures and historic maps. See also Western Reserve, Cleveland Public Library.

OH —OHIO DEPT DEVELOPMENT, Library, 30 E Broad St, PO Box 1001, Columbus, 43216. Jean Fisher, Librn
Holdings: Vols (5000)
Notes: Economic data and census data.

OHIO—ANTIQUITIES

OH —OHIO HISTORICAL SOCIETY, Archives Library Division, 1982 Velma Ave, Columbus, 43211. Dennis East, Division Chief
Holdings: Mss Maps Pix
Notes: Collection begun in 1885 to support work of the Division of Archaeology, Ohio Historical Society.
See also entry under Ohio - History

OHIO—GENEALOGY

FL —ORLANDO PUBLIC LIBRARY, Local History & Genealogy Dept, 100 Block of Central Ave, Orlando, 32806. Eileen B Willis, Librn
Holdings: Vols 11,000 Cat Maps Microforms
Budget: $8000
Notes: Genealogy collection on Md, Del, W Va, NC, SC, Ala, Miss, La, Texas, Ark, Ky, Ohio, Ill, Ind, and Mich are well represented. Most other states are covered by smaller collections.
See also entry under Genealogy - Collections.

MI —MONROE COUNTY LIBRARY SYSTEM, Ellis Reference and Information Center, 3700 S Custer Rd, Monroe, 48161. Marie D Chulski, Head of Reference Services
Notes: Incl individual county histories, atlases, biographies, etc. The Monroe County history collection contains veteran records, plat books, oral history tapes, family histories, church records, cemetery index, atlases and census records. Genealogy emphasis is not only Monroe County but incl surrounding counties and the states with large migration to the area, such as Ohio, Kentucky, Tennessee and the New England states.

OH —OHIO UNIVERSITY, Vernon R Alden Library, Department of Archives and Special Collections, Athens, 45701. Gary A Hunt, Head
Holdings: Vols 825 Cat Mss Maps Pix Microforms VF
Notes: The Ohio Historical Collections can be divided into 4 major parts: Ohio

University Archives, containing institutional records, dating from 1804, of the oldest university West of the Alleghenies; Local Government Records Collection, containing birth, death, marriage, tax and other public records from an 18-county region of Southeastern Ohio; Ohioana Collection, consisting of published books, periodicals, newspapers, documents, directories and other printed materials (incl imprints) relating to this region; and the Manuscript Collections, containing both personal papers as well as family, business and organizational records pertaining to Southeastern Ohio.

OH —PUBLIC LIBRARY OF CINCINNATI & HAMILTON COUNTY, History Dept, 800 Vine St, Cincinnati, 45202. J Richard Abell, Head
Holdings: Vols 9996 Cat Microforms
Notes: Collection emphasizes Ohio, neighboring states, and Eastern seaboard states. Some material on Great Britain and Ireland. There is a genealogical index of family histories by surname only.

OH —COSHOCTON PUBLIC LIBRARY, 655 Main St, Coshocton, 43812. Susan Anderson, Librn
Holdings: Vols (875) Cat Mss Maps Pix Microforms
Budget: ($1000)
Notes: Local history and genealogy of Coshocton, Guernsey, Holmes, Knox, Tuscarawas, Licking and Muskingum counties. Incl published works, censuses (microfilm), cemetery index (Muskingum Co). Incl, for Coshocton Co, directories, newspapers, obituary and cemetery indexes, local authors and imprints, photographs, clippings, letters, personal papers. Building collection of histories and genealogies from areas of high migration to Coshocton Co.

OH —DAYTON & MONTGOMERY COUNTY PUBLIC LIBRARY, Dayton Collection, 215 E Third St, Dayton, 45402. Kevin Smith, Librn
Holdings: Vols (4500) Cat Mss Maps Pix
Notes: Contains materials on Dayton, Montgomery County and the Miami Valley, Ohio, area, incl materials relative to Dayton authors, inventors, political figures, etc, eg, Paul Laurence Dunbar, Wright Brothers, Clement Vallandigham, as well as materials on the geography, history, genealogy and political structure of the area.

OH —GRANVILLE PUBLIC LIBRARY, 217 E Broadway, Granville, 43023. Nadine Robson, Librn
Holdings: Vols 150 Cat Pix Microforms
Notes: Genealogy and local history of Licking County, Ohio and related areas. A bibliography of the collection is being prepared. Incl biographical material of early residents of Granville and Licking County; cemetery records; rosters of Ohio Soldiers in various wars; *Granville Times* on microfilm, 1880-1941 (complete); DAR materials, etc.

OH —KENT STATE UNIVERSITY, University Archives, Kent, 44242. Stephen C Morton, University Archivist
Holdings: Uncat Mss Maps Pix Phonorecords Filmstrips Microforms
Notes: Diocese of Youngstown Chancery Office and Parish Files. Collection on deposit. Some materials are restricted. Contains materials on the second Vatican Council and Council Review Days, Cathedral records and plans, parochial school photography collection, Canon Law collection. The parish records are especially valuable for researching births, marriages, and deaths. A large amount of ethnic material is also found in the files.

OH —WARREN COUNTY HISTORICAL SOCIETY, Museum Library, 105 S Broadway, PO Box 223, Lebanon, 45036. Victoria Visintainer, Dir
Holdings: Vols (1030) Cat Microforms
Budget: ($3500)
Notes: Warren County, Ohio history and genealogy. Incl 690 general information files; 879 family files; 21 vols of cemetery, marriage and birth records; 75,000 index cards on individuals; 317 microfilm reels of local newspapers (1807-1976); court and census records; file of *Ohio Historical Society Quarterly*; ledgers; diaries; and 4

vols of oral history. Society also holds Shaker Collection, incl books, periodicals, pamphlets, maps and pictures (600 pieces).

OH —ALLEN COUNTY HISTORICAL SOCIETY, Elizabeth M MacDonell Memorial Library, 620 W Market St, Lima, 45801. Raymond F Schuck, Cur, Allen County Museum; Anna B Selfridge, Asst Cur, Manuscripts & Archives
Holdings: Vols (6824) Cat Mss Maps Pix Slides Audiotapes Microforms
Notes: Includes history of Allen County; railroad; railroad labor history; genealogy.

OH —LAKE COUNTY HISTORICAL SOCIETY, Percy Kendall Smith Library, 8095 Mentor Ave, Mentor, 44060. Carl Thomas Engel, Librn
Holdings: Vols (2400) Cat Mss Maps Pix Microforms
Notes: Collection covers people, events, and the heritage homes and historic sites of Lake County, Ohio.

OH —TOLEDO-LUCAS COUNTY PUBLIC LIBRARY, Local History & Genealogy Dept, 325 Michigan St, Toledo, 43624. James Marshall, Head
Holdings: Vols 7500 Cat Mss Maps Pix Slides Microforms

OH —JOHN MCINTIRE PUBLIC LIBRARY, 220 N Fifth St, Zanesville, 43701. Peg Harmon, Librn
Holdings: Vols 150 Cat Mss Maps Videotapes
Notes: Wide spectrum of Ohio history, with special emphasis on Zanesville and Muskingum County history & genealogy.

OH —ZANESVILLE CAMPUS, Herrold Hall Learning Resources Center, 1425 Newark Rd, Zanesville, 43701. Roberta Armstrong, Librn
Holdings: Vols 500 Cat Maps Microforms

OHIO—HISTORY

KY —UNIVERSITY OF KENTUCKY, Margaret I King Library, Dept of Special Collections, Lexington, 40506. William Marshall, Head
Holdings: Vols 310 // Cat Mss Pix
Notes: Collection assembled by Dr Emmet Field Horine to document the work and writings on Daniel Drake in medicine and history and education; includes Drake's own publications. (Daniel Drake is important to Ohio and Kentucky history in particular.) Incl oil portrait and bust.

NY —ALFRED UNIVERSITY, Herrick Memorial Library, Alfred, 14802. June E Brown, Head Librn
Notes: The Howells/Frechette Collection. Family documents, 7000 letters of William Cooper Howells (American consul to Quebec, later to Toronto), William Dean Howells, his sister Annie Frechette, Achille Frechette (official translator, Canadian House of Commons), and Louis Frechette (poet laureate of Canada).

OH —AKRON-SUMMIT COUNTY PUBLIC LIBRARY, 55 S Main St, Akron, 44326. Steven Hawk, Dir
Holdings: Vols 875 Cat Microforms
Notes: The collection aims at being exhaustive relative to printed histories of Ohio's counties, towns, and townships. We do not solicit gifts or make purchases of mss.

OH —OHIO UNIVERSITY, Vernon R Alden Library, Department of Archives and Special Collections, Athens, 45701. Gary A Hunt, Head
Holdings: Vols 825 Cat Mss Maps Pix Microforms VF
Notes: The Ohio Historical Collections can be divided into 4 major parts: Ohio University Archives, containing institutional records, dating from 1804, of the oldest university West of the Alleghenies; Local Government Records Collection, containing birth, death, marriage, tax and other public records from an 18-county region of Southeastern Ohio; Ohioana Collection, consisting of published books, periodicals, newspapers, documents, directories and other printed materials (incl imprints) relating to this region; and the Manuscript Collections, containing both personal papers as well as family, business and organizational records pertaining to Southeastern Ohio.

OHIO—HISTORY (cont.)

OH —OHIO UNIVERSITY, Vernon R Alden Library, Athens, 45701. Kent Mulliner, Africana Specialist
Notes: Civil War letters and mss of the Brown and Van Voorhis families, both among the earliest settlers in southeastern Ohio. Mostly written by three members of the family serving in the Union armies between 1861 and 1865.

OH —BOWLING GREEN STATE UNIVERSITY, Jerome Library, Center for Archival Collections, Bowling Green, 43403. Paul D Yon, Dir; Elaine R Ezell, Reference Archivist; Nancy Steen, Rare Books Librn
Holdings: Vols (4000) Cat Mss Pix Slides Maps Microforms
Budget: ($25,000)
Notes: Incl County records and newspapers. Secondary and primary sources documenting the history of the state, especially the northwestern section.

OH —CINCINNATI HISTORICAL SOCIETY, Library, (formerly Historical & Philosophical Society of Ohio), Eden Park, Cincinnati, 45202. Laura L Chace, Librn
Holdings: Vols 60,000 Cat Mss Maps Pix Slides Microforms
Budget: ($8000)
Notes: Regional history relating to Cincinnati, the Northwest Territory and Ohio River Valley.

OH —PUBLIC LIBRARY OF CINCINNATI & HAMILTON COUNTY, Films and Recordings Center, 800 Vine St, Cincinnati, 45202. Robert Hudzik, Head
Holdings: Vols 2500 Cat Maps Pix Slides
Notes: There is a card catalog index and a printed subject index to the entire slide collection. Printed catalog does not break down Cincinnati History Collection. 2000 of the Cincinnati History Slides were originally on 3x4 glass slides and transferred to the more standard 2x2 size. Original slides are still in the collection.

OH —PUBLIC LIBRARY OF CINCINNATI & HAMILTON COUNTY, History Dept, 800 Vine St, Cincinnati, 45202. J Richard Abell, Head
Holdings: Vols 9996 Cat Microforms
Notes: Collection emphasizes Ohio, neighoring states, and Eastern seaboard states. Some material on Great Britain and Ireland. There is a genealogical index of family histories by surname only.

OH —CLEVELAND PUBLIC LIBRARY, History and Geography Department, 325 Superior Ave, Cleveland, 44114. JoAnn Petrello, Head
Holdings: Cat Maps Pix
Notes: Library collection in the subject departments incl: state history, archaeology directories; business and industry; canals and waterworks; technology; art and literature; tourist and travel information; photographs; vital statistics. Early Ohio pictures and historic maps. Depository for state documents, performing arts, sports and recreation.

OH —PLAIN DEALER LIBRARY, 1801 Superior Ave, Cleveland, 44114. Patti A Graziano, Library Dir
Holdings: Vols 3800 Cat
Notes: Ohio history, with emphasis on Cleveland. Incl 3 million newspaper clippings; 1 million pictures, 1858-date; 100 maps; and 6000 microforms.

†OH —UKRAINIAN MUSEUM-ARCHIVES, INC, 1202 Kenilworth Ave, Cleveland, 44113.

OH —OHIO HISTORICAL SOCIETY, Archives Library Division, 1982 Velma Ave, Columbus, 43211. Dennis East, Division Chief
Holdings: Vols (96,000) Cat Mss Maps Pix Slides Microforms
Budget: ($18,000)
Notes: This library is the primary collection for Ohio. Most purchases are on the rare and op market. Collecting area is early American history, esp relating to exploration into the Northwest Territory. Major subject areas are Ohio politics and government (8 presidents) military history (good collection of regimental histories and Ohio narratives of the Civil War), economic and social history, local history, esp county histories & atlases and city directories. Also, Ohio archaeology, natural history, artifacts. Major media collections are books (96,000), newspapers (25,000 vols and 22,000 microfilm), pictures (50,000), maps (2500), manuscripts (1,500,000). Library is noncirculating except through interlibrary loan of microfilm.

OH —COSHOCTON PUBLIC LIBRARY, 655 Main St, Coshocton, 43812. Susan Anderson, Librn
Holdings: Vols (875) Cat Mss Maps Pix Microforms
Budget: ($1000)
Notes: Local history and genealogy of Coshocton, Guernsey, Holmes, Knox, Tuscarawas, Licking and Muskingum counties. Incl published works, censuses (microfilm), cemetery index (Muskingum Co). Incl, for Coshocton Co, directories, newspapers, obituary and cemetery indexes, local authors and imprints, photographs, clippings, letters, personal papers. Building collection of histories and genealogies from areas of high migration to Coshocton Co.

OH —DAYTON & MONTGOMERY COUNTY PUBLIC LIBRARY, Dayton Collection, 215 E Third St, Dayton, 45402. Kevin Smith, Librn
Holdings: Vols (4500) Cat Mss Maps Pix
Notes: Contains materials on Dayton, Montgomery County and the Miami Valley, Ohio, area, incl materials relative to Dayton authors, inventors, political figures, etc, eg, Paul Laurence Dunbar, Wright Brothers, Clement Vallandigham, as well as materials on the geography, history, genealogy and political structure of the area.

OH —WRIGHT STATE UNIVERSITY, Greater Miami Valley Research Center, University Library, Dayton, 45431. Patrick B Nolan, Head of Archives
Holdings: Vols 3000 Mss
Notes: Local records, private papers, business and labor records and institutional records from southwest Ohio and the Miami Valley. Incl 2000 linear ft of records and manuscripts.

OH —RUTHERFORD B HAYES LIBRARY, 1337 Hayes Ave, Fremont, 43420. Watt P Marchman, Dir
Holdings: Vols 10,000 Cat Mss Maps Pix Slides Audiotapes Microforms
Notes: The Rutherford B Hayes Family Collections. The collections comprise papers, books, correspondence, diaries, speeches, account books, financial and real estate records, law cases, ephemera, and memorabilia of members of the Rutherford B Hayes family; his wife, Lucy Webb Hayes; their children: Birchard Austin Hayes; Webb C Hayes I; Rutherford Platt Hayes; Scott Russell Hayes; Fanny Hayes; grandchildren: Dalton Hayes; Webb C Hayes, II; daughter-in-law, Mary Miller Hayes. Mss of the collection are described in *Guide to Manuscripts of the Ohio Historical Society*, 208, 209, 210, 211, 212, 214, 216, 217, 218, 219. Indexed, listed. The collections are housed in the mss division and newspapers division. Ms materials of 256 linear feet; 50, 000 pictures; slides; tapes; moving pictures, maps. The papers ofRutherford Birchard Hayes available on 304 rolls of microfilm. The collection described in *Guide to the Microfilm Edition of the Papers of Rutherford Birchard Hayes, the Nineteenth President of the United States*. Fremont, Ohio: The Rutherford B Hayes Presidential Center, 1983.

OH —GRANVILLE PUBLIC LIBRARY, 217 E Broadway, Granville, 43023. Nadine Robson, Librn
Holdings: Vols 150 Cat Pix Microforms
Notes: Genealogy and local history of Licking County, Ohio and related areas. A bibliography of the collection is being prepared. Incl biographical material of early residents of Granville and Licking County; cemetery records; rosters of Ohio Soldiers in various wars; *Granville Times* on microfilm, 1880-1941 (complete); DAR materials, etc.

OH —HIRAM COLLEGE, Teachout-Price Memorial Library, Hiram, 44234. Joanne M Sawyer, Archivist; Marjorie M Adams, Music Librn
Holdings: Vols 90 Cat Mss Maps Microforms
Notes: Collection incl antiquarian items in this subject area; general collection also emphasizes this subject; incorporates previous subject headings Ohio History and Western Reserve; restricted hours: call or write in advance.

OH —KENT STATE UNIVERSITY, American History Research Center, Kent, 44242. Stephen C Morton, Dir
Holdings: Vols 1000 Cat Mss
Notes: Incl collections of Cowles and Fuller families (qv).

OH —WARREN COUNTY HISTORICAL SOCIETY, Museum Library, 105 S Broadway, PO Box 223, Lebanon, 45036. Victoria Visintainer, Dir
Holdings: Vols (1030) Cat Microforms
Budget: ($3500)
Notes: Warren County, Ohio history and genealogy. Incl 690 general information files; 879 family files; 21 vols of cemetery, marriage and birth records; 75,000 index cards on individuals; 317 microfilm reels of local newspapers (1807-1976), court and census records; file of *Ohio Historical Society Quarterly*; ledgers; diaries; and 4 vols of oral history. Society also holds Shaker Collection, incl books, periodicals, pamphlets, maps and pictures (600 pieces).

OH —ALLEN COUNTY HISTORICAL SOCIETY, Elizabeth M MacDonell Memorial Library, 620 W Market St, Lima, 45801. Raymond F Schuck, Cur, Allen County Museum; Anna B Selfridge, Asst Cur, Manuscripts & Archives
Holdings: Vols (6824) Cat Mss Maps Pix Slides Audiotapes Microforms
Notes: Includes history of Allen County; railroad; railroad labor history; genealogy.

OH —MASSILLON PUBLIC LIBRARY, 208 Lincoln Way E, Massillon, 44646. Camille Leslie, Dir
Holdings: // Mss Maps
Notes: 22 linear ft. Correspondence and business papers of Thomas Rotch and Arvine Wales who migrated in 1811 from New England to Ohio; and of Arvine C Wales, his son, lawyer and civic leader in Massillon, Ohio. Covers period ca 1780-1880; contains much Quaker and anti-slavery material, as well as material on early Ohio. Index in preparation.

OH —LAKE COUNTY HISTORICAL SOCIETY, Percy Kendall Smith Library, 8095 Mentor Ave, Mentor, 44060. Carl Thomas Engel, Librn
Holdings: Vols (2400) Cat Mss Maps Pix Microforms
Notes: Collection covers people, events, and the heritage homes and historic sites of Lake County, Ohio.

OH —MUSKINGUM COLLEGE, Library, New Concord, 43762. Herbert D Safford, Dir; Richard M Cochron, Reference Librn
Holdings: Cat Mss Maps Pix Microforms
Notes: Ohio and local history; Presbyterian Church.

OH —MIAMI UNIVERSITY, King Library, Walter Havighurst Special Collections Library, Oxford, 45056. Helen Ball, Cur of Special Collections
Holdings: Vols (6000) Cat Mss Maps
Notes: Regional history of the Old Northwest Territory and especially of the Ohio River Valley. Incl periodicals.

OH —TOLEDO-LUCAS COUNTY PUBLIC LIBRARY, Local History & Genealogy Dept, 325 Michigan St, Toledo, 43624. James Marshall, Head
Holdings: Vols 8500 Cat Mss Maps Pix Slides Audiotapes Microforms
Budget: $5000
Notes: Departmental catalog and biographical index available. Special unpublished indexes and finding aids available for the following materials: mss, pictures, maps, scrapbooks and VF clippings, and oral history tapes and architectural drawings.

OH —GREENE COUNTY DISTRICT LIBRARY, 76 E Market St, PO Box 520, Xenia, 45385. Julie M Overton, Local

OHIO—HISTORY (cont.)

History Coordr
Holdings: // Uncat
Notes: Galloway Collection of Ohio history is housed in a five-drawer filing cabinet, incl letters, some at the time of the Gold Rush; family letters of the Galloways, Lyons, Worthingtons and others; material about William Maxwell, editor and publisher of the first newspaper in the Northwest Territory, also legal papers concerning him; papers, some legal, concerning Galloways, incl "The Galloway Lands in 1812," and papers about the Worthingtons and Lyons; indentures; Civil War diary of Clark Galloway, MD, a surgeon in the war; pictures of families, covered bridges, mills etc; material about Tecumseh and some other Indians and their traditions; galley sheets and correspondence concerning the publishing of the New Testament in the Shawnee language; material about the railroad, OVCH (formerly OS&OS Home), Antioch College, Wilberforce University and other items about Ohiohistory. Also collection of papers of Raymond Higgins editor emeritus of the Xenia Daily Gazette and historian for the Xenia area until the mid-1970's. Many notes, papers and correspondence acquired when William Galloway was preparing to write the book "Old Chillicothe," published posthumously in 1934.
OH —JOHN MCINTIRE PUBLIC LIBRARY, 220 N Fifth St, Zanesville, 43701. Peg Harmon, Librn
Holdings: Vols 150 Cat Mss Maps Videotapes
Notes: Wide spectrum of Ohio history, with special emphasis on Zanesville and Muskingum County history & genealogy.
OH —ZANESVILLE CAMPUS, Herrold Hall Learning Resources Center, 1425 Newark Rd, Zanesville, 43701. Roberta Armstrong, Librn
Holdings: Vols 500 Cat Maps Microforms
RI —BROWN UNIVERSITY, John Hay Library, 20 Prospect St, Providence, 02912. Mark N Brown, Cur Mss
Holdings: // Mss
Notes: Solomon Drowne papers. He was a physician and Professor of Botany at Brown, Class of 1773. Mss incl accounts, invoices, receipts; originals and copies of prose and poetry; notes of Dr Drowne; sketches and valentines; political, legal, and military documents; and ships' papers. Subjects incl Colonial and Revolutionary history of Rhode Island and Brown University; medicine and botany 1770-1834; the early history of Morgantown, Virginia; Union, Pennsylvania; and Marietta, Ohio; business and trade in the Colonial period; and the Continental Congress. Correspondence with most persons of importance in his time.

OHIO—IMPRINTS

OH —COSHOCTON PUBLIC LIBRARY, 655 Main St, Coshocton, 43812. Susan Anderson, Librn
Holdings: Vols (875) Cat Mss Maps Pix Microforms
Budget: ($1000)
Notes: Local history and genealogy of Coshocton, Guernsey, Holmes, Knox, Tuscarawas, Licking and Muskingum counties. Incl published works, censuses (microfilm), cemetery index (Muskingum Co). Incl, for Coshocton Co, directories, newspapers, obituary and cemetery indexes, local authors and imprints, photographs, clippings, letters, personal papers. Building collection of histories and genealogies from areas of high migration to Coshocton Co.

OHIO—LAWS AND LEGISLATION

OH —CLEVELAND PUBLIC LIBRARY, Social Sciences Department, 325 Superior Ave, Cleveland, 44114. Thelma Morris, Head
Holdings: Vols 1000 Cat
Notes: Incl "Laws of Ohio" (sessional laws) House and Senate Journals of the Ohio General Assembly, Bulletins of the General Assembly, and House and Senate Bills of the General Assembly since 1937. Ohio Executive Documents.
OH —CLEVELAND PUBLIC LIBRARY, Public Administration Library, City Hall, 601 Lakeside Ave NE Rm 100, Cleveland, 44114. Janice Ryan Novak, Head
Holdings: Vols 20,000 Cat
Notes: Incl Ohio laws and the law of municipal corporations, case law and reporter systems. (The Law Library of the Cleveland City Law Department is administered and operated by the Public Administration Library under a contract between the city of Cleveland and the Cleveland Public Library.)

OHIO—MAPS

OH —PUBLIC LIBRARY OF CINCINNATI & HAMILTON COUNTY, Map Collection, History Dept, 800 Vine St, Cincinnati, 45202. Carl G Marquette Jr, Librn
Notes: The collection consists of 137,951 maps (uncataloged); 1250 atlases, with emphasis on Ohio county atlases, national atlases and facsimiles of important cartographic works; 125 bibliographies of maps or collections of maps and atlases; 400 gazetteers and other works, monographs series and journals (partially cataloged) relating to cartography and maps. The library is a depository for USGS and Defense Mapping Agency. Concentration of maps is Ohio, Hamilton County and Cincinnati. No catalog for flat maps.
OH —CLEVELAND PUBLIC LIBRARY, Science & Technology Dept, 325 Superior Ave, Cleveland, 44114. Jean Z Piety, Head
Notes: Unbound geologic maps organized to provide information on what is on, under or within an area incl soils, oil and gas, mine and mineral resources. Special emphasis on Ohio. Card index. Also large collection of weather maps and US statistical meteorological data.
OH —CLEVELAND PUBLIC LIBRARY, General Reference Dept, 325 Superior Ave, Cleveland, 44114. Donald Tipka, Head
Notes: Incl extensive collection of Cleveland and Cuyahoga County maps. Depository for Army Map Service and US Geological Survey topographic maps. Large collection of historical reproductions, national and international. Great Lakes navigation charts. Some aeronautical navigation charts.
OH —HIRAM COLLEGE, Teachout-Price Memorial Library, Hiram, 44234. Joanne M Sawyer, Archivist; Marjorie M Adams, Music Librn
Notes: The Fox Collection of Antique, Regional Maps concentrates on Ohio's Western Reserve, Ohio, Upper Midwest, eastern Canada; earliest maps are of the New World; does not circulate; restricted hours: call or write in advance. Incl 66 maps.

OHIO—POLITICS AND GOVERNMENT

DC —LIBRARY OF CONGRESS, Manuscript Division, Washington, 20540. John C Broderick, Chief
Notes: Papers of Robert Taft, Jr.
OH —CLEVELAND PUBLIC LIBRARY, 325 Superior Ave, Cleveland, 44114.
Holdings: Cat Maps Microforms
Notes: Depository of documents of the United States, Ohio, the United Nation, Organization of American States, and related organizations. Extensive holdings of other domestic and foreign publications. Congressional serial set incl Hearings, US and Great Britain Parliamentary papers.

OHIO—SOCIAL LIFE AND CUSTOMS

†OH —UKRAINIAN MUSEUM-ARCHIVES, INC, 1202 Kenilworth Ave, Cleveland, 44113.

OHIO ART see Art, Ohio

OHIO ARTISTS see Artists, Ohio

OHIO AUTHORS see Authors, Ohio

OHIO LAW see Law, Ohio

OHIO NEWSPAPERS see Newspapers, Ohio

OHIO RIVER

IN —INDIANA STATE UNIVERSITY, EVANSVILLE, Library, 8600 University Blvd, Evansville, 47712. Gina R Walker, Acting Archivist
Holdings: Cat Mss
Notes: Ohio River traffic and operating logs for now deactivated locks and dams No 43, No 44, and No 45, 1927-1972. Unpublished list.
LA —LOUISIANA STATE UNIVERSITY, SHREVEPORT, Library-Archives, 8515 Youree Dr, Shreveport, 71129. Patricia L Meador, Archivist & Asst Librn
Notes: See Louisiana - History entry for LSU Archives.

OHIO SOLDIERS AND SAILORS' ORPHANS HOME

OH —GREENE COUNTY DISTRICT LIBRARY, 76 E Market St, PO Box 520, Xenia, 45385. Julie M Overton, Local History Coordr
Notes: Earliest electrostatic copies of admission records, 1869-ca 1890 of the Ohio Soldiers and Sailors' Orphans Home (now called the Ohio Veterans' Children's Home).

OHIO VALLEY

IL —UNIVERSITY OF CHICAGO LIBRARY, Dept of Special Collections, 1100 E 57 St, Chicago, 60637.
KY —UNIVERSITY OF KENTUCKY, Margaret I King Library, Dept of Special Collections, Lexington, 40506. William Marshall, Head
Holdings: Cat Mss Maps Pix
Notes: History of Kentucky, Ohio Valley and Presbyterian Church. Consists of books, letters, maps, etc; about 10,000 pieces.
MO —WASHINGTON UNIVERSITY, John M Olin Library, Campus Box 1061, St Louis, 63130.
Holdings: Vols (1800) Cat Mss
Notes: Incl material from the Arthur C Hoskins, Richard S Hawes, Ernst C Krohn, George N Meissner, Stratford Lee Morton, and Edgar M Queeny collections; strong in early travel literature of the US and Latin America; accounts of exploration in the Mississippi Valley and Trans-Mississippi West; miscellaneous accounts of history, pioneer life, and travel in the Ohio Valley, Old Southwest, and California; material on the American Indian; 18th century American music; early American imprints.
OH —CINCINNATI HISTORICAL SOCIETY, Library, (formerly Historical & Philosophical Society of Ohio), Eden Park, Cincinnati, 45202. Laura L Chace, Librn
Holdings: Vols 60,000 Cat Mss Maps Pix Slides Microforms
Budget: ($8000)
Notes: Regional history relating to Cincinnati, the Northwest Territory and Ohio River Valley.
OH —MIAMI UNIVERSITY, King Library, Walter Havighurst Special Collections Library, Oxford, 45056. Helen Ball, Cur of Special Collections
Holdings: Vols (6000) Cat Mss Maps
Notes: Regional history of the Old Northwest Territory and especially of the Ohio River Valley. Incl periodicals.
PA —UNIVERSITY OF PITTSBURGH, Darlington Memorial Library, Special Collections, 601 Cathedral of Learning, Pittsburgh, 15260. Dennis Lambert, Darlington Librn
Holdings: Vols (17,000) Cat Mss Maps Pix
Notes: The Darlington Collection is especially rich in American history of the colonial period, the French and Indian War, the Revolution, and the War of 1812 with geographical emphasis on Western Pennsylvania and Ohio Valley history to 1870 and on Pittsburgh history to 1900. Indian treaties, captivity accounts, US and Pennsylvania travel and description, and early American fiction and prose are represented. A partial guide to the Darlington Manuscript Collections is available by writing for *Darlington Memorial Library: A Descriptive Checklist of its Manuscript Collections*, University of Pittsburgh Bibliographic Series 5, 1969. Noncirculating.

OHLINGER FAMILY

OH —RUTHERFORD B HAYES LIBRARY,
1337 Hayes Ave, Fremont, 43420. Watt P
Marchman, Dir
Holdings: Uncat Mss Pix Microforms
Notes: The Frank Ohlinger Family
Collection: American religion; Chinese
missionary; education (9 linear feet). Index
in collections.

OIL see Oils and Fats; Petroleum

OIL AND GAS LAW see Petroleum Law and Legislation

OIL ENGINES see Gas and Oil Engines

OIL INDUSTRY AND TRADE see Petroleum Industry and Trade

OIL PAINTING see Painting

OIL PIONEERS

TX —AMARILLO PUBLIC LIBRARY, 413 E
Fourth, Amarillo, 79101. Mary Kay Snell,
Librn
Holdings: Vols Cat Mss Maps Pix
Notes: The southwest collections incl
materials on the history of Texas, Louisiana,
New Mexico, Arkansas, Missouri and
Kansas. General subjects covered incl
overland journeys, early narratives, early
biographies, Indian captivities, outlaws, US
government reports, Mississippi and Ohio
Rivers, the Mexican War, reports of Catholic
missionaries, Niles Register, early
publications, fur trade, western trails, Texas
Rangers, sheriffs and Texas as a sovereign
state, buffalo hunting, Indian wars, cowboys,
the arrival of farmers, fences, and towns.
Over 1600 items which incl books,
documents, maps, mss, pamphlets,
unpublished theses, interviews and
photographs. The three major collections are
the William Henry Bush Collection, the
Laurence J Fitzsimon Collection and the
Calendar of John L McCarty.
TX —UNIVERSITY OF TEXAS LIBRARIES,
General Libraries, Barker Texas History
Center, PO Box P, Austin, 78712. Don
Carleton, Dir
Holdings: Vols (132,000) Cat Mss Maps Pix
Slides Phonorecords Audiotapes Microforms
Notes: See description of collection under
Texas-History.

OIL POLLUTION OF RIVERS, HARBORS, ETC.

CA —UNIVERSITY OF CALIFORNIA,
SANTA BARBARA, Library, Dept of
Special Collections, Santa Barbara, 93106.
Christian F Brun, Head
Holdings: Pix Clippings
Notes: Santa Barbara Oil Spill Jan 1969.
WA —URS ENGINEERS, Library, 2615
Fourth Ave, Seattle, 98121. Jill Phelps,
Librn
Holdings: Vols (3100) Cat
Budget: ($5000)
Notes: Environmental impact assessment,
hazardous materials disposal, oil spill
cleanup and environmental effects of
waterborne pollutants, especially with regard
to California and the western environment.

OIL REFINERIES see Petroleum Refineries

OIL SPILLS AND WILDLIFE

CA —UNIVERSITY OF CALIFORNIA,
SANTA BARBARA, Library, Dept of
Special Collections, Santa Barbara, 93106.
Christian F Brun, Head
Holdings: Pix Clippings
Notes: Santa Barbara Oil Spill Jan 1969.
WA —URS ENGINEERS, Library, 2615
Fourth Ave, Seattle, 98121. Jill Phelps,
Librn
Holdings: Vols (3100) Cat
Budget: ($5000)
Notes: Environmental impact assessment,

hazardous materials disposal, oil spill
cleanup and environmental effects of
waterborne pollutants, especially with regard
to California and the western environment.

OILS, ESSENTIAL see Essences and Essential Oils

OILS AND FATS

NY —BORDEN FOODS INC, Research
Centre Library, 600 N Franklin St, Syracuse,
13204. Carol Lenz-Taylor, Librn
Holdings: Vols (1800) Cat
Notes: Incl 10 vertical file drawers and 6100
patents.
PA —FRANKLIN INSTITUTE LIBRARY, 20
& The Parkway, Philadelphia, 19103.
Miriam Padusis, Dir; Charles Wilt, Readers
Servs Librn
Holdings: Vols (300,000) Cat Maps Pix
Microforms

OIRAT LANGUAGE (MONGOLIAN) see Kalmuck Language

OJIBWA INDIANS see Chippewa Indians

O'KEEFE CENTER, TORONTO

†ON —METROPOLITAN TORONTO
LIBRARY, Theatre Dept, Toronto, M4W
2G8, Can.
Notes: Papers of Jack Karr, Canadian film
and theatre critic, and public relations
director for Stratford Festival and O'Keefe
Centre.

OKHRANA

CA —HOOVER INSTITUTION ON WAR,
REVOLUTION & PEACE, Stanford
University, Stanford, 94305. Milorad M
Drachkovitch, Archivist
Holdings: // Mss
Notes: Records of the Imperial Russian
Secret Police (Okhrana) headquarters in
Paris, 1883-1917. Materials incl reports of
agents in the field, Paris office reports,
dispatches, circulars, studies,
correspondence, and other material. 203 ms
boxes, 10 clipping volumes, 163,802
biographical and reference cards, and 16
boxes of photographs. Unpublished register
is available in repository.

OKINAWA

DC —LIBRARY OF CONGRESS, African and
Middle Eastern Division, Washington,
20540.
Holdings: Cat Mss Microforms
Notes: Orientalia: the Orientalia Division
contains 1,400,000 vols in Oriental
languages. Chinese: more than 422,000 vols,
espec strong in local histories and Ch'ing
(1644-1911) period material. Japanese: over
574,000 vols, espec strong in economics,
statistics, history, literature; 12,000
government, learned society, and university
periodical titles, particularly science,
technology, and social sciences. Korean: 56,
000 vols, espec strong in social sciences and
modern history.
HI —UNIVERSITY OF HAWAII, Library,
2550 The Mall, Honolulu, 96822. Joyce
Wright, Head, Asia Collection; Masato
Matsu, Head, East Asia Vernacular
Collection
Holdings: Vols (400,000) Cat Microforms
See also entry under Ryukyu Islands.
NY —SYRACUSE UNIVERSITY
LIBRARIES, Ernest S Bird Library, George
Arents Research Library for Special
Collections, Syracuse, 13210. Carolyn A
Davis, Manuscripts Librn; Amy S Doherty,
University Archivist; Mark F Weimer, Rare
Book Librn
Holdings: Vols 2000 Cat Pix Microforms
Notes: Collection of material relating to
Okinawa and the Southern Ryukyus, largely
in Japanese. Library has published *Catalog of
the Ryukyu Research Collection*, compiled
by Douglas G Haring, 1969.

OKLAHOMA—GENEALOGY

OK —WILL ROGERS MEMORIAL
LIBRARY, W Will Rogers Blvd, Box 157,

Claremore, 74017. Reba N Collins, Dir
Holdings: Vols 100 Cat Microforms Serials
Notes: Includes Cherokee Indian Records,
local area histories.
OK —LAWTON PUBLIC LIBRARY, 110 SW
4th St, Lawton, 73501. Bernice Jackson, Dir;
Alene Simpson, Genealogical Research Dir
Holdings: Vols Documents Microforms Cat
Budget: $5000
Notes: This collection is primarily for
genealogical research for Southwestern
Oklahoma, but also contains general
genealogical research material.
TX —ECTOR COUNTY LIBRARY, Texas-
Southwest History & Genealogy Dept, 321
W 5th St, Odessa, 79761. Jan Carter, Head
Holdings: Vols (6968) Cat Phonorecords
Microforms
Budget: ($4000)
Notes: The genealogy collection is non-
circulating. The materials are arranged by
state and all periodicals for that state are
shelved with the books. National Archives
Census Microfilm is held, mainly, for
Southern States and migratory routes into
Texas.

OKLAHOMA—HISTORY

KS —UNIVERSITY OF KANSAS, Kenneth
Spencer Research Library, Kansas
Collection, Lawrence, 66045. Sheryl K
Williams, Cur
Holdings: Vols (92,000) Cat Mss Maps Pix
Notes: All aspects of the American West
and trans-Mississippi history, especially
northern and central regions. Overland
diaries, cartographic history, Indians,
emigration and immigration, printing history,
cattle industry, agriculture and farm life,
conservation are some special interests, in
addition to the usual political, economic,
military and social interests.
LA —LOUISIANA STATE UNIVERSITY,
SHREVEPORT, Library-Archives, 8515
Youree Dr, Shreveport, 71129. Patricia L
Meador, Archivist & Asst Librn
Notes: The collection's primary emphasis is
the history of North Louisiana, particularly
Northwest Louisiana.
NM —ROSWELL PUBLIC LIBRARY, 301 N
Pennsylvania Ave, Roswell, 88201. Sarah
Beth Galloway, Library Dir
Holdings: Vols (2000) Cat Maps
Budget: $1000
Notes: Covers literature (fiction and
nonfiction), history, biography, geography, of
Oklahoma, Texas, Colorado, New Mexico
and Arizona.
OK —ARDMORE PUBLIC LIBRARIES,
Grand at E St NW, Ardmore, 73401.
Carolyn Franks, Dir
Holdings: Vols 4000 Cat Mss Maps Pix
Notes: McGallird collection of local history
incl photographs and other printed material.
OK —WILL ROGERS MEMORIAL
LIBRARY, W Will Rogers Blvd, Box 157,
Claremore, 74017. Reba N Collins, Dir
Holdings: Vols (2800) Cat Microforms VF
OK —CENTRAL STATE UNIVERSITY,
Library, 100 N University Dr, Edmond,
73034. Andrew Peters, Reference Librn
Holdings: Vols 500 Cat
Notes: Copies of Town Site cases.
OK —PHILLIPS UNIVERSITY, Zollars
Memorial Library, University Sta, Enid,
73701. John L Sayre, Dir of University
Libraries
Holdings: Audiotapes Cat
Notes: *Living Legends* (Oral History
Collection) Interviews with 282 early
Northwest Oklahoma residents. Includes
reminiscences of the Cherokee Outlet Land
Run in 1893 and experiences in early
statehood and depression periods of
Oklahoma. Also includes recollections of
early Phillips University history.
OK —US ARMY FIELD ARTILLERY
SCHOOL LIBRARY, Morris Swett Library,
Snow Hall, Fort Sill, 73503. Lester L Miller
Jr, Chief Librn
Notes: Incl data on Fort Sill, Indian
Territory, settlement of Kiowa, Apache and
Commanche tribes, imprisonment of
Geronimo, Oklahoma territory, settlement of
Lawton. Unit histories, incl 10th Cavalry

OKLAHOMA—HISTORY (cont.)

(Buffalo Soldiers, a black unit that built Fort Sill); working papers of Sheridan, Grierson and other commanders; Field Artillery School. Photographs on army subjects, Fort Sill, Indians, Indian Territory, settlement of Southwest Oklahoma.

OK —LAWTON PUBLIC LIBRARY, 110 SW 4th St, Lawton, 73501. Bernice Jackson, Dir; Alene Simpson, Genealogical Research Dir
Holdings: Vols (500) Cat Maps Pix
Budget: ($1000)

OK —MUSEUM OF THE GREAT PLAINS, Research Center, 601 Ferris, PO Box 68, Lawton, 73502. Steve Wilson, Dir; Paula Williams, Special Collections
Holdings: Vols 20,000 Documents Pix Maps
Notes: Settlement of southwestern Oklahoma. Incl Charles Black and L M Gensman collections on law and politics in early Lawton; Harry Buckingham collection on business in early Lawton; Mildred Chrisman collection on show business 1900-1940; Fred Harris collection on politics in 1960's. 30,000 photographs.

OK —UNIVERSITY OF OKLAHOMA, Bizzell Memorial Library, Western History Collections, 401 W Brooks, Norman, 73069. John Ezell, Cur
Holdings: Cat Mss Maps Pix Microforms

OK —OKLAHOMA DEPT OF LIBRARIES, Law Library, 109 State Capital, Oklahoma City, 73105. Robert Clark, Dir; Betty Brown, Okla Collection Librn; Virginia Collier, US Documents; Jan Blakely, State Documents; Blane Dessy, Library Science
Holdings: Vols 18,000 Cat
Notes: Noncirculating.

OK —OKLAHOMA HISTORICAL SOCIETY, Library, Historical Bldg, Oklahoma City, 73105. Andrea Clark, Dir, Library Resources Division
Holdings: Vols (43,000) Cat Mss Maps Pix Microforms
Notes: The Society also has the Indian Archives Collection of 2,500,000 pieces (Mary Lee Boyle, Archivist). This is an extensive collection of records, particularly of the Five Civilized Tribes. Incl tribal rolls, agency reports, manuscripts, etc.

OK —OKLAHOMA STATE UNIVERSITY, Library, Stillwater, 74708. Roscoe Rouse, Dir
Holdings: Vols 1000 Cat Mss Maps Pix Microforms

OK —CHEROKEE NATIONAL HISTORICAL SOCIETY, Archives & Library, PO Box 515 TSA-LA-GI, Tahlequah, 74464. Duane King, Dir
Holdings: Vols (1000) Uncat Mss Maps Pix Slides Audiotapes Microforms
Notes: An embryonic collection, directly or indirectly related to Cherokee history, culture and genealogy. Slide collection depicts copies of material from the collection, from the Cherokee National Museum Village (Cherokee, 1650 AD) and the Cultural Theatre ("Trail of Tears Drama"). Newspaper collection incl several hundred newspapers dating back to 1762, each of which contains some reference to the Cherokees. The Cherokee National Archives also contains the non-current 1975 files of the Cherokee Nation of Oklahoma and the Keeler Collection (papers and personal files of W W Keeler, former Principal Chief of the Cherokee Nation for 26 years).

OK —PHILBROOK ART CENTER, Library, 2727 S Rockford Rd, Tulsa, 74114. Thomas E Young, Librn
Holdings: Vols (1000) Uncat Pix
Notes: The Roberta C Lawson Collection is mainly books, with some serials, and an uncounted group of photographs. The books are organized and partially cataloged; photographs are not. They deal with Indians and western Americana.

OK —THOMAS GILCREASE INSTITUTE OF AMERICAN HISTORY & ART LIBRARY, 1400 North 25th West Ave, Tulsa, 74127. Sarah Hirsch, Librn
Holdings: Vols Cat Mss Maps Pix
Notes: Trans-Mississippi West, US, Indian and Hispanic history. The Gilcrease Library contains a total of about 40,000 mss; 10,000 imprints; 5000 photographs; 600 maps and 50,000 vols.

OK —UNIVERSITY OF TULSA, McFarlin Library, Dept of Rare Books and Special Collections, 600 S College, Tulsa, 74104. David Farmer, Dir; Toby Murray, Archivist; Caroline Swinson, Cur of Manuscripts & Art
Holdings: Cat
Notes: The Indian collection of John W Shleppey. Indian materials of some 6000 bibliographic items, excl of mss and photographs. Emphasis on Indian Territory imprints, laws, Cherokee and Choctaw tribes, etc.

TX —UNIVERSITY OF TEXAS LIBRARIES, General Libraries, Barker Texas History Center, PO Box P, Austin, 78712. Don Carleton, Dir
Holdings: Vols (132,000) Cat Mss Maps Pix Slides Phonorecords Audiotapes Microforms
Notes: See description of collection under Texas-History.

TX —ECTOR COUNTY LIBRARY, Texas-Southwest History & Genealogy Dept, 321 W 5th St, Odessa, 79761. Jan Carter, Head
Holdings: Vols (8500) Cat Maps Pix
Budget: ($4000)
Notes: A card catalog of Texas-History; Southwest, New-History; Oklahoma-History is located in the Texas-Southwest History Dept. A card file by subject is a guide to vertical file materials and Texas, New Mexico, Oklahoma, Arizona periodicals. The Texas-History collection has reference, closed shelf, and circulating books.

OKLAHOMA—IMPRINTS

OK —UNIVERSITY OF TULSA, McFarlin Library, Dept of Rare Books and Special Collections, 600 S College, Tulsa, 74104. David Farmer, Dir; Toby Murray, Archivist; Caroline Swinson, Cur of Manuscripts & Art
Holdings: Cat
Notes: The Indian collection of John W Shleppey. Indian materials of some 6000 bibliographic items, excl of mss and photographs. Emphasis on Indian Territory imprints, laws, Cherokee and Choctaw tribes, etc.

OKLAHOMA—MAPS

OK —UNIVERSITY OF OKLAHOMA, Geology Library, 830 Van Vleet Oval Rm 102, Norman, 73019. Claren Kidd, Geology Librn
Notes: Most are received as the result of Oklahoma Geological Survey exchanges or a depository status. 90,000 maps.

OK —TULSA CITY-COUNTY LIBRARY, Business & Technology Dept, 400 Civic Center, Tulsa, 74103. Craig Buthod, Head
Notes: Original General Land Office survey maps for the states of Arizona, Arkansas, Colorado, Illinois, Indiana, Idaho, Kansas, Michigan, Missouri, Montana, Nebraska, Nevada, New Mexico, North Dakota, Ohio, Oklahoma, South Dakota, Utah and Wyoming. Incomplete coverage of each state.

OKLAHOMA—POLITICS AND GOVERNMENT

OK —CENTRAL STATE UNIVERSITY, Library, 100 N University Dr, Edmond, 73034. Andrew Peters, Reference Librn
Holdings: Vols Cat
Notes: 5000 periodicals and pamphlet documents.
See also entry under Alternative Press.

OK —MUSEUM OF THE GREAT PLAINS, Research Center, 601 Ferris, PO Box 68, Lawton, 73502. Steve Wilson, Dir; Paula Williams, Special Collections
Holdings: Vols 20,000 Documents Maps Pix VF
Notes: Settlement of southwestern Oklahoma. Incl Charles Black and L M Gensman collections on law and politics in early Lawton; Harry Buckingham collection on business in early Lawton; Mildred Chrisman collection on show business 1900-1940; Fred Harris collection on politics in 1960's. 30,000 photographs.

OK —UNIVERSITY OF OKLAHOMA, Bizzell Memorial Library, Western History Collections, 401 W Brooks, Norman, 73069. John Ezell, Cur

Notes: Subject scope covers all aspects of history and culture of American Trans-Mississippi West and the North American Indians with special emphasis on Oklahoma and adjacent states, the Southwest and Spanish borderlands. Printed and non-print holdings cover Indians, explorations and surveys, range cattle industry, fur-trade, transportation, overland travels, emigration and immigration, frontier life, agriculture, mining, oil gas industry, conservation, literature, and the social-cultural history as well as the usual political and economic interests. The large holdings of U.S. Congressional papers also reflect other national and international affairs.

OKLAHOMA AUTHORS see Authors, Oklahoma

OKLAHOMA NEWSPAPERS see Newspapers, Oklahoma

OKUMA PAPERS

IL —CENTER FOR RESEARCH LIBRARIES, 6050 S Kenwood Ave, Chicago, 60637. Donald B Simpson, Dir; Esther Smith, Collection Development Librn
Holdings: Cat Microforms
Notes: Japanese foreign ministry archives 1868-1945, archives of army, navy, and other government agencies 1868-1945, Cabinet archives, Tokugawa docuemnts, Okuma papers, other archival materials. Descriptive pamphlet available.

OLANDER, VICTOR A.

IL —CHICAGO HISTORICAL SOCIETY, Library, Clark St at North Ave, Chicago, 60614. Archie Motley, Manuscript Librn
Notes: Papers of labor leader.
See also entry under Labor-History.

OLBRECHTS, FRANS M.

PA —AMERICAN PHILOSOPHICAL SOCIETY, Library, 105 S Fifth St, Philadelphia, 19106. Edward C Carter II, Librn
Notes: Papers, incl American Indian anthropological studies.

OLD AGE see Aging and Aged

OLD AGE BENEFITS see Old Age Pensions

OLD AGE PENSIONS

FL —FLORIDA STATE UNIVERSITY, Robert Manning Strozier Library, Special Collections Dept, Tallahassee, 32306. Opal M Free, Head, Special Collections
Notes: The official papers, documents, photographs, recordings, and memorabilia of US Representative Claude Pepper. Incl the papers, photographs, and memorabilia of his wife, Mildred Irene Webster Pepper (706, 536 items).

MD —US SOCIAL SECURITY ADMINISTRATION, Library, Library Information & Graphics Services Branch, Altmeyer Bldg Rm 571, 6401 Security Blvd, Baltimore, 21235. Rowena S Sadler, Chief
Holdings: Vols Cat
Notes: All phases of social insurance incl OASI pensions, welfare health insurance and medical economics.

OLD BACTRIAN LANGUAGE see Avesta Language and Literature

OLD BULGARIAN LANGUAGE see Church Slavic Languages and Literature

OLD CHURCH SLAVIC LANGUAGE see Church Slavic Languages and Literature

OLD ENGLISH LANGUAGE see Anglo-Saxon Language and Literature

OLD ENGLISH LITERATURE see English Literature—Middle English

OLD ERIE ACADEMY

PA —ERIE COUNTY HISTORICAL SOCIETY LIBRARY, 417 State St, Erie, 16501. Helen Andrews, Librn
Notes: Original research materials in 16 legal size drawers, including Pennsylvania Population Company papers, Old Erie Academy papers, Erie Street railway papers, Harry Burleigh (black singer & composer) transcripts and research papers; also four letter size drawers with old account books.

OLD FRENCH LITERATURE see French Language and Literature—Old French

OLD FICTION see Fiction, Old

OLD ICELANDIC LANGUAGE AND LITERATURE see Icelandic and Old Norse Languages and Literature

OLD NORSE LANGUAGE AND LITERATURE see Icelandic and Old Norse Languages and Literature

OLD NORTHWEST see Northwest, Old

OLD PERSIAN LANGUAGE

NY —NEW YORK PUBLIC LIBRARY, Oriental Div, Fifth Ave & 42 St, New York, 10018. E Christian Filstrup, Chief
Holdings: Cat Mss Microforms
Budget: ($56,455)
Notes: Published catalog of holdings.

OLD PRUSSIAN LANGUAGE see Prussian Language and Literature

OLD SLOVENIAN LANGUAGE see Church Slavic Languages and Literature

OLD UZBEK LANGUAGE see Jagataic Language and Literature

OLDFIELD, CLAUDE HOUGHTON, 1889-

CA —CLAREMONT COLLEGES, Honnold Library, Ninth & Dartmouth, Claremont, 91711. Tania Rizzo, Special Collections Dept Head
Holdings: Vols 30 // Cat Mss
Notes: First and special British and American editions; 17 with original dust jackets; 9 inscribed; one ALS.
See also entry under Houghton, Claude
BC —UNIVERSITY OF VICTORIA, McPherson Library, Victoria, V8W 3H5, Can.

OLDS, RANSOM ELI

MI —R E OLDS MUSEUM LIBRARY, 240 Museum Drive, Lansing, 48933.
Notes: Emphasizes the contributions that Lansing has made to transportation history; materials on Oldsmobile, Reo, Star, Durant, and Bates cars. Incl books, manuals, magazines, advertisements, photographs, films, slides, audiotapes, videotapes, VF, and art reproductions.

OLEFACTION

CT —YALE MEDICAL LIBRARY, 333 Cedar St, New Haven, 06510.
Notes: A special subject emphasis.

OLIPHANT, MARGARET (WILSON), 1828-1897

CA —UNIVERSITY OF CALIFORNIA, LOS ANGELES, Research Library, Dept of Special Collections, 405 Hilgard Ave, Los Angeles, 90024. Edward Shreeves, Chairman, Bibliographers Group; David S Zeidberg, Head
Holdings: Vols 100
Notes: 100 first and other editions of her books; 17 letters.

OLIVE, LINDSEY S.

†NC —UNIVERSITY OF NORTH CAROLINA, CHAPEL HILL, Department of Botany Library, 301 Coker Hall 010-A, Chapel Hill, 27514. William R Burk, Botany Librn
Notes: The mycology collection incl some 6000 pamphlets. It contains papers of the following scientists: William C Coker, John N Couch, Lindsay F Olive, mycologists; also, Victor A Greulach, plant pathologist. The mycology catalog is in preparation (1983), and will provide author, title, and subject access.

OLIVER, ELI L.

DC —GEORGE WASHINGTON UNIVERSITY, Gelman Library, 2130 H St NW, Washington, 20052.
Holdings: Cat Mss Pix
Notes: The Eli L Oliver labor papers cover the period 1930-1952 and particularly concern labor's involvement in politics. The correspondence contains letters from union officials nationwide. Organizational papers of Labor's Non-Partisan League include financial records, memos, campaign pamphlets, press releases, etc. Oliver's papers also include reports discussing primary and general election strategies for 1938 and 1940; similar material is present for the American Labor Party of New York relating to the 1940 campaign and for the Labor Committee's backing of the Truman-Barkley and the Stevenson-Sparkman campaigns of 1948 and 1952, respectively. The collection also contains some of Oliver's speeches, addresses, etc and some personal files including photos, financial records, clippings, etc. Cataloged as a collection with unpublished inventory for access.

OLIVER FAMILY

MA —MASSACHUSETTS HISTORICAL SOCIETY LIBRARY, 1154 Boylston St, Boston, 02215. John D Cushing, Librn
Notes: Papers. One of more than 5000 individual collections in the Library. Collection of mss has been cataloged and issued in nine folio vols by G K Hall & Co of Boston. It is widely distributed throughout the United States and Europe.

OLIVER OPTIC

DC —LIBRARY OF CONGRESS, Children's Literature Center, Washington, 20540. Sybille Jagusch, Chief
Notes: Extensive holdings of works by Jacob Abbott, Oliver Optic (Adams, William T), Alden (Pansy), Samuel G Goodrich (Peter Parley), many in Rare Book and Special Collections Division.
IL —NORTHERN ILLINOIS UNIVERSITY, Founders Memorial Library, Rare Books and Special Collections Dept, De Kalb, 60115. William R DuBois, Dept Head
Holdings: Vols (1000)
Budget: ($5000)
Notes: Mass-appeal publications, ca 1865-1920. Includes Horatio Alger, "Oliver Optic" and other popular writers.
MA —BRANDEIS UNIVERSITY, Goldfarb Library, 415 South St, Waltham, 02154. Bessie Hahn, Dir
Holdings: Vols
Notes: Dime Novel and Juvenile Literature Collection. This collection consists of over 1000 dime novels, an extensive collection of the works of Horatio Alger, Harry Castleman, Oliver Optic and other boys and girls literature of the 19th and early 20th century. Access to this collection is through the card catalog in Special Collections.
MS —UNIVERSITY OF SOUTHERN MISSISSIPPI, William David McCain Graduate Library, Box 5148, Southern Sta, Hattiesburg, 39406.
Holdings: Vols 146
Notes: The Lena Y de Grummond Collection of Children's Literature. Incl the Robert L Dartt Collection of over 1800 books for boys from the late 19th and early 20th centuries. Extensive Henty (over 550 vols), Alger, Brereton, Castlemon, Fenn, Kingston, Optic, and Stratemeyer holdings. Catalog in progress.
OH —OHIO UNIVERSITY, Vernon R Alden Library, Department of Archives and Special Collections, Athens, 45701. Gary A Hunt, Head
Holdings: Vols (1400) Uncat
Notes: A miscellaneous collection of children's books by American and English authors, with most imprint dates in the period 1870-1930; numerous series books. Authors incl Jacob Abbott (196 v), "Oliver Optic" (84 v), Horatio Alger (89 v), J H Ewing (53 v), Martha Finley (47 v), G A Henty (46 v), Frank V Webster (38 v), and many others.

OLLAS, SINHALESE (MEDICINE)

MD —JOHNS HOPKINS UNIVERSITY, Institute of the History of Medicine, 1900 E Monument St, Baltimore, 21205. Doris Thibodeau, Librn
Holdings: Vols 25

OLMSTEAD, FREDERICK LAW

MA —UNIVERSITY OF LOWELL, Library, One University Ave, Lowell, 01854. Martha Mayo, Special Collections Librn
Notes: Papers of the Manning family, incl the correspondence of Warren H Manning, founder of the American Society of Landscape Architects, with small amount of materials on Frederick Law Olmstead.

OLMSTED ASSOCIATES

DC —LIBRARY OF CONGRESS, Manuscript Division, Washington, 20540. John C Broderick, Chief
Notes: More than 150,000 items added to the records of Olmsted Associates, Inc, of Brookline, Massachusetts, landscape architects.

OLPIN, A. RAY, 1898-

UT —UNIVERSITY OF UTAH, Marriott Library, Special Collections, Salt Lake City, 84112. Gregory C Thompson, Cur
Notes: Papers (1946-1964).

OLSEN, NILS A.

IA —IOWA STATE UNIVERSITY, Library, Dept of Special Collections, Ames, 50011. Stanley M Yates, Head
Holdings: // Mss
Notes: Nils A Olsen (1886-1940) Papers. Collection contains correspondence, diary (1925-1935), printed matter and newspaper clippings relating to his work as Chief of Bureau of Agricultural Economics of the USDA (1928-1935). 750 items. Finding aid available.

OLSEN, OLE

CA —UNIVERSITY OF SOUTHERN CALIFORNIA, Edward L Doheny Memorial Library, Archives of Performing Arts, University Park, Los Angeles, 90089. Robert Knutson, Librn
Holdings: Mss Pix
Notes: Personal collection of papers, pictures, etc.

OLSEN, PAUL

MA —BOSTON UNIVERSITY, Mugar Memorial Library, Special Collections Dept,

OLSEN, PAUL (cont.)

771 Commonwealth Ave, Boston, 02215.
Howard B Gotlieb, Dir
Holdings: Cat Mss Correspondence

OLSON, CHARLES, 1910-1970

CT —UNIVERSITY OF CONNECTICUT,
Library, Storrs, 06268. George F Butterick,
Cur of Literary Archives
Holdings: Mss Maps Pix Phonorecords
Audiotapes 16mm Films
Notes: Repository for the poet's papers. Incl
writings by and about him.
MA —SAWYER FREE LIBRARY, 2 Dale
Ave, Gloucester, 01930. Stillman P Hilton,
Librn
Holdings: Vols 76 Cat Pix
Notes: Also 6 vertical file folders.
MO —WASHINGTON UNIVERSITY, John
M Olin Library, Campus Box 1061, St Louis,
63130.
Notes: Extensive collection of books,
correspondence and mss.
NY —STATE UNIVERSITY OF NEW
YORK, STONY BROOK, Melville Library,
Dept of Special Collections, Stony Brook,
11794. Evert Volkersz, Head
Holdings: Cat Mss
BC —SIMON FRASER UNIVERSITY,
Library, Burnaby, V5A 1S6, Can. Percilla
Groves, Special Collections Librn
Holdings: Cat Mss
Notes: Letters of Charles Olson to Robin
Blaser, Andrew Crozier, Barry Hall, Le Roi
Jones (Amiri Baraka), Ed Sanders.
Typescript and galleys for *Maximus IV, V,
VI*, mss published in *Pacific Nation* and
Wivenhoe Park Review. See *Line*, vol 1, no
1, spring 1983, for a complete list of Olson
mss at SFU.

OLYMPIC GAMES

CA —UNIVERSITY OF CALIFORNIA,
BERKELEY, Bancroft Library, Manuscripts
Division, Berkeley, 94720. James D Hart,
Dir
Notes: Wide scope but emphasis on the
University's teams.
CA —FIRST INTERSTATE BANK, Athletic
Foundation, 2141 W Adams, Los Angeles,
90018. W R Schroeder, Managing Dir
Notes: One of the most extensive library and
museum collections relating to sports, the
Olympic Games, etc. Bound vols of sports
sections from several newspapers. Large
collection of college and university annuals
and yearbooks; souvenir publications from
amateur, college, and professional sporting
events. Also, large museum collection of
sports memorabilia, ledger of halls of fame
with thousands of names of outstanding
athletes in all sports. Repository for the
Association of Sports Museums and Halls of
Fame. Noncirculating.
CA —LOS ANGELES PUBLIC LIBRARY,
Art, Music & Recreation Dept, 630 W Fifth
St, Los Angeles, 90071. Melvin H
Rosenberg, Mgr & Principal Librn
Notes: Large collection.
FL —INTERNATIONAL SWIMMING HALL
OF FAME LIBRARY, 1 Hall of Fame Dr,
Fort Lauderdale, 33316. Marion Washburn,
Librn
Holdings: Vols (3000) Cat Mss Audiotapes
Videotapes 16mm Films
Notes: All aspects of swimming: history,
instruction, competition. Incl rare and out of
print editions, complete set of *NCAA
Swimming Guides* (1915-date), numerous
periodicals (eg, *Swimming World*, 1951-
date), and small collection of materials on
related aquatic sports: diving, synchronized
swimming, etc. Also have materials on
Olympic Games, 1896-date, covering
history, results, pictorial essays, programs,
etc
IL —UNIVERSITY OF ILLINOIS,
URBANA/CHAMPAIGN, Library,
University Archives, 19 Library, 1408 W
Gregory Drive, Urbana, 61801. Maynard
Brichford, University Archivist
Holdings: Vols (1663)// Cat Mss Pix
Notes: The Avery Brundage Collection. Incl

his papers and material on amateur athletics,
Olympic games, and sports. Published guide
is available: *Avery Brundage Collection,
1908-1975* (Cologne: Karl Hofmann
Schorndorf, 1977). 517,000 ms pieces. There
is also a collection on Olympic sports and
other aspects of sports kept in the Brundage
Room.
NY —COLUMBIA UNIVERSITY
LIBRARIES, Rare Book & Manuscript
Library, 801 Butler Library, 535 W 114 St,
New York, 10027. Kenneth A Lohf, Librn
Notes: The L S Alexander Gumby
Collection, which incl material on Blacks in
sports. Restricted use.
WI —MILWAUKEE PUBLIC LIBRARY, 814
W Wisconsin Ave, Milwaukee, 53233.
Donald J Sager, City Librn
Holdings: Vols Cat
Notes: All official publications of the US
Olympic Committee as well as all major
publications from the host countries.

OMAN

CA —HOOVER INSTITUTION ON WAR,
REVOLUTION & PEACE, Stanford
University, Stanford, 94305. Peter Duignan,
Cur; Karen Fung, Deputy Cur
Holdings: Vols (100,000)
Notes: For full description of collection, see
Hoover Institution entry under Near East.

OMAR KHAYYAM

AZ —ARIZONA STATE UNIVERSITY,
Library, Tempe, 85287. Marilyn
Wurzburger, Special Collections Librn
Holdings: Vols 487 Cat
Notes: Incl reference works and parodies of
the *Rubaiyat* and versions in several
languages.
CA —CLAREMONT COLLEGES, Honnold
Library, Ninth & Dartmouth, Claremont,
91711. Tania Rizzo, Special Collections
Dept Head
Holdings: Vols 200 Uncat
Notes: Special and limited published and
privately printed editions, some with unique
illustrations; five versions of Edward
Fitzgerald in different printings; other
translations, paraphrases and parodies;
biographies of Omar; historical and critical
studies of the *Rubaiyat*. Restricted use.
CA —UNIVERSITY OF CALIFORNIA, SAN
DIEGO, Central University Library,
Mandeville Dept of Special Collections, La
Jolla, 92093. Lynda Corey Claassen, Head
Holdings: Vols 563 // Cat
Notes: Incl 500 editions of *The Rubaiyat*.
CA —UNIVERSITY OF CALIFORNIA, LOS
ANGELES, Research Library, Dept of
Special Collections, 405 Hilgard Ave, Los
Angeles, 90024. Edward Shreeves,
Chairman, Bibliographers Group; David S
Zeidberg, Head
Holdings: Vols 450 Mss
Notes: Based on A G Potter's Collection.
450 volumes; 2 linear feet of
correspondence, mss, and ephemera relating
to various editions of the *Rubaiyat*.
IN —INDIANA UNIVERSITY, Lilly Library,
Seventh St, Bloomington, 47405. William R
Cagle, Librn
Holdings: Vols 650 // Cat Mss
Notes: Largely printings of the English
translations by Fitzgerald, Eben Thompson,
etc.
†OH —OHIO NORTHERN UNIVERSITY,
Heterick Memorial Library, 525 S Main St,
Ada, 45810.
Notes: Editions of the *Rubaiyat*, icnl English
translations, critical analyses, and
biographies. Noncirculating.
OH —CLEVELAND PUBLIC LIBRARY, Fine
Arts and Special Collections Department,
325 Superior Ave, Cleveland, 44114. Alice
N Loranth, Head
Holdings: Vols 1050 Cat Mss
Notes: One of the outstanding collections of
Omariana in the United States, holding
many editions and versions in 48 languages.
Incl the first edition of 1859, the first
American edition, published in Columbus,
Ohio, in 1870; and many unique editions
brought together by the late Clarke W

Walton of Monroe, North Carolina. Forms
part of the Chess Collection.. Separate
edition file is maintained. See also Chess,
Cleveland Public Library.
See also entries under Oriental Languages
and Literatures; Rare Books.

O'MEARA, WALTER

MA —BOSTON UNIVERSITY, Mugar
Memorial Library, Special Collections Dept,
771 Commonwealth Ave, Boston, 02215.
Howard B Gotlieb, Dir
Holdings: Cat Mss Pix
Notes: Mss, correspondence, etc collected in
depth; incl publications by or about.

OMEGA DELTA PROFESSIONAL
OPTOMETRIC FRATERNITY

MI —FERRIS STATE COLLEGE
ARCHIVES, 901 S State St, Big Rapids,
49307. R Lawrence Martin, Coordr
Holdings: Vols 26 Cat Mss Pix
Notes: 4 boxes of papers and books of Dr
Chauncey J Howe, OD, practicing
optometrist in Hillsdale, Mich, 1920-1968,
secretary, Michigan Board of Examiners in
Optometry, 1941-1972, founder of Omega
Delta, professional optometric fraternity.
Includes professional papers of Dr Howe,
papers of the State Board and 7 vols of
minutes of the State Board, 1909-1970.

OMENS

OH —CLEVELAND PUBLIC LIBRARY, Fine
Arts and Special Collections Department,
325 Superior Ave, Cleveland, 44114. Alice
N Loranth, Head
Holdings: Vols (2500) Cat
Notes: Part of the Occult Sciences
Collection. Emphasis is on historical
treatises, folklore aspects and the classic
texts pertaining to apparitions, ghosts,
divinations, oracles, omens, witchcraft,
magic, and sorcery in various civilizations.
Astrology, palmistry, psychical research and
contemporary manifestations are slmost
entirely omitted.
See also entries under Folklore; Occult
Sciences.

OMNIBUS SERVICE see Motor Bus Lines

ONCOLOGY

CA —UNIVERSITY OF CALIFORNIA, LOS
ANGELES, Biomedical Library, Center for
the Health Sciences, Los Angeles, 90024.
Alison Bunting, Acting Biomedical Librn;
Victoria Steele, Head, History & Special
Collections Div
Holdings: Vols (400,000) Cat Slides
Phonorecords Audiotapes Videotapes 16mm
Films Microforms

Notes: The UCLA Biomedical Library serves
primarily the Schools of Medicine, Dentistry,
Nursing, and Public Health, the UCLA Medical
Center, the Departments of Microbiology and
Biology in the College of Letters and Science, and
related institutes in biomedicine. The collections of
the Library are broad in scope, designed not only
to support the teaching and research needs of its
many users, but also to function as a resource for
the health sciences-biological field as a whole. The
outstanding feature of the collection is the strength
of its periodical holdings, both current and
retrospective. The Library also has an excellent
reference collection, a comprehensive historical
section, and gives special emphasis to the fields of
neuroscience, psychiatry, ophthalmology, radiation
biology, molecular biology, and vertebrate
zoology. Increased emphasis is being given to the
acquisition of audiovisual materials.

ONCOLOGY (cont.)

†CT —YALE UNIVERSITY, Medical Library,
333 Cedar St, New Haven, 06520.
Notes: An extensive collection.

IL —ARGONNE NATIONAL
LABORATORY, Biological and Medical
Research Branch Library, 9700 S Cass Ave,
Argonne, 60439. Rebecca Smith, Librn
Notes: Incl 14,000 vols monographs, 250
current journals. Materials may be used by
the public in the library by prior
arrangement. Photocopies may be supplied
for interlibrary loan, for which a processing
and handling charge is made.

MA —FRANCIS A COUNTWAY LIBRARY
OF MEDICINE, Boston Medical Library/
Harvard Medical Library, 10 Shattuck St,
Boston, 02115. C Robin LeSueur, Librn;
Richard J Wolfe, Cur, Rare Books &
Manuscripts
Holdings: Cat Pix Microforms

MA —SOUTHWOOD COMMUNITY
HOSPITAL, Medical Library, 111 Dedham
St, Norfolk, 02056.
Holdings: Vols (800) Cat Audiotapes
Filmstrips
Budget: ($4500)
Notes: The present emphasis is on human
and animal research, diagnosis and
treatment. Journals cataloged v 1-19, 1941-
59; v 20, 1960-.

NE —UNIVERSITY OF NEBRASKA
MEDICAL CENTER, Library, 42 & Dewey
Ave, Omaha, 68105. Robert M Braude, Dir
Notes: Eppley Institute research collection
on cancer now part of Medical Center
Library.

NY —COLD SPRING HARBOR
LABORATORY, Library, PO Box 100,
Cold Spring Harbor, 11724. Susan Gensel,
Library Dir; Genemary Falvey, Librn
Holdings: Vols (30,000)
Budget: ($103,500)
Notes: The highly technical collection is
comprised of 20,000 serial vols and 10,000
monographs. The library receives 500
current serial titles. Subjects covered incl
molecular and cellular biology, virology,
biochemistry, microbiology, oncology,
neurobiology, biological risk assessment and
genetic engineering/biotechnology. Special
collections in eugenics and genetics are
primarily historical dealing with the
development of genetics in the US which
had its beginnings here.

NY —MEMORIAL SLOAN KETTERING
CANCER CENTER, Lee Coombe
Memorial Library, 1275 York Ave, New
York, 10021. Angelina Harmon, Dir
Holdings: Vols (25,000) Cat Mss Pix Slides
Phonorecords Audiotapes Videotapes 16mm
Films Microforms
Budget: ($450,000)
Notes: Incl an developing archives
collection, with some rare materials. An
extensive bibliography of the institution's
professional staff is maintained along with
reprints. The main collection is concentrated
in cancer and related fields of research and
therapy.

TN —SAINT JUDE CHILDREN'S
RESEARCH HOSPITAL, Medical Library,
323 N Lauderdale, PO Box 318, Memphis,
38101. Mary Edith Walker, Librn; Cindy
Suter, Asst Librn
Holdings: Vols (10,000)
Notes: The collection of pediatric oncology
is intermingled with general clinical and
research materials. Published description of
collection in International Directory of
Specialized Cancer Research and Treatment
Establishments (Geneva: International Union
Against Cancer, 1976), p 442.

TX —UNIVERSITY OF TEXAS, M D
Anderson Hospital and Tumor Institute,
Research Medical Library, Texas Medical
Center, Houston, 77030. Marie Harvin,
Research Medical Library
Holdings: Vols (48,000) Cat
Notes: Library attempts to collect every
publication in all languages related to clinical
cancer (or oncology) Aim is an exhaustive
collection in this field. Collect heavily
(research level) in pathology, radiology,
nuclear medicine, genetics and cell biology.

ONE-ACT PLAYS

KY —HOPKINSVILLE COMMUNITY
COLLEGE, Library, North Dr,
Hopkinsville, 42240. Marjanna J Frising,
Librn
Holdings: Vols (500) Cat Phonorecords
Audiotapes Filmstrips
Notes: Incl most notable Broadway plays,
both musical and non-musical, with sound-
tracks available for most. Also a large
collection of children's and one-act plays as
well as non-musical but best known 3-act
plays, incl comedy and mystery plays.

O'NEAL, COTHBURN

MA —BOSTON UNIVERSITY, Mugar
Memorial Library, Special Collections Dept,
771 Commonwealth Ave, Boston, 02215.
Howard B Gotlieb, Dir
Holdings: Cat Mss
Notes: Mss, correspondence, etc collected in
depth; incl publications by or about.

O'NEAL, REP. MASTON

GA —UNIVERSITY OF GEORGIA,
Libraries, Special Collections Division,
Athens, 30602. Vesta Lee Gordon, Asst Dir
for Special Collections
Notes: Collection contains 1394.8 linear feet
of mss: papers of US Senator Richard B
Russell; US Congressmen John W Davis,
Maston O'Neal, Robert G Stephens Jr, John
L Pilcher, Dudley M Hughes; Governors
Hoke Smith, Lester Maddox, Carl Sanders.

ONEIDA COMMUNITY

MA —AMHERST COLLEGE, Library,
Amherst, 01002. John Lancaster, Special
Collections Librn
Holdings: Vols 78 Cat

MI —UNIVERSITY OF MICHIGAN, Library,
Dept of Rare Books & Special Collections,
Ann Arbor, 48109. Robert J Starring, Head
Holdings: Vols 64 Cat
Notes: Holdings incl 49 vols of rare serials;
also early monographs.

NY —NEW YORK STATE LIBRARY, State
Education Bldg Annex, Washington Ave,
Albany, 12224.
Holdings: Cat
Notes: Strong collection of Oneida
Community publications.

NY —SYRACUSE UNIVERSITY
LIBRARIES, Ernest S Bird Library, George
Arents Research Library for Special
Collections, Syracuse, 13210. Carolyn A
Davis, Manuscripts Librn; Amy S Doherty,
University Archivist; Mark F Weimer, Rare
Book Librn
Holdings: Vols 180 Cat Pix
Notes: Extensive collection on Oneida
Community and John Humphrey Noyes.
Library has published The Oneida
Community Collection in the Syracuse
University Library, 1961.

O'NEILL, EUGENE

CA —AZUSA PACIFIC COLLEGE,
Marshburn Memorial Library, Citrus &
Alosta, Azusa, 91702. Edward Peterman,
Librn
Holdings: Vols (150) Uncat
Notes: The Odo B Stade Collection of
Literary First Editions. No photocopying.

CT —YALE UNIVERSITY, Beinecke Rare
Book & Manuscript Library, Osborn
Collection, New Haven, 06520. Stephen R
Parks, Cur
Holdings: Mss

CT —CONNECTICUT COLLEGE, Library,
Mohegan Ave, New London, 06320. Brian
Rogers, College Librn
Holdings: Vols 200 Cat Mss
Notes: O'Neill lived in New London. No
photocopying.

MA —AMHERST COLLEGE, Library,
Amherst, 01002. John Lancaster, Special
Collections Librn
Holdings: Vols 125 Cat Mss Pix

NH —DARTMOUTH COLLEGE, Baker
Memorial Library, Hanover, 03755.
Holdings: Cat Mss Pix
Notes: First editions, mss, etc.
Noncirculating.

NY —C W POST CENTER OF LONG
ISLAND UNIVERSITY, B Davis Schwartz
Memorial Library, Greenvale, 11548. Jean
Goldberg, Special Collections Librn
Holdings: Vols 1522 Cat
Notes: The private library of Eugene and
Carlotta O'Neill. By appointment.
Noncirculating.

RI —BROWN UNIVERSITY, John Hay
Library, Harris Collection, Prospect St,
Providence, 02912. Rosemary L Cullen, Cur
Holdings: Vols (200,000) Cat Mss Pix
Phonorecords Microforms
Budget: ($15,000)
Notes: The Harris Collection of American
Poetry and Plays is principally composed of
American and Canadian poetry and plays,
17th century-date. Extensive holdings in
songsters, gift books and annuals, hymnals,
pageants, broadside verse, carriers'
addresses, women poets, juvenile poetry,
(incl Mother Goose and The Night Before
Christmas), sheet music with lyrics, small
press publications, fine printing, black poets,
"little magazines," Yiddish-American
literature. All movements or schools of
American poetry are represented. Incl first
editions of most American poets and
playwrights, notably Whitman, Poe, Wallace
Stevens, Eugene O'Neill, Edward Albee,
Ezra Pound, T S Eliot, William Carlos
Williams, Amy Lowell, Phyllis Wheatley,
Robert Frost, Allen Ginsberg, Bliss Carman,
and Stephen Foster sheet music. Also incl
the Saunders Walt Whitman Collection
(1300 vols); the LangdonCollection of
Pageants (250 vols); the Asa Cushman
Collection of plays in ms and prompt copies;
the MacDougall Collection of Psalters and
Hymnals; 4000 plays issued by Walter H
Baker Co, Boston (1890-1957); the Vaxer
Collection of Yiddish Poetry, Plays and
Music (1700 vols). Collections incl 200,000
vols, 30,000 broadsides, 55,000 mss, 170,000
pieces of sheet music, 450 phonorecords, and
375 microfilm reels. See Dictionary Catalog
of the Harris Collection of American Poetry
and Plays (Boston: G K Hall, 1972), 13 vols;
Supplement (1977), 3 vols. See also,
American Poetry, 1609-1900, A Collection
on Microfilm, Segment I (1609-1820);
Segment II (1821-1850); Segment III (1851-
1870) (Woodbridge, Conn: Research
Publications). Separate catalog.

TX —UNIVERSITY OF HOUSTON, M D
Anderson Memorial Library, University
Park, Houston, 77004. David Farmer, Cur,
Special Collections; Jean Jackson, Assistant
Cur
Holdings: Vols 125 Cat
Notes: Emphasis is on textual studies. Only
reprints, variants, and periodical appearances
of his dramatic works are sought.

VA —UNIVERSITY OF VIRGINIA,
Alderman Library, Clifton Waller Barrett
Collection, Charlottesville, 22901. Joan St C
Crane, Cur of American Literature
Collections
Notes: Papers.

WI —UNIVERSITY OF WISCONSIN,
MADISON, Memorial Library, British &
American Language & Literature Collection,
728 State St, Madison, 53706. Yvonne
Schofer, Bibliographer
Holdings: Cat
Notes: 25 first editions of Eugene O'Neill's
plays, many signed by the author, some
holograph letters, photographs and other
miscellaneous emphemera.

O'NEILL, EUGENE, MEMORIAL
THEATRE CENTER

NY —NEW YORK PUBLIC LIBRARY,
Performing Arts Research Center, Billy Rose
Theatre Collection, 111 Amsterdam Ave,

O'NEILL, EUGENE, MEMORIAL THEATRE CENTER (cont.)

New York, 10023. Dorothy L Swerdlove, Cur
Holdings: Cat
Notes: Material on the activities at the Center, such as the annual playwrights' conference and the Critics Institute.

O'NOLAN, BRIAN

IL —SOUTHERN ILLINOIS UNIVERSITY, CARBONDALE, Delyte W Morris Library, Special Collections Dept, Carbondale, 62901. David V Koch, Cur of Special Collections; Louisa Bowen, Cur of Manuscripts
Holdings: Mss
Notes: Personal papers, 1939-1966, and literary mss, 6 linear feet. Inventory and name index available at library.

ONTARIO

ON —METROPOLITAN TORONTO LIBRARY, Canadian History Dept, Baldwin Room Section, 789 Yonge St, Toronto, M4W 2G8, Can. David B Kotin, Head
Holdings: Vols (52,000) Mss Pix
Notes: This collection consists of material on Canadian history, geography, travel, archaeology, genealogy, retrospective city and telephone directories, collective biographies, native peoples (excluding customs, rights and social conditions), Arctic regions, military history and theory. It is an extremely strong collection of both current and retrospective material. Particular strengths are national and local history (especially Ontario), Arctic regions, native peoples, travel (especially Ontario), and military history. Incl 78,000 historical pictures, 235 linear meters mss, 14,000 broadsides and 3800 bound newspapers.

ONTARIO—DESCRIPTION AND TRAVEL

ON —METROPOLITAN TORONTO LIBRARY, Canadian History Dept, Baldwin Room Section, 789 Yonge St, Toronto, M4W 2G8, Can. David B Kotin, Head
Holdings: Vols (52,000) Mss Pix
Notes: This collection consists of material on Canadian history, geography, travel, archaeology, genealogy, retrospective city and telephone directories, collective biographies, native peoples (excluding customs, rights and social conditions), Arctic regions, military history and theory. It is an extremely strong collection of both current and retrospective material. Particular strengths are national and local history (especially Ontario), Arctic regions, native peoples, travel (especially Ontario), and military history. Incl 78,000 historical pictures, 235 linear meters mss, 14,000 broadsides and 3800 bound newspapers.

ONTARIO—DIRECTORIES

ON —METROPOLITAN TORONTO LIBRARY, Canadian History Dept, 789 Yonge St, Toronto, M4W 2G8, Can.
Notes: Bell Canada Telephone Historical Collection of 448 reels of microfilm of Ontario and Quebec telephone books from 1878 to 1979. The collection will be updated. Toronto city directories from 1868-1949 are available also.

ONTARIO—HISTORY

MI —DETROIT PUBLIC LIBRARY, Burton Historical Collection, 5201 Woodward Ave, Detroit, 48202. Alice Dalligan, Chief
MB —UNIVERSITY OF MANITOBA, Elizabeth Dafoe Library, Government Publications Section, Winnipeg, R3T 2N2, Can. June Dutka, Head
Holdings: Uncat Maps Pix Microforms
Notes: The Canadian National Energy Board's Polar Gas Project documentation provides an extremely useful source of information describing the proposed

construction of the pipeline route which would generally pass from the Arctic Islands through the Northwest Territories, northern Manitoba and into Ontario, Canada.
ON —FORT MALDEN NATIONAL HISTORIC PARK, Library, 100 Laird Ave, Box 38, Amherstburg, N9V 2Z2, Can. Sally E Snyder, Librn
Notes: History of Essex County and Fort Malden (300 vols).
ON —CHATHAM PUBLIC LIBRARY, 120 Queen St, Chatham, N7M 2G6, Can. Arlene Mason, Head of Reference
Holdings: Cat Mss Maps Pix Slides Microforms
Notes: Collection incl books on Black history, especially the Underground Railroad pertaining to the Chatham and Windsor area; many articles, and a few pictures of these subjects; also Indians of Kent County. Kent County and Southern Ontario History is also a subject of this collection, especially United Empire Loyalists in Southern Ontario.
ON —YORK UNIVERSITY, Scott Library, Downsview, M3J 2R2, Can. Hartwell Bowsfield, University Archivist
Notes: A collection of 10,000 Canadian pamphlets, providing a continuum of information about political and cultural events in Canada, especially Quebec and Ontario between 1880 and 1950.
ON —UNIVERSITY OF GUELPH, McLaughlin Library, Guelph, N1G 2W1, Can. Margaret Beckman, Head Librn; David Hull, Sciences Librn
Holdings: Vols 20,000 Cat Maps Mss Pix Slides Phonorecords Audiotapes Videotapes 16mm Films Microforms
Notes: Documents and monographs. 75 periodical titles. Special mss collection related to The Canada Company, John Galt, settlement of Huron Tract Lands. Also incl history of the Bruce, Grey, Halton, Wellington, Co.'s Region.
ON —HURON COLLEGE, Silcox Memorial Library, 1349 Western Rd, London, N6G 1H3, Can. Pamela MacKay, Chief Librn
Holdings: Uncat Mss Maps Pix
Notes: Archives of the Anglican Diocese of Huron. Plan to begin organizing, cataloguing and developing collection in 1978/79. We advise any interested party to write ahead. Records date back to before the creation of the diocese including parish registers, account books, synod reports.
ON —LONDON PUBLIC LIBRARIES & MUSEUMS, London Room, 305 Queen's Ave, London, N6B 1X2, Can. W Glen Curnoe, Librn
Holdings: Cat Mss Maps Pix Slides Phonorecords Audiotapes 16mm Films Microforms
Budget: ($3700)
Notes: History of Ontario, with emphasis on London and region, from early 19th century onward. Separate catalog for books, films and microforms. Various subject indexes to materials. Special interest in London, Ontario authors and publishers.
ON —ONTARIO MINISTRY OF TOURISM & RECREATION, Huronia Historical Resource Centre, PO Box 160, Midland, L4R 4K8, Can. M Quealey, Supervisor, Library Services
Holdings: Vols 11,000 Cat Mss Maps Pix Slides Phonorecords Audiotapes Filmstrips Microforms Videotapes
Notes: Reference collection; interlibrary loan; non-circulating. Research facility for reconstruction of historic sites: Historic Naval and Military Establishments, 19th century British base on the Great Lakes; and Sainte-Marie among the Hurons, an early 17th century French Jesuit mission to the Huron Indians. Also, local history collection and archaeological reports for Simcoe County, Ont, Canada.
ON —MISSISSAUGA PUBLIC LIBRARY, 110 Dundas St W, Mississauga, L5B 1H3, Can. Albert Spratt, Librn
Holdings: Vols 3000 Cat Mss Maps Slides
Budget: $2000
Notes: The Ruth Konrad Collection was originally rare Canadiana but the scope has been narrowed to Southern Ontariana and

local history of the Peel Region (formerly Peel County) and the city of Mississauga (formerly Township of Toronto). Published catalog. Unpublished bibliography of Mississauga on cards. 10,000 slides of Mississauga buildings, sites, views, etc.
ON —SAULT SAINTE MARIE PUBLIC LIBRARY, 50 East St, Sault Sainte Marie, P6A 3C3, Can. Brian R Ingram, Dir
Notes: Sault Sainte Marie Local History Collection incl books, city directories, newspapers, scrapbooks, photographs and a local history index.
ON —THUNDER BAY PUBLIC LIBRARY, Brodie Branch, 216 S Braindie, Thunder Bay, P7C 1E2, Can. Laraine Tapak, Reference Librn
Holdings: Vols 1100 Cat Maps Pix Microforms
Notes: No separate index, except for photographs. There is a bibliography of cataloged items and a subject authority file for clippings, taken from local newspapers.
ON —METROPOLITAN TORONTO LIBRARY, Canadian History Dept, Baldwin Room Section, 789 Yonge St, Toronto, M4W 2G8, Can. David B Kotin, Head
Holdings: Vols (52,000) Mss Pix
Notes: This collection consists of material on Canadian history, geography, travel, archaeology, genealogy, retrospective city and telephone directories, collective biographies, native peoples (excluding customs, rights and social conditions), Arctic regions, military history and theory. It is an extremely strong collection of both current and retrospective material. Particular strengths are national and local history (especially Ontario), Arctic regions, native peoples, travel (especially Ontario), and military history. Incl 78,000 historical pictures, 235 linear meters mss, 14,000 broadsides and 3800 bound newspapers.
ON —NORTH YORK PUBLIC LIBRARY, Canadiana Collection, 35 Fairview Mall Dr, Willowdale, M2J 4S4, Can. Ian C Ross, Head
Holdings: Vols (70,000) Cat Microforms
See also entry under Canada.

ONTARIO—MAPS

ON —ONTARIO MINISTRY OF NATURAL RESOURCES, Mines Library, 77 Grenville St, Rm 812, Toronto, M5S 1B3, Can. Nancy Thurston, Librn
Notes: Geology of Ontario. Incl 20,000 maps. Depository for US and Canadian federal publications in geology and mining.
ON —UNIVERSITY OF TORONTO, Library, Map Library, 130 St George St, Toronto, M5S 1A5, Can. Joan Winearls, Map Librn
Holdings: Vols (10,376) Cat
Notes: A collection of 183,000 current topographic and thematic maps for all parts of the world; strong in Canada, Ontario, Toronto, Europe, US, parts of Latin America and Africa, Near East and Far East. Good atlas and cartography collection; 205,283 aerial photos, 1977-date, for Toronto, 1952-date for southern Ontario and parts of northern Ontario; files maintained of the following: publishers catalogs; maps clipped from newspapers and reports; articles on cartography, particularly the history of cartography; and base maps. In-house bibliographies on Toronto maps, climate and map interpretation. Map catalog is separate and housed only in the Map Library. Equipment, facilities for use of materials.

ONTARIO—RELIGION

†ON —METROPOLITAN TORONTO LIBRARY, Social Sciences Dept, 789 Yonge St, Toronto, M4W 2G8, Can. Abdus Salam, Head
Holdings: Vols Cat Maps Phonorecords Audiotapes 16mm Films Microforms
Notes: The collection is strong in the history and philosophy of religion and comparative religions; literature of all the major religions of the world; works on the devotional and practical aspects of religion; and books on such sacred scripture as the Bible. In addition, our holdings contain many

ONTARIO—RELIGION (cont.)

denominational studies on religion in Canada, as well as more than 300 congregational histories, particularly Ontario churches and synagogues.

ONTARIO-QUEBEC ATHLETIC ASSOCIATION

ON —UNIVERSITY OF WINDSOR, Leddy Library, Windsor, N9B 3P4, Can. P Jerome Malone, Librn
Notes: Human kinetics, with emphasis on the history, psychology, sociology, philosophy, and administration of sports and their organization. Also hold archival records, etc of numerous Canadian sports organizations: Canadian Intercollegiate Athletic Union (CIAU), Ontario-Quebec AA, Ontario Universities AA, etc. Local and Regional history. 40 feet of materials.

ONTARIO UNIVERSITIES ATHLETIC ASSOCIATION

ON —UNIVERSITY OF WINDSOR, Leddy Library, Windsor, N9B 3P4, Can. P Jerome Malone, Librn
Notes: Human kinetics, with emphasis on the history, psychology, sociology, philosophy, and administration of sports and their organization. Also hold archival records, etc of numerous Canadian sports organizations: Canadian Intercollegiate Athletic Union (CIAU), Ontario-Quebec AA, Ontario Universities AA, etc. Local and Regional history. 40 feet of materials.

OOLOGY

CA —WESTERN FOUNDATION OF VERTEBRATE ZOOLOGY, Library, 1100 Glendon Ave, Los Angeles, 90024. Lloyd F Kiff, Dir
Holdings: Vols (4000) Uncat Mss Pix Slides 16mm Films
Budget: ($10,000)
Notes: This is probably the third largest collection on birds in the Western US. It incl the combined resources of 10 former private libraries on this topic, plus additions made by us during the past 20 years. There is special emphasis on oology, or the study of bird eggs. The collection is freely available for use by any interested researcher.

OPEC see Organization of Petroleum Exporting Countries (OPEC)

OPEN COURT PUBLISHING COMPANY

IL —SOUTHERN ILLINOIS UNIVERSITY, CARBONDALE, Delyte W Morris Library, Special Collections Dept, Carbondale, 62901. David V Koch, Cur of Special Collections; Louisa Bowen, Cur of Manuscripts
Holdings: Vols 140 Cat Mss Pix
Notes: Twenty Collections related to 20th century American philosophy incl company archives, 1886-1930, 72 linear feet. The archives of Dr Paul Carus and the Open Court Publishing Company of LaSalle, Illinois, major publishing center for philosophy for more than 30 years, consist of more than 100,000 letters and ms pages. Dr Carus and his associates conducted a voluminous correspondence with philosophers, scientists, and men of letters throughout the world, so that the archives offer a major source of historical study of philosophy from 1880 to 1920.

OPEN PIT MINING see Strip Mining

OPEN SPACES

MD —MARYLAND-NATIONAL CAPITAL PARK & PLANNING COMMISSION, Montgomery County Planning Department Library, 8787 Georgia Ave, Silver Spring, 20907. Janice C Holt, Librn
Holdings: Vols (5000) Cat Microforms
Notes: Specific subject areas include: community facilities, conservation, economics, flood control, highways, housing, human and natural resources. landscape architecture, open space, parks, pollution, population, recreation, transportation, urban renewal, and zoning. Commission's publications are maintained by Records Management (not Library).

OPEN THEATRE

NY —NEW YORK PUBLIC LIBRARY, Performing Arts Research Center, Billy Rose Theatre Collection, 111 Amsterdam Ave, New York, 10023. Dorothy L Swerdlove, Cur
Holdings: Cat
See also entry under Theatre.
OH —KENT STATE UNIVERSITY, Libraries, Dept of Special Collections, Kent, 44242. Dean H Keller, Cur
Holdings: Vols 25 Cat Mss Pix
Notes: The archive of The Open Theatre group, incl notebooks, correspondence, business papers, publicity material, and clippings.

OPERA

CA —UNIVERSITY OF CALIFORNIA, BERKELEY, Humanities-Social Sciences Libraries, Music Library, 24 Morrison Hall, Berkeley, 94720. Michael A Keller, Head Librn
Holdings: Vols 12,000 Cat Mss Microforms Sound recordings
Notes: The Music Library incorporates the opera collections of Harris D H Connick, Sigmund Romberg, and Alfred Cortot, as well as a special collection of ca 5000 opera libretti.
CA —CLAREMONT COLLEGES, Honnold Library, Ninth & Dartmouth, Claremont, 91711. Tania Rizzo, Special Collections Dept Head
Holdings: Vols (606) Cat
Notes: Opera scores, librettos, books about opera, principally of the 17th and 18th centuries. Gift of John Laurence Seymour. Many librettos (uncataloged) in 2 languages, with programs collected by the donor, 1920s to 60s. Restricted use.
CA —UNIVERSITY OF CALIFORNIA, LOS ANGELES, Music Library, Schonberg Hall, Los Angeles, 90024. Stephen M Fry, Music Librn
Holdings: Vols Cat Mss Microforms
Notes: Approx 6000 scores for European and American operas, ca 1700-present. Published descriptions of collection: University of California Music Libraries, Berkeley, Los Angeles, Catalog of the Opera Collections, (Boston: G K Hall, 1983).
CA —UNIVERSITY OF CALIFORNIA, SANTA BARBARA, Arts Library, Music Section, Santa Barbara, 93106. Susan Sonnet Bower, Asst Music Librn
Holdings: Cat Phonorecords
Notes: The Archive of Recorded Vocal Music: 20,000 78 rpm discs, containing representative performances by almost every opera and lieder singer recorded.
CT —YALE UNIVERSITY, Music Library, 98 Wall St, New Haven, 06520. Harold E Samuel, Librn
Holdings: Vols (118,000) Cat Mss Pix Phonorecords Audiotapes Microforms
Notes: General reference and research materials. Performing editions. Strong in theoretical literature, opera, 17-18th century music (incl mss), J S Bach and sons in early editions and mss, Russian liturgical music (Tkaczenko Collection), hymnology, American music. Also collection of musical pictures and portraits.
CT —YALE UNIVERSITY, Drama Library, 222 York St, Box 1903A, Yale Station, New Haven, 06520. Pamela C Jordan, Librn
Holdings: Vols (24,000) Cat Pix Slides Audiotapes
Budget: ($6000)
Notes: Book collection covers all phases of the dramatic arts: theatre, film, opera, dance, etc, with an emphasis on 20th century theatre. Incl audiotapes of Yale Drama School and Repertory Theatre productions, other plays and dramatic readings, and dialect tapes. Incl 1200 slides on costume design and 2000 slides on architecture, interiors, and furniture. Also incl more than 80,000 pictures on set and costume design.
CT —UNIVERSITY OF HARTFORD, Hartt School of Music, Allen Memorial Library, 200 Bloomfield Ave, West Hartford, 06117. Ethel Bacon, Music Librn
Holdings: Vols (56,806) Cat Slides Phonorecords Audiotapes Filmstrips Microforms
Budget: ($14,500)
Notes: Cataloged materials incl 12,000 books on music, 66 slides, 17,000 phonorecords, 1000 audiotapes, 57 filmstrips, 683 microforms, and 26,000 music scores. Also, the Kalmen Opperman Collection: 350 vols of clarinet music, solo through ensemble. Also, the Robert E Smith Collections of 34,000 phonorecords, 150 audiotapes with 80 vols of transcripts from his two radio programs: Your Box At The Opera; Theater of Melody (uncataloged).
IN —INDIANA UNIVERSITY, Music Library, Bloomington, 47401. David E Fenske, Head
Holdings: Vols 4000 Cat
Notes: Have opera scores and parts.
NY —STATE UNIVERSITY OF NEW YORK, BINGHAMTON, Glenn G Bartle Library, Binghamton, 13901. Marion Hanscom, Special Collections Librn
Notes: Frances R Conole Archive. A collection of 50,000 plus sound recordings devoted to the preservation of 20th century vocal art as recorded over the last ninety years. Emphasis is on opera singers from 1900-1960. Over 3000 singers are represented with an excess of 4000 complete performances of over 400 operas.
NY —CORNELL UNIVERSITY LIBRARIES, Music Library, 225 Lincoln Hall, Ithaca, 14853. Lenore Coral, Music Librn
Holdings: Vols (106,022) Cat
See also entry under Music.
NY —AMERICAN INSTITUTE FOR VERDI STUDIES, New York University, Bobst Library, Music Div, New York, 10023. Ruth B Hilton, Librn
Holdings: Mss Maps Pix Slides Microforms
Notes: Contains the archives of the Institute for Verdi Studies.
NY —NANANNE PORCHER OSPREY DESIGNS, Library, 49 W 96 St, New York, 10028.
Notes: Lighting records for Lyric Opera of Chicago, 1961-1966; Dallas Civic Opera, 1959-1964; American Ballet Theatre, 1965-1966, 1971-1977; etc.
NY —SYRACUSE UNIVERSITY LIBRARIES, Music Collection, 222 Waverly Ave, Syracuse, 13210. Donald Seibert, Librn
Holdings: Vols 1349 // Cat
Notes: Collection of 19th century Italian opera and ballet librettos. An annotated catalog of the collection has been published by the Syracuse University Libraries: 19th Century Italian Opera and Ballet Libretti, ed by Aubrey S Garlington. The catalog is arranged by title, with indices of composers, librettists, ballets, ballet creators, places of performance and publishers.
NC —UNIVERSITY OF NORTH CAROLINA, CHAPEL HILL, Music Library, Hill Hall, Chapel Hill, 27514.
Holdings: Vols (90,000) Cat Mss Pix Slides Phonorecords Audiotapes Microforms
Budget: ($60,000)
Notes: Extensive holdings of early theoretical treatises; complete editions; performing scores; music periodicals; reference works.
OH —OBERLIN COLLEGE, Oberlin Conservatory of Music, Mary M Vial Library, Oberlin, 44074. John E Druesedow Jr, Dir
Holdings: Vols (75,000) Cat Phonorecords Audiotapes Filmstrips Microforms
Budget: ($60,000)
Notes: Special emphases: history and literature of the organ; music before 1700; music since 1950; music education; opera; American music; chamber and solistic music. Published catalog: Mr and Mrs C W Best Collection of Autographs in the Mary M

OPERA (cont.)

Vial Music Library of the Oberlin College Conservatory of Music (Oberlin, Ohio: Oberlin College, 1967).

TX —UNIVERSITY OF TEXAS LIBRARIES, Music Library, PO Box P, Austin, 78712. Olga Buth, Librn
Holdings: Vols (21,862) Cat Phonorecords Audiotapes Microforms
Notes: Collection incl 36,462 scores, 3505 bound periodicals, 4506 microforms, 289 periodical subscriptions, 312 serials and monographs, 13,706 phonodiscs, and 922 phonotapes.

VA —SWEET BRIAR COLLEGE, Library, Sweet Briar, 24595. John Jaffe, Librn
Holdings: Vols 175 // Cat Phonorecords
Notes: Sigred Onegin Collection. Incl 18th and 19th century opera scores; 4000 songs; and phonorecords.

OPERA—LIBRETTOS see
Operas—Librettos

OPERA, CHINESE

CA —UNIVERSITY OF CALIFORNIA, LOS ANGELES, Music Dept, Ethnomusicology Archive, 405 Hilgard Ave, Los Angeles, 90024. Ann Briegleb, Ethnomusicology Librn
Notes: Minimal collection of recordings, uncataloged.

OPERA, COMIC, AND OPERETTA

DC —LIBRARY OF CONGRESS, Music Division, Washington, 20540.
Notes: Music and music mss of Victor Herbert and Sigmund Romberg.

WI —UNIVERSITY OF WISCONSIN, MADISON, Mills Music Library, 728 State St, Madison, 53706. Arne Arneson, Music Librn
Holdings: // Uncat Mss
Notes: Tams-Witmark Collection formed part of the rental collection of the firm bearing that name. Includes piano-conductor scores (some in mss); ca 65 sets of orchestral parts for operas; 70 vocal scores of works by American composers including Herbert, Sousa, Edwards and De Koven; ca 100 sets of orchestral parts of comic operas; ca 4000 vocal scores of European operas. Restricted use.

OPERA, FRENCH

IN —INDIANA UNIVERSITY, Lilly Library, Seventh St, Bloomington, 47405. William R Cagle, Librn
Holdings: Cat
Notes: First and early printings of works by major and minor composers, largely 19th century. French opera is especially well represented.

NY —EASTMAN SCHOOL OF MUSIC, Sibley Music Library, 44 Swan St, Rochester, 14604. Ruth Watanabe, Librn

OPERAS—LIBRETTOS

CA —UNIVERSITY OF CALIFORNIA, BERKELEY, Humanities-Social Sciences Libraries, Music Library, 24 Morrison Hall, Berkeley, 94720. Michael A Keller, Head Librn
Holdings: Vols 9000 Cat Mss Microforms
Notes: The Music Library incorporates the opera collections of Harris D H Connick, Sigmund Romberg, and Alfred Cortot, as well as a special collection of ca 7500 opera libretti.

CA —CLAREMONT COLLEGES, Honnold Library, Ninth & Dartmouth, Claremont, 91711. Tania Rizzo, Special Collections Dept Head
Holdings: Vols (606) Cat
Notes: Opera scores, librettos, books about opera, principally of the 17th and 18th centuries. Gift of John Laurence Seymour. Many librettos (uncataloged) in 2 languages, with programs collected by the donor, 1920s to 60s. Restricted use.

DC —LIBRARY OF CONGRESS, Music Division, Washington, 20540.
Holdings: Cat
Notes: Albert Schatz Collection, an outstanding selection of German and Italian texts, particularly from the 17th and 18th centuries. Chronological list of opera performances from 1541 to 1901. Sixty card files contain information (title, composer, librettist, genre, number of acts, and date, city, and theater of the premiere performance) for as many productions as Schatz could document. Schatz also compiled in ledgers detailed chronological lists, complete with dates of first and subsequent performances, of operas by 14 18th-century composers.

IL —NEWBERRY LIBRARY, 60 W Walton St, Chicago, 60610. Diana Haskell, Cur of Modern Mss
Holdings: Vols 800 Cat
Notes: Ranging from Peri's L'Euridice to the major works of Richard Strauss. Restricted use: noncirculating.

NY —NEW YORK PUBLIC LIBRARY, Music Div, 111 Amsterdam Ave, New York, 10023. Frank C Campbell, Chief
Holdings: Vols (300,000) Cat Mss Pix Microforms
Notes: Described in Dictionary Catalog of the Music Collection, The Research Libraries of the New York Public Library, 33 vols (532,000 cards), 1964, $2190; Supplement 1, 1 vol (17,000 cards), 1966, $100. Also, Bibliographic Guide to Music, 2 vols, 1975-1976, $70 ea. Literature pertaining to virtually all musical subjects, and scores covering the broadest range of musical style and history are represented in this catalog. Special strengths of the collection incl folk songs, 18th and 19th-century librettos, full scores of operas, complete works, historical editions, Beethoven, Americana, American music, periodicals, vocal music, literature on the voice, programs, record catalogs, and mss in detail; sheet music, 355,414; sound recordings, 400,000; clippings and programs, 2 million; broadsides, 1821; songsters, 375; pictures, 51,002; ms, 29,877.

NY —YONKERS PUBLIC LIBRARY, Grinton I Will Library, 1500 Central Park Ave, Yonkers, 10701. Joan W Stevenson, Head of Fine Arts Dept
Holdings: Vols (12,000) Cat
Budget: ($36,000)
Notes: Incl periodicals, 70 titles (ca 15 yr back issues); 27 vertical file drawers (18 on artists & musicians); 1230 slides; 2200 music scores; cat; sheet music, ca 1200 titles; 140 libretti; 13,000 phonograph albums; cat; 1000 cassettes. Books, scores, phonograph albums, cassettes are cataloged. Rare collection of 57 test pressings of Geraldine Farrar, some of which have never been issued.

ON —UNIVERSITY OF TORONTO, Thomas Fisher Rare Book Library, 120 Saint George St, Toronto, M5S 1A5, Can. Richard G Landon, Head
Holdings: Vols 6500 Cat Mss
Notes: Italian Play Collection comprises editions of Italian plays performed before 1815, with particular emphasis on the Renaissance period. Holdings partially described in Corrigan, Beatrice. Catalogue of Italian Plays, 1500-1700, in the Library of the University of Toronto (Toronto, 1961). Some unpublished ms material. Libretti collection comprises libretti for operas performed in Italian after 1815.

OPERAS—SCORES AND PARTS

CA —CLAREMONT COLLEGES, Honnold Library, Ninth & Dartmouth, Claremont, 91711. Tania Rizzo, Special Collections Dept Head
Holdings: Vols (606) Cat
Notes: Opera scores, librettos, books about opera, principally of the 17th and 18th centuries. Gift of John Laurence Seymour. Many librettos (uncataloged) in 2 languages, with programs collected by the donor, 1920s to 60s. Restricted use.

CA —OAKLAND PUBLIC LIBRARY, Art, Music and Recreation Section, 125 14 St,

Oakland, 94612. Richard Colvig, Senior Librn
Notes: Vocal scores and miniature scores only.
See also entry under music.

CA —SAN DIEGO PUBLIC LIBRARY, Art, Music & Recreation Sect, 820 E St, San Diego, 92101. Barbara A Tuhill, Supvr
Holdings: Cat
Notes: Score collection of 17,000 pieces covers all types of music incl religious works, opera scores, musical plays, miniature scores. Complete works of Bach, Berlioz, Beethoven, Mozart, and others are added as published in German reprint. Also, thematic indexes, and study and instructions for playing various musical instruments. General circulation.

CA —SANTA CRUZ PUBLIC LIBRARY, Art, Music, Film Dept, 224 Church St, Santa Cruz, 95060. Alma Westberg, Librn
Holdings: Vols (1500) Cat Mss
Budget: ($750)
Notes: The music collection is in a catalog separate from the general one. It consists of approx 1700 cataloged books about music; 2100 bound, cataloged books of music incl opera and musical comedy scores; 2700 pieces of sheet music which incl sacred, art and popular songs, and instrumental solos. Good collection of chamber music from baroque to contemporary composers. Also a special collection of 10,000 pieces of American popular sheet music of the period from the 1860s to 1970s incl songs of California. The record collection, primarily classical, consists of about 5500 records.

DC —LIBRARY OF CONGRESS, Music Division, Washington, 20540.
Holdings: Cat Mss Maps Pix Slides Microforms
Notes: Incl full scores, piano scores, librettos.

IL —CHICAGO PUBLIC LIBRARY, Music Section, Fine Arts Division, 78 E Washington St, Chicago, 60602. Rosalinda I Hack, Fine Arts Division Chief; Richard C Schwegel, Head, Music Section
Holdings: Vols (10,000) Cat Pix Microforms
Notes: Collection also incl pamphlets & clippings, periodicals, approx 17,000 cataloged pieces of sheet music and 9000 cataloged bound vols of music, approx 28,000 cataloged recordings. Have indexed (but uncataloged) collection of over 5000 sheets of old popular music in original covers, dating from early 19th century. Growing reference collection of full scores of orchestral and operatic works, setsof complete works of 17 major composers in printed and microfiche editions. Services: issue monthly lists of new materials and annotated reading lists; monthly exhibits relating to music; semi-weekly concerts and music appreciation programs from October to May, by Chicago area musicians and speakers as a free public service.

IL —NEWBERRY LIBRARY, 60 W Walton St, Chicago, 60610. Diana Haskell, Cur of Modern Mss
Holdings: Cat Mss
Notes: Collection primarily musicological, not performance. 55,000 scores; 100,000 pieces of sheet music. Primary and secondary materials for the study of Western European music from the Middle Ages through the 19th century, and of American music from its beginnings. Strongest holdings are: early theory, music literature and scores of the Renaissance and Baroque periods, opera scores (3600), and libretti, early American psalmody and religious music, music periodicals, monumental editions and monographs, popular sheet music and music mss. See article by Donald W Krummel, "The Newberry Library, Chicago" in Fontes artis musicae, 1969/3. Restricted use: noncirculating.

IN —INDIANA UNIVERSITY, Lilly Library, Seventh St, Bloomington, 47405. William R Cagle, Librn
Holdings: Cat
Notes: First and early printings or works by major and minor composers, largely 19th century. French opera is especially well represented.

OPERAS—SCORES AND PARTS (cont.)

IN —INDIANA UNIVERSITY, Music
Library, Bloomington, 47401. David E
Fenske, Head
Holdings: Vols 6000 Cat
Budget:
Notes: Designed eventually to be an
exhaustive collection of full piano-vocal
scores of operas.

MA —BOSTON UNIVERSITY, Mugar
Memorial Library, Special Collections Dept,
771 Commonwealth Ave, Boston, 02215.
Howard B Gotlieb, Dir
Holdings: Mss
Notes: Mss of 19th century Italian opera
scores of deposit from Boston Symphony
Orchestra.

MI —UNIVERSITY OF MICHIGAN, School
of Music, Music Library, Moore Bldg, Ann
Arbor, 48109. Peggy Daub, Head
Holdings: Vols (90,000) Cat Mss Microforms
Notes: Reference and research materials, as
well as performing editions. Rare materials
(including the Stellfeld Collection) are strong
in early editions of works by the sons of J S
Bach and 18th-19th century opera scores,
particularly French. Includes 1200
microfilms of important European and
American primary sources. See L Cuyler, H
David & G Sutherland: "The University of
Michigans's Purchase of the Stellfeld Music
Library," *MLA Notes* 12 (1954-5), 3-19.

MI —DETROIT PUBLIC LIBRARY, Music &
Performing Arts Dept, 5201 Woodward,
Detroit, 48202. Agatha Pfeiffer Kalkanis,
Chief
Holdings: Vols 19,000 Cat Mss Pix
Microforms
Notes: Also incl (77,000) scores. General
collection intended for practical use in
performance and for scholarly research.
Good working collection of bibliographies,
thematic catalogs, dictionaries and
encyclopedias, periodical indexes. Many sets
of collected works, monumental editions,
historical anthologies. Good representation
of opera and operetta, art song and folk
song, solo instrumental literature and
chamber music in practical editions. 2575
titles of choral music, chiefly sacred, for use
by choirs. 17,000 titles of popular sheet
music, uncataloged but thoroughly indexed.
Considerable recent holdings of books and
periodicals in foreign languages. Special
collections of black and local materials. 25,
000 recordings and extensive discographical
literature. Collection of publishers' trade
catalogs.

NY —STATE UNIVERSITY OF NEW
YORK, BUFFALO, Baird Music Library,
Baird Hall, Amherst, 14260. James B
Coover, Dir
Holdings: Vols (104,000) Cat Mss Pix Slides
Phonorecords Microforms
Notes: Nearly complete collections of
Denkmaeler and Gesamtausgaben and other
historical sets. Strong collection of
dictionaries, bibliographies, biographies,
facsimiles, works on the "new" music,
organology and ethnomusicology. Special
emphasis on operas, scores of the avant-
garde, jazz and urban popular music,
discography and music librarianship. Good
collection of medieval and Renaissance
anthologies, contemporary and avant-garde
recordings. Houses Archives of the Center of
the Creative and Performing Arts.
Collections incl 2100 slides, 22,000
phonorecords, 46,000 scores and parts, 29,
000 books, 4900 microforms. Computerized
record catalog in process.

NY —NEW YORK PUBLIC LIBRARY, Music
Div, 111 Amsterdam Ave, New York,
10023. Frank C Campbell, Chief
Holdings: Vols (300,000) Cat Mss Pix
Microforms
Notes: Described in *Dictionary Catalog of
the Music Collection, The Research
Libraries of the New York Public Library*,
33 vols (532,000 cards), 1964, $2190;
Supplement 1, 1 vol (17,000 cards), 1966,
$100. Also, *Bibliographic Guide to Music*, 2
vols, 1975-1976, $70 ea. Literature
pertaining to virtually all musical subjects,
and scores covering the broadest range of
musical style and history are represented in
this catalog. Special strengths of the
collection incl folk songs, 18th and 19th-
century librettos, full scores of operas,
complete works, historical editions,
Beethoven, Americana, American music,
periodicals, vocal music, literature on the
voice, programs, record catalogs, and mss in
detail; sheet music, 355,414; sound
recordings, 400,000; clippings and programs,
2 million; broadsides, 1821; songsters, 375;
pictures, 51,002; ms, 29,877.

OH —CLEVELAND PUBLIC LIBRARY, Fine
Arts and Special Collections Department,
325 Superior Ave, Cleveland, 44114. Alice
N Loranth, Head
Holdings: Vols (72,050) Cat
Notes: Incl 37,850 scores, 20,430 pieces of
sheet music. Every type of score from opera,
piano orchestral, instrumental, etc. Large
editions and anthologies. Primarily classical
in scope, scores are also available for musical
comedies with a sampling of popular music
incl, particularly in older sheet music. Incl
are 2500 miniature and study scores. Misc
collections (songs, hymns, piano, violin and
organ) are indexed for contents.

PA —WEST CHESTER UNIVERSITY, Music
Library, Swope Hall, University Ave, West
Chester, 19383. Ruth I Weidner, Music
Librn
Budget: ($26,000)
Notes: Large basic music collection (scores,
sheet music, and 21,000 phonorecords)
which is especially strong in collected works,
historical editions, opera, keyboard music,
and miniature scores. Incl 24,000 music
scores. All music is fully cataloged. Scope of
collection is broad and excludes only music
education and curriculum materials.
Collection does not include books about
music or periodicals but does have about 500
reference books. For the most part collection
is music published during or availalbe within
the past twenty years.

TX —FORT WORTH PUBLIC LIBRARY,
Arts Division, 300 Taylor St, Fort Worth,
76102. Heather Gobel, Head
Holdings: Vols (21,500) Cat Mss
Phonorecords
Budget: ($26,700)
Notes: Emphasis is on older popular music
and musical comedies, folk songs, operas,
music composed by Fort Worth and Texas
composers, and music about Texas. Sheet
music has a separate index.

WA —UNIVERSITY OF WASHINGTON
LIBRARIES, Music Library, DN-10, Seattle,
98195. David A Wood, Music Libn
Holdings: Vols (46,212) Cat Mss Microforms
Budget: ($44,522)
Notes: Collection of 17th-19th century opera
scores.

WI —UNIVERSITY OF WISCONSIN,
MADISON, Mills Music Library, 728 State
St, Madison, 53706. Arne Arneson, Music
Librn
Holdings: // Uncat Mss
Notes: Tams-Witmark Collection formed
part of the rental collection of the firm
bearing that name. Includes piano-conductor
scores (some in mss); ca 65 sets of orchestral
parts for operas; 70 vocal scores of works by
American composers including Herbert,
Sousa, Edwards and De Koven; ca 100 sets
of orchestral parts of comic operas; ca 4000
vocal scores of European operas. Restricted
use.

OPERAS, COMIC, AND OPERETTAS—SCORES AND PARTS

MI —DETROIT PUBLIC LIBRARY, Music &
Performing Arts Dept, 5201 Woodward,
Detroit, 48202. Agatha Pfeiffer Kalkanis,
Chief
Holdings: Vols 19,000 Cat Mss Pix
Microforms
Notes: Also incl (77,000) scores. General
collection intended for practical use in
performance and for scholarly research.
Good working collection of bibliographies,
thematic catalogs, dictionaries and
encyclopedias, periodical indexes. Many sets
of collected works, monumental editions,
historical anthologies. Good representation
of opera and operetta, art song and folk
song, solo instrumental literature and
chamber music in practical editions. 2575
titles of choral music, chiefly sacred, for use
by choirs. 17,000 titles of popular sheet
music, uncataloged but thoroughly indexed.
Considerable recent holdings of books and
periodicals in foreign languages. Special
collections of black and local materials. 25,
000 recordings and extensive discographical
literature. Collection of publishers' trade
catalogs.

OPERATING RATIOS

NY —DUN & BRADSTREET BUSINESS
LIBRARY, 99 Church St, New York, 10007.
Carol Stankiewicz, Librn
Holdings: Vols (400) Cat
Budget: ($2500)
Notes: A collection of industry financial
ratios (or operating ratios) showing such
items as current assets, net profits, debt,
fixed assets, etc--components of composite
company balance sheets--not individual
companies.

OPERATION DIXIE

NC —DUKE UNIVERSITY, William R
Perkins Library, Manuscript Dept, Durham,
27706. Ellen Gartrell, Cur of Mss
Holdings: Cat Mss
Notes: Emphasis on US South, especially
CIO Organizing Committee papers, 1946-53
(ca 143,00 items). Large percentage have
been commercially microfilmed under title
"Operation Dixie." Also papers of Lucy
Randolph Mason, Frank deVyver, Frank
Morrison.

OPERATIONAL ANALYSIS see
Operations Research

OPERATIONAL RESEARCH see
Operations Research

OPERATIONS RESEARCH

AL —UNIVERSITY OF ALABAMA, Business
Library, Box 2937, University, 35486.
Dorothy Eady Brown, Librn; Linda Suttle
Harris, Ref Librn and Data Base Searcher

CA —UNIVERSITY OF CALIFORNIA, LOS
ANGELES, Graduate School of
Management Library, UCLA Campus, Los
Angeles, 90024. Robert Bellanti, Head Librn
Holdings: Vols (128,000) Cat Mss
Microforms
Notes: The

CA —LOGICON INC, Strategic & Information
Systems Division, Information Center, 255
W Fifth St, Box 471, San Pedro, 90731.
Constance B Davenport, Supervisor
Holdings: Vols (3000) Cat Mss Microforms
Notes: Incl about 3000 books, 250 periocial
titles, 5000 technical reports, 10,000
microfiche, 750 standards and specifications.
Catalog is computerized. Interactive search
capability with Dialog, Orbit, DMS on-line,
NASA Recon. Material on computer
programming, systems analysis, military
systems and operations research.

CA —STANFORD UNIVERSITY
LIBRARIES, Mathematical & Computer
Sciences Library, Stanford, 94305. Harry
Llull, Branch Librn
Holdings: Vols (42,000) Cat

CT —YALE UNIVERSITY, Social Science
Library, 140 Prospect St, New Haven,
06520. Billie I Salter, Librn
Holdings: Vols (40,000) Cat Microforms
See also entry under Social Sciences.

PA —FRANKLIN INSTITUTE LIBRARY, 20
& The Parkway, Philadelphia, 19103.
Miriam Padusis, Dir; Charles Wilt, Readers
Servs Librn
Holdings: Vols (300,000) Cat Maps Pix
Microforms

TX —UNIVERSITY OF TEXAS LIBRARIES,
Richard W McKinney Engineering Library,
1.3 ECJ, Austin, 78712. Susan B Ardis,
Librn
Holdings: Vols (83,548) Cat Microforms

OPERATIONS RESEARCH (cont.)

VA —MITRE CORPORATION, Information
Services, 1820 Dolley Madison Blvd,
McLean, 22102. Paula M Strain, Mgr
Holdings: Vols (10,000) Cat Microforms
Budget: ($142,000)
Notes: Collection incl current and back files
of periodicals in bound and microfilm form,
approx 70,000 technical reports mostly in
microfiche format and 10,000 vols, all of
which are cataloged and indexed. Collection
deals with systems engineering as a
methodology with special emphasis on its
applications in these areas: civil systems;
communication systems; energy; incl
alternate energy sources; environmental
problems; mass and urban transportation;
and aviation operation incl collision
avoidance, landing systems, and traffic
scheduling.

WY —US AIR FORCE INSTITUTE OF
TECHNOLOGY, Library, Dept 9 Bldg 831,
FE, Warren AFB, 82001. Patricia A
Johnson, Librn
Holdings: Vols (7000) Cat Microforms
Budget: ($9000)
Notes: The Library supports graduate
programs for students (Air Force Missle-
Combat Crewmen) seeking a Master of
Business Administration Degree. Civilian
students and other military personnel are
also admitted.

OPERETTAS see Opera, Comic, and Operetta

OPHIOLOGY see Snakes

OPHTHALMIC LENSES

NY —STATE UNIVERSITY OF NEW
YORK, State College of Optometry, Harold
Kohn Vision Science Library, 100 E 24 St,
New York, 10010. Margaret S Lewis, Librn
Holdings: Vols (23,000) Cat Audiotapes
Microforms
Notes: All subjects related to visual
disabilities; much on vision disorders among
children.

OPHTHALMOLOGY

AL —UNIVERSITY OF ALABAMA,
BIRMINGHAM, Lister Hill Library of the
Health Sciences, University Sta,
Birmingham, 35294. Richard B Fredericksen,
Dir
CA —UNIVERSITY OF CALIFORNIA,
BERKELEY, General Library, Optometry
Library, 490 Minor Hall, Berkeley, 94720.
Alison Howard, Librn
Holdings: Vols (8000) Cat Pix Microforms
Budget: ($13,500)
Notes: Specialized collection of Library
materials complemented by significant,
related holdings in the Biology and Public
Health Libraries on campus.
CA —SOUTHERN CALIFORNIA COLLEGE
OF OPTOMETRY, 2001 Associated Rd,
Fullerton, 92631. Pat Carlson, Librn
Holdings: Vols (10,000) Cat Mss Pix Slides
Microforms
Notes: Collection deals with vision and all
that pertains to training optometrists. Core
of the collection leans heavily towards
optometry; rest of collection deals with
ophthalmology and related fields.
CA —UNIVERSITY OF CALIFORNIA, LOS
ANGELES, Biomedical Library, Center for
the Health Sciences, Los Angeles, 90024.
Alison Bunting, Acting Biomedical Librn;
Victoria Steele, Head, History & Special
Collections Div
Holdings: Vols (400,000) Cat Slides
Phonorecords Audiotapes Videotapes 16mm
Films Microforms

Notes: The UCLA Biomedical Library serves
primarily the Schools of Medicine, Dentistry,
Nursing, and Public Health, the UCLA Medical
Center, the Departments of Microbiology and
Biology in the College of Letters and Science, and
related institutes in biomedicine. The collections of
the Library are broad in scope, designed not only
to support the teaching and research needs of its
many users, but also to function as a resource for
the health sciences-biological field as a whole. The
outstanding feature of the collection is the strength
of its periodical holdings, both current and
retrospective. The Library also has an excellent
reference collection, a comprehensive historical
section, and gives special emphasis to the fields of
neuroscience, psychiatry, ophthalmology, radiation
biology, molecular biology, and vertebrate
zoology. Increased emphasis is being given to the
acquisition of audiovisual materials.

CA —STANFORD UNIVERSITY
LIBRARIES, Lane Medical Library,
Stanford University, Medical Center,
Stanford, 94305. Peter Stangl, Librn
Notes: Collections incl the Barkan Library of
Ophthalmology and Otolaryngology and the
Barkan History of Medicine library.
CT —YALE MEDICAL LIBRARY, 333 Cedar
St, New Haven, 06510.
Holdings: Vols (334,215) Cat Mss Pix Slides
Microforms
Budget: ($361,650)
Notes: Incl films, audiotapes, artifacts, etc.
FL —UNIVERSITY OF MIAMI, School of
Medicine, Louis Calder Memorial Library,
PO Box 520875, Miami, 33152. Henry L
Lemkau, Jr, Dir
Holdings: Vols (127,843) Cat Mss Maps Pix
Slides Phonorecords Audiotapes Videotapes
16mm Films Filmstrips Microforms
Budget: ($915,000)
Notes: Ophthalmology Branch Library of
6969 vols incl in total count; University of
Miami School of Medicine dissertations; 209
medical medallions; physicians' bookplates;
postage stamps with medical themes.
IL —ILLINOIS COLLEGE OF
OPTOMETRY, Carl F Shepard Memorial
Library, 3241 S Michigan Ave, Chicago,
60616. Kevin K Wah, Dir of Library and
Instructional Services
Holdings: Vols (13,000) Cat Slides
Phonorecords Audiotapes Videotapes 16mm
Films Filmstrips Microforms
Budget: ($25,000)
Notes: Research and teaching collection on
every aspect of the eye and vision and their
disorders, excl surgery. Incl historical and
current materials; excl foreign-language
materials. Library participates in Midwest
Health Sciences Library Network and
ILLINET.
IN —INDIANA UNIVERSITY, Optometry
Branch Library, Bloomington, 47405. Roger
Deckman, Head; Elizabeth Egan, Branch
Librn
Holdings: Vols (11,000) Cat Slides
Microforms
Budget:
Notes: Incl all aspects of vision: anatomy,
physiology, pathology of the eye,
neurophysiology, perception, colorimetry,
illumination, safety, etc. Interlibrary loans
through Main Library, Indiana University,
Bloomington.
MA —HARVARD UNIVERSITY, Lucien
Howe Library of Ophthalmology, 243
Charles St, Boston, 02114. Judith C Nims,
Library Dir
Holdings: Vols (10,162) Cat
MA —NEW ENGLAND COLLEGE OF
OPTOMETRY, Library, 420 Beacon St,
Boston, 02115. F Eleanor Warner, Librn
Holdings: Vols (7750) Cat Mss Slides
Phonorecords Audiotapes Videotapes 16mm
Films Microforms
Budget: ($30,000)
Notes: Acquisitions in optometry and

ophthalmology are comprehensive; they are
selective in areas of surgery and the
therapeutic use of drugs. Collection incl 75
slide/tape programs; 75 videotapes; 11 VF
drawers of pamphlets and reprints; 16 units
of realia; 275 periodical subscriptions.
Publishes periodicals holdings list,
audiovisual holdings list and an acquisitions
list. Open to the public for reference use.
MO —INTERNATIONAL LIBRARY,
ARCHIVES AND MUSEUM OF
OPTOMETRY, 243 N Lindbergh, Saint
Louis, 63141. Maria Dablemont, Librn
Holdings: Vols (12,000) Cat Mss Pix Slides
Phonorecords Audiotapes Videotapes 16mm
Films Filmstrips
Notes: Established to collect, preserve, and
make available for researchers materials
related to optometry and the visual sciences;
the oldest special library of vision science in
this country, serving the public worldwide
with reference services and materials. The
archives contain documents pertaining to the
history of optometry and the history of the
American Optometric Association. In the
museum are found antique eyeglasses and
optical instruments as well as artifacts from
the history of the optometric profession and
items associated with its leaders.
NY —COLUMBIA UNIVERSITY
LIBRARIES, Rare Book & Manuscript
Library, 801 Butler Library, W 114 St,
New York, 10027. Kenneth A Lohf, Librn
Holdings: Mss
Notes: Nearly 6000 letters, notes and mss
relating to Cornelius Rea Agnew, professor
of diseases of the eye and ear at Columbia's
College of Physicians and Surgeons, and a
founder of the Manhattan Eye and Ear
Hospital. Much of the material relates to the
treatment of eye diseases during the latter
half of the 19th century. Restricted use.
NY —NATIONAL SOCIETY FOR THE
PREVENTION OF BLINDNESS, Conrad
Berens Library, 79 Madison Ave, New York,
10016. Dede Silverston, Librn
Holdings: Vols (3000) Cat
Notes: Includes complete and up-to-date
ophthalmology collection. Current vertical
file of 21 drawers on phases of eye care.
NY —PRESBYTERIAN HOSPITAL, Edward
S Harkness Eye Institute, John M Wheeler
Library, 635 W 165 St, New York, 10032.
Albertina F Mount, Library Supvr
Holdings: Vols 12,600 Cat Pix Slides
Phonorecords Audiotapes
Notes: Rare books; museum of ophthalmic
instruments; rare paintings of eye diseases by
former staff member Dr E Gustav Bethke.
OK —DEAN A MCGEE EYE INSTITUTE,
Library, 606 Stanton L Young Blvd,
Oklahoma City, 73104. Sheri Taylor, Librn
OR —PACIFIC UNIVERSITY LIBRARY,
Forest Grove, 97116. Laurel Gregory,
Science/Optometry Librn
Holdings: Vols (133,000) Cat Slides
Microforms
Budget: ($49,000)
PA —COLLEGE OF PHYSICIANS OF
PHILADELPHIA, Library, 19 S 22 St,
Philadelphia, 19103. Anthony Aguirre, Libr
Dir
Holdings: Vols (316,223) Cat Mss
Microforms
Budget: ($1,096,557)
Notes: Incl 13,515 pamphlets; 1435 mss;
326,367 reports, dissertations, and reprints.
Strong historical and bibliographical
collections, as well as current materials.
Medical documentation service provides
current alerting, incl abstracting, etc.
PA —WILLS EYE HOSPITAL, Library, Ninth
& Walnut Sts, Philadelphia, 19107. Fleur
Weinberg, Library Dir
Holdings: Vols 9000 Cat Maps Slides
Audiotapes Videotapes Microforms
Budget: $40,000
PA —EYE & EAR HOSPITAL OF
PITTSBURGH, Blair-Lippincott Library,
230 Lothrop St, Pittsburgh, 15213. Bruce A
Johnston, Medical Librn
Holdings: Vols (6000) Cat
Notes: Special emphasis on ophthalmology,
otorhinolaryngology, audiology, and speech
pathology.
TX —UNIVERSITY OF TEXAS HEALTH
SCIENCE CENTER, SAN ANTONIO,

OPHTHALMOLOGY (cont.)

7703 Floyd Curl Dr, San Antonio, 78284.
Joyce M Ray, Archivist/Special Collections
Librn; JoAnn Glisson, Library Asst
PQ —McGILL UNIVERSITY, Medical
Library, 3655 Drummond St, Montreal,
H3G 1Y6, Can. Frances Groen, Librn
Holdings: Vols (176,000) Cat Slides
Audiotapes Videotapes
Notes: General medicine collection, covering
all phases of medicine; emphasis on
ophthalmology.

OPHTHALMOLOGY—HISTORY

AL —UNIVERSITY OF ALABAMA,
BIRMINGHAM, Lister Hill Library of the
Health Sciences, University Sta,
Birmingham, 35294. Richard B Fredericksen,
Dir
CA —UNIVERSITY OF CALIFORNIA, LOS
ANGELES, Biomedical Library, Center for
the Health Sciences, Los Angeles, 90024.
Alison Bunting, Acting Biomedical Librn;
Victoria Steele, Head, History & Special
Collections Div
Holdings: Vols 44// Cat
Notes: Collection of Dr M N Beigelman.
Classics of ophthalmology.
IL —UNIVERSITY OF CHICAGO
LIBRARY, Dept of Special Collections,
1100 E 57 St, Chicago, 60637.
Notes: E V L Brown Collection.
MO —WASHINGTON UNIVERSITY, School
of Medicine, Library, 660 South Euclid Ave,
Saint Louis, 63110. Christopher Hoolihan,
Rare Book Librn
Holdings: Vols 650 Cat
Budget: ($40,000)
Notes: The Bernard Becker, MD Library of
Ophthalmology. Incl many of the most
important works in ophthalmology and
optics published between the 15th and 20th
centuries. The second edition of an
annotated catalog of the collection was
published in 1983.
PA —WILLS EYE HOSPITAL, Library, Ninth
& Walnut Sts, Philadelphia, 19107. Fleur
Weinberg, Library Dir
Holdings: Vols 9000 Cat Maps Slides
Audiotapes Videotapes Microforms
Budget: $40,000

OPHTHALMOSCOPE AND
OPHTHALMOSCOPY—HISTORY

MN —MAYO MEDICAL LIBRARY, History
of Medicine Collection, Rochester, 55905.
Nancy R Hensel, Librn
Holdings: Vols 140 Cat
Notes: Very specialized collection incl nearly
all atlases of ophthalmoscopy published;
augmented by classics of interest to
ophthalmologists incl first English and first
Latin edition of Newton's *Opticks*.
Collection described: Keys, Thomas E &
Rucker, C Wilbur: "The Atlases of
Ophthalmoscopy: a Bibliography, 1850-
1960." *Am J Ophthalmol.* 49:881-894, May,
1960.

OPIATES see Drugs

OPISTHOBRANCHIATA

CA —STANFORD UNIVERSITY, Hopkins
Marine Station Library, Cabrillo Point,
Pacific Grove, 93950. Alan Baldridge, Librn
Holdings: // Cat
Notes: The Opisthobranchiata Molluscan
Library of Frank Mace MacFarland; 800
items.

OPIUM WAR, 1840-1842 see
China—History_War of 1840-1842

OPPANOL see Rubber, Artificial

OPPEL, REINHARD

CA —UNIVERSITY OF CALIFORNIA,
RIVERSIDE, University Library, 4045
Canyon Crest Dr, Box 5900, Riverside,
92517.
Notes: The Oswald Jonas Memorial

Collection holds the musicological mss,
letters, biographical materials, and notebooks
of Heinrich Schenker and also the papers of
the late Oswald Jonas, musicologist and
leading authority on the life and work of
Schenker. Incl Schenker's diary;
correspondence with Anthony van Hoboken,
Reinhard Oppel, Moriz Violin, Eugen
d'Albert, and Oswald Jonas; the proofs and
mss of his published works; printed editions
from his library with notes, marginalia, and
critical annotations; *Urlinie* tables; and
miscellanea. A guide to the collection will be
published by the library.

OPPENHEIMER, J. ROBERT

DC —LIBRARY OF CONGRESS, Manuscript
Division, Washington, 20540. John C
Broderick, Chief
Holdings: Cat Mss Pix
Notes: His papers; about 75,000 pieces, incl
correspondence with world leaders; US
Atomic Energy Commission, etc.
DC —LIBRARY OF CONGRESS, Motion
Pictures, Broadcasting and Recorded Sound
Div, Washington, 20540.
Notes: Disc recordings of Dr J Robert
Oppenheimer's lectures and interviews. Incl
a 3-hour discussion between Niels Bohr and
Dr Oppenheimer taped in Denmark in 1958
and a conference held at Seven Springs
Farm in Mount Kisco, NY, that featured
addresses by Nicolas Nabokov and Robert
Lowell.
NY —AMERICAN INSTITUTE OF
PHYSICS, Center for the History of Physics,
Niels Bohr Library, 335 E 45 St, New York,
10017. John Aubry, Librn
Notes: Oppenheimer's unique collection of
offprints of journal articles by physicists,
begun at Harvard in the 1920s and
continued until his death in 1967. Arranged
by author.

OPPENHEIMER, JOEL

CT —UNIVERSITY OF CONNECTICUT,
Library, Storrs, 06268. George F Butterick,
Cur of Literary Archives
Holdings: Mss
Notes: Repository for the poet's papers.

OPPORTUNITY, ECONOMIC see
Economic Opportunity

OPTIC, OLIVER see Oliver Optic

OPTICAL INSTRUMENTS

NY —UNIVERSITY OF ROCHESTER, Rush
Rhees Library, Department of Rare Books
and Special Collections, Rochester, 14627.
Peter Dzwonkoski, Librn
Notes: A large collection of trade catalogs.
See also entry under Trade Catalogs -
Collections.
PA —CARNEGIE LIBRARY OF
PITTSBURGH, Science & Technology Dept,
4400 Forbes Ave, Pittsburgh, 15213.
Catherine M Brosky, Dept Head
Notes: Incl much of the material in *Index to
Handicrafts.* Books for the home owner,
repairman and craftsman and the general
builder and mechanics are emphasized.
Information on the use of tools and materials
especially for woodworking and metal crafts;
also optical instruments, clocks, guns, and
other mechanic trades.
See also entry under Science.

OPTICAL STORAGE

CA —INTERNATIONAL BUSINESS
MACHINES RESEARCH LIBRARY, 5600
Cottle Rd, San Jose, 95193. Phil Grincewich,
Mgr Technical Information
Holdings: Vols (13,500) Cat
Notes: Principally electronic computer
storage system architecture. Incl 21,000 vols
of 770 journals. On-line search facility. Vols
are divided into three libraries, Technical
Research, Technical Information, and
Programing. Not open to public.

OPTICIANS

CA —UNIVERSITY OF CALIFORNIA,
BERKELEY, General Library, Optometry

Library, 490 Minor Hall, Berkeley, 94720.
Alison Howard, Librn
Holdings: Vols (8000) Cat Pix Microforms
Budget: ($13,500)
Notes: Incl 350 microfiches.

OPTICS

CA —BECKMAN INSTRUMENTS, Research
Library, 2500 Harbor Blvd, Fullerton, 92634.
Jean R Miller, Librn
Holdings: Vols (7000) Cat Slides Audiotapes
Videotapes Microforms
Budget: ($9000)
Notes: Strong collections in scientific and
analytic instrumentation, electrochemistry,
analytical chemistry, optics and
spectroscopy, chromatography, clinical
chemistry and biochemistry.
CA —SOUTHERN CALIFORNIA COLLEGE
OF OPTOMETRY, 2001 Associated Rd,
Fullerton, 92631. Pat Carlson, Librn
Holdings: Vols (10,000) Cat Mss Pix Slides
Microforms
Notes: Collection deals with vision and all
that pertains to training optometrists. Core
of the collection leans heavily towards
optometry; rest of collection deals with
ophthalmology and related fields.
CA —R & D ASSOCIATES, Technical
Information Center, 4640 Admiralty Way,
PO Box 9695, Marina del Rey, 90291.
Margaret R Anderson, Mgr
Holdings: Vols (10,000) Cat Mss Maps
Microforms
Notes: Military arts and sciences, tactical
and strategic studies, and defense systems.
Incl 45,000 government contractor and
technical reports; and briefing charts
(transparencies).
CA —GTE COMMUNICATIONS PRODUCT
CORP, Sylvania Systems Group, Western
Division Library, MC-2201, PO Box 7188,
Mountain View, 94039. J B Fierro,
Supervisor Library Services
Holdings: Vols (10,000) Cat
Notes: Interlibrary loan.
MA —NEW ENGLAND COLLEGE OF
OPTOMETRY, Library, 420 Beacon St,
Boston, 02115. F Eleanor Warner, Librn
Holdings: Vols (7750) Cat Mss Slides
Phonoreocrds Audiotapes Videotapes 16mm
Films Micorforms
Budget: ($30,000)
Notes: Acquisitions in optometry and
ophthalmology are comprehensive; they are
selective in areas of surgery and the
therapeutic use of drugs. Collection incl 75
slide/tape programs; 75 videotapes; 11 VF
drawers of pamphlets and reprints; 16 units
of realia; 275 periodical subscriptions.
Publishes periodicals holdings list,
audiovisual holdings list and an acquisitions
list. Open to the public for reference use.
MA —SMITHSONIAN INSTITUTION
LIBRARIES, Astrophysical Observatory
Branch, 60 Garden St, Cambridge, 02138.
Joyce Rey, Librn
Holdings: Vols (10,000) Cat Maps Pix
Microforms
MO —INTERNATIONAL LIBRARY,
ARCHIVES AND MUSEUM OF
OPTOMETRY, 243 N Lindbergh, Saint
Louis, 63141. Maria Dablemont, Librn
Holdings: Vols (12,000) Cat Mss Pix Slides
Phonorecords Audiotapes Videotapes 16mm
Films Filmstrips
Notes: Established to collect, preserve, and
make available for researchers materials
related to optometry and the visual sciences;
the oldest special library of vision science in
this country, serving the public worldwide
with reference services and materials. The
archives contain documents pertaining to the
history of optometry and the history of the
American Optometric Association. In the
museum are found antique eyeglasses and
optical instruments as well as artifacts from
the history of the optometric profession and
items associated with its leaders.
NY —ENGINEERING SOCIETIES
LIBRARY, 345 E 47 St, New York, 10017.
S Kirk Cabeen, Dir
Holdings: Vols 250,000 Cat Maps 16mm
Films Microforms
Notes: One of the largest, most

OPTICS (cont.)

comprehensive engineering libraries in the world. Covers all engineering disciplines; particularly strong in electrical and electronic, mechanical, mining annd metallurgical, petroleum, chemical, industrial, air conditioning and refrigeration engineering. Incl Wheeler Collection of early materials on magnetism and electricity. 125,000 bound periodical volumes; 10,000 maps; 5000 serial subscriptions (many foreign-language). Virtually all materials abstracted in *Engineering Index* (1884-date) are incl in Library. Noncirculating, except to members of professional engineering societies which support the Library. See *Engineering Societies Library, New York, Classed Subject Catalog and Index* (Boston: G K Hall, 1963); and *Supplements*, 1-10, 1964-1973.

NY —STATE UNIVERSITY OF NEW YORK, State College of Optometry, Harold Kohn Vision Science Library, 100 E 24 St, New York, 10010. Margaret S Lewis, Librn
Holdings: Vols (23,000) Cat Audiotapes Microforms
Notes: All subjects related to visual disabilities; much on vision disorders among children.

NY —EASTMAN KODAK COMPANY, Research Library, Research Laboratories, Bldg 83, Rochester, 14650. E W Kraus, Head
Holdings: Vols 1900 Cat Microforms

NY —UNIVERSITY OF ROCHESTER, Rush Rhees Library, Department of Rare Books and Special Collections, Rochester, 14627. Peter Dzwonkoski, Librn
Holdings: Vols Cat
Notes: Large collection of trade catalogs 30 early cataloged volumes.

NY —VISUAL STUDIES WORKSHOP, Research Center, 31 Prince St, Rochester, 14607. Linn Underhill, Coordr; Robert Bretz, Librn
Holdings: Vols (8000) Cat pix Slides Audiotapes Videotapes
Notes: Strong emphasis on photography (over 1,000,000 pictures) and the photographic arts in many subject areas incl in this volume. Heavy emphasis on early photographic processes and collections of examples of them. Also collections of individual photographers' works.

OR —PACIFIC UNIVERSITY LIBRARY, Forest Grove, 97116. Laurel Gregory, Science/Optometry Librn
Holdings: Vols (133,000) Cat Slides Microforms
Budget: ($49,000)

PA —FRANKLIN INSTITUTE LIBRARY, 20 & The Parkway, Philadelphia, 19103. Miriam Padusis, Dir; Charles Wilt, Readers Servs Librn
Holdings: Vols (300,000) Cat Maps Pix Microforms

PA —GRAPHIC ARTS TECHNICAL FOUNDATION, Edward H Wadewitz Memorial Library, 4615 Forbes Ave, Pittsburgh, 15213. Janice L Lloyd, Librn
Holdings: Vols (3500) Cat Slides Microforms
Notes: All printing processes. Also, books and periodicals on paper, ink, photography, optics, color theory, environmental control. Approximately 250 periodical titles and 35,000 classified abstracts of selected periodical articles. Approximately 15,000 slides within the organization. Research reports from foreign graphic arts research institutes.

OPTICS—HISTORY

MA —LASER HISTORY PROJECT, 25 Stoddard St, Woburn, 01801. Joan Lisa Bromberg, Dir
Notes: Four professional societies--the American Physical Society, The Laser Institute of America, The Optical Society of America and the IEEE Quantum Electronics and Applications Society have joined with the American Institute of Physics' Center for History of Physics and the Institute of Electrical and Electronics Engineers' Center for the History of Electrical Engineering to initiate a project on the history of lasers. The project's central activities will be the taking of oral histories, and the locating of papers, photographs, tapes, and equipment of historical significance.

MO —WASHINGTON UNIVERSITY, School of Medicine, Library, 660 South Euclid Ave, Saint Louis, 63110. Christopher Hoolihan, Rare Book Librn
Holdings: Vols 650 Cat
Budget: ($40,000)
Notes: The Bernard Becker, MD Collection in Ophthalmology. Incl many of the most important works in ophthalmology and optics published between the 15th and 20th centuries. The second edition of an annotated catalog of the collection was published in 1983.

OPTICS, ELECTRONIC see Electron Optics

OPTICS, PHYSIOLOGICAL

AL —UNIVERSITY OF ALABAMA, BIRMINGHAM, Lister Hill Library of the Health Sciences, University Sta, Birmingham, 35294. Richard B Fredericksen, Dir

CA —UNIVERSITY OF CALIFORNIA, BERKELEY, General Library, Optometry Library, 490 Minor Hall, Berkeley, 94720. Alison Howard, Librn
Holdings: Vols (8000) Cat Pix Microforms
Budget: ($13,500)
Notes: Specialized collection of Library materials complemented by significant, related holdings in the Biology and Public Health Libraries on campus.

IL —ILLINOIS COLLEGE OF OPTOMETRY, Carl F Shepard Memorial Library, 3241 S Michigan Ave, Chicago, 60616. Kevin K Wah, Dir of Library and Instructional Services
Holdings: Vols (13,000) Cat Slides Phonorecords Audiotapes Videotapes 16mm Films Filmstrips Microforms
Budget: ($25,000)
Notes: Research and teaching collection on every aspect of the eye and vision and their disorders, excl surgery. Incl historical and current materials; excl foreign-language materials. Library participates in Midwest Health Sciences Library Network and ILLINET.

NY —STATE UNIVERSITY OF NEW YORK, State College of Optometry, Harold Kohn Vision Science Library, 100 E 24 St, New York, 10010. Margaret S Lewis, Librn
Holdings: Vols (23,000) Cat Audiotapes Microforms
Notes: All subjects related to visual disabilities; much on vision disorders among children.

†NY —UNIVERSITY OF ROCHESTER, Rush Rhees Library, Rochester, 14627.

OPTOMETRY

AL —UNIVERSITY OF ALABAMA, BIRMINGHAM, Lister Hill Library of the Health Sciences, University Sta, Birmingham, 35294. Richard B Fredericksen, Dir

CA —UNIVERSITY OF CALIFORNIA, BERKELEY, General Library, Optometry Library, 490 Minor Hall, Berkeley, 94720. Alison Howard, Librn
Holdings: Vols (8000) Cat Pix Microforms
Budget: ($13,500)
Notes: Specialized collection of Library materials complemented by significant, related holdings in the Biology and Public Health Libraries on campus.

CA —SOUTHERN CALIFORNIA COLLEGE OF OPTOMETRY, 2001 Associated Rd, Fullerton, 92631. Pat Carlson, Librn
Holdings: Vols (10,000) Cat Mss Pix Slides Microforms
Notes: Collection deals with vision and all that pertains to training optometrists. Core of the collection leans heavily towards optometry; rest of collection deals with ophthalmology and related fields.

IL —ILLINOIS COLLEGE OF OPTOMETRY, Carl F Shepard Memorial Library, 3241 S Michigan Ave, Chicago, 60616. Kevin K Wah, Dir of Library and Instructional Services
Holdings: Vols (13,000) Cat Slides Phonorecords Audiotapes Videotapes 16mm Films Filmstrips Microforms
Budget: ($25,000)
Notes: Research and teaching collection on every aspect of the eye and vision and their disorders, excl surgery. Incl historical and current materials; excl foreign-language materials. Library participates in Midwest Health Sciences Library Network and ILLINET.

IN —INDIANA UNIVERSITY, Optometry Branch Library, Bloomington, 47405. Roger Deckman, Head; Elizabeth Egan, Branch Librn
Holdings: Vols (11,000) Cat Slides Microforms
Budget:
Notes: Incl all aspects of vision: anatomy, physiology, pathology of the eye, neurophysiology, perception, colorimetry, illumination, safety, etc. Interlibrary loans through Main Library, Indiana University, Bloomington.

MA —NEW ENGLAND COLLEGE OF OPTOMETRY, Library, 420 Beacon St, Boston, 02115. F Eleanor Warner, Librn
Holdings: Vols (7500) Cat Mss Slides Phonoreocrds Audiotapes Videotapes 16mm Films Micorforms
Budget: ($30,000)
Notes: Acquisitions in optometry and ophthalmology are comprehensive; they are selective in areas of surgery and the therapeutic use of drugs. Collection incl 75 slide/tape programs; 75 videotapes; 11 VF drawers of pamphlets and reprints; 16 units of realia; 275 periodical subscriptions. Publishes periodicals holdings list, audiovisual holdings list and an acquisitions list. Open to the public for reference use.

MI —FERRIS STATE COLLEGE ARCHIVES, 901 S State St, Big Rapids, 49307. R Lawrence Martin, Coordr
Holdings: Vols 26 Cat Mss Pix
Notes: 4 boxes of papers and books of Dr Chauncey J Howe, OD, practicing optometrist in Hillsdale, Mich, 1920-1968, secretary, Michigan Board of Examiners in Optometry, 1941-1972, founder of Omega Delta, professional optometric fraternity. Includes professional papers of Dr Howe, papers of the State Board and 7 vols of minutes of the State Board, 1909-1970. *See also* entry under Omega Delta Professional Optometric Fraternity.

MO —INTERNATIONAL LIBRARY, ARCHIVES AND MUSEUM OF OPTOMETRY, 243 N Lindbergh, Saint Louis, 63141. Maria Dablemont, Librn
Holdings: Vols (12,000) Cat Mss Pix Slides Phonorecords Audiotapes Videotapes 16mm Films Filmstrips
Notes: Established to collect, preserve, and make available for researchers materials related to optometry and the visual sciences; the oldest special library of vision science in this country, serving the public worldwide with reference services and materials. The archives contain documents pertaining to the history of optometry and the history of the American Optometric Association. In the museum are found antique eyeglasses and optical instruments as well as artifacts from the history of the optometric profession and items associated with its leaders.

NY —STATE UNIVERSITY OF NEW YORK, State College of Optometry, Harold Kohn Vision Science Library, 100 E 24 St, New York, 10010. Margaret S Lewis, Librn
Holdings: Vols (23,000) Cat Audiotapes Microforms
Notes: All subjects related to visual disabilities; much on vision disorders among children.

OR —PACIFIC UNIVERSITY LIBRARY, Forest Grove, 97116. Laurel Gregory, Science/Optometry Librn
Holdings: Vols (133,000) Cat Slides Microforms
Budget: ($49,000)

ORACLE BONES

NY —COLUMBIA UNIVERSITY LIBRARIES, C V Strarr East Asian Library,

ORACLE BONES (cont.)

300 Kent Hall, New York, 10027. James
Reardon-Anderson, Librn
Notes: Incl 67 bone and shell items
registered in Chou, Hung-hsaing's *Oracle
Bone Collections in the United States.*
(Berkeley: University of California Press,
1976) and approx 30 counterfeit and
unevaluated bones.

ORACLES

OH —CLEVELAND PUBLIC LIBRARY, Fine
Arts and Special Collections Department,
325 Superior Ave, Cleveland, 44114. Alice
N Loranth, Head
Holdings: Vols (2500) Cat
Notes: Part of the Occult Sciences
Collection. Emphasis is on historical
treatises, folklore aspects and the classic
texts pertaining to apparitions, ghosts,
divinations, oracles, omens, witchcraft,
magic, and sorcery in various civilizations.
Astrology, palmistry, psychical research and
contemporary manifestations are almost
entirely omitted.
See also entries under Folklore; Occult
Sciences.

ORAL BIOLOGY

PA —UNIVERSITY OF PENNSYLVANIA,
School of Dental Medicine, Leon Levy
Library, 4001 Spruce St, Philadelphia,
19104. John M Whittock Jr, Librn
Holdings: Vols (45,000) Cat Pix Slides
Notes: Collection is comprised of 15,250
monographs, 25,250 bound periodical vols.
Library currently receives about 700 dental
and medical journals. Houses S S White
Dental Manufacture Co collection of U S
dental patents, 1797-1966, and U S and
foreign dental catalogs. 1000 rare books on
dentistry and oral biology. 3000 pictures and
1000 slides.

ORAL HISTORY—COLLECTIONS

AL —WHEELER BASIN REGIONAL
LIBRARY, 504 Cherry St NE, PO Box
1766, Decatur, 35602. Margarete Lange,
Reference Librn
Holdings: Vols 5 Cat Mss Pix Slides
Audiotapes VF
Notes: North Alabama Folklore and Folklife
Archive. Primarily oral history on North
Alabama, incl history, politics, folklore.
AZ —NORTHERN ARIZONA
UNIVERSITY, Special Collection Library,
CU Box 6022, Flagstaff, 86011. Peter M
Whiteley, Coordr/Archivist; William
Mullane, Librn
Notes: Flagstaff City-Coconino County
Public Library Oral History Project: 89
interviews conducted with people that had
been in the Flagstaff area at least before the
1930's. A representative number of
individuals from a cross section of Flagstaff
in the past was interviewed, such as
businessmen, lumbermen, doctors,
housewives, lawyers, government employees,
teachers, newspapermen, scientists, ranchers,
Flagstaff natives and minority groups.
Outline of topics covered in each interview
is available, 1976-1977 (5 feet). Also,
collection of materials acquired as a result of
the Oral History projects conducted in 1975-
1976. Part of collection of approx 150
interviews of Arizonans, primarily in the
northern section of the state, incl such
prominent Arizonans as Jack Williams,
Howard Pyle, and Emery Kolb.
CA —JUDAH L MAGNES MEMORIAL
MUSEUM, Morris Goldstein Library, 2911
Russell St, Berkeley, 94705. Jane Levy,
Archivist
Holdings: Vols 7000 Cat Mss Maps Pix
Slides Audiotapes Microforms
Notes: Most of our special collections have
been deposited in our archives by Western
Jewish families or institutions. The collection
focuses on the contribution of Western Jews
and Jewish institutions (California, Nevada,
Oregon, Utah, Washington, Colorado, Texas,

New Mexico, and Latin America) to the
cultural, intellectual, commercial, civic, etc
growth of the American West. 135 ms
collections. The collection is cataloged,
many of the documents being indexed and
inventoried. The collection has been noted in
the Western Jewish History Center's
published bibliographies by Sara Cogan,
Pioneer Jews of the California Mother Lode
and *The Jews of San Francisco and the
Greater Bay Area, 1849-1919,* also, *A
Selective History of San Francisco Eastern
European Jewish Life, 1880-1940,* by Ruth
Kelson Rafael (Berkeley: Magnes Museum,
1976; rev 1977);*Catalog of Manuscripts
Collections in the Western Jewish History
Center, Judah L Magnes Memorial Museum,
Berkeley,* by Suzanne Nemiroff (Berkeley:
Magnes Museum, 1977); and *Catalog of
Western Jewish Periodicals, 1849-1945, at
the Western Jewish History Center...,* by
Suzanne Nemiroff (Berkeley: Magnes
Museum, 1976).
CA —LONG BEACH PUBLIC LIBRARY,
101 Pacific Ave, Long Beach, 90802.
Douglas Kermode, Librn
Holdings: Vols (700) Cat Mss Maps Pix
Notes: Records the development of Long
Beach from its beginnings as a city (ca
1887). Picture file (ca 3400) and negative
collection from local Winstead Bros,
Photographers (ca 10,000).
CA —AMERICAN FILM INSTITUTE, Louis
B Mayer Library, 2021 N Western Ave, PO
Box 27999, Los Angeles, 90027. Anne G
Schlosser, Dir
Holdings: Vols (3500) Cat
Notes: American Film Institute Louis B
Mayer Oral History Program includes over
40 interviews with pioneers of the film
industry.
CA —UNIVERSITY OF CALIFORNIA, LOS
ANGELES, Theater Arts Library, Los
Angeles, 90024. Edward Shreeves,
Chairman, Bibliographers Group; Audree
Malkin, Head, Theater Arts Library
Holdings: Vols (12,500) Cat Mss Films
Notes: Over 4,000,000 moving picture stills;
over 32,636 screenplays and scripts from
American and British films; Incl radio (1740)
scripts, television script collection (3000).
Extensive poster collection (over 7000, 1915
to date); many for Polish and Czech
productions.
CA —UNIVERSITY OF SOUTHERN
CALIFORNIA, Edward L Doheny
Memorial Library, Archives of Performing
Arts, University Park, Los Angeles, 90089.
Robert Knutson, Librn
Holdings: Vols (15,000) Cat Mss Pix Films
Audiotapes Videotape
Notes: Approx 15,000 vols of books and
serials about film, incl a large collection of
foreign language books and periodicals.
Current subscriptions to over 200 serials.
Large collection of clippings about motion
pictures and television. Warner Brothers
Films Collection (1920-1968) incl 700,000
stills and negatives; 3,000 titles of feature,
short subject and television screenplays,
script materials, set designs, engineering
drawings, production records, patent records,
music and legal files. Over 1000 bound vols
describing the inventory and 100 bound vols
of index to the inventory. Universal Pictures
Corporation Collection incl 600 boxes of
production and publicity department records,
incl 1,500 screenplays. Metro-Goldwyn-
Mayer Collection incl screenplays from
1919-1958. Twentieth Century-Fox
Collection incl screenplays and story
department notes from 1919-1967.Hal
Roach Studio Collection contains studio
records from 1916-mid fifties. More than
150 personal collections from actors,
directors, producers, writers, etc. Also have
2,000 additional screenplays; 1,000 posters,
110,000 photographs; 750 recorded
soundtracks; 1,500 interview tapes; 400
David Wolper videotapes. A collection of
feature films on videotape is being created.
There is also a historical collection of motion
picture cameras, projectors and other
equipment from the earliest times to present.
CA —POMONA PUBLIC LIBRARY, Special
Collections, 625 S Garey Ave, PO Box 2271,

Pomona, 91766. David Streeter, Librn
Holdings: Cat Audiotapes
Notes: Oral, taped interviews with Pomona
Valley settlers and residents.
CA —A K SMILEY PUBLIC LIBRARY, 125
W Vine St, Redlands, 92373. Larry E
Burgess, Archivist
Holdings: Vols (3500) Mss Maps Pix
Phonorecords Microforms
Budget: ($45,000)
Notes: Emphasis on San Bernadino County
and the Redlands area. Especially prized is
The Citrograph, 1887-1908 (bound vols and
microfilm) edited by Scipio Craig, prominent
in state, national, and newspaper circles. The
ms collection (250,000 pieces) incl the
Smiley Family papers, much on water
development, and on the citrus industry. The
photograph collection (over 5000) covers the
history of the area; there are many
stereographs and glass slides. The collection
on Indians of California and the Southwest
was begun from a special gift by Andrew
Carnegie honoring his friend, Albert K
Smiley.
CA —ROSEMEAD PUBLIC LIBRARY, 8800
Valley Blvd, Rosemead, 91770. Sally Colby,
Ref Librn
Holdings: Vols 11,012 Cat Mss
Budget: $7500
Notes: Los Angeles County Public Library
System cooperates with the Oral History
Program, Claremont Colleges, Claremont,
California, in the policy, planning,
interviewing and funding of oral histories on
the San Gabriel Valley and greater Los
Angeles area. Collection incl 25 mss
(cataloged). No photocopying.
CA —FOREST HISTORY SOCIETY INC,
Library, 109 Coral St, Santa Cruz, 95060.
Mary E Johnson, Librn
Holdings: Vols (4000) Cat Mss Maps Pix
Slides Audiotapes Microforms Serials Films
VF
Budget: ($2000)
Notes: Incl archives of the Society of
American Foresters, the American Forestry
Association, the National Lumber
Manufacturers Association, National Forest
Products Association, and the American
Forest Institute.
CO —FORT COLLINS PUBLIC LIBRARY,
201 Peterson, Fort Collins, 80524. Jane B
Davis, Library Dir
Holdings: Vols 1600 Cat Mss Maps Pix
Audiotapes
Budget: $14,273
Notes: Local history collection, primarily
Fort Collins and Larimer County. Incl local
newspapers (1874-date; some on microform;
partially indexed); clipping file, and 130,000
old photographs. Incl 75 mss, 25 maps, and
350 audiotapes (oral history).
CO —FORT MORGAN PUBLIC LIBRARY,
414 Main, Fort Morgan, 80701. Jo Ann
Kruglet, Dir
Holdings: Vols 500
Notes: Lute Johnson Collection contains
books about Colorado by Colorado authors,
many autographed, written at the turn of the
century. Noncirculating. No photocopying.
Also, 40 oral history tapes, collected during
the Bicentennial, predominantly about the
history of Fort Morgan and Morgan County,
Colorado.
DC —BROADCAST PIONEERS LIBRARY,
1771 N St NW, Washington, 20036.
Catharine Heinz, Dir
Holdings: Vols (6500) Uncat Pix
Phonorecords Audiotapes
Notes: Special collections: Oral History
(750); Havrilla (photos, radio performers);
William S Hedges Collection; Elmo Neale
Pickerill Collection; Joseph E Baudino
Collection; Archive of Federal
Communications Bar Association. Incl 20,
000 pictures, 1450 phonorecords and 1200
audiotapes.
DC —DISTRICT OF COLUMBIA PUBLIC
LIBRARY, Martin Luther King Memorial
Library, Washingtoniana Div and
Washington Star Collection, 901 G St NW,
Washington, 20001. Roxanna Deane, Chief
Notes: Oral History Research Center
collects information on projects being
conducted throughout the city and, when

ORAL HISTORY—COLLECTIONS (cont.)

possible, has copies of tapes and transcripts from oral history projects.

DC —HOWARD UNIVERSITY, Moorland-Spingarn Research Center, 500 Howard Place NW, Washington, 20059. Clifford L Muse, Jr, Acting Dir
Holdings: Vols (106,086) Cat Mss Maps Pix Slides Phonorecords Audiotapes 16mm Films Filmstrips Microforms
Budget: ($854,753)
Notes: *The Glenn Carrington Collection: A Guide to the Books, Manuscripts, Music and Recordings* (DC MSRC, 1977). *Dictionary Catalog of the Jesse E Moorland Collection of Negro Life and History*, 9 vols and Supplement, 3 vols (Boston: G K Hall, 1970, 1977). *Dictionary Catalog of the Arthur Spingarn Collection of Negro Authors*, 2 vols (Boston: G K Hall, 1970). Guide to Processed Collections in the Manuscript Division of the Moorland-Spingarn Research Center (DC, MSRC, 1983). The Moorland-Spingran Research Center is recognized as one of the largest and most comprehensive repositories in the world for the collection, preservation and dissemination of historical materials documenting from antiquity to the present the history and culture of Black people in Africa, Europe, the Caribbean and the US. Since 1973, the Research Center has greatly expanded its facilitiesand resources and currently provides research services in all aspects of library and archival research, including manuscripts, oral history, music, prints and photographs and general library materials. The Research Center also maintains professional zerographic, micrographic, photographic and similar reproduction laboratories.

GA —MARTIN LUTHER KING, JR, CENTER FOR NONVIOLENT SOCIAL CHANGE, INC, King Library and Archives, 449 Auburn Ave, Atlanta, 30312. D Louise Cook, Dir of Library and Archives
Holdings: Vols 4000 Cat Mss Audiotapes Microforms
Notes: The philosophy of Martin Luther King and the movement he led. Emphasis on obscure information and ephemeral pieces. Oral history project has over 500 tapes. Incl collection of mss of various civil rights organizationsof the 1950s and 1960s. All materials are noncirculating.

IL —NORTHERN ILLINOIS REGIONAL HISTORY CENTER, Sven Parson Hall, Northern Illinois University, De Kalb, 60115. Glen Gildemeister, Dir
Holdings: Cat Mss Maps Pix Slides Phonorecords Audiotapes 16mm Films Microforms
Notes: "A research center for advanced research in the humanities. This northern area of Illinois (excluding Cook County) has been virtually untouched by collecting agencies and we hope to fill that void. We will be strong in agribusiness, agricultural implement business, and hybrid farming mechanics....Will be primarily a ms repository, but (have) already taken responsibility for many artifacts and books, some rare."

IL —UNIVERSITY OF ILLINOIS, URBANA/CHAMPAIGN, Library, University Archives, 19 Library, 1408 W Gregory Drive, Urbana, 61801. Maynard Brichford, University Archivist
Holdings: Uncat Mss Maps Pix Slides Phonorecords Microforms
Notes: In addition to the university archives and the collections of academic and administrative staff, the archives have numerous other series of institutional and personal papers. Published guide to the collections is available: *Manuscripts Guide to Collections at the University of Illinois at Urbana-Champaign* (University of Illinois Press, 1976). Control cards and ADP control on 3644 record series; 5132 pages of supplementary finding aids. Probably the largest ms collection in the state. Holdings on the history of librarianship and faculty and student life are particularly strong. Incl

original mss and 91 tapes of interviews for anthropological work, the gift of Oscar Lewis, largely concerning his studies of the culture of poverty.

KS —FORT HAYS STATE UNIVERSITY, Forsyth Library, Folklore and Oral History Collection, 600 Park St, Hays, 67601. Esta Lou Riley, Archivist/Special Collections Librn
Holdings: //
Notes: Kansas folklore, personal reminiscences (dust storms, depression, war experiences) collected by students. Consists principally of oral interviews on tape (cassettes, reels) and beliefs, superstitions, autograph verses, etc in standard folklore form. Incl (725) tapes with transcriptions; (10 linear feet) of vertical file material. Partially cataloged.

KY —WESTERN KENTUCKY UNIVERSITY, Kentucky Building, Folklore, Folklife & Oral History Archives, Bowling Green, 42101. Patricia M Hodges, Archivist
Holdings: Cat Mss Audiotapes Videotapes
Notes: Archive contains manuscripts of field collection projects done by students and faculty. There is a large folk song collection in manuscript and tapes of local performers of traditional songs and music. Materials generally relate to Kentucky and surrounding areas; or to country music and traditional music. 3500 tapes; 135 linear ft of manuscripts.

LA —LOUISIANA STATE UNIVERSITY, Troy H Middleton Library, Baton Rouge, 70803. Lance E Dickson, Acting Dir
Holdings: Vols (1000) Cat Mss Maps Pix Audiotapes
Notes: The Troy H Middleton Collection. Contains vols on military history and tactics. Letters, documents, photographs, and mementos belonging to Troy H Middleton, former President of LSU and distinguished military leader. Also, tape recordings by some of Gen Middleton's associates in the Army, incl Gen Eisenhower, and on civilian life and reminiscences by Gen Middleton. The Library has other materials on military history also.

ME —MAINE STATE LIBRARY, Special Collections Dept, Cultural Bldg, Station 64, Augusta, 04333. Shirley Thayer, Librn
Holdings: // Audiotapes
Budget: ($2,500,000)
Notes: Oral history of Aroostook County on over 100 cassette tapes.

ME —UNIVERSITY OF MAINE AT PRESQUE ISLE LIBRARY, 181 Main St, Presque Isle, 04769. Anna McGrath, Technical Services Librn
Holdings: Vols 1100
Budget: $500
Notes: Aroostook County, Maine. Vertical file material, photographs, artifacts, tapes (oral history), maps, scrapbooks, diaries, journals.

MD —UNIVERSITY OF MARYLAND, Library, Archives & Manuscripts Dept, College Park, 20742. Mary A Boccaccio, Head
Holdings: Mss Pix
Notes: University of Maryland publications and archives; collections of organizational papers (eg Baltimore & Ohio Railroad; various organizations concerned with the Chesapeake Bay and environs; various labor unions, particularly those involving the tobacco industry); collections of papers and mss associated with literary and public figures (eg the late Senator Millard Tydings); oral histories relating to the archival and mss collections; associated memorabilia; photographs, mainly associated with Maryland. A guide to collections of personal, family, and organizational papers relating to Maryland is being prepared.

†MD —UNIVERSITY OF MARYLAND, Library, Music Educators National Conference Historical Center, College Park, 20742. Bruce Wilson, Cur
Holdings: Cat Mss Pix Audiotapes
Notes: The official archive of the Music Educators' National Conference (MENC), and a repository for the documentation of music education. Incl the papers of the

MENC, state units, and associated organizations and committees; personal papers and association items (notably, relating to Frances Elliot Clark, Lowell Mason, and Luther Whiting Mason); published proceedings of MENC and other groups; oral histories, numerous school music textbooks, and the archives of the Contemporary Music Project.

†MA —JOHN F KENNEDY LIBRARY, Columbia Point, Boston, 02125. Dan H Fenn Jr, Dir
Holdings: Vols 20,000 Cat Mss Maps Pix Slides Phonorecords Audiotapes Videotapes 16mm Films Microforms
Notes: The major collection about JFK, his life, family and administration. It contains personal papers, audiovisual materials, books, oral history interviews. Collection is described in "Historical Materials in the John F Kennedy Library." "The Kennedy Collection," a subject guide to the book collection, is available for sale.

MA —JOHN F KENNEDY LIBRARY, Columbia Point, Boston, 02125. Henry J Gwiazda II, Cur
Notes: The Robert F Kennedy Papers cover the period from 1937-1968 and are divided into four subcollections: the Pre-Administration, Attorney General's, Senate, and 1968 Presidential Campaign Papers. In the Pre-Administration Papers, over 140 archives boxes or 70 percent of the materials are open to research. The Personal and Political Papers of this subcollection are almost entirely open. Most of the unprocessed mss are in the Working Files and involve investigative work on labor racketeering. Seventy five percent or 185 archives boxes of the Attorney General's Papers are open, incl the correspondence, the John F Kennedy Library File, the Speech and Trip Files for 1961-1964. For the Senate Papers, 200 boxes are open for the 1964 Senate Campaign, the Legislative Subject File, and the Speech and Trip Files for 1964-1968. The speeches and press releases(incl in the Senate subcollection Speech File) and "The Black Books" (16 boxes) on state and delegate information are open for the 1968 campaign. Each subcollection has its own finding aid. The Library also has available for research about 100 audiotapes of Robert F Kennedy's public addresses from 1962-1966 and some 50 oral history interviews on RFK and one (1000 pages) by RFK. There are also available the major documentaries on RFK and a number of films donated by the major networks for research use in the Library.

MA —RADCLIFFE COLLEGE, Arthur & Elizabeth Schlesinger Library on the History of Women in America, 3 James St, Cambridge, 02138. Patricia Miller King, Dir; Eva Moseley, Cur of Mss
Notes: Tapes and transcripts of three projects sponsored by the Schlesinger Library: Family Planning Oral History Project, Black Women Oral History Project, and Women in the Federal Government Oral History Project (in progress, 1984); also transcripts of oral history projects conducted elsewhere, and of individual interviews sponsored by the Schlesinger Library or other institutions.

MA —PEABODY INSTITUTE LIBRARY, Danvers Archival Center, 15 Sylvan St, Danvers, 01923. Richard B Trask, Archivist, Rare Books & Special Collections
Holdings: Vols 5000 Cat Mss
Notes: The Ellerton J Brehaut Collection on New England witchcraft, especially Salem witchcraft. (Danvers, where the library is located, was part of Salem at the time of the witchcraft trials.) 17th and 18th century English and American books on witchcraft; transcripts of all known trial records. Manuscript records of the First Church of Salem Village. Special catalog to collection. Danvers History Collection consists of 5000 volumes, 250,000 mss, numerous photos, newspaper clippings, maps, audiotapes, and visual tapes.

MA —BRANDEIS UNIVERSITY, Goldfarb Library, 415 South St, Waltham, 02154. Bessie Hahn, Dir
Notes: Holocaust Survivors Collection. 20

ORAL HISTORY—COLLECTIONS
(cont.)

linear feet of recorded interviews with survivors of the Holocaust, now living in the US. The tapes are not transcribed and the collection is unprocessed, but the tapes are arranged alphabetically by interviewee.

MA —LASER HISTORY PROJECT, 25 Stoddard St, Woburn, 01801. Joan Lisa Bromberg, Dir
Notes: Four professional societies--the American Physical Society, The Laser Institute of America, The Optical Society of America and the IEEE Quantum Electronics and Applications Society have joined with the American Institute of Physics' Center for History of Physics and the Institute of Electrical and Electronics Engineers' Center for the History of Electrical Engineering to initiate a project on the history of lasers. The project's central activities will be the taking of oral histories, and the locating of papers, photographs, tapes, and equipment of historical significance.

MI —SUOMI COLLEGE, Finnish-American Historical Archives, Hancock, 49930. Kenneth Niemi, Archives Librn
Notes: Collection incl 8000 vols, 152,000 mss, 2000 photographs, 760 audiotapes; microforms and maps; 14,000 holdings are cataloged. Subject interests: coop movement, labor, pioneer library of rare books and church records, socialist and communist movements, temperance societies. Special Collections: Finnish language newspapers (includes 100 titles from 1876-present); Suomi Synod Archives; Finnish-American Oral History.

MI —MONROE COUNTY LIBRARY SYSTEM, Ellis Reference and Information Center, 3700 S Custer Rd, Monroe, 48161. Marie D Chulski, Head of Reference Services
Notes: Historic Monroe County, tracing its beginnings to 1780, is a definite part of Michigan's history. Many events of the area and citizens are part of Michigan's heritage. The Michigan collection besides general works contains individual county histories, atlases, biographies, etc. The Monroe County history collection contains veteran records, plat books, oral history tapes, family histories, church records, cemetery index, atlases and census records. Genealogy emphasis is not only Monroe County but includes surrounding counties and the states with large migration to the area, such as Ohio, Kentucky, Tennessee and the New England states.

MI —GENERAL MOTORS, Research Laboratories Library, General Motors Technical Center, Warren, 48090. Robert W Gibson, Librn
Notes: The Oral History Project incl taped interviews with people who knew and worked with Charles F Kettering. Collection available to serious students of the history of science and technology.

MN —MINNESOTA HISTORICAL SOCIETY LIBRARY, 690 Cedar St, Saint Paul, 55101. Patricia C Harpole, Chief of Reference Library; Bonnie G Wilson, Head of Special Libraries
Holdings: Mss
Notes: The Minnesota Historical Society conducts its own oral history program, sponsors special projects, and collects materials of other sponsoring groups and individuals. The collection of oral history tapes contains, among others, the following notable series: (1) Interviews with every governor (except Floyd B Olson) from J A O Preus (1921-25) to Harold LeVander (1967-71). (2) Representatives of ethnic groups in Minnesota interviewed as a part of special projects include Blacks, Mexican-Americans, Finns in Northern Minnesota, and Jews in Minneapolis. (3) Leaders of both state houses have been interviewed during each legislative session from 1969 to 1976. State politics in the 1930's and 1940's is a recurring subject. Interviews with Minnesotans in government, including congressmen, United States ambassadors,

state officers, and others, are also a part of thisseries. (4) Industries in Minnesota which have been documented in interviews include lumbering, commercial fishing on the North Shore of Lake Superior, and printing and graphics in the Twin Cities. (5) Activities of such groups as the Women's International League for Peace and Freedom, labor organizations, and the Izaak Walton League are discussed in interviews. (6) Interviews with Minnesota's educational leaders, expecially in the area of higher education, are in this series. (7) Interviews with these early builders of Minnesota touch on a wide range of subjects.

MS —UNIVERSITY OF SOUTHERN MISSISSIPPI, William David McCain Graduate Library, Box 5148, Southern Sta, Hattiesburg, 39406.
Holdings: Vols 200 Cat
Notes: More than 200 complete vols and over 700 other interviews dealing with a broad range of subjects related to Mississippi life and culture, incl politics and government, ethnic history, civil rights, agriculture, labor, education, the arts, prisoners of war, and native Mississippians of national prominence.

MO —UNIVERSITY OF MISSOURI-KANSAS CITY, General Library, State Historical Society of Missouri Manuscripts, 5100 Rockhill Road, Kansas City, 64110. Kenneth J LaBudde, Dir; Gordon Hendrickson, Assoc Dir
Holdings: Mss

Notes: Joint Collection Western Historical Manuscript Collection and the State Historical of Missouri Manuscripts, University of Missouri-Kansas City General Library, 5100 Rockhill Road, Kansas City, MO 64110. Ca 2,500 linear feet of manuscripts, blueprints and oral history tapes.
Notes: The manuscript collection includes material which documents the history, growth and development of Missouri, especially the Greater Kansas City area. The personal papers of business, civic, cultural, political and community leaders; local historians and other individuals of families from the area are within the collection as are the records of associations, organizations and institutions which reflect the history of the area. Prominent among the collections are the papers of Charles B. Wheeler, Jr., Charles N. Kimball, Arthur Mag, Oscar D. Nelson, Lou B. Holland, J. C. Nichols, Perry Cookingham, Blevins Davis and Daniel Macmorris and the records of the Kansas City Board of Trade. Architectural designs and plans for approximately 3,500 Kansas City buildings and the records of the Hoit, Price and Barnes architectural firm and the papers of Asa Beebe Cross, early Kansas City architect as well as a number of oral histories with Kansas City Jazz figures are in the collection.

NE —DANA COLLEGE, C A Dana-Life Library, Blair, 68008. Ronald D Johnson, Head Librn
Holdings: Vols (10,000) Cat Audiotapes
Notes: Strong emphasis on Danish literature although we include other Scandinavian countries. Have an oral history tape collection with recordings of Danish emigrants to the midwest. Our book collection is strongest in the literature area with history a close second.

NE —UNIVERSITY OF NEBRASKA-LINCOLN, Don L Love Library, Czech

Heritage Collection, Lincoln, 68588. Joseph G Svoboda, University Archivist
Holdings: Vols (3000) Cat Mss Pix Audiotapes Microforms
Notes: The Czech Heritage Collection.

NE —YORK COLLEGE, Levitt Library, York, 67467. Charles Van Baucom, Dir
Holdings: Vols 80 Cat Mss Pix Audiotapes
Notes: Yorkana Collection incl titles on the college, the city and the county. There is also an active oral history program that has produced 51 tapes. It is to be cataloged and continued.

NV —UNIVERSITY OF NEVADA, RENO, University Library, Special Collections Dept, Reno, 89557. Robert E Blesse, Head
Notes: Incl 2100 cubic feet of mss, 25,000 photographs, maps, VF, microforms, and oral histories. Both primary and secondary materials are collected which document the history and development of Nevada and the Great Basin region from its beginnings to the present day. Areas of strength incl mining, politics, water resources, railroads, biography, land use, anthropology, architecture, Lake Tahoe, lumbering, and early Nevada imprints. Major emphasis is on the prehistory and history of Nevada with lesser emphasis on bordering states and the Great Basin region. Specialized catalogs and indexes are available in the department.

†NM —SUOMI CONFERENCE OF THE LUTHERAN CHURCH IN AMERICA, 516 Villa Verde, Rio Rancho, 87124.
Notes: Contains mss, correspondence, dissertations, documents, pictorial material, and oral history for the use of scholars conducting research on Finnish-Americans.

NY —CITY UNIVERSITY OF NEW YORK, BROOKLYN COLLEGE, Library, Special Collections Div, Bedford Ave & Ave H, Brooklyn, 11210. Antoinette Ciolli, Chief
Holdings: // Uncat Audiotapes
Notes: The Brooklyn College Oral Archives project incl interviews with prominent Brooklyn individuals who were involved in the early development of the College. Among the tapes are interviews with Randolph E Evans, the architect who designed all the original buildings on the Brooklyn College Midwood campus; Mrs Mary S Ingraham and Mrs Pearl B Max, formerly of the New York City Board of Higher Education; Harry D Gideonse, Francis P Kilcoyne, Presidents Emeriti; and Walter Mais and Abraham S Goodhartz, Deans Emeriti. No transcipts.

†NY —STATE UNIVERSITY OF NEW YORK, COLLEGE AT BUFFALO, Vietnamese Immigration Collection, Buffalo, 14260.
Notes: Oral history, interviews, orientation materials, and refugee camp newspapers.

NY —STATE UNIVERSITY OF NEW YORK, COLLEGE AT FREDONIA, Daniel A Reed Library, Fredonia, 14063. John P Saulitis, Dir of Library Services; Joanne L Schweik, Supv of Special Collections; Joseph Chouinard, Music Librn
Holdings: Audiotapes Videotapes
Notes: The Oral History Collection (ca 160 audiotapes and videotapes), part of Reed Library's Local History Collection, focuses on the history of education in the local area, particularly rural education, and incl audiotapes and a few videotapes of events important in the College's history.

NY —CORNELL UNIVERSITY, New York State School of Industrial & Labor Relations, Martin P Catherwood Library, Ives Hall, Ithaca, 14853. Shirley F Harper, Dir
Holdings: Vols (150,000) Cat Mss Pix Phonorecords Microforms
Notes: Collection incl approx 1000 periodicals and union journals currently received, and ms collections of labor unions, arbitrators, and scholars. 6000 linear ft. *Library Catalog of the New York State School of Industrial and Labor Relations* (Boston: G K Hall, 1967), 12 volumes; *Cumulation of the Library Catalog Supplements of the New York State School of Industrial and Labor Relations* (Boston: G K Hall, 1976), 8 volumes.

NY —CORNELL UNIVERSITY LIBRARIES, Collection of Regional History, Dept of

ORAL HISTORY—COLLECTIONS (cont.)

Manuscripts and Univ Archives, Ithaca, 14853.
Notes: Incl 3 tape recordings of Thomas Everal Milliman speaking about agricultural subjects, and 3 tape recordings of Malvina Harlan Shanklin reminiscing about her early life.

NY —CORNELL UNIVERSITY LIBRARIES, Collection of Regional History, Dept of Manuscripts and Univ Archives, Ithaca, 14853.
Notes: Tape recordings of interviews, programs and public events at Cornell University, NY.

NY —AMERICAN INSTITUTE OF PHYSICS, Center for the History of Physics, Niels Bohr Library, 335 E 45 St, New York, 10017. John Aubry, Librn
Holdings: Vols (16,000) Cat Mss Pix Slides Phonorecords Audiotapes 16mm Films Microforms
Notes: The Library contains an extensive collection of published works relating to the history of modern physics and astronomy. Its archives incl letter, notebooks and other papers of physicists, as well as the records of leading American physics societies and institutions. Its collections of ms autobiographies, oral history interviews, and other tape recordings, and pictorial materials (incl unpublished film footage) are unrivaled in the field of history of science. It maintains the International Catalog of Sources for History of Physics and and Astronomy.

†NY —AMERICAN JEWISH COMMITTEE, William E Wiener Oral History Library, 165 E 56 St, New York, 10022.
Notes: All aspects of the American Jewish experience in the 20th century. Other materials located in the Blaustein Library.

NY —COLUMBIA UNIVERSITY LIBRARIES, Rare Book & Manuscript Library, 801 Butler Library, 535 W 114 St, New York, 10027. Kenneth A Lohf, Librn
Notes: Transcipts of recorded reminiscences of political figures, writers, journalists, diplomats, film and theater personalities and other prominent figures. Restricted use.

NY —NEW YORK PUBLIC LIBRARY, Performing Arts Research Center, Dance Collection, 111 Amsterdam Ave, New York, 10023. Genevieve Oswald, Cur

Notes: Oral History Archive of 1600 audiotapes and cassettes. Chiefly Oral Biographies of persons associated with the dance—dancers, choreographers, teachers, composers, and writers; radio programs including those of Irving Deakin, Marian Horosko, Walter Terry, Robert Sherman, and John Gruen; lectures, symposiums, and conferences, The Oral History Project, begun in 1974, provides original documentation concentrating on interviewing clusters of distinguished artists asssociated with eight seminal figures in the dance: Frederick Ashton, George Balanchine, Lucia Chase, Alexandra Danilova, Ninette De Valois, Martha Graham, Alicia Markova, and Leonide Massine. Over 130 interviews completed by early 1984 include: Aaron Copland, Anton Dolin, Andre Eglevsky, Frederic Franklin, Tamara Geva, Arnold Haskell, Robert Irving, Maria Karnilova, Gene Kelly, Bertran Ross, Vera Stravinsky, Twyla Tharp, Violette Verdy, and Lavinia Williams. Archive also contains original documentation of Indonesian, Thai, Indian, and Philippine dance artists, and transcripts of tapes made for the Oral History Project. Cataloged items appear in Dictionary Catalog of the Dance Collection, published by G K Hall, Boston 1974, and its annual supplement, Bibliographic Guide to dance.

NY —NEW YORK PUBLIC LIBRARY, Performing Arts Research Center, Rodgers & Hammerstein Archives of Recorded Sound, 111 Amsterdam Ave, New York, 10023.
Holdings: Cat Tapes
Notes: A collection of taped interviews, representing over 400 prominent figures. Incl are voices of Richard Nixon, Billy Graham, Maurice Chevalier, Sammy Davis, Jr, Dr Albert Sabin, etc. Also, 57 audiotapes of interviews conducted in 1967 by Margaret Fairbanks Jory with American composers. Transcripts are available for the greater part of these interviews.

NC —GREENSBORO PUBLIC LIBRARY, Oral History Program Library, Drawer X-4, Greensboro, 27402. Eugene Edwin Pfaff, Jr, Librn
Holdings: Videotapes Audiotapes
Notes: Oral history on the cultural, social, and economic development of Greensboro and Guilford County; the program is expanding to incl prominent North Carolinians throughout the State. Collection consists of 42 videotapes and 93 audiotapes which are uncataloged.

OH —OHIO UNIVERSITY, Vernon R Alden Library, Department of Archives and Special Collections, Athens, 45701. Gary A Hunt, Head
Holdings: Vols 67 Cat
Notes: The Cornelius Ryan Memorial Collection of World War II Papers, containing the research files, correspondence and working library assembled by Ryan in the course of writing his three major books on World War II. The research papers incl some 3,072 files for individual participants in the Normandy invasion, the battle for Berlin, and the Market-Garden operation. Also incl are 166 audio recordings of interviews conducted by Ryan,many with leading figures associated with the war, such as Eisenhower, Chuikov, Gavin, Montgomery, and Prince Bernhard of the Netherlands.

OK —PHILLIPS UNIVERSITY, Zollars Memorial Library, University Sta, Enid, 73701. John L Sayre, Dir of University Libraries
Holdings: Audiotapes Cat
Notes: Living Legends (Oral History Collection) Interviews with 282 early Northwest Oklahoma residents. Includes reminiscences of the Cherokee Outlet Land Run in 1893 and experiences in early statehood and depression periods of Oklahoma. Also includes recollections of early Phillips University history.

OR —UMATILLA COUNTY LIBRARY, 214 N Main St, Pendleton, 97801. Barbara L Bishop, Dir
Holdings: Vols (675) Cat Mss Pix Audiotapes 16mm Films Microforms
Notes: Oregon history, especially Umatilla County. Lee Moorehouse photos (glass negatives)--1004 negatives, use restricted to professional photographers, copies may be made on premises only, also 3 rolls of microfilm of Moorehouse photos. Dr William McKay papers, 1830-1900, 14 folders, uncataloged, letters, coroner's reports (1885-86), miscellaneous papers, notes, memos and rough drafts, Army statements, receipts, accounts and business and personal receipts, accounts, 8 letters written by Donald McKay, one letter written December 7, 1880, by William F Cody. Early brands of Eastern Oregon, 1/2 reel microfilm. Some cassette recordings of interviews with early pioneers.

PA —LIGONIER VALLEY LIBRARY ASSOCIATION, Library, 120 W Main St, Ligonier, 15658. Janet Hudson, Cur
Holdings: Vols (3800) Cat Mss Audiotapes Microforms
Notes: Have entire microfilmed contents of the Ligonier Echo (weekly newspaper) from Sept 1888 to the present. There is a complete cross-reference file index to the microfilm. The Pennsylvania Room also contains an obituary file. A complete bibliography of materials in the collection is being compiled.

PA —PENNSYLVANIA STATE UNIVERSITY, Fred Lewis Pattee Library, Labor History Collection, University Park, 16802. Peter Gottlieb, Archivist
Holdings: Cat Mss Pix
Notes: Penn State is "provisional repository" for papers and records of the United Steel Workers of America, incl records from the USWA international headquarters in Pittsburgh and from 29 district offices. A comprehensive oral history program with union members is underway.

PA —PENNSYLVANIA STATE UNIVERSITY, Fred Lewis Pattee Library, University Park, 16802.
Holdings: Cat
Notes: Repository for tapes of speeches by distinguished visiting lecturers.

RI —US NAVAL WAR COLLEGE, Historical Collection & Museum, Newport, 02841. Anthony S Nicolosi, Dir; Evelyn Cherpak, Cur
Holdings: Mss
Notes: Collections incl over 200,000 separate pieces; chiefly papers of naval officers and records of organizations associated with the US Navy, the Naval War College, the college's major study areas, and the Navy in the Narragansett Bay region; oral history collection; Naval War College Archives, 1884-present; records of conferences held at the College; newspaper collections dealing with naval themes and military conflicts.

SD —SOUTH DAKOTA HISTORICAL RESOURCE CENTER, Library, Soldiers Memorial Bldg, Pierre, 57501. Rosemary Evetts, Librn
Holdings: Vols 1000 Cat Pix
Budget: $2000
Notes: Collection is about evenly divided between Sioux and other tribes and Indian subjects in general, such as art, wars, etc, 1650 audiotapes duplicating one-third of the Indian history project at the University of South Dakota, Vermillion.

†SD —SOUTH DAKOTA SCHOOL OF MINES & TECHNOLOGY, Devereaux Library, Rapid City, 57701.
Holdings: Vols 1000 Cat Mss Maps Microforms Audiotapes
Notes: Microfilm copy (complete set) of the US Bureau of Mines "Mine Map Depository (Denver)" material. Also, there are about a half-dozen periodicals that we subscribe to that relate to this subject (in general or specifically). Lastly, there are a few private collections, of varying size, that we are in process of acquiring for this area. Have collection of cave maps, also. Further, oral history program underway.

TN —MEMPHIS STATE UNIVERSITY, John Willard Brister Library, Memphis, 38152. John Terreo, Special Collections Librn
Notes: 1968 Memphis Sanitation Workers Strike. A collection of audiotape interviews with Memphis governmental officals and administrators, strikers, union leaders, religious leaders, and other significant persons involved in the strike, during which civil rights leader Dr Martin Luther King, Jr was assassinated. Also incl are photographic prints and negatives and the news outakes from the news departments of the three Memphis television stations as well as clippings from newspapers and periodicals. Published finding aid can be found in the Mississippi Valley Collection.

TX —UNIVERSITY OF TEXAS, ARLINGTON, Library, Arlington, 76019. Charles A Colley, Dir of Special Collections; Robert A Gamble, Head of Archives
Holdings: Mss Pix Microforms
Notes: History of organized labor in Texas, along with movements. This collection contains primary sources documenting the history of organized labor in Texas. Scope incl original records such as minute books, correspondence, photographs, broadsides,

ORAL HISTORY—COLLECTIONS (cont.)

agreements, contracts, leaflets, posters, scrapbooks, and press releases dealing with the growth of organized labor in the state. The earliest records date from 1870. Donors incl individual labor leaders, labor law firms, local unions, city and county labor councils, state councils, and district offices of international unions. Through its oral history program, the Archives interviews union leaders and others involved in the labor movement. 1000 linear ft of mss. Detailed finding aids have been compiled for all collections. A brochure and a guide are available upon request. All prospective researchers are interviewed.

TX —UNIVERSITY OF TEXAS LIBRARIES, General Libraries, Barker Texas History Center, PO Box P, Austin, 78712. Don Carleton, Dir
Holdings: Vols (132,000) Cat Mss Maps Pix Slides Phonorecords Audiotapes Microforms
Notes: See description of collection under Texas-History.

TX —LEE COLLEGE, Library, PO Box 818, Baytown, 77522. William K Peace, Librn
Notes: Oral history tapes covering the area of east Harris County, Texas. Early history of Baytown, Goose Creek, and Pelly, with some relating to the early development of Humble Oil and Refining Company as remembered by early residents of the area. Also in the western area of Chambers County, Texas, known as Barbers Hill. The original tapes are housed in the Lee College Library, with copies located in the Sterling Municipal Library of Baytown. Incl 75 tapes; 50 transcripts.

TX —PANHANDLE-PLAINS HISTORICAL MUSEUM, Research Center, Box 967, WT Sta, Canyon, 79016. Claire R Kuehn, Archivist-Librn
Holdings: Vols 8000 Cat Mss Maps Pix Microforms
Budget: $2000
Notes: History of the Texas Panhandle. Incl interviews with early settlers taken over a 50-year period, ranch reocrds, and business records relating to the Texas Panhandle and surrounding states.

TX —NORTH TEXAS STATE UNIVERSITY, Archives, NT Station Box 5188, Denton, 76203. Robert LaForte, University Archivist
Holdings: Vols 700 Uncat
Notes: The NTSU Archives houses the patron's copy of oral history interviews that are part of the Oral History Collection, an independent project not part of the Archives. This collection of interviews covers, in part, the following subject areas: World War II Pearl Harbor survivors, World War II prisoners of war, Texas legislators, ex-governors of Texas, Texans employed by the administrations of FDR, Texas businessmen and businesswomen, development of the Coastal Bend area of south Texas, and Mexican-American social action activities. Cataloged. Transcriptions available. See *Oral History Collection,* North Texas State University Bulletin, April 1981.

TX —UNIVERSITY OF TEXAS, EL PASO, Library, Special Collections Dept, El Paso, 79968. Cesar Caballero, Dept Head
Notes: Oral History Collection. A product of the Oral History Institute at U T El Paso, this collection consists of tapes and transcripts of interviews with prominent and not so prominent persons of the community of El Paso, Juarez and other parts of the Border region.

TX —TEXAS TECH UNIVERSITY, Library, Lubbock, 79409. David J Murrah, Assoc Dir for Special Collections

TX —BAYLOR UNIVERSITY, Moody Memorial Library, Texas History Collection, Waco, 76706. Kent Keeth, Librn
Holdings: Vols (80,000) Cat Mss Maps Pix Slides Phonorecords Audiotapes Microforms
Notes: The Texas Collection gathers materials which relate to life in Texas in all its aspects, from earliest days to the present. Incl Baylor University Archives.

VA —ARLINGTON COUNTY LIBRARIES, Virginiana Collection, 1015 N Quincy St, Arlington, 22201. Sara Collins, Librn
Holdings: Vols (6800) Cat Mss Maps Pix Audiotapes Microforms VF
Notes: Collection incl books, magazines, pamphlets, clippings and maps on Virginia history, especially local history of the northern Virginia area. Incl a number of rare pamphlets and leaflets concerning Arlington County history in the early part of the century, as well as county and state documents on matters of current concern. One feature is the Oral and Video History collection, aimed at collecting personal recollections and programs on Arlington's development and history from all members of the community, including Blacks. A special community archive project is collecting and organizing manuscripts of collections donated by individuals and community groups. Researchers should make an appointment for use of special materials.

VA —VIRGINIA POLYTECHNIC INSTITUTE AND STATE UNIVERSITY LIBRARY, Blacksburg, 24061. Glenn L McMullen, Special Collections Librn
Holdings: Vols (2000) Cat Mss Maps Pix Audiotapes
Notes: Primarily Southwest Virginia materials. Collection incl ca 200 mss, account books and other archival records of nineteenth century area businesses and other mining operations; the extant archival records of several Southwest Virginia railroads, incl the Virginia and Tennessee Railroad and the Norfolk and Western Railroad; and papers of historically prominent Southwest Virginians, incl John Apperson, Dr Harvy Black, James P Charlton, W Graham Claytor, Henley Fugate, Clement D Johnston, Germanicus Kent, William Preston, J Hoge Tyler, and William C Wampler. Several oral history collections incl material on Appalachian customs and folklore, particularly in Patrick County.

VA —VIRGINIA UNION UNIVERSITY, William J Clark Library, 1500 N Lombardy St, Richmond, 23220. Verdelle V Bradley, Librn
Holdings: Vols 9905 Cat Pix Slides Phonorecords Audiotapes Filmstrips Microforms
Notes: Incl 1369 microforms. Special collection on slavery is not cataloged; oral history tapes of Black Virginians, especially in religious contexts.

†WA —UNIVERSITY OF WASHINGTON LIBRARIES, Seattle, 98195.

AB —UNIVERSITY OF CALGARY, Libraries, Special Collections Div, 2500 University Dr, Calgary, T2N 1N4, Can.
Holdings: Cat Mss Pix Audiotapes 16mm Films Microforms
Notes: The Canadian Architectural Archives at the University of Calgary include collections of drawings, records, sketches, renderings, correspondence, project files of the following Canadian architects (qv separate entries): Raymond T Affleck, J Francis Brown and F Bruce Brown, J A Cawston, Arthur C Erickson, Long Mayell & Associates, Hugh McMillan Architects Ltd, Raymond Moriyama, John B Parkin Associates/NORR, Rule Wynn & Rule (Edmonton and Calgary), Stevenson Raines Barrett Hutton Seton & Partners, The Thom Partnership, Thompson Berwick Pratt & Partners, and H M Whiddington. Dates from 1891 to about 1974. The Archives also incl photographs, microfilmed material (16mm and 35mm, film strip and aperture cards), and Oral History Interviews on tape. Project lists and/or inventories are on hand.

MB —MANITOBA MUSEUM OF MAN & NATURE, Library, 190 Rupert Ave, Winnipeg, R3B 0N2, Can. V Hatten, Librn
Holdings: Audiotapes
Notes: Human and natural history of Manitoba. Incl 720 audiotapes.

ORAL HYGIENE see Dental Hygiene

ORAL TRADITION AND LITERATURE

MA —HARVARD UNIVERSITY LIBRARY, Widener Library, Milman Parry Collection of Oral Literature & the James A Notopoulos Collection, Cambridge, 02138. Albert B Lord, Cur
Holdings: Cat Mss

ORANGUTANS

OR —OREGON REGIONAL PRIMATE RESEARCH CENTER, Library, 505 NW 185 Ave, Beaverton, 97006. Isabel McDonald, Librn
Holdings: Vols (765) Cat Audiotapes 16mm Films Microforms
Notes: Incl small collection of dissertations and theses.

ORATORIOS

MI —UNIVERSITY OF MICHIGAN, William L Clements Library, Ann Arbor, 48109. John C Dann, Dir

NC —UNIVERSITY OF NORTH CAROLINA, CHAPEL HILL, Music Library, Hill Hall, Chapel Hill, 27514.
Holdings: Vols (90,000) Cat Mss Pix Slides Phonorecords Audiotapes Microforms
Budget: ($60,000)

Notes: Extensive holdings of early theoretical treatises; complete editions; performing scores; music periodicals; reference works. Special interests reflected in holdings of sonatas; oratorios; requiems; operas; microfilms of Vatican Library holdings of mss containing hymns; microfilms from the Deutsches Musikgeschichtliches Archiv; microfilms of important European primary sources; contemporary chamber music. Approx 5000 pieces of early American sheet music,

ORATORIOS (cont.)

primarily antebellum. Substantial collection of shape-note hymnals, 19th and 20th century. Dictionary catalog of books, scores, microforms and recordings. Separate card catalog of early American music and song anthologies held by Music Library. Partial book catalog of libretto collection.

ORBITING VEHICLES see Artificial Satellites

ORCHARDS see Fruit Culture

ORCHESTRAL MUSIC

CA —CLAREMONT COLLEGES, Honnold Library, Ninth & Dartmouth, Claremont, 91711. Tania Rizzo, Special Collections Dept Head
Holdings: Vols 500 // Uncat Mss Pix Slides
Notes: Joseph W Clokey Collection. 250 mss items, scores, opaques, transparencies and transcriptions of church choral music, often with orchestral and organ accompaniments; 195 printed copies of published works; 15 folders of correspondence with his publishers, miscellaneous notes and typescripts. Restricted use. No photocopies permitted. On deposit.

†DC —CATHOLIC UNIVERSITY OF AMERICA, Music Library, Washington, 20064. Betty Libbey, Head Music Library
Holdings: Cat Microforms
Notes: A large collection to support advanced degree study. Emphasis on church music, musicology, history and criticism, instrumental and vocal music, solo music for all voices, instruments, and musical forms.

DC —LIBRARY OF CONGRESS, Music Division, Washington, 20540.
Notes: A collection of 120 historic high-fidelity and stereophonic recordings of Leopold Stokowski conducting the Philadelphia Orchestra made in 1931 and 1932.

IL —CHICAGO PUBLIC LIBRARY, Music Section, Fine Arts Division, 78 E Washington St, Chicago, 60602. Rosalinda I Hack, Fine Arts Division Chief; Richard C Schwegel, Head, Music Section
Notes: Collection mainly of miniature scores. Growing number of orchestral sets, 100 titles.

IL —UNIVERSITY OF ILLINOIS, URBANA/CHAMPAIGN, Library, Music Library, Urbana, 61801. William M McClellan, Librn
Holdings: Vols (200,000) Cat Mss Slides Sound Recordings Microforms Books Scores
Budget: ($65,000)
Notes: Introductory, instructive, research and reference materials to support work at graduate level in ethnomusicology,, musicology, music education, performance areas. Special areas incl about 2500 pre-1800 music mss and editions of music on microfilm, 2400 graduate music theses on microfilm, a special collection of 30,000 titles of American vocal sheet music covering the period 1790-1970, the Rafael Joseffy Collection of about 2000 pieces of 19th century piano music (incl performer markings), the Joseph Szigeti Collection (700 items: published music, mss, recordings), mainly violin and piano music by various commposers. Also incl a special collection of 45,000 78 rpm sound recordings (uncat) of classical music and jazz; a collection of 2900 titles from Chicago radio station WGN. Incl orchestrations, a collection of 500,000 items (uncat) from stock of Hunleth Music Store, St Louis, Missouri, mainly early 20th century imprints of songs, wind music, string music, piano, sets of theatre orchestra parts, dance band orchestrations. A separate collection of choral octavos and instrumental parts is maintained, incl 135,000 pieces of choral music, 30,500 orchestral parts, and 5500 wind ensemble parts. Also, music publishers' catalogues (mainly European and American), ca 126 cubic feet, 1860s-1950s.

IN —INDIANA UNIVERSITY, Music Library, Bloomington, 47401. David E

Fenske, Head
Holdings: Cat Slides Phonorecords Audiotapes Videotapes Filmstrips Microforms
Budget:
Notes: 120,000 books and scores; 185,583 choral and orchestral parts; 33,000 phonorecords; 37,000 audiotapes.

MD —PEABODY CONSERVATORY LIBRARY, 21 E Mt Vernon Place, Baltimore, 21202. Edwin A Quist, Librn
Holdings: Vols 70,000 Cat Mss Pix Phonorecords Audiotapes Videotapes Microforms
Budget: $30,000
Notes: The Peabody Conservatory Library, formerly a part of the Peabody Institute Library (now the George Peabody Library of the Johns Hopkins University) supplies the library needs of the faculty and student body of the Peabody Conservatory of Music. While the collection has numerous research capabilities, it is basically a collection of musical scores. The entire history of Western music is represented through collected editions, monumental anthologies, study scores, performing editions and a large collection of books and music periodicals. This collection is supplemented by a listening facility containing 14,000 discs and an ensembles library containing scores and parts of orchestral, band and chorus works.

MA —BOSTON UNIVERSITY, Mugar Memorial Library, Special Collections Dept, 771 Commonwealth Ave, Boston, 02215. Howard B Gotlieb, Dir
Notes: Tape recordings and some videotapes of the Boston Symphony Orchestra performances.

MI —DETROIT PUBLIC LIBRARY, Music & Performing Arts Dept, 5201 Woodward, Detroit, 48202. Agatha Pfeiffer Kalkanis, Chief
Holdings: Cat
Notes: One of the oldest record collections in a public library (established 1921). Consists of circulating rental collection (all LPs, 19,000) and reference and archive collections (LPs and 78s, 6000). Emphasis is on broad range of concert music in all mediums and from all periods. Also folk music, literary, and documentary recordings, instructional recordings. Main library collection supplemented by independent collections in 15 branch libraries and by a collection in the Children's Library. No tapes or taping facilities. No taping or other copying permitted.

NJ —PRINCETON UNIVERSITY, Library, Rare Books Dept, Princeton, 08544. Stephen Ferguson, Cur
Notes: The Valva Collection (gift of the Worcester, Massachusetts Public Library). Orchestral parts and conductors' scores for several thousand popular songs and musical effects used in movie houses and vaudeville from the turn of the century to the end of the silent movie era.

NY —BUFFALO & ERIE COUNTY PUBLIC LIBRARY, Music Dept, Lafayette Sq, Buffalo, 14203. Norma Jean Lamb, Head
Holdings: Cat
Notes: 76,400 bound vols of music and music literature. Complete works of the great composers, and historical editions. Orchestral scores and parts.

NY —NEW YORK PUBLIC LIBRARY, Music Div, 111 Amsterdam Ave, New York, 10023. Frank C Campbell, Chief
Notes: The 33,925 orchestral sets incl the Thomas Sherman Collection, the CBS Music Library Collection, and the Opera Collection.

NY —NEW YORK PUBLIC LIBRARY, General Library and Museum of the Performing Arts, 111 Amsterdam Ave, New York, 10023. George Louis Mayer, Coordinator; Kris Shuman, Music Specialist
Budget: ($15,000)
Notes: Circulating collections incl 6,115 scores; 28,000 orchestral sets. Incl Thomas Sherman Collection, CBS Music Library Collection, Opera Collection.

OH —CLEVELAND PUBLIC LIBRARY, Fine Arts and Special Collections Department, 325 Superior Ave, Cleveland, 44114. Alice

N Loranth, Head
Holdings: Vols 1750 Cat
Notes: Scores and parts ranging in size from theatre to symphony orchestra. Incl symphonies, concertos, incidental music, light classical and 3080 dance band orchestrations. Indexed. Available for circulation in Cuyahoga County area.

TX —UNIVERSITY OF TEXAS LIBRARIES, Music Library, PO Box P, Austin, 78712. Olga Buth, Librn
Holdings: Vols (21,862) Cat Phonorecords Audiotapes Microforms
Notes: Emphasis on symphony. Collection incl 36,462 scores, 3505 bound periodicals, 4506 microforms, 289 periodical subscriptions, 312 serials and monographs, 13,706 phonodiscs, and 922 phonotapes.

ORCHESTRA—HISTORY

IL —CHICAGO PUBLIC LIBRARY, Music Section, Fine Arts Division, 78 E Washington St, Chicago, 60602. Rosalinda I Hack, Fine Arts Division Chief; Richard C Schwegel, Head, Music Section
Notes: Many programs of US orchestras incl Chicago Symphony. Special collections incl Balaban & Katz Orchestral collection, 15,000 titles of arranged classical and dance band music from 1920-50s used at Chicago Theatre (primarily in storage).

MA —BOSTON UNIVERSITY, Mugar Memorial Library, Special Collections Dept, 771 Commonwealth Ave, Boston, 02215. Howard B Gotlieb, Dir
Notes: Personal collection of Arthur Fiedler, incl 6000 scores and sound recordings, manuscripts, photographs, memorabilia, library, and test pressings of Fiedler's performances.

ORCHIDACEAE see Orchids

ORCHIDS

CA —UNIVERSITY OF CALIFORNIA, IRVINE, Library, Irvine, 92664. Roger Berry, Dept Head
Notes: The Emma D Menninger extensive collection of 19th and 20th century information on horticulture, with special emphasis on orchids.

CA —SAN DIEGO STATE UNIVERSITY, Malcolm A Love Library, 5300 Campanile Dr, San Diego, 92182. D Dickinson, Univ Librn; Don L Bosseau, Dir
Holdings: Vols Journals Pamphlets Prints Cat
Notes: Reginald S Davis Orchid Collection. Includes books, journals, pamphlets, prints, catalogs about orchids throughout the world.

†CO —DENVER BOTANIC GARDENS, Helen Fowler Library, 909 York St, Denver, 80206. Solange G Gignac, Librn
Notes: Emphasis on Bromeliada Literature; horticulture; Colorado, Oregon, and Rocky Mountains Region botany; landscape architecture; juvenile horticultural and botanical literature. Incl over 5000 pamphlets on botany and horticulture; also, 197 watercolors of Colorado wildflowers by Emma Irvine, and 250 of Oregon by Lillian Hallock.

IN —UNIVERSITY OF NOTRE DAME, University Libraries, Notre Dame, 46556.
Notes: The collection (500 items) contains books on orchids, botany, gardening, horticulture and other related subjects. The collection is particularly rich in color plates of orchids in such works as Frederick Sander's *Reichenbachia* and periodicals such as *Lindenia, Orchid Album, and Orchid* Bulletin.

MA —HARVARD UNIVERSITY LIBRARY, Oakes Ames Orchid Library, University Herbarium, 22 Divinity Ave, Cambridge, 02138. Herman R Sweet, Librn
Holdings: Vols 4387 Cat Mss Microforms
Budget: $100

PA —LONGWOOD GARDENS, INC, Library, Kennett Square, 19348. Enola Jane N Teeter, Librn

ON —CIVIC GARDEN CENTRE LIBRARY, 777 Lawrence Ave E, Don Mills, M3C 1P2, Can. Pamela MacKenzie, Librn
Holdings: Vols 5000

ORDER OF RAILWAY CONDUCTORS

PA —PENNSYLVANIA STATE
UNIVERSITY, Fred Lewis Pattee Library,
Labor History Collection, University Park,
16802. Peter Gottlieb, Archivist
Holdings: Cat Mss
Notes: Trade union's archives, etc.

ORDERS, MONASTIC see Monasticism and Religious Orders

ORDERS OF KNIGHTHOOD AND CHIVALRY

CO —AMERICAN NUMISMATIC
ASSOCIATION LIBRARY, 818 N Cascade
Ave, Colorado Springs, 80903. Nancy W
Green, Librn
Holdings: Vols (20,000) Cat Slides
Notes: One of the largest numismatic
libraries, the collection incl books,
periodicals and auction catalogs on coins and
coin collecting, medals, tokens, military
orders and decorations, paper money,
primitive money, banks and banking, seals
and scarabs. ANA publishes a classified
subject catalog of its collection and is open
to the public for research and reference
services. Only members may check books
out.

DC —GEORGETOWN UNIVERSITY,
Library, Special Collections Div, 37 & O Sts
NW, Washington, 20057. George M
Barringer, Special Collections Librn;
Nicholas B Sheetz, Mss Librn
Holdings: Vols 800 Uncat Mss
Notes: Deals most extensively with
Continental orders, both secular and
ecclesiastical.

NY —AMERICAN NUMISMATIC SOCIETY
LIBRARY, Broadway between 155 & 156
Sts, New York, 10032. Francis D Campbell
Jr, Chief Librn
Holdings: Vols (50,000) Cat Mss Maps Pix
Slides 16mm Films Microforms
Budget: ($6000)
Notes: Incl materials devoted to coins,
medals, decorations, orders, tokens, paper
money, seals, heraldry. Aids materials incl
history, economic history, art history,
archaeology, inscriptions and a number of
encyclopedias and biographical dictionaries.
Dictionary card catalog provides access to
the materials: *Dictionary Catalogue of the
Library of the American Numismatic
Society.* (Boston: G K Hall, 1962). 6 vols
and vol listing the auction catalogs in our
collection; *First Supplement: 1962-1967;
Second Supplement: 1968-1972; Third
Supplement: 1973-1977* (Boston: G K Hall,
1967, 1973, 1978). Noncirculating.

RI —BROWN UNIVERSITY, John Hay
Library, Anne S K Brown Military
Collection, 20 Prospect St, Providence,
02912. Richard B Harrington, Cur
Holdings: Vols (40,000) Cat Mss Pix
Notes: The Anne S K Brown Military
Collection has been formed over the past
forty or more years by Mrs John Nicholas
Brown, now of Newport, and contains
approximately 40,000 volumes and 60,000
prints, drawings and watercolors as well as a
number of oil paintings and about 5000
miniature model soldiers. At its beginning
(and still today) the emphasis or focus of this
collection has been upon the history of, and
the accurate contemporary illustration of,
military and naval uniforms of all nations
from the early XVII century to the present.
In the course of time, however, the
collection has come to incl also a vast and
related amount of material on military and
naval history, military and naval arts and
tactics, wars, campaigns, ceremonies,
biography, portraits and caricatures of this
and earlier periods. It has been probably the
largest private collection of such a nature
inthe world, and it contains much ms and
graphic documentation which is unique. It
has been useful to numerous scholars and
historians, editors, filmmakers and publishers
for research and for illustrative material and
has also contributed to many museum

exhibitions. In 1982 the entire collection,
with its complete card catalog and subject
index, has been presented to Brown
University, where it is located in the John
Hay Library. Special requests are taken care
of by phone, mail and appointments with the
curator.

ORDNANCE

CA —AEROJET ORDNANCE &
MANUFACTURING CO, Library, 2521
Michelle Dr, Tustin, 92680. Norman J
Storrer, Database Manager
Holdings: Vols 7000 Cat
Budget: $50,000
Notes: Ordnance and weapons systems. Also
150,000 documents; 80,000 microforms.

KY —NAVAL ORDNANCE SYSTEMS
COMMAND, Technical Library, Code
50122, Louisville, 40214. Libby Miles, Librn
Holdings: Vols 5500 Cat Maps Microforms
Notes: Excel in Government specifications,
ordnance pamphlets, and all types of other
Government documents. Large service in
Industry Standard on film, some volumes.

NM —UNIVERSITY OF CALIFORNIA, Los
Alamos National Laboratory, Libraries, PO
Box 1663, MSP 362, Los Alamos, 87545. J
Arthur Freed, Head Librn
Holdings: Vols (800,000) Cat Films
Microforms
Budget: ($700,000)
Notes: Incl 500,000 classified and
unclassified reports. There are 25 branch
libraries and a central collection. The
Medical Library contains about 40,000 vols
in the areas of biomedical research.

NY —FORT ONTARIO HISTORIC SITE,
Oswego, 13126. Shelley B Weinreb, Historic
Site Mgr
Holdings: Vols (400) Cat Mss Maps Pix
Slides
Notes: Primary focus is upon military
activities at the mouth of the Oswego River
and the utilization of fortifications (Fort
Ontario, Fort Oswego, and Fort George) at
that point which served to control the outlet
of the traditional Mohawk-Oneida-Oswego
route to the Great Lakes. A limited number
of sources on fortification design, weapons,
uniforms, and military equipment are
included. Also incl 4000 slides and 400
pictures.

NY —US MILITARY ACADEMY LIBRARY,
West Point, 10996. Egon A Weiss, Librn
Holdings: Vols (100,000) Cat Mss Maps Pix
Slides Phonorecords Videotapes 16mm Films
Filmstrips Microforms
Notes: Described in *Subject Catalog of the
Military Art and Science Collection in the
Library of the US Military Academy*
(Greenwood Publishing Corp, 1969).

OK —US ARMY FIELD ARTILLERY
SCHOOL LIBRARY, Morris Swett Library,
Snow Hall, Fort Sill, 73503. Lester L Miller
Jr, Chief Librn
Holdings: Vols (265,958) Documents Pix
Maps Slides Microforms
Notes: Field artillery; artillery; ordnance;
military history; military science; weapons
and weapons systems; ammunition; ballistics;
missiles; Field Artillery unit histories;
military periodicals analytical index file
(VF). Incl US and foreign artillery; survey
data; photographs on army subjects.

†WA —WASHINGTON STATE
UNIVERSITY, Library, Manuscripts,
Archives & Special Collections, Pullman,
99164. John F Guido, Head
Holdings: Cat Mss Maps Pix
Notes: The Carl Parcher Russell papers, a
vast resource (24,916 items; 45 linear feet)
on American Indian and Western pioneer
activities and artifacts. Much on the fur
trade; pioneer life; mountain men and
trapping; wildlife; primitive life in detail.
Also the National Park Service, parks,
monuments, etc. Described in *Carl Parcher
Russell: An Indexed Register of His
Scholarly and Professional Papers, 1920-
1967, in the Washington State University
Library* (Pullman, 1970), 149 pp.

ON —FORT MALDEN NATIONAL
HISTORIC PARK, Library, 100 Laird Ave,
Box 38, Amherstburg, N9V 2Z2, Can. Sally

E Snyder, Librn
Holdings: Vols (400) Cat Mss Pix Slides
Notes: British and Canadian military life,
weaponry, uniforms, from about 1760 to
1860.

ORDNANCE, NAVAL

KY —NAVAL ORDNANCE SYSTEMS
COMMAND, Technical Library, Code
50122, Louisville, 40214. Libby Miles, Librn
Holdings: Vols 5500 Cat Maps Microforms
Notes: Excel in Government specifications,
ordnance pamphlets, and all types of other
Government documents. Large service in
Industry Standard on film, some volumes.

OREGON

OR —UNIVERSITY OF OREGON, Map
Library, Eugene, 97403. Peter L Stark, Map
Librarian
Holdings: Cat Maps Aerial Photographs
Budget: ($4000)
Notes: Incl 82 atlases, 52,000 maps, 330,000
aerial photographs. Atlases are fully
cataloged; maps are classified with shelf list
cards; aerial photographs are fully indexed.

OR —OREGON STATE LIBRARY, State
Library Bldg, Salem, 97310. Alden Moberg,
Oregoniana Consultant
Holdings: Vols 70,000 Cat Mss Maps Pix
Microforms
Budget: $11,635
Notes: Main body of the collection is
cataloged books, state and federal
documents, and periodicals. Also incl are
newspapers, maps, pamphlets and clippings,
mss, pictures, published books by Oregon
authors. Files of clippings, biographical
information, and pictures are kept for
Oregon authors. There is a card index for
newspaper articles and other selected
materials. Scope: Oregon territorial and state
history, government, economics, natural
resources, social conditions, biography,
authors.

WA —WASHINGTON STATE LIBRARY,
Washington/Northwest Rm, State Library
Bldg, Olympia, 98504. Nancy B Pryor,
Research Consultant
Holdings: Vols 8000 Cat Mss Maps Pix
Microforms
Notes: Mss, photographs and microfilm
largely limited to Washington territorial and
state materials as is the file of pamphlets and
newspaper clippings, which includes both
historical and current material. The book
collection incl works on the four Pacific
Northwest States, Alaska, and British
Columbia, and books by Washington
authors.

WA —UNIVERSITY OF WASHINGTON
LIBRARIES, Pacific Northwest Collection,
Seattle, 98195. Andrew F Johnson, Librn
Holdings: Vols (50,000) Cat Mss Maps Pix
Budget: ($12,000)
Notes: The Pacific Northwest Collection
contains printed materials documenting the
historic and contemporary life and culture of
the region in a broad range of subject areas.
The Pacific Northwest is defined as the
geographic region including Washington,
Oregon, Idaho, Montana, British Columbia,
Yukon Territory, and Alaska. Printed
materials including books, periodicals,
government documents, maps, weekly and
local regional newspapers, theses and
dissertations, as well as photographs and
architectural drawings are included in the
Pacific Northwest Collection. Photographic
works of over 200 photographers active in
the Pacific Northwest, Alaska, and the
Yukon Territory (Canada) during the period
1860-1930, including Asahel and Edward S
Curtis, Eric Hegg, and Clark Kinsey, are
represented in a print collection of more
than 300,000 images. The
architecturaldrawings collection includes
over 19,000 original plans, drawings,
sketches, renderings and blue prints
pertaining to the history of architecture and
urban planning and landscape gardening in
the Pacific Northwest ca 1880-1940. Areas
of particular strength are the holdings of
over 1100 published journals of Pacific

OREGON (cont.)

Northwest exploration expeditions, photographs of Northwest Coast Native Americans and of historic Seattle, newspapers issued within the Japanese-American relocation camps, 1942-1945, materials relating to the 1980 eruption of Mt St Helens, and Sanborne fire insurance maps for Washington. A unique feature of the Collection is the subject index to regional periodicals and local newspapers maintained by the PNW Collection staff; over 100 titles are currently indexed. G K Hall Company published a books catalog of the Pacific Northwest Collectionin 1973.

OREGON—GENEALOGY

OR —BAKER COUNTY PUBLIC LIBRARY, 2400 Resort St, Baker, 97814. Paul C Crouthamal, Librn
Holdings: Vols (1700) Cat Mss Maps Pix Microforms
Budget: ($2000)
Notes: Baker County, Oregon materials, historical and current, emphasizing genealogy, mining, agriculture and the people. Incl any fiction with Oregon as the locale. Local newspapers on microfilm, 1870-date, but incomplete for early years. 50 files on local plants, 1953-date, with separate catalog. Incl 300 maps.

OREGON—HISTORY

CA —AZUSA PACIFIC COLLEGE, Marshburn Memorial Library, Citrus & Alosta, Azusa, 91702. Edward Peterman, Librn
Holdings: Vols (6000) Uncat
Budget: ($30,000)
Notes: Significant holdings in the George E Fullerton Library of Californiana and Western Americana.

CA —UNIVERSITY OF CALIFORNIA, BERKELEY, Bancroft Library, Manuscripts Division, Berkeley, 94720. James D Hart, Dir
Holdings: Vols Mss Maps Pix Slides Microforms

Notes: Approxi. twelve million pieces, with primary emphasis on California, with a lesser emphasis on the other Pacific States, incl. Alaska and the Province of British Columbia. In general, the Bancroft Library seeks to acquire historical and biographical works and primary source materials, documenting: the development of a geographic area or political unit; man and his activities, and his impact on the land and on his institutions. Methodological and theoretical work and texts in the physical and biological sciences are not collected, as a rule; exceptions here are publications essential to the study of an area's historical development and those providing general background information. Hubert Howe Bancroft's own distinguished holdings, assembled 1860-1880, constitute the core of the collection. The Bancroft Library's collections are noncirculating. A. G. K. Hall catalog has been published. The Bolton Collection (146,000 pages of archival material) contains ms. materials for the history of the Pacific Coast and the Southwest, gathered by Herbert Eugene Bolton. There is a comprehensive key to the arrangement of the collection.

IN —INDIANA UNIVERSITY, Lilly Library, Seventh St, Bloomington, 47405. William R

Cagle, Librn
Holdings: // Cat Mss
Notes: 19th and early 20th century printings. Mss incl the papers of several 19th century Oregon political figures.

OR —ASTORIA PUBLIC LIBRARY, Astor Library, 450 Tenth St, Astoria, 97103. Bruce Berney, Dir
Holdings: Vols 500 Cat Pix Audiotapes Microforms Newspapers
Budget: $300
Notes: History of Lower Columbia River area. Incl file of local newspapers, 1873 to date. 1,000 photographs of Fort Stevens and other coastal defense facilities.

OR —BAKER COUNTY PUBLIC LIBRARY, 2400 Resort St, Baker, 97814. Paul C Crouthamal, Librn
Holdings: Vols (1700) Cat Mss Maps Pix Microforms
Budget: ($2000)
Notes: Baker County, Oregon materials, historical and current, emphasizing genealogy, mining, agriculture and the people. Incl any fiction with Oregon as the locale. Local newspapers on microfilm, 1870-date, but incomplete for early years. 50 files on local plants, 1953-date, with separate catalog. Incl 300 maps.

OR —LANE COUNTY MUSEUM, Library, 740 W 13 Ave, Eugene, 94701. Margret West, Cur of Special Collections
Holdings: Vols 250 Cat Mss Maps Pix Slides Audiotapes 16mm Films Microforms
Budget: $2000
Notes: Emphasis on Oregon and Lane County history. Collection of 10,000 photographs of Lane County; Kennell-Ellis photographers, 3500 commercial photographs of Eugene area, 1927-42. Also papers of John Whiteaker 1858-1944. Incl records (1887-1940) of Meyer & Kyle; William Kyle & Sons, Co; Florence, Oregon.

OR —UNIVERSITY OF OREGON LIBRARY, Special Collections Div, Eugene, 97403. Kenneth W Duckett, Curator
Holdings: Vols (35,000) Cat Mss Pix
Notes: Extensive mss collections of diaries and correspondence relating primarily to Oregon history and politics, files and drawings of primarily Oregon architects, and business and organization records.
Publication: Martin Schmitt, *Catalogue of Manuscripts in the University of Oregon Library.* (Eugene, Oregon: University of Oregon Books, 1971). The Oregon Collection contains ca 35,000 vols relating to Oregon history, life and letters, incl Oregon State documents.
See also entry under Architects

OR —SOUTHERN OREGON HISTORICAL SOCIETY, Jacksonville Museum Library, 206 N Fifth St, PO Box 480, Jacksonville, 97530. Richard H Engeman, Librn
Holdings: Vols 900 Cat Mss Maps Pix Slides Audiotapes 16mm Films Microforms
Budget: ($5200)
Notes: Emphasis on Southern Oregon history.

OR —WESTERN OREGON STATE COLLEGE, College Library, 345 N Monmouth St, Monmouth, 97361. Clarence Gorchels, Dir
Holdings: Vols 8500 Cat Mss Maps Pix Slides 16mm Films Filmstrips Microforms
Budget: $4000
Notes: The John C Higgins Memorial Collection on the history and culture of the Pacific Northwest.

OR —UMATILLA COUNTY LIBRARY, 214 N Main St, Pendleton, 97801. Barbara L Bishop, Dir
Holdings: Vols (675) Cat Mss Pix Audiotapes 16mm Films Microforms
Notes: Oregon history, especially Umatilla County. Lee Moorehouse photos (glass negatives)--1004 negatives, use restricted to professional photographers, copies may be made on premises only, also 3 rolls of microfilm of Moorehouse photos. Dr William McKay papers, 1830-1900, 14 folders, uncataloged, letters, coroner's reports (1885-86), miscellaneous papers, notes, memos and rough drafts, Army statements, receipts, accounts and business and personal receipts, accounts, 8 letters

written by Donald McKay, one letter written December 7, 1880, by William F Cody. Early brands of Eastern Oregon, 1/2 reel microfilm. Some cassette recordings of interviews with early pioneers.

OR —LIBRARY ASSOCIATION OF PORTLAND, 801 SW Tenth St, Portland, 97205. James Burghardt, Head Librn
Holdings: Vols 22,500 Cat Maps Microforms
Notes: Official publications of the State of Oregon and other governmental bodies within the State; books and pamphlets relating to Oregon and the Oregon Territory; periodicals; maps.

OR —OREGON STATE LIBRARY, State Library Bldg, Salem, 97310. Alden Moberg, Oregoniana Consultant
Holdings: Vols 70,000 Cat Mss Maps Pix Microforms
Budget: $11,635
Notes: Main body of the collection is cataloged books, state and federal documents, and periodicals. Also incl are newspapers, maps, pamphlets, and clippings, mss, pictures, published books by Oregon authors. Files of clippings, biographical information, and pictures are kept for Oregon authors. There is a card index for newspaper articles and other selected materials. Scope: Oregon territorial and state history, government, economics, natural resources, social conditions, biography, authors.

†WA —WASHINGTON STATE UNIVERSITY, Library, Manuscripts, Archives & Special Collections, Pullman, 99164. John F Guido, Head
Holdings: // Mss Maps Pix
Notes: Papers, 1821-1873, covering Father De Smet's early sojourns at Whitemarsh and St Louis, his founding of the Rocky Mountain Missions, his long service as Procurator and Socius of the Missouri Province, and his many travels. Correspondence with his family in Belgium, mss of his published journals, 2 small maps, sketches and engravings used to illustrate his books. Incl about 100 small pencil sketches by Father Nicholas Point depicting the 1841 journey from Westport to St Mary's Mission in the Bitterroot Valley. Described in *The Record*, 30 (1969) 6-40; and 32 (1971) 47-63.

WA —UNIVERSITY OF WASHINGTON LIBRARIES, Pacific Northwest Collection, Seattle, 98195. Andrew F Johnson, Librn
Holdings: Vols (50,000) Cat Maps Pix
Budget: ($12,000)
Notes: The Pacific Northwest Collection contains printed materials documenting the historic and contemporary life and culture of the region in a broad range of subject areas. The Pacific Northwest is defined as the geographic region including Washington, Oregon, Idaho, Montana, British Columbia, Yukon Territory, and Alaska. Printed materials including books, periodicals, government documents, maps, weekly and local regional newspapers, theses and dissertations, as well as photographs and architectural drawings are included in the Pacific Northwest Collection. Photographic works of over 200 photographers active in the Pacific Northwest, Alaska, and the Yukon Territory (Canada) during the period 1860-1930, including Asahel and Edward S Curtis, Eric Hegg, and Clark Kinsey, are represented in a print collection of more than 300,000 images. The architecturaldrawings collection includes over 19,000 original plans, drawings, sketches, renderings and blue prints pertaining to the history of architecture and urban planning and landscape gardening in the Pacific Northwest ca 1880-1940. Areas of particular strength are the holdings of over 1100 published journals of Pacific Northwest exploration expeditions, photographs of Northwest Coast Native Americans and of historic Seattle, newspapers issued within the Japanese-American relocation camps, 1942-1945, materials relating to the 1980 eruption of Mt St Helens, and Sanborne fire insurance maps for Washington. A unique feature of the Collection is the subject index to regional

OREGON—HISTORY (cont.)

periodicals and local newspapers maintained by the PNW Collection staff; over 100 titles are currently indexed. G K Hall Company published a books catalog of the Pacific Northwest Collectionin 1973.

OREGON—IMPRINTS

OR —UNIVERSITY OF OREGON LIBRARY, Special Collections Div, Eugene, 97403. Kenneth W Duckett, Curator
Holdings: Vols 500 Cat
Notes: An important collection of materials printed in Oregon during its "incunable" period, 1845-1870.

OREGON—PICTURES, ILLUSTRATIONS, ETC.

OR —LANE COUNTY MUSEUM, Library, 740 W 13 Ave, Eugene, 94701. Margret West, Cur of Special Collections
Holdings: Vols 250 Cat Mss Maps Pix Slides Audiotapes 16mm Films Microforms
Budget: $2000
Notes: Emphasis on Oregon and Lane County history. Collection of 10,000 photographs of Lane County; Kennell-Ellis photographers, 3500 commercial photographs of Eugene area, 1927-42. Also papers of John Whiteaker 1858-1944.

OREGON AUTHORS see Authors, Oregon

OREGON NEWSPAPERS see Newspapers, Oregon

OREGON PINE see Douglas Fir

O'REILLY, LEONORA, 1870-1927

MA —RADCLIFFE COLLEGE, Arthur & Elizabeth Schlesinger Library on the History of Women in America, 3 James St, Cambridge, 02138. Patricia Miller King, Dir; Eva Moseley, Cur of Mss
Holdings: Cat Mss
Notes: Correspondence, speeches, diaries, writings, etc of a factory worker, labor organizer, and social reformer who became vice-president of the New York Women's Trade Union League.

O'REILLY, PATRICK

CA —UNIVERSITY OF CALIFORNIA, SANTA CRUZ, University Library, Special Collections, Santa Cruz, 95064. Rita Bottoms, Special Collections Librn; Margaret Felts, South Pacific Collection Bibliographer
Notes: South Pacific Collection. Extensive Collection. His personal library and collected material on New Caledonia.

ORGAN

†DC —CATHOLIC UNIVERSITY OF AMERICA, Music Library, Washington, 20064. Betty Libbey, Head Music Library
Holdings: Cat Microforms
Notes: A large collection to support advanced degree study. Emphasis on church music, musicology, history and criticism, instrumental and vocal music, solo music for all voices, instruments, and musical forms.
OH —OHIO WESLEYAN UNIVERSITY, Delaware, 43015. John Reed, Librn
Holdings: Vols 700
Notes: Organ Historical Society of America Archives. Collection of organ building data and a master list of extant organs built before 1900. Collection will be moved to Pennsylvania in the near future.
OH —OBERLIN COLLEGE, Oberlin Conservatory of Music, Mary M Vial Library, Oberlin, 44074. John E Druesedow Jr, Dir
Holdings: Vols (75,000) Cat Phonorecords Audiotapes Filmstrips Microforms
Budget: ($60,000)
Notes: Special emphases; history and literature of the organ; music before 1700;

music since 1950; music education; opera; American music; chamber and solistic music.
Published catalog: *Mr and Mrs C W Best Collection of Autographs in the Mary M Vial Music Library of the Oberlin College Conservatory of Music* (Oberlin, Ohio: Oberlin College, 1967).

ORGAN, BARREL see Orchestrions

ORGAN MUSIC

CA —CLAREMONT COLLEGES, Honnold Library, Ninth & Dartmouth, Claremont, 91711. Tania Rizzo, Special Collections Dept Head
Holdings: Vols 500 // Uncat Mss Pix Slides
Notes: Joseph W Clokey Collection. 250 mss items, scores, opaques, transparencies and transcriptions of church choral music, often with orchestral and organ accompaniments; 195 printed copies of published works; 15 folders of correspondence with his publishers, miscellaneous notes and typescripts. Restricted use. No photocopies permitted. On deposit.
CA —OAKLAND PUBLIC LIBRARY, Art, Music and Recreation Section, 125 14 St, Oakland, 94612. Richard Colvig, Senior Librn
Holdings: Vols (5000) Cat Phonorecords Audiotapes
Budget: ($6700)
Notes: 10,000 scores, incl chamber music, instrumental music (piano and organ collections especially strong), minature scores, opera scores, songs and song collections; 30,000 octavos (anthems and choral music of all kinds); 5000 books about music; 8000 phonorecords; and audiocassettes.
CT —YALE UNIVERSITY, Music Library, 98 Wall St, New Haven, 06520. Harold E Samuel, Librn
Holdings: Vols (118,000) Cat Mss Pix Phonorecords Audiotapes
Notes: Manuscript and archive collection comprising over 500 individual musical mss as well as the personal papers and musical mss of such American musicians and composers as Charles Ives, Carl Ruggles, Haratio Parker, Quincy Porter, Richard Donovan and David Stanley Smith, Leo Ornstein, Armin Loos, Duane Davidson, Alonzo Elliott, John Rosamund Johnson, Hope Leroy Baumgartner, Gustave Stoeckel, Hershy Kay, Virgil Thomson, Kurt Weill, Lotte Lenya, Lowell Mason, Parker Bailey, Henry Gilbert, Seymour Shifrin, Lehman Engel, Ernest Trow Carter, and Alec Templeton. Extensive Paul Hindemith Collection. Also ca 35,000 pieces of American sheet music, both instrumental and vocal as well as extensive holdings of 17th & 18th century American hymn books.
†DC —CATHOLIC UNIVERSITY OF AMERICA, Music Library, Washington, 20064. Betty Libbey, Head Music Library
Holdings: Cat Microforms
Notes: A large collection to support advanced degree study. Emphasis on church music, musicology, history and criticism, instrumental and vocal music, solo music for all voices, instruments, and musical forms.
IN —INDIANA UNIVERSITY, Music Library, Bloomington, 47401. David E Fenske, Head
Holdings: Vols 400 // Cat Microforms
Notes: Keyboard music to 1800. See Dominique-Rene de Lerma, *An Annotated Catalog of Early Keyboard Literature Contained within the Apel Collection.* Bloomington (Indiana): The Music Library, Indiana University, 1973.
NJ —WESTMINSTER CHOIR COLLEGE, Talbott Library, Hamilton Ave at Walnut Lane, Princeton, 08540. Sherry L Vellucci, Acting Dir
Holdings: Vols (43,500) Cat Scores Periodicals Phonorecords Audiotapes Videotapes Microforms
Budget: ($30,000)
Notes: Talbott Library supports the curriculum of a music college which grants undergraduate and graduate degrees in church music, music education and music

performance (voice, piano, organ and choral conducting), with an emphasis on choral music. Incl 7000 phonorecords, 3500 titles in quantity of choral music, 30,000 single copies of choral music.
OH —CLEVELAND PUBLIC LIBRARY, Fine Arts and Special Collections Department, 325 Superior Ave, Cleveland, 44114. Alice N Loranth, Head
Holdings: Vols 2210 Cat
Notes: Bound scores, miscellaneous collections and sheet music. Indexed.
OH —OBERLIN COLLEGE, Oberlin Conservatory of Music, Mary M Vial Library, Oberlin, 44074. John E Druesedow Jr, Dir
Holdings: Vols (75,000) Cat Phonorecords Audiotapes Filmstrips Microforms
Budget: ($60,000)
Notes: Special emphases; history and literature of the organ; music before 1700; music since 1950; music education; opera; American music; chamber and solistic music.
Published catalog: *Mr and Mrs C W Best Collection of Autographs in the Mary M Vial Music Library of the Oberlin College Conservatory of Music* (Oberlin, Ohio: Oberlin College, 1967).

ORGAN TRANSPLANTS see Transplantation of Organs, Tissues, Etc.

ORGANIC CHEMISTRY see Chemistry, Organic

ORGANIC PHOTOMATERIAL see Photomaterial, Organic

ORGANIZATION, INTERNATIONAL see International Organization

ORGANIZATION FOR ECONOMIC COOPERATION AND DEVELOPMENT

CT —YALE UNIVERSITY, Social Science Library, Economic Growth Center Collection, 140 Prospect St, New Haven, 06520. Billie I Salter, Librn
Holdings: Microforms

ORGANIZATION OF AMERICAN STATES (OAS)

DC —LIBRARY OF CONGRESS, General Reading Rooms Division, Microform Reading Room, Washington, 20540.
Holdings: Cat Mss Maps Pix Microforms
Notes: Microform materials only in this LC Division. Works of individual authors; holdings of collections; archival records, etc, press releases and translations, etc.
†MA —BOSTON PUBLIC LIBRARY, Copley Sq, Boston, 02117.
Holdings: Cat Microforms
Notes: Microform Publication by NCR Microcard Editions. Organization of American States Documents.
NY —NEW YORK STATE LIBRARY, State Education Bldg Annex, Washington Ave, Albany, 12224.
Holdings: Cat Microforms
Notes: Official depository of New York State publications; regional depository of US documents, also in microfilm; depository for Canadian government documents; strong collections of state documents, New York City documents; British sessional papers; also League of Nations, United Nations, OAS documents. Extensive holdings of other domestic and foreign publications. Congressional serial set, incl hearings (1946-date).
NY —NEW YORK PUBLIC LIBRARY, Research Libraries, Economic & Public Affairs Div, Fifth Ave & 42 St, New York, 10018. Edward DiRoma, Chief
Holdings: Vols (1,500,000) Cat Microforms
PA —UNIVERSITY OF PITTSBURGH, Hillman Library, Pittsburgh, 15260. Glenora E Rossell, Head
Holdings: Vols 2050 Cat Microforms
Notes: A collection of books and documents on Inter-American relations, with emphasis on the relations between the US and Mexico,

ORGANIZATION OF AMERICAN STATES (OAS) (cont.)

Peru, Chile, Guatemala, Dominican Republic and Cuba. It covers international affairs, boundary problems, inter-American politics.
TX —NORTH TEXAS STATE UNIVERSITY, Government Documents Dept, NT Station Box 5188, Denton, 76203. Melody Kelley, Librn
Notes: 2000 documents regarding Organization of American States (OAS) in Document Section of main library.

ORGANIZATION OF PETROLEUM EXPORTING COUNTRIES (OPEC)

MA —HARVARD UNIVERSITY, Center for Middle Eastern Studies, Library, Coolidge Hall, 1737 Cambridge St, Cambridge, 02138. Barbara Mitchell, Librn
Holdings: Vols (5000) Periodicals
Notes: Some history of countries of the Middle East; increasingly emphasizes culture and politics of the current Middle Eastern area. Special collection of Energy Economics Research. Library currently receives 15 periodical titles.

ORGANIZATIONAL DEVELOPMENT

CA —UNIVERSITY OF CALIFORNIA, LOS ANGELES, Graduate School of Management Library, UCLA Campus, Los Angeles, 90024. Robert Bellanti, Head Librn
Holdings: Vols (128,000) Cat Mss Microforms
Notes: The
MA —HARVARD UNIVERSITY, Graduate School of Business Administration, Baker Library, Soldiers Field, Boston, 02163. Mary V Chatfield, Librn; Florence Bartoshesky, Cur of Manuscripts and Archives
Notes: Organizations, organizational behavior and planning.
NY —CORNELL UNIVERSITY, New York State School of Industrial & Labor Relations, Martin P Catherwood Library, Ives Hall, Ithaca, 14853. Shirley F Harper, Dir
Notes: Collection incl approx 1000 periodicals and union journals currently received, and ms collections of labor unions, arbitrators, and scholars. 6000 linear ft. *Library Catalog of the New York State School of Industrial and Labor Relations* (Boston: G K Hall, 1967), 12 volumes; *Cumulation of the Library Catalog Supplements of the New York State School of Industrial and Labor Relations* (Boston: G K Hall, 1976), 8 volumes.

ORGANIZATIONS see Associations, Institutions, Etc.

ORGANIZATIONS, INTERNATIONAL see International Agencies

ORGANOMETALLIC COMPOUNDS

†DC —CATHOLIC UNIVERSITY OFF AMERICA, Nursing & Biology Library, Washington, 20064. N L Powell, Head
Holdings: Vols (16,000) Cat
Notes: Espec strong in organometallic, Moessbauer and physical chemistry.
IL —ARGONNE NATIONAL LABORATORY, Chemistry Branch Library, 9700 S Cass Ave, Argonne, 60439. Betty Guttman, Librn
Notes: Organo-metallic compounds. Incl 20, 000 vols monographs, 190 current journals. Materials may be used by the public in the library by prior arrangement. Photocopies may be supplied for interlibrary loan, for which a processing and handling charge is made.
NY —UNIVERSITY OF ROCHESTER, Carlson Library, Hutchison Hall, River Campus, Rochester, 14627. Michael W Poulin, Librn
Holdings: Vols (48,720) Cat Microforms
Notes: Strong collection in the field and related areas.

ORGASM

IN —INDIANA UNIVERSITY, Institute for Sex Research Library, 416 Morrison Hall,
Bloomington, 47401. Douglas Freeman, Collections and Services Librn; Joan Brewer, Information Services Librn
Holdings: Vols (62,000) Cat Mss Pix Microforms
See also entry under Sex.

ORGONE ENERGY see Orgonomy

ORGONOMY

AZ —WORLD UNIVERSITY, Library, 711 E Blacklidge Dr, Tucson, 85719. Howard John Zitko, Cur
Holdings: Vols (15,000) Cat Mss Maps Audiotapes
Notes: Collection concerns what are generally called the "frontier sciences." No interlibrary loan.

ORIENT AND OCCIDENT see East and West

ORIENT QUESTION, 1877-1878

DC —LIBRARY OF CONGRESS, Washington, 20540.
Notes: Project of a consortium to microfilm about 200,000 pp of material on Great Britain, France, Russia, and Prussia, for the period 1848-1918 in the ms and documentary collections of the Austrian State Archives. The collection will incl among others, documents on the Austro-Prussian War of 1866, the treaty negotiations between France and Italy in 1868-1870, the Orient Question of 1877-1878, the persecution of Jews in Russia in 1882, the Congo Conference in Berlin, 1884-1887 and the British-Portuguese conflict in East Africa, 1889-1891. Copies are available at LC, the Center for Research Libraries, the Hampshire Inter-Library Center, and the libraries of Boston College, Yale, Harvard, Duke, Stanford and the University of Virginia.

ORIENTAL ANTIQUITIES

MO —SCHOOL OF THE OZARKS, Lois Brownell Research Library, Ralph Foster Museum, Point Lookout, 65726. Robert Esworthy, Librn
Holdings: Vols (1300) Cat
Notes: Oriental antiques and art.
NY —BUFFALO MUSEUM OF SCIENCE, Buffalo Society of Natural Sciences, Research Library, Humboldt Park, Buffalo, 14211. Marcia T Morrison, Chief Librn
Holdings: Vols 900 Cat Mss Pix
Notes: The Elizabeth W Hamlin Oriental Library of Art and Archaeology. Incl 75 scrolls.
OH —CLEVELAND PUBLIC LIBRARY, Fine Arts and Special Collections Department, 325 Superior Ave, Cleveland, 44114. Alice N Loranth, Head
Holdings: Vols (54,000) Cat Mss Maps Microforms
Notes: Research and reference collection on Orientalia contains scholarly books, periodicals, and serials in Western and in the vernacular languages of Asia, Africa, Pacific Ocean, Australia and native cultures of Latin America. Incl all aspects of Oriental civilization: archaeology, history, language, literature, philology, philosophy and religion prior to the impact of Western influence. (Exception: History of British India extended to 1859). Strong holdings in scholarly editions of classic texts, their versions and translations. Some museum objects.
See also entries under Egyptology; Near East.

ORIENTAL ART see Art, Oriental

ORIENTAL DANCE

NY —NEW YORK PUBLIC LIBRARY, Performing Arts Research Center, Dance Collection, 111 Amsterdam Ave, New York, 10023. Genevieve Oswald, Cur
Holdings: Vols (40,000) Cat Mss Pix
Audiotapes Videotapes 16mm Films Microforms
Budget: ($9280)
See also entry under Asian Dance

ORIENTAL FOLKLORE see Folklore, Oriental

ORIENTAL LANGUAGES AND LITERATURES

AZ —UNIVERSITY OF ARIZONA, Library, Oriental Studies Collection, Tucson, 85721. Mary J McWhorter, Actg Head Librn
Holdings: Vols (95,000) Cat Microforms
Budget: ($30,000)
Notes: The Oriental Studies Collection houses Chinese, Japanese, Arabic, Persian, Hindu, Urdu, Turkish, and other Oriental language books, periodicals and newspapers. The collection incl a broad range of subject areas with emphasis on reference and bibliography, history, literature, linguistics, social sciences, Chinese and Japanese classics, and Oriental art. The collection is a depository library for Library of Congress PL-480 programs for Middle East and South Asian languages. Also incl is a section of Western language reference and bibliographic sources. The Oriental Studies Collection maintains its own combined author-title-subject catalogs for each language represented in the collection. Cards for each item are also filed in the Central Reference area of the Main Library.
CA —UNIVERSITY OF CALIFORNIA, BERKELEY, University Library, East Asiatic Library, Room 208, Durant Hall, Berkeley, 94720. Donald Shively, Head
Holdings: Vols (500,000) Cat Mss Maps Pix Microforms
Notes: Library materials are mainly on humanities and social sciences covering the ancient and the modern periods and selectively in natural sciences; substantial in various fields but particularly notable in literary works, fine arts, rare books, folklore, wood-block printed editions, Chinese stone rubbings, Japanese old maps, first editions of Meiji literature, Buddhist texts, and Tibetan xylographs. Estimated 160,000 vols in Chinese, 150,000 vols in Japanese, 14,000 vols in Korean, the remainder in Manchu, Mongol or Tibetan.
CA —CLAREMONT COLLEGES, Honnold Library, Ninth & Dartmouth, Claremont, 91711. Tania Rizzo, Special Collections Dept Head
Holdings: Vols 150 // Uncat
Notes: Grammars and dictionaries (some dual-language with French or Dutch) of mainly Malayo-Polynesian, some Sino-Tibetan, and other languages, dating from the late 19th to mid-20th centuries. Checklisted.
CT —TRINITY COLLEGE LIBRARY, 300 Summit St, Hartford, 06106. Ralph S Emerick, Librn
Holdings: Cat
Notes: Moore Collection of the Far East.
CT —YALE UNIVERSITY, American Oriental Society Library, 120 High St, New Haven, 06520. Rutherford B Rogers, Librarian
Holdings: Vols 22,000 Cat Mss
Notes: On deposit.
DC —LIBRARY OF CONGRESS, African and Middle Eastern Division, Washington, 20540.
Holdings: Cat Mss Microforms
Notes: Orientalia. The Orientalia Division contains over 1,400,000 vols in Oriental languages. Chinese: more than 422,000 vols, espec strong in local histories and Ch'ing (1644-1911) period material. Japanese: over 574,000 vols, espec strong in economics, statistics, history, literature; 12,000 government, learned society, and university periodicals titles, espec strong in science, technology, and social sciences. Korean: 56, 000 vols, espec strong in social sciences and modern history. Hebraic: about 109,000 vols in Hebrew, Yiddish, Judeo-Arabic, Judeo-Persian, Ladino, Syriac, Ethiopic, espec strong in biblical subjects, responsa literature and socio-political aspects. Near Eastern:

ORIENTAL LANGUAGES AND LITERATURES (cont.)

over 104,000 vols, Arabic, Armenian, Persian, Turkish, and fringe languages. Special subject strength Muslim theology, history and literature. Southern Asian: over 137,000 vols,literature of South and Southeast Asia from Pakistan to Philippines. Oriental maps are in the custody of Library's Geography & Map Division; pictorial materials, slides, etc, are in the custody of Prints & Photographs Division.

IL —UNIVERSITY OF ILLINOIS, URBANA/CHAMPAIGN, Asian Library, Urbana, 61801. William S Wong, Asian Librn
Holdings: Vols 82,000 Cat
Notes: South and West Asian Collection. Primarily a collection of South Asian and Middle Eastern language materials.

MD —JOHNS HOPKINS UNIVERSITY, Milton S Eisenhower Library, Charles & 34 Sts, Baltimore, 21218. Ann S Gwyn, Assistant Dir for Special Collections
Holdings: Vols 4000 Cat
Notes: The August Dillmann Collection of Oriental Literature. Very strong and complete collection of Ethiopic until 1900. Dillmann was the greatest scholar in his field. Catalog published at Johns Hopkins. Also contains Biblical philology.

NY —HEMPSTEAD PUBLIC LIBRARY, Foreign Language Collection, 115 Nichols Court, Hempstead, 11550. Irene A Duszkiewicz, Dir
Notes: Mainly French, German, Italian, Spanish, Polish, Yiddish, Hebrew. Holdings in other languages, including Asian.

NY —NEW YORK PUBLIC LIBRARY, Oriental Div, Fifth Ave & 42 St, New York, 10018. E Christian Filstrup, Chief
Holdings: Cat Mss Microforms
Budget: ($56,455)
Notes: Described in *Dictionary Catalog of the Oriental Collection*, The Research Libraries of the New York Public Library, 1960, 16 vols, and *First Supplement*, 1976, 8 vols (144,000 cards). This catalog incl 318,000 entries for works in about 100 languages of the East, and all works in Western languages on Oriental subjects. The Oriental Collection numbers about 120,000 vols; its Arabic and Indic holdings and those on ancient Egypt and the ancient Near East are among the largest in the US. There is also a collection of 30,000 vols of PL 480 material from Egypt, Pakistan, and India to which there is main entry access, but which is not incorporated into the dictionary catalog. Other outstanding features of the Oriental Collection incl extensive holdings of Japanese technical and scientific periodicals; a unique collection of linguistic works, grammars, anddictionaries; and unusually good coverage of the field of Oriental religions and philosophies. The catalog contains numerous subject references to periodical articles in all languages. All entries are arranged alphabetically according to the Roman alphabet.

NY —NEW YORK PUBLIC LIBRARY, Donnell Foreign Language Library, 20 W 53 St, New York, 10019. Bosiljka Stevanovic, Supvr Librn
Notes: Listings under each separate language.

NY —US MILITARY ACADEMY LIBRARY, Special Collections Division, West Point, 10996. Angela H Kao, Orientalia Librn
Notes: Primarily military and general history of China, incl biographies of Chinese military leaders of different political backgrounds from the early years of the Chinese Republic to recent times. Books as well as periodicals are mostly in Chinese with a few additional works in English and Japanese. Described in *Catalog of the Orientalia Collection of the USMA Library, West Point, 1978.*

OH —CLEVELAND PUBLIC LIBRARY, Fine Arts and Special Collections Department, 325 Superior Ave, Cleveland, 44114. Alice N Loranth, Head
Holdings: Vols (54,400) Cat Mss Maps

Microforms
Notes: Research and reference collection on Orientalia contains scholarly books, periodicals and serials in Western and in the vernacular languages of Asia, Africa, Pacific Ocean, Australia and native cultures of Latin America. Incl all aspects of Oriental civilization: archaeology, history, language, literature, philology, philosophy and religion prior to the impact of Western influence. (Exception: History of British India extended to 1859). Strong holdings in scholarly editions of classic texts, their versions and translations. Some museum objects.
See also entry under Folklore

OR —UNIVERSITY OF OREGON LIBRARY, Social Science Dept, Eugene, 97403. Holway R Jones, Head Dept Librn
Holdings: Vols (40,000) Cat
Budget: ($39,300)
Notes: In Chinese and Japanese. The collection covers all periods, with major exphasis on modern period. Subject areas incl novel, fiction, poetry, essay, language, and drama. Extensive holdings on modern literature of China and Japan. Strong collection of resources on the White Birch School (Shirakabaha) literature.

RI —BROWN UNIVERSITY, John Hay Library, 20 Prospect St, Providence, 02912. Mark N Brown, Cur Mss
Holdings: Vols (74,000) Cat Microforms
Budget: ($10,000)
Notes: East Asia Collection. The primary focus is on Chinese studies with a small segment of approx 700 vols devoted to Japanese studies. Major subject areas, in descending order of strength, are: literature, incl classics, history, geography, social sciences, philosophy and religion, fine arts, science and technolgoy. This incl the personal collection (20,000 vols) formed by Harvard University Sinologist Dr Charles Sidney Gardner, which is especially rich in materials relating to the Ch'ing Dynasty (1644-1912). In addition to books, there are 500 reels of microfilm, plus runs of 8 Chinese newspapers and 26 current Chinese periodicals. Also, Indic Manuscripts Collection--53 codices written in Burmese, Cambodian, Telugu, Skandhas, Bengali, and Sinhalese script on palm leaves and encased within wood covers, some lacquered. Subjects include: Buddhist canon, Pali grammar andlexicons, epics, dance drama, and a treatise on midwifery. Recorded in *A Census of Indic Manuscripts in the United States and Canada* compiled by Horace I Poleman (New Haven: American Oriental Society, 1938).

ORIENTAL MANUSCRIPTS see Manuscripts, Oriental

ORIENTAL MEDICINE see Medicine, Oriental

ORIENTAL RELIGIONS see Religion, Oriental

ORIENTAL RUGS see Rugs, Oriental

ORIENTAL SCROLLS see Scrolls, Oriental

ORIENTALIA

CT —YALE UNIVERSITY, American Oriental Society Library, 120 High St, New Haven, 06520. Rutherford B Rogers, Librarian
Holdings: Vols 22,000 Cat Mss
Notes: On deposit.

NY —NEW YORK PUBLIC LIBRARY, Oriental Div, Fifth Ave & 42 St, New York, 10018. E Christian Filstrup, Chief
Holdings: Cat Mss Microforms
Notes: Published catalog of holdings.

ORIENTATION (STUDENTS) see Students

ORIENTATION (TEACHERS) see Teachers, Training of

ORIGAMI

†CT —UNIVERSITY OF CONNECTICUT LIBRARY, Special Collections Dept, Storrs,

06268. Richard H Schimmelpfeng, Dir of Special Collections
Notes: Good and unusual collection.

ORIGIN OF LIFE see Life—Origin

ORNAMENT see Decoration and Ornament

ORNAMENTAL PLANTS see Plants, Ornamental

ORNITHOLOGICAL PERIODICALS see Periodicals, Ornithological

ORNITHOLOGY

CA —LOS ANGELES PUBLIC LIBRARY, Science & Technology Dept, 630 W Fifth St, Los Angeles, 90071. Billie M Connor, Dept Head
Holdings: Vols 2250 Cat
Notes: Extensive collection of handbooks, identification manuals and monographs. Many classical illustrated works, materials on domesticated birds.

CA —UNIVERSITY OF CALIFORNIA, LOS ANGELES, Biomedical Library, Center for the Health Sciences, Los Angeles, 90024. Alison Bunting, Acting Biomedical Librn; Victoria Steele, Head, History & Special Collections Div
Holdings: Vols (4000) Cat
Notes: Incl the Donald R Dickey Library of Vertebrate Zoology. Classics of ornithology and mammalogy and related materials.

CA —WESTERN FOUNDATION OF VERTEBRATE ZOOLOGY, Library, 1100 Glendon Ave, Los Angeles, 90024. Lloyd F Kiff, Dir
Holdings: Vols (4000) Uncat Mss Pix Slides 16mm Films
Budget: ($10,000)
Notes: This is probably the third largest collection on birds in the Western US. It incl the combined resources of 10 former private libraries on this topic, plus additions made by us during the past 20 years. There is special emphasis on oology, or the study of bird eggs. The collection is freely available for use by any interested researcher.

CA —CALIFORNIA ACADEMY OF SCIENCES, J W Mailliard Jr Library, Golden Gate Park, San Francisco, 94118. Ray Brian, Librn
Notes: Downs No 2160.

†CA —STANFORD UNIVERSITY LIBRARIES, Stanford, 94305.
Notes: In collection of English and American Literature.

CT —TRINITY COLLEGE LIBRARY, Watkinson Library, 300 Summit St, Hartford, 06106. Jeffrey Kaimowitz, Cur
Holdings: Vols (7000) Cat
Notes: Incl the Ostrom Enders and Gurdon Russell Collections of Ornithology.

CT —YALE UNIVERSITY, Ornithology Library, Peabody Museum of Natural History, 170 Whitney Ave, New Haven, 06520. Eleanor Stickney, Senior Museum Asst
Holdings: Vols 8200 Cat Slides
Notes: The William R Coe Collection is held in this library. There is also a reprint collection of 10,000. Incl 120 journals.

†CT —UNIVERSITY OF CONNECTICUT LIBRARY, Special Collections Dept, Storrs, 06268. Richard H Schimmelpfeng, Dir of Special Collections

DE —UNIVERSITY OF DELAWARE, Agriculture Library, 2 Townsend Hall, Newark, 19717. Frederick Getze, Assoc Librn
Holdings: Vols (32,500) Cat Pix Microforms
Notes: Strong in entomology and ornamental horticulture. Extensive collection of state agriculture documents for each US state and Puerto Rico. Library subscribes to 600 serials (English and foreign).

DC —NATIONAL GEOGRAPHIC SOCIETY, Library, 1146 16th St NW, Washington, 20036. Susan Fifer Canby, Dir
Holdings: Vols (63,000) Cat Mss Maps Pix
Notes: Material concerning land, sea, and space exploration--past and present. All

ORNITHOLOGY (cont.)

fields of anthropology, natural history, geography, etc.

DC —SMITHSONIAN INSTITUTION, Archives Div, Washington, 20560. William W Moss, Archivist
Holdings: Cat Mss Pix
Notes: The Archives holds the official records of the National Museum of Natural History's Division of Birds and some of the papers of associated ornithologists Spencer F Baird, Robert Ridgway, and Alexander Wetmore, in addition to the records of the American Ornithologists' Union.
See also entries under Baird, Spencer F; Wetmore, Alexander; Natural History

DC —SMITHSONIAN INSTITUTION LIBRARIES, Natural History Branch, Washington, 20560. Sylvia Churgin, Chief Librn
Holdings: Vols 4600 Cat Maps Pix Slides

FL —EVERGLADES NATIONAL PARK, South Florida Research Center, PO Box 279, Homestead, 33030. Gary Hendrix, Librn
Holdings: Vols (5500) Cat Microforms
Notes: Emphasis on South Florida, birds, water problems. This is a special reference collection maintained for the Park Staff only. Noncirculating. ILL available.

HI —BERNICE P BISHOP MUSEUM, Library, PO Box 19000-A, Honolulu, 96819. Cynthia Timberlake, Librn
Holdings: Vols (90,000) Cat Mss Maps Pix Slides Microforms
Budget: ($30,000)
Notes: Only American library devoted exclusively to the Pacific region. Collection reflects historical and contemporary research emphases of Bishop Museum; ie the natural and cultural history of the Pacific. Areas of concentration incl archaeology, ethnology, linguistics, voyages and explorations, history, vertebrate and invertebrate zoology, botany and museology. Strong special collections incl photographs, mss and archives, maps and art. Publications: Quarterly "Additions to the Catalog," Dictionary Catalog of the Library (9 vols and 2 suppl; Boston: G K Hall, 1964-69).

IL —FIELD MUSEUM OF NATURAL HISTORY, Edward E Ayer Ornithology Library Collection, Roosevelt Rd & Lake Shore Dr, Chicago, 60605. W Peyton Fawcett, Librn
Holdings: Vols 3500 Cat
Notes: John T Zimmer's concluding note: "In the works cataloged...there are, approximately, 50,995 plates of birds (39,888 in colors and 11,107 plain), 39,347 text figures of ornithological subjects (987 in colors and 38,360 plain), and 1981 plates of birds' eggs (1914 in colors and 67 plain)." Downs 2333.

IA —IOWA STATE UNIVERSITY, Library, Ames, 50011. Warren B Kuhn, Dean of Library Services
Holdings: Cat
Notes: Extensive serial holdings supplement this strong collection.

LA —LOUISIANA STATE UNIVERSITY, Troy H Middleton Library, E A McIlhenny Natural History Collection, Baton Rouge, 70803. Kathryn N Morgan, Cur
Holdings: Vols (6000) Maps Pix
Notes: Collection of rare and valuable works on natural history with emphasis on ornithology and botany. Noncirculating collection open to researchers and visitors.

LA —LOUISIANA STATE UNIVERSITY, Troy H Middleton Library, Louisiana Room, Baton Rouge, 70803. Evangeline Mills Lynch, Head Librn; Ruth Murray, Associate Librn
Holdings: Vols (33,500) Cat Maps VF
Notes: Louisiana Collection of history, description and travel, biography, agriculture, literature, politics and government, folklore, anthropology, geography, geology, education, language, music and natural history. Especially large subject collections may be found on Louisiana, the history of the lower Mississippi Valley, Abraham Lincoln, Romance languages and literatures, sugar

culture and technology, Southern history, petroleum engineering, plant pathology, micropaleontology, ornithology, and various aspects of crawfish life, biology and culture. Complete depository of Louisiana State Documents; extensive newspapers clipping files; separate card catalog; items listed in Louisiana Union Catalog; restricted use (research and reference). Incl both materials about Louisiana and by Louisianians without regard to subject. LSU Press Collection(preservation copy of each title kept for exhibit purposes only). LSU theses and dissertations from 1900-date. LSU Faculty Collection. Also, 1300 maps, 104 VF drawers, 250 boxes of uncataloged pamphlets.

LA —R W NORTON ART GALLERY, Library, 4747 Creswell Ave, Shreveport, 71106. Jerry M Bloomer, Librn
Holdings: Cat
Notes: Many rare works, such as Audubon's elephant folio ed of The Birds of America, (also the octavo edition), Catesby, John Gould (a complete collection), Alexander Wilson and Rex Brasher.

ME —BOWDOIN COLLEGE, Library, Brunswick, 04011. Dianne M Gutscher, Cur of Special Collections
Holdings: Vols Mss Pix
Notes: The Alfred Otto Gross collection consists of several thousand pieces of mss, incl correspondence, journals, notes, etc, most of which relate to Professor Gross' career as an ornithologist on the Bowdoin College faculty. His extensive collection of photographs of birds and nesting sites, as well as his books, are also part of the collection.
See also entry under Natural History

ME —BATES COLLEGE, George & Helen Ladd Library, Special Collections, Bardwell St, Lewiston, 04240. Mary Riley, Special Collections Librn
Holdings: Vols 602// Cat
Notes: Ornithological and natural history books from the collections of Bates Professor Jonathan Young Stanton, 1834-1918.

MD —JOHNS HOPKINS UNIVERSITY, Milton S Eisenhower Library, Special Collections, John Work Garrett Library, 4545 N Charles St, Baltimore, 21210. Jane Katz, Garrett Librn
Holdings: Vols Cat Mss Maps
Notes: The John Work Garrett Library incl ornithology and natural history (complete set of Gould's Birds).

MA —UNIVERSITY OF MASSACHUSETTS AT AMHERST, Library, Amherst, 01003. Siegfried Feller, Assoc Dir for Collection Development
Holdings: Cat
Notes: Incl the Arthur Cleveland Bent Ornithology Collection.

MA —HARVARD UNIVERSITY, Museum of Comparative Zoology, Library, 26 Oxford St, Cambridge, 02138. Eva S Jonas, Librn
Holdings: Cat Mss Pix Microforms

†MA —WILLIAMS COLLEGE, Chapin Library of Rare Books, PO Box 426, Williamstown, 01267. Robert L Volz, Custodian
Holdings: Vols 220 Cat
Budget: $3500
Notes: Comprehensive collection of illustrated bird books. 17th-20th centuries.

MI —UNIVERSITY OF MICHIGAN, Museums Library, Ann Arbor, 48109. Patricia B Yocum, Librn
Holdings: Vols 11,000 Cat

MN —MINNEAPOLIS PUBLIC LIBRARY & INFORMATION CENTER, 300 Nicollet Mall, Minneapolis, 55401. Richard J Hofstad, Athenaeum Librn
Holdings: Vols 700 Cat Pix
Notes: Incl rare books in natural history. Emphasis on botany and ornithology.

NY —NEW YORK ZOOLOGICAL SOCIETY LIBRARY, Bronx Zoo, Bronx, 10460. Steven P Johnson, Archivist and Librn
Holdings: Vols (6000) Cat Mss
Budget: ($50,000)
Notes: Collection consists primarily of journals in captive management of animals, vertebrate zoology, and veterinary medicine. Primarily intended for the scientific staff, the

collection is open to the public on a noncirculating basis, by appointment, (212) 220-6874.

NY —CORNELL UNIVERSITY LIBRARIES, Albert R Mann Library, Ithaca, 14853. Henry T Murphy, Librn
Holdings: Vols 4000 Cat Pix Microforms
Notes: There are about 1500 additional vols in the Ornithology Library, a branch of the Mann Library, at the Cornell Laboratory of Ornithology. About 75 percent of these are duplicates of the Mann Library collection.

NY —CORNELL UNIVERSITY LIBRARIES, Collection of Regional History, Dept of Manuscripts and Univ Archives, Ithaca, 14853.
Notes: Incl records, 1934-52; coursework, recommendations, reports of summer field work made by students and their employers, and many student records.

NY —AMERICAN MUSEUM OF NATURAL HISTORY, Library Services Dept, Central Park W & 79th St, New York, 10024. Nina J Root, Chairwoman; Mary Genett, Asst Librn for Reference Services
Holdings: Vols (385,000) Cat Mss Maps Pix Slides Microforms
Notes: Nearly all collections are outstanding for depth of coverage and international range. Early and historic works, rare books, colored illustrations, and relevant serial publications supplement the modern scientific publications necessary to the researches of the scientific staff and the work of the educational division. Open to the public.

OH —OHIO HISTORICAL SOCIETY, Archives Library Division, 1982 Velma Ave, Columbus, 43211. Dennis East, Division Chief
Holdings: Vols 800 Cat
Notes: Collection based on the William L Dawson Library; more than local coverage; good for scarce periodicals. Supports Natural History Division of the Society.

PA —ACADEMY OF NATURAL SCIENCES LIBRARY, 19 Benjamin Franklin Parkway, Philadelphia, 19103.
Holdings: Vols (180,000) Cat Mss Maps Pix Slides Microforms
Notes: Incl (250,000) mss. Described in Academy of Natural Sciences of Philadelphia: Catalog (Boston: G K Hall, 1972); Guide to the Manuscript Collections in the Academy of Natural Sciences of Philadelphia, by Venia T Phillips (Philadelphia: Academy of Natural Sciences, 1963).

PA —ZOOLOGICAL SOCIETY OF PHILADELPHIA, Library, 34 & Girard Ave, Philadelphia, 19104. Alyssa N Scheuermann, Librn
Holdings: Vols (500) Cat
Notes: Photocopying with permission.

PA —CARNEGIE LIBRARY OF PITTSBURGH, Science & Technology Dept, 4400 Forbes Ave, Pittsburgh, 15213. Catherine M Brosky, Dept Head
Holdings: Vols (380,000) Cat Maps Microforms
Budget: ($240,000)
Notes: Incl both modern and classic works. Indexes, bibliographies, and standard reference books. Many journals and society publications complete from the beginning.

SC —COLLEGE OF CHARLESTON LIBRARY, Special Collections Dept, Charleston, 29401.
Notes: 42 illustrations by John Henry Dick for Marjory Bartlett Sanger's World of the Great White Heron (1967); biographical material of Wendell Mitchel Levi; correspondence concerning pigeons and camellias; notes, photographs, mss, typescripts, and galleys of published works; and other materials relating to pigeons and camellias.

SC —UNIVERSITY OF SOUTH CAROLINA, Thomas Cooper Library, Columbia, 29208. Kenneth E Toombs, Dir of Libraries; Roger Mortimer, Rare Book Librn
Holdings: Vols 500 Cat
Notes: Especially rare items incl the Elephant folio Audubon, and rare editions of Catesby, Wilson, Selby, Gould and Brasher.

SD —AUGUSTANA COLLEGE, Mikkelsen Library & Learning Resource Center, Center

ORNITHOLOGY (cont.)

for Western Studies, Sioux Falls, 57197.
Ronelle Thompson, Dir Library
Holdings: Vols (40,000) Cat Mss Maps Pix
Slides Microforms
Budget: ($130,000)
Notes: The Center for Western Studies,
located in the Mikkelsen Library, is an
archival and research agency of Augustana
College. Dedicated to the history and culture
of the Great Plains and the Trans-Mississippi
West, the Center collects and preserves
materials relating to Plains Indians,
immigrant settlers, Norwegiana, Western
Americana, Herbert Krause, Frederick
Manfred, Donald Parker, Richard F
Pettigrew, Augustana College, the Episcopal
Diocese of South Dakota, the South Dakota
District of the American Lutheran Church,
the South Dakota Penitentiary and
Minnehaha County.

TN —PUBLIC LIBRARY OF NASHVILLE &
DAVIDSON COUNTY, Nashville Room,
Eighth Ave N & Union St, Nashville, 37203.
Mary Glenn Hearne, Head
Holdings: Vols 300 // Uncat Mss Maps Pix
Notes: A 60-year collection of books,
journals, diaries, and notes on birds, kept by
Harry C Monk. It incl 1916-1966 Nashville
bird sightings; 1922-1974 correspondence
with Mrs Amelia Laskey of Nashville; book
blurbs; government documents; Tennessee
Ornithological Society minutes, finance, and
membership reports. Partially cataloged. *The
Carrie Mae Weil Ornithological Collection*
(Nashville: Public Library of Nashville and
Davidson County, 1977).

VA —CHRISTOPHER NEWPORT
COLLEGE, Captain John Smith Library, 50
Shoe Lane, PO Box 6070, Newport News,
23606.
Holdings: Vols 264 // Cat
Notes: Ray J Beasley Memorial Collection
incl the Virginia Ornithological Society
Journal, *The Raven*, 1945-1970.

WI —UNIVERSITY OF WISCONSIN,
MADISON, Memorial Library, 728 State St,
Madison, 53706. Erwin K Welsch, Social
Studies Bibliographer
Notes: Incl the Warner Taylor Collection,
167 titles largely of British and American
ornithology, incl color-plate items and
scholarly studies, acquired in 1959; and the
Thordarson Collection, over 10,000 vols in
fine condition pertaining to the history and
development of English science, particularly
strong in ornithology and botany.

ON —ROYAL BOTANICAL GARDENS,
Library, Box 399, Hamilton, L8N 3H8, Can.
Ina Vrugtman, Librn
Holdings: Vols (5000)
Notes: Strengths in ornamental horticulture,
botany, ornithology, entomology, natural
history.

ON —NATIONAL MUSEUMS OF
CANADA, Library Services Directorate,
Ottawa, K1A 0M8, Can. Valerie
Monkhouse, Director
Holdings: Vols (90,000) Cat Mss Microforms
Budget: ($81,000)
Notes: Emphasis on Canadian and
circumpolar natural history. Collection incl
botany, herpetology, ichthyology,
invertebrate zoology, malacology,
mammology, mineralogy, ornithology,
paleobiology, zooarchaeology. Exceptional
collections in lichenology, bryology,
malacology, ornithology. Research
collection, interlibrary loans available, public
may use on the premises.

ON —ROYAL ONTARIO MUSEUM, Main
Library and Archives, 100 Queen's Park,
Toronto, M5S 2C6, Can. Julia Matthews,
Head Librn
Holdings: Vols (85,000) Cat
Notes: Since January 1977, acquisitions have
been entered in UTLAS.

ON —UNIVERSITY OF TORONTO, Thomas
Fisher Rare Book Library, 120 Saint George
St, Toronto, M5S 1A5, Can. Richard G
Landon, Head
Holdings: Vols 3000 Mss
Notes: Baillie Collection named for James L
Baillie, Canadian ornithologist. Particularly

significant for pamphlet and offprint material
on both Canadian and American
ornithology; extensive holdings of Ontario
naturalists' club newsletters and reports;
extensive manuscript collection consisting of
field notes compiled by J L Baillie recording
his observations in Southern Ontario over a
fifty-year period.

PQ —MCGILL UNIVERSITY, Blacker-Wood
Library of Zoology & Ornithology, 3459
McTavish St, Montreal, H3A 1Y1, Can.
Eleanor MacLean, Librn
Holdings: Vols (77,600) //
Notes: Special features of collection incl:
Robert Gurney Collection of reprints on
Crustaceana; 3000 folders of letters from
naturalists; over 9000 original paintings of
wildlife; a small collection of falconry
equipment; the archives of the Montreal
Natural History Society; the archives of the
North American Falconry Association; 156
17th-century feather pictures of birds and
people. Does not incl entomology collection.
See also entry under Falconry and Falcons.

ORNITHOLOGY—HISTORY

CT —LEE ASH, (personal collection), 66
Humiston Dr, Bethany, 06525.
Holdings: Mss Maps Pix
Notes: First editions, mss, ephemera,
memorabilia.

OH —CLEVELAND PUBLIC LIBRARY,
Science & Technology Dept, 325 Superior
Ave, Cleveland, 44114. Jean Z Piety, Head
Holdings: Cat
Notes: Many early volumes.

PA —BRYN MAWR COLLEGE, Canaday
Library, Bryn Mawr, 19010. James Tanis,
Dir
Notes: Rare books: Michaelis, Zirkle
(Botony) and Castle (Ornithology and
Botanical Illustration) Collections.

ORNSTEIN, LEO

CT —YALE UNIVERSITY, Music Library, 98
Wall St, New Haven, 06520. Harold E
Samuel, Librn
Notes: Personal papers and musical mss.
See also entry under Music, American.

OROGRAPHY see Mountains

OROLOGY see Mountains

ORPEN, SIR WILLIAM, 1878-1931

BC —UNIVERSITY OF VICTORIA,
McPherson Library, Victoria, V8W 3H5,
Can.
Notes: 36 letters to Beatrice Elvery all
illustrated with ink or pencil sketches; 1 ink
sketch titled, "Howth."

ORPHANS AND ORPHANAGES

NJ —NEW JERSEY HISTORICAL
SOCIETY, Library and Museum, 230
Broadway, Newark, 07104. Joan C Hull,
Exec Dir; Barbara S Irwin, Library Dir; Alan
R Fraser, Cur
Holdings: Mss
Budget: ($100,000)
Notes: Records of eight Newark orphanages
and child service organizations dating back
to 1847. Incl records, casebooks, registers,
adoption contracts, minutes of meetings,
financial and administrative records, case
studies by student interns in social work, and
related printed materials.

NY —HAMPDEN-BOOTH THEATRE
LIBRARY AT THE PLAYERS, 16
Gramercy Park, New York, 10003. Louis A
Rachow, Librn/Cur
Holdings: // Uncat Mss
Notes: The British Actors Orphanage Fund was
incorporated in Los Angeles, California, in July
1940 "To promote and effect the transfer of male
and female minor orphans of deceased British
actors and actresses from their present home or
homes in Great Britain to America...and to
provide and pay for their complete maintenance,
housing and schooling therein, during the
pendency of the present war between Great Britain
and Germany, to the end that these orphans may be
removed from the horrors and perils of such war.
"The duties and activities of the Fund came to a
successful conclusion in 1946 when forty-eight of
the original fifty-four orphans returned to
England and the remaining six either became self-
supporting or their care was assumed by others.
The collection consists of copies of the charter and
by-laws, minutes, journals and ledgers, children's
travel arrangements, working files and preliminary
and general correspondence for the years
1940–1946 featuring such luminaries as Noel
Coward, Dame May Whitty, Boris Karloff,
Maurice Evans, Cole Porter, Peggy Wood and
Margaret Webster.

ORRERIES see Planetaria

ORSETTI FAMILY, TUSCANY

KS —UNIVERSITY OF KANSAS, Kenneth
Spencer Research Library, Special
Collections Dept, Lawrence, 66045.
Alexandra Mason, Librn
Holdings: Vols 289
Notes: The Rubinstein Collection of the
papers of the Orsetti Family of Lucca,
Tuscany, 1180-1850 (mostly before 1650).
117 linear ft.

ORSINI FAMILY, ITALY

CA —UNIVERSITY OF CALIFORNIA, LOS
ANGELES, Research Library, Dept of
Special Collections, 405 Hilgard Ave, Los
Angeles, 90024. Edward Shreeves,
Chairman, Bibliographers Group; David S
Zeidberg, Head
Holdings: Mss
Notes: 266 linear feet of the family archives,
13th-20th century, formerly in the
possession of Cardinal Orsini.

ORTELIUS, ABRAHAM

AL —BIRMINGHAM PUBLIC LIBRARY,
2020 Seventh Ave N, Birmingham, 35203.
Virginia K Scott, Librn
Holdings: Vols (2000) Cat Maps Pix
Notes: History and development of
cartography. 19th-century US atlases. Maps
of eastern US with most emphasis on
southeastern US. The Rucker Agee Map
Collection incl over 2000 maps. See *The
Rucker Agee Collection of the Birmingham
Public Library*, Birmingham Public Library,
1964; *Atlas Maior, Sive Cosmographia
Blaviana, Qva Solvm, Salvm, Coelvm,
Accvratissime Describvntvr*, Birmingham
Public Library, nd; 1570-1970. *An Exhibit in
Commemoration of the 400th Anniversary
of Publication by Abraham Ortelius of
Theatrum Orbis Terrarum; the World's First
Atlas*, Birmingham Public Library, 1970;
George Ray Stewart, *The Special Collections
In the Birmingham Public Library*, MA
thesis, Emory University, 1971; and *A List
of Nineteenth Century Maps of the State of
Alabama*, Birmingham Library, 1973.

IN —INDIANA UNIVERSITY, Lilly Library,
Seventh St, Bloomington, 47405. William R
Cagle, Librn
Holdings: Vols 22 Cat
Notes: Extensive collection of editions of
Ortelius from 1570 to 1684.

ORTEGA Y GASSET, JOSE

DC —LIBRARY OF CONGRESS, Manuscript
Division, Washington, 20540. John C

ORTEGA Y GASSET, JOSE (cont.)

Broderick, Chief
Notes: 82 microfilm reels of his papers, the originals being in Madrid.

ORTHODONTIA

NJ —FAIRLEIGH DICKINSON UNIVERSITY, School of Dentistry, Library, 110 Fuller Place, Hackensack, 07601. Ruth Schwartz, Dir
Holdings: Vols (550) Cat Slides Microforms
Notes: Emphasis on graduate level orthodontics. Dental equipment--museum pieces; masters theses in orthodontics from 1964; over 486 current periodical subscriptions. About 700 slides.

ORTHODONTICS see Orthodontia

ORTHODOX (ORTHODOX EASTERN CHURCH) IN THE U.S.

NJ —SAINT SOPHIA UKRAINIAN ORTHODOX THEOLOGICAL SEMINARY, PO Box 240, South Bound Brook, 08880. Iwan Korowytzky, Dir; Fr Wasyl Iwashchuk, Librn
Holdings: 4000 Vols Cat Mss
Budget: ($10,000)
Notes: Open to all.
NY —ARCHIVES OF THE ORTHODOX CHURCH IN AMERICA, PO Box 675, Syosset, 11791. Dennis Rhodes, Archivist
Notes: Incl material on Orthodox Churches in the Western Hemisphere espec in North America.
NY —SAINT VLADIMIRS' ORTHODOX THEOLOGICAL SEMINARY, 575 Scarsdale Rd, Yonkers, 10707. Paul D Garrett, Librn
Holdings: Vols 36,000 Pix
Notes: Incl 250 periodicals. A major source of materials on Orthodox Church theology. Much on works of art.
WI —SAINT SAVA SERBIAN ORTHODOX CATHEDRAL LIBRARY, 3201 S 51 St, Milwaukee, 53219. Dijo Radisich, Librn
Holdings: Vols 1500

ORTHODOX EASTERN CHURCH, RUSSIAN

†CA —UNIVERSITY OF CALIFORNIA, BERKELEY, LIBRARIES, Berkeley, 94720.
Notes: Comprehensive collection of indexes to more than 40 provincial Russian periodicals dealing with the Russians Orthodox Church during the Imperial period. More than 200 photocopies of letters, telegrams, sketches, and photographs from the collection of the Grand Duchess Mariia Alexandrovna, daughter of Emperor Alexander II of Russia. Dating from last third of the 19th century. Incl correspondence from her parents, court, and other friends. Copies made available by the Executive Committee of the Museum of Russian Culture in San Francisco.
DC —LIBRARY OF CONGRESS, American Folklife Center, Archive of Folk Culture, Washington, 20540.
Notes: The Sidney Robertson Cowell Collection of her folk music recordings, 1937 to 1957. Incl very unusual contributions by the Molokan community in the Potrero Hill neighborhood of San Francisco, a breakaway sect from the Russian Orthodox Church.
NY —ARCHIVES OF THE ORTHODOX CHURCH IN AMERICA, PO Box 675, Syosset, 11791. Dennis Rhodes, Archivist
Notes: Incl material on Orthodox Churches in the Western Hemisphere espec in North America.
NY —SAINT VLADIMIRS' ORTHODOX THEOLOGICAL SEMINARY, 575 Scarsdale Rd, Yonkers, 10707. Paul D Garrett, Librn
Holdings: Vols (36,000) Pix
Notes: Incl 250 periodicals. A major source of materials on Orthodox Church theology. Much on works of art.
PA —HOLY TRINITY BENEDICTINE BYZANTINE RITE MONESTERY, PO Box 990, Butler, 16002.

ORTHOEPY see Phonetics

ORTHOPEDICS

CA —ORTHOPAEDIC HOSPITAL, Lt Robert J Rubel Memorial Library, 2400 S Flower St, Los Angeles, 90007. Veena Vyas, Librn
Holdings: Vols 1725 Cat
CT —NEWINGTON CHILDREN'S HOSPITAL, Professional Library, 181 E Cedar St, Newington, 06111. Jean Long, Librn
Holdings: Vols (3500) Cat
Budget: ($6500)
MA —NEW ENGLAND BAPTIST HOSPITAL, Medical Staff Library, 91 Parker Hill Ave, Boston, 02120. Paul E Woodard, Librn
Holdings: Vols 108 Cat
Budget: ($17,487)
Notes: No photocopying.
MI —REHABILITATION INSTITUTE, Learning Resources Center, 261 Mack Blvd, Detroit, 48201. Daria Drobny, Medical Librn
Holdings: Vols (2600) Cat Slides
Notes: Physical medicine and rehabilitation.
NY —HOSPITAL FOR SPECIAL SURGERY, Kim Barrett Memorial Library, 535 E 70 St, New York, 10021. Munir U Din, Librn
Holdings: Vols 2520 Cat Slides Audiotapes Videotapes 16mm Films
Budget: $12,000
Notes: Incl 2520 Books, 2493 Bound Journals, 98 Videotapes, 117 Sound Slide Programs, 7 Motion Pictures, 22 Audiotapes. No photocopying.
NY —UNIVERSITY OF ROCHESTER, School of Medicine and Dentistry, Edward G Miner Library, 601 Elmwood Ave, Rochester, 14642. Lucretia McClure, Medical Librn; Janet Brady Berk, History of Medicine Librn
Notes: Strong in yellow fever, cholera, orthopaedics, anatomy and original historic medical photographs.
RI —MIRIAM HOSPITAL MEDICAL LIBRARY, 164 Summit Ave, Providence, 02906. Ann LeClaire, Dir of Library Services
Holdings: Cat Cassettes
Notes: Special collection on the renal system with emphasis on kidney transplantation and dialysis.
TX —SHRINERS HOSPITAL FOR CRIPPLED CHILDREN, Houston Unit Orthopedic Library, 1402 Outer Belt Dr, Houston, 77030. Patti Martin, Librn
Holdings: Vols 600 Cat Microforms
TX —SANTA ROSA MEDICAL CENTER, Health Science Library, PO Box 7330 Sta A, San Antonio, 78285. Marjorie McFarland, Librn
Holdings: Vols (6500) Cat
Budget: ($5000)
Notes: Special emphasis on pediatrics and orthopedics. Incl 947 audiotapes. Access to Medline.
VT —PUTNAM MEMORIAL HOSPITAL, Medical Library, 100 Hospital Dr, Bennington, 05201. Lynn Crandall, Library Coordinator
Holdings: Vols (1000) Cat Audiotapes
Notes: Incl 10,000 journals (earliest 1975) and 8 titles in audiotapes.

ORTHOPEDICS—HISTORY

GA —MEDICAL COLLEGE OF GEORGIA, Library, Laney Walker Blvd, Augusta, 30902. Dorothy H Mims, Librn for Special Collections
Holdings: Vols (2500) Cat
Notes: Special collection of late 18th and early 19th century medical books, incl typical texts, classics and atlases in orthopedics.
NY —UNIVERSITY OF ROCHESTER, School of Medicine and Dentistry, Edward G Miner Library, 601 Elmwood Ave, Rochester, 14642. Lucretia McClure, Medical Librn; Janet Brady Berk, History of Medicine Librn
Notes: Strong in yellow fever, cholera, orthopaedics, anatomy and original historic medical photographs.

ORTON, SAMUEL T.

NY —COLUMBIA UNIVERSITY LIBRARIES, Health Sciences Library, 701 W 168 St, New York, 10032. Rachael K Goldstein, Librn
Notes: Ca 3000 fiche. Incl the June Lyday and Samuel T Orton collection of patient records dating from 1928-77. Photocopying limited. Restricted.

ORTON FAMILY

TX —STEPHEN F AUSTIN STATE UNIVERSITY, Ralph W Steen Library, Special Collections Dept, Box 13055, SFA Sta, Nacogdoches, 75962. Linda Cheves Nicklas, Special Collections Librn
Holdings: Mss Maps Pix
Budget: ($5000)
Notes: Incl personal and business papers, letters, diaries, and other records of East Texans and East Texas institutions and businesses. Major collections incl papers of Karl Wilson Baker, George L Crocket, Bennett Blake, McFarland-Russell family, Orton family, Samuel E Asbury; and records of Nacogdoches University, East Texas Historical Association, Kelly Plow Company and many local organizations; 60 Thomas J Rusk letters. Indexes, calendars and inventories are available. Description: SFASU, A Guide to Special Collections, 1980.

ORWELL, GEORGE

NV —UNIVERSITY OF NEVADA, RENO, University Library, Special Collections Dept, Reno, 89557. Robert E Blesse, Head
Holdings: Vols (57) Cat Other appearances 145 Cat
Notes: Includes individual works by author in all editions including translations; also prefaces, introductions, published correspondence, appearances in anthologies, periodicals, etc. Bibliographical research collection, part of Modern Authors Collection.
OH —MIAMI UNIVERSITY, King Library, Walter Havighurst Special Collections Library, Oxford, 45056. Helen Ball, Cur of Special Collections
Holdings: Vols 300 Cat
Notes: First publications of almost all of George Orwell's writings. Include periodical publications and critical works.

OSAGE INDIANS

KS —UNIVERSITY OF KANSAS, Kenneth Spencer Research Library, Kansas Collection, Lawrence, 66045. Sheryl K Williams, Cur
Holdings: Vols (92,000) Cat Mss Maps Pix
Notes: Several photographic collections devoted exclusively to American Indian subjects, collections of personal papers, contemporary American Indian periodicals, 19th century tracts and treatises. Wars, missionary contracts, reservation life, etc in Kansas, Oklahoma and Nebraska. Good holdings treating Potawatomie Indians (Prairie Band), Sauk, Fox, Osage. Incl pamphlets, serials, and state publications.

OSBORN, CHASE S.

MI —LAKE SUPERIOR STATE COLLEGE, Library, College Dr, Sault Sainte Marie, 49783. Frederick A Michels, Dir
Holdings: Vols (400) Cat Maps Pix Slides Clippings
Notes: Michigan History with emphasis on Sault Ste Marie, Eastern end of Upper Peninsula, and area Indians (Chippewa or Ojibway).

OSBORN, HENRY FAIRFIELD

NY —AMERICAN MUSEUM OF NATURAL HISTORY, Library Services Dept, Central Park W & 79th St, New York, 10024. Nina J Root, Chairwoman; Mary Genett, Asst Librn for Reference Services
Holdings: Cat Mss Maps Pix Slides

OSBORN, HENRY FAIRFIELD (cont.)

Microforms
Notes: The Henry Fairfield Osborn
Archives, incl his personal papers concerning
his family and the many years of his
association with the Museum. About 500,
000 pieces. Paleontology is a major
emphasis.
NY —NEW YORK HISTORICAL SOCIETY,
Library, 170 Central Park W, New York,
10024. James Gregory, Librn
Notes: Papers of the president of American
Museum of Natural History from 1908-1933;
also of his family. Additional papers are in
the museum's library across the street.

OSBORN, JOHN

DC —LIBRARY OF CONGRESS, Manuscript
Division, Washington, 20540. John C
Broderick, Chief
Notes: His papers; 45,000 items.

OSBORN, STELLA BRUNT

MI —LAKE SUPERIOR STATE COLLEGE,
Library, College Dr, Sault Sainte Marie,
49783. Frederick A Michels, Dir
Holdings: Vols (400) Cat Maps Pix Slides
Clippings
Notes: Michigan History with emphasis on
Sault Ste Marie, Eastern end of Upper
Peninsula, and area Indians (Chippewa or
Objibway).

OSLER, WILLIAM, 1849-1919

CA —LOS ANGELES COUNTY MEDICAL
ASSOCIATION, Library, 634 S Westlake
Ave, Los Angeles, 90057. Elizabeth S
Crahan, Chief Librn
Holdings: Cat Pix
CA —UNIVERSITY OF CALIFORNIA, SAN
FRANCISCO, Library, Special Collections,
San Francisco, 94143. Nancy Witten Zinn,
Librn
Holdings: Vols 530 Cat Mss Pix
Notes: His writings, etc.
CT —YALE UNIVERSITY, Medical Historical
Library, Klebs Collection, 333 Cedar St,
New Haven, 06520. Ferenc A Gyorgyey,
Librn
Notes: Correspondence with Harvey
Cushing; partly in Historical Library and
partly in Manuscripts and Archives Division.
IA —UNIVERSITY OF IOWA, Health
Sciences Library, John Martin Rare Book
Room, Iowa City, 52242. Richard Eimas,
Librn
Holdings: Vols (2200) Cat Slides
Notes: Catalog: Iowa, University, Health
Sciences Library. *Heirs of Hippocrates* (Iowa
City, IA, Friends of the University of Iowa
Libraries, 1980). Collection is particularly
strong in areas of anatomy and surgery. It
also contains 300 books and reprints by and
about Sir William Osler as well as over 80
letters written by Osler.
MD —JOHNS HOPKINS UNIVERSITY,
Institute of the History of Medicine, 1900 E
Monument St, Baltimore, 21205. Doris
Thibodeau, Librn
Holdings: Vols 333 Cat
MD —MEDICAL & CHIRURGICAL
FACULTY OF THE STATE OF
MARYLAND, Library, 1211 Cathedral St,
Baltimore, 21201. Joseph E Jensen, Librn
Holdings: Vols (10,000) // Cat Mss Maps
Pix
Notes: Nearly a complete collection. Part of
the history of medicine and rare medical
book collection.
PA —COLLEGE OF PHYSICIANS OF
PHILADELPHIA, Library, 19 S 22 St,
Philadelphia, 19103. Christine Ruggere, Cur,
Historical Collections
Holdings: Vols (316,223) Cat Mss
Budget: ($1,096,557)
Notes: Very strong collection.
See also entry under Medicine
PQ —MCGILL UNIVERSITY, Osler Library,
3655 Drummond St, Montreal, H3G 1Y6,
Can. Philip M Teigen, Librn
Holdings: Vols (35,000) Cat Mss Pix Slides

Microforms
Notes: The Osler Library is a research
library in the history of medicine and allied
sciences. Its scope incl the history of medical
practice, medical sciences (eg anatomy,
pathology), medical specialities (eg
psycholoy, genetics, biochemistry), and
medical statistics, historical demography,
and medical institutions. Partial listing in
Bibliotheca Osleriana, 1929, reprinted 1969;
Library publishes *Osler Library Newsletter,*
free on request.

OSMANIC LANGUAGE see Turkish Language and Literature

OSMANLI LANGUAGE see Turkish Language and Literature

OSMOSIS

MA —ABCOR, INC, Library, 850 Main St,
Wilmington, 01887. Eileen Smith, Librn
Holdings: Vols (2000) Cat
Budget: ($10,000)
Notes: Reverse osmosis technology.
Particularly strong in government technical
reports.

OSMOSIS TECHNOLOGY RESEARCH see Reverse Osmosis Technology

OSRIN, RAY

OH —OHIO STATE UNIVERSITY, Library
for Communication and Graphic Arts, 242
W 18th St, Columbus, 43210. Lucy S
Caswell, Curator
Notes: The original works of editorial
cartoonists Art Poinier, Scott Willis, Brian
Basset, Billy Ireland, Frank Williams,
Charles Werner, Ned Beard, L D Warren,
Edward D Kuekes, Ray Osrin, Mike Peters,
Draper Hill, Eugene Craig and Bert
Whitman.

OSSETIC LANGUAGE AND LITERATURE

NY —NEW YORK PUBLIC LIBRARY,
Oriental Div, Fifth Ave & 42 St, New York,
10018. E Christian Filstrup, Chief
Holdings: Cat Mss Microforms
Budget: ($56,455)
Notes: Published catalog of holdings.

OSSOLI, MARGARET FULLER, 1872-1959

CT —YALE UNIVERSITY, Box 1603A, Yale
Station, New Haven, 06520.
Holdings: Mss
CT —CONNECTICUT COLLEGE, Library,
Mohegan Ave, New London, 06320. Brian
Rogers, College Librn
Holdings: // Uncat
Notes: Preliminary sorting has taken place.
About 12 linear ft.
MA —HARVARD UNIVERSITY LIBRARY,
Houghton Library, Cambridge, 02138.
Rodney G Dennis, Cur of Manuscripts
Holdings: Cat Mss
MA —CONCORD FREE PUBLIC LIBRARY,
129 Main St, Concord, 01742. Rose Marie
Mitten, Dir
Holdings: Cat Mss Pix
Notes: Her close association with the
Concord Authors is very important.
WI —UNIVERSITY OF WISCONSIN,
MADISON, Memorial Library, British &
American Language & Literature Collection,
728 State St, Madison, 53706. Yvonne
Schofer, Bibliographer
Holdings: Vols 2200 Mss Microforms
Documents Periodicals
Notes: A collection of primary and
secondary materials for nine major American
women writers: Anne Bradstreet; Louisa
May Alcott, Emily Dickinson, Kate Chopin,
Mary Williams Freeman, Margaret Fuller,
Sarah Orne Jewett, Charlotte Perkins
Gilman, Harriet Beecher Stowe. Primary
materials also collected for a list of less well
known authors together with manuscripts

and archives of letters of special research
interest. Variety of holdings: fiction, poetry,
drama, biography and autobiography, letters,
memoirs, diaries, travel, domestic economy
and other kinds of writings by women
mostly of the 19th century. Held in Dept of
Rare Books and Special Collections.

OSTEOLOGY

NY —AMERICAN MUSEUM OF
NATURAL HISTORY, Library Services
Dept, Central Park W & 79th St, New York,
10024. Nina J Root, Chairwoman; Mary
Genett, Asst Librn for Reference Services
Holdings: Vols (385,000) Cat Mss Maps Pix
Slides Microforms
Notes: Nearly all collections are outstanding
for depth of coverage and international
range. Early and historic works, rare books,
colored illustrations, and relevant serial
publications supplement the modern
scientific publications necessary to the
researches of the scientific staff and the
work of the educational division. Open to
the public.

OSTEOPATHY

IL —CHICAGO COLLEGE OF
OSTEOPATHIC MEDICINE, Library,
1122 E 53 St, Chicago, 60615. Sandra
Worley, Dir of Libraries
Holdings: Vols 300 Uncat Pix
MO —KIRKSVILLE COLLEGE OF
OSTEOPATHIC MEDICINE, A T Still
Memorial Library, Kirksville, 63501.
Georgia Walter, Librn
Holdings: Vols (53,000) Cat Mss Pix
Notes: The oldest osteopathic library has
one of the most complete collections on
osteopathy, incl most of the original works
to date. Incl papers, pictures and other
materials of the College's founder, A T Still.
All newly published materials on the subject
are obtained and most national and state
osteopathic periodicals received. A card
catalog has been prepared for an osteopathic
periodical index.
NY —BAPTIST MEDICAL CENTER OF
NEW YORK, Alyn M Steinhardt Library,
2749 Linden Blvd, Brooklyn, 11208. Ana
McBean, Librn
Holdings: Vols (150) Cat Slides
Phonorecords Audiotapes 16mm Films
Filmstrips
PA —PHILADELPHIA COLLEGE OF
OSTEOPATHIC MEDICINE, O J Snyder
Memorial Library, Evans Hall, 4150 City
Ave, Philadelphia, 19131. Shanker H Vyas,
Dir of Libraries
Holdings: Vols (50,000) Cat Audiotapes
Videotapes 16mm Films Microforms
Notes: Osteopathy and all medical fields.
Osteopathy collection incl 387 books, 98
theses, 66 pamphlets and periodicals, 1103
audiotapes and 946 videotapes.

OSTEOPATHY—HISTORY

OH —OHIO UNIVERSITY, Vernon R Alden
Library, Department of Archives and Special
Collections, Athens, 45701. Gary A Hunt,
Head
Holdings: Vols 90 Cat Mss
Notes: History of Osteopathic Medicine,
concentrating on books published prior to
1940. Incl records of the Ohio Osteopathic
Association and its predecessor, the Ohio
Osteopathic Society, 1890-1970.

OSTERMAN, MARJORIE

MA —BOSTON UNIVERSITY, Mugar
Memorial Library, Special Collections Dept,
771 Commonwealth Ave, Boston, 02215.
Howard B Gotlieb, Dir
Holdings: Cat Mss Correspondence

OSTERTAG, HAROLD CHARLES, 1896-

NY —CORNELL UNIVERSITY LIBRARIES,
Collection of Regional History, Dept of
Manuscripts and Univ Archives, Ithaca,
14853.
Notes: US Congressman, assemblyman. Incl

OSTERTAG, HAROLD CHARLES, 1896- (cont.)

papers, 1937-64; public statements, press releases, questionnaires, films, tapes, photos, newspaper clippings, copies of bills he introduced, and much correspondence.

OSTRAKA

FL —FLORIDA STATE UNIVERSITY, Robert Manning Strozier Library, Special Collections Dept, Tallahassee, 32306. Opal M Free, Head, Special Collections
Holdings: Vols 83 // Uncat
Notes: Babylonian clay tablets (2100-2300 BC), 25 items. Papyri, 26 fragments, with Greek text. Ostraka, 32 items, 29 in Greek text, 3 in Latin text. Noncirculating.

OSTRY, ETHEL

MB —UNIVERSITY OF MANITOBA, Elizabeth Dafoe Library, Archives and Special Collections Dept, Winnipeg, R3T 2N2, Can. Richard E Bennett, Dept Head; Corrado A Santoro, Reference Archivist
Notes: A journal entitled After the Holocaust: My work with UNRRA (1970).

O'SULLIVAN, TIM

AZ —NORTHERN ARIZONA UNIVERSITY, Special Collection Library, CU Box 6022, Flagstaff, 86011. Peter M Whiteley, Coordr/Archivist; William Mullane, Librn
Notes: Wyant Alexander Collection; diary of Wyant's journey with photographer Tim O'Sullivan as part of the Wheeler Expedition through Northeastern Arizona and Southern Utah and New Mexico, 1873. Wyant was an artist.

OSUSKY, STEFAN, 1889-1973

CA —HOOVER INSTITUTION ON WAR, REVOLUTION & PEACE, Stanford University, Stanford, 94305. Milorad M Drachkovitch, Archivist
Holdings: Mss Pix
Notes: Papers of S Osusky consisting of correspondence, memoranda, reports, clippings, printed matter, memorabilia, photographs, etc, pertaining to his career as Czechoslovak Ambassador to Great Britain, 1918-1920; and to France, 1920-1940; foreign and domestic affairs of Czechoslovakia; and international relations, primarily in Western and central Europe between the world wars. 42 mss boxes, 1 oversize album and 2 card files.

OSWALD, LEE HARVEY

TX —TEXAS CHRISTIAN UNIVERSITY, Mary Couts Burnett Library, Fort Worth, 76129.
Notes: The Marguerite Oswald Collection (mother of Lee Harvey Oswald), incl the full Warren Commission Report, with her own annotations and comments. Also, some 200 vols, many inscribed or dedicated to her.

OSWEGO COLLEGE

NY —STATE UNIVERSITY OF NEW YORK, COLLEGE AT OSWEGO, Penfield Library, Oswego, 13126. Anne Commerton, Dir
Holdings: Cat Mss Pix
Notes: Edward Austin Sheldon was an educator and first president of the Oswego College. Incl about 100 letters. 2 ft. Unpublished guide.

OTCHIPWE INDIANS see Chippewa Indians

OTERO, MIGUEL A.

MS —UNIVERSITY OF SOUTHERN MISSISSIPPI, William David McCain Graduate Library, Box 5148, Southern Sta, Hattiesburg, 39406.
Holdings: Cat Mss Pix
Notes: Correspondence and records (1847-1892) relating to Alexander Melvorne Jackson's participation in the Mexican War, his service as Secretary of the State of the New Mexico Territory (1857-1861), and his participation in the Civil War on the side of the Confederacy. Among his correspondents were Albert Gallatin Brown, Reuben Davis, Miguel A Otero, Jacob Thompson, and John Ireland. Incl are photographs of Austin, Texas, ca 1890. 1.1 cubic feet holdings.

OTEY, RT. REV. JAMES HERVEY

TN —UNIVERSITY OF THE SOUTH ARCHIVES, Jessie Ball DuPont Library, Sewanee, 37375. Gertrude French Mignery, Archivist
Holdings: Vols (3000) Cat Mss
Notes: His papers, etc.

OTITIS see Ear—Diseases

OTOLARYNGOLOGY see Otorhinolaryngology

OTOLOGY see Ear—Diseases; Otorhinolaryngology

OTORHINOLARYNGOLOGY

MA —HARVARD UNIVERSITY, Lucien Howe Library of Ophthalmology, 243 Charles St, Boston, 02114. Judith C Nims, Library Dir
Holdings: Vols (10,162) Cat
NY —COLUMBIA UNIVERSITY LIBRARIES, Rare Book & Manuscript Library, 801 Butler Library, 535 W 114 St, New York, 10027. Kenneth A Lohf, Librn
Holdings: Mss
Notes: Nearly 6000 letters, notes and mss relating to Cornelius Rea Agnew, professor of diseases of the eye and ear at Columbia's College of Physicians and Surgeons, and a founder of the Manhattan Eye and Ear Hospital. Much of the material relates to the treatment of eye diseases during the latter half of the 19th century. Restricted use.
PA —EYE & EAR HOSPITAL OF PITTSBURGH, Blair-Lippincott Library, 230 Lothrop St, Pittsburgh, 15213. Bruce A Johnston, Medical Librn
Holdings: Vols (6000) Cat
Notes: Special emphasis on ophthalmology, otorhinolaryngology, audiology, and speech pathology.

OTROSIMOV, YURII

CT —YALE UNIVERSITY, Box 1603A, Yale Station, New Haven, 06520.
Holdings: Mss
Notes: 500 letters; also some of his unpublished mss.

OTTAWA, ONTARIO

ON —OTTAWA PUBLIC LIBRARY, 120 Metcalfe St, Ottawa, K1P 5M2, Can. Thomas Rooney, Librn
Holdings: Vols (7000) Cat Mss Maps
Notes: Incl pamphlets, ephemera and postcards. Ottawa subjects, imprints and authors. Municipal and regional government publications, incl bylaws, minutes, and planning studies. Also incl Ottawa - Carleton (Ont); Outaouais, Region De L' (Quebec); Ottawa Valley (Quebec and Ont).

OUIDA

CA —UNIVERSITY OF CALIFORNIA, LOS ANGELES, Research Library, Dept of Special Collections, 405 Hilgard Ave, Los Angeles, 90024. Edward Shreeves, Chairman, Bibliographers Group; David S Zeidberg, Head
Notes: 100 first and other editions of the books of "Ouida" (Marie Louise de la Ramee, 1839-1908); also 28 letters, 5 mss, and 100 items from her solicitor.
NJ —PRINCETON UNIVERSITY, Library, Morris L Parrish Collection, Princeton, 08540. Alexander D Wainwright, Cur
Holdings: Vols 43
Notes: The collection contains over 6500 vols, as well as many theatre programs, playbills, photographs, clippings and other miscellanea. Parrish's goal was to assemble in both the English and the American first editions, in the original condition as issued, everything that a given author published. He was also interested in a high standard of condition for his books. Many additions have been acquired since the Parrish collection came to the Library as a bequest in 1944. The collection is an assemblage of author collections, consisting of books by: William Harrison Ainsworth, James Matthew Barrie, William Black, The Brontes, William Wilkie Collins, Dinah Mulock Craik, Marie de la Ramee ("Ouida"), Benjamin Disraeli, Charles Dickens, Charles Dodgson, George du Maurier, George Eliot (ie Mary Ann Evans), Elizabeth Gaskell, Thomas Hardy, Thomas Hughes, Charles Kingsley, Charles Lever, Edward George Earle Bulwer-Lytton, Mary Maxwell, George Meredith, Charles Reade, Walter Scott, Robert Louis Stevenson, William Makepeace Thackeray, Trollope Family, Ellen Wood, and Charlotte Yonge.

OUR GANG

CA —UNIVERSITY OF CALIFORNIA, LOS ANGELES, Theater Arts Library, Los Angeles, 90024. Edward Shreeves, Chairman, Bibliographers Group; Audree Malkin, Head, Theater Arts Library
Holdings: Cat Mss Pix
Notes: Script Collection, Screenplays: a collection of more than 32,636 unpublished scripts for American, British and some foreign language films. An important part of the collection is the Metro-Goldwyn-Mayer Screenplay Collection which covers the period 1924-1947. Incl are the Andy Hardy, Dr Kildare, and Maisie film series which are virtually complete, and a number of short features, such as Robert Benchley Series, Pete Smith Specialties, and Our Gang Comedies.

OURSLER, FULTON

DC —GEORGETOWN UNIVERSITY, Library, Special Collections Div, 37 & O Sts NW, Washington, 20057. George M Barringer, Special Collections Librn; Nicholas B Sheetz, Mss Librn
Holdings: // Cat Mss Pix
Notes: Papers of Fulton Oursler, editor of Liberty and, later, Reader's Digest, including substantial correspondences with Upton Sinclair, H L Mencken, Franklin D Roosevelt, Madame Chiang Kai-shek, J Edgar Hoover, Houdini, Herbert Hoover, and Immanuel Velikousky.

OURY, WILLIAM S. AND GRANVILLE H.

AZ —NORTHERN ARIZONA UNIVERSITY, Special Collection Library, CU Box 6022, Flagstaff, 86011. Peter M Whiteley, Coordr/Archivist; William Mullane, Librn
Notes: Typescript of "Some Unpublished History of the Southwest," by Colonel C C Smith. Incl are the stories of William S and Granville H Oury, brothers who arrived in Tucson, Ariz, in the 1850's.

OUSAMAQUIN, CHIEF see Massasoit (Indian Chief)

OUSPENSKAYA, MARIA

CA —UNIVERSITY OF CALIFORNIA, LOS ANGELES, Research Library, Dept of Special Collections, 405 Hilgard Ave, Los Angeles, 90024. Edward Shreeves, Chairman, Bibliographers Group; David S Zeidberg, Head
Holdings: Mss Pix
Notes: 2 linear feet of publicity, scripts and ephemera.

OUTAGAMI INDIANS see Fox Indians

OUTDOOR ADVERTISING see Advertising, Outdoor

OUTDOOR EDUCATION

GA —FERNBANK SCIENCE CENTER LIBRARY, 156 Heaton Park Dr NE,

OUTDOOR EDUCATION (cont.)

Atlanta, 30307. Mary Larsen, Librn; Janice MacLeod, Bibliographic Instructor
Holdings: Vols (12,000) Cat Maps Pix Slides Microforms
Budget: ($35,000)
Notes: Science with emphasis on astronomy, biology, outdoor education. Incl 5500 color slides; periodicals on microfilm.

IL —UNIVERSITY OF ILLINOIS, URBANA/CHAMPAIGN, Library, Applied Life Studies Library, 1408 W Gregory Dr, Urbana, 61801.
Holdings: Vols (38,000) Cat Microforms
Notes: Special emphasis on leisure studies, recreation surveys and plans, outdoor education, recreation programs, theories of play, supervision, and therapeutic recreation.
See also entry under Physical Education

OUTDOOR LIFE

MA —HARVARD UNIVERSITY, Harvard Forest Library, Petersham, 01366. Catherine M Danahar, Librn
Holdings: Cat
Notes: Emphasis on National Forest recreation, with related subjects incl wildlife and economics.

NY —ADIRONDACK HISTORICAL ASSOCIATION, Museum Library, Blue Mountain Lake, 12812. Jerold Pepper, Librn
Holdings: Vols (7500) Cat Mss Maps Pix Phonorecords Audiotapes 16mm Films Microforms
Notes: Anything about the Adirondacks-- history, people, economics, places, things. Strong in Adirondack art, outdoor recreation, logging, small boats. Resources incl more than 1000 maps, 40,000 pictures, 1600 microfilm reels, 576 linear ft of ms material, and 12 cabinets of VF ephemera, etc.

OUTDOOR RECREATION

CT —YALE UNIVERSITY, Forestry Library, 205 Prospect St, New Haven, 06511. Joseph A Miller, Librn
Holdings: Vols (115,000) Cat Microforms
Notes: Forestry is construed broadly to incl underlying or closely related social, physical, and biological sciences.

OUTDOOR RELIEF see Public Welfare

OUTER SPACE EXPLORATION

DC —US NAVAL OBSERVATORY LIBRARY, 30th & Massachusetts Ave, NW, Washington, 20016. Brenda G Corbin, Librn
Holdings: Vols (75,000) Cat Mss Maps Pix Slides Microforms
Notes: Incl 1000 journals, with monograph and serial publications in the fields of celestial mechanics, fundamental astronomy, time determination, photographic astrometry and astrophysics, data processing, mathematics.

NY —EXPLORERS CLUB, James B Ford Memorial Library, 46 E 70 St, New York, 10021. Janet Baldwin, Librn
Holdings: Vols (24,000) Cat Maps
Notes: Additions to the collection depend upon gifts. Access by appointment only.

TX —DALLAS PUBLIC LIBRARY, Central Library, Humanities Division, 1515 Young St, Dallas, 75201. Richard L Waters, Acting Dir; Ron Boyd, Fiction Librn
Holdings: Vols Cat Microforms
Notes: Cited in Tymn, Marshall, Roger C Schlobin, and L W Currey. A Research Guide to Science Fiction New York: Garland, 1977. The science fiction collection now exceeds 8000 circulating vols. In addition, the Library purchased in 1983 the personal library and archives of Brian Aldiss (which will be for reference use only). This collection consists of 350 books by Aldiss, 1900 other books by other science fiction writers, 800 issues of science fiction and fantasy periodicals, 100 vols concerning astronautics and space travel, over 1000 typescript pages of mss(incl 6 corrected mss), several sound recordings (incl BBC tapes), and a considerable amount of correspondence.

TX —TRINITY UNIVERSITY, Elizabeth Coates Maddux Library, 715 Stadium Dr, San Antonio, 78284. Richard Hume Werking, Library Dir; Craig Likness, Head Bibliographer
Holdings: Vols 1461
Notes: Paul A Campbell Man and Space Collection. Collection of primary and secondary materials, incl press releases and photographs documenting space exploration efforts.

OUTLAWS

IL —NEWBERRY LIBRARY, 60 W Walton St, Chicago, 60610. Diana Haskell, Cur of Modern Mss
Holdings: Vols 150 Cat
Notes: The Collection falls into two groups. Western Americana (which includes some pictures, biographies, broadsides and rare pamphlets) and English (mostly 18th and 19th century broadsides and poems).

TX —AMARILLO PUBLIC LIBRARY, 413 E Fourth, Amarillo, 79101. Mary Kay Snell, Librn
Holdings: Vols Cat Mss Maps Pix
Notes: The southwest collections incl materials on the history of Texas, Louisiana, New Mexico, Arkansas, Missouri and Kansas. General subjects covered incl overland journeys, early narratives, early biographies, Indian captivities, outlaws, US government reports, Mississippi and Ohio Rivers, the Mexican War, reports of Catholic missionaries, Niles Register, early publications, fur trade, western trails, Texas Rangers, sheriffs and Texas as a sovereign state, buffalo hunting, Indian wars, cowboys, the arrival of farmers, fences, and towns. Over 1600 items which incl books, documents, maps, mss, pamphlets, unpublished theses, interviews and photographs. The three major collections are the William Henry Bush Collection, the Laurence J Fitzsimon Collection and the Calendar of John L McCarty.

TX —UNIVERSITY OF TEXAS LIBRARIES, General Libraries, Barker Texas History Center, PO Box P, Austin, 78712. Don Carleton, Dir
Holdings: Vols (132,000) Cat Mss Maps Pix Slides Phonorecords Audiotapes Microforms
Notes: See description of collection under Texas-History.

VA —VIRGINIA POLYTECHNIC INSTITUTE AND STATE UNIVERSITY LIBRARY, Blacksburg, 24061. Glenn L McMullen, Special Collections Librn
Holdings: Vols (4000)
Notes: Collection largely consists of nineteenth century and early twentieth century imprints, emphasizing the role of native Virginians in the development of the trans-Mississippi West, particularly Texas; cowboys and the cattle industry; outlaws and lawlessness; and emigrants' guidebooks to states, cities, and regions in the West.

OUTLOOK (MAGAZINE) ARCHIVES

ME —BOWDOIN COLLEGE, Library, Brunswick, 04011. Dianne M Gutscher, Cur of Special Collections
Holdings: Mss Pix
Notes: The Abbott Memorial Collection contains both printed and manuscript materials relating to Jacob Abbott, John S C Abbott, Edward Abbott and Lyman Abbott, as well as other members of the family. It consists of approximately 25,000 items, including correspondence, sermons, diaries and journals, addresses, the archives of both the Literary World and Outlook magazines, and the Lyman Abbott autograph collection. First and subsequent editions of almost all of the family's published writings are also present.

OUTPATIENT SERVICES IN HOSPITALS see Hospitals—Outpatient Services

OVERLAND JOURNEYS

CA —AZUSA PACIFIC COLLEGE, Marshburn Memorial Library, Citrus & Alosta, Azusa, 91702. Edward Peterman, Librn
Holdings: Vols (600) Uncat
Budget: ($30,000)
Notes: Significant holdings in the George E Fullerton Library of California and Western Americana.

CA —UNIVERSITY OF CALIFORNIA, SAN DIEGO, Central University Library, Mandeville Dept of Special Collections, La Jolla, 92093. Lynda Corey Claassen, Head
Holdings: Vols (2400) Cat Mss Maps
Notes: The Hill Collection of Pacific Voyages, including reports and commentaries of important voyages in the Pacific, from those of Magellan and Sir Francis Drake to exploration through the first half of the 19th century. Includes many rare overland accounts to the Pacific across North America, Mexico, and Panama.
Bibliography: Silveira de Braganza, Ronald, The Hill Collection of Pacific Voyages (La Jolla: Calif, 1974-1983).

CA —LONG BEACH PUBLIC LIBRARY, Historic Sites Section, Rancho Los Cerritos, 4600 Virginia Rd, Long Beach, 90807. Ellen Calomiris, Historical Cur
Holdings: Vols (3000) Cat Mss Maps Pix Audiotapes
Budget: $1000
Notes: Emphasis on rancho, Long Beach, and Southern California history; incl materials on the westward movement. Incl 250 maps and 3000 pictures. Additional historic site: Rancho Los Alamitos, 6400 Bixby Hill Rd, Long Beach, Calif, 90815.

CA —POMONA PUBLIC LIBRARY, Special Collections, 625 S Garey Ave, PO Box 2271, Pomona, 91766. David Streeter, Librn
Holdings: Cat Maps Microforms
Notes: Complete California census through 1900 on microfilm; 1850 California Census index; reconstructed passenger lists; overland arrivals. Scattered censuses on microfilm from other states. All printed indexes to US Census; general US research collection. Basic heraldry and coats-of-arms.

CA —CALIFORNIA HISTORICAL SOCIETY, Schubert Hall Library, 2099 Pacific Ave, San Francisco, 94109. Bruce L Johnson, Library Dir
Holdings: Vols (50,000) Cat Mss Maps Pix

CA —SOCIETY OF CALIFORNIA PIONEERS, Library, 456 McAllister St, San Francisco, 94102. Grace E Baker, Librn
Holdings: Vols (12,000) Cat Mss Maps Pix Microforms
Notes: California history, especially the gold rush and the San Francisco earthquake, Sherman collection of early California music, business letterheads of early California firms, San Francisco City Directories 1850-1944, records of California Battalion 1846-47, ms material on overland diaries, ships' logs and passenger lists. Also, large photograph collection.

CO —COLORADO HISTORICAL SOCIETY, Research Collections, 1300 Broadway, Denver, 80203. Catherine Kane, Head Public Service and Access
Holdings: Cat Pix Slides
Notes: 250,000 photographs of western and Colorado subjects incl gold rush, mining, Indians, natural features, transportation, cities and towns, portraits. William Henry Jackson photographs of area west of Mississippi.

CO —DENVER PUBLIC LIBRARY, Western History Department, 1357 Broadway, Denver, 80203. Eleanor M Gehres, Head
Holdings: Vols (50,000) Cat Mss Maps Pix Audiotapes Microforms
Notes: Western US History. The department has a separate catalog, published in 1970 in 7 vols by G K Hall Co. First supplement published in 1975 in 1 vol. There is a subject index of some 3 million entries to newspapers and magazines of the Rocky Mountain region, added to daily. The Western Newspaper Microfilm Center contains approx 7000 reels of Western US newspapers. Collection has ca 275,000 negatives and prints of Western life; and ca 2500 maps, cataloged and classified.

IL —NEWBERRY LIBRARY, 60 W Walton St, Chicago, 60610. Diana Haskell, Cur of

OVERLAND JOURNEYS (cont.)

Modern Mss
Holdings: Vols 25 Cat Mss
Notes: Edward E Ayer and D Graff collections.

IL —NORTHERN ILLINOIS UNIVERSITY, Founders Memorial Library, Rare Books and Special Collections Dept, De Kalb, 60115. William R DuBois, Dept Head
Holdings: Vols (1000) Cat Maps Pix
Notes: Collection deals with all aspects of Colorado: early travel narratives, history, literature, geology, ecology, maps and some bibliography.

IL —KNOX COLLEGE, Henry M Seymour Library, Galesburg, 61401. Douglas L Wilson, Dir
Holdings: Vols 4780 Cat Mss Maps Pix
Notes: Special emphasis on the earliest European contacts in the upper Mississippi, early settlement in Illinois.

IN —INDIANA UNIVERSITY, Lilly Library, Seventh St, Bloomington, 47405. William R Cagle, Librn
Holdings: // Cat Mss Maps
Notes: Description and travel of the US Plains and Rockies; overland accounts; issues of California newspapers of the gold rush era, etc.

KS —UNIVERSITY OF KANSAS, Kenneth Spencer Research Library, Kansas Collection, Lawrence, 66045. Sheryl K Williams, Cur
Holdings: Vols (92,000) Cat Mss Maps Pix
Notes: All aspects of the American West and trans-Mississippi history, especially northern and central regions. Overland diaries, cartographic history, Indians, emigration and immigration, printing history, cattle industry, agriculture and farm life, conservation are some special interests, in addition to the usual political, economic, military and social interests.

KY —UNIVERSITY OF KENTUCKY, Margaret I King Library, Dept of Special Collections, Lexington, 40506. William Marshall, Head
Holdings: Cat Mss Maps Pix Microforms
Notes: Kentucky history and travel. Incl the Samuel M Wilson Library, Kentucky imprints, Kentucky authors, biography and autobiography, regional history (Ohio Valley), Kentucky maps. Also sheet music, clippings, etc.

MA —AMERICAN ANTIQUARIAN SOCIETY LIBRARY, 185 Salisbury St, Worcester, 01609. Marcus A McCorison, Dir & Librn
Holdings: Vols 1500 Cat
Notes: Narratives especially. Incl the Donald McKay Frost Collection.

MO —SAINT LOUIS PUBLIC LIBRARY, Gardner Rare Book Room, 1301 Olive St, Saint Louis, 63103. Julanne M Good, Supervisor; Martha Riley, Rare Books Librn
Holdings: Vols 100 Cat Maps
Budget: ($5573)
Notes: Small growing collection of travels incl St Louis or Missouri, largely transferred from the general stacks, although an occasional purchase is made. Incl early business directories of St Louis, river pilots' handbooks and maps. Noncirculating.

MO —WASHINGTON UNIVERSITY, John M Olin Library, Campus Box 1061, St Louis, 63130.
Holdings: Vols (1800) Cat Mss
Notes: Incl material from the Arthur C Hoskins, Richard S Hawes, Ernst C Krohn, George N Meissner, Stratford Lee Morton, and Edgar M Queeny collections; strong in early travel literature of the US and Latin America; accounts of exploration in the Mississippi Valley and Trans-Mississippi West; miscellaneous accounts of history, pioneer life, and travel in the Ohio Valley, Old Southwest, and California; material on the American Indian; 18th century American music; early American imprints.

NE —KEARNEY STATE COLLEGE, Calvin T Ryan Library, Kearney, 68847. John Mayeski, Dir; Anita Norman, Reference Librn
Holdings: Vols (1700) Cat Mss Maps Pix

Slides Microforms
Notes: Collection attempts to cover total historical development of Nebraska. Special strengths incl overland journeys, pony express, sod houses, and the Union Pacific. Special consideration has been given to Indians of Nebraska and the cattle industry. The collection is well supported by the library's general strength of Western Americana.

NE —UNIVERSITY OF NEBRASKA-LINCOLN, Don L Love Library, University Archives and Special Collections, Lincoln, 68588. Joseph G Svoboda, University Archivist
Holdings: Vols (1000) // Cat Mss Maps Pix Audiotapes 16mm Films

Notes: The Mari Sandoz Collection consists of four basic parts. The first contains correspondence files, 25,000 letters in all, including letters received from 1925 on and carbon copies of letters sent. The correspondence files are a rich source of information about the author's life and career, creative writing, and Plains Indian and western American history. The second portion of the collection is the author's personal library of books and periodicals, many annotated. Part three contains the author's published works, including most of the editions, foreign and domestic and some unpublished manuscripts as well. Many of the early drafts of books, copy-edited manuscripts, and galley and proofs are also contained in this portion of the collection. The final part of the collections consists of the author's resource files, research and reading notes, clippings, and related materials. These materials fill over fifty standard letter boxes. In addition, the prepared 45,000 index cards refering to information contained both in and out of the collection.

NV —UNIVERSITY OF NEVADA, RENO, University Library, Special Collections Dept, Reno, 89557. Robert E Blesse, Head
Holdings: Vols 800 Cat
Notes: The Women in the West Collection contains materials which document experience of women in the trans-Mississippi West. Major emphasis is on first-hand experience, diaries, letters and autobiographies, but major biographies of women who were prominent or greatly influenced others are also collected. Emphasis is the 19th and 20th centuries.

NY —NEW YORK PUBLIC LIBRARY, Research Libraries, American History Div, Fifth Ave & 42 St, New York, 10018.
Holdings: Vols (14,000) Cat
Notes: Outstanding collection of material on the Old West, incl early settlement, the lawless era, and the resulting vigilantism.

OK —THOMAS GILCREASE INSTITUTE OF AMERICAN HISTORY & ART LIBRARY, 1400 North 25th West Ave, Tulsa, 74127. Sarah Hirsch, Librn
Holdings: Vols Cat Mss Maps Pix
Notes: Trans-Mississippi West, US, Indian and Hispanic history. The Gilcrease Library contains a total of about 40,000 mss; 10,000 imprints; 5000 photographs; 600 maps and 50,000 vols.

PA —UNIVERSITY OF PENNSYLVANIA, Van Pelt Library, Rare Books Collection, 34 & Walnut Sts, Philadelphia, 19104. Daniel Traister, Special Collections Librn
Holdings: Vols 2500 //
Notes: Robert Dechert Collection: early exploration, 17th and 18th centuries; western Americana, 19th century; Canadiana, incl Jesuit relations.

RI —BROWN UNIVERSITY, John Hay Library, 20 Prospect St, Providence, 02912.

Mark N Brown, Cur Mss
Holdings: Vols (350) // Uncat
Notes: Eberstadt Collection of Narratives of California Pioneers--personal narratives written by pioneers who crossed the Plains to California after the discovery of gold in 1849. A large portion of the books were printed in the late 19th and early 20th centuries and deal with: Indian contacts, captivities, frontier lore, travel routes, topography, fauna and flora, outlaws, traders and trappers, and frontier army life.

TX —AMARILLO PUBLIC LIBRARY, 413 E Fourth, Amarillo, 79101. Mary Kay Snell, Librn
Holdings: Vols Cat Mss Maps Pix
Notes: The southwest collections incl materials on the history of Texas, Louisiana, New Mexico, Arkansas, Missouri and Kansas. General subjects covered incl overland journeys, early narratives, early biographies, Indian captivities, outlaws, US government reports, Mississippi and Ohio Rivers, the Mexican War, reports of Catholic missionaries, Niles Register, early publications, fur trade, western trails, Texas Rangers, sheriffs and Texas as a sovereign state, buffalo hunting, Indian wars, cowboys, the arrival of farmers, fences, and towns. Over 1600 items which incl books, documents, maps, mss, pamphlets, unpublished theses, interviews and photographs. The three major collections are the William Henry Bush Collection, the Laurence J Fitzsimon Collection and the Calendar of John L McCarty.

TX —TEXAS A&M UNIVERSITY, Sterling C Evans Library, Special Collections Div, College Station, 77843. Donald H Dyal, Librn
Holdings: Vols (16,000) Mss Pix
Notes: Jeff Dykes Range Livestock Collection (incl a 600-item collection of J Frank Dobie works). Part of the Dobie Collection is described in Dykes, Jeff C *My Dobie Collection* (College Station, Tex: Friends of the Texas A & M University Library).

TX —SOUTHERN METHODIST UNIVERSITY, DeGolyer Library, Box 396, SMU, Dallas, 75275. Clifton H Jones, Dir
Holdings: Vols 50,000 Cat Mss Maps Pix
Notes: History of the trans-Mississippi West and Mexico, from discovery to present. Original editions of most of the important early collections of travels.

TX —LUBBOCK CITY-COUNTY LIBRARY, 1306 Ninth St, Lubbock, 79401. Marlene M Harp, Dir, Adult Services
Holdings: Vols (10,000) Mss Microforms
Notes: Emphasis on the South and the various immigration routes used by settlers or their descendents from the Virginia-Georgia coast to west Texas. Very few periodical holdings prior to 1955. Material is not available for circulation or interlibrary loan.

UT —PROVO CITY PUBLIC LIBRARY, 13 N 100 E, Provo, 84601. Larry Hortin, Dir
Holdings: Vols (600) Cat
Notes: Western states history with emphasis on Utah State and Utah County.

UT —UNIVERSITY OF UTAH, Marriott Library, Special Collections, Salt Lake City, 84112. Gregory C Thompson, Cur
Holdings: Cat Mss Microfilm Rare Books Maps
Notes: Extensive collection.

†WA —WASHINGTON STATE UNIVERSITY, Library, Manuscripts, Archives & Special Collections, Pullman, 99164. John F Guido, Head
Holdings: Cat Mss Maps Pix
Notes: The Carl Parcher Russell papers, a vast resource (24,916 items; 45 linear feet) on American Indian and Western pioneer activities and artifacts. Much on the fur trade; pioneer life; mountain men and trapping; wildlife; primitive life in detail. Also the National Park Service, parks, monuments, etc. Described in *Carl Parcher Russell: An Indexed Register of His Scholarly and Professional Papers, 1920-1967, in the Washington State University Library* (Pullman, 1970), 149 pp. Also, papers, 1821-1873, covering Father De

OVERLAND JOURNEYS (cont.)

Smet's early sojourns at Whitemarsh and St Louis, his founding of the Rocky Mountain Missions, his long service as Procurator and Socius of the Missouri Province, and his many travels. Correspondence with his family in Belgium, mss of his published journals, 2 small maps, sketches and engravings usedto illustrate his books. Incl about 100 small pencil sketches by Father Nicholas Point depicting the 1841 journey from Westport to St Mary's Mission in the Bitterroot Valley. Described in *The Record*, 30 (1969) 6-40; and 32 (1971) 47-63.

ON —QUEEN'S UNIVERSITY, Douglas Library, Kingston, K7L 5C4, Can. William F E Morley, Cur, Special Collections
Holdings: Vols (50,000) Cat Mss Maps Pix Microforms
Budget: ($12,000)
Notes: The Edith and Lorne Pierce Collection of Canadiana. Also over 15,000 titles in Canadian Pamphlet Collection. Strong in humanities and social sciences, special strength in English and French Canadian literature; discovery and exploration narratives; Loyalists; War of 1812; opening of the West; local history, 19th century pamphlets and association items. Described in *A Catalogue of Canadian Manuscripts Collected by Lorne Pierce and Presented to Queen's University* (Toronto: Ryerson, 1946); and in *Canadiana 1698-1900 in the Possession of the Douglas Library*, comp by Janet S Porteous, foreword by Lorne Pierce (Kingston, 1932). Also later monographs and articles on parts of the collection.

ON —UNIVERSITY OF TORONTO, Thomas Fisher Rare Book Library, 120 Saint George St, Toronto, M5S 1A5, Can. Richard G Landon, Head
Holdings: Vols 30,000 Mss Maps Pix
Notes: Great variety of material relating to early exploration and settlement of Canada, including the search for the Northwest Passage and the subsequent exploration of the Arctic. Manuscript and printed material pertaining to the overland exploration of northwestern Canada and the Barren Lands. Manuscript and printed material documenting early emigration schemes and colonization attempts, including Selkirk's Red River settlement.

OVERTON, RICHARD

PA —TEMPLE UNIVERSITY LIBRARIES, Special Collections Dept, Rare Books & Mss Section, Philadelphia, 19122. Thomas M Whitehead, Cur
Holdings: Vols Cat Mss
Notes: Seventeeth and 18th century books and pamphlets on political, religious, social and intellectual life and history of England. Strong holdings of John Cotton, Gilbert Burnet, Richard Overton, John Lilburne; Civil War pamphlets, ranters and levellers. The Nordell and Simpson Collections.

OVID

VT —UNIVERSITY OF VERMONT, Guy W Bailey/David W Howe Library, Burlington, 05405. John Buehler, Asst Dir for Special Collections
Notes: Illustrated editions.

OWEN, ALBERT KIMSEY

CA —CALIFORNIA STATE UNIVERSITY, FRESNO, Henry Madden Library, Dept of Special Collections, Fresno, 93740. Ronald J Mahoney, Head
Holdings: Vols 130 Cat Mss Maps Pix
Notes: Archives of Albert Kimsey Owen, founder of the utopian colony at Topolobampo, Sinaloa, Mexico. Over 10,000 letters, maps, documents, pictures, newspapers, pamphlets, and plans, relating to the colony and the Credit Foncier Company already represented in the Library by the Viola Gabriel Collection of about 800 similar items and nearly 400 photographs. See *Cat's*

Paw Utopia, by Ray Reynolds (El Cajon, Calif, 1971). Incl 20 linear feet of ms material. Partially cataloged.
CA —UNIVERSITY OF CALIFORNIA, SAN DIEGO, Central University Library, Mandeville Dept of Special Collections, La Jolla, 92093. Lynda Corey Claassen, Head
Holdings: Vols 15 // Uncat Mss Maps Pix
Notes: Largely manuscript materials, pamphlets, newspapers.

OWEN, RICHARD, ROBERT, AND ROBERT DALE

IL —UNIVERSITY OF ILLINOIS, URBANA/CHAMPAIGN, Library, Illinois Historical Survey Library, 1408 W Gregory Dr, 1A Library, Urbana, 61801.
Holdings: Vols 50 Cat Mss Maps Pix Microforms
Notes: Communitarianism in America. The ms material, contained in 30 separate collections (10 cubic feet), concentrates on the period 1840-70. It incl correspondence, records, minutes, ledgers and diaries. Communal societies such as Bishop Hill, Brook Farm, New Harmony, the North American Phalanx and the Sodus Bay Phalanx are represented. Among the correspondents are Albert Brisbane, Parke Godwin, Sarah Grimke, Richard Owen, Robert Owen, Robert Dale Owen, and George Ripley. Numerous pictures. Guide to the collections published in 1976.
IN —INDIANA UNIVERSITY, Lilly Library, Seventh St, Bloomington, 47405. William R Cagle, Librn
Holdings: // Cat Mss
Notes: Contemporary printings.
NY —CORNELL UNIVERSITY LIBRARIES, Collection of Regional History, Dept of Manuscripts and Univ Archives, Ithaca, 14853.
Notes: Incl mss and letters from 19th century British comparative anatomist Richard Owen.

OWEN, ROBERT LATHAM

OK —UNIVERSITY OF OKLAHOMA, Bizzell Memorial Library, Western History Collections, 401 W Brooks, Norman, 73069. John Ezell, Cur
Holdings: Mss Documents
Notes: US Senator. His papers. Guide available.

OWEN, WILFRED

NY —HOFSTRA UNIVERSITY, Library, 1000 Fulton Ave, Hempstead, 11550. Charles R Andrews, Dean of Library Services

OWEN FAMILY

IN —INDIANA HISTORICAL SOCIETY, Library, 315 W Ohio St, Indianapolis, 46202. Robert K O'Neill, Dir
Holdings: Cat Mss Maps Pix Slides Microforms

OWENISM

IN —PURDUE UNIVERSITY LIBRARIES, Graduate School of Management, Krannert Library, West Lafayette, 47907. Gordon Law, Librn
Notes: An important resource at the Krannert Library is its Special Collection of Business and Economics, consisting of some 8000 rare pre-20th century strengths in books, journals, tracts and pamphlets covering primarily the early literature of economic thought and business practices in America and abroad, 1500-1870. A catalog was issued in 1979.

OWENS, CLAIRE MYERS

TX —TEXAS WOMAN'S UNIVERSITY, Bralley Memorial Library, Box 23715, TWU Sta, Denton, 76204. Metta Nicewarner, Spec Collections Libn
Holdings: Uncat Mss Pix
Notes: The Claire Myers Owens Papers

belong to the Texas author, religious philosopher, Zen Buddhist. Includes correspondence, edited mss, galleys and personal items.

OWENS, ROCHELLE

MA —BOSTON UNIVERSITY, Mugar Memorial Library, Special Collections Dept, 771 Commonwealth Ave, Boston, 02215. Howard B Gotlieb, Dir
Holdings: Cat Mss Pix
Notes: Mss, correspondence, etc collected in depth; incl publications by or about.

OWENS, REP. WAYNE

UT —UNIVERSITY OF UTAH, Marriott Library, Special Collections, Salt Lake City, 84112. Gregory C Thompson, Cur
Holdings: Cat Mss Microfilm Film Oral History
Notes: Papers.

OWENS FAMILY

TX —NORTH TEXAS STATE UNIVERSITY, Archives, NT Station Box 5188, Denton, 76203. Robert LaForte, University Archivist
Notes: Part of the Business Archive Project. Interviews with C B Owens, founder of Owens Country Sausage, and with Jerry Owens. Incl views on family-owned businesses.

OWLS

CT —LEE ASH, (personal collection), 66 Humiston Dr, Bethany, 06525.
PA —TEMPLE UNIVERSITY LIBRARIES, Special Collections Dept, Conwellana-Templana Collection, 13 & Berks St, Philadelphia, 19122. Miriam I Crawford, Cur
Holdings: Mss Pix
Budget: ($30,000)
Notes: The owl is the mascot and symbol of Temple University, which makes the Templana Collection (the University archives) the collector and recipient of information and images of owls in their many representations. Chief holdings are 4 typed, illustrated notebooks, titled "Owlana," compiled around 1954 by Edna DeFrehn, and a collection of 25 sculpture pieces, presented by University Chancellor Millard E Gladfelter.

OWSLEY, ALVIN M.

TX —NORTH TEXAS STATE UNIVERSITY, Archives, NT Station Box 5188, Denton, 76203. Robert LaForte, University Archivist
Notes: 72 linear feet. Texas political manuscript collections housed in the NTSU Archives incl the Fred H Minor Collection (former Texas Speaker of the House), the Alvin M Owsley Collection (former US diplomat from Texas), and the Bullock Hyder Collection (former representative to Texas House from Lewisville). The collections cover Texas politics from the 1920's to the 1970's. Published Description: Fred H Minor Collection, *The National Union Catalog of Manuscript Collections: Catalog 1979* Washington: Library of Congress, 1980. Alvin M Owsley Collection, Ibid, Hermine Tobolowsky Equal Legal Rights Collection, Ibid.

OXFORD MOVEMENT

CA —SAINT MARY'S COLLEGE, Library, Moraga, 94575. Brother Casimir Reichlin, Dir of the Library; Brother Richard Lemberg FSC, Asst Librn
Holdings: Vols 1746
Notes: Biographical information on Oxford Movement figures, esp John Henry Newman.
CT —YALE UNIVERSITY, Beinecke Rare Book & Manuscript Library, Osborn Collection, New Haven, 06520. Stephen R Parks, Cur
Holdings: Mss
NY —GENERAL THEOLOGICAL SEMINARY, Saint Marks Library, 175

OXFORD MOVEMENT (cont.)

Ninth Ave, New York, 10011. David Green, Dir
Holdings: Vols (200,000) Cat
Notes: Extensive collection.

OXFORD UNIVERSITY AND CITY

CA —CLAREMONT COLLEGES, Honnold Library, Eighth & Dartmouth, Claremont, 91711. Catharine K Firman, Cur, Oxford Collection
Holdings: Vols 4500 Cat Mss Pix
Notes: History, university life, Oxford printing, biography, philosophy, religion, literature, and periodicals. Restricted use. Downs 945. Published catalogs: *The William W Clary Oxford Collection: A Descriptive Catalogue*, ed by Grace M Briggs (Honnold Library, 1956); *The William W Clary Oxford Collection: A Supplementary Catalogue*, ed by Catharine K Firman (Honnold Library, 1965).

CT —YALE UNIVERSITY, Beinecke Rare Book & Manuscript Library, Osborn Collection, New Haven, 06520. Stephen R Parks, Cur
Holdings: Mss

DC —GEORGETOWN UNIVERSITY, Library, Special Collections Div, 37 & O Sts NW, Washington, 20057. George M Barringer, Special Collections Librn; Nicholas B Sheetz, Mss Librn
Holdings: Cat Mss
Notes: The papers of the English author, journalist, and historian Douglas Woodruff (1897-1978), containing correspondence, mss, and photographs. Incl is considerable material concerning his years at Oxford University; his editorship for many years of The "Tablet"; English Catholic society in general and English Catholic literature in particular. Also present are research files on the Tichborne Claimant, one of the most famous cases of impersonation in English legal history. There is extensive correspondence from such figures as: Hilaire Belloc; Tom Burns; Rev Martin D'Arcy, SJ; Christopher Dawson; Sir Roy Harrod; Christopher Hollis; Msgr Ronald Knox; Sir Shane Leslie; Sir Arnold Lunn; Rebecca West; and Evelyn Waugh.

IL —CHICAGO PUBLIC LIBRARY, Special Collections Div, Cultural Center, 78 E Washington St, Chicago, 60602. Laura Linard, Cur
Holdings: Cat
Notes: Since Thomas Hughes, MP and author of *Tom Brown's Schooldays*, was instrumental in the founding of The Chicago Public Library in 1871, the Library has begun to collect him in depth. The collection is small at present but several bookdealers in the US and Great Britain are searching for Hughes material and we purchase nearly 90 per cent of what is quoted. The Hughes Collection supplements the English Book Donation of 1871, originally about 7000 volumes (now only 500 are preserved), sponsored by Hughes. The Donation comprises primarily books donated by Oxford University and bears Oxford's gift-stamp and bookplate; the other extant books are late editions of Victorian literary and historical writers.

OXIDATION

NY —PENNWALT CORPORATION, Lucidol Division, Research Library, 1740 Military Road, Buffalo, 14240. Brenda L Cassoni Asst Librn
Holdings: Vols 8000 Books Per
Notes: There is a separate catalog of subject references to articles in periodicals.

OXYMURIATIC ACID see Chlorine

OZANAM, ANTOINE FREDERIC, 1813-1853

MO —SAINT LOUIS UNIVERSITY, Pius XII Memorial Library, 3655 W Pine Blvd, Saint Louis, 63108. William Cole, Dir
Holdings: Vols 250 Cat
Notes: Antoine Frederic Ozanam, 11813-1853, was the Catholic answer to Karl Marx. St Louis University owns almost everything by and about Ozanam, due to the kindness of the local St Vincent de Paul Society.

OZARK FOLK SONGS see Folk Songs, Ozark

OZARK REGION

AR —UNIVERSITY OF ARKANSAS, Library, Special Collections Dept, Fayetteville, 72701. Michael J Dabrishus, Cur
Holdings: Vols (40,299) Cat Mss Maps Pix Phonorecords Audiotapes Microforms
Notes: Material pertaining to the political, governmental, economic, social, cultural, educational, religious, scientific and literary history of Arkansas, its people and its institutions, incl the "natural history," anthropological development, and folk traditions of the area, from prehistoric times to the present. Holdings described in: Samuel A Sizer, *A Guide to Selected Manuscript Collections in the University of Arkansas Library* (Fayetteville, Ark, 1976) and in supplementary catalogs, inventories, indexes and other unpublished finding aids in the library.

DC —LIBRARY OF CONGRESS, American Folklife Center, Archive of Folk Culture, Washington, 20540.
Notes: Vance Randolph's papers, photographs, and field recordings of Ozark folk music, 1930s - 1960s.

MO —SPRINGFIELD-GREENE COUNTY PUBLIC LIBRARY, 397 E Central, PO Box 737, Springfield, 65801. Jewell Smith, Administrative Librn
Holdings: Vols 7100 Cat Maps Pix Microforms
Notes: Missouri and Ozarks collection. Incl uncataloged pamphlets. Special indexes have been prepared.

OZONE

MA —MASSACHUSETTS INSTITUTE OF TECHNOLOGY, Institute Archives, Special Collections, Cambridge, 02139.
Notes: Correspondence, newsletters, fact-sheets, newspaper and magazine articles, books and reports of the Citizens' League Against the Sonic Boom, established in 1967 by William Shurcliff to oppose the sonic boom, stop commercial supersonic transport production, and influence public opinion and policy decisions on the SST. Major correspondents incl Bo Lundberg, Richard Wiggs, several US congressmen, and CLASB members.

OH —EMERY INDUSTRIES, Research Library, 4900 Este Ave, Cincinnati, 45232. B A Bernard, Librn
Holdings: Cat
Notes: Special subjects: fatty acids and organic chemical derivatives, ozone, plasticizers, polymers, synthetic lubricants.

P

P.T. BOATS

TN —PT BOATS MUSEUM & LIBRARY, PO
Box 109, Memphis, 38101. J M "Boats"
Newberry, Librn
Holdings: Vols (2000) Uncat Maps Pix
Slides Phonorecords Audiotapes 16mm
Films Microforms Videotapes Biographies
Budget: ($25,000)
Notes: PT Boats, Inc is an 8000 man
organization of PT boat veterans, families,
modelers and history buffs who have
donated a sizable collection of artifacts and
records pertaining to their PT boat service.
The collection also contains an 80-foot Elco
PT boat and a 78-foot Higgins PT boat, both
restored. National headquarters and archives
are in Memphis, and the display collection is
located on board the USS Massachusetts at
Battleship Cove, Fall River, Mass, 02721. To
use the library, write PT Boat Coordinator,
William C Hindle and/or Don Rhoads, Chief
Administrative Officer in Memphis.
Memphis headquarters has some 10,000
photos and line drawings with specifications.

PABST, G.W.

NY —MUSEUM OF MODERN ART, Dept of
Film, 11 W 53 St, New York, 10019. Eileen
Bowser, Cur
Holdings: Mss Pix
Notes: Papers, correspondence, scrapbooks,
pictures, etc. Partially cataloged.

PACFORNET

WA —UNIVERSITY OF WASHINGTON
LIBRARIES, Forest Resources Library, AQ-
15, Seattle, 98195. Barbara B Gordon, Head
Holdings: Vols 63,000 Cat Maps Microforms
Budget: $12,500
Notes: Modern imprints only. Mostly in
English, some German, Slavic, and East
Asian languages. No geographical limits but
emphasis is on Pacific Northwest. Northern
service center for Pacific Forestry Research
Information Network (PACFORNET);
southern center is at USFS Pacific Southwest
Experiment Station, Berkeley, California.
Partially cataloged.

PACHUCO

CA —CALIFORNIA STATE UNIVERSITY,
FULLERTON, Library, Box 4150,
Fullerton, 92634. Alfredo H Zuniga, Coord
Notes: Some materials on the subject; not
maintained as a separate collection.

PACIFIC AMERICAN FISHERIES

WA —WESTERN WASHINGTON
UNIVERSITY, Center for Pacific Northwest
Studies, High St, Bellingham, 98225. James
W Scott, Dir
Holdings: // Cat Mss Maps Pix
Notes: The Archie W Shiels Collection.
Archie W Shiels, who died in his 95th year
in 1974, was formerly Managing Dir of
Pacific American Fisheries and an author of
some note on Alaskan topics. A few papers
of his company are incl in the collection,
which is primarily focused on Alaska,
particularly its history and its seal and other
fisheries. See also entry for Galen A Biery.

PACIFIC COAST—HISTORY

CA —NATIONAL MARITIME MUSEUM,
SAN FRANCISCO, J Porter Shaw Library,
Golden Gate National Recreation Area, Fort
Mason, San Francisco, 94123. David A Hull,
Librn; Herbert Beckwith, Catalog Librn;
Irene Stachura, Ref Librn; John Maounis,
Photo Librn
Holdings: Vols (12,000) Mss Maps Pix Slides
Microforms Periodicals VF
Budget: ($4000)
Notes: Pacific Coast maritime history. The
photo collection of 160,000 is partly
cataloged and classified. The library has
complete runs of *Merchant Vessels of US*
and *Lloyd's Register of Shipping* to 1970.
The collection is particularly strong on
Pacific Coast and San Francisco maritime
history. About 250 log books; scrapbooks.
Oral history interviews, nautical charts,
vertical files. 60 percent of books are
cataloged.

PACIFIC FORESTRY RESEARCH INFORMATION NETWORK (PACFORNET) see Pacfornet

PACIFIC IMPROVEMENT COMPANY

CA —STANFORD UNIVERSITY, Graduate
School of Business, J Hugh Jackson Library,
Stanford, 94305.
Holdings: Vols (316,994) Cat Microforms
Corporate Reports
Budget: ($255,000)
Notes: Incl 590,027 microforms, 300,000
corporate reports, and 2344 periodical
subscriptions. Library Publications: *Selected
Additions to the J Hugh Jackson Library*
(bimonthly); and *Catalog of Jackson Library
Periodicals and Annuals on Standing Order*
(annual).

PACIFIC ISLANDS see Islands of the Pacific

PACIFIC NORTHWEST see Northwest, Pacific

PACIFIC OCEAN

CA —UNIVERSITY OF CALIFORNIA,
SANTA CRUZ, University Library, Special
Collections, Santa Cruz, 95064. Rita
Bottoms, Special Collections Librn; Margaret
Felts, South Pacific Collection Bibliographer
Notes: South Pacific Collection. Ryerson,
Carlton, Skinner and Malinowski, O'Reilly
and Firth Collections.

HI —BERNICE P BISHOP MUSEUM,
Library, PO Box 19000-A, Honolulu, 96819.
Cynthia Timberlake, Librn
Holdings: Vols (90,000) Cat Mss Pix Slides
Microforms
Budget: ($30,000)
Notes: Only American library devoted
exclusively to the Pacific region. Collection
reflects historical and contemporary research
emphases of Bishop Museum; ie the natural
and cultural history of the Pacific. Areas of
concentration incl archaeology, ethnology,
linguistics, voyages and explorations, history,
vertebrate and invertebrate zoology, botany
and museology. Strong special collections
incl photographs, mss and archives, maps
and art. Publications: Quarterly "Additions
to the Catalog," *Dictionary Catalog of the
Library* (9 vols and 2 suppl; Boston: G K
Hall, 1964-69).

HI —HAWAII STATE LIBRARY, Hawaii &
Pacific Collection, 478 S King St, Honolulu,
96813. Proserfina Strona, Acting Head
Holdings: Vols (93,834) Cat Microforms
Budget: ($30,000)
Notes: Publish cumulative index of Hawaii
State Documents biennially and an Index to
the *Honolulu Advertiser* and *Honolulu
Star-Bulletin* annually. Also print
bibliographies of special interest, such as
ethnic bibliographies, Aloha Week
celebrations, etc. Depository for county and
state documents.

HI —PACIFIC SCIENTIFIC INFORMATION
CENTER, Bernice P Bishop Library,
Geography and Map Division, PO Box
19000A, Honolulu, 96819. Lee S Motteler,
Geographer; Valerie T Higa, Asst
Geographer
Holdings: Vols (2000) Cat Mss Maps Pix
Notes: Incl 20,000 maps and 70,000 aerial
photos of Hawaii and the Pacific.

IN —BUTLER UNIVERSITY, Irwin Library,
Hugh Thomas Miller Rare Book Room,
4600 Sunset Ave, Indianapolis, 46208.
Gisela Terrell, Rare Books Librn
Holdings: Vols (2500) Cat Maps Pix
Notes: *Gaar Williams/Kin Hubbard*
Collection. This collection was presented to
the library by Blanche Stillson in 1964. It
contains original cartoons and other
drawings, books (many of them inscribed),
magazines, letters and other manuscripts,
photographs, and memorabilia by both
Hoosier cartoonists and humorists. A
catalogue of the Gaar Williams ("Abe
Martin") items was printed in 1981. It is
available upon request.

MN —UNIVERSITY OF MINNESOTA,
James Ford Bell Library, 309 19th Ave S,
Minneapolis, 55455. John Parker, Cur
Holdings: Vols (11,000) Cat Mss Maps
Notes: Collection of original materials
relating to European expansion, 1400-1800.

PA —PENNSYLVANIA STATE
UNIVERSITY, Fred Lewis Pattee Library,
University Park, 16802. Stuart Forth, Dean
of Libraries
Holdings: Vols Cat Mss Maps Pix
Notes: The Pennsylvania State University
has for several years had a strong interest in
the South Pacific, based on Australia but
extending to New Zealand and other island
groups, together with an interest in voyages
of exploration and scientific discovery. The
collection is particularly strong in literature
but extends to history, political science, the
arts and humanities generally. Holdings
housed in Special Collections includes the
Moody gift of 90 prints and paintings, press
collections including the Wattle Grove press,
and Fanfrolico Press publications associated
with Norman Lindsay. The special collection
of Australiana is dedicated to Bruce
Sutherland and was described in his
publication *Australiana in the PSU Libraries*
(Pennsylvania State University Libraries,
1969), 390 pp.

PACIFIC RIM COUNTRIES

CA —AZUSA PACIFIC COLLEGE,
Marshburn Memorial Library, Citrus &
Alosta, Azusa, 91702. Edward Peterman,
Librn
Holdings: Vols (6000) Uncat
Budget: ($30,000)
Notes: Significant holdings in the George E
Fullerton Library of Californiana and
Western Americana.

CA —UNIVERSITY OF CALIFORNIA,
BERKELEY, University Library, Slavic
Collections, Berkeley, 94720. Edward
Kasinec, Librn
Notes: Russian Pacifica collection, the best
on the West coast, incl materials in the
folowing areas: Russian exploration and
settlement of the North American continent;
Russian exploration and settlement and
colonization of Siberia; Russian exploration
of the Pacific; Russian communities in
Manchuria and other parts of the Far East.
While many items pertaining to the
geographical area are found in the Main
Library's stack collection, the bulk of
Russian Pacifica holdings is concentrated in
the Bancroft Library. The Bancroft
collections contain the greater number of
items listed in the two major bibliographies
of Russian Pacifica: Valentin Lada-
Macarski's *Bibliography of Books on Alaska
Published before 1868* (Yale Univ Press,
1969), and V I Mezhov's *Sibirskaia
bibliografiia* (S Petersburg: Semenov, 1903).
During 1983-84, with the assistance of Title
II-C funding, a major project of collection
evaluation and development was undertaken
in the area of Russian Racifica, resulting in
the acquisition on microfilm of several
hundred items, incl a part of the holdings of
the Museum of Russian Culture in San
Francisco relating to Siberia and Russian
communities in China.

CA —UNIVERSITY OF CALIFORNIA, SAN
DIEGO, Central University Library,
Mandeville Dept of Special Collections, La
Jolla, 92093. Lynda Corey Claassen, Head
Notes: Pacific Collection: Various cultures of
the Pacific rim and Pacific islands are
described in these works. The Kingdom of
Tonga is a special focus of the collection.
The Melanesian Archive preserves published
and unpublished research materials
documenting the culture of this archipelago.

CA —UNIVERSITY OF CALIFORNIA, LOS
ANGELES, Research Library, Indo/Pacific

PACIFIC RIM COUNTRIES (cont.)

Collection, 405 Hilgard Ave, Los Angeles, 90024. Edward Shreeves, Chairman, Bibliographers Group; Charlotte Spence, Indo/Pacific Bibliographer
Holdings: Vols Cat Mss Maps Pix Microforms
Notes: The Pacific area collection has been developed on a combination of the research and teaching levels. It focuses on the cultural, economic, political and social history of Australia, New Zealand and the various island groups. The accounts of the early European voyagers are well represented, with the highlight being the Captain Cook collection. An effort has also been made to collect the novels, poetry, drama, etc, of Australian and New Zealand authors.

CA —UNIVERSITY OF CALIFORNIA, SANTA CRUZ, University Library, Special Collections, Santa Cruz, 95064. Rita Bottoms, Special Collections Librn; Margaret Felts, South Pacific Collection Bibliographer

CA —HOOVER INSTITUTION ON WAR, REVOLUTION & PEACE, Stanford University, Stanford, 94305. Milorad M Drachkovitch, Archivist
Holdings: Mss Pix
Notes: Collection of correspondence, reports, memoranda, study papers, press releases, printed matter and photographs, 1925-1960, relating to the study of political, social and economic conditions in the Far East by the American Council of the Institute of Pacific Relations, collected by Ray Lyman Wilbur. 21 ms boxes, 1 album, 1 envelope.

HI —BERNICE P BISHOP MUSEUM, Library, PO Box 19000-A, Honolulu, 96819. Cynthia Timberlake, Librn
Holdings: Vols (90,000) Cat Mss Maps Pix Slides Microforms
Budget: ($30,000)
Notes: Only American library devoted exclusively to the Pacific region. Collection reflects historical and contemporary research emphases of Bishop Museum; ie the natural and cultural history of the Pacific. Areas of concentration incl archaeology, ethnology, linguistics, voyages and explorations, history, vertebrate and invertebrate zoology, botany and museology. Strong special collections incl photographs, mss and archives, maps and art. Publications: Quarterly "Additions to the Catalog," *Dictionary Catalog of the Library* (9 vols and 2 suppl; Boston: G K Hall, 1964-69).

†HI —EAST-WEST POPULATION INSTITUTE RESOURCE MATERIALS COLLECTION, 1777 East-West Rd, Honolulu, 96848.
Notes: Demography, population problems and policy in Hawaii, Asian countries and Pacific area, family planning programs, environment.

HI —HAWAII STATE LIBRARY, Hawaii & Pacific Collection, 478 S King St, Honolulu, 96813. Proserfina Strona, Acting Head
Holdings: Vols (93,834) Cat Microforms
Budget: ($30,000)
Notes: Publish cumulative index of Hawaii State Documents biennially and index to the *Honolulu Advertiser* and *Honolulu Star-Bulletin* annually. Also print bibliographies of special interest, such as ethnic bibliographies, Aloha Week celebrations, etc. Depository for county and state documents.

†HI —PACIFIC AND ASIAN AFFAIRS COUNCIL, Pacific House Library, 2004 University Ave, Honolulu, 96816.
Notes: Asia and the Pacific. Pacific and Asian foreign policy.

IL —NEWBERRY LIBRARY, 60 W Walton St, Chicago, 60610. Diana Haskell, Cur of Modern Mss
Holdings: Vols 400 Cat Mss Maps Pix
Notes: Incl circumnavigations of the world, the many travelers to the Philippines and the Northwest Coast.

NE —UNIVERSITY OF NEBRASKA-LINCOLN, Don L Love Library, University Archives and Special Collections, Lincoln, 68588. Joseph G Svoboda, University

Archivist
Notes: Collection consists mainly of pamphlets, clippings, posters, and other World War II ephemera; 2000 items.

PA —PENNSYLVANIA STATE UNIVERSITY, Fred Lewis Pattee Library, University Park, 16802. Stuart Forth, Dean of Libraries
Holdings: Vols Cat Mss Maps Pix
Notes: The Pennsylvania State University has for several years had a strong interest in the South Pacific, based on Australia but extending to New Zealand and other island groups, together with an interest in voyages of exploration and scientific discovery. The collection is particularly strong in literature but extends to history, political science, the arts and humanities generally. Holdings housed in Special Collections include the Moody gift of 90 prints and paintings, press collections including the Wattle Grove press, and Golden Cockerell Press publications associated with Norman Lindsay. The special collection of Australiana is dedicated to Bruce Sutherland and was described in his publication *Australiana in the PSU Libraries* (Pennsylvania State University Libraries, 1969), 390 pp. A separate card file is maintained.

PACIFIC STATES

CA —UNIVERSITY OF CALIFORNIA, BERKELEY, Bancroft Library, Manuscripts Division, Berkeley, 94720. James D Hart, Dir
Holdings: Vols Mss Maps Pix Slides Microforms
Notes: Approx

CA —UNIVERSITY OF CALIFORNIA, BERKELEY, Museum of Vertebrate Zoology, Grinnell-Miller Library, Berkeley, 94720.
Holdings: Vols (2000) Cat
Notes: Vertebrate zoology, with emphasis on birds and mammals of the Pacific States.

WA —UNIVERSITY OF WASHINGTON LIBRARIES, Pacific Northwest Collection, Seattle, 98195. Andrew F Johnson, Librn
Holdings: Vols (50,000) Cat Maps Pix
Budget: ($12,000)
Notes: The Pacific Northwest Collection contains printed materials documenting the historic and contemporary life and culture of the region in a broad range of subject areas. The Pacific Northwest is defined as the geographic region including Washington, Oregon, Idaho, Montana, British Columbia, Yukon Territory, and Alaska. Printed materials including books, periodicals, government documents, maps, weekly and local regional newspapers, theses and dissertations, as well as photographs and architectural drawings are included in the Pacific Northwest Collection. Photographic works of over 200 photographers active in the Pacific Northwest, Alaska, and the Yukon Territory (Canada) during the period 1860-1930, including Asahel and Edward S Curtis, Eric Hegg, and Clark Kinsey, are represented in a print collection of more than 300,000 images. The architecturaldrawings collection includes over 19,000 original plans, drawings, sketches, renderings and blue prints pertaining to the history of architecture and urban planning and landscape gardening in the Pacific Northwest ca 1880-1940. Areas of particular strength are the holdings of over 1100 published journals of Pacific Northwest exploration expeditions, photographs of Northwest Coast Native Americans and of historic Seattle, newspapers issued within the Japanese-American relocation camps, 1942-1945, materials relating to the 1980 eruption of Mt St Helens, and Sanborne fire insurance maps for Washington. A unique feature of the Collection is the subject index to regional periodicals and local newspapers maintained by the PNW Collection staff; over 100 titles are currently indexed. G K Hall Company published a books catalog of the Pacific Northwest Collectionin 1973.

PACIFIC STEAMSHIP COMPANY

CA —CLAREMONT COLLEGES, Honnold Library, Ninth & Dartmouth, Claremont,

91711. Tania Rizzo, Special Collections Dept Head
Holdings: Vols 353 Calendared Mss Maps Pix
Notes: Ms and typescript volumes of account books, ledgers, log books, journals, annual reports, cargo lists, correspondence, etc. Given to Pomona College by the Robert Dollar Co upon the liquidation of the Pacific Steamship Co Thompson, R C, comp, *Calendar of Archives and Records of Certain Pacific Coast steamship companies* (typescript prepared 1940-1941). Restricted use.

PACIFIC VOYAGES

CA —AZUSA PACIFIC COLLEGE, Marshburn Memorial Library, Citrus & Alosta, Azusa, 91702. Edward Peterman, Librn
Holdings: Vols (6000) Uncat
Budget: ($30,000)
Notes: Significant holdings in the George E Fullerton Library of Californiana and Western Americana.

CA —UNIVERSITY OF CALIFORNIA, SAN DIEGO, Central University Library, Mandeville Dept of Special Collections, La Jolla, 92093. Lynda Corey Claassen, Head
Holdings: Vols (2400) Cat Mss Maps
Notes: The Hill Collection of Pacific Voyages, including reports and commentaries of important voyages in the Pacific, from those of Magellan and Sir Francis Drake to exploration through the first half of the 19th century. Includes many rare overland accounts to the Pacific across North America, Mexico, and Panama. Bibliography: Silveira de Braganza, Ronald, *The Hill Collection of Pacific Voyages* (La Jolla: Calif, 1974-1983).

CA —PACIFIC GROVE PUBLIC LIBRARY, 550 Central Ave, Pacific Grove, 93950. Margaret McBride, Library Dir
Holdings: Vols (1200) // Cat
Notes: Alvin Seale South Seas Collection, incl rare and unusual items, accounts of early voyages, ships' logs and artifacts. Separate catalog. Gift of Alvin Seale, curator of Steinhart Aquarium, San Francisco, 1937.

HI —PACIFIC SCIENTIFIC INFORMATION CENTER, Bernice P Bishop Library, Geography and Map Division, PO Box 19000A, Honolulu, 96819. Lee S Motteler, Geographer; Valerie T Higa, Asst Geographer
Holdings: Vols (2000) Cat Mss Maps Pix
Notes: Incl 20,000 maps and 70,000 aerial photos of Hawaii and the Pacific.

MA —PEABODY MUSEUM OF SALEM, Phillips Library, E India Sq, Salem, 01970. Gregor Trinkaus-Randall, Librn
Holdings: Vols (100,000) Cat Mss Maps Pix
Notes: Pacific and Artic voyages.

ON —UNIVERSITY OF TORONTO, Thomas Fisher Rare Book Library, 120 Saint George St, Toronto, M5S 1A5, Can. Richard G Landon, Head
Notes: Sheldon Collection of Australiana, named for collector William Sheldon. Especially rich in 19th century accounts of the exploration of the South Pacific and the interior of the Australian continent. Includes narratives of exiled Canadians who took part in the Rebellion of 1837 in Canada. Includes works on colonization and settlement, the gold-rush of the mid 19th century, and on the life of the indigenous peoples. Includes literature written by Australians or about Australia.

PACIFISM

CA —HOOVER INSTITUTION ON WAR, REVOLUTION & PEACE, Stanford University, Stanford, 94305. Milorad M Drachkovitch, Archivist
Holdings: Mss Pix
Notes: Two collections: (1) Records of *National Republic* magazine, incl newspapers clippings, printed matter, pamphlets, reports, indices, notes, bulletins, letter, and photographs, 1905-1960, relating to pacifist, communist, fascist, and other radical movements as well as political developments

PACIFISM (cont.)

in the US and Soviet Russia. 826 ms boxes.
(2) Papers of Alice Park, 1883-1957, incl
diaries, correspondence, pamphlets,
clippings, and leaflets, relating to Pacifism
and the peace movement, the Ford Peace
Ship Expedition of 1915-1916, feminism,
socialism, the labor movement, prison
reform, child labor legislation, civil liberties,
and a variety of other reform movements in
the US. 30 ms boxes, 3 envelopes.
MA —RADCLIFFE COLLEGE, Arthur &
Elizabeth Schlesinger Library on the History
of Women in America, 3 James St,
Cambridge, 02138. Patricia Miller King, Dir;
Eva Moseley, Cur of Mss
Holdings: Cat Mss Audiotapes 16mm Films
Microforms
Notes: Incl papers from Jeannette Rankin's
two terms in Congress (1917-19, 1941-43),
mainly about her votes against US entry into
World Wars I and II, from her (mainly
pacifist) activities in the 1960s and 1970s,
and family papers. Also records of the
Massachusetts affiliate of the Women's
International League for Peace and
Freedom.
MA —NEW ENGLAND QUAKER
RESEARCH LIBRARY, PO Box 655,
North Amherst, 01059. Francis W Holmes,
Librn
Holdings: Vols (6000) Cat Mss Pix Slides
Phonorecords Audiotapes Microforms
Budget: ($300)
Notes: No photocopying on premises.
Subject emphases: Quakers and Quaker
concerns; Pacifism; Racism; Feminism;
Religion; Bible; Poverty.
MI —UNIVERSITY OF MICHIGAN, Dept of
Rare Books & Special Collections, Ann
Arbor, 48109. Edward C Weber, Head,
Labadie Collection
Holdings: Vols (40,000) Cat Mss Pix
Phonorecords Audiotapes Microforms
Notes: Emphasis is on radical aspects of
pacifism, incl civil disobedience. Also have
papers of Mary Hays Weik (1898-1979).
OH —WILMINGTON COLLEGE, Watson
Library, Quaker Collection, Pyle Center,
Box #1227, Wilmington, 45177. Audrey
Haines, Cur
Holdings: Vols (6000) Cat Mss Maps Pix
Microforms
Notes: Collection houses Wilmington
College archives, 1870-present, and serves as
repository for the records of the Wilmington
and Ohio Valley Yearly Meetings of the
Religious Society of Friends (Quakers), ca
1800-present. Also incl 120 Quaker
periodical and newsletter titles, ca 1828-
present; several hundred pamphlets, tracts,
and epistles; 220 genealogical works,
primarily Quaker families; and 3900 vols on
Quaker history, philosophy, thought, and
practice, particularly peace, war, slavery,
education, and biography, ca 1750-present.
Incl some fiction, poetry and children's
books. Rare or fragile materials, reference
works, pamphlets, and genealogies do not
circulate. Please notify prior to visiting.
WI —BELOIT COLLEGE LIBRARIES, Beloit,
53511. Dennis W Dickinson, Dir
Holdings: Vols 700 Cat
Notes: The Martin Luther King Jr Collection
on Nonviolence. This small collection was
given by H Vail Deale, Director, at the time
of the assassination of Dr King in 1968.
Comprises books by and about: M K
Gandhi, H D Thoreau, M L King, world
peace, pacifism, nonviolence, etc. Contains a
35-year bound file of Fellowship, the
magazine of US pacifism. At present time
there is only a local card index of the
collection, though items are fully cataloged
in the Public Card Catalog. A specially
designed bookplate by local artist, O Vernon
Shaffer, is used for books in this collection.

PACIFISM—HISTORY

PA —SWARTHMORE COLLEGE, Peace
Collection, Swarthmore, 19081. Jean R
Soderlund, Cur of Peace Collection
Holdings: Vols (10,000) Cat Mss Pix
Microforms
Notes: The history of pacifism has been one
of the major subject emphases of the Peace
Collection since its inception in 1930. In
addition to books, pamphlets, and current
materials of all kinds on the subject, the
Peace Collection is the official depository for
many 20th century pacifist organizations and
papers of individual peace leaders. These incl
Women's International League for Peace
and Freedom; War Resisters League;
Fellowship of Reconciliation; SANE, A
Committee for a Sane Nuclear Policy;
Friends Committee on National Legislation;
CCCO1 An Agency for Military and Draft
Counseling; National Interreligious Service
Board for Conscientious Objectors; A J
Muste (1885-1967); and Devere Allen
(1891-1955). Other materials collected incl
records and memorabilia of 19th and early
20th century peace leaders and
organizations, such as the American Peace
Society and itsbranches, Jane Addams
(1860-1935), the Wisbech Local Peace
Association (England), Emily Greene Blach
(1867-1961), English and American Friends'
Peace Societies, the Universal Peace Union,
William Ladd (1778-1841), Elihu Burritt
(1810-1879), and Benjamin F Trueblood
(1847-1916). The Peace Collection has been
described in Downs 972, 978, 4633, and in
Downs 1950-1961 Supplement 507 and 916.
For descriptions of major document groups,
see the Guide to the Swarthmore College
Peace Collection, 2nd ed (1981).

PACIFIST PERIODICALS see Periodicals,
Pacifist

PACKAGING

DC —LIBRARY OF CONGRESS, Prints &
Photographs Div, Washington, 20540.
Notes: Packaging for American tobacco
products, 1840s-1880s. Approx 1000 tobacco
labels, arranged by subject.
MN —MTS SYSTEMS CORP, Information
Services, PO Box 24012, Minneapolis,
55424. Kathleen Werner, Technical Librn
Holdings: Cat Mss Pix Slides Phonorecords
Audiotapes Videotapes 16mm Films
Microforms
Notes: Material testing machines. Incl 2000
ms reports, 10,000 pictures, 6000 slides.
NY —INTERNATIONAL PAPER CO,
Corporate Information Center, 77 W 45 St,
New York, 10036. Elizabeth Skerritt,
Corporate Librn
Holdings: Vols 220 Cat Maps Pix Slides
Microforms
Notes: Extensive statistics and VF on paper
industry.
NC —R J REYNOLDS TOBACCO CO,
Scientific Information Services Library,
Bowman Gray Technical Center, BGTC
611-12/205, Winston-Salem, 27102. Nellie
W Sizemore, Librn
Holdings: Vols 1000 Cat Microforms
SC —CRYOVAC TECHNICAL LIBRARY,
PO Box 464, Duncan, 29334. M M Ezell,
Libn
Holdings: Vols (6000) Cat
Notes: Library supports corporate research,
development, and engineering. Incl materials
on chemical and mechanical engineering,
polymers and polymerization, plastics, and
food packaging. 175 periodical titles
received. Library open by appointment or
through ILL.
WI —UNIVERSITY OF WISCONSIN-
STOUT, Library Learning Center,
Menomonie, 54751. Philip Sawin Jr, Coll
Develop Librn
Notes: Supports the Packaging concentration
of the Master's Degree in Industrial
Management. Concentration was authorized
at the graduate level in 1974, but specialized
collection since 1965.

PADDLEFORD, CLEMENTINE

KS —KANSAS STATE UNIVERSITY,
Library, Special Collections & University
Archives, Manhattan, 66506. Antonia Q
Pigno, Coordr; John J Vander Velde, Librn;
Anthony R Crawford, Univ Archivist
Holdings: Vols 4500 Cat Mss
Budget: ($10,000)
Notes: Cookbooks and related items on
home economics, nutrition and domestic
economy. Nucleus of the collection is from
the Abbey Lillian Marlatt collection
augmented by a sizable bequest from the
estate of Clementine Paddleford. Includes
about 600 volumes of rare cookbooks from
the 16th, 17th, and 18th centuries as well as
unprocessed papers (scrapbooks, recipe files
and correspondence of Clementine
Paddleford). A chronological bibliography is
available for the pre-1900 portion of the
collection: The Kansas State University
Receipt Book and Household Manual (1968)
by G A Rudolph.

PADEN, JOHN

IL —NORTHWESTERN UNIVERSITY,
Melville J Herskovits Library of African
Studies, Evanston, 60201. Hans E Panofsky,
Cur
Holdings: Vols (85,000) Mss
Budget: ($70,000)
Notes: Papers, incl Arabic and Hausa mss.
See also entry under Africa

PADEREWSKI, IGNACY JAN

CA —HOOVER INSTITUTION ON WAR,
REVOLUTION & PEACE, Stanford
University, Stanford, 94305. Milorad M
Drachkovitch, Archivist
Holdings: Mss
Notes: Papers of I J Paderewski, Polish
statesman and pianist, incl correspondence,
speeches, clippings, printed matter, and
photographs, 1894-1941, relating to his
political and musical careers. 6 1/2 ms
boxes.

PADUA THEATER

CA —POMONA PUBLIC LIBRARY, Special
Collections, 625 S Garey Ave, PO Box 2271,
Pomona, 91766. David Streeter, Librn
Holdings: Uncat Mss
Notes: 14 linear feet of theater archives incl
original play scripts, original music
compositions, tape recordings of play
performances, theater advertising,
photographs of players, play bills, etc.
Theatrical group was also known as The
Mexican Players. Period covered: 1930's-
1960's.

PAETEL, KARL OTTO, 1906-1975

NY —STATE UNIVERSITY OF NEW YORK
AT ALBANY, Library, Special Collections
Dept, 1400 Washington Ave, Albany, 12222.
Marion P Munzer, Coordr
Notes: Correspondence regarding Karl Otto
Paetel and his German language newspaper,
Aufbau; mss and letters concerning the
German youth movement, Ernst Jünger,
German resistance, and the refugee question
(3.8 linear feet). Part of the Library's
German Exile Collection.
See also entries under Journalists; German
Youth Movement; Exiles, Political; Jünger,
Ernst; Newspapers, German;
Jugendbewegung

PAGAN CIVILIZATION see Civilization,
Pagan

PAGANY/ A NATIVE QUARTERLY,
1930-1933

DE —UNIVERSITY OF DELAWARE, Hugh
M Morris Library, S College Ave, Newark,
19711. T Stuart Dick, Special Collections
Holdings: Mss
Notes: Includes all of the remaining
manuscripts and correspondence pertaining
to the publication of Pagany: A Native
Quarterly, 1930-1933. Among others,
important groups of letters from Sherwood
Anderson, Richard Blackmur, Erskine
Caldwell, Edward Dahlberg, Charles Henri
Ford, Albert Halper, Robert McAlmon, John

PAGANY/ A NATIVE QUARTERLY, 1930-1933 (cont.)

Sherry Mangon, Ezra Pound, Gertrude Stein, William Carlos Williams, and Louis Zykofsky.

PAGE, RUTH

IL —CHICAGO PUBLIC LIBRARY, Art Section, Fine Arts Division, 78 E Washington St, Chicago, 60602. Rosalinda I Hack, Fine Arts Division Chief; Yvonne S Brown, Head, Art Section
Holdings: Vols 2500
Notes: Reference and circulating collection of books, periodicals, pamphlets, and videotapes on all aspects of the dance eg ballet, social dance, square dance, jazz and folkdance. Focus of the collection is on ballet, history, biographies of dancers, and dance instruction. Subject is supplemented by a dance videotape collection, the *Folk Dance Index* a comprehensive index to descriptions of folkdances of all nations. Special Collections: Eliza Stigler Dance Collection of 200 dance books on ballet and dance history with particular emphasis on Spanish Dance. Ruth Page Archives: small collection of memorabilia documents the career of Ms Page. Reference collection of 85 dance videotapes that document notable dance performances, from the past and present by well known dancers and dance groups. Subject concentration is that of ballet, with some examples of ethnic dance. There is alsoa collection of tapes that document Chicago area dance groups, dancers, and choreographers. A file to the contents of the tapes is available.

NY —NEW YORK PUBLIC LIBRARY, Performing Arts Research Center, Dance Collection, 111 Amsterdam Ave, New York, 10023. Genevieve Oswald, Cur
Notes: Extensive biographical and visual material. The Ruth Page Collection includes manuscripts, business correspondence, letters, programs, clippings, scrapbooks, posters, photographs, over 750 original designs by Clave, Delfau, Wakhevitch, Noguchi, Dayde, Robert Fletcher, Nicholas Remisoff, and Sviatoslav Roerich, tape-recorded interviews, and motion pictures. A register of the Ruth Page Collection of ms material was published in the *Bulletin of Research in the Humanities*, vol 83, no 1, Spring 1980.

PAGE, THOMAS NELSON

NC —DUKE UNIVERSITY, William R Perkins Library, Manuscript Dept, Durham, 27706. Ellen Gartrell, Cur of Mss
Notes: Papers, correspondence, etc.

VA —UNIVERSITY OF VIRGINIA, Alderman Library, Clifton Waller Barrett Collection, Charlottesville, 22901. Joan St C Crane, Cur of American Literature Collections
Holdings: Vols 109 Cat Mss
Notes: Includes first editions. Over 43,000 manuscript pieces.

PAGEANTS

NY —NEW YORK PUBLIC LIBRARY, Performing Arts Research Center, Billy Rose Theatre Collection, 111 Amsterdam Ave, New York, 10023. Dorothy L Swerdlove, Cur
Holdings: Cat
Notes: See entry under Theatre.
See also entry under Theatre

RI —BROWN UNIVERSITY, John Hay Library, 20 Prospect St, Providence, 02912. Mark N Brown, Cur Mss
Holdings: Vols (4000) Mss Pix
Notes: Papers of William Chauncey Langdon (1871-1947), incl over 300 pageants, some written and directed by him, 1911-1921.

RI —BROWN UNIVERSITY, John Hay Library, Harris Collection, Prospect St, Providence, 02912. Rosemary L Cullen, Cur
Holdings: Vols (200,000) Cat Mss Pix Phonorecords Microforms
Budget: ($15,000)
Notes: The Harris Collection of American

Poetry and Plays is principally composed of American and Canadian poetry and plays from the 17th century to the present. Extensive holdings in pageants, incl the Langdon Collection of Pageants, containing 250 vols and portfolios of English and American pageants for the period 1898-1940. Many pageants, drills, exercises, incl in 4000 printed plays issued by Walter H Baker Company of Boston for the period 1890-1957. See *Dictionary Catalog of The Harris Collection of American Poetry and Plays* (Boston: G K Hall, 1972), 13 vols; Supplement (1977), 3 vols. Separate catalog.

VA —GEORGE MASON UNIVERSITY, Fenwick Library, Special Collections Dept, 4400 University Drive, Fairfax, 22030. Ruth Kerns, Public Services Librn
Notes: The Federal Theatre Project (FTP) was established in August 1935 as a part of the arts program of the Works Progress Administration (renamed Work Projects Administration in 1939). Supporting 150 separate units throughout the United States, the FTP produced over 830 major stage plays, 6000 radio programs, and innumerable marionette plays, vaudeville shows, outdoor pageants, and circuses. At the conclusion of the project in June 1939, the "product materials" generated by the FTP were sent to the Library of Congress, and the administrative records to the National Archives. The Library's Federal Theatre Project collection was placed on deposit at George Mason University in Fairfax, Virginia, in 1974.

PAHLAVI LANGUAGE AND LITERATURE

NY —NEW YORK PUBLIC LIBRARY, Oriental Div, Fifth Ave & 42 St, New York, 10018. E Christian Filstrup, Chief
Holdings: Cat Mss Microforms
Budget: ($56,455)
Notes: Published catalog of holdings.

PAINE, THOMAS

IN —INDIANA UNIVERSITY, Lilly Library, Seventh St, Bloomington, 47405. William R Cagle, Librn
Holdings: Vols 225 // Cat
Notes: First and early editions, by and about Paine.

MI —UNIVERSITY OF MICHIGAN, William L Clements Library, Ann Arbor, 48109. John C Dann, Dir

Notes: The William L. Clements Library of Americana is a non-circulating rare book library of original source material, printed and manuscript, dealing with America, from the discovery period into the late nineteenth century. The collection includes approximately 55,000 books and pamphlets, 550 linear feet of manuscripts, 4,100 volumes of newspapers, 36,000 maps, 40,000 pieces of sheet music, and 1,000 prints. The collection is strongest for the period of the American Revolution, and includes the papers of Thomas Gage, Sir Henry Clinton, and the Earl of Shelburne. Other areas of strength include antislavery, cartography and geography, discovery and exploration, American Indians, The Civil War, tune-books, sermons and orations, and the War of 1812. There are selective research collections dealing with Christopher Columbus, Thomas Paine, Benjamin Franklin, George Washington, Thomas Jefferson, and the Federalist Papers. Publications describing the collections of the library are: Author/Title catalog of Americana 1493-1860 in the William L. Clements Library... 7 volumes, Boston, G. K. Hall, 1970; Guide to the manuscript collections of the William L. Clements Library, by Arlene P. Shy 3d edition, Boston, G. K. Hall, 1978; Guide to the manuscript maps in the William L. Clements Library, compiled by Christian Burn, Ann Arbor, U. of Michigan, 1959; and Research catalog of maps of America, to 1860 in the William L. Clements Library...,edited by Douglas W. Marshall, 4 volumes, Boston, G. K. Hall, 1972.

PA —AMERICAN PHILOSOPHICAL SOCIETY, Library, 105 S Fifth St, Philadelphia, 19106. Edward C Carter II, Librn
Holdings: Vols Cat Mss Microforms
Notes: The Thomas Paine Collection of Richard Gimbel. Approx 4000 vols.

PAINE, TIMOTHY OTIS

ME —COLBY COLLEGE, Miller Library, Colby Archives, Waterville, 04901.
Holdings: Mss
Notes: Family papers or other correspondence.

PAINT

PA —FRANKLIN INSTITUTE LIBRARY, 20 & The Parkway, Philadelphia, 19103. Miriam Padusis, Dir; Charles Wilt, Readers Servs Librn
Holdings: Vols (300,000) Cat Maps Pix Microform

ON —C-I-L PAINTS INC, Library, Paint Research Laboratory, 1330 Castlefield Ave, Toronto, M6B 4B3, Can. M Elaine Fitzpatrick, Librn
Holdings: Vols 5000 Cat
Notes: Plus 50 file drawers of reports and microfiche.

PAINTED GLASS see Glass Painting and Staining

PAINTERS

CA —SACRAMENTO PUBLIC LIBRARY, 828 I St, Sacramento, 95814. Dorothy Harvey, Librn, Special Collections
Holdings: Vols 26,000 Cat
Notes: Picture files and card indexes. Extensive collection on painters and their works.

OH —CLEVELAND PUBLIC LIBRARY, Fine Arts and Special Collections Department, 325 Superior Ave, Cleveland, 44114. Alice N Loranth, Head
Holdings: Vols (10,500) Cat Pix
Notes: Part of the collection on Painting, which incl techniques and materials in painting, biographies of painters and discussion of their works. All countries and periods represented.

PAINTERS UNION see Brotherhood of Painters, Decorators, and Paperhangers Union

PAINTING

CA —J PAUL GETTY MUSEUM, Research Library, 17985 Pacific Coast Highway, Malibu, 90265. Anne-Mieke Halbrook, Head Librn
Holdings: Vols (140,000) Cat
Notes: Western European paintings; French 18th century decorative art; classical art.

CA —J PAUL GETTY MUSEUM, Photo Archives, 17985 Pacific Coast Hwy, Malibu, 90265. William Reeder, Cur
Holdings: Pix
Notes: Incl photographs of works of art at the Museum (180,000 cataloged, 500,000 uncataloged), incl ancient art, western

PAINTING (cont.)

European art (painting, sculpture, graphics) and European decorative arts, medieval and Renaissance to 19th century, and antiquities.

CA —CALIFORNIA COLLEGE OF ARTS & CRAFTS, Meyer Library, Broadway at College, Oakland, 94618. Robert L Harper, Head Librn
Holdings: Vols (29,000) Cat Pix
Budget: ($10,000)
Notes: All fields of arts and crafts.

CA —PASADENA PUBLIC LIBRARY, Fine Arts Division, Reference Services, 285 E Walnut St, Pasadena, 91101. Anne Cain, Principal Librn
Holdings: Vols (109,000) Cat Pix Films
Notes: Library has 55 vertical drawers of pictures and clippings, constantly revised and added to. Incl over 130,000 pictures, 64 films

CA —SACRAMENTO PUBLIC LIBRARY, 828 I St, Sacramento, 95814. Dorothy Harvey, Librn, Special Collections
Holdings: Vols 26,000 Cat
Notes: Picture files and card indexes. Extensive collection on painters and their works.

CA —STANFORD UNIVERSITY LIBRARIES, Art & Architecture Library, 102 Cummings Art Bldg, Stanford, 94305. Alexander D Ross, Art Librarian
Holdings: Vols (110,000) Cat
Notes: Incl materials of scholarly interest on the history of the visual arts: painting, sculpture, architecture, drawing, printmaking, etc, for all regions and periods.

DC —SMITHSONIAN INSTITUTION, Hirshhorn Museum & Sculpture Garden Library, Eighth & Independence Ave SW, Washington, 20560. Anna Brooke, Librn
Holdings: Vols (12,000) Cat Pix Slides Microforms Audiotapes 16mm Films VF
Budget: ($79,000)
Notes: Twentieth century painting and sculpture. Incl 1200 pictures and 1300 slides.

IL —ART INSTITUTE OF CHICAGO, Ryerson & Burnham Libraries, Michigan Ave & Adams St, Chicago, 60603. Daphne C Roloff, Dir
Holdings: Vols (136,000) Cat Mss Slides Microforms
Budget: ($167,000)
Notes: Total collection incl 300,000 slides.

IL —CHICAGO PUBLIC LIBRARY, Art Section, Fine Arts Division, 78 E Washington St, Chicago, 60602. Rosalinda I Hack, Fine Arts Division Chief; Yvonne S Brown, Head, Art Section
Notes: 14 drawers of color mounted paintings arranged by artist's name.

KY —BOWLING GREEN PUBLIC LIBRARY, 1225 State St, Bowling Green, 42101. Karen A Turner, Dir
Holdings: Vols 1012 Cat Pix Slides Filmstrips

LA —R W NORTON ART GALLERY, Library, 4747 Creswell Ave, Shreveport, 71106. Jerry M Bloomer, Librn
Holdings: Vols 500 Cat

MA —MELROSE PUBLIC LIBRARY, 69 W Emerson St, Melrose, 02176. Diane E Shaw, Art Librn
Holdings: Vols (8500) Cat Pix Slides Phonorecords
Budget: ($6900)
Notes: Framed and unframed art reproductions (110), slides (2773), periodicals, clippings, sound recordings (3000). Incl the Mary Livermore Collection of Sacred Art, the Odlin Collection, and the Pierre Gendrot Collection of Fine Art.

MA —OLD STURBRIDGE VILLAGE, Research Library, Sturbridge, 01566. Theresa Rini Percy, Librn
Holdings: Cat Pix
Notes: Folk and academic art in New England, to 1850.

MI —CRANBROOK ACADEMY OF ART, 500 Lone Pine Rd, Box 801, Bloomfield Hills, 48013. Diane Gunn, Librn
Holdings: Vols (25,000) Slides

MI —KALAMAZOO INSTITUTE OF ARTS LIBRARY, 314 S Park St, Kalamazoo, 49006. Marianne Cavanaugh, Librn
Holdings: Vols (5000) Cat Slides
Budget: $2000
Notes: Incl (8000) slides. Vertical file on artists. Collection is supplemented by 55 current subscriptions to periodicals in visual arts. Emphasis is on 20th century art and on American art. Collection supports permanent collection in prints, paintings, photography and sculpture.

MN —MINNEAPOLIS COLLEGE OF ART & DESIGN, Library, 200 E 25 St, Minneapolis, 55404. Richard Kronstedt, Head Librn
Holdings: Vols 3800 Cat Slides
Notes: Incl exhibition catalogs; collection emphasis on 20th century painting and painters.

MN —WALKER ART CENTER, Staff Reference Library, Vineland Place, Minneapolis, 55403. Rosemary Furtak, Librn
Holdings: Vols 5000 Cat Pix
Notes: Incl 10,000 catalogs of individual artists; museum gallery catalogs-10,000 catalogs of major exhibitions from all over the world dating back to 1940. VF material and tapes.

MO —SAINT LOUIS ART MUSEUM, Richardson Memorial Library, Saint Louis, 63110. Ann B Abid, Librn
Holdings: Vols (30,000) Cat Pix Slides Microforms
Notes: Art history, incl decorative arts, catalogs, exhibitions, etc.

NY —PRATT INSTITUTE LIBRARY, Art & Architecture Dept, 200 Willoughby Ave, Brooklyn, 11205. Sydney Star Keaveney, Prof
Holdings: Vols (30,000) Cat Pix Slides
Budget: ($50,000)
Notes: Art and architecture, incl sculpture, photography, painting, design, costume, and commercial art. Incl 60,000 art slides. Use restricted to Pratt faculty and students.

NY —CITY UNIVERSITY OF NEW YORK, City College, Library, 138 St & Convent Ave, New York, 10031. Vira C Hinds, Assoc Prof
Notes: In general reference library.

NY —FRICK ART REFERENCE LIBRARY, 10 E 71 St, New York, 10021. Helen Sanger, Librn
Holdings: Vols (154,384) Cat Pix Per
Notes: History of painting, drawing, sculpture and illuminated mss of US and western Europe from 4th century AD to about 1860. 54,862 art auction catalogs; 420,507 study photographs.

NY —METROPOLITAN MUSEUM OF ART, Thomas J Watson Library, Fifth Ave & 82 St, New York, 10028. William B Walker, Chief Librn
Holdings: Vols (250,000) Cat Mss Microforms
Notes: All fields of art: 1400 periodicals, incl bulletins and annual reports, catalogs, etc of American and foreign art societies, museums, etc; incl sales catalogs, exhibition catalogs, clipping file on individual artists and subjects, autograph letters. See *Library Catalog of the Metropolitan Museum of Art, New York*, second ed, rev and enl (Boston, G K Hall, 1980, 48 v and first supplement, 1982). Since 1980, holdings have been cataloged in RLIN.

†NY —METROPOLITAN MUSEUM OF ART, Photograph & Slide Library, 82 St & Fifth Ave, New York, 10028. Margaret P Nolan, Chief Librn
Holdings: Cat Slides
Notes: Over 286,000 (125,000 in 2 x 2 color). The slides illustrate the history of architecture, sculpture, painting and the decorative arts from prehistoric times to the present. Incl a representative coverage of the Metropolitan Museum collections as well as objects from other museums and private collections. Slides available for rental to the public.

NY —MUSEUM OF MODERN ART, Library, 11 W 53 St, New York, 10019. Clive Phillpot, Library Dir
Notes: Art of the 20th and latter half of the 19th century (painting, sculpture, drawings and prints, architecture, photography, film).

NY —NEW YORK HISTORICAL SOCIETY, Library, 170 Central Park W, New York, 10024. James Gregory, Librn
Holdings: Mss
Notes: Incl original mss, illustrative materials, etc.

NY —NEW YORK PUBLIC LIBRARY, Art, Prints, and Photographs Div, Fifth Ave & 42 St, New York, 10018. Donald Anderle, Chief
Holdings: Cat Mss Pix

NC —UNIVERSITY OF NORTH CAROLINA, CHAPEL HILL, Art Library, Art Classroom Studio Bldg, 079A, Chapel Hill, 27514. Philip A Rees, Art Librn
Holdings: Vols (47,000) Cat Microforms
Budget: ($52,000)
Notes: Emphasis on European and American art and architecture, ancient to modern. Special strengths: Rubens and 19th century French painting.

OH —CLEVELAND PUBLIC LIBRARY, Fine Arts and Special Collections Department, 325 Superior Ave, Cleveland, 44114. Alice N Loranth, Head
Holdings: Vols 10,500 Cat Pix
Notes: Techniques and materials in painting, biographies of painters, and discussion of their works. All countries and periods represented.

PA —PHILADELPHIA COLLEGE OF ART, Library, Broad & Spruce Sts, Philadelphia, 19102. Hazel Gustow, Dir
Holdings: Vols 25,000 Cat Periodicals Pix Slides Microforms VF
Notes: Printed materials on the arts (history, techniques, aesthetics, etc.). Current buying incl most significant books coming into print or being reprinted, mainly in English. Incl about 22,000 titles, periodicals, 30 cabinets vertical file materials, etc.

PA —UNIVERSITY OF PITTSBURGH, Henry Clay Frick Fine Arts Library, Pittsburgh, 15260. Anne W Gordon, Fine Arts Librn
Holdings: Vols (55,000) Cat Pix Slides Microforms
Notes: Emphasis is on the art of the Western World--architecture, sculpture, painting, minor arts, archaeology, with special strength in the Byzantine, early Christian, medieval, renaissance and modern periods. The Oriental field is represented, incl replicas of scrolls. Studio arts are also covered. Illuminated ms facsimiles. Extensive collections of slides and photographs for study of art history are available in the building but not administered by the art library.

TX —UNIVERSITY OF TEXAS LIBRARIES, Fine Arts Library, PO Box P, Austin, 78712. Carole L Cable, Fine Arts Librn
Holdings: Vols (55,000) Cat Pix

WI —UNIVERSITY OF WISCONSIN, MADISON, Kohler Art Library, 800 University Ave, Madison, 53706. William C Bunce, Chief; Louise Hunning, Ref Librn
Holdings: Vols (83,000) Cat Microforms
Notes: Incl over 10,000 exhibition and auction catalogs.

WI —MILWAUKEE ART MUSEUM, Library, 750 N Lincoln Memorial Dr, Milwaukee, 53202. Betty Karow, Librn
Notes: Also, small collection on 19th century German painting and on Meissen porcelain.

AB —SOUTHERN ALBERTA INSTITUTE OF TECHNOLOGY, Learning Resources Centre, 1301 16 Ave NW, Calgary, T2M 0L4, Can. Tom Skinner, Historian
Holdings: Vols (5000) Cat Pix Slides Films Audiotapes Filmstrips Videotapes
Notes: Serves Alberta College of Art (4-year professional course).

BC —VANCOUVER PUBLIC LIBRARY, Art Div, 750 Burrard St, Vancouver, V6Z 1X5, Can.
Holdings: Cat Pix
Notes: Book and pamphlet collection. Also, (1) Newspaper Clippings File: 31 drawers of relevant clippings from major newspapers, incl the *Sun, Province, Toronto Globe and Mail, Christian Science Monitor, New York Times*, etc on arts, music, architecture; incl biographical material (16 drawers). (2) Picture File about 500,000 pictures in 150 cabinet drawers, strong in architecture, costume, interior decoration, painting, sculpture, also portraits. (3) Exhibition Catalogs File: British Columbia and elsewhere. (4) Association and Organization File: organizations in the Lower Mainland in

PAINTING (cont.)

arts, music, city planning, etc, begun in
1940s; (5) Canadian Artists Index: begun in
1964, alphabetically by artist, with about
300,000 citationsto reproductions of work
and biographical material on Canadian artist
from the division's books and other sources;
(6) Miscellaneous Index: material not
covered in other special or published
indexes, primarily of Canadian and local
cultural events, hard-to-find informations,
etc. Local newspapers, special Canadian
publications and British film journals are the
most regularly indexed items. (7) Song Index
started in the 1930s. (8) Title Index to song
collections and sheet music in the VPL
collection, approx 100,000 entries.

ON —NATIONAL GALLERY OF
CANADA, Library, National Museums of
Canada, Ottawa, K1A 0M8, Can. J Hunter,
Chief Librn

ON —METROPOLITAN TORONTO
LIBRARY, Fine Arts Dept, 789 Yonge St,
Toronto, M4W 2G8, Can. Alan Suddon,
Head
Holdings: Vols (42,000) Cat Pix Microforms
Notes: Extensive collection.

PAINTING, AMERICAN

DE —HENRY F DUPONT WINTERTHUR
MUSEUM LIBRARY, Winterthur, 19735.
Frank H Sommer, III, Head
Holdings: Cat
Notes: Strong collections.

MI —MONROE COUNTY LIBRARY
SYSTEM, Bedford Branch, 8575 Jackman
Road, Temperance, 48182. Paula
Kaczmarek, Head, Bedford Branch
Holdings: Vols 6500 Cat Periodicals AV
Budget: $8000
Notes: Circulating general collection of
popular art books, especially Western
European and American painting; also
includes technique, graphic arts,
photography, sculpture, architecture.
Periodicals held five years.

NJ —MONTCLAIR ART MUSEUM
LIBRARY, 3 South Mountain Ave, PO Box
1582, Montclair, 07042. Edith A Rights,
Librn
Holdings: Vols (10,000) Cat Pix Slides
Audiotapes
Budget: ($3500)
Notes: American painting and sculpture. Incl
5000 pictures; 10,000 slides; posters.
Audiotapes on American art and artists.

NY —BROOKLYN MUSEUM, Art Reference
Library, 188 Eastern Parkway, Brooklyn,
11238.
Holdings: Vols (130,000)

NY —MUNSON-WILLIAMS-PROCTOR
INSTITUTE, Reference Library, 310
Genessee St, Utica, 13502. Linda Lott, Librn
Holdings: Cat Slides Monographs Exhibition
Catalogues
Notes: Specifically 19th and 20th century
American art and history of art. Incl 16,500
slides. Separate catalog.

PAINTING, BRITISH

CT —YALE UNIVERSITY, Yale Center for
British Art, Rare Book Dept, New Haven,
06520. Joan Friedman, Cur
Notes: One of the greatest assemblages of
British Art of the 17th-19th centuries.

PAINTING, DECORATIVE see Art,
Decorative; Decoration and Ornament

PAINTING, HOUSE see House Painting

PAINTING, JAPANESE

MA —HARVARD UNIVERSITY LIBRARY,
Fine Arts Library, Rubel Asiatic Research
Collection, Sackler Museum, 38 Quincy
Street, Cambridge, 02138. Yen-Shew Lynn
Chao, Librn
Holdings: Vols (12,000)
Notes: Rubel Asiatic Research Collection;
specializes exclusively in the acquisition of
Oriental language (Chinese, Japanese, and

Korean) materials. Particular strengths incl
the areas of Buddhist arts, Chinese bronzes
and painting, Japanese painting and prints,
and Chinese and Japanese ceramics. Also
large holdings of oriental art periodicals,
reprints, and exhibition and sales catalogs.

MO —THE NELSON-ATKINS MUSEUM OF
ART, Kenneth & Helen Spencer Art
Reference Library, 4525 Oak St, Kansas
City, 64111. Stanley W Hess, Librn

WA —UNIVERSITY OF WASHINGTON
LIBRARIES, East Asia Library, DO-27,
Seattle, 98195. Karl Lo, Head
Holdings: Vols (300,000) Cat Microforms
Budget: ($200,000)
Notes: Southwest China: Joseph Rock
Collection, ca 2000 vols; modern Chinese
poetry, 1919 to date: ca 700 titles; Asian art
esp Japanese painting: 4097 vols; Tiao-yu-
t'ai movement in the US: ca 499 items of
periodicals and pamphlets; modern Korean
poetry, ancient and modern: ca 1000 titles;
Mu-yu-shu folk literature: ca 1000 items.

PAINTING, MODERN—20TH CENTURY

CA —CALIFORNIA INSTITUTE OF THE
ARTS, Library, 24700 McBean Pkwy,
Valencia, 91355. James Elrod, Dir
Holdings: Vols (61,000) Slides
Budget: ($11,000)
Notes: Modern art, incl abstract, conceptual,
concrete, environment, minimal, and pop art;
art; dadaism; surrealism; happenings; and
caricatures and cartoons. Slides (61,683).

PAINTING, NAIVE

NY —NEW YORK STATE HISTORICAL
ASSOCIATION, Library, Lake Rd,
Cooperstown, 13326. Amy Barnum, Librn
Holdings: Vols (55,000) Cat Slides
Notes: Emphasis on folk art, naive painting.
Noncirculating.

PAINTING, PORTRAIT see Portrait Painting

PAINTING, RELIGIOUS see Christian Art and Symbolism

PAINTING, TRAY see Tray Painting

PAINTINGS—COLOR REPRODUCTIONS see Color Prints

PAINTINGS, FORE-EDGE see Fore-Edge Paintings

PAINTS see Paint

PAIUTE INDIANS

NV —UNIVERSITY OF NEVADA, RENO,
University Library, Special Collections Dept,
Reno, 89557. Robert E Blesse, Head
Holdings: Vols 1100 Mss Pix
Notes: Incl over 5000 photographs,
government documents, periodicals, 80 cubic
feet, mss, and audiotapes. The Great Basin
Indian Collection contains materials on the
anthropology, archaeology, and ethnohistory
of the Great Basin region. Materials are
collected for a defined group of 65 tribes incl
Washo, Shoshone, Northern and Southern
Paiute, the major tribes of the region.
Collection of importance incl the Sven
Liljeblad Collection, linguistics and
ethnography; papers of US agent Lorenzo D
Greel, 1902-22; Robert Leland Collection,
Indian water rights.

PAKISTAN

CA —UNIVERSITY OF CALIFORNIA,
BERKELEY, University Library, 438 Main
Library, Berkeley, 94720. Kenneth R Logan,
South Asia Librn
Notes: South Asia collection (India,
Pakistan, Bangladesh, Nepal, Sri Lanka)
contain 150,000-200,000 titles. Covers at
research level the social sciences and
humanities in western languages and 20

South Asian languages. Subject areas:
history, political science, lanuage and
literature (especially strong in Hindi, Urdu,
Tamil, Sanskrit and Nepali), art and art
history, sociology, education, music,
environmental design, philosophy and
religion, anthropology, geography, national
and local government publications. Formats:
monographs, periodicals, newspapers,
microforms, maps, sound recordings, videotapes, pamphlets. Special strengths: modern
Hindi literature; history of South Asian
countries; government publications of India,
late 19th and 20th centuries. Member of
South Asia Microform Project; Participant in
Library of Congress AcquisitionsPrograms
for India, Pakistan, Nepal, and Bangladesh.

HI —UNIVERSITY OF HAWAII, Library,
2550 The Mall, Honolulu, 96822. Joyce
Wright, Head, Asia Collection; Masato
Matsu, Head, East Asia Vernacular
Collection
Holdings: Vols 75,215 Cat Microforms
Notes: The Asia Collection holds material
from and relating to Bangladesh, India,
Nepal, Pakistan, and Sri Lanka in western
and Asian languages. South Asian languages
currently acquired: Bengali, Hindi, Marathi,
Nepali, Pali, Prakrit, Sanskrit, Tamil. Period
emphasis is post-World War II. Subject
emphases: social sciences and the humanities
(literature, economics, history, religion/
philosophy). Holdings are supplemented by a
large uncataloged backlog, much of it
accessible through the Library of Congress
Accessions Lists for the area and by over
7000 cataloged titles in the main library
collection. *South Asian Library Resources in
North America: A Survey Prepared for the
Boston Conference*, 1974, ed by M L P
Patterson (Zug, Switzerland: Tutes
Documentation Compnay, 1975).(Bibliotheca
Asiatica 12-), "University of Hawaii," pp
103-114.

IL —CENTER FOR RESEARCH
LIBRARIES, 6050 S Kenwood Ave,
Chicago, 60637. Donald B Simpson, Dir;
Esther Smith, Collection Development Librn
Holdings: Uncat Microforms
Notes: Monographs and serials from 1969,
government documents from 1964, received
on PL 480. 16 newspapers on microfilm,
mostly from 1962.

MI —UNIVERSITY OF MICHIGAN,
Graduate Library, South Asian Dept, Ann
Arbor, 48109. Om P Sharma, Librn
Holdings: Vols (365,000) Cat Maps Slides
Microforms
Notes: The major emphasis is on social
sciences and humanities. Besides materials in
classical languages, South Asian vernaculars
being retained are Hindi, Bengali, Urdu,
Marathi and Tamil; strong in classical
languages, especially Sanskrit, Pali, and
Prakrit.

MI —MICHIGAN STATE UNIVERSITY,
International Library, South and Southeast
Asia Collection, East Lansing, 48824.
Clinton Lockert, Bibliographer
Holdings: Vols 55,700 Cat Mss Maps
Audiotapes Microforms
Notes: Serials and monographs of South
Asia received on PL 480 for India, Pakistan,
Sri Lanka, and Nepal since 1968. Emphasis
is upon Social Sciences, Humanities, and
Science. Areas of strength are Anthropology
and rural development.

MO —UNIVERSITY OF MISSOURI-
COLUMBIA, Ellis Library, Ninth and
Lowry, Columbia, 65201. Murari Lal Nagar,
Librn
Holdings: Vols 100,000 Maps Slides
Phonorecoords 16mm Films Filmstrips
Microforms
Notes: The South Asia Studies Program at
the University of Missouri-Columbia, is an
interdepartmental, multi-disciplinary area
studies program on India, Pakistan,
Bangladesh, Sri Lanka and Nepal.
Depository for the PL480 Program of the
Library of Congress in many languages from
South Asia. There are library resources in
Sankskrit, Hindi, Bengali, Panjabi, and
Malayalam. The library is particularly strong
in Baroda, Bengal and the Punjab.

NY —NEW YORK PUBLIC LIBRARY,
Oriental Div, Fifth Ave & 42 St, New York,

PAKISTAN (cont.)

10018. E Christian Filstrup, Chief
Holdings: Cat Mss Microforms
Budget: ($56,455)
Notes: Described in *Dictionary Catalog of the Oriental Collection*, The Research Libraries of the New York Public Library, 1960, 16 vols, and *First Supplement*, 1976, 8 vols (144,000 cards). This catalog incl 318,000 entries for works in about 100 languages of the East, and all works in Western languages on Oriental subjects. The Oriental Collection numbers about 120,000 vols; its Arabic and Indic holdings and those on ancient Egypt and the ancient Near East are among the largest in the US. There is also a collection of 30,000 vols of PL 480 material from Egypt, Pakistan, and India to which there is main entry access, but which is not incorporated into the dictionary catalog. Other outstanding features of the Oriental Collection incl extensive holdings of Japanese technical and scientific periodicals; a unique collection of linguistic works, grammars, anddictionaries; and unusually good coverage of the field of Oriental religions and philosophies. The catalog contains numerous subject references to periodical articles in all languages. All entries are arranged alphabetically according to the Roman alphabet.

TX —UNIVERSITY OF TEXAS LIBRARIES, General Libraries, PO Box P, Austin, 78713. Carolyn Bucknell, Asst Dir for Collection Development
Holdings: Cat Microforms

PAKISTAN—CENSUSES

TX —UNIVERSITY OF TEXAS LIBRARIES, Asian Collection, PO Box P, Austin, 78712. Kevin Lin, Asian Librn; Merry Burlingham, South Asian Librn
Holdings: Vols (58,000) Cat Microforms
Notes: Materials in Hindi, Sanskrit, Urdu, Prakrit, and Pali (acquired chiefly through the Special Foreign Acquisitions Program) and selected English-language materials, incl Indian censuses and district gazetteers and Pakistani censuses.

PAKISTAN, EAST see Bangladesh

PALA LANGUAGE see Palaic Language

PALAIC LANGUAGE

NY —NEW YORK PUBLIC LIBRARY, Oriental Div, Fifth Ave & 42 St, New York, 10018. E Christian Filstrup, Chief
Holdings: Cat Mss Microforms
Budget: ($56,455)
Notes: Published catalog of holdings.

PALAITE LANGUAGE see Palaic Language

PALAWI LANGUAGE see Palaic Language

PALEOASIATIC LANGUAGES see Hyperborean Languages and Literatures

PALEOASIATICS see Arctic Races

PALEOBIOLOGY

DC —SMITHSONIAN INSTITUTION, Archives Div, Washington, 20560. William W Moss, Archivist
Holdings: Cat Mss Pix
Notes: The Archives holds the official records of the National Museum of Natural History's Division of Vertebrate Paleontology, 1882-1957.
See also entry under Walcott, Charles Doolittle.

PALEOBOTANY

IL —UNIVERSITY OF ILLINOIS, URBANA/CHAMPAIGN, Library, Geology Library, 223 Natural History Bldg, Urbana, 61801. Dederick Ward, Librn
Holdings: Vols (105,186) Cat Maps Microforms

NY —NEW YORK BOTANICAL GARDEN LIBRARY, Bronx, 10458. Charles R Long, Asst Vice Pres & Dir
Holdings: Vols 7000 Cat Mss Pix Slides Microforms VF
Budget: ($356,000)
Notes: One of the largest botanical collections in the world. Covers botany (150,000 vols), botanists (3000), horticulture (45,000), plant diseases (25,000), plant physiology (15,000), history of botany (1500), conservation of natural resources (15,000), gardening (13,000), paleobotany (7000), ecology (20,000), forestry (5000), medical botany (3000), agriculture (9000) and biology (20,000). Reference library; materials do not circulate, except via standard inter-library loan. About 5000 vols uncataloged. Incl archives, art and vertical files. An OCLC library.

OR —UNIVERSITY OF OREGON, Library, Eugene, 97403. Kenneth W Duckett, Curator
Notes: Ralph W Chaney's books; about 12,000 letters; and mss for books and articles. Largely concerned with various aspects of paleontology, paleobotany, and the fossil Redwoods.

PA —CARNEGIE LIBRARY OF PITTSBURGH, Science & Technology Dept, 4400 Forbes Ave, Pittsburgh, 15213. Catherine M Brosky, Dept Head
Notes: Subject of secondary interest with emphasis on North America. Covers paleobotany, vertebrates and invertebrates, foraminifera, mollusks, fish, reptiles, mammals. Abstracts, indexes, catalogs, bibliographies, journals, continuations, federal, state and society publications available.

PALEOCLIMATOLOGY

NY —COLUMBIA UNIVERSITY LIBRARIES, Geoscience Library, Lamont-Doherty Geological Observatory, Palisades, 10964. Susan Klimley, Librn
Holdings: Vols (20,000) Cat
Notes: Geosciences, incl geochemistry, marine geology, seismology and paleoclimatology.

PALEOETHNOGRAPHY see Archaeology

PALEOGEOGRAPHY

IL —UNIVERSITY OF ILLINOIS, URBANA/CHAMPAIGN, Library, Geology Library, 223 Natural History Bldg, Urbana, 61801. Dederick Ward, Librn
Holdings: Vols (105,186) Cat Maps Microforms

PALEOGRAPHY

IL —NEWBERRY LIBRARY, John M Wing Foundation on the History of Printing, 60 W Walton St, Chicago, 60610. Diana Haskell, Cur of Modern Mss
Holdings: Vols (30,000) Cat Mss
Budget: ($50,000)
Notes: Part of the John M Wing Foundation on the History of Printing, which collects western European and American printing from the invention to the present day. Includes some 2,000 incunabula, excellent collections of the major printers, modern illustrated books, etc. Especially strong in periodicals and illustrated books of the Victorian period, G K Hall has published *A Dictionary Catalogue of the John M. Wing Foundation and two Supplements*. Parts have been described in various articles, etc., notable J.M. Wells, *The Scholar Printers* and an article by Wells in *The Book Collector*.

IN —VOLHYNIAN BIBLIOGRAPHIC CENTER, 307 N Overhill Drive, Bloomington, 47401. Max Boyko, Mgr
Notes: Collect materials on Volhynia in Western Ukraine. Compile and publish bibliographies on the region.

KS —UNIVERSITY OF KANSAS, Kenneth Spencer Research Library, Special Collections Dept, Lawrence, 66045.

Alexandra Mason, Librn
Holdings: Cat Mss
Notes: Mss (see entry for Manuscripts) and reference collection on paleography and manuscript studies incl catalogs, facsimiles, incipit indices, and other reference books. Noncirculating.

KY —UNIVERSITY OF KENTUCKY, Margaret I King Library, Dept of Special Collections, Lexington, 40506. William Marshall, Head
Holdings: Cat Mss Pix Slides Microforms
Notes: Comprehensive collection of books on typography and history of printing; fine press books (incl Lexington imprints); ms books and illumination, paleography; mss of W A Dwiggins (gift of C H Griffith); James Anderson papers; bookbinding; 2 hand-presses and working collection for summer seminars in hand-press printing; bookplates, bookmarks, book jackets, etc.

MN —SAINT JOHN'S ABBEY & UNIVERSITY, Hill Monastic Manuscript Library, Collegeville, 56321. Julian G Plante, Dir
Holdings: Vols (61,000) Microfilms
Notes: Films of 61,000 mss. The total number of codices or bound handwritten mss represents the holdings of several hundred libraries in Europe, mostly Austria, Spain, Ethiopia, West Germany, Portugal, and also Italy, Hungary, Poland, Great Britain, Belgium, Yugoslavia, France, Switzerland, and the Netherlands.

MO —SAINT LOUIS UNIVERSITY, Pius XII Memorial Library, Vatican Film Library Collection, 3655 W Pine Blvd, Saint Louis, 63108. Charles J Ermatinger, Librn
Holdings: Mss Slides Microforms
Notes: Vatican Film Library has 75 percent of the Greek, Latin and western European vernacular holdings in the Vatican Library, plus all the Hebrew, Arabic and Ethiopic holdings on film. Covers 5th-19th centuries. Sizable collection of western European books. In addition, has largest collection on the work of the Jesuits in Latin America, the US and the Philippines, filmed from European Jesuit archives. Excellent catalogs and guides to all collections. Also, 50,608 slides of illuminated mss; 26,470 reels of microfilm.

MO —SAINT LOUIS UNIVERSITY, Pius XII Memorial Library, 3655 W Pine Blvd, Saint Louis, 63108. William Cole, Dir
Holdings: Slides Microforms
Notes: Collection covers all areas of learning and European history from Classical Antiquity to early modern period. Researchers using collection receive assistance in paleography, bibliography and reference search. Approx 10,000 1000-foot reels of microfilm (not counting master negatives) reproducing Vatican Library's Latin, Greek, Hebrew, Arabic and Ethiopic mss. Some 8000 100-foot reels of microfilm (again not counting master negative) reproducing rare and out of print books relating to subject areas in the mss. Over 50,000 color slides of medieval and Renaissance mss illuminations. A reference collection of modern materials relating to mss research.

NY —NEW YORK PUBLIC LIBRARY, Rare Books and Manuscripts Div, Fifth Ave & 42 St, New York, 10018. William L Joyce, Asst Dir; Susan E Davis, Cur of Mss
Holdings: Cat Mss

NY —PIERPONT MORGAN LIBRARY, 29 E 36 St, New York, 10016. Herbert Cahoon, Librn
Holdings: Cat Mss Pix

PA —UNIVERSITY OF PITTSBURGH, Hillman Library, Pittsburgh, 15260. Glenora E Rossell, Head
Holdings: Vols (11,550) Cat
Notes: The classics collection is particularly strong in Greek and Latin literature, Greek and Roman history, Greek philosophy, Greek and Latin language, and Greek epigraphy. In combination with the Frick Fine Arts collection it has a good collection in Greek and Roman art and archaeology. The collection of journals is also quite strong in these areas. There has been an emphasis in collecting books by and about Homer, Aristotle, Euripides, Vergil, Cicero and

PALEOGRAPHY (cont.)

Pertronius. It has a unique collection of unpublished PhD dissertations and Master's theses on Petronius. It has a basic collection on Greek and Latin paleography and papyrology.

RI —BROWN UNIVERSITY, John Hay Library, 20 Prospect St, Providence, 02912. Mark N Brown, Cur Mss
Holdings: Vols (53) //
Notes: Indic Manuscripts Collection. Codices written in Burmese, Cambodian, Telugu, Skandhas, Bengali, and Sinhalese script on palm leaves, encased within wood covers, some lacquered. Subjects include: Buddhist canon, Pali grammar and lexicons, epics, dance drama, and a treatise on midwifery. Recorded in *A Census of Indic Manuscripts in the United States and Canada* compiled by Horace I Poleman (New Haven: American Oriental Society, 1938).

VA —UNIVERSITY OF VIRGINIA, Alderman Library, Manuscripts Dept, Charlottesville, 22901. Edmund Berkeley Jr, Cur
Notes: Collection of mediaeval paleography. Practically all Western scripts are represented; 235 pieces.

PALEOLOG, SERGEI N.

CA —HOOVER INSTITUTION ON WAR, REVOLUTION & PEACE, Stanford University, Stanford, 94305. Milorad M Drachkovitch, Archivist
Holdings: // Mss
Notes: Office files, incl correspondence, memoranda, are reports of Serge N Paleolog, chairman of the board of the Government Plenipotentiary of the Resettlement of Russian Refugees in Yugoslavia, 1920-1933. 12 ft.

PALEONTOLOGICAL SOCIETY

IL —UNIVERSITY OF ILLINOIS, URBANA/CHAMPAIGN, Library, University Archives, 19 Library, 1408 W Gregory Drive, Urbana, 61801. Maynard Brichford, University Archivist
Holdings: Cat Mss Maps Pic Slides Microfmorms
Notes: Papers archival reords, etc.

PALEONTOLOGY

CA —UNIVERSITY OF CALIFORNIA, BERKELEY, Physical Sciences Libraries, Earth Sciences Library, 230 Earth Sciences Bldg, Berkeley, 94720. Julie F Rinaldi, Librn
Holdings: Vols (83,202) Cat Microforms
Budget: ($74,880)
Notes: A strong collection, giving particular emphasis to vertebrates and invertebrates. Especially rich in serials; approx (2850) current titles received on subscription, and in foreign-language publications.

CA —UNIVERSITY OF CALIFORNIA, DAVIS, Physical Sciences Library, Davis, 95616. Scott Kennedy, Head
Holdings: Vols (25,000) Cat Maps
Notes: Complete files of US Geological Survey and California State geology series. Strong collection of western US geologic guide books. Excellent paleontology collection represented by catalogs of foramnifera, ostracoda and radialania. About 4000 geologic maps including western US and basic collection of worldwide maps. Access to onine reference service.

CA —UNIVERSITY OF CALIFORNIA, LOS ANGELES, Biomedical Library, Center for the Health Sciences, Los Angeles, 90024. Alison Bunting, Acting Biomedical Librn; Victoria Steele, Head, History & Special Collections Div

CA —UNIVERSITY OF CALIFORNIA, LOS ANGELES, Geology-Geophysics Library, 4697 Geology Bldg, Los Angeles, 90024. Sarah E How, Geology-Geophysics Librn
Holdings: Vols (85,000) Cat Maps Microforms
Notes: Incl theses and dissertations of UCLA Dept of Earth and Space Sciences; and (2000) serial titles.

CA —UNIVERSITY OF CALIFORNIA, RIVERSIDE, University Library, 4045 Canyon Crest Dr, Box 5900, Riverside, 92517.
Holdings: Vols (88,500) Cat Mss Maps Pix Microforms
Notes: Files of the US Geological Survey and California State Geology series. Strong collections of western US geological guidebooks, paleontological studies and geological maps.

CA —CALIFORNIA ACADEMY OF SCIENCES, J W Mailliard Jr Library, Golden Gate Park, San Francisco, 94118. Ray Brian, Librn
Notes: Downs No 2160.

CO —COLORADO SCHOOL OF MINES, Arthur Lakes Library, 14 & Illinois Sts, Golden, 80401. Hartley K Phinney, Jr, Head Librn
Holdings: Vols (270,557) Cat Mss Maps Microforms

CT —YALE UNIVERSITY, Geology Library, 210 Whitney Ave, PO Box 6666, New Haven, 06511. Harry Scammell, Librn
Holdings: Vols (100,000) Cat Maps Pix Microforms
Budget: ($115,000)
Notes: The O C Marsh Collection (vertebrate paleontology) is also here.

DC —NATIONAL GEOGRAPHIC SOCIETY, Library, 1146 16th St NW, Washington, 20036. Susan Fifer Canby, Dir
Holdings: Vols (63,000) Cat Mss Maps Pix
Notes: Material concerning land, sea, and space exploration--past and present. All fields of anthropology, natural history, geography, etc.

DC —SMITHSONIAN INSTITUTION, Archives Div, Washington, 20560. William W Moss, Archivist
Holdings: Mss Maps Pix
Notes: Papers of William H Dall (1865-1927), naturalist and paleontologist. Incl material on the Western Union Telegraph Expedition to Alaska (1865-1868), and reports on the Alaskan boundary disputes in 1885 and 1888.

DC —SMITHSONIAN INSTITUTION LIBRARIES, Natural History Branch, Washington, 20560. Sylvia Churgin, Chief Librn
Holdings: Vols (75,550) Cat Mss Maps Pix Slides Microforms
Notes: Incl vertebrate and invertebrate paleontology; vertebrate zoology: systematics and taxonomy.

ID —IDAHO MUSEUM OF NATURAL HISTORY, Research Library, Campus Box 8096, Pocatello, 83209. Michael L Perry, Dir
Holdings: Vols 8300 Cat Mss Maps Pix Slides

IL —FIELD MUSEUM OF NATURAL HISTORY, Library, Roosevelt Rd & Lake Shore Dr, Chicago, 60605. W Peyton Fawcett, Librn; Benjamin W Williams, Assoc Librn
Holdings: Vols (210,000) Cat
Budget: ($100,000)
Notes: Extensive collections-publications of learned societies and institutions and monographic works-in all fields of natural history, with emphasis on taxonomy and evolutionary biology; and on museum publications, American and foreign: anthropology, especially archaeology and ethnology of the Americas, Africa, East Asia, and Oceania; botany, particularly strong for the Americas; geology, chiefly paleontology and meteoritic studies; and zoology, worldwide (birds, fishes, insects, mammals, mollusks, reptiles and amphibians).

IL —UNIVERSITY OF ILLINOIS, URBANA/CHAMPAIGN, Library, Geology Library, 223 Natural History Bldg, Urbana, 61801. Dederick Ward, Librn
Holdings: Vols (105,186) Cat Maps Microforms

MD —CALVERT MARINE MUSEUM, Library, PO Box 97, Solomons, 20688.
Holdings: Vols (2000) Uncat Maps Pix Slides 16mm Films
Notes: Paleontology of southern Maryland. Primarily professional research papers, reports and Maryland State Geological Surveys.

MA —HARVARD UNIVERSITY, Museum of Comparative Zoology, 26 Oxford St, Cambridge, 02138. Eva S Jonas, Librn
Holdings: Cat Mss
Notes: Catalog, in 8 vols, published in 1968. For description, see *Harvard Library Bulletin*, VI (1952): pp 202-218.

MI —UNIVERSITY OF MICHIGAN, Museums Library, Ann Arbor, 48109. Patricia B Yocum, Librn
Holdings: Vols 8000 Cat

NV —FORESTA INSTITUTE FOR OCEAN AND MOUNTAIN STUDIES, Library, 6205 Franktown Rd, Carson City, 89701. Shannon Porter, Librn
Holdings: Vols 500 Cat Maps Slides
Notes: Collection is international in scope; incl material on fish of the far western US espec Nevada from prehistoric times to the present. Also, about 1000 pamphlets, etc.

NJ —PRINCETON UNIVERSITY, Library, Rare Books Dept, Princeton, 08544. Stephen Ferguson, Cur
Holdings: Cat

NY —AMERICAN TEILHARD ASSOCIATION FOR THE FUTURE OF MAN, Dept of Religious Studies, Manhattan College, Bronx, 10471. Donald P Gray, Librn
Holdings: Vols 450 Cat Slides
Notes: Material by and about Teilhard de Chardin, philosopher and paleontologist.

NY —PALEONTOLOGICAL INSTITUTION, Library, 1259 Trumansburg Rd, Ithaca, 14850. Peter Hoover, Dir
Holdings: Vols (60,000) Maps Pix

NY —AMERICAN MUSEUM OF NATURAL HISTORY, Library Services Dept, Central Park W & 79th St, New York, 10024. Nina J Root, Chairwoman; Mary Genett, Asst Librn for Reference Services
Holdings: Vols (385,000) Cat Mss Maps Pix Slides Microforms
Notes: Nearly all collections are outstanding for depth of coverage and international range. Early and historic works, rare books, colored illustrations, and relevant serial publications supplement the modern scientific publications necessary to the researches of the scientific staff and the work of the educational division. The Henry Fairfield Osborn Archives incl material on paleontology. Open to the public.

NY —UNIVERSITY OF ROCHESTER, Rush Rhees Library, Geology/Map Library, Rochester, 14627. Arleen N Somerville, Librn
Holdings: Vols (12,424) Cat Maps
Notes: Strong collection in the field and related areas.

NC —CAMPBELL COLLEGE, Carrie Rich Memorial Library, Box 98, Buies Creek, 27506. Helen Sistrunk, Asst to Dir
Holdings: Vols 15,000 Cat Maps Pix
Budget: $717
Notes: Emphasis on Paleontology. Large collection of Geological Survey Bulletins and professional papers. Collection in process of cataloging (255,000 pieces).

NC —UNIVERSITY OF NORTH CAROLINA, CHAPEL HILL, Geology Library, Mitchell Hall 029A, Chapel Hill, 27514. Miriam L Sheaves, Librn
Holdings: Vols (41,000) Cat Maps
Notes: Earth sciences, paleontology, oceanography, geology, geophysics. Incl theses and dissertations; 103,000 map sheets.

NC —GEO-TECH INTERNATIONAL LTD, Paleontological Research Laboratory, Library, 3616 Garden Club Lane, Charlotte, 28210. Elizabeth Carson, Librn
Holdings: Maps Pix Slides
Budget: $12,000
Notes: Special emphasis on paleoanthropological collection devoted to reprints, source materials, and all current publications and journals on paleoanthropology and evolution.

OR —UNIVERSITY OF OREGON, Library, Eugene, 97403. Kenneth W Duckett, Curator
Notes: Ralph W Chaney's books; about 12,000 letters; and mss for books and articles.

PALEONTOLOGY (cont.)

Largely concerned with various aspects of paleontology, paleobotany, and the fossil Redwoods.

PA —ACADEMY OF NATURAL SCIENCES LIBRARY, 19 Benjamin Franklin Parkway, Philadelphia, 19103.
Holdings: Vols (180,000) Cat Mss Maps Pix Slides Microforms
Notes: (250,000) mss. Described in *Academy of Natural Sciences of Philadelphia: Catalog* (Boston: G K Hall, 1972); *Guide to the Manuscript Collections in the Academy of Natural Sciences of Philadelphia*, by Venia T Phillips (Philadelphia: Academy of Natural Sciences, 1963).

PA —CARNEGIE LIBRARY OF PITTSBURGH, Science & Technology Dept, 4400 Forbes Ave, Pittsburgh, 15213. Catherine M Brosky, Dept Head
Notes: Subject of secondary interest with emphasis on North America. Covers paleobotany, vertebrates and invertebrates, foraminifera, mollusks, fish reptiles, mammals. Abstracts, indexes, catalogs, bibliographies, journals, continuations, federal, state and society publications available.

PA —UNIVERSITY OF PITTSBURGH, Langley Library, A-217 Langley Hall, Pittsburgh, 15260. D L Johnston, Librn

†SD —SOUTH DAKOTA SCHOOL OF MINES & TECHNOLOGY, Devereaux Library, Rapid City, 57701.
Holdings: Vols (166,200) Cat Mss Maps Pix Microforms
Notes: Emphasis on the White River Badlands. The Museum has an extensive collection of reprint materials in this specific area (which is supportive of, and complimentary to, the resources of the Library).

TX —UNIVERSITY OF TEXAS LIBRARIES, General Libraries, Geology Dept, PO Box P, Austin, 78712. Chestalene Pintozzi, Librn
Holdings: Vols (59,349) Cat Maps Microforms

TX —SOUTHERN METHODIST UNIVERSITY, Science/Engineering Library, Dallas, 75275. Devertt D Bickston, Librn
Holdings: Vols (140,000) Cat Maps Pix Microforms
Budget: ($150,000)
Notes: Also maintain an herbarium.

TX —FORT WORTH PUBLIC LIBRARY, 300 Taylor St, Fort Worth, 76102. John R McCracken, Manager
Holdings: Vols (4000) Cat
Budget: ($21,000)

UT —UNIVERSITY OF UTAH, Marriott Library, Special Collections, Salt Lake City, 84112. Gregory C Thompson, Cur
Notes: Papers of Earl Douglass, discoverer of Dinosaur National Monument. (some restrictions apply to collection).

WI —MILWAUKEE PUBLIC MUSEUM, Reference Library, 800 W Wells St, Milwaukee, 53233. Judith Campbell Turner, Museum Librn
Holdings: Vols (90,000) Cat Maps Microforms

WI —UNIVERSITY OF WISCONSIN, MILWAUKEE, Greene Memorial Museum, 3367 N Downer Ave, PO Box 413, Milwaukee, 53201. Robert E Gernand, Acting Cur
Holdings: Vols (250) Uncat
Notes: Noncirculating collection of books used by Thomas A Greene in his study of minerals and fossils, 1860-1894. Incl 150,000 specimens.

ON —NATIONAL MUSEUMS OF CANADA, Library Services Directorate, Ottawa, K1A 0M8, Can. Valerie Monkhouse, Director
Holdings: Vols (90,000) Cat Mss Microforms
Budget: ($81,000)
Notes: Emphasis on Canadian and circumpolar natural history. Collection incl botany, herpetology, ichthyology, invertebrate zoology, malacology, mammology, mineralogy, ornithology, paleobiology, zooarchaeology. Exceptional collections in lichenology, bryology, malacology, ornithology. Paleobiology, palynology, paleoclimatology. A library of reprints, consisting of approx 6000 items presented by C S Sternberg. The reprints are restricted to the subj of vertebrate paleontology, (and form a definitive collection for Canada); incl, many early papers. The National Museums Library is gradually binding the collection, and filling gaps whenever possible. Recently added; J F Grayson Collection. Approx 5000 reprints plus textbooks, catalogues, periodicals, and transparencies presented by him. Research collection, interlibrary loans available, public may use onthe premises.

ON —ROYAL ONTARIO MUSEUM, Main Library and Archives, 100 Queen's Park, Toronto, M5S 2C6, Can. Julia Matthews, Head Librn
Holdings: Vols (85,000) Cat
Notes: Since January 1977, acquisitions have been entered in UTLAS.

PQ —MCGILL UNIVERSITY, Blacker-Wood Library of Zoology & Ornithology, 3459 McTavish St, Montreal, H3A 1Y1, Can. Eleanor MacLean, Librn
Holdings: Vols (77,600) Cat Mss
Notes: Special features of collection incl: Robert Gurney Collection of reprints on Crustaceana ; 3000 folders of letters from naturalists ; over 9000 original paintings of wildlife; a small collection of falconry equipment ; the archives of the Montreal Natural History Society ; the archives of the North American Falconry Association; 156 17th-century feather pictures of birds and people . Does not incl entomology collection.

PALEONTOLOGY, BOTANICAL see Paleobotany

PALEONTOLOGY, HUMAN see Fossil Man

PALEONTOLOGY, ZOOLOGICAL see Paleontology

PALEOSIBERIAN LANGUAGES see Hyperborean Languages and Literatures

PALEOSIBERIANS see Arctic Races

PALEOZOOLOGY see Paleontology

PALESTINE

CA —PACIFIC SCHOOL OF RELIGION, Bade Institute of Biblical Archeology, 1798 Scenic Ave, Berkeley, 94709. Kay Schellhase, Cur
Holdings: Vols (2500) Cat
Budget: ($700)
Notes: Syro-Palestinian archaeology.

DC —LIBRARY OF CONGRESS, Prints & Photographs Div, Washington, 20540.
Notes: The Matson Photo Service Collection contains photographs of the Middle East, 1896-1946.

FL —UNIVERSITY OF FLORIDA LIBRARY, Isser and Rae Price Library of Judaica, 18 Libr East, Gainesville, 32611. Robert Singerman, Head Librn
Budget: ($30,000)
Notes: Total holdings estimated at 55,000 vols dealing with the political, social, economic and intellectual history of the Jews in the ancient, medieval and modern periods and in all geographic areas. The following areas are especially well represented by printed matter in all relevant languages: Bibliography, Festschriften, History, Bible, Judaism and Jewish theology, liturgy, responsa, rabbinical literature, Jewish law, Hebrew language and literature, Yiddish language and literature, anti-semitism, Zionism, Palestine and the *Yishuv*, and the State of Israel. German and American Judaica form a collecting emphasis with holdings for all the standard histories as well as histories of individual synagogues, institutions and local communities. Works in Hebrew and Yiddish comprise about 60 percent of the collection (estimated 30,000 vols). With few exceptions, holdingsare limited to nineteenth and twentieth century imprints, with complete sets of journals and thousands of ephemeral pamphlets, many of them commemorating anniversaries, enhancing the research value of the collection, the largest Judaica research library in the southeastern United States. Only about half of the collection is cataloged; the collection is a circulating one and vols may be borrowed on interlibrary loan. Incl the Leonard C Mishkin Collection (40,000 vols), the largest personal Judaica collection in the United States, the Shlomo Marenof Collection (3500 vols), and the inventory of Bernard Morgenstern's Lower East Side Book Store (8000 vols). Scholars should inquire in advance of their visit. *The Isser and Rae Price Library of Judaica* Report (circulation 2900 copies) is mailed gratis twice a year to all interested parties. Special catalogs:Pre-1881 Hebrew imprints recorded in a chronological card file.

OH —HEBREW UNION COLLEGE-JEWISH INSTITUTE OF RELIGION, Klau Library, 3101 Clifton Ave, Cincinnati, 45220. David J Gilner, Reference Librn
Holdings: Uncat Maps
Notes: About 200 pre-1900 maps, some as old as early 16th century. About 400 post-1900, most in color. Primarily of Israel/Palestine.

PA —LIBRARY COMPANY OF PHILADELPHIA, 1314 Locust St, Philadelphia, 19107. Edwin Wolf II, Librn; Kenneth Finkel, Cur of Prints
Notes: The Edwin Wolf Collection of Judaica, consisting of 165 manuscripts and more than 500 books and broadsides printed in the US between 1718 and 1875. Incl literature, prayer books, Hebrew schoolbooks, reports of Jewish organizations, missionary tracts, narratives of travel to Palestine, and books on medicine. Most of the manuscripts consists of correspondence of the Gratz family, American pioneers.

PALFI, MARION

AZ —UNIVERSITY OF ARIZONA, Center for Creative Photography, 843 E University Blvd, Tucson, 85721. James Enyeart, Dir; Terence Pitts, Cur and Librn
Holdings: Pix
Notes: Center has significant collections consisting of more than 25 photographs plus other archival material such as negatives, contact sheets, work prints, correspondence, financial records, diaries, project files, etc. Inventories of the collections are available to researchers. Published guides available for some collections.

PALI LANGUAGE AND LITERATURE

CA —UNIVERSITY OF CALIFORNIA, LOS ANGELES, Research Library, Indo/Pacific Collection, 405 Hilgard Ave, Los Angeles, 90024. Edward Shreeves, Chairman, Bibliographers Group; Charlotte Spence, Indo/Pacific Bibliographer
Holdings: Vols Cat Mss Maps Pix Microforms
Notes: The South Asian collection has been developed on two levels. On the research level it focuses on (1) the cultural, economic, political and social history of India from about 1859 to 1947; (2) linguistic and literary studies, with particular emphasis given to Sanskrit and Pali; and (3) the history of the Portuguese experience in South Asia. On the teaching level, materials are collected which relate to India before 1859, and from 1947 to date, as well as materials relating to the other political entities of South Asia. A description of the South Asian collection is included in the May, 1977 issue of *The Librarian*, and in *South Asian Library Resources in North America* (1975).

HI —UNIVERSITY OF HAWAII, Library, 2550 The Mall, Honolulu, 96822. Joyce Wright, Head, Asia Collection; Masato Matsu, Head, East Asia Vernacular Collection
Holdings: Vols 75,215 Cat Microforms
Notes: The Asia Collection holds material

PALI LANGUAGE AND LITERATURE (cont.)

from and relating to Bangladesh, India, Nepal, Pakistan, and Sri Lanka in western and Asian languages. South Asian languages currently acquired: Bengali, Hindi, Marathi, Nepali, Pali, Prakrit, Sanskrit, Tamil. Period emphasis is post-World War II. Subject emphasis: social sciences and the humanities (literature, economics, history, religion/philosophy). Holdings are supplemented by a large uncataloged backlog, much of it accessible through the Library of Congress Accessions Lists for the area and by over 7000 cataloged titles in the main library collection. *South Asian Library Resources in North America: A Survey Prepared for the Boston Conference*, 1974, ed by M L P Patterson (Zug, Switzerland: Tutes Documentation Compnay, 1975).(Bibliotheca Asiatica 12-), "University of Hawaii," pp 103-114.

MA —HARVARD UNIVERSITY LIBRARY, Widener Library, Cambridge, 02138.
Holdings: Cat Mss

MI —UNIVERSITY OF MICHIGAN, Graduate Library, South Asian Dept, Ann Arbor, 48109. Om P Sharma, Librn
Holdings: Vols (365,000) Cat Maps Slides Microforms
Notes: The major emphasis is on social sciences and humanities. Besides materials in classical languages, South Asian vernaculars being retained are Hindi, Bengali, Urdu, Marathi and Tamil; strong in classical languages, especially Sanskrit, Pali, and Prakrit.

NY —NEW YORK PUBLIC LIBRARY, Oriental Div, Fifth Ave & 42 St, New York, 10018. E Christian Filstrup, Chief
Holdings: Cat Mss Microforms
Budget: ($56,455)
Notes: Published catalog of holdings.

OH —CLEVELAND PUBLIC LIBRARY, Fine Arts and Special Collections Department, 325 Superior Ave, Cleveland, 44114. Alice N Loranth, Head
Holdings: Vols 1200 Cat Mss
Notes: Emphasis is on language, literature, religion; classic texts and their Western translations. Incl 1100 vols in Pali. Separate catalog of author entries for titles in Pali is maintained.
See also entry under Oriental Languages and Literatures.

TX —UNIVERSITY OF TEXAS LIBRARIES, Asian Collection, PO Box P, Austin, 78712. Kevin Lin, Asian Librn; Merry Burlingham, South Asian Librn
Holdings: Vols (56,000)
Notes: Materials in Hindi, Sanskrit, Urdu, Prakrit, and Pali (acquired chiefly through the Special Foreign Acquisitions Program) and selected English-language materials, including Indian censuses and district gazetteers and Pakistani censuses.

PALIMPSESTS see Manuscripts (Palimpsests)

PALM LEAF INSCRIPTIONS

RI —BROWN UNIVERSITY, John Hay Library, 20 Prospect St, Providence, 02912. Mark N Brown, Cur Mss
Holdings: Vols (53) //
Notes: Indic Manuscripts Collection--codices written in Burmese, Cambodian, Telugu Skandhas, Bengali, and Sinhalese script on palm leaves, encased within wood covers, some lacquered. Subjects include: Buddhist canon, Pali grammar and lexicons, epics, dance drama, and a treatise on midwifery. Recorded in *A Census of Indic Manuscripts in the United States and Canada* compiled by Horace I Poleman (New Haven: American Oriental Society, 1938).

PQ —McGILL UNIVERSITY, McLennan Library, Rare Books and Special Collections Dept, 3459 McTavish St, Montreal, H3A 1Y1, Can.
Notes: 100 items in Arabic, Persian, Indian illuminated manuscripts and Pali palm leaf manuscripts.

PALMER, ALBERT MARSHMAN

NY —HAMPDEN-BOOTH THEATRE LIBRARY AT THE PLAYERS, 16 Gramercy Park, New York, 10003. Louis A Rachow, Librn/Cur
Holdings: Mss Pix
Notes: The Union Square Theatre Collection, incl correspondence, original contracts for plays produced, autobiographies by many actors and actresses who had performed at The Union Square Theatre, sheetmusic, photographs, illustrations, playbills. This collection was made by Albert Marshman Palmer and covers the years of his career as Manager of The Union Square Theatre. Described in Palmer's *Catalog of the Library of Albert M Palmer* (published in 1906), pp 100-109. Described in *Theatre & Performing Arts Collections* (New York: Haworth Press, 1981).

PALMER, BRUCE

MA —BOSTON UNIVERSITY, Mugar Memorial Library, Special Collections Dept, 771 Commonwealth Ave, Boston, 02215. Howard B Gotlieb, Dir
Holdings: Cat Mss Correspondence

PA —US ARMY MILITARY HISTORY INSTITUTE, Carlisle Barracks, 17013. Richard J Sommers, Chief Archivist-Historian
Holdings: Mss Cat
Notes: 2000 boxes mss. The Viet Nam War collection, personal letters, daily logs, memoirs, speeches, and official papers of American officers and soldiers serving in Viet Nam or elsewhere in the world during the era. Almost all these papers are from Generals, incl William DePuy, Harold K Johnson, Bruce Palmer, Jonathan Seaman, and William Westmoreland.

PALMER, CHARLES FORREST

GA —EMORY UNIVERSITY, Robert W Woodruff Library, Special Collections Dept, Atlanta, 30322. Linda M Matthews, Head Special Collections; Virginia J H Cain, Processing Archivist; Richard H F Lindemann, Reference Archivist
Holdings: Vols (16,000) Cat Mss Maps Pix Slides
Notes: Personal books, papers, diaries and printed materials of Charles Forrest Palmer of Atlanta. About 15,000 pieces.

PALMER, POTTER

IL —CHICAGO HISTORICAL SOCIETY, Library, Clark St at North Ave, Chicago, 60614. Archie Motley, Manuscript Librn
Notes: Papers of Potter Palmer and Bertha Honore Palmer.

PALMER, SOPHIA

MA —SIMMONS COLLEGE ARCHIVES, 300 The Fenway, Boston, 02115. Megan Sniffin-Marinoff, College Archivist
Notes: Archives of the Simmons College School of Public Health Nursing (later reorganized into the School of Nursing) cover the years 1902-1970. Important correspondents in the collection incl M Adelaide Nutting, Mary Beard, Isabel Stewart, and Anne Hervey Strong, etc. Incl Strong's records of activity with regard to nursing education in the National Organization for Public Health Nursing, 1918-22. 1000 linear feet in institution, incl special collections nursing and photographs, nursing.

PALMER FAMILY

MA —NEW ENGLAND HISTORIC GENEALOGICAL SOCIETY, Library, 101 Newbury St, Boston, 02116. Ralph J Crandell, Dir
Notes: Family papers, likely to incl personal correspondence, diaries, business records, etc.

PAMMEL, LOUIS H.

IA —IOWA STATE UNIVERSITY, Library, Dept of Special Collections, Ames, 50011.

Stanley M Yates, Head
Holdings: Vols 49// Cat Mss
Notes: Louis H Pammel (1862-1931) was professor of botany (1889-1931) and head of department of botany. Collection incl correspondence, collected works, speeches, interviews and articles. Collection is 39 linear feet.

PAMPHLETS—COLLECTIONS

CA —UNIVERSITY OF CALIFORNIA, SAN DIEGO, Central University Library, Mandeville Dept of Special Collections, La Jolla, 92093. Lynda Corey Claassen, Head
Notes: Rare Book Collection incl 8000 English-language political pamphlets, 17th to 20th centuries.

CA —UNIVERSITY OF CALIFORNIA, LOS ANGELES, Research Library, Dept of Special Collections, 405 Hilgard Ave, Los Angeles, 90024. Edward Shreeves, Chairman, Bibliographers Group; David S Zeidberg, Head
Notes: Collection of 300 Mexican pamphlets, the bulk dating from the 1820s.

CT —YALE UNIVERSITY, Beinecke Rare Book & Manuscript Library, Osborn Collection, New Haven, 06520. Stephen R Parks, Cur
Holdings: Mss

IL —LOYOLA UNIVERSITY OF CHICAGO, E M Cudahy Memorial Library, 6525 N Sheridan Rd, Chicago, 60626.
Notes: Dorr E Felt Pamphlet and Clipping Collection. Emphasizes political and economic issues, 1902-35, and documents Illinois Manufacturers Association Conference, September 8-9, 1919; Air Board of Chicago, April 16, 1921-August 1, 1930; Allied Debts to the US, May 15, 1923-September 30, 1926; Bolshevism, Communism, "Red" Russia, 1924-27; Child Labor Bill, March 30, 1915, 1914-20; Labor, March, 1902-March, 1932; Railroad Strike, August 25, 1916-August 7, 1920; The War, August, 1914-October 23, 1930; War Industries Commission, June, 1918-November 23, 1928. A pamphlet list is available for each topic.

MI —UNIVERSITY OF MICHIGAN, Dept of Rare Books & Special Collections, Ann Arbor, 48109. Edward C Weber, Head, Labadie Collection
Notes: The Labadie Collection of radical materials, containing papers, tracts, handbills, and publications of minority political and social reform organizations from the mid-1800s to the present, incl 8000 serial titles and 20,000 uncataloged pamphlets.

NY —CORNELL UNIVERSITY LIBRARIES, Collection of Regional History, Dept of Manuscripts and Univ Archives, Ithaca, 14853.
Notes: Incl ca 600 items; centennial and other commemorative or descriptive publications issued throughout New York State.

NC —DUKE UNIVERSITY, William R Perkins Library, Rare Book Room, Durham, 27706. John L Sharpe, III, Cur
Notes: English pamphlet collection of about 10,000 items. In the main, 17th and 18th century "political history and international relations of Great Britain." French pamphlet collection. Relating to the political, economic and social life of France from the early 18th century down to 1830.

NS —DALHOUSIE UNIVERSITY LIBRARY, Halifax, B3H 4H8, Can.
Holdings: Vols 2000
Notes: Nova Scotia history pamphlets. Compiled by a Nova Scotia newspaper editor, J J Stewart, the pamphlet collection provides a comprehensive view of Nova Scotia society in the 19th century, religious, political, educational, economic, and moral issues are all hotly debated in the collection's pamphlets. Many unique items are to be found in the collection.

PAN AMERICAN EXPOSITION

NY —BUFFALO & ERIE COUNTY HISTORICAL SOCIETY, 25 Nottingham Court, Buffalo, 14216. Herman Sass, Librn

PAN-AMERICAN GAMES

ON —UNIVERSITY OF WESTERN
ONTARIO, Dept of Special Collections,
London, N6A 5B9, Can. Beth Miller, Librn
Notes: Large and important collection on
Canadian participation in pre-Olympic and
other Game series. Incl minutes of annual
meetings of the Athletic Union of Canada,
1884-1898, 1908-1954.

PAN AMERICAN HEALTH ORGANIZATION

MI —UNIVERSITY OF MICHIGAN, Public
Health Library, Ann Arbor, 48109. Mary
Townsend, Head
Holdings: Vols (55,000) Cat Maps Pix
Budget: ($24,000)

PAN AMERICAN SOCIETY, SAN FRANCISCO

CA —UNIVERSITY OF THE PACIFIC,
Library, Stockton, 95211. Hiram L Davis,
Dir of Libraries
Holdings: //
Notes: Records, 1945-1964, incl
correspondence, business records, minutes of
meeting, membership rosters, programs,
invitations, newsletters, special reports,
photographs, flag sets, scraps and related
papers. Twelve document boxes.

PAN AMERICAN UNION

NY —NEW YORK PUBLIC LIBRARY,
Research Libraries, Economic & Public
Affairs Div, Fifth Ave & 42 St, New York,
10018. Edward DiRoma, Chief
Holdings: Vols (1,500,000) Cat Microforms
TX —UNIVERSITY OF TEXAS LIBRARIES,
Nettie Lee Benson Latin American
Collection, Sid Richardson Hall 1.109,
Austin, 78712. Laura Gutierrez-Witt, Head
Librn
Holdings: Vols (450,000) Cat Mss Maps Pix
Phonorecords Filmstrips Microforms
See also entry under Latin America.
TX —NORTH TEXAS STATE UNIVERSITY,
Government Documents Dept, NT Station
Box 5188, Denton, 76203. Melody Kelley,
Librn
Notes: 2000 documents regarding
Organization of American States (OAS) in
Document Section of main library.

PAN AMERICAN WOMEN'S ASSOCIATION

NJ —RUTGERS, THE STATE UNIVERSITY
OF NEW JERSEY, Alexander Library,
Special Collections and Archives, College
Ave & Huntington St, New Brunswick,
08903. Ronald L Becker, Cur of Manuscripts
and Rare Books
Notes: Papers of the Inter-American
Association for Democracy and Freedom,
the Pan American Women's Association,
and their director, Frances Grant (1930-).
Also papers of Robert Alexander, incl
transcripts of several thousand interviews
with Latin American political leaders,
students, etc (1950-).

PAN AMERICANISM see Pan-Americanism

PANAMA

AZ —UNIVERSITY OF ARIZONA, Library,
Tucson, 85721. W David Laird, Librn
Notes: The collection of the noted
Panamanian historian, Professor Ernesto J
Castillero, concerning all aspects of life and
history in Panama.
CT —YALE UNIVERSITY, Sterling Memorial
Library, Latin American Collections, New
Haven, 06520. Lee H Williams Jr, Cur
Holdings: Vols (300,000) Cat Maps Pix
Slides Phonorecords 16mm Films Filmstrips
See also entry under Latin America
FL —UNIVERSITY OF MIAMI, Otto G
Richter Library, PO Box 248214, Coral

Gables, 33124. Frank Rodgers, Dir of
Libraries
Holdings: Vols 800 Cat
Notes: Additional materials in US
government publications, periodicals, etc,
and in cataloged collection of Darien.
Described in part in Catalog of the Cuban
and Caribbean Library, University of Miami
(Boston: G K Hall, 1977).
KS —UNIVERSITY OF KANSAS, Watson
Library, Lawrence, 66045. George Jerkovich,
Cur Slavic Collections
Notes: Over 6000 valuable Central
American titles, of which fewer than half in
a random sample are presently located in
OCLC, and over half not incl in published
holdings of the University of Texas or
Tulane University. A special grant is
supporting cataloging of the collection.
MA —PAN AMERICAN SOCIETY OF NEW
ENGLAND, Shattuck Library, 152 North
Street, Boston, 02109. Vivian Ingrao, Dir
Holdings: Vols (10,000) Cat Slides
Phonorecords
Notes: Books on art, literature, history, and
economy of Pan American countries.
RI —BROWN UNIVERSITY, John Carter
Brown Library, Providence, 02912. Norman
Fiering, Librn; Everett C Wilkie Jr,
Bibliographer; Susan Danforth, Cur Maps &
Prints
Notes: A substantial part of the collection of
John Scott of Edinburgh. The company was
to establish a colony on the coast of Panama.

PANAMA—HISTORY

AZ —UNIVERSITY OF ARIZONA, Library,
Tucson, 85721. W David Laird, Librn
Notes: Latin American materials in the
University of Arizona Library system may
be found in all of the campus libraries. The
largest collection is located in the Main
Library and concentrates primarily on the
history, literature, political science and
economics in Mexico, Panama, Colombia,
Argentina, Brazil and Chile. Special
Collections specializes in the colonial period
in the areas of law, religion, and economics.
They also incl numerous manuscript
collections, photographs, and 4000
broadsides from Mexico covering the late
18th century through the 20th century
revolutionary period. There are also strong
map, music and phonorecord collections
primarily on Mexico. The greatest collecting
effort is current materials on contemporary
Latin America. Materials are fully accessible
through the main card catalog as there is no
separate catalog of the collection.

PANAMA CANAL

AL —GADSDEN PUBLIC LIBRARY, 254
College St, Gadsden, 35999. Margaret C
Rouse, Reference Librn
Holdings: Vols 269// Cat Mss Maps Pix
Notes: Sibert Collection, the papers of
William Luther Sibert, director of
construction of the Panama Canal. Mr Sibert
was Etowah County native and Gadsden
resident, 1860-1935. Collection received
from Mrs Mary Papoi (Aug 1976) and John
Freeman (Aug 1977). Separate card index.
CA —CLAREMONT COLLEGES, Honnold
Library, Ninth & Dartmouth, Claremont,
91711. Tania Rizzo, Special Collections
Dept Head
Holdings: Vols (70,000) Cat
Notes: Subject strength.
DC —GEORGETOWN UNIVERSITY,
Library, Special Collections Div, 37 & O Sts
NW, Washington, 20057. George M
Barringer, Special Collections Librn;
Nicholas B Sheetz, Mss Librn
Holdings: Cat Pix
Notes: Collection of photographs taken by
Captain Donald C Kemp, Signal Corps. The
photographs document the people, land and
culture of Panama (ca 1928-32). Includes
papers of Tomas Heran, Earl Harding,
Thomas E Martin, William McCan, Clark
Thompson, Leonor K Sullivan, and Capt
Miles Duval. Correspondence, memoranda,
texts of addresses and congressional
testimony, articles, publications,

photographs, and newspaper clippings from
the House Subcommittee on the Panama
Canal.
MA —HARVARD UNIVERSITY LIBRARY,
Widener Library, Cambridge, 02138.
Holdings: Cat
MI —UNIVERSITY OF MICHIGAN,
Engineering-Transportation Library, 312
Undergraduate Library, Ann Arbor, 48109.
Sharon A Balius, Assoc Librn
Holdings: Mss Pix
Notes: The collection contains 475 items
covering the construction of the Panama
Canal, incl 24 vols of photographs compiled
by John G Clayburn, a superintendent of the
Dredging Division.
NY —STATE UNIVERSITY OF NEW
YORK, COLLEGE OF ARTS & SCIENCE
AT GENESEO, Milne Library, Geneseo,
14454. William T Lane, Head of Information
Services & Archivist
Holdings: // Pix
Notes: The Martha Blow Wadsworth
Collection. Photographs taken or collected
by Mrs Wadsworth from the 1890s to
around 1910. There are 33 albums
containing 4561 mounted photographs, and
3 boxes containing 345 hand-tinted lantern
slides. Subjects include horseback rides from
Washington, DC to Avon, NY (1905-1909);
US Army packtrain trips in the
Southwestern US (1907-1910); Hopi,
Navajo, and Zuni Indians (1910); motor trip
through France and England (1909); Panama
Canal Construction; Alaskan boundary
survey trip; and the Wadsworth family of
Livingston County, NY. There are no
negatives. Inventory in repository. Open to
qualified investigators with permission of
archivist. Gift of Michael Moukhanoff,
Ashantee, NY, 1976.
NY —NEW YORK PUBLIC LIBRARY,
Research Libraries, General Research
Division, Fifth Ave & 42 St, New York,
10018. Rodney Phillips, Chief
Holdings: Vols (2,225,000) Cat Maps Pix
Microforms
Budget: ($775,718)
NY —CANAL MUSEUM, Research Library,
318 Erie Blvd E, Syracuse, 13202. Todd S
Weseloh, Librn & Archivist
Holdings: Vols (6000) Uncat Mss Maps Pix
Slides
Notes: Collections on American Canals,
English Canals and Panama Canal. Main
focus on canals of New York State from
1793 to present. Engineering, finance,
maintenance, construction, canal life, canal
boats and impact of canals on New York.
Limited genealogical value. 954 linear feet
mss, 46,000 photos and slides, 7000 mss,
maps and plans.
BC —LEGISLATIVE LIBRARY
(PROVINCIAL), Parliament Bldgs, Victoria,
V8V 1X4, Can. J H MacEachern, Head,
Government Documents Division
Holdings: Cat Maps Microforms

PAN-AMERICANISM

PA —UNIVERSITY OF PITTSBURGH,
Hillman Library, Pittsburgh, 15260. Glenora
E Rossell, Head
Holdings: Vols 2050 Cat Microforms
Notes: A collection of books and documents
on Inter-American relations, with emphasis
on the relations between the US and Mexico,
Peru, Chile, Guatemale, Dominican Republic
and Cuba. It covers international affairs,
boundary problems, inter-American politics.

PANCHATANTRA

OH —CLEVELAND PUBLIC LIBRARY, Fine
Arts and Special Collections Department,
325 Superior Ave, Cleveland, 44114. Alice
N Loranth, Head
Holdings: Vols (700) Cat Mss Pix
Notes: Part of the Fables Collection, which
is strong in Medieval European and Oriental
works. Numerous rare and early editions of
Reynard the Fox (200 vols), Panchatantra,
Bidpai, Hitopadesa, etc, are incl. Aesop and
the modern fabulists are incl only by
representative editions.
See also entries under Fables; Oriental
Languages and Literatures.

PANEGYRICS

KS —UNIVERSITY OF KANSAS, Kenneth Spencer Research Library, Special Collections Dept, Lawrence, 66045. Alexandra Mason, Librn
Holdings: Vols 300 Cat Mss
Notes: In addition to Marlborough holdings throughout the 18th century collections, the department has particular strength in satire and panegyric on John Churchill, Duke of Marlborough, in the Robert Horn Collection (over 150 vols). See Hyde, Ann, *The Queen's General: John Churchill, First Duke of Marlborough, 1650-1722, an exhibition... in the Kenneth Spencer Research Library* (Lawrence: Univsersity of Kansas Libraries) 1972. Noncirculating.

PANGBORN, CLYDE EDWARD

†WA —WASHINGTON STATE UNIVERSITY, Library, Manuscripts, Archives & Special Collections, Pullman, 99164. John F Guido, Head
Holdings: Vols Cat Mss Maps Pix
Notes: The papers of Clyde Edward Pangborn, barnstormer, round-the-world aviator, and test pilot are in the Washington State University Library. The collection has been described by Mary W Avery in *The Record* (1963): pp 68-70.

PANGBORN, EDGAR

MA —BOSTON UNIVERSITY, Mugar Memorial Library, Special Collections Dept, 771 Commonwealth Ave, Boston, 02215. Howard B Gotlieb, Dir
Holdings: Cat Mss
Notes: Mss Correspondence, etc collected in depth; incl publications by or about.

PANGENESIS see Heredity; Reproduction

PANICS see Depressions—1929—U.s.

PANJABI LANGUAGE AND LITERATURE

AZ —UNIVERSITY OF ARIZONA, Library, Oriental Studies Collection, Tucson, 85721. Mary J McWhorter, Actg Head Librn
Holdings: Vols (95,000) Cat Microforms
Budget: ($30,000)
See also entry under Oriental Languages and Literatures
MO —UNIVERSITY OF MISSOURI-COLUMBIA, Ellis Library, Ninth and Lowry, Columbia, 65201. Murari Lal Nagar, Librn
Holdings: Vols 100,000 Maps Microforms
Notes: The South Asia Studies Program at the University of Missouri-Columbia, is an interdepartmental, multi-disciplinary area studies program on India, Pakistan, Bangladesh, Sri Lanka and Nepal. Depository for the PL480 Program of the Library of Congress in many languages from South Asia. There are library resources in Sanskrit, Hindi, Bengali, Panjabi, and Malayalam. The library is particularly strong in Baroda, Bengal and the Punjab.
NY —NEW YORK PUBLIC LIBRARY, Oriental Div, Fifth Ave & 42 St, New York, 10018. E Christian Filstrup, Chief
Holdings: Cat Mss Microforms
Budget: ($56,455)
Notes: Published catalog of holdings.
NY —NEW YORK PUBLIC LIBRARY, Donnell Foreign Language Library, 20 W 53 St, New York, 10019. Bosiljka Stevanovic, Supvr Librn
Holdings: Vols 213 Cat
Notes: Panjabi collection incl Panjabi authors of Panjabi expression. No separate catalog.

PANKHURST, EMMELINE

NC —UNIVERSITY OF NORTH CAROLINA, GREENSBORO, Walter Clinton Jackson Library, Special Collections Dept, 1000 Spring Garden St, Greensboro, 27412. Emilie W Mills, Librn
Holdings: Cat Mss
Notes: 78 letters by the English composer Dame Ethel Mary Smyth, chiefly to Emmeline Pankhurst, written from Helouan, Egypt, 1913-1914. Other letters incl several from Empress Eugenie and members of her circle, and several letters to Lady Ponsonby. This group of letters mainly traces the composer's interest in the suffrage movement and the development of her musical career. No photocopying.

PANS see Kettles

PANTACLES see Talismans

PANTOMIME see Mimes and Miming

PANUNZIO, CONSTANTINE MARIA

CA —HOOVER INSTITUTION ON WAR, REVOLUTION & PEACE, Stanford University, Stanford, 94305. Milorad M Drachkovitch, Archivist
Holdings: // Mss
Notes: Papers, 1921-1945, of Constantine Maria Panunzio, author and sociologist. Letters, articles, news clippings, bibliographies and booklists relating to Italian politics. Topics incl fascism, church and state, Mussolini, anti-Semitism and racism. About 75 percent of the material printed. 12 boxes. Unpublished preliminary inventory in repository.

PAPACY AND ANTI-PAPACY

CA —UNIVERSITY OF CALIFORNIA, LOS ANGELES, Research Library, Dept of Special Collections, 405 Hilgard Ave, Los Angeles, 90024. Edward Shreeves, Chairman, Bibliographers Group; David S Zeidberg, Head
Holdings: Mss
Notes: Various single mss and service books. The Orsini family papers, 13th to 20th century, incl material relating to their relationships with the Catholic Church and the Papal Throne.
CO —UNIVERSITY OF COLORADO, Libraries, Special Collections, Boulder, 80309. Nora J Quinlan, Head
Holdings: Vols 800
Notes: The Mandell Creighton Library. Renaissance papacy, Protestant reform and the Conciliar movement. Separate catalog.
MO —SAINT LOUIS UNIVERSITY, Pius XII Memorial Library, 3655 W Pine Blvd, Saint Louis, 63108. William Cole, Dir
Holdings: Slides Microforms
Notes: Collection covers all areas of learning and European history from Classical Antiquity to early modern period. Researchers using collection receive assistance in paleography, bibliography and reference search. Approx 10,000 1000-foot reels of microfilm (not counting master negatives) reproducing Vatican Library's Latin, Greek, Hebrew, Arabic and Ethiopic mss. Some 8000 100-foot reels of microfilm (again not counting master negative) reproducing rare and out of print books relating to subject areas in the mss. Over 50,000 color slides of medieval and Renaissance mss illuminations. A reference collection of modern materials relating to ms research.
PA —LUTHERAN THEOLOGICAL SEMINARY, Krauth Memorial Library, 7301 Germantown Ave, Philadelphia, 19119. Rev David J Wartluft, Dir Libr
Holdings: Cat
Notes: The Otto Louis Schreiber Collection of Martin Luther and the Reformation in Numismatic Art. Also limited items in Melanchthon, Johann Sebastian Bach, and Anti-papal medals. This is most complete collection on the subject in America--1000 items. A printed descriptive catalog is available.

PAPAGO INDIANS

AZ —NORTHERN ARIZONA UNIVERSITY, Special Collection Library, CU Box 6022, Flagstaff, 86011. Peter M Whiteley, Coordr/Archivist; William Mullane, Librn
Notes: Dean Saxton Collection; corrected Papago Hymnal, first edition, 1959. Concise Papago-English dictionary with corrections, dated ca 1950's or 1960's.
AZ —UNIVERSITY OF ARIZONA, Center for Creative Photography, 843 E University Blvd, Tucson, 85721. James Enyeart, Dir; Terence Pitts, Cur and Librn
Holdings: Pix
Notes: The Marion Palfi Photo Archive. Famous portrayals of, espec, poverty-stricken and victimized persons in the US, 1940 through 1970s, incl Hopi, Navajo, and Papago Indians on reservations, in urban relocation, and acculturation centers. Over 1500 master prints, 10,000 work prints, hundreds of glass plate and film negatives, manuscripts, etc.

PAPAL BULLS see Bulls, Papal

PAPAL DOCUMENTS

MA —COLLEGE OF THE HOLY CROSS, Dinand Library, College St, Worcester, 01610. James M Mahoney, Cur of Special Collection
Holdings: Uncat Mss Pix
Notes: 48 signed papal documents and letters of 31 popes, 1181-1946; about 100 portrait engravings of the popes. Restricted use.

PAPER

CA —AVERY INTERNATIONAL CORP, Information Center, 325 N Altadena Dr, Pasadena, 91107. Louanne A Kalvinskas, Information Specialist
Holdings: Vols 800 Cat
Notes: Also many reports.
NY —XEROX CORP, Technical Information Center, PO Box 305, Webster, 14580. Michael D Majcher, Mgr
Holdings: Vols (30,000) Cat Microforms
OH —OWENS-ILLINOIS, Information Research Department, One Seagate, Toledo, 43666. Patricia Ajemian, Librn
Holdings: Vols (24,000) Cat Pix Microforms
Notes: Requests for use are handled on an individual basis. Incl information on packaging.
PA —CARNEGIE LIBRARY OF PITTSBURGH, Science & Technology Dept, 4400 Forbes Ave, Pittsburgh, 15213. Catherine M Brosky, Dept Head
Holdings: Vols (380,000) Cat Maps Microforms
Budget: ($240,000)
Notes: Incl many journals, encyclopedias, general reference books, abstracts, indexes and bibliographies.
PQ —MCGILL UNIVERSITY, McLennan Library, Rare Books and Special Collections Dept, 3459 McTavish St, Montreal, H3A 1Y1, Can.
Notes: 47,604 items, old and new, mostly contemporary, Canadian and non-Canadian, organized by form. Housed within the William Colgate History of Printing Collection.

PAPER DOLLS

PA —CHESTER COUNTY HISTORICAL SOCIETY, 225 N High St, West Chester, 19380. Rosemary B Philips, Librn; Jack McCarthy, Archivist; Laurie Rofini, Asst Archivist
Notes: Books, photographs, mss on early art, architecture, material culture of Chester County. Espec large collection of paper dolls and paper toys (not limited to Chester County, PA).

PAPER MAKING AND TRADE

AL —INTERNATIONAL PAPER CO, Science & Technology-Information Services, Erling Riis Research Laboratory, PO Box

PAPER MAKING AND TRADE (cont.)

2787, Mobile, 36601. Fran Row, Sr Library
Clerk; J Pope, Superv
Holdings: Vols (9000) Cat Audiotapes
Microforms

CT —DEXTER CORP, C H Dexter Div,
Technical Library, Windsor Locks, 06096.
Fred N Masters, Librn
Holdings: Vols 1500 Cat

DC —LIBRARY OF CONGRESS,
Preservation Office, Washington, 20540.
Notes: Extensive gift of Japanese ancient
and modern paper making equipment, from
Mr Tokuyoshi Kono, of Kamakura, Japan.
Complements the Library's great interest in
the problems of paper manufacture and
preservation.

GA —TECHNICAL ASSOCIATION OF THE
PULP & PAPER INDUSTRY, James d'A
Clark Library, PO Box 105113, Atlanta,
30348. Elizabeth A Bibby, Information
Services Adminr
Holdings: Vols 2500 Cat Audiotapes Slides
Microforms
Budget: $3500
Notes: Collection open to public, call for
times/hours. FEC-Based reference service
available.

MA —STONE & WEBSTER ENGINEERING
CORP, Technical Information Center,
Library, 245 Summer St, PO Box 2325,
Boston, 02107. Nancy M Pellini, Mgr
Holdings: Vols (10,000) Cat Pix Microforms
Notes: Also over 1200 periodicals. Extensive
vertical file collection, and 5 on-line system
for search.

MI —WESTERN MICHIGAN UNIVERSITY,
Dwight B Waldo Library, Kalamazoo,
49008. Michael Buckner, Science Librn
Holdings: Vols 5000 Cat

NJ —NEWARK PUBLIC LIBRARY, Art &
Music Dept, 5 Washington St, Newark,
07101. William J Dane, Supv
Holdings: Vols (3500) Cat
Notes: R C Jenkinson Collection of Finely
Printed Books. Shows the physical form of
the book and its development through the
centuries. There is always a related exhibit in
this section of the library covering such
subjects as letter forms, printing, individual
presses and publishers, papermaking, etc.
Extensive Bruce Rogers collection.

NY —COLUMBIA UNIVERSITY
LIBRARIES, Rare Book & Manuscript
Library, 801 Butler Library, 535 W 114 St,
New York, 10027. Kenneth A Lohf, Librn
Holdings: Vols (15,000) Cat
Notes: Covers all phases of bookmaking,
bookbinding, book illustrations, book design,
development of writing, paper, type, etc.
Books about books as well as examples of
fine printing.

NY —INTERNATIONAL PAPER CO,
Corporate Information Center, 77 W 45 St,
New York, 10036. Elizabeth Skerritt,
Corporate Librn
Holdings: Vols 390 Cat Maps Pix Slides
Microforms
Notes: Extensive statistics and VF on paper
industry.

NY —NEW YORK PUBLIC LIBRARY,
Research Libraries, Science and Technology
Research Center, Fifth Ave & 42 St, New
York, 10018.
Holdings: Vols (1,100,000) Cat Microforms
Budget: ($647,259)

NY —ROCHESTER INSTITUTE OF
TECHNOLOGY, Melbert B Cary Jr
Graphic Arts Collection, School of Printing,
One Lomb Memorial Drive, Rochester,
14623. David Pankow, Cur
Holdings: Vols (11,000) Cat Pix
Notes: Incl most of the volumes produced by
Dard Hunter; also specimens.

NY —STATE UNIVERSITY OF NEW
YORK, COLLEGE OF
ENVIRONMENTAL SCIENCE AND
FORESTRY, F Franklin Moon Library,
Syracuse, 13210. Donald F Webster, Librn
Holdings: Vols (86,430) Cat
Budget: ($120,000)

NC —NORTH CAROLINA STATE
UNIVERSITY, Forest Resources Library,
4012 Biltmore Hall, Raleigh, 27650. Pamela

E Puryear, Head
Holdings: Vols (9000) Cat Microforms
Notes: Forestry, wood and paper sciences;
recreation; remote sensing; FAO and forest
service and forest products labs. Publications
and audiovisual materials.

PA —FRANKLIN INSTITUTE LIBRARY, 20
& The Parkway, Philadelphia, 19103.
Miriam Padusis, Dir; Charles Wilt, Readers
Servs Librn
Holdings: Vols (300,000) Cat Maps Pix
Microforms

PA —CARNEGIE LIBRARY OF
PITTSBURGH, Science & Technology Dept,
4400 Forbes Ave, Pittsburgh, 15213.
Catherine M Brosky, Dept Head
Holdings: Vols (380,000) Cat Maps
Microforms
Budget: ($240,000)
See also entry under Paper.

PA —GRAPHIC ARTS TECHNICAL
FOUNDATION, Edward H Wadewitz
Memorial Library, 4615 Forbes Ave,
Pittsburgh, 15213. Janice L Lloyd, Librn
Holdings: Vols (3500) Cat Slides Microforms
Notes: All printing processes. Also, books
and periodicals on paper, ink, photography,
optics, color theory, environmental control.
Approximately 250 periodical titles and 35,
000 classified abstracts of selected periodical
articles. Approximately 15,000 slides within
the organization. Research reports from
foreign graphic arts research institutes.

PA —P H GLATFELTER CO, Research
Library, Dept of Research, Spring Grove,
17362. Jean M Bailey, Librn
Holdings: Vols (2000) Cat Microfilms
Notes: Pulp and paper technology.

RI —BROWN UNIVERSITY, John Hay
Library, 20 Prospect St, Providence, 02912.
Mark N Brown, Cur Mss
Holdings: Vols 75 Cat
Notes: All works by or about artists,
papermaker, and paper historian Dard
Hunter are incl in the Dard Hunter
Collection.

SC —SONOCO PRODUCTS CO, Research
Laboratory, Technical Information Center,
One N Second St, Hartsville, 29550. Ken
Chavis, Dir
Holdings: Vols (4000) Cat Mss Slides
Microforms
Notes: Restricted to Sonoco employees. No
Photocopying.

SC —WOFFORD COLLEGE, Sandor Teszler
Library, N Church St, Spartanburg, 29301.
Frank J Anderson, Librn
Holdings: Vols (500) Cat
Budget: ($500)
Notes: Books about the history and practice
of printing, hand papermaking, bookbinding,
book collecting, fine press and private press
books used in conjunction with instruction at
the Wofford Library Press, an experimental
and bibliographic press which has been in
operation since 1969. Collection contains
materials on printmaking methods and
related graphic arts.

WA —UNIVERSITY OF WASHINGTON
LIBRARIES, Suzzallo Library, Special
Collections Division, Rare Book Collection,
FM-25, Seattle, 98195. Gary Menges,
Coordinator for Special Collections
Holdings: Vols 63,000 Cat Maps Microforms
Budget: $12,500
Notes: Modern imprints only. Mostly in
English, some German, Slavic, and East
Asian languages. No geographical limits but
emphasis is on Pacific Northwest. Northern
service center for Pacific Forestry Research
Information Network (PACFORNET);
southern center is at USFS Pacific Southwest
Experiment Station, Berkeley, California.
Partially cataloged.

WI —US FOREST SERVICE, Forest Products
Laboratory Library, Box 5130, Madison,
53705. Roger Schurmer, Librn; Dr Regis
Miller, Librn; Dr Harold H Burdsall, Jr,
Librn
Holdings: Vols (136,240) Cat Microforms
Budget: ($122,083)
Notes: Forest products utilization research.
KWIC index of FPL reports; centralized title
service from Forestry Bureau, Oxford,
England (card and microfilm). Incl 53,000
specimens of wood from all over the world;
and 2500 genera and many more species.

ON —CIP RESEARCH, Library, 179 Main St
W, Hawkesbury, K6A 2H4, Can. Margaret
Higginson, Librn
Holdings: Vols (12,000) Cat
Budget: ($40,000)
Notes: Pulp and paper technology.

ON —UNIVERSITY OF WESTERN
ONTARIO, Schoool of Library and
Information Science, Library, London, N6G
1H1, Can. Victoria Ripley, Librn
Holdings: Vols (50,000)
Notes: Auction and antiquarian booksellers'
catalogs from Canadian, American and
European firms, some dating back to the
18th century. A special strength is 19th and
early 20th century American booksellers'
catalogs, recently augmented by a collection
of pre-1920 catalogs formed by the late H O
Teisberg. Current emphasis is on Canadian
catalogs.

ON —METROPOLITAN TORONTO
LIBRARY, Fine Arts Dept, 789 Yonge St,
Toronto, M4W 2G8, Can. Alan Suddon,
Head
Holdings: Vols (42,000) Cat Pix Microforms
Notes: Extensive collection.

ON —UNIVERSITY OF TORONTO, Massey
College, Robertson Davies Library, 4
Devonshire Place, Toronto, M5S 2E1, Can.
Desmond G Neill, Librn
Holdings: Vols (12,000) Cat Mss Microforms
Notes: Library contains Bibliography Room
(11 hand presses, type and equipment) and
Papermaking Room. Book collections incl
Ruari McLean Collection of 19th-century
books on, and representative of, color
printing (approx 4300 items).

PQ —MCGILL UNIVERSITY, McLennan
Library, Rare Books and Special Collections
Dept, 3459 McTavish St, Montreal, H3A
1Y1, Can.
Notes: 47,604 items, old and new, mostly
contemporary, Canadian and non-Canadian,
organized by form. Housed within the
William Colgate History of Printing
Collection.

PQ —PULP AND PAPER RESEARCH
INSTITUTE OF CANADA, Library, Saint
John's Rd, Pointe-Claire, H9R 3J9, Can.
Alison Finnemore, Librn
Holdings: Vols (14,000) Cat Microforms
Budget: ($16,000)
Notes: Book catalog.

PQ —TROIS-RIVIERES COLLEGE
LIBRARY, CEGEP de Trois-Rivieres-
Bibliotheque, 3500 de Courval, Trois-
Rivieres, G9A 5E6, Can. Denis Simard,
Librn
Holdings: Vols 4000
Notes: 4000 volumes to support the
curriculum.

PAPER MAKING AND TRADE—HISTORY

CA —CLAREMONT COLLEGES, Ella Strong
Denison Library, Scripps College,
Claremont, 91711. Judy Harvey Sahak,
Librn
Holdings: Vols (200) Uncat
Notes: In addition to books, the Kimberly
Stuart Collection on the history of paper and
papermaking includes trade journals,
examples of handmade papers and
watermarks and a distinguished collection of
Dard Hunter books and ephemera.

CA —MILLS COLLEGE LIBRARY, Oakland,
94613. Steven P Pandolfo, Librn
Holdings: Vols (1000) Cat
Notes: Books on typography, the history of
books and printing, bookbinding and
papermaking. Representative examples of
fine printing, 15th-20th centuries.

CA —UNIVERSITY OF CALIFORNIA,
SANTA BARBARA, Library, Dept of
Special Collections, Santa Barbara, 93106.
Christian F Brun, Head
Holdings: Cat Pix
Notes: A small but distinctive Dard Hunter
collection. Skofield Printers Collection.

CA —STANFORD UNIVERSITY
LIBRARIES, Cecil H Green Library,
Stanford, 94305. Michael T Ryan, Cur
Holdings: Vols (12,000) Cat
Notes: The Morgan A & Aline D Gunst

PAPER MAKING AND TRADE—HISTORY (cont.)

Memorial Library. The book arts in every century with some of the best examples. Strong collection of examples of California printers and graphic artists. Complete or nearly complete collections of works by the Kelmscott, Doves, Ashendene, Colt, Grabhorn, and Grabhorn-Hoyem presses.

CT —LEE ASH, (personal collection), 66 Humiston Dr, Bethany, 06525.
Holdings: Cat Mss Pix
Notes: Incl books, letters, ephemera, etc.

DC —LIBRARY OF CONGRESS, Washington, 20540.
Holdings: Cat Mss Maps Pix
Notes: An extensive collection, celebrated by publication of a special and exhibit catalog, 1968/69. Also incl the Harrison Elliott Collection of Paperiana; historic examples of paper and materials related to paper making, etc. Described in LC *Press Release*, vol 68, p 31.

IL —NEWBERRY LIBRARY, 60 W Walton St, Chicago, 60610. Diana Haskell, Cur of Modern Mss
Holdings: Cat Mss Pix
Notes: Emphasis on hand-made paper, incl watermarks. A small working collection on modern papermaking, mainly for use of our conservation department. A few mss on early papermaking machinery.

IL —NEWBERRY LIBRARY, John M Wing Foundation on the History of Printing, 60 W Walton St, Chicago, 60610. Diana Haskell, Cur of Modern Mss
Holdings: Vols (26,500) Cat Mss
Budget: ($50,000)
Notes: The collection covers printing and printing history of Western Europe and the Americas from its invention to the present. It is particularly rich in incunabula (about 2000); the works of the great printers, among others Aldus, Bodoni, Baskerville, and Rogers. Printed catalog: *A Dictionary Catalogue . . .*(Boston: G K Hall, 1961); *Supplement* (1971). Brief descriptions: James M Wells, "The John M Wing Foundation of The Newberry Library." *The Book Collector*, VIII, 2 (Summer 1959), pp 157-162; Lawrence W Towner, *An Uncommon Collection of Uncommon Collections* (Chicago: The Newberry Library, 1977), pp 25-26.

MA —AMERICAN ANTIQUARIAN SOCIETY LIBRARY, 185 Salisbury St, Worcester, 01609. Marcus A McCorison, Dir & Librn
Notes: Some 800 examples of watermarks in early American paper, from 1699.

NY —BUFFALO & ERIE COUNTY PUBLIC LIBRARY, Rare Book Room, Lafayette Sq, Buffalo, 14203. William H Loos, Cur
Holdings: Vols 25 Cat Mss
Notes: Nearly all Dard Hunter's major works, incl some letters.

NY —INTERNATIONAL PAPER CO, Corporate Information Center, 77 W 45 St, New York, 10036. Elizabeth Skerritt, Corporate Librn
Holdings: Vols 75 Cat Maps Pix Slides Microforms
Notes: Extensive statistics and VF on paper industry.

OR —GEORGIA-PACIFIC HISTORICAL MUSEUM, Library, 900 SW Fifth, Portland, 97204. Richard Thompson, Museum Dir
Holdings: Vols (300) Uncat Videotapes 16mm Films Pix
Notes: Use of collection is by written request for specific information or materials.

VA —COLLEGE OF WILLIAM AND MARY, Earl Gregg Swem Library, Williamsburg, 23185. Margaret C Cook, Cur of Manuscripts & Rare Books
Holdings: Vols 100 // Cat
Notes: Beinbrink Collection.

PAPER MONEY

CO —AMERICAN NUMISMATIC ASSOCIATION LIBRARY, 818 N Cascade Ave, Colorado Springs, 80903. Nancy W Green, Librn
Holdings: Vols (20,000) Cat Slides
Notes: One of the largest numismatic

libraries, the collection incl books, periodicals and auction catalogs on coins and coin collecting, medals, tokens, military orders and decorations, paper money, primitive money, banks and banking, seals and scarabs. ANA publishes a classified subject catalog of its collection and is open to the public for research and reference services. Only members may check books out.

DC —SMITHSONIAN INSTITUTION LIBRARIES, National Museum of American History Branch, Washington, 20560. Rhoda S Ratner, Branch Librn
Holdings: (7700) Cat Maps Pix

MD —MARYLAND HISTORICAL SOCIETY, Library, 201 W Monument St, Baltimore, 21201. William B Keller, Head Librn
Holdings: Cat Mss Maps Pix Slides Microforms
Notes: Espec relating to Maryland and Baltimore. Extensive collection

MA —AMERICAN ANTIQUARIAN SOCIETY LIBRARY, 185 Salisbury St, Worcester, 01609. Marcus A McCorison, Dir & Librn
Notes: Colonial American currency; also Confederate money, and State Bank notes.

NY —AMERICAN MUSEUM OF NATURAL HISTORY, Library Services Dept, Central Park W & 79th St, New York, 10024. Nina J Root, Chairwoman; Mary Genett, Asst Librn for Reference Services

NY —AMERICAN NUMISMATIC SOCIETY LIBRARY, Broadway between 155 & 156 Sts, New York, 10032. Francis D Campbell Jr, Chief Librn
Holdings: Vols (50,000) Cat Mss Maps Pix Slides 16mm Films Microforms
Budget: ($6000)
Notes: Incl materials devoted to coins, medals, decorations, orders, tokens, paper money, seals, heraldry. Aids materials incl history, economic history, art history, archaeology, inscriptions and a number of encyclopedias and biographical dictionaries. Dictionary card catalog provides access to the materials: *Dictionary Catalogue of the Library of the American Numismatic Society.* (Boston: G K Hall, 1962). 6 vols and vol listing the auction catalogs in our collection; *First Supplement: 1962-1967; Second Supplement: 1968-1972; Third Supplement: 1973-1977* (Boston: G K Hall, 1967, 1973, 1978). Noncirculating.

NY —NEW YORK PUBLIC LIBRARY, Research Libraries, General Research Division, Fifth Ave & 42 St, New York, 10018. Rodney Phillips, Chief
Holdings: Vols (2,225,000) Cat Maps Pix Microforms
Budget: ($775,718)

PAPERBACK BOOKS see Bibliography—Paperback Editions

PAPERBACK (MASS MARKET) PUBLISHING

CA —UNIVERSITY OF CALIFORNIA, LOS ANGELES, Research Library, Dept of Special Collections, 405 Hilgard Ave, Los Angeles, 90024. Edward Shreeves, Chairman, Bibliographers Group; David S Zeidberg, Head
Notes: American Paperback Fiction Collection: 3500 turn-of-the-century American paperback novels and 1000 boys' books published in series.

NY —GRADUATE CENTER OF THE CITY UNIVERSITY OF NEW YORK, William H and Gwynne K Crouse Library for Publishing Arts, 33 W 42 St, New York, 10036. Alfred H Lane, Dir
Notes: Recently established and still growing, but intended to become the authoritative source of materials in the field, of particular value in research about the publishing industry. Open to staff members of publishing houses, students, scholars, authors, printers, and booksellers. Primarily 20th century materials, and particularly useful for research on technical, financial, and historical matters. Much on the history

of individual houses, economics of authorship; marketing and distribution of books; etc.

PAPERHANGERS UNION see Brotherhood of Painters, Decorators, and Paperhangers Union

PAPERMAKING see Paper Making and Trade

PAPINEAU REBELLION see Canada—History—Rebellion, 1837-1838

PAPYRI see Manuscripts (Papyri); Manuscripts, Greek

PARACELSUS

PA —COLLEGE OF PHYSICIANS OF PHILADELPHIA, Library, 19 S 22 St, Philadelphia, 19103. Anthony Aguirre, Libr Dir
Holdings: Vols (316,223) Cat Mss Microforms
Budget: ($1,096,557)
Notes: Incl 13,515 pamphlets; 1435 mss; 326,367 reports, dissertations, and reprints. Strong historical and bibliographical collections, as well as current materials. Medical documentation service provides current alerting, incl abstracting, etc.

PARACHUTING

IN —THE MICHAEL HORAN PARACHUTING RESOURCES LIBR, 115 N 13 St, Richmond, 47374. Michael Horan, Librn
Holdings: Vols 250 Uncat
Notes: Current, out of print, and rare books on parachuting, incl periodicals from the US, Canada, and Great Britain, 1950-date. Also, material on skydiving. The "largest collection of (parachuting) books in the US."

NY —RACQUET & TENNIS CLUB, Library, 370 Park Ave, New York, 10022. Gerald Belliveau, Jr, Librn
Holdings: Vols (17,500) Cat
Budget: ($6000)
Notes: Specializes in court tennis, lawn tennis, early American sport. See *Dictionary Catalogue of the Library of Sports in the Racquet and Tennis Club* (Boston: G K Hall, 1971). Also, Robert W Henderson, *Early American Sport*, 3rd ed. (Cranbury, NJ: Fairleigh Dickinson University Press, 1977).

PARACLETE see Holy Spirit

PARADE MUSIC see Marches

PARADES see Processions

PARAGUAY

CA —UNIVERSITY OF CALIFORNIA, RIVERSIDE, University Library, 4045 Canyon Crest Dr, Box 5900, Riverside, 92517.
Holdings: Vols (1,000) Cat Mss Maps Pix
Notes: General research collection in the humanities and social sciences, with special strengths in history (mainly 19th and 20th centuries), literature, folklore and economic conditions, many books from the library of Julio Cesar Chaves. The Special Collections contains the papers of Juan Silvano Godoi, statesman and historian, his diaries (1897-1903, 1905-1921), the papers and correspondence of the historians Nicolas Diaz Perez, Viriato Diaz Perez, and of Hugo Rodriguez Alcala. See Thomas L Whigham and Jerry W Cooney, *Paraguayan History: Manuscript Sources in the United States*, in *Latin American Review*, vol 18 (1983) no 1: p 104-108.

CT —YALE UNIVERSITY, Sterling Memorial Library, Latin American Collections, New Haven, 06520. Lee H Williams Jr, Cur
Holdings: Vols (300,000) Cat Maps Pix Slides Phonorecords 16mm Films Filmstrips
See also entry under Latin America

PARAGUAY—HISTORY

CA —UNIVERSITY OF CALIFORNIA, RIVERSIDE, University Library, 4045

PARAGUAY—HISTORY (cont.)

Canyon Crest Dr, Box 5900, Riverside, 92517.
Holdings: Vols (1,000) Cat Mss Maps Pix
Notes: General research collection in the humanities and social sciences, with special strengths in history (mainly 19th and 20th centuries), literature, folklore and economic conditions, many books from the library of Julio Cesar Chaves. The Special Collections contains the papers of Juan Silvano Godoi, statesman and historian, his diaries (1897-1903, 1905-1921), the papers and correspondence of the historians Nicolas Diaz Perez, Viriato Diaz Perez, and of Hugo Rodriguez Alcala. See Thomas L Whigham and Jerry W Cooney, *Paraguayan History: Manuscript Sources in the United States*, in *Latin American Review*, vol 18 (1983) no 1: p 104-108.

NE —AMERICAN HISTORICAL SOCIETY OF GERMANS FROM RUSSIA (AHSGR), 615 Twelfth St, Lincoln, 68502. Mary Lynn Tuck, Librn
Holdings: Vols (1900) Mss Maps Pix Phonorecords Videotapes Audiotapes Microforms VF
Notes: History of German people from Russia and history of people of German-Russian ancestry. Including times in Russia, Germany, US, Canada, Mexico, Argentina, Brazil, Paraguay, Korea, and Japan. This Society has fifty-six chapters in the United States. 1900 volumes, 100 maps; 500 mss; 1200 vertical files; 2000 pictures; 40,000 obituary files, 40,000 family group charts, 50 phonorecords, 20 videotapes, 50 audiotapes, 15 reel-to-reel tapes, 150 periodicals, 250 microforms, 250 family histories-published and unpublished.

TX —UNIVERSITY OF TEXAS LIBRARIES, Nettie Lee Benson Latin American Collection, Sid Richardson Hall 1.109, Austin, 78712. Laura Gutierrez-Witt, Head Librn
Holdings: Vols (450,000) Cat Mss Maps
Notes: Private library of Manual Gondra, former President of Paraguay. Incl 10,000 books, pamphlets, journals and maps and 2000 mss, relating to the Rio de la Plata area and Brazil.
See also entry under Latin America

PARALYSIS, ANTERIOR SPINAL see Poliomyelitis

PARALYSIS, CEREBRAL see Cerebral Palsy

PARALYSIS, INFANTILE see Poliomyelitis

PARAMEDICS see Allied Health Personnel

PARAMOUNT STUDIOS

CA —ACADEMY OF MOTION PICTURE ARTS & SCIENCES, Margaret Herrick Library, 8949 Wilshire Blvd, Beverly Hills, 90211. Linda Harris Mehr, Library Administrator
Notes: Scripts and stills archive.
See also entry under Moving Pictures.

CA —UNIVERSITY OF CALIFORNIA, LOS ANGELES, Research Library, Dept of Special Collections, 405 Hilgard Ave, Los Angeles, 90024. Edward Shreeves, Chairman, Bibliographers Group; David S Zeidberg, Head
Notes: 23 linear feet of correspondence, ephemera, slides, etc, concerning Walter Beyer's work as an engineer at Paramount Pictures, the development of VistaVision, the Motion Picture Research Council, and Universal Pictures.

PARAPHILIAS, MINOR

IN —INDIANA UNIVERSITY, Institute for Sex Research Library, 416 Morrison Hall, Bloomington, 47401. Douglas Freeman, Collections and Services Librn; Joan Brewer,

Information Services Librn
Holdings: Vols (62,000) Cat Mss Pix Microforms
See also entry under Sex.

PARAPSYCHOLOGY

CA —LOS ANGELES PUBLIC LIBRARY, Philosophy & Religion Dept, 630 W Fifth St, Los Angeles, 90071. Marilyn C Wherley, Librn
Holdings: Vols 600 Cat
Budget: ($60,000)
Notes: Part of the comprehensive collection on Occult Sciences.

NY —PARAPSYCHOLOGY SOURCES OF INFORMATION CENTER, 2 Plane Tree Lane, Dix Hills, 11746. Rhea A White, Dir
Holdings: Vols (4000)
Notes: The PSI Center includes 4000 books, 100 periodical titles, cassette tapes, and unpublished mss dealing with parapsychology and the transformation of consciousness, also 12,000 articles, reprints, etc. There is a charge for reference service and bibliographies.

NY —NEW YORK PUBLIC LIBRARY, Research Libraries, General Research Division, Fifth Ave & 42 St, New York, 10018. Rodney Phillips, Chief
Notes: See *Bibiographic Guide to Psychology, 1976* (Boston: G K Hall 1977). Incl publications cataloged during the year, with additional entries from MARC tapes.

NY —PARAPSYCHOLOGY FOUNDATION, Eileen J Garrett Library, 228 E 71st St, New York, 10021. Wayne Norman, Librn
Holdings: Vols (9300) Cat
Notes: One of the largest libraries on parapsychology. Main emphasis is on the literature of contemporary parapsychology; also a strong collection on the history of parapsychology (early spiritualism, mysticism, relevant philosophical works, etc). Rare book collection incl early rare books and periodicals on psychical research and psychical phenomena. Receives about 100 titles of periodicals and binds the more significant titles. The library maintains its own periodicals index to parapsychological literature, dating from 1966. Main emphasis literature is on experimental parapsychology, or those publications that approach the subject with an objective and/or analytic point of view.

NY —UNITED LODGE OF THEOSOPHISTS LIBRARY, 347 E 72 St, New York, 10021.
Notes: Ancient and modern philosophy and psychology; comparative religion and mythology; parapsychology; reincarnation research in science and religion.

NC —DUKE UNIVERSITY, William R Perkins Library, Manuscript Dept, Durham, 27706. Ellen Gartrell, Cur of Mss
Holdings: Mss
Notes: Correspondence, research notes, financial records, reprints of J B Rhine and Parapsychology Laboratory at Duke (200,000 items, 1934-1962)

NC —FOUNDATION FOR RESEARCH ON THE NATURE OF MAN (FRNM), Institute for Parapsychology, 402 Buchanan Blvd, Box 6847, College Sta, Durham, 27708. K Ramakrishna Rao, Dir
Holdings: Vols (2500) Cat Mss Pix 16mm Films
Budget: ($12,000)
Notes: There is also a large body of early "psychical research" literature as well as most of the latest books in the field of parapsychology. Since the Foundation's activities are primarily devoted to the quantitative investigation of psi phenomena, the library in general does not stock books on occult topics (magic, witchcraft, astrology, etc).

VA —ASSOCIATION FOR RESEARCH & ENLIGHTENMENT, Library, 67 & Atlantic Avenue, PO Box 595, Virginia Beach, 23451. Stephen Jordan, Library Mgr
Holdings: Vols (1800) Cat
Notes: ARE Library Booklist incl 6000 items in 24 subject categories. This special collection is especially strong in the following subjects: astrology, spiritualism,

reincarnation, healing arts, Theosophy, Atlantis, parapsychology and transpersonal psychology.

MB —UNIVERSITY OF MANITOBA, Elizabeth Dafoe Library, Archives and Special Collections Dept, Winnipeg, R3T 2N2, Can. Richard E Bennett, Dept Head; Corrado A Santoro, Reference Archivist
Notes: Papers of Thomas Glendenning Hamilton, physician and surgeon, member of the Manitoba Legislative Assembly, psychic researcher. Winnipeg, Manitoba. Important collection, emphasis is on psychic research with limited amount of materials regarding his medical and political careers. Seance attendance registers, records and affidavits, lecture notes, correspondence, newspaper clippings, books and journal articles. Photographs, slides and ca 50 boxes of glass plate negatives.

PARASITOLOGY

CA —UNIVERSITY OF CALIFORNIA, BERKELEY, Life Sciences Library, Entomology Library, 201 Wellman Hall, Berkeley, 94720. Nancy Axelrod, Librn
Holdings: Vols (12,000) Cat Microforms
Notes: A highly specialized collection limited to materials on insects, arachnida and animal parasites. Special emphasis is given to works on pest control, particularly on biological methods of control. The library's holdings in the field of parasitology emphasize medical parasitology. Incl over (17,000) pamphlets.

CA —UNIVERSITY OF CALIFORNIA, DAVIS, General Library, Davis, 95616. Bernard Kreissman, University Librn; C Danial Elliott, Asst Head, Dept Special Collections
Notes: Relatively strong in materials published from 1920 to date. Areas of entomology that are emphasized incl bees (apiculture), nematology, parasitology and the control of insect publications. The slides and specimens in the collection are housed in the research collection of the Department of Entomology.

CT —YALE UNIVERSITY, Medical Historical Library, Klebs Collection, 333 Cedar St, New Haven, 06520. Ferenc A Gyorgyey, Librn
Notes: The Arnold Carl Klebs Medical Collection books, pamphlets, etc, incl the library of his father, Edwin T A Klebs, pathologist. Strong in bibliography of early printed medical books, herbals, plague tracts, inoculation, vaccination and tubercular diseases.

IA —IOWA STATE UNIVERSITY, Library, Ames, 50011. Warren B Kuhn, Dean of Library Services
Holdings: Cat
Notes: Extensive serial holdings supplement this strong collection.

MS —GULF COAST RESEARCH LABORATORY, Gordon Gunter Library, E Beach Rd, Ocean Springs, 39564. Malcolm Ware, Sr, Librn
Holdings: Vols (9000) Uncat Mss Pix Microforms
Notes: Also have reprint collection of 30,000 cataloged reprints, indexed by card catalog, on all aspects of marine biology.

NY —CORNELL UNIVERSITY LIBRARIES, Comstock Memorial Library of Entomology, Ithaca, 14853. Edwin Spragg, Librn
Holdings: Vols (30,000) Cat Maps Pix Audiotapes Microforms
Budget: ($13,500)
Notes: Major topics: general and applied entomology. Minor topics: parasitology, medical entomology, ecology, zoological nomenclature and allied orders of arthropods. Separate catalog to the collection, also extensive collection of reprints. Apiculture material kept at nearby A R Mann Library.

OH —OHIO STATE UNIVERSITY, Biological Sciences Library, 1735 Neil Ave, Columbus, 43210. Victoria Welborn, Librn
Holdings: Vols (85,000) Cat Mss Maps Microforms

TX —SOUTHWEST FOUNDATION FOR RESEARCH AND EDUCATION

PARASITOLOGY (cont.)

LIBRARY, Preston C Northrup Memorial
Library, Baboon Information Center, W
Loop 410 at Military Dr, PO Box 28147,
San Antonio, 78284. Dorothy M Brooks,
Baboon
Notes: Principle field of research: Birth
defects, atherosclerosis, reproductive
physiology, cancer, genetics, organic
chemistry, parasitology, primatology and
behavioral sciences and their application to
problems of drug abuse, alcoholism and
ecology. Maintains the largest baboon colony
in the world.
ON —ONTARIO MINISTRY OF HEALTH,
Laboratory Services Branch, Library, Box
9000, Terminal A, Toronto, M5W 1R5, Can.
Doris A Standing, Librn
Holdings: Vols (4000) Cat
Budget: ($50,000)
Notes: Medical laboratory technology and
related subjects: microbiology; environmental
bacteriology (limited to testing of milk, food
and water for bacterial quality, etc);
biological chemistry (clinical); mycology;
parasitology; virology; immunology;
serology; automated laboratory techniques;
biohazard control.

PARBATE LANGUAGE see Nepali
Language and Literature

PARBUTTI LANGUAGE see Nepali
Language and Literature

PARTCH, HARRY

TX —NORTH TEXAS STATE UNIVERSITY,
Audio Center, Box 5188, NT Station,
Denton, 76203. Morris Martin, Music Librn
Notes: Emphasis on Contemporary and
Avant Garde music. More than 450 musical
compositions (mostly manuscript, many
multi-media). This is an archive of materials
published in, or submitted for publication to,
the contemporary music magazine Source,
the Music of the Avant Garde which
appeared from 1967-1977 (although bearing
dates only through 1973). Composers
represented are the editors (Larry Austin
and Stanley Lunetta), John Cage, Steve
Reich, Pauline Oliveros, Harry Partch,
Morton Feldman, Lukas Foss, Barney
Childs, David Cope, Peter Garland, Philip
Glass, Ben Johnston, Alcides Lanza, Alvin
Lucier, David Rosenboom, Dane Rudhyar,
and Nicolas Slonimsky.

PARDUE, LOUIS A., 1900-1963

†VA —VIRGINIA POLYTECHNIC
INSTITUTE AND STATE UNIVERSITY,
Blacksburg, 24061.

PARENT AND CHILD

CT —PERROT MEMORIAL LIBRARY, 90
Sound Beach Ave, Old Greenwich, 06870.
Michael F Hagan, Dir
Notes: Child rearing, discipline, child
development.
NY —MATERNITY CENTER
ASSOCIATION, Library, 48 E 92 St, New
York, 10028. Esther Hanchett, Acting Librn
Holdings: Vols 2000 Cat
Notes: No photocopying.
NY —YWCA NATIONAL BOARD, Library,
726-730 Broadway, New York, 10012.
Elizabeth Norris, Librn
Holdings: Vols (3000) Cat Mss
Budget: ($2400)
Notes: Women and their contemporary
interest.
ON —UNIVERSITY OF GUELPH, Library,
Guelph, N1G 2W1, Can. Margaret
Beckman, Chief Librn; Ellen Pearson, Ref
Librn
Holdings: Vols 30,000 Cat Audiotapes
Videotapes 16mm Films Microforms
Budget: ($21,500)
Notes: 320 periodical titles. Special cats can
be produced for any part of the collection.
Additional historical material in archives on
early rural movements, such as the women's

institutes.
See also entry under Rural Sociology

PARIS, FRANCE

CA —UNIVERSITY OF CALIFORNIA,
RIVERSIDE, University Library, 4045
Canyon Crest Dr, Box 5900, Riverside,
92517.
Holdings: Vols 1,000
Notes: Books on the history of Paris, historic
buildings, and the Paris Commune of 1871;
rich in works of political and social
caricature of the 19th century.
NY —FRENCH INSTITUTE-ALLIANCE
FRANCAISE, Library, 22 E 60 St, New
York, 10022. Fred J Gitner, Librn
Holdings: Vols (40,000) Cat Phonorecords
Audiotapes
Budget: ($23,000)
Notes: Special collections of art books,
books about Paris. Rich in bibliographical,
biographical and lexicographical works.
Standard editions of all major French
authors. Name has been changed from
French Institute in the United States Library
since merger with the Alliance Francaise de
New York.

PARIS, RENEE

AB —UNIVERSITY OF CALGARY,
Libraries, Special Collections Div, 2500
University Dr, Calgary, T2N 1N4, Can.
Holdings: Cat Mss
Notes: The papers include manuscripts for
George Ryga's poetry, short stories, novels,
feature film screenplays, radio and television
scripts, stage plays, musicals, essays, and
public addresses. The correspondence covers
the years 1960-1975, and includes a set of
files of Ryga's literary agent, Renee Paris,
for the years 1963-1976.

PARIS COMMUNE, 1871

IL —NORTHWESTERN UNIVERSITY,
Library, Special Collections Dept, 1937
Sheridan Rd, Evanston, 60201. R Russell
Maylone, Cur
Holdings: Cat Mss Pix
Notes: Large collection of material from the
Siege of Paris, 1870, and the Paris
Commune, 1871, incl 1500 posters, 3000
caricatures and drawings, books, pamphlets,
newspapers, journals, letters, and 800
photographs. Literature: Pardo and Press,
"Siege and Paris Commune, "Special
Collections Department, Northwestern
University Library, 1973.

PARIS CONSERVATORIE DE
MUSIQUE

MA —BOSTON UNIVERSITY, Mugar
Memorial Library, Special Collections Dept,
771 Commonwealth Ave, Boston, 02215.
Howard B Gotlieb, Dir
Holdings: Cat Mss
Notes: Scores, correspondence and mss in
the archives of the Paris Conservatoire de
Musique, mainly latter half of 19th century.

PARIS MUSIC HALL

GA —UNIVERSITY OF GEORGIA,
Libraries, Special Collections Division,
Athens, 30602. Vesta Lee Gordon, Asst Dir
for Special Collections
Notes: Theater Collection contains the Paris
Music Hall set and costume designs with
original drawings by Erte, Barbier, Zig and
others; British Music Hall Papers; European
toy theater collection; Charles Coburn
papers; television script collection; Tennessee
Williams papers. Collection contains 16,000
pieces.

PARIS PEACE CONFERENCE, 1919

CA —HOOVER INSTITUTION ON WAR,
REVOLUTION & PEACE, Stanford
University, Stanford, 94305. Milorad M
Drachkovitch, Archivist
Holdings: Mss
Notes: Records of the Russian Embassy in

France, incl correspondence, reports,
memoranda, and notes, 1917-24, relating to
relations between France and the Russian
Provisional Government, the Russian
Revolution, counter-revolutionary
movements, the Paris Peace Conference, and
Russian emigres after the revolution. In
Russian and French. 36 1/2 ms boxes.
CT —YALE UNIVERSITY, Box 1603A, Yale
Station, New Haven, 06520.
Holdings: Cat
Notes: Incl the diaries, notebooks, etc of
Charles Seymour.
DC —GEORGETOWN UNIVERSITY,
Library, Special Collections Div, 37 & O Sts
NW, Washington, 20057. George M
Barringer, Special Collections Librn;
Nicholas B Sheetz, Mss Librn
Holdings: Mss Cat Pix
Notes: The papers of James Brown Scott
(1866-1945), internationalist and authority in
international law, consisting of
correspondence, memoranda, documents,
minutes, printed material, manuscripts of
articles and addresses, photographs, and
newspaper clippings. Incl is material from
Scott's activities as Solicitor (1906-1910)
and Special Advisor (1914-1917) for the
State Department, as delegate to the Second
Hague Conference (1907) and the Paris
Peace Conference (1919), his membership
and offices in the Carnegie Endowment for
International Peace, the American Society of
International Law, and the Institut de Droit
International, as well as Scott's involvement
in numerous courts of international
arbitration. Also incl is material relating to
Pan-American law. Correspondence incl
letters from Charles Evans Hughes, Robert
Bacon, William Jennings Bryan, James
Bryce, Nicholas Murray Bulter, Andrew
Carnegie, Charles Francis Adams, Frank B
Kellogg, Robert Lansing, Franklin Roosevelt,
Elihu Root, and Woodrow Wilson, among
many others.
MI —EASTERN MICHIGAN UNIVERSITY,
Center of Educational Resources, Ypsilanti,
48197.
Notes: Collection of Mark S W Jefferson's
correspondence, papers and notes--also incl
the Paris Peace Conference Diary.

PARISH, DAVID

NY —SAINT LAWRENCE UNIVERSITY,
Owen D Young Library, Canton, 13617.
Mahlon Peterson, Librn
Holdings: Cat Mss Maps Pix
Notes: The Parish-Rosseel Papers. The bulk
of the material falls within the period 1807-
1816 and consists of the correspondence of
David Parish and Joseph Rosseel. Very
valuable source of information on the
settlement of the North Country and the
War of 1812 as well as the general social and
economic conditions of the time. Approx
1600 items.

PARISH, JAMES ROBERT

OH —KENT STATE UNIVERSITY, Libraries,
Dept of Special Collections, Kent, 44242.
Dean H Keller, Cur
Holdings: Vols (2000) Uncat Mss Pix

PARISH FAMILY

NY —SAINT LAWRENCE COUNTY
HISTORICAL ASSOCIATION, 3 1/2 E
Main St, PO Box 8, Canton, 13617. John A
Baule, Dir
Holdings: Vols 55
Notes: Major land speculator in New York
State. Have business correspondence,
personal papers, account book from the
1820's-70's.

PARISH REGISTERS see Church Records
and Registers; Registers of Births, Etc.

PARK, ALICE, 1861-1961

CA —HOOVER INSTITUTION ON WAR,
REVOLUTION & PEACE, Stanford
University, Stanford, 94305. Milorad M

PARK, ALICE, 1861-1961 (cont.)

Drachkovitch, Archivist
Holdings: Mss
Notes: Papers of Alice Park, 1883-1957, incl diaries, correspondence, pamphlets, clippings, and leaflets, relating to Pacifism and the peace movement, the Ford Peace Ship Expedition of 1915-1916, feminism, socialism, the labor movement, prison reform, child labor legislation, civil liberties, and a variety of other reform movements in the US. 30 ms boxes, 3 envelopes.

PARK, MAUD WOOD, 1871-1955

DC —LIBRARY OF CONGRESS, Manuscript Division, Washington, 20540. John C Broderick, Chief
Notes: Papers of Maud Wood Park (1871-1955), first president of the League of Women Voters. 3500 items, incl personal and professional correspondence, family papers, speeches and lectures, reports, photographs, and an autograph collection, documenting the women's rights movement in the US, particularly in the first half of the 20th century.
MA —RADCLIFFE COLLEGE, Arthur & Elizabeth Schlesinger Library on the History of Women in America, 3 James St, Cambridge, 02138. Patricia Miller King, Dir; Eva Moseley, Cur of Mss
Holdings: Cat Mss
Notes: Personal papers and mss, records of suffrage and other organizations in which Park was active. Also reports on condition of women in Asia. Park was first president of National League of Women Voters. Her papers are part of the Woman's Rights Collection, of which she was the donor.

PARKER, B. G.

BC —UNIVERSITY OF VICTORIA, McPherson Library, Victoria, V8W 3H5, Can.

PARKER, DONALD

SD —AUGUSTANA COLLEGE, Mikkelsen Library & Learning Resource Center, Center for Western Studies, Sioux Falls, 57197. Ronelle Thompson, Dir Library
Notes: The Center for Western Studies, located in the Mikkelsen Library, is an archival and research agency of Augustana College. Dedicated to the history and culture of the Great Plains and the Trans-Mississippi West, the Center collects and preserves materials relating to Plains Indians, immigrant settlers, Norwegiana, Western Americana, Herbert Krause, Frederick Manfred, Donald Parker, Richard F Pettigrew, Augustana College, the Episcopal Diocese of South Dakota, the South Dakota District of the American Lutheran Church, the South Dakota Penitentiary and Minnehaha County.

PARKER, DOROTHY (ROTHSCHILD)

NV —UNIVERSITY OF NEVADA, RENO, University Library, Special Collections Dept, Reno, 89557. Robert E Blesse, Head
Holdings: Vols (24) Cat
Notes: Includes individual works by author in all editions including translations; also prefaces, introductions, published correspondence, appearances in anthologies, periodicals, etc. Bibliographical research collection, part of Modern Authors Collection. Other appearances 230 cataloged.

PARKER, ELY S.

PA —AMERICAN PHILOSOPHICAL SOCIETY, Library, 105 S Fifth St, Philadelphia, 19106. Edward C Carter II, Librn
Notes: Papers, incl American Indian anthropological studies.

PARKER, HORATIO

CT —YALE UNIVERSITY, Music Library, 98 Wall St, New Haven, 06520. Harold E

Samuel, Librn
Holdings: Vols (118,000) Cat Mss Pix Phonorecords Audiotapes
Notes: Personal papers and musical mss.
See also entry under Music, American
DC —LIBRARY OF CONGRESS, Music Division, Washington, 20540.
Notes: The business papers and music mss of the Arthur P Schmidt Company. Numerous works by important composers.

PARKER, JOHN C.

ME —BOWDOIN COLLEGE, Library, Brunswick, 04011. Dianne M Gutscher, Cur of Special Collections
Holdings: Mss Pix
Notes: A miscellaneous collection of ten logs and journals kept by members of the Bowdoin expeditions to Labrador in 1860 and 1891; as well as 29 letters, a log book, and about 100 newsclippings from the John C Parker Papers, concerning the Labrador expedition of 1891; and about 200 nitrate negatives and 200 mounted prints of those negatives done by Alfred O Gross, professor of biology at Bowdoin, when he accompanied Donald B MacMillan on an expedition to Labrador in 1934. Most of the pictures are of native birds and nesting sites.

PARKER, JOHN ROWE

RI —BROWN UNIVERSITY, John Hay Library, 20 Prospect St, Providence, 02912. Mark N Brown, Cur Mss
Holdings: Mss
Notes: Papers of William O Fuller (1828-1910), music teacher of Providence, comprising letters 1848 from Europe, incl a letter from Franz Liszt; papers of Johann Christian Gottlieb Graupner (1767-1836) and John Rowe Parker (fl 1820s) collected by Horace Mason Reynolds, relating to the music-publishing business in Boston, 1802-1838; papers of the American folklorist Mellinger Edward Henry (1873-1946) relating to his research and publications on American folk-songs 1910-1942; papers, 1912-1948, of Providence composer Hugh Frederick MacColl (1885-1953); papers of Frances Herriot Sargent, stage manager for "Porgy" and "Porgy and Bess", relating to productions of these, 1928-1942.

PARKER, MATHEW ARCHIBALD, 1871-1953

MB —UNIVERSITY OF MANITOBA, Elizabeth Dafoe Library, Archives and Special Collections Dept, Winnipeg, R3T 2N2, Can. Richard E Bennett, Dept Head; Corrado A Santoro, Reference Archivist
Holdings: Pix
Notes: Photographs taken by Prof Parker and his father, John Parker, of Scotland, England and Europe before and at the turn of the century. Rural scenes are highlighted.

PARKER, PETER

CT —YALE UNIVERSITY, Medical Historical Library, 333 Cedar St, New Haven, 06510. Ferenc A Gyorgyey, Librn
Holdings: Pix
Notes: Pictures of 86 patients with pronounced pathological conditions, painted in China by Lam-Qua in the 19th century, commissioned by Dr Peter Parker, a medical missionary.

PARKIN, JOHN B., ASSOCIATES

AB —UNIVERSITY OF CALGARY, Libraries, Special Collections Div, 2500 University Dr, Calgary, T2N 1N4, Can.
Holdings: Cat Mss Pix Audiotapes 16mm Films Filmstrips
Notes: Collection consists of 16,499 architectural drawings, office files, records, correspondence, design notes, etc, from 1938 onwards, of the architectural firm of John B Parkin, and its successor firms. 35mm microfilm of early project drawings, as well as an extensive photographic record of

buildings in progress and completed, and oral history taped interviews are included. Projects: Toronto City Hall; Toronto International Airport; SunLife Office Building, Toronto; Simpsons Tower, Toronto, etc. Project lists and inventories are on hand. 461 meters of documents.

PARKINSON'S DISEASE

MI —LAFAYETTE CLINIC LIBRARY, 951 E Lafayette, Detroit, 48207. Nancy E Ward, Librn
Holdings: Vols (7000) Cat
Notes: Special emphasis on epilepsy, movement disorders, Parkinson's Disease and the biological aspects, causes and treatment of mental illness.

PARKMAN, FRANCIS

MA —HARVARD UNIVERSITY LIBRARY, Houghton Library, Cambridge, 02138. Rodney G Dennis, Cur of Manuscripts
Holdings: Cat Mss

PARKS

CA —UNIVERSITY OF CALIFORNIA, BERKELEY, Environmental Design Library, (The General Library), 210 Wurster Hall, Berkeley, 94720. Arthur B Waugh, Head
Holdings: Vols (9000) Cat
Budget: ($4900)
Notes: Research collection emphasizing the following areas: Park and garden design; site planning; spatial planning; professional practice. Lesser emphasis on horticulture. The Library also includes the Beatrix Farrand Collection of rare books in the field of landscape architecture.
DC —METROPOLITAN WASHINGTON COUNCIL OF GOVERNMENTS, Research Library, 1875 Eye St NW, Suite 200, Washington, 20006. Suan Kalish, Librn
Holdings: Vols (3000) Cat Microforms
Notes: Contains (on 75 reels of microfilm) archives of Maryland-National Park and Planning Commission, archives of the Council of Governments, and audits and financial reports of local governments (1950-date). Also incl annual reports planning reports and budgets from each jurisdiction (1973-date).
IL —UNIVERSITY OF ILLINOIS, URBANA/CHAMPAIGN, Library, Applied Life Studies Library, 1408 W Gregory Dr, Urbana, 61801.
Holdings: Vols (38,000) Cat Microforms
Notes: Special emphasis on leisure studies, recreation surveys and plans, outdoor education, recreation programs, theories of play, supervision, and therapeutic recreation.
See also entry under Physical Education and Training
IA —IOWA STATE UNIVERSITY, Library, Dept of Special Collections, Ames, 50011. Stanley M Yates, Head
Notes: Louis H Pammel (1862-1931) was professor of botany (1889-1931) and head of department of botany. Collection incl correspondence, collected works, speeches, interviews and articles. Collection is 39 linear feet. Important in conservation movement; founder of Iowa State Park System; teacher and friend of George Washington Carver.
MD —MARYLAND-NATIONAL CAPITAL PARK & PLANNING COMMISSION, Montgomery County Planning Department Library, 8787 Georgia Ave, Silver Spring, 20907. Janice C Holt, Librn
Holdings: Vols (5000) Cat
Notes: Specific subject areas include: community facilities, conservation, economics, flood control, highways, housing, human and natural resources. landscape architecture, open space, parks, pollution, population, recreation, transportation, urban renewal, and zoning. Commission's publications are maintained by Records Management (not Library).
MA —HARVARD UNIVERSITY, Graduate School of Design, Frances Loeb Library, Gund Hall, Cambridge, 02138. James

PARKS (cont.)

Hodgson, Librn
Holdings: Cat Mss Microforms
Notes: Particularly strong in park commission reports; *Catalogue* of library published in 1968 (44 volumes), with supplements, 1970, 1974 and 1979.

NJ —MIDDLESEX COUNTY PLANNING BOARD, Library, 40 Livingston Ave, New Brunswick, 08901. Lou Mattei, Planning Supervisor, Data Mgt
Holdings: Vols (3500) Cat
Budget: ($500)

NY —ROCKEFELLER UNIVERSITY, Rockefeller Archive Center, Hillcrest, Pocantico Hills, North Tarrytown, 10591. Joseph W Ernst, Dir; J William Hess, Assoc Dir
Notes: The Rockefeller Archive Center, a division of The Rockefeller University, preserves and makes available to scholars the records of the University, the Rockefeller Foundation, the Rockefeller Brothers Fund, members of the family, and those of other individuals and organizations associated with their endeavors. Collections at the Center document a century of philanthropy by legions of associated social and scientific pioneers, providing a unique window into the past.

†NY —UNION COLLEGE, Adirondack Research Center, Schenectady, 12308.
Notes: Books, periodicals, maps, and historical and political records of the Adirondack Park area.

NC —NORTH CAROLINA STATE UNIVERSITY, D H Hill Library, Box 7111, Raleigh, 27695. I T Littleton, Dir
Holdings: Vols 3940 Cat
Budget: $2000
Notes: Covers parks and recreation management. Incl monographs.
See also entry under Recreation.

AB —CANADIAN FORESTRY SERVICE, Northern Forest Research Centre Library, 5320 122nd, Edmonton, T6H 3S5, Can. David J S Robinson, Librn
Holdings: Vols (7000) Cat Microforms
Budget: ($25,000)
Notes: Also 23,000 government documents, 2600 research reports, 3000 pamphlets and reprints.

ON —ONTARIO MINISTRY OF NATURAL RESOURCES, Natural Resources Library, Whitney Block 4540, Toronto, M5S 1B3, Can. Sandra Louet, Librn
Holdings: Cat

PARKS, GORDON

KS —KANSAS STATE UNIVERSITY, Library, Special Collections & University Archives, Manhattan, 66506. Antonia Q Pigno, Coordr; John J Vander Velde, Librn; Anthony R Crawford, Univ Archivist
Holdings: Vols 20 Cat Mss
Budget: ($10,000)
Notes: Photographs of filming *The Learning Tree* and the ms of *The Learning Tree.*

PARLEY, PETER see Goodrich, Samuel Griswold, 1793-1860

PARLOA, MARIA

MA —SIMMONS COLLEGE ARCHIVES, 300 The Fenway, Boston, 02115. Megan Sniffin-Marinoff, College Archivist
Notes: (I) Minutes of the Industrial Committee of the Woman's Education Association (1873-1929) from Feb 15, 1872 to Dec 5, 1882. Primarily concerned with the Committee's development of the Boston Cooking School. Figuring prominently in the minutes are Maria Parloa (1843-1909), one of the first instructors at the school, and Mary Johnson Bailey Lincoln (1844-1921), under whose leadership the Boston Cooking School began to attain a national reputation. For further information on these women, see *Notable American Women.* The Committee's relationship with the NY Diet Kitchen, the North Bennett St Industrial School (Boston), and the Massachusetts

Institute of Technology also are discussed in the minutes. In addition to organizing a school for cooking, the Committee concerned itself with the education for women in dressmaking, nursing, phonography, andwoodcarving (based on the Cincinnati carving school). (II) Account books of the Household Aid Co (The Domestic Economy Committee) of the Woman's Education Association from August, 1903 to May, 1905. Organized by the Association of Collegiate Alumnae and the Woman's Education Association, the company was a cooperative residence for 20 servants with a training and placement program and a mediation service to deal with employers.

PARNIN, JOHN ROSS

PA —US ARMY MILITARY HISTORY INSTITUTE, Carlisle Barracks, 17013. Richard J Sommers, Chief Archivist-Historian
Holdings: Cat // Mss
Notes: The John Ross Parnin papers, relating to his tour with the Anti-Aircraft Artillery Headquarters/Tenth Army, 1945 and earlier service, 1917-19.
See also entries under World War, 1914-1918; World War, 1939-1945.

PAROLE

DC —FEDERAL BUREAU OF PRISONS, Library, 320 First St NW, Washington, 20001. Lloyd W Hooker, Librn
Holdings: Vols (2500) Cat
Budget: ($20,000)

MO —SAINT LOUIS POLICE LIBRARY, 315 S Tucker Blvd, Saint Louis, 63102. Cathy Reilly, Librn
Holdings: Vols (21,000) Cat Mss Pix Microforms
Budget: ($18,400)
Notes: Library on all subjects of police work is open to the public for general reference use.

NJ —RUTGERS, THE STATE UNIVERSITY OF NEW JERSEY, John Cotton Dana Library, 185 University Ave, Newark, 07102. Phyllis Schultze, Librn
Holdings: Vols 40,000 Cat
Notes: National Council on Crime and Delinquency. Criminology, as applied, means all phases of crime and delinquency prevention, control and treatment, ie, the whole "criminal justice" gamut: police, courts, probation and parole, prisons, community rehabilitation centers, etc. In short, everything except police laboratory materials. Collection completely cataloged; all criminological and correctional journals indexed. Incl many reports of correctional agencies, research reports, unpublished monographs, publications in the field by all government agencies, federal, state, county and local. Information file contains over 40,000 such items, as well as about 10,000 uncataloged clippings and other pieces of information stored by specific subjects.

ON —ONTARIO MINISTRY OF CORRECTIONAL SERVICES, Library, 2001 Eglinton Ave E, Scarborough, M1L 4P1, Can. T J B Anderson, Chief Librn
Holdings: Vols (4676) Cat VF
Budget: ($16,000)
Notes: Approx 135 periodicals received. Library services also provided in approx 50 jails and adult institutions.

PARRAVICINI FAMILY

IL —NEWBERRY LIBRARY, 60 W Walton St, Chicago, 60610. Diana Haskell, Cur of Modern Mss
Notes: Papers (3600 documents) of the Parravicini family of Ardenno (northern Italy); 15th-19th centuries.

PARRISH, EDWARD J.

NC —DUKE UNIVERSITY, William R Perkins Library, Manuscript Dept, Durham, 27706. Ellen Gartrell, Cur of Mss
Holdings: Cat Mss
Notes: Tobacco culture, marketing, trade,

especially US South, 19th-20th century, incl papers of Duke Family, Richard H Wright, British-American Tobacco Co, James A Thomas, Edward J Parrish, United Cigarette Machine Co; also tobacco advertising (trade cards, etc).

PARRISH, MAXFIELD

NC —UNIVERSITY OF NORTH CAROLINA, GREENSBORO, Walter Clinton Jackson Library, Special Collections Dept, 1000 Spring Garden St, Greensboro, 27412. Emilie W Mills, Librn
Notes: All but nine of the titles published by Way and Williams of Chicago, 1895-1898. First, variant editions, many autographed by authors or publisher. Many association items. Letters to Chauncey Williams from William Allen White, Maxfield Parrish, Charles Lummis, Opie Read, etc. Photographs of Williams and several authors. Original artwork by Parrish, Will Bradley and ephemeral printing incl in the scrapbook compiled by Chauncey L Williams, ca 1919. Major part of the collection the gift of John M Williams in memory of Chauncey L Williams.

PA —FREE LIBRARY OF PHILADELPHIA, Rare Book Dept, Logan Sq, Philadelphia, 19103. Marie E Korey, Rare Book Librn
Holdings: Vols (1000) Cat Mss Pix
Notes: The Thornton Oakley Collection containing 1000 pieces of original art, autograph letters, and books and periodicals, illustrated by Howard Pyle and his students, incl Maxfield Parrish, Frank Schoonover, Jessie Wilcox Smith, and N C Wyeth.

PARRISH, ROBERT

MA —BOSTON UNIVERSITY, Mugar Memorial Library, Special Collections Dept, 771 Commonwealth Ave, Boston, 02215. Howard B Gotlieb, Dir
Holdings: Cat Mss
Notes: Mss, correspondence, etc collected in depth; incl publications by or about.

PARRY, HUGH

MA —BOSTON UNIVERSITY, Mugar Memorial Library, Special Collections Dept, 771 Commonwealth Ave, Boston, 02215. Howard B Gotlieb, Dir
Holdings: Cat Mss Correspondence

PARSI LANGUAGE see Pahlavi Language and Literature

PARSONS, EDWARD S.

NV —UNIVERSITY OF NEVADA, RENO, University Library, Special Collections Dept, Reno, 89557. Robert E Blesse, Head
Holdings: Cat Mss Pix
Notes: Approximately 15,000 drawings, along with papers and photographs of three major Nevada architects. Frederic DeLongchamps, 1882-1969, was Nevada's most important for the first half of the 20th century designing many major public buildings. Edward S Parsons, Nevada's most prolific architect, did over 725 jobs between 1935 and 1983. Hewitt Wells designed the Washoe County Library, an internationally known building. These collections constitute the major holdings of the Nevada Architectural Archives.

PARSONS, ELSIE CLEWS

PA —AMERICAN PHILOSOPHICAL SOCIETY, Library, 105 S Fifth St, Philadelphia, 19106. Edward C Carter II, Librn
Notes: Papers, incl American Indian anthropological studies.

PARSONS, USHER, 1788-1868

RI —BROWN UNIVERSITY, John Hay Library, 20 Prospect St, Providence, 02912. Mark N Brown, Cur Mss
Notes: Papers of Usher Parsons, Professor of

PARSONS, USHER, 1788-1868 (cont.)

Anatomy and Surgery at Brown University. About 950 items for the period 1611 to 1919 with two major subdivisions: 1) the papers of Usher Parsons and family (ca 575 items) consisting of correspondence, autograph mss, notebooks, notebooks, and documents; 2) genealogical and other materials (ca 375 items), original and copy, gathered by Usher Parsons and his son, Charles William, and consisting of correspondence, deeds of land, wills, indentures, court documents, warrants, and receipts, etc.

PARSONS, REV. WILFRID, S.J.

DC —GEORGETOWN UNIVERSITY, Library, Special Collections Div, 37 & O Sts NW, Washington, 20057. George M Barringer, Special Collections Librn; Nicholas B Sheetz, Mss Librn
Holdings: Cat Mss
Notes: His papers, etc.

PARTICLE ACCELERATORS

CA —STANFORD LINEAR ACCELERATOR CENTER, Library, PO Box 4349, Stanford, 94305. Robert C Gex, Librn
Holdings: Cat Microforms
Notes: High energy physics and particle accelerators.
NM —UNIVERSITY OF CALIFORNIA, Los Alamos National Laboratory, Libraries, PO Box 1663, MSP 362, Los Alamos, 87545. J Arthur Freed, Head Librn
Holdings: Vols (800,000) Cat Films Microforms
Budget: ($700,000)
Notes: Incl 500,000 classified and unclassified reports. There are 25 branch libraries and a central collection. The Medical Library contains about 40,000 vols in the areas of biomedical research.

PARTICLES (NUCLEAR PHYSICS)

IL —FERMI NATIONAL ACCELERATOR LABORATORY (FERMILAB), Library, PO Box 500, Batavia, 60510. Roger S Thompson, Manager, Technical Information
Holdings: Vols 12,000 Cat
Budget: ($140,000)

PARTIES, POLITICAL see Political Parties

PARTRIDGE, ERIC

IN —INDIANA UNIVERSITY, Lilly Library, Seventh St, Bloomington, 47405. William R Cagle, Librn
Holdings: Mss
Notes: Papers of lexicographer and phiologist Eric Partridge, 1894-1979. Correspondence, research materials for publications, and mss of writings. 6757 items.

PARTURITION see Childbirth

PASADENA PLAYHOUSE

CA —CALIFORNIA STATE UNIVERSITY, LONG BEACH, Library, Dept of Special Collections & Archives, 1250 Bellflower Blvd, Long Beach, 90840. John Ahouse, Special Collections Librn
Holdings: Vols (5000) Cat Pix
Notes: Incl playbills, scripts, scrapbooks from the former Pasadena Playhouse, together with the former Hidebrand Collection of English and American Drama before 1830.
CA —UNIVERSITY OF CALIFORNIA, LOS ANGELES, Research Library, Dept of Special Collections, 405 Hilgard Ave, Los Angeles, 90024. Edward Shreeves, Chairman, Bibliographers Group; David S Zeidberg, Head
Notes: 15 linear feet of correspondence and business records of the Pasadena Playhouse, Community Playhouse Association of Pasadena.

PASCAL, BLAISE

MA —BOSTON UNIVERSITY, Mugar Memorial Library, Special Collections Dept, 771 Commonwealth Ave, Boston, 02215. Howard B Gotlieb, Dir
Holdings: Vols Cat
Notes: Incl 105 vols by and about him, the collections of Mary Arms Edmonds, donated by her son, Dean S Edmonds, Jr.
NY —HOFSTRA UNIVERSITY, Library, 1000 Fulton Ave, Hempstead, 11550. Charles R Andrews, Dean of Library Services
Holdings: Vols 156 // Uncat
Notes: The Morris Bishop Collection. Incl many early editions. No photocopying.

PASHTO LANGUAGE

NY —NEW YORK PUBLIC LIBRARY, Oriental Div, Fifth Ave & 42 St, New York, 10018. E Christian Filstrup, Chief
Holdings: Cat Mss Microforms
Budget: ($56,455)
Notes: Published catalog of holdings.

PASSAMAQUODDY INDIANS

ME —BOWDOIN COLLEGE, Library, Brunswick, 04011. Dianne M Gutscher, Cur of Special Collections
Holdings: Mss
Notes: The Kellogg Collection contains the diaries of Elijah Kellogg (1761-1842) for the years of 1821, 1822, and 1825-1827, during the time of his missionary work with the Passamaquoddies.
MA —COLLEGE OF THE HOLY CROSS, Dinand Library, College St, Worcester, 01610. James M Mahoney, Cur of Special Collection
Holdings: Uncat Mss Pix
Notes: The John J Williams SJ collection contains correspondence, notes on history of Passamaquoddy tribe; (86) letters and copies of documents concerning Maine Indians from 1778-1913; pictures and 3 notebooks. Restricted use, noncirculating.

PASSIVE RESISTANCE

PA —SWARTHMORE COLLEGE, Peace Collection, Swarthmore, 19081. Jean R Soderlund, Cur of Peace Collection
Holdings: Vols (10,000) Cat
Notes: Incl peace plays which date mostly from 1912-40, in print or mimeographed; about 1/4 are juvenile; most are American. Book and pamphlet collections incl drama, poetry, fiction and juvenile literature on the subjects of peace, nonviolence and biographies of peace leaders. The aims of current acquisitions incl collecting as much as possible in this area, in order to amplify the main body of the collection. The Peace Collection has been described in Downs 972, 978, 4633, and in Downs 1950-1961 Supplement 507 and 916.
See also entry under Pacifism - History.
WI —BELOIT COLLEGE LIBRARIES, Beloit, 53511. Dennis W Dickinson, Dir
Holdings: Vols 700 Cat
Notes: The Martin Luther King Jr Collection on Nonviolence. This small collection was given by H Vail Deale, Director, at the time of the assassination of Dr King in 1968. Comprises books by and about: M K Gandhi, H D Thoreau, M L King, world peace, pacifism, nonviolence, etc. Contains a 35-year bound file of Fellowship, the magazine of US pacifism. At present time there is only a local card index of the collection, though items are fully cataloged in the Public Card Catalog. A specially designed bookplate by local artist, O Vernon Shaffer, is used for books in this collection.

PASTERNAK, BORIS

CA —UNIVERSITY OF CALIFORNIA, BERKELEY, Bancroft Library, Manuscripts Division, Berkeley, 94720. James D Hart, Dir
Holdings: Uncat Mss
Notes: Letters in Stephen Spencer Collection.

PASTERNAK, JOE

CA —UNIVERSITY OF SOUTHERN CALIFORNIA, Edward L Doheny Memorial Library, Archives of Performing Arts, University Park, Los Angeles, 90089. Robert Knutson, Librn
Holdings: Mss Pix
Notes: Personal collection of papers, pictures, etc.

PASTEUR, LOUIS, 1822-1895

CT —BURNDY LIBRARY, Electra Square, Norwalk, 06856. Philip J Weimerskirch, Asst Dir
Holdings: Vols 150
Notes: Includes mss, photographs and his own copies of his publications some with mss notes.
MD —JOHNS HOPKINS UNIVERSITY, Institute of the History of Medicine, 1900 E Monument St, Baltimore, 21205. Doris Thibodeau, Librn
Holdings: Vols 225 Cat
†MA —FRANCIS A COUNTWAY LIBRARY OF MEDICINE, Boston, 02115.

PASTIMES see Games; Sports

PASTORAL COUNSELING

KS —MENNINGER FOUNDATION, Archives, 5600 W Sixth St, Box 829, Topeka, 66601. Alice Brand, Librn; Mark West, Archivist
Holdings: Vols (33,000) Cat Pix Audiotapes Microforms
Notes: Incl journals. Literature searches and document delivery available for a fee.
NY —INSTITUTES OF RELIGION AND HEALTH LIBRARY, 3 W 29 St, New York, 10001. Frank P DeGeorges, Librn
Holdings: Vols 4000 Cat
Budget: $1000
Notes: Library not open to the general public. Incl 50 journals.

PASTORAL PSYCHIATRY see Pastoral Psychology

PASTORAL PSYCHOLOGY

CT —YALE UNIVERSITY, Beinecke Rare Book & Manuscript Library, Osborn Collection, New Haven, 06520. Stephen R Parks, Cur
Holdings: Mss
NC —SOUTHEASTERN BAPTIST THEOLOGICAL SEMINARY LIBRARY, PO Box 752, Wake Forest, 27587. H Eugene McLeod, Librn
Holdings: Cat Audiotapes Microforms
SC —BAPTIST MEDICAL CENTER, Amelia White Pitts Memorial Library, Taylor at Marion Sts, Columbia, 29220. Lois W Smith, Medical Librn
Holdings: Vols (3000) Cat

PASTORAL THEOLOGY

AZ —COOK CHRISTIAN TRAINING SCHOOL, Mary M McCarthy Library, 708 S Lindon Lane, Tempe, 85281. Mark E Thomas, Librn
Holdings: Vols 2500 Cat Audiotapes Videotapes Filmstrips
NY —GENERAL THEOLOGICAL SEMINARY, Saint Marks Library, 175 Ninth Ave, New York, 10011. David Green, Dir
Holdings: Vols (200,000) Cat
ON —HURON COLLEGE, Silcox Memorial Library, 1349 Western Rd, London, N6G 1H3, Can. Pamela MacKay, Chief Librn
Holdings: Vols (28,000) Cat
Budget: ($24,710)
Notes: Covers Bible, church history, church music, liturgics, pastoralia, religious education, philosophy of religion, religious studies, systematics. 95 periodical subscriptions including foreign language materials. Rare books collection of 750 volumes, including collections of sermons,

PASTORAL THEOLOGY (cont.)

commentaries, particularly rare bibles, many in foreign languages.

PASTORAL WORK

NC —SOUTHEASTERN BAPTIST THEOLOGICAL SEMINARY LIBRARY, PO Box 752, Wake Forest, 27587. H Eugene McLeod, Librn
Holdings: Cat Slides Audiotapes Videotapes Microforms

OR —MULTNOMAH SCHOOL OF THE BIBLE, Library, 8435 NE Gilsan St, Portland, 97220. James F Scott, Dir of Library; Susan Johnson, Asst Librn
Holdings: Vols (40,686) Cat Slides Phonorecords Audiotapes Filmstrips
Budget: ($33,950)
Notes: Multnomah School of the Bible is an evangelical school that educates students through a program of instruction having the Bible as its center. It supports this centralized Bible major with several ancillary, pertinent supporting minors, ie, Christian education, pastoral, missions and New Testament Greek.

PASTUHOV, VLADIMIR D., 1898-1967

CA —HOOVER INSTITUTION ON WAR, REVOLUTION & PEACE, Stanford University, Stanford, 94305. Milorad M Drachkovitch, Archivist
Holdings: Mss Maps Pix
Notes: Papers of Vladimir D Pastuhov, 1927-1938, incl correspondence, memoranda, reports, interviews, maps, photographs, and printed matter, relating to the investigation of the Manchurian incident of 1931 by the Lytton Commission of the League of Nations, of which V D Pastuhov was Secretary. Most of the material is in English; some in French, Russian and Chinese. 58 ms boxes and 3 oversize packages. 13 photograph albums.

PASTURES

SK —CANADA PRAIRIE FARM REHABILITATION ADMINISTRATION LIBRARY, Motherwell Bldg, Regina, S4P 0R5, Can. C Kosack, Head
Holdings: Vols (10,000) Cat
Budget: ($8000)
Notes: PFRA is a Canadian federal government agency initiated to alleviate the effects of drought and water shortages on the prairies. The collection covers engineering (dams), agricultural economics, hydrology, irrigation, community pastures, and soil and water conservation.

PATAYAN CULTURE

AZ —COLORADO RIVER INDIAN TRIBES MUSEUM/LIBRARY, Rte One, Box 23-B, Parker, 85344. Priscilla Johnson, Librn
Holdings: Cat Mss Maps Pix Slides Audiotapes Microforms
Notes: Library deals with the four tribes of the Colorado River Indian Reservation: Mojave, Chemehuevi, Navajo, and Hopi. Emphasis is also given to the prehistoric cultures of this area; Patayan and Hohokam. Library collections include original manuscripts and other documents, photographs, oral history tape recordings, cultural items and copies of many documents relating to the reservation are in bound volumes, microfilm, and photocopies. Photos relative to the reservation from various other collections are copied in our collection. Of particular interest is the museum basket collection which incl about 1000 Chemehuevi baskets--the largest Chemehuevi basket collection. Other artifacts give special emphasis to the Mojave culture.

PATCHEN, KENNETH

CA —FRANCIS BACON LIBRARY, 655 N Dartmouth Ave, Claremont, 91711. Elizabeth S Wrigley, Dir
Holdings: Mss Pix
Notes: Arensberg's miscellaneous

correspondence with American literary figures (1920's-50's) including Bruce Bliven, Catherine Drinker Bowen, Kay Boyle, Witter Bynner, Edwin Corle, Helen A Keller, Lysander Kemp, Kenneth Macgowan, John Macy, Henry Miller, Lewis Mumford, Clifford Odets, Kenneth Patchen, Irving Stone, and William Carlos Williams.

CA —UNIVERSITY OF CALIFORNIA, SANTA CRUZ, University Library, Special Collections, Santa Cruz, 95064. Rita Bottoms, Special Collections Librn; Margaret Felts, South Pacific Collection Bibliographer
Holdings: Mss Poems Pub Works
Notes: Noncirculating; scholarly research only.

NV —UNIVERSITY OF NEVADA, RENO, University Library, Special Collections Dept, Reno, 89557. Robert E Blesse, Head
Holdings: // Vols (81) Cat Other appearances 440 Cat
Notes: Includes individual works by author in all editions including translations; also prefaces, introductions, published correspondence, appearances in anthologies, periodicals, etc. Bibliographical research collection, part of Modern Authors Collection.

TX —UNIVERSITY OF HOUSTON, M D Anderson Memorial Library, University Park, Houston, 77004. David Farmer, Cur, Special Collections; Jean Jackson, Assistant Cur
Holdings: Cat Mss Phonorecords
Notes: The collection is intended to be as complete a bibliographical holding as possible. Incl 3 original Patchen paintings. Reprints, proofs, and ephemera are actively sought.

PATE, MAURICE, 1894-1965

NJ —PRINCETON UNIVERSITY, Seeley G Mudd Manuscript Library, Public Affairs Papers Collection, Princeton, 08544. Nancy Bressler, Cur
Notes: Incl 34 boxes. The papers cover the period 1909-65. An unpublished 3p checklist is available in the Library.

PATENT CEREALS COMPANY

NY —CORNELL UNIVERSITY LIBRARIES, Collection of Regional History, Dept of Manuscripts and Univ Archives, Ithaca, 14853.
Notes: Incl papers, 1888-1950; correspondence, legal documents, reports and other business papers relating to this firm's processing of corn grits and flakes and other cereal products, chiefly for the brewing industry.

PATENT LAWS AND LEGISLATION

MA —HARVARD UNIVERSITY LIBRARY, Law School Library, Langdell Hall, Cambridge, 02138. Harry S Martin III, Librn
Holdings: Cat
Budget: Patent law

PATENT MEDICINES see Medicines, Patent, Proprietary, Etc.

PATENTS—COLLECTIONS

CA —AVERY INTERNATIONAL CORP, Information Center, 325 N Altadena Dr, Pasadena, 91107. Louanne A Kalvinskas, Information Specialist
Holdings: Vols 800 Cat
Notes: Also many reports.

IN —INLAND STEEL RESEARCH LABORATORIES, Research Library, 3001 E Columbus Dr, East Chicago, 46312. Barbara Minne Banek, Librn
Holdings: Vols (4500) Cat 16mm Films Filmstrips Microforms
Notes: Emphasis on metallurgy and steel. Also 7000 bound periodical vols; 3500 government publications, 47 vertical file drawers of translations, 15 vertical file drawers of patents.

IA —ARCHER DANIELS MIDLAND, Research Library, PO Box 340, Clinton,

52732. Carol L Kolk, Research Librn
Holdings: Vols 2200 Cat Microforms
Notes: Card index to patent file. Keydex index to Research Experiment Reports.

MA —HARVARD UNIVERSITY LIBRARY, Law School Library, Langdell Hall, Cambridge, 02138. Harry S Martin III, Librn
Holdings: Cat
Notes: Patent law.

MI —ACHESON COLLOIDS, Library, 511 Port St, Port Huron, 48060. Myles T Musgrave, Librn
Holdings: Vols (5000) Cat Mss Microforms
Notes: Solid lubricants: graphite, molybdenum disulfide and related organic and inorganic compounds used as solid lubricants (in films, liquids, greases, etc) for industrial applications. Incl extensive patent collection (US and foreign).

MN —3M COMPANY, Mertle Library, 3M Center, Bldg 235-1D, Saint Paul, 55101.
Holdings: Vols (4000) // Cat Mss Pix
Notes: The collection of Joseph S Mertle, includes patents, portraits, a clipping file, and other historical graphic arts books and periodicals.

NJ —EXXON RESEARCH AND ENGINEERING CO, Linden Information Center, PO Box 121, Linden, 07036. PA Lorenz, Section Head
Holdings: Vols (40,000) Cat Maps Pix Microforms
Notes: No photocopying.

NY —NEW YORK PUBLIC LIBRARY, Annex Section, 521 W 43 St, New York, 10036. Richard L Hill, First Asst
Holdings: Vols 250,000 Cat Microforms
Notes: Complete files of US and British patents; partial coverage for other countries. Abstracts, indexes, patent literature.

NY —MARGARET WOODBURY STRONG MUSEUM, 1 Manhattan Square, Rochester, 14607.
Holdings: Vols (20,000) Periodicals
Notes: The Margaret Woodbury Strong Museum Library contains a collection of approx 20,000 books, periodicals and ephemera of and concerning the 19th and early 20th centuries. A large part of the library's holdings reflect the interests of Margaret Strong and her family: domestic life and literature of the 19th century and world travel, with particular emphasis on the Orient. The library's resources are available to all visitors for research. Book stacks and rare book storage are not open for browsing and do not circulate, but facilities are provided in reading room for study.

NY —YONKERS PUBLIC LIBRARY, Information Services, 7 Main St, Yonkers, 10701. Martita Schwarz, Dept Head
Holdings: Vols (21,500) Cat Maps Microforms
Budget: ($30,000)

PA —FRANKLIN INSTITUTE LIBRARY, 20 & The Parkway, Philadelphia, 19103. Miriam Padusis, Dir; Charles Wilt, Readers Servs Librn
Holdings: Cat
Notes: Espec US Patents (3,643,000); British (1,273,000); Swiss (510,000).

PA —CARNEGIE LIBRARY OF PITTSBURGH, Science & Technology Dept, 4400 Forbes Ave, Pittsburgh, 15213. Catherine M Brosky, Dept Head
Holdings: Vols (380,000) Cat Maps Microforms
Budget: ($240,000)
Notes: US Patent Depository Library. Complete US and UK patents, manual of classification, indexes. CASSIS capability (Patent and Trademark Office online system).

PA —CABOT CORPORATION, Reading Technology Library, PO Box 1296, Reading, 19603. Pamela L Hehr, Librn
Holdings: Vols (3800) Cat Mss Slides Microforms
Notes: Copper-beryllium and special metals and alloys. Incl 2100 patents, 9000 reports and articles.

VA —US PATENT OFFICE, Science Library, 2021 Jefferson Davis Hwy, Arlington, 22202. Henry Rosicky, Chief Librn
Holdings: Vols 350,000 Cat Pix Microforms
Notes: Strengths are in applied sciences and

PATENTS—COLLECTIONS (cont.)

technology. Public card catalog in Reading Room listing books by author, title, and subject, and periodicals by title amd subject. Over 77,000 additional volumes of periodicals.

WV —US DEPT OF ENERGY, Morgantown Energy Technology Center, Library, PO Box 880, Morgantown, 26505. Elaine Pasini, Librn
Holdings: Cat Maps Microforms

ON —METROPOLITAN TORONTO LIBRARY, Science & Technology Dept, 789 Yonge St, Toronto, M4W 2G8, Can. Margaret Walshe, Head
Holdings: Vols Cat Maps Microforms
Notes: Collection incl books, patents, periodicals, standards, and Geological Survey of Canada publications.

PATENTS—COLLECTIONS—CANADA

OH —PUBLIC LIBRARY OF CINCINNATI & HAMILTON COUNTY, Science & Technology Dept, 800 Vine St, Cincinnati, 45202. Rosemary Gaiser, Head
Notes: Canadian Patent Office Record, 1896 to date. Noncirculating.

OH —TOLEDO-LUCAS COUNTY PUBLIC LIBRARY, 325 Michigan St, Toledo, 43624. Mary B Hubbard, Head, Science-Technology Dept; Paula Baker, Head, Fine Arts Dept
Holdings: Vols 500 //
Notes: Canadian Patent Office Record, 1911-1920; 1928-1983.

ON —METROPOLITAN TORONTO LIBRARY, Science & Technology Dept, 789 Yonge St, Toronto, M4W 2G8, Can. Margaret Walshe, Head
Holdings: Vols (10,000) Cat Microforms
Notes: Canada, Patent Office, Patent Office Record, 1824 to present, abstracts only. Patent literature, incl classification manuals, vertical files, and contacts to other sources.

PATENTS—COLLECTIONS—FOREIGN

CA —LOS ANGELES PUBLIC LIBRARY, Science & Technology Dept, 630 W Fifth St, Los Angeles, 90071. Billie M Connor, Dept Head
Holdings: Cat Microforms
Budget: $4500
Notes: Complete collection of US chemical, utility, and plant patent specifications, including drawings, beginning with 1790 to date. Extensive files of patent abstracts from six foreign countries including Great Britain (1533-1969), Germany (1880-1940 and 1962-1978), Canada (1890-), Cuba (1915-1971), and USSR (1962-1978). Full patents for Great Britain, old and new law, (1970-). Over 4 million patents.

NY —NEW YORK PUBLIC LIBRARY, Annex Section, 521 W 43 St, New York, 10036. Richard L Hill, First Asst
Holdings: Vols 90,000 Cat Microforms
Notes: Comprehensive New York (City) coverage; selective coverage of other US and foreign countries. Incl 24,000 bound volumes; 86,000 microfilm reels.

PA —CARNEGIE LIBRARY OF PITTSBURGH, Science & Technology Dept, 4400 Forbes Ave, Pittsburgh, 15213. Catherine M Brosky, Dept Head
Holdings: Vols (380,000) Cat Maps Microforms
Budget: ($240,000)
Notes: Complete United Kingdom patents.

VA —US PATENT OFFICE, Science Library, 2021 Jefferson Davis Hwy, Arlington, 22202. Henry Rosicky, Chief Librn
Holdings: Vols 95,000 Uncat Microforms
Notes: Substantially complete collection of approximately 9,000,000 numerically arranged foreign patents. Foreign patents are acquired by exchange agreements with foreign patent offices.

PATENTS—COLLECTIONS—GERMANY

MO —SAINT LOUIS PUBLIC LIBRARY, 1301 Olive St, Saint Louis, 63103. Therese F Dawson, Librn, Applied Science Dept
Holdings: // Cat Pix Microforms
Notes: 1894-1939 (incomplete). On microfilm now; books not available.

PATENTS—COLLECTIONS—GREAT BRITAIN

IL —CHICAGO PUBLIC LIBRARY, Business/Science/Technology Div, Science/Technology Information Center, 425 North Michigan Ave, Chicago, 60611. Lynda Sanford, Head; John R Moore, Environment Collection Coordinator & Engineering Librn
Notes: US patents, 1970-date; Great Britain, 1617-date; German, 1912-38. Patent abstracts and journals for US, Great Britain, Canada, Australia and USSR. All tools available for conducting patent searches, assistance provided by trained reference staff. Self-service copy machines on premises or copies available through interlibrary loan.

MO —SAINT LOUIS PUBLIC LIBRARY, 1301 Olive St, Saint Louis, 63103. Therese F Dawson, Librn, Applied Science Dept
Holdings: Cat Pix
Notes: Complete file, 1617-date. On microfilm now; books not available.

NY —NEW YORK PUBLIC LIBRARY, Annex Section, 521 W 43 St, New York, 10036. Richard L Hill, First Asst
Holdings: Cat Microforms
Notes: Complete files of US and British patents; partial coverage for other countries. Abstracts, indexes, patent literature.

OH —PUBLIC LIBRARY OF CINCINNATI & HAMILTON COUNTY, Science & Technology Dept, 800 Vine St, Cincinnati, 45202. Rosemary Gaiser, Head
Notes: Specifications of inventions, 1844 to 1957. Offical Journal, 1864 to date. Abridgement of specifications, 1617 to date. Noncirculating.

WI —MILWAUKEE PUBLIC LIBRARY, 814 W Wisconsin Ave, Milwaukee, 53233. Donald J Sager, City Librn
Holdings: Cat
Notes: Complete set of British patents, all in full-sized copies. Staff trained to guide general public in patent searches and do some reference searching. British Official Patent Journal Abridgement, 1617 to date (being completed). Canadian Patent Office Record and Register of Copyrights and Trademarks, 1873 to date. (British Specifications, 1617 to date.)

ON —METROPOLITAN TORONTO LIBRARY, Science & Technology Dept, 789 Yonge St, Toronto, M4W 2G8, Can. Margaret Walshe, Head
Holdings: Vols (5900) Cat
Notes: Great Britain, Official Journal, 1963 to date (abstracts only).

PATENTS—COLLECTIONS—U.S.

CA —LOS ANGELES PUBLIC LIBRARY, Science & Technology Dept, 630 W Fifth St, Los Angeles, 90071. Billie M Connor, Dept Head
Holdings: Cat Microforms
Budget: $4500
Notes: Complete collection of US chemical, utility, and plant patent specifications, including drawings, beginning with 1790 to date. Extensive files of patent abstracts from six foreign countries including Great Britain (1533-1969), Germany (1880-1940 and 1962-1978), Canada (1890-), Cuba (1915-1971), and USSR (1962-1978). Full patents for Great Britain, old and new law, (1970-). Over 4 million patents.

CA —SUNNYVALE PUBLIC LIBRARY, Patent Library, 665 W Olive Ave, Sunnyvale, 94086. Margreta Nisbett, Supvr
Holdings: Cat Microforms
Budget: $2500
Notes: Perhaps the only subject classified patent collection in the US outside of Washington, DC. Seventeen years of patents in paper form as of March, 1984. Incl nearly 1,140,707 patents. 4,435,850 patents starting with number 1 on microfilm in numerical order. Full set of gazettes from 1836 also available. Each week's newly issued patents rearranged into main classes. Library used by researchers from all over the western states.

IL —CHICAGO PUBLIC LIBRARY, Business/Science/Technology Div, Science/Technology Information Center, 425 North Michigan Ave, Chicago, 60611. Lynda Sanford, Head; John R Moore, Environment Collection Coordinator & Engineering Librn
Notes: US patents, 1970-date; Great Britain, 1617-date; German, 1912-38. Patent abstracts and journals for US, Great Britain, Canada, Australia and USSR. All tools available for conducting patent searches, assistance provided by trained reference staff. Self-service copy machines on premises or copies available through interlibrary loan.

MA —MERRIMACK VALLEY TEXTILE MUSEUM, Library, 800 Massachusetts Ave, North Andover, 01845. Clare Sheridan, Librn; Laurence Gross, Cur
Holdings: Vols (35,000) Cat Mss Maps Pix Slides
Notes: Checklist of Prints, Drawings and Painting in the Merrimack Valley Textile Museum, Helena E Wright, 1972; Checklist of Finished Textiles, Katherine R Koob, 1980; New City on the Merrimack: Prints of Lawrence 1845-1876, Helena Wright, 1974; Homespun to Factory Made: Woolen Textiles in America 1776-1876 (exhibit catalog) 1978; Textile Technology Prints: A Checklist of Prints, Drawings and Paintings in the Merrimack Valley Textile Museum, Helena E Wright, 1980; All Sorts of Good Sufficient Cloth: Linen-making in New England, 1640-1860, (exhibit catalogue) 1980; The Merrimack Valley Textile Museum: A Guide to the Manuscript Collections Helena E Wright, Garland Press 1983.

MA —OLD STURBRIDGE VILLAGE, Research Library, Sturbridge, 01566. Theresa Rini Percy, Librn
Holdings: Cat
Notes: To 1900.

MO —SAINT LOUIS PUBLIC LIBRARY, 1301 Olive St, Saint Louis, 63103. Therese F Dawson, Librn, Applied Science Dept
Holdings: Cat Pix
Notes: Annual reports, 1837-1925; specifications and drawings, 1871 to date. On microfilm now; books not available.

NY —NEW YORK STATE LIBRARY, State Education Bldg Annex, Washington Ave, Albany, 12224.
Holdings: Uncat
Notes: All US patents from no 115,266 (about 1870) to date. US patent Gazette, 1872 to date.

NY —BUFFALO & ERIE COUNTY PUBLIC LIBRARY, Science and Technology Dept, Lafayette Sq, Buffalo, 14203. Stanley P Zukowski, Head
Holdings: Uncat Microforms

NY —NEW YORK PUBLIC LIBRARY, Annex Section, 521 W 43 St, New York, 10036. Richard L Hill, First Asst
Holdings: Vols 160,000 Cat Microforms
Notes: Complete files of US and British patents; partial coverage for other countries. Abstracts, indexes, patent literature.

NC —NORTH CAROLINA STATE UNIVERSITY, D H Hill Library, Box 7111, Raleigh, 27695. J Porter, Librn
Notes: Collection is complete from 1790.

OH —PUBLIC LIBRARY OF CINCINNATI & HAMILTON COUNTY, Science & Technology Dept, 800 Vine St, Cincinnati, 45202. Rosemary Gaiser, Head
Notes: Complete specifications and drawings, 1871 to date. Annual Reports of the Commissioner of Patents, 1842 to 1871. Official Gazette, 1872 to date. Noncirculating.

OH —TOLEDO-LUCAS COUNTY PUBLIC LIBRARY, 325 Michigan St, Toledo, 43624. Mary B Hubbard, Head, Science-Technology Dept; Paula Baker, Head, Fine Arts Dept
Holdings: Vols 15,222 16mm Film
Notes: Patent Depository Library. US Patent Specifications, 1871-1911; Feb 1934-date; Official Gazette, 1872-date.

OK —OKLAHOMA STATE UNIVERSITY, Library, Stillwater, 74708. Roscoe Rouse, Dir
Notes: Complete collection of US patents, 1790-date.

PA —FRANKLIN INSTITUTE LIBRARY, 20 & The Parkway, Philadelphia, 19103. Miriam Padusis, Dir; Charles Wilt, Readers Servs Librn
Holdings: Cat

PATENTS—COLLECTIONS—U.S. (cont.)

TX —RICE UNIVERSITY, Fondren Library, 6100 S Main St, PO Box 1892, Houston, 77251. Dr Samuel M Carrington, Jr, University Librn
Notes: All US patents since 1962.

WA —UNIVERSITY OF WASHINGTON LIBRARIES, Engineering Library, FH-15, Seattle, 98195. Harold N Wiren, Engineering Librn
Holdings: Vols (108,313) Cat Microforms
Budget: ($314,409)
Notes: Patent specifications, 1966 to date, on microfilm.

WI —UNIVERSITY OF WISCONSIN, MADISON, Kurt F Wendt Library, 215 N Randall Ave, Madison, 53706. LeRoy G Zweifel, Librn
Holdings: Vols (95,000) Cat Microforms
Notes: Complete US patent collection.

WI —MILWAUKEE PUBLIC LIBRARY, 814 W Wisconsin Ave, Milwaukee, 53233. Donald J Sager, City Librn
Holdings: Cat
Notes: US Patent Specifications and Drawings, 1871 to date. *US Patent Gazette*, 1872 to date. The library is a depository for the US Patent publications. Patents all in full-sized copies. Staff trained to guide general public in patent searches and do some reference searching. CASSIS on-line potent classification information available to public.

ON —METROPOLITAN TORONTO LIBRARY, Science & Technology Dept, 789 Yonge St, Toronto, M4W 2G8, Can. Margaret Walshe, Head
Holdings: Vols (10,000) Cat Microforms
Notes: US Patent Office, *Official Gazette*, 1851 to date. US Patents, complete specifications, on microfilm, 1970 to date; etc.

PATENTS—DENTISTRY

PA —UNIVERSITY OF PENNSYLVANIA, School of Dental Medicine, Leon Levy Library, 4001 Spruce St, Philadelphia, 19104. John M Whittock Jr, Librn
Holdings: Vols (45,000) Cat Pix Slides
Notes: Collection is comprised of 15,250 monographs, 25,250 bound periodical vols. Library currently receives about 700 dental and medical journals. Houses S S White Dental Manufacture Co collection of U S dental patents, 1797-1966, and U S and foreign dental catalogs. 1000 rare books on dentistry and oral biology. 3000 pictures and 1000 slides.

PATENTS—LAWS AND LEGISLATION see Patent Laws and Legislation

PATER, WALTER HORATIO

MI —UNIVERSITY OF MICHIGAN, Library, Dept of Rare Books & Special Collections, Ann Arbor, 48109. Robert J Starring, Head
Holdings: Vols 151 Cat Mss
Notes: Incl two complete sets of first editions, one in the original cloth; later editions, especially limited, and association items.

NS —DALHOUSIE UNIVERSITY LIBRARY, Halifax, B3H 4H8, Can.
Notes: The collection of numerous editions from Dr Henry Hicks, past president of Dalhousie.

PATERSON, WILLIAM, 1745-1806

NJ —RUTGERS, THE STATE UNIVERSITY OF NEW JERSEY, Alexander Library, Special Collections and Archives, College Ave & Huntington St, New Brunswick, 08903. Ronald L Becker, Cur of Manuscripts and Rare Books
Holdings: // Mss
Notes: Papers, etc (10 linear feet).

NJ —WILLIAM PATERSON COLLEGE OF NEW JERSEY, Sarah Byrd Askew Library, 300 Pompton Rd, Wayne, 07470. Robert Lopresti, Librn
Notes: The professional papers of William Paterson, second governor of New Jersey. Incl more than a thousand letters, ledgers, and legal papers, most of which were written in Paterson's own hand during his political life and in his legal practice. Bibliography of cataloged items available.

PATHOLOGICAL BOTANY see Plant Diseases

PATHOLOGICAL CHEMISTRY see Chemistry, Medical and Pharmaceutical

PATHOLOGY

AR —NATIONAL CENTER FOR TOXICOLOGICAL RESEARCH, Library, Jefferson, 72079. Susan Laney-Sheehan, Supvr Librn
Holdings: Vols (15,000) Cat Mss Slides Audiotapes 16mm Films Microforms
Notes: Incl (860) journal titles, (230) current subscriptions.

CA —UNIVERSITY OF CALIFORNIA, LOS ANGELES, Research Library, Dept of Special Collections, 405 Hilgard Ave, Los Angeles, 90024. Edward Shreeves, Chairman, Bibliographers Group; David S Zeidberg, Head
Notes: Marcus E Crahan's medical files relating to Los Angeles County court cases. Closed to access until 2004 AD.

CT —YALE MEDICAL LIBRARY, 333 Cedar St, New Haven, 06510.
Holdings: Vols (334,215) Cat Mss Pix Slides Microforms
Budget: ($361,650)
Notes: Incl films, audiotapes, artifacts, etc.

CT —YALE UNIVERSITY, School of Medicine, Section of Neuropathology Library, Brain Tumor Registry, New Haven, 06520. Dr Elias Manuelidis, Cur
Holdings: Cat Slides
Notes: The Ernest Sachs Collection of about 8000 microscopic slides of brain tumors. Also the Harvey Cushing Collection of 800 jars of brain tissue in Formalin, and about 2500 microscopic slides. Another collection, belonging to the Pathology Department, consists of brain sections from about 100 monkeys, with 30 slides from each brain. Not cataloged, in boxes and inaccessible.

CT —YALE UNIVERSITY, School of Medicine, Dept of Obstetrics & Gynecology Library, Farnam Memorial Bldg, New Haven, 06510.
Holdings: Cat Mss Pix Slides
Notes: X-ray plates, 10,000 slides of monkey and human tissue and about 1000 slides of gynecological and obstetrical pathology, used as teaching and research materials. Other large collections of X-rays and radiotherapy photographs are in the Hunter Radiation Therapy Center.

DC —SMITHSONIAN INSTITUTION LIBRARIES, National Zoological Park Branch, Washington, 20008. Kay Kenyon, Chief Librn
Holdings: Vols (5500) Cat
Notes: Collection incl animal nutrition, capture and care of animals in captivity, conservation and endangered species, pathology, veterinary medicine, zoology.

IN —PURDUE UNIVERSITY LIBRARIES, Veterinary Medical Library, C J Lynn Hall of Veterinary Medicine, West Lafayette, 47907. Gretchen Stephens, Librn
Holdings: Vols (31,022) Cat
Budget: ($106,381)
Notes: The collection contains the outstanding books and serials in English that are germane to comparative and veterinary medicine. Foreign language materials are added selectively. Subjects of particular strength are laboratory animal medicine, pathology, comparative anatomy, animal behavior and clinical veterinary medicine.

MD —US ARMED FORCES RADIOBIOLOGY RESEARCH INSTITUTE, Naval Medical Command, Bethesda, 20014. Nannette M Pope, Head, Library Division
Holdings: Vols (50,000)
Budget: ($150,000)
Notes: Collection consists of monographs, technical reports, serials, and microfiche related to radiation effects on human and animal biology.

MA —UNIVERSITY OF MASSACHUSETTS AT AMHERST, Library, Amherst, 01003. Siegfried Feller, Assoc Dir for Collection Development
Holdings: Cat
Notes: Microbiology, incl bacteriology, immunology, virology, and pathology.

MA —HARVARD MEDICAL SCHOOL, New England Primate Research Center Library, 1 Pine Hill Dr, Southborough, 01772. Sydney Fingold, Librn
Holdings: Vols (4000)

MI —WARNER-LAMBERT/PARKE-DAVIS, Research Library, 2800 Plymouth Rd, Ann Arbor, 48106. Katherine C Owen, Mgr, Library Services
Holdings: Vols (27,977) Cat

NY —BOOTH MEMORIAL MEDICAL CENTER, Health Education Library, Main St at Booth Memorial Ave, Flushing, 11355. Rita Maier, Library Dir
Holdings: Vols (3000) Cat Audiotapes
Notes: Incl 7000 bound journals; software slide tape programs.

NY —NASSAU COUNTY DEPARTMENT OF HEALTH, Division of Laboratories & Research, 209 Main St, Hempstead, 11550. Madeline Burston, Librn; Beatrice R Sewald, Asst Librn
Holdings: Vols (4076) Cat Mss Slides Microforms

NY —MILTON HELPERN LIBRARY OF LEGAL MEDICINE, 520 First Ave, New York, 10016. Barry W Seaver, Librn
Holdings: Vols (2480) Cat Pix Slides Microforms
Notes: Forensic (legal) medicine (incl forensic pathology, serology, toxicology and criminalistics).

ND —UNIVERSITY OF NORTH DAKOTA, Harley E French Medical Library, Grand Forks, 58202. David W Boilard, Dir; Lila Pedersen, Asst Dir
Holdings: Vols (56,000) Cat
Budget: ($206,000)
Notes: 1075 current periodical subscriptions.

TX —UNIVERSITY OF TEXAS, M D Anderson Hospital and Tumor Institute, Research Medical Library, Texas Medical Center, Houston, 77030. Marie Harvin, Research Medical Librn
Holdings: Vols (48,000) Cat
Notes: Library attempts to collect every publication in all languages related to clinical cancer (or oncology). Aim is an exhaustive collection in this field. Collect heavily (research level) in pathology, radiology, nuclear medicine, genetics and cell biology.

PATHOLOGY—HISTORY

CT —YALE UNIVERSITY, Medical Historical Library, Klebs Collection, 333 Cedar St, New Haven, 06520. Ferenc A Gyorgyey, Librn
Notes: Incl the collections of Harvey Cushing, John F Fulton, Arnold C Klebs and the historical collections of the Yale Medical Library. Also, keep pictures of 86 patients with pronounced pathological conditions, painted in China by Lam-Qua in the 19th century, commissioned by Dr Peter Parker, a medical missionary.

GA —MEDICAL COLLEGE OF GEORGIA, Library, Laney Walker Blvd, Augusta, 30902. Dorothy H Mims, Librn for Special Collections
Holdings: Vols (2500) // Cat
Notes: Special collection of late 18th and early 19th century medical books, incl pathology classics such as Cruveilhier, Virchow and Rokitansky. Also early works on the use of the microscope in pathology.

MN —UNIVERSITY OF MINNESOTA, Owen H Wangensteen Historical Library of Biology & Medicine, Diehl Hall, Minneapolis, 55455. Judith Overmier, Cur
Holdings: Vols (35,000) Cat Mss
Budget: ($80,000)
Notes: Pathology Archives.

PATHOLOGY, DENTAL see Teeth—Diseases

PATHOLOGY, VEGETABLE see Plant Diseases

PATHOLOGY, VETERINARY see Veterinary Pathology

PATMORE, BRIGIT, 1882-1965

BC —UNIVERSITY OF VICTORIA, McPherson Library, Victoria, V8W 3H5, Can.

PATMORE, COVENTRY

MA —BOSTON COLLEGE LIBRARIES,
Thomas P O'Neill Library, Chestnut Hill,
02167. Frank J Seegraber, Special
Collections Libation
Holdings: Vols 1300 Cat Mss Pix
Phonorecords Audiotapes Microforms
Notes: This, the most commplete collection
of Thompsoniana in existence, incl incl
notebooks, mss, letters, and rare editions,
and collateral material relating to poet, his
times and his work. The notebooks are the
chief source of clues to the identification of
300 of Thompson's unsigned contributions
to periodicals. *An Account of the Books and
Manuscripts of Francis Thompson,* ed by
Rev Terence L Connolly (Boston College,
1937). Works of Wilfrid and Alice Meynell
and their children, Viola, Sir Francis, and
Everard, are incl in this collection. The items
give a well-rounded view of this remarkable
family as poets, fiction writers, essayists,
biographers, prefacers, and editors. This
collection incl mss, poems, correspondence,
articles, and book reviews by Coventry
Patmore, an English poet, essayist, and
critic, and a good friend of Francis
Thompson. Among thecorrespondents are
Robert Browning, Alfred Tennyson,
Matthew Arnold, Ralph Waldo Emerson,
Nathaniel Hawthorne, Thomas Carlyle, and
William Makepeace Thackeray. For
reference use only, by arrangement with
librarian.

PATON, ALAN

NV —UNIVERSITY OF NEVADA, RENO,
University Library, Special Collections Dept,
Reno, 89557. Robert E Blesse, Head
Holdings: Vols (42) Cat
Notes: Includes individual works by author
in all editions including translations; also
prefaces, introductions, published
correspondence, appearances in anthologies,
periodicals, etc. Bibliographical research
collection, part of Modern Authors
Collection. Other appearances 40 cataloged.

PATRIARCHY see Family

PATRICK, JOHN

MA —BOSTON UNIVERSITY, Mugar
Memorial Library, Special Collections Dept,
771 Commonwealth Ave, Boston, 02215.
Howard B Gotlieb, Dir
Holdings: Cat Mss Pix
Notes: Mss correspondence, etc collected in
depth; incl publications by or about.

PATRICK, LEE

MA —BOSTON UNIVERSITY, Mugar
Memorial Library, Special Collections Dept,
771 Commonwealth Ave, Boston, 02215.
Howard B Gotlieb, Dir
Holdings: Pix Scrapbooks

PATRIOT WAR, 1837-1842 see
Canada—History—Rebellion, 1837-1838

PATRIOTIC LETTER WRITERS see
Network of Patriotic Letter Writers

PATRIOTIC MUSIC, AMERICAN

IL —CHICAGO PUBLIC LIBRARY, Special
Collections Div, Cultural Center, 78 E
Washington St, Chicago, 60602. Laura
Linard, Cur
Holdings: Vols (7000) Cat Mss Maps Pix
Notes: The Civil War and American History
Research Collection at the Chicago Public
Library is our largest collection. It spans the
pre-war sectional crisis as well as
Reconstruction. Scarce slavery pamphlets;
large collection of regimental histories;
manuscripts of US Grant, Sherman,
Breckinridge; letters and diaries of soldiers
and other officers; original photographs of
individuals and field shots; Confederate
Battle Plan for the Battle of Shiloh (original);

swords, rifles, uniforms, flags and other
military accessories. A substantial part of
this collection has been cataloged. The
museum objects are inventoried (Grand
Army Hall and Memorial Association of
Illinois Collection).See *Treasures of The
Chicago Public Library,* comp by Thomas A
Oriando and Marie Gecik, 1977, pp 36-79.

IN —INDIANA UNIVERSITY, Lilly Library,
Seventh St, Bloomington, 47405. William R
Cagle, Libation
Holdings: // Uncat
Notes: 19th and 20th century sheet music in
the Starr Collection

NY —BARNARD A & MORRIS N YOUNG
LIBRARY OF EARLY AMERICAN
POPULAR MUSIC, 270 Riverside Dr, New
York, 10025. Morris N Young, Cur
Holdings: Cat Mss Pix Phonorecords
Audiotapes Microforms
Notes: 48,000 items of American popular
music, mostly 1790-1910. Incl books, serials,
sheet music, broadsides, anthologies, air
checks, broadcasting and music business
memorabilia, and correspondence.

NC —DUKE UNIVERSITY, William R
Perkins Library, Rare Book Room, Durham,
27706. John L Sharpe, III, Cur
Notes: Collection of more than 3500 titles of
Confederate imprints. Possibly the largest
such collection in the country, it includes
broadsides, maps, music, newspapers, Union
and Confederate regimental histories, and
sheet music.

PA —FREE LIBRARY OF PHILADELPHIA,
Sheet Music Collection, Logan Sq,
Philadelphia, 19103. Connie Jessum, Libation
Budget: ($2000)
Notes: Covers entire span of American
popular expression in song and instrumental
music (piano) from colonial times to the
present. Incl Newland-Zeuner and Edward I
Keffer Collections on loan from the Musical
Fund Society. Items printed before 1825
indexed in Sonneck-Upton and Wolfe.
Checklists for cover illustrations, musical
shows or films and special subjects. Songs
are filed by title; piano music by composer.
Examples of special materials not filed in
regular collection incl early Philadelphia
composers and publications, national
(centennial and state), patriotic ("Star-
Spangled Banner"), political (Presidents), and
war (1861; 1914; 1939) songs. Most of the
ms materials are anonymous. Collection
contains 138,360 pieces of sheet music.

PATRIOTIC POETRY, AMERICAN

RI —BROWN UNIVERSITY, John Hay
Library, 20 Prospect St, Providence, 02912.
Mary T Russo, Cur of Broadsides
Notes: A very large selection of patriotic
verse appears in the Broadside Collection. It
is particularly strong in World War I
material. Partial catalog.

PATRIOTISM

CA —UNIVERSITY OF CALIFORNIA, LOS
ANGELES, Research Library, Dept of
Special Collections, 405 Hilgard Ave, Los
Angeles, 90024. Edward Shreeves,
Chairman, Bibliographers Group; David S
Zeidberg, Head
Holdings: Cat Mss Pix
Notes: 11 cartons of materials, recordings,
etc relating to the John Birch Society, with
runs of relevant periodicals, government
documents, etc; 6.5 linear feet on Loyalty
Oaths incl in other collections; 6 transcribed
Oral History interviews.

TX —ABILENE CHRISTIAN UNIVERSITY,
Margaret & Herman Brown Library, ACU
Sta, Abilene, 79601. Callie Faye Milliken,
Assoc Dir
Holdings: Vols 5000 // Cat
Notes: Donner Library of Americanism.
Books, pamphlets, documents, and periodical
materials dealing with American politics of
the far right collected by Robert Donner
during and after World War II. Also incl
materials on Jews and Freemasonry.

PATRISTICS see Fathers of the Church

PATROL TORPEDO BOATS see P.T. Boats

PATRONYMS see Names, Personal

PATTEE, FRED LEWIS

PA —PENNSYLVANIA STATE
UNIVERSITY, Fred Lewis Pattee Library,

Special Collections Dept, University Park,
16802. Charles Mann, Chief, Special
Collections
Holdings: Vols 1862 // Cat Mss
Budget: ($37,000)
Notes: The private library of Fred Lewis
Pattee, Professor and Historian of American
Literature, including his own publications
and correspondence. Early 20th century
literary connections.

PATTERNS FOR CROCHETING see
Crocheting—Patterns

PATTERNS FOR EMBROIDERY see
Embroidery—Patterns

PATTERNS FOR NEEDLEWORK see
Needlework—Patterns

PATTERNS FOR WEAVING see
Weaving—Patterns

PATTERSON, GEORGE A.

IL —CHICAGO HISTORICAL SOCIETY,
Library, Clark St at North Ave, Chicago,
60614. Archie Motley, Manuscript Libation
Notes: Papers of steel workers union
organize.

PATTERSON, JOSEPH MEDILL

IL —LAKE FOREST COLLEGE, Donnelley
Library, Lake Forest, 60045. Arthur H
Miller Jr, College Libation
Holdings: Vols (1000) Mss Pix
Notes: Working files (1919-1946) of Capt
Joseph Medill Patterson, founder of the New
York *News.*

PATTERSON, LINDSAY

MA —BOSTON UNIVERSITY, Mugar
Memorial Library, Special Collections Dept,
771 Commonwealth Ave, Boston, 02215.
Howard B Gotlieb, Dir
Holdings: Cat Mss Pix Correspondence
Audiotapes

PATTERSON, RICHARD NORTH

MA —BOSTON UNIVERSITY, Mugar
Memorial Library, Special Collections Dept,
771 Commonwealth Ave, Boston, 02215.
Howard B Gotlieb, Dir
Holdings: Mss

PATTON, FRANCES GRAY

NC —DUKE UNIVERSITY, William R
Perkins Library, Rare Book Room, Durham,
27706. John L Sharpe, III, Cur
Notes: A collection of Duke University
authors, established around 1963, with the
writings of the students of William
Blackburn and greatly enhanced by the gift
of Professor Blackburn's collection.
Represented are James Applewhite, Fred
Chappell, Guy Davenport, Reynolds Price,
William Styron, Frances Gray Patton, and
Anne Tyler. Printed works are in the Rare
Book Room and manuscripts are in the
Manuscript Department.

PAUL, BARBARA

MA —BOSTON UNIVERSITY, Mugar
Memorial Library, Special Collections Dept,
771 Commonwealth Ave, Boston, 02215.
Howard B Gotlieb, Dir
Holdings: Mss

PAUPERISM see Poor

PAVING see Pavements

PAVLOVA, ANNA, 1882-1931

NY —NEW YORK PUBLIC LIBRARY,
Performing Arts Research Center, Dance
Collection, 111 Amsterdam Ave, New York,
10023. Genevieve Oswald, Cur
Holdings: Vols (36,752)
Notes: Extensive biographical and visual

PAVLOVA, ANNA, 1882-1931 (cont.)

material. Incl 400 photographs, scrapbooks, clippings, programs, original drawings, and silent motion picture footage filmed 1915-1924. Over 200 cataloged items listed in published catalog: *Dictionary Catalog of the Dance Collection,* (Boston, G K Hall), 1974, 10 vols.

PAXTON, JOHN, 1911-

CA —UNIVERSITY OF CALIFORNIA, LOS ANGELES, Research Library, Dept of Special Collections, 405 Hilgard Ave, Los Angeles, 90024. Edward Shreeves, Chairman, Bibliographers Group; David S Zeidberg, Head
Holdings: Mss
Notes: 2 linear feet of mss and screenplays.

PAYNE, B. IDEN

†TX —UNIVERSITY OF TEXAS LIBRARIES, Hoblitzelle Theatre Arts Library, Austin, 78712.
Notes: Memorabilia of B Iden Payne, internationally known Shakespearean director.

PAYNE, EUGENE G.

NC —UNIVERSITY OF NORTH CAROLINA, CHARLOTTE, J Murrey Atkins Library, UNCC Station, Charlotte, 28223. Robert F Brabham Jr, Special Collections Librn
Holdings: Cat
Notes: 1059 cartoons by Eugene G Payne, Pulitzer Prize-winning cartoonist of *The Charlotte Observer.*

PAYNE, MITCHELL

AZ —UNIVERSITY OF ARIZONA, Center for Creative Photography, 843 E University Blvd, Tucson, 85721. James Enyeart, Dir; Terence Pitts, Cur and Librn
Notes: Center has significant collections consisting of more than 25 collections plus other archival material such as negatives, contact sheets, work prints, correspondence, financial records, diaries, project files, etc. Inventories of the collections are available to researchers. Published guides available for some collections.

PAYNE, ROBERT, 1911-1983

CA —UNIVERSITY OF CALIFORNIA, LOS ANGELES, Research Library, Dept of Special Collections, 405 Hilgard Ave, Los Angeles, 90024. Edward Shreeves, Chairman, Bibliographers Group; David S Zeidberg, Head
Holdings: Mss
Notes: 6 linear feet of books, mss, letters, and ephemera.
NY —STATE UNIVERSITY OF NEW YORK, STONY BROOK, Melville Library, Dept of Special Collections, Stony Brook, 11794. Evert Volkersz, Head
Holdings: Vols 200 Cat
Notes: Author writes under the name of Robert Payne and has also used a number of pseudonyms. Photocopying.

PAYTON, BOYD E.

NC —UNIVERSITY OF NORTH CAROLINA, CHARLOTTE, J Murrey Atkins Library, UNCC Station, Charlotte, 28223. Robert F Brabham Jr, Special Collections Librn
Holdings: Vols Cat Mss Pix
Notes: Papers of Boyd E Payton, documenting strike (1958-61) at Harriett-Henderson Textile Mill in Henderson, NC; Payton's imprisonment for conspiring to dynamite the mill; and the ensuing controversy over the legitimacy of Payton's conviction amidst allegations of a state-supported frame-up.

PAZEND see Pahlavi Language and Literature

PEABODY, ELIZABETH

MA —CONCORD FREE PUBLIC LIBRARY, 129 Main St, Concord, 01742. Rose Marie Mitten, Dir
Holdings: Cat Mss Pix
Notes: Extensive collection of her own library and of her "store" on West Street in Boston.
OH —ANTIOCH COLLEGE, Olive Kettering Library, Livermore St, Yellow Springs, 45387. Nina Myatt, Cur
Holdings: Vols 14 // Mss
Notes: Letters of the Peabody, Mann, Hawthorne and related families. Collected by Robert Straker from many sources, arranged in chronological order and well indexed.

PEABODY, HENRY

MA —SOCIETY FOR THE PRESERVATION OF NEW ENGLAND ANTIQUITIES, Library, 141 Cambridge St, Boston, 02114. Ellie Reichlin, Librn & Cur of Photographic Collections
Holdings: Vols (3000) Cat Pix Microforms
Budget: ($75,000)
Notes: Photograph collections, all media (incl daguerreotypes, ambrotypes, etc, stereographic views, carte de visite) depicting New England buildings; interiors; street and town views; occupations; pastimes; transport and personalities. Covers 1840s-1930s, with some more recent additons. Amateur and professional photographers represented. Cataloged in part, otherwise arranged by localities, subject, personal name. Special collections incl: marine photographs by N L Stebbins and Henry Peabody (1880s-1920s); Boston and Albany railroad photographic archive, early 1900s; Quabbin Valley views; historic American Buildings Survey photographs (17th to early 19th century architecture) by Arthur Haskell; Baldwin Coolidge collection, and many others. Size: 500,000 prints, ca 75,000 negatives (glass plates and copy negs). These are cataloged. Some special indexes incllandscape design (arbors, conservatories, flower beds, bandstands etc); photographers represented; architects represented (partial), and pending, interiors (specific features of); occupations.

PEACE

ME —BOWDOIN COLLEGE, Library, Brunswick, 04011. Dianne M Gutscher, Cur of Special Collections
Holdings: Mss
Notes: The Rowland Bailey Howard Papers contain about 250 letters, as well as diaries, newsclippings, and ephemera, primarily for the period 1848-1891, of this clergyman and Secretary of the American Peace Society. The collection contains almost exclusively family letters and complements those of Rowland's brothers, Oliver Otis Howard and Charles Henry Howard.
MA —RADCLIFFE COLLEGE, Arthur & Elizabeth Schlesinger Library on the History of Women in America, 3 James St, Cambridge, 02138. Patricia Miller King, Dir; Eva Moseley, Cur of Mss
Notes: Papers of Congresswoman Jeannette Rankin (1880-1973), peace educator Fannie Fern (Phillips) Andrews (1867-1950); of Helen (Lamb) Lamont (1906-1975), Florence Hope Luscomb (1887-), and other opponents of the Vietnam War; and some correspondence of Jane Addams (1860-1935) and records of the Massachusetts affiliate of the Women's International League for Peace and Freedom.
NY —ALFRED UNIVERSITY, Herrick Memorial Library, Alfred, 14802. June E Brown, Head Librn
Notes: The Evelyn Tennyson Openhym Collection of modern British literature and social history. Correspondence addressed to Ursula Roberts ("Susan Miles"), many pieces concerning the British peace movement of the 1930s.
NY —CARNEGIE ENDOWMENT FOR INTERNATIONAL PEACE, James Thomson Shotwell Library, Formerly, New York, 10017.
Notes: This important collection has been dispersed (Summer 1983). The United Nations documents collection has gone to the University of the West Indies, St Augustine, Trinidad. The rest of the library has been given to special collections in the New York area or to the USBE.
OH —WILMINGTON COLLEGE, Peace Resource Center, Hiroshima/Nagasaki Memorial Collection, Pyle Center Box 1183, Wilmington, 45177. Helen Redding, Librn
Holdings: Vols Pix Slides Audiotapes Videotapes Film Slides Art Reproductions VF
Notes: The Hiroshima/Nagasaki Memorial Collection is nationally known and respected as a major source of information, films, slides and audiotapes about the atomic bombings of Hiroshima and Nagasaki. An especially signifciant part of the Collection is a continually growing library in Japanese currently numbering more than 500 vols. Here are recorded eyewitness account of the atomic bombings, as well as details of what life has been like in the intervening years for the thousands of survivors (*hibakusha*). Also incl are books of poetry, photo books, juvenile literature, and books dealing with medical information, peace research, peace education, nuclear power, etc. All books in the Hiroshima/Nagasaki Memorial Collection are available for interlibrary loan. An *Annotated Bibliography of Japanese A-Bomb Literature* may be purchased or borrowed from the PRC. In it are briefsummaries in English of each book in the Collection.
PA —CARLOW COLLEGE, Grace Library, Fifth Ave, Pittsburgh, 15213. Joan M Mitchell, Dir of Library Services
Holdings: Vols (977) Cat Pamphlets
Budget: ($300)
Notes: The Peace Studies Collection is a collection of books which deals with the search for peace in the modern world from the perspective of the Judeo-Christian tradition. It is especially strong in the area of social justice, civil rights and world politics.
PA —FRIENDS HISTORICAL LIBRARY OF SWARTHMORE COLLEGE, Swarthmore, 19081. J William Frost, Dir
Holdings: Vols (35,000) Cat Mss Pix Microforms
Notes: Library's collections contain information on the history and doctrine of the Society of Friends, Quaker contributions to literature, science, business, education, and government, plus reform efforts in peace, Indian rights, women's rights, and abolition of slavery. Among the more than 250 mss collections are the personal papers of Quaker pacifists, conscientious objectors, workers for international peace, and participants in relief and reconstruction projects following the Civil War and World War I.
PA —SWARTHMORE COLLEGE, Peace Collection, Swarthmore, 19081. Jean R Soderlund, Cur of Peace Collection
Holdings: Vols (10,000) Cat Mss Pix Microforms
Notes: The history of pacifism has been one of the major subject emphases of the Peace Collection since its inception in 1930. In addition to books, pamphlets, and current materials of all kinds on the subject, the Peace Collection is the official depository for many 20th century pacifist organizations and papers of individual peace leaders. These incl Women's International League for Peace and Freedom; War Resisters League; Fellowship of Reconciliation; SANE, A Committee for a Sane Nuclear Policy; Friends Committee on National Legislation; CCCO1 An Agency for Military and Draft Counseling; National Interreligious Service Board for Conscientious Objectors; A J Muste (1885-1967); and Devere Allen (1891-1955). Other materials collected incl records and memorabilia of 19th and early 20th century peace leaders and organizations, such as the American Peace Society and itsbranches, Jane Addams (1860-1935), the Wisbech Local Peace Association (England), Emily Greene Blach (1867-1961), English and American Friends' Peace Societies, the Universal Peace Union, William Ladd (1778-1841), Elihu Burritt (1810-1879), and Benjamin F Trueblood

PEACE (cont.)

(1847-1916). For descriptions of major document groups, see the *Guide to the Swarthmore College Peace Collection*, 2nd ed (1981).

RI —BROWN UNIVERSITY, John Hay Library, 20 Prospect St, Providence, 02912. Mark N Brown, Cur Mss
Holdings: Mss
Notes: The Isabel Harris Metcalf Peaceana Collection, 1918-1942, consists of mounted and loose newspaper clippings (in 57 vols and numerous boxed envelopes) attempting to document the peace issue in the world and the world and the New Deal in the US. The clippings are classified by country, topic, and date. Also incl related correspondence, pamphlets, and broadsides.

WI —STATE HISTORICAL SOCIETY OF WISCONSIN, Archives, 816 State St, Madison, 53706. Harold L Miller, Reference Archivist
Holdings: Mss Pix Audiotapes Microforms
Notes: Records and papers of organizations and individuals engages in social and political reform activities. Major focus areas are civil rights, 1950s to the present, and anti-Vietnam war and other protest movements of the 1960s to the present. Also covered are other reform movements, socialism, and communism from the 1930s to the present. Collections are described in *Social Action Collection at the State Historical Society of Wisconsin: A Guide*, (1983) and in current accession notes in the *Wisconsin Magazine of History*. Major collections are also listed in Hamer, *Guide to Manuscripts and Archives in the United States*, (1961) and in the *National Union Catalog of Manuscript Collections*, (1959-date).

PEACE—BIOGRAPHY

PA —SWARTHMORE COLLEGE, Peace Collection, Swarthmore, 19081. Jean R Soderlund, Cur of Peace Collection
Holdings: Vols (10,000) Cat Mss Pix Microforms
Notes: The Peace Collection has biographical material on thousands of individual pacifists, advocates of nonviolence, and past and present leaders of peace movements.
See also entry under Pacifism - History.

PEACE CORPS

DC —ACTION, Photo Library, 806 Connecticut Ave NW, Washington, 20525.
Holdings: Pix Slides
Notes: Volunteer photos for ACTION, VISTA, and older American programs. 15,000 photographs.

DC —PEACE CORPS, Information Services Division, 806 Connecticut Ave NW, Room M407, Washington, 20526. Rita C Warpeha, Chief Librn
Holdings: Vols (35,000) Cat
Budget: ($10,000)
Notes: Social, political, economic and health topics related to the countries of Asia, the Pacific, Africa, Latin America and the Caribbean where Peace Corp volunteers work. Includes materials from its beginning in 1961.

†MA —JOHN F KENNEDY LIBRARY, Columbia Point, Boston, 02125. Dan H Fenn Jr, Dir
Holdings: // Cat Mss Microforms
Notes: Papers of JFK; microfilm copies (20 rolls) of papers of Public Information Director Edwin Bayley, General Counsel William Josephson; and records of the Peace Corps, 1961-1966. 2 linear ft of mss. Holdings are described in "Historical Materials in the John F Kennedy Library." Copies may be obtained by writing the Research Archivist.

PEACE RIVER, CANADA

BC —LIBRARY SERVICES BRANCH, Peace River Associated Libraries, 1017 105th Ave, Dawson Creek, V1G 2L3, Can. Mary E Grant, Librn
Holdings: Vols (350) Cat Mss Pix
Notes: Incl relevant newspaper files.

PEACOCK, THOMAS LOVE

NC —DUKE UNIVERSITY, William R Perkins Library, Durham, 27706. Elvin E Strowd, University Librn
Notes: The Shelley-Goodwin Collection of Lord Abinger is a microfilm copy of the Shelley and Godwin collection. Lord Abinger's entire manuscript collection, representing the last portion of the papers of Sir Percy Florence Shelley which is still in private hands, has been reproduced on 16 reels of film. The Bodleian Library is the only other location for this film.

PEAKE, MERVYN

CT —LEE ASH, (personal collection), 66 Humiston Dr, Bethany, 06525.
Holdings: Mss Maps Pix
Notes: First editions, mss, ephemera, memorabilia.

PEALE, CHARLES WILLSON

PA —AMERICAN PHILOSOPHICAL SOCIETY, Library, 105 S Fifth St, Philadelphia, 19106. Edward C Carter II, Librn
Holdings: Cat Mss Pix Microforms
Notes: Charles Willson Peale and family.

PEALE, TITIAN RAMSAY

NY —AMERICAN MUSEUM OF NATURAL HISTORY, Library Services Dept, Central Park W & 79th St, New York, 10024. Nina J Root, Chairwoman; Mary Genett, Asst Librn for Reference Services
Holdings: Mss
Notes: Incl oil paintings, self-portrait, mss, sketches, watercolors.

PEARKES, GEORGE RANDOLPH

BC —UNIVERSITY OF VICTORIA, McPherson Library, Victoria, V8W 3H5, Can.
Notes: Cabinet minister. Interviews; confidential papers. Restricted until 1985.

PEARL, RAYMOND

NY —STATE UNIVERSITY OF NEW YORK, STONY BROOK, Biology Library, Stony Brook, 11794. Doris Williams, Biology Librn
Holdings: Vols 625 // Uncat
Notes: Raymond Pearl Collection. The collection contains reprints collected by Raymond Pearl, founder of the *Quarterly Review of Biology*. The reprints are indexed by author and arranged by twenty subjects relating to biology and the history of science.

PEARL HARBOR, ATTACK ON, 1941

CA —HOOVER INSTITUTION ON WAR, REVOLUTION & PEACE, Stanford University, Stanford, 94305. Milorad M Drachkovitch, Archivist
Notes: Two collections: (1) Typewritten documentation of events and conditions leading up to the Japanese attack on Pearl Harbor, December 7, 1941, assembled by Lt Gen W C Short, Commanding General, US Army, Hawaiian Department, for his defense before the "Roberts Commission," which investigated the attack. 1/2 ms box. (2) Papers of Robert A Theobald, Rear Admiral, US Navy; Destroyer Commander, Pacific Fleet, 1940-41; and Commander, Northern Pacific Force in Alaskan Operations, May 1942-January 1943; incl correspondence, speeches and writings, war diaries, dispatches, operations plans and orders, manuals, service lists, memoranda, reports, and war estimates. 1908-59, relating to his career in the US Navy; naval operations in Alaska, May 1942-January 1943; incl the Japanese invasion of the Aleutians, June 1942; and the Japanese attack on Pearl Harbor. 12 ms boxes.

TX —NORTH TEXAS STATE UNIVERSITY, Archives, NT Station Box 5188, Denton, 76203. Robert LaForte, University Archivist
Notes: Oral History Collection. Incl interviews with survivors of attack on Pearl Harbor, incl soldiers, sailors, nurses, civilians, family members present during the attack. Cataloged. Transcriptions available.

PEARSON, EDMUND LESTER

IN —INDIANA UNIVERSITY, Lilly Library, Seventh St, Bloomington, 47405. William R Cagle, Librn
Holdings: Vols 21 Cat Mss
Notes: A complete collection of Pearson's works, including many with the author's annotations. Manuscripts include extensive correspondence between Pearson and two Brittish crime enthusiast, William Roughead and Marie Belloc-Lowndes.

PEARY, JOSEPHINE D. (MRS. ROBERT EDWIN)

ME —WESTBROOK COLLEGE, Library, 716 Stevens Ave, Portland, 04103. Dorothy M Healy, Special Collections Librn
Holdings: Vols (3000) Cat Mss Pix Memorabilia
Notes: Collection incl work of Maine women writers. Many mss and scrapbooks are incl. Memorabilia of Mrs Robert E Peary, Mary Ellen Chase, Florence B Jacobs, Celia Thaxter, and Edna St Vincent Millay are notable items. Some rare books, ie Madame Wood novels, are part of the collection.

PEARY, ROBERT EDWIN, 1856-1920

ME —BOWDOIN COLLEGE, Library, Brunswick, 04011. Dianne M Gutscher, Cur of Special Collections
Holdings: Mss
Notes: The papers (about 15,000 items) of Robert A Bartlett, arctic explorer and shipmaster for Admirals Robert E Peary and Donald B MacMillan, contain more than 15,000 manuscripts, photographs, clippings, diaries, logbooks and some printed material relating to Bartlett's arctic voyages.

MI —UNIVERSITY OF MICHIGAN, Library, Dept of Rare Books & Special Collections, Ann Arbor, 48109. Robert J Starring, Head
Holdings: Cat Mss Maps Pix
Notes: Includes over 100 books, mostly autographed presentation copies from polar explorers to donor William H Hobbs, and 62 scrapbooks, notebooks, albums, and made-up volumes of pamphlets, documents and correspondence, 11 relating to Admiral Peary. Also there are such primary records from Professor Hobbs' own expeditions as his journals, radio logs, purchase requisitions, pilot balloon ascension reports and graphs, and anemoscope records. In addition there are an estimated 3500 items of correspondence with explorers and other notables, 800 photographs, and maps.

NY —EXPLORERS CLUB, James B Ford Memorial Library, 46 E 70 St, New York, 10021. Janet Baldwin, Librn
Holdings: Vols (24,000) Cat Maps
Notes: Additions to the collection depend upon gifts. Access by appointment only.

VA —UNIVERSITY OF VIRGINIA, Alderman Library, Manuscripts Dept, Charlottesville, 22901. Edmund Berkeley Jr, Cur
Holdings: Cat Mss Pix
Notes: Papers of Edwin Swift Balch, author of *The North Pole* and *Bradley Land*, and *Antarctica*, and authority on the Cook-Peary controversy incl scrapbooks and correspondence.

PEASANT ART see Art Industries and Trade; Folk Art

PEATTIE, DONALD CULROSS, 1898-1964

CA —UNIVERSITY OF CALIFORNIA, SANTA BARBARA, Library, Dept of

PEATTIE, DONALD CULROSS, 1898-1964 (cont.)

Special Collections, Santa Barbara, 93106. Christian F Brun, Head
Holdings: Cat Mss Pix
Notes: Letters and mss of American naturalist and author Donald Culross Peattie; 15,343 items.

PECK, GRAHAM

MA —BOSTON UNIVERSITY, Mugar Memorial Library, Special Collections Dept, 771 Commonwealth Ave, Boston, 02215. Howard B Gotlieb, Dir
Holdings: Mss Pix

PECKINPAH, SAM

CA —AMERICAN FILM INSTITUTE, Louis B Mayer Library, 2021 N Western Ave, PO Box 27999, Los Angeles, 90027. Anne G Schlosser, Dir
Holdings: Vols (3500) Cat

PECKINPAUGH, WILLIAM H., AND FAMILY

IN —INDIANA STATE UNIVERSITY, EVANSVILLE, Library, 8600 University Blvd, Evansville, 47712. Gina R Walker, Acting Archivist
Holdings: // Cat Mss Pix
Notes: Family letters, 1861-1916, consisting mainly of letters (1 linear foot) exchanged during and after the Civil War between William Henry Peckinpaugh (1835-1875) and Mary Ann (Mollie) Emmick (1843-post 1910). Also one letter written on linen by William's younger brother, Nicholas Rice (1846-1911) to his family from Sitka, Alaska, when he served as one of the acting Governors of the Territory, 1890-1894. Unpublished guide.

PEDAGOGY see Education; Education—Study and Teaching

PEDEN, PRESTON

OK —UNIVERSITY OF OKLAHOMA, Bizzell Memorial Library, Western History Collections, 401 W Brooks, Norman, 73069. John Ezell, Cur
Holdings: Mss Documents Maps
Notes: US Representative. His papers. Guide available.

PEDEN, RACHEL

MA —BOSTON UNIVERSITY, Mugar Memorial Library, Special Collections Dept, 771 Commonwealth Ave, Boston, 02215. Howard B Gotlieb, Dir
Holdings: Cat Mss

PEDIATRIC PSYCHIATRY see Child Psychiatry

PEDIATRICS

AL —UNIVERSITY OF ALABAMA, BIRMINGHAM, Lister Hill Library of the Health Sciences, University Sta, Birmingham, 35294. Richard B Fredericksen, Dir
CA —CHILDRENS HOSPITAL OF LOS ANGELES, Health Sciences Library, 4650 Sunset Blvd, Los Angeles, 90027. Harvey Hammond, Medical Librn
Holdings: Vols 15,000 Cat Slides Audiotapes Filmstrips
Budget: $90,000
Notes: Current material on clinical pediatrics.
CT —YALE MEDICAL LIBRARY, 333 Cedar St, New Haven, 06510.
Holdings: Vols (334,215) Cat Mss Pix Slides Microforms
Budget: ($361,650)
Notes: Incl films, audiotapes, artifacts, etc.
CT —NEWINGTON CHILDREN'S HOSPITAL, Professional Library, 181 E Cedar St, Newington, 06111. Jean Long, Librn
Holdings: Vols (3500) Cat
Budget: ($6500)
IN —BRISTOL-MYERS PHARMACEUTICAL R&D DIVISION, Scientific Information Dept, 2404 W Pennsylvania St, Evansville, 47721. Alice Weisling, Mgr
Holdings: Vols 33,000 Cat Microforms
IN —INDIANA UNIVERSITY, School of Dentistry, Library, 1121 W Michigan St, Indianapolis, 46202. Marie Sparks, Librn
Holdings: Vols (50,000) Cat Mss Slides Audiotapes Films Microforms
Budget: ($41,790)
Notes: Juvenile dentistry, scanning electron microscopy, pediatrics and basic sciences.
MI —CHILDREN'S HOSPITAL OF MICHIGAN, Medical Library, 3901 Beaubien, Detroit, 48201. Michele S Klein, Dir of Library Services; Nancy T Bulgarelli, Co-Dir
Holdings: Vols 8000 Cat
Budget: $78,000
Notes: Encompasses all aspects of the subject. Clinical Pediatric medicine is covered in depth. The hospital is affiliated with Wayne State University Medical School and is the resource for the pediatric literature.
NY —FLUSHING HOSPITAL & MEDICAL CENTER, Medical Library, Parsons Blvd & 45 Ave, Flushing, 11355. Maria Czechowicz, Dir
Holdings: Vols (5741) Cat Audiotapes
Budget: ($11,000)
PA —CHILDREN'S HOSPITAL OF PHILADELPHIA, Medical Library, 34th and Civic Center Blvd, Philadelphia, 19104. Sharon Chopa, Dir
Holdings: Vols 6000 Cat Audiotapes
PA —COLLEGE OF PHYSICIANS OF PHILADELPHIA, Library, 19 S 22 St, Philadelphia, 19103. Anthony Aguirre, Libr Dir
Holdings: Vols (316,223) Cat Mss Microforms
Budget: ($1,096,557)
Notes: Incl 13,515 pamphlets; 1435 mss; 326,367 reports, dissertations, and reprints. Strong historical and bibliographical collections, as well as current materials. Medical documentation service provides current alerting, incl abstracting, etc.
TN —SAINT JUDE CHILDREN'S RESEARCH HOSPITAL, Medical Library, 323 N Lauderdale, PO Box 318, Memphis, 38101. Mary Edith Walker, Librn; Cindy Suter, Asst Librn
Holdings: Vols (10,000)
Notes: The collection of pediatric oncology is intermingled with general clinical and research materials. Published description of collection in *International Directory of Specialized Cancer Research and Treatment Establishments* (Geneva: International Union Against Cancer, 1976), p 442.
TX —SANTA ROSA MEDICAL CENTER, Health Science Library, PO Box 7330 Sta A, San Antonio, 78285. Marjorie McFarland, Librn
Holdings: Vols (6500) Cat
Budget: ($5000)
Notes: Special emphasis on pediatrics and orthopedics. Incl 947 audiotapes. Access to Medline.
WA —CHILDREN'S ORTHOPEDIC HOSPITAL & MEDICAL CENTER, Medical Library, 4800 Sand Point Way NE, Seattle, 98105. Tamara A Turner, Librn
Holdings: Vols (2000)
Notes: Specialize in pediatric texts and journals.
ON —HOSPITAL FOR SICK CHILDREN, Medical Library, 555 University Ave, Toronto, M5G 1X8, Can. Irene Jeryn, Medical Librn
Holdings: Vols 23,000 // Cat
PQ —UNIVERSITY OF MONTREAL, Bibliotheque Para-medicale, 2375 Chemin de la Cote Ste Catherine, Montreal, H3C 3J7, Can. Johanne Hopper, Head Librn
Holdings: Vols 700 Cat Filmstrips
Notes: 15 percent of collection in French.

PEDIATRICS—HISTORY

CA —UNIVERSITY OF THE PACIFIC, Holt-Atherton Pacific Center for Western Studies, Stockton, 95211. Hiram L Davis, Dir of Libraries
Holdings: // Uncat Mss Pix Slides
Notes: The Bolt family papers comprise primarily the diaries of Beatrice Rebecca (French) Bolt, and the papers of her husband, Dr Richard Authur Bolt (1880-1959), a noted US child health authority. 19 linear ft. (42 document boxes).
GA —MEDICAL COLLEGE OF GEORGIA, Library, Laney Walker Blvd, Augusta, 30902. Dorothy H Mims, Librn for Special Collections
Holdings: Vols (2500) // Cat
Notes: Special collection of late 18th and early 19th century medical books, incl classics on diseases of children and advice to mothers on care of children.
MD —MEDICAL & CHIRURGICAL FACULTY OF THE STATE OF MARYLAND, Library, 1211 Cathedral St, Baltimore, 21201. Joseph E Jensen, Librn
Holdings: Vols (10,000) // Cat Mss Maps Pix
See also entry under Medicine - History and Historic
OH —CLEVELAND MEDICAL LIBRARY ASSOCIATION/CASE WESTERN RESERVE UNIVERSITY, Cleveland Health Sciences Library, Historical Division, Allen Memorial Medical Library, 11000 Euclid Ave, Cleveland, 44106. Glen Jenkins, Rare Book Librarian & Archivist
Notes: Incl 15,000 historical vols, 6000 in the supporting collection. Incl about 1000 16th-18th century titles. Strength of collection: diseases, epidemiology, anatomy, surgery, medicine, obstetrics, gynecology, pediatrics and yellow fever. Incl also medical Americana, listed in Robert B Austin *Early American Medical Imprints*, 1668-1820 (Washington, DC, HEW, Public Health Service, 1961) and ca 7000 19th century works. Our total medical Americana collection also incl journals (not counted), mss and archives (900 linear ft) and 5000 pictures, especially of the Western Reserve. Anatomical works discussed in I Ebner and G Jenkins *Skeletons in Our Closet* (Cleveland, Cleveland Health Sciences Library, 1983).

PEDIGREES see Heraldry

PEDOLOGY (CHILD STUDY) see Child Development; Children

PEDOLOGY (SOIL SCIENCE) see Soil Science

PEDOPHILIA AND PEDERASTY

†CA —INSTITUTE FOR THE ADVANCED STUDY OF HUMAN SEXUALITY, 1523 Franklin St, San Francisco, 94109.
IN —INDIANA UNIVERSITY, Institute for Sex Research Library, 416 Morrison Hall, Bloomington, 47401. Douglas Freeman, Collections and Services Librn; Joan Brewer, Information Services Librn
Holdings: Vols (62,000) Cat Mss Pix Microforms
See also entry under Sex.

PEI, MARIO

MA —BOSTON UNIVERSITY, Mugar Memorial Library, Special Collections Dept, 771 Commonwealth Ave, Boston, 02215. Howard B Gotlieb, Dir
Holdings: Cat Mss
Notes: Mss, correspondence, etc collected in depth; incl publications by or about.

PEIRCE, CHARLES SANDERS

TX —TEXAS TECH UNIVERSITY, Library, Lubbock, 79409. David J Murrah, Assoc Dir for Special Collections

PEIRCE, DANIEL, 1709-1773

NH —PORTSMOUTH ATHENAEUM, 9 Market Sq, Box 848, Portsmouth, 03801. Joseph P Copley, Cur
Holdings: Vols Cat Mss
Notes: Incl Larkin Papers, 1758-1798 (235

PEIRCE, DANIEL, 1709-1773 (cont.)

items); papers of Daniel and John Peirce, ca 1730-1800 (115 items); and papers of N H Fire and Marine Insurance Co, 1803-1823 (1800 items).

PEIRCE, NEAL R.

MA —BOSTON UNIVERSITY, Mugar Memorial Library, Special Collections Dept, 771 Commonwealth Ave, Boston, 02215. Howard B Gotlieb, Dir
Holdings: Cat Mss
Notes: Mss, correspondence, etc collected in depth; incl publications by or about.

PELAGIC FAUNA see Marine Fauna

PELAGIC FLORA see Marine Flora

PELHAM, PETER

MA —AMERICAN ANTIQUARIAN SOCIETY LIBRARY, 185 Salisbury St, Worcester, 01609. Marcus A McCorison, Dir & Librn
Notes: A rare collection relating to the beginnings of the art among Anglo-Americans. Incl copies of all of Paul Revere's engravings, and nearly all of Peter Pelham's mezzotints, as well as most of the works by other early American engravers. Examples of about half the works in Stauffer and Fielding subject and engraver catalog.

PELL, SEN. CLAIBORNE

RI —UNIVERSITY OF RHODE ISLAND, Library, Special Collections, Kingston, 02881. David Maslyn, Head
Notes: His papers.

PELLAGRA

TN —VANDERBILT UNIVERSITY, Medical Center Library, Nashville, 37232. Mary H Teloh, Special Collections Librn
Holdings: Uncat Mss Pix Videotapes
Notes: The nucleus of the developing nutrition collection at Vanderbilt is the papers of medical researcher Joseph Goldberger, MD, and his associate W Henry Sebrell, Jr, MD. The collection consists of first editions and translations of classic books on pellagra, and the letters, mss, and notebooks compiled by Dr Goldberger and Dr Sebrell during the years of research on pellagra. See *Nutrition Reviews*, 33(10):310-312, Oct 1975. 10 linear ft of mss.

PELLY, THOMAS

WA —UNIVERSITY OF WASHINGTON LIBRARIES, Suzzallo Library, Manuscripts Section, FM-25, Seattle, 98195. Karyl Winn, Librn
Notes: Incl 192 linear ft, circa 1953-1972.

PELLY, WILLIAM DUDLEY

AZ —WORLD UNIVERSITY, Library, 711 E Blacklidge Dr, Tucson, 85719. Howard John Zitko, Cur
Holdings: Vols (15,000) Cat Mss Maps Audiotapes
Notes: Collection concerns the "frontier sciences." No interlibrary loan.

PELOQUIN, CLAUDE, 1940-

AB —UNIVERSITY OF CALGARY, Libraries, Special Collections Div, 2500 University Dr, Calgary, T2N 1N4, Can.
Holdings: Cat Mss
Notes: The collection comprises draft manuscripts, galley proofs, research notes and correspondence relating to a number of Claude Peloquin's works. Also included are scrapbooks, photographs, cassette tapes of readings and filmed interviews.

PENAL CODES see Criminal Law

PENAL INSTITUTIONS see Prisons and Prisoners

PENAL LAW see Criminal Law

PENDLETON FARMERS' SOCIETY

SC —CLEMSON UNIVERSITY, Libraries, Clemson, 29631. Michael F Kohl, Head of Special Collections
Holdings: // Cat Mss
Notes: Scrapbooks, ledgers, books, magazines of the Pendleton Farmers' Association; 3954 ms pieces from the South Carolina Farmers' Alliance; 1800 items from the South Carolina State Grange, 1872-1895 (Patrons of Husbandry).

PENETRANT INSPECTION

IL —CHICAGO BRIDGE & IRON CO, Technical Library, 800 Jorie Blvd, Oak Brook, 60521. Susan Beatty, Librn
Holdings: Vols (7500) Cat
Budget: ($39,500)
Notes: Quality control and nondestructive testing.

PENGUIN BOOKS

WY —UNIVERSITY OF WYOMING, William Robertson Coe Library, 13 & Ivinson, Laramie, 82071.
Notes: Archives of publishers Penguin Books and New American Library.

†ON —UNIVERSITY OF WESTERN ONTARIO, School of Library and Information Science, Special Collections Room, London, N6A 5B9, Can.
Holdings: Vols 295
Notes: The collection consists of Penguin's Specials, ranging from Number 1, published in 1937, to the present.

PENITENTIARIES see Prisons and Prisoners

PENMANSHIP

IL —NEWBERRY LIBRARY, 60 W Walton St, Chicago, 60610. Diana Haskell, Cur of Modern Mss
Holdings: Vols (2000) Cat Mss Pix
Notes: John M Wing Collection of printed writing-books and calligraphic mss chosen to show the evolution of letter-forms and their relationship to printing types. Over 1000 writing-books, probably the largest collection extant, incl about 200 from the 16th and 17th centuries. Calligraphic examples by Arrighi, Beauchesne, Jarry and Johnston. Also materials on Platt R Spencer, incl writing specimen books and about 7000 ms pieces on American handwriting, espec the Spencerian hand.

IL —NEWBERRY LIBRARY, John M Wing Foundation on the History of Printing, 60 W Walton St, Chicago, 60610. Diana Haskell, Cur of Modern Mss
Holdings: Vols (26,500) Cat Mss
Budget: ($50,000)
Notes: The collection covers printing and printing history of Western Europe and the Americas from its invention to the present. It is particularly rich in incunabula (about 2000); the works of the great printers, among others Aldus, Bodoni, Baskerville, and Rogers. Printed catalog: *A Dictionary Catalogue...* (Boston: G K Hall, 1961); *Supplement* (1971). Brief descriptions: James M Wells, "The John M Wing Foundation of The Newberry Library," *The Book Collector*, VIII, 2 (Summer 1959), pp 157-162; Lawrence W Towner, *An Uncommon Collection of Uncommon Collections* (Chicago: The Newberry Library, 1977), pp 25-26.

MA —HARVARD UNIVERSITY LIBRARY, Widener Library, Cambridge, 02138.
Holdings: Cat Mss
Notes: English copybooks of the 18th century are described in *Harvard Library* Bulletin, XIV (1960), pp 12-19.

MA —AMERICAN ANTIQUARIAN SOCIETY LIBRARY, 185 Salisbury St, Worcester, 01609. Marcus A McCorison, Dir & Librn
Holdings: Cat Maps Pix Slides
Notes: About 90,000 postal cards and 60,000 stereophotographs. Arranged geographically or by subject. Postal cards date from 1893; stereos 1860-1890. Also some rare copybook covers of views, 1794-1860. Extensive slide collection.

NY —COLUMBIA UNIVERSITY

NY —COLUMBIA UNIVERSITY LIBRARIES, Rare Book & Manuscript Library, 801 Butler Library, 535 W 114 St, New York, 10027. Kenneth A Lohf, Librn
Holdings: Vols Mss
Notes: The Plimpton Collection. One of the best collections in existence. Particularly rich in American examples, but most of the old masters are well represented.

PA —FREE LIBRARY OF PHILADELPHIA, Rare Book Dept, Logan Sq, Philadelphia, 19103. Marie E Korey, Rare Book Librn
Holdings: Vols (5600) Uncat Mss
Notes: A collection of printed writing books (200), as well as the David N Carvalho Collection of examples of handwriting from the 9th to the 20th century.

PENN, WILLIAM

PA —FRIENDS HISTORICAL LIBRARY OF SWARTHMORE COLLEGE, Swarthmore, 19081. J William Frost, Dir
Holdings: Vols (31,340) Cat Mss Pix
Notes: Comprehensive collection of writings by and about the founder of Pennsylvania, exponent of Friends' teachings and writer on social and political philosophy.

PENN FAMILY

PA —HISTORICAL SOCIETY OF PENNSYLVANIA, Library, 1300 Locust St, Philadelphia, 19107. David Fraser, Librn
Holdings: Vols (230,000) Mss Maps Pix Microforms
Notes: Incl over 14,000,000 ms pieces. The Library Company of Philadelphia mss are on deposit with the Historical Society of Pennsylvania. Many of the Society's rare books are on deposit with the Library Company. The Society maintains the collections of the Genealogicl Society of Pennsylvania, incl some 20,000 printed genealogies, original mss, family, church, and civil records.

PENN VIRGINIA CORPORATION

DE —HAGLEY MUSEUM AND LIBRARY, Eleutherian Mills-Hagley Foundation Inc, PO Box 3630, Greenville, 19807. Richmond D Williams, Dir; Heddy A Richter, Imprints Librn
Notes: Westmoreland Coal Company records (1854-1982; 350 cubic feet) document the history of the nation's oldest bituminous coal mining company which operated in the Connellsville, Pa area (1880-89) and southern West Virginia (1906-56). Penn Virginia Corporation records (1864-1970; 120 cubic feet) document the history of one of Virginia's most significant coal mining companies. Also, Saint Clair Coal Company (1895-1930; 15 cubic feet). Records document the history of an important Schuylkill County, Pa anthracite coal producer. The colleciton incl minute books, financial records and photographs.

PENNELL, ELIZABETH ROBBINS, 1855-1936

DC —LIBRARY OF CONGRESS, Rare Book & Special Collections Div, Washington, 20540. William Matheson, Chief
Notes: Personal library of Elizabeth Robins Pennell, magazine journalist and wife of artist Joseph Pennell, incl about 430 cookbooks in English, French and German 16th to 18th century, described in Mrs. Pennell's *My Cookery Books* (Boston, Houghton-Mifflin, 1903).
See also entry under Gastronomy

DC —LIBRARY OF CONGRESS, Prints & Photographs Div, Washington, 20540.
Notes: Graphic art, papers, and cookbook collection of Joseph and Elizabeth Pennell. Cookbooks are in the Rare Books Division.

PENNELL, JOSEPH JUDD

DC —LIBRARY OF CONGRESS, Prints & Photographs Div, Washington, 20540.
Notes: Graphic art, papers, and cookbook

PENNELL, JOSEPH JUDD (cont.)

collection of Joseph and Elizabeth Pennell.
Cookbooks are in the Rare Books Division.
KS —UNIVERSITY OF KANSAS, Kenneth
Spencer Research Library, Kansas
Collection, Lawrence, 66045. Sheryl K
Williams, Cur
Holdings: Cat Pix
Notes: The J J Pennell Collection. Joseph
Judd Pennell (1866-1922) was a commercial
photographer living and working in Junction
City, Kansas from 1888 to 1922. This
collection of more than 30,000 glass
negatives and nearly 6000 prints is a
pictorial record of Junction City, Kansas and
nearby Ft Riley. The residents of Junction
City have been photographed in their various
business, professional, social, and cultural
activities, while the army post, Fort Riley,
has been documented as a cavalry and light
artillery post, as well as an important
military post during the First World war and
after. The various ethnic groups which made
up the population of Junction City, whites,
blacks, and Mexican-Americans are
represented in the collection. Pennell's day
books accompany the photographic
collection.

PENNSYLVANIA

PA —LAUGHLIN MEMORIAL LIBRARY,
11 & Maplewood Sts, Ambridge, 15003.
Alyce Grubbs, Dir
Holdings: Vols 1250 Cat Maps Microforms
Notes: Pennsylvania Collection incl 1000
pamphlets (partially cataloged), local
newspaper, 1904-date (microfilm), and
material on Beaver County history. Separate
catalog.
PA —PENNSYLVANIA GEOLOGICAL
SOCIETY, Library, 916 Executive House,
Second & Chestnut Sts, Harrisburg, 17120.
Sandra Blust, Librn
Holdings: Vols (7600) Cat Mss Maps
Microforms
Notes: Incl 20,000 aerial photographs and
250,000 maps.
PA —FREE LIBRARY OF PHILADELPHIA,
Social Science and History Dept, Map
Collection, Logan Sq, Philadelphia, 19103.
Holdings: Vols (30,000) Cat Mss Maps
Notes: Map collection incl atlases, maps,
pamphlets, and aerial views. Incl a
representative collection of early atlases
(1534-1827). The collection emphasizes the
Philadelphia, Pennsylvania and Delaware
Valley areas in particular and the eastern
seaboard in general. Low altitude oblique
aerial photographs have been transferred to
the Print and Picture Dept; high altitude
vertical aerial photographs have been
retained; some volumes and pamphlets
reassigned within the Social Science and
History Dept.
PA —UNIVERSITY OF PITTSBURGH,
Library, Graduate School of Public and
International Affairs, Forbes Quadrangle, 1st
floor West, Pittsburgh, 15260. Nicholas C
Caruso, Librn
Holdings: Vols (80,000) Cat
Budget: ($150,000)
Notes: The library attempts to collect as
many national economic and social
development plans as possible from the
developing countries of the world. It also
holds city, regional and state plans for
Pennsylvania, particularly the 9
southwestern counties of Pennsylvania.
PA —SCRANTON PUBLIC LIBRARY, Local
History & Genealogical Section, Vine St &
Washington Ave, Scranton, 18503. Bettina
Manzo, Librn
Holdings: Vols (2000) Cat Mss Maps Pix
Microforms
Notes: Emphasis on northeastern
Pennsylvania. Also, historical materials
about local churches, schools, businesses,
architecture, clubs and organizations,
demographics, geography and geology, and
biographies.
PA —PENNSYLVANIA STATE
UNIVERSITY, Fred Lewis Pattee Library,
Special Collections Dept, University Park,

16802. Charles Mann, Chief, Special
Collections
Holdings: Vols (122,533) Cat Mss Maps Pix
Slides Phonorecords Audiotapes Videotapes
16mm Films Microforms
Budget: ($37,000)
Notes: Special Collections and Rare Books
includes several collections described
separately. The holdings are particularly
strong in literature, the 18th century,
aeronautics, facsimiles, atlases, 19th century
illustrated works on birds, botany and
traveller's views. Special strengths are
Emblem Books, Utopias, Fantastic Fiction,
Australiana, Fine Presses, Labor Archives,
Landscape Architecture, Pennsylvaniana.
These collections are strengthened by
parallel holdings in the open stacks. It also
includes the collections of the Penn State
Room. Several mimeographed lists are
available. Audiotapes are listed in Voices
and Events, A Catalog of Audio Tapes
(Pennsylvania State University Libraries,
1975), 45 pp.

PENNSYLVANIA—DESCRIPTION AND TRAVEL

PA —UNIVERSITY OF PITTSBURGH,
Darlington Memorial Library, Special
Collections, 601 Cathedral of Learning,
Pittsburgh, 15260. Dennis Lambert,
Darlington Librn
Holdings: Vols (17,000) Cat Mss Maps Pix
Notes: The Darlington Collection is
especially rich in American history of the
colonial period, the French and Indian war,
the Revolution and the War of 1812 with
geographical emphasis on Western
Pennsylvania and Ohio Valley history to
1870 and on Pittsburgh history to 1900.
Indian treaties, captivity accounts, US and
Pennsylvania travel and description and
early Americn fiction and prose are
represented. A partial guide to the
Darlington Manuscript Collections is
available by writing for Darlington Memorial
Library: A Descriptive Checklist of its
Manuscripts Collections, University of
Pittsburgh Bibliographic Series 5, 1969.
Noncirculating.

PENNSYLVANIA—DESCRIPTION AND TRAVEL—VIEWS

PA —PENNSYLVANIA STATE
UNIVERSITY, Fred Lewis Pattee Library,
Special Collections Dept, University Park,
16802. Charles Mann, Chief, Special
Collections
Holdings: Pix
Budget: ($37,000)
Notes: City views of Pennsylvania.

PENNSYLVANIA—GENEALOGY

FL —ORLANDO PUBLIC LIBRARY, Local
History & Genealogy Dept, 100 Block of
Central Ave, Orlando, 32806. Eileen B
Willis, Librn
Notes: Strong collection in local genealogy
materials on Mass, NY, Va, Ga, and Florida.
Contains exceptional holdings on all New
England States, Penn, and NJ.
See also entry under Genealogy -
Collections.
NY —ONONDAGA COUNTY PUBLIC
LIBARY, Local History and Genealogy
Dept, 335 Montgomery St, Syracuse, 13202.
Gerald James Parsons, Head
Holdings: Vols (30,000) Cat Mss Maps Pix
Microforms
Budget: ($12,000)
Notes: Collection of local history and
genealogy covers primarily Syracuse,
Onondaga County, New York State and the
northeast, ie, New England, New Jersey and
Pennsylvania.
PA —CARNEGIE FREE LIBRARY, Resource
& Research Center for Beaver County &
Local History, 1301 Seventh Ave, Beaver
Falls, 15010. Vivian C McLaughlin, Dir
Holdings: Vols (2000) Cat Maps Pix
Microforms
Budget: ($7000)
Notes: Local and Pennsylvania history; also

bordering states. Acquire every possible
history and atlas of Pennsylvania. Separate
catalog. Affiliated with Carnegie Library;
project of Beaver County commissioners and
Beaver Falls public school system. Also
Beaver County newspapers on microfilm
complete Beaver County census.
PA —BUCKS COUNTY HISTORICAL
SOCIETY, Spruance Library, Pine &
Ashland Sts, Doylestown, 18901. Terry A
McNealy, Librn
Holdings: Vols (18,000) Cat Mss Maps Pix
Slides Microforms
Notes: Pennsylvania history and genealogy,
especially the Bucks County area.
PA —EASTON AREA PUBLIC LIBRARY,
Reference & Special Collections, Sixth &
Church Sts, Easton, 18042. Guentin de
Streel, Head
Holdings: Vols (10,000) Cat Mss Maps Pix
Microforms
Budget: ($800)
Notes: The Henry Marx Historical and
Genealogical Collection, especially
Northampton County. Incl microfilmed
newspapers, 1799-date. Reference only.
PA —CAMBRIA COUNTY HISTORICAL
SOCIETY MUSEUM & LIBRARY, 521 W
High St, Edensburg, 15931. Sara C
Leishman, Cur
Holdings: Vols (2000) Cat Maps
PA —EMMAUS PUBLIC LIBRARY, Ridge
and Main Sts, Emmaus, 18049. Elaine B
Timbers, Librn
Holdings: Vols 180 Cat
Notes: Given by local Shelter House Society,
a group devoted to the preservation of the
historical log-cabin called the Shelter House.
Many members are from long-time local
families, whose books, pamphlets, etc
became the nucleus of this collection.
PA —LANCASTER MENNONITE
CONFERENCE HISTORICAL SOCIETY
LIBRARY, 2215 Millstream Rd, Lancaster,
17602. Lloyd Zeager, Librn; David J
Smucker, Genealogist
Holdings: Vols (55,000) Cat Mss Maps Pix
Microforms
Budget: ($3186)
Notes: Specializes in southeastern
Pennsylvania genealogy and history.
Genealogical card file of over 200,000 cards.
Cemetery records for all Lancaster County,
Pa, cemeteries. Periodical index compiled
from historical, genealogical, and theological
periodicals. Census records on microfilm for
1790, 1800, 1810, 1820, 1830, 1840, 1850,
1860, 1870, 1880, 1900, and 1910 for
Lancaster County and incomplete census
records for other southeastern Pennsylvania
counties. Complete 1850 for Pennsylvania.
PA —SNYDER COUNTY HISTORICAL
SOCIETY, Library, 30 E Market St, PO Box
276, Middleburg, 17842. Kathryn G Gift,
Librn
Holdings: Vols 200 Cat Microforms
Notes: Unpublished notes on genealogy by
Dr C H Fisher, given to the Society some
years ago. They incl genealogies of many
families in the Snyder (Union-
Northumberland) County area.
PA —OIL CITY LIBRARY, 2 Central Ave, Oil
City, 16301. Richard A Speer, Dir
Holdings: Vols 600 Cat Pix Microforms
PA —BALCH INSTITUTE FOR ETHNIC
STUDIES, Library, 18 S Seventh St,
Philadelphia, 19106. R Joseph Anderson,
Library Dir
Notes: The Amandus Johnson Collection of
his papers, incl biographical material on 20th
century Swedish-Americans, records from
the American Swedish Historical Museum in
South Philadelphia, and source documents
on the early Swedish settlement of the
Delaware Valley, and historical writings
based on these documents.
PA —HISTORICAL SOCIETY OF
PENNSYLVANIA, Library, 1300 Locust St,
Philadelphia, 19107. David Fraser, Librn
Holdings: Vols (230,000) Mss Maps Pix
Microforms
Notes: Incl over 14,000,000 ms pieces. The
Library Company of Philadelphia mss are on
deposit with the Historical Society of
Pennsylvania. Many of the Society's rare
books are on deposit with the Library

PENNSYLVANIA—GENEALOGY (cont.)

Company. The Society maintains the collections of the 20,000 printed genealogies, original mss, family, church, and civil records.

PA —CARNEGIE LIBRARY OF PITTSBURGH, Pennsylvania Div, 4400 Forbes Ave, Pittsburgh, 15213. Maria Zini, Head
Holdings: Vols (24,000) Cat Mss Maps Pix Microforms
Budget: ($6000)
Notes: Collection contains at least one history of each county; historical atlases; biography; church histories; sociological and economic studies; journals of the General Assembly; state documents. The Pittsburgh section of the collection includes Pittsburgh directories 1815-date; newspapers on microfilm 1786-date, 30,000 photographs relating to Pittsburgh. A 65-drawer clipping collection supplements the published works. The genealogical materials (approx 5000 vols) incl individual family histories; regional and general genealogical works; periodicals; US. Census enumerations for Pennsylvania 1790-1910 (microfilm); indexes to biography, deaths and marriages. Separate catalog to entire Division. Collection is reference only.

PA —HISTORICAL SOCIETY OF WESTERN PENNSYLVANIA, 4338 Bigelow Blvd, Pittsburgh, 15213. Helen M Wilson, Librn
Holdings: Vols (28,850) Cat Mss Maps Pix Slides Microforms
Budget: ($3000)
Notes: Western Pennsylvania emphasis. Mss: 487 ft, 875 bound vols. Collection incl name index from Western Pennsylvania Genealogical Society. Genealogical collection, 1100 vols. For archives description, see John W Harpster, "The Manuscript and Miscellaneous Collections of the Historical Society of Western Pennsylvania, A Preliminary Guide," *Western Pennsylvania Historical Society*, vol 49, pp 67-78, 345-358 (1966); vol 50, pp 161-170, 256-268, 339-359 (1967); vol 51, pp 80-97, 198-208, 309-326, 417-430 (1968); vol 52, pp 89-98, 293-310 (1969); vol 53, pp 90-104, 199-206, 305-315, 400-407 (1970); vol 54, pp 88- 109, 224-243, 327-339, 430- 441 (1971); vol 55, pp 103-116, 203-211 (1972). Guide being revised and indexed.

PA —SCRANTON PUBLIC LIBRARY, Local History & Genealogical Section, Vine St & Washington Ave, Scranton, 18503. Bettina Manzo, Librn
Holdings: Vols (2000) Cat Mss Maps Pix Microforms
Notes: Emphasis on northeastern Pennsylvania. Also, historical materials about local churches, schools, businesses, architecture, clubs and organizations, demographics, geography and geology, and biographies.

PA —FRIENDS HISTORICAL LIBRARY OF SWARTHMORE COLLEGE, Swarthmore, 19081. J William Frost, Dir
Holdings: Vols (35,000) Cat Mss Microforms
Notes: As an official depository for the records of Philadelphia and Baltimore Yearly Meetings, the library holds either in the original manuscript or on microfilm the largest collection in the world of Quaker meeting archives, incl some records of Ohio and Illinois Yearly Meetings (Hicksite), and microfilm copies of minutes and registers of many meetings in New England, New York, North Carolina, Indiana, and Great Britain. Many, but by no means all, Friends meetings are incl in the *William Wade Hinshaw Index to Quaker Meeting Records*, a card index to genealogical data from the records of 307 Quaker meetings in the US, which supplements Hinshaw's well-known *Encyclopedia of American Quaker Genealogy*. Among the library's more than 250 mss collections are the papers of many Quaker families.

PA —UNIONTOWN PUBLIC LIBRARY, 24 Jefferson St, Uniontown, 15401. Barry R Laine, Head Librn
Holdings: Vols 100 Cat Mss Maps Pix
Notes: Especially Fayette County region history and genealogy.

PA —CHESTER COUNTY HISTORICAL SOCIETY, 225 N High St, West Chester, 19380. Rosemary B Philips, Librn; Jack McCarthy, Archivist; Laurie Rofini, Asst Archivist
Holdings: Cat Mss Maps Pix Microforms
Notes: Focus on Chester Countians. Very inclusive for Chester County. 100,000 clippings go back to 1808; 80,000 mss back to William Penn charters.

PA —JAMES V BROWN LIBRARY, 19 E Fourth St, Williamsport, 17701. Janice Trapp, Dir
Holdings: Vols 2000 Cat Pix Microforms
Notes: Pennsylvania history and genealogy, with emphasis on Lycoming County and Williamsport. Incl local newspapers, 1807-date (separate index, 1807-1900; selectively indexed, 1900-date); Pennsylvania historical and genealogical periodicals and publications of historical societies (indexed).

TN —CHATTANOOGA-HAMILTON COUNTY, Bicentennial Library, Local History and Genealogy Dept, 1001 Broad St, Chattanooga, 37402. Clara W Swann, Librn
Holdings: Vols (24,561) Cat Mss Maps Pix Microforms
Budget: ($7000)
Notes: Emphasis on southern states, and eastern Tennessee counties, with considerable material on New England, Pennsylvania, and Maryland genealogy and history. Census records on microfilm. Special indexes and clipping files. Noncirculating.

PENNSYLVANIA—GOVERNMENT PUBLICATIONS

PA —PENNSYLVANIA STATE UNIVERSITY, Fred Lewis Pattee Library, Documents Section, University Park, 16802. Diane H Smith, Head
Notes: Depository for US Government publications; depository for Pennsylvania documents; collect United Nations and related international and intergovernmental organization publications; selected publications from Australia, Great Britain, including Parliamentary Papers; census materials; a large microform collection, including Department of Energy (formerly ERDA, AEC), Congressional publications, Patents, OAS, UN. Incl 900,000 documents. Pennsylvania books are uncataloged.

PENNSYLVANIA—HISTORY

AL —BIRMINGHAM PUBLIC LIBRARY, Southern History Dept, 2020 Seventh Ave N, Birmingham, 35203. Virginia K Scott, Head
Holdings: Vols (50,000) Cat Microforms
Notes: History and social conditions of the southeastern US. Significant holdings on border areas such as Texas, Pennsylvania, Maryland. Strong genealogical collection with emphasis on the southeastern area of the US. Very strong Civil War Collection and early southern travel accounts. See George Ray Stewart, *The Special Collections in the Birmingham Public Library*. MA Thesis, Emory University, 1971.

DE —UNIVERSITY OF DELAWARE, Hugh M Morris Library, S College Ave, Newark, 19711. T Stuart Dick, Special Collections
Holdings: // Mss
Notes: Three collections: (1) Personal and business letters and receipts of the Albertson family a Quaker lumber and lime merchants (1782-1862) residing in Plymouth, Montgomery Co, Pa. Included are many letters concerning the Plymouth RR and rules and regulations for its administration. (2) Correspondence (1782-1832) relating to all phases of David Lenox's career subsequent to the Revolution, ie, land speculation, duties in the Whiskey Rebellion, executorship of the estate of John Lukens, his banking career, household receipts and settlement of his estate. (3) The Lukens Family papers cover the years 1745-1789 concerning John Lukens, Surveyor-General of Pennsylvania and Delaware, 1761-1776; of Pennsylvania, 1781-1789. Included are such official papers as deputy surveyors'

indentures andwarrants, maps, survey returns for Pennsylvania and Delaware.

MD —JOHNS HOPKINS UNIVERSITY, Milton S Eisenhower Library, Charles & 34 Sts, Baltimore, 21218. Ann S Gwyn, Assistant Dir for Special Collections

NJ —GLASSBORO STATE COLLEGE, Savitz Library, Stewart Room, Glassboro, 08028. Clara Kirner, Special Collection Librn
Holdings: Cat Mss Maps Pix
Notes: Emphasis on Eastern Pennsylvania and Philadelphia in the Colonial Period. Mss incl papers of Frank H Stewart Electric Co (circa 1900-1925). Diary of Jacob Elfreth.

NY —COLUMBIA UNIVERSITY LIBRARIES, Rare Book & Manuscript Library, 801 Butler Library, 535 W 114 St, New York, 10027. Kenneth A Lohf, Librn
Holdings: Mss
Notes: Consisting of music mss of the Ephrata Community, by the founder of the community, Conrad Beissel. Restricted use.

NY —ONONDAGA COUNTY PUBLIC LIBARY, Local History and Genealogy Dept, 335 Montgomery St, Syracuse, 13202. Gerald James Parsons, Head
Holdings: Vols (30,000) Cat Mss Maps Pix Microforms
Budget: ($12,000)
Notes: Collection of local history and genealogy covers primarily Syracuse, Onondaga County, New York State and the northeast, ie, New England, New Jersey and Pennsylvania.

PA —PARKLAND COMMUNITY LIBRARY, Allentown, 4422 Walbert Ave, Orefield, 18104. Marjorie Stevens, Library Dir
Holdings: Vols 241 Cat Slides
Notes: This library is 10 years old with just the beginnings of a special emphasis collection on Lehigh County.

PA —LAUGHLIN MEMORIAL LIBRARY, 11 & Maplewood Sts, Ambridge, 15003. Alyce Grubbs, Dir
Holdings: Vols 1250 Cat Maps Microforms
Notes: Pennsylvania Collection incl 1000 pamphlets (partially cataloged), local newspaper, 1904-date (microfilm), and material on Beaver County history. Separate catalog.

PA —CARNEGIE FREE LIBRARY, Resource & Research Center for Beaver County & Local History, 1301 Seventh Ave, Beaver Falls, 15010. Vivian C McLaughlin, Dir
Holdings: Vols (2000) Cat Maps Pix Microforms
Budget: ($7000)
Notes: Local and Pennsylvania history; also bordering states. Acquire every possible history and atlas of Pennsylvania. Separate catalog. Affiliated with Carnegie Library; project of Beaver County commissioners and Beaver Falls public school system. Also Beaver County newspapers on microfilm complete Beaver County census.

PA —SHAW PUBLIC LIBRARY, 6 S Frank St, Clearfield, 16830. Margaret Barton, Librn
Holdings: Vols 1500 Cat Maps
Notes: Pennsylvania and Clearfield County.

PA —BUCKS COUNTY HISTORICAL SOCIETY, Spruance Library, Pine & Ashland Sts, Doylestown, 18901. Terry A McNealy, Librn
Holdings: Vols (18,000) Cat Mss Maps Pix Slides Microforms
Notes: Pennsylvania history and genealogy, especially the Bucks County area.

PA —PENNSYLVANIA STATE UNIVERSITY, Du Bois Campus Library, College Place, Du Bois, 15801. Karen Fuller, Librn
Holdings: Cat Maps
Notes: Extensive collection incl local and county history emphasis.

PA —EASTON AREA PUBLIC LIBRARY, Reference & Special Collections, Sixth & Church Sts, Easton, 18042. Guentin de Streel, Head
Holdings: Vols (10,000) Cat Mss Maps Pix Microforms
Budget: ($800)
Notes: The Henry Marx Historical and Genealogical Collection, especially Northampton County. Incl microfilmed newspapers, 1799-date. Reference only.

PENNSYLVANIA—HISTORY (cont.)

PA —CAMBRIA COUNTY HISTORICAL SOCIETY MUSEUM & LIBRARY, 521 W High St, Edensburg, 15931. Sara C Leishman, Cur
Holdings: Vols (2000) Cat Maps

PA —EMMAUS PUBLIC LIBRARY, Ridge and Main Sts, Emmaus, 18049. Elaine B Timbers, Librn
Holdings: Vols 180 Cat
Notes: Given by local Shelter House Society, a group devoted to the preservation of the historical log-cabin called the Shelter House. Many members are from long-time local families, whose books, pamphlets, etc became the nucleus of this collection.

PA —PENNSYLVANIA HISTORICAL & MUSEUM COMMISSION, Ephrata Cloister, 632 W Main St, Ephrata, 17522. James Lewars, Adminr; John L Kraft, Librn
Holdings: Vols (150) Cat Mss Maps Pix Slides Phonorecords
Notes: Ephrata Cloister and early Pennsylvania imprints.

PA —ERIE COUNTY HISTORICAL SOCIETY LIBRARY, 417 State St, Erie, 16501. Helen Andrews, Librn
Notes: Archives of the Sobel family papers in 24 file cases. Olds family papers in 40 Hollinger boxes and 100 collections boxes mostly dealing with real estate and attorney's papers, estates, civil suits and bankruptcies. Original research materials in 16 legal size drawers, including Pennsylvania Population Company papers, Old Erie Academy papers, Erie Street railway papers, Harry Burleigh (black singer and composer) transcripts and research papers; also four letter size drawers with old account books. Ephemeral material, pamphlets, clippings, research papers. Postcard collection of 1712 cards relating to Erie city and county. Iconographics of 11,000 glass negatives (mostly photos of Erie people). World War II and Korean War veterans, 66 vertical file drawers containing mostly newspaper clippings. Erie Newspapers, 36 titles.

PA —ADAMS COUNTY HISTORICAL SOCIETY, Drawer A, Gettysburg, 17325. Charles H Glatfelter, Dir
Holdings: Vols 50 Cat Mss Maps Pix
Notes: Emphasis on Adams County and the Gettysburg area. Strength of collection in mss, maps, and pictorial items.

PA —GREENSBURG LIBRARY, 237 S Pennsylvania Ave, Greensburg, 15601. Helen K Yockman, Librn
Holdings: Vols 1500 Cat
Notes: Separate catalog in Pennsylvania Historical Room.

PA —PENNSYLVANIA DIV OF ARCHIVES & MANUSCRIPTS, State Archives, PO Box 1026, Harris, 17108. Roland M Baumann, Chief, History & Museums
Holdings: Vols (3000) // Uncat Mss Maps Pix
Budget: ($40,000)
Notes: The Harmony Society (1785-1905), a German communistic and spiritual community, which immigrated to the US in 1805 and established their community in Harmony, Pennsylvania, moved to New Harmony, Indiana, and returned to Pennsylvania to set up the town of Economy, 20 miles north of Pittsburgh on the Ohio River. The Harmonists had a vast impact on the economy of the areas in which they lived. They were involved in agriculture, manufacturing and investing. 300,000 cu ft.

PA —ABINGTON LIBRARY SOCIETY, Jenkintown Library, York & Vista Rds, Jenkintown, 19046. Joan Greenberg, Librn
Holdings: Vols 900 Cat Maps
Notes: Emphasis on southeastern Pennsylvania.

PA —FRANKLIN & MARSHALL COLLEGE, Library, Lancaster, 17604. Kathleen J Moretto, Library Dir
Holdings: Vols (3300) Cat

PA —LIGONIER VALLEY LIBRARY ASSOCIATION, Library, 120 W Main St, Ligonier, 15658. Janet Hudson, Cur
Holdings: Vols (3800) Cat Mss Audiotapes Microforms
Notes: Have entire microfilmed contents of the *Ligonier Echo* (weekly newspaper) from Sept 1888 to the present. There is a complete cross-reference file index to the microfilm. The Pennsylvania Room also contains an obituary file. A complete bibliography of materials in the collection is being compiled.

PA —CARNEGIE FREE LIBRARY, 1507 Library Ave, McKeesport, 15132. Ruth Richards, Head Librn
Holdings: Vols 169 Cat Maps Pix
Notes: Western Pennsylvania Collection.

PA —CRAWFORD COUNTY HISTORICAL SOCIETY, Meadville Public Library, N Main St, Meadville, 16335. Robert D Ilisevich, Librn
Holdings: Vols 1500 Cat Mss Maps Pix Slides Audiotapes Microforms
Notes: History of Meadville and Crawford County, Pennsylvania. Incl 26 linear ft of mss, 750 maps, thousands of pictures, slides, audiotapes, microforms and postcards.

PA —MONTGOMERY COUNTY-NORRISTOWN PUBLIC LIBRARY, Swede & Elm Sts, Norristown, 19401. James G Gear, Exec Dir
Holdings: Vols 3000 Cat Mss Maps Pix Phonorecords Microforms
Notes: Emphasis is on Montgomery County and Norristown. Collection is retrospective and current. Local authors and publishers plus materials relating to local area are represented. Genealogies are not included in order not to duplicate the excellent collection of the Montgomery County Historical Society.

PA —OIL CITY LIBRARY, 2 Central Ave, Oil City, 16301. Richard A Speer, Dir
Holdings: Vols 600 Cat Pix Microforms

†PA —GERMAN SOCIETY OF PENNSYLVANIA, Joseph Horner Memorial Library, 611 Spring Garden St, Philadelphia, 19123.
Notes: All subjects with special emphasis on history, biography, literature (85 per cent in German); juvenile literature.

PA —HISTORICAL SOCIETY OF PENNSYLVANIA, Library, 1300 Locust St, Philadelphia, 19107. David Fraser, Librn
Holdings: Vols (230,000) Mss Maps Pix Microforms
Notes: Incl over 14,000,000 ms pieces. The Library Company of Phildelphia mss are on deposit with the Historical Society of Pennsylvania. Many of the Society's rare books are on deposit with the Library Company. The Society maintains the collections of the Genealogical Society of Pennsylvania, incl some 20,000 printed genealogies, original mss, family, church, and civil records.

PA —INDEPENDENCE NATIONAL HISTORICAL PARK, Library, 313 Walnut St, Philadelphia, 19106. David C G Dutcher, Chief Historian; Shirley A Mays, Librn
Holdings: Vols 5000 Cat Mss Videotapes Films
Budget: ($25,000)
Notes: Emphasis on Pennsylvania and Philadelphia, incl arts and crafts to early 19th century. Incl some 2000 ms pieces; 25, 000 pictures; 3000 slides; 600 microfilm reels. No photocopying.

PA —PENNSYLVANIA HORTICULTURAL SOCIETY, Library, 325 Walnut St, Philadelphia, 19106. Mary Lou Wolfe, Librn
Notes: Publications: *Selected Books From the Library of the Pennsylvania Horticultural Society*, 1976; *From Seed to Flower, Philadelphia 1681-1876*, 1976.

PA —PHILADELPHIA MARITIME MUSEUM, Library, 321 Chestnut St, Philadelphia, 19106. Dorothy H Mueller, Librn
Holdings: Vols (8000) Cat Mss Maps Pix Slides 16mm Films
Notes: Maritime history of Bay and River Delaware and of the port of Philadelphia. Includes shipbuilding and shipbuilders on the Delaware River, mercantile activity, recreational activity, maritime-related organizations, institutions and people, development of Philadelphia as a port, vessel registers 1878-1970s. Artifacts & prints.

PA —UNION LEAGUE OF PHILADELPHIA, Library, 140 S Broad St, Philadelphia, 19102. James G Mundy Jr, Librn
Holdings: Vols (23,000) Cat Mss Pix
Notes: Emphasis on Civil War, Philadelphia, Philadelphia history and biographies.

PA —CARNEGIE LIBRARY OF PITTSBURGH, Pennsylvania Div, 4400 Forbes Ave, Pittsburgh, 15213. Maria Zini, Head
Holdings: Vols (24,000) Cat Mss Maps Pix Microforms
Budget: ($6000)
Notes: Collection contains at least one history of each county; historical atlases; biography; church histories; sociological and economic studies; journals of the General Assembly; state documents. The Pittsburgh section of the collection includes Pittsburgh directories 1815-date; newspapers on microfilm 1786-date, 30,000 photographs relating to Pittsburgh. A 65-drawer clipping collection supplements the published works. The genealogical materials (approx 5000 vols) incl individual family histories; regional and general genealogical works; periodicals; US. Census enumerations for Pennsylvania 1790-1910 (microfilm); indexes to biography, deaths and marriages. Separate catalog to entire Division. Collection is reference only.

PA —HISTORICAL SOCIETY OF WESTERN PENNSYLVANIA, 4338 Bigelow Blvd, Pittsburgh, 15213. Helen M Wilson, Librn
Holdings: Vols (28,850) Cat Mss Maps Pix Slides Microforms
Budget: $3000
Notes: Western Pennsylvania emphasis. Mss: 487 ft, 875 bound vols. Collection incl name index from Western Pennsylvania Genealogical Society. Genealogical collection, 1100 vols. For archives description, see John W Harpster, "The Manuscript and Miscellaneous Collections of the Historical Society of Western Pennsylvania, A Preliminary Guide," *Western Pennsylvania Historical Society*, vol 49, pp 67-78, 345-358 (1966); vol 50, pp 161-170, 256-268, 339-359 (1967); vol 51, pp 80-97, 198-208, 309-326, 417-430 (1968); vol 52, pp 89-98, 293-310 (1969); vol 53, pp 90-104, 199-206, 305-315, 400-407 (1970); vol 54, pp 88- 109, 224-243, 327-339, 430-441 (1971); vol 55, pp 103-116, 203-211 (1972). Guide being revised and indexed.

PA —UNIVERSITY OF PITTSBURGH, Hillman Library, Archives of Industrial Society, 363 Hillman Library, Pittsburgh, 15260. Frank A Zabrosky, Cur
Holdings: Mss Maps Pix Slides Audiotapes Microforms
Notes: Broad subject area covers the history of urban, industrial society since ca 1850. Incl primary source material from Pittsburgh, Western Pennsylvania and West Virginia areas. Comprised of business, industrial, church, ethnic, labor, fraternal and social organization, political party, political/social movement,and city government records and private papers of individuals and families. Primarily a manuscript collection for graduate and post-graduate research. Unique collection: Allegheny, Pa, city records, 3000 vols, incl tax assessment records (1840-1907); Pittsburgh schools system, 150 vols, incl minutes, pupil enrollment records; voter registration records for Allegheny County, and Pittsburgh, 1935-1960; election return books, Allegheny County and Pittsburgh, 1926 date; Pittsburgh and Lake Erie Railroad and Photograph Collection; Pittsburgh City Photographers Photo Collection;1000 city directories for US cities, 1955-71; and political papers of US Congressmen Corbett, Fulton and Holland. Archives of the national headquarters, districts and locals of the United Electrical, Radio and Machine Workers of America (UE); printed and manuscript material on Blacks and ethnic groups in Pittsburgh.

PA —UNIVERSITY OF PITTSBURGH, Darlington Memorial Library, Special Collections, 601 Cathedral of Learning, Pittsburgh, 15260. Dennis Lambert, Darlington Librn
Holdings: Vols (17,000) Cat Mss Maps Pix
Notes: The Darlington Collection is

PENNSYLVANIA—HISTORY (cont.)

especially rich in American history of the colonial period, the French and Indian War, the Revolution, and the War of 1812 with geographical emphasis on Western Pennsylvania and Ohio Valley history to 1870 and on Pittsburgh history to 1900. Indian treaties, captivity accounts, US and Pennsylvania travel and description, and early American fiction and prose are represented. A partial guide to the Darlington Manuscript Collections is available by writing for *Darlington Memorial Library: A Descriptive Checklist of its Manuscript Collections,* University of Pittsburgh Bibliographic Series 5, 1969. Noncirculating.

PA —ROSEMONT COLLEGE, Gertrude Kistler Memorial Library, Rosemont, 19010. Sister Mary Dennis Lynch, SHCJ, Dir of Library Services
Holdings: Cat Maps Microforms

PA —SCRANTON PUBLIC LIBRARY, Local History & Genealogy Section, Vine St & Washington Ave, Scranton, 18503. Bettina Manzo, Librn
Holdings: Vols (2000) Cat Mss Maps Pix Microforms
Notes: Emphasis on northeastern Pennsylvania. Also, historical materials about local churces, schools, businesses, architecture, clubs and organizations, demographics, geography and geology, and biographies.

PA —FRIENDS HISTORICAL LIBRARY OF SWARTHMORE COLLEGE, Swarthmore, 19081. J William Frost, Dir
Holdings: Vols (35,000) Cat Mss Pix Microforms
Notes: Library's collection contain information on the history and doctrine of the Society of Friends, Quaker contributions to literature, science, business, education, and government, plus their reform efforts in peace, Indian rights, women's rights, and abolition of slavery. As an official depository of the records of the Philadelphia Yearly Meeting, the library holds, either in the original manuscript or on microfilm, records of Friends meetings in Pennsylvania. Among the over 250 mss collections are several which concern Pennsylvania Quaker leaders, families, and organizations.

PA —UNIONTOWN PUBLIC LIBRARY, 24 Jefferson St, Uniontown, 15401. Barry R Laine, Head Librn
Holdings: Vols 100 Cat Mss Maps Pix
Notes: Especially Fayette County region history and genealogy.

PA —PENNSYLVANIA STATE UNIVERSITY, Fred Lewis Pattee Library, Special Collections Dept, University Park, 16802. Charles Mann, Chief, Special Collections
Holdings: Vols (1976) Cat Mss Pix Slides
Budget: ($37,000)
Notes: Includes the Beaver Collection (576 vols) in honor of James Beaver, Governor of Pennsylvania, mostly county histories, atlases and Regimental Civil War histories; John M Read Pamphlets (1400 titles), 1830-1890, relating to canals, railroads and civil law. No photocopying.

PA —WASHINGTON AND JEFFERSON COLLEGE, Library, Washington, 15301. Robert E Connell, Librn
Holdings: Vols 2100 Cat Mss Maps Pix
Notes: A general subject and author card catalog has been prepared for the ms collection. Published description of the collection appears in: Pennsylvania, Historical and Museum Commission, *Historical Manuscript Depositories in Pennsylvania* (Harrisburg, 1965), compiled by Irwin Richman. Incl are materials concerning the "Westward movement"--letters, land grants, etc. Much on the Revolutionary War, the "Whiskey Rebellion" of 1794. Many other small collections of mss, some containing American Indian and Western Pennsylvania history.

PA —CHESTER COUNTY HISTORICAL SOCIETY, 225 N High St, West Chester, 19380. Rosemary B Philips, Librn; Jack

McCarthy, Archivist; Laurie Rofini, Asst Archivist
Holdings: Cat Mss Maps Pix Microforms
Notes: Emphasis on West Chester region. Incl 80,000 mss; 100,000 clippings and 100,000 pieces of vertical file materials. Chester County Archives with government records of county government, 1681 to 20th century. Albert Cook Myers collection of William Penn books, pamphlets, mss and Penn history; early Chester County postal history (Robert Brinton collection).

PA —JAMES V BROWN LIBRARY, 19 E Fourth St, Williamsport, 17701. Janice Trapp, Dir
Holdings: Vols 2000 Cat Pix Microforms
Notes: Pennsylvania history and genealogy, with emphasis on Lycoming County and Williamsport. Incl local newspapers, 1807-date (separate index, 1807-1900; selectively indexed, 1900-date); Pennsylvania historical and genealogical periodicals and publications of historical societies (indexed).

RI —BROWN UNIVERSITY, John Hay Library, 20 Prospect St, Providence, 02912. Mark N Brown, Cur Mss
Holdings: // Mss
Notes: Solomon Drowne papers. He was a physician and Professor of Botany at Brown, Class of 1773. Mss incl accounts, invoices, receipts; originals and copies of prose and poetry; notes of Dr Drowne; sketches and valentines; political, legal, and military documents; and ships' papers. Subjects incl Colonial and Revolutionary history of Rhode Island and Brown University; medicine and botany 1770-1834; the early history of Morgantown, Virginia; Union, Pennsylvania; and Marietta, Ohio, business and trade in the Colonial period; and the Continental Congress. Correspondence with most persons of importance in his time.

TN —CHATTANOOGA-HAMILTON COUNTY, Bicentennial Library, Local History and Genealogy Dept, 1001 Broad St, Chattanooga, 37402. Clara W Swann, Librn
Holdings: Vols (24,561) Cat Mss Maps Pix Microforms
Budget: ($7000)
Notes: Emphasis on southern states, and eastern Tennessee counties, with considerable material on New England, Pennsylvania, and Maryland genealogy and history. Census records on microfilm. Special indexes and clipping files. Noncirculating.

VA —UNIVERSITY OF VIRGINIA, Alderman Library, Charlottesville, 22901.
Holdings: Mss
Notes: Papers of Gen John Forbes, 1757-1759, on operations against the French at Fort Duquesne (Pittsburgh).

PENNSYLVANIA—HISTORY—INSURRECTION OF 1794 see Whiskey Insurrection, 1794

PENNSYLVANIA—IMPRINTS

PA —PENNSYLVANIA HISTORICAL & MUSEUM COMMISSION, Ephrata Cloister, 632 W Main St, Ephrata, 17522. James Lewars, Adminr; John L Kraft, Librn
Holdings: Vols (150) Cat Mss Maps Pix Slides Phonorecords
Notes: Ephrata Cloister and early Pennsylvania imprints.

PA —JUNIATA COLLEGE LIBRARY, Huntingdon, 16652. David Eyman, Dir
Holdings: Vols 5000 // Cat Mss
Notes: Early Pennsylvania imprints, many in German. Large collection of imprints from Christopher Sauer's press. Early Brethren and other German sectarian (Schwenkfelders, Anabaptists) tracts from Pennsylvania and Europe. Several of the collections have been described in *American German Review* (1941), *Pennsylvania History* (1940, 1959), and *Pennsylvania Magazine* (1943).

PA —LIBRARY COMPANY OF PHILADELPHIA, 1314 Locust St, Philadelphia, 19107. Edwin Wolf II, Librn; Kenneth Finkel, Cur of Prints
Holdings: Vols (400,000) Cat Maps
Budget: ($25,000)
Notes: Any book, pamphlet or broadside

printed in or relating to Pennsylvania history, to 1820. Along with the Historical Society of Pennsylvania, the major collection of early Pennsylvania imprints and related books.

PA —PENNSYLVANIA HORTICULTURAL SOCIETY, Library, 325 Walnut St, Philadelphia, 19106. Mary Lou Wolfe, Librn
Holdings: Vols (200) Cat Pix Slides
Notes: Books about horticulture published by Pennsylvanians, about Pennsylvania, or which bear a Philadelphia imprint. Descriptive catalog which highlights the collection: *From Seed to Flower: Philadelphia 1681-1876; A Horticultural Point of View* (Philadelphia: Pennsylvania Horticultural Society, 1976).

PA —PENNSYLVANIA STATE UNIVERSITY, Fred Lewis Pattee Library, Special Collections Dept, University Park, 16802. Charles Mann, Chief, Special Collections
Holdings: Vols 2922 Cat
Budget: ($37,000)
Notes: Pre-1840 imprints; includes much Pennsylvania German material; at this time (1978) there are 900 additional imprints uncataloged. No photocopying.

PENNSYLVANIA—INDUSTRIES

DE —HAGLEY MUSEUM AND LIBRARY, Eleutherian Mills-Hagley Foundation Inc, PO Box 3630, Greenville, 19807. Richmond D Williams, Dir; Heddy A Richter, Imprints Librn
Notes: Westmoreland Coal Company records (1854-1982; 350 cubic feet) document the history of the nation's oldest bituminous coal mining company which operated in the Connellsville, Pa area (1880-89) and southern West Virginia (1906-56). Penn Virginia Corporation records (1864-1970; 120 cubic feet) document the history of one of Virginia's most significant coal mining companies. Also, Saint Clair Coal Company (1895-1930; 15 cubic feet). Records document the history of an important Schuylkill County, Pa anthracite coal producer. The colleciton incl minute books, financial records and photographs.

PENNSYLVANIA—MAPS

DC —LIBRARY OF CONGRESS, Geography and Map Division, Washington, 20540. John A Wolter, Chief
Notes: The American Map Collection incl 167 works produced between 1750 and 1790 incl copies of *A Map of the Most Inhabited Part of Virginia* by Joshua Fry and Peter Jefferson (1755 and 1775 editions), John Montresor's *A Map of the Province of New York* (1777), William Gerard De Brahm's *A Map of South Carolina and a Part of Georgia* (1757), and *A Plan of the City of Philadelphia* (1776) by Benjamin Easburn.

PA —CARNEGIE FREE LIBRARY, Resource & Research Center for Beaver County & Local History, 1301 Seventh Ave, Beaver Falls, 15010. Vivian C McLaughlin, Dir
Holdings: Vols (2000) Cat Maps Pix Microforms
Budget: ($7000)
Notes: Local and Pennsylvania history; also bordering states. Acquire every possible history and atlas of Pennsylvania. Separate catalog. Affiliated with Carnegie Library; project of Beaver County commissioners and Beaver Falls public school system. Also Beaver County newspapers on microfilm complete Beaver County census.

PA —FREE LIBRARY OF PHILADELPHIA, Social Science and History Dept, Map Collection, Logan Sq, Philadelphia, 19103. Notes: Map collection incl atlases, maps, pamphlets, and aerial views. Incl a representative collection of early atlases (1534-1827). The collection emphasizes the Philadelphia, Pennsylvania and Delaware Valley areas in particular and the eastern seaboard in general. Low altitude oblique aerial photographs have been transferred to the Print and Picture Dept; high altitude vertical aerial photographs have been retained; some volumes and pamphlets

PENNSYLVANIA—MAPS (cont.)

reassigned within the Social Science and History Dept.

PA —PENNSYLVANIA STATE UNIVERSITY, Fred Lewis Pattee Library, Maps Section, University Park, 16802. Karl Proehl, Head
Holdings: Vols (274,000) Maps
Budget: ($3000)
Notes: Depositories for US Geological Survey topographic maps; Defense mapping agency topographic maps and nautical charts; National Ocean Survey nautical and aeronautical charts; Canadian topographic maps. Sanborn Fire Insurance maps for Pennsylvania villages and towns. 1970 and 1980 census maps for Pennsylvania counties, townships, and cities. General coverage for foreign countries-topographic and thematic maps. Map catalog by area and subdivided by subject; atlas catalog by author-title and area-subject; shelf list catalogs for maps and atlases. See *Pennsylvania Maps and Atlases in The Pennsylvania State University* Libraries, by Ruby M Miller (Pennsylvania State University Libraries, 1971. 682 pp).

PENNSYLVANIA—POLITICS AND GOVERNMENT

CT —TRINITY COLLEGE LIBRARY, 300 Summit St, Hartford, 06106. Peter J Knapp, Archivist
Holdings: Uncat Mss Pix
Notes: Late 18th and 19th century mss, letter, diaries, etc of the Curtis Family of Connecticut and New York, with emphasis on: William Edmond (1755-1838), US Congressman from Conn; Holbrook Curtis (1787-1858); William Edmond Curtis (1823-1880), Chief Justice of Superior Court of New York; Mary Ann Scovill Curtis (1831-1908); and William Edmond Curtis Jr, (1855-1923), US Asst Secy of the Treasury. Incl on basis of relation through marriage are late 18th and 19th century mss, letters and diaries of the Hiester, McLanahan and Muhlenberg Families of Pennsylvania, with emphasis on Joseph Hiester (1752-1832), US Congressman and Governor of Pennsylvania; and Andrew Gregg (1755-1835), US Congressman and Senator from Pennsylvania. 12 linear feet.

PENNSYLVANIA—RELIGION

PA —KING'S COLLEGE, D Leonard Corgan Library, 14 W Jackson St, Wilkes-Barre, 18711. Judith Tierney, Special Collections Librn
Holdings: Mss Pix
Notes: The St Stephen's Historical Files, 1813-1979, 16 linear ft. Collection focuses on historical development of the Episcopal Diocese of Bethlehem, Pennsylvania, and on the development of St Stephen's Episcopal Church, Wilkes-Barre, within that context. Material was collected by Dr George Raddin in preparation of his book *The Wilderness and the City* (Wilkes-Barre, Pa: St Stephen's Church, 1968). Another collection focuses on the histories of the various parishes in the Roman Catholic Diocese of Scranton, Pennsylvania and other churches in northeastern Pennsylvania. Collection indexed by name, location, denomination, and ethnic group. 9 linear ft.

PENNSYLVANIA ABOLITION SOCIETY

SC —COLLEGE OF CHARLESTON LIBRARY, Special Collections Dept, Charleston, 29401.
Notes: This collection consists of photocopied material from the papers of the Pennsylvania Abolition Society housed at the Historical Society of Pennsylvania, dealing with the establishment (1866), maintenance and eventual relinquishing of the Laing School to the local Public School Board (1940). Collection guide available.

PENNSYLVANIA ACADEMY OF THE FINE ARTS

PA —PENNSYLVANIA ACADEMY OF THE FINE ARTS, ARCHIVES, Broad &

Cherry Sts, Philadelphia, 19102. Marietta Bushnell, Librn
Holdings: Mss Pix
Notes: Incl material relating to the history of the school and museum, exhibition catalogs and records, limited biographical information about former students, faculty, and exhibitors. Open to serious scholars by appointment only.

PENNSYLVANIA ART see Art, Pennsylvania

PENNSYLVANIA ARTISTS see Artists, Pennsylvania

PENNSYLVANIA AUTHORS see Authors, Pennsylvania

PENNSYLVANIA COMPOSERS see Composers, Pennsylvania

PENNSYLVANIA DUTCH see Pennsylvania Germans

PENNSYLVANIA GERMANS

PA —MUHLENBERG COLLEGE, Haas Library, 2400 Chew St, Allentown, 18104. Linda Bowers
Holdings: Vols 1450 Cat Mss Maps Pix Audiotapes
Budget: $300
Notes: Incl in main catalog.

PA —BALCH INSTITUTE FOR ETHNIC STUDIES, Library, 18 S Seventh St, Philadelphia, 19106. R Joseph Anderson, Library Dir
Holdings: Vols 140 Cat

†PA —GERMAN SOCIETY OF PENNSYLVANIA, Joseph Horner Memorial Library, 611 Spring Garden St, Philadelphia, 19123.
Notes: All subjects with special emphasis on history, biography, literature (85 per cent in German); juvenile literature.

PA —LIBRARY COMPANY OF PHILADELPHIA, 1314 Locust St, Philadelphia, 19107. Edwin Wolf II, Librn; Kenneth Finkel, Cur of Prints
Holdings: Vols (400,000) Cat Maps
Budget: ($25,000)
Notes: With the Historical Society of Pennsylvania, the largest collection of Pennsylvania-German imprints in the United States.

PA —PENNSYLVANIA STATE UNIVERSITY, Arts Library, 405 E Pattee Library, University Park, 16802. Daniel Zager, Music Librn
Holdings: Vols (14,000) Cat Phonorecords
Notes: The music collection supports a School of Music curriculum which is comprehensive at the undergraduate and masters degree levels. The collection includes scores (collected works and performance editions), books, periodicals, and recordings. The Special Collections area of the library includes the following music collections: the manuscripts, published scores, personal papers, and some recordings of the American composer Charles Wakefield Cadman; 18th and 19th century American tunebooks and 18th and 19th century Pennsylvania German hymnbooks and songbooks; and the Doyle Guntharp collection of field recordings of fiddler's performances and interviews from Central Pennsylvania.

PENNSYLVANIA GERMANS—IMPRINTS

MA —AMERICAN ANTIQUARIAN SOCIETY LIBRARY, 185 Salisbury St, Worcester, 01609. Marcus A McCorison, Dir & Librn
Holdings: Vols 18,000 Cat
Notes: Strongest for New York, Pennsylvania, Massachusetts, and Connecticut. Incl Canada, Hawaii, Mexico, the West Indies; also Pennsylvania German. About 18,000 or 90 percent of the almanacs and yearbooks known to have been printed

in the United States before 1850; The Latin American and Canadian collections are the most complete in this country.

PA —JUNIATA COLLEGE LIBRARY, Huntingdon, 16652. David Eyman, Dir
Holdings: Vols 5000 // Cat Mss
Notes: Early Pennsylvania imprints, many in German. Large collection of imprints from Christopher Sauer's press. Early Brethren and other German sectarian (Schwenkfelders, Anabaptists) tracts from Pennsylvania and Europe. Several of the collections have been described in *American German Review* (1941), *Pennsylvania History* (1940, 1959), and *Pennsylvania Magazine* (1943).

PA —FRANKLIN & MARSHALL COLLEGE, Library, Lancaster, 17604. Kathleen J Moretto, Library Dir
Notes: German-American imprints. Primarily monographs (books and pamphlets) dating from 1739 to 1900. The collection contains a large proportion of bibles, catechisms, almanacs and hymn books, as well as books dealing with political and agricultural subjects.

PA —FREE LIBRARY OF PHILADELPHIA, Rare Book Dept, Logan Sq, Philadelphia, 19103. Marie E Korey, Rare Book Librn
Holdings: Uncat
Notes: 2400 books, pamphlets and broadsides in the German language printed in the US and Canada from 1732 to 1850 for the use of the Pennsylvania Germans and their descendants. Numerous Christopher Sauer imprints.

PA —FREE LIBRARY OF PHILADELPHIA, Music Dept, Logan Sq, Philadelphia, 19103. Frederick James Kent, Head
Holdings: Vols (2000)
Notes: The American Humnody Collection incl early psalters, hymn books and anthologies of sacred music published in the 18th and 19th centuries. Examples of holdings are Lyon's *Urania* (1761), Billings' *Singing Master's Assistant* (1778), and Wyeth's *Repository of Sacred Music*. Arrangements to use the collection should be made in advance.

RI —BROWN UNIVERSITY, John Hay Library, Harris Collection, Prospect St, Providence, 02912. Rosemary L Cullen, Cur
Holdings: Vols (200,000) Cat Mss Pix Phonorecords Microforms
Budget: ($15,000)
Notes: The Harris Collection of American Poetry and Plays is principally composed of American and Canadian poetry and plays from the 17th century to the present. Extensive holdings in hymnals of the 17th to the 20th centuries, incl a number of Pennsylvania German hymnals. Collection incl the MacDougall Collection of Psalters and Hymnals. See *Dictionary Catalog of The Harris Collection of American Poetry and Plays* (Boston: G K Hall, 1972), 13 vols; Supplement (1977), 3 vols. Separate catalog.

PENNSYLVANIA GERMANS—MANUSCRIPTS

PA —FREE LIBRARY OF PHILADELPHIA, Rare Book Dept, Logan Sq, Philadelphia, 19103. Marie E Korey, Rare Book Librn
Holdings: Vols (1100) Cat Mss Pix
Notes: A collection of 1100 pieces of Pennsylvania German folk art on paper in manuscript and printed form, incl birth and baptismal certificates, writing examples, and bookplates.

PENNSYLVANIA INSURRECTION OF 1794 see Whiskey Insurrection, 1794

PENNSYLVANIA POWER AND LIGHT COMPANY

DE —HAGLEY MUSEUM AND LIBRARY, Eleutherian Mills-Hagley Foundation Inc, PO Box 3630, Greenville, 19807. Richmond D Williams, Dir; Heddy A Richter, Imprints Librn
Notes: Records of Pennsylvania Power & Light Company (1853-1955; 1000 cubic feet). The archive consists of the records of

PENNSYLVANIA POWER AND LIGHT COMPANY (cont.)

1050 predecessor companies that merged over a 75-year period (1880-1955) to form the present-day PP&L. The collection describes the industry's tentative beginnings using the Edison system of direct current, the technological innovations which allowed small, innercity utilities to expand beyond their original urban centers, and the consolidation movement that culminated with the formation of a great regional power network.

PENNY DREADFULS see Dime Novels; Fiction, Gothic

PENOBSCOT BAY, MAINE

ME —PENOBSCOT MARINE MUSEUM, Library, Church St, Searsport, 04974. Charles Howard, Librn
Holdings: Vols (4000) Cat Mss Maps Pix
Budget: ($5000)
Notes: Maine maritime history, log books, journals, diaries, marine charts, ships registers, photographs, archives & mss, and books relating to world navigation. The greatest emphasis is placed on the Penobscot Bay region.

PENOLOGY see Corrections; Prisons and Prisoners

PENSIONS

CA —UNIVERSITY OF SOUTHERN CALIFORNIA, Crocker Business Library, Hoffman Hall, University Park, Los Angeles, 90007. Judith A Truelson, Head Librn
Holdings: Vols (100,000) Cat Microforms
Notes: The Roy P Crocker Library of Business Administration, located in Hoffman Hall, houses more than 100,000 volumes and regularly receives approximately 1500 trade, financial, economics, labor, and general business periodicals and newspapers. The areas of subject concentration include business economics, finance and investments, general management/management theory, international business, finance and management, marketing/food marketing, and quantitative business analysis.
DC —US DEPT OF LABOR, Library, 200 Constitution Ave NW, Washington, 20210. Sabina Jacobson, Dir
Holdings: Vols (550,000) Cat
MN —NORTHWESTERN NATIONAL LIFE INSURANCE CO, Library, Box 20, Minneapolis, 55440. Beth Soener, Librn
Holdings: Vols (8000) Cat
Notes: Incl a small collection of annuities and life insurance published 1731-1864. Also materials about employee benefits.
ON —CANADA DEPT OF LABOUR, Library, Ottawa, K1A 0J2, Can. Monique Marchand, Chief Librn
Holdings: Vols (100,000) Cat Microforms
PQ —CENTRE DE DOCUMENTATION, REGIE DES RENTES DU QUEBEC, CP 5200, Quebec, G1K 7S9, Can. Michel Dupuis, Bibliothecaine en Chef; Nicole Paquin, Bibliotechnicienne
Holdings: Vols 5000 Cat
Budget: $60,500
Notes: Social security, incl private pension plans literature. 80 vertical file drawers.

PENSIONS, MILITARY

NE —NEBRASKA STATE HISTORICAL SOCIETY, Archives, 1500 R St, Box 82554, Lincoln, 68501. James E Potter, State Archivist
Holdings: Uncat Mss
Notes: Silver and the money question; also material on the Greenback Party. Printed speeches and tracts relating to the money question, 1890-1895. Many written by prominent politcal figures of the day. Also, pamphlets which relate to income tax, tariffs, free trade, soldiers' pensions, railroads, election laws and public lands. Collection of John Davis, Congressman from Kansas, 1891-1895.

PENSIONS, OLD AGE see Old Age Pensions

PENTACLES see Talismans

PENTECOSTAL CHURCHES see Holiness and Pentecostal Churches

PEOPLE'S DEMOCRATIC REPUBLIC OF YEMEN (SOUTH YEMEN) see Yemen, South

PEOPLE'S REPUBLIC OF BENIN see Benin

PEPPER, REP. CLAUDE

FL —FLORIDA STATE UNIVERSITY, Robert Manning Strozier Library, Special Collections Dept, Tallahassee, 32306. Opal M Free, Head, Special Collections
Notes: The official papers, documents, photographs, recordings, and memorabilia of US Representative Claude Pepper. Incl the papers, photographs, and memorabilia of his wife, Mildred Irene Webster Pepper (706, 536 items).

PEPPER, STEPHEN C.

IL —SOUTHERN ILLINOIS UNIVERSITY, CARBONDALE, Delyte W Morris Library, Special Collections Dept, Carbondale, 62901. David V Koch, Cur of Special Collections; Louisa Bowen, Cur of Manuscripts
Holdings: Mss Pix
Notes: Personal papers and mss. 13 linear feet.

PEPPERRELL FAMILY

MA —NEW ENGLAND HISTORIC GENEALOGICAL SOCIETY, Library, 101 Newbury St, Boston, 02116. Ralph J Crandell, Dir
Notes: Family papers, likely to incl personal correspondence, diaries, business records, etc.

PEPYS, SAMUEL

MA —HARVARD UNIVERSITY LIBRARY, Houghton Library, Cambridge, 02138. Rodney G Dennis, Cur of Manuscripts
Holdings: Cat Mss

PERCEPTION, EXTRASENSORY see Extrasensory Perception (ESP)

PERCEPTION, VISUAL see Visual Perception

PERCEPTUAL LEARNING

NY —VISUAL STUDIES WORKSHOP, Research Center, 31 Prince St, Rochester, 14607. Linn Underhill, Coordr; Robert Bretz, Librn
Holdings: Vols (8000) Cat Pix Slides Audiotapes Videotapes
Notes: Strong emphasis on photography (over 1,000,000 pictures) and the photographic arts in many subject areas incl in this volume. Heavy emphasis on early photographic processes and collections of examples of them. Also collections of individual photographers' works.

PERCIVAL, JAMES GATES

CT —YALE UNIVERSITY, Box 1603A, Yale Station, New Haven, 06520.
Holdings: Cat Mss

PERCUSSION INSTRUMENTS AND MUSIC

AZ —ARIZONA STATE UNIVERSITY, Music Library, Tempe, 85281. Arlys L McDonald, Music Librn
Holdings: Vols 2500 Cat
Notes: The International Percussion

Reference Library is a collection of scores and instructional materials featuring percussion instruments. It is a perusal collection available for 14-day loan. A catalog is available for sale. No photocopying.
IL —UNIVERSITY OF ILLINOIS, URBANA/CHAMPAIGN, Library, Bands & Busch Instrument Collection, 1103 S Sixth St, Champaign, 61820. John Cranford, Librn
Notes: This collection of 212 old and unusual wind and percussion instruments comes from two sources: The Carl Busch collection, and instruments collected by the late Director of University Bands Emeritus, Dr A A Harding. The museum is open from 8 to 5 Monday through Friday, by appointment only.
†MD —UNIVERSITY OF MARYLAND, Library, The National Association of College Wind & Percussion Instructors Library, College Park, 20742. Pearl Z Tubiash, Supvr
Holdings: Cat
Notes: Primarily scores, along with some organizational papers and publications.
MD —TOWSON STATE UNIVERSITY, Fine Arts Bldg, Room 457, Towson, 21204. Edwin L Gerhardt, Curator
Notes: The Gerhardt Library of Musical Information is a segregated representative collection of music literature, phonograph and tape recordings, pictures and artifacts. It incl special sections on Thomas Alva Edison and the phonograph, John Philip Sousa and bands, old popular songs and percussion. Most of the material is out of print and hard to find. It is not a collection of scores or manuscripts. A detailed outline is available upon request. Direct all correspondence to the curator, Edwin L Gerhardt, 4926 Leeds Ave, Baltimore, MD 21227, (301) 242-0328. See also entry under Musical Instruments

PERCY, SEN. CHARLES H.

IL —CHICAGO HISTORICAL SOCIETY, Library, Clark St at North Ave, Chicago, 60614. Archie Motley, Manuscript Librn
Notes: Papers of business executive, US Senator.

PERCY, WALKER

NV —UNIVERSITY OF NEVADA, RENO, University Library, Special Collections Dept, Reno, 89557. Robert E Blesse, Head
Holdings: // Vols (8) Cat Other appearances 22 Cat
Notes: Includes individual works by author in all editions including translations; also prefaces, introductions, published correspondence, appearances in anthologies, periodicals, etc. Bibliographical research collection, part of Modern Authors Collection.
NC —UNIVERSITY OF NORTH CAROLINA, CHAPEL HILL, Louis Round Wilson Academic Affairs Library, Southern Historical Collection, Chapel Hill, 27514. Carolyn Wallace, Librn
Notes: Manuscripts and papers of Walker Percy. Primarily mss from work on his published novels, etc.

PERELMUTER, SHOLEM

NY —YIVO INSTITUTE FOR JEWISH RESEARCH, Library & Archives, 1048 Fifth Ave, New York, 10028. Dina Abramowicz, Librn; Marek Web, Archivist
Holdings: Cat Mss Pix Slides
Notes: Yiddish drama in the original and in English translation from its 19th-century beginnings to the present; the Yiddish theatre in the Soviet Union and the theatrical activities in the ghettos during the Nazi regime; special collections of Sholem Perelmuter, Mendl Elkin, Maurice Schwartz, Abraham Goldfaden, Jacob Gordin, and Mark Schweid; records of the Union of Jewish Actors in Poland between the two world wars; the Vilna YIVO Collection of posters, playbills, and photographs; recordings.

PERFECTION (CATHOLIC)

DC —GEORGETOWN UNIVERSITY, Woodstock Theological Center Library, Box

PERFECTION (CATHOLIC) (cont.)

37445, Washington, 20013. Thomas a Marshall, SJ, Librn
Holdings: Vols (165,000)
Notes: On Catholic spirituality.
WI —DERANCE FOUNDATION, 7700 W Blue Mound Rd, Milwaukee, 53213. Harry John, Pres
Holdings: Vols (5200)
Notes: On Catholic spirituality. Private non-circulating collection.

PERFECTION (MONASTIC) see Perfection (Catholic)

PERFECTION (THEOLOGY)

CA —POINT LOMA NAZARENE COLLEGE, Ryan Library, 3900 Lomaland Dr, San Diego, 92106. Esther Schandorff, Librn
Holdings: Vols 1600 Cat Mss Pix
Notes: Person and work of the Holy Spirit and the doctrine of Christian Perfection.

PERFECTIONISTS see Oneida Community

PERFORMING ARTS FOUNDATION

NY —STATE UNIVERSITY OF NEW YORK, STONY BROOK, Melville Library, Dept of Special Collections, Stony Brook, 11794. Evert Volkersz, Head
Holdings: Mss
Notes: The Performing Arts Foundation of Huntington, NY, existed from 1964 to 1982. The partially cataloged collection incl records of the affiliated Arts in Education and the Performing Arts Curriculum Enrichment Project. No photocopying.

PERFUMES AND PERFUMERY

DE —UNIVERSITY OF DELAWARE, Hugh M Morris Library, S College Ave, Newark, 19711. T Stuart Dick, Special Collections
Holdings: Cat
Notes: Part of the Unidel Collection of the History of Chemistry.
NY —REVLON RESEARCH CENTER, Research Bldg Library, 945 Zerega Ave, Bronx, 08818. Lee J Tanen, Library Services Mgr
Holdings: Vols 200 Cat

PERINATAL HEALTH CARE see Maternal Health Services

PERINATALOGY see Pediatrics

PERIODICALS—COLLECTIONS

CA —LOS ANGELES PUBLIC LIBRARY, Art, Music & Recreation Dept, 630 W Fifth St, Los Angeles, 90071. Melvin H Rosenberg, Mgr & Principal Librn
Notes: Very extensive with very long runs in some cases in all subjects the department covers.
CA —UNIVERSITY OF CALIFORNIA, SAN FRANCISCO, Library, San Francisco, 94143. David Bishop, University Librn
Notes: Health Science periodicals.
CO —NATIONAL WRITERS CLUB LIBRARY, 1450 S Havana, Suite 620, Aurora, 80012. Donald E Bower, Dir
Holdings: Vols 500 Uncat
Notes: Rare issues of literary periodicals.
DC —LIBRARY OF CONGRESS, Serial and Government Publications Division, Washington, 20540.
Notes: Serials. One of the largest and most extensive collections in the world, incl periodicals; scientific and learned journals in all languages and in all fields except agriculture and medicine; US Government serials (Federal, State, County, and Muncipal); national foreign government serials from all countries; provincial serials from provinces possessing autonomy; municipal serials from principal cities; newspapers (850,000 unbound issues, 75,000 bound vols, 270,000 microfilm reels), 12,000

microprint cards of early American newspapers, 1704-1820, incl 1500 titles currently received, 500 of these being representative titles from all States of the Union and 1000 from all foreign countries.
FL —MIAMI-DADE PUBLIC LIBRARY SYSTEM, 1 Biscayne Blvd, Miami, 33132. Carol A Stone, Serials Librn
Holdings: Vols 53,794 Cat Microforms
Budget: $250,000
Notes: Incl 38,392 bound vols and 46,133 microforms.
IL —CENTER FOR RESEARCH LIBRARIES, 6050 S Kenwood Ave, Chicago, 60637. Donald B Simpson, Dir; Esther Smith, Collection Development Librn
ME —PORTLAND PUBLIC LIBRARY, 5 Monument Sq, Portland, 04101. Edward V Chenevert, Library Dir
Notes: Collection incl 5000 phonorecords, 400 cassettes. Other collections within the department include sheet music, songbooks, picture file, periodicals, and choral music.
NY —COLD SPRING HARBOR LABORATORY, Library, PO Box 100, Cold Spring Harbor, 11724. Susan Gensel, Library Dir; Genemary Falvey, Librn
Holdings: Vols (30,000)
Budget: ($103,500)
Notes: The highly technical collection is comprised of 20,000 serial vols and 10,000 monographs. The library receives 500 current serial titles. Subjects covered incl molecular and cellular biology, virology, biochemistry, microbiology, oncology, neurobiology, biological risk assessment and genetic engineering/biotechnology. Special collections in eugenics and genetics are primarily historical dealing with the development of genetics in the US which had its beginnings here.
NY —NEW YORK PUBLIC LIBRARY, Research Libraries, General Research Div, Fifth Ave & 42 St, New York, 10018. Keith McKinney, Assistant Div Chief
Holdings: Cat
Notes: Current periodicals. Subjects incl advertising, business and professional periodicals, international affairs, labor and trade unions, political and social sciences, humanities in general. Division holds 10,000 titles. Incl little magazines.
NC —DUKE UNIVERSITY, William R Perkins Library, Durham, 27706. Elvin E Strowd, University Librn
Notes: The Flowers Collection of Southern Americana currently consists of 4,300,500 items. Additions are ongoing. Included in this collection are several types of materials, which are housed in appropriate sections of the library. The various types of materials are: manuscripts, books, pamphlets, maps, music, broadsides, newspapers, photographs, engravings, prints and memorabilia.
OH —PUBLIC LIBRARY OF CINCINNATI & HAMILTON COUNTY, History Dept, 800 Vine St, Cincinnati, 45202. J Richard Abell, Head
Holdings: Vols 17,969 Cat Microforms
Notes: Incl 342 19th-century titles (bound).
OH —PUBLIC LIBRARY OF CINCINNATI & HAMILTON COUNTY, Literature Dept, 800 Vine St, Cincinnati, 45202. Donna S Monnig, Head
Holdings: Vols 12,004 Cat Microforms
Notes: Includes 197 19th century American literary periodicals (bound), 233 English literary periodicals (microform), as APS I, II, and III (microform).
OH —CASE WESTERN RESERVE UNIVERSITY, M A Baxter School of Information and Library Science, 10900 Euclid Ave, Cleveland, 44106. Bettina MacAyeal, Librn; Gretchen Larson, Librn
Holdings: Vols (1100)
Notes: Incl collection of 1100 historical children's books and periodicals, housed in the Special Collections Dept of Freiberger Library, and can be used by the public. Incl *The Holy Bible Abridged* published by Isaiah Thomas in 1786, *The Life and Strange Surprising Adventures of Robinson Crusoe* of 1790, and a *Cinderella* dated 1809. There are examples of the work of illustrators Walter Crane, Randolph Caldecott, Kate Greenaway and Maurice Boutet de Monvel.

The periodical collection incl a complete run of St. Nicholas Magazine.
OH —OHIO HISTORICAL SOCIETY, Archives Library Division, 1982 Velma Ave, Columbus, 43211. Dennis East, Division Chief
Holdings: Vols (96,000) Cat Mss Maps Pix Slides Microforms
Budget: ($18,000)
Notes: This library is the primary collection for Ohio. Most purchases are on the rare and op market. Collecting area is early American history, esp relating to exploration into the Northwest Territory. Major subject areas are Ohio politics and government (8 presidents) military history (good collection of regimental histories and Ohio narratives of the Civil War), economic and social history, local history, esp county histories & atlases and city directories. Also, Ohio archaeology, natural history, artifacts. Major media collection are books (96,000), newspapers (25,000 vols and 22,000 microfilm), pictures (50,000), maps (2500), manuscripts (1,500,000). Library is noncirculating except through interlibrary loan of microfilm.
OK —CENTRAL STATE UNIVERSITY, Library, 100 N University Dr, Edmond, 73034. Andrew Peters, Reference Librn
Holdings: Cat Maps Audiotapes Microforms
Notes: Microforms Research Center for newspapers and periodicals, incl ERIC, LAC, LEL, HRAF, and annual reports, etc. Vols on microfilm reels, microfiche; microcards; academic and music audiotapes; and maps.
PA —ZOOLOGICAL SOCIETY OF PHILADELPHIA, Library, 34 & Girard Ave, Philadelphia, 19104. Alyssa N Scheuermann, Librn
Holdings: Mss Maps Pix Slides
Notes: 150 journals received annually on subjects of natural history, zoology, biology, etc. Approx 100 publications received annually on zoological gardens and aquariums housed by city of origin (English and non-English publications). Photocopying with permission.
RI —BROWN UNIVERSITY, John Carter Brown Library, Providence, 02912. Norman Fiering, Librn; Everett C Wilkie Jr, Bibliographer; Susan Danforth, Cur Maps & Prints
Notes: Runs of European and American periodicals, incl some American newspapers, printed before 1833.
RI —PROVIDENCE ATHENAEUM, 251 Benefit St, Providence, 02903. Sally Duplaix, Dir
Holdings: (152,000) Vols
Notes: Material available on interlibrary loan under certain conditions.
ON —UNIVERSITY OF TORONTO, Thomas Fisher Rare Book Library, 120 Saint George St, Toronto, M5S 1A5, Can. Richard G Landon, Head
Holdings: Vols 6535 Uncat
Notes: Maclean-Hunter and Southam Press Collections contain periodicals issued by these two Canadian publishers. These are largely trade journlas. Many long and complete runs of items like *Canadian Footwear, Electrical News and Engineering; Gift Buyer; Canadian Home Journal; Chatelaine; Macleans;* etc. Many runs originate in 1880s and 1890s. Also include current publications. Approx 268 titles. Fisher Library designated the official archives for published material by Maclean-Hunter and Southam Press.

PERIODICALS, AFRICAN

CA —UNIVERSITY OF CALIFORNIA, LOS ANGELES, Research Library, African Studies Collection, 405 Hilgard Ave, Los Angeles, 90024. Edward Shreeves, Chairman, Bibliographers Group; Joseph J Lauer, African Studies Bibliographer
Holdings: Maps Pix Slides Phonorecords Audiotapes Microforms
Notes: General collection mainly in the humanities and social sciences, covering prehistoric times to the present. Particular strengths include: early travel and

PERIODICALS, AFRICAN (cont.)

exploration, mission field, literature, vernacular languages and literatures, Portuguese Africa, slavery (have the British Foreign Office's *General Correspondence. Slave Trade* on microfilm). Extensive holdings of journals, newspapers and government publications. The collection was described in the *Handbook of American Resources for African Studies* (1967).

CA —HOOVER INSTITUTION ON WAR, REVOLUTION & PEACE, Stanford University, Stanford, 94305. Peter Duignan, Cur; Karen Fung, Deputy Cur
Holdings: Vols (60,000) Cat Mss Maps Pix Slides Microforms
Notes: Politics, economics, and history from 1870 to the present. About 500 current periodicals titles, about 90 current newspaper titles. Legislative debates, political ephemera. Have microfilm of Portuguese African nationalist material, confidential prints of Great Britian's foreign and colonial offices 1870 through 1922. Nigerian pamphlets (market literature, political and historical tracts), collection of the correspondence pamphlets and ephemera of Alfred B Xuma, collections on Zaire (1955-1963), South African nationalist publications on microfilm. Descriptions of the Collection: *African and Middle East Collections* pub by Hoover Institute, *Handbook of American Resources for African Studies* pub by Hoover. Holdings of the Collection in *Hoover Institute on War, Revolution, and Peace Library Catalog* pub by G K Hall, *Emerging Nationalism in Portuguese Africa: A Bibliography* pub by Hoover, *German Africa* pub by Hoover. *The Treason Trail in South Africa: A Guide to the Microfilm Record of the Trial* pub by Hoover. *History of the Library and Archives of the Hoover Institution on War, Revolution and Peace*, edited by Peter Duignan (Hoover Institution Press), *Guide to Non-federal Archives and Manuscripts in the United States Relating to Africa*, compiled Aloha P Smith (East Ardsley, Eng, Microform Ltd).

DC —HOWARD UNIVERSITY, Moorland-Spingarn Research Center, 500 Howard Place NW, Washington, 20059. Clifford L Muse, Jr, Acting Dir

MI —MICHIGAN STATE UNIVERSITY, International Library, Africana Collection, East Lansing, 48824. Eugene de Benko, Librn; Onuma Ezera, Bibliographer for Africana
Holdings: Vols (82,700) Cat Mss Maps Pix Slides Phonorecords Audiotapes Videotapes Filmstrips
Budget: ($78,000)
See also entry under Africa for full description.

†MB —UNIVERSITY OF MANITOBA, Library, Winnipeg, R3T 2N2, Can.
Notes: Statistical serials from Botswana, Malawi, Mauritius, Nigeria, South Africa, Togo, United Arab Republic, and Zimbabwe in the *African Official Statistical Serials on Microfiche Collection.*

PERIODICALS, AGRICULTURAL

CA —UNIVERSITY OF CALIFORNIA, BERKELEY, Science Libraries, Natural Resources Library, 40 Giannini Hall, Berkeley, 94720. Norma Kobzina, Head Librn
Holdings: Vols (100,000) Cat Maps Microforms
Budget: ($40,000)
Notes: Subject emphasis is on basic agricultural and pest management research, particularly in the areas of tropical and subtropical agriculture and plantation crops, ie, cotton, rice, tobacco, and sugar. Materials in agricultural engineering, farm machinery, and veterinary medicine are not acquired for the Berkeley campus. Serials, especially the extensive holdings of foreign titles, constitute the collection's major strength. Over 5700 serials are being received currently.

PA —UNIVERSITY OF PENNSYLVANIA, Van Pelt Library, Rare Books Collection, 34 & Walnut Sts, Philadelphia, 19104. Daniel Traister, Special Collections Librn
Holdings: Vols 685 Cat Mss
Notes: Incl 18th and early 19th century English and American texts and periodicals on agriculture and animal husbandry; with mss vols of contemporary correspondence of the Philadelphia Society for Promoting Agriculture.

PERIODICALS, AMERICAN

CT —TRINITY COLLEGE LIBRARY, Watkinson Library, 300 Summit St, Hartford, 06106. Jeffrey Kaimowitz, Cur
Holdings: Cat
Notes: Strong in 19th century material, including women's and children's periodicals.

DC —LIBRARY OF CONGRESS, General Reading Rooms Division, Microform Reading Room, Washington, 20540.
Holdings: Cat Mss Maps Pix Microforms
Notes: Microform materials only in this LC Division. Works of individual authors; holdings of collections; archival records, etc, press releases and translations, etc.

DC —LIBRARY OF CONGRESS, Prints & Photographs Div, Washington, 20540.
Holdings: Cat Pix
Notes: Complete photographic files of *Look* magazine: the history of 35 years in pictures. Incl 17.5 million black and white negatives, 1.5 million color transparencies, 450,000 contact sheets, and 25,000 movie stills. Effective October 1, 1983, the Library's Prints and Photographs Division has discontinued reproduction and reference service on its collection of photographs which appeared in *Look* magazine from 1937 to 1971. This limitation on service will remain in effect until questions of rights and permissions affecting these photographs can be clarified. The Library acquired the *Look* archive in 1971 as additional resources for research in American life by scholars and other investigators. It was anticipated that the photographs would serve as a study collection for researchers in many fields, but the major use of the collection has been by publishers, advertisers, andmakers of documentary films. Such picture users require clear rights to reproduce the images. The Library has been unable to satisfy these requests because of the donor's stipulation precluding such use. Until some accommodation can be made with the donor to free the collection for a wider range of public use, the collection will remain in remote cold storage to retard deterioration of sensitive films, especially color films. This policy will remain in effect until further notice. LC Information Bulletin, 10 Oct 83.

IL —NEWBERRY LIBRARY, 60 W Walton St, Chicago, 60610. Diana Haskell, Cur of Modern Mss
Notes: American periodicals before 1930.

†MA —BOSTON PUBLIC LIBRARY, Copley Sq, Boston, 02117.
Holdings: Microforms
Notes: Microform Publication by University Microfilms. American periodical Series, Series I, II and II. 1000 reels.

NY —NEW YORK PUBLIC LIBRARY, Rare Books and Manuscripts Div, Fifth Ave & 42 St, New York, 10018. William L Joyce, Asst Dir; Francis O Mattson, Curator
Holdings: Cat
Budget: ($7161)
Notes: Specialties incl 18th century American periodicals. Described in *Dictionary Catalog of the Rare Book Division, The Research Libraries of the New York Public Library.*

NC —DUKE UNIVERSITY, William R Perkins Library, Jay B Hubbell Center for American Literary Historiography, Durham, 27706. Erma Whittington, Librn
Notes: 77,312 items, including manuscripts, pictures, clippings, and correspondence. "The objective of the Center is to gather the papers and materials of significant scholars and critics in American literary history." The Center is a part of the Perkins Library Manuscripts Department.

PA —ATHENAEUM OF PHILADELPHIA, 219 S Sixth St, Philadelphia, 19106. Roger W Moss Jr, Librn
Holdings: Vols 20,000 Cat
Notes: Victorian Periodicals Collection. Anglo-American periodicals of the 19th century particularly relating to social and cultural history and literature.

RI —BROWN UNIVERSITY, John Carter Brown Library, Providence, 02912. Norman Fiering, Librn; Everett C Wilkie Jr, Bibliographer; Susan Danforth, Cur Maps & Prints
Notes: Runs of European and American periodicals, incl some American newspapers, printed before 1833.

PERIODICALS, AMERICAN—19TH CENTURY

MA —AMERICAN ANTIQUARIAN SOCIETY LIBRARY, 185 Salisbury St, Worcester, 01609. Marcus A McCorison, Dir & Librn
Holdings: Vols 60,000 Cat
Notes: Sixty percent of the total of books and pamphlets known to have been printed in the United States before 1821. Source of Readex Microprint Corp project called *Early American Imprints, 1639-1800*, a Microprint edition of every extant book, pamphlet, and broadside printed in what is now the United States. Keyed to Evans *American Bibliography* it reprints in full the texts of nearly 50,000 titles and includes all of Shipton's revision of Evans. A second series, keyed to Shaw and Shoemaker's *American Bibliography* will bring these Microprint reproductions up to 1820. One of the great strengths of the collection is its broadsides and American newspapers--the best anywhere. From it emerged Clarence Brigham's monumental *History and Bibliography of American Newspapers, 1690-1820*, which locates every surviving copy of every newspaper printed in the United States before 1821. ReadexMicroprint Corp is also reproducing this collection. The Society's collections extend beyond 1820, in special strengths, to the turn of the century. The collection incl unusual strengths in Amateur Newspapers (about 50,000 issues), and Bolivian, Chilean, and West Indian newspapers.

PERIODICALS, AMERICAN INDIAN

NJ —PRINCETON UNIVERSITY, Library, Rare Books Dept, Princeton, 08544. Stephen Ferguson, Cur
Holdings: Cat
Notes: A large collection of publications issued by American Indian groups, etc.

PA —TEMPLE UNIVERSITY LIBRARIES, Special Collections Dept, Contemporary Culture Collection, Philadelphia, 19122. Patricia J Case, Cur
Notes: The Contemporary Culture Collection. See full entry under US-Social Life and Customs.

PERIODICALS, ANTHROPOLOGICAL

CA —UNIVERSITY OF CALIFORNIA, BERKELEY, Humanities-Social Sciences Libraries, Anthropology Library, 230 Kroeber Hall, Berkeley, 94720. Dorothy A Koenig, Librn
Holdings: Vols (55,000) Cat Microforms
Notes: The library maintains general research collections covering all aspects of social and physical anthropology, anthropological linguistics and archaeology (excluding classical archaeology). Serials constitute the collection's special strength.

PERIODICALS, ARABIC

TX —UNIVERSITY OF TEXAS LIBRARIES, Middle East Collection, PO Box P, Austin, 78712. Abazar Sepehri, Librn
Holdings: Vols (45,000) Cat Microforms
Notes: Arabic, Persian and Turkish materials in the humanities and social sciences. Incl 350 periodical and 45 newspaper titles from most of the countries of the Arab League, Turkey, Iran and Afghanistan.

PERIODICALS, ARABIC (cont.)

UT —UNIVERSITY OF UTAH, Middle East
Library, Salt Lake City, 84112. Ragai N
Makar, Librn
Holdings: Vols 8000
Budget: ($40,000)

PERIODICALS, ARCHAEOLOGICAL

OH —CLEVELAND PUBLIC LIBRARY,
History and Geography Department, 325
Superior Ave, Cleveland, 44114. JoAnn
Petrello, Head
Holdings: Cat
Notes: General, exclusive of oriental
archaeology in White Collection and biblical
archaeology in the Social Sciences
department. Especially strong in British and
French archaeological serials.

PERIODICALS, ARCHITECTURAL

CA —UNIVERSITY OF CALIFORNIA,
BERKELEY, Environmental Design
Library, (The General Library), 210 Wurster
Hall, Berkeley, 94720. Arthur B Waugh,
Head
Holdings: Vols (90,000) Cat Pix Microforms
Budget: ($17,400)
Notes: A research collection devoted to the
following aspects of the field of architecture:
working details, drawing, theory, standards
and professional practice; building materials,
building types, earthquake resistant
architecture, contemporary architecture of
all countries, history of architecture, and
architecture as a profession. A small rare
book collection in the field of architecture is
maintained. Approximately 1500 serials, incl
many foreign-language titles, are currently
being received. A collection of photographs
(of buildings) and a slide collection are
administered by the department of
architecture.
OH —OBERLIN COLLEGE LIBRARY,
Clarence Ward Art Library, Allen Art Bldg,
Oberlin, 44074. Jeffrey Weidman, Librn
Holdings: Vols (62,000) Cat Microforms
Notes: Strong in medieval European
architecture and American architecture. Incl
the Jefferson Collection, an almost complete
duplication of the architectural books in
Thomas Jefferson's library. Also incl
Frederick B Artz Collection of books on
architecture and gardening dating from the
16th through the 19th centuries. Significant
holdings in early serials (see *ARLO Union
List of Serials*).

PERIODICALS, ARMENIAN

CA —UNIVERSITY OF CALIFORNIA, LOS
ANGELES, Research Library, Armenian
Collection, 405 Hilgard Ave, Los Angeles,
90024. Edward Shreeves, Chairman,
Bibliographers Group; Gia Aivazian,
Armenian Bibliographer
Holdings: Mss
Notes: Incl one of the largest collections in
the US of publications in Armenian and
relating to Armenia. Approx 150 titles.

PERIODICALS, ART

AZ —TUCSON MUSEUM OF ART
LIBRARY, 140 N Main, Tucson, 85705.
Dorcas Worsley, Librn
Holdings: Vols (2000)
Notes: Extensive file of biographical and
critical information on Arizona artists which
is continually being increased. Subject card
index to magazines on Western art and
artists in magazines not indexed in *Art
Index 12* drawers in 1984, and continues to
grow. Have a collection of 15,000 slides.
CA —SAN FRANCISCO ART INSTITUTE,
Anne Bremer Memorial Library, 800
Chestnut St, San Francisco, 94133. Jeff
Gunderson, Librn
Holdings: Vols (23,144) Cat Pix Slides
Audiotapes 16mm Films Microforms
Budget: ($15,000)
IL —NORTHWESTERN UNIVERSITY,
Library, Special Collections Dept, 1937

Sheridan Rd, Evanston, 60201. R Russell
Maylone, Cur
Holdings: Cat
Notes: The collection includes 70 titles of
the major Art Nouveau journals published in
Belgium and France, among them *Van Nu
en Straks, La Wallonie, La Jeune Litteraire,
Le Centaure, Le Chat-Noir, L'Ermitage,
L'Estampe et l'Affiche, Gil Blas Illustree,
Le Mercure de France, La Revue
Contemporaine* and *Le Symboliste*.
Literature: Howe, Jeffery W, *Belgian and
French Journals of the Fin-de-Siecle in the
Northwestern University Library: A
Bibliographical Study from an Art Historical
Point of View* (Evanston: Northwestern
University Library, 1977).

PERIODICALS, ART, EARLY

OH —OBERLIN COLLEGE LIBRARY,
Clarence Ward Art Library, Allen Art Bldg,
Oberlin, 44074. Jeffrey Weidman, Librn
Holdings: Vols (62,000) Cat Microforms
Notes: Incl approx 18,000 uncataloged
exhibition catalogues and major sales
catalogues. Significant holdings in early
serials (see *ARLO Union List of Serials*).

PERIODICALS, ASIAN

NY —CORNELL UNIVERSITY LIBRARIES,
John M Olin Library, John M Echols
Collection on Southeast Asia, Ithaca, 14853.
Giok Po Oey, Curator
See also entry under Asia, Southeast.

PERIODICALS, ASTRONOMICAL

PA —UNIVERSITY OF PENNSYLVANIA,
Mathematics-Physics-Astronomy Library, 33
& Walnut Sts, Philadelphia, 19104. Marion
A Kreiter, Librn
Holdings: Cat
Notes: Incl astronomical observatory
publications.

PERIODICALS, AUSTRIAN

CA —STANFORD UNIVERSITY
LIBRARIES, Cecil H Green Library,
Stanford, 94305. Peter R Frank, Cur, CDP-
Germanic Collection
Holdings: Cat
Notes: Extensive holdings, covering Austrian
history of the Habsburg Empire to the
present. Especially strong for the period of
Maria Theresia and Joseph II, 19th and 20th
century. Extremely rich in the Josephinic
pamphlets (Broschuren-Literatur),
broadsheets of the Napoleonic Wars and of
the Revolution 1848-1849, rare periodicals.
This and other rare material in the Stanford
Collection of German, Austrian and Swiss
Culture, Special Collections. Over 4,000 vols
entered in RLIN. Description: "Narrative on
a Good Meal: A Collection of Austriaca at
Stanford University Libraries" by Peter R
Frank.

PERIODICALS, BASQUE

NV —UNIVERSITY OF NEVADA, RENO,
Noble H Getchell Library, Reno, 89557.
William A Douglass, Coordinator
Holdings: Vols (15,000)
Notes: America's largest collection of
Basque materials, both retrospective and
current. Semi-annual *Newsletter*.

PERIODICALS, BIOLOGICAL

PQ —MCGILL UNIVERSITY, Institute of
Oceanography, Oceanography Library, 3620
University St, Montreal, H3A 2B2, Can.
Yvonne Mahocks, Librn
Holdings: Vols (10,848) Cat Mss Maps Pix
Microforms
Budget: ($1200)
Notes: Extensive periodical collection. 12,
332 government documents, , 322 microtech,
321 microfiche, 25,000 reprints.

PERIODICALS, BLACK

DC —HOWARD UNIVERSITY, Moorland-
Spingarn Research Center, 500 Howard

Place NW, Washington, 20059. Clifford L
Muse, Jr, Acting Dir
MA —UNIVERSITY OF MASSACHUSETTS
AT AMHERST, Library, Archives and
Manuscripts, Amherst, 01003. Siegfried
Feller, Assoc Dir for Collection
Development
Holdings: Mss Pix
Notes: Papers of the NAACP's *The Crisis*
during W E B Du Bois' editorship, 1910-34.
Incl W E B Du Bois papers.
TX —FORT WORTH PUBLIC LIBRARY,
Southeast Branch, 4300 E Berry, Fort
Worth, 76105. Michael Roseborough,
Special Collections Librn
Holdings: Vols 2500 Cat Mss Pix
Phonorecords Audiotapes Filmstrips
Microforms
Budget: ($6000)
Notes: Studies Collection incl most titles by
and about Blacks published since 1972, plus
many older titles on Afro-American history.
Library also maintains up-to-date index to
more than 20 Black periodicals.

PERIODICALS, BOTANICAL

IA —IOWA STATE UNIVERSITY, Library,
Ames, 50011. Warren B Kuhn, Dean of
Library Services
Notes: Specific strengths: botanical
taxonomy, ferns, mycology and plant
pathology. Extensive serial holdings.
MD —NATIONAL LIBRARY OF
MEDICINE, 8600 Rockville Pike, Bethesda,
20209. Harold M Schoolinam, Actg Dir
Notes: The world's largest medical library.
Materials are collected exhaustively in some
40 biomedical areas and, to a lesser degree,
in related subject areas such as general
chemistry, physics, zoology, botany, and
instrumentation. Holdings include 80,000
monographic volumes, pre-1871; 368,000
monographic volumes, 1871-present; 545,000
bound serial volumes; 281,000 theses; 172,
000 pamphlets; 822,000 manuscripts; 32,000
microforms; 5000 audiovisuals; and 72,000
prints and photographs. Pre-1871 material is
in a separate historical collection.
Approximately 26,000 serial titles are
currently received.

PERIODICALS, BRAZILIAN

AZ —UNIVERSITY OF ARIZONA, Library,
Tucson, 85721. W David Laird, Librn
Notes: The greatest strength of this
collection is in long back-runs of periodicals.

PERIODICALS, BRITISH

DC —CATHOLIC UNIVERSITY OF
AMERICA, Canon Law Library, 300B
Mullen Library, Washington, 20064. R
Bruce Miller, Librn
Holdings: Vols (22,000)
Notes: The collection includes extensive
16th, 17th, and 18th century works in both
Latin and Italian. There are many printed
editions of pre-16th century sources. Both
the 19th and 20th century materials are well
represented. This collection is also rich in
materials relating to the Second Vatican
Council and its aftermath and is up-to-date
on the new (1983) Code of Canon Law.
Current periodical subscriptions to journals
in English, German, French, Italian, and
Spanish.
DC —LIBRARY OF CONGRESS, General
Reading Rooms Division, Microform
Reading Room, Washington, 20540.
Holdings: Cat Mss Maps Pix Microforms
Notes: Microform materials only in this LC
Division. Works of individual authors;
holdings of collections; archival records, etc,
press releases and translations, etc.
WI —UNIVERSITY OF WISCONSIN,
MADISON, Memorial Library, 728 State St,
Madison, 53706. Erwin K Welsch, Social
Studies Bibliographer
Holdings: Vols (25,000) Microforms
Notes: Covers all fields of English and Irish
life, literary, historical, scientific and social
scientific. Also incl special collections of gift
annuals, eg *Aunt Judy's Annual*, on
Temperance, Free Thought, labor literature

PERIODICALS, BRITISH (cont.)

and periodicals from various groups and organizations, eg *Charity Organization Review*. Notably strong in the serial publicatons of scholarly societies, eg Manchester Statistical Society. Collection partly described in Erwin K Welsch, "A Preliminary Checklist of English and Irish Periodcials Published between 1800 and 1914 in the Memorial Library University of Wisconsin-Madison" (Madison, 1982).

PERIODICALS, BRITISH—17TH-18TH CENTURIES

KS —UNIVERSITY OF KANSAS, Kenneth Spencer Research Library, Special Collections Dept, Lawrence, 66045. Alexandra Mason, Librn
Holdings: Vols 1600 Cat
Notes: English periodicals, 17th and 18th centuries, especially literary, especially *Tatler, Spectator, Guardian*. Noncirculating. Based on Richard P and Marjorie N Bond Collection with additional material.
Described in: Bond, Richmond P. *The Tatler and The Spectator and the development of the early periodic press in England; a checklist of the collection of Richmond P Bond and Marjorie N Bond*. Chapel Hill, NC, 1965. *Books and Libraries at the University of Kansas*, v 7:1, Feb 1970.

PERIODICALS, BRITISH—19TH CENTURY

IL —NEWBERRY LIBRARY, 60 W Walton St, Chicago, 60610. Diana Haskell, Cur of Modern Mss
Holdings: Cat
Notes: A strong collection.

PERIODICALS, BRUNEI

IL —CENTER FOR RESEARCH LIBRARIES, 6050 S Kenwood Ave, Chicago, 60637. Donald B Simpson, Dir; Esther Smith, Collection Development Librn
Holdings: Uncat Microforms
Notes: Receive serials and monographs fromm Indonesia, Malaysia and Singapore under NPAC (formerly PL 480). Collection starts 1969 for Indonesia, 1971 for Malaysia, Singapore and Brunei. Buy 14 newspapers on microfilm. Also incl Southeast Asia Microform Project. Borrowing is restricted to members of the project.

PERIODICALS, BULGARIAN

IL —UNIVERSITY OF ILLINOIS, URBANA/CHAMPAIGN, Slavic and East European Library, Urbana, 61801. Marianna Tax Choldin, Head
Holdings: Vols (9200) Cat Microforms
Notes: Extensive coverage.

PERIODICALS, BUSINESS

OH —PUBLIC LIBRARY OF CINCINNATI & HAMILTON COUNTY, Government and Business Dept, 800 Vine St, Cincinnati, 45202. Paul T Hudson, Head
Holdings: Vols 120,000 Cat
Notes: Department receives over 1200 periodical and loose-leaf service titles, 1500 serial titles and over 1500 telephone directories. Subjects include political science, especially foreign relations, economics, law, public administration and business management. Dept houses Murray Seasongood collection of local government. Dept has extensive census material from 1790. Library is a full depository for US Government Publications, 1884 to date.

PERIODICALS, CALIFORNIA

CA —A K SMILEY PUBLIC LIBRARY, 125 W Vine St, Redlands, 92373. Larry E Burgess, Archivist
Holdings: Vols (3500) Mss Maps Pix Phonorecords Microforms
Budget: ($45,000)
Notes: Emphasis on San Bernadino County and the Redlands area. Especially prized is *The Citrograph*, 1887-1908 (bound vols and microfilm) edited by Scipio Craig, prominent in state, national, and newspaper circles. The ms collection (250,000 pieces) incl the Smiley Family papers, much on water development, and on the citrus industry. The photograph collection (over 5000) covers the history of the area; there are many stereographs and glass slides. The collection on Indians of California and the Southwest was begun from a special gift by Andrew Carnegie honoring his friend, Albert K Smiley.

PERIODICALS, CANADIAN

AB —UNIVERSITY OF CALGARY, Libraries, Special Collections Div, 2500 University Dr, Calgary, T2N 1N4, Can.
Holdings: Mss
Notes: The Division has extensive collections of the papers of modern Canadian authors (qv individuals), incl Hugh MacLennan, Mordecai Richler, Brian Moore, W O Mitchell, Cliff Faulknor, Christie Harris, Robert Kroetsch, Rudy Wiebe, Claude Peloquin, George Ryga, Andre Langevin, Malcolm Ross, Bruce Hutchison, John Mellor, Grant MacEwan, James Gray, Ernest Watkins, Len Peterson, Michael Cook, & Joanna Glass. The papers of musician Morris Surdin contain hundreds of Canadian Broadcasting Corporation scripts, and constitute a valuable addition to the purely literary ms collections. The Division's holdings also incl collections of scores by Canadian musicians R Murray Schafer and Bruce Mather. In addition, the records of the following Canadian publishing houses are on deposit: E C W Press, Hancock House Publishers Ltd and Coach House Press. The Division alsohouses small collections of letters and mss of Canadian poets such as Earle Birney and George Bowering as well as the archives of the literary periodicals *Tish, Imago, Ariel, Descant, Canadian Review Magazine*, and *Canadian Short Story Magazine*. The ms collections are complemented by a book collection of some 5000 vols.

ON —NATIONAL LIBRARY OF CANADA, 395 Wellington St, Ottawa, K1A 0N4, Can. Andre Preibish, Dir
Budget: $315,000
Notes: Collection consists of over 33,000 Canadian titles in all subject fields, received on legal deposit, plus over 6000 foreign titles in the social sciences and humanities. Canadian serials have been received on legal deposit since 1966. Earlier serials were purchased. Collection of Canadian serials covers all subjects and aims to be comprehensive; Foreign serials are acquired in the fields of social sciences and humanities only.

ON —UNIVERSITY OF TORONTO, Thomas Fisher Rare Book Library, 120 Saint George St, Toronto, M5S 1A5, Can. Richard G Landon, Head
Holdings: Vols 6535 Uncat
Notes: Maclean-Hunter and Southam Press Collections contain periodicals issued by these two Canadian publishers. These are largely trade journlas. Many long and complete runs of items like *Canadian Footwear, Electrical News and Engineering; Gift Buyer; Canadian Home Journal; Chatelaine; Macleans;* etc. Many runs originate in 1880s and 1890s. Also include current publications. Approx 268 titles. Fisher Library designated the official archives for published material by Maclean-Hunter and Southam Press.

PERIODICALS, CHEMICAL

MA —HARVARD UNIVERSITY LIBRARY, Converse Memorial Library, Chemistry Library, 12 Oxford St, Cambridge, 02138. Ludmila Birladeanu, Supv
Holdings: Vols (50,000) Cat Microforms
Budget: ($110,000)
Notes: Also, 13,000 bound periodical vols; 23,000 foreign chemical theses.

OH —PUBLIC LIBRARY OF CINCINNATI & HAMILTON COUNTY, Science & Technology Dept, 800 Vine St, Cincinnati, 45202. Rosemary Gaiser, Head
Holdings: Vols (250,000) Cat
Notes: Pure and applied science. Incl over 1600 periodicals and serial titles and more than 100 abstracting and indexing services in major fields of science and technology.

OH —CASE WESTERN RESERVE UNIVERSITY LIBRARIES, Chemistry Department Library, Cleveland, 44106.
Notes: Chemistry department subscribes to chemistry abstracts. Current periodicals in Sears Library; with some old periodicals in special collections.

PERIODICALS, CHESS

NY —BROOKLYN PUBLIC LIBRARY, Art & Music Div, Grand Army Plaza, Brooklyn, 11238. Sue H Sharma, Chief
Holdings: Vols (4500) Cat Mss
Notes: "One of the finest collections of literature on chess and checkers in the world...incl some of the rarest books that exist on the subject..." Second largest collection of its kind, after that of the Cleveland Public Library. Incl private collections of William T Call (checkers), Melvin Brown, and R H Rimington-Wilson. Books are in many languages, from the 15th century to date. Incl many valuable mss, complete runs of most of the best-known periodicals, and over 100 scrapbooks of newspaper and periodical clippings. Many first editions and rare titles.

PERIODICALS, CHILDREN'S

CA —LOS ANGELES PUBLIC LIBRARY, Children's Literature Dept, 630 W 5th St, Los Angeles, 90071. Serenna Day, Sr Librn
Holdings: Cat
Notes: Fourteen 19th century juvenile magazines, some complete runs.

CT —TRINITY COLLEGE LIBRARY, Watkinson Library, 300 Summit St, Hartford, 06106. Jeffrey Kaimowitz, Cur
Holdings: Cat
Notes: Strong in 19th century material, including women's and children's periodicals.

DC —LIBRARY OF CONGRESS, Children's Literature Center, Washington, 20540. Sybille Jagusch, Chief
Holdings: Cat
Notes: Many bound runs of 19th-century magazines. Items in general collection and in Rare Book and Special Collections Division.

FL —FLORIDA STATE UNIVERSITY, Robert Manning Strozier Library, Childhood in Poetry Collection, Tallahassee, 32306. Frederick Korn, Cur
Holdings: Vols (25,000) Cat
Notes: The Childhood in Poetry Collection consists of the books of all the great poets and hundreds of minor poets of all periods, in first or other early and illustrated editions, in children's periodicals and "juveniles." There are more than 300 hymnals, incl the personal collection of Dr Robert Lowry, author of "Shall We Gather at the River" and other popular hymns. There are also nearly 500 annuals and gift books. The Collection is strong, as well, in works of criticism, biography and reference. An eleven-volume, illustrated catalog (1967-1980) is available from Gale Research. Over 200,000 poems are listed in a key-word index, keyed to the books in which they appear. The nucleus of the Collection was assembled as the lifetime leisure activity of the donor, John Mackay Shaw, who now serves as curator emeritus. His object has been to gather in one place the books inwhich poems relating to childhood first appeared.

MI —WAYNE STATE UNIVERSITY, Kresge Library (Education), Detroit, 48202. Theodore Manheim, Librn
Holdings: Vols (65,000) Cat Mss Microforms
Budget: ($2000)
Notes: The Eloise Ramsey Collection (10, 000 vols). See, *The Eloise Ramsey Collection of Literature for Young People: A Catalogue;* compiled by Joan Cusenza (Detroit: Wayne State University Libraries,

PERIODICALS, CHILDREN'S (cont.)

1967). Besides the Ramsey Collection, which is housed separately and does not circulate, the Education Library has approx 55,000 volumes of children's and young adults' literature, with a very large picture-book collection, a large poetry collection; all with special emphasis on urban and ethnic materials.

MN —UNIVERSITY OF MINNESOTA, Libraries, Children's Literature Research Collections, 109 Walter Library, Minneapolis, 55455. Karen Nelson Hoyle, Cur
Holdings: Cat
Notes: 19th and 20th century, primarily American and British; 150 titles. No photocopying. Kerlan Collection

MS —UNIVERSITY OF SOUTHERN MISSISSIPPI, William David McCain Graduate Library, Box 5148, Southern Sta, Hattiesburg, 39406.
Notes: Over 125 titles (1788-1950s), incl *Aunt Judy's Magazine, The Captain, Chatterbox, Demorest's Young America, Girl's Own Paper, Good Words for the Young, Juvenile Magazine, Little Folks, Our Young Folks, St Nicholas, The Union Jack, Wide Awake,* and *Youth's Companion.*

OH —CASE WESTERN RESERVE UNIVERSITY, M A Baxter School of Information and Library Science, 10900 Euclid Ave, Cleveland, 44106. Bettina MacAyeal, Librn; Gretchen Larson, Librn
Holdings: Vols (1100)
Notes: Incl collection of 1100 historical children's books and periodicals, housed in the Special Collections Dept of Freiberger Library, and can be used by the public. Incl *The Holy Bible Abridged* published by Isaiah Thomas in 1786, *The Life and Strange Surprising Adventures of Robinson Crusoe* of 1790, and a *Cinderella* dated 1809. There are examples of the work of illustrators Walter Crane, Randolph Caldecott, Kate Greenaway and Maurice Boutet de Monvel. The periodical collection incl a complete run of St. Nicholas Magazine.

TX —NORTH TEXAS STATE UNIVERSITY, Libraries, NT Station Box 5188, Denton, 76203. Margaret Galloway, General Librn; Pat Stinson, Library Science Librn
Holdings: Vols (29,776)
Notes: Juvenile Collection. Incl 1500 rare items located in the Rare Book Room. Card catalogs for both regular and rare collections. Rare items cover primarily 1800-1940.

WI —UNIVERSITY OF WISCONSIN, MADISON, Cooperative Children's Book Center, Helen C White Hall, Rm 4290, 600 N Park St, Madison, 53706. Ginny Moore Kruse, Dir
Holdings: Vols (25,000) Cat
Notes: Cooperative Children's Book Center collections incl most US trade books published for children in last 24 months; first editions of recommended US children's trade books published since 1965; over 400 alternative press books published for children in US and Canada since 1970; children's books about Wisconsin and by Wisconsin authors and illustrators; representative 19th and early 20th century American children's books; 19th century children's periodicals; first and significant editions of Newbury and Caldecott Medal books; historical and contemporary toybooks; 75 vols of Mother Goose published since 1828; 160 vols of Thorton Burgess books, many first editions; ms and original artwork for Ellen Raskin's *The Westing Game* and *The Mysterious Disappearance of Leon (I Mean Noel);* juvenile mass market and traderomance fiction.

PERIODICALS, CHINESE

IL —CENTER FOR RESEARCH LIBRARIES, 6050 S Kenwood Ave, Chicago, 60637. Donald B Simpson, Dir; Esther Smith, Collection Development Librn
Holdings: Microforms
Notes: 2000 reels of microfilm of mainland Chinese newspapers, periodicals and clippings. Microfilm and reprints of serials from Center for Chinese research materials.

RI —BROWN UNIVERSITY, John Hay Library, 20 Prospect St, Providence, 02912. Mark N Brown, Cur Mss
Holdings: Vols (74,000) Cat Microforms
Budget: ($10,000)
Notes: East Asia Collection--the primary focus is on Chinese studies with a small segment of approx 700 vols devoted to Japanese studies. Major subject areas, in descending order of strength, are: literature (incl classics), history, geography, social sciences, philosophy and religion, fine arts, science and technology. This incl the personal collection (20,000 vols) formed by Harvard University Sinologist Dr Charles Sideny Gardner, which is especially rich in materials relating to the Ch'ing Dynasty (1644-1912). In addition to books, there are 500 reels of microfilm, plus runs of 8 Chinese newspapers and 25 current Chinese periodicals.

TX —UNIVERSITY OF TEXAS LIBRARIES, Asian Collection, PO Box P, Austin, 78712. Kevin Lin, Asian Librn; Merry Burlingham, South Asian Librn
Holdings: Vols Cat Microforms
Notes: Anthropology, economics, government, history, and language and literature of China. Incl 230 periodical titles.

SK —UNIVERSITY OF SASKATCHEWAN, Library, Saskatoon, S7N 0W0, Can. S Perkins, Librn
Notes: *Documents on Contemporary China,* 1949-1975, 525 microfiches; material from a wide variety of sources. Much on Red Guard and the Cultural Revolution. The Library also holds the *Survey of China Mainland Press.*

PERIODICALS, CUBAN AMERICAN

FL —UNIVERSITY OF MIAMI, Otto G Richter Library, PO Box 248214, Coral Gables, 33124. Frank Rodgers, Dir of Libraries
Notes: 412 Cuban exile periodicals, 381 of which have been published in Miami, Florida.

PERIODICALS, CUBAN EXILES'

FL —UNIVERSITY OF MIAMI, Otto G Richter Library, PO Box 248214, Coral Gables, 33124. Frank Rodgers, Dir of Libraries
Notes: The Cuban exile periodicals incl 412 titles of which 381 have been published in Miami, Florida. The archival material incl 54 cubic ft of mss, invitations, programs, braodsides, posters, postcards, prints, reports, maps, etc. This collection incl personal and corporate papers of Cubans settled in the US or in other countries. The truth about Cuban Committee Papers. 40 cubic ft. Contains records and correspondence of intellectual and professional Cuban and American leaders in the US dedicated to the course of eliminating Communism from the Western Hemisphere.

PERIODICALS, CZECH

IL —UNIVERSITY OF ILLINOIS, URBANA/CHAMPAIGN, Slavic and East European Library, Urbana, 61801. Marianna Tax Choldin, Head
Holdings: Vols (35,000) Cat
Notes: Extensive coverage.

NE —UNIVERSITY OF NEBRASKA-LINCOLN, Don L Love Library, Czech Heritage Collection, Lincoln, 68588. Joseph G Svoboda, University Archivist
Holdings: Vols (3000) Cat Mss Pix Audiotapes Microforms
Notes: The Czech Heritage Collection.

PERIODICALS, DUTCH EAST INDIAN

OH —CLEVELAND PUBLIC LIBRARY, Fine Arts and Special Collections Department, 325 Superior Ave, Cleveland, 44114. Alice N Loranth, Head
Holdings: Vols (2000) Cat Mss Maps
Notes: Emphasis is on materials concerning Dutch East India. Complete runs of the Dutch serials and periodicals, such as the publications of the *Indisch Genootschnap, Instituut voor Taal-, Land- en Volkenkunde,* etc are the strengths of this collection. *See also* entry under Oriental Languages and Literatures.

PERIODICALS, EARLY

DC —LIBRARY OF CONGRESS, General Reading Rooms Division, Microform Reading Room, Washington, 20540.
Holdings: Cat Mss Maps Pix Microforms
Notes: Microform materials only in this LC Division. Works of individual authors; holdings of collections; archival records, etc, press releases and translations, etc.

NY —BUFFALO & ERIE COUNTY PUBLIC LIBRARY, Rare Book Room, Lafayette Sq, Buffalo, 14203. William H Loos, Cur
Holdings: Vols 500 Cat

PERIODICALS, EARLY ART see Periodicals, Art, Early

PERIODICALS, EARTH SCIENCES

CA —UNIVERSITY OF CALIFORNIA, BERKELEY, Physical Sciences Libraries, Earth Sciences Library, 230 Earth Sciences Bldg, Berkeley, 94720. Julie F Rinaldi, Librn
Holdings: Vols (83,202) Cat Microforms Maps
Budget: ($74,880)
Notes: Library maintains a strong research collection in all aspects of geology. The collection is particularly rich in serial holdings; long runs of periodicals; approx (2850) current serial titles, and extensive foreign (espec Slavic) language coverage. Whereas coverage is world-wide in scope, emphasis is given to materials dealing with the geology of the western United States.

PERIODICALS, ECUADOREAN

NC —DUKE UNIVERSITY, William R Perkins Library, Durham, 27706. Elvin E Strowd, University Librn
Notes: The Leonardo Jenaro Munoz collection of material on Ecuador consists of more than 2000 volumes (with additions continuing) primarily history, politics and economics; it contains numbers of special documents, journals, and government publications largely 19th and 20th century material.

PERIODICALS, EDUCATION

MI —WAYNE STATE UNIVERSITY, Kresge Library (Education), Detroit, 48202. Theodore Manheim, Librn
Holdings: Vols (297,000) Cat Microforms
Budget: ($105,000)
Notes: Incl complete ERIC microfiche file. 1191 current serial subscriptions. Also 35 drawers of vertical file material. Separate catalog to the collection.

OH —CLEVELAND PUBLIC LIBRARY, Social Sciences Department, 325 Superior Ave, Cleveland, 44114. Thelma Morris, Head
Notes: Strength of collection is in long runs of periodical sets spanning years from early 1800s. Majority of journals in the *Education Index* are held.

PERIODICALS, FOREIGN

IL —UNIVERSITY OF ILLINOIS, URBANA/CHAMPAIGN, Slavic and East European Library, Urbana, 61801. Marianna Tax Choldin, Head
Holdings: Vols (420,000) Cat
Notes: One of the largest Slavic and East European collections. Strong in Russian and Soviet materials-humanities, sciences, and social sciences; languages and literatures; periodicals, newspapers, and microforms. Ca 260,000 volumes in languages of the Soviet Union plus 20,000 Russian and Ukrainian titles on microform. Extensive coverage of Czechoslovakia (35,000 vols); Yugoslavia

PERIODICALS, FOREIGN (cont.)

(31,000 vols); Bulgaria (9200 vols); Poland (34,600 vols); Romania (13,000 vols); and Hungary (18,000 vols) and the languages, literatures, and history of these countries.

MA —BOSTON PUBLIC LIBRARY, South End Branch, Multilingual Library, 685 Tremont St, Boston, 02118. Laura H Reyes, Librn
Holdings: Cat

MA —HARVARD UNIVERSITY LIBRARY, Widener Library, Modern Greek Collection, Cambridge, 02138. Evangelie Flessas, Librn
Holdings: Vols (80,000) Cat Mss Microforms
Notes: In Greek language.

PA —CARNEGIE LIBRARY OF PITTSBURGH, Science & Technology Dept, 4400 Forbes Ave, Pittsburgh, 15213. Catherine M Brosky, Dept Head
Notes: This department serves as the Resource Library for Science and Technology in the Commonwealth of Pennsylvania. Agreements with other Resource Libraries in the Commonwealth and with certain institutions in Pittsburgh for sharing resources, cooperative acquisition of materials, provision of services and information. Collections described in *Guide to the Regional Library Resource Centers of Pennsylvania*, compiled by Ralph W McComb, 1967.

PA —SCRANTON PUBLIC LIBRARY, Vine & N Washington Sts, Scranton, 18503. Thomas McHale, Dir
Holdings: Vols (192) Cat
Budget: ($7000)
Notes: Foreign trade information service.

ON —METROPOLITAN TORONTO LIBRARY, Languages Centre, 789 Yonge St, Toronto, M4W 2G8, Can. Barbara Gunther, Head
Holdings: Vols (90,000) Cat Phonorecords Audiotapes
Notes: Original literature in over 80 languages; books, records, cassettes, microfilm on language studies; newspapers and periodicals from 50 counties. Language study materials. Issue quarterly additions lists by language. Collect North American Indian and Eskimo language materials. Occasional bibliographies.

PERIODICALS, FOREIGN LANGUAGE (AMERICAN)

PA —BALCH INSTITUTE FOR ETHNIC STUDIES, Library, 18 S Seventh St, Philadelphia, 19106. R Joseph Anderson, Library Dir
Holdings: Vols Microforms
See also entry under Ethnic Newspapers - North America.

PERIODICALS, FRENCH

CA —UNIVERSITY OF CALIFORNIA, BERKELEY, University Library, French and Italian Collections, Berkeley, 94720. Donald G Williams, Librn
See also entry under French Language and Literature.

CA —UNIVERSITY OF CALIFORNIA, LOS ANGELES, Research Library, Western European Collection, Los Angeles, 90024. Edward Shreeves, Chairman, Bibliographers Group; Mary E Greco, Western European Bibliographer
Holdings: Microforms
Notes: Microfilm records (8 reels) of 51 newspapers and periodicals of the French Resistance, from 1940 to 1944.

DC —CATHOLIC UNIVERSITY OF AMERICA, Canon Law Library, 300B Mullen Library, Washington, 20064. R Bruce Miller, Librn
Holdings: Vols (22,000)
Notes: The collection includes extensive 16th, 17th, and 18th century works in both Latin and Italian. There are many printed editions of pre-16th century sources. Both the 19th and 20th century materials are well represented. This collection is also rich in materials relating to the Second Vatican Council and its aftermath and is up-to-date on the new (1983) Code of Canon Law. Current periodical subscriptions to journals in English, German, French, Italian, and Spanish.

NY —FRENCH INSTITUTE-ALLIANCE FRANCAISE, Library, 22 E 60 St, New York, 10022. Fred J Gitner, Librn
Holdings: Vols (40,000) Cat Phonorecords Audiotapes
Budget: ($23,000)
Notes: Receive approx 85 current titles and hold back-files of many French periodicals no longer published.

WI —UNIVERSITY OF WISCONSIN, MADISON, Memorial Library, 728 State St, Madison, 53706. Erwin K Welsch, Social Studies Bibliographer
Holdings: Cat Microforms
Notes: French Socialism Collection, 1871-1914. Collection of pamphlets, periodicals, and monographs on French socialism and the working-class movement. Incl the reports of 81 socialist congresses held from 1876 to 1914 (original, manuscript or microfilm), manuscripts and other materials from the First International, and a very large collection (in microform) of periodicals, together with a substantial number of volumes in the original. Described in Jack A Clarke, "French Social Congresses," *Journal of Modern History*, 31 (June, 1959), pp 124-129; Robert Brecy, *Le Mouvement syndical en France 1871-1921* (Paris, 1963) can also be used as a guide since 90 percent of the items cited are in the collection.

PERIODICALS, GEOLOGICAL

CA —UNIVERSITY OF CALIFORNIA, BERKELEY, Physical Sciences Libraries, Earth Sciences Library, 230 Earth Sciences Bldg, Berkeley, 94720. Julie F Rinaldi, Librn
Holdings: Vols (83,202) Cat Maps Microforms
Budget: ($74,880)
Notes: Library maintains a strong research collection in all aspects of geology. The collection is particularly rich in serial holdings; long runs of periodicals; approx (2850) current serial titles, and extensive foreign (espec Slavic) language coverage. Whereas coverage is world-wide in scope, emphasis is given to materials dealing with the geology of the western United States.

IL —UNIVERSITY OF ILLINOIS, URBANA/CHAMPAIGN, Library, Geology Library, 223 Natural History Bldg, Urbana, 61801. Dederick Ward, Librn
Holdings: Vols (105,186) Cat Maps Microforms
Notes: Incl complete sets of outstanding geological surveys of the US, states, Canada and most foreign countries; espec strong for India and Latin America; the same is true for geological journals, incl Russia-- a special strength since 1960. Extensive collection of early geological literature and rare books, perhaps the most extensive. Library houses the university's collection of 21,000 cataloged geological maps, incl many rarities. Special collection of aerial photographs.

PERIODICALS, GERMAN

CA —HOOVER INSTITUTION ON WAR, REVOLUTION & PEACE, Stanford University, Stanford, 94305. Milorad M Drachkovitch, Archivist
Holdings: Vols (16,000) Cat Mss Pix Microforms
Notes: The German history collections extend from a set of Reichstage Debates, 1870-1918, the Revolution of 1918-1919, the Weimar Government, the National Socialist State, World War II, the period of Allied Occupation to the present, incl materials for both the Federal Republic of Germany and the Democratic Republic. Particulary noteworthy are holdings of newspapers, incl *Vorwaerts*, *Voelkischer Beobachter*, and periodicals, incl *Sueddeutsche Monatshefte*, *Einheit*. Of archival interest are the microfilms of the NSDAP Hauptarchiv (155 reels). Guides: *The Hoover Library Collections on Germany*, Hildegard R Boeninger (Stanford, 1955) and *Western Europe*, Agnes F Peterson (Stanford, 1970).

CA —STANFORD UNIVERSITY LIBRARIES, Cecil H Green Library, Stanford, 94305. Peter R Frank, Cur, CDP-Germanic Collection
Holdings: Vols 4605 Cat
Notes: Stanford has an extensive collection of periodicals from the German area, rare original periodicals from the Baroque, Enlightenment and later periods, reprints and on microform. Rare items are in the Stanford Collection of German, Austrian and Swiss Culture. Description: "New Look at Old Times: Early German Periodicals and German Periodicals from the late 18th Century to the Thirties" by Peter R Frank.

DC —CATHOLIC UNIVERSITY OF AMERICA, Canon Law Library, 300B Mullen Library, Washington, 20064. R Bruce Miller, Librn
Holdings: Vols (22,000)
Notes: The collection includes extensive 16th, 17th, and 18th century works in both Latin and Italian. There are many printed editions of pre-16th century sources. Both the 19th and 20th century materials are well represented. This collection is also rich in materials relating to the Second Vatican Council and its aftermath and is up-to-date on the new (1983) Code of Canon Law. Current periodical subscriptions to journals in English, German, French, Italian, and Spanish.

WI —UNIVERSITY OF WISCONSIN, MADISON, Memorial Library, 728 State St, Madison, 53706. Erwin K Welsch, Social Studies Bibliographer
Holdings: Vols (50,000)
Notes: Periodicals from all humanistic, historical, social scientific and scientific fields from all periods with noticeable strength in the 19th and 20th centuries. Incl periodicals of literary groups as well as political parties and academies of science (almost complete) and similar organizations. *See also* entries under German Democratic Republic; National Socialism.

PERIODICALS, HAWAIIAN

HI —BERNICE P BISHOP MUSEUM, Library, PO Box 19000-A, Honolulu, 96819. Cynthia Timberlake, Librn
Notes: Early voyages, natural and general history, archaeology, and ethnology of the Pacific area. Hawaiian materials incl mss, maps, 360,000 photographs dating from 1845, and Hawaiian language newspapers.

PERIODICALS, INDIAN (NORTH AMERICA AND MEXICO) see Periodicals, American Indian

PERIODICALS, INSURANCE

NY —COLLEGE OF INSURANCE, Library, 123 William St, New York, 10038. Donald Carson, Chief Librn
Holdings: Vols (52,543) Cat Pix
Budget: ($50,000)
Notes: Collection contains 53,322 pieces of VF material. Included in the collection are 6374 bound vols of US and foreign periodicals dating back to 19th century; laws and regulations of the insurance departments of all 50 states, as well as those of Canada and other foreign countries; 16th century treatise on marine insurance.

PERIODICALS, INTERNATIONAL LAW

DC —LIBRARY OF CONGRESS, Law Library, 101 Independence Ave, SE, Washington, 20540. Carleton W Kenyon, Dir
Holdings: Vols Microforms
Notes: The Law Library receives 270 national, state, provincial, regional, and municipal gazettes from 118 countries.

PERIODICALS, IRISH

WI —UNIVERSITY OF WISCONSIN, MADISON, Memorial Library, 728 State St, Madison, 53706. Erwin K Welsch, Social

PERIODICALS, IRISH (cont.)

Studies Bibliographer
Holdings: Vols (25,000) Microforms
Notes: Covers all fields of English and Irish life, literary, historical, scientific and social scientific. Also incl special collections of gift annuals, eg *Aunt Judy's Annual,* on Temperance, Free Thought, labor literature and periodicals from various groups and organizations, eg *Charity Organization Review.* Notably strong in the serial publicatons of scholarly societies, eg Manchester Statistical Society. Collection partly described in Erwin K Welsch, "A Preliminary Checklist of English and Irish Periodcials Published between 1800 and 1914 in the Memorial Library University of Wisconsin-Madison" (Madison, 1982).

ON —MCMASTER UNIVERSITY, Mills Memorial Library, Div of Archives & Research Collections, Hamilton, L8S 4L6, Can. G R Hill, Univ Librn
Holdings: Cat Mss
Notes: The main part of this collection consists of works from the Anglo-Irish renaissance, 1890 to 1939. There is also a small archival collection, as well as extensive runs of some Irish periodicals.

PERIODICALS, ITALIAN

DC —CATHOLIC UNIVERSITY OF AMERICA, Canon Law Library, 300B Mullen Library, Washington, 20064. R Bruce Miller, Librn
Holdings: Vols (22,000)
Notes: The collection includes extensive 16th, 17th, and 18th century works in both Latin and Italian. There are many printed editions of pre-16th century sources. Both the 19th and 20th century materials are well represented. This collection is also rich in materials relating to the Second Vatican Council and its aftermath and is up-to-date on the new (1983) Code of Canon Law. Current periodical subscriptions to journals in English, German, French, Italian, and Spanish.

MI —MICHIGAN STATE UNIVERSITY, Libraries, Special Collections Div, East Lansing, 48824. Jannette Fiore, Librn
Notes: The primary emphasis of this collection is on the central period of the Italian Risorgimento, 1845-1870. It includes accounts by eyewitnesses, works by significant political figures, many scarce political pamphlets and complete runs of several key serial publications. The library is actively acquiring additional materials to support and expand this subject collection. 1500 pamphlets; 7000 issues of newspapers and periodicals.

PERIODICALS, JAPANESE

IL —CENTER FOR RESEARCH LIBRARIES, 6050 S Kenwood Ave, Chicago, 60637. Donald B Simpson, Dir; Esther Smith, Collection Development Librn
Holdings: Vols Cat
Notes: About 520 current scientific journal subscriptions.

MI —GENERAL MOTORS, Research Laboratories Library, General Motors Technical Center, Warren, 48090. Robert W Gibson, Librn

TX —UNIVERSITY OF TEXAS LIBRARIES, Asian Collection, PO Box P, Austin, 78712. Kevin Lin, Asian Librn; Merry Burlingham, South Asian Librn
Holdings: Vols Cat Microforms
Notes: Anthropology, economics, government, history, and language and literature of Japan. Incl 120 periodical titles.

PERIODICALS, JEWISH

NY —YIVO INSTITUTE FOR JEWISH RESEARCH, Library & Archives, 1048 Fifth Ave, New York, 10028. Dina Abramowicz, Librn; Marek Web, Archivist
Holdings: Cat Mss Pix

OH —HEBREW UNION COLLEGE-JEWISH INSTITUTE OF RELIGION, Klau Library,

3101 Clifton Ave, Cincinnati, 45220. David J Gilner, Reference Librn
Holdings: Cat Microforms
Notes: American Jewish Periodical Center aims to microfilm every American Jewish newspaper and periodical up to 1925 and selectively since. See: American Jewish Periodical Center, *Jewish Newspapers and Periodicals on Microfilm Available at the AJPC* (Cincinnati, 1983).

PERIODICALS, JUVENILE see Periodicals, Children'S

PERIODICALS, LABOR

CA —UNIVERSITY OF CALIFORNIA, BERKELEY, University Library, Social Science Library, 30 Stephens Hall, Berkeley, 94720. Bette Erskine, Librn
Holdings: Vols 11,000 Cat Mss Microforms
Notes: The Labor Union Collection consists primarily of labor union journals, newspapers, proceedings and constitutions. Holdings are largely national in scope, with emphasis on Northern California. Approximately 850 current serials are being received. This collection is complemented by labor union materials in the Institute of Industrial Relations Library and in The Bancroft Library, and by holdings in Labor History in the Main Library. Incl 1683 microfilm reels.

OK —UNIVERSITY OF TULSA, McFarlin Library, Dept of Rare Books and Special Collections, 600 S College, Tulsa, 74104. David Farmer, Dir; Toby Murray, Archivist; Caroline Swinson, Cur of Manuscripts & Art
Holdings: Vols 2000
Notes: A major collection of Proletarian literature based on Walter Rideout's *The Radical Novel in the United States,* 1900-1954.

PERIODICALS, LANGUAGE

NY —NEW YORK PUBLIC LIBRARY, Mid-Manhattan Library, Literature and Language Dept, 455 Fifth Ave, New York, 10016. Eric Steele, Sr Principal Librn
Holdings: Vols (160,000) Cat Phonorecords Microforms Audiotapes
Budget: ($92,000)
Notes: Broad coverage for the study of over 100 languages and dialects, materials on most areas of theoretical and applied linguistics. Extensive runs of major journals. 3000 records and cassettes aid in the learning of 40 languages, in addition to English.

PERIODICALS, LATIN AMERICAN

IL —SOUTHERN ILLINOIS UNIVERSITY, CARBONDALE, Delyte W Morris Library, Carbondale, 62901.
Holdings: Vols (19,000) Cat
Notes: Especially strong in Ecuadorean and Mexican literature; complete or almost complete files of many important literary journals published in Spanish America. Described in Woodbridge, Hensley C, "Faculty and library collaboration in developing the Latin American collection for area studies programs at Southern Illinois University," Twelfth Seminar on the Acquisition of Latin American Library Materials, Final Report and Working Papers, vol 2, pp 99-108 (1967).

IA —UNIVERSITY OF IOWA, University Libraries, Iowa City, 52242. Frank Paluka, Head, Special Collections Dept
Holdings: Vols (13,170) Cat
Notes: F M Lauritsen, "Rare 19th-Century Latin American Periodicals", *Books at Iowa,* November 1969.

MO —UNIVERSITY OF MISSOURI-COLUMBIA, Ellis Library, Language and Literature Dept, Columbia, 65201. Jeaneice Brewer, Librn
Holdings: Vols Cat
Notes: Greatest strength of this collection is in long back-runs of periodicals, especially those dealing with Mexico.

TX —UNIVERSITY OF TEXAS LIBRARIES, Nettie Lee Benson Latin American

Collection, Sid Richardson Hall 1.109, Austin, 78712. Laura Gutierrez-Witt, Head Librn
Holdings: Vols Cat Periodicals
Notes: Ca 25,000 periodical titles, cataloged. *Benson Latin American Collection Serials* List published in microfiche by The General Libraries, University of Texas.
See also entry under Latin America.

PERIODICALS, LATVIAN

NY —NEW YORK PUBLIC LIBRARY, Slavonic Div, Fifth Ave & 42 St, New York, 10018. Edward Kasinec, Chief
Holdings: Cat Microforms
Notes: See: New York Public Library, Slavonic Div, *Dictionary Catalog of the Slavonic Collection,* 2nd ed, rev and enl (Boston: G K Hall, 1974), 44 vols; and New York Public Library, *Dictionary Catalog of the Research Libraries* (New York, 1972-).

PERIODICALS, LAW

DC —LIBRARY OF CONGRESS, Law Library, 101 Independence Ave, SE, Washington, 20540. Carleton W Kenyon, Dir
Holdings: Vols Microforms
Notes: The Law Library receives 270 national, state, provincial, regional, and municipal gazettes from 118 countries.

PERIODICALS, LITERARY

DC —LIBRARY OF CONGRESS, General Reading Rooms Division, Microform Reading Room, Washington, 20540.
Holdings: Cat Mss Maps Pix Microforms
Notes: Microform materials only in this LC Division. Works of individual authors; holdings of collections; archival records, etc, press releases and translations, etc.

ME —BOWDOIN COLLEGE, Library, Brunswick, 04011. Dianne M Gutscher, Cur of Special Collections
Holdings: Mss Pix
Notes: The Abbott Memorial Collection contains both printed and manuscript materials relating to Jacob Abbott, John S C Abbott, Edward Abbott and Lyman Abbott, as well as other members of the family. It consists of approximately 25,000 items, including correspondence, sermons, diaries and journals, addresses, the archives of both the *Literary World* and *Outlook* magazines, and the Lyman Abbott autograph collection. First and subsequent editions of almost all of the family's published writings are also present.

RI —BROWN UNIVERSITY, John Hay Library, Harris Collection, Prospect St, Providence, 02912. Rosemary L Cullen, Cur
Holdings: Vols (200,000) Cat Mss Pix Phonorecords Microforms
Budget: ($15,000)
Notes: The Harris Collection of American Poetry and Plays is principally composed of American and Canadian poetry and plays, 17th century-date. Extensive holdings in songsters, gift books and annuals, hymnals, pageants, broadside verse, carriers' addresses, women poets, juvenile poetry, (incl Mother Goose and *The Night Before Christmas*), sheet music with lyrics, small press publications, fine printing, black poets, "little magazines," Yiddish-American literature. All movements or schools of American poetry are represented. Incl first editions of most American poets and playwrights, notably Whitman, Poe, Wallace Stevens, Eugene O'Neill, Edward Albee, Ezra Pound, T S Eliot, William Carlos Williams, Amy Lowell, Phyllis Wheatley, Robert Frost, Allen Ginsberg, Bliss Carman, and Stephen Foster sheet music. Also incl the Saunders Walt Whitman Collection (1300 vols); the LangdonCollection of Pageants (250 vols); the Asa Cushman Collection of plays in ms and prompt copies; the MacDougall Collection of Psalters and Hymnals; 4000 plays issued by Walter H Baker Co, Boston (1890-1957); the Vaxer Collection of Yiddish Poetry, Plays and Music (1700 vols). Collections incl 200,000

PERIODICALS, LITERARY (cont.)

vols, 30,000 broadsides, 55,000 mss, 170,000 pieces of sheet music, 450 phonorecords, and 375 microfilm reels. See *Dictionary Catalog of the Harris Collection of American Poetry and Plays* (Boston: G K Hall, 1972), 13 vols; *Supplement* (1977), 3 vols. See also, *American Poetry, 1609-1900, A Collection on Microfilm, Segment I* (1609-1820); *Segment II* (1821-1850); *Segment III* (1851-1870)* (Woodbridge, Conn: Research Publications). Separate catalog.

PERIODICALS, LITHUANIAN

MN —UNIVERSITY OF MINNESOTA, Immigration History Research Center, 826 Berry St, Saint Paul, 55114. Susan Griegs, Cur
Notes: 500 separate titles of Lithuanian immigrant publications; materials published in displaced persons' camps by Lithuanians during and after World War II.

NY —NEW YORK PUBLIC LIBRARY, Slavonic Div, Fifth Ave & 42 St, New York, 10018. Edward Kasinec, Chief
Holdings: Cat Microforms
Notes: See: New York Public Library, Slavonic Div, *Dictionary Catalog of the Slavonic Collection*, 2nd ed, rev and encl (Boston: G K Hall, 1974), 44 vols; and New York Public Library, *Dictionary Catalog of the Research Libraries* (New York, 1972-).

PERIODICALS, MALAYSIAN

IL —CENTER FOR RESEARCH LIBRARIES, 6050 S Kenwood Ave, Chicago, 60637. Donald B Simpson, Dir; Esther Smith, Collection Development Librn
Holdings: Uncat Microforms
Budget: $15,000
Notes: Receive serials and monographs fromm Indonesia, Malaysia and Singapore under NPAC (formerly PL 480). Collection starts 1969 for Indonesia, 1971 for Malaysia, Singapore and Brunei. Buy 14 newspapers on microfilm. Also incl Southeast Asia Microform Project. Borrowing is restricted to members of the project.

PERIODICALS, MARINE

NY —STATE UNIVERSITY OF NEW YORK, Maritime College, Stephen B Luce Library, Fort Schuyler, Bronx, 10465. Richard H Corson, Librn
Holdings: Vols (68,000)
Budget: ($90,000)
Notes: Extensive holdings in periodical literature with long and complete of many titles.

PERIODICALS, MATHEMATICS

CA —UNIVERSITY OF CALIFORNIA, LOS ANGELES, Engineering & Mathematical Sciences Library, 405 Hilgard, Los Angeles, 90024. Rosalee I Wright, Librn
Holdings: Vols (180,000) Cat Microforms
See also entry under Engineering

IL —UNIVERSITY OF ILLINOIS, URBANA/CHAMPAIGN, Library, Mathematics Library, 216 Altgeld Hall, Urbana, 61801. Nancy D Anderson, Librn
Holdings: Vols 63,000 Cat Microforms
Budget: ($56,600)
Notes: The Mathematics Library is a comprehensive research collection. Subscribe to 450 periodical titles and 500 continuation titles. We collect essentially all monographs reviewed in Mathematical Reviews. Other strong areas are the collected works of the major mathematicians, arithmetics published prior to 1900, lecture notes, the publications of the major mathematical and scientific soceites, 1890 to date, and Easern European mathematical works. Library has not collected as extensively in applied mathematics, statistics, mathematics of computation, and the teaching of mathematics.

PERIODICALS, MEDICAL

AL —UNIVERSITY OF ALABAMA, BIRMINGHAM, Lister Hill Library of the Health Sciences, University Sta, Birmingham, 35294. Richard B Fredericksen, Dir

IL —CENTER FOR RESEARCH LIBRARIES, 6050 S Kenwood Ave, Chicago, 60637. Donald B Simpson, Dir; Esther Smith, Collection Development Librn
Holdings: Vols 190,000 Cat
Notes: Extensive collection of older medical journals, both US and foreign.

KS —UNIVERSITY OF KANSAS MEDICAL CENTER, College of Health Sciences & Hospital, Clendening History of Medicine Library, Rainbow Blvd at 39th, Kansas City, 66103. Robert P Hudson, Chmn/Cur
Holdings: Vols (15,725) Cat Mss
Notes: Strong in all fields of medical history. Incl incunabula and serials. Mss incl Jakob Henle, 1809-1885, papers (ca 4050 items); Howard Atwood Kelly, 1858-1943, correspondence (ca 90 items); Joseph Lister, 1827- 1912, letters (7); Florence Nightingale, 1820-1910, letters (20); and Samuel Jay Crumbine, 1862-1954, papers (ca 2365 items).

MD —MEDICAL & CHIRURGICAL FACULTY OF THE STATE OF MARYLAND, Library, 1211 Cathedral St, Baltimore, 21201. Joseph E Jensen, Librn
Holdings: Vols (110,000) Cat Mss Maps Pix Slides Audiotapes Videotapes Microforms
Budget: ($250,000)
Notes: Library for the state medical society. Open to the public, but circulation is restricted to members. The current acquisitions policy emphasizes English language monographs and periodicals on all aspects of clinical medicine, and on the social, economic, legal and administrative aspects of medical practice in the United States. The library subscribes to all state medical society journals in the United States. Holdings include a very fine history of medicine and rare medical book collection, and a strong collection of medical monographs and serials prior to 1900.

MD —NATIONAL LIBRARY OF MEDICINE, 8600 Rockville Pike, Bethesda, 20209. Harold M Schoolinam, Actg Dir
Holdings: Vols (3,150,000) Cat Mss Audiotapes Videotapes 16mm Films Filmstrips Microforms
Budget: ($46,400)
Notes: The world's largest medical library. Materials are collected exhaustively in some 40 biomedical areas and, to a lesser degree, in related subject areas such as general chemistry, physics, zoology, botany, and instrumentation. Holdings include 82,000 monographic volumes, pre-1871; 438,000 monographic volumes, 1871-present; 714,000 bound serial volumes; 281,000 theses; 172,000 pamphlets; 1,207,000 manuscripts; 156,000 microforms; 12,000 audiovisuals; and 75,000 prints and photographs. Pre-1871 material is in a separate historical collection. Approximately 24,000 serial titles are currenly received.

MA —FRANCIS A COUNTWAY LIBRARY OF MEDICINE, Boston Medical Library/ Harvard Medical Library, 10 Shattuck St, Boston, 02115. C Robin LeSueur, Librn; Richard J Wolfe, Cur, Rare Books & Manuscripts
Holdings: Vols (500,000) Cat Mss Maps Pix Microforms
Notes: Combines resources of the Harvard Medical School and the Boston Medical Library. Strong in serials and medical history in all fields of medicine, incl incunabula, non-medical books by doctors, travel books by doctors. 500,000 medical dissertations and theses. Special strength in all medical subjects listed in this volume. Over 21,000 periodicals titles for all periods.

MA —SOUTHWOOD COMMUNITY HOSPITAL, Medical Library, 111 Dedham St, Norfolk, 02056.
Holdings: Vols (800) Cat Audiotapes Filmstrips
Budget: ($4500)
Notes: The present emphasis is on human and animal research, diagnosis and treatment. Journals cataloged v 1-19, 1941-59; v 20, 1960-.

MN —MAYO MEDICAL LIBRARY, History of Medicine Collection, Rochester, 55905.

Nancy R Hensel, Librn
Notes: Incl 200 titles of early medical or scientific periodicals published before 1875; 34 titles from Ebert.

NY —COLD SPRING HARBOR LABORATORY, Library, PO Box 100, Cold Spring Harbor, 11724. Susan Gensel, Library Dir; Genemary Falvey, Librn
Holdings: Vols (30,000)
Budget: ($103,500)
Notes: The highly technical collection is comprised of 20,000 serial vols and 10,000 monographs. The library receives 500 current serial titles. Subjects covered incl molecular and cellular biology, virology, biochemistry, microbiology, oncology, neurobiology, biological risk assessment and genetic engineering/biotechnology. Special collections in eugenics and genetics are primarily historical dealing with the development of genetics in the US which had its beginnings here.

NY —UNIVERSITY OF ROCHESTER, School of Medicine and Dentistry, Edward G Miner Library, 601 Elmwood Ave, Rochester, 14642. Lucretia McClure, Medical Librn; Janet Brady Berk, History of Medicine Librn
Holdings: Vols (185,000) Cat
Notes: The Edward G Miner Library serves the School of Medicine & Dentistry, the School of Nursing, and Strong Memorial Hospital. The collection encompasses all the biomedical fields, nursing and dental research, and is designed to serve the teaching, patient care and research needs of persons in the Medical Center. The Library subscribes to more than 2900 current journals and serials, has an excellent reference collection and an extensive collection of rare and historical works in medicine and nursing.

PA —COLLEGE OF PHYSICIANS OF PHILADELPHIA, Library, 19 S 22 St, Philadelphia, 19103. Anthony Aguirre, Libr Dir
Holdings: Vols (316,223) Cat Mss Microforms
Budget: ($1,096,557)
Notes: Incl 13,515 pamphlets; 1435 mss; 326,367 reports, dissertations, and reprints. Strong historical and bibliographical collections, as well as current materials. Medical documentation service provides current alerting, incl abstracting, etc.

PA —PENNSYLVANIA HOSPITAL HISTORICAL LIBRARY, Eighth & Spruce Sts, Philadelphia, 19107. Caroline Morris, Librn
Holdings: Vols (12,963) // Cat Mss
Notes: First medical library in the US. Rich in runs of 19th century medical journals. Some early botany books. Some incunabula. Printed catalog was made in 1876. This collection is important because it reflects the history of medicine by the nature of the materials that were acquired. However, *no attempt is made to keep a current history of medicine library*.

TX —UNIVERSITY OF TEXAS, DALLAS, Health Science Center, Reference Dept & History of Health Sciences Dept, 5323 Harry Hines Blvd, Dallas, 75235. Helen Mayo, Head
Holdings: Vols (10,000) Cat Pix Slides Audiotapes Videotapes Microforms
Notes: History of Medicine collection contains ca 10,000 vols. This total is comprised of pre-1900 journals, primary materials in the History of Medicine and the History of Science, and secondary studies in these two areas. The major strengths of this collection are in the areas of epidemics and plagues, military medicine, and collected works of famous medical pioneers. Incl in this collection are the medical journals published by the county medical societies in Texas, local publications by Dallas County medical organizations, and ephemeral material in a similar vein. The university archives contain all theses and dissertations form UTHSCD and miscellaneous institutional documents circulated by the school's administration.

ON —CANADIAN MEDICAL ASSOCIATION, Library, PO Box 8650,

PERIODICALS, MEDICAL (cont.)

Ottawa, K1G 0G8, Can. Kathleen Beaudoin, Librn
Holdings: Vols 4000 Uncat
Notes: Mainly medical journals.

PERIODICALS, MOVING PICTURE

CA —ACADEMY OF MOTION PICTURE ARTS & SCIENCES, Margaret Herrick Library, 8949 Wilshire Blvd, Beverly Hills, 90211. Linda Harris Mehr, Library Administrator
Holdings: Vols (16,000) Cat Mss Pix Slides
Budget: ($250,000)
Notes: Also posters, scrapbooks, clippings and press books. Collection emphases are the moving picture industry, moving picture history, biographical material on actors, actresses and industry personnel. Files on specific films, reviews, cast and credits, production data, etc, on more than 65,000 moving pictures. (Over 5000 films, incl early 28mm films in Film Archive). Over 5 million pictures. Special collections: papers of Mary Pickford, Mack Sennett, Adolph Zukor, Lewis Milestone, George Stevens, George Cukor, John Huston, Edith Head; Paramount scripts and stills archive, MGM stills archive, RKO stills archive, Thomas H Ince stills collection, Cecil B DeMille stills collection.

CA —AMERICAN FILM INSTITUTE, Louis B Mayer Library, 2021 N Western Ave, PO Box 27999, Los Angeles, 90027. Anne G Schlosser, Dir
Notes: Rare periodical holdings: *Film Daily* newspaper (1923-1969); *Radio-TV Daily* newspaper (1939-1964); *RKO Radio Flash,* house organ for RKO (1932-1955); *TV Guide* (1948 to date).

CA —INSTITUTE OF THE AMERICAN MUSICAL, Library, 121 N Detroit St, Los Angeles, 90036. Miles Kreuger, Cur
Holdings: Cat Mss Maps Pix Slides Phonorecords
Notes: Reference materials on the American musical theatre and motion pictures incl 40,000 phonograph records, sound tapes, and cylinders dating back to the 1890s; record catalogs to 1900; thousands of theatre and film programs, periodicals, sheet music and vocal scores as early as 1830; thousands of motion picture press books and over 200,000 stills from 1914 to the present; every musical comedy script published in America and dozens in ms form, original or photocopy materials from the archives of movie palaces, films and record companies, incl discographies of many major Broadway and Hollywood stars; and thousands of books on theatre, film, broadcasting, world's fairs and other allied areas of showmanship.

NY —NEW YORK PUBLIC LIBRARY, Performing Arts Research Center, Billy Rose Theatre Collection, 111 Amsterdam Ave, New York, 10023. Dorothy L Swerdlove, Cur
Holdings: Cat
See also entries under Moving Pictures Industry; Moving Pictures - History; Theatre - History.

TX —SOUTHERN METHODIST UNIVERSITY, Fondren Library, McCord Theater Collection, Room 301, Dallas, 75275. Edyth Renshaw, Cur; Linda Sellers, Pub Serv
Holdings: Vols (2000) Uncat Mss Pix Slides Phonorecords
Notes: See *Theatre Collections in Libraries and Museums,* Gilder and Freedley (Theatre Arts, 1936). The McCord Theatre Collection encompasses the entire spectrum of the performing arts. The central purpose is to gather records of our regional theater before such ephemeral material is lost. Records of over two hundred early Texas theaters, some fragmentary and some relatively complete, are in the files. These records incl photographs of buildings, stagehands, orchestras, and performers. Local theatre history incl the once famous Dallas Little Theatre and the Margo Jones Theatre. The national theatre, opera, ballet, and circus archives incl pictures (some autographed), programs, posters, throw-aways, tear sheets, clippings, and letters. Our international archives are small, but we have some excellent material, eg, artifacts from Max Reinhardt's production of "The Miracle" which happened to go bankrupt in Dallas. After a few years the items were given to us. There are posters, tear-sheets, souvenir programs, and other colorful items from Morris Gest and the Artef Collection. We have about 200 19th century English playbills and a few from the 18th century. There is a collection of modern English, French, and other European programs, many of them illustrated souvenir programs. Also, magazines on theater, cinema, and television (1800). Scrapbooks covering both southwest and Dallas theater, 1890s-1950s. Special Collections: artifacts and documents on puppets; masks; costume design; circus; and ballet and dance. The Harriet Bacon MacDonald Collection of over 200 photographs of musicians appearing in Dallas during the first three decades of the 20th century. Many autographed. Affiliated with Meadow Theatre of the Arts.

ON —NATIONAL FILM, TELEVISION AND SOUND ARCHIVES, Documentation & Public Service, 395 Wellington St, Ottawa, K1A 0N3, Can. Jana Vosikovska, Chief; Gloria Grant, Librn; Sylvie Robitaille, Stills and Posters Librn
Notes: Several collections supporting the documentation on film, television and recorded sound: 1060 periodical titles (450 current), some on microfilm. Picture-stills, 265,000; moving picture posters, 6000; cataloged microfiche, 33,000 (vertical file material put on microfilm, then into a fiche format). Index cards (periodical references, credits): 334,000 cards (Film Title Index: 250,000 cards; Personalities Index: 84,000 cards).

PERIODICALS, MUSEUM

DC —SMITHSONIAN INSTITUTION LIBRARIES, General Library, Washington, 20560. Mary Claire Grey, Chief Cent Ref & Loan Servs
Holdings: Vols (79,000) Cat Mss Maps Pix Slides Microforms
Notes: Incl publications of foreign and domestic museums, and all phases of museum work.

PERIODICALS, MUSIC

CA —SANTA CRUZ PUBLIC LIBRARY, Art, Music, Film Dept, 224 Church St, Santa Cruz, 95060. Alma Westberg, Librn
Holdings: Phonorecords Videotapes
Notes: The Edward Podesta Jazz Collection incl about 250 jazz periodicals of the 1960s and 1970s and about 200 jazz records, all cataloged. For reference use only.

IL —CHICAGO PUBLIC LIBRARY, Music Section, Fine Arts Division, 78 E Washington St, Chicago, 60602. Rosalinda I Hack, Fine Arts Division Chief; Richard C Schwegel, Head, Music Section
Holdings: Vols 6000
Notes: 600 Titles in all areas of music with emphasis on popular music, rock, jazz, and music business. Complete runs of *Billboard* and *Variety.* Also programs from major US orchestras and complete Chicago Symphony programs.

IL —NEWBERRY LIBRARY, 60 W Walton St, Chicago, 60610. Diana Haskell, Cur of Modern Mss
Holdings: Cat
Notes: Strong collection, particularly in periodicals of the 19th century.

MI —DETROIT PUBLIC LIBRARY, Music & Performing Arts Dept, 5201 Woodward, Detroit, 48202. Agatha Pfeiffer Kalkanis, Chief
Notes: Collection of discographical material- -500 discographies, manufacturers' catalogs, indexes to reviews, histories of recording industry, runs of American and European record magazines.

NM —NEW MEXICO STATE UNIVERSITY, Library, Box 3475, Las Cruces, 88003.

James Dyke, Dir
Holdings: Vols 4000 // Cat
Notes: Jazz, Blues, and music history. Collection of music periodicals and monographs of the 1930s, 1940s and 1950s.

NY —CORNELL UNIVERSITY LIBRARIES, Music Library, 225 Lincoln Hall, Ithaca, 14853. Lenore Coral, Music Librn
Holdings: Vols (106,022) Cat
See also entry under Music.

NY —COLUMBIA UNIVERSITY LIBRARIES, Music Library, 701 Dodge, Broadway & 116 St, New York, 10027. M Haefliger, Librn
Holdings: Vols (55,020) Cat Phonorecords Audiotapes Microforms
Notes: Incl extensive holdings of early music treatises and journals.

NY —NEW YORK PUBLIC LIBRARY, Music Div, 111 Amsterdam Ave, New York, 10023. Frank C Campbell, Chief
Holdings: Vols (300,000) Cat Mss Pix Microforms
Notes: Described in *Dictionary Catalog of the Music Collection, The Research Libraries of the New York Public Library,* 33 vols (532,000 cards), 1964, $2190; Supplement 1, 1 vol (17,000 cards), 1966, $100. Also, *Bibliographic Guide to Music,* 2 vols, 1975-1976, $70 ea. Literature pertaining to virtually all musical subjects, and scores covering the broadest range of musical style and history are represented in this catalog. Special strengths of the collection incl folk songs, 18th and 19th-century librettos, full scores of operas, complete works, historical editions, Beethoven, Americana, American music, periodicals, vocal music, literature on the voice, programs, record catalogs, and mss in detail; sheet music, 355,414; sound recordings, 400,000; clippings and programs, 2 million; broadsides, 1821; songsters, 375; pictures, 51,002; ms, 29,877.

PA —CARNEGIE LIBRARY OF PITTSBURGH, Music and Art Dept, 4400 Forbes Ave, Pittsburgh, 15213. Ida Reed, Dept Head
Holdings: Vols 96,000 Cat Mss Pix Phonorecords
Notes: Emphasis in lending collection on practical editions of music since 1600. Reference collection incl early and first editions, monumental sets, historical anthologies, bibliographies. Thematic catalogs, dictionaries, encyclopedias, etc. Files of periodicals begin with year 1722 and incl notable collection of 19th century American music journals. Also, 30,000 phonorecords. Library compiles indexes of orchestral performances, piano, song, organ, and violin materials.

SD —UNIVERSITY OF SOUTH DAKOTA, Shrine to Music Museum, USD Box 194, Vermillion, 57069. Andre P Larson, Dir
Budget: ($205,036)
Notes: The Shrine to Music Museum is one of America's major collections of musical resource materials, incl more than 4000 antique musical instruments from all over the world, plus an extensive supporting library of several thousand books, music, periodicals, recordings, photographs, and related musical memorabilia. The collection of 19th and early 20th-century sheet music and music for wind instruments is probably the most extensive in the country. Inquiries and visits are welcomed.

TX —SOUTHWESTERN BAPTIST THEOLOGICAL SEMINARY, Music Library, Fort Worth, 76122. Phillip W Sims, Librn
Holdings: Vols (19,000) Cat
Budget: ($30,000)
Notes: Incl in the Treasure Section are approx 250 tune books, plus many very old hymnals and other antiquarian items. Incl 97,000 pieces of sheet music, 24,000 scores, 7500 phonograph records and 3500 audiocassettes. The entire collection is cataloged except the periodicals and about one fourth of the sheet music.

ON —NATIONAL LIBRARY OF CANADA, 395 Wellington St, Ottawa, K1A 0N4, Can. Andre Preibish, Dir
Notes: Includes 2000 pieces of Canadian

PERIODICALS, MUSIC (cont.)

sheet music (mostly 19th century imprints), 40,000 cylinders, discs, tapes; over 600 serials titles devoted to music; 200 archival collections of composers, musicians and conductors, eg papers of Healy Willan, eminent composer; Glen Gould, well-known pianist; Sir Ernest MacMillan, conductor, director and composer. Since 1950 the Canadian imprints have been received on legal deposit. Intensive purchases aim at a comprehensive collection of Canadian music.

ON —METROPOLITAN TORONTO LIBRARY, Music Dept, 789 Yonge St, Toronto, M4W 2G8, Can. Isabel Rose, Head
Holdings: Cat
Budget: ($54,000)
Notes: 14,800 books, 40,000 scores; 1900 pieces of retrospective Canadian sheet music; 500 pieces of American and British sheet music, pre-1980; 17,000 phonorecords; 180 current periodical titles; 2800 bound peiodicals; 340 reels of microfilmed periodicals; 16,000 concert programs, chiefly Toronto city; 8850 newspaper clipping files; music picture files integrated with Fine Art Dept picture collection.

PERIODICALS, NEW JERSEY

NJ —SOMERSET COUNTY LIBRARY, Northbridge & Vogt Dr, Box 6700, Bridgewater, 08807. Elizabeth Griesbach, Head Reference Librn
Holdings: Vols (2500) Cat Mss Maps Pix Audiotapes
Notes: Historical and modern history; state (NJ) depository documents; juvenile collection; New Jersey periodicals; vertical files (26 drawers); and landmark survey on each county municipality. Separate catalog in New Jersey Room. Restricted use; noncirculating.

PERIODICALS, NORTHWEST (PACIFIC)

WA —UNIVERSITY OF WASHINGTON LIBRARIES, Pacific Northwest Collection, Seattle, 98195. Andrew F Johnson, Librn
Holdings: Vols (50,000) Cat Mss Maps Pix
Budget: ($12,000)
Notes: The Pacific Northwest Collection contains printed materials documenting the historic and contemporary life and culture of the region in a broad range of subject areas. The Pacific Northwest is defined as the geographic region including Washington, Oregon, Idaho, Montana, British Columbia, Yukon Territory, and Alaska. Printed materials including books, periodicals, government documents, maps, weekly and local regional newspapers, theses and dissertations, as well as photographs and architectural drawings are included in the Pacific Northwest Collection. Photographic works of over 200 photographers active in the Pacific Northwest, Alaska, and the Yukon Territory (Canada) during the period 1860-1930, including Asahel and Edward S Curtis, Eric Hegg, and Clark Kinsey, are represented in a print collection of more than 300,000 images. The architecturaldrawings collection includes over 19,000 original plans, drawings, sketches, renderings and blue prints pertaining to the history of architecture and urban planning and landscape gardening in the Pacific Northwest ca 1880-1940. Areas of particular strength are the holdings of over 1100 published journals of Pacific Northwest exploration expeditions, photographs of Northwest Coast Native Americans and of historic Seattle, newspapers issued within the Japanese-American relocation camps, 1942-1945, materials relating to the 1980 eruption of Mt St Helens, and Sanborne fire insurance maps for Washington. A unique feature of the Collection is the subject index to regional periodicals and local newspapers maintained by the PNW Collection staff; over 100 titles are currently indexed. G K Hall Company published a books catalog of the Pacific Northwest Collectionin 1973.

PERIODICALS, ORNITHOLOGICAL

OH —OHIO HISTORICAL SOCIETY, Archives Library Division, 1982 Velma Ave, Columbus, 43211. Dennis East, Division Chief
Holdings: Vols 800 Cat
Notes: Collection based on the William L Dawson Library; more than local coverage; good for scarce periodicals. Supports Natural History Division of the Society.

PERIODICALS, PACIFIST

CA —HOOVER INSTITUTION ON WAR, REVOLUTION & PEACE, Stanford University, Stanford, 94305. Milorad M Drachkovitch, Archivist
Holdings: Mss Pix
Notes: Records of *National Republic* magazine, incl newspaper clippings, printed matter, pamphlets, reports, indices, notes, bulletins, lettergrams, weekly letters and photographs, 1905-1960, relating to pacifist, communist, fascist, and other radical movements as well as political developments in the US and Soviet Russia. 826 ms boxes.

PA —SWARTHMORE COLLEGE, Peace Collection, Swarthmore, 19081. Jean R Soderlund, Cur of Peace Collection
Holdings: Vols 2000 Cat Microforms
Notes: Periodicals are cataloged by title; a card index to organizations is also available. Scope of periodical collection: incl US and foreign periodicals in the fields of peace and nonviolence from the 19th century to the present.
See also entry under Pacifism - History.

PERIODICALS, PERSIAN

TX —UNIVERSITY OF TEXAS LIBRARIES, Middle East Collection, PO Box P, Austin, 78712. Abazar Sepehri, Librn
Holdings: Vols (45,000) Cat Microforms
Notes: Arabic, Persian and Turkish materials in the humanities and social sciences. Incl 350 periodical and 45 newspaper titles from most of the countries of the Arab League, Turkey, Iran and Afghanistan.

UT —UNIVERSITY OF UTAH, Middle East Library, Salt Lake City, 84112. Ragai N Makar, Librn
Budget: ($40,000)

PERIODICALS, PHOTOGRAPHY

NY —VISUAL STUDIES WORKSHOP, Research Center, 31 Prince St, Rochester, 14607. Linn Underhill, Coordr; Robert Bretz, Librn
Holdings: Vols (8000) Cat Pix Slides Audiotapes Videotapes
Notes: Strong emphasis on photography (over 1,000,000 pictures) and the photographic arts in many subject areas incl in this volume. Heavy emphasis on early photographic processes and collections of examples of them. Also collections of individual photographers' works.

NC —UNIVERSITY OF NORTH CAROLINA, CHARLOTTE, J Murrey Atkins Library, UNCC Station, Charlotte, 28223. Robert F Brabham Jr, Special Collections Librn
Notes: Papers of John A Tennant, 1868-1957, publisher of *The Photo-Miniature,* and early photographic journal. Incl Tennant's marked copy of the journal, 1899-1904.

PERIODICALS, POETRY

DC —GEORGETOWN UNIVERSITY, Library, Special Collections Div, 37 & O Sts NW, Washington, 20057. George M Barringer, Special Collections Librn; Nicholas B Sheetz, Mss Librn
Holdings: Vols (3000) Uncat Mss
Notes: The Murray L Marshall Collection, including several thousand issues of American poetry magazines; a complete run of *Sonnet Sequences,* 1929-58; and Mr Marshall's editorial files for *Sonnet Sequences.*

NM —NEW MEXICO STATE UNIVERSITY, Library, Box 3475, Las Cruces, 88003.

James Dyke, Dir
Holdings: Cat
Notes: The collection contains 38,630 items--a vast quantity of little magazines and Anglo-American Modernism published between 1900-1975. Little poetry magazines are an exceptionally strong part of this collection.

VA —UNIVERSITY OF VIRGINIA, Alderman Library, Rare Book Dept, Charlottesville, 22901. Julius P Barclay, Cur
Holdings: Vols (6500) Cat
Notes: The Marvin Tatum Collection of Contemporary Prose and Poetry contains some extremely rare items (mostly paperback) of American and British poetry and prose in the 1960s and 1970s. Some of Lawrence Ferlinghetti's earliest publications in mimeograph form are here. Poster, portfolios.

PERIODICALS, POLISH

IL —UNIVERSITY OF ILLINOIS, URBANA/CHAMPAIGN, Slavic and East European Library, Urbana, 61801. Marianna Tax Choldin, Head
Holdings: Vols (34,600) Cat
Notes: Extensive coverage.

NY —NEW YORK PUBLIC LIBRARY, Slavonic Div, Fifth Ave & 42 St, New York, 10018. Edward Kasinec, Chief
Holdings: Cat Microforms
Notes: See: New York Public Library, Slavonic Div, *Dictionary Catalog of the Slavonic Collection,* 2nd ed, rev and enl (Boston: G K Hall, 1974), 44 vols; and New York Public Library, *Dictionary Catalog of the Research Libraries* (New York, 1972-).

PERIODICALS, POPULAR

CA —UNIVERSITY OF CALIFORNIA, LOS ANGELES, Research Library, Dept of Special Collections, 405 Hilgard Ave, Los Angeles, 90024. Edward Shreeves, Chairman, Bibliographers Group; David S Zeidberg, Head
Notes: Various collections, incl almanacs, comic books, commercial catalogs, fantasy fiction, pulp magazines, trade cards, and 19th century American paperbacks.

IL —CENTER FOR RESEARCH LIBRARIES, 6050 S Kenwood Ave, Chicago, 60637. Donald B Simpson, Dir; Esther Smith, Collection Development Librn
Holdings: Vols 6000 Uncat
Notes: A random sample of representative comic books and popular magazines, selected twice yearly, 1951-1983.

PERIODICALS, PORTUGUESE

WI —UNIVERSITY OF WISCONSIN, MADISON, Memorial Library, Ibero-American Studies Collection, 728 State St, Madison, 53706. Suzanne Hodgman, Bibliographer
Holdings: Vols (20,000) Cat Maps Pix Microforms
Notes: This collection of strictly Portuguese, as opposed to Brazilian, language and literature has been built up over more than a century. It contains many rare items, including several serials found nowhere else in the US. Not separately housed; no listing available.

PERIODICALS, PRESBYTERIAN

NC —HISTORICAL FOUNDATION OF THE PRESBYTERIAN & REFORMED CHURCHES, Library, Box 847, Montreat, 28757. Jerrold Lee Brooks, Exec Dir
Holdings: Vols (90,000) Cat Mss Maps Pix Slides Phonorecords Audiotapes Videotapes 16mm Films Filmstrips Microforms
Budget: ($350,000)
Notes: Presbyterian and Reformed Churches of the World. History, archives, etc.

PERIODICALS, PRISON see Prison Periodicals

PERIODICALS, PROFESSIONAL

NY —NEW YORK PUBLIC LIBRARY, Research Libraries, General Research Div,

PERIODICALS, PROFESSIONAL (cont.)

Fifth Ave & 42 St, New York, 10018. Keith McKinney, Assistant Div Chief
Holdings: Cat
Notes: Current periodicals. Subjects incl advertising, business and professional periodicals, international affairs, labor and trade unions, political and social sciences, humanities in general. Division holds 10,000 titles.

PERIODICALS, PUBLISHING OF—HISTORY—U.S.

IN —INDIANA UNIVERSITY, Lilly Library, Seventh St, Bloomington, 47405. William R Cagle, Librn
Holdings: Mss Pix
Notes: Ms collections incl editorial and correspondence files of the following periodicals: *American Magazine*, 1906-15; *Athenaeum*, Jan 1853-Aug 1869 (Wm Hepworth Dixon); *Aylesford Review*, 1955-68; *Floating Bear*, 1961 (LeRoi Jones); *McClure's Magazine*, 1893-1925; *Northwest Review*, 1961-67 (Wm Wroth); *Origin*, 1960-62 (Cid Corman); *Poetry*, 1954-80 (Henry Rago; Darly Hine); *Tree*, 1969-74 (David Meltzer); *X: A Quarterly Review*, 1959-61; and *Yugen*, 1958-61 (LeRoi Jones). Also, correspondence and papers of the Association of Literary Magazines of American, 1961-64 (164 items).

NY —GRADUATE CENTER OF THE CITY UNIVERSITY OF NEW YORK, William H and Gwynne K Crouse Library for Publishing Arts, 33 W 42 St, New York, 10036. Alfred H Lane, Dir
Notes: Recently established and still growing, but intended to become the authoritative source of materials in the field, of particular value in research about the publishing industry. Open to staff members of publishing houses, students, scholars, authors, printers, and booksellers. Primarily 20th-century materials, and particularly useful for research on technical, financial, and historical matters. Much on the history of individual houses, economics of authorship; marketing and distribution of books; etc.

PERIODICALS, RADICAL

CA —HOOVER INSTITUTION ON WAR, REVOLUTION & PEACE, Stanford University, Stanford, 94305. Milorad M Drachkovitch, Archivist
Holdings: Mss Pix
Notes: Records of *National Republic* magazine, incl newspaper clippings, printed matter, pamphlets, reports, indices, notes, bulletins, lettergrams, weekly letters, and photographs, 1905-1960, relating to pacifist, communist, fascist, and other radical movements as well as political developments in the US and Soviet Russia. 826 ms boxes.

PERIODICALS, RADIO

NY —NEW YORK PUBLIC LIBRARY, Performing Arts Research Center, Billy Rose Theatre Collection, 111 Amsterdam Ave, New York, 10023. Dorothy L Swerdlove, Cur
Holdings: Cat
See also entry under Radio.

PERIODICALS, RAILROAD

IL —LAKE FOREST COLLEGE, Donnelley Library, Lake Forest, 60045. Arthur H Miller Jr, College Librn
Holdings: Vols (1500) Cat Mss Maps Pix
Budget: ($1000)
Notes: Elliott Donnelley Collection (received 1976) of mostly mid-20th century books and periodicals on Western railroads and mountain narrow gauge, world narrow gauge and short lines, steam, live steam, model railroading, and some traction. Purchases keep collection emphasis current (50-75 new books per year, 22 periodical subscriptions). Also, the Munson Paddock

Collecction (received 1977) of train illustrations, maps, and timetables, 1850-1950. In addition to American technical and historical books and periodicals, the collection contains books of views, narrations of rail travel (particularly American West), and US local histories--all with illustrations of trains. Most titles are late 19th century Americna. The 1550 volumes are supplemented by related holdings of more than 150 pamphlets, 600 timetables, 2000 unbound periodical issues, 200 maps, 75 diagrams (engines, cars) hundreds of clippings of train illustrations, and 1000 photographs. In progress is a card index of illustrations by wheel type line, and manufacturer. Together, the collections contain about 7000 items.

PERIODICALS, RELIGIOUS see Religious Periodicals

PERIODICALS, RUMANIAN

IL —UNIVERSITY OF ILLINOIS, URBANA/CHAMPAIGN, Slavic and East European Library, Urbana, 61801. Marianna Tax Choldin, Head
Holdings: Vols (13,000) Cat
Notes: Extensive coverage.

PERIODICALS, RUSSIAN

†CA —UNIVERSITY OF CALIFORNIA, BERKELEY, LIBRARIES, Berkeley, 94720.
Notes: Comprehensive collection of indexes to more than 40 provincial Russian periodicals dealing with the Russians Orthodox Church during the Imperial period. More than 200 photocopies of letters, telegrams, sketches, and photographs from the collection of the Grand Duchess Mariia Alexandrovna, daughter of Emperor Alexander II of Russia. Dating from last third of the 19th century. Incl correspondence from her parents, court, and other friends. Copies made available by the Executive Committee of the Museum of Russian Culture in San Francisco.

CA —UNIVERSITY OF CALIFORNIA, LOS ANGELES, Library, Slavic Collection, 405 Hilgard Ave, Los Angeles, 90024. Edward Shreeves, Chairman, Bibliographers Group; Leon Ferder, Slavic Bibliographer
Holdings: Vols (250,000) Cat
Notes: The Slavic Collection at UCLA consists of materials from and relating to Russia and the Soviet Union, Poland, Czechoslovakia, Yugoslavia, Bulgaria, the Sorbians in East Germany, and works by Slavic emigres. The collection contains nearly 250,000 vols, and is particularly strong in linguistics, literature, history and social sciences, and reference materials. Slavic materials are collected in hard copy and microform, and incl monographs, serials (incl newspapers), reference works, proceedings of Slavistic congresses and symposia, and also *Festschriften* and dissertations.

IL —CENTER FOR RESEARCH LIBRARIES, 6050 S Kenwood Ave, Chicago, 60637. Donald B Simpson, Dir; Esther Smith, Collection Development Librn
Notes: Several hundred current subscriptions to infrequently held serials, especially those published by Akademiia Nauk SSSR. Also extensive collection of backfiles of Akademiia SSSR journals.

IL —UNIVERSITY OF ILLINOIS, URBANA/CHAMPAIGN, Slavic and East European Library, Urbana, 61801. Marianna Tax Choldin, Head
Holdings: Vols (420,000) Cat Microforms
Notes: One of the largest Slavic and East European collections. Strong in Russian and Soviet materials-humanities, sciences, and social sciences; languages and literatures; periodicals, newspapers, and microforms. Ca 260,000 volumes in languages of the Soviet Union plus 20,000 Russian and Ukrainian titles on microform. Extensive coverage of Czechoslovakia (35,000 vols); Yugoslavia (31,000 vols); Bulgaria (9200 vols); Poland (34,600 vols); Romania (13,000 vols); and

Hungary (18,000 vols) and the languages, literatures, and history of these countries.

†NY —US ARMY RUSSIAN INSTITUTE (USARI), APO, New York, 09053.
Holdings: Vols (24,841)
Notes: A research and language facility of the Army Foreign Affairs Officers Speciality (USSR), located in Garmisch, West Germany. 65 percent of the collection is in Russian; 35 percent in English and other languages. Contains most representative Soviet Newspapers and periodicals, as well as American and other English language publications.

PERIODICALS, SAILSHIP

NY —STATE UNIVERSITY OF NEW YORK, Maritime College, Stephen B Luce Library, Fort Schuyler, Bronx, 10465. Richard H Corson, Librn
Holdings: Vols (68,000)
Budget: ($90,000)
Notes: Incl history of ships with special emphasis on US sailing ships of the 19th century. Extensive holdings in periodical literature wih long and complete runs of many titles.

PERIODICALS, SATIRICAL

†CT —UNIVERSITY OF CONNECTICUT LIBRARY, Special Collections Dept, Storrs, 06268. Richard H Schimmelpfeng, Dir of Special Collections
Notes: Good and unusual collection.

PERIODICALS, SCANDINAVIAN

WI —UNIVERSITY OF WISCONSIN, MADISON, Memorial Library, 728 State St, Madison, 53706. Erwin K Welsch, Social Studies Bibliographer
Holdings: Vols (20,000) Cat
Notes: Strongest in 19th-century and 20th-century Danish, Norwegian and Swedish literary and historical periodicals. Special collection incl the "Mimer's Collection," consisting of 1000 vols collected by Rasmus B Anderson, founder of the UW Scandinavian Studies Department, with the aid of the Norwegian violinist Ole Bull and which consists largely of Old Norse materials, and the "Olson Collection," about 400 vols of Scandinavian literary classics from the 19th century. The holdings in Icelandic and Old Norse are substantial (although the modern Icelandic collection is not) with some unique manuscript materials from the 17th and 18th centuries collected by Chester Thordarson. There is also a collection of experimental literature, particularly Danish poetry, from the 1960s.

PERIODICALS, SCIENCE FICTION

CA —CALIFORNIA STATE UNIVERSITY, FULLERTON, Library, Box 4150, Fullerton, 92634. Linda Herman, Special Collections Librn
Notes: A major collection of science fiction magazines dating from the 1930s. Incl a complete run from 1926 to 1940 of *Amazing*, the first major science fiction magazine. Also incl are short-span publications and runs of British s/f publications.

MD —UNIVERSITY OF MARYLAND, BALTIMORE COUNTY, Albin O Kuhn Library and Gallery, 5401 Wilkens Ave, Baltimore, 21228. Ann Copeland, Special Collections Librn
Holdings: Vols (4500) Cat Mss Pix Phonorecords
Notes: The Azriel Rosenfeld Science Fiction Research Collection of about 20,000 items, incl over 4000 issues of science fiction periodicals such as *Analog, Galaxy,* and a complete run of *Amazing Stories*, as well as 4500 hard cover and paperback books, and criticisms of science fiction. A valuable research collection. Complementing these resources is the Walter Coslet Collection of 10,000 fanzines. The Library provides reference service (by mail or in person) to scholars and other persons interested in the

PERIODICALS, SCIENCE FICTION (cont.)

area of research.
See also entry under Science Fiction.

PERIODICALS, SCIENTIFIC AND TECHNICAL

CA —NASA, Ames Research Center, Libraries, Library Br 202-3, Moffett Field, 94035. Sarah Dueker, Chief, Library Branch
Holdings: Cat Audiotapes Microforms
Notes: Main library collections cover physical sciences, engineering and mathematical fields related to research programs in aeronautics-space research. Life sciences library collections cover medical, physiological, behavioral and biological sciences related to research programs. Also emphases on remote sensing of earth resources and the search for extraterrestrial life. 950 journal titles and 85,000 monographs. Reports collection includes 60,000 hard copy reports and 900,000 microfiche.

CA —UNIVERSITY OF CALIFORNIA, SAN FRANCISCO, Library, San Francisco, 94143. David Bishop, University Librn

DC —SMITHSONIAN INSTITUTION LIBRARIES, General Library, Washington, 20560. Mary Claire Grey, Chief Cent Ref & Loan Servs
Holdings: Vols (79,000) Cat Mss Maps Pix Slides Microforms
Notes: Incl publications of foreign and domestic museums, and all phases of museum work.

IL —CENTER FOR RESEARCH LIBRARIES, 6050 S Kenwood Ave, Chicago, 60637. Donald B Simpson, Dir; Esther Smith, Collection Development Librn
Holdings: Vols Cat
Notes: Very extensive holdings of older scientific journals, especially in medicine, applied science, technology, industry and trade. Currently 5,000 titles.

IL —UNIVERSITY OF ILLINOIS, URBANA/CHAMPAIGN, Library, Biology Library, 101 Burrill Hall, 407 S Goodwin, Urbana, 61801. Elisabeth B Davis, Librn
Holdings: Vols (115,000) Cat Microforms
Budget: ($200,000)
Notes: The Biology Library incl books, periodicals, and reference works that cover the fields of anatomy, biophysics, brain, ecology, entomology, genetics, immunology, microbiology, physiology and zoology. About three-quarters of the total collection is made up of journals and other serials representing 2000 distinctive titles. The serial list is comprehensive for the biological sciences, contains most of the major international titles and consists of complete runs for almost all titles. Additional materials (approx 90,000 vols) in the biological sciences are available in the Natural History Survey Library and the bookstacks at the Main Library on the Urbana campus. Professional assistance is available for reference service, online searching, and library instruction. Interlibrary loan service is provided. Photocopying.

IN —INDIANA STATE LIBRARY, John Shepard Wright Memorial Library, 140 N Senate Ave, Indianapolis, 46204. M Harzler, Librn
Holdings: Vols 10,733 Cat
Notes: Scientific and technical journals received on exchange with the Academy.

MD —UNIVERSITY OF MARYLAND, BALTIMORE COUNTY, Albin O Kuhn Library and Gallery, 5401 Wilkens Ave, Baltimore, 21228. Ann Copeland, Special Collections Librn
Holdings: Vols (3000) Cat
Notes: The Archives of the American Society for Microbiology (ASM) are strong in 20th century English-language immunological and bacteriological works, incl nearly every edition of every major microbiological title published in England and the US. The reprint collection is also excellent, incl significant material published in non-bacteriological journals. The theses are largely European, pre-1900 inaugural dissertations. The collection also incl mss, proceedings, memorabilia and correspondence of the Society.

MI —GENERAL MOTORS, Research Laboratories Library, General Motors Technical Center, Warren, 48090. Robert W Gibson, Librn

NY —COLD SPRING HARBOR LABORATORY, Library, PO Box 100, Cold Spring Harbor, 11724. Susan Gensel, Library Dir; Genemary Falvey, Librn
Holdings: Vols (30,000)
Budget: ($103,500)
Notes: The highly technical collection is comprised of 20,000 serial vols and 10,000 monographs. The library receives 500 current serial titles. Subjects covered incl molecular and cellular biology, virology, biochemistry, microbiology, oncology, neurobiology, biological risk assessment and genetic engineering/biotechnology. Special collections in eugenics and genetics are primarily historical dealing with the development of genetics in the US which had its beginnings here.

NY —AMERICAN MUSEUM OF NATURAL HISTORY, Library Services Dept, Central Park W & 79th St, New York, 10024. Nina J Root, Chairwoman; Mary Genett, Asst Librn for Reference Services
Holdings: Vols (385,000) Cat Mss Maps Pix Slides Microforms
Notes: Nearly all collections are outstanding for depth of coverage and international range. Early and historic works, rare books, colored illustrations, and relevant serial publications supplement the modern scientific publications necessary to the researches of the scientific staff and the work of the educational division. Open to the public.

NY —NEW YORK PUBLIC LIBRARY, Research Libraries, Science and Technology Research Center, Fifth Ave & 42 St, New York, 10018.
Holdings: Vols (1,100,000) Cat Microforms
Budget: ($647,259)
Notes: Currently receiving over 5000 periodicals on an international basis.

OH —PUBLIC LIBRARY OF CINCINNATI & HAMILTON COUNTY, Science & Technology Dept, 800 Vine St, Cincinnati, 45202. Rosemary Gaiser, Head
Holdings: Cat
Notes: Over 1100 periodicals currently being received. Extensive holdings incl many 19th century titles.

OH —CLEVELAND PUBLIC LIBRARY, Science & Technology Dept, 325 Superior Ave, Cleveland, 44114. Jean Z Piety, Head
Holdings: Cat
Notes: Primarily an engineering collection with basic sciences; strong in 19th and 20th century American, British, and Canadian technical societies' publications; comprehensive bibliography, standards and specifications; Rand Corp; 4400 periodicals and serial; extensive collections in chemistry, pamphlets (60,000). Incl collections on geology, aeronautics and agriculture.

OK —UNIVERSITY OF OKLAHOMA, University Libraries, 401 W Brooks, Norman, 73019. Duane Roller, Cur
Holdings: Vols (61,000)
Notes: The History of Science Collections hold more than 61,000 vols. Incl the first printed editions of most major scientific works, all editions of many works; several thousand vols of early scientific journals; biographies of scientists; histories of science and of the sciences; encyclopedias and dictionaries; all the scholarly resources needed for the study of the history of science.

PA —FRANKLIN INSTITUTE LIBRARY, 20 & The Parkway, Philadelphia, 19103. Miriam Padusis, Dir; Charles Wilt, Readers Servs Librn
Holdings: Vols 8000 Cat

PA —CARNEGIE LIBRARY OF PITTSBURGH, Science & Technology Dept, 4400 Forbes Ave, Pittsburgh, 15213. Catherine M Brosky, Dept Head
Holdings: Vols (380,000) Cat Maps Microforms
Budget: ($240,000)
See also entries under Engineering; Science; Chemistry; Technology.

ON —METROPOLITAN TORONTO LIBRARY, Science & Technology Dept, 789 Yonge St, Toronto, M4W 2G8, Can. Margaret Walshe, Head
Holdings: Vols (40,000) Cat Microforms
Notes: Department has over 1300 current subscriptions. Acquires most titles indexed in *Applied Science and Technology Index*. Some back files of periodicals from 1800s. Newsletters are also collected; emphasis is on Canadian content.

PQ —MCGILL UNIVERSITY, Institute of Oceanography, Oceanography Library, 3620 University St, Montreal, H3A 2B2, Can. Yvonne Mahocks, Librn
Holdings: Vols (10,848) Cat Mss Maps Pix Microforms
Budget: ($1200)
Notes: Extensive periodical collection. 12,332 government documents, , 322 microtech, 321 microfiche, 25,000 reprints.

PERIODICALS, SERBIAN

NY —NEW YORK PUBLIC LIBRARY, Slavonic Div, Fifth Ave & 42 St, New York, 10018. Edward Kasinec, Chief
Holdings: Cat Microforms
Notes: See: New York Public Library, Slavonic Div, *Dictionary Catalog of the Slavonic Collection*, 2nd ed, rev and enl (Boston: G K Hall, 1974), 44 vols; and New York Public Library, *Dictionary Catalog of the Research Libraries* (New York, 1972-).

PERIODICALS, SINGAPORE

IL —CENTER FOR RESEARCH LIBRARIES, 6050 S Kenwood Ave, Chicago, 60637. Donald B Simpson, Dir; Esther Smith, Collection Development Librn
Holdings: Uncat Microforms
Budget: $15,000
Notes: Receive serials and monographs fromm Indonesia, Malaysia and Singapore under NPAC (formerly PL 480). Collection starts 1969 for Indonesia, 1971 for Malaysia, Singapore and Brunei. Buy 14 newspapers on microfilm. Also incl Southeast Asia Microform Project. Borrowing is restricted to members of the project.

PERIODICALS, SLAVIC

CA —UNIVERSITY OF CALIFORNIA, BERKELEY, University Library, Slavic Collections, Berkeley, 94720. Edward Kasinec, Librn
Holdings: Vols (210,000) Cat Maps Microforms
Budget: ($40,000)
Notes: Incl about 100 current Ukrainian periodical titles.
See also entry under Ukraine - History.

CA —UNIVERSITY OF CALIFORNIA, LOS ANGELES, Library, Slavic Collection, 405 Hilgard Ave, Los Angeles, 90024. Edward Shreeves, Chairman, Bibliographers Group; Leon Ferder, Slavic Bibliographer
Holdings: Vols (250,000)
Notes: The Slavic Collection at UCLA consists of materials from and relating to Russia and the Soviet Union, Poland, Czechoslovakia, Yugoslavia, Bulgaria, the Sorbians in East Germany, and works by Slavic emigres. The collection contains nearly 250,000 vols, and is particularly strong in linguistics, literature, history and social sciences, and reference materials. Slavic materials are collected in hard copy and microform, and incl monographs, serials (incl newspapers), reference works, proceedings of Slavistic congresses and symposia, and also *Festschriften* and dissertations.

IL —UNIVERSITY OF ILLINOIS, URBANA/CHAMPAIGN, Slavic and East European Library, Urbana, 61801. Marianna Tax Choldin, Head
Holdings: Vols (420,000) Cat Microforms
Notes: One of the largest Slavic and East European collections. Strong in Russian and

PERIODICALS, SLAVIC (cont.)

Soviet materials-humanities, sciences, and social sciences; languages and literatures; periodicals, newspapers, and microforms. Ca 260,000 volumes in languages of the Soviet Union plus 20,000 Russian and Ukrainian titles on microform. Extensive coverage of Czechoslovakia (35,000 vols); Yugoslavia (31,000 vols); Bulgaria (9200 vols); Poland (34,600 vols); Romania (13,000 vols); and Hungary (18,000 vols) and the languages, literatures, and history of these countries.

NY —NEW YORK PUBLIC LIBRARY, Slavonic Div, Fifth Ave & 42 St, New York, 10018. Edward Kasinec, Chief
Holdings: Cat Microforms
Notes: Described in *Dictionary Catalog of the Slavonic Collection* (Boston: G K Hall, 1974), 44 vols.

OH —BATTELLE MEMORIAL INSTITUTE LIBRARY, 505 King Ave, Columbus, 43201. Carol Young, Librn
Holdings: Vols (150,000) Cat Maps Microforms
Notes: Large collection of Russian and Eastern European science and technology. Over 1600 current journal titles and extensive monography and serial holdings in Slavic languages.

PA —JANKOLA LIBRARY AND SLOVAK ARCHIVES, Danville, 17821.
Holdings: Vols 2000
Notes: Learned journals, language arts, fine arts, religion, customs, and literature.

PERIODICALS, SOCIALIST

WI —UNIVERSITY OF WISCONSIN, MADISON, Memorial Library, 728 State St, Madison, 53706. Erwin K Welsch, Social Studies Bibliographer
Holdings: Vols (50,000)
Notes: The collection dates from the turn of the century and incl materials gathered and donated to the library by such activists as William Henry Walling and Heinrich Schl1ter. The materials incl periodicals from national organizations as well as regional groups from England, France and Germany and some titles that existed for only a few issues from minor groups.
See also entry under Socialism - France.

PERIODICALS, SOLDIERS'

PA —TEMPLE UNIVERSITY LIBRARIES, Special Collections Dept, Contemporary Culture Collection, Philadelphia, 19122. Patricia J Case, Cur
Notes: The Contemporary Culture Collection. See full entry under US-Social Life and Customs.

PERIODICALS, SOUTH ASIAN

IL —CENTER FOR RESEARCH LIBRARIES, 6050 S Kenwood Ave, Chicago, 60637. Donald B Simpson, Dir; Esther Smith, Collection Development Librn
Holdings: Microforms
Notes: Receive journals from India, Pakistan, Ceylon and Nepal, on PL 480. Buy 88 newspapers and serials on microfilm. Collection begins 1969 in most cases. Have newspaper microfilms for some earlier years.

PERIODICALS, SOUTHEAST ASIAN

IL —CENTER FOR RESEARCH LIBRARIES, 6050 S Kenwood Ave, Chicago, 60637. Donald B Simpson, Dir; Esther Smith, Collection Development Librn
Holdings: Microforms
Budget: $15,000
Notes: Receive serials and monographs fromm Indonesia, Malaysia and Singapore under NPAC (formerly PL 480). Collection starts 1969 for Indonesia, 1971 for Malaysia, Singapore and Brunei. Buy 14 newspapers on microfilm. Also incl Southeast Asia Microform Project. Borrowing is restricted to members of the project.

PERIODICALS, SOUTHERN STATES

NC —DUKE UNIVERSITY, William R Perkins Library, Durham, 27706. Elvin E Strowd, University Librn
Notes: The Flowers Collection of Southern Americana currently consists of 4,300,500 items. Additions are ongoing. Included in this collection are several types of materials, which are housed in appropriate sections of the library. The various types of materials are: manuscripts, books, pamphlets, maps, music, broadsides, newspapers, photographs, engravings, prints and memorabilia.

PERIODICALS, SPANISH

CT —UNIVERSITY OF CONNECTICUT, Library, Storrs, 06268. R H Schimmelpfeng, Dir of Special Collections
Holdings: Cat
Notes: Collection of newspapers and periodicals formerly belonging to the Duque de T'Serclaes. Ranging from the 17th century through the 20th, the bulk of titles are from 1800-1840, covering the Napoleonic period and the Latin American wars of independence.

DC —CATHOLIC UNIVERSITY OF AMERICA, Canon Law Library, 300B Mullen Library, Washington, 20064. R Bruce Miller, Librn
Holdings: Vols (22,000)
Notes: The collection includes extensive 16th, 17th, and 18th century works in both Latin and Italian. There are many printed editions of pre-16th century sources. Both the 19th and 20th century materials are well represented. This collection is also rich in materials relating to the Second Vatican Council and its aftermath and is up-to-date on the new (1983) Code of Canon Law. Current periodical subscriptions to journals in English, German, French, Italian, and Spanish.

PERIODICALS, SUGAR

LA —LOUISIANA STATE UNIVERSITY, Troy H Middleton Library, Baton Rouge, 70803. Lance E Dickson, Acting Dir
Holdings: Vols 1200 Cat Mss
Notes: Extensive holdings on all aspects of sugar cane growing and cane sugar production, especially in Louisiana and the Southern States. Some archival material from Cuba, Puerto Rico, Trindad, and other areas of the world.

PERIODICALS, TELEVISION

CA —AMERICAN FILM INSTITUTE, Louis B Mayer Library, 2021 N Western Ave, PO Box 27999, Los Angeles, 90027. Anne G Schlosser, Dir
Notes: Rare periodical holdings: *Film Daily* newspaper (1923-1969); *Radio-TV Daily* newspaper (1939-1964); *RKO Radio Flash,* house organ for RKO (1932-1955); *TV Guide* (1948 to date).

NY —NEW YORK PUBLIC LIBRARY, Performing Arts Research Center, Billy Rose Theatre Collection, 111 Amsterdam Ave, New York, 10023. Dorothy L Swerdlove, Cur
Holdings: Cat
See also entry under Television.

TX —SOUTHERN METHODIST UNIVERSITY, Fondren Library, McCord Theater Collection, Room 301, Dallas, 75275. Edyth Renshaw, Cur; Linda Sellers, Pub Serv
Holdings: Vols (2000) Uncat Mss Pix Slides Phonorecords
Notes: See *Theatre Collections in Libraries and Museums,* Gilder and Freedley (Theatre Arts, 1936). The McCord Theatre Collection encompasses the entire spectrum of the performing arts. The central purpose is to gather records of our regional theater before such ephemeral material is lost. Records of over two hundred early Texas theaters, some fragmentary and some relatively complete, are in the files. These records incl photographs of buildings, stagehands, orchestras, and performers. Local theatre history incl the once famous Dallas Little Theatre and the Margo Jones Theatre. The national theatre, opera, ballet, and circus archives incl pictures (some autographed), programs, posters, throw-aways, tear sheets, clippings, and letters. Our international archives are small, but we have some excellent material, eg, artifacts from Max Reinhardt's production of"The Miracle" which happened to go bankrupt in Dallas. After a few years the items were given to us. There are posters, tear sheets, souvenir programs, and other colorful items from Morris Gest and the Artef Collection. We have about 200 19th century English playbills and a few from the 18th century. There is a collection of modern English, French, and other European programs, many of them illustrated souvenir programs. Also, magazines on theater, cinema, and television (1800). Scrapbooks covering both southwest and Dallas theater, 1890s-1950s. Special Collections: artifacts and documents on puppets; masks; costume design; circus; and ballet and dance. The Harriet Bacon MacDonald Collection of over 200 photographs of musicians appearing in Dallas during the first three decades of the 20th century. Many autographed. Affiliated with Meadow Theatre of the Arts.

PERIODICALS, THEATRE

CA —INSTITUTE OF THE AMERICAN MUSICAL, Library, 121 N Detroit St, Los Angeles, 90036. Miles Kreuger, Cur
Holdings: Cat Mss Maps Pix Slides Phonorecords
Notes: Reference materials on the American musical theatre and motion pictures incl 40,000 phonograph records, sound tapes, and cylinders dating back to the 1890s; record catalogs to 1900; thousands of theatre and film programs, periodicals, sheet music and vocal scores as early as 1830; thousands of motion picture press books and over 200,000 stills from 1914 to the present; every musical comedy script published in America and dozens in ms form, original or photocopy materials from the archives of movie palaces, films and record companies, incl discographies of many major Broadway and Hollywood stars; and thousands of books on theatre, film, broadcasting, world's fairs and other allied areas of showmanship.

NY —NEW YORK PUBLIC LIBRARY, Performing Arts Research Center, Billy Rose Theatre Collection, 111 Amsterdam Ave, New York, 10023. Dorothy L Swerdlove, Cur
Holdings: Cat
See also entry under Theatre - History.

TX —SOUTHERN METHODIST UNIVERSITY, Fondren Library, McCord Theater Collection, Room 301, Dallas, 75275. Edyth Renshaw, Cur; Linda Sellers, Pub Serv
Holdings: Vols (2000) Uncat Mss Pix Slides Phonrecords
Notes: See *Theatre Collections in Libraries and Museums,* Gilder and Freedley (Theatre Arts, 1936). The McCord Theatre Collection encompasses the entire spectrum of the performing arts. The central purpose is to gather records of our regional theater before such ephemeral material is lost. Records of over two hundred early Texas theaters, some fragmentary and some relatively complete, are in the files. These records incl photographs of buildings, stagehands, orchestras, and performers. Local theatre history incl the once famous Dallas Little Theatre and the Margo Jones Theatre. The national theatre, opera, ballet, and circus archives incl pictures (some autographed), programs, posters, throw-aways, tear sheets, clippings, and letters. Our international archives are small, but we have some excellent material, eg, artifacts from Max Reinhardt's production of"The Miracle" which happened to go bankrupt in Dallas. After a few years the items were given to us. There are posters, tear-sheets, souvenir programs, and other colorful items from Morris Gest and the Artef Collection. We have about 200 19th century English playbills and a few from the 18th century. There is a collection of modern English, French, and other European programs, many of them illustrated souvenir programs. Also,

PERIODICALS, THEATRE (cont.)

magazines on theater, cinema, and television (1800). Scrapbooks covering both southwest and Dallas theater, 1890s-1950s. Special Collections: artifacts and documents on puppets; masks; costume design; circus; and ballet and dance. The Harriet Bacon MacDonald Collection of over 200 photographs of musicians appearing in Dallas during the first three decades of the 20th century. Many autographed. Affiliated with Meadow Theatre of the Arts.

WA —UNIVERSITY OF WASHINGTON LIBRARIES, Drama Library, BH-20, Seattle, 98195. Liz Fugate, Drama Librn
Holdings: Vols
Budget: ($13,182)
Notes: Collection incl history; criticism; costume; make-up; scene design; lighting; creative dramatics; children's theatre; directing; playwriting; acting. Special Collections include 19th century acting editions, contemporary acting editions and local theatre posters. 17,731 items cataloged, 24,255 uncataloged.

PERIODICALS, TRADE

ON —UNIVERSITY OF TORONTO, Thomas Fisher Rare Book Library, 120 Saint George St, Toronto, M5S 1A5, Can. Richard G Landon, Head
Holdings: Vols 6535 Uncat
Notes: Maclean-Hunter and Southam Press Collections contain periodicals issued by these two Canadian publishers. These are largely trade journlas. Many long and complete runs of items like *Canadian Footwear, Electrical News and Engineering; Gift Buyer; Canadian Home Journal; Chatelaine; Macleans;* etc. Many runs originate in 1880s and 1890s. Also include current publications. Approx 268 titles. Fisher Library designated the official archives for published material by Maclean-Hunter and Southam Press.

PERIODICALS, TRANSPORTATION

NY —STATE UNIVERSITY OF NEW YORK, Maritime College, Stephen B Luce Library, Fort Schuyler, Bronx, 10465. Richard H Corson, Librn
Holdings: Vols (68,000) Cat Maps Pix Slides Audiotapes Videotapes 16mm Films Filmstrips Microforms
Budget: ($90,000)
Notes: Incl the *Transportation Masterfile* (1921-1971), comprising a collection of 700,000 abstracts and annotated entries contained on 140 reels of 35mm microfilm, a subject guide to the microfilm, and a periodicals directory listing in alphabetical arrangement the 2000 current and discontinued international periodicals abstracted and indexed.
ON —CANADIAN TRANSPORT COMMISSION, Library, Ottawa, K1A 0N9, Can. Marty H Lovelock, Librn
Holdings: Cat Microforms
Budget: ($50,000)
Notes: Books, documents, periodicals. Emphasis on transportation law and economics.

PERIODICALS, TURKISH

TX —UNIVERSITY OF TEXAS LIBRARIES, Middle East Collection, PO Box P, Austin, 78712. Abazar Sepehri, Librn
Holdings: Vols (45,000) Cat Microforms
Notes: Arabic, Persian and Turkish materials in the humanities and social sciences. Incl 350 periodical and 45 newspaper titles from most of the countries of the Arab League, Turkey, Iran and Afghanistan.

PERIODICALS, UKRAINIAN

NY —NEW YORK PUBLIC LIBRARY, Slavonic Div, Fifth Ave & 42 St, New York, 10018. Edward Kasinec, Chief
Holdings: Cat Microforms
Notes: See: New York Public Library,

Slavonic Div, *Dictionary Catalog of the Slavonic Collection,* 2nd ed, rev and enl (Boston: G K Hall, 1974), 44 vols; and New York Public Library, *Dictionary Catalog of the Research Libraries* (New York, 1972-).

PERIODICALS, U.S. see Periodicals, American

PERIODICALS, WOMEN'S

CA —WOMEN'S HISTORY RESEARCH CENTER, Microfilm Library, 2325 Oak St, Berkeley, 94708. Laura X, Librn
Holdings: Microforms
Notes: Microfilm (90 reels; reel guides) of collection on women's periodicals, 1956-1974, "Herstory," housed at Northwestern University Library, Special Collections Dept, Evanston, Ill 60201, c/o Sarah Sherman. Available at many universities and for purchase at the Women's History Research Center, 2325 Oak St, Berkeley, Ca 94708.
CT —TRINITY COLLEGE LIBRARY, Watkinson Library, 300 Summit St, Hartford, 06106. Jeffrey Kaimowitz, Cur
Holdings: Cat
Notes: Strong in 19th century material, including women's and children's periodicals.
NY —YWCA NATIONAL BOARD, Library, 726-730 Broadway, New York, 10012. Elizabeth Norris, Librn
Holdings: Vols (3000) Cat Mss
Budget: ($2400)
Notes: Women and their contemporary interests.

PERIODICALS, YOUTH

NY —SCHOLASTIC MAGAZINES, Editorial Library, 730 Broadway, New York, 10003. Lucy Evankow, Chief Librn

PERIODICALS, YUGOSLAV

IL —UNIVERSITY OF ILLINOIS, URBANA/CHAMPAIGN, Slavic and East European Library, Urbana, 61801. Marianna Tax Choldin, Head
Holdings: Vols (31,000) Cat Microforms
Notes: Extensive coverage.

PERKINS, FRANCES, 1882-1965

CT —CONNECTICUT COLLEGE, Library, Mohegan Ave, New London, 06320. Brian Rogers, College Librn
Holdings: Mss
Notes: Three boxes mss; other papers relating to the Dept of Labor.
MA —RADCLIFFE COLLEGE, Arthur & Elizabeth Schlesinger Library on the History of Women in America, 3 James St, Cambridge, 02138. Patricia Miller King, Dir; Eva Moseley, Cur of Mss
Notes: Government official specializing in labor, Frances Perkins was the first woman in the Cabinet (Secy of Labor, 1933-45). Papers, which are part of the Woman's Rights Collection, concern the ILO, Committee on Economic Security, etc.
NY —CORNELL UNIVERSITY LIBRARIES, Collection of Regional History, Dept of Manuscripts and Univ Archives, Ithaca, 14853.
Notes: Secretary of Labor, 1933-45. Incl one personal letter.
NY —COLUMBIA UNIVERSITY LIBRARIES, Rare Book & Manuscript Library, 801 Butler Library, 535 W 114 St, New York, 10027. Kenneth A Lohf, Librn
Holdings: Mss
Notes: Her papers. 69,000 items. Restricted use.

PERLES, ALFRED

BC —UNIVERSITY OF VICTORIA, McPherson Library, Victoria, V8W 3H5, Can.
Notes: *Alien Corn* carbon typescripts and corrected page proof; *Art & Outrage* (Henry Miller, Lawrence Durrell, Alfred Perles - a correspondence); typescripts and carbon

typescripts, galley proof, corrected page proof: *My Friend Henry Miller;* corrected galley proof; untitled, unidentified ms, holograph; miscellaneous correspondence.

PERMIAN LANGUAGES AND LITERATURES

NY —NEW YORK PUBLIC LIBRARY, Slavonic Div, Fifth Ave & 42 St, New York, 10018. Edward Kasinec, Chief
Holdings: Cat Microforms
Notes: See New York Public Library, *Dictionary Catalog of the Slavonic Collection* (Boston: G K Hall, 1974), 44 vols.

PERON, JUAN DOMINGO AND EVA

CA —UNIVERSITY OF CALIFORNIA, RIVERSIDE, University Library, 4045 Canyon Crest Dr, Box 5900, Riverside, 92517.
Holdings: Vols 5000
Notes: General research collection in the humanities and social sciences, with special strengths in history, literature, folklore and economic conditions, especially 20th century. Significant collection of material about and by the Perons, incl complete set of *Mundo Peronista* (1951-1955).
CA —HOOVER INSTITUTION ON WAR, REVOLUTION & PEACE, Stanford University, Stanford, 94305. Milorad M Drachkovitch, Archivist
Holdings: Vols 1400 Pix
Notes: The Peron period in Argentina is represented by a wide range of published materials, especially the writings and speeches of Juan and Eva Peron, covering political, social and economic aspects of the regime. General description of the Latin American Collection and complete listing of the serial and newspaper holdings available in: Joseph W Bingaman, *Latin America; a Survey of Holdings at the Hoover Institution on War, Revolution and Peace.* Stanford, California: Hoover Institution, Stanford University, 1972. 96 pp.
MO —WASHINGTON UNIVERSITY, John M Olin Library, Campus Box 1061, St Louis, 63130.
Holdings: Vols (50,000) Cat
Notes: Strong collection. Much unusual material.
NY —STATE UNIVERSITY OF NEW YORK, STONY BROOK, Melville Library, Dept of Special Collections, Stony Brook, 11794. Evert Volkersz, Head
Holdings: // Uncat
Notes: Pamphlets (380) of speeches by Juan and Eva Peron, as well as materials about them or promoting their regime. A list of titles is available.

PEROXIDES

NY —PENNWALT CORPORATION, Lucidol Division, Research Library, 1740 Military Road, Buffalo, 14240. Brenda L Cassoni Asst Librn
Holdings: Vols 8000
Notes: There is a separate catalog of subject references to articles in periodicals.

PERRET LIBRARY

DC —SMITHSONIAN INSTITUTION, National Museum of American Art & the National Portrait Gallery Library, Eighth & F Sts, NW, Washington, 20560. Cecilia Chin, Librn
Notes: The "Ferninand Perret Library"; 180 scrapbooks (with card index) on California art and artists, incl clippings, catalogs, reproductions, etc.

PERRIER, EDMOND, 1844-1921

NY —CORNELL UNIVERSITY LIBRARIES, Collection of Regional History, Dept of Manuscripts and Univ Archives, Ithaca, 14853.
Notes: French zoologist, director of the Museum National d'Histoire Naturelle of

PERRIER, EDMOND, 1844-1921 (cont.)

Paris. Letters, 1873-1917, from colleagues, students, the public, and relatives. Also, about 200 drafts from the hand of Perrier, from 1876-1919.

PERRIN, EDWARD

AZ —NORTHERN ARIZONA UNIVERSITY, Special Collection Library, CU Box 6022, Flagstaff, 86011. Peter M Whiteley, Coordr/Archivist; William Mullane, Librn
Notes: Edward Perrin (1873-1945) Collection; entrepreneur, rancher in Seligman and Williams, Ariz. Incl correspondence, business records, records of the '63 Gold and Silver Mining Company, 1873-1879, Mohave County, Ariz; Baca Float Number 5, Yavapai County; Babacomari Ranch, Cochise County; San Francisco Mountain Forest Reserve, Coconino County; and mining in Mohave, Yavapai and Coconino Counties, Ariz. Inventory available.

PERROTT, GEORGE ST. JOHN

MD —NATIONAL LIBRARY OF MEDICINE, 8600 Rockville Pike, Bethesda, 20209. Harold M Schoolinam, Actg Dir
Budget: ($46,400)
Notes: Papers of the eminent biostatistician, who conducted the National Health Survey of 1935-36.

PERRY, ANNE

MA —BOSTON UNIVERSITY, Mugar Memorial Library, Special Collections Dept, 771 Commonwealth Ave, Boston, 02215. Howard B Gotlieb, Dir
Holdings: Mss

PERRY, JAMES DE WOLF

RI —UNIVERSITY OF RHODE ISLAND, Library, Special Collections, Kingston, 02881. David Maslyn, Head
Holdings: Mss
Notes: Archive of the papers of the Rt Rev James De Wolf Perry.

PERRY, MATTHEW CALBRAITH

DC —NATIONAL ARCHIVES AND RECORDS SERVICE, National Archives Library, Pennsylvania Ave & Eighth St NW, Washington, 20408.
Notes: Journals kept by Commodore Matthew C Perry (1794-1858) on his expidition to Japan in 1852-1854. The three journals were kept by Perry as his personal account of the trip, undertaken as a diplomatic mission to establish trade relations with Japan. Incl numerous illustrations of rare birds, flowers, fish, animals, and the life and ceremonies of trade ports along Perry's route.
MA —HARVARD UNIVERSITY LIBRARY, Houghton Library, Cambridge, 02138. Rodney G Dennis, Cur of Manuscripts
Holdings: Cat Mss

PERRY, RITCHIE

MA —BOSTON UNIVERSITY, Mugar Memorial Library, Special Collections Dept, 771 Commonwealth Ave, Boston, 02215. Howard B Gotlieb, Dir
Holdings: Cat Mss
Notes: Mss, correspondence, etc collected in depth; incl publications by or about.

PERSECUTION OF JEWS see
Jews—Persecutions

PERSHING, JOHN JOSEPH, 1860-1948

DC —GEORGETOWN UNIVERSITY, Library, Special Collections Div, 37 & O Sts NW, Washington, 20057. George M Barringer, Special Collections Librn; Nicholas B Sheetz, Mss Librn
Holdings: Mss Cat
Notes: Correspondence written to Edythe Patten Corbin, prominent Washington socialite and wife of General Henry Clark Corbin. Extensive correspondence, spanning numerous years, is incl from William Howard Taft, Philip Bunau-Varilla, Myron T Herrick, General John Pershing, and Elihu Root, among others. The correspondence contains extensive discussions of national and international affairs.
DC —LIBRARY OF CONGRESS, Manuscript Division, Washington, 20540. John C Broderick, Chief
Holdings: 14,000 Items
Notes: The papers of General John Joseph Pershing.

PERSIA

DC —LIBRARY OF CONGRESS, African and Middle Eastern Division, Washington, 20540.
Holdings: Cat Mss Microforms
Notes: Near East: Over 75,000 vols, Arabic, Armenian, Turkish, Persian, and related languages. Special subject strengths incl Islamic philosophy, history, and literature.
NJ —PRINCETON UNIVERSITY, Library, Near East Collections, Princeton, 08540. James Weinberger, Cur
Holdings: Vols (100,000) Cat Mss Maps Phonorecords Audiotapes Microforms
Budget: ($72,000)
Notes: Princeton has the largest collection of Arabic mss in the US. Collections are particularly rich in classical Arabic and Persian texts, encomposing all the traditional genres. Of special note are the collections in Arabic and Persian literature, language, history, philosophy and theology and the religious sciences of Islam, both in ms and printed formats. A separate, additional collection of Arabic mss (about 2000 items) is being cataloged. It is especially rich in theology and philosophy of the classical Islamiuc period. Two printed catalogs are available: *Descriptive Catalog of the Garrett Collection of Arabic Manuscripts*, Philip K Hitti et al (Princeton: Princeton Univ Press, 1938): and *Catalogue of Arabic Manuscripts (Yahuda Section) in the Garrett Collection, Princeton University*. Rudolf Mach (Princeton: Princeton Univ Press, 1977).

PERSIAN LANGUAGE—DIALECTS, JUDAEO-PERSIAN see Judaeo-Persian Language and Literature

PERSIAN LANGUAGE—MIDDLE PERSIAN (PAHLAVI) see Pahlavi Language and Literature

PERSIAN LANGUAGE—OLD PERSIAN see Old Persian Language

PERSIAN LANGUAGE—PAHLAVI see Pahlavi Language and Literature

PERSIAN LANGUAGE AND LITERATURE

AZ —UNIVERSITY OF ARIZONA, Library, Oriental Studies Collection, Tucson, 85721. Mary J McWhorter, Actg Head Librn
Holdings: Vols (95,000) Cat Microforms
Budget: ($30,000)
See also entry under Oriental Languages and Literatures.
CA —LOS ANGELES PUBLIC LIBRARY, Foreign Languages Dept, 630 W Fifth St, Los Angeles, 90071. Sylva Manoogian, Principal Librn
Holdings: Vols 250 Cat
Budget: ($41,500)
CA —UNIVERSITY OF CALIFORNIA, LOS ANGELES, Research Library, Near Eastern Collection, Los Angeles, 90024. Edward Shreeves, Chairman, Bibliographers Group; Dunning Wilson, Near Eastern Bibliographer
Holdings: Vols (200,000) Cat Mss Maps Microforms
Notes: Incl ancient cultures and history.
CA —HOOVER INSTITUTION ON WAR, REVOLUTION & PEACE, Stanford University, Stanford, 94305. Peter Duignan, Cur; Karen Fung, Deputy Cur
Holdings: Vols (100,000)
Notes: For full description of collection, see Hoover Institution entry under Near East.
DC —LIBRARY OF CONGRESS, African and Middle Eastern Division, Washington, 20540.
Holdings: Cat Mss Microforms
Notes: Near East: Over 75,000 vols, Arabic, Armenian, Turkish, Persian, and related languages. Special subject strengths incl Islamic philosophy, history, and literature.
MA —HARVARD UNIVERSITY LIBRARY, Widener Library, Middle Eastern Dept, Cambridge, 02138. David H Partington, Librn
Holdings: Cat Mss Microforms
Budget: ($55,000)
Notes: The Library's published *Catalogue of Arabic, Persian, and Ottoman Turkish Books* (1968) lists some 5500 volumes in Persian; see also *Harvard Library Bulletin*, XVI (1968), 313-325.
MI —UNIVERSITY OF MICHIGAN, Graduate Library, Near East Dept, Ann Arbor, 48109. John A Eilts, Bibliographer
Holdings: Vols Cat Mss Maps Microforms
Notes: Excludes Islam in the Far East, Judaism in general, though it does incl specifically Near Eastern Judaism. Incl Bahaism and Arab philosophy, fields of study connected with Islamic or Arabic studies, Turkish language and literature.
NJ —PRINCETON UNIVERSITY, Library, Near East Collections, Princeton, 08540. James Weinberger, Cur
Holdings: Vols (100,000) Cat Mss Maps Phonorecords Audiotapes Microforms
Budget: ($72,000)
Notes: Princeton has the largest collection of Arabic mss in the US. Collections are particularly rich in classical Arabic and Persian texts, encompassing all the traditional genres. Of special note are the collections in Arabic and Persian literature, language, history, philosophy and theology and the religious sciences of Islam, both in ms and printed formats. A separate, additional collection of Arabic mss (about 2000 items) is being cataloged. It is especially rich in theology and philosophy of the classical Islamic period. Two printed catalogs are available: *Descriptive Catalog of the Garrett Collection of Arabic Manuscripts*, Philip K Hitti et al (Princeton: Princeton Univ Press, 1938); and *Catalogue of Arabic Manuscripts (Yahuda Section) in the Garrett Collection, Princeton University*, Rudolf Mach (Princeton: Princeton Univ Press, 1977).
NY —COLUMBIA UNIVERSITY LIBRARIES, Rare Book & Manuscript Library, 801 Butler Library, 535 W 114 St, New York, 10027. Kenneth A Lohf, Librn
Holdings: Vols (5000)
Notes: Incl numerous photographic copies of mss in various Middle Eastern libraries.
NY —NEW YORK PUBLIC LIBRARY, Oriental Div, Fifth Ave & 42 St, New York, 10018. E Christian Filstrup, Chief
Holdings: Cat Mss Microforms
Budget: ($56,455)
Notes: Published catalog of holdings.
NY —NEW YORK PUBLIC LIBRARY, Donnell Foreign Language Library, 20 W 53 St, New York, 10019. Bosiljka Stevanovic, Supvr Librn
Holdings: Vols 159 Cat
Notes: Persian collection incl Persian authors of Persian expression. No separate catalog.
OH —CLEVELAND PUBLIC LIBRARY, Fine Arts and Special Collections Department, 325 Superior Ave, Cleveland, 44114. Alice N Loranth, Head
Holdings: Vols (1600) Cat Mss
Notes: Classic texts and translations of literature, history, philosophy and religion prior to the impact of Western influence are emphasized in addition to works on linguistics. 1000 vols in Persian. Separate catalog of main entries for titles in Persian is maintained.
See also entries under Manuscripts, Persian; Oriental Languages and Literatures.
OH —OHIO STATE UNIVERSITY, Library, 1858 Neil Mall, Columbus, 43210. Dona

PERSIAN LANGUAGE AND LITERATURE (cont.)

Straley, Islamica Librn
Holdings: Vols (25,000) Cat Maps Microforms
Budget: ($30,000)
Notes: The bulk of the Arabic language collection is in the field of language and literature, with large and medium collections in the fields of Islamica and Middle East history. There are also approx 2000 Persian language vols and approx 3000 vols in Turkish. Scholarly translations of Arabic, Persian and Turkish materials are acquired as available. Also a substantial supporting collection of materials on Arabic language and literature, Islamica, and Middle East history in all of the major European languages. PL 480 recipient since 1975. No ms holdings.

TX —UNIVERSITY OF TEXAS LIBRARIES, Middle East Collection, PO Box P, Austin, 78712. Abazar Sepehri, Librn
Holdings: Vols (45,000) Cat Microforms
Notes: Arabic, Persian and Turkish materials in the humanities and social sciences. Incl 350 periodical and 45 newspaper titles from most of the countries of the Arab League, Turkey, Iran and Afghanistan.

UT —UNIVERSITY OF UTAH, Middle East Library, Salt Lake City, 84112. Ragai N Makar, Librn
Holdings: Vols 4000
Budget: ($40,000)

WA —UNIVERSITY OF WASHINGTON LIBRARIES, Suzzallo Library, Near East Section, FM-25, Seattle, 98195. Fawzi W Khoury, Head
Holdings: Vols 10,000 Cat
Budget: ($52,752)
Notes: Includes a collection of 10,000 titles in the Persian language.

PERSIAN MANUSCRIPTS see Manuscripts, Persian

PERSIANS see Iranians

PERSIUS FLACCUS, AULUS

MA —HARVARD UNIVERSITY LIBRARY, Widener Library, Cambridge, 02138.
Holdings: Cat
Notes: Collection of 1029 titles listed in Harvard University Library, *Bibliographical Contributions*, 58 (1909).

PERSONAL DEVELOPMENT see Personality

PERSONAL HYGIENE see Hygiene, Public

PERSONAL LOANS see Loans, Personal

PERSONAL NAMES see Names, Personal

PERSONALITY

MA —HARVARD UNIVERSITY, Graduate School of Education, Monroe C Gutman Library, 6 Appian Way, Cambridge, 02138. Susan S Baughman, Associate Librn
Holdings: Vols (150,000) Cat Mss Microforms
Budget: ($95,000)
Notes: A comprehensive research collection that seeks to acquire all scholarly works published in the English language in the fields of education, educational administration, educational psychology, and human development. Selective coverage in the related areas of counseling and psychology, business administration, finance, forecasting, statistical analysis and survey design, public and social policy, linguistics, demographics, and international and economic development. Incl 4000 educational and psychological tests.

OH —OHIO STATE UNIVERSITY, Home Economics Library, Campbell Hall Rm 325, 1787 Neil Ave, Columbus, 43210. Neosha Mackey, Librn
Holdings: Vols (14,000) Cat Microforms
Notes: Separate catalog. Also, book catalog:

Catalog of the Home Economics Library (Boston: G K Hall, 1976), 3 vols.

PERSONALITY, DISORDERS OF

NC —DUKE UNIVERSITY, William R Perkins Library, Manuscript Dept, Durham, 27706. Ellen Gartrell, Cur of Mss
Notes: The personal papers of Chris Costner Sizemore, who is widely known as the subject of the book and movie, "The Three Faces of Eve." Incl poems and other writings, diaries, drawings, photographs, tapes of interviews, and some printed material.

PERSONALITY, MULTIPLE see Multiple Personality

PERSONALITY TESTS

IL —UNIVERSITY OF ILLINOIS, URBANA/CHAMPAIGN, Library, University Archives, 19 Library, 1408 W Gregory Drive, Urbana, 61801. Maynard Brichford, University Archivist
Holdings: Vols (6000) Cat
Budget: $1500
Notes: The Odell Test Collection contains 3150 items comprising intelligence, achievement, subject, and character and personality tests. Almost every educational and psychological test of consequence prior to the early 1950s is included. The collection is located in the Education and Social Science Library and is integrated into a comprehensive collection of current and recent standardized tests. The indexing of the collection follows the scheme created and used by Oscar K Buros in his *Mental Measurement Yearbooks* and in the predecessors to the Yearbooks which appeared in the Rutgers Studies in Education series. The collection was a gift in 1960 of Charles Watters Odell, Professor Emeritus of Education. No photocopying.

PERSONNEL ADMINISTRATION see Personnel Management

PERSONNEL MANAGEMENT

AZ —TUCSON PUBLIC LIBRARY, Governmental Reference Library, PO Box 27210, City Hall, Tucson, 85726. Ann Strickland, Librn
Holdings: Vols (4000) Cat Maps Audiotapes Microforms
Notes: Special emphasis on public administration, including public finance, public personnel management, social services, urban planning, public transportation, public works, water management, solid waste management, public recreation and government of growing southwestern US cities in 200,000 to 500,000 population range.

CA —UNIVERSITY OF CALIFORNIA, BERKELEY, Institute of Governmental Studies Library, 109 Moses Hall, Berkeley, 94720. Jack Leister, Head Librn
Holdings: Vols (350,000) Cat Mss Maps Microforms
Budget: ($160,000)
Notes: The library collects primarily pamphlets. Incl in the library's holdings are documents from all levels of government, as well as publications issued by professional associations and special interest groups. A G K Hall catalog covering the Institute's Library holdings is available. Since 1937, Library has been depository for all California local documents (city, county & special district). Formerly: Bureau of Public Administration.

CA —ALAMEDA COUNTY LIBRARY SYSTEM, Business & Government Library, 2201 Broadway, Oakland, 94612. David Lewallen, Manager
Holdings: Vols (10,000) Cat Maps Microforms
Budget: ($50,000)

DC —US OFFICE OF PERSONNEL MANAGEMENT, Library, 1900 E St NW, Washington, 20415. Betty B Guerin, Supv Librn
Holdings: Vols 75,000 Cat Microforms
Notes: US Civil Service Commission terminated by Act of Congress, 10/78. US Office of Personnel Management created and effective, 1/79. Library houses a comprehensive collection of materials in all phases of federal personnel administration, both historical and current and incl federal documents and other pamphlets. It is supplemented by collections in general personnel administration, public administration, management, and state, local and foreign Civil Service.

MI —UNIVERSITY OF MICHIGAN, Graduate School of Business Administration, Business Administration Library, Institute for International Commerce Reading Rm, Ann Arbor, 48109. Carol Holbrook, Dir
Notes: The collection contains historical and current materials published by business, government, US labor unions and associations on employer-employee relationship, absenteeism, employee benefits, executive compensation, fair employment practices, job satisfaction, management development and performance appraisal. Labor union publications incl convention proceedings, constitutions, histories, manuals for officers and stewards, newspapers, and research reports. Incl approx (61,000) cataloged vertical file items.

MI —UNIVERSITY OF MICHIGAN, Bureau of Government Library, 100A Rackman Bldg, Ann Arbor, 48109. Barbara Landay, Technical Libr Assistant
Holdings: Vols (66,000) Cat
Budget: ($10,000)
Notes: Established in 1914 to serve faculty and students of Institute of Public Policy Studies. Particularly concerned with state and local documents, but incl some federal documents. Also has a pamphlet and newspaper clipping collection on Michigan. Some information on foreign governments.

NY —CORNELL UNIVERSITY, New York State School of Industrial & Labor Relations, Martin P Catherwood Library, Ives Hall, Ithaca, 14853. Shirley F Harper, Dir
Notes: Incl periodicals and oral history tapes.

NC —GREENSBORO PUBLIC LIBRARY, Business Library, 201 Greene St, Drawer X-4, Greensboro, 27402. Lebby B Lamb, Business Librn
Holdings: Vols (6000) Cat Microforms
Budget: ($12,000)

WY —US AIR FORCE INSTITUTE OF TECHNOLOGY, Library, Dept 9 Bldg 831, FE, Warren AFB, 82001. Patricia A Johnson, Librn
Holdings: Vols (7000) Cat Microforms
Budget: ($9000)
Notes: The Library supports graduate programs for students (Air Force Missile-Combat Crewman) seeking a Master of Business Administration Degree. Civilian students and other military personnel are also admitted.

ON —CANADA PUBLIC SERVICE COMMISSION, Library, Room 930 W Tower, Esplande Laurier, Ottawa, K1A 0M7, Can. A Campbell, Chief Librn
Notes: Subject interests: linguistics, educational psychology, personnel management, psychology, public administration, sociology.

PERSPECTIVE (MAGAZINE)

MO —WASHINGTON UNIVERSITY, Libraries, Special Collections Dept, Campus Box 1061, St Louis, 63130.
Notes: The Archives of this American literary journal.

PERSUASION (PSYCHOLOGY)

CA —GRADUATE THEOLOGICAL UNION LIBRARY, New Religious Movements Research Collection, Public Services and Special Collections Dept, 2400 Ridge Road, Berkeley, 94709. Diane Choquette, Dept Head
Holdings: Vols (3000) Mss Pix
Notes: Begun in 1977, the collection focuses

PERSUASION (PSYCHOLOGY) (cont.)

on religious movements new to America since 1960, and unorthodox religious movements resurgent since 1960. American forms of Hinduism, Buddhism, Sikhism, and Sufism are included along with occultism, New-Paganism, esoteric and alternative forms of Christianity, feminist spirituality, and human potential movements having a spiritual aspect. Legal issues, such as deprogramming, and the question of church/state relations are an important part of the collection. The Library is a depository for publications of the Unification Church in America, the Church of Scientology, and the International Society for Krishna Consciousness (America). The *responses* of mainstream religions and concerned citizens groups are also included. Besides 3000 monographs, the library has 350 periodical titles, 200 posters from the San FranciscoBay Area, 1965-77, 300 research papers, and 24 linear feet of ephemera.

PERU

CA —UNIVERSITY OF CALIFORNIA, BERKELEY, University Library, Hispanic Collections, Berkeley, 94720. Gaston Somoshegyi-Szokol, Librn
Holdings: Vols (14,000)
Notes: General research collection in the humanities and social sciences, with special strengths in history, literature, economics, and political developments. Main library holdings are supplemented by subject coverage in branch libraries. Extensive government document holdings are maintained in the Government Documents Department.
CT —YALE UNIVERSITY, Sterling Memorial Library, Latin American Collections, New Haven, 06520. Lee H Williams Jr, Cur
Holdings: Vols (300,000) Cat Maps Pix Slides Phonorecords 16mm Films Filmstrips
See also entry under Latin America
NY —AMERICAN MUSEUM OF NATURAL HISTORY, Library Services Dept, Central Park W & 79th St, New York, 10024. Nina J Root, Chairwoman; Mary Genett, Asst Librn for Reference Services
NY —COLUMBIA UNIVERSITY LIBRARIES, Rare Book & Manuscript Library, 801 Butler Library, 535 W 114 St, New York, 10027. Kenneth A Lohf, Librn
Notes: More than 32,000 items documenting the rise of William Russell Grace's shipping business and other materials relating to his career as mayor of New York. Incl records and correspondence relating to all aspects of the shipping business in New York and South America, mining interest in Peru and Chile, and transportation in Costa Rica and Nicaragua. Family memorabilia and photographs, materials concerning New York Politics, banking and insurance, real estate interests and Catholic charities, and letters from Chester A Arthur, John Jacob Astor, Andrew Carnegie, Grover Cleveland, Hamilton Fish, John Hay and J Pierpont Morgan. Restricted use.
NC —DUKE UNIVERSITY, William R Perkins Library, Durham, 27706. Elvin E Strowd, University Librn
Notes: The Perez de Velasco collection of 3000 titles relates to all phases of Latin American life. Emphasis is on colonial Peru.
PA —UNIVERSITY OF PITTSBURGH, Hillman Library, Pittsburgh, 15260. Glenora E Rossell, Head
Holdings: Vols (172,000) Cat Microforms
Notes: A general collection on Peruvian studies, but particularly strong in the history of the conquest, the discovery, the colonial period, and indian civilizations and cultures. Emphasis also is on contemporary history, politics, sociology, and anthropology.

PERU—HISTORY

CA —UNIVERSITY OF CALIFORNIA, BERKELEY, University Library, Hispanic Collections, Berkeley, 94720. Gaston Somoshegyi-Szokol, Librn
Holdings: Vols (5000)
Notes: A well balanced research collection covering both various types of historical literature (published documents, monographs, periodical articles, etc) and specific periods. Special emphasis on the development of Peruvian agrarian structure since the colonial period and on Peruvian ethnohistory.
CA —CALIFORNIA STATE UNIVERSITY, FRESNO, Henry Madden Library, Dept of Special Collections, Fresno, 93740. Ronald J Mahoney, Head
Holdings: // Uncat Mss Maps
Notes: Promotional material and correspondence of an unsuccessful attempt by Americans to raise capital to exploit the Toronty, or Cercada-de-San Antonio Estate in southern Peru. The estate was said to have been the source of ancient Peruvian gold. 50 ms items.
CT —YALE UNIVERSITY, Sterling Memorial Library, Latin American Collections, New Haven, 06520. Lee H Williams Jr, Cur
Holdings: Vols (300,000) Cat Maps Pix Slides Phonorecords 16mm Films Filmstrips
See also entry under Latin America
DC —LIBRARY OF CONGRESS, Manuscript Division, Washington, 20540. John C Broderick, Chief
Notes: The Harkness Collection contains documents relating to the first 200 years of Spanish rule in Mexico and Peru.
IN —INDIANA UNIVERSITY, Lilly Library, Seventh St, Bloomington, 47405. William R Cagle, Librn
Holdings: Vols (40,000) Cat Mss Maps
Notes: Research and rare book collection (Bernardo Mendel) of first or only editions, mostly printed in Latin America, from the discovery of the New World through 1830. Special strength in discoveries and exploration, history (mainly period of independence), Inquisition, missionary works by the Augustinians, Dominicans, Franciscans, and the Jesuits, and the history of the Catholic Church in these countries. Major geographic concentration is on the three great viceroyalties of Mexico (ca 10,000 titles, plus over 10,000 official Mexican broadsides), Peru (2000 titles), and Argentina (4000 titles), incl in Argentina a substantial amount of printings from the Imprenta de Ninos Expositos, and the Coleccion Santamaria. A special Bolivian Collection (2500 titles), mostly history, from the establishment of the press there, ca 1826, through the beginning of the 20th century. Part of theMendel Collection is the select Bibliotheca Boxeriana from Charles R Boxer (1000 titles) on Europeann expansion into Asia, and into the New World, mainly Brazil, during the 16th-18th centuries. The collection supplemented by substantial material from the private collection of Josiah K Lilly.
LA —TULANE UNIVERSITY, Howard-Tilton Memorial Library, Latin American Library, New Orleans, 70118. Thomas Niehaus, Dir
Holdings: Vols (150,000) Cat Mss Maps Pix Microforms VF
Budget: ($67,000)
Notes: *Catalog of the Latin American Library* (Boston: G K Hall, 1970, suppl. 1973,1975,1978); Downs 5338-41; suppl (1961), 2727, 2737. The Latin American Library is a general collection, but specializes in Central American, Mexican, and Brazilian materials. The disciplines which are most strongly represented are history, anthropology, and archaeology. The Viceregal Ecclesiastical Mexican Collection contains manuscripts from the colonial period. The France V Scholes Collection contains a large number of photoprints and microfilm of colonial documents from the archives of Spain and Mexico. The Merle Greene Robertson Rubbings Collection contains nearly five hundred rubbings of relief sculpture from Mayan archaeological sites in Mexico and Guatemala. The Photographic Collection contains photos of archaeological sites inMeso-America, of pre-Columbian Peruvian architecture, and a general group of historic photos from Latin America.
NC —DUKE UNIVERSITY, William R Perkins Library, Durham, 27706. Elvin E Strowd, University Librn
Notes: The Perez de Velasco collection of 3000 titles relates to all phases of Latin American life. Emphasis is on colonial Peru.
PA —PENNSYLVANIA STATE UNIVERSITY, Fred Lewis Pattee Library, Library Hispanic Program, University Park, 16802. Donald C Henderson, Head
Holdings: Vols 15,000 Cat Mss
Budget: ($21,000)
Notes: An outstanding collection from the colonial era through the 20th century including the APRA and social and political history; contains materials not to be found in other US institutions and is superbly backed by holdings in Peruvian literature, anthropology and related fields. Holdings incorporate the personal libraries of Dr Luis Alberto Sanchez and other eminent scholars; supports doctoral programs.
TX —UNIVERSITY OF TEXAS LIBRARIES, Nettie Lee Benson Latin American Collection, Sid Richardson Hall 1.109, Austin, 78712. Laura Gutierrez-Witt, Head Librn
Holdings: Vols (450,000) Cat Mss Maps Microforms
Notes: Private collection of Diego Munoz relating to Chile, Bolivia, Peru and Ecuador. Incl extensive coverage of the laws of Chile and of the Congress of Chile during the 19th century; also, 200 volumes of works of Jose Toribio Medina.
See also entry under Latin America

PERU—INDUSTRIES

CA —CALIFORNIA STATE UNIVERSITY, FRESNO, Henry Madden Library, Dept of Special Collections, Fresno, 93740. Ronald J Mahoney, Head
Holdings: // Uncat Mss Maps
Notes: Promotional material and correspondence of an unsuccessful attempt by Americans to raise capital to exploit the Torontoy, or Cercada-de-San Antonio Estate in southern Peru. The estate was said to have been the source of ancient Peruvian gold. 50 ms items.

PERUVIAN LITERATURE

PA —PENNSYLVANIA STATE UNIVERSITY, Fred Lewis Pattee Library, Library Hispanic Program, University Park, 16802. Donald C Henderson, Head
Holdings: Vols 15,000 Cat Mss
Budget: ($21,000)
Notes: An outstanding collection covering all periods, colonial to contemporary, with materials not found elsewhere in the US, superbly backed by holdings in Peruvian history, anthropology and related fields. Holdings incorporate the personal libraries of Dr Luis Alberto Sanchez and other eminent scholars; supports doctoral programs.

PERUVIAN MANUSCRIPTS see Manuscripts, Peruvian

PERUVIAN POETRY

CA —UNIVERSITY OF CALIFORNIA, BERKELEY, University Library, Hispanic Collections, Berkeley, 94720. Gaston Somoshegyi-Szokol, Librn
See also entry under Spanish Language and Literature.

PESSL, YELLA, 1906-

NY —STATE UNIVERSITY OF NEW YORK AT ALBANY, Library, Special Collections Dept, 1400 Washington Ave, Albany, 12222. Marion P Munzer, Coordr
Holdings: Vols Phonorecords
Notes: Music scores; recordings; reviews of Yella Pessl's music performances (1.2 linear feet; 30 volumes from her personal library). Part of the Library's German Exile Collection.
See also entry under Musicians

PESTICIDES

AR —NATIONAL CENTER FOR TOXICOLOGICAL RESEARCH, Library,

PESTICIDES (cont.)

Jefferson, 72079. Susan Laney-Sheehan, Supvr Librn
Holdings: Vols (15,000) Cat Mss Slides Audiotapes 16mm Films Microforms
Notes: Incl (860) journal titles, (230) current subscriptions.

CA —UNIVERSITY OF CALIFORNIA, DAVIS, Environmental Toxicology Library, Davis, 95616. Ming-yu Li, Documentation Specialist
Holdings: Vols (5000) Cat
Notes: Library is open to the public for reference only. In addition to the cataloged holdings, the library also maintains a pamphlet collection of 50 file drawers on agricultural chemicals, environmental pollution, heavy metals, food toxicants, toxicology, pesticides and trace elements.

MD —INSECT CONTROL & RESEARCH, Library, 1330 Dillon Heights Ave, Baltimore, 21228. Eugene J Gerberg, Librn
Holdings: Vols (3000) Uncat Slides Microforms

MD —RACHEL CARSON COUNCIL INC, Library, 8940 Jones Mill Rd, Chevy Chase, 20815. Shirley A Briggs, Exec Dir
Notes: Bioassays of pesticides and other toxic substances for carcinogenicity by National Cancer Institute; government regulatory documents. Holdings approx 1500 books; 1000 documents and unbound reports; 40 drawers of specialized files. Also have Environmental Protection Agency Pesticide Product Information. Subscribe to 54 journals and others serials. Also publish on pesticides, toxic substances and alternatives to use of pesticides. Have index to pesticides by chemical formula, trade names and CAS number.

MI —MICHIGAN STATE UNIVERSITY, Science Library, East Lansing, 48824. Carole S Armstrong, Head
Holdings: Vols 700 Cat
Notes: Both books and journals include titles in English, French, German and Russian, with a few in other languages. The scope includes general toxicology, industrial toxicology, veterinary toxicology, the toxicology of metals and insecticides, and poisons as studied in experimental pharmacology.

MO —US FISH & WILDLIFE SERVICE, Columbia National Fisheries Research Laboratory, Rte One, Columbia, 65201. Axie Hindman, Librn
Holdings: Vols (2000) Cat Microforms
Budget: ($7000)
Notes: Pesticides in aquatic biota; fisheries research; fresh-water ecology. Also incl collection in water pollution, acid rain, aquatic invertebrets, environment and 10,000 reprints.

NY —BOYCE THOMPSON INSTITUTE FOR PLANT RESEARCH, Library, Cornell University, Tower Rd, Ithaca, 14853. Greta Colavito, Librn
Holdings: Vols (5300) Cat
Budget: ($46,000)
Notes: Mainly plant physiology, biochemistry, entomology, air and water pollution, pesticides, and plant pathology.

PESTILENCES see Epidemics

PESTS AND PEST CONTROL

CA —UNIVERSITY OF CALIFORNIA, BERKELEY, Science Libraries, Natural Resources Library, 40 Giannini Hall, Berkeley, 94720. Norma Kobzina, Head Librn
Holdings: Vols (100,000) Cat Maps Microforms
Budget: ($40,000)
Notes: Subject emphasis is on basic agricultural and pest management research, particularly in the areas of tropical and subtropical agriculture and plantation crops, ie, cotton, rice, tobacco, and sugar. Materials in agricultural engineering, farm machinery, and veterinary medicine are not acquired for the Berkeley campus. Serials, especially the extensive holdings of foreign titles, constitute

the collection's major strength. Over 5700 serials are being received currently.

CA —UNIVERSITY OF CALIFORNIA, BERKELEY, Life Sciences Library, Entomology Library, 201 Wellman Hall, Berkeley, 94720. Nancy Axelrod, Librn
Holdings: Vols (12,000) Cat Microforms
Notes: A highly specialized collection limited to materials on insects, arachnida and animal parasites. Special emphasis is given to works on pest control, particularly on biological methods of control. The library's holdings in the field of parasitology emphasize medical parasitology. Incl over (17,000) pamphlets.

IA —IOWA STATE UNIVERSITY, Library, Ames, 50011. Warren B Kuhn, Dean of Library Services
Holdings: Cat
Notes: Incl: economic entomology, parasitology, pest management, systematic entomology and toxicology. Particular strengths: flies, mosquitoes and ticks. Extensive serial holdings.

IA —IOWA STATE UNIVERSITY, Library, Dept of Special Collections, Ames, 50011. Stanley M Yates, Head
Holdings: // Mss
Notes: Papers of Dwight Isley (1887-1974) who worked at the Bureau of Entomology at the USDA (1915-1921), then at the University of Arkansas (1921-1951), and finally as the Associate Director of the Agriculture Experiment Station at the University of Arkansas (1951-1953). Seven linear feet; finding aid available.

MD —INSECT CONTROL & RESEARCH, Library, 1330 Dillon Heights Ave, Baltimore, 21228. Eugene J Gerberg, Librn
Holdings: Vols (3000) Uncat Slides Microforms

BC —CANADIAN FORESTRY SERVICE, Pacific Forest Research Centre, Library, 506 West Burnside Rd, Victoria, V8Z 1M5, Can. Alice Solyma, Librn
Holdings: Vols (60,500) Cat Microforms
Notes: Incl rearing, biological control, identification, dispersal, insect pest management, comprehensive collection re Mountain Pine Beetle, Western Spruce Budworm, Douglas Fir Tussack Moth.

PE —AGRICULTURE CANADA, Research Station Library, PO Box 1210, Charlottetown, C1A 7M8, Can. Barrie Stanfield, Librn
Holdings: Vols (2300) Cat
Budget: ($5000)

PETAIN, MARSHALL HENRI PHILLIPPE

CA —HOOVER INSTITUTION ON WAR, REVOLUTION & PEACE, Stanford University, Stanford, 94305. Milorad M Drachkovitch, Archivist
Holdings: // Mss
Notes: The Rene Chambrun Collection. Depositions concerning the government of Marshall Petain and Pierre Laval, by persons who held important official positions in France during the German occupation. Unpublished register available in repository.

PETER, JOHN DESMOND

BC —UNIVERSITY OF VICTORIA, McPherson Library, Victoria, V8W 3H5, Can.
Notes: Mss, galleys, etc for three novels, *Along that Coast, Take Hands in Winter*, *Runaway*.

PETERKIN, WILBUR J., 1904-

CA —HOOVER INSTITUTION ON WAR, REVOLUTION & PEACE, Stanford University, Stanford, 94305. Milorad M Drachkovitch, Archivist
Holdings: Mss Maps 16mm Films
Notes: Papers of Wilbur J Peterkin, executive and commanding officer of the US Observer Mission to the Chinese Communists, 1944-1945, incl diary transcripts, reports, maps, 16mm film, and other material, 1944-1945, relating to

Chinese communist forces and the Japanese occupation of China during World War II. Also incl are rifle, bayonet, pistol, and hand grenade used by the Chinese communists during the Sino-Japanese Conflict. 1 1/2 ms boxes.

PETERICH, GERDA

NY —SYRACUSE UNIVERSITY LIBRARIES, Ernest S Bird Library, George Arents Research Library for Special Collections, Syracuse, 13210. Carolyn A Davis, Manuscripts Librn; Amy S Doherty, University Archivist; Mark F Weimer, Rare Book Librn
Notes: The George Arents Research Library for Special Collections at Syracuse University contains the papers of Margaret Bourke-White, Clara Sipprell, Gerda Peterich, Edward John Wall, Louis Fabian Bachrach, Joseph Costa (National Press Photographers Association), the University Archives Photographic Collection, and other misc photographs.

PETERS, FRITZ

MA —BOSTON UNIVERSITY, Mugar Memorial Library, Special Collections Dept, 771 Commonwealth Ave, Boston, 02215. Howard B Gotlieb, Dir
Holdings: Mss Pix Correspondence

PETERS, MIKE

OH —OHIO STATE UNIVERSITY, Library for Communication and Graphic Arts, 242 W 18th St, Columbus, 43210. Lucy S Caswell, Curator
Notes: The original works of editorial cartoonists Art Poinier, Scott Willis, Brian Basset, Billy Ireland, Frank Williams, Charles Werner, Ned Beard, L D Warren, Edward D Kuekes, Ray Osrin, Mike Peters, Draper Hill, Eugene Craig and Bert Whitman.

PETERSBURG, VIRGINIA—SIEGE, 1864-1865

VA —PETERSBURG NATIONAL BATTLEFIELD, Library, Box 549, Petersburg, 23804. C M Calkins, Librn
Holdings: Vols 2000 Cat Mss Maps Pix Slides
Notes: Information on following engagements during siege: Battle for Petersburg, June 1864; Jerusalem Plank Road, June 1864; Battle of the Crater, July 1864; Weldon Railroad, August 1864; Reams Station, August 1864; Peebles Farm, Sept-Oct 1864; Boydton Plant Road, Oct 1864; Hatchers Run, Feb 1864; Fort Stedman, March 1865; Five Forks, April 1865; Assault on Petersburg, April 1865. Noncirculating.

PETERSEN, CHRISTIAN

IA —IOWA STATE UNIVERSITY, Library, Dept of Special Collections, Ames, 50011. Stanley M Yates, Head
Holdings: // Mss Pix
Notes: The Christian Petersen (1885-1961) Papers. Petersen was on Iowa State University faculty 1937-1961; executed many pieces of sculpture. Collection incl correspondence, articles about Petersen, original sketches and about 400 photographs. Collection is 9 linear ft.

PETERSEN, HOWARD

†MA —JOHN F KENNEDY LIBRARY, Columbia Point, Boston, 02125. Dan H Fenn Jr, Dir
Holdings: // Cat Mss
Notes: Files and papers of JFK and his key foreign trade advisors Christian Herter and Howard Petersen, 1961-1967. 40 linear ft of mss. Holdings are described in "Historical Materials in the John F Kennedy Library." Copies may be obtained by writing the Research Archivist.

PETERSHAM FAMILY

MA —PETERSHAM HISTORICAL SOCIETY, Library, N Main St, Petersham,

PETERSHAM FAMILY (cont.)

01366. Delight G Haines, Librn
Holdings: Vols (900) Cat Mss Maps Pix
Notes: The Petersham area. Genealogical
files on Petersham families. Incl Daniel
Sharp Rebellion.

PETERSON, ESTHER (EGGERTSEN), 1906-

MA —RADCLIFFE COLLEGE, Arthur &
Elizabeth Schlesinger Library on the History
of Women in America, 3 James St,
Cambridge, 02138. Patricia Miller King, Dir;
Eva Moseley, Cur of Mss
Holdings: Mss Pix
Notes: Correspondence of Esther
(Eggertsen) Peterson with family and
friends; correspondence and printed material
re work in Industrial Union Dept of AFL-
CIO (1958-1961); ILO; International
Confederation of Free Trade Unions;
Democratic political campaigns (1960-);
National Committee on Household
Employment; National Women's Committee
on Civil Rights. Correspondence, speeches,
and printed material re work as Dir, US
Women's Bureau (1961-1964); Asst Sec of
Labor (1962-1969); Special Asst to the Pres
for Consumer Affairs (1964-1967, 1977-
1981); Exec Vice Chmn of President's
Commission on the Status of Women (1961-
1963); Consumer Advisor to Giant Food
(1970-1976). Other papers re Peterson's re
Peterson's work for rights of women,
minorities, labor, consumers.

PETERSON, LEONARD BYRON, 1917-

AB —UNIVERSITY OF CALGARY,
Libraries, Special Collections Div, 2500
University Dr, Calgary, T2N 1N4, Can.
Holdings: Cat Mss
Notes: The papers of Len Peterson include
research material, manuscripts and
correspondence for his first novel Chipmunk
(1949), and his plays Burlap Bags (1946),
and The Great Hunger (1958).

PETERSON, VIRGILIA

MA —BOSTON UNIVERSITY, Mugar
Memorial Library, Special Collections Dept,
771 Commonwealth Ave, Boston, 02215.
Howard B Gotlieb, Dir
Holdings: Cat Mss Pix Correspondence

PETIEVICH, GERALD

MA —BOSTON UNIVERSITY, Mugar
Memorial Library, Special Collections Dept,
771 Commonwealth Ave, Boston, 02215.
Howard B Gotlieb, Dir
Holdings: Mss

PETIGRU, J. L.

SC —COLLEGE OF CHARLESTON
LIBRARY, Special Collections Dept,
Charleston, 29401.
Notes: Papers, 1842-1853, incl
correspondence of Mitchell King with Henry
C King (son), F S Holmes, J L Petigru, and
John Pennington.

PETRARCH

CA —UNIVERSITY OF CALIFORNIA,
BERKELEY, University Library, French
and Italian Collections, Berkeley, 94720.
Donald G Williams, Librn
Notes: Research collection with special
strengths in early Italian literature (to 1400),
and Italian literature of the Renaissance.
Strong holdings for such authors as Dante,
Petrarch, Boccaccio, Ariosto, Machiavelli,
Tasso, and many others. The collections in
the Main Library are complemented by
significant incunabula, rare books and ms
holdings in the Bancroft Library.
CT —YALE UNIVERSITY, Box 1603A, Yale
Station, New Haven, 06520.
DC —LIBRARY OF CONGRESS, General
Reading Rooms Division, Microform

Reading Room, Washington, 20540.
Holdings: Cat Mss Maps Pix Microforms
Notes: Microform materials only in this LC
Division. Works of individual authors,
holdings of collections; archival records, etc,
press releases and translations, etc.
MA —HARVARD UNIVERSITY LIBRARY,
Houghton Library, Cambridge, 02138.
Rodney G Dennis, Cur of Manuscripts
Holdings: Cat Mss
Notes: For manuscripts, see Harvard Library
Bulletin, XII (1958), 320-325.
MO —SAINT LOUIS UNIVERSITY, Pius XII
Memorial Library, Saint Louis Room
Collection, 3655 W Pine Blvd, Saint Louis,
63108. Catherine E Weidle, Rare Books
Librn
Holdings: Mss Uncat
NY —CORNELL UNIVERSITY LIBRARIES,
John M Olin Library, Dept of Rare Books,
Ithaca, 14853. Donald D Eddy, Librn
Holdings: Vols 5190 Cat Mss
Notes: Downs 3685. See Petrarch: Catalogue
of the Petrarch Collection in Cornell
University Library (Millwood, NY: KTO
Press, 1974).
NC —DUKE UNIVERSITY, William R
Perkins Library, Durham, 27706. Elvin E
Strowd, University Librn
Notes: The Mazzoni collection of
approximately 23,000 books and 67,000
reprints and pamphlets is strong in, but not
limited by any means to, Italian literature. A
special aspect of this collection is a group of
essays, studies, or small works published on
the occasion of a marriage. These "per la
nozze di" range from a poem published in
post card form to a scientific or literary
work. The manuscript catalog of the
pamphlet collection has been published by
the library in book form; the 23,000 volumes
have been cataloged and are shelved in the
library's bookstacks.

PETROCHEMICALS

IL —STANDARD OIL CO (INDIANA),
Central Research Library, PO Box 400,
Naperville, 60540. Cammille Stryek, Staff
Librn
Holdings: Vols (30,000) Cat Microforms
NJ —EXXON RESEARCH AND
ENGINEERING CO, Linden Information
Center, PO Box 121, Linden, 07036. PA
Lorenz, Section Head
Holdings: Vols (40,000) Cat Maps Pix
Microforms
Notes: No photocopying.
NJ —WITCO CHEMICAL CORP, Corporate
Research Center Library, 100 Bauer Dr,
Oakland, 07436. Jo Therese Smith, Mgr,
Information Services
Holdings: Vols (9000) Cat
Budget: ($52,000)
AB —ALBERTA OIL SANDS
INFORMATION CENTRE, 6th Floor,
Highfield Place, 10010-106 St, Edmonton,
T5J 3L8, Can. Helga Radvanyi, Mgr
Notes: "Major activity of the Centre has
been preparation of the Alberta Oil Sands
Index. However...scope has broadened to
include the Heavy Oil/Enhanced Recovery
Index," and other informative literature.

PETROGRAPHY see Petrology

PETROLEUM

CA —KERN COUNTY LIBRARY SYSTEM,
1315 Truxtun Ave, Bakersfield, 93301. Mary
Haas, Geology, Mining, Petroleum Librn
Holdings: Vols (28,256) Cat Maps
Microforms
Notes: Deals with California and western
states primarily. Incl 500 maps.
CA —UNION OIL CO OF CALIFORNIA,
Library, 376 S Valencia Ave, Brea, 92621.
Barbara Orosz, Head Librn
Holdings: Vols (40,000) Cat Maps
Microforms Books Documents Journals
†CA —STANDARD OIL COMPANY OF
CALIFORNIA, 225 Bush St, San Francisco,
92104.
Holdings: Maps
Notes: 8000 maps and charts.
CO —COLORADO SCHOOL OF MINES,
Arthur Lakes Library, 14 & Illinois Sts,

Golden, 80401. Hartley K Phinney, Jr, Head
Librn
Holdings: Vols (270,557) Cat Mss Maps
Microforms
DE —HAGLEY MUSEUM AND LIBRARY,
Eleutherian Mills-Hagley Foundation Inc,
PO Box 3630, Greenville, 19807. Richmond
D Williams, Dir; Heddy A Richter, Imprints
Librn
Notes: Records of Sun Oil Company (1889-
1966; 750 cubic feet) contain both
administrative and operating records as well
as papers of key executive officers: Joseph N
Pew, Joseph N Pew Jr, and Arthur Pew.
IL —STANDARD OIL CO (INDIANA),
Central Research Library, PO Box 400,
Naperville, 60540. Cammille Stryek, Staff
Librn
Holdings: Vols (30,000) Cat Microforms
NM —ROSWELL PUBLIC LIBRARY, 301 N
Pennsylvania Ave, Roswell, 88201. Sarah
Beth Galloway, Library Dir
Holdings: Vols 600 Cat Maps
Notes: Great majority of collection consists
of bound copies of professional journals.
Many items on petroleum and minerals, with
emphasis on Southwestern US.
PA —FRANKLIN INSTITUTE LIBRARY, 20
& The Parkway, Philadelphia, 19103.
Miriam Padusis, Dir; Charles Wilt, Readers
Servs Librn
Holdings: Vols (300,000) Cat Maps Pix
Microforms
PA —CARNEGIE LIBRARY OF
PITTSBURGH, Science & Technology Dept,
4400 Forbes Ave, Pittsburgh, 15213.
Catherine M Brosky, Dept Head
Holdings: Vols (380,000) Cat Maps
Microforms
Budget: ($240,000)
Notes: Incl many long runs and journals.
Encyclopedias, general reference books,
abstracts, indexes and bibliographies.
See also entry under Technology.
TX —MIDLAND COUNTY PUBLIC
LIBRARY, Petroleum Dept, 301 W
Missouri, PO Box 1191, Midland, 79701.
Sandra Wagner, Librn
Holdings: Vols (27,000) Cat Maps
Budget: ($2000)
Notes: Scout tickets covering W Texas and
New Mexico, driller's logs for the same area,
Lockwood reports 1947-1970, over one
hundred industry-related periodicals,
publications of many State Surveys, USGS,
USBM, and Geological Societies. Incl 7600
maps.

PETROLEUM—GEOLOGY

AR —MURPHY OIL USA, INC, LIBRARY,
Library, 200 Peach St, El Dorado, 71730.
Peggy A Makepeace, Librn
Holdings: Vols (6300) Cat Maps
Notes: Incl 2000 maps.
CA —LOS ANGELES PUBLIC LIBRARY,
Science & Technology Dept, 630 W Fifth St,
Los Angeles, 90071. Billie M Connor, Dept
Head
Holdings: Vols 18,000 Maps Microforms
Notes: Extensive holdings of state geology
department publications and maps of the
Western states including Alaska and Hawaii,
US Geological Survey, US Bureau of Mines,
and the geology departments of major
universities. Complete sets of publications
and indexes of major geological societies
including the Geological Society of America
and the American Association of Petroleum
Geologists. Partially cataloged.
IL —UNIVERSITY OF ILLINOIS,
URBANA/CHAMPAIGN, Library,
Geology Library, 223 Natural History Bldg,
Urbana, 61801. Dederick Ward, Librn
Holdings: Vols (105,186) Cat Maps
Microforms
IN —INDIANA STATE UNIVERSITY,
EVANSVILLE, Library, 8600 University
Blvd, Evansville, 47712. Gina R Walker,
Acting Archivist
Holdings: Uncat Mss Maps Pix
Phonorecords Microforms
Notes: 120 file cabinet drawers of material
pertaining to Tri-State (Indiana, Illinois,
Kentucky) area donated by Sun Oil
Company; 10 drawers, a gift of a local

PETROLEUM—GEOLOGY (cont.)

geologist. Objective: to collect and preserve materials pertaining to the development of the petroleum industry in this area. Restricted use: noncirculating.

OK —UNIVERSITY OF OKLAHOMA, Geology Library, 830 Van Vleet Oval Rm 102, Norman, 73019. Claren Kidd, Geology Librn
Holdings: Vols 70,000 Cat Maps Microforms
Budget: $22,000
Notes: Geology Library is also the Oklahoma Geological Survey Library.

OK —AMOCO PRODUCTION CO RESEARCH CENTER, Library, 4502 E 41 St, Tulsa, 74102. Carolyn Beson, Research Librn
Holdings: Vols (25,000) Cat Maps Microforms
Notes: Petroleum exploration and production research.

OK —TULSA CITY-COUNTY LIBRARY, Business & Technology Dept, 400 Civic Center, Tulsa, 74103. Craig Buthod, Head
Holdings: Vols (1600) Cat
Notes: The A I Levorsen Geology Collection. The department has a major emphasis on geology and petroleum geology. There is a catalog of the collection which was given to the library in 1968.

PA —PENNSYLVANIA GEOLOGICAL SOCIETY, Library, 916 Executive House, Second & Chestnut Sts, Harrisburg, 17120. Sandra Blust, Librn
Holdings: Vols (7600) Cat Mss Maps Microforms
Notes: Incl 200,000 aerial photographs and 250,000 maps.

TX —UNIVERSITY OF TEXAS LIBRARIES, General Libraries, Geology Dept, PO Box P, Austin, 78712. Chestalene Pintozzi, Librn
Holdings: Vols (59,349) Cat Maps Microforms

AB —AMOCO CANADA PETROLEUM LTD, Library, Rm 1013, 444 Seventh Ave, SW, Calgary, T2P 0Y2, Can. Frances M Drummond, Librn
Holdings: Vols (40,000) Cat Maps
Notes: Petroleum geology, engineering, and economics.

PETROLEUM—HISTORY

WY —UNIVERSITY OF WYOMING, William Robertson Coe Library, Archives - American Heritage Center, Laramie, 82071.
Holdings: Vols 6000 Cat Mss Maps Pix
Notes: The Petroleum History & Research Center has been active since 1958 as one of the subject areas of the University of Wyoming Archival program. Main emphasis has been in the collection of ms collections, and accessions are going forward at better than 15 percent per year. Incl 2000 linear feet of ms material in over 100 separate collections.

PETROLEUM—LAW see Petroleum Law and Legislation

PETROLEUM—PIPE LINES

AK —ALASKA STATE LIBRARY, Alaska Historical Library Collection, Pouch G, Juneau, 99811. Phyllis Demuth, Readers Services Librn
Holdings: Vols (24,000) Cat Mss Maps Pix Slides Phonorecords Audiotapes Videotapes 16mm Films Microforms

PETROLEUM—REFINING

AR —MURPHY OIL USA, INC, LIBRARY, Library, 200 Peach St, El Dorado, 71730. Peggy A Makepeace, Librn
Holdings: Vols (6300) Cat Maps
Notes: Incl 2000 maps.

NJ —EXXON RESEARCH AND ENGINEERING CO, Research Library, Clinton Township, Rt 22 E, Annandale, 08801.

NJ —EXXON RESEARCH AND ENGINEERING CO, Research Information Center (RIC), PO Box 121, Linden, 07036.

R G M Cosgrave, Head
Holdings: Vols (35,000) Cat Maps Pix Microforms
Notes: No photocopying.

PETROLEUM CONSTRUCTION

OH —MARATHON OIL CO, Law Library, 539 S Main St, Room 854-M, Findlay, 45840. Durand S Dudley, Sr Law Librn
Holdings: Vols (18,000) Cat
Budget: ($100,000)
Notes: Library serves the informational needs of the staff attorneys of a major oil company operating in both domestic and foreign areas. Includes all of the domestic law reports and digests. Includes statutes of 25 states. Particular emphasis is given to the acquisition of mineral (petroleum) law and energy legislation and regulation. Library open to the public by permission.

PETROLEUM ENGINEERING

CA —STANFORD UNIVERSITY, School of Earth Sciences, Branner Earth Sciences Library, Stanford, 94305. Charlotte Derksen, Head Librn
Holdings: Vols (70,000) Cat Microforms
Notes: Incl SPE Technical Papers collection on microfiche. Also incl SUPRI reports.

LA —LOUISIANA STATE UNIVERSITY, Troy H Middleton Library, Louisiana Room, Baton Rouge, 70803. Evangeline Mills Lynch, Head Librn; Ruth Murray, Associate Librn
Holdings: Vols (33,500) Cat Maps VF
Notes: Louisiana Collection of history, description and travel, biography, agriculture, literature, politics and government, folklore, anthropology, geography, geology, education, language, music and natural history. Especially large subject collections may be found on Louisiana, the history of the lower Mississippi Valley, Abraham Lincoln, Romance languages and literatures, sugar culture and technology, Southern history, petroleum engineering, plant pathology, micropaleontology, ornithology, and various aspects of crawfish life, biology and culture. Complete depository of Louisiana State Documents; extensive newspapers clipping files; separate card catalog; items listed in Louisiana Union Catalog; restricted use (research and reference). Incl both materials about Louisiana and by Louisianians without regard to subject. LSU Press Collection(preservation copy of each title kept for exhibit purposes only). LSU theses and dissertations from 1900-date. LSU Faculty Collection. Also, 1300 maps, 104 VF drawers, 250 boxes of uncataloged pamphlets.

MA —STONE & WEBSTER ENGINEERING CORP, Technical Information Center, Library, 245 Summer St, PO Box 2325, Boston, 02107. Nancy M Pellini, Mgr
Holdings: Vols (10,000) Cat Pix Microforms
Notes: Also over 1200 periodicals. Extensive vertical file collection, and 5 on-line system for search.

NJ —EXXON RESEARCH AND ENGINEERING CO, Research Library, Clinton Township, Rt 22 E, Annandale, 08801.

NJ —EXXON RESEARCH AND ENGINEERING CO, Research Information Center (RIC), PO Box 121, Linden, 07036. R G M Cosgrave, Head
Holdings: Vols (35,000) Cat Maps Pix Microforms
Notes: No photocopying.

NY —ENGINEERING SOCIETIES LIBRARY, 345 E 47 St, New York, 10017. S Kirk Cabeen, Dir
Holdings: Vols 250,000 Cat Maps 16mm Films Microforms
Notes: One of the largest, most comprehensive engineering libraries in the world. Covers all engineering disciplines; particularly strong in electrical and electronic, mechanical, mining and metallurgical, petroleum,, chemical, industrial, air conditioning and refrigeration engineering. Incl Wheeler Collection of early

materials on magnetism and electricity. 125,000 bound periodical volumes; 10,000 maps; 5000 serial subscriptions (many foreign-language). Virtually all materials abstracted in *Engineering Index* (1884-date) are incl in Library. Noncirculating, except to members of professional engineering societies which support the Library. See *Engineering Societies Library, New York, Classed Subject Catalog and Index* (Boston: G K Hall, 1963); and *Supplements*, 1-10, 1964-1973.

OK —AMOCO PRODUCTION CO RESEARCH CENTER, Library, 4502 E 41 St, Tulsa, 74102. Carolyn Beson, Research Librn
Holdings: Vols (25,000) Cat Maps Microforms
Notes: Petroleum exploration and production research.

PA —FRANKLIN INSTITUTE LIBRARY, 20 & The Parkway, Philadelphia, 19103. Miriam Padusis, Dir; Charles Wilt, Readers Servs Librn
Holdings: Vols (300,000) Cat Maps Pix Microforms

PA —PENNSYLVANIA STATE UNIVERSITY, Earth & Mineral Sciences Library, 105 Deike Bldg, University Park, 16802. Emilie McWilliams, Head Librn
Holdings: Vols (58,000) Cat Maps Microforms
Budget: ($49,750)
Notes: This collection includes substantial numbers of geological maps, and strong periodical holdings including microform.

TX —UNIVERSITY OF TEXAS LIBRARIES, Richard W McKinney Engineering Library, 1.3 ECJ, Austin, 78712. Susan B Ardis, Librn
Holdings: Vols (83,548) Cat Microforms
Notes: Chemical Engineering - at University of Texas, Chemistry Library.

TX —MIDLAND COUNTY PUBLIC LIBRARY, Petroleum Dept, 301 W Missouri, PO Box 1191, Midland, 79701. Sandra Wagner, Librn
Holdings: Vols (27,000) Cat Maps
Budget: ($2000)
Notes: Scout tickets covering W Texas and New Mexico, driller's logs for the same area, Lockwood reports 1947-1970, over one hundred industry-related periodicals, publications of many State Surveys, USGS, USBM, and Geological Societies. Incl 7600 Maps.

TX —ECTOR COUNTY LIBRARY, Department of Business and Technology, 321 W 5th St, Odessa, 79760. Pat Jones, Dept Head
Holdings: Vols 100 Cat

AB —AMOCO CANADA PETROLEUM LTD, Library, Rm 1013, 444 Seventh Ave, SW, Calgary, T2P 0Y2, Can. Frances M Drummond, Librn
Holdings: Vols (40,000) Cat Maps
Notes: Petroleum geology, engineering, and economics.

PETROLEUM ENGINES see Gas and Oil Engines

PETROLEUM GEOLOGY see Petroleum—Geology

PETROLEUM INDUSTRY AND TRADE

AR —MURPHY OIL USA, INC, LIBRARY, Library, 200 Peach St, El Dorado, 71730. Peggy A Makepeace, Librn
Holdings: Vols (6300) Cat Maps
Notes: Incl 2000 maps.

IN —INDIANA STATE UNIVERSITY, EVANSVILLE, Library, 8600 University Blvd, Evansville, 47712. Gina R Walker, Acting Archivist
Holdings: Uncat Mss Maps Pix Phonorecords Microforms
Notes: 120 file cabinet drawers of material pertaining to Tri-State (Indiana, Illinois, Kentucky) area donated by Sun Oil Company; 10 drawers, a gift of a local geologist. Objective: to collect and preserve materials pertaining to development of the petroleum industry in this area. Restricted use: noncirculating.

PETROLEUM INDUSTRY AND TRADE (cont.)

LA —UNIVERSITY OF SOUTHERN LOUISIANA, Dupre Library, Jefferson Caffery Louisiana Room, 302 East St Mary Blvd, Lafayette, 70504. Cynthia J Rice, Louisiana Room Ref Librn
Holdings: Vols 50 Mss
Notes: Fifty linear feet mss.

MA —HARVARD UNIVERSITY, Center for Middle Eastern Studies, Library, Coolidge Hall, 1737 Cambridge St, Cambridge, 02138. Barbara Mitchell, Librn
Holdings: Vols (5000) Periodicals
Notes: Some history of countries of the Middle East; increasingly emphasizes culture and politics of the current Middle Eastern area. Special collection of Energy Economics Research. Library currently receives 15 periodical titles.

NY —MOBIL CORP, Secretariat Library, 150 E 42 St, New York, 10017. Patricia K Marshall, Mgr Analytic Research
Holdings: Vols (8000) Cat Maps Microforms
Notes: Economics and statistics. Does not incl technical and scientific aspects, except superficially.

PA —FRANKLIN INSTITUTE LIBRARY, 20 & The Parkway, Philadelphia, 19103. Miriam Padusis, Dir; Charles Wilt, Readers Servs Librn
Holdings: Vols (300,000) Cat Maps Pix Microforms

PA —CARNEGIE LIBRARY OF PITTSBURGH, Science & Technology Dept, 4400 Forbes Ave, Pittsburgh, 15213. Catherine M Brosky, Dept Head
Holdings: Vols (380,000) Cat Maps Microforms
Budget: ($240,000)
Notes: General information acquired. Manufacturers directories, including old editions, standards and specifications, basic periodicals, indexes, and bibliographies. *See also* entry under Technology.

TX —UNIVERSITY OF TEXAS LIBRARIES, General Libraries, Barker Texas History Center, PO Box P, Austin, 78712. Don Carleton, Dir
Holdings: Vols (132,000) Cat Mss Maps Pix Slides Phonorecords Audiotapes Microforms
Notes: Materials pertaining to the historical, social, economic, scientific, humanistic and literary development of Texas. Rich in early state imprints, as well as the period of the Republic. Texas archival and ms holdings number over 18,000,000 items. Texas history prior to the Republic is covered by the Bexar Archives.

TX —MIDLAND COUNTY PUBLIC LIBRARY, Petroleum Dept, 301 W Missouri, PO Box 1191, Midland, 79701. Sandra Wagner, Librn
Holdings: Vols (27,000) Cat Maps
Budget: ($2000)
Notes: Scout tickets covering W Texas and New Mexico, driller's logs for the same area, Lockwood reports 1947-1970, over one hundred industry-related periodicals, publications of many State Surveys, USGS, USBM, and Geological Societies. Incl 7600 maps.

TX —ECTOR COUNTY LIBRARY, Department of Business and Technology, 321 W 5th St, Odessa, 79760. Pat Jones, Dept Head
Holdings: Vols 100 Cat
Notes: Incl 100 vertical files, 25 periodicals, 250 Trade Standards. Collections concentrated on the Drilling and Production industries. Also included are Exploration methods Reservoir Development, Pipeline, Construction, Well Servicing, Well Logging, and Well Control. Complete collection of the API Specifications, and Complete Welding "library".

AB —AMOCO CANADA PETROLEUM LTD, Library, Rm 1013, 444 Seventh Ave, SW, Calgary, T2P 0Y2, Can. Frances M Drummond, Librn
Holdings: Vols (40,000) Cat Maps
Notes: Petroleum geology, engineering, and economics.

AB —ALBERTA OIL SANDS INFORMATION CENTRE, 6th Floor, Highfield Place, 10010-106 St, Edmonton, T5J 3L8, Can. Helga Radvanyi, Mgr
Notes: "Major activity of the Centre has been preparation of the Alberta Oil Sands Index. However...scope has broadened to include the Heavy Oil/Enhanced Recovery Index," and other informative literature.

MB —UNIVERSITY OF MANITOBA, Elizabeth Dafoe Library, Government Publications Section, Winnipeg, R3T 2N2, Can. June Dutka, Head
Holdings: Vols 1300 // Uncat Maps Pix
Notes: The collection, which dates from 1975, consists of written dialect testimonies and responses with supporting exhibits from over 100 oil and gas companies, Indian and native associations and concerned citizen groups. The content of these documents incl construction plans, financial statements, alternate corridors, and describes the social and economic impact of the Arctic Gas Pipeline in northern Canada. The *Biological Report Series* offers vital information on soils and vegetation, movements of porcupine, caribou herds, bird distribution and fisheries research. An index listing the various company exhibits accompanies this collection.

ON —ENERGY, MINES & RESOUCES CANADA, Headquarters, 580 Booth St, Ottawa, K1A 0E4, Can. F B Scollie, Chief Librn
Holdings: Vols (65,000) Cat Microforms
Budget: ($200,000)
Notes: EMR Libraries Network includes the Headquarters, Conservation and Non-Petroleum Branch, and Petroleum Incentives Branch. Topics incl energy and mineral economics, especially Canadian.

PETROLEUM INDUSTRY AND TRADE—HISTORY

CA —LONG BEACH PUBLIC LIBRARY, Science and Technology Dept, 101 Pacific Ave, Long Beach, 90802. James Jackson, Librn
Holdings: Vols 2000 Uncat Mss Maps Pix Slides
Notes: California Petroleum Industry Collection incl 2000 government publications, 700 petroleum company documents, 750 pamphlets, 1000 tool catalogs and brochures, 93 periodical titles, mss, 400 maps, 3000 pictures, and slides. Cataloged and indexed. Open to serious researchers by appointment.

KY —UNIVERSITY OF LOUISVILLE, Ekstrom Library, Photographic Archives, Louisville, 40292. J C Anderson, Cur; David G Horvath, Asst Cur
Holdings: Vols (750,000) Cat Pix Slides
Budget: ($60,000)
Notes: Standard Oil of New Jersey Collection, 85,000 pictures of oil industry's effect on life in the 20th century (1943-1950, directed by Roy Stryker).

PA —PENNSYLVANIA HISTORICAL & MUSEUM COMMISSION, Drake Well Museum Library, RD 3, Titusville, 16354. Vance Packard, Adminr
Holdings: Vols 7000 Cat Mss Maps Pix Slides
Notes: The most complete library collection relative to the subject of the 19th century oil industry, with a large amount of materials relative to the 20th century. Incl 4000 pictures by John Mather.

TX —LEE COLLEGE, Library, PO Box 818, Baytown, 77522. William K Peace, Librn
Notes: Oral history tapes covering the area of east Harris County, Texas. Early history of Baytown, Goose Creek, and Pelly, with some relating to the early development of Humble Oil and Refining Company as remembered by early residents of the area. Also in the western area of Chambers County, Texas, known as Barbers Hill. The original tapes are housed in the Lee College Library, with copies located in the Sterling Municipal Library of Baytown. Incl 75 tapes; 50 transcripts.

TX —SPINDLETOP MEMORIAL MUSEUM, Library, 950 E Florida, PO Box 10082, Lamar Univ, Beaumont, 77710. David L Hartman, Dir; Christy Stutz, Secy
Holdings: Vols 200 Uncat Mss Maps Pix Audiotapes 16mm Films
Notes: Oil History of Southeast Texas 1901 to present. Artifacts include furniture and socio-economic examples housed in a "Boomtown" for the time period 1901-1906. Other artifacts are housed in the temporary indoor museum and cover from 1907 to the present time.

TX —SOUTHERN METHODIST UNIVERSITY, DeGolyer Library, Box 396, SMU, Dallas, 75275. Clifton H Jones, Dir
Holdings: Cat Mss Maps Pix
Notes: Transportation, especially railroads and trans-Atlantic steamboats.

TX —RICE UNIVERSITY, Fondren Library, Woodson Research Center, 6100 S Main St, PO Box 1892, Houston, 77251. Nancy Parker, Dir Woodson Research Center
Notes: The papers of Walter Benona Sharp and Estelle Boughton Sharp. His papers consist of letters written to his wife and family from 1890 to 1912 as well as papers relating to his involvement in the oil business. Her papers cover a variety of topics, incl United Charities, the peace movement, Rice University, her business and financial affairs, and her efforts to record the history of the oil industry in the Southwest.

WY —UNIVERSITY OF WYOMING, William Robertson Coe Library, Archives - American Heritage Center, Laramie, 82071. Holdings: Vols 6000 Cat Mss Maps Pix
Notes: The Petroleum History & Research Center has been active since 1958 as one of the subject areas of the University of Wyoming Archival program. Main emphasis has been in the collection of ms collections, and accessions are going forward at better that 15 percent per year. Incl 2000 linear feet of ms material in over 100 separate collections.

AB —ALBERTA OIL SANDS INFORMATION CENTRE, 6th Floor, Highfield Place, 10010-106 St, Edmonton, T5J 3L8, Can. Helga Radvanyi, Mgr
Notes: "Major activity of the Centre has been preparation of the Alberta Oil Sands Index. However...scope has broadened to include the Heavy Oil/Enhanced Recovery Index," and other informative literature.

PETROLEUM LAW AND LEGISLATION

OH —MARATHON OIL CO, Law Library, 539 S Main St, Room 854-M, Findlay, 45840. Durand S Dudley, Sr Law Librn
Holdings: Vols (18,000) Cat
Budget: ($100,000)
Notes: Library serves the informational needs of the staff attorneys of a major oil company operating in both domestic and foreign areas. Includes all of the domestic law reports and digests. Includes statutes of 25 states. Particular emphasis is given to the acquisition of mineral (petroleum) law and energy legislation and regulation. Library open to the public by permission.

AB —UNIVERSITY OF ALBERTA, John Weir Memorial Law Library, Law Centre, Second Floor, Edmonton, T6G 2H5, Can. Lillian MacPherson, Law Librn
Holdings: Vols (140,000) Cat Maps Audiotapes Microforms
Budget: ($400,000)
Notes: Emphases on Canadian Government Publications, oil and gas, Canadian and US, UK, Australian, New Zealand primary materials. Separate catalog.

PETROLEUM PIPE LINES see Petroleum—Pipe Lines

PETROLEUM REFINERIES

KY —UNIVERSITY OF KENTUCKY, Robert E Shaver Library of Engineering, 355 Anderson Hall, Lexington, 40506. Russell H Powell, Engineering Librn
Holdings: Vols (48,000) Cat Microforms

PETROLEUM REFINING see Petroleum—Refining

PETROLOGY

IL —UNIVERSITY OF ILLINOIS, URBANA/CHAMPAIGN, Library,

PETROLOGY (cont.)

Geology Library, 223 Natural History Bldg, Urbana, 61801. Dederick Ward, Librn
Holdings: Vols (105,186) Cat Maps Microforms

MA —HARVARD UNIVERSITY LIBRARY, Geological Sciences Library, 24 Oxford St, Cambridge, 02138. Constance Wick, Librn
Holdings: Vols (51,000) Cat Mss Maps Pix 16mm Films Microforms
Notes: The Geological Sciences Library supports the research efforts of faculty, graduate students, and upper-level undergraduate and graduate instruction in the geological sciences. Subjects collected deal with the earth sciences in general, mineralogy, petrology, geochemistry, geophysics, crystallography, structural geology, regional geology, economic geology, some geomorphology, and some gemology. The collection incl 850 serial publications and 15,000 maps.

OK —AMOCO PRODUCTION CO RESEARCH CENTER, Library, 4502 E 41 St, Tulsa, 74102. Carolyn Beson, Research Librn
Holdings: Vols (25,000) Cat Maps Microforms
Notes: Petroleum exploration and production research.

PETRONIUS

PA —UNIVERSITY OF PITTSBURGH, Hillman Library, Pittsburgh, 15260. Glenora E Rossell, Head
Holdings: Vols (11,550) Cat
Notes: The classic collection is particularly strong in Greek and Latin literature, Greek and Roman history, Greek Philosophy, Greek and Latin language, and Greek epigraphy. In combination with the Fricke Fine Arts collection it has a good collection in Greek and Roman art and archaeology. The collection of journals is also quite strong in these areas. There has been an emphasis in collecting books by and about Homer, Aristotles, Euripides, Vergil, Cicero and Petronius. It has a basic collection on Greek and Latin paleography and papyrology.

ON —UNIVERSITY OF TORONTO, Thomas Fisher Rare Book Library, 120 Saint George St, Toronto, M5S 1A5, Can. Richard G Landon, Head
Holdings: Vols 200 Cat
Notes: Bagnani Collection contains editions of the works of Petronius published from 15th century to present day; some critical works. Collection named for its donor Gilbert Bagnani, Professor of Classics, University of Toronto.

PETROVA, OLGA

NY —NEW YORK PUBLIC LIBRARY, Performing Arts Research Center, Billy Rose Theatre Collection, 111 Amsterdam Ave, New York, 10023. Dorothy L Swerdlove, Cur
Holdings: Cat Mss Pix
Notes: Papers, scrapbooks, mss, photographs, memorabilia, etc.

PETRY, ANN

MA —BOSTON UNIVERSITY, Mugar Memorial Library, Special Collections Dept, 771 Commonwealth Ave, Boston, 02215. Howard B Gotlieb, Dir
Holdings: Cat Mss Pix
Notes: Mss, correspondence, etc collected in depth; incl publications by or about.

PETS see Cats and Catlore; Dogs; Domestic Animals

PETTIGREW, RICHARD F.

SD —AUGUSTANA COLLEGE, Mikkelsen Library & Learning Resource Center, Center for Western Studies, Sioux Falls, 57197. Ronelle Thompson, Dir Library
Notes: The Center for Western Studies, located in the Mikkelsen Library, is an archival and research agency of Augustana College. Dedicated to the history and culture of the Great Plains and the Trans-Mississippi West, the Center collects and preserves materials relating to Plains Indians, immigrant settlers, Norwegiana, Western Americana, Herbert Krause, Frederick Manfred, Donald Parker, Richard F Pettigrew, Augustana College, the Episcopal Diocese of South Dakota, the South Dakota District of the American Lutheran Church, the South Dakota Penitentiary and Minnehaha County.

SD —SIOUXLAND HERITAGE MUSEUMS, Pettigrew Museum Library, 131 N Duluth Ave, Sioux Falls, 57104. Ms Lee N McLaird, Cur of Collections
Holdings: Vols (7500) Cat Mss Maps Pix
Budget: ($900)
Notes: Pettigrew Museum Library is a support service of the Siouxland Heritage Museums. US Senator R F Pettigrew established the core collection in 1926, covering natural history (incl North American Indian anthropology) and state-local history (concentrating on exploration and settlement to about 1900). The collection also incl the Senator's private papers (ca 1870-1926). Additions to the collection since 1926 have emphasized Plains Indian anthropology, state-local history, baseball and museology, supporting the work of the Museum staff. The collection is mostly cataloged and is inter-indexed with Augustana College, Sioux Falls College, and Sioux Falls Public Libraries (as well as having its own catalog). The photograph collection includes prints by D F Barry as well as other photographers' work with native peoples.The photograph collection incl photos of Pettigrew, his family, and his business enterprises.

PEW FAMILY

DE —HAGLEY MUSEUM AND LIBRARY, Eleutherian Mills-Hagley Foundation Inc, PO Box 3630, Greenville, 19807. Richmond D Williams, Dir; Heddy A Richter, Imprints Librn
Notes: Records of Sun Oil Company (1889-1966; 750 cubic feet) contain both administrative and operating records as well as papers of key executive officers: Joseph N Pew, Joseph N Pew, Jr and Arthur Pew.

PEWTER

IN —ALLEN COUNTY PUBLIC LIBRARY, 900 Webster St, Fort Wayne, 46802. Paul Deane, Reader Services Dept Head; Kay Lynn Isca, Art Music & AV Dept Head
Holdings: Vols 1257 Cat Pix

MA —OLD STURBRIDGE VILLAGE, Research Library, Sturbridge, 01566. Theresa Rini Percy, Librn
Holdings: Cat Pix
Notes: New England, 1790-1850, and some English sources.

PEYOTE

CA —FITZ HUGH LUDLOW MEMORIAL LIBRARY, PO Box 99346, San Francisco, 94109. Michael R Aldrich, Exec Cur
Holdings: Vols Cat Mss Maps Pix Slides Phonorecords Audiotapes Videotapes
Notes: Collection stored. Important mail inquiries only. No interlibrary lending or telephone inquiries. Hallucinogens as used in historical and contemporary cultures. Nearly complete collection of books and articles by or about Timothy Leary, incl manuscripts; also nearly complete collection of the writings of Aldous Huxley concerning drugs. Much autographed or inscribed material, mostly popular music from the 1960s but also incl ethnographic music. Emphasis on psychoactive drugs relative to religion, literature, art. Also an excellent collection of research papers (chemistry, pharmacology, epidemiology, sociology, ethnobotany) in this field, as well as artifacts and artwork relating to the field.

PGHO DIALECT see Karen Language

PHANTOMS see Apparitions; Ghosts

PHARMACEUTICAL CHEMISTRY see Chemistry, Medical and Pharmaceutical

PHARMACEUTICAL INDUSTRY see Drug Trade

PHARMACEUTICAL RESEARCH

DC —GEORGETOWN UNIVERSITY, Medical Center, John Vinton Dahlgren Memorial Library, 3900 Reservoir Rd NW, Washington, 20057. Clementine Pellegrino, Librn
Notes: Being developed.

IN —INDIANA STATE UNIVERSITY, EVANSVILLE, Library, 8600 University Blvd, Evansville, 47712. Gina R Walker, Acting Archivist
Holdings: Cat Mss Pix Slides Phonorecords 16mm Films Filmstrips
Notes: Historical documents, 1895 to the present, related to the growth and development of the Mead Johnson Company (a pharmaceutical company engaged in manufacture and research in Evansville, Indiana); papers concerning Company administration and organization; industrial and public relations; marketing and merchandising; product histories of Mead products, both past and present; research and development; Johnson family pictures; product samples and memorabilia. Unpublished guide.

IN —PURDUE UNIVERSITY LIBRARIES, Pharmacy, Nursing and Health Sciences Library, Pharmacy Bldg, West Lafayette, 47907. Theodora Andrews, Librn
Holdings: Vols (36,279) Cat Audiotapes Microforms
Budget: ($86,791)
Notes: Pharmaceutical Science. There is a separate catalog to the collection. Contains research level materials as well as undergraduate.

NY —REVLON HEALTH CARE GROUP, Information Services, One Scarsdale Ave, Tuckahoe, 10707. Rena Radovich, Manager
Holdings: Cat
Notes: Book vols & periodicals.

PHARMACEUTICALS—ADVERTISING see Advertising—Pharmaceuticals

PHARMACISTS see Pharmacy

PHARMACODYNAMICS see Pharmacology

PHARMACOGNOSY

OH —LLOYD LIBRARY & MUSEUM, 917 Plum St, Cincinnati, 45202. John B Griggs, Librn
Notes: Extensive holdings on drug plants, plant drugs, pharmacognosy, and plant chemistry.

OH —OHIO STATE UNIVERSITY, College of Pharmacy Library, 500 W 12 Ave, Columbus, 43210. Virginia B Hall, Head
Holdings: Vols (29,000) Cat Audiotapes 16mm Films Microforms

PHARMACOLOGY

CT —YALE MEDICAL LIBRARY, 333 Cedar St, New Haven, 06510.
Holdings: Vols (334,215) Cat Mss Pix Slides Microform
Budget: ($361,650)
Notes: Incl films, audiotapes, artifacts, etc.

DC —GEORGETOWN UNIVERSITY, Medical Center, John Vinton Dahlgren Memorial Library, 3900 Reservoir Rd NW, Washington, 20057. Clementine Pellegrino, Librn
Notes: Being developed.

IN —MILES LABORATORIES, Library Resources and Services, 1127 Myrtle St, PO Box 40, Elkhart, 46515. Allam Hagopian, Mgr
Holdings: Vols (16,500) Cat Audiotapes Microforms
Notes: Incl files of pharmaceutical product advertising pieces, extensive literature files on company related drugs; domestic and international marketing files. 32,000 bound periodicals.

IN —BRISTOL-MYERS PHARMACEUTICAL R&D DIVISION, Scientific Information Dept, 2404 W Pennsylvania St, Evansville, 47721. Alice Weisling, Mgr
Holdings: Vols 33,000 Cat Microforms

IN —ELI LILLY AND COMPANY, Scientific Library, 307 E McCarty St, Indianapolis,

PHARMACOLOGY (cont.)

46285. Adele Hoskin, Chief Librn
Holdings: Vols (35,000) Cat Microforms
Notes: Drug product information (1.7 million cards); drug encyclopedias, foreign and domestic; foreign pharmacopoeias. Restricted use: company employees and approved outsiders.

IN —PURDUE UNIVERSITY LIBRARIES, Pharmacy, Nursing and Health Sciences Library, Pharmacy Bldg, West Lafayette, 47907. Theodora Andrews, Librn
Holdings: Vols (36,279) Cat Audiotapes Microforms
Budget: ($86,791)
Notes: Pharmaceutical Science. There is a separate catalog to the collection. Contains research level materials as well as undergraduate.

MD —MEDICAL & CHIRURGICAL FACULTY OF THE STATE OF MARYLAND, Library, 1211 Cathedral St, Baltimore, 21201. Joseph E Jensen, Librn
Holdings: Vols (10,000) // Cat Mss Maps Pix
See also entry under Medicine - History and Historic

MA —HARVARD UNIVERSITY LIBRARY, Botanical Museum Library, Cambridge, 02138.
Holdings: Vols (2400) Mss Pix
Notes: The Tina and Gordon Wisson Ethnomycological Collection, one of the most important modern collections, acquired as an adjunct to the Museum's Economic Botany Library of Oakes Ames. From 15th to 20th century, it deals with hallucinogenic mushrooms in art, religion, and folklore; chemistry, pharmacology, linguistics, archaeological artifacts of Mexico, Guatemala, India, Japan, China, etc. Personal papers, etc.

MA —RADCLIFFE COLLEGE, Arthur & Elizabeth Schlesinger Library on the History of Women in America, 3 James St, Cambridge, 02138. Patricia Miller King, Dir; Eva Moseley, Cur of Mss
Holdings: // Cat Mss Pix Microforms
Notes: Business records of the (Lydia E) Pinkham Medicine Co incl financial and advertising records and miscellaneous materials on formulas, manufacturing, labelling, packaging, litigation, transactions with regulatory agencies, etc; some restricted materials on clinical tests; and a small amount of family papers, incl notebooks of Lydia E Pinkham. Partly microfilmed. Inventory published by G K Hall; see Hamilton Family for citation.

MI —WARNER-LAMBERT/PARKE-DAVIS, Research Library, 2800 Plymouth Rd, Ann Arbor, 48106. Katherine C Owen, Mgr, Library Services
Holdings: Vols (27,977) Cat

MI —MICHIGAN STATE UNIVERSITY, Science Library, East Lansing, 48824. Carole S Armstrong, Head
Holdings: Vols 700 Cat
Notes: Both books and journals include titles in English, French, German and Russian, with a few in other languages. The scope includes general toxicology, industrial toxicology, veterinary toxicology, the toxicology of metals and insecticides, and poisons as studied in experimental pharmacology.

MI —THE UPJOHN COMPANY, Corporate Technical Library, 301 Henrietta St, Kalamazoo, 49001. Lorraine Schulte, Manager
Holdings: Cat Microforms Books Journals

MN —UNIVERSITY OF MINNESOTA, Bio-Medical Library, Diehl Hall, Minneapolis, 55455. Gertrude Foreman, Acting Dir
Holdings: Vols (19,122) Uncat Slides Audiotapes Microforms
Budget: $13,000

NE —UNIVERSITY OF NEBRASKA MEDICAL CENTER, Library, 42 & Dewey Ave, Omaha, 68105. Robert M Braude, Dir
Holdings: Vols (196,313)
Budget: ($320,000)
Notes: Serves the Colleges of Medicine, Nursing, Pharmacy, and the School of Allied Health Professions; the Hospital and Clinics; and several research institutes with a collection that is broad in scope and both current and retrospective.

NJ —BERLEX LABORATORIES, Research & Development Library, 110 E Hanover Ave, Cedar Knolls, 07927. Lorene Lingelbach, Librn
Holdings: Vols (10,000) Cat Microforms
Notes: The library was established in 1972 by consolidating the collections of companies which merged with Berlex Laboratories. 425 periodical titles are received currently.

NJ —ORTHO PHARMACEUTICAL CORP, Hartman Library, U S Highway 202, Raritan, 08869. June Bente, Mgr
Holdings: Vols (15,000) Cat Microforms

NY —MEDICAL LETTER, Library, 56 Harrison St, New Rochelle, 10801. Donna Goodstein, Librn
Holdings: Vols (1000) Cat
Budget: $5000
Notes: No separate catalog or index. Main holdings are in medical journals. Book collection consists of standard texts in medicine, pharmacology and therapeutics, plus many on specific drugs and adverse effects and interactions of drugs. Library is maintained primarily for in-house use.

NY —AYERST LABORATORIES, Medical Information Center, 685 Third Ave, New York, 10017. Mimi Golob, Head Librn
Holdings: Vols (4000) Uncat Microforms
Notes: Publications on Ayerst drug products (microfiche); 50,000 journal articles; (400) periodical titles.

NY —CREEDMOOR PSYCHIATRIC CENTER, Health Sciences Library, Bldg 51, 80-45 Winchester Blvd, Queens Village, 11427. Susan Taubman, Dir of Library; Pushpa Bhati, Sr Librn
Holdings: Vols (12,000) Cat Slides Phonorecords Audiotapes Filmstrips Microforms
Budget: ($50,000)
Notes: Particularly strong in the areas of neurology, pharmacology, psychoanalysis, and psychopharmacology.

NY —REVLON HEALTH CARE GROUP, Information Services, One Scarsdale Ave, Tuckahoe, 10707. Rena Radovich, Manager
Holdings: Cat
Notes: Book vols & periodicals.

NY —MASONIC MEDICAL RESEARCH LIBRARY, 2150 Bleecker St, Utica, 13501. Irma A Tuttle, Librn
Holdings: Vols (2000) Cat Slides Microforms
Notes: Biochemical gerontology collection represents 10 percent of total holdings in basic medical research fields of physiology, pharmacology, vision and circulation. Incl 16,000 periodicals.

NC —NATIONAL INSTITUTE OF ENVIRONMENTAL HEALTH SCIENCES, Library, PO Box 12233, Research Triangle Park, 27709. W Davenport Robertson, Head Librn
Holdings: Vols (9000) Cat Mss Audiotapes Microforms
Notes: The subject, "environmental health," incl toxicology, carcinogenesis, pharmacology, genetics, biophysics, and biochemistry. Special emphasis is placed on cell biology. The collection does not incl works on pollution control or law. In addition to the collection there are some 2500 vols in the laboratories. The library has an automated catalog.

ND —UNIVERSITY OF NORTH DAKOTA, Harley E French Medical Library, Grand Forks, 58202. David W Boilard, Dir; Lila Pedersen, Asst Dir
Holdings: Vols (56,000) Cat
Budget: ($206,000)
Notes: 1075 current periodical subscriptions.

OH —OHIO STATE UNIVERSITY, College of Pharmacy Library, 500 W 12 Ave, Columbus, 43210. Virginia B Hall, Head
Holdings: Vols 29,000 Cat Audiotapes 16mm Films Microforms
Notes: Pharmaceutics, pharmacognosy, clinical pharmacy, pharmacy administration.

PA —PHILADELPHIA COLLEGE OF PHARMACY & SCIENCE, Joseph W England Library, 42 St & Woodland Ave, Philadelphia, 19104. Carol H Fenichel, Dir of Library Services
Holdings: Vols (53,000) Cat Slides Phonorecords Audiotapes Videotapes 16mm Films Filmstrips Microforms
Budget: ($132,000)
Notes: Pharmacy and related subjects, incl pharmacology, international drug information history of pharmacy and toxicology. Incl 320 periodical titles, vertical files.

PA —MERCK SHARP & DOHME, Research Laboratories, Literature Resource Center, West Point, 19486. Evelyn W Armstrong, Dir, Literature Resource Centers
Holdings: Cat Microforms
Notes: Monographs (3000) and journals (15,000 vols).

WA —WASHINGTON STATE UNIVERSITY, Veterinary Medical & Pharmacy Library, 701 Wegner Hall, Pullman, 99164. Vicki F Croft, Head
Holdings: Vols (42,000) Cat Mss Microforms
Budget: ($146,667)

WA —UNIVERSITY OF WASHINGTON LIBRARIES, Chemistry-Pharmacy Library, BG-10, Seattle, 98195. Heidi Mercado, Librn
Holdings: Vols (47,500) Cat
Budget: ($195,000)
Notes: Includes primarily books and journals on medicinal chemistry and pharmacokinetics. Most of the pharmacy material is located in the University of Washington's Health Sciences Library.

WI —UNIVERSITY OF WISCONSIN, MADISON, School of Pharmacy, F B Power Pharmaceutical Library, 425 N Charter St, Madison, 53706. Dolores Nemec, Librn
Holdings: Vols 33,290 Cat Microforms
Notes: Library incl and administers the unique national historical pharmaceutical collection known as the Kremers Reference Files, and various special historical collections--historical drug catalogs; historical college catalogs (pharmacy); the Kremers manuscript encyclopedia of historical pharmacy; pharmaceutical corporation reports; representative prescription books of pharmacies; and the pharmaco-literary collection. These collections are regularly supplemented with new materials, but are not incl in the library's holdings statement. The special collections contain about 800 volumes in book form; the Kremers Reference Files presently consist of 360 legal-size file drawers; and the Kremers manuscript encyclopedia comprises 145 file boxes. The Kremers Reference Files--which contain materials from 1850 to date in the form of letters, laboratoryrecords, minute books of organizations, biographical sketches, prescriptions, pictures, pamphlets, circulars, reprints, broadsides, and other printed matter--provide detailed historical information mainly relating to pharmaceutical subjects. Published catalog: Catalog of the F B Power Pharmaceutical Library, School of Pharmacy, University of Wisconsin, Madison, Wisconsin (Boston: G K Hall, 1976), 4 vols.

PHARMACOLOGY—HISTORY

CA —UNIVERSITY OF SOUTHERN CALIFORNIA, School of Medicine, Norris Medical Library, 2025 Zonal Ave, Los Angeles, 90033. Nelson J Gilman, Librn
Holdings: Vols 275 Cat
Budget: $200
Notes: The Collection of American Indian Ethnopharmacology.

CA —FITZ HUGH LUDLOW MEMORIAL LIBRARY, PO Box 99346, San Francisco, 94109. Michael R Aldrich, Exec Cur
Holdings: Vols (500) Cat Pix Slides Phonorecords Videotapes
Notes: Collection stored. Important mail inquiries only. No interlibrary loan or telephone queries. We collect many old pharmacopoeias, dispensatories, formularies, medical history books and records, old pharmaceutical bottles and labels, etc valuable for researching the history of

PHARMACOLOGY—HISTORY (cont.)

psychoactive drug use. Incl a small but valuable collection of works on anesthesia and toxicology.

GA —MEDICAL COLLEGE OF GEORGIA, Library, Laney Walker Blvd, Augusta, 30902. Dorothy H Mims, Librn for Special Collections
Holdings: Vols (2500) // Cat
Notes: Special collection of late 18th and early 19th century medical books, incl texts on *materia medica* and early American pharmacopoeias and dispensatories.

PHARMACOLOGY—RESEARCH see Pharmaceutical Research

PHARMACOLOGY, EXPERIMENTAL

CT —YALE MEDICAL LIBRARY, 333 Cedar St, New Haven, 06510.
Notes: A special subject emphasis.

PHARMACOLOGY, PRIMITIVE

AZ —NORTHERN ARIZONA UNIVERSITY, Special Collection Library, CU Box 6022, Flagstaff, 86011. Peter M Whiteley, Coordr/Archivist; William Mullane, Librn
Notes: Handwritten recipe book containing many recipes for cures, often for farm animals, late 1800's.

CA —UNIVERSITY OF SOUTHERN CALIFORNIA, School of Medicine, Norris Medical Library, 2025 Zonal Ave, Los Angeles, 90033. Nelson J Gilman, Librn
Holdings: Vols 275 Cat
Budget: $200
Notes: The Collection of American Indian Ethnopharmacology.

PHARMACOPOEIAS AND FORMULARIES

CA —FITZ HUGH LUDLOW MEMORIAL LIBRARY, PO Box 99346, San Francisco, 94109. Michael R Aldrich, Exec Cur
Holdings: Vols (500) Cat Pix Slides Phonorecords Videotapes
Notes: Collection stored. Important mail inquiries only. No interlibrary loan or telephone queries. We collect many old pharmacopoeias, dispensatories, formularies, medical history books and records, old pharmaceutical bottles and labels, etc valuable for researching the history of psychoactive drug use. Incl a small but valuable collection of works on anesthesia and toxicology.

IL —UNIVERSITY OF ILLINOIS AT CHICAGO, Library of the Health Sciences, 1750 W Polk St, PO Box 7509, Chicago, 60612. Robert J Adelsperger, Cur, Special Collections
Holdings: Vols (6000) Cat Mss
Notes: Emphasis on pharmacopoeias, formularies and dispensatories, and American and foreign herbals. Description of collection in *Pharmacopeias, Formularies, Dispensatories*, (Chicago: Library of the Health Sciences, 1975).

IN —ELI LILLY AND COMPANY, Scientific Library, 307 E McCarty St, Indianapolis, 46285. Adele Hoskin, Chief Librn
Holdings: Vols (35,000) Cat Microforms
Notes: Drug product information (1.7 million cards); drug encyclopedias, foreign and domestic; foreign pharmacopoeias. Restricted use: company employees and approved outsiders.

MD —UNIVERSITY OF MARYLAND, BALTIMORE, Health Sciences Library, 111 S Greene St, Baltimore, 21201. Cyril C H Feng, Dir
Notes: The Pharmacy Historical Collection contains a very good collection of pharmacopoeias, dispensatories and herbals.

MA —MASSACHUSETTS COLLEGE OF PHARMACY AND ALLIED HEALTH SCIENCES, Sheppard Library, 179 Longwood Ave, Boston, 02115. Barbara M Hill, Librn
Holdings: Vols (56,000) Cat Mss Pix Slides Microforms
Notes: Worldwide representation.

MN —UNIVERSITY OF MINNESOTA, Bio-Medical Library, Diehl Hall, Minneapolis, 55455. Gertrude Foreman, Acting Dir
Holdings: Vols (263,361)
Budget: ($500,000)

OH —LLOYD LIBRARY & MUSEUM, 917 Plum St, Cincinnati, 45202. John B Griggs, Librn
Notes: Said to be the world's largest collection of pharmacopoeias, formularies and dispensatories.

PHARMACY

CA —UNIVERSITY OF CALIFORNIA, SAN FRANCISCO, Library, San Francisco, 94143. David Bishop, University Librn
Holdings: Vols (502,261) Cat
Budget: ($602,604)

CT —UNIVERSITY OF CONNECTICUT, Pharmacy Library, Box U-92, Storrs, 06268. Georgia Scura, Librn
Holdings: Vols 18,000 Cat Mss Slides Audiotapes Videotapes 16mm Films Filmstrips Microforms
Notes: Separate catalogs for print and nonprint collections.

DE —UNIVERSITY OF DELAWARE, Hugh M Morris Library, S College Ave, Newark, 19711. T Stuart Dick, Special Collections
Holdings: Cat
Notes: Part of the Unidel Collection of the History of Chemistry.

DC —HOWARD UNIVERSITY, Health Sciences Libraries, Pharmacy Library, 2300 Fourth St, NW, Washington, 20059. Jei Whan Kim, Librn
Holdings: Vols 13,000 Cat Mss Audiotapes Microforms
Budget: $50,000
Notes: Incl 5000 ms pieces.

GA —MERCER UNIVERSITY SOUTHERN SCHOOL OF PHARMACY, H Custer Naylor Library, 345 Boulevard NE, Atlanta, 30312. Elizabeth Christian Jackson, Librn
Holdings: Vols 6000 Cat Pix Slides Microforms Audiotapes
Notes: Incl 250 current journal subscriptions.

IN —MILES LABORATORIES, Library Resources and Services, 1127 Myrtle St, PO Box 40, Elkhart, 46515. Allam Hagopian, Mgr
Holdings: Vols (16,500) Cat Audiotapes Microforms
Notes: Incl files of pharmaceutical product advertising pieces, extensive literature files on company related drugs; domestic and international marketing files. 32,000 bound periodicals.

IN —BRISTOL-MYERS PHARMACEUTICAL R&D DIVISION, Scientific Information Dept, 2404 W Pennsylvania St, Evansville, 47721. Alice Weisling, Mgr
Holdings: Vols 33,000 Cat Microforms

IN —ELI LILLY AND COMPANY, Scientific Library, 307 E McCarty St, Indianapolis, 46285. Adele Hoskin, Chief Librn
Holdings: Vols (35,000) Cat Microforms
Notes: Drug product information (1.7 million cards); drug encyclopedias, foreign and domestic; foreign pharmacopoeias. Restricted use: company employees and approved outsiders.

IN —PURDUE UNIVERSITY LIBRARIES, Pharmacy, Nursing and Health Sciences Library, Pharmacy Bldg, West Lafayette, 47907. Theodora Andrews, Librn
Holdings: Vols (36,279) Cat Audiotapes Microforms
Budget: ($86,791)
Notes: Pharmaceutical Science. There is a separate catalog to the Collection. Contains research level materials as well as undergraduate. Incl 1 file cabinet full of microforms.

LA —NORTHEAST LOUISIANA UNIVERSITY, Library, 700 University Ave, Monroe, 71201. Clarrissa Pickett, Librn
Holdings: Vols 6500 Cat Microforms

MD —UNIVERSITY OF MARYLAND, BALTIMORE, Health Sciences Library, 111 S Greene St, Baltimore, 21201. Cyril C H Feng, Dir
Holdings: Vols 3028

MA —MASSACHUSETTS COLLEGE OF PHARMACY AND ALLIED HEALTH SCIENCES, Sheppard Library, 179 Longwood Ave, Boston, 02115. Barbara M Hill, Librn
Holdings: Vols (56,000) Cat Mss Pix Slides Microforms
Notes: Worldwide representation.

MI —WARNER-LAMBERT/PARKE-DAVIS, Research Library, 2800 Plymouth Rd, Ann Arbor, 48106. Katherine C Owen, Mgr, Library Services
Holdings: Vols (27,977) Cat

MI —WAYNE STATE UNIVERSITY, Vera Parshall Shiffman Medical Library, 4325 Brush St, Detroit, 48201. Faith Van Toll, Acting Head Librn
Holdings: Vols (158,612)
Budget: ($381,153)
Notes: Resource Library in Greater Midwest Regional Medical Library Network Program.

MI —THE UPJOHN COMPANY, Corporate Technical Library, 301 Henrietta St, Kalamazoo, 49001. Lorraine Schulte, Manager
Holdings: Cat Microforms Books Journals

MN —UNIVERSITY OF MINNESOTA, Bio-Medical Library, Diehl Hall, Minneapolis, 55455. Gertrude Foreman, Acting Dir
Holdings: Vols (263,361)
Budget: ($500,000)

MN —3M COMPANY, 3M Center, Riker Laboratories, Saint Paul, 55101.
Holdings: Vols (6100) Cat
Budget: ($13,000)
Notes: Covers medical and pharmaceutical chemistry and medical botany. Incl 2600 books (175 drug directories) and 3500 bound journal vols.

NE —UNIVERSITY OF NEBRASKA MEDICAL CENTER, Library, 42 & Dewey Ave, Omaha, 68105. Robert M Braude, Dir
Holdings: Vols (196,313)
Budget: ($320,000)
Notes: Serves the Colleges of Medicine, Nursing, Pharmacy, and the School of Allied Health Professions; the Hospital and Clinics; and several research institutes with a collection that is broad in scope and both current and retrospective.

NM —UNIVERSITY OF NEW MEXICO, Medical Center Library, North Campus, Albuquerque, 87131. Erika Love, Dir
Notes: Health sciences collection, principally medicine, but incl nursing, pharmacy, and allied health sciences, in book, journal, and multimedia formats. Library holdings include 33,427 book titles; 37,266 vols; 2,260 periodical subscriptions; 71,303 bound vols.

NY —LONG ISLAND UNIVERSITY, Brooklyn Center, Pharmacy Library Collection, University Plaza, Brooklyn, 11201. Barbara Chanton, Dir & Health Sciences Librn
Holdings: Vols (17,500) Cat Mss
Notes: Pharmacy, drug abuse, hospital pharmacy, medicinal chemistry.

NY —STATE UNIVERSITY OF NEW YORK, COLLEGE AT BUFFALO, Health Sciences Library, Stockton Kimball Tower, Buffalo, 14214. C K Huang, Dir
Holdings: Vols (222,108) Cat
Budget: ($493,931)

NC —UNIVERSITY OF NORTH CAROLINA, CHAPEL HILL, Health Sciences Library, 223 H, Chapel Hill, 27514. Samuel Hitt, Dir
Holdings: Vols (200,000) Cat Slides Journals Audiotapes Videotapes Microforms
Budget: ($560,000)

OH —LLOYD LIBRARY & MUSEUM, 917 Plum St, Cincinnati, 45202. John B Griggs, Librn
Notes: Extensive holdings in pharmacy. Incl John Uri Lloyd's writings.

OH —OHIO STATE UNIVERSITY, College of Pharmacy Library, 500 W 12 Ave, Columbus, 43210. Virginia B Hall, Head
Holdings: Vols 29,000 Cat Audiotapes 16mm Films Microforms
Notes: Pharmaceutics, pharmacognosy, clinical pharmacy, pharmacy administration.

OK —UNIVERSITY OF OKLAHOMA, Health Sciences Center, Library, 1000 Stanton L Young Blvd, PO Box 26901, Oklahoma City, 73190. C M Thompson, Jr, Dir
Holdings: Vols (155,434) Cat Slides

PHARMACY (cont.)

Audiotapes Videotapes 16mm Films
Microforms
Budget: ($374,000)
OR —OREGON STATE UNIVERSITY,
Library, Corvallis, 97331. Melvin George,
Dir
Holdings: Vols 7000 Cat
PA —COLLEGE OF PHYSICIANS OF
PHILADELPHIA, Library, 19 S 22 St,
Philadelphia, 19103. Christine Ruggere, Cur,
Historical Collections
Holdings: Vols (316,223)4
Budget: ($1,096,557)
Notes: Very strong collection.
See also entry under Medicine.
PA —PHILADELPHIA COLLEGE OF
PHARMACY & SCIENCE, Joseph W
England Library, 42 St & Woodland Ave,
Philadelphia, 19104. Carol H Fenichel, Dir
of Library Services
Holdings: Vols (53,000) Cat Slides
Phonorecords Audiotapes Videotapes 16mm
Films Filmstrips Microforms
Budget: ($132,000)
Notes: Pharmacy and related subjects, incl
pharmacology, international drug
information history of pharmacy and
toxicology. Incl 320 periodical titles, vertical
files.
PA —TEMPLE UNIVERSITY, Health
Sciences Center Library, Broad & Tioga Sts,
Philadelphia, 19140. Ruth Diamond, Dir
Holdings: Vols (87,480) Cat Slides
Microforms
Budget: ($340,950)
PA —UNIVERSITY OF PITTSBURGH, Falk
Library of the Health Professions, History of
Medicine Collection, Scaife Hall, Pittsburgh,
15261. Jonathon Erlen, Cur
Holdings: Vols (13,500) Cat Pix
Budget: ($425,269)
Notes: Medicine, dentistry, nursing,
pharmacy, public health, psychiatry
materials, incl some rare books and 300
pamphlets on anesthesia.
TX —UNIVERSITY OF TEXAS LIBRARIES,
Science Library, PO Box P, Austin, 78712.
Betty White, Librn
Holdings: Vols (103,000) Cat Microforms
†VA —VIRGINIA COMMONWEALTH
UNIVERSITY/MEDICAL COLLEGE OF
VIRGINIA, Tompkins-McCaw Library, Box
667, MCV Sta, Richmond, 23298. J Craig
McLean, Asst Dir of University Libraries
Holdings: Vols (155,000) Cat Mss
Microforms
Budget: ($281,200)
Notes: Graduate sciences (biomedical
emphasis). All newly cataloged books and
journals are reported in the *Abridged Book*
Catalog. Citations are limited to main entry
and two subject entries. The catalog is
cumulated monthly in 42x microfiche
format. A cumulated Union Catalog covering
6 years and parts of 5 library collections is in
preparation.
WA —WASHINGTON STATE
UNIVERSITY, Veterinary Medical &
Pharmacy Library, 701 Wegner Hall,
Pullman, 99164. Vicki F Croft, Head
Holdings: Vols (42,000) Cat Mss Microforms
Budget: ($146,667)
WA —UNIVERSITY OF WASHINGTON
LIBRARIES, Health Sciences Library, SB-
55, Seattle, 98195. Gerald J Oppenheimer,
Dir
Holdings: Vols (232,000) Cat Slides
Audiotapes Microforms
Budget: ($550,000)
See also entry under Pharmacology.
WI —UNIVERSITY OF WISCONSIN,
MADISON, School of Pharmacy, F B
Power Pharmaceutical Library, 425 N
Charter St, Madison, 53706. Dolores
Nemec, Librn
Holdings: Vols 33,290 Cat Microforms
Notes: Library incl and administers the
unique national historical pharmaceutical
collection known as the Kremers Reference
Files, and various special historical
collections--historical drug catalogs;
historical college catalogs (pharmacy); the
Kremers manuscript encyclopedia of

historical pharmacy; pharmaceutical
corporation reports; representative
prescription books of pharmacies; and the
pharmaco-literary collection. These
collections are regularly supplemented with
new materials, but are not incl in the
library's holdings statement. The special
collections contain about 800 volumes in
book form; the Kremers Reference Files
presently consist of 360 legal-size file
drawers; and the Kremers manuscript
encyclopedia comprises 145 file boxes. The
Kremers Reference Files--which contain
materials from 1850 to date in the form
ofletters, laboratory records, minute books of
organizations, biographical sketches,
prescriptions, pictures, pamphlets, circulars,
reprints, broadsides, and other printed
matter--provide detail historical information
mainly relating to pharmaceutical subjects.
Published catalog: *Catalog of the F B Power
Pharmaceutical Library, School of Pharmacy,
University of Wisconsin, Madison,
Wisconsin* (Boston: G K Hall, 1976), 4 vols.
MB —UNIVERSITY OF MANITOBA,
Science Library, Machray Hall, Winnipeg,
R3T 2N2, Can. V Simosko, Head
Holdings: Vols (90,000) Cat Microforms

PHARMACY—HISTORY

CA —FITZ HUGH LUDLOW MEMORIAL
LIBRARY, PO Box 99346, San Francisco,
94109. Michael R Aldrich, Exec Cur
Holdings: Vols (500) Cat Pix Slides
Phonorecords Videotapes
Notes: Collection stored. Important mail
inquiries only. No interlibrary loan or
telephone queries. We collect many old
pharmacopoeias, dispensatories, formularies,
medical history books and records, old
pharmaceutical bottles and labels, etc
valuable for researching the history of
psychoactive drug use. Incl a small but
valuable collection of works on anesthesia
and toxicology.
CA —UNIVERSITY OF CALIFORNIA, SAN
FRANCISCO, Library, Special Collections,
San Francisco, 94143. Nancy Witten Zinn,
Librn
Holdings: Vols (23,000) Cat Mss Pix
Budget: ($8500)
CT —YALE UNIVERSITY, Medical Historical
Library, 333 Cedar St, New Haven, 06510.
Ferenc A Gyorgyey, Librn
Holdings: Uncat
Notes: Incl model early pharmacy room; gift
of Dr Edward Clark Streeter.
DE —UNIVERSITY OF DELAWARE, Hugh
M Morris Library, S College Ave, Newark,
19711. T Stuart Dick, Special Collections
Holdings: Cat Mss
Notes: The Unidel History of Chemistry
Collection. 60 percent of the collection deals
with chemistry prior to 1780. Particularly
strong in alchemical works incl some 6
alchemical mss. Also works on mining,
medicine and pharmacy. Notable chemical
pioneers of the 1780-1860 period are well
represented by such men as Lavoisier,
Avogardo, Chaptal, Davy, Faraday,
Fourcroy, Liebig and Volta. Majority of the
collection in French and Italian.
IL —UNIVERSITY OF ILLINOIS AT
CHICAGO, Library of the Health Sciences,
1750 W Polk St, PO Box 7509, Chicago,
60612. Robert J Adelsperger, Cur, Special
Collections
Holdings: Vols (6000) Cat Mss
Notes: Emphasis on pharmacopoeias,
formularies and dispensatories, and
American and foreign herbals. Description of
collection in *Pharmacopeias, Formularies,
Dispensatories,* (Chicago: Library of the
Health Sciences, 1975).
MD —UNIVERSITY OF MARYLAND,
BALTIMORE, Health Sciences Library, 111
S Greene St, Baltimore, 21201. Cyril C H
Feng, Dir
Holdings: Vols (550) Cat Mss Documents
Pix Art Reproductions VF
Budget: $300
Notes: The Pharmacy Historical Collection
contains a very good collection of
pharmacopoeias, dispensatories and herbals.
MN —UNIVERSITY OF MINNESOTA, Bio-
Medical Library, Diehl Hall, Minneapolis,

55455. Gertrude Foreman, Acting Dir
Holdings: Vols (263,361)
Budget: ($500,000)
OH —LLOYD LIBRARY & MUSEUM, 917
Plum St, Cincinnati, 45202. John B Griggs,
Librn
Notes: Large collection of original materials
on the history of pharmacy.
WI —UNIVERSITY OF WISCONSIN,
MADISON, School of Pharmacy, F B
Power Pharmaceutical Library, 425 N
Charter St, Madison, 53706. Dolores
Nemec, Librn
Holdings: Vols 33,290 Cat Microforms
Notes: Library incl and administers the
unique national historical pharmaceutical
collection known as the Kremers Reference
Files, and various special historical
collections--historical drug catalogs;
historical college catalogs (pharmacy); the
Kremers manuscript encyclopedia of
historical pharmacy; pharmaceutical
corporation reports; representative
prescription books of pharmacies; and the
pharmaco-literary collection. These
collections are regularly supplemented with
new materials, but are not incl in the
library's holdings statement. The special
collections contain about 800 volumes in
book form; the Kremers Reference Files
presently consist of 360 legal-size file
drawers; and the Kremers manuscript
encyclopedia comprises 145 file boxes. The
Kremers Reference Files--which contain
materials from 1850 to date in the form of
letters, laboratoryrecords, minute books of
organizations, biographical sketches,
prescriptions, pictures, pamphlets, circulars,
reprints, broadsides, and other printed
matter--provide detailed historical
information mainly relating to
pharmaceutical subjects. Published catalog:
*Catalog of the F B Power Pharmaceutical
Library, School of Pharmacy, University of
Wisconsin, Madison, Wisconsin* (Boston: G
K Hall, 1976), 4 vols.

PHARMACY—RESEARCH see
Pharmaceutical Research

PHARMACY ADMINISTRATION see
Pharmacy Management

PHARMACY MANAGEMENT

OH —OHIO STATE UNIVERSITY, College
of Pharmacy Library, 500 W 12 Ave,
Columbus, 43210. Virginia B Hall, Head
Holdings: Vols (29,000) Cat Audiotapes
16mm Films Microforms

PHARR, ROBERT DEANE

MA —BOSTON UNIVERSITY, Mugar
Memorial Library, Special Collections Dept,
771 Commonwealth Ave, Boston, 02215.
Howard B Gotlieb, Dir
Holdings: Mss Cat

PHELYPEAUX, JEAN FREDERIC see
Maurepas, Jean Frederic Phelypeaux,
Comte De, 1701-1781

PHENOMENA, UNEXPLAINED see
Unexplained Phenomena

PHENOMENOLOGY

NY —NEW SCHOOL FOR SOCIAL
RESEARCH, Raymond Fogelman Library,
65 Fifth Ave, New York, 10003. Michael
Lordi, Director
Holdings: Mss
Notes: The papers, etc, of Edmund Husserl.
Copies of unpublished notebooks.

PHILADELPHIA, PENNSYLVANIA

†PA —TEMPLE UNIVERSITY LIBRARIES,
Special Collections Dept, Urban Archives
Center, Philadelphia, 19122. Thomas
Whitehead, Cur of Mss
Holdings: Cat Mss Pix Maps
Notes: Incl the records of several separate

PHILADELPHIA, PENNSYLVANIA (cont.)

collections which are deposited in the Urban Archives Center. Many collections contain photographs, maps and pamphlets, in addition to manuscripts. All collections in the Urban Archives are separately cataloged.

PHILADELPHIA, PENNSYLVANIA—DESCRIPTION—VIEWS

PA —FREE LIBRARY OF PHILADELPHIA, Rare Book Dept, Logan Sq, Philadelphia, 19103. Marie E Korey, Rare Book Librn
Holdings: Uncat Pix
Notes: The Evan Randolph Collection of 450 Philadelphia views: engravings, etchings and lithographs.

PA —LIBRARY COMPANY OF PHILADELPHIA, 1314 Locust St, Philadelphia, 19107. Edwin Wolf II, Librn; Kenneth Finkel, Cur of Prints
Notes: 40,000 items. The Print Dept has prints, maps and photographs of Philadelphia, chiefly 18th and 19th centuries. Incl 2500 prints by Joseph J Kelly's firm. The Photo-Illustrators; with a large proportion on the Sesquicentennial and other Philadelphia views.

PHILADELPHIA, PENNSYLVANIA—HISTORY

DC —LIBRARY OF CONGRESS, Geography and Map Division, Washington, 20540. John A Wolter, Chief
Notes: The American Map Collection incl 167 works produced between 1750 and 1790 incl copies of *A Map of the Most Inhabited Part of Virginia* by Joshua Fry and Peter Jefferson (1755 and 1775 editions), John Montresor's *A Map of the Province of New York* (1777), William Gerard De Brahm's *A Map of South Carolina and a Part of Georgia* (1757), and *A Plan of the City of Philadelphia* (1776) by Benjamin Easburn.

MD —JOHNS HOPKINS UNIVERSITY, Milton S Eisenhower Library, Charles & 34 Sts, Baltimore, 21218. Ann S Gwyn, Assistant Dir for Special Collections

PA —FREE LIBRARY OF PHILADELPHIA, Art Dept, Logan Sq, Philadelphia, 19103. Marianne Promos, Head
Holdings: Cat
Notes: The Old Philadelphia Survey, 1931-1932, (368 measured drawings of principal 18th-century Philadelphia buildings bound in 14 vols), The Historic American Building Survey, 1933-1941, (9 vols of measured drawings 1668 through mid-19th century) and architectural pattern books from 16th-century European through 19th-century American. Noncirculating, for use of graduate students and adult users in the department only.

PA —HISTORICAL SOCIETY OF PENNSYLVANIA, Library, 1300 Locust St, Philadelphia, 19107. David Fraser, Librn
Holdings: Vols (230,000) Mss Maps Pix Microforms
Notes: Incl over 14,000,000 ms pieces. The Library Company of Philadelphia mss are on deposit with the Historical Society of Pennsylvani. Many of the Society's rare books are on deposit with the Library Company. The Society maintains the collections of the Genealogical Society of Pennsylvania, incl some 20,000 printed genealogies, original mss, family church, and civil records.

PA —INDEPENDENCE NATIONAL HISTORICAL PARK, Library, 313 Walnut St, Philadelphia, 19106. David C G Dutcher, Chief Historian; Shirley A Mays, Librn
Holdings: Vols 5000 Cat Mss Videotapes Films
Budget: ($25,000)
Notes: Emphasis on Pennsylvania and Philadelphia, incl arts and crafts to early 19th century. Incl some 2000 ms pieces; 25,000 pictures; 3000 slides; 600 microfilm reels. No photocopying.

PA —PHILADELPHIA MARITIME MUSEUM, Library, 321 Chestnut St,

Philadelphia, 19106. Dorothy H Mueller, Librn
Holdings: Vols (8000) Cat Mss Maps Pix Slides 16mm Films
Notes: Maritime history of Bay and River Delaware and of the port of Philadelphia. Includes shipbuilding and shipbuilders on the Delaware River, mercantile activity, recreational activity, maritime-related organizations, institutions and people, development of Philadelphia as a port, vessel registers 1878-1970s. Also, artifacts and prints.

PA —SAINT JOSEPH'S UNIVERSITY, Drexel Library, 5600 City Ave, Philadelphia, 19131. Josephine Savaro, Dir of Library
Notes: The collection of Martin I J Griffin (1842-1911), leading figure in Catholic historiography, and founder of the American Catholic Historical Society of Philadelphia. Correspondence, scrapbooks, and pamphlets.

PA —SCHOOL DISTRICT OF PHILADELPHIA, Pedagogical Library, 21 St & Pkwy, Philadelphia, 19103. Helen E Howe, Librn; Patricia K Buck, Asst Librn
Holdings: Vols (47,000) Cat Pix Microforms
Budget: ($25,000)
Notes: Collection emphasis on public school education K-12 with the main areas including Afro-American history and culture, elementary and early childhood education, secondary education, educational administration, educational research, reading, school law, educational psychology. Special Collections: ERIC (140,000 documents), Archives of the School District of Philadelphia. Approx 500 periodical subscriptions.

PA —TEMPLE UNIVERSITY, Samuel Paley Library, Berks & 13 Sts, Philadelphia, 19122. Notes: 150 oral history interviews of individuals prominently associated with the Philadelphia Renaissance era from the 1940s to the early 1970s.

PA —TEMPLE UNIVERSITY LIBRARIES, Special Collections Dept, Conwellana-Templana Collection, 13 & Berks St, Philadelphia, 19122. Miriam I Crawford, Cur
Holdings: Vols (2200) Cat Mss Maps Pix Slides Phonorecords Audiotapes Videotapes 16mm Films VF
Budget: ($30,000)
Notes: The Conwellana Collection is a memorial to Dr Russell H Conwell, founder of Temple University and pastor of the Baptist Temple (Grace Baptists Church) of Philadelphia from 1882 to his death in 1925. The Collection contains almost all of his published works; his personal library of almost 2000 books, emphasizing Biblical and religious thoughts; mss both by Conwell and about his development of the institutional church; letters, including a large number written to his assistant pastor, Arthur E Harris; a near-complete bound set of his sermons and of the *Temple Review* of the Baptist Temple in which they appeared over a 36-year period; and an extensive file of articles, photographs and information on his activities. Card catalog of the Conwellana-Templana Collection incl books by and about Russell Conwell. Separate card files index his sermons, quotationsfrom his sermons, and items in the *Temple Review*. *Russell Herman Conwell, 1843-1925, A Bibliography*, by Maurice F Tauber (Philadelphia Temple University Library, 1935. 40 leaves mimeographed). *Russell Herman Conwell: The Individual and His Influence: Catalog of an Exhibition*, by Miriam I Crawford (Temple University General Alumni Association, 1977); unpaged. Also a collection of Frank Brookhouser, news reporter, columnist, and film and book critic. He emphasized the human interest in his stories, which incl daily columns in the Philadelphia newspapers, 1936 to 1975, and a large number of magazine stories. Philadelphia and its people provide the focus of his writing.

†PA —TEMPLE UNIVERSITY LIBRARIES, Special Collections Dept, Urban Archives Center, Philadelphia, 19122. Thomas Whitehead, Cur of Mss
Holdings: Mss
Notes: Ms collection focusing on urban life

and development and drawing on the Philadelphia metropolitan area since the Civil War. Incl the papers of several private organizations, such as the Philadelphia Housing Association (1909-1972); Delaware Valley Regional Planning Commission (1965-1972); Greater Philadelphia Movement (1949-1976); YWCA of Philadelphia (1870-1960); YMCA of Philadelphia (1854-1970); Health and Welfare Council of Philadelphia (1922-1969); United Fund of Philadelphia and Vicinity (1920-1975); Philadelphia Urban League (1935-1967); ACLU-Philadelphia Chapter (1948-1975); Legal Aid Society of Philadelphia (1933-1976); etc.

PA —UNION LEAGUE OF PHILADELPHIA, Library, 140 S Broad St, Philadelphia, 19102. James G Mundy Jr, Librn
Holdings: Vols (23,000) Cat Mss Pix
Notes: Emphasis on Civil War, American social and political history, Philadelphia and Pennsylvania history.

PA —FRIENDS HISTORICAL LIBRARY OF SWARTHMORE COLLEGE, Swarthmore, 19081. J William Frost, Dir
Holdings: Vols (35,000) Cat Mss Pix Microforms
Notes: Library's collection contain information on the history and doctrine of the Society of Friends, Quaker contributions to literature, science, business, education, and government, plus their reform efforts in peace, Indian rights, women's rights, and abolition of slavery. As an official depository of the records of the Philadelphia Yearly Meeting, the library holds, either in the original manuscript or on microfilm, records of Friends meetings in Philadelphia. Among the over 250 mss collections are several which concern Philadelphia Quaker leaders, families, and organizations.

PHILADELPHIA, PENNSYLVANIA—IMPRINTS

PA —ATHENAEUM OF PHILADELPHIA, 219 S Sixth St, Philadelphia, 19106. Roger W Moss Jr, Librn
Holdings: Vols 75 Cat
Notes: French Language Philadelphia Imprints. Separate catalog by date. Collection formed originally by Samuel Breck, 1771-1862, and presented to the Athenaeum at his death.

PA —PENNSYLVANIA HORTICULTURAL SOCIETY, Library, 325 Walnut St, Philadelphia, 19106. Mary Lou Wolfe, Librn
Holdings: Vols (200) Cat Pix Slides
Notes: Books about horticulture published by Pennsylvanians, about Pennsylvania, or which bear a Philadelphia imprint. Descriptive catalog which highlights the collection: *From Seed to Flower: Philadelphia 1681-1876; A Horticultural Point of View* (Philadelphia: Pennsylvania Horticultural Society, 1976).

PHILADELPHIA, PENNSYLVANIA—SOCIAL LIFE AND CUSTOMS

DE —UNIVERSITY OF DELAWARE, Hugh M Morris Library, S College Ave, Newark, 19711. T Stuart Dick, Special Collections
Holdings: // Mss
Notes: Personal and business letters and receipts of six generations of the Brintons of Philadelphia, a Quaker family (1786-1930) prominent in mercantile and medical circles. Included are household receipts for the 1808-1827 period. Also, a collection of Samuel Meredith's household, farming, and business receipts, representing quite fully the day-to-day expenses of a wealthy Philadelphian of the 1780s and 1790s. Meredith was a member of the Continental Congress, 1787-1788 and first Treasurer of the United States, 1789-1801. The papers cover the years 1764-1814.

PA —HAVERFORD COLLEGE, Magill Library, Special Collections Dept, Haverford, 19041. Diana Alteu, Manuscripts Librn; E Rotau Sargent, Cricket Collection

PHILADELPHIA, PENNSYLVANIA—SOCIAL LIFE AND CUSTOMS (cont.)

Librn
Notes: The C C Morris Cricket Library Association Collection. Perhaps the largest cricket collection in the Western Hemisphere. Incl books, periodicals, photographs, both foreign and American. Much on cricket in the Philadelphia area.

PHILADELPHIA CENTENNIAL EXPOSITION, 1876

CT —YALE UNIVERSITY, Box 1603A, Yale Station, New Haven, 06520.
Notes: World's Fair Collection.
NY —CORNELL UNIVERSITY LIBRARIES, Collection of Regional History, Dept of Manuscripts and Univ Archives, Ithaca, 14853.
Notes: Guidebook and scrapbook, 1876-77; 2 items.

PHILADELPHIA EVENING BULLETIN

PA —TEMPLE UNIVERSITY LIBRARIES, Special Collections Dept, Rare Books & Mss Section, Philadelphia, 19122. Thomas M Whitehead, Cur
Holdings: Vols (10,000) Mss Pix
Notes: The private library of Charles Blockson established as a collection at Temple University. Approximately 25,000 items of Afro-American literature, history of slavery and African and Carribbean histroy and history and culture. Selective catalog (exhibition) available.

PHILADELPHIA INQUIRER

PA —TEMPLE UNIVERSITY LIBRARIES, Special Collections Dept, Rare Books & Mss Section, Philadelphia, 19122. Thomas M Whitehead, Cur
Holdings: Vols (10,000) Mss Pix
Notes: The private library of Charles Blockson established as a collection at Temple University. Approximately 25,000 items of Afro-American literature, history of slavery and African and Carribbean histroy and history and culture. Selective catalog (exhibition) available.

PHILADELPHIA NATIONAL BANK

DE —HAGLEY MUSEUM AND LIBRARY, Eleutherian Mills-Hagley Foundation Inc, PO Box 3630, Greenville, 19807. Richmond D Williams, Dir; Heddy A Richter, Imprints Librn
Notes: Philadelphia National Bank (1890-1935; 300 cubic feet).

PHILADELPHIA ORCHESTRA

DC —LIBRARY OF CONGRESS, Music Division, Washington, 20540.
Notes: A collection of 120 historic high-fidelity and stereophonic recordings of Leopold Stokowski conducting the Philadelphia Orchestra made in 1931 and 1932.

PHILADELPHIA RENAISSANCE

PA —TEMPLE UNIVERSITY, Samuel Paley Library, Berks & 13 Sts, Philadelphia, 19122.
Notes: 150 oral history interviews of individuals prominently associated with the Philadelphia Renaissance era from the 1940s to the early 1970s.

PHILADELPHIA SESQUICENTENNIAL

PA —LIBRARY COMPANY OF PHILADELPHIA, 1314 Locust St, Philadelphia, 19107. Edwin Wolf II, Librn; Kenneth Finkel, Cur of Prints
Holdings: 2500 Prints
Notes: Incl 2500 prints by Joseph J Kelly's firm, The Photo-Illustrators; with a large proportion on the Sesquicentennial and other Philadelphia views.

PHILADELPHIA SOCIETY FOR PROMOTING AGRICULTURE

PA —UNIVERSITY OF PENNSYLVANIA, Van Pelt Library, Rare Books Collection, 34 & Walnut Sts, Philadelphia, 19104. Daniel Traister, Special Collections Librn
Holdings: Vols 685 Cat Mss
Notes: Incl 18th and early 19th century English and American texts and periodicals on agriculture and animal husbandry; with mss vols of contemporary correspondence of the Philadelphia Society for Promoting Agriculture.

PHILANTHROPY see Charitable Uses, Trusts, and Foundations; Endowments; Social Service

PHILANTHROPY—U.S.

†PA —LIBRARY COMPANY OF PHILADELPHIA, 1314 Locust St, Philadelphia, 19107. Edwin Wolf II, Librn
Holdings: Vols (450,000)

PHILATELIC AGENCIES

FL —LIBRARY OF THE PHILATELIC JOURNALIST, 154 Laguna Court, Saint Augustine Shores, 32086. Gustav Detjen Jr, Editor
Holdings: Vols 400 Cat Slides
Budget: $400
Notes: Incl books on stamp collecting, US and foreign philatelic periodicals and lists of philatelic libraries, museums and journalists (1200).

PHILATELY AND PHILATELISTS see Postage Stamps—Collections

PHILBRICK, CHARLES, 1922-1971

RI —BROWN UNIVERSITY, John Hay Library, 20 Prospect St, Providence, 02912. Mark N Brown, Cur Mss
Notes: Papers of the poet and Professor of English Literature at Brown University. Brown class of 1944. Drafts, mss, and typescripts of poems for the period 1946 to 1963 in 12 portfolios. See also the Winfield Townley Scott Papers containing 54 letters from Philbrick to Scott, and 35 from Scott to Philbrick for the period 1948 to 1966 concerning their poetry, literature and personal affairs.

PHILIPP, ISIDOR

KY —UNIVERSITY OF LOUISVILLE, School of Music, Dwight Anderson Memorial Music Library, 2301 S Third St, Louisville, 40292. Marion Korda, Librn
Holdings: Vols 361 Cat Mss Pix
Notes: Consists of his compositions, pedagogical works, compositions he was edited. Isidor Philipp Archive. Described in: *The American Liszt Society*, vol 1, no 2, June, 1977; vol II, December, 1977; and vol 34, no 1, Sept, 1977.

PHILIPPINE FOUNDATION OF AMERICA

DC —LIBRARY OF CONGRESS, Washington, 20540.
Holdings: Mss Pix
Notes: Correspondence, photographs, records of its post-World War II activities. Archival gift from Lee Ash.

PHILIPPINE LANGUAGES AND LITERATURE

CA —LOS ANGELES PUBLIC LIBRARY, Foreign Languages Dept, 630 W Fifth St, Los Angeles, 90071. Sylva Manoogian, Principal Librn
Holdings: Vols 100 Cat
Budget: ($41,500)
CA —UNIVERSITY OF CALIFORNIA, LOS ANGELES, Research Library, Indo/Pacific Collection, 405 Hilgard Ave, Los Angeles, 90024. Edward Shreeves, Chairman, Bibliographers Group; Charlotte Spence, Indo/Pacific Bibliographer
Holdings: Vols Cat Mss Maps Pix Microforms
Notes: The Southeast Asian collection has been developed on a combination of the research and teaching levels; it focuses on the cultural, economic, political and social history of the area from ancient times to the present day. Although all the individual countries of the region are represented, some priority is given to Malaysia, Singapore, Indonesia and the Philippines. The majority of the materials is in Western languages except for a collection of several thousand books in Thai, and a smaller collection of materials in Vietnamese, Indonesian, Malaysian, and the Philippine languages.
IL —NEWBERRY LIBRARY, 60 W Walton St, Chicago, 60610. Diana Haskell, Cur of Modern Mss
Holdings: Cat Mss
Notes: The Ayer Collection.

PHILIPPINE ISLANDS

CA —UNIVERSITY OF CALIFORNIA, LOS ANGELES, Research Library, Indo/Pacific Collection, 405 Hilgard Ave, Los Angeles, 90024. Edward Shreeves, Chairman, Bibliographers Group; Charlotte Spence, Indo/Pacific Bibliographer
Holdings: Vols Cat Mss Maps Pix Microforms
Notes: The Southeast Asian collection has been developed on a combination of the research and teaching levels; it focuses on the cultural, economic, political and social history of the area from ancient times to the present day. Although all the individual countries of the region are represented, some priority is given to Malaysia, Singapore, Indonesia and the Philippines. The majority of the materials is in Western languages except for a collection of several thousand books in Thai, and a smaller collection of materials in Vietnamese, Indonesian, Malaysian, and the Philippine languages.
HI —UNIVERSITY OF HAWAII, Library, 2550 The Mall, Honolulu, 96822. Joyce Wright, Head, Asia Collection; Masato Matsu, Head, East Asia Vernacular Collection
Holdings: Vols 331,620 Cat Microforms
Notes: The Asia Collection includes materials from and about the Philippines, mainly 20th century English imprints in the social sciences and humanities. Emphasis on the post-World War II period, supplemented by retrospective resources in the main library collection. Minimal holdings in Spanish and Philippine languages. Microfiche collection of theses and dissertations from various Philippine institutions. Philippine Research/ Resource File; a depository collection for fugitive unpublished materials. "A Survey of Philippine Research Materials at the University of Hawaii Libraries, January 1975," by Shiro Saito, Supplement 2 to *Philippine Studies Program Feasibility Report*, by B Aquerro and others, Honolulu, 1975.
IL —NEWBERRY LIBRARY, 60 W Walton St, Chicago, 60610. Diana Haskell, Cur of Modern Mss
Holdings: Cat Mss Maps Pix
Notes: The Ayer Collection incl the Worcester Collection of 6000 photographs. Emphasis on Philippine history, to 1900 (some later). Several checklists published.
IL —NORTHERN ILLINOIS UNIVERSITY, Founders Memorial Library, Southeast Asia

PHILIPPINE ISLANDS (cont.)

Collection, Normal Rd, De Kalb, 60115. Lee S Dutton Dr, Cur
Holdings: Vols (34,000) Cat Mss Maps Microforms
Notes: An extensive collection of books, periodicals, newspapers, maps, and microforms from or about Southeast Asia. Areas of concentration incl Thailand, Malaysia, Indonesia, Singapore, Brunei, Philippines, Laos, and Burma. Holdings (except rare books, maps, and microforms) are housed in a separate area collection within the Founders Library. A departmental card catalog and specialized reference collection support reference services. A Thai collection of several thousand vols is the largest vernacular component. Extensive Malaysia, Indonesia, Singapore, and Brunei holdings have been acquired through the NPAC program. A collection of Filipino-American newspapers, and a growing collection of children's literature in common and uncommon Southeast Asian languages are available. Resources are accessible to borrowers through OCLC.

MI —UNIVERSITY OF MICHIGAN, Library, Dept of Rare Books & Special Collections, Ann Arbor, 48109. Robert J Starring, Head
Holdings: Vols 1718 Cat Mss Pix
Notes: The Worcester Philippine Collection contains much of Dean Conant Worcester's official and personal correspondence as a Philippine Commissioner and later as Secretary of the Interior of the Islands. Between three and four thousand mss and printed items on government, history, politics, ethnology and archaeology. 12 photo albums. Covers chiefly the period 1899-1915. Ms collection partially described in *Balita mula Maynila* (1971) by Thomas Powers (Bulletin No 19 of the Michigan Historical Collections and Special Publication No 1 of the Center for South and Southeast Asia Studies).

MI —MICHIGAN STATE UNIVERSITY, International Library, South and Southeast Asia Collection, East Lansing, 48824. Clinton Lockert, Bibliographer
Holdings: Vols (13,500) Cat Mss Maps Pix Audiotapes Microforms
Notes: Emphasis is upon South Vietnam (1955-1962), Thailand (1964-1968) and the Philippines (1898-). Complete holdings of MSU Vietnam Advisory Group, *Reports and Documents*. Extensive materials related to Thailand Project in Educational Planning, 1964-1968. Extensive holdings of the Institute of Pacific Relations.

NY —CORNELL UNIVERSITY LIBRARIES, John M Olin Library, John M Echols Collection on Southeast Asia, Ithaca, 14853. Giok Po Oey, Curator
Holdings: Vols (167,000) Cat Mss Maps Pix Microforms
Budget: ($90,000)
Notes: Additions published in the collection's monthly accessions list (Ithaca: Cornell University, Southeast Asia Program, 1959-). Holdings through December 1980 listed in *Cornell University Libraries Southeast Asia Catalog* (Boston: G K Hall, 1976, First supplement, 1983), 10 vols.

†NY —PHILIPPINE ASSOCIATION LIBRARY, 501 Madison Ave, New York, 10022.
Notes: Collection concentrates on economics, law and government in the Philippines.

NC —DUKE UNIVERSITY, William R Perkins Library, Durham, 27706. Elvin E Strowd, University Librn
Notes: The Philippines collection is made up of more than 8300 books and manuscripts.

OH —OHIO UNIVERSITY, Vernon R Alden Library, Southeast Asia Collection, Athens, 45701. Lian The-Mulliner, Head
Holdings: Vols (68,000) Cat Maps Slides Phonorecords Videotapes 16mm Films Filmstrips Microforms
Budget: ($35,000)
Notes: Emphasis on Indonesia, Malaysia, Singapore, Brunei and the Philippines. Incl language and literature, history, civilization and culture, art, medicine, philosophy and economic conditions. Separate catalog.

PHILIPPINE ISLANDS—COMMERCE

†CA —FAR EAST MERCHANTS ASSOCIATION, Femas Trade Library, 1597 Curtis St, Berkeley, 94702.
Notes: Trade with Far Eastern countries, esp China, Japan, Philippine Islands and Singapore.

PHILIPPINE ISLANDS—HISTORY

†CT —PHILIPPINE-AMERICAN RESEARCH CENTER, Library, PO Box507, Sharoni, 06069. John Silva, Dir
Holdings: Vols 200 Maps Pix
Notes: Philippine history and culture from pre-colonial times to the present, as well as under Spanish, Japanese, and American regimes, and post-independence. Mostly rare works of the late 19th and early 20th century; history and anthropology. Over 2, 500 photographs. Incl maps, posters, memorabilia. Limited copying. Visits by appointment.

CT —UNIVERSITY OF CONNECTICUT, Library, Storrs, 06268. R H Schimmelpfeng, Dir of Special Collections
Holdings: // Uncat Mss
Notes: Manuscript material relating to activities in the Philippines and Spain of Valeriano Weyler y Nicolau, Duque de Rubi ("Butcher Weyler").

DC —AMERICAN HISTORICAL COLLECTION, US Embassy, Manilla, Philippines, c/o US Dept of State, Washington, 20525. Aurora P Galvez, Librn; Lewis E Gleeck Jr, Cur
Holdings: Vols 10,000 Cat Mss Pix
Notes: The American Historical Collection is located at 1201 Roxas Blvd, Metro Manila, Philippines. Incl the William Cameron Forbes, Eugene A Perkins Memorial Library, Leonard Dawson, and Sternberg Collections. Some Spanish Period materials and much on later history, espec Commonwealth Period (except 1942-45). Considerable on Japanese in World War II and the Japanese-supported "Philippine Republic" (approx 1946-53), incl political and trade relations, and on military bases. Strong on Philippines during the American period. Collections incl mss, documents, reports, theses. Library maintains special picture-file collections. Also incl bound periodicals published during the American period 1900-1930. Complete reports of the Philippine Commission (1900-1915); reportsof the Governor-General (1916-1930); High Commissioner Reports (1931-1935); original minutes and memoranda of the internees of the US Internment Camp. Mailing address: OB-442 US Embassy, Roxas Blvd, Manila.

DC —GEORGETOWN UNIVERSITY, Library, Special Collections Div, 37 & O Sts NW, Washington, 20057. George M Barringer, Special Collections Librn; Nicholas B Sheetz, Mss Librn
Holdings: Mss Cat
Notes: Principally a collection of typescripts containing Fr Repetti's unpublished history of the Society of Jesus in the Philippines, 1589-1615; with other mss material and correspondence dealing with Fr Repetti's researches in Philippine Jesuit and seismological history and on the life of Pye Neale.

IN —INDIANA UNIVERSITY, Lilly Library, Seventh St, Bloomington, 47405. William R Cagle, Librn
Holdings: Vols (2000) // Cat Mss
Notes: The core of the collection is the specialized library of Charles R Boxer (1000) dealing with the history of the Iberians in the East, 16th-18th century. Mainly incl works on China, Japan and the Philippines during the period of their early intercourse with the West through 1800, as well as materials on the English and Dutch East India Companies, and the 17th century Anglo-Dutch naval wars. Special mention should be made of the valuable letters from missions by the Jesuits, and the works in this area by the Augustinians, Franciscans, and Dominicans, from the time of the arrival of the Iberians in Asia. The collection is a valuable source of information for the study of the European expansion into the area, including Southeast Asia.

MA —HARVARD UNIVERSITY LIBRARY, Cambridge, 02138.
Notes: Incl the William Cameron Forbes Collection.

NE —UNIVERSITY OF NEBRASKA LINCOLN, Don L Love Library, University Archives and Special Collections, Lincoln, 68588. Joseph G Svoboda, University Archivist
Notes: Collection consists mainly of pamphlets, clippings, posters, and other World War II ephemera; 2000 items.

OR —UNIVERSITY OF OREGON LIBRARY, Special Collections Div, Eugene, 97403. Kenneth W Duckett, Curator
Holdings: Cat Mss Pix
Notes: Ca 15 mss collections of soldiers serving in the Philippine Constabulary, ca 1899-1920, consisting mainly of letters, diaries, reports, documents, and some photographs. Publication: Martin Schmitt, comp, *Catalogue of Manuscripts in the University of Oregon Library* (Eugene: University of Oregon Books, 1971).

VA —MACARTHUR MEMORIAL, Library & Archives, MacArthur Sq, Norfolk, 23510. Ellen E Folkama, Asst Archivist
Holdings: Vols (4000) Cat Maps Pix Slides Phonorecords Audiotapes 16mm Films Microforms
Notes: Everything relating to the life and related activities of MacArthur. The Archives of the collection consist of 600 shelf-feet of documents from Gen MacArthur's official headquarters files over the period 1941-1951. These papers pertain to all matters with which his various commands were involved: military, naval and air matters; international relations; political science; Japanese occupation, peace treaty and Constitution, etc. Each Record Group is indexed. The indexes are retained here since they are being expanded. They are available for researchers.

PHILIPPINE ISLANDS—PICTURES, ILLUSTRATIONS, ETC.

†CT —PHILIPPINE-AMERICAN RESEARCH CENTER, Library, PO Box507, Sharoni, 06069. John Silva, Dir
Holdings: Vols 200 Maps Pix
Notes: Philippine history and culture from pre-colonial times to the present, as well as under Spanish, Japanese, and American regimes, and post-independence. Mostly rare works of the late 19th and early 20th century; history and anthropology. Over 2, 500 photographs. Incl maps, posters, memorabilia. Limited copying. Visits by appointment.

PHILIPPINE ISLANDS—POLITICS AND GOVERNMENT

DC —AMERICAN HISTORICAL COLLECTION, US Embassy, Manilla, Philippines, c/o US Dept of State, Washington, 20525. Aurora P Galvez, Librn; Lewis E Gleeck Jr, Cur
Notes: The American Historical Collection is located at 1201 Roxas Blvd, Metro Manila, Philippines. Incl the William Cameron Forbes, Eugene A Perkins Memorial Library, Leonard Dawson, and Sternberg Collections. Some Spanish Period materials and much on later history, espec Commonwealth Period (except 1942-45). Considerable on Japanese in World War II and the Japanese-supported "Philippine Republic" (approx 1946-53), incl political and trade relations, and on military bases. Strong on Philippines during the American period. Collections incl mss, documents, reports, theses. Library maintains special picture-file collections. Also incl bound periodicals published during the American period 1900-1930. Complete reports of the Philippine Commission (1900-1915); reportsof the Governor-General (1916-1930); High Commissioner Reports

PHILIPPINE ISLANDS—POLITICS AND GOVERNMENT (cont.)

(1931-1935); original minutes and memoranda of the internees of the US Internment Camp. Mailing address: OB-442 US Embassy, Roxas Blvd, Manila.

PHILIPPINOS IN THE U.S.

IL —NORTHERN ILLINOIS UNIVERSITY, Founders Memorial Library, Southeast Asia Collection, Normal Rd, De Kalb, 60115. Lee S Dutton Dr, Cur
Holdings: Vols (34,000) Cat Maps Microforms
Notes: An extensive collection of books, periodicals, newspapers, maps, and microforms from or about Southeast Asia. Areas of concentration incl Thailand, Malaysia, Indonesia, Singapore, Brunei, Philippines, Laos, and Burma. Holdings (except rare books, maps, and microforms) are housed in a separate area collection within the Founders Library. A departmental card catalog and specialized reference collection support reference services. A Thai collection of several thousand vols is the largest vernacular component. Extensive Malaysia, Indonesia, Singapore, and Brunei holdings have been acquired through the NPAC program. A collection of Filipino-American newspapers, and a growing collection of children's literature in common and uncommon Southeast Asian languages are available. Resources are accessible to borrowers through OCLC.
PA —BALCH INSTITUTE FOR ETHNIC STUDIES, Library, 18 S Seventh St, Philadelphia, 19106. R Joseph Anderson, Library Dir

PHILLIPPS, SIR THOMAS

ON —UNIVERSITY OF TORONTO, Thomas Fisher Rare Book Library, 120 Saint George St, Toronto, M5S 1A5, Can. Richard G Landon, Head
Holdings: Vols 300
Notes: Middle Hill Press Collection contains items published by the private press established by Sir Thomas Phillipps, the 19th century bibliophile, and named after his estate. Phillipps used the Press to publish his discoveries in early English topographical and genealogical history. Press was active at periods between 1822 and 1872. Some proof sheets with annotations by Phillipps.

PHILLIPS, CABELL, 1904-1976

MA —BOSTON UNIVERSITY, Mugar Memorial Library, Special Collections Dept, 771 Commonwealth Ave, Boston, 02215. Howard B Gotlieb, Dir
Holdings: Mss Pix
Notes: Mss, correspondence, etc collected in depth; incl publications by or about.

PHILLIPS, MRS. HAMES (CARRIE)

DC —LIBRARY OF CONGRESS, Manuscript Division, Washington, 20540. John C Broderick, Chief
Notes: Over 100 letters in the controversial series of "love letters" and "love poems" to and from President Harding to Mrs Hames (Carrie) Phillips: unpublished (except for some unauthorized phrases in newspapers), and under seal until the year 2014.

PHILOLOGY

CA —LOS ANGELES PUBLIC LIBRARY, Literature and Philology Dept, 630 W Fifth St, Los Angeles, 90071. Helene G Mochedlover, Dept Librn
Holdings: Cat
Notes: Foreign Language Collection. Approximately 450 languages and dialects are represented, most of which are not included in Foreign Languages Department collection. Emphasis is on breadth of reference collection, which includes dictionaries, grammars, phrase books, and many important encyclopedias.

CA —DEFENSE LANGUAGE INSTITUTE FOREIGN LANGUAGE CENTER, Academic Library, Presidio of Monterey, Monterey, 93944. Gary D Walter, Librn
Holdings: Vols (85,000) Cat Videotapes
Budget: ($90,000)
Notes: Linguistics and foreign materials. Formerly US Army Language School Technical Library, Monterey, Calif.
CA —STANFORD UNIVERSITY LIBRARIES, Cecil H Green Library, Stanford, 94305. Peter R Frank, Cur, CDP-Germanic Collection
Notes: Library of Prof Rudolf Hildebran, Leipzig, the first large collection acquired by Stanford in 1895/1896, laid the foundation for an extensive German collection. Hildebrand's library is especially strong in German and Austrian philology (rare dictionaries, etc.), but also in literary works. The collection is now especially strong for the period of the Reformation and Baroque, up to the present, with many rare editions, journals, almanacs, and the like. Sizable collections of women's working class and popular literature, dissertations and Schulschriften. Rare and valuable items in the Stanford Collection of German, Austrian and Swiss Culture, Special Collections. Catalog: *Katalog der Bibliothek des Herrn Prof Dr Rudolf Hildebrand.* Description: *The German Area Collection: A Stanford Tradition* by Peter R Frank.
IN —INDIANA UNIVERSITY, Lilly Library, Seventh St, Bloomington, 47405. William R Cagle, Librn
Holdings: Mss
Notes: Papers of lexicographer and philologist Eric Partridge, 1894- . Correspondence, research materials for publications, and mss of writings. 6757 items.
LA —LOUISIANA STATE UNIVERSITY, Library, Baton Rouge, 70803. Anna H Perrault, Humanities Bibliographer
Holdings: Cat Mss
Notes: Espec strong in philology, French language, and literature.
NY —NEW YORK PUBLIC LIBRARY, Mid-Manhattan Library, Literature and Language Dept, 455 Fifth Ave, New York, 10016. Eric Steele, Sr Principal Librn
Holdings: Vols (160,000) Cat Phonorecords Microforms Audiotapes
Budget: ($92,000)
Notes: Extensive collection of works, criticism and biographies of major and minor American writers for undergraduate study; special attention directed towards Black American literature. Collection includes material on the teaching of literature, the techniques of creative writing, and the history of the theater when relevant to the study of dramatic literature. Substantial or complete runs of the major journals. Representative collection of literary magazines. Recordings of prose, poetry and drama.
NC —DUKE UNIVERSITY, William R Perkins Library, Durham, 27706. Elvin E Strowd, University Librn
Notes: The James W Bright collection on Philology contains monographs collected by James Bright of Johns Hopkins; it is valuable for its philological monographs and numerous files of literary periodicals. It is cataloged as a separate collection.
OH —CLEVELAND PUBLIC LIBRARY, Fine Arts and Special Collections Department, 325 Superior Ave, Cleveland, 44114. Alice N Loranth, Head
Holdings: Vols (15,000) Cat Mss
Notes: Part of the Language and Languages Collection. Contains many grammars, dictionaries, and works on linguistics in African, Asian and Western languages and dialects. Material in the Dewey/Brett collection is classified by an extensively expanded language classification scheme. Its special feature is the "Language File," indexing samples of over 7000 languages and dialects housed in Special Collections. *See also* entry under Language and Languages.
RI —BROWN UNIVERSITY, John Hay Library, 20 Prospect St, Providence, 02912.

Mark N Brown, Cur Mss
Holdings: Mss Microforms
Notes: See the Horace Mann Manuscript Collection; the Franz Clemens Brentano, 1838-1917, Collection--Austrian philosopher (approximately 8000 items); and the Mary Ann Smith Atwood Collection--English theosophist (700 items). See also Transcendentalism.
†WA —UNIVERSITY OF WASHINGTON LIBRARIES, Seattle, 98195.
WI —UNIVERSITY OF WISCONSIN, MADISON, Seminary of Medieval Spanish Studies, 1130 Van Hise Hall, Madison, 53706. Lloyd A Kasten, Emeritus Prof of Spanish
Holdings: Vols (7500)// Cat Mss Pix Slides Microforms
Notes: Medieval materials and subjects. 100 reels of microfilm, 2500 pamphlets and reprints. Incl a 300-volume collection on 13th century Spanish law. Other emphases: language studies (incl 616,247 vocabulary cards), dictionaries, bibliographies, periodicals. The nucleus of the collection is photostats of the mss of unpublished works of Alfonso X. Restricted circulation.
WI —UNIVERSITY OF WISCONSIN, MADISON, Memorial Library, Slavic Studies Collection, 728 State St, Madison, 53706. Aleksander Rolich, Bibliographer for Slavic Studies; Robert P Gakovich, Slavic Cataloger; Valdis J Zeps, Baltic Studies Center
Holdings: Cat
Notes: Memorial Library has been collecting Polish materials since before WWII and now has a Polonistyka collection of more than 40,000 vols, primarily in philology and history. among its rare books are Maciej Stryjkowski's *Kronika polska* and Jan Dlugosz's *Historia Polonica.*
WI —UNIVERSITY OF WISCONSIN, MADISON, Memorial Library, Western European Humanities Collection, 728 State St, Madison, 53706. Charles Szabo, Bibliographer
Notes: Germanic Seminary Library. The basis for Wisconsin's great Germanic collections, acquired from 1899 on and containing materials on the whole range of German culture. Strongest in German philology.
BC —VANCOUVER PUBLIC LIBRARY, Language & Literature Div, 750 Burrard St, Vancouver, V6Z 1X5, Can. B Kinnear, Head
Notes: A good general collection of language dictionaries supplemented by clippings and a word file compiled by the staff.
ON —CANADA PUBLIC SERVICE COMMISSION, Library, Room 930 W Tower, Esplande Laurier, Ottawa, K1A 0M7, Can. A Campbell, Chief Librn
Holdings: Vols 7000 Cat
Budget: $20,000
Notes: Library supports the research, administrative, and instructional needs of the Commission. English and French materials.
ON —CANADA PUBLIC SERVICE COMMISSION, Library, Room 930 W Tower, Esplande Laurier, Ottawa, K1A 0M7, Can. A Campbell, Chief Librn
Notes: Subject interests: linguistics, educational psychology, personnel management, psychology, public administration, sociology.
PQ —MCGILL UNIVERSITY, McLennan Library, Rare Books and Special Collections Dept, 3459 McTavish St, Montreal, H3A 1Y1, Can.
Notes: 5600 pamphlets, located in the Ribbeck Collection. Pamphlets, mostly in German, on Greek and Latin literature and philology.

PHILOLOGY, CLASSICAL see Classical Philology

PHILOSOPHERS—CORRESPONDENCE, REMINISCENCES, ETC.

IL —SOUTHERN ILLINOIS UNIVERSITY, CARBONDALE, Delyte W Morris Library, Special Collections Dept, Carbondale, 62901. David V Koch, Cur of Special Collections;

PHILOSOPHERS—CORRESPONDENCE, REMINISCENCES, ETC. (cont.)

Louisa Bowen, Cur of Manuscripts
Holdings: Vols 140 Cat Mss Pix
Notes: Twenty collections related to 20th
century American philosophy incl company
archives, 1886-1930, 72 linear feet. The
archive of Dr Paul Carus and the Open
Court Publishing Company of LaSalle,
Illinois, major publishing center for
philosophy for more than 30 years, consist of
more than 100,000 letters and ms pages. Dr
Carus and his associates conducted a
voluminous correspondence with
philosophers, scientists, and men of letters
throughout the world, so that the archives
offer a major source of historical study of
philosophy from 1888 to 1920. There is
correspondence with John Dewey and C S
Pierce, whose early writings were published
by Open Court, J M Baldwin, Couturat,
DeVries, Höffding, Husserl, Eucken,
Harnack, Hasegawa, Levy-Bruhl, Lovejoy,
Lombroso, Lutoslawski, Mach, Morgan,
Poincare, Royce, Sarton, Suzuki, Thorndike.

PHILOSOPHERS' EGG see Alchemy

PHILOSOPHERS' STONE see Alchemy

PHILOSOPHY

AZ —WORLD UNIVERSITY, Library, 711 E
Blacklidge Dr, Tucson, 85719. Howard John
Zitko, Cur
Holdings: Vols (15,000) Cat Mss Maps
Audiotapes
Notes: Collection concerns the "frontier
sciences." No interlibrary loan.

CA —CLAREMONT COLLEGES, Honnold
Library, Ninth & Dartmouth, Claremont,
91711. Tania Rizzo, Special Collections
Dept Head
Holdings: Cat Mss
Notes: 362 ALsS to the Viennese
philosophers Theodor and Heinrich
Gomperz from Heinrich and Lily Braun,
Hermann Diels, Robert Lytton, Ernst Mach,
and other correspondents. Some letters have
been published in the 2-vol biography of
Theodor Gomperz (Vienna, 1936 and 1974).
Philip and Franziszka Merlan, donors.
Restricted use.

†CA —HEBREW UNION COLLEGE, Jewish
Institute of Religion, 3077 University Ave,
Los Angeles, 90007.
Notes: Bible, Talmud, Rabbinics, Jewish
history, philosophy, art and communal
science, Hebrew literature, religion, Zionism.

CA —LOS ANGELES PUBLIC LIBRARY,
Philosophy & Religion Dept, 630 W Fifth St,
Los Angeles, 90071. Marilyn C Wherley,
Librn
Holdings: Vols 2450 Cat
Budget: ($60,000)
Notes: Comprehensive coverage of popular
and scholarly works on historically
significant systems of philosophy for all time
periods and geographical distribution.
Particular strengths in oriental philosophies,
classical catholic thinkers, and general
history of philosophy.

CA —THEOSOPHICAL BOOK
ASSOCIATION FOR THE BLIND, Baker
Memorial Library, Route 2 Krotona 54, Ojai,
93023. Dennis Gotschalk, Dir
Holdings: Vols 1200
Notes: Free lending library for the blind;
Braille books, tapes, cassettes concerning
philosophy, religion and theosophical.

CA —STANFORD UNIVERSITY, Dept of
Philosophy, Tanner Memorial Library of
Philosophy, Bldg 90, Inner Quad, Stanford,
94305. Margaret Harvey, Librn
Holdings: Vols (5000) Cat Mss
Notes: Tanner Library is a branch of
Stanford University Libraries. Some older
parts of collection are unique. Incl separately
shelved collection of books which belonged
to C I Lewis. Incl in Stanford University
Libraries' catalogs; also separate catalogs.

CT —YALE UNIVERSITY, Box 1603A, Yale
Station, New Haven, 06520.
Holdings: Vols (3000) Cat Mss
Budget: ($700)
Notes: Trigant Burrow Manuscript
Collection.

DC —CENTER FOR BIOETHICS, Library,
Kennedy Institute, Georgetown University,
3520 Prospect St NW, Washington, 20057.
Doris Goldstein, Dir; Judith Mistichelli,
Senior Librn
Holdings: Vols (8200)
Notes: Largest library of its kind. Incl 31,
000 journal articles on applied ethics.
Produces computer database *Bioethicsline*,
available through MEDLARS; and the
printed annual *Bibliography of Bioethics*.
Other library publications are: *New Titles in
Bioethics* (monthly); *Scope Notes* series on
current topics.

DC —LIBRARY OF CONGRESS, Manuscript
Division, Washington, 20540. John C
Broderick, Chief
Notes: 82 microfilm reels of the papers of
Ortega Y Gasset, the originals being in
Madrid.

IL —SOUTHERN ILLINOIS UNIVERSITY,
CARBONDALE, Delyte W Morris Library,
Special Collections Dept, Carbondale, 62901.
David V Koch, Cur of Special Collections;
Louisa Bowen, Cur of Manuscripts
Holdings: Cat Mss Pix
Notes: Twenty collections relating to 20th
century American philosophy incl four
collections: (1) The archives of Henry
Nelson Wieman, American theologian and
philosopher, consist of some 30 vols which
Wieman authored or co-authored, together
with mss (published and unpublished),
autobiographical materials, letters, lecture
notes, and other papers. See Martin Luther
King, *A Comparison of the Conception of
God in the Thinking of Paul Tillich and
Henry Nelson Wieman*, 1955. Inventory and
name index available at the library. (2)
Company archives, 1886-1930, 72 linear
feet. The archives of Dr Paul Carus and the
Open Court Publishing Company of LaSalle,
Illinois, major publishing center for
philosophy for more than 30 years, consist of
more than 100,000 letters and ms pages. Dr
Carus and his associates conducted a
voluminous correspondence with
philosophers, scientists, and men of letters
throughout the world, so that the archives
offer a source of historical study of
philosophy from 1888 to 1920. There is
correspondence with John Dewey and C S
Pierce, whose early writings were published
by Open Court, J M Baldwin, Couturat,
Devries, Höffing, Husserl, Eucken, Harnack,
Hasegwa, Levy-Bruhl, Lovejoy, Lombroso,
Lutoslawski, Mach, Morgan, Poincare,
Royce, Sarton, Suzuki, Thorndike, and
Wundt. (3) The papers and library of John
Dewey, incl letters, mss, photographs, etc.
(4) The library and papers of Dewey's
colleague, George S Counts, authority on
education in Russia; incl much
correspondence with Charles and Mary
Beard.

IL —MORTON GROVE PUBLIC LIBRARY,
6140 Lincoln Ave, Morton Grove, 60053.
Joan Stewart, Librn
Holdings: Vols (4200) Cat
Notes: Maintained as philosophy and
psychology subject center.

IL —HEBREW THEOLOGICAL COLLEGE,
Saul Silber Memorial Library, 7135 N
Carpenter Rd, Skokie, 60077. Leah Mishkin,
Head Librn/Cur
Holdings: Vols (58,000) Cat Mss Microforms
Notes: Main subject is rabbinics (Halachic
literature). We also have a very large and
important Holocaust Collection.

IN —INDIANA UNIVERSITY, Lilly Library,
Seventh St, Bloomington, 47405. William R
Cagle, Librn
Notes: The Mary-Margaret Barr Koon
Collection contains extensive holdings of
works by and about Voltaire.

MD —JOHNS HOPKINS UNIVERSITY,
Milton S Eisenhower Library, George
Peabody Collection, 17 E Mt Vernon Place,
Baltimore, 21201. Lyn Hart, Peabody Librn
Notes: Emphasis on materials published
before 1950. Strength is a good collection
through the 19th century.

MD —SAINT MARY'S SEMINARY &
UNIVERSITY, School of Theology Library,
5400 Roland Ave, Baltimore, 21210. David
Siemen, Dir
Holdings: Vols (170,000) Cat Mss Maps Pix
Audiotapes Videotapes Microforms

MA —HARVARD UNIVERSITY LIBRARY,
Widener Library, Cambridge, 02138.
Holdings: Cat
Notes: The Kant Collection is outstanding;
there are significant ms materials of Franz
Brentano, Hegal, William James, and
Santayana. *Widener Library Shelflist* Nos
42-43 (1973) lists some 53,000 volumes on
philosophy and psychology.

MA —HARVARD UNIVERSITY LIBRARY,
Robbins Library of Philosophy, Dept of
Philosophy, Emerson Hall, Cambridge,
02138. M Pakaluk, Asst in Charge
Holdings: Vols (8677) Cat Mss
Budget: ($9000)
Notes: In the care of the library is the
Bechtel Collection of first edition 19th and
20th century works in philosophy (430
volumes) and a special collection of
Kierkegaard's works and important
secondary literature, largely in Danish and
German (140 volumes). Major research
collection for philosophy is in general
collection of Harvard Library.

MI —ANDREWS UNIVERSITY, James White
Library, Berrien Springs, 49104. Marley H
Soper, Dir
Holdings: Cat Mss
Notes: The George McCready Price
Collection on the theory of Creation,
geology, etc. Much of this material was
gathered by this author and educator in
preparation for numerous books and
pamphlets. He is described as an ardent
creationist and a vigorous opponent of the
theory of evolution. Over 900 items. Not
available by interlibrary loan, but may be
used at this library.

MN —MINNEAPOLIS PUBLIC LIBRARY &
INFORMATION CENTER, Sociology
Dept, 300 Nicollet Mall, Minneapolis,
55401. Eileen Scwartzbauer, Dept Head
Holdings: Vols (90,000) Cat Phonorecords
Audiotapes Microforms
Budget: ($69,890)
Notes: Special collections: Foundation
Center Regional Collection; college catalogs
on fiche; adult basic education collection.
Separate department catalog.

MN —UNIVERSITY OF MINNESOTA, O
Meredith Wilson Library, 309 19 Ave S,
Minneapolis, 55455. Austin J McLean,
Chief, Special Collections
Holdings: Vols 800 Cat
Notes: Classical, medieval, and modern
philosophy; consisting primarily of the
George P Conger Philosophy Collection.

NJ —PRINCETON UNIVERSITY, Library,
Rare Books Dept, Princeton, 08544. Stephen
Ferguson, Cur
Holdings: Cat

NY —AMERICAN SOCIETY FOR
PSYCHICAL RESEARCH LIBRARY, 5 W
73 St, New York, 10023. Rhea A White,
Consultant to the Library
Holdings: Vols (7000) Cat Mss Pix
Budget: ($1500)
Notes: Incl books on spiritualism, as well as
works in psychology, religion, philosophy,
physics, anthropology, etc which have a
possible bearing on parapsychology. An
attempt is made to obtain all serious books
on parapsychology in English.

NY —NEW SCHOOL FOR SOCIAL
RESEARCH, Raymond Fogelman Library,
65 Fifth Ave, New York, 10003. Michael
Lordi, Director
Holdings: Mss
Notes: The papers, etc, of Edmund Husserl.
Copies of unpublished notebooks.

NY —NEW YORK PUBLIC LIBRARY,
Research Libraries, General Research
Division, Fifth Ave & 42 St, New York,
10018. Rodney Phillips, Chief
Holdings: Vols (2,225,000) Cat Maps Pix
Microforms
Budget: ($775,718)

NY —PARAPSYCHOLOGY FOUNDATION,
Eileen J Garrett Library, 228 E 71st St, New
York, 10021. Wayne Norman, Dir
Holdings: Vols (9300) Cat
Notes: One of the largest libraries on
parapsychology. Main emphasis is on the
literature of contemporary parapsychology;
also a strong collection on the history of
parapsychology (early spiritualism,

PHILOSOPHY (cont.)

mysticism, relevant philosophical works, etc). Rare book collection incl early rare books and periodicals on psychical research and psychical phenomena. Receives about 100 titles of periodicals and binds the more significant titles. The library maintains its own periodicals index to parapsychological literature, dating from 1966. Main emphasis literature is on experimental parapsychology, or those publications that approach the subject with an objective and/or analytic point of view.

NY —UNION THEOLOGICAL SEMINARY, Library, 3041 Broadway at Reinhold Niebuhr Place, New York, 10027. Richard D Spoor, Dir
Holdings: Vols (580,000) Cat Mss Microforms
Budget: ($750,000)

NY —US MILITARY ACADEMY LIBRARY, West Point, 10996. Elaine B Eatroff, Rare Book Cur
Holdings: Vols 1500 Cat
Notes: Thayer Collection, incl rare editions of 19th century science.

NC —BELMONT ABBEY COLLEGE, Abbot Vincent Taylor Library, Belmont, 28012. Marjorie McDermott, Dir
Holdings: Vols (10,000) Cat Mss Pix
Notes: Patristics (incl Migne's *Patrologie*), Roman Catholic Church history, philosophy, literature (American and British), and both US and North Carolina history. A substantial number of the books date from the 15th, 16th, and 17th centuries. Most of the source material in Catholic studies particularly could not be obtained elsewhere in the Southeast.

NC —SOUTHEASTERN BAPTIST THEOLOGICAL SEMINARY LIBRARY, PO Box 752, Wake Forest, 27587. H Eugene McLeod, Librn
Holdings: Cat Microforms

OH —CLEVELAND PUBLIC LIBRARY, Social Sciences Department, 325 Superior Ave, Cleveland, 44114. Thelma Morris, Head
Holdings: Cat

†OH —UNIVERSITY OF DAYTON LIBRARY, Dayton, 45469.
Notes: Major part of the library of the former St Leonard's Franciscan Seminary in Centerville, Ohio. Incl some 1600 rare books, 2500 reference books, 5500 journal volumes, and about 33,000 books of theology and philosophy.

†PA —LIBRARY COMPANY OF PHILADELPHIA, 1314 Locust St, Philadelphia, 19107. Edwin Wolf II, Librn
Holdings: Vols (450,000)

PA —UNIVERSITY OF PITTSBURGH, Hillman Library, Pittsburgh, 15260. Glenora E Rossell, Head
Holdings: Vols 20,870 Cat Microforms
Notes: The collection covers all periods and philosophical disciplines. Its strength is in modern and contemporary philosophy. The approval program keeps the support for the collection up to date. The rare books, as part of the British philosophy to 1900, are located in Special Collections.

†RI —UNIVERSITY OF RHODE ISLAND, Library, Kingston, 02881.
Notes: Strong collection.

TX —UNIVERSITY OF TEXAS LIBRARIES, General Libraries, PO Box P, Austin, 78713. Carolyn Bucknell, Asst Dir for Collection Development
Holdings: Cat Microforms

TX —TRINITY UNIVERSITY, Elizabeth Coates Maddux Library, 715 Stadium Dr, San Antonio, 78284. Richard Hume Werking, Library Dir; Craig Likness, Head Bibliographer
Notes: General reference.

WA —SEATTLE PUBLIC LIBRARY, 1000 Fourth Ave, Seattle, 98104. Ronald A Dubberly, City Librn
Holdings: Cat

WA —UNIVERSITY OF WASHINGTON LIBRARIES, Philosophy Library, 331 Savery, DK-50, Seattle, 98195. Carolyn Mateer, Acting Selector
Holdings: Vols (18,302) Cat
Budget: ($27,516)
Notes: Collection includes materials in philosophy of language, law, mind, ethics, logic, mataphysics, religion, science, epistemology, social and political philosophy and the history of philosophy.

WI —MARQUETTE UNIVERSITY, Memorial Library, 1415 W Wisconsin Ave, Milwaukee, 53233. Jay Kirk, Health Sciences Librn
Notes: The Philosophy/Theology Collection has particular strengths in the areas of ancient, partistic and medieval thought and in scholastic philosophy and theology after the Middle Ages. This Collection also has an added dimension in its classification arrangement, which brings together into one unified grouping both the works and the criticisms of an individual philosopher or theologian.

BC —VANCOUVER PUBLIC LIBRARY, Sociology Div, 750 Burrard St, Vancouver, V6Z 1X5, Can.
Holdings: Cat
Notes: Incl special files of pamphlets, clippings, etc.

ON —HURON COLLEGE, Silcox Memorial Library, 1349 Western Rd, London, N6G 1H3, Can. Pamela MacKay, Chief Librn
Holdings: Vols (28,000) Cat
Budget: ($24,710)
Notes: Covers Bible, church history, church music, liturgics, pastoralia, religious education, philosophy of religion, religious studies, systematics. 95 periodical subscriptions including foreign language materials. Rare book collection of 750 volumes, including collections of sermons, commentaries, particularly rare bibles, many in foreign languages.

ON —UNIVERSITY OF OTTAWA, Morisset Library, 65 Hastey St, Ottawa, K1N 9A5, Can. Yvon Richer, University Chief Librn
Holdings: Vols (17,000) Cat Maps Slides Microforms
Notes: Only a small portion of this material is housed in Special Collections, but it is one of the strongest elements of our regular collection. Incl 125 cataloged periodical sets. Additional support, particulary in archaeology, philosophy and religion is also available at the affiliated St Paul University, 223 Main Street, Ottawa.

†ON —METROPOLITAN TORONTO LIBRARY, Social Sciences Dept, 789 Yonge St, Toronto, M4W 2G8, Can. Abdus Salam, Head
Holdings: Vols Cat Maps Phonorecords Audiotapes 16mm Films Microforms
Notes: Includes general histories of philosophy. The collection is especially strong in the works of individual philosophers, both ancient and modern, and critical works about them; also, in studies of the various schools of philosophy.

ON —UNIVERSITY OF TORONTO, Thomas Fisher Rare Book Library, 120 Saint George St, Toronto, M5S 1A5, Can. Richard G Landon, Head
Notes: Harcourt Brown Voltaire Collection, named for donor. Chiefly 18th century editions of Voltaire's works, including rare piracies; also includes contemporary and later works relating to Voltaire.

SK —UNIVERSITY OF REGINA, Campion College, Library, Regina, S4S 0A2, Can. Myfanwy Truscott, Librn
Holdings: Vols (50,000) Cat
Budget: ($100,000)

PHILOSOPHY—HISTORY

CA —CLAREMONT COLLEGES, Norman F Sprague Memorial Library, 12 & Dartmouth, Claremont, 91711. David Kuhner, Librn
Holdings: Vols (1000) Cat Mss Pix VF
Notes: President Herbert Hoover's personal collection of rare technical books of the 15th-19th centuries. *Bibliotheca De Re Metallica: The Herbert Clark Hoover Collection of Mining and Metallurgy* (Claremont, 1980). Restricted use.

IL —SOUTHERN ILLINOIS UNIVERSITY, CARBONDALE, Delyte W Morris Library, Special Collections Dept, Carbondale, 62901. David V Koch, Cur of Special Collections; Louisa Bowen, Cur of Manuscripts
Holdings: Cat Mss
Notes: Twenty Collections relating to 20th century American philosophy incl the papers of John Dewey, Henry Nelson Wieman, Stephen C Pepper, and Toyohiko Kagawa; the archives of the *Library of Living Philosophers* and the Open Court Publishing Company; and small collections James H Tufts, Edward Scribner Ames and Sidney Hook.

MO —SAINT LOUIS UNIVERSITY, Pius XII Memorial Library, 3655 W Pine Blvd, Saint Louis, 63108. William Cole, Dir
Holdings: Slides Microforms
Notes: Collection covers all areas of learning and European history from Classical Antiquity to early modern period. Researchers using collection receive assistance in paleography, bibliography and reference search. Approx 10,000 1000-foot reels of microfilm (not counting master negatives) reproducing Vatican Library's Latin, Greek, Hebrew, Arabic and Ethiopic mss. Some 8000 100-foot reels of microfilm (again not counting master negative) reproducing rare and out of print books relating to subject areas in the mss. Over 50,000 color slides of medieval and Renaissance mss illuminations. A reference collection of modern materials relating to ms research.

†NY —ISTITUTO ITALIANO DI CULTURA LIBRARY, 686 Park Ave, New York, 10021.
Notes: Italian philosophy, social sciences concerning Italy, Italian language and literature, science and technology, Italian arts, history, geography and biography.

NC —DUKE UNIVERSITY, William R Perkins Library, Durham, 27706. Elvin E Strowd, University Librn
Holdings: Vols Mss
Notes: The James Ray Newman collection of several thousand books and more than 8000 manuscripts is broad in scope and particularly strong in mathematics, philosophy, logic and history and philosophy of science.

†RI —UNIVERSITY OF RHODE ISLAND, Library, Kingston, 02881.
Notes: Strong collection.

WA —UNIVERSITY OF WASHINGTON LIBRARIES, Philosophy Library, 331 Savery, DK-50, Seattle, 98195. Carolyn Mateer, Acting Selector
Holdings: Vols (18,302) Cat
Budget: ($27,516)
Notes: Collection includes materials in philosophy of language, law, mind, ethics, logic, mataphysics, religion, science, epistemology, social and political philosophy and the history of philosophy.

WI —UNIVERSITY OF WISCONSIN, MADISON, Memorial Library, Western European Humanities Collection, 728 State St, Madison, 53706. Charles Szabo, Bibliographer
Notes: Chwalibog Collection. Contemporary editions of the principal European theologians of the 17th and 18th centuries. The bulk of the collection consists of standard sets of Roman Catholic writers such as Bossuet, Fenelon, and Cardinal Fleury. There are also a number of rare and unusual items dealing with other Christian demoninations. There is also a good representation of titles by the philosophers of the 18th century enlightenment. Supplements the Tank Collection (Calvinism) and the Montauban Collection (French Protestantism).

PHILOSOPHY, ARABIC

MI —UNIVERSITY OF MICHIGAN, Graduate Library, Near East Dept, Ann Arbor, 48109. John A Eilts, Bibliographer
Holdings: Vols (150,000) Cat Mss Maps Microforms
Notes: Excludes Islam in the Far East, Judaism in general, though it does incl specifically Near Eastern Judaism. Incl Bahaism and Arab philosophy, fields of study connected with Islamic or Arabic studies, Turkish language and literature.

NJ —PRINCETON UNIVERSITY, Library, Near East Collections, Princeton, 08540. James Weinberger, Cur
Holdings: Vols (100,000) Cat Mss Maps

PHILOSOPHY, ARABIC (cont.)

Phonorecords Audiotapes Microforms
Budget: ($72,000)
Notes: Princeton has the largest collection of
Arabic mss in the US. Collections are
particularly rich in classical Arabic and
Persian texts, encompassing all the
traditional genres. Of special note are the
collections in Arabic and Persian literature,
language, history, philosophy and theology
and the religious science of Islam, both in ms
and printed formats. A separate, additional
collection of Arabic mss (about 2000 items)
is being cataloged. It is especially rich in
theology and philosophy of the classical
Islamic period. Two printed catalogs are
available: *Descriptive Catalog of Garrett
Collection of Arabic Manuscripts*, Philip K
Hitti et al (Princeton: Princeton Univ Press,
1938); and *Catalogue of Arabic Manuscripts
(Yahuda Section) in the Garrett Collection,
Princeton University*, Rudolf Mach
(Princeton: Princeton Univ Press, 1977).

PHILOSOPHY, CHINESE

OH —OHIO UNIVERSITY, Vernon R Alden
Library, Athens, 45701. Kent Mulliner,
Africana Specialist
Notes: A collection of 634 vols of Chinese
books covering a wide range of subjects incl
art, culture, economics, geography, history,
language, literature, martial arts, medical
science, philosophy, and technology.

PHILOSOPHY, COMPARATIVE

CA —CALIFORNIA INSTITUTE OF
INTEGRAL STUDIES, Library, 3494 21st
St, San Francisco, 94110. Vern Haddick,
Library Dir
Holdings: Vols (23,000) Cat Maps
Phonorecords Audiotapes
Budget: ($10,000)
Notes: Comparative philosophy, psychology
and counseling and comparative religions of
East and West. Incl 550 audiotapes.

PHILOSOPHY, FRENCH

IN —INDIANA UNIVERSITY, Lilly Library,
Seventh St, Bloomington, 47405. William R
Cagle, Librn
Notes: The Mary-Margaret Barr Koon
Collection contains extensive holdings of
works by and about Voltaire.

PHILOSOPHY, ISLAMIC

NJ —PRINCETON UNIVERSITY, Library,
Near East Collections, Princeton, 08540.
James Weinberger, Cur
Holdings: Vols (100,000) Cat Mss Maps
Phonorecords Audiotapes Microforms
Budget: ($72,000)
Notes: Princeton has the largest collection of
Arabic mss in the US. Collections are
particularly rich in classical Arabic and
Persian texts, encompassing all the
traditional genres. Of special note are the
collections in Arabic and Persian literature,
language, history, philosophy and theology
and the religious sciences of Islam, both in
ms and printed formats. A separate,
additional collection of Arabic mss (about
2000 items) is being cataloged. It is
especially rich in theology and philosophy of
the classical Islamic period. Two printed
catalogs are available: *Descriptive Catalog of
the Garrett Collection of Arabic
Manuscripts*, Philip K Hitti et al (Princeton:
Princeton Univ Press, 1938); and *Catalogue
of Arabic Manuscripts (Yahuda Section) in
the Garrett Collection, Princeton University*,
Rudolf Mach (Princeton: Princeton Univ
Press, 1977).

PHILOSOPHY, JEWISH

NY —NEW YORK PUBLIC LIBRARY,
Jewish Division, Fifth Ave & 42 St, New
York, 10018. Leonard S Gold, Chief
Holdings: Vols (200,000) Cat Mss
Microforms
Budget: ($33,383)
Notes: A collection of material in all
languages on Judaism, Jewish history,
literature and traditions from the earliest
times to date and works in the Hebrew
alphabet (mainly Hebrew and Yiddish) on a
variety of subjects. The division has
extensive files of Jewish periodicals and
newspapers. The collection of rare Hebraica
incl medieval texts, cabalistic works, ethical
and philosophical tracts in book form. See
Dictionary Catalog of the Jewish Collection
(Boston: G K Hall, 1960), 14 vols. First
Supplement (Boston: G K Hall, 1975), 8
vols.

PA —DUQUESNE UNIVERSITY, Library,
Pittsburgh, 15282. Dena F Jacobson, Music
and Reference Librn
Holdings: Vols 3000 Cat
Notes: Main emphasis of collection is on
history of Jewish philosophy in the Middle
Ages and relationship between Jewish and
Christian scholars; collection incl works by
14th century writer Nicholas de Lyra and
general Judaica, history of the Jews,
theology, Bible texts and commentaries,
literature, grammatical works and
dictionaries, etc.

TX —UNIVERSITY OF TEXAS, EL PASO,
Library, El Paso, 79968. Fred W Hanes, Dir
Holdings: Vols 1730 Cat
Budget: ($5000)
Notes: The Judaica Collection. Jewish
history and culture, as well as religion,
philosophy and literature are documented by
the collection.

PHILOSOPHY, MEDIEVAL

PA —DUQUESNE UNIVERSITY, Library,
Pittsburgh, 15282. Dena F Jacobson, Music
and Reference Librn
Holdings: Vols 3000 Cat
Notes: Main emphasis of collection is on
history of Jewish philosophy in the Middle
Ages and relationship between Jewish and
Christian scholars; collection incl works by
14th century writer Nicholas de Lyra and
general Judaica, history of the Jews,
theology, Bible texts and commentaries,
literature, grammatical works and
dictionaries, etc.

PHILOSOPHY, MODERN

†IL —SOUTHERN ILLINOIS UNIVERSITY,
CARBONDALE, Library, Special
Collections Dept, Carbondale, 62901.
Notes: Archives of the Library of Living
Philosophers, a publishing project founded
by Paul Arthur Schilpp in 1938 to provide a
forum for contemporary philosophers to
reply to their critics. Incl correspondence
from John Dewey, George Santayana, Alfred
North Whitehead, G E Moore, and Albert
Einstein.

MD —JOHNS HOPKINS UNIVERSITY,
Milton S Eisenhower Library, George
Peabody Collection, 17 E Mt Vernon Place,
Baltimore, 21201. Lyn Hart, Peabody Librn
Notes: Noncirculating.

NY —AMERICAN TEILHARD
ASSOCIATION FOR THE FUTURE OF
MAN, Dept of Religious Studies, Manhattan
College, Bronx, 10471. Donald P Gray,
Librn
Holdings: Vols 450 Cat Slides
Notes: Material by and about Teilhard de
Chardin, philosopher and paleontologist.

NY —UNITED LODGE OF
THEOSOPHISTS LIBRARY, 347 E 72 St,
New York, 10021.
Notes: Ancient and modern philosophy and
psychology; comparative religion and
mythology; parapsychology; reincarnation
research in science and religion.

ON —UNIVERSITY OF WATERLOO,
Library, Waterloo, N2L 3G1, Can. Susan
Bellingham, Special Collections Librn
Holdings: Vols 350
Notes: Collection consists of Santayana's
personal library. Most books contain
extensive annotations. Also contains copies
of books by and about Santayana. Collection
described in *A Catalogue of the Library of
George Santayana in the University of
Waterloo Library*. University of Waterloo
Library Bibliography #8, 1980.

PHILOSOPHY, MOHAMMEDAN see
Philosophy, Islamic

PHILOSOPHY, MORAL see Ethics

PHILOSOPHY, MOSLEM see Philosophy,
Islamic

PHILOSOPHY, NATURAL see Physics

PHILOSOPHY, NON-ARISTOTELIAN
see General Semantics

PHILOSOPHY, ORIENTAL

†CA —CALIFORNIA INSTITUTE OF
ASIAN STUDIES LIBRARY, 3494 21 St,
San Francisco, 94110.
Notes: Philosophy, psychology, religion,
Hindu and Buddhist literature, Yoga and
Zen discipline, art, Asian languages.

PHILOSOPHY, PATRISTIC see Fathers of
the Church

PHILP, WILLIAM RUSSELL

CA —HOOVER INSTITUTION ON WAR,
REVOLUTION & PEACE, Stanford
University, Stanford, 94305. Milorad M
Drachkovitch, Archivist
Holdings: // Mss
Notes: Collection of material relating to
World War II with emphasis on Germany,
gathered mostly by the US Forces in the
European Theater, 1939-1945. 7 boxes.
Unpublished register in the repository.

PHILPOTTS, EDEN, 1862-1960

CA —UNIVERSITY OF CALIFORNIA, LOS
ANGELES, Research Library, Dept of
Special Collections, 405 Hilgard Ave, Los
Angeles, 90024. Edward Shreeves,
Chairman, Bibliographers Group; David S
Zeidberg, Head
Holdings: Vols 125
Notes: 125 first and other editions of his
books; 4 linear feet of correspondence and
mss.

MA —BOSTON UNIVERSITY, Mugar
Memorial Library, Special Collections Dept,
771 Commonwealth Ave, Boston, 02215.
Howard B Gotlieb, Dir
Holdings: Vols 57 Cat Mss
Notes: Books, mss and letters.

PHLEGER, HERMAN, 1890-

NJ —PRINCETON UNIVERSITY, Library,
Manuscript Collection, Nassau St, Princeton,
08540. Jean F Preston, Cur
Holdings: Mss
Notes: 3 cartons of paper. The collection
relates to the Bricker Amendment and the
treaty-making power of the United States,
1952-57.

PHOENIX STEEL CORPORATION

DE —HAGLEY MUSEUM AND LIBRARY,
Eleutherian Mills-Hagley Foundation Inc,
PO Box 3630, Greenville, 19807. Richmond
D Williams, Dir; Heddy A Richter, Imprints
Librn
Notes: Records of the Lukens Steel Co of
Coatsville, Pa (1798-1944; 750 cubic feet)
incl administrative, accounting, payroll,
production and sales records documenting
the history of one of America's oldest iron
and steel companies. Records of the Phoenix
Steel Corporation (1827-1962; 335 cubic
feet) incl minute books, financial records,
payroll and production records documenting
the history of this important Delaware
Valley steel producer. Also, Alan Wood
Steel Company of Conshohocken, Pa (1728-
1937; 250 cubic feet).

PHOENIX THEATRE COMPANY

NY —NEW YORK PUBLIC LIBRARY,
Performing Arts Research Center, Billy Rose
Theatre Collection, 111 Amsterdam Ave,

PHOENIX THEATRE COMPANY (cont.)

New York, 10023. Dorothy L Swerdlove, Cur
Notes: Incl the archives of The Company from its beginning in 1953. Partially cataloged.

PHONOGRAPH—HISTORY

MD —TOWSON STATE UNIVERSITY, Fine Arts Bldg, Room 457, Towson, 21204. Edwin L Gerhardt, Curator
Notes: The Gerhardt Library of Musical Information is a segregated representative collection of music literature, phonograph and tape recordings, pictures and artifacts. It incl special sections on Thomas Alva Edison and the phonograph, John Philip Sousa and bands, old popular songs and percussion. Most of the material is out of print and hard to find. It is *not* a collection of scores or manuscripts. A detailed outline is available upon request. Direct all correspondence to the curator, Edwin L Gerhardt, 4926 Leeds Ave, Baltimore, MD 21227, (301) 242-0328. *See also* entry under Edison, Thomas Alva

MI —DETROIT PUBLIC LIBRARY, Music & Performing Arts Dept, 5201 Woodward, Detroit, 48202. Agatha Pfeiffer Kalkanis, Chief
Notes: Collection of discographical material--500 discographies, manufacturers' catalogs, indexes to reviews, histories of recording industry, runs of American and European record magazines.

NJ —YESTERYEAR MUSEUM, Library, Box 1890-M, Morristown, 07960. Lee R Munsick, Dir
Holdings: Vols (300) Uncat Mss Pix Slides Phonorecords Audiotapes 16mm Films Filmstrips
Budget: ($30,000)
Notes: Mechanical and automatic music; Edisonia; etc.

PHONOGRAPHY see Shorthand

PHONOLOGY see Phonetics

PHONORECORDS—COLLECTIONS see Sound Recordings and Reproductions—Collections

PHOSPHATES

IN —INTERNATIONAL MINERALS & CHEMICAL CORP, R & D Library, 1331 S First St, PO Box 207, Terre Haute, 47808. Ruth Smedlund, Librn
Holdings: Vols (50,000) Cat Maps Microforms
Notes: Phosphate and potash fertilizers.

PHOTOBIOLOGY

TX —UNIVERSITY OF TEXAS, Marine Science Institute Library, Port Aransas, 78373. Ruth Grundy, Librn
Holdings: Vols (45,000) Cat Maps Pix
Budget: ($70,000)
Notes: Current researches in marine science, especially concerning the Gulf of Mexico, the Texas Coastal Zone, and the Continental Shelf. Incl journals.

PHOTOCHEMISTRY

IL —ARGONNE NATIONAL LABORATORY, Chemistry Branch Library, 9700 S Cass Ave, Argonne, 60439. Betty Guttman, Librn
Notes: Incl 20,000 vols monographs, 190 current journals. Materials may be used by the public in the library by prior arrangement. Photocopies may be supplied for interlibrary loan, for which a processing and handling charge is made.

PHOTOCOPIERS

NY —XEROX CORP, Technical Information Center, PO Box 305, Webster, 14580. Michael D Majcher, Mgr
Holdings: Vols (30,000) Cat Microforms

PHOTOCOPYING PROCESSES

NY —XEROX CORP, Technical Information Center, PO Box 305, Webster, 14580. Michael D Majcher, Mgr
Holdings: Vols (30,000) Cat Microforms

PHOTOGRAPHERS

AL —BIRMINGHAM PUBLIC LIBRARY, Dept of Archives & Mss, 2020 Seventh Ave N, Birmingham, 35203. Marvin Y Whiting, Archivist & Cur
Holdings: Mss Pix Slides Audiotapes Microforms
Notes: Especially Birmingham history. Largest available collections are the Robert Jemison, Jr Papers (ca 1.2 million items) and the Donald Comer Papers (ca 390,000 items). Photographs incl ca one million negatives from the collection of Birmingham photographer Charles Preston.

AZ —NORTHERN ARIZONA UNIVERSITY, Special Collection Library, CU Box 6022, Flagstaff, 86011. Peter M Whiteley, Coordr/Archivist; William Mullane, Librn
Notes: Kolb Collection of Photographs; very extensive collection of Kolb's photographs (over 250,000) which concentrate on the Grand Canyon, between 1902-1975. Incl an undetermined amount of photographs, motion pictures, correspondence, mss cameras, and other museum objects of Emery and Ellsworth Kolb's photographic studio at the Grand Canyon from the early 1900's to 1976. Incl the first motion picture film of the running of the Colorado River Rapids. This collection is subject to restrictions pending the cataloging of the collection. Also, Alexander Wyant Collection; diary of Wyant's journey with photographer Tim O'Sullivan as part of the Wheeler Expedition through Northeastern Ariz, Southern Utah, and New Mexico, 1873. Wyant was an artist.

AZ —UNIVERSITY OF ARIZONA, Center for Creative Photography, 843 E University Blvd, Tucson, 85721. James Enyeart, Dir; Terence Pitts, Cur and Librn
Notes: Center has significant collections consisting of more than 25 photographs plus other archival material such as negatives, contact sheets, work prints, correspondence, financial records, diaries, project files, etc. Photographers incl Ansel E Adams, Ernest Bloch, Dean Brown, Wynn Bullock, Harry Callahan, Andreas Feininger, Aaron Siskind, W Eugene Smith, Frederick Sommer, Edward Weston, Jerry Uelsmann, Henry Holmes Smith, Marion Palfi, Ben Rose, Mitchell Payne, Stephen Sprague, Johan Hagemeyer, Robert Heinecken, Garry Winogrand, Paul Strand, Esta Nesbitt, Edward Steichen, Weegee, Sonya Noskowiak. Inventories of the collections are available to researchers. Published guides available for some collections.

CA —HARRISON MEMORIAL LIBRARY, Ocean & Lincoln Sts, Carmel, 93921. Keith Brehmer, Ref Librn
Holdings: // Uncat Pix
Notes: 125 original Edward Weston photographs, which may be viewed in library under staff supervision. No photocopying.

CA —CALIFORNIA STATE UNIVERSITY, LONG BEACH, Library, Dept of Special Collections & Archives, 1250 Bellflower Blvd, Long Beach, 90840. John Ahouse, Special Collections Librn
Holdings: Vols 600
Notes: Libraries of Dr Fred Modern and photojournalist Richard Cross, and incl signed books and photographs of photographer Ansel Adams.

CA —UNIVERSITY OF CALIFORNIA, LOS ANGELES, Research Library, Dept of Special Collections, 405 Hilgard Ave, Los Angeles, 90024. Edward Shreeves, Chairman, Bibliographers Group; David S Zeidberg, Head
Holdings: Vols 1000 Cat Pix
Notes: 1000 books; 2,000,000 pieces. Various collections incl Albert Boni collection of early photography; individual images and albums of work by George Barnard, A Beato, Isabella Bird Bishop, Felix Bonfils, Julia Margaret Cameron, Maxime du Camp, Francis Frith, Alexander Gardner, W Hammerschmidt, Eadweard Muybridge, William Henry Fox Talbot, Edward Vischer, and Carleton E Watkins; 300 books illustrated with original photographs; photography as documentation, incl images of Australasia, 1700 images of the Middle East, and extensive holdings reflecting local history incl 6000 architectural photographs of Southern California and the *Los Angeles Daily News* and *Los Angeles Times* morgues; images by California Pictorialists Will Connell, Louis Fleckenstein, Ernest Pratt, Roland and Florence Schneider, and Louis J Stellman; 2000 19th century cabinet cards of theater personalities; 10,000 20th century theater photographs by Jerome Robinson; 300,000 negatives of Los Angeles commercial photographer Otto Rothschild. Also, Community Playhouse of Pasadena, George P Johnson Negro Film, Jerome Robinson, theatrical programs, and turn-of-the-century cabinet cards collections.

CA —POMONA PUBLIC LIBRARY, Special Collections, 625 S Garey Ave, PO Box 2271, Pomona, 91766. David Streeter, Librn
Holdings: Cat Pix Slides
Notes: Together, about 100,000 photographs. Burton Frasher collection, 60,000 negatives and prints of California, Arizona, New Mexico, Colorado, Utah, and Nevada, 1920-1940; Loyd Cooper collection, 20,000 negatives and prints of California, 1920-1940; Brooking Tatum, 125 color prints, 50 color 35mm transparencies of California flora; Percy Everett, 4000 color 35mm transparencies of world travels, 1960s.

CA —CALIFORNIA HISTORICAL SOCIETY, Schubert Hall Library, 2099 Pacific Ave, San Francisco, 94109. Bruce L Johnson, Library Dir
Holdings: Pix
Notes: San Francisco CHS Photographic Archives holds 300,000 images on California statewide; The CHS Title Insurance and Trust Corporation Collection of Historical Photographs in Los Angeles contains 20,000 photographs centered around pictures of Southern California by noted photographer C C Pierce. Copies of photographs by other pioneer Los Angeles photographers, such as Godfrey, Wolfenstein and Parker are incl, as well as 2000 glass plate negatives of local Indians by George Wharton James.

CO —DENVER PUBLIC LIBRARY, Western History Department, 1357 Broadway, Denver, 80203. Eleanor M Gehres, Head
Holdings: Vols (50,000) Cat Mss Maps Pix Audiotapes Microforms
Notes: Western US History. The department has a separate catalog, published in 1970 in 7 vols by G K Hall Co. First supplement published in 1975 in 1 vol. There is a subject index of some 3 million entries to newspapers and magazines of the Rocky Mountain region, added to daily. The Western Newspaper Microfilm Center contains approx 7000 reels of Western US newspapers. Collection has ca 275,000 negatives and prints of Western life; and ca 2500 maps, cataloged and classified.

DE —DELAWARE ART MUSEUM, Library, 2301 Kentmere Pkwy, Wilmington, 19806. Anne Hoslam, Librn
Holdings: Vols (25,000) Cat Mss Pix
Notes: The collection is rich in the following subjects: Howard Pyle and his pupils; John Sloan and the eight; history of the book and printing; and English and American illustrated books. There is also a section on contemporary photography. Archival material on Albert Mumford Lindsay, Jerome Myers, Everett Shinn, Gayle Porter Hoskins, Frank Schoonover.

DC —LIBRARY OF CONGRESS, Washington, 20540.
Notes: The Charles Eames Collection of original negatives and prints of each of the 106 films he created, business correspondence from 1944 to 1978, approximately 400,000 color slides, 31,000 black-and-white photographs, production materials for exhibits, and drawings for all

PHOTOGRAPHERS (cont.)

the major furniture designs. Acquired on a grant of $500,000 from IBM.

DC —LIBRARY OF CONGRESS, Prints & Photographs Div, Washington, 20540.
Notes: Incl photographs by Mathew B Brady, Levin C Handy, Frances Benjamin Johnston, and others.

FL —FLORIDA DEPT OF STATE, Florida State Archives, Florida Photographic Collection, R A Gray Bldg, Tallahassee, 32301. Mrs Allen Morris, Archives Supervisor
Holdings: Maps Pix Slides Films Audiotapes
Notes: Areas of emphasis within the collection: (1) Florida government. There is a complete file of governors' photos, and many photos of legislative sessions and legislators going back to the late 1800s. (2) Stanley J Morrow. Mr Morrow learned his craft under Mathew B Brady. He worked in Florida from 1882-1887. Collection has several hundred of his glass negatives that document a period of southward expansion in Florida. (3) Alvan S Harper, Tallahassee portrait artist; 1700 glass negatives of Tallahassee people between 1885-1910. (4) W A Fishbaugh. Several thousand photographs of the "boom," Miami and Coral Gables in the 1920s. (5) Charles A Mosier, Charles Torrey Simpson and J K Small; 500 photographs of Florida flora, made by these famous naturalists, mostly in South Dade County. (6) Added March, 1983; 2200 glass and nitrate negatives by J K Small. (7) Collectionalso incl 40,000 negatives (4x5) made by Harvey Slade in Tallahassee, 1946-1975, predominantly portraits; also 15,000 news story negatives (4x5 and 2x2) relative to local and state government, 1957-1969, unprinted, from *The Tallahassee Democrat*. (8) 39,000 (4x5) negatives and contact prints deposited by the Florida Dept of Commerce, 1946-late 1970s. Subjects incl Florida cities, attractions, industries, beaches, festivals, boating, fishing, forts, gardens, hotels, highways, lighthouses, monuments, museums and recreations. (9) 25,000 (8x10, 4x5 & 35mm) negatives by Jacksonville commercial photographer Gordon Spottswood & Son, 1916-1967. Subjects incl Jacksonville people (individuals and groups), street scenes, commercial buildings, Atlantic Coast Line & Seaboard Airline Railroads, and Boy Scout Activities. (10) 15,000 (4x5) negativesfrom Seldomridge portrait studio in Tampa. Tampa people from the 1940s to the 1970s.

IL —CHICAGO PUBLIC LIBRARY, Art Section, Fine Arts Division, 78 E Washington St, Chicago, 60602. Rosalinda I Hack, Fine Arts Division Chief; Yvonne S Brown, Head, Art Section
Holdings: Vols 6000
Notes: Includes all aspects of photography, materials, techniques, as well as artistic, scientific and technical application in cinamatography, animation, and photomechinical processes. Collection concentrates on the history of photography and works of significant photographers past and present. Collection is supplemented by the microfilm edition of the *History of Photography*.

IN —INDIANA STATE UNIVERSITY, EVANSVILLE, Library, 8600 University Blvd, Evansville, 47712. Gina R Walker, Acting Archivist
Holdings: // Cat Pix Slides
Notes: Collection of photographs, negatives and slides by John Waring Doane (1915-1972), Mt Vernon, Indiana, photographer. Also a group of glass negatives taken by earlier photographers; people, places, and events of Posey County and Evansville, Indiana. 1900-1972. Unpublished index.

KS —KANSAS STATE UNIVERSITY, Library, Special Collections & University Archives, Manhattan, 66506. Antonia Q Pigno, Coordr; John J Vander Velde, Librn; Anthony R Crawford, Univ Archivist
Notes: Photographs of filming Gordon Park's *The Learning Tree*.

KS —WICHITA PUBLIC LIBRARY, Local History Dept, 223 S Main, Wichita, 67202.

William Clark Ellington, Jr, Dept Head & City Historian
Notes: The Local History collection consists of a photographic archive of Wichita and Sedgwick county subjects and views. Many early Wichita and Sedgwick county town builders are represented in this extensive collection. The photographic archive also includes the prints and glass plates of pioneer photographers, W S Rogers of Wichita and John R Salmon of Mount Hope, Ks. Manuscripts, diarys and a general file of historical information covering Wichita and Sedgwick county history are maintained for public use. Rare early editions of the Wichita Beacon are also part of the Local History section.

KY —UNIVERSITY OF LOUISVILLE, Ekstrom Library, Photographic Archives, Louisville, 40292. J C Anderson, Cur; David G Horvath, Asst Cur
Holdings: Vols (750,000) Cat Pix Slides
Budget: ($60,000)
Notes: Photographs in three broad areas: works of outstanding photographers; examples of major developments in the art and technology of photography; photographs important as sociological, historical, or behavioral documents. Actors and actresses, Louisville's Macauley Theatre. Standard Oil of New Jersey Collection, 85,000 pictures of oil industry's effect on life in the 20th century (1943-1950, directed by Roy Stryker); Stryker's collection from Farm Security Administration series on rural conditions, 1935-1942; Jones and Laughlin Steel Corp. Picture Library, by Stryker. Stryker manuscripts, 1934-1972. Caufield and Shook commercial photographs, Louisville area, 1920-1949. Jean Thomas "The Traipsin' Woman" photographs of Kentucky mountain folkways. Kate Matthews' (1870-1956) photographs incl prototypes for "Little Colonel" Series. Other collections described in unpublishedbrochure. Print duplication service.

MD —US NAVAL ACADEMY, Nimitz Library, Annapolis, 21402. Alice S Creighton, Assistant Librn for Special Collections
Holdings: Vols (420) Cat Pix 16mm Films
Notes: Edward J Steichen Collection was established in honor of Steichen's 90th birthday. Collection incl approximately 10,000 photographs, about 3/4 of which are World War II naval combat photographs and 1/4 of which cover American life as viewed through the eyes of such 20th century American photographers as Edward and Brett Weston, Ansel Adams, Margaret Bourke-White, and many others. Incl 420 books, chiefly on American photography. No photocopying.

MA —SOCIETY FOR THE PRESERVATION OF NEW ENGLAND ANTIQUITIES, Library, 141 Cambridge St, Boston, 02114. Ellie Reichlin, Librn & Cur of Photographic Collections
Holdings: Vols (3000) Cat Pix Microforms
Budget: ($75,000)
Notes: Photograph collections, all media (incl daguerreotypes, ambrotypes, etc, stereographic views, carte de visite) depicting New England buildings; interiors; street and town views; occupations; pastimes; transport and personalities. Covers 1840s-1930s, with some more recent additons. Amateur and professional photographers represented. Cataloged in part, otherwise arranged by localities, subject, personal name. Special collections incl: marine photographs by N L Stebbins and Henry Peabody (1880s-1920s); Boston and Albany railroad photographic archive, early 1900s; Quabbin Valley views; historic American Buildings Survey photographs (17th to early 19th century architecture) by Arthur Haskell; Baldwin Coolidge collection, and many others. Size: 500,000 prints, ca 75,000 negatives (glass plates and copy negs) that are cataloged. Some special indexes incllandscape design (arbors, conservatories, flower beds, bandstands etc); photographers represented; architects represented (partial), and pending, interiors (specific features of); occupations.

MA —LENOX LIBRARY ASSOCIATION, Main St, Lenox, 01240. Denis J Lesieur, Dir
Holdings: Pix
Notes: Edwin Hale Lincoln, (1848-1938), Pittsfield photographer. Collection contains glass plate negatives and platinum prints concentrating on Lenox estates, ca 1883-1933. Publication: *A Pride of Places; Lenox Summer Cottages 1883-1933*, Donald T Oakes, ed (Lenox Library Association, 1981).

NM —MUSEUM OF NEW MEXICO, Photo Archives, Box 2087, Santa Fe, 87503. Arthur L Olivas, Cur; Richard Rudisill, Photo Historian
Holdings: Cat Pix Slides
Budget: ($9000)
Notes: 90,000 photographs, cataloged, and 1000 slides. Photographs may be ordered as research copies for set fees. Reproduction or publication requires written permission plus additional required fees. Incl. special groups of photographs, e.g. T. Harmon Parkhurst Collection-ca. 15,000 photos, 1915-1950, Southwest Indians, scenic views, town views; H. F. Robinson Collection-ca. 1000 items, ca. 1910-1920, Southwest Indians, esp. Hopi and Blackfoot; Ben Wittick Collection-ca. 1500 items, 1879-1903, Southwest Indians, military, town views. Many other of the important early photographers are represented, especially large collections of the work of G. C. Bennett, William H. Brown, Dana B. Chase, Edward S. Curtis, H. H. Dorman, Rev. J. C. Gullette, P. E. Harroun, William H. Jackson, Charles F. Lummis, Jesse L. Nussbaum, Henry A. Schmidt, and about a hundred others.

NY —STATE UNIVERSITY OF NEW YORK AT ALBANY, Library, Special Collections Dept, 1400 Washington Ave, Albany, 12222. Marion P Munzer, Coordr
Notes: Mss, publications, photographs relating to the work of Fritz Neugass as art correspondent for foreign newspapers and periodicals, specializing in the American art market (53 linear feet, 25 feet of auction catalogs). Part of the Library's German Exile Collection.
See also entry under Neugass, Fritz; Journalists

NY —BROOKLYN PUBLIC LIBRARY, Brooklyn Collection, Grand Army Plaza, Flatbush Ave and Eastern Parkway, Brooklyn, 11238.
Notes: Over 3000 books, pamphlets, and documents. Strong collections on the six original towns which made up Brooklyn. Also microfilm copies of defunct Brooklyn newspapers as well as recent issues of local community papers. A great treasure is the *Brooklyn Daily Eagle* morgue published from 1841-1955, the morgue's contents dating from 1904. Collection incl more than 25,000 photographs of people, place, and things from 1870 to the present; nearly a quarter of the photographs are by George Brainard and Daniel Berry Austin. Further, there are more than 500 Brooklyn maps from the earliest times. Incl records of the Brooklyn Mercantile Library Association.

NY —VISUAL STUDIES WORKSHOP, Research Center, 31 Prince St, Rochester, 14607. Linn Underhill, Coordr; Robert Bretz, Librn
Holdings: Vols (8000) Cat Pix Slides Audiotapes Videotapes
Notes: Strong emphasis on photography (over 1,000,000 pictures) and the photographic arts in many subject areas incl in this volume. Heavy emphasis on early photographic processes and collections of examples of them. Also collections of individual photographers' works.

OR —LANE COUNTY MUSEUM, Library, 740 W 13 Ave, Eugene, 94701. Margret

PHOTOGRAPHERS (cont.)

West, Cur of Special Collections
Holdings: Vols 250 Cat Mss Maps Pix Slides Audiotapes 16mm Films Microforms
Budget: $2000
Notes: Emphasis on Oregon and Lane County history. Collection of 10,000 photographs of Lane County; Kennell-Ellis photographers, 3500 commercial photographs of Eugene area, 1927-42. Also papers of John Whiteaker 1858-1944.

OR —UMATILLA COUNTY LIBRARY, 214 N Main St, Pendleton, 97801. Barbara L Bishop, Dir
Holdings: Vols (675) Cat Mss Pix Audiotapes 16mm Films Microforms
Notes: Oregon history, especially Umatilla County. Photographs (glass negatives)--1004 negatives, use restricted to professional photographers, copies may be made on premises only. Also 3 rolls of microfilm of Moorehouse photos.

PA —LIBRARY COMPANY OF PHILADELPHIA, 1314 Locust St, Philadelphia, 19107. Edwin Wolf II, Librn; Kenneth Finkel, Cur of Prints
Notes: 40,000 items. Print Dept has items (albumen and platinum prints and daguerreotypes) from beginning of photography through the Depression. Incl 2500 prints by Joseph J Kelly's firm, The Photo-Illsutrators; with a large proportion on the Sesquicentennial and other Philadelphia views. Also incl genre photographs by the 19th-century Germantown photographer, George Bacon Wood. Incl numerous photographs of earlier members of the Wood Family; 541 platinum prints.

SD —SIOUXLAND HERITAGE MUSEUMS, Pettigrew Museum Library, 131 N Duluth Ave, Sioux Falls, 57104. Ms Lee N McLaird, Cur of Collections
Notes: Pettigrew Museum Library is a support service of the Siouxland Heritage Museums. US Senator R F Pettigrew established the core collection in 1926, covering natural history (incl North American Indian anthropology) and state-local history (concentrating on exploration and settlement to about 1900). The collection also incl the Senator's private papers (ca 1870-1926). Additions to the collection since 1926 have emphasized Plains Indian anthropology, state-local history, baseball and museology, supporting the work of the Museum staff. The collection is mostly cataloged and is inter-indexed with Augustana College, Sioux Falls College, and Sioux Falls Public libraries (as well as having its own catalog). The photograph collection includes prints by D F Barry as well as other photographs work with native peoples.

TX —AMON CARTER MUSEUM, 3501 Camp Bowie Blvd, PO Box 2365, Fort Worth, 76113. Jan K Muhlert, Dir; Marni Sandweiss, Cur of Photographs
Holdings: Cat Mss Pix
Notes: Laura Gilpin (1891-1979) was equally adept as a portraitist, an architectural photographer, a chronicler of Southwestern Indian life, and a landscape photographer. Her bequest of her photographic estate to the Amon Carter Museum includes 26,000 negatives, 20,000 prints, a substantial photographic library, and extensive personal correspondence.

VA —GEORGE MASON UNIVERSITY, Fenwick Library, Special Collections Dept, 4400 University Drive, Fairfax, 22030. Ruth Kerns, Public Services Librn
Notes: The Ollie Atkins Photographic Collection. Atkins, award-winning photographer with the *Saturday Evening Post*, was also White House photographer under several administrations. The collection incl more than 15,000 prints, negatives, contact sheets, slides and 4000 images covering subjects of historical, artistic and social significance from 1948 to 1968.

WA —UNIVERSITY OF WASHINGTON LIBRARIES, Pacific Northwest Collection, Seattle, 98195. Andrew F Johnson, Librn
Holdings: Vols (50,000) Cat Maps Pix
Budget: ($12,000)
Notes: The Pacific Northwest Collection contains printed materials documenting the historic and contemporary life and culture of the region in a broad range of subject areas. The Pacific Northwest is defined as the geographic region including Washington, Oregon, Idaho, Montana, British Columbia, Yukon Territory, and Alaska. Printed materials including books, periodicals, government documents, maps, weekly and local regional newspapers, theses and dissertations, as well as photographs and architectural drawings are included in the Pacific Northwest Collection. Photographic works of over 200 photographers active in the Pacific Northwest, Alaska, and the Yukon Territory (Canada) during the period 1860-1930, including Asahel and Edward S Curtis, Eric Hegg, and Clark Kinsey, are represented in a print collection of more than 300,000 images. The architecturaldrawings collection includes over 19,000 original plans, drawings, sketches, renderings and blue prints pertaining to the history of architecture and urban planning and landscape gardening in the Pacific Northwest ca 1880-1940. Areas of particular strength are the holdings of over 1100 published journals of Pacific Northwest exploration expeditions, photographs of Northwest Coast Native Americans and of historic Seattle, newspapers issued within the Japanese-American relocation camps, 1942-1945, materials relating to the 1980 eruption of Mt St Helens, and Sanborne fire insurance maps for Washington. A unique feature of the Collection is the subject index to regional periodicals and local newspapers maintained by the PNW Collection staff; over 100 titles are currently indexed. G K Hall Company published a books catalog of the Pacific Northwest Collectionin 1973.

WI —DOUGLAS COUNTY HISTORICAL MUSEUM, 906 E Second St, Superior, 54880. James E Lundsted, Dir
Notes: Photographs by David Barry, of Sioux Indians at time of Custer fiasco, 1875-1888.

PHOTOGRAPHERS—CALIFORNIA

CA —UNIVERSITY OF CALIFORNIA, LOS ANGELES, Research Library, Dept of Special Collections, 405 Hilgard Ave, Los Angeles, 90024. Edward Shreeves, Chairman, Bibliographers Group; David S Zeidberg, Head
Notes: 1000 books; 2,000,000 pieces. Various collections incl Albert Boni collection of early photography; individual images and albums of work by George Barnard, A Beato, Isabella Bird Bishop, Felix Bonfils, Julia Margaret Cameron, Maxime du Camp, Francis Frith, Alexander Gardner, W Hammerschmidt, Eadweard Muybridge, William Henry Fox Talbot, Edward Vischer, and Carleton E Watkins; 300 books illustrated with original photographs; photography as documentation, incl images of Australasia, 1700 images of the Middle East, and extensive holdings reflecting local history incl 6000 architectural photographs of Southern California and the *Los Angeles Daily News* and *Los Angeles Times* morgues; images by California Pictorialists Will Connell, Louis Fleckenstein, Ernest Pratt, Roland and Florence Schneider, and Louis J Stellman; 2000 19th century cabinet cards oftheater personalities; 10,000 20th century theater photographs by Jerome Robinson; 300,000 negatives of Los Angeles commercial photographer Otto Rothschild.

PHOTOGRAPHERS, WOMEN see Women Photographers

PHOTOGRAPHIC DUPLICATION see Photomechanical Processes

PHOTOGRAPHIC MEASUREMENTS see Photogrammetry

PHOTOGRAPHIC MEASUREMENTS OF STARS see Stars—Photographic Measurements

PHOTOGRAPHS—COLLECTIONS

AL —BIRMINGHAM PUBLIC LIBRARY, Dept of Archives & Mss, 2020 Seventh Ave N, Birmingham, 35203. Marvin Y Whiting, Archivist & Cur
Holdings: Mss Pix Slides Audiotapes Microforms
Notes: Collections concentrate on the history of Birmingham and Jefferson County, Alabama, and to a lesser extent, the state of Alabama, 1819-1960. Records of real estate companies, coal, steel, and iron industries, city government, and selected prominent individuals. Extensive photograph collections showing general views of the city, photographic portraits of prominent individuals, major buildings and streets, and development of mass transit. Also incl articles, brochures, correspondence, family genealogies, maps, newspaper clippings, pamphlets, and programs concerning significant families, individuals, organizations, and events.

AK —TONGASS HISTORICAL SOCIETY, Library, 629 Dock St, Ketchikan, 99901. Marjorie Anne Voss, Librn
Holdings: Vols 400 Cat Pix
Notes: Alaskan and regional history and art, as well as Northwest Coast Indian history and art. Extensive photograph collection.

AZ —NORTHERN ARIZONA UNIVERSITY, Special Collection Library, CU Box 6022, Flagstaff, 86011. Peter M Whiteley, Coordr/Archivist; William Mullane, Librn
Notes: Various collections, incl (1) Kolb Collection; very extensive collection of Kolb's photographs (over 250,000) which concentrate on the Grand Canyon, 1901-1975. (2) Stuart M Young Collection; photographs from the Utah Archeological Expedition of 1909, incl the first photographs of Rainbow Bridge and many Anasazi ruins of Northern Arizona and Southern Utah. (3) Phillip Johnston Collection; incl thousands of photo negatives of the Navajo Reservation, 1920's-1930's and slide shows of the Navajo Reservation and Mexico.

AZ —NORTHERN ARIZONA UNIVERSITY, Special Collection Library, CU Box 6022, Flagstaff, 86011. Peter M Whiteley, Coordr/Archivist; William Mullane, Librn
Notes: Northern Arizona Pioneers' Historican Society and NAU Collections have combined holdings of over 12,000 photos. Both collections contain photos depicting many aspects of all areas of Arizona, but the majority are of people and places in Flagstaff, Coconino County, Jerome, the Verde Valley, and the Navajo Indian Reservation. The photos span from the 1880's to the present. A catalog to these collections is currently in progress. Special Collections also holds approx 200,000 negatives of the *Arizona Daily Sun* newspaper of Flagstaff, 1947-1970.

AZ —ARIZONA STATE UNIVERSITY, Library, Arizona Collection, Tempe, 85281. Edward C Oetting, Head
Holdings: Pix
See also entry under Arizona - History

AZ —TUCSON MUSEUM OF ART LIBRARY, 140 N Main, Tucson, 85705. Dorcas Worsley, Librn
Holdings: Vols (2000)
Budget: ($1500)
Notes: Extensive file of biographical and critical information on Arizona artists which is continually being increased. Subject card index to magazines on Western art and artists in magazines not indexed in *Art Index* 12 drawers in 1984, and continues to grow. Have a collection of 15,000 slides.

AZ —UNIVERSITY OF ARIZONA, University Library, Special Collections, Tucson, 85721. Louis A Hieb, Head
Budget: ($40,000)
Notes: The collection incl Arizona general periodicals and fiction, and books of the history, biography, travel, Indians, the arts, physical and natural resources, politics and government, business and industry, and social problems of Arizona. There are also over 450 processed ms collections varying in size from a single volume to hundreds of boxes. Also, incl are the Arizona photograph and pamphlet collections.

PHOTOGRAPHS—COLLECTIONS (cont.)

AZ —UNIVERSITY OF ARIZONA, Center for Creative Photography, 843 E University Blvd, Tucson, 85721. James Enyeart, Dir; Terence Pitts, Cur and Librn
Holdings: Pix
Notes: Center has significant collections consisting of more than 25 photographs plus other archival material such as negatives, contact sheets, work prints, correspondence, financial records, diaries, project files, etc. Inventories of the collections are available to researchers. Published guides available for some collections.
See also entry under Photographers.

CA —ACADEMY OF MOTION PICTURE ARTS & SCIENCES, Margaret Herrick Library, 8949 Wilshire Blvd, Beverly Hills, 90211. Linda Harris Mehr, Library Administrator
Holdings: Vols (16,000) Cat Mss Maps Pix Slides
Budget: ($250,000)
Notes: Also posters, scrapbooks, clippings and press books. Collection emphases are the moving picture industry, moving picture history, biographical material on actors, actresses and industry personnel. Files on specific films, reviews, cast and credits, production data, etc, on more than 65,000 moving pictures. (Over 5000 films, incl early 28mm films in Film Archive). Over 5 million pictures. Special collections: papers of Mary Pickford, Mack Sennett, Adolph Zukor, Lewis Milestone, George Stevens, George Cukor, John Huston, Edith Head; Paramount scripts and stills archive, MGM stills archive, RKO stills archive, Thomas H Ince stills collection, Cecil B DeMille stills collection.

CA —BURBANK PUBLIC LIBRARY, 110 N Glenoaks Blvd, Burbank, 91502. Mary Ann Grasso, Coordr; Barbara Stones, Coordr, Media Project
Holdings: Vols (32,000) Cat Clippings Pix VF

Notes: The Warner Research Collection is a full service research division designed to serve the production needs of the motion picture, television, theatrical, and creative arts communities. This is a see-based service available by appointment only. Subject specialties include costumes, U.S. military, crime and criminals, transportation, license plates, and Sears catalogues.

CA —LONG BEACH PUBLIC LIBRARY, 101 Pacific Ave, Long Beach, 90802. Douglas Kermode, Librn
Holdings: Vols (700) Cat Mss Maps Pix
Notes: Reocrds the development of Long Beach from its beginnings as a city (ca 1867). Picture file (ca 3400) and negative collection from local Winstead Bros, Photographers (ca 10,000).

CA —CRAFT AND FOLK ART MUSEUM, Library, 5814 Wilshire Blvd, Los Angeles, 90036. Joan M Benedetti, Museum Librn
Holdings: Vols (2000) Slides VF
Notes: Incl 2000 books; 70 journal subscriptions; artists' biographical files: 6 file drawers; clipping files: 8 file drawers; 20,000 slides. Representation of the material culture of all people, traditional and contemporary expressions. Incl visual and printed information on ethnic, traditional, popular, decorative, idiosyncratic, and contemporary crafts as well as vernacular architecture, handmade houses, and design. Information about and for professional artists on health hazards, conservation, and career management. Anthropological and art historical works; exhibition catalogues; slides, photographs, audiocassettes; clipping and pamphlet files. Contemporary Slide Registry of Craftspeople and extensive biographical files of contemporary craft artists.
Information and referral files of craft related galleries, shops, festivals, organizations, etc.

CA —LOS ANGELES PUBLIC LIBRARY, Central Library, Audio Visual Dept, 630 W Fifth St, Los Angeles, 90071. Richard V Partlow, Principal Librn
Budget: ($71,989)
Notes: Includes 16mm film (4300), VHS video (300), audio recordings (20,000), audio cassettes (5500), picture file (220,000 cstimated clippings), filmstrips (60), periodicals (65). Material on all subject areas are included.

CA —LOS ANGELES PUBLIC LIBRARY, History Dept, 630 W 5th St, Los Angeles, 90071. Bettye H Ellison, Librn in Charge, California Room
Holdings: Vols 8000 Cat Pix
Budget:
Notes: The California Collection is a reference and circulating collection consisting of state, county and city histories, volumes of travel and description, periodicals, and publications of state and local historical societies. Over 260,000 historic photographs from the turn of the century to the mid-1950s. Portraits are incl. The majority of the views are of Los Angeles and Southern California. Special subject and biographical indexes provide references to a wide variety of California related books, periodicals and Los Angeles area newspapers. A separate index is maintained for photographs.

CA —UNIVERSITY OF CALIFORNIA, LOS ANGELES, Research Library, Dept of Special Collections, 405 Hilgard Ave, Los Angeles, 90024. Edward Shreeves, Chairman, Bibliographers Group; David S Zeidberg, Head
Notes: 1000 books; 2,000,000 pieces. Various collections incl Albert Boni collection of early photography; individual images and albums of work by George Barnard, A Beato, Isabella Bird Bishop, Felix Bonfils, Julia Margaret Cameron, Maxime du Camp, Francis Frith, Alexander Gardner, W Hammerschmidt, Eadweard Muybridge, William Henry Fox Talbot, Edward Vischer, and Carleton E Watkins; 300 books illustrated with original photographs; photography as documentation, incl images of Australasia, 1700 images of the Middle East, and extensive holdings reflecting local history incl 6000 architectural photographs of Southern California and the Los Angeles Daily News and Los Angeles Times morgues; images by California Pictorialists \'ill Connell, Louis Fleckenstein, Ernest Pratt, Roland and Florence Schneider, and Louis J Stellman; 2000 19th century cabinet cards oftheater personalities; 10,000 20th century theater photographs by Jerome Robinson; 300,000 negatives of Los Angeles commercial photographer Otto Rothschild. Also, much of the work of Louis J Stellman, a San Francisco photographer, in the Richard Dillon Collection of photographs. Incl 98 examples of Chinatown photographs (1910s and 1920s), in addition to 62 of the Mother Lode country, during the early 1930s.

CA —UNIVERSITY OF CALIFORNIA, LOS ANGELES, Theater Arts Library, Los Angeles, 90024. Edward Shreeves, Chairman, Bibliographers Group; Audree Malkin, Head, Theater Arts Library
Holdings: Cat Mss Pix Slides
Notes: Photograph Collection: A collection of approximately 4,000,000 production stills, scene stills, portraits, publicity stills, and other miscellaneous photographs spanning the history of motion pictures 1905 to the present. Notable features are the Jessen Faragoh Collection which consists of 2169 production stills and photographs of such early studios as Biograph, Keystone, Selig, Triangle, and Vitagraph, and 901 portraits of performers such as Thomas Ince, D W Griffith, and Jesse Lasky from 1905-1929; the Richard Dix Collection of 5217 stills from Richard Dix films; Columbia Pictures Still Collection consisting of over 200,000 stills from Columbia films; portraits of performers and keybooks dating 1940-present. Twentieth Century Fox Motion Picture Still Collection comprises photographs from 288 American

andEuropean films released by Twentieth Century Fox, primarily during the 1950s and 1960s. The collection contains 80,751 production stills, 71 keysets, 2763 individual proof sheets, 415 individual proof sheets, 349 proof sheet books, 309 Rollei proof sheet books, 164 color transparencies, 37 portraits, and a number of publicity news releases.

CA —UNIVERSITY OF CALIFORNIA, LOS ANGELES, Music Library, Schonberg Hall, Los Angeles, 90024. Stephen M Fry, Music Librn
Notes: The Philip Kahgan Collection of music films, letters, programs, and photographs important to the Southern California classical music scene. Incl 16mm "home movies" of more than thirty renowned conductors and performers during Hollywood Bowl rehearsals in the late 1930s. Incl Kahgan correspondence, memorabilia, 35 scrapbooks, etc.

CA —UNIVERSITY OF CALIFORNIA, LOS ANGELES, Art Library, Los Angeles, 90024. Max Marmor, Library Assistant
Holdings: Pix Microforms
Notes: Art; Art History; Early Christian and Byzantine Art; Medieval Art; Apostolic Age to 1400; Iconography; Photo Archive; Christian Art and Symbolism.

CA —UNIVERSITY OF SOUTHERN CALIFORNIA, Edward L Doheny Memorial Library, Archives of Performing Arts, University Park, Los Angeles, 90089. Robert Knutson, Librn
Holdings: Vols (15,000) Cat Mss Pix Videotapes Film Audiotapes
Notes: Approx 15,000 vols of books and serials about film, incl a large collection of foreign language books and periodicals. Current subscriptions to over 200 serials. Large collection of clippings about motion pictures and television. Warner Brothers Films Collection (1920-1968) incl 700,000 stills and negatives; 3,000 titles of feature, short subject and television screenplays, script materials, set designs, engineering drawings, production records, patent records, music and legal files. Over 1000 bound vols describing the inventory and 100 bound vols of index to the inventory. Universal Pictures Corporation Collection incl 600 boxes of production and publicity department records, incl 1,500 screenplays. Metro-Goldwyn-Mayer Collection incl screenplays from 1919-1958. Twentieth Century-Fox Collection incl screenplays and story department notes from 1919-1967.Hal Roach Studio Collection contains studio records from 1916-mid fifties. More than 150 personal collections from actors, directors, producers, writers, etc. Also have 2,000 additional screenplays; 1,000 posters, 110,000 photographs; 750 recorded soundtracks; 1,500 interview tapes; 400 David Wolper videotapes. A collection of feature films on videotape is being created. There is also a historical collection of motion picture cameras, projectors and other equipment from the earliest times to present.

CA —J PAUL GETTY MUSEUM, Photo Archives, 17985 Pacific Coast Hwy, Malibu, 90265. William Reeder, Cur
Holdings: Pix
Notes: Incl photographs of works of art at the Museum (180,000 cataloged, 500,000 uncataloged), incl ancient art, western European art (painting, sculpture, graphics) and European decorative arts, medieval and Renaissance to 19th century, and antiquities.

CA —CALIFORNIA INSTITUTE OF TECHNOLOGY, Robert A Millikan Memorial Library, Archives, 1201 E California Blvd, Pasadena, 91125. Judith R Goodstein, Archivist
Holdings: Vols (3000) Uncat Mss Maps Pix Slides Phonorecords Audiotapes Viotapes 16mm Films Microforms
Notes: Over 60 collections (1830s-present) relating to history of 19th-20th centuries science and technology and the history of the Institute. Included are over 5000 photographs of American and European scientists.

CA —POMONA PUBLIC LIBRARY, Special Collections, 625 S Garey Ave, PO Box 2271,

PHOTOGRAPHS—COLLECTIONS (cont.)

Pomona, 91766. David Streeter, Librn
Holdings: Cat Pix Slides
Notes: About 100,000 photographs: Loyd Cooper collection, 20,000 negatives and prints of California, 1920-1940; Percy Everett collection, 4000 color 35mm transparencies of world travel, 1960s; Burton Frasher collection, 60,000 negatives and prints of California, Arizona, New Mexico, Colorado, Utah, Nevada, 1920-1940; Brooking Tatum collection, 125 color prints and 50 color 35mm transparencies of California flora; Pomona Valley collection, 20,000 photographs, 1880-date; California post card collection, 4000 views; world post card collection, 30,000 views; stereoptican collection, 900 views; lantern slide collection 450 views; glass plate negative collection, 2500 views of the Pomona Valley, 1900-1920.

CA —A K SMILEY PUBLIC LIBRARY, 125 W Vine St, Redlands, 92373. Larry E Burgess, Archivist
Holdings: Vols (3500) Mss Maps Pix Phonorecords Microforms
Budget: ($45,000)
Notes: Emphasis on San Bernadino County and the Redlands area. Especially prized is *The Citrographic*, 1887-1908 (bound vols and microfilm) edited by Scipio Craig, prominent in state, national, and newspaper circles. The ms collection (250,000 pieces) incl the Smily Family papers, much on water development, and onthe citrus industry. The photograph collection (over 5000) covers the history of the area; there are many stereographs and glass slides. The collection on Indians of California and the Southwest was begun from a special gift by Andrew Carnegie honoring his friend, Albert K Smiley.

CA —UNIVERSITY OF CALIFORNIA, RIVERSIDE, University Library, 4045 Canyon Crest Dr, Box 5900, Riverside, 92517.
Holdings: Vols 2,500 Pix
Notes: A broad collection representing history and aesthetics of photography, incl volumes of examples of individual photographers' work. Supports the photograph collections of the California Museum of Photography and the Keystone Mast Archive of stereographic photographs.

CA —SAN DIEGO HISTORICAL SOCIETY, Research Archives, Casa de Balboa 1649 El Prado, Balboa Park PO Box 81825, San Diego, 92138. Sylvia Arden, Head Librn & Archivist
Holdings: Cat Mss Maps Pix Audiotapes
Notes: Emphasis on San Diego County and early materials of Riverside and Imperial counties. Over 10,000 photographs also.

CA —CALIFORNIA HISTORICAL SOCIETY, Schubert Hall Library, 2099 Pacific Ave, San Francisco, 94109. Bruce L Johnson, Library Dir
Holdings: Pix
Notes: San Francisco CHS Photographic Archives holds 300,000 images on California statewide; The CHS Title Insurance and Trust Corporation Collection of Historical Photographs in Los Angeles contains 20,000 photographs centered around pictures of Southern California by noted photographer C C Pierce. Copies of photographs by other pioneer Los Angeles photographers, such as Godfrey, Wolfenstein and Parker are incl, as well as 2000 glass plate negatives of local Indians by George Wharton James.

CA —THE POLISH ARTS AND CULTURE FOUNDATION, 1290 Sutter St, San Francisco, 94109. Wanda Tomczykowska, President
Holdings: Pix
Notes: Portraits of Polish personalities in art and culture, photographs of costumes, dances, observance of traditions, historical events. Color photographs of California.

CA —SOCIETY OF CALIFORNIA PIONEERS, Library, 456 McAllister St, San Francisco, 94102. Grace E Baker, Librn
Holdings: Vols (12,000) Cat Mss Maps Pix Microforms
Notes: California history, especially the gold rush and the San Francisco earthquake, Sherman collection of early California music, business letterheads of early California firms, San Francisco City Directories 1850-1944, records of California Battalion 1846-47, ms material on overland diaries, ships' logs and passenger lists. Also, large photograph collection.

CA —SAN JOSE HISTORICAL MUSEUM, Repository, 635 Phelan Ave, San Jose, 95112. Mignon Gibson, Museum Dir
Holdings: Cat Mss Maps Pix Phonorecords 16mm Films
Notes: Collection of about 2500 cu ft relates to the history of the Santa Clara Valley. Holdings incl Spanish documents from Pueblo de San Jose, ca 1790-1840: Spanish and Mexican landgrant maps for the area; official city and county records, from 1860s on; local newspapers, from 1878 on; maps; personal papers of prominent local figures; local business and organizational records; miscellaneous ephemera; and over 4000 historic photographs. Limited photocopying.

CA —CALIFORNIA POLYTECHNIC STATE UNIVERSITY LIBRARY, Special Collections and University Archives, San Luis Obispo, 93407. Nancy E Loe, Head Librn
Holdings: Vols 100 Cat Mss Pix Slides
Notes: The Fairs Collection incl 56,000 mss materials (correspondence, scrapbooks, legislative opinions, and memoranda), photographs and slides documenting the Western Fairs Association of Sacramento, California, and the management and growth of fairs in California and around the world (materials in rough sorting stage).

CA —UNIVERSITY OF CALIFORNIA, SANTA BARBARA, Map and Imagery Laboratory, Santa Barbara, 93106. Larry Carver, Dept Head
Notes: Worldwide coverage of Landsat imagery donated by US Dept of Agriculture Aerial Photography Field Office. Consists of 153,000 scenes, covering most of the earth's surface between the years 1975 and 1980. Incl 300,000 maps, 1800 atlases, 9 globes, 300 relief models, 1,500,000 satellite imagery and aerial photographs, 700 reference books and gazetteers, 25 serials (titles received), and 21,000 microforms.

CA —THE HAGGIN MUSEUM, Petzinger Library of Californiana, 1201 N Pershing Ave, Stockton, 95203. Diane Freggiaro, Librn/Archivist
Holdings: Vols (7000) Cat Mss Maps Pix Slides Audiotapes 16mm Films
Notes: The Petzinger Library is open by appointment only. Special emphasis on Stockton and San Joaquin County and Valley area, local biography, agriculture, agricultural history, industrial history, farm machinery (especially Holt Manufacturing Co, Stockton). There is a photograph collection of 8500 pictures, and extensive manuscript holdings (about 17,000 pieces).

CA —WHITTIER COLLEGE, Wardman Library, Whittier, 90608. Christine Erdmann, Special Collections Librn
Holdings: // Cat Pix
Notes: Aerial photographs of California, 1927-1963. 100,000 aerial photo negatives (40,000 nitrate-base), 300,000 aerial photo prints, 1000 photomosaics, 750 orthophoto maps. Concentration in California, particularly in the Los Angeles region, and elsewhere in metropolitan areas. Many flights are among the earliest available and cover areas since developed. Sequential photos often allow documentation of the history of development or of natural effects. Prints may be borrowed for 2-week periods. Purchase of prints only through Teledyne-Geotronics, Long Beach, California. An inventory list of flights can be purchased through the Dept of Geology.

CO —DENVER PUBLIC LIBRARY, Western History Department, 1357 Broadway, Denver, 80203. Eleanor M Gehres, Head
Holdings: Vols (50,000) Cat Mss Maps Pix Audiotapes Microforms
Notes: Western US History. The department has a separate catalog, published in 1970 in 7 vols by G K Hall Co. First supplement published in 1975 in 1 vol. There is a subject index of some 3 million entries to newspapers and magazines of the Rocky Mountain region, added to daily. The Western Newspaper Microfilm Center contains approx 7000 reels of Western US newspapers. Collection has ca 275,000 negatives and prints of Western life; and ca 2500 maps, cataloged and classified.

CT —YALE UNIVERSITY, Box 1603A, Yale Station, New Haven, 06520.
Notes: Papers of Walter Camp, father of American football and foremost authority on sports and physical fitness. 48 microfilm reels; incl also over 20,000 clippings, etc on sports, providing virtual history, 1866-1925. Published guide to the collection for sale.

CT —YALE UNIVERSITY, Music Library, 98 Wall St, New Haven, 06520. Harold E Samuel, Librn
Holdings: Vols (118,000) Cat Mss Pix Phonorecords Audiotapes Microforms
Notes: General reference and research materials. Performing editions. Strong in theoretical literature, opera, 17-18th century music (incl mss), J S Bach and sons in early editions and mss, Russian liturgical music (Tkaczenko Collection), hymnology, American music. Also collection of musical pictures and portraits.

†CT —PHILIPPINE-AMERICAN RESEARCH CENTER, Library, PO Box507, Sharoni, 06069. John Silva, Dir
Holdings: Vols 200 Maps Pix
Notes: Philippine history and culture from pre-colonial times to the present, as well as under Spanish, Japanese, and American regimes, and post-independence. Mostly rare works of the late 19th and early 20th century; history and anthropology. Over 2,500 photographs. Incl maps, posters, memorabilia. Limited copying. Visits by appointment.

CT —UKRAINIAN MUSEUM AND LIBRARY, 161 Glenbrook Rd, Stamford, 06902. Wasyl Lencyk, Dir
Notes: Over 600 photographs.

DE —HENRY F DUPONT WINTERTHUR MUSEUM LIBRARY, Winterthur, 19735. Frank H Sommer, III, Head
Holdings: Cat
Notes: Strong collections.

DC —ACTION, Photo Library, 806 Connecticut Ave NW, Washington, 20525.
Holdings: Pix Slides
Notes: Volunteer photos for ACTION, VISTA, and older Americans programs. 15,000 photographs.

DC —BROADCAST PIONEERS LIBRARY, 1771 N St NW, Washington, 20036. Catharine Heinz, Dir
Holdings: Vols (6500) Uncat Pix Phonorecords Audiotapes
Notes: Special collections: Oral History (750); Havrilla (photos, radio performers); William S Hedges Collection; Elmo Neale Pickerill Collection; Joseph E Baudino Collection; Archive of Federal Communications Bar Association. Incl 20,000 pictures, 1450 phonorecords and 1200 audiotapes.

DC —DISTRICT OF COLUMBIA PUBLIC LIBRARY, Martin Luther King Memorial Library, Washingtoniana Div and Washington Star Collection, 901 G St NW, Washington, 20001. Roxanna Deane, Chief
Holdings: Vols (20,000) Cat Maps Pix Slides
Budget: ($5500)
Notes: *Washington Star* Collection was the working morgue and photo library of the *Washington Star* newspaper. There are an estimated one million photos dating from about 1930 to 1981. These are arranged by subject and personal name and cover international, national and local news. There are approx 13 million news clippings arranged by subject and personal name for the same period. Each *Star* article was clipped and placed in as many different files as was necessary to cover all topics or personal names mentioned in the article. Reproductions from the photo collection may be purchased.

DC —FREER GALLERY OF ART, Library, 12th & Jefferson Dr SW, Washington,

PHOTOGRAPHS—COLLECTIONS (cont.)

20560. Ellen A Nollman, Librn
Holdings: Cat Pix Slides
Notes: Incl 50,000 slides; 8000 photographs. Catalog published by G K Hall, Boston.

DC —GEORGETOWN UNIVERSITY, Library, Special Collections Div, 37 & O Sts NW, Washington, 20057. George M Barringer, Special Collections Librn; Nicholas B Sheetz, Mss Librn
Holdings: Vols 500 Cat Pix
Notes: Incorporates the picture "morgue" of the Quigley Publishing Company and archival runs of its publications. Over 50,000 pictures. The library has additional picture resources of over 100,000 photographs.

DC —HOWARD UNIVERSITY, Moorland-Spingarn Research Center, 500 Howard Place NW, Washington, 20059. Clifford L Muse, Jr, Acting Dir
Holdings: Vols (106,086) Cat Mss Maps Pix Slides Phonorecords Audiotapes 16mm Films Filmstrips Microforms
Budget: ($854,753)
Notes: *The Glenn Carrington Collection: A Guide to the Books, Manuscripts, Music and Recordings* (DC MSRC, 1977). *Dictionary Catalog of the Jesse E Moorland Collection of Negro Life and History*, 9 vols and Supplement, 3 vols (Boston: G K Hall, 1970, 1977). *Dictionary Catalog of the Arthur Spingarn Collection of Negro Authors*, 2 vols (Boston: G K Hall, 1970). Guide to Processed Collections in the Manuscript Division of the Moorland-Spingarn Research Center (DC, MSRC, 1983). The Moorland-Spingran Research Center is recognized as one of the largest and most comprehensive repositories in the world for the collection, preservation and dissemination of historical materials documenting from antiquity to the present the history and culture of Black people in Africa, Europe, the Caribbean and the US. Since 1973, the Research Center has greatly expanded its facilitiesand resources and currently provides research services in all aspects of library and archival research, including manuscripts, oral history, music, prints and photographs and general library materials. The Research Center also maintains professional zerographic, micrographic, photographic and similar reproduction laboratories.

DC —INTERNATIONAL LABOR ORGANIZATION, International Labor Office, Washington Branch Library, 1750 New York Ave NW, Rm 330, Washington, 20006. Karen J Mark, Librn
Holdings: Vols (13,500) Cat Pix 16mm Films Monographs
Notes: Wide range of titles dealing with worldwide labor and social matters. The library contains ILO publications and documentation only, dating back to 1919. Also, a collection of ILO films and photos. See *Subject Guide to Publications of the ILO, 1919-1964 and ILO Catalogue of Publications in Print, 1982* (ILO).

DC —LIBRARY OF CONGRESS, Geography and Map Division, Washington, 20540. John A Wolter, Chief

DC —LIBRARY OF CONGRESS, Washington, 20540.
Notes: Papers and working materials of Charles Eames (1907-1978), American architect and designer. Incl are original negatives and prints of the 106 education films he created, business correspondence 1944 to 1978, some 400,000 color slides, 31,000 black and white photographs, production materials for exhibits, and drawings for all his major furniture designs. Acquired on a grant of $500,000 from IBM.

DC —LIBRARY OF CONGRESS, Prints & Photographs Div, Washington, 20540.
Holdings: Vols 51 Pix
Notes: The Abdul-Hamid II Collection of photographs of Turkey. Formal views of military installations and personnel, naval vessels, schools, hospitals, historic monuments, fire-fighting and lif▪ iving equipment, major cities, palaces and stables of the Imperial Court, and other subjects of official interest. 2500 pictures.

DC —LIBRARY OF CONGRESS, Prints & Photographs Div, Washington, 20540.
Holdings: 11,427 Items
Notes: The Joseph S Allen Collection of architectural photographs. Covering the period 1945 to 1967, the collection consists of photographs of churches, colleges, government buildings, residential structures, and historic monuments in 27 eastern and mid-western states.

DC —LIBRARY OF CONGRESS, Prints & Photographs Div, Washington, 20540.
Notes: The George Grantham Bain Collection documents New York City sports events, theater, celebrities, crime, disasters, political activities, conventions, and public celebrations of the early 20th century with approximately 120,000 glass plate negatives and 240,000 photoprints acquired from the Bain News Service. The National Photo Company Collection contains news photographs of Washington, DC, 1910s-1930s.

DC —LIBRARY OF CONGRESS, Prints & Photographs Div, Washington, 20540.
Notes: The Brady-Handy Collection consists of some 10,000 negatives from the files of photographers Levin C Handy (1855?-1932) and Mathew B Brady (1823?-1896), most of which are portrait photographs and views of Washington, DC from the 19th and early 20th centuries. Incl portraits of congressmen and government leaders (1855-90).

DC —LIBRARY OF CONGRESS, Prints & Photographs Div, Washington, 20540.
Notes: The F Holland Day Collection of Day's photographs. 640 photoprints.

DC —LIBRARY OF CONGRESS, Prints & Photographs Div, Washington, 20540.
Notes: Photographs by Arnold Genthe and other great photographers.

DC —LIBRARY OF CONGRESS, Prints & Photographs Div, Washington, 20540.
Notes: The Edward S Curtis collection of photographs of North American Indians, early 20th century. About 1600 photoprints.

DC —LIBRARY OF CONGRESS, Prints & Photographs Div, Washington, 20540.
Notes: The Charles Henry Currier Collection of photographs of homes, offices, factories, charitable institutions, and recreational organizations in the Boston area, 1890s-1910s.

DC —LIBRARY OF CONGRESS, Prints & Photographs Div, Washington, 20540.
Notes: Civil War Photograph Collection incl photographs commissioned by Mathew Brady and others. Brady employed 20 photographers at the height of his operations. His staff incl Alexander and James Gardner, James F Gibson, and Thomas C Roche.

DC —SMITHSONIAN INSTITUTION LIBRARIES, National Air & Space Museum Branch, NASM Bldg, Sixth & Independence Ave SW, Washington, 20560. Frank A Pietropaoli, Branch Chief
Holdings: Vols (39,000) Cat Mss Maps Pix Slides Microforms
Notes: History of flight and aerospace development, incl biographical material on aviation pioneers, balloons and ballooning. Extensive photographic collection (600,000 pictures). Incl the Sherman Fairchild Collection of aeronautical photographs (transferred from the American Institute of Aeronautics and Astronautics). Also incl the Bella Landauer Aeronautical Sheet Music Collection (1500 pieces). 2000 films; 800,000 microforms; 9000 volumes bound.

FL —FLORIDA DEPT OF STATE, Florida State Archives, Florida Photographic Collection, R A Gray Bldg, Tallahassee, 32301. Mrs Allen Morris, Archives Supervisor
Holdings: Maps Pix Slides Films Audiotapes
Notes: Areas of emphasis within the collection: (1) Florida government. There is a complete file of governors' photos, and many photos of legislative sessions and legislators going back to the late 1800s. (2) Stanley J Morrow. Mr Morrow learned his craft under Mathew B Brady. He worked in Florida from 1882-1887. Collection has several hundred of his glass negatives that document a period of southward expansion in Florida. (3) Alvan S Harper, Tallahassee portrait artist; 1700 glass negatives of Tallahassee people between 1885-1910. (4) W A Fishbaugh. Several thousand photographs of the "boom," Miami and Coral Gables in the 1920s. (5) Charles A Mosier, Charles Torrey Simpson and J K Small; 500 photographs of Florida flora, made by these famous naturalists, mostly in South Dade County. (6) Added March, 1983; 2200 glass and nitrate negatives by J K Small. (7) Collectionalso incl 40,000 negatives (4x5) made by Harvey Slade in Tallahassee, 1946-1975, predominantly portraits; also 15,000 news story negatives (4x5 and 2x2) relative to local and state government, 1957-1969, unprinted, from *The Tallahassee Democrat*. (8) 39,000 (4x5) negatives and contact prints deposited by the Florida Dept of Commerce, 1946-late 1970s. Subjects incl Florida cities, attractions, industries, beaches, festivals, boating, fishing, forts, gardens, hotels, highways, lighthouses, monuments, museums and recreations. (9) 25,000 (8x10, 4x5 & 35mm) negatives by Jacksonville commercial photographer Gordon Spottswood & Son, 1916-1967. Subjects incl Jacksonville people (individuals and groups), street scenes, commercial buildings, Atlantic Coast Line & Seaboard Airline Railroads, and Boy Scout Activities. (10) 15,000 (4x5) negativesfrom Seldomridge portrait studio in Tampa. Tampa people from the 1940s to the 1970s.

FL —UNIVERSITY OF SOUTH FLORIDA, Library, Tampa, 33620. J B Dobkin, Special Collections Librn
Notes: Public and private papers of Nelson Poynter, Chairman of the board of Times Publishing Company. Incl political correspondence, photographs, and Pulitzer Prize commendation records.

HI —BERNICE P BISHOP MUSEUM, Library, PO Box 19000-A, Honolulu, 96819. Cynthia Timberlake, Librn
Notes: Only American library devoted exclusively to the Pacific region. Collection reflects historical and contemporary research emphases of Bishop Museum; ie the natural and cultural history of the Pacific. Areas of concentration incl archaeology, ethnology, linguistics, voyages and explorations, history, vertebrate and invertebrate zoology, botany and museology. Strong special collections incl photographs, mss and archives, maps and art. Publications: Quarterly "Additions to the Catalog," *Dictionary Catalog of the Library* (9 vols and 2 suppl; Boston: G K Hall, 1964-69).

IL —CHICAGO HISTORICAL SOCIETY, Library, Graphics Collection, Clark St at North Ave, Chicago, 60614. Larry A Viskochil, Cur
Holdings: Pix
Notes: About 750,000 pieces. Chiefly concern Chicago, but incl many portraits of national leaders and other materials concerning American history. Incl many early daguerreotypes, ambrotypes, tintypes, stereographs; negatives and photographs from Chicago newspaper morgues, 1900-1965 (250,000); photographs from Chicagoland-in-Pictures, a project for historical photography sponsored by the Society and the Chicago Area Camera Clubs Association since 1948 (22,000); and other photographic materials.

IL —CHICAGO PUBLIC LIBRARY, Art Section, Fine Arts Division, 78 E Washington St, Chicago, 60602. Rosalinda I Hack, Fine Arts Division Chief; Yvonne S Brown, Head, Art Section
Holdings: Vols 6000
Notes: Reference and circulating collection, with special emphasis on general architectural history, modern architecture, architecture of the United States, and Chicago architectural history. Collection is supported by the Chicago Architecture File, a card file that lists citations to information on buildings that been recognized for their architectural significance. The Section's picture Collection has extensive documentation on Chicago area architecture, and incorporates a collection of architectural photographs by Stephen Beal. Archival copies of these photographs are to be found

PHOTOGRAPHS—COLLECTIONS
(cont.)

in Special Collections. The collections is also supplemented by the microform collections of *The Historic American Buildings Survey,* and *American Architectural Books.*

IL —CHICAGO PUBLIC LIBRARY, Special Collections Div, Cultural Center, 78 E Washington St, Chicago, 60602. Laura Linard, Cur
Holdings: Vols (7000) Cat Mss Maps Pix
Notes: The Civil War and American History Research Collection at the Chicago Public Library is our largest collection. It spans the pre-war sectional crisis as well as Reconstruction. Scarce slavery pamphlets; large collection of regimental histories; manuscripts of US Grant, Sherman, Breckinridge; letters and diaries of soldiers and other officers; original photographs of individuals and field shots; Confederate Battle Plan for the Battle of Shiloh (original); swords, rifles, uniforms, flags and other military accessories. A substantial part of this collection has been cataloged. The museum objects are inventoried (Grand Army Hall and Memorial Association of Illinois Collection).See *Treasures of The Chicago Public Library,* comp by Thomas A Oriando and Marie Gecik, 1977, pp 36-79.

IL —NEWBERRY LIBRARY, 60 W Walton St, Chicago, 60610. Diana Haskell, Cur of Modern Mss
Holdings: Cat Mss Maps Pix
Notes: The Ayer Collection. Incl the Worcester Collection of 6000 photographs. Emphasis on Philippine history, to 1900 (some later). Several checklists published.

†IL —NEWBERRY LIBRARY, 60 W Walton St, Chicago, 60610.
Notes: Collection of color slides of the early 1950s. Photographs by the eight-year Superintendent of the Fort Belknap Indian Reservation in Montana, J W "Duke" Wellington, who was allowed to take pictures of some of the most important rituals of the Assiniboine and Gros Ventres Indians, dances, renewals, etc. An annotated collection.

IL —NORTHWESTERN UNIVERSITY, Library, Special Collections Dept, 1937 Sheridan Rd, Evanston, 60201. R Russell Maylone, Cur
Holdings: Vols 1500 Cat Maps Pix
Notes: Newspapers, magazines, books, pamphlets, mimeographed and printed government documents and journals, 1200 photographs, 50 posters, 30 scrapbooks of clippings from Dutch newspapers concerning the war.

IL —LAKE FOREST COLLEGE, Donnelley Library, Lake Forest, 60045. Arthur H Miller Jr, College Librn
Holdings: Vols (1500) Cat Mss Maps Pix
Budget: ($1000)
Notes: Elliott Donnelley Collection (received 1976) of mostly mid-20th century books and periodicals on Western railroads and mountain narrow gauge, world narrow gauge and short lines, steam, live steam, model railroading, and some traction. Purchases keep collection emphasis current (50-75 new books per year, 22 periodical subscriptions). Also, the Munson Paddock Collecction (received 1977) of train illustrations, maps, and timetables, 1850-1950. In addition to American technical and historical books and periodicals, the collection contains books of views, narrations of rail travel (particularly American West), and US local histories--all with illustrations of trains. Most titles are late 19th century Americna. The 1550 volumes are supplemented by related holdings of more than 150 pamphlets, 600 timetables, 2000 unbound periodical issues, 200 maps, 75 diagrams (engines, cars) hundreds of clippings of train illustrations, and 1000 photographs. In progress is a card index of illustrations by wheel type line, and manufacturer. Together, the collections contain about 7000 items.

IN —INDIANA UNIVERSITY, Institute for Sex Research Library, 416 Morrison Hall,

Bloomington, 47401. Douglas Freeman, Collections and Services Librn; Joan Brewer, Information Services Librn
Holdings: Vols (62,000) Cat Mss Pix Microforms
See also entry under Sex.

IN —INDIANA STATE UNIVERSITY, Cunningham Memorial Library, Dept of Rare Books & Special Collections, Terre Haute, 47809. Lawrence J McCrank, Head
Holdings: Vols 750 Mss
Budget: $500
Notes: The University Archives holds copies of all publications of the Indiana Normal School which became the Indiana State Teachers College and Indiana State University, plus collections of faculty publications and papers. The K Martin sub-collection contains 10,000 photographs relating to ISU from the 1890s to the 1950s. Incl 300 feet of mss.

KS —KANSAS STATE UNIVERSITY, Library, Special Collections & University Archives, Manhattan, 66506. Antonia Q Pigno, Coordr; John J Vander Velde, Librn; Anthony R Crawford, Univ Archivist
Notes: Collection of 128 photographs by Gordon Parks.

KS —MENNINGER FOUNDATION, Archives, 5600 W Sixth St, Box 829, Topeka, 66601. Alice Brand, Librn; Mark West, Archivist
Notes: Over 10,000 photographs. Many of these are portraits of staff members of the Menninger Foundation. Also incl are photographs of the Foundation's buildings and grounds.

KY —WESTERN KENTUCKY UNIVERSITY, Kentucky Library, Bowling Green, 42101. Riley Handy, Head, Special Collections; Connie Mills, Maps & Music Librn; Nancy Baird, Photographs Librn; Nancy Solley, Conservation Librn
Holdings: Vols (25,000) Cat Mss Maps Pix Microforms
Notes: Besides Kentucky history, other strengths are Mammoth Cave, South Union Shakers, Kentucky religion; and steamboat photos (3300 cataloged pictures); 8000 Kentucky postal cards, etc.

KY —UNIVERSITY OF KENTUCKY, Margaret I King Library, Dept of Special Collections, Lexington, 40506. William Marshall, Head
Holdings: Cat Pix
Notes: Incl original prints, negatives and direct positives. Most of the images are Kentucky-related; period covered: 1840's to present. Index to majority of collection. Ca 60,000 pieces.

KY —UNIVERSITY OF LOUISVILLE, Ekstrom Library, Photographic Archives, Louisville, 40292. J C Anderson, Cur; David G Horvath, Asst Cur
Holdings: Vols (750,000) Cat Pix Slides
Budget: ($60,000)
Notes: Photographs in three broad areas: works of outstanding photographers; examples of major developments in the art and technology of photography; photographs important as sociological, historical, or behavioral documents. Actors and actresses, Louisville's Macauley Theatre. Standard Oil of New Jersey Collection, 85,000 pictures of oil industry's effect on life in the 20th century (1943-1950, directed by Roy Stryker); Stryker's collection from Farm Security Administration series on rural conditions, 1935-1942; Jones and Laughlin Steel Corp Picture Library, by Stryker. Stryker manuscripts, 1934-1972. Caufield and Shook commercial photographs, Louisville area, 1920-1949. Jean Thomas "The Traipsin' Woman" photographs of Kentucky mountain folkways. Kate Matthews' (1870-1956) photographs incl prototypes for "Little Colonel" Series. Other collections described in unpublishedbrochure. Print duplication service.

LA —LOUISIANA STATE MUSEUM, Louisiana Historical Center, 400 Esplanade Ave, (Mailing add: 751 Chartres St, New Orleans, 70116). Edward F Haas, Chief Cur
Holdings: Vols 2000 Cat Pix Slides Phonorecords Audiotape's
Notes: New Orleans Jazz Museum and

Archives Collection. Donated to the Louisiana State Museum by the New Orleans Jazz Club in 1977. It was formerly a private museum sponsored by the Jazz Club and housed at 833 Conti St, New Orleans, La 70130. Emphasis is New Orleans jazz, incl 8000 pieces of sheet music; 12,000 phonorecords; 15,000 pictures; 1000 slides; and 200 audiotapes. A guide to the collection is in preparation.

LA —NEW ORLEANS PUBLIC LIBRARY, Louisiana Div & City Archives Dept, Louisiana History Collection, 219 Loyola Ave, New Orleans, 70140. Collin B Hamer Jr, Head
Holdings: Mss Maps Pix
Notes: Maps incl 3000 mss and printed maps, mostly for Greater New Orleans area. Also 16,700 aerial photographs.

LA —NEW ORLEANS PUBLIC LIBRARY, Louisiana Div, 219 Loyola Ave, New Orleans, 70140. Collin B Hamer Jr, Head; Brenda M Osbey, Library Associate
Notes: Louisiana and New Orleans Picture File Collection ranges from the late 19th century-date and incl the following separate collections: Alexander Allison (ca 1898-1951, 337 pieces); Charles Franck (ca 1920-50, 170 pieces); Leda Plauche (ca 1935-53, 220 pieces); C Milo Williams (ca 1910, 85 pieces); Wilson S Howell (ca 1890, 49 pieces); Grauman Marks (ca 1960, 268 pieces); Robert Tallant (ca 1940-50, 70 pieces); Robert E Tracy (1959, 87 pieces); Anthony J Flaherty (ca 1970-84, 83 pieces); George F Mugnier (1880-1920, 186 pieces); Color Slides (ca 1945-date, 500 pieces); 30,000 photographs incl 500 color slides and 104 negatives. Use of the material is restricted to on-site research. Publication must be accompanied by credit cut line.

LA —TULANE UNIVERSITY, Howard-Tilton Memorial Library, Latin American Library, New Orleans, 70118. Thomas Niehaus, Dir
Holdings: Vols (150,000) Cat Mss Maps Pix Microforms VF
Budget: ($67,000)
Notes: *Catalog of the Latin American Library* (Boston: G K Hall, 1970, suppl. 1973,1975,1978); Downs 5338-41; suppl (1961), 2727, 2737. The Latin American Library is a general collection, but specializes in Central American, Mexican, and Brazilian materials. The disciplines which are most strongly represented are history, anthropology, and archaeology. The Viceregal Ecclesiastical Mexican Collection contains manuscripts from the colonial period. The France V Scholes Collection contains a large number of photoprints and microfilm of colonial documents from the archives of Spain and Mexico. The Merle Greene Robertson Rubbings Collection contains nearly five hundred rubbings of relief sculpture from Mayan archaeological sites in Mexico and Guatemala. The Photographic Collection contains photos of archaeological sites inMeso-America, of pre-Columbian Peruvian architecture, and a general group of historic photos from Latin America.

LA —TULANE UNIVERSITY, Howard-Tilton Memorial Library, Southeast Architectural Archives, 7001 Freret St, New Orleans, 70118. William R Cullison, Cur of Prints & Drawings
Holdings: Pix
Notes: Southeast Architectural Archives Collection incl over 5000 photographic prints and over 12,000 negatives. Views are mostly of Louisiana buildings, scenes and personages, with emphasis on New Orleans. Negatives are available for most of the photographic prints.

LA —TULANE UNIVERSITY, Howard-Tilton Memorial Library, Special Collections Div, William Ransom Hogan Jazz Archive, 7001 Freret, New Orleans, 70118. Richard B Allen, Acting Cur; Alma D Williams, Assistant to the Cur
Holdings: Pix
Budget: ($90,000)
Notes: A major collection of photographs (6,273) relating to New Orleans Jazz, other jazz music, and history of jazz.
See also entry under Jazz

PHOTOGRAPHS—COLLECTIONS
(cont.)

ME —MAINE STATE LIBRARY, Special Collections Dept, Cultural Bldg, Station 64, Augusta, 04333. Shirley Thayer, Librn
Holdings: // Pix
Budget: ($2,500,000)
Notes: A very large photograph collection (incl glass slides) on lumbering in northern Maine, 1876-1936.

ME —MAINE MARITIME MUSEUM, Library and Archives, 963 Washington St, Bath, 04530. Nathan R Lipfert, Asst Cur
Holdings: Vols (5000) Cat Maps Pix Slides
Notes: The collection is limited primarily to shipbuilding in Bath, Maine, and to a lesser extent Maine as a whole. The unique aspects of the collection are a large collection of photographs of wooden shipbuilding and related trades, photographs of the vessels themselves, and a large collection of papers of a shipbuilding company in Bath active throughout the 19th century.

ME —BOOTHBAY THEATRE MUSEUM, Library, Corey Lane, Boothbay, 04537. Franklyn Lenthall, Cur
Holdings: Vols 6000 Cat Mss Pix Slides Phonorecords Audiotapes
Notes: The only Theatre Museum, as such, in America. Very extensive photo collection.

ME —BOWDOIN COLLEGE, Library, Brunswick, 04011. Dianne M Gutscher, Cur of Special Collections
Holdings: Mss Pix
Notes: A miscellaneous collection of ten logs and journals kept by members of the Bowdoin expeditions to Labrador in 1860 and 1891; as well as 29 letters, a log book, and about 100 newsclippings from the John C Parker Papers, concerning the Labrador expedition of 1891; and about 200 nitrate negatives and 200 mounted prints of those negatives done by Alfred O Gross, professor of biology at Bowdoin, when he accompanied Donald B MacMillan on an expedition to Labrador in 1934. Most of the pictures are of native birds and nesting sites.

MD —US NAVAL ACADEMY, Nimitz Library, Annapolis, 21402. Alice S Creighton, Assistant Librn for Special Collections
Holdings: Pix
Notes: Approximately 15,000 pictures, incl portraits of naval officers and photographs of ships; also naval news photos.

MD —PEALE MUSEUM, Municipal Museum of Baltimore, 225 Holiday St, Baltimore, 21202. Nancy Brennan, Dir; Richard Flint, Cur Prints and Photos
Holdings: Cat Maps Pix
Notes: Pictorial history of Baltimore. Collection of 100,000 items incl: T E Hambleton Collection of Historical Prints; A Aubrey Bodine Photographic Collection; John Dubas Collection of Photographs. Many original photographic negatives.

MD —STEAMSHIP HISTORICAL SOCIETY OF AMERICA (SSHSA), University of Baltimore Library, 1420 Maryland Ave, Baltimore, 21201.
Holdings: Vols (3500) Cat Maps Pix Slides 16mm Films
Budget: ($15,000)
Notes: Powered Maritime Transportation Collection. Photo bank of over 15,000 negatives and 25,000 prints, arranged alphabetically by vessel name. Extensive blueprint and tracing collection. Collection documents history of steam navigation from the early 19th century to the present. Emphasis upon East Coast American vessels of late 19th and early 20th centuries and upon transatlantic vessels. Some coverage of Great Lakes and inland river steamboats. Very little about sailing vessels. No published catalog. Books listed in OCLC. Collection located at University of Baltimore. Address for Society is 414 Pelton Ave, Staten Island, NY 10310, attention: Alice S Wilson, Secretary and SSHSA Librn.

MD —UNIVERSITY OF BALTIMORE, Langsdale Library, 1420 Maryland Ave, Baltimore, 21201. Gerry Watkins, Head of Special Collections Dept
Holdings: Pix
Notes: Photographs, plates and pictures of Baltimore and other areas (1890-1909); many on the Baltimore fire.

MD —UNIVERSITY OF MARYLAND, BALTIMORE COUNTY, Albin O Kuhn Library and Gallery, Edward L Bafford Photography Collection, 5401 Wilkens Ave, Baltimore, 21228. Tom Beck, Cur
Holdings: Vols (3000) Cat Pix Slides Uncat
Notes: The Edward L Bafford Photography Collection contains more than 200,000 images, negatives, cameras and books representing the entire history and aesthetics of photography. The theme of the collection is photography as a social force, as represented by the 4000 photographs and negatives by Lewis Hine and by William Henry Jackson's *Photographs of the Yellowstone National Park and Views of Montana and Wyoming Territories*. John Thomson's *Street Life in London* and Alexander Gardner's *Photographic Sketchbook of the War* are representative of the book collections. There are also a large number of photographs by both 19th and 20th century photographers, such as Ansel Adams, Diane Arbus, Edward Bafford, Felice Beato, George Bretz, Lucien Clergue, Barbara Crane, Edward Curtis, Robert Frank, Roland Freeman, John Gossage, Lotte Jacobi, Eadweard Muybridge, AddisonScurlock, Jaromir Stephany, Alfred Stieglitz, Gary Winogrand and many others. In addition, UMBC has extensive collections of news and wire photographs, over 500 photographs form the Arctic expeditions of Admiral Robert Peary, and images of Baltimore from the Hughes Company studio ca 1910 and the East Baltimore Documentary Project, 1980.

MD —NATIONAL LIBRARY OF MEDICINE, 8600 Rockville Pike, Bethesda, 20209. Harold M Schoolinam, Actg Dir
Holdings: Vols (3,150,000) Cat Mss Pix Audiotapes Videotapes 16mm Films Filmstrips Microforms
Budget: ($46,400)
Notes: The world's largest medical library. Materials are collected exhaustively in some 40 biomedical areas and, to a lesser degree, in related subject areas such as general chemistry, physics, zoology, botany, and instrumentation. Holdings include 82,000 monographic volumes, pre-1871; 438,000 monographic volumes, 1871-present; 714,000 bound serial volumes; 281,000 theses; 172,000 pamphlets; 1,207,000 manuscripts; 156,000 microforms; 12,000 audiovisuals; and 75,000 prints and photographs. Pre-1871 material is in a separate historical collection. Approximately 24,000 serial titles are currenlty received.

MD —UNIVERSITY OF MARYLAND, Library, Archives & Manuscripts Dept, College Park, 20742. Mary A Boccaccio, Head
Holdings: Mss Pix
Notes: University of Maryland publications and archives; collections of organizational papers (eg, Baltimore & Ohio Railroad; various organizations concerned with the Chesapeake Bay and environs; various labor unions, particularly those involving the tobacco industry), mostly associated with Maryland; collections of papers and mss associated with literary and public figures (eg, the late Senator Miliard Tydings); oral histories relating to the archival and mss collections; associated memorabilia; photographs, mainly associated with Maryland. A guide to collections of personal, family, and organizational papers relating to Maryland is being prepared.

†MA —JOHN F KENNEDY LIBRARY, Columbia Point, Boston, 02125. Dan H Fenn Jr, Dir
Holdings: Vols 20,000 Cat Mss Maps Pix Slides Phonorecords Audiotapes Videotapes 16mm Films Microforms
Notes: The major collection about JFK, his life, family and administration. It contains personal papers, audiovisual materials, books, oral history interviews. Collection is described in "Historical Materials in the John F Kennedy Library." "The Kennedy Collection," a subject guide to the book collection, is available for sale.

MA —SOCIETY FOR THE PRESERVATION OF NEW ENGLAND ANTIQUITIES, Library, 141 Cambridge St, Boston, 02114. Ellie Reichlin, Librn & Cur of Photographic Collections
Holdings: Vols (3000) Cat Pix Microforms
Budget: ($75,000)
Notes: Photograph collections, all media (incl daguerreotypes, ambrotypes, etc, stereographic views, carte de visite) depicting New England buildings; interiors; street and town views; occupations; pastimes; transport and personalities. Covers 1840s-1930s, with some more recent additons. Amateur and professional photographers represented. Cataloged in part, otherwise arranged by localities, subject, personal name. Special collections incl: marine photographs by N L Stebbins and Henry Peabody (1880s-1920s); Boston and Albany railroad photographic archive, early 1900s; Quabbin Valley views; historic American Buildings Survey photographs (17th to early 19th century architecture) by Arthur Haskell; Baldwin Coolidge collection, and many others. Size: 500,000 prints, ca 75,000 negatives (glass plates and copy negs). These are cataloged. Some special indexes incllandscape design (arbors, conservatories, flower beds, bandstands etc); photographers represented; architects represented (partial), and pending, interiors (specific features of); occupations.

MA —SOCIETY FOR THE PRESERVATION OF NEW ENGLAND ANTIQUITIES, Library, 141 Cambridge St, Boston, 02114. Ellie Reichlin, Librn & Cur of Photographic Collections
Notes: (1) Halliday Historic Photograph Company (1800-ca 1912): emphasis on 17th-19th century structures in Massachusetts. Some original negatives. 3000 pieces; no index. (2) New England News Company (ca 1904-1913): views of vernacular housing, business districts, public buildings and manufacturing plants in southern and eastern Massachusetts, New Hampshire and Maine prepared for eventual use as postcards; publicizes small towns which might have otherwise remained obscure. Ca 3500 pieces. (3) SPNEA-owned Historic Properties (1910-present): inventory photographs, primarily of interiors and construction details. Ca 3000 pieces; continually updated.

MA —HARVARD UNIVERSITY LIBRARY, Theatre Collection, Cambridge, 02138. Jeanne T Newlin, Cur
Notes: One of the largest existing collections of playbills, programs, prints, photographs, promptbooks, and other materials relating to the performing arts, the scope is worldwide; resources on the English-speaking stage of the 18th and 19th centuries are unequalled. Incl materials on ballet and modern dance, the circus, magic, minstrel shows, cinema, and pantomime. For description, see *Harvard Library Bulletin*, VI (1925): pp 281-301. Also, papers of Robert E Sherwood (1896-1955), John Mason Bowers, George Pierce Baker, Edward Sheldon, Percy Mackaye; Angus McBean collection of photographs of the London Stage, 1937-1965; Alix Jeffry collection of photographs of the Off-Broadway Theatre; and others.

MA —MASSACHUSETTS INSTITUTE OF TECHNOLOGY MUSEUM, Hart Nautical Collections, 77 Massachusetts Ave, Rm 5-329, Cambridge, 02139. John W Waterhouse, Cur
Holdings: Vols (800) Cat Maps Pix
Notes: Ship and marine engineering development. Museum is under jurisdiction of MIT's Dept of Ocean Engineering. Collection incl various collections of prints and photographs of ships and yachts; working drawings from the Herreshoff Manufacturing Co, 1870-1945, and of the George Lawley and Son Corp; working drawings and models from the Munro, Owen, and Paine Collections.

MA —CONCORD FREE PUBLIC LIBRARY, 129 Main St, Concord, 01742. Rose Marie Mitten, Dir
Holdings: Cat Mss Maps Pix Slides
Notes: Extensive collection.

MA —HISTORIC DEERFIELD-POCUMTUCK VALLEY MEMORIAL

PHOTOGRAPHS—COLLECTIONS
(cont.)

ASSOCIATION, Libraries, Memorial St, Box 53, Deerfield, 01342. David R Proper, Librn
Holdings: Vols (17,000) Cat Mss Maps Pix Microforms
Notes: Local and regional history, especially western Massachusetts. Also, remnants of several collection of books available to early Deerfield and Greenfield residents. Strong ms collection dealing with the region's families, businesses, etc. These consist of sermons, diaries, town and church records, voluntary societies' archives, etc. Extensive collection of photographs of the people and buildings of Deerfield and its environs, and travels in Maine, California, and England (1880s to 1920s). Also, large collection of glassplate negatives. Houses the Connecticut Valley Bibliography, a comprehensive card file on the history and culture of the Connecticut Valley of Massachusetts.

MA —LENOX LIBRARY ASSOCIATION, Main St, Lenox, 01240. Denis J Lesieur, Dir
Holdings: Pix
Notes: Edwin Hale Lincoln, (1848-1938), Pittsfield photographer. Collection contains glass plate negatives and platinum prints concentrating on Lenox estates, ca 1883-1933. Publication: *A Pride of Places; Lenox Summer Cottages 1883-1933*, Donald T Oakes, ed (Lenox Library Association, 1981).

MA —CHINA TRADE MUSEUM, Library, 215 Adams St, Milton, 02186. Lisa L Gwirtzman, Librn
Notes: Incl an indexed masterpiece collection of photographs of China.

MA —BRANDEIS UNIVERSITY, Goldfarb Library, 415 South St, Waltham, 02154. Bessie Hahn, Dir
Notes: Approx 8 linear ft of photographs of famous American personage taken by Carl Van Vechten. The collection is unprocessed, spring 1984.

MI —UNIVERSITY OF MICHIGAN, Library, Dept of Rare Books & Special Collections, Ann Arbor, 48109. Robert J Starring, Head
Holdings: Cat Mss Maps Pix
Notes: Includes

MI —UNIVERSITY OF MICHIGAN, Bentley Historical Library, Michigan Historical Collections, 1150 Beal Ave, Ann Arbor, 48109. Francis X Blovin Jr, Dir
Holdings: Vols (45,000) Cat Mss Maps Pix Phonorecords Audiotapes Videotapes 16mm Films Microforms
Budget: ($302,000)
Notes: A modern ms archives collecting original source material pertaining to Michigan, its people, its institutions and the University of Michigan. Emphasizes the accumulations of personal papers of historically important persons, incl files of correspondence, diaries and journals as well as the records of significant Michigan institutions. At present the collections contain 45,000 printed vols, 40,000,000 mss items, 3500 maps and 500,000 photographs. The library maintains its own catalog and published in 1976 a revised, 2nd updated *Guide to the Michigan Historical Collections*. Special areas of interest to the collections are Philippine Islands history, the history of the temperance and prohibition movement in the US. Immigration to Michigan, business history, church history, and US-China relations.

MI —DETROIT PUBLIC LIBRARY, Burton Historical Collection, 5201 Woodward Ave, Detroit, 48202. Alice Dalligan, Chief
Notes: Thousands of pictures of Detroit scenes and people make up the Burton picture files. Many books, magazines, and newspapers have been indexed for illustrations. A large collection of postcards shows how city and state looked to tourists of earlier days.

MI —WAYNE STATE UNIVERSITY, Walter P Reuther Library, Archives of Labor & Urban Affairs, Detroit, 48202. Philip Mason, Dir
Notes: An inconographic collection, containing more than 12,000 photographs, closely parallels the events and people described in the labor collections. Tapes, films, and phonograph records pertaining to a myriad of labor topics are also available. Interested researchers are invited to utilize these audio-visual materials in their studies.

MI —AMERICAN MUSEUM OF MAGIC, 107 East Michigan Ave, Mar·hall, 49608. Robert Lund; Elaine Lund
Notes: The Irving Desfor Collection of 40,000 photographs of magicians. In addition to the Desfor photographs, this collection consists of approx 250,000 books, magazines, newspaper clippings, letters, programs, advertising material, posters, films, authors' manuscripts, paintings and prints, apparatus, coins and tokens, toys, phonograph records and tape recordings, statuary, sheet music, costumes and other material, all on the subject of magic and magicians. The collection is privately owned by Robert and Elaine Lund.

MN —NORTHEAST MINNESOTA HISTORICAL CENTER, University of Minnesota, Duluth, Library 375, Duluth, 55812. Patricia Maus, Administrator
Notes: The Northeast Minnesota Historical Center is jointly maintained by the University of Minnesota, Duluth, and the St Louis County Historical Society. Local and regional history collections with emphasis on transportation, lumbering, mining. Photograph collection. Photocopy service available.

MN —MINNEAPOLIS PUBLIC LIBRARY & INFORMATION CENTER, Minneapolis History Collection, 300 Nicollet Mall, Minneapolis, 55401. Dorothy M Burke, Librn
Holdings: Vols (20,000) Cat Mss Maps Pix Slides Phonorecords Audiotapes
Budget: ($850)
Notes: Collection contains print and film materials pertaining to Minneapolis, includes some Minnesota history. Also have 29 five-drawer legal files of clips and ephemeral materials, and direct access to the 119-file morgue of the old *Minneapolis Times*, a newspaper which ceased publishing in 1948. This is especially useful for items covering the 20s, 30s and 40s. Special card indexes to plates in architectural serials (local), houses, buildings, streets, parks, etc; also indexes to 10-20 local newspapers and magazines. Collection of about 60 neighborhood newspapers (current and retrospective) and about 1000 maps and atlases; nearly 250,000 pictures; early (1859-1920) city directories.

MN —MINNESOTA HISTORICAL SOCIETY LIBRARY, 690 Cedar St, Saint Paul, 55101. Patricia C Harpole, Chief of Reference Library; Bonnie G Wilson, Head of Special Libraries
Notes: Photographs, posters, art - over 150,000 pictorial works - can be found in the Audio-Visual Library of the Minnesota Historical Society. The collection's emphasis is on Minnesota from the mid-1880's to the present day. Many aspects of American life can be researched in this collection.

MO —WASHINGTON UNIVERSITY, Libraries, Special Collections Dept, Campus Box 1061, St Louis, 63130.
Holdings: //
Notes: Records of the St Louis Car Company, 1887-1973, incl the transportation manufacturing enterprise's files of over 20,000 photographs and negatives of the firm's products; over 2000 original tracings of railroad and street car equipment. Also printed material about the firm, and catalogs published by the company from 1904 to 1965.

NE —ADAMS COUNTY HISTORICAL SOCIETY, Library, 1330 N Burlington Ave, Hastings, 68901. Corinne Cody, Secretary
Holdings: Vols (200) Cat Mss Maps Pix Slides Phonorecords Audiotapes Videotapes 16mm Films Microforms
Budget: ($5000)
Notes: The most noteworthy portions of the Adams County Collection are the church and school records from the county, useful for case studies on many aspects of life on the Great Plains. The photographic collection is intensively indexed. A catalog and a guide to Adams County material available locally are in progress.

NE —WESTERN HERITAGE MUSEUM, 801 S Tenth St, Omaha, 68108. Jane G Murray, Photo-Archivist
Holdings: Pix
Budget: ($750,000)
Notes: Approximately 120,000 photographs and glass negatives from the: Bostwick-Frohardt Photography Collection, The John S Savage Collection and the Rinehart-Marsden Collection.

NV —UNIVERSITY OF NEVADA, RENO, University Library, Special Collections Dept, Reno, 89557. Robert E Blesse, Head
Holdings: Vols 1100 Mss Pix
Notes: Incl over 5000 photographs, government documents, periodicals, 80 cubic feet, mss, and audiotapes. The Great Basin Indian Collection contains materials on the anthropology, archaeology, and ethnohistory of the Great Basin region. Materials are collected for a defined group of 65 tribes incl Washo, Shoshone, Northern and Southern Paiute, the major tribes of the region. Collection of importance incl the Sven Liljeblad Collection, linguistics and ethnography; papers of US agent Lorenzo D Greel, 1902-22; Robert Leland Collection, Indian water rights.
See also entries under Mines and Mining; Nevada - History.

NH —MANCHESTER HISTORIC ASSOCIATION, Library, 129 Amherst St, Manchester, 03104. Elizabeth Lessard, Librn
Notes: Business and production records of the Amoskeag Manufacturing Company (1831-1936); incl real estate holdings; personnel name index (70,000 pieces; biographies of employees); insurance surveys, etc. Photographs, glass negatives (1414 pieces), cynotypes, reproductions of glass negatives (3 volumes), prints (3 volumes and 500 items).

NH —STRAWBERY BANKE, Thayer Cumings Historical Reference Library, Portsmouth, 03801. Nicole R Osborn, Librn
Notes: The Library is a small, highly specialized library with holdings in American art, architecture and decorative arts. The collection is especially strong in the American decorative arts, with additional concentration in European decorative arts. In addition, the collection contains books on American painting, American architecture, archaeology, technology, maritime history and boatbuilding, landscape gardening and design, as well as books on local and regional history and social and material culture of the 17th-19th centuries. Collection of mss microfilm and documents is related to important properties and personages of Portsmouth and the surrounding area. Incl over 2000 photographs of Portsmouth in early 1900's.

NM —UNIVERSITY OF NEW MEXICO, Zimmerman Library, Albuquerque, 87131.
Holdings: Mss Pix
Notes: Entire professional library and archives of John Gaw Meem, architect of the Southwest. Incl pictures of many buildings taken by noted photographers.

NM —MUSEUM OF NEW MEXICO, Photo Archives, Box 2087, Santa Fe, 87503. Arthur L Olivas, Cur; Richard Rudisill, Photo Historian
Holdings: Cat Pix Slides
Budget: ($9000)

Notes: 90,000 photographs, cataloged, and 1000 slides. Photographs may be ordered as research copies for set fees. Reproduction or publication requires written permission plus additional required fees. Incl. special groups of photographs, e.g. T. Harmon Parkhurst Collection-ca. 15,000 photos, 1915-1950, Southwest Indians, scenic views, town views; H. F. Robinson Collection-ca. 1000 items, ca. 1910-1920, Southwest Indians, esp. Hopi and Blackfoot; Ben Wittick Collection-ca. 1500 items, 1879-1903, Southwest Indians, military, town

PHOTOGRAPHS—COLLECTIONS (cont.)

views. Many other of the important early photographers are represented, especially large collections of the work of G. C. Bennett, William H. Brown, Dana B. Chase, Edward S. Curtis, H. H. Dorman, Rev. J. C. Gullette, P. E. Harroun, William H. Jackson, Charles F. Lummis, Jesse L. Nussbaum, Henry A. Schmidt, and about a hundred others.

NY —STATE UNIVERSITY OF NEW YORK, BINGHAMTON, Glenn G Bartle Library, Binghamton, 13901. Marion Hanscom, Special Collections Librn
Holdings: Cat Pix
Budget: ($8000)
Notes: Max Reinhardt Archive. Library has extensive (approx 250,000 items) archival material relating to Max Reinhardt, as well as his personal library. This personal library is not a subject collection per se, but contains much information about German theater in the 20th century. The archival material contains letters, prompt books, photographs, playbills, etc.

NY —ADIRONDACK HISTORICAL ASSOCIATION, Museum Library, Blue Mountain Lake, 12812. Jerold Pepper, Librn
Holdings: Vols (7500) Cat Mss Maps Pix Phonorecords Audiotapes 16mm Films Microforms
Notes: Anything about the Adirondacks--history, people, economics, places, things. Strong in Adirondack art, outdoor recreation, logging, small boats. Resources incl more than 1000 maps, 40,000 pictures, 1600 microfilm reels, 576 linear ft of ms material, and 12 cabinets of VF ephemera, etc.

NY —NEW YORK BOTANICAL GARDEN LIBRARY, Bronx, 10458. Charles R Long, Asst Vice Pres & Dir
Notes: One of the largest botanical collections in the world. Over 900,000 items. Covers botany (150,000 vols), botanists (3000), horticulture (45,000) plant diseases (25,000), plant physiology (15,000), history of botany (1500), conservation of natural resources (15,000), gardening (13,000), paleobotany (7000), ecology (20,000), forestry (5000) medical botany (3000), agriculture (9000) and biology (20,000). Reference library; materials do not circulate, except for member circulating collection (1200) and standard inter-library loan. About 5000 vols uncataloged. Incl art, books, serials, pamphlets, archives and manuscripts, vertical files, microfiche and microfilm, nursery and seed catalogs, photographs, paintings, prints, drawings and engravings. Covers all areas of botanical sciences. This is an OCLC library with fullresource services incl photocopying and photography.

NY —BROOKLYN PUBLIC LIBRARY, Brooklyn Collection, Grand Army Plaza, Flatbush Ave and Eastern Parkway, Brooklyn, 11238.
Notes: More than 3000 books, pamphlets, and documents cover such topics as history, religion, literature, and politics. Microfilm copies of now defunct Brooklyn daily newspapers as well as recent issues of local Brooklyn papers. Incl the morgue of the *Brooklyn Daily Eagle* (1841-1955). Also, more than 25,000 photographs of Brooklyn people, places, and things dating from 1870 to the present, incl those by George Brainard and Daniel Berry Austin. Old town records, vertical files, maps, and institutional archives.

NY —LONG ISLAND HISTORICAL SOCIETY, 128 Pierrepont St, at Clinton St, Brooklyn, 11201.
Notes: Books and pamphlets relating to the history of Brooklyn. Over 350 newspapers and periodical resources, incl *The Long Island Star* (1809-1863) and *Williamsburgh*

Gazette (1835-1853). 10,000 photographs. Paintings, prints, and broadsides. More than 1400 mss collections relating primarily to Brooklyn, dating from 1650 to 1980s. 750 maps and atlases, artifacts, archives, and Decorative Arts collections. Two published guides to Manuscripts: *Calendar of Manuscripts: 1783-1783*, LIHS by Karin N Mango. 1980. Also, *A Guide to Brooklyn Manuscripts in the Long Island Historical Society*. Prepared by Brooklyn Rediscovery, a program of the Brooklyn Educational and Cultural Alliance. 1980. Also, guide to Museum Exhibit, *Brooklyn Before the Bridge - American paintings from the Long Island Historical Society*. Published by Brooklyn Museum. 1982.

NY —STATE UNIVERSITY OF NEW YORK, STONY BROOK, Health Sciences Library, PO Box 66, East Setauket, 11733.
Notes: Slide collection of Historical Medical Photographs is an archive of 3000 slides pertaining to the history of medical care in America--Medical and public health activities from the 1850s to the 1950s. An illustrated catalogue, published by Greenwood Press, is scheduled for 1984.

NY —STATE UNIVERSITY OF NEW YORK, COLLEGE OF ARTS & SCIENCE AT GENESEO, Milne Library, Geneseo, 14454. William T Lane, Head of Information Services & Archivist
Holdings: // Pix
Notes: The Martha Blow Wadsworth Collection. Photographs taken or collected by Mrs Wadsworth from the 1890s to around 1910. There are 33 albums containing 4561 mounted photographs, and 3 boxes containing 345 hand-tinted lantern slides. Subjects include horseback rides from Washington, DC to Avon, NY (1905-1909); US Army packtrain trips in the Southwestern US (1907-1910); Hopi, Navajo, and Zuni Indians (1910); motor trip through France and England (1909); Panama Canal Construction; Alaskan boundary survey trip; and the Wadsworth family of Livingston County, NY. There are no negatives. Inventory in repository. Open to qualified investigators with permission of archivist. Gift of Michael Moukhanoff, Ashantee, NY, 1976.

NY —CORNELL UNIVERSITY LIBRARIES, Collection of Regional History, Dept of Manuscripts and Univ Archives, Ithaca, 14853.
Notes: Incl photos (1865-1962) relating to all phases of activities at Cornell University, NY.

NY —AMERICAN INSTITUTE OF PHYSICS, Center for the History of Physics, Niels Bohr Library, 335 E 45 St, New York, 10017. John Aubry, Librn
Holdings: Vols (16,000) Cat Mss Pix Slides Phonorecords Audiotapes 16mm Films Microforms
Notes: The Library contains an extensive collection of published works relating to the history of modern physics and astronomy. Its archives incl letter, notebooks and other papers of physicists, as well as the records of leading American physics societies and institutions. Its collections of ms autobiographies, oral history interviews, and other tape recordings, and pictorial materials (incl unpublished film footage) are unrivaled in the field of history of science. It maintains the International Catalog of Sources for History of Physics and and Astronomy.

NY —AMERICAN MUSEUM OF NATURAL HISTORY, Library Services Dept, Central Park W & 79th St, New York, 10024. Nina J Root, Chairwoman; Mary Genett, Asst Librn for Reference Services
Holdings: Cat Pix
Notes: The Photographic Collection consist of over 500,000 black-and-white prints and almost 50,000 color transparencies and slides in this and many other subjects. Many from Museum expeditions and fieldwork. Examples of human beings, scenery, animals, plants and minerals from all over the world, as well as visual documentation of scientific phenomena. Subject areas covered incl anthropology, archeology, astronomy, some botany, ecology, geography and travel,

geology, the history of natural history, mineralogy, gemstones, paleontology, fossils, primitive art, scientists, and zoology.

NY —THE CLOISTERS, Metropolitan Museum of Art (Branch), Fort Tryon Park, New York, 10040. Suse C Childs, Librn
Holdings: Vols (5000) Cat Mss Pix Slides
Notes: A branch of the Metropolitan Museum of Art devoted solely to the literature of medieval art. Incl 16,000 slides and 5000 photographs with unique strengths in certain aspects of medieval art.

NY —COLUMBIA UNIVERSITY LIBRARIES, Avery Architectural and Fine Arts Library, 201 Avery Hall, New York, 10027. Angela Giral, Librn
Notes: Photograph albums which show the steps in the constructionof a building from the excavation to the finished structure ("A Progress series"). Other photograph albums which record the work of architectural firms.

†NY —COLUMBIA UNIVERSITY LIBRARIES, Butler Library, Rare Book and Manuscript Library, 535 W 114 St, New York, 10027.
Notes: Papers of the American Bureau for Medical Aid to China, incl correspondence, memoranda, reports, minutes, membership and financial records, photographs, posters and printed material. Approx 45,000 pieces. Also, some 6000 photographs of Chinese medical colleges, hospitals, laboratories, and personnel.

NY —MUSEUM OF MODERN ART, Library, 11 W 53 St, New York, 10019. Clive Phillpot, Library Dir
Notes: Art of the 20th and latter half of the 19th century (painting, sculpture, drawings and prints, architecture, photography, film).

NY —MUSEUM OF THE CITY OF NEW YORK, Photo Archives, Fifth Ave & 103 St, New York, 10029. Esther Brumberg, Librn
Holdings: Mss Maps Pix
Notes: All aspects of New York City--history, costume, social life and customs, etc. Also, Byron Collection--about 10,000 prints, 1880-1930, of views of New York, commercial interiors, interiors and exteriors of private residences, social events, shipping, immigration; Wurts Collection--15,000 glass negatives, 1890-1940, mostly architectural; 100,000 Wurts Architectural Photographs, to be cataloged. Underhill Collection--about 900 glass negatives, mostly architectural, 1896-1936; McKim, Mead & White Collection--1000 glass negatives of the work of the firm, 1880-1915; and Berenice Abbott Collection, Changing New York--about 350 negatives taken by Miss Abbott for the Federal Arts Project, 1930s. Other FAP photographs incl a series on Coney Island, one on Harlem, Sewing Project, and Sabbath Studies.

NY —NEW YORK HISTORICAL SOCIETY, Library, 170 Central Park W, New York, 10024. James Gregory, Librn
Holdings: Mss Pix
Notes: Incl original mss, illustrative materials, etc.

NY —NEW YORK PUBLIC LIBRARY, Performing Arts Research Center, Billy Rose Theatre Collection, 111 Amsterdam Ave, New York, 10023. Dorothy L Swerdlove, Cur
Holdings: Cat
Notes: Theatre Collection received part of the Friedman-Abeles photograph archive when the partners decided to split up into separate companies.

NY —NEW YORK PUBLIC LIBRARY, Performing Arts Research Center, Dance Collection, 111 Amsterdam Ave, New York, 10023. Genevieve Oswald, Cur

PHOTOGRAPHS—COLLECTIONS
(cont.)

NY —NEW YORK PUBLIC LIBRARY, Local History and Genealogy Div, Fifth Ave & 42 St, New York, 10018. Gunther E Pohl, Chief
Holdings: Vols (160,000) Cat Pix
Budget: ($38,548)
Notes: Extensive collection of county, city, town and village histories of the United States. All other local, state, and national histories are part of the General Research and Humanities Division. Collection includes over 60,000 mounted photographs of New York City views arranged by address and/or subject. 20,000 film and glass plate negatives depicting NYC tenement housing conditions (1902-1938). Also the Lloyd L Acker collection of 48,000 film negatives depicting NYC buildings, 1935-1975. Collection of Lewis W Hine photographic prints made by the photographer on immigration, child labor, women at work and men at work. Eugene Armbruster Collection of Long Island views; D B Austin's photographs of Long Island and western Americana; scrapbooks, and postcards of NYC and other US localities (200,000). See United States Local History Catalog (Boston: GK Hall, 1974), 2 vols. Stereophotographic collection (18,000 items), housed in the Art, Prints and Photographs Division, is worldwide in scope of subjects. Stereoscopes are available for viewing purposes.

NY —SCHOLASTIC MAGAZINES, Editorial Library, 730 Broadway, New York, 10003. Lucy Evankow, Chief Librn
Holdings: Cat
Notes: TV back to the 1950s; 1940s motion pictures; black and white photographs; political cartoons back to the 1940s-50s; curriculum educations; software.

NY —YIVO INSTITUTE FOR JEWISH RESEARCH, Library & Archives, 1048 Fifth Ave, New York, 10028. Dina Abramowicz, Librn; Marek Web, Archivist
Holdings: Cat Mss Pix Slides
Notes: Yiddish drama in the original and in English translation from its 19th-century beginnings to the present; the Yiddish theatre in the Soviet Union and the theatrical activities in the ghettos during the Nazi regime; special collections of Sholem Pereimuter, Mendl Elkin, Maurice Schwartz, Abraham Goldfaden, Jacob Gordin, and Mark Schweid; records of the Union of Jewish Actors in Poland between the two world wars; the Vilna YIVO Collection of posters, playbills, and photographs; recordings.

NY —STATE UNIVERSITY OF NEW YORK, COLLEGE AT PLATTSBURGH, Feinberg Library, Special Collections, 153 Hawkins Hall, Plattsburgh, 12901. Joseph G Swinyer, Librn
Holdings: Vols (3355) Cat
See also entry under New York (State) - History

NY —SUFFOLK COUNTY HISTORICAL SOCIETY, Library, 300 W Main St, Riverhead, 11901. Betty Carpenter, Librn
Holdings: Vols (15,000) Cat Mss Maps Pix
Notes: Fullerton Photograph Collection. Approx 2000 photographic plate negatives.

NY —MARGARET WOODBURY STRONG MUSEUM, 1 Manhattan Square, Rochester, 14607.

Holdings: Vols (20,000) Periodicals
Notes: The Margaret Woodbury Strong Museum Library contains a collection of approx 20,000 books, periodicals and ephemera of and concerning the 19th and early 20th centuries. A large part of the library's holdings reflect the interests of Margaret Strong and her family: domestic life and literature of the 19th century and world travel, with particular emphasis on the Orient. The library's resources are available to all visitors for research. Book stacks and rare book storage are not open for browsing and do not circulate, but facilities are provided in reading room for study.

NY —UNIVERSITY OF ROCHESTER, Rush Rhees Library, Department of Rare Books and Special Collections, Rochester, 14627. Peter Dzwonkoski, Librn
Holdings: Vols 600 Cat Pix
Notes: Hubbell Collection of books illustrated with mounted photographs, 1850-1875, also photographs in several manuscript collections and including George Eastman Papers, Henry A Ward Papers; photographs of Rochester, New York and other upstate New York areas.

NY —VISUAL STUDIES WORKSHOP, Research Center, 31 Prince St, Rochester, 14607. Linn Underhill, Coordr; Robert Bretz, Librn
Holdings: Vols (8000) Cat Pix Slides Audiotapes Videotapes
Notes: Strong emphasis on photography (over 1,000,000 pictures) and the photographic arts in many subject areas incl in this volume. Heavy emphasis on early photographic processes and collections of examples of them. Also collections of individual photographers' works.

NY —STATE UNIVERSITY OF NEW YORK, STONY BROOK, Melville Library, Dept of Special Collections, Stony Brook, 11794. Evert Volkersz, Head
Holdings: Vols 40 Cat Pix
Notes: Forty albums combining detailed pencil drawings of Long Island Railroad tracks and explanatory notes with more than 5000 identified photographs; 300 timetables, 1895-date; and related materials.

NY —SYRACUSE UNIVERSITY LIBRARIES, Ernest S Bird Library, George Arents Research Library for Special Collections, Syracuse, 13210. Carolyn A Davis, Manuscripts Librn; Amy S Doherty, University Archivist; Mark F Weimer, Rare Book Librn
Notes: The George Arents Research Library for Special Collections at Syracuse University contains the papers of Margaret Bourke-White, Clara Sipprell, Gerda Peterich, Edward John Wall, Louis Fabian Bachrach, Joseph Costa (National Press Photographers Association), the University Archives Photographic Collection, and other misc photographs.

NC —PACK MEMORIAL PUBLIC LIBRARY, North Carolina Collection, 67 Haywood St, Asheville, 28801. John Toms, Dept Head
Holdings: Pix
Notes: Collection incl early ms accounts of western North Carolina; Civil War letters; letters, diary, and mss of Horace Kephart; mss of Thomas Dixon; Thomas Wolfe Collection; contemporary North Carolina authors; North Carolina censuses, 1790-1910; rare newspapers and runs of local newspapers, and clippings from Asheville newspapers, from 1920s; early maps; information on Cherokee Indians; approx

400 vols of North Carolina genealogy and file of unpublished genealogies. Collection concentrates on western North Carolina, with some general Appalachian materials. Incl 4000 local and state photographs, separate catalog.

ND —NORTH DAKOTA STATE UNIVERSITY, Library, Fargo, 58105. John E Bye, Archivist
Holdings: Vols (2500) Cat Mss Maps Pix
Budget: ($14,000)
Notes: The Collection is administered by the North Dakota Institute for Regional Studies. It contains materials on North Dakota history, especially the Red River Valley, with emphasis on bonanza farming, pioneer life, agriculture, local history, literary figures, business, Fargo, ND, and some political collections, particularly of the Nonpartisan League. Also, there is an extensive photographic collection covering the pioneer to post-World War I period and includes the "Hultstrand 'History in Pictures' Collection" of sod houses, pioneer life and farming. For the small collections, there has been published, Guide to the Small Collection Manuscripts of the North Dakota Institute for Regional Studies, by John E Bye, 1977.

OH —BOWLING GREEN STATE UNIVERSITY, Library, Popular Culture Library, Bowling Green, 43403.
Notes: Extensive holdings of Big-Little books, comic books, matchbook covers, picture postcards, personal scrapbooks, trading cards, posters, magazines, film pressbooks, juvenile series novels and popular literature.

OH —CLEVELAND PUBLIC LIBRARY, History and Geography Department, 325 Superior Ave, Cleveland, 44114. JoAnn Petrello, Head
Notes: This collection of 200,000 newsworthy glossy photographs from the Newspaper Enterprise Association spans five decades 1920-1970. The collection is a social and historical pictorial exposition, international in scope.

OH —RUTHERFORD B HAYES LIBRARY, 1337 Hayes Ave, Fremont, 43420. Watt P Marchman, Dir
Holdings: Vols 10,000 Cat Mss Maps Pix Slides Audiotapes Microforms
Notes: The Rutherford B Hayes Family Collections. The collections comprise papers, books, correspondence, diaries, speeches, account books, financial and real estate records, law cases, ephemera, and memorabilia of members of the Rutherford B Hayes family; his wife, Lucy Webb Hayes; their children: Birchard Austin Hayes; Webb C Hayes I; Rutherford Platt Hayes; Scott Russell Hayes; Fanny Hayes; grandchildren: Dalton Hayes; Webb C Hayes, II; daughter-in-law, Mary Miller Hayes. Mss of the collection are described in Guide to Manuscripts of the Ohio Historical Society, 208, 209, 210, 211, 212, 214, 216, 217, 218, 219. Indexed, listed. The collections are housed in the mss division and newspapers division. Ms materials of 256 linear feet; 50,000 pictures; slides; tapes; moving pictures, maps. The papers of Rutherford Birchard Hayes available on 304 rolls of microfilm. The collection described in Guide to the Microfilm Edition of the Papers of Rutherford Birchard Hayes, the Nineteenth President of the United States. Fremont, Ohio: The Rutherford B Hayes Presidential Center, 1983. In addition, the Great Lakes Marine Collection, incl Capt Frank E Hamilton Collection; Great Lakes boats and shipping. Incl 300 charts, over 20,000 pictures (with 2500 negatives, 30 glass plates). Index and finding aids with the collection.

OH —OBERLIN COLLEGE LIBRARY, Clarence Ward Art Library, Slide Library, Oberlin, 44074.
Holdings: Vols (62,000) Cat Pix Microforms
Notes: Original photographs of works of art collected by Prof Ellen Johnson. Formerly mounted photographs were part of the Art Library; now, however, they are under the care of the Slide Library, which is part of the Art Department.

OK —US ARMY FIELD ARTILLERY SCHOOL LIBRARY, Morris Swett Library,

PHOTOGRAPHS—COLLECTIONS
(cont.)

Snow Hall, Fort Sill, 73503. Lester L Miller Jr, Chief Librn
Notes: Incl data on Fort Sill, Indian Territory, settlement of Kiowa, Apache and Commanche tribes, imprisonment of Geronimo, Oklahoma territory, settlement of Lawton. Unit histories, incl 10th Cavalry (Buffalo Soldiers, a black unit that built Fort Sill); working papers of Sheridan, Grierson and other commanders; Field Artillery School. Photographs on army subjects, Fort Sill, Indians, Indian Territory, settlement of Southwest Oklahoma.

OK —MUSEUM OF THE GREAT PLAINS, Research Center, 601 Ferris, PO Box 68, Lawton, 73502. Steve Wilson, Dir; Paula Williams, Special Collections
Notes: Incl 30,000 photographs. Especially about settlement and Indians of Southwestern Oklahoma and Southern Plains.
See also entries under Great Plains; Oklahoma - History

OK —HTB TECHNICAL INFORMATION CENTER, PO Box 1845, Oklahoma City, 73101. Retha Robertson, Librn
Holdings: Vols (100) Cat Documents Pix Slides Audiotapes 16mm Films Filmstrips VF
Notes: Architecture and engineering of the US, especially. Extensive photograph collection, incl 3000 slides.

OR —LANE COUNTY MUSEUM, Library, 740 W 13 Ave, Eugene, 94701. Margret West, Cur of Special Collections
Holdings: Vols 250 Cat Mss Maps Pix Slides Audiotapes 16mm Films Microforms
Budget: $2000
Notes: Emphasis on Oregon and Lane County history. Collection of 10,000 photographs of Lane County; Kennell-Ellis photographers, 3500 commercial photographs of Eugene area, 1927-42. Also papers of John Whiteaker 1858-1944.

OR —UNIVERSITY OF OREGON LIBRARY, Special Collections Div, Eugene, 97403. Kenneth W Duckett, Curator
Holdings: Photographs
Notes: Incl 90,000 photographs and negatives. Areas of strength are Oregon, Pacific Northwest, Alaska, and the Yukon Territory, with lesser concentrations relating to Appalachia and the Far East, particularly China and Japan.

OR —UMATILLA COUNTY LIBRARY, 214 N Main St, Pendleton, 97801. Barbara L Bishop, Dir
Holdings: Vols (675) Cat Mss Pix Audiotapes 16mm Films Microforms
Notes: Oregon history, especially Umatila County. Lee Moorehouse photos (glass negatives)--1004 negatives, use restricted to professional photographers, copies may be made on premises only, also 3 rolls of microfilm of Moorehouse photos. Dr William McKay papers, 1830-1900, 14 folders, uncataloged, letters, coroner's reports (1885-86), miscellaneous papers, notes, memos and rough drafts, Army statements, receipts, accounts and business and personal receipts, accounts, 8 letters written by Donald McKay, one letter written December 7, 1880, by William F Cody. Early brands of Eastern Oregon, 1/2 reel microfilm. Some cassette recordings of interviews with early pioneers.

PA —ERIE COUNTY HISTORICAL SOCIETY LIBRARY, 417 State St, Erie, 16501. Helen Andrews, Librn
Notes: Iconographics of 11,000 glass negatives (mostly photos of Erie people.)

PA —ATHENAEUM OF PHILADELPHIA, 219 S Sixth St, Philadelphia, 19106. Roger W Moss Jr, Librn
Notes: Incl 450 drawings of Thomas Ustick Walter from 1804-1887; nineteenth century architecture and decorative art; 30,000 mss drawings; 20,000 photographs; one billion mss.

PA —COLLEGE OF PHYSICIANS OF PHILADELPHIA, Library, 19 S 22 St, Philadelphia, 19103. Christine Ruggere, Cur, Historical Collections
Holdings: Pix

PA —FRANKLIN INSTITUTE LIBRARY, Dept of Historical Programs, 20th St and Parkway, Philadelphia, 19103.
Holdings: 2500 Items
Notes: Julian P Scott Collection of photographs of scientists (1920-1938).

PA —LIBRARY COMPANY OF PHILADELPHIA, 1314 Locust St, Philadelphia, 19107. Edwin Wolf II, Librn; Kenneth Finkel, Cur of Prints
Notes: Incl 2500 prints by Joseph J Kelly's firm, The Photo-Illustrators; with a large proportion on the Sesquicentennial and other Philadelphia views.

PA —TEMPLE UNIVERSITY LIBRARIES, Special Collections Dept, Rare Books & Mss Section, Philadelphia, 19122. Thomas M Whitehead, Cur
Holdings: 15,000 Images
Notes: "Photojournalism Collection". Curated by George Brightbill and Elaine Clever. News photography archives: News films from two Philadelphia television stations WPVI (nee WFIL) 1947-date, and KYW, 1950-1960's; 1937-1972 photo-archives of the Philadelphia Inquirer newspaper and the Index, clipping file, photo-archive and library of the Evening Bulletin newspaper. Archival set of the Bulletin, 1847-1982.

PA —TEMPLE UNIVERSITY LIBRARIES, Special Collections Dept, Conwellana-Templana Collection, 13 & Berks St, Philadelphia, 19122. Miriam I Crawford, Cur
Holdings: Mss Pix Audiotapes 16mm Films
Budget: ($30,000)
Notes: Chiefly photographs, both negative and prints, scrapbooks and play programs, plus a few scripts, stage designs and promptbooks, the bulk of which document the productions of the Temple University Theater, 1930-1969, under the direction of Paul Randall. A small supplementary collection of miscellaneous theatrical programs given at the school, and a continuing collection of play programs and publicity materials of the University Theater since Randall's departure.

PA —PENNSYLVANIA STATE UNIVERSITY, Fred Lewis Pattee Library, Special Collections Dept, University Park, 16802. Charles Mann, Chief, Special Collections
Holdings: Vols (122,533) Cat Mss Maps Pix Slides Phonorecords Audiotapes Videotapes 16mm Films Microforms
Budget: ($37,000)
Notes: Special Collections and Rare Books includes several collections described separately. The holdings are particularly strong in literature, the 18th century, aeronautics, and traveller's views. Special strengths are Emblem Books, Utopias, Fantastic Fiction, Australiana, Fine Presses, Labor Archives, Landscape Architecture, Pennsylvaniana. These collections are strengthened by parallel holdings in the open stacks. It also includes the collections of the Penn State Room. Several mimeographed lists are available. Audiotapes are listed in Voices and Events, A Catalog of Audio Tapes (Pennsylvania State University Libraries, 1975), 45 pp.

PA —PENNSYLVANIA STATE UNIVERSITY, Fred Lewis Pattee Library, Life Sciences Library, University Park, 16802. Keith Roe, Head
Holdings: Vols (108,000) Cat Slides Microforms
Budget: ($147,170)
Notes: This collection is strong in periodical runs, particularly European learned societies and agriculture. It contains extensive collections of Experiment Station publications and has developed specialities in Mycology and Fusaria. There is also a special collection of 1105 glass slides on early Pennsylvania lumbering.

RI —PROVIDENCE PUBLIC LIBRARY, Rhode Island Collection, 150 Empire St, Providence, 02903. Jeanne L Richardson, Librn
Holdings: Vols (7400) Cat Maps Pix Microforms
Budget: ($1500)
Notes: Rhode Island Collection is divided

into five categories: books; maps; pictures and pamphlets; plus the Rhode Island Index: 4 catalog cases (total of 185 drawers) containing index to material on Rhode Island. This is primarily a subject index. Author cards made only for books and articles by Rhode Island authors; title cards for periodicals in collection. Providence Journal and Evening Bulletin are indexed daily for all pertinent articles about the state and its people. Incl are cards for pertinent articles in books and periodicals in other parts of the library.

RI —RHODE ISLAND SCHOOL OF DESIGN, Library, Two College St, Providence, 02903. James A Findlay, Dir
Holdings: Vols (70,000) Cat Pix Slides Phonorecords
Budget: ($50,000)
Notes: All fields of art incl 92,000 slides; 30,000 mounted photographs; 1100 posters and color reproductions; and 280,000 clippings.

TN —MEMPHIS STATE UNIVERSITY, John Willard Brister Library, Memphis, 38152. John Terreo, Special Collections Librn
Notes: Theatre Collection, 1789-1972. Correspondence, scripts, programs, handbills, musical scores, clippings, drawings, sketches, and photographs, documenting careers of artists, production of plays, ballett and theatre companies, and theaters and opera houses centering in New York and London, England. Incl drawings, prints, publications, and other personal papers of British producer and designer Edward Gordon Craig (1872-1966), relating to his career, radio talks (1951-1961) for the BBC, acting school in Florence, Italy, and his mother, actress Ellen Terry; and correspondence, scripts, programs, reviews, scrapbooks, photos, and other materials, of American producer Jed Harris (?)-1979, relating to his stage productions (1926-1945).

†TX —UNIVERSITY OF TEXAS LIBRARIES, General Libraries, Humanities Research Center, PO Box 7219, Austin, 78712. John Chalmers, Librn

TX —DALLAS PUBLIC LIBRARY, Texas/Dallas History and Archives Division, 1515 Young St, Dallas, 75201. Richard L Waters, Acting Dir; Wayne Gray, Manager
Notes: Emphasis on historic photographs of Dallas, Texas. Incl 5000 items.

TX —SOUTHERN METHODIST UNIVERSITY, DeGolyer Library, Box 396, SMU, Dallas, 75275. Clifton H Jones, Dir
Holdings: Vols (15,000) Cat Mss Maps Pix
Notes: One of the largest railroad photograph collections in the world; about 230,000 prints and 70,000 negatives, all countries. Accompanied by a major collection (12,000 vols), of railroadiana; much on locomotives. All languages.

TX —SOUTHERN METHODIST UNIVERSITY, Fondren Library, McCord Theater Collection, Room 301, Dallas, 75275. Edyth Renshaw, Cur; Linda Sellers, Pub Serv
Holdings: Vols (2000) Uncat Mss Pix Slides Phonorecords
Notes: See Theatre Collections in Libraries and Museums, Gilder and Freedley (Theatre Arts, 1936). The McCord Theatre Collection encompasses the entire spectrum of the performing arts. The central purpose is to gather records of our regional theater before such ephemeral material is lost. Records of over two hundred early Texas theaters, some fragmentary and some relatively complete, are in the files. These records incl photographs of buildings, stagehands, orchestras, and performers. Local theatre history incl the once famous Dallas Little Theatre and the Margo Jones Theatre. The national theatre, opera, ballet, and circus archives incl pictures (some autographed), programs, posters, throw-aways, tear sheets, clippings, and letters. Our international archives are small, but we have some excellent material, eg, artifacts from Max Reinhardt's production of"The Miracle" which happened to go bankrupt in Dallas. After a few years the items were given to us. There are posters, tear-sheets, souvenir programs, and other colorful items from Morris Gest and the Artef Collection. We

PHOTOGRAPHS—COLLECTIONS (cont.)

have about 200 19th century English playbills and a few from the 18th century. There is a collection of modern English, French, and other European programs, many of them illustrated souvenir programs. Also, magazines on theater, cinema, and television (1800). Scrapbooks covering both southwest and Dallas theater, 1890s-1950s. Special Collections: artifacts and documents on puppets; masks; costume design; circus; and ballet and dance. The Harriet Bacon MacDonald Collection of over 200 photographs of musicians appearing in Dallas during the first three decades of the 20th century. Many autographed. Affiliated with Meadow Theatre of the Arts.

TX —EL PASO PUBLIC LIBRARY, Southwest Collection, 501 N Oregon, El Paso, 79901. Mary A Sarber, Head
Holdings: Vols (12,000) Cat Mss Maps Pix
Budget: ($11,000)
Notes: Research collection includes rare books and mss journals, vertical files, index to El Paso newspapers, microfilmed newspapers, photographs, and architectural plans. Separate catalog. Limited to materials on Texas, New Mexico, Arizona and Mexico. Special collections of material by and about Tom Lea Jr, and Carl Hertzog. Aultman Collection of photographs includes 3500 on El Paso Southwest and 2500 on Mexican Revolution. Cited in Lovelace, Lisa, "The Southwest Collection of the El Paso Public Library". *Great Plains Journal*, vol 2, no 2, pp 161-166; Aultman, Otis A *Photographs from the Border: The Otis A Aultman Collection,* El Paso Public Library Association, 1977.

TX —AMON CARTER MUSEUM, 3501 Camp Bowie Blvd, PO Box 2365, Fort Worth, 76113. Jan K Muhlert, Dir; Marni Sandweiss, Cur of Photographs
Holdings: Cat Pix Slides
Notes: American photography from the beginning to the present with particular strength in photographs of the 19th century West. Includes the photographic estates of Laura Gilpin and Karl Struss. Incl 250,000 pictures; 55,000 slides.

TX —STEPHEN F AUSTIN STATE UNIVERSITY, Ralph W Steen Library, Special Collections Dept, Box 13055, SFA Sta, Nacogdoches, 75962. Linda Cheves Nicklas, Special Collections Librn
Holdings: Vols (13,500) Cat Mss Maps Pix
Budget: ($5000)
Notes: Emphasis on local and university-related subjects, especially people, culture, events, buildings of Texas, East Texas, and historic Nacogdoches. Extensive ms collection (1200 linear ft); 344 maps; 1600 pictures. Published description: SFASU, *A Guide to Special Collections,* 1980.

TX —INSTITUTE OF TEXAN CULTURES, Library, 801 S Bowie Street, PO Box 1226, San Antonio, 78294. Deborah Large, Dir of Library Services
Holdings: Vols (4500) Cat Pix Slides
Budget: ($60,000)
Notes: Incl 88,000 pictures and 7000 slides.

TX —BAYLOR UNIVERSITY, Moody Memorial Library, Texas History Collection, Waco, 76706. Kent Keeth, Librn
Holdings: Vols (80,000) Cat Mss Maps Pix Slides Phonorecords Audiotapes Microforms
Notes: The Texas Collection gathers materials which relate to life in Texas in all its aspects, from earliest days to the present. Incl Baylor University Archives.

UT —UNIVERSITY OF UTAH, Marriott Library, Special Collections, Salt Lake City, 84112. Gregory C Thompson, Cur
Notes: Approx 35,000 photos, covering all aspects of Utah and the west.

VA —GEORGE MASON UNIVERSITY, Fenwick Library, Special Collections Dept, 4400 University Drive, Fairfax, 22030. Ruth Kerns, Public Services Librn
Notes: The Ollie Atkins Photographic Collection. Atkins, award-winning photographer with the *Saturday Evening Post*, was also White House photographer

under several administrations. The collection incl more than 15,000 prints, negatives, contact sheets, slides and 4000 images covering subjects of historical, artistic and social significance from 1948 to 1968.

WA —WASHINGTON STATE HISTORICAL SOCIETY LIBRARY, 315 N Stadium Way, Tacoma, 98403. Frank L Green, Librn
Holdings: Vols 15,000 Cat Mss Maps Pix Microforms
Notes: Curtis Collection Frederick and Engerman, *Asahel Curtis: Photographs of the Great Northwest* pub 1983. Scope is entire Pacific Northwest, with emphasis on Washington.

WV —WEST VIRGINIA UNIVERSITY, Library, West Virginia and Regional History Collection, Morgantown, 26506. George P Parkinson Jr, Cur
Holdings: Vols 30,000 Cat Mss Maps Pix Audiotapes 16mm Films Filmstrips Microforms
Budget: ($20,000)
Notes: The West Virginia Collection contains over 10,000 linear ft of mss, broadsides, pictures, photographs, and other items relating to West Virginia and the Appalachian region. There are published guides to the collections.

WI —UNIVERSITY OF WISCONSIN, LA CROSSE, Murphy Library, 1631 Pine St, La Crosse, 54601. Edwin L Hill, Special Collections Librn
Holdings: Vols 50 Cat Pix
Budget: $9000
Notes: The steamboat project undertakes to collect photographs, sketches, and basic information on upper Mississippi River steamboats. Collection now incl about 20,000 photographs and sketches, with data file. Most photos are copy prints; some are protected by copyright and may not be used for commercial purposes. Most photos are unpublished. Collecting and data searching actively pursued. Boats from tributary rivers included. Collection is supplemented by primary and secondary sources and active field research. Overall arrangement is alphabetical by boat name, with notation of special categories of boats.

WI —MILWAUKEE PUBLIC LIBRARY, 814 W Wisconsin Ave, Milwaukee, 53233. Donald J Sager, City Librn
Notes: Collection incl local history and archival photographs of the greater Milwaukee area, instruction manuals and history of photography.

WI —UNIVERSITY OF WISCONSIN, MILWAUKEE, American Geographical Society Collection, 2311 E Hartford Ave, PO Box 399, Milwaukee, 53201. Roman Drazniowsky, Cur
Holdings: Vols (196,800)
Budget: ($270,000)
Notes: The largest special collection in the field of geography, cartography, and related fields in the Western Hemisphere. Incl 6469 atlases; 385,610 maps; 72 globes; 33,700 pamphlets; 79,000 photographs; 99,000 Landsat Images. Catalog published by G K Hall, Boston.

PR —UNIVERSITY OF PUERTO RICO, Jose M Lazaro Memorial Library, Sala Zenobia y Juan Ramon Jimenez, Rio Piedras, 00931. Raquel Sarraga, Librn
Holdings: Vols (8000) Cat Mss Pix Phonorecords Audiotapes Filmstrips
Notes: This special collection was created because Juan Ramon Jimenez, Nobel Prize for Literature, and one of the leading Spanish poets of this century, donated his personal library and papers to the University of Puerto Rico. It's main importance is that its contents represent the best Spanish literature of this century and the bibliographical data on the "Modernismo" period is very rich. The papers bring the opportunity to study the creative process of Juan Ramon Jimenez as well as the historical literary period in which they were written. The collection incl rare books, first editions autographed by their authors, magazines (some are rare collections), thousands of Juan Ramon's originals and manuscripts, letters of some of the top literary writers of this century, photographs (3061), paper

clippings (32,000), paintings, furniture and personal belongings.

AB —ALPINE CLUB OF CANADA LIBRARY, Archives of the Canadian Rockies, Box 160, Banff, T0L 0C0, Can. E J Hart, Head Archivist
Holdings: Vols (2429) Cat Mss Maps Slides Audiotapes
Budget: ($1000)
Notes: Covers the Canadian Rocky Mountains from international border in the south to the St Elias Range in the North; eastern slopes of the Rockies, incl foothills, to the western slopes of the interior ranges of British Columbia. Include physical, natural, and human history. The Archives of the Canadian Rockies is the custodian of the library and archival collection of The Alpine Club of Canada. The materials cover mountaineering all over the world. Subject areas incl history, personal records, mountain rescue and medicine, alpine flora and fauna, guide books, manuals and handbooks. A large part of the archival collection is concentrated on the Canadian Rocky Mountains, as in Banff, Alberta.

AB —PETER WHYTE FOUNDATION, Archives of the Canadian Rockies, Box 160, Banff, T0L 0C0, Can. Mary Andrews, ACR Librn
Holdings: Vols (4247) Cat Mss Maps Pix Slides Phonorecords Audiotapes Videotapes 16mm Films Filmstrips
Budget: ($1500)
Notes: Collect all available material which touches on the Rocky Mountains of Canada (from the US border to the Peach River in the north; from west of Calgary on the east to the town of Revelstoke, BC on the west) This material incl history (the early explorers, Indians, construction of the railroads, mountaineering, and development of the national parks), natural history (geology, botany, wildlife) and poetry and fiction with the Rockies as a setting. Collect maps of the area, photographs, tape recordings of the pioneers. We also house on our premises the Alpine Club of Canada's library, which is one of the most comprehensive collections on the subject of mountaineering worldwide. Noncirculating.

AB —UNIVERSITY OF CALGARY, Libraries, Special Collections Div, 2500 University Dr, Calgary, T2N 1N4, Can. Holdings: Cat Mss Pix Audiotapes 16mm Films Microforms
Notes: The Canadian Architectural Archives at the University of Calgary include collections of drawings, records, sketches, renderings, correspondence, project files of the following Canadian architects (qv separate entries): Raymond T Affleck, J Francis Brown and F Bruce Brown, J A Cawston, Arthur C Erickson, Long Mayell & Associates, Hugh McMillan Architects Ltd, Raymond Moriyama, John B Parkin Associates/NORR Rule Wynn & Rule (Edmonton and Calgary), Stevenson Raines Barrett Hutton Seton & Partners, The Thom Partnership, Thompson Berwick Pratt & Partners, and H M Whiddington. Dates from 1891 to about 1974. The Archives also incl photographs, microfilmed material (16mm and 35mm, film strip and aperture cards), and Oral History Interviews on tape. Project lists and/or inventories are on hand.

BC —UNIVERSITY OF BRITISH COLUMBIA, Library, 1956 Main Mall, Vancouver, V6T 1Y3, Can. Anne Yandle, Special Collections Librn
Notes: British Columbia Mountaineering Club photograph collection covering many years of activities. Incl 420 negatives, 2 albums (photos), 1 book.

MB —UNIVERSITY OF MANITOBA, Elizabeth Dafoe Library, Archives and Special Collections Dept, Winnipeg, R3T 2N2, Can. Richard E Bennett, Dept Head; Corrado A Santoro, Reference Archivist
Holdings: Pix
Notes: (1) Photographs of western prairie Canada as collected by Heather Robertson from archives and museums across Canada for use in her book *Salt from the Earth*. Pictures are between 1880-1915, showing such things as immigrant families, farms,

PHOTOGRAPHS—COLLECTIONS (cont.)

towns and city life on the prairies, churches, schools, railroads, homestead residences and other aspects of life in the developing Canadian West. (2) Photographs relating to soil surveys, crop experimentation and land development projects conducted primarily in rural Manitoba by Joseph Henry Ellis. (3) Barkwell Collection incl photographs of Treherne, Manitoba, and environs taken in the early part of the 20th century. (4) 317 b/w prints taken by Mathew Archibald Parker at turn of the century of England and Europe. Rural scenes are highlighted. (5) Postcards and photographs showing details of Nazi Germany'sbombings and occupation of Holland in 1940.

†MB —UNIVERSITY OF MANITOBA, Library, Winnipeg, R3T 2N2, Can.
Notes: Complete research archive of ninety years of the Winnipeg *Times*, defunct in 1980. Millions of newspaper clippings, indexed and in chronological order; about one million photographs, identified and dated; 10,000 books, etc.

ON —NATIONAL FILM BOARD, CANADA, Tunney's Pasture Area, Ottawa, K1A 0M9, Can.
Notes: Photo library of 225,000 Canadian images, incl 33,000 slides.

ON —PUBLIC ARCHIVES OF CANADA, Library, 395 Wellington St, Ottawa, K1A 0N3, Can. Dawn E Monroe, Collections Development Officer
Holdings: Vols (80,000) Cat
Notes: R J Cyriax Collection (280 items). An impressive collection of books forms the backbone of this multi-media collection which also incl maps, photographs, notes and correspondence relating to Arctic explorations. Dr Cyriax visited places connected with the Franklin Expeditions, taking photographs and obtaining what are now rare guide books. He also spent time in Sweden and could read the several Danish and Norwegian items which remain in the collection. The collection is incl in the main library catalog.

ON —METROPOLITAN TORONTO LIBRARY, Theatre Dept, 789 Yonge St, Toronto, M4W 2G8, Can. Heather McCallum, Head
Notes: 55,000 photographs document Canadian theatre, film and dance productions, performing arts personalities and British and American film stills.

ON —METROPOLITAN TORONTO LIBRARY, Music Dept, 789 Yonge St, Toronto, M4W 2G8, Can. Isabel Rose, Head
Budget: ($54,000)
Notes: 14,800 books, 40,000 scores; 1900 pieces of retrospective Canadian sheet music; 500 pieces of American and British sheet music, pre-1980; 17,000 phonorecords; 180 current periodical titles; 2800 bound peiodicals; 340 reels of microfilmed periodicals; 16,000 concert programs, chiefly Toronto city; 8850 newspaper clipping files; music picture files integrated with Fine Art Dept picture collection.

ON —UNIVERSITY OF TORONTO, Art History Reference Library, Dept of Fine Art, 100 Saint George St, Toronto, M5S 1A1, Can. Andrea Retfalvi, Research Librn
Holdings: Vols (20,000) Cat Pix
Notes: The collection specializes in art history catalogs of various types: temporary exhibition catalogs, from the major institutions in Europe and North America; permanent collection catalogs, again for all the major institutions; dealer catalogs; and auction catalogs. The collection of auction catalogs is primarily French, covering 1870-1970, with particular strength from ca 1900 on. There is a catalog for all these types of catalogs. 90,000 photographs, black and white only. Primarily mediaeval, with some classical and renaissance coverage. The photographs are not cataloged.

PHOTOGRAPHY

CA —CALIFORNIA STATE UNIVERSITY, LONG BEACH, Library, Dept of Special Collections & Archives, 1250 Bellflower Blvd, Long Beach, 90840. John Ahouse, Special Collections Librn
Holdings: Vols 600
Notes: Libraries of Dr Fred Modern and photojournalist Richard Cross, and incl signed books and photographs of photographer Ansel Adams.

CA —UNIVERSITY OF CALIFORNIA, LOS ANGELES, Research Library, Dept of Special Collections, 405 Hilgard Ave, Los Angeles, 90024. Edward Shreeves, Chairman, Bibliographers Group; David S Zeidberg, Head
Holdings: Vols 1000 Pix
Notes: 1000 books; 2,000,000 pieces. Various collections incl Albert Boni collection of early photography; individual images and albums of work by George Barnard, A Beato, Isabella Bird Bishop, Felix Bonfils, Julia Margaret Cameron, Maxime du Camp, Francis Frith, Alexander Gardner, W Hammerschmidt, Eadweard Muybridge, William Henry Fox Talbot, Edward Vischer, and Carleton E Watkins; 300 books illustrated with original photographs; photography as documentation, incl images of Australasia, 1700 images of the Middle East, and extensive holdings reflecting local history incl 6000 architectural photographs of Southern California and the *Los Angeles Daily News* and *Los Angeles Times* morgues; images by California Pictorialists Will Connell, Louis Fleckenstein, Ernest Pratt, Roland and Florence Schneider, and Louis J Stellman; 2000 19th century cabinet cards oftheater personalities; 10,000 20th century theater photographs by Jerome Robinson; 300,000 negatives of Los Angeles commercial photographer Otto Rothschild. Also various collections on color photography, incl Edward Bower Hesser, originator of Hessercolor, and Bela Gaspar collection of patents relating to color photography.

CA —UNIVERSITY OF CALIFORNIA, LOS ANGELES, Theater Arts Library, Los Angeles, 90024. Edward Shreeves, Chairman, Bibliographers Group; Audree Malkin, Head, Theater Arts Library
Holdings: Cat Mss Pix Slides
Notes: 23 linear feet of correspondence, ephemera, slides, etc, concerning Walter Beyer's work as an engineer at Paramount Pictures, the development of VistaVision, the Motion Picture Research Council, and Universal Pictures.

CA —UNIVERSITY OF CALIFORNIA, RIVERSIDE, University Library, 4045 Canyon Crest Dr, Box 5900, Riverside, 92517.
Holdings: Vols 2,500 Pix
Notes: A broad collection representing history and aesthetics of photography, incl volumes of examples of individual photographers' work. Supports the photograph collections of the California Museum of Photography and the Keystone Mast Archive of stereographic photographs.

CA —SAN FRANCISCO ART INSTITUTE, Anne Bremer Memorial Library, 800 Chestnut St, San Francisco, 94133. Jeff Gunderson, Librn
Holdings: Vols (23,114) Cat Pix Slides Audiotapes 16mm Films Microforms
Budget: ($15,000)

CT —GREENWICH LIBRARY, 101 W Putnam Ave, Greenwich, 06830. Wayne T Campbell Jr, Film Services Coordr
Holdings: Vols 874 Cat Videotapes Films
Notes: Collection is very broad. Supplemented by books on film making in both this collection and the photographic collection. Also supplemented by 16mm film collection and videocassettes.

DC —NATIONAL GEOGRAPHIC SOCIETY, Library, 1146 16th St NW, Washington, 20036. Susan Fifer Canby, Dir
Holdings: Vols (63,000) Cat Mss Maps Pix
Notes: Material concerning land, sea, and space exploration--past and present. All fields of anthropology, natural history, geography, etc.

HI —BERNICE P BISHOP MUSEUM, Library, PO Box 19000-A, Honolulu, 96819. Cynthia Timberlake, Librn
Holdings: Vols (90,000) Cat Mss Maps Pix Slides Microforms
Budget: ($30,000)
Notes: Only American library devoted exclusively to the Pacific region. Collection reflects historical and contemporary research emphases of Bishop Museum; ie the natural and cultural history of the Pacific. Areas of concentration incl archaeology, ethnology, linguistics, voyages and explorations, history, vertebrate and invertebrate zoology, botany and museology. Strong special collections incl photographs, mss and archives, maps and art. Publications: Quarterly "Additions to the Catalog," *Dictionary Catalog of the Library* (9 vols and 2 suppl; Boston: G K Hall, 1964-69).

IL —CHICAGO PUBLIC LIBRARY, Art Section, Fine Arts Division, 78 E Washington St, Chicago, 60602. Rosalinda I Hack, Fine Arts Division Chief; Yvonne S Brown, Head, Art Section
Holdings: Vols 6000
Notes: Includes all aspects of photography, materials, techniques, as well as artistic, scientific and technical application in cinamatography, animation, and photomechinical processes. Collection concentrates on the history of photography and works of significant photographers past and present. Collection is supplemented by the microfilm edition of the *History of Photography*.

IL —UNIVERSITY OF ILLINOIS, URBANA/CHAMPAIGN, Library, Communications Library, 122 Gregory Hall, Urbana, 61801. Nancy Allen, Librn
Holdings: Vols (18,000) Cat
Budget: ($27,000)
Notes: Photojournalism theory and methods.

IN —INDIANA LAW ENFORCEMENT ACADEMY, David F Allen Memorial Learning Resources Center, Rd 700 E, PO Box 313, Plainfield, 46168. Donna K Zimmerman, Librn
Holdings: Vols (4500) Cat Slides 16mm Films
Budget: ($8500)
Notes: Concentrated in the areas of police science, criminology, and law.

KY —UNIVERSITY OF LOUISVILLE, Ekstrom Library, Photographic Archives, Louisville, 40292. J C Anderson, Cur; David G Horvath, Asst Cur
Holdings: Vols (750,000) Cat Pix Slides
Budget: ($60,000)
Notes: Photographs in three broad areas: works of outstanding photographers; examples of major developments in the art and technology of photography; photographs important as sociological, historical, or behavioral documents. Actors and actresses, Louisville's Macauley Theatre. Standard Oil of New Jersey Collection, 85,000 pictures of oil industry's effect on life in the 20th century (1943-1950, directed by Roy Stryker); Stryker's collection from Farm Security Administration series on rural conditions, 1935-1942; Jones and Laughlin Steel Corp Picture Library, by Stryker. Stryker manuscripts, 1934-1972. Caufield and Shook commercial photographs, Louisville area, 1920-1949. Jean Thomas "The Traipsin' Woman" photographs of Kentucky mountain folkways. Kate Matthews' (1870-1956) photographs incl prototypes for "Little Colonel" Series. Other collections described in unpublishedbrochure. Print duplication service.

MA —SOCIETY FOR THE PRESERVATION OF NEW ENGLAND ANTIQUITIES, Library, 141 Cambridge St, Boston, 02114. Ellie Reichlin, Librn & Cur of Photographic Collections
Holdings: Vols (3000) Cat Pix Microforms
Budget: ($75,000)
Notes: Photograph collections, all media (incl daguerreotypes, ambrotypes, etc, stereographic views, carte de visite) depicting New England buildings; interiors; street and town views; occupations; pastimes; transport and personalities. Covers 1840s-1930s, with some more recent additons. Amateur and professional photographers represented. Cataloged in part, otherwise arranged by localities, subject, personal

PHOTOGRAPHY (cont.)

name. Special collections incl: marine photographs by N L Stebbins and Henry Peabody (1880s-1920s); Boston and Albany railroad photographic archive, early 1900s; Quabbin Valley views; historic American Buildings Survey photographs (17th to early 19th century architecture) by Arthur Haskell; Baldwin Coolidge collection, and many others. Size: 500,000 prints, ca 75,000 negatives (glass plates and copy negs). These are cataloged. Some special indexes incllandscape design (arbors, conservatories, flower beds, bandstands etc); photographers represented; architects represented (partial), and pending, interiors (specific features of); occupations.

MA —HARVARD UNIVERSITY, Harvard College Library, Fine Arts Library, Fogg Museum, 32 Quincy St, Cambridge, 02138. Wolfgang M Freitag, Librn
Holdings: Cat Pix Slides
Notes: See *Harvard Library Bulletin*, VII (1953), 208-220.

MA —MELROSE PUBLIC LIBRARY, 69 W Emerson St, Melrose, 02176. Diane E Shaw, Art Librn
Holdings: Vols (8500) Cat Pix Slides Phonorecords
Budget: ($6900)
Notes: Framed and unframed art reproductions (110), slides (2773), periodicals, clippings, sound recordings (3000). Incl the Mary Livermore Collection of Sacred Art, the Odlin Collection, and the Pierre Gendrot Collection of Fine Art.

MA —SPRINGFIELD CITY LIBRARY, Art & Music Dept, 220 State St, Springfield, 01103. Karen A Dorval, Supvr & Art Librn; Sylvia A Saint Amand, Music Librn
Holdings: Vols (22,000) Cat Pix Phonorecords Audiotapes Microforms
Budget: ($183,000)
Notes: Art: books (17,500), pamphlets (8000), pictures (120,000); music: books (5000), music scores (10,000), phonorecords (18,000), Audiocassettes (288 titles). Also microfilm (75 reels). Separate catalogs for art, music, and phonorecords and audiocassettes.

MI —CRANBROOK ACADEMY OF ART, 500 Lone Pine Rd, Box 801, Bloomfield Hills, 48013. Diane Gunn, Librn
Holdings: Vols (25,000) Slides

MI —MICHIGAN STATE UNIVERSITY, Art Library, East Lansing, 48824. Shirlee A Studt, Librn
Holdings: Vols (45,000) Cat
Notes: The Illuminated Manuscript Facsimile Collection includes examples of religious and secular works from the earliest codex to the age of printing. It has particular strengths in Carolingian, Ottonian, French Gothic and works from the British Isles. The facsimile collection is strengthened by related research materials (biographical material, critical studies, etc) The facsimile collection and related materials are part of a 45,000 volume separately housed and staffed collection on the visual and decorative arts (including photography) serving the curricular and research needs of the University community. A guide to full facsimiles in the collection is available in the Art Library and in the Special Collections division. A strong collection of architectural history.

MI —KALAMAZOO INSTITUTE OF ARTS LIBRARY, 314 S Park St, Kalamazoo, 49006. Marianne Cavanaugh, Librn
Holdings: Vols (5000) Cat Slides
Notes: Incl (8000) slides. Vertical file on artists. Collection is supplemented by 55 current subscriptions to periodicals in visual arts. Emphasis is on 20th century art and on American art. Collection supports permanent collection in prints, paintings, photography, and sculpture.

MI —MONROE COUNTY LIBRARY SYSTEM, Bedford Branch, 8575 Jackman Road, Temperance, 48182. Paula Kaczmarek, Head, Bedford Branch
Holdings: Vols 6500 Cat Periodicals AV
Budget: $8000
Notes: Circulating general collection of popular art books, especially Western European and American painting; also includes technique, graphic arts, photography, sculpture, architecture. Periodicals held five years.

MN —MINNEAPOLIS COLLEGE OF ART & DESIGN, Library, 200 E 25 St, Minneapolis, 55404. Richard Kronstedt, Head Librn
Holdings: Vols 1750 Cat Slides
Notes: Incl art exhibition catalogs.

MN —3M COMPANY, Mertle Library, 3M Center, Bldg 235-1D, Saint Paul, 55101.
Holdings: Vols (4000) // Cat Mss Pix
Notes: The collection of Joseph S Mertle, includes patents, portraits, a clipping file, and other historical graphic arts books and periodicals.

MO —SAINT LOUIS ART MUSEUM, Richardson Memorial Library, Saint Louis, 63110. Ann B Abid, Librn
Holdings: Vols (30,000) Cat Pix Slides Microforms
Notes: Art history, incl decorative arts, catalogs, exhibitions, etc.

NH —DARTMOUTH COLLEGE, Sherman Art Library, Hanover, 03755. Jeffrey L Horrell, Art Librn
Holdings: Vols (52,000) Cat
Notes: Incl art, architecture and photography. Access is available through OCLC and RLIN.

NY —PRATT INSTITUTE LIBRARY, Art & Architecture Dept, 200 Willoughby Ave, Brooklyn, 11205. Sydney Star Keaveney, Prof
Holdings: Vols (30,000) Cat Pix Slides
Budget: ($50,000)
Notes: Art and architecture, incl sculpture, photography, painting, design, costume, and commercial art. Incl 60,000 art slides. Use restricted to Pratt faculty and students.

NY —ALBRIGHT-KNOX ART GALLERY, Art Reference Library, 1285 Elmwood Ave, Buffalo, 14222. Annette Masling, Librn
Holdings: Vols (20,000) Cat
Notes: Special strength in American 19th and 20th century art. Excellent collection of exhibition catalogs for contemporary art.

NY —PARAPSYCHOLOGY SOURCES OF INFORMATION CENTER, 2 Plane Tree Lane, Dix Hills, 11746. Rhea A White, Dir
Holdings: Vols (4000)
Notes: The PSI Center includes 4000 books, 100 periodical titles, cassette tapes, and unpublished mss dealing with parapsychology and the transformation of consciousness, also 12,000 articles, reprints, etc. There is a charge for reference service and bibliographies.

NY —NEW YORK PUBLIC LIBRARY, Research Libraries, General Research Division, Fifth Ave & 42 St, New York, 10018. Rodney Phillips, Chief
Holdings: Vols (2,225,000) Cat Maps Pix Microforms
Budget: ($775,718)

NY —NEW YORK PUBLIC LIBRARY, Art, Prints, and Photographs Div, Fifth Ave & 42 St, New York, 10018. Donald Anderle, Chief
Holdings: Vols (150,000) Cat Mss Pix Microforms
Notes: History and design in the fine and applied arts. Architecture, painting, drawing, sculpture, costume, furniture, advertising art, prints, photography, crafts, and jewelry are among the subjects covered from ancient times to the present. See New York Public Library *Dictionary Catalog of the Art and Architecture Division* (Boston, G K Hall, 1975), 30 vols. Holdings after that time are incl in the *Dictionary Catalog of the Research Libraries*. African Art and Afro-American Art are collected by the Schomburg Center for Research in Black Culture. Books on the history of photography and photographs representing all processes from daguerreotypes and silver prints to color prints in all formats as well as stereoscopic views will be selectively acquired by the Art, Prints and Photographs Division as examples of the work ofindividual artists or groups of artists and/or for subject interest. Photographs relating to Black culture are acquired by the Schomburg Center; New York City views are acquired by the US Local History and Genealogy Division; and photographs relating to the performing arts are acquired by the divisions and collections at the Performing Arts Research Center.

NY —EASTMAN KODAK COMPANY, Research Library, Research Laboratories, Bldg 83, Rochester, 14650. E W Kraus, Head
Holdings: Vols 12,500 Cat Microforms
Notes: Incl all technical aspects of photography.

NY —ROCHESTER INSTITUTE OF TECHNOLOGY, Technical & Education Center of the Graphic Arts, Graphic Arts Information Service, One Lomb Memorial Dr, Rochester, 14623. Susan Clark, Technical Librn
Holdings: Vols (1500) Cat Microforms
Notes: Graphic arts (photographic and applied art aspects) with emphasis on science and technology of printing. Periodicals (265) and technical reports, pertinent to the graphic arts, are routinely scanned for articles of significant information content; articles are classified and keyworded, if needed, and the complete reference is published in *Graphic Arts Literature* Abstracts, a monthly publication of the Graphic Arts Research Center. All abstracted articles are microfilmed and in individual fiche jackets for easy storage and retrieval.

NY —UNIVERSITY OF ROCHESTER, Fine Arts Library and Gallery, Rochester, 14627. Stephanie J Frontz, Librn
Holdings: Vols (35,000) Cat
Budget: ($15,000)

NY —VISUAL STUDIES WORKSHOP, Research Center, 31 Prince St, Rochester, 14607. Linn Underhill, Coordr; Robert Bretz, Librn
Holdings: Vols (8000) Cat Pix Slides Audiotapes Videotapes
Notes: Strong emphasis on photography (over 1,000,000 pictures) and the photographic arts in many subject areas incl in this volume. Heavy emphasis on early photographic processes and collections of examples of them. Also collections of individual photographers' works.

NC —NORTH CAROLINA STATE UNIVERSITY, Harry B Lyons Design Library, P. O. Box 7701, Raleigh, 27607. Maryellen LoPresti, Librn
Notes: Collection covers architecture, landscape architecture, design and related professions. Additional materials maybe found on art, painting sculpture photography and solar energy design. The library presently houses a total of 28,000 books, periodical and serial volumes to support the curriculum. A product and trade literature file and a vertical file of pamplets are also locally cataloged in the library representing an additional 3000 items of materials available for use. A significant collections of over 50,000 cataloged slides primarily representing the areas of art and architectural history are also contained in the library facility. See *Directory of Special Libraries and Information Centers.*

OH —OHIO UNIVERSITY, Vernon R Alden Library, Fine Arts Library, Athens, 45701. Anne Braxton, Fine Arts Librn
Holdings: Vols (40,000) Cat Pix Slides Microforms
Notes: Strong collection in history of film and photography; general art collection incl some 2000 exhibition catalogs.

OH —PUBLIC LIBRARY OF CINCINNATI & HAMILTON COUNTY, Art & Music Dept, 800 Vine St, Cincinnati, 45202. R Jayne Craven, Head
Holdings: Vols (122,185) Cat Pix
Budget: ($56,100)
Notes: Special collections: Eda Kuhn Loeb, "Artist and the Book, 1875-Date" (now shelved in Rare Book Room); music librettos (2345); exhibition catalogs (5474); large prints and posters (5051); Cincinnati artists vertical files; picture collection (673,906 clippings).

OH —CLEVELAND PUBLIC LIBRARY, Science & Technology Dept, 325 Superior

PHOTOGRAPHY (cont.)

Ave, Cleveland, 44114. Jean Z Piety, Head
Holdings: Cat
Notes: Incl the Charles Abel Collection of Photographic Literature intershelved with other books on photography.

PA —GRAPHIC ARTS TECHNICAL FOUNDATION, Edward H Wadewitz Memorial Library, 4615 Forbes Ave, Pittsburgh, 15213. Janice L Lloyd, Librn
Holdings: Vols (3500) Cat Slides Microforms
Notes: All printing processes. Also, books and periodicals on paper, ink, photography, optics, color theory, environmental control. Approximately 250 periodical titles and 35,000 classified abstracts of selected periodical articles. Approximately 15,000 slides within the organization. Research reports from foreign graphic arts research institutes.

RI —RHODE ISLAND SCHOOL OF DESIGN, Library, Two College St, Providence, 02903. James A Findlay, Dir
Holdings: Vols (70,000) Cat
Budget: ($50,000)

WI —UNIVERSITY OF WISCONSIN-STOUT, Library Learning Center, Menomonie, 54751. Philip Sawin Jr, Coll Develop Librn
Notes: Comprehensive collection since the graduate program began in 1959.

WI —MILWAUKEE PUBLIC LIBRARY, 814 W Wisconsin Ave, Milwaukee, 53233. Donald J Sager, City Librn
Holdings: Vols 6300 Cat
Notes: Collection incl local history and archival photographs of the greater Milwaukee area, instruction manuals and history of photography.

AB —PETER WHYTE FOUNDATION, Gallery, Box 160, Banff, T0L 0C0, Can. Mary Andrews, Librn
Holdings: Vols (935)
Budget: ($800)

MB —UNIVERSITY OF MANITOBA, Architecture & Fine Arts Library, Winnipeg, R3T 2N2, Can. Peter Anthony, Head
Holdings: Vols (54,000)

ON —NATIONAL GALLERY OF CANADA, Library, National Museums of Canada, Ottawa, K1A 0M8, Can. J Hunter, Chief Librn

ON —NATIONAL MUSEUMS OF CANADA, Library Services Directorate, Ottawa, K1A 0M8, Can. Valerie Monkhouse, Director
Holdings: Vols 15,500
Budget: $25,000
Notes: History and technology of agriculture, astronomy, aviation, chemistry, communications, computers, electrical engineering, exploration and surveying, fire prevention, forestry, industrial technology, mathematics, medicine, mining, photography, physics, printing, space and transportation. research collection, interlibrary loans available, public may use on the premises.

ON —METROPOLITAN TORONTO LIBRARY, Fine Arts Dept, 789 Yonge St, Toronto, M4W 2G8, Can. Alan Suddon, Head
Holdings: Vols (42,000) Cat Pix Microforms
Notes: Extensive collection.

PHOTOGRAPHY—ANIMATED PICTURES see Cinematography; Moving Pictures

PHOTOGRAPHY—HIGH SPEED see Photography, High Speed

PHOTOGRAPHY—HISTORY

AZ —NORTHERN ARIZONA UNIVERSITY, Special Collection Library, CU Box 6022, Flagstaff, 86011. Peter M Whiteley, Coordr/Archivist; William Mullane, Librn
Holdings: Cat Mss Pix
Notes: More than 15,000 photographs of the Grand Canyon taken by the Kolb Brothers, 1902-1970.
See also entry under Kolb, Emery

CA —UNIVERSITY OF CALIFORNIA, LOS ANGELES, Research Library, Dept of Special Collections, 405 Hilgard Ave, Los Angeles, 90024. Edward Shreeves, Chairman, Bibliographers Group; David S Zeidberg, Head
Notes: The Albert Boni Collection covers the early history of photography, incl an extensive collection of early photographic books and 19th century photographic images.

CA —CALIFORNIA HISTORICAL SOCIETY, Schubert Hall Library, 2099 Pacific Ave, San Francisco, 94109. Bruce L Johnson, Library Dir
Holdings: Pix
Notes: San Francisco CHS Photographic Archives holds 300,000 images on California statewide; The CHS Title Insurance and Trust Corporation Collection of Historical Photographs in Los Angeles contains 20,000 photographs centered around pictures of Southern California by noted photographer C C Pierce. Copies of photographs by other pioneer Los Angeles photographers, such as Godfrey, Wolfenstein and Parker are incl, as well as 2000 glass plate negatives of local Indians by George Wharton James.

CA —SAN FRANCISCO ART INSTITUTE, Anne Bremer Memorial Library, 800 Chestnut St, San Francisco, 94133. Jeff Gunderson, Librn
Holdings: Vols (23,114) Cat Pix Slides Audiotapes 16mm Films Microforms
Budget: ($15,000)

DE —DELAWARE ART MUSEUM, Library, 2301 Kentmere Pkwy, Wilmington, 19806. Anne Hoslam, Librn
Holdings: Vols (25,000) Cat Mss
Notes: The collection is rich in the following subjects: Howard Pyle and his pupils; John Sloan and the eight; history of the book and printing; and English and American illustrated books. There is also a section on contemporary photography. Archival material on Albert Mumford Lindsay, Jerome Myers, Everett Shinn, Gayle Porter Hoskins, Frank Schoonover.

MD —US NAVAL ACADEMY, Nimitz Library, Annapolis, 21402. Alice S Creighton, Assistant Librn for Special Collections
Holdings: Vols (420) Cat Pix 16mm Films
Notes: Edward J Steichen Collection was established in honor of Steichen's 90th birthday. Collection incl approximately 10,000 photographs, about 3/4 of which are World War II naval combat photographs and 1/4 of which cover American life as viewed through the eyes of such 20th century American photographers as Edward and Brett Weston, Ansel Adams, Margaret Bourke-White, and many others. Incl 420 books, chiefly on American photography. No photocopying.

MD —UNIVERSITY OF MARYLAND, BALTIMORE COUNTY, Albin O Kuhn Library and Gallery, Edward L Bafford Photography Collection, 5401 Wilkens Ave, Baltimore, 21228. Tom Beck, Cur
Holdings: Vols (3000) Cat Pix Slides
Notes: The Edward L Bafford Photography Collection contains 200,000 images, negatives, cameras, and books representing the entire history and aesthetics of photography. The theme of the collection is photography as a social force, as represented by the 5000 photographs and negatives by Lewis Hine and by William Henry Jackson's *Photographs of the Yellowstone National Park and Views of Montana and Wyoming Territories*. Another important historical document is the rare *Photographic Sketchbook of the Civil War* by Alexander Gardner. There are also a large number of photographs by both 19th and 20th century photographers, such as Edward Curtis, Eadweard Muybridge, Alfred Stieglitz, Diane Arbus, Lotte Jacobi, and many others. In addition, UMBC has been awarded the photographic archives of the *News American*.

MA —WELLESLEY COLLEGE, Art Library, Wellesley, 02181. Katherine D Finkelpearl, Art Librn
Holdings: Vols (30,000) Cat Pix Slides
Budget: ($22,000)
Notes: Primarily the art and architecture of Western Europe, the Far East, and classical antiquity. However, efforts are being made to expand the collection in the areas of photography, primitive art, and ancient (non-classical) art. The Art Department maintains a separate collection of 62,500 mounted pictures and 90,000 slides.

MN —3M COMPANY, Mertle Library, 3M Center, Bldg 235-1D, Saint Paul, 55101.
Holdings: Vols (4000) // Cat Mss Pix
Notes: The collection of Joseph S Mertle, includes patents, portraits. a clipping file, and other historical graphic arts books and periodicals.

NE —WESTERN HERITAGE MUSEUM, 801 S Tenth St, Omaha, 68108. Jane G Murray, Photo-Archivist
Holdings: Pix
Budget: ($750,000)
Notes: Approximately 120,000 photographs and glass negatives from the: Bostwick-Frohardt Photography Collection, The John S Savage Collection and the Rinehart-Marsden Collection.

NJ —PRINCETON UNIVERSITY, Marquand Library, McCormick Hall, Princeton, 08544. Mary M Schmidt, Librn
Holdings: Vols (130,000) Cat Microforms
Notes: Especially strong in classical archaeology and medieval art and architecture and photography history.

NY —COLUMBIA UNIVERSITY LIBRARIES, Rare Book & Manuscript Library, 801 Butler Library, 535 W 114 St, New York, 10027. Kenneth A Lohf, Librn
Holdings: Vols 4594 Cat
Notes: Restricted use: noncirculating.

NY —NEW YORK PUBLIC LIBRARY, Art, Prints, and Photographs Div, Fifth Ave & 42 St, New York, 10018. Donald Anderle, Chief
Holdings: Vols (150,000) Cat Mss Pix Microforms
Notes: History and design in the fine and applied arts. Architecture, painting, drawing, sculpture, costume, furniture, advertising art, prints, photography, crafts, and jewelry are among the subjects covered from ancient times to the present. See: New York Public Library *Dictionary Catalog of the Art and Architecture Division* (Boston, G K Hall, 1975), 30 vols. Holdings after that time are incl in the *Dictionary Catalog of the Research Libraries*. African Art and Afro-American Art are collected by the Schomburg Center for Research in Black Culture.

NY —INTERNATIONAL MUSEUM OF PHOTOGRAPHY AT GEORGE EASTMAN HOUSE, Archives, 900 East Ave, Rochester, 14607. Rachel Stuhlman, Head Librn
Holdings: Vols (30,000) Cat Mss Microforms
Budget: ($104,000)
Notes: History, aesthetics and technology of photography and cinematography, incl the Gabriel Cromer, Josef Maria Eder, Alden Scott Boyer, Louis Walton Sipley/3M Collections, and the James Card Collection from 1893. Covers photographic, especially cinematographic history; also hundreds of negatives of Edward Muybridge as well as his notebooks. Incl 450,000 pictures and slides. Also the Lewis Hine Collection of social documentary photography.

NY —UNIVERSITY OF ROCHESTER, Rush Rhees Library, Department of Rare Books and Special Collections, Rochester, 14627. Peter Dzwonkoski, Librn
Holdings: Cat Mss
Notes: Five collections of materials relating to the life and career of George Eastman. Incl materials by Roger Butterfield and Lawrence Bachmann in preparation of proposed Eastman biographies. Eastman's correspondence, and architectural details and letters on Eastman House construction. Also Hubbell Collection of books with mounted photographs, 1850-1875. No photocopying.

NY —VISUAL STUDIES WORKSHOP, Research Center, 31 Prince St, Rochester, 14607. Linn Underhill, Coordr; Robert Bretz, Librn
Holdings: Vols (8000) Cat Pix Slides Audiotapes Videotapes
Notes: Strong emphasis on photography

PHOTOGRAPHY—HISTORY (cont.)

(over 1,000,000 pictures) and the photographic arts in many subject areas incl in this volume. Heavy emphasis on early photographic processes and collections of examples of them. Also collections of individual photographers' works.

NC —UNIVERSITY OF NORTH CAROLINA, CHARLOTTE, J Murrey Atkins Library, UNCC Station, Charlotte, 28223. Robert F Brabham Jr, Special Collections Librn
Holdings: Cat Mss
Notes: Papers of John A Tennant, 1868-1957, publisher of *The Photo-Miniature,* and early photographic journal. Incl Tennant's marked copy of the journal, 1899-1904.

TX —AMON CARTER MUSEUM, 3501 Camp Bowie Blvd, PO Box 2365, Fort Worth, 76113. Jan K Muhlert, Dir; Marni Sandweiss, Cur of Photographs
Holdings: Cat Pix Slides
Notes: American photography from the beginning to the present with particular strength in photographs of the 19th century West. Includes the photographic estates of Laura Gilpin and Karl Struss. Incl 250,000 pictures; 55,000 slides.

WA —UNIVERSITY OF WASHINGTON LIBRARIES, Pacific Northwest Collection, Seattle, 98195. Andrew F Johnson, Librn
Holdings: Vols (50,000) Cat Maps Pix
Budget: ($12,000)
Notes: The Pacific Northwest Collection contains printed materials documenting the historic and contemporary life and culture of the region in a broad range of subject areas. The Pacific Northwest is defined as the geographic region including Washington, Oregon, Idaho, Montana, British Columbia, Yukon Territory, and Alaska. Printed materials including books, periodicals, government documents, maps, weekly and local regional newspapers, theses and dissertations, as well as photographs and architectural drawings are included in the Pacific Northwest Collection. Photographic works of over 200 photographers active in the Pacific Northwest, Alaska, and the Yukon Territory (Canada) during the period 1860-1930, including Asahel and Edward S Curtis, Eric Hegg, and Clark Kinsey, are represented in a print collection of more than 300,000 images. The architecturaldrawings collection includes over 19,000 original plans, drawings, sketches, renderings and blue prints pertaining to the history of architecture and urban planning and landscape gardening in the Pacific Northwest ca 1880-1940. Areas of particular strength are the holdings of over 1100 published journals of Pacific Northwest exploration expeditions, photographs of Northwest Coast Native Americans and of historic Seattle, newspapers issued within the Japanese-American relocation camps, 1942-1945, materials relating to the 1980 eruption of Mt St Helens, and Sanborne fire insurance maps for Washington. A unique feature of the Collection is the subject index to regional periodicals and local newspapers maintained by the PNW Collection staff; over 100 titles are currently indexed. G K Hall Company published a books catalog of the Pacific Northwest Collectionin 1973.

PHOTOGRAPHY—MOVING PICTURES
see Cinematography; Moving Pictures

PHOTOGRAPHY, AERIAL

CA —UNIVERSITY OF CALIFORNIA, LOS ANGELES, Map Library, Los Angeles, 90024. Carlos B Hagen, Head
Holdings: Vols (5566) Cat Maps Pix
Notes: The Library is a depository for the publications of many world-wide mapping agencies. The collection incl 507,097 maps of all areas of the world (subject and topographic maps, nautical and aeronautical charts, historical maps, and city plans), gazetteers, atlases, aerial photographs, periodicals and other basic cartographic reference tools. Incl 2550 atlases; 10,424 aerial maps; 1035 technical reports; and 311 (titles) serials subscriptions.

CA —UNIVERSITY OF CALIFORNIA, SANTA BARBARA, Map and Imagery Laboratory, Santa Barbara, 93106. Larry Carver, Dept Head
Notes: Worldwide coverage of Landsat imagery donated by US Dept of Agriculture Aerial Photography Field Office. Consists of 153,000 scenes, covering most of the earth's surface between the years 1975 and 1980. Incl 300,000 maps, 1800 atlases, 9 globes, 300 relief models, 1,500,000 satellite imagery and aerial photographs, 700 reference books and gazetteers, 25 serials (titles received), and 21,000 microforms. *See also* entry under California - Maps.

CA —WHITTIER COLLEGE, Dept of Geology, Fairchild Aerial Photograph Collection, Whittier, 90608. Dallas D Rhodes, Dir, Fairchild Collection
Holdings: // Cat
Notes: Aerial photographs of California, 1927-1963. 100,000 aerial photo negatives (40,000 nitrate-base), 300,000 aerial photo prints, 1000 photomosaics, 750 orthophoto maps. Concentration in California, particularly in the Los Angeles region, and elsewhere in metropolitan areas. Many flights are among the earliest available and cover areas since developed. Sequential photos often allow documentation of the history of development or of natural effects. Prints may be borrowed for 1-month periods. Purchase of prints can be arranged. An inventory list of flights can be purchased through the Dept of Geology.

CT —UNIVERSITY OF CONNECTICUT, University Library, Map Room, Storrs, 06268. Thornton P McGalmery, Librn
Holdings: Vols (903) Cat Maps Pix
Budget: ($5000)
Notes: The Map Room is the largest publicly supported map library in any Connecticut institution of higher education. It is a depository library for the US Geological Survey, the Defense Mapping Agency, and the Metropolitan District (Hartford, Conn). Incl over 100,000 maps and 8523 aerial photographs. Of particular interest is the *Petersen Collection*, a group of photostats of old town maps of New England.

DC —GEORGETOWN UNIVERSITY, Library, Special Collections Div, 37 & O Sts NW, Washington, 20057. George M Barringer, Special Collections Librn; Nicholas B Sheetz, Mss Librn
Holdings: Cat
Notes: The Ernest Larue Jones Collection consists of seven large volumes of photographs which document the development of American aeronautics from 1863-1917. The majority of the pictures are of the period 1907-1915 when Jones was publisher of the pioneer technical journal "Aeronautics".

DC —LIBRARY OF CONGRESS, Geography and Map Division, Washington, 20540. John A Wolter, Chief

GA —UNIVERSITY OF GEORGIA, Libraries, Map Collection, Athens, 30602. John Sutherland, Cur of Maps
Holdings: Cat Maps
Budget: ($20,000)
Notes: Sheet maps, 285,000; aerial photographs, 186,000; three-dimensional maps, 40; atlases, 800 (note: the Libraries contain other atlases; these are part of the map collection as such). The collection contains maps from all countries and in all languages, although the area of specialization is the US, with particular emphasis on the southeastern sector. The collection is a depository for maps from the US Geological Survey, DMATC, NOAA, and Georgia's Dept of Transportation. Collection has 7100 sheets of Sanborn maps for Georgia. Bibliographies available for atlases, Sanborn sheets, and air photo holdings.

IL —NORTHWESTERN UNIVERSITY, Library, Map Collection, Evanston, 60201. Mary Fortney, Librn
Notes: Incl 170,104 maps, cataloged; 1540 aerial photographs, cataloged.

MN —MANKATO STATE UNIVERSITY, Memorial Library, Maywood & Ellis, Mankato, 56001. Russell K Amling, Map Librn
Holdings: Cat Maps
Budget: ($2000)
Notes: 74,736 maps and 685 atlases (mostly topographic and thematic) of the US, especially Minnesota (3000 maps). 16,369 aerial photos (incl Minnesota). Separate catalog.

NM —UNIVERSITY OF NEW MEXICO, Technology Application Center, 2500 Central SE, Albuquerque, 87131. Amy Budge, Photo Search Service
Notes: Remote sensing; aerial photography; all earth-oriented satellite photography; NCIC affiliate.

OR —UNIVERSITY OF OREGON, Map Library, Eugene, 97403. Peter L Stark, Map Librarian
Holdings: Cat Maps Aerial Photographs
Budget: ($4000)
Notes: 330,000 aerial photographs covering Oregon from 1929-present. Remainder of collection covers National Forests of adjoining states and teaching examples. Collection fully indexed.

PA —PENNSYLVANIA GEOLOGICAL SOCIETY, Library, 916 Executive House, Second & Chestnut Sts, Harrisburg, 17120. Sandra Blust, Librn
Notes: Incl 200,000 aerial photographs and 250,000 maps.

PA —FREE LIBRARY OF PHILADELPHIA, Social Science and History Dept, Map Collection, Logan Sq, Philadelphia, 19103.
Holdings: Vols (30,000) Cat Mss Maps
Notes: Map collection incl atlases, maps, pamphlets, and aerial views. Incl a representative collection of early atlases (1534-1827). The collection emphasizes the Philadelphia, Pennsylvania and Delaware Valley areas in particular and the eastern seaboard in general. Low altitude oblique aerial photographs have been transferred to the Print and Picture Dept; high altitude vertical aerial photographs have been retained; some volumes and pamphlets reassigned within the Social Science and History Dept.

TX —TEXAS A&M UNIVERSITY, Sterling C Evans Library, College Station, 77843. Judith Rieke, Map Librn; Irene B Hoadley, Dir of Libraries
Notes: Maps of all areas of the world with geographic emphasis on the US and Texas. Subject emphasis on geology, petroleum, soils, highways and streets. Depository for NOS coastal and bathymetric charts, DMA maps, and USGS topographic and geologic maps. An extensive file of publisher's catalogs is available to the public. Collection incls aerial photographs (1100), atlases and gazetteers (1500), maps (82,600).

WA —UNIVERSITY OF WASHINGTON LIBRARIES, Suzzallo Library, Map Section, FM-25, Seattle, 98195. Steve Hiller, Head
Holdings: Pix
Budget: ($8953)
Notes: Includes 39,164 aerial photos.

WI —UNIVERSITY OF WISCONSIN, MILWAUKEE, American Geographical Society Collection, 2311 E Hartford Ave, PO Box 399, Milwaukee, 53201. Roman Drazniowsky, Cur
Holdings: Vols (196,800)
Budget: ($270,000)
Notes: The largest special collection in

PHOTOGRAPHY, AERIAL (cont.)

geography, cartography and related fields in the Western Hemisphere. Incl 6469 atlases; 385,610 maps; 71 globes; 33,700 pamphlets; 79,000 photographs; 99,000 Landsat Images. Catalog published by G K Hall, Boston.

ON —UNIVERSITY OF TORONTO, Library, Map Division, 130 St George St, Toronto, M5S 1A5, Can. Joan Winearls, Map Librn
Holdings: Vols (10,376) Cat Maps
Notes: A collection of 183,000 current topographic and thematic maps for all parts of the world; strong in Canada, Ontario, Toronto, Europe, US, parts of Latin America and Africa, Near East and Far East. Good atlas and cartography collection; 205,283 aerial photos, 1977-date, for Toronto, 1952-date for southern Ontario and parts of northern Ontario; files maintained of the following: publishers catalogs; maps clipped from newspapers and reports; articles on cartography, particularly the history of cartography; and base maps. In-house bibliographies on Toronto maps, climate and map interpretation. Map catalog is separate and housed only in the Map Library. Equipment, facilities for use of materials.

PHOTOGRAPHY, ARTISTIC

DC —LIBRARY OF CONGRESS, Prints & Photographs Div, Washington, 20540.
Notes: The F Holland Day Collection of Day's photographs. 640 photoprints.

NY —INTERNATIONAL MUSEUM OF PHOTOGRAPHY AT GEORGE EASTMAN HOUSE, Archives, 900 East Ave, Rochester, 14607. Rachel Stuhlman, Head Librn
Holdings: Vols (20,000) Cat Mss Pix Slides Microforms
Budget: ($73,000)
Notes: Photographic, especially cinematographic history; incl The James Card Collection from 1893; also other special items and hundreds of negatives of Eadweard Muybridge as well as his notebooks. Incl 450,000 pictures and slides. Also the Lewis Hine Collection of social documentary photography.

ON —NATIONAL GALLERY OF CANADA, Library, National Museums of Canada, Ottawa, K1A 0M8, Can. J Hunter, Chief Librn
Holdings: Vols (72,000) Cat Pix Slides Microforms
Budget: ($190,000)
Notes: History of art (postmediaeval, Western). Public reference only. Circulating only to gallery staff and on interlibrary loan. 1000 periodical titles currently received. 50,000 pamphlets, mostly exhibition and sales catalogs (not cataloged). 40,000 items in documentation files: clippings, notices of exhibitions and other ephemera. Exchange of National Gallery publications with other art galleries. Special section on history of Canadian art. Emphasis of collection on painting, sculpture, graphic arts and photography. Study collection of photographs and slides. See Catalogue of the National Gallery of Canada, 8 vols (Boston: G K Hall, 1973) and Supplement, 6 vols (Boston: G K Hall, 1981).

PHOTOGRAPHY, CRIME see Photography, Legal

PHOTOGRAPHY, DOCUMENTARY

KY —UNIVERSITY OF LOUISVILLE, Ekstrom Library, Photographic Archives, Louisville, 40292. J C Anderson, Cur; David G Horvath, Asst Cur
Holdings: Vols (750,000) Cat Pix Slides
Budget: ($60,000)
Notes: Photographs in three broad areas: works of outstanding photographers; examples of major developments in the art and technology of photography; photographs important as sociological, historical, or behavioral documents. Actors and actresses, Louisville's Macauley Theatre. Standard Oil of New Jersey Collection, 85,000 pictures of oil industry's effect on life in the 20th century (1943-1950, directed by Roy Stryker); Stryker's collection from Farm Security Administration series on rural conditions, 1935-1942; Jones and Laughlin Steel Corp Picture Library, by Stryker. Stryker manuscripts, 1934-1972. Caufield and Shook commercial photographs, Louisville area, 1920-1949. Jean Thomas "The Traipsin' Woman" photographs of Kentucky mountain folkways. Kate Matthews' (1870-1956) photographs incl prototypes for "Little Colonel" Series. Other collections described in unpublishedbrochure. Print duplication service.

NY —INTERNATIONAL MUSEUM OF PHOTOGRAPHY AT GEORGE EASTMAN HOUSE, Archives, 900 East Ave, Rochester, 14607. Rachel Stuhlman, Head Librn
Holdings: Vols (30,000) Cat Mss Microforms
Budget: ($104,000)
Notes: History, aesthetics and technology of photography and cinematography, incl the Gabriel Cromer, Josef Maria Eder, Alden Scott Boyer, Louis Walton Sipley/3M Collections, and the James Card Collection from 1893. Covers photographic, especially cinematographic history; also hundreds of negatives of Edward Muybridge as well as his notebooks. Incl 450,000 pictures and slides. Also the Lewis Hine Collection of social documentary photography.

PHOTOGRAPHY, EROTIC

KY —UNIVERSITY OF LOUISVILLE, Ekstrom Library, Photographic Archives, Louisville, 40292. J C Anderson, Cur; David G Horvath, Asst Cur
Holdings: Vols (750,000) Cat Pix Slides
Budget: ($60,000)
Notes: Photographs in three broad areas: works of outstanding photographers; examples of major developments in the art and technology of photography; photographs important as sociological, historical, or behavioral documents. Other collections described in unpublished brochure. Print duplication service.

PHOTOGRAPHY, FORENSIC see Photography, Legal

PHOTOGRAPHY, HIGH SPEED

NM —UNIVERSITY OF CALIFORNIA, Los Alamos National Laboratory, Libraries, PO Box 1663, MSP 362, Los Alamos, 87545. J Arthur Freed, Head Librn
Holdings: Vols (800,000) Cat Films Microforms
Budget: ($700,000)
Notes: Incl 500,000 classified and unclassified reports. There are 25 branch libraries and a central collection. The Medical Library contains about 40,000 vols in the areas of biomedical research.

PHOTOGRAPHY, INFRA-RED

MB —UNIVERSITY OF MANITOBA, Elizabeth Dafoe Library, Archives and Special Collections Dept, Winnipeg, R3T 2N2, Can. Richard E Bennett, Dept Head; Corrado A Santoro, Reference Archivist
Notes: Papers of Thomas Glendenning Hamilton, physician and surgeon, member of the Manitoba Legislative Assembly, psychic researcher. Winnipeg, Manitoba. Important collection, emphasis is on psychic research with limited amount of materials regarding his medical and political careers. Seance attendance registers, records and affidavits, lecture notes, correspondence, newspaper clippings, books and journal articles. Photographs, slides and ca 50 boxes of glass plate negatives.

PHOTOGRAPHY, KIRLIAN see Kirlian Photography

PHOTOGRAPHY, LEGAL

KY —UNIVERSITY OF LOUISVILLE, Ekstrom Library, Photographic Archives, Louisville, 40292. J C Anderson, Cur; David G Horvath, Asst Cur
Holdings: Vols (750,000) Cat Pix Slides
Budget: ($60,000)
Notes: Photographs in three broad areas: works of outstanding photographers; examples of major developments in the art and technology of photography; photographs important as sociological, historical, or behavioral documents. Other collections described in unpublished brochure. Print duplication service.

PHOTOGRAPHY, MEDICAL X-RAY see Tomography

PHOTOGRAPHY, POLICE see Photography, Legal

PHOTOGRAPHY, SATELLITE

DC —LIBRARY OF CONGRESS, Geography and Map Division, Washington, 20540. John A Wolter, Chief
Notes: Not a comprehensive collection. Samples of Landsat imagery.

NM —UNIVERSITY OF NEW MEXICO, Technology Application Center, 2500 Central SE, Albuquerque, 87131. Amy Budge, Photo Search Service
Notes: Remote sensing; aerial photography; all earth-oriented satellite photography; NCIC affiliate.

PHOTO-ILLUSTRATORS, INC.

PA —LIBRARY COMPANY OF PHILADELPHIA, 1314 Locust St, Philadelphia, 19107. Edwin Wolf II, Librn; Kenneth Finkel, Cur of Prints
Holdings: 2500 Items
Notes: Incl 2500 prints by Joseph J Kelly's firm, The Photo-Illustrators; with a large proportion on the Sesquicentennial and other Philadelphia views.

PHOTOJOURNALISM see Journalism, Pictorial

PHOTOMATERIAL, ORGANIC

CA —INTERNATIONAL BUSINESS MACHINES RESEARCH LIBRARY, 5600 Cottle Rd, San Jose, 95193. Phil Grincewich, Mgr Technical Information
Holdings: Vols (13,500) Cat
Notes: Collection includes emphasis on laser spectroscopy, organic photomaterial and chemical dynamics. Incl 21,000 vols of 770 journals. On-line search facility. Vols are divided into three libraries, Technical Research, Technical Information, and Programing. Not open to public.

PHOTOMECHANICAL PROCESSES

MN —3M COMPANY, Mertle Library, 3M Center, Bldg 235-1D, Saint Paul, 55101.
Holdings: Vols (4000) // Cat Mss Pix
Notes: The collection of Joseph S Mertle, includes patents, portraits, a clipping file, and other historical graphic arts books and periodicals.

PHOTOMETRY, ASTRONOMICAL

CA —UNIVERSITY OF CALIFORNIA, SANTA CRUZ, University Library, Special Collections, Santa Cruz, 95064. Rita Bottoms, Special Collections Librn; Margaret Felts, South Pacific Collection Bibliographer
Notes: Astronomy Library.

DC —US NAVAL OBSERVATORY LIBRARY, 30th & Massachusetts Ave, NW, Washington, 20016. Brenda G Corbin, Librn
Holdings: Vols (75,000) Cat Mss Maps Pix Slides Microforms
Notes: Incl 1000 journals, with monograph and serial publications in the fields of celestial mechanics, fundamental astronomy, time determination, photographic astrometry and astrophysics, data processing, mathematics.

PHOTOPSYCHOGRAPHY see Kirlian Photography

PHOTOSYNTHESIS

CA —UNIVERSITY OF CALIFORNIA, BERKELEY, Bancroft Library, Manuscripts

PHOTOSYNTHESIS (cont.)

Division, Berkeley, 94720. James D Hart, Dir
Notes: Extensive collections of papers and archives relative to the history of modern chemistry.

PHRENOLOGY

CA —SAN DIEGO PUBLIC LIBRARY, Literature & Language Sect, 820 E St, San Diego, 92101. Alyce Archuleta, Senior Librn
Holdings: Vols 20 Cat
Notes: Early texts in English and French dating back to 1810.

CT —YALE UNIVERSITY, Medical Historical Library, Klebs Collection, 333 Cedar St, New Haven, 06520. Ferenc A Gyorgyey, Librn
Notes: Incl 120 vols from the defunct British Phrenological Society.

KY —UNIVERSITY OF LOUISVILLE, Kornhauser Health Sciences Library, 520 S Preston St, PO Box 35260, Louisville, 40292. Leonard M Eddy, Dir; Sherrill R McConnell, Archivist
Holdings: Vols 100 Cat Mss
Notes: Phrenology and the Charles Caldwell Collection. Have phrenological and head charts. See E Horine, *Sketch and Guide to the Writings of Charles Caldwell* (1960).

MA —FRANCIS A COUNTWAY LIBRARY OF MEDICINE, Boston Medical Library/ Harvard Medical Library, 10 Shattuck St, Boston, 02115. C Robin LeSueur, Librn; Richard J Wolfe, Cur, Rare Books & Manuscripts
Holdings: Vols (500,000) Cat Mss Maps Pix Microforms
Notes: Combines resources of the Harvard Medical School and the Boston Medical Library. Strong in serials and medical history in all fields of medicine, incl incunabula, non-medical books by doctors, travel books by doctors. 300,000 medical dissertations and theses. Special strength in all medical subjects listed in this volume.

NY —AMERICAN MUSEUM OF NATURAL HISTORY, Library Services Dept, Central Park W & 79th St, New York, 10024. Nina J Root, Chairwoman; Mary Genett, Asst Librn for Reference Services
Holdings: Uncat
Notes: Incl a large, classified collection of human skulls as phrenological phenomena.

PHYCOLOGY see Algology

PHYSICAL ANTHROPOLOGY see Anthropology, Physical; Somatology

PHYSICAL CHEMISTRY see Chemistry, Physical and Theoretical

PHYSICAL CULTURE see Physical Education and Training

PHYSICAL EDUCATION AND TRAINING

CT —YALE UNIVERSITY, Box 1603A, Yale Station, New Haven, 06520.
Notes: Papers of Walter Camp, father of American football and foremost authority on sports and physical fitness. 48 microfilm reels; incl also over 20,000 clippings, etc on sports, providing virtual history, 1866-1925. Published guide to the collection for sale.

IL —UNIVERSITY OF ILLINOIS, URBANA/CHAMPAIGN, Library, Applied Life Studies Library, 1408 W Gregory Dr, Urbana, 61801.
Holdings: Vols (38,000) Cat Microforms
Notes: Library has own card catalog and shelf list for this collection; it is also represented in the main card catalog and shelf list of the University of Illinois Library. Card indexes to games and sports are incl in books in the collection, also to folk and national dances. Try to have fairly complete coverage of books published in all aspects of the field of physical education which would be of interest to students, as well as a lot of

more general books on sports. Coverage of health education and recreation is also quite complete. This is one of the few (if not only) departmental libraries in the US devoted to this field. Published catalog: *Dictionary Catalog of the Applied Life Studies Library* (formerly *Physical Education Library*), *University of Illinois at Urbana-Champaign* v 1-4 (Boston: G K Hall, 1977) and *First Supplement* v 1-2 (Boston: G K Hall, 1982).

KY —UNIVERSITY OF KENTUCKY, Margaret I King Library, Dept of Special Collections, Lexington, 40506. William Marshall, Head
Holdings: Vols (400) Uncat
Notes: Early physical education manuals and textbooks to 1925; 18th and 19th century sports, games.

MA —UNIVERSITY OF MASSACHUSETTS AT AMHERST, Library, Amherst, 01002.
Notes: Strong collections in physical education, sports studies, exercise, gymnastics, etc.

MA —SPRINGFIELD COLLEGE LIBRARY, Babson Library, Springfield, 01109. Henry Dutcher, Reference Librn
Holdings: Vols (130,000) Cat
Budget: ($65,000)

NJ —MONTCLAIR STATE COLLEGE, Harry A Sprague Library, Upper Montclair, 07043.
Holdings: // Cat
Notes: Collection of over 150 physical education textbooks; 19th to early 20th century.

NC —UNIVERSITY OF NORTH CAROLINA, GREENSBORO, Walter Clinton Jackson Library, Special Collections Dept, 1000 Spring Garden St, Greensboro, 27412. Emilie W Mills, Librn
Holdings: Vols 100 Uncat Mss Pix
Notes: Incl papers of the Project Movement Education, Plattsburg, New York (1966-69), and papers and publications of Laurie Campbell, Gladys Andrews Fleming, Bonnie Gilliom, James H Humphrey, Elizabeth A Ludwig, Ruth Morison and Lorena Porter.

OR —UNIVERSITY OF OREGON LIBRARY, Education-Psychology Dept, Eugene, 97403. Rose Marie Service, Head Dept Librn
Holdings: Microforms
Budget: ($4000)
Notes: General and research collection in health, physical education, recreation and dance incl serials. An important series is *Microforms Publications,* produced by the College of Health, Physical Education and Recreation, University of Oregon, which is comprised of 3632 microcards or microfiche of unpublished research of national significance.

PA —PENNSYLVANIA STATE UNIVERSITY, Fred Lewis Pattee Library, University Park, 16802.
Notes: Numerous and large collections on many sports. Also, materials supporting every aspect of the program of the Center for Women and Sport, incl research into kinetics, endocrinology, physiology, psychology, etc.

PA —WEST CHESTER UNIVERSITY, Francis Harvey Green Library, West Chester, 19380. R Gerald Schoelkopf, Special Collections Librn
Holdings: Vols 600 Cat
Notes: Comprehensive collection of works (1890-1947) which are indicative of the development of physical education. The Allen-Ehinger Collection.

TN —VANDERBILT UNIVERSITY, George Peabody College for Teachers, Education Library, Box 325, Nashville, 37203. Mary Beth Blalock, Librn
Holdings: Vols (192,541) Cat Pix Slides Phonorecords Filmstrips Microforms
Budget: ($59,000)
Notes: The Education Library (192,541 vols) collects in all areas relating to education with special emphasis on Child Study and Exceptional Children. Special funds are available for continuing purchases in these areas. The collection is strong in curriculum materials, physical education, applied art, psychology related to education and all areas of education. Amoung special papers are

over 300 papers by and about Jean Piaget and an extensive author and subject file referring to the location of these papers and books and journal articles by and about Piaget in the rest of the Education Library collection. The Education Library is a Division of the Vanderbilt University Library.

MB —UNIVERSITY OF MANITOBA, Faculty of Education, D S Woods Education Library, Winnipeg, R3T 2N2, Can. Doreen Shanks, Head
Holdings: Vols (57,000) Cat

ON —SPORT INFORMATION RESOURCE CENTER (SIRC), 333 River Rd, Ottawa, K1L 8H9, Can. Gilles Chiasson, Director
Notes: The database "SPORT" created by this institution is available for searching on SDC Search Services. Incl 20,000 monographs, 1400 current periodical subscriptions and 130,000 bibliographical references.

ON —SIRLS, Faculty of Human Kinetics & Leisure Studies, University of Waterloo, Waterloo, N2L 3G1, Can. Betty Smith, Database Mgr
Notes: Information Retrieval System for the Sociology of Leisure and Sport (SIRLS) is a computerized online database of about 13,000 entries (1983). Incl dance as a leisure time activity.

PQ —UNIVERSITY OF MONTREAL, Physical Education Library, Montreal, H3C 3J7, Can. Lisa Mayrand, Dir
Holdings: Vols 15,000
Notes: Perhaps Canada's largest university library sports collection. Collection is bilingual (in English and French). 441 periodical subscriptions, 890 periodical titles, 4000 microfiche and 317 microfilms. On line with Ottawa's SIRC data base (qv).

PHYSICAL EDUCATION AND TRAINING—HISTORY

NC —UNIVERSITY OF NORTH CAROLINA, GREENSBORO, Walter Clinton Jackson Library, Special Collections Dept, 1000 Spring Garden St, Greensboro, 27412. Emilie W Mills, Librn
Holdings: Vols 2000 // Cat
Notes: Incl 1000 pamphlets. The Homans Collection of historical materials acquired from Wellesley College, dating from 16th century to early 1900s. Emphasis on history of physical education for women. Incl early dance books and landmark works on all types of physcial activity, training, theory; gymnastics books date from the 16th century.

PHYSICAL EDUCATION AND TRAINING—MEDICAL ASPECTS see Sports Medicine

PHYSICAL GEOGRAPHY

CA —NASA, Ames Research Center, Libraries, Library Br 202-3, Moffett Field, 94035. Sarah Dueker, Chief, Library Branch
Holdings: Cat Audiotapes Microforms
Notes: Main library collections cover physical sciences, engineering and mathematical fields related to research programs in aeronautics-space research. Life sciences library collections cover medical, physiological, behavioral and biological sciences related to research programs. Also emphases on remote sensing of earth resources and the search for extraterrestrial life. 950 journal titles and 85,000 monographs. Reports collection includes 60,000 hard copy reports and 900,000 microfiche.

ON —GEOLOGICAL SURVEY OF CANADA, Library, Dept of Energy, Mines, & Resouces, 601 Booth St, Ottawa, K1A 0E8, Can. Annette E Bourgeois, Librn
Holdings: Vols (300,000) Cat Mss Maps Microforms
Notes: All aspects of Geology are collected and an attempt is made to collect all Canadian geology information. The library is a national resource collection in the geosciences. Incl 40,000 book titles

PHYSICAL GEOGRAPHY (cont.)

(monographs), 4000 personals, 35,000 microfiche, 300,000 maps, 2000 translations of reports, 20 verrtical files, 300,000 vols of bound periodicals.

PHYSICAL OCEANOGRAPHY see Oceanography

PHYSICAL SCIENCES

CA —COGSWELL COLLEGE, Library, 600 Stockton St, San Francisco, 94108. Judith Carson-Croes, Dir
Holdings: Vols (12,000) Cat

PHYSICAL THERAPY

CA —LOS ANGELES PUBLIC LIBRARY, Science & Technology Dept, 630 W Fifth St, Los Angeles, 90071. Billie M Connor, Dept Head
Holdings: Vols (7500)
Notes: A well-rounded collection of materials related to consumer health, medicine and drugs as well as materials for the allied health and medical professions. Includes a sound representative selection of basic texts covering various aspects of medical treatment, drugs, diseases and syndromes. Indexes are collected as well as a basic collection of journals. The directories collection is strong. The broadest possible collection of books oriented toward consumer health, medicine, diets and nutrition is maintained, both traditional and alternative. Texts and examination study books are collected for nurses, laboratory technicians, physcial therapists, speech therapists, paramedics and other allied health professions.
IL —UNIVERSITY OF ILLINOIS, URBANA/CHAMPAIGN, Library, Applied Life Studies Library, 1408 W Gregory Dr, Urbana, 61801.
Holdings: Vols (38,000) Cat Pix Microforms
See also entry under Physical Education and Training.
MI —REHABILITATION INSTITUTE, Learning Resources Center, 261 Mack Blvd, Detroit, 48201. Daria Drobny, Medical Librn
Holdings: Vols (2600) Cat Slides
Notes: Physical medicine and rehabilitation.
†NY —MEDICAL RESEARCH LIBRARY OF BROOKLYN, Academy of Medicine of Brooklyn & The State University of New York Downstate Medical Center, 450 Clarkson St, Brooklyn, 11203. Kenneth E Moody, Dir
Holdings: Vols 1000 Cat
See also entry under Medicine.
ND —UNIVERSITY OF NORTH DAKOTA, Harley E French Medical Library, Grand Forks, 58202. David W Boilard, Dir; Lila Pedersen, Asst Dir
Holdings: Vols (56,000) Cat
Budget: ($206,000)
Notes: 1075 current periodical subscriptions.
OH —SAINT ELIZABETH MEDICAL CENTER, Health Sciences Library, 601 Miami Blvd W, Dayton, 45408. Ann Lewis, Librn
Holdings: Vols (13,000) Cat Slides Audiotapes Filmstrips
WI —MARQUETTE UNIVERSITY, Memorial Library, 1415 W Wisconsin Ave, Milwaukee, 53233. Jay Kirk, Health Sciences Librn
Notes: Supports curriculum and research.
PQ —UNIVERSITY OF MONTREAL, Bibliotheque Para-medicale, 2375 Chemin de la Cote Ste Catherine, Montreal, H3C 3J7, Can. Johanne Hopper, Head Librn
Holdings: Vols 1475 Cat Pix
Budget: $4000

PHYSICAL TRAINING see Physical Education and Training

PHYSICALLY HANDICAPPED

DC —LIBRARY OF CONGRESS, National Library Service for Blind Physically Handicapped, 1291 Taylor St NW, Washington, 20542. Frank Kunt Cylke, Director; Hylda Kamisar, Head Reference Section
Holdings: Vols 3000 Cat
Notes: A reference collection about blindness and physical handicapping conditions. Excludes medicine. Collection consists of books, periodicals, and vertical file items. Machine-readable data laser accessed through DIALOG and BRS. Available for use by libraries, organizations, and individuals.
NY —JEWISH GUILD FOR THE BLIND, Cassette Library, 15 W 65 St, New York, 10023. Bruce Edward Massis, Dir
Holdings: Cat Audiotapes
Budget: $115,000
Notes: This 40,000 audiocassette library records and circulates fiction and non-fiction best sellers in their unabridged form on standard cassettes to blind and physically handicapped persons free of charge worldwide.

PHYSICALLY HANDICAPPED—BIOGRAPHY

MN —MAYO MEDICAL LIBRARY, History of Medicine Collection, Rochester, 55905. Nancy R Hensel, Librn
Holdings: Vols 800 Cat
Notes: The Walter C Alvarez Collection of autobiographies of the physically and mentally handicapped. Collection described in *Mayo Clin Proc*, 47:125-127, Feb 1972.

PHYSICALLY HANDICAPPED—EMPLOYMENT see Vocational Rehabilitation

PHYSICIANS

IN —INDIANA UNIVERSITY, Lilly Library, Seventh St, Bloomington, 47405. William R Cagle, Librn
Holdings: Cat Mss
Notes: First appearances in print of great medical discoveries. Mss incl papers of various 19th century midwestern physicians.
LA —TULANE UNIVERSITY, Rudolph Matas Medical Library, 1430 Tulane Ave, New Orleans, 70112. W D Postell Jr, Librn
Holdings: Cat Mss Pix
Notes: Incl the Elizabeth Bass Collection of personalized material on women doctors (3640 vols).
MA —RADCLIFFE COLLEGE, Arthur & Elizabeth Schlesinger Library on the History of Women in America, 3 James St, Cambridge, 02138. Patricia Miller King, Dir; Eva Moseley, Cur of Mss
Holdings: // Cat Mss
Notes: Mss collections of or about women physicians, incl Elizabeth (1821-1910) and Emily (1826-1910) Blackwell, founders of New York Infirmary; Martha May Eliot (1891-1978), a pediatrician who was head of the US Children's Bureau and Asst Dir-General of WHO; industrial toxicologist Alice Hamilton (1869-1970); Yale Pediatrician and psychiatrist Edith Banfield Jackson (1895-1977); New York physician Mary (Putnam) Jacobi (1842-1906); and Ida Sophia Scudder (1870-1960), medical missionary in India. Also several collections concerning New England Hospital for Women and Children, and oral history interviews in the Family Planning Oral History Project.
MO —WASHINGTON UNIVERSITY, School of Medicine, Archives, 660 S Euclid Ave, Saint Louis, 63110. Paul G Anderson, Archivist
Holdings: Mss Pix Audiotapes
Budget: ($38,000)
Notes: Institutional records and papers of faculty of Washington University School of Medicine and its predecessors and associated hospitals. Contains records of St Louis Medical College, Missouri Medical Barnard Free Skin and Cancer Hospital, Barnes Hospital, St Louis Children's Hospital and Jewish Hospital of St Louis. Incl papers of William Beaumont, Joseph Erlanger, Leo Loeb, Evarts Graham, Edmund V Cowdry, Helen Graham, Carl V Moore, Margaret Smith and others. Oral history program. See also: Anderson, Paul G and Hoolihan, Christopher, eds. *Special Collections* (St Louis: Washington University School of Medicine, 1981). 960 linear feet.
NY —CORNELL UNIVERSITY LIBRARIES, Collection of Regional History, Dept of Manuscripts and Univ Archives, Ithaca, 14853.
Notes: French surgeon, Maurice Augusto Chevassu, author and editor of medical publications. Incl 265 publications. Incl 265 letters and notes to Chevassu.
SC —COLLEGE OF CHARLESTON LIBRARY, Special Collections Dept, Charleston, 29401.
Notes: Journal kept by an unidentified physician (I.F.R.) as a medical student at the University of Pennsylvania and at the University of Louisiana in New Orleans, as a ship's surgeon for two years in the Caribbean, and as a private practitioner. Incl notes of lectures by Dr Samuel Jackson of the University of Pennsylvania.
TX —UNIVERSITY OF TEXAS, DALLAS, Health Science Center, Reference Dept & History of Health Sciences Dept, 5323 Harry Hines Blvd, Dallas, 75235. Helen Mayo, Head
Holdings: Vols (10,000) Cat Pix Slides Audiotapes Videotapes Microforms
Notes: History of Medicine collection contains ca 10,000 vols. This total is comprised of pre-1900 journals, primary materials in the History of Medicine and the History of Science, and secondary studies in these two areas. The major strengths of this collection are in the areas of epidemics and plagues, military medicine, and collected works of famous medical pioneers. Incl in this collection are the medical journals published by the county medical societies in Texas, local publications by Dallas County medical organizations, and ephemeral material in a similar vein. The university archives contain all theses and dissertations form UTHSCD and miscellaneous institutional documents circulated by the school's administration.

PHYSICIANS—BIOGRAPHY

CT —YALE UNIVERSITY, Medical Historical Library, 333 Cedar St, New Haven, 06510. Ferenc A Gyorgyey, Librn
Holdings: Vols 6500 Cat

PHYSICIANS—CARICATURES AND CARTOONS

MN —MAYO MEDICAL LIBRARY, History of Medicine Collection, Rochester, 55905. Nancy R Hensel, Librn
Holdings: Pix
Notes: The Comfort Collection of caricatures of physicians and scientists from *Vanity Fair*. Description: Mann. Ruth J: "The unheroic representation of heroes." *Mayo Clin Proc*. 46:197-199, Mar 1971.

PHYSICIANS—PORTRAITS

LA —TULANE UNIVERSITY, Rudolph Matas Medical Library, 1430 Tulane Ave, New Orleans, 70112. W D Postell Jr, Librn
Holdings: Cat
Notes: Pictures of doctors-3400; Medical art-700.
MD —JOHNS HOPKINS UNIVERSITY, Institute of the History of Medicine, 1900 E Monument St, Baltimore, 21205. Doris Thibodeau, Librn
Holdings: Pix
Notes: Holdings contain 15,000 items.
NY —NEW YORK ACADEMY OF MEDICINE, Library, 2 E 103 St, New York, 10029. Brett A Kirkpatrick, Librn
Notes: Incl 250,000 separate items as well as portraits appearing in publications.

PHYSICIANS, WOMEN see Women Physicians

PHYSICIANS AS AUTHORS

LA —TULANE UNIVERSITY, Rudolph Matas Medical Library, 1430 Tulane Ave,

PHYSICIANS AS AUTHORS (cont.)

New Orleans, 70112. W D Postell Jr, Librn
Holdings: Vols (1400) Cat
Notes: B B Weinstein Collection of
nonmedical material written by doctors and
fiction about doctors.

PHYSICIANS IN LITERATURE

LA —TULANE UNIVERSITY, Rudolph
Matas Medical Library, 1430 Tulane Ave,
New Orleans, 70112. W D Postell Jr, Librn
Holdings: Vols (1400) Cat
Notes: B B Weinstein Collection of
nonmedical material by doctors and fiction
about doctors.

PHYSICISTS

CA —CALIFORNIA INSTITUTE OF
TECHNOLOGY, Robert A Millikan
Memorial Library, Archives, 1201 E
California Blvd, Pasadena, 91125. Judith R
Goodstein, Archivist
Notes: The Lee A DuBridge papers, incl 228
boxes of correspondence, documents,
reports, and memorabilia reflecting his
tenure as head of MIT Radiation Laboratory,
1940-1946; as president of Caltech, 1946-
1969; and his participation in professional
and governmental organizations.
IA —HERBERT HOOVER PRESIDENTIAL
LIBRARY, West Branch, 52358. Dale C
Mayer, Archivist
Notes: Papers.
MA —MASSACHUSETTS INSTITUTE OF
TECHNOLOGY, Institute Archives, Special
Collections, Cambridge, 02139.
Notes: Papers of Bernard Feld, nuclear
physicist at MIT and a world leader in
disarmament activities. Graduate student
under Leo Szilard and Enrico Fermi and
continued as a physicist with the Manhattan
Engineer District in Los Alamos, New
Mexico. The collection incl extensive
documentation of national and international
arms control efforts which Feld initiated in
the Cold War which followed the destruction
of Hiroshima and Nagasaki. Founder and
Editor-in-Chief of the Bulletin of Atomic
Scientists.
NY —CORNELL UNIVERSITY LIBRARIES,
Manuscript and Archives Division, Ithaca,
14853. H Thomas Hickerson, Special
Collections Librn
Notes: Raymond Bowers' papers, 1950-78.

PHYSICS

AR —UNIVERSITY OF ARKANSAS,
Technology Campus Library, 1201
McAlmont St, PO Box 3017, Little Rock,
72203. Brent Nelson, Librn
Holdings: Vols (20,849) Cat Slides
Microforms
Budget: ($35,000)
CA —UNIVERSITY OF CALIFORNIA,
DAVIS, Physical Sciences Library, Davis,
95616. Scott Kennedy, Head
Holdings: Vols (17,372) Cat Microforms
Budget: ($11,000)
Notes: Strong in journal runs and reference
materials. Nuclear physics represented by
microcopy depository collection of US Dept
of Energy (AEC and ERDA) technical
reports (est 462,574). Selected NASA
reports on microfiche since 1975. Access to
online information bases.
CA —UNIVERSITY OF CALIFORNIA, LOS
ANGELES, Physics Library, 213 Kinsey
Hall, Los Angeles, 90024. J Wally Pegram,
Librn
Holdings: Vols (37,000) Cat
Notes: UCLA physics theses; current SLAC
preprints in high-energy physics. (592)
current serials subscriptions. Pure physics is
emphasized. Strong collections in high
energy physics, nuclear physics, plasma
physics, and solid state physics. Acoustics,
astrophysics, biophysics, geophysics, optics,
and spectroscopy also collected.
CA —UNIVERSITY OF SOUTHERN
CALIFORNIA, Seaver Science Library,
University Park, Los Angeles, 90089. A

Albert Baker, Head
Holdings: Vols (200,000) Microforms
Budget: ($700,000)
Notes: Includes technical reports (12,000),
serial and periodical titles (3600).
CA —R & D ASSOCIATES, Technical
Information Center, 4640 Admiralty Way,
PO Box 9695, Marina del Rey, 90291.
Margaret R Anderson, Mgr
Holdings: Vols (10,000) Cat Mss Maps
Microforms
Notes: Military arts and sciences, tactical
and strategic studies, and defense systems.
Incl 45,000 government contractor and
technical reports; and briefing charts
(transparencies).
CA —NASA, Ames Research Center, Libraries,
Library Br 202-3, Moffett Field, 94035.
Sarah Dueker, Chief, Library Branch
Holdings: Cat Audiotapes Microforms
Notes: Main library collections cover
physical sciences, engineering and
mathematical fields related to research
programs in aeronautics-space research. Life
sciences library collections cover medical,
physiological, behavioral and biological
sciences related to research programs. Also
emphases on remote sensing of earth
resources and the search for extraterrestrial
life. 950 journal titles and 85,000
monographs. Reports collection includes 60,
000 hard copy reports and 900,000
microfiche.
CA —UNIVERSITY OF CALIFORNIA,
RIVERSIDE, Physical Sciences Library,
Riverside, 92517. Richard W Vierich, Librn
Holdings: Vols (89,000) Cat Microforms
Budget: ($347,000)
CA —LOGICON INC, Strategic & Information
Systems Division, Information Center, 255
W Fifth St, Box 471, San Pedro, 90731.
Constance B Davenport, Supervisor
Holdings: Vols (3000) Cat Mss Microforms
Notes: Incl about 3000 books, 250 periodical
titles, 5000 technical reports, 10,000
microfiche, 750 standards and specifications.
Catalog is computerized. Interactive search
capability with Dialog, Orbit, DMS on-line,
NASA Recon. Material on computer
programming, systems analysis, military
systems and operations research.
CA —UNIVERSITY OF CALIFORNIA,
SANTA CRUZ, University Library, Special
Collections, Santa Cruz, 95064. Rita
Bottoms, Special Collections Librn; Margaret
Felts, South Pacific Collection Bibliographer
CO —IBM, Boulder Library, PO Box 1900,
Boulder, 80302. Beverly Jorman, Library
Mgr
Holdings: Vols (10,000) Cat Microforms
Reports
Notes: Emphasis in chemistry, physics,
computer sciences and technology.
CO —UNIVERSITY OF COLORADO, Duane
Physical Laboratories G140, Mathematics-
Physics Library, Boulder, 80309. Allen
Wynne, Head Librn
Holdings: Vols Cat Microforms
Notes: All areas of mathematics and physics
with special emphasis on astrophysics,
astrogeophysics, theoretical high energy
physics and theoretical computer science.
Also basic astronomy. The most
comprehensive general mathematics and
physics collection in the Rocky Mountain
area, although not having sufficient depth to
allow doctoral research in some specific
areas. Excellent bibliographic control for
current and retrospective searching as
complete runs of most major subject
indexing and abstracting services are present.
ILL for businesses through the Colorado
Technical Reference Center in main library
building.
CO —COLORADO SCHOOL OF MINES,
Arthur Lakes Library, 14 & Illinois Sts,
Golden, 80401. Hartley K Phinney, Jr, Head
Librn
Holdings: Vols (270,557) Cat Mss Maps
Microforms
CT —YALE UNIVERSITY, Observatory
Library, 260 Whitney Ave, Box 6666, New
Haven, 06511.
Holdings: Vols (15,000) Cat Maps Pix
Budget: ($15,000)
Notes: Also an extensive collection of
domestic and foreign observatory
publications.

CT —YALE UNIVERSITY, Kline Science
Library, Kline Biology Tower Rm C-8, PO
Box 6666, New Haven, 06511. Richard J
Dionne, Head
Holdings: Vols (175,480) Cat 16mm Films
Microforms
Budget: ($340,000)
Notes: Comprehensive collection on
biological sciences, physics, and chemistry.
Incl Evans Collection of Bryology and
Lichenology (with catalog cards in both
Kline Science Library and Sterling Memorial
Library). Also incl AEC reports (hardcopy
and microform) to 1970.
FL —UNIVERSITY OF FLORIDA,
Engineering & Physics Library, 410 Weil
Hall, Gainesville, 32611. Roger V Krumm,
Librn
Holdings: Cat Microforms
Notes: Incl AEC, ERDA, DOE, NASA
reports.
GA —GEORGIA INSTITUTE OF
TECHNOLOGY, Price Gilbert Memorial
Library, 225 North Ave, Atlanta, 30332.
Edward Graham Roberts, Dir
Holdings: Vols (1,661,559) Cat Maps Slides
Microforms
Budget: ($1,383,302)
Notes: Incl (4,307,996) patents and (568,
490) government documents.
IL —ARGONNE NATIONAL
LABORATORY, Library, Technical
Information Services Dept, 9700 Cass Ave,
Argonne, 60439. Hillis L Griffin, Dir
Notes: The ANL library system consists of
eight branch libraries with centralized
processing services. The entire collection
numbers 70,000 monographic titles, 3700
journal titles, and over 1 million scientific
and technical reports. Materials may be used
by the public in the library by prior
arrangement. Photocopies may be supplied
for interlibrary loan, for which a processing
and handling charge is made.
IL —ARGONNE NATIONAL
LABORATORY, Mathematics/Physics/
Computer Science Branch Library, 9700 S
Cass Ave, Argonne, 60439.
Notes: Theoretical, medium and low-energy
physics. Incl 30,000 vols monographs, 190
current journals. Materials may be used by
the public in the library prior arrangement.
Photocopies may be supplied for interlibrary
loan, for which a processing and handling
charge is made.
IL —UNIVERSITY OF CHICAGO
LIBRARIES, John Crerar Library
Collections, 1100 E 57th St, Chicago, 60637.
Robert Rosenthal, Special Collections Librn
Notes: The John Crerar Library's extensive
science, medicine, and engineering
collections have been transferred in trust to
the University of Chicago Libraries. Incl rare
books and special collections as listed here.
IL —NORTHWESTERN UNIVERSITY,
Seeley G Mudd Library for Science &
Engineering, 2233 Sheridan Rd, Evanston,
60201. Robert C Michaelson, Head
Holdings: Vols (200,000) Cat Microforms
Notes: Collection emphasizes graduate and
research level material.
IL —UNIVERSITY OF ILLINOIS,
URBANA/CHAMPAIGN, Slavic and East
European Library, Urbana, 61801. Marianna
Tax Choldin, Head
Holdings: Vols (420,000) Cat Microforms
Notes: One of the largest Slavic and East
European collections. Strong in Russian and
Soviet materials-humanities, sciences, and
social sciences; languages and literatures;
periodicals, newspapers, and microforms. Ca
260,000 volumes in languages of the Soviet
Union plus 20,000 Russian and Ukrainian
titles on microform. Extensive coverage of
Czechoslovakia (35,000 vols); Yugoslavia
(31,000 vols); Bulgaria (9200 vols); Poland
(34,600 vols); Romania (13,000 vols); and
Hungary (18,000 vols) and the languages,
literatures, and history of these countries.
IN —INDIANA STATE UNIVERSITY,
Science Library, Terre Haute, 47809. Susan
J Thompson, Science Librn
Holdings: Vols (40,000) Cat Microforms
Budget: ($160,846)
IN —PURDUE UNIVERSITY LIBRARIES,
Physics Library, Physics Bldg, West

PHYSICS (cont.)

Lafayette, 47907. Janet Huettner, Librn
Holdings: Vols (35,000) Cat Microforms

IA —IOWA STATE UNIVERSITY, Library,
Ames, 50011. Warren B Kuhn, Dean of
Library Services
Holdings: Cat
Notes: Extensive serial holdings.

IA —UNIVERSITY OF IOWA, Physics
Library, Iowa City, 52242. Jack W Dickey,
Physics Librn
Holdings: Vols (36,199)
Budget: ($79,000)
Notes: General physics and space physics.

KY —UNIVERSITY OF KENTUCKY,
Chemistry-Physics Library, 150 Chemistry-
Physics Bldg, Lexington, 40506. Jane M
Lane, Acting Librn
Holdings: Vols (41,500) Cat Audiotapes
Budget: ($164,700)
Notes: One shelflist is maintained. No
record of volumes in each collection.
Combined library has its own catalog, as well
as entires in the public catalog in the main
library.

ME —COLLEGE OF THE ATLANTIC,
Thorndike Library, Bar Harbor, 04609.
Marcie L Dworak, Libr Dir
Notes: A rebuilding, fire-destroyed library
(1983).

MD —JOHNS HOPKINS UNIVERSITY,
Milton S Eisenhower Library, Charles & 34
Sts, Baltimore, 21218. Ann S Gwyn,
Assistant Dir for Special Collections
Holdings: Vols 25,000 Cat Microforms
Notes: Strong, espec in journals in
theoretical fields. Long runs back to 19th
and 18th centuries of many foreign and
American serials.

MD —NATIONAL LIBRARY OF
MEDICINE, 8600 Rockville Pike, Bethesda,
20209. Harold M Schoolinam, Actg Dir
Holdings: Vols (3,150,000) Cat Mss
Audiotapes Videotapes 16mm Films
Filmstrips Microforms
Budget: ($46,400)
Notes: The world's largest medical library.
Materials are collected exhaustively in some
40 biomedical areas and, to a lesser degree,
in related subject areas such as general
chemistry, physics, zoology, botany, and
instrumentation. Holdings include 82,000
monographic volumes, pre-1871; 438,000
monographic volumes, 1871-present; 714,000
bound serial volumes; 281,000 theses; 172,
000 pamphlets; 1,207,000 manuscripts; 156,
000 microforms; 12,000 audiovisuals; and 75,
000 prints and photographs. Pre-1871
material is in a separate historical collection.
Approximately 24,000 serial titles are
currenlty received.

MA —UNIVERSITY OF MASSACHUSETTS
AT AMHERST, Physical Sciences Library,
Amherst, 01003. Siegfried Feller, Assoc Dir
for Collection Development
Holdings: Cat Microforms
Notes: Incl extensive holdings of journals,
NACA and NASA publications, and AEC
documents (microfiche).

MA —HARVARD UNIVERSITY LIBRARY,
Gordon McKay Library, Division of Applied
Sciences, Pierce Hall, Oxford St, Cambridge,
02138. Julie Sandall Barlas, Librn
Holdings: Vols (100,000) Cat Microforms

MA —HARVARD UNIVERSITY LIBRARY,
Physics Research Library, 450 Jefferson
Laboratory, 17 Oxford St, Cambridge,
02138. Nina McMaster, Librn
Holdings: Vols (18,000) Cat Microforms

MA —SMITHSONIAN INSTITUTION
LIBRARIES, Astrophysical Observatory
Branch, 60 Garden St, Cambridge, 02138.
Joyce Rey, Librn
Holdings: Vols (10,000) Cat Maps Pix
Microforms

MA —BOSTON COLLEGE LIBRARIES,
Science Library, Devlin Hall, Chestnut Hill,
02167. F Clifford McElroy, Science Librn
Holdings: Vols (54,508) Cat Maps
Microforms
Budget: ($94,270)
Notes: Library is being absorbed into the
general collection.

MA —AVCO EVERETT RESEARCH
LABORATORY, INC, Library, 2385 Revere

Beach Parkway, Everett, 02149. Lorraine T
Nazzaro, Librn
Holdings: Vols (24,000) Cat Maps Slides
Microforms
Budget: ($50,000)
Notes: Incl 32,000 reports.

MA —TUFTS UNIVERSITY, Mathematics-
Physics Library, Medford, 02155. Pauline
Boucher, Librn
Holdings: Vols 6000
Notes: Incl also 1500 preprints.

MA —WELLESLEY COLLEGE, Margaret
Clapp Library, College Archives, Wellesley,
02181.
Notes: Records of the Departments of
Astronomy, Biological Sciences, Botany,
Chemistry, Geology, Physics, Zoology, and
individuals connected with these
departments at Wellesley College (27 linear
feet).

MI —UNIVERSITY OF MICHIGAN, Physics-
Astronomy Library, 290 Dennison Bldg,
Ann Arbor, 48109. Jack W Weigel, Physical
Sciences Librn
Holdings: Vols 38,500 Microforms
Budget: $100,000

MO —WASHINGTON UNIVERSITY,
Physics Dept Library, 6600 Millbrook Blvd,
Saint Louis, 63130. Betty Eickhoff, Librn
Holdings: Vols 26,000 Cat

NV —UNIVERSITY OF NEVADA, RENO,
Physical Sciences Library, Chemistry Bldg,
Rm 316, Reno, 89557. Roberta Kiefer
Orcutt, Librn
Holdings: Vols (24,000) Cat Slides
Microforms

NJ —AT&T BELL LABORATORIES,
Libraries and Information Systems Center,
600 Mountain Ave, Murray Hill, 07974. W
D Penniman, Dir
Holdings: Vols (346,000) Cat Microforms
Notes: Restricted use to AT&T employees.
Catalogs/Indexes: Bell Laboratories Library
Network and Book Serial Catalogs; Bell
Laboratories Translations. Bell Laboratories
Library Network with New Jersey libraries
located in Holmdel, Murray Hill,
Piscataway, Whippany, Princeton, Short
Hills, Summit, West Long Branch, Crawford
Hill; libraries also in Allentown,
Pennsylvania; Reading, Pennsylvania; New
York, New York; Atlanta, Georgia;
Columbus, Ohio; Naperville, Illinois;
Indianapolis, Indiana; North Andover,
Massachusetts.

NJ —PRINCETON UNIVERSITY, Fine Hall
Library of Mathematics, Physics & Statistics,
Princeton, 08540. Peter Cziffra, Librn
Holdings: Vols (82,000) Cat Microforms
Budget: ($155,000)
Notes: All aspects of pure mathematics;
applied mathematics, numerical methods,
linear programming, etc are collected
selectively. Emphasis on pure, as opposed to
applied, physics; few acquisitions in plasma
physics. Also, mathematical statistics.
Separate catalog; most titles also in main
catalog of Firestone Library.

NM —UNIVERSITY OF CALIFORNIA, Los
Alamos National Laboratory, Libraries, PO
Box 1663, MSP 362, Los Alamos, 87545. J
Arthur Freed, Head Librn
Holdings: Vols (800,000) Cat Films
Microforms
Budget: ($700,000)
Notes: Incl 500,000 classified and
unclassified reports. There are 25 branch
libraries and a central collection. The
Medical Library contains about 40,000 vols
in the areas of biomedical research.

NY —POLYTECHNIC INSTITUTE OF NEW
YORK, Long Island Center Library, Route
110, Farmingdale, 11735. Lorraine Schein,
Branch Librn
Holdings: Vols 2800 Cat

NY —CORNELL UNIVERSITY LIBRARIES,
Physical Sciences Library, Clark Hall,
Ithaca, 14853. Ellen S Thomas, Librn
Holdings: Vols (73,701) Cat Microforms
Budget: ($244,185)

NY —AMERICAN SOCIETY FOR
PSYCHICAL RESEARCH LIBRARY, 5 W
73 St, New York, 10023. Rhea A White,
Consultant to the Library
Holdings: Vols (7000) Cat Mss Pix
Budget: ($1500)
Notes: Incl books on spiritualism, as well as

works in psychology, religion, philosophy,
physics, anthropology, etc which have a
possible bearing on parapsychology. An
attempt is made to obtain all serious books
on parapsychology in English.

NY —COLUMBIA UNIVERSITY
LIBRARIES, Physics Library, 810 Pupin,
535 W 114 St, New York, 10027. Mary Kay,
Librn
Holdings: Vols 26,000 Cat
Notes: Theoretical aspects of physics,
particularly atomic and nuclear physics.

NY —ENGINEERING SOCIETIES
LIBRARY, 345 E 47 St, New York, 10017.
S Kirk Cabeen, Dir
Holdings: Vols 250,000 Cat Maps 16mm
Films Microforms
Notes: One of the largest, most
comprehensive engineering libraries in the
world. Covers all engineering disciplines;
particularly strong in electrical and
electronic, mechanical, mining and
metallurgical, petroleum, chemical,
industrial, air conditioning and refrigeration
engineering. Incl Wheeler Collection of early
materials on magnetism and electricity. 125,
000 bound periodical volumes; 10,000 maps;
5000 serial subscriptions (many foreign-
language). Virtually all materials abstracted
in *Engineering Index* (1884-date) are incl in
Library. Noncirculating, except to members
of professional engineering societies which
support the Library. See *Engineering
Societies Library, New York, Classed
Subject Catalog and Index* (Boston: G K
Hall, 1963); and *Supplements*, 1-10, 1964-
1973.

NY —NEW YORK PUBLIC LIBRARY,
Research Libraries, Science and Technology
Research Center, Fifth Ave & 42 St, New
York, 10018.
Holdings: Vols (1,100,000) Cat Microforms
Budget: ($647,259)

NY —NEW YORK UNIVERSITY, Courant
Institute of Mathematical Sciences Library,
251 Mercer St, New York, 10012. Nancy
Gubman, Librn
Holdings: Vols (52,000) Cat Audiotapes
Microforms
Notes: Collection covers all aspects of
mathematics, theoretical computer science,
and mathematical physics on the level of
graduate research. Catalog is located in
Courant Institute Library.

†NY —TECHNICAL CAREER INSTITUTE
LIBRARY, 320 W 31st Street, New York,
10001. Michael Brent, Librn
Holdings: Vols (3500)

NY —EASTMAN KODAK COMPANY,
Research Library, Research Laboratories,
Bldg 83, Rochester, 14650. E W Kraus,
Head
Holdings: Vols 7700 Cat Microforms

NY —UNIVERSITY OF ROCHESTER,
Physics-Optics-Astronomy Library, Bausch
& Lomb Bldg, River Campus, Rochester,
14627. Loretta Caren, Librn
Holdings: Vols (20,000) Cat
Notes: Strong research level collection in the
field and related areas.

NC —DUKE UNIVERSITY, Mathematics-
Physics Library, Durham, 27706. Mary Ann
Southern, Librn
Holdings: Vols 69,171
Notes: A special collection is the Microwave
Catalog from the University of Ulm, a
bibliography of microwave literature divided
into molecule types, ie radicals, linear,
diatomic, symmetric tops, asymmetric tops,
and hindered rotation; it is regularly updated
by supplements.

NC —NORTH CAROLINA STATE
UNIVERSITY, D H Hill Library, Box 7111,
Raleigh, 27695. I T Littleton, Dir
Holdings: Vols 22,685 Cat
Budget: $11,000
Notes: Incl monographs.

OH —FIRESTONE TIRE & RUBBER CO,
1200 Firestone Pkwy, Akron, 44317. S Koo,
Librn
Holdings: Vols (6000) Cat
Notes: Collection centered on engineering,
mathematics, physics, and manufacturing
(metal processing); no rubber or tires. Incl
several hundred government reports. No
index.

PHYSICS (cont.)

OH —SAINT THOMAS INSTITUTE, Library,
1842 Madison Rd, Cincinnati, 45206. Sister
M Virgil Ghering, O P Librn
Holdings: Vols 6000 Cat
Budget: ($39,878)

OK —OKLAHOMA STATE UNIVERSITY,
Library, Stillwater, 74708. Roscoe Rouse,
Dir
Holdings: Vols 24,430 Cat

OR —OREGON STATE UNIVERSITY,
Library, Corvallis, 97331. Melvin George,
Dir
Holdings: Vols 30,000 Cat

PA —COLLEGE OF PHYSICIANS OF
PHILADELPHIA, Library, 19 S 22 St,
Philadelphia, 19103. Anthony Aguirre, Libr
Dir
Holdings: Vols (316,223) // Cat Mss
Microforms
Budget: ($1,096,557)
Notes: Incl 13,515 pamphlets; 1435 mss;
326,367 reports, dissertations, and reprints.
Strong historical and bibliographical
collections, as well as current materials.
Medical documentation service provides
current alerting, incl abstracting, etc.

PA —FRANKLIN INSTITUTE LIBRARY, 20
& The Parkway, Philadelphia, 19103.
Miriam Padusis, Dir; Charles Wilt, Readers
Servs Librn
Holdings: Vols (300,000) Cat Maps Pix
Microforms

PA —UNIVERSITY OF PENNSYLVANIA,
Mathematics-Physics-Astronomy Library, 33
& Walnut Sts, Philadelphia, 19104. Marion
A Kreiter, Librn
Holdings: Cat

PA —CARNEGIE LIBRARY OF
PITTSBURGH, Science & Technology Dept,
4400 Forbes Ave, Pittsburgh, 15213.
Catherine M Brosky, Dept Head
Holdings: Vols (380,000)
Budget: ($240,000)
Notes: Incl guides to the literature, abstracts,
indexes, tables, dictionaries, compilations of
data, bibliographies, handbooks,
encyclopedias, government reports and
documents, annual reviews, major journals
and serials.

PA —ROCKWELL INTERNATIONAL,
General Industries Operations, Technical
Information Center, 400 N Lexington Ave,
Pittsburgh, 15208. Kathleen H Witkowski,
Library Coordr
Holdings: Vols Cat Microforms Mss
Documents Periodicals VF
Budget: ($5100)

PA —UNIVERSITY OF PITTSBURGH,
Physics Library, 208 Engineering Hall,
Pittsburgh, 15260. Paul J Kobulnicky,
Physical Sciences Librn
Holdings: Vols (25,000) Cat Microforms
Budget: ($100,000)
Notes: The Physics Library collection is both
a graduate student research-level collection
in basic experimental and theoretical physics
with emphasis on solid-state, nuclear, upper-
atmosphere, space, and crystallography, and
also a collection in the earth and planetary
sciences, serving both graduate and
undergraduate students. The collection is
cataloged in both the University of
Pittsburgh, Hillman Library union catalog
and in a separate catalog in the Physics
Library.

PA —PENNSYLVANIA STATE
UNIVERSITY, Physical Sciences Library,
230 Davey Laboratory, University Park,
16802. Cornelius J McKown, Librn
Notes: 77,317 items.

†RI —UNIVERSITY OF RHODE ISLAND,
Library, Kingston, 02881.
Notes: Extensive collections.

SC —UNIVERSITY OF SOUTH CAROLINA,
Thomas Cooper Library, Columbia, 29208.
Kenneth E Toombs, Dir of Libraries; Roger
Mortimer, Rare Book Librn
Holdings: Vols 1250 Cat
Notes: Especially for 1750-1850.

†SD —SOUTH DAKOTA SCHOOL OF
MINES & TECHNOLOGY, Devereaux
Library, Rapid City, 57701.
Holdings: Vols (166,200) Cat Maps

Audiotapes Filmstrips Microforms
Notes: Supportive collection incl periodicals
and technical reports (NASA, ACRL, JPL,
etc); and extensive government document
materials (NBS, Dept of Commerce, HEW,
etc).

TN —UNIVERSITY OF TENNESSEE, Space
Institute Library, Tullahoma, 37388. Helen B
Mason, Librn
Holdings: Vols (14,000) Cat Microforms
Budget: ($50,000)
Notes: Incl NASA and other series of
technical reports.

TX —UNIVERSITY OF TEXAS LIBRARIES,
Physics-Mathematics-Astronomy Library,
PO Box P, Austin, 78712. John Fandey,
Librn
Holdings: Vols (55,000) Cat Microforms

TX —SOUTHERN METHODIST
UNIVERSITY, Fondren Library, Dallas,
75275. Curt Holleman, Librn for Collection
Development

TX —GENERAL DYNAMICS/FORT
WORTH DIV, Technical Library &
Information Services, PO Box 748, Mail
Zone 2246, Fort Worth, 76101. P Rogers de
Tonnancour, Dir
Holdings: Vols 36,000 Cat Maps Slides
Microforms Technical Documents
Budget: $100,000
Notes: Incl 500,000 microforms. Catalogs for
books and documents are separate.
Collection is strong in mathematics, nuclear
physics, materials and aerodynamics.
Emphasis on the mission of the division-the
development and production of manned
aircraft. Division also involved in electronic
manufacturing (avionic components), so
collection strength in this area is growing
very rapidly.

TX —RICE UNIVERSITY, Fondren Library,
6100 S Main St, PO Box 1892, Houston,
77251. Dr Samuel M Carrington, Jr,
University Librn
Holdings: Vols 2500 Cat
Budget: $69,900
Notes: Each serial title counted once.

TX —TEXAS TECH UNIVERSITY, Library,
Lubbock, 79409. David J Murrah, Assoc Dir
for Special Collections

VT —UNIVERSITY OF VERMONT,
Chemistry/Physics Library, Burlington,
05405. Craig A Robertson, Librn
Holdings: Vols (23,000) Cat Microforms
Notes: The collection consists largely of
periodicals, having about 12,000 bound
periodical volumes. The number of periodical
titles currently received is approximately
210.

WA —BATTELLE-PACIFIC NORTHWEST
LABORTORIES, Technical Library, PO
Box 999, Richland, 99352. Wayne Snyder,
Librn
Holdings: Vols (50,000) Cat Microforms
Budget: ($500,000)
Notes: Holdings: 50,000 books; 35,000
bound periodical volumes; 200,000 technical
reports; 200,000 technical reports in
microform. Subscriptions: 1800 journals and
other serials. Services: interlibrary loans;
literature searching; translation; library open
to public with restrictions.

WI —MILWAUKEE PUBLIC LIBRARY, 814
W Wisconsin Ave, Milwaukee, 53233.
Donald J Sager, City Librn
Holdings: Vols Cat
Notes: Strong collection acquired to support
state interlibrary loan. Covers all the pure
and applied sciences. Incl over (1600)
periodicals and serial titles and more than
(100) abstracting and indexing services in
major fields of science and technology.
Strong general reference service.

MB —UNIVERSITY OF MANITOBA,
Science Library, Machray Hall, Winnipeg,
R3T 2N2, Can. V Simosko, Head
Holdings: Vols (90,000) Cat Microforms

ON —ONTARIO RESEARCH
FOUNDATION, Library, Sheridan Park,
Mississauga, L5K 1B3, Can. Carl K Wei,
Librn
Holdings: Vols (13,000) Cat
Budget: ($14,000)

PHYSICS—HISTORY

CA —UNIVERSITY OF CALIFORNIA,
BERKELEY, Bancroft Library, Manuscripts

Division, Berkeley, 94720. James D Hart,
Dir
Notes: Extensive collections of papers and
archives relative to the history of modern
physics.
See also entry under Cyclotron.

CA —CALIFORNIA INSTITUTE OF
TECHNOLOGY, Robert A Millikan
Memorial Library, Archives, 1201 E
California Blvd, Pasadena, 91125. Judith R
Goodstein, Archivist
Holdings: Vols (3000) Cat Mss Maps Pix
Slides Phonorecords Audiotapes Videotapes
16mm Films Microforms
Notes: Ms sources for the history of
astrophysics, cosmology, mathematical
physics, experimental physics, radio
astronomy, geophysics and biophysics.
Collections incl the papers of: George Ellery
Hale, Jesse Greenstein, H P Robertson,
Richard Feynman, Paul Epstein, Max
Delbruck, and Beno Gutenberg. Candid
photos of physicists at meetings; etchings
and photographs of Einstein; scientific
medals; selected pieces of scientific
apparatus (including the oil-drop machine
constructed by Millikan at Caltech in the
early 1920s); the reprint collection of Paul
Epstein; over 3000 landmark books in the
history of 20th century physics and
mathematics. Printed publications include:
Daniel Kevles, Guide to the Microfilm
Edition of the George Ellery Hale Papers
(Pasadena, Carnegie Institute of Washington
and Caltech), 1968; Judith R Goodstein,
TheRobert Andrews Millikan Collection at
the California Institute of Technology: Guide
to a Microfilm Edition (Pasadena, Caltech),
1977; Judith R Goodstein and Carolyn
Kopp, The Theodore von Karman
Collections at the California Institute of
Technology (Pasadena, Archives), 1981.

†CA —CALIFORNIA INSTITUTE OF
TECHNOLOGY, Robert A Millikan
Memorial Library, Archives, 1201 E
California Blvd, Pasadena, 91125.
Notes: Geophysicist Charles Richter's
lecture notes and oral history interview. Incl
notes from courses at Caltech taught by
physicist Paul Epstein (1883-1966), such as
higher dynamics, 1925; thermodynamics,
1925/26; quantum theory, 1926-28, 1940.

IA —HERBERT HOOVER PRESIDENTIAL
LIBRARY, West Branch, 52358. Dale C
Mayer, Archivist
Notes: Unpublished papers of physicists and
astronomers, 1917-1969.

MI —UNIVERSITY OF MICHIGAN, Library,
Dept of Rare Books & Special Collections,
Ann Arbor, 48109. Robert J Starring, Head
Holdings: Cat Mss Pix
Notes: Chiefly pre-1800 imprints.

NY —CORNELL UNIVERSITY LIBRARIES,
John M Olin Library, History of Science
Collections, Ithaca, 14853. Lillian A Clark,
Administrative Supervisor; David W Corson,
History of Science Librn
Holdings: Vols (33,000) Cat
Notes: Early printed source materials in all
physical sciences, 16th through 19th
centuries, with special emphases on latter
17th and 18th centuries, Newton and his
influence. Noncirculating.
See also entry under Science - History

NY —AMERICAN INSTITUTE OF
PHYSICS, Center for the History of Physics,
Niels Bohr Library, 335 E 45 St, New York,
10017. John Aubry, Librn
Holdings: Vols (16,000) Cat Mss Pix Slides
Phonorecords Audiotapes 16mm Films
Microforms
Notes: The Library contains an extensive
collection of published works relating to the
history of modern physics and astronomy.
Its archives incl letter, notebooks and other
papers of physicists, as well as the records of
leading American physics societies and
institutions. Its collections of ms
autobiographies, oral history interviews, and
other tape recordings, and pictorial materials
(incl unpublished film footage) are unrivaled
in the field of history of science. It maintains
the International Catalog of Sources for
History of Physics and and Astronomy.

NY —AMERICAN INSTITUTE OF
PHYSICS, Center for the History of Physics,

PHYSICS—HISTORY (cont.)

Niels Bohr Library, 335 E 45 St, New York, 10017. John Aubry, Librn
Notes: Darrow Collection: Physicist Karl Kelchner Darrow's professional correspondence (1928-73), diaries (1911-75), and early undergraduate notes, as well as materials on lectures, speeches, offprints, and family correspondence. Most of Dr Darrow's career was with the Bell Telephone Laboratories, and he was Secretary of the American Physical Society for 25 years. Van Vleck Collection: Primarily professional correspondence from the 1920s to the 1970s of Prof John Hasbrouck Van Vleck, first American awarded a PhD in theoretical physics (1922). Won the Nobel Prize for his work in quantum physics theory and on solid state physics. Others of his papers are deposited in the Harvard University Archives.Goudsmit Collection: Papers, incl correspondence, notebooks, awards, photographs, and other materials originated by Samuel A Goudsmit. Oral history interviews dealing with the discovery of and subsequent work on pulsars, collected by Steve Woolgar. Permission needed for use of the latter.

NY —US MILITARY ACADEMY LIBRARY, West Point, 10996. Egon A Weiss, Librn
Holdings: Mss
Notes: Records of the Department of Chemistry, Mechanics, and Physics (1881-1971), of the US Military Academy at West Point. 9.75 ft of mss.

OH —CLEVELAND PUBLIC LIBRARY, Science & Technology Dept, 325 Superior Ave, Cleveland, 44114. Jean Z Piety, Head
Holdings: Cat
Notes: Many early volumes.

PA —AMERICAN PHILOSOPHICAL SOCIETY, Library, 105 S Fifth St, Philadelphia, 19106. Edward C Carter II, Librn
Holdings: Cat Mss Microforms
Notes: 20th century physicists.

PA —UNIVERSITY OF PITTSBURGH, Hillman Library, Pittsburgh, 15260. Glenora E Rossell, Head
Holdings: Vols (6100) Cat Microforms
Notes: The History and Philosophy of Science collection is rapidly growing to support research interests in a very new synoptic approach in the integration of history of science, philosophy of science, and history of philosophy, and the intensive new program of instruction. The trend of collection is to include works in philosophical foundations of contemporary physics and cosmology, the philosophical problems of the social sciences, science and theology in the 17th century, the relation between science and epistemology in the 18th and 19th centuries; problems of microphysics, history of molecular biology, theories of scientific explanation, and relation between science and metaphysics.

RI —BROWN UNIVERSITY, John Hay Library, 20 Prospect St, Providence, 02912. Mark N Brown, Cur Mss
Holdings: // Mss
Notes: About 750 letters chiefly to Carl Barus from physicists in the US, Canada, and Europe; drafts of his contributions to scientific journals; University and faculty correspondence; and his autobiography in 269 typed pages with ms revisions. Register available.

†TX —UNIVERSITY OF TEXAS LIBRARIES, General Libraries, Humanities Research Center, PO Box 7219, Austin, 78712. John Chalmers, Librn
Notes: Some of Albert Einstein's mathematical-physics topics, 230 pages, written by Albert Einstein during the period 1950-1955. These complement 250 pages of similar manuscripts notes from the same period already in the Einstein collection. Also, papers of Alfred Schild (1921-1977), physicist, especially strong in documenting the formation and activities of the "Texas Group" of relativists.

ON —UNIVERSITY OF TORONTO, Thomas Fisher Rare Book Library, 120 Saint George St, Toronto, M5S 1A5, Can. Richard G Landon, Head
Holdings: Vols 4000
Notes: The Science Collection is especially rich in works on Renaissance astronomy, physics and mechanics and has noteworthy holdings of works of English experimental scientists in the 17th and 18th centuries with excellent collections of the works of Robert Boyle, Robert Hooke, and Sir Isaac Newton. Includes virtually all important early editions of Euclid; alchemical works of the 16th and 17th centuries together with the works of 18th century chemists like Lavoisier and Priestly; works on agriculture with special emphasis on British agriculture in the 18th century; and a variety of other works important in the history of science in all its branches. In addition the Fisher Library has many other specialized scientific collections which are listed separately.

PQ —MCGILL UNIVERSITY, McLennan Library, University Archives, 3459 McTavish St, Montreal, H3A 1Y1, Can. Martha Caya, Archivist
Holdings: Vols (7) notebooks
Notes: The papers of the McGill Physical Society, 1897-1959. Original mss and handwritten work available for Scholarly research only. Microfilm available to public.

PHYSICS—STUDY AND TEACHING

NY —US MILITARY ACADEMY LIBRARY, West Point, 10996. Egon A Weiss, Librn
Holdings: Mss
Notes: Records of the Department of Chemistry, Mechanics, and Physics (1881-1971), of the US Military Academy at West Point. 9.75 ft of mss.

PHYSICS, ASTRONOMICAL see Astrophysics

PHYSICS, BIOLOGICAL see Biological Physics

PHYSICS, HIGH ENERGY see High Energy Physics

PHYSICS, MEDICAL see Medical Physics

PHYSICS, MEDIUM ENERGY see Medium Energy Physics

PHYSICS, MOLECULAR see Molecular Physics

PHYSICS, NUCLEAR see Nuclear Physics

PHYSICS, SOLID STATE see Solid State Physics

PHYSICS, SPACE see Space Physics

PHYSICS, STATISTICAL see Statistical Physics

PHYSICS, TERRESTRIAL see Geophysics

PHYSIOCRACY

DE —HAGLEY MUSEUM AND LIBRARY, Eleutherian Mills-Hagley Foundation Inc, PO Box 3630, Greenville, 19807. Richmond D Williams, Dir; Heddy A Richter, Imprints Librn
Holdings: Vols 6000 Pamphlets
Notes: The French history collection is especially good in pamphlets of the Revolutionary and Napoleonic periods; French 18th Century economic theory, especially Physiocracy; and the works of or concerning P S du Pont de Nemours.

PHYSIOGRAPHY see Physical Geography

PHYSIOLOGICAL ACOUSTICS see Hearing

PHYSIOLOGICAL ASPECTS OF SPORTS see Sports—Physiological Aspects

PHYSIOLOGICAL EFFECT OF CHEMICALS see Pharmacology

PHYSIOLOGICAL OPTICS see Optics, Physiological

PHYSIOLOGICAL PSYCHOLOGY see Psychology, Physiological

PHYSIOLOGY

AL —UNIVERSITY OF ALABAMA, BIRMINGHAM, Lister Hill Library of the Health Sciences, University Sta, Birmingham, 35294. Richard B Fredericksen, Dir

CA —UNIVERSITY OF CALIFORNIA, DAVIS, Health Sciences Library, Davis, 95616. Marjan Merala, Health Sciences Librn
Holdings: Vols (164,000) Cat Microforms
Budget: ($509,737)
Notes: Human medicine: ca 82,000 vols; veterinary medicine: ca 19,700 vols; allied sciences (biochemistry, physiology, etc); reference works: ca 62,300 vols.

CA —UNIVERSITY OF CALIFORNIA, LOS ANGELES, Biomedical Library, Center for Health Sciences, Los Angeles, 90024. Louise Darling, Biomedical Librn

CA —NASA, Ames Research Center, Libraries, Library Br 202-3, Moffett Field, 94035. Sarah Dueker, Chief, Library Branch
Holdings: Cat Audiotapes Microforms
Notes: Main library collections cover physical sciences, engineering and mathematical fields related to research programs in aeronautics-space research. Life sciences library collections cover medical, physiological, behavioral and biological sciences related to research programs. Also emphases on remote sensing of earth resources and the search for extraterrestrial life. 950 journal titles and 85,000 monographs. Reports collection includes 60,000 hard copy reports and 900,000 microfiche.

CT —YALE MEDICAL LIBRARY, 333 Cedar St, New Haven, 06510.
Holdings: Vols (334,215) Cat Mss Pix Slides Microforms
Budget: ($361,650)
Notes: Incl films, audiotapes, artifacts, etc.

†DC —CATHOLIC UNIVERSITY OFF AMERICA, Nursing & Biology Library, Washington, 20064. N L Powell, Head
Holdings: Vols (17,000) Cat Microforms

IL —UNIVERSITY OF CHICAGO LIBRARIES, John Crerar Library Collections, 1100 E 57th St, Chicago, 60637. Robert Rosenthal, Special Collections Librn
Notes: The John Crerar Library's extensive science, medicine, and engineering collections have been transferred in trust to the University of Chicago Libraries. Incl rare books and special collections as listed here.

IL —UNIVERSITY OF ILLINOIS, URBANA/CHAMPAIGN, Library, Biology Library, 101 Burrill Hall, 407 S Goodwin, Urbana, 61801. Elisabeth B Davis, Librn
Holdings: Vols (115,000) Cat Microforms
Budget: ($200,000)
Notes: The Biology Library incl books, periodicals, and reference works that cover the fields of anatomy, biophysics, botany, ecology, entomology, genetics, immunology, microbiology, physiology and zoology. About three-quarters of the total collection is made up of journals and other serials representing 2000 distinctive titles. The serial list is comprehensive for the biological sciences, contains most of the major international titles and consists of complete runs for almost all titles. Additional materials (approx 90,000 vols) in the biological sciences are available in the Natural History Survey Library and the bookstacks at the Main Library on the Urbana campus. Professional assistance is available for reference service, online searching, and library instruction. Interlibrary loan service is provided. Photocopying.

MD —JOHNS HOPKINS UNIVERSITY, Milton S Eisenhower Library, Charles & 34 Sts, Baltimore, 21218. Ann S Gwyn, Assistant Dir for Special Collections
Holdings: Vols (46,500) Cat
Notes: Very strong in all biological fields except taxonomy. Strongest in molecular biology, cell physiology and premedical areas. Strong in journals, espec in biochemistry. Many long runs of rare journals. Natural science not as strong as biochemistry. Contemporary monographs better than earlier ones.

MD —US ARMED FORCES RADIOBIOLOGY RESEARCH INSTITUTE, Naval Medical Command,

PHYSIOLOGY (cont.)

Bethesda, 20014. Nannette M Pope, Head, Library Division
Holdings: Vols (50,000)
Budget: ($150,000)
Notes: Collection consists of monographs, technical reports, serials, and microfiche related to radiation effects on human and animal biology.

MA —UNIVERSITY OF MASSACHUSETTS AT AMHERST, Library, Amherst, 01003. Siegfried Feller, Assoc Dir for Collection Development
Holdings: Cat
Notes: Special emphasis on cellular, developmental and physiological zoology.

MA —UNIVERSITY OF MASSACHUSETTS AT AMHERST, Library, Amherst, 01002.
Notes: Strong collections in physical education, sports studies, exercise, gymnastics, etc.

MA —FRANCIS A COUNTWAY LIBRARY OF MEDICINE, Boston Medical Library/Harvard Medical Library, 10 Shattuck St, Boston, 02115. C Robin LeSueur, Librn; Richard J Wolfe, Cur, Rare Books & Manuscripts
Holdings: Vols (500,000) Cat Mss Maps Pix Microforms
Notes: Combines resources of the Harvard Medical School and the Boston Medical Library. Strong in serials and medical history in all fields of medicine, incl incunabula, non-medical books by doctors, travel books by doctors. 500,000 medical dissertations and theses. Special strength in all medical subjects listed in this volume.

MA —HARVARD UNIVERSITY LIBRARY, Biological Laboratories Library, 16 Divinity Ave, Cambridge, 02138. Dorothy Solbrig, Librn
Holdings: Vols (20,000) Cat Films
Notes: Materials in all areas of biology, emphasizing biochemistry and cellular and developmental biology. There is little in systematic biology and morphology.

NY —COLUMBIA UNIVERSITY LIBRARIES, Health Sciences Library, 701 W 168 St, New York, 10032. Rachael K Goldstein, Librn
Holdings: Vols 1900
Notes: Landmark works, incl the John Green Curtis collection. Restricted.

NY —CORNELL UNIVERSITY MEDICAL COLLEGE, Samuel J Wood Library, 1300 York Ave, New York, 10021. Erich Meyerhoff, Dir
Holdings: Vols (9000) Cat Films
Notes: All aspects of muscle diseases.

NY —MUSCULAR DYSTROPHY ASSOCIATION, 810 Seventh Ave, New York, 10019. Marianthe Pappas, Librn
Holdings: Vols 8770 Cat
Budget: $55,000
Notes: All phases of muscular diseases. Incl some films.

NY —MASONIC MEDICAL RESEARCH LIBRARY, 2150 Bleecker St, Utica, 13501. Irma A Tuttle, Librn
Holdings: Vols (2000) Cat Slides Microforms
Notes: Biochemical gerontology collection represents 10 percent of total holdings in basic medical research fields of physiology, pharmacology, vision and circulation. Incl 16,000 periodicals.

NC —UNIVERSITY OF NORTH CAROLINA, CHAPEL HILL, Zoology Dept Library, Wilson Hall 046A, Chapel Hill, 27514. John B Darling, Librn
Holdings: Vols (31,000) Cat
Notes: Collection incl theses and dissertations.

ND —UNIVERSITY OF NORTH DAKOTA, Harley E French Medical Library, Grand Forks, 58202. David W Boilard, Dir; Lila Pedersen, Asst Dir
Holdings: Vols (56,000) Cat
Budget: ($206,000)
Notes: 1075 current periodical subscriptions.

PA —COLLEGE OF PHYSICIANS OF PHILADELPHIA, Library, 19 S 22 St, Philadelphia, 19103. Christine Ruggere, Cur, Historical Collections
Holdings: Vols (316,223)
Budget: ($1,096,557)
Notes: Very strong collection.
See also entry under Medicine

PA —UNIVERSITY OF PENNSYLVANIA, Archives and Records Center, North Facade - Franklin Field, Philadelphia, 19104. Mark Frazier Lloyd, Archivist
Notes: R Tait McKenzie's personal papers, and the J William White Collection of personal papers--sealed until 2016. Incl materials relating to McKenzie's sculpting and the sports medallions and medals which he sculpted. Biographical and reserved materials for two books about him. Incl 39 cu ft.

PA —CARNEGIE LIBRARY OF PITTSBURGH, Science & Technology Dept, 4400 Forbes Ave, Pittsburgh, 15213. Catherine M Brosky, Dept Head
Notes: Except for certain special areas, such as entomology and ornithology and a few others that are emphasized, this general subject is of secondary interest. Incl both modern and classic works. Kept up to date in cooperation with the Library of Carnegie Museum of Natural History. Materials available on the various phyla, classes, orders and species. Abstracts, indexes, bibliographies, taxonomic manuals and standard reference books. Many journals and society publications complete from the beginning.

PA —PENNSYLVANIA STATE UNIVERSITY, Fred Lewis Pattee Library, University Park, 16802.
Notes: Numerous and large collections on many sports. Also, materials supporting every aspect of the program of the Center for Women and Sport, incl research into kinetics, endocrinology, physiology, psychology, etc.

TN —UNIVERSITY OF TENNESSEE, KNOXVILLE, Library, Knoxville, 37996. John Dobson, Special Collections Librn
Holdings: Mss
Notes: Papers of the eminent physiologist Arthur H Steinhaus (1897-1974).

TX —US AIR FORCE, School of Aerospace Medicine, Strughold Aeromedical Library, Brooks AFB, 78235. Fred W Todd, Chief Librn
Holdings: Vols (119,188) Cat Mss Maps Pix Microforms
Budget: ($499,000)
Notes: Aviation and space medicine and physiology, including the physiological effects of altitude and decompression. Biomedical and and human engineering. Military medicine, including chemical and biological warfare. Emergency medicine in both professional and technical areas. Radiobiology, including atomic medicine, nuclear medicine, and space radiation. Material not oriented to the School of Aerospace Medicine are excluded. Incl also 45,787 microforms and 142,371 technical documents.

TX —UNIVERSITY OF TEXAS, Marine Science Institute Library, Port Aransas, 78373. Ruth Grundy, Librn
Holdings: Vols (45,000) Cat Maps Pix
Budget: ($70,000)
Notes: Current researches in marine science, especially concerning the Gulf of Mexico, the Texas Coastal Zone, and the Continental Shelf. Incl journals.

WI —UNIVERSITY OF WISCONSIN-STOUT, Library Learning Center, Menomonie, 54751. Philip Sawin Jr, Coll Develop Librn
Notes: Supports graduate program in Foods and Nutrition, which was begun in 1960. Quite specific collection with emphasis on the clinical aspects of nutrition.

ON —UNIVERSITY OF WINDSOR, Leddy Library, Windsor, N9B 3P4, Can. P Jerome Malone, Librn
Notes: Human kinetics, with emphasis on the history, psychology, sociology, philosophy, and administration of sports and their organization. Also hold archival records, etc of numerous Canadian sports organizations: Canadian Intercollegiate Athletic Union (CIAU), Ontario-Quebec AA, Ontario Universities AA, etc. Local and Regional history. 40 feet of materials.

PHYSIOLOGY, ANIMAL see Animal Physiology

PHYSIOLOGY, MOLECULAR see Biological Physics

PHYSIOLOGY, NEURAL see Neurophysiology

PHYSIOLOGY, VETERINARY see Veterinary Physiology

PHYSIOLOGY OF PLANTS see Plant Physiology

PHYSIOPHILOSOPHY see Natural History

PHYSIOTHERAPY see Physical Therapy

PHYTOCHEMISTRY see Botanical Chemistry

PHYTOGRAPHY see Botany

PHYTOLOGY see Botany

PHYTOPATHOLOGY see Plant Diseases

PHYTOPLANKTON

ME —BIGELOW LABORATORY FOR OCEAN SCIENCES & MAINE DEPT OF MARINE RESOURCES, Library, McKown Point, West Boothbay Harbor, 04575. Pamela Shephard-Lupo, Librn
Holdings: Vols Cat Mss
Budget: ($55,000)
Notes: This library presently serves two institutions. The Maine Dept of Marine Resources has maintained the library since 1957 and thus the majority of our holdings are geared to their needs, ie fish biology and stock assessment on a local, national and international level. In 1973 Bigelow Laboratory for Ocean Sciences came to West Boothbay Harbor and began to contribute to the library with a very specialized collection on the Gulf of Maine marine chemistry, phytoplankton and nutrient cycles.

PIAGET, JEAN

NY —HOFSTRA UNIVERSITY, Library, 1000 Fulton Ave, Hempstead, 11550. Charles R Andrews, Dean of Library Services
Notes: Strong collection. Incl some mss.

PA —TEMPLE UNIVERSITY LIBRARIES, Special Collections Dept, Rare Books & Mss Section, Philadelphia, 19122. Thomas M Whitehead, Cur
Holdings: Vols 800 Cat
Budget: $500
Notes: Contains all available works by and about Jean Piaget and those of his principal associates. Incl over 500 journal articles and 70 dissertations. Collection originally developed as the research collection of the Jean Piaget Society.

TN —VANDERBILT UNIVERSITY, George Peabody College for Teachers, Education Library, Box 325, Nashville, 37203. Mary Beth Blalock, Librn
Holdings: Vols (192,541) Cat Pix Slides Phonorecords Filmstrips Microforms
Budget: ($59,000)
Notes: The Education Library (192,541 vols) collects in all areas relating to education with special emphasis on Child Study and Exceptional Children. Special funds are available for continuing purchases in these areas. The collection is strong in curriculum materials, physical education, applied art, psychology related to education and all areas of education. Amoung special papers are over 300 papers by and about Jean Piaget and an extensive author and subject file referring to the location of these papers and books and journal articles by and about Piaget in the rest of the Education Library collection. The Education Library is a Division of the Vanderbilt University Library.

PIANO

†DC —CATHOLIC UNIVERSITY OF AMERICA, Music Library, Washington, 20064. Betty Libbey, Head Music Library
Holdings: Cat Microforms
Notes: A large collection to support advanced degree study. Emphasis on church music, musicology, history and criticism, instrumental and vocal music, solo music for all voices, instruments, and musical forms.

PIANO—INSTRUCTION AND STUDY

†DC —CATHOLIC UNIVERSITY OF AMERICA, Music Library, Washington, 20064. Betty Libbey, Head Music Library
Holdings: Cat Microforms
Notes: A large collection to support advanced degree study. Emphasis on church music, musicology, history and criticism, instrumental and vocal music, solo music for all voices, instruments, and musical forms.

TN —VANDERBILT UNIVERSITY, Music Library, 419 21st Ave South, Nashville, 37203. Shirley Marie Watts, Librn
Holdings: Vols (23,000) Cat Phonorecords Audiotapes Microforms
Budget: ($10,600)
Notes: Tapes of lectures, master classes and recitals incl in Seminars in Piano Teaching held at George Peabody College for Teachers, 1970-76. Also, Francis Robinson Collection of Sound Recordings. 23,000

PIANO—INSTRUCTION AND STUDY (cont.)

books and musical scores, 10,000 phonorecords, 350 audiotapes, 1650 microforms. All materials cataloged.

PIANO MUSIC

CA —OAKLAND PUBLIC LIBRARY, Art, Music and Recreation Section, 125 14 St, Oakland, 94612. Richard Colvig, Senior Librn
Holdings: Vols (5000) Cat Phonorecords Audiotapes
Budget: ($6700)
Notes: 10,000 scores, incl chamber music, instrumental music (piano and organ collections especially strong), miniature scores, opera scores, songs and song collections; 30,000 octavos (anthems and choral music of all kinds); 5000 books about music; 8000 phonorecords; and audiocassettes.

IL —UNIVERSITY OF ILLINOIS, URBANA/CHAMPAIGN, Library, Music Library, Urbana, 61801. William M McClellan, Librn
Holdings: Vols (200,000) Cat Mss Slides Sound Recordings Microforms Books Scores
Budget: ($65,000)
Notes: Introductory, instructive, research and reference materials to support work at graduate level in ethnomusicology,, musicology, music education, performance areas. Special areas incl about 2500 pre-1800 music mss and editions of music on microfilm, 2400 graduate music theses on microfilm, a special collection of 30,000 titles of American vocal sheet music covering the period 1790-1970, the Rafael Joseffy Collection of about 2000 pieces of 19th century piano music (incl performer markings), the Joseph Szigeti Collection (700 items: published music, mss, recordings), mainly violin and piano music by various commposers. Also incl a special collection of 45,000 78 rpm sound recordings (uncat) of classical music and jazz; a collection of 2900 titles from Chicago radio station WGN. Incl orchestrations, a collection of 500,000 items (uncat) from stock of Hunleth Music Store, St Louis, Missouri, mainly early 20th century imprints of songs, wind music, string music, piano, sets of theatre orchestra parts, dance band orchestrations. A separate collection of choral octavos and instrumental parts is maintained, incl 135,000 pieces of choral music, 30,500 orchestral parts, and 5500 wind ensemble parts. Also, music publishers' catalogues (mainly European and American), ca 126 cubic feet, 1860s-1950s.

MD —UNIVERSITY OF MARYLAND, Music Library, International Piano Archives at Maryland, College Park, 20742. Neil Ratliff, Head Librn; Morgan Cundiff, Piano Archives Librn
Holdings: Cat Mss Pix Phonorecords Audiotapes VF
Notes: A collection centered around the performance of piano music. Incl 90 percent of all disc and cylinder recordings of serious piano music ever issued. (16,000 phonorecords, 1200 audiotapes, 4000 music scores, 2300 piano rolls, all cataloged.) *Catalog of the Reproducing Piano Rolls in the International Piano Archives at Maryland.* College Park: University of Maryland Music Library, 1983. 280 p. (Publications of the Music Library, University of Maryland College Park, 2) *Microfiche Catalog of the Disc Recordings in the International Piano Archives at Maryland.* College Park: University of Maryland Music Library, 1984. 1031 microfiche. (Publications of the Music Library, University of Maryland College Park, 3)

MA —UNIVERSITY OF MASSACHUSETTS AT AMHERST, Music Library, Fine Arts Center, Amherst, 01003.
Holdings: Uncat
Notes: The personal library of Howard M Lebow (once an outstanding concert pianist). The collection (over 5000 items) incl

primarily keyboard music, as well as many unusual early editions.

NJ —WESTMINSTER CHOIR COLLEGE, Talbott Library, Hamilton Ave at Walnut Lane, Princeton, 08540. Sherry L Vellucci, Acting Dir
Holdings: Vols (43,500) Cat Scores Periodicals Phonorecords Audiotapes Videotapes Microforms
Budget: ($30,000)
Notes: Talbott Library supports the curriculum of a music college which grants undergraduate and graduate degrees in church music, music education and music performance (voice, piano, organ and choral conducting), with an emphasis on choral music. Incl 7000 phonorecords, 3500 titles in quantity of choral music, 30,000 single copies of choral music.

NY —BROOKLYN PUBLIC LIBRARY, Art & Music Div, Grand Army Plaza, Brooklyn, 11238. Sue H Sharma, Chief
Holdings: Vols (4500) Cat Mss
Notes: Over 50,000 items, most of which circulate to the public. The collection contains some reference materials, incl the complete works of many composers; over 3500 popular song folios with our own in-house index for locating individual songs; some rare editions and mss of local composers; and a small collection of rare sheet music beginning with the 18th century. The circulating collection incl standard vocal scores, methods, piano music, etc, and is one of the largest public library collections in the country.

NY —NEW YORK PUBLIC LIBRARY, Performing Arts Research Center, Rodgers & Hammerstein Archives of Recorded Sound, 111 Amsterdam Ave, New York, 10023.
Holdings: // Phonorecords Audiotapes
Notes: The Jan Holcman Collection of commercial phonodiscs representing the great piano virtuosi of Europe and the US from 1900 to 1967, on both 78 rpm and LP formats. Many rare items include representations of Busoni, d'Albert, Hofmann, Plante, and most of the Liszt pupils who made recordings. Incl 2250 phonorecords.

PA —FREE LIBRARY OF PHILADELPHIA, Sheet Music Collection, Logan Sq, Philadelphia, 19103. Connie Jessum, Librn
Budget: ($2000)
Notes: Covers entire span of American popular expression in song and instrumental music (piano) from colonial times to the present. Incl Newland-Zeuner and Edward I Keffer Collections on loan from the Musical Fund Society. Items printed before 1825 indexed in Sonneck-Upton and Wolfe. Checklists for cover illustrations, musical shows or films and special subjects. Songs are filed by title; piano music by composer. Examples of special materials not filed in regular collection incl early Philadelphia composers and publications, national (centennial and state), patriotic ("Star-Spangled Banner"), political (Presidents), and war (1861; 1914; 1939) songs. Most of the ms materials are anonymous. Collection contains 138,360 pieces of sheet music.

RI —BROWN UNIVERSITY, John Hay Library, 20 Prospect St, Providence, 02912. Mark N Brown, Cur Mss
Holdings: Uncat
Notes: The Sheet Music Collection concentrates on music of American imprint, incl 170,000 vocal pieces filed by title, plus 80,000 instrumental pieces filed by composer. Major strengths are in 19th century music, especially prior to 1830; Civil War music, both Union and Confederate; lithographic covers; World War I songs; political campaign music; and band music. An additional 100,000 pieces of American and European imprint remain unprocessed.

WI —UNIVERSITY OF WISCONSIN, MADISON, Mills Music Library, 728 State St, Madison, 53706. Arne Arneson, Music Librn
Holdings: // Uncat Mss
Notes: Tams-Witmark Collection formed part of the rental collection of the firm bearing that name. Includes piano-conductor

scores (some in mss); ca 65 sets of orchestral parts for operas; 70 vocal scores of works by American composers including Herbert, Sousa, Edwards and De Koven; ca 100 sets of orchestral parts of comic operas; ca 4000 vocal scores of European operas. Restricted use.

PIANO—VOCAL SCORES

IL —NEWBERRY LIBRARY, 60 W Walton St, Chicago, 60610. Diana Haskell, Cur of Modern Mss
Holdings: Vols 3000 Cat
Notes: Scores of operas to 1930.

NY —BROOKLYN PUBLIC LIBRARY, Art & Music Div, Grand Army Plaza, Brooklyn, 11238. Sue H Sharma, Chief
Holdings: Vols (4500) Cat Mss
Notes: Over 50,000 items, most of which circulate to the public. The collection contains some reference materials, incl the complete works of many composers; over 3500 popular song folios with our own in-house index for locating individual songs; some rare editions and mss of local composers; and a small collection of rare sheet music beginning with the 18th century. The circulating collection incl standard vocal scores, methods, piano music, etc, and is one of the largest public library collections in the country.

OH —CLEVELAND PUBLIC LIBRARY, Fine Arts and Special Collections Department, 325 Superior Ave, Cleveland, 44114. Alice N Loranth, Head
Holdings: Vols (10,550) Cat
Notes: Part of Vocal Music Collection, which incl oratorios, masses, cantatas, etc, with mostly single copies, piano-vocal scores and about 200 orchestral scores.

RI —BROWN UNIVERSITY, John Hay Library, 20 Prospect St, Providence, 02912. Mark N Brown, Cur Mss
Notes: The Sheet Music Collection concentrates on music of American imprint, incl 170,000 vocal pieces filed by title, plus 80,000 instrumental pieces filed by composer. Major strengths are in 19th century music, especially prior to 1830; Civil War music, both Union and Confederate; lithographic covers; World War I songs; political campaign music; and band music. An additional 100,000 pieces of American and European imprint remain unprocessed. *See also* entry under Song Books - Collections

PICABIA, FRANCIS

CA —FRANCIS BACON LIBRARY, 655 N Dartmouth Ave, Claremont, 91711. Elizabeth S Wrigley, Dir
Holdings: Mss Pix
Notes: Correspondence of Walter Arensberg with artists John Covert, Marcel Duchamp, Francis Picabia and his wife Gabrielle Buffet Picabia, and psychiatrist Elmer Ernest Southard, 1876-1920.

PICASSO, PABLO

CA —CLAREMONT COLLEGES, Honnold Library, Ninth & Dartmouth, Claremont, 91711. Tania Rizzo, Special Collections Dept Head
Notes: Working papers of Irving Wallace and his family. Incl audio and video taped interviews with Wallace, Marlene Dietrich, Raymond Chandler, and Pablo Picasso.

PICKENS, GEN. ANDREW, 1739-1817

SC —CLEMSON UNIVERSITY, Libraries, Clemson, 29631. Michael F Kohl, Head of Special Collections
Holdings: // Cat Mss
Notes: This collection, presented by Alice Noble Waring (*The Fighting Elder: Andrew Pickens, 1739-1817*), consists entirely of photostatic copies of original mss in various repositories. Use by scholars must be governed by the regulations of each repository.

PICKERILL, ELMO NEALE

DC —BROADCAST PIONEERS LIBRARY, 1771 N St NW, Washington, 20036.

PICKERILL, ELMO NEALE (cont.)

Catharine Heinz, Dir
Holdings: Mss
Notes: Incl the papers of Elmo Neale
Pickerill, pioneer in wireless telegraphy and
air-to-ground radio communications. Open
to public by appointment.

PICKERING, WILLIAM

CA —CALIFORNIA INSTITUTE OF
TECHNOLOGY, Robert A Millikan
Memorial Library, Archives, 1201 E
California Blvd, Pasadena, 91125. Judith R
Goodstein, Archivist
Notes: Interviewed for the Oral History
Program of the Archives.

PICKERING FAMILY

†MA —UNIVERSITY OF
MASSACHUSETTS AT AMHERST,
Library, Amherst, 01003.
Notes: Microform collections of materials in
other American libraries.

PICKFORD, MARY

CA —ACADEMY OF MOTION PICTURE
ARTS & SCIENCES, Margaret Herrick
Library, 8949 Wilshire Blvd, Beverly Hills,
90211. Linda Harris Mehr, Library
Administrator
Notes: Papers.
See also entry under Moving Pictures.
DC —LIBRARY OF CONGRESS, Motion
Pictures, Broadcasting and Recorded Sound
Div, Washington, 20540.
Notes: Films of Mary Pickford.
NY —NEW YORK PUBLIC LIBRARY,
Performing Arts Research Center, Billy Rose
Theatre Collection, 111 Amsterdam Ave,
New York, 10023. Dorothy L Swerdlove,
Cur
Holdings: Cat Mss Pix
Notes: Papers, scrapbooks, mss, photographs,
memorabilia, etc.
†TX —UNIVERSITY OF TEXAS
LIBRARIES, Hoblitzelle Theatre Arts
Library, Austin, 78712.
Notes: A 100,000-item collection of
correspondence and documents related to
the career and personal life of Gloria
Swanson, one of the largest archives from
1913 to 1983. Correspondence with Mary
Pickford, William Faulkner, and the
Kennedy Family, the latter to remain sealed
until the year 2000.

PICKLING see Canning and Preserving

PICK'S DISEASE OF THE BRAIN see
Presenile Dementia

PICKTHALL, MARJORIE L.C.

ON —VICTORIA UNIVERSITY, Library, 71
Queen's Park Crescent, Toronto, M5S 1K7,
Can. Robert C Brandeis, Chief Librn
Notes: The collection is very strong in 19th-
20th century poetry, drama and fiction; it
contains gazetteers, travel books,
biographies, and works on history and
geography. Nucleus of collection listed in
James, C C, *A Bibliography of Canadian
Poetry (English)* (Victoria University Library
Publication No 1, Toronto, 1899); and
Horning, L E and Burpee, L J, *A
Bibliography of Canadian Fiction (English)*
(Victoria University Library Publication No
2, Toronto, 1904). Collection incl mss and
vols by Canadian writers Helena Coleman,
Raymond Knister, and Marjorie L C
Pickthall and letters of Bliss Carman, and
Duncan Campbell Scott.

PICTOGRAPHS AND PICTOGRAPHY
see Picture Writing

PICTURE BOOKS FOR CHILDREN see
Illustrated Books, Children's

PICTURE POSTCARDS see Postal Cards;
Postal Cards—Collections

PICTURE POSTERS see
Posters—Collections

PICTURE WRITING

OH —CLEVELAND PUBLIC LIBRARY, Fine
Arts and Special Collections Department,

325 Superior Ave, Cleveland, 44114. Alice
N Loranth, Head
Holdings: Vols (1500) Cat
Notes: Part of the Manuscripts Collection.
Special emphasis is on chess, and on British
India, 1750-1850. More than 250 vols. (19,
000 pages) are incl in the East India
Company ms collection. Important Arabic
texts, illuminated Persian mss, Mosu
pictographs, and some unpublished Latin
medieval compilations of legends and
romances deserve special attention. The
collection of original mss is well
supplemented by several hundred copies of
chess mss and facsimile editions with
emphasis on Medieval texts and Mexican
and Maya codices in addition to the bound
vols, extensive archival holdings are incl in
the chess and folklore collections.

PICTURES—COLLECTIONS

AK —UNIVERSITY OF ALASKA, Elmer E
Rasmuson Library, Fairbanks, 99701. Robert
H Geiman, Dir
Holdings: Vols Cat Mss Maps Pix Slides
Phonorecords Audiotapes Films Microforms
Notes: The Alaska Collection is strong in all
disciplines concerning Alaska. Main
strengths are exploration and travel, pioneer
memoirs, and materials on Alaska natives.
Bulk of collection is in English with
significant holdings in Russian, Native
American, and European languages. Archival
holdings incl 6000 cu ft of mss, 110,000
historic photographs, 2319 tape recordings,
727 films and videotapes, 200 rare maps and
1273 microfilms. Ms collection strongest in
political and economic areas. A Guide to the
Collections is available in hard copy and
microfiche. About 1000 special collections,
some 300 quite significant.
AZ —NORTHERN ARIZONA
UNIVERSITY, Special Collection Library,
CU Box 6022, Flagstaff, 86011. Peter M
Whiteley, Coordr/Archivist; William
Mullane, Librn
Holdings: Cat Mss Maps Pix Slides
Audiotapes Microforms
Notes: Northern Arizona history and
Arizona economic history. Depository of
Forest History Society of America; custodian
for Northern Arizona Pioneers Historical
Society Manuscript Collection. Various
collections, incl (1) Kolb Collection; very
extensive collection of Kolb's photographs
(over 250,000) which concentrate on the
Grand Canyon, 1901-1975. (2) Stuart M
Young Collection; photographs from the
Utah Archeological Expedition of 1909, incl
the first photographs of Rainbow Bridge and
many Anasazi ruins of Northern Arizona
and Southern Utah. (3) Phillip Johnston
Collection; incl thousands of photo negatives
of the Navajo Reservation, 1920's-1930's
and slide shows of the Navajo Reservation
and Mexico.
AZ —ARIZONA STATE UNIVERSITY,
Library, Tempe, 85287. Marilyn
Wurzburger, Special Collections Librn
Notes: The Jimmy Starr Film History
Collection contains the personal library and
working materials of Jimmy Starr,
Hollywood movie columnist from the 1920s-
1960s. In addition to working as a press
agent, Mr Starr was a columnist for the now
defunct *Los Angeles Record* and the *Los
Angeles Herald & Express,* and his
columnswere widely syndicated; he also
wrote silent comedies for Mack Sennett,
scripts for the talkies, as well as several
mystery novels. The collection incl over
2100 biographical files of entertainers
containing well over 20,000 contemporary
newspaper and periodical clippings; over
3000 stills; reviews, premiere invitations and
other ephemera for over 6000 films; and
other writers. Also, there are reference
books, selected film periodicals and
scrapbooks which round out the collection.
The material is partially cataloged; finding
guides are available.
AZ —ARIZONA DAILY STAR, Library, 4850
S Park Ave, PO Box 26807, Tucson, 85726.
Elaine Y Raines, Librn; Michele R Canney,
Asst Librn
Holdings: Cat Maps Pix Microforms
Budget: ($110,000)
Notes: Main resource is 1,800,000 piece

clipping collection of Tucson and Arizona,
from 1939. Holdings incl Tucson telephone
books, from 1940; Tucson city directories,
from 1918; 1500 books on Tucson and
Arizona; daily newspaper (microfilm), from
1877. Index prepared by Univ of Arizona,
1953-1965 and 1979, with plans to index
missing years. Picture collection (150,000)
and VF of ephemera (5000 pieces) are
valuable historical sources.
AZ —TUCSON MUSEUM OF ART
LIBRARY, 140 N Main, Tucson, 85705.
Dorcas Worsley, Librn
Holdings: Vols (2000)
Budget: ($1500)
Notes: Extensive file of biographical and
critical information on Arizona artists which
is continually being increased. Subject card
index to magazines on Western art and
artists in magazines not indexed in *Art
Index* 12 drawers in 1984, and continues to
grow. Have a collection of 15,000 slides.
AZ —NAVAJO TRIBAL MUSEUM, Navajo
Historical Library, Window Rock, 86515.
Russell P Hartman, Cur
Notes: Navajo history, art, social life and
customs.
CA —ANAHEIM PUBLIC LIBRARY, 500 W
Broadway, Anaheim, 92805.
Holdings: Vols (2000) Cat Mss Maps Pix
Microforms
Notes: Our specialty is local history,
especially that of Anaheim and Orange
County. In addition to many books on
California, we have photographs, maps,
directories, organization histories, ephemera,
journals; books published by The Fine Arts
Press, Santa Ana; periodicals, original
minute books and records of the Los
Angeles Vineyard Society. The Walt Disney
Archives has designated the library as an
official depository of material on Walt
Disney, with an emphasis on Disneyland.
This collection incl Disney books, Disney
periodicals, press releases, operating
manuals, guide-books, posters, photographs,
Disney character merchandise and examples
of ephemeral materials such as tickets, hand-
bills, and advertising matter.
CA —BERKELEY PUBLIC LIBRARY, Art
and Music Div, 2090 Kittredge St, Berkeley,
97404. Diane Davenport, Reference
Holdings: Vols (20,000) Cat Pix Slides
Audiotapes
CA —UNIVERSITY OF CALIFORNIA,
BERKELEY, Environmental Design
Library, (The General Library), 210 Wurster
Hall, Berkeley, 94720. Arthur B Waugh,
Head
Holdings: Vols (90,000) Cat Pix Microforms
Budget: ($17,400)
Notes: A research collection devoted to the
following aspects of the field of architecture:
working details, drawing, theory standards
and professional practice; building materials,
building types, earthquake resistant
architecture, contemporary architecture of
all countries, history of architecture, and
architecture as a profession. A small rare
book collection in the field of architecture is
maintained. Approximately 1500 serials, incl
many foreign-language titles, are currently
being received. A collection of photographs
(of buildings) and a slide collection are
administered by the department of
architecture.
CA —ACADEMY OF MOTION PICTURE
ARTS & SCIENCES, Margaret Herrick
Library, 8949 Wilshire Blvd, Beverly Hills,
90211. Linda Harris Mehr, Library
Administrator
Holdings: Vols (16,000) Cat Mss Pix Slides
Budget: ($250,000)
Notes: Also posters, scrapbooks, clippings
and press books. Collection emphases are the
moving picture industry, moving picture
history, biographical material on actors,
actresses and industry personnel. Files on
specific films, reviews, cast and credits,
production data, etc, on more than 65,000
moving pictures. (Over 5000 films, incl early
28mm films in Film Archive). Over 5 million
pictures. Special collections: papers of Mary
Pickford, Mack Sennett, Adolph Zukor,
Lewis Milestone, George Stevens, George
Cukor, John Huston, Edith Head;

PICTURES—COLLECTIONS (cont.)

Paramount scripts and stills archive, MGM stills archive, RKO stills archive, Thomas H Ince stills collection, Cecil B DeMille stills collection.

CA —CLAREMONT COLLEGES, Honnold Library, Ninth & Dartmouth, Claremont, 91711. Tania Rizzo, Special Collections Dept Head
Holdings: Vols (7000) Uncat Music Mss Pix Ephemera
Notes: The Schumann-Heink Bequest made to Pomona College in 1938. Collection consists of music and professional and personal memorabilia, 1885-1936. Nearly 10,000 items total, mostly music, some in manuscript (printed scores partly catalogued among general library holdings); 350 letters and cards; journals, diaries, and day books; 175 photographs; and clippings, programs, awards, and other items. Complete inventory in preparation. Restricted use.

CA —UNIVERSITY OF CALIFORNIA, DAVIS, Shields Library, Dept of Special Collections, Davis, 95616. Donald Kunitz, Head; C Danial Elliott, Asst Head
Holdings: Vols (112,000) Cat Mss Pix
Notes: Programs, playbills, posters, designs, and scripts from 19th and 20th century American and British theatre. American materials incl the eastern United States (NYC) and California. Production groupings center in Sir Henry Irving, McKee Rankin, Sir John Martin-Harvey, E L Davenport. Clippings, photographs, and correspondence of theatre personalities; records of the Bread and Puppet Theatre, San Francisco Mime Troupe, Living Theatre, Firehouse Theatre, Squat Theatre, papers of Toby Cole. Described in: Sarlos, Robert K, "The Theatre Collection at Davis," *American Society for Theatre Research Newsletter,* vol 3, no 1, fall 1974, pp 2-3, 9-10.

CA —CALIFORNIA STATE UNIVERSITY, FRESNO, Henry Madden Library, Dept of Special Collections, Fresno, 93740. Ronald J Mahoney, Head
Holdings: // Uncat Pix
Notes: The Harry Pidgeon Collection of photographs of logging in the Sugar Pine area of the Sierra Nevada mountains, Madera County, California. Also a collection of photographs on all international expositions, 1851-1940, especially the Panama-Pacific International Exposition, San Francisco, 1915.

CA —UNIVERSITY OF CALIFORNIA, IRVINE, Library, Irvine, 92664. Roger Berry, Dept Head
Holdings: Cat Mss Maps Pix Slides
Notes: The Meadows Collection, an extensive collection of California. Rich in material on the history of Orange County, Southern California and Baja, California. Incl more than 3500 vols, thousands of pieces of printed ephemera, over 10,000 mss items, significant runs of California historical periodicals and of rare early Orange County newspapers, maps and several hundred local historical photographs.

CA —LOMA LINDA UNIVERSITY, Dell E Webb Memorial Library, Loma Linda, 92354. James R Nix, Assoc University Archivist
Holdings: Vols 16,000 Cat Mss Maps Pix Slides Phonorecords Audiotapes 16mm Films Microforms
Notes: Materials by and about Seventh-day Adventists, as well as the history of Christianity. Larger collection at Loma Linda campus.

CA —AMERICAN FILM INSTITUTE, Louis B Mayer Library, 2021 N Western Ave, PO Box 27999, Los Angeles, 90027. Anne G Schlosser, Dir
Holdings: Vols (3500) Cat
Notes: Collection contains 2500 American film scripts and 1000 television scripts; oral histories conducted in the American Film Institute Louis B Mayer Oral History Program; the MGM Script Collection of 400 MGM scripts from the silent period up to the mid-1950's; Columbia Stills Collection covering the period 1930-1950; special mss collections of Henry Hathaway (director), Harry Horner, Buster Keaton, George Byron Sage and Stewart Stern (writer). Also clipping files on motion pictures, personalities, television shows, production organizations and technical topics; film festival file of all US and foreign festivals. Rare periodical holdings incl *Film Daily* newspaper (1923-1969); *Radio-TV Daily* newspaper (1939-1964); *RKO Radio Flash,* house organ of RKO (1932-1955); *TV Guide* (1948 to date).

CA —INSTITUTE OF THE AMERICAN MUSICAL, Library, 121 N Detroit St, Los Angeles, 90036. Miles Kreuger, Cur
Holdings: Cat Mss Maps Pix Slides Phonorecords
Notes: Reference materials on the American musical theatre and motion pictures incl 40,000 phonograph records, sound tapes, and cylinders dating back to the 1890s; record catalogs to 1900; thousands of theatre and film programs, periodicals, sheet music and vocal scores as early as 1830; thousands of motion picture press books and over 200,000 stills from 1914 to the present; every musical comedy script published in America and dozens in ms form, original or photocopy materials from the archives of movie palaces, films and record companies, incl discographies of many major Broadway and Hollywood stars; and thousands of books on theatre, film, broadcasting, world's fairs and other allied areas of showmanship.

CA —LOS ANGELES PUBLIC LIBRARY, Central Library, Audio Visual Dept, 630 W Fifth St, Los Angeles, 90071. Richard V Partlow, Principal Librn
Budget: ($71,989)
Notes: Includes 16mm film (4300), VHS video (300), audio recordings (20,000), audio cassettes (5500), picture file (220,000 estimated clippings), filmstrips (60), periodicals (65). Material on all subject areas are included.

CA —UNIVERSITY OF CALIFORNIA, LOS ANGELES, Research Library, Dept of Special Collections, 405 Hilgard Ave, Los Angeles, 90024. Edward Shreeves, Chairman, Bibliographers Group; David S Zeidberg, Head
Holdings: Cat Mss Pix
Notes: 2 million pictures, incl original photographs and ephemera of California people and places, images by California Pictorialists, and news photographs from the morgues of the *Los Angeles Daily News* and the *Los Angeles Times.* Also 150 images by Louis Stellman of San Francisco Chinatown and the Mother Lode country.

CA —UNIVERSITY OF CALIFORNIA, LOS ANGELES, Theater Arts Library, Los Angeles, 90024. Edward Shreeves, Chairman, Bibliographers Group; Audree Malkin, Head, Theater Arts Library
Holdings: Vols (12,500) Cat Mss Films
Notes: Over 4,000,000 moving picture stills; over 32,636 screenplays and scripts from American and British films; Incl radio (1740) scripts, television script collection (3000). Extensive poster collection (over 7000, 1915 to date); many for Polish and Czech productions.

CA —UNIVERSITY OF CALIFORNIA, LOS ANGELES, Theater Arts Library, Los Angeles, 90024. Edward Shreeves, Chairman, Bibliographers Group; Audree Malkin, Head, Theater Arts Library
Holdings: Cat Mss Pix Slides
Notes: Photograph Collection: A collection of approximately 4,000,000 production stills, scene stills, portraits, publicity stills, and other miscellaneous photographs spanning the history of motion pictures 1905 to the present. Notable features are the *Jessen Faragoh Collection* which consists of 2169 production stills and photographs of such early studios as Biograph, Keystone, Selig, Triangle, and Vitagraph, and 901 portraits of performers such as Thomas Ince, D W Griffith, and Jesse Lasky from 1905-1929; the *Richard Dix Collection* of 5217 stills from Richard Dix films; *Columbia Pictures Still Collection* consisting of over 200,000 stills from Columbia films; portraits of performers and keybooks dating 1940-present. *Twentieth Century Fox Motion Picture Still Collection* comprises photographs from 288 American andEuropean films released by Twentieth Century Fox, primarily during the 1950s and 1960s. The collection contains 80,751 production stills, 71 keysets, 2763 individual proof sheets, 415 individual proof sheets, 349 proof sheet books, 309 Rollei proof sheet books, 164 color transparencies, 37 portraits, and a number of publicity news releases.

CA —OAKLAND PUBLIC LIBRARY, Art, Music and Recreation Section, 125 14 St, Oakland, 94612. Richard Colvig, Senior Librn
Holdings: Pix
Budget: ($500)
Notes: About 350,000 mounted pictures, posters, pictorial maps, postal cards, art reproductions, framed and unframed.

CA —OAKLAND PUBLIC LIBRARY, Oakland History Room, 125 14th St, Oakland, 94612. William W Sturm, Librn
Holdings: Vols (20,000) Cat Mss Maps Pix Microforms
Notes: The Oakland History Room Collection is a reference collection of books, pamphlets, periodicals, pictures, and newspaper clippings. California items incl as much biographical material as possible clipped from the *Oakland Tribune, Oakland Post, California Voice,* the *Montclarion,* and *Alameda Times-Star.* (Library no longer clips *San Francisco Chronicle* or *Examiner*). These clippings are filed by subjects. An index of all the subjects with many cross references are made. An index of articles from about 75 magazines dealing with California subjects is kept up to date. The log books of the Coast Guard Cutter *Bear* from 1889 to 1932 are in the collection. The Jack London collection is listed separately. Ms pages and letters from Joaquin Miller and a fewmiscellaneous letters from other authors are also incl. A set of George Sterling, both inscribed and not inscribed, is owned by the Room.

CA —PASADENA PUBLIC LIBRARY, Fine Arts Division, Reference Services, 285 E Walnut St, Pasadena, 91101. Anne Cain, Principal Librn
Holdings: Vols (10,000) Cat Pix Films
Notes: Plus clipping files and scrapbooks emphasizing Pasadena and California architecture; Greene & Greene, Architects. Incl over 130,000 pictures, 64 films. Special index of *Architectural Digest,* vols I-III and VI-XII for southern California homes and architects.

CA —SACRAMENTO PUBLIC LIBRARY, 828 I St, Sacramento, 95814. Dorothy Harvey, Librn, Special Collections
Holdings: Vols 26,000 Cat
Notes: Picture files and card indexes. Extensive collection on painters and their works.

CA —SAN DIEGO PUBLIC LIBRARY, Art, Music & Recreation Sect, 820 E St, San Diego, 92101. Barbara A Tuhill, Supvr
Notes: Mainly 423,012 unmounted and 5396 mounted pictures filed under 11,400 subjects ranging from Aardvark through Zulu grouped in manila folders. Large collection of "portraits" of the famous and pictures of historical events, such as World War II, etc. For general circulation.

CA —ASIAN ART MUSEUM OF SAN FRANCISCO, Library, Golden Gate Park, San Francisco, 94118. Fred A Cline Jr, Librn
Holdings: Vols (16,000) Cat Mss Pix Microforms Clippings
Notes: The Avery Brundage Collection of Oriental Art. Emphasis on East Asian, Southeast Asian and East Indian art. Also building a microform library; collecting pictures and clipping files. Noncirculating. No interlibrary loans. Hours 1-4:45 (city holidays excepted).

CA —CALIFORNIA HISTORICAL SOCIETY, Schubert Hall Library, 2099 Pacific Ave, San Francisco, 94109. Bruce L Johnson, Library Dir
Holdings: Vols (30,000) Cat Mss Maps Pix
See also entry under California - History

PICTURES—COLLECTIONS (cont.)

CA —FITZ HUGH LUDLOW MEMORIAL
LIBRARY, PO Box 99346, San Francisco,
94109. Michael R Aldrich, Exec Cur
Holdings: Vols Caat Mss Maps Pix Slides
Phonorecords Audiotapes Videotapes
Notes: Collection stored. Important mail
inquiries only. No interlibrary lending or
telephone queries. Index to hundreds of
drug-related illustrations, filed in several
binders by topic (Cannabis, Hallucinogens,
Cocaine, Music, etc). We have photostats of
about 500 of the best illustrations available
to researchers and writers as a graphics
archive; copyright and reproduction
permission must however be obtained by the
user of publisher, in addition to a nominal
fee (per illustration) paid to the Library. We
also collect original art works, artifacts,
paraphernalia, comic books, newspaper
illustrations, and drug advertisements
relating to psychoactive drug use and abuse.
In addition we have available many
illustrations pertinent to mythology (ancient
and modern) peripherally related to drug
history and folklore.

CA —NATIONAL MARITIME MUSEUM,
SAN FRANCISCO, J Porter Shaw Library,
Golden Gate National Recreation Area, Fort
Mason, San Francisco, 94123. David A Hull,
Librn; Herbert Beckwith, Catalog Librn;
Irene Stachura, Ref Librn; John Maounis,
Photo Librn
Holdings: Vols (12,000) Mss Maps Pix Slides
Microforms
Budget: ($4000)
Notes: Pacific Coast maritime history. The
photo collection of 160,000 is partly
cataloged and classified. The library has
complete runs of *Merchant Vessels of US*
and *Lloyd's Register of Shipping* to 1970.
The collection is particularly strong on
Pacific Coast and San Francisco maritime
history. About 250 log books; scrapbooks.
Ca 250 oral history interviews. 60 percent of
books cataloged.

CA —SAN FRANCISCO ART INSTITUTE,
Anne Bremer Memorial Library, 800
Chestnut St, San Francisco, 94133. Jeff
Gunderson, Librn
Holdings: Vols (23,114) Cat Pix Slides
Audiotapes 16mm Films Microforms
Budget: ($15,000)

CA —SAN JOSE PUBLIC LIBRARY, 180 W
San Carlos St, San Jose, 95113. Homer
Fletcher, Dir
Holdings: Vols (11,000) Cat Mss Maps Pix
Slides Microforms
Notes: Extensive collection of California.

CA —WHITTIER COLLEGE, Wardman
Library, Whittier, 90608. Christine
Erdmann, Special Collections Librn
Holdings: Vols 1400 Cat Mss Pix

CO —COLORADO HISTORICAL SOCIETY,
Research Collections, 1300 Broadway,
Denver, 80203. Catherine Kane, Head
Public Service and Access
Holdings: Cat Pix Slides
Notes: 250,000 photographs of western and
Colorado subjects incl gold rush, mining,
Indians, natural features, transportation,
cities and towns, portraits. William Henry
Jackson photographs of area west of
Mississippi.

CO —DENVER PUBLIC LIBRARY, Western
History Department, 1357 Broadway,
Denver, 80203. Eleanor M Gehres, Head
Holdings: Vols (50,000) Cat Mss Maps Pix
Audiotapes Microforms
Notes: Western US History. The department
has a separate catalog, published in 1970 in
7 vols by G K Hall Co. First supplement
published in 1975 in 1 vol. There is a subject
index of some 3 million entries to
newspapers and magazines of the Rocky
Mountain region, added to daily. The
Western Newspaper Microfilm Center
contains approx 7000 reels of Western US
newspapers. Collection has ca 275,000
negatives and prints of Western life; and ca
2500 maps, cataloged and classified.

CT —MARK TWAIN MEMORIAL, 351
Farmington Ave, Hartford, 06105. Wynn
Lee, Dir
Holdings: Vols 1500 Cat Mss Pix Slides
Microforms
Notes: The Samuel L Clemens Family
Collection, 1867 to date. Very large
collection of photographs of S L Clemens,
his family, friends, houses, etc, plus period
photographs filed chronologically and
categorically--no catalog; large collection of
related clippings filed under subject
headings--no catalog; correspondence,
literary mss, documents and other papers--
over 1000 items. Card catalog for books
(many with SLC's marginalia), magazines,
periodicals, pamphlets, letters, mss and
documents. Published description of the
collection in the Library of Congress Union
Catalog of Manuscript Collections. Also
have memorabilia and audio recordings. No
photocopying.

CT —NEW HAVEN COLONY HISTORICAL
SOCIETY, Whitney Library, 114 Whitney
Ave, New Haven, 06510. M Ottilia Koel,
Librn & Cur of Mss
Holdings: Vols 25,000 Cat Mss Maps Pix
Microforms
Notes: 25,000 printed books and pamphlets;
ca 15,000 linear feet of manuscript material
including historic manuscripts, records of
education, maritime and harbor industry,
private papers, business and family records;
40,000 photographic images; maps and
microforms relating to the early settlement
and subsequent history of New Haven and
vicinity.

CT —YALE UNIVERSITY, Art Library, 180
York St, New Haven, 06520. Nancy S
Lambert, Art Librn
Holdings: Cat Pix Slides
Notes: About 140,000 slides, and 120,000
b&w and color photographs accumulating
since the 1890s.

CT —YALE UNIVERSITY, Dept of
Astronomy Library, 260 Whitney Ave, Box
6666, New Haven, 06511.
Holdings: Cat Pix Slides
Notes: Over 3000 plates of asteroids,
pictures taken with Yale telescopes in the
Northern and Southern Hemispheres. Also
about 65,000 stellar parallax plates and about
1000 (17 x 17 in) zone catalog plates
recording some 200,000 star positions. There
is also a collection of about 500 plates
recording the location of the north celestial
pole among the stars. Of this latter, only one
other similar collection exists, at the Pulkova
Observatory, near Leningrad.

CT —YALE UNIVERSITY, School of
Medicine, Dept of Obstetrics & Gynecology
Library, Farnam Memorial Bldg, New
Haven, 06510.
Holdings: Cat Mss Pix Slides
Notes: X-ray plates, 10,000 slides of monkey
and human tissue and about 1000 slides of
gynecological and obstetrical pathology, used
as teaching and research materials. Other
large collections of X-rays and radiotherapy
photographs are in the Hunter Radiation
Therapy Center.

CT —STAMFORD HISTORICAL SOCIETY,
Library, 713 Bedford St, Stamford, 06901.
Ronald Marcus, Librn
Holdings: Vols (1200) Cat Mss Maps Pix
Slides
Notes: Connecticut history, with emphasis
on Fairfield County area and Stamford. Over
3000 Stamford pictures. Numerous
manuscript business records and archives.

DE —DELAWARE ART MUSEUM, Library,
2301 Kentmere Pkwy, Wilmington, 19806.
Anne Hoslam, Librn
Holdings: Vols (25,000) Cat Mss Pix
Notes: The collection is rich in the following
subjects: Howard Pyle and his pupils; John
Sloan and the eight; history of the book and
printing; and English and American
illustrated books. There is also a section on
contemporary photography. Archival
material on Albert Mumford Lindsay,
Jerome Myers, Everett Shinn, Gayle Porter
Hoskins, Frank Schoonover.

DC —CHRONICLE OF HIGHER
EDUCATION, INC, 1333 New Hampshire
Ave NW, Suite 500, Washington, 20036.
Edith H Uunila, Sr Editor
Holdings: Cat Pix
Notes: *Chronicle of Higher Education*
published weekly. Library is for editorial
research.

DC —GEORGETOWN UNIVERSITY,
Library, Special Collections Div, 37 & O Sts
NW, Washington, 20057. George M
Barringer, Special Collections Librn;
Nicholas B Sheetz, Mss Librn
Holdings: Vols 500 Cat Pix
Notes: Incorporates the picture "morgue" of ·
the Quigley Publishing Company and
archival runs of its publications. Over 50,000
pictures. The library has additional picture
resources of over 100,000 photographs.

DC —HARVARD UNIVERSITY, Dumbarton
Oaks, Research Library, 1703 32nd St NW,
Washington, 20007. Irene Vaslef, Librn
Holdings: Vols (91,000) Cat Maps Pix Slides
Microforms
Budget: ($219,000)
Notes: Byzantine civilization (including art,
archaeology, literature, history, religion, law,
music, etc). Extensive supplemental material
on Classical, Hellenistic, Medieval, Islamic,
Medieval Slavic cultures. 62,000 b/w
photographs, 25,000 slides and
transparencies, 1000 microfilms of books and
manuscripts. Printed description of collection
in *Harvard Library Bulletin*, vol 19, no 1
(Jan 1971), pp 25-35 and vol 19, no 2 (April
1971), pp 204-214, pp 25-35 and vol 19, no
2 (April 1971), pp 204-214.

DC —HOWARD UNIVERSITY, Founders
Library, Channing Pollock Theatre
Collection, 500 Howard Place NW,
Washington, 20059. Marilyn Mahanand,
Librn
Holdings: Vols (16,440) Cat Mss Maps Pix
Slides Microforms
Notes: Much on the Black Theatre.

DC —LIBRARY OF CONGRESS, Prints &
Photographs Div, Washington, 20540.
Notes: Effective October 1, the Library's
Prints and Photographs Division has
discontinued reproduction and reference
service on its collection of photographs
which appeared in *Look* magazine from 1937
to 1971. This limitation on service will
remain in effect until questions of rights and
permissions affecting these photographs can
be clarified. The Library acquired the *Look*
archive in 1971 as additional resources for
research in American life by scholars and
other investigators. It was anticipated that
the photographs would serve as a study
collection for researchers in many fields, but
the major use of the collection has been by
publishers, advertisers, and makers of
documentary films. Such picture users
require clear rights to reproduce the images.
The Library has been unable to satisfy these
requests because of the donor's stipulation
precluding such use. Until some
accommodation canbe made with the donor
to free the collection for a wider range of
public use, collection will remain in remote
cold storage to retard deterioration of
sensitive films, especially color films. This
policy will remain in effect until further
notice. LC Information Bulletin, 10 Oct 83.

DC —LIBRARY OF CONGRESS, Prints &
Photographs Div, Washington, 20540.
Holdings: Cat Pix
Notes: Prints & Photographs. Artists prints
from the 15th through the 20th century
(approx 70,000) in the J & E R Pennell, the
Gardiner Greene Hubbard & the George
Lothrop Bradley collections. Historical prints
of the 18th and 19th centuries (approx 75,
000 engravings & lithographs by Currier and
Ives and other printmakers of views,
portraits, battles, theater posters,
advertisements, etc). Cabinet of American
Illustration (original drawings by the Civil
War artists, Alfred R Waud and Edwin
Forbes, and work produced during the 1890s
through the 1920s); Archives of American
Graphic Humor (genre and political
cartoons--original lithographs and drawings
by McCutcheon, Nast, Kirby, etc).
Photograph collections: Brady-Handy and
Mathew B Brady (Civil War, portraits),
Frances Benjamin Johnston (early American
architecture), George Grantham Bain
(portraits and events, 1898-1916),Detroit
Photographic Company (views, human
interest pictures, 1898-1914), Herbert E
French (photographs of the Washington, D
C scene, 1919-1932), American Red Cross

PICTURES—COLLECTIONS (cont.)

(1900 through World War I), Erwin E Smith (cowboys and the western range), Farm Security Administration-- Office of War Information (survey of America, 1935-1943), Historic American Buildings Survey (measured drawings, photographs, data pages), Archive of Hispanic Culture (Latin American art and architecture), Look Magazine collection (American life and culture, 1937-1971), Toni Frissell collection (society and fashion), Rizzuto collection (New York City, ca 1950-1966), Matson collection (Palestine and the middle east, 1890s to 1946). Master Photographs collection (items of particular esthetic or historical importance). Extensive portrait and geographic files. Poster collection World WarsI and II, Art Nouveau, Contemporary poster art. Total: Over 20,000,000 items.

DC —LIBRARY OF CONGRESS, Prints & Photographs Div, Washington, 20540.
Notes: The Roger Fenton Collection of 265 original Crimean War photoprints.

DC —LIBRARY OF CONGRESS, Prints and Photographs Div, Historic American Buildings Survey, Washington, 20540.
Holdings: Cat Mss Pix Drawings
Notes: Details of some 17,000 American buildings in 81,000 photographs, 42,000 measured drawings and 44,000 pp of written documentation.

DC —LIBRARY OF CONGRESS, Motion Pictures, Broadcasting and Recorded Sound Div, Washington, 20540.
Holdings: Cat Mss Pix
Notes: Motion Picture Film. Early film dating from 1894; paper print collection of early film (1897-1915) deposited for copyright, converted to projectable film. George Kleine Collection (1900-1920); Edison Laboratories Collection; Theodore Roosevelt Memorial Association Collection; American Film Institute Collection (theatrical films from 1897 to 1956 and theatrical shorts from all periods); German, Japanese, and Italian collections received through transfer from other Government governments; American Copyright Collection of films (incl television shows) selected from those registered for copyright from 1942 to the present. Collection of stills; poster collection; script and continuity collection. Holdings: motion pictures, 50,000 titles; 300,000 stills, 8000 posters; 137,000 scripts and continuities.

DC —NATIONAL GALLERY OF ART, Library, Sixth & Constitution Ave NW, Washington, 20565. J M Edelstein, Chief Librn
Holdings: Cat Mss Pix Slides Microforms
Notes: Incl art sale and exhibition catalogs, catalogs of private art collections, and photographic archives of western European and US art (798,229 photographs).

DC —NATIONAL GEOGRAPHIC SOCIETY, Library, 1146 16th St NW, Washington, 20036. Susan Fifer Canby, Dir
Holdings: Vols (63,000) Cat Mss Maps Pix
Notes: Material concerning land, sea, and space exploration--past and present. All fields of anthropology, natural history, geography, etc.

DC —SMITHSONIAN INSTITUTION LIBRARIES, Anthropology Branch, Washington, 20560. Jean C Smith, Asst Dir for Bureau Services
Holdings: Vols (54,000) Cat Mss Maps Pix Slides Microforms
Budget: ($7041)
Notes: Physical anthropology, archaeology, ethnology, language and languages; Indians of both continents.

DC —SMITHSONIAN INSTITUTION LIBRARIES, General Library, Washington, 20560. Mary Claire Grey, Chief Cent Ref & Loan Servs
Holdings: Vols (79,000) Cat Mss Maps Pix Slides Microforms
Notes: Incl publications of foreign and domestic museums, and all phases of museum work.

DC —SMITHSONIAN INSTITUTION LIBRARIES, Business & Industry Collections, Washington, 20560.
Notes: The Warshaw Collection of illustrative materials.

†DC —SMITHSONIAN INSTITUTION LIBRARIES, Washington, 20560.
Notes: The published guide to the numerous Smithsonian Institution museums and deposits is one of the most helpful and successfully (and well-indexed) complementary vols that can be used with this edition of Subject Collections. Refer to Lynda Corey Claassen's Finder's Guide to Prints and Drawings in the Smithsonian Institution, 210 pp, (Washington: Smithsonian Institution Press, 1981), Los Angeles. An index of artists lists about 10,000 names represented in the Smithsonian's collections in the Archives of American Art, Cooper-Hewitt Museum, Freer Gallery of Art, Hirshhorn Museum and Sculpture Garden, Museum of African Art, National Air and Space Museum, National Museum of American Art, National Museum of American History, National Museum of Natural History and National Museum of Man, National Portrait Gallery, Smithsonian Institution Archives, andSmithsonian Institution Libraries, and their subject departments, all of which are described.

FL —HISTORICAL ASSOCIATION OF SOUTHERN FLORIDA, Charlton W Tebeau Library of Florida History, 101 W Flager St, Miami, 33130. Rebecca A Smith, Cur of Research Materials
Holdings: Vols (3000) Cat Mss Maps Pix Slides Audiotapes 16mm Films Microforms
Notes: History of Florida, with emphasis on southern area. Less extensively, history of the Caribbean area, especially as related to Florida. Florida materials incl anthropology, archaeology, Indians of south Florida, incl Seminole Indians, Dade County history, and a complete run of the newspaper The American Eagle (1906-date), printed by Koreshan Unity, Estero, Florida. Incl 90 feet of mss, 400 maps, 20,000 pictures, 2000 slides, 125 audiotapes, 25 16mm films, 20 microforms, 50 feet of vertical files, and 7000 postcards. Work in progress on guide to ms collection and on indexing of photographs. Also incl some books and journals on museum science: conservation and preservation of museum materials.

FL —MIAMI-DADE PUBLIC LIBRARY SYSTEM, One Biscayne Blvd, Miami, 33132. Don Chauncey, AV Librn; Barbara Young, Art & Music Dept Librn
Holdings: Cat Pix Films
Notes: Picture file; portrait file; painting picture file; costume picture file; 1,733 framed pictures, approximately half of which are available for public circulation.

FL —ORLANDO PUBLIC LIBRARY, 100 Block of Central Ave, Orlando, 32806. Helen M Struthers, AV Librn
Holdings: Cat Pix Slides
Budget: $150
Notes: The picture file collection (38,000 pictures) is made up of mounted pictures, pamphlets (10,000), and other vertical file material related to subjects in the Dewey 700's. 438 slides are available for circulation, as well as 340 framed art reproductions.

FL —UNIVERSITY OF WEST FLORIDA, John C Pace Library, Pensacola, 32514. Dean Debolt, Head, Special Collections
Holdings: Vols 1550 Cat Mss Maps Pix Slides Microforms
Notes: History of Florida before 1865; almost exclusively West Florida and Pensacola after 1865. Catalog of ms collection: The First One Hundred and an article describing the collection in Manuscripts, vol 25, no 1, Winter 1973; and The Second One Hundred (pamphlet, 1978). Collection incl 800,000 ms pieces, 3000 maps, 10,000 pictures (chiefly photographs of early 20th century Pensacola). Also incl speeches of early 20th century legislators.

FL —FLORIDA DEPT OF NATURAL RESOURCES BUREAU OF MARINE RESEARCH, Library, 100 Eighth Ave SE, Saint Petersburg, 33701. Keir Gray, Archivist
Holdings: Vols (3400) Cat Maps Pix Slides 16mm Films Microforms
Budget: ($27,500)
Notes: The library supports the research of approx 50 biologists and technicians, with emphasis on the marine resources of Florida and nearby areas. An archives section houses original research data, reports, publications,, etc, developed by the scientific staff. Marine biological literature is received on exchange from laboratories and libraries throughout the world. There are approx 1400 journal titles in the collection. Current titles received number approx 600. The 33,000 reprints are cataloged by author and subject. Current laboratory activities incl marine studies in aquaculture, descriptive biology, ecological studies, fisheries biology, and oceanography.

FL —FLORIDA DEPT OF STATE, Florida State Archives, Florida Photographic Collection, R A Gray Bldg, Tallahassee, 32301. Mrs Allen Morris, Archives Supervisor
Holdings: Maps Pix Slides Films Audiotapes
Notes: Areas of emphasis within the collection: (1) Florida government. There is a complete file of governors' photos, and many photos of legislative sessions and legislators going back to the late 1800s. (2) Stanley J Morrow. Mr Morrow learned his craft under Mathew B Brady. He worked in Florida from 1882-1887. Collection has several hundred of his glass negatives that document a period of southward expansion in Florida. (3) Alvan S Harper, Tallahassee portrait artist; 1700 glass negatives of Tallahassee people between 1885-1910. (4) W A Fishbaugh. Several hundred photographs of the "boom," Miami and Coral Gables in the 1920s. (5) Charles A Mosier, Charles Torrey Simpson and J K Small; 500 photographs of Florida flora, made by these famous naturalists, mostly in South Dade County. (6) Added March, 1983; 2200 glass and nitrate negatives by J K Small. (7) Collectionalso incl 40,000 negatives (4x5) made by Harvey Slade in Tallahassee, 1946-1975, predominantly portraits; also 15,000 news story negatives (4x5 and 2x2) relative to local and state government, 1957-1969, unprinted, from The Tallahassee Democrat. (8) 39,000 (4x5) negatives and contact prints deposited by the Florida Dept of Commerce, 1946-late 1970s. Subjects incl Florida cities, attractions, industries, beaches, festivals, boating, fishing, forts, gardens, hotels, highways, lighthouses, monuments, museums and recreations. (9) 25,000 (8x10, 4x5 & 35mm) negatives by Jacksonville commercial photographer Gordon Spottswood & Son, 1916-1967. Subjects incl Jacksonville people (individuals and groups), street scenes, commercial buildings, Atlantic Coast Line & Seaboard Airline Railroads, and Boy Scout Activities. (10) 15,000 (4x5) negativesfrom Seldomridge portrait studio in Tampa. Tampa people from the 1940s to the 1970s.

GA —UNIVERSITY OF GEORGIA, Libraries, Special Collections Division, Athens, 30602. Vesta Lee Gordon, Asst Dir for Special Collections
Holdings: Vols (75,000) Cat Mss Maps Pix
Notes: Materials on Georgia history, incl approx 3,000,000 items in 2000 collections of mss; 1200 maps; 6000 pictures and over 200 pieces of sheet music.

GA —ATLANTA COLLEGE OF ART LIBRARY, 1280 Peachtree St N E, Atlanta, 30309. Jean Haskell, Librn
Holdings: Vols (16,000) Cat Pix Slides Phonorecords Videotapes Microforms
Notes: Visual arts, with 20th-century emphasis. There is a catalog to the books and the exhibition catalogs.The library is the only collection devoted totally to the visual arts in the Atlanta area. Rare book collection and extensive artists' books collection.

GA —COLQUITT-THOMAS REGIONAL LIBRARY, Moultrie-Colquitt County Library, 204 Fifth St SE, PO Box 1110, Moultrie, 31768. Melody Jenkins, Dir
Holdings: Maps Pix Slides Microforms
Notes: Emphasis on Colquitt County area.

HI —BERNICE P BISHOP MUSEUM, Library, PO Box 19000-A, Honolulu, 96819. Cynthia Timberlake, Librn
Notes: Only American library devoted exclusively to the Pacific region. Collection reflects historical and contemporary research

PICTURES—COLLECTIONS (cont.)

emphases of Bishop Museum; ie the natural and cultural history of the Pacific. Areas of concentration incl archaeology, ethnology, linguistics, voyages and explorations, history, vertebrate and invertebrate zoology, botany and museology. Strong special collections incl photographs, mss and archives, maps and art. Publications: Quarterly "Additions to the Catalog," *Dictionary Catalog of the Library* (9 vols and 2 suppl; Boston: G K Hall, 1964-69).

HI —HONOLULU ACADEMY OF ARTS, Robert Allerton Library, 900 S Beretania St, Honolulu, 96814. Anne T Seaman, Librn
Holdings: Vols (40,000) Cat Pix Slides VF
Notes: Incl 7000 pictures, 300 slides, 12 VF drawers.

IL —SOUTHERN ILLINOIS UNIVERSITY, CARBONDALE, Delyte W Morris Library, Special Collections Dept, Carbondale, 62901. David V Koch, Cur of Special Collections; Louisa Bowen, Cur of Manuscripts
Holdings: Vols 110 Uncat Mss Pix
Notes: The personal papers (75 linear feet) and art work of Mordecai Gorelik, stage designer, director, and playwright, incl a large volume of correspondence with persons of the theater, in the US and abroad, scripts of plays, and thousands of sketches, drawings, and photographs of stage settings.

IL —UNIVERSITY OF ILLINOIS, URBANA/CHAMPAIGN, Library, Ricker Library of Architecture & Art, 208 Architecture Bldg, 608 East Lorado Taft Dr, Champaign, 61820. Dee Wallace, Architecture & Art Librn
Holdings: Vols Cat Pix
Notes: Incl 32,901 mounted photos and reproductions. Cataloged. Also incl noncirculating collection of exhibition catalogs.

IL —AMERICAN LIBRARY ASSOCIATION, Headquarters Library, 50 E Huron St, Chicago, 60611. Joel M Lee, Librn
Holdings: Vols (21,000) Cat Audiotapes Videotapes Microforms
Budget: ($12,000)
Notes: Collections incl such specialized material as building programs, programs, plans, pictures, and slides of libraries.

IL —ART INSTITUTE OF CHICAGO, Ryerson & Burnham Libraries, Michigan Ave & Adams St, Chicago, 60603. Daphne C Roloff, Dir
Holdings: Vols (136,000) Cat Mss Slides Microforms
Budget: ($167,000)
Notes: Total collection incl 300,000 slides.

IL —BURSON-MARSTELLER LIBRARY, Information Services, One E Wacker Dr, Chicago, 60601. Ellen Steininger, Librn
Holdings: Vols 1000 Cat Pix
Notes: Incl 10,000 pictures.

IL —CHICAGO HISTORICAL SOCIETY, Library, Graphics Collection, Clark St at North Ave, Chicago, 60614. Larry A Viskochil, Cur
Notes: About 1,000,000 pieces. Chiefly concern Chicago, but incl many portraits of national leaders and other materials concerning American history. Incl many early daguerreotypes, ambrotypes, tintypes, stereographs; negatives and photographs from Chicago newspaper morgues, 1900-1965 (250,000); photographs from Chicagoland-in-Pictures, a project for historical photography sponsored by the Society and the Chicago Area Camera Clubs Association since 1948 (22,000); and other photographic materials.

IL —CHICAGO PUBLIC LIBRARY, Art Section, Fine Arts Division, 78 E Washington St, Chicago, 60602. Rosalinda I Hack, Fine Arts Division Chief; Yvonne S Brown, Head, Art Section
Holdings: Vols 6000
Notes: Reference and circulating collection, with special emphasis on general architectural history, modern architecture, architecture of the United States, and Chicago architectural history. Collections is supported by the Chicago Architecture File, a card file that lists citations to information

on buildings that been recognized for their architectural significance. The Section's picture Collection has extensive documentation on Chicago area architecture, and incorporates a collection of architectural photographs by Stephen Beal. Archival copies of these photographs are to be found in Special Collections. The collections is also supplemented by the microform collections of *The Historic American Buildings Survey*, and *American Architectural Books*.

IL —DE PAUL UNIVERSITY, Library, 2323 N Seminary, Chicago, 60614. Kathryn De Graff, Special Collections Librn
Holdings: Vols (598) Uncat Pix
Budget: $1500
Notes: The Jack Davidson and Nathan Schwartz Collection. Numerous editions of Dickens' works in the original publisher parts, first complete editions, first American editions and special editions. Also about 300 books about Dickens incl *The Dickension*, 500 prints, posters and photographs, an interesting collection of memorabilia such as figurines, etc. The extra-illustrated volumes, with over 7000 illustrations, were prepared by Mr Bradford, the original owner of the collection, and contain the conceptions of scenes and characters in Dicken's novels by various illustrators.

IL —NEWBERRY LIBRARY, 60 W Walton St, Chicago, 60610. Diana Haskell, Cur of Modern Mss
Holdings: Cat Mss Pix
Notes: Inventoried collection of 1572 items, incl 346 letters from various Indian villages of the West and Southwest. Approx 1200 crayon drawings and 26 oil paintings of Indians and Indian life.

†IL —NORTHWESTERN UNIVERSITY, Medical School, Archibald Church Library, 303 E Chicago Ave, Chicago, 60611. Cecile E Kramer, Librn
Holdings: Cat Mss Pix Slides
Notes: Incl about 3000 vols, 5100 pictures and 1200 slides concerning the history of medicine.

IL —NORTHWESTERN UNIVERSITY, Melville J Herskovits Library of African Studies, Evanston, 60201. Hans E Panofsky, Cur
Holdings: Vols 59,122 Mss Maps Pix Slides Microforms Audiotapes
Budget: $60,000
Notes: Emphasis on social sciences and humanities in Africa and about Africa. Primary and secondary sources. Printed catalog of 8 vols published by the G K Hall Co in 1972. This incl cumulation of *Joint Acquisition List of Africana* (JALA) through 1971. *JALA* continues to be issued bimonthly.

IL —AMERICAN SOCIETY OF ANESTHESIOLOGISTS, Wood Library-Museum of Anesthesiology, 515 Busse Hwy, Park Ridge, 60068. Patrick Sim, Librn
Holdings: Vols 7000 Cat Mss Pix Slides Audiotapes
Notes: History of anesthesiology.

IL —ILLINOIS STATE HISTORICAL SOCIETY, Library, Old State Capitol, Springfield, 62706. Roger D Bridges, Head Librn
Holdings: Cat Pix
Notes: Incl an unusual collection of Illnois pictorial history-some 12,000 scenes and portraits preserved on glass photographic negatives dating from the 1890s to the 1920s acquired from the estate of Herbert W Georg, Springfield photographer. Also, a collection of 180,000 pictures.
See also entry under Illinois - History

IL —UNIVERSITY OF ILLINOIS, URBANA/CHAMPAIGN, Library, University Archives, 19 Library, 1408 W Gregory Drive, Urbana, 61801. Maynard Brichford, University Archivist
Holdings: Uncat Mss Maps Pix Slides Phonorecords Microforms
Notes: In addition to the university archives and the collections of academic and administrative staff, the archives have numerous other series of institutional and personal papers. Published guide to the collections is available: *Manuscripts Guide to Collections at the University of Illinois at*

Urbana-Champaign (University of Illinois Press, 1976). Control cards and ADP control on 3644 records series; 5132 pages of supplementary finding aids. Probably the largest ms collection in the state. Holdings on the history of librarianship and faculty and student life are particularly strong.

IL —UNIVERSITY OF ILLINOIS, URBANA/CHAMPAIGN, Library, Illinois Historical Survey Library, 1408 W Gregory Dr, 1A Library, Urbana, 61801.
Holdings: Vols (6500) Cat Mss Maps Pix Microforms
Notes: Important ms collections incl: Randolph County Records, 1720-1853, 91 items, 59 reels of microfilm; St Clair County Records, 1722-1809, 6 items, 5 reels of microfilm; George Morgan, papers, 1766-1826, 280 items, 5 reels of microfilm; William Morrison, papers, 1805-1855, 7 reels of microfilm. Pierre Menard, papers, 1780, 1802-1859, 155 items, 27 volumes, 29 reels microfilm; Illinois Surveyors' field notes and plat maps, 1805-1850, 56 reels microfilm. Numerous county and local histories and plat books. 1733 maps, and thousands of Illinois pictures. Guide to the collections published in 1976.

IL —LAKE COUNTY MUSEUM LIBRARY, Lakewood Forest Preserve, Wauconda, 60084. Rebecca Goldberg, Dir; Katherine Hamilton-Smith, Cur
Notes: "The world's largest postcard collection. The Curt Teich Industries assets, consisting of several million postcards and associated artwork depicting local communities around the world, cards donated by Regensteiner Enterprises Inc. Curt Teich is considered one of the originators of present day postcards. Project funded by the Curt Teich Foundation."

IN —INDIANA UNIVERSITY, Lilly Library, Seventh St, Bloomington, 47405. William R Cagle, Librn
Holdings: // Mss Pix
Notes: Photographs, etc, of actors and actresses are located in ms collections: (1) Johnson, William Spencer, 1813-1897, printer. Correspondence and photographs from actors and actresses, 1846-1894. 129 items; (2) Stock, Keith Lievesley, 1911-, professor. Autographs, etc of people associated with 19th-early 20th century theatre in England. 279 items; and (3) Woodward, Sidney C, journalist. Correspondence, autographs, and pictures, 1769-1961, of actors, actresses, and other theatre people, mostly American and British. 1235 items. Also, in Printed Books Division: small pictures (largely engravings excerpted from books) of Shakespearean actors and actresses, 18th into 20th century. The Hohenberger collection includes the negatives and original prints of Brown County, Indiana photographer Frank M Hohenberger, 1876-1963.

IN —INDIANA UNIVERSITY, Institute for Sex Research Library, 416 Morrison Hall, Bloomington, 47401. Douglas Freeman, Collections and Services Librn; Joan Brewer, Information Services Librn
Holdings: Vols (62,000) Cat Mss Pix Microforms
See also entry under Sex.

IN —HENRY BLOMMEL AUTOMOTIVE DATA COLLECTION, Library, Route 5, Connersville, 47331. Henry Blommel, Librn
Holdings: Uncat Pix
Notes: Automotive industry data.

IN —LOUIS A WARREN LINCOLN LIBRARY AND MUSEUM, 1300 S Clinton St, Fort Wayne, 46801. Mark E Neely Jr, Dir
Holdings: Vols (17,000) Cat Mss Maps Pix Artifacts
Notes: Acquire all books on Abraham Lincoln, most on his contemporaries, as many as possible on his times, and historical journals. Constantly acquiring unpublished mss on Lincoln, Lincoln's associates, correspondents, and collateral figures. Have some Kentucky Court Records, Richard Thompson Papers. Publish a monthly bulletin of historical research on Lincoln's life and times called *Lincoln Lore*, which includes an annually updated bibliography of Lincolniana.

PICTURES—COLLECTIONS (cont.)

IN —DEPAUW UNIVERSITY, Roy O West Library, University Archives, PO Box 137, Greencastle, 46135. Virginia C Brann, Sr Archives Asst
Holdings: Vols (2000) Cat Mss Maps Pix Slides Microforms
Notes: Archives of DePauw University and Indiana United Methodism. *Select Bibliographic Guide* available upon request.

IN —INDIANA HISTORICAL SOCIETY, Library, 315 W Ohio St, Indianapolis, 46202. Robert K O'Neill, Dir
Holdings: Cat Mss Maps Pix Slides Microforms

IN —MORRISSON-REEVES LIBRARY, 80 N Sixth St, Richmond, 47374. Harriet E Bard, Librn
Notes: Books on art covering a broad range of subject headings. Also, 1030 lantern slides of European sculpture, painting and architecture, particularly emphasizing the Italian Renaissance.

IN —INDIANA STATE UNIVERSITY, Cunningham Memorial Library, Dept of Rare Books & Special Collections, Terre Haute, 47809. Lawrence J McCrank, Head
Notes: The University Archives holds copies of all publications of the Indiana Normal School which became the Indiana State Teachers College and Indiana State University, plus collections of faculty publications and papers. The K Martin sub-collection contains 10,000 photographs relating to ISU from the 1890s to the 1950s. Incl 300 feet of mss.

IA —UNIVERSITY OF IOWA, University Libraries, Iowa City, 52242. Robert A McCown, Mss Librn
Holdings: Mss Pix

Notes: Five collections: Robert Blees collection of motion picture and television material, 1925-65, inc, including stories, still production photos, and motion picture and television scripts of a motion picture and television script writer; David Swift collection of motion picture and television material, 1951-65, including scripts, posters, photos, drawings, and blueprints for final set construction of a motion picture and television producer and writer; the Albert Jay Cohen collection of motion picture and television production material, 1948-58, including correspondence, film scripts, stories, photos, financial and production papers, and censorship records; the Arthur A. Ross collection of motion picture and television material, 1943-65, including correspondence, scripts, photos, production records, and artists' sketches of a motion picture and television script writer; and the Norman Felton Papers, 1937-1978, including correspondence, notes, notebooks, subject files, budgets, other financial records, photographs, and scripts relating to such television series as The Eleventh Hour, The Lieutenant, The Man From U.N.C.L.E., Jericho, The Strange Report, The Psychiatrist, Hawkins, and Dr. Kildare, produced by Felton, 124 ft. of mss.

KS —SANTA FE TRAIL CENTER, Library, Rte 3, Larned, 67550. Kim Keiswetter, Archivist/Education Dir
Holdings: Cat Mss Maps Pix Slides
Budget: ($2500)
Notes: Archives and history of Pawnee County, Kansas, and the Santa Fe Trail. Strong slide and picture collections.

KS —UNIVERSITY OF KANSAS, Kenneth Spencer Research Library, Kansas Collection, Lawrence, 66045. Sheryl K Williams, Cur
Holdings: Cat Pix
Notes: The J J Pennell Collection. Joseph Judd Pennell (1866-1922) was a commerical photographer living and working in Junction City, Kansas from 1888 to 1922. This collection of more than 30,000 glass negatives and nearly 6000 prints is a pictorial record of Junction City, Kansas and nearby Ft Riley. The residents of Junction City have been photographed in their various business, professional, social, and cultural activities, while the army post, Fort Riley, has been documented as a cavalry and light artillery post, as well as an important military post during the First World War and after. The various ethnic groups which made up the population of Junction City, whites, blacks, and Mexican-Americans are represented in the collection. Pennell's day books accompany the photographic collection.

LA —NEW ORLEANS PUBLIC LIBRARY, Art & Music Div, 219 Loyola Ave, New Orleans, 70140. Marilyn Wilkins, Head
Holdings: Cat Pix
Notes: Over 100,000 pictures-broad in subject coverage, some arranged geographically; 21,244 postal cards-mainly geographical, some subjects.

LA —NEW ORLEANS PUBLIC LIBRARY, Louisiana Div, 219 Loyola Ave, New Orleans, 70140. Collin B Hamer Jr, Head; Brenda M Osbey, Library Associate
Holdings: Cat Maps Pix
Notes: Louisiana and New Orleans Picture File Collection ranges from the late 19th century-date and incl the following separate collections: Alexander Allison (ca 1898-1951, 337 pieces); Charles Franck (ca 1920-50, 170 pieces); Leda Plauche (ca 1935-53, 220 pieces); C Milo Williams (ca 1910, 85 pieces); Wilson S Howell (ca 1890, 49 pieces); Grauman Marks (ca 1960, 268 pieces); Robert Tallant (ca 1940-50, 70 pieces); Robert E Tracy (1959, 87 pieces); Anthony J Flaherty (ca 1970-84, 83 pieces); George F Mugnier (1880-1920, 186 pieces); Color Slides (ca 1945-date, 500 pieces); 30,000 photographs incl 500 color slides and 104 negatives. Use of the material is restricted to on-site research. Publication must be accompanied by credit cut line.

ME —MAINE HISTORICAL SOCIETY, Library, 485 Congress St, Portland, 04101.
Holdings: Vols (60,000) Cat Mss Maps Pix
Notes: The Society's holdings cover all of Maine in its scope, with special emphasis on the Portland region.

ME —PORTLAND PUBLIC LIBRARY, 5 Monument Sq, Portland, 04101. Edward V Chenevert, Library Dir
Holdings: Vols 85,000 Cat Maps Pix Microforms
Notes: State of Maine Collection. Books by Maine authors or about Maine-related subjects, and Maine imprints. Maine and Portland government documents dating back to 1829. Collection strong in Maine history and Maine literature and poetry.

MD —JOHNS HOPKINS UNIVERSITY, Institute of the History of Medicine, 1900 E Monument St, Baltimore, 21205. Doris Thibodeau, Librn
Holdings: Vols (50,000) Cat Mss Pix Slides Audiotapes 16mm Films Microforms
Notes: One of the strongest history of medicine collections in the U S. Very strong for Osler, Billings, etc.

MD —CALVERT MARINE MUSEUM, Library, PO Box 97, Solomons, 20688.
Holdings: Cat Mss Maps Pix Slides Audiotapes 16mm Films
Notes: Local maritime history, estuarine biology, and paleontology of southern Maryland. Large picture collection (1800), blueprints (358) and slides (1100).

MA —JONES LIBRARY, 43 Amity St, Amherst, 01002. Daniel J Lombardo, Cur of Special Collections
Holdings: Vols (2710) Cat Maps Pix
Notes: The Boltwood Collection. Several thousand documents, cataloged, 18th and 19th centuries. The scope is primarily local, then regional, Massachusetts, New England. Several thousand local pictures, chiefly post-1926.

MA —BOSTON PUBLIC LIBRARY, Copley Sq, Boston, 02117. Theresa D Cederholm, Cur of Fine Arts
Holdings: Vols 390,000 Cat Pix
Notes: Collections incl original prints, photographs, reproductions on many subjects, and on art architecture and decorative arts.

MA —MASSACHUSETTS COLLEGE OF ART, Library, 364 Brookline Ave, Boston, 02215. Benjamin Hopkins, Head Librn
Holdings: Vols 45,000 Cat Pix Slides
Notes: Incl 55,000 slides, 12 vertical file drawers of pictures.

MA —HARVARD UNIVERSITY, Harvard College Library, Fine Arts Library, Fogg Museum, 32 Quincy St, Cambridge, 02138. Wolfgang M Freitag, Librn
Holdings: Vols (202,000) Cat Mss Pix Slides Microforms
Budget: ($176,500)
Notes: Catalog, in 15 volumes, published 1971, with supplementary volume listing auction catalogs. First supplement, 3 volumes, 1976. Incl 700,000 pictures; 220,000 slides.

MA —RADCLIFFE COLLEGE, Arthur & Elizabeth Schlesinger Library on the History of Women in America, 3 James St, Cambridge, 02138. Patricia Miller King, Dir; Eva Moseley, Cur of Mss
Holdings: Pix Microforms
Notes: About 33,000 photographs, mainly of US women, document 19th and 20th century women's political movements; women's organizations; schools and settlement houses; women in politics, government, and in medicine and other professions; the family (including children and pets); domestic interiors; women at work; recreation and travel (in the US and abroad); and women in the armed forces. About half have been microfilmed. Also drawings, photographs of sculpture by various women.

MA —BOSTON COLLEGE LIBRARIES, Thomas P O'Neill Library, Brehaut Bostonian Collection, Chestnut Hill, 02167. Frank J Seegraber, Special Collections Librn
Holdings: Cat Mss Maps Pix
Notes: Over 5000 items, incl 85 scrapbooks, and 100 maps of Boston and vicinity, 1850-1900. Emphasis on political history, incl the Boston fire, 1872; Boston police strike, 1919; development of the Boston transit system; career of James Michael Curley. For reference use only, by arrangement with librarian.

MA —UNIVERSITY OF LOWELL, Library, One University Ave, Lowell, 01854. Martha Mayo, Special Collections Librn
Holdings: 15,000 Cat Pix
Notes: Lowell History Collection contains photographs, lithographs, post cards, stereoviews, and lanternslides pertaining to the history of the area with special focus on the textile industry and the men and women who worked in the mills from New England Yankee farm girls to the Irish, French-Canadian, and Greek immigrants. The Locks and Canals Collection contains photographs taken from 1875-1947 showing the day to day operations of the company.

MA —SMITH COLLEGE, Hillyer Art Library, Fine Arts Center, Northampton, 01063. Karen Harvey, Librn
Holdings: Vols (45,000) Cat Pix Slides

MA —MERRIMACK VALLEY TEXTILE MUSEUM, Library, 800 Massachusetts Ave, North Andover, 01845. Clare Sheridan, Librn; Laurence Gross, Cur
Holdings: Vols (35,000) Cat Mss Maps Pix Slides
Notes: *Checklist of Prints, Drawings and Painting in the Merrimack Valley Textile Museum*, Helena E Wright, 1972; *Checklist of Finished Textiles*, Katherine R Koob, 1980; *New City on the Merrimack: Prints of Lawrence 1845-1876*, Helena Wright, 1974; *Homespun to Factory Made: Woolen Textiles in America 1776-1876* (exhibit catalog) 1978; *Textile Technology Prints: A Checklist of Prints, Drawings and Paintings*

PICTURES—COLLECTIONS (cont.)

in the Merrimack Valley Textile Museum, Helena E Wright, 1980; *All Sorts of Good Sufficient Cloth: Linen-making in New England, 1640-1860,* (exhibit catalogue) 1980; *The Merrimack Valley Textile Museum: A Guide to the Manuscript* Collections Helena E Wright, Garland Press 1983.

MA —SPRINGFIELD CITY LIBRARY, Art & Music Dept, 220 State St, Springfield, 01103. Karen A Dorval, Supvr & Art Librn; Sylvia A Saint Amand, Music Librn
Holdings: Vols (22,500) Cat Pix Phonorecords Audiotapes Microforms
Budget: ($183,000)
Notes: Art: books (17,500), pamphlets (8000), pictures (120,000); music: books (5000), music scores (10,000), phonorecords (18,000), Audiocassettes (288 titles). Also microfilm (75 reels). Separate catalogs for art, music, and phonorecords and audiocassettes.

MA —SPRINGFIELD CITY LIBRARY, Genealogy and Local History Dept, 220 State St, Springfield, 01103. Joseph Carvalho III, Supervisor
Holdings: Vols (17,000) Cat Mss Maps Pix Microforms VF
Budget: ($8000)
Notes: New England, Massachusetts, local history, and genealogy collections. 18,000 pictures, 3200 microforms, ca 15,000 clippings, pamphlets, etc (280 ft of vertical files).

MA —WELLESLEY COLLEGE, Art Library, Wellesley, 02181. Katherine D Finkelpearl, Art Librn
Holdings: Vols (30,000) Cat Pix Slides
Budget: ($22,000)
Notes: Primarily the art and architecture of Western Europe, the Far East, and classical antiquity. However, efforts are being made to expand the collection in the areas of photography, primitive art, and ancient (non-classical) art. The Art Department maintains a separate collection of 62,500 mounted pictures and 90,000 slides.

MA —AMERICAN ANTIQUARIAN SOCIETY LIBRARY, 185 Salisbury St, Worcester, 01609. Marcus A McCorison, Dir & Librn
Holdings: Cat Mss Maps Pix Slides Microforms
Notes: Over half a million manuscript pieces; extensive collection of contemporary imprints before 1850 (with supplementary supporting studies); over 10,000 maps (weak for 15th-17th centuries; excellent for 18th, strongest in 19th century, especially maps of local nature). Strongest collection of portraits of early New Englanders; paintings, engravings, and miniatures. Further, the largest collection of regional, state, county, and local histories.

MI —EDISON INSTITUTE, Greenfield Village and Henry Ford Museum, Archives & Research Library, PO Box 1970, Dearborn, 48121. Steve Hamp, Dir; Joan W Gartland, Librn
Holdings: Vols (400,000) Cat Mss Maps Microforms
Notes: 400,000 vols incl pamphlets. The Archives and research library supports the program of Greenfield Village and the Henry Ford Museum. Special collections incl: automotive literature, ephemera, McGuffey Readers, trade catalogs, photographs and graphics.

MI —DETROIT PUBLIC LIBRARY, Fine Arts Department, 5201 Woodward Ave, Detroit, 48202. Shirley Solvick, Chief
Holdings: Vols 60,000 Cat Pix
Budget: ($20,000)
Notes: Downs number 2882, 2923, 2938. Book collection covers all phases of art. Picture collection of over 500,000 items covers all subjects; especially strong in the fine and decorative arts, portraits, costume, and Detroit.

MI —DETROIT PUBLIC LIBRARY, Burton Historical Collection, 5201 Woodward Ave, Detroit, 48202. Alice Dalligan, Chief
Notes: Thousands of pictures of Detroit

scenes and people make up the Burton picture files. Many books, magazines, and newspapers have been indexed for illustrations. A large collection of postcards shows how city and state looked to tourists of earlier days.

MI —MICHIGAN TECHNOLOGICAL UNIVERSITY, Archives, Copper County Historical Collections, Houghton, 49931. Theresa Sanderson Spence, University Archivist
Holdings: Vols (1500) Cat Mss Maps Pix Slides Microforms
Notes: Michigan-Copper Country. Description of collection in *Michigan Chronicle,* 1st quarter, 1973. Accession lists are available for some of the collections. The collecting program embraces the university and all areas of the economic, cultural and social life of the people and institutions of the Copper Country (Baraga, Houghton, Keweenaw, and Ontonogan Counties). Special strength is in the mining history and mining company reports. Personal and business records, maps and photographs, broadsides, family histories, newspapers and oral materials as well as slides and film have been collected. Extensive holdings in area newspapers. As a regional depository for the state archives, provides access to a variety of research materials. Also, Keweenaw Historical Society Collection, see *Michigan History Magazine,*vols 1 (1917), 129-155.

MI —SAINT CLAIR COUNTY LIBRARY, 210 McMorran Blvd, Port Huron, 48060. Frances A Marshall, Local History Librn
Holdings: Vols 5116 Cat Mss Maps Pix Microforms
Notes: The

MI —GENERAL MOTORS, Design Staff Library, General Motors Technical Center, Warren, 48090. Billie Delevich, Librn
Holdings: Vols 3500
Notes: Incl 130 magazine titles, 85 drawers of automotive catalogs.

MN —SAINT JOHN'S ABBEY & UNIVERSITY, Hill Monastic Manuscript Library, Collegeville, 56321. Julian G Plante, Dir
Holdings: Vols Cat Mss Slides Microforms
Notes: Wherever miniatures and illuminations appear in a ms these are microfilmed in color. In addition to the usual ms catalogs of the collections, a partial iconographic card catalog is available. Reasonable requests will be honored. Incl 70, 000 exposures.

MN —MINNEAPOLIS COLLEGE OF ART & DESIGN, Library, 200 E 25 St, Minneapolis, 55404. Richard Kronstedt, Head Librn

MN —MINNEAPOLIS PUBLIC LIBRARY & INFORMATION CENTER, Art, Music & Films Dept, 300 Nicollet Mall, Minneapolis, 55401. Mary Alice Walker, Music Specialist
Holdings: Vols (94,200) Cat Pix Slides
Budget: ($111,642)
Notes: Art collection incl 1,196,865 pictures; 46,560 slides; and 10,650 stereographs.

MN —MTS SYSTEMS CORP, Information Services, PO Box 24012, Minneapolis, 55424. Kathleen Werner, Technical Librn
Holdings: Cat Mss Pix Slides Phonorecords Audiotapes Videotapes 16mm Films Microforms
Notes: Material testing machines. Incl 2000 ms reports, 10,000 pictures, 6000 slides.

MN —MAYO MEDICAL LIBRARY, History of Medicine Collection, Rochester, 55905. Nancy R Hensel, Librn
Holdings: Vols (18,000) Cat Mss Maps Pix Slides
Notes: The collection consists of over 18,000 vols, 6500 of which are considered source material (rare or reprint editions of classics). 4308 items from Garrison-Morton are available in the collection. Appropriate bibliographies, biographies and histories of medicine are a part of the collection. Fields of collecting interest are anesthesiology, dermatology, cardiology, neurology, immunology and radiology. Eight medical incunabula.

MN —SAINT PAUL PUBLIC LIBRARY, Arts & Audiovisual Services, 90 W Fourth St, Saint Paul, 55102. Delores Sundbye,

Supervising Librn
Holdings: Cat Pix Slides Phonorecords Audiotapes
Budget: ($20,000)
Notes: The Art and Music Dept incl 10,000 books on art and architecture, 4000 books on music and 10,000 cataloged music scores. Collection of 650 color reproduction, 10,000 mounted pictures and 500 exhibit catalogs. Complete set of first edition of Arundel Prints (color lithographic copies of Renaissance paintings, published by the Arundel Society, 1849-1897).

MO —HALLMARK CARDS, Creative Research Library, 25 & McGee, Kansas City, 64141. Sara E Wallace, Mgr of Library Services
Holdings: Vols (12,000) Cat Mss Pix Slides
Notes: Picture research collection for greeting card artists.

MO —CONCORDIA HISTORICAL INSTITUTE, 801 DeMun Ave, Saint Louis, 63105. Aug R Suelflow, Dir
Holdings: Vols (58,000) Mss Maps Pix Slides Films Microforms
Budget: ($100,000)
Notes: A centralized collection of all information media pertaining to the history and theology of Lutheranism in North America; also German-Americana; indexes and finding aids are available; extensive microfilm collection of mss, books, periodicals, church records; the ms collection exceeds 2,500,000 pages.

MO —MISSOURI HISTORICAL SOCIETY, Library, Jefferson Memorial Bldg, Saint Louis, 63112. Stephanie Klein, Librn-Archivist; Peter Michel, Cur of Manuscripts
Holdings: Cat Mss Maps Pix
Notes: Extensive ms holdings relating to Missouri, US history, etc. Also ms collections of many noted persons (all but subsequent additions listed in Hamer, 1961). Library holdings described in Whitehall, Walter Muir, *Independent Historical* Societies (Boston, 1962).

MO —SPRINGFIELD ART MUSEUM, Reference Library, 1111 E Brookside Dr, Springfield, 65807. Greg G Thielen, Cur of Collections
Holdings: Vols 3000 Cat Pix Slides Art Reproductions
Notes: Art history and related fields. Growing emphasis on contemporary arts. Incl 1000 slides.

NE —NEBRASKA STATE HISTORICAL SOCIETY, Museum, Fort Robinson, Box 304, Crawford, 69339. Vance Nelson, Cur
Holdings: Vols (1500) Cat Mss Maps Pix Slides Phonorecords Audiotapes 16mm Films Microforms
Notes: Materials related to the history of Fort Robinson, and incl the Post Medical Library, reference books on state government, etc, Western Americana: books on ranching, homesteaders, Indian wars, etc; microfilm records for Fort Robinson records, Red Cloud and Spotted Tail Indian Agency records, Crawford and Chadron, Nebraska newspapers, diaries and interviews. Library incl the E Kopac Collection of books dealing with Western Americana; particularly Indian wars, transportation, guns and railroads.

NE —NEBRASKA STATE HISTORICAL SOCIETY, Library, 1500 R St, Box 82554, Lincoln, 68501. M Ann Reinert, Library Dept Head
Holdings: Vols (100,000) Cat Maps Pix Microforms
Budget: ($200,000)
Notes: Approx 120,000 photographs of Nebraska and Nebraskans.
See also entry under Great Plains

NV —NORTHEASTERN NEVADA MUSEUM, Library, 1515 Idaho St, PO Box 2550, Elko, 89801. Howard Hickson, Museum Dir
Holdings: Vols 2000 Cat Mss Maps Pix Slides Audiotapes
Budget: $8000
Notes: Emphasis on northeastern Nevada and Elko County. Incl 140 mss, 65 maps, 1500 pictures, 2000 slides, and 35 audiotapes.

NV —NEVADA STATE HISTORICAL SOCIETY, Library, 1650 N Virginia St,

PICTURES—COLLECTIONS (cont.)

Reno, 89503. Eric N Moody, Cur of Manuscripts; Lee Mortensen, Librn
Holdings: Vols 15,000 Cat Mss Maps Pix Slides Microforms
Budget: ($156,994)
Notes: Incl 2800 mss, 1500 maps and 70,000 pictures.

NV —UNIVERSITY OF NEVADA, RENO, Desert Research Institute, PO Box 60220, Reno, 89557. Roberta Kiefer Orcutt, Librn
Holdings: Vols (10,480) Cat Maps Microforms
Notes: Incl materials in atmospheric physics, meteorology, climatology, weather modification, antarctic studies and related materials in basic sciences. Over 3000 microforms; also 1300 technical reports and 18,000 government publications.

NH —NEW HAMPSHIRE HISTORICAL SOCIETY, Library, 30 Park St, Concord, 03301. William Copeley, Assoc Librn
Holdings: Uncat Pix
Budget: ($9000)
Notes: 20,000 pictures incl views of New Hampshire towns, New Hampshire buildings and photographs of New Hampshire notables. Incl stereoscopic views and postcards.

NJ —ELIZABETH PUBLIC LIBRARY, Art & Music Dept, 11 S Broad St, Elizabeth, 07202. Roman Sawycky, Head
Holdings: Vols (20,000) Cat Pix Phonorecords 16mm Films Filmstrips
Budget: ($10,000)
Notes: Incl 200,000 pictures, 12,000 phonorecords and 700 films and filmstrips.

NJ —ENGLEWOOD LIBRARY, 31 Engle St, Englewood, 07631. N E Rhoades, Reference Librn
Holdings: Vols (1750) Cat

NJ —FAIRLEIGH DICKINSON UNIVERSITY, Friendship Library, 285 Madison Ave, Madison, 07940. James Fraser, Library Dir; Renee Weber, Cur
Holdings: Vols 1200 Cat Mss Pix Slides Phonorecords 16mm Films
Notes: Official depository for the Outdoor Advertising industry. Collection initiated in August 1972. About 100,000 items. It is the concern of the Outdoor Advertising Association of America that this collection become the definitive collection on the industry in this country. Incl 20,000 mss, 10,000 pictures, 30,000 slides. 15 original billboards.

NJ —UNITED METHODIST CHURCH, Commission on Archives and History, 36 Madison Ave, PO Box 127, Madison, 07940. Charles Yrigoyen, Jr, General Secy
Holdings: Vols 40,000 Cat Mss Maps Pix Slides Microforms
Budget: $110,000
Notes: The United Methodist Church Collection includes these churches and dates: The United Evangelical Church, 1891-1922; The Evangelical Association, 1800-1922; The Evangelical Church, 1922-1946; The United Brethren in Christ, 1800-1946; The Evangelical United Brethren Church, 1946-1968; The Methodist Episcopal Church, 1773-1939; The Methodist Episcopal Church, South, 1844-1939; The Methodist Church, 1939-1968; The United Methodist Church, 1968-date. There is no published catalog. The Depository is a specialized collection pertaining to manuscript and published material dealing with the United Methodist Church and its antecedent bodies. It is the official church depository for preservation of records-over 2 million items.

NJ —MONTCLAIR ART MUSEUM LIBRARY, 3 South Mountain Ave, PO Box 1582, Montclair, 07042. Edith A Rights, Librn
Holdings: Vols (10,000) Cat Pix Slides Audiotapes
Budget: ($3500)
Notes: American painting and sculpture. Incl 5000 pictures; 10,000 slides; posters. Audiotapes on American art and artists.

NJ —NEWARK PUBLIC LIBRARY, Art & Music Dept, 5 Washington St, Newark, 07101. William J Dane, Supv
Holdings: Mss Maps Pix Slides
Notes: 1,000,000 pictures with supporting

collections of postcards, 2000 portfolios of plates of design, fine and circulating print collections (incl Japanese), 1400 illustrated books, 4000 posters. The classification scheme and headings used are listed in *The Picture Collection Subject Headings* (Shoe String Press, 1968).

NJ —NEW JERSEY HISTORICAL SOCIETY, Library and Museum, 230 Broadway, Newark, 07104. Joan C Hull, Exec Dir; Barbara S Irwin, Library Dir; Alan R Fraser, Cur
Budget: ($100,000)
Notes: Incl 75,000 photographs.

NJ —RUTGERS, THE STATE UNIVERSITY OF NEW JERSEY, Alexander Library, Special Collections and Archives, College Ave & Huntington St, New Brunswick, 08903. Ronald L Becker, Cur of Manuscripts and Rare Books
Holdings: Pix
Notes: The pictorial collection of Special Collections, dating from the 18th century to the present, incl foreign, US and New Jersey material: portraits, local views, historical scenes. Special groups: George Washington and Benjamin Franklin engraved portraits; photos of New Jersey Dutch houses and New Jersey localities (among these about 10,000 postal cards).

NJ —PRINCETON UNIVERSITY, Library, Manuscript Collection, Nassau St, Princeton, 08540. Jean F Preston, Cur
Holdings: Mss Pix
Notes: The papers of the late Edwin W Kemmerer. Incl are papers spanning nearly a half-century dating from student days in 1897--letters, diaries, drafts of articles, speech texts, financial records, offprints, clippings, academic notes, photographs, and personal copies of numerous reports. Also incl are scrapbooks, diplomas, maps and charts, books from his own library, and a wealth of memoranda and mementos. Incl 147 letter boxes; 240 boxes; 4 cartons; appprox 125 vols. Limited photocopying.

NM —MUSEUM OF NEW MEXICO, Photo Archives, Box 2087, Santa Fe, 87503. Arthur L Olivas, Cur; Richard Rudisill, Photo Historian
Holdings: Cat Pix Slides
Budget: ($9000)

Notes: 90,000 photographs, cataloged, and 1000 slides. Photographs may be ordered as research copies for set fees. Reproduction or publication requires written permission plus additional required fees. Incl. special groups of photographs, e.g. T. Harmon Parkhurst Collection-ca. 15,000 photos, 1915-1950, Southwest Indians, scenic views, town views; H. F. Robinson Collection-ca. 1000 items, ca. 1910-1920, Southwest Indians, esp. Hopi and Blackfoot; Ben Wittick Collection-ca. 1500 items, 1879-1903, Southwest Indians, military, town views. Many other of the important early photographers are represented, especially large collections of the work of G. C. Bennett, William H. Brown, Dana B. Chase, Edward S. Curtis, H. H. Dorman, Rev. J. C. Gullette, P. E. Harroun, William H. Jackson, Charles F. Lummis, Jesse L. Nussbaum, Henry A. Schmidt, and about a hundred others.

NY —NEW YORK STATE LIBRARY, General Reference Library, Albany, 12224. Christian Beauregard, Librn
Holdings: Pix
Notes: Incl clippings, prints, postcards, photographs, reproductions, some mounted or laminated or both 100,000 items.

NY —ALBRIGHT-KNOX ART GALLERY, Art Reference Library, 1285 Elmwood Ave, Buffalo, 14222. Annette Masling, Librn
Holdings: Vols (20,000) Cat
Notes: Special strength in American 19th

and 20th century art. Excellent collection of exhibition catalogs for contemporary art.

NY —BUFFALO MUSEUM OF SCIENCE, Buffalo Society of Natural Sciences, Research Library, Humboldt Park, Buffalo, 14211. Marcia T Morrison, Chief Librn
Holdings: Vols 37,000 Cat Mss Pix
Notes: Natural sciences, anthropology, archaeology.

NY —NEW YORK STATE HISTORICAL ASSOCIATION, Library, Lake Rd, Cooperstown, 13326. Amy Barnum, Librn
Holdings: Vols (55,000) Cat Mss Maps Pix Slides Audiotapes
Notes: Emphasis on Otsego County area. Incl Smith-Telfer Collection of 60,000 glass plate negatives, Otsego County, ca 1850-1950; also, picture collection (14 file drawers); also, postal cards Noncirculating.

NY —CORNING MUSEUM OF GLASS LIBRARY, Corning, 14831. Norma P H Jenkins, Librn
Holdings: Vols (30,000) Cat Slides Videotapes Microforms
Notes: Extensive and comprehensive coverage of the art, archaeology, history and early manufacture of glass, with supporting materials in art, archaeology, and the decorative arts. Collection incl some 1800 manufacturers' trade catalogs on microfiche, 10,000 periodical vols and documents. 130 videotapes, 1000 microforms. Some incumabula. Research library primarily for use on the premises.

NY —MUSICAL MUSEUM AND LIBRARY, Deansboro, 13328. Arthur H Sanders, Cur
Holdings: Vols 1000 Uncat Pix Slides
Notes: Antique musical instruments and music boxes.

NY —EASTCHESTER HISTORICAL SOCIETY LIBRARY, Box 37, Eastchester, 10709. Madeline D Schaeffer, Librn
Holdings: Vols (6000) Cat Mss Maps Pix Slides
Notes: New York State history with emphasis on Westchester County and local area. Also children's literature, 1750-1910, and juvenile textbooks, 1790-1910. No photocopying.

NY —NASSAU COUNTY MUSEUM, Reference Library, Eisenhower Park, East Meadow, 11554. Richard Winsche, Historian; Monica Albala, Museum Cur
Holdings: Vols 5000 Cat Mss Maps Pix Slides Phonorecords Audiotapes Micorforms
Notes: Incl 10,000 mss; 300 maps; 10,000 pictures; 500 slides; 10 records; 20 audiotapes; and 3000 microforms. Mss, slides, and half of pictures are uncataloged. Cooperstown, NY.

NY —STATE UNIVERSITY OF NEW YORK, COLLEGE OF ARTS & SCIENCE AT GENESEO, Milne Library, Geneseo, 14454. William T Lane, Head of Information Services & Archivist
Holdings: // Cat Mss Pix Slides
Notes: The Carl Schmidt Collection on Local Architecture. Mss for Schmidt's books and folios on cobblestone architecture, Octagon House, Victorian architecture, colonial and post-colonial architecture, mouldings, etc. Notebooks; 2000 measured drawings of architecture and architectural detail in the Rochester, New York, area; 10,000 slides. 60 ms storage boxes; 12 drawers of drawings.

NY —HALL OF FAME OF THE TROTTER, Library, 240 Main St, Goshen, 10924. Philip Pines, Dir
Holdings: Vols 2000 Cat Mss Pix Slides
Notes: Harness horses (trotters and pacers). Incl history of harness racing. Assembling videotape collection of famous races, interviews with prominent horsemen, film-to-tape. Not yet cataloged.

NY —QUEENS BOROUGH PUBLIC LIBRARY, Art & Music Div, 89-11 Merrick Blvd, Jamaica, 11432. Dorothea Wu, Head
Holdings: Vols (85,000) Cat Maps Pix Phonorecords Audiotapes Microforms
Budget: ($44,000)
Notes: The Picture Collection, covering all subjects, consists of approximately 1,500,000 pictures, mainly reproductions and clippings from books and magazines, photographs, and postcards on all subjects; The Framed

PICTURES—COLLECTIONS (cont.)

Picture Collection, approx 180 framed pictures, mostly reproductions of paintings from various periods; and The Phonorecord and Cassette Collection consists of approx 3500 reference phonorecords and 6500 circulating records as well as 1000 reference cassettes and 1500 circulating cassettes.

NY —QUEENS BOROUGH PUBLIC LIBRARY, Long Island Div, 89-11 Merrick Blvd, Jamaica, 11432. Nicholas Falco, Head
Holdings: Vols (22,000) Cat Mss Maps Pix Microforms
Budget: ($13,000)
Notes: Files of Long Island community newspapers, with strong holdings for Queens Borough. Also, 550 glass negatives of Long Island scenes, 1895-1915; with 32,750 other pictures; 5300 maps; 36,000 ms pieces. Extensive name indexes of births, deaths and marriages mainly from 19th century Long Island books and newspapers. Many cemetery records, etc. 60 VF drawers of clippings; over 500 broadsides, 1795-date, relating to Long Island, with chronological and community name indexes; books published by Marion Press, a private press in Jamaica, NY.

NY —NEWSDAY, INC, Library, 235 Pine Lawn Rd, Melville, 11747. Andrew Ippolito, Dir of Library & Research
Holdings: Vols 2000 Cat Pix Microforms
Notes: Over two million news clippings and pictures of Newsday and other newspapers and magazines since 1940.

NY —NEW ROCHELLE PUBLIC LIBRARY, Fine Arts Dept, Library Plaza, New Rochelle, 10801. Eugene L Mittelgluck, Library Dir
Holdings: Vols (13,000) Cat Pix Slides
Budget: ($10,000)
Notes: Incl (430,000) pictures and (6300) slides.
See also entries under Art; Ballet and the Dance; Costume; Music.

NY —AMERICAN CRAFT COUNCIL, Library and Artists Registry, 44 W 53 St, New York, 10019. Joanne Polster, Librn
Holdings: Vols 3300 Cat Pix Slides Films
Notes: Crafts and craft-related subjects, incl portfolios for approx 2000 contemporary American craftspeople consisting of biographical material and photographs, indexed by media, geographic location, and a visual index. Over 1500 exhibition catalogs. The collection incl 35mm slide kits available for purchase. Catagories covered are: exhibitions of ACC's American Craft Museum from 1958 to date; kits in all media: fiber, metal, wood, clay, glass and multimedia; kits covering crafts processes. The Library also holds catalogs of craft school and art centers offering craft courses; newsletters, by-laws, and other materials of craft organizations and groups; the Archives and Photo-Archives of the American Craft Museum. No photocopying.

NY —ELECTRIC RAILROADERS ASSOCIATION, Frank J Sprague Memorial Library, 89 E 42nd St, New York, 10018. Hugh A Dunne, First VP
Notes: Private library. Incl all forms of railroads operated by electricity. Forms of electric railroads included: street railways, subways & elevated lines, high-speed interurbans, suburban commuter lines, electrified trunk lines, monorails, mountain climbing inclines, etc. Also railroad timetables.

NY —FRICK ART REFERENCE LIBRARY, 10 E 71 St, New York, 10021. Helen Sanger, Librn
Holdings: Vols (154,384) Cat Pix Per
Notes: History of painting, drawing, sculpture and illuminated mss of US and western Europe from 4th century AD to about 1860. 54,862 art auction catalogs; 420,507 study photographs.

NY —HAMPDEN-BOOTH THEATRE LIBRARY AT THE PLAYERS, 16 Gramercy Park, New York, 10003. Louis A Rachow, Librn/Cur
Holdings: Vols 12,000 Cat Mss Pix Slides Phonorecords
Notes: A strong collection on theatre

history, with special emphasis on 19th and 20th century English and American stage. Large collection of English playbills of the 18th and 19th centuries; important collection of prompt books (mainly 19th century); Edwin Booth, incl memorabilia rare books, association items, his 2nd, 3rd, and 4th Shakespeare Folios, etc. Large collection of English and American biographies and pictures of actors and actresses; the Chuck Callahan Burlesque Collection (qv Burlesque); and other specialties described elsewhere in this volume. The library is chartered by the Regents of the State of New York and is open to all qualified researchers upon application. Described in Theatre & Performing Arts Collections (New York: Haworth Press, 1981).

NY —HISPANIC SOCIETY OF AMERICA, Library, 613 W 155 St, New York, 10032. Martha M de Narvaez, Cur of Mss; Irene S Frye, Asst Librn
Holdings: Vols (150,000) Cat Mss Maps Pix Slides Phonorecords Microforms
Notes: History, art, literature and general culture of the Hispanic countries (where Spanish or Portuguese is spoken). Incl (18,000) vols printed before 1701, incl (250) incunabula; over (100,000) later vols, plus thousands of periodicals. About (200,000) mss incl ms maps. Printed atlases are in the Book Collection. Some microfilms, chiefly of our early books. Engraved and printed separate maps; reference collection of over 100,000 photographs; slides: all in Department of Iconography, not in library. Catalogs: Catalogue of the Hispanic Society of America (Boston: G K Hall, 1962), 10 vols; First Supplement (Boston, 1970), 4 vols. Early books: Printed Books 1468-1700; Mss: Catalogo de los Manuscritos Poeticos Castellanos (15th-17th centuries; 3 vols); Medieval Manuscripts in the Library; Golden Age Drama Manuscripts (the latter in press).

NY —LEO BAECK INSTITUTE, Library, 129 E 73 St, New York, 10021. Fred Grubel, Secretary & Dir
Holdings: Vols 6000 Cat Pix Microforms
Notes: History and philosophy of European German-speaking Jewry, 18th to 20th century. Publications: LBI Archives and Library News, free, 2 issues a year. Provides an update of collections. Also, LBI News incl more general info for members only. $35.00 per year dues.

†NY —METROPOLITAN MUSEUM OF ART, Photograph & Slide Library, 82 St & Fifth Ave, New York, 10028. Margaret P Nolan, Chief Librn
Holdings: Cat Pix
Notes: 252,000 black and white photographs; 6000 color prints. A reference collection of photographs covering the history of architecture, sculpture, painting and the decorative arts from prehistoric times to the 20th century; photographic records of the Metropolitian Museum collections available for study and for use in ordering photographic prints.

NY —METROPOLITAN MUSEUM OF ART, Robert Goldwater Library, Fifth Ave at 82nd St, New York, 10028. Allan D Chapman, Librn
Holdings: Vols (27,000) Cat Pix
Notes: Primitive art: African, Indians of the Americans (incl Pre-Columbian), Oceanic, Polynesian, etc. 150,000 photographs.

NY —NEW YORK HISTORICAL SOCIETY, Library, 170 Central Park W, New York, 10024. James Gregory, Librn
Holdings: Mss
Notes: Incl original mss, illustrative materials, etc.

NY —NEW YORK PUBLIC LIBRARY, Performing Arts Research Center, Billy Rose Theatre Collection, 111 Amsterdam Ave, New York, 10023. Dorothy L Swerdlove, Cur
Holdings: Cat
See also entry under Theatre-History.

NY —NEW YORK PUBLIC LIBRARY, Research Libraries, General Research Division, Fifth Ave & 42 St, New York, 10018. Rodney Phillips, Chief
Holdings: Vols (2,225,000) Cat Maps Pix

Microforms
Budget: ($775,718)
Notes: Fields of strength have been listed specifically throughout this vol. Much material for most subjects is supplemented by microfilm and picture resources.

NY —NEW YORK PUBLIC LIBRARY, Art, Prints, and Photographs Div, Fifth Ave & 42 St, New York, 10018. Donald Anderle, Chief
Holdings: Uncat Pix
Notes: The collection is made up primarily of 2,500,000 clippings from books and magazines arranged by subject. To facilitate problems of copyright the collection has a source catalog for the pictures in addition to special subject indexes. Subject coverage is comprehensive.

NY —NEW YORK PUBLIC LIBRARY, Local History and Genealogy Div, Fifth Ave & 42 St, New York, 10018. Gunther E Pohl, Chief
Holdings: Vols (160,000) Cat Pix
Budget: ($38,548)
Notes: Extensive collection of county, city, town and village histories of the United States. All other local, state, and national histories are part of the General Research and Humanities Division. Collection includes over 60,000 mounted photographs of New York City views arranged by address and/or subject. 20,000 film and glass plate negatives depicting NYC tenement housing conditions (1902-1938). Also the Lloyd L Acker collection of 48,000 film negatives depicting NYC buildings, 1935-1975. Collection of Lewis W Hine photographic prints made by the photographer on immigration, child labor, women at work and men at work. Eugene Armbruster Collection of Long Island views; D B Austin's photographs of Long Island and western Americana; scrapbooks, and postcards of NYC and other US localities (200,000). See United States Local History Catalog (Boston: GK Hall, 1974), 2 vols.

NY —NEW YORK PUBLIC LIBRARY, Music Div, 111 Amsterdam Ave, New York, 10023. Frank C Campbell, Chief
Holdings: Vols (300,000) Cat Mss Pix Microforms
Notes: Described in Dictionary Catalog of the Music Collection, The Research Libraries of the New York Public Library, 33 vols (532,000 cards), 1964, $2190; Supplement 1, 1 vol (17,000 cards), 1966, $100. Also, Bibliographic Guide to Music, 2 vols, 1975-1976, $70 ea. Literature pertaining to virtually all musical subjects, and scores covering the broadest range of musical style and history are represented in this catalog. Special strengths of the collection incl folk songs, 18th and 19th-century librettos, full scores of operas, complete works, historical editions, Beethoven, Americana, American music, periodicals, vocal music, literature on the voice, programs, record catalogs, and mss in detail; sheet music, 355,414; sound recordings, 400,000; clippings and programs, 2 million; broadsides, 1821; songsters, 375; pictures, 51,002; ms, 29,877.

NY —US COMMITTEE FOR UNICEF, Information Center on Children's Cultures, 331 E 38 St, New York, 10016. Melinda Greenblatt, Chief Librn
Holdings: Vols (17,500) Cat Pix Slides Films Filmstrips
Notes: Social and cultural aspects of lives of children from developing countries. Especially strong in the area of school textbooks from Near Eastern Asian, African, Latin American, Caribbean, and Pacific Area countries; holidays and celebrations related to children all over the world; children's books in English which describe child life in other countries. Especially strong collection of folklore, and folklore of children, from all regions mentioned above.

NY —WHITNEY MUSEUM OF AMERICAN ART, Library, 945 Madison Ave, New York, 10021. May Castleberry, Librn
Holdings: 20,000 Uncat Pix
Notes: Vertical files on individual American artists; incl clippings, catalogs, exhibitions, letters, pictures, etc. Also, 1050 bound periodical titles.

PICTURES—COLLECTIONS (cont.)

NY —YIVO INSTITUTE FOR JEWISH
RESEARCH, Library & Archives, 1048
Fifth Ave, New York, 10028. Dina
Abramowicz, Librn; Marek Web, Archivist
Holdings: Cat Mss Pix Slides
Notes: Special collection of books and
periodicals, incl government publications,
which appeared in Germany between the
years 1933-1945. Extensive library and
archives collections on history of Jews under
Nazi rule in Europe, 1933-1945, in all
languages. Hundreds of memorial volumes
for towns destroyed by Nazis.

NY —SHAKER MUSEUM, Emma B King
Library, Shaker Museum Rd, Old Chatham,
12136. Viki Sand, Dir; Ann Kelly, Archivist
Holdings: Vols 2500 Cat Mss Maps Pix
Slides Phonorecords Audiotapes 16mm
Films Filmstrips Microforms
Budget: ($11,200)
Notes: Incl also about 750 mss of Shaker
interest; 150 maps or drawings; and 1800
deeds, letters, and indentures. Also about
5000 pictures.

NY —FORT ONTARIO HISTORIC SITE,
Oswego, 13126. Shelley B Weinreb, Historic
Site Mgr
Holdings: Vols (400) Cat Mss Maps Pix
Slides
Notes: Primary focus is upon military
activities at the mouth of the Oswego River
and the utilization of fortifications (Fort
Ontario, Fort Oswego, and Fort George) at
the point which served to control the outlet
of the traditional Mohawk-Onedia-Oswego
route to the Great Lakes. A limited number
of sources on fortification design, weapons,
uniforms, and military equipment are
included. Also incl 4000 slides and 400
pictures.

NY —STATE UNIVERSITY OF NEW
YORK, COLLEGE AT PURCHASE,
Library, Lincoln Ave, Purchase, 10577.
Robert W Evans, Dir
Holdings: Vols (1400) Mss Pix Slides
Notes: The Gerald D McDonald Collection.
Over 1400 books on moving pictures and all
aspects of the industry: production,
directing, acting. Thousands of pictures of
actors and actresses, directors, etc. Also
about 2000 slides picturing movie
personalities, etc; stereoptican pictures,
buttons, bottle caps, playing cards, etc. Also,
the George Rickey collection of
constructivist art works has been given to the
Neuberger Museum at the College at
Purchase. The collection consist largely of
over 1000 announcements and catalogs of
exhibitions of constructivist works and
material about the artists.

NY —INTERNATIONAL MUSEUM OF
PHOTOGRAPHY AT GEORGE
EASTMAN HOUSE, Archives, 900 East
Ave, Rochester, 14607. Rachel Stuhlman,
Head Librn
Holdings: Vols (30,000) Cat Mss Microforms
Budget: ($104,000)
Notes: History, aesthetics and technology of
photography and cinematography, incl the
Gabriel Cromer, Josef Maria Eder, Alden
Scott Boyer, Louis Walton Sipley/3M
Collections, and the James Card Collection
from 1893. Covers photographic, especially
cinematographic history; also hundreds of
negatives of Edward Muybridge as well as
his notebooks. Incl 450,000 pictures and
slides. Also the Lewis Hine Collection of
social documentary photography.

NY —LANDMARK SOCIETY OF
WESTERN NEW YORK, Wenrich
Memorial Library, 130 Spring Rd,
Rochester, 14608.
Holdings: Vols (2000) Cat Maps Pix Slides
Budget: ($500)
Notes: Paintings, slides, drawings, as well as
the Society's archives of local architecture
and information on preservation and
restoration techniques. Much on
preservations ordinances; legal, physical and
financial aspects of building preservation;
local and regional history, especially of
Rochester and Monroe County.

NY —VISUAL STUDIES WORKSHOP,
Research Center, 31 Prince St, Rochester,

14607. Linn Underhill, Coordr; Robert
Bretz, Librn
Holdings: Vols (8000) Cat Pix Slides
Audiotapes Videotapes
Notes: Strong emphasis on photography
(over 1,000,000 pictures) and the
photographic arts in many subject areas incl
in this volume. Heavy emphasis on early
photographic processes and collections of
examples of them. Also collections of
individual photographers's works.

NY —SKIDMORE COLLEGE, Lucy Scribner
Library, Saratoga Springs, 12866. Jane
Graves, Fine Arts Librn
Holdings: Vols 7500 Cat Pix Slides
Notes: Also 40,000 art slides.

NY —CANAL MUSEUM, Research Library,
318 Eric Blvd E, Syracuse, 13202. Todd S
Weseloh, Librn & Archivist
Holdings: Vols 7000 Mss Maps Pix Slides
Notes: Covers US canals, English canals,
Panama Canal, Canadian canals, and
Syracuse, NY. Emphasis on New York State
canals: Erie Canal and lateral canals.
Complete photo coverage of construction of
Western Division of New York State Barge
Canal (1904-1925). Mss collection (7000)
contains printed maps, plans, and views
mostly of engineering nature. Incl ca 46,000
images: 8000 original photos, 6000 copy
photos and newspaper clipping photos. Also
incl 2500 postcards, 800 prints, 641 pen and
ink drawings; 8000 35mm transparencies;
7000 glass plate negatives; 700 4x5 copy
negatives. Mss 954 linear feet.

NC —APPALACHIAN STATE
UNIVERSITY, Belk Library, Appalachian
Collection, Boone, 28608. Eric J Olson,
Librn
Holdings: Vols (12,000) Cat Mss Maps Pix
Slides Phonorecords Audiotapes
Budget: ($4000)
Notes: The Appalachian Collection incl the
Fry Collectin of handmade quilts and
coverlets; the York Collection of folk songs
and ballads, plus tapes; the I G Greer
Collection of Folk Songs and Ballads; the
Amos Abrams ballad collection; artifacts,
incl the Tatum Collection of household
items, furniture, and farm implements;
Daniel Boone loom; oral history tapes; the
Jack Guy Collection of tapes of area music
and photographs; and regional genealogy.
This is a very comprehensive study on the
Southern Appalachian Region. Separate
catalog for the collection.

NC —DUKE UNIVERSITY, William R
Perkins Library, Manuscript Dept, Durham,
27706. Ellen Gartrell, Cur of Mss
Holdings: Pix
Notes: Incl 15,000 items (prints, photos,
drawings, posters, etc.) 19th-20th centuries;
geography and history, especially US South;
military scenes (especially Civil War);
people; Socialist Party of America; early
western landscape photos (O'Sullivan,
Jackson, Hillers, Bell); advertisements and
postcards.

NC —MARS HILL COLLEGE, Memorial
Library, Appalachian Room, Mars Hill,
28754. Richard Dillingham, Dir, Special
Collections
Holdings: Vols (9600) Cat Mss Maps Pix
Slides Phonorecords Audiotapes Microforms
Budget: ($4000)
Notes: Collection strong on local history,
folklore, fiction. Incl Bascom Lamar
Lunsford papers, books, sound recordings.
Separate catalog.

ND —THEODORE ROOSEVELT
NATIONAL PARK, Library, PO Box 7,
Medora, 58645. Susan Snow, Librn; Miki
Hellickson, Chief Naturalist
Holdings: Vols (1500) Cat Mss Maps Pix
Slides Audiotapes 16mm Films
Notes: Theodore Roosevelt, cattle country
history, natural history. Also 2400 pictures
and 2200 slides.

OH —AKRON-SUMMIT COUNTY PUBLIC
LIBRARY, Science & Technology Div, 55 S
Main St, Akron, 44326. Joyce McKnight,
Head
Holdings: Vols 820 Cat Pix
Notes: The Lighter-Than-Air Society book
collection is in the Akron Public Library.
Incl foreign language books.

OH —AKRON-SUMMIT COUNTY PUBLIC
LIBRARY, 55 S Main St, Akron, 44326.
Steven Hawk, Dir
Holdings: Cat Pix Phonorecords
Budget: ($9600)
Notes: General music and fine arts
collection, incl 16,515 phonorecords, 2951
music scores, 3000 pieces of sheet music and
55,472 pictures.

OH —CINCINNATI ART MUSEUM, Library,
Eden Park, Cincinnati, 45202. Patrician P
Rutledge, Librn
Holdings: Vols (45,850) Cat Microforms
Notes: Art library containing all subjects on
art-history, graphic arts, advertising art, etc;
special strength in prints, ie engravings, etc.
Near Eastern art and decorative arts are also
strong. At least 90,000 art exhibition
catalogs. Emphasis on artists of Cincinnati
and vicinity in vertical file material.

OH —PUBLIC LIBRARY OF CINCINNATI
& HAMILTON COUNTY, Dept of Rare
Books & Special Collections, 800 Vine St,
Library Square, Cincinnati, 45202. Yeatman
Anderson III, Cur
Holdings: Cat Mss Maps Pix Slides
Microforms
Notes: Inland River Collection. Incl
logbooks, account books, personal
correspondence, diaries, etc. Also, a picture
collection on 14,000 items (steamboats,
towboats, river views, crews, construction,
barges, etc).

OH —PUBLIC LIBRARY OF CINCINNATI
& HAMILTON COUNTY, Art & Music
Dept, 800 Vine St, Cincinnati, 45202. R
Jayne Craven, Head
Holdings: Vols (122,185)
Budget: ($56,100)
Notes: Special collections: Eda Kuhn Loeb,
"Artist and the Book, 1875-Date" (now
shelved in Rare Book Room); music librettos
(2345); exhibition catalogs (5474); large
prints and posters (5051); Cincinnati artists
vertical files; picture collection (673,906
clippings).

OH —CLEVELAND MUSEUM OF ART,
Library, 11150 E Blvd, Cleveland, 44106.
Jack Perry Brown, Librn
Holdings: Vols (120,000) Cat Pix Slides
Microforms
Notes: 1500 serial titles incl museum
bulletins. Also 200,000 slides; 250,000
photographs. Special photograph collections:
Decimal Index Art of Low Countries
(DIAL); Gernsheim Corpus Photographicum
of drawings; Archive of Biblioteca Berenson;
National Palace Collection, Victoria and
Albert Museum. Index of Ohio artists.

OH —CLEVELAND PUBLIC LIBRARY,
Literature Dept, 325 Superior Ave,
Cleveland, 44114. Evelyn Ward, Head
Holdings: Cat Mss Pix
Notes: Large collection of stills and
photographs from cinema and television.
Personal library and other collections of W
Ward Marsh, former film critic of the
Cleveland *Plain Dealer*. The major categories
of the bequest are: production stills which
begin with the films of the Thirties and
concentrate on those of the Forties and
Fifties; an actor/actress file of folders for
individual personalities containing studio and
agent biographies, clippings and publicity
photos; "pressbooks" (kits of advertising
materials used for promoting a specific
movie); a review file numbering over 20,000
critiques clipped from *Boxoffice, Variety,*
and miscellaneous trade journals, incl
Marsh's own reviews; and his
correspondence. Also incl are a specially
bound copy of shooting script (accompanied
by color transparencies) for Cecil B
deMille's remake of *The Ten
Commandments;* and acollection of more
than 700 46g x 56g glass slides (dating from
the silent era) which were used by theatre
owners to promote their upcoming
attractions.

OH —CLEVELAND PUBLIC LIBRARY, 325
Superior Ave, Cleveland, 44114.
Holdings: Cat Maps Pix
Notes: Library collection in the subject
departments incl: state and local history; city
directories; business and industry; canals and
waterworks; technology; local authors and

PICTURES—COLLECTIONS (cont.)

artists; tourist and travel information (only advisory), vital statistics. Early Ohio pictures and historic maps. See also Western Reserve, Cleveland Public Library.

OH —OHIO HISTORICAL SOCIETY, Archives Library Division, 1982 Velma Ave, Columbus, 43211. Dennis East, Division Chief
Holdings: Vols (96,000) Cat Mss Maps Pix Slides Microforms
Budget: ($18,000)
Notes: This library is the primary collection for Ohio. Most purchases are on the rare and out of print market. Collection area is early American history, esp relating to exploration into the Northwest Territory. Also, Ohio archaeology, natural history, and artifacts. Major media collections are books (96,000), newspapers (25,000 vols and 22,000 microfilm), pictures (50,000), maps (2500), manuscripts (1,500,000). Library is noncirculating except through interlibrary loan of microfilm.

OH —OHIO STATE UNIVERSITY, Fine Arts Library, 1813 N High St, Columbus, 43210. Susan Wyngaard, Head, Fine Arts Library
Holdings: Vols (75,000) Cat Microforms
Budget: ($60,000)
Notes: Also have 1000 uncataloged exhibition catalogs. Book collection strong in history of art especially in area of medieval & Northern Renaissance art. Good collection of portfolios. Photographic collections on microfiche. Receive Slavic titles, many on Byzantine frescoes. Online catalog. Decimal Index of the Art of the Low Countries, as well as Marburger Index; Index Photographique de i' Arten France; Alinari Archives on microfiche and other major microform collections in art.

OH —OHIO STATE UNIVERSITY, Library for Communication and Graphic Arts, 242 W 18th St, Columbus, 43210. Lucy S Caswell, Curator
Notes: Original comic art of Caniff, Foster, Dunn, Dudley T Fisher. Extensive original cartoon art. Shel Dorf Collection of comic strips and related material. A small but growing collection of comic books especially those featuring *Katy Keene,* is available in the Library. Movie posters and stills, 110,000. Incl Milton Caniff Research Room.

OH —DAYTON ART INSTITUTE LIBRARY, 405 W Riverview Ave, PO Box 941, Dayton, 45401. Helen L Pinkney, Librn and Assoc Cur
Holdings: Vols (23,220) Cat Mss Pix Slides Microforms VF
Budget: ($7000)
Notes: Incl museum catalogs and bulletins and collection of slides of stained glass.

OH —UNIVERSITY OF DAYTON, Marian Library, 300 College Park Ave, Dayton, 45469. Rev Theodore Koehler, SM, Dir/Cur
Holdings: Cat Pix
Notes: Part of largest and most comprehensive collection in the world of literature on the Virgin Mary. Incl Vloberg collection of pictures, ms notes and offprints on Marian iconography; 10,000 holy cards from 19th and 20th centuries; 2600 postcard views of shrines; 3000 postcards of Marian art; philatelic collection of 1000 stamps and 200 first-day covers; 3000 photographs.
See also entry under Mary, Virgin

†OH —KINGWOOD CENTER, Library, 900 Park Ave W, Mansfield, 44906.
Notes: Espec ornamental horticulture, home gardening, landscaping, and floral arrangements. Incl 12,000 35mm slides of plants.

OK —PHILLIPS UNIVERSITY, John Rogers Graduate Seminary Library, Library, University Sta, Enid, 73701. John L Sayre, Dir of University Libraries
Holdings: Vols 3000 Cat Mss Maps Pix Slides Microforms Tapes Games
Budget: $500
Notes: Disciples of Christ Collection.

OK —PHILLIPS UNIVERSITY, Zollars Memorial Library, University Sta, Enid, 73701. John L Sayre, Dir of University Libraries
Holdings: Vols 2050 Cat Pix Slides

Microforms Games
Notes: Works on speech and hearing disorders, research, and therapy.

OK —UNIVERSITY OF OKLAHOMA, Bizzell Memorial Library, Western History Collections, 401 W Brooks, Norman, 73069. John Ezell, Cur
Holdings: Vols 40,000 Cat Mss Maps Pix Slides Microforms

OK —THOMAS GILCREASE INSTITUTE OF AMERICAN HISTORY & ART LIBRARY, 1400 North 25th West Ave, Tulsa, 74127. Sarah Hirsch, Librn
Holdings: Pix 5000
Notes: Trans-Mississippi West, US, Indian and Hispanic history. The Gilcrease Library contains a total of about 40,000 mss; 10,000 imprints; 5000 photographs; 600 maps and 50,000 vols.

OR —COLLIER STATE PARK LOGGING MUSEUM LIBRARY, PO Box 428, Klamath Falls, 97601. Alfred D Collier, Cur; Lowell N Jones, Asst Cur
Holdings: Uncat Mss Maps Pix Slides
Notes: 600 pieces of equipment showing evolution of logging. 800 pictures of logging. 15 pioneer log cabins. 500 Indian Stone artifacts. Collection of cruisers marks and sleighs.

OR —LIBRARY ASSOCIATION OF PORTLAND, Art & Music Dept, 801 S W Tenth Ave, Portland, 97205. Barbara K Padden, Librn
Holdings: Vols Cat Pix Slides Phonorecords
Notes: Art book titles: 21,325; music book titles (incl dance books): 10,800; sheet music titles: 19,550; slides on art subjects: about 12,000; phonorecord albums: 27,000; picture clippings: about 2 million; color reproductions of old and modern masters: about 640.

PA —BUCKS COUNTY HISTORICAL SOCIETY, Spruance Library, Pine & Ashland Sts, Doylestown, 18901. Terry A McNealy, Librn
Holdings: Vols (18,000) Cat Mss Maps Pix Slides Microforms
Notes: Pennsylvania history and genealogy, especially the Bucks County area.

PA —NEWCOMEN SOCIETY OF THE UNITED STATES, Thomas Newcomen Library of Steam Technology and Industrial History, 412 Newcomen Rd, Exton, 19341.
Holdings: Vols 3500 Cat Mss Pix Slides Microforms
Notes: Steam history and technology. Also, over 1100 trade catalogs.

PA —FREE LIBRARY OF PHILADELPHIA, Automobile Reference Collection, Logan Sq, Philadelphia, 19103. Louis G Helverson, Jr, Librn in Charge
Holdings: Vols (14,000) Cat Pix Slides
Notes: Collection is concerned with all aspects of automotive industry and its history. Includes shop manuals, instruction books, parts books, and periodicals dealing with all types of bicycles, tricylces and motor vehicles. Industry statistics, corporate annual reports, environmental problems, safety. Incl 18,000 pictures, 1700 slides, 648 microfilm reels, 23,000 sales catalogs, 5000 pieces of ephemera.

PA —UNIVERSITY OF PENNSYLVANIA, Archives and Records Center, North Facade - Franklin Field, Philadelphia, 19104. Mark Frazier Lloyd, Archivist

PA —CARNEGIE LIBRARY OF PITTSBURGH, Science & Technology Dept, 4400 Forbes Ave, Pittsburgh, 15213. Catherine M Brosky, Dept Head
Notes: This department serves as the Resource Library for Science and Technology in the Commonwealth of Pennsylvania. Agreements with other Resource Libraries in the Commonwealth and with certain institutions in Pittsburgh for sharing resources, cooperative acquisition of materials, provision of services and information. Collections described in *Guide to the Regional Library Resource Centers of Pennsylvania,* compiled by Ralph W McComb, 1967.

PA —CARNEGIE LIBRARY OF PITTSBURGH, Pennsylvania Div, 4400 Forbes Ave, Pittsburgh, 15213. Maria Zini, Head
Holdings: Vols (24,000) Cat Mss Maps Pix

Microforms
Budget: ($6000)
Notes: Collection contains at least one history of each county; historical atlases; biography; church histories; sociological and economic studies; journals of the General Assembly; state documents. The Pittsburgh section of the collection includes Pittsburgh directories 1815-date; newspapers on microfilm 1786-date, 30,000 photographs relating to Pittsburgh. A 65-drawer clipping collection supplements the published works. The genealogical materials (approx 5000 vols) incl individual family histories; regional and general genealogical works; periodicals; US. Census enumerations for Pennsylvania 1790-1910 (microfilm); indexes to biography, deaths and marriages. Separate catalog to entire Division. Collection is reference only.

PA —CARNEGIE LIBRARY OF PITTSBURGH, Music and Art Dept, 4400 Forbes Ave, Pittsburgh, 15213. Ida Reed, Dept Head
Holdings: Uncat Pix
Notes: 300,000 pictures, both art reproductions and general subjects; circulating.

PA —HUNT INSTITUTE FOR BOTANICAL DOCUMENTATION, Hunt Botanical Library, Carnegie-Mellon University, Pittsburgh, 15213. Bernadette G Callery, Librn
Holdings: Vols (23,000) Cat Pix
Notes: Collection of primarily historical botany and plant taxonomy, especially 1730-1840. Includes approximately 500 15th through 17th century herbals, extensive collection of 18th and 19th century color-plate works, floras and monographic works, and other works on natural history, early gardening and horticulture, and travel, particularly that dealing with plant exploration and introduction. Extensive biographical materials, on people in plant sciences. Reference collection and extensive documentation in botanical bibliography, especially concerning books published before 1850. Includes as separate collections, the Strandell Collection of Linnaeana and the Michel Adanson Library. Over 800 items described in *Catalogue of Botanical Books in the Collection of Rachel McMasters Miller Hunt, 1477-1800* (Pittsburgh, 1958-1960).

PA —UNIVERSITY OF PITTSBURGH, Henry Clay Frick Fine Arts Library, Pittsburgh, 15260. Anne W Gordon, Fine Arts Librn
Holdings: Vols (55,000) Cat Pix Slides Microforms
Notes: Emphasis is on the art of the Western World--Architecture, sculpture, painting, minor arts, archaeology, with special strength in the Byzantine, early Christian, medieval, renaissance and modern periods. The Oriental field is represented, incl replicas of scrolls. Studio arts are also covered. Illuminated ms facsimiles. Extensive collections of slides and photographs for study of art history are available in the building but not administered by the art library.

PA —UNIVERSITY OF PITTSBURGH, Special Collections Dept, Curtis Theatre Collection, 363 Hillman Library, Pittsburgh, 15260. Jeanette Blanco, Cur
Notes: The legitimate theatre of plays, musicals and vaudeville, chiefly of New York City and Pittsburgh, from 1865, and other US, community, summer, college and foreign theatre. Incl 500,000 programs, 12,000 pictures, 300 posters, the Oliver P Merriman Scrapbooks and 300 other scrapbooks, clippings and other ephemera. Vols incl over 3000 acting editions and playscripts. Separate collections: Ralph G Allen Burlesque Skits Collection; Michael Ellis Papers; William P Halstead Theatre Collection; Kenyon Family Papers; Philip Dunning Playscripts Collection; Pittsburgh Playhouse Records; Pittsburgh Savoyards Records. Noncirculating.

PA —READING SCHOOL DISTRICT PLANETARIUM, Library, 1211 Parkside Dr S, Reading, 19611. Bruce L Dietrich, Dir
Holdings: Vols (640) Cat Maps Pix Slides Phonorecords Audiotapes 16mm Films
Budget: ($1000)
Notes: Incl 400 maps, 1000 pictures, 7300 slides and 110 audiotapes.

PICTURES—COLLECTIONS (cont.)

PA —SHIPPENSBURG STATE COLLEGE, Lehman Library, Media/Curricular Center, Shippensburg, 17257. Gene R Hanson, Dir
Holdings: Vols 23,700 Cat Maps Pix Slides
Budget: ($20,000)
Notes: Extensive curriculum collection.

PA —FRIENDS HISTORICAL LIBRARY OF SWARTHMORE COLLEGE, Swarthmore, 19081. J William Frost, Dir
Holdings: Vols (35,000) Cat Mss Pix Slides Films Microforms
Notes: Library has an extensive collection of pictures, largely photographs, of individual Quakers and Quaker groups, meeting houses, and other buildings such as residences, schools, colleges, and institutions. In addition to photographs, the library has prints, silhouettes, drawings, and a few paintings. Highlighting the library's art works are drawings by Benjamin West, and paintings by West, Edward Hicks, James Sharples, and Howard Pyle.

PA —PENNSYLVANIA HISTORICAL & MUSEUM COMMISSION, Drake Well Museum Library, RD 3, Titusville, 16354. Vance Packard, Adminr
Holdings: Vols 7000 Cat Mss Maps Pix Slides
Notes: The most complete library collection relative to the subject of the 19th century oil industry, with a large amount of materials relative to the 20th century. Incl 4000 pictures by John Mather.

RI —BROWN UNIVERSITY, John Hay Library, Anne S K Brown Military Collection, 20 Prospect St, Providence, 02912. Richard B Harrington, Cur
Notes: The Anne S K Brown Military Collection has been formed over the past forty or more years by Mrs John Nicholas Brown, now of Newport, and contains approximately 40,000 volumes and 60,000 prints, drawings and watercolors as well as a number of oil paintings and about 5000 miniature model soldiers. At its beginning (and still today) the emphasis or focus of this collection has been upon the history of, and the accurate contemporary illustration of, military and naval uniforms of all nations from the early XVII century to the present. In the course of time, however, the collection has come to incl also a vast and related amount of material on military and naval history, military and naval arts and tactics, wars, campaigns, ceremonies, biography, portraits and caricatures of this and earlier periods. It has been probably the largest private collection of such a nature inthe world, and it contains much ms and graphic documentation which is unique. It has been useful to numerous scholars and historians, editors, filmmakers and publishers for research and for illustrative material and has also contributed to many museum exhibitions. In 1982 the entire collection, with its complete card catalog and subject index, has been presented to Brown University, where it is located in the John Hay Library. Special requests are taken care of by phone, mail and appointments with the curator.

RI —RHODE ISLAND SCHOOL OF DESIGN, Library, Two College St, Providence, 02903. James A Findlay, Dir
Holdings: Vols (70,000) Cat Pix Slides Phonorecords
Budget: ($50,000)
Notes: All fields of art incl 92,000 slides; 30,000 mounted photographs; 1100 posters and color reproductions; and 280,000 clippings.

SC —CHARLESTON LIBRARY SOCIETY, Library, 164 King St, Charleston, 29401. Catherine Sadler, Librn
Holdings: Vols 20,000 Cat Mss Maps Pix Microforms
Notes: South Caroliniana. Also, more than 500 bound pamphlet vols; 2000 rolls of microfilm.

SC —CHARLESTON MUSEUM LIBRARY, 360 Meeting St, Charleston, 29403. John Brumgardt, Museum Dir
Holdings: Vols 30,000 Cat Mss Maps Pix

SC —SOUTH CAROLINA HISTORICAL SOCIETY LIBRARY, Fireproof Bldg, 100 Meeting St, Charleston, 29401. Gene Widdell, Dir
Holdings: Vols (50,000) Cat Mss Maps Pix Slides Microforms
Notes: No photocopying. Pamphlets; 2.5 million pages of mss.

SC —GREENVILLE COUNTY LIBRARY, 300 College St, Greenville, 29601. Joan Sorensen, Asst Dir of Public Servs
Holdings: Vols 6000 Cat Mss Maps Pix Microforms
Notes: An index to local South Carolina newspapers is maintained; also a picture collection.

SD —SOUTH DAKOTA HISTORICAL RESOURCE CENTER, Library, Soldiers Memorial Bldg, Pierre, 57501. Rosemary Evetts, Librn
Holdings: Vols 1020 Cat Mss Maps Pix
Budget: $2000
Notes: South Dakota state and territorial materials. Picture collection has been cataloged and numbers approximately 20,000 items, of which we have negatives for about half. South Dakota materials include items on general state and territorial history, biographical, autobiographical, political, geological, economic and county and town materials.

†SD —SOUTH DAKOTA SCHOOL OF MINES & TECHNOLOGY, Devereaux Library, Rapid City, 57701.
Holdings: Vols 400 Cat
Notes: Also, about 7400 hard copies of NASA Technical Reports. Have a Lunar Orbiter Photograph Collection.

SD —UNIVERSITY OF SOUTH DAKOTA, Shrine to Music Museum, USD Box 194, Vermillion, 57069. Andre P Larson, Dir
Holdings: Pix Slides
Budget: ($205,036)
Notes: The Shrine to Music Museum is one of America's major collections of musical resource materials, incl more than 4000 antique musical instruments from all over the world, plus an extensive supporting library of several thousand books, music, periodicals, recordings, photographs, and related musical memorabilia. The collection of 19th and early 20th-century sheet music and music for wind instruments is probably the most extensive in the country. Inquiries and visits are welcomed.

TN —STUDENTS' MUSEUM, Library, 516 Beaman St, Chihowee Park, Knoxville, 37914. Sylvia Gloeckner, Librn
Holdings: Vols 877 Cat Mss Maps Pix Slides Phonorecords Audiotapes Videotapes
Notes: The materials are all related to objects exhibitions, and programs of the Student's Museum. Incl 200 ms pieces, 100 maps, 1500 pictures, 5000 slides, etc.

TN —PT BOATS MUSEUM & LIBRARY, PO Box 109, Memphis, 38101. J M "Boats" Newberry, Librn
Holdings: Vols (2000) Uncat Maps Pix Slides Phonorecords Audiotapes 16mm Films Microforms Videotapes Biographies
Budget: ($25,000)
Notes: PT Boats, Inc is an 8000 man organization of PT boat veterans, families, modelers and history buffs who have donated a sizable collection of artifacts and records pertaining to their PT boat service. The collection also contains an 80-foot Elco PT boat and a 78-foot Higgins PT boat, both restored. National headquarters and archives are in Memphis, and the display collection is located on board the USS Massachusetts at Battleship Cove, Fall River, Mass, 02721. To use the library, write PT Boat Coordinator, William C Hindle and/or Don Rhoads, Chief Administrative Officer in Memphis. Memphis headquarters has some 10,000 photos and line drawings with specifications.

TN —UNIVERSITY OF THE SOUTH ARCHIVES, Jessie Ball DuPont Library, Sewanee, 37375. Gertrude French Mignery, Archivist
Holdings: Vols (3000) Cat Mss Maps Pix Slides Microforms
Notes: Collection is comprised almost entirely of materials relating to the Episcopal Church and the University and its relationship to the 24 owning Southern dioceses. This collection is not duplicated in the library of the School of Theology. The collection encompasses some 250 cubic feet of official University records, mss (ca 15,000 pieces), bound vols (ca 3000), pamphlets (ca 700), audiovisual resources (ca 100 tape recordings, 100 motion picture films, 5000 loose photographs, and 950 slides), microfilms (ca 90 reels), maps (ca 100 of Sewanee and Franklin County), scrapbooks (ca 100), and museum pieces (ca 300 objects). Almost all of the larger collections have been reported to the National Union Catalog of Manuscript Collections. Such collections incl the papers of Bishops Leonidas Polk, Charles Todd Quintard, James Hervey Otey, as well as extensive collections of all pastVice-Chancellors. A collection of letters of the American Episcopate, 1784-1953 (ca 1200 pieces) has recently been processed for the collection. A master name and subject for the entire holdings.

TX —TEXAS STATE LIBRARY, Archives Div, 1201 Brazos, PO Box 12927, Capitol Sta, Austin, 78711. David B Gracy II, State Archivist
Holdings: Vols 30,000 Cat Mss Maps Pix Microforms
Notes: Collections are limited to Texas history, primarily archives of the Texas state government. Mss, 25,000 cubic ft; 3000 maps; 35,000 pictures; 5000 microforms.

TX —UNIVERSITY OF TEXAS LIBRARIES, Nettie Lee Benson Latin American Collection, Sid Richardson Hall 1.109, Austin, 78712. Laura Gutierrez-Witt, Head Librn
Holdings: Vols (450,000) Cat Mss Maps Pix Phonorecords Filmstrips Microforms
Notes: See entry under Latin America.

TX —EAST TEXAS STATE UNIVERSITY, James G Gee Library, Special Collections Dept, East Texas Station, Commerce, 75428. James Conrad, Dept Head
Holdings: Vols (3000) Cat Mss Pix Slides
Budget: ($3000)
Notes: Extensive collection of county histories of Texas. In the process of classifying and preparing catalog cards for archival materials (photographs, non-photographic materials such as deeds, commencement programs, business records, etc and various items relating to the East Texas State University from its beginning as a private school in 1894 as East Texas Normal College). Photographs and mss have been processed and finding aids prepared.

TX —DALLAS PUBLIC LIBRARY, Texas/Dallas History and Archives Division, 1515 Young St, Dallas, 75201. Richard L Waters, Acting Dir; Wayne Gray, Manager
Notes: Dallas and Texas history.

TX —SOUTHERN METHODIST UNIVERSITY, Fondren Library, McCord Theater Collection, Room 301, Dallas, 75275. Edyth Renshaw, Cur; Linda Sellers, Pub Serv
Holdings: Vols (2000) Uncat Mss Pix Slides Phonorecords
Notes: See *Theatre Collections in Libraries and Museums*, Gilder and Freedley (Theatre Arts, 1936). The McCord Theatre Collection encompasses the entire spectrum of the performing arts. The central purpose is to gather records of our regional theater before such ephemeral material is lost. Records of over two hundred early Texas theaters, some fragmentary and some relatively complete, are in the files. These records incl photographs of buildings, stagehands, orchestras, and performers. Local theatre history incl the once famous Dallas Little Theatre and the Margo Jones Theatre. The national theatre, opera, ballet, and circus archives incl pictures (some autographed), programs, posters, throw-aways, tear sheets, clippings, and letters. Our international archives are small, but we have some excellent material, eg, artifacts from Max Reinhardt's production of"The Miracle" which happened to go bankrupt in Dallas. After a few years the items were given to us. There are posters, tear sheets, souvenir programs, and other colorful items from Morris Gest and the Artef Collection. We have about 200 19th century English

PICTURES—COLLECTIONS (cont.)

playbills and a few from the 18th century.
There is a collection of modern English,
French, and other European programs, many
of them illustrated souvenir programs. Also,
magazines on theater, cinema, and television
(1800). Scrapbooks covering both southwest
and Dallas theater, 1890s-1950s. Special
Collections: artifacts and documents on
puppets; masks; costume design; circus; and
ballet and dance. The Harriet Bacon
MacDonald Collection of over 200
photographs of musicians appearing in Dallas
during the first three decades of the 20th
century. Many autographed. Affiliated with
Meadow Theatre of the Arts.

TX —AMON CARTER MUSEUM, 3501
Camp Bowie Blvd, PO Box 2365, Fort
Worth, 76113. Jan K Muhlert, Dir; Marni
Sandweiss, Cur of Photographs
Holdings: Cat Pix Slides
Notes: American photography from the
beginning to the present with particular
strength in photographs of the 19th century
West. Includes the photographic estates of
Laura Gilpin and Karl Struss. Incl 250,000
pictures; 55,000 slides.

TX —FORT WORTH PUBLIC LIBRARY,
Arts Division, 300 Taylor St, Fort Worth,
76102. Heather Gobel, Head
Holdings: Pix
Notes: This special picture collection
provides research service materials for
requests in all subjects areas requiring
pictorial illustrations. Includes postal cards
and poster collections. The fine arts
reproductions comprise another separate
collection of framed & matted and portfolio-
contained pictures not included in the
Subjects collection.

TX —ROSENBERG LIBRARY, Galveston and
Texas History Center, 2310 Sealy Ave,
Galveston, 77550. Jane Kenamore, Archivist
Holdings: Cat Pix
Notes: 16,000 photographs of Galveston and
Texas subjects, private scrapbooks and
postcards.

TX —HOUSTON POST LIBRARY, 4747
Southwest Freeway, Houston, 77001. Kathy
Foley, Librn
Holdings: Cat Maps Pix Microforms
Notes: Incl 5,000,000 clippings and 3,000,
000 pictures.

TX —RICE UNIVERSITY, Fondren Library,
Woodson Research Center, 6100 S Main St,
PO Box 1892, Houston, 77251. Nancy
Parker, Dir Woodson Research Center
Holdings: Mss Maps Pix
Notes: Incl Texas family papers, letters,
diaries, business records in several
collections. Also, letters, broadsides,
clippings, photographs, memorabilia, and
microfilm, relating to the Maximilian era in
Mexico. Incl letters from Carlotta as a young
girl to members of her family.

TX —BOY SCOUTS OF AMERICA, Library,
1325 Walnut Hill Lane, Irving, 75062. Ann
Lamont McVicar, Librn
Holdings: Vols 3000 Cat Pix Slides
Notes: Early and current books on the Boy
Scouts of America, and on the subjects of
scouts and scouting.

UT —UTAH STATE UNIVERSITY, Merrill
Library, Department of Special Collections
& Archives, Logan, 84322. A J Simmonds,
Curator; Jeanie F Simmonds, Archivist;
Bradford R Cole, Mss Librn
Holdings: Vols 1100 Uncat Mss Pix Slides
Notes: The Austin E and Alla S Fife folklore
archive of western, cowboy, and folksong
materials. Over 300 pictures; 4200 slides;
800 field recordings; 75 ft of ms items.
Complete card index to folklore themes in
the collection. See Catalog of recordings in
"A Bibiliography of the Archives of the Utah
Humanities Research Foundation," *Bulletin
of the University of Utah*, vol XXXVIII, no
9 (Dec 1947): pp 26-35; description of Fife
Mormon collection in *Western Folklore
Quarterly*, vol VII, no 3 (July 1948): pp 299-
301; description of "Fife Collection of
Western American Folksong and Folklore"
in *The Folklore and Folk Music Archivist*,
vol VII, no 2 (Spring 1964): pp 41-44.

UT —UTAH STATE UNIVERSITY, Merrill
Library, Department of Special Collections
& Archives, Logan, 84322. A J Simmonds,
Curator; Jeanie F Simmonds, Archivist;
Bradford R Cole, Mss Librn
Notes: 8000 cataloged photographs and 15,
000 uncataloged. Collections deals heavily
with Western America, especially southern
Idaho and Utah. Also contains substantial
collection of World War II Italian campaign,
ranch life, Western parks and national
forests. Photographers represented by
substantial numbers of photos include
Charles Ellis Johnson, C R Savage, John C
H Grabil, W H Jackson, A J Russell. Also in
excess of 5000 photographs on the history of
Utah State University, 1890 to the present.
In addition, books and pamphlets on the
history of western grazing (cattle and sheep).
Incl manuscript of WPA-produced history of
grazing, 1540-1936; supported by 800
photographs.

VA —EASTERN MENNONITE COLLEGE,
Menno Simons Historical Library &
Archives, Harrisonburg, 22801. Grace
Showalter, Librn
Holdings: Vols (15,318) Cat Maps Pix Slides
Budget: ($30,500)
Notes: Anabaptist, Mennonite, and local
history and genealogy. Incl art reproductions
and prints.

†VA —GEORGE C MARSHALL
RESEARCH FOUNDATION AND
LIBRARY, Drawer 920, Lexington, 24450.
Royster Lyle Jr, Cur Collections
Holdings: Vols Cat Mss Maps Pix
Phonorecords Audiotapes Films Filmstrips
Microforms
Notes: About 400 posters-American,
German, French; complete *Stars and Stripes*
for WWII; approx 5000 cataloged
photographs, over 5000 uncataloged Office
of War information photos, and over 10,000
US Signal Corps photos (uncat). Approx 250
regimental histories, operation reports, and
army manuals; published memoirs and letters
of Marshall associates; official military
histories (American, British); over 1200
maps-approx 300 newsmaps, 800 daily
situation maps (European Theatre), 37
bound vols of daily situation maps 1944-
1945; seven of the *Why We Fight* series
(films). Major ms collections incl the papers
of generals George C Marshall, Marshall S
Carter, William T Sexton, Lucian Truscott,
William R Arnold, Paul M Robinett, Frank
McCarthy; Forrest C Pogue; colonels Collas
Harris, Francis P Miller, William F
Friedman; officers of the Women's Army
Corps. Hearingsand government documents.
Agency records copied from NARS. Vertical
file arranged by subject.

VA —MOUNT VERNON LADIES'
ASSOCIATION OF THE UNION,
Research & Reference Library, Mount
Vernon, 22121. Ellen McCallister Clark,
Librn; John Rhodehamel, Dir of Education
Holdings: Vols (12,000) Cat Mss Maps Pix
Slides
Notes: The Washington family and Mount
Vernon. The history of the Mount Vernon
Ladies' Association and historic
preservation.

VA —MARINERS MUSEUM, Library,
Newport News, 23606. Ardie L Kelly, Librn
Holdings: Vols (60,000) Cat Mss Maps Pix
Slides
Notes: Incl collections of over 150,000
photographs of merchant ships, naval vessels,
sailing ships, lighthouses, portraits of naval
men, harbors, canals, etc, and maps, ships'
papers, and log books. Catalogs of various
parts of the collection published by G K
Hall, Boston.

VA —NORFOLK PUBLIC LIBRARY,
Sargeant Memorial Room, 301 E City Hall
Ave, Norfolk, 23510. Lucile B Portlock, Cur
Holdings: Vols (14,600) Cat Mss Maps Pix
Microforms
Budget: $1500
Notes: Incl microfilms (2494) of local
newspapers, 1736-1969. Incl 8000 pictures,
indexed; 50,000 negatives; chronological
index to maps. Separate catalog. Also incl
published and unpublished genealogies;
county records; indexes to family names; and

census records on microfilm of all counties
of Virginia and North Carolina, 1790-1910;
Maryland, West Virginia and District of
Columbia 1800-1910; South Carolina 1900-
1910.

VA —PORTSMOUTH PUBLIC LIBRARY,
601 Court St, Portsmouth, 23704. Dean
Burgess, Library Dir
Holdings: Vols 55 Cat Pix
Notes: This collection is in connection with
the lightship Museum of the US Coast
Guard located on the lightship
PORTSMOUTH moored permanently on
the Portsmouth waterfront and with the
headquarters of the Coast Guard located in
Portsmouth (headquarters for the 5th Coast
Guard district). We are most interested in
Lightships but also buy materials on
lighthouses. The scope is international and
dealing with all periods. We hope to find all
types of materials but now hold only printed
books. Pictures and materials other than
books are housed in the lightship Portsmouth
(Alice Hanes, Curator), 1 High Street,
Portsmouth, Va 23704.

VA —VIRGINIA STATE LIBRARY, 12 &
Capitol Sts, Richmond, 23219.
Holdings: Cat Pix
Notes: Incl 86,960 prints, photographs, etc,
chiefly of Virginia, the Civil War, and the
Confederacy.

VA —COLONIAL WILLIAMSBURG
FOUNDATION, Abby Aldrich Rockefeller
Folk Art Center, PO Box C, Williamsburg,
23187. Anne E Watkins, Registrar
Holdings: Vols 1200 Cat Maps Pix Slides
Notes: American folk art emphasis

WA —WESTERN WASHINGTON
UNIVERSITY, Center for Pacific Northwest
Studies, High St, Bellingham, 98225. James
W Scott, Dir
Holdings: Cat Mss Maps Pix
Notes: The percival R Jeffcott Collection of
Local History is particularly rich in
photographic materials, incl about 1800
negatives and about 1100 photographs,
which deal with pioneer settlement and
economic and culture developments in
Whatcom County, Washington, and a few
adjacent areas, such as the Lower Mainland
of British Columbia to the north and
neighboring counties of Washington to the
south and west. Incl also ms versions of
Jeffcott's published works: *Nooksack Tales
and Trails, Chechaco and Sourdough and
Blanket Bill Jarmen* and numerous
unpublished papers and workbooks. A small
collection of Jeffcott materials is housed in
the Washington State Historical Society,
Tacoma, and for this there is an unpublished
inventory. An inventory of the present
collection is being prepared for publication
by the Center for Pacific Northwest Studies.

WA —WASHINGTON STATE LIBRARY,
Washington/Northwest Rm, State Library
Bldg, Olympia, 98504. Nancy B Pryor,
Research Consultant
Holdings: Vols 8000 Cat Mss Maps Pix
Microforms
Notes: Mss, photographs and microfilm
largely limited to Washington territorial and
state materials as is the file of pamphlets and
newspaper clippings, which includes both
historical and current material. The book
collection incl works on the four Pacific
Northwest States, Alaska, and British
Columbia, and books by Washington
authors.

†WA —WASHINGTON STATE
UNIVERSITY, Library, Manuscripts,
Archives & Special Collections, Pullman,
99164. John F Guido, Head
Holdings: Cat Mss Maps Pix
Notes: The manuscript collection incl
business and financial records of banks,
breweries, fisheries, insurance, land, lumber
and livestock companies, trade and
commodity associations; as well as the
personal and professional papers of authors,
aviators, educators, engineers, farmers,
historians, pioneers, politicians and scientists;
especially rich in documents relating to the
exploration, settlement and development of
the Palouse Country, the Inland Empire, the
Columbia Basin and the Pacific Northwest.
Described in *Selected Manuscript Resources*

PICTURES—COLLECTIONS (cont.)

in the Washington State University Library (Pullman, 1974); and other published and unpublished inventories and registers. Also, the Robert Cushman Butler Collection of Theatrical Illustrations contains: approx 1600 illustrations, sheet music covers, programs and playbills; approx 100 mss of actors, actresses and playwrights;and approx 200 volumes of theatrical history and reminiscesces, several extra-illustrated, concentrating on 18th-19th century British and American drama. A guide to the collection is in preparation.

WA —HISTORICAL SOCIETY OF SEATTLE AND KING COUNTY, Sophie Frye Bass Library, 2161 E Hamlin, Seattle, 98112. Rick Caldwell, Librn
Holdings: Vols (20,000) Cat Mss Maps Pix Slides
Notes: Incl 15,000 pictures on Pacific Northwest.

WA —SEATTLE PUBLIC LIBRARY, 1000 Fourth Ave, Seattle, 98104. Ronald A Dubberly, City Librn
Holdings: Vols 70,000 Cat Pix
Notes: Incl 28,000 photographs of Seattle and Pacific Northwest architecture and views. Balance of picture collection about 650,000 items. Also, the Balch Autograph Collection of contemporary autographs (about 2000 //) and photographs of newsworthy persons in all fields. Worldwide scope. Collection begun in late 1920s.

WA —WASHINGTON STATE HISTORICAL SOCIETY LIBRARY, 315 N Stadium Way, Tacoma, 98403. Frank L Green, Librn
Holdings: Vols 15,000 Cat Mss Maps Pix Microforms
Notes: Curtis Collection Frederick and Engerman, *Asahel Curtis: Photographs of the Great Northwest* pub 1983. Scope is entire Pacific Northwest, with emphasis on Washington.

WV —WEST VIRGINIA UNIVERSITY, Library, West Virginia and Regional History Collection, Morgantown, 26506. George P Parkinson Jr, Cur
Holdings: Vols 30,000 Cat Mss Maps Pix Audiotapes 16mm Films Filmstrips Microforms
Budget: ($20,000)
Notes: The West Virginia Collection contains over 10,000 linear ft of mss, broadsides, pictures, photographs, and other items relating to West Virginia and the Appalachian region. There are published guides to the collections.

WI —CIRCUS WORLD MUSEUM LIBRARY, 415 Lynn St, Baraboo, 53913. Robert L Parkinson, Research Center Dir
Holdings: Vols (1800) Cat Mss Pix Slides Phonorecords 16mm Films
Notes: Circus and "Wild West" shows. Owned by State Historical Society of Wisconsin. Incl 1800 books on circus subject; 400 route books; 1200 programs, 8000 circus lithographs, 20,000 photo negatives, 50,000 photo prints, heralds, couriers, tickets, letterheads, route cards, original circus artwork, records and documents of circus business, movies, newspaper ads, circus band music and periodicals of show business such as *Billboard, New York Clipper, White Tops,* Bandwagon, etc. Partially cataloged.

WI —DOUGLAS COUNTY HISTORICAL MUSEUM, 906 E Second St, Superior, 54880. James E Lundsted, Dir
Notes: Photographs by David Barry, of Sioux Indians at time of Custer fiasco, 1875-1888.

WY —UNIVERSITY OF WYOMING, William Robertson Coe Library, Western History Research Center, Laramie, 82071. Gene M Gressley, Dir, Asst to Pres
Holdings: Vols (35,000) Cat Mss Maps Pix Microforms
Notes: The Western History Research Center of the University of Wyoming's William Robertson Coe Library has sizable ms collections in several areas pertaining to the history and development of the American West. Principal ms collection

areas incl; cattle industry history, western literature, mining and petroleum history, transportation history, conservation history, water resources history, and related western history topics. The collections are supplemented by a fine Western Americana book collection cataloged by the main library but located at the Western History Research Center.

AB —GLENBOW-ALBERTA INSTITUTE, Historical Library & Archives, 130 9th Avenue SE, Calgary, T2G 0P3, Can. Leonard J Gottseleg, Chief Librn
Holdings: Vols (60,000) Cat Mss Maps Pix Microforms
Notes: Main emphasis is on Western Canadian history. Equally important emphasis is placed on the Canadian Arctic and Alaska, Northwest Coast explorations, Aboriginal peoples of the North and Canadian West, and the furs trade in the US Northwest.

AB —SOUTHERN ALBERTA INSTITUTE OF TECHNOLOGY, Learning Resources Centre, 1301 16 Ave NW, Calgary, T2M 0L4, Can. Tom Skinner, Historian
Holdings: Vols (5000) Cat Pix Slides Films Audiotapes Filmstrips Videotapes
Notes: Serves Alberta College of Art (4-year professional course).

BC —BRITISH COLUMBIA TEACHERS' FEDERATION, Resources Center, 2235 Burrand St, Vancouver, V6J 3H9, Can. T M Murphy, Librn
Holdings: Vols (10,000) Cat Mss Maps Pix Slides Audiotapes Films Microforms
Notes: Emphasis is on teacher's professional in-service training. Borrowing privileges to BCTF members and Affiliation Library and Institution. Subject bibliographies of the collection are available. Data-Bases, searching available.

BC —VANCOUVER PUBLIC LIBRARY, Art Div, 750 Burrard St, Vancouver, V6Z 1X5, Can.
Holdings: Cat Pix
Notes: Book and pamphlet collection. Also, (1) Newspaper Clippings File: 31 drawers of relevant clippings from major newspapers, incl the *Sun, Province, Toronto Globe and Mail, Christian Science Monitor, New York Times,* etc on arts, music, architecture; incl biographical material (16 drawers). (2) Picture File about 500,000 pictures in 150 cabinet drawers, strong in architecture, costume, interior decoration, painting, sculpture, also portraits. (3) Exhibition Catalogs File: British Columbia and elsewhere. (4) Association and Organization File: organizations in the Lower Mainland in arts, music, city planning, etc, begun in 1940s; (5) Canadian Artists Index: begun in 1964, alphabetically by artist, with about 300,000 citationsto reproductions of work and biographical material on Canadian artist from the division's books and other sources; (6) Miscellaneous Index: material not covered in other special or published indexes, primarily of Canadian and local cultural events, hard-to-find informations, etc. Local newspapers, special Canadian publications and British film journals are the most regularly indexed items. (7) Song Index started in the 1930s. (8) Title Index to song collections and sheet music in the VPL collection, approx 100,000 entries.

BC —MARITIME MUSEUM OF BRITISH COLUMBIA, 28 Bastion Sq, Victoria, V8W 1H9, Can. C H Shaw, Dir
Holdings: Vols (2500) Cat Mss Maps Pix Slides Microforms
Budget: ($110,000)
Notes: Also 4000 registration cards; 6000 pictures.

MB —HUDSON'S BAY CO, Library, 77 Main St, Winnipeg, R3C 2R1, Can. Carol Preston, Librn Hudson's Bay House
Holdings: Vols (6000) Cat Mss Maps Pix Slides
Notes: Main purpose is to provide research materials for production of the historical quarterly *The Beaver,* and to answer inquiries about the Company's history. Incl 250,000 pictures and 7000 VF pieces. No published catalog, but Library maintains author/subject/title card catalog. Limited

photocopying. Mss of HBC Archives held by the Manitoba Provincial Archives. Published descriptions: Dowdall, Judi, "Hudson's Bay Company Library," *Canadian Library Journal,* June 1974, p 179; Preston, Carol, "Hudson's Bay Company Library," *Manitoba Library Association Bulletin,* June 1976, pp 24-25.

ON —ROYAL BOTANICAL GARDENS, Library, Box 399, Hamilton, L8N 3H8, Can. Ina Vrugtman, Librn
Holdings: Vols (5000) Cat
Budget: ($13,000)
Notes: Botany and ornamental horticulture. Incl 10,000 slides. Periodicals are not yet union listed. Collection of nursery and seed trade catalogs; *Gray Herbarium Index; Centre for Canadian Historical Horitcultural Studies.* The library is located in the headquarters building of the Royal Botanical Gradens, 680 Plains Road West (Highway No 2) Burlington, Ontario. Phone: (416) 527-1158. Road West (Highway No 2) Burlington, Ontario. Phone: (416) 527-1158.

ON —QUEEN'S UNIVERSITY, Douglas Library, Kingston, K7L 5C4, Can. William F E Morley, Cur, Special Collections
Holdings: Vols 3400 Uncat Pix
Notes: 2854 pictures and 2520 pictures postcards, almost all Canadian.

ON —NATIONAL FILM BOARD, CANADA, Tunney's Pasture Area, Ottawa, K1A 0M9, Can.
Notes: Photo library of 225,000 Canadian images, incl 33,000 slides.

ON —NATIONAL FILM, TELEVISION AND SOUND ARCHIVES, Documentation & Public Service, 395 Wellington St, Ottawa, K1A 0N3, Can. Jana Vosikovska, Chief; Gloria Grant, Librn; Sylvie Robitaille, Stills and Posters Librn
Notes: Several collections supporting the documentation on film, television and recorded sound: 1060 periodical titles (450 current), some on microfilm. Picture-stills, 265,000; moving picture posters, 6000; cataloged microfiche, 33,000 (vertical file material put on microfilm, then into a fiche format). Index cards (periodical references, credits): 334,000 cards (Film Title Index: 250,000 cards; Personalities Index: 84,000 cards).

ON —NATIONAL GALLERY OF CANADA, Library, National Museums of Canada, Ottawa, K1A 0M8, Can. J Hunter, Chief Librn

ON —NATIONAL MUSEUMS OF CANADA, Library Services Directorate, Ottawa, K1A 0M8, Can. Valerie Monkhouse, Director
Holdings: Vols 400,000 Pix Cat
Notes: Archaeology, ethnology, history, National Collection of Nature Photographs, representative holdings in natural sciences, science and technology. Prints may be ordered and used in publication with credit to the National Museums of Canada.

ON —UNIVERSITY OF OTTAWA, Morisset Library, 65 Hastey St, Ottawa, K1N 9A5, Can. Yvon Richer, University Chief Librn
Holdings: Vols (17,000) Cat Maps Slides Microforms
Notes: Only a small portion of this material is housed in Special Collections, but is is one of the strongest elements of our regular collections. Additional support, particularly in archaeology, philosophy and religion is also available at the affiliated St Paul University, 223 Main Street, Ottawa.

ON —CANADIAN ASSOCIATION IN SUPPORT OF THE NATIVE PEOPLES, Library, 277 Victoric St, Toronto, M5V 1W2, Can. Frances Davidson-Arnott, Librn
Holdings: Vols 4000 Cat Mss Maps Pix Slides Microforms
Notes: Native peoples of North America, especially of Canada.

ON —METROPOLITAN TORONTO LIBRARY, Theatre Dept, 789 Yonge St, Toronto, M4W 2G8, Can. Heather McCallum, Head
Notes: 55,000 photographs document Canadian theatre, film and dance productions, performing arts personalities and British and American film stills.

ON —METROPOLITAN TORONTO LIBRARY, Fine Arts Dept, 789 Yonge St,

PICTURES—COLLECTIONS (cont.)

Toronto, M4W 2G8, Can. Alan Suddon, Head
Holdings: Uncat Pix
Notes: Incl circulating picture collections (clippings) on all subjects. Reference picture collection, mainly 19th century Canadian, but non-Toronto. Postcards. Printed ephemera. 100,000 reference pictures 750,00 circulating pictures. Loose pictures from magazines and books.

ON —METROPOLITAN TORONTO LIBRARY, Canadian History Dept, Baldwin Room Section, 789 Yonge St, Toronto, M4W 2G8, Can. David B Kotin, Head
Holdings: Vols (52,000) Mss Pix
Notes: This collection consists of material on Canadian history, geography, travel, archaeology, genealogy, retrospective city and telephone directories, collective biographies, native peoples (excluding customs, rights and social conditions), Arctic regions, military history and theory. It is an extremely strong collection of both current and retrospective material. Particular strengths are national and local history (especially Ontario), Arctic regions, native peoples, travel (especially Ontario), and military history. Incl 78,000 historical pictures, 235 linear meters mss, 14,000 broadsides and 3800 bound newspapers.

PQ —SPECIAL LIBRARY FOR LA SOCIETE HISTORIQUE DU SAGUENAY, 930 est, Jacques-Cartier, PO Box 456, Chicoutimi, G7H 5C8, Can. Roland Belanger, Archivist
Holdings: Vols 850 Uncat Mss Maps Pix
Notes: All concerning the history and geography of the Saguenay Region. Incl about 50,000 pictures.

PQ —MUSEE D'ART CONTEMPORAIN, Bibliotheque, Cite du Havre, Montreal, H3C 3R4, Can. Isabelle Montplaisir, Librn
Holdings: Vols (5780) Cat Pix Slides Audiotapes Videotapes Microforms
Budget: ($12,000)
Notes: 7050 exhibition catalogs on a basic exchange from art galleries, museums, etc of many countries. Also 2000 pictures; 32,000 slides; and 2500 files relating to artists, galleries, museums, etc. Also, the Archives Paul-Emile Borduas (painter) of 12,500 items, incl his writings, correspondence, exhibition catalogs, etc. Plus 150 periodical subscriptions.

SK —SASKATCHEWAN ARCHIVES BOARD, University of Regina, Regina, S4S 0A2, Can. Ian E Wilson, Provincial Archivist
Holdings: Mss Maps Pix Audiotapes Videotapes 16mm Films Microforms
Budget: $900,000
Notes: The Saskatchewan Archives Board attempts to document the history of the area now the Province of Saskatchewan and its communities through all archival media. Collection incl 5800 meters of mss, 4800 maps, 250,000 pictures, 10,000 architectural drawings, 4400 audiotapes, 1648 16mm films and 9400 microfilm reels. Individual collections are listed in *The Union List of Manuscripts in Canadian Repositories* (Ottawa, 1975 & 1976). Detailed catalogs, indexes and inventories are available in two offices. (Second office is located at University of Saskatchewan, Saskatoon, Sask S7N 0W0 Canada.)

†SK —UNIVERSITY OF REGINA, Library, Regina, S4S 0A2, Can. Margarett Hammond, Librn
Notes: Native peoples of North America, especially of Canada. Collection formerly held by Canadian Association in Support of the Native Peoples.

SK —WESTERN DEVELOPMENT MUSEUM, George Shepherd Library, 2935 Melville St, PO Box 1910, Saskatoon, S7K 3S5, Can. Warren Clubb, Research Coordr
Holdings: Vols Pix Audiotapes Film Maps
Notes: Staff reference library. Open to the public although not a lending library. Extensive holdings of agricultural machinery catalogs, from Canadian and American manufacturers and distributors. Other holdings incl automobiles, aviation, museology and Western Canadian history. Partially cataloged.

YT —YUKON ARCHIVES, Box 2703, Whitehorse, Y1A 3C6, Can. Miriam McTiernan, Territorial Archivist
Holdings: Vols (8000) Cat Mss Maps Pix Phonorecords Audiotapes Videotapes 16mm Films Microforms
Budget: $15,000
Notes: Yukon and regional history and development. Incl also 500 mss; 10,000 maps; 30,000 pictures; 1200 microfilm rolls; 1115 oral history tapes, etc; Yukon newspapers.

PICTURES, HUMOROUS see Caricatures and Cartoons

PICTURES, TYPE see Type Pictures

PIDGIN ENGLISH

MA —HARVARD UNIVERSITY LIBRARY, Cambridge, 02138.
Holdings: Cat

PIEDRA-BUENO, ANDRES DE

OH —KENT STATE UNIVERSITY, Libraries, Dept of Special Collections, Kent, 44242. Dean H Keller, Cur
Holdings: Vols 1800 // Cat
Notes: Private library of Dr Andres de Piedra-Bueno incl most of his own work.

PIERCE, C. C.

CA —CALIFORNIA HISTORICAL SOCIETY, Schubert Hall Library, 2099 Pacific Ave, San Francisco, 94109. Bruce L Johnson, Library Dir
Holdings: Pix
Notes: San Francisco CHS Photographic Archives holds 300,000 images on California statewide; The CHS Title Insurance and Trust Corporation Collection of Historical Photographs in Los Angeles contains 20,000 photographs centered around pictures of Southern California by noted photographer C C Pierce. Copies of photographs by other pioneer Los Angeles photographers, such as Godfrey, Wolfenstein and Parker are incl, as well as 2000 glass plate negatives of local Indians by George Wharton James.

PIERCE, FRANKLIN, 1804-1869

DC —LIBRARY OF CONGRESS, Manuscript Division, Washington, 20540. John C Broderick, Chief
Notes: The Presidential Papers collection incl the papers, etc, of numerous Presidents.

ME —BOWDOIN COLLEGE, Library, Brunswick, 04011. Dianne M Gutscher, Cur of Special Collections
Holdings: Mss
Notes: The Franklin Pierce Papers consist of 29 letters, mss, and documents of this member of Bowdoin's class of 1824.

NH —NEW HAMPSHIRE HISTORICAL SOCIETY, Manuscripts Library, 30 Park St, Concord, 03301. Thomas E Camden, Cur
Holdings: Cat Mss
Notes: Franklin Pierce Papers incl correspondence, scrapbook of newspaper clippings, drafts of Pierce's message to Congress in December 1855. Much of the correspondence is between Pierce and his sister, Elizabeth and her husband, Gen John McNeil. Emphasis of the collection, in general, is on the presidential election of 1852. About 1500 items. Index to the collection available at the New Hampshire Historical Society.

NH —FRANKLIN PIERCE COLLEGE, Frank S DiPietro Library, College Rd, Rindge, 03461. Robert W Chatfield, Dir
Holdings: Cat
Notes: Material about President Pierce.

PIERCE, GEORGE WASHINGTON, 1898-1955

MA —HARVARD UNIVERSITY LIBRARY, Cambridge, 02138.

Notes: The papers of George Washington Pierce (1898-1955).

PIERCE, OVID W.

NC —DUKE UNIVERSITY, William R Perkins Library, Manuscript Dept, Durham, 27706. Ellen Gartrell, Cur of Mss
Holdings: Cat Mss
Notes: Papers, correspondence, etc.

PIERCE AND BICKFORD, ARCHITECTS

NY —CORNELL UNIVERSITY LIBRARIES, Collection of Regional History, Dept of Manuscripts and Univ Archives, Ithaca, 14853.
Notes: Incl records, ca 1892-ca 1931; bills, receipts, contracts, indexes of negatives and photos, negatives, printing blocks and blueprints.

PIERCE-ARROW AUTOMOBILE

MI —UNIVERSITY OF MICHIGAN, Engineering-Transportation Library, 312 Undergraduate Library, Ann Arbor, 48109. Sharon A Balius, Assoc Librn
Holdings: Pix
Notes: The collection contains original advertising material, owners' manuals, and 1500 factory photographs.

PIERCE FAMILY

CA —UNIVERSITY OF CALIFORNIA, DAVIS, Shields Library, Dept of Special Collections, Davis, 95616. Donald Kunitz, Head; C Daniel Elliott, Asst Head
Holdings: Cat Mss Pix
Notes: The Pierce Papers contain general and family correspondence, business and legal papers, photographs, and related printed material of an early Davis, California, family, as well as material relating to the purchase to the University of California, Davis, and to the California Almond Growers' Exchange (1075 items).

PIERPONT, HEZEKIAH BEERS, 1768-1838

NY —NEW YORK PUBLIC LIBRARY, Rare Books and Manuscripts Div, Fifth Ave & 42 St, New York, 10018. William L Joyce, Asst Dir; Susan E Davis, Cur of Mss
Budget: ($7161)
Notes: Papers.

PIETISM

PA —LUTHERAN THEOLOGICAL SEMINARY, Krauth Memorial Library, 7301 Germantown Ave, Philadelphia, 19119. Rev David J Wartluft, Dir Libr
Holdings: Vols 1000 Cat
Notes: Strongest in 18th century German pietism.

PIEZOELECTRIC TRANSDUCERS

MA —HARVARD UNIVERSITY LIBRARY, Cambridge, 02138.
Notes: The papers of George Washington Pierce (1891-1955).

PIG see Swine

PIGEONS

OH —CLEVELAND PUBLIC LIBRARY, Science & Technology Dept, 325 Superior Ave, Cleveland, 44114. Jean Z Piety, Head
Holdings: Cat
Notes: Collection contains much on history and many early and rare volumes.

SC —COLLEGE OF CHARLESTON LIBRARY, Special Collections Dept, Charleston, 29401.
Notes: Contains biographical and family history material of Wendell Mitchel Levi; invertebrate anatomy course notes from the College of Charleston; University of Chicago Law School casebooks; correspondence

PIGEONS (cont.)

concerning pigeons and camellias; notes, photographs, mss, typescripts, and galleys of published works; and other materials relating to pigeons and camellias. Among the more prominent correspondents are B F Skinner, Madame Chiang Kai-Shek, and Mary Bonner.

PIGS see Swine

PIKES PEAK REGION

CO —HORTICULTURAL ART SOCIETY OF COLORADO SPRINGS, Library, Orchard House, 3202 Chambers Way, Colorado Springs, 80904. Ernestine H Fagan, Librn
Holdings: Vols (950)
Notes: Horticulture of the Pikes Peak Region.

PILCHER, REP. JOHN L.

GA —UNIVERSITY OF GEORGIA, Libraries, Special Collections Division, Athens, 30602. Vesta Lee Gordon, Asst Dir for Special Collections
Notes: Collection contains 1394.8 linear feet of mss: papers of US Senator Richard B Russell; US Congressmen John W Davis, Maston O'Neal, Robert G Stephens Jr, John L Pilcher, Dudley M Hughes; Governors Hoke Smith, Lester Maddox, Carl Sanders.

PILGRIM FATHERS

MA —BRIDGEWATER PUBLIC LIBRARY, 15 South St, Bridgewater, 02324. Maryellen Remmert, Dir
Holdings: Cat Mss Maps Pix
Notes: Incl some genealogical material of considerable interest since Bridgewater was the first inland colony of the Plymouth (Pilgrim) Colony, being known as the Duxbury Plantation.

PILGRIMAGE THEATRE, LOS ANGELES

CA —LOS ANGELES PUBLIC LIBRARY, Frances Howard Goldwyn Hollywood Regional Library, 1623 Ivar Ave, Los Angeles, 90028. Sally Dumaux, Librn
Holdings: Vols (100,000) Cat Pix VF
Budget: ($60,000)
Notes: Over 2000 playbills, photographs, posters, and programs of Los Angeles area theatre from the 1920s to the present. Collection includes *Turnabout Theatre Monthly Bulletin,* 1942-48, souvenir programs and flyers. Also Pilgrimage Theatre and Hollywood Bowl programs, 1922 to present. Gladys Littell Collection. Hollywood Bowl Sunrise Services, 1920s-1940s. Hollywood Conservatory of Music, 1920s. Hollywood Chamber of Commerce. Including correspondence, programs, working papers, and photographs.

PILLION, JOHN RAYMOND, 1904-

NY —CORNELL UNIVERSITY LIBRARIES, Collection of Regional History, Dept of Manuscripts and Univ Archives, Ithaca, 14853.
Notes: US Congressman, assemblyman, attorney. Incl papers, 1947-65; copies of bills he introduced, speeches, news releases, tape recordings, questionnaires, clipping scrapbooks, loose clippings from newspapers and periodicals, and much correspondence.

PILOT CHARTS see Nautical Charts

PILOTING—AIRPLANES see Airplanes—Piloting

PILOTLESS AIRCRAFT see Guided Missiles

PILOTS—SPACE SHIPS see Astronauts

PILOTS, WOMEN see Women in Aeronautics

PILSUDSKI, JOZEF

NY —JOZEF PILSUDSKI INSTITUTE FOR RESEARCH IN THE MODERN

HISTORY OF POLAND, INC, 381 Park Ave, South, New York, 10016.
Holdings: 12,000 Vols Mss Maps Pix Archive
Notes: Said to be the fourth largest Polish collection of documents in the world outside of Poland. Materials emphasize history since 1863. Incl 2000 periodicals.

PINCKNEY, CHARLES COTESWORTH

SC —COLLEGE OF CHARLESTON LIBRARY, Special Collections Dept, Charleston, 29401.
Notes: Papers incl Pinckney's plantation diary which contains lists of slaves, crop yields for 1817-19, listings of acreage owned, an account of a steamboat trip, and a tally of drum fish caught.

PINE, WILLIAM BLISS

OK —UNIVERSITY OF OKLAHOMA, Bizzell Memorial Library, Western History Collections, 401 W Brooks, Norman, 73069. John Ezell, Cur
Holdings: Mss Documents
Notes: US Senator. His papers. Guide available.

PINE TREE INDUSTRY

GA —UNIVERSITY OF GEORGIA, Libraries, Athens, 30602. Arlene E Luchsinger, Asst Dir Branch Libraries
Notes: Collection of over 1000 photographs on Southern forestry and the Southern logging industry, 1939-46. This gift, from the Southern Forest Institute, includes the records and files of four groups formed to solve specific problems of Southern forests.

PINE TREES

BC —CANADIAN FORESTRY SERVICE, Pacific Forest Research Centre, Library, 506 West Burnside Rd, Victoria, V8Z 1M5, Can. Alice Solyma, Librn
Holdings: Vols (60,500) Cat Microforms
Notes: Incl rearing, biological control, identification, dispersal, insect pest management, comprehensive collection re Mountain Pine Beetle, Western Spruce Budworm, Douglas Fir Tussack Moth.

PINERO, ARTHUR WING

NY —UNIVERSITY OF ROCHESTER, Rush Rhees Library, Department of Rare Books and Special Collections, Rochester, 14627. Peter Dzwonkoski, Librn
Holdings: Cat Mss Pix
Notes: Papers, etc, incl books by and about, etc.

PINKER, JAMES B., AND SONS

IL —SOUTHERN ILLINOIS UNIVERSITY, CARBONDALE, Delyte W Morris Library, Special Collections Dept, Carbondale, 62901. David V Koch, Cur of Special Collections; Louisa Bowen, Cur of Manuscripts
Holdings: Vols 850 Cat Mss Pix Tapes
Notes: The Dr H K Croessmann Collection of James Joyce (17 linear ft) incl the papers of Joyce's biographer, Herbert Gorman, his literary agent, James Pinker, and his German translator, Georg Goyert, and more than 200 of Joyce's letters. Inventory available in library.
IL —NORTHWESTERN UNIVERSITY, Library, Special Collections Dept, 1937 Sheridan Rd, Evanston, 60201. R Russell Maylone, Cur
Holdings: (9000) Cat Mss
Notes: First, limited, special editions, letters, ephemera of major 20th century Anglo-Irish and English writers such as James Joyce, W B Yeats, T S Eliot, W H Auden and Lawrence Durrell, as well as representative minor writers. Correspondence files of James B Pinker & Sons, literary agents: 50,000 pieces, 1900-1934 inclusive.

PINKHAM MEDICINE CO.

MA —RADCLIFFE COLLEGE, Arthur & Elizabeth Schlesinger Library on the History

of Women in America, 3 James St, Cambridge, 02138. Patricia Miller King, Dir; Eva Moseley, Cur of Mss
Holdings: // Cat Mss Pix Microforms
Notes: Business records of the (Lydia E) Pinkham Medicine Co incl financial and advertising records and miscellaneous materials on formulas, manufacturing, labelling, packaging, litigation, transactions with regulatory agencies, etc; some restricted materials on clinical tests; and a small amount of family papers, incl notebooks of Lydia E Pinkham. Partly microfilmed. Inventory published by G K Hall; see Hamilton Family for citation.

PINKLEY, FRANK

AZ —NORTHERN ARIZONA UNIVERSITY, Special Collection Library, CU Box 6022, Flagstaff, 86011. Peter M Whiteley, Coordr/Archivist; William Mullane, Librn
Notes: J C Clarke Collection; correspondence between the Department of the Interior and Clarke when he was custodian of Wupatki National Monument near Flagstaff, Ariz. Incl letters from Frank Pinkley, who was the Superintendent of Southwestern Monuments, National Park Service, 1924-1926, 1932.

PINTER, HAROLD

NY —HOFSTRA UNIVERSITY, Library, 1000 Fulton Ave, Hempstead, 11550. Charles R Andrews, Dean of Library Services
Notes: Strong collection. Incl some mss.

PIONEER LIFE see Frontier and Pioneer Life

PIONEER SOCIETY, COLORADO see Colorado Pioneer Society

PIONEER VALLEY, MASSACHUSETTS

MA —GREENFIELD COMMUNITY COLLEGE, Pioneer Valley Resource Center, One College Drive, Greenfield, 01301. Margaret E C Howland, Dir; Carol Letson, Librn
Notes: Houses a special collection of primary and secondary material on the area surrounding the Connecticut River in Western Massachusetts. Covers every aspect of the Pioneer Valley, past and present, incl art and artists, authors, census data, environment, ethnicity, geology, history, industry and commerce, literature, politics and government, etc. Separately housed. Open 20 hours a week.

PIONEERS see Frontier and Pioneer Life

PIONEERS, OIL see Oil Pioneers

PIOZZI, HESTER LYNCH THRALE AND GABRIEL

MA —HARVARD UNIVERSITY LIBRARY, Houghton Library, Cambridge, 02138. Rodney G Dennis, Cur of Manuscripts
Holdings: Cat Mss
†NY —COLUMBIA UNIVERSITY LIBRARIES, Butler Library, Rare Book and Manuscript Library, 535 W 114 St, New York, 10027.
Notes: Autographed diaries.

PIPE LINES

AK —ALASKA STATE LIBRARY, Alaska Historical Library Collection, Pouch G, Juneau, 99811. Phyllis Demuth, Readers Services Librn
Holdings: Vols (24,000) Cat Mss Maps Pix Slides Phonorecords Audiotapes Videotapes 16mm Films Microforms
MO —NATIONAL MUSEUM OF TRANSPORT, Reference Library, 3105 Barrett Station Rd, Saint Louis, 63122. John P Roberts, Secretary
Holdings: Vols (10,000) Cat Mss Maps Pix Slides

PIPE LINES (cont.)

TX —TRANSCONTINENTAL GAS PIPE LINE CORP, Corporate Library, PO Box 1396, Houston, 77251. Cheryl L Watson, Librn; Jane Mascher, Library Specialist
Holdings: Vols (8000) Cat

TX —ECTOR COUNTY LIBRARY, Department of Business and Technology, 321 W 5th St, Odessa, 79760. Pat Jones, Dept Head
Notes: Incl 100 vertical files, 25 periodicals, 250 Trade Standards. Collections concentrated on the Drilling and Production industries. Also included are Exploration methods Reservoir Development, Pipeline, Construction, Well Servicing, Well Logging, and Well Control. Complete collection of the API Specifications, and Complete Welding "library".

MB —UNIVERSITY OF MANITOBA, Elizabeth Dafoe Library, Government Publications Section, Winnipeg, R3T 2N2, Can. June Dutka, Head
Holdings: Uncat Maps Pix Microforms
Notes: The Canadian National Energy Board's Polar Gas Project documentation provides an extremely useful source of information describing the proposed construction of the pipeline route which would generally pass from the Arctic Islands through the Northwest Territories, northern Manitoba and into Ontario Canada.

PIPE-ORGAN see Organ

PIPES, TOBACCO see Tobacco Pipes

PIRACY see Pirates and Piracy

PIRANESI, GIOVANNI BATTISTA

NY —COLUMBIA UNIVERSITY LIBRARIES, Avery Architectural and Fine Arts Library, 201 Avery Hall, New York, 10027. Angela Giral, Librn
Notes: Drawings (24) for proposed rebuilding of the Church of Saint Giovanni in Laterano, Rome (Sackler Collections). Ms account book of rebuilding of the Church of Santa Maria Aventino, Rome. Extensive collection of Piransei etchings, featuring the Dr Arthur M Sackler Collection. Restricted use. Appointment necessary.

PIRATES AND PIRACY

IL —MILLIKIN UNIVERSITY, Staley Library, 1184 W Main St, Decatur, 62522. Charles E Hale, Librn
Holdings: Vols 50 Cat Mss Pix
Budget: $100
Notes: The Stephen Decatur Collection. The core of this collection was given by John Valentine (1895-1955) to the Millkin University Library in 1947. Also have realia of coins, busts, etc.

KS —WICHITA PUBLIC LIBRARY, 223 S Main, Wichita, 67202. Richard Rademacher, Librn
Holdings: Vols 1600 Mss Maps
Notes: The Driscoll Piracy Collection is one of the largest on the subject, incl miscellaneous Parliamentary acts, books, broadsides, scrapbooks, etc; many rarities in books, logs, and some mss. Collection was begun by Charles Driscoll, author. Not loaned.

MA —BOSTON COLLEGE LIBRARIES, Thomas P O'Neill Library, Nicholas M Williams Ethnological Collection, Chestnut Hill, 02167. Frank J Seegraber, Special Collections Librn
Holdings: Vols 10,000 // Cat Mss Maps
Notes: Collection emphasizes Caribbeana, especially Jamaica, to 1940. Incl discovery, exploration and natural history of the British, French and Spanish settlements; the slave question; piracy. There are over 6000 mss, 5000 of which are Anansi folk tales recorded by native school children. Also small ancillary sections of Africana and Judaica. For reference use only, by arrangement with librarian.

NY —NEW YORK PUBLIC LIBRARY, Research Libraries, Science and Technology Research Center, Fifth Ave & 42 St, New York, 10018.
Holdings: Vols (1,100,000) Cat Microforms
Budget: ($647,259)

PIRNIE, ALEXANDER, 1903-

NY —CORNELL UNIVERSITY LIBRARIES, Collection of Regional History, Dept of Manuscripts and Univ Archives, Ithaca, 14853.
Notes: Papers, (1965-70)-72; 38 ft. Attorney, Congressman. Restricted.

PISCATOR, ERWIN

IL —SOUTHERN ILLINOIS UNIVERSITY, CARBONDALE, Delyte W Morris Library, Special Collections Dept, Carbondale, 62901. David V Koch, Cur of Special Collections; Louisa Bowen, Cur of Manuscripts
Holdings: Vols 160 Cat Mss Pix
Notes: The personal papers and business records of Erwin Piscator, internationally known producer, director and playwright, associated with the epic theater. This extensive collection consists of scripts, playbills, photographs, business records of various productions abroad, correspondence with actors, directors and playwright (incl Bertold Brecht), both in America and Europe, and family papers. Also the papers of his widow, Dr Maria Piscator, ballerine, playwright, directors and novelist. (Akademie der Kunste, Berlin, *Erwin Piscator, 1893-1966*, 1971.) Detailed inventory and name index available at the library.

PISCES see Fishes

PISCICULTURE see Fish Culture

PISE, REV. CHARLES CONSTANTINE

DC —GEORGETOWN UNIVERSITY, Library, Special Collections Div, 37 & O Sts NW, Washington, 20057. George M Barringer, Special Collections Librn; Nicholas B Sheetz, Mss Librn
Holdings: Mss Cat
Notes: Correspondence, mss, and related materials concerning Fr Pise's voyage to Rome in 1820; his Senate chaplaincy (1832); and his later pastoral and literary career in New York City.

PISTOLS

†WA —WASHINGTON STATE UNIVERSITY, Library, Manuscripts, Archives & Special Collections, Pullman, 99164. John F Guido, Head
Holdings: Cat Mss Maps Pix
Notes: The Carl Parcher Russell papers, a vast resource (24,916 items; 45 linear feet) on American Indian and Western pioneer activities and artifacts. Much on the fur trade; pioneer life; mountain men and trapping; wildlife; primitive life in detail. Also the National Park Service, parks, monuments, etc. Described in *Carl Parcher Russell: An Indexed Register of His Scholarly and Professional Papers, 1920-1967, in the Washington State University Library* (Pullman, 1970), 149 pp.

PISTON, WALTER

MA —BOSTON PUBLIC LIBRARY, Rare Books and Manuscripts, Copley Square, Boston, 02117. Laura V Monti, Keeper of Rare Books
Notes: Gift of the composer, the collection represents Piston's library as it was maintained in his home in Belmont, Mass. The collection is housed in a replica of his study in a room adjoining the Koussevitzky Room. In addition to the collection of books and scores in the Piston Room, papers, correspondence, scrapbooks, and holographs are kept in the Rare Books and Manuscripts Department.

PIT RIVER INDIANS

CA —UNIVERSITY OF CALIFORNIA, LOS ANGELES, Research Library, Dept of Special Collections, 405 Hilgard Ave, Los Angeles, 90024. Edward Shreeves, Chairman, Bibliographers Group; David S Zeidberg, Head
Holdings: Vols Mss Pix
Notes: Books, letters, mss, and photographs collected by Jaime de Angulo.

PITCAIRN ISLANDS

CA —PACIFIC UNION COLLEGE, Nelson Memorial Library, Angwin, 94508. Taylor D Ruhl, Dir

PITTS, JAMES A.

AZ —NORTHERN ARIZONA UNIVERSITY, Special Collection Library, CU Box 6022, Flagstaff, 86011. Peter M Whiteley, Coordr/Archivist; William Mullane, Librn
Notes: Seligman, Ariz. Incl correspondence, 1912, 1918, with Henry F Ashurst and a pioneer reminiscence of his childhood in Flagstaff, and friendship with Ashurst.

PITTSBURGH, PENNSYLVANIA—HISTORY

PA —CARNEGIE LIBRARY OF PITTSBURGH, Pennsylvania Div, 4400 Forbes Ave, Pittsburgh, 15213. Maria Zini, Head
Holdings: Vols (24,000) Cat Mss Maps Pix Microforms
Budget: ($6000)
Notes: Collection contains at least one history of each county; historical atlases; biography; church histories; sociological and economic studies; journals of the General Assembly; state documents. The Pittsburgh section of the collection includes Pittsburgh directories 1815-date; newspapers on microfilm 1786-date, 30,000 photographs relating to Pittsburgh. A 65-drawer clipping collection supplements the published works. The genealogical materials (approx 5000 vols) incl individual family histories; regional and general genealogical works; periodicals; US. Census enumerations for Pennsylvania 1790-1910 (microfilm); indexes to biography, deaths and marriages. Separate catalog to entire Division. Collection is reference only.

PA —HISTORICAL SOCIETY OF WESTERN PENNSYLVANIA, 4338 Bigelow Blvd, Pittsburgh, 15213. Helen M Wilson, Librn
Holdings: Vols 500 Cat Mss Maps Pix
See also entry under Pennsylvania - History

PA —UNIVERSITY OF PITTSBURGH, Hillman Library, Archives of Industrial Society, 363 Hillman Library, Pittsburgh, 15260. Frank A Zabrosky, Cur
Holdings: Mss Maps Pix Microforms Audiotapes
Notes: Broad subject area covers the history of urban, industrial society since ca 1850. Incl primary source material from Pittsburgh, Western Pennsylvania and West Virginia areas. Comprised of business, industrial, church, ethnic, labor, fraternal and social organization, political party, political/social movement,and city government records and private papers of individuals and families. Primarily a manuscript collection for graduate and post-graduate research. Unique collection: Allegheny, Pa, city records, 3000 vols, incl tax assessment records (1840-1907); Pittsburgh schools system, 150 vols, incl minutes, pupil enrollment records; voter registration records for Allegheny County, and Pittsburgh, 1935-1960; election return books, Allegheny County and Pittsburgh, 1926 date; Pittsburgh and Lake Erie Railroad and Photograph Collection; Pittsburgh City Photographers Photo Collection;1000 city directories for US cities, 1955-71; and political papers of US Congressmen Corbett, Fulton and Holland. Archives of the national headquarters, districts and locals of the United Electrical, Radio and Machine Workers of America (UE); printed and manuscript material on Blacks and ethnic groups in Pittsburgh.

PA —UNIVERSITY OF PITTSBURGH, Darlington Memorial Library, Special

PITTSBURGH, PENNSYLVANIA—HISTORY (cont.)

Collections, 601 Cathedral of Learning, Pittsburgh, 15260. Dennis Lambert, Darlington Librn
Holdings: Vols (17,000) Cat Mss Maps Pix
Notes: The Darlington Collection is especially rich in American history of the colonial period, the French and Indian war, the Revolution and the War of 1812 with geographical emphasis on Western Pennsylvania and Ohio Valley history to 1870 and on Pittsburgh history to 1900. Indian treaties, captivity accounts, US and Pennsylvania travel and description and early American fiction and prose are represented. A partial guide to the Darlington Manuscripts Collections is available by writing for *Darlington Memorial Library: A Descriptive Checklist of its Manuscripts Collections*, University of Pittsburgh Bibliographic Series 5, 1969. Noncirculating.

PITTSBURGH, SHAWMUT AND NORTHERN RAILROAD COMPANY

NY —CORNELL UNIVERSITY LIBRARIES, Collection of Regional History, Dept of Manuscripts and Univ Archives, Ithaca, 14853.
Notes: Papers, 1872-1960. Materials included are for PS&N, predecessors, affiliates, and otherwise connected lines. Among them are the Lackawanna & Southwestern; Allegany Central; Brookville & Mahoning; Buffalo and Susquehanna; Buffalo, St Marys & Southwestern; Central New York and Western; Clarion River Railway; Erie Narrow Guage System; Friendship Rail Road Company; Genesee River, Lackawanna & Pittsburgh; Kane and Elk; Lackawanna & Pittsburgh; Mt Jewett and Smethport; Mt Jewett, Kinzua & Riterville; New York & Pennsyulvania; Olean Rail Road Company; Rochester, Hornellsville & Lackawanna; Rochester, Hornellsville & Lackawanna; Rochester, New York and Pennsylvania; and Tionesta Valley Railway.

PITTSBURGH LANDING, BATTLE OF, 1862 see Shiloh, Battle of, 1862

PITTSBURGH PLAYHOUSE

PA —UNIVERSITY OF PITTSBURGH, Special Collections Dept, Curtis Theatre Collection, 363 Hillman Library, Pittsburgh, 15260. Jeanette Blanco, Cur
Holdings: Mss Documents Pix
Notes: Records incl board minutes, pressbooks, correspondence, programs, photographs, etc, 1934-1974.

PITTSBURGH SAVOYARDS

PA —UNIVERSITY OF PITTSBURGH, Special Collections Dept, Curtis Theatre Collection, 363 Hillman Library, Pittsburgh, 15260. Jeanette Blanco, Cur
Holdings: Mss Pix
Notes: Pittsburgh Savoyards records.
See also entry under Theatre - Pittsburgh.

PLACE-NAMES see Names, Geographical

PLACE, WILLIAM

MA —SOCIETY FOR THE PRESERVATION OF NEW ENGLAND ANTIQUITIES, Library, 141 Cambridge St, Boston, 02114. Ellie Reichlin, Librn & Cur of Photographic Collections
Notes: Original drwaings by this Rhode Island architect for vernacular, residential, and commercial buildings. 100 pieces.

PLAGEMANN, BENTZ

MA —BOSTON UNIVERSITY, Mugar Memorial Library, Special Collections Dept, 771 Commonwealth Ave, Boston, 02215. Howard B Gotlieb, Dir
Holdings: Cat Mss Pix
Notes: Mss, correspondence, etc collected in depth; incl publications by or about.

PLAGUE

MD —MEDICAL & CHIRURGICAL FACULTY OF THE STATE OF MARYLAND, Library, 1211 Cathedral St, Baltimore, 21201. Joseph E Jensen, Librn
Holdings: Vols (10,000) // Cat Mss Maps Pix
See also entry under Medicine - History and Historic

OH —MIAMI UNIVERSITY, Science Library, Oxford, 45056.
Notes: Zoonoses and related diseases. Collection partially transferred from Parker-Davis Memorial Library, Hamilton, Mont.

TX —UNIVERSITY OF TEXAS, DALLAS, Health Science Center, Reference Dept & History of Health Sciences Dept, 5323 Harry Hines Blvd, Dallas, 75235. Helen Mayo, Head
Holdings: Vols (10,000) Cat Pix Slides Audiotapes Videotapes Microforms
Notes: History of Medicine collection contains ca 10,000 vols. This total is comprised of pre-1900 journals, primary materials in the History of Medicine and the History of Science, and secondary studies in these two areas. The major strengths of this collection are in the areas of epidemics and plagues, military medicine, and collected works of famous medical pioneers. Incl in this collection are the medical journals published by the county medical societies in Texas, local publications by Dallas County medical organizations, and ephemeral material in a similar vein. The university archives contain all theses and dissertations form UTHSCD and miscellaneous institutional documents circulated by the school's administration.

PLAGUE TRACTS

CT —YALE UNIVERSITY, Medical Historical Library, Klebs Collection, 333 Cedar St, New Haven, 06520. Ferenc A Gyorgyey, Librn
Notes: The Arnold Carl Klebs Medical Collection books, pamphlets, etc, incl the library of his father, Edwin T A Klebs, pathologist. Strong in bibliography of early printed medical books, herbals, plague tracts, inoculation, vaccination and tubercular diseases.

TX —UNIVERSITY OF TEXAS, DALLAS, Health Science Center, Reference Dept & History of Health Sciences Dept, 5323 Harry Hines Blvd, Dallas, 75235. Helen Mayo, Head
Holdings: Vols (10,000) Cat Pix Slides Audiotapes Videotapes Microforms
Notes: History of Medicine collection contains ca 10,000 vols. This total is comprised of pre-1900 journals, primary materials in the History of Medicine and the History of Science, and secondary studies in these two areas. The major strengths of this collection are in the areas of epidemics and plagues, military medicine, and collected works of famous medical pioneers. Incl in this collection are the medical journals published by the county medical societies in Texas, local publications by Dallas County medical organizations, and ephemeral material in a similar vein. The university archives contain all theses and dissertations form UTHSCD and miscellaneous institutional documents circulated by the school's administration.

PLAINS, THE GREAT see Great Plains

PLAINS INDIANS

CT —LEE ASH, (personal collection), 66 Humiston Dr, Bethany, 06525.
Holdings: Mss Maps Pix

IA —IOWA FALLS PUBLIC LIBRARY, 520 Rocksylvania, Iowa Falls, 50126. Deanne Keller, Librn
Holdings: Vols (500) Cat

NE —NEIHARDT STUDY CENTER, Library, Bancroft, 68004. John Lindahl, Cur; Ann Reinert, Librn
Notes: The Center will preserve the published works and papers of John G Neihardt, State Poet Laureate and authority on Plains Indians.

NE —NEBRASKA STATE HISTORICAL SOCIETY, Archives, 1500 R St, Box 82554, Lincoln, 68501. James E Potter, State Archivist
Holdings: Uncat Mss
Notes: Collection and mss of Judge E S Ricker of Dawes County, Nebraska, concerning Indians of the Great Plains and their final conflict with the white man. Interviews with soldiers, cowboys, trappers, and Indians.

NE —UNIVERSITY OF NEBRASKA-LINCOLN, Don L Love Library, Lincoln, 68588. Joseph G Svoboda, University Archivist
Holdings: Vols (1000) // Uncat Mss Maps Pix Audiotapes 16mm Films
Notes: The

NV —UNIVERSITY OF NEVADA, RENO, University Library, Special Collections Dept, Reno, 89557. Robert E Blesse, Head
Holdings: Vols 1100 Mss Pix
Notes: Incl over 5000 photographs, government documents, periodicals, 80 cubic feet, mss, and audiotapes. The Great Basin Indian Collection contains materials on the anthropology, archaeology, and ethnohistory of the Great Basin region. Materials are collected for a defined group of 65 tribes incl Washo, Shoshone, Northern and Southern Paiute, the major tribes of the region. Collection of importance incl the Sven Liljeblad Collection, linguistics and ethnography; papers of US agent Lorenzo D Greel, 1902-22; Robert Leland Collection, Indian water rights.

SD —AUGUSTANA COLLEGE, Mikkelsen Library & Learning Resource Center, Center for Western Studies, Sioux Falls, 57197. Ronelle Thompson, Dir Library
Notes: The Center for Western Studies, located in the Mikkelsen Library, is an archival and research agency of Augustana College. Dedicated to the history and culture of the Great Plains and the Trans-Mississippi West, the Center collects and preserves materials relating to Plains Indians, immigrant settlers, Norwegiana, Western Americana, Herbert Krause, Frederick Manfred, Donald Parker, Richard F Pettigrew, Augustana College, the Episcopal Diocese of South Dakota, the South Dakota District of the American Lutheran Church, the South Dakota Penitentiary and Minnehaha County.

SD —SIOUXLAND HERITAGE MUSEUMS, Pettigrew Museum Library, 131 N Duluth Ave, Sioux Falls, 57104. Ms Lee N McLaird, Cur of Collections
Holdings: Vols (7500) Cat Mss Maps Pix
Budget: ($900)
Notes: Pettigrew Museum Library is a support service of the Siouxland Heritage Museums. US Senator R F Pettigrew established the core collection in 1926, covering natural history (incl North American Indian anthropology) and state-local history (concentrating on exploration and settlement to about 1900). The collection also incl the Senator's private papers (ca 1870-1926). Additions to the collection since 1926 have emphasized Plains Indian anthropology, state-local history, baseball and museology, supporting the work of the Museum staff. The collection is mostly cataloged and is inter-indexed with Augustana College, Sioux Falls College, and Sioux Falls Public Libraries (as well as having its own catalog). The photograph collection includes prints by D F Barry as well as other photographers' work with native peoples.The photograph collection incl photos of Petigrew, his family, and his business enterprises.

PLANETARIA

CA —GRIFFITH OBSERVATORY, Library, 2800 E Observatory Rd, Los Angeles, 90027. E C Krupp, Dir
Holdings: Vols Cat Pix Slides Phonorecords
Budget: ($1000)
Notes: No separate catalog. No photocopying.

PLANETARIA (cont.)

IL —ADLER PLANETARIUM, Reference Library, 1300 S Lake Shore Dr, Chicago, 60605. Tim Blackman, Librn
Holdings: Vols (6500) Cat Maps
Budget: ($5000)
Notes: Noncirculating; no photocopying.

NC —SCHIELE MUSEUM OF NATURAL HISTORY, Library, 1500 E Garrison Blvd, Gastonia, 28052. Dot Gray, Librn; Margaret Summerill, Librn
Holdings: Vols (3800) Cat Maps Pix Slides Phonorecords Audiotapes 16mm Films Filmstrips Microforms
Budget: ($2800)
Notes: Listed on RECON computer with Library of Congress as Reference Center in Southeast in subject areas of natural sciences, aerospace and planetarium technology, and anthropology.

PA —READING SCHOOL DISTRICT PLANETARIUM, Library, 1211 Parkside Dr S, Reading, 19611. Bruce L Dietrich, Dir
Holdings: Vols (640) Cat Maps Pix Slides Phonorecords Audiotapes 16mm Films
Budget: ($1000)
Notes: Incl 400 maps, 1000 pictures, 7300 slides and 110 audiotapes.

AB —CENTENNIAL PLANETARIUM, Library, PO Box 2100, 701 Eleventh St, Calgary, T2P 2M5, Can. Sig Wieser, Librn
Holdings: Vols (400) Uncat Pix Audiotapes 16mm Films
Notes: Also western Canadian aviation history with bias towards technology; and history of space technology.

PLANETARY GEOLOGY see Geology, Planetary

PLANETS

CA —CALIFORNIA INSTITUTE OF TECHNOLOGY, Geology Library, Pasadena, 91125. Daphne Plane, Geology Librn
Holdings: Vols 25,000 Cat Maps Microforms
Notes: Incl 1000 microforms, 11,750 books, and 879 serials.

DC —SMITHSONIAN INSTITUTION LIBRARIES, National Air & Space Museum Branch, NASM Bldg, Sixth & Independence Ave SW, Washington, 20560. Frank A Pietropaoli, Branch Chief
Holdings: Vols (39,000) Cat Mss Maps Pix Slides Microforms
Notes: History of flight and aerospace development, incl biographical material on aviation pioneers, balloons and ballooning. Extensive photographic collection (600,000 pictures). Incl the Sherman Fairchild Collection of aeronautical photographs (transferred from the American Institute of Aeronautics and Astronautics). Also incl the Bella Landauer Aeronautical Sheet Music Collection (1500 pieces). 2000 films; 800,000 microforms; 9000 volumes bound.

TX —LUNAR & PLANETARY INSTITUTE, Library/Information Center, 3303 Nasa Rd One, Houston, 77058. Frances B Waranius, Library/Information Center Mgr
Holdings: Cat Mss Maps Pix Slides Microforms
Notes: Development of collection begun in 1972 to incl lunar studies from approx 1950 forward. Planets, meteorites, asteroids and comets added 1978. Seek to become as inclusive as possible.

PLANETS, MINOR see Asteroids

PLANKTON RESEARCH

ME —BIGELOW LABORATORY FOR OCEAN SCIENCES & MAINE DEPT OF MARINE RESOURCES, Library, McKown Point, West Boothbay Harbor, 04575. Pamela Shephard-Lupo, Librn
Holdings: Vols Cat Periodicals Mss
Budget: ($55,000)
Notes: This library presently serves two institutions. The Maine Dept of Marine Resources has maintained the library since 1957 and thus the majority of our holdings

are geared to their needs, ie fish biology and stock assessment on a local, national and international level. In 1973 Bigelow Laboratory for Ocean Sciences came to West Boothbay Harbor and began to contribute to the library with a very specialized collection on the Gulf of Maine marine chemistry, phytoplankton and nutrient cycles.

PLANNING

CA —UNIVERSITY OF CALIFORNIA, BERKELEY, Institute of Governmental Studies Library, 109 Moses Hall, Berkeley, 94720. Jack Leister, Head Librn
Holdings: Vols (350,000) Cat Mss Maps Microforms
Budget: ($160,000)
Notes: The library collects primarily pamphlets. Incl in the library's holdings are documents from all levels of government, as well as publication issued by professional associations and special interest groups. A G K Hall catalog covering the Institute's Library holdings is available. Since 1937, Library has been depository for all California local documents (city, county & special district). Formerly: Bureau of Public Administration.

MA —HARVARD UNIVERSITY, Graduate School of Business Administration, Baker Library, Soldiers Field, Boston, 02163. Mary V Chatfield, Librn; Florence Bartoshesky, Cur of Manuscripts and Archives
Notes: Organizations, organizational behavior and planning.

OR —UNIVERSITY OF OREGON, Library, Eugene, 97403. Kenneth W Duckett, Curator
Notes: Papers of Prof Charles McKinley, incl files of correspondence, minutes, reports, position papers concerning (largely) public administration and planning.

PLANNING, CITY see Cities and Towns—Planning

PLANNING, ECONOMIC see Economic Policy

PLANNING, NATIONAL see Economic Policy

PLANNING, REGIONAL see Regional Planning

PLANNING, SOCIAL see Social Policy

PLANNING, STATE see Economic Policy; Regional Planning

PLANS see Architectural Drawings; Maps and Atlases—Collections; Mechanical Drawing

PLANT, RICHARD, 1911-

NY —STATE UNIVERSITY OF NEW YORK AT ALBANY, Library, Special Collections Dept, 1400 Washington Ave, Albany, 12222. Marion P Munzer, Coordr
Notes: Correspondence of Richard Plant (0.5 linear feet); incl mss, reviews of moving pictures and plays. Part of the Library's German Exile Collection.
See also entry under Theatre

PLANT BREEDING

CA —UNIVERSITY OF CALIFORNIA, DAVIS, General Library, Davis, 95616. Bernard Kreissman, University Librn; C Danial Elliott, Asst Head, Dept Special Collections
Notes: The collection emphasizes general works on genetics, evolution and variation. The collection is particularly strong in works dealing with plant and animal breeding.

NY —CORNELL UNIVERSITY LIBRARIES, Collection of Regional History, Dept of Manuscripts and Univ Archives, Ithaca, 14853.
Notes: Incl records, (1907-1948)-1964; correspondence, reports, and data relating to

research conducted at Cornell University's Department of Plant Breeding, agricultural assistance work undertaken by the department in the Phillipines, and consideration of similar work in Taiwan and Thailand.

PA —CARNEGIE LIBRARY OF PITTSBURGH, Science & Technology Dept, 4400 Forbes Ave, Pittsburgh, 15213. Catherine M Brosky, Dept Head
Holdings: Vols (380,000) Cat Maps Microforms
Budget: ($240,000)
Notes: Now of secondary importance, this subject was extensively developed from 1902 to 1945. Abstracts, indexes, bibliographis and the important reference books. There are some old and rare items in the original and some important compilations, sets and journals are available. Covers plant classification, physiology, nutrition, breeding, pathology, structural botany, plant chemistry, economic botany, plant history and geography.

PLANT CHEMISTRY see Botanical Chemistry

PLANT CHEMISTRY

OH —LLOYD LIBRARY & MUSEUM, 917 Plum St, Cincinnati, 45202. John B Griggs, Librn
Notes: Extensive holdings in plant chemistry.

PLANT CLASSIFICATION see Botany—Classification

PLANT DISEASES

CA —CALIFORNIA STATE POLYTECHNIC UNIVERSITY, POMONA, University Library, 3801 W Temple Ave, Pomona, 91768. Harold Schleiser, Actg Dir
Notes: General reference materials on agricultural business management, agricultural engineering, animal science, horticulture and plant and soil science.

CA —UNIVERSITY OF CALIFORNIA, RIVERSIDE, University Library, Bio-Agricultural Library, Batchelor Hall, Riverside, 92521. Barbara Montanary, Head
Holdings: Vols (130,000) Cat Mss Maps Pix Microforms
Notes: The Bio-Agricultural Library (formerly the Library of Citrus Experiment Station of the University of California) is well known for its complete collections in the fields of the agriculture sciences. It is especially known for its emphasis on entomology, incl bio-control; botany, citriculture, plant sciences, nematology and plant pathology; arid and semi-arid lands research and subtropical agriculture. Specific areas of interest are avocados, dates, desert flora, jojoba, guayule and carob.

FL —FLORIDA DEPARTMENT OF AGRICULTURE & CONSUMER SERVICES, Div of Plant Industry, Library, PO Box 1269, Gainesville, 32602. June B Jacobson, Librn; Alice Richards, Asst Librn
Holdings: Vols (11,455) Cat Mss Microforms
Budget: ($23,798)
Notes: Collection is primarily taxonomic. 464 periodical, current and antiquariat titles.

IL —ILLINOIS NATURAL HISTORY SURVEY LIBRARY, 196 Natural Resources Bldg, Champaign, 61820. Carla G Heister, Librn
Holdings: Vols (36,000) Cat Microforms
Budget: ($25,500)
Notes: A Research and Science Branch of the State of Illinois, the Natural History Survey maintains a library of books, journals and reports on various aspects of natural history. Material is collected in all major languages. The library maintains its own exchange arrangements with some 600 worldwide institutions and organizations. Interlibrary loans and photocopy services are available through the University of Illinois Library. Publications issued regularly by the Survey incl *Biological Notes, The Bulletin, and Circulars.*

PLANT DISEASES (cont.)

IL —MORTON ARBORETUM, Sterling
Morton Library, Lisle, 60532. Ian MacPhail,
Librn
Holdings: Vols (20,000) Cat Maps Pix
Budget: ($10,000)
Notes: The library is especially concerned
with the literature of woody plants (trees
and shrubs) of north temperate zones but has
substantial holdings in the taxonomy and
systematics of plants in general, both wild
and cultivated, flora of different parts of the
world, and a growing collection on plant
monographs. Also about 2000 pictures.
Described in *The Morton Arboretum
Quarterly*, vol 9, no 4 (Winter 1973), pp 56-
61.

IA —IOWA STATE UNIVERSITY, Library,
Ames, 50011. Warren B Kuhn, Dean of
Library Services
Holdings: Cat Mss
Notes: Specific strengths: botanical
taxonomy, ferns, mycology and plant
pathology. Extensive serial holdings.

IA —BICKELHAUPT ARBORETUM FREE
LENDING LIBRARY, 340 S Fourteenth St,
Clinton, 52732. Francie B Hill, Librn
Notes: Strong on indoor plants, horticulture,
ecology, energy conservation, plant
entomology and pathology, urban tree
planting; also curriculum materials. Over
3000 slides available for lending.

KY —UNIVERSITY OF KENTUCKY,
Agricultural Library, Agricultural Science
Center North, Lexington, 40506. Antoinette
Paris Powell, Librn
Holdings: Vols (90,000) Cat Microforms
Budget: ($110,385)

LA —LOUISIANA STATE UNIVERSITY,
Troy H Middleton Library, Louisiana Room,
Baton Rouge, 70803. Evangeline Mills
Lynch, Head Librn; Ruth Murray, Associate
Librn
Holdings: Vols (33,500) Cat Maps VF
Notes: Louisiana Collection of history,
description and travel, biography,
agriculture, literature, politics and
government, folklore, anthropology,
geography, geology, education, language,
music and natural history. Especially large
subject collections may be found on
Louisiana, the history of the lower
Mississippi Valley, Abraham Lincoln,
Romance languages and literatures, sugar
culture and technology, Southern history,
petroleum engineering, plant pathology,
micropaleontology, ornithology, and various
aspects of crawfish life, biology and culture.
Complete depository of Louisiana State
Documents; extensive newspapers clipping
files; separate card catalog; items listed in
Louisiana Union Catalog; restricted use
(research and reference). Incl both materials
about Louisiana and by Louisianians without
regard to subject. LSU Press
Collection(preservation copy of each title
kept for exhibit purposes only). LSU theses
and dissertations from 1900-date. LSU
Faculty Collection. Also, 1300 maps, 104 VF
drawers, 250 boxes of uncataloged
pamphlets.

LA —US FOREST SERVICE, Southern Forest
Experiment Station Library, T-10210 Postal
Service Bldg, 701 Loyola Ave, New Orleans,
70113. Linda A Korb, Librn
Holdings: Vols (50,000) Cat 16mm Films VF
Budget: ($100,000)
Notes: Field library of the National
Agricultural Library (USDA), serving
research scientists of the Southern Forest
Experiment Station at headquarters in New
Orleans and in seven states of the Mid-South
and Puerto Rico.

MA —UNIVERSITY OF MASSACHUSETTS
AT AMHERST, Library, Amherst, 01003.
Siegfried Feller, Assoc Dir for Collection
Development
Holdings: Cat
Notes: Botanical taxonomy, physiology,
pathology and mycology.

MI —MICHIGAN STATE UNIVERSITY,
Science Library, East Lansing, 48824. Carole
S Armstrong, Head
Holdings: Vols 18,900 Cat
Notes: Collection has 390 journal titles with
9300 vols and 9600 monographs.

NY —NEW YORK BOTANICAL GARDEN
LIBRARY, Bronx, 10458. Charles R Long,
Asst Vice Pres & Dir
Holdings: Vols 25,000 Cat Mss Pix Slides
Microforms VF
Budget: ($356,000)
Notes: One of the largest botanical
collections in the world. Covers botany (150,
000 vols), botanists (3000), horticulture (45,
000), plant diseases (25,000), plant
physiology (15,000), history of botany
(1500), conservation of natural resources
(15,000), gardening (13,000), paleobotany
(7000), ecology (20,000), forestry (5000),
medical botany (3000), agriculture (9000)
and biology (20,000). Reference library;
materials do not circulate, except via
standard inter-library loan. About 5000 vols
uncataloged. Incl archives, art and vertical
files. An OCLC library.

NY —BOYCE THOMPSON INSTITUTE
FOR PLANT RESEARCH, Library, Cornell
University, Tower Rd, Ithaca, 14853. Greta
Colavito, Librn
Holdings: Vols (5300) Cat
Budget: ($46,000)
Notes: Mainly plant physiology,
biochemistry, entomology, air and water
pollution, pesticides, and plant pathology.

NY —CORNELL UNIVERSITY LIBRARIES,
Collection of Regional History, Dept of
Manuscripts and Univ Archives, Ithaca,
14853.
Notes: Records (1908-59) of the Cornell
University Department of Plant Pathology.
Incl a seminar book, class record books,
exams, class registrations and other records.
Also incl field reports, 1919-29, concerning
control of insect pests and plant diseases;
also, one vol of summaries of final reports.
Unpublished guide available.

†NC —UNIVERSITY OF NORTH
CAROLINA, CHAPEL HILL, Department
of Botany Library, 301 Coker Hall 010-A,
Chapel Hill, 27514. William R Burk, Botany
Librn
Notes: The mycology collection incl some
6000 pamphlets. It contains papers of the
following scientists: William C Coker, John
N Couch, Lindsay F Olive, mycologists;
also, Victor A Greulach, plant pathologist.
The mycology catalog is in preparation
(1983), and will provide author, title, and
subject access.

OH —OHIO STATE UNIVERSITY, Biological
Sciences Library, 1735 Neil Ave, Columbus,
43210. Victoria Welborn, Librn
Holdings: Vols (85,000) Cat Mss Maps
Microforms

OH —OHIO AGRICULTURAL RESEARCH
& DEVELOPMENT CENTER, Dept of
Plant Pathology, Madison Ave, Wooster,
44691. Richard M Ritter
Holdings: Vols 2000 Papers Journal Reprints
Notes: Virus diseases of corn. "Maize Virus
Information Service."

PA —UNIVERSITY OF PENNSYLVANIA,
Morris Arboretum Library, 9414
Meadowbrook Ave, Philadelphia, 19118.
Holdings: Vols 6000

PA —CARNEGIE LIBRARY OF
PITTSBURGH, Science & Technology Dept,
4400 Forbes Ave, Pittsburgh, 15213.
Catherine M Brosky, Dept Head
Notes: Now of secondary importance, this
subject was extensively developed from 1902
to 1945. Abstracts, indexes, bibliographies
and the important reference books. There are
some old and rare items in the original and
some important compilations, sets and
journals are available. Covers plant
classification, physiology, nutrition, breeding,
pathology, structural botany, plant
chemistry, economic botany, plant history
and geography.

WA —WASHINGTON STATE
UNIVERSITY, Owen Science &
Engineering Library, Pullman, 99164.
Elizabeth P Roberts, Head
Holdings: Vols 8900 Cat Microforms
Notes: Collection of books and journals on
mycology, plant pathology, and related
subjects. In addition, there are 63,800
reprints of articles accessible through author
and title.

WI —UNIVERSITY OF WISCONSIN,
MADISON, College of Agricultural & Life
Sciences, Steenbock Memorial Library, 550
Babcock Dr, Madison, 53706. Jan Kennedy,
Dir
Holdings: Vols (186,312) Cat Docs Slides
Notes: Collection emphasizes genetics,
pathology and physiology of horticultural
plants, forests, and food crops.

BC —CANADIAN FORESTRY SERVICE,
Pacific Forest Research Centre, Library, 506
West Burnside Rd, Victoria, V8Z 1M5, Can.
Alice Solyma, Librn
Holdings: Vols (60,500) Cat Microforms
Notes: Incl general materials related to plant
pathology and comprehensive collection on
tree diseases.

ON —ROYAL BOTANICAL GARDENS,
Library, Box 399, Hamilton, L8N 3H8, Can.
Ina Vrugtman, Librn
Holdings: Vols (4200)
Notes: Strengths in ornamental horticulture,
botany, ornithology, entomology, natural
history.

PE —AGRICULTURE CANADA, Research
Station Library, PO Box 1210,
Charlottetown, C1A 7M8, Can. Barrie
Stanfield, Librn
Holdings: Vols (2300) Cat
Budget: ($5000)

PLANT GENETICS

NY —CORNELL UNIVERSITY LIBRARIES,
Collection of Regional History, Dept of
Manuscripts and Univ Archives, Ithaca,
14853.
Notes: Incl records, 1925-26; tentative
schedules, notes, and memoranda concerning
the International Congress of Plant Sciences
(Fourth International Botanical Congress),
held in August, 1926 at Cornell University,
NY.

WI —UNIVERSITY OF WISCONSIN,
MADISON, College of Agricultural & Life
Sciences, Steenbock Memorial Library, 550
Babcock Dr, Madison, 53706. Jan Kennedy,
Dir
Holdings: Vols (186,312) Cat Docs

PLANT HUNTING

PA —LONGWOOD GARDENS, INC,
Library, Kennett Square, 19348. Enola Jane
N Teeter, Librn

PA —HUNT INSTITUTE FOR BOTANICAL
DOCUMENTATION, Hunt Botanical
Library, Carnegie-Mellon University,
Pittsburgh, 15213. Bernadette G Callery,
Librn
Holdings: Vols (23,000) Cat Pix
Notes: Collection of primarily historical
botany and plant taxonomy, especially 1730-
1840. Includes approximately 500 15th
through 17th century herbals, extensive
collection of 18th and 19th century color-
plate works, floras and monographic works,
and other works on natural history, early
gardening and horticulture, and travel,
particularly that dealing with plant
exploration and introduction. Extensive
biographical materials, on people in plant
sciences. Reference collection and extensive
documentation in botanical bibliography,
especially concerning books published before
1850. Includes as separate collections, the
Strandell Collection of Linnaeana and the
Michel Adanson Library. Over 800 items
described in *Catalogue of Botanical Books in
the Collection of Rachel McMasters Miller
Hunt, 1477-1800* (Pittsburgh, 1958-1960).

PLANT INSPECTION

FL —FLORIDA DEPARTMENT OF
AGRICULTURE & CONSUMER
SERVICES, Div of Plant Industry, Library,
PO Box 1269, Gainesville, 32602. June B
Jacobson, Librn; Alice Richards, Asst Librn
Holdings: Vols (11,455) Cat Mss Microforms
Budget: ($23,798)
Notes: Collection is primarily taxonomic.
464 periodical, current and antiquariat titles.

PLANT-LICE

NY —AMERICAN MUSEUM OF
NATURAL HISTORY, Library Services

PLANT-LICE (cont.)

Dept, Central Park W & 79th St, New York, 10024. Nina J Root, Chairwoman; Mary Genett, Asst Librn for Reference Services
Notes: A major literature collection supplements the museum's entomology collections; perhaps the largest in the world.

PLANT PATHOLOGY see Plant Diseases

PLANT PHYSIOLOGY

CA —UNIVERSITY OF CALIFORNIA, LOS ANGELES, Biomedical Library, Center for Health Sciences, Los Angeles, 90024. Louise Darling, Biomedical Librn
MD —SMITHSONIAN ENVIRONMENTAL RESEARCH CENTER, Branch Library, 12441 Parklawn Dr, Rockville, 20852. Angela N Haggins, Chief
Holdings: Vols (3300) Cat Maps Pix Slides
MA —UNIVERSITY OF MASSACHUSETTS AT AMHERST, Library, Amherst, 01003. Siegfried Feller, Assoc Dir for Collection Development
Holdings: Cat
Notes: Botanical taxonomy, physiology, pathology and mycology.
MA —HARVARD UNIVERSITY LIBRARY, Biological Laboratories Library, 16 Divinity Ave, Cambridge, 02138. Dorothy Solbrig, Librn
Holdings: Vols (20,000) Cat Films
Notes: Materials in all areas of biology, emphasizing biochemisty and cellular and developmental biology. There is little in systematic biology and morphology.
NY —NEW YORK BOTANICAL GARDEN LIBRARY, Bronx, 10458. Charles R Long, Asst Vice Pres & Dir
Holdings: Vols 15,000 Cat Mss Pix Slides Microforms VF
Budget: ($356,000)
Notes: One of the largest botanical collections in the world. Covers botany (150,000 vols), botanists (3000), horticulture (45,000), plant diseases (25,000), plant physiology (15,000), history of botany (1500), conservation of natural resources (15,000), gardening (13,000), paleobotany (7000), ecology (20,000), forestry (5000), medical botany (3000), agriculture (9000) and biology (20,000). Reference library; materials do not circulate, except via standard inter-library loan. About 5000 vols uncataloged. Incl archives, art and vertical files. An OCLC library.
NY —BOYCE THOMPSON INSTITUTE FOR PLANT RESEARCH, Library, Cornell University, Tower Rd, Ithaca, 14853. Greta Colavito, Librn
Holdings: Vols (5300) Cat
Budget: ($46,000)
Notes: Mainly plant physiology, biochemistry, entomology, air and water pollution, pesticides, and plant pathology.
NY —UNIVERSITY OF ROCHESTER, Carlson Library, Hutchison Hall, River Campus, Rochester, 14627. Michael W Poulin, Librn
Holdings: Vols (48,720) Cat Microforms
Notes: Strong collection in the field and related areas.
PA —CARNEGIE LIBRARY OF PITTSBURGH, Science & Technology Dept, 4400 Forbes Ave, Pittsburgh, 15213. Catherine M Brosky, Dept Head
Notes: Now of secondary importance, this subject was extensively developed from 1902 to 1945. Abstracts, indexes, bibliographies and the important reference books. There are some old and rare items in the original and some important compilation, sets and journals are available. Covers plant classification, physiology, nutrition, breeding, pathology, structural botany, plant chemistry, economic botany, plant history and geography.
PE —AGRICULTURE CANADA, Research Station Library, PO Box 1210, Charlottetown, C1A 7M8, Can. Barrie Stanfield, Librn
Holdings: Vols (2300) Cat
Budget: ($5000)

PLANT TAXONOMY see Botany—Classification

PLANTATION CROPS

AL —TROY STATE UNIVERSITY, Library, Troy, 36081. Kenneth Croslin, Dir of University Libraries
Holdings: // Mss
Notes: Incl the John Horry Dent Papers, 1851-1892, 25 vols, mss, farm journals, account books, letters, legal documents, clippings and miscellaneous memorabilia of a planter, plantation owner, investor, who lived in Barbour County, Alabama from 1837 to 1867 and in Floyd County, Georgia from 1867 to 1892. Typescript from tape "Sharecropping farming in Pike County, Alabama in early 1900's" (56p). Typescript of tapes of "Source material extracted from Troy, Alabama newspapers, 1871-1935" indexed under 9 subjects by color code.
CA —UNIVERSITY OF CALIFORNIA, BERKELEY, Science Libraries, Natural Resources Library, 40 Giannini Hall, Berkeley, 94720. Norma Kobzina, Head Librn
Holdings: Vols (100,000) Cat Maps Microforms
Budget: ($40,000)
Notes: Subject emphasis is on basic agricultural and pest management research, particularly in the areas of tropical and subtropical agriculture and plantation crops, ie, cotton, rice, tobacco, and sugar. Materials in agriculture engineering, farm machinery, and veterinary medicine are not acquired for the Berkeley campus. Serials, especially the extensive holdings of foreign titles, constitute the collection's major strength. Over 5700 serials are being received currently.
LA —NICHOLLS STATE UNIVERSITY, Ellender Memorial Library, Thibodaux, 70310. Randall A Detro, Dir; Philip D Uzee, Archivist
Notes: South Louisiana sugar plantations (1838-1926), Martin - Pugh Collection (1838-1935), J Wilson Lepine Collection (1890-1926).

PLANTATION RECORDS

LA —LOUISIANA STATE MUSEUM, Louisiana Historical Center, 400 Esplanade Ave, (Mailing add: 751 Chartres St, New Orleans, 70116). Edward F Haas, Chief Cur
Holdings: Mss Maps Pix
Budget: ($1,200,000)
Notes: Archives and Manuscripts Collections. Special guides and indices are in preparation. The single most important collection in this section is the Louisiana Colonial Archives, consisting of the judicial records of the French Superior and the Spanish Cabildo in Louisiana dating from 1714 to 1803. There are approximately 500,000 pages of documents in this collection. Also, 19th century collections of personal papers, plantation records, business ledgers, etc. Incl 3500 maps and 15,000 pictures.
LA —LOUISIANA STATE UNIVERSITY, SHREVEPORT, Library-Archives, 8515 Youree Dr, Shreveport, 71129. Patricia L Meador, Archivist & Asst Librn
Notes: Archives incl catalogued manuscripts and records, 500 maps, more than 5000 photographs, 1000 architectural drawings, slides. The collection's primary emphasis is the history of North Louisiana, particularly Northwest Louisiana. The 1500 linear ft incl area plantation records and ledgers; personal papers of area pioneers, planters, legislators, politicians, educators, businessmen, and architects; papers and records of longtime (1919-1961) Caddo Parish Coroner, Willis P Butler; the Samuel G Wiener, Sr architectual records (1921-1976) with drawings and photographs; the Ted Flaxman architectual records (1919-1968); the papers (1860-1921) of architect Nathaniel S Allen; the collection of Dewey A Somdal, Shreveport architect, historian and collector, with emphasis on steamboats, travel on the Red River and Louisiana history, 1780-1972.

LA —NICHOLLS STATE UNIVERSITY, Ellender Memorial Library, Thibodaux, 70310. Randall A Detro, Dir; Philip D Uzee, Archivist
Notes: South Louisiana sugar plantations (1838-1926), Martin - Pugh Collection (1838-1935), J Wilson Lepine Collection (1890-1926).
MS —MISSISSIPPI STATE UNIVERSITY, Mitchell Memorial Library, Box 5408, Mississippi State, 39762. Frances N Coleman, Head, Special Collections
Holdings: Mss
Notes: Papers of the Delta and Pine Land Co, 1886-1980, once the largest cotton plantation in the world.
NC —DUKE UNIVERSITY, William R Perkins Library, Durham, 27706. Elvin E Strowd, University Librn
Notes: The Plantations collection consists of material illustrating the historical, economic and sociological aspects of the plantation system, not only in the South, but throughout the world. Additions are ongoing.
NC —DUKE UNIVERSITY, William R Perkins Library, Manuscript Dept, Durham, 27706. Ellen Gartrell, Cur of Mss
Holdings: Cat Mss
Notes: Especially US South, incl slavery and slave trade, abolition movement, freedmen, civil rights. Notable are papers of black educator Charles N Hunter, many plantation records, and British antislavery papers of William Wilberforce and William Smith.
SC —COLLEGE OF CHARLESTON LIBRARY, Special Collections Dept, Charleston, 29401.
Notes: (1) The account book of the John Cordes estate, 1764-1798, with a family history of the years 1695-1728. (2) Another collection, possibly gathered in 1851 by William Henry Trescott for his history of the Cuthbert family, consists of papers dealing with property owned by the family in Beaufort County, SC. The deeds, etc, do not all involve Cuthbert family members, but do pertain to property held by one or more of the family at some time. Among those landowners not of the Cuthbert family were Hugh Bryan, Thomas Corbett, Henry William De Saussure, Charles Heyward, Charles Palmer, Thomas Rutledge, and William Stoutenburg. These documents may come from Beaufort district and county judgment roles. (3) Pinkney papers incl Pinckney's plantation diary which contains lists of slaves, crop yields for 1817-1819, listings of acreage owned, anaccount of a steamboat trip, and a tally of drum fish caught. (4) The Porcher plantation account book (1774-1834) begun by Philip Porcher, and the memoirs (1809-1859). (5) Thomas Robert's plantation journal of receipts, lists of slaves, expenses, and "recipe for a consumption." (6) Plowden Weston's business ledger (1764-1769) and plantation journal (1802-1820). The ledger also contains the plantation accounts kept by his son, Francis Weston, at a later date.
TX —UNIVERSITY OF TEXAS LIBRARIES, General Libraries, Barker Texas History Center, PO Box P, Austin, 78712. Don Carleton, Dir
Notes: Louisiana and Virginia plantation records.
VA —UNIVERSITY OF VIRGINIA, Alderman Library, Manuscripts Dept, Charlottesville, 22901. Edmund Berkeley Jr, Cur
Holdings: Cat Mss Pix
Notes: Material in over 420 collections documents the history and culture of Afro-Americans incl letters and narratives by slaves and masters, plantation accounts, letters from Liberian immigrants, folklore, literture, the desegregation movement in Virginia in the 1960s and 1970s and the "massive resistance" of Virginia political leaders. Michael F Plunkett (ed) *A Guide to Materials on the History, Literature, and Culture of Afro-Americans in the Manuscripts Department, University of Virginia Library.*

PLANTING see Agriculture; Gardens and Gardening; Landscape Gardening

PLANTS

CA —LOS ANGELES PUBLIC LIBRARY, Science & Technology Dept, 630 W Fifth St,

PLANTS (cont.)

Los Angeles, 90071. Billie M Connor, Dept Head
Holdings: Vols (14,000) Cat Maps
Notes: Includes agricultural publications of the US Department of Agriculture, California and other state experiment station publications on all aspects of plant and animal husbandry, soil science and analysis, including Soil Surveys. Emphasis is on the Western states and semi-tropical areas.

CA —UNIVERSITY OF CALIFORNIA, LOS ANGELES, Biomedical Library, Center for Health Sciences, Los Angeles, 90024. Louise Darling, Biomedical Librn

DE —UNIVERSITY OF DELAWARE, Agriculture Library, 2 Townsend Hall, Newark, 19717. Frederick Getze, Assoc Librn
Holdings: Vols (32,500)
Notes: Strong in entomology and ornamental horticulture. Extensive collection of state agriculture documents for each US state and Puerto Rico. Library subscribes to 600 serials (English and foreign).

DE —WILMINGTON GARDEN CENTER LIBRARY, 503 Market Street Mall, Wilmington, 19801. Bonnie J Swan Day, Admin Asst; Karen Bidus, Librn
Holdings: Vols (1500)
Notes: Library open to the public, only circulates to members.

DC —SMITHSONIAN INSTITUTION LIBRARIES, Botany Branch, Washington, 20560. Ruth Schallert, Branch Librn
Notes: Taxonomic botany; with the J D Smith Collection of general botany, the Dawson Collection on algae, and the Hitchcock-Chase Collection on grasses.

FL —UNIVERSITY OF FLORIDA, Institute of Food & Agricultural Sciences, Hume Library, Gainesville, 32611. Albert C Strickland, Librn
Holdings: Vols (135,000) Cat Mss Microforms
Notes: Including journals and monographs, this collection is a general agricultural one. The emphasis is on tropical agriculture, especially Latin America. Entomology is very strong. The library offers on-line information retrieval using Lockheed and SDC data bases.

FL —ARCHBOLD BIOLOGICAL STATION, Library, Rt 2, Box 180, Lake Placid, 33852. Fred E Lohrer, Librn
Holdings: Cat Slides
Notes: Florida natural history. Emphasis on south central peninsular Florida. Habitats, plants, vertebrates, land use changes. About 8000 2x2 color transparencies and 35mm films.

IL —MORTON ARBORETUM, Sterling Morton Library, Lisle, 60532. Ian MacPhail, Librn
Holdings: Vols (20,000) Cat Maps Pix
Budget: ($10,000)
Notes: The library is especially concerned with the literature of woody plants (trees and shrubs) of north temperate zones but has substantial holdings in the taxonomy and systematics of plants in general, both wild and cultivated, flora of different parts of the world, and a growing collection on plant monographs. Also about 2000 pictures. Descibed in *The Morton Arboretum Quarterly*, vol 9, no 4 (Winter 1973), pp 56-61.

MA —HARVARD UNIVERSITY LIBRARY, Gray Herbarium Library, 22 Divinity Ave, Cambridge, 02138. Barbara A Callahan, Librn
Holdings: Vols (61,445) Cat Pix Microforms
Notes: Flowering plants and ferns are emphasized. *Gray Herbarium Index*, 10 volumes (published 1968) reproduces 265,000 cards giving names and literature citations of newly described or established vascular plants of the Western Hemisphere.

MA —MASSACHUSETTS AUDUBON SOCIETY, Hathaway Environmental Education Institute, Lincoln, 01773. Louise C Maglione, Librn
Notes: Largest and most comprehensive collection in the field of environmental education; especially good in the curriculum area. Extensive sections on animal, behavioral and environmental issues, and quality of environment.

NY —NEW YORK BOTANICAL GARDEN LIBRARY, Bronx, 10458. Charles R Long, Asst Vice Pres & Dir
Holdings: Vols (385,000) Cat Mss Pix Slides Microforms VF
Budget: ($356,000)
Notes: One of the largest botanical collections in the world. Covers botany (150,000 vols), botanists (3000), horticulture (45,000), plant diseases (25,000), plant physiology (15,000), history of botany (1500), conservation of natural resources (15,000), gardening (13,000), paleobotany (7000), ecology (20,000), forestry (5000), medical botany (3000), agriculture (9000) and biology (20,000). Reference library; materials do not circulate, except via standard inter-library loan. About 5000 vols uncataloged. Incl archives, art and vertical files. An OCLC library.

OH —CLEVELAND PUBLIC LIBRARY, Science & Technology Dept, 325 Superior Ave, Cleveland, 44114. Jean Z Piety, Head
Holdings: Cat
Notes: Part of the Gardening Collection, which emphasizes the history of gardens around the world, domestic landscape planning and planting, incl flower gardening, annuals and perennials and indoor plants.

PA —CARNEGIE LIBRARY OF PITTSBURGH, Science & Technology Dept, 4400 Forbes Ave, Pittsburgh, 15213. Catherine M Brosky, Dept Head
Holdings: Vols (380,000) Cat Maps Microforms
Budget: ($240,000)
Notes: Now of secondary importance, this subject was extensively developed from 1902 to 1945. Abstracts, indexes, bibliographies and the important reference books. Covers plant classification, physiology, nutrition, breeding, pathology, structural botany, plant chemistry, economic botany, plant history and geography.

VA —NORFOLK BOTANICAL GARDENS LIBRARY, Airport Rd, Norfolk, 23518. Marian Cole, Librn
Holdings: Vols 1903 Cat Pix

MB —UNIVERSITY OF MANITOBA, Agriculture Library, Dafoe Rd, Winnipeg, R3T 2N2, Can. Judy Harper, Head
Holdings: Vols (9000) Cat

ON —AGRICULTURE CANADA, Plant Research Library, Research Branch, Central Experimental Farm 49, Ottawa, K1A 0C6, Can. Mrs E Gavora, Librn
Holdings: Vols (10,500) Cat Maps Microforms
Notes: One of the most extensive botanical collections in Canada, especially in the Taxonomy of higher plants and fungi. Contains many of the basic works from the starting point of botany in 1753 to date. Major botanical works of Linnaeus and others, covering flora of land areas of most parts of the world.

ON —LAURENTIAN UNIVERSITY LIBRARY, Ramsey Lake Rd, Sudbury, P3E 2C6, Can. Suzanne Brunette, Special Collection Librn; Sue Vongpeisal, Head Librn
Notes: Materials on northern Canada, incl 2200 books and pamphlets, 60,000 press clippings on northern topics 75 series of periodicals and over 1500 maps, plus photographs and thousands of samples of arctic and subarctic plants incl mosses, lichens, algae and wood sections. Much of the material is in French.

PLANTS—AUSTRALIA see Botany—Australia

PLANTS—CALIFORNIA see Botany—California

PLANTS—CANADA see Botany—Canada

PLANTS—CLASSIFICATION see Botany—Classification

PLANTS—COLORADO see Botany—Colorado

PLANTS—DISEASES see Plant Diseases

PLANTS—ECOLOGY see Botany—Ecology

PLANTS—INSPECTION see Plant Inspection

PLANTS—MEXICO see Botany—Mexico

PLANTS—OREGON see Botany—Oregon

PLANTS—PATHOLOGY see Plant Diseases

PLANTS—SOUTH AFRICA see Botany—South Africa

PLANTS, FOSSIL see Paleobotany

PLANTS, MEDICINAL see Botany, Medical

PLANTS, ORNAMENTAL

DE —UNIVERSITY OF DELAWARE, Agriculture Library, 2 Townsend Hall, Newark, 19717. Frederick Getze, Assoc Librn
Holdings: Vols (32,500) Cat Pix Microforms
Notes: Strong in entomology and ornamental horticulture. Extensive collection of state agriculture documents for each US state and Puerto Rico. Library subscribes to 600 serials (English and foreign).

IA —IOWA STATE UNIVERSITY, Library, Ames, 50011. Warren B Kuhn, Dean of Library Services
Holdings: Cat
Notes: Extensive serial holdings.

MI —MICHIGAN STATE UNIVERSITY, Science Library, East Lansing, 48824. Carole S Armstrong, Head
Holdings: Vols 6500 Cat
Notes: The collection has 107 journal titles with 2900 vols and 3600 monographs.

VA —NORFOLK BOTANICAL GARDENS LIBRARY, Airport Rd, Norfolk, 23518. Marian Cole, Librn
Holdings: Vols 1903 Cat Pix

ON —ROYAL BOTANICAL GARDENS, Library, Box 399, Hamilton, L8N 3H8, Can. Ina Vrugtman, Librn
Holdings: Vols (5000) Cat
Budget: ($13,000)
Notes: Books are union cataloged in card catalog of Mills Library. McMaster University, Hamilton, Ontario. Periodicals are not yet union listed. Interlibrary loans are handled through Mills Library Collection of nursery and seed trade catalogs; *Gray Herbarium Index*. The library is located in the Headquarters Building of the Royal Botanical Gardens, 680 Plains Road West (Highway No 2), Burlington, Ontario.

PLANTS, TEXTILE see Textile Fibers

PLANTS, TROPICAL see Tropical Crops

PLANTS, USEFUL see Botany, Economic

PLANTS, WOODY see Woody Plants

PLASMA PHYSICS

CA —UNIVERSITY OF CALIFORNIA, LOS ANGELES, Physics Library, 213 Kinsey Hall, Los Angeles, 90024. J Wally Pegram, Librn
Holdings: Vols (37,000) Cat
Notes: UCLA physics theses; current SLAC preprints in high-energy physics. (592) current serials subscriptions.

MA —AVCO EVERETT RESEARCH LABORATORY, INC, Library, 2385 Revere Beach Parkway, Everett, 02149. Lorraine T Nazzaro, Librn
Holdings: Vols (24,000) Cat Maps Microforms
Budget: ($150,000)
Notes: Incl 50,000 reports.

NJ —PRINCETON UNIVERSITY, Library, Rare Books Dept, Princeton, 08544. Stephen Ferguson, Cur
Holdings: Vols 4500 Cat Microforms

NM —UNIVERSITY OF CALIFORNIA, Los Alamos National Laboratory, Libraries, PO Box 1663, MSP 362, Los Alamos, 87545. J Arthur Freed, Head Librn
Holdings: Vols (800,000) Cat Film Microforms
Budget: ($700,000)
Notes: Incl 500,000 classified and unclassified reports. There are 25 branch libraries and a central collection. The Medical Library contains about 40,000 vols in the areas of biomedical research.

NY —UNIVERSITY OF ROCHESTER, Physics-Optics-Astronomy Library, Bausch & Lomb Bldg, River Campus, Rochester, 14627. Loretta Caren, Librn
Holdings: Vols (20,000) Cat
Notes: Strong research level collection in the field and related areas.

PLASMOGENY see Life—Origin

PLASTIC ADDITIVES see Plasticizers

PLASTIC MATERIALS see Plastics

PLASTIC PRODUCTS see Plastics

PLASTIC SURGERY see Surgery, Plastic

PLASTICIZERS

OH —EMERY INDUSTRIES, Research Library, 4900 Este Ave, Cincinnati, 45232.

PLASTICIZERS (cont.)

B A Bernard, Librn
Holdings: Cat
Notes: Special subjects: fatty acids and organic chemical derivatives, ozone, plasticizers, polymers, synthetic lubricants.

PLASTICS

CT —ROGERS CORP, Lurie Library, One Technology Drive, Rogers, 06263. Myrna D Riquier, Librn; Nini S Davis, Librn
Holdings: Vols (650) Cat
Notes: Emphasis on materials science, plastics, polymers, resins.

NY —PENNWALT CORPORATION, Lucidol Division, Research Library, 1740 Military Road, Buffalo, 14240. Brenda L Cassoni Asst Librn
Holdings: Vols 8000
Notes: There is a separate catalog of subject references to articles in periodicals.

NY —ENGINEERING SOCIETIES LIBRARY, 345 E 47 St, New York, 10017. S Kirk Cabeen, Dir
Holdings: Vols 250,000 Cat Maps 16mm Films Microforms
Notes: One of the largest, most comprehensive engineering libraries in the world. Covers all engineering disciplines; particularly strong in electrical and electronic, mechanical, mining and metallurgical, petroleum, chemical, industrial, air conditioning and refrigeration engineering. Incl Wheeler Collection of early materials on magnetisn and electricity. 125,000 bound periodical volumes; 10,000 maps; 5000 serial subscriptions (many foreign-language). Virtually all materials abstracted in *Engineering Index* (1884-date) are incl in Library. Noncirculating, except to members of professional engineering societies which support the Library. See *Engineering Societies Library, New York, Classed Subject Catalog and Index* (Boston: G K Hall, 1963); and *Supplements*, 1-10, 1964-1973.

OH —AKRON-SUMMIT COUNTY PUBLIC LIBRARY, Science & Technology Div, 55 S Main St, Akron, 44326. Joyce McKnight, Head
Holdings: Vols 880 Cat
Budget: ($24,000)

OH —OWENS-ILLINOIS, Information Research Department, One Seagate, Toledo, 43666. Patricia Ajemian, Librn
Holdings: Vols (24,000) Cat Pix Microforms
Notes: Requests for use are handled on an individual basis. Incl information on packaging.

PA —FRANKLIN INSTITUTE LIBRARY, 20 & The Parkway, Philadelphia, 19103. Miriam Padusis, Dir; Charles Wilt, Readers Servs Librn
Holdings: Vols (300,000) Cat Maps Pix Microforms

PA —CARNEGIE LIBRARY OF PITTSBURGH, Science & Technology Dept, 4400 Forbes Ave, Pittsburgh, 15213. Catherine M Brosky, Dept Head
Holdings: Vols (380,000) Cat Maps Microforms
Budget: ($240,000)
Notes: Incl many journals. Encyclopedias, general reference books, abstracts, indexes, monographs, and bibliographies.

SC —CRYOVAC TECHNICAL LIBRARY, PO Box 464, Duncan, 29334. M M Ezell, Libn
Holdings: Vols (6000) Cat
Notes: Library supports corporate research, development, and engineering. Incl materials on chemical and mechanical engineering, polymers and polymerization, plastics, and food packaging. 175 periodical titles received. Library open by appointment or through ILL.

SC —SONOCO PRODUCTS CO, Research Laboratory, Technical Information Center, One N Second St, Hartsville, 29550. Ken Chavis, Dir
Holdings: Vols (4000) Cat Mss Slides Microforms
Notes: Restricted to Sonoco employees. No photocopying.

PLASTICS—ADDITIVES

OH —FERRO CORP, Ferro Chemical Library, 7050 Krick Rd, Bedford, 44146. Mary Jane Campbell, Librn
Holdings: Vols 3500 Cat Audiotapes Microforms
Notes: Incl audiotapes (10) and microforms (52,750).

PLASTICS INDUSTRY AND TRADE

PA —CARNEGIE LIBRARY OF PITTSBURGH, Science & Technology Dept, 4400 Forbes Ave, Pittsburgh, 15213. Catherine M Brosky, Dept Head
Holdings: Vols (380,000) Cat Maps Microforms
Budget: ($240,000)
Notes: General information acquired. Manufactures directories, including old editions, standards and specifications. *See also* entry under Plastics.

PLATH, SYLVIA

NV —UNIVERSITY OF NEVADA, RENO, University Library, Special Collections Dept, Reno, 89557. Robert E Blesse, Head
Holdings: Vols (31) Cat
Notes: Includes individual works by author in all editions including translations; also prefaces, introductions, published correspondence, appearances in anthologies, periodicals, etc. Bibliographical research collection, part of Modern Authors Collection. Other appearances 320 cataloged.

PLATO AND PLATONISM

CA —UNIVERSITY OF CALIFORNIA, IRVINE, Library, Irvine, 92664. Roger Berry, Dept Head
Notes: Incl the library of Professor Paul Friedlander (3000 vols). Located in general circulation collection.

IL —NORTHWESTERN UNIVERSITY, Library, Special Collections Dept, 1937 Sheridan Rd, Evanston, 60201. R Russell Maylone, Cur
Holdings: Vols 65 Cat
Notes: Thomas Taylor Collection. No published description of the collection, which incl many articles by Taylor extracted from journals.

MO —UNIVERSITY OF MISSOURI-COLUMBIA, Ellis Library, Special Collections Dept, Ninth & Lowry, Columbia, 65201. Margaret A Howell, Head, Special Collections
Holdings: Vols 1700 // Cat
Notes: The Thomas Moore Johnson Collection. There is a printed catalog.

PLATONIC ACADEMY

†CA —CLAREMONT COLLEGES, Honnold Library, Claremont, 91711.
Notes: Florentine Renaissance, particularly 1450-1500. Angelo Poliziano (1454-1494), the humanist scholars and writers of the Medici circle, and the Platonic Academy.

PLATT, KIN

MA —BOSTON UNIVERSITY, Mugar Memorial Library, Special Collections Dept, 771 Commonwealth Ave, Boston, 02215. Howard B Gotlieb, Dir
Holdings: Mss
Notes: Mss, correspondence, etc collected in depth; incl publications by or about.

PLAUCHE, LEDA

LA —NEW ORLEANS PUBLIC LIBRARY, Louisiana Div, 219 Loyola Ave, New Orleans, 70140. Collin B Hamer Jr, Head; Brenda M Osbey, Library Associate
Holdings: Cat Maps Pix
Notes: Louisiana and New Orleans Picture File Collection ranges from the late 19th century-date and incl the following separate collections: Alexander Allison (ca 1898-1951, 337 pieces); Charles Franck (ca 1920-50, 170 pieces); Leda Plauche (ca 1935-53, 220 pieces); C Milo Williams (ca 1910, 85 pieces); Wilson S Howell (ca 1890, 49 pieces); Grauman Marks (ca 1960, 268 pieces); Robert Tallant (ca 1940-50, 70 pieces); Robert E Tracy (1959, 87 pieces); Anthony J Flaherty (ca 1970-84, 83 pieces); George F Mugnier (1880-1920, 186 pieces); Color Slides (ca 1945-date, 500 pieces); 30,000 photographs incl 500 color slides and 104 negatives. Use of the material is restricted to on-site research. Publication must be accompanied by credit cut line.

PLAY

IL —UNIVERSITY OF ILLINOIS, URBANA/CHAMPAIGN, Library, Applied Life Studies Library, 1408 W Gregory Dr, Urbana, 61801.
Holdings: Vols (38,000) Cat Microforms
Notes: Speical emphasis on leisure studies, recreation surveys and plans, outdoor education, recreation programs, theories of play, supervision, and therapeutic recreation. *See also* entry under Physical Education and Training.

ON —SIRLS, Faculty of Human Kinetics & Leisure Studies, University of Waterloo, Waterloo, N2L 3G1, Can. Betty Smith, Database Mgr
Notes: Information Retrieval System for the Sociology of Leisure and Sport (SIRLS) is a computerized online database of about 13,000 entries (1983). Incl dance as a leisure time activity.

PLAY CENTERS see Community Centers

PLAYBILLS—COLLECTIONS

CA —UNIVERSITY OF CALIFORNIA, DAVIS, Shields Library, Dept of Special Collections, Davis, 95616. Donald Kunitz, Head; C Danial Elliott, Asst Head
Holdings: Uncat Broadsides
Notes: Playbills from 19th and 20th century British theatre.

CA —CALIFORNIA STATE UNIVERSITY, LONG BEACH, Library, Dept of Special Collections & Archives, 1250 Bellflower Blvd, Long Beach, 90840. John Ahouse, Special Collections Librn
Holdings: Vols (5000) Cat Pix
Notes: Incl playbills, scripts, scrapbooks from the former Pasadena Playhouse, together with the former Hildebrand Collection of English and American Drama before 1830.

CA —LOS ANGELES PUBLIC LIBRARY, Literature and Philology Dept, 630 W Fifth St, Los Angeles, 90071. Helene G Mochedlover, Dept Librn
Holdings: Vols (50,000) Cat Pix Slides Microforms
Notes: Incl theatre programs, playbills, clippings, play reviews on 19th and 20th century plays produced in or near Los Angeles. Play collection of over 30,000 vols is particularly strong in 19th and 20th centuries. Annotated subject index to plays is kept up-to-date. A file of local as well as New York and London play reviews is kept. Collection incl microprints and microcards. There are a number of long files of important dramatic periodicals.

CA —LOS ANGELES PUBLIC LIBRARY, Frances Howard Goldwyn Hollywood Regional Library, 1623 Ivar Ave, Los Angeles, 90028. Sally Dumaux, Librn
Holdings: Vols (100,000) Cat Mss Pix VF
Budget: ($60,000)
Notes: A general and a research collection on theatre history, US and foreign, with special emphasis on Los Angeles, Chicago, and New York theatre from the late 1800s to the present. Other aspects of the collection include theatre design, make-up, costume, and acting and directing techniques. Also includes biographies of actors and actresses (many signed). The play collection of over 15,000 titles covers mainly English and American plays of the 19th and 20th century. There are over 5000 playbills, scrapbooks, posters, and programs. Special Collections: "Hellzapoppin," NY, 1938-40.

PLAYBILLS—COLLECTIONS (cont.)

Includes photographs, clippings, and programs; *Turnabout Theatre Monthly* Bulletin, 1942-48, souvenir programs and flyers. Also Pilgrimage Theatre and Hollywood Bowl programs, 1922 to present.

CA —UNIVERSITY OF CALIFORNIA, LOS ANGELES, Research Library, Dept of Special Collections, 405 Hilgard Ave, Los Angeles, 90024. Edward Shreeves, Chairman, Bibliographers Group; David S Zeidberg, Head
Holdings: Cat
Notes: 5 linear feet of theatrical playbills from California, Europe (incl 80 relating to Charles Dickens), and New York.

CT —YALE UNIVERSITY, Box 1603A, Yale Station, New Haven, 06520.

DC —HOWARD UNIVERSITY, Founders Library, Channing Pollock Theatre Collection, 500 Howard Place NW, Washington, 20059. Marilyn Mahanand, Librn
Holdings: Vols (16,440) Cat Mss Maps Pix Slides Microforms
Notes: Much on the Black Theatre.

DC —LIBRARY OF CONGRESS, Rare Book & Special Collections Div, Washington, 20540. William Matheson, Chief
Holdings: Cat
Notes: The Theatre Playbill Collection consists of 7500 playbills relating to performances in Washington (largely), New York, Boston, Philadelphia, Cincinnati, Buffalo, Charlestown, etc between 1823 and 1930, with a concentration in late 19th and early 20th century performances. Incl a large number of theatre playbills for productions in London, Birmingham, Liverpool, Newcastle, Manchester, etc between 1810 and 1880 (especially Shakespearean performances).

IL —CHICAGO HISTORICAL SOCIETY, Library, Clark St at North Ave, Chicago, 60614. Robert L Brubaker, Librn
Holdings: Vols (150,000) Cat Mss Pix
Notes: Chicago theatre programs (5000); scrapbooks containing reviews and other clippings; a few letters, reminiscences, account books, and other records of theatres, actors and actresses, and managers; theatre posters; Thomas Conolly Collection of Theatrical Portraits; other photographs of theatres, productions, and casts.

IL —CHICAGO PUBLIC LIBRARY, Special Collections Div, Cultural Center, 78 E Washington St, Chicago, 60602. Laura Linard, Cur
Holdings: Mss Pix
Notes: Special Collections maintains a scarce collection of theatre broadsides, playbills, programs and other ephemera for Chicago productions, 1880-1930. These are described in *Treasures of The Chicago Public Library*, compiled by Thomas A Orlando and Marie Gecik, 1977, pp 121-33. The Archives of the Publicity Department of the Goodman Theatre (formerly of the Art Institute of Chicago) are maintained by Special Collections at The Chicago Public Library. We also have a nearly complete collection of the plays of Kenneth Sawyer Goodman, after whom the Goodman Theatre is named. A finding aid to the Theatre Arts Collection will be prepared in 1978-79. Some unique pre-fire material is also to be found in these collections.

IN —INDIANA UNIVERSITY, Lilly Library, Seventh St, Bloomington, 47405. William R Cagle, Librn
Holdings: // Cat
Notes: 19th and 20th century British and American playbills.

IN —INDIANA UNIVERSITY, SOUTH BEND, Library, 1700 Mishawaka Ave, South Bend, 46615. James L Mullins, Dir
Holdings: Vols (1490) Cat Mss Maps Pix Phonorecords
Notes: Incl design materials, scripts, theatre music, rare editions, theatre programs, playbills, clippings and periodicals from the 1850s to the 1940s.

MD —MARYLAND HISTORICAL SOCIETY, Library, 201 W Monument St, Baltimore, 21201. William B Keller, Head Librn
Holdings: Cat Mss Maps Pix Slides Microforms
Notes: Espec relating to Maryland and Baltimore. Extensive collection.

MA —HARVARD UNIVERSITY LIBRARY, Theatre Collection, Cambridge, 02138. Jeanne T Newlin, Cur
Holdings: Uncat
Notes: See *Harvard Library Bulletin*, VI (1952), 281-301. Playbills for the fifteen major London theatres of the 18th and 19th centuries have been published on microfilm by Research Publications Inc.

MA —BRANDEIS UNIVERSITY, Goldfarb Library, 415 South St, Waltham, 02154. Bessie Hahn, Dir
Notes: American Theater Programs Collection consists of 14 linear ft of American theater and stage programs of the late 19th and early 20th century with particular emphasis on the Boston dramatic scene. This collection is unprocessed, spring 1984.

MI —UNIVERSITY OF MICHIGAN, Library, Dept of Rare Books & Special Collections, Ann Arbor, 48109. Robert J Starring, Head
Holdings: Cat Mss Pix
Notes: Extensive holdings of books on the theatre. Also, in the Charles Sanders Collection, about 14,000 British and American playbills and programs mostly of the 19th century, as well as scrapbooks, posters, and about 750 photographs and prints of actors and actresses. In the Ellen Van Volkenburg-Maurice Browne Collection, about 4000 photographs of stage productions and friends and associates, as well as programs, posters, scrapbooks of mounted clippings, about 200 original stage and costume designs, promptbooks, and play manuscripts, representing the American and British careers of this husband-wife team from 1912-1917, to about 1940. The Chicago Little Theatre, 1912-1917, is well represented. Also contains more than 6000 items of correspondence with theatrical and literary figures. Another collection contains 143 Alfred Lunt letters, mainly from 1909-1915.

MI —DETROIT PUBLIC LIBRARY, Burton Historical Collection, 5201 Woodward Ave, Detroit, 48202. Alice Dalligan, Chief

NJ —PRINCETON UNIVERSITY, Library, William Seymour Theatre Collection, Princeton, 08544. Mary Ann Jensen, Cur
Budget: ($10,000)
Notes: Plus scrapbooks, playbills, posters.

NY —NEW YORK STATE LIBRARY, State Education Bldg Annex, Washington Ave, Albany, 12224.
Holdings: Cat
Notes: Printed handbills and posted announcements of historic and everyday events; Theatre performances; auctions; advertisements; land sales; slave sales, reward posters for runaways; inducements to enlist for military service. Over 2000 pieces. Also over 1300 poetic broadside ballads.

NY —STATE UNIVERSITY OF NEW YORK, BINGHAMTON, Glenn G Bartle Library, Binghamton, 13901. Marion Hanscom, Special Collections Librn
Holdings: Cat
Budget: ($8000)
Notes: Max Reinhardt Archive. Library has extensive (approx 250,000 items) archival material relating to Max Reinhardt, as well as his personal library. This personal library is not a subject collection per se, but contains much information about German theatre in the 20th century. The archival material contains letters, prompt books, photographs, playbills, etc.

NY —HAMPDEN-BOOTH THEATRE LIBRARY AT THE PLAYERS, 16 Gramercy Park, New York, 10003. Louis A Rachow, Librn/Cur
Holdings: Vols 43 //
Notes: The Henderson Collection of English Theatre Playbills, 1734-1888. The collection is indexed and comprises 4000 playbills. This collection is no longer added to, but the library does continue to collect playbills. Described in *Theatre & Performing Arts Collections* (New York: Haworth Press, 1981).

NY —NEW YORK PUBLIC LIBRARY, Performing Arts Research Center, Billy Rose Theatre Collection, 111 Amsterdam Ave, New York, 10023. Dorothy L Swerdlove, Cur
Holdings: Cat
See also entry under Theatre.

NY —NEW YORK PUBLIC LIBRARY, Performing Arts Research Center, Dance Collection, 111 Amsterdam Ave, New York, 10023. Genevieve Oswald, Cur
Notes: About 4400 dance playbills and posters. The playbills date from the late 18th century to the present, with heaviest concentration on 19th century English items. They also include some 18th century French items, Fanny Elssler's appearances at the Park Theatre, New York, in the 1840s, and late 19th century productions at Niblo's Garden, notably *The Black Crook*. The posters are chiefly of the 20th century with greatest emphasis on American dance. Extensive collection of posters for the New York City Ballet, Ballet Theatre prior to 1957, the Denishawn Dancers, and Anna Pavlova. Also numerous posters and playbills for Les Ballets Russes de Diaghilev and Isadora Duncan. Mostly uncataloged.
See also entry under Programs, Dance

NY —YIVO INSTITUTE FOR JEWISH RESEARCH, Library & Archives, 1048 Fifth Ave, New York, 10028. Dina Abramowicz, Librn; Marek Web, Archivist
Holdings: Cat Mss Pix Slides
Notes: Yiddish drama in the original and in English translation from its 19th-century beginnings to the present; the Yiddish thatre in the Soviet Union and the theatrical activities in the ghettos during the Nazi regime; special collections of Sholem Perelmuter, Mendl Elkin, Maurice Schwartz, Abraham Goldfaden, Jacob Gordin, and Mark Schweid; records of the Union of Jewish Actors in Poland between the two world wars; the Vilna YIVO Collection of posters, playbills, and photographs; recordings.

NY —UNIVERSITY OF ROCHESTER, Rush Rhees Library, Department of Rare Books and Special Collections, Rochester, 14627. Peter Dzwonkoski, Librn
Notes: 18th and 19th century English and 19th century American plays and works on theatre. Also incl ms colleciton on theatre, and papers of Clement William Scott, John Lawrence Toole, Arthur Wing Pinero, Charles Kean, Lillian Russell and Leon Marks Lion, collection of 130 lithographic theatre posters, and collection of programs and playbills, chiefly Rochester and New York City, NY, 1900-1950. Unpublished guides to ms collections available in repository.

NY —STATE UNIVERSITY OF NEW YORK, STONY BROOK, Melville Library, Dept of Special Collections, Stony Brook, 11794. Evert Volkersz, Head
Holdings: // Uncat
Notes: Nineteenth century Chilean playbills, plays and libretti. A list of holdings is available. About 570 pamphlets bound in 57 vols.

OH —CLEVELAND PUBLIC LIBRARY, Literature Dept, 325 Superior Ave, Cleveland, 44114. Evelyn Ward, Head
Holdings: Cat
Notes: The theatre program collection consists of some 22,000 items, incl nearly complete sets for existing local theatres and resident companies, as well as substantial holdings, particularly in the Wertheimer Collection, for older theatres that have passed from the scene, dating back to the 19th century. The Leo and Lillie Weidenthal Memorial Collection also contains many rare programs and playbills, particularly from London theatres of the 19th century. Indexed by title, theatre, season, and some performers.

PA —FREE LIBRARY OF PHILADELPHIA, Theatre Collection, Logan Sq, Philadelphia, 19103. Geraldine Duclow, Librn-in-Charge
Holdings: Vols (1,250,000) Uncat Pix
Notes: The Theatre Collection contains books, magazines, playbills, broadsides, posters, photographs, and other memorabilia

PLAYBILLS—COLLECTIONS (cont.)

covering theatre, motion pictures, minstrels, vaudeville, circus, radio and television. The Library's Philadelphia Theatre Index lists the major productions here since 1855, and partially indexes the collection of local playbills which date back to 1803. There are also programs from many other cities, incl New York; some from London date back to 1800. Early film companies as well as the present movie industry are represented by advertising materials and over 30,000 film stills. The Lubin Film Co (1910-1916) Archive has been established with over 600 photographs and related items. Circus programs and route books date back to 1900. There are minstrel programs as early as 1865. Most significant are the mss from Philadelphia's Dumont Minstrels. Variousfiles contain autographs, photographs, newspaper articles and reviews in all pertinent subject areas. Noncirculating.

PA —UNIVERSITY OF PENNSYLVANIA, Van Pelt Library, Rare Books Collection, 34 & Walnut Sts, Philadelphia, 19104. Daniel Traister, Special Collections Librn
Holdings: Cat
Notes: Principally 18th century London and 18th and 19th century Philadelphia theatres.

PA —UNIVERSITY OF PITTSBURGH, Special Collections Dept, Curtis Theatre Collection, 363 Hillman Library, Pittsburgh, 15260. Jeanette Blanco, Cur
Holdings: Vols (4000) Cat Mss Documents Microforms Pix Slides VF
Notes: The legitimate theatre of plays, musicals and vaudeville, chiefly of New York City and Pittsburgh, from 1865, and other US, community, summer, college and foreign theatre. Incl 500,000 programs, 12,000 pictures, 300 posters, the Oliver P Merriman Scrapbooks and 300 other scrapbooks, clippings and other ephemera. Vols incl over 3000 acting editions and playscripts. Separate collections: Ralph G Allen Burlesque Skits Collection; Michael Ellis Papers; William P Halstead Theatre Collection; Kenyon Family Papers; Philip Dunning Playscripts Collection; Pittsburgh Playhouse Records; Pittsburgh Savoyards Records. Noncirculating.

TX —DALLAS PUBLIC LIBRARY, Fine Arts Div, 1515 Young St, Dallas, 75201. Richard L Waters, Acting Dir; Jane Holahan, Manager
Holdings: // Uncat Mss Pix
Notes: The Margo Jones Theatre Collection (75 linear ft) contains the office papers of this theatre: financial, business, legal records, scripts, programs, photos of productions, reviews and clippings, personal correspondence; organizational records. Gift of Dallas Civic Theatre, Inc, 1962 after theatre ceased operation. Described in LC card catalog MS 66-1622. Also The W E Hill Theatre Collection, 18th-20th centuries, ca 75,000 items. Contains letters, portraits, and photos of leading American, British, and European dramatists, actors, managers, and other persons associated with the stage or the performing arts, particularly music; playbills, posters of stage plays, minstrel shows, and circuses; and newspaper and magazine clippings. The bulk of the collection consists of 19th and 20th century items. Described in LC card catalog MS 66-1621. Partiallydescribed in the "Fine Arts Department of the Dallas Public Library presents an exhibit of selected material from the W E Hill theatre collection on the occasion of the opening of the collection..." (1966). Gift of estate of William Ely Hill, 1963. Also The John Rosenfield Collection consisting of ca 2000 playbills assembled by this Amusements Critic of the *Dallas Morning News*, from both his travels and local productions. Also correspondence with various important artists in the theatre. There are also photographs, telegrams, etc of these people. The Dallas Little Theatre Collection consists of printed programs of this group which won the Belasco Cup three consecutive years in New York City; many clippings, photographs and other related

newspaper articles. Oral histories are being assembled from persons connected with the theatre during its lifetimefrom 1922-1944.

TX —SOUTHERN METHODIST UNIVERSITY, Fondren Library, McCord Theater Collection, Room 301, Dallas, 75275. Edyth Renshaw, Cur; Linda Sellers, Pub Serv
Holdings: Vols (2000) Uncat Mss Pix Slides Phonorecords
Notes: See *Theatre Collections in Libraries and Museums*, Gilder and Freedley (Theatre Arts, 1936). The McCord Theatre Collection encompasses the entire spectrum of the performing arts. The central purpose is to gather records of our regional theater before such ephemeral material is lost. Records of over two hundred early Texas theaters, some fragmentary and some relatively complete, are in the files. These records incl photographs of buildings, stagehands, orchestras, and performers. Local theatre history incl the once famous Dallas Little Theatre and the Margo Jones Theatre. The national theatre, opera, ballet, and circus archives incl pictures (some autographed), programs, posters, throw-aways, tear sheets, clippings, and letters. Our international archives are small, but we have some excellent material, eg, artifacts from Max Reinhardt's production of"The Miracle" which happened to go bankrupt in Dallas. After a few years the items were given to us. There are posters, tear sheets, souvenir programs, and other colorful items from Morris Gest and the Artef Collection. We have about 200 19th century English playbills and a few from the 18th century. There is a collection of modern English, French, and other European programs, many of them illustrated souvenir programs. Also, magazines on theater, cinema, and television (1800). Scrapbooks covering both southwest and Dallas theater, 1890s-1950s. Special Collections: artifacts and documents on puppets; masks; costume design; circus; and ballet and dance. The Harriet Bacon MacDonald Collection of over 200 photographs of musicians appearing in Dallas during the first three decades of the 20th century. Many autographed. Affiliated with Meadow Theatre of the Arts.

†WA —WASHINGTON STATE UNIVERSITY, Library, Manuscripts, Archives & Special Collections, Pullman, 99164. John F Guido, Head
Holdings: // Cat Mss Pix
Notes: The Robert Cushman Butler Collection of Theatrical Illustrations contains: approx 1600 illustrations, sheet music covers, programs and playbills; approx 100 mss of actors and actresses and playwrights; and approx 200 vols of theatrical history and reminiscences, several extra-illustrated, concentrating on the 18th-19th century British and American drama. A guide to the collection is in preparation.

AB —UNIVERSITY OF ALBERTA, Cameron Library, The Bruce Peel Special Collections Room, Edmonton, T6G 2J8, Can. John Charles, Special Collections Librn
Holdings: Cat
Notes: Several hundred theatre posters and playbills.

ON —NATIONAL LIBRARY OF CANADA, 395 Wellington St, Ottawa, K1A 0N4, Can. Andre Preibish, Dir
Holdings: Vols 8000
Notes: Includes 100 serial titles, also programs, play bills etc on microfilm. Performing arts collection consists of Canadian titles received on legal deposit and purchased. Areas of concentration: Canadian theatre and dance; European and American performing arts tradition; theatre architecture; stage craft; costume history; dance history and notation etc.

ON —METROPOLITAN TORONTO LIBRARY, Theatre Dept, 789 Yonge St, Toronto, M4W 2G8, Can. Heather McCallum, Head
Holdings: Vols (30,500) Mss Pix Slides Phonorecords Microforms
Notes: Collections of playbills, clippings and correspondence document the career of Charles Manny (1890-1962) in both England

and the United States; interviews and reminiscences on tape are available for the first all-sister act in vaudeville, the Canadian born O'Conner Sisters.

THE PLAYERS

NY —HAMPDEN-BOOTH THEATRE LIBRARY AT THE PLAYERS, 16 Gramercy Park, New York, 10003. Louis A Rachow, Librn/Cur
Holdings: Cat Mss Pix
Notes: "The Players Revivals Collection" incl 8 linear feet of mss, playbills, photographs. The series of revivals produced by The Players began with *The Rivals* in 1922. In subsequent years productions incl *The School for Scandal* (1923), *Trelawny of the Wells* (1925), *The Way of the World* (1931), *Uncle Tom's Cabin* (1933), and others. The last revival in the series was a production of *Love for Love* in 1940. All business details, staging and publicity were undertaken exclusively by members of The Players. Actors such as John Drew, Otis Skinner, Walter Hampden, Charles Coburn, George M Cohan, and Howard Lindsay, and actresses such as Ethel Barrymore, Helen Hayes, Laurette Taylor, Pauline Lord, Dorothy Stickney, and others contributed their services. "The Players Pipe Nights Collection" incl 20 linear ft ofindexed phonotapes of guests of honor's recollections, etc, incl Alfred Lunt and Lynn Fontanne, Howard Lindsay, William L Laurence, George Abbott, Maurice Chevalier, Sol Hurok, and many others. Archives of the British Actors Orphanage Fund; also of La Mama Experimental Theatre Club. Described in *Theatre & Performing Arts Collections* (New York: Haworth Press, 1981).

NY —NEW YORK PUBLIC LIBRARY, Performing Arts Research Center, Billy Rose Theatre Collection, 111 Amsterdam Ave, New York, 10023. Dorothy L Swerdlove, Cur
Holdings: Cat
See also entry under Theatre.

PLAYFAIR, GILES

MA —BOSTON UNIVERSITY, Mugar Memorial Library, Special Collections Dept, 771 Commonwealth Ave, Boston, 02215. Howard B Gotlieb, Dir
Holdings: Cat Mss Pix
Notes: Mss, correspondence, etc collected in depth; incl publications by or about.

PLAYING CARDS see Cards

PLAYS see Drama

PLAYS, CHILDREN'S see Children's Plays

PLAYSCRIPTS

VA —GEORGE MASON UNIVERSITY, Fenwick Library, Special Collections Dept, 4400 University Drive, Fairfax, 22030. Ruth Kerns, Public Services Librn
Notes: The Federal Theatre Project Collection includes 5000 playscripts, 2500 radio scripts, 25,000 photographs, 40 blueprints, 1000 posters, over 1600 costume designs, 350 scene designs, 750 production notebooks, 1700 programs and heralds, 26 musical scores and 18 cubic feet of research materials and play readers reports.

PLAYWRIGHTS, AMERICAN

DE —UNIVERSITY OF DELAWARE, Hugh M Morris Library, S College Ave, Newark, 19711. T Stuart Dick, Special Collections
Holdings: Cat Mss Pix
Notes: Mss, etc incl literary correspondence, playscripts, screenplays, production notes, playbills of Tennessee Williams.

MA —BRANDEIS UNIVERSITY, Goldfarb Library, 415 South St, Waltham, 02154. Bessie Hahn, Dir
Notes: Arthur Laurents Collection:

PLAYWRIGHTS, AMERICAN (cont.)

Collection contains six linear ft of dramatic mss in various draft forms. Access to the collection is through the Main Card Catalog and a finding list in Special Collections. Louis Kronenberger Collection: Consists of 5 linear ft of literary mss. Mr Kronenberger was a former drama and literary critic. The collection is unprocessed.

VA —GEORGE MASON UNIVERSITY, Fenwick Library, Special Collections Dept, 4400 University Drive, Fairfax, 22030. Ruth Kerns, Public Services Librn
Notes: Some 275,000 items (incl administrative, play service and research, library and production records) pertaining to the WPA Federal Theatre Project, on permanent loan from the Library of Congress.

WA —UNIVERSITY OF WASHINGTON LIBRARIES, Drama Library, BH-20, Seattle, 98195. Liz Fugate, Drama Librn
Holdings: Vols
Budget: ($13,182)
Notes: Collection incl history; criticism; costume; make-up; scene design; lighting; creative dramatics; children's theatre; directing; playwriting; acting. Special Collections include 19th century acting editions, contemporary acting editions and local theatre posters. 17,731 items cataloged, 24,255 uncataloged.

PLAYWRIGHTS, CANADIAN

BC —SIMON FRASER UNIVERSITY, Library, Burnaby, V5A 1S6, Can. Percilla Groves, Special Collections Librn
Holdings: Cat Mss
Notes: Playscripts, prose and poetry mss, correspondence, proofs and notebooks of the British Columbia poet and playwright.

ON —METROPOLITAN TORONTO LIBRARY, Theatre Dept, 789 Yonge St, Toronto, M4W 2G8, Can. Heather McCallum, Head
Holdings: Vols (30,500) Mss Pix Slides Phonorecords Microforms
Notes: Theatre Department is one of 11 subject departments of the Metropolitan Toronto Library. The department balances book and nonbook materials in all areas of the performing arts except music. the collection is international in scope and is particularly strong in materials relating to Canadian theatre history and drama. A comprehensive collection of Canadian plays is supplemented by extensive files of newspaper clippings and photographs, as well as indexes for biographical/critical material about performing arts personalities.

PLAYWRIGHTS, IRISH

PA —CARLOW COLLEGE, Grace Library, Fifth Ave, Pittsburgh, 15213. Joan M Mitchell, Dir of Library Services
Holdings: Vols 543 // Cat Phonorecords Audiotapes
Notes: The Gladys Wholey Curran Collection, which consists primarily of titles in the area of Irish Literature, specifically those titles concerned with the study of the Irish playwrights and poets. The collection is particularly strong in volumes related to the study of Jonathan Swift, John M Synge, and William B Yeats. In addition, there is notable focus upon Irish history of the 17th and 18th centuries. No photocopying.

PLAYWRIGHTS, WOMEN see Women Playwrights

PLAYWRIGHTS COMPANY

NY —NEW YORK PUBLIC LIBRARY, Performing Arts Research Center, Billy Rose Theatre Collection, 111 Amsterdam Ave, New York, 10023. Dorothy L Swerdlove, Cur
Holdings: Cat
Notes: Files covering period 1938-1960.

PLEASANTS, HENRY

MA —BOSTON UNIVERSITY, Mugar Memorial Library, Special Collections Dept, 771 Commonwealth Ave, Boston, 02215. Howard B Gotlieb, Dir
Holdings: Cat Mss Correspondence

PLECTRAL INSTRUMENTS see Stringed Instruments

PLESSEN, ELISABETH

MA —BOSTON UNIVERSITY, Mugar Memorial Library, Special Collections Dept, 771 Commonwealth Ave, Boston, 02215. Howard B Gotlieb, Dir
Holdings: Cat Mss

PLINIUS SECUNDUS, C.

MN —MAYO MEDICAL LIBRARY, History of Medicine Collection, Rochester, 55905. Nancy R Hensel, Librn
Holdings: Vols 50 Cat
Notes: The C Wilbur Rucker "Pliny" Collection, incl 43 14th, 15th and 16th century editions of the more than 200 editions of *Historia naturalis* by C Plinius Secundus.

PLOWDEN FAMILY

DC —GEORGETOWN UNIVERSITY, Library, Special Collections Div, 37 & O Sts NW, Washington, 20057. George M Barringer, Special Collections Librn; Nicholas B Sheetz, Mss Librn
Holdings: Mss Cat
Notes: Property leases, deeds, legal briefs, warrants, land surveys, and genealogical records pertaining to the Plowden family of Maryland, dating primarily from the 17th and 18th centuries.

PLOWING

AL —US DEPT OF AGRICULTURE, SCIENCE & EDUCATION ADMINISTRATION, National Tillage Machinery Laboratory, Library, PO Box 792, Auburn, 36830. William A Gill, Collaborator
Holdings: Vols (39,000) Cat Mss Maps Pix Slides 16mm Films Microforms
Budget: ($20,000)
Notes: The National Tillage Machinery Laboratory (NTML) has a special technical library comprised of highly selective engineering and physical science materials pertinent to soil-machine relations, such as tillage, earthmoving, mining, soil trafficability, and vehicle mobility. A high percentage of the library material comes from sources outside the US and outside agriculture. Particularly strong in Russian-language literature.

PLUMBAGO see Graphite

PLUMBING

NY —YONKERS PUBLIC LIBRARY, Information Services, 7 Main St, Yonkers, 10701. Martita Schwarz, Dept Head
Holdings: Vols (21,500) Cat Maps Microforms
Budget: ($30,000)

PA —CARNEGIE LIBRARY OF PITTSBURGH, Science & Technology Dept, 4400 Forbes Ave, Pittsburgh, 15213. Catherine M Brosky, Dept Head
Notes: Collection incl material on general construction, carpentry, masonry, plumbing, heating, air conditioning, corrosion and painting and numerous other building trades. Sweets Architectural File complete except for a few years. *Car Builders Encyclopedia of American Practice*, most editions since 1879.

PLUNKETT, EDWARD J.M.D. see Dunsany, Edward J.M.D. Plunkett, Lord, 1878-1957

PLUNKETT, SIR HORACE

DC —GEORGETOWN UNIVERSITY, Library, Special Collections Div, 37 & O Sts NW, Washington, 20057. George M Barringer, Special Collections Librn; Nicholas B Sheetz, Mss Librn
Holdings: Mss Cat Pix
Notes: The papers of the Irish man-of-letters Sir Shane Leslie (1885-1971) containing letters, mss, diaries, notebooks, clippings, and photographs. Extensive correspondence by Margot Asquith, countess of Oxford and Asquith; Lady Violet Bonham-Carter; Burke Cochran; Lord Alfred Douglas; Moreton Frewen; Cardinal Gasquet; Vyvyan Holland; Lady Leonie Leslie; Sir Wilfrid Meynell; Sir Horace Plunkett; John Quinn; Frederick Rolfe (Baron Corvo); and Elizabeth Russell, among others. Also incl are research files on Sir Winston Churchill (Leslie's first cousin); Leonard Jerome; Maria Anne Fitzherbet (wife of King George IV); Ghosts and Ghost stories; and Eton College.

PLUTZIK, HYMAN

NY —UNIVERSITY OF ROCHESTER, Rush Rhees Library, Department of Rare Books and Special Collections, Rochester, 14627. Peter Dzwonkoski, Librn
Holdings: Vols Cat Mss
Notes: Extant archive including manuscripts, worksheets, correspondence, and lecture notes. Described in exhibition catalogue, "The Hyman Plutzik Archive," University of Rochester Library, 5 December-5 June, 1982.

PLYMOUTH COLONY

MA —BRIDGEWATER PUBLIC LIBRARY, 15 South St, Bridgewater, 02324. Maryellen Remmert, Dir
Holdings: Cat Mss Maps Pix
Notes: Incl some genealogical material of considerable interest since Bridgewater was the first inland colony of the Plymouth (Pilgrim) Colony, being known as the Duxbury Plantation.

MA —PLYMOUTH PUBLIC LIBRARY, North St, Plymouth, 02360. Anne Clark, Reference Librn
Holdings: Vols 600 Cat Mss Maps Pix
Notes: Most of the collection deals with pre-1800 Plymouth. Includes facsimiles and/or printed editions of early journals, diaries, laws, records of Plymouth Colony and town.

RI —BROWN UNIVERSITY, John Hay Library, 20 Prospect St, Providence, 02912. Mark N Brown, Cur Mss
Holdings: // Mss
Notes: 8 mss in the hand of Roger Williams incl his copy of Chief Osamaquin's deed of land (1646), letters to the Plymouth Colony, a copy of *Proceedings of the General Assembly* (1655), and his proposals to resolve the Pawtuxet-Providence boundary dispute.

POCKET PLANTATION

VA —UNIVERSITY OF VIRGINIA, Alderman Library, Manuscripts Dept, Charlottesville, 22901. Edmund Berkeley Jr, Cur
Holdings: Cat Mss Maps Pix
Notes: 19th century Virginia Family Papers Collections enable a researcher to obtain an excellent picture of the economic and social interactions on large plantations in Virginia during the 19th century. They are invaluable as research sources in the study of slavery, women's history, economic history, agrarian and political history.

PODAGRA see Gout

PODIATRY

CA —CALIFORNIA COLLEGE OF PODIATRIC MEDICINE, Schmidt Medical Library, 1210 Scott St, San Francisco, 94115. Leonard P Shapiro, Library Dir
Holdings: Vols (20,000) Cat Mss Slides Phonorecords Audiotapes Videotapes
Budget: $99,762
Notes: General medical library with special emphasis on the foot and podiatry (500 vols). Also orthopedics, lower extremity materials, sports medicine.

PODIATRY (cont.)

NJ —SAINT MICHAEL'S MEDICAL
CENTER, Aquinas Medical Library, 268
High St, Newark, 07102. Betty L Garrison,
Dir; Valerie Manuel, Library Asst
Holdings: Vols (4500) Cat
Notes: Primarily bound journals, 1958-date.

NY —UNIVERSITY OF ROCHESTER,
School of Medicine and Dentistry, Edward
G Miner Library, 601 Elmwood Ave,
Rochester, 14642. Lucretia McClure,
Medical Librn; Janet Brady Berk, History of
Medicine Librn
Holdings: Slides
Notes: Very rare historical collection of
some 300 glass slides, most of which relate
to human gait, the foot, footwear, and
myodynamics.

OH —OHIO COLLEGE OF PODIATRIC
MEDICINE LIBRARY, 10515 Carnegie
Ave, Cleveland, 44106. Judy Cowell, Librn
Holdings: Vols 1000 Slides Audiotapes
Videotapes
Notes: Incl podiatric medicine.

PA —PENNSYLVANIA COLLEGE OF
PODIATRIC MEDICINE, Charles E
Krausz Library, Race at Eighth St,
Philadelphia, 19107. John C Harris, Librn;
Frances E Peters, Librn; Lisabeth M
Holloway, Archivist
Holdings: Vols (15,000) Cat
Budget: $125,000
Notes: Emphasis on podiatry and chiropody.
Numerous rare books in collection.

POE, EDGAR ALLAN

CA —UNIVERSITY OF CALIFORNIA, SAN
DIEGO, Central University Library,
Mandeville Dept of Special Collections, La
Jolla, 92093. Lynda Corey Claassen, Head
Notes: First and/or important editions of his
writings.

IN —INDIANA UNIVERSITY, Lilly Library,
Seventh St, Bloomington, 47405. William R
Cagle, Librn
Holdings: Vols 300 // Cat Mss Pix
Notes: First and early editions. Mss incl
correspondence and papers relating to Poe
and correspondence of Sarah Helen
Whitman concerning her friendship with
Poe, 1846-1878. 311 items.

IA —UNIVERSITY OF IOWA, University
Libraries, Iowa City, 52242. Frank Paluka,
Head, Special Collections Dept
Holdings: Vols 160 Cat
Notes: Nucleus of collection consists of the
Poe-related books and articles collected by
the late Thomas Olive Mabbott.

MD —JOHNS HOPKINS UNIVERSITY,
Milton S Eisenhower Library, Special
Collections, John Work Garrett Library,
4545 N Charles St, Baltimore, 21210. Jane
Katz, Garrett Librn
Holdings: // Cat Mss
Notes: Music related to the works of Poe.
Cataloged in *Music and Edgar Allan Poe: a
Bibliographical Study*, by May Garrettson
Evans (Baltimore: Johns Hopkins Univ
Press, 1939).

MA —HARVARD UNIVERSITY LIBRARY,
Houghton Library, Cambridge, 02138.
Rodney G Dennis, Cur of Manuscripts
Holdings: Cat Mss
Budget: mss

NY —BRONX COUNTY HISTORICAL
SOCIETY, Bronx County Research Library,
3309 Bainbridge Ave, Bronx, 10467. Gary
Hermalyn, Exec Dir
Holdings: Vols (100) Cat Mss Pix Slides
Audiotapes 16mm Films Filmstrips
Notes: Historical Bronx. Publishes *The
Bronx County Historical Society Journal*.

PA —FREE LIBRARY OF PHILADELPHIA,
Rare Book Dept, Logan Sq, Philadelphia,
19103. Marie E Korey, Rare Book Librn
Holdings: Vols 1500 Cat Mss Pix
Notes: The Colonel Richard Gimble
Collection of Edgar Allan Poe, incl first
editions, manuscripts, autograph letters,
reprints, illustrated editions, foreign editions,
periodicals and newspapers as well as
biographical and critical reference materials.
The Free Library of Philadelphia also owns

the house at 530 N 7th Street, in which Poe
lived from 1843 to 1844.

RI —BROWN UNIVERSITY, John Hay
Library, 20 Prospect St, Providence, 02912.
Mark N Brown, Cur Mss
Holdings: // Mss
Notes: Sarah Helen Whitman, 1803-1898, an
American poet and friend of Edgar Allan
Poe. A group of about 500 mss for the
period 1835-192, chiefly correspondence,
notes, and articles by Mrs Whitman.
Subjects include: Poe, English and American
literature, spiritualism, and personal matters.
Also incl correspondence and copies of
letters, mss, and reminiscences of Mrs
Whitman gathered by her literary heirs;
letters to and from James Albert Harrison
(1848-1911) regarding his books on Poe; and
letters from Maria Clemm Poe to Mrs
Whitman about Poe.

RI —BROWN UNIVERSITY, John Hay
Library, Harris Collection, Prospect St,
Providence, 02912. Rosemary L Cullen, Cur
Holdings: Vols (200,000) Cat Mss Pix
Phonorecords Microforms
Budget: ($15,000)
Notes: Extensive collection of first editions,
biographical and critical material, ephemera,
portraits, association items, sheet music.
Collections incl 200,000 vols 30,000
broadsides, 55,000 mss, 170,000 pieces of
sheet music, 450 phonorecords, and 375
microfilm reels. See *Dictionary Catalog of
the Harris Collection of American Poetry
and Plays* (Boston: G K Hall, 1972), 13 vols;
Supplement (1977), 3 vols. See also,
*American Poetry, 1609-1900, A Collection
on Microfilm, Segment I (1609-1820);
Segment II (1821-1850); Segment III
(1851-1870)* (Woodbridge, Conn: Research
Publications). Separate catalog.

VA —UNIVERSITY OF VIRGINIA,
Alderman Library, Manuscripts Dept,
Charlottesville, 22901. Edmund Berkeley Jr,
Cur
Holdings: // Cat Mss Pix
Notes: The Poe-Ingram Collection includes
letters and other manuscripts, photographs,
printed matter, biographical source materials,
collected by Poe biographer John Henry
Ingram, including many otherwise unknown
copies of Poe letters. About 10,000 ms
pieces. Bibliography: John Carl Miller, *John
Henry Ingram's Poe Collection at the
University of Virginia* (Charlottesville:
University of Virginia Press, 1960).

VA —UNIVERSITY OF VIRGINIA,
Alderman Library, Clifton Waller Barrett
Collection, Charlottesville, 22901. Joan St C
Crane, Cur of American Literature
Collections
Holdings: Vols 30 Cat Mss
Notes: Rare editions of Poe, many in fine
state. Incl mss and letters.

POE, JAMES, 1921-

CA —UNIVERSITY OF CALIFORNIA, LOS
ANGELES, Research Library, Dept of
Special Collections, 405 Hilgard Ave, Los
Angeles, 90024. Edward Shreeves,
Chairman, Bibliographers Group; David S
Zeidberg, Head
Holdings: Mss Pix
Notes: 13 linear feet of radio, television, and
moving picture scripts, correspondence, etc.

POE SOCIETY see Edgar Allan Poe
Society

POELKER, JOHN H.

MO —WASHINGTON UNIVERSITY,
Libraries, Special Collections Dept, Campus
Box 1061, St Louis, 63130.
Notes: St Louis Mayoral Papers Collection:
Papers of Aloys P Kaufmann, 1944-49;
Raymond R Tucker, 1953-65; Alphonso J
Cervantes, 1965-73; John H Poelker, 1973-
77; James F Conway, 1977-81.

POETESSES see Women Poets

POETICAL MISCELLANIES—ENGLISH

KS —UNIVERSITY OF KANSAS, Kenneth
Spencer Research Library, Special

Collections Dept, Lawrence, 66045.
Alexandra Mason, Librn
Holdings: Vols 500 Cat
Notes: Mostly 18th century. Noncirculating.
Index to first-lines in repository (Boys-
Mizener index).

POETRY—COLLECTIONS

CA —UNIVERSITY OF CALIFORNIA,
DAVIS, Shields Library, Dept of Special
Collections, Davis, 95616. Donald Kunitz,
Head; C Danial Elliott, Asst Head
Notes: 7500 ephemeral and rare titles in
experimental or post-1946 American or
innovative poetry; 10,000 vols of minor
British poets (1789-1950s).

CA —LOS ANGELES COUNTY PUBLIC
LIBRARY, Huntington Park Library, 6518
Miles Ave, Huntington Park, 90255. Michael
McClintock, Librn
Holdings: Vols 1350 Cat
Notes: The Granger Collection.

CA —UNIVERSITY OF CALIFORNIA, SAN
DIEGO, Central University Library,
Mandeville Dept of Special Collections, La
Jolla, 92093. Lynda Corey Claassen, Head;
Michael Davidson, Cur, Archive for New
Poetry
Notes: An extensive collection of modern
English-language poetry published since
World War II, the Archive contains over 28,
000 books, over 1000 magazine titles, and
some 900 tapes and records. The Archive
maintains substantial collections of papers
from Paul Blackburn, Charles Reznikoff,
Lew Welch, Jerome Rothenberg, Louis
Zukofsky, and other major contemporary
American poets. The collection of papers
belonging to editor and publisher Donald
Allen represents the work of one of the first
publishers to make innovative poetry
available through his anthology, *The New
American Poetry, 1945-1960*, and through
his two presses, The Four Seasons
Foundation and Grey Fox Press.

CA —CALIFORNIA STATE UNIVERSITY,
NORTHRIDGE, Delmar T Oviatt & South
Libraries, 1811 Nordhoff St, Northridge,
91330. Donald L Read, Special Collections
Dept
Holdings: Vols 2500 Cat
Notes: McDermott collection of
contemporary writers of American fiction
and poetry, signed, first editions. Emphasis is
upon both established and new
contemporary writers. Collection fully
cataloged.

CA —CONTRA COSTA COUNTY
LIBRARY, 1750 Oak Park Blvd, Pleasant
Hill, 94523. Barbara Potter, Librn

CA —SAN DIEGO PUBLIC LIBRARY,
Literature & Language Sect, 820 E St, San
Diego, 92101. Alyce Archuleta, Senior Librn
Holdings: Cat
Notes: Collection of both well-known and
lesser known American contemporary poets.

CT —TRINITY COLLEGE LIBRARY,
Watkinson Library, 300 Summit St,
Hartford, 06106. Jeffrey Kaimowitz, Cur
Holdings: Cat Mss
Notes: Incl the Reif Collection of modern
poetry and separate poetry collections, such
as Frost, Millay, Moore, Robinson, etc.

CT —YALE UNIVERSITY, Box 1603A, Yale
Station, New Haven, 06520.

CT —YALE UNIVERSITY, Beinecke Rare
Book & Manuscript Library, Osborn
Collection, New Haven, 06520. Stephen R
Parks, Cur
Holdings: Mss
Notes: English poetry, especially 17th-18th
centuries. Incl first-line index of all poems.

CT —UNIVERSITY OF CONNECTICUT,
Library, Storrs, 06268. George F Butterick,
Cur of Literary Archives
Holdings: Mss Pix
Notes: Post-modern American poets. Incl
books and mss of writers Charles Olson,
Robert Creeley, Robert Duncan, Edward
Dorn, Joel Oppenheimer, John Wieners, as
well as documents pertaining to Black
Mountain College.

DC —LIBRARY OF CONGRESS, Rare Book
& Special Collections Div, Washington,
20540. William Matheson, Chief
Holdings: Cat
See also entry under Broadsides - Collections

POETRY—COLLECTIONS (cont.)

DC —LIBRARY OF CONGRESS, Motion
Pictures, Broadcasting and Recorded Sound
Div, Washington, 20540.
Notes: Archive of Recorded Poetry and
Literature is a collection of nearly 1200
spoken recordings. Among the major literary
figures represented by noncommercial
recordings are Conrad Aiken, John
Berryman, E E Cummings, Robert Frost,
and Robert Lowell.

FL —FLORIDA STATE UNIVERSITY,
Robert Manning Strozier Library, Childhood
in Poetry Collection, Tallahassee, 32306.
Frederick Korn, Cur
Holdings: Vols (25,000) Cat
Notes: The Childhood in Poetry Collection
consists of the books of all the great poets
and hundreds of minor poets of all periods,
in first or other early and illustrated editions,
in children's periodicals and "juveniles".
There are more than 300 hymnals, incl the
personal collection of Dr Robert Lowry,
author of "Shall We Gather at the River"
and other popular hymns. There are also
nearly 500 annuals and gift books. The
Collection is strong, as well, in works of
criticism, biography and reference. An
eleven-volume, illustrated catalog (1967-
1980) is available from Gale Research. Over
200,000 poems are listed in a key-word
index, keyed to the books in which they
appear. The nucleus of the Collection was
assembled as the lifetime leisure activity of
the donor, John Mackay Shaw, who now
serves as curator emeritus. His object has
been to gather in one place the books
inwhich poems relating to childhood first
appeared.

FL —ROLLINS COLLEGE, Mills Memorial
Library, Winter Park, 32789. Patricia J
Delks, Dir of Libraries
Holdings: Vols 1775 // Cat Mss
Notes: Poetry collection of Jessie B
Rittenhouse. Poetry and letters (to and
from). Noncirculating.

IL —NEWBERRY LIBRARY, 60 W Walton
St, Chicago, 60610. Diana Haskell, Cur of
Modern Mss
Holdings: Cat
Notes: First editions of English and
American poetry by recognized poets.

IN —INDIANA UNIVERSITY, Lilly Library,
Seventh St, Bloomington, 47405. William R
Cagle, Librn
Holdings: Cat Mss
Notes: Extensive holdings of British and
American first editions and of the writings
and correspondence of poets and of poetry
publications, especially of modern literary
magazines.
See also entry under Periodicals, Publishing
of - History - US

IN —INDIANA UNIVERSITY, Institute for
Sex Research Library, 416 Morrison Hall,
Bloomington, 47401. Douglas Freeman,
Collections and Services Librn; Joan Brewer,
Information Services Librn
Holdings: Vols (62,000) Cat Mss Pix
Phonorecords Audiotapes Slides Films
Microforms
Budget: ($20,000)
Notes: One of the greatest and most
extensive collections on sexual behavior, the
library collects materials on all aspects of sex
activity, with special emphasis on behavioral
and social aspects. Also collects erotic
literature and sexual ephemera. Incl 105
audiotapes, 23 vertical file drawers, 108
phonorecords, 55,000 pictures, 500 slides,
and 1700 films. Rich in French, German and
American sources; also much Oriental.
Semitraditional erotic poetry and song of
17th-18th century England. Bawdy
limericks, double-entendre, puns, slang,
erotic literature, graffiti, slang and special
dictionaries, proverbs and sayings, epigrams
and research materials of the Kinsey Studies,
etc. Contact Information Service for:
literature searching, preparation of
bibliographies, permission to use collection.
Limited photocopying.

KY —BEREA COLLEGE, Hutchins Library,
Berea, 40404. Gerald F Roberts, Librn

Special Collections
Notes: In the general collection.

MA —AMHERST COLLEGE, Library,
Amherst, 01002. John Lancaster, Special
Collections Librn
Holdings: Vols (500) Uncat Mss
Notes: Concentration on the Georgian poets
Lascelles Abercrambie, Edmund Blunden, W
H Davies, John Drinkwater, Wilifred
Gibson, Harold Monro, Edward Thomas.

MA —BOSTON UNIVERSITY, Mugar
Memorial Library, Special Collections Dept,
771 Commonwealth Ave, Boston, 02215.
Howard B Gotlieb, Dir
Holdings: Vols Cat Mss Pix
Notes: Incl the publications, mss and
personal papers of ca 25 people. Researchers
should inquire.

MA —HARVARD UNIVERSITY LIBRARY,
Lamont Library, Woodberry Poetry Rm,
Cambridge, 02138. Stratis Haviaras, Cur
Holdings: Vols 4000 Cat Phonorecords
Notes: See Harvard Library Bulletin, III
(1949), 441-445, and VIII (1954), 65-73.
Photocopying restricted and discouraged.

MA —PINE MANOR COLLEGE, Library,
310 Heath St, Chestnut Hill, 02167. Linda
Denners, Head Librn
Holdings: Vols (500) Cat
Notes: French symbolist poets.

MA —CARY MEMORIAL LIBRARY, 1874
Massachusetts Ave, Lexington, 02173.
Robert C Hilton, Dir
Holdings: Cat
Notes: Strong in modern American poetry,
the collection also incl ancient, foreign, and
English poetry.

MA —WHEATON COLLEGE, Library,
Norton, 02766. Sherrie S Bergman, College
Librn
Holdings: Vols (2100) Cat
Notes: The Cole Collection. English and
American literature and poetry based on the
personal library of Dr Samuel Valentine
Cole.

MI —DETROIT PUBLIC LIBRARY,
Language and Literature Dept, 5201
Woodward Ave, Detroit, 48202. Ann
Rabjohns, Chief
Holdings: Vols 28,500 Cat
Notes: The collection is strong in English
and American poetry with emphasis on
modern English-speaking poets. But it also
incl significant foreign poetry in translation,
occasionally in the original language. Many
contemporary small press publications are
incl.

MI —WAYNE STATE UNIVERSITY, Kresge
Library (Education), Detroit, 48202.
Theodore Manheim, Librn
Holdings: Vols (65,000) Cat Mss Microforms
Budget: ($2000)
Notes: The Eloise Ramsey Collection (10,
000 vols). See, The Eloise Ramsey
Collection of Literature for Young People: A
Catalogue; compiled by Joan Cusenza
(Detroit: Wayne State University Libraries,
1967). Besides the Ramsey Collection, which
is housed separately and does not circulate,
the Education Library has approx 55,000
volumes of children's and young adults'
literature, with a very large picture-book
collection, a large poetry collection; all with
special emphasis on urban and ethnic
materials.

MI —MICHIGAN STATE UNIVERSITY,
Libraries, Special Collections Div, East
Lansing, 48824. Jannette Fiore, Librn
Notes: Several thousand vols of American
small press poetry, ca 1965 to present, being
augmented at the rate of 350 to 450 vols per
year.

NJ —MONTCLAIR STATE COLLEGE,
Harry A Sprague Library, Upper Montclair,
07043.
Holdings: Vols 1357 // Uncat
Notes: Collection comprises Webster
Collection, Margaret B Pennick Collection,
Arthur M Sullivan Collection, and William
Carlos Williams Collection. Collection. Incl
many first editions, presentation copies and
signed and limited editions. There are
separate shelf-lists for each collection.

NM —NEW MEXICO STATE UNIVERSITY,
Library, Box 3475, Las Cruces, 88003.
James Dyke, Dir
Notes: The collection contains 38,630 items-

-a vast quantity of little magazines and
Anglo-American Modernism published
between 1900-1975. Little poetry magazines
are an exceptionally strong part of this
collection.

NY —NEW YORK STATE LIBRARY, State
Education Bldg Annex, Washington Ave,
Albany, 12224.
Holdings: Vols (10,000) Cat
Notes: American poetry of more than 10,000
vols. Strong in minor poetry, extensive to
1900. Over 1300 broadside ballads.

NY —STATE UNIVERSITY OF NEW
YORK, COLLEGE AT BUFFALO, Poetry/
Rare Books Collection, 420 Capen Hall,
Buffalo, 14260. Robert J Bertholf, Cur
Holdings: Vols (75,000) Cat Mss Pix
Phonorecords Audiotapes Microforms
Notes: The Poetry Collection, founded in
1937 by the late Charles D Abbott, is
devoted to 20th century poetry in English
and in translation. It contains some 75,000
vols in first and variant editions, 600
phonorecords and 400 audiotapes presenting
poets who read from their own work; more
than 3500 sets of little magazines covering
the last 80 years; a unique collection of mss,
letters, notebooks, worksheets, and noted by
contemporary poets, explaining their
methods of composition; and a number of
portraits, sculptures and photographs. "The
Poetry Collection is internationally known
for its importance in the field of James Joyce
(qv), Dylan Thomas, William Carlos
Williams, Robert Graves, Martin Seymour-
Smith and Robert Kelley."

NY —NATIONAL BASEBALL HALL OF
FAME AND MUSEUM, National Baseball
Library, Cooperstown, 13326. Thomas R
Heitz, Librn
Notes: An extensive collection of verse
devoted to baseball by amateur and
professional poets.

NY —CITY UNIVERSITY OF NEW YORK,
City College, Morris R Cohen Library,
North Academic Center, Convent Ave &
137th St, New York, 10031. Barbara J
Dunlap, Archivist
Holdings: Vols 75 // Phonorecords
Audiotapes
Notes: Kimball Flaccus Collection of
Recordings made at City College between
1938 and 1941 under the direction of faculty
member Flaccus, himself a poet. Incl are
recordings by Edgar Lee Masters, Richard
Aldington, Marianne Moore, Robinson
Jeffers, Allen Tate, John Peale Bishop, and
W H Auden. In some cases these were the
first recordings made by the poets reading
from their own works. In addition to the
recordings, the collection comprises some
seventy-five vols of poetry from the period,
many of them signed first editions. The
original 99 discs (some of aluminum) have
been transcribed onto cassette tape so
patrons may hear them without damage to
the originals.

†NY —NEIGHBORHOOD PLAYHOUSE
SCHOOL OF THE THEATRE, Irene
Lewisohn Library, 340 E 54 St, New York,
10022. Alice G Owen, Librn
Holdings: Vols Cat Mss Pix
See also entry under Theatre - History

NY —NEW YORK PUBLIC LIBRARY,
Research Libraries, General Research
Division, Fifth Ave & 42 St, New York,
10018. Rodney Phillips, Chief
Holdings: Vols (2,225,000) Cat Maps Pix
Microforms
Budget: ($775,718)

NY —POETRY SOCIETY OF AMERICA,
Van Voorhis Library, 15 Gramercy Park,
New York, 10003. Jason Shinder, Dir
Holdings: Vols 5000 Cat Mss
Notes: The American poetry ranges from the
turn of the century to contemporary poets.
There is a separate catalog for American
poetry. American and other poetry
anthologies, biography, criticism, essays, and
poetics. A large holograph collection and
memorabilia of the Poetry Society of
America are included in the Rare Book
Division of the NY Public Library.

NY —STATE UNIVERSITY OF NEW
YORK, COLLEGE AT ONEONTA, James
M Milne Library, Oneonta, 13820. Richard

POETRY—COLLECTIONS (cont.)

D Johnson, Librn
Holdings: Vols (427,646) Cat Mss Maps Pix Slides Phonorecords Audiotapes 16mm Films Filmstrips Microforms
Budget: ($338,299)
Notes: New York State Collection; 19th and early 20th century popular fiction; New York State Verse Collection; Early Textbook & Early Educational Theory Collection.

NC —APPALACHIAN STATE UNIVERSITY, Belk Library, Instructional Materials Center, Boone, 28608. Selma P Farthing, Librn
Holdings: Vols (20,000) Cat Pix
Notes: The collection is especially strong in poetry and folklore, chosen for the use of classes in children's literature. It also includes many old children's books, used in Critical History courses.

NC —PUBLIC LIBRARY OF CHARLOTTE & MECKLENBURG COUNTY, Literature and Drama Dept, 310 N Tryon St, Charlotte, 28202. Anne McNair, Reference Librn
Holdings: Cat Phonorecords
Notes: Large collection of poetry in English and other languages in translation or original. Biographies of poets, indexes, criticisms, recordings.

NC —DUKE UNIVERSITY, William R Perkins Library, Rare Book Room, Durham, 27706. John L Sharpe, III, Cur
Notes: Paul Hamilton Hayne collection of American poets and poetry (1800 books, pamphlets and periodicals).

OH —CLEVELAND PUBLIC LIBRARY, Literature Dept, 325 Superior Ave, Cleveland, 44114. Evelyn Ward, Head
Holdings: Vols Cat Phonorecords
Notes: A large collection of poetry, incl virtually all the works of every American poet who has received critical recognition, as well as a substantial representation of English poets, early through modern, and foreign poets in English translation. Extensive critical and biographical material. Extensive card index to individual poems, by author, title, first line, and subject.

PA —ATHENAEUM OF PHILADELPHIA, 219 S Sixth St, Philadelphia, 19106. Roger W Moss Jr, Librn
Holdings: Vols 2000 Uncat Mss Pix
Notes: The Charles Wharton Stork Collection of 20th Century Poetry. Charles Wharton Stork (d 1972) was editor of the all poetry journal, *Contemporary Verse*. His entire library of first editions and inscribed works by American poets, in addition to correspondence files for the journal, were presented to the Athenaeum in 1972. In the process of being cataloged. Mss and correspondence, approx 30 large Hollinger cases. the Athenaeum will add to this collection in the area of American poets, c 1900-1925. No photocopying until cataloged.

RI —BROWN UNIVERSITY, John Hay Library, Harris Collection, Prospect St, Providence, 02912. Rosemary L Cullen, Cur
Holdings: Vols (200,000) Cat Mss Phonorecords Microforms
Budget: ($15,000)
Notes: The Harris Collection of American Poetry and Plays is principally composed of American and Canadian poetry and plays, 17th century-date. Extensive holdings in songsters, gift books and annuals, hymnals, pageants, broadside verse, carriers' addresses, women poets, juvenile poetry, (incl Mother Goose and *The Night Before Christmas*), sheet music with lyrics, small press publications, fine printing, black poets, "little magazines," Yiddish-American literature. All movements or schools of American poetry are represented. Incl first editions of most American poets and playwrights, notably Whitman, Poe, Wallace Stevens, Eugene O'Neill, Edward Albee, Ezra Pound, T S Eliot, William Carlos Williams, Amy Lowell, Phyllis Wheatley, Robert Frost, Allen Ginsberg, Bliss Carman, and Stephen Foster sheet music. Also incl the Saunders Walt Whitman Collection (1300 vols); the LangdonCollection of

Pageants (250 vols); the Asa Cushman Collection of plays in ms and prompt copies; the MacDougall Collection of Psalters and Hymnals; 4000 plays issued by Walter H Baker Co, Boston (1890-1957); the Vaxer Collection of Yiddish Poetry, Plays and Music (1700 vols). Collections incl 200,000 vols, 30,000 broadsides, 55,000 mss, 170,000 pieces of sheet music, 450 phonorecords, and 375 microfilm reels. See *Dictionary Catalog of the Harris Collection of American Poetry and Plays* (Boston: G K Hall, 1972), 13 vols; *Supplement* (1977), 3 vols. See also, *American Poetry, 1609-1900, A Collection on Microfilm, Segment I* (1609-1820); *Segment II* (1821-1850); *Segment III* (1851-1870) (Woodbridge, Conn: Research Publications). Separate catalog.

RI —BROWN UNIVERSITY, John Hay Library, 20 Prospect St, Providence, 02912. Mary T Russo, Cur of Broadsides
Holdings: Vols (30,000)
Notes: A major collection of 30,000 pieces of American verse in broadside form dating from the 18th through the 20th century. Ephemeral in nature and all inclusive, it covers a broad spectrum of American life. Numerous examples of early American poetry, admonishing, proclaiming, celebrating, advertising and mourning are represented. Poets range from the anonymous to major figures, incl Cummings, Eliot, Emerson, Frost, Pound, and Whitman as well as countemporary authors. The Beat Movement, Black Mountain School, Concrete Poetry and poetry of the Harlem Renaissance are represented as well as that of the young black poets published by the Detroit Broadside Press and a good selection of poetry by women. Retrospective and current pieces are added annually. Partial catalog.

TN —VANDERBILT UNIVERSITY, Library, Nashville, 37240. Marice Wolfe, Special Collections Librn
Holdings: Vols 1000 Cat Mss Pix
Notes: Collection relating to the Fugitive poets of the 1920s, the Agrarian writers of the 1930s and their subsequent careers, as a complement to extensive mss collections in this field. Chief figures incl Allen Tate, John Crowe Ransom, Robert Penn Warren, Andrew Lytle, Donald Davidson, Merrill Moore, Laura Riding, et al.

WA —UNIVERSITY OF WASHINGTON LIBRARIES, Suzzallo Library, Special Collections Division, Rare Book Collection, FM-25, Seattle, 98195. Gary Menges, Coordinator for Special Collections
Holdings: Vols (12,000) Cat Maps
Notes: American, British, French, German and Italian books printed before 1800, chiefly in the fields of history and literature. Fine bindings and illustrated works are represented. Incl incunabula, emblemata, history of travel, and first editions of the works of major poets: Spenser, Blake, Whitman, Yeats, Roethke, etc.

WI —BELOIT COLLEGE LIBRARIES, Beloit, 53511. Dennis W Dickinson, Dir
Holdings: Vols 3000 Cat
Budget: $500
Notes: This is a collection of contemporary American poetry. Format of material varies from very slim to regular book-size vols; also backfiles of numerous poetry magazines. Kept together as a "special collection" for those interested in studying the tenor of contemporary American poetry (good and bad). Incl the *Beloit Poetry Journal* Collection.

BC —SIMON FRASER UNIVERSITY, Library, Burnaby, V5A 1S6, Can. Percilla Groves, Special Collections Librn
Holdings: Vols (12,000) Cat Mss
Notes: This collection concentrates on avant-garde American poetry since World War II. Incl some Canadian poetry (particularly West Coast poets), some British and certain of the International Concrete school. It particularly features the Black Mountain and San Francisco schools and those American and Canadian poets influenced by them. There is a relatively complete collection of works by Ezra Pound (qv), William Carlos Williams, Charles

Olson, Gertrude Stein and Louis Zukofsky together with considerable criticism on these authors. Also incl certain underground newspapers and 1600 periodical titles.

BC —VANCOUVER PUBLIC LIBRARY, Language & Literature Div, 750 Burrard St, Vancouver, V6Z 1X5, Can. B Kinnear, Head
Notes: General collection of poetry, drama criticism, novels, pamphlets. Index files of author biographies, poetry in periodicals, criticism in periodicals; also poetry index, both compiled by the staff to books unindexed periodicals. Partially cataloged. Also incl audiotapes.

BC —UNIVERSITY OF VICTORIA, McPherson Library, Victoria, V8W 3H5, Can.
Notes: Stony Brook Poetics Foundation. Incl 7 leaves, 1968; Stony Brook Holographs 1968 no 3/10; folder of 7 cardboard sheets (35 cm x 28 cm) with holograph poems, signed by Robert Duncan, Jim Harrison, Denise Levertov, Jerome Rothenberg, Charles Simic, Louis Simpson, John Wieners.

ON —QUEEN'S UNIVERSITY, Douglas Library, Kingston, K7L 5C4, Can. William F E Morley, Cur, Special Collections
Holdings: Vols 650 Uncat
Notes: Incl F R Scott Collection, incl Canadian poetry and poetry magazines. Checklist of holdings is available.

ON —VICTORIA UNIVERSITY, Library, 71 Queen's Park Crescent, Toronto, M5S 1K7, Can. Robert C Brandeis, Chief Librn
Holdings: Vols (5000) Cat
See also entry under Canada - History

POETRY—RECORDINGS

CT —YALE UNIVERSITY, Sterling Memorial Library, Yale Collection of Historical Sound Recordings, 120 High St, New Haven, 06520. Richard Warren Jr, Cur
Holdings: Mss Pix Phonorecords Audiotapes
Notes: Incl "classical music" ("concert music") of all types from Western culture, jazz, the American Musical Theatre, spoken material (literary, dramatic, documentary). The aim of the Collection is to document performance practice in the fields collected. See the article by Karol Berger in the *Journal of the Association for Recorded Sound Collections*, vol VI, no 1, pp 13-25. Partially cataloged.

POETRY—SELECTIONS see Poetry—Collections

POETRY, AMERICAN see American Poetry

POETRY, AMERICAN PATRIOTIC see Patriotic Poetry, American

POETRY, CALIFORNIA

CA —CALIFORNIA STATE UNIVERSITY, HAYWARD, Library, Hayward, 94542. Melissa Rose, Dir
Holdings: Vols 8000 Cat Phonorecords
Budget: $2469
Notes: Covers San Francisco Bay Area poetry publishing from early 1960s to date, incl key writers and works of the era of the Beat Generation. Incl books, periodicals, broadsides, records, with extensive collection of titles from Black Sparrow, Oyez, and Unicorn presses. Noncirculating.

POETRY, CHILDREN'S see Children's Poetry

POETRY, CHINESE

WA —UNIVERSITY OF WASHINGTON LIBRARIES, East Asia Library, DO-27, Seattle, 98195. Karl Lo, Head
Holdings: Vols (300,000) Cat Microforms
Budget: ($200,000)
Notes: Southwest China: Joseph Rock Collection, ca 2000 vols; modern Chinese poetry, 1919 to date: ca 700 titles; Asian art, esp Japanese painting: 4097 vols; Tiao-yu-t'ai movement in the US: ca 400 items of periodicals and pamphlets; modern Korean

POETRY, CHINESE (cont.)

poetry, ancient and modern: ca 1000 titles; Mu-yu-shu folk literature: ca 1000 items.

POETRY, CONCRETE see Concrete Poetry

POETRY, ENGLISH see English Poetry

POETRY, EXPERIMENTAL see Experimental Poetry

POETRY, FRENCH see French Poetry

POETRY, IMAGIST see Imagist Poetry

POETRY, INNOVATIVE see Innovative Poetry

POETRY, KOREAN

WA —UNIVERSITY OF WASHINGTON LIBRARIES, East Asia Library, DO-27, Seattle, 98195. Karl Lo, Head
Holdings: Vols (300,000) Cat Microforms
Budget: ($200,000)
Notes: Southwest China: Joseph Rock Collection, ca 2000 vols; modern Chinese poetry, 1919 to date; ca 700 titles; Asian art, esp Japanese painting; 4097 vols; Tiao-yu-t'ai movement in the US: ca 400 items of periodicals and pamphlets; modern Korean poetry, ancient and modern: ca 1000 titles; Mu-yu-shu folk literature: ca 1000 items.

POETRY, MODERN

CA —UNIVERSITY OF CALIFORNIA, BERKELEY, Bancroft Library, Manuscripts Division, Berkeley, 94720. James D Hart, Dir
Holdings: Vols 2000 Cat Mss
Notes: The Contemporary Poetry Collection covers the San Francisco publishing scene, from the period of the Beat Movement through the present day. In addition to printed materials, The Bancroft Library contains the important printer/publisher/bookseller archives of the Untide Press, City Lights, and the Auerhahn Press.
CA —UNIVERSITY OF CALIFORNIA, DAVIS, Shields Library, Dept of Special Collections, Davis, 95616. Donald Kunitz, Head; C Danial Elliott, Asst Head
Holdings: Vols 7500 Cat Mss
Notes: 7500 ephemeral and rare titles in experimental or innovative post-1946 American poetry. Incl papers of Gary Snyder (5500 items), cataloged.
CA —CALIFORNIA STATE UNIVERSITY, HAYWARD, Library, Hayward, 94542. Melissa Rose, Dir
Holdings: Vols 8000 Cat Phonorecords
Budget: $2469
Notes: Covers San Francisco Bay Area poetry publishing from early 1960s to date, incl key writers and works of the era of the Beat Generation. Incl books, periodicals, broadsides, records, with extensive collection of titles from Black Sparrow, Oyez, and Unicorn presses. Noncirculating.
CA —UNIVERSITY OF CALIFORNIA, SAN DIEGO, Central University Library, Mandeville Dept of Special Collections, La Jolla, 92093. Lynda Corey Claassen, Head; Michael Davidson, Cur, Archive for New Poetry
Notes: An extensive collection of modern English-language poetry published since World War II, the Archive contains over 28,000 books, over 1000 magazine titles, and some 900 tapes and records. The Archive maintains substantial collections of papers from Paul Blackburn, Charles Reznikoff, Lew Welch, Jerome Rothenberg, Louis Zukofsky, and other major contemporary American poets. The collection of papers belonging to editor and publisher Donald Allen represents the work of one of the first publishers to make innovative poetry available through his anthology, The New American Poetry, 1945-1960, and through his two presses, The Four Seasons Foundation and Grey Fox Press.

CA —CALIFORNIA STATE UNIVERSITY, NORTHRIDGE, Delmar T Oviatt & South Libraries, 1811 Nordhoff St, Northridge, 91330. Donald L Read, Special Collections Dept
Holdings: Vols 2500 Cat
Notes: McDermott collection of contemporary writers of American fiction and poetry, signed, first editions. Emphasis is upon both established and new contemporary writers. Collection fully cataloged.
CA —SAN DIEGO PUBLIC LIBRARY, Literature & Language Sect, 820 E St, San Diego, 92101. Alyce Archuleta, Senior Librn
Holdings: Cat
Notes: Collection of both well-known and lesser known American contemporary poets.
CT —TRINITY COLLEGE LIBRARY, Watkinson Library, 300 Summit St, Hartford, 06106. Jeffrey Kaimowitz, Cur
Holdings: Cat Mss
Notes: Incl the Reif Collection of modern poetry and separate poetry collections, such as Frost, Millay, Moore, Robinson, etc.
CT —UNIVERSITY OF CONNECTICUT, Library, Storrs, 06268. R H Schimmelpfeng, Dir of Special Collections
Holdings: Cat Mss Pix Audiotapes
Notes: Focuses on poets brought to attention by Donald Allen's New American Poetry anthology: the Black Mountain, New York, San Francisco, Beat poets, and their successors; the Postmodern American poets, such as Charles Olson, Robert Creeley, Robert Duncan, Allen Ginsberg, Edward Dorn, Frank O'Hara, Gary Snyder, LeRoi Jones/Imamu Baraka, and Denise Levertov.
DC —GEORGETOWN UNIVERSITY, Library, Special Collections Div, 37 & O Sts NW, Washington, 20057. George M Barringer, Special Collections Librn; Nicholas B Sheetz, Mss Librn
Holdings: Vols (3000) Uncat Mss
Notes: The Murray L Marshall Collection, including several thousand issues of American poetry magazines; a complete run of Sonnet Sequences, 1929-58; and Mr Marshall's editorial files for Sonnet Sequences.
FL —UNIVERSITY OF MIAMI, Otto G Richter Library, PO Box 248214, Coral Gables, 33124. Frank Rodgers, Dir of Libraries
Notes: Innovative and experimental writing of the 1960s and 1970s. Incl generous proportion of press books: Black Sparrow, Auerhahn, and many others; also other private publications ranging from the best to the least attractive. Format incl postcards and broadsides as well as periodical and book form. Writers incl Charles Bukowski, Diane Wakoski, Jerome Rothenberg, Clayton Eshleman, and many of their contemporaries. 2400 items.
FL —UNIVERSITY OF FLORIDA, Libraries, Special Collections, W University Ave, Gainesville, 32611. Sidney Ives, Librn & Rare Books
Holdings: Vols 10,000 Cat Mss Audiotapes
Notes: First editions of American and English poets from 1900 to date; strong after 1930.
IL —NEWBERRY LIBRARY, 60 W Walton St, Chicago, 60610. Diana Haskell, Cur of Modern Mss
Notes: English and American to 1950.
IL —UNIVERSITY OF CHICAGO LIBRARY, Dept of Special Collections, 1100 E 57 St, Chicago, 60637.
Notes: Harriet Monroe Collection.
IN —BALL STATE UNIVERSITY, Libraries, Special Collections Dept, University Ave, Muncie, 47306. David C Tambo, Head of Special Collections
Holdings: Cat Mss Pix Phonorecords Audiotapes
Notes: Primarily American poets.
KS —UNIVERSITY OF KANSAS, Kenneth Spencer Research Library, Special Collections Dept, Lawrence, 66045. Alexandra Mason, Librn
Holdings: Vols 3000 Cat Mss
Notes: Modern American poetry, 1960 to date. Nonacademic, especially fugitive and ephemeral. Noncirculating.

MD —UNIVERSITY OF MARYLAND, Library, Archives & Manuscripts Dept, College Park, 20742. Mary A Boccaccio, Head
Holdings: Mss Pix
MA —BOSTON UNIVERSITY, Mugar Memorial Library, Special Collections Dept, 771 Commonwealth Ave, Boston, 02215. Howard B Gotlieb, Dir
Holdings: Cat Mss Pix
Notes: Contemporary literary criticism and poetry, incl literary and personal papers of numerous modern authors; first editions, translations, etc. A complete list is available.
MA —SUFFOLK UNIVERSITY, College Library, Beacon Hill, Boston, 02114. Edmund G Hamann, College Librn
Holdings: Vols 4000 // Cat
Notes: The Irving Zieman library of 19th and 20th century British and American poetry.
MA —HARVARD UNIVERSITY LIBRARY, Lamont Library, Woodberry Poetry Rm, Cambridge, 02138. Stratis Haviaras, Cur
Holdings: Vols 4000 Cat Phonorecords
Notes: See Harvard Library Bulletin, III (1949), 441-445, and VIII (1954), 65-73. Photocopying restricted and discouraged.
MA —CARY MEMORIAL LIBRARY, 1874 Massachusetts Ave, Lexington, 02173. Robert C Hilton, Dir
Holdings: Cat
Notes: Strong in modern American poetry, the collection also incl ancient, foreign, and English poetry.
MA —BRANDEIS UNIVERSITY, Goldfarb Library, 415 South St, Waltham, 02154. Bessie Hahn, Dir
Notes: Frank Zwillinger Collection: 12 linear ft of drafts, revised drafts and final drafts of poetry and dramatic presentations in German by this Austrian literary figure. Incl in the collection are 3 linear ft of tape recordings of poetry readings by this author. A finding list to the collection is located in Special Collections. Lizette W Reese Collection: Consists of 6 linear ft of first editions, ms poetry and correspondence of this American poetess. The collection is unprocessed.
MI —DETROIT PUBLIC LIBRARY, Language and Literature Dept, 5201 Woodward Ave, Detroit, 48202. Ann Rabjohns, Chief
Holdings: Vols 28,500 Cat
Notes: The collection is strong in English and American poetry with emphasis on modern English-speaking poets. But it also incl significant foreign poetry in translation, occasionally in the original language. Many contemporary small press publications are incl.
MO —WASHINGTON UNIVERSITY, John M Olin Library, Campus Box 1061, St Louis, 63130.
Holdings: Mss
Notes: First, later, special editions; copies corrected or inscribed by the author; critical studies; little magazines and other printed materials, of a select group of American and British authors and representative minor figures. Extensive collections and/or mss, correspondence of Conrad Aiken, Lee Anderson, Basil Bunting, Robert Creeley, James Dickey, Robert Duncan, William Everson, Donald Finkel, Ted Hughes, Robert Lowell, James Merrill, Marianne Moore, Howard Nemerov, Charles Olson, William Jay Smith, Gary Snyder, Mona Van Duyn, William Carlos Williams, Louis Zukofsky and others. Incl printed works.
MO —WASHINGTON UNIVERSITY, Libraries, Special Collections Dept, Campus Box 1061, St Louis, 63130.
Notes: A major collection, incl books, mss, correspondence, literary papers, photographs, etc. Described in Special Collections: an Annotated Guide to the Holdings of the Manuscript Division and the University Archives and Research Collection.
NM —NEW MEXICO STATE UNIVERSITY, Library, Box 3475, Las Cruces, 88003. James Dyke, Dir
Holdings: Cat
Notes: The collection contains 38,630 items--a vast quantity of little magazines and

POETRY, MODERN (cont.)

Anglo-American Modernism published between 1900-1975. Little poetry magazines are an exceptionally strong part of this collection.

NY —STATE UNIVERSITY OF NEW YORK, COLLEGE AT BUFFALO, Poetry/ Rare Books Collection, 420 Capen Hall, Buffalo, 14260. Robert J Bertholf, Cur
Holdings: Vols (75,000) Cat Mss Pix Phonorecords Audiotapes Microforms
Notes: The Poetry Collection, founded in 1937 by the late Charles D Abbott, is devoted to 20th century poetry in English and in translation. It contains some 75,000 vols in first and variant editions, 600 phonorecords and 400 audiotapes presenting poets who read from their own work; more than 3500 sets of little magazines covering the last 80 years; a unique collection of mss, letters, notebooks, worksheets, and noted by contemporary poets, explaining their methods of composition; and a number of portraits, sculptures and photographs. "The Poetry Collection is internationally known for its importance in the field of James Joyce (qv), Dylan Thomas, William Carlos Williams, Robert Graves, Martin Seymour-Smith and Robert Kelley." In addition, extensive archive of Jack Shoemaker, a prominent bookseller, publisher and poet. Incl mss, work sheets, correspondence, ephemera, andbusiness records of the Sand Dollar and Unicorn bookshops and the Maya Press. Also incl mss and letters of prominent modern poets.

NY —POETRY SOCIETY OF AMERICA, Van Voorhis Library, 15 Gramercy Park, New York, 10003. Jason Shinder, Dir
Holdings: Vols 5000 Cat Mss
Notes: The American poetry ranges from the turn of the century to contemporary poets. There is a separate catalog for American poetry. American and other poetry anthologies, biography, criticism, essays, and poetics. A large holograph collection and memorabilia of the Poetry Society of America are included in the Rare Book Division of the NY Public Library.

NY —STATE UNIVERSITY OF NEW YORK, STONY BROOK, Melville Library, Dept of Special Collections, Stony Brook, 11794. Evert Volkersz, Head
Holdings: Cat
Notes: Publications and ms materials of poets who studied with Charles Olson at Black Mountain College, incl Robert Creeley, who also edited *Black Mountain Review*, and those associated with that generation of writers. In addition, authors and poets associated with The Perishable Press Ltd of Wisconsin, which started publication in 1966 and has published Paul Blackburn, David Kherdian, Galway Kinnell, Toby Olson, Joel Oppenheimer, W D Snodgrass, William Stafford, Diane Wakoski, Keith and Mary Waldrop, and Perishable Press owners Walter and Mary Hamady.

NY —RUSSELL SAGE COLLEGE LIBRARY, James Wheelock Clark Library, Ferry St, Troy, 12180. Joseph Menditto, Dir of Tech Services
Holdings: Vols (8000) Cat Mss Phonorecords
Notes: Incl 20th-century traditional and avant-garde poetry in first editions. Also, the Hamilton Finlay Collection of Concrete Poetry archives.

OH —OHIO UNIVERSITY, Vernon R Alden Library, Department of Archives and Special Collections, Athens, 45701. Gary A Hunt, Head
Holdings: Vols 1300 Uncat
Notes: A collection of 19th and 20th century poetry by lesser-known and unknown English and American authors.

OH —BOWLING GREEN STATE UNIVERSITY, Jerome Library, Center for Archival Collections, Bowling Green, 43403. Paul D Yon, Dir; Elaine R Ezell, Reference Archivist; Nancy Steen, Rare Books Librn
Holdings: Vols 600 Cat Periodicals
Budget: ($3000)
Notes: The Thomas F Eckman Memorial Collection of selected modern poetry. Many volumes signed.

PA —TEMPLE UNIVERSITY LIBRARIES, Special Collections Dept, Contemporary Culture Collection, Philadelphia, 19122. Patricia J Case, Cur
Notes: The Contemporary Culture Collection. See full entry under US-Social Life and Customs.

PA —UNIVERSITY OF PITTSBURGH, Hillman Library, Special Collections Dept, Hervey Allen Collection, Pittsburgh, 15260. Charles E Aston, Jr, Coordr
Holdings: Vols 2100 Cat
Notes: Emphasis on American and British poetry of the 20th century with special focus on the period 1950-date.

RI —UNIVERSITY OF RHODE ISLAND, Library, Special Collections, Kingston, 02881. David Maslyn, Head
Notes: Extensive collections.

RI —REDWOOD LIBRARY & ATHENAEUM, 50 Bellevue Ave, Newport, 02840. Donald T Gibbs, Librn
Holdings: Vols 3500 Cat
Budget: $300
Notes: Greenvale Collection of Contemporary Poetry.

RI —BROWN UNIVERSITY, John Hay Library, Harris Collection, Prospect St, Providence, 02912. Rosemary L Cullen, Cur
Holdings: Vols (200,000) Cat Mss Phonorecords Microforms
Budget: ($15,000)
Notes: The Harris Collection of American Poetry and Plays is principally composed of American and Canadian poetry and plays, 17th century-date. Extensive holdings in songsters, gift books and annuals, hymnals, pageants, broadside verse, carriers' addresses, women poets, juvenile poetry, (incl Mother Goose and *The Night Before Christmas*), sheet music with lyrics, small press publications, fine printing, black poets, "little magazines," Yiddish-American literature. All movements or schools of American poetry are represented. Incl first editions of most American poets and playwrights, notably Whitman, Poe, Wallace Stevens, Eugene O'Neill, Edward Albee, Ezra Pound, T S Eliot, William Carlos Williams, Amy Lowell, Phyllis Wheatley, Robert Frost, Allen Ginsberg, Bliss Carman, and Stephen Foster sheet music. Also incl the Saunders Walt Whitman Collection (1300 vols); the LangdonCollection of Pageants (250 vols); the Asa Cushman Collection of plays in ms and prompt copies; the MacDougall Collection of Psalters and Hymnals; 4000 plays issued by Walter H Baker Co, Boston (1890-1957); the Vaxer Collection of Yiddish Poetry, Plays and Music (1700 vols). Collections incl 200,000 vols, 30,000 broadsides, 55,000 mss, 170,000 pieces of sheet music, 450 phonorecords, and 375 microfilm reels. See *Dictionary Catalog of the Harris Collection of American Poetry and Plays* (Boston: G K Hall, 1972), 13 vols; *Supplement* (1977), 3 vols. See also, *American Poetry, 1609-1900, A Collection on Microfilm, Segment I* (1609-1820); *Segment II* (1821-1850); *Segment III* (1851-1870) (Woodbridge, Conn: Research Publications). Separate catalog.

RI —BROWN UNIVERSITY, John Hay Library, 20 Prospect St, Providence, 02912. Mary T Russo, Cur of Broadsides
Notes: A major collection of 30,000 pieces of American verse in broadside form dating from the 18th through the 20th century. Ephemeral in nature and all inclusive, it covers a broad spectrum of American life. Numerous examples of early American poetry, admonishing, proclaiming, celebrating, advertising and mourning are represented. Poets range from the anonymous to major figures, incl Cummings, Eliot, Emerson, Frost, Pound, and Whitman as well as contemporary authors. The Beat Movement, Black Mountain School, Concrete Poetry and poetry of the Harlem Renaissance are represented as well as that of the young black poets published by the Detroit Broadside Press and a good selection of poetry by women. Retrospective and current pieces are added annually. Partial catalog.

TX —UNIVERSITY OF TEXAS LIBRARIES, General Libraries, PO Box P, Austin, 78713. Carolyn Bucknell, Asst Dir for Collection Development
Holdings: Cat Microforms

TX —SAM HOUSTON STATE UNIVERSITY, Library, PO Box 2179, Huntsville, 77340. Chas Dwyer, Librn
Holdings: Cat Mss
Notes: The *Wild Dog* was a little magazine which published 20 issues from April 1963 to January 1964. The *Wild Dog* Collection consists of the typescripts for the published issues; correspondence with contributors, would-be contributors, bookshops, and individual subscribers; and the original cover art work with correspondence with the artists. There are approximately 600 letters and cards from the above mentioned sources; approximately 450 typescripts, some signed and corrected, by the authors who were published in the *Wild Dog;* and approximately 25 letters from artists accompanying the original cover art work. In connection with this archival material, additional separately published works by the contributing authors (approximately 120 volumes). No photocopying.

VT —UNIVERSITY OF VERMONT, Guy W Bailey/David W Howe Library, Burlington, 05405. John Buehler, Asst Dir for Special Collections
Notes: Poetic manuscripts of John Engels.

VA —VIRGINIA COMMONWEALTH UNIVERSITY, James Branch Cabell Library, Richmond, 23284. Daniel Yanchisin, Special Collections Librn
Holdings: Vols (3600)
Notes: A collection of approximately 3600 volumes by post 1945 American poets including some bibliography and criticism. 2000 books are cataloged and the remainder are accessible by author. The collection includes the library and archival holdings of two literary support organizations, New Virginia Review, Inc and the Poetry Society of Virginia.

WI —BELOIT COLLEGE LIBRARIES, Beloit, 53511. Dennis W Dickinson, Dir
Holdings: Vols 3000 Cat
Budget: $500
Notes: This is a collection of contemporary American poetry. Format of material varies from very slim to regular book-size vols; also backfiles of numerous poetry magazines. Kept together as a "special collection" for those interested in studying the tenor of contemporary American poetry (good and bad). Incl the *Beloit Poetry Journal* Collection.

WI —UNIVERSITY OF WISCONSIN, LA CROSSE, Murphy Library, 1631 Pine St, La Crosse, 54601. Edwin L Hill, Special Collections Librn
Holdings: Vols 1000 Cat Mss
Notes: Center for Contemporary Poetry (a collection of contemporary midwestern poetry). Emphasis on purchase of trade and small press publications of midwestern amd especially Wisconsin poets. Unpublished materials are collected for a few poets and incl comprehensive papers, mss, reviews, letters, etc. Collection also incl various midwestern and Wisconsin little magazines. Several fine midwestern private presses, especially Perishable Press. Collection is largely regional and contemporary. Most is cataloged and/or indexed. Collection incl records and papers of *Margins* (1972-1976), a review of little magazines and small press books. The Center for Contemporary Poetry published an annual volume, *Voyages to the Inland Sea*, from 1971-1979, featuring the poetry and essays of prominent midwestern poets.

WI —UNIVERSITY OF WISCONSIN, MILWAUKEE, Library, Box 604, Milwaukee, 53201. William C Roselle, Dir
Holdings: Vols (68,000) Cat Mss Phonorecords Audiotapes
Notes: Special strengths of the literature collection include Shakespeare Research Collection (1800 vols), 17th Century Collection (600 vols), William Blake, James Joyce, Howard Fast (English-language editions and unique collection of foreign-

POETRY, MODERN (cont.)

language translations), contemporary small press poetry publications, etc.

BC —SIMON FRASER UNIVERSITY, Library, Burnaby, V5A 1S6, Can. Percilla Groves, Special Collections Librn
Holdings: Vols (13,000) Cat Mss
Notes: This collection concentrates on avant-garde American poetry since World War II. Incl some Canadian poetry (particularly West Coast poets), some British and certain of the International Concrete school. It particularly features the Black Mountain and San Francisco schools and those American and Canadian poets influenced by them. There is a relatively complete collection of works by Ezra Pound (qv), William Carlos Williams, Charles Olson, Gertrude Stein and Louis Zukofsky together with considerable criticism on these authors. Also incl certain underground newspapers and 1600 periodical titles.

NB —MOUNT ALLISON UNIVERSITY, Ralph Pickard Bell Library, Sackville, E0A 3C0, Can. M Fancy, Librn
Holdings: Vols (13,372) Cat
Notes: The Mary Mellish Archibald Memorial Library incl folklore, folk music; children's literature. Incl phonorecords, with special emphasis on Canadian folklore and folk music.

†ON —UNIVERSITY OF TORONTO, Thomas Fisher Rare Book Library, Toronto, M5S 1A5, Can.
Notes: In addition to the special collections the library's extensive holdings in Canadian literature and history should be noted. One copy of all currently published Canadian poetry and fiction is placed in the Rare Book Library now as are copies of most significant works on Canadian art and most historical and biographical studies. Our retrospective literary holdings are comprehensive for Canadian poetry and extensive for Canadian fiction.

POETRY, PATRIOTIC AMERICAN see Patriotic Poetry, American

POETRY, PERUVIAN see Peruvian Poetry

POETRY, SYMBOLIST see Symbolist Poetry

POETRY, UKRAINIAN

PA —SLAVIA LIBRARY, 418 W Nittany Ave, State College, 16801. W O Luciw, Founder & Dir; Jurij A Luciw, Asst Dir
Holdings: Vols (45,000) Mss Pix
Budget: ($3500)
Notes: Incl 5000 periodicals, 3000 av materials, 4000 artifacts, and 200 art works. Also 16,000 letters, etc from Slavic and other personages.

POETRY, WAR see War Poetry

POETRY BOOK SOCIETY

MO —WASHINGTON UNIVERSITY, Libraries, Special Collections Dept, Campus Box 1061, St Louis, 63130.
Notes: A small but significant collection.

POETRY FOR CHILDREN see Children's Poetry

POETRY PERIODICALS see Periodicals, Poetry

POETRY SOCIETY OF AMERICA

NY —POETRY SOCIETY OF AMERICA, Van Voorhis Library, 15 Gramercy Park, New York, 10003. Jason Shinder, Dir
Holdings: Vols 5000 Cat Mss
Notes: The American poetry ranges from the turn of the century to contemporary poets. There is a separate catalog for American poetry. American and other poetry anthologies, biography, criticism, essays, and poetics. A large holograph collection and memorabilia of the Poetry Society of America are included in the Rare Book Division of the NY Public Library.

POETS

CT —YALE UNIVERSITY, Box 1603A, Yale Station, New Haven, 06520.

DC —LIBRARY OF CONGRESS, Motion Pictures, Broadcasting and Recorded Sound Div, Washington, 20540.
Notes: Archive of Recorded Poetry and Literature is a collection of nearly 1200 spoken recordings. Among the major literary figures represented by noncommercial recordings are Conrad Aiken, John Berryman, E E Cummings, Robert Frost, and Robert Lowell.

IN —INDIANA UNIVERSITY, Lilly Library, Seventh St, Bloomington, 47405. William R Cagle, Librn
Holdings: Cat mss
Notes: Extensive holdings of British and American first editions and of the writings and correspondence of poets and of poetry publications, especially of modern literary magazines.
See also entry under Periodicals, Publishing of - History - US

MA —BOSTON UNIVERSITY, Mugar Memorial Library, Special Collections Dept, 771 Commonwealth Ave, Boston, 02215. Howard B Gotlieb, Dir
Holdings: Cat Mss Pix
Notes: Incl the publications, mss and personal papers of ca 25 poets. Researchers should inquire.

NY —NEW YORK PUBLIC LIBRARY, Research Libraries, General Research Division, Fifth Ave & 42 St, New York, 10018. Rodney Phillips, Chief
Holdings: Vols (2,225,000) Cat Maps Pix Microforms
Budget: ($775,718)

NY —POETRY SOCIETY OF AMERICA, Van Voorhis Library, 15 Gramercy Park, New York, 10003. Jason Shinder, Dir
Holdings: Vols 5000 Cat Mss
Notes: The American poetry ranges from the turn of the century to contemporary poets. There is a separate catalog for American poetry. American and other poetry anthologies, biography, criticism, essays, and poetics. A large holograph collection and memorabilia of the Poetry Society of America are included in the Rare Book Division of the NY Public Library.

NY —SYRACUSE UNIVERSITY LIBRARIES, Ernest S Bird Library, George Arents Research Library for Special Collections, Syracuse, 13210. Carolyn A Davis, Manuscripts Librn; Amy S Doherty, University Archivist; Mark F Weimer, Rare Book Librn
Holdings: Mss
Notes: Personal papers of the poet, A E Johnson, incl correspondence with many notable "modern" literary persons.

NC —PUBLIC LIBRARY OF CHARLOTTE & MECKLENBURG COUNTY, Literature and Drama Dept, 310 N Tryon St, Charlotte, 28202. Anne McNair, Reference Librn
Holdings: Cat Phonorecords
Notes: Large collectin of poetry in English and other languages in translation or original. Biographies of poets, indexes, criticism, recordings.

BC —UNIVERSITY OF VICTORIA, McPherson Library, Victoria, V8W 3H5, Can.
Notes: Stony Brook Poetics Foundation. Incl 7 leaves, 1968; Stony Brook Holographs 1968 no 3/10; folder of 7 cardboard sheets (35 cm x 28 cm) with holograph poems, signed by Robert Duncan, Jim Harrison, Denise Levertov, Jerome Rothenberg, Charles Simic, Louis Simpson, John Wieners.

POETS, AMERICAN

CA —UNIVERSITY OF CALIFORNIA, DAVIS, Shields Library, Dept of Special Collections, Davis, 95616. Donald Kunitz, Head; C Daniel Elliott, Asst Head
Holdings: Vols 5500 Cat Mss
Notes: The Gary Snyder Papers contains ms worksheets and notebooks, copies of publications with works by Snyder, and correspondence to Snyder by many well-known poets of his generation--Robert Bly, Kirby Congdon, Cid Corman, Gregory Corso, Robert Creeley, Lawrence Ferlinghetti, Anselm Hollo, Joanne Kyger, John Montgomery, Philip Whalen, etc.

CA —UNIVERSITY OF CALIFORNIA, SAN DIEGO, Central University Library, Mandeville Dept of Special Collections, La Jolla, 92093. Lynda Corey Claassen, Head; Michael Davidson, Cur, Archive for New Poetry
Notes: An extensive collection of modern English-language poetry published since World War II, the Archive contains over 28,000 books, over 1000 magazine titles, and some 900 tapes and records. The Archive maintains substantial collections of papers from Paul Blackburn, Charles Reznikoff, Lew Welch, Jerome Rothenberg, Louis Zukofsky, and other major contemporary American poets. The collection of papers belonging to editor and publisher Donald Allen represents the work of one of the first publishers to make innovative poetry available through his anthology, *The New American Poetry, 1945-1960*, and through his two presses, The Four Seasons Foundation and Grey Fox Press.

CT —TRINITY COLLEGE LIBRARY, Watkinson Library, 300 Summit St, Hartford, 06106. Jeffrey Kaimowitz, Cur
Holdings: Cat
Notes: Incl Emily Dickinson, Robert Frost, Edna St Vincent Millay, Marianne Moore, Edwin Arlington Robinson, Wallace Stevens, Elinor Wylie, and other 19th and 20th century American poets.

CT —UNIVERSITY OF CONNECTICUT, Library, Storrs, 06268. George F Butterick, Cur of Literary Archives
Holdings: Mss Pix
Notes: American poets since World War II (post-modern American poets). Incl books and mss of writers Charles Olson, Robert Creeley, Robert Duncan, Edward Dorn, Joel Oppenheimer, John Wieners, Tom Clark, Ed Sanders, James Koller, Tom Raworth, Frank O'Hara, as well as documents pertaining to Black Mountain College.

DE —UNIVERSITY OF DELAWARE, Hugh M Morris Library, S College Ave, Newark, 19711. T Stuart Dick, Special Collections
Holdings: Cat Mss
Notes: Mss, notebooks, drafts, galleys and page proofs of all published works of Pulitzer Prize poet Donald Justice. Incl literary correspondence from 1953-1982.

DC —LIBRARY OF CONGRESS, Motion Pictures, Broadcasting and Recorded Sound Div, Washington, 20540.
Notes: The Archive of Recorded Poetry and Literature contains discs and tapes of readings of American literary figures from the 1940s to the present.

IN —BALL STATE UNIVERSITY, University Libraries, Special Collections Dept, University Ave, Muncie, 47306. David C Tambo, Head of Special Collections
Holdings: Cat Mss Pix Phonorecords Audiotapes

MA —GREENFIELD COMMUNITY COLLGE, The Archibald MacLeish Collection, One College Dr, Greenfield, 01301. Margaret E C Howland, Cur
Holdings: Vols 1662 Cat Mss Pix Slides Phonorecords Audiotapes Videotapes
Notes: The only authorized collection in the world devoted exclusively to the study of Archibald MacLeish, the man, his works, and his life. Contains all his published works plus clippings, galley proofs, letters, memorabilia, playbills and programs, posters, etc. Separately housed. Open by appointment.

MA —BRANDEIS UNIVERSITY, Goldfarb Library, 415 South St, Waltham, 02154. Bessie Hahn, Dir
Notes: Lizette W Reese Collection. Consists of 6 linear ft of first editions, ms poetry and correspondence of this American poetess. The collection is unprocessed, spring 1984.

MO —UNIVERSITY OF MISSOURI-COLUMBIA, Ellis Library, Language and

POETS, AMERICAN (cont.)

Literature Dept, Columbia, 65201. Jeaneice
Brewer, Librn
Holdings: Vols (3500) Cat
Notes: Consists of the personal library of
John G Neihardt, 1881-1973, poet, literary
critic, and lecturer. Lived among Omaha
Indians and Ogalala Sioux Indians to study
their character and history. Poet laureate of
Nebraska. Literary editor of *St Louis
Post-Dispatch*, 1926-38. Poet in residence
and lecturer in English, U of Missouri, 1949-
66. Manuscripts are housed separately in
Western Historical Manuscripts Collection of
Ellis Library.

MO —WASHINGTON UNIVERSITY,
Libraries, Special Collections Dept, Campus
Box 1061, St Louis, 63130.
Notes: A major collection, incl books, mss,
correspondence, literary papers, photographs,
etc. Described in *Special Collections: an
Annotated Guide to the Holdings of the
Manuscript Division and the University
Archives and Research Collection*.

NC —DUKE UNIVERSITY, William R
Perkins Library, Rare Book Room, Durham,
27706. John L Sharpe, III, Cur
Notes: Paul Hamilton Hayne collection of
American poets and poetry (1800 books,
pamphlets and periodicals).

NC —DUKE UNIVERSITY, William R
Perkins Library, Jay B Hubbell Center for
American Literary Historiography, Durham,
27706. Erma Whittington, Librn
Notes: 77,312 items, including manuscripts,
pictures, clippings, and correspondence. "The
objective of the Center is to gather the
papers and materials of significant scholars
and critics in American literary history." The
Center is a part of the Perkins Library
Manuscripts Department.

OH —CLEVELAND PUBLIC LIBRARY,
Literature Dept, 325 Superior Ave,
Cleveland, 44114. Evelyn Ward, Head
Holdings: Vols Cat Phonorecords
Notes: A large collection of poetry, incl
virtually all the works of every American
poet who has received critical recognition, as
well as a substantial representation of
English poets, early through modern, and
foreign poets in English translation.
Extensive critical and biographical material.
Extensive card index to individual poems, by
author, title, first line, and subject.

RI —BROWN UNIVERSITY, John Hay
Library, 20 Prospect St, Providence, 02912.
Mark N Brown, Cur Mss
Notes: Numerous mss involving American
poets, incl collections of Margaret Emerson
Bailer, Howard Blake, Anne Charlotte
Lynch Botta, George Shepherd Burleigh,
Harry Crosby, Bloodgood Haviland Cutter, S
Foster Damon, David Cornel DeJong,
Thomas Stearns Eliot, Edward Fenner, Hugh
Bernard Fox, Richard Watson Gilder, Albert
Gorton Greene, John Hay, Edwin Honig,
William Lewis Kinter, Harry Lyman
Koopman, William James Linton, Howard
Phillips Lovecraft, Nancy Luce, Willard
Maas, Edgar Lee Masters, William Douglas
O'Connor, Charles Horace Philbrick, Ezra
Loomis Pound, Winfield Townley Scott,
Benjamin Franklin Sours, Edmund Clarence
Stedman, William Leroy Stidger, Theodore
Tilton, Lucia De Fox Ungaro, Oscar
Wegelin, John Brooks Wheelwright, Sarah
Helen Whitman, Walt Whitman, William
Carlos Williams, Clement Wook, and Clarke
Ashton Smith (unprocessed). These
collections vary greatly insize and depth.

RI —BROWN UNIVERSITY, John Hay
Library, Harris Collection, Prospect St,
Providence, 02912. Rosemary L Cullen, Cur
Holdings: Vols (200,000) Cat Mss Pix
Phonorecords Microforms
Budget: ($15,000)
Notes: The Harris Collection of American
Poetry and Plays is principally composed of
American and Canadian poetry and plays,
17th century-date. Extensive holdings in
songsters, gift books and annuals, hymnals,
pageants, broadside verse, carriers'
addresses, women poets, juvenile poetry,
(incl Mother Goose and *The Night Before

Christmas*), sheet music with lyrics, small
press publications, fine printing, black poets,
"little magazines," Yiddish-American
literature. All movements or schools of
American poetry are represented. Incl first
editions of most American poets and
playwrights, notably Whitman, Poe, Wallace
Stevens, Eugene O'Neill, Edward Albee,
Ezra Pound, T S Eliot, William Carlos
Williams, Amy Lowell, Phyllis Wheatley,
Robert Frost, Allen Ginsberg, Bliss Carman,
and Stephen Foster sheet music. Also incl
the Saunders Walt Whitman Collection
(1300 vols); the LangdonCollection of
Pageants (250 vols); the Asa Cushman
Collection of plays in ms and prompt copies;
the MacDougall Collection of Psalters and
Hymnals; 4000 plays issued by Walter H
Baker Co, Boston (1890-1957); the Vaxer
Collection of Yiddish Poetry, Plays and
Music (1700 vols). Collections incl 200,000
vols, 30,000 broadsides, 55,000 mss, 170,000
pieces of sheet music, 450 phonorecords, and
375 microfilm reels. See *Dictionary Catalog
of the Harris Collection of American Poetry
and Plays* (Boston: G K Hall, 1972), 13 vols;
Supplement (1977), 3 vols. See also,
*American Poetry, 1609-1900, A Collection
on Microfilm, Segment I* (1609-1820);
Segment II (1821-1850); *Segment III* (1851-
1870) (Woodbridge, Conn: Research
Publications). Separate catalog.

†TX —UNIVERSITY OF TEXAS
LIBRARIES, General Libraries, Humanities
Research Center, PO Box 7219, Austin,
78712. John Chalmers, Librn
Notes: Complete archives of the Pulitzer
Prize poet, Anne Sexton (1928-1974).
Includes some of her suicide notes; also
correspondence with Maxine Kumin, another
Pulitzer winner.

†TX —UNIVERSITY OF TEXAS
LIBRARIES, General Libraries, Humanities
Research Center, PO Box 7219, Austin,
78712. John Chalmers, Librn
Holdings: Mss
Notes: A collection of documents relating to
the poet, Robert Lowell (1917-77). Incl 8000
ms pages of his works, galley and page
proofs of his last five books of poetry, and
nearly 2000 pages of literary correspondence
with his contemporaries.

WA —UNIVERSITY OF WASHINGTON
LIBRARIES, Suzzallo Library, Special
Collections Division, Rare Book Collection,
FM-25, Seattle, 98195. Gary Menges,
Coordinator for Special Collections
Holdings: Vols 12,000 Cat Maps
Notes: American, British, French, German
and Italian books printed before 1800,
chiefly inthe fields of history and literature.
Fine bindings and illustrated works are
represented. Incl incunabula, emblemata,
history of travel, and first editions of the
works of major poets: Spenser, Blake,
Whitman, Yeats, Roethke, etc.

BC —SIMON FRASER UNIVERSITY,
Library, Burnaby, V5A 1S6, Can. Percilla
Groves, Special Collections Librn
Holdings: Vols (12,000) Cat Mss
Notes: This collection concentrates on
avant-garde American poetry since World
War II. Incl some Canadian poetry
(particularly West Coast poets), some British
and certain of the International Concrete
school. It particularly features the Black
Mountain and San Francisco schools and
those American and Canadian poets
influenced by them. There is a relatively
complete collection of works by Ezra Pound
(qv), William Carlos Williams, Charles
Olson, Gertrude Stein and Louis Zukofsky
together with considerable criticism on these
authors. Also incl certain underground
newspapers and 1600 periodical titles.

POETS, AMERICAN, POSTMODERN
see Postmodern American Poets

POETS, AUSTRIAN

MA —BRANDEIS UNIVERSITY, Goldfarb
Library, 415 South St, Waltham, 02154.
Bessie Hahn, Dir
Notes: Frank Zwillinger Collection: 12 linear

ft of drafts, revised drafts and final drafts of
poetry and dramatic presentations in
German by this Austrian literary figure. Incl
in the collection are 3 linear ft of tape
recordings of poetry readings by this author.
A finding list to the collection is located in
Special Collections.

POETS, BLACK

IL —CHICAGO PUBLIC LIBRARY, G
Woodson Regional Library, George C Hall
Branch, 9525 S Halsted, Chicago, 60628.
Steven C Newsome, Cur; Hattie L Power,
Regional Library Dir
Notes: The Vivian G Harsh Collectioon on
Afro-American History and Literature, in
the George Cleveland Hall Branch of the
Chicago Public Library, contains books, in
print and on microfilm, periodicals,
recordings, tapes, pamphlets and mss.
Specializes in Afro-Americana, but contains
a sizeable number of books on Africa. Also
contains these noteworthy items: *The Negro
in Illinois: the Illinois Writers Project Files;
The Chicago Afro-American Union Analytic
Catalog; Big Boy Leaves Home*, by Richard
Wright (an original typewritten ms); *The Big
Sea*, by Langston Hughes (3 original
typewritten mss of this work). 7800 vols on
microfilm.

LA —AMISTAD RESEARCH CENTER, 400
Esplanade Ave, New Orleans, 70116. Clifton
H Johnson, Exec Dir; Florence E Borders,
Senior Archivist
Notes: Papers of Countee Cullen.

MA —UNIVERSITY OF MASSACHUSETTS
AT AMHERST, Library, Archives and
Manuscripts, Amherst, 01003. Siegfried
Feller, Assoc Dir for Collection
Development
Notes: Papers of W E B Du Bois.

RI —BROWN UNIVERSITY, John Hay
Library, Harris Collection, Prospect St,
Providence, 02912. Rosemary L Cullen, Cur
Holdings: Vols (200,000) Cat Mss Pix
Phonorecords Microforms
Budget: ($15,000)
Notes: The Harris Collection of American
Poetry and Plays is principally composed of
American and Canadian poetry and plays,
17th century-date. Extensive holdings in
songsters, gift books and annuals, hymnals,
pageants, broadside verse, carriers'
addresses, women poets, juvenile poetry,
(incl Mother Goose and *The Night Before
Christmas*), sheet music with lyrics, small
press publications, fine printing, black poets,
"little magazines," Yiddish-American
literature. All movements or schools of
American poetry are represented. Incl first
editions of most American poets and
playwrights, notably Whitman, Poe, Wallace
Stevens, Eugene O'Neill, Edward Albee,
Ezra Pound, T S Eliot, William Carlos
Williams, Amy Lowell, Phyllis Wheatley,
Robert Frost, Allen Ginsberg, Bliss Carman,
and Stephen Foster sheet music. Also incl
the Saunders Walt Whitman Collection
(1300 vols); the LangdonCollection of
Pageants (250 vols); the Asa Cushman
Collection of plays in ms and prompt copies;
the MacDougall Collection of Psalters and
Hymnals; 4000 plays issued by Walter H
Baker Co, Boston (1890-1957); the Vaxer
Collection of Yiddish Poetry, Plays and
Music (1700 vols). Collections incl 200,000
vols, 30,000 broadsides, 55,000 mss, 170,000
pieces of sheet music, 450 phonorecords, and
375 microfilm reels. See *Dictionary Catalog
of the Harris Collection of American Poetry
and Plays* (Boston: G K Hall, 1972), 13 vols;
Supplement (1977), 3 vols. See also,
*American Poetry, 1609-1900, A Collection
on Microfilm, Segment I* (1609-1820);
Segment II (1821-1850); *Segment III* (1851-
1870) (Woodbridge, Conn: Research
Publications). Separate catalog.

POETS, BLACK MOUNTAIN see Black
Mountain Poets

POETS, CANADIAN

RI —BROWN UNIVERSITY, John Hay
Library, Harris Collection, Prospect St,

POETS, CANADIAN (cont.)

Providence, 02912. Rosemary L Cullen, Cur
Holdings: Vols (175,000) Cat Mss
Phonorecords Microforms
Budget: ($15,000)
Notes: The Harris Collection of American
Poetry and Plays is principally composed of
American and Canadian poetry and plays,
17th century-date. Extensive holdings in
songsters, gift books and annuals, hymnals,
pageants, broadside verse, carriers'
addresses, women poets, juvenile poetry,
(incl Mother Goose and *The Night Before
Christmas*), sheet music with lyrics, small
press publications, fine printing, black poets,
"little magazines," Yiddish-American
literature. All movements or schools of
American poetry are represented. Incl first
editions of most American poets and
playwrights, notably Whitman, Poe, Wallace
Stevens, Eugene O'Neill, Edward Albee,
Ezra Pound, T S Eliot, William Carlos
Williams, Amy Lowell, Phyllis Wheatley,
Robert Frost, Allen Ginsberg, Bliss Carman,
and Stephen Foster sheet music. Also incl
the Saunders Walt Whitman Collection
(1300 vols); the LangdonCollection of
Pageants (250 vols); the Asa Cushman
Collection of plays in ms and prompt copies;
the MacDougall Collection of Psalters and
Hymnals; 4000 plays issued by Walter H
Baker Co, Boston (1890-1957); the Vaxer
Collection of Yiddish Poetry, Plays and
Music (1700 vols). Collections incl 200,000
vols, 30,000 broadsides, 55,000 mss, 170,000
pieces of sheet music, 450 phonorecords, and
375 microfilm reels. See *Dictionary Catalog
of the Harris Collection of American Poetry
and Plays* (Boston: G K Hall, 1972), 13 vols;
Supplement (1977), 3 vols. See also,
*American Poetry, 1609-1900, A Collection
on Microfilm, Segment I* (1609-1820);
Segment II (1821-1850); *Segment III* (1851-
1870) (Woodbridge, Conn: Research
Publications). Separate catalog.

AB —UNIVERSITY OF CALGARY,
Libraries, Special Collections Div, 2500
University Dr, Calgary, T2N 1N4, Can.
Holdings: Vols (5000) Cat Mss
Notes: The Division has extensive
collections of the papers of modern
Canadian authors (qv individuals), incl Hugh
MacLennan, Mordecai Richler, Brian
Moore, W O Mitchell, Cliff Faulknor,
Christie Harris, Robert Kroetsch, Rudy
Wiebe, Claude Peloquin, George Ryga,
Andre Langevin, Malcolm Ross, Bruce
Hutchison, John Mellor, Grant MacEwan,
James Gray, Ernest Watkins, Len Peterson,
Michael Cook, and Joanna Glass. The papers
of musician Morris Surdin contain hundreds
of Canadian Broadcasting Corporation
scripts, and constitute a valuable addition to
the purely literary ms collections. The
Division's holdings also incl collections of
scores by Canadian musicians R Murray
Schafer and Bruce Mather. In addition, the
records of the following Canadian publishing
houses are on deposit: E C W Press,
Hancock House Publishers Ltd and Coach
House Press. The Division alsohouses small
collections of letters and mss of Canadian
poets such as Earle Birney and George
Bowering as well as the archives of the
literary periodicals *Tish, Imago, Ariel,
Descant, Canadian Review Magazine*, and
Canadian Short Story Magazine. The ms
collections are complemented by a book
collection of some 5000 vols.

BC —SIMON FRASER UNIVERSITY,
Library, Burnaby, V5A 1S6, Can. Percilla
Groves, Special Collections Librn
Holdings: Vols (12,000) Cat Mss
Notes: This collection concentrates on
avant-garde American poetry since World
War II. Incl some Canadian poetry
(particularly West Coast poets), such as BP
Nichol, George Rouering, Dephne Marlett,
Margaret Atwood, Fred Wah, Phyllis Webb,
some British and certain of the International
Concrete school. It particularly features the
Black Mountain and San Francisco schools
and those American and Canadian poets
influenced by them. There is a relatively

complete collection of works by Ezra Pound
(qv) and William Carlos Williams together
with considerable criticism on both. Also
incl certain underground newspapers and
1600 periodical titles.

POETS, ENGLISH

CA —UNIVERSITY OF CALIFORNIA,
DAVIS, Shields Library, Dept of Special
Collections, Davis, 95616. Donald Kunitz,
Head; C Danial Elliott, Asst Head
Holdings: Vols 10,000 Uncat
Notes: Printed books by minor British poets
for the period 1789-1950s.

CT —TRINITY COLLEGE LIBRARY,
Watkinson Library, 300 Summit St,
Hartford, 06106. Jeffrey Kaimowitz, Cur
Holdings: Cat
Notes: Incl Rupert Brooke, Robert
Browning, Lord (George Gordon) Byron,
Geoffrey Chaucer, Walter De la Mare, John
Keats, Rudyard Kipling, John Masefield,
Alexander Pope, Sir Walter Scott, Robert
Louis Stevenson, Algernon Charles
Swinburne, and other 19th and 20th century
English poets.

MA —BOSTON COLLEGE LIBRARIES,
Thomas P O'Neill Library, Chestnut Hill,
02167. Frank J Seegraber, Special
Collections Librn
Holdings: Vols 1300 Cat Mss Pix
Phonorecords Audiotapes Microforms
Notes: This, the most commplete collection
of Thompsoniana in existence, incl incl
notebooks, mss, letters, and rare editions,
and collateral material relating to poet, his
times and his work. The notebooks are the
chief source of clues to the identification of
300 of Thompson's unsigned contributions
to periodicals. *An Account of the Books and
Manuscripts of Francis Thompson*, ed by
Rev Terence L Connolly (Boston College,
1937). Works of Wilfrid and Alice Meynell
and their children, Viola, Sir Francis, and
Everard, are incl in this collection. The items
give a well-rounded view of this remarkable
family as poets, fiction writers, essayists,
biographers, prefacers, and editors. This
collection incl mss, poems, correspondence,
articles, and book reviews by Coventry
Patmore, an English poet, essayist, and
critic, and a good friend of Francis
Thompson. Among thecorrespondents are
Robert Browning, Alfred Tennyson,
Matthew Arnold, Ralph Waldo Emerson,
Nathaniel Hawthorne, Thomas Carlyle, and
William Makepeace Thackeray. For
reference use only, by arrangement with
librarian.

NC —DUKE UNIVERSITY, William R
Perkins Library, Rare Book Room, Durham,
27706. John L Sharpe, III, Cur
Notes: Thomas J Wise collection. Many rare
pieces, including works of Byron, Coleridge,
Dryden, Pope and Hardy. 135 political and
religious broadsides, mostly of the 17th
century.

OH —OHIO UNIVERSITY, Vernon R Alden
Library, Department of Archives and Special
Collections, Athens, 45701. Gary A Hunt,
Head
Holdings: Vols 372 Cat Mss Audiotapes
Notes: A comprehensive collection of
Tennyson's published works, in first and
later editions, incl a few mss and related
material. Incl 22 different sets (1870-1908)
of collected editions; some 30 editions
(1878-1913) of the one-volume *Works;* many
editions of each of the individual titles; and
the ms journal (1870-1872) of Tennyson's
neighbor, J H Mangles, recording or
summarizing many conversations with the
poet. All editions of all titles are collected,
except those published posthumously.

OH —CLEVELAND PUBLIC LIBRARY,
Literature Dept, 325 Superior Ave,
Cleveland, 44114. Evelyn Ward, Head
Holdings: Vols Cat Phonorecords
Notes: A large collection of poetry,
substantial representation of English poets,
early through modern. Extensive critical and
biographical materials. Extensive card index
to individual poems, by author, title, first
line, and subject.

WA —UNIVERSITY OF WASHINGTON
LIBRARIES, Suzzallo Library, Special

Collections Division, Rare Book Collection,
FM-25, Seattle, 98195. Gary Menges,
Coordinator for Special Collections
Holdings: Vols (12,000) Cat Maps
Notes: American, British, French, German
and Italian books printed before 1800,
chiefly in the field of history and literature.
Fine bindings and illustrated works are
represented. Incl incunabula, emblemata,
history of travel, and first editions of the
works of major poets: Spenser, Blake,
Whitman, Yeats, Roethke, etc.

BC —UNIVERSITY OF VICTORIA,
McPherson Library, Victoria, V8W 3H5,
Can.

POETS, FOREIGN

OH —CLEVELAND PUBLIC LIBRARY,
Literature Dept, 325 Superior Ave,
Cleveland, 44114. Evelyn Ward, Head
Holdings: Vols Cat Phonorecords
Notes: A large collection of poetry, incl
foreign poets in English translation. Critical
and biographical material. Extensive card
index to individual poems, by author, title,
first line and subject.

PA —SLAVIA LIBRARY, 418 W Nittany Ave,
State College, 16801. W O Luciw, Founder
& Dir; Jurij A Luciw, Asst Dir
Holdings: Vols (45,000) Mss Pix
Budget: ($3500)
Notes: Incl 5000 periodicals, 3000 av
materials, 4000 artifacts, and 200 art works.
Also 16,000 letters, etc from Slavic and
other personages.

†TN —VANDERBILT UNIVERSITY, Library,
Special Collections Dept, 419 21st Ave S,
Nashville, 37203.
Notes: The Baudelaire Collection contains
extensive materials by and about Charles
Baudelaire.

POETS, FUGITIVE see Fugitive Poets

POETS, GEORGIAN

NY —HOFSTRA UNIVERSITY, Library,
1000 Fulton Ave, Hempstead, 11550.
Charles R Andrews, Dean of Library
Services
Notes: Strong collection. Incl some mss.

OH —OHIO UNIVERSITY, Vernon R Alden
Library, Department of Archives and Special
Collections, Athens, 45701. Gary A Hunt,
Head
Holdings: Vols (10,191) Uncat Mss
Notes: The Edmund Blunden Collection of
Romantic and Modern Literature, being the
private library assembled by Blunden during
6 decades of active collecting. The bulk of
the collection (6,264 titles) consists of
English imprints from the period 1750-1850,
concentrating on literature but also incl
contemporary works on art, natural history,
philosophy and other subjects important for
understanding the background of English
Romanticism. Among the authors most
heavily represented by first and other early
editions are: Allington, Barnes, Bloomfield,
Byron, Clare, Coleridge, Cowper, Dyer,
Edgeworth, Goldsmith, Hazlitt, Hunt, Lamb,
Landor, Scott, Thompson and Wordsworth.
Books written by Blunden himself, together
with his Georgian contemporaries
(particularly W H Davies, Walter De la
Mare, and Sigfried Sassoon) form a second
major area of strength. Many ofthe modern
books are inscribed to Blunden, and nearly
all the volumes in the collection bear his
annotations.

POETS, MIDWESTERN

WI —UNIVERSITY OF WISCONSIN, LA
CROSSE, Murphy Library, 1631 Pine St, La
Crosse, 54601. Edwin L Hill, Special
Collections Librn
Holdings: Vols 1000 Cat Mss
Notes: Center for Contemporary Poetry (a
collection of contemporary midwestern
poetry). Emphasis on purchase of trade and
small press publications of midwestern amd
especially Wisconsin poets. Unpublished
materials are collected for a few poets and
incl comprehensive papers, mss, reviews,

POETS, MIDWESTERN (cont.)

letters, etc. Collection also incl various midwestern and Wisconsin little magazines. Several fine midwestern private presses, especially Perishable Press. Collection is largely regional and contemporary. Most is cataloged and/or indexed. Collection incl records and papers of *Margins* (1972-1976), a review of little magazines and small press books. The Center for Contemporary Poetry published an annual volume, *Voyages to the Inland Sea*, from 1971-1979, featuring the poetry and essays of prominent midwestern poets.

POETS, POSTMODERN AMERICAN
see Postmodern American Poets

POETS, WOMEN see Women Poets

POFF, RICHARD HARDING

VA —UNIVERSITY OF VIRGINIA, Alderman Library, Manuscripts Dept, Charlottesville, 22901. Edmund Berkeley Jr, Cur
Holdings: Cat Mss Pix Audiotapes 16mm Films
Notes: Papers, personal and political, etc.

POGUE, FORREST C.

†VA —GEORGE C MARSHALL RESEARCH FOUNDATION AND LIBRARY, Drawer 920, Lexington, 24450. Royster Lyle Jr, Cur Collections
Holdings: Vols Cat Mss Pix
Notes: Papers of Forrest C Pogue, Army historian, Marshall biographer. Also over 300 German propaganda and military handbooks, and miscellaneous German pre-War books; French, German and American WW II newspapers (approx 300).

POHL, FREDERICK

CA —SAN DIEGO STATE UNIVERSITY, Malcolm A Love Library, 5300 Campanile Dr, San Diego, 92182. D Dickinson, Univ Librn; Don L Bosseau, Dir
Holdings: Mss Cassettes
Notes: Elizabeth Chater Collection in Science Fiction. Includes Tolkien Collection, fantasy, folklore, Gothic novels, mostly autographed first editions, some rare and scarce, includes manuscripts, graphics, cassette tapes. Examples: authors included, Isaac Asimov, Ray Bradbury, Joan Vinge, Greg Baer, Frederick Pohl, Andre Norton, etc. Examples of periodicals, Amazing Stories, Famous Fantastic Mysteries of the 1940s, The Black Cat, 1895. (3000 items)
MD —UNIVERSITY OF MARYLAND, BALTIMORE COUNTY, Albin O Kuhn Library and Gallery, 5401 Wilkens Ave, Baltimore, 21228. Ann Copeland, Special Collections Librn
Holdings: Cat Mss
Notes: Science fiction mss.
See also entry under Science Fiction.

POINDEXTER, MILES

VA —UNIVERSITY OF VIRGINIA, Alderman Library, Manuscripts Dept, Charlottesville, 22901. Edmund Berkeley Jr, Cur
Holdings: Cat Mss Pix
Notes: Papers, personal and political, etc.

POINIER, ART

OH —OHIO STATE UNIVERSITY, Library for Communication and Graphic Arts, 242 W 18th St, Columbus, 43210. Lucy S Caswell, Curator
Notes: The original works of editorial cartoonists Art Poinier, Scott Willis, Brian Basset, Billy Ireland, Frank Williams, Charles Werner, Ned Beard, L D Warren, Edward D Kuekes, Ray Osrin, Mike Peters, Draper Hill, Eugene Craig and Bert Whitman.

POINSETT, ALEX

MA —BOSTON UNIVERSITY, Mugar Memorial Library, Special Collections Dept,

771 Commonwealth Ave, Boston, 02215. Howard B Gotlieb, Dir
Holdings: Mss Correspondence

POINT, FATHER NICHOLAS

†WA —WASHINGTON STATE UNIVERSITY, Library, Manuscripts, Archives & Special Collections, Pullman, 99164. John F Guido, Head
Holdings: // Mss Maps Pix
Notes: Papers, 1821-1873, covering Father De Smet's early sojourns at Whitemarsh and St Louis, his founding of the Rocky Mountain Missions, his long service as Procurator and Socius of the Missouri Province, and his many travels. Correspondence with his family in Belgium, mss of his published journals, 2 small maps, sketches and engravings used to illustrate his books. Incl about 100 small pencil sketches by Father Nicholas Point depicting the 1841 journey from Westport to St Mary's Mission in the Bitterroot Valley. Described in *The Record*, 30 (1969) 6-40; and 32 (1971) 47-63.

POISONING, FOOD see Food Poisoning

POISONS

MI —MICHIGAN STATE UNIVERSITY, Science Library, East Lansing, 48824. Carole S Armstrong, Head
Holdings: Vols 700 Cat
Notes: Both books and journals include titles in English, French, German and Russian, with a few in other langauges. The scope includes general toxicology, industrial toxicology, veterinary toxicology, the toxicology of metals and insecticides, and poisons as studied in experimental pharmacology.

POISONS, ECONOMIC see Pesticides

POISONS, INDUSTRIAL see Industrial Toxicology

POISTER, ARTHUR

NY —SYRACUSE UNIVERSITY LIBRARIES, Ernest S Bird Library, George Arents Research Library for Special Collections, Syracuse, 13210. Carolyn A Davis, Manuscripts Librn; Amy S Doherty, University Archivist; Mark F Weimer, Rare Book Librn
Notes: American Music Collection. Papers of Ernst Bacon, Louis Krasner, Franklin Morris, William Henry Berwald, Earl George, and Arthur Polster.

POKER

LA —LOUISIANA STATE UNIVERSITY, Troy H Middleton Library, Baton Rouge, 70803. Lance E Dickson, Acting Dir
Notes: About two thirds of all the known books and other materials published on the subject of poker. Some 500 pieces. Gift of former Judge Oliver P "Ike" Carriere, of New Orleans.

POL, NICOLAUS

OH —CLEVELAND MEDICAL LIBRARY ASSOCIATION/CASE WESTERN RESERVE UNIVERSITY, Cleveland Health Sciences Library, Historical Division, Allen Memorial Medical Library, 11000 Euclid Ave, Cleveland, 44106. Glen Jenkins, Rare Book Librarian & Archivist
Holdings: Cat Mss
Notes: Incl the 40 vol Nicolaus Pol Collection of Incunabula; see Max H Fisch, *Nicolaus Pol Doctor 1494* (Bibliography) (New York: Reicher, 1947). Includes 14th century mss *Geometria*.

POLAND

CA —UNIVERSITY OF CALIFORNIA, BERKELEY, University Library, Slavic Collections, Berkeley, 94720. Edward

Kasinec, Librn
Holdings: Vols (210,000) Cat Maps Microforms
Budget: ($40,000)
Notes: Strong research collections for Bulgaria, Czechoslavakia, Poland, Russia-USSR, and Yugoslavia. Holdings are excellent in economics, folklore, history, linguistics, and literature. Publications issued by academies, major universities, and principal scholarly institutions are well represented. Extensive periodical holdings have been built up, largely as a result of early exchange arrangements. More than 4000 Slavic-language serials are currently being received. Farmington Plan and PL480 commitments have augmented Yugoslav resources. Sizable Slavic-language collections are to be found in Branch Libraries as well, in such subjects as agriculture, biology, earth sciences, forestry, and mathematics.
DC —GEORGETOWN UNIVERSITY, Library, Special Collections Div, 37 & O Sts NW, Washington, 20057. George M Barringer, Special Collections Librn; Nicholas B Sheetz, Mss Librn
Holdings: Mss Pix
Notes: Correspondence, documents, journals, diaries, financial accounts, mss, photographs, and art work comprising the personal and professional papers of McCeney Werlich, diplomat, as well as those of his wife, Gladys Hinckley Werlich; Thomas Hinckley; and Robert O'Donnel Hinckley, both diplomats; papers of Eleanor O'Donnell Hinckley, mother of Gladys Werlich, and her husband Robert Hinckley, noted portrait painter. The papers incl: State Department correspondence and other material relating to McCeney Werlich's posts in Latvia (1926-1927), Poland (1927-1931), Costa Rica (1931-1932), Liberia (1932-1933), and France (1934-1936); correspondence from Robert O'Donnell Hinckley from his travels in the Orient, 1919; correspondence from Thomas Hinckley, incl accounts of the Austro-Hungarian empire, 1914-1915; as well as numerous journalsand diaries kept by Gladys Werlich regarding her extensive travels and variety of experiences.
IL —UNIVERSITY OF ILLINOIS, URBANA/CHAMPAIGN, Slavic and East European Library, Urbana, 61801. Marianna Tax Choldin, Head
Holdings: Vols (34,600) Cat Microforms
Notes: Extensive coverage.
NY —STATE UNIVERSITY OF NEW YORK, COLLEGE AT BUFFALO, Poetry/ Rare Books Collection, 420 Capen Hall, Buffalo, 14260. Robert J Bertholf, Cur
Holdings: Vols 5000 Mss Maps Pix Films Filmstrips
Budget: $4000
Notes: Strong on history of Polish settlement in Buffalo, NY and US Rare collection of documents from Polish Royal court from the 16th to 18th century. University maintains exchange with Polish Academy of Science.
NY —NEW YORK PUBLIC LIBRARY, Slavonic Div, Fifth Ave & 42 St, New York, 10018. Edward Kasinec, Chief
Holdings: Vols 35,000 Cat Microforms
Notes: Subject strength is in literature (especially of the 19th and early 20th centuries and literary criticism). Linguistics and folklore are well represented, as are history and especially Polish miltary history. In the fields of social sciences publications on statistics and government documents are strong. See New York Public Library, *Dictionary Catalog of the Slavonic Collection* (Boston: G K Hall, 1974), 44 vols.
NC —DUKE UNIVERSITY, William R Perkins Library, Durham, 27706. Elvin E Strowd, University Librn

POLAND—CIVILIZATION AND CULTURE

FL —AMERICAN INSTITUTE OF POLISH CULTURE, INC, 110 Bricknell Ave Suite 600, Miami, 33131.
Holdings: 3000 Vols
IL —POLISH MUSEUM OF AMERICA, Library, 984 N Milwaukee Ave, Chicago,

POLAND—CIVILIZATION AND CULTURE (cont.)

60622. Donald Bilinski, OFM, Cur/Librn
Holdings: 25,000 Vols

IL —POLISH NATIONAL ALLIANCE OF THE UNITED STATES OF NORTH AMERICA (PNA), 6100 N Cicero Ave, Chicago, 60646. Josephine Rzewska, Librn
Holdings: Vols 18,000
Notes: This fraternal society also supports Alliance College, Cambridge Springs, PA. Also publish *Polish Daily Zgoda*, 1908- , Daily.

IL —POLISH WOMEN'S ALLIANCE OF AMERICA, 205 S Northwest Highway, Park Ridge, 60068.
Holdings: 1500 Vols

NY —STATE UNIVERSITY OF NEW YORK, COLLEGE AT BUFFALO, Lockwood Memorial Library, Polish Collection, Buffalo, 14260. William Borodacz, Cur
Holdings: 10,000 Vols Mss Pix
Notes: Incl theses and dissertations. Exchange with Polish Academy of Science, Warsaw. Poles and Polish-Americans are largest Buffalo ethnic group. Slides and films also.

NY —POLISH INSTITUTE OF ARTS & SCIENCES OF AMERICA, Library and Archives, 59 E 66 St, New York, 10021. Francis Puslowski, Deputy Director
Holdings: 12,000 Vols Pix
Notes: Very extensive exchange program with Polish Universities and cultural institutions.

NY —POLISH SINGERS ALLIANCE OF AMERICA, 180 2nd Ave, New York, 10003.
Notes: About 2000 pieces of music. Cataloged.

PA —ALLIANCE COLLEGE, Washington Hall Library, Fullerton Ave, Cambridge Springs, 16403. Stanley J Kozaczka, Head Librn
Holdings: Vols (23,000) Cat Mss Maps Pix Slides Phonorecords Audiotapes Videotapes 16mm Films Filmstrips Microforms
Notes: Polish and Polish-American history, literature and culture. Current publications of world press in Polish. Collection founded in 1912 under patronage of the Polish National Alliance was lost to fire in 1931, but rebuilding began immediately. Incl 100 maps, 1000 pictures, 1000 slides and 100 phonorecords.

PA —HOLY FAMILY COLLEGE LIBRARY, Grant & Frankford Aves, Philadelphia, 19114. Sister M Kathryn Dobbs, CSFN, Dir
Holdings: Vols (3362) Cat Maps
Notes: A mimeographed list, *Polonica; Polish History, Literature, and Culture*, available at the library. This list is divided into three sections: Cataloged books arranged by call number, selected uncataloged books arranged alphabetically by author, periodicals listed by title.

PA —ALVERNIA COLLEGE, Library, Reading, 19607. Sister Mary Edwinette, Librn
Holdings: Vols (2000) Cat

PA —POLISH NATIONAL UNION OF AMERICA, 1004 Pittston Ave, Scranton, 18505.

POLAND—GOVERNMENT IN EXILE

CA —HOOVER INSTITUTION ON WAR, REVOLUTION & PEACE, Stanford University, Stanford, 94305. Milorad M Drachkovitch, Archivist
Holdings: Mss
Notes: Records of the Polish Government in Exile in London, incl correspondence, memoranda, and reports, 1918-1945, relating primarily to foreign relations and other governmental functions of the Polish Government in Exile during World War II, and secondarily to political conditions in Poland and to Polish foreign relations between the two world wars. In Polish. 970 ms boxes. Also, minutes of the meetings of the Polish National Council, advisory body to the Government in Exile, at Angers, London, and Paris, 1940-1941. 1 ms box.

POLAND—HISTORY

CA —POLAND'S MILLENIUM LIBRARY, 3424 W Adams Blvd, Los Angeles, 90018.
Holdings: Vols 6000 Mss
Notes: Nearly all in Polish. Many published before WWII.

CA —UNIVERSITY OF CALIFORNIA, LOS ANGELES, Library, Slavic Collection, 405 Hilgard Ave, Los Angeles, 90024. Edward Shreeves, Chairman, Bibliographers Group; Leon Ferder, Slavic Bibliographer
Holdings: Vols (250,000) Cat Mss Maps
Notes: The entire range of humanities, social sciences, and the arts. One of the most comprehensive US collections for material not only on Russia and the Soviet Union, but also on Bulgaria, Czechoslovakia, Poland, Yugoslavia, the non-Slavic countries of Eastern Europe (Romania, Hungary, Albania) and Soviet Central Asia. Holdings in Russian and Slavic linguistics, Russian literature, and Russian history are particularly strong, covering all periods. The collections are described in some detail in Paul Horecky's book on US Slavic collections.

CA —THE POLISH ARTS AND CULTURE FOUNDATION, 1290 Sutter St, San Francisco, 94109. Wanda Tomczykowska, President
Holdings: Vols (1000)
Notes: Incl much on the Polish contribution to California.

CA —HOOVER INSTITUTION ON WAR, REVOLUTION & PEACE, Stanford University, Stanford, 94305. Milorad M Drachkovitch, Archivist
Holdings: Mss
Notes: Four collections: (1) Papers of I J Paderewski, Polish statesman and pianist, incl correspondence, speeches, clippings, printed matter, and photographs, 1894-1941, relating to his political and musical careers. 6 1/2 ms boxes. (2) Records of the Polish Embassy in the US incl reports, correspondence, bulletins, communiques, memoranda, dispatches and instructions, speeches and writings, and printed matter, 1918-56, relating to the establishment of the Republic of Poland; the Poland-Soviet War of 1920; Polish politics and foreign relations; national minorities in Poland; the territorial questions of Danzig, Memel, the Polish Corridor, and Galicia; the Polish emigration abroad; Poland during World War II; and the Polish Government in Exile in London. In Polish. 118 ms boxes. Also, records of the Consulate General in New York City, 1940-1948, of similar substance. 7 ms boxes.(3) Records of the Polish Embassy at Moscow and Kuibyshev, incl reports, correspondence, accounts, lists, testimonies, questionaires, certificates, petitions, card files, maps, circulars, graphs, protocols, and clippings, 1941-1944, relating to World War II, the Soviet occupation of Poland, the Polish-Soviet military and diplomatic agreements of 1941, the reestablishment of the Polish Embassy in Moscow, Polish prisoners-of-war in the USSR, deportations of Polish citizens to the USSR, labor camps and settlements, relief work by Polish Social Welfare Department delegations among the deportees, the Polish Armed Forces formed in the USSR, evacuation of the Polish Embassy to Kuibyshev, evacuation of Polish citizens to the Middle East, the Katyn massacre of Polish officers, and the break-down of Polish-Soviet relations in April, 1943. Also inclmaterial on the Communist Party of the Soviet Union and the Soviet government, 1928-1929. 54 ms boxes. (4) Papers of Tadeusz Romer (microfilm), Polish statesman, diplomat and professor; Polish Ambassador to the USSR, 1942-43; and Polish Minister of Foreign Affairs in the Polish Government in Exile (London), 1943-44; incl correspondence, memoranda, speeches and writings, reports, telegrams, minutes of meetings, clippings, printed matter and other materials, 1913-1975, relating to his government service in Poland and abroad, his subsequent years after emigration, political events in Poland, and

Polish foreign relations. Originals located at the Public Archives of Canada.

CA —STANFORD UNIVERSITY LIBRARIES, Cecil H Green Library, Stanford, 94305. Wojciech Zalewski, Cur, Russian & East European Collection
Holdings: Vols (200,000) Cat Maps Microforms
Budget: ($90,000)
Notes: Strong collection prior to 20th century, but Stanford University Libraries' collecting effort is coordinated with Hoover Institution, Stanford, and holdings are not duplicated. Collection descriptions: Wojciech Zalewski, *Russian Materials in the Main Library of Stanford University, A Collection Survey* (Stanford: Stanford University Libraries, 1974). Wojciech Zalerski, "Stanford University" in P L Horecky, ed, *East Central and Southeast Europe, A Handbook of Library and Archival Resources in North America* (Santa Barbara: Clio Press, 1976).

DC —LIBRARY OF CONGRESS, European Division, Washington, 20540.
Notes: The Library of Congress collection of "Solidarity" and other uncensored Polish materials incl books, periodicals, documents, bulletins, cartoons, and posters, most of which are photocopies of originals held by other libraries.

IL —POLISH MUSEUM OF AMERICA, Library, 984 N Milwaukee Ave, Chicago, 60622. Donald Bilinski, OFM, Cur/Librn
Holdings: Vols (25,000) Cat Mss Maps Pix Slides Phonorecords 16mm Films Filmstrips Microforms
Notes: Material on Poland and Polish-Americans; works written by Polish-Americans, regardless of subject. About 80 percent of the works are in Polish. Extensive juvenile section in Polish for youngsters. The collection contains books not only of Poles in US but Poles beyond the borders of Poland. It contains Polish literature, incl translations into English.

IL —POLISH NATIONAL ALLIANCE OF THE UNITED STATES OF NORTH AMERICA (PNA), 6100 N Cicero Ave, Chicago, 60646. Josephine Rzewska, Librn
Holdings: Vols 18,000
Notes: This fraternal society also supports Alliance College, Cambridge Springs, PA. Also publish *Polish Daily Zgoda*, 1908- , Daily.

IL —POLISH WOMEN'S ALLIANCE OF AMERICA, 205 S Northwest Highway, Park Ridge, 60068.
Holdings: 1500 Vols

IN —INDIANA UNIVERSITY, University Libraries, Bloomington, 47401. Murlin Croucher, Librn for Slavic Studies
Holdings: Vols (300,000) Cat Maps Microforms
Budget: ($63,000)
Notes: The collection, established after World War II, covers material of, and on, the Soviet Union (55 percent) and Eastern Europe (45 percent) in the languages of the area and in western European languages as well. Material is chiefly in the fields of humanities and social sciences. Many other Slavic and East European books are located in the Lilly Library (rare book library).

KS —UNIVERSITY OF KANSAS, Kenneth Spencer Research Library, Special Collections Dept, Lawrence, 66045. Alexandra Mason, Librn
Holdings: Vols 650 Cat Mss Maps
Notes: Especially strong for 16th and 17th centuries, incl Polish and other imprints. Papers of Antonio Maria Graziani, Vatican emissary to court of Poland in later 16th century. Noncirculating. Unpublished list in repository. Also see Hoskins, Janina W, *Early and rare Polonica of the 15th-17th centuries in American libraries*, Boston, G K Hall, 1973.

KS —UNIVERSITY OF KANSAS, Watson Library, Lawrence, 66045. George Jerkovich, Cur Slavic Collections
Notes: The Polish collection is particulary strong in history, politics, and economics, and includes a special group of rare 16th and 17th century Polonica. Over 30,000 vols.

MD —POLISH NOBILITY ASSOCIATION, Villa Anneslie, 529 Dunkirk Road,

POLAND—HISTORY (cont.)

Baltimore, 21212.
Notes: Publish *Voice of the White Eagle*, 1965- , Annual.

MD —SOVEREIGN HOSPITALLER ORDER OF SAINT JOHN, Villa Annenslie, 529 Dunkirk Road, Baltimore, 21212.
Holdings: Vols 1500
Notes: The Sovereign Hospitaller Order of Saint John is an ecumenical Christian religious Order founded in the 11th century; successor Order to the Knights of Rhodes and the Knights of Malta.

MA —HARVARD UNIVERSITY LIBRARY, Widener Library, Slavic Collections, Cambridge, 02138. Hugh M Olmsted, Slavic Dept Head
Holdings: Vols Cat Mss Pix Microforms
Notes: Polish history shelflist through June, 1976 lists 9685 titles (earlier version was incl in *Widener Library Shelflist,* volumes 28-31, 1971). The collections continue to be developed actively, and are strong both in current and in antiquarian materials. See also *East Central and Southeast Europe; A Handbook of Library and Archival Resources in North America,* edited by P L Horecky and D H Kraus, 1976, pp 141-148.

MI —SAINT MARY'S COLLEGE, Alumni Memorial Library, Orchard Lake, 48033. Sister Mary Ellen Lampe, Librn
Holdings: Vols (6000)

NY —SAINT STANISLAUS KOSTKA LIBRARY, 607 Humboldt St, Brooklyn, 11222. Jan Jachniewicz, Librn
Holdings: 1500 Vols

NY —STATE UNIVERSITY OF NEW YORK, COLLEGE AT BUFFALO, Lockwood Memorial Library, Polish Collection, Buffalo, 14260. William Borodacz, Cur
Holdings: 10,000 Vols Cat Maps Mss Pix
Budget: $1500
Notes: Strong on history of Polish settlement in Buffalo, New York and US Rare collection of documents from Polish Royal court from the 16th to 18th century. Incl theses and dissertations. University maintains exchange with Polish Academy of Science. Curator publishes bibliographies on various aspects of Polish life in US. Poles and Polish-Americans are largest Buffalo ethnic group. Slides and films also.

NY —JOZEF PILSUDSKI INSTITUTE FOR RESEARCH IN THE MODERN HISTORY OF POLAND, INC, 381 Park Ave, South, New York, 10016.
Holdings: 12,000 Vols Mss Maps Pix Archive
Notes: Said to be the fourth largest Polish collection of documents in the world outside of Poland. Materials emphasize history since 1863. Incl 2000 periodicals.

NY —KOSCIUSZKO FOUNDATION, Book Service, 15 E 65 St, New York, 10021.
Holdings: Vols 1500
Notes: Published guide available. Materials on Tadeusz Kosciuszko (1746-1817), Polish history, and Poles in the United States.

NY —NEW YORK PUBLIC LIBRARY, Slavonic Div, Fifth Ave & 42 St, New York, 10018. Edward Kasinec, Chief
Holdings: Cat Microforms
Notes: Polish history, and especially military history, are well represented. See New York Public Library, *Dictionary Catalog of the Slavonic Collection* (Boston: G K Hall, 1974), 44 vols.

NY —POLISH INSTITUTE OF ARTS & SCIENCES OF AMERICA, Library and Archives, 59 E 66 St, New York, 10021. Francis Puslowski, Deputy Director

OH —OHIO STATE UNIVERSITY, William Oxley Thompson Memorial Library, Hilander Room, 1858 Neil Ave Mall, Columbus, 43210. Predrag Matejic, Cur; G Koolemans Beynen, Slavic Bibliographer
Holdings: Vols (200,000) Cat Maps Microforms
Budget: ($45,000)
Notes: Area studies of Central, Southeastern and Eastern Europe. Emphasis on on Slavic literatures, languages and history. At present economics, sociology, law (Russian only)

have been added. Within this framework the following priorities have been established: Material in Russian problems; then Medieval Slavic (Cyrillic); then Polish, then Serbo-Croatian, then Bulgarian, and now Romanian. Special attention is paid to serials, bibliographies, ms descriptions and dictionaries (incl biographical and encyclopedias). Apart from materials in native languages, materials in the following languages are acquired: Old Church Slavonic, Greek, English, French, German, Italian, a few in Scandinavian languages, incl Finnish, and a few in Baltic languages. The Hillandar Room holds approx 2000 Slavic mss, 1050 from Hilandar Monastery, Mount Athos, on microform and a related referencecollection.

PA —ALLIANCE COLLEGE, Washington Hall Library, Fullerton Ave, Cambridge Springs, 16403. Stanley J Kozaczka, Head Librn
Holdings: Vols (23,000) Cat Mss Maps Pix Slides Phonorecords Audiotapes Videotapes 16mm Films Filmstrips Microforms
Notes: Polish and Polish-American history, literature and culture. Current publications of world press in Polish. Collection founded in 1912 under patronage of the Polish National Alliance was lost to fire in 1931, but rebuilding began immediately. Incl 100 maps, 1000 pictures, 1000 slides and 100 phonorecords.

PA —HOLY FAMILY COLLEGE LIBRARY, Grant & Frankford Aves, Philadelphia, 19114. Sister M Kathryn Dobbs, CSFN, Dir
Holdings: Vols (3362) Cat Maps
Notes: A mimeographed list, *Polonica; Polish History, Literature, and Culture,* available at the library. This list is divided into three sections: Cataloged books arranged by call number, selected uncataloged books arranged alphabetically by author, periodicals listed by title.

WA —UNIVERSITY OF WASHINGTON LIBRARIES, Suzzallo Library, Slavic & East European Section, FM-25, Seattle, 98195. Barbara A Galik, Head
Holdings: Vols (250,000) Cat Mss Maps Pix Phonorecords Audiotapes Microforms
Budget: ($85,000)
Notes: Strong research collections for the history of Poland. Holdings are excellent in historical source materials. There are extensive holdings of the publications of academies, major universities, and principal scholarly institutions, especially of long serial runs.

WI —UNIVERSITY OF WISCONSIN, MADISON, Memorial Library, Slavic Studies Collection, 728 State St, Madison, 53706. Aleksander Rolich, Bibliographer for Slavic Studies; Robert P Gakovich, Slavic Cataloger; Valdis J Zeps, Baltic Studies Center
Holdings: Cat
Notes: Memorial Library has been collecting Polish materials since before WWII and now has a Polonistyka collection of more than 40,000 vols, primarily in philology and history. among its rare books are Maciej Stryjkowski's *Kronika polska* and Jan Dlugosz's *Historia Polonica.*

POLAND—NOBILITY

MD —POLISH NOBILITY ASSOCIATION, Villa Anneslie, 529 Dunkirk Road, Baltimore, 21212.
Notes: Publish *Voice of the White Eagle,* 1965-date, Annual.

POLAND—PICTURES, ILLUSTRATIONS, ETC.

CA —THE POLISH ARTS AND CULTURE FOUNDATION, 1290 Sutter St, San Francisco, 94109. Wanda Tomczykowska, President
Notes: 1000 slides covering architecture, art, religion, traditions, history, and Polish contributions to California.

POLAND—POLITICS AND GOVERNMENT

DC —LIBRARY OF CONGRESS, European Division, Washington, 20540.
Notes: The Library of Congress collection of

"Solidarity" and other uncensored Polish materials incl books, periodicals, documents, bulletins, cartoons, and posters, most of which are photocopies of originals held by other libraries.

NY —POLISH INSTITUTE OF ARTS & SCIENCES OF AMERICA, Library and Archives, 59 E 66 St, New York, 10021. Francis Puslowski, Deputy Director

POLANYI, MICHAEL

IL —UNIVERSITY OF CHICAGO LIBRARY, Dept of Special Collections, 1100 E 57 St, Chicago, 60637.
Notes: Papers.

POLAR GAS PROJECT

MB —UNIVERSITY OF MANITOBA, Elizabeth Dafoe Library, Government Publications Section, Winnipeg, R3T 2N2, Can. June Dutka, Head
Holdings: Uncat Maps Pix Microforms
Notes: The Canadian National Energy Board's Polar Gas Project documentation provides an extremely useful source of information describing the proposed construction of the pipeline route which would generally pass from the Arctic Islands through the Northwest Territories, northern Manitoba and into Ontario, Canada.

POLAR REGIONS see Antarctic Regions; Arctic Regions; Libris Polaris; North Pole; South Pole

POLE LINE HARDWARE

NJ —AT&T BELL LABORATORIES, Libraries and Information Systems Center, 600 Mountain Ave, Murray Hill, 07974. W D Penniman, Dir
Holdings: Vols (273,100) Cat Mss Audiotapes Videotapes Microforms
Budget: ($670,000)
Notes: Restricted use to AT&T employees. Catalogs/*Indexes:* Bell Laboratories Library Network and Book Serial Catalogs; Bell Laboratories Translations. Bell Laboratories Library Network with New Jersey libraries located in Holmdel, Murray Hill, Piscataway, Whippany, Princeton, Short Hills, Summit, West Long Branch, Crawford Hill; libraries also in Allentown, Pennsylvania; Reading, Pennsylvania; New York, New York; Atlanta, Georgia; Columbus, Ohio; Naperville, Illinois; Indianapolis, Indiana; North Andover, Massachusetts.

OH —PREFORMED LINE PRODUCTS CO, Research & Engineering Library, 660 Beta Drive, Mayfield Village, (Mailing add: PO Box 91129, Cleveland, 44101). Edwina T Barron, Librn
Holdings: Vols (11,500) Cat Mss Microfiche Pix VF
Budget: ($30,500)
Notes: Library covering research and engineering fields emphasizing this subject. Aerodynamic characteristics and electrical characteristics of power cables, communication cables (including fiber optics), cable support systems, as well as associated fittings and hardware; in service behavior of manufactured products and materials as it relates to its static and dynamic forces and environmental conditions; oceanographic cable fittings and terminations.

POLES IN CANADA

NY —STATE UNIVERSITY OF NEW YORK, COLLEGE AT BUFFALO, Lockwood Memorial Library, Polish Collection, Buffalo, 14260. William Borodacz, Cur
Holdings: Vols 4600 Cat Maps
Budget: $1500
Notes: Strong on history of Polish settlement in Buffalo, New York and US Rare collection of documents from Polish Royal court from the 16th to 18th century. University maintains exchange with Polish

POLES IN CANADA (cont.)

Academy of Science. Curator publishes bibliographies on various aspects of Polish life in US.

PA —BALCH INSTITUTE FOR ETHNIC STUDIES, Library, 18 S Seventh St, Philadelphia, 19106. R Joseph Anderson, Library Dir

POLES IN RUSSIA

CA —HOOVER INSTITUTION ON WAR, REVOLUTION & PEACE, Stanford University, Stanford, 94305. Milorad M Drachkovitch, Archivist
Holdings: Mss Maps
Notes: Records

POLES IN THE U.S.

CA —THE POLISH ARTS AND CULTURE FOUNDATION, 1290 Sutter St, San Francisco, 94109. Wanda Tomczykowska, President
Holdings: Vols (1000)
Notes: Archival materials on Polish organizations and people in Northern California, detailed documentation of PACF's work, some manuscripts, and books from Poland dating from the 16th century. Materials in Polish and English.

CA —HOOVER INSTITUTION ON WAR, REVOLUTION & PEACE, Stanford University, Stanford, 94305. Milorad M Drachkovitch, Archivist
Holdings: Mss
Notes: Records of the Polish Embassy in the US incl reports, correspondence, bulletins, communiques, memoranda, dispatches and instructions, speeches and writings, and printed matter, 1918-56, relating to the establishment of the Republic of Poland; the Polish-Soviet War of 1920; Polish politics and foreign relations; national minorities in Poland; the territorial questions of Danzig, Memel, th Polish Corridor, and Galicia; the Polish emigration abroad; Poland during World War II; and the Polish Government in Exile in London. In Polish. 118 ms boxes. Also, records of the Consulate General in New York City, 1940-1948, of similar substance. 7 ms boxes.

IL —POLISH MUSEUM OF AMERICA, Library, 984 N Milwaukee Ave, Chicago, 60622. Donald Bilinski, OFM, Cur/Librn
Holdings: Vols (25,000) Cat Mss Maps Pix Slides Phonorecords 16mm Films Filmstrips Microforms
Notes: Material on Poland and Polish-Americans; works written by Polish-Americans, regardless of subject. About 80 percent of the works are in Polish. Extensive juvenile section in Polish for youngsters. The collection contains books not only of Poles in US but Poles beyond the borders of Poland. It contains Polish literature, incl translations into English.

IL —POLISH NATIONAL ALLIANCE OF THE UNITED STATES OF NORTH AMERICA (PNA), 6100 N Cicero Ave, Chicago, 60646. Josephine Rzewska, Librn
Holdings: Vols 18,000
Notes: This fraternal society also supports Alliance College, Cambridge Springs, PA. Also publish *Polish Daily Zgoda*, 1908- , Daily.

IL —POLISH WOMEN'S ALLIANCE OF AMERICA, 205 S Northwest Highway, Park Ridge, 60068.
Holdings: 1500 Vols

MD —POLISH NOBILITY ASSOCIATION, Villa Anneslie, 529 Dunkirk Road, Baltimore, 21212.
Notes: Publish *Voice of the White Eagle*, 1965- , Annual.

MI —SAINT MARY'S COLLEGE, Alumni Memorial Library, Orchard Lake, 48033. Sister Mary Ellen Lampe, Librn

MN —UNIVERSITY OF MINNESOTA, Immigration History Research Center, 826 Berry St, Saint Paul, 55114. Susan Griegs, Cur
Holdings: Vols (35,000) Mss Maps Pix Phonorecords Audiotapes 16mm Films Microforms
See also entry under - US - Emigration and Immigration

NY —STATE UNIVERSITY OF NEW YORK, COLLEGE AT BUFFALO, Lockwood Memorial Library, Polish Collection, Buffalo, 14260. William Borodacz, Cur
Holdings: 10,000 Vols Cat Maps Mss Pix
Budget: $1500
Notes: Strong on history of Polish settlement in Buffalo, New York and US Rare collection of documents from Polish Royal court from the 16th to 18th century. Incl theses and dissertations. University maintains exchange with Polish Academy of Science. Curator publishes bibliographies on various aspects of Polish life in US. Poles and Polish-Americans are largest Buffalo ethnic group. Slides and films also.

NY —STATE UNIVERSITY OF NEW YORK, COLLEGE AT BUFFALO, Library, The Francis E Fronczak Collection, Buffalo, 14222. Lucien E Palmieri, Head Collections Dept
Holdings: 1000 Vols
Notes: Collection of Buffalo's noted Polish-American, Francis E Fronczak.

NY —JOZEF PILSUDSKI INSTITUTE FOR RESEARCH IN THE MODERN HISTORY OF POLAND, INC, 381 Park Ave, South, New York, 10016.
Holdings: 12,000 Vols Mss Maps Pix Archive
Notes: Said to be the fourth largest Polish collection of documents in the world outside of Poland. Materials emphasize history since 1863. Incl 2000 periodicals.

NY —KOSCIUSZKO FOUNDATION, Book Service, 15 E 65 St, New York, 10021.
Holdings: Vols 1500
Notes: Published guide available. Materials on Tadeusz Kosciuszko (1746-1817), Polish history, and Poles in the United States.

NY —NEW YORK PUBLIC LIBRARY, Slavonic Div, Fifth Ave & 42 St, New York, 10018. Edward Kasinec, Chief
Holdings: Cat Microforms
Notes: See: New York Public Library, Slavonic Div, *Dictionary Catalog of the Slavonic Collection*, 2nd ed, rev and enl (Boston: G K Hall, 1974), 44 vols; and New York Public Library, *Dictionary Catalog of the Research Libraries* (New York, 1972-).

NY —POLISH INSTITUTE OF ARTS & SCIENCES OF AMERICA, Library and Archives, 59 E 66 St, New York, 10021. Francis Puslowski, Deputy Director

PA —ALLIANCE COLLEGE, Washington Hall Library, Fullerton Ave, Cambridge Springs, 16403. Stanley J Kozaczka, Head Librn
Holdings: Vols (23,000) Cat Mss Maps Pix slides Phonorecords Audiotapes Videotapes 16mm Films Filmstrips Microforms
Notes: Polish and Polish-American history, literature and culture. Current publications of world press in Polish. Collection founded in 1912 under patronage of the Polish National Alliance was lost to fire in 1931, but rebuilding began immediately. Incl 100 maps, 1000 pictures, 1000 slides and 100 phonorecords.

PA —BALCH INSTITUTE FOR ETHNIC STUDIES, Library, 18 S Seventh St, Philadelphia, 19106. R Joseph Anderson, Library Dir
Holdings: Vols 630 Cat Mss Pix Microforms

PA —UNIVERSITY OF PITTSBURGH, Hillman Library, Archives of Industrial Society, 363 Hillman Library, Pittsburgh, 15260. Frank A Zabrosky, Cur
Holdings: Mss Maps Pix Slides Audiotapes Microforms
Notes: Incl documents; newspapers; records of churches, fraternal/beneficial societies; social/cultural organizations.

PA —ALVERNIA COLLEGE, Library, Reading, 19607. Sister Mary Edwinette, Librn
Holdings: Vols 2000 Cat

PA —POLISH NATIONAL UNION OF AMERICA, 1004 Pittston Ave, Scranton, 18505.

POLICE

CA —SACRAMENTO PUBLIC LIBRARY, 828 I St, Sacramento, 95814. Dorothy Harvey, Librn, Special Collections
Holdings: Vols (4000) Cat
Notes: Incl books on public administration and police science, local government (city and county). Have over 4000 Sacramento city and county documents.

IL —MUNICIPAL REFERENCE LIBRARY, City Hall, Rm 1004, Chicago, 60602. Joyce Malden, Librn
Notes: Municipal government.

IL —NORTHWESTERN UNIVERSITY, Transportation Center Library, Evanston, 60201. Mary Roy, Librn
Notes: Emphasizing police operations administration and training, traffic law enforcement, police traffic operations.

IN —INDIANA LAW ENFORCEMENT ACADEMY, David F Allen Memorial Learning Resources Center, Rd 700 E, PO Box 313, Plainfield, 46168. Donna K Zimmerman, Librn
Holdings: Vols (4500) Cat Slides 16mm Films
Budget: ($8500)
Notes: Concentrated in the areas of police science, criminology, and law.

MD —INTERNATIONAL ASSOCIATION OF CHIEFS OF POLICE, 13 Firstfield Rd, PO Box 6010, Gaithersburg, 20760.
Holdings: Vols (6000) Cat Mss
Notes: Collection heavy in criminal investigation, crime prevention, police administration and management. Collecting in public sector labor relations, family violence, terrorism.

MO —SAINT LOUIS POLICE LIBRARY, 315 S Tucker Blvd, Saint Louis, 63102. Cathy Reilly, Librn
Holdings: Vols (21,000) Cat Mss Pix Microforms
Budget: ($18,400)
Notes: Collection covers police administration, criminology, penology, juvenile delinquency, probation and parole, criminalistics, criminal law, sociology, psychology, race relations, traffic, narcotics, alcoholism, police science and technology, etc.

NJ —RUTGERS, THE STATE UNIVERSITY OF NEW JERSEY, John Cotton Dana Library, 185 University Ave, Newark, 07102. Phyllis Schultze, Librn
Holdings: Vols 40,000 Cat
Notes: National Council on Crime and Delinquency. Criminology, as applied, means all phases of crime and delinquency prevention, control and treatment, ie, the whole "criminal justice" gamut: police, courts, probation and parole, prisons, community rehabilitation centers, etc. In short, everything except police laboratory materials. Collection completely cataloged; all criminological and correctional journals indexed. Incl many reports of correctional agencies, research reports, unpublished monographs, publications in the field by all government agencies, federal, state, county and local. Information file contains over 40,000 such items, as well as about 10,000 uncataloged clippings and other pieces of information stored by specific subjects.

OH —CLEVELAND PUBLIC LIBRARY, Public Administration Library, City Hall, 601 Lakeside Ave NE Rm 100, Cleveland, 44114. Janice Ryan Novak, Head
Holdings: Vols 800 Cat
Notes: Emphasize practical police work and law enforcement as well as aspects of criminology.

TX —SAM HOUSTON STATE UNIVERSITY, Library, PO Box 2179, Huntsville, 77340. Chas Dwyer, Librn

WI —UNIVERSITY OF WISCONSIN, MADISON, Law School Library, Criminal Justice Reference & Information Center, Madison, 53706. Sue Center, Librn
Holdings: Vols (29,000) Cat Mss
Budget: ($45,000)
Notes: In-depth subject access is provided to collection by our own cataloging and classification systems. Incl are periodical articles which are selectively cataloged to supplement the collection. Special items in collection incl penal press (prisoner newspapers); annual and statistical reports from criminal justice agencies throughout the

POLICE (cont.)

US and Canada; theses and dissertations; and 280 periodical titles in the field of criminal justice.

†ON —METROPOLITAN TORONTO LIBRARY, Social Sciences Dept, 789 Yonge St, Toronto, M4W 2G8, Can. Abdus Salam, Head
Holdings: Vols Cat Maps Phonorecords Audiotapes 16mm Films Microforms
Notes: The criminology collection includes contemporary and historical material on theories of criminality, police work, criminal law, corrections, and the rehabilitation of offenders.

ON —UNIVERSITY OF TORONTO, Centre of Criminology, Library, 130 St George St, Rm 8001, Toronto, M5S 1A5, Can. Catherine J Matthews, Librn
Holdings: Vols (20,000) Cat
Notes: Over 4500 research reports, article reprints, theses, etc. Extensive newspaper clippings file from 1963 to the present indexed under 350 subject headings. The collection covers criminology, law enforcement and policing, delinquency, criminal justice system, penology and corrections. Acquisitions list is published three times a year; subscription.

POLICE PHOTOGRAPHY see Photography, Legal

POLICE UNIFORMS see Uniforms, Police

POLICY, MEDICAL see Medical Policy

POLIOMYELITIS

CT —YALE UNIVERSITY, Medical Historical Library, Klebs Collection, 333 Cedar St, New Haven, 06520. Ferenc A Gyorgyey, Librn
Notes: The Arnold Carl Klebs Medical Collection books, pamphlets, etc, incl the library of his father, Edwin T A Klebs, pathologist. Strong in bibliography of early printed medical books, herbals, plague tracts, inoculation, vaccination and tubercular diseases.

NH —DARTMOUTH COLLEGE, Dartmouth-Hitchcock Medical Center, Dana Biomedical Library, Hanover, 03756. Shirley J Grainger, Librn
Holdings: Vols (6000) Cat Mss
Notes: Collection incl the *Henry Kumm Index to Papers on Poliomyelitis and Tropical Medicine.*

POLISH AMERICAN AUTHORS see Authors, Polish American

POLISH AMERICAN NEWSPAPERS see Newspapers, Polish American

POLISH ART see Art, Polish

POLISH CHILDREN'S LITERATURE see Children'S Literature, Polish

POLISH COMPOSERS see Composers, Polish

POLISH JEWS see Jews, Polish

POLISH LANGUAGE AND LITERATURE

CA —LOS ANGELES PUBLIC LIBRARY, Foreign Languages Dept, 630 W Fifth St, Los Angeles, 90071. Sylva Manoogian, Principal Librn
Holdings: Vols 4843 Cat
Budget: ($41,500)

CA —POLAND'S MILLENIUM LIBRARY, 3424 W Adams Blvd, Los Angeles, 90018.
Holdings: Vols 6000 Mss
Notes: Nearly all in Polish. Many published before WWII.

CA —UNIVERSITY OF CALIFORNIA, LOS ANGELES, Library, Slavic Collection, 405 Hilgard Ave, Los Angeles, 90024. Edward Shreeves, Chairman, Bibliographers Group;

Leon Ferder, Slavic Bibliographer
Holdings: Vols (250,000) Cat Mss Maps
Notes: The Slavic Collection at UCLA consists of materials from and relating to Russia and the Soviet Union, Poland, Czechoslovakia, Yugoslavia, Bulgaria, the Sorbians in East Germany, and works by Slavic emigres. The collection contains nearly 250,000 vols, and is particularly strong in linguistics, literature, history and social sciences, and reference materials. Slavic materials are collected in hard copy and microform, and incl monographs, serials (incl newspapers), reference works, proceedings of Slavistic congresses and symposia, and also *Festschriften* and dissertations.

CA —THE POLISH ARTS AND CULTURE FOUNDATION, 1290 Sutter St, San Francisco, 94109. Wanda Tomczykowska, President
Holdings: Vols (1000)
Notes: Archival materials on Polish organizations and people in Northern California, detailed documentation of PACF's work, some manuscripts, and books from Poland dating from the 16th century. Materials in Polish and English. Also incl Polish reference books pertaining to all aspects and subjects, plus dictionaries on most subjects.

CA —STANFORD UNIVERSITY LIBRARIES, Cecil H Green Library, Stanford, 94305. Wojciech Zalewski, Cur, Russian & East European Collection
Holdings: Vols (200,000) Cat Maps Microforms
Budget: ($90,000)
Notes: Strong collection prior to 20th century, but Stanford University Libraries' collecting effort is coordinated with Hoover Institution, Stanford, and holdings are not duplicated. Collection descriptions: Wojciech Zalewski, *Russian Materials in the Main Library of Stanford University, A Collection Survey* (Stanford: Stanford University Libraries, 1974). Wojciech Zalerski, "Stanford University" in P L Horecky, ed, *East Central and Southeast Europe, A Handbook of Library and Archival Resources in North America* (Santa Barbara: Clio Press, 1976).

CT —YALE UNIVERSITY, Box 1603A, Yale Station, New Haven, 06520.

IL —POLISH MUSEUM OF AMERICA, Library, 984 N Milwaukee Ave, Chicago, 60622. Donald Bilinski, OFM, Cur/Librn
Holdings: Vols (25,000) Cat Mss Maps Pix Slides Phonorecords 16mm Films Filmstrips Microforms
Notes: Material on Poland and Polish-Americans; works written by Polish-Americans, regardless of subject. About 80 percent of the works are in Polish. Extensive juvenile section in Polish for youngsters. The collection contains books not only of Poles in US but Poles beyond the borders of Poland. It contains Polish literature, incl translations into English.

IL —UNIVERSITY OF ILLINOIS, URBANA/CHAMPAIGN, Slavic and East European Library, Urbana, 61801. Marianna Tax Choldin, Head
Holdings: Vols (34,600) Cat Microforms
Notes: Extensive coverage.

KS —UNIVERSITY OF KANSAS, Watson Library, Lawrence, 66045. George Jerkovich, Cur Slavic Collections
Notes: Collection incl most of the standard materials. Among 17th century writers covered are Twardowsk, Potock, Opalinski and Kollataj. Holdings of romantic period are well balanced, with works by Mickiewicz and his rival Slowacki as well as by Krasinski and Norwid. The positivist movement and hisotircal novel are represented by works of Kraszewski, Lozinski, Sienkiewicz, Prus, Glowacki, and Orzeszkowa. Late 19th and 20th centuries works incl those of Zeromski and Nobel prizewinner Reymont, as well as those of the Tatraists and the modernists, such as Przybyszewski, Wyspianski, and Zelenski. Realism and the postwar period, and emigre literture, are represented by works of Maria Kuncewicz, Szczepanska; Maria Dabrowska, Szumska; Milosz,

Andrzejewski, Rozewicz, and others. Polonica also includes literary criticism by Juliusz Kleiner.

MA —HARVARD UNIVERSITY LIBRARY, Widener Library, Slavic Collections, Cambridge, 02138. Hugh M Olmsted, Slavic Dept Head
Holdings: Vols Cat Microforms
Notes: Polish literature shelflist through June, 1976 lists 9404 titles (earlier version was incl in *Widener Library Shelflist*, volumes 28-31, 1971). The language and literature collections continue to be developed actively, and are strong both in current and in antiquarian materials.

MA —SAINT HYACINTH COLLEGE & SEMINARY, Kolbe Memorial Library, 66 School St, Granby, 01033. Brother Christian Katusz, OFM Conv, Librn
Holdings: Microforms
Notes: Partially cataloged.

MI —SAINT MARY'S COLLEGE, Alumni Memorial Library, Orchard Lake, 48033. Sister Mary Ellen Lampe, Librn

NY —STATE UNIVERSITY OF NEW YORK, COLLEGE AT BUFFALO, Lockwood Memorial Library, Polish Collection, Buffalo, 14260. William Borodacz, Cur
Holdings: 10,000 Vols Mss Pix
Notes: Incl theses and dissertations. Exchange with Polish Academy of Science, Warsaw. Poles and Polish-Americans are largest Buffalo ethnic group. Slides and films also.

NY —HEMPSTEAD PUBLIC LIBRARY, Foreign Language Collection, 115 Nichols Court, Hempstead, 11550. Irene A Duszkiewicz, Dir
Notes: Mainly French, German, Italian, Spanish, Polish, Yiddish, Hebrew. Holdings in other languages, including Asian.

NY —KOSCIUSZKO FOUNDATION, Book Service, 15 E 65 St, New York, 10021.
Holdings: Vols 4000
Notes: Collection incl *Polish-English, English-Polish Dictionary, Introduction to the Polish Language.* Book catalog available:

NY —NEW YORK PUBLIC LIBRARY, Donnell Foreign Language Library, 20 W 53 St, New York, 10019. Bosiljka Stevanovic, Supvr Librn
Holdings: Vols 1156 Cat
Notes: Polish collection incl Polish authors of Polish expression. No separate catalog.

NY —NEW YORK PUBLIC LIBRARY, Slavonic Div, Fifth Ave & 42 St, New York, 10018. Edward Kasinec, Chief
Holdings: Vols 35,000 Cat Microforms
Notes: Subject strength is in literature (especially of the 19th and early 20th centuries and literary criticism). Linguistics and folklore are well represented, as are history and especially Polish military history. In the fields of social sciences publications on statistics and government documents are strong. See New York Public Library, *Dictionary Catalog of the Slavonic Collection* (Boston: G K Hall, 1974), 44 vols.

NY —POLISH INSTITUTE OF ARTS & SCIENCES OF AMERICA, Library and Archives, 59 E 66 St, New York, 10021. Francis Puslowski, Deputy Director
Holdings: 12,000 Vols Pix
Notes: Very extensive exchange program with Polish Universities and cultural institutions.

NC —CUMBERLAND COUNTY PUBLIC LIBRARY, North Carolina Foreign Language Center, 328 Gillespie St, Fayetteville, 28301. Patrick M Valentine, Coordinator
Holdings: Vols 450 Cat
Budget: $400
Notes: The largest book collections are, in descending order of size, German Spanish, French, Japanese, Korean and Vietnamese, with fair sized collections in Italian, Russian, Chinese, Arabic, Greek, Hungarian, Polish, Hebrew, Thai, and Hindi. The Center has several shelves each of books in Bengali, Dutch, Marathi, Portuguese, Urdu, and Yiddish. Smaller collections of one to three shelves each incl Catalan, Croatian, Czech, Danish, Finnish, Gujarati, Icelandic,

POLISH LANGUAGE AND LITERATURE (cont.)

Kannada, Latin, Lithuanian, Malayalam, Norwegian, Panjabi, Persian (Farsi), Romanian, Slovak, Swedish, Tagalog, Tamil, Telegu, and Ukrianian. The Center has grammars, dictionaries and occasionally other readings in languages from Afrikaans and Albanian to Welsh, Yoruba and Zulu.

OH —CLEVELAND PUBLIC LIBRARY, Foreign Literature Dept, 325 Superior Ave, Cleveland, 44114. Natalia Bezugloff, Head
Holdings: Vols 9640 Cat
Notes: A popular circulating collection containing classics and the standard works with emphasis on belles lettres, history and biography. A variety of other subjects such as learning languages, how to do books, art, children's books, spoken phonodiscs and cassettes, periodicals, etc. Incl 580 ephemera.
See also entry under Foreign Language Collections

OH —KENT STATE UNIVERSITY, Libraries, Ethnic Collections, Kent, 44242.
Holdings: Vols 725 Cat
See also entry under Foreign Language Collections

PA —ALLIANCE COLLEGE, Washington Hall Library, Fullerton Ave, Cambridge Springs, 16403. Stanley J Kozaczka, Head Librn
Holdings: Vols 23,000 Cat Mss Maps Pix Slides Phonorecords Audiotapes Videotapes 16mm Films Filmstrips Microforms
Notes: Polish and Polish-American history, literature and culture. Current publications of world press in Polish. Collection founded in 1912 under patrongage of the Polish National Alliance was lost to fire in 1931, but rebuilding began immediately. Incl 100 maps, 1000 pictures, 1000 slides and 100 phonorecords.

PA —HOLY FAMILY COLLEGE LIBRARY, Grant & Frankford Aves, Philadelphia, 19114. Sister M Kathryn Dobbs, CSFN, Dir
Holdings: Vols (3362) Cat Maps
Notes: A mimeographed list, Polonica; Polish History, Literature, and Culture, available at the library. This list is divided into three sections: Cataloged books arranged by call number, selected uncataloged books arranged alphabetically by author, periodicals listed by title.

PA —ALVERNIA COLLEGE, Library, Reading, 19607. Sister Mary Edwinette, Librn
Holdings: Vols 2000 Cat

PA —PENNSYLVANIA STATE UNIVERSITY, Fred Lewis Pattee Library, Slavic Library Program, University Park, 16802. Wasyl O Luciw, Head
Holdings: Vols (75,000) Cat Mss Pix
Budget: ($18,000)
Notes: The collection covers a wide range of languages Slavic and East European but its principal strengths are in Russian and Ukrainian. A special collection of 1576 volumes includes pre-revolutionary Russian, fine press publications, in our rare collection and children's literature. Besides book volumes, we have quite a large collection of manuscripts, documents, photographs and many periodicals, also including out of print books on microforms.

WI —UNIVERSITY OF WISCONSIN, MADISON, Memorial Library, Slavic Studies Collection, 728 State St, Madison, 53706. Aleksander Rolich, Bibliographer for Slavic Studies; Robert P Gakovich, Slavic Cataloger; Valdis J Zeps, Baltic Studies Center
Holdings: Cat
Notes: Memorial Library has been collecting Polish materials since before WWII and now has a Polonistyka collection of more than 40,000 vols, primarily in philology and history. among its rare books are Maciej Stryjkowski's Kronika polska and Jan Dlugosz's Historia Polonica.

MB —UNIVERSITY OF MANITOBA, Elizabeth Dafoe Library, Slavic Collection, Winnipeg, R3T 2N2, Can. John S Muchin, Librn
Holdings: Vols (33,000) Cat Mss Microforms

Budget: ($5000)
Notes: Material in all Slavic languages, mostly in Russian (approx 15,000 vols), Ukrainian (approx 15,000 vols), Polish, Old Church Slavic; mainly literature, language, history, art, geography, economics, statistics, political science; newspapers and periodicals; over 20,000 vols of microforms. Cited in Slavic Collection of the University of Manitoba Libraries, John S Muchin (Winnipeg: University of Manitoba Libraries and UVAN, 1970).

POLISH NEWSPAPERS see Newspapers, Polish

POLISH NOBILITY see Poland—Nobility

POLISH PERIODICALS see Periodicals, Polish

POLISH MUSIC see Music, Polish

POLISH WOMEN see Women, Polish

POLITENESS see Etiquette

POLITICAL ASSASSINATIONS see Assassination

POLITICAL BALLADS AND SONGS

MA —AMERICAN ANTIQUARIAN SOCIETY LIBRARY, 185 Salisbury St, Worcester, 01609. Marcus A McCorison, Dir & Librn
Holdings: Cat Maps Pix
Notes: Over 6000 American prints, arranged by lithographer. Incl political caricatures and cartoons, maps, sheet music. Also advertising cards, Valentines, etc.

PA —FREE LIBRARY OF PHILADELPHIA, Music Dept, Logan Sq, Philadelphia, 19103. Frederick James Kent, Head
Holdings: Vols 400 Cat
Notes: The Songster Collection contains songbooks of all types, campaign songsters, union songbooks and patriotic song collections, covering most of American music history. There is also a collection of 400 slip sheet and broadside ballads dating from the Civil War period.

RI —BROWN UNIVERSITY, John Hay Library, 20 Prospect St, Providence, 02912. Mark N Brown, Cur Mss
Notes: The Sheet Music Collection concentrates on music of American imprint, incl 170,000 vocal pieces filed by title, plus 80,000 instrumental pieces filed by composer. Major strengths are in 19th century music, especially prior to 1830; Civil War music, both Union and Confederate; lithographic covers; World War I music; political campaign music; and band music. An additional 100,000 pieces of American and European imprint remain unprocessed. See also entries under Lincoln, Abraham; Broadsides - Collections; American Ballads and Songs

RI —BROWN UNIVERSITY, John Hay Library, Harris Collection, Prospect St, Providence, 02912. Rosemary L Cullen, Cur
Holdings: Vols (200,000) Cat Mss Pix Phonorecords Microforms
Budget: ($15,000)
Notes: The Harris Collection of American Poetry and Plays is principally composed of American and Canadian poetry and plays from the 17th century to the present. Extensive holdings in songsters, sheet music with lyrics (170,000 pieces), and broadsides (30,000 pieces). Incl large collection of Stephen Foster sheet music and music by Rhode Island composers and lyricists. See Dictionary Catalog of the Harris Collection of American Poetry and Plays (Boston: G K Hall, 1972), 13 vols: Supplement (1977), 3 vols. Separate catalog.

RI —BROWN UNIVERSITY, John Hay Library, 20 Prospect St, Providence, 02912. Mary T Russo, Cur of Broadsides
Notes: A major collection of 30,000 pieces of American verse in broadside form dating from the 18th through the 20th century. Ephemeral in nature and all inclusive, it

covers a broad spectrum of American life. It incl many examples of political ballads, particularly in the section of the collection represented by slip or sheet ballads which were published from 1830 to 1870.

RI —BROWN UNIVERSITY, John Hay Library, McLellan Lincoln Collection, 20 Prospect St, Providence, 02912. Jennifer B Lee, Special Collections Librn
Notes: Sheet music collection has almost every piece of Lincoln sheet music known to exist from minstrel tunes to funeral marches, memorial songs and campaign songs. Statuary is well represented and incl two Rogers groups, an original Truman Bartlett plaster statuette of Lincoln, and replicas of Leonard Volk's work.

POLITICAL ECONOMY see Economics

POLITICAL EXILES see Exiles, Political

POLITICAL MISCELLANIES—ENGLISH

NY —CORNELL UNIVERSITY LIBRARIES, Collection of Regional History, Dept of Manuscripts and Univ Archives, Ithaca, 14853.
Notes: Political campaign materials, 1976; .4 ft.

POLITCAL MURDER see Assassination

POLITICAL PAMPHLETS, FRENCH, 1547-1648 see French Political Pamphlets, 1547-1648

POLITICAL PARTIES

CA —LOS ANGELES PUBLIC LIBRARY, Social Sciences Dept, 630 W Fifth St, Los Angeles, 90071. Marilyn C Wherley, Principal Librn
Holdings: Vols 3000 Cat
Budget: ($150,000)
Notes: Pamphlets, bound periodicals, incl political parties (US and some foreign), practical politics, elections statistics, extensive pamphlet file of California and Los Angeles City/County elections materials dating from the early 1900s. Scholarly and popular works.

DC —LIBRARY OF CONGRESS, Prints & Photographs Div, Washington, 20540.
Notes: The Gary Yonker Collection of political propaganda posters, late 1960s to present. Strongest for US materials but incl about 50 other countries' work. Over 4500 items, arranged geographically.

MA —JOHN F KENNEDY LIBRARY, Columbia Point, Boston, 02125. Henry J Gwiazda II, Cur
Notes: The Robert F Kennedy Papers cover the period from 1937-1968 and are divided into four subcollections: the Pre-Administration, Attorney General's, Senate, and 1968 Presidential Campaign Papers. In the Pre-Administration Papers, over 140 archives boxes or 70 percent of the materials are open to research. The Personal and Political Papers of this subcollection are almost entirely open. Most of the unprocessed mss are in the Working Files and involve investigative work on labor racketeering. Seventy five percent or 185 archives boxes of the Attorney General's Papers are open, incl the correspondence, the John F Kennedy Library File, the Speech and Trip Files for 1961-1964. For the Senate Papers, 200 boxes are open for the 1964 Senate Campaign, the Legislative Subject File, and the Speech and Trip Files for 1964-1968. The speeches and press releases(incl in the Senate subcollection Speech File) and "The Black Books" (16 boxes) on state and delegate information are open for the 1968 campaign. Each subcollection has its own finding aid. The Library also has available for research about 100 audiotapes of Robert F Kennedy's public addresses from 1962-1966 and some 50 oral history interviews on RFK and one (1000 pages) by RFK. There are also available the major documentaries on RFK

POLITICAL PARTIES (cont.)

and a number of films donated by the major networks for research use in the Library.

MA —BRANDEIS UNIVERSITY, Goldfarb Library, 415 South St, Waltham, 02154. Bessie Hahn, Dir
Notes: Hall-Hoag Archives on Extremism in the U.S. Approx 5000 pieces of Extremist literature, both Right and Left, dealing with various social, religious and political aspects of the US from the 1960s, 1970s and 1980s. A finding list is in Special Collections. Material is arranged by the name of the sponsoring organization in alphabetical order.

UT —UNIVERSITY OF UTAH, Marriott Library, Special Collections, Salt Lake City, 84112. Gregory C Thompson, Cur

WI —UNIVERSITY OF WISCONSIN, MILWAUKEE, Library, Box 604, Milwaukee, 53201. William C Roselle, Dir
Holdings: Vols 2500 Cat Mss Pix
Notes: Fromkin Memorial Collection, emphasizing third party forces in American politics. Restricted use: noncirculating. Special subject catalog of pamphlet material.

POLITICAL PLATFORMS see Political Parties

POLITICAL SATIRE

DC —LIBRARY OF CONGRESS, Prints & Photographs Div, Washington, 20540.
Notes: The British Cartoon collection contains 10,000 British political caricatures and satires dating from the 17th through mid 19th centuries. Incl the work of Henry Bunbury, George Cruikshank, Issac Cruikshank, Matthew Darly, James Gillray, and Thomas Rowlandson.

POLITICAL SCIENCE

AL —MILES COLLEGE, C A Kirkendoll Library, Birmingham, 35208. Mattie Jackson, Librn
Holdings: Vols (3000) Cat
Notes: Books from the private library of Dr Clinton Rossiter, well-known political scientist, historian, lecturer, writer and one of the foremost authorities on American constitutional history and political theory.

CA —FRANCIS BACON LIBRARY, 655 N Dartmouth Ave, Claremont, 91711. Elizabeth S Wrigley, Dir
Holdings: Vols 300 Cat Pix Microforms
Notes: American political theory (Lee-Bernard Collection). Contains a significant part of "statesman's library", incl periodicals, that James Madison and Thomas Jefferson listed in 1783 and urged the Continental Congress to buy. Collection made by the late Dr Douglass Adair, professor of history at the Claremont Graduate School and was given by him to the Francis Bacon Library. Long-title catalog of the collection published by the Library in 1972.

CA —CALIFORNIA STATE UNIVERSITY, FULLERTON, Library, Box 4150, Fullerton, 92634. Linda Herman, Special Collections Librn
Holdings: Vols 8000 Cat Mss
Notes: Aim is to cover the entire spectrum of political controversy for the Freedom Center of Polemic Political Ephemera. Incl 4000 serial titles and extensive ephemera.

CA —LOS ANGELES PUBLIC LIBRARY, Social Sciences Dept, 630 W Fifth St, Los Angeles, 90071. Marilyn C Wherley, Principal Librn
Holdings: Vols 3000 Cat
Budget: ($150,000)
Notes: Pamphlets, bound periodicals, incl political parties (US and foreign), practical politics, elections statistics, extensive pamphlet file of California and Los Angeles City/County elections materials dating from the early 1900s. Scholarly and popular works on all aspects of political science.

CA —SACRAMENTO PUBLIC LIBRARY, 828 I St, Sacramento, 95814. Dorothy Harvey, Librn, Special Collections
Holdings: Vols (4000) Cat
Notes: Incl books on public administration and police science, local government (city and county). Have over 4000 Sacramento city and county documents.

CA —COMMONWEALTH CLUB OF CALIFORNIA, Library, 681 Market St, San Francisco, 94105. Virginia Rees, Librn
Holdings: Vols (6500) Cat Maps Pix
Budget: ($2000)

CA —BIBLIOGRAPHIC RESEARCH LIBRARY, 964 Chapel Hill Way, San Jose, 95122. Robert B Harmon, Bibliographer
Holdings: Vols 759 Uncat Microforms
Budget: $500
Notes: Private research library emphasizing bibliography, political science, John Steinbeck and Ernest Hemingway.

CA —ABC-CLIO, Inge Boehm Library, 2040 Alameda Padre Serra, PO Box 4397, Santa Barbara, 93103. Hope Smith, Librn
Holdings: Uncat
Budget: $600
Notes: 300 current serials in political science; part of collection on history and history-related social sciences and humanities. These serials are used in the production of ABC POL SCI, an index of article titles in political science and government.

CT —YALE UNIVERSITY, Social Science Library, 140 Prospect St, New Haven, 06520. Billie I Salter, Librn
Holdings: Vols (40,000) Cat Microforms
See also entry under Social Sciences.

DC —COMMISSION OF THE EUROPEAN COMMUNITIES, European Community Information Service Library, 2100 M St NW Suite 707, Washington, 20037. Barbara Sloan, Head of Public Inquiries
Holdings: Vols (35,000) Cat Maps Pix Microforms
Notes: Library contains all of the official documents and occasional publications of the Institutions of the European Communities: ie, European Economic Community (Common Market), European Atomic Energy Community (Euratom), European Coal and Steel Community (ECSC). It collects non-Community publications about European integration, international trade and monetary affairs. Also, has the publications of the General Agreements for Tariffs and Trade (GATT), Western European Union, and Council of Europe. Also 1000 vertical files.

DC —GEORGETOWN UNIVERSITY, Library, Special Collections Div, 37 & O Sts NW, Washington, 20057. George M Barringer, Special Collections Librn; Nicholas B Sheetz, Mss Librn
Holdings: Mss Cat
Notes: The papers of Heinrich A Rommen (1897-1967), educator and authority on political philosphy and international law, consisting of correspondence, mss, clippings, photographs, and printed material. Incl material on religious opposition, in particular Catholic opposition, within Germany to the Hitler regime.

DC —US DEPT OF STATE, Library, Rm 3239 NS, Washington, 20520. Conrad P Eaton, Librn
Holdings: Vols (750,000) Cat Microforms
Notes: Incl 7200 microfilm reels.

DC —US OFFICE OF PERSONNEL MANAGEMENT, Library, 1900 E St NW, Washington, 20415. Betty B Guerin, Supv Librn
Holdings: Vols 75,000 Cat Microforms
Notes: US Civil Service Commission terminated by Act of Congress, 10/78. US Office of Personnel Management created and effective, 1/79. Library houses a comprehensive collection of materials in all phases of federal personnel administration, both historical and current and incl federal documents and other pamphlets. It is supplemented by collections in general personnel administration, public administration, management, and state, local and foreign Civil Service.

GA —UNIVERSITY OF GEORGIA, Libraries, Special Collections Division, Athens, 30602. Vesta Lee Gordon, Asst Dir for Special Collections
Notes: The Arbitron Collection of television and radio program ratings, 1949-date (except past year). In-depth, statistical analyses of the listening public by age, sex, county, some ethnic groups, farm population, listening preferences, etc. 26,302 bound vols. 2 reports, 1949-81. To be added to annually.

GA —ATLANTA PUBLIC LIBRARY, Ivan Allen Jr Dept of Science, Industry & Government, One Margaret Mitchell Square, Atlanta, 30303. William D Munro, Head
Holdings: Vols (2000) Cat
Budget: ($180,000)
Notes: Collection concentrates on Georgia state documents in the areas of law, business, industry, and science. Major series incl Georgia Laws (1825 to date); Georgia Reports and Georgia Appeals Reports. Annual reports, bulletins and circulars for selected state agencies and departments are also included.

IL —NORTHWESTERN UNIVERSITY, Library, Special Collections Dept, 1937 Sheridan Rd, Evanston, 60201. R Russell Maylone, Cur
Holdings: Vols (14,000) Cat
Notes: Periodicals and pamphlets concerning many social and political movements in the 20th century, with emphasis on anarchism, struggles of the working class, women's rights, and student protest of the 1960s. Foreign material incl. An additional 10,000 pieces arranged by subject.

LA —TULANE UNIVERSITY, Howard-Tilton Memorial Library, Special Collections Div, 7001 Freret St, New Orleans, 70118. Wilbur E Meneray, Librn
Holdings: Cat Audiotapes Microforms
Notes: Books, pamphlets, serial publications and circualrs from over 2000 individuals and organizations representing the fringe of 20th century US political opinion.

MD —JOHNS HOPKINS UNIVERSITY, Milton S Eisenhower Library, Charles & 34 Sts, Baltimore, 21218.
Holdings: Vols 53,000 Cat
Notes: Fairly balanced collection.

MA —HARVARD UNIVERSITY LIBRARY, Widener Library, Cambridge, 02138.
Holdings: Cat Microforms
Notes: Widener Library Shelflist No 22 (1969) lists 10,941 vols on government, but this does not incl document collections or extensive holdings of law school.

MI —UNIVERSITY OF MICHIGAN, Library, Dept of Rare Books & Special Collections, Ann Arbor, 48109. Robert J Starring, Head
Holdings: Cat Microforms
Notes: Incl the library of Professor Karl Heinrich Rau of the University of Heidelberg, acquired in 1871, containing 6076 vols especially rich in works on political economics and European statistics before 1850.

MI —UNIVERSITY OF MICHIGAN, Bureau of Government Library, 100A Rackman Bldg, Ann Arbor, 48109. Barbara Landay, Technical Libr Assistant
Holdings: Vols (66,000) Cat
Budget: ($10,000)
Notes: Established in 1914 to serve faculty and students of Institute of Public Policy Studies. Particularly concerned with state and local documents, but incl some federal documents. Also has a pamphlet and newspaper clipping collection on Michigan. Some information on foreign governments.

NJ —PRINCETON UNIVERSITY, Woodrow Wilson School Library, Princeton, 08544. Linda Oppenheim, Special Librn
Holdings: Vols 17,345
Budget: $30,000
Notes: This is a convenience collection primarily for Woodrow Wilson School of Public and International Affairs students. It is a functional special library, intended to support courses by providing reserve readings, journals and reference works. Faculty and students alike are expected to use the central campus library for research.

NY —NEW YORK STATE DEPT OF STATE, Community Affairs Library, 162 Washington Ave, Albany, 12231. M L Johnson, Librn
Holdings: Vols (28,600) Cat
Notes: Local government. Serves as research arm for official activities. 26,000 items in vertical files; 400 periodicals. Unique

POLITICAL SCIENCE (cont.)

Community File collection of about 8000 communities arranged by the 62 countries, towns, and villages in the state.

NY —NEW YORK STATE LIBRARY, State Education Bldg Annex, Washington Ave, Albany, 12224.
Holdings: Vols 700,000 Cat Microforms
Notes: Comprehensive; heavy concentration of official publications.

NY —COLUMBIA UNIVERSITY LIBRARIES, Rare Book & Manuscript Library, 801 Butler Library, 535 W 114 St, New York, 10027. Kenneth A Lohf, Librn
Holdings: Mss
Notes: Incl the papers (5000 items) of Professor Robert Morrison MacIver: correspondence, notes, drafts of mss, etc on sociology, political power and juvenile delinquency, incl his participation on the City of New York Juvenile Delinquency Evaluation Project, on which he served after his retirement from Columbia University. Restricted use.

NY —NEW YORK PUBLIC LIBRARY, Research Libraries, Economic & Public Affairs Div, Fifth Ave & 42 St, New York, 10018. Edward DiRoma, Chief
Holdings: Vols (1,500,000) Cat Microforms

OH —PUBLIC LIBRARY OF CINCINNATI & HAMILTON COUNTY, Government and Business Dept, 800 Vine St, Cincinnati, 45202. Paul T Hudson, Head
Holdings: Vols 120,000 Cat
Notes: Department receives over 1200 periodical and loose-leaf service titles, 1500 serial titles and over 1500 telephone directories. Subjects include political science, especially foreign relations, economics, law, public administration and business management. Dept houses Murray Seasongood collection of local government. Dept has extensive census material from 1790. Library is a full depository for US Government Publications, 1884 to date.

OH —CLEVELAND PUBLIC LIBRARY, Social Sciences Department, 325 Superior Ave, Cleveland, 44114. Thelma Morris, Head
Holdings: Cat
Notes: Extensive collection. Full runs of periodicals.

OR —UNIVERSITY OF OREGON, Library, Eugene, 97403. Kenneth W Duckett, Curator
Notes: Papers of Prof Charles McKinley, incl files of correpsondence, minutes, reports, position papers concerning (largely) public administration and planning.

PA —UNIVERSITY OF PITTSBURGH, Hillman Library, Pittsburgh, 15260. Glenora E Rossell, Head
Holdings: Vols (700) Cat Pix Microforms
Notes: Advanced industrial societies of Europe. At Hillman Library are cataloged the publications of political parties and interest organizations of Austria (7), Belgium (5), Denmark (8), Finland (6), France (12), Germany (9), Great Britain (6), Italy (6), Netherlands (12), Norway (4), Switzerland (10), Sweden (6). Supplementing this collection is the general political science collection which incl OECD publications, statistics, parliamentary records and government documents of these countries. This collection was developed in cooperation with the 8 university Council on European Studies.

PA —SCRANTON PUBLIC LIBRARY, Vine & N Washington Sts, Scranton, 18503. Thomas McHale, Dir
Holdings: Vols (975) Cat
Budget: ($6000)

TX —ABILENE CHRISTIAN UNIVERSITY, Margaret & Herman Brown Library, ACU Sta, Abilene, 79601. Callie Faye Milliken, Assoc Dir
Notes: The Omar Burleson Congressional Papers. Includes correspondence, hearings, books, memorabilia.

TX —UNIVERSITY OF DALLAS, Kendall Memorial Library, Univeristy of Dallas Sta, Irving, 75061. Caroline Silhman, SSND Head Librn
Holdings: Vols 1050 // Cat Audiotapes
Notes: Political philosphy.

WA —UNIVERSITY OF WASHINGTON LIBRARIES, Political Science Library, 220 Smith Hall, DP-25, Seattle, 98195. Alvin Fritz, Librn
Holdings: Vols (57,344) Cat
Budget: ($57,792)

WI —UNIVERSITY OF WISCONSIN, GREEN BAY, Library/Learning Center, Green Bay, 54301. Marian A Gould, Acting Dir, Special Collections/University Archives
Holdings: Vols 700 // Cat
Notes: This represents the collection of Leon Kramer, "idealist, philosophical anarchist and bookseller." Much of the material concerns radical literature and small socialist and communist parties in the US, although there is a considerable amount of books, booklets, and pamphlets published in Germany, Italy, and other parts of Europe. Incl uncounted pamphlets.

WI —UNIVERSITY OF WISCONSIN, MILWAUKEE, Library, Box 604, Milwaukee, 53201. William C Roselle, Dir
Holdings: Vols 2500 Cat Mss Pix
Notes: Fromkin Memorial Collection, emphasizing third party forces in American politics. Restricted use: noncirculating. Special subject catalog of pamphlet material.

BC —LEGISLATIVE LIBRARY (PROVINCIAL), Parliament Bldgs, Victoria, V8V 1X4, Can. J H MacEachern, Head, Government Documents Division
Holdings: Cat Maps Microforms

ON —CANADA DEPT OF EXTERNAL AFFAIRS, Library Services Div, 125 Sussex Dr, Ottawa, K1A 0G2, Can. Ruth Margaret Thompson, Dir
Holdings: Vols (40,000) Cat Maps Phonorecords Audiotapes Microforms
Notes: Incl 1000 maps, 250,000 microforms, and 550,000 documents.

ON —LIBRARY OF PARLIAMENT, Parliament Bldgs, Ottawa, K1A 0A9, Can. Erik J Spicer, Parliamentary Librn
Holdings: Vols 45,000 Cat
Notes: Incl periodicals.

ON —NATIONAL LIBRARY OF CANADA, 395 Wellington St, Ottawa, K1A 0N4, Can. Andre Preibish, Dir
Holdings: Vols 10,000
Notes: Includes 130 serial titles, theses, pamphlets, government publications relating to family and marriage. The following disciplines covered: anthropology, psychology and psychiatry, law, economics, religion, sociology, demography, education, political science and biology. Earliest title 1630.

SK —SASKATCHEWAN LEGISLATIVE LIBRARY, 234 Legislative Bldg, Regina, S4S 0B3, Can. Marian Powell, Librn
Holdings: Vols 2350 Cat Microforms
Notes: Emphasis on books published in Canada.

POLITICAL SCIENCE—ANECDOTES, FACETIAE, SATIRE, ETC. see Political Satire

POLITICAL SCIENCE—HISTORY

DC —LIBRARY OF CONGRESS, Manuscript Division, Washington, 20540. John C Broderick, Chief
Notes: Papers of Hannah Arendt; now unrestricted, except for the Judah L Magnes correspondence.

NY —UNIVERSITY OF ROCHESTER, Rush Rhees Library, Department of Rare Books and Special Collections, Rochester, 14627. Peter Dzwonkoski, Librn
Holdings: Vols 450 Cat
Notes: Collection of materials on 16th and 17th century European law and political theory with special emphasis on works emanating from the French Civil Wars of the late 16th century. Particularly notable are the editions of the works of Francois Hotman and the editions of the Corpus Juris Civilis printed in Lyon. No photocopying.

PA —UNIVERSITY OF PENNSYLVANIA, Lea Library, 3420 Walnut St, Philadelphia, 19104. Daniel Traister, Special Collections Librn
Holdings: Vols (20,000) Cat Mss
Notes: Collection incl works on Church

history, the history of jurisprudence, political theory. Byzantine history, the Crusades and medieval urban history. See Downs 4241, 4234.

POLITICAL SCIENCE ASSOCIATION, AMERICAN see American Political Science Association

POLITICAL SONGS see Political Ballads and Songs

POLITICAL VIOLENCE see Assassination

POLITICIANS see Statesmen and Stateswomen

POLITICS, AMERICAN see U.S.—Politics and Government

POLITICS, PRACTICAL

CA —WOMEN'S HISTORY RESEARCH CENTER, Microfilm Library, 2325 Oak St, Berkeley, 94708. Laura X, Librn
Holdings: Microforms
Notes: Incl 500 subject files of material on Women and Law (General); Politics; Employment; Education; Rape/Prison/ Prostitution; Black and Third World women. Collection at University of Wyoming, Archive of Contemporary History, PO Box 3334, Laramie, Wyoming 82071, c/o David Crosson. Reasearch inquiries accepted. Microfilm of collection (40 reels & reel guides) available through Women's History Research Center, 2325 Oak St, Berkeley, CA 94708. No collections housed at this address.

CA —CALIFORNIA STATE UNIVERSITY, FULLERTON, Library, Box 4150, Fullerton, 92634. Linda Herman, Special Collections Librn
Holdings: Vols 8000 Cat Mss
Notes: Aim is to cover the entire spectrum of political controversy for the Freedom Center of Polemic Political Ephemera. Incl 4000 serial titles and extensive ephemera.

CA —UNIVERSITY OF CALIFORNIA, LOS ANGELES, Research Library, Public Affairs Service, 405 Hilgard Ave, Los Angeles, 90024. Edward Shreeves, Chairman, Bibliographers Group; Eugenia Eaton, Head, Public Affairs Service
Holdings: Uncat
Notes: Current non-governmental English-language pamphlets (192,819), broadsides, leaflets and other ephemera on public affairs, from 1960, representing a wide spectrum of political and social opinions. Social welfare and industrial relations are strong fields. Legal loose-leaf labor services, such as the *Daily Labor Report*, the *Government Employee Relations Report* and the *Labor Relations Reporter*, as well as labor pamphlets from the mid-1940s, reflect a long-standing responsibility to the University's Institute of Industrial Relations.

LA —TULANE UNIVERSITY, Howard-Tilton Memorial Library, Special Collections Div, 7001 Freret St, New Orleans, 70118. Wilbur E Meneray, Librn
Holdings: Cat Audiotapes Microforms
Notes: Books, pamphlets, serial publications and circulars from over 2000 individuals and organizations representing the fringe of 20th century US political opinion.

MA —RADCLIFFE COLLEGE, Arthur & Elizabeth Schlesinger Library on the History of Women in America, 3 James St, Cambridge, 02138. Patricia Miller King, Dir; Eva Moseley, Cur of Mss
Notes: Papers of several women who have held elective office and the local, state, or federal level, and of both Democratic and Republican national committee women. Also papers of Mary William Dewson (1874-1962), who reorganized and headed the Women's Division of the Democratic National Committee in 1933.

NY —STATE UNIVERSITY OF NEW YORK, STONY BROOK, Melville Library, Dept of Special Collections, Stony Brook, 11794. Evert Volkersz, Head
Holdings: Cat Mss
Notes: Printed and ms materials relating to

POLITICS, PRACTICAL (cont.)

local and regional Long Island history. Ms collections focus on women, environment, social welfare, and politics.

OH —AKRON-SUMMIT COUNTY PUBLIC LIBRARY, Business, Labor & Government Div, 55 S Main St, Akron, 44326. William G Johnson, Head
Holdings: Vols (10,000) Cat Microforms
Budget: ($20,000)

RI —BROWN UNIVERSITY, John Hay Library, 20 Prospect St, Providence, 02912. Mark N Brown, Cur Mss
Holdings: Mss
Notes: The Brown University Manuscript Collection contains several large collections relating to politics, incl collections involving Rhode Island, United States, and even international politics. Collections incl the papers of Benjamin Bourne, 1755-1808, soldier, jurist, and US Congressman from RI (200 items); Zechariah Chafee Jr, 1885-1957, (qv); Samuel Sullivan Cox, 1824-1889, (qv); Thomas Wilson Dorr, 1805-1854, (qv); John Hay, 1838-1905, (qv); Charles Evans Hughes, 1818-1875, RI lawyer and US Congressman (100 items); Charles Warren Lippitt, 1846-1924 (qv); John G Nocolay, 1832-1901 (300 items); Whitelaw Reid, 1837-1912; John Hay Collection, (qv); the Sidney S Rider Papers (qv); the Thomas Rodney, 1744-1811, Collection, member Continental Congress and jurist (70 items); Jonathan Russell (qv); William and Catherine Chase Sprague--governor and US Senator(250 items); Eli Thayer, 1819-1899 (qv); Jonah Titus, lawyer and Rhode Island legislator; and Samuel Wyllys, 1632-1709, colonial magistrate (125 items).

UT —UNIVERSITY OF UTAH, Marriott Library, Special Collections, Salt Lake City, 84112. Gregory C Thompson, Cur
Holdings: Cat Mss Microfilm Film Oral History
Notes: Papers of Senators Frank Moss, Jake Garn, Wallace Bennet, William King, Reed Smoot; Representatives Allan Howe, Sherman Lloyd, Reva Beck Bosone, Wayne Owens; Utah Governors J Bracken Lee, Calvin Rampton, Herbert Maw; US Treasurer Ivy Baker Priest.

PR —CARIBBEAN REGIONAL LIBRARY, General Library, University of Puerto Rico, Rio Piedras, (Mailing add: PO Box 21917, University Station, San Juan, 00931). Carmen M Costa de Ramos, Librn
Holdings: Vols (115,605) Cat Maps Pix Microforms
Notes: Collection is specialized in the Caribbean with emphasis in the areas of interest to developing countries: social sciences, politics, economics, labor, education, commerce, tourism, literature, etc. The Current Caribbean Bibliography is compiled at the Caribbean Regional Library, with card contributions from all countries of the Caribbean; it also lists all the new additions to the library.

POLITICS, WOMEN IN see Women in Politics

POLITICS, WORLD see World Politics

POLIZIANO, ANGELO, 1454-1494

†CA —CLAREMONT COLLEGES, Honnold Library, Claremont, 91711.
Notes: Collection given by Mr and Mrs Harold Bodman, who owned a villa in Florence, once the home of Poliziano, Renaissance humanist and friend of Lorenzo de Medici. Works in Italian or Renaissance Latin by and about Poliziano, both contemporary and later publications.

POLK, JAMES K.

DC —LIBRARY OF CONGRESS, Manuscript Division, Washington, 20540. John C Broderick, Chief
Notes: The Presidential Papers collection incl the papers, etc, of numerous Presidents.

POLK, RT. REV. LEONIDAS

TN —UNIVERSITY OF THE SOUTH ARCHIVES, Jessie Ball DuPont Library,

Sewanee, 37375. Gertrude French Mignery, Archivist
Holdings: Vols (3000) Cat Mss

POLLAND, MADELEINE

MA —BOSTON UNIVERSITY, Mugar Memorial Library, Special Collections Dept, 771 Commonwealth Ave, Boston, 02215. Howard B Gotlieb, Dir
Holdings: Cat Mss Pix Correspondence

POLLARD, JOHN GARLAND

VA —COLLEGE OF WILLIAM AND MARY, Earl Gregg Swem Library, Williamsburg, 23185. Margaret C Cook, Cur of Manuscripts & Rare Books
Holdings: // Cat Mss Pix
Notes: John Garland Pollard Papers, 1850-1937. Collection of personal, family, and professional papers of Pollard (1871-1937), governor of Virginia during period 1930-1934 and chairman, US Board of Veterans Appeals, 1934-1937. 18,000 items.

POLLARD AND REDGRAVE, STC BOOKS

CA —UNIVERSITY OF CALIFORNIA, LOS ANGELES, William Andrews Clark Memorial Library, 2520 Cimarron St, Los Angeles, 90018.
Holdings: Cat

†MA —BOSTON PUBLIC LIBRARY, Copley Sq, Boston, 02117.
Holdings: Uncat Microforms
Notes: Microform publication by University Microfilms. Early English Books, 1475-1640, based on Pollard and Redgrave Short-Title Catalog. 1927 reels.

NY —NEW YORK STATE LIBRARY, State Education Bldg Annex, Washington Ave, Albany, 12224.
Holdings: Microforms
Notes: English books, 1475-1640. University Microfilms collection. Access thru Pollard and Redgrave, Short-title Catalogue. English books, 1641-1700. University Microfilms collection. Access thru Wing, Short-title Catalogue.

PA —UNIVERSITY OF PENNSYLVANIA, Van Pelt Library, Rare Books Collection, 34 & Walnut Sts, Philadelphia, 19104. Daniel Traister, Special Collections Librn
Holdings: Cat Microforms
Notes: The University Library has acquired approx 20,000 editions of the University Microfilms Xerox Collection of STC (Pollard and Redgrave) books. See (University of Pennsylvania) Library Chronicle, vol 34, no 1, winter 1968, Frye, Roland M "The new photocopy library of British Renaissance Books at the University of Pennsylvania."

POLLS see Elections; Public Opinion Polls

POLLUTION

CA —UNIVERSITY OF CALIFORNIA, BERKELEY, Giannini Foundation of Agricultural Economics, Library, 248 Giannini Hall, Berkeley, 94720. Grace Dote, Librn
Holdings: Vols (18,000) Cat Mss Maps Microforms
Notes: Noncirculating collection. No interlibrary loans. Also about 124,000 unbound vols. Open to graduate students and faculties of universities and colleges, research workers and interested public. Mostly English language materials, primarily 1900 to date. Card catalog published by G K Hall Co. Dictionary Catalog of the Giannini Foundation of Agricultural Economics Library, Univ of California, 12 vols. (holdings thru 7/71).

CA —UNIVERSITY OF CALIFORNIA, DAVIS, Environmental Toxicology Library, Davis, 95616. Ming-yu Li, Documentation Specialist
Holdings: Vols (5000) Cat
Notes: Library is open to the public for reference only. In addition to the cataloged holdings, the library also maintains a

pamphlet collection of 50 file drawers on agricultural chemicals, environmental pollution, heavy metals, food toxicants, toxicology, pesticides and trace elements.

CA —UNIVERSITY OF CALIFORNIA, LOS ANGELES, Engineering & Mathematical Sciences Library, 405 Hilgard, Los Angeles, 90024. Rosalee I Wright, Librn
Notes: Partial depository for NTIS (pollution, environment, meteorology, and bioengineering) since 1970.
See also entry under Engineering

CA —UNIVERSITY OF CALIFORNIA, LOS ANGELES, Biomedical Library, Center for Health Sciences, Los Angeles, 90024. Louise Darling, Biomedical Librn

CA —ASSOCIATION OF BAY AREA GOVERNMENTS, MTC/ABAG Library, 101 Eighth St, Oakland, 94607. Diane Gillman, Information Coord
Notes: Concentrates heavily on the nine-county Bay Area region. About 10,000 monographs and serials. Title catalog, OCLC/ATS. Central collection of documents for six transit properties in Bay Area.

CA —CALIFORNIA DEPT OF TRANSPORTATION, Transportation Library, 5900 Folsom Blvd, PO Box 19128, Sacramento, 95819. Eva Caro, Librn
Holdings: Vols (10,000) Cat Mss Pix Slides Phonorecords Audiotapes Videotapes 16mm Films Filmstrips Microforms

CA —ENVIRONMENTAL PROTECTION AGENCY, Library, 215 Fremont St, San Francisco, 94105. Jean Circiello, Librn
Holdings: Vols 115,000 Cat Maps Microforms
Budget: $30,000
Notes: Especially strong in environmental pollution in California, Arizona, Nevada, and Hawaii.

CT —YALE UNIVERSITY, Forestry Library, 205 Prospect St, New Haven, 06511. Joseph A Miller, Librn
Holdings: Vols (115,000) Cat Microforms
Notes: The Forestry Library is a unit of the Yale University Library, housed in and serving primarily the School of Forestry and Environmental Studies. Founded in 1900, it has become one of the largest forestry libraries in the world. Forestry is construed broadly to incl underlying or closely related social, physical, and biological sciences. The literature of North American forestry and forest products is most completely covered, though other countries and foreign languages are well represented. Environmental studies and allied fields of natural resources management have been emphasized during the past 10 years. See Dictionary Catalog of the Yale Forestry Library, 12 vols (Boston: G K Hall, 1962).

DC —CONSERVATION FOUNDATION, Library, 1717 Massachusetts Ave NW, Washington, 20036. Barbara K Rodes, Librn
Holdings: Vols (8000) Cat Maps
Notes: Collection incl natural resources, ecology, population, city and regional planning, recreation, transportation, energy resources, education, economics, pollution, agriculture, etc.

DC —US ENVIRONMENTAL PROTECTION AGENCY, 401 M St SW, Washington, 20460. Sarah T Kadec, Dir Information Management & Services Division
Holdings: Vols (480,000) Cat Maps Pix Microforms

IL —CHICAGO PUBLIC LIBRARY, Business/Science/Technology Div, Science/Technology Information Center, 425 North Michigan Ave, Chicago, 60611. Lynda Sanford, Head; John R Moore, Environment Collection Coordinator & Engineering Librn
Holdings: Vols 2000 Cat Maps Films Slides Phonorecords Audiotapes Microforms
Budget: $7000
Notes: Incl Aaron Montgomery Ward Collection.

MD —RACHEL CARSON COUNCIL INC, Library, 8940 Jones Mill Rd, Chevy Chase, 20815. Shirley A Briggs, Exec Dir
Notes: Bioassays of pesticides and other toxic substances for carcinogenicity by National Cancer Institute; government

POLLUTION (cont.)

regulatory documents. Holdings approx 1500 books; 1000 documents and unbound reports; 40 drawers of specialized files. Also have Environmental Protection Agency Pesticide Product Information. Subscribe to 54 journals and others serials. Also publish on pesticides, toxic substances and alternatives to use of pesticides. Have index to pesticides by chemical formula, trade names and CAS number.

MD —CHARLES COUNTY COMMUNITY COLLEGE, Learning Resource Center, PO Box 910, La Plata, 20646. J Elaine Ryan, Dean
Holdings: Vols (1500) // Uncat 16mm Films Microforms
Notes: Primarily composed of government documents, this collection emphasizes the technical aspects of waste water treatment. Additional point of emphasis is desalination.

MD —MARYLAND-NATIONAL CAPITAL PARK & PLANNING COMMISSION, Montgomery County Planning Department Library, 8787 Georgia Ave, Silver Spring, 20907. Janice C Holt, Librn
Holdings: Vols (5000) Cat Microforms
Notes: Specific subject areas include: community facilities, conservation, economics, flood control, highways, housing, human and natural resources. landscape architecture, open space, parks, pollution, population, recreation, transportation, urban renewal, and zoning. Commission's publications are maintained by Records Management (not Library).

MA —CAMP, DRESSER & MCKEE, Herman G Dresser Library, One Center Plaza, Boston, 02108. Virginia L Carroll, Librn
Holdings: Vols (15,000) Cat Maps Slides Microforms
Notes: Air, land, and water pollution; environmental engineering; hazardous wastes; water resources; solid wastes; resource recycling.

NJ —WITCO CHEMICAL CORP, Corporate Research Center Library, 100 Bauer Dr, Oakland, 07436. Jo Therese Smith, Mgr, Information Services
Holdings: Vols (9000)
Budget: ($52,000)

NY —ENGINEERING SOCIETIES LIBRARY, 345 E 47 St, New York, 10017. S Kirk Cabeen, Dir
Holdings: Vols 250,000 Cat Maps 16mm Films Microforms
Notes: One of the largest, most comprehensive engineering libraries in the world. Covers all engineering disciplines; particularly strong in electrical and electronic, mechanical, mining and metallurgical, petroleum, chemical, industrial, air conditioning and refrigeration engineering. Incl Wheeler Collection of early materials on magnetism and electricity. 125,000 bound periodical volumes; 10,000 maps; 5000 serial subscriptions (many foreign-language). Virtually all materials abstracted in *Enginering Index* (1884-date) are incl in Library. Noncirculating, except to members of professional engineering societies which support the Library. See *Engineering Societies Library, New York, Classed Subject Catalog and Index* (Boston: G K Hall, 1963); and *Supplements*, 1-10, 1964-1973.

OH —CLEVELAND PUBLIC LIBRARY, Science & Technology Dept, 325 Superior Ave, Cleveland, 44114. Jean Z Piety, Head
Holdings: Cat Pix
Notes: Special collection covers the environmental sciences concerned with the Great Lakes-St Lawrence drainage basins. Emphasis is on limnology, ecology, meteorology, hydraulics, biology, pollution of air and water, natural history and general research. Most of the material indexed has been donated by numerous agencies around the Great Lakes.

AB —CANADIAN FORESTRY SERVICE, Northern Forest Research Centre Library, 5320 122nd, Edmonton, T6H 3S5, Can. David J S Robinson, Librn
Holdings: Vols (7000) Cat Microforms
Budget: ($25,000)
Notes: Also 23,000 government documents,

2600 research reports, 3000 pamphlets and reprints.

ON —AGRICULTURE CANADA, Research Branch, Neatby Library, Rm 3032, K W Neatby Bldg, CEF, Ottawa, K1A 0C6, Can. Marcel Charette, Library Technician
Holdings: Vols 600 Cat

ON —METROPOLITAN TORONTO LIBRARY, Science & Technology Dept, 789 Yonge St, Toronto, M4W 2G8, Can. Margaret Walshe, Head
Holdings: Vols (120,000) Cat VF
Notes: All aspects of science and technology for the specialist, the student and the general public. The department gives high priority to Canadian materials.

ON —METROPOLITAN TORONTO LIBRARY, Municipal Reference Library, City Hall, Toronto, M5H 2N1, Can. Margot Hewings, Head
Holdings: Vols (60,000) Cat Maps Pix Microforms Slides VF
Budget: ($112,600)
Notes: Community development; municipal finance; local municipal government; housing; urban pollution; urban transportation; urban affairs; urban geography.

PQ —UNIVERSITY OF MONTREAL, Bibliotheque Para-medicale, 2375 Chemin de la Cote Ste Catherine, Montreal, H3C 3J7, Can. Johanne Hopper, Head Librn
Holdings: Vols 1700 Cat
Notes: Social medicine, preventive medicine, epidemiology, industrial health and hygiene, and environmental factors (pollution) as related to health. Depository for World Health Organization publications.

PQ —NORANDA RESEARCH CENTRE, Library, 240 Hymus Blvd, Pointe-Claire, H9R 1G5, Can. Shirley Courtis, Librn
Holdings: (7000) Cat Microforms

PQ —SERVICE DE LA DOCUMENTATION ET DES RENSEIGNEMENTS MINISTERE DE L'ENERGIE ET DES RESSOURCES, 2000B, chemin Sainte-Foy, 7th floor, Quebec, G1R 4X7, Can. Normand Guerette, Dir
Holdings: Vols (114,800) Slides Videotapes
Notes: In 1979, the Bibliotheque du ministere des Richesses naturelles du Quebec merged with the Bibliotheque du ministere des Terres et Forets. The result of this merger was the creation of the service de la Documentation et des Renseignements du ministere de l'Energie et des Ressources. Publications: Info-Biblio Terres et Forets; Mines; Energy.

POLLUTION CONTROL DEVICES (MOTOR VEHICLES) see Motor Vehicles—Pollution Control Devices

POLLUTION OF WATER see Oil Pollution of Rivers, Harbors, Etc.; Water—Pollution and Control

POLO

WV —SALEM COLLEGE, Library, Salem, 26426. Myron J Smith, Jr, Librn
Notes: Collection supports "the most complete equestrian studies program available anywhere". *Myron J Smith, Equestrian Studies:* the Salem College [Bibliographical] Guide to Sources in English, 1950-1980. Metuchen, NJ: Scarecrow Press, 1981; 4645 entries.

POLO, MARCO

CA —CALIFORNIA STATE UNIVERSITY, HAYWARD, Library, Hayward, 94542. Melissa Rose, Dir
Holdings: Vols 175 Cat Maps Pix
Budget: ($7408)
Notes: Editions in several languages of works by and about Marco Polo, originally in the library of Henry Hart, San Fransicso scholar whose extensive writings in the field of early voyages and travels incl a biography of Marco Polo. Noncirculating.

IN —INDIANA UNIVERSITY, Lilly Library, Seventh St, Bloomington, 47405. William R Cagle, Librn
Holdings: Cat
Notes: Research and rare book collection (Bernardo Mendel) of first or only editions, mostly printed in Latin America, from the discovery of the New World through 1830. Special strength in discoveries and exploration, history (mainly period of independence), Inquisition, missionary works by the Augustinians, Dominicans, Franciscans, and the Jesuits, and the history of the Catholic Church in these countries. Major geographic concentration is on the three great viceroyalties of Mexico (ca. 10,000 titles, plus over 10,000 official Mexican broadsides), Peru (2000 titles), and Argentina (4000 titles), incl. in Argentina a substantial amount of printings from the Imprenta de Ninos Expositos, and the Coleccion Santamarina. A special Bolivian Collection (2500 titles), mostly history, from the establishment of the press there, ca. 1826, through the beginning of the 20th century. Part of the Mendel Collection is the select Bibliotheca Boxeriana from Charles R. Boxer (1000 titles) on European expansion into Asia, and into the New World, mainly Brazil, during the 16th-18th centuries. The collection is supplemented by substantial material from the private collection of Josiah K. Lilly. See also entries under Spain-History, Portugal-History, and Mexico-History.

POLYGAMY

UT —UTAH STATE UNIVERSITY, Merrill Library, Department of Special Collections & Archives, Logan, 84322. A J Simmonds, Curator; Jeanie F Simmonds, Archivist; Bradford R Cole, Mss Librn
Holdings: Vols 3000 Cat Mss Maps Microforms
Notes: Incl all LDS Churches, though major emphasis is on the Salt Lake based Church of Jesus Christ of Latterday Saints and on the Mormon fundamentalists (Polygamists). Additional material in the Library's Utah Collection.

UT —UNIVERSITY OF UTAH, Marriott Library, Special Collections, Salt Lake City, 84112. Gregory C Thompson, Cur

POLYMERIZATION see Polymers and Polymerization

POLYMERS AND POLYMERIZATION

CA —AVERY INTERNATIONAL CORP, Information Center, 325 N Altadena Dr, Pasadena, 91107. Louanne A Kalvinskas, Information Specialist
Holdings: Vols 800 Cat
Notes: Also many reports.

CA —KELCO DIV OF MERCK, Library, 8355 Aero Dr, San Diego, 92123. Ann A Jenkins, Librn
Holdings: Cat Mss Maps Pix Slides Microforms
Notes: Kelco, as the largest producer of algin and xanthan gum in the world, supports a library specialized in the subject of natural gums and polysaccharides, incl all aspects of the subject: chemistry, biology, microbiology, applications (food, industrial, petroleum), etc.

CA —INTERNATIONAL BUSINESS MACHINES RESEARCH LIBRARY, 5600 Cottle Rd, San Jose, 95193. Phil Grincewich, Mgr Technical Information
Holdings: Vols (13,500) Cat
Notes: Principally electronic computer

POLYMERS AND POLYMERIZATION (cont.)

storage system architecture. Incl 21,000 vols of 770 journals. On-line search facility. Vols are divided into three libraries, Technical Research, Technical Information, and Programing. Not open to public.

CT —UPJOHN CO, D S Gilmore Library, 410 Sacketts Point Rd, North Haven, 06473. A M Nashu, Supvr
Holdings: Vols 6000 Cat
Budget: $60,000
Notes: Polymers chemistry.

CT —BELDING HEMINWAY CO, Belding Corticelli Research Center Library, Grosvenordale, PO Drawer 28, Putnam, 06260.
Holdings: Vols (4500) Cat
Notes: Restricted access.

CT —ROGERS CORP, Lurie Library, One Technology Drive, Rogers, 06263. Myrna D Riquier, Librn; Nini S Davis, Librn
Holdings: Vols (650) Cat
Notes: Emphasis on materials science, plastics, polymers, resins.

IL —CHEMPLEX CO LIBRARY, 3100 Golf Rd, Rolling Meadows, 60008. Frieda R Oetting, Head Librn
Holdings: Vols 2031 Cat 16mm Films Microforms

IL —UNIVERSITY OF ILLINOIS, URBANA/CHAMPAIGN, Chemistry Library, 255 Noyes Laboratory, Urbana, 61801. Lucille M Wert, Chemistry Librn; Susan Eilering, Asst Chemistry Librn
Holdings: Vols (150,000) Cat Microforms
Budget: ($224,660)
Notes: Collection incl monographs, treatises and serials in all languages covering all the fields of polymer chemistry. It is designed to serve the instructional and research needs of the School of Chemical Sciences and the University Community.

KY —UNIVERSITY OF KENTUCKY, Robert E Shaver Library of Engineering, 355 Anderson Hall, Lexington, 40506. Russell H Powell, Engineering Librn
Holdings: Vols (48,000) Cat Microforms

MD —GILLETTE MEDICAL EVALUATION LABORATORIES, Information Center, 1413 Reasearch Blvd, Rockville, 20034. Patrick Dexter, Librn

MA —UNIVERSITY OF MASSACHUSETTS AT AMHERST, Physical Sciences Library, Amherst, 01003. Siegfried Feller, Assoc Dir for Collection Development
Holdings: Cat

MA —ABCOR, INC, Library, 850 Main St, Wilmington, 01887. Eileen Smith, Librn
Holdings: Vols (2000) Cat
Budget: ($10,000)
Notes: Reverse osmosis technology. Particularly strong in government technical reports.

MA —NORTON COMPANY, Library, 1 New Bond St, Worcester, 01606. Joan K Chaffey, Librn
Holdings: Cat
Notes: Abrasive industry collection.

MS —UNIVERSITY OF SOUTHERN MISSISSIPPI, William David McCain Graduate Library, Box 5148, Southern Sta, Hattiesburg, 39406.
Holdings: Mss
Notes: Collections incl the research records (1934-1977) of Dr James S Long and the research records and organizational records of the American Tung Oil Institute and its predecessor organizations. 33 cubic feet of mss.

NJ —WITCO CHEMICAL CORP, Corporate Research Center Library, 100 Bauer Dr, Oakland, 07436. Jo Therese Smith, Mgr, Information Services
Holdings: Vols (9000) Cat
Budget: ($52,000)

NY —POLYTECHNIC INSTITUTE OF NEW YORK, Spicer Library, 333 Jay St, Brooklyn, 11201.
Notes: An extensive collection.

NY —PENNWALT CORPORATION, Lucidol Division, Research Library, 1740 Military Road, Buffalo, 14240. Brenda L Cassoni, Asst Librn
Holdings: Vols 8000
Notes: There is a separate catalog of subject references to articles in periodicals.

NY —SCHENECTADY CHEMICALS INC, W H Wright Research Center, Library, 2750 Balltown Rd, Schenectady, 12309. Elizabeth H Groot, Mgr Tech Information Serv
Holdings: Vols (1000) Cat Microforms
Notes: Also incl patents. Open by appointment only.

NY —STATE UNIVERSITY OF NEW YORK, COLLEGE OF ENVIRONMENTAL SCIENCE AND FORESTRY, F Franklin Moon Library, Syracuse, 13210. Donald F Webster, Librn
Holdings: Vols (86,430) Cat
Budget: ($120,000)

NC —NORTH CAROLINA STATE UNIVERSITY, Burlington Textile Library, Box 8301 NCSU, Raleigh, 27695. Georgia H Rodeffer, Librn
Holdings: Vols (15,200) Cat Microforms
Notes: Specially housed library covering all phases of the textile industry incl textile chemistry, machinery, weaving, management, apparel manufacture, etc.

OH —FERRO CORP, Ferro Chemical Library, 7050 Krick Rd, Bedford, 44146. Mary Jane Campbell, Librn
Holdings: Vols 3500 Cat Audiotapes Microforms
Notes: Incl audiotapes (10) and microforms (52,750).

OH —EMERY INDUSTRIES, Research Library, 4900 Este Ave, Cincinnati, 45232. B A Bernard, Librn
Holdings: Cat
Notes: Special subjects: fatty acids and organic chemical derivatives, ozone, plasticizers, polymers, synthetic lubricants.

PA —FRANKLIN INSTITUTE LIBRARY, 20 & The Parkway, Philadelphia, 19103. Miriam Padusis, Dir; Charles Wilt, Readers Servs Librn
Holdings: Vols (300,000) Cat Maps Pix Microforms

PA —UNIVERSITY OF PENNSYLVANIA, Towne Scientific Library, 220 S 33 St, Philadelphia, 19104. Charles Meyers, Librn
Holdings: Vols (65,000) Cat

PA —PENNSYLVANIA STATE UNIVERSITY, Earth & Mineral Sciences Library, 105 Deike Bldg, University Park, 16802. Emilie McWilliams, Head Librn
Holdings: Vols (58,000) Cat Maps Microforms
Budget: ($49,750)
Notes: This collection includes substantial numbers of geological maps, and strong periodical holdings including microform.

SC —CRYOVAC TECHNICAL LIBRARY, PO Box 464, Duncan, 29334. M M Ezell, Libn
Holdings: Vols (6000) Cat
Notes: Library supports corporate research, development, and engineering. Incl materials on chemical and mechanical engineering, polymers and polymerization, plastics, and food packaging. 175 periodical titles received. Library open by appointment or through ILL.

TX —UNIVERSITY OF TEXAS LIBRARIES, John W Mallet Chemistry Library, Welch Hall 2132, Austin, 78712. A E Skinner, Chemistry Librn
Holdings: Vols (44,000) Cat Microforms
Notes: Described in *The John W Mallet Chemistry Library (The University of Texas at Austin)* (Austin: The General Libraries, 1975).

ON —DUNLOP RESEARCH CENTRE, Sheridan Park Research Community, Mississauga, L5K 1Z8, Can. Shirley A Morrison, Librn
Holdings: Vols 2000 Cat
Budget: ($4000)
Notes: Mainly current materials. Not open to the public except by appointment.

POLYNESIA see Islands of the Pacific

POLYNESIAN ART see Art, Oceanic

POLYNESIAN LANGUAGES AND LITERATURE

CA —CLAREMONT COLLEGES, Honnold Library, Ninth & Dartmouth, Claremont, 91711. Tania Rizzo, Special Collections Dept Head
Holdings: Vols 150 // Uncat
Notes: Grammars and dictionaries (some dual-language with French or Dutch) of mainly Malayo-Polynesian, some Sino-Tibetan, and other languages, dating from the late 19th to mid-20th centuries. Checklisted.

POMARE, ELEO

KS —WICHITA PUBLIC LIBRARY, Art & Music Division, 223 S Main, Wichita, 67202. Leonard Messineo, Jr, Head, Art & Music Division; Deborah Hamilton, Special Collections Librn
Holdings: Uncat Audiotapes Videotape Pix
Notes: Alice Bauman Dance Symposia Collection. Contains 300 hours of audio tapes, 1 hour-long video tape, several hundred photographs, and fugitive material of the American Dance Symposia held in Wichita from 1968-1972. The symposia covered all dance idioms-ballet, modern, jazz, folk, ethnic, dance education and therapy-and featured such notable figures such as Leonide Massine, Martha Hill, William Christensen, Alfonso Cimber, Toni Intravaia, James Clouser, Eleo Pomare, Juana de Laban, and many others. Characterized by the *Kansas City Star* as the "most distinguished faculties of fine artists ever assembled in the contemporary world of dance."

POMERENE, ATLEE

OH —KENT STATE UNIVERSITY, Libraries, Dept of Special Collections, Kent, 44242. Dean H Keller, Cur
Holdings: // Mss Pix
Notes: Collection incl letters, clippings, scrapbooks, government reports, diaries, personal effects of Senator Pomerene.

POMEROY, MIGGS

MA —BOSTON UNIVERSITY, Mugar Memorial Library, Special Collections Dept, 771 Commonwealth Ave, Boston, 02215. Howard B Gotlieb, Dir
Holdings: Cat Mss Pix
Notes: Mss, correspondence, etc collected in depth; incl publications by or about.

POMO INDIANS

CA —LAKE COUNTY LIBRARY, 200 Park St, Lakeport, 95453. Kathleen Jansen, Librn
Holdings: Vols (50)Cat
Notes: Collection of books and articles dealing with the Pomo Indians of California.

POMOLOGY see Fruit; Fruit Culture

POMONA VALLEY REGION

CA —POMONA PUBLIC LIBRARY, Special Collections, 625 S Garey Ave, PO Box 2271, Pomona, 91766. David Streeter, Librn
Holdings: Vols 43,000 Cat Mss Maps Pix Slides Audiotapes Microforms
Notes: Collections consist of printed materials; manuscripts; diaries; oral history interviews; photographs (100,000 images); societies and organizations; Pomona Valley business records. 48 linear feet of city records: Acessors records 1888-1933; various police records (Police Docket, Civil Docket) 1891-1960. Considerable emphasis on the Pomona Valley Region (Los Angeles-San Bernadino Counties).

POMPEII

MD —UNIVERSITY OF MARYLAND, Library, Rare Book Collection, College Park, 20742. Donald Farren, Assoc Dir for Special Collections
Holdings: Vols (10,000) Cat
Notes: Ranging from incunabula to modern first editions, the Rare Book Collection is particularly strong in materials relating to the history of France and in *exempla* of interest to students of bibliography. Related

POMPEII (cont.)

collections include sizable groups of books and other items relating to the Savoy, to *Expressionismus,* and to Pompeii. Pamphlet collections include many Mazarinades, many pamphlets relating to slavery and abolition, numerous French plays, and press books.

POMPONIUS MELA

IN —INDIANA UNIVERSITY, Lilly Library, Seventh St, Bloomington, 47405. William R Cagle, Librn
Holdings: Vols 33 Cat
Notes: Extensive collection of *De Situ Orbis* from 1478 to 1782.

POND, INEZ HENDERSON

†CA —UNIVERSITY OF THE PACIFIC, Library, Stockton, 95211.
Notes: Papers.

PONICSAN, DARRYL

MA —BOSTON UNIVERSITY, Mugar Memorial Library, Special Collections Dept, 771 Commonwealth Ave, Boston, 02215. Howard B Gotlieb, Dir
Holdings: Cat Mss Pix
Notes: Mss, correspondence, etc collected in depth; incl publications by or about.

PONIES—STUD-BOOKS

ON —CANADIAN TROTTING ASSOCIATION, Standardbred Canada Library, 233 Evans Ave, Toronto, M8Z 1J6, Can. David Hornell, Librn; Margaret Neal, Coordinator
Notes: Books, magazines, photographs, etc relating to harness racing in Canada.

PONS, MAURICE

MA —BOSTON UNIVERSITY, Mugar Memorial Library, Special Collections Dept, 771 Commonwealth Ave, Boston, 02215. Howard B Gotlieb, Dir
Holdings: Cat Mss

PONY EXPRESS

NE —KEARNEY STATE COLLEGE, Calvin T Ryan Library, Kearney, 68847. John Mayeski, Dir; Anita Norman, Reference Librn
Holdings: Vols (1700) Cat Mss Maps Pix Slides Microforms
Notes: Collection attempts to cover total historical development of Nebraska. Special strengths incl overland journeys, pony express, sod houses, and the Union Pacific. Special consideration has been given to Indians of Nebraska and the cattle industry. The collection is well supported by the library's general strength of Western Americana.

POOR

AZ —UNIVERSITY OF ARIZONA, Center for Creative Photography, 843 E University Blvd, Tucson, 85721. James Enyeart, Dir; Terence Pitts, Cur and Librn
Holdings: Pix
Notes: The Marion Palfi Photo Archive. Famous portrayals of, espec, poverty-stricken and victimized persons in the US, 1940 through 1970s, incl Hopi, Navajo, and Papago Indians on reservations, in urban relocation, and acculturation centers. Over 1500 master prints, 10,000 work prints, hundreds of glass plate and film negatives, manuscripts, etc.
NY —COLUMBIA UNIVERSITY LIBRARIES, Rare Book & Manuscript Library, 801 Butler Library, 535 W 114 St, New York, 10027. Kenneth A Lohf, Librn
Holdings: Mss
Notes: Papers of the Community Service Society of New York. Incl files, books, photographs (1000) and bound volumes of periodicals and conference proceedings.

Among the papers are central and district administrative records, committee correspondence and minutes, and files of programs sponsored by the organization. Also more than 1000 photographs by Jessie Tarbox Beals and Lewis W Hine depicting conditions of the poor. 276,000 items. Restricted use.
NY —MUSEUM OF THE CITY OF NEW YORK, Library, Fifth Ave & 103 St, New York, 10025.
Notes: The Jacob A Riis Collection of New York City photographs, especially of slum life at about the turn of the century.
NY —NEW YORK CITY HUMAN RESOURCES ADMINISTRATION, McMillan Library, 109 E 16 St, New York, 10003. Harold Benson, Librn
Holdings: Vols (13,000) Cat Mss
Budget: ($18,000)
Notes: Public welfare in all aspects; the poor in America, administration, management, child welfare, social services, social work in contemporary society, and urban affairs.
NY —NEW YORK PUBLIC LIBRARY, Rare Books and Manuscripts Div, Fifth Ave & 42 St, New York, 10018. William L Joyce, Asst Dir; Susan E Davis, Cur of Mss
Notes: The papers of Jacob A Riis, incl diaries, mss, etc.
†PA —TEMPLE UNIVERSITY LIBRARIES, Special Collections Dept, Urban Archives Center, Philadelphia, 19122. Thomas Whitehead, Cur of Mss
Holdings: Cat
Notes: Incl the records of several separate collections which are deposited in the Urban Archives Center. Many collections contain photographs, maps and pamphlets, in addition to manuscripts. All collections in the Urban Archives are separately cataloged.

POOR RELIEF see Public Welfare

POP ART

CA —CALIFORNIA INSTITUTE OF THE ARTS, Library, 24700 McBean Pkwy, Valencia, 91355. James Elrod, Dir
Holdings: Vols (61,000) Slides
Budget: ($11,000)
Notes: Modern art, incl abstract, conceptual, concrete, environment, minimal, and pop art; art; dadaism; surrealism; happenings; and caricatures and cartoons. Slides (61,683).

POPE, ALEXANDER

AZ —UNIVERSITY OF ARIZONA, University Library, Special Collections, Tucson, 85721. Louis A Hieb, Head
Holdings: Vols (7000) Cat Mss Microforms
Budget: ($30,000)
Notes: Strong in Restoration and 18th century drama. Major author strengths of the 18th century are Dryden, Fielding, Pope, Richardson, and Smollett.
CA —UNIVERSITY OF CALIFORNIA, LOS ANGELES, William Andrews Clark Memorial Library, 2520 Cimarron St, Los Angeles, 90018.
Holdings: Cat Mss
Notes: Extensive collection, first editions, etc.
†CA —STANFORD UNIVERSITY LIBRARIES, Stanford, 94305.
Notes: In collection of English and American Literature.
CO —UNIVERSITY OF COLORADO, Libraries, Special Collections, Boulder, 80309. Nora J Quinlan, Head
Holdings: Vols 800
Notes: The Mandell Creighton Library. Renaissance papacy, Protestant reform and the Conciliar movement. Separate catalog.
MA —HARVARD UNIVERSITY LIBRARY, Widener Library, Cambridge, 02138.
Holdings: Cat Mss
Notes: Catalog of Marshall C Lefferts collection, published in 1910, lists special collection acquired by Harvard.
NY —CORNELL UNIVERSITY LIBRARIES, John M Olin Library, Dept of Rare Books, Ithaca, 14853. Donald D Eddy, Librn
Notes: A collection of materials by and about Alexander Pope.

NC —DUKE UNIVERSITY, William R Perkins Library, Rare Book Room, Durham, 27706. John L Sharpe, III, Cur
Notes: Thomas J Wise collection. Many rare pieces, including works of Byron, Coleridge, Dryden, Pope and Hardy. 135 political and religious broadsides, mostly of the 17th century.

POPES

MD —JOHNS HOPKINS UNIVERSITY, Milton S Eisenhower Library, George Peabody Collection, 17 E Mt Vernon Place, Baltimore, 21201. Lyn Hart, Peabody Librn
Notes: Emphasis on materials published before 1950. Strength is a good collection through the 19th century.

POPES—BULLS see Bulls, Papal

POPES—PORTRAITS

MA —COLLEGE OF THE HOLY CROSS, Dinand Library, College St, Worcester, 01610. James M Mahoney, Cur of Special Collection
Holdings: Uncat Mss Pix
Notes: 48 signed papal documents and letters of 31 popes, 1181-1946; about 100 portrait engravings of the popes. Restricted use.
MO —SAINT LOUIS UNIVERSITY, Pius XII Memorial Library, 3655 W Pine Blvd, Saint Louis, 63108. William Cole, Dir
Holdings: Vols 246 // Uncat
Notes: The Haren Medal collection contains 246 medals of popes, etc. Not available to public.

POPISH PLOT, 1678

†ON —UNIVERSITY OF TORONTO, Thomas Fisher Rare Book Library, Toronto, M5S 1A5, Can.

POPKIN, ZELDA

MA —BOSTON UNIVERSITY, Mugar Memorial Library, Special Collections Dept, 771 Commonwealth Ave, Boston, 02215. Howard B Gotlieb, Dir
Holdings: Mss Correspondence

POPULAR ART see Art Industries and Trade

POPULAR MUSIC see Music, Popular

POPULAR PERIODICALS see Periodicals, Popular

POPULAR SONGS see Music, Popular

POPULATION

CA —LOS ANGELES PUBLIC LIBRARY, Social Sciences Dept, 630 W Fifth St, Los Angeles, 90071. Marilyn C Wherley, Principal Librn
Budget: ($150,000)
Notes: Nearly complete set of US Census, mainly population and housing statistics, current reports, from 1790. Depository (selective) since 1891.
CA —ASSOCIATION OF BAY AREA GOVERNMENTS, MTC/ABAG Library, 101 Eighth St, Oakland, 94607. Diane Gillman, Information Coord
Notes: Concentrates heavily on the nine-county Bay Area region. About 10,000 monographs and serials. Title catalog, OCLC/ATS. Central collection of documents for six transit properties in Bay Area.
DC —CENTER FOR BIOETHICS, Library, Kennedy Institute, Georgetown University, 3520 Prospect St NW, Washington, 20057. Doris Goldstein, Dir; Judith Mistichelli, Senior Librn
Holdings: Vols 8200
Notes: Largest library of its kind. Incl 31,000 journal articles. Collects in the following subject areas: applied ethics; medical ethics; philosophy of medicine; science, technology

POPULATION (cont.)

and society; sociology of medicine; patient-physician care; sexuality; contraception; abortion; population policy; reproductive technologies; in vitro fertilization; genetic counseling and screening; genetic engineering; mental organ transplantation; death and dying; "baby doe" issues; euthanasia; suicide; use of chemical and biological weapons. Produces computer database *Bioethicsline,* available through MEDLARS; and the printed annual *Bibliography of Bioethics.* Other library publications are: *New Titles in Bioethics* (monthly); *Scope Notes* series on current topics.

DC —POPULATION REFERENCE BUREAU, Joseph Sunnen Library, 1337 Connecticut Ave NW, Washington, 20037. Janice Beattie, Dir, Library & Information Servs
Holdings: Vols 10,000
Notes: Data search: Popline, Dialog. Incl 460 journals.

MA —HARVARD UNIVERSITY, Center for Population Studies, 665 Huntington Ave, Boston, 02115. Wilma E Winters, Librn
Holdings: Vols (20,000) Cat
Notes: Incl books and pamphlets.

NY —STATE UNIVERSITY OF NEW YORK AT ALBANY, Library, Special Collections Dept, 1400 Washington Ave, Albany, 12222. Marion P Munzer, Coordr
Notes: Correspondence, lecture notes, speeches, mss, clippings dealing with work by Robert Rienow and his wofe, Leona Train, on wildlife conservation, anti-nuclear movement, and population control (15 linear feet).

NY —STATE UNIVERSITY OF NEW YORK, STONY BROOK, Biology Library, Stony Brook, 11794. Doris Williams, Biology Librn
Holdings: Vols 625 // Uncat
Notes: Raymond Pearl Collection. The collection contains reprints collected by Raymond Pearl, founder of the *Quarterly Review of Biology.* The reprints are indexed by author and arranged by twenty subjects relating to biology and the history of science.

NC —CAROLINA POPULATION CENTER, Library, University Sq E, Chapel Hill, 27514. Patricia Shipman, Head Librn
Holdings: Vols 20,000 Cat Mss Microforms
Budget: $10,500
Notes: Try to acquire everything published in English on population, with particular emphasis on the US and developing countries. Also acquire conference proceedings, seminar papers. These and journal articles are indexed and the analytics are incl in the catalog. Incl 13,000 reprints and other pieces of ephemera. Most extensive area files are on India, Africa, Thailand, Iran, Korea, and Latin America. Holdings are recorded on an automated data base. A microfiche catalog is available for use in the Library and for purchase. Access by subject & geographic area are available through the Library's own thesaurus-based indexing systems.

TX —UNIVERSITY OF TEXAS LIBRARIES, Population Research Center Library, 1701 Main Bldg Tower, Austin, 78712. Doreen S Goyer, Librn
Holdings: Vols (20,000) Cat Microforms
Budget: ($3000)
Notes: The International Census Collection contains population censuses of 200 nations and territories, current and retrospective. Combined holdings of several University of Texas libraries constitute 80 percent of the items cited in the *International Population Census Bibliography* (original 6 volumes with 1 supplement and other revisions and updates), with the majority of items in the Population Research Center. Other books, monographs, journals and reprints also support this subject.

†ON —METROPOLITAN TORONTO LIBRARY, Social Sciences Dept, 789 Yonge St, Toronto, M4W 2G8, Can. Abdus Salam, Head
Holdings: Vols Cat Maps Phonorecords

Audiotapes 16mm Films Microforms
Notes: Collection includes material on the size, growth, density, distribution and ecology of human populations. Covers general theory to research materials. International in scope.

POPULATION—RESEARCH see Population Research

POPULATION—STATISTICS

DC —US BUREAU OF THE CENSUS, Library, Federal Office Bldg 3, Rm 2451, Washington, 20233. Betty Baxtresser, Chief, ASD Library Branch
Holdings: Cat Microforms
Notes: Emphasizes on statistics of agriculture, business, construction, economics, foreign trade, governments, housing, industry, population, transportation, statistical methodology, and data processing. Library holdings are largely current materials covering the Bureau's programs. Outdated materials are withdrawn regularly.

POPULATION, FOREIGN see Emigration and Immigration

POPULATION BIOLOGY, ANIMAL see Animal Populations

POPULATION RESEARCH

CA —WOMEN'S HISTORY RESEARCH CENTER, Microfilm Library, 2325 Oak St, Berkeley, 94708. Laura X, Librn
Holdings: Mss Pix Microforms
Notes: Incl material (150 subject files) on physical and mental health and illnesses; sex roles; biology; women and the life cycle; birth/population control; sex and sexuality; black and Third World women. Collection at University of Wyoming. Archive of Contemporary History, PO Box 3334, Laramie, Wyoming 82701, c/o David Crosson. Research inquiries accepted. Microfilm of collection (14 reels and reel guides) available at many universities and through Women's History Research Center, 2325 Oak St, Berkeley, CA 94708. No collections housed at this address.

GA —UNIVERSITY OF GEORGIA, Libraries, Special Collections Division, Athens, 30602. Vesta Lee Gordon, Asst Dir for Special Collections
Notes: The Arbitron Collection of television and radio program ratings, 1949-date (except past year). In-depth, statistical analyses of the listening public by age, sex, county, some ethnic groups, farm population, listening preferences, etc. 26,302 bound vols. 2 reports, 1949-81. To be added to annually.

NJ —PRINCETON UNIVERSITY, Office of Population Research, Library, 21 Prospect Ave, Princeton, 08540. Thomas Holzmann, Librn
Holdings: Vols (25,000) Cat Mss Maps Microforms
Notes: The library is attached to the Office of Population Research, which publishes the *Population Index.* Library is particularly strong in statistical materials, such as worldwide population censuses and vital statistics; it is less strong in the biomedical aspects of population research. Incl 10,000 reprints, Pamphlets, mss, etc ILL requests should be addressed to Princeton University Library, Interlibrary Services.

NY —UNIVERSITY OF ROCHESTER, Carlson Library, Hutchison Hall, River Campus, Rochester, 14627. Michael W Poulin, Librn
Holdings: Vols (48,720) Cat Microforms
Notes: Strong collection in the field and related areas.

POPULATIONS, ANIMAL see Animal Populations

POPULIST MOVEMENT

TX —UNIVERSITY OF TEXAS LIBRARIES, General Libraries, PO Box P, Austin, 78713. Carolyn Bucknell, Asst Dir for Collection Development
Holdings: Cat Microforms

PORCELAIN

IN —ALLEN COUNTY PUBLIC LIBRARY, 900 Webster St, Fort Wayne, 46802. Paul Deane, Reader Services Dept Head; Kay Lynn Isca, Art Music & AV Dept Head
Holdings: Vols 570 Cat Pix

LA —R W NORTON ART GALLERY, Library, 4747 Creswell Ave, Shreveport, 71106. Jerry M Bloomer, Librn
Holdings: Cat
Notes: Primarily histories on pottery and porcelain-making in America and Europe and books of interest to collectors.

MO —THE NELSON-ATKINS MUSEUM OF ART, Kenneth & Helen Spencer Art Reference Library, 4525 Oak St, Kansas City, 64111. Stanley W Hess, Librn

NY —NEW YORK STATE COLLEGE OF CERAMICS AT ALFRED UNIVERSITY, Scholes Library, Harder Hall, Alfred, 14802. Bruce E Connolly, Library Dir
Holdings: Vols (70,000) Cat Mss Slides Microforms
Budget: ($134,000)
Notes: Very specialized collection incl all phases of the arts and sciences related to ceramics. Incl 1112 subscriptions.

NY —GENEVA HISTORICAL SOCIETY, James Luckett Memorial Archives, 543 S Main St, Geneva, 14456. Eleanore Clise, Librn

NC —MINT MUSEUM OF ART, Delhom-Gambrell Reference Library, 501 Hempstead Place, Charlotte, 28207. Sara H Wolf, Librn
Holdings: Vols (3430) Cat Pix Slides
Notes: Library has added 2 private collections on Oriental ceramics (approx 800 volumes, not cataloged) and on decorative arts, mostly French Ceramics (approx 500 volumes, not cataloged). No photocopying.

WI —MILWAUKEE ART MUSEUM, Library, 750 N Lincoln Memorial Dr, Milwaukee, 53202. Betty Karow, Librn
Notes: Also, small collection on 19th century German painting and on Meissen porcelain.

WI —MILWAUKEE PUBLIC LIBRARY, 814 W Wisconsin Ave, Milwaukee, 53233. Donald J Sager, City Librn
Holdings: Vols Cat
Notes: Strength in American and European decorative arts incl ceramics, glassware, jewelry, porcelain, silverware, furniture, interior decoration, textile arts and handicraft.
See also entry under Art, Decorative.

PORCELAIN DESIGN

NY —FASHION INSTITUTE OF TECHNOLOGY, Edward C Blum Design Laboratory, 227 W 27 St, New York, 10001. Laura Sinderbrand, Dir
Holdings: Cat Pix Slides
Notes: The largest resource of it kind consisting of 4 million indexed swatches and 300 swatch books, jacquard point paper, croquis, quilts, rug samples, laces, embroideries, and color swatch cards. A collection of international scope incl antique and contemporary textiles; woven and printed patterns created for apparel and home furnishings which may be adapted to china, giftware, floor covering, wallpaper, and package design. A comprehensive research facility comprised of over one million articles of dress dating from the 17th Century to the present, incl men's, women's, children's clothes, furs, foundation garments and lingerie, as well as an outstanding grouping of 19th and 20th century designer clothing. Accessories as diverse as hats, handbags, gloves, hosiery, shoes, shawls, and costume jewelry offer an additonal resource to this international collection.

PORCELAIN ENAMELS see Enamel and Enameling

PORCHER, NANANNE

NY —NANANNE PORCHER OSPREY DESIGNS, Library, 49 W 96 St, New York,

PORCHER, NANANNE (cont.)

10028.
Notes: Lighting records for Lyric Opera of Chicago, 1961-1966; Dallas Civic Opera, 1959-1964; American Ballet Theatre,1965-1966, 1971-1977; etc.

PORCHER FAMILY

SC —COLLEGE OF CHARLESTON LIBRARY, Special Collections Dept, Charleston, 29401.
Notes: Papers, 1774-1884. Contains the Porcher plantation account book (1774-1884) begun by Philip Porcher, and the memoirs (1809-1859), and lecture notes of Frederick A Porcher, a professor at the College of Charleston.

PORNOGRAPHY

CA —FITZ HUGH LUDLOW MEMORIAL LIBRARY, PO Box 99346, San Francisco, 94109. Michael R Aldrich, Exec Cur
Holdings: Vols 600 Mss Maps Pix Slides Phonorecords Audiotapes Videotapes
Notes: Collection stored. Important mail inquiries only. No interlibrary lending or telephone queries. The heart of this special collection of psychoactive drug literature is about 400 vols of memoirs or lightly-disguised fiction concerning psychoactive drugs, plus about 600 vols related to Beat writers of the 1950s-60s, plus about 300 vols related to the "Hippie" movement of the 1960s, plus 600 vols (mostly paperback) of drug-related pornography, and several hundred vols related to drug slang, drugs and music, drug art, drug cuisine, etc. In addition we have many boxes of offprints, files of newspaper clippings, complete runs to underground newspapers, and many artifacts related to this area. Much of the 1950s-60s-70s literature is autographed or inscribed.

†CA —INSTITUTE FOR THE ADVANCED STUDY OF HUMAN SEXUALITY, 1523 Franklin St, San Francisco, 94109.

CA —INTERNATIONAL MUSEUM OF EROTIC ART, Formerly, San Francisco, 94108.
Notes: Unfortunately this renowned collection has been dispersed and no longer (1984) exists, including the Phyllis and Eberhard Kronhausen Collection, according to the information we have been given.

IN —INDIANA UNIVERSITY, Institute for Sex Research Library, 416 Morrison Hall, Bloomington, 47401. Douglas Freeman, Collections and Services Librn; Joan Brewer, Information Services Librn
Holdings: Vols (62,000) Cat Mss Pix Phonorecords Audiotapes Slides Films Microforms
Budget: ($20,000)
Notes: One of the greatest and most extensive collections on sexual behavior, the library collects materials on all aspects of sex activity, with special emphasis on behavioral and social aspects. Also collects erotic literature and sexual ephemera. Incl 105 audiotapes, 23 vertical file drawers, 108 phonorecords, 55,000 pictures, 5000 slides, and 1700 films. Rich in French, German and American sources; also much Oriental. Semitraditional erotic poetry and song of 17th-18th century England. Bawdy limericks, double-entendre, puns, slang, erotic literature, graffiti, slang and special dictionaries, proverbs and sayings, epigrams and research materials of the Kinsey Studies, etc. Contact Information Service for: literature searching, preparation of bibliographies, permission to use collection. Limited photocopying.

PORTEOUS, JOHN

MI —DETROIT PUBLIC LIBRARY, Burton Historical Collection, 5201 Woodward Ave, Detroit, 48202. Alice Dalligan, Chief

PORTER, COLE

CT —YALE UNIVERSITY, Sterling Memorial Library, Yale Collection of Historical Sound Recordings, 120 High St, New Haven, 06520. Richard Warren Jr, Cur
Holdings: Mss Sheet Music Scores Phonorecords Audiotapes
Notes: His papers, publications, scrapbooks, photographs, recordings, notebooks, lyric books, etc. See Yale University Library Gazette, July 1969.

PORTER, ADM. DAVID DIXON

MD —US NAVAL ACADEMY, Nimitz Library, Annapolis, 21402. Alice S Creighton, Assistant Librn for Special Collections
Holdings: Mss Pix
Notes: Papers, etc.

PORTER, JANE, 1776-1850

CA —UNIVERSITY OF CALIFORNIA, LOS ANGELES, Research Library, Dept of Special Collections, 405 Hilgard Ave, Los Angeles, 90024. Edward Shreeves, Chairman, Bibliographers Group; David S Zeidberg, Head
Holdings: Vols 25
Notes: 25 first and other editions of her books; diary and account books (1830-1840, 1842); 38 letters.

PORTER, KATHERINE ANNE

†MD —UNIVERSITY OF MARYLAND, Library, College Park, 20742. Donald Farren, Assoc Dir for Special Collections
Holdings: Cat Mss Pix Phonorecords
Notes: Her private library and working collection along with personal papers, mss, and memorabilia. Incl translations and anthology appearances. Incl works of her contemporaries (many presentation copies, many with her annotations).

NV —UNIVERSITY OF NEVADA, RENO, University Library, Special Collections Dept, Reno, 89557. Robert E Blesse, Head
Holdings: // Vols (55) Cat Other appearances 200 Cat
Notes: Includes individual works by author in all editions including translations; also prefaces, introductions, published correspondence, appearances in anthologies, periodicals, etc. Bibliographical research collection, part of Modern Authors Collection.

PORTER, QUINCY

CT —YALE UNIVERSITY, Music Library, 98 Wall St, New Haven, 06520. Harold E Samuel, Librn
Holdings: Vols (118,000) Cat Mss Pix Phonorecords Audiotapes
Notes: Personal papers and musical mss.
See also entry under Music, American.

PORTER, WILLIAM SYDNEY see O. Henry

PORTER FAMILY PAPERS

NY —UNIVERSITY OF ROCHESTER, Rush Rhees Library, Department of Rare Books and Special Collections, Rochester, 14627. Peter Dzwonkoski, Librn
Holdings: Cat Mss
Notes: Letters to Samuel Drummond Porter and Susan Farley Porter from family members, fellow abolitionists Frederick Douglass and Gerritt Smith, and their son while a soldier during the Civil War.

PORTO RICO see Puerto Rico

PORTOLAN CHARTS

DC —LIBRARY OF CONGRESS, Geography and Map Division, Washington, 20540. John A Wolter, Chief
Notes: Rare nautical charts on vellum.

IL —NEWBERRY LIBRARY, Hermon Dunlap Smith Center, 60 W Walton St, Chicago, 60610. David Buisseret, Head
Holdings: Cat Maps
Notes: Historical map collection, with cut-off date of about 1900, incl 1600 atlases and 13,000 separate maps (in 1984). Rich in nautical cartography, incl some exceptional portolan charts.
See also entry under Maps and Atlases - Collections.

PORTRAIT PAINTING

DC —SMITHSONIAN INSTITUTION, National Museum of American Art & the National Portrait Gallery Library, Eighth & F Sts, NW, Washington, 20560. Cecilia Chin, Librn
Holdings: Vols (47,000) Cat Microforms
Budget: ($60,000)
Notes: Subscribe to 600 foreign and domestic periodicals on art and American history. Holdings of older bound periodicals. Collection emphasizes American art, contemporary American and European painting, portraiture, American biography. Uncataloged material incl: 350 vertical file drawers of clippings, small catalogs and other ephemera on artists, art organizations, museums, etc; mss and archival material on American artists; the "Ferdinand Perret Library"--180 scrapbooks with card index on California art and artists, incl clippings, catalogs, reproductions, etc; card bibliography of books and periodical literature on portaiture--international, retrospective and current--in progress.

MO —THE NELSON-ATKINS MUSEUM OF ART, Kenneth & Helen Spencer Art Reference Library, 4525 Oak St, Kansas City, 64111. Stanley W Hess, Librn

PQ —MCGILL UNIVERSITY, McLennan Library, Rare Books and Special Collections Dept, 3459 McTavish St, Montreal, H3A 1Y1, Can.
Holdings: Vols 2680
Notes: Incl books on the puppet theatre, puppets, toy theatres and their theatrical portraits, pantins, prints and posters, located in the Rosalynde Stearn Puppet Collection. A catalogue is available: The Rosalynde Stearn Puppet Collection. Montreal, 1961. Incl 171 puppets.

PORTRAITS—COLLECTIONS

CA —LOS ANGELES PUBLIC LIBRARY, History Dept, 630 W 5th St, Los Angeles, 90071. Bettye H Ellison, Librn in Charge, California Room
Holdings: Vols 8000 Cat Pix
Notes: The California Collection is a reference and circulating collection consisting of state, county and city histories, volumes of travel and description, periodicals, and publications of state and local historical societies. Over 260,000 historic photographs from the turn of the century to the mid-1950s. Portraits are incl. The majority of the views are of Los Angeles and Southern California. Special subject and biographical indexes provide references to a wide variety of California related books, periodicals and Los Angeles area newspapers. A separate index is maintained for photographs.

CA —SAN DIEGO PUBLIC LIBRARY, Art, Music & Recreation Sect, 820 E St, San Diego, 92101. Barbara A Tuhill, Supvr
Notes: Mainly 423,012 unmounted and 5396 mounted pictures filed under 11,400 subjects ranging from Aardvark through Zulu grouped in manila folders. Large collection of "portraits" of the famous and pictures of historical events, such as World War II, etc. For general circulation.

CA —UNIVERSITY OF CALIFORNIA, SANTA CRUZ, Shane Archives of Lick Observatory, Santa Cruz, 95064. Dorothy Schauberg, Archivist
Notes: Dr Edward S Holden (first director of Lick Observatory) Collection of portraits of every famous astronomer from Galileo to the present. Open for scholarly research by appointment.

CA —STANFORD UNIVERSITY LIBRARIES, Cecil H Green Library, Stanford, 94305. Michael T Ryan, Cur
Holdings: Cat Pix
Notes: The Dr and Mrs Leon Kolb Portrait

PORTRAITS—COLLECTIONS (cont.)

Collection. Over 1600 portraits (engravings, etchings, mezzotints, lithographs) of rulers, statesmen, authors, scholars and other famous personages from ancient times to the 19th century. A catalog of the collection, compiled by Dr Susan Lenkey, was published in 1972.

CO —COLORADO HISTORICAL SOCIETY, Research Collections, 1300 Broadway, Denver, 80203. Catherine Kane, Head Public Service and Access
Holdings: Cat Pix Slides
Notes: 250,000 photographs of western and Colorado subjects incl gold rush, mining, Indians, natural features, transportation, cities and towns, portraits. William Henry Jackson photographs of area west of Mississippi.

CT —YALE UNIVERSITY, Box 1603A, Yale Station, New Haven, 06520.
Holdings: Pix
Notes: Incl a collection of 116 photographs of leaders of the Nazi Party, 1941-1944.

CT —YALE UNIVERSITY, Music Library, 98 Wall St, New Haven, 06520. Harold E Samuel, Librn
Holdings: Vols (118,000) Cat Mss Pix Phonorecords Audiotapes Microforms
Notes: General reference and research materials. Performing editions. Strong in theoretical literature, opera, 17-18th century music (incl mss), J S Bach and sons in early editions and mss, Russian liturgical music (Tkaczenko Collection), hymnology, American music. Also collection of musical pictures and portraits.

DC —LIBRARY OF CONGRESS, Prints & Photographs Div, Washington, 20540.
Notes: The Brady-Handy Collection consists of some 10,000 negatives from the files of photographers Levin C Handy (1855?-1932) and Mathew B Brady (1823?-1896), most of which are portrait photographs and views of Washington, DC from the 19th and early 20th centuries. Incl portraits of congressmen and government leaders (1855-90). Also, the F Holland Day Collection of Day's photographs. 640 photoprints.

DC —LIBRARY OF CONGRESS, Prints & Photographs Div, Washington, 20540.
Notes: The James T Mitchell Collection contains American book illustrations and portrait prints, 1770 to 1840s.

IL —CHICAGO HISTORICAL SOCIETY, Library, Clark St at North Ave, Chicago, 60614. Robert L Brubaker, Librn
Holdings: Vols (150,000) Cat Mss Pix
Notes: Chicago theatre programs (5000); scrapbooks containing reviews and other clippings; a few letters, reminiscences, account books, and other records of theatres, actors and actresses, and managers; theatre posters; Thomas Conolly Collection of Theatrical Portraits; other photographs of theatres, production, and casts.

IL —ILLINOIS STATE HISTORICAL SOCIETY, Library, Old State Capitol, Springfield, 62706. Roger D Bridges, Head Librn
Holdings: Cat Pix
Notes: Incl an unusual collection of Illinois pictorial history--some 12,000 scenes and portraits preserved on glass photographic negatives dating from the 1890s to the 1920s acquired from the estate of Herbert W Georg, Springfield photographer. Also, a collection of 180,000 pictures.
See also entry under Illinois - History

IN —INDIANA UNIVERSITY, Lilly Library, Seventh St, Bloomington, 47405. William R Cagle, Librn
Holdings: // Cat
Notes: Portraits of literary figures from the J K Lilly collection; War of 1812; and Lincoln. Also thousands in the Starr Collection of American Sheet Music.

KY —UNIVERSITY OF LOUISVILLE, Kornhauser Health Sciences Library, 520 S Preston St, PO Box 35260, Louisville, 40292. Leonard M Eddy, Dir; Sherrill R McConnell, Archivist
Holdings: Cat Mss Pix
Notes: Kentucky physicians and medical

hitory (pictures and mss). Over 10,000 pages of source material compiled under WPA for history of medicine in Kentucky, plus collection of photographs of Kentucky physicians. WPA material being microfilmed. Partly cataloged.

LA —TULANE UNIVERSITY, Howard-Tilton Memorial Library, Southeast Architectural Archives, 7001 Freret St, New Orleans, 70118. William R Cullison, Cur of Prints & Drawings
Holdings: Pix
Notes: Southeast Architectural Archives Collection incl over 5000 photographic prints and over 12,000 negatives. Views are mostly of Louisiana buildings, scenes and personages, with emphasis on New Orleans. Negatives are available for most of the photographic prints.

MD —US NAVAL ACADEMY, Nimitz Library, Annapolis, 21402. Alice S Creighton, Assistant Librn for Special Collections
Holdings: Pix
Notes: Approximately 15,000 pictures, incl portraits of naval officers and photographs of ships; also naval news photos.

MA —ROBBINS LIBRARY, 700 Massachusetts Ave, Arlington, 02174. Peter L Fenton, Dir
Holdings: Cat Pix
Notes: 150,000 graphic works in all media, emphasizing portrait prints from the 15th century to the present day.

MA —BOSTON PUBLIC LIBRARY, Print Collection, Dartmouth St at Copley Sq, Boston, 02117. Sinclair H Hitchings, Keeper of Prints
Holdings: Cat
Notes: The Americana collection is especially strong in the 19th century. Incl 250 prints of American views, tradesmen's calling cards, illustrated diplomas and advertisements. Also in it is the McGreevey Baseball Collection of 225 photos, photoreproductions and paintings from the period 1870 to 1914. The American portrait collection contains 300 engravings, etchings and lithographs of prominent figures of the 18th and 19th century. In addition there are 200 portraits of Benjamin Franklin. Items cataloged by subject. Prints also by artist/ publisher.

MA —COLLEGE OF THE HOLY CROSS, Dinand Library, College St, Worcester, 01610. James M Mahoney, Cur of Special Collection
Holdings: Uncat Mss Pix
Notes: 48 signed papal documents and letters of 31 popes. 1181-1946; about 100 portrait engravings of the popes. Restricted use.

MI —DETROIT PUBLIC LIBRARY, Fine Arts Department, 5201 Woodward Ave, Detroit, 48202. Shirley Solvick, Chief
Holdings: Vols 60,000 Cat Pix
Budget: ($20,000)
Notes: Downs number 2882, 2923, 2938. Book collection covers all phases of art. Picture collection of over 500,000 items covers all subjects; especially strong in the fine and decorative arts, portraits, costume, and Detroit.

MN —MAYO MEDICAL LIBRARY, History of Medicine Collection, Rochester, 55905. Nancy R Hensel, Librn
Holdings: // Cat Pix
Notes: Feldman portrait photographs of Nobel laureates and selected Mayo Clinic staff. Collection partially described in "'The Pleasurable Recreation' of Dr William H Feldman," by Ruth J Mann, Mayo Clin Proc, vols 48, 1973, pp 738-740.

MO —THE NELSON-ATKINS MUSEUM OF ART, Kenneth & Helen Spencer Art Reference Library, 4525 Oak St, Kansas City, 64111. Stanley W Hess, Librn

NM —MUSEUM OF NEW MEXICO, Photo Archives, Box 2087, Santa Fe, 87503. Arthur L Olivas, Cur; Richard Rudisill, Photo Historian
Notes: Photographic collection. Portraits (identified and unidentified), filed by last name.

NY —AMERICAN MUSEUM OF NATURAL HISTORY, Library Services

Dept, Central Park W & 79th St, New York, 10024. Nina J Root, Chairwoman; Mary Genett, Asst Librn for Reference Services
Holdings: Cat Pix
Notes: Incl a card index of about 800 entries of portraits of named American Indians, indexed from various publications. Indexing ended, apparently, about 1955.

NY —HAMPDEN-BOOTH THEATRE LIBRARY AT THE PLAYERS, 16 Gramercy Park, New York, 10003. Louis A Rachow, Librn/Cur
Holdings: Vols 12,000 Cat Mss Pix Slides Phonotapes
Notes: A strong collection on theatre history, with special emphasis on 19th and 20th century English and American stage. Large collection of English playbills of the 18th and 19th centuries; important collection of prompt books (mainly 19th century); Edwin Booth, incl memorabilia rare books, association items, his 2nd, 3rd, and 4th Shakespeare Folios, etc. Large collection of English and American biographies and pictures of actors and actresses; the Chuck Callahan Burlesque Collection (qv Burlesque); and other specialties described elsewhere in this volume. The library is chartered by the Regents of the State of New York and is open to all qualified researchers upon application. Described in Theatre & Performing Arts Collections (New York: Haworth Press, 1981).

NY —NEW YORK ACADEMY OF MEDICINE, Library, 2 E 103 St, New York, 10029. Brett A Kirkpatrick, Librn
Notes: Portraits of physicians, incl 250,000 separate items as well as portraits appearing in publications.

NY —NEW YORK HISTORICAL SOCIETY, Library, 170 Central Park W, New York, 10024. James Gregory, Librn
Holdings: Mss
Notes: Incl original mss, illustrative materials, etc.

NY —NEW YORK PUBLIC LIBRARY, Music Div, 111 Amsterdam Ave, New York, 10023. Frank C Campbell, Chief
Holdings: Vols (300,000) Cat Mss Pix Microforms
Notes: Described in Dictionary Catalog of the Music Collection, The Research Libraries of the New York Public Library, 33 vols (532,000 cards), 1964, $2190; Supplement 1, 1 vol (17,000 cards), 1966, $100. Also, Bibliographic Guide to Music, 2 vols, 1975-1976, $70 ea. Literature pertaining to virtually all musical subjects, and scores covering the broadest range of musical style and history are represented in this catalog. Special strengths of the collection incl folk songs, 18th and 19th-century librettos, full scores of operas, complete works, historical editions, Beethoven, Americana, American music, periodicals, vocal music, literature on the voice, programs, record catalogs, and mss in detail; sheet music, 355,414; sound recordings, 400,000; clippings and programs, 2 million; broadsides, 1821; songsters, 375; pictures, 51,002; ms, 29,877.

OH —CLEVELAND PUBLIC LIBRARY, History and Geography Department, 325 Superior Ave, Cleveland, 44114. JoAnn Petrello, Head
Holdings: Cat Pix
Notes: Cleveland Picture Collection: 13,500 pictures incl the Standiford Portrait Collection (500 pictures); the Edmondson Portrait Collection of Clevelanders (2425 glass plates and prints); the Ohio Collection (430 pictures); the Ketteringham Collection (250 glass plates and prints). Cleveland Picture Collection is now on microfiche. Reproduction of the photos may be arranged.

PA —PENNSYLVANIA HOSPITAL HISTORICAL LIBRARY, Eighth & Spruce Sts, Philadelphia, 19107. Caroline Morris, Librn
Holdings: Vols (12,963)// Cat Mss
Notes: First medical library in US. Rich in runs of 19th century medical journals. Some early botany books. Some incunabula. Printed catalog was made in 1876. This collection is important because it reflects the

PORTRAITS—COLLECTIONS (cont.)

history of medicine by the nature of the materials that were acquired. However, *no attempt is made to keep a current history of medicine library.*

RI —BROWN UNIVERSITY, John Hay Library, McLellan Lincoln Collection, 20 Prospect St, Providence, 02912. Jennifer B Lee, Special Collections Librn
Holdings: Vols (15,000) Cat Mss Pix Phonorecords
Notes: Prints, arranged according to Meserve numbers, contain most of the known photographs of Lincoln, rare engravings, caricatures, Currier and Ives prints, and original oil portraits done by artists of Lincoln's day, as well as original paintings of Lincoln's deathbed by Alonzo Chappel and Alexander Ritchie; some original drawings, as well as a scrapbook of Thomas Nast's Civil War sketches.

RI —BROWN UNIVERSITY, John Hay Library, Anne S K Brown Military Collection, 20 Prospect St, Providence, 02912. Richard B Harrington, Cur
Notes: The Anne S K Brown Military Collection has been formed over the past forty or more years by Mrs John Nicholas Brown, now of Newport, and contains approximately 40,000 volumes and 60,000 prints, drawings and watercolors as well as a number of oil paintings and about 5000 miniature model soldiers. At its beginning (and still today) the emphasis or focus of this collection has been upon the history of, and the accurate contemporary illustration of, military and naval uniforms of all nations from the early XVII century to the present. In the course of time, however, the collection has come to incl also a vast and related amount of material on military and naval history, military and naval arts and tactics, wars, campaigns, ceremonies, biography, portraits and caricatures of this and earlier periods. It has been probably the largest private collection of such a nature in the world, and it contains much ms and graphic documentation which is unique. It has been useful to numerous scholars and historians, editors, filmmakers and publishers for research and for illustrative material and has also contributed to many museum exhibitions. In 1982 the entire collection, with its complete card catalog and subject index, has been presented to Brown University, where it is located in the John Hay Library. Special requests are taken care of by phone, mail and appointments with the curator.

†TX —UNIVERSITY OF TEXAS LIBRARIES, General Libraries, Humanities Research Center, PO Box 7219, Austin, 78712. John Chalmers, Librn

TX —FORT WORTH PUBLIC LIBRARY, Arts Division, 300 Taylor St, Fort Worth, 76102. Heather Gobel, Head
Holdings: Pix
Notes: Photographs of concert artists appearing on Fort Worth stages (many are autographed). Nucleus collection from the estate of the late Mrs John F Lyons. Additions are made as performing artists make their appearances in this area.

BC —VANCOUVER PUBLIC LIBRARY, Art Div, 750 Burrard St, Vancouver, V6Z 1X5, Can.
Holdings: Cat Pix
Notes: Book and pamphlet collection. Also, (1) Newspaper Clippings File: 31 drawers of relevant clippings from major newspapers, incl the *Sun, Province, Toronto Globe and Mail, Christian Science Monitor, New York Times,* etc on arts, music, architecture; incl biographical material (16 drawers). (2) Picture File about 500,000 pictures in 150 cabinet drawers, strong in architecture, costume, interior decoration, painting, sculpture, also portraits. (3) Exhibition Catalogs File: British Columbia and elsewhere. (4) Association and Organization File: organizations in the Lower Mainland in arts, music, city planning, etc, begun in 1940s; (5) Canadian Artists Index: begun in 1964, alphabetically by artist, with about

300,000 citations to reproductions of work and biographical material on Canadian artist from the division's books and other sources; (6) Miscellaneous Index: material not covered in other special or published indexes, primarily of Canadian and local cultural events, hard-to-find informations, etc. Local newspapers, special Canadian publications and British film journals are the most regularly indexed items. (7) Song Index started in the 1930s. (8) Title Index to song collections and sheet music in the VPL collection, approx 100,000 entries.

ON —MACLEAN HUNTER LIBRARY, Maclean Hunter Bldg, 777 Day St, Toronto, M5W 1A7, Can. Theresa Butcher, Librn
Holdings: Vols 1500 Cat Pix
Notes: Mainly a resource for the journalists of the *Financial Post,* Canada's foremost financial paper. The library is basically made up of vertical files divided into (1) general subject files, (2) Canadian public companies, (3) biographical (mainly photographic). The Toronto *Globe and Mail* (daily) and other Canadian publications are selectively clipped. In addition, the library houses all Maclean-Hunter publications (over 80 and constantly growing). The *Financial Post* is indexed by the library staff.

ON —METROPOLITAN TORONTO LIBRARY, Theatre Dept, 789 Yonge St, Toronto, M4W 2G8, Can. Heather McCallum, Head
Notes: A collection of several thousand prints incl British and American engraved dramatic portraits, engravings of British theatres, and a growing collection of 18th and 19th century prints of dancers.

PQ —MCGILL UNIVERSITY, McLennan Library, Rare Books and Special Collections Dept, 3459 McTavish St, Montreal, H3A 1Y1, Can.
Notes: 12,680 original prints and posters dating from the 16th century to the present. Prints representing many graphic techniques; special subject areas such as: early railways, Japanese woodblocks, Napoleon, early Canadian portraits.

PORTRAITS, AMERICAN

DC —LIBRARY OF CONGRESS, Prints & Photographs Div, Washington, 20540.
Notes: The James T Mitchell Collection contains American book illustrations and portrait prints, 1770 to 1840s.

DC —SMITHSONIAN INSTITUTION, National Museum of American Art & the National Portrait Gallery Library, Eighth & F Sts, NW, Washington, 20560. Cecilia Chin, Librn
Holdings: Vols (47,000) Cat Microforms
Budget: ($60,000)
Notes: Subscribe to 600 foreign and domestic periodicals on art and American history. Holdings of older bound periodicals. Collection emphasizes American art, contemporary American and European painting, portraiture, American biography. Uncataloged material incl: 350 vertical file drawers of clippings, small catalogs and other ephemera on artists, art organizations, museums, etc; mss and archival material on American artists; the "Ferdinand Perret Library"--180 scrapbooks with card index on California art and artists, incl clippings, catalogs, reproductions, etc; card bibliography of books and periodical literature on portraiture--international, retrospective and current--in progress.

PORTRAITURE

DC —SMITHSONIAN INSTITUTION, National Museum of American Art & the National Portrait Gallery Library, Eighth & F Sts, NW, Washington, 20560. Cecilia Chin, Librn
Holdings: Vols (47,000) Cat Microforms
Budget: ($60,000)
Notes: Subscribe to 600 foreign and domestic periodicals on art and American history. Holdings of older bound periodicals. Collection emphasizes American art, contemporary American and European painting, portraiture, American biography.

Uncataloged material incl: 350 vertical file drawers of clippings, small catalogs and other ephemera on artists, art organizations, museums, etc; mss and archival material on American artists; the "Ferdinand Perret Library"--180 scrapbooks with card index on California art and artists, incl clippings, catalogs, reproductions, etc; card bibliography of books and periodical literature on portraiture--international, retrospective and current--in progress.

PORTS see Harbors and Ports

PORTSMOUTH, VIRGINIA

VA —PORTSMOUTH PUBLIC LIBRARY, 601 Court St, Portsmouth, 23704. Dean Burgess, Library Dir
Holdings: Vols 500 Cat Mss Maps Pix Slides Microforms
Notes: Portsmouth was founded in 1752 and was the headquarters for the British army throughout the Revolution. It has the oldest and now the largest American Navy Shipyard dating to before the Revolution and called the Norfolk Naval Shipyard. It also was the site of the building of the Merimac (which battled the Monitor off Portsmouth's waterfront). Several pre-revolutionary houses remain in the historic downtown area although most are from the Federal period 1800-1830. Portsmouth is often neglected in American history books perhaps because it was a Tory town.

PORTUGAL

CA —UNIVERSITY OF CALIFORNIA, SAN DIEGO, Central University Library, Mandeville Dept of Special Collections, La Jolla, 92093. Lynda Corey Claassen, Head
Notes: Hispanic Collection: Approx 6000 vols describe cultures of Spain, Portugal, Mexico, Latin America, and South America. Works of literature, history, philosophy and art date from the 15th to the mid-19th century. Highlights of the collection include rare 18th century Spanish provincial dramas and works on the history of Seville and Andalusia.

MO —WASHINGTON UNIVERSITY, John M Olin Library, Campus Box 1061, St Louis, 63130.
Holdings: Vols (7500) Cat Microforms
Budget: $200
Notes: Major subject concentration.

NY —HISPANIC SOCIETY OF AMERICA, Library, 613 W 155 St, New York, 10032. Martha M de Narvaez, Cur of Mss; Irene S Frye, Asst Librn
Holdings: Vols (150,000) Cat Mss Maps Pix Slides Phonorecords Microforms
Notes: History, art, literature and general culture of the Hispanic countries (where Spanish or Portuguese is spoken). Incl (18,000) vols printed before 1701, incl (250) incunabula; over (100,000) later vols, plus thousands of periodicals. About (200,000) mss incl ms maps. Printed atlases are in the Book Collection. Some microfilms, chiefly of our early books. Engraved and printed separate maps; reference collection of over 100,000 photographs; slides: all in Department of Iconography, not in library. Catalogs: *Catalogue of the Hispanic Society of America* (Boston: G K Hall, 1962), 10 vols; *First Supplement* (Boston, 1970), 4 vols. Early books: *Printed Books 1468-1700; Mss: Catalogo de los Manuscritos Poeticos Castellanos* (15th-17th centuries; 3 vols); *Medieval Manuscripts in the Library; Golden Age Drama Manuscripts* (the latter in press).

TX —SOUTHERN METHODIST UNIVERSITY, Fondren Library, Dallas, 75275. Curt Holleman, Librn for Collection Development

PORTUGAL—EXPATRIATES

OK —UNIVERSITY OF TULSA, McFarlin Library, Dept of Rare Books and Special Collections, 600 S College, Tulsa, 74104. David Farmer, Dir; Toby Murray, Archivist; Caroline Swinson, Cur of Manuscripts & Art

PORTUGAL—EXPATRIATES (cont.)

Holdings: Vols 2500
Notes: The only known extant lending library from the 19th century. It was formed by British subjects in Oporto, Portugal between 1820-1890. 70 percent not in Sadlier.

PORTUGAL—EXPLORING EXPEDITIONS

†DC —CATHOLIC UNIVERSITY OF AMERICA, Oliveira Lima Library, Washington, 20064.
Notes: Brazilian and Portuguese history, literature, church history, Portuguese colonial expansion, Portuguese diplomatic history, Brazilian travel.
IL —NEWBERRY LIBRARY, 60 W Walton St, Chicago, 60610. Diana Haskell, Cur of Modern Mss
Holdings: Cat
Notes: The Greenlee Collection of materials on discovery, exploration and colonization by the Portuguese.
IN —INDIANA UNIVERSITY, Lilly Library, Seventh St, Bloomington, 47405. William R Cagle, Librn
Holdings: Cat
Notes: First and early printings of 15th through 17th century European voyages to the western hemisphere, incl such collections as the *Decades* of Peter Martyr, the *Grands* and *Petits Voyages* gathered by DeBry, and Hakluyt's *Principall Navigations*; travels to the Orient, incl first printed accounts of Marco Polo; the Portuguese in India from the time of the arrival of Vasco da Gama; 18th century voyages by Captain James Cook, Le Comte de Laperouse and others; and the great scientific expeditions of the 18th and 19th centuries.
NY —NEW YORK PUBLIC LIBRARY, Research Libraries, General Research Division, Fifth Ave & 42 St, New York, 10018. Rodney Phillips, Chief
Holdings: Vols (2,225,000) Cat Maps Pix Microforms
Budget: ($775,718)

PORTUGAL—HISTORY

CA —UNIVERSITY OF CALIFORNIA, SAN DIEGO, Central University Library, Mandeville Dept of Special Collections, La Jolla, 92093. Lynda Corey Claassen, Head
Holdings: Vols 1500 Cat Maps
Notes: Largely 19th century history, plus many travel accounts, also largely 19th century.
†DC —CATHOLIC UNIVERSITY OF AMERICA, Oliveira Lima Library, Washington, 20064.
Notes: Brazilian and Portuguese history, literature, church history, Portuguese colonial expansion, Portuguese diplomatic history, Brazilian travel.
DC —LIBRARY OF CONGRESS, Manuscript Division, Washington, 20540. John C Broderick, Chief
Notes: Mss relating to Portuguese history and literature.
DC —LIBRARY OF CONGRESS, Washington, 20540.
Notes: Project of a consortium to microfilm about 200,000 pp of material on Great Britian, France, Russia and Prussia, for the period 1848-1918 in the ms and documentary collections of the Austrian State Archives, The collection will incl, among others, documents on the Austro-Prussian War of 1866, the treaty negotiations between France and Italy in 1868-1870, the Orient Question of 1877-1878, the persecution of Jews in Russia in 1882, the Congo Conference in Berlin, 1884-1887 and the British-Portuguese conflict in East Africa, 1889-1891. Copies are available at LC, the Center for Research Libraries, the Hampshire Inter-Library Center, and the libraries of Boston College, Yale, Harvard, Duke, Stanford and the University of Virginia.
FL —UNIVERSITY OF MIAMI, Otto G Richter Library, PO Box 248214, Coral

Gables, 33124. Frank Rodgers, Dir of Libraries
Holdings: Vols 2000
Notes: Incl valuable collection of books, rare offprints, microfilms, and miscellaneous items pertaining to medieval and early modern Portuguese history from the collection of Dr Bailey W Diffie.
IL —NEWBERRY LIBRARY, 60 W Walton St, Chicago, 60610. Diana Haskell, Cur of Modern Mss
Holdings: Cat
Notes: The Greenlee Collection, espec 1300-1825.
IN —INDIANA UNIVERSITY, Lilly Library, Seventh St, Bloomington, 47405. William R Cagle, Librn
Holdings: Cat Mss
Notes: First and early printings of 15th through 17th century European voyages to the western hemisphere, incl such collections as the *Decades* of Peter Martyr, the *Grands* and *Petits Voyages* gathered and by DeBry, and Hakluyt's *Principall Navigations*, travels to the Orient, incl first printed accounts of Marco Polo; the Portuguese in India from the time of the arrival of Vasco da Gama; 18th century voyages by Captain James Cook, Le Comte de Laperouse and others; and the great scientific expeditions of the 18th and 19th centuries.
KS —UNIVERSITY OF KANSAS, Kenneth Spencer Research Library, Special Collections Dept, Lawrence, 66045. Alexandra Mason, Librn
Holdings: Vols 500 Uncat Mss
Notes: Boehrer Collection. Portuguese and Brazilian history in first half of 19th century, incl over 4000 manuscripts. Noncirculating.
MA —FRANCIS A COUNTWAY LIBRARY OF MEDICINE, Boston Medical Library/ Harvard Medical Library, 10 Shattuck St, Boston, 02115. C Robin LeSueur, Librn; Richard J Wolfe, Cur, Rare Books & Manuscripts
Holdings: Cat Mss Microforms
Notes: Early Portuguese medicine and the role of Portugal in disseminating knowledge of Western medicine and science in Africa, Asia, and America.
MA —HARVARD UNIVERSITY LIBRARY, Widener Library, Cambridge, 02138. Ellen H Brow, Specialist in Book Selection
Holdings: Cat Mss Microforms
Notes: Catalog of Palha library (4 vols, Lisbon, 1896) lists collection acquired by Harvard, incl several hundred mss of Joao III and his court.
MO —WASHINGTON UNIVERSITY, John M Olin Library, Campus Box 1061, St Louis, 63130.
Holdings: Vols (7500) Cat Microforms
Notes: Major subject concentration.
NY —HISPANIC SOCIETY OF AMERICA, Library, 613 W 155 St, New York, 10032. Martha M de Narvaez, Cur of Mss; Irene S Frye, Asst Librn
Holdings: Vols (150,000) Cat Mss Maps Pix Slides Phonorecords Microforms
Notes: History, art, literature and general culture of the Hispanic countries (where Spanish or Portuguese is spoken). Incl (18, 000) vols printed before 1701, incl (250) incunabula; over (100,000) later vols, plus thousands of periodicals. About (200,000) mss incl ms maps. Printed atlases are in the Book Collection. Some microfilms, chiefly of our early books. Engraved and printed separate maps; reference collection of over 100,000 photographs; slides: all in Department of Iconography, not in library.
Catalogs: *Catalogue of the Hispanic Society of America* (Boston: G K Hall, 1962), 10 vols; *First Supplement* (Boston, 1970), 4 vols. Early books: *Printed Books 1468-1700;* Mss: *Catalogo de los Manuscritos Poeticos Castellanos* (15th-17th centuries; 3 vols); *Medieval Manuscripts in the Library; Golden Age Drama Manuscripts*(the latter in press).
NY —NEW YORK PUBLIC LIBRARY, Research Libraries, General Research Division, Fifth Ave & 42 St, New York, 10018. Rodney Phillips, Chief
Holdings: Vols (2,225,000) Cat Maps Pix Microforms
Budget: ($775,718)

OH —HEBREW UNION COLLEGE-JEWISH INSTITUTE OF RELIGION, Klau Library, 3101 Clifton Ave, Cincinnati, 45220. David J Gilner, Reference Librn
Holdings: Cat Mss
Notes: Incl papal bulls, edicts of inquisitions, royal letters, inquisitorial instructions, sermons preached at the autos-da-fe held by the Portuguese Inquisition at Lisbon, Columbia, etc. Early and late histories.
WI —UNIVERSITY OF WISCONSIN, MADISON, Memorial Library, Ibero-American Studies Collection, 728 State St, Madison, 53706. Suzanne Hodgman, Bibliographer
Holdings: Vols (230,000) Cat Maps Pix Phonorecords Microforms
Budget: ($50.000)
Notes: Materials on Latin America, Spain, and Portugal may be found in all the campus libraries. The largest single collection is located in the Memorial Library, and the above holdings and budget statements refer only to this collection. Strongest holdings are in language and literature and in history, although many other disciplines in the humanities and social sciences are well represented: political science, sociology, economics, anthropology, statistics, etc. Geographically, primary emphasis is on Brazil. The collection of materials on the history of Portugal is outstanding and that of Portuguese language and literature is one of the largest in the US. The collection is fully integrated into the general collections of the libraries. There is no separate catalog.
ON —QUEEN'S UNIVERSITY, Douglas Library, Kingston, K7L 5C4, Can. William F E Morley, Cur, Special Collections
Notes: Incl the W C Atkinson (of Glasgow) Collection.

PORTUGAL—IMPRINTS

NY —HISPANIC SOCIETY OF AMERICA, Library, 613 W 155 St, New York, 10032. Martha M de Narvaez, Cur of Mss; Irene S Frye, Asst Librn
Holdings: Vols (150,000) Cat Mss Maps Pix Slides Phonorecords Microforms
Notes: History, art, literature and general culture of the Hispanic countries (where Spanish or Portuguese is spoken). Incl (18, 000) vols printed before 1701, incl (250) incunabula; over (100,000) later vols, plus thousands of periodicals. About (200,000) mss incl ms maps. Printed atlases are in the Book Collection. Some microfilms, chiefly of our early books. Engraved and printed separate maps; reference collection of over 100,000 photographs; slides: all in Department of Iconography, not in library.
Catalogs: *Catalogue of the Hispanic Society of America* (Boston: G K Hall, 1962), 10 vols; *First Supplement* (Boston, 1970), 4 vols. Early books: *Printed Books 1468-1700;* Mss: *Catalogo de los Manuscritos Poeticos Castellanos* (15th-17th centuries; 3 vols); *Medieval Manuscripts in the Library; Golden Age Drama Manuscripts*(the latter in press).
See also entry under Spain

PORTUGAL—LIBRARIES

MN —SAINT JOHN'S ABBEY & UNIVERSITY, Hill Monastic Manuscript Library, Collegeville, 56321. Julian G Plante, Dir
Notes: Films of 61,000 mss. The total number of codices (bound handwritten mss) represents the holdings of several hundred libraries in Europe and elsewhere: Austria, Spain, Malta, Ethiopia, West Germany, Portugal, England, but also with concentrations of holdings from Italy, Hungary, Poland, Great Britain, Belgium, Yugoslavia, France, Switzerland and the Netherlands, and Vatican City. Also incl 70, 000 exposures.

PORTUGAL—POLITICS AND GOVERNMENT

RI —BROWN UNIVERSITY, John Hay Library, 20 Prospect St, Providence, 02912.

PORTUGAL—POLITICS AND GOVERNMENT (cont.)

Mark N Brown, Cur Mss
Notes: The Jose Rodrigues Migueis Collection of his works, personal library, correspondence, some manuscripts, diaries, drawings, notebooks, photographs, etc. Incl reprints, and thousands of newspaper clippings relating to him, Portugal's most important 20th century writer. Much of the correspondence is with Portuguese and other writers, academics, and political figures. Migueis was very active in modern Portuguese politics and Portuguese American studies.

PORTUGAL—RELIGION

†DC —CATHOLIC UNIVERSITY OF AMERICA, Oliveira Lima Library, Washington, 20064.
Notes: Brazilian and Portuguese history, literature, church history, Portuguese colonial expansion, Portuguese diplomatic history, Brazilian travel.

PORTUGAL—SOCIAL LIFE AND CUSTOMS

NY —HISPANIC SOCIETY OF AMERICA, Library, 613 W 155 St, New York, 10032. Martha M de Narvaez, Cur of Mss; Irene S Frye, Asst Librn
Holdings: Vols (150,000) Cat Mss Maps Pix Slides Phonorecords Microforms
Notes: History, art, literature and general culture of the Hispanic countries (where Spanish or Portuguese is spoken). Incl (18, 000) vols printed before 1701, incl (250) incunabula; over (100,000) later vols, plus thousands of periodicals. About (200,000) mss incl ms maps. Printed atlases are in the Book Collection. Some microfilms, chiefly of our early books. Engraved and printed separate maps; reference collection of over 100,000 photographs; slides: all in Department of Iconography, not in library.
Catalogs: *Catalogue of the Hispanic Society of America* (Boston: G K Hall, 1962), 10 vols; *First Supplement* (Boston, 1970), 4 vols. Early books: *Printed Books 1468-1700;* Mss: *Catalogo de los Manuscritos Poeticos Castellanos* (15th-17th centuries; 3 vols); *Medieval Manuscripts in the Library; Golden Age Drama Manuscripts*(the latter in press).
See also entry under Spain

PORTUGUESE AMERICAN STUDIES

RI —BROWN UNIVERSITY, John Hay Library, 20 Prospect St, Providence, 02912. Mark N Brown, Cur Mss
Notes: The Jose Rodrigues Migueis Collection of his works, personal library, correspondence, some manuscripts, diaries, drawings, notebooks, photographs, etc. Incl reprints, and thousands of newspaper clippings relating to him, Portugal's most important 20th century writer. Much of the correspondence is with Portuguese and other writers, academics, and political figures. Migueis was very active in modern Portuguese politics and Portuguese American studies.

PORTUGUESE ART see Art, Portuguese

PORTUGUESE AUTHORS see Authors, Portuguese

PORTUGUESE COLONIZATION

CA —UNIVERSITY OF CALIFORNIA, LOS ANGELES, Research Library, African Studies Collection, 405 Hilgard Ave, Los Angeles, 90024. Edward Shreeves, Chairman, Bibliographers Group; Joseph J Lauer, African Studies Bibliographer
Holdings: Maps Pix Slides Phonorecords Audiotapes Microforms
Notes: General collection mainly in the humanities and social sciences, covering prehistoric times to the present. Particular

strengths include: early travel and exploration, mission field, literature, vernacular languages and literatures, Portuguese Africa, slavery (have the British Foreign Office's *General Correspondence. Slave Trade* on microfilm). Extensive holdings of journals, newspapers and government publications. The collection was described in the *Handbook of American Resources for African Studies* (1967).

CA —UNIVERSITY OF CALIFORNIA, LOS ANGELES, Research Library, Indo/Pacific Collection, 405 Hilgard Ave, Los Angeles, 90024. Edward Shreeves, Chairman, Bibliographers Group; Charlotte Spence, Indo/Pacific Bibliographer
Holdings: Vols Cat Mss Maps Pix Microforms
Notes: The South Asian collection has been developed on two levels. On the research level it focuses on (1) the cultural, economic, political and social history of India from about 1859 to 1947; (2) linguistic and literary studies, with particular emphasis given to Sanskrit and Pali; and (3) the history of the Portuguese experience in South Asia. On the teaching level, materials are collected which relate to India before 1859, and from 1947 to date, as well as materials relating to the other political entities of South Asia. A description of the South Asian collection is included in the May, 1977 issue of *The Librarian,* and in *South Asian Library Resources in North America* (1975).

†DC —CATHOLIC UNIVERSITY OF AMERICA, Oliveira Lima Library, Washington, 20064.
Notes: Brazilian and Portuguese history, literature, church history, Portuguese colonial expansion, Portuguese diplomatic history, Brazilian travel.

IL —NEWBERRY LIBRARY, 60 W Walton St, Chicago, 60610. Diana Haskell, Cur of Modern Mss
Holdings: Cat
Notes: The Greenlee Collection of materials on discovery, exploration and colonization by the Portuguese.

IN —INDIANA UNIVERSITY, Lilly Library, Seventh St, Bloomington, 47405. William R Cagle, Librn
Holdings: Cat
Notes: First and early printings of 15th through 17th century European voyages to the western hemisphere, incl such collections as the *Decades* of Peter Martyr, the *Grands* and *Petis Voyages* gathered by DeBry, and Haklayt's *Principall Navigations;* travels to the Orient, incl first printed accounts of Marco Polo; the Portuguese in India from the time of the arrival of Vasco da Gama; 18th century voyages by Captain James Cook, Le Comte de Laperouse and others; and the great scientific expeditions of the 18th and 19th centuries.

PORTUGUESE DRAMA

NY —CENTER FOR INTER-AMERICAN RELATIONS, Library, 680 Park Ave, New York, 10021.
Notes: Most, but not all, of the 1000 plays and reference books are in Spanish or Portuguese.

NY —HISPANIC SOCIETY OF AMERICA, Library, 613 W 155 St, New York, 10032. Martha M de Narvaez, Cur of Mss; Irene S Frye, Asst Librn
Holdings: Vols (150,000) Cat Mss Maps Pix Slides Phonorecords Microforms
Notes: History, art, literature and general culture of the Hispanic countries (where Spanish or Portuguese is spoken). Incl (18, 000) vols printed before 1701, incl (250) incunabula; over (100,000) later vols, plus thousands of periodicals. About (200,000) mss incl ms maps. Printed atlases are in the Book Collection. Some microfilms, chiefly of our early books. Engraved and printed separate maps; reference collection of over 100,000 photographs; slides: all in Department of Iconography, not in library.
Catalogs: *Catalogue of the Hispanic Society of America* (Boston: G K Hall, 1962), 10 vols; *First Supplement* (Boston, 1970), 4

vols. Early books: *Printed Books 1468-1700;* Mss: *Catalogo de los Manuscritos Poeticos Castellanos* (15th-17th centuries; 3 vols); *Medieval Manuscripts in the Library; Golden Age Drama Manuscripts*(the latter in press).
See also entry under Spain

NY —NEW YORK PUBLIC LIBRARY, Performing Arts Research Center, Billy Rose Theatre Collection, 111 Amsterdam Ave, New York, 10023. Dorothy L Swerdlove, Cur
See also entry under Theatre - History.

PORTUGUESE FOLK MUSIC see Folk Music, Portuguese

PORTUGUESE IN AFRICA

CA —HOOVER INSTITUTION ON WAR, REVOLUTION & PEACE, Stanford University, Stanford, 94305. Milorad M Drachkovitch, Archivist
Notes: Collection of sound recordings of interviews with British, Portuguese and South African diplomats, politicians, economic advisors, journalists, and businessmen, 1970-76, relating to political events in Portugal and Southern Africa, collected by Keith Middlemas, Professor at the University of Sussex, England. Also incl are documents and correspondence pertaining to British, Portuguese and South African relations and various political events, 1966-1973. 7 ms boxes.

CA —HOOVER INSTITUTION ON WAR, REVOLUTION & PEACE, Stanford University, Stanford, 94305. Peter Duignan, Cur; Karen Fung, Deputy Cur
Notes: History, politics and economics from 1870 to the present. Extensive collection on Portuguese colonial history incl monographs, government publications, photographs, microforms, journals, newspapers. Incl journals such as *Revista Portugueza Colonial e Maritima, Revista de Angola, Defesa Nacional, Revista Militar, Angola in Arms, Kwacha-Angola, Mozambique Revolution.* Special collections incl the 15 reel Ronald Chilcote collection "Emerging Nationalism in Portuguese Africa", the 12 reel Immanuel Wallerstein Collection of Political Ephemera of the Liberation Movements of Lusophone Africa..., and the Robert Keith Middlemas Collection on Portugal and South Africa 1966-1976. Descriptions of the Collection in *Handbook of American Resources for African Studies* pub by Hoover. Holdings of the Collection in*Hoover Institution on War, Revolution, and Peace Library Catalog* pub by G K Hall, *Emerging Nationalism in Portuguese Africa: A Bibliography* pub by Hoover, *German Africa* pub by Hoover, *The Treason Trial in South Africa: A Guide to the Microfilm Record of the Trial* pub by Hoover. Also, *History of the Library and Archives of the Hoover Institution on War, Revolution and Peace,* edited by Peter Duignan (Hoover Institution Press), *Guide to Non-federal Archives and Manuscripts in the United States Relating to Africa,* compiled by Aloha P South (East Ardsley, Eng, Microform Ltd).

PORTUGUESE IN THE U.S.

PA —BALCH INSTITUTE FOR ETHNIC STUDIES, Library, 18 S Seventh St, Philadelphia, 19106. R Joseph Anderson, Library Dir
Holdings: Vols Cat

PORTUGUESE INDIA see Goa

PORTUGUESE LANGUAGE AND LITERATURE

AZ —UNIVERSITY OF ARIZONA, Library, Tucson, 85721. W David Laird, Librn
Notes: The greatest strength of this collection is in long back-runs of periodicals.

CA —UNIVERSITY OF CALIFORNIA, SAN DIEGO, Central University Library, Mandeville Dept of Special Collections, La Jolla, 92093. Lynda Corey Claassen, Head
Notes: Approximately 6000 volumes

PORTUGUESE LANGUAGE AND LITERATURE (cont.)

describe the cultures of Spain, Portugal, Mexico, Latin America, and South America. Works of literature, history, philosophy, and art date from the 15th to the mid-19th century. Highlights of the collection include rare 18th century Spanish provincial dramas.

CA —LOS ANGELES PUBLIC LIBRARY, Foreign Languages Dept, 630 W Fifth St, Los Angeles, 90071. Sylva Manoogian, Principal Librn
Holdings: Vols 1710 Cat
Budget: ($41,500)

CA —UNIVERSITY OF CALIFORNIA, LOS ANGELES, Research Library, Medieval and Renaissance Collection, 405 Hilgard Ave, Los Angeles, 90024. Edward Shreeves, Chairman, Bibliographers Group; Frances K Zeitlin, Medievan and Renaissance Bibliographer
Holdings: Mss
Notes: Particular strength in medieval literature and in 19th century continental Portuguese literature. Incorporates the libraries of Joseph Benoliel and Xavier da Cunha. 19th century literary periodicals.

CA —UNIVERSITY OF CALIFORNIA, SANTA BARBARA, Library, Dept of Special Collections, Santa Barbara, 93106. Christian F Brun, Head

CT —UNIVERSITY OF CONNECTICUT, Library, Storrs, 06268. R H Schimmelpfeng, Dir of Special Collections
Holdings: Vols 258 Cat

†DC —CATHOLIC UNIVERSITY OF AMERICA, Oliveira Lima Library, Washington, 20064.
Notes: Brazilian and Portuguese history, literature, church history, Portuguese colonial expansion, Portuguese diplomatic history, Brazilian travel.

DC —LIBRARY OF CONGRESS, Manuscript Division, Washington, 20540. John C Broderick, Chief
Notes: Mss relating to Portuguese history and literature.

DC —LIBRARY OF CONGRESS, Hispanic Division, Washington, 20540.
Notes: The Archive of Hispanic Literature on Tape is a repository of recorded poetry and prose from the Spanish- and Portuguese-speaking world. Most of the outstanding Hispanic literary figures of the last 30 years are included.

IL —SOUTHERN ILLINOIS UNIVERSITY, CARBONDALE, Delyte W Morris Library, Carbondale, 62901.
Holdings: Vols (19,000) Cat
Notes: Especially strong in Ecuadorean and Mexican literature; complete or almost complete files of many important literary journals published in Spanish America. Described in Woodbridge, Hensley C, "Faculty and library collaboration in developing the Latin American collection for area studies programs at Southern Illinois University," Twelfth Seminar on the Acquisition of Latin American Library Materials, Final Report and Working Papers, vols 2, pp-108 (1967).

IL —NEWBERRY LIBRARY, 60 W Walton St, Chicago, 60610. Diana Haskell, Cur of Modern Mss
Holdings: Cat Mss Maps
Notes: Incl the Greenlee Collection of Portuguese history and literature.

IN —INDIANA UNIVERSITY, Lilly Library, Seventh St, Bloomington, 47405. William R Cagle, Librn

MA —BOSTON PUBLIC LIBRARY, South End Branch, Multilingual Library, 685 Tremont St, Boston, 02118. Laura H Reyes, Librn
Holdings: Cat

MA —HARVARD UNIVERSITY LIBRARY, Widener Library, Cambridge, 02138. Ellen H Brow, Specialist in Book Selection
Holdings: Cat Mss Microforms
Notes: Catalog of Palha library (4 vols, Lisbon, 1896) lists collection acquired by Harvard. The Camoens collection is noteworthy, as is the collection of *autos*.

MA —SOUTHEASTERN MASSACHUSETTS UNIVERSITY, North Dartmouth, 02747.
Notes: Collections incl American Imprints,

Hansard Parliamentary Debates, and Poruguese Language and Literature.

MO —WASHINGTON UNIVERSITY, John M Olin Library, Campus Box 1061, St Louis, 63130.
Holdings: Vols (7500) Cat Microforms
Notes: Major subject concentration.

NY —HISPANIC SOCIETY OF AMERICA, Library, 613 W 155 St, New York, 10032. Martha M de Narvaez, Cur of Mss; Irene S Frye, Asst Librn
Holdings: Vols (150,000) Cat Mss Maps Pix Slides Phonorecords Microforms
Notes: History, art, literature and general culture of the Hispanic countries (where Spanish or Portuguese is spoken). Incl (18, 000) vols printed before 1701, incl (250) incunabula; over (100,000) later vols, plus thousands of periodicals. About (200,000) mss incl ms maps. Printed atlases are in the Book Collection. Some microfilms, chiefly of our early books. Engraved and printed separate maps; reference collection of over 100,000 photographs; slides: all in Department of Iconography, not in library.
Catalogs: *Catalogue of the Hispanic Society of America* (Boston: G K Hall, 1962), 10 vols; *First Supplement* (Boston, 1970), 4 vols. Early books: *Printed Books 1468-1700*; Mss: *Catalogo de los Manuscritos Poeticos Castellanos* (15th-17th centuries; 3 vols); *Medieval Manuscripts in the Library*; *Golden Age Drama Manuscripts* (the latter in press).

NY —NEW YORK PUBLIC LIBRARY, Donnell Foreign Language Library, 20 W 53 St, New York, 10019. Bosiljka Stevanovic, Supvr Librn
Holdings: Vols 662 Cat
Notes: Portuguese collection incl Portuguese authors of Portuguese expression. No separate catalog.

NY —STATE UNIVERSITY OF NEW YORK, STONY BROOK, Melville Library, Stony Brook, 11794. John B Smith, Dir
Holdings: Vols 11,000 Cat
Notes: The Brasiliana Collection of literature and all fields of the social sciences.

OH —CLEVELAND PUBLIC LIBRARY, Foreign Literature Dept, 325 Superior Ave, Cleveland, 44114. Natalia Bezugloff, Head
Holdings: Vols 2460 Cat
Notes: A popular circulating collection containing classics and the standard works with emphasis on belles lettres, history and biography. A variety of other subjects such as learning languages, how to do books, art, children's books, spoken phonodiscs and cassettes, periodicals, etc. Incl 110 ephemera.
See also entry under Foreign Language Collections

PA —PENNSYLVANIA STATE UNIVERSITY, Fred Lewis Pattee Library, Library Hispanic Program, University Park, 16802. Donald C Henderson, Head
Holdings: Vols (50,000) Cat Mss
Budget: ($31,000)
Notes: A good general collection covers all periods; supports doctoral programs.

RI —BROWN UNIVERSITY, John Hay Library, 20 Prospect St, Providence, 02912. Mark N Brown, Cur Mss
Notes: The Jose Rodrigues Migueis Collection of his works, personal library, correspondence, some manuscripts, diaries, drawings, notebooks, photographs, etc. Incl reprints, and thousands of newspaper clippings relating to him, Portugal's most important 20th century writer. Much of the correspondence is with Portuguese and other writers, academics, and political figures. Migueis was very active in modern Portuguese politics and Portuguese American studies.

TN —VANDERBILT UNIVERSITY, Library, Nashville, 37240. Marice Wolfe, Special Collections Librn

TX —UNIVERSITY OF TEXAS LIBRARIES, Nettie Lee Benson Latin American Collection, Sid Richardson Hall 1.109, Austin, 78712. Laura Gutierrez-Witt, Head Librn
Holdings: Vols (450,000) Cat Mss Maps Pix Phonorecords Filmstrips Microforms
See also entry under Latin America.

WI —UNIVERSITY OF WISCONSIN, MADISON, Memorial Library, Ibero-American Studies Collection, 728 State St, Madison, 53706. Suzanne Hodgman, Bibliographer
Holdings: Vols (20,000) Cat Maps Pix Microforms
Notes: This collection of strictly Portuguese, as opposed to Brazilian, language and literature has been built up over more than a century. It contains many rare items, including several serials found nowhere else in the US. Not separately housed; no listing available.

ON —QUEEN'S UNIVERSITY, Douglas Library, Kingston, K7L 5C4, Can. William F E Morley, Cur, Special Collections
Notes: Incl the W C Atkinson (of Glasgow) Collection.

PORTUGUESE LANGUAGE AND LITERATURE—BRAZIL

AZ —UNIVERSITY OF ARIZONA, Library, Tucson, 85721. W David Laird, Librn
Notes: The greatest strength of this collection is in long back-runs of periodicals.

CA —UNIVERSITY OF CALIFORNIA, RIVERSIDE, University Library, 4045 Canyon Crest Dr, Box 5900, Riverside, 92517.
Holdings: Vols 2,500
Notes: General research collection in the humanities and social sciences, with special strengths in history, literature, folklore and economic conditions, chiefly 20th century.

PORTUGUESE TIMOR see Timor, Portuguese

POSADA, JOSE GUADALUPE

DC —LIBRARY OF CONGRESS, Prints & Photographs Div, Washington, 20540.
Notes: Swann Collection is strong in the work of contemporary cartoonists. Among the 400 artists represented are Peter Arno, Bil Canfield, Al Capp, Miguel Covarrubias, Louis Dalrymple, Whitney Darrow, Rube Goldberg, Thomas Nast, Jose Guadalupe Posada, Edward Sorel, and John Tenniel.

POSITIVIST CHURCH OF BRAZIL

WI —UNIVERSITY OF WISCONSIN, MADISON, Memorial Library, Ibero-American Studies Collection, 728 State St, Madison, 53706. Suzanne Hodgman, Bibliographer
Holdings: Vols (394) Uncat
Notes: Brazilian Positivist Collection. The collection consists of a nearly complete set of the official publications of the Positivist Church of Brazil. It includes first editions of pamphlets and booklets from the late 19th century, in addition to later reprints. A typescript listing of the collection is available. Collection is housed in the Rare Book Department.

POSSIBLE ART see Art, Conceptual

POST, AMY

NY —UNIVERSITY OF ROCHESTER, Rush Rhees Library, Department of Rare Books and Special Collections, Rochester, 14627. Peter Dzwonkoski, Librn
Holdings: Cat Mss Pix
Notes: Approximately 300 letters including correspondence with Rachel Foster Avery (178 letters); Harriet Taylor Upton, Amy Post, Elizabeth Cady Stanton, and others. Also includes photographs, printed ephemera, and museum pieces.

POST, ISAAC, AND FAMILY

NY —UNIVERSITY OF ROCHESTER, Rush Rhees Library, Department of Rare Books and Special Collections, Rochester, 14627. Peter Dzwonkoski, Librn
Holdings: Mss
Notes: Autograph letters and other mss incl in the Amy and Issac Post family papers.

POST, ISAAC, AND FAMILY (cont.)

Amy (1802-1889) and Isaac (1798-1872). Both were abolitionists, spriitualists, temperance and women's rights advocates. Correspondents include Susan B Anthony, Elizabeth Cady Stanton. Frederick Douglass, and William C Nell.

POST CARDS see Postal Cards

POST OFFICE see Postal Service

POST WAR WORLD COUNCIL

PA —SWARTHMORE COLLEGE, Peace Collection, Swarthmore, 19081. Jean R Soderlund, Cur of Peace Collection
Holdings: Vols (10,000) Cat Mss Pix Microforms
Notes: International arbitration has been one of the central subject emphases of the Peace Collection since its inception in 1930. A large proportion of the total book collection deals with international arbitration. In addition, major records and document collections in this area incl those of the Women's Peace Party (1915-1919), and its successor, the Women's International League for Peace and Freedom (1919-); the Lake Mohonk (New York) Arbitration Conferences (1895-1917); the American Peace Society and its branches (1828-1947); the World Peace Foundation (1911-); the Post War World Council (1942-1967); also, books and other materials on the Hague Peace Conferences of 1899 and 1907, and other peace congresses and conventions. The Peace Collection has been described in Downs 972, 978, 4633, and in Downs 1950-1961 Supplement 507 and 916. Fordescriptions of major document groups, see the *Guide to the Swarthmore College Peace Collection*, 2nd ed (1981).
See also entry under Pacifism - History.

POSTAGE METERS

CT —PITNEY BOWES, Technical Information Center, Walten Wheeler Drive, Stamford, 06923. Mary Lynn Ainsworth, Mgr
Notes: US Postal Service. Partially cataloged.

POSTAGE STAMP CATALOGS see Catalogs, Postage Stamp

POSTAGE STAMPS

CA —SUNNYVALE PUBLIC LIBRARY, 665 W Olive Ave, Sunnyvale, 94086. Evelyn J Johnson, Librn
Holdings: Vols 2600 Cat
Budget: $300
Notes: Books and periodicals associated with origin, history, the making and collecting of postage stamps. Most materials donated by the Friends of the Western Philatelic Library. Collection also incl extensive pamphlet and tear sheet files maintained by the Friends of the Western Philatelic Library.

MA —BOSTON UNIVERSITY, Mugar Memorial Library, Special Collections Dept, 771 Commonwealth Ave, Boston, 02215. Howard B Gotlieb, Dir
Holdings: Cat Mss Pix

MA —CARDINAL SPELLMAN PHILATELIC MUSEUM, Library, 235 Wellesley St, Weston, 02193. Ruth Koved, Librn
Holdings: Vols (20,000) Cat
Notes: Library privileges available to members in person or by mail.

NJ —NATIONAL ASSOCIATION OF PRECANCEL COLLECTORS, Chester Davis Memorial Library, 5121 Park Blvd, Wildwood, 08260. Glenn W Dye, Secretary
Holdings: Vols 5000 Uncat Pix
Notes: Precancelled postage stamps; pictures of stamps in color; pictures of old post offices in New Jersey and New Hampshire. No photocopying. Publish monthly journal Precancel Stamp Collector.

NY —COLLECTORS CLUB, Library, 22 E 35 St, New York, 10016. Werner Elias, Librn
Holdings: Cat Mss Maps Pix Slides
Notes: Incl a special area of essays and proof which may be of interest to people desiring knowledge of art and engravers. Incl photographs of stamps. 100,000 items.

NY —NEW YORK PUBLIC LIBRARY, Research Libraries, General Research Division, Fifth Ave & 42 St, New York, 10018. Rodney Phillips, Chief
Holdings: Vols (2,225,000) Cat Maps Pix Microforms
Budget: ($775,718)

PA —FREE LIBRARY OF PHILADELPHIA, Business, Science & Industry Dept, Logan Sq, Philadelphia, 19103. Alex S Weinbaum, Head Librn
Holdings: Vols 6000 Cat Microforms
Budget: $1500
Notes: Philatelic Literature Collections incl catalogs, periodicals, etc. Mostly limited to English-language materials.

PA —AMERICAN PHILATELIC RESEARCH LIBRARY, PO Box 8338, State College, 16801. Keith A Wagner, Exec Dir
Holdings: Vols (25,000) Periodicals Mss
Notes: An educational affiliate of the American Philatelic Society, PO Box 8000, State College, PA 16803. Holdings incl catalogs, documents, records.

WI —MILWAUKEE PUBLIC LIBRARY, 814 W Wisconsin Ave, Milwaukee, 53233. Donald J Sager, City Librn
Holdings: Vols 1755 Cat
Notes: The major area resource for stamps. An excellent basic collection incl long runs of stamp catalogs and the majority of current material published.

ON —METROPOLITAN TORONTO LIBRARY, Fine Arts Dept, 789 Yonge St, Toronto, M4W 2G8, Can. Alan Suddon, Head
Holdings: Vols (42,000) Cat Pix Microforms
Notes: Extensive collection.

POSTAGE STAMPS—COLLECTIONS

CA —CALIFORNIA STATE UNIVERSITY, FRESNO, Henry Madden Library, Dept of Special Collections, Fresno, 93740. Ronald J Mahoney, Head
Holdings: // Uncat
Notes: The Frank J Homan Memorial Stamp Collection. Nearly complete collection of regular, air mail, and commemorative issues, 1847-1956.

CA —POMONA PUBLIC LIBRARY, Special Collections, 625 S Garey Ave, PO Box 2271, Pomona, 91766. David Streeter, Librn
Holdings: Vols 1000 Cat
Notes: Willis Kerr Philatelic collection covers all phases of philately and philatelic history; stresses North American subjects.

CA —LINCOLN MEMORIAL SHRINE, A K Smiley Public Library, 125 W Vine St, Redlands, 92373. Larry E Burgess, Archivist
Holdings: Vols (3000) Cat Mss Maps Pix Slides Phonorecords 16mm Films Microforms
Budget: ($18,000)
Notes: One of the larger collections on Lincoln and his times. Incl broadsides, letters, prints, campaign badges, stamps, coins, medals; bust, by George Grey Bernard. Endowment of Watchorn Lincoln Memorial Association. There is an additional pamphlet collection of more than 3000 pieces; an extensive philately collection incl first-day covers, commemorative and foreign issues, and Civil War envelopes.

CA —JAPANESE-AMERICAN PHILATELIC SOCIETY, Library, PO Box 24561, San Jose, 95154.
Notes: Philatelic history of the Japanese empire and associated areas. Research materials in English, Japanese, French and German available to society members only.

CT —MOLESWORTH INSTITUTE, Memorial Library, 143 Hanks Hill Rd, Storrs, 06268. Norman D Stevens, Dir, Cur, and Librn
Holdings: Vols (1000) Uncat Mss
Notes: Incl material relating to the Molesworth Family, books by and about any person named Molesworth as well as original materials upon which the legendary Molesworth Institute was founded. In addition the collections now contain over 20,000 library postcards and approx 375 library commemoratives acquired as part of the Institute's research work.

DC —SMITHSONIAN INSTITUTION LIBRARIES, National Museum of American History Branch, Washington, 20560. Rhoda S Ratner, Branch Librn
Holdings: Vols 7500 Cat Mss Maps Pix
Notes: International in scope. Covers all phases of philately and postal history. Incl auction and dealers' catalogs.

FL —UNIVERSITY OF MIAMI, School of Medicine, Louis Calder Memorial Library, PO Box 520875, Miami, 33152. Henry L Lemkau, Jr, Dir
Holdings: Vols (127,843) Cat Mss Maps Pix Slides Phonorecords Audiotapes Videotapes 16mm Films Filmstrips Microforms
Budget: ($915,000)
Notes: Ophthalmology Branch Library of 6969 vols incl in total count; University of Miami School of Medicine dissertations; 209 medical medallions; physicians' bookplates; postage stamps with medical themes.

FL —LIBRARY OF THE PHILATELIC JOURNALIST, 154 Laguna Court, Saint Augustine Shores, 32086. Gustav Detjen Jr, Editor
Holdings: Vols 400 Cat Slides
Budget: $400
Notes: Incl books on stamp collecting, US and foreign philatelic periodicals and lists of philatelic libraries, museums and journalists (1200).

KS —WICHITA PUBLIC LIBRARY, Reference Dept, 223 S Main, Wichita, 67202. Myrna Hudson, General Ref Librn
Holdings: Vols (5000)// Cat
Notes: Harrie S Mueller Collection. International in scope. Extensive collection of books, booklets, some long run periodicals and handbooks. Covers all phases of philately and postal history. Additional books in the general collection of the library.

NE —BOYS TOWN PHILAMATIC CENTER, Box One, Boys Town, 68010. Ivan E Sawyer, Asst Cur
Holdings: Vols 2600

NJ —NATIONAL ASSOCIATION OF PRECANCEL COLLECTORS, Chester Davis Memorial Library, 5121 Park Blvd, Wildwood, 08260. Glenn W Dye, Secretary
Holdings: Vols 5000 Uncat Pix
Notes: Precancelled postage stamps; pictures of stamps in color; pictures of old post offices in New Jersey and New Hampshire. No photocopying. Publish nonthly journal Precancel Stamp Collector.

NY —COLLECTORS CLUB, Library, 22 E 35 St, New York, 10016. Werner Elias, Librn
Holdings: Cat Mss Maps Pix Slides
Notes: Incl a special area of essays and proof which may be of interest to people desiring knowledge of art and engravers. Incl photographs of stamps. 100,000 items.

OH —HEBREW UNION COLLEGE-JEWISH INSTITUTE OF RELIGION, Klau Library, 3101 Clifton Ave, Cincinnati, 45220. David J Gilner, Reference Librn
Holdings: Uncat
Notes: Consists of early issues of Israeli stamps and numerous first day covers and special cancellations; current Israeli issues; and stamps of other countries that portray Jewish personalities and other themes of Jewish interest.

PA —AMERICAN PHILATELIC RESEARCH LIBRARY, PO Box 8338, State College, 16801. Keith A Wagner, Exec Dir
Notes: An educational affiliate of the American Philatelic Society, PO Box 8000, State College, PA 16803. Holdings incl catalogs, documents, records.

RI —BROWN UNIVERSITY, John Hay Library, 20 Prospect St, Providence, 02912. Mark N Brown, Cur Mss
Holdings: Vols 100 Uncat
Notes: Arthur I Andrews Collection--12 albums of American first day covers 1924-1958; Webster Knight Collection--5 mounting cases of US stamps (1846-date) (additions made). William L L Peltz Collection--10 albums of US Special Delivery stamps and covers; Henry H Morriss Collection--3 albums of world-wide Special Delivery stamps; World-wide

POSTAGE STAMPS—COLLECTIONS
(cont.)

Collection--60 albums of world-wide postage stamps (additions made).
See also entry under Lincoln, Abraham

WI —MILWAUKEE PUBLIC LIBRARY, 814 W Wisconsin Ave, Milwaukee, 53233. Donald J Sager, City Librn
See also entry under Postage Stamps.

BC —VANCOUVER PUBLIC LIBRARY, Art Div, 750 Burrard St, Vancouver, V6Z 1X5, Can.
Holdings: Vols (3000) Cat Maps Pix Vert File
Notes: An extensive collection, supported by local philatelic groups.

ON —NATIONAL POSTAL MUSEUM, Philatelic Library, Ottawa, K1A 0B1, Can. Cimon Morin, Librn
Holdings: Vols 6000 Cat Maps Slides Audiotapes Videotapes Microforms
Notes: Philatelic and postal history materials

POSTAGE STAMPS—HISTORY

CA —POMONA PUBLIC LIBRARY, Special Collections, 625 S Garey Ave, PO Box 2271, Pomona, 91766. David Streeter, Librn
Holdings: Vols 1000 Cat
Notes: Willis Kerr Philatelic collection covers all phases of philately and philatelic history; stresses North American subjects.

DC —SMITHSONIAN INSTITUTION LIBRARIES, National Museum of American History Branch, Washington, 20560. Rhoda S Ratner, Branch Librn
Holdings: Vols 7500 Cat Mss Maps Pix
Notes: International in scope. Covers all phases of philately and postal history. Incl auction and dealers' catalogs.

ON —NATIONAL POSTAL MUSEUM, Philatelic Library, Ottawa, K1A 0B1, Can. Cimon Morin, Librn
Holdings: Vols 6000 Cat Maps Pix Slides Audiotapes Videotapes Microforms
Notes: Philatelic and postal history materials.

POSTAGE STAMPS—ISRAEL

OH —HEBREW UNION COLLEGE-JEWISH INSTITUTE OF RELIGION, Klau Library, 3101 Clifton Ave, Cincinnati, 45220. David J Gilner, Reference Librn
Holdings: Uncat
Notes: Consists of early issues of Israeli stamps and numerous first day covers and special cancellations; current Israeli issues; and stamps of other countries that portray Jewish personalities and other themes of Jewish interest.

POSTAGE STAMPS—U.S.

NY —NEW YORK PUBLIC LIBRARY, Research Libraries, General Research Division, Fifth Ave & 42 St, New York, 10018. Rodney Phillips, Chief
Holdings: Vols (2,225,000) Cat Maps Pix Microforms
Budget: ($775,718)

POSTAL CARDS

IL —LAKE COUNTY MUSEUM LIBRARY, Lakewood Forest Preserve, Wauconda, 60084. Rebecca Goldberg, Dir; Katherine Hamilton-Smith, Cur
Notes: "The world's largest postcard collection. The Curt Teich Industries assets, consisting of several million postcards and associated artwork depicting local communities around the world, cards donated by Regensteiner Enterprises Inc. Curt Teich is considered one of the originators of present day postcards. Project funded by the Curt Teich Foundation."

POSTAL CARDS—COLLECTIONS

AZ —NORTHERN ARIZONA UNIVERSITY, Special Collection Library, CU Box 6022, Flagstaff, 86011. Peter M Whiteley, Coordr/Archivist; William Mullane, Librn
Notes: Ed McGonigle Family Collection. Incl files on the McGonigle Lumber Company, Flagstaff; Flagstaff Lumber Company and Oatman Amalgamated Gold Mining Company. Also Incl hundreds of early 1900's post cards of holidays and places.

AZ —UNIVERSITY OF ARIZONA, University Library, Special Collections, Tucson, 85721. Louis A Hieb, Head

CA —CALIFORNIA STATE UNIVERSITY, FRESNO, Henry Madden Library, Dept of Special Collections, Fresno, 93740. Ronald J Mahoney, Head
Holdings: Uncat
Notes: The Alexander Pronin Collection of Russian Postcards of approx 1500 Russian postcards, 1890-1920, illustrating Russian art, architecture and life. Approx 150 are partially used, incl various World War I censors' marks.

CA —OAKLAND PUBLIC LIBRARY, Art, Music and Recreation Section, 125 14 St, Oakland, 94612. Richard Colvig, Senior Librn
Holdings: Pix
Budget: $500
Notes: About 350,000 mounted pictures, posters, pictorial maps, postal cards, art reproductions, framed and unframed.

CA —POMONA PUBLIC LIBRARY, Special Collections, 625 S Garey Ave, PO Box 2271, Pomona, 91766. David Streeter, Librn
Holdings: Uncat Slides
Notes: Contains 550 lantern slides (mostly of California) and 4200 color 35mm transparencies of world travel, 1960s. Also, the Burton Frasher Postal Card Collection of 60,000 negatives and prints of California, Arizona, Colorado, New Mexico, Nevada, and Utah; 30,000 world views; 8000 California views. There are also world views in nearly 1000 stereophotographs.

CA —SAN DIEGO PUBLIC LIBRARY, Art, Music & Recreation Sect, 820 E St, San Diego, 92101. Barbara A Tuhill, Supvr
Notes: Collection of 24,935 postal cards derived from numerous gifts and organized directly under subjects which correspond to similar subjects in the picture collection. Art reproductions, scenic European and American views, and architecture are incl. For general circulation.

CA —SAN JOSE PUBLIC LIBRARY, 180 W San Carlos St, San Jose, 95113. Homer Fletcher, Dir
Holdings: Vols (11,000) Cat Mss Maps Pix Slides Microforms
Notes: Extensive collection of Californiana.

CT —MOLESWORTH INSTITUTE, Memorial Library, 143 Hanks Hill Rd, Storrs, 06268. Norman D Stevens, Dir, Cur, and Librn
Holdings: Vols (1000) Uncat Mss
Notes: Incl material relating to the Molesworth Family, books by and about any person named Molesworth as well as original materials upon which the legendary Molesworth Institute was founded. In addition the collections now contain over 20,000 library postcards and approx 375 library commemoratives acquired as part of the Institute's research work.

FL —HISTORICAL ASSOCIATION OF SOUTHERN FLORIDA, Charlton W Tebeau Library of Florida History, 101 W Flager St, Miami, 33130. Rebecca A Smith, Cur of Research Materials
Holdings: Vols (3000) Cat Mss Maps Pix Slides Audiotapes 16mm Films Microforms

IL —UKRAINIAN NATIONAL MUSEUM, Library, 2453 W Chicago Ave, Chicago, 60622. Emil Basiuk, Librn
Notes: Department has been organized in collaboration with the Ukrainian Librarians of America Association, Ukrainian Bibliographic-Reference Center. Interlibrary loans. Collection of books and pamphlets incl material in Ukrainian and other languages on Ukrainian history, geography, literature, language, art, social sciences, religion and Ukrainian fiction. Large collection of Ukrainian calendars and almanacs. Around 100 current periodicals. Collection of serials and monographs of the Ukrainian scholarly institutions, collection of publications of the Institute for the Study of the USSR. There is a large collection of Ukrainian postcards showing all aspects of Ukrainian civilization and culture.

IL —LAKE COUNTY MUSEUM LIBRARY, Lakewood Forest Preserve, Wauconda, 60084. Rebecca Goldberg, Dir; Katherine Hamilton-Smith, Cur
Notes: "The world's largest postcard collection. The Curt Teich Industries assets, consisting of several million postcards and associated artwork depicting local communities around the world, cards donated by Regensteiner Enterprises Inc. Curt Teich is considered one of the originators of present day postcards. Project funded by the Curt Teich Foundation."

KY —WESTERN KENTUCKY UNIVERSITY, Kentucky Library, Bowling Green, 42101. Riley Handy, Head, Special Collections; Connie Mills, Maps & Music Librn; Nancy Baird, Photographs Librn; Nancy Solley, Conservation Librn
Holdings: Vols (25,000) Cat Mss Maps Pix Microforms
Notes: Besides Kentucky history, other strengths are Mammoth Cave, South Union Shakers, Kentucky religion; and steamboat photos (3300 cataloged pictures); 8000 Kentucky postal cards, etc.

KY —UNIVERSITY OF KENTUCKY, Margaret I King Library, Dept of Special Collections, Lexington, 40506. William Marshall, Head
Holdings: Mss Uncat
Notes: Ca 220,000 pieces, incl views of animals, lighthouses, modes of transportation, holiday motifs, works of art, illuminated mss, special materials (leather, wood, metal and silk), buildings and scenes in the US and Europe. Especially strong in Kentucky cities.

LA —NEW ORLEANS PUBLIC LIBRARY, Art & Music Div, 219 Loyola Ave, New Orleans, 70140. Marilyn Wilkins, Head
Holdings: Cat Pix
Notes: Over 100,000 pictures--broad in subject coverage, some arranged geographically; 21,244 postal cards--mainly geographical, some subjects.

MA —BOSTON PUBLIC LIBRARY, Print Collection, Dartmouth St at Copley Sq, Boston, 02117. Sinclair H Hitchings, Keeper of Prints
Holdings: Maps Pix Slides
Notes: The Boston Pictorial Archive (especially strong from 1850 to 1910) contains views, aerial views, buildings, and events depicted in fine art prints, 19th and 20th century photos, and early 20th century postcards: 18 original town plans, 3000 old photos, 600 old glass negatives, 2500 old postcards, 100 prints, 100 stereopticon views. Material of the 18th and 20th century is also incl to a lesser degree. Items are cataloged by subject matter. Prints are also cataloged by artist and/or by publisher.

MA —SOCIETY FOR THE PRESERVATION OF NEW ENGLAND ANTIQUITIES, Library, 141 Cambridge St, Boston, 02114. Ellie Reichlin, Librn & Cur of Photographic Collections
Notes: Stereographic views (1850s-1890s) are particularly rich in architectural coverage for Boston, Oak Bluffs, Newburyport, Lowell, and the White Mountains (10,000 pieces). Postcards and small photographs (1880s-1920s) emphasize historic, commercial buildings throughout New England, with many small towns represented (6000 pieces). Photographic albums (mid-19th-1920s) are notable for their coverage of historic structures, Victorian interiors, and landscaping.
See also entry under Photographs - Collections.

MA —AMERICAN ANTIQUARIAN SOCIETY LIBRARY, 185 Salisbury St, Worcester, 01609. Marcus A McCorison, Dir & Librn
Holdings: Cat Maps Pix Slides
Notes: About 90,000 postal cards and 60,000 stereophotographs. Arranged geographically or by subject. Postal cards date from 1893; stereos 1860-1890. Also some rare copybook covers of views, 1794-1860. Extensive slide collection.

POSTAL CARDS—COLLECTIONS (cont.)

NJ —ATLANTIC CITY FREE PUBLIC LIBRARY, Illinois & Pacific Aves, Atlantic City, 08401. Paul Nee, Adult Serv Librn
Holdings: Cat Maps
Notes: Incl 2000 postcards.

NJ —NEWARK PUBLIC LIBRARY, Art & Music Dept, 5 Washington St, Newark, 07101. William J Dane, Supv
Holdings: Mss Maps Pix Slides
Notes: 1,000,000 pictures with supporting collections of postcards, 2000 portfolios of plates of design, fine and circulating print collections (incl Japanese), 1400 illustrated books, 4000 posters. The classification scheme and headings used are listed in *The Picture Collection Subject Headings* (Shoe String Press, 1968).

NJ —RUTGERS, THE STATE UNIVERSITY OF NEW JERSEY, Alexander Library, Special Collections and Archives, College Ave & Huntington St, New Brunswick, 08903. Ronald L Becker, Cur of Manuscripts and Rare Books
Notes: Over 18,000 postal cards, some from 1900; about 10,000 depict New Jersey scenes.

NY —NEW YORK STATE LIBRARY, General Reference Library, Albany, 12224. Christian Beauregard, Librn
Notes: Incl clippings, prints, postcards, photographs, reproductions, some mounted or laminated or both. 10,000 items.

NY —NEW YORK STATE HISTORICAL ASSOCIATION, Library, Lake Rd, Cooperstown, 13326. Amy Barnum, Librn
Holdings: Vols (55,000) Cat Mss Maps Pix Slides Tapes
Notes: Emphasis on Otsego County area. Incl Smith-Telfer Collection of 60,000 glass plate negatives, Otsego County, ca 1850-1950; also, picture collection (14 file drawers); also, postal cards Noncirculating.

NY —QUEENS BOROUGH PUBLIC LIBRARY, Art & Music Div, 89-11 Merrick Blvd, Jamaica, 11432. Dorothea Wu, Head

NY —NEW YORK PUBLIC LIBRARY, Local History and Genealogy Div, Fifth Ave & 42 St, New York, 10018. Gunther E Pohl, Chief
Notes: Over 350,000 photographs and postcard views of New York City and other local areas of the US. Incl 10,000 postal cards, arranged by state for the US; arranged by country for other areas of the world. Collection is worldwide in scope. Added to selectively.

NY —STATE UNIVERSITY OF NEW YORK, COLLEGE AT PURCHASE, Library, Lincoln Ave, Purchase, 10577. Robert W Evans, Dir
Holdings: Vols (1400) Mss Pix Slides
Notes: The Gerald D McDonald Collection. Over 1400 books on moving pictures and all aspects of the industry: production, directing, acting. Thousands of pictures of actors and actresses, directors, etc. Also about 2000 slides picturing movie personalities, etc; stereoptican pictures, buttons, bottle caps, playing cards, etc.

NY —MARGARET WOODBURY STRONG MUSEUM, 1 Manhattan Square, Rochester, 14607.
Holdings: Vols (20,000) Periodicals
Notes: The Margaret Woodbury Strong Museum Library contains a collection of approx 20,000 books, periodicals and ephemera of and concerning the 19th and early 20th centuries. A large part of the library's holdings reflect the interests of Margaret Strong and her family: domestic life and literature of the 19th century and world travel, with particular emphasis on the Orient. The library's resources are available to all visitors for research. Book stacks and rare book storage are not open for browsing and do not circulate, but facilities are provided in reading room for study.

NY —VISUAL STUDIES WORKSHOP, Research Center, 31 Prince St, Rochester, 14607. Linn Underhill, Coordr; Robert Bretz, Librn
Holdings: Vols (8000) Cat Pix Slides Audiotapes Videotapes
Notes: Strong emphasis on photography

(over 1,000,000 pictures) and the photographic arts in many subject areas incl in this volume. Heavy emphasis on early photographic processes and collections of examples of them. Also collections of individual photographers' works.

NC —DUKE UNIVERSITY, William R Perkins Library, Manuscript Dept, Durham, 27706. Ellen Gartrell, Cur of Mss
Notes: Estimate 35,000 US (especially South) and foreign, plus some subjects, early 20th century to present.

OH —BOWLING GREEN STATE UNIVERSITY, Library, Popular Culture Library, Bowling Green, 43403.
Notes: Extensive holdings of Big-Little books, comic books, matchbook covers, picture postcards, personal scrapbooks, trading cards, posters, magazines, film pressbooks, juvenile series novels and popular literature.

OH —OHIO STATE UNIVERSITY, Library for Communication and Graphic Arts, 242 W 18th St, Columbus, 43210. Lucy S Caswell, Curator
Notes: Library will receive collection of materials on this subject at a future date.

OH —UNIVERSITY OF DAYTON, Marian Library, 300 College Park Ave, Dayton, 45469. Rev Theodore Koehler, SM, Dir/Cur
Holdings: Cat
Notes: Part of largest and most comprehensive collection in the world of literature on the Virgin Mary. Incl Vloberg collection of pictures, ms notes and offprints on Marian iconography; 10,000 holy cards from 19th and 20th centuries; 2600 postcard views of shrines; 3000 postcards of Marian art; philatelic collection of 1000 stamps and 200 first-day covers; 1000 photographs.
See also entry under Mary, Virgin

PA —ERIE COUNTY HISTORICAL SOCIETY LIBRARY, 417 State St, Erie, 16501. Helen Andrews, Librn
Notes: 1712 postcards relating to Erie city and county.

TN —TENNESSEE STATE LIBRARY & ARCHIVES, 403 Seventh Ave N, Nashville, 37219. Olivia K Young, State Librn & Archivist
Holdings: Uncat Pix
Notes: Mainly picture postcards of Tennessee and southern scenes, but largest part of the collection is the Mrs Joseph H Thompson Collection incl cards from Europe, Africa, Asia and North and South America.

TX —FORT WORTH PUBLIC LIBRARY, Arts Division, 300 Taylor St, Fort Worth, 76102. Heather Gobel, Head
Notes: This special picture collection provides research service materials for requests in all subject areas requiring pictorial illustrations. Includes postal cards and poster collections. The fine arts reproductions comprise another separate collection of framed and matted and portfolio-contained pictures not included in the Subjects collection.

TX —ROSENBERG LIBRARY, Galveston and Texas History Center, 2310 Sealy Ave, Galveston, 77550. Jane Kenamore, Archivist
Holdings: Cat Pix
Notes: 16,000 photographs of Galveston and Texas subjects, private scrapbooks and postcards.

ON —QUEEN'S UNIVERSITY, Douglas Library, Kingston, K7L 5C4, Can. William F E Morley, Cur, Special Collections
Holdings: Vols 3400 Uncat Pix
Notes: 2850 pictures and 2520 picture postcards, almost all Canadian.

ON —METROPOLITAN TORONTO LIBRARY, Fine Arts Dept, 789 Yonge St, Toronto, M4W 2G8, Can. Alan Suddon, Head
Holdings: Uncat Pix
Notes: Incl circulating picture collections (clippings) on all subjects. Reference picture collection, mainly 19th century Canadian, but non-Toronto. Postcards. Printed ephemera. 100,000 reference pictures 750,00 circulating pictures. Loose pictures from magazines and books.

ON —METROPOLITAN TORONTO LIBRARY, Canadian History Dept, Baldwin

Room Section, 789 Yonge St, Toronto, M4W 2G8, Can. David B Kotin, Head
Holdings: Vols (52,000) Mss Pix
Notes: This collection consists of material on Canadian history, geography, travel, archaeology, genealogy, retrospective city and telephone directories, collective biographies, native peoples (excluding customs, rights and social conditions), Arctic regions, military history and theory. It is an extremely strong collection of both current and retrospective material. Particular strengths are national and local history (especially Ontario), Arctic regions, native peoples, travel (especially Ontario), and military history. Incl 78,000 historical pictures, 235 linear meters mss, 14,000 broadsides and 3800 bound newspapers.

PQ —MCGILL UNIVERSITY, McLennan Library, Rare Books and Special Collections Dept, 3459 McTavish St, Montreal, H3A 1Y1, Can.
Notes: 5524 sheet maps, 370 atlases, 571 folded maps, 629 guide books, 248 reference books. The coverage is worldwide, specializing in North America, Canada, Quebec, Montreal. Includes a collection of guide books from the 1800s to the present day, as well as a reference collection; there is also a large collection of modern topographical literature with worldwide coverage, and an important collection of postcards particularly of Montreal and the Province of Quebec. A finding list is available for 19th century guide books on Canada: *A Preliminary Guide to Nineteenth Century Canadian Guide Books: a Survey of the Holdings of the McLennan Library with an Historical Introduction*. Montreal, 1982.

POSTAL CARDS—RUSSIAN

CA —CALIFORNIA STATE UNIVERSITY, FRESNO, Henry Madden Library, Dept of Special Collections, Fresno, 93740. Ronald J Mahoney, Head
Holdings: Uncat
Notes: The Alexander Pronin Collection of Russian Postcards of approx 1500 Russian postcards, 1890-1920, illustrating Russian art, architecture and life. Approx 150 are partially used, incl various World War I censors' marks.

POSTAL LIFE INSURANCE see Insurance, Life

POSTAL RECORDS

AZ —NORTHERN ARIZONA UNIVERSITY, Special Collection Library, CU Box 6022, Flagstaff, 86011. Peter M Whiteley, Coordr/Archivist; William Mullane, Librn
Notes: Flagstaff Arizona Postal Records Collection; 1909-1936. Also, postal records of Fort Apache, Ariz, 1888-1919, Cottonwood, Ariz, 1885-1912, and Woodruff, Ariz, 1902-1953.

POSTAL SERVICE

CO —US AIR FORCE ACADEMY, Library, USAF Academy, Colorado Springs, 80840. Reiner H Schaeffer, Dir
Holdings: // Cat Microforms
Notes: Air letter sheets issued by all countries throughout the world, and the United Nations, from 1941 to 1974. Incl are sheets used by Germany and given to captive prisoners of war during World War II.

CT —PITNEY BOWES, Technical Information Center, Walten Wheeler Drive, Stamford, 06923. Mary Lynn Ainsworth, Mgr
Notes: US Postal Service. Partially cataloged.

BC —VANCOUVER PUBLIC LIBRARY, Art Div, 750 Burrard St, Vancouver, V6Z 1X5, Can.
Holdings: Cat Slides
Notes: An extensive collection, supported by local philatelic groups.

POSTAL SERVICE—BUILDINGS

NJ —NATIONAL ASSOCIATION OF PRECANCEL COLLECTORS, Chester

POSTAL SERVICE—BUILDINGS (cont.)

Davis Memorial Library, 5121 Park Blvd, Wildwood, 08260. Glenn W Dye, Secretary
Holdings: Vols 5000 Uncat Pix
Notes: Precancelled postage stamps; pictures of stamps in color; pictures of old post offices in New Jersey and New Hampshire. No photocopying. Publish monthly journal Precancel Stamp Collector.

POSTAL SERVICE—HISTORY

DC —SMITHSONIAN INSTITUTION LIBRARIES, National Museum of American History Branch, Washington, 20560. Rhoda S Ratner, Branch Librn
Holdings: Vols 7500 Cat Mss Maps Pix
Notes: International in scope. Covers all phases of philately and postal history. Incl auction and dealers' catalogs.

IL —STAMP COLLECTORS CLUB OF CHICAGO, Library, 1029 N Dearborn St, Chicago, 60610. Lester Winick, Lib Comm
Notes: 4000 books; 2000 bound periodicals; 100 periodical subscriptions.

MA —CARDINAL SPELLMAN PHILATELIC MUSEUM, Library, 235 Wellesley St, Weston, 02193. Ruth Koved, Librn
Holdings: Vols (20,000) Cat
Notes: Library privileges available to members in person or by mail.

NY —COLLECTORS CLUB, Library, 22 E 35 St, New York, 10016. Werner Elias, Librn
Holdings: Cat Mss Maps Pix Slides
Notes: Incl a special area of essays and proof which may be of interest to people desiring knowledge of art and engravers. Incl photographs of stamps. 100,000 items.

PA —AMERICAN PHILATELIC RESEARCH LIBRARY, PO Box 8338, State College, 16801. Keith A Wagner, Exec Dir
Holdings: Vols (25,000) Periodicals Mss
Notes: An educational affiliate of the American Philatelic Society, PO Box 8000, State College, PA 16803. Holdings incl catalogs, documents, records.

ON —NATIONAL POSTAL MUSEUM, Philatelic Library, Ottawa, K1A 0B1, Can. Cimon Morin, Librn
Holdings: Vols 6000 Cat Maps Pix Slides Audiotapes Videotapes Microforms
Notes: Philatelic and postal history materials.

POSTAL SERVICE—U.S.

NJ —NATIONAL ASSOCIATION OF PRECANCEL COLLECTORS, Chester Davis Memorial Library, 5121 Park Blvd, Wildwood, 08260. Glenn W Dye, Secretary
Holdings: Vols 5000 Uncat Pix
Notes: Precancelled postage stamps; pictures of stamps in color; pictures of old post offices in New Jersey and New Hampshire. No photocopying. Published monthly journal, Precancel Stamp Collector.

POST CARDS see Postal Cards—Collections

POSTERS—COLLECTIONS

CA —GRADUATE THEOLOGICAL UNION LIBRARY, New Religious Movements Research Collection, Public Services and Special Collections Dept, 2400 Ridge Road, Berkeley, 94709. Diane Choquette, Dept Head
Holdings: Vols (3000) Mss Pix
Notes: Begun in 1977, the collection focuses on religious movements new to America since 1960, and unorthodox religious movements resurgent since 1960. American forms of Hinduism, Buddhism, Sikhism, and Sufism are included along with occultism, Neo-Paganism, esoteric and alternative forms of Christianity, feminist spirituality, and human potential movements having a spiritual aspect. Legal issues, such as deprogramming, and the question of church/ state relations are an important part of the collection. The Library is a depository for publications of the Unification Church in America, the Church of Scientology, and the International Society for Krishna Consciousness (America). The responses of mainstream religions and concerned citizens groups are also included. Besides 3000 monographs, the library has 400 periodical titles, 200 posters from the San FranciscoBay Area, 1965-77, 300 research papers, and 31 linear feet of ephemera.

CA —ACADEMY OF MOTION PICTURE ARTS & SCIENCES, Margaret Herrick Library, 8949 Wilshire Blvd, Beverly Hills, 90211. Linda Harris Mehr, Library Administrator
Holdings: Vols (10,000) Cat Mss Pix Slides
Budget: ($250,000)
Notes: Plus posters, scrapbooks, clippings and press books. Collection emphases are the moving picture industry, moving picture history, biographical material on actors, actresses and industry personnel. Files on specific films, reviews, cast and credits, production data, etc. on more than 40,000 moving pictures. Over 2000 films, incl early 28mm films. Over 1 million pictures.

CA —CLAREMONT COLLEGES, Honnold Library, Ninth & Dartmouth, Claremont, 91711. Tania Rizzo, Special Collections Dept Head
Holdings: Vols (250) Uncat Mss Maps Doc Pix Rec Posters Scrapbooks
Notes: Combined holdings of memorabilia of both world wars, primarily WWII. The Howard D Mills Collection on War Bonds occupies 33 linear ft of scrapbooks, documents, mss, and photographs, in addition to several dozen War Bond, Liberty Bond, and recruitment posters. Nazi propaganda and German medals. Soldiers' handbooks, maps, pamphlets, scrapbooks of clippings, photographs, and recordings. Restricted use.

CA —UNIVERSITY OF CALIFORNIA, DAVIS, Shields Library, Dept of Special Collections, Davis, 95616. Donald Kunitz, Head; C Danial Elliott, Asst Head
Holdings: Vols (112,000) Cat Mss Pix
Notes: Programs, playbills, posters, designs, and scripts from 19th and 20th century American and British theatre. American materials incl the eastern United States (NYC) and California. Production groupings center in Sir Henry Irving, McKee Rankin, Sir John Martin-Harvey, E L Davenport. Clippings, photographs, and correspondence of theatre personalities; records of the Bread and Puppet Theatre, San Francisco Mime Troupe, Living Theatre, Firehouse Theatre, Squat Theatre, papers of Toby Cole.
Described in: Sarlos, Robert K, "The Theatre Collection at Davis," American Society for Theatre Research Newsletter, vol 3, no 1, fall 1974, pp 2-3, 9-10.

CA —LOS ANGELES PUBLIC LIBRARY, Frances Howard Goldwyn Hollywood Regional Library, 1623 Ivar Ave, Los Angeles, 90028. Sally Dumaux, Librn
Holdings: Vols (100,000) Cat Mss Pix VF
Budget: ($60,000)
Notes: A general and a research collection on theatre history, US and foreign, with special emphasis on Los Angeles, Chicago, and New York theatre from the late 1800s to the present. Other aspects of the collection include theatre design, make-up, costume, and acting and directing techniques. Also includes biographies of actors and actresses (many signed). The play collection of over 15,000 titles covers mainly English and American plays of the 19th and 20th century. There are over 5000 playbills, scrapbooks, posters, and programs. Special Collections: "Hellzapoppin," NY, 1938-40. Includes photographs, clippings, and programs.

CA —UNIVERSITY OF CALIFORNIA, LOS ANGELES, Research Library, Dept of Special Collections, 405 Hilgard Ave, Los Angeles, 90024. Edward Shreeves, Chairman, Bibliographers Group; David S Zeidberg, Head
Holdings: Cat
Notes: 1000 American and foreign examples incl dance, exhibitions, student protest movements, theater, travel, and World Wars I and II.

CA —UNIVERSITY OF CALIFORNIA, LOS ANGELES, Theater Arts Library, Los Angeles, 90024. Edward Shreeves, Chairman, Bibliographers Group; Audree Malkin, Head, Theater Arts Library
Holdings: Cat Mss Pix Slides
Notes: Film posters and programs: A diverse collection of rare and early film posters, programs, and advertising compaign books for American films dating from 1915. Posters and programs for Polish and Czechoslovakian productions are also represented. Also a collection of original comic books, color comic books, storyboards, and posters illustrated by Clyde Geronimi.

CA —UNIVERSITY OF SOUTHERN CALIFORNIA, Edward L Doheny Memorial Library, Archives of Performing Arts, University Park, Los Angeles, 90089. Robert Knutson, Librn
Holdings: Vols (15,000) Cat Mss Pix Films Audiotapes Videotapes
Notes: Approx 15,000 vols of books and serials about film, incl a large collection of foreign language books and periodicals. Current subscriptions to over 200 serials. Large collection of clippings about motion pictures and television. Warner Brothers Films Collection (1920-1968) incl 700,000 stills and negatives; 3,000 titles of feature, short subject and television screenplays; script materials, set designs, engineering drawings, production records, patent records, music and legal files. Over 1000 bound vols describing the inventory and 100 bound vols of index to the inventory. Universal Pictures Corporation Collection incl 600 boxes of production and publicity department records, incl 1,500 screenplays. Metro-Goldwyn-Mayer Collection incl screenplays from 1919-1958. Twentieth Century-Fox Collection incl screenplays and story department notes from 1919-1967.Hal Roach Studio Collection contains studio records from 1916-mid fifties. More than 150 personal collections from actors, directors, producers, writers, etc. Also have 2,000 additional screenplays; 1,000 posters, 110,000 photographs; 750 recorded soundtracks; 1,500 interview tapes; 400 David Wolper videotapes. A collection of feature films on videotape is being created. There is also a historical collection of motion picture cameras, projectors and other equipment from the earliest times to present.

CA —OAKLAND PUBLIC LIBRARY, Art, Music and Recreation Section, 125 14 St, Oakland, 94612. Richard Colvig, Senior Librn
Holdings: Pix
Budget: ($500)
Notes: About 350,000 mounted pictures, posters, pictorial maps, postal cards, art reproductions, framed and unframed.

CA —CALIFORNIA HISTORICAL SOCIETY, Schubert Hall Library, 2099 Pacific Ave, San Francisco, 94109. Bruce L Johnson, Library Dir
Holdings: Vols (50,000) Cat Mss Maps Pix
See also entry under California - History

CT —YALE UNIVERSITY, Box 1603A, Yale Station, New Haven, 06520.
Notes: War Posters.

DC —HOWARD UNIVERSITY, Founders Library, Channing Pollock Theatre Collection, 500 Howard Place NW, Washington, 20059. Marilyn Mahanand, Librn
Holdings: Vols (16,440) Cat Mss Maps Pix Slides Microforms
Notes: Much on the Black Theatre.

DC —LIBRARY OF CONGRESS, Prints & Photographs Div, Washington, 20540.
Notes: Poster collection numbers about 70, 000 American and foreign items from the 1850s to the present. Incl Art Nouveau of WWI and WWII, WPA, propaganda, performing arts, and psychedelic posters.

DC —LIBRARY OF CONGRESS, Prints & Photographs Div, Washington, 20540.
Notes: The Gary Yonker Collection of political propaganda posters, late 1960s to present. Strongest for US materials but incl

POSTERS—COLLECTIONS (cont.)

about 50 other countries' work. Over 4500 items, arranged geographically.

DC —LIBRARY OF CONGRESS, Motion Pictures, Broadcasting and Recorded Sound Div, Washington, 20540.
Holdings: Cat Mss Pix
Notes: Motion Picture Film. Early film dating from 1894; paper print collection of early film (1897-1915) deposited for copyright, converted to projectable film. George Kleine Collection (1900-1920); Edison Laboratories Collection; Theodore Roosevelt Memorial Association Collection; American Film Institute Collection (theatrical films from 1897 to 1956 and theatrical shorts from all periods); German, Japanese, and Italian collections received through transfer from other Government agencies and by exchange with foreign governments; American Copyright Collection of films (incl television shows) selected from those registered for copyright from 1942 to the present. Collection of stills; poster collection; script and continuity collection. Holdings: motion pictures, 50,000 titles; 300,000 stills; 8000 posters;137,000 scripts and continuities.,

GA —US ARMY INFANTRY CENTER, National Infantry Museum, Fort Benning, 31905. Dick D Grube, Dir; Z Frank Hanner, Cur; Carol Sims, Librn
Holdings: Vols (6000) Cat Mss Maps Pix Slides
Notes: Published and unpublished works dealing with infantry history, equipment, and units, for research on the Museum's collections of artifacts. Items cannot be checked out except under unusual and compelling circumstances. The collection traces the two centuries of history of the US Infantry. Of special interest are: unpublished reports of tests conducted on US Army Infantry equipment; photographs showing the history of Fort Benning; books and periodical articles dealing with Infantry small arms, both American and foreign, especially Japanese, Soviet, Chinese, and British; US Army manuals, incl many from the early 20th and late 19th centuries; WWII battlefield maps; WWI and WWII posters; histories of WWI; US Army insignia and medals; WWII era German uniforms and insignia. Also, over 2500 weapons.

IL —CHICAGO HISTORICAL SOCIETY, Library, Clark St at North Ave, Chicago, 60614. Robert L Brubaker, Librn
Holdings: Vols (150,000) Cat Mss Pix
Notes: Chicago theatre programs (5000); scrapbooks containing reviews and other clippings; a few letters, reminiscences, account books, and other records of theatres, actors and actresses, and managers; theatre posters; Thomas Conolly Collection of Theatrical Portraits; other photographs of theatres, productions, and casts.

IL —CHICAGO PUBLIC LIBRARY, Special Collections Div, Cultural Center, 78 E Washington St, Chicago, 60602. Laura Linard, Cur
Holdings: // Cat
Notes: A mint collection of 500 World War I posters, the greater part of which are from Great Britain. Several of the posters were only recently removed from their original packages, dated 1919, and distributed to public libraries by the British Information Service. See *Take Up the Sword of Justice: An Exibition of British World War I Posters from the Special Collections of The Chicago Public Library*, compiled by Marie Gecik and Thomas A Orlando, 1976. A similar collection of World War II posters (500) is almost exclusively American in origin.

IL —NORTHWESTERN UNIVERSITY, Library, Special Collections Dept, 1937 Sheridan Rd, Evanston, 60201. R Russell Maylone, Cur
Notes: Four collections: (1) 14,000 French Revolution pamphlets; 1560 mazarinades; 2500 Brabant Revolution pamphlets. Large collection of material from the Siege of Paris, 1870, and the Paris Commune, 1871, incl posters, caricatures and drawings, books,

pamphlets, newspapers, journals, letters and photographs. Documentation of the May-June Revolt, Paris, 1968, incl film, books, pamphlets and over 350 original posters. (2) Over 350 original posters produced at the schools of the Sorbonne, Beaux Arts and other ad hoc ateliers during the student and worker uprising, May-June Revolt, Paris, 1968. French posters from World War I; Russian posters from the 1920s and 1930s. Broadside poems produced in England and America during the 20th century. Fillmore West posters (500). (3) Periodicals, posters, leaflets, and street sheets documentingthe Free Speech Movement, University of California at Berkeley, 1964. (4) Chicago Women's Graphic Collective, other women's liberation movement posters from Europe, England and Australia.

IA —UNIVERSITY OF IOWA, University Libraries, Iowa City, 52242. Robert A McCown, Mss Librn
Holdings: Mss Pix

Notes: Five collections: Robert Blees collection of motion picture and television material, 1925-65, inc, including stories, still production photos, and motion picture and television scripts of a motion picture and television script writer; David Swift collection of motion picture and television material, 1951-65, including scripts, posters, photos, drawings, and blueprints for final set construction of a motion picture and television producer and writer; the Albert Jay Cohen collection of motion picture and television production material, 1948-58, including correspondence, film scripts, stories, photos, financial and production papers, and censorship records; the Arthur A. Ross collection of motion picture and television material, 1943-65, including correspondence, scripts, photos, production records, and artists' sketches of a motion picture and television script writer; and the Norman Felton Papers, 1937-1978, including correspondence, notes, notebooks, subject files, budgets, other financial records, photographs, and scripts relating to such television series as The Eleventh Hour, The Lieutenant, The Man From U.N.C.L.E., Jericho, The Strange Report, The Psychiatrist, Hawkins, and Dr. Kildare, produced by Felton, 124 ft. of mss.

KY —UNIVERSITY OF KENTUCKY, Margaret I King Library, Dept of Special Collections, Lexington, 40506. William Marshall, Head
Notes: Ca 1400 pieces, partially cataloged. Incl travel, theater, World Wars I and II, art nouveau, Atelier Populaire's posters from the 1968 Parisian student riots.

KY —UNIVERSITY OF LOUISVILLE, Allen R Hite Art Institute, Library, Belknap Campus, Louisville, 40292. Gail Gilbert, Librn
Holdings: Vols (40,000) Cat Pix
Budget: ($29,000)
Notes: Incl books on art, architecture, landscape architecture and gardening, prints, printing, illustrated books and brass rubbings. Library subscribes to 200 periodical titles in these and other areas. Collection circulates to faculty and staff only, with same restrictions placed on interlibrary loan. Library also has collections of bookplates, posters, original prints, hand-made Christmas cards and clippings file filling 56 VF drawers.

MD —UNIVERSITY OF BALTIMORE, Langsdale Library, 1420 Maryland Ave,

Baltimore, 21201. Gerry Watkins, Head of Special Collections Dept
Notes: Collection contains 71 posters on a variety of topics.

MA —BOSTON PUBLIC LIBRARY, Print Collection, Dartmouth St at Copley Sq, Boston, 02117. Sinclair H Hitchings, Keeper of Prints
Holdings: Cat
Notes: There are especially large number of French and American lithographs, incl a large collection of proofs of the Prang Company, Boston, from 1858 to 1900; also, 300 mid-19th century American illustrated music sheets; and vast collections of early Parisian lithography (several thousand items); and of the lithographs of Daumier, Gavarni, Charlet and others. In addition there are turn-of-the-century posters, 400 American and 100 European. Mostly lithographs are cataloged by artist or by country.

MA —BOSTON UNIVERSITY, Mugar Memorial Library, Special Collections Dept, 771 Commonwealth Ave, Boston, 02215. Howard B Gotlieb, Dir
Holdings: // Cat Pix
Notes: Over 500 war posters; primarily World War I.

MA —AMERICAN JEWISH HISTORICAL SOCIETY, Library, 2 Thornton Rd, Waltham, 02154. Nathan M Kaganoff, Librn-Editor
Holdings: Vols 78,000 Cat Mss Pix Microforms
Budget: ($9000)
Notes: American Jewish history; incl paintings (100), theatre posters (500), sheet music (3500), mss (4 million). Calendar to individual collection published (2 vols).

MA —AMERICAN ANTIQUARIAN SOCIETY LIBRARY, 185 Salisbury St, Worcester, 01609. Marcus A McCorison, Dir & Librn
Holdings: Pix
Notes: About 1300 theatre posters, from the late 1870s to the mid-90s.

MI —UNIVERSITY OF MICHIGAN, Library, Dept of Rare Books & Special Collections, Ann Arbor, 48109. Robert J Starring, Head
Holdings: Pix
Notes: Incl about 320 American and French World War I posters, and about 500 election posters of German, covering the years 1950-1957. Partially checklisted on cards.

MN —MINNEAPOLIS PUBLIC LIBRARY & INFORMATION CENTER, 300 Nicollet Mall, Minneapolis, 55401. Richard J Hofstad, Athenaeum Librn
Holdings: Vols 5000 Cat Mpas Pix Periodicals
Notes: Incl 2000 posters of World War II era.

MN —UNIVERSITY OF MINNESOTA, O Meredith Wilson Library, 309 19 Ave S, Minneapolis, 55455. Austin J McLean, Chief, Special Collections
Holdings: Vols (6000)// Uncat
Notes: Extensive collection of multi-lingual propaganda pamphlets, political cartoons and posters. Complete listing available in the Division.

MN —MINNESOTA HISTORICAL SOCIETY LIBRARY, 690 Cedar St, Saint Paul, 55101. Patricia C Harpole, Chief of Reference Library; Bonnie G Wilson, Head of Special Libraries
Notes: Photographs, posters, art - over 150, 000 pictorial works - can be found in the Audio-Visual Library of the Minnesota Historical Society. The collection's emphasis is on Minnesota from the mid-1880's to the present day. Many aspects of American life can be researched in this collection.

NE —UNIVERSITY OF NEBRASKA-LINCOLN, Don L Love Library, University Archives and Special Collections, Lincoln, 68588. Joseph G Svoboda, University Archivist
Holdings: // Uncat
Notes: Collection consists mainly of pamphlets, clippings, posters, and other World War II ephemera; 1000 items.

NJ —FAIRLEIGH DICKINSON UNIVERSITY, Friendship Library, 285 Madison Ave, Madison, 07940. James

POSTERS—COLLECTIONS (cont.)

Fraser, Library Dir; Renee Weber, Cur
Holdings: Vols 1200 Cat Mss Pix Slides
Phonorecords 16mm Films
Notes: Official depository for the Outdoor
Advertising industry. Collection initiated in
August 1972. About 100,000 items. It is the
concern of the Outdoor Advertising
Association of America that this collection
become the definitive collection on the
industry in this country. Incl 20,000 mss, 10,
000 pictures, 30,000 slides. 15 original
billboards.

NJ —MONTCLAIR ART MUSEUM
LIBRARY, 3 South Mountain Ave, PO Box
1582, Montclair, 07042. Edith A Rights,
Librn
Holdings: Vols (10,000) Cat Pix Slides
Audiotapes
Budget: ($3500)
Notes: American painting and sculpture, Incl
5000 pictures; 10,000 slides; posters.
Audiotapes on American art and artists.

NJ —NEWARK PUBLIC LIBRARY, Art &
Music Dept, 5 Washington St, Newark,
07101. William J Dane, Supv
Notes: 4000 selected examples of poster art
and history, indexed, with groupings for
World Wars I and II, travel posters, and
many representative of the poster revival of
recent years; incl works by individual artists;
museum, gallery, and special event posters.

NJ —PRINCETON UNIVERSITY, Library,
William Seymour Theatre Collection,
Princeton, 08544. Mary Ann Jensen, Cur
Holdings: Vols (7000) Cat
Budget: ($10,000)
Notes: Plus scrapbooks, playbills, posters.

NY —NEW YORK STATE LIBRARY, State
Education Bldg Annex, Washington Ave,
Albany, 12224.
Holdings: Cat
Notes: World War I (including Benjamin
Walworth Arnold collection), World War II
(including war industries and civilian
cooperation); UN posters; a few theater
posters, miscellaneous items.

NY —BUFFALO & ERIE COUNTY PUBLIC
LIBRARY, Rare Book Room, Lafayette Sq,
Buffalo, 14203. William H Loos, Cur
Holdings: // Uncat
Notes: The collection of 3000 posters
consists primarily of World War I posters
with a few from World War II, as well as
some modern posters.

NY —NEW YORK PUBLIC LIBRARY,
Performing Arts Research Center, Billy Rose
Theatre Collection, 111 Amsterdam Ave,
New York, 10023. Dorothy L Swerdlove,
Cur
Holdings: Cat
See also entries under Circus; Moving
Picture Industry.

NY —NEW YORK PUBLIC LIBRARY,
Research Libraries, General Research
Division, Fifth Ave & 42 St, New York,
10018. Rodney Phillips, Chief
Holdings: Vols (2,225,000) Cat Maps Pix
Microforms
Budget: ($775,718)
Notes: See Subject Catalog of the World
War I Collection, The Research Libraries of
The Subject Catalog of The New York
Public Library's World War I Collection
forms an outstanding bibliography of the
subject, incl as it does, works in many
languages, analytical entries for important
articles in scholarly journals, and thousands
of pamphlets. Under the main heading
"European War, 1914-1918", there are over
one thousand subdivisions running from
"Addresses, sermons, etc" through "Women's
work."

NY —NEW YORK PUBLIC LIBRARY,
Performing Arts Research Center, Dance
Collection, 111 Amsterdam Ave, New York,
10023. Genevieve Oswald, Cur
Notes: About 4400 dance playbills and
posters. The posters are chiefly of the 20th
century, with greatest emphasis on American
dance. Extensive collection of posters for the
New York City Ballet, Ballet Theatre prior
to 1957, the Denishawn Dancers, and Anna
Pavlova. Also numerous posters and playbills

for Les Ballets Russes de Diaghilev and
Isadora Duncan. Mostly uncataloged.

NY —YIVO INSTITUTE FOR JEWISH
RESEARCH, Library & Archives, 1048
Fifth Ave, New York, 10028. Dina
Abramowicz, Librn; Marek Web, Archivist
Holdings: Cat Mss Pix Slides
Notes: Yiddish drama in the original and in
English translation from its 19th-century
beginnings to the present; the Yiddish
theatre in the Soviet Union and the
theatrical activities in the ghettos during the
Nazi regime; special collections of Sholem
Perelmuter, Mendl Elkin, Maurice Schwartz,
Abraham Goldfaden, Jacob Gordin, and
Mark Schweid; records of the Union of
Jewish Actors in Poland between the two
world wars; the Vilna YIVO Collection of
posters, playbills, and photographs;
recordings.

NY —MARGARET WOODBURY STRONG
MUSEUM, 1 Manhattan Square, Rochester,
14607.
Holdings: Vols (20,000) Periodicals
Notes: The Margaret Woodbury Strong
Museum Library contains a collection of
approx 20,000 books, periodicals and
ephemera of and concerning the 19th and
early 20th centuries. A large part of the
library's holdings reflect the interests of
Margaret Strong and her family: domestic
life and literature of the 19th century and
world travel, with particular emphasis on the
Orient. The library's resources are available
to all visitors for research. Book stacks and
rare book storage are not open for browsing
and do not circulate, but facilities are
provided in reading room for study.

NY —UNIVERSITY OF ROCHESTER, Rush
Rhees Library, Department of Rare Books
and Special Collections, Rochester, 14627.
Peter Dzwonkoski, Librn
Holdings: Vols (300) Cat Mss Pix
Notes: 19th century English and American
plays and works on theatre. Also includes
manuscript collections on theatre, and papers
of Clement William Scott, John Lawrence
Toole, Arthur Wing Pinero, Charles Kean,
Lillian Russell and Leon Marks Lion,
collection of 130 lithographic theatre
posters, and collection of programs and
playbills, chiefly Rochester, NY and New
York City, 1900-1950. Unpublished guides
to mss collections available in repository.

NY —VISUAL STUDIES WORKSHOP,
Research Center, 31 Prince St, Rochester,
14607. Linn Underhill, Coordr; Robert
Bretz, Librn
Holdings: Vols (8000) Cat Pix Slides
Audiotapes Videotapes
Notes: Strong emphasis on photography
(over 1,000,000 pictures) and the
photographic arts in many subject areas incl
in this volume. Heavy emphasis on early
photographic processes and collections of
examples of these. Also collections of
individual photographers' works.

NY —MUSEUM OF CARTOON ART
LIBRARY, Comly Avenue, Rye Brook,
10573.
Notes: Original comics and cartoon art, 60,
000 pieces. 800 animated cartoons. Disney
collection extensive. Samples of Big-Little
Books, foreign comics, fanzines, cartoon
related games, posters, pulps, undergrounds.
Hal Foster, Walt Kelly, Gene Byrns, Tad
Dorgan, Chester Gould extensive original art
collections.

OH —BOWLING GREEN STATE
UNIVERSITY, Library, Popular Culture
Library, Bowling Green, 43403.
Notes: Extensive holdings of Big-Little
books, comic books, matchbook covers,
picture postcards, personal scrapbooks,
trading cards, posters, magazines, film
pressbooks, juvenile series novels and
popular literature.

OH —CINCINNATI ART MUSEUM, Library,
Eden Park, Cincinnati, 45202. Patrician P
Rutledge, Librn
Holdings: Vols (45,850) Cat Mss Microforms
Notes: Art library containing all subjects on
art--history, graphic arts, advertising art, etc;
special strength in prints, ie engravings, etc.
Near Eastern art and decorative arts are also
strong. At least 90,000 art exhibition

catalogs. Emphasis on artists of Cincinnati
and vicinity in vertical file material.

OH —HEBREW UNION COLLEGE-JEWISH
INSTITUTE OF RELIGION, Klau Library,
3101 Clifton Ave, Cincinnati, 45220. David
J Gilner, Reference Librn
Holdings: Uncat
Notes: Incl 5000 posters, broadsides, leaflets
and various ephemera, mostly from Israel
and the US. Subjects incl charity, politics,
religion, culture, education, theatre, Zionism,
anti-Semitism, all of Jewish content.

OH —PUBLIC LIBRARY OF CINCINNATI
& HAMILTON COUNTY, Art & Music
Dept, 800 Vine St, Cincinnati, 45202. R
Jayne Craven, Head
Holdings: Vols (122,185) Cat Pix
Budget: ($56,100)
Notes: Special collections: Eda Kuhn Loeb,
"Artist and the Book, 1875-Date" (now
shelved in Rare Book Room); music librettos
(2345); exhibition catalogs (5474); large
prints and posters (5051); Cincinnati artists
vertical files; picture collection (673,906
clippings).

OH —OHIO STATE UNIVERSITY, Library
for Communication and Graphic Arts, 242
W 18th St, Columbus, 43210. Lucy S
Caswell, Curator
Notes: Original comic art of Caniff, Foster,
Dunn, Dudley T Fisher. Extensive original
cartoon art. Shel Dorf Collection of comic
strips and related material. A small but
growing collection of comic books especially
those featuring Katy Keene, is available in
the Library. Movie posters and stills, 110,
000. Incl Milton Caniff Research Room.

PA —FRANKLIN & MARSHALL
COLLEGE, Library, Lancaster, 17604.
Kathleen J Moretto, Library Dir
Holdings: Mss Pix
Notes: The Franklin J Schaffner Film
Library consists of shooting scripts in various
drafts, still photos, posters and other
memorabilia of all the motion picture films
directed by Mr Schaffner. Actual prints of
all the films incl, but not circulated.

PA —BALCH INSTITUTE FOR ETHNIC
STUDIES, Library, 18 S Seventh St,
Philadelphia, 19106. R Joseph Anderson,
Library Dir
Notes: War posters. Collections open in
1976.

PA —FREE LIBRARY OF PHILADELPHIA,
Theatre Collection, Logan Sq, Philadelphia,
19103. Geraldine Duclow, Librn-in-Charge
Holdings: Vols (1,250,000) Uncat Pix
Notes: The Theatre Collection contains
books, magazines, playbills, broadsides,
posters, photographs, and other memorabilia
covering theatre, motion pictures, minstrels,
vaudeville, circus, radio and television. The
Library's Philadelphia Theatre Index lists
the major productions here since 1855, and
partially indexes the collection of local
playbills which date back to 1803. There are
also programs from many other cities, incl
New York; some from London date back to
1800. Early film companies as well as the
present movie industry are represented by
advertising materials and over 30,000 film
stills. The Lubin Film Co (1910-1916)
Archive has been established with over 600
photographs and related items. Circus
programs and route books date back to 1900.
There are minstrel programs as early as
1865. Most significant are the mss from
Philadelphia's Dumont Minstrels.
Variousfiles contain autographs, photographs,
newspaper articles and reviews in all
pertinent subject areas. Noncirculating.

PA —TEMPLE UNIVERSITY LIBRARIES,
Special Collections Dept, Rare Books & Mss
Section, Philadelphia, 19122. Thomas M
Whitehead, Cur
Notes: 3000 posters of World War I and II,
and the Vietnam Conflict; US and foreign.
Card guide to World War I posters.

PA —UNIVERSITY OF PITTSBURGH,
Special Collections Dept, Curtis Theatre
Collection, 363 Hillman Library, Pittsburgh,
15260. Jeanette Blanco, Cur
Holdings: Vols (4000) Cat Mss Documents
Microforms Pix Slides VF
Notes: The legitimate theatre of plays,
musicals and vaudeville, chiefly of New

POSTERS—COLLECTIONS (cont.)

York City and Pittsburgh, from 1865, and other US, community, summer, college and foreign theatre. Incl 500,000 programs, 12,000 pictures, 300 posters, the Oliver P Merriman Scrapbooks and 300 other scrapbooks, clippings and other ephemera. Vols incl over 3000 acting editions and playscripts. Separate collections: Ralph G Allen Burlesque Skits Collection; Michael Ellis Papers; William P Halstead Theatre Collection; Kenyon Family Papers; Philip Dunning Playscripts Collection; Pittsburgh Playhouse Records; Pittsburgh Savoyards Records. Noncirculating.

PA —SWARTHMORE COLLEGE, Peace Collection, Swarthmore, 19081. Jean R Soderlund, Cur of Peace Collection
Holdings: Pix Cat
Notes: The poster collection, about 3000 items, incl material issued by the Peace Pledge Union and the Friends' peace societies of England, national branches of the Women's International League for Peace and Freedom, the League of Nations Association, the Emergency Peace Campaign (US, 1937), Clergy and Laity Concerned, American Friends Service Committee, SANE, and the 1932 disarmament campaign in France. Also included are World War I US government recruiting and food conservation posters, Red Cross posters, and some foreign items from the 1915-1931 period. Many recent posters of the anti Vietnam War and nuclear disarmament movements have been acquired through the issuing organizations through gift or deposit. The Peace Collection has been described in Downs 972, 978, 4633, and in Downs 1950-1961 Supplement 507 and 916.

RI —BROWN UNIVERSITY, John Hay Library, 20 Prospect St, Providence, 02912. Mary T Russo, Cur of Broadsides
Holdings: Vols (700)
Notes: The Broadside Collection holds a collection of posters of World War I and World War II, American and some foreign. Misc posters, some dealing with labor and temperance are also available.

RI —RHODE ISLAND SCHOOL OF DESIGN, Library, Two College St, Providence, 02903. James A Findlay, Dir
Holdings: Vols (70,000) Cat Pix Slides Phonorecords
Budget: ($50,000)
Notes: All fields of art incl 92,000 slides; 30,000 mounted photographs; 1100 posters and color reproductions; and 280,000 clippings.

TN —PUBLIC LIBRARY OF NASHVILLE & DAVIDSON COUNTY, Nashville Room, Eighth Ave N & Union, Nashville, 37203. David Marshall Stewart, Chief Librn
Holdings: Vols Pix
Notes: The Naff Collection of programs, autographed photographs, posters, etc tells the story of professional theatre in Nashville between 1900 and 1960. All materials noncirculating.

TX —EAST TEXAS STATE UNIVERSITY, James G Gee Library, Special Collections Dept, East Texas Station, Commerce, 75428. James Conrad, Dept Head
Holdings: Vols (3500) Cat Mss Pix Slides
Notes: The books on Black Literature (with the exception of those on Texas folklore) and Slavery in the US have been transferred to the general stack area of the library; however, our collection of county histories of Texas, which is still housed in the Special Collections, continues to grow. In addition, we have acquired sizeable collections of books on Texas folklore and Texas place names; and World War II posters. Another new area is printing arts in Texas. There is a separate dictionary card catalog for the book collection in the Special Collections Department.

TX —DALLAS PUBLIC LIBRARY, Fine Arts Div, 1515 Young St, Dallas, 75201. Richard L Waters, Acting Dir; Jane Holahan, Manager
Notes: 18th-20th century.

TX —FORT WORTH PUBLIC LIBRARY, Arts Division, 300 Taylor St, Fort Worth,

76102. Heather Gobel, Head
Notes: This special picture collection provides research service materials for requests in all subject areas requiring pictorial illustrations. Includes postal cards and poster collections. The fine arts reproductions comprise another separate collection of framed and matted and portfolio-contained pictures not included in the Subjects collection.

VA —GEORGE MASON UNIVERSITY, Fenwick Library, Special Collections Dept, 4400 University Drive, Fairfax, 22030. Ruth Kerns, Public Services Librn
Notes: The Federal Theatre Project Collection includes 5000 playscripts, 2500 radio scripts, 25,000 photographs, 40 blueprints, 1000 posters, over 1600 costume designs, 350 scene designs, 750 production notebooks, 1700 programs and heralds, 26 musical scores and 18 cubic feet of research materials and play readers reports.

†VA —GEORGE C MARSHALL RESEARCH FOUNDATION AND LIBRARY, Drawer 920, Lexington, 24450. Royster Lyle Jr, Cur Collections
Holdings: Vols Cat Mss Maps Pix Phonorecords Audiotapes Films Filmstrips Microforms
Notes: About 400 posters-American, German, French; complete Stars and Stripes for WWII; approx 5000 cataloged photographs, over 5000 uncataloged Office of War information photos, and over 10,000 US Signal Corps photos (uncat). Approx 250 regimental histories, operation reports, and army manuals; published memoirs and letters of Marshall associates; official military histories (American, British); over 1200 maps-approx 300 newsmaps, 800 daily situation maps (European Theatre), 37 bound vols of daily situation maps 1944-1945; seven of the Why We Fight series (films). Major ms collections incl the papers of generals George C Marshall, Marshall S Carter, William T Sexton, Lucian Truscott, William R Arnold, Paul M Robinett, Frank McCarthy; Forrest C Pogue; colonels Collas Harris, Francis P Miller, William F Friedman; officers of the Women's Army Corps. Hearingsand government documents. Agency records copied from NARS. Vertical file arranged by subject.

WA —UNIVERSITY OF WASHINGTON LIBRARIES, Drama Library, BH-20, Seattle, 98195. Liz Fugate, Drama Librn
Holdings: Vols
Budget: ($13,182)
Notes: Collection incl history; criticism; costume; make-up; scene design; lighting; creative dramatics; children's theatre; directing; playwriting; acting. Special Collections include 19th century acting editions, contemporary acting editions and local theatre posters. 17,731 items cataloged, 24,255 uncataloged.

WA —TACOMA PUBLIC LIBRARY, 1102 Tacoma Ave S, Tacoma, 98402. Kevin Hegarty, Dir
Holdings: Vols 1300 Mss Maps Posters
Notes: Collection of World War I propaganda pamphlets and posters. 1000 posters,, mostly US, but some French.

WI —MILWAUKEE PUBLIC LIBRARY, 814 W Wisconsin Ave, Milwaukee, 53233. Donald J Sager, City Librn
Holdings: Vols 15,000
Notes: Emphasis on historical posters (World Wars I and II), travel, safety, art exhibitions, and Milwaukee events. Theatrical, including minstrel and magicians.

AB —UNIVERSITY OF ALBERTA, Cameron Library, The Bruce Peel Special Collections Room, Edmonton, T6G 2J8, Can. John Charles, Special Collections Librn
Holdings: Cat
Notes: Several hundred theatre posters and playbills, 19th century British, and Vienna State Opera, 1940s.

ON —QUEEN'S UNIVERSITY, Douglas Library, Kingston, K7L 5C4, Can. William F E Morley, Cur, Special Collections
Holdings: Cat
Notes: Canadian Broadside Collection. 1100 broadsides, incl posters.

ON —NATIONAL FILM, TELEVISION AND SOUND ARCHIVES, Documentation

& Public Service, 395 Wellington St, Ottawa, K1A 0N3, Can. Jana Vosikovska, Chief; Gloria Grant, Librn; Sylvie Robitaille, Stills and Posters Librn
Notes: Several collections supporting the documentation on film, television and recorded sound: 1060 periodical titles (450 current), some on microfilm. Picture-stills, 265,000; moving picture posters, 6000; cataloged microfiche, 33,000 (vertical file material put on microfilm, then into a fiche format). Index cards (periodical reference credits): 334,000 cards (Film Title Index: 250,000 cards; Personalities Index: 84,000 cards).

ON —METROPOLITAN TORONTO LIBRARY, Theatre Dept, 789 Yonge St, Toronto, M4W 2G8, Can. Heather McCallum, Head
Holdings: Vols (30,500) Mss Pix Slides Phonorecords Microforms
Notes: A collection of over 4700 theatre, film, dance and circus posters incl a good record of Canadian professional theatre, British and American posters from the late 19th century, and Polish theatre and circus posters.

PQ —MCGILL UNIVERSITY, McLennan Library, Rare Books and Special Collections Dept, 3459 McTavish St, Montreal, H3A 1Y1, Can.
Notes: 12,680 original prints and posters dating from the 16th century to the present. Prints representing many graphic techniques; special subject areas such as: early railways, Japanese woodblocks, Napoleon, early Canadian portraits.
See also entry under Puppets and Puppet Plays.

POSTMODERN AMERICAN POETS

CT —UNIVERSITY OF CONNECTICUT, Library, Storrs, 06268. R H Schimmelpfeng, Dir of Special Collections
Holdings: Cat Mss Pix Audiotapes
Notes: Focuses on poets brought to attention by Donald Allen's New American Poetry anthology: the Black Mountain, New York, San Francisco, Beat poets, and their successors; the Postmodern American poets, such as Charles Olson, Robert Creeley, Robert Duncan, Allen Ginsberg, Edward Dorn, Frank O'Hara, Gary Snyder, LeRoi Jones/Imamu Baraka, and Denise Levertov.

POST-OBJECT ART see Art, Conceptual

POST-OFFICE BUILDINGS see Postal Service—Buildings

POTASH

IN —INTERNATIONAL MINERALS & CHEMICAL CORP, R & D Library, 1331 S First St, PO Box 207, Terre Haute, 47808. Ruth Smedlund, Librn
Holdings: Vols (50,000) Cat Maps Microforms
Notes: Phosphate and potash fertilizers.

POTAWATOMI INDIANS

KS —UNIVERSITY OF KANSAS, Kenneth Spencer Research Library, Kansas Collection, Lawrence, 66045. Sheryl K Williams, Cur
Holdings: Cat Pix
Notes: The Floyd Schultz Photographic Collection mainly treating Potawatomie Indians (Prairie Band). About 450 photographs.

ON —CHATHAM PUBLIC LIBRARY, 120 Queen St, Chatham, N7M 2G6, Can. Arlene Mason, Head of Reference
Notes: Material on the Indians of Kent County, Ont, incl articles and books on the Potawatomis and Chippewas of Walpole Island Reserve and on the Delaware Indians brought to Canada by the Moravian Missionaries in 1792 (the Fairfield Mission).

POTS see Kettles

POTSHERDS (OSTRAKA) see Ostraka

POTTAWATAMIE INDIANS see Potawatomi Indians

POTTER, ALBERT F.

AZ —NORTHERN ARIZONA UNIVERSITY, Special Collection Library,

POTTER, ALBERT F. (cont.)

CU Box 6022, Flagstaff, 86011. Peter M Whiteley, Coordr/Archivist; William Mullane, Librn
Notes: Diary of A F Potter, apparently a government official, written while touring the cattle and sheep ranges of Texas, New Mexico, and Arizona, 1904.

POTTER, BEATRIX

PA —FREE LIBRARY OF PHILADELPHIA, Rare Book Dept, Logan Sq, Philadelphia, 19103. Marie E Korey, Rare Book Librn
Holdings: Vols 350 Cat Mss Pix
Notes: The H Bacon Collamore Collection, with additions, containing first editions, association copies, manuscripts, autograph letters, and original art.

POTTER FAMILY

DE —UNIVERSITY OF DELAWARE, Hugh M Morris Library, S College Ave, Newark, 19711. T Stuart Dick, Special Collections
Holdings: // Mss
Notes: Personal and business papers of the Potter Family, a Philadelphia merchant family prominent in the import trade with Central America, particularly Nicaragua (1801-1943).

POTTERY

CA —CALIFORNIA COLLEGE OF ARTS & CRAFTS, Meyer Library, Broadway at College, Oakland, 94618. Robert L Harper, Head Librn
Holdings: Vols (29,132) Cat Pix
Budget: ($10,000)
Notes: All fields of arts and crafts.

IN —ALLEN COUNTY PUBLIC LIBRARY, 900 Webster St, Fort Wayne, 46802. Paul Deane, Reader Services Dept Head; Kay Lynn Isca, Art Music & AV Dept Head
Holdings: Vols Cat Pix

LA —R W NORTON ART GALLERY, Library, 4747 Creswell Ave, Shreveport, 71106. Jerry M Bloomer, Librn
Holdings: Cat
Notes: Primary histories on pottery and porcelain-making in America and Europe and books of interest to collectors.

MA —OLD STURBRIDGE VILLAGE, Research Library, Sturbridge, 01566. Theresa Rini Percy, Librn
Holdings: Cat Mss Pix
Notes: Craft and product, especially in New England, 1790-1850; some English works.

MO —THE NELSON-ATKINS MUSEUM OF ART, Kenneth & Helen Spencer Art Reference Library, 4525 Oak St, Kansas City, 64111. Stanley W Hess, Librn

NY —NEW YORK STATE COLLEGE OF CERAMICS AT ALFRED UNIVERSITY, Scholes Library, Harder Hall, Alfred, 14802. Bruce E Connolly, Library Dir
Holdings: Vols (70,000) Cat Mss Slides Microforms
Budget: ($134,000)
Notes: Very specialized collection incl all phases of the arts and sciences related to ceramics. Incl 1112 subscriptions.

NC —MINT MUSEUM OF ART, Delhom-Gambrell Reference Library, 501 Hempstead Place, Charlotte, 28207. Sara H Wolf, Librn
Holdings: Vols (3430) Cat Pix Slides
Notes: Library has added 2 private collections on Oriental ceramics (approx 800 volumes, not cataloged) and on decorative arts, mostly French Ceramics (approx 500 volumes, not cataloged). No photocopying.

OH —JOHN MCINTIRE PUBLIC LIBRARY, 220 N Fifth St, Zanesville, 43701. Peg Harmon, Librn
Holdings: Vols 100 Cat

RI —RHODE ISLAND SCHOOL OF DESIGN, Library, Two College St, Providence, 02903. James A Findlay, Dir
Holdings: Vols (70,000) Cat
Budget: ($50,000)

WI —MILWAUKEE PUBLIC LIBRARY, 814 W Wisconsin Ave, Milwaukee, 53233. Donald J Sager, City Librn
Holdings: Vols Cat
Notes: Special strength.
See also entry under Art, Decorative.

POTTERY, CHINESE

KS —OTTAWA UNIVERSITY, Myers Library, Ottawa, 66067. J Marion Rioth, Head Librn
Holdings: Vols 2350 Cat Maps Pix
Budget: $150
Notes: This started as a collection of studies about Chinese ceramics, art, and related areas. Incl 800 vols on general Asian studies. If this collection has any unique feature it is in the field of 19th century ceramics trade, especially Chinese. There is a bibliography of the collection.

POTTOWATOMIE INDIANS see Potawatomi Indians

POULENC, FRANCIS

DC —LIBRARY OF CONGRESS, Music Division, Washington, 20540.
Notes: Mss in Koussevitzky Archives.

POULSON, NORRIS

CA —UNIVERSITY OF CALIFORNIA, LOS ANGELES, Research Library, Dept of Special Collections, 405 Hilgard Ave, Los Angeles, 90024. Edward Shreeves, Chairman, Bibliographers Group; David S Zeidberg, Head
Notes: 5 linear feet of correspondence and photographs, mostly relating to his two terms and mayor of Los Angeles.

POULTRY

IA —IOWA STATE UNIVERSITY, Library, Dept of Special Collections, Ames, 50011. Stanley M Yates, Head
Holdings: Mss
Notes: Papers of Poultry Science Association. Organized in 1908, its members are engaged in teaching, research or extension and in technical services to the poultry industry. 11 linear ft, finding aid available.

KS —KANSAS STATE UNIVERSITY, Library, Special Collections & University Archives, Manhattan, 66506. Antonia Q Pigno, Coordr; John J Vander Velde, Librn; Anthony R Crawford, Univ Archivist
Holdings: Vols 1000
Budget: ($10,000)
Notes: Collection bequeathed by Leonora C Hering and contains rare first editions. Focus is on poultry breeding with peripheral materials featuring poultry, such as children's books and poetry.

MD —US DEPT OF AGRICULTURE, National Agricultural Library, 10301 Baltimore Blvd, Beltsville, 20705. Joseph H Howard, Director
Notes: NAL has acquired the poultry library of Dr James M Gwin, incl such rarities as the 1843 and 1844 American Poultry Book and the original 1750 French edition of The Art of Hatching Fowls.

NY —CORNELL UNIVERSITY LIBRARIES, James E Rice Memorial Poultry Library, Ithaca, 14853. Jan Olsen, Librn
Holdings: Vols 4500 Cat

OH —CLEVELAND PUBLIC LIBRARY, Science & Technology Dept, 325 Superior Ave, Cleveland, 44114. Jean Z Piety, Head
Holdings: Cat
Notes: Collection contains much on history and many early and rare volumes.

TX —AMARILLO PUBLIC LIBRARY, 413 E Fourth, Amarillo, 79101. Mary Kay Snell, Librn
Holdings: Vols 1210 Cat Maps Filmstrips VF
Notes: The Meat Industry Collection contains documents, periodicals, pamphlets, AV materials on the production of processing and marketing of cattle, swine, sheep, poultry and rabbits. Most of the collection circulates except for the magazines.

WI —UNIVERSITY OF WISCONSIN, MADISON, College of Agricultural & Life Sciences, Steenbock Memorial Library, 550 Babcock Dr, Madison, 53706. Jan Kennedy, Dir
Holdings: Vols (186,312) Cat Microforms
Notes: Extensive general agricultural collection supporting the College of Agricultural and Life Sciences in agronomy, dairy science, agricultural engineering, entomology, botany, natural resources, nutrition, forestry, genetics, veterinary science, meat and animal science, poultry science, soils. Collection incl USDA, USDI, experiment station and state documents.

POULTRY BREEDING

IA —IOWA STATE UNIVERSITY, Library, Dept of Special Collections, Ames, 50011. Stanley M Yates, Head
Holdings: Mss
Notes: Papers of Poultry Science Association. Organized in 1908, its members are engaged in teaching, research or extension and in technical services to the poultry industry. 11 linear ft, finding aid available.

MA —UNIVERSITY OF MASSACHUSETTS AT AMHERST, Library, Amherst, 01003. Siegfried Feller, Assoc Dir for Collection Development
Holdings: Cat
Notes: Veterinary medicine and animal sciences. Special emphases: reproductive physiology, poultry genetics, animal nutrition.

POULTRY SCIENCE ASSOCIATION

IA —IOWA STATE UNIVERSITY, Library, Dept of Special Collections, Ames, 50011. Stanley M Yates, Head
Holdings: Mss
Notes: Organized in 1908, its members are engaged in teaching, research or extension and in technical services to the poultry industry. 11 linear ft, finding aid available.

POUND, DOROTHY SHAKESPEARE

IN —INDIANA UNIVERSITY, Lilly Library, Seventh St, Bloomington, 47405. William R Cagle, Librn
Notes: Incl more than 12,000 letters from the estate of Dorothy Shakespeare Pound, widow of Ezra Pound, ranging from 1900 to 1973, but concentrated between 1946 and 1958, the years of his confinement at St Elizabeths Hospital.

POUND, EZRA LOOMIS, 1885-1972

CA —UNIVERSITY OF CALIFORNIA, BERKELEY, Bancroft Library, Manuscripts Division, Berkeley, 94720. James D Hart, Dir
Holdings: Uncat Mss
Notes: Collection off letters and a few mss; also letters from Pound in various collections.

CA —UNIVERSITY OF CALIFORNIA, LOS ANGELES, Research Library, Dept of Special Collections, 405 Hilgard Ave, Los Angeles, 90024. Edward Shreeves, Chairman, Bibliographers Group; David S Zeidberg, Head
Holdings: Vols 175 Mss
Notes: 175 first and other editions of his books; 1 linear foot of correspondence and mss. No photocopying without permission of his literary heirs.

CA —UNIVERSITY OF CALIFORNIA, RIVERSIDE, University Library, 4045 Canyon Crest Dr, Box 5900, Riverside, 92517.
Holdings: Vols 700
Notes: Comprehensive collection of works by and about Pound, primarily works in print, incl books, pamphlets, dissertations, editions of his works, first and rare editions.

CA —UNIVERSITY OF CALIFORNIA, SANTA BARBARA, Library, Dept of Special Collections, Santa Barbara, 93106. Christian F Brun, Head
Holdings: Vols 150 Cat Mss
Notes: Books, pamphlets, correspondence by and about Ezra Pound, Many editions.

CA —UNIVERSITY OF CALIFORNIA, SANTA CRUZ, University Library, Special

POUND, EZRA LOOMIS, 1885-1972 (cont.)

Collections, Santa Cruz, 95064. Rita Bottoms, Special Collections Librn; Margaret Felts, South Pacific Collection Bibliographer

CT —YALE UNIVERSITY, Box 1603A, Yale Station, New Haven, 06520.
Holdings: Cat Mss

DE —UNIVERSITY OF DELAWARE, Hugh M Morris Library, S College Ave, Newark, 19711. T Stuart Dick, Special Collections
Holdings: Cat Mss Pix
Notes: Manuscripts, etc, incl literary correspondence.

ID —UNIVERSITY OF IDAHO, Library, Dept of Special Collections & Archives, Moscow, 83843.
Holdings: Vols 305 Cat Phonorecords Audiotapes Microforms
Budget: $1000
Notes: Incl rare, first, signed, and limited editions; also, association copies. Contains the FBI files (photocopies) of Pound's trials, described in *A Bibliography of Material by and about Ezra Pound Held by the University of Idaho Library*, Milo G Nelson (Moscow: Univ of Idaho, 1975).

IL —NORTHWESTERN UNIVERSITY, Library, Special Collections Dept, 1937 Sheridan Rd, Evanston, 60201. R Russell Maylone, Cur
Holdings: Vols 225 Cat Mss
Notes: First editions, letters, works by and about him.

IN —INDIANA UNIVERSITY, Lilly Library, Seventh St, Bloomington, 47405. William R Cagle, Librn
Holdings: Vols 157 Cat Mss
Notes: An extensive collection of original editions of Ezra Pound. Ms incl more than 12,000 letters from the estate of Dorothy Shakespeare Pound, widow of Ezra Pound, ranging from 1900 to 1973, but concentrated between 1946 and 1958, the years of his confinement at St Elizabeths Hospital. Letters from Pound to his friend and mentor, Agnes Bedford. 1919-1933. Correspondence with William Bird of Three Mountains Press, 1922-1947. Letters to Pound, 1919-1924 from various friends and literary figures including Hemingway, T S Eliot, D G Bridson and John Quinn. Manuscript drafts of Pound's translations of French novelist Paul Morand's stories.

MA —HARVARD UNIVERSITY LIBRARY, Houghton Library, Cambridge, 02138. Rodney G Dennis, Cur of Manuscripts
Holdings: Cat Mss

MO —WASHINGTON UNIVERSITY, John M Olin Library, Campus Box 1061, St Louis, 63130.
Notes: Extensive collection of printed material, some correspondence and mss.

MO —WASHINGTON UNIVERSITY, Libraries, Special Collections Dept, Campus Box 1061, St Louis, 63130.
Notes: A small but significant collection.

NY —HAMILTON COLLEGE, Daniel Burke Library, Special Collections Dept, Clinton, 13323. Frank K Lorenz, Cur
Holdings: Vols 1000 Cat Mss Pix Phonorecords Audiotapes 16mm Films Microforms
Notes: Comprehensive collection of works by and about him. Primarily works in print, incl books, pamphlets, articles, dissertations. Incl numerous editions of Pound's works.

NY —NEW YORK PUBLIC LIBRARY, Fifth Ave & 42 St, New York, 10018.
Holdings: Cat Mss

NY —STATE UNIVERSITY OF NEW YORK, STONY BROOK, Melville Library, Dept of Special Collections, Stony Brook, 11794. Evert Volkersz, Head
Holdings: Vols 105 Cat

NC —UNIVERSITY OF NORTH CAROLINA, GREENSBORO, Walter Clinton Jackson Library, Special Collections Dept, 1000 Spring Garden St, Greensboro, 27412. Emilie W Mills, Librn
Holdings: // Cat Mss
Notes: Letters of Ezra, Omar and Dorothy Pound to the late Elizabeth Winslow of Asheboro, NC. The letters of 1945-1948

were written by Ezra Pound when he was a patient at St Elizabeth's Hospital, where Miss Winslow visited the author. No photocopying.

RI —UNIVERSITY OF RHODE ISLAND, Library, Special Collections, Kingston, 02881. David Maslyn, Head
Notes: Extensive collections.

RI —BROWN UNIVERSITY, John Hay Library, 20 Prospect St, Providence, 02912. Mark N Brown, Cur Mss
Holdings: //
Notes: A small collection of 24 letters, chiefly from Pound, 1917-1956, to younger writers stating his position on poetry, censorship, criticism, government, and economics. Also 6 printed broadsides by or about Pound. Register available.

RI —BROWN UNIVERSITY, John Hay Library, Harris Collection, Prospect St, Providence, 02912. Rosemary L Cullen, Cur
Holdings: Vols (200,000) Cat Mss Pix Phonorecords Microforms
Budget: ($15,000)
Notes: The Harris Collection of American Poetry and Plays is principally composed of American and Canadian poetry and plays, 17th century-date. Extensive holdings in songsters, gift books and annuals, hymnals, pageants, broadside verse, carriers' addresses, women poets, juvenile poetry, (incl Mother Goose and *The Night Before Christmas*), sheet music with lyrics, small press publications, fine printing, black poets, "little magazines," Yiddish-American literature. All movements or schools of American poetry are represented. Incl first editions of most American poets and playwrights, notably Whitman, Poe, Wallace Stevens, Eugene O'Neill, Edward Albee, Ezra Pound, T S Eliot, William Carlos Williams, Amy Lowell, Phyllis Wheatley, Robert Frost, Allen Ginsberg, Bliss Carman, and Stephen Foster sheet music. Also incl the Saunders Walt Whitman Collection (1300 vols); the LangdonCollection of Pageants (250 vols); the Asa Cushman Collection of plays in ms and prompt copies; the MacDougall Collection of Psalters and Hymnals; 4000 plays issued by Walter H Baker Co, Boston (1890-1957); the Vaxer Collection of Yiddish Poetry, Plays and Music (1700 vols). Collections incl 200,000 vols, 30,000 broadsides, 55,000 mss, 170,000 pieces of sheet music, 450 phonorecords, and 375 microfilm reels. See *Dictionary Catalog of the Harris Collection of American Poetry and Plays* (Boston: G K Hall, 1972), 13 vols; *Supplement* (1977), 3 vols. See also, *American Poetry, 1609-1900, A Collection on Microfilm, Segment I* (1609-1820); *Segment II* (1821-1850); *Segment III* (1851-1870) (Woodbridge, Conn: Research Publications). Separate catalog.

VA —UNIVERSITY OF VIRGINIA, Alderman Library, Clifton Waller Barrett Collection, Charlottesville, 22901. Joan St C Crane, Cur of American Literature Collections
Holdings: Vols 300

BC —SIMON FRASER UNIVERSITY, Library, Burnaby, V5A 1S6, Can. Percilla Groves, Special Collections Librn
Holdings: Cat Mss
Notes: Incl a collection of 75 letters to Agnes Bedford and 5 letters to Wyndham Lewis, 1950-1959, plus 46 letters to Denis Goacher, an English poet and actor who supported Pound during his years in St Elizabeths, and 140 pages to Sinologist Willis Hawley, with carbons of Hawley's letters to Pound; also graphics for *Confucius: The Great Digest and Unwobbling Pivot,* and for *The Cantos.*

BC —UNIVERSITY OF VICTORIA, McPherson Library, Victoria, V8W 3H5, Can.
Notes: Mss, "Nils Lykke," "A Prologue," "That Audience, or the Bugaboo of the Public," *Personae;* corrected proofs *Personae, Lustra, Canzoni* and *Ripostes;* correspondence: St John Adcock, Montgomery Belgion, British Union of Fascists, Clifford Gessler, Michael Harald, Elkin Mathews, Else Seel, Louis Zukofsky.

POUND, LOUISE

NE —UNIVERSITY OF NEBRASKA-LINCOLN, Don L Love Library, University

Archives and Special Collections, Lincoln, 68588. Joseph G Svoboda, University Archivist
Notes: Virginia Faulkner was recognized as one of Nebraska's most distinguished writers and scholars. The Virginia Faulkner Collection, containing over 2000 titles, is housed in the Special Collections Department of Love Library. It is especially strong in twentieth century writers and in University of Nebraska Press publications. Of especial value to scholars are her extensive holdings of Willa Cather, Wright Morris, and John Neihardt. Her correspondence with S N Behrman, E B White, Edward Wagenknecht, Donald Sutherland, Wright Morris, Louise Pound, Mari Sandoz, Hazel Barnes, Alfred A and Blanche Knopf, and others provide insight into the literary development of these figures, as well as chronicle the intellectual thought of the period. Amassed in a separate file, these letters are available to interested scholars.

POUND, ROSCOE, 1870-1964

MA —HARVARD UNIVERSITY LIBRARY, Law School Library, Langdell Hall, Cambridge, 02138. Erika S Chadbourn, Cur of Mss
Holdings: Cat Mss
Notes: Personal-professional papers; memorabilia. Typed inventory in repository. Inclusive dates: 1889-1964.

POVERTY

CA —UNIVERSITY OF CALIFORNIA, BERKELEY, Institute of Governmental Studies Library, 109 Moses Hall, Berkeley, 94720. Jack Leister, Head Librn
Holdings: Vols (350,000) Cat Mss Maps Microforms
Budget: ($160,000)
Notes: The library collects primarily pamphlets. Incl in the library's holdings are documents from all levels of government, as well as publications issued by professional associations and special interest groups. A G K Hall catalog covering the Institute's Library holdings is available. Since 1937, Library has been depository for all California local documents (city, county & special district). Formerly: Bureau of Public Administration.

IL —UNIVERSITY OF ILLINOIS, URBANA/CHAMPAIGN, Library, University Archives, 1408 W Gregory Drive, Urbana, 61801. Maynard Brichford, Univ Archivist
Holdings: Cat Mss Pix
Notes: Original mss and 91 tapes of interviews for anthropological work, the gift of Oscar Lewis, largely concerning his studies of the culture of poverty.

†MA —JOHN F KENNEDY LIBRARY, Columbia Point, Boston, 02125. Dan H Fenn Jr, Dir
Holdings: // Cat Mss
Notes: Daniel Knapp's background materials for his book *Scouting the War on Poverty* and his papers relating to the President's Commission on Juvenile Delinquency, late 1950s-late 1960s. 19 linear ft of mss. Holdings are described in "Historical Materials in the John F Kennedy Library." Copies may be obtained by writing the Research Archivist.

MA —NEW ENGLAND QUAKER RESEARCH LIBRARY, PO Box 655, North Amherst, 01059. Francis W Holmes, Librn
Holdings: Vols (6000) Cat Mss Pix Slides Phonorecords Audiotapes Microforms
Budget: ($300)
Notes: No photocopying on premises. Subject emphases: Quakers and Quaker concerns; Pacifism; Racism; Feminism; Religion; Bible; Poverty.

POWDER METALLURGY

MI —GENERAL ELECTRIC COMPANY, Carboloy Systems Department, Library, Box 237, GPO, Detroit, 48232.
Holdings: Vols (4500) Cat Maps Slides

POWDER METALLURGY (cont.)

16mm Films Filmstrips Microforms
Budget: ($5000)
Notes: Collection covers cemented carbide cutting tools, powder metallurgy, metal cutting, metalworking, machining, and related subjects. Also numerical control, statistics (related to the cutting tool industry) and general management. Incl 500 maps, 4000 slides, 61 films, 261 filmstrips, 700 microfiche, 7000 patents, and 300 periodical titles.
PA —COLT INDUSTRIES, Crucible Research Center Library, Box 88, Pittsburgh, 15230. Patricia J Aducci, Technical Librn

POWELL, ANTHONY

†CA —STANFORD UNIVERSITY LIBRARIES, Stanford, 94305.
Notes: In collection of English and American Literature.
NV —UNIVERSITY OF NEVADA, RENO, University Library, Special Collections Dept, Reno, 89557. Robert E Blesse, Head
Holdings: Vols (65) Cat Other appearances 225 Cat
Notes: Includes individual works by author in all editions including translations; also prefaces, introductions, published correspondence, appearances in anthologies, periodicals, etc. Bibliographical research collection, part of Modern Authors Collection.

POWELL, EDWARD B.

CA —UNIVERSITY OF CALIFORNIA, LOS ANGELES, Music Library, Schonberg Hall, Los Angeles, 90024. Stephen M Fry, Music Librn
Notes: Mss

POWELL, JOHN

VA —UNIVERSITY OF VIRGINIA, Alderman Library, Music Collection, Charlottesville, 22901. Evan Bonds, Music Librn
Holdings: Vols (38,000) Cat Mss Microforms
Budget: ($22,000)
Notes: Sizeable amount of rare book material: extensive ms collections, principally of traditional music; extensive collection of miscellaneous imprints of performing editions; valuable collection of 18th-century imprints incl rare tutors, etc in the Alexander MacKay-Smith Collection; the Monticello Music Collection; printed and ms collection of the music of John Powell; extensive collections, ms and typescript, and discs of traditional music; some Randall Thompson mss; 250 tapes; 9000 phonorecords.

POWELL, LAWRENCE CLARK, 1906-

CA —CLAREMONT COLLEGES, Ella Strong Denison Library, Scripps College, Claremont, 91711. Judy Harvey Sahak, Librn
Holdings: Vols 200 // Cat
Notes: Gift of W W Robinson includes books, many inscribed to Robinson; articles, reviews, and typescripts.
CA —UNIVERSITY OF CALIFORNIA, LOS ANGELES, Research Library, Dept of Special Collections, 405 Hilgard Ave, Los Angeles, 90024. Edward Shreeves, Chairman, Bibliographers Group; David S Zeidberg, Head
Holdings: Cat Mss
Notes: 55 linear feet of mss, correspondence, memorabilia, etc.
CT —YALE UNIVERSITY, Box 1603A, Yale Station, New Haven, 06520.

POWELL, THOMAS REED, 1880-1955

MA —HARVARD UNIVERSITY LIBRARY, Law School Library, Langdell Hall, Cambridge, 02138. Erika S Chadbourn, Cur of Mss
Holdings: Cat Mss
Notes: Personal-professional papers. Typed

inventory in repository. Inclusive dates: 1905-1955.

POWER (MECHANICS)

PA —FRANKLIN INSTITUTE LIBRARY, 20 & The Parkway, Philadelphia, 19103. Miriam Padusis, Dir; Charles Wilt, Readers Servs Librn
Holdings: Vols (300,000) Cat Maps Pix Micrforms
WA —WESTERN WASHINGTON UNIVERSITY, Center for Pacific Northwest Studies, High St, Bellingham, 98225. James W Scott, Dir
Holdings: Vols 400 // Cat Mss
Notes: Puget Sound Power and Light Company Records Collection consists of the complete company records of 41 former companies, which were bought out, amalgamated with or in other ways came under the control of Puget Sound Power and Light Company. Most of the companies were concerned with transportation or the production of power--both gas and electricity. Among the companies represented are street railways, interuban railways, traction companies and gas companies, all of which operated in the region west of the Cascades, especially in the Puget Sound area but with a few as far south as Vancouver, Washington. The collection has been placed in the Center for Pacific Northwest Studies by the Puget Sound Power and Light Company on a permanent loan basis.

POWER (SOCIAL SCIENCES)

MA —HARVARD UNIVERSITY, Graduate School of Business Administration, Baker Library, Soldiers Field, Boston, 02163. Mary V Chatfield, Librn; Florence Bartoshesky, Cur of Manuscripts and Archives
Holdings: Cat
Notes: List of special collection (*Power & Morality* by Benjamin M Selekman) published by the library, 1963.
NY —COLUMBIA UNIVERSITY LIBRARIES, Rare Book & Manuscript Library, 801 Butler Library, 535 W 114 St, New York, 10027. Kenneth A Lohf, Librn
Holdings: Mss
Notes: Incl the papers (5000 items) of Professor Robert Morrison MacIver: correspondence, notes, drafts of mss, etc on sociology, political power and juvenile delinquency, incl his participation on the City of New York Juvenile Delinquency Evaluation Project, on which he served after his retirement from Columbia University. Restricted use.

POWER, ELECTRIC see Electric Power

POWER, POLITICAL see Power (Social Sciences)

POWER PLANTS

CO —STONE & WEBSTER ENGINEERING CORP, Technical Information Center, PO Box 5406, Denver, 80217. Sue Newhams, Librn
Holdings: Vols (5000) Cat Microforms
Notes: The subject emphasis of this collection is centered around the power industry and energy resources.
OH —PREFORMED LINE PRODUCTS CO, Research & Engineering Library, 660 Beta Drive, Mayfield Village, (Mailing add: PO Box 91129, Cleveland, 44101). Edwina T Barron, Librn
Holdings: Vols (11,500) Cat Mss Microfiche Pix VF
Budget: ($30,500)
Notes: Library covering research and engineering fields emphasizing this subject. Aerodynamic characteristics and electrical characteristics of power cables, communication cables (including fiber optics), cable support systems, as well as associated fittings and hardware; in service behavior of manufactured products and materials as it relates to its static and

dynamic forces and environmental conditions; oceanographic cable fittings and terminations.
TN —TENNESSEE VALLEY AUTHORITY (TVA), Technical Library, 400 W Summit Hill Dr, E2 B7, Knoxville, 37902. Jesse C Mills, Chief Librn
Holdings: Vols (106,900) Cat Mss Maps Pix Audiotapes Microforms
Budget: ($2,025,000)
Notes: The Technical Library Headquarters Staff (order, cataloging, information, and administration) is located in Knoxville, Tenn. In addition there are branch libraries in Knoxville, Norris, and Chattanooga, Tennessee, and Muscle Shoals, Alabama.
WA —WESTERN WASHINGTON UNIVERSITY, Center for Pacific Northwest Studies, High St, Bellingham, 98225. James W Scott, Dir
Holdings: Vols 400 // Cat Mss
Notes: Puget Sound Power and Light Company Records Collection consists of the complete company records of 41 former companies, which were bought out, amalgamated with or in other ways came under the control of Puget Sound Power and Light Company. Most of the companies were concerned with transportation or the production of power--both gas and elecricity. Among the companies represented are street railways, interurban railways, traction companies and gas companies, all of which operated in the region west of the Cascades, especially in the Puget Sound area but with a few as far south as Vancouver, Washington. The collection has been placed in the Center for Pacific Northwest Studies by the Puget Sound Power and Light Company on a permanent loan basis.

POWER PLANTS, ATOMIC see Atomic Power Plants

POWER PLANTS, GAS see Gas Power Plants

POWER RESOURCES

AL —SOUTHERN NATURAL GAS CO, Corporate Library, PO Box 2563, Birmingham, 35202. Regina Hinkle, Librn
Holdings: Vols 2500 Cat Mss Maps
CA —UNIVERSITY OF CALIFORNIA, BERKELEY, Giannini Foundation of Agricultural Economics, Library, 248 Giannini Hall, Berkeley, 94720. Grace Dote, Librn
Holdings: Cat Microforms
Notes: Energy resources (oil, gas, geothermal, etc). Material dates primarily from 1972.
CA —UNIVERSITY OF CALIFORNIA, LOS ANGELES, Research Library, Dept of Special Collections, 405 Hilgard Ave, Los Angeles, 90024. Edward Shreeves, Chairman, Bibliographers Group; David S Zeidberg, Head
Holdings: // Uncat Mss
Notes: In various collections, incl the John Randolph Haynes and Dora Haynes Foundation Collections.
CA —UNIVERSITY OF CALIFORNIA, RIVERSIDE, Physical Sciences Library, Riverside, 92517. Richard W Vierich, Librn
Holdings: Vols (89,000) Cat Microforms
Budget: ($247,700)
CA —HOOVER INSTITUTION ON WAR, REVOLUTION & PEACE, Stanford University, Stanford, 94305. Milorad M Drachkovitch, Archivist
Holdings: Mss
Notes: Papers of John A Busterud, US attorney and public official, Deputy Assistant Secretary of Defense for Environmental Quality, 1971-72, Chairman of the Council on Environmental Quality, Executive Office of the President, 1972-77, incl correspondence, speeches and writings, memoranda, reports, studies, printed matter, and other material, 1972-77, relating to his government service in the US, and to international and domestic energy and environmental programs. 22 ms boxes.
CO —STONE & WEBSTER ENGINEERING CORP, Technical Information Center, PO

POWER RESOURCES (cont.)

Box 5406, Denver, 80217. Sue Newhams, Librn
Holdings: Vols (5000) Cat Microforms
Notes: The subject emphasis of this collection is centered around the power industry and energy resources.

DC —EDISON ELECTRIC INSTITUTE, Library-8th Floor, 1111 19th St NW, Washington, 20036. Ethel Tiberg, Mgr, Library Services
Holdings: Vols (13,321) Cat Maps Pix Microforms

DC —FOSTER ASSOCIATES, Library, 1101 17th St NW, Washington, 20036. A Blandamer, Librn
Notes: The principal subject areas are public utility regulation and economics, and energy economics.

IL —PEOPLES GAS, LIGHT & COKE COMPANY, Library, 122 S Michigan Ave Rm 727, Chicago, 60603. Rosann Meagher, Librn
Holdings: Vols 5000 Cat Maps
Notes: The gas industry, incl production and distribution.

IL —UNIVERSITY OF ILLINOIS, URBANA/CHAMPAIGN, Library, Geology Library, 223 Natural History Bldg, Urbana, 61801. Dederick Ward, Librn
Holdings: Vols (105,186) Cat Maps Microforms

KS —WICHITA PUBLIC LIBRARY, 223 S Main, Wichita, 67202. Larry DePiesse, Head, Business & Technology Dept; Jayne F Young, Business & Technology Dept
Holdings: Vols 800 Cat
Budget: $700
Notes: 456 of our holdings are circulating books. The remaining 344 books are in a special non-circulating collection, the "Energy Collection." Includes solar, wind, nuclear, etc.

MA —NEW ENGLAND ELECTRIC SYSTEM, Technical Information Center, 25 Research Dr, Westborough, 01581. William J McCall, Librn
Holdings: Vols 2350 Cat Microforms
Notes: Compile KWIC index to our special and technical reports. Also compile indexes to industry newsletters. Collection reflects R&D interests of electric utility industry.

MI —US ENVIRONMENTAL PROTECTION AGENCY, Motor Vehicle Emission Laboratory Library, 2565 Plymouth Rd, Ann Arbor, 48105. Debra Talsma, Librn
Holdings: // Uncat Microforms
Notes: No separate catalog. Collection described in: US EPA, Library System Branch, Guide to EPA Libraries, July, 1977. Collection includes 9500 technical reports on air pollution from mobile sources (especially automobiles); air pollution legislation (350 vols); fuel economy and conservation (800 technical reports); automobile engineering (300 vols); emission control technology for mobile source (8000 reports and papers); use of methanol and other alternative fuels in motor vehicles (600 technical reports).

NE —NORTHERN NATURAL GAS CO, 2223 Dodge St, Omaha, 68102. Marvin E Lauver, Librn

NH —TOTAL ENVIRONMENTAL ACTION, INC. (TEA), Library of Conservation, Environmental Studies, and Renewable Energy, 7 Church Hill, Harrisville, 03450. Bruce Anderson, Pres
Holdings: 10,000 Vols
Notes: Available for sale. Library in temporary storage, summer 1983. One of the most extensive private collections. Reports, surveys, monographs, technical papers, bibliographies, and indexes to highly specialized studies.

NM —NATIONAL ATOMIC MUSEUM, Library & Public Document Room, Kirtland AFB-E, Albuquerque, 87115. Philip P Larragoite, Librn
Holdings: Vols (50) Cat
Budget: ($600)
Notes: Alternative energy resources.

NM —UNIVERSITY OF CALIFORNIA, Los Alamos National Laboratory, Libraries, PO Box 1663, MSP 362, Los Alamos, 87545. J Arthur Freed, Head Librn
Holdings: Vols (800,000) Cat Films Microforms
Budget: ($700,000)
Notes: Incl 500,000 classified and unclassified reports. There are 25 branch libraries and a central collection. The Medical Library contains about 40,000 vols in the areas of biomedical research.

NY —CARY ARBORETUM OF THE NEW YORK BOTANICAL GARDEN, Library, Box AB, Millbrook, 12545. Fred Strum, Librn
Notes: This collection of alternative energy sources consists of publications concerned with solar energy, wind power, biofuel, methanol, small hydroelectric projects, and wood power.

NY —NATIONAL ECONOMIC RESEARCH ASSOCIATES, INC, Library, 123 Main St, White Plains, 10601. Debra Gaffey, Asst Librn
Holdings: Vols 7500 Cat
Notes: Energy economics, power resources, anti-trust legislation, and public policy.

OH —MARATHON OIL CO, Law Library, 539 S Main St, Room 854-M, Findlay, 45840. Durand S Dudley, Sr Law Librn
Holdings: Vols (18,000) Cat
Budget: ($100,000)
Notes: Library serves the informational needs of the staff attorneys of a major oil company operating in both domestic and foreign areas. Includes all of the domestic law reports and digests. Includes statutes of 25 states. Particular emphasis is given to the acquisition of mineral (petroleum) law and energy legislation and regulation. Library open to the public by permission.

OR —UNIVERSITY OF OREGON, Library, Eugene, 97403. Kenneth W Duckett, Curator
Holdings: Cat Mss
Notes: Over 15 mss collections of public power officials (specifically with the Bonneville Power Administration); government officials with a special interest in the public-private power issue, incl Congressman Walter Pierce and Senator Richard Neuberger; and records of utility companies in Oregon. Publication: Martin Schmitt, comp, Catalog of Manuscripts in the University of Oregon Library (Eugene: University of Oregon Books, 1971).

OR —PORTLAND STATE UNIVERSITY LIBRARY, 934 SW Harrison, PO Box 1151, 97207, Portland, 97201. Kenneth W Butler, Asst Dir
Holdings: Vols (669,592) Uncat Mss Maps Pix Microforms
Budget: ($1,321,288)
Notes: Northwest natural resources and electrical power development. Incl the Ivan Bloch Collection.

OR —US DEPT OF ENERGY, Bonneville Power Administration Library, 1002 NE Holladay St, PO Box 3621, Portland, 97232. Karen Hadman, Chief of Library Branch
Holdings: Vols (15,000) // Cat Microforms
Budget: ($8000)

†PA —GILBERT ASSOCIATES, Library Information Services, PO Box 1498, Reading, 19603. Debra Bosler, Supervisor
Notes: Energy conversion technology. Many government technical reports are received regularly, particularly those on fossil fuel technology.

TN —TENNESSEE VALLEY AUTHORITY (TVA), Technical Library, 400 W Summit Hill Dr, E2 B7, Knoxville, 37902. Jesse C Mills, Chief Librn
Holdings: Vols (106,900) Cat Mss Maps Pix Audiotapes Microforms
Budget: ($2,025,000)
Notes: The Technical Library Headquarters Staff (order, cataloging, information, and administration) is located in Knoxville, Tenn. In addition there are branch libraries in Knoxville, Norris and Chattanooga, Tennessee, and Muscle Shoals, Alabama.

TN —US DEPT OF ENERGY, Technical Information Center, PO Box 62, Oak Ridge, 37831. Joseph G Coyne, Manager
Notes: TIC manages the technical information program of the DOE through which the DOE scientific research and development information is disseminated for offical and public use. TIC is also responsible for producing the DOE Energy Data Base and a number of abstracting and indexing journals which provide worldwide coverage of the energy literature. Cataloged holdings incl 500,000 reports, 94,000 engineering drawings and 10,000 books. 800 journal titles are received, with most not being retained.

TX —UNIVERSITY OF TEXAS LIBRARIES, Richard W McKinney Engineering Library, 1.3 ECJ, Austin, 78712. Susan B Ardis, Librn
Holdings: Vols (83,548) Cat Microforms
Notes: All US Patents since 1977.

TX —SOUTHERN UNION CO, Library, Inter-First II, Suite 1800, Dallas, 75270. Charles Woodard, Research Librn
Holdings: Vols (50) Uncat
Notes: Incl periodicals (43 subscriptions), and annual reports (1500).

TX —MCDERMOTT HUDSON ENGINEERING, Library, 5900 Hillcroft, Houston, 77036. Chris Ramirez, Librn
Holdings: Vols (750) Uncat Microforms
Notes: Emphasis is on all forms of alternative energy sources and energy conversion.

WI —UNIVERSITY OF WISCONSIN, MILWAUKEE, Library, Box 604, Milwaukee, 53201. William C Roselle, Dir
Holdings: Cat Microforms
Notes: Wisconsin Legislative Reference Bureau Clippings File. Special strength in a collection mostly of Wisconsin emphasis. 440 reels of 16mm microfilm. A subject-chronological arrangement (approximately 1200 subjects covering the years from the 1890s through 1970) of pamphlets and a variety of fugitive materials and of clippings from national and Wisconsin newspapers, popular magazines and scholarly journals, and federal, state, and local government documents.

WY —NATRONA COUNTY PUBLIC LIBRARY, 307 E Second St, Casper, 82601. Kathleen Nowak, Earth Sciences/Reference Librn
Holdings: Vols (3000) Cat Maps
Notes: The earth sciences collection consists of technical literature published in energy-related fields. A map collection of topographic and geologic maps of Wyoming is maintained. State geological survey documents for the states surrounding Wyoming are collected. Also some thirty periodicals in the earth sciences.

MB —UNIVERSITY OF MANITOBA, Elizabeth Dafoe Library, Government Publications Section, Winnipeg, R3T 2N2, Can. June Dutka, Head
Holdings: Uncat Maps Pix Microforms
Notes: The Canadian National Energy Board's Polar Gas Project documentation provides an extremely useful source of information describing the proposed construction of the pipeline route which would generally pass from the Artic Islands through the Northwest Territories, northern Manitoba and into Ontario, Canada.

ON —METROPOLITAN TORONTO LIBRARY, Science & Technology Dept, 789 Yonge St, Toronto, M4W 2G8, Can. Margaret Walshe, Head
Holdings: Vols (120,000) Cat VF
Notes: All aspects of science and technology for the specialist, the student and the general public. The department gives high priority to Canadian materials.

POWER RESOURCES—RESEARCH

MO —UNIVERSITY OF MISSOURI-COLUMBIA, Research Park Library, 131 Dalton Research Center, Columbia, 65211. Janice Dysart, Librn
Holdings: Uncat Microforms
Notes: An almost complete collection of the AEC-ERDA-DOE research and development reports, as well as reports from foreign organizatons with which AEC-ERDA-DOE had/has agreeements for technical cooperation, covering the years 1948 to date. The collection consists

POWER RESOURCES—RESEARCH
(cont.)

primarily of 750,000 microcards and
microfiche, with some hard copies supplied
from the UMC Library Government
Documents collection. The collection is
indexed in *Nuclear Science Abstracts,
Energy Research Abstracts,* and *INIS
Atomindex.*

POWER TRANSMISSION, ELECTRIC
see Electric Power

POWERS, JAMES FARL

NV —UNIVERSITY OF NEVADA, RENO,
University Library, Special Collections Dept,
Reno, 89557. Robert E Blesse, Head
Holdings: // Vols (10) Cat
Notes: Includes individual works by author
in all editions including translations; also
prefaces, introductions, published
correspondence, appearances in anthologies,
periodicals, etc. Bibliographical research
collection, part of Modern Authors
Collection. Other appearances 50 cataloged.

POWYS, JOHN COWPER, 1872-1963

CT —UNIVERSITY OF CONNECTICUT,
Library, Storrs, 06268. R H Schimmelpfeng,
Dir of Special Collections
Holdings: Vols (225) Cat Mss Pix
IL —ILLINOIS STATE UNIVERSITY, Milner
Library, Dept of Special Collections,
Normal, 61761. Robert Sokan, Librn
Notes: First editions, limited editions,
ephemera, etc.
NV —UNIVERSITY OF NEVADA, RENO,
University Library, Special Collections Dept,
Reno, 89557. Robert E Blesse, Head
Holdings: // Vols (75) Cat Other
appearances 35 Cat
Notes: Includes individual works by author
in all editions including translations; also
prefaces, introductions, published
correspondence, appearances in anthologies,
periodicals, etc. Bibliographical research
collection, part of Modern Authors
Collection.
NY —COLGATE UNIVERSITY, Everett
Needham Case Library, Hamilton, 13346.
Bruce M Brown, Collections Librn
Holdings: Vols 245 Uncat Mss Pix
Notes: Collection includes 913 letters from J
C Powys; about 550 to him. There are 3
original drawings, 2 busts, and books from
his library. Also, books by other members of
the family (Littleton, Philippa, Laurence,
Marion). See other entries for his brothers
Llewelyn and Theodore Francis. Also,
material by close friends--Kenneth Hopkins,
Louis U Wilkinson, John Redwood
Anderson, John Gawsworth (Terence Ian
Fytton Armstrong), and E N Visiak.
Description in various issued of *Philobiblon:
The Journal of the Friends of the Colgate
University Library.*
NY —HOFSTRA UNIVERSITY, Library,
1000 Fulton Ave, Hempstead, 11550.
Charles R Andrews, Dean of Library
Services
Notes: Strong collection. Incl some mss.
BC —UNIVERSITY OF VICTORIA,
McPherson Library, Victoria, V8W 3H5,
Can.
Notes: Letters to Alfred Perles and Henry
Miller about Perles.

POWYS, LLEWELYN, 1884-1939

CT —UNIVERSITY OF CONNECTICUT,
Library, Storrs, 06268. R H Schimmelpfeng,
Dir of Special Collections
Holdings: Vols (225) Cat Mss Pix
NY —COLGATE UNIVERSITY, Everett
Needham Case Library, Hamilton, 13346.
Bruce M Brown, Collections Librn
Holdings: Vols 75 Uncat Mss
Notes: See entry for John Cowper Powys.
Two manuscripts, 45 letters.
NY —HOFSTRA UNIVERSITY, Library,
1000 Fulton Ave, Hempstead, 11550.
Charles R Andrews, Dean of Library

Services
Notes: Strong collection. Incl some mss.

POWYS, THEODORE FRANCIS, 1875-1953

CT —UNIVERSITY OF CONNECTICUT,
Library, Storrs, 06268. R H Schimmelpfeng,
Dir of Special Collections
Holdings: Vols (225) Cat Mss Pix
NY —COLGATE UNIVERSITY, Everett
Needham Case Library, Hamilton, 13346.
Bruce M Brown, Collections Librn
Holdings: Vols 115
Notes: See entry for John Cowper Powys.
One manuscript, 15 letters.
NY —HOFSTRA UNIVERSITY, Library,
1000 Fulton Ave, Hempstead, 11550.
Charles R Andrews, Dean of Library
Services
Notes: Strong collection. Incl some mss.

POWYS FAMILY

CT —UNIVERSITY OF CONNECTICUT,
Library, Storrs, 06268. R H Schimmelpfeng,
Dir of Special Collections
Holdings: Vols 225 Cat Mss Pix
Notes: The collection consists primarily of
the writings of John Cowper, Llewelyn, and
Theodore Franics Powys, but also incl
writings, of other members of the family and
secondary sources.
†NC —WAKE FOREST UNIVERSITY, Z
Smith Reynolds Library, Box 7777, Reynold
Sta, Winston-Salem, 27109.
Notes: A significant collection.

POYNTER, NELSON

FL —UNIVERSITY OF SOUTH FLORIDA,
Library, Tampa, 33620. J B Dobkin, Special
Collections Librn
Notes: Public and private papers of Nelson
Poynter, Chairman of the board of Times
Publishing Company. Incl political
correspondence, photographs, and Pulitzer
Prize commendation records.

PRACTICAL NURSING

NC —TECHNICAL INSTITUTE OF
ALAMANCE, Learning Resources Center,
Jimmy Kerr Rd, PO Box 623, Haw River,
27258. Ron Plummer, Coordr
Holdings: Vols (1605) Cat Pix Audiotapes
16mm Films Filmstrips Microforms
Notes: Practical nursing only.
SC —BAPTIST MEDICAL CENTER, Amelia
White Pitts Memorial Library, Taylor at
Marion Sts, Columbia, 29220. Lois W Smith,
Medical Librn
Holdings: Vols (3000) Cat

PRACTICAL POLITICS see Politics,
Practical

PRACTICAL PSYCHOLOGY see
Psychology, Applied

PRAGER, STANLEY, MEMORIAL
FUND

NY —NEW YORK PUBLIC LIBRARY,
Performing Arts Research Center, Billy Rose
Theatre Collection, 111 Amsterdam Ave,
New York, 10023. Dorothy L Swerdlove,
Cur
Holdings: Cat Videotapes

PRAGMATICISM

TX —TEXAS TECH UNIVERSITY, Library,
Lubbock, 79409. David J Murrah, Assoc Dir
for Special Collections

PRAIRIES

ND —NORTHERN PRAIRIE WILDLIFE
RESEARCH CENTER, Library, PO Box
1747, Jamestown, 58401.
Holdings: Vols (2500) Cat Pix Slides
Budget: ($10,000)
Notes: Wildlife management and research,
incl avian biology, plant and animal ecology

as related to wetlands and prairies, waterfowl
research, and effects of predators on
waterfowl.

PRAKRIT LANGUAGES AND
LITERATURES

HI —UNIVERSITY OF HAWAII, Library,
2550 The Mall, Honolulu, 96822. Joyce
Wright, Head, Asia Collection; Masato
Matsu, Head, East Asia Vernacular
Collection
Holdings: Vols 75,215 Cat Microforms
Notes: The Asia Collection holds material
from and relating to Bangladesh, India,
Nepal, Pakistan, and Sri Lanka in western
and Asian languages. South Asian languages
currently acquired: Bengali, Hindi, Marathi,
Nepali, Pali, Prakrit, Sanskrit, Tamil. Period
emphasis is post-World War II. Subject
emphases: social sciences and the humanities
(literature, economics, history, religion/
philosophy). Holdings are supplemented by a
large uncataloged backlog, much of it
accessible through the Library of Congress
Accessions Lists for the area and by over
7000 cataloged titles in the main library
collection. *South Asian Library Resources in
North America: A Survey Prepared for the
Boston Conference, 1974,* ed by M L P
Patterson (Zug, Switzerland: Tutes
Documentation Company, 1975).
(Bibliotheca Asiatica 12-), "University of
Hawaii," pp 103-114.
MA —HARVARD UNIVERSITY LIBRARY,
Widener Library, Cambridge, 02138.
Holdings: Cat Mss
MI —UNIVERSITY OF MICHIGAN,
Graduate Library, South Asian Dept, Ann
Arbor, 48109. Om P Sharma, Librn
Holdings: Vols (365,000) Cat Maps Slides
Microforms
Notes: The major emphasis is on social
sciences and humanities. Besides materials in
classical languages, South Asian vernaculars
being retained are Hindi, Bengali, Urdu,
Marathi and Tamil; strong in classical
languages, especially Sanskrit, Pali, and
Prakrit.
NY —NEW YORK PUBLIC LIBRARY,
Oriental Div, Fifth Ave & 42 St, New York,
10018. E Christian Filstrup, Chief
Holdings: Cat Mss Microforms
Budget: ($56,455)
Notes: Published catalog of holdings.
TX —UNIVERSITY OF TEXAS LIBRARIES,
Asian Collection, PO Box P, Austin, 78712.
Kevin Lin, Asian Librn; Merry Burlingham,
South Asian Librn
Holdings: Vols (56,000) Microforms
Notes: Materials in Hindi, Sanskrit, Urdu,
Prakrit, and Pali (acquired chiefly through
the Special Foreign Acquisitions Program)
and selected English-language materials,
including Indian censuses and district
gazetteers and Pakistani censuses.

PRANG, LOUIS, 1824-1909

PA —TEMPLE UNIVERSITY LIBRARIES,
Special Collections Dept, Rare Books & Mss
Section, Philadelphia, 19122. Thomas M
Whitehead, Cur
Holdings: Vols (200) Cat Mss Pix
Notes: The lithography collection
emphasizes the technical process rather than
the artistic medium and stresses the years
1800-1835. Significant are the early manuals,
the Kubilius Louis Prang Collection and the
documentation of early Mexican lithography.
Some holdings are listed in the 1972
publication: *Aloys Senefelder 1771-1834: A
Catalogue of Early Technical Literature and
Selected Lithograph.* A register of the
Mexican documents is available.

PRATT, DEANE WINTHROP

NY —MOUNT PLEASANT PUBLIC
LIBRARY, 350 Bedford Rd, Pleasantville,
10570. Charlotte Miller, Dir
Holdings: Vols 3000 Cat Mss Pix
Notes: The Deane Winthrop Pratt collection
of acting editions of mostly 19th-20th
century British plays. Incl some 200 prompt

PRATT, DEANE WINTHROP (cont.)

books, most of them comprehensively marked with production notes. The collection was the product of a 19th-early 20th century professional actor who turned to direction of suburban amateur acting groups and the prompt books reflect that activity. There are several ms plays by Mr Pratt in the collection. Theatre memorabilia mainly tipped into the various vols. The collection of John W Frost is especially strong in 17th and 18th century drama.

PRATT, E. J.

ON —VICTORIA UNIVERSITY, Library, 71 Queen's Park Crescent, Toronto, M5S 1K7, Can. Robert C Brandeis, Chief Librn
Holdings: Cat Mss Pix Phonorecords Audiotapes Microforms
Notes: A comprehensive collection of E J Pratt's published works and a major collection of mss, lecture notes, etc. Victoria's ms holdings are listed in "Shortlist of E J Pratt Manuscripts," a section of Lila Laakso, "E J Pratt: A Preliminary Checklist," *Canadian Library Journal* 34: 4(August 1977), 273-94 (repr from: *The E J Pratt Symposium.* Ed Glenn Clever. Ottawa: University of Ottawa Press, 1977). *E J Pratt: An Annotated Bibliography* by Lila Laakso, Downsview, Ont. ECW Press 1980, p 147-220. (Offprint from vol 2 of *The Annotated Bibliography of Canada's Major Authors*).

PRATT, ERNEST

CA —UNIVERSITY OF CALIFORNIA, LOS ANGELES, Research Library, Dept of Special Collections, 405 Hilgard Ave, Los Angeles, 90024. Edward Shreeves, Chairman, Bibliographers Group; David S Zeidberg, Head
Notes: Large collection of California photographers' works, incl Will Connell, Ernest Pratt, and 136 pictures of Los Angeles architect Mark Daniels' work.

PRATT, GEORGE R., 1876-

MB —UNIVERSITY OF MANITOBA, Elizabeth Dafoe Library, Archives and Special Collections Dept, Winnipeg, R3T 2N2, Can. Richard E Bennett, Dept Head; Corrado A Santoro, Reference Archivist
Notes: Unpublished literary manuscript entitled *Creation* with text and 13 handmade illustrated plates.

PRATT, THEODORE

FL —FLORIDA ATLANTIC UNIVERSITY LIBRARY, Boca Raton, 33431. Elaine K Kelly, Librn
Holdings: Cat Mss Pix
Notes: Incl mss, paintings, animations, short stories, articles, speeches, first editions, and foreign editions of his novels, correspondence, notes, clippings, personal memorabilia. Also, a 16mm color print of motion picture made from *The Barefoot Mailman*, etc. There is a separate catalog to the collection. Restricted use: noncirculating.

PRATT, ADM. WILLIAM V.

RI —US NAVAL WAR COLLEGE, Historical Collection & Museum, Newport, 02841. Anthony S Nicolosi, Dir; Evelyn Cherpak, Cur
Holdings: Mss
Notes: Personal papers consisting of official correspondence, writings and speeches and official orders, reports and memoranda. Adm Pratt was president of the Naval War College, head of the US Fleet and Chief of Naval Operations. This collection is a primary source for research on the US Navy in the early twentieth century, the Naval War College, the Washington Naval Conference, international disarmament and China.

PRATT, ZADOCK, 1790-1871

MA —BOSTON UNIVERSITY, Mugar Memorial Library, Special Collections Dept,

771 Commonwealth Ave, Boston, 02215. Howard B Gotlieb, Dir
Holdings: // Cat Mss
Notes: Part of Ralph Ingersoll Collection. Correspondence, scrapbooks.

PRAYER, MENTAL see Meditation

PRAYER BOOKS see Bibles and Prayer Books

PREACHING

NC —SOUTHEASTERN BAPTIST THEOLOGICAL SEMINARY LIBRARY, PO Box 752, Wake Forest, 27587. H Eugene McLeod, Librn
Holdings: Cat Audiotapes Videotapes Microforms

PREACHING FRIARS see Dominicans

PRECANCELS

NJ —NATIONAL ASSOCIATION OF PRECANCEL COLLECTORS, Chester Davis Memorial Library, 5121 Park Blvd, Wildwood, 08260. Glenn W Dye, Secretary
Holdings: Vols 5000 Uncat Pix
Notes: Precancelled postage stamps; pictures of stamps in color; pictures of old post offices in New Jersey and New Hampshire. No photocopying. Published monthly journal Precancel Stamp Collector.

PRECIOUS STONES

RI —PROVIDENCE PUBLIC LIBRARY, 150 Empire St, Providence, 02903. Lance J Bauer, Special Collections Librn
Notes: Works dating from 1670 on the history, lore, and legends of precious stones, and the history and practice of jewelry-making and silversmithing. Restricted use.

PRECISIANS see Puritans

PRECOCITY see Gifted Children

PRE-COLUMBIAN ART see Art, Pre-Columbian

PREDICADORES see Dominicans

PREGNANCY AND ULTRASOUND see Ultrasound in Pregnancy

PREGNANT SCHOOLGIRLS see Teenage Women—Pregnancy

PREHISTORIC ANTIQUITIES see Archaeology

PREHISTORIC ART see Art, Primitive

PREHISTORIC FAUNA see Paleontology

PREHISTORY see Archaeology

PREISLER, PAUL

MO —UNIVERSITY OF MISSOURI-SAINT LOUIS, Thomas Jefferson Library, Manuscript and Historical Society Collection, 8001 Natural Bridge Rd, Saint Louis, 63121.

PRELUDES AND FIGURES see Canons, Fugues, Etc.

PRENTICE, ROYAL A.

NM —MUSEUM OF NEW MEXICO, Photo Archives, Box 2087, Santa Fe, 87503. Arthur L Olivas, Cur; Richard Rudisill, Photo Historian
Holdings: Cat Pix Slides
Notes: Extensive collection of his work.

PREPAID MEDICAL CARE see Medical Care, Prepaid

PRERAPHAELITES AND PRERAPHAELITISM

AZ —ARIZONA STATE UNIVERSITY, Library, Tempe, 85287. Marilyn

Wurzburger, Special Collections Librn
Holdings: Vols 553 Cat Mss
Notes: 203 letters.
CA —UNIVERSITY OF THE PACIFIC, Library, Stockton, 95211. Hiram L Davis, Dir of Libraries
Holdings: Vols (350) Uncat Pix
Notes: A general collection of Victorian literature and life given to the University by James M Perrin in 1968-1970. The primary specialization is material by and about William Morris and the Kelmscott Press, but the collection also is rich in Victorian first editions, Pre-Raphaelites and Pre-Raphaelitism, and early colored illustrations and chromolithography.
DE —DELAWARE ART MUSEUM, Library, 2301 Kentmere Pkwy, Wilmington, 19806. Anne Hoslam, Librn
Holdings: Vols 1000 Cat Mss Pix
Notes: Catalog of the Samuel and Mary R Bancroft Pre-Raphaelite collection of paintings and books is to come out the spring of 1978. Collection is described in *Pre-Raphaelitism; A Bibliocritical Study*, by William Fredeman (Harvard University Press, 1965).
KS —UNIVERSITY OF KANSAS, Kenneth Spencer Research Library, Special Collections Dept, Lawrence, 66045. Alexandra Mason, Librn
Holdings: Cat Mss
Notes: Strongest in 18th and 19th century. Old English (Clubb Collection); 18th-century plays, poems, sermons. English Poetical Miscellanies collection. Literary periodicals and newspapers (18th century). Noncirculating.
NJ —PRINCETON UNIVERSITY, Library, Rare Books Dept, Princeton, 08544. Stephen Ferguson, Cur
Holdings: Cat
Notes: Rosetti Collection of Janet Camp Troxell. 728 vols concerning various members of the Rossetti family, though the collection has grown considerably since the original purchase. One entire issue of the *Princeton University Library Chronicle* has been devoted to the Rossetti collection. See especially the article: Robert S Fraser, "The Rossetti Collection of Janet Camp Troxell: A Survey with Some Sidelights" in the *Princeton University Library Chronicle* XXXIII, 3 (spring, 1972) pp 146-175. The most substantial single part of the collection contains material by or relating to Dante Gabriel Rossetti, with 227 titles in 262 vols. Also notable is *The Torch: A Journal of International Socialism.* London, 1891-1896. This socialist-anarchist paper was published by Helen, Olivia and Arthur Rossetti. Princeton holdings for this publication begin with the issue believed to be forSeptember 1891 and conclude with that for December 1895. However, the Library lacks as many as 23 nubmers. A typescript catalog of all printed books in the Troxell collection was prepared by R S Fraser (Ex)Z5948.P9 xF7. Also see the 5 boxes of material by Janet Troxell relating to her Rossetti Collection. The boxes are held by the Manuscript Division and are mentioned on p 1 of the checklist of the Troxell Collection of Rossetti Manuscripts.
BC —UNIVERSITY OF BRITISH COLUMBIA, Library, Special Collections Div, 1956 Main Mall, Vancouver, V6T 1Y3, Can. Anne Yandle, Head
Holdings: Vols Cat Mss

PRESBYTERIAN CHURCH

GA —AGNES SCOTT COLLEGE, McCain Library, E College Ave, Decatur, 30030. Judith Bourgeois Jensen, Librn
Holdings: Vols (945) Uncat
Budget: $300
Notes: The Frontier Religion Collection, which was given by Prof Walter Brownlow Posey, traces the effects of slavery on religion in the Old South Frontier prior to 1860. A catalog file (by author entry only) accompanies the collection at present. Noncirculating.
IL —JESUIT-KRAUSS-MCCORMICK LIBRARY, 1100 E 55th St, Chicago, 60615.

PRESBYTERIAN CHURCH (cont.)

Donald Vorp, Dir; Elvire Hilgert, Librn
Holdings: Vols (375,000)
Notes: Collections contain merger of Jesuit Library, Lutheran School of Theology of Chicago (Krauss Library), and McCormick Theological Seminary. McCormick: Presbyteriana; historical record of Synod of Illinois (United Presbyterian Church of USA); Church Federation of Chicago archives prior to 1969; USA imprints of the Bible (Simms Collection).
See also entries under Religion; Catholic Church; Lutheran Church

KY —UNIVERSITY OF KENTUCKY, Margaret I King Library, Dept of Special Collections, Lexington, 40506. William Marshall, Head
Holdings: Cat Mss Maps Pix
Notes: History of Kentucky, Ohio Valley and Presbyterian Church. Consists of books, letters, maps, etc; about 10,000 pieces.

NY —CORNELL UNIVERSITY LIBRARIES, Collection of Regional History, Dept of Manuscripts and Univ Archives, Ithaca, 14853.
Holdings: Pix
Notes: Papers, 1804-1945; incl accounts of the women's society, manuals, anniversity publications, historical sketches, eulogies, sermons, photos, proceedings of the Washington County Bible Society, etc.

NC —HISTORICAL FOUNDATION OF THE PRESBYTERIAN & REFORMED CHURCHES, Library, Box 847, Montreat, 28757. Jerrold Lee Brooks, Exec Dir
Holdings: Vols (90,000) Cat Mss Maps Pix Slides Phonorecords Audiotapes Videotapes 16mm Films Filmstrips Microforms Archives
Budget: ($350,000)
Notes: Presbyterian and Reformed Churches of the World; Presbyterian Church in the South; Presbyterian Church (USA). History, archives, etc.

OH —MUSKINGUM COLLEGE, Library, New Concord, 43762. Herbert D Safford, Dir; Richard M Cochron, Reference Librn
Holdings: Cat Mss Maps Pix Microforms
Notes: Ohio and local history; Presbyterian Church.

ON —QUEEN'S UNIVERSITY, Douglas Library, Kingston, K7L 5C4, Can. William F E Morley, Cur, Special Collections
Holdings: Mss Maps Pix
Notes: About 3500 linear feet of mss material with special emphasis on families and businesses of eastern Ontario; Presbyterian Church; Canadian politics and public affairs, university and city of Kingston records, literary figures.

ON —TORONTO SCHOOL OF THEOLOGY, Consortium of Libraries, University of Toronto, Toronto, M5S 1A5, Can. R Grane Bracewell, Library Coordr
Holdings: Cat
Notes: A consortium of 7 theological college and faculty libraries at the University of Toronto.

PRESBYTERIAN CHURCH, CUMBERLAND see Cumberland Presbyterian Church

PRESBYTERIAN CHURCH, REFORMED see Reformed Presbyterian Church

PRESBYTERIAN PERIODICALS see Periodicals, Presbyterian

PRESCHOOL READERS AND SPEAKERS see Readers and Speakers

PRESERVATION OF ART OBJECTS see Art Objects—Conservation and Restoration

PRESENILE DEMENTIA

MI —LAFAYETTE CLINIC LIBRARY, 951 E Lafayette, Detroit, 48207. Nancy E Ward, Librn
Holdings: Vols (7000) Cat
Notes: Special emphasis on memory

disorder, dementia and Alzheimer's disease (presenile dementia). Library's emphasis is on the biological aspects, causes and treatments of mental illness.

PRESERVATION OF BOOKS see Books—Conservation and Restoration

PRESERVATION OF FOOD see Food—Preservation

PRESERVATION OF FORESTS see Forests and Forestry; Natural Resources

PRESERVATION OF HISTORIC HOUSES, SITES, ETC.

IL —LAKE FOREST COLLEGE, Donnelley Library, Lake Forest, 60045. Arthur H Miller Jr, College Librn
Holdings: Vols (500) Cat Maps
Budget: ($1200)
Notes: Focus on development of suburban fringe areas, particularly Lake Co, Ill, and Chicago region: local documents (plans, transit, zoning maps, etc), US documents, and special studies of suburban issues, such as historic preservation and land use.

MI —DETROIT PUBLIC LIBRARY, Burton Historical Collection, 5201 Woodward Ave, Detroit, 48202. Alice Dalligan, Chief

VA —MARY WASHINGTON COLLEGE, E Lee Trinkle Library, Fredericksburg, 22401. Ruby Y Weinbrecht, Librn
Holdings: Vols 6000
Budget: $1500

PRESERVATION OF HISTORICAL RECORDS see Archives

PRESERVATION OF MANUSCRIPTS see Manuscripts—Conservation and Restoration

PRESERVATION OF TISSUES see Tissues—Preservation

PRESERVATION OF VEGETABLES see Canning and Preserving

PRESERVATION OF WILDLIFE see Wildlife Conservation

PRESERVING see Canning and Preserving

PRESIDENTS—U.S.

†AL —MUSEUMS OF THE CITY OF MOBILE, Reference Library, 355 Government St, Mobile, 36602. Caldwell Delaney, Adminr

CA —CLAREMONT COLLEGES, Norman F Sprague Memorial Library, 12 & Dartmouth, Claremont, 91711. David Kuhner, Librn
Holdings: Vols (1000) Cat Mss Pix VF
Notes: President Herbert Hoover's personal collection of rare technical books of the 15th-19th centuries. Bibliotheca De Re Metallica: The Herbert Clark Hoover Collection of Mining and Metallurgy (Claremont, 1980). Restricted use.

CA —LINCOLN MEMORIAL SHRINE, A K Smiley Public Library, 125 W Vine St,

Redlands, 92373. Larry E Burgess, Archivist
Holdings: Vols (3000) Cat Mss Maps Pix Slides Phonorecords 16mm Films Microforms
Budget: ($18,000)
Notes: One of the larger collections on Lincoln and his times. Incl broadsides, letters, prints, campaign badges, stamps, coins, medals; bust, by George Grey Bernard. Endowment of Watchorn Lincoln Memorial Association. There is an additional pamphlet collection of more than 3000 pieces; an extensive philately collection incl first-day covers, commemorative and foreign issues, and Civil War envelopes.

CA —UNIVERSITY OF CALIFORNIA, SANTA BARBARA, Library, Dept of Special Collections, Santa Barbara, 93106. Christian F Brun, Head
Holdings: Vols 24,500 Cat Mss Maps Pix Microforms
Budget: $7000
Notes: The William Wyles Collection of Americana. Incl American Civil War, Abraham Lincoln, Westward Movement, Americans for the Orient, slavery, abolition movement, etc.

CA —HOOVER INSTITUTION ON WAR, REVOLUTION & PEACE, Stanford University, Stanford, 94305. Milorad M Drachkovitch, Archivist
Holdings: Mss
Notes: Two collections: (1) Correspondence between Herbert Hoover and Woodrow Wilson, 1915-1920. 152 items. Also the Paul A Hill Collection of some 300 letters from famous people concerning their opinions of Wilson. (2) Papers, 1900-1967, of Raymond Moley, political adviser to Franklin D Roosevelt and political columnist. Correspondence, reports, memoranda, speeches and writings, notes, and printed matter. The most prominent part of the collection consists of ms drafts of 81 Roosevelt speeches with annotations by both Moley and Roosevelt. 220 ms boxes. Unpublished register is available in repository.

CA —UNIVERSITY OF THE PACIFIC, Library, Stockton, 95211. Hiram L Davis, Dir of Libraries
Holdings: Vols 316 Cat Pix
Notes: Books, pamphlets, periodicals, and illustrative material and scraps relating to the life and times of Lincoln. Gift of Dr and Mrs Milton Henry Shutes. Incl over 200 miscellaneous items.

DC —LIBRARY OF CONGRESS, Rare Book & Special Collections Div, Washington, 20540. William Matheson, Chief
Notes: Books and personal mementos of President Woodrow Wilson, incl his personal library.

DC —LIBRARY OF CONGRESS, Manuscript Division, Washington, 20540. John C Broderick, Chief
Notes: The Presidential Papers collection incl the papers, etc, of numerous Presidents.

IL —SOUTHERN ILLINOIS UNIVERSITY, CARBONDALE, Delyte W Morris Library, Carbondale, 62901.
Notes: Scrapbook collection (15) on Ulysses S Grant

IL —CHICAGO HISTORICAL SOCIETY, Library, Clark St at North Ave, Chicago, 60614. Archie Motley, Manuscript Librn
Notes: Papers of these Presidents and other officials of the executive branch of the federal government: John Cabell Breckinridge (Representative and Senator Vice President, Confederate Secretary of War); John C Calhoun (Representative and Senator, Secretary of War, Vice President and Secretary of State); Schuyler Colfax (Representative, Vice President); Henry Dearborn (Representative, Secretary of War, War of 1812 officer); Henry A S Dearborn (Representative, political leader); Zebina Eastman (journalist, abolitionist); Ulysses S Grant (US Army officer, US President); Andrew Jackson (Representative, Senator, US Army officer, President); Joseph R Jones (businessman, member of US Diplomatic Corps, associate of Ulysses S Grant); Abraham Lincoln (Representative, US President); Robert Todd Lincoln papers in

PRESIDENTS—U.S. (cont.)

the Library ofCongress; Henry Crittenden
Morris (lawyer, US Consul at Ghent);
George Washington (US President); All
other Presidents and many other federal
officers are represented in small quantities.

IL —NORTHWESTERN UNIVERSITY,
Library, Special Collections Dept, 1937
Sheridan Rd, Evanston, 60201. R Russell
Maylone, Cur
Holdings: Vols 1064 Cat Mss Pix
Notes: The Unger Collection of Franklin D
Roosevelt (qv) and the Wilson Collection of
Woodrow Wilson (qv).

IL —ILLINOIS STATE HISTORICAL
SOCIETY, Library, Old State Capitol,
Springfield, 62706. James T Hickey, Lincoln
Cur
Holdings: Cat Mss Pix
Notes: Downs 2605, 2610, 2492. Incl 1319
mss concerning Lincoln.

IN —INDIANA UNIVERSITY, Lilly Library,
Seventh St, Bloomington, 47405. William R
Cagle, Librn
Holdings: Vols 5000 Cat Mss
Notes: Emphasis on materials printed during
Lincoln's lifetime. Mss incl papers and
correspondence of Lincoln, members of his
family, and members of his cabinet.

KS —DWIGHT D EISENHOWER LIBRARY,
226 SE Fourth, Abilene, 67410. John E
Wickman, Dir
Holdings: Vols 28,000 Cat Mss Maps Pix
Slides
Notes: Dwight D Eisenhower and the
Eisenhower Presidential Administration.
Also, about 20,000,000 ms pieces.

KS —EMPORIA STATE UNIVERSITY,
William Allen White Library, Emporia,
66801. Mary E Bogan, Special Collections
Librn
Holdings: Vols (277) // Cat Mss Pix
Phonorecords Audiotapes
Notes: The William Allen White Collection
contains books by and about Mr White as
well as inscribed volumes from his personal
library, manuscripts, photographs, newspaper
and periodical articles, memorabilia, as well
as letters and telegrams exchanged between
Mr White and such national figures as
Herbert Hoover, Calvin Coolidge, Theodore
Roosevelt, Franklin D Roosevelt, William
Dean Howells, William Howard Taft, Robert
Taft and many others.
See also entry under White, William Allen

LA —LOUISIANA STATE UNIVERSITY,
Troy H Middleton Library, Baton Rouge,
70803. Lance E Dickson, Acting Dir
Holdings: Vols 5000 Uncat Maps Pix
Notes: Core is composed of the Warren L
Jones Lincoln Collection. Incl the major
Lincoln biographies, pamphlets, photographs,
periodicals, broadsides, museum objects,
special editions, and some items pertaining
to the Civil War.

†MA —BOSTON PUBLIC LIBRARY, Copley
Sq, Boston, 02117.
Holdings: Cat Microforms
Notes: Microform Publication by Library of
Congress. The Presidential Papers Program
of the Library of Congress.

†MA —JOHN F KENNEDY LIBRARY,
Columbia Point, Boston, 02125. Dan H Fenn
Jr, Dir
Holdings: Vols 20,000 Cat Mss Maps Pix
Slides Phonorecords Audiotapes Videotapes
16mm Films Microforms
Notes: The major collection about JFK, his
life, family and administration. It contains
personal papers, audiovisual materials, books,
oral history interviews. Collection is
described in "Historical Materials in the
John F Kennedy Library." "The Kennedy
Collection," a subject guide to the book
collection, is available for sale.

MA —STATE LIBRARY OF
MASSACHUSETTS, 341 State House,
Boston, 02133. Gaspar Caso, State Librn
Holdings: Vols (750) Cat Mss Pix

MA —FORBES LIBRARY, 20 West St,
Northampton, 01060. Lawrence E
Wikander, Cur
Holdings: Vols 4000 Cat Mss Maps Pix
Slides Microforms
Budget: $200
Notes: Collection incl portraits, cartoons,
furniture, Indian gear, and other
memorabilia.

MA —BRANDEIS UNIVERSITY, Goldfarb
Library, 415 South St, Waltham, 02154.
Bessie Hahn, Dir
Notes: Approx 125 letters to and from
Eleanor Roosevelt dating from 1929 through
1962. There is a finding list to the
correspondence in Special Collections.

†MA —WILLIAMS COLLEGE, Chapin
Library of Rare Books, PO Box 426,
Williamstown, 01267. Robert L Volz,
Custodian
Holdings: Vols 160 Cat Mss
Notes: No material available on interlibrary
loan.

MI —NATIONAL HAMILTONIAN PARTY,
Library, 3314 Dillon Rd, Flushing, 48433.
Holdings: Vols 4670 Cat Mss
Notes: The life and writings of Alexander
Hamilton. The National Hamiltonian Library
is a part of the offices of the Hamiltonian
National Committee, the governing body of
the National Hamiltonian Party, a Neo-
Federalist political movement. Incl 4835
vols. Also the Kelly Collection, a group of
over 10,000 pieces of American political
memorabilia covering presidents and
presidential hopefuls of major and minor
parties as well as special sectons on women,
minorities and families in politics.

MI —CENTRAL MICHIGAN UNIVERSITY,
Clarke Historical Library, Mount Pleasant,
48859. William H Mulligan, Jr, Dir; William
Miles, Biography Collections Librn
Holdings: Vols 600
Notes: Biography collection of books written
during campaigns of both successful and
unsuccessful candidates for presidential
nomination.

MN —UNIVERSITY OF MINNESOTA, O
Meredith Wilson Library, 309 19 Ave S,
Minneapolis, 55455. Austin J McLean,
Chief, Special Collections
Holdings: Vols (879) Uncat Mss Pix 16mm
Films
Notes: Publications by Franklin Delano
Roosevelt and works written about him and
his political career. Incl is a large collection
of memorabilia, such as commemorative
china, campaign buttons, posters, etc. A
complete listing is available in the Division.

MO —HARRY S TRUMAN LIBRARY,
Independence, 64050. Benedict K Zobrist,
Dir
Holdings: Mss
Notes: Papers of Harry S Truman's
administration; also papers of Edwin G
Arnold, James P Aylword, Willa Mae
Roberts. Approx 13,000,000 pages on hand.

NH —NEW HAMPSHIRE HISTORICAL
SOCIETY, Manuscripts Library, 30 Park St,
Concord, 03301. Thomas E Camden, Cur
Holdings: Cat Mss
Notes: Franklin Pierce Papers incl
correspondence, scrapbook of newspapers
clippings, drafts of Pierce's message to
Congress in December 1855. Much of the
correspondence is between Pierce and his
sister, Elizabeth, and her husband, Gen John
McNeil. Emphasis of the collection, in
general, is on the presidential election of
1852. About 1500 items. Index to the
collection available at the New Hampshire
Historical Society.

NH —FRANKLIN PIERCE COLLEGE,
Frank S DiPietro Library, College Rd,
Rindge, 03461. Robert W Chatfield, Dir
Holdings: Cat
Notes: Material about President Pierce.

NJ —GLASSBORO STATE COLLEGE,
Savitz Library, Stewart Room, Glassboro,
08028. Clara Kirner, Special Collection
Librn
Holdings: Vols 90 Cat Mss Pix
Notes: Incl mss of letters of military
campaign in New Jersey and portraits of
Washington by Gilbert Stuart and Rembrant
Peale (originals).

NJ —PRINCETON UNIVERSITY, Library,
Manuscript Collection, Nassau St, Princeton,
08540. Jean F Preston, Cur
See also entries under George Washington;
Abraham Lincoln; Theodore Roosevelt;
Woodrow Wilson; Franklin Delano
Roosevelt.

NY —BUFFALO & ERIE COUNTY
HISTORICAL SOCIETY, 25 Nottingham
Court, Buffalo, 14216. Herman Sass, Librn

NY —COLUMBIA UNIVERSITY
LIBRARIES, Rare Book & Manuscript
Library, 801 Butler Library, 535 W 114 St,
New York, 10027. Kenneth A Lohf, Librn
Holdings: Vols 59 Uncat
Notes: The Jacob J Padell Collection. Letters
and books from Franklin Delano Roosevelt's
personal library. 89 items. Restricted use.

NY —NEW YORK HISTORICAL SOCIETY,
Library, 170 Central Park W, New York,
10024. James Gregory, Librn
Notes: Miscellaneous papers,
correspondence, etc, of George Washington
and John Quincy Adams. Also,
correspondence between John Quincy
Adams, James Madison, James Monroe and
Robert Fulton (qv).

NY —NEW YORK PUBLIC LIBRARY,
Research Libraries, General Research
Division, Fifth Ave & 42 St, New York,
10018. Rodney Phillips, Chief
Holdings: Vols (2,225,000) Cat Maps Pix
Microforms
Budget: ($775,718)

NY —NEW YORK PUBLIC LIBRARY, Rare
Books and Manuscripts Div, Fifth Ave & 42
St, New York, 10018. William L Joyce, Asst
Dir; Susan E Davis, Cur of Mss
Holdings: Cat Mss
Budget: ($7161)
Notes: Includes the only extant copy of
Washington's Farewell Address written in
his own hand; 236 letters written during the
period 1792 to 1799, several volumes of
Washington's letterpress copybooks, and an
orderly book, also a military journal written
during his colonelcy in the Virginia militia,
1757, and many other documents of US
Presidents.

NY —NEW YORK PUBLIC LIBRARY,
Research Libraries, American History Div,
Fifth Ave & 42 St, New York, 10018.
Holdings: Vols (45,000) Cat Maps
Microforms
Notes: Collection incl publications of
national and state historical societies.
Comprehensive, particularly when viewed in
conjunction with the parent institution's
documents collection and monographs and
serials elsewhere in the Library which are
available through use of the American
History Division catalog or through use of
bibliographies within the division. Strong on
Colonial and Revolutionary periods, War of
1812, Mexican War, Civil War, Spanish
American War, and the Slavery Controversy.
Incl collection of the papers of American
statesmen. Fine collection of books by
European travellers to the United States
during the 19th century. See Dictionary
Catalog of the History of Americas
Collection (Boston: G K Hall, 1961), 28
vols.

NY —NEW YORK PUBLIC LIBRARY, Fifth
Ave & 42 St, New York, 10018.
Notes: Supported by a special Lyndon
Baines Johnson Memorial Fund, to acquire
materials by and about him. Supported by a
special Harry S Truman Memorial Fund, to
collect materials relating to his life and work.

NY —STATE UNIVERSITY OF NEW
YORK, COLLEGE AT OSWEGO, Penfield
Library, Oswego, 13126. Anne Commerton,
Dir
Holdings: Cat Mss
Notes: President Millard Fillmore
Collection. Incl about 9000 items, with legal
papers relating to Fillmore's law practice;
personal letters of family, relatives and
friends; political correspondence during
career as State legislator, Congressman,
Comptroller of New York, Vice-President,
President and during retirement. Among
Fillmore's correspondents were his two law
partners and long time political associates,
Nathan K Hall and Solomon G Haven as
well as Anna Ella Carroll and Dorothea Dix.
Papers cover the period 1824-1889.
Unpublished calendar.

NY —SAGAMORE HILL NATIONAL
HISTORIC SITE, Library, 304 Cove Neck
Rd, Oyster Bay, 11771.
Holdings: Vols 250 Pix Videotapes 16mm
Films Filmstrips
Notes: Life and times of Theodore
Roosevelt. Partially cataloged.

PRESIDENTS—U.S. (cont.)

ND —DICKINSON STATE COLLEGE,
Stoxen Library, Dickinson, 58601. James
Martz, Acquisitions Librn
Holdings: Vols 229 Cat Mss Pix Microforms

**ND —THEODORE ROOSEVELT
NATIONAL PARK,** Library, PO Box 7,
Medora, 58645. Susan Snow, Librn; Miki
Hellickson, Chief Naturalist
Holdings: Vols (1500) Cat Mss Maps Pix
Slides Audiotapes 16mm Films
Budget: ($5000)
Notes: Theodore Roosevelt, cattle country
history, natural history. Also 2400 pictures
and 2200 slides.

OH —OHIO UNIVERSITY, Vernon R Alden
Library, Department of Archives and Special
Collections, Athens, 45701. Gary A Hunt,
Head
Notes: The DeWitt Collection of
Presidential Campaign Artifacts, containing
drawings, cartoons, textiles, lapel devices,
jewelry, glassware, and other artifacts
relating to US Presidential campaigns from
1824-1968.

OH —OHIO HISTORICAL SOCIETY,
Archives Library Division, 1982 Velma Ave,
Columbus, 43211. Dennis East, Division
Chief
Holdings: Vols 2000 Cat Mss Pix
Microforms
Notes: This is essentially the "Presidential"
library for Harding. The papers have been
microfilmed (1971) and are available by loan
or purchase from the Ohio Historical
Society. The microfilm edition totals 263
reels; a printed inventory to the microfilm
edition is available. Also, other materials on
the 8 Ohio Presidents.

OH —RUTHERFORD B HAYES LIBRARY,
1337 Hayes Ave, Fremont, 43420. Watt P
Marchman, Dir
Holdings: Vols 10,000 Cat Mss Maps Pix
Slides Microforms Audiotapes
Notes: The Rutherford B Hayes Family
Collections. The collections comprise papers,
books, correspondence, diaries, speeches,
account books, financial and real estate
records, law cases, ephemera, and
memorabilia of members of the Rutherford B
Hayes family; his wife, Lucy Webb Hayes;
their children: Birchard Austin Hayes; Webb
C Hayes I; Rutherford Platt Hayes; Scott
Russell Hayes; Fanny Hayes; grandchildren:
Dalton Hayes; Webb C Hayes, II; daughter-
in-law, Mary Miller Hayes. Mss of the
collection are described in *Guide to
Manuscripts of the Ohio Historical Society*,
208, 209, 210, 211, 212, 214, 216, 217, 218,
219. Indexed, listed. The collections are
housed in the mss division and newspapers
division. Ms materials of 256 linear feet; 50,
000 pictures; slides; tapes; moving pictures,
maps. The papers of Rutherford Birchard
Hayes available on 304 rolls of microfilm.
The collection described in *Guide to the
Microfilm Edition of the Papers of
Rutherford Birchard Hayes, the Nineteenth
President of the United States*. Fremont,
Ohio: The Rutherford B Hayes Presidential
Center, 1983. In addition, the Great Lakes
Marine Collection, incl Capt Frank E
Hamilton Collection; Great Lakes boats and
shipping. Incl 300 charts, over 20,000
pictures (with 2500 negatives, 30 glass
plates). Index and finding aids with the
collection.

**OH —LAKE COUNTY HISTORICAL
SOCIETY,** Percy Kendall Smith Library,
8095 Mentor Ave, Mentor, 44060. Carl
Thomas Engel, Librn
Holdings: Vols (2400) Cat Mss Pix
Notes: James Abram Garfield, 1831-1881.

OH —MIAMI UNIVERSITY, King Library,
Walter Havighurst Special Collections
Library, Oxford, 45056. Helen Ball, Cur of
Special Collections
Holdings: Uncat
Notes: Microfilms and some memorabilia.
Papers of William Henry Harrison and
Benjamin Harrison.

**PA —FRANKLIN & MARSHALL
COLLEGE,** Library, Lancaster, 17604.
Kathleen J Moretto, Library Dir
Holdings: Uncat Pix
Notes: The W W Griest Collection of

Lincoln Pictures contains 300 photographs,
lithographs, wood engravings, half-tone
engravings, mezzotints and etchings of
Lincoln. The Ralph E Stine Lincoln
Collection.

**PA —BALCH INSTITUTE FOR ETHNIC
STUDIES,** Library, 18 S Seventh St,
Philadelphia, 19106. R Joseph Anderson,
Library Dir

**PA —HISTORICAL SOCIETY OF
PENNSYLVANIA,** Library, 1300 Locust St,
Philadelphia, 19107. David Fraser, Librn
Holdings: Vols (230,000) Mss Maps Pix
Microforms
Notes: Incl over 14,000,000 ms pieces. The
Library Company of Philadelphia mss are on
deposit with the Historical Society of
Pennsylvania. Many of the Society's rare
books are on deposit with the Library
Company. The Society maintains the
collections of the Genealogical Society of
Pennsylvania, incl some 20,000 printed
genealogies, original mss, family, church, and
civil records.

RI —BROWN UNIVERSITY, John Hay
Library, McLellan Lincoln Collection, 20
Prospect St, Providence, 02912. Jennifer B
Lee, Special Collections Librn
Holdings: Vols (15,000) Cat Mss Pix
Phonorecords
Notes: The McLellan Lincoln Collection was
originally the property of Charles Woodberry
McLellan, one of 5 great Lincoln collectors
at the turn of the century. It was acquired
for Brown University in 1923 by John D
Rockefeller and others. Increased steadily
since that time, the book collection is
especially strong in biographies and early
editions of the campaign lives. About 85
percent of the titles in *Lincoln Bibliography,
1829-1939,* by Jay Monaghan, are in the
collection. Of the 218 foreign titles listed in
this bibliography, the collection has some
167 books and 16 films or photostats. In
conjunction with The Harris Collection, the
John Hay Library holds what is probably the
largest number of poems on Lincoln in any
one place. There is also a good selection of
representative titles of the books which
Lincoln read. The ms collection incl original
letters, notes and documents,over 950 of
which were written or signed by Lincoln;
from 1838 on, there is something for every
year of his life. The Lincoln mss appear in
The Collected Works of Abraham Lincoln
edited by Roy P Basler, and its supplement.
Ms material of Lincoln's family and
associates as well as ms facsimiles of
holdings of Lincoln material in other
libraries are in the collection. The broadsides
incl many song sheets, contemporary
political sheets, ballots, and posters; also 27
of the 52 printed editions of the
"Emancipation Proclamation" listed by
Charles Eberstadt in *Lincoln's Emancipation
Proclamation.* There is a selection of
newspapers for the war years, 1860-1865,
and an index of over 11,300 entries for
Lincoln items in all existing files of the
Illinois newspapers down through the Civil
War. The prints, arranged according to
Meserve numbers, contains most of
theknown photographs of Lincoln, rare
engravings, caricatures, Currier and Ives
prints, and original oil portraits done by
artists of Lincoln's day, as well as original
paintings of Lincoln's deathbed by Alonzo
Chappel and Alexander Ritchie; some
original drawings, as well as a scrapbook of
Thomas Nast's Civil War sketches. Sheet
music collection has almost every piece of
Lincoln sheet music known to exist from
minstrel songs to funeral marches, memorial
songs and campaign songs. Statuary is well
represented and incl two Rogers groups, an
original Truman Bartlett plaster statuette of
Lincoln, and replicas of Leonard Volk's
work. The museum objects incl over 550
medals, mourning and campaign badges,
coins, postage stamps and other miscellany.
For a more detailed description of the
collection, see Esther C Cushman: The
McLellan Lincoln Collection at
BrownUniversity (Brown University Library,
1928). The collection is housed in two
separate rooms plus stack space. It has its
own catalog and is restricted to reference
use.

TN —LINCOLN MEMORIAL UNIVERSITY,
Carnegie Library with Bert Vincent
Memorial Wing, Harrogate, 37752. Edgar
Archer, Dir
Holdings: Vols 18,000 Cat Maps Pix
Phonorecords 16mm Films
Notes: The Abraham Lincoln Center for
Lincoln studies located at Abraham Lincoln
Museum on the campus of Lincoln
University established to display one of the
largest collections of Lincoln and Civil War
materials in the United States. Described
fully in the Lincoln Herald, summer, 1973
(entire issue). National Lincoln Civil War
Council Center for study of military surgery
and medicine from the Civil War. National
headquarters for the Society of Civil War
surgeons. Also the center for the study of
military music. 7000 pieces of sheet music
dating from the War of 1812.

**TN —UNIVERSITY OF TENNESSEE,
KNOXVILLE,** Library, Knoxville, 37996.
John Dobson, Special Collections Librn
Holdings: Mss
Notes: Joint member in a project planning a
comprehensive new edition of the papers of
Andrew Jackson.

TX —UNIVERSITY OF TEXAS, Lyndon
Baines Johnson Presidential Library, 2813
Red River St, Austin, 78712. Harry J
Middleton, Dir
Holdings: Vols (14,164) Cat Mss Pix
Phonorecords Audiotapes Videotapes Films
VF
Budget: ($856,500)
Notes: A collection containing the papers
and materials of President Lyndon Baines
Johnson; his life, associates, family and
administration. Incl 34,699,837 ms pages;
593,417 still photographs; 824,076 feet of
motion picture film; 5711 videotapes; 11,146
audiotapes; 607 audio disks; oral history
transcripts; 37,836 museum objects. 7731
cataloged vertical files.

**TX —SAM RAYBURN FOUNDATION
LIBRARY,** 800 W Sam Rayburn Dr, Box
123, Bonham, 75418.
Holdings: Vols 8000 Cat Mss Pix
Microforms
Notes: Historical research library--contains
all of Speaker Rayburn's papers. Incl books
on American history, biography, politics and
government, and the Presidents and their
writings.

TX —WEST TEXAS STATE UNIVERSITY,
Cornette Library, PO Box 748 WT Sta,
Canyon, 79016. Faye Hendrickson, Special
Collections Asst
Holdings: Vols (451,253) Uncat Microforms
Notes: Includes microform collections.

TX —TEXAS CHRISTIAN UNIVERSITY,
Mary Couts Burnett Library, Fort Worth,
76129.
Notes: The Marguerite Oswald Collection
(mother of Lee Harvey Oswald), incl the full
Warren Commission Report, with her own
annotations and comments. Also, some 200
vols, many inscribed or dedicated to her.

TX —HOUSTON POST LIBRARY, 4747
Southwest Freeway, Houston, 77001. Kathy
Foley, Librn

TX —PRESIDENTIAL MUSEUM, 622 N Lee
Ave, Odessa, 79761.
Holdings: Vols 3000 Cat Mss Maps Pix
Slides
Budget: ($95,057)
Notes: Books incl first editions, rare editions,
those written and/or signed by the
presidents as well as authors.

VA —UNIVERSITY OF VIRGINIA,
Alderman Library, Manuscripts Dept,
Charlottesville, 22901. Edmund Berkeley Jr,
Cur
Notes: The papers of Maj Gen Edwin M
Watson (Pres Franklin D Roosevelt's
military aide in the years before and during
World War II). Incl some 16,000 documents
and other articles, reflect both the full scope
of Watson's duties as an aide to Roosevelt
and his personal associations with the
president and other national leaders during
his years of service.

VA —UNIVERSITY OF VIRGINIA,
Alderman Library, Tracy W McGregor
Collection, Charlottesville, 22901. William H
Runge, Cur
Holdings: Vols 300 // Cat
Notes: All pamphlets owned by Madison
and donated to the University of Virginia.

PRESIDENTS—U.S. (cont.)

VA —MOUNT VERNON LADIES'
ASSOCIATION OF THE UNION,
Research & Reference Library, Mount
Vernon, 22121. Ellen McCallister Clark,
Librn; John Rhodehamel, Dir of Education
Holdings: Vols (12,000) Cat Mss Maps Pix
Slides
Notes: The Washington family and Mount
Vernon. The history of the Mount Vernon
Ladies' Association and historic
preservation.

VA —VIRGINIA STATE LIBRARY, 12 &
Capitol Sts, Richmond, 23219.
Holdings: Vols 9050 Cat Mss Maps Pix
Notes: Incl George Washington (5500 vols);
Thomas Jefferson (2700 vols); and James
Madison (500 vols).

VA —WOODROW WILSON BIRTHPLACE,
PO Box 24, Staunton, 24401. Gertrude
Davis, Librn
Holdings: Vols 3500 Cat Mss Pix
Budget: $500

VA —COLLEGE OF WILLIAM AND
MARY, Earl Gregg Swem Library,
Williamsburg, 23185. Margaret C Cook, Cur
of Manuscripts & Rare Books
Holdings: Cat
Notes: Papers, letters, etc of Thomas
Jefferson (qv), James Monroe (qv).

†WA —WASHINGTON STATE
UNIVERSITY, Library, Manuscripts,
Archives & Special Collections, Pullman,
99164. John F Guido, Head
Holdings: Vols // Cat Mss
Notes: Bissett-Witherspoon Collection incl a
Lincoln ms, approx 2000 monographs, and
about 500 pamphlets, bibliographies,
facsimiles, clippings, photographs and
illustrations, programs, brochures and other
ephemera on Lincoln and the Lincoln theme.
Described in *The Record* (October 1945), pp
10-11.

WA —TACOMA PUBLIC LIBRARY, 1102
Tacoma Ave S, Tacoma, 98402. Kevin
Hegarty, Dir
Holdings: Vols 1500 Cat Pix
Notes: Based on collection of Marion L
Saunders.

WI —BELOIT COLLEGE LIBRARIES, Beloit,
53511. Dennis W Dickinson, Dir
Holdings: Vols (1200) Cat Pix
Notes: The Joseph P Rheingold Collection
on Franklin Delano Roosevelt (qv) and The
Irving S Kull Collection on Woodrow Wilson
(qv).

PRESIDENTS—U.S.—AUTOGRAPHS

IL —SOUTHERN ILLINOIS UNIVERSITY,
CARBONDALE, Delyte W Morris Library,
Special Collections Dept, Carbondale, 62901.
David V Koch, Cur of Special Collections;
Louisa Bowen, Cur of Manuscripts
Holdings: // Cat Mss
Notes: Incl the Philip D Sang and the Alfred
C Berol collections of documents of
American presidents; the James S Schoff
collection of letters of Civil War generals;
and the Elbridge Gerry Collection of Elsie O
and Philip D Sang. Separate catalogs exist
for each collection.

ME —BOWDOIN COLLEGE, Library,
Brunswick, 04011. Dianne M Gutscher, Cur
of Special Collections
Holdings: Mss
Notes: The Franklin Pierce Papers consist of
29 letters, mss, and documents of this
member of Bowdoin's class of 1824.

MA —WILLIAMS COLLEGE, Sawyer
Library, Williamstown, 01267. Phyllis L
Cutler, Dir
Holdings: Cat Mss Pix
Notes: Incl the Gates W McGarrah
Collection of Presidential Autographs,
originally assembled by William Henry Poor,
containing handwritten letters and
documents by every President from
Washington to Theodore Roosevelt. The
Library has numerous other presidential
autograph pieces as well.

PA —FREE LIBRARY OF PHILADELPHIA,
Rare Book Dept, Logan Sq, Philadelphia,
19103. Marie E Korey, Rare Book Librn
Holdings: Uncat Mss
Notes: The Norman H and Charlotte A

Strouse Collection of 100 selected autograph
letters of presidents of the US.

PRESIDENTS—U.S.—PICTURES, ILLUSTRATIONS, ETC.

VA —GEORGE MASON UNIVERSITY,
Fenwick Library, Special Collections Dept,
4400 University Drive, Fairfax, 22030. Ruth
Kerns, Public Services Librn
Notes: The Ollie Atkins Photographic
Collection. Atkins, award-winning
photographer with the *Saturday Evening
Post*, was also White House photographer
under several administrations. The collection
incl more than 15,000 prints, negatives,
contact sheets, slides and 4000 images
covering subjects of historical, artistic and
social significance from 1948 to 1968.

PRESIDENT'S COMMISSION ON THE ACCIDENT AT THREE MILE ISLAND (MAY-DECEMBER 1979)

DC —NATIONAL ARCHIVES AND
RECORDS SERVICE, Civil Archives
Division, Washington, 20408.
Notes: Records of the President's
Commission on the Accident at Three Mile
Island (May-December 1979).

PRESNAL, BILL

TX —TEXAS A&M UNIVERSITY, Sterling C
Evans Library, University Archives, College
Station, 77843. Charles R Schultz,
University Archivist
Notes: The Archives of Modern Politics:
Texas Legislator Bill Presnal 1974-1983.

PRESS, FREEDOM OF THE see Liberty of the Press

PRESS AGENTS

NY —NEW YORK PUBLIC LIBRARY,
Performing Arts Research Center, Billy Rose
Theatre Collection, 111 Amsterdam Ave,
New York, 10023. Dorothy L Swerdlove,
Cur
Holdings: Cat
See also entry under Theatre - History.

PRESS BOOKS

AL —MOBILE PUBLIC LIBRARY, Special
Collections Div, 701 Government St,
Mobile, 36602.
Holdings: Vols 500 Cat
Notes: The Harris Collection.

AZ —UNIVERSITY OF ARIZONA, Library,
Tucson, 85721. W David Laird, Librn
Notes: Theatre collection incl works by and
about Thomas Wood Stevens and the theater
in Pittsburgh and Chicago. Mss of pageants,
programs, scrapbooks, prompt books, private
press imprints, personal correspondence.

CA —UNIVERSITY OF CALIFORNIA,
BERKELEY, Bancroft Library, Manuscripts
Division, Berkeley, 94720. James D Hart,
Dir
Holdings: Vols Cat Mss
Notes: Materials are collected to serve as
specimens for the study of printing history
and the development of fine printing.
English and American fine presses of the
19th and 20th centuries are particularly well
represented. Comprehensive coverage for
San Francisco Bay Area printers such as
Grabhorn, Grabhorn-Hoyem, and John
Henry Nash.

CA —BURBANK PUBLIC LIBRARY, 110 N
Glenoaks Blvd, Burbank, 91502. Mary Ann
Grasso, Coordr; Barbara Stones, Coordr,
Media Project
Holdings: Vols (2600) Cat Maps Pix
Notes: Strong in Grabhorn Press imprints
and other California press items of historical
interest. Also, strong collection of pamphlets
and ephemera concerning California.
Separate catalog in preparation. Collection
well described in "The Burbank Western
History Collection," by Thomas F Parker, in
California Librarian (April 1965).

CA —CLAREMONT COLLEGES, Ella Strong
Denison Library, Scripps College,

Claremont, 91711. Judy Harvey Sahak,
Librn
Holdings: Vols (10,000) Cat Mss Pix
Notes: Emphasizes the history of the books
and fine printings; includes illuminated
manuscripts, incunabula, fine bindings,
representative examples of modern fine
presses, first editions, and literary ALS.

CA —CLAREMONT COLLEGES, Honnold
Library, Ninth & Dartmouth, Claremont,
91711. Tania Rizzo, Special Collections
Dept Head
Holdings: Vols (70,000) Cat VF
Notes: Books on typography, bibliography,
and history of printing; incunabula; specimen
books; fine press books, esp Kelmscott,
Doves, Daniel, Mosher, Grabhorn, Nash,
and Arion presses and many Southern
California printers. A comprehensive
collection of Zamorano Club publications
and keepsakes, partial source for George E
Fulleton, *The Zamorano Club: The First
Half Century* (Los Angeles, 1978). Extensive
files of ephemera. Fine bindings and fore-
edge paintings. Samples of Oriental type and
printing.

CA —CALIFORNIA STATE UNIVERSITY,
FULLERTON, Library, Box 4150,
Fullerton, 92634. Linda Herman, Special
Collections Librn
Holdings: Vols 4600 Cat
Notes: Press books and fine printing of the
20th century incl vols from the Grabhorn
Press of San Francisco (Dr William B
Langsdorf Anniversary Collection; 613 vols)
and the Fine Arts Press of Santa Ana, Calif
(67 vols). It is supplemented by a group of
related collections on printing, binding, and
book history reference, which incl
representative examples of most modern fine
presses.

CA —CALIFORNIA STATE UNIVERSITY,
HAYWARD, Library, Hayward, 94542.
Melissa Rose, Dir

CA —UNIVERSITY OF CALIFORNIA, SAN
DIEGO, Central University Library,
Mandeville Dept of Special Collections, La
Jolla, 92093. Lynda Corey Claassen, Head
Notes: The Press Collection comprises
examples of fine printing from numerous
private presses operating during the 19th and
20th centuries. Incl extensive holdings of the
Golden Cockerel Press, the Cuala Press, the
Hogarth Press, the Eucalyptus Press, and the
Plantin Press.

CA —UNIVERSITY OF CALIFORNIA, LOS
ANGELES, Research Library, Dept of
Special Collections, 405 Hilgard Ave, Los
Angeles, 90024. Edward Shreeves,
Chairman, Bibliographers Group; David S
Zeidberg, Head
Notes: Ephemera. 200 linear feet of
mailings, announcements, keepsakes, sample
leaves, etc, relating to small presses and
graphic arts.

CA —UNIVERSITY OF CALIFORNIA, LOS
ANGELES, William Andrews Clark
Memorial Library, 2520 Cimarron St, Los
Angeles, 90018.
Holdings: Cat Mss Pix
Notes: Extensive collection, first editions,
etc.

CA —MILLS COLLEGE LIBRARY, Oakland,
94613. Steven P Pandolfo, Librn
Holdings: Vols 4550 Cat
Notes: Books and ephemera from English
and American fine presses. Strong interest in
collecting the work of women printers.

CA —SAN DIEGO PUBLIC LIBRARY,
Wangenheim Rm, 820 E St, San Diego,
92101. Eileen Boyle, Librn
Holdings: Vols (7500) Cat
Notes: A collection on the history of the
book and the development of printing with
specimens ranging from Babylonian tablets
to cassettes.

CA —UNIVERSITY OF SAN FRANCISCO,
Richard A Gleeson Library, The Countess
Bernardine Murphy Donohue Rare Book
Room, San Francisco, 94117. D Steven
Corey, Special Collections Librn
Notes: Major collections of John Henry
Nash, the Grabhorns, Allen Press, The Book
Club of California, Peregrine Press, plus the
archives for the Cranium Press, Five Trees
Press, Tamalpais Press, and extensive

PRESS BOOKS (cont.)

holdings of all other presses in the San Francisco Bay area, extensive ephemera. 2, 500 items.

CA —UNIVERSITY OF CALIFORNIA, SANTA BARBARA, Library, Dept of Special Collections, Santa Barbara, 93106. Christian F Brun, Head
Notes: Incl Skofield Printers Collection.

CA —SOLANO COUNTY LIBRARY, John F Kennedy Library, Donovan J McCune Collection, 505 Santa Clara St, Vallejo, 94590.
Holdings: Vols (1500) // Cat Mss
Notes: The Donovan J McCune Collection.

CO —DENVER PUBLIC LIBRARY, Douglas Collection of Fine Printing, 1357 Broadway, Denver, 80203.
Holdings: Vols 1700 Cat
Notes: Books from private presses, limited editions and books about private presses. Incl a complete set of vols from William Morris' Kelmscott Press and a virtually complete collection of Ashendene Press books. Most major presses are well represented and minor presses have representative works in the collection.

CT —LEE ASH, (personal collection), 66 Humiston Dr, Bethany, 06525.
Holdings: Cat Mss Pix
Notes: Incl books, letters, ephemera, etc.

CT —TRINITY COLLEGE LIBRARY, Watkinson Library, 300 Summit St, Hartford, 06106. Jeffrey Kaimowitz, Cur
Holdings: Cat
Notes: Separate collection indexed by press plus file of private press ephemera.

CT —YALE UNIVERSITY, Box 1603A, Yale Station, New Haven, 06520.
Notes: Excellent representation of numerous private or famous presses. Inquire.

DC —LIBRARY OF CONGRESS, Rare Book & Special Collections Div, Washington, 20540. William Matheson, Chief
Notes: Books dating from the 1890s to the present, printed by American and British fine presses. Collection is rapidly growing.

FL —UNIVERSITY OF MIAMI, Otto G Richter Library, PO Box 248214, Coral Gables, 33124. Frank Rodgers, Dir of Libraries
Notes: 3500 items. Black Sparrow, Auerhahn and other press books of the 1960s and 1970s, within the general area of contemporary poetry. Also, separate from this group, are many Cuala, Mosher, Kelmscott imprints, and all of the Trianon Press Blake facsimiles. Noncirculating.

FL —FLORIDA STATE UNIVERSITY, Robert Manning Strozier Library, Special Collections Dept, Tallahassee, 32306. Opal M Free, Head, Special Collections
Holdings: Vols (12,254) Cat Mss Maps
Notes: Noncirculating. No photocopying.

GA —UNIVERSITY OF GEORGIA, Libraries, Special Collections Division, Athens, 30602. Vesta Lee Gordon, Asst Dir for Special Collections
Holdings: Vols (8000)
Notes: One of the larger collections of private press books, pamphlets, and ephemera. The Elmore H Mundell Collection of materials from over 1200 different private printers.

IL —SOUTHERN ILLINOIS UNIVERSITY, CARBONDALE, Delyte W Morris Library, Special Collections Dept, Carbondale, 62901. David V Koch, Cur of Special Collections; Louisa Bowen, Cur of Manuscripts
Holdings: Vols 2000 Cat Mss

IL —CHICAGO PUBLIC LIBRARY, Special Collections Div, Cultural Center, 78 E Washington St, Chicago, 60602. Laura Linard, Cur
Holdings: Vols (800) Cat
Budget: ($3000)
Notes: The Special Collections Division endeavors to collect all Chicago imprints produced before 1900, and all Chicago private press productions 1900-50. An exceptional collection of books and keepsakes designed by Norman Forgue. We actively purchase in this area. Outstanding items in the Chicago Imprints Inventory are

described in the recent catalog, *Treasures of The Chicago Public Library*, compiled by Thomas A Orlando and Marie Gecik, 1977, pp 93-120.

IL —NEWBERRY LIBRARY, John M Wing Foundation on the History of Printing, 60 W Walton St, Chicago, 60610. Diana Haskell, Cur of Modern Mss
Holdings: Vols (30,000) Cat Mss
Budget: ($50,000)
Notes: The collection covers printing and printing history of Western Europe and the Americas from its invention to the present. It is particularly rich in incunabula (about 2000); the works of the great printers, among others Aldus, Bodoni, Baskerville, and Rogers. Printed catalog: *A Dictionary Catalogue.* (Boston: G K Hall, 1961); *Supplements* (1981). Brief descriptions: James M Wells, "The John M Wing Foundation of the Newberry Library," *The Book Collector, VIII,* 2 (Summer 1959), pp 157-162; Lawrece W Towner, *An Uncommon Collection of Uncommon Collections* (Chicago: The Newberry Library, 1977), pp 25-26.

IL —NORTHERN ILLINOIS UNIVERSITY, Founders Memorial Library, Rare Books and Special Collections Dept, De Kalb, 60115. William R DuBois, Dept Head
Holdings: Vols 1500 Cat
Notes: Midwestern Private Presses Collection. Incl private press books from private presses in Illinois, Indiana, Iowa, Michigan and Wisconsin. Noncirculating.

IL —NORTHWESTERN UNIVERSITY, Library, Special Collections Dept, 1937 Sheridan Rd, Evanston, 60201. R Russell Maylone, Cur
Holdings: Vols 27,000 Cat Mss
Notes: Representative collection with emphasis on the humanities and 19th century English and American literature in first edtions. Incl Elzeviers, Aldines, Deism, German classics, Fichte, Gruntvig, Ibsen, Kant, Kierkegaard, Mark Twain, Walt Whitman, economic history, Siege and Commune of Paris, 1870-1871, etc. Also rare law books (4000)-- British, European, Roman, Canon, American law; incunabula; Blackstone collection. Incl representative examples of the work of the modern private press from Strawberry Hill to the current small printers. Incl such presses as Cuala, Essex House, Golden Cockerel, Grabhorn, Nonesuch, Roxburghe, etc. Also 15,000 "little magazine" titles exclusive of runs in the general library collections.

IL —LAKE FOREST COLLEGE, Donnelley Library, Lake Forest, 60045. Arthur H Miller Jr, College Librn
Holdings: Vols (1000) Cat
Notes: Examples of many late 19th century and early 20th century presses, from Alfred Hamill Collection. Much mid-20th century ephemera (including printers' Christmas gifts, in Richard Templeton collection of 500 items, received 1977). Largely from the collection of Mr and Mrs DeWitt O'Kieffe, the collection has a range of items from landmarks (*Grabhorn Leaves of Grass.*) to ephemera of private presses. Among those incl are Grabhorn Press, Lawton and Alfred Kennedy, Book Club of California, and Carl Hertzog.

IL —ILLINOIS STATE UNIVERSITY, Milner Library, Dept of Special Collections, Normal, 61761. Robert Sokan, Librn
Holdings: Vols (2800) Cat
Notes: Emphasis thus far on Black Sparrow, Golden Cockerel, Grabhorn, Nonesuch, Roycroft and St Dominc's.

IN —INDIANA UNIVERSITY, Lilly Library, Seventh St, Bloomington, 47405. William R Cagle, Librn
Holdings: Cat
Notes: Usually acquired for content rather than as a press book; nevertheless, the collection is extensive, especially with regard to Americn and British authors and poets.

IN —INDIANA STATE UNIVERSITY, Cunningham Memorial Library, Dept of Rare Books & Special Collections, Terre Haute, 47809. Lawrence J McCrank, Head
Holdings: Vols (2800) Cat Maps
Budget: ($1500)
Notes: The Indiana collection covers entire

state with special emphasis on Terre Haute and the Wabash Valley in the following categories: first or special limited editions of major writers associated with Indiana for a significant portion of their productive lives; publications of private presses in Indiana; early Indiana imprints; other materials pertinent to Indiana, eg diaries, broadsides, early travel literature, etc; county, local and regional histories-chiefly 18th and 19th century; early atlases of Indiana locations; other materials (not rare) which depict the life of the state in a significant way in such areas as education, religion, industry, sports, social life, etc.

KS —EMPORIA STATE UNIVERSITY, William Allen White Library, Emporia, 66801. Mary E Bogan, Special Collections Librn
Holdings: Vols (1400) Phonorecords

KS —KANSAS STATE UNIVERSITY, Library, Special Collections & University Archives, Manhattan, 66506. Antonia Q Pigno, Coordr; John J Vander Velde, Librn; Anthony R Crawford, Univ Archivist
Holdings: Vols 700 Mss
Notes: Collection includes books and correspondence from Don Drenner, owner and printer of the Zauberberg Press, Coffeyville, Kansas.

MD —WALTERS ART GALLERY, Library & Manuscripts & Rare Book Collection, 600 N Charles St, Baltimore, 21201. Muriel L Toppan, Reference Librn; Lilian M C Randall, Cur of Mss & Rare Books
Holdings: Vols (80,000) Cat Mss
Budget: ($35,000)
Notes: The collection supports the gallery's collections of art objects which date from 4000 BC to the end of the 19th century. The collection of medieval and renaissance illuminated mss (782 in number), incunabula (about 1400) and rare books are considered art objects. There are card catalogs providing indexing to the collection. The mss are listed in De Ricci and the incunabula in Goff. Photocopying permitted for Reference Library materials only.

†MD —UNIVERSITY OF MARYLAND, Library, R D Remley Collection, College Park, 20742. Donald Farren, Cur Rare Books
Holdings: Vols (2000) Cat
Notes: *Exempla* and secondary works in the areas of typography, calligraphy, book design, book illustration, the history of books, and of publishing, etc. Catalog entries for designers, printing types, private presses, etc.

MA —BOSTON UNIVERSITY, Mugar Memorial Library, Special Collections Dept, 771 Commonwealth Ave, Boston, 02215. Howard B Gotlieb, Dir
Holdings: Cat Mss Pix
Notes: The Silver Private Press Book Collection; also the archives of The Society of Printers.

MA —SMITH COLLEGE, Library, Northampton, 01063. Ruth Mortimer, Cur of Rare Books
Holdings: Vols (10,000) Cat
Notes: Representative examples: incunabula, 16th century printers, through modern fine press books; Northampton imprints; typographic ephemera.

MI —DETROIT PUBLIC LIBRARY, Rare Books Department, 5201 Woodward Ave, Detroit, 48202.
Holdings: Cat
Notes: Restricted use. Reference collection.

MN —MINNEAPOLIS PUBLIC LIBRARY & INFORMATION CENTER, 300 Nicollet Mall, Minneapolis, 55401. Richard J Hofstad, Athenaeum Librn
Holdings: Vols (300) Cat
Notes: A wide selection of books from the outstanding twentieth century fine presses of the United States and Great Britain.

MN —UNIVERSITY OF MINNESOTA, O Meredith Wilson Library, 309 19 Ave S, Minneapolis, 55455. Austin J McLean, Chief, Special Collections
Holdings: Vols 4545 Cat
Notes: Publications of the modern private press movement, including ephemera.

MO —UNIVERSITY OF MISSOURI-COLUMBIA, Ellis Library, Special

PRESS BOOKS (cont.)

Collections Dept, Ninth & Lowry, Columbia, 65201. Margaret A Howell, Head, Special Collections
Holdings: Vols Cat
Notes: Examples from 15th century to the present. Includes works from over 500 modern private presses.

MO —SAINT LOUIS PUBLIC LIBRARY, Gardner Rare Book Room, 1301 Olive St, Saint Louis, 63103. Julanne M Good, Supervisor; Martha Riley, Rare Books Librn
Holdings: Vols (2300) Cat
Budget: ($5573)
Notes: Specimen items from such presses as Grabhorn, Grabhorn-Hoyem, John Henry Nash, Prairie Press, Torch Press, Merrymount Press, Kelmscott Press, Chiswick Press, Derrydale Press, Nonesuch Press, etc. Collections of materials published by Thomas Bird Mosher, Elbert Hubbard, and William K Bixby are more in depth, as are collections of regional St Louis presses like the Printery, Autolycus Press, Singing Wind, Singing Bone and Ronart Press. Noncirculating.

MO —WASHINGTON UNIVERSITY, John M Olin Library, Campus Box 1061, St Louis, 63130.
Holdings: Vols (3700) Cat Mss
Notes: The Isador Mendle Memorial Collection contains representative examples from the 15th century to the present. Specializes in technical and aesthetic aspects of printing in the 19th and 20th centuries incl private presses. The materials assembled support study and research on design, art history, economics, textual and analytical bibliography, and a variety of other topics. No photocopying.

NJ —FAIRLEIGH DICKINSON UNIVERSITY, Friendship Library, 285 Madison Ave, Madison, 07940. James Fraser, Library Dir; Renee Weber, Cur
Holdings: Vols 100 Cat Mss Pix
Notes: Books printed and bound by Loyd Haberly; also original drawings and sketches for illustrated bindings and page layouts for various books. Private funds are provided for purchase of books on the subject of Haberly's interests: hand binding and fine printing, not only his own.

NJ —NEWARK PUBLIC LIBRARY, Art & Music Dept, 5 Washington St, Newark, 07101. William J Dane, Supv
Holdings: Vols (3500) Cat
Notes: R C Jenkinson Collection of Finely Printed Books. Shows the physical form of the book and its development through the centuries. There is always a related exhibit in this section of the library covering such subjects as letter forms, printing, individual presses and publishers, papermaking, etc. Extensive Bruce Rogers collection.

NJ —PRINCETON UNIVERSITY, Library, Graphic Arts Collection, Princeton, 08540. Dale Roylance, Cur
Holdings: Vols
Notes: Very large collection (7000-8000 vols) of Private Press Books, mainly 20th century.

NY —BUFFALO & ERIE COUNTY PUBLIC LIBRARY, Rare Book Room, Lafayette Sq, Buffalo, 14203. William H Loos, Cur
Holdings: Vols 2200 Cat
Notes: Representative collection of modern press books, American, British, and European.

NY —HOFSTRA UNIVERSITY, Library, 1000 Fulton Ave, Hempstead, 11550. Charles R Andrews, Dean of Library Services
Notes: Strong collection. Incl some mss.

NY —CARL H PFORZHEIMER LIBRARY, 41 E 42 St, New York, 10017. Mihai H Handrea, Librn
Holdings: Cat Mss Pix
Notes: Extensive collections of numerous press books. Some unique materials.

NY —COLUMBIA UNIVERSITY LIBRARIES, Rare Book & Manuscript Library, 801 Butler Library, 535 W 114 St, New York, 10027. Kenneth A Lohf, Librn
Holdings: Cat

NY —GRADUATE CENTER OF THE CITY UNIVERSITY OF NEW YORK, William H and Gwynne K Crouse Library for Publishing Arts, 33 W 42 St, New York, 10036. Alfred H Lane, Dir
Notes: Recently established and intended as a source of 20th century materials, in hard form or microfilm, incl books, pamphlets, reprints, translations, dissertations, periodicals, indexing and abstracting services, yearbooks, reports and directories of organizations, publishers' and antiquarian dealers' catalogs (particularly those who deal in books about books), periodicals, legislative materials, and clippings pertaining to the book industry. Sections of the library deal with printing, including typography, specimen books, history of printing and printing techniques, book design and small press and alternative publishing.

NY —NEW YORK PUBLIC LIBRARY, Rare Books and Manuscripts Div, Fifth Ave & 42 St, New York, 10018. William L Joyce, Asst Dir; Francis O Mattson, Curator
Holdings: Cat
Budget: ($7161)
Notes: Extensive collection of modern fine printing. Complete or nearly complete files of Kelmscott Press; books of the major private and special presses such as Allen, Ashendene, Doves, Golden Cockerel, Grabhorn, Kelmscott, Nonesuch, Vale, etc; one of the finest institutional collections of books designed by Bruce Rogers. See Catalog of Special and Private Presses in the Rare Book Division, (G K Hall, 1978), 2 vols.

NY —UNIVERSITY CLUB, Library, One W 54 St, New York, 10019. Guy St Clair, Library Dir
Holdings: Vols (100,000) Cat Mss Maps Pix
Notes: A private library for the members of the University Club, their guests, and serious scholars upon written application to the Library Director. Holds the Edward Larocque Tinker Collection of Illustrated Books Between the Two World Wars, A Milton Runyon Collection on the History of Printing and Publishing, the Frederic R Coudert "Les Bibliophiles des Paris" Collection, The University Club Rare Book Collection, and the Frederick G Rudge Collection of Books Designed by William E Rudge and Bruce Rogers.

NY —ROCHESTER INSTITUTE OF TECHNOLOGY, Melbert B Cary Jr Graphic Arts Collection, School of Printing, One Lomb Memorial Drive, Rochester, 14623. David Pankow, Cur
Holdings: Vols (11,000) Cat Mss Pix

NY —VISUAL STUDIES WORKSHOP, Research Center, 31 Prince St, Rochester, 14607. Linn Underhill, Coordr; Robert Bretz, Librn
Holdings: Vols (8000) Cat Pix Slides Audiotapes Videotapes
Notes: Strong emphasis on photography (over 1,000,000 pictures) and the photographic arts in many subject areas incl in this volume. Heavy emphasis on early photographic processes and collections of examples of them. Also collections of individual photographers' works.

NC —UNIVERSITY OF NORTH CAROLINA, CHAPEL HILL, Wilson Library, Rare Book Collection, Chapel Hill, 27514. Paul S Koda, Cur of Rare Books
Holdings: Vols 1000 Cat
Notes: Books from private or special presses, incl a large collection of books from the Limited Editions Club, Heritage Press, and Kelmscott Press. Subjects incl the history of printing, bibliographical information, and books by authors whose works are collected.

NC —UNIVERSITY OF NORTH CAROLINA, GREENSBORO, Walter Clinton Jackson Library, Special Collections Dept, 1000 Spring Garden St, Greensboro, 27412. Emilie W Mills, Librn
Holdings: Vols (800) Cat
Notes: Emphasis is on English and American presses from the 1890s to the present. Selections from the major presses are included as are the lesser known presses. Periodicals incl The Dolphin, The Fleuron, The Colophon and The Imprint. Extensive

holdings of American presses currently operating incl Penumbra Press, The Perishable Press Limited, Jargon Society, and Unicorn Press.

OH —MOUNT UNION COLLEGE, Library, Alliance, 44601. Yost Osborne, Librn
Holdings: Vols 785 Cat
Budget: $350
Notes: No photocopying.

OH —PUBLIC LIBRARY OF CINCINNATI & HAMILTON COUNTY, Dept of Rare Books & Special Collections, 800 Vine St, Library Square, Cincinnati, 45202. Yeatman Anderson III, Cur
Holdings: Cat Mss
Notes: A collection of examples of fine printing from Gutenberg to date.

OH —CLEVELAND PUBLIC LIBRARY, Literature Dept, 325 Superior Ave, Cleveland, 44114. Evelyn Ward, Head
Holdings: Vols Cat
Notes: Comprehensive collection of literary texts, with a large body of literary history, criticism and biography. Strong in drama and poetry. Many first editions, books from special presses, and rarities. Microprint. Reference aids.

OK —UNIVERSITY OF TULSA, McFarlin Library, Dept of Rare Books and Special Collections, 600 S College, Tulsa, 74104. David Farmer, Dir; Toby Murray, Archivist; Caroline Swinson, Cur of Manuscripts & Art
Holdings: Cat
Notes: Incl the John Bennett Shaw Collection of Books About Books.

OR —AMERICAN PRIVATE PRESS ASSOCIATION, 112 E Burnett St, Stayton, 97383. Martin M Horvat, Librn
Notes: The collection is divided into two primary segments: the first is the traditional one of Amateur Journalism, the second is science fiction and fantasy oriented. The collection was once at New York University Libraries but moved in 1981.

PA —FREE LIBRARY OF PHILADELPHIA, Rare Book Dept, Logan Sq, Philadelphia, 19103. Marie E Korey, Rare Book Librn
Holdings: Vols (550) Uncat
Notes: Selected examples of fine printing and binding from many presses, and a collection of books and pamphlets issued by Henry Morris's Bird and Bull Press.

PA —PHILIP H & A S W ROSENBACH FOUNDATION LIBRARY, 2010 DeLancey Pl, Philadelphia, 19103. Clive E Driver, Dir
Holdings: Cat Mss Maps Pix

PA —TEMPLE UNIVERSITY, Samuel Paley Library, Berks & 13 Sts, Philadelphia, 19122.
Notes: Collection of works of the City of Birmingham School of Printing (England). Books and ephemera of the students and Leonard Jay, Master Printer. Also the William Danner Collection of periodical issues from amateur printers and presses.

PA —TEMPLE UNIVERSITY LIBRARIES, Special Collections Dept, Rare Books & Mss Section, Philadelphia, 19122. Thomas M Whitehead, Cur
Holdings: Vols (5000) Mss Pix
Notes: The printing and graphic arts collections stress the technological developments within the printing industry and the achievements in fine printing in the 19th and 20th centuries. Selected additions are continually made of examples and secondary works. Holdings include the Library and archives of Richard W Ellis, typographer, archives of Philadelphia printers and photoengravers. Partially cataloged. Collections of all major private press imprints.

PA —EASTERN COLLEGE, Frank Warner Memorial Library, Saint Davids, 19087. James L Sauer, Librn
Holdings: Uncat Mss Pix
Notes: The Harry C Goebel Collection. Incl Bruce Rogers printings (over 460); press books (about 350); oriental art (over 250); bookplates (with a separate collection of an almost complete set of bookplates designed by Edwin Davis French); Christmas Books; art and graphic arts (incl the French Graphic Arts Collection of Adolph DeMilly); first editions of Christopher Morley; Print Collection (1315 prints); Oriental art realia and artifacts.

PRESS BOOKS (cont.)

PA —SWARTHMORE COLLEGE, Library, Swarthmore, 19081. Michael J Durkan, Librn
Holdings: Vols 3073 Cat
Notes: Mostly private presses and private press books.

PA —PENNSYLVANIA STATE UNIVERSITY, Fred Lewis Pattee Library, Special Collections Dept, University Park, 16802. Charles Mann, Chief, Special Collections
Holdings: Vols (989) Uncat
Budget: ($37,000)
Notes: No photocopying.

RI —UNIVERSITY OF RHODE ISLAND, Library, Special Collections, Kingston, 02881. David Maslyn, Head
Notes: Extensive collections.

RI —BROWN UNIVERSITY, John Hay Library, 20 Prospect St, Providence, 02912. Mark N Brown, Cur Mss
Holdings: Vols (1000) Cat
Notes: Incl many examples of 19th and 20th century private and small presses of American and English imprint. Some of the presses represented are: Aldine, Anthoensen, Black Sun, Bodini, Catnatch, Cuala, Doves, Elzevier, Essex House, Golden Cockerel, Grabhorn, Kelmscott, Merrymount, Mosher, Nonesuch, Perishable, Stinehour, Trianon, plus many Rhode Island small presses such as Burning Deck, Turkey, and Hell Coal. See also entries under Printing History; Little Magazines

RI —BROWN UNIVERSITY, John Hay Library, Harris Collection, Prospect St, Providence, 02912. Rosemary L Cullen, Cur
Holdings: Vols (200,000) Cat Mss Pix Phonorecords Microforms
Budget: ($15,000)
Notes: The Harris Collection of American Poetry and Plays is principally composed of American and Canadian poetry and plays from the 17th century to the present. Extensive holdings in small press publications, fine printing, and "little magazines". All movements or schools of American poetry are represented. Over 600 "little magazines" received currently; 2500 back titles. See Dictionary Catalog of The Harris Collection of American Poetry and Plays (Boston: G K Hall, 1972), 13 vols; Supplement (1977), 3 vols. Separate catalog.

RI —PROVIDENCE PUBLIC LIBRARY, 150 Empire St, Providence, 02903. Lance J Bauer, Special Collections Librn
Holdings: Vols 400 // Cat
Notes: The Wetmore Illustrated Books Collection. This historical collection of more than 400 volumes was given to Providence Public Library in 1955 by Newport, Rhode Island, Collector Edith Wetmore. An extremely fine collection of livres d'artiste, examples of fine illustration, printing and bindings. This collection incl the works of such notable artists as William Blake, Pablo Picasso, Giorgio DiChirico, Aubrey Beardsley, Jean Cocteau, William Hogarth, Raoul Dufy, Pierre Bonnard and numerous others. Although especially strong in the French illustrated books, English and German illustrated books are amply represented also. Partially cataloged. Material must be used in-house.

SC —WOFFORD COLLEGE, Sandor Teszler Library, N Church St, Spartanburg, 29301. Frank J Anderson, Librn
Holdings: Vols 1,000 Cat
Budget: ($500)
Notes: Books about the history and practice of printing, hand papermaking, bookbinding, book collecting, fine press and private press books used in conjunction with instruction at the Wofford Library Press, an experimental and bibliographic press which has been in operation since 1969. Collection contains materials on printmaking methods and related graphic arts. Collection incl imprints of: Briarpatch Press, Anthoensen Press, Mosher Press, Kitmang Press, Windhover Press, Penman Press, Unicorn Press, Wofford Library Press and others.

TX —HARDIN-SIMMONS UNIVERSITY, Richardson Library, Abilene, 79601. Joe F Dahlstrom, Dir
Holdings: Vols (10,000) Cat Mss Maps Pix Microforms
Notes: Special collection name is Richardson Research Center, named in honor of Dr Rupert N Richardson. Collect in the areas of his own research interests, especially that portion of the US that was once a part of Mexico. Emphases on the history of ranching, railroads, discovery and exploration, Texas county histories, etc. Incl 350 items printed and/or designed by El Paso printer Carl Hertzog; the Judge R C Crane collection of Texana and a similar collection of Louise Kelley's and the Research Publication's Western Americana collection (microfilm).

TX —DALLAS PUBLIC LIBRARY, Fine Arts Div, 1515 Young St, Dallas, 75201. Richard L Waters, Acting Dir; Jane Holahan, Manager
Holdings: Vols 1400 Uncat Mss
Budget: $12,000
Notes: Fine printing and the history of printing. No photocopying.

TX —ROSENBERG LIBRARY, Fox Rare Book Room, 2310 Sealy Ave, Galveston, 77550. Fernando Basilza, Rare Book Librn
Holdings: Vols (2000) Cat Mss Pix
Notes: The Col Milo Pitcher Fox and Agnes Peel Fox Rare Book Room contains 2000 vols incunabula, first printings, and modern fine printing. Incl clay tablets, horn books, parchment material, illuminated books and mss, fine printing (principally 15th-18th centuries), fine binding, fore-edge paintings, etc.

TX —UNIVERSITY OF HOUSTON, M D Anderson Memorial Library, University Park, Houston, 77004. David Farmer, Cur, Special Collections; Jean Jackson, Assistant Cur
Holdings: Vols 600 Cat
Notes: This collection is confined to books in some way distinguished by their typographic qualities and produced within the borders of Texas at any time, past or present. Larger portions of the collection incl the work of the Encino Press, William Holman, Carl Hertzog, Edwin Hill, and other private and fine printers.

WA —UNIVERSITY OF WASHINGTON LIBRARIES, Suzzallo Library, Special Collections Division, Rare Book Collection, FM-25, Seattle, 98195. Gary Menges, Coordinator for Special Collections
Notes: Printing history, including early printed books and modern fine printing; book arts, including papermaking, decorated papers, bookbinding, book design, and artist's books; American literature, 19th century includes: Stephen Crane, Ralph Waldo Emerson, Nathaniel Hawthorne, Henry James, Henry Wadsworth Longfellow, Herman Melville, Frank Norris, Harriet Beecher Stowe and Walt Whitman and 20th century includes: Theodore Roethke; illustrated books, including emblem books, historical children's illustration, books illustrated with prints, and artist's books; costume history; voyages and travels; preservation of library materials.

WI —UNIVERSITY OF WISCONSIN, LA CROSSE, Murphy Library, 1631 Pine St, La Crosse, 54601. Edwin L Hill, Special Collections Librn
Holdings: Vols 1000 Cat Mss
Notes: Center for Contemporary Poetry (a collection of contemporary midwestern poetry). Emphasis on purchase of trade and small press publications of midwestern amd especially Wisconsin poets. Unpublished materials are collected for a few poets and incl comprehensive papers, mss, reviews, letters, etc. Collection also incl various midwestern and Wisconsin little magazines. Several fine midwestern private presses, especially Perishable Press. Collection is largely regional and contemporary. Most is cataloged and/or indexed. Collection incl records and papers of Margins (1972-1976), a review of little magazines and small press books. The Center for Contemporary Poetry published an annual volume, Voyages to the Inland Sea, from 1971-1979, featuring the poetry and essays of prominent midwestern poets.

WI —UNIVERSITY OF WISCONSIN, MADISON, Memorial Library, 728 State St, Madison, 53706. Erwin K Welsch, Social Studies Bibliographer
Notes: Incl the Limited Editions Club Collection, an extensive collection of these privately printed books, mostly literature.

WI —UNIVERSITY OF WISCONSIN, MADISON, Memorial Library, Rare Books Collection, 728 State St, Madison, 53706. Gretchen Lagana, Cur
Holdings: Vols 6000 Cat
Notes: Private Press Collection. Strong collection of the major fine presses, modern fine printing, as well as books from Wisconsin private presses. Also includes a large collection of small press books up to 1980. Especially strong in Golden Cockerel and Perishable Press imprints. Housed in the Dept of Rare Books and Special Collections.

WI —MILWAUKEE PUBLIC LIBRARY, 814 W Wisconsin Ave, Milwaukee, 53233. Donald J Sager, City Librn
Holdings: Vols 5000 Cat
Notes: Extensive collection of author, imprint, subject, press, library, bibliographies.

ON —QUEEN'S UNIVERSITY, Douglas Library, Kingston, K7L 5C4, Can. William F E Morley, Cur, Special Collections
Holdings: Vols 6980 Cat Mss Pix
Notes: Subject strength of the collections.

†ON —UNIVERSITY OF WESTERN ONTARIO, School of Library and Information Science, Special Collections Room, London, N6A 5B9, Can.
Holdings: Vols 776
Notes: A representative collection incl early materials of private presses and fine press books. Also incl publications of bibliophile clubs and societies.

ON —NATIONAL LIBRARY OF CANADA, 395 Wellington St, Ottawa, K1A 0N4, Can. Andre Preibish, Dir
Holdings: Vols 10,000
Notes: The collection on History and Art of the Book consists of over 10,000 volumes. Areas of concentration are: early imprints, special editions, examples of private presses works, book industry and trade books illustrating the aesthetic and technical aspects of the field, collection of books illustrated by Bartlett.

ON —METROPOLITAN TORONTO LIBRARY, Fine Arts Dept, 789 Yonge St, Toronto, M4W 2G8, Can. Alan Suddon, Head
Holdings: Vols (42,000) Cat Pix Microforms
Notes: Joseph Henry Jackson's personal library. Strong in Californiana.

ON —UNIVERSITY OF WATERLOO, Library, Waterloo, N2L 3G1, Can. Susan Bellingham, Special Collections Librn
Notes: Incl Canadian, American and British presses. Strengths incl St Dominic's, Nonesuch and Golden Cockerel Presses. Collection contains 5600 titles.

PRESS BOOKS—ABATTOIR EDITIONS

NE —UNIVERSITY OF NEBRASKA, OMAHA, Library, 60 & Dodge Sts, Omaha, 68132. Mel Bohn, Librn
Holdings: Vols 100 Cat
Notes: One of the most complete collections of Cummington Press and Abattoir Editions publications. 100 bound vols and 218 other pieces; including broadsheets, proofsheets, woodblocks, etc. No photocopying.

PRESS BOOKS—ACHILLE I. ST. ONGE

†NY —COLUMBIA UNIVERSITY LIBRARIES, Butler Library, Rare Book and Manuscript Library, 535 W 114 St, New York, 10027.

PRESS BOOKS—ALDINE PRESS

CA —UNIVERSITY OF CALIFORNIA, LOS ANGELES, Research Library, Dept of Special Collections, 405 Hilgard Ave, Los Angeles, 90024. Edward Shreeves, Chairman, Bibliographers Group; David S Zeidberg, Head
Notes: 500 books printed by Aldus Manutius, his father-in-law, his son, and his grandson, incl 21 printed before 1501.

PRESS BOOKS—ALDINE PRESS (cont.)

CT —YALE UNIVERSITY, Box 1603A, Yale
Station, New Haven, 06520.
Notes: A distinguished collection.

IL —NEWBERRY LIBRARY, John M Wing
Foundation on the History of Printing, 60 W
Walton St, Chicago, 60610. Diana Haskell,
Cur of Modern Mss
Holdings: Vols (30,000) Cat Mss
Budget: ($50,000)
See also entry under Printing - History

IL —NORTHWESTERN UNIVERSITY,
Library, Special Collections Dept, 1937
Sheridan Rd, Evanston, 60201. R Russell
Maylone, Cur
Holdings: Vols 73 Cat

†MA —WILLIAMS COLLEGE, Chapin
Library of Rare Books, PO Box 426,
Williamstown, 01267. Robert L Volz,
Custodian
Holdings: Vols 134 Cat
Budget: ($3500)
Notes: 93 titles; 52 published before 1516;
30 in Greek and 11 in Italian.

PA —BUCKNELL UNIVERSITY, Ellen
Clarke Bertrand Library, Lewisburg, 17837.
Ann de Klerk, Librn

PRESS BOOKS—ALLEN PRESS

CA —UNIVERSITY OF SAN FRANCISCO,
Richard A Gleeson Library, The Countess
Bernardine Murphy Donohue Rare Book
Room, San Francisco, 94117. D Steven
Corey, Special Collections Librn
Holdings: Vols 43
Notes: Complete collection of one of the
most important presses of the US in current
operation. Extensive collection of ephemera,
original art work for several titles.

CT —YALE UNIVERSITY, Box 1603A, Yale
Station, New Haven, 06520.

NY —NEW YORK PUBLIC LIBRARY, Rare
Books and Manuscripts Div, Fifth Ave & 42
St, New York, 10018. William L Joyce, Asst
Dir; Francis O Mattson, Curator
Holdings: Cat
Budget: ($7161)
Notes: Complete or nearly complete file of
publications, incl books, pamphlets,
broadsides and other ephemera.

UT —UNIVERSITY OF UTAH, Marriott
Library, Special Collections, Salt Lake City,
84112. Gregory C Thompson, Cur
Notes: The publications of Utah presses are
also acquired. These presses are Olympus,
Peregrine, Smith, Real Peoples, Horizon,
Canticle, and Westwater. For the Rare
Books collection materials from certain
outside presses are also included. These
presses are Northland, Allen, Grabhorn,
Black Sparrow, Lime Kiln and Black
Mountain. Books on Freemasonry are also
collected.

PRESS BOOKS—AMERICANA HOUSE

IL —CHICAGO PUBLIC LIBRARY, Special
Collections Div, Cultural Center, 78 E
Washington St, Chicago, 60602. Laura
Linard, Cur
Holdings: Vols (800) Cat
Budget: ($3000)
Notes: The Special Collections Division
endeavors to collect all Chicago imprints
produced before 1900, and all Chicago
private press productions 1900-50. An
exceptional collection of books and
keepsakes designed by Norman Forgue. We
actively purchase in this area. Outstanding
items in the Chicago Imprints Inventory are
described in the recent catalog, *Treasures of
The Chicago Public Library*, compiled by
Thomas A Orlando and Marie Gecik, 1977,
pp 93-120.

PRESS BOOKS—ANGEL HAIR PRESS

BC —SIMON FRASER UNIVERSITY,
Library, Burnaby, V5A 1S6, Can. Percilla
Groves, Special Collections Librn
Holdings: // Cat Mss
Notes: Letters from Anne Waldman to
Lewis Warsh, many concerned with *Silo* and
Angel Hair Press, 1965-1973; some mss
enclosed.

PRESS BOOKS—ANTHOENSEN PRESS

ME —BOWDOIN COLLEGE, Library,
Brunswick, 04011. Dianne M Gutscher, Cur
of Special Collections
Holdings: Vols 1200 Cat
Notes: Incl nearly all items printed since
1923 and many before that date (when press
was known as Southworth Press); also
Records of the press from 1925 to 1951.

ME —PORTLAND PUBLIC LIBRARY, 5
Monument Sq, Portland, 04101. Edward V
Chenevert, Library Dir
Holdings: Vols 448 Cat
Notes: Originated as the Southworth
Printing Company and was concerned with
producing religious tracts. The scope of the
press broadened under the later ownership
(ca 1923) of Fred Anthoensen; it is still
publishing.

ME —UNIVERSITY OF MAINE AT
PORTLAND-GORHAM, Portland Campus
Library, 96 Falmouth St, Portland, 04103.
Albert A Howard, Special Collections Librn
Holdings: Vols 900 Cat
Notes: Collection incl broadsides,
prospectuses and other printed ephemera
(not cataloged). Also some imprints of
Southworth-Anthoensen. Collection is
comprehensive. Collection is in main catalog
and there is a separate shelf list.

SC —WOFFORD COLLEGE, Sandor Teszler
Library, N Church St, Spartanburg, 29301.
Frank J Anderson, Librn
Holdings: Vols 1000 Cat
Notes: Books about the history and practice
of printing, hand papermaking, bookbinding,
book collecting, fine press and private press
books used in conjunction with instruction at
the Wofford Library Press, an experimental
and bibliographic press which has been in
operation since 1969. Collection contains
materials on printmaking methods and
related graphic arts. Collection incl imprints
of: Briarpatch Press, Anthoensen Press,
Mosher Press, Kitmang Press, Windhover
Press, Penman Press, Unicorn Press,
Wofford Library Press and others.

PRESS BOOKS—ANVIL PRESS

†CA —UNIVERSITY OF SAN FRANCISCO,
Richard A Gleeson Library, The Countess
Bernardine Murphy Donohue Rare Book
Room, San Francisco, 94117. D Steven
Corey, Special Collections Librn
Holdings: Vols (75) Uncat Mss
Notes: A complete collection of Victor
Hammer with unique items. Incl the
Stamperia del Santuccio, Wells College
Press, Hammer Press, and Anvil Press. Also
present are a number of Hammer's original
drawings and sketches, as well as a printed
triptych.

KY —UNIVERSITY OF KENTUCKY,
Margaret I King Library, Dept of Special
Collections, Lexington, 40506. William
Marshall, Head
Holdings: Cat Mss
Notes: Complete sets of Stamperia del
Santuccio imprints (C and V Hammer); The
Anvil Press; the Gravesend Press (Joseph
Graves); The Bur Press; King Library Press;
Gnoman Press; Buttonwood Press.

PRESS BOOKS—APPLEDORE PRESS

CT —YALE UNIVERSITY, Box 1603A, Yale
Station, New Haven, 06520.
See also entry under Linton, Williams.

PRESS BOOKS—ARCHETYPE PRESS

CA —UNIVERSITY OF CALIFORNIA, LOS
ANGELES, William Andrews Clark
Memorial Library, 2520 Cimarron St, Los
Angeles, 90018.

PRESS BOOKS—ARIES PRESS

NY —BUFFALO & ERIE COUNTY PUBLIC
LIBRARY, Rare Book Room, Lafayette Sq,
Buffalo, 14203. William H Loos, Cur
Holdings: Vols 8 Cat

PRESS BOOKS—ARION PRESS

CA —CLAREMONT COLLEGES, Honnold
Library, Ninth & Dartmouth, Claremont,

91711. Tania Rizzo, Special Collections
Dept Head
Holdings: Vols (75) Cat VF
Notes: The combined holdings of Honnold
and Denison Libraries at the Claremont
Colleges contain a complete set but one of
the books published by the Arion Press as
well as commissioned books and pamphlets,
and a comprehensive collection of books
printed by Andrew Hoyem for Grabhorn-
Hoyem and others. Complete ephemera
since 1979. Extensive files of advertising,
prospectuses, correspondence, and
broadsides.

PRESS BOOKS—ARKHAM HOUSE

IN —INDIANA UNIVERSITY, Lilly Library,
Seventh St, Bloomington, 47405. William R
Cagle, Librn
Holdings: Cat Mss
Notes: Extensive holdings. Mss include some
letters by August Derleth discussing Arkham
House.

SC —UNIVERSITY OF SOUTH CAROLINA,
Thomas Cooper Library, Columbia, 29208.
Kenneth E Toombs, Dir of Libraries; Roger
Mortimer, Rare Book Librn
Holdings: Vols 175 Cat
Notes: Perhaps one of the most complete
collections available.

WI —UNIVERSITY OF WISCONSIN, LA
CROSSE, Murphy Library, 1631 Pine St, La
Crosse, 54601. Edwin L Hill, Special
Collections Librn
Holdings: Vols 1000 Cat
Notes: The Paul W Skeeters Collection of
science fiction, fantasy, and horror literature.
Complements the library's complete
collection of Arkham House books, which
contains many titles autographed by August
Derleth, and H P Lovecraft's complete
fiction and poetic works.

PRESS BOOKS—ARMITAGE, MERLE

CA —UNIVERSITY OF CALIFORNIA, LOS
ANGELES, William Andrews Clark
Memorial Library, 2520 Cimarron St, Los
Angeles, 90018.

PRESS BOOKS—ASHANTILLY PRESS

GA —UNIVERSITY OF GEORGIA,
Libraries, Special Collections Division,
Athens, 30602. Vesta Lee Gordon, Asst Dir
for Special Collections
Holdings: Vols (8000)
Notes: One of the larger collections of
private press books, pamphlets, and
ephemera. The Elmore H Mundell
Collection of materials from over 1200
different private printers.

PRESS BOOKS—ASHENDENE PRESS

CA —CLAREMONT COLLEGES, Ella Strong
Denison Library, Scripps College,
Claremont, 91711. Judy Harvey Sahak,
Librn
Holdings: Vols (1100) Cat

CA —STANFORD UNIVERSITY
LIBRARIES, Cecil H Green Library,
Stanford, 94305. Michael T Ryan, Cur
Holdings: Vols (12,000) cat
Notes: The Morgan A & Aline D Gunst
Memorial Library. The book arts in every
century with some of the best examples.
Strong collection of examples of California
printers and graphic artists. Complete or
nearly complete collections of works by the
Kelmscott, Doves, Ashendene, Colt,
Grabhorn, and Grabhorn-Hoyem presses.

CO —DENVER PUBLIC LIBRARY, Douglas
Collection of Fine Printing, 1357 Broadway,
Denver, 80203.
Holdings: Vols 1700 Cat
Notes: Books from private presses, limited
editions and books about private presses.
Incl a complete set of vols from William
Morris' Kelmscott Press and a virtually
complete collection of Ashendene Press
books. Most major presses are well
represented and minor presses have
representative works in the collection.

CT —TRINITY COLLEGE LIBRARY,
Watkinson Library, 300 Summit St,

PRESS BOOKS—ASHENDENE PRESS (cont.)

Hartford, 06106. Jeffrey Kaimowitz, Cur
Holdings: Cat Mss
Notes: Gift of Allerton C Hickmott. 39 of the major pieces, 16 on vellum, and 8 of the minor pieces. Also limited ephemera and mss.

NY —BUFFALO & ERIE COUNTY PUBLIC LIBRARY, Rare Book Room, Lafayette Sq, Buffalo, 14203. William H Loos, Cur
Holdings: Vols 6 Cat

NY —NEW YORK PUBLIC LIBRARY, Rare Books and Manuscripts Div, Fifth Ave & 42 St, New York, 10018. William L Joyce, Asst Dir; Francis O Mattson, Curator
Holdings: Cat
Budget: ($7161)
Notes: Complete or nearly complete file of publications, incl books, pamphlets, broadsides and other ephemera.

NY —ROCHESTER INSTITUTE OF TECHNOLOGY, Melbert B Cary Jr Graphic Arts Collection, School of Printing, One Lomb Memorial Drive, Rochester, 14623. David Pankow, Cur
Holdings: Vols (11,000) Cat

PRESS BOOKS—AUERHAHN PRESS

CA —UNIVERSITY OF CALIFORNIA, BERKELEY, Bancroft Library, Manuscripts Division, Berkeley, 94720. James D Hart, Dir
Holdings: Vols 2000 Cat Mss
Notes: The Contemporary Poetry Collection covers the San Francisco publishing scene, from the period of the Beat Movement through the present day. In addition to printed materials, The Bancroft Library contains the important printer/publisher/bookseller archives of the Untide Press, City Lights, and the Auerhahn Press.

FL —UNIVERSITY OF MIAMI, Otto G Richter Library, PO Box 248214, Coral Gables, 33124. Frank Rodgers, Dir of Libraries
Notes: 3500 items. Black Sparrow, Auerhahn and other press books of the 1960s and 1970s, within the general area of contemporary poetry. Also, separate from this group, are many Cuala, Mosher, Kelmscott imprints, and all of the Trianon Press Blake facsimiles. Noncirculating.

PRESS BOOKS—AUTOLYCUS PRESS

MO —SAINT LOUIS PUBLIC LIBRARY, Gardner Rare Book Room, 1301 Olive St, Saint Louis, 63103. Julanne M Good, Supervisor; Martha Riley, Rare Books Librn
Holdings: Vols (2300) Cat
Budget: ($5573)

PRESS BOOKS—BANDAR LOG PRESS

AZ —UNIVERSITY OF ARIZONA, Library, Tucson, 85721. W David Laird, Librn
Notes: Frank Holme and 2 complete collections of books from the Bandarlog Press, numerous original drawings for newspapers and other media, books from Holme's art library.

CA —UNIVERSITY OF CALIFORNIA, LOS ANGELES, Research Library, Dept of Special Collections, 405 Hilgard Ave, Los Angeles, 90024. Edward Shreeves, Chairman, Bibliographers Group; David S Zeidberg, Head
Notes: 1.5 linear feet of publications, correspondence, and ephemera.

PRESS BOOKS—BASKERVILLE PRESS

IL —NEWBERRY LIBRARY, John M Wing Foundation on the History of Printing, 60 W Walton St, Chicago, 60610. Diana Haskell, Cur of Modern Mss
Holdings: Vols (30,000) Cat Mss
Budget: ($50,000)
See also entry under Printing - History

PRESS BOOKS—BEAUMONT PRESS

IL —ILLINOIS STATE UNIVERSITY, Milner Library, Dept of Special Collections,
Normal, 61761. Robert Sokan, Librn
Holdings: Vols (2800) Cat

PRESS BOOKS—BELLEVUE PRESS

NY —STATE UNIVERSITY OF NEW YORK, BINGHAMTON, Glenn G Bartle Library, Binghamton, 13901. Marion Hanscom, Special Collections Librn
Holdings: Cat

PRESS BOOKS—BERKELEY PRESS

†NY —COLUMBIA UNIVERSITY LIBRARIES, Butler Library, Rare Book and Manuscript Library, 535 W 114 St, New York, 10027.

PRESS BOOKS—BIGUS, RICHARD

CA —UNIVERSITY OF SAN FRANCISCO, Richard A Gleeson Library, The Countess Bernardine Murphy Donohue Rare Book Room, San Francisco, 94117. D Steven Corey, Special Collections Librn
Notes: Comprehensive collection of his early posters and broadsides, most of his later work. 45 items.

PRESS BOOKS—BIRD AND BULL PRESS

GA —UNIVERSITY OF GEORGIA, Libraries, Special Collections Division, Athens, 30602. Vesta Lee Gordon, Asst Dir for Special Collections
Holdings: Vols (8000)
Notes: One of the larger collections of private press books, pamphlets, and ephemera. The Elmore H Mundell Collection of materials from over 1200 different private printers.

PA —FREE LIBRARY OF PHILADELPHIA, Rare Book Dept, Logan Sq, Philadelphia, 19103. Marie E Korey, Rare Book Librn
Holdings: Vols (550) Uncat
Notes: Selected examples of fine printing and binding from many presses, and a collection of books and pamphlets issued by Henry Morris's Bird and Bull Press.

PA —PENNSYLVANIA STATE UNIVERSITY, Fred Lewis Pattee Library, Special Collections Dept, University Park, 16802. Charles Mann, Chief, Special Collections
Holdings: Vols (989) Uncat
Budget: ($37,000)
Notes: No photocopying.

PRESS BOOKS—BIRMINGHAM SCHOOL OF PRINTING

IL —ILLINOIS STATE UNIVERSITY, Milner Library, Dept of Special Collections, Normal, 61761. Robert Sokan, Librn
Holdings: Vols 191 Cat
Notes: The city of Birmingham, School of Printing collection incl all the items that were produced by the School of Printing under the direction of Leonard Jay from 1925-1953.

PRESS BOOKS—BIXBY, WILLIAM K.

MO —SAINT LOUIS PUBLIC LIBRARY, Gardner Rare Book Room, 1301 Olive St, Saint Louis, 63103. Julanne M Good, Supervisor; Martha Riley, Rare Books Librn
Holdings: Vol (2300) Cat
Budget: ($5573)

PRESS BOOKS—BLACK CAT PRESS

IL —CHICAGO PUBLIC LIBRARY, Special Collections Div, Cultural Center, 78 E Washington St, Chicago, 60602. Laura Linard, Cur
Holdings: Vols (800) Cat
Budget: ($3000)
Notes: The Special Collections Division endeavors to collect all Chicago imprints produced before 1900, and all Chicago private press productions 1900-50. An exceptional collection of books and keepsakes designed by Norman Forgue. We
actively purchase in this area. Outstanding items in the Chicago Imprints Inventory are described in the recent catalog, Treasures of The Chicago Public Library, compiled by Thomas A Orlando and Marie Gecik, 1977, pp 93-120.

†NY —COLUMBIA UNIVERSITY LIBRARIES, Butler Library, Rare Book and Manuscript Library, 535 W 114 St, New York, 10027.

PRESS BOOKS—BLACK MANIKIN PRESS

IL —ILLINOIS STATE UNIVERSITY, Milner Library, Dept of Special Collections, Normal, 61761. Robert Sokan, Librn
Holdings: Vols (2800) Cat

PRESS BOOKS—BLACK MOUNTAIN PRESS

UT —UNIVERSITY OF UTAH, Marriott Library, Special Collections, Salt Lake City, 84112. Gregory C Thompson, Cur
Notes: The publications of Utah presses are also acquired. These presses are Olympus, Peregrine, Smith, Real Peoples, Horizon, Canticle, and Westwater. For the Rare Books collection materials from certain outside presses are also included. These presses are Northland, Allen, Grabhorn, Black Sparrow, Lime Kiln and Black Mountain. Books on Freemasonry are also collected.

PRESS BOOKS—BLACK SPARROW PRESS

AZ —UNIVERSITY OF ARIZONA, University Library, Special Collections, Tucson, 85721. Louis A Hieb, Head

CA —UNIVERSITY OF CALIFORNIA, SAN DIEGO, Central University Library, Mandeville Dept of Special Collections, La Jolla, 92093. Lynda Corey Claassen, Head
Holdings: Vols 425 Cat

CA —UNIVERSITY OF CALIFORNIA, LOS ANGELES, Research Library, Dept of Special Collections, 405 Hilgard Ave, Los Angeles, 90024. Edward Shreeves, Chairman, Bibliographers Group; David S Zeidberg, Head
Notes: All publications and issues; 25 letters to publisher, John Martin.

CA —SAN DIEGO STATE UNIVERSITY, Malcolm A Love Library, 5300 Campanile Dr, San Diego, 92182. D Dickinson, Univ Librn; Don L Bosseau, Dir
Notes: Collected publications of certain fine presses and illustrators as: Golden Cockerel, Black Sparrow, Roycroft, Mosher, Bruce Rogers, Janus Press.

FL —UNIVERSITY OF MIAMI, Otto G Richter Library, PO Box 248214, Coral Gables, 33124. Frank Rodgers, Dir of Libraries
Notes: 3500 items. Black Sparrow, Auerhahn and other press books of the 1960s and 1970s, within the general area of contemporary poetry. Also, separate from this group, are many Cuala, Mosher, Kelmscott imprints, and all of the Trianon Press Blake facsimiles. Noncirculating.

IL —ILLINOIS STATE UNIVERSITY, Milner Library, Dept of Special Collections, Normal, 61761. Robert Sokan, Librn
Holdings: Vols (2800) Cat

IN —INDIANA UNIVERSITY, Lilly Library, Seventh St, Bloomington, 47405. William R Cagle, Librn
Holdings: Cat Mss
Notes: Extensive holdings. Mss include Black Sparrow Press printing records Noel Young, printer, 1968-1974.

MA —BOSTON UNIVERSITY, Mugar Memorial Library, Special Collections Dept, 771 Commonwealth Ave, Boston, 02215. Howard B Gotlieb, Dir
Holdings: Vols 750

NM —UNIVERSITY OF NEW MEXICO, General Library, Special Collections Dept, Albuquerque, 87131.
Notes: Selected items (150 pieces) from the Black Sparrow Press, incl original mss, correspondence, galleys and page proofs.

PRESS BOOKS—BLACK SPARROW PRESS (cont.)

NY —HOFSTRA UNIVERSITY, Library, 1000 Fulton Ave, Hempstead, 11550. Charles R Andrews, Dean of Library Services
Notes: Strong collection.

PA —PENNSYLVANIA STATE UNIVERSITY, Fred Lewis Pattee Library, Special Collections Dept, University Park, 16802. Charles Mann, Chief, Special Collections
Holdings: Vols (989) Uncat
Budget: ($37,000)
Notes: No photocopying.

UT —UNIVERSITY OF UTAH, Marriott Library, Special Collections, Salt Lake City, 84112. Gregory C Thompson, Cur
Notes: The publications of Utah presses are also acquired. These presses are Olympus, Peregrine, Smith, Real Peoples, Horizon, Canticle, and Westwater. For the Rare Books collection materials from certain outside presses are also included. These presses are Northland, Allen, Grabhorn, Black Sparrow, Lime Kiln and Black Mountain. Books on Freemasonry are also collected.

AB —UNIVERSITY OF ALBERTA, Cameron Library, The Bruce Peel Special Collections Room, Edmonton, T6G 2J8, Can. John Charles, Special Collections Librn
Notes: The press archives, 1966-70, for their first 94 books.

PRESS BOOKS—BLACK STONE PRESS

CA —UNIVERSITY OF SAN FRANCISCO, Richard A Gleeson Library, The Countess Bernardine Murphy Donohue Rare Book Room, San Francisco, 94117. D Steven Corey, Special Collections Librn
Holdings: Vols 40
Notes: Complete collection, archives for several books, unique items, extensive ephemera of this San Francisco press operated by Peter Koch and Shelley Hoyt-Koch.

PRESS BOOKS—BLACK SUN PRESS

IL —SOUTHERN ILLINOIS UNIVERSITY, CARBONDALE, Delyte W Morris Library, Special Collections Dept, Carbondale, 62901. David V Koch, Cur of Special Collections; Louisa Bowen, Cur of Manuscripts
Holdings: Vols 225 Cat Mss Pix
Notes: Incl archives of the press, 12 linear feet.

IN —INDIANA UNIVERSITY, Lilly Library, Seventh St, Bloomington, 47405. William R Cagle, Librn
Holdings: Vols 24 Cat

RI —BROWN UNIVERSITY, John Hay Library, 20 Prospect St, Providence, 02912. Mark N Brown, Cur Mss
Holdings: // Mss
Notes: Harry Crosby, American poet and founder with Caresse Crosby of the Black Sun Press in Paris. 13 portfolios containing proofs of *Chariot of the Sun* and *Shadows of the Sun*, typescripts of poems; 10 diaries and notebooks, 1926 to 1929; biographical notes by Caresse Crosby; 9 letters about Harry Crosby and the Black Sun Press; and a copy of Crosby's will. Also a sizable collection of the imprints of the Press. See "The Black Sun Press: 1927 to the Present," by Millicent Bell, in *Books at Brown*, vol XVII, no 1-2, (January 1955), pp [1]-24; and "Harry Crosby: A Heliograph," by Hugh Fox, in *Books at Brown*, vol XXII (1969), pp 95-100.

PRESS BOOKS—BODONI PRINTINGS

CA —UNIVERSITY OF CALIFORNIA, BERKELEY, Bancroft Library, Manuscripts Division, Berkeley, 94720. James D Hart, Dir
Holdings: Cat

CA —UNIVERSITY OF CALIFORNIA, LOS ANGELES, Research Library, Dept of Special Collections, 405 Hilgard Ave, Los Angeles, 90024. Edward Shreeves, Chairman, Bibliographers Group; David S Zeidberg, Head
Holdings: Vols 300

CT —YALE UNIVERSITY, Box 1603A, Yale Station, New Haven, 06520.

IL —NEWBERRY LIBRARY, John M Wing Foundation on the History of Printing, 60 W Walton St, Chicago, 60610. Diana Haskell, Cur of Modern Mss
Holdings: Vols (30,000) Cat Mss
Budget: ($50,000)
See also entry under Printing - History

NY —COLUMBIA UNIVERSITY LIBRARIES, Rare Book & Manuscript Library, 801 Butler Library, 535 W 114 St, New York, 10027. Kenneth A Lohf, Librn
Holdings: Cat

NY —GROLIER CLUB OF NEW YORK LIBRARY, 47 E 60 St, New York, 10022. Robert Nikirk, Librn
Holdings: Cat

NY —NEW YORK PUBLIC LIBRARY, Fifth Ave & 42 St, New York, 10018.
Holdings: Cat

OR —UNIVERSITY OF OREGON, Library, Eugene, 97403. Kenneth W Duckett, Curator
Holdings: Vols 50 Cat
Notes: Also much secondary source material on Bodoni printings in the Robert Carr Hall Collection.

RI —PROVIDENCE PUBLIC LIBRARY, 150 Empire St, Providence, 02903. Lance J Bauer, Special Collections Librn
Holdings: Vols (6300) Cat Mss Pix
Notes: The

PRESS BOOKS—BOOK CLUB OF CALIFORNIA

CA —UNIVERSITY OF SAN FRANCISCO, Richard A Gleeson Library, The Countess Bernardine Murphy Donohue Rare Book Room, San Francisco, 94117. D Steven Corey, Special Collections Librn
Holdings: Vols 170
Notes: A complete collection of this San Francisco publishing institution, all of whose books are printed by Western Fine Printers. Extensive collection of ephemera. Incl material from 1915 to date.

CA —SOLANO COUNTY LIBRARY, John F Kennedy Library, Donovan J McCune Collection, 505 Santa Clara St, Vallejo, 94590.
Holdings: Vols 150 //
Notes: The Donovan J McCune Collection (3000) vols //.

IL —LAKE FOREST COLLEGE, Donnelley Library, Lake Forest, 60045. Arthur H Miller Jr, College Librn
Holdings: Vols (350)
Notes: Largely from the collection of Mr and Mrs DeWitt O'Kieffe, the collection has a range of items from landmarks (Grabhorn *Leaves of Grass* for example) to ephemera of private presses. Among those incl are Grabhorn Press, Lawton and Alfred Kennedy, Book Club of California and Carl Hertzog.

OK —UNIVERSITY OF TULSA, McFarlin Library, Dept of Rare Books and Special Collections, 600 S College, Tulsa, 74104. David Farmer, Dir; Toby Murray, Archivist; Caroline Swinson, Cur of Manuscripts & Art
Notes: Complete collection of publications issued by the Book Club of California.

PRESS BOOKS—BOOKSTORE PRESS

†CT —UNIVERSITY OF CONNECTICUT LIBRARY, Special Collections Dept, Storrs, 06268. Richard H Schimmelpfeng, Dir of Special Collections
Notes: Press archives.

PRESS BOOKS—BRIARPATCH PRESS

SC —WOFFORD COLLEGE, Sandor Teszler Library, N Church St, Spartanburg, 29301. Frank J Anderson, Librn
Holdings: Vols 1000 Cat
Notes: Books about the history and practice of printing, hand papermaking, bookbinding, book collecting, fine press and private press books used in conjunction with instruction at the Wofford Library Press, an experimental and bibliographic press which has been in operation since 1969. Collection contains materials on printmaking methods and related graphic arts. Collection incl imprints of: Briarpatch Press, Anthoensen Press, Mosher Press, Kitmang Press, Windhover Press, Penman Press, Unicorn Press, Wofford Library Press and others.

PRESS BOOKS—BRITISH COLUMBIA PRESS

BC —SIMON FRASER UNIVERSITY, Library, Burnaby, V5A 1S6, Can. Percilla Groves, Special Collections Librn
Holdings: Cat Mss
Notes: Mss for published and unpublished works, plus a complete collection of published books, chapbooks and broadsides by Canadian and American writers, plus correspondence and business records of the British Columbia Press run by poet and teacher Barry McKinnon from 1972 to 1980.

PRESS BOOKS—BROADSIDE PRESS

MA —UNIVERSITY OF MASSACHUSETTS AT AMHERST, Library, Amherst, 01003. Siegfried Feller, Assoc Dir for Collection Development
Holdings: Cat
Notes: A nearly complete collection of imprints of The Broadside Press, Detroit, Mich. In Special Collections and Rare Books.

PRESS BOOKS—BRUCE ROGERS see Rogers, Bruce

PRESS BOOKS—BUR PRESS

KY —UNIVERSITY OF KENTUCKY, Margaret I King Library, Dept of Special Collections, Lexington, 40506. William Marshall, Head
Holdings: Cat Mss
Notes: Complete sets of Stamperia del Santuccio imprints (C and V Hammer); The Anvil Press; the Gravesend Press (Joseph Graves); The Bur Press; King Library Press; Gnoman Press; Buttonwood Press.

PRESS BOOKS—BURNING DECK PRESS

RI —BROWN UNIVERSITY, John Hay Library, 20 Prospect St, Providence, 02912. Mark N Brown, Cur Mss
Holdings: Vols (1000) Cat
Notes: Many examples of 19th and 20th century private and small presses of American and English imprint. Some of the presses represented are: Anthoensen, Bayberry Hill, Black Sun, Catnatch, Cuala, Doves, Essex House, Golden Cockerel, Grabhorn, Kelmscott, Merrymount, Mosher, Nonesuch, Perishable, Stinehour, Trianon, Unicorn, Vagabond, plus many Rhode Island small presses such as Burning Deck, Turkey, and Hall Coal.

PRESS BOOKS—BUTTONWOOD PRESS

KY —UNIVERSITY OF KENTUCKY, Margaret I King Library, Dept of Special Collections, Lexington, 40506. William Marshall, Head
Holdings: Cat Mss
Notes: Complete sets of Stamperia del Santuccio imprints (C and V Hammer); The Anvil Press; the Gravesend Press (Joseph Graves); The Bur Press; King Library Press; Gnoman Press; Buttonwood Press.

PRESS BOOKS—CANADA see Press Books, Canadian

PRESS BOOKS—CANTICLE PRESS

UT —UNIVERSITY OF UTAH, Marriott Library, Special Collections, Salt Lake City,

PRESS BOOKS—CANTICLE PRESS (cont.)

84112. Gregory C Thompson, Cur
Notes: The publications of Utah presses are also acquired. These presses are Olympus, Peregrine, Smith, Real Peoples, Horizon, Canticle, and Westwater. For the Rare Books collection materials from certain outside presses are also included. These presses are Northland, Allen, Grabhorn, Black Sparrow, Lime Kiln and Black Mountain. Books on Freemasonry are also collected.

PRESS BOOKS—CAPRA PRESS

IN —INDIANA UNIVERSITY, Lilly Library, Seventh St, Bloomington, 47405. William R Cagle, Librn
Holdings: Cat Mss
Notes: Nearly complete. Mss incl the office and publishing files of Capra Press, 1955- . Additions made yearly. Incl correspondence, mss, book design and art work, business records, contracts, binding records, etc.

PRESS BOOKS—CASTLE PRESS

CA —UNIVERSITY OF CALIFORNIA, LOS ANGELES, William Andrews Clark Memorial Library, 2520 Cimarron St, Los Angeles, 90018.

PRESS BOOKS—CAXTON PRINTERS

ID —UNIVERSITY OF IDAHO, Library, Dept of Special Collections & Archives, Moscow, 83843.
Holdings: Vols 1000 Uncat
Notes: All books published by Caxton Printers and catalogs and other promotional material on their books.

PRESS BOOKS—CENTAUR PRESS

CA —UNIVERSITY OF SAN FRANCISCO, Richard A Gleeson Library, The Countess Bernardine Murphy Donohue Rare Book Room, San Francisco, 94117. D Steven Corey, Special Collections Librn
Holdings: Vols 15
Notes: Complete collection of this short-lived (1948-1952) San Francisco press, operated by Kermit Sheets.

PRESS BOOKS—CHENEY, WILLIAM MURRAY

CA —UNIVERSITY OF CALIFORNIA, LOS ANGELES, William Andrews Clark Memorial Library, 2520 Cimarron St, Los Angeles, 90018.
Holdings: Cat Mss Pix
Notes: Incl correspondence and printed ephemera.

PRESS BOOKS—COLT PRESS

†CA —UNIVERSITY OF SAN FRANCISCO, Richard A Gleeson Library, The Countess Bernardine Murphy Donohue Rare Book Room, San Francisco, 94117. D Steven Corey, Special Collections Librn
Holdings: Vols 50
Notes: A complete collection of Jane Grabhorn items. Incl Jumbo and Colt Press imprints; extensive ephemera.
CA —STANFORD UNIVERSITY LIBRARIES, Cecil H Green Library, Stanford, 94305. Michael T Ryan, Cur
Holdings: Vols (12,000) Cat
Notes: The Morgan A & Aline D Gunst Memorial Library. The book arts in every century with some of the best examples. Strong collection of examples of California printers and graphic artists. Complete or nearly complete collections of works by the Kelmscott, Doves, Ashendene, Colt, Grabhorn, and Grabhorn-Hoyem presses.

PRESS BOOKS—COPELAND AND DAY

NC —UNIVERSITY OF NORTH CAROLINA, GREENSBORO, Walter

Clinton Jackson Library, Special Collections Dept, 1000 Spring Garden St, Greensboro, 27412. Emilie W Mills, Librn
Notes: Emphasis is on American small publishers since late 19th century attention to fine printing, sound production and textual content are exemplary. Significant holdings of books published by The Typophiles, Stinehour Press, David R Godine, Jargon Society and Way and Williams are included with selective holdings of other small commercial publishers and printers, incl R H Russell, Copeland and Day, Stone and Kimball.

PRESS BOOKS—COVICI-MCGEE

IL —CHICAGO PUBLIC LIBRARY, Special Collections Div, Cultural Center, 78 E Washington St, Chicago, 60602. Laura Linard, Cur
Holdings: Vols (800) Cat
Budget: ($3000)
Notes: The Special Collections Division endeavors to collect all Chicago imprints produced before 1900, and all Chicago private press productions 1900-50. An exceptional collection of books and keepsakes designed by Norman Forgue. We actively purchase in this area. Outstanding items in the Chicago Imprints Inventory are described in the recent catalog, *Treasures of The Chicago Public Library*, compiled by Thomas A Orlando and Marie Gecik, 1977, pp 93-120.

PRESS BOOKS—CRANACH PRESS

IL —NEWBERRY LIBRARY, John M Wing Foundation on the History of Printing, 60 W Walton St, Chicago, 60610. Diana Haskell, Cur of Modern Mss
Holdings: Vols 50 Cat Mss Pix
Notes: Incl correspondence among Kessler and Eric Gill, Gordon Craig, Emery Walker, Edward Johnson, et al; proofs and sketchs for Cranach books and types. Complements the Kessler collection at Cambridge, with which microfilms have been exchanged.

PRESS BOOKS—CRANIUM PRESS

CA —UNIVERSITY OF SAN FRANCISCO, Richard A Gleeson Library, The Countess Bernardine Murphy Donohue Rare Book Room, San Francisco, 94117. D Steven Corey, Special Collections Librn
Holdings: Vols 110 Mss
Notes: The proprietor Clifford Burke operated the press in San Francisco from 1967 to 1976. This is the complete archive of the press and incl mss, correspondence, trials, and proofs. Also present is a virtually complete collection of books, broadsides, and emphemera of the press.

PRESS BOOKS—CUALA PRESS

CA —CLAREMONT COLLEGES, Ella Strong Denison Library, Scripps College, Claremont, 91711. Judy Harvey Sahak, Librn
Holdings: Vols 49 // Cat
Notes: Includes 2 collections of broadsides.
CA —UNIVERSITY OF CALIFORNIA, SAN DIEGO, Central University Library, Mandeville Dept of Special Collections, La Jolla, 92093. Lynda Corey Claassen, Head
Holdings: Cat Mss
CA —UNIVERSITY OF CALIFORNIA, LOS ANGELES, William Andrews Clark Memorial Library, 2520 Cimarron St, Los Angeles, 90018.
CA —MILLS COLLEGE LIBRARY, Oakland, 94613. Steven P Pandolfo, Librn
Holdings: Vols 65 Cat Mss
Notes: Books and ephemera from the Press; ms correspondence between Albert M Bender and the Yeats family.
CA —STANFORD UNIVERSITY LIBRARIES, Cecil H Green Library, Stanford, 94305. Michael T Ryan, Cur
Holdings: Vols (2300) Uncat Mss Pix
Notes: The James A Healy Collection of Irish Literature. Incl books, magazines, prints, photgraphs, ephemera, and about

3000 unpublished letters. Among the books are complete sets of Dun Emer and Cuala Press publications. Individuals represented in the Healy ms collection incl: A E, Oliver St John Gogarty, James Joyce, Elizabeth C Yeats, George Yeats, and William Butler Yeats.
CT —CONNECTICUT COLLEGE, Library, Mohegan Ave, New London, 06320. Brian Rogers, College Librn
Holdings: Vols (80) Uncat Mss Pix
Notes: Cuala Press and first editions.
FL —UNIVERSITY OF MIAMI, Otto G Richter Library, PO Box 248214, Coral Gables, 33124. Frank Rodgers, Dir of Libraries
Notes: 3500 items. Black Sparrow, Auerhahn and other press books of the 1960s and 1970s, within the general area of contemporary poetry. Also, separate from this group, are many Cuala, Mosher, Kelmscott imprints, and all of the Trianon Press Blake facsimiles. Noncirculating.
IL —SOUTHERN ILLINOIS UNIVERSITY, CARBONDALE, Delyte W Morris Library, Special Collections Dept, Carbondale, 62901. David V Koch, Cur of Special Collections; Louisa Bowen, Cur of Manuscripts
Holdings: Vols 93 Cat
Notes: Also 152 broadsides and cards from the Cuala Press.
IL —NORTHWESTERN UNIVERSITY, Library, Special Collections Dept, 1937 Sheridan Rd, Evanston, 60201. R Russell Maylone, Cur
Holdings: Vols (5000) Cat
Notes: Representative examples of the work of the modern private press from Strawberry Hill to the current small printers. Incl such presses as Cuala, Essex House, Golden Cockerel, Grabhorn, Nonesuch, Roxburghe, etc. Also 15,000 "little magazine" titles exclusive of runs in the general library collections.
IN —INDIANA UNIVERSITY, Lilly Library, Seventh St, Bloomington, 47405. William R Cagle, Librn
Holdings: // Cat
Notes: Extensive holdings.
ME —BOWDOIN COLLEGE, Library, Brunswick, 04011. Dianne M Gutscher, Cur of Special Collections
Holdings: Vols 55 Cat
Notes: Incl most of the first editions.
ME —PORTLAND PUBLIC LIBRARY, 5 Monument Sq, Portland, 04101. Edward V Chenevert, Library Dir
Holdings: Vols 66 // Cat Pix
Notes: Incl greeting cards and hand-colored prints.
MA —BOSTON COLLEGE LIBRARIES, Thomas P O'Neill Library, Irish Collection, Chestnut Hill, 02167. Ralph Coffman, Cur
Holdings: Vols (10,000) Cat Mss Maps Pix
Notes: Nearly every aspect of Irish history and literature are covered in this collection. Items of special interest are the many papers of Patrick Andrew Collins, president of the Irish Land League, and letters of Jeremiah O'Donovan Rossa, poet, editor and leader in the Fenian and related organizations. Holdings also incl a facsimile of the famous illuminated ms of the Gospels, the *Book of Kells;* a complete vol of *Malton's Views of Dublin, 1799; The Ordinance Surveys;* a complete set of the *Irish Bulletin;* and Colgan's *Acta Sanctorum Hiberniae* describing the lives of the Irish saints.
NY —BUFFALO & ERIE COUNTY PUBLIC LIBRARY, Rare Book Room, Lafayette Sq, Buffalo, 14203. William H Loos, Cur
Holdings: Vols 16 Cat
NY —ADELPHI UNIVERSITY, Library, Garden City, 11530. Jerome Yavarkovsky, Dean of Libraries
Holdings: Vols 110 Cat
†NC —WAKE FOREST UNIVERSITY, Z Smith Reynolds Library, Box 7777, Reynold Sta, Winston-Salem, 27109. Richard J Murdoch, Rare Book Librn
Holdings: Vols 90 Cat
AB —UNIVERSITY OF ALBERTA, Cameron Library, The Bruce Peel Special Collections Room, Edmonton, T6G 2J8, Can. John Charles, Special Collections Librn
Notes: 82 items, lacking only 12 booklets and 1 issue of a 1937 broadside.

PRESS BOOKS—CUALA PRESS (cont.)

ON —QUEEN'S UNIVERSITY, Douglas Library, Kingston, K7L 5C4, Can. William F E Morley, Cur, Special Collections
Holdings: Vols (3250) Cat
Notes: Collection incl all the original vols in the Cuala Press series and a facsimile reprint of each plus about 170 other works by and about W B Yeats, 200 by and about James Joyce, 240 by and about G B Shaw, 100 by and about "A E," George W Russell.

PRESS BOOKS—CUMMINGTON PRESS

IA —UNIVERSITY OF IOWA, University Libraries, Iowa City, 52242. Frank Paluka, Head, Special Collections Dept
Holdings: Vols 66 Cat
Notes: Mary L Richmond, "The Cummington Press," in *Books at Iowa*, Nov 1967.
NE —UNIVERSITY OF NEBRASKA, OMAHA, Library, 60 & Dodge Sts, Omaha, 68132. Mel Bohn, Librn
Holdings: Vols 55 Uncat
Notes: One of the most complete collections of Cummington Press and Abattoir Editions publications. 100 bound vols and 218 other pieces; including broadsheets, proofsheets, woodblocks, etc. No photocopying.

PRESS BOOKS—CURWEN PRESS

AB —UNIVERSITY OF ALBERTA, Cameron Library, The Bruce Peel Special Collections Room, Edmonton, T6G 2J8, Can. John Charles, Special Collections Librn
Notes: Curwen's own in-house collection of materials, 1919-56, incl 1000 books, 2500 items of ephemera.

PRESS BOOKS—DANIEL PRESS

CA —CLAREMONT COLLEGES, Honnold Library, Ninth & Dartmouth, Claremont, 91711. Tania Rizzo, Special Collections Dept Head
Holdings: Vols (70,000) Cat VF
Notes: Books on typography, bibliography, and history of printing; incunabula; specimen books; fine press books, esp Kelmscott, Doves, Daniel, Mosher, Grabhorn, Nash, and Arion presses and many Southern California printers. A comprehensive collection of Zamorano Club publications and keepsakes, partial source for George E Fulleton, *The Zamorano Club: The First Half Century* (Los Angeles, 1978). Extensive files of ephemera. Fine bindings and fore-edge paintings. Samples of Oriental type and printing.
CA —UNIVERSITY OF SAN FRANCISCO, Richard A Gleeson Library, The Countess Bernardine Murphy Donohue Rare Book Room, San Francisco, 94117. D Steven Corey, Special Collections Librn
Holdings: Vols 70
Notes: Almost complete collection of the Oxford imprints, lacking 3 items, plus two Frome imprints, ephemera.
†MA —WILLIAMS COLLEGE, Chapin Library of Rare Books, PO Box 426, Williamstown, 01267. Robert L Volz, Custodian
Holdings: Vols 115 Cat Mss
Budget: ($3500)
Notes: Almost complete collection of major and minor Oxford works, Frome books, and bibliographical and critical works. Also, 24 autograph letters.
NY —BUFFALO & ERIE COUNTY PUBLIC LIBRARY, Rare Book Room, Lafayette Sq, Buffalo, 14203. William H Loos, Cur
Holdings: Vols 37 Cat

PRESS BOOKS—DEAN, MALLETTE

CA —UNIVERSITY OF SAN FRANCISCO, Richard A Gleeson Library, The Countess Bernardine Murphy Donohue Rare Book Room, San Francisco, 94117. D Steven Corey, Special Collections Librn
Holdings: Vols 50
Notes: Archive with virtually complete

collection of books he printed or illustrated plus his own archival collection of trials, proofs and copies of his many wood engravings and other graphic art work (over 500 items).

PRESS BOOKS—DERRYDALE PRESS

NY —BUFFALO & ERIE COUNTY PUBLIC LIBRARY, Rare Book Room, Lafayette Sq, Buffalo, 14203. William H Loos, Cur
Holdings: Vols 35 Cat
OH —PUBLIC LIBRARY OF CINCINNATI & HAMILTON COUNTY, Dept of Rare Books & Special Collections, 800 Vine St, Library Square, Cincinnati, 45202. Yeatman Anderson III, Cur
Notes: Large hunting and fishing collection, and a nearly complete set of Derrydale Press publications.
OH —CLEVELAND PUBLIC LIBRARY, Fine Arts and Special Collections Department, 325 Superior Ave, Cleveland, 44114. Alice N Loranth, Head
Holdings: Vols 180 Cat
Notes: Complete collection of Derrydale Press publications (165 titles). See *Publications of the Derrydale Press, 1927-1941*, by W C Thompson (Minneapolis, 1953).

PRESS BOOKS—DIVERS PRESS

MO —WASHINGTON UNIVERSITY, Libraries, Special Collections Dept, Campus Box 1061, St Louis, 63130.
Notes: A small but significant collection of mss, correspondence and printed materials.

PRESS BOOKS—DOVES PRESS

CA —CLAREMONT COLLEGES, Ella Strong Denison Library, Scripps College, Claremont, 91711. Judy Harvey Sahak, Librn
Holdings: Vols (1100) Cat
CA —CLAREMONT COLLEGES, Honnold Library, Ninth & Dartmouth, Claremont, 91711. Tania Rizzo, Special Collections Dept Head
Holdings: Vols (70,000) Cat VF
Notes: Books on typography, bibliography, and history of printing; incunabula; specimen books; fine press books, esp Kelmscott, Doves, Daniel, Mosher, Grabhorn, Nash, and Arion presses and many Southern California printers. A comprehensive collection of Zamorano Club publications and keepsakes, partial source for George E Fulleton, *The Zamorano Club: The First Half Century* (Los Angeles, 1978). Extensive files of ephemera. Fine bindings and fore-edge paintings. Samples of Oriental type and printing.
CA —UNIVERSITY OF CALIFORNIA, LOS ANGELES, William Andrews Clark Memorial Library, 2520 Cimarron St, Los Angeles, 90018.
Holdings: Cat Mss Pix
Notes: Extensive collection, first editions, etc, described in the Library's *Kelmscott and Doves Presses* (1921).
CA —STANFORD UNIVERSITY LIBRARIES, Cecil H Green Library, Stanford, 94305. Michael T Ryan, Cur
Holdings: Vols (12,000) Cat
Notes: The Morgan A & Aline D Gunst Memorial Library. The book arts in every century with some of the best examples. Strong collection of examples of California printers and graphic artists. Complete or nearly complete collections of works by the Kelmscott, Doves, Ashendene, Colt, Grabhorn, and Grabhorn-Hoyem presses.
CO —UNIVERSITY OF COLORADO, Libraries, Special Collections, Boulder, 80309. Nora J Quinlan, Head
Notes: Samuel Goldman Collection. Composed of the Limited Editions Club Collection, the Kelmscott Press Collection (both virtually complete) and examples of works from other major fine presses incl the Doves Press, Golden Cockerel, Nonesuch, etc.
MA —WHEATON COLLEGE, Library, Norton, 02766. Sherrie S Bergman, College

Librn
Holdings: Vols (300) Cat
Notes: The Paul H Smart Collection of Private Press Books, Espec strong in Bruce Rogers and Doves Press.
NY —BUFFALO & ERIE COUNTY PUBLIC LIBRARY, Rare Book Room, Lafayette Sq, Buffalo, 14203. William H Loos, Cur
Holdings: Vols 31 Cat
NY —NEW YORK PUBLIC LIBRARY, Rare Books and Manuscripts Div, Fifth Ave & 42 St, New York, 10018. William L Joyce, Asst Dir; Francis O Mattson, Curator
Holdings: Cat
Budget: ($7161)
Notes: Complete or nearly complete file of publications, incl books, pamphlets, broadsides and other ephemera.

PRESS BOOKS—DUN EMER PRESS

CA —UNIVERSITY OF CALIFORNIA, SAN DIEGO, Central University Library, Mandeville Dept of Special Collections, La Jolla, 92093. Lynda Corey Claassen, Head
Holdings: Cat Mss
Notes: Complete collection.
CA —UNIVERSITY OF CALIFORNIA, LOS ANGELES, William Andrews Clark Memorial Library, 2520 Cimarron St, Los Angeles, 90018.
CA —STANFORD UNIVERSITY LIBRARIES, Cecil H Green Library, Stanford, 94305. Michael T Ryan, Cur
Holdings: Vols (2300) Uncat Mss Pix
Notes: The James A Healy Collection of Irish Literature. Incl books, magazines, prints, photgraphs, ephemera, and about 3000 unpublished letters. Among the books are complete sets of Dun Emer and Cuala Press publications. Individuals represented in the Healy ms collection incl: A E, Oliver St John Gogarty, James Joyce, Elizabeth C Yeats, George Yeats, and William Butler Yeats.
ME —PORTLAND PUBLIC LIBRARY, 5 Monument Sq, Portland, 04101. Edward V Chenevert, Library Dir
Holdings: Vols 11 // Cat
MA —BOSTON COLLEGE LIBRARIES, Thomas P O'Neill Library, Irish Collection, Chestnut Hill, 02167. Ralph Coffman, Cur
Holdings: Vols (10,000) Cat Mss Maps Pix
Notes: Nearly every aspect of Irish history and literature are covered in this collection. Items of special interest are the many papers of Patrick Andrew Collins, president of the Irish Land League, and letters of Jeremiah O'Donovan Rossa, poet, editor and leader in the Fenian and related organizations. Holdings also incl a facsimile of the famous illuminated ms of the Gospels, the *Book of Kells*; a complete vol of *Malton's Views of Dublin, 1799; The Ordinance Surveys;* a complete set of the *Irish Bulletin;* and Colgan's *Acta Sanctorum Hiberniae* describing the lives of the Irish saints.

PRESS BOOKS—ELDER, PAUL

CA —UNIVERSITY OF CALIFORNIA, LOS ANGELES, William Andrews Clark Memorial Library, 2520 Cimarron St, Los Angeles, 90018.
CA —UNIVERSITY OF CALIFORNIA, SANTA BARBARA, Library, Dept of Special Collections, Santa Barbara, 93106. Christian F Brun, Head
Holdings: Vols 250 Cat Ephemera
Notes: Excellent collection; some very scarce imprint.

PRESS BOOKS—ELSTON PRESS

†MA —WILLIAMS COLLEGE, Chapin Library of Rare Books, PO Box 426, Williamstown, 01267. Robert L Volz, Custodian
Holdings: Vols 24 Cat
Budget: ($3500)
Notes: Nearly complete collection.

PRESS BOOKS—ELZEVIER PRESS

IL —NORTHWESTERN UNIVERSITY, Library, Special Collections Dept, 1937

PRESS BOOKS—ELZEVIER PRESS (cont.)

Sheridan Rd, Evanston, 60201. R Russell Maylone, Cur
Holdings: Vols 263 Cat

MI —UNIVERSITY OF MICHIGAN, Library, Dept of Rare Books & Special Collections, Ann Arbor, 48109. Robert J Starring, Head
Holdings: Vols 1700 Cat
Notes: Nucleus is the Copinger Collection of 1446 volumes, which are checked in a copy of H B Copinger's *The Elzevier Press* (London: 1927). Approximately 230 volumes not in the Copinger Collection are fully cataloged.

PA —UNIVERSITY OF PENNSYLVANIA, Van Pelt Library, Rare Books Collection, 34 & Walnut Sts, Philadelphia, 19104. Daniel Traister, Special Collections Librn
Holdings: Vols 1600 Cat
Notes: Incl 400 Elzevier Press Leyden dissertations. Downs (Suppl) 311.

WI —UNIVERSITY OF WISCONSIN, MADISON, Memorial Library, Rare Books Collection, 728 State St, Madison, 53706. Gretchen Lagana, Cur
Holdings: Vols (58) Cat
Notes: Grotius Collcetion. Some 58 volumes by, about, or associated with the Dutch jurist and humanist Hugo Grotius. A number of the volumes comprise classical writings edited by Grotius. Certain of the volumes issued by Jansson, Elzevier, and Estienne are, in addition, valuable as specimens illustrating the history of printing. Restricted use: Rare Bok Department.

PRESS BOOKS—ENCINO PRESS

TX —UNIVERSITY OF HOUSTON, M D Anderson Memorial Library, University Park, Houston, 77004. David Farmer, Cur, Special Collections; Jean Jackson, Assistant Cur
Holdings: Vols 600 Cat
Notes: This collection is confined to books in some way distinguished by their typographic qualities and produced within the borders of Texas at any time, past or present. Larger portions of the collection incl the work of the Encino Press, William Holman, Carl Hertzog, Edwin Hill, and other private and fine printers.

TX —TRINITY UNIVERSITY, Elizabeth Coates Maddux Library, 715 Stadium Dr, San Antonio, 78284. Richard Hume Werking, Library Dir; Craig Likness, Head Bibliographer
Holdings: Vols 107
Notes: Materials published by William Wittliff at the Encino Press, Austin, Texas. *See also* entry under Wittliff, William.

PRESS BOOKS—ENITHARMON PRESS

AB —UNIVERSITY OF ALBERTA, Cameron Library, The Bruce Peel Special Collections Room, Edmonton, T6G 2J8, Can. John Charles, Special Collections Librn
Notes: Variant copies of all publications, incl ephemera.

PRESS BOOKS—EQUINOX COOPERATIVE PRESS

DC —GEORGETOWN UNIVERSITY, Library, Special Collections Div, 37 & O Sts NW, Washington, 20057. George M Barringer, Special Collections Librn; Nicholas B Sheetz, Mss Librn
Notes: The papers, files, art works, etc of Lynd Ward and his wife, May McNeer.

PRESS BOOKS—ERAGNY PRESS

†NY —UNIVERSITY OF ROCHESTER, Rush Rhees Library, Rochester, 14627.

PRESS BOOKS—ESSEX HOUSE PRESS

IL —NORTHWESTERN UNIVERSITY, Library, Special Collections Dept, 1937 Sheridan Rd, Evanston, 60201. R Russell Maylone, Cur
Holdings: Vols (5000) Cat
Notes: Representative examples of the work of the modern private press from Strawberry Hill to the current small printers. Incl such presses as Cuala, Essex House, Golden Cockerel, Grabhorn, Nonesuch, Roxburghe, etc. Also 15,000 "little magazine" titles exclusive of runs in the general library collections.

PRESS BOOKS—ESTIENNE PRINTING

WI —UNIVERSITY OF WISCONSIN, MADISON, Memorial Library, Rare Books Collection, 728 State St, Madison, 53706. Gretchen Lagana, Cur
Holdings: Vols (58) Cat
Notes: Grotius Collection. Some 58 volumes by, about, or associated with the Dutch jurist and humanist Hugo Grotius. A number of the volumes comprise classical writings edited by Grotius. Certain of the volumes issued by Jansson, Elzevier, and Estienne are, in addition, valuable as specimens illustrating the history of printing. Restricted use: Rare Books Department.

PRESS BOOKS—EUCALYPTUS PRESS

CA —UNIVERSITY OF CALIFORNIA, SAN DIEGO, Central University Library, Mandeville Dept of Special Collections, La Jolla, 92093. Lynda Corey Claassen, Head
Notes: The press collection comprises examples of fine printing from numerous private presses operating during the 19th and 20th centuries. Incl extensive holdings of the Golden Cockerel Press, the Cuala Press, the Hogarth Press, the Eucalyptus Press, and the Plantin Press.

CA —MILLS COLLEGE LIBRARY, Oakland, 94613. Steven P Pandolfo, Librn
Holdings: Vols 200 Cat

PRESS BOOKS—EVANS, HENRY

†CA —UNIVERSITY OF SAN FRANCISCO, Richard A Gleeson Library, The Countess Bernardine Murphy Donohue Rare Book Room, San Francisco, 94117. D Steven Corey, Special Collections Librn
Holdings: Vols 75 Uncat
Notes: With ephemera.

PRESS BOOKS—FANFROLICO PRESS

IL —ILLINOIS STATE UNIVERSITY, Milner Library, Dept of Special Collections, Normal, 61761. Robert Sokan, Librn
Holdings: Vols (2800) Cat

PRESS BOOKS—FILIGIA PRESS

†CT —UNIVERSITY OF CONNECTICUT LIBRARY, Special Collections Dept, Storrs, 06268. Richard H Schimmelpfeng, Dir of Special Collections
Notes: Press archives.

PRESS BOOKS—FINE ARTS PRESS

CA —ANAHEIM PUBLIC LIBRARY, 500 W Broadway, Anaheim, 92805.
Holdings: Vols (2000) Cat

CA —CALIFORNIA STATE UNIVERSITY, FULLERTON, Library, Box 4150, Fullerton, 92634. Linda Herman, Special Collections Librn
Holdings: Vols 4600 Cat
Notes: Press books and fine printing of the 20th century incl vols from the Grabhorn Press of San Francisco (Dr William B Langsdorf Anniversary Collection; 613 vols) and the Fine Arts Press of Santa Ana, Calif (67 vols). It is supplemented by a group of related collections on printing, binding, and book history reference, which incl representative examples of most modern fine press.

PRESS BOOKS—FIRST CASUALTY PRESS

CT —UNIVERSITY OF CONNECTICUT, Library, Storrs, 06268. R H Schimmelpfeng, Dir of Special Collections
Holdings: // Uncat Mss Pix
Notes: The archives consist of the business records and mss, published and unpublished, of the press which was deeply involved with Vietnam veterans' experiences in Vietnam. Volumes issued by the press were *Winning Hearts and Minds and Free Fire Zone*, both literary.

PRESS BOOKS—FIVE TREES PRESS

CA —UNIVERSITY OF SAN FRANCISCO, Richard A Gleeson Library, The Countess Bernardine Murphy Donohue Rare Book Room, San Francisco, 94117. D Steven Corey, Special Collections Librn
Holdings: Vols 25
Notes: Archive with a complete collection, plus the archival business files of the firm, much ephemera.

PRESS BOOKS—FORTUNE PRESS

NY —STATE UNIVERSITY OF NEW YORK, STONY BROOK, Melville Library, Dept of Special Collections, Stony Brook, 11794. Evert Volkersz, Head
Holdings: Vols 110 Cat
Notes: The Fortune Press commenced publishing in London in 1925, but holdings reflect primarily publications of 1940-1946.

PRESS BOOKS—FOULIS PRESS

†NY —COLUMBIA UNIVERSITY LIBRARIES, Butler Library, Rare Book and Manuscript Library, 535 W 114 St, New York, 10027.
Notes: The Franklin H Kissner Collection of 121 editions printed in Glasgow by Robert and Andrew Foulis brings the Library's holdings close to completion.

PRESS BOOKS—FOUR SEASONS FOUNDATION

CA —UNIVERSITY OF CALIFORNIA, SAN DIEGO, Central University Library, Mandeville Dept of Special Collections, La Jolla, 92093. Lynda Corey Claassen, Head; Michael Davidson, Cur, Archive for New Poetry
Notes: The collection of papers belonging to editor and publisher Donald Allen represents the work of one of the first publishers to make innovative poetry available through his landmark anthology, *The New American Poetry, 1945-1960*, and through his two presses, The Four Seasons Foundation and Grey Fox Press.

PRESS BOOKS—GEHENNA PRESS

CT —TRINITY COLLEGE LIBRARY, Watkinson Library, 300 Summit St, Hartford, 06106. Jeffrey Kaimowitz, Cur
Holdings: Cat

CT —YALE UNIVERSITY, Box 1603A, Yale Station, New Haven, 06520.

GA —UNIVERSITY OF GEORGIA, Libraries, Special Collections Division, Athens, 30602. Vesta Lee Gordon, Asst Dir for Special Collections
Holdings: Vols (8000)
Notes: One of the larger collections of private press books, pamphlets, and ephemera. The Elmore H Mundell Collection of materials from over 1200 different private printers.

MA —SMITH COLLEGE, Library, Northampton, 01063. Ruth Mortimer, Cur of Rare Books
Holdings: Vols 50 Cat
Notes: Incl ephemeral pieces. No photocopying.

†NY —COLUMBIA UNIVERSITY LIBRARIES, Butler Library, Rare Book and Manuscript Library, 535 W 114 St, New York, 10027.

PRESS BOOKS-GIOLITO DE FERRARI

CA —UNIVERSITY OF CALIFORNIA, LOS ANGELES, Research Library, Dept of Special Collections, 405 Hilgard Ave, Los Angeles, 90024. Edward Shreeves, Chairman, Bibliographers Group; David S Zeidberg, Head
Holdings: Vols 100

PRESS BOOKS—GIUNTA PRINTINGS

CA —UNIVERSITY OF CALIFORNIA, LOS
ANGELES, Research Library, Dept of
Special Collections, 405 Hilgard Ave, Los
Angeles, 90024. Edward Shreeves,
Chairman, Bibliographers Group; David S
Zeidberg, Head
Holdings: Vols 100
Notes: 100 books, printed in Florence and
Venice, 1491-1550.

PRESS BOOKS—GNOMAN PRESS

KY —UNIVERSITY OF KENTUCKY,
Margaret I King Library, Dept of Special
Collections, Lexington, 40506. William
Marshall, Head
Holdings: Cat Mss
Notes: Complete sets of Stamperia del
Santuccio imprints (C and V Hammer); The
Anvil Press; the Gravesend Press (Joseph
Graves); The Bur Press; King Library Press;
Gnoman Press; Buttonwood Press.

PRESS BOOKS—GOLDEN COCKEREL PRESS

CA —UNIVERSITY OF CALIFORNIA,
DAVIS, Shields Library, Dept of Special
Collections, Davis, 95616. Donald Kunitz,
Head; C Danial Elliott, Asst Head
Holdings: Vols 120 Cat
Notes: Substantial holdings of the principal
editions.
CA —UNIVERSITY OF CALIFORNIA, SAN
DIEGO, Central University Library,
Mandeville Dept of Special Collections, La
Jolla, 92093. Lynda Corey Claassen, Head
Holdings: Vols 100 Cat Mss
CA —UNIVERSITY OF CALIFORNIA, LOS
ANGELES, William Andrews Clark
Memorial Library, 2520 Cimarron St, Los
Angeles, 90018.
Notes: The papers and library of Eric Gill,
incl business correspondence, accounts,
Gill's diary in 27 volumes, many of his
writings in typescript or holograph, and
more than 500 original drawings. Also, the
Joseph Kelly Vodrey Collection of Robert
Gibbings material. Consists of Gibbings'
books, illustrations, wood engravings,
drawings, and mss. Director of the Golden
Cockerel Press (1924-1933), Gibbings
worked closely with Eric Gill. The collection
is described in *The Clark Newsletter,*
number 5 (1983).
CA —SAN DIEGO STATE UNIVERSITY,
Malcolm A Love Library, 5300 Campanile
Dr, San Diego, 92182. D Dickinson, Univ
Librn; Don L Bosseau, Dir
Notes: Collected publications of certain fine
presses and illustrators as: Golden Cockerel,
Black Sparrow, Roycroft, Mosher, Bruce
Rogers, Janus Press.
CO —UNIVERSITY OF COLORADO,
Libraries, Special Collections, Boulder,
80309. Nora J Quinlan, Head
Notes: Samuel Goldman Collection.
Composed of the Limited Editions Club
Collection, the Kelmscott Press Collection
(both virtually complete) and examples of
works from other major fine presses incl the
Doves Press, Golden Cockerel, Nonesuch,
etc.
IL —NORTHWESTERN UNIVERSITY,
Library, Special Collections Dept, 1937
Sheridan Rd, Evanston, 60201. R Russell
Maylone, Cur
Holdings: Vols (5000) Cat
Notes: Representative examples of the work
of the modern private press from Strawberry
Hill to the current small printers. Incl such
presses as Cuala, Essex House, Golden
Cockerel, Grabhorn, Nonesuch, Roxburghe,
etc. Also 15,000 "little magazine" titles
exclusive of runs in the geneal library
collections.
IL —ILLINOIS STATE UNIVERSITY, Milner
Library, Dept of Special Collections,
Normal, 61761. Robert Sokan, Librn
Holdings: Vols (2800) Cat
IN —INDIANA UNIVERSITY, Lilly Library,
Seventh St, Bloomington, 47405. William R

Cagle, Librn
Holdings: // Cat
Notes: Large holdings.
NY —BUFFALO & ERIE COUNTY PUBLIC
LIBRARY, Rare Book Room, Lafayette Sq,
Buffalo, 14203. William H Loos, Cur
Holdings: Vols 62 Cat
NY —HOFSTRA UNIVERSITY, Library,
1000 Fulton Ave, Hempstead, 11550.
Charles R Andrews, Dean of Library
Services
Notes: Strong collection. Incl some mss.
NY —NEW YORK PUBLIC LIBRARY, Rare
Books and Manuscripts Div, Fifth Ave & 42
St, New York, 10018. William L Joyce, Asst
Dir; Francis O Mattson, Curator
Holdings: Cat
Budget: ($7161)
Notes: Complete or nearly complete file of
publications, incl books, pamphlets,
broadsides and other ephemera.
NY —ROCHESTER INSTITUTE OF
TECHNOLOGY, Melbert B Cary Jr
Graphic Arts Collection, School of Printing,
One Lomb Memorial Drive, Rochester,
14623. David Pankow, Cur
Holdings: Vols (11,000) Cat
NY —UNIVERSITY OF ROCHESTER, Rush
Rhees Library, Department of Rare Books
and Special Collections, Rochester, 14627.
Peter Dzwonkoski, Librn
Holdings: Vols 110 Cat
PA —PENNSYLVANIA STATE
UNIVERSITY, Fred Lewis Pattee Library,
Special Collections Dept, University Park,
16802. Charles Mann, Chief, Special
Collections
Holdings: Vols (989) Uncat
Budget: ($37,000)
Notes: No photocopying.
WI —UNIVERSITY OF WISCONSIN,
MADISON, Memorial Library, Rare Books
Collection, 728 State St, Madison, 53706.
Gretchen Lagana, Cur
Holdings: Vols 6000 Cat
Notes: Private Press Collection. Strong
collection of the major fine presses, modern
fine printing, as well as books from
Wisconsin private presses. Also includes a
large collection of small press books up to
1980. Especially strong in Golden Cockerel
and Perishable Press imprints. Housed in the
Dept of Rare Books and Special Collections.
ON —UNIVERSITY OF WATERLOO,
Library, Waterloo, N2L 3G1, Can. Susan
Bellingham, Special Collections Librn
Notes: Incl 133 titles.

PRESS BOOKS—GRABHORN, JANE

CA —UNIVERSITY OF SAN FRANCISCO,
Richard A Gleeson Library, The Countess
Bernardine Murphy Donohue Rare Book
Room, San Francisco, 94117. D Steven
Corey, Special Collections Librn
Holdings: Vols 50
Notes: A complete collection of Jane
Grabhorn's Jumbo and Colt Press imprints;
extensive ephemera, mss material, photos.

PRESS BOOKS—GRABHORN-HOYEM PRESS

CA —STANFORD UNIVERSITY
LIBRARIES, Cecil H Green Library,
Stanford, 94305. Michael T Ryan, Cur
Holdings: Vols (12,000) Cat
Notes: The Morgan A & Aline D Gunst
Memorial Library. The book arts in every
century with some of the best examples.
Strong collection of examples of California
printers and graphic artists. Complete or
nearly complete collections of works by the
Kelmscott, Doves, Ashendene, Colt,
Grabhorn, and Grabhorn-Hoyem presses.

PRESS BOOKS—GRABHORN PRESS

CA —UNIVERSITY OF CALIFORNIA,
BERKELEY, Bancroft Library, Manuscripts
Division, Berkeley, 94720. James D Hart,
Dir
Holdings: Vols Cat Mss
Notes: Materials are collected to serve as
specimans for the study of printing history

and the development of fine printing.
English and American fine presses of the
19th and 20th centuries are particularly well
represented. Comprehensive coverage for
San Francisco Bay Area printers such as
Grabhorn, Grabhorn-Hoyem, and John
Henry Nash.
CA —BURBANK PUBLIC LIBRARY, 110 N
Glenoaks Blvd, Burbank, 91502. Mary Ann
Grasso, Coordr; Barbara Stones, Coordr,
Media Project
Holdings: Vols (2600) Cat Maps Pix
Notes: Strong in Grabhorn Press imprints
and other California press items of historical
interest. Also, strong collection of pamphlets
and ephemera concerning California.
Separate catalog in preparation. Collection
well described in "The Burbank Western
History Collection," by Thomas F Parker, in
California Librarian (April 1965).
CA —CLAREMONT COLLEGES, Honnold
Library, Ninth & Dartmouth, Claremont,
91711. Tania Rizzo, Special Collections
Dept Head
Holdings: Vols (75) Cat VF
Notes: The combined holdings of Honnold
and Denison Libraries at the Claremont
Colleges contain a complete set but one of
the books published by the Arion Press as
well as commissioned books and pamphlets,
and a comprehensive collection of books
printed by Andrew Hoyem for Grabhorn-
Hoyem and others. Complete ephemera
since 1979. Extensive files of advertising,
prospectuses, correspondence, and
broadsides.
CA —CALIFORNIA STATE UNIVERSITY,
FULLERTON, Library, Box 4150,
Fullerton, 92634. Linda Herman, Special
Collections Librn
Holdings: Vols 4600 Cat
Notes: Press books and fine printing of the
20th century incl vols from the Grabhorn
Press of San Francisco (Dr William B
Langsdorf Anniversary Collection; 613 vols)
and the Fine Arts Press of Santa Ana, Calif
(67 vols). It is supplemented by a group of
related collections on printing, binding, and
book history reference, which incl
representative examples of most modern fine
presses.
CA —UNIVERSITY OF CALIFORNIA, LOS
ANGELES, William Andrews Clark
Memorial Library, 2520 Cimarron St, Los
Angeles, 90018.
CA —MILLS COLLEGE LIBRARY, Oakland,
94613. Steven P Pandolfo, Librn
Holdings: Vols 500 Cat
CA —UNIVERSITY OF SAN FRANCISCO,
Richard A Gleeson Library, The Countess
Bernardine Murphy Donohue Rare Book
Room, San Francisco, 94117. D Steven
Corey, Special Collections Librn
Holdings: Vols 600
Notes: A comprehensive collection of Edwin
and Robert Grabhorn incl unique items,
extensive ephemera, photos.
CA —STANFORD UNIVERSITY
LIBRARIES, Cecil H Green Library,
Stanford, 94305. Michael T Ryan, Cur
Holdings: Vols (12,000) Cat
Notes: The Morgan A & Aline D Gunst
Memorial Library. The book arts in every
century with some of the best examples.
Strong collection of examples of California
printers and graphic artists. Complete or
nearly complete collections of works by the
Kelmscott, Doves, Ashendene, Colt,
Grabhorn, and Grabhorn-Hoyem presses.
GA —UNIVERSITY OF GEORGIA,
Libraries, Special Collections Division,
Athens, 30602. Vesta Lee Gordon, Asst Dir
for Special Collections
Holdings: Vols (8000)
Notes: One of the larger collections of
private press books, pamphlets, and
ephemera. The Elmore H Mundell
Collection of materials from over 1200
different private printers.
IL —NORTHWESTERN UNIVERSITY,
Library, Special Collections Dept, 1937
Sheridan Rd, Evanston, 60201. R Russell
Maylone, Cur
Holdings: Vols (5000) Cat
Notes: Representative examples of the work
of the moden private press from Strawberry

PRESS BOOKS—GRABHORN PRESS (cont.)

Hill to the current small printers. Incl such presses as Cuala, Essex House, Golden Cockerel, Grabhorn, Nonesuch, Roxburghe, etc. Also 15,000 "little magazine" titles exclusive of runs in the general library collections.

IL —LAKE FOREST COLLEGE, Donnelley Library, Lake Forest, 60045. Arthur H Miller Jr, College Librn
Notes: Largely from the collection of Mr and Mrs DeWitt O'Kieffe, the collection has a range of items from landmarks (Grabhorn *Leaves of Grass* for example) to ephemera of private presses. Among those incl are Grabhorn Press, Lawton and Alfred Kennedy, Book Club of California and Carl Hertzog.

IL —ILLINOIS STATE UNIVERSITY, Milner Library, Dept of Special Collections, Normal, 61761. Robert Sokan, Librn
Holdings: Vols (2800) Cat

IN —INDIANA UNIVERSITY, Lilly Library, Seventh St, Bloomington, 47405. William R Cagle, Librn
Holdings: // Cat
Notes: Large holdings.

NY —COLUMBIA UNIVERSITY LIBRARIES, Rare Book & Manuscript Library, 801 Butler Library, 535 W 114 St, New York, 10027. Kenneth A Lohf, Librn
Holdings: Cat

NY —NEW YORK PUBLIC LIBRARY, Rare Books and Manuscripts Div, Fifth Ave & 42 St, New York, 10018. William L Joyce, Asst Dir; Francis O Mattson, Curator
Holdings: Cat
Budget: ($7161)
Notes: Complete or nearly complete file of publications, incl books, pamphlets, broadsides and other ephemera.

NY —UNIVERSITY OF ROCHESTER, Rush Rhees Library, Department of Rare Books and Special Collections, Rochester, 14627. Peter Dzwonkoski, Librn
Holdings: Vols 100 Cat

UT —UNIVERSITY OF UTAH, Marriott Library, Special Collections, Salt Lake City, 84112. Gregory C Thompson, Cur
Notes: The publications of Utah presses are also acquired. These presses are Olympus, Peregrine, Smith, Real Peoples, Horizon, Canticle, and Westwater. For the Rare Books collection materials from certain outside presses are also included. These presses are Northland, Allen, Grabhorn, Black Sparrow, Lime Kiln and Black Mountain. Books on Freemasonry are also collected.

AB —UNIVERSITY OF ALBERTA, Cameron Library, The Bruce Peel Special Collections Room, Edmonton, T6G 2J8, Can. John Charles, Special Collections Librn
Notes: 750 books and ephemera.

PRESS BOOKS—GRAF KESSLER ARCHIVE

IL —NEWBERRY LIBRARY, John M Wing Foundation on the History of Printing, 60 W Walton St, Chicago, 60610. Diana Haskell, Cur of Modern Mss
Holdings: Vols (30,000) Cat Mss
Budget: ($50,000)
See also entry under Printing - History

PRESS BOOKS—GRAVESEND PRESS

KY —UNIVERSITY OF KENTUCKY, Margaret I King Library, Dept of Special Collections, Lexington, 40506. William Marshall, Head
Holdings: Cat Mss
Notes: Complete sets of Stamperia del Santuccio imprints (C and V Hammer); The Anvil Press; the Gravesend Press (Joseph Graves); The Bur Press; King Library Press; Gnoman Press; Buttonwood Press.

PRESS BOOKS—GREENWICH BOOKS

NY —STATE UNIVERSITY OF NEW YORK, STONY BROOK, Melville Library, Dept of Special Collections, Stony Brook, 11794. Evert Volkersz, Head
Holdings: Vols 130 Uncat
Notes: An incomplete collection of this vanity/subsidy publisher, 1955-1959.

PRESS BOOKS—GREY BOW PRESS

NJ —FAIRLEIGH DICKINSON UNIVERSITY, Friendship Library, 285 Madison Ave, Madison, 07940. James Fraser, Library Dir; Renee Weber, Cur
Holdings: Vols 100 Cat Mss Pix
Notes: Books printed and bound by Loyd Haberly; also original drawings and sketches for illustrated bindings and page layouts for various books. Private funds are provided for purchase of books on the subject of Haberly's interests: hand binding and fine printing, not only his own.

NY —COLUMBIA UNIVERSITY LIBRARIES, Rare Book & Manuscript Library, 801 Butler Library, 535 W 114 St, New York, 10027. Kenneth A Lohf, Librn

PRESS BOOKS—GREY FOX PRESS

CA —UNIVERSITY OF CALIFORNIA, SAN DIEGO, Central University Library, Mandeville Dept of Special Collections, La Jolla, 92093. Lynda Corey Claassen, Head; Michael Davidson, Cur, Archive for New Poetry
Notes: The collection of papers belonging to editor and publisher Donald Allen represents the work of one of the first publishers to make innovative poetry available through his landmark anthology, *The New American Poetry, 1945-1960*, and through his two presses, The Four Seasons Foundation and Grey Fox Press.

PRESS BOOKS—HAMMER, VICTOR

CA —UNIVERSITY OF SAN FRANCISCO, Richard A Gleeson Library, The Countess Bernardine Murphy Donohue Rare Book Room, San Francisco, 94117. D Steven Corey, Special Collections Librn
Holdings: Vols 75 Mss
Notes: A complete collection of Victor Hammer with unique items. Incl the Stamperia del Santuccio, Wells College Press, Hammer Press, and Anvil Press. Also present are a number of Hammer's original drawings and sketches for a painted triptych in the collection and a self-portrait.

PRESS BOOKS—HAMMER CREEK PRESS

CA —UNIVERSITY OF SAN FRANCISCO, Richard A Gleeson Library, The Countess Bernardine Murphy Donohue Rare Book Room, San Francisco, 94117. D Steven Corey, Special Collections Librn
Holdings: Vols 75
Notes: Comprehensive collection, extensive ephemera. John Fass, proprietor.

†NY —COLUMBIA UNIVERSITY LIBRARIES, Butler Library, Rare Book and Manuscript Library, 535 W 114 St, New York, 10027.

PRESS BOOKS—HAND AND FLOWER PRESS

MO —WASHINGTON UNIVERSITY, Libraries, Special Collections Dept, Campus Box 1061, St Louis, 63130.
Notes: A small but significant collection.

PRESS BOOKS—HARBOR PRESS

MA —AMHERST COLLEGE, Library, Amherst, 01002. John Lancaster, Special Collections Librn
Holdings: Vols 225 Cat

†NY —COLUMBIA UNIVERSITY LIBRARIES, Butler Library, Rare Book and Manuscript Library, 535 W 114 St, New York, 10027.

PRESS BOOKS—HARRIS, JOHN

CA —UNIVERSITY OF CALIFORNIA, LOS ANGELES, Research Library, Dept of Special Collections, 405 Hilgard Ave, Los Angeles, 90024. Edward Shreeves, Chairman, Bibliographers Group; David S Zeidberg, Head
Holdings: Vols 500

PRESS BOOKS—HAWTHORN HOUSE

CA —UNIVERSITY OF CALIFORNIA, SANTA BARBARA, Library, Dept of Special Collections, Santa Barbara, 93106. Christian F Brun, Head
Holdings: Vols 55 Cat Mss
Notes: Incl ephemera.

CT —TRINITY COLLEGE LIBRARY, Watkinson Library, 300 Summit St, Hartford, 06106. Jeffrey Kaimowitz, Cur
Holdings: Vols 70 Cat

PRESS BOOKS—HELL COAL PRESS

RI —BROWN UNIVERSITY, John Hay Library, 20 Prospect St, Providence, 02912. Mark N Brown, Cur Mss
Holdings: Vols (1000) Cat
Notes: Many examples of 19th and 20th century private and small presses of American and English imprint. Some of the presses represented are: Anthoensen, Bayberry Hill, Black Sun, Catnatch, Cuala, Doves, Essex House, Golden Cockerel, Grabhorn, Kelmscott, Merrymount, Mosher, Nonesuch, Perishable, Stinehour, Trianon, Unicorn, Vagabond, plus many Rhode Island small presses such as Burning Deck, Turkey, and Hall Coal.

PRESS BOOKS—HERITAGE PRESS

NC —UNIVERSITY OF NORTH CAROLINA, CHAPEL HILL, Wilson Library, Rare Book Collection, Chapel Hill, 27514. Paul S Koda, Cur of Rare Books
Holdings: Vols 1000 Cat
Notes: Books from private or special presses, incl a large collection of books from the Limited Editions Club, Heritage Press, and Kelmscott Press. Subject incl the history of printing, bibliographical information, and books by authors whose works are collected.

PRESS BOOKS—HERTZOG, CARL

CA —UNIVERSITY OF CALIFORNIA, LOS ANGELES, William Andrews Clark Memorial Library, 2520 Cimarron St, Los Angeles, 90018.

IL —LAKE FOREST COLLEGE, Donnelley Library, Lake Forest, 60045. Arthur H Miller Jr, College Librn
Holdings: Vols (350)
Notes: Largely from the collection of Mr and Mrs DeWitt O'Kieffe, the collection has a range of items from landmarks (Grabhorn *Leaves of Grass* for example) to ephemera of private presses. Among those incl are Grabhorn Press, Lawton and Alfred Kennedy, Book Club of California and Carl Hertzog.

TX —UNIVERSITY OF TEXAS, EL PASO, Library, Special Collections Dept, El Paso, 79968. Cesar Caballero, Dept Head
Budget: ($6000)
Notes: Carl Hertzog Collection. More than three hundred books produced by the prominent printer/book designer Carl Hertzog and over a thousand books on books about books, typography, and the history of printing make up this collection. It also contains many Southwestern classics by Frank Dobie and Tom Lea.

TX —UNIVERSITY OF HOUSTON, M D Anderson Memorial Library, University Park, Houston, 77004. David Farmer, Cur, Special Collections; Jean Jackson, Assistant Cur
Holdings: Vols 600 Cat
Notes: This collection is confined to books in some way distinguished by their typographic qualities and produced within the borders of Texas at any time, past or present. Larger portions of the collection incl the work of the Encino Press, William Holman, Carl Hertzog, Edwin Hill, and other private and fine printers.

PRESS BOOKS—HIGH HOUSE PRESS

IL —ILLINOIS STATE UNIVERSITY, Milner Library, Dept of Special Collections,

PRESS BOOKS—HIGH HOUSE PRESS (cont.)

Normal, 61761. Robert Sokan, Librn
Holdings: Vols (2800) Cat

PRESS BOOKS—HILL, EDWIN (PRINTER)

TX —UNIVERSITY OF HOUSTON, M D
Anderson Memorial Library, University
Park, Houston, 77004. David Farmer, Cur,
Special Collections; Jean Jackson, Assistant
Cur
Holdings: Vols 600 Cat
Notes: This collection is confined to books
in some way distinguished by their
typographic qualities and produced within
the borders of Texas at any time, past or
present. Larger portions of the collection incl
the work of the Encino Press, William
Holman, Carl Hertzog, Edwin Hill, and othe
private and fine printers.

PRESS BOOKS—HILLSIDE PRESS

†NY —COLUMBIA UNIVERSITY
LIBRARIES, Butler Library, Rare Book and
Manuscript Library, 535 W 114 St, New
York, 10027.

PRESS BOOKS—HOGARTH PRESS

CA —UNIVERSITY OF CALIFORNIA, SAN
DIEGO, Central University Library,
Mandeville Dept of Special Collections, La
Jolla, 92093. Lynda Corey Claassen, Head
Holdings: Vols 175 Cat
DE —UNIVERSITY OF DELAWARE, Hugh
M Morris Library, S College Ave, Newark,
19711. T Stuart Dick, Special Collections
Holdings: Cat
Notes: Incl first and variant editions of
publications issued by the Hogarth Press,
founded by Leonard and Virginia Woolf.
IL —NORTHWESTERN UNIVERSITY,
Library, Special Collections Dept, 1937
Sheridan Rd, Evanston, 60201. R Russell
Maylone, Cur
Holdings: Vols 230 Cat
IN —INDIANA UNIVERSITY, Lilly Library,
Seventh St, Bloomington, 47405. William R
Cagle, Librn
Holdings: // Cat
Notes: The bulk of the Lilly Library's
holdings came from the Mary Gaither
Collection of 221 vols printed 1917-1938.
Lilly now owns examples of all but one of
the hand-printed pieces.
NY —HOFSTRA UNIVERSITY, Library,
1000 Fulton Ave, Hempstead, 11550.
Charles R Andrews, Dean of Library
Services
Notes: Strong collection. Incl some mss.
OH —OHIO UNIVERSITY, Vernon R Alden
Library, Department of Archives and Special
Collections, Athens, 45701. Gary A Hunt,
Head
Holdings: Vols 100 Cat
Notes: A small collection of the publications
of Virginia and Leonard Woolf's Hogarth
Press, mostly 1920s and 1930s.
†WA —WASHINGTON STATE
UNIVERSITY, Library, Manuscripts,
Archives & Special Collections, Pullman,
99164. John F Guido, Head
Holdings: Vols Mss Pix
Notes: The library of Virginia and Leonard
Woolf (from Monk's House and Victoria Sq)
forms the nucleus of the collection, which
incorporates the library of Sir Leslie
Stephen, Virginia's father. Leonard's
interests are reflected by works concerning
the Labour Party, the Fabian Society, as well
as Ceylon. Their interest in printing and
publishing works of significance is reflected
by the collection of Hogarth Press
publications (1917-1941). Incl works by
Virginia and Leonard Woolf, the Bloomsbury
Group, as well as by other friends eg,
Elizabeth Robins, Victoria Sackville-West,
Harold Nicholson, etc. Many of these are
unique copies, ie, of association and textual
interest. Other 20th century English authors
incl the Sitwells, Margaret Sackville, Rose

Macaulay, D H Lawrence, John Masefield,
Rupert Croft-Cooke, and Charles Williams.
Partially cataloged.
ON —VICTORIA UNIVERSITY, Library, 71
Queen's Park Crescent, Toronto, M5S 1K7,
Can. Robert C Brandeis, Chief Librn
Holdings: Vols Cat
Notes: A collection of first editional and
others of Virginia Woolfe and Bloomsbury
writers: Clive Bell, Roger Fry, E M Forster,
V Sackville-West, K Mansfield, etc. Contains
a significant collection of Hogarth Press
books (over 340 vols), and many of those
handprinted by the Woolfs.

PRESS BOOKS—HOLIDAY HOUSE

CA —CLAREMONT COLLEGES, Ella Strong
Denison Library, Scripps College,
Claremont, 91711. Judy Harvey Sahak,
Librn
Holdings: Vols 78 Cat
Notes: Works designed by Miss Gentry,
primarily for Holiday House. Also incl
Holiday House. Also incl correspondence,
ephemera and items printed by Miss Gentry.

PRESS BOOKS—HOLMAN, WILLIAM (PRINTER)

TX —UNIVERSITY OF HOUSTON, M D
Anderson Memorial Library, University
Park, Houston, 77004. David Farmer, Cur,
Special Collections; Jean Jackson, Assistant
Cur
Holdings: Vols 600 Cat
Notes: This collection is confined to books
in some way distinguished by their
typographic qualities and produced with the
borders of Texas at any time, past or
present. Larger portions of the collection incl
the work of the Encino Press, William
Holman, Carl Hertzog, Edwin Hill, and
other private and fine printers.

PRESS BOOKS—HORIZON PRESS

UT —UNIVERSITY OF UTAH, Marriott
Library, Special Collections, Salt Lake City,
84112. Gregory C Thompson, Cur
Notes: The publications of Utah presses are
also acquired. These presses are Olympus,
Peregrine, Smith, Real Peoples, Horizon,
Canticle, and Westwater. For the Rare
Books collection materials from certain
outside presses are also included. These
presses are Northland, Allen, Grabhorn,
Black Sparrow, Lime Kiln and Black
Mountain. Books on Freemasonry are also
collected.

PRESS BOOKS—IRIS PRESS

NY —STATE UNIVERSITY OF NEW
YORK, BINGHAMTON, Glenn G Bartle
Library, Binghamton, 13901. Marion
Hanscom, Special Collections Librn
Holdings: Cat

PRESS BOOKS—JANSSON PRINTING

WI —UNIVERSITY OF WISCONSIN,
MADISON, Memorial Library, Rare Books
Collection, 728 State St, Madison, 53706.
Gretchen Lagana, Cur
Holdings: Vols (58) Cat
Notes: Grotius Collection. Some 58 voumes
by, about, or associated with the Dutch jurist
and humanist Higo Grotius. A number of the
volumes comprise classical writings edited by
Grotius. Certain of the volumes issued by
Jansson, Elzevier, and Estienne are, in
addition, valuable as specimens illustrating
the history of printing. Restricted use: Rare
Book Department.

PRESS BOOKS—JANUS PRESS

CA —SAN DIEGO STATE UNIVERSITY,
Malcolm A Love Library, 5300 Campanile
Dr, San Diego, 92182. D Dickinson, Univ
Librn; Don L Bosseau, Dir
Notes: Collected publications of certain fine
presses and illustrators as: Golden Cockerel,
Black Sparrow, Roycroft, Mosher, Bruce
Rogers, Janus Press.

PRESS BOOKS—JARGON SOCIETY

NY —STATE UNIVERSITY OF NEW
YORK, COLLEGE AT BUFFALO, Poetry/
Rare Books Collection, 420 Capen Hall,
Buffalo, 14260. Robert J Bertholf, Cur
Notes: Extensive holdings of the
publications, mss, correspondence, working
mss, ephemera, business records for the
Jargon Society, a small press publisher. The
holdings also incl the private papers,
correspondence and mss of Jonathan
Williams, owner of the Jargon Society.
NC —UNIVERSITY OF NORTH
CAROLINA, GREENSBORO, Walter
Clinton Jackson Library, Special Collections
Dept, 1000 Spring Garden St, Greensboro,
27412. Emilie W Mills, Librn
Holdings: Vols (800) Cat
Notes: Emphasis is on English and
American presses from the 1890s to the
present. Selections from the major presses
are included as are the lesser known presses.
Periodicals incl *The Dolphin*, *The Fleuron*,
The Colophon and *The Imprint*. Extensive
holdings of American presses currently
operating incl Penumbra Press, The
Perishable Press Limited, Jargon Society,
and Unicorn Press.

PRESS BOOKS—JUMBO PRESS

†CA —UNIVERSITY OF SAN FRANCISCO,
Richard A Gleeson Library, The Countess
Bernardine Murphy Donohue Rare Book
Room, San Francisco, 94117. D Steven
Corey, Special Collections Librn
Holdings: Vols 50
Notes: A complete collection of Jane
Grabhorn items. Incl Jumbo and Colt Press
imprints; extensive ephemera.

PRESS BOOKS—KAYAK PRESS

FL —UNIVERSITY OF MIAMI, Otto G
Richter Library, PO Box 248214, Coral
Gables, 33124. Frank Rodgers, Dir of
Libraries
Notes: 3500 items. Nineteenth century well
represented by Longfellow and Thoreau
collections organized by Thomas DeValcourt
at Longfellow House. Additional Thoreau
items were purchased later. Innovative and
experimental writing of 1960s and 1970s,
incl press books from Black Sparrow,
Unicorn, Kayak and other small presses, as
well as privately published works and many
small magazines. Format ranges from
postcard and poster to fine limited editions
of codex form.

PRESS BOOKS—KELMSCOTT PRESS

AZ —ARIZONA STATE UNIVERSITY,
Library, Tempe, 85287. Marilyn
Wurzburger, Special Collections Librn
Holdings: Cat
Notes: 53 titles (Chaucer in facsimile).
Ephemera incl the rare trial pages of
Froissart's Chronicles, the Wayzgoose
Programs, and numerous specimen leaves. In
addition are 135 volumes by and about
Willaim Morris.
CA —CLAREMONT COLLEGES, Ella Strong
Denison Library, Scripps College,
Claremont, 91711. Judy Harvey Sahak,
Librn
Holdings: // Cat
Notes: In addition to all volumes produced
at the Press, includes original drawings,
proof sheets, and other ephemera.
CA —CLAREMONT COLLEGES, Honnold
Library, Ninth & Dartmouth, Claremont,
91711. Tania Rizzo, Special Collections
Dept Head
Holdings: Vols (70,000) Cat VF
Notes: Books on typography, bibliography,
and history of printing; incunabula; specimen
books; fine press books, esp Kelmscott,
Doves, Daniel, Mosher, Grabhorn, Nash,
and Arion presses and many Southern
California printers. A comprehensive
collection of Zamorano Club publications
and keepsakes, partial source for George E
Fulleton, *The Zamorano Club: The First*

PRESS BOOKS—KELMSCOTT PRESS (cont.)

Half Century (Los Angeles, 1978). Extensive files of ephemera. Fine bindings and fore-edge paintings. Samples of Oriental type and printing.

CA —UNIVERSITY OF CALIFORNIA, LOS ANGELES, William Andrews Clark Memorial Library, 2520 Cimarron St, Los Angeles, 90018.
Holdings: Cat Mss Pix
Notes: Extensive collection, first editions, etc, described in the Library's *Kelmscott and Doves Presses* (1921).

CA —STANFORD UNIVERSITY LIBRARIES, Cecil H Green Library, Stanford, 94305. Michael T Ryan, Cur
Holdings: Vols (12,000) Cat
Notes: The Morgan A & Aline D Gunst Memorial Library. The book arts in every century with some of the best examples. Strong collection of examples of California printers and graphic artists. Complete or nearly complete collections of works by the Kelmscott, Doves, Ashendene, Colt, Grabhorn, and Grabhorn-Hoyem presses.

CA —UNIVERSITY OF THE PACIFIC, Library, Stockton, 95211. Hiram L Davis, Dir of Libraries
Holdings: Vols (350) Uncat Pix
Notes: A general collection of Victorian literature and life given to the University by James M Perrin in 1968-1970. The primary specialization is material by and about William Morris and the Kelmscott Press, but the collection also is rich in Victorian first editions, Pre-Raphaelites and Pre-Raphaelitism, and early colored illustrations and chromolithography.

CO —UNIVERSITY OF COLORADO, Libraries, Special Collections, Boulder, 80309. Nora J Quinlan, Head
Notes: Samuel Goldman Collection. Composed of the Limited Editions Club Collection, the Kelmscott Press Collection (both virtually complete) and examples of works from other major fine presses incl the Doves Press, Golden Cockerel, Nonesuch, etc.

CO —DENVER PUBLIC LIBRARY, Douglas Collection of Fine Printing, 1357 Broadway, Denver, 80203.
Holdings: Vols 1700 Cat
Notes: Books from private presses, limited editions and books about private presses. Incl a complete set of vols from William Morris' Kelmscott Press and a virtually complete collection of Ashendene Press books. Most major presses are well represented and minor presses have representative works in the collection.

FL —UNIVERSITY OF MIAMI, Otto G Richter Library, PO Box 248214, Coral Gables, 33124. Frank Rodgers, Dir of Libraries
Notes: 3500 items. Black Sparrow, Auerhahn and other press books of the 1960s and 1970s, within the general area of contemporary poetry. Also, separate from this group, are many Cuala, Mosher, Kelmscott imprints, and all of the Trianon Press Blake facsimiles. Noncirculating.

FL —FLORIDA STATE UNIVERSITY, Robert Manning Strozier Library, Special Collections Dept, Tallahassee, 32306. Opal M Free, Head, Special Collections
Holdings: Vols 64 // Cat
Notes: Complete collection of Howard A Storrs. Noncirculating.

IN —INDIANA UNIVERSITY, Lilly Library, Seventh St, Bloomington, 47405. William R Cagle, Librn
Holdings: // Cat
Notes: Complete collection of items printed at the Kelmscott Press.

NY —BUFFALO & ERIE COUNTY PUBLIC LIBRARY, Rare Book Room, Lafayette Sq, Buffalo, 14203. William H Loos, Cur
Holdings: Vols 46 Cat
Notes: Collection incl a Kelmscott Chancer.

†NY —COLUMBIA UNIVERSITY LIBRARIES, Butler Library, Rare Book and Manuscript Library, 535 W 114 St, New York, 10027.

NY —NEW YORK PUBLIC LIBRARY, Rare Books and Manuscripts Div, Fifth Ave & 42 St, New York, 10018. William L Joyce, Asst Dir; Francis O Mattson, Curator
Holdings: Cat
Budget: ($7161)
Notes: Complete or nearly complete file of publications, incl books, pamphlets, broadsides and other ephemera.

NY —ROCHESTER INSTITUTE OF TECHNOLOGY, Melbert B Cary Jr Graphic Arts Collection, School of Printing, One Lomb Memorial Drive, Rochester, 14623. David Pankow, Cur
Holdings: Vols (11,000) Cat

NC —UNIVERSITY OF NORTH CAROLINA, CHAPEL HILL, Wilson Library, Rare Book Collection, Chapel Hill, 27514. Paul S Koda, Cur of Rare Books
Holdings: Vols 1000 Cat
Notes: Books from private or special presses, incl a large collection of books from the Limited Editions Club, Heritage Press, and Kelmscott Press. Subjects incl the history of printing, bibliographical information, and books by authors whose works are collected.

PA —PENNSYLVANIA STATE UNIVERSITY, Fred Lewis Pattee Library, Special Collections Dept, University Park, 16802. Charles Mann, Chief, Special Collections
Holdings: Vols (989) Uncat
Budget: ($37,000)
Notes: No photocopying.

PRESS BOOKS—KENNEDY, LAWTON AND ALFRED

CA —UNIVERSITY OF SAN FRANCISCO, Richard A Gleeson Library, The Countess Bernardine Murphy Donohue Rare Book Room, San Francisco, 94117. D Steven Corey, Special Collections Librn
Holdings: Vols 150
Notes: About 1000 items in the archival collection of this San Francisco firm. Extensive ephemera.

IL —LAKE FOREST COLLEGE, Donnelley Library, Lake Forest, 60045. Arthur H Miller Jr, College Librn
Holdings: Vols (350)
Notes: Largely from the collection of Mr and Mrs DeWitt O'Kieffe, the collection has a range of items from landmarks (Grabhorn *Leaves of Grass* for example) to ephemera of private presses. Among those incl are Grabhorn Press, Lawton and Alfred Kennedy, Book Club of California and Carl Hertzog.

PRESS BOOKS—KENNEDY, LAWTON R.

CA —UNIVERSITY OF CALIFORNIA, LOS ANGELES, William Andrews Clark Memorial Library, 2520 Cimarron St, Los Angeles, 90018.

PRESS BOOKS—KING LIBRARY PRESS

KY —UNIVERSITY OF KENTUCKY, Margaret I King Library, Dept of Special Collections, Lexington, 40506. William Marshall, Head
Holdings: Cat Mss
Notes: Complete sets of Stamperia del Santuccio imprints (C and V Hammer); The Anvil Press; the Gravesend Press (Joseph Graves); The Bur Press; King Library Press; Gnoman Press; Buttonwood Press.

PRESS BOOKS—KITIMAUG PRESS

SC —WOFFORD COLLEGE, Sandor Teszler Library, N Church St, Spartanburg, 29301. Frank J Anderson, Librn
Holdings: Vols 1000 Cat
Notes: Books about the history and practice of printing, hand papermaking, bookbinding, book collecting, fine press and private press books used in conjunction with instruction at the Wofford Library Press, an experimental and bibliographic press which has been in operation since 1969. Collection contains

materials on printmaking methods and related graphic arts. Collection incl imprints of: Briarpatch Press, Anthoensen Press, Mosher Press, Kitimaug Press, Windhover Press, Penman Press, Unicorn Press, Wofford Library Press and others.

PRESS BOOKS—KLINGSPOR PRESS

†NY —COLUMBIA UNIVERSITY LIBRARIES, Butler Library, Rare Book and Manuscript Library, 535 W 114 St, New York, 10027.

PRESS BOOKS—LABORATORY PRESS

CA —UNIVERSITY OF CALIFORNIA, LOS ANGELES, William Andrews Clark Memorial Library, 2520 Cimarron St, Los Angeles, 90018.

PRESS BOOKS—LAKESIDE PRESS

IL —CHICAGO PUBLIC LIBRARY, Special Collections Div, Cultural Center, 78 E Washington St, Chicago, 60602. Laura Linard, Cur
Holdings: Vols (800) Cat
Budget: ($3000)
Notes: The Special Collections Division endeavors to collect all Chicago imprints produced before 1900, and all Chicago private press productions 1900-50. An exceptional collection of books and keepsakes designed by Norman Forgue. We actively purchase in this area. Outstanding items in the Chicago Imprints Inventory are described in the recent catalog, *Treasures of The Chicago Public Library*, compiled by Thomas A Orlando and Marie Gecik, 1977, pp 93-120.

IL —LAKE FOREST COLLEGE, Donnelley Library, Lake Forest, 60045. Arthur H Miller Jr, College Librn
Holdings: Vols (500)
Notes: Limited editions, privately printed books (William Kittredge), ephemera, Lakeside Classics; examples of work from R R Donnelley extra bindery.

PRESS BOOKS—LIME KILN PRESS

UT —UNIVERSITY OF UTAH, Marriott Library, Special Collections, Salt Lake City, 84112. Gregory C Thompson, Cur
Notes: The publications of Utah presses are also acquired. These presses are Olympus, Peregrine, Smith, Real Peoples, Horizon, Canticle, and Westwater. For the Rare Books collection materials from certain outside presses are also included. These presses are Northland, Allen, Grabhorn, Black Sparrow, Lime Kiln and Black Mountain. Books on Freemasonry are also collected.

PRESS BOOKS—LIMITED EDITIONS CLUB

CA —SOLANO COUNTY LIBRARY, John F Kennedy Library, Donovan J McCune Collection, 505 Santa Clara St, Vallejo, 94590.
Holdings: Vols 700 //
Notes: The Donovan J McCune Collection (3000) vols //.

CO —UNIVERSITY OF COLORADO, Libraries, Special Collections, Boulder, 80309. Nora J Quinlan, Head
Notes: Samuel Goldman Collection. Composed of the Limited Editions Club Collection, the Kelmscott Press Collection (both virtually complete) and examples of works from other major fine presses incl the Doves Press, Golden Cockerel, Nonesuch, etc.

IN —DEPAUW UNIVERSITY, Roy O West Library, PO Box 137, Greencastle, 46135. James A Martindale, Dir
Holdings: Vols 397 // Cat

†MA —WILLIAMS COLLEGE, Chapin Library of Rare Books, PO Box 426, Williamstown, 01267. Robert L Volz, Custodian
Holdings: Vols 200 Cat
Notes: Incl archives.

PRESS BOOKS—LIMITED EDITIONS CLUB (cont.)

MO —UNIVERSITY OF MISSOURI-COLUMBIA, Ellis Library, Special Collections Dept, Ninth & Lowry, Columbia, 65201. Margaret A Howell, Head, Special Collections
Holdings: Vols (250) Cat
Notes: Limited Editions Club titles are of exceptional quality both in content and craft. These fine examples of bookmaking are sought by collectors.

NY —COLUMBIA UNIVERSITY LIBRARIES, Rare Book & Manuscript Library, 801 Butler Library, 535 W 114 St, New York, 10027. Kenneth A Lohf, Librn
Holdings: Cat

NC —UNIVERSITY OF NORTH CAROLINA, CHAPEL HILL, Wilson Library, Rare Book Collection, Chapel Hill, 27514. Paul S Koda, Cur of Rare Books
Holdings: Vols 1000 Cat
Notes: Books from private or speical presses, incl a large collection of books from the Limited Editions Club, Heritage Press, and Kelmscott Press. Subjects incl the history of printing, bibligrahical information, and books by authors whose works are collected.

OH —PUBLIC LIBRARY OF CINCINNATI & HAMILTON COUNTY, Dept of Rare Books & Special Collections, 800 Vine St, Library Square, Cincinnati, 45202. Yeatman Anderson III, Cur
Holdings: Uncat
Notes: Complete set.

PA —UNIVERSITY OF PITTSBURGH, Hillman Library, Special Collections Dept, 363 Hillman Library, Pittsburgh, 15260. Charles E Aston Jr, Coordinator
Holdings: Vols Cat
Notes: Limited editions of 20th-century British and US authors; also a representative collection of Limited Editions Club imprints. Incl over 5000 vols.

WI —UNIVERSITY OF WISCONSIN, MADISON, Memorial Library, Rare Books Collection, 728 State St, Madison, 53706. Gretchen Lagana, Cur
Holdings: Vols 285 Cat
Notes: Extensive collection. Restricted use: Rare Book Department.

PRESS BOOKS—LOUJON PRESS

IL —NORTHWESTERN UNIVERSITY, Library, Special Collections Dept, 1937 Sheridan Rd, Evanston, 60201. R Russell Maylone, Cur
Holdings: Vols 165 Cat Mss Paintings
Notes: Henry Miller: first editions letters, ephemera. Incl mss, correspondence, and production files from the Loujon Press.

IN —INDIANA UNIVERSITY, Lilly Library, Seventh St, Bloomington, 47405. William R Cagle, Librn
Holdings: Cat Mss
Notes: Extensive holdings. Mss incl a file of correspondence of Jon and Louise Webb on operation of the Press, 1962-69. 127 items.

PRESS BOOKS—MCCALLISTER, BRUCE

CA —UNIVERSITY OF CALIFORNIA, LOS ANGELES, William Andrews Clark Memorial Library, 2520 Cimarron St, Los Angeles, 90018.

PRESS BOOKS—MCLOUGHLIN BROTHERS

†NY —COLUMBIA UNIVERSITY LIBRARIES, Butler Library, Rare Book and Manuscript Library, 535 W 114 St, New York, 10027.

PRESS BOOKS—MCMURTRIE PRINTINGS

AL —SAMFORD UNIVERSITY, Special Collections Library, 800 Lakeshore Dr, Birmingham, 35229. Annie Ford Wheeler, Acting Head Librn
Holdings: Vols 420 Cat
Notes: Albert T Scroggins Collection. Many limited editions.

PRESS BOOKS—MAGPIE PRESS

†CA —UNIVERSITY OF CALIFORNIA, Library, Los Angeles, 90024.
Notes: Magpie Press, jointly owned and operated by Margaret Gustafson and Roberta Nixon.

PRESS BOOKS—MAYA PRESS

NY —STATE UNIVERSITY OF NEW YORK, COLLEGE AT BUFFALO, Poetry/Rare Books Collection, 420 Capen Hall, Buffalo, 14260. Robert J Bertholf, Cur
Notes: Extensive archive of Jack Shoemaker, a prominent bookseller, publisher, and poet. Incl mss, work sheets, correspondence, ephemera, and business records of the Sand Dollar and Unicorn bookshops and the Maya Press. Also incl mss and letters of prominent modern poets.

PRESS BOOKS—MEADOW PRESS

CA —UNIVERSITY OF SAN FRANCISCO, Richard A Gleeson Library, The Countess Bernardine Murphy Donohue Rare Book Room, San Francisco, 94117. D Steven Corey, Special Collections Librn
Notes: Virtually complete collection of Leigh McLellan's books and ephemera. 50 items.

PRESS BOOKS—MERIDEN GRAVURE COMPANY

CT —TRINITY COLLEGE LIBRARY, Watkinson Library, 300 Summit St, Hartford, 06106. Jeffrey Kaimowitz, Cur
Holdings: Cat

PRESS BOOKS—MERRYMOUNT PRESS

RI —PROVIDENCE PUBLIC LIBRARY, 150 Empire St, Providence, 02903. Lance J Bauer, Special Collections Librn
Holdings: Vols (6300) Cat Mss Pix
Notes: The

PRESS BOOKS—MIDDLE HILL PRESS

CT —YALE UNIVERSITY, Box 1603A, Yale Station, New Haven, 06520.
Notes: Nearly complete collection of the production of the private press operated by Sir Thomas Phillipps at Middle Hill, Worcestershire, 1822-72. The Hans P Kraus Collection.

ON —UNIVERSITY OF TORONTO, Thomas Fisher Rare Book Library, 120 Saint George St, Toronto, M5S 1A5, Can. Richard G Landon, Head
Holdings: Vols 300
Notes: Middle Hill Press Collection contains items published by the private press established by Sir Thomas Phillipps, the 19th century bibliophile, and named after his estate. Phillipps used the Press to publish his discoveries in early English topographical and genealogical history. Press was active at periods between 1822 and 1872. Some proof sheets with annotations by Phillipps.

PRESS BOOKS—MINERVA PRESS

CA —UNIVERSITY OF CALIFORNIA, LOS ANGELES, Research Library, Dept of Special Collections, 405 Hilgard Ave, Los Angeles, 90024. Edward Shreeves, Chairman, Bibliographers Group; David S Zeidberg, Head
Holdings: Vols 35

PRESS BOOKS—MOSHER PRESS

AZ —ARIZONA STATE UNIVERSITY, Library, Tempe, 85287. Marilyn Wurzburger, Special Collections Librn
See also entry under Mosher, Thomas Bird.

CA —CLAREMONT COLLEGES, Honnold Library, Ninth & Dartmouth, Claremont, 91711. Tania Rizzo, Special Collections Dept Head
Holdings: Vols (70,000) Cat VF
Notes: Books on typography, bibliography, and history of printing; incunabula; specimen books; fine press books, esp Kelmscott, Doves, Daniel, Mosher, Grabhorn, Nash, and Arion presses and many Southern California printers. A comprehensive collection of Zamorano Club publications and keepsakes, partial source for George E Fulleton, *The Zamorano Club: The First Half Century* (Los Angeles, 1978). Extensive files of ephemera. Fine bindings and fore-edge paintings. Samples of Oriental type and printing.

CA —SAN DIEGO STATE UNIVERSITY, Malcolm A Love Library, 5300 Campanile Dr, San Diego, 92182. D Dickinson, Univ Librn; Don L Bosseau, Dir
Notes: Collected publications of certain fine presses and illustrators as: Golden Cockerel, Black Sparrow, Roycroft, Mosher, Bruce Rogers, Janus Press.

CT —TRINITY COLLEGE LIBRARY, Watkinson Library, 300 Summit St, Hartford, 06106. Jeffrey Kaimowitz, Cur
Holdings: Cat

FL —UNIVERSITY OF MIAMI, Otto G Richter Library, PO Box 248214, Coral Gables, 33124. Frank Rodgers, Dir of Libraries
Notes: 3500 items. Black Sparrow, Auerhahn and other press books of the 1960s and 1970s, within the general area of contemporary poetry. Also, separate from this group, are many Cuala, Mosher, Kelmscott imprints, and all of the Trianon Press Blake facsimiles. Noncirculating.

FL —UNIVERSITY OF SOUTH FLORIDA, Library, Tampa, 33620. J B Dobkin, Special Collections Librn
Holdings: Vols 550 Uncat
Budget: ($7500)
Notes: Thomas Bird Mosher Collection of over 400 editions of the publications of the Mosher Press. Arranged in accordance with B L Hatch's *A Checklist of the Publications of Thomas Bird Mosher*. Hatch numbers serve as access points to items in collection.

KY —UNIVERSITY OF LOUISVILLE, Ekstrom Library, Rare Books & Special Collections, 2301 S Third St, Louisville, 40208. George T McWhorter, Cur; Delinda Stephens Buie, Asst Cur
Holdings: Vols 1000 Uncat Mss
Budget: ($1500)
Notes: Press books in limited and fine editions, mss, bibliographies.

ME —MAINE STATE LIBRARY, Special Collections Dept, Cultural Bldg, Station 64, Augusta, 04333. Shirley Thayer, Librn
Holdings: Vols 600 //
Budget: ($2,500,000)
Notes: A collection of imprints by the Mosher Press, Portland, Maine.

ME —BOWDOIN COLLEGE, Library, Brunswick, 04011. Dianne M Gutscher, Cur of Special Collections
Holdings: Vols 400 Cat

ME —PORTLAND PUBLIC LIBRARY, 5 Monument Sq, Portland, 04101. Edward V Chenevert, Library Dir
Holdings: Vols 626 Cat
Notes: Press of Thomas Bird Mosher (1852-1923) of Portland. Incl complete *Bibelot* (monthly pamphlet/20 years). Nearly complete collection.

MO —SAINT LOUIS PUBLIC LIBRARY, Gardner Rare Book Room, 1301 Olive St, Saint Louis, 63103. Julanne M Good, Supervisor; Martha Riley, Rare Books Librn
Holdings: Vols (2300) Cat
Budget: ($5573)

NY —COLUMBIA UNIVERSITY LIBRARIES, Rare Book & Manuscript Library, 801 Butler Library, 535 W 114 St, New York, 10027. Kenneth A Lohf, Librn
Holdings: Cat

SC —WOFFORD COLLEGE, Sandor Teszler Library, N Church St, Spartanburg, 29301. Frank J Anderson, Librn
Holdings: Vols 500 Cat
Notes: Books about the history and practice of printing, hand papermaking, bookbinding, book collecting, fine press and private press books used in conjunction with instruction at the Wofford Library Press, an experimental and bibliographic press which has been in operation since 1969. Collection contains

PRESS BOOKS—MOSHER PRESS (cont.)

materials on printmaking methods and related graphic arts. Collection incl imprints of: Briarpatch Press, Anthoensen Press, Mosher Press, Kitmang Press, Windhover Press, Penman Press, Unicorn Press, Wofford Library Press and others.

†ON —UNIVERSITY OF WESTERN ONTARIO, School of Library and Information Science, Special Collections Room, London, N6A 5B9, Can.
Notes: Small collection of examples of Mosher's printing.

PRESS BOOKS—NASH, JOHN HENRY

CA —UNIVERSITY OF CALIFORNIA, BERKELEY, Bancroft Library, Manuscripts Division, Berkeley, 94720. James D Hart, Dir
Holdings: Vols Cat Mss
Notes: Materials are collected to serve as specimens for the study of printing history and the development of fine printing. English and American fine presses off the 19th and 20th centuries are particularly well represented. Comprehensive coverage for San Francisco Bay Area printers such as Grabhorn, Grabhorn-Hoyem, and John Henry Nash.
CA —CLAREMONT COLLEGES, Ella Strong Denison Library, Scripps College, Claremont, 91711. Judy Harvey Sahak, Librn
Holdings: Vols (1100) Cat
CA —CLAREMONT COLLEGES, Honnold Library, Ninth & Dartmouth, Claremont, 91711. Tania Rizzo, Special Collections Dept Head
Holdings: Vols (70,000) Cat VF
Notes: Books on typography, bibliography, and history of printing; incunabula; specimen books; fine press books, esp Kelmscott, Doves, Daniel, Mosher, Grabhorn, Nash, and Arion presses and many Southern California printers. A comprehensive collection of Zamorano Club publications and keepsakes, partial source for George E Fulleton, *The Zamorano Club: The First Half Century* (Los Angeles, 1978). Extensive files of ephemera. Fine bindings and fore-edge paintings. Samples of Oriental type and printing.
CA —MILLS COLLEGE LIBRARY, Oakland, 94613. Steven P Pandolfo, Librn
Holdings: Vols 300 Cat
CA —UNIVERSITY OF SAN FRANCISCO, Richard A Gleeson Library, The Countess Bernardine Murphy Donohue Rare Book Room, San Francisco, 94117. D Steven Corey, Special Collections Librn
Holdings: Vols 350
Notes: The collection formed by Norman H Strouse based on the collection of Nash's compositor, Joseph Fauntleroy. Unique items, extensive ephemera.
IL —SOUTHERN ILLINOIS UNIVERSITY, CARBONDALE, Delyte W Morris Library, Special Collections Dept, Carbondale, 62901. David V Koch, Cur of Special Collections; Louisa Bowen, Cur of Manuscripts
Holdings: Vols 400 Cat
Notes: Also 300 broadsides.

PRESS BOOKS—NASH PRINTINGS see Press Books—Nash, John Henry

PRESS BOOKS—NEWBERY, JOHN

CA —UNIVERSITY OF CALIFORNIA, LOS ANGELES, Research Library, Dept of Special Collections, 405 Hilgard Ave, Los Angeles, 90024. Edward Shreeves, Chairman, Bibliographers Group; David S Zeidberg, Head
Holdings: Vols 300

PRESS BOOKS—NONESUCH PRESS

CA —UNIVERSITY OF CALIFORNIA, LOS ANGELES, William Andrews Clark Memorial Library, 2520 Cimarron St, Los Angeles, 90018.

CA —SOLANO COUNTY LIBRARY, John F Kennedy Library, Donovan J McCune Collection, 505 Santa Clara St, Vallejo, 94590.
Holdings: 91 Vols //
Notes: The Donovan J McCune Collection (3000) vols //.
CO —UNIVERSITY OF COLORADO, Libraries, Special Collections, Boulder, 80309. Nora J Quinlan, Head
Notes: Samuel Goldman Collection. Composed of the Limited Editions Club Collection, the Kelmscott Press Collection (both virtually complete) and examples of works from other major fine presses incl the Doves Press, Golden Cockerel, Nonesuch, etc.
IL —NORTHWESTERN UNIVERSITY, Library, Special Collections Dept, 1937 Sheridan Rd, Evanston, 60201. R Russell Maylone, Cur
Holdings: Vols (5000) Cat
Notes: Representative examples of the work of the modern private press from Strawberry Hill to the current small printers. Incl such presses as Cuala, Essex House, Golden Cockerel, Grabhorn, Nonesuch, Roxburghe, etc. Also 15,000 little magazines titles exclusive of runs in the general library collections.
IL —ILLINOIS STATE UNIVERSITY, Milner Library, Dept of Special Collections, Normal, 61761. Robert Sokan, Librn
Holdings: Vols (2800) Cat
†MA —WILLIAMS COLLEGE, Chapin Library of Rare Books, PO Box 426, Williamstown, 01267. Robert L Volz, Custodian
Holdings: Vols 85 Cat
Notes: No material available on interlibrary loan.
NY —HOFSTRA UNIVERSITY, Library, 1000 Fulton Ave, Hempstead, 11550. Charles R Andrews, Dean of Library Services
Notes: Strong collection. Incl some mss.
NY —NEW YORK PUBLIC LIBRARY, Rare Books and Manuscripts Div, Fifth Ave & 42 St, New York, 10018. William L Joyce, Asst Dir; Francis O Mattson, Curator
Holdings: Cat
Budget: ($7161)
Notes: Complete or nearly complete file of publications, incl books, pamphlets, broadsides and other ephemera.
ON —UNIVERSITY OF WATERLOO, Library, Waterloo, N2L 3G1, Can. Susan Bellingham, Special Collections Librn
Notes: Incl 89 titles.

PRESS BOOKS—NORMAN PRESS

IL —CHICAGO PUBLIC LIBRARY, Special Collections Div, Cultural Center, 78 E Washington St, Chicago, 60602. Laura Linard, Cur
Holdings: Vols (800) Cat
Budget: ($3000)
Notes: The Special Collections Division endeavors to collect all Chicago imprints produced before 1900, and all Chicago private press productions 1900-50. An exceptional collection of books and keepsakes designed by Norman Forgue. We actively purchase in this area. Outstanding items in the Chicago Imprints Inventory are described in the recent catalog, *Treasures of The Chicago Public Library*, compiled by Thomas A Orlando and Marie Gecik, 1977, pp 93-120.

PRESS BOOKS—NORMANDIE HOUSE

IL —CHICAGO PUBLIC LIBRARY, Special Collections Div, Cultural Center, 78 E Washington St, Chicago, 60602. Laura Linard, Cur
Holdings: Vols (800) Cat
Budget: ($3000)
Notes: The Special Collections Division endeavors to collect all Chicago imprints produced before 1900, and all Chicago private press productions 1900-50. An exceptional collection of books and keepsakes designed by Norman Forgue. We actively purchase in this area. Outstanding

items in the Chicago Imprints Inventory are described in the recent catalog, *Treasures of The Chicago Public Library*, compiled by Thomas A Orlando and Marie Gecik, 1977, pp 93-120.

PRESS BOOKS—NORTHLAND PRESS

UT —UNIVERSITY OF UTAH, Marriott Library, Special Collections, Salt Lake City, 84112. Gregory C Thompson, Cur
Notes: The publications of Utah presses are also acquired. These presses are Olympus, Peregrine, Smith, Real Peoples, Horizon, Canticle, and Westwater. For the Rare Books collection materials from certain outside presses are also included. These presses are Northland, Allen, Grabhorn, Black Sparrow, Lime Kiln and Black Mountain. Books on Freemasonry are also collected.

PRESS BOOKS—OLYMPUS PRESS

UT —UNIVERSITY OF UTAH, Marriott Library, Special Collections, Salt Lake City, 84112. Gregory C Thompson, Cur
Notes: The publications of Utah presses are also acquired. These presses are Olympus, Peregrine, Smith, Real Peoples, Horizon, Canticle, and Westwater. For the Rare Books collection materials from certain outside presses are also included. These presses are Northland, Allen, Grabhorn, Black Sparrow, Lime Kiln and Black Mountain. Books on Freemasonry are also collected.

PRESS BOOKS—ORIOLE PRESS

NJ —BERKELEY HEIGHTS PUBLIC LIBRARY, 290 Plainfield Ave, Berkeley Heights, 07922. Caren Brown, Dir
Holdings: Vols 250 //
Notes: Joseph Ishill had his press in Berkeley Heights for many years. The collection incl examples of most of his work from 1931 to 1966. Also a tape of an interview with him.

PRESS BOOKS—OVERBROOK PRESS

CA —UNIVERSITY OF SAN FRANCISCO, Richard A Gleeson Library, The Countess Bernardine Murphy Donohue Rare Book Room, San Francisco, 94117. D Steven Corey, Special Collections Librn
Holdings: Vols 150
Notes: All the major books, ephemera.
†MA —WILLIAMS COLLEGE, Chapin Library of Rare Books, PO Box 426, Williamstown, 01267. Robert L Volz, Custodian
Holdings: Vols 184 Cat
Budget: ($3500)
Notes: Nearly complete collection of books, pamphlets, broadsides, and ephemera.
NY —HOFSTRA UNIVERSITY, Library, 1000 Fulton Ave, Hempstead, 11550. Charles R Andrews, Dean of Library Services
Notes: Strong collection. Incl some mss.

PRESS BOOKS—OYEZ PRESS

CT —UNIVERSITY OF CONNECTICUT, Library, Storrs, 06268. R H Schimmelpfeng, Dir of Special Collections
Holdings: Uncat Mss Pix
Notes: The archives, consisting of the business papes, mss, printing proofs, and printed books and pamphlets of the Berkley, California, press. Although not cataloged, a checklist to the collection is available.

PRESS BOOKS—PEAR TREE PRESS

CA —UNIVERSITY OF CALIFORNIA, SANTA BARBARA, Library, Dept of Special Collections, Santa Barbara, 93106. Christian F Brun, Head
Holdings: Vols 110 Cat Mss Pix
Notes: An outstanding colection, incl ephemera.

PRESS BOOKS—PENNYROYAL PRESS

IL —ILLINOIS STATE UNIVERSITY, Milner Library, Dept of Special Collections,

PRESS BOOKS—PENNYROYAL PRESS (cont.)

Normal, 61761. Robert Sokan, Librn
Holdings: Vols (2800) Cat

PRESS BOOKS—PENUMBRA PRESS

NC —UNIVERSITY OF NORTH
CAROLINA, GREENSBORO, Walter
Clinton Jackson Library, Special Collections
Dept, 1000 Spring Garden St, Greensboro,
27412. Emilie W Mills, Librn
Holdings: Vols (800) Cat
Notes: Emphasis is on English and
American presses from the 1890s to the
present. Selections from the major presses
are included as are the lesser known presses.
Periodicals incl *The Dolphin, The Fleuron,
The Colophon* and *The Imprint*. Extensive
holdings of American presses currently
operating incl. Penumbra Press, The
Perishable Press Limited, and Unicorn Press.

PRESS BOOKS—PEREGRINE PRESS

CA —UNIVERSITY OF CALIFORNIA, LOS
ANGELES, William Andrews Clark
Memorial Library, 2520 Cimarron St, Los
Angeles, 90018.
Holdings: Cat Mss Pix
Notes: Incl an extensive collection Henry
Evans' botanical prints.
CA —UNIVERSITY OF SAN FRANCISCO,
Richard A Gleeson Library, The Countess
Bernardine Murphy Donohue Rare Book
Room, San Francisco, 94117. D Steven
Corey, Special Collections Librn
Holdings: Vols 75
Notes: San Francisco press operated by
Henry Evans, extensive ephemera.
UT —UNIVERSITY OF UTAH, Marriott
Library, Special Collections, Salt Lake City,
84112. Gregory C Thompson, Cur
Notes: The publications of Utah presses are
also acquired. These presses are Olympus,
Peregrine, Smith, Real Peoples, Horizon,
Canticle, and Westwater. For the Rare
Books collection materials from certain
outside presses are also included. These
presses are Northland, Allen, Grabhorn,
Black Sparrow, Lime Kiln and Black
Mountain. Books on Freemasonry are also
collected.

PRESS BOOKS—PERISHABLE PRESS

GA —UNIVERSITY OF GEORGIA,
Libraries, Special Collections Division,
Athens, 30602. Vesta Lee Gordon, Asst Dir
for Special Collections
Holdings: Vols (8000)
Notes: One of the larger collections of
private press books, pamphlets, and
ephemera. The Elmore H Mundell
Collection of materials from over 1200
different private printers.
IL —ILLINOIS STATE UNIVERSITY, Milner
Library, Dept of Special Collections,
Normal, 61761. Robert Sokan, Librn
Holdings: Vols (2800)
NY —STATE UNIVERSITY OF NEW
YORK, STONY BROOK, Melville Library,
Dept of Special Collections, Stony Brook,
11794. Evert Volkersz, Head
Holdings: Vols 100 Cat Mss
Notes: The Perishable Press Ltd is the
private press of Walter and Mary Hamady.
This collection is the most complete
institutional collection of printed works; also
incl a substantial amount of the archives of
the Press since its beginning in 1965.
NC —UNIVERSITY OF NORTH
CAROLINA, GREENSBORO, Walter
Clinton Jackson Library, Special Collections
Dept, 1000 Spring Garden St, Greensboro,
27412. Emilie W Mills, Librn
Holdings: Vols (800) Cat
Notes: Emphasis is on English and
American presses from the 1890s to the
present. Selections from the major presses
are included as are the lesser known presses.
Periodicals incl *The Dolphin, The Fleuron,
The Colophon* and *The Imprint*. Extensive
holdings of American presses currently
operating incl Penumbra Press, The
Perishable Press Limited, and Unicorn Press.
WI —UNIVERSITY OF WISCONSIN,
MADISON, Memorial Library, Rare Books
Collection, 728 State St, Madison, 53706.
Gretchen Lagana, Cur
Holdings: Vols 6000 Cat
Notes: Private Press Collection. Strong
collection of the major fine presses, modern
fine printing, as well as books from
Wisconsin private presses. Also includes a
large collection of small press books up to
1980. Especially strong in Golden Cockerel
and Perishable Press imprints. Housed in the
Dept of Rare Books and Special Collections.

PRESS BOOKS—PETER PAUPER PRESS

CA —UNIVERSITY OF CALIFORNIA, LOS
ANGELES, Research Library, Dept of
Special Collections, 405 Hilgard Ave, Los
Angeles, 90024. Edward Shreeves,
Chairman, Bibliographers Group; David S
Zeidberg, Head
Holdings: Vols 100

PRESS BOOKS—PICKERING, WILLIAM

CA —UNIVERSITY OF CALIFORNIA, LOS
ANGELES, Research Library, Dept of
Special Collections, 405 Hilgard Ave, Los
Angeles, 90024. Edward Shreeves,
Chairman, Bibliographers Group; David S
Zeidberg, Head
Holdings: Vols 300

PRESS BOOKS—PLANTIN PRESS (MODERN)

CA —UNIVERSITY OF CALIFORNIA, SAN
DIEGO, Central University Library,
Mandeville Dept of Special Collections, La
Jolla, 92093. Lynda Corey Claassen, Head
Holdings: Uncat Mss Pix
Notes: 2000 scrapbooks, portfolios,
ephemera representing every type of press
work.
CA —UNIVERSITY OF CALIFORNIA, LOS
ANGELES, Research Library, Dept of
Special Collections, 405 Hilgard Ave, Los
Angeles, 90024. Edward Shreeves,
Chairman, Bibliographers Group; David S
Zeidberg, Head
Holdings: Cat Mss Pix
Notes: Incl correspondence, proofs, and
original drawings.
CA —UNIVERSITY OF CALIFORNIA, LOS
ANGELES, Biomedical Library, Center for
Health Sciences, Los Angeles, 90024. Louise
Darling, Biomedical Librn
Notes: Incl a unique set of 42 anatomical
facsimile plants from Juan de Valverde's
Vivae Imagines...printed by the Plantin Press
in 1969. Described in *UCLA Librarian*, vol
25, no 3, March 1972.

PRESS BOOKS—PORPOISE BOOKSHOP PRESS

†CA —UNIVERSITY OF SAN FRANCISCO,
Richard A Gleeson Library, The Countess
Bernardine Murphy Donohue Rare Book
Room, San Francisco, 94117. D Steven
Corey, Special Collections Librn
Holdings: Vols 75 Uncat
Notes: With ephemera.

PRESS BOOKS—PRAIRIE PRESS

IA —UNIVERSITY OF IOWA, University
Libraries, Iowa City, 52242. Frank Paluka,
Head, Special Collections Dept
Holdings: Vols 175 Cat
Notes: L O Cheever, "The Prairie Press: a
Thirty-Year Record," in *Books at Iowa*, Nov
1965; Emerson G Wulling, "Carroll Coleman
on Printing, with a Prairie Press Checklist,
1965-1975," in *Books at Iowa*, Nov 1975.

PRESS BOOKS—THE PRINTERY

MO —SAINT LOUIS PUBLIC LIBRARY,
Gardner Rare Book Room, 1301 Olive St,
Saint Louis, 63103. Julanne M Good,
Supervisor; Martha Riley, Rare Books Librn
Holdings: Vols (2300) Cat
Budget: ($5573)

PRESS BOOKS—PRIORY PRESS

CT —YALE UNIVERSITY, Box 1603A, Yale
Station, New Haven, 06520.

PRESS BOOKS—PYM RANDALL PRESS

RI —UNIVERSITY OF RHODE ISLAND,
Library, Special Collections, Kingston,
02881. David Maslyn, Head
Notes: Press established to print first books
of new poets; business records,
correspondence, galleys, first editions (10
linear ft, 1964-).

PRESS BOOKS—PYNSON PRINTERS

NJ —PRINCETON UNIVERSITY, Library,
Manuscript Collection, Nassau St, Princeton,
08540. Jean F Preston, Cur
Holdings: Vols Mss
Notes: The mss, consisting largely of the
working papers of Pynson Printers, are
housed in over 150 archival cartons.

PRESS BOOKS—RAMPART LIONS PRESS

IL —ILLINOIS STATE UNIVERSITY, Milner
Library, Dept of Special Collections,
Normal, 61761. Robert Sokan, Librn
Holdings: Vols (2800) Cat
BC —UNIVERSITY OF VICTORIA,
McPherson Library, Victoria, V8W 3H5,
Can.
Notes: Correspondence. Alexander
Hutchinson with George Woodcock re
reviews of Robin Skelton's poetry and with
Will and Sebastian Carter (The Rampant
Lions Press) re printing a collection of
broadsides.

PRESS BOOKS—REAL PEOPLES PRESS

UT —UNIVERSITY OF UTAH, Marriott
Library, Special Collections, Salt Lake City,
84112. Gregory C Thompson, Cur
Notes: The publications of Utah presses are
also acquired. These presses are Olympus,
Peregrine, Smith, Real Peoples, Horizon,
Canticle, and Westwater. For the Rare
Books collection materials from certain
outside presses are also included. These
presses are Northland, Allen, Grabhorn,
Black Sparrow, Lime Kiln and Black
Mountain. Books on Freemasonry are also
collected.

PRESS BOOKS—RITCHIE, WARD, PRESS

CA —CLAREMONT COLLEGES, Ella Strong
Denison Library, Scripps College,
Claremont, 91711. Judy Harvey Sahak,
Librn
Holdings: Vols (1100) Cat
CA —OCCIDENTAL COLLEGE, Library,
1600 Campus Rd, Los Angeles, 90041.
Michael C Sutherland, Special Collections
Librn
Holdings: Vols 750 Cat
Notes: A nearly complete and growing
collection of books published over 40 years
by the Ward Ritchie Press and printed by
Anderson, Ritchie, and Simon.
CA —UNIVERSITY OF CALIFORNIA, LOS
ANGELES, Research Library, Dept of
Special Collections, 405 Hilgard Ave, Los
Angeles, 90024. Edward Shreeves,
Chairman, Bibliographers Group; David S
Zeidberg, Head
Holdings: Cat Mss Pix
Notes: Extensive collection, incl ephemera,
correspondence and original job dockets.

PRESS BOOKS—ROGERS, BRUCE see Rogers, Bruce

PRESS BOOKS—RONART PRESS

MO —SAINT LOUIS PUBLIC LIBRARY,
Gardner Rare Book Room, 1301 Olive St,

PRESS BOOKS—RONART PRESS (cont.)

Saint Louis, 63103. Julanne M Good,
Supervisor; Martha Riley, Rare Books Librn
Holdings: Vols (2300) Cat
Budget: ($5573)

PRESS BOOKS—ROXBURGHE PRESS

IL —NORTHWESTERN UNIVERSITY,
Library, Special Collections Dept, 1937
Sheridan Rd, Evanston, 60201. R Russell
Maylone, Cur
Holdings: Vols (5000) Cat
Notes: Representative examples of the work
of the modern private press from Strawberry
Hill to the current small printers. Incl such
presses as Cuala, Essex House, Golden
Cockerel, Grabhorn, Nonesuch, Roxburghe,
etc. Also 15,000 "little magazine" titles
exclusive of runs in the general library
collections.
PA —PENNSYLVANIA STATE
UNIVERSITY, Fred Lewis Pattee Library,
Special Collections Dept, University Park,
16802. Charles Mann, Chief, Special
Collections
Holdings: Vols (989) Uncat
Budget: ($37,000)
Notes: No photocopying.

PRESS BOOKS—ROYCROFT PRESS

AZ —NORTHERN ARIZONA
UNIVERSITY, Special Collection Library,
CU Box 6022, Flagstaff, 86011. Peter M
Whiteley, Coordr/Archivist; William
Mullane, Librn
Holdings: Vols 650 // Cat
Notes: Lloyd C Henning Collection:
extensive collection of Roycroft Press Books,
incl several unique and several very rare
items.
CA —UNIVERSITY OF CALIFORNIA, SAN
DIEGO, Central University Library,
Mandeville Dept of Special Collections, La
Jolla, 92093. Lynda Corey Claassen, Head
Holdings: Vols 425 // Uncat
CA —UNIVERSITY OF CALIFORNIA, LOS
ANGELES, Research Library, Dept of
Special Collections, 405 Hilgard Ave, Los
Angeles, 90024. Edward Shreeves,
Chairman, Bibliographers Group; David S
Zeidberg, Head
Notes: 4 linear feet of publications and
ephemera.
CA —SAN DIEGO STATE UNIVERSITY,
Malcolm A Love Library, 5300 Campanile
Dr, San Diego, 92182. D Dickinson, Univ
Librn; Don L Bosseau, Dir
Notes: Collected publications of certain fine
presses and illustrators as: Golden Cockerel,
Black Sparrow, Roycroft, Mosher, Bruce
Rogers, Janus Press.
IL —ILLINOIS STATE UNIVERSITY, Milner
Library, Dept of Special Collections,
Normal, 61761. Robert Sokan, Librn
Holdings: Vols (2800) Cat
MO —SAINT LOUIS PUBLIC LIBRARY,
Gardner Rare Book Room, 1301 Olive St,
Saint Louis, 63103. Julanne M Good,
Supervisor; Martha Riley, Rare Books Librn
Holdings: Vols (2300) Cat
Budget: ($5573)
NY —BUFFALO & ERIE COUNTY PUBLIC
LIBRARY, Rare Book Room, Lafayette Sq,
Buffalo, 14203. William H Loos, Cur
Holdings: Vols 450 Cat Mss Pix
NY —AURORA HISTORICAL SOCIETY,
Library-Museum, 571 Main St, Village Hall,
East Aurora, 14052. Genevieve Steffen, Cur
Holdings: Vols 1500 Cat Mss Pix Audiotapes
Notes: A one-room Library-Museum
dedicated to the preservation of Hubbard/
Roycroft memorabilia. In addition to
beautifully printed and bound books, we
have collections of metalcraft and
leathercraft items and furniture made in the
Roycroft shops 1895-1938. The collection
belongs to the Village of East Aurora. Check
for opening hours.
NY —UNIVERSITY OF ROCHESTER, Rush
Rhees Library, Department of Rare Books
and Special Collections, Rochester, 14627.
Peter Dzwonkoski, Librn
Holdings: Vols 1100 Uncat Mss Pix
Notes: First editions, limited editions;

complete runs of The Philistine, Fra, and
Little Journey series; correspondence,
ephemera, etc.
OH —OHIO UNIVERSITY, Vernon R Alden
Library, Department of Archives and Special
Collections, Athens, 45701. Gary A Hunt,
Head
Holdings: Vols 13 Cat
Notes: Dard Hunter's books on paper, incl
some presentation copies. Also a number of
the Roycrofters books designed by Hunter.
†ON —UNIVERSITY OF WESTERN
ONTARIO, School of Library and
Information Science, Special Collections
Room, London, N6A 5B9, Can.
Holdings: Vols 246
Notes: Representative colection incl some
early items from the Roycrofters private
press.

PRESS BOOKS—RUDGE PRINTINGS

CA —UNIVERSITY OF CALIFORNIA,
SANTA BARBARA, Library, Dept of
Special Collections, Santa Barbara, 93106.
Christian F Brun, Head
Holdings: Vols 774 Cat Mss Pix
Notes: Skofield Printers Collection.
Attempting to collect all of the imprints,
printing and ephemera of William Edwin
Rudge. Incl the working library of the
printing house of William Edwin Rudge.

PRESS BOOKS—RUSSELL, R. H.

NC —UNIVERSITY OF NORTH
CAROLINA, GREENSBORO, Walter
Clinton Jackson Library, Special Collections
Dept, 1000 Spring Garden St, Greensboro,
27412. Emilie W Mills, Librn
Notes: Emphasis is on American small
publishers since late 19th century attention
to fine printing, sound production and
textual content are exemplary. Significant
holdings of books published by The
Typophiles, Stinehour Press, David R
Godine, Jargon Society and Way and
Williams are included with selective holdings
of other small commercial publishers and
printers, incl R H Russell, Copeland and
Day, Stone and Kimball.

PRESS BOOKS—ST. DOMINIC'S PRESS

CA —UNIVERSITY OF SAN FRANCISCO,
Richard A Gleeson Library, The Countess
Bernardine Murphy Donohue Rare Book
Room, San Francisco, 94117. D Steven
Corey, Special Collections Librn
Holdings: Mss Pix
Notes: Very large collection containing
much correspondence of Eric Gill, a number
of original wood engravings, and over half of
his total output of wood engravings
represented by about 400 prints. Nearly all
of the published works are present, incl
many unique items.
DC —GEORGETOWN UNIVERSITY,
Library, Special Collections Div, 37 & O Sts
NW, Washington, 20057. George M
Barringer, Special Collections Librn;
Nicholas B Sheetz, Mss Librn
Holdings: Cat
IL —ILLINOIS STATE UNIVERSITY, Milner
Library, Dept of Special Collections,
Normal, 61761. Robert Sokan, Librn
Holdings: Vols (2800) Cat
ON —UNIVERSITY OF WATERLOO,
Library, Waterloo, N2L 3G1, Can. Susan
Bellingham, Special Collections Librn
Notes: Incl 140 titles.

PRESS BOOKS—SCHOLARTIS PRESS

CA —UNIVERSITY OF SAN FRANCISCO,
Richard A Gleeson Library, The Countess
Bernardine Murphy Donohue Rare Book
Room, San Francisco, 94117. D Steven
Corey, Special Collections Librn
Holdings: Vols 122 Mss
Notes: Good collection of books published
plus mss for five books by Eric Partridge and
a large group of ALS's.

PRESS BOOKS—SCRIPPS COLLEGE PRESS

CA —CLAREMONT COLLEGES, Ella Strong
Denison Library, Scripps College,

Claremont, 91711. Judy Harvey Sahak,
Librn
Holdings: Cat Mss Pix
Notes: In addition to books and ephemera,
collection includes original drawings, paper
and metal pattens, matrices, and fonts for
types that Frederic S Goudy designed for
the Scripps College Press.

PRESS BOOKS—SEIZIN PRESS

IL —NORTHWESTERN UNIVERSITY,
Library, Special Collections Dept, 1937
Sheridan Rd, Evanston, 60201. R Russell
Maylone, Cur
Holdings: Vols 130 Cat Mss
Notes: Robert Graves' letters, first editions,
Seizin Press Books.

PRESS BOOKS—SINGING BONE

MO —SAINT LOUIS PUBLIC LIBRARY,
Gardner Rare Book Room, 1301 Olive St,
Saint Louis, 63103. Julanne M Good,
Supervisor; Martha Riley, Rare Books Librn
Holdings: Vols (2300) Cat
Budget: ($5573)

PRESS BOOKS—SINGING WIND

MO —SAINT LOUIS PUBLIC LIBRARY,
Gardner Rare Book Room, 1301 Olive St,
Saint Louis, 63103. Julanne M Good,
Supervisor; Martha Riley, Rare Books Librn
Holdings: Vols (2300) Cat
Budget: ($5573)

PRESS BOOKS—SMITH PRESS

UT —UNIVERSITY OF UTAH, Marriott
Library, Special Collections, Salt Lake City,
84112. Gregory C Thompson, Cur
Notes: The publications of Utah presses are
also acquired. These presses are Olympus,
Peregrine, Smith, Real Peoples, Horizon,
Canticle, and Westwater. For the Rare
Books collection materials from certain
outside presses are also included. These
presses are Northland, Allen, Grabhorn,
Black Sparrow, Lime Kiln and Black
Mountain. Books on Freemasonry are also
collected.

PRESS BOOKS—SOMETHING ELSE PRESS

TX —TRINITY UNIVERSITY, Elizabeth
Coates Maddux Library, 715 Stadium Dr,
San Antonio, 78284. Richard Hume
Werking, Library Dir; Craig Likness, Head
Bibliographer
Holdings: Vols 125
Notes: Avant garde poetry and other writing
from Dick Higgins' Something Else Press
and the Fluxus group. Incl some ephemera.

PRESS BOOKS—SOUTHAM PRESS

ON —UNIVERSITY OF TORONTO, Thomas
Fisher Rare Book Library, 120 Saint George
St, Toronto, M5S 1A5, Can. Richard G
Landon, Head
Holdings: Vols 6535 Uncat
Notes: Maclean-Hunter and Southam Press
Collections contain periodicals issued by
these two Canadian publishers. Many largely
trade journals. Many long and
complete runs of items like Canadian
Footwear, Electrical News and Engineering;
Gift Buyer; Canadian Home Journal;
Chatelaine; Macleans; etc. Many runs
originate in 1880s and 1890s. Also include
current publications. Approx 268 titles.
Fisher Library designated the official
archives for published material by Maclean-
Hunter and Southam Press.

PRESS BOOKS—SOUTHWORTH-ANTHOENSEN

ME —UNIVERSITY OF MAINE AT
PORTLAND-GORHAM, Portland Campus
Library, 96 Falmouth St, Portland, 04103.
Albert A Howard, Special Collections Librn
Holdings: Vols 900 Cat
Notes: Collections incl broadsides,

PRESS BOOKS—SOUTHWORTH-ANTHOENSEN (cont.)

prospectuses and other printed ephemera (not cataloged). Also some imprints of Southworth-Anthoensen. Collection is comprehensive. Collection is in main catalog and there is a separate shelf list.

PRESS BOOKS—STAMPERIA DEL SANTUCCIO

†CA —UNIVERSITY OF SAN FRANCISCO, Richard A Gleeson Library, The Countess Bernardine Murphy Donohue Rare Book Room, San Francisco, 94117. D Steven Corey, Special Collections Librn
Holdings: Vols (75) Uncat Mss
Notes: A complete collection of Victor Hammer with unique items. Incl the Stamperia del Santuccio, Wells College Press, Hammer Press, and Anvil Press. Also present are a number of Hammer's original drawings and sketches, as well as a painted triptych.

PRESS BOOKS—STAMPERIA VALDONEGA

CT —YALE UNIVERSITY, Box 1603A, Yale Station, New Haven, 06520.

PRESS BOOKS—STANBROOK ABBEY PRESS

MD —UNIVERSITY OF MARYLAND, Library, Stanbrook Abbey Collection, College Park, 20742. Donald Farren, Assoc Dir
Holdings: Vols 200
Notes: The library has acquired samples of nearly all material published since 1876 by the Stanbrook Abbey Press, Worcester, England. The press was originally created to provide religious texts but has expanded its work to incl poetry, essays and other secular work.

MA —BOSTON COLLEGE LIBRARIES, Chestnut Hill, 02167.
Notes: An extensive collection of materials printed by the Stanbrook Abbey Press. Some 175 examples of fine printing, incl greeting cards, hardbound books, booklets, folders, broadsides, and correspondence.

ON —UNIVERSITY OF TORONTO, Thomas Fisher Rare Book Library, 120 Saint George St, Toronto, M5S 1A5, Can. Richard G Landon, Head
Holdings: Vols 125 Cat
Notes: Stanbrook Abbey Press Collection of books, pamphlets, broadsides printed by the cloistered order of Benedictine nuns at Stanbrook Abbey, Worcester, England. Dates from 1950s to present. Ephemera include Christmas cards, advertising brochures, etc. Texts are both literary and religious.

PRESS BOOKS—STONE AND KIMBALL

DC —LIBRARY OF CONGRESS, Rare Book & Special Collections Div, Washington, 20540. William Matheson, Chief
Notes: The collection was drawn from the Library's general collections and incl many copyright deposit copies.

IL —NEWBERRY LIBRARY, John M Wing Foundation on the History of Printing, 60 W Walton St, Chicago, 60610. Diana Haskell, Cur of Modern Mss
Holdings: Vols 1000 Cat Mss Pix
Notes: Incl collection formed by Herbert S Stone, Jr, which was the basis for Sidney Kramer's published history and bibliography of the firm. Has mss by authors published; the Firm's publications, incl posters and magazines, esp the *Chap Book* original art for illustrations and posters, and other art by those who were part of the group; memorabilia and correspondence. Also materials on successors firms.

NC —UNIVERSITY OF NORTH CAROLINA, GREENSBORO, Walter Clinton Jackson Library, Special Collections Dept, 1000 Spring Garden St, Greensboro, 27412. Emilie W Mills, Librn
Notes: Emphasis is on American small publishers since late 19th century attention to fine printing, sound production and textual content are exemplary. Significant holdings of books published by The Typophiles, Stinehour Press, David R Godine, Jargon Society and Way and Williams are included with selective holdings of other small commercial publishers and printers, incl R H Russell, Copeland and Day, Stone and Kimball.

PRESS BOOKS—STONE WALL PRESS

IA —UNIVERSITY OF IOWA, University Libraries, Iowa City, 52242. Frank Paluka, Head, Special Collections Dept
Holdings: Vols 32 Cat
Notes: James Lamar Weygand, "The Stone Wall Press," in the *American Book Collector*, Oct 1964; Kay Amert and others, "Works Printed by K K Merker: The Stone Wall Press, the Windhover Press, and Others," in *Books at Iowa*, Nov 1976.

PRESS BOOKS—STRAWBERRY HILL PRESS

IL —NORTHWESTERN UNIVERSITY, Library, Special Collections Dept, 1937 Sheridan Rd, Evanston, 60201. R Russell Maylone, Cur
Holdings: Vols (5000) Cat
Notes: Representative examples of the work of the modern private press from Strawberry Hill to the current small printers. Incl such presses as Cuala, Essex House, Golden Cockerel, Grabhorn, Nonesuch, Roxburghe, etc. Also 15,000 "little magazine" titles exclusive of runs in the general library collections.

PRESS BOOKS—THREE MOUNTAINS PRESS

IN —INDIANA UNIVERSITY, Lilly Library, Seventh St, Bloomington, 47405. William R Cagle, Librn
Holdings: Cat Mss
Notes: Extensive holdings. Mss incl correspondence of William Bird and Ezra Pound on Three Mountains Press publications. 135 items.

PRESS BOOKS—TORCH PRESS

IA —LORAS COLLEGE, Wahlert Memorial Library, 14 & Alta Vista, Dubuque, 52001. Robert F Klein, Librn
Holdings: Vols 530 Cat
Notes: Maddigan, Mike, "The Torch Press: Addenda to a Checklist," in *Books at Iowa*, November, 1979.

IA —UNIVERSITY OF IOWA, University Libraries, Iowa City, 52242. Frank Paluka, Head, Special Collections Dept
Holdings: Vols 300 Cat
Notes: Thomas L Carney and Joyce Crawford, "The Torch Press: A Preliminary History," in *Books at Iowa*, Nov 1974. Also Mike Maddigan, "The Torch Press: Addenda to a Checklist", *Books at Iowa*, November 1979.

PRESS BOOKS—TWOWINDOWS PRESS

CA —UNIVERSITY OF SAN FRANCISCO, Richard A Gleeson Library, The Countess Bernardine Murphy Donohue Rare Book Room, San Francisco, 94117. D Steven Corey, Special Collections Librn
Holdings: Vols 45
Notes: Complete collection, ephemera, of this Berkeley press operated by Don Gray.

PRESS BOOKS—TRIANON PRESS

CA —UNIVERSITY OF CALIFORNIA, RIVERSIDE, University Library, 4045 Canyon Crest Dr, Box 5900, Riverside, 92517.
Holdings: Vols 900
Notes: Works by and about Blake, incl some contemporary printed editions and all the Trianon Press facsimiles of his illuminated books.

CA —UNIVERSITY OF CALIFORNIA, SANTA CRUZ, University Library, Special Collections, Santa Cruz, 95064. Rita Bottoms, Special Collections Librn; Margaret Felts, South Pacific Collection Bibliographer
Notes: The archives of Trianon Press. All major publications of the Press. Under the direction of Arnold Fawcus from the late 1940s through the 1970s, Trianon Press was noted for its replica editions of the works of early authors with special emphasis on the works of William Blake Marcel Duchamp.

FL —UNIVERSITY OF MIAMI, Otto G Richter Library, PO Box 248214, Coral Gables, 33124. Frank Rodgers, Dir of Libraries
Notes: Incl all of the Trianon Press facsimiles on William Blake works.

PRESS BOOKS—TROVILLION PRIVATE PRESS

IL —SOUTHERN ILLINOIS UNIVERSITY, CARBONDALE, Delyte W Morris Library, Special Collections Dept, Carbondale, 62901. David V Koch, Cur of Special Collections; Louisa Bowen, Cur of Manuscripts
Holdings: Vols 200 Cat Mss Pix
Notes: Incl the archives of the press and Hal W Trovillion's personal papers, inventory in library.

PRESS BOOKS—TURKEY PRESS

RI —BROWN UNIVERSITY, John Hay Library, 20 Prospect St, Providence, 02912. Mark N Brown, Cur Mss
Holdings: Vols (1000) Cat
Notes: Many examples of 19th and 20th century private and small presses of American and English imprint. Some of the presses represented are: Anthoensen, Bayberry Hill, Black Sun, Catnatch, Cuala, Doves, Essex House, Golden Cockerel, Grabhorn, Kelmscott, Merrymount, Mosher, Nonesuch, Perishable, Stinehour, Trianon, Unicorn, Vagabond, plus many Rhode Island small presses such as Burning Deck, Turkey, and Hall Coal.

PRESS BOOKS—THE TYPOPHILES

†NY —COLUMBIA UNIVERSITY LIBRARIES, Butler Library, Rare Book and Manuscript Library, 535 W 114 St, New York, 10027.

NY —STATE UNIVERSITY OF NEW YORK, STONY BROOK, Melville Library, Dept of Special Collections, Stony Brook, 11794. Evert Volkersz, Head
Holdings: Vols 110 Cat
Notes: Typophile chapbooks and monographs, as well as other volumes printed by and for members of The Typophiles, New York.

PRESS BOOKS—UNICORN PRESS

FL —UNIVERSITY OF MIAMI, Otto G Richter Library, PO Box 248214, Coral Gables, 33124. Frank Rodgers, Dir of Libraries
Notes: 3500 items. Nineteenth century well represented by Longfellow and Thoreau collections organized by Thomas DeValcourt at Longfellow House. Additional Thoreau items were purchased later. Innovative and experimental writing of 1960s and 1970s, incl press books from Black Sparrow, Unicorn, Kayak and other small presses, as well as privately published works and many small magazines. Format ranges from postcard and poster to fine limited editions of codex form.

NC —UNIVERSITY OF NORTH CAROLINA, GREENSBORO, Walter Clinton Jackson Library, Special Collections Dept, 1000 Spring Garden St, Greensboro, 27412. Emilie W Mills, Librn
Holdings: Vols (800) Cat
Notes: Emphasis is on English and American presses from the 1890s to the

PRESS BOOKS—UNICORN PRESS (cont.)

present. Selections from the major presses are included as are the lesser known presses. Periodicals incl *The Dolphin, The Fleuron, The Colophon* and *The Imprint.* Extensive holdings of American presses currently operating incl Penumbra Press, The Perishable Press Limited, Jargon Society, and Unicorn Press.

SC —WOFFORD COLLEGE, Sandor Teszler Library, N Church St, Spartanburg, 29301. Frank J Anderson, Librn
Holdings: Vols 1000 Cat
Notes: Books about the history and practice of printing, hand papermaking, bookbinding, book collecting, fine press and private press books used in conjunction with instruction at the Wofford Library Press, an experimental and bibliographic press which has been in operation since 1969. Collection contains materials on printmaking methods and related graphic arts. Collection incl imprints of: Briarpatch Press, Anthoensen Press, Mosher Press, Kitmang Press, Windhover Press, Penman Press, Unicorn Press, Wofford Library Press and others.

PRESS BOOKS—UNTIDE PRESS

CA —UNIVERSITY OF CALIFORNIA, BERKELEY, Bancroft Library, Manuscripts Division, Berkeley, 94720. James D Hart, Dir
Holdings: Vols 2000 Cat Mss
Notes: The Contemporary Poetry Collection covers the San Francisco publishing scene, from the period of the Beat Movement through the present day. In addition to printed materials, The Bancroft Library contains the important printer/publisher/bookseller archives of the Untide Press, City Lights, and the Auerhahn Press.

PRESS BOOKS—VAGABOND PRESS

RI —BROWN UNIVERSITY, John Hay Library, 20 Prospect St, Providence, 02912. Mark N Brown, Cur Mss
Holdings: Vols 83 Mss
Notes: Records of the Vagabond Press, containing approximately 3000 items. Vagabond magazine, chapbooks, etc, were published and edited, 1965-80, by John Bennett (1938-).

PRESS BOOKS—VALE PRESS

CA —UNIVERSITY OF CALIFORNIA, LOS ANGELES, William Andrews Clark Memorial Library, 2520 Cimarron St, Los Angeles, 90018.
Holdings: Cat Mss Pix
Notes: Incl original designs and artwork by Charles Ricketts.

IL —ILLINOIS STATE UNIVERSITY, Milner Library, Dept of Special Collections, Normal, 61761. Robert Sokan, Librn
Holdings: Vols (2800) Cat

NY —NEW YORK PUBLIC LIBRARY, Rare Books and Manuscripts Div, Fifth Ave & 42 St, New York, 10018. William L Joyce, Asst Dir; Francis O Mattson, Curator
Holdings: Cat
Budget: ($7161)
Notes: Complete or nearly complete file of publications, incl books, pamphlets, broadsides and other ephemera.

PRESS BOOKS—WATTLE GROVE PRESS

PA —PENNSYLVANIA STATE UNIVERSITY, Fred Lewis Pattee Library, Special Collections Dept, University Park, 16802. Charles Mann, Chief, Special Collections
Holdings: Vols (989) Uncat
Budget: ($37,000)
Notes: No photocopying.

PRESS BOOKS—WEED AND FLOWER PRESS

†ON —McMASTER UNIVERSITY, Library, Hamilton, L8S 4L6, Can.
Notes: Nelson Ball manuscript poems,

correspondence, and files relating to Weed and Flower Press, 1964-1967.

PRESS BOOKS—WELLS COLLEGE PRESS

†CA —UNIVERSITY OF SAN FRANCISCO, Richard A Gleeson Library, The Countess Bernardine Murphy Donohue Rare Book Room, San Francisco, 94117. D Steven Corey, Special Collections Librn
Holdings: Vols (75) Uncat Mss
Notes: A complete collection of Victor Hammer with unique items. Incl the Stamperia del Santuccio, Wells College Press, Hammer Press, and Anvil Press. Also present are a number of Hammer's original drawings and sketches, as well as a painted triptych.

PRESS BOOKS—WESTWATER PRESS

UT —UNIVERSITY OF UTAH, Marriott Library, Special Collections, Salt Lake City, 84112. Gregory C Thompson, Cur
Notes: The publications of Utah presses are also acquired. These presses are Olympus, Peregrine, Smith, Real Peoples, Horizon, Canticle, and Westwater. For the Rare Books collection materials from certain outside presses are also included. These presses are Northland, Allen, Grabhorn, Black Sparrow, Lime Kiln and Black Mountain. Books on Freemasonry are also collected.

PRESS BOOKS—WHIPPORWILL PRESS

KY —BOYD COUNTY PUBLIC LIBRARY, 1740 Central Ave, Ashland, 41101. Juliette Bryson, Dir
Notes: Kentucky authors.

PRESS BOOKS—WHITTINGHAM PRINTING

VT —UNIVERSITY OF VERMONT, Guy W Bailey/David W Howe Library, Burlington, 05405. John Buehler, Asst Dir for Special Collections
Notes: Imprints of Charles Whittingham, the younger.

PRESS BOOKS—WILKE, WILLIAM

CA —UNIVERSITY OF CALIFORNIA, SANTA BARBARA, Library, Dept of Special Collections, Santa Barbara, 93106. Christian F Brun, Head
Holdings: Uncat Mss Pix
Notes: Important collection of drawings, plates, imprints, etc, of this San Francisco designer who worked for John Henry Nash, etc.

PRESS BOOKS—WINDHOVER PRESS

IA —LORAS COLLEGE, Wahlert Memorial Library, 14 & Alta Vista, Dubuque, 52001. Robert F Klein, Librn
Holdings: Vols 31 Cat

IA —UNIVERSITY OF IOWA, University Libraries, Iowa City, 52242. Frank Paluka, Head, Special Collections Dept
Holdings: Vols 18 Cat

SC —WOFFORD COLLEGE, Sandor Teszler Library, N Church St, Spartanburg, 29301. Frank J Anderson, Librn
Holdings: Vols 1000 Cat
Notes: Books about the history and practice of printing, hand papermaking, bookbinding, book collecting, fine press and private press books used in conjunction with instruction at the Wofford Library Press, an experimental and bibliographic press which has been in operation since 1969. Collection contains materials on printmaking methods and related graphic arts. Collection incl imprints of: Briarpatch Press, Anthoensen Press, Mosher Press, Kitmang Press, Windhover Press, Penman Press, Unicorn Press, Wofford Library Press and others.

PRESS BOOKS—WOFFORD LIBRARY PRESS

SC —WOFFORD COLLEGE, Sandor Teszler Library, N Church St, Spartanburg, 29301.

Frank J Anderson, Librn
Holdings: Vols 1000 Cat
Notes: Books about the history and practice of printing, hand papermaking, bookbinding, book collecting, fine press and private press books used in conjunction with instruction at the Wofford Library Press, an experimental and bibliographic press which has been in operation since 1969. Collection contains materials on printmaking methods and related graphic arts. Collection incl imprints of: Briarpatch Press, Anthoensen Press, Mosher Press, Kitmang Press, Windhover Press, Penman Press, Unicorn Press, Wofford Library Press and others.

PRESS BOOKS—WOOLLY WHALE PRESS

NY —BUFFALO & ERIE COUNTY PUBLIC LIBRARY, Rare Book Room, Lafayette Sq, Buffalo, 14203. William H Loos, Cur
Holdings: Vols 23 Cat

PRESS BOOKS—YELLOW KID PRESS

ME —PORTLAND PUBLIC LIBRARY, 5 Monument Sq, Portland, 04101. Edward V Chenevert, Library Dir
Holdings: Vols 17 Cat
Notes: The Yellow Kid Press is privately operated by David W Serette. Specialty is miniature books.

PRESS BOOKS, CANADIAN

ON —NORTH YORK PUBLIC LIBRARY, Canadiana Collection, 35 Fairview Mall Dr, Willowdale, M2J 4S4, Can. Ian C Ross, Head
Holdings: Vols (70,000) Cat Microforms //
See also entry under Canada.

PRESS BOOKS—ZAMORANO CLUB

CA —CLAREMONT COLLEGES, Honnold Library, Ninth & Dartmouth, Claremont, 91711. Tania Rizzo, Special Collections Dept Head
Holdings: Vols (70,000) Cat VF
Notes: Books on typography, bibliography, and history of printing; incunabula; specimen books; fine press books, esp Kelmscott, Doves, Daniel, Mosher, Grabhorn, Nash, and Arion presses and many Southern California printers. A comprehensive collection of Zamorano Club publications and keepsakes, partial source for George E Fulleton, *The Zamorano Club: The First Half Century* (Los Angeles, 1978). Extensive files of ephemera. Fine bindings and fore-edge paintings. Samples of Oriental type and printing.

PRESS BOOKS—ZAUBERBERG PRESS

KS —KANSAS STATE UNIVERSITY, Library, Special Collections & University Archives, Manhattan, 66506. Antonia Q Pigno, Coordr; John J Vander Velde, Librn; Anthony R Crawford, Univ Archivist
Holdings: Vols 700 Mss
Notes: Collection incl books and correspondence from Don Drenner, owner and printer of the Zauberberg Press, Coffeyville, Kansas.

PRESS CENSORSHIP see Liberty of the Press

PRESSES, COLLEGE see University Presses

PRESSES, LITTLE see Little Presses

PRESSES, UNIVERSITY see University Presses

PRESTIDIGITATION see Magic and Magicians

PRESTON, CHARLES

AL —BIRMINGHAM PUBLIC LIBRARY, Dept of Archives & Mss, 2020 Seventh Ave

PRESTON, CHARLES (cont.)

N, Birmingham, 35203. Marvin Y Whiting, Archivist & Cur
Holdings: Mss Pix Slides Audiotapes Microforms
Notes: Especially Birmingham history. Largest available collections are the Robert Jemison, Jr. Papers (ca 1.2 million items) and the Donald Comer Papers (ca 390,000 items). Photographs incl ca one million negatives from the collection of Brimingham photographer Charles Preston.

PRESTON, WILLIAM THOMAS ROCHESTER, 1851-1942

VA —VIRGINIA POLYTECHNIC INSTITUTE AND STATE UNIVERSITY LIBRARY, Blacksburg, 24061. Glenn L McMullen, Special Collections Librn
Holdings: Vols (2000) Cat Mss Maps Pix Audiotapes
Notes: Primarily Southwest Virginia materials. Collection incl ca 200 mss, account books and other archival records of nineteenth century area businesses and other mining operations; the extant archival records of several Southwest Virginia railroads, incl the Virginia and Tennessee Railroad and the Norfolk and Western Railroad; and papers of historically prominent Southwest Virginians, incl John Apperson, Dr Harvy Black, James P Charlton, W Graham Claytor, Henley Fugate, Clement D Johnston, Germanicus Kent, William Preston, J Hoge Tyler, and William C Wampler. Several oral history collections incl material on Appalachian customs and folklore, particularly in Patrick County.
MB —UNIVERSITY OF MANITOBA, Elizabeth Dafoe Library, Archives and Special Collections Dept, Winnipeg, R3T 2N2, Can. Richard E Bennett, Dept Head; Corrado A Santoro, Reference Archivist
Holdings: Ms
Notes: Unsigned, undated manuscript critique (5 pages) ow W T R Preston's highly critical biography of Lord Strathcona.

PREVENTION OF ACCIDENTS see Accidents—Prevention

PREVENTION OF CRUELTY TO ANIMALS see Animals, Treatment of

PREVENTIVE INOCULATION see Inoculation—History

PREVENTIVE MEDICINE see Medicine, Preventive

PREVIN, ANDRE

CA —UNIVERSITY OF CALIFORNIA, LOS ANGELES, Music Library, Schonberg Hall, Los Angeles, 90024. Stephen M Fry, Music Librn
Notes: Mss.

PRICE, ERNEST B., 1890-1973

CA —HOOVER INSTITUTION ON WAR, REVOLUTION & PEACE, Stanford University, Stanford, 94305. Milorad M Drachkovitch, Archivist
Holdings: Mss Pix
Notes: Papers of Ernest B Price, 1914-1950, incl correspondence, diary, dispatches, manuscripts, lecture material, photographs, and printed matter relating to Japanese military intervention in China and Manchuria, 1931-1945; political and economic development in China, 1914-1929; and E B Price's career in the US Foreign Service in China, 1914-1929, in business, and in education. 13 ms boxes.

PRICE, EUGENIA

MA —BOSTON UNIVERSITY, Mugar Memorial Library, Special Collections Dept, 771 Commonwealth Ave, Boston, 02215.

Howard B Gotlieb, Dir
Holdings: Cat Mss Correspondence Pix

PRICE, PERCIVAL

ON —NATIONAL LIBRARY OF CANADA, 395 Wellington St, Ottawa, K1A 0N4, Can. Andre Preibish, Dir
Notes: Books, papers, and artifacts from Percival Price, renowned authority on campanology and first Dominion carilloneur (1927-39). Incl designs of bells and bell towers around the world, sound recordings, programs, etc. Some bells. About a third of the collection refers to Canadian carillons and carilloneurs.

PRICE, REYNOLDS

NC —DUKE UNIVERSITY, William R Perkins Library, Rare Book Room, Durham, 27706. John L Sharpe, III, Cur
Notes: A collection of Duke University authors, established around 1963, with the writings of the students of William Blackburn and greatly enhanced by the gift of Professor Blackburn's collection. Represented are James Applewhite, Fred Chappell, Guy Davenport, Reynolds Price, William Styron, Frances Gray Patton, and Anne Tyler. Printed works are in the Rare Book Room and manuscripts are in the Manuscript Department.

PRICE, VINCENT

DC —LIBRARY OF CONGRESS, Manuscript Division, Washington, 20540. John C Broderick, Chief
Holdings: Vols 7000
Notes: His papers incl items of correspondence 1961-1967: miscellaneous correspondence, personal correspondence and requests and invitations.

PRICES

CA —UNIVERSITY OF CALIFORNIA, BERKELEY, Giannini Foundation of Agricultural Economics, Library, 248 Giannini Hall, Berkeley, 94720. Grace Dote, Librn
Holdings: Vols (18,000) Cat Mss Maps Microforms
Notes: Noncirculating collection. No interlibrary loans. Also about 124,000 unbound vols. Open to graduate students and faculties of universities and colleges, research workers and interested public. Mostly English language materials, primarily 1900 to date. Card catalog published by G K Hall Co Dictionary Catalog of the Giannini Foundation of Agricultural Economics Library, Univ of California, 12 vols (Holdings thru 7/71).

PRIEST, IVY BAKER

UT —UNIVERSITY OF UTAH, Marriott Library, Special Collections, Salt Lake City, 84112. Gregory C Thompson, Cur
Holdings: Cat Mss Microfilm Film Oral History
Notes: Her papers.

PRIESTLEY, JOSEPH, 1733-1804

NY —ALFRED UNIVERSITY, Herrick Memorial Library, Alfred, 14802. June E Brown, Head Librn
Notes: The Evelyn Tennyson Openhym Collection of modern British literature and social history. Papers, incl correspondence of authors concerned with the business aspects of authorship. Gift of Evelyn Tennyson Openhym of Wellsville, NY. Also, 5300 volumes of British literature.
PA —UNIVERSITY OF PENNSYLVANIA, Van Pelt Library, Edgar Fahs Smith Memorial Collection in the History of Chemistry, 3420 Walnut St, Philadelphia, 19104. Arnold W Thackray, Cur
Holdings: Vols 250 Cat
Notes: The Smith Collection, 15,000 vols, is one of the most comprehensive collections on the history of chemistry in North

America, covering chemistry and its allied disciplines, from the Renaissance to the early 20th century. The Collection's traditional strengths lie in classical history of chemistry, ie pre-1800. However acquisitions over the past 15 years have substantially built up the post-1800 holdings, especially in areas of chemical technology. News of the Collection may be found in the Center's twice yearly newsletter CHOC News which is available free of charge to interested persons. A convenient description is provided in Herbert S Klickstein, "Edgar Fahs Smith-His Contributions to the History of Chemistry," Chymia, 5 (1959), 11-30. A published catalog of our holdings now needs considerable revision, due to continued acquisitions:Catalog of the Edgar Fahs Smith Memorial Collection (Boston: G K Hall and Co, 1960). Portions of our manuscript collection have been described in Norman P Zacour and Rudolf Hirsch, Catalogue of the Manuscripts in the Libraries of the University of Pennsylvania to 1800 (Philadelphia: University of Pennsylvania Press, 1965), 231-243; and R Hirsch, "Catalogue of Manuscripts...Supplement a (5)," Library Chronicle, 37 (1971), 91-115.
WI —UNIVERSITY OF WISCONSIN, MADISON, Memorial Library, History of Science Collection, 728 State St, Madison, 53706. John Neu, Bibliographer
Holdings: Cat
Notes: Extensive collection of editions of Priestley's scientific and theological works. Restricted use: Rare Book Department.

PRIMARY BATTERIES see Electric Batteries

PRIMARY STRUCTURES see Minimal Sculpture

PRIMATES AND PRIMATOLOGY

AL —UNIVERSITY OF ALABAMA, BIRMINGHAM, Lister Hill Library of the Health Sciences, University Sta, Birmingham, 35294. Richard B Fredericksen, Dir
CA —UNIVERSITY OF CALIFORNIA, DAVIS, California Primate Research Center, Library, Davis, 95616. Pauline R Frederick, Librn
Notes: Collection distributed to other libraries. Now primarily a reference service.
MA —HARVARD MEDICAL SCHOOL, New England Primate Research Center Library, 1 Pine Hill Dr, Southborough, 01772. Sydney Fingold, Librn
Holdings: Vols (4000)
NY —AMERICAN MUSEUM OF NATURAL HISTORY, Library Services Dept, Central Park W & 79th St, New York, 10024. Nina J Root, Chairwoman; Mary Genett, Asst Librn for Reference Services
OR —OREGON REGIONAL PRIMATE RESEARCH CENTER, Library, 505 NW 185 Ave, Beaverton, 97006. Isabel McDonald, Librn
Holdings: Vols (765) Cat Audiotapes 16mm Films Microforms
Notes: Incl small collection of dissertations and theses.
TX —SOUTHWEST FOUNDATION FOR RESEARCH AND EDUCATION LIBRARY, Preston C Northrup Memorial Library, Baboon Information Center, W Loop 410 at Military Dr, PO Box 28147, San Antonio, 78284. Dorothy M Brooks, Baboon
Notes: Principle field of research: Birth defects, atherosclerosis, reproductive physiology, cancer, genetics, organic chemistry, parasitology, primatology and behavioral sciences and their application to problems of drug abuse, alcoholism and ecology. Maintains the largest baboon colony in the world.
WI —UNIVERSITY OF WISCONSIN, MADISON, Wisconsin Regional Primate Research Center, Primate Center Library, 1223 Capitol Court, Madison, 53715. Lawrence Jacobsen, Librn
Holdings: Vols (15,000) Cat Pix
Notes: Research in reproductive physiology,

PRIMATES AND PRIMATOLOGY (cont.)

neurosciences, and behavior. Extensive subject orientated primate reprint file, audiovisual collection on primates. Current research uses approximately 25 species of nonhuman primates. Publications: *Primate Library Report*: print and non-print editions, biomonthly.

PRIMEROSE, ROBERT

SC —COLLEGE OF CHARLESTON LIBRARY, Special Collections Dept, Charleston, 29401.
Notes: Papers, 1810, 1835.

PRIMERS

PA —UNIVERSITY OF PITTSBURGH, Hillman Library, Special Collections Dept, John A Nietz Textbook Collection, 363 Hillman Library, Pittsburgh, 15260. Charles E Aston, Jr, Coordr
Holdings: Vols 13,480 Cat Vols 3000 Uncat Mss
Notes: The John A Nietz Textbook Collection of primarily American textbooks in 3 areas; primary school books to 1900, secondary texts to ca 1930 and pedagogical books (1000 vols on the history and theory of education incl writings of the key figures in the field of education). Books are cataloged via an inhouse computer printout, and are accessible via name, title, subject, place, publisher and date. Late 18th and all of the 19th century are well represented. Important titles in each subject are discussed in John A Nietz's *Old Textbooks* (Pittsburgh, 1961) and in his *The Evolution of American Secondary School Textbooks* (Rutland, Vt, 1966). Collection also incl the papers (noncirculating) of Prof John A Nietz.

PRIMITIVE ARCHITECTURE see Architecture, Primitive

PRIMITIVE ART see Art, Primitive

PRIMITIVE MUSIC see Music, Primitive

PRIMITIVE PHARMACOLOGY see Pharmacology, Primitive

PRIMITIVE SOCIETIES

PA —CARNEGIE LIBRARY OF PITTSBURGH, Science & Technology Dept, 4400 Forbes Ave, Pittsburgh, 15213. Catherine M Brosky, Dept Head
Notes: Of secondary interest in acquisitions because of the department's role in cooperation with Pittsburgh institutions and others across the Commonwealth in sharing resources, the cooperative acquistion of materials, and the provision of services and information. However, some aspects of the subject are emphasized. There are separate entries for each of these specialties in this vol.

PRINCE EDWARD ISLAND

PE —CONFEDERATION CENTRE PUBLIC LIBRARY, PO Box 7000, Charlestown, C1A 8G8, Can. Elinor Vass, Cur of Special Collection
Holdings: Vols (1300) Cat Phonorecords Microforms
Notes: Material pertaining to PEI and works by PEI authors. The book and pamphlet collection of approximately 1300 items is cataloged and a separate catalogue is maintained. The microforms incl Prince Edward Island newspapers dating from 1792, PEI government documents and publications dating from 1770, 3 early census records, 1841, 1861 (incomplete) and 1881 at the Public Archives, PEI. The Prince Edward Island Heritage Foundation is preparing a vital statistics index (births, marriages, deaths) and a complete names index for the Island newspapers.

PE —AGRICULTURE CANADA, Research Station Library, PO Box 1210, Charlottetown, C1A 7M8, Can. Barrie Stanfield, Librn
Holdings: Vols 50 Cat Pix
Budget: ($5000)
Notes: History and agriculture of Prince Edward Island.

PE —CONFEDERATION CENTRE PUBLIC LIBRARY, PO Box 7000, Charlottetown, C1A 8G8, Can. William Masselink, Chief Librn
Holdings: Vols 1300 Cat Mss
Notes: There is a separate catalog. Materials held separately from PEI Archives.

†PE —PUBLIC ARCHIVES OF PRINCE EDWARD ISLAND, PO Box 1000, Charlottetown, C1A 7N3, Can.
Notes: Correspondence, business records, school records, photographs, maps, government documents (some vital statistics, land registry records, etc), manuscripts, etc.

PRINCETON INDEX OF CHRISTIAN ART

CA —UNIVERSITY OF CALIFORNIA, LOS ANGELES, Art Library, Los Angeles, 90024. Max Marmor, Library Assistant
Holdings: Pix Microforms
Notes: 1 of 4 copies existing in the world of the Princeton Index of Christian Art. Art; Art History; Early Christian and Byzantine Art; Medieval Art; Apostolic Age to 1400; Iconography; Photo Archive; Christian Art and Symbolism.

PRINCETON RADIO PROJECT (1937-40)

NY —ROCKEFELLER UNIVERSITY, Rockefeller Archive Center, Hillcrest, Pocantico Hills, North Tarrytown, 10591. Joseph W Ernst, Dir; J William Hess, Assoc Dir
Notes: Papers relative to the Rockefeller Family, Foundations, University, and other specific enterprises and contributions to particular areas of social, physical, educational, and historic reform, preservation, conservation, or development. Extensive records of administrative, financial, physical, or intellectual relationships.

PRINGSHEIM, KLAUS, 1883-1973

ON —MCMASTER UNIVERSITY, Mills Memorial Library, Div of Archives & Research Collections, Hamilton, L8S 4L6, Can. G R Hill, Univ Librn
Holdings: // Mss
Notes: Correspondence mss and original musical compositions.

PRINT MAKERS see Print Artists

PRINT MAKING see Prints—Techniques

PRINTERS' MARKS

DC —LIBRARY OF CONGRESS, Rare Book & Special Collections Div, Washington, 20540. William Matheson, Chief
Holdings: Uncat
Notes: The Otto H Vollbehr Collection of Publishers' and Printer's Marks. The collection covers Western European countries from the 15th to the 18th centuries, with extension into the 19th century for Germany, Austria and Scandinavia. Features espec early marks designed by Cranach, Holbein, Urs Graf, Amman, Beham, Flotner and others. About 10,700 pieces.

NY —GRADUATE CENTER OF THE CITY UNIVERSITY OF NEW YORK, William H and Gwynne K Crouse Library for Publishing Arts, 33 W 42 St, New York, 10036. Alfred H Lane, Dir
Notes: Recently established and intended as a source of 20th century materials, in hard form or microfilm, incl books, pamphlets, reprints, translations, dissertations, periodicals, indexing and abstracting services, yearbooks, reports and directories of organizations, publishers' and antiquarian dealers' catalogs (particularly those who deal in books about books), periodicals, legislative materials, and clippings pertaining to the book industry. Sections of the library deal with printing, including typography, specimen books, history of printing and printing techniques, book design and small press and alternative publishing.

PA —FREE LIBRARY OF PHILADELPHIA, Rare Book Dept, Logan Sq, Philadelphia, 19103. Marie E Korey, Rare Book Librn
Holdings: // Uncat
Notes: The John Ashhurst Collection of 5500 printers marks and title-pages.

UT —BRIGHAM YOUNG UNIVERSITY, Harold B Lee Library, Unversity Hill, Provo, 84602. Sterling Albrecht, Dir
Holdings: Vols 275 Cat

PRINTERS' ORNAMENTS see Printers' Marks

PRINTING

CA —UNIVERSITY OF CALIFORNIA, SAN DIEGO, Central University Library, Mandeville Dept of Special Collections, La Jolla, 92093. Lynda Corey Claassen, Head
Notes: The Reference Collection: More than 2500 bibliographies guides, and catalogues to rare book and manuscript collections, auction records, histories of book collecting, and important works on the social and technological history of books and printing are included.

CA —UNIVERSITY OF CALIFORNIA, SANTA BARBARA, Library, Dept of Special Collections, Santa Barbara, 93106. Christian F Brun, Head
Holdings: Vols 11,000 Cat Mss Pix
Notes: Skofield Printers Collection.

CO —DENVER PUBLIC LIBRARY, Douglas Collection of Fine Printing, 1357 Broadway, Denver, 80203.
Holdings: Vols 1700 Cat
Notes: Books from private presses, limited editions and books about private presses. Incl a complete set of vols from William Morris' Kelmscott Press and a virtually complete collection of Ashendene Press books. Most major presses are well represented and minor presses have representative works in the collection.

CT —TRINITY COLLEGE LIBRARY, Watkinson Library, 300 Summit St, Hartford, 06106. Jeffrey Kaimowitz, Cur
Holdings: Cat
Notes: Incl Private Press Collection and Trumbull-Prime Collection of early illustrated books.

CT —YALE UNIVERSITY, Sterling Memorial Library, Arts of the Book Collection, New Haven, 06520. Gay Walker, Cur
Holdings: Vols 3000
Notes: 3000 books on practical printing and private press publications, type design books, etc.

GA —UNIVERSITY OF GEORGIA, Libraries, Special Collections Division, Athens, 30602. Vesta Lee Gordon, Asst Dir for Special Collections
Holdings: Vols (8000)
Notes: One of the larger collections of private press books, pamphlets, and ephemera. The Elmore H Mundell Collection of materials from over 1200 different private printers.

IL —NEWBERRY LIBRARY, John M Wing Foundation on the History of Printing, 60 W Walton St, Chicago, 60610. Diana Haskell, Cur of Modern Mss
Holdings: Vols (30,000) Cat Mss Pix
Budget: ($50,000)
Notes: Part of the John M Wing Foundation on the History of Printing, which collects western European and American printing from the invention to the present day. Includes some 2,000 incunabula, excellent collections of the major printers, modern illustrated books, etc. Especially strong in periodicals and illustrated books of the Victorian period, G K Hall has published *A Dictionary Catalogue of the John M. Wing*

PRINTING (cont.)

Foundation and two Supplements. Parts have been described in various articles, etc., notable J.M. Wells, *The Scholar Printers* and an article by Wells in *The Book Collector*.

IL —UNIVERSITY OF ILLINOIS, URBANA/CHAMPAIGN, Library, Communications Library, 122 Gregory Hall, Urbana, 61801. Nancy Allen, Librn
Holdings: Vols (18,000) Cat
Budget: ($27,000)

IN —PURDUE UNIVERSITY LIBRARIES, Special Collections Dept, West Lafayette, 47907. Keith Dowden, Asst Dir, Special Collections
Holdings: Vols 925 Cat Mss Pix
Notes: Bruce Rogers Collection. Incl book design examples and books about fine printing. The nucleus of the collection is Bruce Rogers' own collection left to his alma mater, Purdue University. Some unique material.

IA —UNIVERSITY OF IOWA, University Libraries, Iowa City, 52242. Frank Paluka, Head, Special Collections Dept
Holdings: Vols 2215// Cat
Notes: The John Springer Collection and the Typographic Laboratory Collection. Harry Duncan, "Bookworms and Type Lice", *Books at Iowa*, April 1965.

KY —UNIVERSITY OF KENTUCKY, Margaret I King Library, Dept of Special Collections, Lexington, 40506. William Marshall, Head
Holdings: Cat Mss Pix Slides Microforms
Notes: Comprehensive collection of books on typography and history of printing; fine press books (incl Lexington imprints); ms books and illumination, paleography; mss of W A Dwiggins (gift of C H Griffith); James Anderson papers; bookbinding; 2 hand-presses and working collection for summer seminars in hand-press printing; bookplates, bookmarks, books jackets, etc.

KY —UNIVERSITY OF LOUISVILLE, Allen R Hite Art Institute, Library, Belknap Campus, Louisville, 40292. Gail Gilbert, Librn
Holdings: Vols (40,000) Cat Pix
Budget: ($29,000)
Notes: Incl books on art, architecture, landscape architecture and gardening, prints, printing, illustrated books and brass rubbings. Library subscribes to 200 periodical titles in these and other areas. Collection circulates to faculty and staff only, with same restrictions placed on interlibrary loan. Library also has collections of bookplates, posters, original prints, hand-made Christmas cards and clippings file filling 56 VF drawers.

†MD —UNIVERSITY OF MARYLAND, Library, R D Remley Collection, College Park, 20742. Donald Farren, Cur Rare Books
Holdings: Vols (2000) Cat
Notes: *Exempla* and secondary works in the areas of typography, calligraphy, book design, book illustration, the history of books, and of publishing, etc. Catalog entries for designers, printing types, private presses, etc.

MA —BOSTON UNIVERSITY, Mugar Memorial Library, Special Collections Dept, 771 Commonwealth Ave, Boston, 02215. Howard B Gotlieb, Dir
Holdings: Cat Mss Pix
Notes: The Silver Private Press Book Collection; also the archives of The Society of Printers, example of other private presses incl Golden Cockerel, Nonesuch, Black Sparrow, Merrymount, Mosher.

MA —MASSACHUSETTS INSTITUTE OF TECHNOLOGY, Institute Archives, Special Collections, Cambridge, 02139.
Notes: Derr and I Austin Kelly collections contain significant monuments of science, technology and printing.

MO —WASHINGTON UNIVERSITY, John M Olin Library, Campus Box 1061, St Louis, 63130.
Holdings: Vols (3700) Cat Mss
Notes: The Isador Mendle Memorial Collection contains representative examples

from the 15th century to the present. Specializes in technical and asthetic aspects of printing in the 19th and 20th centuries incl private presses. The materials assembled support study and research on design, art history, economics, textual and analytical bibliography, and a variety of others topics. No photocopying.

NJ —NEWARK PUBLIC LIBRARY, Art & Music Dept, 5 Washington St, Newark, 07101. William J Dane, Supv
Holdings: Vols (3500) Cat
Notes: R C Jenkinson Collction of Finely Printed Books Shows the physical form of the book and its development through the centuries. There is always a related exhibit in this section of the library covering such subjects as lettes forms, printing, individual preses and publishers, papermaking, etc. Extensive Bruce Rogers collection.

NY —COLUMBIA UNIVERSITY LIBRARIES, Rare Book & Manuscript Library, 801 Butler Library, 535 W 114 St, New York, 10027. Kenneth A Lohf, Librn
Holdings: Mss
Notes: 10,500 pieces of archival material of the printing firm of R Hoe & Co. Restricted use.

NY —GRADUATE CENTER OF THE CITY UNIVERSITY OF NEW YORK, William H and Gwynne K Crouse Library for Publishing Arts, 33 W 42 St, New York, 10036. Alfred H Lane, Dir
Notes: Recently established and still growing, but intended to become the authoritative source of materials in the field, of particular value in research about the publishing industry. Open to staff members of publishing houses, students, scholars, authors, printers, and booksellers. Particularly useful for research on technical, financial, and historical matters. Much on the history of individual houses, economics of authorship; marketing and distribution of books; etc. Primarily 20th century material in hard form or microfilm, incl books, pamphlets, reprints, translations, dissertations, periodicals, indexing and abstracting services, yearbooks, reports and directories of organizations, publishers' and antiquarian dealers' catalogs (particularly those who deal in books about books), periodicals, legislative materials, and clippingspertaining to the book industry. Sections of the library deal with printing, incl typography, specimen books, history of printing and printing techniques, book design and small press and alternative publishing.

NY —GROLIER CLUB OF NEW YORK LIBRARY, 47 E 60 St, New York, 10022. Robert Nikirk, Librn

NY —NEW YORK PUBLIC LIBRARY, Research Libraries, General Research Division, Fifth Ave & 42 St, New York, 10018. Rodney Phillips, Chief
Holdings: Vols (2,225,000) Cat Maps Pix Microforms
Budget: ($775,718)

NY —UNIVERSITY CLUB, Library, One W 54 St, New York, 10019. Guy St Clair, Library Dir
Holdings: Vols (100,000) Cat Mss Maps Pix
Notes: A private library for the members of the University Club, their guests, and serious scholars upon written application to the Library Director.

NY —ROCHESTER INSTITUTE OF TECHNOLOGY, Technical & Education Center of the Graphic Arts, Graphic Arts Information Service, One Lomb Memorial Dr, Rochester, 14623. Susan Clark, Technical Librn
Holdings: Vols (1500) Cat Microforms
Notes: Graphic arts (photographic and applied art aspects) with emphasis on science and technology of printing. Periodicals (265) and technical reports, pertinent to the graphic arts, are routinely scanned for articles of significant information content; articles are classified and keyworded, if needed, and the complete reference is published in *Graphic Arts Literature Abstracts*, a monthly publication of the Graphic Arts Research Center. All abstracted articles are microfilmed and in individual fiche jackets for easy storage and retrieval.

OH —CLEVELAND PUBLIC LIBRARY, Business, Economics and Labor Department, 325 Superior Ave, Cleveland, 44114. Joan Sorger, Head
Holdings: Cat
Notes: Currently receiving over 1700 periodicals and 1300 serial titles; 1000 individual trade, industrial and professional directories, worldwide; 324 file drawers annual reports of old companies, many local; 24 drawers historical information on Clevleand companies. Annual reports, 10-K's, Proxy Statements (disclosure SEC filings on fiche); over 200 loose-leaf services; 1700 current telephone and city directories. Emphasis on current material. Areas of special strength are banking, investments, marketing and management. Also strong insurance, accounting, real estate and transportation collections. Computerized sources available incl Dow Jones News Service and a variety of Dialog business-related databases.

PA —GRAPHIC ARTS TECHNICAL FOUNDATION, Edward H Wadewitz Memorial Library, 4615 Forbes Ave, Pittsburgh, 15213. Janice L Lloyd, Librn
Holdings: Vols (3500) Cat Slides Microforms
Notes: The Lee Augustine Collection. All printing processes. Also, books and periodicals on paper, ink photography, optics, color theory, environmntal control. Approximately 250 periodical titles and 35,000 classified abstracts of selected periodical articles. Approximately 15,000 slides within the organization. Research reports from foreign graphic arts research institutes.

†PA —UNIVERSITY OF PITTSBURGH, Graduate School of Library & Information Sciences Library, L I S Bldg, Third Fl, Pittsburgh, 15260. Jean Kindlin, Librn
Notes: Rare book collection of 1800 titles dealing with the history of the book and printing.

RI —BROWN UNIVERSITY, John Hay Library, Harris Collection, Prospect St, Providence, 02912. Rosemary L Cullen, Cur
Holdings: Vols (200,000) Cat Mss Pix Phonorecords Microforms
Budget: ($15,000)
Notes: The Harris Collection of American Poetry and Plays is principally composed of American and Canadian poetry and plays, 17th century-date. Extensive holdings in songsters, gift books and annuals, hymnals, pageants, broadside verse, carriers' addresses, women poets, juvenile poetry, (incl Mother Goose and *The Night Before Christmas*), sheet music with lyrics, small press publications, fine printing, black poets, "little magazines," Yiddish-American literature. All movements or schools of American poetry are represented. Incl first editions of most American poets and playwrights, notably Whitman, Poe, Wallace Stevens, Eugene O'Neill, Edward Albee, Ezra Pound, T S Eliot, William Carlos Williams, Amy Lowell, Phyllis Wheatley, Robert Frost, Allen Ginsberg, Bliss Carman, and Stephen Foster sheet music. Also incl the Saunders Walt Whitman Collection (1300 vols); the LangdonCollection of Pageants (250 vols); the Asa Cushman Collection of plays in ms and prompt copies; the MacDougall Collection of Psalters and Hymnals; 4000 plays issued by Walter H Baker Co, Boston (1890-1957); the Vaxer Collection of Yiddish Poetry, Plays and Music (1700 vols). Collections incl 200,000 vols, 30,000 broadsides, 55,000 mss, 170,000 pieces of sheet music, 450 phonorecords, and 375 microfilm reels. See *Dictionary Catalog of the Harris Collection of American Poetry and Plays* (Boston: G K Hall, 1972), 13 vols; *Supplement* (1977), 3 vols. See also, *American Poetry, 1609-1900, A Collection on Microfilm, Segment I* (1609-1820); *Segment II* (1821-1850); *Segment III* (1851-1870) (Woodbridge, Conn: Research Publications). Separate catalog.

RI —PROVIDENCE PUBLIC LIBRARY, 150 Empire St, Providence, 02903. Lance J Bauer, Special Collections Librn
Holdings: Vols (6300) Cat Mss Pix
Notes: The

SC —WOFFORD COLLEGE, Sandor Teszler Library, N Church St, Spartanburg, 29301.

PRINTING (cont.)

Frank J Anderson, Librn
Holdings: Vols (500) Cat
Budget: ($500)
Notes: Books about the history and pratice of printing, hand papermaking, bookbinding, book collecting, fine press and private press books used in conjunction with instruction at the Wofford Library Press, an experimental and bibliographic press which has been in operation since 1969. Collection contains materials on printmaking methods and related graphic arts.

TX —UNIVERSITY OF TEXAS, EL PASO, Library, Special Collections Dept, El Paso, 79968. Cesar Caballero, Dept Head
Budget: ($6000)
Notes: Carl Hertzog Collection. More than three hundred books produced by the prominent printer/book designer Carl Hertzog and over a thousand books on books about books, typography, and the history of printing make up this collection. It also contains many Southwestern classics by Frank Dobie and Tom Lea.

ON —NATIONAL MUSEUMS OF CANADA, Library Services Directorate, Ottawa, K1A 0M8, Can. Valerie Monkhouse, Director
Holdings: Vols 15,500
Budget: $25,000
Notes: History and technology of agriculture, astronomy, aviation, chemistry, communications, computers, electrical engineering, exploration and surveying, fire prevention, forestry, industrial technology, mathematics, medicine, mining, photography, physics, printing, space and transportation. research collection, interlibrary loans available, public may use on the premises.

ON —METROPOLITAN TORONTO LIBRARY, Fine Arts Dept, 789 Yonge St, Toronto, M4W 2G8, Can. Alan Suddon, Head
Holdings: Vols (42,000) Cat Pix Microforms
Notes: Extensive collection.

ON —UNIVERSITY OF TORONTO, Massey College, Robertson Davies Library, 4 Devonshire Place, Toronto, M5S 2E1, Can. Desmond G Neill, Librn
Holdings: Vols (12,000) Cat Mss Microforms
Notes: Library contains Bibliography Room (11 hand presses, type and equipment) and Papermaking Room. Book collections incl Ruari McLean Collection of 19th-century books on, and representative of, color printing (approx 4300 items).

PQ —MCGILL UNIVERSITY, McLennan Library, Rare Books and Special Collections Dept, 3459 McTavish St, Montreal, H3A 1Y1, Can.
Holdings: Vols 13,159
Notes: 13,159 volumes and 47,604 items of printed ephemera. Incl early printing manuals, type specimens, books on the history of printing, particularly colour printing, paper, and examples of modern fine printing. Located in the William Colgate History of Printing Collection.

PRINTING—HISTORY

CA —UNIVERSITY OF CALIFORNIA, BERKELEY, Bancroft Library, Manuscripts Division, Berkeley, 94720. James D Hart, Dir
Holdings: Vols 237,000 Cat Mss
Notes: Materials are collected to serve as specimens for the study of printing history and the development of fine printing. English and American fine presses of the 19th and 20th centuries are particularly well represented. Comprehensive coverage for San Francisco Bay Area printers such as Grabhorn, Grabhon-Hoyem, and John Henry Nash.

CA —UNIVERSITY OF CALIFORNIA, BERKELEY, Humanities-Social Sciences Libraries, Library School Library, 2 South Hall, Berkeley, 94720. Virginia Pratt, Head
Holdings: Vols (41,500) Cat Microforms
Notes: Research collection with special strengths in general library science; history of libraries; history of printing and book arts, and publishing; information systems and services; history, criticism, and bibliography of children's literature. The collections in printing and the book arts are complemented by significant holdings both in the Main Library and in the Bancroft Library. Incl collection of 5000 pamphlets.

CA —SAINT JOHN'S SEMINARY, Edward Laurence Doheny Memorial Library, The Estelle Doheny Collection, 5012 E Seminary Rd, Camarillo, 93010. Rita S Faulders, Cur

CA —CLAREMONT COLLEGES, Ella Strong Denison Library, Scripps College, Claremont, 91711. Judy Harvey Sahak, Librn
Holdings: Cat Mss Pix
Notes: In addition to books and ephemera, collection includes original drawings, paper and metal patterns, matrices, and fonts for types that Frederic S Goudy designed for the Scripps College Press.

CA —CLAREMONT COLLEGES, Honnold Library, Ninth & Dartmouth, Claremont, 91711. Tania Rizzo, Special Collections Dept Head
Holdings: Vols (70,000) Cat VF
Notes: Books on typography, bibliography, and history of printing; incunabula; specimen books; fine press books, esp Kelmscott, Doves, Daniel, Mosher, Grabhorn, Nash, and Arion presses and many Southern California printers. A comprehensive collection of Zamorano Club publications and keepsakes, partial source for George E Fulleton, *The Zamorano Club: The First Half Century* (Los Angeles, 1978). Extensive files of ephemera. Fine bindings and fore-edge paintings. Samples of Oriental type and printing.

CA —UNIVERSITY OF CALIFORNIA, SAN DIEGO, Central University Library, Mandeville Dept of Special Collections, La Jolla, 92093. Lynda Corey Claassen, Head
Notes: The Reference Collection: More than 2500 bibliographies guides, and catalogues to rare book and manuscript collections, auction records, histories of book collecting, and important works on the social and technological history of books and printing are included.

CA —LOS ANGELES PUBLIC LIBRARY, Literature and Philology Dept, 630 W Fifth St, Los Angeles, 90071. Helene G Mochedlover, Dept Librn
Holdings: Cat
Notes: Basic works on modern printing and machinery, plus many rare items on the history of printing and the book.

CA —UNIVERSITY OF CALIFORNIA, LOS ANGELES, Research Library, Dept of Special Collections, 405 Hilgard Ave, Los Angeles, 90024. Edward Shreeves, Chairman, Bibliographers Group; David S Zeidberg, Head
Holdings: Vols (70) Cat Pix
Notes: Books with color illustrations, and color prints, printed by George Baxter. Restricted use: scholarly research only.

CA —UNIVERSITY OF CALIFORNIA, LOS ANGELES, William Andrews Clark Memorial Library, 2520 Cimarron St, Los Angeles, 90018.
Holdings: Cat Mss Pix
Notes: The papers and library of Eric Gill, incl business correspondence, accounts, Gill's diary in 27 volumes, many of his writings in typescript or holograph, and more than 500 original drawings. Also, the Joseph Kelly Vodrey Collection of Robert Gibbings material. Consists of Gibbings' books, illustrations, wood engravings, drawings, and mss. Director of the Golden Cockerel Press (1924-1933), Gibbings worked closely with Eric Gill. The collection is described in *The Clark Newsletter*, number 5 (1983).

CA —UNIVERSITY OF CALIFORNIA, LOS ANGELES, Research Library, Medieval and Renaissance Collection, 405 Hilgard Ave, Los Angeles, 90024. Edward Shreeves, Chairman, Bibliographers Group; Frances K Zeitlin, Medievan and Renaissance Bibliographer
Notes: Early printing history, catalogs of ms collections. Incorporates the reference library of the antiquarian bookselling firm of Ulrice Hoepli of Milan.

CA —MILLS COLLEGE LIBRARY, Oakland, 94613. Steven P Pandolfo, Librn
Holdings: Vols 5000 Cat Pix
Notes: Printed books representative of the history of book; research collection on all aspects of the history of printing and bookmaking. Books and ephemera from English and American fine presses. Strong interest in collecting the work of women printers.

CA —SAN DIEGO PUBLIC LIBRARY, Wangenheim Rm, 820 E St, San Diego, 92101. Eileen Boyle, Librn
Holdings: Vols (7500) Cat Pix
Notes: A collection on the history of the book and the development of printing with specimens ranging from Babylonian tablets to cassettes.

CA —CALIFORNIA HISTORICAL SOCIETY, Schubert Hall Library, 2099 Pacific Ave, San Francisco, 94109. Bruce L Johnson, Library Dir
Holdings: Vols 4400 Cat Mss Pix Microforms
Notes: The Edward C Kemble Collections. Not collections of fine printing, but of the history of printing and publishing with emphasis on the Pacific Coast, although the full scope of the collection is not limited to this area. In addition to bibliographic tools and reference works, it contains type specimen books and several long runs of trade periodicals and house organs of San Francisco typefounders. The Taylor & Taylor Archives, a part of this collection, contain the working record of a major San Francisco printing firm. The *Kemble Occasional*, published three times a year from the Kemble Collections, presents scholarly articles on the history of printing. Edward C Kemble was the first historian of printing in California.

†CA —UNIVERSITY OF SAN FRANCISCO, Richard A Gleeson Library, The Countess Bernardine Murphy Donohue Rare Book Room, San Francisco, 94117. D Steven Corey, Special Collections Librn
Holdings: Vols 40 Cat
Notes: None of the incunabula are recorded in Golf.

CA —HUNTINGTON LIBRARY, Art Gallery & Botanical Gardens, 1151 Oxford Rd, San Marino, 91108. Robert L Middlekauff, Dir; Daniel H Woodward, Librn
Holdings: Mss Maps Pix Slides Microforms
Notes: Approx 350,000 rare books, 250,000 reference books, manuscript collection of nearly 2,500,000 pieces and between 200,000 and 300,000 prints, rare photographs and other related materials. The fullest available survey is now *Guide to Literary Manuscripts in the Huntington Library*, a 539-page handlist published by the Library in 1979.

CA —UNIVERSITY OF CALIFORNIA, SANTA BARBARA, Library, Dept of Special Collections, Santa Barbara, 93106. Christian F Brun, Head
Holdings: Cat Mss Pix
Notes: Skofield Printers Collection.

CA —UNIVERSITY OF CALIFORNIA, SANTA CRUZ, University Library, Special Collections, Santa Cruz, 95064. Rita Bottoms, Special Collections Librn; Margaret Felts, South Pacific Collection Bibliographer
Notes: Archives of Arnold Fawcus's Trianon Press, users of a unique process in the evolution of printing combining collotyping and hand stenciling to make almost perfect replicas. The press is known especially for its replica editions of the works of William Blake.

CA —STANFORD UNIVERSITY LIBRARIES, Cecil H Green Library, Stanford, 94305. Michael T Ryan, Cur
Holdings: Vols (12,000) Cat
Notes: The Morgan A & Aline D Gunst Memorial Library. The book arts in every century with some of the best examples. Strong collection of examples of California printers and graphic artists. Complete or nearly complete collections of works by the Kelmscott, Doves, Ashendene, Colt, Grabhorn, and Grabhorn-Hoyem presses.

PRINTING—HISTORY (cont.)

CA —SOLANO COUNTY LIBRARY, John F
Kennedy Library, Donovan J McCune
Collection, 505 Santa Clara St, Vallejo,
94590.
Holdings: Vols (1500)// Cat Mss

CT —TRINITY COLLEGE LIBRARY,
Watkinson Library, 300 Summit St,
Hartford, 06106. Jeffrey Kaimowitz, Cur
Holdings: Cat
Notes: Broad range of materials in depth
including histories, bibliographies,
periodicals, and monographs on special
subjects.

CT —YALE UNIVERSITY, Box 1603A, Yale
Station, New Haven, 06520.

CT —YALE UNIVERSITY, Sterling Memorial
Library, Arts of the Book Collection, New
Haven, 06520. Gay Walker, Cur
Holdings: Vols 1000
Notes: 1000 books, historical printing
manuals, type specimen books and related
articles.

CT —CONNECTICUT COLLEGE, Library,
Mohegan Ave, New London, 06320. Brian
Rogers, College Librn
Notes: Collection includes material relating
to New London and surrounding
communities including Groton, Norwich and
Stonington. Includes pamphlets and
broadsides printed in New London by
Timothy Green during the Revolutionary
period. Also "Atlantic Neptune" facsimiles.

DE —DELAWARE ART MUSEUM, Library,
2301 Kentmere Pkwy, Wilmington, 19806.
Anne Hoslam, Librn
Holdings: Vols (25,000) Cat Mss
Notes: The collection is rich in the following
subjects: Howard Pyle and his pupils; John
Sloan and the eight; history of the book and
printing; and English and American
illustrated books. There is also a section on
contemporary photography. Archival
material on Albert Mumford Lindsay,
Jerome Myers, Everett Shinn, Gayle Porter
Hoskins, Frank Schoonover.

DC —LIBRARY OF CONGRESS, Rare Book
& Special Collections Div, Washington,
20540. William Matheson, Chief
Holdings: Vols 1791 Cat Mss
Notes: The Frederic and Bertha Goudy
Collection was purchased directly from the
Goudys in 1944. Apart from the books,
pamphlets, magazine articles, clippings, etc
that constitute a working library, the
collection includes correspondence, type
specimens and typefounding equipment. This
purchase was supplemented in 1975 by the
acquisition of a substantial collection of
Goudyana, consisting largely of
correspondence and other original source
material.

DC —LIBRARY OF CONGRESS, Manuscript
Division, Washington, 20540. John C
Broderick, Chief
Notes: Papers of Richard Hoe and
Company, printers.

FL —FLORIDA STATE UNIVERSITY,
Robert Manning Strozier Library, Special
Collections Dept, Tallahassee, 32306. Opal
M Free, Head, Special Collections
Holdings: Vols (12,254) Cat Mss Maps
Notes: Noncirculating. No photocopying.

GA —UNIVERSITY OF GEORGIA,
Libraries, Special Collections Division,
Athens, 30602. Vesta Lee Gordon, Asst Dir
for Special Collections
Holdings: Vols (8000)
Notes: One of the larger collections of
private press books, pamphlets, and
ephemera. The Elmore H Mundell
Collection of materials from over 1200
different private printers.

IL —CHICAGO PUBLIC LIBRARY, Special
Collections Div, Cultural Center, 78 E
Washington St, Chicago, 60602. Laura
Linard, Cur
Holdings: Vols (1000) Cat
Notes: A general collection on the history of
typography, including a specimen collection
of works printed before 1700, books about
books, private press productions (primarily
Chicago), limited editions, illustrated and
extra-illustrated books and fine bindings.

Outstanding items described in *Treasures of
The Chicago Public Library*, compiled by
Thomas A Orlando and Marie Gecik, 1977,
pp 6-29.

IL —DE PAUL UNIVERSITY, Library, 2323
N Seminary, Chicago, 60614. Kathryn De
Graff, Special Collections Librn
Holdings: Vols (170)// Uncat
Notes: The Louis Silver Collection. Incl
materials describing the history of printing,
typography, book binding, book plates,
bibliographies, exhibition catalogs, private
collections, and subject-related periodicals.

IL —NEWBERRY LIBRARY, John M Wing
Foundation on the History of Printing, 60 W
Walton St, Chicago, 60610. Diana Haskell,
Cur of Modern Mss
Holdings: Vols (30,000) Cat Mss
Budget: ($50,000)
Notes: The collection covers printing and
printing history of Western Europe and the
Americas from its invention to the present.
It is particularly rich in incunabula (about
2000); the works of the great printers,
among others Aldus, Bodoni, Baskerville,
and Rogers. Printed catalog: *A Dictionary
Catalogue.* (Boston: G K Hall, 1961);
Supplements (1981). Brief descriptions:
James M Wells, "The John M Wing
Foundation of the Newberry Library," *The
Book Collector, VIII*, 2 (Summer 1959), pp
157-162; Lawrece W Towner, *An
Uncommon Collection of Uncommon
Collections* (Chicago: The Newberry Library,
1977), pp 25-26.

IL —NORTHERN ILLINOIS UNIVERSITY,
Founders Memorial Library, Rare Books and
Special Collections Dept, De Kalb, 60115.
William R DuBois, Dept Head
Holdings: Vols (450) Cat
Notes: Works on the history of books and
printing and representative examples of fine
printing. Includes more than 50 titles
published in Chicago by Way & Williams.

IL —NORTHWESTERN UNIVERSITY,
Library, Special Collections Dept, 1937
Sheridan Rd, Evanston, 60201. R Russell
Maylone, Cur
Holdings: Vols 2000 Cat Mss Drawings
Layouts
Notes: The John J Louis Memorial
Collection: works dealing with the
typographic arts and extensive collections of
the major typographers, especially Rogers,
Dwiggins, Goudy, Clelland and Kittedge.
5000 representative examples of the work of
the modern private press from Strawberry
Hill to the current small printers. Additional
material in the general collection.

IL —ILLINOIS STATE UNIVERSITY, Milner
Library, Dept of Special Collections,
Normal, 61761. Robert Sokan, Librn
Holdings: Vols 191 // Cat
Notes: The city of Birmingham, School of
Printing collection incl all the items that
were produced by the School of Printing
under the direction of Leonard Jay from
1925-1953.

IN —INDIANA UNIVERSITY, Lilly Library,
Seventh St, Bloomington, 47405. William R
Cagle, Librn
Holdings: Vols 6000 // Cat
Notes: The Lilly Library collection of
incunables (books printed before January
1501) now numbers over 700 titles and is
being added to on a selective basis, primarily
in the major works of the humanities and
sciences. Presses from the sixteenth century
to the present are well represented, and to
aid the user there is a separate printers and
presses file which will lead to the major
books of all periods from Gutenburg to
Grabhorn. It is a selective rather than a
comprehensive collection.

KS —BAKER UNIVERSITY, Library, Quayle
Rare Bible Collection, Eighth St, Baldwin
City, 66006. John Forbes, Dir
Holdings: Vols (600) Cat Mss
Notes: This collection of rare Bibles was
given by Bishop William A Quayle (1860-
1925), representative collection of books and
other writings before advent (in the westen
world) of printing by moveable type,
incunabula, Biblical works since 1501, and a
few non-Biblical works since 1500. See *The
William Alfred Quayle Bible Collection: A*

Descriptive Catalog, by Margaret Stutzman;
also *The William A Quayle Rare Bible
Collection: A Self-Guided Tour Manual*
(preliminary ed) by Ray Firestone. Persons
desiring to visit the collection are advised to
make an appointment or phone ahead to
Baker University (913-594-6451 ext 4141) to
assure that collection is open.

KS —EMPORIA STATE UNIVERSITY,
William Allen White Library, Emporia,
66801. Mary E Bogan, Special Collections
Librn
Holdings: Vols (1400) Phonorecords

KY —UNIVERSITY OF KENTUCKY,
Margaret I King Library, Dept of Special
Collections, Lexington, 40506. William
Marshall, Head
Holdings: Cat Mss Pix Slides Microforms
Notes: Comprehensive collection of books
on typography and history of printing; fine
press books (incl Lexington imprints); ms
books and illumination, paleography; mss of
W A Dwiggins (gift of C H Griffith); James
Anderson papers; bookbinding; 2 hand-
presses and working collection for summer
seminars in hand-press printing; bookplates,
bookmarks, book jackets, etc.

†MD —UNIVERSITY OF MARYLAND,
Library, R D Remley Collection, College
Park, 20742. Donald Farren, Cur Rare
Books
Holdings: Vols (2000) Cat
Notes: *Exempla* and secondary works in the
areas of typography, calligraphy, book
design, book illustration, the history of
books, and of publishing, etc. Catalog entries
for designers, printing types, private presses,
etc.

MA —BOSTON UNIVERSITY, Mugar
Memorial Library, Special Collections Dept,
771 Commonwealth Ave, Boston, 02215.
Howard B Gotlieb, Dir
Holdings: // Cat Mss
Notes: Papers of Society of Printers and
correspondence of Rollo G Silver with
various private presses.

MA —FRANCIS A COUNTWAY LIBRARY
OF MEDICINE, Boston Medical Library/
Harvard Medical Library, 10 Shattuck St,
Boston, 02115. C Robin LeSueur, Librn;
Richard J Wolfe, Cur, Rare Books &
Manuscripts
Holdings: Vols (500,000) Cat Mss Maps Pix
Microforms
Notes: Combines resources of the Harvad
Medical School and the Boston Medical
Library. Strong in serials and medical history
in all fields of medicine, incl incunabula,
non-medical books by doctors, travel books
by doctors. 500,000 medical dissertations
and theses. Special strength in all medical
subjects listed in this volume.

MA —HARVARD UNIVERSITY LIBRARY,
Houghton Library, Printing and Graphic
Arts Dept, Cambridge, 02138. Eleanor M
Garvey, Cur
Holdings: Cat
Notes: Collection incl illustrated books, fine
printing, type specimens, illuminated and
calligraphic manuscripts, and drawings for
book illustration.

MA —SMITH COLLEGE, Library,
Northampton, 01063. Ruth Mortimer, Cur
of Rare Books
Holdings: Vols (10,000) Cat
Notes: Representative examples: incunabula,
16th century printers, through modern fine
press books; Northampton imprints;
typographic ephemera.

MA —OLD STURBRIDGE VILLAGE,
Research Library, Sturbridge, 01566.
Theresa Rini Percy, Librn
Holdings: Vols (23,000) Cat Microforms
Notes: New England to 1850. Incl printers'
manuals.

MA —BRANDEIS UNIVERSITY, Goldfarb
Library, 415 South St, Waltham, 02154.
Bessie Hahn, Dir
Budget:
Notes: About 300 ephemeral items
exemplifying the printing process from the
Victorian period. No finding list or catalog
present.

†MA —WILLIAMS COLLEGE, Chapin
Library of Rare Books, PO Box 426,
Williamstown, 01267. Robert L Volz,

PRINTING—HISTORY (cont.)

Custodian
Holdings: Vols 3000 Cat Maps Pix
Notes: No material available on interlibrary loan.

MA —AMERICAN ANTIQUARIAN SOCIETY LIBRARY, 185 Salisbury St, Worcester, 01609. Marcus A McCorison, Dir & Librn
Holdings: Cat Mss
Notes: US printing is remarkably represented by some 60,000 volumes, about 60 percent of the number known to have been printed before 1821. Incl the Isaiah Thomas Papers, his imprinted books, and his printing press. The Library is also especially strong in early English type-specimen books, and American examples to 1860.

MI —UNIVERSITY OF MICHIGAN, Library, Dept of Rare Books & Special Collections, Ann Arbor, 48109. Robert J Starring, Head
Holdings: Cat
Notes: Many examples of early prints and printing and famous private presses.

MI —DETROIT PUBLIC LIBRARY, Rare Books Department, 5201 Woodward Ave, Detroit, 48202.
Holdings: Cat
Notes: A substantial collection of books about books and the history of printing as well as examples from the 15th to 20th centuries. Restricted use. Reference collection.

MI —MICHIGAN STATE UNIVERSITY, Libraries, Special Collections Div, East Lansing, 48824. Jannette Fiore, Librn
Holdings: Mss
Notes: Outstanding collection of over 100,000 items, including Douglas C McMurtrie's published pamphlets and monographs, with manuscript, typescript, galleys, etc, material for the unfinished *History of Printing in the United States*, and his vast correspondence on printing and its history. Supported by a collection of works on printing.

MO —UNIVERSITY OF MISSOURI-COLUMBIA, Ellis Library, Special Collections Dept, Ninth & Lowry, Columbia, 65201. Margaret A Howell, Head, Special Collections
Holdings: Vols Cat
Notes: Examples from 15th century to the present. Includes works from over 500 modern private presses.

MO —KANSAS CITY PUBLIC LIBRARY, 311 E 12, Kansas City, 64106. Daniel J Bradbury, Dir
Holdings: Vols 1500 Cat
Notes: Graphic arts collection contains the "rare book" section of the library with emphasis on book arts and printing. Additions made as desired items become available.

MO —SAINT LOUIS PUBLIC LIBRARY, Gardner Rare Book Room, 1301 Olive St, Saint Louis, 63103. Julanne M Good, Supervisor; Martha Riley, Rare Books Librn
Holdings: Vols 1300 Cat Mss
Budget: ($5573)
Notes: Collection of rare materials, 350 specimen leaves and supporting reference materials on history of the book, history of printing, bibliography, book collecting, book and document conservation, papermaking, and bookbinding. The 350 specimen leaves are from illuminated manuscript books and incunabula. Noncirculating.

MO —WASHINGTON UNIVERSITY, John M Olin Library, Campus Box 1061, St Louis, 63130.
Holdings: Vols (3700) Cat Mss
Notes: The Isador Mendle Memorial Collection contains representative examples from the 15th century to the present. Specializes in technical and aesthetic aspects of printing in the 19th and 20th centuries incl private presses. The materials assembled support study and research on design, art, history, economics, textual and analytical bibliography, and a variety of other topics. No photocopying.

MO —WASHINGTON UNIVERSITY, Libraries, Special Collections Dept, Campus Box 1061, St Louis, 63130.
Holdings: //
Notes: The Gast Banknote Company's

records, 1884-1952. Incl general ledgers, sales ledgers, payroll books, equipment inventories, and selected sample books of printing work of this lithography and printing firm.

NY —PRATT INSTITUTE LIBRARY, 200 Willoughby Ave, Brooklyn, 11205.

NY —TYPOPHILES INC, Typographic Reference Library, 140 Lincoln Rd, Brooklyn, 11225. Robert L Leslie, Dir
Holdings: 4800 Vols
Notes: History of printing in all languages. Special collection of French and German type specimen books since 1888.

NY —MANHASSET PUBLIC LIBRARY, 30 Onderdonk Ave, Manhasset, 11030. Sylvia Levin, Dir
Holdings: Vols 400
Notes: A checklist of the collection is available.

NY —COLUMBIA UNIVERSITY LIBRARIES, Rare Book & Manuscript Library, 801 Butler Library, 535 W 114 St, New York, 10027. Kenneth A Lohf, Librn
Holdings: Vols 25,000 Cat
Notes: Incl allied crafts. Books arts, graphic arts and typographic libraries. Restricted use: noncirculating.

NY —GENERAL THEOLOGICAL SEMINARY, Saint Marks Library, 175 Ninth Ave, New York, 10011. David Green, Dir
Holdings: Vols (200,000) Cat Mss Maps Pix Slides Microforms
Notes: Extensive collection.

NY —GRADUATE CENTER OF THE CITY UNIVERSITY OF NEW YORK, William H and Gwynne K Crouse Library for Publishing Arts, 33 W 42 St, New York, 10036. Alfred H Lane, Dir
Notes: Recently established and still growing, but intended to become the authoritative source of materials in the field, of particular value in research about the publishing industry. Open to staff members of publishing houses, students, scholars, authors, printers, and booksellers. Particularly useful for research on technical, financial, and historical matters. Much on the history of individual houses, economics of authorship; marketing and distribution of books; etc. Primarily 20th century material in hard form or microfilm, incl books, pamphlets, reprints, translations, dissertations, periodicals, indexing and abstracting services, yearbooks, reports and directories of organizations, publishers' and antiquarian dealers' catalogs (particularly those who deal in books about books), periodicals, legislative materials, and clippingspertaining to the book industry. Sections of the library deal with printing, incl typography, specimen books, history of printing and printing techniques, book design and small press and alternative publishing.

NY —GROLIER CLUB OF NEW YORK LIBRARY, 47 E 60 St, New York, 10022. Robert Nikirk, Librn
Notes: Subject strength.

NY —NEW YORK HISTORICAL SOCIETY, Library, 170 Central Park W, New York, 10024. James Gregory, Librn
Holdings: Mss
Notes: Incl original mss, illustrative materials, etc.

NY —NEW YORK PUBLIC LIBRARY, Research Libraries, General Research Division, Fifth Ave & 42 St, New York, 10018. Rodney Phillips, Chief
Holdings: Vols (2,225,000) Cat Maps Pix Microforms
Budget: ($775,718)

NY —NEW YORK PUBLIC LIBRARY, Rare Books and Manuscripts Div, Fifth Ave & 42 St, New York, 10018. William L Joyce, Asst Dir; Susan E Davis, Cur of Mss
Holdings: Cat Mss Pix
Budget: ($7161)
Notes: The personal and scientific papers of Chester F Carlson, inventor of xerography, and many other collections pertaining to the history of the book trades.

NY —NEW YORK PUBLIC LIBRARY, Rare Books and Manuscripts Div, Fifth Ave & 42 St, New York, 10018. William L Joyce, Asst Dir; Francis O Mattson, Curator
Holdings: Vols 95,000 Cat Maps
Budget: ($7161)
Notes: The Division contains a large number

of bibliographies, monographs, and other materials relating to printing history and the history of the American book trades generally.

NY —UNIVERSITY CLUB, Library, One W 54 St, New York, 10019. Guy St Clair, Library Dir
Holdings: Vols (100,000) Cat Mss Maps Pix
Notes: A private library for the members of the University Club, their guests, and serious scholars upon written application to the Library Director. Holds the Edward Larocque Tinker Collection of Illustrated Books Between the Two World Wars, A Milton Runyon Collection on the History of Printing and Publishing, the Frederic R Coudert "Les Bibliophiles de Paris" Collection, The University Club Rare Book Collection, and the Frederick G Rudge Collection of Books Designed by William E Rudge and Bruce Rogers.

NY —ROCHESTER INSTITUTE OF TECHNOLOGY, Melbert B Cary Jr Graphic Arts Collection, School of Printing, One Lomb Memorial Drive, Rochester, 14623. David Pankow, Cur
Holdings: Vols (11,000) Cat Mss Pix
Notes: An extensive collection of the work of typographic artist Albert Schiller. Incl type pictures, their type forms, correspondence, sketches, books, proofs, and ephemera. Incl the *New York Times Museum of the Printed Word*.

NY —VISUAL STUDIES WORKSHOP, Research Center, 31 Prince St, Rochester, 14607. Linn Underhill, Coordr; Robert Bretz, Librn
Holdings: Vols (8000) Cat Pix Slides Audiotapes Videotapes
Notes: Strong emphasis on photography (over 1,000,000 pictures) and the photographic arts in many subject areas incl in this volume. Heavy emphasis on early photographic processes and collections of examples of them. Also collections of individual photographers' works.

NC —UNIVERSITY OF NORTH CAROLINA, CHAPEL HILL, Wilson Library, Rare Book Collection, Chapel Hill, 27514. Paul S Koda, Cur of Rare Books
Holdings: Vols 1000 Cat Mss
Notes: The Hanes Collection of the History of the Book consists of Sumerian and Babylonian clay tablets, papyri in Egyptian and in Greek, stone inscriptions, 24 olas, manuscripts, and 600 items of 16th, 17th, and 18th century printing, incl many landmarks in the history of printing. It also contains many books about books, incl some rare bibliographies, histories of presses and technology, and books on collecting.

OH —PUBLIC LIBRARY OF CINCINNATI & HAMILTON COUNTY, Dept of Rare Books & Special Collections, 800 Vine St, Library Square, Cincinnati, 45202. Yeatman Anderson III, Cur
Holdings: Cat Mss
Notes: A collection of examples of fine printing from Gutenberg to date.

OH —CASE WESTERN RESERVE UNIVERSITY, M A Baxter School of Information and Library Science, 10900 Euclid Ave, Cleveland, 44106. Bettina MacAyeal, Librn; Gretchen Larson, Librn
Holdings: Vols (15,000) Cat

OH —KENT STATE UNIVERSITY, Libraries, Dept of Special Collections, Kent, 44242. Dean H Keller, Cur
Holdings: Vols 650 Cat Mss
Notes: Incl books about printers and printing and examples of printing from the incunable period to the present.

OK —UNIVERSITY OF TULSA, McFarlin Library, Dept of Rare Books and Special Collections, 600 S College, Tulsa, 74104. David Farmer, Dir; Toby Murray, Archivist; Caroline Swinson, Cur of Manuscripts & Art
Holdings: Cat
Notes: Incl the John Bennett Shaw Collection of Books About Books.

PA —TEMPLE UNIVERSITY, Samuel Paley Library, Berks & 13 Sts, Philadelphia, 19122.
Notes: Collection of works of the City of Birmingham School of Printing (England). Books and ephemera of the students and Leonard Jay, Master Printer. Also the

PRINTING—HISTORY (cont.)

William Danner Collection of periodical issues from amateur printers and presses.

PA —TEMPLE UNIVERSITY LIBRARIES, Special Collections Dept, Rare Books & Mss Section, Philadelphia, 19122. Thomas M Whitehead, Cur
Holdings: Vols (5000) Mss Pix
Notes: The printing and graphic arts collections stress the technological developments within the printing industry and the achievements in fine printing in the 19th and 20th centuries. Selected additions are continually made of examples and secondary works. Holdings include the Library and archives of Richard W Ellis, typographer, archives of Philadelphia printers and photoengravers. Partially cataloged.

PA —UNIVERSITY OF PENNSYLVANIA, Van Pelt Library, Rare Books Collection, 34 & Walnut Sts, Philadelphia, 19104. Daniel Traister, Special Collections Librn
Holdings: Vols 10,000 Cat
Notes: *Sixteenth-Century Imprints in the Libraries of the University of Pennsylvania,*, by M A Shaaber (University of Pennsylvania Press, 1976).

PA —GRAPHIC ARTS TECHNICAL FOUNDATION, Edward H Wadewitz Memorial Library, 4615 Forbes Ave, Pittsburgh, 15213. Janice L Lloyd, Librn
Notes: The Lee Augustine Collection.

†PA —UNIVERSITY OF PITTSBURGH, Graduate School of Library & Information Sciences Library, L I S Bldg, Third Fl, Pittsburgh, 15260. Jean Kindlin, Librn
Notes: Rare book collection of 1800 titles dealing with the history of the book and printing.

PA —EASTERN COLLEGE, Frank Warner Memorial Library, Saint Davids, 19087. James L Sauer, Librn
Holdings: Uncat Mss Pix
Notes: The Harry C Goebel Collection. Incl Bruce Rogers printings (over 460); press books (about 350); oriental art (over 250); bookplates (with a separate collection of an almost complete set of bookplates designed by Edwin Davis French); Christmas Books; art and graphic arts (incl the French Graphics Arts Collection of Adolph DeMilly); first editions of Christopher Morely; Print Collection (1315 prints); Oriental art realia and artifacts.

PA —SWARTHMORE COLLEGE, Library, Swarthmore, 19081. Michael J Durkan, Librn
Holdings: Vols 3073 Cat
Notes: Mostly private presses and private press books.

RI —BROWN UNIVERSITY, John Hay Library, 20 Prospect St, Providence, 02912. Mark N Brown, Cur Mss
Holdings: Vols 9000 Cat Mss Pix
Notes: The

RI —PROVIDENCE PUBLIC LIBRARY, 150 Empire St, Providence, 02903. Lance J Bauer, Special Collections Librn
Holdings: Vols 400 // Cat
Notes: The Wetmore Illustrated Books Collection. This historical collection of more than 400 volumes was given to Providence Public Library in 1955 by Newport, Rhode Island, Collector Edith Wetmore. An extremely fine collection of *livres d'artiste,* examples of fine illustration, printing and bindings. This collection incl the works of such notable artists as William Blake, Pablo Picasso, Giorgio DiChirico, Aubrey Beardsley, Jean Cocteau, William Hogarth, Raoul Dufy, Pierre Bonnard and numerous others. Although especially strong in the French illustrated books, English and German illustrated books are amply represented also. Partially cataloged. Material must be used in-house.

SC —UNIVERSITY OF SOUTH CAROLINA, Thomas Cooper Library, Columbia, 29208. Kenneth E Toombs, Dir of Libraries; Roger Mortimer, Rare Book Librn
Holdings: Vols 1000 Cat
Notes: Collection contains examples of bookmaking for the 15th-20th centuries,

especially, noteworthy bindings and fore-edge paintings.

SC —WOFFORD COLLEGE, Sandor Teszler Library, N Church St, Spartanburg, 29301. Frank J Anderson, Librn
Holdings: Vols (500) Cat
Budget: ($500)
Notes: Books about the history and practice of printing, hand papermaking, bookbinding, book collecting, fine press and private press used in conjunction with instruction at the Wofford Library Press, and experimental and bibliographic press which has been in operation since 1969. Collection contains mateials on printmaking methods and related graphic arts.

TX —EAST TEXAS STATE UNIVERSITY, James G Gee Library, Special Collections Dept, East Texas Station, Commerce, 75428. James Conrad, Dept Head
Holdings: Vols (3500) Cat Mss Pix Slides
Notes: The books on Black Literature (with the exception of those on Texas folklore) and Slavery in the US have been transferred to the general stack area of the library; however, our collection of country histories of Texas, which is still housed in the Special Collections, continues to grow. In addition, we have acquired sizable collections of books on Texas folklore and Texas placenames; and World War II posters. Another new area is printing arts in Texas. There is a separate dictionary card catalog for the book collection in the Special Collections Department.

TX —DALLAS PUBLIC LIBRARY, Fine Arts Div, 1515 Young St, Dallas, 75201. Richard L Waters, Acting Dir; Jane Holahan, Manager
Holdings: Vols 1400 Uncat Mss
Budget: $12,000
Notes: Fine printing and the history of printing. No photocopying.

TX —UNIVERSITY OF TEXAS, EL PASO, Library, Special Collections Dept, El Paso, 79968. Cesar Caballero, Dept Head
Budget: ($6000)
Notes: Carl Hertzog Collection. More than three hundred books produced by the prominent printer/book designer Carl Hertzog and over a thousand books on books about books, typography, and the history of printing make up this collection. It also contains many Southwestern classics by Frank Dobie and Tom Lea.

TX —ROSENBERG LIBRARY, Fox Rare Book Room, 2310 Sealy Ave, Galveston, 77550. Fernando Basilza, Rare Book Librn
Holdings: Vols (2000) Cat Mss Pix
Notes: The Col Milo Pitcher Fox and Agnes Peel Fox Rare Book Room contains 2000 vols incuabula, first printings, and moden fine printing. Incl clay tablets, horn books, parchment material, illuminated books and mss, fine printing (principally 15th-18th centuries), fine binding, fore-edge paintings, etc.

TX —UNIVERSITY OF HOUSTON, M D Anderson Memorial Library, University Park, Houston, 77004. David Farmer, Cur, Special Collections; Jean Jackson, Assistant Cur
Holdings: Vols 225 Cat
Notes: The collection follows, to a degree, the checklist prepared by Charles Heartman in 1942 (supplement, 1946), but contains many items not included by Heartman.

UT —BRIGHAM YOUNG UNIVERSITY, Harold B Lee Library, Unversity Hill, Provo, 84602. Sterling Albrecht, Dir
Holdings: Vols 2000 Cat
Notes: A large collection covering all phases of literature and life in the Age of Queen Victoria. Incl an unusual collection of "Yellow Backs" (1750 printer's proofs for yellow-back covers of original paperbacks of the 19th century). Also, Marco Heidner Collection of representative works (275 vols) of the great printers of the 15th-16th centuries.

VA —UNIVERSITY OF VIRGINIA, Alderman Library, Rare Book Dept, Charlottesville, 22901. Julius P Barclay, Cur
Holdings: Vols (6500) // Mss
Notes: The Oscar Ogg Collection of Book Arts covers calligraphy, letterforms,

typography, printing, and graphic arts. Contains early writing books and printed works, as well as modern manuals and other works on printing, publishing, and promotion through graphic arts. The Dept also has the Edward L Stone Collection of Printing Specimens, 3000 items. Contains materials tracing the history of printing, inks, binding styles and materials, types. Also the Tompkins Collection (2000 vols), and the Stevens Watts collection (900 vols).

VA —COLLEGE OF WILLIAM AND MARY, Earl Gregg Swem Library, Williamsburg, 23185. Margaret C Cook, Cur of Manuscripts & Rare Books
Holdings: Vols 336// Cat Pix
Notes: The Ralph Green Collection, incl his notes, notebooks, and blueprints.

WA —UNIVERSITY OF WASHINGTON LIBRARIES, Suzzallo Library, Special Collections Division, Rare Book Collection, FM-25, Seattle, 98195. Gary Menges, Coordinator for Special Collections
Holdings: Vols (12,000) Cat Maps
Notes: American, British, French, German and Italian books printed before 1800, chiefly in the fields of history and literature. Fine bindings and illustrated works are represented. Incl incunabula, emblemata, history of travel, and first editions of the works of major poets: Spenser, Blake, Whitman, Yeats, Roethke, etc.

WA —UNIVERSITY OF WASHINGTON LIBRARIES, Suzzallo Library, Special Collections Division, Rare Book Collection, FM-25, Seattle, 98195. Gary Menges, Coordinator for Special Collections
Notes: Printing history, including early printed books and modern fine printing; book arts, including papermaking, decorated papers, bookbinding, book design, and artist's books; American literature, 19th century includes: Stephen Crane, Ralph Waldo Emerson, Nathaniel Hawthorne, Henry James, Henry Wadsworth Longfellow, Herman Melville, Frank Norris, Harriet Beecher Stowe and Walt Whitman and 20th century includes: Theodore Roethke; illustrated books, including emblem books, historical children's illustration, books illustrated with prints, and artist's books; costume history; voyages and travels; preservation of library materials.

WI —UNIVERSITY OF WISCONSIN, MADISON, Memorial Library, Rare Books Collection, 728 State St, Madison, 53706. Gretchen Lagana, Cur
Holdings: Vols (58) Cat
Notes: Grotius Collection. Some 58 volumes by, about, or associated with the Dutch jurist and humanist Hugo Grotius. A number of the volumes comprise classical writings edited by Grotius. Certain of the volumes issued by Jansson. Elzevier, and Estienne are, in addition, valuable as specimens illustrating the history of printing. Restricted use: Rare Book Department.

PR —LA CASA DEL LIBRO, Library, Calle del Cristo 255, PO Box 2265, San Juan, 00903. David Jackson McWilliams, Dir
Holdings: Vols 5000 Uncat Mss Maps Slides
Notes: History and art of the book.

ON —UNIVERSITY OF WESTERN ONTARIO, Schoool of Library and Information Science, Library, London, N6G 1H1, Can. Victoria Ripley, Librn
Holdings: Vols (50,000)
Notes: Auction and antiquarian booksellers' catalogs from Canadian, American and European firms, some dating back to the 18th century. A special strength is 19th and early 20th century American booksellers' catalogs, recently augmented by a collection of pre-1920 catalogs formed by the late H O Teisberg. Current emphasis is on Canadian catalogs.

ON —NATIONAL LIBRARY OF CANADA, 395 Wellington St, Ottawa, K1A 0N4, Can. Andre Preibish, Dir
Holdings: Vols 10,000
Notes: The collection on History and Art of the Book consists of over 10,000 volumes. Areas of concentration are: early imprints, special editions, examples of private presses works, book industry and trade books illustrating the aesthetic and technical

PRINTING—HISTORY (cont.)

aspects of the field, collection of books illustrated by Bartlett.

ON —METROPOLITAN TORONTO LIBRARY, Fine Arts Dept, 789 Yonge St, Toronto, M4W 2G8, Can. Alan Suddon, Head
Holdings: Vols (42,000) Cat Pix Microforms
Notes: Extensive collection.

ON —VICTORIA UNIVERSITY, Library, Centre for Reformation and Renaissance Studies, 71 Queen's Park Crescent, Toronto, M5S 1K7, Can. Robert C Brandeis, Chief Librn; James Estes, Dir
Holdings: Vols (15,000) Cat Slides
Notes: The CRRS concentrates on the northern European countries and France; its chief strengths are Erasmus, 650 vols; early printed books, especially 16th century editions of Latin classics; bibliography and the history of printing. The Erasmus holdings are cataloged in W T McCready et al, "The Erasmus Collection in the Centre for Reformation and Renaissance Studies...A Catalogue"...*Reformation and Renaissance* 7 (1971), 32-76 and "A Supplementary List"...*Reformation and Renaissance*, 10 (1974), 116-119. Published catalogs. Humanist Editions of the Classics at CRRS, Toronto, 1979; Humanist Editions of Statutes and History at CRRS, Toronto, 1980; Bibles, Theological Treatises and Other Religious Literature 1491-1700 at CRRS, Toronto, 1981.

PQ —MCGILL UNIVERSITY, McLennan Library, Rare Books and Special Collections Dept, 3459 McTavish St, Montreal, H3A 1Y1, Can.
Holdings: Vols 13,159
Notes: 13,159 volumes and 47,604 items of printed ephemera. Incl early printing manuals, type specimens, books on the history of printing, particularly colour printing, paper, and examples of modern fine printing. Located in the William Colgate History of Printing Collection.

PRINTING—LATIN AMERICA

TX —UNIVERSITY OF TEXAS LIBRARIES, Nettie Lee Benson Latin American Collection, Sid Richardson Hall 1.109, Austin, 78712. Laura Gutierrez-Witt, Head Librn
Holdings: Vols (450,000) Cat Mss Maps Pix Phonorecords Filmstrips Microforms
See also entry under Latin America.

PRINTING—LITTLE PRESSES see Little Presses

PRINTING—SAMPLE BOOKS

MO —WASHINGTON UNIVERSITY, Libraries, Special Collections Dept, Campus Box 1061, St Louis, 63130.
Holdings: //
Notes: The Gast Banknote Company's records, 1884-1952. Incl general ledgers, sales ledgers, payroll books, equipment inventories, and selected sample books of printing work of this lithography and printing firm.

PRINTING—SPECIMENS

CA —CLAREMONT COLLEGES, Honnold Library, Ninth & Dartmouth, Claremont, 91711. Tania Rizzo, Special Collections Dept Head
Holdings: Vols (70,000) Cat VF
Notes: Books on typography, bibliography, and history of printing; incunabula; specimen books; fine press books, esp Kelmscott, Doves, Daniel, Mosher, Grabhorn, Nash, and Arion presses and many Southern California printers. A comprehensive collection of Zamorano Club publications and keepsakes, partial source for George E Fulleton, *The Zamorano Club: The First Half Century* (Los Angeles, 1978). Extensive files of ephemera. Fine bindings and fore-edge paintings. Samples of Oriental type and printing.

CA —UNIVERSITY OF CALIFORNIA, SAN DIEGO, Central University Library, Mandeville Dept of Special Collections, La Jolla, 92093. Lynda Corey Claassen, Head
Notes: The Press Collection comprises examples of fine printing from numerous private presses operating during the 19th and 20th centuries. Incl extensive holdings of the Golden Cockerel Press, the Cuala Press, the Hogarth Press, the Eucalyptus Press, and the Plantin Press.

CA —SAN DIEGO PUBLIC LIBRARY, Wangenheim Rm, 820 E St, San Diego, 92101. Eileen Boyle, Librn
Holdings: Vols (7500) Cat Pix
Notes: A collection on the history of the book and the development of printing.

CA —CALIFORNIA HISTORICAL SOCIETY, Schubert Hall Library, 2099 Pacific Ave, San Francisco, 94109. Bruce L Johnson, Library Dir
Holdings: Vols 4400 Cat Mss Pix Microforms
Notes: The Edward C Kemble Collections. Not collections of fine printing, but of the history of printing and publishing with emphasis on the Pacific Coast, although the full scope of the collection is not limited to this area. In addition to bibliographic tools and reference works, it contains type specimen books and several long runs of trade periodicals and house organs of San Francisco typefounders. The Taylor & Taylor Archives, a part of this collection, contain the working record of a major San Francisco printing firm. The *Kemble Occasional*, published three times a year from the Kemble Collections, presents scholarly articles on the history of printing. Edward C Kemble was the first historian of printing in California.

CA —SOLANO COUNTY LIBRARY, John F Kennedy Library, Donovan J McCune Collection, 505 Santa Clara St, Vallejo, 94590.
Holdings: Vols (3000) //
Notes: The Donovan J McCune Collection.

DC —LIBRARY OF CONGRESS, Rare Book & Special Collections Div, Washington, 20540. William Matheson, Chief
Holdings: Vols 1791 Cat Mss
Notes: The Frederic and Bertha Goudy Collection incl original type designs, mss, personal correspondence, type specimens, ephemeral material and a small section of typefounding equipment.
See also entry under Goudy, Frederick W.

DC —LIBRARY OF CONGRESS, Prints & Photographs Div, Washington, 20540.
Notes: Packaging for American tobacco products, 1840s-1880s. Approx 1000 tobacco labels, arranged by subject. Graphic Design Collection contains specimens of commercial and ornamental printing produced in Europe and America between 1875-1925.

IL —CHICAGO PUBLIC LIBRARY, Special Collections Div, Cultural Center, 78 E Washington St, Chicago, 60602. Laura Linard, Cur
Holdings: Vols (800) Cat
Budget: ($3000)
Notes: The Special Collections Division endeavors to collect all Chicago imprints produced before 1900, and all Chicago private press productions 1900-50. An imprint is defined as any printed item; thus we have a fine collection of pre-fire theatre broadsides and other ephemeral material. Private presses well-represented are Black Cat Press, Norman Press, Normandie House, Americana House, Covici-McGee and Lakeside Press. An exceptional collection of books and keepsakes designed by Norman Forgue. We actively purchase in this area. Outstanding items in the Chicago Imprints Inventory are described in *Treasures of the Chicago Public Library*, compiled by Thomas A Orlando and Marie Gecik, 1977,pp 93-120.

IL —NEWBERRY LIBRARY, John M Wing Foundation on the History of Printing, 60 W Walton St, Chicago, 60610. Diana Haskell, Cur of Modern Mss
Holdings: Vols (30,000) Cat Mss Pix
Budget: ($50,000)
Notes: Part of the John M Wing Foundation on the History of Printing, which collects western European and American printing from the invention to the present day. Includes some 2,000 incunabula, excellent collections of the major printers, modern illustrated books, etc. Especially strong in periodicals and illustrated books of the Victorian period, G K Hall has published *A Dictionary Catalogue of the John M. Wing Foundation and two Supplements*. Parts have been described in various articles, etc., notable J.M. Wells, *The Scholar Printers* and an article by Wells in *The Book Collector*.

IN —INDIANA UNIVERSITY, Lilly Library, Seventh St, Bloomington, 47405. William R Cagle, Librn
Holdings: Vols (40,000) Cat Mss Maps
Notes: The Lilly Library collection of incunables (books printed before January 1501) now numbers over 700 titles and is being added to on a selective basis, primarily in the major works of the humanities and sciences. Presses from the sixteenth century to the present are well represented, and to aid the user there is a separate printers and presses file which will lead to the major books of all periods from Gutenburg to Grabhorn. It is a selective rather than a comprehensive collection.

KS —UNIVERSITY OF KANSAS, Kenneth Spencer Research Library, Special Collections Dept, Lawrence, 66045. Alexandra Mason, Librn
Holdings: Vols 4400 Uncat Mss
Notes: Strongest in 18th and 19th century. Old English (Clubb Collection); 18th-century plays, poems, sermons. English Poetical Miscellanies collection. Tennyson, Yeats, Joyce. Literary periodicals and newspapers (18th century). Noncirculating.

ME —PORTLAND PUBLIC LIBRARY, 5 Monument Sq, Portland, 04101. Edward V Chenevert, Library Dir
Holdings: Vols 427 Cat
Notes: Originated as the Southworth Printing Company and was concerned with producing religious tracts. The scope of the press broadened under the later ownership (ca 1923) of Fred Anthoensen; it is still publishing.

MA —OLD STURBRIDGE VILLAGE, Research Library, Sturbridge, 01566. Theresa Rini Percy, Librn
Holdings: Vols (23,000) Cat Microforms
Notes: New England to 1850. Incl printers' manuals.

MA —AMERICAN ANTIQUARIAN SOCIETY LIBRARY, 185 Salisbury St, Worcester, 01609. Marcus A McCorison, Dir & Librn
Holdings: Cat Mss
Notes: US printing is remarkably represented by some 60,000 volumes, about 60 percent of the number known to have been printed before 1821. Incl the Isaiah Thomas Papers, his imprinted books, and his printing press. The Library is also especially strong in early English type-specimen books, and American examples to 1860.

MO —WASHINGTON UNIVERSITY, John M Olin Library, Campus Box 1061, St Louis, 63130.
Holdings: Vols (3700) Cat Mss
Notes: The Isador Mendle Memorial Collection contains representative examples from the 15th century to the present. Specializes in technical and aesthetic aspects of printing in the 19th and 20th centuries incl private presses. The Materials assembled support study and research on design, art history, economics, textual and analytical bibliography, and a variety of other topics. No photocopying.

NY —GRADUATE CENTER OF THE CITY UNIVERSITY OF NEW YORK, William H and Gwynne K Crouse Library for Publishing Arts, 33 W 42 St, New York, 10036. Alfred H Lane, Dir
Notes: Recently established and still growing, but intended to become the authoritative source of materials in the field, of particular value in research about the publishing industry. Open to staff members of publishing houses, students, scholars, authors, printers, and booksellers. Particularly useful for research on technical,

PRINTING—SPECIMENS (cont.)

financial, and historical matters. Much on
the history of individual houses, economics
of authorship; marketing and distribution of
books; etc. Primarily 20th century material
in hard form or microfilm, incl books,
pamphlets, reprints, translations,
dissertations, periodicals, indexing and
abstracting services, yearbooks, reports and
directories of organizations, publishers' and
antiquarian dealers' catalogs (particularly
those who deal in books about books),
periodicals, legislative materials, and
clippingspertaining to the book industry.
Sections of the library deal with printing,
incl typography, specimen books, history of
printing and printing techniques, book design
and small press and alternative publishing.

OR —AMERICAN PRIVATE PRESS
ASSOCIATION, 112 E Burnett St, Stayton,
97383. Martin M Horvat, Librn
Notes: The collection is divided into two
primary segments: the first is the traditional
one of Amateur Journalism, the second is
science fiction and fantasy oriented. The
collection was once at New York University
Libraries but moved in 1981.

PA —FREE LIBRARY OF PHILADELPHIA,
Rare Book Dept, Logan Sq, Philadelphia,
19103. Marie E Korey, Rare Book Librn
Holdings: Vols (1500) // Uncat
Notes: The Charles J Biddle Collection of
early 19th century American pamphlets.

PA —TEMPLE UNIVERSITY LIBRARIES,
Special Collections Dept, Rare Books & Mss
Section, Philadelphia, 19122. Thomas M
Whitehead, Cur
Holdings: Vols (5000) Mss Pix
Notes: The printing and graphic arts
collections stress the technological
developments within the printing industry
and the achievements in fine printing in the
19th and 20th centuries. Selected additions
are continually made of examples and
secondary works. Holdings include the
Library and archives of Richard W Ellis,
typographer, archives of Philadelphia
printers and photoengravers. Partially
cataloged.

PA —GRAPHIC ARTS TECHNICAL
FOUNDATION, Edward H Wadewitz
Memorial Library, 4615 Forbes Ave,
Pittsburgh, 15213. Janice L Lloyd, Librn
Notes: The Lee Augustine Collection.

RI —BROWN UNIVERSITY, John Hay
Library, 20 Prospect St, Providence, 02912.
Mary T Russo, Cur of Broadsides
Notes: Broadside specimens of fine printing
such as invitations, private press offerings,
specimen leaves and other examples of fine
typography and design appear. The
collection is strong in examples of modern
limited editions of poetry containing fine
graphics. Partial catalog.

TX —HARDIN-SIMMONS UNIVERSITY,
Richardson Library, Abilene, 79601. Joe F
Dahlstrom, Dir
Holdings: Vols (10,000) Cat Mss Maps Pix
Microforms
Notes: Special collection name is Richardson
Research Center, named in honor or Dr
Rupert N Richardson. Collect in the areas of
his own research interests, especially that
portion of the US that was one a part of
Mexico. Emphases on the history or
ranching, railroads, discovery and
exploration, Texas county histories, etc. Incl
350 items printed and/or designed by El
Paso printer Carl Hertzog; the Judge R C
Crane collection of Texana and a similar
collection of Louise Kelley's and the
Research Publication's Western Americana
collection (microfilm).

TX —UNIVERSITY OF HOUSTON, M D
Anderson Memorial Library, University
Park, Houston, 77004. David Farmer, Cur,
Special Collections; Jean Jackson, Assistant
Cur
Holdings: Vols 150 Cat
Notes: This relatively young collection is not
a collection of cornerstone books in printing
history, fine printing or presses, but rather a
collection of technical manuals, specimen
books, and literature on the processes of
bookmaking.

UT —BRIGHAM YOUNG UNIVERSITY,
Harold B Lee Library, Unversity Hill, Provo,
84602. Sterling Albrecht, Dir
Holdings: Vols 550 Cat

VA —UNIVERSITY OF VIRGINIA,
Alderman Library, Rare Book Dept,
Charlottesville, 22901. Julius P Barclay, Cur
Holdings: Vols (6500) // Mss
Notes: The Oscar Ogg Collection of Book
Arts covers calligraphy, letterforms,
typography, printing, and graphic arts.
Contains early writing books and printed
works, as well as modern manuals and other
works on printing, publishing, and promotion
through graphic arts. The Dept also has the
Edward L Stone Collection of Printing
Specimens, 3000 items. Contains materials
tracing the history of printing, inks, binding
styles and materials, types. Also the
Tompkins Collection (2000 vols), and the
Stevens Watts collection (900 vols).

WA —UNIVERSITY OF WASHINGTON
LIBRARIES, Suzzallo Library, Special
Collections Division, Rare Book Collection,
FM-25, Seattle, 98195. Gary Menges,
Coordinator for Special Collections
Notes: Printing history, including early
printed books and modern fine printing;
book arts, including papermaking, decorated
papers, bookbinding, book design, and
artist's books; American literature, 19th
century includes: Stephen Crane, Ralph
Waldo Emerson, Nathaniel Hawthorne,
Henry James, Henry Wadsworth Longfellow,
Herman Melville, Frank Norris, Harriet
Beecher Stowe and Walt Whitman and 20th
century includes: Theodore Roethke;
illustrated books, including emblem books,
historical children's illustration, books
illustrated with prints, and artist's books;
costume history; voyages and travels;
preservation of library materials.

ON —VICTORIA UNIVERSITY, Library, 71
Queen's Park Crescent, Toronto, M5S 1K7,
Can. Robert C Brandeis, Chief Librn
Holdings: Vols (400) // Cat
Notes: A major collection of George
Baxter's woodblock and metal plate prints
and book illustrations in watercolor and oil
color. Listed in *Star Collection of Baxter*
Prints. Toronto: Ryerson Press, 1946.

PQ —MCGILL UNIVERSITY, McLennan
Library, Rare Books and Special Collections
Dept, 3459 McTavish St, Montreal, H3A
1Y1, Can.
Notes: 47,604 items, old and new, mostly
contemporary, Canadian and non-Canadian,
organized by form. Housed within the
William Colgate History of Printing
Collection.

PRINTING—UKRAINE

IN —VOLHYNIAN BIBLIOGRAPHIC
CENTER, 307 N Overhill Drive,
Bloomington, 47401. Max Boyko, Mgr
Notes: Collect materials on Volhynia in
Western Ukraine. Compile and publish
bibliographies on the region.

PRINTING—UNIVERSITY PRESSES see
University Presses

PRINTING, PRACTICAL

CA —LOS ANGELES PUBLIC LIBRARY,
Literature and Philology Dept, 630 W Fifth
St, Los Angeles, 90071. Helene G
Mochedlover, Dept Librn
Holdings: Cat
Notes: Basic works on modern printing and
machinery, plus many rare items on the
history of printing and the book.

DC —LIBRARY OF CONGRESS, Prints &
Photographs Div, Washington, 20540.
Notes: Graphic Design Collection contains
specimens of commercial and ornamental
printing produced in Europe and America
between 1875-1925.

NY —GRADUATE CENTER OF THE CITY
UNIVERSITY OF NEW YORK, William H
and Gwynne K Crouse Library for
Publishing Arts, 33 W 42 St, New York,
10036. Alfred H Lane, Dir
Notes: Recently established and still

growing, but intended to become the
authoritative source of materials in the field,
of particular value in research about the
publishing industry. Open to staff members
of publishing houses, students, scholars,
authors, printers, and booksellers. Primarily
20th century materials, and particularly
useful for research on technical, financial,
and historical matters. Much on the history
of individual houses, economics of
authorship; marketing and distribution of
books; etc.

PA —GRAPHIC ARTS TECHNICAL
FOUNDATION, Edward H Wadewitz
Memorial Library, 4615 Forbes Ave,
Pittsburgh, 15213. Janice L Lloyd, Librn
Holdings: Vols (3500) Cat Slides Microforms
Notes: All printing proceses. Also, books
and periodicals on paper, ink photography,
optics, color theory, environmental control.
Approximately 250 periodical titles and 35,
000 classified abstracts of selected peiodical
articles. Approximately 15,000 slides within
the organization. Research reports from
foreign graphic arts research institutes.

TX —UNIVERSITY OF HOUSTON, M D
Anderson Memorial Library, University
Park, Houston, 77004. David Farmer, Cur,
Special Collections; Jean Jackson, Assistant
Cur
Holdings: Vols 150 Cat
Notes: This relatively young collection is not
a collection of cornerstone books in printing
history, fine printing or presses, but rather a
collection of technical manuals, specimen
books, and literature on the processes of
bookmaking.

PRINTING CLUBS see Book Clubs

PRINTING CRAFTS UNION

PA —PENNSYLVANIA STATE
UNIVERSITY, Fred Lewis Pattee Library,
University Park, 16802.
Holdings: Cat Mss
Notes: Archives of the now defunct Printing
Crafts Union.

PRINTING FOR THE BLIND see
Blind—Printing and Writing Systems

PRINTING INDUSTRY

CA —CALIFORNIA HISTORICAL
SOCIETY, Schubert Hall Library, 2099
Pacific Ave, San Francisco, 94109. Bruce L
Johnson, Library Dir
Holdings: Vols 4400 Cat Mss Pix
Microforms
Notes: The Edward C Kemble Collections.
Not collections of fine printing, but of the
history of printing and publishing with
emphasis on the Pacific Coast, although the
full scope of the collection is not limited to
this area. In addition to bibliographic tools
and reference works, it contains type
specimen books and several long runs of
trade periodicals and house organs of San
Francisco typefounders. The Taylor &
Taylor Archives, a part of this collection,
contain the working record of a major San
Francisco printing firm. The *Kemble
Occasional*, published three times a year
from the Kemble Collections, presents
scholarly articles on the history of printing.
Edward C Kemble was the first historian of
printing in California.

NY —GRADUATE CENTER OF THE CITY
UNIVERSITY OF NEW YORK, William H
and Gwynne K Crouse Library for
Publishing Arts, 33 W 42 St, New York,
10036. Alfred H Lane, Dir
Notes: Recently established and still
growing, but intended to become the
authoritative source of materials in the field,
of particular value in research about the
publishing industry. Open to staff members
of publishing houses, students, scholars,
authors, printers, and booksellers. Primarily
20th century materials, and particularly
useful for research on technical, financial,
and historical matters. Much on the history
of individual houses, economics of
authorship; marketing and distribution of
books; etc.

PRINTING INDUSTRY (cont.)

NY —ROCHESTER INSTITUTE OF
TECHNOLOGY, Technical & Education
Center of the Graphic Arts, Graphic Arts
Information Service, One Lomb Memorial
Dr, Rochester, 14623. Susan Clark,
Technical Librn

PA —PENNSYLVANIA STATE
UNIVERSITY, Fred Lewis Pattee Library,
University Park, 16802.
Holdings: Cat Mss
Notes: Archives of the now defunct Printing
Crafts Union.

TX —UNIVERSITY OF HOUSTON, M D
Anderson Memorial Library, University
Park, Houston, 77004. David Farmer, Cur,
Special Collections; Jean Jackson, Assistant
Cur
Holdings: Vols 150 Cat
Notes: This relatively young collection is not
a collection of cornerstone books in printing
history, fine printing or presses, but rather a
collection of technical manuals, specimen
books, and literature on the processes of
bookmaking.

PRINTING TRADE see Printing,
Practical; Printing Industry

PRINTMAKING see
Prints—Techniques

PRINTS—COLLECTIONS

†CA —UNIVERSITY OF SAN FRANCISCO,
Richard A Gleeson Library, The Countess
Bernardine Murphy Donohue Rare Book
Room, San Francisco, 94117. D Steven
Corey, Special Collections Librn
Notes: Some highly specialized materials.

CA —HUNTINGTON LIBRARY, Art Gallery
& Botanical Gardens, 1151 Oxford Rd, San
Marino, 91108. Robert L Middlekauff, Dir;
Daniel H Woodward, Librn
Notes: Some 1500 scarce books on English
and American sports from the Renaissance
to modern times. Many English and
American sporting prints.

CA —STANFORD UNIVERSITY
LIBRARIES, Cecil H Green Library,
Stanford, 94305. Michael T Ryan, Cur
Holdings: Cat Pix
Notes: The Dr and Mrs Leon Kolb Portrait
Collection. Over 1600 portraits (engravings,
etchings, mezzotints, lithographs) of rulers,
statesmen, authors, scholars and other
famous personages from ancient times to the
19th century. A catalog of the collection,
compiled by Dr Susan Lenkey, was
published in 1972.

CA —SOLANO COUNTY LIBRARY, John F
Kennedy Library, Donovan J McCune
Collection, 505 Santa Clara St, Vallejo,
94590.
Holdings: Cat
Notes: The Donovan J McCune Collection
(3000) vols //. Incl 32 folios; prints.

CT —TRINITY COLLEGE LIBRARY,
Watkinson Library, 300 Summit St,
Hartford, 06106. Jeffrey Kaimowitz, Cur
Holdings: // Uncat
Notes: Incl 40 scrapbooks, mostly of early
German engravers.

CT —YALE UNIVERSITY, Medical Historical
Library, 333 Cedar St, New Haven, 06510.
Ferenc A Gyorgyey, Librn
Holdings: Cat Pix
Notes: The Clements C Fry Collection of
Medical Prints and Drawings. About 2000
items. Also, about 3000 bookplates of
physicians, many of medical interest.

CT —YALE UNIVERSITY, Sterling Memorial
Library, Arts of the Book Collection, New
Haven, 06520. Gay Walker, Cur
Notes: 8000 posters, broadsides and
examples of all printmaking methods.

DC —HOWARD UNIVERSITY, Moorland-
Spingarn Research Center, 500 Howard
Place NW, Washington, 20059. Clifford L
Muse, Jr, Acting Dir
Holdings: Vols (106,086) Cat Mss Maps Pix
Slides Phonorecords Audiotapes 16mm
Films Filmstrips Microforms
Budget: $854,753
Notes: *The Glenn Carrington Collection: A*

Guide to the Books, Manuscripts, Music and
Recordings (DC MSRC, 1977). *Dictionary
Catalog of the Jesse E Moorland Collection
of Negro Life and History,* 9 vols and
Supplement, 3 vols (Boston: G K Hall, 1970,
1977). *Dictionary Catalog of the Arthur
Spingarn Collection of Negro Authors,* 2
vols (Boston: G K Hall, 1970). Guide to
Processed Collections in the Manuscript
Division of the Moorland-Spingarn Research
Center (DC, MSRC, 1983). The Moorland-
Spingran Research Center is recognized as
one of the largest and most comprehensive
repositories in the world for the collection,
preservation and dissemination of historical
materials documenting from antiquity to the
present the history and culture of Black
people in Africa, Europe, the Caribbean and
the US. Since 1973, the Research Center has
greatly expanded its facilitiesand resources
and currently provides research services in
all aspects of library and archival research,
including manuscripts, oral history, music,
prints and photographs and general library
materials. The Research Center also
maintains professional zerographic,
micrographic, photographic and similar
reproduction laboratories.

DC —LIBRARY OF CONGRESS, Prints &
Photographs Div, Washington, 20540.
Holdings: Cat Pix
Notes: Prints & Photographs. Artists prints
from the 15th through the 20th century
(approx 70,000) in the J & E R Pennell, the
Gardiner Greene Hubbard & the George
Lothrop Bradley collections. Historical prints
of the 18th and 19th centuries (approx 75,
000 engravings & lithographs by Currier and
Ives and other printmakers of views,
portraits, battles, theater posters,
advertisements, etc). Cabinet of American
Illustration (original drawings by the Civil
War artists, Alfred R Waud and Edwin
Forbes, and work produced during the 1890s
through the 1920s); Archives of American
Graphic Humor (genre and political
cartoons-original lithographs and drawings
by McCutcheon, Nast, Kirby, etc).
Photograph collections: Brady-Handy and
Mathew B Brady (Civil War, portraits and
events, 1898-1916), Detroit Photographic
Company (views, human interest pictures,
1898-1914), Herbert E French(photographs
of the Washington, DC scene, 1919-1932),
American Red Cross (1900 through World
War I), Erwin E Smith (cowboys and the
western range), Farm Security
Administration-Office of War Information
(survey of America, 1935-1943), Historic
American Buildings Survey (measured
drawings, photographs, data pages), Archive
of Hispanic Culture (Latin American art and
architecture), Look Magazine collection
(American life and culture, 1937-1971), Toni
Frissell collection (society and fashion),
Rizzuto collection (New York City, ca 1950-
1966), Matson collection (Palestine and the
middle east, 1890s to 1946). Master
Photographs collection (items of particular
esthetic or historical importance). Extensive
portrait and geographic files. Poster
collection: World War I and II, Art
Nouveau, Contemporary poster art. Total:
Over 10,000,000 items.

†DC —SMITHSONIAN INSTITUTION
LIBRARIES, Washington, 20560.
Notes: The published guide to the numerous
Smithsonian Institution museums and
deposits is one of the most helpful and
successfully (and well-indexed)
complementary vols that can be used with
this edition of *Subject Collections.* Refer to
Lynda Corey Claassen's *Finder's Guide to
Prints and Drawings in the Smithsonian
Institution,* 210 pp, (Washington:
Smithsonian Institution Press, 1981), Los
Angeles. An index of artists lists about 10,
000 names represented in the Smithsonian's
collections in the Archives of American Art,
Cooper-Hewitt Museum, Freer Gallery of
Art, Hirshhorn Museum and Sculpture
Garden, Museum of African Art, National
Air and Space Museum, National Museum
of American Art, National Museum of
American History, National Museum of
Natural History and National Museum of

Man, National Portrait Gallery, Smithsonian
Institution Archives, andSmithsonian
Institution Libraries, and their subject
departments, all of which are described.

IL —CHICAGO HISTORICAL SOCIETY,
Library, Graphics Collection, Clark St at
North Ave, Chicago, 60614. Larry A
Viskochil, Cur
Notes: About 50,000 pieces. Emphasis on
Chicago, Illinois, and the Midwest, but
includes many views of other cities and
localities and substantial holdings concerning
important leaders and events in the history
of the US.

IL —DE PAUL UNIVERSITY, Library, 2323
N Seminary, Chicago, 60614. Kathryn De
Graff, Special Collections Librn
Holdings: Vols (598) Uncat Pix
Budget: $1500
Notes: The Jack Davidson and Nathan
Schwartz Collection. Numerous editions of
Dickens' works in the original publisher
parts, first complete editions, first American
editions and special editions. Also about 300
books about Dickens incl *The Dickension,*
500 prints, posters and photographs, an
interesting collection of memorabilia such as
figurines, etc. The extra-illustrated volumes,
with over 7000 illustrations, were prepared
by Mr Bradford, the original owner of the
collection, and contain the conceptions of
scenes and characters in Dicken's novels by
various illustrators.

IL —MORTON ARBORETUM, Sterling
Morton Library, Lisle, 60532. Ian MacPhail,
Librn
Holdings: Vols (22,000)
Notes: Emphasis is on Woody plants. Print
collection of 3000 pieces; 2000 botanical and
horticultural rare books; Linnaeana. The Jens
Jensen Archive of letters, photographs,
blueprints, landscape plans.

IN —INDIANA UNIVERSITY, Lilly Library,
Seventh St, Bloomington, 47405. William R
Cagle, Librn
Holdings: // Cat
Notes: Portraits of literary figures from the J
K Lilly collection; War of 1812; and Lincoln.
Also thousands in the Star Collection of
American Sheet Music.

IN —INDIANA UNIVERSITY, Institute for
Sex Research Library, 416 Morrison Hall,
Bloomington, 47401. Douglas Freeman,
Collections and Services Librn; Joan Brewer,
Information Services Librn
Holdings: Vols (62,000) Cat Mss Pix
Microforms
See also entry under Sex.

IN —BUTLER UNIVERSITY, Irwin Library,
Hugh Thomas Miller Rare Book Room,
4600 Sunset Ave, Indianapolis, 46208.
Gisela Terrell, Rare Books Librn
Holdings: Uncat
Notes: Zoological print colection tracing the
history and development of zoological
illustration from the 15th through the mid-
19th centuries.

MD —BALTIMORE MUSEUM OF ART
LIBRARY, Art Museum Dr, Baltimore,
21218. Anita Gilden, Librn
Holdings: Vols (40,000) Cat
Notes: General reference sources with
emphasis on 19th and 20th century art and
American decorative art. Incl prints and
drawings. Photocopying.

MD —PEALE MUSEUM, Municipal Museum
of Baltimore, 225 Holiday St, Baltimore,
21202. Nancy Brennan, Dir; Richard Flint,
Cur Prints and Photos
Holdings: Cat Maps
Notes: Pictorial history of Baltimore.
Collection of 100,000 items incl: T E
Hambleton Collection of Historical Prints; A
Aubrey Bodine Photographic Collection;
John Dubas Collection of Photographs.
Many original photographic negatives.

MD —UNIVERSITY OF MARYLAND,
BALTIMORE, Health Sciences Library, 111
S Greene St, Baltimore, 21201. Cyril C H
Feng, Dir
Holdings: Vols (1000) Cat Mss Pix VF
Notes: The Clarence J Grieves Dental
Historical Collection is one of the strongest
collections of its kind in the United States. It
includes some of the most significant early
dental imprints; early records of the

PRINTS—COLLECTIONS (cont.)

Maryland State Dental Association; and an excellent collection of prints on early dentistry and St Apollonia.

MD —NATIONAL LIBRARY OF MEDICINE, 8600 Rockville Pike, Bethesda, 20209. Harold M Schoolinam, Actg Dir
Holdings: Vols (3,150,000) Cat Mss Audiotapes Videotapes 16mm Films Filmstrips Microforms
Budget: ($46,400)
Notes: The world's largest medical library. Materials are collected exhaustively in some 40 biomedical areas and, to a lesser degree, in related subject areas such as general chemistry, physics, zoology, botany, and instrumentation. Holdings include 82,000 monographic volumes, pre-1871; 438,000 monographic volumes, 1871-present; 714,000 bound serial volumes; 281,000 theses; 172,000 pamphlets; 1,207,000 manuscripts; 156,000 microforms; 12,000 audiovisuals; and 75,000 prints and photographs. Pre-1871 material is in a separate historical collection. Approximately 24,000 serial titles are currenlty received.

MD —HOOD COLLEGE, Joseph Henry Apple Library, Rosemont Ave, Frederick, 21701.
Notes: The Samuel J Cole Hogarth Print Collection (116 prints).

MA —ROBBINS LIBRARY, 700 Massachusetts Ave, Arlington, 02174. Peter L Fenton, Dir
Holdings: Cat Pix
Notes: 150,000 graphic works in all media emphasizing portrait prints from the 15th century to the present day.

MA —BOSTON PUBLIC LIBRARY, Print Collection, Dartmouth St at Copley Sq, Boston, 02117. Sinclair H Hitchings, Keeper of Prints
Holdings: Cat
Notes: The collection of about 70,000 prints and 4500 drawings as well as a few oil paintings. There is a small collection of Old Master prints and drawings and a large and growing collection of French, British, and American prints (as well as some drawings) especially of the 19th century, also 18th and 20th century. Some German and Spanish artists are also represented. An overview of the entire collection appears in *Artist's Proof*, Vol XI. Arrangements can be made for professional photocopying.

MA —FRANCIS A COUNTWAY LIBRARY OF MEDICINE, Boston Medical Library/ Harvard Medical Library, 10 Shattuck St, Boston, 02115. C Robin LeSueur, Librn; Richard J Wolfe, Cur, Rare Books & Manuscripts
Holdings: Vols (50,000) Cat Mss Maps Pix Microforms
Notes: Combines resources of the Harvard Medical School and the Boston Medical Library. Strong in serials and medical history in all fields of medicine, incl incunabula, non-medical books by doctors, travel books by doctors. 500,000 medical dissertations and theses. Special strength in all medical subjects listed in this volume.

MA —HARVARD UNIVERSITY, Baker Library of the Graduate School of Business Administration, Kress Library of Business and Economics, Soldiers Field, Boston, 02163. Ruth E Rogers, Cur
Holdings: Cat
Notes: Bleichroder print collection of over 1000 engravings, etchings, and lithographs from the 15th-19th centuries, relating to money, banking, and financial history.

MA —MASSACHUSETTS HORTICULTURAL SOCIETY, 300 Massachusetts Ave, Boston, 02115. Becky Ellis, Librn
Holdings: Vols (37,000)
Notes: Garden history, pomology, flora, landscape design. Print collection of many centuries; nursery catalogues from the mid-18th century. In storage, remodeling, will be available in about a year. Open to the public.

MA —SOCIETY FOR THE PRESERVATION OF NEW ENGLAND ANTIQUITIES, Library, 141 Cambridge St, Boston, 02114.

Ellie Reichlin, Librn & Cur of Photographic Collections
Holdings: Vols (3000) Cat Pix Microforms
Budget: ($75,000)
Notes: Photograph collections, all media (incl daguerreotypes, ambrotypes, etc, stereographic views, carte de visite) depicting New England buildings; interiors; street and town views; occupations; pastimes; transport and personalities. Covers 1840s-1930s, with some more recent additons. Amateur and professional photographers represented. Cataloged in part, otherwise arranged by localities, subject, personal name. Special collections incl: marine photographs by N L Stebbins and Henry Peabody (1880s-1920s); Boston and Albany railroad photographic archive, early 1900s; Quabbin Valley views; historic American Buildings Survey photographs (17th to early 19th century architecture) by Arthur Haskell; Baldwin Coolidge collection, and many others. Size: 500,000 prints, ca 75,000 negatives (glass plates and copy negs). These are cataloged. Some special indexes incllandscape design (arbors, conservatories, flower beds, bandstands etc); photographers represented; architects represented (partial), and pending, interiors (specific features of); occupations.

MA —SOCIETY FOR THE PRESERVATION OF NEW ENGLAND ANTIQUITIES, Library, 141 Cambridge St, Boston, 02114. Ellie Reichlin, Librn & Cur of Photographic Collections
Notes: Prints (lithographs, wood engravings) of town views provide visual documentation of architecture from the 1830s-1860s (1000 pieces). Original artworks (1870s-1920s) emphasize historic structures, especially in Massachusetts (500 pieces).

MA —MASSACHUSETTS INSTITUTE OF TECHNOLOGY MUSEUM, Hart Nautical Collections, 77 Massachusetts Ave, Rm 5-329, Cambridge, 02139. John W Waterhouse, Cur
Holdings: Vols (800) Cat Maps Pix
Notes: Ship and marine engineering development. Museum is under jurisdiction of MIT's Dept of Ocean Engineering. Collection incl various collections of prints and photographs of ships and yachts; working drawings from the Herreshoff Manufacturing Co, 1870-1945, and of the George Lawley and Son Corp; working drawings and models from the Munro, Owen, and Paine Collections.

MA —MELROSE PUBLIC LIBRARY, 69 W Emerson St, Melrose, 02176. Diane E Shaw, Art Librn
Holdings: Vols (8500) Cat Pix Slides Phonorecords
Budget: ($6900)
Notes: Framed and unframed art reproductions (110), slides (2773), periodicals, clippings, sound recordings (3000). Incl the Mary Livermore Collection of Sacred Art, the Odlin Collection, and the Pierre Gendrot Collection of Fine Art.

MA —MERRIMACK VALLEY TEXTILE MUSEUM, Library, 800 Massachusetts Ave, North Andover, 01845. Clare Sheridan, Librn; Laurence Gross, Cur
Notes: *Checklist of Prints, Drawings and Painting in the Merrimack Valley Textile Museum*, Helena E Wright, 1972; *Checklist of Finished Textiles*, Katherine R Koob, 1980; *New City on the Merrimack: Prints of Lawrence 1845-1876*, Helena Wright, 1974; *Homespun to Factory Made: Wollen Textiles in America 1776-1876* (exhibit catalog) 1978; *Textile Technology Prints: A Checklist of Prints, Drawings and Paintings in the Merrimack Valley Textile Museum*, Helena E Wright, 1980; *All Sorts of Good Sufficient Cloth: Linen-making in New England, 1640-1860*, (exhibit catalogue) 1980; *The Merrimack Valley Textile Museum: A Guide to the Manuscript Collections* Helena E Wright, Garland Press 1983.

MA —AMERICAN ANTIQUARIAN SOCIETY LIBRARY, 185 Salisbury St, Worcester, 01609. Marcus A McCorison, Dii & Librn
Holdings: Cat Maps Pix
Notes: Over 6000 American prints, arranged by lithographer. Incl political caricatures and cartoons, maps, sheet music. Also advertising cards, Valentines, etc.

MI —UNIVERSITY OF MICHIGAN, Engineering-Transportation Library, 312 Undergraduate Library, Ann Arbor, 48109. Sharon A Balius, Assoc Librn
Holdings: Pix
Budget:
Notes: The print files cover all areas of transportation. The collection contains 12,000 pieces incl 18th century engravings, lithographs, photographs, reproductions, and originals. Two separate collections of note are the 250 Currier and Ives prints of transportation topics and 100 original drawings by Otto Kuhler, designer of the first streamlined trains.

MI —UNIVERSITY OF MICHIGAN, William L Clements Library, Ann Arbor, 48109. John C Dann, Dir

Notes: The William L. Clements Library of Americana is a non-circulating rare book library of original source material, printed and manuscript, dealing with America, from the discovery period into the late nineteenth century. The collection includes approximately 55,000 books and pamphlets, 550 linear feet of manuscripts, 4,100 volumes of newspapers, 36,000 maps, 40,000 pieces of sheet music, and 1,000 prints. The collection is strongest for the period of the American Revolution, and includes the papers of Thomas Gage, Sir Henry Clinton, and the Earl of Shelburne. Other areas of strength include antislavery, cartography and geography, discovery and exploration, American Indians, The Civil War, tune-books, sermons and orations, and the War of 1812. There are selective research collections dealing with Christopher Columbus, Thomas Paine, Benjamin Franklin, George Washington, Thomas Jefferson, and the Federalist Papers. Publications describing the collections of the library are: Author/Title catalog of Americana 1493-1860 in the William L. Clements Library... 7 volumes, Boston, G. K. Hall, 1970; Guide to the manuscript collections of the William L. Clements Library, by Arlene P. Shy 3d edition, Boston, G. K. Hall, 1978; Guide to the manuscript maps in the William L. Clements Library, compiled by Christian Burn, Ann Arbor, U. of Michigan, 1959; and Research catalog of maps of America, to 1860 in the William L. Clements Library..., edited by Douglas W. Marshall, 4 volumes, Boston, G. K. Hall, 1972.

MI —EDISON INSTITUTE, Greenfield Village and Henry Ford Museum, Archives & Research Library, PO Box 1970, Dearborn, 48121. Steve Hamp, Dir; Joan W Gartland, Librn
Holdings: Vols 400,000 Cat Mss Maps Microforms
Notes: 400,000 vols incl pamphlets. The Archives and research library supports the program of Greenfield Village and the Henry Ford Museum. Special collections incl: automotive literature, ephemera, McGuffey Readers, trade catalogs, photographs and graphics.

MI —KALAMAZOO INSTITUTE OF ARTS LIBRARY, 314 S Park St, Kalamazoo, 49006. Marianne Cavanaugh, Librn
Holdings: Vols (5000) Cat Slides
Budget: $2000
Notes: Incl (8000) slides. Vertical file on

PRINTS—COLLECTIONS (cont.)

artists. Collection is supplemented by 55 current subscriptions to periodicals in visual art. Collection supports permanent collection in prints, paintings, photography, and sculpture.

MN —MINNEAPOLIS COLLEGE OF ART & DESIGN, Library, 200 E 25 St, Minneapolis, 55404. Richard Kronstedt, Head Librn

MN —MAYO MEDICAL LIBRARY, History of Medicine Collection, Rochester, 55905. Nancy R Hensel, Librn
Holdings: Pix
Notes: The Comfort Collection of caricatures of physicians and scientists from *Vanity Fair.*
Description: Mann, Ruth J: "The unheroic representation of heroes." *Mayo Clin Proc.* 46:197-199, Mar 1971.

MO —SAINT LOUIS ART MUSEUM, Richardson Memorial Library, Saint Louis, 63110. Ann B Abid, Librn
Holdings: Vols (30,000) Cat Pix Slides Microforms
Notes: Art history, incl decorative arts, catalogs, exhibitions, etc.

MO —SAINT LOUIS PUBLIC LIBRARY, Art Dept, 1301 Olive St, Saint Louis, 63103. Martha Hilligoss, Librn
Holdings: Vols 44,000 Cat Pix Slides
Notes: Plus more than 1400 framed prints, 250 pieces of sculpture, 29,000 slides, and 470,000 pictures.

NJ —NEWARK PUBLIC LIBRARY, Art & Music Dept, 5 Washington St, Newark, 07101. William J Dane, Supv
Holdings: Mss Maps Pix Slides
Notes: 1,000,000 pictures with supporting collections of postcards, 2000 portfolios of plates of design, fine and circulating print collections (incl Japanese), 1400 illustrated books, 4000 posters. The classification scheme and headings used are listed in *The Picture Collection Subject Headings* (Shoe String Press, 1968).

NJ —PRINCETON UNIVERSITY, Library, Graphic Arts Collection, Princeton, 08540. Dale Roylance, Cur
Notes: Large collection of prints and drawings.

NY —BARNARD A & MORRIS N YOUNG LIBRARY OF EARLY AMERICAN POPULAR MUSIC, 270 Riverside Dr, New York, 10025. Morris N Young, Cur
Holdings: Cat Mss Pix Phonorecords Audiotapes Microforms
Notes: 48,000 items of American popular music, mostly 1790-1910. Incl books, serials, sheet music, mostly 1790-1910. Incl books, serials, sheet music business memorabilia, and correspondence.

NY —COLUMBIA UNIVERSITY LIBRARIES, Rare Book & Manuscript Library, 801 Butler Library, 535 W 114 St, New York, 10027. Kenneth A Lohf, Librn
Holdings: Pix
Notes: William Barclay Parsons Collection of Railroad Prints, relating primarily to American and English railroads. 235 items. Restricted use.

NY —METROPOLITAN MUSEUM OF ART, Dept of Prints & Photographs, 82 St & Fifth Ave, New York, 10028. Colta Ives, Cur
Holdings: Vols (10,000)
Notes: Contained in a collection of 500,000 prints from 15th to 20th century. Approx 10,000 illustrated books; European and American. No photocopying.

NY —NEW YORK HISTORICAL SOCIETY, Library, 170 Central Park W, New York, 10024. James Gregory, Librn
Holdings: Mss
Notes: Incl original mss, illustrative materials, etc.

NY —NEW YORK PUBLIC LIBRARY, Performing Arts Research Center, Billy Rose Theatre Collection, 111 Amsterdam Ave, New York, 10023. Dorothy L Swerdlove, Cur
Holdings: Cat
See also entry under Theatre - History.

NY —NEW YORK PUBLIC LIBRARY, Performing Arts Research Center, Dance Collection, 111 Amsterdam Ave, New York,

10023. Genevieve Oswald, Cur
Notes: Approximately 6000 prints, i e lithographs, engravings, woodcuts, and etchings record scenes of both social and theatrical dance, with a heavy concentration in the Romantic period of the 19th century. The Cia Fornaroli Collection includes several hundred Italian prints, many by Alessandro Sanquirico, fully documenting the visual aspects of productions at La Scala, Milan, in the early 19th century. Well-represented in the collection are depictions of 19th century dancers such as Carlotta Grisi, Fanny Cerrito, Fanny Elssler, Lucile Grahn, Marie Taglioni, and members of the Vestris family. Also included are a significant number of 15th-20th century depictions of the Dance of Death. Descriptions of individual prints listed in *Dictionary Catalog of the Dance Collection,* published by G K Hall, Boston, 1974, in 10 vols. Annualsupplements: *Bibliographic Guide to Dance,* also published by G K Hall, 1975-.

NY —NEW YORK PUBLIC LIBRARY, Art, Prints, and Photographs Div, Fifth Ave & 42 St, New York, 10018. Donald Anderle, Chief
Holdings: Vols (150,000) Cat Mss Pix Microforms
Notes: History and design in the fine and applied arts. Architecture, painting, drawing, sculpture, costume, furniture, advertising art, prints, photography, crafts, and jewelry are among the subjects covered from ancient times to the present. See: New York Public Library *Dictionary Catalog of the Art and Architecture Division* (Boston, G K Hall, 1975), 30 vols. Holdings after that time are incl in the *Dictionary Catalog of the Research Libraries.* African Art and Afro-American Art are collected by the Schomburg Center for Research in Black Culture.

NY —NEW YORK PUBLIC LIBRARY, Print Collection, Fifth Ave & 42 St, New York, 10018. Robert Rainwater, Keeper
Holdings: Vols 12,000 Cat
Notes: Incl 175,000 prints and drawings. A representative collection of fine prints from the 15th century to the present, cataloged by artist, with strong holdings in 19th century French prints and Americana. See Stokes-Haskell, *American Historical Prints, Etc New York* (New York Public Library, 1933) and Weitenkampf, Frank, *The Eno Collection of New York City Views* (New York Public Library, 1925). See *Dictionary Catalog of the Prints Division* (Boston: G K Hall, 1975), 5 vols.

NY —STATE UNIVERSITY OF NEW YORK, COLLEGE AT PLATTSBURGH, Feinberg Library, Special Collections, 153 Hawkins Hall, Plattsburgh, 12901. Joseph G Swinyer, Librn
Holdings: Vols (100) Cat
See also entry under New York (State) - History

NC —DUKE UNIVERSITY, William R Perkins Library, Durham, 27706. Elvin E Strowd, University Librn
Notes: The Thomas collection relating to China and the Far East contains more than 1500 items. It is a comprehensive body of books, newspapers, prints and other materials dealing with many phases of the culture of the Orient. Additions are ongoing.

OH —CINCINNATI ART MUSEUM, Library, Eden Park, Cincinnati, 45202. Patrician P Rutledge, Librn
Holdings: Vols (45,850) Cat Mss Microforms
Notes: Art library containing all subjects on art--history, graphic arts, advertising art, etc; special strength in prints, ie engravings, etc. Near Eastern art and decorative arts are also strong. At least 90,000 art exhibition catalogs. Emphasis on artists of Cincinnati and vicinity in vertical file material.

OH —PUBLIC LIBRARY OF CINCINNATI & HAMILTON COUNTY, Art & Music Dept, 800 Vine St, Cincinnati, 45202. R Jayne Craven, Head
Holdings: Vols (122,185) Cat Pix
Budget: ($56,100)
Notes: Special collections: Eda Kuhn Loeb, "Artist and the Book, 1875-Date" (now

shelved in Rare Book Room); music librettos (2345); exhibition catalogs (5474); large prints and posters (5051); Cincinnati artists vertical files; picture collection (673,906 clippings).

OR —LIBRARY ASSOCIATION OF PORTLAND, Art & Music Dept, 801 S W Tenth Ave, Portland, 97205. Barbara K Padden, Librn
Holdings: Vols Cat Pix Slides Phonorecords
Notes: Art book titles: 21,325; music book titles (incl dance books): 10,800; sheet music titles: 19,550; slides on art subjects: about 12,000; phonorecord albums: 27,000; picture clippings: about 2 million; color reproductions of old and modern masters: about 640.

PA —FREE LIBRARY OF PHILADELPHIA, Rare Book Dept, Logan Sq, Philadelphia, 19103. Marie E Korey, Rare Book Librn
Holdings: Uncat Pix
Notes: The Evan Randolph Collection of 450 Philadelphia views: engravings, etching and lithographs.

PA —HISTORICAL SOCIETY OF PENNSYLVANIA, Library, 1300 Locust St, Philadelphia, 19107. David Fraser, Librn
Holdings: lVols (230,000) Mss Maps Pix Microforms
Notes: Incl over 14,000,000 ms pieces. The Library Company of Philadelphia mss are on deposit with the Historical Society of Pennsylvania. Many of the Society's rare books are on deposit with the Library Company. The Society maintains the collections of the Genealogical Society of Pennsylvania, incl some 20,000 church, and civil records.

†PA —LIBRARY COMPANY OF PHILADELPHIA, 1314 Locust St, Philadelphia, 19107. Edwin Wolf II, Librn
Holdings: Vols (450,000)

PA —UNIVERSITY OF PITTSBURGH, Hillman Library, Pittsburgh, 15260.
Holdings: Vols (10,000)
Notes: The entire contents of the oldest used book shop in Pittsburgh, the John C Daub Book Store. The collection deals mainly in the areas of military history; works dealing with the Civil War, the World Wars and other military topics; and local history; county histories, city, state or regional histories. Also incl are military works containing colored plates; a large group of Americana; and many framed, colored prints on military subjects.

PA —EASTERN COLLEGE, Frank Warner Memorial Library, Saint Davids, 19087. James L Sauer, Librn
Holdings: Uncat Mss Pix
Notes: The Harry C Goebel Collection. Incl Bruce Rogers printings (over 460); press books (about 350); oriental art (over 250); bookplates (with a separate collection of an almost complete set of bookplates designed by Edwin Davis French); Christmas Books; art and grapic arts (incl the French Graphic Arts Collection of Adolph DeMilly); first editions of Christopher Morley; Print Collection (1315 prints); Oriental art realia and artifacts.

PA —PENNSYLVANIA STATE UNIVERSITY, Arts Library, 405 E Pattee Library, University Park, 18602. Jean Smith, Arts and Architecture Librn
Holdings: 500 Prints
Notes: Collection includes mainly American artists of the mid-20th century.

RI —BROWN UNIVERSITY, John Carter Brown Library, Providence, 02912. Norman Fiering, Librn; Everett C Wilkie Jr, Bibliographer; Susan Danforth, Cur Maps & Prints
Holdings: Vols 1000
Notes: Separately published sheet engravings; most of these are European depictions of events in the New World, particularly British American colonies.
See also entry under Engravings.

RI —RHODE ISLAND SCHOOL OF DESIGN, Library, Two College St, Providence, 02903. James A Findlay, Dir
Holdings: Vols (70,000) Cat Pix Slides Phonorecords
Budget: ($50,000)
Notes: All fields of art incl 92,000 slides; 30,

PRINTS—COLLECTIONS (cont.)

000 mounted photographs; 1100 posters and color reproductions; and 280,000 clippings.

TN —THE BOTANICAL GARDENS AND FINE ARTS CENTER, Fine Arts Library, Forrest Park Drive, Nashville, 37205. Muriel H Connell, Librn
Holdings: Vols (3500) Cat Pix Slides
Budget: $2500

TX —UNIVERSITY OF TEXAS LIBRARIES, Fine Arts Library, PO Box P, Austin, 78712. Carole L Cable, Fine Arts Librn
Holdings: Vols (55,000) Cat Pix
Notes: Emphasis is on historical as well as practical aspects.

TX —AMON CARTER MUSEUM, 3501 Camp Bowie Blvd, PO Box 2365, Fort Worth, 76113. Jan K Muhlert, Dir; Marni Sandweiss, Cur of Photographs
Holdings: Cat Pix
Notes: Emphasis of American prints dating from the sixteenth century through the twentieth century. Includes book illustrations, documentary records of important scientific explorations, renderings of landscape and city views, and fine art prints produced by artists seeking to exploit the expressive qualities inherent in the materials and techniques of the medium. Large collections of Audubon, Currier and Ives, nineteenth century city views, and early American modern fine art prints.

WI —CIRCUS WORLD MUSEUM LIBRARY, 415 Lynn St, Baraboo, 53913. Robert L Parkinson, Research Center Dir
Holdings: Vols (1800) Cat Mss Pix Slides Phonorecords 16mm Films
Notes: Circus and "Wild West" shows. Owned by State Historical Society of Wisconsin. Incl 1800 books on circus subject; 400 route books; 1200 programs, 8000 circus lithographs, 20,000 photo negatives, 50,000 photo prints, heralds, couriers, tickets, letterheads, route cards, original circus artwork, records and documents of circus business, movies, newspapers ads, circus band music and periodical of show business such as *Billboard, New York Clipper, White Tops*, Bandwagon, etc. Partially cataloged.

NS —DALHOUSIE UNIVERSITY LIBRARY, Halifax, B3H 4H8, Can.
Holdings: Cat Pix
Notes: Approx 2000 lithographs, steel engravings, fine prints and illustrated historical maps from the 18th and 19th centuries are in the collection. Subject coverage is primarily of Nova Scotia, New Brunswick, Prince Edward Island, and Newfoundland scenery, street scenes, and portrayals of prominent people, buildings and events. Generally rich in illustrations of the working and social life of the period. Artists represented incl: J E Woolford, J F W Desbarres, William Eagar, William Bartlett and Richard Short. Historical maps incl some of the earliest visual depictions of the Atlantic coast. Material available for editorial reproduction. Print fee charged. No loans.

ON —METROPOLITAN TORONTO LIBRARY, Theatre Dept, 789 Yonge St, Toronto, M4W 2G8, Can. Heather McCallum, Head
Notes: A collection of several thousand prints incl British and American engraved dramatic portraits, engravings of British theatres, and a growing collection of 18th and 19th century prints of dancers.

ON —VICTORIA UNIVERSITY, Library, 71 Queen's Park Crescent, Toronto, M5S 1K7, Can. Robert C Brandeis, Chief Librn
Holdings: Vols (400) // Uncat
Notes: A major collection of George Baxter's woodblock and metal plate prints and book illustrations in watercolor and oil color. Listed in *Starr Collection of Baxter* Prints. Toronto: Ryerson Press, 1946.

PQ —MCGILL UNIVERSITY, McLennan Library, Rare Books and Special Collections Dept, 3459 McTavish St, Montreal, H3A 1Y1, Can.
Notes: 12,680 original prints and posters dating from the 16th century to the present.

Prints representing many graphic techniques; special subject areas such as: early railways, Japanese woodblocks, Napoleon, early Canadian portraits.

PRINTS—TECHNIQUES

CA —CALIFORNIA STATE UNIVERSITY, HAYWARD, Library, Hayward, 94542. Melissa Rose, Dir

CA —CALIFORNIA COLLEGE OF ARTS & CRAFTS, Meyer Library, Broadway at College, Oakland, 94618. Robert L Harper, Head Librn
Holdings: Vols (29,000) Cat Pix
Budget: ($10,000)
Notes: All fields of arts and crafts.

MI —CRANBROOK ACADEMY OF ART, 500 Lone Pine Rd, Box 801, Bloomfield Hills, 48013. Diane Gunn, Librn
Holdings: Vols (25,000) Slides

SC —WOFFORD COLLEGE, Sandor Teszler Library, N Church St, Spartanburg, 29301. Frank J Anderson, Librn
Holdings: Vols (500) Cat
Budget: ($500)
Notes: Books about the history and practice of printing, hand papermaking, bookbinding, book collecting, fine press and private press books used in conjunction with instruction at the Wofford Library Press, an experimental and bibliographic press which has been in operation since 1969. Collection contains materials on printmaking methods and related graphic arts.

WA —UNIVERSITY OF WASHINGTON LIBRARIES, Suzzallo Library, Special Collections Division, Rare Book Collection, FM-25, Seattle, 98195. Gary Menges, Coordinator for Special Collections
Notes: Printing history, including early printed books and modern fine printing; book arts, including papermaking, decorated papers, bookbinding, book design, and artist's books; American literature, 19th century includes: Stephen Crane, Ralph Waldo Emerson, Nathaniel Hawthorne, Henry James, Henry Wadsworth Longfellow, Herman Melville, Frank Norris, Harriet Beecher Stowe and Walt Whitman and 20th century includes: Theodore Roethke; illustrated books, including emblem books, historical children's illustration, books illustrated with prints, and artist's books; costume history; voyages and travels; preservation of library materials.

PRINTS, BAXTER

ON —VICTORIA UNIVERSITY, Library, 71 Queen's Park Crescent, Toronto, M5S 1K7, Can. Robert C Brandeis, Chief Librn
Holdings: Vols (400) // Cat
Notes: A major collection of George Baxter's woodblock and metal plate prints and books illustrations in watercolor and oil color. Listed in *Starr Collection of Baxter* Prints. Toronto: Ryerson Press, 1946.

PRINTS, JAPANESE

MA —HARVARD UNIVERSITY LIBRARY, Fine Arts Library, Rubel Asiatic Research Collection, Sackler Museum, 38 Quincy Street, Cambridge, 02138. Yen-Shew Lynn Chao, Librn
Holdings: Vols (12,000)
Notes: Rubel Asiatic Research Collection; specializes exclusively in the acquisition of Oriental language (Chinese, Japanese, and Korean) materials. Particular strengths incl the areas of Buddhist arts, Chinese bronzes and painting, Japanese painting and prints, and Chinese and Japanese ceramics. Also large holdings of oriental art periodicals, reprints, and exhibition and sales catalogs.

PRIOLEAU, SAMUEL

SC —COLLEGE OF CHARLESTON LIBRARY, Special Collections Dept, Charleston, 29401.
Notes: Papers, incl correspondence between Thomas Henderson and Samuel Prioleau regarding political and financial matters, June 23 and August 31, 1832.

PRIOLEAU FAMILY

SC —COLLEGE OF CHARLESTON LIBRARY, Special Collections Dept, Charleston, 29401.
Notes: Papers, 1811, incl marriage settlement trust deed, involving transfer of ownership of slaves from Samuel and Hannah Motte Prioleau to James Hamilton, Jr.

PRISON ASSOCIATION, NATIONAL see National Prison Association

PRISON EMPLOYEES see Correctional Personnel

PRISON LITERATURE

DC —LIBRARY OF CONGRESS, Washington, 20540.
Notes: "An unrivaled prison periodical collection." See *Quarterly Journal of the Library of Congress*, Spring 1983, pp 151-61.

PRISON PERIODICALS

DC —LIBRARY OF CONGRESS, Washington, 20540.
Notes: "An unrivaled prison periodical collection." See *Quarterly Journal of the Library of Congress*, Spring 1983, pp 151-61.

WI —UNIVERSITY OF WISCONSIN, MADISON, Law School Library, Criminal Justice Reference & Information Center, Madison, 53706. Sue Center, Librn
Holdings: Vols (29,000) Cat Mss
Budget: ($45,000)
Notes: In-depth subject access is provided to collection by our own cataloging and classification systems. Incl are periodical articles which are selectively cataloged to supplement the collection. Special items in collection incl penal press (prisoner newspapers); annual and statistical reports from criminal justice agencies throughout the US and Canada; theses and dissertations; and 280 periodical titles in the field of criminal justice.

PRISONERS' PERIODICALS see Prison Periodicals

PRISONS AND PRISONERS

CA —WOMEN'S HISTORY RESEARCH CENTER, Microfilm Library, 2325 Oak St, Berkeley, 94708. Laura X, Librn
Holdings: Microforms
Notes: Incl 500 subject files of material on Women and Law (General); Politics; Employment; Education; Rape/Prison/Prostitution; Black and Third World women. Collection at University of Wyoming, Archive of Contemporary History, PO Box 3334, Laramie, Wyoming 82071, c/o David Crosson. Reasearch inquiries accepted. Microfilm of collection (40 reels & reel guides) available through Women's History Research Center, 2325 Oak St, Berkeley, CA 94708. No collections housed at this address.

CA —HOOVER INSTITUTION ON WAR, REVOLUTION & PEACE, Stanford University, Stanford, 94305. Milorad M Drachkovitch, Archivist
Holdings: Mss
Notes: Papers of Alice Park, 1883-1957, incl diaries, correspondence, pamphlets, clippings, and leaflets, relating to Pacifism and the peace movement, the Ford Peace Ship Expedition of 1915-1916, feminism, socialism, the labor movement, prison reform, child labor legislation, civil liberties, and a variety of other reform movements in the US 30 ms boxes, 3 envelopes.

CA —STANFORD UNIVERSITY LIBRARIES, Lane Medical Library, Stanford University, Medical Center, Stanford, 94305. Peter Stangl, Librn
Notes: 48 feet of mss incll Leo L Stanley's records of his years as resident physician at San Quentin prison. Volumes from 1916-23 and 1931-50.

DE —DELAWARE CORRECTIONAL CENTER, Main Library, Education Bldg,

PRISONS AND PRISONERS (cont.)

Smyrna, 19977. Chris Tack, Librn
Holdings: Vols 2200 Uncat
Budget: $1500
Notes: Federal and state laws pertaining to prisons and prisoners

DC —FEDERAL BUREAU OF PRISONS, Library, 320 First St NW, Washington, 20001. Lloyd W Hooker, Librn
Holdings: Vols (2500) Cat
Budget: ($20,000)

DC —LIBRARY OF CONGRESS, Washington, 20540.
Notes: "An unrivaled prison periodical collection." See *Quarterly Journal of the Library of Congress*, Spring 1983, pp 151-66.

FL —UNION CORRECTIONAL INSTITUTION LIBRARY, PO Box 221, Raiford, 32083. Harry Rabe, Librn
Holdings: Vols 16,000 Cat Mss Maps

IL —NORTHWESTERN UNIVERSTY, School of Law, Library, 357 E Chicago Ave, Chicago, 60611. George S Grossman, Dir
Notes: Comprehensive collections of Anglo-American and foreign (especially European) law; Roman and Canon law (selective); international law; European Common Market; Williams Collection of Legal Instruments (AD 1300-1700); George W Shaw Collection of Early European Law. Incl 500 ms legal documents.

IN —INDIANA LAW ENFORCEMENT ACADEMY, David F Allen Memorial Learning Resources Center, Rd 700 E, PO Box 313, Plainfield, 46168. Donna K Zimmerman, Librn
Holdings: Vols (4500) Cat Slides 16mm Films
Budget: ($8500)
Notes: Concentrated in the areas of police science, criminology, and law.

MA —HARVARD UNIVERSITY LIBRARY, Law School Library, Langdell Hall, Cambridge, 02138. Harry S Martin III, Librn
Holdings: Cat

MO —SAINT LOUIS POLICE LIBRARY, 315 S Tucker Blvd, Saint Louis, 63102. Cathy Reilly, Librn
Holdings: Vols (18,000) Cat Mss Pix Microforms
Budget: ($25,000)
Notes: Library on all subjects of police work is open to the public for general reference use.

NJ —RUTGERS, THE STATE UNIVERSITY OF NEW JERSEY, John Cotton Dana Library, 185 University Ave, Newark, 07102. Phyllis Schultze, Librn
Holdings: Vols 40,000 Cat
Notes: National Council on Crime and Delinquency. Criminology, as applied, means all phases of crime and delinquency prevention, control and treatment, ie, the whole "criminal justice" gamut: police, courts, probation and parole, prisons, community rehabilitation centers, etc. In short, everything except police laboratory materials. Collection completely cataloged; all criminological and correctional journals indexed. Incl many reports of correctional agencies, research reports, unpublished monographs, publications in the field by all government agencies, federal, state, county and local. Information file contains over 40,000 such items, as well as about 10,000 uncataloged clippings and other pieces of information stored by specific subjects.

NY —CORNELL UNIVERSITY LIBRARIES, Collection of Regional History, Dept of Manuscripts and Univ Archives, Ithaca, 14853.
Notes: *Inspectors of State Prisons of the State of New York.* Fourth annual report, 1852; 1 vol.

NC —DUKE UNIVERSITY, William R Perkins Library, Durham, 27706. Elvin E Strowd, University Librn
Notes: The Bruno Lasker collection contains 51 portfolios; the Perkins Library general collection and other collections contain a significant amount of material on the subject of slavery and antislavery.

PA —BALCH INSTITUTE FOR ETHNIC STUDIES, Library, 18 S Seventh St, Philadelphia, 19106. R Joseph Anderson, Library Dir

PA —FRIENDS HISTORICAL LIBRARY OF SWARTHMORE COLLEGE, Swarthmore, 19081. J William Frost, Dir
Holdings: Vols (35,000) Cat Mss Pix Microforms
Notes: Library's collections contain information on the history and doctrine of the Society of Friends, Quaker contributions to literature, science, business, education, and government, plus their reform efforts in peace, Indian rights, women's rights, abolition of slavery, and prison reform. Among the more than 250 mss collections are the papers of several Quaker advocates of prison reform, some of whom observed prison conditions and provided assistance to prisoners.

ON —ONTARIO MINISTRY OF CORRECTIONAL SERVICES, Library, 2001 Eglinton Ave E, Scarborough, M1L 4P1, Can. T J B Anderson, Chief Librn
Holdings: Vols (3676) Cat VF
Budget: ($16,000)
Notes: Approx 135 periodicals received. Library services also provided in approx 50 jails and adult institutions.

ON —UNIVERSITY OF TORONTO, Centre of Criminology, Library, 130 St George St, Rm 8001, Toronto, M5S 1A5, Can. Catherine J Matthews, Librn
Holdings: Vols (20,000) Cat
Notes: Over 4500 research reports, article reprints, theses, ect. Extensive newspaper clippings file from 1963 to present indexed under 350 subjects headings. The collection covers criminology, law enforcement and policing, delinquency, criminal justice system, penology and corrections. Acquistitons list published three times a year; subscription.

PRIVATE HOUSEHOLD WORKERS see Servants

PRIVATELY PRINTED BOOKS see Press Books

PRIZEFIGHTING see Boxing

PROBABILITIES (STATISTICS)

CA —UNIVERSITY OF CALIFORNIA, BERKELEY, Science Libraries, Astronomy-Mathematics-Statistics-Computer Science Library, 100 Evans Hall, Berkeley, 94720. Kimiyo Hom, Head
Holdings: Vols (53,000) Cat Maps Microforms
Budget: ($117,301)
Notes: A research collection in the fields of astronomy, mathematics, statistics and computer science. In the field of astronomy, emphasis is given to star charts, atlases and catalogs. In mathematics, the collection's strengths are in pure mathematics, mathematical statistics and probability theory. The computer science holdings emphasize the mathematics the theory of the field. The Library's serial holdings are particularly rich in foreign-language materials. Some 1300 serial titles are currently being received; over 4000 pamphlets. (Holdings in the AMSCS Library are complemented by approx 15,000 additional vols in the Main Library, as well as rare book materials in The Bancroft Library.)

CA —ESL, SUBSIDIARY OF TRW, Research Library, 495 Java Dr, PO Box 3510, Sunnyvale, 94086. Verna Van Valzer, Head Librn
Holdings: Vols 100 Cat
Budget: $1000

CT —YALE UNIVERSITY, Statistics Library, Dana House, 24 Hillhouse Ave, New Haven, 06520. Billie I Salter, Librn
Holdings: Vols 3695 Cat
Budget: $5130

IL —NORTHWESTERN UNIVERSITY, Mathematics Library, 2033 Sheridan Rd, Evanston, 60201. Zita Hayward, Library Asst
Holdings: Vols (25,000) Cat
Notes: Collection emphasizes pure mathematics on the graduate and research level.

PROBABILITIES (STATISTICS) —HISTORY

PA —UNIVERSITY OF PITTSBURGH, Hillman Library, Pittsburgh, 15260.
Notes: Economic and philosophical papers of the English scholar Frank Plumpton Ramsey (1903-1930), incl mss of published and unpublished writings, reading notes, etc. Significant because of his work in modern mathematics, logic, probability, and economics. Complementary to the Library's holdings of the papers of the logical empiricists, Rudolf Carnap and Hans Reichenback.

PROBATION

DC —FEDERAL BUREAU OF PRISONS, Library, 320 First St NW, Washington, 20001. Lloyd W Hooker, Librn
Holdings: Vols (2500) Cat
Budget: ($20,000)

MO —SAINT LOUIS POLICE LIBRARY, 315 S Tucker Blvd, Saint Louis, 63102. Cathy Reilly, Librn
Holdings: Vols (21,000) Cat Mss Pix Microforms
Budget: ($18,400)
Notes: Library on all subjects of police work is open to the public for general reference use.

NJ —RUTGERS, THE STATE UNIVERSITY OF NEW JERSEY, John Cotton Dana Library, 185 University Ave, Newark, 07102. Phyllis Schultze, Librn
Holdings: Vols 40,000 Cat
Notes: National Council on Crime and Delinquency. Criminology, as applied, means all phases of crime and delinquency prevention, control and treatment, ie, the whole "criminal justice" gamut: police, courts, probation and parole, prisons, community rehabilitation centers, etc. In short, everything except police laboratory materials. Collection completely cataloged; all criminological and correctional journals indexed. Incl many reports of correctional agencies, research reports, unpublished monographs, publications in the field by all government agencies, federal, state, county and local. Information file contains over 40,000 such items, as well as about 10,000 uncataloged clippings and other pieces of information stored by specific subjects.

OH —OHIO STATE UNIVERSITY, Social Work Library, 1947 N College Rd, Columbus, 43210. Toyo S Kawakami, Librn
Holdings: Vols (46,410) Cat
Budget: ($11,960)
Notes: VF incl approx 4500 pamphlets, arranged by LC subject headings. 278 serial titles on social work, social and public service, crime and delinquency, corrections, criminal justice, marriage and the family, probation, and related topics, are received.

ON —ONTARIO MINISTRY OF CORRECTIONAL SERVICES, Library, 2001 Eglinton Ave E, Scarborough, M1L 4P1, Can. T J B Anderson, Chief Librn
Holdings: Vols (3676) Cat VF
Budget: ($16,000)
Notes: Approx 135 periodicals received. Library services also provided in approx 50 jails and adult institutions.

PROBLEM CHILDREN

PQ —HOPITAL SAINTE-JUSTINE POUR LES ENFANTS, Centre d'Information sur la Sante de l'Enfant, 3175 Cote Sainte-Catherine, Montreal, H3T 1C5, Can. Louis LucLecompte, Librn
Holdings: Vols (7000) Cat Audiotapes Videotapes 16mm Films Microforms
Budget: ($11,000)
Notes: 40 percent of collection in French.

PROBLEMS OF THE CITY (RADIO PROGRAMS)

IL —CHICAGO HISTORICAL SOCIETY, Library, Clark St at North Ave, Chicago, 60614. Archie Motley, Manuscript Librn
Notes: Audiotapes of 73 "Problems of the

PROBLEMS OF THE CITY (RADIO PROGRAMS) (cont.)

City" programs broadcast over Chicago radio station WAIT.

PROCESS CONTROL

PA —COLT INDUSTRIES, Crucible Research Center Library, Box 88, Pittsburgh, 15230. Patricia J Aducci, Technical Librn

PROCESS ENGINEERING see Production Engineering

PROCESSIONS

RI —BROWN UNIVERSITY, John Hay Library, Anne S K Brown Military Collection, 20 Prospect St, Providence, 02912. Richard B Harrington, Cur
Holdings: Vols (40,000) Cat Mss Pix
Notes: The Anne S K Brown Military Collection has been formed over the past forty or more years by Mrs John Nicholas Brown, now of Newport, and contains approximately 40,000 volumes and 60,000 prints, drawings and watercolors as well as a number of oil paintings and about 5000 miniature model soldiers. At its beginning (and still today) the emphasis or focus of this collection has been upon the history of, and the accurate contemporary illustration of, military and naval uniforms of all nations from the early XVII century to the present. In the course of time, however, the collection has come to incl also a vast and related amount of material on military and naval history, military and naval arts and tactics, wars, campaigns, ceremonies, biography, portraits and caricatures of this and earlier periods. It has been probably the largest private collection of such a nature inthe world, and it contains much ms and graphic documentation which is unique. It has been useful to numerous scholars and historians, editors, filmmakers and publishers for research and for illustrative material and has also contributed to many museum exhibitions. In 1982 the entire collection, with its complete card catalog and subject index, has been presented to Brown University, where it is located in the John Hay Library. Special requests are taken care of by phone, mail and appointments with the curator.

PROCLAMATIONS

NY —NEW YORK STATE LIBRARY, State Education Bldg Annex, Washington Ave, Albany, 12224.
Holdings: Cat
Notes: Printed handbills and posted announcements of historic and everyday events; Theater performances; auctions; advertisements; land sales; slave sales, reward posters for runaways; inducements to enlist for military service. Over 2000 pieces. Also over 3000 poetic broadside ballads.

PROCTER, MAURICE

MA —BOSTON UNIVERSITY, Mugar Memorial Library, Special Collections Dept, 771 Commonwealth Ave, Boston, 02215. Howard B Gotlieb, Dir
Holdings: Cat Mss
Notes: Mss, correspondence, etc collected in depth incl publications by or about.

PRODIGIES, MEMORY

NY —MORRIS N & CHESLEY V YOUNG LIBRARY OF MNEMONICS, 270 Riverside Dr, New York, 10025. Morris N Young, Cur
Holdings: Cat Mss Maps Pix Phonorecords Audiotapes 16mm Films Microforms
Notes: Collection of 5000 books, pamphlets, pictures, memorabilia, etc incl medieval art of memory; psychology of memory, forgetting and reading; medical aspects of memory, amnesia, dyslexia; biomedical aspects of learning and memory; information storage, retrieval and cybernetics; memory prodigies, lightning calculators, calendars; remembrance cups and memory mementos. All languages. Memorabilia incl engravings, posters, programs, advertisements, birthday cards, teaching cards, ASLs, and Mark Twain's Memory Builder game and other games. Items range from 1410 to 1980s.

PRODUCE EXCHANGES see Commodity Exchanges

PRODUCER GAS see Gas and Oil Engines

PRODUCTION, COOPERATIVE see Cooperative Societies

PRODUCTION CONTROL

PA —COLT INDUSTRIES, Crucible Research Center Library, Box 88, Pittsburgh, 15230. Patricia J Aducci, Technical Librn

PRODUCTION ENGINEERING

CA —CALIFORNIA STATE POLYTECHNIC UNIVERSITY, POMONA, University Library, 3801 W Temple Ave, Pomona, 91768. Harold Schleiser, Actg Dir
Notes: General reference materials on aerospace, chemical, civil, electrical, electronics, industrial, mechanical and manufacturing engineering.
DC —US DEPT OF LABOR, Library, 200 Constitution Ave NW, Washington, 20210. Sabina Jacobson, Dir
Holdings: Vols (550,000) Cat
NY —ENGINEERING SOCIETIES LIBRARY, 345 E 47 St, New York, 10017. S Kirk Cabeen, Dir
Holdings: Vols 250,000 Cat Maps 16mm Films Microforms
Notes: One of the largest, most comprehensive engineering libraries in the world. Covers all engineering disciplines; particularly strong in electrical and electronic, mechanical, mining and metallurgical, petroleum, chemical, industrial, air conditioning and refrigeration engineering. Incl Wheeler Collection of early materials on magnetisn and electricity. 125, 000 bound periodical volumes; 10,000 maps; 5000 serial subscriptions (many foreign-language). Virtually all materials abstracted in *Engineering Index* (1884-date) are incl in Library. Noncirculating, except to members of professional engineering societies which support the Library. See *Engineering Societies Library, New York, Classed Subject Catalog and Index* (Boston: G K Hall, 1963); and *Supplements*, 1-10, 1964-1973.
NY —GENERAL ELECTRIC CO, Main Library, One River Rd, Schenectady, 12345. Julia Hewitt, Mgr
Holdings: Vols (56,000) Cat
NC —TECHNICAL INSTITUTE OF ALAMANCE, Learning Resources Center, Jimmy Kerr Rd, PO Box 623, Haw River, 27258. Ron Plummer, Coordr
Holdings: Vols 250 Cat 16mm Films Microforms
Notes: Manufacturing technology.
PA —CARNEGIE LIBRARY OF PITTSBURGH, Science & Technology Dept, 4400 Forbes Ave, Pittsburgh, 15213. Catherine M Brosky, Dept Head
Holdings: Vols (380,000) Cat Maps Microforms
Budget: ($240,000)
Notes: General information acquired in various subject areas especially those relating to iron and steel and other metals, rubber, leather, pulp, and paper, textiles, glass, petroleum and coal tar by-products, lumber, plastics, etc.
WA —PUGET SOUND NAVAL SHIPYARD, Engineering Library, Code 202.5, Bremerton, 98314. Carol J Swanson, Engineering Librn
Holdings: Vols (1000) Cat
WY —US AIR FORCE INSTITUTE OF TECHNOLOGY, Library, Dept 9 Bldg 831, FE, Warren AFB, 82001. Patricia A Johnson, Librn
Holdings: Vols (7000) Cat Microforms
Budget: ($9000)
Notes: The Library supports graduate programs for students (Air Force Missile-Combat Crewman) seeking a Master of Business Administration Degree. Civilian students and other military personnel are also admitted.
ON —CANADA DEPT OF LABOUR, Library, Ottawa, K1A 0J2, Can. Monique Marchand, Chief Librn
Holdings: Vols (100,000) Cat Microforms

PRODUCTIVITY CENTERS see Industrial Productivity Centers

PRODUCTS, DAIRY see Dairy Products

PRODUCTS, WASTE see Waste Products

PROETZ, ARTHUR

MO —WASHINGTON UNIVERSITY, Libraries, Special Collections Dept, Campus Box 1061, St Louis, 63130.
Notes: Family and business correspondence.

PROFESSIONAL PERIODICALS see Periodicals, Professional

PROFESSIONS

NY —CATALYST, Library, 14 E 60 St, New York, 10022. Gurley Turner, Dir of Information Services
Holdings: Vols (6000) Cat Mss VF
Notes: Working Women (current information); career and family issues plus career library.
NC —FORSYTH COUNTY PUBLIC LIBRARY, Adult Continuing Education (ACE) Div, 660 W Fifth St, Winston-Salem, 27101. Ann R Gehlen, Librn
Holdings: Vols 3500 Phonorecords Audiotapes Videotapes 16mm Films Filmstrips Microforms
Budget: $6900
Notes: Special emphasis on high school equivalency preparation, adult new readers, improvement in language and math, secretarial skills, job-hunting techniques, college alternatives, test preparation, and support to independent study in popular subject areas. Extensive pamphlet files of up-to-date career information, indexed. Some 600 bound college catalogs plus national microfiche collection. Current local job openings on microfiche. Information and referral files maintained to relevant local resources (courses, etc). Partially cataloged.

PROFIT AND LOSS STATEMENTS see Financial Statements

PROGRAMMED INSTRUCTION

NY —COLUMBIA UNIVERSITY LIBRARIES, Teachers College, Milbank Memorial Library, 525 W 120 St, New York, 10027. Jane P Franck, Dir
Holdings: Vols 800 Uncat
Notes: Programmed instruction texts. Basic collection gift of Center for Programmed Instruction in 1963.

PROGRAMMED TEXTBOOKS see Programmed Instruction

PROGRAMMING LANGUAGES (ELECTRONIC COMPUTERS)

CA —LOS ANGELES PUBLIC LIBRARY, Science & Technology Dept, 630 W Fifth St, Los Angeles, 90071. Billie M Connor, Dept Head
Holdings: Vols (12,000) Cat
Notes: Materials on the application of electronic devices, circuits and systems in various fields such as computers, automatic control, sound productions and reproduction, radio and telecommunications. Extensive holdings of materials on computers, peripherals, and software including many texts pertaining to specific programming languages. Complete collection of Howard Sams schematics for radio television, and other electronic equipment repair as well as

PROGRAMMING LANGUAGES (ELECTRONIC COMPUTERS) (cont.)

historical sets of Rider's Radio and Television schematics.

CA —LOGICON INC, Strategic & Information Systems Division, Information Center, 255 W Fifth St, Box 471, San Pedro, 90731. Constance B Davenport, Supervisor
Holdings: Vols (3000) Cat Mss Microforms
Notes: Incl about 3000 books, 250 periocial titles, 5000 technical reports, 10,000 microfiche, 750 standards and specifications. Catalog is computerized. Interactive search capability with Dialog, Orbit, DMS on-line, NASA Recon. Material on computer programming, systems analysis, military systems and operations research.

OH —CASE WESTERN RESERVE UNIVERSITY, M A Baxter School of Information and Library Science, 10900 Euclid Ave, Cleveland, 44106. Bettina MacAyeal, Librn; Gretchen Larson, Librn
Holdings: Vols (15,000) Cat

PROGRAMS, CIRCUS

NY —NEW YORK PUBLIC LIBRARY, Performing Arts Research Center, Billy Rose Theatre Collection, 111 Amsterdam Ave, New York, 10023. Dorothy L Swerdlove, Cur
Holdings: Cat

WI —CIRCUS WORLD MUSEUM LIBRARY, 415 Lynn St, Baraboo, 53913. Robert L Parkinson, Research Center Dir
Holdings: Vols (1800) Cat Mss Pix Slides Phonorecords 16mm Films
Notes: Circus and "Wild West" shows. Owned by State Historical Society of Wisconsin. Incl 1800 books on circus subjects; 400 route books; 1200 programs, 8000 circus lithographs, 20,000 photo negatives, 50,000 photo prints, heralds, couriers, tickets, letterheads, route cards, original circus business, movies, newspaper ads, circus band music and periodicals of show business such as *Billboard, New York Clipper, White Tops, Bandwagon,* etc. Partially cataloged.

PROGRAMS, CONCERT see Concerts—Programs

PROGRAMS, DANCE

CA —LOS ANGELES PUBLIC LIBRARY, Frances Howard Goldwyn Hollywood Regional Library, 1623 Ivar Ave, Los Angeles, 90028. Sally Dumaux, Librn
Holdings: Vols (100,000) Uncat Pix VF
Budget: ($60,000)
Notes: There is both a general and reference collection covering the history of dance, mainly Europe and the US. Special Collections: Gladys Littell-Ruth St Denis, 1880-1968, covering circa 1941-1957 incl photographs, programs, flyers, and brochures; Dance Programs, over 400 programs and playbills, mainly Los Angeles and New York from the 1930s to the present.

CA —UNIVERSITY OF CALIFORNIA, LOS ANGELES, Research Library, Dept of Special Collections, 405 Hilgard Ave, Los Angeles, 90024. Edward Shreeves, Chairman, Bibliographers Group; David S Zeidberg, Head
Holdings: Vols 250 Cat Mss Pix
Notes: 1000 in the Arthur Todd collection; many others in various collections.

IL —UNIVERSITY OF ILLINOIS, URBANA/CHAMPAIGN, Library, Applied Life Studies Library, 1408 W Gregory Dr, Urbana, 61801.
Holdings: Vols (38,000) Cat Pix Microforms
Notes: Contains books on ballet, contemporary dance, folk and national dances, ethnic dance, dance history, choreography, dance notation, dance therapy. Also collected are programs of dance concerts and performances of the 20th century.

NY —NEW YORK PUBLIC LIBRARY, Performing Arts Research Center, Dance Collection, 111 Amsterdam Ave, New York, 10023. Genevieve Oswald, Cur
Budget: ($9,280)
Notes: About 90,000 programs. The Collection maintains comprehensive sets of house programs from American dance companies, including their foreign tours; foreign companies are represented primarily by programs for their American tours. New York programs are most strongly represented. Numerous souvenir programs of American and foreign companies. Ethnic dance companies and individual dancers also are documented. Good collection of the programs of Les Ballets Russes de Diaghilev, De Basil's Ballet Russe, Ballet Russe de Monte Carlo, Royal Ballet (Covent Garden), and of dancers Anna Pavlova, Isadora Duncan, Jose Limon, Ruth St Denis, Ted Shawn, Martha Graham, Doris Humphrey, Charles Weidman, and Helen Tamiris.
See also entry under Playbills - Collections

PA —FREE LIBRARY OF PHILADELPHIA, Music Dept, Drinker Library of Choral Music, Logan Sq, Philadelphia, 19103. Frederick James Kent, Head
Notes: Musical and dance programs given in Philadelphia area. Partially indexed. Programs cover all phases of musical entertainment, such as ballet, choir, musical theatre, orchestra, organ, recitals, etc. Early Academy of Music concerts (1850-1900) filed chronologically. Some valuable scrapbooks, unindexed.

PROGRAMS, MUSIC

MA —BOSTON PUBLIC LIBRARY, Music Division, 666 Boylston St, Box 286, Boston, 02117. Ruth Bleecker, Cur of Music
Notes: The Handel and Haydn Society officially transferred its collection to the library in 1978. The Society gave its books, scores, and archives to the Trustees of the Library to be maintained and preserved as part of the permanent research collection. Presently the collection ranges from early imprints of Handel's music and copies of the *Handel and Haydn Society Collection of Church Music* to the holographs of commissioned works. The archives incl copies off bills and disbursements dating back to 1815, printers' plates for tickets, programs from 1815-1912, membership lists, and by-laws.

NY —NEW YORK PUBLIC LIBRARY, Music Div, 111 Amsterdam Ave, New York, 10023. Frank C Campbell, Chief
Holdings: Vols (300,000) Cat Mss Pix Microforms
Notes: Described in *Dictionary Catalog of the Music Collection, The Research Libraries of the New York Public Library,* 33 vols (532,000 cards), 1964, $2190; Supplement 1, 1 vol (17,000 cards), 1966, $100. Also, *Bibliographic Guide to Music,* 2 vols, 1975-1976, $70 ea. Literature pertaining to virtually all musical subjects, and scores covering the broadest range of musical style and history are represented in this catalog. Special strengths of the collection incl folk songs, 18th and 19th-century librettos, full scores of operas, complete works, historical editions, Beethoven, Americana, American music, periodicals, vocal music, literature on the voice, programs, record catalogs, and mss in detail; sheet music, 355,414; sound recordings, 400,000; clippings and programs, 2 million; broadsides, 1821; songsters, 375; pictures, 51,002; ms, 29,877.

OH —CLEVELAND PUBLIC LIBRARY, Fine Arts and Special Collections Department, 325 Superior Ave, Cleveland, 44114. Alice N Loranth, Head
Holdings: Vols 5000
Notes: Programs of performances in the Cleveland area (1871-1976) are filed chronologically and indexed by performer, giving date and place of performance. After 1976 programs are filed under performers' names in music VF.

PA —FREE LIBRARY OF PHILADELPHIA, Music Dept, Drinker Library of Choral Music, Logan Sq, Philadelphia, 19103. Frederick James Kent, Head
Notes: Musical and dance programs given in Philadelphia area. Partially indexed. Programs cover all phases of musical entertainment, such as ballet, choir, musical theatre, orchestra, organ, recitals, etc. Early Academy of Music concerts (1850-1900) filed chronologically. Some valuable scrapbooks, unindexed.

PA —UNIVERSITY OF PITTSBURGH, Music Library, B-31 Music Bldg, Pittsburgh, 15260. Norris L Stephens, Music Librn
Notes: Concert programs of local performing organizations.

†WA —SEATTLE PUBLIC LIBRARY, Music Dept, Fourth & Madison, Seattle, 98104. Carolyn Holmquist, Head
Holdings: Vols 22,300 Cat
Notes: Books 11,000, music 10,000, dance 1300 vols, 14,000 phonorecords, 28,000 pieces of sheet music. Special indexes: symphony orchestra program notes. World, National and local premiere dates. Song titles in collections, 60,000 cards. Music literature, printed music and sheet music, and phonograph record collections all have separate catalogs.

WI —MILWAUKEE PUBLIC LIBRARY, 814 W Wisconsin Ave, Milwaukee, 53233. Donald J Sager, City Librn
Notes: Concert programs of local performing organizations.

ON —METROPOLITAN TORONTO LIBRARY, Music Dept, 789 Yonge St, Toronto, M4W 2G8, Can. Isabel Rose, Head
Budget: ($54,000)
Notes: 14,800 books, 40,000 scores; 1900 pieces of retrospective Canadian sheet music; 500 pieces of American and British sheet music, pre-1980; 17,000 phonorecords; 180 current periodical titles; 2800 bound peiodicals; 340 reels of microfilmed periodicals; 16,000 concert programs, chiefly Toronto city; 8850 newspaper clipping files; music picture files integrated with Fine Art Dept picture collection. Programs indexed by performer, date, location.

PROGRAMS, RADIO see Radio Programs

PROGRAMS, TELEVISION see Television Programs

PROGRAMS, THEATRE—COLLECTIONS

CA —UNIVERSITY OF CALIFORNIA, DAVIS, Shields Library, Dept of Special Collections, Davis, 95616. Donald Kunitz, Head; C Danial Elliott, Asst Head
Holdings: Vols Uncat
Notes: Programs from 19th and 20th century American and British theatre.

CA —INSTITUTE OF THE AMERICAN MUSICAL, Library, 121 N Detroit St, Los Angeles, 90036. Miles Kreuger, Cur
Holdings: Cat Mss Maps Pix Slides Phonorecords
Notes: Reference materials on the American musical theatre and motion pictures incl 40, 000 phonograph records, sound tapes, and cylinders dating back to the 1890s; record catalogs to 1900; thousands of theatre and film programs, periodicals, sheet music and vocal scores as early as 1830; thousands of motion picture press books and over 200,000 stills from 1914 to the present; every musical comedy script published in America and dozens in ms form, original or photocopy materials from the archives of movie palaces, films and record companies, incl discographies of many major Broadway and Hollywood stars; and thousands of books on theatre, film, broadcasting, world's fairs and other allied areas of showmanship.

CA —LOS ANGELES PUBLIC LIBRARY, Frances Howard Goldwyn Hollywood Regional Library, 1623 Ivar Ave, Los Angeles, 90028. Sally Dumaux, Librn
Holdings: Vols (100,000) Cat Mss Pix VF
Budget: ($60,000)
Notes: A general and a research collection on theatre history, US and foreign, with special emphasis on Los Angeles, Chicago, and New York theatre from the late 1800s to the present. Other aspects of the collection include theatre design, make-up,

PROGRAMS, THEATRE—COLLECTIONS (cont.)

costume, and acting and directing techniques. Also includes biographies of actors and actresses (many signed). The play collection of over 15,000 titles covers mainly English and American plays of the 19th and 20th century. There are over 5000 playbills, scrapbooks, posters, and programs. Special Collections: "Hellzapoppin," NY, 1938-40. Includes photographs, clippings, and programs.

CA —UNIVERSITY OF CALIFORNIA, LOS ANGELES, Research Library, Dept of Special Collections, 405 Hilgard Ave, Los Angeles, 90024. Edward Shreeves, Chairman, Bibliographers Group; David S Zeidberg, Head
Notes: 125 linear feet, mostly Los Angeles programs, but incl California, New York, Boston, and Europe.

CA —SAN DIEGO PUBLIC LIBRARY, Art, Music & Recreation Sect, 820 E St, San Diego, 92101. Barbara A Tuhill, Supvr
Holdings: Vols 500 Cat
Notes: The gift of Elwyn B Gould, the collection consists of many first editions of biographies of famous actors and actresses and histories of the American, London and European stages. Theatre program scrapbooks dating from 1890 to 1928, some of local events. For reference use only.

CA —SAN DIEGO STATE UNIVERSITY, Malcolm A Love Library, 5300 Campanile Dr, San Diego, 92182. D Dickinson, Univ Librn; Don L Bosseau, Dir
Notes: Theatre and Film Programs Collection. Includes programs from theatrical performances and film showings; theatre programs date from 1850 to the present; the film programs date from the beginning of silent films to the present. (2500 items)

IL —CHICAGO HISTORICAL SOCIETY, Library, Clark St at North Ave, Chicago, 60614. Robert L Brubaker, Librn
Holdings: Vols (150,000) Cat Mss Pix
Notes: Chicago theatre programs (5000); scrapbooks containing reviews and other clippings; a few letters, reminiscences, account books, and other records of theatres, actors and actresses, and managers; theatre posters; Thomas Conolly Collection of Theatrical Portraits; other photographs of theatres, productions, and casts.

IL —CHICAGO PUBLIC LIBRARY, Special Collections Div, Cultural Center, 78 E Washington St, Chicago, 60602. Laura Linard, Cur
Holdings: Mss Pix
Notes: Special Collections maintains a scarce collection of theatre broadsides, playbills, programs and other ephemera for Chicago productions, 1880-1930 as well as a recently acquired collection of contemporary material (1971-1981). These are described in *Treasures of The Chicago Public Library*, compiled by Thomas A Orlando and Marie Gecik, 1977, pp 121-33. The Archives of the Publicity Department of the Goodman Theatre (formerly of the Art Institute of Chicago) are maintained by Special Collections at The Chicago Public Library. We also have a nearly complete collection of the plays of Kenneth Sawyer Goodman, after whom the Goodman Theatre is named. Some unique pre-fire material is also to be found in these collections. A finding aid to these collections has been prepared.

IN —INDIANA UNIVERSITY, SOUTH BEND, Library, 1700 Mishawaka Ave, South Bend, 46615. James L Mullins, Dir
Holdings: Vols (1490) Cat Mss Maps Pix Phonorecords
Notes: Incl design materials, scripts, theatre music, rare editions, theatre programs, playbills, clipping and periodicals from the 1850s to the 1940s.

MD —MARYLAND HISTORICAL SOCIETY, Library, 201 W Monument St, Baltimore, 21201. William B Keller, Head Librn
Holdings: Cat Mss Maps Pix Slides Microforms
Notes: Espec relating to Maryland and Baltimore. Extensive collection.

MA —HARVARD UNIVERSITY LIBRARY, Theatre Collection, Cambridge, 02138. Jeanne T Newlin, Cur
Holdings: Uncat
Notes: See *Harvard Library Bulletin*, VI (1952), 281-301. Playbills for the fifteen major London theatres of the 18th and 19th centuries have been published on microfilm by Research Publications Inc.

MA —BRANDEIS UNIVERSITY, Goldfarb Library, 415 South St, Waltham, 02154. Bessie Hahn, Dir
Notes: American Theater Programs Collection. Consists of 14 linear ft of American theater and stage programs of the late 19th and early 20th century with particular emphasis on the Boston dramatic scene. This collection is unprocessed, spring 1984.

MI —UNIVERSITY OF MICHIGAN, Library, Dept of Rare Books & Special Collections, Ann Arbor, 48109. Robert J Starring, Head
Holdings: Cat Mss Pix
Notes: Extensive holdings of books on the theatre. Also, in the Charles Sanders Collection, about 14,000 British and American playbills and programs mostly of the 19th century, as well as scrapbooks, posters, and about 750 photographs and prints of actors and actresses. In the Ellen Van Volkenburg-Maurice Browne Collection, about 4000 photographs of stage productions and friends and associates, as well as programs, posters, scrapbooks of mounted clippings, about 200 original stage and costume designs, promptbooks, and play manuscripts, representing the American and British careers of this husband-wife team from 1912 to about 1940. The Chicago Little Theatre, 1912-1917, is well represented. Also contains more than 6000 items of correspondence with theatrical and literary figures. Another collection contains 143 Alfred Lunt letters, mainly from 1901-1915.

MI —DETROIT PUBLIC LIBRARY, Music & Performing Arts Dept, 5201 Woodward, Detroit, 48202. Agatha Pfeiffer Kalkanis, Chief
Holdings: Mss Pix
Notes: Extensive bound files of programs for Detroit theatres, 1890 to present, partially indexed by names and titles. Supplemented by manuscript history of Detroit theatre 1811-1908, and Bonstelle theatre 1910-1929. Also clipping files.

NY —CORNELL UNIVERSITY LIBRARIES, Collection of Regional History, Dept of Manuscripts and Univ Archives, Ithaca, 14853.
Notes: From 1885. Incl Broadway, summer stock, repertory theatre, opera, concerts, recitals, ballet, vaudeville, motion pictures, drama, comedy, farce, fable, musicals, variety shows and others. Mainly from New York City.

NY —NEW YORK PUBLIC LIBRARY, Performing Arts Research Center, Billy Rose Theatre Collection, 111 Amsterdam Ave, New York, 10023. Dorothy L Swerdlove, Cur
Holdings: Cat
Notes: See entry under Theatre-History.

†NY —SHUBERT ARCHIVE, Lyceum Theatre, 149 W 45th St, New York, 10036. Brigitte Kueppers, Archivist
Notes: The vast Shubert Archive, mostly unexplored is the largest collection in the world representative of the "business" of the theatre. It includes almost all of the Shubert empire's correspondence from the turn of the century to the 1950s, road company records, thousands of playscripts (American and European), set and costume designs, music scores for Shubert productions, business, financial, and legal records, actors' contracts, etc.

NY —UNIVERSITY OF ROCHESTER, Rush Rhees Library, Department of Rare Books and Special Collections, Rochester, 14627. Peter Dzwonkoski, Librn
Notes: 18th and 19th century English and 19th century American plays and works on theatre. Also incl ms collection on theatre, and papers of Clement William Scott, John Lawrence Toole, Arthur Wing Pinero, Charles Kean, Lillian Russell and Leon

Marks Lion, collection of 130 lithographic theatre posters, and collection of programs and playbills, chiefly Rochester and New York City, NY, 1900-1950. Unpublished guides to ms collections available in repository.

NC —UNIVERSITY OF NORTH CAROLINA, CHAPEL HILL, Wilson Library, Rare Book Collection, Chapel Hill, 27514. Paul S Koda, Cur of Rare Books
Holdings: // Uncat Pix
Notes: The Roland Holt Collection of American Theater Memorabilia incl 15,000 clippings, programs, pictures, photographs, and articles on the American theater, 1881-1931. Thirteen scrapbooks arranged chronologically, 19 letter files, 250 photographs in albums, 100 opera libretti. Sixty miscellaneous books on drama, chiefly biographical.

NC —DUKE UNIVERSITY, William R Perkins Library, Durham, 27706. Elvin E Strowd, University Librn
Holdings: Cat Mss Pix
Notes: Montrose J Moses' collection of books, mss, and papers, mostly concerned with men and women of the theatre, and creative writers of the first third of the century. 3000 books; 22,000 mss.

OH —CLEVELAND PUBLIC LIBRARY, Literature Dept, 325 Superior Ave, Cleveland, 44114. Evelyn Ward, Head
Holdings: Cat
Notes: The theatre program collection consists of some 22,000 items, incl nearly complete sets for existing local theatres and resident companies, as well as substantial holdings, particularly in the Wertheimer Collection, for older theatres that have passed from the scene, dating back to the 19th century. The Leo and Lillie Weidenthal Memorial Collection also contains many rare programs and playbills, particularly from London theatres of the 19th century. Indexed by title, theatre, season, and some performers.

PA —FREE LIBRARY OF PHILADELPHIA, Theatre Collection, Logan Sq, Philadelphia, 19103. Geraldine Duclow, Librn-in-Charge
Holdings: Vols (1,250,000) Uncat Pix
Notes: The Theatre Collection contains books, magazines, playbills, broadsides, posters, photographs, and other memorabilia covering theatre, motion pictures, minstrels, vaudeville, circus, radio and television. The Library's Philadelphia Theatre Index lists the major productions here since 1855, and partially indexes the collection of local playbills which date back to 1803. There are also programs from many other cities, incl New York; some from London date back to 1800. Early film companies as well as the present movie industry are represented by advertising materials and over 30,000 film stills. The Lubin Film Co (1910-1916) Archive has been established with over 600 photographs and related items. Circus programs and route books date back to 1900. There are minstrel programs as early as 1865. Most significant are the mss from Philadelphia's Dumont Minstrels. Various files contain autographs, photographs, newspaper articles and reviews in all pertinent subject areas. Noncirculating.

PA —TEMPLE UNIVERSITY LIBRARIES, Special Collections Dept, Conwellana-Templana Collection, 13 & Berks St, Philadelphia, 19122. Miriam I Crawford, Cur
Holdings: Mss Pix Audiotapes 16mm Films
Budget: ($30,000)
Notes: Chiefly photographs, both negative and prints, scrapbooks and play programs, plus a few scripts, stage designs and promptbooks, the bulk of which document the productions of the Temple University Theatre, 1930-1969, under the direction of Paul Randall. A small supplementary collection of miscellaneous theatrical programs given at the school, and a continuing collection of play programs and publicity materials of the University Theater since Randall's departure.

PA —UNIVERSITY OF PITTSBURGH, Special Collections Dept, Curtis Theatre Collection, 363 Hillman Library, Pittsburgh, 15260. Jeanette Blanco, Cur
Holdings: Vols (4000) Cat Mss Documents

PROGRAMS, THEATRE—COLLECTIONS (cont.)

Microforms Pix Slides VF
Notes: The legitimate theatre of plays, musicals and vaudeville, chiefly of New York City and Pittsburgh, from 1865, and other US, community, summer, college and foreign theatre. Incl 500,000 programs, 12,000 pictures, 300 posters, the Oliver P Merriman Scrapbooks and 300 other scrapbooks, clippings and other ephemera. Vols incl over 3000 acting editions and playscripts. Separate collections: Ralph G Allen Burlesque Skits Collection; Michael Ellis Papers; William P Halstead Theatre Collection; Kenyon Family Papers; Philip Dunning Playscripts Collection; Pittsburgh Playhouse Records; Pittsburgh Savoyards Records. Noncirculating.

TN —MEMPHIS STATE UNIVERSITY, John Willard Brister Library, Memphis, 38152. John Terreo, Special Collections Librn
Notes: Theatre Collection, 1789-1972. Correspondence, scripts, programs, handbills, musical scores, clippings, drawings, sketches, and photographs, documenting careers of artists, production of plays, ballett and theatre companies, and theaters and opera houses centering in New York and London, England. Incl drawings, prints, publications, and other personal papers of British producer and designer Edward Gordon Craig (1872-1966), relating to his career, radio talks (1951-1961) for the BBC, acting school in Florence, Italy, and his mother, actress Ellen Terry; and correspondence, scripts, programs, reviews, scrapbooks, photos, and other materials, of American producer Jed Harris (?)-1979, relating to his stage productions (1926-1945).

TN —PUBLIC LIBRARY OF NASHVILLE & DAVIDSON COUNTY, Nashville Room, Eighth Ave N & Union, Nashville, 37203. David Marshall Stewart, Chief Librn
Holdings: Vols Cat Maps Pix
Notes: The Naff Collection of programs, autographed photographs, posters, etc tells the story of professional theatre in Nashville between 1900 and 1960. All materials noncirculating.

TX —SOUTHERN METHODIST UNIVERSITY, Fondren Library, McCord Theater Collection, Room 301, Dallas, 75275. Edyth Renshaw, Cur; Linda Sellers, Pub Serv
Holdings: Vols (2000) Uncat Mss Pix Slides Phonorecords
Notes: See *Theatre Collections in Libraries and Museums*, Gilder and Freedley (Theatre Arts, 1936). The McCord Theatre Collection encompasses the entire spectrum of the performing arts. The central purpose is to gather records of our regional theater before such ephemeral material is lost. Records of over two hundred early Texas theaters, some fragmentary and some relatively complete, are in the files. These records incl photographs of buildings, stagehands, orchestras, and performers. Local theatre history incl the once famous Dallas Little Theatre and the Margo Jones Theatre. The national theater, opera, ballet, and circus archives incl pictures (some autographed), programs, posters, throw-aways, tear sheets, clippings, and letters. Our international archives are small, but we have some excellent material, eg, artifacts from Max Reinhardt's production of "The Miracle" which happened to go bankrupt in Dallas. After a few years the items were given to us. There are posters, tear sheets, souvenir programs, and other colorful items from Morris Gest and the Artef Collection. We have about 200 19th century English playbills and a few from the 18th century. There is a collection of modern English, French, and other European programs, many of them illustrated souvenir programs. Also, magazines on theater, cinema, and television (1800). Scrapbooks covering from southwest and Dallas theater, 1890s-1950s. Special Collections: artifacts and documents on puppets; masks; costume design; circus; and ballet and dance. The Harriet Bacon

MacDonald Collection of over 200 photographs of musicians appearing in Dallas during the first three decades of the 20th century. Many autographed. Affiliated with Meadow Theatre of the Arts.

VA —GEORGE MASON UNIVERSITY, Fenwick Library, Special Collections Dept, 4400 University Drive, Fairfax, 22030. Ruth Kerns, Public Services Librn
Notes: The Federal Theatre Project Collection includes 5000 playscripts, 2500 radio scripts, 25,000 photographs, 40 blueprints, 1000 posters, over 1600 costume designs, 350 scene designs, 750 production notebooks, 1700 programs and heralds, 26 musical scores and 18 cubic feet of research materials and play readers reports.

WA —SEATTLE PUBLIC LIBRARY, 1000 Fourth Ave, Seattle, 98104. Ronald A Dubberly, City Librn
Holdings: Vols 12,000 // Cat
Notes: Incl programs or copies of programs of plays, musical concerts, etc, performed in Seattle 1864-1958. Known as Sayre-Carkeek Theatre Program collection. Indexed by play, player, and chronilogically.

WI —MILWAUKEE PUBLIC LIBRARY, 814 W Wisconsin Ave, Milwaukee, 53233. Donald J Sager, City Librn
Holdings: Vols Cat
Notes: Collection incl programs from old local area theatres from 1850s incl early German theatre to the present; also current programs of all local theatre events.

ON —NATIONAL LIBRARY OF CANADA, 395 Wellington St, Ottawa, K1A 0N4, Can. Andre Preibish, Dir
Holdings: Vols 8000
Notes: Includes 100 serial titles, also programs, play bills etc on microfilm. Performing arts collection consists of Canadian titles received on legal deposit and purchased. Areas of concentration: Canadian theatre and dance; European and American performing arts tradition; theatre architecture; stage craft; costume history, dance history and notation etc.

ON —METROPOLITAN TORONTO LIBRARY, Theatre Dept, 789 Yonge St, Toronto, M4W 2G8, Can. Heather McCallum, Head
Holdings: Vols (30,500) Mss Pix Slides Phonorecords Microforms
Notes: Over 22,000 theatre programs provide a full record of professional productions in Canada, incl a collection of 19th century playbills for eastern Canada. British and American theatres are collected but not as extensively.
See also entry under Theatre - Canada.

PROGRESSIVE EDUCATION ASSOCIATION

IL —UNIVERSITY OF ILLINOIS, URBANA/CHAMPAIGN, Library, University Archives, 19 Library, 1408 W Gregory Drive, Urbana, 61801. Maynard Brichford, University Archivist
Holdings: Cat Mss Maps Pix Slides Microforms
Notes: Papers, archival records, etc.

PROGRESSIVE LEAGUE (LONDON)

MO —WASHINGTON UNIVERSITY, Libraries, Rare Book Department, Skinker & Lindell Blvds, Saint Louis, 63130. Holly Hall, Chief, Rare Books & Special Collections
Holdings: Cat Mss
Notes: Papers of this London political and literary forum, 1949-1963, incl correspondence of W H Auden, C Day Lewis, Robert Graves, and Julian Huxley in correspondence with the League's secretaries.

PROHIBITION

ME —BOWDOIN COLLEGE, Library, Brunswick, 04011. Dianne M Gutscher, Cur of Special Collections
Holdings: Mss
Notes: The Neal Dow Papers contain 110 letters, 1852-1887, of this temperance reformer, known as "father of the Maine Law." The Hubbard Family Papers contain more than 12,000 pieces of correspondence and other mss materials relating to the Hubbard Family, for the period 1794-1915. Of principal interest are extensive files of letters to and from John Hubbard (1794-1869), governor of Maine, who signed the "Maine Law" (prohibition law) in 1851, and was a commissioner under the Reciprocity Treaty with Great Britain.

†MA —UNIVERSITY OF MASSACHUSETTS AT AMHERST, Library, Amherst, 01003.
Notes: The history of the temperance and prohibition movement in the US.

NY —NEW YORK PUBLIC LIBRARY, Research Libraries, General Research Division, Fifth Ave & 42 St, New York, 10018. Rodney Phillips, Chief
Holdings: Vols (2,225,000) Cat Maps Pix Microforms
Budget: ($775,718)

NY —ROCKEFELLER UNIVERSITY, Rockefeller Archive Center, Hillcrest, Pocantico Hills, North Tarrytown, 10591. Joseph W Ernst, Dir; J William Hess, Assoc Dir
Notes: Papers relative to the Rockefeller Family, Foundations, University, and other specific enterprises and contributions to particular areas of social, physical, educational, and historic reform, preservation, conservation or development. Extensive records of administrative, financial, physical, or intellectual relationships.

RI —BROWN UNIVERSITY, John Hay Library, 20 Prospect St, Providence, 02912. Mark N Brown, Cur Mss
Holdings: // Mss
Notes: Eli H Canfield mss reflect issues of the day and incl the subjects of mission, religious education, temperance, Prohibition, and Reconstruction. There are also 300 letters from Canfield to his son and grandchildren; letters from Europe and the South during and after the Civil War; and papers relating to Christ Church, Brooklyn. Register available. See "The Rev Eli Canfield (1817-1898): Low-church Yankee Episcopalian," ed by William G McLoughlin, Jr, in *Books at Brown*, vol XXIII (1969), pp 135-68.

PROJECT BLUE BOOK

CA —UNIVERSITY OF CALIFORNIA, LOS ANGELES, Research Library, Dept of Special Collections, 405 Hilgard Ave, Los Angeles, 90024. Edward Shreeves, Chairman, Bibliographers Group; David S Zeidberg, Head
Notes: 72 linear feet of the records of the US Air Force Project Blue Book, the group responsible for investigating reported UFO sightings in the US and around the world. Incl scripts for the television program, *Project UFO*.

PROJECT MATTERHORN

NJ —PRINCETON UNIVERSITY, Library, University Archives, Princeton, 08540.
Holdings: 2 Boxes
Notes: Records of Project Matterhorn, 1951-1966.

PROJECT MOVEMENT EDUCATION

NC —UNIVERSITY OF NORTH CAROLINA, GREENSBORO, Walter Clinton Jackson Library, Special Collections Dept, 1000 Spring Garden St, Greensboro, 27412. Emilie W Mills, Librn
Holdings: Vols 100 Uncat
Notes: Incl papers of the Project Movement Education, Plattsburg, New York (1966-69), and papers and publications of Laurie Campbell, Gladys Andrews Fleming, Bonnie Gilliom, James H Humphrey, Elizabeth A Ludwig, Ruth Morison and Lorena Porter.

PROJECT SIGMA

MO —WASHINGTON UNIVERSITY, Libraries, Special Collections Dept, Campus

PROJECT SIGMA (cont.)

Box 1061, St Louis, 63130.
Notes: Extensive collection.

PROJECT WHIRLWIND

MA —MASSACHUSETTS INSTITUTE OF
TECHNOLOGY, Institute Archives, Special
Collections, Cambridge, 02139.
Notes: The materials in the Magnetic Core
Memory collection assembled in support of
MIT during the patent litigation over the
magnetic core memory. Invented in 1947 by
Jay Forrester during the development of the
Whirlwind Computer, magnetic core
memory set the stage for the development of
high-speed digital computers. Though
Whirlwind was originally begun as an
aircraft simulator project during World War
II, the computer which resulted became the
prototype for most large scale general
purpose computers. The collection dates
mostly from the 1940s and 1950s.

PROKOSCH, FREDERIC, 1908-

CA —UNIVERSITY OF CALIFORNIA, LOS
ANGELES, Research Library, Dept of
Special Collections, 405 Hilgard Ave, Los
Angeles, 90024. Edward Shreeves,
Chairman, Bibliographers Group; David S
Zeidberg, Head
Holdings: Vols 30
Notes: 30 first and other editions of his
books; 40 letters; 2 mss. No photocopying.

PROLETARIAN LITERATURE

OK —UNIVERSITY OF TULSA, McFarlin
Library, Dept of Rare Books and Special
Collections, 600 S College, Tulsa, 74104.
David Farmer, Dir; Toby Murray, Archivist;
Caroline Swinson, Cur of Manuscripts & Art
Holdings: Vols 2000
Notes: A major collection of Proletarian
literature based on Walter Rideout's *The
Radical Novel in the United States,
1900-1954.*

PROLONGED-RELEASE DRUGS see
Delayed-Action Preparations

PRONZINI, BILL

MA —BOSTON UNIVERSITY, Mugar
Memorial Library, Special Collections Dept,
771 Commonwealth Ave, Boston, 02215.
Howard B Gotlieb, Dir
Holdings: Cat Mss Correspondence

PROPAGANDA, AMERICAN

DC —GEORGETOWN UNIVERSITY,
Library, Special Collections Div, 37 & O Sts
NW, Washington, 20057. George M
Barringer, Special Collections Librn;
Nicholas B Sheetz, Mss Librn
Holdings: Mss Cat
Notes: The papers of Ambassador Martin F
Herz (1917-1983), containing
correspondence, reports, memoranda,
posters, propaganda leaflets, and other
ephemeral material relating to psychological
warfare in World War II and Vietnam; also
much material on the Cold War and
American foreign policy in the years
following World War II.
DC —LIBRARY OF CONGRESS, Prints &
Photographs Div, Washington, 20540.
Notes: The Gary Yonker Collection of
political propaganda posters, late 1960s to
present. Strongest for US materials but incl
about 50 other countries' work. Over 4500
items, arranged geographically.
IL —CENTER FOR RESEARCH
LIBRARIES, 6050 S Kenwood Ave,
Chicago, 60637. Donald B Simpson, Dir;
Esther Smith, Collection Development Librn
IL —NORTHWESTERN UNIVERSITY,
Library, Special Collections Dept, 1937
Sheridan Rd, Evanston, 60201. R Russell
Maylone, Cur
Holdings: Vols 300 Uncat
Notes: Propaganda--OSS, WW II material
for both Europe and Asia.

LA —TULANE UNIVERSITY, Howard-Tilton
Memorial Library, Special Collections Div,
7001 Freret St, New Orleans, 70118. Wilbur
E Meneray, Librn
Holdings: Cat Audiotapes Microforms
Notes: Books, pamphlets, serial publications
and circulars from over 2000 individuals and
organizations representing the fringe of 20th
century US political opinion.
MD —UNIVERSITY OF MARYLAND,
BALTIMORE COUNTY, Albin O Kuhn
Library and Gallery, 5401 Wilkens Ave,
Baltimore, 21228. Ann Copeland, Special
Collections Librn
Holdings: // Uncat
Notes: The collection incl more than 1000
pamphlets and broadsides on communism,
fascism, Trotskyism, socialism, etc.
NE —UNIVERSITY OF NEBRASKA-
LINCOLN, Don L Love Library, University
Archives and Special Collections, Lincoln,
68588. Joseph G Svoboda, University
Archivist
Notes: Collection consists mainly of
pamphlets, clippings, posters, and other
World War II ephemera; 2000 items.
NY —COLUMBIA UNIVERSITY
LIBRARIES, Lehman Library, Bureau of
Applied Social Research Archive, 420 W
118th St, New York, 10027. David Lewis,
Librn
Holdings: Uncat
Notes: Current information file of Radio
Free Europe publications. There is
significant coverage of the period 1956-1973.
The current file incl Radio Free Europe
Situation Reports, which are published for
selected countries on a weekly basis,
Background Reports dealing with themes of
broader significance, and Media Surveys
which are translations of important East
European press articles. The retrospective
files incl these research products arranged on
a country-by-country basis.
WA —TACOMA PUBLIC LIBRARY, 1102
Tacoma Ave S, Tacoma, 98402. Kevin
Hegarty, Dir
Holdings: Vols 1300 Mss Maps Posters
Notes: Collection of World War I
propaganda pamphlets and posters. 1000
posters, mostly US, but some French.

PROPAGANDA, ANTI-RUSSIAN

DC —GEORGETOWN UNIVERSITY,
Library, Special Collections Div, 37 & O Sts
NW, Washington, 20057. George M
Barringer, Special Collections Librn;
Nicholas B Sheetz, Mss Librn
Holdings: Mss Cat
Notes: The papers of Ambassador Martin F
Herz (1917-1983), containing
correspondence, reports, memoranda,
posters, propaganda leaflets, and other
ephemeral material relating to psychological
warfare in World War II and Vietnam; also
much material on the Cold War and
American foreign policy in the years
following World War II.

PROPAGANDA, FRENCH

CA —HOOVER INSTITUTION ON WAR,
REVOLUTION & PEACE, Stanford
University, Stanford, 94305. Milorad M
Drachkovitch, Archivist
Holdings: Vols 3500 Cat Mss Microforms
Notes: History of the Fifth Republic of
France. Noteworthy among ephemera is a
collection of offical French election
propaganda for the general elections of
1958-1978. Bibliography: *The French Fifth
Republic, Established and Consolidation
(1958-1965): An Annotated Bibliography of
the Holdings at the Hoover Insititution* and
the sequel *The French Fifth Republic,
Continutiy and Charge (1966-1970),* Grete
Heinz and Agnes F Peterson (Stanford,
1970, 1974).
WA —TACOMA PUBLIC LIBRARY, 1102
Tacoma Ave S, Tacoma, 98402. Kevin
Hegarty, Dir
Holdings: Vols 1300 Mss Maps Posters
Notes: Collection of World War I
propaganda pamphlets and posters. 1000
posters. 1000 posters, mostly US, but some
French.

PROPAGANDA, GERMAN

CA —HOOVER INSTITUTION ON WAR,
REVOLUTION & PEACE, Stanford
University, Stanford, 94305. Milorad M
Drachkovitch, Archivist
Holdings: Mss Pix
Notes: Two collections: (1) Collection of
clippings, 1903-42, relating to the literary
career of GS Viereck, his arrest and trail as a
pro-German propagandist in the US during
World War II, German-American relations,
and US foreign policy during World War I.
Many of the clippings are articles by GS
Viereck. 32 scrapbooks. (2) Papers of Karl H
von Wiegand, Hearst newspaper foreign
correspondent, 1917-61, incl
correspondence, dispatches, mss of writings,
photos, clippings, and printed matter, 1911-
61, relating to European diplomacy and
German politics between the world war, the
Sino-Japanese War, the European theater in
World War II, the Cold War, the postwar
Middle Eastern situation, and US foreign
policy. In English and German. 88 ms boxes,
6 binders, 1 stack of oversize mounted
clippings, 2 swords, 1 shield.
DC —GEORGETOWN UNIVERSITY,
Library, Special Collections Div, 37 & O Sts
NW, Washington, 20057. George M
Barringer, Special Collections Librn;
Nicholas B Sheetz, Mss Librn
Holdings: Mss Cat
Notes: The papers of Ambassador Martin F
Herz (1917-1983), containing
correspondence, reports, memoranda,
posters, propaganda leaflets, and other
ephemeral material relating to psychological
warfare in World War II and Vietnam; also
much material on the Cold War and
American foreign policy in the years
following World War II.
DC —LIBRARY OF CONGRESS, Motion
Pictures, Broadcasting and Recorded Sound
Div, Washington, 20540.
Notes: German films, 1930s and 1940s, incl
silent and sound features, newsreels, and
educational, entertainment, documentary,
and propaganda shorts.
MN —UNIVERSITY OF MINNESOTA, O
Meredith Wilson Library, 309 19 Ave S,
Minneapolis, 55455. Austin J McLean,
Chief, Special Collections
Holdings: Vols (6000) // Uncat
Notes: Extensive collection of multi-lingual
propaganda pamphlets, political cartoons and
posters. Complete listing available in the
Division.
†VA —GEORGE C MARSHALL
RESEARCH FOUNDATION AND
LIBRARY, Drawer 920, Lexington, 24450.
Royster Lyle Jr, Cur Collections
Holdings: Vols Cat Mss Pix
Notes: Papers of Forrest C Pogue, Army
historian, Marshall biographer. Also over
300 German propaganda and military
handbooks, and miscellaneous German pre-
War books; French, German and American
WW II newspapers (approx 300).

PROPAGANDA, JAPANESE

NE —UNIVERSITY OF NEBRASKA-
LINCOLN, Don L Love Library, University
Archives and Special Collections, Lincoln,
68588. Joseph G Svoboda, University
Archivist
Notes: Collection consists mainly of
pamphlets, clippings, posters, and other
World War II ephemera; 2000 items.

PROPAGANDA AND
PROPAGANDISTS

CA —HOOVER INSTITUTION ON WAR,
REVOLUTION & PEACE, Stanford
University, Stanford, 94305. Milorad M
Drachkovitch, Archivist
Holdings: Mss
Notes: Collection of clippings, 1903-42,
relating to the literary career of GS Viereck,
his arrest and trial as a pro-German
propagandist in the US during World War II,
German-American relations, and US foreign

PROPAGANDA AND PROPAGANDISTS (cont.)

policy during World War I. Many of the clippings are articles by GS Viereck. 32 scrapbooks.

MA —EDWARD L BERNAYS PUBLIC RELATIONS LIBRARY, 7 Lowell St, Cambridge, 02138.
Holdings: Vols (3000) Cat
Notes: Said to be one of the largest collections on the subject of public relations, publicity, and propaganda. Many pamphlets. No photocopying.

NC —US ARMY SPECIAL WARFARE CENTER, Marquat Library, Fort Bragg, 28307. Frank Lundgren, Librn
Holdings: Vols (45,000) Cat Microforms
Notes: Guerilla warfare, unconventional warfare, strategy, etc. International aspect in political science. 425 periodicals, serial subject collections; newspapers, HRAF microfiche subscription.

PROPAGANDA AND PROPAGANDISTS—PICTURES, ILLUSTRATIONS, ETC.

DC —LIBRARY OF CONGRESS, Prints & Photographs Div, Washington, 20540.
Notes: Poster collection numbers about 70,000 American and foreign items from the 1850s to the present. Incl *Art Nouveau* of World War I and World War II, WPA, propaganda, performing arts, and psychedelic posters.

PROPERTY—VALUATION see Valuation

PROPERTY, LITERARY see Copyright

PROPERTY INSURANCE see Insurance, Property

PROPERTY TAX

IL —INTERNATIONAL ASSOCIATION OF ASSESSING OFFICERS, Research & Technical Services Dept, 1313 E 60 St, Chicago, 60637. Stuart W Miller, Librn
Holdings: Vols 6000 Cat Documents Microforms
Budget: ($3500)
Notes: Extensive collection of materials relating to the property tax and its administration, incl assessment studies, reports of legislative and civic groups, manuals, judicial decisions and other works. Subscription information service available. Library is an OCLC member and lends on ILL. The Library is open to the public (at least 24 hours notice required) and accepts telephone inquiries.

PROPHECIES

NY —COLUMBIA UNIVERSITY LIBRARIES, Rare Book & Manuscript Library, 801 Butler Library, 535 W 114 St, New York, 10027. Kenneth A Lohf, Librn
Holdings: Mss
Notes: Conditions, methods, history and case studies of prophetic prediction.

NY —COLUMBIA UNIVERSITY LIBRARIES, C V Starr East Asian Library, 300 Kent Hall, New York, 10027. James Reardon-Anderson, Librn
Notes: Incl 67 bone and shell items registered in Chou, Hung-hsaing's *Oracle Bone Collections in the United States*. (Berkeley: University of California Press, 1976) and approx 30 counterfeit and unevaluated bones.

PROPRIETARY MEDICINES see Medicines, Patent, Proprietary, Etc.

PROPULSION

KY —UNIVERSITY OF KENTUCKY, Robert E Shaver Library of Engineering, 355 Anderson Hall, Lexington, 40506. Russell H Powell, Engineering Librn
Holdings: Vols (48,000) Cat Microforms

TN —UNIVERSITY OF TENNESSEE, Space Institute Library, Tullahoma, 37388. Helen B Mason, Librn
Holdings: Vols (14,000) Cat Microforms
Budget: ($50,000)
Notes: Incl NASA and other series of technical reports.

PROSCENIUM PRESS PAPERS

DE —UNIVERSITY OF DELAWARE, Hugh M Morris Library, S College Ave, Newark, 19711. T Stuart Dick, Special Collections
Holdings: Cat Mss Pix
Notes: Manuscripts, etc, incl 20th century Irish literary and theatrical correspondence.

PROSPECTING

CA —UNIVERSITY OF THE PACIFIC, Library, Stockton, 95211. Hiram L Davis, Dir of Libraries
Holdings: Vols (25,000) Cat Mss Maps Pix Slides Microforms
Budget: ($1000)
Notes: The Stuart Library of Western Americana accounts for the bulk of the special collections in the university library. Established to support the research activities of the California History Foundation under the leadership of Rockwell D Hunt in 1947 and named after Reginald R Stuart and his late wife Grace who directed the Foundation from 1956 to 1965 and contributed the nucleus of the collection. While the collection covers all of the Trans-Mississippi West, special emphasis is upon original documents and accounts of the California gold rush and subsequent development of the Central Valley of California. The most notable holdings are the John Muir papers. Research papers are published in the *Pacific Historian*, a quarterly journal.

PA —CARNEGIE LIBRARY OF PITTSBURGH, Science & Technology Dept, 4400 Forbes Ave, Pittsburgh, 15213. Catherine M Brosky, Dept Head
Holdings: Vols (380,000) Cat Maps Microforms
Budget: ($240,000)
Notes: Subject area well developed with emphasis on North American geology; other continents of secondary interest. Long runs of journals, reports of geological surveys and society publications. Incl abstracts, indexes, bibliographies, literature guides, dictionaries, handbooks, manuals, compilations of data, maps, history and biography. Complete sets of US topographic maps and geologic folios, climatological data, water supply papers and soil surveys.

PROSTAGLANDINS

MI —THE UPJOHN COMPANY, Corporate Technical Library, 301 Henrietta St, Kalamazoo, 49001. Lorraine Schulte, Manager
Holdings: Cat Microforms
Notes: Complete collection of books, journals, articles, and patents; current bibliography.

PROSTITUTION

CA —WOMEN'S HISTORY RESEARCH CENTER, Microfilm Library, 2325 Oak St, Berkeley, 94708. Laura X, Librn
Holdings: Microforms
Notes: Incl 500 subject files of material on Women and Law (General); Politics; Employment; Education; Rape/Prison/Prostitution; Black and Third World women. Collection at University of Wyoming, Archive of Contemporary History, PO Box 3334, Laramie, Wyoming 82071, c/o David Crosson. Reasearch inquiries accepted. Microfilm of collection (40 reels & reel guides) available through Women's History Research Center, 2325 Oak St, Berkeley, CA 94708. No collections housed at this address.

CA —CALIFORNIA STATE UNIVERSITY, NORTHRIDGE, Delmar T Oviatt & South Libraries, 1811 Nordhoff St, Northridge, 91330. Donald L Read, Special Collections Dept
Holdings: Vols 1800 Cat
Notes: Books and other materials devoted to

all aspects of human sexuality, particularly strong in prostitution and homosexuals and homosexuality.

IN —INDIANA UNIVERSITY, Institute for Sex Research Library, 416 Morrison Hall, Bloomington, 47401. Douglas Freeman, Collections and Services Librn; Joan Brewer, Information Services Librn
Holdings: Vols (62,000) Cat Mss Pix Microforms
See also entry under Sex.

OH —CLEVELAND PUBLIC LIBRARY, Social Sciences Department, 325 Superior Ave, Cleveland, 44114. Thelma Morris, Head
Holdings: Vols 300 Cat
Notes: The Walton collection of prostitution consists mainly of 19th-century publications in English and French, plus a few in German and other languages.

PROTECTION OF CHILDREN see Child Welfare

PROTECTION OF ENVIRONMENT see Environmental Protection

PROTECTION OF NATURE see Nature Conservation

PROTECTION OF WILDLIFE see Wildlife Conservation

PROTECTIVE COATINGS

IN —UNION CARBIDE CORP, Coatings Service Dept, Technical Library, 1500 Polco St, PO Box 24166, Indianapolis, 46224. Mary Ann Brady, Librn
Holdings: Vols 6000 Cat
Notes: Coating technology. Restricted use: corporate personnel.

SC —SONOCO PRODUCTS CO, Research Laboratory, Technical Information Center, One N Second St, Hartsville, 29550. Ken Chavis, Dir
Holdings: Vols (4000) Cat Mss Slides Microforms
Notes: Restricted to Sonoco employees. No photocopying.

PROTEST MOVEMENTS AND DEMONSTRATIONS

IL —NORTHWESTERN UNIVERSITY, Library, Special Collections Dept, 1937 Sheridan Rd, Evanston, 60201. R Russell Maylone, Cur
Holdings: Vols 1000 Cat
Notes: Very large collection of original journals from the 1960s and 1970s, mostly American and Canadian, but also several English and French. Also high school papers. Subjects incl left-wing politics, American Indian ecology, drug culture, anti-war and environmental issues. Women's collection of serial holdings largest in country. All hard copy with exception of some of the Women's collection.

MD —UNIVERSITY OF MARYLAND, BALTIMORE COUNTY, Albin O Kuhn Library and Gallery, 5401 Wilkens Ave, Baltimore, 21228. Ann Copeland, Special Collections Librn
Holdings: Vols 1000 // Uncat
Notes: The Hugh Davis Graham papers relate toDr Graham's works as Co-Director of the Task Force on the History of Violence in America (for the National Commission on the Causes and Prevention of Violence). The Collection consists of materials dealing with all aspects of violence as well as movements specifically related to the 1960s ("Ban the Bomb," etc). The collection is topically arranged and available for research use.

WI —STATE HISTORICAL SOCIETY OF WISCONSIN, Archives, 816 State St, Madison, 53706. Harold L Miller, Reference Archivist
Holdings: Mss Pix Audiotapes Microforms
Notes: Records and papers of organizations and individuals engages in social and political reform activities. Major focus areas are civil rights, 1950s to the present, and

PROTEST MOVEMENTS AND DEMONSTRATIONS (cont.)

anti-Vietnam war and other protest movements of the 1960s to the present. Also covered are other reform movements, socialism, and communism from the 1930s to the present. Collections are described in *Social Action Collection at the State Historical Society of Wisconsin: A Guide*, (1983) and in current accession notes in the *Wisconsin Magazine of History*. Major collections are also listed in Hamer, *Guide to Manuscripts and Archives in the United States*, (1961) and in the *National Union Catalog of Manuscript Collections*, (1959-date).

ON —MCMASTER UNIVERSITY, Mills Memorial Library, Div of Archives & Research Collections, Hamilton, L8S 4L6, Can. G R Hill, Univ Librn
Holdings: Mss
Notes: Office files of the Combined Universities Campaign for Nuclear Disarmament (1959-1964) and its successor The Student Union for Peace Action (1964-1967). Correspondence between branches and with others.

PROTESTANT CHURCHES

CA —AZUSA PACIFIC COLLEGE, Marshburn Memorial Library, Citrus & Alosta, Azusa, 91702. Edward Peterman, Librn
Holdings: Vols 175 Cat Mss
Notes: The Clifford M Drury Collection on the Protestant Missionary in the Far West. No photocopying.

MS —MISSISSIPPI STATE UNIVERSITY, Mitchell Memorial Library, Box 5408, Mississippi State, 39762. Frances N Coleman, Head, Special Collections
Holdings: Vols (15,000) Cat Mss Maps Pix Microforms
Notes: Social and political history of Mississippi, incl University Archives (now separate branch). Microfilms of Protestant Church records. There are strong collections on history of the Southern States, Mississippi authors (especially Faulkner, Williams, Carter, Welty, and Young); also the John C Stennis Collection of over 2 million items, his books, papers, photographs, etc. Incl 400 collections of mss; papers of US Rep David R Bowen 1973-1983; papers of US Rep G V Montgomery 1967-.

PROTESTANT EPISCOPAL CHURCH IN THE U.S.A.

MA —EPISCOPAL DIOCESE OF MASSACHUSETTS, Diocesan Library, 1 Joy St, Boston, 02108. Mark J Duffy, Archivist; Margaret A Dempsey, Asst Archivist
Holdings: Mss Pix
Budget: $37,000
Notes: Official material of the Diocese of Massachusetts, incl parish histories, biographies and writings of bishops and clergymen; prayer books and hymnals of the American Church; Americana; colonial Church histories; materials relating to the Society for the Propagation of the Gospel (SPG); 18th and 19th century pamphlets.

NJ —DREW UNIVERSITY, Library, Madison, 07940. Caroline Coughlin, Assoc Dir
Notes: The Maser Collection of the *Book of Common Prayer*. Incl 152 versions, ranging from a 1522 *Psalter and Hymnal of the Sarum Use* to the 1977 version of the prayer book of the Protestant Episcopal Church of the USA.

NY —GENERAL THEOLOGICAL SEMINARY, Saint Marks Library, 175 Ninth Ave, New York, 10011. David Green, Dir
Holdings: Vols (200,000) Cat Mss
Notes: Extensive collection.

PA —KING'S COLLEGE, D Leonard Corgan Library, 14 W Jackson St, Wilkes-Barre, 18711. Judith Tierney, Special Collections Librn
Holdings: Mss Pix
Notes: The St Stephen's Historical Files,

1813-1979, 16 linear ft. Collection focuses on historical development of the Episcopal Diocese of Bethlehem, Pennsylvania, and on the development of St Stephen's Episcopal Church, Wilkes-Barre, within that context. Material was collected by Dr George Raddin in preparation of his book *The Wilderness and the City* (Wilkes-Barre, Pa: St Stephen's Church, 1968). Another collection focuses on the histories of the various parishes in the Roman Catholic Diocese of Scranton, Pennsylvania and other churches in northeastern Pennsylvania. Collection indexed by name, location, denomination, and ethnic group. 9 linear ft.

RI —UNIVERSITY OF RHODE ISLAND, Library, Special Collections, Kingston, 02881. David Maslyn, Head
Holdings: Mss
Notes: Archive of the Episcopal Diocese of Rhode Island.

SD —AUGUSTANA COLLEGE, Mikkelsen Library & Learning Resource Center, Center for Western Studies, Sioux Falls, 57197. Ronelle Thompson, Dir Library
Notes: The Center for Western Studies, located in the Mikkelsen Library, is an archival and research agency of Augustana College. Dedicated to the history and culture of the Great Plains and the Trans-Mississippi West, the Center collects and preserves materials relating to Plains Indians, immigrant settlers, Norwegiana, Western Americana, Herbert Krause, Frederick Manfred, Donald Parker, Richard F Pettigrew, Augustana College, the Episcopal Diocese of South Dakota, the South Dakota District of the American Lutheran Church, the South Dakota Penitentiary and Minnehaha County.

TN —UNIVERSITY OF THE SOUTH ARCHIVES, Jessie Ball DuPont Library, Sewanee, 37375. Gertrude French Mignery, Archivist
Holdings: Vols (3000) Cat Mss Maps Pix Slides Microforms
Notes: Collection is comprised almost entirely of materials relating to the Episcopal Church and the University and its relationship to the 24 owning Southern dioceses. This collection is not duplicated in the library of the School of Theology. The collection encompasses some 250 cubic feet of official University records, mss (ca 15,000 pieces), bound vols (ca 3000), pamphlets (ca 700), audiovisual resources (ca 100 tape recordings, 100 motion picture films, 5000 loose photographs, and 950 slides), microfilms (ca 90 reels), maps (ca 100 of Sewanee and Franklin County), scrapbooks (ca 100), and museum pieces (ca 300 objects). Almost all of the larger collections have been reported to the National Union Catalog of Manuscript Collections. Such collections incl the papers of Bishops Leonidas Polk, Charles Todd Quintard, James Hervey Otey, as well as extensive collections of all pastVice-Chancellors. A collection of letters of the American Episcopate, 1784-1953 (ca 1200 pieces) has recently been processed for the collection. A master name and subject for the entire holdings.

TX —ROSENBERG LIBRARY, Galveston and Texas History Center, 2310 Sealy Ave, Galveston, 77550. Jane Kenamore, Archivist
Holdings: Vols 7368 Cat Mss Maps Pix Slides Microforms
Budget: $1000
Notes: Emphasis on upper Texas coast material; Republic of Texas period; Civil War period; Shipping; Texas Navy; Jean Laffite; Freemasonry in Texas; Texas politics, 19th-20th century; Railroads; Episcopal Church in Texas. Texas journalism, incl microfilms of Galveston newspapers, 1838-date. In addition to the 7368 cataloged volumes, collection also has approximately 100,000 uncataloged pamphlets, state documents, reports, invitations, etc.

PROTESTANT DISSENTERS see Dissenters, Religious

PROTESTANT REFORMATION see Reformation and Counter-Reformation

PROTESTANTISM

CA —UNIVERSITY OF CALIFORNIA, LOS ANGELES, Research Library, Western

European Collection, Los Angeles, 90024. Edward Shreeves, Chairman, Bibliographers Group; Mary E Greco, Western European Bibliographer
Holdings: Mss Maps Pix Microforms
Notes: Good general coverage. Special strengths in the religious history of the 17th and 18th centuries.

CA —STANFORD UNIVERSITY LIBRARIES, Cecil H Green Library, Stanford, 94305. Michael T Ryan, Cur
Holdings: Vols Cat
Notes: An emphasis in the Rare Book Collection.

MD —JOHNS HOPKINS UNIVERSITY, Milton S Eisenhower Library, George Peabody Collection, 17 E Mt Vernon Place, Baltimore, 21201. Lyn Hart, Peabody Librn
Notes: Noncirculating.

MA —HARVARD UNIVERSITY, Harvard Divinity School, Andover-Harvard Theological Library, 45 Francis Ave, Cambridge, 02138. Maria Grossmann, Librn
Holdings: Vols (370,000) Cat Mss Microforms
Notes: European Protestantism especially.

NY —GENERAL THEOLOGICAL SEMINARY, Saint Marks Library, 175 Ninth Ave, New York, 10011. David Green, Dir
Holdings: Vols (200,000) Cat Mss Maps Pix Slides Microforms

†NY —COLGATE ROCHESTER DIVINITY SCHOOL, Ambrose Swasey Library, 1100 S Goodman St, Rochester, 14620.
Notes: Incl general works about worship, its history and practice and contains manuals of worship, liturgies of primarily Protestant denomination, a sizable collection of hymn books, with particular emphasis upon the Anglican tradition.

OH —PUBLIC LIBRARY OF CINCINNATI & HAMILTON COUNTY, Education & Religion Dept, 800 Vine St, Cincinnati, 45202. Susan F Hettinger, Head
Holdings: Vols (45,000) Cat
Budget: ($10,000)
Notes: Theological and religious collection: religion, church history, theology, 18th and 19th century Protestant writings and sermons.

WI —UNIVERSITY OF WISCONSIN, MADISON, Memorial Library, Western European Humanities Collection, 728 State St, Madison, 53706. Charles Szabo, Bibliographer
Notes: Montauban Collection. Formerly the private library of a prominent Huguenot family long connected with the University of Montauban and organized to document the origin and development of Calvinism in France. Includes a large number of pamphlets, sermons, and other fugitive materials. Supplements the Tank Collection (Calvinism) and the Chwalibog Collection (theology).

PROTOCOL

WI —UNIVERSITY OF WISCONSIN, MADISON, Memorial Library, Slavic Studies Collection, 728 State St, Madison, 53706. Aleksander Rolich, Bibliographer for Slavic Studies; Robert P Gakovich, Slavic Cataloger; Valdis J Zeps, Baltic Studies Center
Notes: The Prince Romanovskii private library reflects his various professional and public interests as a member of the Suite of Tsar Alexander II, as President of the Mineralogical Society and as General of the Cavalry and General-Adjutant. Books on protocol, religion, science, technology, military science, transportation and mining are among the 1000 volumes in his library, as well as an unusual array of maps.

PROTOPHYTA see Cryptogams

PROVENCAL LANGUAGE AND LITERATURE

MA —HARVARD UNIVERSITY LIBRARY, Widener Library, Cambridge, 02138. Assunta S Pisani, Specialist in Book Selection
Holdings: Cat

PROVENCAL LANGUAGE AND LITERATURE (cont.)

NY —HAMILTON COLLEGE, Daniel Burke Library, Special Collections Dept, Clinton, 13323. Frank K Lorenz, Cur
Holdings: Cat
Notes: Outstanding collection described in Rouben C Cholakian's excellent book, *The William P Shepard Collection of Provencalia: A Critical Bibliography* (Clinton, NY: Hamilton College, 1971), with over 500 entries.

NY —NEW YORK PUBLIC LIBRARY, Fifth Ave & 42 St, New York, 10018.
Holdings: Cat

PROVERBS see Aphorisms, Apothegms, Epigrams, Maxims, and Proverbs

PROVIDENCE PUBLIC LIBRARY HISTORICAL COLLECTION

RI —PROVIDENCE PUBLIC LIBRARY, 150 Empire St, Providence, 02903. Lance J Bauer, Special Collections Librn
Holdings: Vols 500 // Cat
Notes: The collection contains the original library of the Providence Public Library. It is very strong in 18th and early 19th century belles-lettres and history.

PROVINCETOWN PLAYERS

NY —NEW YORK PUBLIC LIBRARY, Performing Arts Research Center, Billy Rose Theatre Collection, 111 Amsterdam Ave, New York, 10023. Dorothy L Swerdlove, Cur
Holdings: Cat Mss Pix
Notes: Papers, scrapbooks, mss, photographs, memorabilia, etc.

PROVISIONAL THEATRE

NE —UNIVERSITY OF NEBRASKA, OMAHA, Library, 60 & Dodge Sts, Omaha, 68132. Mel Bohn, Librn
Holdings: Mss
Notes: Provisional Theatre Archives. 30 linear ft of mss and printed works.

PROXMIRE, WILLIAM, 1915-

MA —MASSACHUSETTS INSTITUTE OF TECHNOLOGY, Institute Archives, Special Collections, Cambridge, 02139.
Notes: Correspondence, newsletters, factsheets, newspaper and magazine articles, books and reports of the Citizens' League Against the Sonic Boom, established in 1967 by William Shurcliff to oppose the sonic boom, stop commercial supersonic transport production, and influence public opinion and policy decisions on the SST. Major correspondents incl Bo Lundberg, Richard Wiggs, several US congressmen, and CLASB members.

PRUSSIA—HISTORY

DC —LIBRARY OF CONGRESS, Washington, 20540.
Holdings: Microforms
Notes: Project of a consortium to microfilm about 200,000 pp of material on Great Britain, France, Russia and Prussia, for the period 1848-1918 in the ms and documentary collections of the Austrian State Archives. The collection will incl among others, documents on the Austro-Prussian War of 1866, the treaty negotiations between France and Italy in 1868-1870, the Orient Question of 1877-1878, the persecution of Jews in Russia in 1882, the Congo Conference in Berlin, 1884-1887, and the British-Portuguese conflict in East Africa, 1889-1891. Microfilm copies are available at LC, the Center for Research Libraries, the Hampshire Inter-Library Center, and the libraries of Boston College, Yale, Harvard, Duke, Stanford and the University of Virginia.

ON —METROPOLITAN TORONTO LIBRARY, History Dept, 789 Yonge St, Toronto, M4W 2G8, Can. Michael Pearson, Head

PRUSSIAN LANGUAGE AND LITERATURE

NY —NEW YORK PUBLIC LIBRARY, Slavonic Div, Fifth Ave & 42 St, New York, 10018. Edward Kasinec, Chief
Holdings: Cat Microforms
Notes: Old Prussian Language and Literature. See New York Public Library, *Dictionary Catalog of the Slavonic Collection* (Boston: GK Hall, 1974), 44 vols.

PRUYSER, PAUL W., 1916-

KS —MENNINGER FOUNDATION, Archives, 5600 W Sixth St, Box 829, Topeka, 66601. Alice Brand, Librn; Mark West, Archivist
Notes: 17 boxes, 1956-date. Incl mss and miscellaneous articles.

PSALMODY AND PSALM BOOKS

CA —UNIVERSITY OF CALIFORNIA, LOS ANGELES, Music Library, Schonberg Hall, Los Angeles, 90024. Stephen M Fry, Music Librn
Holdings: Vols 900
Notes: 17th-18th century Dutch song and psalm books.

IL —NEWBERRY LIBRARY, 60 W Walton St, Chicago, 60610. Diana Haskell, Cur of Modern Mss
Holdings: Cat Mss
Notes: 18th and 19th century secular songbooks, hymnody and psalmody. Small selection of ms song books. Noncirculating.

MA —AMERICAN ANTIQUARIAN SOCIETY LIBRARY, 185 Salisbury St, Worcester, 01609. Marcus A McCorison, Dir & Librn
Holdings: Vols (10,000) Cat
Notes: Presumably the most extensive collection of American psalmody in the country. Over 5000 volumes before 1880. Incl the Bay Psalm Book.

PSALTERS

RI —BROWN UNIVERSITY, John Hay Library, Harris Collection, Prospect St, Providence, 02912. Rosemary L Cullen, Cur
Holdings: Vols (200,000) Cat Mss Pix Phonorecords Microforms
Budget: ($15,000)
Notes: The Harris Collection of American Poetry and Plays is principally composed of American and Canadian poetry and plays from the 17th century to the present. Extensive holdings in hymnals of the 17th to the 20th centuries, incl a number of Pennsylvania German hymnals. Collection incl the MacDougall Collections of Psalters and Hymnals. See *Dictionary Catalog of The Harris Collection of American Poetry and Plays* (Boston: G K Hall, 1972), 13 vols; Supplement (1977), 3 vols. Separate catalog.

PSEUDO-ROMANTICISM see Romanticism

PSYCHAGOGY see Psychology, Applied; Psychotherapy

PSYCHEDELIC ART see Art, Psychedelic

PSYCHIATRIC HOSPITALS

CT —INSTITUTE OF LIVING, Medical Library, 400 Washington St, Hartford, 06106. Helen Lansberg, Librn
Holdings: Vols (30,000) Cat Mss Maps Pix
Notes: Three special collections in psychiatry, neurology and related subjects. *See also* entry under Psychiatary

MO —MISSOURI INSTITUTE OF PSYCHIATRY LIBRARY, 5400 Arsenal St, Saint Louis, 63139. Connie Wolf, Librn
Holdings: Vols (18,000) Cat
Notes: St Louis State Hospital patient records and annals, 1869-1914. The data are hand-written, bound in 14 1/2 x 22 1/2 vols. Incl detailed admission, readmission, and discharge data, plus clinical information, for all patients treated during the years covered. Other data incl restraint records, expenditures, staff member, and other medical records. There is no separate catalog or index. No photocopying.

PA —WESTERN PSYCHIATRIC INSTITUTE & CLINIC, Library, 3811 O'Hara St, Pittsburgh, 15261. Lucile Stark, Dir
Holdings: Vols 50,000 Cat Mss Pix Films Microforms Audiotapes
Budget: ($180,000)
Notes: Also incl the archives of the Institute and other ms material relating to the development of psychiatry in Western Pennsylvania, specifically in Pittsburgh. Incl 12,000 pamphlets on all aspects on psychiatry, etc. Rich in bibliographies and reference materials. Incl 750 journal titles.

PSYCHIATRIC NURSING

CT —CONNECTICUT VALLEY HOSPITAL, Hallock Medical Library, Silver St, Middletown, 06457. Mildred Asbell, Medical Librn
Holdings: Vols (3400) Cat

IL —JACKSONVILLE STATE HOSPITAL, Training & Research Library, 1201 S Main St, Jacksonville, 62650. Lois E Wells, Librn
Notes: Concerned particularly with developmental disabilities.

†MA —UNIVERSITY OF MASSACHUSETTS AT AMHERST, Library, Amherst, 01003.
Notes: Special emphases: medical-surgical, psychiatric and mental health, and community health.

MA —BOSTON COLLEGE LIBRARIES, School of Nursing, Library, Cushing Hall, Chestnut Hill, 02167. Mary L Pekarski, Librn
Holdings: Vols 30,000 Cat Slides Audiotapes Videotapes Filmstrips Microforms
Budget: $24,650
Notes: This collection is being absorbed in the general collection.

MA —MEDFIELD STATE HOSPITAL, Medical Library, Hospital Rd, Medfield, 02052. Jeanne M Migliacci, Sr Librn
Holdings: Vols (2063) Cat Audiotapes 16mm Films
Notes: Covers all aspects of psychiatry: clinical, descriptive, and historical plus related subjects; psychiatric nursing, psychiatric social casework, etc.

MI —LAFAYETTE CLINIC LIBRARY, 951 E Lafayette, Detroit, 48207. Nancy E Ward, Librn
Holdings: Vols (7000) Cat
Notes: Library's special emphasis is on the biological aspects, causes and treatment of mental illness.

PA —WESTERN PSYCHIATRIC INSTITUTE & CLINIC, Library, 3811 O'Hara St, Pittsburgh, 15261. Lucile Stark, Dir
Holdings: Vols 50,000 Cat Mss Pix Films Microforms Audiotapes
Budget: ($180,000)
Notes: Also incl the archives of the Institute and other ms material relating to the development of psychiatry in Western Pennsylvania, specifically in Pittsburgh. Incl 12,000 pamphlets on all aspects of psychiatry, etc. Rich in bibliographies and reference materials. Incl 750 journal titles.

VA —CENTRAL STATE HOSPITAL, Medical Library, PO Box 4030, Petersburg, 23803. P D Upadyaya, Medical Librn
Holdings: Vols (10,000) Cat

WA —WESTERN STATE HOSPITAL, Library, Fort Steilacoom, 98494. Neal Van Der Voorn, Librn
Holdings: Vols (5900) Cat Audiotapes
Notes: Collection incl 5500 journal vols, 1800 pamphlets and 420 audiotapes.

PSYCHIATRIC SOCIAL WORK

CA —REISS-DAVIS CHILD STUDY CENTER, Research Library, 3200 Motor Ave, Los Angeles, 90034. Lee Freehling, Librn
Holdings: Vols (12,000) Cat
Notes: Child study, child psychiatry, psychoanalysis, clinical psychology, psychiatric social work. Incl 500 audiotapes; 25 16mm Films.

PSYCHIATRIC SOCIAL WORK (cont.)

MA —MEDFIELD STATE HOSPITAL,
Medical Library, Hospital Rd, Medfield,
02052. Jeanne M Migliacci, Sr Librn
Holdings: Vols (2063) Cat Audiotapes 16mm
Films
Notes: Covers all aspects of psychiatry:
clinical, descriptive, and historical plus
related subjects: psychiatric nursing,
psychiatric social casework, etc.

WA —WESTERN STATE HOSPITAL,
Library, Fort Steilacoom, 98494. Neal Van
Der Voorn, Librn
Holdings: Vols (5900) Cat Audiotapes
Notes: Collection incl 5500 journal vols,
1800 pamphlets and 420 audiotapes.

PSYCHIATRISTS

DC —LIBRARY OF CONGRESS, Manuscript
Division, Washington, 20540. John C
Broderick, Chief
Notes: Papers of the psychiatrist, William G
Niederland; 4000 items.

†MA —FRANCIS A COUNTWAY LIBRARY
OF MEDICINE, Boston, 02115.

†NJ —ADELPHI UNIVERSITY, Library,
Garden City, 11530.
Notes: Marie Beynon (Lyons) Ray
Collection incl mss, correspondence with
prominent psychiatrists and others during
the years 1937-1958.

PSYCHIATRY

CA —CAMARILLO STATE HOSPITAL,
Professional Library, Camarillo, 93010. Kaye
Schmitt, Acting Librn
Holdings: Vols 11,000 Cat
Budget: $8000
Notes: Incl 2000 pamphlets.

CA —LOS ANGELES PSYCHOANALYTIC
SOCIETY AND INSTITUTE, The Simmel-
Fenichel Library, 2014 Sawtelle Blvd, Los
Angeles, 90025.
Holdings: Cat Mss Pix Phonorecords
Notes: The Freudiana Special Collection
(150 vols photocopied letters, translations,
etc; voice recordings), is part of the library's
main collection on psychoanalysis and
psychiatry.

CA —UNIVERSITY OF CALIFORNIA, LOS
ANGELES, Biomedical Library, Center for
the Health Sciences, Los Angeles, 90024.
Alison Bunting, Acting Biomedical Librn;
Victoria Steele, Head, History & Special
Collections Div
Holdings: Vols (400,000) Cat Slides
Phonorecords Audiotapes Videotapes 16mm
Films Microforms

Notes: The UCLA Biomedical Library serves
primarily the Schools of Medicine, Dentistry,
Nursing, and Public Health, the UCLA Medical
Center, the Departments of Microbiology and
Biology in the College of Letters and Science, and
related institutes in biomedicine. The collections of
the Library are broad in scope, designed not only
to support the teaching and research needs of its
many users, but also to function as a resource for
the health sciences-biological field as a whole. The
outstanding feature of the collection is the strength
of its periodical holdings, both current and
retrospective. The Library also has an excellent
reference collection, a comprehensive historical
section, and gives special emphasis to the fields of
neuroscience, psychiatry, ophthalmology, radiation
biology, molecular biology, and vertebrate
zoology. Increased emphasis is being given to the
acquisition of audiovisual materials.

CA —PATTON STATE HOSPITAL, Medical
Library, 26802 E Highland Ave, Patton,
92369. Mary Stumberg, Sr Librn
Holdings: Vols (6000) Cat
Notes: Incl abnormal psychiatry.

†CA —INSTITUTE FOR THE ADVANCED
STUDY OF HUMAN SEXUALITY, 1523
Franklin St, San Francisco, 94109.

CA —LANGLEY PORTER PSYCHIATRIC
INSTITUTE LIBRARY, University of
California, 401 Parnassus Ave Box 13-B, San
Francisco, 94143. Lisa M Dunkel, Librn
Holdings: Vols (11,700) Cat
Notes: Attempt to cover, selectively,
literature in psychiatry, psychoanalysis,
clinical psychology, and allied fields for an
institute which is involved in clinical work,
training and research.

CT —INSTITUTE OF LIVING, Medical
Library, 400 Washington St, Hartford,
06106. Helen Lansberg, Librn
Holdings: Vols (30,000) Cat Mss Maps Pix
Notes: Psychiatry, neurology and related
subjects. There are 3 special collections in
the Library in addition to the regular
collection, which contains about 19,500
books and journals and a quantity of
historical material incl letters and papers of
Dr Eli Todd. The following collections are
complete: (1) The Smith Ely Jelliffe
Collection. Slighty over 10,000 books and
journals on psychoanalysis, psychiatry,
neurology and related subjects, almost all
published before 1940, and some of great
historical interest. (2) The Gregory Zilboorg
Collection. About 300 books from the 16th,
17th, 18th and 19th centuries, most of them
landmarks in the history of psychiatry,
especially psychiatric theory. (3) The Hubert
J Norman Collection. About 300 books from
the 18th, 19th and 20th centuries, relating to
or illustrating mental illness. Incl many
pamphlets, pictures, etc.Emphasis is on legal
psychiatry, the development of hospitals, and
the experience of the patient. No
photocopying.

CT —CONNECTICUT VALLEY HOSPITAL,
Hallock Medical Library, Silver St,
Middletown, 06457. Mildred Asbell, Medical
Librn
Holdings: Vols (3400) Cat

CT —YALE MEDICAL LIBRARY, 333 Cedar
St, New Haven, 06510.
Holdings: Vols (334,215) Cat Mss Pix Slides
Microforms
Budget: ($361,650)
Notes: Incl films, audiotapes, artifacts, etc.
Also Trigant Burow Manuscript Collection
transferred from Lifwynn Foundation.

DC —AMERICAN PSYCHIATRIC
MUSEUM ASSOCIATION, Library and
Archives, 1400 K Street NW, Washington,
20009. Zing Jung, Dir, Library and Archives
Holdings: Vols (17,000) Cat Mss Audiotapes
Videotapes

GA —US VETERANS ADMINISTRATION
HOSPITAL, Medical Library, Lenwood Div,
Augusta, 30904.
Holdings: Vols (3000) Cat Audiotapes
Videotapes
Budget: ($8000)

GA —CENTRAL STATE HOSPITAL, Mental
Health Library, Milledgeville, 31062.
Katherine J Ridley, Librn
Holdings: Vols 450 Cat Audiotapes
Filmstrips
Budget: ($5000)

HI —HAWAII STATE HOSPITAL, Medical
Library, 45-710 Keaahala Rd, Kaneohe,
96744. Diana Stephens, Medical Librn
Holdings: Vols 6000
Budget: $15,200

IL —INSTITUTE FOR PSYCHOANALYSIS,
McLean Library, 180 N Michigan Ave,
Chicago, 60601. Glenn Miller, Librn
Holdings: Vols (10,000) Cat Mss Pix
Audiotapes Videotapes 16mm Films
Microforms
Budget: ($87,000)
Notes: The collection is the data base for the
Chicago Psychoanalytic Literature Index, a
computer-generated quarterly subject guide
to books, monographs, journals, symposia,
tapes, films, and unpublished material
indexed to a depth determined by the quality
of the data. The Index is published by the

Institute in Chicago; a sample is available on
request.

IL —ILLINOIS DEPT OF MENTAL
HEALTH & DEVELOPMENTAL
DISABILITIES, Adolf Meyer Mental
Health Center, Professional Library, 2310 E
Mound Rd, Decatur, 62526.
Holdings: Vols (1000) Cat Audiotapes
Videotapes Microforms
Budget: ($4500)
Notes: Mental health, in general, incl
personal mental health and community
mental health, the behavioral science
(biomedical, psychological, and social), and
treatment modalities of mental illness, with
primary emphasis on community mental
health.

IL —JACKSONVILLE STATE HOSPITAL,
Training & Research Library, 1201 S Main
St, Jacksonville, 62650. Lois E Wells, Librn
Notes: Concerned particularly with
developmental disabilities.

IN —INDIANA UNIVERSITY, Institute for
Sex Research Library, 416 Morrison Hall,
Bloomington, 47401. Douglas Freeman,
Collections and Services Librn; Joan Brewer,
Information Services Librn
Holdings: Vols (62,000) Cat Mss Pix
Microforms
See also entry under Sex.

IN —CENTRAL STATE HOSPITAL, Medical
Library, 3000 W Washington St,
Indianapolis, 46222. Aurella S Baker, Librn
Holdings: Vols (10,400) Cat Audiotapes
Budget: ($41,000)

IN —LARUE D CARTER MEMORIAL
HOSPITAL, Medical Library, 1315 W
Tenth St, Indianapolis, 46202. Philip I Enz,
Librn
Holdings: Vols (14,600) Audiotapes
Budget: ($15,500)
Notes: Incl 100 audiotapes and 219 journal
subscriptions.

IN —LOGANSPORT STATE HOSPITAL,
Staff Library, Logansport, 46947. Terra
Newton, Librn
Holdings: Vols (3000) Cat

IA —US VETERANS ADMINISTRATION
HOSPITAL, Medical Library, Knoxville,
50138. Roger B Sayers, Chief, Library
Service
Holdings: Vols (3000) Cat
Budget: ($2000)

KS —JOHNSON COUNTY MENTAL
HEALTH CENTER, John R Keach
Memorial Library, 6000 Lamar Ave,
Mission, 66202. Krista Hilton-Ross, Librn
Holdings: Vols (1000) Cat Mss

KS —TOPEKA STATE HOSPITAL STAFF
LIBRARY, 2700 W Sixth St, Topeka,
66606. Laura Schafer, Librn
Holdings: Vols (10,000) Cat

KY —NKC HOSPITALS, Medical Library, PO
Box 35070, Louisville, 40232. Holly Shipp
Buchanan, Dir
Holdings: Vols (4500) Cat Audiotapes 16mm
Films
Budget: $200,000
Notes: The Library has a special historical
collection, corporate archives in honor of Dr
Morris Flexner.

LA —CENTRAL LOUISIANA STATE
HOSPITAL, Medical & Professional Library,
PO Box 31, Pineville, 71360. B Carol
McGee, Librn
Holdings: Vols 9400 Cat Audiotapes 16mm
Films
Budget: $25,000

MD —UNION MEMORIAL HOSPITAL,
Nursing Library, 3301 N Calvert St,
Baltimore, 21218. Carolyn Daugherty, Librn
Holdings: Vols (4000) Cat Mss Pix

MD —SPRING GROVE HOSPITAL
CENTER, Sulzbacher Memorial Library,
Catonsville, 21228. Charles H Johnson, Dir
Holdings: Vols (3800) Cat Slides
Phonorecords Audiotapes

MD —CROWNSVILLE HOSPITAL
CENTER, Medical Staff Library,
Crownsville, 21032. Joyce E Munsey, Librn
Holdings: Vols (1500) Cat
Budget: $2000
Notes: Behavior therapy, clinical psychology,
and family therapy.

MD —SPRINGFIELD HOSPITAL CENTER,
Medical Library, Sykesville, 21784.

PSYCHIATRY (cont.)

Elizabeth D Mercer, Librn
Holdings: Vols 3232 Cat

MA —MCLEAN HOSPITAL MEDICAL
LIBRARY, 115 Mill St, Belmont, 02178.
Hector Bossange, Dir
Holdings: Vols 25,611 Cat
Notes: Extensive collection.

MA —BOSTON STATE HOSPITAL, Library,
591 Morton St, Boston, 02124. John Picott,
Librn
Holdings: Vols (3000) Audiotapes
Budget: ($6000)

MA —FRANCIS A COUNTWAY LIBRARY
OF MEDICINE, Boston Medical Library/
Harvard Medical Library, 10 Shattuck St,
Boston, 02115. C Robin LeSueur, Librn;
Richard J Wolfe, Cur, Rare Books &
Manuscripts
Holdings: Vols (500,000) Cat Mss Maps Pix
Microforms
Notes: Combines resources of the Harvard
Medical School and the Boston Medical
Library. Strong in serials and medical history
in all fields of medicine, incl inclunabula,
non-medical books by doctors, travel books
by doctors. 500,000 medical dissertations
and theses. Special strength in all medical
subjects listed in this volume.

MA —SIMMONS COLLEGE, School of Social
Work Library, 51 Commonwealth Ave,
Boston, 02115. Marilyn Bregoni, Librn
Holdings: Vols (20,000) Cat Mss

MA —MEDFIELD STATE HOSPITAL,
Medical Library, Hospital Rd, Medfield,
02052. Jeanne M Migliacci, Sr Librn
Holdings: Vols (2063) Cat Audiotapes 16mm
Films
Notes: Covers all aspects of psychiatry:
clinical, descriptive, and historical plus
related subjects: psychiatric nursing,
psychiatric social casework, etc.

†MA —CLARK UNIVERSITY, Robert
Hutchings Goddard Library, Worcester,
01610. Dorothy Mosa Kowski, Rare Books
Librn
Holdings: Vols Cat
Notes: Particularly strong in earlier
psychological works, 1880-1920.
Approximately 100 current journal
subscriptions, with supporting journals in
psychiatry, and the social and biological
sciences.

MI —LAFAYETTE CLINIC LIBRARY, 951
E Lafayette, Detroit, 48207. Nancy E Ward,
Librn
Holdings: Vols (7000) Cat
Notes: Special emphasis on the biological
aspects, causes and treatment of mental
illness. Also geriatrics.

MO —SAINT JOSEPH STATE HOSPITAL,
Professional Library, 3400 Frederick Ave,
Box 263, Saint Joseph, 64502. Martha
Goodding, Librn
Holdings: Vols (3000) Cat Slides
Phonorecords Audiotapes 16mm Films
Filmstrips Videotapes

MO —SAINT LOUIS PSYCHOANALYTIC
INSTITUTE, Betty Golde Smith Memorial
Library, 4524 Forest Park Blvd, Saint Louis,
63108. Rheba Symeonoglou, Librn
Holdings: Vols (6019) Cat
Budget: ($4000)
Notes: Primarily a psychoanalytic library.
Considerable material in the fields of
psychiatry, psychology and sociology.
Special section (about 400 books) for the lay
reader. who is also welcome to read any of
the other material in the library. Library has
incorporated the *Index of the Chicago
Institute for Psychoanalysis of American
Psychology and Psychiatry*, Barry T Klein,
ed 3655 W Pine Blvd, St Louis, Mo 63108.

MO —WASHINGTON UNIVERSITY,
Libraries, Dept of Psychiatry, 4940 Audubon
Ave, Saint Louis, 63110. Nora Bennett,
Acting Librn
Holdings: Vols 6500 Cat
Notes: Not open to the public; medical
department personnel only.

NV —NEVADA MENTAL HEALTH
INSTITUTE, Library, 480 Galletti Way,
Reno, 89512. Robert D Armstrong, Librn
Holdings: Vols (2500) Cat Audiotapes

NJ —ESSEX COUNTY HOSPITAL, Hamilton
Memorial Medical Library, PO Box 500,
Cedar Grove, 07009. Elizabeth B Guarducci,
Librn
Holdings: Vols (6500) Cat Audiotapes
Budget: $20,000
Notes: Covers all modes of psychotherapy,
incl psychiatry, and some psychology and
sociology. Incl 135 journal titles.

NJ —GREYSTONE PSYCHIATRIC
HOSPITAL, Medical Library, PO Box A,
Greystone Park, 07950. Brian C Hamilton,
Medical Librn
Holdings: Vols (900)

NM —NEW MEXICO STATE HOSPITAL,
Ella P Kief Memorial Library, Hot Spring
Blvd, PO Box 1388, Las Vegas, 87701.
Hazel Hurley, Librn
Holdings: Vols (5000) Cat
Budget: ($2500)
Notes: Partially cataloged.

NY —LONG ISLAND JEWISH-HILLSIDE
MEDICAL CENTER, Hillside Div, Health
Sciences Library, PO Box 38, Glen Oaks,
11004. Joan L Kauff, Librn
Holdings: Vols (9000) Cat Audiotapes

NY —ANALYTICAL PSYCHOLOGY CLUB
OF NEW YORK, Kristine Mann Library, 28
E 39 St, New York, 10016. Doris Albrecht,
Librn
Holdings: Vols 7800 audiotapes
Notes: Material areas in religion, art
mythology, fairy tales and alchemy.

NY —COLUMBIA UNIVERSITY
LIBRARIES, Whitney M Young Jr
Memorial Library of Social Work, 420 W
118 St, New York, 10027. Tyrone Cannon,
Librn
Holdings: Vols (118,646) Cat
Notes: The collection covers the history and
philosophy of social work, social work
methodology, and all aspects of social
welfare services, especially child welfare,
mental hygiene, correction, the aging, social
security and medical care, rehabilitation,
aspects and problems of civil rights and
automation. There is also a substantial
representation of literature in psychiatry and
the behavioral and social sciences. The
reference section includes more than 419
periodicals, publications issued by voluntary
agencies, government publications, doctoral
dissertations and masters' essays in the field
and standard reference works. Reference
service is available.

NY —MORRIS N & CHESLEY V YOUNG
LIBRARY OF MNEMONICS, 270
Riverside Dr, New York, 10025. Morris N
Young, Cur
Holdings: Cat Mss Maps Pix Phonorecords
Audiotapes 16mm Films Microforms
Notes: Collection of 5000 books, pamphlets,
pictures, memorabilia, etc incl medieval art
of memory; psychology of memory,
forgetting and reading; medical aspects of
memory, amnesia, dyslexia; biomedical
aspects of learning and memory; information
storage, retrieval and cybernetics; memory
prodigies, lightning calculators, calendars;
remembrance cups and memory mementos.
All languages. Memorabilia incl engravings,
posters, programs, advertisements, birthday
cards, teaching cards, ASLs, and Mark
Twain's Memory Builder game and other
games. Items range from 1410 to 1980s.

NY —CREEDMOOR PSYCHIATRIC
CENTER, Health Sciences Library, Bldg 51,
80-45 Winchester Blvd, Queens Village,
11427. Susan Taubman, Dir of Library;
Pushpa Bhati, Sr Librn
Holdings: Vols (12,000) Cat Slides
Phonorecords Audiotapes Filmstrips
Microfiche
Budget: ($50,000)
Notes: Particularly strong in the areas of
neurology, pharmacology, psychoanalysis,
and psychopharmacology.

NY —UTICA-MARCY PSYCHIATRIC
CENTER, MARCY CAMPUS, Professional
Library, 1213 Court St, Utica, 13502. Janina
Strife, Librn
Holdings: Vols (3000) Cat
Budget: ($6000)

NY —UTICA-MARCY PSYCHIATRIC
CENTER, UTICA CAMPUS, Library
Services-Medical, 1213 Court St, Utica,

13502. Toms E Smith, Sr Librn
Holdings: Vols 2500 Cat
Budget: $2000
Notes: Available to health care professionals
and students.

NY —NEW YORK HOSPITAL-CORNELL
MEDICAL CENTER, Westchester
Division, Medical Library, 21 Bloomingdale
Rd, White Plains, 10605. Lillian A Wahrow,
Librn
Holdings: Vols (9970) Cat
Budget: ($30,000)

NY —WILLARD PSYCHIATRIC CENTER,
Medical Library, Willard, 14588. Helen
Bunting, Chief Library Services
Holdings: Vols (2078) Cat Audiotapes

NC —JOHN UMSTEAD HOSPITAL,
Learning Resource Center, Butner, 27509.
Brenda M Ellis, Librn
Holdings: Vols 7528 Cat Mss

NC —DUKE UNIVERSITY, William R
Perkins Library, Manuscript Dept, Durham,
27706. Ellen Gartrell, Cur of Mss
Notes: The personal papers of Chris Costner
Sizemore, who is widely known as the
subject of the book and movie, "The Three
Faces of Eve." Incl poems and other
writings, diaries, drawings, photographs,
tapes of interviews, and some printed
material.

ND —NEUROPSYCHIATRIC INSTITUTE,
Medical Library, 700 First Ave S, Fargo,
58103. Diane Nordeng, Librn
Holdings: Vols (1000) Cat
Budget: ($8000)

ND —UNIVERSITY OF NORTH DAKOTA,
Harley E French Medical Library, Grand
Forks, 58202. David W Boilard, Dir; Lila
Pedersen, Asst Dir
Holdings: Vols (56,000) Cat
Budget: ($206,000)
Notes: 1075 current periodical subscriptions.

ND —NORTH DAKOTA STATE
HOSPITAL, Staff Library, Box 476,
Jamestown, 58401. Gertrude Berndt, Head
Librn
Holdings: Vols 6000 Cat

OH —ATHENS MENTAL HEALTH &
MENTAL RETARDATION CENTER,
Staff Library, Richland Ave, Athens, 45701.
Judy McGinn, Librn
Holdings: Vols (3000) Cat Audiotapes

OH —ROLLMAN PSYCHIATRIC
INSTITUTE, Clinical Library, 3009 Burnet
Ave, Cincinnati, 45219. M Glassmann, Dir
Holdings: Vols (3000) Cat

OH —CLEVELAND PSYCHIATRIC
INSTITUTE, Karnosh Library, 1708 Aiken
Ave, Cleveland, 44109. Anna L Harris,
Librn
Holdings: Vols 5000 Cat

PA —UNIVERSITY OF PITTSBURGH, Falk
Library of the Health Professions, History of
Medicine Collection, Scaife Hall, Pittsburgh,
15261. Jonathon Erlen, Cur
Holdings: Vols (13,500) Cat Pix
Budget: ($425,269)
Notes: Medicine, dentistry, nursing,
pharmacy, public health, psychiatry
materials, incl some rare books and 300
pamphlets on anesthesia.

PA —WESTERN PSYCHIATRIC INSTITUTE
& CLINIC, Library, 3811 O'Hara St,
Pittsburgh, 15261. Lucile Stark, Dir
Holdings: Vols 50,000 Cat Mss Pix Films
Microforms Audiotapes
Budget: ($180,000)
Notes: Also incl the archives of the Institute
and other ms material relating to the
development of psychiatry in Western
Pennsylvania, specifically in Pittsburgh. Incl
12,000 pamphlets on all aspects of
psychiatry, etc. Rich in bibliographies and
reference materials. Incl 750 journal titles.

PA —DIXMONT STATE HOSPITAL,
Personnel Library, Sewickley, 15143. Daisy
Ta-liang Yao Tang, Librn
Holdings: Vols 1150 Cat

PA —WARREN STATE HOSPITAL, Library,
Box 249, Warren, 16365. Darryl G
Ellsworth, Librn
Holdings: Vols 22,000 Cat Audiotapes
Budget: $51,000
Notes: Union catalog identifying materials
held in clinical laboratory collections.

RI —BROWN UNIVERSITY, John Hay
Library, 20 Prospect St, Providence, 02912.

PSYCHIATRY (cont.)

Mark N Brown, Cur Mss
Holdings: Mss
Notes: Papers of Earl F Zinn, American psychiatrist, comprising medical records of 350 hours of analytical interviews with a schizophrenic patient for a period of about four years in the 1930s; also a portfolio of art work by the same patient and a letter from Freud.

RI —MIRIAM HOSPITAL MEDICAL LIBRARY, 164 Summit Ave, Providence, 02906. Ann LeClaire, Dir of Library Services
Holdings: Cat Cassettes
Notes: Special collection on the renal system with emphasis on kidney transplatation and dialysis.

TN —WESTERN MENTAL HEALTH INSTITUTE, Edwin M Levy Professional Library, Bolivar, 38074. Lee Oda Chambers, Librn
Holdings: Vols 1500

TX —TEXAS DEPT OF MENTAL HEALTH & MENTAL RETARDATION, Central Office Library, 909 W 45, Box 12668, Austin, 78711. Becky Renfro, Librn
Holdings: Vols (4600) Cat

TX —UNIVERSITY OF TEXAS HEALTH SCIENCE CENTER, SAN ANTONIO, 7703 Floyd Curl Dr, San Antonio, 78284. Joyce M Ray, Archivist/Special Collections Librn; JoAnn Glisson, Library Asst

VA —CENTRAL STATE HOSPITAL, Medical Library, PO Box 4030, Petersburg, 23803. P D Upadyaya, Medical Librn
Holdings: Vols (10,000) Cat

WA —WESTERN STATE HOSPITAL, Library, Fort Steilacoom, 98494. Neal Van Der Voorn, Librn
Holdings: Vols (5900) Cat Audiotapes
Notes: Collection incl 5500 journal vols, 1800 pamphlets and 420 audiotapes.

WI —UNIVERSITY OF WISCONSIN, MADISON, W S Middleton Health Sciences Library, 1305 Linden Dr, Madison, 53706. Virginia Holtz, Dir
Holdings: Vols (200,000) Cat Pix Slides Audiotapes Videotapes Microforms

WI —MILWAUKEE COUNTY MENTAL HEALTH COMPLEX, Michael Kasak Library, 9455 Watertown Plank Rd, Milwaukee, 53226. Anna M Green, Librn
Holdings: Vols (12,000) Cat Audiotapes Videotapes 16mm Films Filmstrips Micorforms
Budget: $34,000
Notes: Incl 500 audiotapes and 150 videotapes.

NF —WATERFORD HOSPITAL, Health Sciences Library, Waterford Bridge Rd, Saint John's, A1E 4J8, Can. Maisie Young, Librn
Holdings: Vols (2000) Cat Pix Phonorecords Audiotapes Videotapes 16mm Films Filmstrips
Notes: Material incl aspects of psychiatry related to medicine, nursing, psychology, social work, etc. Also incl manuscript work on a history of the hospital, which closely parallels a history of psychiatry in Newfoundland. Journals are only kept for ten years.

ON —NATIONAL LIBRARY OF CANADA, 395 Wellington St, Ottawa, K1A 0N4, Can. Andre Preibish, Dir
Holdings: Vols 10,000
Notes: Includes 130 serial titles, theses, pamphlets, government publications relating to family and marriage. The following disciplines covered: anthropology, psychology and psychiatry, law, economics, religion, sociology, demography, education, political science and biology. Earliest title 1630.

ON —CLARKE INSTITUTE OF PSYCHIATRY, Farrar Library, 250 College St, Toronto, M5T 1R8, Can. Dawn Stewardson, Librn/Archivist
Holdings: Vols 12,000 Cat Audiotapes

PQ —MCGILL UNIVERSITY, Nursing/Social Work Library, 3506 University St, Montreal, H3A 1Y1, Can. Wendy Patrick, Librn
Holdings: Vols (35,000) Cat

PQ —UNIVERSITY OF MONTREAL, Bibliotheque Para-medicale, 2375 Chemin de la Cote Ste Catherine, Montreal, H3C 3J7, Can. Johanne Hopper, Head Librn
Holdings: Vols 1475 Cat Audiotapes
Notes: Special emphasis on psychotherapy. 15 percent in French.

PSYCHIATRY—HISTORY

CA —STOCKTON STATE HOSPITAL, Professional Library, 510 Magnolia, Stockton, 95202. Walter L Greening, Senior Librn
Holdings: Vols (7000) Cat Microforms Audiotapes
Budget: ($6000)
Notes: Incl both historical and current materials on care and treatment of the mentally retarded: residential care; nursing and medical care; rehabilitation; recreational and occupational therapy; teaching; social services; psychological services. Current emphasis on the care and treatment of the multiply handicapped.

CT —INSTITUTE OF LIVING, Medical Library, 400 Washington St, Hartford, 06106. Helen Lansberg, Librn
Holdings: Vols (30,000) Cat Mss Maps Pix
Notes: Three special collections in psychiatry, neurology and related subjects.
See also entry under Psychiatry

DC —LIBRARY OF CONGRESS, Manuscript Division, Washington, 20540. John C Broderick, Chief
Holdings: Cat Mss Pix
Notes: The papers of Alfred Adler, incl a number of professional studies; a selection of letters by him (1891-1937); documents, photographs, etc.

DC —LIBRARY OF CONGRESS, Washington, 20540.
Notes: The Rudolf Dreikurs papers, incl material on the behavioral sciences and psychiatry.

IL —SOUTHERN ILLINOIS UNIVERSITY, CARBONDALE, Delyte W Morris Library, Special Collections Dept, Carbondale, 62901. David V Koch, Cur of Special Collections; Louisa Bowen, Cur of Manuscripts
Holdings: Cat Mss
Notes: Papers and correspondence of Theodore A Schroeder, constitutional lawyer and founder, with Lincoln Steffens, of the Free Speech League, a forerunner of the American Civil Liberties Union. Contains extensive correspondence with Comstock, Gompers, Debs, H Ellis, Sanger, Sinclair, John Dewey, Darrow, Mencken, A G Hays, Emma Goldman, W E B Dubois, etc. Incl several thousand letters; notes and mss, records of legal cases and extensive files relating to the early history of psychiatry.

IL —UNIVERSITY OF ILLINOIS AT CHICAGO, Library of the Health Sciences, 1750 W Polk St, PO Box 7509, Chicago, 60612. Robert J Adelsperger, Cur, Special Collections
Holdings: Vols 750 // Cat
Notes: The Percival Bailey Collection on Neurology and Psychiatry is closed. Printed catalog: A Catalog of the Percival Bailey Collection of Neurology and Psychiatry (Chicago, 1973).

IN —INDIANA MEDICAL HISTORY MUSEUM, Old Pathology Bldg, 3000 W Washington St, Indianapolis, 46222. Katherine Mandusic McDonell, Cur
Budget: ($24,000)
Notes: Over 1000 volumes of mid-to-late 19th century medical works; bound volumes of the proceedings of Indiana State Medical Society (1857-1907); 100 volumes pertaining to the history of medicine; 50 volumes pertaining to museum studies; approximately 200 prints, paintings, and photographs relating to history of medicine in Indiana; early medical school diplomas; vertical files on history of medicine; materials (printed and manuscripts) pertaining to state's first mental hosptial-Central State Hospital.

KS —MENNINGER FOUNDATION, Archives, 5600 W Sixth St, Box 829, Topeka, 66601. Alice Brand, Librn; Mark West, Archivist
Holdings: Cat Mss Pix
Notes: Records of the Menninger Foundation, Menninger Family Archives, Clifford Beers Papers, Dorothea Dix Papers, Sigmund Freud Papers, Gardner Murphy Papers, etc.

KY —UNIVERSITY OF LOUISVILLE, Kornhauser Health Sciences Library, 520 S Preston St, PO Box 35260, Louisville, 40292. Leonard M Eddy, Dir; Sherrill R McConnell, Archivist
Holdings: Vols 500 Cat
Notes: The Gardner Collection of the History of Psychiatry.

MD —MEDICAL & CHIRURGICAL FACULTY OF THE STATE OF MARYLAND, Library, 1211 Cathedral St, Baltimore, 21201. Joseph E Jensen, Librn
Holdings: Vols (10,000) // Cat Mss Maps Pix
See also entry under Medicine - History and Historic

MA —MEDFIELD STATE HOSPITAL, Medical Library, Hospital Rd, Medfield, 02052. Jeanne M Migliacci, Sr Librn
Holdings: Vols (2063) Cat Audiotapes 16mm Films
Notes: Covers all aspects of psychiatry: clinical, descriptive, and historic plus related subjects: psychiatric nursing, psychiatric social casework, etc.

MO —MISSOURI INSTITUTE OF PSYCHIATRY LIBRARY, 5400 Arsenal St, Saint Louis, 63139. Connie Wolf, Librn
Holdings: Vols (18,000) Cat
Notes: St Louis State Hospital patient records and annals, 1869-1914. The data are hand-written, bound in 14 1/2 x 22 1/2 vols. Incl detailed admission, readmission, and discharge data, plus clinical information, for all patients treated during the years covered. Other data incl restraint records, expenditures, staff members, and other medical records. There is no separate catalog or index. No photocopying.

NY —CORNELL UNIVERSITY MEDICAL COLLEGE, Oskar Diethelm Historical Library, 525 E 68 St, New York, 10021. Phyllis Rubinton, Librn
Holdings: Vols (14,000) Cat Mss
Notes: History of psychiatry and the behavioral sciences. 14,000 historical vols, incl hospital annual reports and theses; 4000 reference vols. Library open to scholars and researchers by appointment. No photocopying.

NY —NEW YORK ACADEMY OF MEDICINE, Library, 2 E 103 St, New York, 10029. Brett A Kirkpatrick, Librn
Holdings: Vols 202 // Cat
Notes: Ernest Harms Collection on 19th century German psychology and psychiatry.

NY —NEW YORK PSYCHOANALYTIC INSTITUE, Abraham A Brill Library, 247 E 82 St, New York, 10028. Ellen D Gilbert, Librn
Holdings: Vols (30,000) Cat Mss Pix Audiotapes
Notes: Subject catalog indexing both book and journal literature. Special collections incl Institute archives, manuscript collections, memorabilia and oral histories. Freud's writings complete in English and German and in part in at least 10 other languages. Open to members and students of Institute and other researchers and students. Photocopying.

NY —UTICA-MARCY PSYCHIATRIC CENTER, UTICA CAMPUS, Library Services-Medical, 1213 Court St, Utica, 13502. Toms E Smith, Sr Librn
Holdings: Vols 400 Uncat Pix
Notes: Contains a number of books from Dr Amariah Brigham's personal library (Dr Brigham was first director of Utica State Hospital), then New York State Lunatic Asylum, and was founder of American Journal of Insanity and its first editor. This journal was the first psychiatric journal in America and became the American Journal of Psychiatry. Also contains volumes on early aspects of psychiatric care, and some general books on medicine. Available to health care professionals and students.

OH —CLEVELAND MEDICAL LIBRARY ASSOCIATION/CASE WESTERN RESERVE UNIVERSITY, Cleveland Health Sciences Library, Historical Division, Allen Memorial Medical Library, 11000 Euclid

PSYCHIATRY—HISTORY (cont.)

Ave, Cleveland, 44106. Glen Jenkins, Rare
Book Librarian & Archivist
Holdings: Vols 420 Cat
Notes: The Sigmund Freud Collection.

PA —WESTERN PSYCHIATRIC INSTITUTE
& CLINIC, Library, 3811 O'Hara St,
Pittsburgh, 15261. Lucile Stark, Dir
Holdings: Vols 50,000 Cat Mss Pix Films
Microforms Audiotapes
Budget: ($180,000)
Notes: Also incl the archives of the Institute
and other ms material relating to the
development of psychiatry in Western
Pennsylvania, specifically in Pittsburgh. Incl
12,000 pamphlets on all aspects of
psychiatry, etc. Rich in bibliographies and
reference materials. Incl 750 journal titles.

VA —COLLEGE OF WILLIAM AND
MARY, Earl Gregg Swem Library,
Williamsburg, 23185. Margaret C Cook, Cur
of Manuscripts & Rare Books
Holdings: Vols 80 // Cat
Notes: Galt Collection of 19th century
European vols of psychiatry and mental
illness.

ON —UNIVERSITY OF TORONTO, Thomas
Fisher Rare Book Library, 120 Saint George
St, Toronto, M5S 1A5, Can. Richard G
Landon, Head
Holdings: Vols (6000) Cat
Notes: Hannah Collection named in honour
of Jason A Hannah, the founder of the
Hannah Institute for the History of Medical
and Related Sciences at the University of
Toronto. Collection comprises a wide range
of works in medicine, surgery, anatomy,
physiology and other related sciences
published in the major European countries
and Great Britain from 1500 to 1900. Areas
of special strength are psychology,
gynecology and obstetrics. Highlights of
collection described in two exhibition
catalogues published by the Thomas Fisher
Rare Book Library: *The Early History of
Medicine; An Exhibition of Books Selected
from the Jason A Hannah Collection in the
History of Medical and Related Sciences*
(March, 1974) and *The Byrth of Mankynd*
(1981).

PSYCHIATRY—RUSSIA

NY —NEW YORK ACADEMY OF
MEDICINE, Library, 2 E 103 St, New
York, 10029. Brett A Kirkpatrick, Librn
Holdings: Uncat
Notes: Over 1000 monographs, pamphlets,
journals, correspondence and personal files
donated by Dr Joseph Wortis. Represents
nearly the entire volume of literature on
Russian psychiatry published between 1950
and 1965 in the Russian, German, and
English languages.

PSYCHIC MEDICINE see Medicine, Psychic

PSYCHICAL RESEARCH

AZ —WORLD UNIVERSITY, Library, 711 E
Blacklidge Dr, Tucson, 85719. Howard John
Zitko, Cur
Holdings: Vols (15,000) Cat Mss Maps
Audiotapes
Notes: Collection concerns what are
generally called the "frontier sciences." No
interlibrary loan.

CA —LOS ANGELES PUBLIC LIBRARY,
Philosophy & Religion Dept, 630 W Fifth St,
Los Angeles, 90071. Marilyn C Wherley,
Librn
Holdings: Vols 600 Cat
Budget: ($60,000)
Notes: Part of the comprehensive collection
on Occult Sciences.

CA —SAN DIEGO PUBLIC LIBRARY,
Literature & Language Sect, 820 E St, San
Diego, 92101. Alyce Archuleta, Senior Librn
Holdings: Cat
Notes: Old and current reference and
circulating works on the subject. Incl
complete works by Blavatsky, much by
Rudolf Steiner, and C Zain. Strong in
astrology, witchcraft, parapsychology.

CA —ROSICRUCIAN ORDER, AMORC,
Research Library, Rosicrucian Park, San
Jose, 95191. Clara Campbell, Librn
Holdings: Cat
Notes: Collection incl materials on
Rosicrucians, ancient Egyptian history,
parapsychology and mysticism. No
interlibrary loans.

IL —UNIVERSITY OF ILLINOIS,
URBANA/CHAMPAIGN, Library,
University Archives, 19 Library, 1408 W
Gregory Drive, Urbana, 61801. Maynard
Brichford, University Archivist
Holdings: Vols (5000) Cat
Budget: ($7000)
Notes: The Mandeville Collection in
Parapsychology and Occult Sciences. Titles
in the Merten J Mandeville Collection are
purchased by funds from an endowment
provided specifically for the collection on its
establishment in 1966 by Merten J
Mandeville, Professor Emeritus of
Management, who donated 400 vols from his
personal library as the nucleus of the
collection. There are currently about 5000
titles in the collection, supplemented by
related materials in the general collection.
Topics include astrology, extrasensory
perception, yoga, magic, satanism, faith
healing, hypnosis, Eastern religions,
witchcraft, fortune telling, reincarnation,
flying saucers, ghosts, dreams, numerology,
graphology, and mysticism. Biographies and
reference books are a part of the collection
as are journals devoted to the scientific study
of parapsychology.

NY —PARAPSYCHOLOGY SOURCES OF
INFORMATION CENTER, 2 Plane Tree
Lane, Dix Hills, 11746. Rhea A White, Dir
Holdings: Vols (4000)
Notes: The PSI Center includes 4000 books,
100 periodical titles, cassette tapes, and
unpublished mss dealing with
parapsychology and the transformation of
consciousness, also 12,000 articles, reprints,
etc. There is a charge for reference service
and bibliographies.

NY —AMERICAN SOCIETY FOR
PSYCHICAL RESEARCH LIBRARY, 5 W
73 St, New York, 10023. Rhea A White,
Consultant to the Library
Holdings: Vols (7000) Cat Mss Pix
Budget: ($1500)
Notes: Incl books on spiritualism, as well as
works in psychology, religion, philosophy,
physics, anthropology, etc which have a
possible bearing on parapsychology. An
attempt is made to obtain all serious books
on parapsychology in English.

NY —NEW YORK PUBLIC LIBRARY,
Research Libraries, General Research
Division, Fifth Ave & 42 St, New York,
10018. Rodney Phillips, Chief
Notes: See *Bibliographic Guide to
Psychology, 1976* (Boston: GK Hall, 1977).
Incl publications cataloged during the year,
with additional entries from MARC tapes.

NY —PARAPSYCHOLOGY FOUNDATION,
Eileen J Garrett Library, 228 E 71st St, New
York, 10021. Wayne Norman, Librn
Holdings: Vols (9300) Cat
Notes: One of the largest libraries on
parapsychology. Main emphasis is on the
literature of contemporary parapsychology;
also a strong collection on the history of
parapsychology (early spiritualism,
mysticism, relevant philosophical works,
etc). Rare book collection incl early rare
books and periodicals on psychical research
and psychical phenomena. Receives about
100 titles of periodicals and binds the more
significant titles. The library maintains its
own periodicals index to parapsychological
literature, dating from 1966. Main emphasis
literature is on experimental parapsychology,
or those publications that approach the
subject with an objective and/or analytic
point of view.

NC —FOUNDATION FOR RESEARCH ON
THE NATURE OF MAN (FRNM),
Institute for Parapsychology, 402 Buchanan
Blvd, Box 6847, College Sta, Durham,
27708. K Ramakrishna Rao, Dir
Holdings: Vols (2500) Cat Mss Pix 16mm
Films
Budget: ($12,000)
Notes: There is also a large body of early

"psychical research" literature as well as
most of the latest books in the field of
parapsychology. Since the Foundation's
activities are primarily devoted to the
quantitative investigation of psi phenomena,
the library in general does not stock books
on occult topics (magic, witchcraft,
astrology, etc).

OH —KENT STATE UNIVERSITY, Libraries,
Dept of Special Collections, Kent, 44242.
Dean H Keller, Cur
Holdings: Vols 67 Cat Mss
Notes: Virginia Glenn Memorial Collection
of Readings in Human Potential.

RI —BROWN UNIVERSITY, John Hay
Library, 20 Prospect St, Providence, 02912.
Mark N Brown, Cur Mss
Holdings: Vols (900) // Mss
Notes: John William Graham Collection of
Literature of Psychic Science--350
predominantly late 19th and early 20th
century books dealing with alchemy, black
magic, dreams, demonology, church history,
mysticism, mediumship, physical and
somatic types of psychic experience.
Collection described in *Index to Psychic
Science* compiled by S R Morgan
(Swathmore, 1950). Also, the Damon
Collection of Occult and Visionary
Literature--550 vols devoted to the
development of western mysticism with
particular emphasis on American and British
thought, incl texts on alchemy, black magic,
esoteric church history, dream
interpretations, mysticism, witchcraft, the
Kabbalah, and visionary testaments and
manifestations of all types printed during the
16th to 20th centuries; and the Samuel
Wyllys Papers--125 mss, transcripts, and
photocopies of legal and government papers
relating to Indianaffairs, colonial wars, civil
and criminal cases, and the witchcraft trials
of 1692-1693. Partially cataloged.

VA —ASSOCIATION FOR RESEARCH &
ENLIGHTENMENT, Library, 67 &
Atlantic Avenue, PO Box 595, Virginia
Beach, 23451. Stephen Jordan, Library Mgr
Holdings: Vols (250) Cat Audiotapes
Notes: Book collection plus Edgar Cayce
Collection of Readings-384 looseleaf binders
with typescripts of 14,250 discourses and
answers given by him in response to
questions while in a trance state. Readings
cover period 1903 to September 1944.
Subjects range from "Attitudes and
Emotions" through "World Affairs" and
"Yoga". Medical files cover common
ailments from "Acne" and "Arthritis"
through "Whooping Cough."

MB —UNIVERSITY OF MANITOBA,
Elizabeth Dafoe Library, Archives and
Special Collections Dept, Winnipeg, R3T
2N2, Can. Richard E Bennett, Dept Head;
Corrado A Santoro, Reference Archivist
Notes: Papers of Thomas Glendenning
Hamilton, physician and surgeon, member of
the Manitoba Legislative Assembly, psychic
researcher. Winnipeg, Manitoba. Important
collection, emphasis is on psychic research
with limited amount of materials regarding
his medical and political careers. Seance
attendance registers, records and affidavits,
lecture notes, correspondence, newspaper
clippings, books and journal articles.
Photographs, slides and ca 50 boxes of glass
plate negatives.

†ON —METROPOLITAN TORONTO
LIBRARY, Social Sciences Dept, 789 Yonge
St, Toronto, M4W 2G8, Can. Abdus Salam,
Head
Holdings: Vols Cat Maps Phonorecords
Audiotapes 16mm Films Microforms
Notes: Includes books on general psychology
and its history. Also, a strong collection of
the works of individual psychologists and
critical works about them. The following
specialized areas of psychology are also well
covered: child psychology, psychology and
mental health, and parapsychology.

PSYCHO-KINESIS see Psychokinesis

PSYCHOANALYSIS

CA —LOS ANGELES PSYCHOANALYTIC
SOCIETY AND INSTITUTE, The Simmel-

PSYCHOANALYSIS (cont.)

Fenichel Library, 2014 Sawtelle Blvd, Los Angeles, 90025.
Holdings: Cat Mss Pix Phonorecords
Notes: The Freudiana Special Collection (150 vols; photocopied letters, translations, etc; voice recordings), is part of the library's main collection of psychoanalysis and psychiatry.

CA —LOS ANGELES PUBLIC LIBRARY, Philosophy & Religion Dept, 630 W Fifth St, Los Angeles, 90071. Marilyn C Wherley, Librn
Holdings: Vols 1000 Cat
Budget: ($60,000)
Notes: General materials in the field including serials and periodicals. Part of comprehensive collection on psychology.

CA —REISS-DAVIS CHILD STUDY CENTER, Research Library, 3200 Motor Ave, Los Angeles, 90034. Lee Freehling, Librn
Holdings: Vols (12,000) Cat
Notes: Child study, child psychiatry, psychoanalysis, clinical psychology, psychiatric social work. Incl 500 audiotapes; 25 16mm Films.

CA —LANGLEY PORTER PSYCHIATRIC INSTITUTE LIBRARY, University of California, 401 Parnassus Ave Box 13-B, San Francisco, 94143. Lisa M Dunkel, Librn
Holdings: Vols (11,700) Cat
Notes: Attempt to cover, selectively, literature in psychiatry, psychoanalysis, clinical psychology, and allied fields for an institute which is involved in clinical work, training and research.

CA —SAN FRANCISCO PSYCHOANALYTIC INSTITUTE, Library, 2420 Sutter St, San Francisco, 94115. Anne L Regner, Librn
Holdings: Vols (5000) Cat
Budget: $5000
Notes: Open to public.

CT —INSTITUTE OF LIVING, Medical Library, 400 Washington St, Hartford, 06106. Helen Lansberg, Librn
Holdings: Vols (30,000) Cat Mss Maps Pix
Notes: Three special collections in psychiatry, neurology and related subjects. *See also* entry under Psychiatry.

DC —LIBRARY OF CONGRESS, Rare Book & Special Collections Div, Washington, 20540. William Matheson, Chief
Holdings: Vols (125) Cat
Notes: The Sigmund Freud Collection of first editions, revised editions, important translations of his writings, etc was formed to complement extensive Freud manuscript holdings previously acquired by the Library. In additions to rare editions of books, eg, the author's first book *Zur Auffassung der Aphasien* (Leipzig & Vienna, 1891) and the first edition of his *Die Traumdeutung* (Leipzig & Vienna, 1900), the collection incl scarce pamphlets and offprints such as his early *Uber Coca* (Vienna, 1885). Associated with this collection, but separately maintained, are ca 50 books from Freud's personal library. Most are presentation copies from such authors as Havelock Ellis, Norman Douglas, Andre Breton, Paul Eluard and Morton Prince. Others which Freud acquired personally are by Pierre Janet, Friedrich Goltz, Daniel Hack Tuke, Carl Wernicke, et al.

DC —LIBRARY OF CONGRESS, Manuscript Division, Washington, 20540. John C Broderick, Chief
Holdings: 9000 Items
Notes: Correspondence, photographs, notes, and reprints of Smith Ely Jelliffe (1896-1944).

IL —INSTITUTE FOR PSYCHOANALYSIS, McLean Library, 180 N Michigan Ave, Chicago, 60601. Glenn Miller, Librn
Holdings: Vols (10,000) Cat Mss Pix Audiotapes Videotapes 16mm Films Microforms
Budget: ($87,000)
Notes: The collection is the data base for the *Chicago Psychoanalytic Literature Index*, a computer-generated quarterly subject guide books, monographs, journals, symposia, tapes, films, and unpublished material indexed to a depth determined by the quality of the data. The *Index* is published by the Institute in Chicago; a sample is available on request.

KS —JOHNSON COUNTY MENTAL HEALTH CENTER, John R Keach Memorial Library, 6000 Lamar Ave, Mission, 66202. Krista Hilton-Ross, Librn
Holdings: Vols (1000) Cat Mss

KS —MENNINGER FOUNDATION, Archives, 5600 W Sixth St, Box 829, Topeka, 66601. Alice Brand, Librn; Mark West, Archivist
Holdings: Vols (33,000) Cat Pix Audiotapes Microforms
Notes: Incl journals. Literature searches and document delivery available for a fee.

MA —MCLEAN HOSPITAL MEDICAL LIBRARY, 115 Mill St, Belmont, 02178. Hector Bossange, Dir
Holdings: Vols 25,611 Cat
Notes: Extensive collection.

MA —AUSTEN RIGGS CENTER, Austen Fox Riggs Library, Main St, Stockbridge, 01262. Helen Linton, Librn
Holdings: Vols (10,556) Cat Audiotapes
Budget: ($10,000)
Notes: Current and historical Literature in psychoanalysis and related fields. Restricted use: open only to staff; to others with written permission. Interlibrary loans to institutions. No photocopying.

MI —LAFAYETTE CLINIC LIBRARY, 951 E Lafayette, Detroit, 48207. Nancy E Ward, Librn
Holdings: Vols (7000) Cat
Notes: Small collection on psychoanalysis. Library's special emphasis is on the biological aspects, causes and treatment of mental illness.

MO —SAINT LOUIS PSYCHOANALYTIC INSTITUTE, Betty Golde Smith Memorial Library, 4524 Forest Park Blvd, Saint Louis, 63108. Rheba Symeonoglou, Librn
Holdings: Vols (5566) Cat
Budget: ($4000)
Notes: Primarily a psychoanalytic library. Considerable material in the fields of psychiatry, psychology and sociology. Special section (about 400 books) for the lay reader, who is also welcome to read any of the other material in the library. Library has incorporated the *Index of the Chicago Institute for Psychoanalysis*, an index of periodical articles by author, title and subject. Collection described in *Reference Encyclopedia of American Psychology and Psychiatry*, Barry T Klein, ed 3655 W Pine Blvd, St Louis, Mo 63108

NY —LONG ISLAND JEWISH-HILLSIDE MEDICAL CENTER, Hillside Div, Health Sciences Library, PO Box 38, Glen Oaks, 11004. Joan L Kauff, Librn
Holdings: Vols (9000) Cat Audiotapes

NY —NEW YORK PSYCHOANALYTIC INSTITUTE, Abraham A Brill Library, 247 E 82 St, New York, 10028. Ellen D Gilbert, Librn
Holdings: Vols (30,000) Cat Mss Pix Audiotapes
Notes: Subject catalog indexing both book and journal literature. Special collections incl Institute archives, manuscript collections, memorabilia and oral histories. Freud's writings complete in English and German and in part in at least 10 other languages. Open to members and students of Institute and other researchers and students. Photocopying.

NY —CREEDMOOR PSYCHIATRIC CENTER, Health Sciences Library, Bldg 51, 80-45 Winchester Blvd, Queens Village, 11427. Susan Taubman, Dir of Library; Pushpa Bhati, Sr Librn
Holdings: Vols (12,000) Cat Slides Phonorecords Audiotapes Filmstrips Microfiche
Budget: ($50,000)
Notes: Particulartly strong in the areas of neurology, pharmacology, psychoanalysis, and psychopharmarcology.

PA —WESTERN PSYCHIATRIC INSTITUTE & CLINIC, Library, 3811 O'Hara St, Pittsburgh, 15261. Lucile Stark, Dir
Holdings: Vols 50,000 Cat Mss Pix Films Microforms Audiotapes
Budget: ($180,000)
Notes: Also incl the archives of the Institute and other ms material relating to the development of psychiatry in Western Pennsylvania, specifically in Pittsburgh. Incl 12,000 pamphlets on all aspects of psychiatry, etc. Rich in bibliographies and reference materials. Incl 750 journal titles.

WI —MILWAUKEE COUNTY MENTAL HEALTH COMPLEX, Michael Kasak Library, 9455 Watertown Plank Rd, Milwaukee, 53226. Anna M Green, Librn
Holdings: Vols (12,000) Cat Audiotapes Videotapes 16mm Films Filmstrip Microforms
Budget: $34,000
Notes: Incl 500 audiotapes and 150 videotapes.

PQ —MCGILL UNIVERSITY, Nursing/Social Work Library, 3506 University St, Montreal, H3A 1Y1, Can. Wendy Patrick, Librn
Holdings: Vols (35,000) Cat

PSYCHOANALYSIS—HISTORY

DC —LIBRARY OF CONGRESS, Manuscript Division, Washington, 20540. John C Broderick, Chief
Holdings: Cat Mss
Notes: The Freud Archives. Also, the papers of Siegfried Bernfeld, one of Freud's pupils and associates. Also incl correspondence, photographs, notes, and reprints of Smith Ely Jelliffe (1896-1944).

IL —SOUTHERN ILLINOIS UNIVERSITY, CARBONDALE, Delyte W Morris Library, Special Collections Dept, Carbondale, 62901. David V Koch, Cur of Special Collections; Louisa Bowen, Cur of Manuscripts
Holdings: Vols 430 Cat Mss Pix
Notes: Personal papers (78 linear feet) of Theodore Schroeder, 1873-1957, founder of the Free Speech League, incl archives of the League. Thousands of letters, mss, and notes, with letters from Anthony Comstock, Samuel Gompers, Eugene V Debs, Havelock Ellis, Margaret Sanger, Upton Sinclair, H L Mencken, and Emma Goldman. The archives reflect Schroeder's crusades in the areas of free speech, sex expression, religion, and psychoanalysis. Inventory and name index available at the Library. Described by Ralph E McCoy, *Theodore Schroeder, the Cold Enthusiast*, Carbondale: Southern Illinois University Libraries, 1973. (Bibliographic Contributions, No 8).

IL —INSTITUTE FOR PSYCHOANALYSIS, Gitelson Film Library, 180 N Michigan Ave, Chicago, 60601. Glenn Miller, Librn
Holdings: Vols 150 Cat Videotapes 16mm Films
Notes: The library contains a "living history" series entitled "Portraits in Psychoanalysis," a group of videotaped interviews with some notable present and past staff members on the Institute. The Film Library is available to other mental health facilities on a rental basis. A catalog of the films is available on request.

MA —AUSTEN RIGGS CENTER, Austen Fox Riggs Library, Main St, Stockbridge, 01262. Helen Linton, Librn
Holdings: Vols (10,556) Cat Audiotapes
Budget: ($10,000)
Notes: Current and historical Literature in psychoanalysis and related fields. Restricted use: open only to staff; to others with written permission. Interlibrary loans to institutions. No photocopying.

MA —BRANDEIS UNIVERSITY, Goldfarb Library, 415 South St, Waltham, 02154. Bessie Hahn, Dir
Notes: Lou Andreas-Salome Collection. 6 linear ft of mss material and books by and about Lou Andreas-Salome, novelist and poet, who took an active interest in psychoanalysis in the early part of the 20th century. There is a finding list to the collection in Special Collections.

OH —CLEVELAND MEDICAL LIBRARY ASSOCIATION/CASE WESTERN RESERVE UNIVERSITY, Cleveland Health Sciences Library, Historical Division, Allen Memorial Medical Library, 11000 Euclid Ave, Cleveland, 44106. Glen Jenkins, Rare

PSYCHOANALYSIS—HISTORY (cont.)

Book Librarian & Archivist
Holdings: Vols 420 Cat
Notes: The Sigmund Freud Collection.

PSYCHOBIOLOGY

MA —MCLEAN HOSPITAL MEDICAL
LIBRARY, 115 Mill St, Belmont, 02178.
Hector Bossange, Dir
Holdings: Vols 25,611 Cat
Notes: Extensive collection.

PSYCHOCYBERNETICS

AZ —WORLD UNIVERSITY, Library, 711 E
Blacklidge Dr, Tucson, 85719. Howard John
Zitko, Cur
Holdings: Vols (15,000) Cat Mss Maps
Audiotapes
Notes: Collection concerns what are
generally called the "frontier sciences." No
interlibrary loan.

PSYCHOKINESIS

NY —PARAPSYCHOLOGY FOUNDATION,
Eileen J Garrett Library, 228 E 71st St, New
York, 10021. Wayne Norman, Librn
Holdings: Vols (9300) Cat
Notes: One of the largest libraries on
parapsychology. Main emphasis is on the
literature of contemporary parapsychology;
also a strong collection on the history of
parapsychology (early spiritualism,
mysticism, relevant philosophical works,
etc). Rare book collection incl early rare
books and periodicals on psychical research
and psychical phenomena. Receives about
100 titles of periodicals and binds the more
significant titles. The library maintains its
own periodicals index to parapsychological
literature, dating from 1966. Main emphasis
literature is on experimental parapsychology,
or those publications that approach the
subject with an objective and/or analytic
point of view.
MB —UNIVERSITY OF MANITOBA,
Elizabeth Dafoe Library, Archives and
Special Collections Dept, Winnipeg, R3T
2N2, Can. Richard E Bennett, Dept Head;
Corrado A Santoro, Reference Archivist
Notes: Papers of Thomas Glendenning
Hamilton, physician and surgeon, member of
the Manitoba Legislative Assembly, psychic
researcher. Winnipeg, Manitoba. Important
collection, emphasis is on psychic research
with limited amount of materials regarding
his medical and political careers. Seance
attendance registers, records and affidavits,
lecture notes, correspondence, newspaper
clippings, books and journal articles.
Photographs, slides and ca 50 boxes of glass
plate negatives.

PSYCHOLINGUISTICS

MI —UNIVERSITY OF MICHIGAN, English
Language Institute/Linguistics Library, 1013
N University Bldg, Ann Arbor, 48109.
Patricia M Aldridge, Librn
Holdings: Vols (4500) Cat Maps VF
Videotapes
Notes: The collection on teaching English as
a foreign language is fairly complete; in
modern language study it is also quite good.
Supporting subjects are linguistics and
English grammar; psychology, American
culture, education, foreign student
adjustment, and bibliography are covered.

PSYCHOLOGICAL MEASUREMENT
see Psychometrics

PSYCHOLOGICAL SCALING see
Psychometrics

PSYCHOLOGICAL STATISTICS see
Psychometrics

PSYCHOLOGICAL TESTS see Character
Tests; Mental Tests

PSYCHOLOGICAL WARFARE

NE —UNIVERSITY OF NEBRASKA-
LINCOLN, Don L Love Library, University

Archives and Special Collections, Lincoln,
68588. Joseph G Svoboda, University
Archivist
Notes: Collection consists mainly of
pamphlets, clippings, posters, and other
World War II ephemera; 2000 items.

PSYCHOLOGY

AZ —ARIZONA STATE UNIVERSITY,
Library, Tempe, 85287. Marilyn
Wurzburger, Special Collections Librn
Notes: Reflecting his roles of reporter,
photographer and novelist, Ted Schwarz's
papers cover subject areas such as
investigative journalism, psychology,
criminal justice, law, numismatics, visual
communication, photography and writing as
a career. Collection incl extensive research
materials from the author's study and
reporting of the "Hillside Strangler" case
which deals with multiple personalities.
Partially cataloged and indexed, the
collection consists of 140 linear feet of multi-
media materials: vols, magazines, newspaper
articles, galley proofs, interviews and
correspondence, reel-to-reel tapes,
audiotapes and videotapes.
AZ —WORLD UNIVERSITY, Library, 711 E
Blacklidge Dr, Tucson, 85719. Howard John
Zitko, Cur
Holdings: Vols (15,000) Cat Mss Maps
Audiotapes
Notes: Collection concerns the "frontier
sciences." No interlibrary loan.
CA —UNIVERSITY OF CALIFORNIA,
BERKELEY, Humanities-Social Sciences
Libraries, Education-Psychology Library,
2600 Tolman Hall, Berkeley, 94720. Sonya
Kaufman, Acting Head
Holdings: Vols (110,000)
Notes: General research collection in fields
of education and psycology. Education
collection's emphases are in the areas of
administration, policy planning, higher
education, science and math education,
language and literacy. Serial holdings are
strong. The library receives approx 2200
current serial titles in education and
psychology.
CA —ESALEN SPORT CENTER, Esalen
Institute, Big Sur, 93920.
Notes: Emphasizes integration of mind and
body.
CA —HUMAN RESOURCES RESEARCH
ORGANIZATION (HUMRRO), Western
Div Library, 27857 Berwick Dr, Carmel,
93923. Dianalee Stickler, Librn
Notes: Citations for HumRRO reports
appear in *HumRRO Bibliography of
Publications*, 1971 and *HumRRO
Bibliography of Publications and
Presentations During FY*, 1972-77. Library
is inactive.
CA —LOS ANGELES PUBLIC LIBRARY,
Social Sciences Dept, 630 W Fifth St, Los
Angeles, 90071. Marilyn C Wherley,
Principal Librn
Holdings: Vols (5000) Cat Mciroforms
Budget: ($150,000)
Notes: Education collection. Over 500
bound periodicals. Collection also includes
government publications, agency reports,
statistics, yearbooks, directories, pamphlets,
bibliographies, child and adolescent, adult
and abnormal psychology theories and
history.
CA —LOS ANGELES PUBLIC LIBRARY,
Philosophy & Religion Dept, 630 W Fifth St,
Los Angeles, 90071. Marilyn C Wherley,
Librn
Holdings: Vols 3500 Cat
Budget: ($60,000)
Notes: Comprehensive coverage of scholarly
and popular works in the various schools of
psychology and their historical development.
Emphases on self-help and conduct of life
materials. Includes psyhoanalysis. Many
periodicals and serials included.
CA —UNIVERSITY OF CALIFORNIA, LOS
ANGELES, Education & Psychology
Library, 390 Powell Library Bldg, Los
Angeles, 90024. Barbara Duke, Librn
Holdings: Vols (133,000) Cat Audiotapes
Microforms
Notes: Research collection serving graduate

students and faculty in Education,
Psychology, Kinesiology and Teaching
English as a Second Language. Areas of
emphasis incl higher education, education
and work, comparative education, early
childhood development, reading, second
language acquisition, cognition, perception,
personality, social psychology, motor control
and learning. Library has Univ of Oregon
microfiche collection of unpublished research
in sports, physical education, and recreation
and is a depository for ERIC microfiche.
†CA —INSTITUTE FOR THE ADVANCED
STUDY OF HUMAN SEXUALITY, 1523
Franklin St, San Francisco, 94109.
CT —YALE MEDICAL LIBRARY, 333 Cedar
St, New Haven, 06510.
Holdings: Vols (334,215) Cat Mss Pix Slides
Microforms
Budget: ($361,650)
Notes: Incl films, audiotapes, artifacts, etc.
Also incl the Trigant Burow Manuscript
Collection transferred from the Lifwynn
Foundation.
DC —US OFFICE OF PERSONNEL
MANAGEMENT, Library, 1900 E St NW,
Washington, 20415. Betty B Guerin, Supv
Librn
Holdings: Vols 75,000 Cat Microforms
Notes: US Civil Service Commission
terminated by Act of Congress, 10/78. US
Office of Personnel Management created
and effective, 1/79. Library houses a
comprehensive collection of materials in all
phases of federal personnel administration,
both historical and current and incl federal
documents and other pamphlets. It is
supplemented by collections in general
personnel administration, public
administration, management, and state, local
and foreign Civil Service.
GA —GEORGIA INSTITUTE OF
TECHNOLOGY, Price Gilbert Memorial
Library, 225 North Ave, Atlanta, 30332.
Edward Graham Roberts, Dir
Holdings: Vols (1,661,559) Cat Maps Slides
Microforms
Budget: ($1,383,302)
Notes: Incl (4,307,996) patents and (568,
490) government documents.
GA —CENTRAL STATE HOSPITAL, Mental
Health Library, Milledgeville, 31062.
Katherine J Ridley, Librn
Holdings: Vols (2100) Cat Audiotapes
Budget: ($5000)
HI —HAWAII STATE HOSPITAL, Medical
Library, 45-710 Keaahala Rd, Kaneohe,
96744. Diana Stephens, Medical Librn
Holdings: Vols 6000
Budget: $15,200
IL —ILLINOIS DEPT OF MENTAL
HEALTH & DEVELOPMENTAL
DISABILITIES, Adolf Meyer Mental
Health Center, Professional Library, 2310 E
Mound Rd, Decatur, 62526.
Holdings: Vols (1000) Cat Audiotapes
Videotapes Microforms
Budget: ($4500)
Notes: Mental health, in general, incl
personal mental health and community
mental health, the behavioral sciences
(biomedical, psychological, and social), and
treatment modalities of mental illness, with
primary emphasis on community mental
health and treatment modalities of mental
illness.
IL —JACKSONVILLE STATE HOSPITAL,
Training & Research Library, 1201 S Main
St, Jacksonville, 62650. Lois E Wells, Librn
Holdings: Vols (10,000) Cat
Notes: Concerned particularly with
developmental disabilities.
IL —MORTON GROVE PUBLIC LIBRARY,
6140 Lincoln Ave, Morton Grove, 60053.
Joan Stewart, Librn
Holdings: Vols (4200) Cat
Notes: Maintained as philosophy and
psychology subject center.
IL —LUTHERAN GENERAL HOSPITAL
LIBRARY, 1775 Dempster St, Park Ridge,
60068. Joanne Crispen, Dir of Library
Services
Holdings: Vols (21,298) Cat Slides
Audiotapes Videotapes 16mm Films
Filmstrips
Budget: ($52,600)

PSYCHOLOGY (cont.)

IN —INDIANA UNIVERSITY, Institute for
Sex Research Library, 416 Morrison Hall,
Bloomington, 47401. Douglas Freeman,
Collections and Services Librn; Joan Brewer,
Information Services Librn
Holdings: Vols (62,000) Cat Mss Pix
Microforms
See also entry under Sex.

IN —CENTRAL STATE HOSPITAL, Medical
Library, 3000 W Washington St,
Indianapolis, 46222. Aurella S Baker, Librn
Holdings: Vols (10,400) Cat Audiotapes
Budget: ($41,000)

IN —LARUE D CARTER MEMORIAL
HOSPITAL, Medical Library, 1315 W
Tenth St, Indianapolis, 46202. Philip I Enz,
Librn
Holdings: Vols (14,600) Audiotapes
Budget: ($15,500)
Notes: Incl 100 audiotapes and 219 journal
subscriptions.

IN —LOGANSPORT STATE HOSPITAL,
Staff Library, Logansport, 46947. Terra
Newton, Librn
Holdings: Vols (3000) Cat

IN —PURDUE UNIVERSITY LIBRARIES,
Pyschological Sciences Library, Stanley
Coulter Annex, West Lafayette, 47907. Pam
Baxter, Librn
Holdings: Vols (17,630) Cat
Budget:

IN —WESTVILLE CORRECTIONAL
CENTER, Library Services, PO Box 473,
Westville, 46391. Catherine M Mohlke, Dir
of Library Services
Holdings: Vols 1000 Cat

IA —IOWA STATE UNIVERSITY, Library,
Ames, 50011. Warren B Kuhn, Dean of
Library Services
Holdings: Cat
Notes: Specific strength: developmental
psychology.

KS —JOHNSON COUNTY MENTAL
HEALTH CENTER, John R Keach
Memorial Library, 6000 Lamar Ave,
Mission, 66202. Krista Hilton-Ross, Librn
Holdings: Vols (1000) Cat Mss

KS —KANSAS NEUROLOGICAL
INSTITUTE, Menninger Professional
Library, 3107 W 21 St, Topeka, 66604.
Richard Gray, Librn
Holdings: Vols 1244 Cat
Notes: Incl development disabilities; special
education; nursing care for the handicapped;
programs for the mentally retarded;
behavioral psychology; supervision in mental
health/mental retardation; staff training in
mental health/mental retardation.

KS —TOPEKA STATE HOSPITAL STAFF
LIBRARY, 2700 W Sixth St, Topeka,
66606. Laura Schafer, Librn
Holdings: Vols (10,000) Cat

LA —CENTRAL LOUISIANA STATE
HOSPITAL, Medical & Professional Library,
PO Box 31, Pineville, 71360. B Carol
McGee, Librn
Holdings: Vols 9400 Cat Audiotapes 16mm
Films
Budget: $25,000

MD —JOHNS HOPKINS UNIVERSITY,
Milton S Eisenhower Library, Charles & 34
Sts, Baltimore, 21218. Ann S Gwyn,
Assistant Dir for Special Collections
Notes: Foreign and American doctoral
dissertations and reprints to 1964. Largest
number in history of science, 85,000. Also
biology, chemistry, geology, meteorology,
psychology, physics and mathematics. Johns
Hopkins not included. Incl 100,000 Western
European doctoral dissertations, espec
French and German; some Scandinavian.
Collection is located in Gillman Storage
Area accessible through Special Collection
Division.

MD —UNION MEMORIAL HOSPITAL,
Nursing Library, 3301 N Calvert St,
Baltimore, 21218. Carolyn Daugherty, Librn
Holdings: Vols (4000) Cat Mss Pix

MD —SPRING GROVE HOSPITAL
CENTER, Sulzbacher Memorial Library,
Catonsville, 21228. Charles H Johnson, Dir
Holdings: Vols (3800) Cat Slides
Phonorecords Audiotapes

MA —UNIVERSITY OF MASSACHUSETTS
AT AMHERST, Library, Amherst, 01002.
Notes: Strong collections in physical
education, sports studies, exercise,
gymnastics, etc.

MA —MCLEAN HOSPITAL MEDICAL
LIBRARY, 115 Mill St, Belmont, 02178.
Hector Bossange, Dir
Holdings: Vols 25,611 Cat
Notes: Extensive collection.

MA —HARVARD UNIVERSITY LIBRARY,
Psychology Research Library, William James
Hall, Cambridge, 02138. Annelise Katz,
Librn
Holdings: Vols 10,700 Cat
Notes: Supplements resources of Harvard
Library's central collection.

†MA —CLARK UNIVERSITY, Robert
Hutchings Goddard Library, Worcester,
01610. Dorothy Mosa Kowski, Rare Books
Librn
Holdings: Vols Cat
Notes: Particularly strong in earlier
psychological works. 1880-1920.
Approximately 100 current journal
subscriptions, with supporting journals in
psychiatry, and the social and biological
sciences.

MI —UNIVERSITY OF MICHIGAN, English
Language Institute/Linguistics Library, 1013
N University Bldg, Ann Arbor, 48109.
Patricia M Aldridge, Librn
Holdings: Vols (4500) Cat Maps VF
Videotapes
Notes: The collection on teaching English as
a foreign language is fairly complete; in
modern language study it is also quite good.
Supporting subjects are linguistics and
English grammar; psychology, American
culture, education, foreign student
adjustment, and bibliography are covered.

MI —LAFAYETTE CLINIC LIBRARY, 951
E Lafayette, Detroit, 48207. Nancy E Ward,
Librn
Holdings: Vols (7000) Cat
Notes: Special emphasis on behavior therapy
and the biological aspects, causes and
treatment of mental illness.

MN —MINNEAPOLIS PUBLIC LIBRARY &
INFORMATION CENTER, Sociology
Dept, 300 Nicollet Mall, Minneapolis,
55401. Eileen Scwartzbauer, Dept Head
Holdings: Vols (90,000) Cat Phonorecords
Audiotapes Microforms
Budget: ($69,890)
Notes: Special collections: Foundation
Center Regional Collection; college catalogs
on fiche; adult basic education collection.
Separate department catalog.

MO —SAINT JOSEPH STATE HOSPITAL,
Professional Library, 3400 Frederick Ave,
Box 263, Saint Joseph, 64502. Martha
Goodding, Librn
Holdings: Vols (3000) Cat Slides
Phonorecords Audiotapes 16mm Films
Filmstrips Videotapes

MO —MISSOURI INSTITUTE OF
PSYCHIATRY LIBRARY, 5400 Arsenal St,
Saint Louis, 63139. Connie Wolf, Librn
Holdings: Vols (18,000) Cat
Notes: Subscribe to 430 journals.

MO —SAINT LOUIS POLICE LIBRARY,
315 S Tucker Blvd, Saint Louis, 63102.
Cathy Reilly, Librn
Holdings: Vols (21,000) Cat Mss Pix
Microforms
Budget: ($18,400)
Notes: Library on all subjects of police work
is open to the public for general reference
use.

MO —SAINT LOUIS PSYCHOANALYTIC
INSTITUTE, Betty Golde Smith Memorial
Library, 4524 Forest Park Blvd, Saint Louis,
63108. Rheba Symeonoglou, Librn
Holdings: Vols (5566) Cat
Budget: ($4000)
Notes: Primarily a psychoanalytic library.
Considerable material in the fields of
psychiatry, psychology and sociology.
Speical section (about 400 books) for the lay
reader, who is also welcome to read any of
the other material in the library. Library has
incorporated the *Index to the Chicago
Institute for Psychoanalysis*, an index of
periodical articles by author, title and
subject. Collection described in *Reference*

Encyclopedia of American Psychology and
Psychiatry, Barry T Klein, ed 3655 W Pine
Blvd, St Louis, Mo 63108

NJ —EAST ORANGE GENERAL
HOSPITAL, Library, 300 Central Ave, East
Orange, 07019. Joann Mehalick, Dir of
Library Services
Holdings: Vols (1500) Cat Videotapes

NJ —GREYSTONE PSYCHIATRIC
HOSPITAL, Medical Library, PO Box A,
Greystone Park, 07950. Brian C Hamilton,
Medical Librn
Holdings: Vols (900)

NJ —RUTGERS, THE STATE UNIVERSITY
OF NEW JERSEY, Center of Alcohol
Studies Library, Smithers Hall, New
Brunswick, 08903. Penny Page, Librn
Holdings: Vols (8075) Cat Mss Microforms
Budget: ($110,000)
Notes: See entry for Rutgers University
under Alcoholism.

NJ —EDUCATIONAL TESTING SERVICE,
Carl Campbell Brigham Library, Princeton,
08540. Janet Williams, Librn
Holdings: Vols 15,000 Cat Microforms
Budget: ($35,000)
Notes: Literature related to tests and
measurements.

NJ —PRINCETON UNIVERSITY,
Psychology Library, Green Hall, Princeton,
08540. Janice D Welburn, Librn
Holdings: Vols (19,839) Cat Microforms
Budget: ($50,000)
Notes: Library receives approx 450 current
serial titles. Primarily serves an experimental
psychology department, with interests in
social, personality, developmental,
physiological and cognitive psychology, as
well as learning and perception. Incl 3886
microforms.

NM —NEW MEXICO STATE HOSPITAL,
Ella P Kief Memorial Library, Hot Spring
Blvd, PO Box 1388, Las Vegas, 87701.
Hazel Hurley, Librn
Holdings: Vols (5000) Cat
Budget: ($2500)
Notes: Partially cataloged.

NY —LONG ISLAND JEWISH-HILLSIDE
MEDICAL CENTER, Hillside Div, Health
Sciences Library, PO Box 38, Glen Oaks,
11004. Joan L Kauff, Librn
Holdings: Vols (9000) Cat

NY —AMERICAN SOCIETY FOR
PSYCHICAL RESEARCH LIBRARY, 5 W
73 St, New York, 10023. Rhea A White,
Consultant to the Library
Holdings: Vols (7000) Cat Mss Pix
Budget: ($1500)
Notes: Incl books on spiritualism, as well as
works in psychology, religion, philosophy,
physics, anthropology, etc which have a
possible bearing on parapsychology. An
attempt is made to obtain all serious books
on parapsychology in English.

NY —ANALYTICAL PSYCHOLOGY CLUB
OF NEW YORK, Kristine Mann Library, 28
E 39 St, New York, 10016. Doris Albrecht,
Librn

NY —BANK STREET COLLEGE OF
EDUCATION LIBRARY, 610 W 112 St,
New York, 10025. Eleanor Kule Seid,
Library Dir
Holdings: Vols (90,000) Cat Microforms
Notes: Education, guidance, pyschology,
educational psychology, curricula, textbooks,
Black Studies, etc. All subjects are integrated
in one professional collection; in addition
there are two separately cataloged and
shelved collections: Children's and
Elementary Curriculm Materials.

NY —CITY UNIVERSITY OF NEW YORK,
City College, Library, 138 St & Convent
Ave, New York, 10031. Vira C Hinds, Assoc
Prof
Notes: In general reference library.

NY —COLUMBIA UNIVERSITY
LIBRARIES, Psychology Library, 409
Schermerhorn, New York, 10027. Barbara A
List, Reference/Collection Development
Librn
Holdings: Vols (25,000) Cat Microforms
Budget: ($23,300)
Notes: Incl material on animal physiology,
cogniton, psycholinguistics, learning theories,
memory, perception, personality, sensation,
sensorimotor activities, vision.

PSYCHOLOGY (cont.)

NY —FAMILY SERVICE, America Library, 44 E 23 St, New York, 10010. Joan Fenton, Librn
Holdings: Vols (3600) Cat
Notes: No photocopying.

NY —MORRIS N & CHESLEY V YOUNG LIBRARY OF MNEMONICS, 270 Riverside Dr, New York, 10025. Morris N Young, Cur
Holdings: Cat Mss Maps Pix Phonorecords Audiotapes 16mm Films Microforms
Notes: Collection of 5000 books, pamphlets, pictures, memorabilia, etc incl medieval art of memory; psychology of memory, forgetting and reading; medical aspects of memory, amnesia, dyslexia; biomedical aspects of learning and memory; information storage, retrieval and cybernetics; memory prodigies, lightning calculators, calendars; remembrance cups and memory mementos. All languages. Memorabilia incl engravings, posters, programs, advertisements, birthday cards, teaching cards, ASLs, and Mark Twain's Memory Builder game and other games. Items range from 1410 to 1980s.

NY —NEW YORK ACADEMY OF MEDICINE, Library, 2 E 103 St, New York, 10029. Brett A Kirkpatrick, Librn
Holdings: Vols 202 // Cat
Notes: Ernest Harms Collection on 19th century German psychology and psychiatry.

NY —NEW YORK PUBLIC LIBRARY, Research Libraries, General Research Division, Fifth Ave & 42 St, New York, 10018. Rodney Phillips, Chief
Notes: See *Bibliographic Guide to Psychology, 1976* (Boston: GK Hall, 1977). Incl publications cataloged during the year, with additional entries from MARC tapes.

NY —NEW YORK PUBLIC LIBRARY, Mid-Manhattan Library, History and Social Sciences Dept, 455 Fifth Ave, New York, 10016. Robert Sheehan, Sr Principal Librn
Holdings: Vols 12,000 Cat Audiotapes Microforms
Budget: $20,000
Notes: Strong undergraduate level collection covering developmental, theoretical, clinical and applied psychology. Duplicate reference and circulating copies. 150 periodicals.

NY —PARAPSYCHOLOGY FOUNDATION, Eileen J Garrett Library, 228 E 71st St, New York, 10021. Wayne Norman, Librn
Holdings: Vols (9300) Cat
Notes: One of the largest libraries on parapsychology. Main emphasis is on the literature of contemporary parapsychology; also a strong collection on the history of parapsychology (early spiritualism, mysticism, relevant philosophical works, etc). Rare book collection incl early rare books and periodicals on psychical research and psychical phenomena. Receives about 100 titles of periodicals and binds the more significant titles. The library maintains its own periodicals index to parapsychological literature, dating from 1966. Main emphasis literature is on experimental parapsychology, or those publications that approach the subject with an objective and/or analytic point of view.

NY —UNION THEOLOGICAL SEMINARY, Library, 3041 Broadway at Reinhold Niebuhr Place, New York, 10027. Richard D Spoor, Dir
Holdings: Vols (580,000) Cat Mss Microforms
Budget: ($750,000)

NY —UNITED LODGE OF THEOSOPHISTS LIBRARY, 347 E 72 St, New York, 10021.
Notes: Ancient and modern philosophy and psychology; comparative religion and mythology; parapsychology; reincarnation research in science and religion.

NC —DUKE UNIVERSITY, William R Perkins Library, Manuscript Dept, Durham, 27706. Ellen Gartrell, Cur of Mss
Notes: The personal papers of Chris Costner Sizemore, who is widely known as the subject of the book and movie, "The Three Faces of Eve." Incl poems and other writings, diaries, drawings, photographs, tapes of interviews, and some printed material.

ND —NEUROPSYCHIATRIC INSTITUTE, Medical Library, 700 First Ave S, Fargo, 58103. Diane Nordeng, Librn
Holdings: Vols (1000) Cat
Budget: ($8000)

OH —UNIVERSITY OF AKRON, Archives of the History of American Psychology, Akron, 44325. John A Popplestone, Dir
Holdings: Cat Mss Pix Slides Films
Notes: Nearly 1200 ft of psychologists' personal papers and documents, as well as organizational records, and over 600 items of historic laboratory aparatus. Also, photographs, films, intelligence and aptitude tests, etc, from the 19th century to date.

OH —ATHENS MENTAL HEALTH & MENTAL RETARDATION CENTER, Staff Library, Richland Ave, Athens, 45701. Judy McGinn, Librn
Holdings: Vols (3000) Cat Audiotapes

OH —ROLLMAN PSYCHIATRIC INSTITUTE, Clinical Library, 3009 Burnet Ave, Cincinnati, 45219. M Glassmann, Dir
Holdings: Vols (3000) Cat

OH —CLEVELAND PSYCHIATRIC INSTITUTE, Karnosh Library, 1708 Aiken Ave, Cleveland, 44109. Anna L Harris, Librn
Holdings: Vols 5000 Cat

OH —CLEVELAND PUBLIC LIBRARY, Social Sciences Department, 325 Superior Ave, Cleveland, 44114. Thelma Morris, Head
Holdings: Cat

OR —UNIVERSITY OF OREGON LIBRARY, Education-Psychology Dept, Eugene, 97403. Rose Marie Service, Head Dept Librn
Holdings: Vols (1,300,000) Cat
Budget: $8000
Notes: General research collection in major fields of psychology and educational psychology. Growing current parapsychology collection. Strong serials holdings. Approximately 1700 standardized tests.

PA —UNIVERSITY OF PENNSYLVANIA, Dept of Psychology, Fernberger Library, 3815 Walnut St, Philadelphia, 19104. Frances Clifford, Head
Holdings: Vols 6000 Cat
Notes: Research library incl 100 journal titles. Restricted use, noncirculating.

PA —UNIVERSITY OF PITTSBURGH, Langley Library, A-217 Langley Hall, Pittsburgh, 15260. D L Johnston, Librn
Holdings: Vols 12,500 Cat
Budget: $20,000

PA —PENNSYLVANIA STATE UNIVERSITY, Fred Lewis Pattee Library, University Park, 16802.
Notes: Numerous and large collections on many sports. Also, materials supporting every aspect of the program of the Center for Women and Sport, incl research into kinetics, endocrinology, physiology, psychology, etc.

SC —SOUTH CAROLINA STATE DEPT OF MENTAL RETARDATION, Whitten Center Library, PO Box 239, Clinton, 29325. H Y Keng, Head Librn
Holdings: Vols (20,000) Cat Phonorecords Audiotapes Videotapes 16mm Films Filmstrips Microforms
Notes: Mental retardation, mental deficiency; mentally handicapped education. Materials for the mentally handicapped, incl toys and games. Incl 15,000 microforms.

TN —WESTERN MENTAL HEALTH INSTITUTE, Edwin M Levy Professional Library, Bolivar, 38074. Lee Oda Chambers, Librn
Holdings: Vols 1500

TX —TEXAS DEPT OF MENTAL HEALTH & MENTAL RETARDATION, Central Office Library, 909 W 45, Box 12668, Austin, 78711. Becky Renfro, Librn
Holdings: Vols (4600) Cat

VA —ASSOCIATION FOR RESEARCH & ENLIGHTENMENT, Library, 67 & Atlantic Avenue, PO Box 595, Virginia Beach, 23451. Stephen Jordan, Library Mgr
Holdings: Vols (1100) Cat
Notes: Dreams and dream psychology.

WA —WESTERN STATE HOSPITAL, Library, Fort Steilacoom, 98494. Neal Van Der Voorn, Librn
Holdings: Vols (5900) Cat Audiotapes
Notes: Collection incl 5500 journal vols, 1800 pamphlets and 420 audiotapes.

WA —SEATTLE PUBLIC LIBRARY, 1000 Fourth Ave, Seattle, 98104. Ronald A Dubberly, City Librn
Holdings: Cat

WI —MENDOTA MENTAL HEALTH INSTITUTE, Library-Media Center, 301 Troy Dr, Madison, 53704. Margaret Tiekle Grinnell, Librn
Holdings: Vols 14,800 Cat Slides Phonorecords Audiotapes Videotapes 16mm Films Filmstrips

WI —UNIVERSITY OF WISCONSIN, MADISON, Wisconsin Regional Primate Research Center, Primate Center Library, 1223 Capitol Court, Madison, 53715. Lawrence Jacobsen, Librn
Holdings: Vols (15,000) Cat Pix
Notes: Research in reproductive physiology, neurosciences, and behavior. Extensive subject orientated primate reprint file, audiovisual collection on primates. Current research uses approximately 25 species of nonhuman primates. Publications: *Primate Library Report*: print and non-print editions, biomonthly.

WI —UNIVERSITY OF WISCONSIN, MADISON, W S Middleton Health Sciences Library, 1305 Linden Dr, Madison, 53706. Virginia Holtz, Dir
Holdings: Vols (200,000) Cat Pix Slides Audiotapes Videotapes Microforms

BC —VANCOUVER PUBLIC LIBRARY, Sociology Div, 750 Burrard St, Vancouver, V6Z 1X5, Can.
Holdings: Cat
Notes: Incl special files of pamphlets, clippings, etc.

NF —WATERFORD HOSPITAL, Health Sciences Library, Waterford Bridge Rd, Saint John's, A1E 4J8, Can. Maisie Young, Librn
Holdings: Vols (2000) Cat Pix Phonorecords Audiotapes Videotapes 16mm Films Filmstrips
Notes: Material incl aspects of psychiatry related to medicine, nursing, psychology, social work, etc. Also incl manuscript work on a history of the hospital, which closely parallels a history of psychiatry in Newfoundland. Journals are only kept for ten years.

ON —CANADA PUBLIC SERVICE COMMISSION, Library, Room 930 W Tower, Esplande Laurier, Ottawa, K1A 0M7, Can. A Campbell, Chief Librn
Holdings: Vols 7000 Cat
Budget: $20,000
Notes: Library supports the research, administrative, and instructional needs of the Commission. English and French materials.

ON —NATIONAL LIBRARY OF CANADA, 395 Wellington St, Ottawa, K1A 0N4, Can. Andre Preibish, Dir
Holdings: Vols 10,000
Notes: Includes 130 serial titles, theses, pamphlets, government publications relating to family and marriage. The following disciplines covered: anthropology, psychology and psychiatry, law, economics, religion, sociology, demography, education, political science and biology. Earliest title 1630.

ON —ONTARIO MINISTRY OF CORRECTIONAL SERVICES, Library, 2001 Eglinton Ave E, Scarborough, M1L 4P1, Can. T J B Anderson, Chief Librn
Holdings: Vols (3676) Cat VF
Budget: ($16,000)
Notes: Approx 135 periodicals received. Library services also provided in approx 50 jails and adult institutions.

†ON —METROPOLITAN TORONTO LIBRARY, Social Sciences Dept, 789 Yonge St, Toronto, M4W 2G8, Can. Abdus Salam, Head
Holdings: Vols Cat Maps Phonorecords Audiotapes 16mm Films Microforms
Notes: Includes books on general psychology and its history. Also, a strong collection of the works of individual psychologists and critical works about them. The following specialized areas of psychology are also well covered: child psychology, psychology and mental health, and parapsychology.

ON —UNIVERSITY OF TORONTO, Thomas Fisher Rare Book Library, 120 Saint George St, Toronto, M5S 1A5, Can. Richard G

PSYCHOLOGY (cont.)

Landon, Head
Holdings: Vols (6000) Cat
Notes: Hannah Collection named in honour of Jason A Hannah, the founder of the Hannah Institute for the History of Medical and Related Sciences at the University of Toronto. Collection comprises a wide range of works in medicine, surgery, anatomy, physiology and other related sciences published in the major European countries and Great Britain from 1500 to 1900. Areas of special strength are psychology, gynecology and obstetrics. Highlights of collection described in two exhibition catalogues published by the Thomas Fisher Rare Book Library: *The Early History of Medicine; An Exhibition of Books Selected from the Jason A Hannah Collection in the History of Medical and Related Sciences* (March, 1974) and *The Byrth of Mankynd* (1981).

ON —SIRLS, Faculty of Human Kinetics & Leisure Studies, University of Waterloo, Waterloo, N2L 3G1, Can. Betty Smith, Database Mgr
Notes: Information Retrieval System for the Sociology of Leisure and Sport (SIRLS) is a computerized online database of about 13,000 entries (1983). Incl dance as a leisure time activity.

PQ —MCGILL UNIVERSITY, Nursing/Social Work Library, 3506 University St, Montreal, H3A 1Y1, Can. Wendy Patrick, Librn
Holdings: Vols (35,000) Cat

PSYCHOLOGY—MEASUREMENTS see Psychometrics

PSYCHOLOGY—SCALING see Psychometrics

PSYCHOLOGY—STATISTICS see Psychometrics

PSYCHOLOGY, APPLIED

CA —LOS ANGELES PUBLIC LIBRARY, Social Sciences Dept, 630 W Fifth St, Los Angeles, 90071. Marilyn C Wherley, Principal Librn
Holdings: Vols 2500 Cat Microforms
Budget: ($150,000)
Notes: Education collection. Over 500 bound periodicals. Collection also includes government publications, agency reports, statistics, yearbooks, directories, pamphlets, bibliographies, child and adolescent, adult and abnormal psychology theories and history.

KS —KANSAS NEUROLOGICAL INSTITUTE, Menninger Professional Library, 3107 W 21 St, Topeka, 66604. Richard Gray, Librn
Holdings: Vols 1244 Cat
Notes: Incl development disabilities; special education; nursing care for the handicapped; programs for the mentally retarded; behavioral psychology; supervision in mental health/mental retardation; staff training in mental health/mental retardation.

MA —FRANCIS A COUNTWAY LIBRARY OF MEDICINE, Boston Medical Library/ Harvard Medical Library, 10 Shattuck St, Boston, 02115. C Robin LeSueur, Librn; Richard J Wolfe, Cur, Rare Books & Manuscripts
Holdings: Cat Mss Microforms
Notes: Incl Frantz Fanon Collection on Black psychology.

MO —UNITY LIBRARY, Unity School of Christianity, Unity Village, 64065. Alfreda Williams, Library Dir
Holdings: Vols (50,000) Cat Mss Maps Pix Slides Microforms
Notes: Incl Archives and Historical collections of the Unity School of Christianity, as well as the archives of the International New Thought Alliance.

NJ —EDUCATIONAL TESTING SERVICE, Carl Campbell Brigham Library, Princeton, 08540. Janet Williams, Librn
Notes: Complete works and papers of Louis L Thurstone, a leading psychometrician of the 20th century.

NY —NEW YORK PUBLIC LIBRARY, Research Libraries, General Research Division, Fifth Ave & 42 St, New York, 10018. Rodney Phillips, Chief
Notes: See *Bibliographic Guide to Psychology, 1976* (Boston: GK Hall, 1977). Incl publications cataloged during the year, with additional entries from MARC tapes.

OR —UNIVERSITY OF OREGON LIBRARY, 1607 Agate St, Eugene, 97403. Ruth M Brewer, Resource Librn
Notes: Social and psychological aspects of aging.

PSYCHOLOGY, BLACK

DC —HOWARD UNIVERSITY, Moorland-Spingarn Research Center, 500 Howard Place NW, Washington, 20059. Clifford L Muse, Jr, Acting Dir

PSYCHOLOGY, CHILD see Child Development

PSYCHOLOGY, CLINICAL see Clinical Psychology

PSYCHOLOGY, EDUCATIONAL see Educational Psychology

PSYCHOLOGY, ENVIRONMENTAL see Environmental Psychology

PSYCHOLOGY, EXPERIMENTAL see Psychology, Physiological

PSYCHOLOGY, INDUSTRIAL

CT —LIFE INSURANCE MARKETING & RESEARCH ASSOCIATION, Library, 170 Sigourney St, PO Box 208, Hartford, 06141. William J Mortimer, Mgr, Library and Reference Services
Holdings: Vols 5000 Cat Audiotapes
Budget: ($10,000)
Notes: Incl 150-drawer vertical file on life insurance marketing and 250 audiotapes.

WY —US AIR FORCE INSTITUTE OF TECHNOLOGY, Library, Dept 9 Bldg 831, FE, Warren AFB, 82001. Patricia A Johnson, Librn
Holdings: Vols (7000) Cat Microforms
Budget: ($9000)
Notes: The Library supports graduate programs for students (Air Force Missile-Combat Crewmen) seeking a Master of Business Administration Degree. Civilian students and other military personnel are also admitted.

PSYCHOLOGY, PASTORAL see Pastoral Psychology

PSYCHOLOGY, PHYSIOLOGICAL

CA —UNIVERSITY OF CALIFORNIA, LOS ANGELES, Biomedical Library, Center for Health Sciences, Los Angeles, 90024. Louise Darling, Biomedical Librn

NJ —PRINCETON UNIVERSITY, Psychology Library, Green Hall, Princeton, 08540. Janice D Welburn, Librn
Holdings: Vols (19,839) Cat Microforms
Budget: ($50,000)
Notes: Library receives approx 450 current serial titles. Primarily serves an experimental psychology department, with interests in social, personality, developmental, physiological and cognitive psychology, as well as learning and perception. Incl 3886 microforms.

NY —COLUMBIA UNIVERSITY LIBRARIES, Psychology Library, 409 Schermerhorn, New York, 10027. Barbara A List, Reference/Collection Development Librn
Holdings: Vols (25,000) Cat Microforms
Budget: ($23,300)
Notes: Incl material on animal physiology, cognition, psycholinguistics, learning theories, memory, perception, personality, sensation, sensorimotor activities, vision.

PSYCHOLOGY, PRACTICAL see Psychology, Applied

PSYCHOLOGY, RELIGIOUS

NC —SOUTHEASTERN BAPTIST THEOLOGICAL SEMINARY LIBRARY, PO Box 752, Wake Forest, 27587. H Eugene McLeod, Librn
Holdings: Cat Microforms

TN —LEE COLLEGE, Library, Ocoee St, Cleveland, 37311. Frances Arrington, Head Librn; JoAnne Sparks, Religion Librn
Holdings: Vols 5086 Cat Slides Phonorecords Audiotapes Filmstrips Microforms
Notes: The Pentecostal Research Center houses two special collections: the Church of God (Cleveland, Tennessee) collection and the Pentecostal collection. The latter includes works about the movement and its history, works by Pentecostal authors, and specific subject areas (Holy Spirit, glossolalia, divine healing).

VA —ASSOCIATION FOR RESEARCH & ENLIGHTENMENT, Library, 67 & Atlantic Avenue, PO Box 595, Virginia Beach, 23451. Stephen Jordan, Library Mgr
Holdings: Vols (3000) Cat
Notes: Emphasis on Christian, Buddhist, Hindu religions, mysticism, comparative religion, psychological approach to biofeedback, autogenics, etc.

PSYCHOLOGY, SOCIAL see Social Psychology

PSYCHOLOGY, SPORTS see Sports Psychology

PSYCHOLOGY, TRANSPERSONAL see Transpersonal Psychology

PSYCHOLOGY AND COUNSELING

CA —CALIFORNIA INSTITUTE OF INTEGRAL STUDIES, Library, 3494 21st St, San Francisco, 94110. Vern Haddick, Library Dir
Holdings: Vols (23,000) Cat Maps Phonorecords Audiotapes
Budget: ($10,000)
Notes: Comparative philosophy, psychology and counseling and comparative religions of East and West. Incl 550 audiotapes.

MA —HARVARD UNIVERSITY, Graduate School of Education, Monroe C Gutman Library, 6 Appian Way, Cambridge, 02138. Susan S Baughman, Associate Librn
Holdings: Vols (150,000) Cat Mss Microforms
Budget: ($95,000)
Notes: A comprehensive research collection that seeks to acquire all scholarly works published in the English language in the fields of education, educational administration, educational psychology, and human development. Selective coverage in the related areas of counseling and psychology, business administration, finance, forecasting, statistical analysis and survey design, public and social policy, linguistics, demographics, and international and economic development. Incl 4000 educational and psychological tests.

PSYCHOLOGY IN HISTORY

†PA —CARNEGIE-MELLON UNIVERSITY, Pittsburgh, 15213.
Notes: Studies of the use of psychology.

PSYCHOMETRICS

NJ —EDUCATIONAL TESTING SERVICE, Carl Campbell Brigham Library, Princeton, 08540. Janet Williams, Librn
Notes: Complete works and papers of Louis L Thurstone, a leading psychometrician of the 20th century.

PSYCHOMETRY (PSYCHOPHYSICS) see Psychometrics

PSYCHOPHARMACOLOGY

MA —MCLEAN HOSPITAL MEDICAL LIBRARY, 115 Mill St, Belmont, 02178. Hector Bossange, Dir
Holdings: Vols 25,611 Cat
Notes: Extensive collection.

MI —LAFAYETTE CLINIC LIBRARY, 951 E Lafayette, Detroit, 48207. Nancy E Ward,

PSYCHOPHARMACOLOGY (cont.)

Librn
Holdings: Vols (7000) Cat
Notes: Special emphasis on the biological aspects, causes and treatment of mental illness.

MO —MISSOURI INSTITUTE OF PSYCHIATRY LIBRARY, 5400 Arsenal St, Saint Louis, 63139. Connie Wolf, Librn
Holdings: Vols (18,000) Cat
Notes: Subscribe to 430 journals.

NY —CREEDMOOR PSYCHIATRIC CENTER, Health Sciences Library, Bldg 51, 80-45 Winchester Blvd, Queens Village, 11427. Susan Taubman, Dir of Library; Pushpa Bhati, Sr Librn
Holdings: Vols (12,000) Cat Slides Phonorecords Audiotapes Filmstrips Microfiche
Budget: ($50,000)
Notes: Particularly strong in the areas of neurology, Pharmacology, psychoanalysis, and psychopharmacology.

PSYCHOPHYSICS AND PSYCHOPHYSIOLOGY see Psychology, Physiological

PSYCHOSOMATIC MEDICINE see Medicine, Psychosomatic

PSYCHOSOMATIC RESEARCH

IL —INSTITUTE FOR PSYCHOANALYSIS, McLean Library, 180 N Michigan Ave, Chicago, 60601. Glenn Miller, Librn
Holdings: Vols (10,000) Cat Mss Pix Audiotapes Videotapes 16mm Films Microforms
Budget: ($87,000)
Notes: The collection is the data base for the *Chicago Psychoanalytic Literature Index*, a computer-generated quarterly subject guide to books, monographs, journals, symposia, tapes, films, and unpublished material indexed to a depth determined by the quality of the data. The *Index* is published by the Institute in Chicago; a sample is available on request.

PSYCHOSYNTHESIS

AZ —WORLD UNIVERSITY, Library, 711 E Blacklidge Dr, Tucson, 85719. Howard John Zitko, Cur
Holdings: Vols (15,000) Cat Mss Maps Audiotapes
Notes: Collection concerns what are generally called the "frontier sciences." No interlibrary loan.

PSYCHOTECHNICS see Psychology, Industrial

PSYCHOTHERAPY

IL —JACKSONVILLE STATE HOSPITAL, Training & Research Library, 1201 S Main St, Jacksonville, 62650. Lois E Wells, Librn
Holdings: Vols (10,000) Cat
Notes: Concerned particularly with developmental disabilities.

IN —SOUTHWEST INDIANA MENTAL HEALTH CENTER, Library, 415 Mulberry, Evansville, 47714. Donna Yuschak, Librn
Holdings: Vols 850 Cat Slides Audiotapes 16mm Films
Budget: $4000
Notes: Also about 500 pamphlets on psychotherapy, social work, and therapeutic recreation.

KS —MENNINGER FOUNDATION, Archives, 5600 W Sixth St, Box 829, Topeka, 66601. Alice Brand, Librn; Mark West, Archivist
Holdings: Vols (33,000) Cat Pix Audiotapes Microforms
Notes: Incl journals. Literature searches and document delivery available for a fee.

MA —MCLEAN HOSPITAL MEDICAL LIBRARY, 115 Mill St, Belmont, 02178. Hector Bossange, Dir
Holdings: Vols 25,611 Cat
Notes: Extensive collection.

NJ —ESSEX COUNTY HOSPITAL, Hamilton Memorial Medical Library, PO Box 500, Cedar Grove, 07009. Elizabeth B Guarducci, Librn
Holdings: Vols (6500) Cat Audiotapes
Budget: $20,000
Notes: Covers all modes of psychotherapy, incl psychiatry, and some psychology and sociology. Incl 135 journal titles.

NM —NEW MEXICO STATE HOSPITAL, Ella P Kief Memorial Library, Hot Spring Blvd, PO Box 1388, Las Vegas, 87701. Hazel Hurley, Librn
Holdings: Vols (5000) Cat
Budget: ($2500)
Notes: Partially cataloged.

BC —CAPILANO COLLEGE, Media Centre, 2055 Purcell Way N, Vancouver, V7J 3H5, Can. Pat Biggins, Reference Librn
Holdings: Vols 3000 Cat Phonorecords Audiotapes Periodicals

PQ —UNIVERSITY OF MONTREAL, Bibliotheque Para-medicale, 2375 Chemin de la Cote Ste Catherine, Montreal, H3C 3J7, Can. Johanne Hopper, Head Librn
Holdings: Vols 1475 Cat Audiotapes
Notes: Special emphasis on psychotherapy. 15 percent in French.

PSYCHOTROPIC DRUGS

ON —ALCOHOLISM & DRUG ADDICTION RESEARCH FOUNDATION, Library, 33 Russell St, Toronto, M5S 2S1, Can. D Fridenberg, Manager, Library Services
Holdings: Vols 8000 Cat
Notes: All aspects of the use and misuse of psychotropic drugs. Incl temperance material.

PTELEON see Macdiarmid, Hugh (Christopher Murray Grieve), 1892-1978

PTOLEMY

IL —NEWBERRY LIBRARY, 60 W Walton St, Chicago, 60610. Robert W Karrow, Jr, Cur of Maps
Holdings: Cat Maps
Notes: Historical map collection, with cut-off date of about 1900, incl 1230 atlases and 11,050 separate maps (in 1973). Rich is classical geography, represented by almost all printed editions of Ptolemy.
See also entry under Maps and Atlases - Collections.

IN —INDIANA UNIVERSITY, Lilly Library, Seventh St, Bloomington, 47405. William R Cagle, Librn
Holdings: Vols 28 Cat
Notes: Ptolemy's Geographia in twenty eight editions printed from 1478 to 1621.

MN —UNIVERSITY OF MINNESOTA, O Meredith Wilson Library, 309 19 Ave S, Minneapolis, 55455. Austin J McLean, Chief, Special Collections
Holdings: Vols (103) // Cat Mss
Notes: Basically mathelmatical astronomy with emphasis on eclipses. Particular strengths are the works of such authors as Delambre, Euclid, Newton, Ptolemy, and Rhaticus. Importnat in this respect are 6 of the 10 known printed editions of the Alphonsine Astronomical Tables.

ON —UNIVERSITY OF TORONTO, Thomas Fisher Rare Book Library, 120 Saint George St, Toronto, M5S 1A5, Can. Richard G Landon, Head
Holdings: Vols 300 Cat
Notes: Stillman Drake Galileo Collection. Comprises early editions of Galileo, of his precursors (Ptolemy and Copernicus) and of his contemporaries in the fields of astronomy and physical science. Also, the Science Collection is especially rich in works on Renaissance astronomy, physics and mechanics and has noteworthy holdings of works of English experimental scientists in the 17th and 18th centuries with excellent collections for the works of Robert Boyle, Robert Hooke, and Sir Isaac Newton. Includes virtually all important early editions of Euclid; alchemical works of the 18th century chemists like Lavoisier and Priestly;

works on agriculture with special emphasis on British agriculture in the 18th century; and a variety of other worksimportant in the history of science in all its branches. In addition the Fisher Library has many other specialized scientific collections which are listed separately.

PUBLIC ADMINISTRATION

AZ —TUCSON PUBLIC LIBRARY, Governmental Reference Library, PO Box 27210, City Hall, Tucson, 85726. Ann Strickland, Librn
Holdings: Vols (4000) Cat Maps Audiotapes Microforms
Notes: Special emphasis on public administration, including public finance, public personnel management, social services, urban planning, public transportation, public works, water management, solid waste management, public recreation and government of growing southwestern US cities in 200,000 to 500,000 population range.

CA —UNIVERSITY OF CALIFORNIA, BERKELEY, Institute of Governmental Studies Library, 109 Moses Hall, Berkeley, 94720. Jack Leister, Head Librn
Holdings: Vols (350,000) Cat Mss Maps Microforms
Budget: ($160,000)
Notes: The library collects primarily pamphlets. Incl in the library's holdings are documents from all levels of government, as well as publications issued by professional association and special interest groups. A GK Hall catalog covering the Institute's Library holdings is available. Since 1937, Library has been depository for all California local documents (city, county & special interest district). Formerly: Bureau of Public Administration.

CA —ALAMEDA COUNTY LIBRARY SYSTEM, Business & Government Library, 2201 Broadway, Oakland, 94612. David Lewallen, Manager
Holdings: Vols (10,000) Cat Maps Microforms
Budget: ($50,000)

CA —SACRAMENTO PUBLIC LIBRARY, 828 I St, Sacramento, 95814. Dorothy Harvey, Librn, Special Collections
Holdings: Vols (4000) Cst
Notes: Incl books on public administration and police science, local government (city and county). Have over 4000 Sacramento city and county documents.

DC —US OFFICE OF PERSONNEL MANAGEMENT, Library, 1900 E St NW, Washington, 20415. Betty B Guerin, Supv Librn
Holdings: Vols 75,000 Cat Microforms
Notes: US Civil Service Commission terminated by Act of Congress, 10/78. US Office of Personnel Management created and effective, 1/79. Library houses a comprehensive collection of materials in all phases of federal personnel administration, both historical and current and incl federal documents and other pamphlets. It is supplemented by collections in general personnel administration, public administration, management, and state, local and foreign Civil Service.

HI —LEGISLATIVE REFERENCE BUREAU, Library, State Capitol, Rm 005, Honolulu, 96813. Ms Hanako Kobayashi, Research Librn
Holdings: Vols (70,000) Cat
Budget: $12,450

IN —INDIANA UNIVERSITY, Business-School of Public and Environmental Affairs (SPEA), Bloomington, 47405. Michael Parrish, Dir
Holdings: Vols (100,000)
Budget: ($200,000)
Notes: Collection covers all phases of business, public administration and environment.

KY —COUNCIL OF STATE GOVERNMENTS, States Information Center, Iron Works Pike, PO Box 11910, Lexington, 40578. Sue Stoltz, Dir
Holdings: Vols 18,000 Cat
Notes: State government administration and

PUBLIC ADMINISTRATION (cont.)

procedures. Major portion of collection is research reports of state legislatures, other state government agencies, and current affairs topics of interest to state governments. Incl 200 current journals.

†MA —JOHN F KENNEDY LIBRARY, Columbia Point, Boston, 02125. Dan H Fenn Jr, Dir
Holdings: // Cat Mss
Notes: Papers of JFK and other holdings of the Kennedy Library, specifically the papers of Louis Brownlow and V O Key, 1902-1963. 70 linear ft of mss. Holdings are described in "Historical Materials in the John F Kennedy Library." Copies may be obtained by writing the Research Archivist.

MA —HARVARD UNIVERSITY LIBRARY, John F Kennedy School of Government Library, Manpower and Industrial Relations Collection, Littauer Library, Cambridge, 02138. James C Damaskos, Librn
Holdings: Vols Cat
Notes: For description see *Harvard Library Bulletin*, IX (1955), 118-128.

MI —UNIVERSITY OF MICHIGAN, Bureau of Government Library, 100A Rackman Bldg, Ann Arbor, 48109. Barbara Landay, Technical Libr Assistant
Holdings: Vols (66,000) Cat
Budget: ($10,000)
Notes: Established in 1914 to serve faculty and students of Institute of Public Policy Studies. Particularly concerned with state and local documents, but incl some federal documents. Also has a pamphlet and newspaper clipping collection on Michigan. Some information on foreign government.

MI —OAKLAND COUNTY REFERENCE LIBRARY, 1200 N Telegraph Rd, Pontiac, 48053. Phyllis Jose, Library Dir
Holdings: Vols (11,000) Cat
Budget: ($34,000)

MO —UNIVERSITY OF MISSOURI-KANSAS CITY, General Library, 5100 Rockhill Road, Kansas City, 64110. Kenneth J LaBudde, Dir; Pamela Jenkins, Business Librn
Holdings: Vols 67,500
Notes: Incl many microforms, cataloged. (4121 current serial subscriptions).

NJ —PRINCETON UNIVERSITY, Library, Rare Books Dept, Princeton, 08544. Stephen Ferguson, Cur
Holdings: Cat

NY —NEW YORK STATE DEPT OF STATE, Community Affairs Library, 162 Washington Ave, Albany, 12231. M L Johnson, Librn
Holdings: Vols (14,640) Cat
Notes: Local government. Serves as research arm for official activities. 16,000 items in vertical files; 150 periodicals. Unique Community File collection of about 1600 local governments arranged by counties in the state.

NY —CORNELL UNIVERSITY LIBRARIES, Graduate School of Management, Malott Hall, Ithaca, 14853. Betsy Ann Olive, Librn
Holdings: Vols (135,000) Cat Microforms
Budget: ($130,000)

OH —PUBLIC LIBRARY OF CINCINNATI & HAMILTON COUNTY, Government and Business Dept, 800 Vine St, Cincinnati, 45202. Paul T Hudson, Head
Holdings: Vols 2000 Cat
Notes: The Murray Seasongood Collection of Government, Law and Public Administration contains works on local government, city management, public finance and municipal law. The collection also houses the collected works of Murray Seasongood.

OH —OHIO LEGISLATIVE SERVICE COMMISSION, Research Library, State House, Columbus, 43215. Barbara J Laughon, Library Administrator
Holdings: Vols 10,000 Cat Microforms
Notes: Collection contains all bills introduced since 1888 and all laws passed since 1803. *Gongwer's Ohio Reports* since 1955, other material related to Ohio legislative procedures. Ohio law is small part of collection of 10,000 vols on public

administration and related subjects of interest to legislators.

OR —UNIVERSITY OF OREGON, Library, Eugene, 97403. Kenneth W Duckett, Curator
Notes: Papers of Prof Charles McKinley, incl files of correspondence (largely) public administration and planning. Papers of James C Rettie, Senior Economist of the Department of the Interior.

OR —UNIVERSITY OF OREGON, Bureau of Governmental Research Library, Box 3177, Eugene, 97403. Katherine G Eaton, Head Librn
Holdings: Vols (25,000) Cat Microforms
Budget: ($5000)
Notes: Separate catalog and classification system.

PA —PENNSYLVANIA ECONOMY LEAGUE, Eastern Div Library, 215 S Broad St, Philadelphia, 19107. Ellen Brennan, Librn
Holdings: Vols (15,000) Cat Maps
Notes: Public finance, charters, constitutions, public education.

PA —UNIVERSITY OF PENNSYLVANIA, Fels Center of Government, 39 & Walnut St, Philadelphia, 19104. Nancy K Smith, Librn
Holdings: Vols (18,180) Cat Maps
Notes: Restricted use: Staff, students and government officials.

PA —UNIVERSITY OF PITTSBURGH, Library, Graduate School of Public and International Affairs, Forbes Quadrangle, 1st floor West, Pittsburgh, 15260. Nicholas C Caruso, Librn
Holdings: Vols (80,000) Cat
Budget: ($150,000)
Notes: The library attempts to collect as many national economic and social development plans as possible from the developing countries of the world. Is also holds city, regional and state plans for Pennsylvania, particularly, the 9 southwestern counties of Pennsylvania.

TX —ECTOR COUNTY LIBRARY, Department of Business and Technology, 321 W 5th St, Odessa, 79760. Pat Jones, Dept Head
Holdings: Vols 300 Cat
Notes: *Specialized Collection to Assist the Small Business* in Government Contracting. Incl 500 vertical files, 6 periodicals, 200 US Government Specifications and MIL Standards.

WA —UNIVERSITY OF WASHINGTON LIBRARIES, Political Science Library, 220 Smith Hall, DP-25, Seattle, 98195. Alvin Fritz, Librn
Holdings: Vols (57,344) Cat
Budget: ($57,792)

PR —UNIVERSITY OF PUERTO RICO, Graduate School of Public Administration, Library, Graduate Social Sciences Bldg, Rio Piedras, 00931. Perfecto Camacho, Library Dir
Holdings: Vols (15,000) Cat
Budget: $22,000
Notes: Public administration, economics, and elections. Especially materials related to or about the separate municipalities of Puerto Rico and the Commonwealth of Puerto Rico. Documents collection.

PR —COMMONWEALTH OF PUERTO RICO, Office of Personnel Library, PO Box 8476 Fernadez Juncos Sta, Santurce, 00910. Jose A Fonseca Molina, Librn
Holdings: Vols (1106) Cat

ON —CANADA PUBLIC SERVICE COMMISSION, Library, Room 930 W Tower, Esplande Laurier, Ottawa, K1A 0M7, Can. A Campbell, Chief Librn
Holdings: Vols 7000 Cat
Budget: $20,000
Notes: Library supports the research, administrative, and instructional needs of the Commission. English and French materials.

ON —CANADIAN HOUSING INFORMATION CENTER, Canada Mortgage and Housing Corp, CMHC Annex Bldg Ground Floor, Montreal Rd, Ottawa, K1A 0P7, Can. Leslie Jones, Mgr
Holdings: Cat

PUBLIC ADMINISTRATION CLEARING HOUSE

†MA —JOHN F KENNEDY LIBRARY, Columbia Point, Boston, 02125. Dan H Fenn

Jr, Dir
Holdings: // Cat Mss
Notes: Louis Brownlow's papers relating to government reorganization during the Roosevelt administration, the District of Columbia, the Public Administration Clearing House, and other topics; and personal and family papers, 1902-1963. 30 linear ft of mss. Holdings are described in "Historical Materials in the John F Kennedy Library." Copies may be obtained by writing the Research Archivist.

PUBLIC ASSISTANCE see Public Welfare

PUBLIC CHARITIES see Public Welfare

PUBLIC DOCUMENTS see Government Publications

PUBLIC EDUCATION see Education, Public

PUBLIC ENTERPRISE

MA —HARVARD UNIVERSITY, Institute for International Development, Library, Coolidge Hall, 1737 Cambridge St, Cambridge, 02138. Barbara Mitchell, Librn
Holdings: Vols (17,000) Periodicals
Notes: Economic development, rural development, statistical material on selected underdeveloped countries. Incl 75 periodical titles.

PUBLIC FINANCE see Finance, Public

PUBLIC HEALTH

CA —UNIVERSITY OF CALIFORNIA, BERKELEY, Life Sciences Libraries, Public Health Library, 42 Earl Warren Hall, Berkeley, 94720. Thomas J Alexander, Librn
Holdings: Vols (75,000) Cat Microforms
Notes: Research collection covering all aspects of public health. Health Department annual reports from all 50 states are acquired, as well as such reports from all California health units and from major US cities. Serial publications issued by Health Departments in the 13 western states are being reveived.

CA —UNIVERSITY OF CALIFORNIA, LOS ANGELES, Biomedical Library, Center for the Health Sciences, Los Angeles, 90024. Alison Bunting, Acting Biomedical Librn; Victoria Steele, Head, History & Special Collections Div
Holdings: Vols (400,000) Cat Slides Phonorecords Audiotapes Videotapes 16mm Films Microforms

Notes: The UCLA Biomedical Library serves primarily the Schools of Medicine, Dentistry, Nursing, and Public Health, the UCLA Medical Center, the Departments of Microbiology and Biology in the College of Letters and Science, and related institutes in biomedicine. The collections of the Library are broad in scope, designed not only to support the teaching and research needs of its many users, but also to function as a resource for the health sciences-biological field as a whole. The outstanding feature of the collection is the strength of its periodical holdings, both current and retrospective. The Library has an excellent reference collection, a comprehensive historical section, and gives special emphasis to the fields of neuroscience, psychiatry, ophthalmology, radiation biology, molecular biology, and vertebrate zoology. Increased emphasis is being given to the acquisition of audiovisual materials.

PUBLIC HEALTH (cont.)

CA —STANFORD UNIVERSITY LIBRARIES, Lane Medical Library, Stanford University, Medical Center, Stanford, 94305. Peter Stangl, Librn
Notes: Lane Library serves the schools of medicine and related basic sciences and the research, patient care and physician training activities of the Stanford University Medical Center. The collections cover clinical medicine and its specialties, the preclinical and basic sciences, public health, nursing and related fields.

CO —WESTERN INTERSTATE COMMISSION FOR HIGHER EDUCATION, Wiche Library, PO Drawer P, Boulder, 80302. Karon M Kelly, Dir Library Services
Holdings: Vols (10,000) Cat Microforms
Notes: Incl medical and nursing education, student exchange programs, minority involvement in education, management systems in higher education.

CT —YALE MEDICAL LIBRARY, 333 Cedar St, New Haven, 06510.
Holdings: Vols (334,215) Cat Mss Pix Slides Microforms
Budget: ($361,650)
Notes: Incl films, audiotapes, artifacts, etc.

CT —YALE UNIVERSITY, Box 1603A, Yale Station, New Haven, 06520.
Holdings: Mss Pix
Notes: The Contemporary Medical Care and Health Pollicy Collection. Letters, memos, records, photographs, etc of the principal stategists of the social medical movement in the US.

DC —LIBRARY OF CONGRESS, Manuscript Division, Washington, 20540. John C Broderick, Chief
Notes: Papers of Robert Ramapatnam Williams (1886-1965), a pioneer in the field of nutrition and public health who synthesized thiamin (vitamin B1), helped to effect the widespread enrichment of foodstuff grains, and developed the Williams-Waterman Fund to combat diseases caused by inadequate nutrition. 20,000 items, incl correspondence, reports, photographs, and glass spectographic plates, document research on and production of vitamin B1, enrichment of cereal products, and the Williams-Waterman Fund.

DC —MANUFACTURING CHEMISTS' ASSOCIATION, Library, 1825 Connecticut Ave NW, Washington, 20009. Rose Clark, Librn
Holdings: Vols 3000 Cat
Notes: Incl extensive files on the business and trade aspects of the chemical industry; also, environmental and health aspects.

DC —PAN AMERICAN HEALTH ORGANIZATION, Library, 525 23 St NW, Washington, 20037. Dr Carlos Gamboa, Chief of Library and Reference Services
Holdings: Vols 50,000 Cat Maps Slides Filmstrips

DC —SUGAR ASSOCIATION LIBRARY, 1511 K Street, NW, Washington, 20005.
Holdings: Vols 1000 Cat Mss Maps Pix Slides Microforms
Budget: $8000
Notes: Sugar utililzation and research, public health, food technology, and source chemistry.

FL —BORLAND HEALTH SCIENCES, Library, 580 W Eighth St, Jacksonville, 32209. M Hinz, Librn
Holdings: Vols 15,000 Cat 16mm Films Filmstrips
Notes: Plus 15,000 bound journal vols.

HI —UNIVERSITY OF HAWAII, School of Public Health Reference Collection, 1960 East-West Rd, D-207, Honolulu, 96822. Carol W Arnold, Librn
Holdings: Vols (15,000) Cat Microforms
Budget: ($8,500)
Notes: Public health; also a microfiche collection of 25,000 items on medical care delivery and health administration.

IL —GLENVIEW PUBLIC LIBRARY, 1930 Glenview Rd, Glenview, 60025. Peter Bury, Librn
Holdings: Vols (3500) Cat Filmstrips
Notes: Maintained as health and domestic science subject center. Incl 1840 cookbooks.

IL —UNIVERSITY OF ILLINOIS, URBANA/CHAMPAIGN, Library, Applied Life Studies Library, 1408 W Gregory Dr, Urbana, 61801.
Holdings: Vols (38,000) Cat Pix Microforms
See also entry under Physical Education and Training

MD —MEDICAL & CHIRURGICAL FACULTY OF THE STATE OF MARYLAND, Library, 1211 Cathedral St, Baltimore, 21201. Joseph E Jensen, Librn
Holdings: Vols (10,000) // Cat Mss Maps Pix
See also entry under Medicine - History and Historic

MA —BOSTON UNIVERSITY, Medical Center, Alumni Medical Library, 80 E Concord St, Boston, 02118. Irene Christopher, Chief Librn
Holdings: Vols 89,448

MA —FRANCIS A COUNTWAY LIBRARY OF MEDICINE, Boston Medical Library/ Harvard Medical Library, 10 Shattuck St, Boston, 02115. C Robin LeSueur, Librn; Richard J Wolfe, Cur, Rare Books & Manuscripts
Holdings: Vols 442,245 Cat Mss Pix Microforms
Budget: $1,160,000
Notes: Unities holdings of Boston Medical Library, Harvard's Faculty of Medicine (incl school of Dental Medicine) and Faculty of Public Health. Rare books include 800 incunabula. In resources for medical research the collection is believed to be surpasses in the United States only by the National Library of Medicine.

MI —UNIVERSITY OF MICHIGAN, Public Health Library, Ann Arbor, 48109. Mary Townsend, Head
Holdings: Vols (55,000) Cat Maps Pix
Budget: ($24,000)

MN —MINNESOTA DEPT OF HEALTH, R N Barr Public Health Library, 717 Delaware St SE, PO Box 9441, Minneapolis, 55440. Barbara Brian, Librn
Holdings: Vols (26,000) Cat Microforms
Notes: Public health.

MN —UNIVERSITY OF MINNESOTA, Bio-Medical Library, Diehl Hall, Minneapolis, 55455. Gertrude Foreman, Acting Dir
Holdings: Vols (263,361)
Budget: (500,000)

NJ —NEW JERSEY DEPT OF HEALTH, Library, CN 360, Trenton, 08625. Cathy A Stout, Librn
Holdings: Vols (7000) // Cat Per Microforms
Budget: $22,000

NY —COLUMBIA UNIVERSITY LIBRARIES, Health Sciences Library, 701 W 168 St, New York, 10032. Rachael K Goldstein, Librn
Notes: Restricted.
See also entry under Medicine

NY —NEW YORK ACADEMY OF MEDICINE, Library, 2 E 103 St, New York, 10029. Brett A Kirkpatrick, Librn
Holdings: Mss
Notes: One

NY —UNITED HOSPITAL FUND OF NEW YORK, Library, 3 E 54th St, New York, 10022. Christine Bahr, Librn
Holdings: Vols (4000) Cat Mss Maps Pix
Notes: Incl 100 journal titles.

NY —ROCKEFELLER UNIVERSITY, Rockefeller Archive Center, Hillcrest, Pocantico Hills, North Tarrytown, 10591. Joseph W Ernst, Dir; J William Hess, Assoc Dir
Notes: Papers relative to the Rockefeller Family, Foundations, University, and other specific enterprises and contributions to particular areas of social, physical, educational, and historic reform, preservation, conservation, or development. Extensive records of administrative, financial, physical, or intellectual relationships.

NC —UNIVERSITY OF NORTH CAROLINA, CHAPEL HILL, Health Sciences Library, 223 H, Chapel Hill, 27514. Samuel Hitt, Dir
Holdings: Vols (200,000) Cat Slides Journals Audiotapes Videotapes Microforms
Budget: ($560,000)

NC —NORTH CAROLINA DEPT OF HUMAN RESOURCES, Div of Health Services, Public Health Library, PO Box 2091, Raleigh, 27602. Elnora H Turner, Librn
Holdings: Vols (15,000) Cat

OK —UNIVERSITY OF OKLAHOMA, Health Sciences Center, Library, 1000 Stanton L Young Blvd, PO Box 26901, Oklahoma City, 73190. C M Thompson, Jr, Dir
Holdings: Vols (155,434) Cat Slides Audiotapes Videotapes 16mm Films Microforms
Budget: ($374,960)
Notes: Incl a collection on the health and well-being of the American Indian-historically and currently.

PA —UNIVERSITY OF PITTSBURGH, Falk Library of the Health Professions, History of Medicine Collection, Scaife Hall, Pittsburgh, 15261. Jonathon Erlen, Cur
Holdings: Vols (13,500) Cat Pix
Budget: ($425,269)
Notes: Medicine, dentistry, nursing, pharmacy, public health, psychiatry materials, incl some rare books and 300 pamphlets on anesthesia.

RI —BROWN UNIVERSITY, John Hay Library, 20 Prospect St, Providence, 02912. Mark N Brown, Cur Mss
Holdings: // Mss
Notes: Three boxes of correspondence of Charles V Chapin and mss, 1900-1939, chiefly with workers in public health in America, Europe, and Australia about Dr Chapin's work in communicable diseases.

SC —SOUTH CAROLINA DEPT OF HEALTH & ENVIRONMENTAL CONTROL, Educational Resource Center, 2600 Bull St, Columbia, 29201. Michael Kronenfeld, Librn
Holdings: Vols 1500

SC —SOUTH CAROLINA DEPT OF HEALTH & ENVIRONMENTAL CONTROL, Materials Library, 2600 Bull St, Columbia, 29201. Marie Horton, Librn
Notes: Incl 250 titles of materials for bulk distribution.

SC —SOUTH CAROLINA DEPT OF HEALTH & ENVIRONMENTAL CONTROL, Film Library, 2600 Bull St, Columbia, 29201.
Holdings: Films
Notes: Incl 1300 films on public health and health related topics.

TN —TENNESSEE DEPARTMENT OF PUBLIC HEALTH, Public Health Library, C2-218 Cordell Hull Bldg, Nashville, 37219. Randall Brady, Librn
Holdings: Vols 11,000 Cat
Notes: Separate Film Library containing 16mm films and other AV materials.

TX —HOUSTON ACADEMY OF MEDICINE-TEXAS MEDICAL CENTER, Library, Jesse H Jones Library Bldg, Houston, 77030. Elizabeth Borst White, Special Collections Librn
Holdings: Vols (900) Cat
Notes: Mading Collection on Public Health. English-language materials dealing with American public health conditions before 1925. Emphasis is on epidemiology and infectious diseases (excluding venereal disease), incl material on sanitation and climatology. Federal, state or municipal reports on health, mortality and sanitation are included. Also 500 pamphlets.

WA —UNIVERSITY OF WASHINGTON LIBRARIES, Health Sciences Library, SB-55, Seattle, 98195. Gerald J Oppenheimer, Dir
Holdings: Vols (232,000) Cat Slides Audiotapes Microforms
Budget: ($550,000)

WA —URS ENGINEERS, Library, 2615 Fourth Ave, Seattle, 98121. Jill Phelps, Librn
Holdings: Vols (3100) Cat
Budget: ($5000)
Notes: Environmental impact assessment, hazardous materials disposal, oil spill cleanup and environmental effects of waterborne pollutants, especially with regard to California and the western environment.

PQ —MCGILL UNIVERSITY, Nursing/Social Work Library, 3506 University St, Montreal,

PUBLIC HEALTH (cont.)

H3A 1Y1, Can. Wendy Patrick, Librn
Holdings: Vols (35,000) Cat
PQ —UNIVERSITY OF MONTREAL,
Bibliotheque Para-medicale, 2375 Chemin de
la Cote Ste Catherine, Montreal, H3C 3J7,
Can. Johanne Hopper, Head Librn
Holdings: Vols 1700 Cat
Budget: $6400
Notes: Social medicine, preventive medicine,
epidemiology, industrial health and hygiene,
and environmental factors (pollution) as
related to health. Depository for World
Health Organization publications.

PUBLIC HEALTH—HISTORY

CA —UNIVERSITY OF CALIFORNIA, LOS
ANGELES, Biomedical Library, Center for
the Health Sciences, Los Angeles, 90024.
Alison Bunting, Acting Biomedical Librn;
Victoria Steele, Head, History & Special
Collections Div
Holdings: Vols (21,000) Cat Mss Pix Slides
Microforms
Notes: The History and Special Collections
Division of the UCLA Biomedical Library
owns close to 13,000 rare books comprising
landmarks in biomedical history, 15th
through 19th centuries. Approx 13,000
supporting monographs and serial volumes
related to the history of medicine, dentistry,
nursing, public health and other life sciences.
CT —YALE MEDICAL LIBRARY, 333 Cedar
St, New Haven, 06510.
Notes: A special subject emphasis.
MD —NATIONAL LIBRARY OF
MEDICINE, 8600 Rockville Pike, Bethesda,
20209. Harold M Schoolinam, Actg Dir
Budget: ($46,400)
Notes: Correspondence of George E Waring,
pioneering American sanitary engineer of the
19th century.
NY —STATE UNIVERSITY OF NEW
YORK, STONY BROOK, Health Sciences
Library, PO Box 66, East Setauket, 11733.
Notes: Slide Collection of Historical Medical
Photographs is an archive of 3000 slides
pertaining to the history of medical care in
America--Medical and public health
activities from the 1850s to the 1950s. An
illustrated catalogue, published by
Greenwood Press, is scheduled for 1984.
†NY —COLUMBIA UNIVERSITY
LIBRARIES, Butler Library, Rare Book and
Manuscript Library, 535 W 114 St, New
York, 10027.
Notes: Papers of the American Bureau for
Medical Aid to China, incl correspondence,
memoranda, reports, minutes, membership
and financial records, photographs, posters
and printed material. Approx 45,000 pieces.
Also, some 6000 photographs of Chinese
medical colleges, hospitals, laboratories, and
personnel.

PUBLIC HEALTH NURSING

MA —SIMMONS COLLEGE ARCHIVES,
300 The Fenway, Boston, 02115. Megan
Sniffin-Marinoff, College Archivist
Notes: Archives of the Simmons College
School of Public Health Nursing (later
reorganized into the School of Nursing)
cover the years 1902-1970. Important
correspondents in the collection incl M
Adelaide Nutting, Mary Beard, Isabel
Stewart, and Anne Hervey Strong, etc. Incl
Strong's records of activity with regard to
nursing education in the National
Organization for Public Health Nursing,
1918-22. 1000 linear feet in institution, incl
special collections nursing and photographs,
nursing.
MI —UNIVERSITY OF MICHIGAN, Public
Health Library, Ann Arbor, 48109. Mary
Townsend, Head
Holdings: Vols (55,000) Cat Maps Pix
Budget: ($24,000)

PUBLIC HEALTH SERVICES see Public Health

PUBLIC HEALTH SURVEYS see Health Surveys

PUBLIC HOUSES see Hotels, Taverns, Etc.

PUBLIC HYGIENE see Public Health

PUBLIC LAW

DC —LIBRARY OF CONGRESS, Law
Library, 101 Independence Ave, SE,
Washington, 20540. Carleton W Kenyon,
Dir
Holdings: Vols 1,800,000 Cat Mss
Microforms
Notes: The collection, comprising the legal
sources and literature of the US and all
foreign nations, covers all legal systems incl
common, civil, international, religious, and
historic law.
MD —JOHNS HOPKINS UNIVERSITY,
Milton S Eisenhower Library, Charles & 34
Sts, Baltimore, 21218. Ann S Gwyn,
Assistant Dir for Special Collections
Holdings: // Cat Mss
Notes: Incl part of library of J C Bluntschli,
his complete works, mss and notebooks.
Annotated works and mss of Francis Lieber.
Ms lecture notes of Edounard Laboulaye.

PUBLIC LAW (CANON LAW) see Canon Law

PUBLIC LIBRARIES see Libraries

PUBLIC OFFICE see Public Officers

PUBLIC OFFICERS—U.S.—PORTRAITS

DC —LIBRARY OF CONGRESS, Prints &
Photographs Div, Washington, 20540.
Notes: The Brady-Handy Collection consists
of some 10,000 negatives from the files of
photographers Levin C Handy (1855?-1932)
and Mathew B Brady (1823?-1896), most of
which are portrait photographs and views of
Washington, DC from the 19th and early
20th centuries. Incl portraits of congressmen
and government leaders (1855-90).

PUBLIC OPINION

MA —MASSACHUSETTS INSTITUTE OF
TECHNOLOGY, Institute Archives, Special
Collections, Cambridge, 02139.
Notes: Correspondence, newsletters, fact-
sheets, newspaper and magazine articles,
books and reports of the Citizens' League
Against the Sonic Boom, established in 1967
by William Shurcliff to oppose the sonic
boom, stop commercial supersonic transport
production, and influence public opinion and
policy decisions on the SST. Major
correspondents incl Bo Lundberg, Richard
Wiggs, several US congressmen, and CLASB
members.

PUBLIC OPINION POLLS

CT —YALE UNIVERSITY, Social Science
Library, 140 Prospect St, New Haven,
06520. Billie I Salter, Librn
Holdings: Vols (40,000) Cat Microforms
See also entry under Social Sciences.
IL —UNIVERSITY OF CHICAGO, National
Opinion Research Center, Library, 6030 S
Ellis Ave, Chicago, 60637.
Holdings: Vols 2000 Cat Mss Maps
Notes: Collection incl book, periodical and
ephemeral materials in public opinion
research with an academic approach
predominant. Methodology is represented
mainly in published works ordinarily
available in any research library. Substantive
works, ie, applications of the method, reports
of findings, are less generally available,
especially the poll and survey releases of
domestic and foreign organizations; we
collect some of these and make them
available to scholars. Collection is not
exhaustive but reflects current and past staff
interests. Incl also about 600 studies
conducted by the National Opinion
Research Center on a wide variety of
subjects.

PUBLIC RECORDS—PRESERVATION see Archives

PUBLIC RELATIONS

CA —ASSOCIATION OF BAY AREA
GOVERNMENTS, MTC/ABAG Library,
101 Eighth St, Oakland, 94607. Diane
Gillman, Information Coord
Notes: Concentrates heavily on the nine-
county Bay Area region. About 10,000
monographs and serials. Title catalog,
OCLC/ATS. Central collection of
documents for six transit properties in Bay
Area.
DC —COUNCIL FOR ADVANCEMENT &
SUPPORT OF EDUCATION, Reference
Center, Eleven Dupont Circle NW, Suite
400, Washington, 20036. Cynthia Snyder,
Dir
Holdings: Vols (600) Cat Mss Audiotapes
Microforms
Notes: A membership service containing
information in educational fund raising,
institutional relations, government relations,
alumni administration, publications, and
management techniques for higher education
and independent schools. Collection, in
addition, contains mss, microfiches, and
tapes. Succeeds the American Alumni
Council, dissolved in 1974.
IL —BURSON-MARSTELLER LIBRARY,
Information Services, One E Wacker Dr,
Chicago, 60601. Ellen Steininger, Librn
Holdings: Vols 5000
Notes: Incl 10,000 pictures, 1200 serial
titles.
KY —ASBURY THEOLOGICAL
SEMINARY, B L Fisher Library, Wilmore,
40390. D William Faupel, Dir of Library
Services
Holdings: Uncat
Notes: A collection of 35 document boxes of
publicity materials on nearly 300 service
organizations (Christian, missionary, social,
educational), fugitive materials which would
serve as primary sources for a study of their
history and work--form letters (strictly fund
raising letters deleted), brochures, etc.
MA —EDWARD L BERNAYS PUBLIC
RELATIONS LIBRARY, 7 Lowell St,
Cambridge, 02138.
Holdings: Vols (3000) Cat
Notes: Said to be one of the largest
collections on the subject of public relations,
publicity, and propaganda. Many pamphlets.
No photocopying.
NJ —PRINCETON UNIVERSITY, Library,
Manuscript Collection, Nassau St, Princeton,
08540. Jean F Preston, Cur
Holdings: // Mss Pix
Notes: The Ivy Lee Collection fills 70 ms
boxes, 387 vols. See Princeton University
Library Chronicle, v 27, p 113-20. An
unpublished typescript guide (17 p) is
available in the Library.
NY —CORNELL UNIVERSITY LIBRARIES,
Collection of Regional History, Dept of
Manuscripts and Univ Archives, Ithaca,
14853.
Notes: Publicity material (1950-59) of the
Cornell University Department of Public
Relations and Information. Incl biographical
material and photos. Unpublished guide
available.
NY —ADAMS & RINEHEART INC, Library,
708 E Third Ave, New York, 10017. Joan M
Reicherter, Chief Librn
Notes: Incl library of Earl Newsom & Co,
which merged into Adams & Rinehart.
NY —PUBLIC RELATIONS SOCIETY OF
AMERICA, Information Center, 845 Third
Ave, New York, 10022. Mary W Wilson,
Information Center Dir
NC —GREENSBORO PUBLIC LIBRARY,
Business Library, 201 Greene St, Drawer
X-4, Greensboro, 27402. Lebby B Lamb,
Business Librn
Holdings: Vols (6000) Cat Microforms
Budget: ($12,000)
WI —STATE HISTORICAL SOCIETY OF
WISCONSIN, Archives, 816 State St,
Madison, 53706. Harold L Miller, Reference
Archivist
Holdings: Mss Pix Films Microforms
Notes: Areas represented in collection incl
radio, television, the press, public relations
and advertising. Emphasis is on development
of media in the 20th century; materials are
mainly professional papers of individuals or
organization or organizational records of
firms or associations in the media.
Collections are described in Sources for
Mass Communications, Film and Theater
Research: A Guide, (1982) and in current
accession notes in the Wisconsin Magazine

PUBLIC RELATIONS (cont.)

of History. Major collections are also listed in Hamer, *Guide to Manuscripts and Archives in the United States,* (1961) and in the *National Union Catalog of Manuscripts* Collections, (1959-date). Also incl, disc recordings and tape recordings.

WI —UNIVERSITY OF WISCONSIN, MADISON, Journalism Reading Room (Nieman-Grant), (formerly Bleyer Memorial Reading Room, School of Journalism), Vilas Communication Hall, Rm 2130, Madison, 53706. Arthur Cran, Librn; Mary Nagel, Asst Librn
Holdings: Vols 750 Cat
Budget: ($500)

PUBLIC RELIEF see Public Welfare

PUBLIC SCHOOLS—FINANCE see Education—Finance

PUBLIC SECURITIES see Securities

PUBLIC SERVICE CORPORATIONS see Public Utilities

PUBLIC SPEAKING AND SPEAKERS

DC —GEORGE WASHINGTON UNIVERSITY, Gelman Library, 2130 H St NW, Washington, 20052.
Holdings: Vols (500) Cat Mss Pix
Notes: The Chauncey Mitchell Depew papers cover the period of ca 1872--1928 and include correspondence (primarily incoming), manuscript speeches and misc papers, photographs, and scrapbooks of his Senate campaigns, travels, and obituary notices. The collection primarily reflects Depew's career as a public speaker and is cataloged as a collection with an unpublished inventory for access. The inventory includes an index of correspondents.

PUBLIC UTILITIES

CA —AZUSA PACIFIC COLLEGE, Marshburn Memorial Library, Citrus & Alosta, Azusa, 91702. Edward Peterman, Librn
Holdings: Vols 5000 // Maps Pix
Notes: Azusa Foothill Citrus and Local History collection is related to the genesis of Azusa, the citrus industry, the Slauson and Macneil families, and such companies as the Azusa Land and Water Company, Azusa Electric Lighting and Power Company, Azusa Foothill Citrus Association, Azusa Agricultural Water Company, and the Azusa Foothill Citrus Company. Includes letters, ledgers, etc.

CA —LOS ANGELES PUBLIC LIBRARY, Municipal Reference Dept, Water and Power Division, Room 518 GOB, Box 111, Los Angeles, 90012. Donald F Hinrichs Sr, Librn
Holdings: Vols 21,336 Cat
Notes: Also 2203 serial titles, 533 periodical titles.

DC —EDISON ELECTRIC INSTITUTE, Library-8th Floor, 1111 19th St NW, Washington, 20036. Ethel Tiberg, Mgr, Library Services
Holdings: Vols (13,321) Cat Maps Pix Microforms

DC —FOSTER ASSOCIATES, Library, 1101 17th St NW, Washington, 20036. A Blandamer, Librn
Notes: The principal subject areas are public utility regulation and economics, and energy economics.

IL —LOYOLA UNIVERSITY OF CHICAGO, E M Cudahy Memorial Library, 6525 N Sheridan Rd, Chicago, 60626.
Holdings: Mss
Notes: General correspondence and personal papers. Collection also incl papers of the Middle West Utilities Company 1913-1933, and misc materials from other Samuel Insull controlled enterprises. Transcript of United States vs Insull and his memoirs are also available. To be used under the direct supervision of the archivist at all times.

IL —PEOPLES GAS, LIGHT & COKE COMPANY, Library, 122 S Michigan Ave Rm 727, Chicago, 60603. Rosann Meagher, Librn
Holdings: Vols 5000 Cat Maps
Notes: The gas industry, incl production and distribution.

NJ —PUBLIC SERVICE ELECTRIC AND GAS CO, Nuclear Library, MC150A, PO Box 236, Hancocks Bridge, 08038. Virginia Swichel, Librn
Holdings: Vols (1000) Cat

NJ —PUBLIC SERVICE ELECTRIC & GAS CO, Library, 80 Park Place Plaza P3C, PO Box 570, Newark, 07101. Florine E Hunt, Corporate Librn
Holdings: Vols (20,000) Cat Microforms

NY —NATIONAL ECONOMIC RESEARCH ASSOCIATES, INC, Library, 123 Main St, White Plains, 10601. Debra Gaffey, Asst Librn
Holdings: Vols (6000) Cat

OH —TOLEDO EDISON CO, Library, 300 Madison Ave, Toledo, 43652. Catherine Witker, Librn
Holdings: Vols (2000) Cat Audiotapes
Budget: ($10,000)

†PA —GILBERT ASSOCIATES, Library Information Services, PO Box 1498, Reading, 19603. Debra Bosler, Supervisor
Notes: The Public Utility Regulation and Finance Collection furnishes information for consultants working directly with public utilities on rate cases, load research and management, and generation planning. Extensive material on this industry has been collected. Many statistical sources on the energy industry in general.

SC —COLLEGE OF CHARLESTON LIBRARY, Special Collections Dept, Charleston, 29401.
Notes: South Carolina Utility Reform Coalistion Papers, 1979-1980, documents a rate increase application submitted by South Carolina Electric & Gas, and the suit brought against them by the coalition.

PUBLIC WELFARE

CA —UNIVERSITY OF CALIFORNIA, BERKELEY, Institute of Governmental Studies Library, 109 Moses Hall, Berkeley, 94720. Jack Leister, Head Librn
Holdings: Vols (350,000) Cat Mss Maps Microforms
Budget: ($160,000)
Notes: The library collects primarily pamphlets. Incl in the library's holdings are documents from all levels of government, as well as publications issued by professional associations and special interest groups. A G K Hall catalog covering the Institute's Library holdings is available. Since 1937, Library has been depository for all California local documents (city, county & special district). Formerly: Bureau of Public Administration.

CA —UNIVERSITY OF CALIFORNIA, LOS ANGELES, Research Library, Public Affairs Service, 405 Hilgard Ave, Los Angeles, 90024. Edward Shreeves, Chairman, Bibliographers Group; Eugenia Eaton, Head, Public Affairs Service
Holdings: Uncat
Notes: Current non-governmental English-language pamphlets (192,819), broadsides, leaflets and other ephemera on public affairs, from 1960, representing a wide spectrum of political and social opinions. Social welfare and industrial relations are strong fields. Legal loose-leaf labor services, such as the *Daily Labor Report,* the *Government Employee Relations Report* and the *Labor Relations Reporter,* as well as labor pamphlets from the mid-1940s, reflect a long-standing responsibility to the University's Institute of Industrial Relations.

CA —UNIVERSITY OF SOUTHERN CALIFORNIA, Social Work Library, University Park, Los Angeles, 90007. Ruth Britton, Librn
Holdings: Vols 25,000 Cat Audiotapes Videotapes
Notes: Social work and social welfare. Incl 129 journal titles.

CO —COLORADO STATE DEPARTMENT OF SOCIAL SERVICES LIBRARY, 1575 Sherman St, Denver, 80203. Maynard Chapman, Librn
Holdings: Vols 9924 Cat

KS —JOHNSON COUNTY MENTAL HEALTH CENTER, John R Keach Memorial Library, 6000 Lamar Ave, Mission, 66202. Krista Hilton-Ross, Librn
Holdings: Vols (1000) Cat Mss

KS —KANSAS STATE DEPT OF SOCIAL & REHABILITATION SERVICES, SRS-Staff Development Library, Feldman Bldg, 2700 W Sixth St, Topeka, 66606. Jean Barton, Librn
Holdings: Vols 5000 Cat Mss Slides Audiotapes Videotapes 16mm Films
Budget: $1000

MA —SIMMONS COLLEGE, School of Social Work Library, 51 Commonwealth Ave, Boston, 02115. Marilyn Bregoni, Librn
Holdings: Vols (20,000) Cat Mss

MA —BOSTON COLLEGE LIBRARIES, Graduate School of Social Work Library, McGuinn Hall, Chestnut Hill, 02167. Harriet J Nemiccolo, Librn
Holdings: Vols (28,300) Cat Audiotapes Microforms Videotapes
Notes: The collection covers specifically all areas of social work education and all aspects of social welfare services. Holdings incl government documents, doctoral dissertations. Library is computerized and offers customized data based literature searches. There are 385 journal titles.

MI —UNIVERSITY OF MICHIGAN, Social Work Library, 1548 Frieze Bldg, Ann Arbor, 48109. Christina W Neal, Head
Holdings: Vols (33,000)

NY —MONTEFIORE HOSPITAL & MEDICAL CENTER, Karl Cherkasky Social Medicine Library, 111 E 210 St, Bronx, 10467. Victor Sidel, Dir
Holdings: Vols (500) Cat
Budget: ($1000)

NY —HUNTER COLLEGE, School of Social Work, Library, 129 E 79 St, New York, 10021. Charles Elder, Head Librn
Holdings: Vols Mss Documents
Notes: Paul Schreiber Collection. Books, mss and related documents dealing with successive periods of growth in social welfare in America and England.

NY —NEW YORK CITY HUMAN RESOURCES ADMINISTRATION, McMillan Library, 109 E 16 St, New York, 10003. Harold Benson, Librn
Holdings: Vols (13,000) Cat Mss
Budget: ($18,000)
Notes: Public welfare in all aspects; the poor in America, administration, management, child welfare, social services, social work in contemporary society, and urban affairs.

NY —ROCKEFELLER UNIVERSITY, Rockefeller Archive Center, Hillcrest, Pocantico Hills, North Tarrytown, 10591. Joseph W Ernst, Dir; J William Hess, Assoc Dir
Notes: Papers relative to the Rockefeller Family, Foundations, University, and other specific enterprises and contributions to particular areas of social, physical, educational, and historic reform, preservation, conservation, or development. Extensive records of administrative, financial, physical, or intellectual relationships.

VA —UNITED WAY OF AMERICA INFORMATION CENTER, 701 North Fairfax St, United Way Plaza, Alexandria, 22314. Henry M Smith, Dir; Barbara L Owen, Librn
Holdings: Vols (1200) Cat Microforms
Notes: Incl 5000 research reports and studies on microfiche; 100 vertical file drawers. Services primarily for United Way organizations--United Funds, Community Chests, Health and Welfare Planning Councils.

WI —STATE HISTORICAL SOCIETY OF WISCONSIN, Archives, 816 State St, Madison, 53706. Harold L Miller, Reference Archivist
Holdings: Mss Pix Audiotapes Microforms
Notes: Records and papers of organizations and individuals engages in social and political reform activities. Major focus areas are civil rights, 1950s to the present, and anti-Vietnam war and other protest movements of the 1960s to the present. Also covered are other reform movements,

PUBLIC WELFARE (cont.)

socialism, and communism from the 1930s to the present. Collections are described in *Social Action Collection at the State Historical Society of Wisconsin: A Guide*, (1983) and in current accession notes in the *Wisconsin Magazine of History*. Major collections are also listed in Hamer, *Guide to Manuscripts and Archives in the United States*, (1961) and in the *National Union Catalog of Manuscript Collections*, (1959-date).

ON —CANADIAN COUNCIL ON SOCIAL DEVELOPMENT, Information Centre, Box 3505 C, Ottawa, K1Y 4G1, Can. Odette Gosselin, Library Technician
Holdings: Vols 20,000 Cat Pix Audiotapes
Budget: $6000
Notes: Historical as well as current materials on Canadian social policy. Part of on-line information system.

†ON —METROPOLITAN TORONTO LIBRARY, Social Sciences Dept, 789 Yonge St, Toronto, M4W 2G8, Can. Abdus Salam, Head
Holdings: Vols Cat Maps Phonorecords Audiotapes 16mm Films Microforms
Notes: Historical and contemporary Canadian material covering federal and provincial policies and programs in the fields of health care, geriatrics, child welfare, corrections and care and rehabilitation of the physically and mentally handicapped.

ON —ONTARIO MINISTRY OF COMMUNITY & SOCIAL SERVICES, Library, 880 Bay St, Rm 663, Toronto, M7A 1E9, Can. Sandra Walsh, Chief Librn
Holdings: Vols (30,000) Cat Slides Videotapes 16mm Films Microforms

PQ —MCGILL UNIVERSITY, Nursing/Social Work Library, 3506 University St, Montreal, H3A 1Y1, Can. Wendy Patrick, Librn
Holdings: Vols (35,000) Cat

PUBLIC WELFARE—HISTORY

IL —CHICAGO HISTORICAL SOCIETY, Library, Clark St at North Ave, Chicago, 60614. Archie Motley, Manuscript Librn
Notes: Social welfare history collections incl these papers: Action Committee for Decent Childcare, Chicago; Clifford W Barnes (industrialist, philanthropist, congregational minister, social reformer, founder of the Chicago Community Trust and the Chicago Sunday Evening Club); Louise Hadduck DeKoven Bowen (social worker, President, Juvenile Protective Association and the Hull House Association); Deton Brooks (social research executive, public welfare official); Chapin Hall for Children, formerly the Chicago Nursery and Half-Orphan Asylum (home for children from broken homes); Chicago Area Project (pioneering juvenile delinquency prevention and research project directed by Clifford R Shaw and Henry D McKay); Files of the Institute for Juvenile Research and the Illinois Department of Corrections; Chicago Boys Clubs; Chicago Community Trust; Chicago Lung Association and predecessor organizations; Citizens Committee on the Juvenile Court; Emily Washburn Dean (social worker, President, Juvenile Protective Association, Vice President, Illinois Society for Mental Hygiene, Republican Party activist); Raymond M Hilliard (welfare administrator, Director Cook County Dept of Public Aid, Commissioner of the Department of Welfare of New York City and the Cook County Department of Public Aid); Infant Welfare Society, Chicago; Jewish Community Centers of Chicago; Jewish Community Centers of Chicago-Max Straus Center; Jewish Home for Aged, BMZ (Orthodox), Chicago; John Howard Association, Chicago (penal reform and legislation organization); Hans W Mattick: criminologist, sociologist, Assistant Warden Cook County Jail, Director Chicago Youth Development Project, Director, Center for Sudies in Criminal Justice, University of Chicago; National Association of Social Workers-Chicago Area Chapter; Wilfred Reynolds (social service

executive, Executive Director, Welfare Council of Metropolitan Chicago); audio tapes of 73 "Problems of the City" programs broadcast over Chicago Radio Station WAIT; Lea Demarest Taylor (social worker, head resident Chicago Commons, President National Federation of Settlements, daughter of Graham Taylor, founder of Chicago Commons); United Charities of Chicago (a union of the Chicago Relief and Aid Society and the Chicago Bureau of Charities); Visiting Nurse Association of Chicago; Welfare Council of Metropolitan Chicago; Welfare Public Relations Forum, Chicago. Papers of these Chicago settlement houses: Association House; Chicago Commons;Christopher House; Emerson House; Erie Neighborhood House; Fellowship House; Gads Hill Center; Marillac House; Mary McDowell Settlement (formerly the University of Chicago Settlement); Olivet Community Center; Parkway Community Center.

IN —PURDUE UNIVERSITY LIBRARIES, Graduate School of Management, Krannert Library, West Lafayette, 47907. Gordon Law, Librn
Notes: An important resource at the Krannert Library is its Special Collection of Business and Economics, consisting of some 8000 rare pre-20th century strengths in books, journals, tracts and pamphlets covering primarily the early literature of economic thought and business practices in America and abroad, 1500-1870. A catalog was issued in 1979.

NY —CITY UNIVERSITY OF NEW YORK, City College, Morris R Cohen Library, North Academic Center, Convent Ave & 137th St, New York, 10031. Barbara J Dunlap, Archivist
Holdings: Vols //
Notes: The Russell Sage Collection of Social Welfare in the United States (ca 1880-1950) consists of *printed* materials only (pamphlets, books, reports). Over 120,000 items incl the annual reports and publications of social service agencies, welfare departments, and state institutions for the deaf, retarded, etc. There is some material on Great Britain.

PUBLIC WORKS

AZ —TUCSON PUBLIC LIBRARY, Governmental Reference Library, PO Box 27210, City Hall, Tucson, 85726. Ann Strickland, Librn
Holdings: Vols (4000) Cat Maps Audiotapes Microforms
Notes: Special emphasis on public administration, including public finance, public personnel management, social services, urban planning, public transportation, public works, water management, solid waste management, public recreation and government of growing southwestern US cities in 200,000 to 500,000 population range.

PA —UNIVERSITY OF PITTSBURGH, Library, Graduate School of Public and International Affairs, Forbes Quadrangle, 1st floor West, Pittsburgh, 15260. Nicholas C Caruso, Librn
Holdings: Vols (80,000) Cat
Budget: ($150,000)
Notes: The library attempts to collect as many national economic and social development plans as possible from the developing countries of the world. It also holds city, regional and state plans for Pennsylvania, particularly the 9 southwestern counties of Pennsylvania.

ON —CANADA DEPT OF PUBLIC WORKS, Library, Sir Charles Tupper Bldg, Ottawa, K1A 0M2, Can. A I S Sinclair, Librn
Holdings: Vols 2000 Cat Mss
Notes: Annual, technical and other reports authored by or for the Department since 1844. Reports are deposited in the Departmental Library as part of the Department's publications program.

PUBLICITY

DC —NATIONAL ENDOWMENT FOR THE ARTS, Library, 1100 Pen Ave NW,

Rm 213, Washington, 20506. Christine Morrison, Arts Librn
Holdings: Vols (1000) Cat

KY —ASBURY THEOLOGICAL SEMINARY, B L Fisher Library, Wilmore, 40390. D William Faupel, Dir of Library Services
Holdings: Uncat
Notes: A collection of 35 document boxes of publicity materials on nearly 300 service organizations (Christian, missionary, social, educational), fugitive materials which would serve as primary sources for a study of their history and work--form letters (strictly fund raising letters deleted). brochures, etc.

MA —EDWARD L BERNAYS PUBLIC RELATIONS LIBRARY, 7 Lowell St, Cambridge, 02138.
Holdings: Vols (3000) Cat
Notes: Said to be one of the largest collections on the subject of public relations, publicity, and propaganda. Many pamplets. No photocopying.

PUBLISHERS, CANADIAN

AB —UNIVERSITY OF CALGARY, Libraries, Special Collections Div, 2500 University Dr, Calgary, T2N 1N4, Can.
Holdings: Mss
Notes: The Division has extensive collections of the papers of modern Canadian authors (qv individuals), incl Hugh MacLennan, Mordecai Richler, Brian Moore, W O Mitchell, Cliff Faulknor, Christie Harris, Robert Kroetsch, Rudy Wiebe, Claude Peloquin, George Ryga, Andre Langevin, Malcolm Ross, Bruce Hutchison, John Mellor, Grant MacEwan, James Gray, Ernest Watkins, Len Peterson, Michael Cook, & Joanna Glass. The papers of musician Morris Surdin contain hundreds of Canadian Broadcasting Corporation scripts, and constitute a valuable addition to the purely literary ms collections. The Division's holdings also incl collections of scores by Canadian musicians R Murray Schafer and Bruce Mather. In addition, the records of the following Canadian publishing houses are on deposit: E C W Press, Hancock House Publishers Ltd and Coach House Press. The Division alsohouses small collections of letters and mss of Canadian poets such as Earle Birney and George Bowering as well as the archives of the literary periodicals *Tish, Imago, Ariel, Descant, Canadian Review Magazine*, and *Canadian Short Story Magazine*. The ms collections are complemented by a book collection of some 5000 vols.

PUBLISHERS AND PUBLISHING

CA —UNIVERSITY OF CALIFORNIA, BERKELEY, Humanities-Social Sciences Libraries, Library School Library, 2 South Hall, Berkeley, 94720. Virginia Pratt, Head
Holdings: Vols (41,500) Cat Microforms
Notes: Research collection with special strengths in general library science; history of libraries; history of printing and book arts, and publishing; information systems and services; history, criticism, and bibliography of children's literature. The collections in printing and the book arts are complemented by significant holdings both in the Main Library and in the Bancroft Library. Incl collection of 5000 pamphlets.

CA —SAINT JOHN'S SEMINARY, Edward Laurence Doheny Memorial Library, The Estelle Doheny Collection, 5012 E Seminary Rd, Camarillo, 93010. Rita S Faulders, Cur

CA —CLAREMONT COLLEGES, Honnold Library, Ninth & Dartmouth, Claremont, 91711. Tania Rizzo, Special Collections Dept Head
Holdings: 1600 Cat Mss
Notes: 1600 items of in and out correspondence between Mary Augusta Ward and her publishers, notably Smith, Elder and Co, 1885-1919. Restricted use. *See also* entry under Ward, Mary Augusta (Arnold)

CA —UNIVERSITY OF CALIFORNIA, LOS ANGELES, Research Library, Dept of Special Collections, 405 Hilgard Ave, Los

PUBLISHERS AND PUBLISHING (cont.)

Angeles, 90024. Edward Shreeves, Chairman, Bibliographers Group; David S Zeidberg, Head
Holdings: Cat Mss
Notes: Various collection incl correspondence, records, mss, and *List of the Principal Publications* of Richard Bentley, London; papers of Alan Swallow; publications of Armed Services Editions, Haldeman Julius, Roycrofters, Tauchnitz, etc.

CA —UPDATA PUBLICATIONS INC, Library, 1756 Westwood Blvd, Los Angeles, 90024. Sara Ferguson, Dir; Judith Harrington, Librn
Holdings: Vols (300) Uncat Maps Microforms
Notes: Incl 800,000 microforms, 35 periodicals.

CA —CALIFORNIA HISTORICAL SOCIETY, Schubert Hall Library, 2099 Pacific Ave, San Francisco, 94109. Bruce L Johnson, Library Dir
Holdings: Vols 4400 Cat Mss Pix Microforms
Notes: The Edward C Kemble Collections. Not collections of fine printing, but of the history of printing and publishing with emphasis on the Pacific Coast, although the full scope of the collection is not limited to this area. In addition to bibliographic tools and reference works, it contains type specimen books and several long runs of trade periodicals and house organs of San Francisco typefounders. The Taylor & Taylor Archives, a part of this collection, contain the working record of a major San Francisco printing firm. The *Kemble Occasional*, published three times a year from the Kemble Collections, presents scholarly articles on the history of printing. Edward C Kemble was the first historian of printing in California.

CA —STANFORD UNIVERSITY LIBRARIES, Cecil H Green Library, Stanford, 94305. Peter R Frank, Cur, CDP-Germanic Collection
Notes: Strong collection, with many first editions, rare journals, etc. The Cassirer Collection (correspondence, autographs and typescripts by Hasenclever, Meidner, printed material) in the Stanford Collection of German, Austrian and Swiss Culture, Special Collections Register of Manuscripts.

DE —UNIVERSITY OF DELAWARE, Hugh M Morris Library, S College Ave, Newark, 19711. T Stuart Dick, Special Collections
Holdings: Cat Mss Pix
Notes: Kurt Vonnegut mss, contract information, royalty statements, foreign movie and reprint rights and correspondence for the period 1966-1982 with the publisher, Seymour Lawrence.

DC —GEORGETOWN UNIVERSITY, Library, Special Collections Div, 37 & O Sts NW, Washington, 20057. George M Barringer, Special Collections Librn; Nicholas B Sheetz, Mss Librn
Holdings: Mss Cat Pix
Notes: A portion of the archives of the English publisher Grant Ricards (1872-1948), containing manuscripts, correspondence, photographs, clippings, and printed ephemera. Incl is extensive correspondence from such artists and authors as Neville Cardus; Frank Harris; Sir Hugh Lane; Lady Augusta Gregory; David Low; T Sturge Moore; and C R W Nevinson.

DC —LIBRARY OF CONGRESS, Rare Book & Special Collections Div, Washington, 20540. William Matheson, Chief
Notes: An archival set of translations sponsored by the Franklin Book Programs (1952-1978), incl 3000 titles translated into Arabic, Persian, Bengali and other languages.

IL —CHICAGO HISTORICAL SOCIETY, Library, Clark St at North Ave, Chicago, 60614. Archie Motley, Manuscript Librn
Notes: Publishing and literary collections incl these papers: *Chicago Journalism Review*; *Chicago Seed*; *The Chicagoan*; Friends of American Writers, Chicago

literary group; Emmett Dedmon (Chicago newspaper executive, journalist, author); Interviews of 97 Chicago journalists conducted by students in Northwestern University's Medill School.

IL —JOHNSON PUBLISHING CO, Library, 820 S Michigan Ave, Chicago, 60605. Pamela J Cash, Librn
Holdings: Vols 8000 Cat Maps Microforms
Notes: Incl all publications of Johnson Publishing Company and many more Black publications.

IL —NEWBERRY LIBRARY, John M Wing Foundation on the History of Printing, 60 W Walton St, Chicago, 60610. Diana Haskell, Cur of Modern Mss
Holdings: Vols (30,000) Cat Mss
Budget: ($50,000)
Notes: The collection covers printing and printing history of Western Europe and the Americas from its invention to the present, as well as various ancillary fields. It is particularly rich in incunabula (about 2000); the works of the great printers, among others Aldus, Bodoni, Baskerville, and Rogers. Incl partial archives of C McClurg and Co, Stone and Kimball; other Chicago publishing history. Printed catalog: *A Dictionary* Catalogue. (Boston: G K Hall, 1961); *Supplements* (1981). Brief descriptions: James M Wells, "The John M Wing Foundation of The Newberry Library," *The Book Collector*, VIII, 2 (Summer 1959), pp 157-162; Lawrence W Towner, *An Uncommon Collection of Uncommon Collection* (Chicago: The Newberry Library, 1977), pp 25-26.

IL —NORTHERN ILLINOIS UNIVERSITY, Founders Memorial Library, Rare Books and Special Collections Dept, De Kalb, 60115. William R DuBois, Dept Head
Holdings: Vols (450) Cat
Notes: Works on the history of books and printing and representative examples of fine printing. Includes more than 50 titles published in Chicago by Way & Williams.

IL —UNIVERSITY OF ILLINOIS, URBANA/CHAMPAIGN, Library, Communications Library, 122 Gregory Hall, Urbana, 61801. Nancy Allen, Librn
Holdings: Vols (18,000) Cat
Budget: ($27,000)

IN —INDIANA UNIVERSITY, Lilly Library, Seventh St, Bloomington, 47405. William R Cagle, Librn
Holdings: Mss Pix
Notes: Mss incl office, editorial records and correspondence for following publishers Appleton-Century & Co, 1846-1962 (6249 items); Bobbs-Merrill, 1885-1957 (131,056 items); Calder and Boyars, London, 1950-1875, (ca 250,000 items); Capra Press, Santa Barbara, 1955-date (ca 6000 items); Loujon Press, 1962-69 (127 items); Methuen & Co, 1899-1944 (12 vols of stock ledgers); Secker, Martin, 1944-1930 (200 items); and Viking Press, 1940-1956 (files relating to Upton Sinclair only, 2504 items).

IA —UNIVERSITY OF IOWA, University Libraries, Iowa City, 52242. Robert A McCown, Mss Librn
Holdings: Mss Pix
Notes: Correspondence, speeches, articles, scrapbooks, pamphlets, clippings, photos and other materials dealing with politics, publishing, farm relief, and land development of a former US Secretary of Agriculture and founder of the Meredith Publishing Company, Des Moines, Iowa. Unpublished index in the library. Described in *Books at Iowa*, no 7 (Nov 1967), pp 32-40, "Some Research Opportunities in the Papers of Edwin T Meredith, 1876-1928," by Peter L Petersen. 38 ft of mss.

†MD —UNIVERSITY OF MARYLAND, Library, R D Remley Collection, College Park, 20742. Donald Farren, Cur Rare Books
Holdings: Vols (2000) Cat
Notes: *Exempla* and secondary works in the areas of typography, calligraphy, book design, book illustration, the history of books, and of publishing, etc. Catalog entries for designers, printing types, private presses, etc.

MA —HOUGHTON MIFFLIN CO, Library, One Beacon St, Boston, 02107. Guest Perry,

Dir
Holdings: Vols (15,000) Cat Pix Microforms
Notes: Incl 5000 pictures.

MA —AMERICAN ANTIQUARIAN SOCIETY LIBRARY, 185 Salisbury St, Worcester, 01609. Marcus A McCorison, Dir & Librn
Holdings: Cat
Notes: Papers of D C Heath & Company.

NJ —PRINCETON UNIVERSITY, Library, Manuscript Collection, Nassau St, Princeton, 08540. Jean F Preston, Cur
Holdings: Mss Pix
Notes: The archive of Harper & Brothers, publishers, fills 34 ms boxes. An unpublished typescript guide is available in the Library. Also the archives of Henry Holt, publishers, and Scribner (qv).

NY —STATE UNIVERSITY OF NEW YORK AT ALBANY, Library, Special Collections Dept, 1400 Washington Ave, Albany, 12222. Marion P Munzer, Coordr
Notes: Correspondence with authors; mss; reviews and publicity of works published by Storm Publishers (5.4 linear feet). Part of the Library's German Exile Collection.
See also entry under Storm Publishers

NY —SAINT LAWRENCE UNIVERSITY, Owen D Young Library, Canton, 13617. Mahlon Peterson, Librn
Holdings: Cat Mss Pix
Notes: Collection consists of letters sent to Edith O'Dell Black and Pomeroy Burton of the New York *World* from 1903 to 1944. Also incl are works by Alexander Black, a novelist, and manuscripts which he wrote for "picture plays," the forerunners of the modern moving pictures. Approx 350 items.

NY —CHILDREN'S BOOK COUNCIL, Library, 67 Irving Place, New York, 10003.
Holdings: Vols (750) Cat
Notes: Besides award-winning books, the Children's Book Council maintains a noncirculating examination collection of children's books published by CBC members during the past year, adding books of the current year as they are published. Collection also incl critical and historical studies of children's books; bibliographies; selection aids and other reference books; biographies of authors and illustrators; facsimile editions and catalogs of collections and exhibitions; and books about publishing, writing, and storytelling. There is an author/title card catalog and a separate illustrator card catalog for this collection. No photocopying.

NY —COLUMBIA UNIVERSITY LIBRARIES, Rare Book & Manuscript Library, 801 Butler Library, 535 W 114 St, New York, 10027. Kenneth A Lohf, Librn
Holdings: Mss
Notes: Publishers' archives: (1) correspondence files of the W W Norton Co, 1923-67 (165,000 items); subsequent files likely to be given to the library. Described in *Wilson Library Bulletin*, March 1968. (2) 23,000 item publishing archive of Harper & Row Publishing Co and 19th century contract files and financial records of Harper & Bros. (13,000 items). (3) Files and library of Random House, publishers 1925-76, (753,000 items). (4) Files of Columbia University Press, 1893-1960 (140,000 items). Restricted use.

†NY —COLUMBIA UNIVERSITY LIBRARIES, Butler Library, Rare Book and Manuscript Library, 535 W 114 St, New York, 10027.
Notes: Over 30,000 papers relating to M Lincoln Schuster and the publishing firm, Simon & Schuster. Incl file of letters written by Simon to Schuster from 1921-53, author and subject files of notes and clippings, advertising notebooks, files relating to the books written and edited by Schuster, galley and page proofs, photographs and memorabilia, and other correspondence. Also, the papers of Jacob W Greenberg of Greenberg Publishers.

NY —GRADUATE CENTER OF THE CITY UNIVERSITY OF NEW YORK, William H and Gwynne K Crouse Library for Publishing Arts, 33 W 42 St, New York, 10036. Alfred H Lane, Dir
Notes: Recently established and still

PUBLISHERS AND PUBLISHING (cont.)

growing, but intended to become the authoritative source of materials in the field, of particular value in research about the publishing industry. Open to staff members of publishing houses, students, scholars, authors, printers, and booksellers. Particularly useful for research on technical, financial, and historical matters. Much on the history of individual houses, economics of authorship; marketing and distribution of books; etc. Primarily 20th century material in hard form or microfilm, incl books, pamphlets, reprints, translations, dissertations, periodicals, indexing and abstracting services, yearbooks, reports and directories of organizations, publishers' and antiquarian dealers' catalogs (particularly those who deal in books about books), periodicals, legislative materials, and clippingspertaining to the book industry. Sections of the library deal with printing, incl typography, specimen books, history of printing and printing techniques, book design and small press and alternative publishing.

NY —GROLIER CLUB OF NEW YORK LIBRARY, 47 E 60 St, New York, 10022. Robert Nikirk, Librn
Notes: Subject strength.

NY —HARCOURT BRACE JOVANOVICH, Editorial Library, 757 Third Ave, New York, 10017. Ron Coplen, Librn
Holdings: Vols 9000 Cat
Notes: Company archive incl all new books published.

NY —R R BOWKER CO, Frederick G Melcher Library, 205 E 42nd St, New York, 10036. Nancy Dvorin, Librn
Holdings: Vols (15,000) Cat
Notes: Also have an 80-drawer vertical file. No photocopying.

NY —UNIVERSITY CLUB, Library, One W 54 St, New York, 10019. Guy St Clair, Library Dir
Holdings: Vols (100,000) Cat Mss Maps Pix
Notes: A private library for the members of the University Club, their guests, and serious scholars upon written application to the Library Director. Holds the Edward Larocque Tinker Collection of Illustrated Books Between the Two World Wars, A Milton Runyon Collection on the History of Printing and Publishing, the Frederic R Coudert "Les Bibliophiles des Paris" Collection, The University Club Rare Book Collection, and the Frederick G Rudge Collection of Books Designed by William E Rudge and Bruce Rogers.

NY —UNIVERSITY OF ROCHESTER, Rush Rhees Library, Department of Rare Books and Special Collections, Rochester, 14627. Peter Dzwonkoski, Librn
Holdings: Vols 1200 // Cat
Notes: Collection of British authors published by the Leipzig firm of Bernhard Tauchnitz from 1840-1908. Much of the collection was originally in the library of the Kings of Hanover, and those volumes are bound in cloth with the arms of the Royal Family. No photocopying permitted.

NY —STATE UNIVERSITY OF NEW YORK, STONY BROOK, Melville Library, Dept of Special Collections, Stony Brook, 11794. Evert Volkersz, Head
Holdings: Vols 110 Cat
Notes: The Fortune Press commenced publishing in London in 1925, but holdings reflect primarily publications of 1940-1946. Also, The Perishable Press Ltd is the private press of Walter and Mary Hamady. This collection is the most complete institutional collection of printed works; also incl a substantial amount of the archives of the Press since its beginning in 1965. Also, incomplete collection of Greenwich Press, 1955-1959.

NC —DUKE UNIVERSITY, William R Perkins Library, Durham, 27706. Elvin E Strowd, University Librn
Holdings: Cat Mss Pix
Notes: Montrose J Moses' collection of books, mss, and papers, mostly concerned with men and women of the theatre, and creative writers of the first third of the century. 3000 books; 22,000 mss.

NC —UNIVERSITY OF NORTH CAROLINA, GREENSBORO, Walter Clinton Jackson Library, Special Collections Dept, 1000 Spring Garden St, Greensboro, 27412. Emilie W Mills, Librn
Holdings: Vols (1800) Cat Slides
Notes: Emphasis is on American small publishers since late 19th century attention to fine printing, sound production and textual content are exemplary. Significant holdings of books published by The Typophiles, Stinehour Press, David R Godine, Jargon Society and Way and Williams are included with selective holdings of other small commercial publishers and printers, incl R H Russell, Copeland and Day, Stone and Kimball.

NC —UNIVERSITY OF NORTH CAROLINA, GREENSBORO, Walter Clinton Jackson Library, Special Collections Dept, 1000 Spring Garden St, Greensboro, 27412. Emilie W Mills, Librn
Notes: All but nine of the titles published by Way and Williams of Chicago, 1895-1898. First, variant editions, many autographed by authors or publisher. Many association items. Letters to Chauncey Williams from William Allen White, Maxfield Parrish, Charles Lummis, Opie Read, etc. Photographs of Williams and several authors. Original artwork by Parrish, Will Bradley and ephemeral printing incl in the scrapbook compiled by Chauncey L Williams, ca 1919. Major part of the collection the gift of John M Williams in memory of Chauncey L Williams.

OH —RUTHERFORD B HAYES LIBRARY, 1337 Hayes Ave, Fremont, 43420. Watt P Marchman, Dir
Holdings: Vols 505 Cat Mss Maps Pix Microforms
Notes: Mss of W D Howells, consisting of correspondence, literary mss, genealogical and biographical materials; clippings, etc. Part is listed in *Guide to Manuscripts of the Ohio Historical Society*, 239. Indexed.

OK —UNIVERSITY OF TULSA, McFarlin Library, Dept of Rare Books and Special Collections, 600 S College, Tulsa, 74104. David Farmer, Dir; Toby Murray, Archivist; Caroline Swinson, Cur of Manuscripts & Art
Notes: The personal library of Martin Secker's books which he published, including volumes with significant inscriptions or letters from his authors.

PA —TEMPLE UNIVERSITY LIBRARIES, Special Collections Dept, Rare Books & Mss Section, Philadelphia, 19122. Thomas M Whitehead, Cur
Holdings: Cat Mss
Notes: Letters and documents (15,000 items) of the archives of the London publishers, Constable and Company. Correspondence with close to 400 authors, most of it with Otto Kyllmann and Michael Sadier, directors. Archives of Thomas Nelson & Sons (USA) and of various Philadelphia publishers and of the William J Campbell Bookstore, Philadelphia, from the mid-19th century.

†PA —UNIVERSITY OF PITTSBURGH, Graduate School of Library & Information Sciences Library, L I S Bldg, Third Fl, Pittsburgh, 15260. Jean Kindlin, Librn
Notes: Rare book collection of 1800 titles dealing with the history of the book and printing.

RI —BROWN UNIVERSITY, John Hay Library, 20 Prospect St, Providence, 02912. Mark N Brown, Cur Mss
Notes: The Koopman Collection contains examples of the work of five centuries of fine printers and representative works by modern fine presses such as Kelmscott, Doves, Ashendene and Merrymount. Also incl are examples of ancient writing, illuminated manuscript books, fine bindings, first editions of American and British authors, auction catalogues of sales of significant collections, photographs of American and British authors, and museum objects once owned by various authors. Also a general working collection of Books on Books reference material.

†RI —BROWN UNIVERSITY, Library, Providence, 02912.
Notes: Papers of William O Buller (1828-

1910), music teach of Providence, comprising letters1848 from Europe, including a letter from Franz Liszt; papers of Johann Christian Gottlieb Graupner (1767-1836) and John Rowe Parker (fl 1820s) collected by Horace Mason Reynolds, relating to the music-ublishing business in Boston, 1802-1838; papers of the American folklorist Mellinger Edward Henry (1873-1946) relating to his resarch and publications on American folk-songs, 1910-1942; papers, 1912-1948, of Providence composer Hugh Frederick MacColl (11885-1953); papers of Frances Herriot Sarget, stage manager for "Porgy" and "Porgy and Bess", relating to productions of these, 1928-1942.

TN —COUNTRY MUSIC FOUNDATION, Library & Media Center, 4 Music Sq E, Nashville, 37203. Charlie Seemann, Dir
Holdings: Vols (6000) Mss Pix Slides Phonorecords Audiotapes Videotapes 16mm Films Microforms
Notes: The largest collection in the world dealing with American country music. Related subject areas are also included-- Anglo-American folksong, popular music in general (soul, jazz, rock and roll, rhythm and blues, etc), recorded sound technology, music law.

†TX —UNIVERSITY OF TEXAS LIBRARIES, General Libraries, Humanities Research Center, PO Box 7219, Austin, 78712. John Chalmers, Librn
Notes: The Alfred A and Blanche Knopf Archive, incl their personal library collection with numerous inscribed and association copies of their own and other publications.

VA —UNIVERSITY OF VIRGINIA, Alderman Library, Rare Book Dept, Charlottesville, 22901. Julius P Barclay, Cur
Holdings: Vols (6500) // Mss
Notes: The Oscar Ogg Collection of Book Arts covers calligraphy, letterforms, typography, printing, and graphic arts. Contains early writing books and printed works, as well as modern manuals and other works on printing, publishing, and promotion through graphic arts. The Dept also has the Edward L Stone Collection of Printing Specimens, 3000 items. Contains materials tracing the history of printing, inks, binding styles and materials, types. Also the Tompkins Collection (2000 vols), and the Stevens Watts collection (900 vols).

WI —UNIVERSITY OF WISCONSIN, MILWAUKEE, Library, Box 604, Milwaukee, 53201. William C Roselle, Dir
Holdings: Uncat Mss
Notes: Correspondence of the *Little Review* with prominent 20th-century writers. Restricted use: Cataloged for use in Rare Book area only. No photocopying.

WY —UNIVERSITY OF WYOMING, William Robertson Coe Library, 13 & Ivinson, Laramie, 82071.
Notes: Archives of publishers Penguin Books and New American Library.

AB —UNIVERSITY OF CALGARY, Libraries, Special Collections Div, 2500 University Dr, Calgary, T2N 1N4, Can.
Holdings: Cat Mss
Notes: The Malcolm Ross papers incl correspondence about Ross's academic career from 1934-date and his correspondence with other scholars. There is an important collection of correspondence with Canadian writers and poets. The major part of the papers consists of Malcolm Ross' editorial correspondence about the New Canadian Library reprint series from 1962-76.

BC —SIMON FRASER UNIVERSITY, Library, Burnaby, V5A 1S6, Can. Percilla Groves, Special Collections Librn
Holdings: // Cat Mss Pix
Notes: Talonbook Archive incl correspondence, mss, photographs, proofs, and business records of this local publisher, 1966-1978.

ON —MCMASTER UNIVERSITY, Mills Memorial Library, Div of Archives & Research Collections, Hamilton, L8S 4L6, Can. G R Hill, Univ Librn
Holdings: Mss
Notes: The archives of McClelland and Stewart Ltd (1955-1980) and Macmillan of

PUBLISHERS AND PUBLISHING (cont.)

Canada (1907-1980), consisting of executive correspondence, editorial files, publicity, author correspondence, some art work.
ON —NATIONAL LIBRARY OF CANADA, 395 Wellington St, Ottawa, K1A 0N4, Can. Andre Preibish, Dir
Holdings: Vols 10,000
Notes: The collection on History and Art of the Book consists of over 10,000 volumes. Areas of concentration are: early imprints, special editions, examples of private presses works, book industry and trade books illustrating the aesthetic and technical aspects of the field, collection of books illustrated by Bartlett.
ON —UNIVERSITY OF TORONTO, Thomas Fisher Rare Book Library, 120 Saint George St, Toronto, M5S 1A5, Can. Richard G Landon, Head
Holdings: Vols 6535 Uncat
Notes: Maclean-Hunter and Southam Press Collections contain periodicals issued by these two Canadian publishers. These are largely trade journlas. Many long and complete runs of items like *Canadian Footwear, Electrical News and Engineering; Gift Buyer; Canadian Home Journal; Chatelaine; Macleans;* etc. Many runs originate in 1880s and 1890s. Also include current publications. Approx 268 titles. Fisher Library designated the official archives for published material by Maclean-Hunter and Southam Press.

PUBLISHING OF PERIODICALS—HISTORY—U.S. see Periodicals, Publishing of—History—U.S.

PUDNEY, JOHN

CT —YALE UNIVERSITY, Box 1603A, Yale Station, New Haven, 06520.
Notes: First editions of his books, or of books with his contributions, all in dust jackets and a number with presentation inscriptions from the author.

PUEBLO INCIDENT

CA —HOOVER INSTITUTION ON WAR, REVOLUTION & PEACE, Stanford University, Stanford, 94305. Milorad M Drachkovitch, Archivist
Holdings: Mss Pix
Notes: Papers of Lloyd M Bucher, Commander, US Navy, and Commander of the USS Pueblo, incl correspondence, newspaper clippings, reports, copies of court inquiries, photographs, plaques, memorabilia, and other materials, 1970-75, relating to the Pueblo incident and its aftermath. Incl is a typewritten manuscript of his memoirs, entitled "Bucher, My Story." 68 ms boxes, 1 oversize package.

PUEBLO INDIANS

NM —ALBUQUERQUE PUBLIC LIBRARY, 501 Copper Ave NW, Albuquerque, 87102. Alan B Clark, Dir
Holdings: Vols (4000) Cat Microforms Records Maps VF
Notes: Large collection of materials on all aspects of New Mexico history and cultures. In-house index accesses VF materials and local and regional periodicals. Special emphasis on Indians of New Mexico and northeastern Arizona, particularly the Navajo, Hopi, Pueblos and Apache. Reference copies of many works are housed at the Special Collections Library, 423 Central Ave NE, Albuquerque, NM 87102.
NM —AZTEC RUINS NATIONAL MONUMENT, Library, PO Box U, Aztec, 87410. William L Schart, Park Ranger
Holdings: Vols (500)// Cat Mss Maps Pix Slides
Notes: Archaeology of the Anasazi ruins.

PUERTO RICAN AUTHORS see Authors, Puerto Rican

PUERTO RICAN LITERATURE

NY —NEW YORK PUBLIC LIBRARY, Donnell Foreign Language Library, 20 W 53 St, New York, 10019. Bosiljka Stevanovic, Supvr Librn
Notes: Puerto Rican collection incl Puerto Rican authors of Puerto Rican expression. No separate catalogs.

PUERTO RICANS IN THE U.S.

NY —HUNTER COLLEGE, Centro de Estudios Puertorriquenos, Library, 695 Park Ave, New York, 10021. Nelida Perez, Librn; Felix Rivera, Asst; Amilcar Tirado, Librn
Holdings: Vols 5000 Cat Microforms
Notes: Materials concerning the historical experience, culture, and present condition of Puerto Ricans. Incl numerous periodicals, pamphlets, reports, over 700 doctoral dissertations, and, on microfilm, government documents and 19th and 20th century newspapers.
PA —BALCH INSTITUTE FOR ETHNIC STUDIES, Library, 18 S Seventh St, Philadelphia, 19106. R Joseph Anderson, Library Dir
Holdings: Vols 140 Cat Mss Pix Microforms
TX —UNIVERSITY OF TEXAS LIBRARIES, Nettie Lee Benson Latin American Collection, Sid Richardson Hall 1.109, Austin, 78712. Laura Gutierrez-Witt, Head Librn
Holdings: Vols (450,000) Cat Slides 16mm Films Microforms
Notes: The Mexican American Library Project has, since 1974, collected materials relating to all aspects of Spanish-speaking people in the US, with emphasis on Mexican Americans.
See also entry under Latin America
PR —UNIVERSITY OF PUERTO RICO, Jose M Lazaro Memorial Library (General Library), Box C, University of Puerto Rico Sta, Rio Piedras, 00931. Denise Perez, Head, Puerto Rican Collection
Holdings: Vols (96,782) Cat
Notes: Seek to collect all materials relating to Puerto Rico or the Puerto Ricans in or out of the island. Materials published in Puerto Rico are also collected. The various formats collected are books, pamphlets, mss, maps, slides, microfilm, periodicals and newspapers, academic thesis, tapes, posters, government documents, leaflets and clippings. Have a rare book collection consisting of about 2741 volumes. These are books published in Puerto Rico or relating to Puerto Rico before the 20th century. The aim of the collection is to preserve Puerto Rico's bibliographical heritage and to serve the researchers on Puerto Rican studies.

PUERTO RICO

CT —YALE UNIVERSITY, Sterling Memorial Library, Latin American Collections, New Haven, 06520. Lee H Williams Jr, Cur
Holdings: Vols (300,000) Cat Maps Pix Slides Phonorecords 16mm Films Filmstrips
See also entry under Latin America
CT —UNIVERSITY OF CONNECTICUT, Library, Storrs, 06268. R H Schimmelpfeng, Dir of Special Collections
Holdings: Vols 3600
Notes: Over 3600 pieces, incl books, pamphlets, periodicals and government documents dealing with all aspects of the Island's history and culture. A collection formed through three generations of the Geigel Family of San Juan.
NY —HUNTER COLLEGE, Centro de Estudios Puertorriquenos, Library, 695 Park Ave, New York, 10021. Nelida Perez, Librn; Felix Rivera, Asst; Amilcar Tirado, Librn
Holdings: Vols 5000 Cat Microforms
Notes: Materials concerning the historical experience, culture, and present condition of Puerto Ricans. Incl numerous periodicals, pamphlets, reports, over 700 doctoral dissertations, and, on microfilm, government documents and 19th and 20th century newspapers.
NY —NEW YORK PUBLIC LIBRARY, Donnell Foreign Language Library, 20 W 53 St, New York, 10019. Bosiljka Stevanovic, Supvr Librn
Notes: A circulating collection of books written in about 80 languages. The collections are general and popular in character - current topics, travel, histories, biography, etc, emphasizing the literature of the country - fiction, drama, poetry, literary criticism. The collections are primarily intended for use of readers whose first language is other than English. Separate catalogs for each language. Collections containing less than 100 volumes are not listed. Translations are moderately included.
PR —CARIBBEAN REGIONAL LIBRARY, General Library, University of Puerto Rico, Rio Piedras, (Mailing add: PO Box 21917, University Station, San Juan, 00931). Carmen M Costa de Ramos, Librn
Holdings: Vols (116,000) Cat Maps Pix
Budget: $5000
Notes: Our collection is specialized in the Caribbean with emphasis in the areas of interest to development countries: social sciences, politics, economics, labor, law, education, commerce, tourism, agriculture, etc. *The Current Caribbean Bibliography* is compiled at the Caribbean Regional Library, with card contributions from all countries of the Caribbean; it also lists all the new additions to the library.
PR —UNIVERSITY OF PUERTO RICO, Graduate School of Public Administration, Library, Graduate Social Sciences Bldg, Rio Piedras, 00931. Perfecto Camacho, Library Dir
Holdings: Vols (15,000) Cat
Budget: $22,000
Notes: Public administration, economics, and elections. Especially materials related to or about the separate municipalities of Puerto Rico and the Commonwealth of Puerto Rico. Documents collection.
PR —UNIVERSITY OF PUERTO RICO, Jose M Lazaro Memorial Library (General Library), Box C, University of Puerto Rico Sta, Rio Piedras, 00931. Denise Perez, Head, Puerto Rican Collection
Holdings: Vols (96,782) Cat
Notes: Seek to collect all materials relating to Puerto Rico or the Puerto Ricans in or out of the island. Materials published in Puerto Rico are also collected. The various formats collected are books, pamphlets, mss, maps, slides, microfilm, periodicals and newspapers, academic thesis, tapes, posters, government documents, leaflets and clippings. Have a rare book collection consisting of about 2741 volumes. These are books published in Puerto Rico or relating to Puerto Rico before the 20th century. The aim of the collection is to preserve Puerto Rico's bibliographical heritage and to serve the researchers on Puerto Rican studies.

PUERTO RICO—CIVILIZATION AND CULTURE

NY —NEW YORK PUBLIC LIBRARY, Research Libraries, General Research Division, Fifth Ave & 42 St, New York, 10018. Rodney Phillips, Chief
Holdings: Vols (2,225,000) Cat Maps Pix Microforms
Budget: ($775,718)

PUERTO RICO—HISTORY

†CT —UNIVERSITY OF CONNECTICUT LIBRARY, Special Collections Dept, Storrs, 06268. Richard H Schimmelpfeng, Dir of Special Collections
Notes: Good and unusual collection.

PUERTO RICO—POLITICS AND GOVERNMENT

CT —UNIVERSITY OF CONNECTICUT, Library, Storrs, 06268. R H Schimmelpfeng, Dir of Special Collections
Holdings: Vols 3600
Notes: Over 3600 pieces, incl books, pamphlets, periodicals and government documents dealing with all aspects of the Island's history and culture. A collection formed through three generations of the Geigel Family of San Juan.

PUGET SOUND POWER AND LIGHT COMPANY

WA —WESTERN WASHINGTON UNIVERSITY, Center for Pacific Northwest

PUGET SOUND POWER AND LIGHT COMPANY (cont.)

Studies, High St, Bellingham, 98225. James W Scott, Dir
Holdings: Vols 400 // Cat Mss
Notes: Puget Sound Power and Light Company Records Collection consists of the complete company records of 41 former companies, which were bought out, amalgamated with or in other ways came under the control of Puget Sound Power and Light Company. Most of the companies were concerned with transportation or the production of power--both gas and electricity. Among the companies represented are street railways, interuban railways, traction companies and gas companies, all of which operated in the region west of the Cascades, especially in the Puget Sound area but with a few as far south as Vancouver, Washington. The collection has been placed in the Center for Pacific Northwest Studies by the Puget Sound Power and Light Company on a permanent loan basis.

PUGH FAMILY

TX —UNIVERSITY OF TEXAS LIBRARIES, General Libraries, Barker Texas History Center, PO Box P, Austin, 78712. Don Carleton, Dir

PUGILISM see Boxing

PUGWASH CONFERENCE

CA —CALIFORNIA INSTITUTE OF TECHNOLOGY, Robert A Millikan Memorial Library, Archives, 1201 E California Blvd, Pasadena, 91125. Judith R Goodstein, Archivist
Notes: Correspondence and printed matter of William A Fowler, Nuclear Science Advisory Committee, 1977-1980; the National Academy of Science's Astronomy Survey Committee, 1979-1980; the National Science Foundation's Astronomy Advisory Committee, 1978-1979; and proceedings of the Pugwash Conference for the years 1960, 1962-1963.

PULITZER PRIZES

FL —UNIVERSITY OF SOUTH FLORIDA, Library, Tampa, 33620. J B Dobkin, Special Collections Librn
Notes: Public and private papers of Nelson Poynter, Chairman of the board of Times Publishing Company. Incl political correspondence, photographs, and Pulitzer Prize commendation records.

PULLMAN CORPORATION

IL —NEWBERRY LIBRARY, 60 W Walton St, Chicago, 60610. Diana Haskell, Cur of Modern Mss
Holdings: Uncat Mss Maps Pix Memorabilia
Notes: The papers consist of 1600 sq feet of ledgers, drawings, work orders and financial records of the Pullman Corporation, from the 1870s until 1959. There are no personal letters of George Pullman nor office correspondence relating to the administration of the company. The material is richest for the daily functions of the company in the 1920s and 30s. There are no catalogs or handlists of the records, although one is being prepared.

PULLMAN STANDARD CAR MANUFACTURING CO.

MO —WASHINGTON UNIVERSITY, Libraries, Special Collections Dept, Campus Box 1061, St Louis, 63130.
Notes: Papers of Charles W Bryan Jr, incl correspondence, personal journals, scrapbooks, photographs, and printed material associated with the Federal Shipbuilding Company from 1917 to 1948, and as president of the Pullman Standard Car Manufacturing Company from 1950 to 1958.

PULP AND PAPER TECHNOLOGY see Paper Making and Trade

PULP MAGAZINES

CA —UNIVERSITY OF CALIFORNIA, LOS ANGELES, Research Library, Dept of Special Collections, 405 Hilgard Ave, Los Angeles, 90024. Edward Shreeves, Chairman, Bibliographers Group; David S Zeidberg, Head
Notes: Virtually complete runs of *Adventure* (1910-1938), *Amazing Stories* (1926-1967), *Argosy* (1895-1920), *Black Mask* (1920-1951); scattered issues or extensive runs of 1000 other titles. No photocopying.

CA —UNIVERSITY OF CALIFORNIA, RIVERSIDE, University Library, 4045 Canyon Crest Dr, Box 5900, Riverside, 92517.
Holdings: Vols (30,000)
Notes: The Eaton Collection of science fiction and fantasy materials, incl 5,600 pulp magazines; also horror, supernatural, and Gothic mystery fiction; boys' books; utopian and dystopian fiction, imaginary voyages, future war and lost race fiction; large holdings in French language science fiction and fantasy; critical and scholarly works pertaining to these genres; videotapes of science fiction/fantasy films and shooting scripts. Collection covers science fiction/fantasy literature from the 16th-17th centuries to the present. Strong individual author collections of Jules Verne, H Rider Haggard, H G Wells, Edgar Rice Burroughs, and Philip K Dick. For a complete description of the collection see: George Slusser, "The J Lloyd Eaton Collection," *Special Collections*, II, 1/2, 25-38 (1983), and *Dictionary Catalog of the J Lloyd Eaton Collection of Science Fiction and Fantasy Literature* (Boston: G K Hall) 1982.

CA —SAN FRANCISCO PUBLIC LIBRARY, Civic Center, San Francisco, 94102. Dennis L Maness, Cur
Holdings: Vols 2000 Cat
Notes: McComas Collection of Fantasy and Science Fiction. In addition to the 2000 vols of fiction, there is incl a complete run (vol 1, no 1) of 92 fantasy and science fiction magazines, starting with *Amazing* in 1926.

CO —COLORADO STATE UNIVERSITY, Libraries, Fort Collins, 80523. John Newman, Special Collections Librn
Holdings: Vols (11,000) Cat Mss Pix
Budget: ($7000)
Notes: The Western American Literature Collection incl fiction, poetry, pictures, art, and other works of the imagination set in the American Frontier West and modern rural West, especially the Rocky Mountain Area. There is also a collection of some 500 pulp magazines. "Westerns" mostly.

DC —LIBRARY OF CONGRESS, Serial and Government Publications Division, Washington, 20540.
Notes: Pulp Fiction Collection. 15,000 issues date from the 1920s to the 1950s. Several famous pulps--*Black Mask, Wierd Tales, Amazing Stories*--are kept in the Rare Book and Special Collections Division.

IL —NORTHERN ILLINOIS UNIVERSITY, Founders Memorial Library, Rare Books and Special Collections Dept, De Kalb, 60115. William R DuBois, Dept Head
Holdings: Cat
Notes: The Western Pulp Magazine Collection. Incl 600 magazines. Noncirculating. Limited photocopying. Mass-appeal publications, ca 1865-1920. Includes Horatio Alger, "Oliver Optic" and other popular writers.

IN —INDIANA UNIVERSITY, Lilly Library, Seventh St, Bloomington, 47405. William R Cagle, Librn
Holdings: Cat
Notes: Collection incl extensive runs of major American science fiction periodicals.

KY —UNIVERSITY OF LOUISVILLE, Ekstrom Library, Rare Books & Special Collections, 2301 S Third St, Louisville, 40208. George T McWhorter, Cur; Delinda Stephens Buie, Asst Cur
Holdings: Mss
Notes: Edgar Rice Burroughs Collection

(7000 items) and pulp magazines (10,000), largely duplicates from UCLA.
See also entry under Burroughs, Edgar Rice.

MD —UNIVERSITY OF MARYLAND, BALTIMORE COUNTY, Albin O Kuhn Library and Gallery, 5401 Wilkens Ave, Baltimore, 21228. Ann Copeland, Special Collections Librn
Holdings: Vols (4500) Cat Mss Pix Phonorecords
Notes: The Azriel Rosenfeld Science Fiction Research Collection of about 20,000 items, incl over 4000 issues of science fiction periodicals such as *Analog, Galaxy*, and a complete run of *Amazing Stories*, as well as 4500 hard cover and paperback books. In addition, the library's Treide Collection incl 1000 issues of story magazines published in the 1930's and 1940's.
See also entries under Science Fiction and Fanzines.

MI —MICHIGAN STATE UNIVERSITY, Libraries, Special Collections Div, East Lansing, 48824. Jannette Fiore, Librn
Holdings: Vols (30,000) Cat
Notes: Collection of 19th/20th century authors, including selected expatriate authors. Popular Culture Collections have four principal categories of materials: Comic Art, ca 23,500 items (comics, aprox 21,000 cataloged issues, big-little books, reprints and anthologies, etc); Popular Fiction, ca 24,000 items (dime novels, story magazines and pulps, juvenile series, detective, science fiction, western and romantic novels); Popular Information, ca 5000 items (over 2000 public school text books, along with almanacs, big and little blue books, "self-education" materials, etc); Popular Performing Arts, ca 2300 items (tent-show materials, including 250 scripts, photographs, handbills, records and correspondence; plays and entertainments for home and popular performance and print materials relating to radio-TV-film). Partially cataloged.

MN —UNIVERSITY OF MINNESOTA, Libraries, Children's Literature Research Collections, 109 Walter Library, Minneapolis, 55455. Karen Nelson Hoyle, Cur
Holdings: Vols 4000 Cat
Notes: American and British. Several published descriptions, Kerlan Collection.

OR —UNIVERSITY OF OREGON LIBRARY, Special Collections Div, Eugene, 97403. Kenneth W Duckett, Curator
Holdings: Vols 5,000 Cat
Notes: Ca 150 runs (of varying completeness) of western, detective and romance magazines, 1920-1960. Also, 3,500 cataloged volumes of paperback western and science-fiction, 1950-1970.

MB —UNIVERSITY OF WINNIPEG, Library, 515 Portage Ave, Winnipeg, R3B 2E9, Can. W R Converse, Chief Librn
Holdings: Vols (1800) Cat Microforms
Notes: Collection incl all major science fiction writers, all science fiction classics, *Amazing Stories Monthly* and *Amazing Stories Quarterly*. Also incl fantasy, eg, Edgar Rice Burroughs' Tarzan stories, as well as his Martian stories. Collection will very soon incl all science fiction periodicals on microfilm.

PULPWOOD see Woodpulp and Woodpulp Industry

PULSARS

NY —AMERICAN INSTITUTE OF PHYSICS, Center for the History of Physics, Niels Bohr Library, 335 E 45 St, New York, 10017. John Aubry, Librn
Notes: Papers, incl correspondence, notebooks, awards, photographs, and other materials originated by Samuel A Goudsmit. Oral history interviews dealing with the discovery of and subsequent work on pulsars, collected by Steve Woolgar. Permission needed for use of the latter.

PULSATING RADIO SOURCES see Pulsars

PUNJAB

MO —UNIVERSITY OF MISSOURI-COLUMBIA, Ellis Library, Ninth and

PUNJAB (cont.)

Lowry, Columbia, 65201. Murari Lal Nagar, Librn
Holdings: Vols 100,000 Maps Microforms
Notes: The South Asia Studies Program at the University of Missouri-Columbia, is an interdepartmental, multi-disciplinary area studies program on India, Pakistan, Bangladesh, Sri Lanka and Nepal.
Depository for the PL480 Program of the Library of Congress in many languages from South Asia. There are library resources in Sankskrit, Hindi, Bengali, Panjabi, and Malayalam. The library is particularly strong in Baroda, Bengal and the Punjab.

PUNS AND PUNNING

IN —INDIANA UNIVERSITY, Institute for Sex Research Library, 416 Morrison Hall, Bloomington, 47401. Douglas Freeman, Collections and Services Librn; Joan Brewer, Information Services Librn
Holdings: Vols (62,000) Cat Mss Pix Phonorecords Audiotapes Slides Films Microforms
Budget: ($20,000)
Notes: One of the greatest and most extensive collections on sexual behavior, the library collects materials on all aspects of sex activity, with special emphasis on behavioral and social aspects. Also collects erotic literature and sexual ephemera. Inc 105 audiotapes, 23 vertical file drawers, 108 phonorecords, audiotapes, 55,000 pictures, 5000 slides, and 1700 films. Rich in French, German and American sources; also much Oriental. Semitraditional erotic poetry and song of 17th-18th century England. Bawdy limericks, double-entendre, puns, slang, erotic literature, graffiti, slang and special dictionaries, proverbs and sayings, epigrams and research materials of the Kinsey Studies, etc. Contact Information Service for literature searching, preparation of bibliographies, permission to use collection. Limited photocopying.

PUPIN, MICHAEL I.

IA —HERBERT HOOVER PRESIDENTIAL LIBRARY, West Branch, 52358. Dale C Mayer, Archivist
Notes: Papers.

PUPPETS AND PUPPET PLAYS

CA —UNIVERSITY OF CALIFORNIA, DAVIS, Shields Library, Dept of Special Collections, Davis, 95616. Donald Kunitz, Head; C Danial Elliott, Asst Head
Holdings: Vols (112,000) Cat Mss Pix
Notes: Programs, playbills, posters, designs, and scripts from 19th and 20th century American and British theatre. American materials incl the eastern United States (NYC) and California. Production groupings center in Sir Henry Irving, McKee Rankin, Sir John Martin-Harvey, E L Davenport. Clippings, photographs, and correspondence of theatre personalities; records of the Bread and Puppet Theatre, San Francisco Mime Troupe, Living Theatre, Firehouse Theatre. Described in: Sarlos, Robert K, "The Theatre Collection at Davis," *American Society for Theatre Research Newsletter*, vol 3, no 1, Fall 1974, pp 2-3, 9-10.
CA —CALIFORNIA POLYTECHNIC STATE UNIVERSITY LIBRARY, Special Collections and University Archives, San Luis Obispo, 93407. Nancy E Loe, Head Librn
Holdings: Vols (100) Cat
Notes: The Puppetry Collection incl many rare European and American imprints in the puppetry field from the 1900s to the 1940s. 2 cubic feet of puppetry journals all from early 1900s to the 1940s.
MA —HARVARD UNIVERSITY LIBRARY, Theatre Collection, Cambridge, 02138. Jeanne T Newlin, Cur
Holdings: Cat Mss Pix Slides Microforms
Notes: One of the largest existing collections of playbills, programs, prints, photographs,

promptbooks, and other materials relating to the performing arts, the scope is worldwide; resources on the English-speaking stage of the 18th and 19th centuries are unequalled. Incl materials on ballet and modern dance, the circus, magic, minstrel shows, cinema, and pantomime. For description, see *Harvard Library Bulletin*, VI (1925): pp 281-301.
NM —UNIVERSITY OF NEW MEXICO, Fine Arts Library, Fine Art Bldg, Albuquerque, 87131. James B Wright, Librn
Notes: The Batchelder-McPharlin Puppetry Collection, one of the world's major private collections. About 2200 items on puppetry of the world.
NY —COOPER-HEWITT MUSEUM, The Smithsonian Institution's National Museum of Design, 2 E 91 St, New York, 10128. David McFadden, Cur of Decorative Arts
Holdings: Cat Mss Pix
Notes: The Haines Marionette Collection. Incl over 200 marionettes, music, scripts, sets and props, all made by the donors and marionetteers Frank and Elizabeth Haines. Also a small collection of 18th and 19th century marionettes, European and English.
NY —NEW YORK PUBLIC LIBRARY, Performing Arts Research Center, Billy Rose Theatre Collection, 111 Amsterdam Ave, New York, 10023. Dorothy L Swerdlove, Cur
Holdings: Cat
Notes: The Theatre Collection maintains current clipping files about activity in the field and acquires photographs and programs of marionette theatre productions. Files are kept on organizations, on individual puppeteers and on associations and organizations in this area of entertainment--professional and amateur, domestic and foreign. The reviews of such productions in New York are entered in the review collection kept seasonally. The collection has been enriched by the gift of books and papers of the late William H Cleveland, Jr.
TX —SOUTHERN METHODIST UNIVERSITY, Fondren Library, McCord Theater Collection, Room 301, Dallas, 75275. Edyth Renshaw, Cur; Linda Sellers, Pub Serv
Holdings: Vols (2000) Uncat Mss Pix Slides Phonorecords
Notes: See *Theatre Collections in Libraries and Museums*, Gilder and Freedley (Theatre Arts, 1936). The McCord Theatre Collection encompasses the entire spectrum of the performing arts. The central purpose is to gather records of our regional theater before such ephemeral material is lost. Records of over two hundred early Texas theaters, some fragmentary and some relatively complete, are in the files. These records incl photographs of buildings, stagehands, orchestras, and performers. Local theatre history incl the once famous Dallas Little Theatre and the Margo Jones Theatre. The national theatre, opera, ballet, and circus archives incl pictures (some autographed), programs, posters, throw-aways, tear sheets, clippings, and letters. Our international archives are small, but we have some excellent material, eg, artifacts from Max Reinhardt's production of "The Miracle" which happened to go bankrupt in Dallas. After a few years the items were given to us. There are posters, tear sheets, souvenir programs, and other colorful items from Morris Gest and the Artef Collection. We have about 200 19th century English playbills and a few from the 18th century. There is a collection of modern English, French, and other European programs, many of them illustrated souvenir programs. Also, magazines on theater, cinema, and television (1800). Scrapbooks covering both southwest and Dallas theater, 1890s-1950s. Special Collections: artifacts and documents on puppets; masks; costume design; circus; and ballet and dance. The Harriet Bacon MacDonald Collection of over 200 photographs of musicians appearing in Dallas during the first three decades of the 20th century. Many autographed. Affiliated with Meadow Theatre of the Arts.
VA —GEORGE MASON UNIVERSITY, Fenwick Library, Special Collections Dept,

4400 University Drive, Fairfax, 22030. Ruth Kerns, Public Services Librn
Notes: The Federal Theatre Project (FTP) was established in August 1935 as a part of the arts program of the Works Progress Administration (renamed Work Projects Administration in 1939). Supporting 150 separate units throughout the United States, the FTP produced over 830 major stage plays, 6000 radio programs, and innumerable marionette plays, vaudeville shows, outdoor pageants, and circuses. At the conclusion of the project in June 1939, the "product materials" generated by the FTP were sent to the Library of Congress, and the administrative records to the National Archives. The Library's Federal Theatre Project collection was placed on deposit at George Mason University in Fairfax, Virginia, in 1974.
WA —UNIVERSITY OF WASHINGTON LIBRARIES, East Asia Library, DO-27, Seattle, 98195. Karl Lo, Head
Holdings: Vols (300,000) Cat Microforms
Budget: ($200,000)
Notes: Southwest China: Joseph Rock Collection, ca 2000 vols; modern Chinese poetry, 1919 to date: ca 700 titles; Asian art, esp. Japanese painting painting: 4097 vols; Tiao-yu-t'ai movement in the US: ca 400 items of periodicals and pamphlets; modern Korean poetry, ancient and modern: ca 1000 titles; Mu-yu-shu folk literature: ca 1000 items.
ON —METROPOLITAN TORONTO LIBRARY, Theatre Dept, 789 Yonge St, Toronto, M4W 2G8, Can. Heather McCallum, Head
Holdings: Vols (30,500) Mss Pix Slides Phonorecords Microforms
Notes: Book and nonbook materials in all areas of the performing arts except music: theatre and drama, moving pictures, dance, television and radio programming, and varieties of popular entertainment such as circus, music hall, vaudeville, puppetry and pantomime. Special collections relating to the history of the performing arts in Canada. Access to the book and periodical collection is provided through a divided dictionary COM catalog on microfiche. In addition, extensive card indexes are available. Published descriptions of the collection: Heather McCallum. Research Collections in Canadian Libraries, Part II. Special Studies no I. *Theatre resources in Canadian collections* (Ottawa: National Library of Canada, 1973); Heather McCallum. "The Theatre Department of the Metropolitan Toronto Library" in *Special Collections*, vol 1 (1), fall 1981.
PQ —MCGILL UNIVERSITY, McLennan Library, Rare Books and Special Collections Dept, 3459 McTavish St, Montreal, H3A 1Y1, Can.
Holdings: Vols 2680
Notes: Incl books on the puppet theatre, puppets, toy theatres and their theatrical portraits, pantins, prints and posters, located in the Rosalynde Stearn Puppet Collection. A catalogue is available: The Rosalynde Stearn Puppet Collection. Montreal, 1961. Incl 171 puppets.

PURCELL, GRAHAM

TX —TEXAS A&M UNIVERSITY, Sterling C Evans Library, University Archives, College Station, 77843. Charles R Schultz, University Archivist
Holdings: Mss
Notes: The Archives of Modern Politics: the papers of Texas Congressmen Graham Purcell, 1961-1971.

PURCELL, WILLIAM

CA —UNIVERSITY OF CALIFORNIA, LOS ANGELES, William Andrews Clark Memorial Library, 2520 Cimarron St, Los Angeles, 90018.
Holdings: Cat Mss
Notes: Small collection, original editions, etc.

PURDOM, TOM

†PA —TEMPLE UNIVERSITY LIBRARY, Philadelphia, 19122. Thomas M Whitehead,

PURDOM, TOM (cont.)

Librn
Notes: More than 100 cubic ft of mss, incl papers of Michael Bishop, Ben Bova, Jack Dann, Gardner Dozois, Lloyd Eshback, Tom Purdom, Pamela Sargent, John Varley, and George Zebrowski.

PURDY, JAMES

NV —UNIVERSITY OF NEVADA, RENO, University Library, Special Collections Dept, Reno, 89557. Robert E Blesse, Head
Holdings: Vols (50) Cat
Notes: Includes individual works by author in all editions including translations; also prefaces, introductions, published correspondence, appearances in anthologies, periodicals, etc. Bibliographical research collection, part of Modern Authors Collection. Other appearances 90 cataloged.

PURIFICATION OF WATER see Water—Purification

PURITANS

MD —JOHNS HOPKINS UNIVERSITY, Milton S Eisenhower Library, George Peabody Collection, 17 E Mt Vernon Place, Baltimore, 21201. Lyn Hart, Peabody Librn
Notes: Emphasis on materials published before 1950. Strength is a good collection through the 19th century.

PURITY, SOCIAL see Sexual Ethics

PUROHIT, SWAMI SHRI

DE —UNIVERSITY OF DELAWARE, Hugh M Morris Library, S College Ave, Newark, 19711. T Stuart Dick, Special Collections
Notes: Extensive Yeats holdings, incl a collection of personal correspondence which features 67 unpublished letters and telegrams written in 1931-39 to Swami Shri Purohit, an Indian mystic, who with Yeats cotranslated the *Upanishads* into English.

PURSER, SARAH, 1848-1943

BC —UNIVERSITY OF VICTORIA, McPherson Library, Victoria, V8W 3H5, Can.

PURUCKER, GOTTFRIED DE

CA —SAN DIEGO PUBLIC LIBRARY, Literature & Language Sect, 820 E St, San Diego, 92101. Alyce Archuleta, Senior Librn
Holdings: Vols (140) Cat

PUSHTU LANGUAGE see Afghan Language and Literature

PUTNAM, GEORGE PALMER

MD —JOHNS HOPKINS UNIVERSITY, Milton S Eisenhower Library, Charles & 34 Sts, Baltimore, 21218. Ann S Gwyn, Assistant Dir for Special Collections
Holdings: Cat Mss
Notes: Letters and other correspondence; cataloged in manuscript room.
MA —RADCLIFFE COLLEGE, Arthur & Elizabeth Schlesinger Library on the History of Women in America, 3 James St, Cambridge, 02138. Patricia Miller King, Dir; Eva Moseley, Cur of Mss
Notes: Cache of correspondence, largely made up of letters to and from Amelia Earhart, her mother, Amy Otis Earhart, sister, and her husband George Palmer Putnam.

PUTNAM, RUFUS

OH —RUTHERFORD B HAYES LIBRARY, 1337 Hayes Ave, Fremont, 43420. Watt P Marchman, Dir
Notes: Correspondence in the Lyman-Lincoln Collection.

PUTNAM, SAMUEL

IL —SOUTHERN ILLINOIS UNIVERSITY, CARBONDALE, Delyte W Morris Library, Special Collections Dept, Carbondale, 62901. David V Koch, Cur of Special Collections; Louisa Bowen, Cur of Manuscripts
Holdings: Cat Mss Pix
Notes: Papers and mss of this American expatriate were acquired from his widow. The Putnam archives consist largely of a record of his later years which were devoted to Latin American literature and translating. (Harvey Gardiner, *Samuel Putnam, Latin Americanist*. Bibliographic Contribution No 5.)

PUZZLES

†NY —COLUMBIA UNIVERSITY LIBRARIES, Butler Library, Rare Book and Manuscript Library, 535 W 114 St, New York, 10027.
Notes: Papers of Dr Ivan Morris, American Section chairman of Amnesty International, his researches into Japanese literature and culture, and his books on puzzles.
RI —BROWN UNIVERSITY, John Hay Library, 20 Prospect St, Providence, 02912. Mark N Brown, Cur Mss
Notes: The Royal Vale Heath Collection of about 200 of his designs, drawings, models, ocular, and verbal descriptions of simultaneous solutions to linear Diophantine equations in such examples as magic squares, Platonic solids, etc. These curious designs often were devised as talismans in ancient India and were first developed as mathematical problems by the Chinese.

PYPER, NANCY

†ON —METROPOLITAN TORONTO LIBRARY, Theatre Collections, 789 Yonge St, Toronto, M4W 2G8, Can.
Notes: Papers covering the career of Nancy Pyper as actress, director, writer, and teacher. Incl photographs, programs, stage designs, etc for her productions at Hart House Theatre in the 1930s, etc.

PWO DIALECT see Karen Language

PYLE, HOWARD

DE —DELAWARE ART MUSEUM, Library, 2301 Kentmere Pkwy, Wilmington, 19806. Anne Hoslam, Librn
Holdings: Vols 400 Cat Pix
Notes: The museum has a large collection of Howard Pyle paintings, drawings, etc. There are also clipping files and books relating to the Pyle pupils. Collection incl part of Pyle's personal library and most of his published works.
PA —FREE LIBRARY OF PHILADELPHIA, Rare Book Dept, Logan Sq, Philadelphia, 19103. Marie E Korey, Rare Book Librn
Holdings: Vols (1000) Cat Mss Pix
Notes: The Thornton Oakley Collection containing 1000 pieces of original art, autograph letters, and books and periodicals, illustrated by Howard Pyle and his students, incl Maxfield Parish, Frank Schoonover, Jessie Wilcox Smith, and N C Wlyeth.
PA —FRIENDS HISTORICAL LIBRARY OF SWARTHMORE COLLEGE, Swarthmore, 19081. J William Frost, Dir
Holdings: Vols (35,000) Cat Mss Pix Slides Microforms
Notes: Library has an extensive collection of pictures, largely photographs, of individual Quakers and Quaker groups, meeting houses, and other buildings such as residences, schools, colleges, and institutions. In addition to photographs, the library has prints, silhouettes, drawings, and a few paintings. Highlighting the library's art works are drawings by Benjamin West, and paintings by West, Edward Hicks, James Sharples, and Howard Pyle.

PYNCHON, THOMAS

NV —UNIVERSITY OF NEVADA, RENO, University Library, Special Collections Dept, Reno, 89557. Robert E Blesse, Head
Holdings: // Vols (11) Cat
Notes: Includes individual works by author in all editions including translations; also prefaces, introductions, published correspondence, appearances in anthologies, periodicals, etc. Bibliographical research collection, part of Modern Authors Collection. Other appearances 459 cataloged.

PYROTECHNICS see Fireworks

Q

'Q' (SIR ARTHUR QUILLER-COUCH)

CT —LEE ASH, (personal collection), 66
Humiston Dr, Bethany, 06525.
Holdings: Mss Maps Pix
Notes: First editions, mss, ephemera,
memorabilia.

QATAR

CA —HOOVER INSTITUTION ON WAR,
REVOLUTION & PEACE, Stanford
University, Stanford, 94305. Peter Duignan,
Cur; Karen Fung, Deputy Cur
Holdings: Vols (100,000)
Notes: For full description of collection, see
Hoover Institution entry under Near East.

QUACKENBUSH, JAN

MA —BOSTON UNIVERSITY, Mugar
Memorial Library, Special Collections Dept,
771 Commonwealth Ave, Boston, 02215.
Howard B Gotlieb, Dir
Holdings: Cat Mss Pix
Notes: Mss correspondence, etc collected in
depth; incl publications by or about.

QUAKERS see Friends, Society of

QUALITY CONTROL

IL —CHICAGO BRIDGE & IRON CO,
Technical Library, 800 Jorie Blvd, Oak
Brook, 60521. Susan Beatty, Librn
Holdings: Vols (7500) Cat
Budget: ($39,500)
Notes: Quality control and nondestructive
testing.

ON —ONTARIO MINISTRY OF HEALTH,
Laboratory Services Branch, Library, Box
9000, Terminal A, Toronto, M5W 1R5, Can.
Doris A Standing, Librn
Holdings: Vols (4000) Cat
Budget: ($50,000)
Notes: Medical laboratory technology and
related subjects: microbiology; environmental
bacteriology (limited to testing of milk, food
and water for bacterial quality, etc);
biological chemistry (clinical); mycology;
parasitology; virology; immunology;
serology; automated laboratory techniques;
biohazard control.

QUALITY OF WATER see Water Quality

QUANTUM MECHANICS see Quantum Theory

QUANTUM THEORY

CA —UNIVERSITY OF CALIFORNIA,
BERKELEY, Bancroft Library, Manuscripts
Division, Berkeley, 94720. James D Hart,
Dir
Holdings: // Cat Microforms
Notes: The Archive for the History of
Quantum Physics contains tape-recorded
interviews, microfilmed documents, and
correspondence (largely unpublished),
relating to the history of quantum and
atomic physics. Coverage centers on the
years 1900 to 1930. The Archive consists of
some 300 reels of microfilm, in conjunction
with the Office for History of Science, UC
Berkeley. A catalog of about one-third of the
holdings is incl in T S Kuhn, J L Heilbron, P
Forman and L Allen, *Sources for the History
of Quantum Physics* (Philadelphia: American
Philosophical Society, 1967).

†CA —CALIFORNIA INSTITUTE OF
TECHNOLOGY, Robert A Millikan
Memorial Library, Archives, 1201 E
California Blvd, Pasadena, 91125.
Notes: Geophysicist Charles Richter's
lecture notes and oral history interview. Incl
notes from courses at Caltech taught by
physicist Paul Epstein (1883-1966), such as
higher dynamics, 1925; thermodynamics,
1925/26; quantum theory, 1926-28, 1940.

NY —AMERICAN INSTITUTE OF
PHYSICS, Center for the History of Physics,
Niels Bohr Library, 335 E 45 St, New York,
10017. John Aubry, Librn
Holdings: Cat Mss Maps Pix Microforms

NY —UNIVERSITY OF ROCHESTER,
Physics-Optics-Astronomy Library, Bausch
& Lomb Bldg, River Campus, Rochester,
14627. Loretta Caren, Librn
Holdings: Vols (20,000) Cat
Notes: Strong research level collection in the
field and related areas.

PA —AMERICAN PHILOSOPHICAL
SOCIETY, Library, 105 S Fifth St,
Philadelphia, 19106. Edward C Carter II,
Librn
Holdings: Cat Mss Microforms

TX —RICE UNIVERSITY, Fondren Library,
6100 S Main St, PO Box 1892, Houston,
77251. Dr Samuel M Carrington, Jr,
University Librn
Holdings: // Cat Mss Pix
Notes: Papers of William V Houston, incl his
research papers in spectroscopy, theory of
solid state, quantum mechanics and
superconductivity (15 linear ft).

QUARANTINE, VETERINARY

NY —US DEPT OF AGRICULTURE,
Agriculture Research Service, Plum Island
Animal Disease Laboratory, PO Box 848,
Greenport, 11944. Stephen Perlman, Librn
Holdings: Vols (15,000) Cat Pix Slides
Microforms
Budget: ($37,000)

QUARRYING, GRANITE see Granite Industry and Trade

QUASARS

CA —GRIFFITH OBSERVATORY, Library,
2800 E Observatory Rd, Los Angeles,
90027. E C Krupp, Dir
Holdings: Vols Cat Pix Slides Phonorecords
Budget: ($1000)
Notes: No separate catalog. No
photocopying.

QUATTLEBAUM, PAUL, 1886-1964

SC —CLEMSON UNIVERSITY, Libraries,
Clemson, 29631. Michael F Kohl, Head of
Special Collections
Holdings: // Cat Mss
Notes: Paul Quattlebaum, South Carolina
State Senator. 31 cubic feet. Unpublished
folder title listing.

QUEBEC (PROVINCE)—DIRECTORIES

ON —METROPOLITAN TORONTO
LIBRARY, Canadian History Dept, 789
Yonge St, Toronto, M4W 2G8, Can.
Notes: Bell Canada Telephone Historical
Collection of 448 reels of microfilm of
Ontario and Quebec telephone books from
1878 to 1979. The collection will be
updated. Toronto city directories from 1868-
1949 are available also.

QUEBEC (PROVINCE)—GENEALOGY

MA —FREE PUBLIC LIBRARY, Genealogy
Room, 613 Pleasant St, Bedford, 02740. Paul
A Cyr, Librn
Holdings: Vols (10,000) Cat Mss Maps Pix
Microforms
Budget: ($1000)
Notes: Extensive collection on the history
and genealogy of New England, with a
strong emphasis on southeastern
Massachusetts. Materials incl books,
periodicals, mss, microfilms, and pictures of
New England life. Unique features of the
collection incl the *Leonard Papers* ms of
vital records of early Bristol County,
Repertoires des Mariages of Province
Quebec, Canada, and a collection on the
Society of Friends, or Quakers.

PQ —MISSISQUOI HISTORICAL SOCIETY,
Missisquoi Museum Library, Box 186,
Stanbridge East, J0J 1A0, Can. R S
McIntosh, Pres
Holdings: Vols (2000) Cat Mss Maps Pix
Slides Phonorecords Audiotapes
Notes: Catalog of 10,000 documents.

QUEBEC (PROVINCE)—HISTORY

PA —BALCH INSTITUTE FOR ETHNIC
STUDIES, Library, 18 S Seventh St,
Philadelphia, 19106. R Joseph Anderson,
Library Dir

ON —YORK UNIVERSITY, Scott Library,
Downsview, M3J 2R2, Can. Hartwell
Bowsfield, University Archivist
Notes: A collection of 10,000 Canadian
pamphlets, providing a continuum of
information about political and cultural
events in Canada, especially Quebec and
Ontario between 1880 and 1950.

PQ —SPECIAL LIBRARY FOR LA
SOCIETE HISTORIQUE DU
SAGUENAY, 930 est, Jacques-Cartier, PO
Box 456, Chicoutimi, G7H 5C8, Can.
Roland Belanger, Archivist
Holdings: Vols 850 Uncat Mss Maps Pix
Notes: All concerning the history and
geography of the Saguenay Region. Incl
about 50,000 pictures.

PQ —BISHOP'S UNIVERSITY, John Bassett
Memorial Library, Laurie Allison Room for
Special Collections, Lennoxville, J1M 1Z7,
Can. Germain Belisle, Chief Librn
Holdings: Vols Mss Maps Pix Microforms
VF
Notes: The P H Scowen Eastern Townships
Historical Collection. In addition to general
works on the history of this region, included
in this collection are historical accounts of
specific localities, institutions, and prominent
townshippers; reports on immigration and
colonization; studies on the geography of the
region; census records on microfilm dating
from 1825; newspapers from the 19th
century from Quebec and eastern townships.

PQ —MCGILL UNIVERSITY, McLennan
Library, Rare Books and Special Collections
Dept, 3459 McTavish St, Montreal, H3A
1Y1, Can.
Holdings: Vols 3000
Notes: 3000 books and a large collection of
newspapers. The Rodolphe Joubert
Collection on French Canada includes
material on economic conditions, history,
politics and government of the province of
Quebec. Also the department includes much
material on the subject throughout its
collections.

PQ —BIBLIOTHEQUE DES ARCHIVES
NATIONALES DU QUEBEC, CP 10450,
Sainte-Foy, G1V 4N1, Can. Collete Barry,
Dir
Holdings: Vols (50,000) Cat Mss Maps Pix
Microforms
Budget: ($25,000)
Notes: Dictionary catalog on cards
(unpublished). Official Quebec documents
published before 1867.

PQ —MISSISQUOI HISTORICAL SOCIETY,
Missisquoi Museum Library, Box 186,
Stanbridge East, J0J 1A0, Can. R S
McIntosh, Pres
Holdings: Vols (2000) Cat Mss Maps Pix
Slides Phonorecords Audiotapes
Notes: Missisquoi County History.

QUEBEC (PROVINCE) —HISTORY—REBELLION, 1837-1838 see Canada—History—Rebellion, 1837-1838

QUEBEC (PROVINCE)—POLITICS AND GOVERNMENT

ON —OTTAWA PUBLIC LIBRARY, 120
Metcalfe St, Ottawa, K1P 5M2, Can.
Thomas Rooney, Librn
Holdings: Vols (7000) Cat Mss Maps
Pamphlets Ephemera Postcards
Notes: Ottawa subjects, imprints and
authors. Municipal and regional government
publications, incl bylaws, minutes, and
planning studies. Also incl Ottawa - Carleton
(Ont); Outaouais, Region De L' (Quebec);
Ottawa Valley (Quebec and Ont).

PQ —MCGILL UNIVERSITY, McLennan
Library, Rare Books and Special Collections
Dept, 3459 McTavish St, Montreal, H3A
1Y1, Can.
Notes: 3000 books and a large collection of

QUEBEC (PROVINCE)—POLITICS AND GOVERNMENT (cont.)

newspapers. The Rodolphe Joubert Collection on French Canada includes material on economic conditions, history, politics and government of the province of Quebec. Also the department includes much material on the subject throughout its collections.

QUEBEC (PROVINCE)—SOCIAL LIFE AND CUSTOMS

PQ —MCGILL UNIVERSITY, McLennan Library, Rare Books and Special Collections Dept, 3459 McTavish St, Montreal, H3A 1Y1, Can.
Notes: 3000 books and a large collection of newspapers. The Rodolphe Joubert Collection on French Canada includes material on economic conditions, history, politics and government of the province of Quebec. Also the department includes much material on the subject throughout its collections.

QUEEN MARY II

CA —LONG BEACH PUBLIC LIBRARY, Literature & History Dept, 101 Pacific Ave, Long Beach, 90802. Harriet J Friis, Head
Holdings: Vols Pamphlets Documents Pix Maps Periodicals Audiotapes Microforms
Notes: Collection documents the history and continuing development of Long Beach. Publications of the City of Long Beach are incl, as well as a selective index to the Long Beach *Independent* and other local newspapers. Also incl material on the steamship *Queen Mary*. Items in the collection do not circulate. Incl city directories.

QUEENS see Rulers (Kings, Queens, Etc.)

QUEENSBORO, NEW YORK—FICTION

NY —STATE UNIVERSITY OF NEW YORK, STONY BROOK, Melville Library, Dept of Special Collections, Stony Brook, 11794. Evert Volkersz, Head
Holdings: Vols Uncat
Notes: A growing collection of fiction and literature with Long Island, incl Queens and Brooklyn, as a fictional setting.

QUEREDO, EDUARDO

CA —STANFORD UNIVERSITY LIBRARIES, Cecil H Green Library, Stanford, 94305. Michael T Ryan, Cur
Notes: Papers of Ernesto Galarza, Bert Corona, Manuel Ruiz, Jr, Eduardo Queredo, Edward Valenzuela.

QUICKSILVER MINES

CA —STANFORD UNIVERSITY LIBRARIES, Cecil H Green Library, Stanford, 94305. Michael T Ryan, Cur
Notes: Research collection.

QUIE, ALBERT H.

MN —MINNESOTA HISTORICAL SOCIETY LIBRARY, 690 Cedar St, Saint Paul, 55101. Patricia C Harpole, Chief of Reference Library; Bonnie G Wilson, Head of Special Libraries
Notes: Materials by such well-known figures as Hubert H. Humphrey, Eugene J. McCarthy, Orville L Freeman, Maurice H. Stans, Donald M Fraser, Albert H Quie, Clark MacGregor and John A Blatnik. A list of these holdings is on file in the Audio-Visual Library, the tapes are housed in the MHS Research Center, 1500 Mississippi Street, St Paul, Minn.

QUIGLEY PUBLISHING COMPANY

DC —GEORGETOWN UNIVERSITY, Library, Special Collections Div, 37 & O Sts NW, Washington, 20057. George M Barringer, Special Collections Librn; Nicholas B Sheetz, Mss Librn
Holdings: Vols 500 Cat Pix
Notes: Incorporates the picture "morgue" of the Quigley Publishing Company and archival runs of its publications. Over 50,000 pictures. The library has additional picture resources of over 100,000 photographs.

QUILLER-COUCH, SIR ARTHUR see Q (Sir Arthur Quiller-Couch)

QUILTS AND QUILTING

KS —WICHITA PUBLIC LIBRARY, Art & Music Division, 223 S Main, Wichita, 67202. Leonard Messineo, Jr, Head, Art & Music Division; Deborah Hamilton, Special Collections Librn
Holdings: Audiotapes
Notes: Joan O'Bryant Kansas Folklore Collection. Contains approximately 200 hours of folkmusic and oral histories on tape; over 27,000 note cards covering topics such as anecdotes, beliefs, customs, games, jokes, medicines and cures, proverbs, recipes, rhymes, riddles, sayings, songs, speech and dialect, etc; 102 research papers covering family histories, town and area histories, biographies, tales, recipes, etc; and well over 70 mounted quilt blocks-covering the folk history of Kansas. This material was collected by Joan O'Bryant and her students from 1947-1964, the period in which she taught Folklore and English at Wichita State University.
NC —APPALACHIAN STATE UNIVERSITY, Belk Library, Appalachian Collection, Boone, 28608. Eric J Olson, Librn
Holdings: Vols (12,000) Cat Mss Maps Pix Slides Phonorecords Audiotapes
Budget: ($4000)
Notes: The Appalachian Collection incl the Fry Collectin of handmade quilts and coverlets; the York Collection of folk songs and ballads, plus tapes; the I G Greer Collection of Folk Songs and Ballads; the Amos Abrams ballad collection; artifacts, incl the Tatum Collection of household items, furniture, and farm implements; Daniel Boone loom; oral history tapes; the Jack Guy Collection of tapes of area music and photographs; and regional genealogy. This is a very comprehensive study on the Southern Appalachian Region. Separate catalog for the collection.
VT —SHELBURNE MUSEUM, Library, Shelburne, 05482. Barbara Reenstierna, Librn
Holdings: Vols (275) Cat Slides

QUIMBY, MOSES

NY —CORNELL UNIVERSITY LIBRARIES, Everett Franklin Phillips Beekeeping Library, Ithaca, 14853. Jan Olsen, Librn
Holdings: Vols 4200 Cat Mss
Notes: Incl collections of Moses Quimby, first commercial beekeeper in America, and Rev L L Langstroth.

QUINLAN, STERLING C.

MA —BOSTON UNIVERSITY, Mugar Memorial Library, Special Collections Dept, 771 Commonwealth Ave, Boston, 02215. Howard B Gotlieb, Dir
Holdings: Cat Mss Correspondence

QUINLEY, HARRIET, 1905-

OK —NINETY-NINES, Library, PO Box 59964, Will Rogers World Airport, Oklahoma City, 73159. Lorretta Craig, Librn
Holdings: Vols 350 Cat Pix
Notes: 10,000 books, periodicals, catalogs on history of aviation. Women's aviation resource center. Collection from the first women aviatrix, Harriet Quinley, 1905-, Matilda Morant, 1925-. 7000 bound periodicals from 1929, 10 issues a year, from the magazine first called "Airwomen" to the "Ninety-Nines". Members of the "Ninety-Nines" incl 7 women astronauts (Betty Smith).

QUINN, JOHN

DC —GEORGETOWN UNIVERSITY, Library, Special Collections Div, 37 & O Sts NW, Washington, 20057. George M Barringer, Special Collections Librn; Nicholas B Sheetz, Mss Librn
Holdings: Mss Cat Pix
Notes: The papers of the Irish man-of-letters Sir Shane Leslie (1885-1971) containing letters, mss, diaries, notebooks, clippings, and photographs. Extensive correspondence by Margot Asquith, countess of Oxford and Asquith; Lady Violet Bonham-Carter; Burke Cochran; Lord Alfred Douglas; Moreton Frewen; Cardinal Gasquet; Vyvyan Holland; Lady Leonie Leslie; Sir Wilfrid Meynell; Sir Horace Plunkett; John Quinn; Frederick Rolfe (Baron Corvo); and Elizabeth Russell, among others. Also incl are research files on Sir Winston Churchill (Leslie's first cousin); Leonard Jerome; Maria Anne Fitzherbet (wife of King George IV); Ghosts and Ghost stories; and Eton College.
IN —INDIANA UNIVERSITY, Lilly Library, Seventh St, Bloomington, 47405. William R Cagle, Librn
Holdings: Vols 10 Cat Mss
Notes: First editions, etc. Mss incl correspondence with Ezra Pound.
NY —NEW YORK PUBLIC LIBRARY, Rare Books and Manuscripts Div, Fifth Ave & 42 St, New York, 10018. William L Joyce, Asst Dir; Susan E Davis, Cur of Mss
Holdings: Cat Mss
Budget: ($7161)
Notes: The John Quinn Memorial Collection, incl 72 letterfile boxes, 16 folders and 30 letterpress copy books of letters, notes, telegrams and cables, 1900-1924.

QUINTARD, RT. REV. CHARLES TODD

TN —UNIVERSITY OF THE SOUTH ARCHIVES, Jessie Ball DuPont Library, Sewanee, 37375. Gertrude French Mignery, Archivist
Holdings: Vols (3000) Cat Mss
Notes: His papers, etc.

QUOTATIONS

OH —CLEVELAND PUBLIC LIBRARY, Fine Arts and Special Collections Department, 325 Superior Ave, Cleveland, 44114. Alice N Loranth, Head
Holdings: Vols (2800) Cat Mss
Notes: One of the most outstanding collections of proverbs in the United States, international in scope but particularly strong in Spanish materials. Forms part of the Folklore Collection.
See also entry under Folklore

R

RABASSA, GREGORY

MA —BOSTON UNIVERSITY, Mugar
Memorial Library, Special Collections Dept,
771 Commonwealth Ave, Boston, 02215.
Howard B Gotlieb, Dir
Holdings: Mss

RABBINICAL LITERATURE

†CA —HEBREW UNION COLLEGE, Jewish
Institute of Religion, 3077 University Ave,
Los Angeles, 90007.
Notes: Bible, Talmud, Rabbinics, Jewish
history, philosophy, art and communal
science, Hebrew literature, religion, Zionism.
FL —UNIVERSITY OF FLORIDA
LIBRARY, Isser and Rae Price Library of
Judaica, 18 Libr East, Gainesville, 32611.
Robert Singerman, Head Librn
Budget: ($30,000)
Notes: Total holdings estimated at 55,000
vols dealing with the political, social,
economic and intellectual history of the Jews
in the ancient, medieval and modern periods
and in all geographic areas. The following
areas are especially well represented by
printed matter in all relevant languages:
Bibliography, Festschriften, History, Bible,
Judaism and Jewish theology, liturgy,
responsa, rabbinical literature, Jewish law,
Hebrew language and literature, Yiddish
language and literature, anti-semitism,
Zionism, Palestine and the *Yishuv,* and the
State of Israel. German and American
Judaica form a collecting emphasis with
holdings for all the standard histories as well
as histories of individual synagogues,
institutions and local communities. Works in
Hebrew and Yiddish comprise about 60
percent of the collection (estimated 30,000
vols). With few exceptions, holdingsare
limited to nineteenth and twentieth century
imprints, with complete sets of journals and
thousands of ephemeral pamphlets, many of
them commemorating anniversaries,
enhancing the research value of the
collection, the largest Judaica research
library in the southeastern United States.
Only about half of the collection is
cataloged; the collection is a circulating one
and vols may be borrowed on interlibrary
loan. Incl the Leonard C Mishkin Collection
(40,000 vols), the largest personal Judaica
collection in the United States, the Shlomo
Marenof Collection (3500 vols), and the
inventory of Bernard Morgenstern's Lower
East Side Book Store (8000 vols). Scholars
should inquire in advance of their visit. *The
Isser and Rae Price Library of Judaica*
Report (circulation 2900 copies) is mailed
gratis twice a year to all interested parties.
Special catalogs:Pre-1881 Hebrew imprints
recorded in a chronological card file.
IL —HEBREW THEOLOGICAL COLLEGE,
Saul Silber Memorial Library, 7135 N
Carpenter Rd, Skokie, 60077. Leah Mishkin,
Head Librn/Cur
Holdings: Vols (58,000) Cat Mss Microforms
Notes: Main subject is rabbinics (Halachic
literature). We also have a very large and
important Holocaust Collection.
MA —HEBREW COLLEGE, Jacob & Rose
Grossman Library and Lawrence Jay &
Anne Cable Rubenstein Library, 43 Hawes
St, Brookline, 02146. Maurice Tuchman,
Librn
Notes: Jewish history, Hebrew literature,
Israel Rabbinic literature.
MA —BRANDEIS UNIVERSITY, Goldfarb
Library, 415 South St, Waltham, 02154.
Bessie Hahn, Dir
Holdings: Mss Microforms
Budget: ($20,000)
†NY —JEWISH THEOLOGICAL
SEMINARY OF AMERICA LIBRARY,
3080 Broadway, New York, 10027.
NY —YESHIVA UNIVERSITY, Library, 500
West 185th Street, New York, 10033. Pearl
Berger
Holdings: Cat Mss

NY —YIVO INSTITUTE FOR JEWISH
RESEARCH, Library & Archives, 1048
Fifth Ave, New York, 10028. Dina
Abramowicz, Librn; Marek Web, Archivist
Notes: Rabbinics collection, embracing
publications from the 16th to the 20th
centuries, incl rare books. Cataloged by
subject and title.
OH —HEBREW UNION COLLEGE-JEWISH
INSTITUTE OF RELIGION, Klau Library,
3101 Clifton Ave, Cincinnati, 45220. David
J Gilner, Reference Librn
Holdings: Cat
†PA —DROPSIE UNIVERSITY, Library,
Broad & York Sts, Philadelphia, 19132.

RABE, DAVID

MA —BOSTON UNIVERSITY, Mugar
Memorial Library, Special Collections Dept,
771 Commonwealth Ave, Boston, 02215.
Howard B Gotlieb, Dir
Holdings: Cat Mss Pix
Notes: Mss, correspondence, etc collected in
depth; incl publications by or about.

RABELAIS, FRANCOIS

MD —JOHNS HOPKINS UNIVERSITY,
Institute of the History of Medicine, 1900 E
Monument St, Baltimore, 21205. Doris
Thibodeau, Librn
Holdings: Vols 213 Cat
OH —CLEVELAND PUBLIC LIBRARY, Fine
Arts and Special Collections Department,
325 Superior Ave, Cleveland, 44114. Alice
N Loranth, Head
Holdings: Vols 245 Cat
Notes: Early and rare editions, translations
and versions of his *Gargantua and
Pantagruel.* Earliest edition: 1558. Separate
"edition" catalog of author entries
maintained.
See also entry under Rare Books.

RABINOWITCH, EUGENE I., 1901-1972

NY —STATE UNIVERSITY OF NEW YORK
AT ALBANY, Library, Special Collections
Dept, 1400 Washington Ave, Albany, 12222.
Marion P Munzer, Coordr
Notes: Eugene I Rabinowitch's
correspondence and administrative files
dealing with his academic and publishing
career; editorship of the *Bulletin of Atomic
Scientists,* establishment of the Center for
Science and the Study of Society at the State
University of New York at Albany (16 linear
feet).
See also entries under Scientists; Bulletin of
Atomic Scientists.

RACE AWARENESS

DC —HOWARD UNIVERSITY, Moorland-
Spingarn Research Center, 500 Howard
Place NW, Washington, 20059. Clifford L
Muse, Jr, Acting Dir
Holdings: Vols (106,086) Mss Maps Pix
Slides Phonorecords Audiotapes 16mm
Films Filmstrips Microforms
Budget: ($854,753)
See also entry under Blacks

RACE DISCRIMINATION

CA —LOS ANGELES PUBLIC LIBRARY,
Social Sciences Dept, 630 W Fifth St, Los
Angeles, 90071. Marilyn C Wherley,
Principal Librn
Holdings: Vols 5000 Cat Microforms
Budget: ($150,000)
Notes: Black Studies Collection. Pamphlets,
bibliographies, indexes, periodicals, with
some historical runs on microfilm, strong
collection on slavery and anti-slavery,
abolition, civil rights movement, with
emphasis on the black experience in the
United States. No separate catalog.
DC —HOWARD UNIVERSITY, Moorland-
Spingarn Research Center, 500 Howard
Place NW, Washington, 20059. Clifford L
Muse, Jr, Acting Dir
Holdings: Vols (106,086) Mss Maps Pix
Slides Phonorecords Audiotapes 16mm
Films Filmstrips Microforms
Budget: ($854,753)
See also entry under Blacks

DC —US COMMISSION ON CIVIL
RIGHTS, National Clearinghouse Library,
1121 Vermont Ave NW, Washington,
20005. Lenora McMillan, Chief Librn
Holdings: Vols (10,200) Cat Slides
Microforms
Notes: The National Clearinghouse Library
has a special collection of the US
Commission on Civil Rights publications
from its inception (1957) to present date.
MA —NEW ENGLAND QUAKER
RESEARCH LIBRARY, PO Box 655,
North Amherst, 01059. Francis W Holmes,
Librn
Holdings: Vols (6000) Cat Mss Pix Slides
Phonorecords Audiotapes Microforms
Budget: ($300)
Notes: No photocopying on premises.
Subject emphases: Quakers and Quaker
concerns; Pacifism; Racism; Feminism;
Religion; Bible; Poverty.
MA —BRANDEIS UNIVERSITY, Goldfarb
Library, 415 South St, Waltham, 02154.
Bessie Hahn, Dir
Notes: Hall-Hoag Archives on Extremism in
the U.S. Approx 5000 pieces of Extremist
literature, both Right and Left, dealing with
various social, religious and political aspects
of the US from the 1960s, 1970s and 1980s.
A finding list is in Special Collections.
Material is arranged by the name of the
sponsoring organization in alphabetical
order.
NY —YWCA NATIONAL BOARD, Library,
726-730 Broadway, New York, 10012.
Elizabeth Norris, Librn
Holdings: Vols (1000) Cat Mss
Budget: ($2400)
Notes: Women and their contemporary
interests.
NC —DUKE UNIVERSITY, William R
Perkins Library, Durham, 27706. Elvin E
Strowd, University Librn
Notes: The Race and Race Relations
collection contains books, pamphlets, letters,
and manuscripts dealing with Southern
problems with the Negro and the subject of
race generally.
PA —BALCH INSTITUTE FOR ETHNIC
STUDIES, Library, 18 S Seventh St,
Philadelphia, 19106. R Joseph Anderson,
Library Dir
Holdings: Vols 100 Cat

RACE IMPROVEMENT see Eugenics

RACE RELATIONS

CA —HOOVER INSTITUTION ON WAR,
REVOLUTION & PEACE, Stanford
University, Stanford, 94305. Milorad M
Drachkovitch, Archivist
Holdings: // Mss
Notes: Records, 1923-1935, on the Survey of
Race Relations at Stanford University,
California. Materials relating to studies on
acculturation patterns of minority groups
on the Pacific coast. The survey attempted a
complete investigation of the economic,
religious, educational, civic, biological, and
social conditions and tendencies prevailing
among the Chinese, Japanese, and other
nonwhite residents of the Pacific coast area
of the US and Canada. 37 boxes.
Unpublished preliminary inventory in the
repository.
IL —NORTHWESTERN UNIVERSITY,
Melville J Herskovits Library of African
Studies, Evanston, 60201. Hans E Panofsky,
Cur
Notes: Historical material and race relations
interpreted very broadly. Also, the
collections of papers assembled by Dennis
Brutus and Gwendolen M Carter.
MO —SAINT LOUIS POLICE LIBRARY,
315 S Tucker Blvd, Saint Louis, 63102.
Cathy Reilly, Librn
Holdings: Vols (21,000) Cat Mss Pix
Microforms
Budget: ($18,400)
Notes: Library on all subjects of police work
is open to the public for general reference
use.
NC —DUKE UNIVERSITY, William R
Perkins Library, Durham, 27706. Elvin E
Strowd, University Librn
Notes: The Race and Race Relations

RACE RELATIONS (cont.)

collection contains books, pamphlets, letters, and manuscripts dealing with Southern problems with the Negro and the subject of race generally.

PA —BALCH INSTITUTE FOR ETHNIC STUDIES, Library, 18 S Seventh St, Philadelphia, 19106. R Joseph Anderson, Library Dir
Holdings: Vols 100 Cat

PA —FRIENDS HISTORICAL LIBRARY OF SWARTHMORE COLLEGE, Swarthmore, 19081. J William Frost, Dir
Holdings: Vols (31,340) Cat Mss Maps Pix Slides Microforms Newspapers Broadsides
Notes: Incl material on all branches of Friends. History, faith, practice, biography, journals from beginning of Quaker movement in England. Concerns of Friends are incl: peace, race relations, Indians, social problems, temperance, education. Records of many Friends' meetings are on deposit.

WA —UNIVERSITY OF WASHINGTON LIBRARIES, Suzzallo Library, Manuscripts Section, FM-25, Seattle, 98195. Karyl Winn, Librn
Holdings: Mss
Notes: Personal papers and organizational records with emphasis on Pacific Northwest history and recent focus on twentieth century Western Washington. Holdings pertain to urban problems and policies, labor history, women's history, natural resource development, environmental politics, race relations, ethnic history, oral hsitory, and the arts. Holdings are complemented by textual records in the University Archives (7045 linear feet) and by graphic and printed holdings in the Pacific Northwest Collection. Described in *Comprehensive Guide to the Manuscripts Collection and to Personal Papers in the University Archives*, 1980 and in *Historical Records of Washington State: Records and Papers Held at Repositories*, 1981 and in unpublished inventories to most accessions. 15,981 linear feet of manuscripts.

RACES OF THE WORLD see Ethnology

RACHMANINOFF, SERGEI

DC —LIBRARY OF CONGRESS, Music Division, Washington, 20540.
Holdings: Cat Mss Maps Pix Slides Microforms

RACHOW, LOUIS A.

CT —LEE ASH, (personal collection), 66 Humiston Dr, Bethany, 06525.
Holdings: Cat Mss Pix
Notes: Mss, notes, letters, pictures, memorabilia, ephemera, etc.

RACIAL AMALGAMATION see Miscegenation

RACIAL AWARENESS see Race Awareness

RACIAL CROSSING see Miscegenation

RACIAL DISCRIMINATION see Race Discrimination

RACIAL SEGREGATION AND DESEGREGATION see Segregation and Desegregation

RACINE, JEAN BAPTISTE

CA —UNIVERSITY OF CALIFORNIA, LOS ANGELES, William Andrews Clark Memorial Library, 2520 Cimarron St, Los Angeles, 90018.
Holdings: Cat
Notes: Original editions.

RACING, AUTOMOBILE see Automobile Racing

RACKHAM, ARTHUR

CA —LOS ANGELES PUBLIC LIBRARY, Children's Literature Dept, 630 W 5th St,

Los Angeles, 90071. Serenna Day, Sr Librn
Holdings: Vols (2120) Cat Phonorecords Filmstrips
Notes: Also includes reference collection, covering some 50 years of published folklore and modern fairy tales. Includes extensive Mother Goose collection, examples of the work of such outstanding illustrators as Edmund Dulac and Arthur Rackham. Many volumes out of print. Index to titles of stories in collection.

CT —CONNECTICUT COLLEGE, Library, Mohegan Ave, New London, 06320. Brian Rogers, College Librn
Holdings: Vols 80 Uncat Mss Pix
Notes: The Arthur Rackham collection is part of the Helen Gildersleeve Collection of Children's Literature. Incl limited, signed editions; also one watercolor (1890). No photocopying.

KY —UNIVERSITY OF LOUISVILLE, Ekstrom Library, Rare Books & Special Collections, 2301 S Third St, Louisville, 40208. George T McWhorter, Cur; Delinda Stephens Buie, Asst Cur
Holdings: Vols 550 Cat Mss Pix
Budget: $600
Notes: Limited, signed first editions, trade editions, original drawings and watercolors, mss, periodical contributions, bibliographical materials, photographs and related materials. Partially cataloged.

NY —COLUMBIA UNIVERSITY LIBRARIES, Rare Book & Manuscript Library, 801 Butler Library, 535 W 114 St, New York, 10027. Kenneth A Lohf, Librn
Holdings: Mss Pix
Notes: Incl sketch books, notebooks, drafts, etc. Probably the most extensive collection in existence. 800 items. Restricted use.

PA —FREE LIBRARY OF PHILADELPHIA, Rare Book Dept, Logan Sq, Philadelphia, 19103. Marie E Korey, Rare Book Librn
Holdings: Cat Mss Pix
Notes: The Grace Clark Haskell Collection, with additions, containig 500 pieces of original art, autograph letters, books and periodicals illustrated by Arthur Rackham.

†TX —UNIVERSITY OF TEXAS LIBRARIES, General Libraries, Humanities Research Center, PO Box 7219, Austin, 78712. John Chalmers, Librn

RACKOWE, ALEC

MA —BOSTON UNIVERSITY, Mugar Memorial Library, Special Collections Dept, 771 Commonwealth Ave, Boston, 02215. Howard B Gotlieb, Dir
Holdings: Cat Mss Correspondence

RADAR

MA —MASSACHUSETTS INSTITUTE OF TECHNOLOGY, Research Laboratory of Electronics, Document Room 36-412, Cambridge, 02139. J E Woore, Head
Holdings: Vols (15,000)
Notes: Incl World War II technical reports on radar. Current electromagnetism and electronic engineering radar, etc.

MA —MASSACHUSETTS INSTITUTE OF TECHNOLOGY, Lincoln Laboratory, Library, 244 Wood St, Lexington, 02173. Jane H Katayama, Library Mgr
Holdings: Vols (70,000) Cat
See also entry under Communications Research

†VA —GEORGE C MARSHALL RESEARCH FOUNDATION AND LIBRARY, Drawer 920, Lexington, 24450. Royster Lyle Jr, Cur Collections
Holdings: Vols Uncat Mss
Notes: Items on secret writing and signaling, radar, telephony and telegraphy, and the study of the Shakespeare-Bacon authorship controversy.

RADIATA see Echinodermata

RADIATION

CA —UNIVERSITY OF CALIFORNIA, BERKELEY, Bancroft Library, Manuscripts Division, Berkeley, 94720. James D Hart, Dir
Notes: Extensive collections of papers and

archives relative to the history of modern physics and chemistry.

CA —UNIVERSITY OF CALIFORNIA, LOS ANGELES, Engineering & Mathematical Sciences Library, 405 Hilgard, Los Angeles, 90024. Rosalee I Wright, Librn
Notes: Collection includes WMO publications (comprehensive); IGY data series on surface observations, radiosonde and rawinsonde observations, upper wind observations, and radiation data (mostly in microform); selected government report or data series, eg from NOAA, NCC and AF Geophysics Laboratory.

CA —UNIVERSITY OF CALIFORNIA, LOS ANGELES, Biomedical Library, Center for the Health Sciences, Los Angeles, 90024. Alison Bunting, Acting Biomedical Librn; Victoria Steele, Head, History & Special Collections Div
Holdings: Vols (400,000) Cat Slides Phonorecords Audiotapes Videotapes 16mm Films Microforms

Notes: The UCLA Biomedical Library serves primarily the Schools of Medicine, Dentistry, Nursing, and Public Health, the UCLA Medical Center, the Departments of Microbiology and Biology in the College of Letters and Science, and related institutes in biomedicine. The collections of the Library are broad in scope, designed not only to support the teaching and research needs of its many users, but also to function as a resource for the health sciences-biological field as a whole. The outstanding feature of the collection is the strength of its periodical holdings, both current and retrospective. The Library also has an excellent reference collection, a comprehensive historical section, and gives special emphasis to the fields of neuroscience, psychiatry, ophthalmology, radiation biology, molecular biology, and vertebrate zoology. Increased emphasis is being given to the acquisition of audiovisual materials.

IL —ARGONNE NATIONAL LABORATORY, Biological and Medical Research Branch Library, 9700 S Cass Ave, Argonne, 60439. Rebecca Smith, Librn
Notes: Incl 14,000 vols monographs, 250 current journals. Materials may be used by the public in the library by prior arrangement. Photocopies may be supplied for interlibrary loan, for which a processing and handling charge is made.

ON —ATOMIC ENERGY OF CANADA LIMITED, Main Library, Technical Information Branch, Chalk River Nuclear Laboratories, Chalk River, K0J 1J0, Can. Harry Greenshields, Chief Librn
Holdings: Vols (128,700) Microforms
Budget: ($662,400)
Notes: The Main Library, Atomic Energy of Canada Limited, is the Canadian repository for the literature of nuclear science and technology. Its collections reflect both fundamental and nuclear aspects of biology, chemistry, electronics, engineering, mathematics, computers, metallurgy, physics and other specific areas of science involving nuclear technology with special emphasis on heavy water reactor systems. 512,000 research reports are available in paper copy and microfiche form. Incl US DOE, INIS and other offshore nuclear research reports. 386,000 microforms.

RADIATION—EFFECTS

KY —UNIVERSITY OF KENTUCKY, Robert E Shaver Library of Engineering, 355 Anderson Hall, Lexington, 40506. Russell H Powell, Engineering Librn
Holdings: Vols (48,000) Cat Microforms

RADIATION—PHYSIOLOGICAL EFFECTS

IL —ARGONNE NATIONAL LABORATORY, Biological and Medical Research Branch Library, 9700 S Cass Ave, Argonne, 60439. Rebecca Smith, Librn
Holdings: Vols (14,000)
Notes: Monographs, 250 current journals. Materials may be used by the public in the library by prior arrangement. Photocopies may be supplied for interlibrary loan, for which a processing and handling charge is made.

MD —US ARMED FORCES RADIOBIOLOGY RESEARCH INSTITUTE, Naval Medical Command, Bethesda, 20014. Nannette M Pope, Head, Library Division
Holdings: Vols (50,000)
Budget: ($150,000)
Notes: Collection consists of monographs, technical reports, serials, and microfiche related to radiation effects on human and animal biology.

MA —MASSACHUSETTS INSTITUTE OF TECHNOLOGY, Institute Archives, Special Collections, Cambridge, 02139.
Holdings: Mss
Notes: The Robley Evans papers, etc.

TX —US AIR FORCE, School of Aerospace Medicine, Strughold Aeromedical Library, Brooks AFB, 78235. Fred W Todd, Chief Librn
Holdings: Vols (119,188) Cat Mss Maps Pix Microforms
Notes: Aviation and space medicine and physiology, including the physiological effects of altitude and decompression. Biomedical and and human engineering. Military medicine, including chemical and biological warfare. Emergency medicine in both professional and technical areas. Radiobiology, including atomic medicine, nuclear medicine, and space radiation. Material not oriented to the School of Aerospace Medicine are excluded. Incl also 45,787 microforms and 142,371 technical documents.

RADIATION—SAFETY MEASURES

CA —UNIVERSITY OF CALIFORNIA, LOS ANGELES, Engineering & Mathematical Sciences Library, 405 Hilgard, Los Angeles, 90024. Rosalee I Wright, Librn
Notes: Complete depository of unclassified technical reports from AEC, ERDA, and DOE; selected IAEA publications, NRC dockets.

KY —UNIVERSITY OF KENTUCKY, Robert E Shaver Library of Engineering, 355 Anderson Hall, Lexington, 40506. Russell H Powell, Engineering Librn
Holdings: Vols (48,000) Cat Microforms

ON —ONTARIO MINISTRY OF LABOUR, Library, 400 University Ave, Toronto, M7A 1T7, Can. Jean Collins-Williams, Librn
Holdings: Vols (80,000) Microforms Films

RADIATION, GRAVITATIONAL see Gravitational Radiation

RADIATION, SOLAR see Solar Radiation

RADIATION BIOLOGY see Radiobiology

RADIATION ECOLOGY see Radioecology

RADIATION FIELD PHOTOGRAPHY see Kirlian Photography

RADICAL PERIODICALS see Periodicals, Radical

RADICALS AND RADICALISM

AZ —NORTHERN ARIZONA UNIVERSITY, Special Collection Library, CU Box 6022, Flagstaff, 86011. Peter M Whiteley, Coordr/Archivist; William Mullane, Librn
Holdings: Vols 9000 Cat Mss Phonorecords

Microforms
Notes: The large Allderdice Collection of thousands of books, pamphlets, periodicals, and organizational files reflects the conservative, communist, socialist, facist, anarchist, and other viewpoints, etc, during the 20th century. Also, papers, 1897-1964. Microfilm collection, also part of the Allderdice Collection.

CA —GRADUATE THEOLOGICAL UNION LIBRARY, New Religious Movements Research Collection, Public Services and Special Collections Dept, 2400 Ridge Road, Berkeley, 94709. Diane Choquette, Dept Head
Holdings: Vols (3000) Mss Pix
Notes: Begun in 1977, the collection focuses on religious movements new to America since 1960, and unorthodox religious movements resurgent since 1960. American forms of Hinduism, Buddhism, Sikhism, and Sufism are included along with occultism, Neo-Paganism, esoteric and alternative forms of Christianity, feminist spirituality, and human potential movements having a spiritual aspect. Legal issues, such as deprogramming, and the question of church/ state relations are an important part of the collection. The Library is a depository for publications of the Unification Church in America, the Church of Scientology, and the International Society for Krishna Consciousness (America). The responses of mainstream religions and concerned citizens groups are also included. Besides 3000 monographs, the library has 400 periodical titles, 200 posters from the San FranciscoBay Area, 1965-77, 300 research papers, and 31 linear feet of ephemera.

CA —UNIVERSITY OF CALIFORNIA, DAVIS, Shields Library, Dept of Special Collections, Davis, 95616. Donald Kunitz, Head; C Danial Elliott, Asst Head
Holdings: Vols 6500 Cat
Notes: Overview of American political movements from the 1890s to the present: socialism, communism, labor, to ecology and women's liberation.

CA —CALIFORNIA STATE UNIVERSITY, LONG BEACH, Library, Dept of Special Collections & Archives, 1250 Bellflower Blvd, Long Beach, 90840. John Ahouse, Special Collections Librn
Holdings: // Cat Pix
Notes: Dorothy Healey Collection of pamphlets, clippings, books and articles on radical politics, especially in Southern California.

CA —SOUTHERN CALIFORNIA LIBRARY FOR SOCIAL STUDIES & RESEARCH, 6120 S Vermont Ave, Los Angeles, 90044. Sarah Cooper, Dir
Holdings: Vols (15,000) Mss Maps Pix Slides Phonorecords Audiotapes 16mm Films
Budget: ($30,000)
Notes: Marxist, non-Marxist and anti-Marxist approaches to social change. Other important functions of the library: to make available source materials to those engaged in the Marxist vs no-Marxist dialog; to aid historians, economists, sociologists, writers, students and labor organizations researching the history of grassroots social movements; and to preserve primary and secondary sources on labor, minorities, women and radicalism. Collection incl 50 mss, 75 maps, 500 pictures, 1000 slides, 100 phonorecords, 2000 audiotapes, 50 16mm films and 150, 000 newspaper clippings.

CA —HOOVER INSTITUTION ON WAR, REVOLUTION & PEACE, Stanford University, Stanford, 94305. Milorad M Drachkovitch, Archivist
Holdings: // Mss
Notes: Two collections (1) Papers, 1913-1918, of Rosa Luxemburg, German revolutionist. Letters and postcards from Mrs Luxemburg to her secretary Mathilde Jacob, diary (1915, 1917-1918), and letters from Mathilde Jacob to Karl Liebknecht, Franz Mehring and Clara Zetkin. 2 boxes. Unpublished preliminary inventory in repository. (2) Records of National Republic Magazine, incl newspaper clippings, printed matter, pamphlets, reports, indices, notes, bulletins, lettergrams, weekly letters, and

photographs, 1905-1960, relating to pacifist, communist, fascist, and other radical movements as well as political developments in the US and Soviet Russia. 826 ms boxes.

CA —HOOVER INSTITUTION ON WAR, REVOLUTION & PEACE, Stanford University, Stanford, 94305. Milorad M Drachkovitch, Archivist
Notes: The New Left Politics Collection consists of monographs and serials on the New Left that are cataloged. In addition, the collection subscribes to numerous underground newspapers and has obtained special subject collections such as the Free Speech Movement at Berkeley 1964-1965, SNCC and Mississippi Summer 1964, and the insurrection at San Francisco State College in 1968-1969. There is also a good collection on the French student revolts of 1968. The collection is a supervised one and not open to browsers. Interested students and scholars are welcome. Only limited photocopying is permitted.

CT —UNIVERSITY OF CONNECTICUT, Library, Storrs, 06268. Ellen Embardo, Cur Special Collections
Holdings: Cat
Notes: Alternative Press Collection. Primarily periodicals and newspapers from the 1960s to today of an alternative or underground nature. Books and pamphlets are incl, representing both the left and the right-wing viewpoints. A catalog is available. Also have archives of the First Casualty Press, which was deeply involved with Vietnam veterans' experiences in Vietnam, as well as the Fat Liberation Movement.

DC —LIBRARY OF CONGRESS, Rare Book & Special Collections Div, Washington, 20540. William Matheson, Chief
Notes: The collection spans the years 1870-1980 but is especially rich for the period 1930-1949. Incl are pamphlets, newspapers, periodicals, broadsides, posters, cartoons, sheet music, and prints relating to American communism, socialism, and anarchism. Incl 2000 items.

DC —LIBRARY OF CONGRESS, Manuscript Division, Washington, 20540. John C Broderick, Chief
Notes: Papers of Hannah Arendt; now unrestricted, except for the Judah L Magnes correspondence.

DC —LIBRARY OF CONGRESS, Washington, 20540.
Notes: Some 4500 pamphlets and sheets dealing primarily with subversive and radical activities in the US from 1900 to 1950. Incl tracts and campaign literature of the Communist and Socialist Parties in the US and works by party leaders; materials on the economic, political, and human rights issues of the pre-World War II, World War II, and early civil rights campaign periods; and pamphlets by various anti-war and anti-communist movement in other countries.

DC —LIBRARY OF CONGRESS, General Reading Rooms Division, Microform Reading Room, Washington, 20540.
Holdings: Cat Mss Maps Pix Microforms
Notes: Microform materials only in this LC Division. Works of individual authors; holdings of collections; archival records, etc, press releases and translations, etc.

DC —LIBRARY OF CONGRESS, Prints & Photographs Div, Washington, 20540.
Notes: The Gary Yonker Collection of political propaganda posters, late 1960s to present. Strongest for US materials but incl about 50 other countries' work. Over 4500 items, arranged geographically.

DC —LIBRARY OF CONGRESS, Music Division, Washington, 20540.
Notes: Musical aspects of the revolutionary workers' movement represented in the Workers Music League's publications and activities; also, the Composers' Collective, etc.

†DC —LIBRARY OF CONGRESS, Rare Book Division, Washington, 20540.
Notes: A collection of considerable strength.

GA —EMORY UNIVERSITY, Robert W Woodruff Library, Atlanta, 30322. Herbert Johnson, Dir
Holdings: Mss Cat
Notes: A collection of materials relating to

RADICALS AND RADICALISM (cont.)

the history of the Communist Party in the US and the Communist International, gathered by author Theodore Draper. Incl periodicals, pamphlets, party documents, and books, as well as taped interviews that Draper conducted with party leaders and correspondence relating to his research. 80 linear ft mss.

HI —HAWAII PACIFIC COLLEGE, Meader Library, 1060 Bishop St, Honolulu, 96813. Barbara Burton Hoefler, Head Librn
Holdings: Vols 900 Cat
Notes: Un-American activities represented by history, biography, political science, and fiction.

IL —SOUTHERN ILLINOIS UNIVERSITY, CARBONDALE, Delyte W Morris Library, Special Collections Dept, Carbondale, 62901. David V Koch, Cur of Special Collections; Louisa Bowen, Cur of Manuscripts
Holdings: Cat Mss
Notes: Papers and correspondence of Theodore A Schroeder, constitutional lawyer and founder, with Lincoln Steffens, of the Free Speech League, a forerunner of the American Civil Liberties Union. Contains extensive correspondence with Comstock, Gompers, Debs, H Ellis, Sanger, Sinclair, John Dewey, Darrow, Mencken, A G Hays, Emma Goldman, W E B DuBois, etc. Incl several thousand letters; notes and mss, records of legal cases and extensive files relating to the early history of psychiatry.

IL —CHICAGO HISTORICAL SOCIETY, Library, Clark St at North Ave, Chicago, 60614. Archie Motley, Manuscript Librn
Notes: Civil liberties and radical history holdings incl these papers: Alliance to End Repression, Chicago; Chicago Committee to Defend the Bill of Rights; Polly Connelly (Marxist activist in political, social, labor, and women's affairs); Sidney Lens (author, Marxist, international peace movement, political and social activist; trade union official); Midwest Committee for Protection of Foreign Born (an affiliate of the American Committee for Protection of Foreign Born).

IL —NEWBERRY LIBRARY, 60 W Walton St, Chicago, 60610. Diana Haskell, Cur of Modern Mss
Holdings: Cat
Notes: 19th century American.

IL —NORTHERN ILLINOIS UNIVERSITY, Founders Memorial Library, Rare Books and Special Collections Dept, De Kalb, 60115. William R DuBois, Dept Head
Holdings: Vols (1350) // Cat
Notes: American, British and Soviet pamphlet publications, ca 1860-1955 by or about the radical labor movement, socialists, communists and the radical right. Some Nazi/anti-Nazi material. Collection is computer-indexed by author, title, series, publisher and date.

IL —NORTHWESTERN UNIVERSITY, Library, Special Collections Dept, 1937 Sheridan Rd, Evanston, 60201. R Russell Maylone, Cur
Holdings: Vols (14,000) Cat
Notes: Periodicals and pamphlets concerning many social and political movements in the 20th century, with emphasis on anarchism, struggles of the working class, women's rights, and student protest of the 1960's. Foreign material incl. An additional 10,000 pieces arranged by subject.

IL —UNIVERSITY OF ILLINOIS, URBANA/CHAMPAIGN, Library, Illinois Historical Survey Library, 1408 W Gregory Dr, 1A Library, Urbana, 61801.
Holdings: Vols 50 Cat Mss Pix Microforms
Notes: Important ms collections on the labor movement and radicalism incl: Adolph Germer, papers, 1918, 1928, 1930-31, 44 folders; Thomas J Morgan, 1880-1910, 64 folders, 19 vols; John H Walker, papers, 1910-1955, 66 boxes. Guide to the collections published in 1976.

IN —INDIANA STATE UNIVERSITY, Cunningham Memorial Library, Dept of Rare Books & Special Collections, Terre Haute, 47809. Lawrence J McCrank, Head
Holdings: Uncat Mss Pix
Budget: ($1350)
Notes: The Debs Collection consists of

aprox 7000 pieces of correspondence between Theodore Debs (brother of E V) and other persons, such as Sinclair Lewis, Upton Sinclair, Ethel Barrymore, Emma Goldman, Robert G Ingersoll, Carl Sandburg, Norman Thomas, Sacco and Vanzetti and many others. Many of the letters are from E V Debs to his brother; a good portion of these are from the federal penitentiary at Atlanta. Entire correspondence file has been microfilmed. 750 pamphlets cover all aspects of the labor movement, socialism and radical thought from the 19th century to appprox 1950. A collection ca 200 related books is also housed in the collection. See: J Robert Constantine and Gail Malmgreen, eds, *The Papers of Eugene V Debs, 1834-1945. A Guide to the Microfilm Edition.* NY: Microfilming Corp of America, 1983 (University Microfilms is the new distributer).

KS —UNIVERSITY OF KANSAS, Kenneth Spencer Research Library, Kansas Collection, Lawrence, 66045. Sheryl K Williams, Cur
Holdings: Vols 6000 Cat Mss Audiotapes
Notes: The Wilcox Collection of Contemporary Political Movements containing American extremist literature from the 1950s to the present, and incl appox 4000 serials, 5000 books and pamplets, 400 audiotapes, and 50,000 pieces of ephemera. Approximately 7000 right and left wing organizations are represented by this material as well as the views of many leaders or prime movers within these organizations. The collection is partially cataloged.

KS —WICHITA STATE UNIVERSITY, Ablah Library, Box 68, Wichita, 67208. Michael T Kelly, Cur of Special Collections
Holdings: Vols Cat Pamphlets

LA —TULANE UNIVERSITY, Howard-Tilton Memorial Library, Special Collections Div, 7001 Freret St, New Orleans, 70118. Wilbur E Meneray, Librn
Holdings: Cat Audiotapes Microforms
Notes: Books, pamphlets, serial publications and circulars from over 2000 individuals and organizations representing the fringe of 20th century US political opinion.

MD —UNIVERSITY OF MARYLAND, BALTIMORE COUNTY, Albin O Kuhn Library and Gallery, 5401 Wilkens Ave, Baltimore, 21228. Ann Copeland, Special Collections Librn
Holdings: Vols 1000 // Uncat
Notes: The Hugh Davis Graham papers relate to Dr Graham's work as Co-Director of the Task Force on the History of Violence in America (for the National Commission on the Causes and Prevention of Violence). The Collection consists of materials dealing with all aspects of violence as well as movements specifically related to the 1960s ("Ban the Bomb," etc). The collection is topically arranged and available for research use. Also, more than 1000 pamphlets and broadsides on communism, fascism, Trotskyism, socialism, etc.

MA —HARVARD UNIVERSITY LIBRARY, Cambridge, 02138.
Holdings: Cat

MA —HARVARD UNIVERSITY LIBRARY, Law School Library, Langdell Hall, Cambridge, 02138. Erika S Chadbourn, Cur of Mss
Notes: Legal documents, pictorial material, microfilms. Incl holograph letters of Sacco and Vanzetti, 1920-1928. Typed chronological list in repository.

MA —BRANDEIS UNIVERSITY, Goldfarb Library, 415 South St, Waltham, 02154. Bessie Hahn, Dir
Notes: Hall-Hoag Archives on Extremism in the U.S. Approx 5000 pieces of Extremist literature, both Right and Left, dealing with various social, religious and political aspects of the US from the 1960s, 1970s and 1980s. A finding list is in Special Collections. Material is arranged by the name of the sponsoring organization in alphabetical order. In addition, the Radical pamphlet collection. Approx 5000 pamphlets from the 1920s through the 1950s dealing with

socialism and communism in the US and Great Britain. There is an author-title card catalog to ca 500 of the items in the Special Collections Card Catalog. Also, the Sacco and Vanzetti Case Collection, 23 linear feet of material collected by both Tom O'Connor and Francis Russell relating to this celebrated American trial. This collection is unprocessed, spring 1984.

MI —UNIVERSITY OF MICHIGAN, Dept of Rare Books & Special Collections, Ann Arbor, 48109. Edward C Weber, Head, Labadie Collection
Holdings: Vols (40,000) Cat Mss Pix Phonorecords Audiotapes Microforms
Notes: Almost entirely radicalism from the 19th century to the present, with strongest holdings in US history. Populism, however, is almost completely excluded. Also, the Labadie Collection of radical materials, containing papers, tracts, handbills, and publications of minority political and social reform organizations from the mid-1800s to the present, incl 8000 serial titles and 20,000 uncataloged pamphlets. Also ms collections of the papers of Mary Hayes Weik, William A Reuben, and the American Committee for the Protection of the Foreign Born.

MI —MICHIGAN STATE UNIVERSITY, Libraries, Special Collections Div, East Lansing, 48824. Jannette Fiore, Librn
Holdings: Vols (10,500) Cat Mss
Notes: Published and unpublished material generated by (1) American left and right, 1900, (2) the New Left, 1969-1970, and (3) current left, right, and alternate life-style groups. (Supported by appropriate secondary material in the Research Library). Also have in microform radical pamphlet literature from the Tamiment Library (New York University), the Right Wing Collection of the University of Iowa, et al.

NY —NEW YORK UNIVERSITY, Elmer Holmes Bobst Library, Div of Special Collections, Tamiment Library of Labor History, Washington Sq, New York, 10012. Dorothy Swanson, Librn
Holdings: Cat Mss Maps Pix Microforms
Notes: Books, pamphlets, newspapers, periodicals and mss. Large microfilm collection. Described in Daniel Bell's *The Tamiment Library* (1969), available free from the Tamiment librarian, and *Elmer Holmes Bobst Library Information Bulletin 8* (updated periodically).

NY —STATE UNIVERSITY OF NEW YORK, STONY BROOK, Melville Library, Dept of Special Collections, Stony Brook, 11794. Evert Volkersz, Head
Holdings: // Uncat
Notes: Radical Education Project. About 120 pamphlets.

NC —UNIVERSITY OF NORTH CAROLINA, CHARLOTTE, J Murrey Atkins Library, UNCC Station, Charlotte, 28223. Robert F Brabham Jr, Special Collections Librn
Holdings: Mss Pix Cat
Notes: Incl pamphlets, newspapers, and ephemera published by various radical groups, 1960s and 1970s, based largely in the Midwest; also papers of T J Reddy, a member of the Charlotte 3, concerning civil rights, the Wilmington 10, and prison reforms.

NC —DUKE UNIVERSITY, William R Perkins Library, Durham, 27706. Elvin E Strowd, University Librn
Notes: The (Quasi)-Nazi collection consists of approximately 7000 items, primarily pamphlets published in the United States by and about Nazi sympathizers Gerald K Smith, Father Coughlin, etc and organizations with Nazi leanings.

NC —DUKE UNIVERSITY, William R Perkins Library, Manuscript Dept, Durham, 27706. Ellen Gartrell, Cur of Mss
Holdings: Cat Mss
Notes: Diverse holdings incl Socialist Party of America Papers, 1900-76 (240,000 items); J B Matthews' extensive files on liberals and radicals, 1930s-60s; papers of mainly conservative southern politicians; Ku Klux Klan papers.

OK —UNIVERSITY OF TULSA, McFarlin Library, Dept of Rare Books and Special

RADICALS AND RADICALISM (cont.)

Collections, 600 S College, Tulsa, 74104.
David Farmer, Dir; Toby Murray, Archivist;
Caroline Swinson, Cur of Manuscripts & Art
Holdings: Vols 2000
Notes: A major collection of Proletarian
literature based on Walter Rideout's *The
Radical Novel in the United States,
1900-1954.*

PA —BALCH INSTITUTE FOR ETHNIC
STUDIES, Library, 18 S Seventh St,
Philadelphia, 19106. R Joseph Anderson,
Library Dir
Holdings: Cat Microforms
Notes: Espec in the US and Canada.

PA —TEMPLE UNIVERSITY, Samuel Paley
Library, Berks & 13 Sts, Philadelphia, 19122.
Notes: Archives of the magazine, *Seven
Days,* which first appeared in 1975 and was
considered the succesor of *Ramparts.*
Leading editor was David Dellinger, one of
the defendants in the Chicago Conspiracy
Trail. Incl office files, correspondence,
editorial files, and a selection of Dellinger's
papers relating to *Seven Days.*

PA —TEMPLE UNIVERSITY LIBRARIES,
Special Collections Dept, Contemporary
Culture Collection, Philadelphia, 19122.
Patricia J Case, Cur
Notes: The Contemporary Culture
Collection. See full entry under US-Social
Life and Customs.

PA —UNIVERSITY OF PITTSBURGH,
Hillman Library, Pittsburgh, 15260. Glenora
E Rossell, Head
Holdings: Vols 3000 Cat Microforms
Notes: Social and political history of Latin
America in the 20th century with emphasis
on revolutionary and radical movements,
and social change.

WI —UNIVERSITY OF WISCONSIN,
GREEN BAY, Library/Learning Center,
Green Bay, 54301. Marian A Gould, Acting
Dir, Special Collections/University Archives
Holdings: Vols 700 // Cat
Notes: This represents the collection of Leon
Kramer, "idealist, philosophical anarchist and
bookseller." Much of the material concerns
radical literature and small socialist and
communist parties in the US, although there
is a considerable amount of books, booklets,
and pamphlets published in Germany, Italy,
and other parts of Europe. Incl uncounted
pamphlets.

WI —STATE HISTORICAL SOCIETY OF
WISCONSIN, Archives, 816 State St,
Madison, 53706. Harold L Miller, Reference
Archivist
Holdings: Mss Pix Microforms
Notes: Records and papers documenting the
history of the labor and Socialist movements
in the United States from 1850s to the
present. Incl are records of labor and
socialist organizations incl American
Federation of Labor and the Socialist Labor
Party, and papers of individual labor and
socialist leaders such as Morris Hillquit and
John L Lewis. Collections are described in *A
Guide to Labor Papers in the State
Historical Society of Wisconsin* (1978) and
in current accession notes in the *Wisconsin
Magazine of History.* Major collections are
also listed in Hamer, *Guide to Manuscripts
and Archives in the United States,* (1961)
and in the *National Union Catalog of
Manuscript Collections,* (1959-date).

WI —UNIVERSITY OF WISCONSIN,
MADISON, Memorial Library, Slavic
Studies Collection, 728 State St, Madison,
53706. Aleksander Rolich, Bibliographer for
Slavic Studies; Robert P Gakovich, Slavic
Cataloger; Valdis J Zeps, Baltic Studies
Center
Holdings: Vols (1000) Cat
Notes: The Komadinich Collection in
Serbian and Yogoslav social and political
history embraces publications and pamphlets
of peasant, socialist and other radical
movements of the last half of the nineteenth
century up to World War II. It consists of
some 1000 items mostly in Serbo-Croatian,
and represents only part of the private
library acquired from the survivors of Milan
Komadinic (1882-1944).

WI —UNIVERSITY OF WISCONSIN,
MADISON, Memorial Library, Rare Books
Collection, 728 State St, Madison, 53706.
Gretchen Lagana, Cur
Holdings: Uncat Pix Microforms
Notes: A collection of pamphlets, posters,
and miscellaneous materials produced by
students and other left-wing groups in
France during the revolt of May-June 1968.
Also included are books on the event and
pictures taken by a UW student in Paris at
the time. Collection partly described in *UW
Library News,* vol 13 (Dec 1968), pp 1-8.
Housed in the Dept of Rare Books and
Special Collections.

WI —UNIVERSITY OF WISCONSIN,
MILWAUKEE, Library, Box 604,
Milwaukee, 53201. William C Roselle, Dir
Holdings: Vols 2500 Cat Mss Pix
Notes: Fromkin Memorial Collection,
emphasizing third party forces in American
politics. Restricted use: noncirculating.
Special subject catalog of pamphlet material.

ON —UNIVERSITY OF TORONTO, Thomas
Fisher Rare Book Library, 120 Saint George
St, Toronto, M5S 1A5, Can. Richard G
Landon, Head
Holdings: Vols 2500 Uncat Mss Pix
Phonorecords
Notes: Kenny Collection named for original
collector, Robert Kenny of Toronto. Chiefly
material on and by the Labor Progressive
Party and the Communist Party of Canada,
including their constitutions, reports of
national conventions, leaflets, posters,
election material, ephemera. Manuscript
material of A E Smith, Tim Buck and other
Canadian communists.

RADICALS AND
RADICALISM—FICTION

PA —BALCH INSTITUTE FOR ETHNIC
STUDIES, Library, 18 S Seventh St,
Philadelphia, 19106. R Joseph Anderson,
Library Dir
Holdings: Vols 850 Cat

RADIN, PAUL

NY —HOFSTRA UNIVERSITY, Library,
1000 Fulton Ave, Hempstead, 11550.
Charles R Andrews, Dean of Library
Services
Notes: The personal library of Paul Radin.
See description of the American
Philosophical Society Library's collection of
his anthropological papers under this entry
(Pa).

PA —AMERICAN PHILOSOPHICAL
SOCIETY, Library, 105 S Fifth St,
Philadelphia, 19106. Edward C Carter II,
Librn
Notes: The anthropological papers of Paul
Radin in fields of ethnology, social
organization, primitive religion, linguistics,
and mythology. He worked mostly amony
the Winnebago, Ojibwa, Fox, Zapotec,
Wappo, Wintun, and Huave Indian tribes;
also Italian and other ethnic minorities of
San Francisco.

RADIO

CA —LOS ANGELES PUBLIC LIBRARY,
Science & Technology Dept, 630 W Fifth St,
Los Angeles, 90071. Billie M Connor, Dept
Head
Holdings: Vols (12,000) Cat
Notes: Materials on the application of
electronic devices, circuits and systems in
various fields such as computers, automatic
control, sound productions and reproduction,
radio and telecommunications. Extensive
holdings of materials on computers,
peripherals, and software including many
texts pertaining to specific programming
languages. Complete collection of Howard
Sams schematics for radio television, and
other electronic equipment repair as well as
historical sets of Rider's Radio and
Television schematics.

CA —UNIVERSITY OF CALIFORNIA, LOS
ANGELES, Theater Arts Library, Los
Angeles, 90024. Edward Shreeves,

Chairman, Bibliographers Group; Audree
Malkin, Head, Theater Arts Library
Holdings: Vols (12,500)
Notes: Major research collections covering
the historical, critical, aesthetic, biographical
and technical aspects of film, television and
radio, and the non-book and primary source
material in these fields. Also 166,000
pamphlets, photographs, microforms and
sound recordings. Incl over 4,000,000
moving picture stills, over 32,636
screenplays, and scripts from American and
British Films. Incl 1740 radio scripts and a
collection of 3000 television scripts. Also
incl portraits, clippings files, film festival
programs, motion picture programs, lobby
cards, original sketches and production
materials; the personal and business papers,
records and correspondence of actors,
directors, producers, art directors and screen
and television writers. Incl 100,000 mss.
Extensive poster collection (over 7000, 1915
to date), many forPolish and Czech
productions. Limited photocopying.

CT —YALE UNIVERSITY, Box 1603A, Yale
Station, New Haven, 06520.
Notes: Papers of Lee De Forest.

IL —WHEATON COLLEGE, Buswell
Memorial Library, Wheaton, 60187. Paul
Snezek, Library Dir
Holdings: Mss
Notes: 5 linear feet of mss material and a
collection of cassette tapes of Mitchell.
Related Topics: Radio.

IN —BUTLER UNIVERSITY, Jordan College
of Music, Library, 4600 Sunset, Indianapolis,
46208. Phyllis J Schoonover, Librn
Holdings: Vols (5383) Cat
Budget: ($16,500)

MI —MICHIGAN STATE UNIVERSITY,
Libraries, Special Collections Div, East
Lansing, 48824. Jannette Fiore, Librn
Notes: The Russel B Nye Popular Culture
Collection in the Michigan State Univ
Libraries incl over (45,000) items. Most of
the collection is organized into 4 categories:
comic art, popular fiction, popular
information materials and materials relating
to the popular performing arts. Materials
relating to popular theatre, music, television,
radio, and film. Theatre is best represented.
A significant collection of primary materials
relating to the tent show incl photographs,
financial and other records of the Henderson
Stock Company, correspondence, leaflets,
handbills and other ephemera from many of
the companies playing in the upper midwest
in the 1920s and 1930s, and photocopies of
250 tent show scripts.

NY —NEW YORK PUBLIC LIBRARY,
Performing Arts Research Center, Billy Rose
Theatre Collection, 111 Amsterdam Ave,
New York, 10023. Dorothy L Swerdlove,
Cur

Holdings: Cat Pix
Notes: As early as 1941 the American Television
Society appointed the Theatre Collection the
official repository of their archives and urged its
members to deposit materials in the Collection.
The Collection maintains clipping files on radio
and television programs, and on the personnel of
these programs. It collects photographs of these
individuals, of television and radio studios,
equipment, etc. There is a collection of television
production scripts, with most of the "Hallmark
Hall of Fame" specials and "Studio One" scripts,
1948-1952. The collection of radio scripts incl.
material regarding the Radio Writers Guild of
America and also runs of several serials written by
Elaine Carrington. The book material incl. the
standard works on the history of broadcasting and
telecasting, vols. on the techniques of the industry.

RADIO (cont.)

*PERIODICAL FILES INCL. DOMESTIC
AND FOREIGN TRADE
PUBLICATIONS.

NY —ROCKEFELLER UNIVERSITY,
Rockefeller Archive Center, Hillcrest,
Pocantico Hills, North Tarrytown, 10591.
Joseph W Ernst, Dir; J William Hess, Assoc
Dir
Notes: Papers relative to the Rockefeller
Family, Foundations, University, and other
specific enterprises and contributions to
particular areas of social, physical,
educational, and historic reform,
preservation, conservation, or development.
Extensive records of administrative,
financial, physical, or intellectual
relationships.

NY —ELIZABETH SETON COLLEGE
LIBRARY, Yonkers, 10701. Sr Margaret
Sullivan, Librn

NY —YONKERS PUBLIC LIBRARY,
Information Services, 7 Main St, Yonkers,
10701. Martita Schwarz, Dept Head
Holdings: Vols (21,500) Cat Maps
Microforms
Budget: ($30,000)

NC —DUKE UNIVERSITY, William R
Perkins Library, Durham, 27706. Elvin E
Strowd, University Librn
Notes: Books, serials and pamphlets (2,820,
527); music scores (31,551); motion pictures
(285); microforms (1,055,627); tapes,
cassettes and phonorecords, the library is a
depository for Radio Canada International
recordings, (2289); and manuscripts, US
Government publications, maps, and
broadsides, additions in all formats are
ongoing.

OH —PUBLIC LIBRARY OF CINCINNATI
& HAMILTON COUNTY, Art & Music
Dept, 800 Vine St, Cincinnati, 45202. R
Jayne Craven, Head
Holdings: Vols (122,185) Cat Pix
Budget: ($56,100)
Notes: Special collections: Eda Kuhn Loeb,
"Artist and the Book, 1875-Date" (now
shelved in Rare Book Room); music librettos
(2345); exhibition catalogs (5474); large
prints and posters (5051); Cincinnati artists
vertical files; picture collection (673,906
clippings).

WI —STATE HISTORICAL SOCIETY OF
WISCONSIN, Archives, 816 State St,
Madison, 53706. Harold L Miller, Reference
Archivist
Holdings: Mss Pix Films Microforms
Notes: Areas represented in collection incl
radio, television, the press, public relations
and advertising. Emphasis is on development
of media in the 20th century; materials are
mainly professional papers of individuals or
organization or organizational records of
firms or associations in the media.
Collections are described in *Sources for
Mass Communications, Film and Theater
Research: A Guide,* (1982) and in current
accession notes in the *Wisconsin Magazine
of History.* Major collections are also listed
in Hamer, *Guide to Manuscripts and
Archives in the United States,* (1961) and in
the *National Union Catalog of Manuscripts
Collections,* (1959-date). Also incl, disc
recordings and tape recordings.

RADIO—APPARATUS AND SUPPLIES

DC —LIBRARY OF CONGRESS, Motion
Pictures, Broadcasting and Recorded Sound
Div, Washington, 20540.
Notes: Recordings, photographs,
correspondence, scrapbooks and other
memorabilia concerning the invention of the
lateral cut disc gramophone record, basis of
the modern recording industry, Emile
Berliner (1851-1929). Devised word
"Gramophone," and invented acoustic tiling.

RADIO—BROADCASTING see Radio Broadcasting

RADIO—HISTORY

CA —UNIVERSITY OF CALIFORNIA,
BERKELEY, Bancroft Library, Manuscripts

Division, Berkeley, 94720. James D Hart,
Dir
Holdings: Mss
Notes: Papers of Samuel Silver, specialist on
applied electromagnetic, microwave, and
radio astronomical problems. Much on the
International Union of Radio Science. 48
linear ft.
See also entry under Technology - History.

CA —ELECTRONICS MUSEUM, Foothill
College, DeForest Memorial Archives,
12345 El Monte Rd, Los Altos Hills, 94022.
Leonard M Lansdowne, Cur
Holdings: Vols 342 Cat Mss Pix Microforms
Notes: The collection was donated by Marie
de Forest, wife of the late Dr Lee De Forest,
known as the "Father of Radio". Awards of
Dr Lee de Forest, presented to him through
the years, are in the collection. The De
Forest mss and papers are cataloged and
microfilmed. Several file cabinets filled with
correspondence, dealing with business and
personal matters are to be cataloged and
microfilmed in the future.

CA —UNIVERSITY OF CALIFORNIA, LOS
ANGELES, Theater Arts Library, Los
Angeles, 90024. Edward Shreeves,
Chairman, Bibliographers Group; Audree
Malkin, Head, Theater Arts Library
Holdings: Vols (12,500)
Notes: Major research collections covering
the historical, critical, aesthetic, biographical
and technical aspects of film, television and
radio, and the non-book and primary source
material in these fields. Also 166,000
pamphlets, photographs, microforms and
sound recordings. Incl over 4,000,000
moving picture stills, over 32,636
screenplays, and scripts from American and
British Films. Incl 1740 radio scripts and a
collection of 3000 television scripts. Also
incl portraits, clippings files, film festival
programs, motion picture programs, lobby
cards, original sketches and production
materials; the personal and business papers,
records and correspondence of actors,
directors, producers, art directors and screen
and television writers. Incl 100,000 mss.
Extensive poster collection (over 7000, 1915
to date), many forPolish and Czech
productions. Limited photocopying.

†CA —SOCIETY OF WIRELESS PIONEERS
(COMMUNICATIONS), PO Box 530,
Santa Rosa, 95402.
Holdings: Vols (2500)
Notes: Museum of early communication
memorabilia and equiptment. Compiles
statistics on shipwrecks where wireless/radio
was involved.

DC —BROADCAST PIONEERS LIBRARY,
1771 N St NW, Washington, 20036.
Catharine Heinz, Dir
Holdings: Vols (6500) Uncat Pix
Phonorecords Audiotapes
Notes: Special collections: Oral History
(750); Havrilla (photos, radio performers);
William S Hedges Collection; Elmo Neale
Pickerill Collection; Joseph E Baudino
Collection; Archive of Federal
Communications Bar Association. Incl 20,
000 pictures, 1450 phonorecords and 1200
audiotapes.

DC —SMITHSONIAN INSTITUTION
LIBRARIES, National Museum of American
History Branch, Washington, 20560. Rhoda
S Ratner, Branch Librn
Holdings: Vols 1500 Cat Mss Pix
Notes: Radio and allied industries. Incl the
Clark Collection of Radioana. Bulk of
material is ms (not incl in vol count).

IN —INDIANA UNIVERSITY, Lilly Library,
Seventh St, Bloomington, 47405. William R
Cagle, Librn
Holdings: Vols (700) Cat Mss
Notes: Extensive collection of scripts. Ms
holdings incl the papers of Lance Sieveking,
BBC producer; Douglas Geoffrey Bridson,
BBC producer and writer; and Douglas
Cleverdon, producer. All three were most
closely connected with The Third Program.
Scripts for many of these programs are in
the collections as well as extensive
correspondence regarding programming.
See also entries under McGreevey, John;
Welles, Orson

†NY —ANTIQUE WIRELESS
ASSOCIATION, Electronic Communication

Museum, Main St, Holcomb, 14469. Bruce
Kelley, Curator
Holdings: Vols (2000)
Notes: Books on radio and electrical material
available for research for members of
association. 15,000 radio, television, and
electrical artifacts.

NY —NEW YORK PUBLIC LIBRARY,
Performing Arts Research Center, Billy Rose
Theatre Collection, 111 Amsterdam Ave,
New York, 10023. Dorothy L Swerdlove,
Cur
Holdings: Cat

NC —DUKE UNIVERSITY, William R
Perkins Library, Durham, 27706. Elvin E
Strowd, University Librn
Notes: Books, serials and pamphlets (2,820,
527); music scores (31,551); motion pictures
(285); microforms (1,055,627); tapes,
cassettes and phonorecords, the library is a
depository for Radio Canada International
recordings, (2289); and manuscripts, US
Government publications, maps, and
broadsides, additions in all formats are
ongoing.

OH —CLEVELAND PUBLIC LIBRARY,
Science & Technology Dept, 325 Superior
Ave, Cleveland, 44114. Jean Z Piety, Head
Holdings: Cat
Notes: Collection contains much on history
and many early and rare volumes.

UT —UNIVERSITY OF UTAH, Marriott
Library, Special Collections, Salt Lake City,
84112. Gregory C Thompson, Cur

ON —QUEEN'S UNIVERSITY, Douglas
Library, Kingston, K7L 5C4, Can. William F
E Morley, Cur, Special Collections
Holdings: Vols (1200) Cat Mss Pix
Notes: McNichol Collection. Books,
pamphlets, journals and ephemera. Origin
and growth to World War II of the
telegraphic, telephonic and radio sciences.
There is a printed catalog of this collection
as originally acquired: *Catalogue of the
McNichol Collection of Books on
Telegraphy, Telephony and Radio Contained
in the Douglas Library,* comp by Janet S
Porteous and edited by Marjorie Sherlock
(Kingston, 1942). Also, the Riche-Covington
Collection, printed catalog in press.

RADIO—REPAIRING

CA —LOS ANGELES PUBLIC LIBRARY,
Science & Technology Dept, 630 W Fifth St,
Los Angeles, 90071. Billie M Connor, Dept
Head
Holdings: Vols (12,000) Cat
Notes: Materials on the application of
electronic devices, circuits and systems in
various fields such as computers, automatic
control, sound productions and reproduction,
radio and telecommunications. Extensive
holdings of materials on computers,
peripherals, and software including many
texts pertaining to specific programming
languages. Complete collection of Howard
Sams schematics for radio television, and
other electronic equipment repair as well as
historical sets of Rider's Radio and
Television schematics.

KS —WICHITA PUBLIC LIBRARY, 223 S
Main, Wichita, 67202. Larry DePiesse,
Head, Business & Technology Dept; Jayne F
Young, Business & Technology Dept
Holdings: Vols 220 Uncat
Budget: $900
Notes: Sams Photofact Schematics. All
service data publications printed since April
11, 1946. Contains listings on over 138,000
chassis and models of home entertainment
equipment: auto radios, CB radios, modular
hi-fis, scanner-monitors, tape recorders,
transistor radios, videocassette recorders,
and videodisc players. No interlibrary loan.

OH —AKRON-SUMMIT COUNTY PUBLIC
LIBRARY, Science & Technology Div, 55 S
Main St, Akron, 44326. Joyce McKnight,
Head
Holdings: Vols 2250 Cat
Budget: ($24,000)
Notes: Incl Howard Sams and John Rider
schematics.

PA —CARNEGIE LIBRARY OF
PITTSBURGH, Science & Technology Dept,

RADIO—REPAIRING (cont.)

4400 Forbes Ave, Pittsburgh, 15213.
Catherine M Brosky, Dept Head
Notes: Radio and television schematics and repair manuals.

SC —HORRY GEORGETOWN
TECHNICAL COLLEGE, Library, Hwy
501, Box 1966, Conway, 29526. Barbara
Brittain, Librn
Holdings: Vols (20,000) Cat Slides
Microforms

WI —MILWAUKEE PUBLIC LIBRARY, 814
W Wisconsin Ave, Milwaukee, 53233.
Donald J Sager, City Librn
Holdings: Vols (2000) Cat
Notes: Incl schematics and pamphlets. No photocopying.

ON —METROPOLITAN TORONTO
LIBRARY, Science & Technology Dept, 789
Yonge St, Toronto, M4W 2G8, Can.
Margaret Walshe, Head
Holdings: Vols (120,000) Cat
Notes: Schematics available for Canadian radio sets, from 1927 to date.

RADIO, FRENCH-ENGLISH

OH —CASE WESTERN RESERVE
UNIVERSITY, Kulas Music Library, 11118
Bellflower Rd, Cleveland, 44106. Timothy
Robson, Music Librn
Notes: Containing deposit of a collection of
some 800 records of music and the spoken
word in French, English, and Spanish
presented by Radio Canada International in
Montreal.

RADIO ADVERTISING

GA —UNIVERSITY OF GEORGIA,
Libraries, Special Collections Division,
Athens, 30602. Vesta Lee Gordon, Asst Dir
for Special Collections
Notes: The Arbitron Collection of television
and radio program ratings, 1949-date (except
past year). In-depth, statistical analyses of
the listening public by age, sex, county, some
ethnic groups, farm population, listening
preferences, etc. 26,302 bound vols. 2
reports, 1949-81. To be added to annually.

RADIO ASTRONOMY

CA —UNIVERSITY OF CALIFORNIA,
BERKELEY, Bancroft Library, Manuscripts
Division, Berkeley, 94720. James D Hart,
Dir
Holdings: Mss
Notes: Papers of Samuel Silver, specialist on
applied electromagnetic, microwave, and
radio astronomical problems. Much of the
International Union of Radio Science. 48
linear ft.

CA —CALIFORNIA INSTITUTE OF
TECHNOLOGY, Robert A Millikan
Memorial Library, Archives, 1201 E
California Blvd, Pasadena, 91125. Judith R
Goodstein, Archivist
Holdings: Vols (3000) Cat Mss Maps Pix
Slides Phonorecords Audiotapes Videotapes
16mm Films Microforms
Notes: Ms sources for the history of
astrophysics, cosmology, mathematical
physics, experimental physics, radio
astronomy, geophysics and biophysics.
Collections incl the papers of: George Ellery
Hale, Jesse Greenstein, H P Robertson,
Richard Feynman, Paul Epstein, Max
Delbruck, and Beno Gutenberg. Candid
photos of physicists at meetings; etchings
and photographs of Einstein; scientific
medals; selected pieces of scientific
apparatus (including the oil-drop machine
constructed by Millikan at Caltech in the
early 1920s); the reprint collection of Paul
Epstein; over 3000 landmark books in the
history of 20th century physics and
mathematics. Printed publications include:
Daniel Kevles, *Guide to the Microfilm
Edition of the George Ellery Hale Papers*
(Pasadena, Carnegie Institute of Washington
and Caltech), 1968; Judith R Goodstein, *The
Robert Andrews Millikan Collection at the
California Institute of Technology: Guide to*

a Microfilm Edition (Pasadena, Caltech),
1977; Judith R Goodstein and Carolyn
Kopp, *The Theodore von Karman
Collections at the California Institute of
Technology* (Pasadena, Archives), 1981.

ON —QUEEN'S UNIVERSITY, Douglas
Library, Kingston, K7L 5C4, Can. William F
E Morley, Cur, Special Collections
Notes: Covington collection on radio
astronomy.

RADIO BROADCASTING

CA —INSTITUTE OF THE AMERICAN
MUSICAL, Library, 121 N Detroit St, Los
Angeles, 90036. Miles Kreuger, Cur
Holdings: Cat Mss Maps Pix Slides
Phonorecords
Notes: Reference materials on the American
musical theatre and motion pictures incl 40,
000 phonograph records, sound tapes, and
cylinders dating back to the 1890s; record
catalogs to 1900; thousands of theatre and
film programs, periodicals, sheet music and
vocal scores as early as 1830; thousands of
motion picture press books and over 200,000
stills from 1914 to the present; every musical
comedy script published in America and
dozens in ms form, original or photocopy
materials from the archives of movie palaces,
films and record companies, incl
discographies of many major Broadway and
Hollywood stars; and thousands of books on
theatre, film, broadcasting, world's fairs and
other allied areas of showmanship.

CA —LOS ANGELES PUBLIC LIBRARY,
Frances Howard Goldwyn Hollywood
Regional Library, 1623 Ivar Ave, Los
Angeles, 90028. Sally Dumaux, Librn
Holdings: Vols (100,000) Cat Mss Pix VF
Budget: ($60,000)
Notes: A general and a research collection
covering motion pictures, radio broadcasting,
and television. Over 2000 motion picture
and television scripts. Biographical
information on actors and actresses. Casts,
credits, and other production information on
over 1500 motion pictures from the 1920s to
the present. Collections also include posters,
lobby cards, souvenir programs, scrapbooks,
vertical files, and over 3000 publicity stills.
Including the following Special Collections:
Fred Archer Collection, photographs,
including the Hunchback of Notre Dame
(1923), and personalities of the stage and
screen, 1907-1930; Gilbert A Adrian,
designer, sketches and photographs; Hazel
Flynn, publicist, correspondence and
photographs.

CA —HOOVER INSTITUTION ON WAR,
REVOLUTION & PEACE, Stanford
University, Stanford, 94305. Milorad M
Drachkovitch, Archivist
Holdings: Mss
Notes: The records of the Stanford Listening
Post, 1940-1945, incl correspondence,
transcripts of radio broadcasts, study papers,
notes, and card indexes relating to a project
to record and study radio broadcasts from
East Asia. 29 ms boxes.

DC —GEORGETOWN UNIVERSITY,
Library, Special Collections Div, 37 & O Sts
NW, Washington, 20057. George M
Barringer, Special Collections Librn;
Nicholas B Sheetz, Mss Librn
Holdings: Mss Cat Pix
Notes: Correspondence, memoranda, reports,
mss of articles and addresses, pamphlets, and
newspaper clippings constituting the papers
of Robert F Kelley (1894-1975). Kelley
served as US Military Attache to the Baltic
Provinces from 1920-22, before entering the
foreign service in 1922. From 1926-37 he
served as Chief of the Division of Eastern
European Affairs in the State Department.
In 1937 he was transferred to Ankara,
Turkey where he remained until his
retirement from foreign service in 1945. The
papers most directly concern USSR internal
affairs as well as US - USSR relations from
the years immediately prior to recognition in
1933 through the cold war years of the early
1960's. Apart from State Department
material, additional material is incl from
Kelley's involvement in the American
Committee for Liberation from Bolshevism
and the establishment of Radio Liberty.

DC —GEORGE WASHINGTON
UNIVERSITY, Gelman Library,
Telecommunications Information Center,
Washington, 20052. Cathy Haworth, Librn
Holdings: Vols (1500) Periodicals
Notes: Incl

GA —UNIVERSITY OF GEORGIA,
Libraries, Special Collections Division,
Athens, 30602. Vesta Lee Gordon, Asst Dir
for Special Collections
Notes: The Arbitron Collection of television
and radio program ratings, 1949-date (except
past year). In-depth, statistical analyses of
the listening public by age, sex, county, some
ethnic groups, farm population, listening
preferences, etc. 26,302 bound vols. 2
reports, 1949-81. To be added to annually.

IL —CENTER FOR RESEARCH
LIBRARIES, 6050 S Kenwood Ave,
Chicago, 60637. Donald B Simpson, Dir;
Esther Smith, Collection Development Librn
Holdings: Microforms
Notes: Microfilms of: *Daily Report of
Foreign Radio Broadcasts*, 1941-1974,
Foreign Broadcast Information Service, (area
editions, 1974-); *Voice of America* scripts
1953-, foreign broadcasts as monitored by
CBS, Aug 1939-March 1945, BBC
monitoring service reports, 1974-date, and
BBC Home Service News 1939-1945.

IL —UNIVERSITY OF ILLINOIS,
URBANA/CHAMPAIGN, Library,
Communications Library, 122 Gregory Hall,
Urbana, 61801. Nancy Allen, Librn
Holdings: Vols (18,000) Cat
Budget: ($27,000)
Notes: Radio broadcasting history, theory
and effects, and skills.

MI —DETROIT PUBLIC LIBRARY, Music &
Performing Arts Dept, 5201 Woodward,
Detroit, 48202. Jean Currie Church, Cur
Holdings: Vols (1375) Cat Mss Pix
Notes: The E Azalia Hackley Collections
document achievements of Blacks in the
fields of music, dance, theatre, motion
pictures, and broadcasting. World-wide in
scope. Extensive clipping files arranged by
personal names, titles and subjects. Incl
musical scores (1500), recordings, and plays.
No taping or other copying of recordings
permitted.

NY —NATIONAL BROADCASTING CO,
Reference Library, 30 Rockefeller Plaza, Rm
1426, New York, 10020. Vera Mayer, Vice-
President Info & Archives
Holdings: Vols (4000) Cat Microforms
Notes: Historical and current materials.
Total collection: 13,000 vols, incl other
subjects such as business, politics and social
issues.

NY —NEW YORK PUBLIC LIBRARY,
Performing Arts Research Center, Billy Rose
Theatre Collection, 111 Amsterdam Ave,
New York, 10023. Dorothy L Swerdlove,
Cur
Holdings: Cat
See also entry under Radio.

NC —DUKE UNIVERSITY, William R
Perkins Library, Durham, 27706. Elvin E
Strowd, University Librn
Notes: Books, serials and pamphlets (2,820,
527); music scores (31,551); motion pictures
(285); microforms (1,055,627); tapes,
cassettes and phonorecords, the library is a
depository for Radio Canada International
recordings, (2289); and manuscripts, US
Government publications, maps, and
broadsides, additions in all formats are
ongoing.

TX —ABILENE CHRISTIAN UNIVERSITY,
Margaret & Herman Brown Library, ACU
Sta, Abilene, 79601. Callie Faye Milliken,
Assoc Dir
Holdings: Mss Audiotapes Videotapes 16mm
Films
Notes: Extensive collection of films,
audiotapes, and scripts used in developing
the religious radio-television program
"Herald of Truth," which has been aired by
Members of Churches of Christ since 1952.

WV —SALEM COLLEGE, Library, Salem,
26426. Myron J Smith, Jr, Librn

WY —UNIVERSITY OF WYOMING,
William Robertson Coe Library, 13 &
Ivinson, Laramie, 82071.
Notes: The papers of Morgan Beatty (1902-

RADIO BROADCASTING (cont.)

1975), an eminent newsman in print and broadcast journalism. Contains several thousand letters, many from prominent personalities, extensive background files of his "News of the World" and other broadcasts, and several thousand radio scripts and feature news stories.

ON —CANADIAN BROADCASTING CORP, Head Office Library, 1500 Bronson Ave, PO Box 8478, Ottawa, K1G 3J5, Can. Normand Deschamps, Librn
Holdings: Vols (6400) Cat
Budget: ($18,000)
Notes: Emphasis on radio and television broadcasting. No holdings on technical aspects.

RADIO BROADCASTING—HISTORY

AZ —NORTHERN ARIZONA UNIVERSITY, Special Collection Library, CU Box 6022, Flagstaff, 86011. Peter M Whiteley, Coordr/Archivist; William Mullane, Librn
Notes: Guy Bensusan Collection; Community Action Broadcasting System, Tucson, Ariz; transcripts of radio programs relating to Arizona subjects, 1972-1973. Also KEOS Radio Station, Flagstaff, Ariz, Collection; program log, 1962.

DC —BROADCAST PIONEERS LIBRARY, 1771 N St NW, Washington, 20036. Catharine Heinz, Dir
Holdings: Vols (6500) Uncat Pix Phonorecords Audiotapes
Notes: Special collections: Oral History (750); Havrilla (photos, radio performers); William S Hedges Collection; Elmo Neale Pickerill Collection; Joseph E Baudino Collection; Archive of Federal Communications Bar Association. Incl 20, 000 pictures, 1450 phonorecords and 1200 audiotapes.

DC —LIBRARY OF CONGRESS, Motion Pictures, Broadcasting and Recorded Sound Div, Washington, 20540.
Notes: Over 5600 papers and broadcast recordings of Raymond Swing (1887-1968).

MA —TUFTS UNIVERSITY, Fletcher School of Law & Diplomacy, Murrow Center of Public Diplomacy, Medford, 02155. Natalie Schatz, Cur of Special Collections
Holdings: Vols (1500) // Cat Mss Pix Phonorecords Audiotapes 16mm Films
Notes: Professional correspondence, reports, speeches, scripts and interviews relating to Edward R Murrow's career in broadcasting: reports, hearings and speeches from his years as Director of USIA, as well as personal correspondence, memorabilia, books, some films and audiotapes. 43,300 pieces.

NY —COLUMBIA UNIVERSITY LIBRARIES, Rare Book & Manuscript Library, 801 Butler Library, 535 W 114 St, New York, 10027. Kenneth A Lohf, Librn
Holdings: Mss
Notes: Some 200,000 papers tracing the career of Edwin Howard Armstrong, inventor of the FM radio, incl correspondence with many of the leading figures in the arts and sciences and numerous legal papers and documentation of his inventive work. Restricted use.

NY —MUSEUM OF BROADCASTING, Library, 1 E 53rd St, New York, 10022. Douglas Gibbons, Dir
Notes: A museum dedicated to the study and preservation of the history of radio and television broadcasting. Maintains a collection of significant radio and television programs from the 1920s to the present. Incl 10,000 TV programs, 10,000 radio programs, 2000 vols, 2550 original scripts.

NY —NEW YORK PUBLIC LIBRARY, Performing Arts Research Center, Billy Rose Theatre Collection, 111 Amsterdam Ave, New York, 10023. Dorothy L Swerdlove, Cur
Holdings: Cat

WA —WESTERN WASHINGTON UNIVERSITY, Center for Pacific Northwest Studies, High St, Bellingham, 98225. James

W Scott, Dir
Holdings: Mss Pix Phonorecords
Notes: The L Rogan Jones Collection: broadcasting executive and community leader, Rogan Jones died in 1972. Owner, operator and senior executive of various radio, TV and cable transmitting companies, Jones was involved during the 1930s in a famous lawsuit brought by various Washington newspapers and Associated Press against Station KVOS, which he then operated. In a case of changing fortunes, first for, then against KVOS, the case was argued before the US Supreme Court in 1936. A unanimous verdict was finally handed down in favor of the station. Is is regarded as a landmark verdict in the history of broadcasting. Papers on this and other radio and television issues are included in he collection. An *Informational Paper* is presently being prepared on this collection. Partially cataloged.

WY —UNIVERSITY OF WYOMING, William Robertson Coe Library, Performing Arts Collections, Laramie, 82071. Gene M Gressley, Dir
Holdings: Mss
Notes: Collections in the Performing Arts area incl some 300 collections of outstanding music composers, arrangers, film industry directors, writers, performers, and individuals prominent in all aspects of music, theatre, radio, television and film industry.

RADIO CANADA INTERNATIONAL

OH —CASE WESTERN RESERVE UNIVERSITY, Kulas Music Library, 11118 Bellflower Rd, Cleveland, 44106. Timothy Robson, Music Librn
Notes: Selected as a full depository for recordings of Radio Canada International. Includes some 800 recordings of music and the spoken word in French, English, and Spanish. Literary, cultural, and political materials are included.

RADIO COMMERCIALS see Radio Advertising

RADIO FREE EUROPE

NY —COLUMBIA UNIVERSITY LIBRARIES, Lehman Library, Bureau of Applied Social Research Archive, 420 W 118th St, New York, 10027. David Lewis, Librn
Holdings: Uncat
Notes: Current information file of Radio Free Europe publications. There is significant coverage of the period 1956-1973. The current file incl Radio Free Europe Situation Reports, which are published for selected countries on a weekly basis, Background Reports dealing with themes of broader significance, and Media Surveys which are translations of important East European press articles. The retrospective files incl these research products arranged on a country-by-country basis.

ON —UNIVERSITY OF TORONTO, Thomas Fisher Rare Book Library, 120 Saint George St, Toronto, M5S 1A5, Can. Richard G Landon, Head
Notes: Background material on communist contries issued by Radio Free Europe. Includes extensive materials on Poland, Czechoslovakia, Hungary, Rumania, Yugoslavia. Also contains material on East Germany, Bulgaria, Albania, Sino-Soviet conflict. Chiefly covers years 1960-1976. Some earlier material from 1950s. Incl 3000 uncataloged items.

RADIO JOURNALISTS see Journalists

RADIO LIBERTY

DC —GEORGETOWN UNIVERSITY, Library, Special Collections Div, 37 & O Sts NW, Washington, 20057. George M Barringer, Special Collections Librn; Nicholas B Sheetz, Mss Librn
Holdings: Mss Cat Pix
Notes: Correspondence, memoranda, reports,

mss of articles and addresses, pamphlets, and newspaper clippings constituting the papers of Robert F Kelley (1894-1975). Kelley served as US Military Attache to the Baltic Provinces from 1920-22, before entering the foreign service in 1922. From 1926-37 he served as Chief of the Division of Eastern European Affairs in the State Department. In 1937 he was transferred to Ankara, Turkey where he remained until his retirement from foreign service in 1945. The papers most directly concern USSR internal affairs as well as US - USSR relations from the years immediately prior to recognition in 1933 through the cold war years of the early 1960's. Apart from State Department material, additional material is incl from Kelley's involvement in the American Committee for Liberation from Bolshevism and the establishment of Radio Liberty.

RADIO PERIODICALS see Periodicals, Radio

RADIO PROGRAMS

CA —UNIVERSITY OF CALIFORNIA, LOS ANGELES, Theater Arts Library, Los Angeles, 90024. Edward Shreeves, Chairman, Bibliographers Group; Audree Malkin, Head, Theater Arts Library
Holdings: Vols (12,500)
Notes: Major research collections covering the historical, critical, aesthetic, biographical and technical aspects of film, television and radio, and the non-book and primary source material in these fields. Also 166,000 pamphlets, photographs, microfilms and sound recordings. Incl over 4,000,000 moving picture stills, over 32,636 screenplays, and scripts from American and British Films. Incl 1740 radio scripts and a collection of 3000 television scripts. Also incl portraits, clippings files, film festival programs, motion picture programs, lobby cards, original sketches and production materials; the personal and business papers, records and correspondence of actors, directors, producers, art directors and screen and television writers. Incl 100,000 mss. Extensive poster collection (over 7000, 1915 to date), many forPolish and Czech productions. Limited photocopying.

DC —BROADCAST PIONEERS LIBRARY, 1771 N St NW, Washington, 20036. Catharine Heinz, Dir
Holdings: Vols (6500) Uncat Pix Phonorecords Audiotapes
Notes: Special collections: Oral History (750); Havrilla (photos, radio performers); William S Hedges Collection; Elmo Neale Pickerill Collection; Joseph E Baudino Collection; Archive of Federal Communications Bar Association. Incl 20, 000 pictures, 1450 phonorecords and 1200 audiotapes.

DC —LIBRARY OF CONGRESS, Motion Pictures, Broadcasting and Recorded Sound Div, Washington, 20540.
Notes: The *Amateur Hour* Collection consists of original radio recordings of the Major Bowes series (1935-1944) and disc, tape, and television coverage of the Ted Mack series (1948-1968). Incl applications to appear on the program and accompanying correspondence and news clippings. The *Arthur Godfrey Time* collection is comprised of recordings of the television and radio programs from the years 1949-57 and recordings of several rehearsals and warm-ups. The American Forces Radio and Television Service (AFRTS) Collection contains disc recordings transferred to the Library as early as 1945 as well as selected early wartime broadcasts. Since 1967 the Library has received AFRTS's complete radio program package. Incl broadcast recordings and scripts of General Foods' radio shows of the 1930s and 1940s, broadcast recordings of National Public Radio's culturalprograms, broadcast recordings of Voice of America music programs. The NBC Radio Collection contains broadcast recordings of NBC radio programs, 1933-70. Duplicated at the

RADIO PROGRAMS (cont.)

Museum of Broadcasting in New York City. Recordings, videotapes, and films of *Meet the Press,* papers of its producer Lawrence E Spivak, and related pictorial material.

GA —UNIVERSITY OF GEORGIA, Libraries, Special Collections Division, Athens, 30602. Vesta Lee Gordon, Asst Dir for Special Collections
Notes: The Arbitron Collection of television and radio program ratings, 1949-date (except past year). In-depth, statistical analyses of the listening public by age, sex, county, some ethnic groups, farm population, listening preferences, etc. 26,302 bound vols. 2 reports, 1949-81. To be added to annually.

IN —INDIANA UNIVERSITY, Lilly Library, Seventh St, Bloomington, 47405. William R Cagle, Librn
Holdings: Vols (700) Cat Mss
Notes: Extensive collection of scripts. Ms holdings incl the papers of Lance Sieveking, BBC producer; Douglas Geoffrey Bridson, BBC producer and writer; and Douglas Cleverdon, producer. All three were most closely connected with The Third Program. Scripts for many of these programs are in the collection as well as extensive correspondence regarding programming.
See also entries under McGreevey, John; Welles, Orson.

IN —MORRISSON-REEVES LIBRARY, 80 N Sixth St, Richmond, 47374. Harriet E Bard, Librn
Holdings: Audiotapes Cat
Notes: Audiotapes (142 //) of Singin' Sam's radio programs from the 1930s and 1940s. Indexed by song title.
See also entry under Music, Popular.

NY —MUSEUM OF BROADCASTING, Library, 1 E 53rd St, New York, 10022. Douglas Gibbons, Dir
Notes: A museum dedicated to the study and preservation of the history of radio and television broadcasting. Maintains a collection of significant radio and television programs from the 1920s to the present. Incl 10,000 TV programs, 10,000 radio programs, 2000 vols, 2550 original scripts.

NY —NEW YORK PUBLIC LIBRARY, Performing Arts Research Center, Billy Rose Theatre Collection, 111 Amsterdam Ave, New York, 10023. Dorothy L Swerdlove, Cur
Holdings: Cat
See also entry under Radio.

NY —NEW YORK PUBLIC LIBRARY, Performing Arts Research Center, Dance Collection, 111 Amsterdam Ave, New York, 10023. Genevieve Oswald, Cur
Notes: The Oral History Archive of 1600 audiotapes and cassettes incl radio programs on dance of Irving Deakin, Marian Horosko, Walter Terry, Robert Sherman, and John Gruen.

PA —FREE LIBRARY OF PHILADELPHIA, Theatre Collection, Logan Sq, Philadelphia, 19103. Geraldine Duclow, Librn-in-Charge
Holdings: Vols (1,250,000) Uncat Pix
Notes: The Theatre Collection contains books, magazines, playbills, broadsides, posters, photographs, and other memorabilia covering theatre, motion pictures, minstrels, vaudeville, circus, radio and television. The Library's Philadelphia Theatre Index lists the major productions here since 1855, and partially indexes the collection of local playbills which date back to 1803. There are also programs from many other cities, incl New York; some from London date back to 1800. Early film companies as well as the present movie industry are represented by advertising materials and over 30,000 film stills. The Lubin Film Co (1910-1916) Archive has been established with over 600 photographs and related items. Circus programs and route books date back to 1900. There are minstrel programs as early as 1865. Most significant are the mss from Philadelphia's Dumont Minstrels. Various files contain autographs, photographs, newspaper articles and reviews in all pertinent subject areas. Noncirculating.

VA —GEORGE MASON UNIVERSITY, Fenwick Library, Special Collections Dept,

4400 University Drive, Fairfax, 22030. Ruth Kerns, Public Services Librn
Notes: The Federal Theatre Project (FTP) was established in August 1935 as a part of the arts program of the Works Progress Administration (renamed Work Projects Administration in 1939). Supporting 150 separate units throughout the United States, the FTP produced over 830 major stage plays, 6000 radio programs, and innumerable marionette plays, vaudeville shows, outdoor pageants, and circuses. At the conclusion of the project in June 1939, the "product materials" generated by the FTP were sent to the Library of Congress, and the administrative records to the National Archives. The Library's Federal Theatre Project collection was placed on deposit at George Mason University in Fairfax, Virginia, in 1974.

ON —METROPOLITAN TORONTO LIBRARY, Theatre Dept, 789 Yonge St, Toronto, M4W 2G8, Can. Heather McCallum, Head
Holdings: Vols (30,500) Mss Pix Slides Phonorecords Microforms
Notes: Book and nonbook materials in all areas of the performing arts except music: theatre and drama, moving pictures, dance, television and radio programming, and varieties of popular entertainment such as circus, music hall, vaudeville, puppetry and pantomime. Special collections relating to the history of the performing arts in Canada. Access to the book and periodical collection is provided through a divided dictionary COM catalog on microfiche. In addition, extensive card indexes are available. Published descriptions of the collection: Heather McCallum. Research Collections in Canadian Libraries, Part II. Special Studies no I. *Theatre resources in Canadian collections* (Ottawa: National Library of Canada, 1973); Heather McCallum. "The Theatre Department of the Metropolitan Toronto Library" in *Special Collections,* vol 1 (1), fall 1981.

RADIO SCRIPTS

CA —UNIVERSITY OF CALIFORNIA, LOS ANGELES, Research Library, Dept of Special Collections, 405 Hilgard Ave, Los Angeles, 90024. Edward Shreeves, Chairman, Bibliographers Group; David S Zeidberg, He ad
Notes: In var. ous collections, incl the Jack Benny, Eddie Cantor, Mort Fine, and David Freeman collections. No photocopying.

CA —UNIVERSITY OF CALIFORNIA, LOS ANGELES, Theater Arts Library, Los Angeles, 90024. Edward Shreeves, Chairman, Bibliographers Group; Audree Malkin, Head, Theater Arts Library
Holdings: Vols (12,500)
Notes: Major research collections covering the historical, critical, aesthetic, biographical and technical aspects of film, television and radio, and the non-book and primary source material in these fields. Also 166,000 pamphlets, photographs, microforms and sound recordings. Incl over 4,000,000 moving picture stills, over 32,636 screenplays, and scripts from American and British Films. Incl 1740 radio scripts and a collection of 3000 television scripts. Also incl portraits, clippings files, film festival programs, motion picture programs, lobby cards, original sketches and production materials; the personal and business papers, records and correspondence of actors, directors, producers, art directors and screen and television writers. Incl 100,000 mss. Extensive poster collection (over 7000, 1915 to date), many for Polish and Czech productions. Limited photocopying.

CA —UNIVERSITY OF CALIFORNIA, LOS ANGELES, Theater Arts Library, Los Angeles, 90024. Edward Shreeves, Chairman, Bibliographers Group; Audree Malkin, Head, Theater Arts Library
Holdings: Cat Mss Pix
Notes: Radio Scripts: a collection of more than 1000 scripts which include the complete *Amos 'n' Andy* radio series, 354 episodes dating from 1943-1953; *Our Miss

Brooks,* 222 scripts from 1948-1954; *The Bob Hope Show,* 29 scripts, 1949-1950; *Philco Radio Time,* starring Bing Crosby, 7 scripts and 6 comedy sketches, 1946-1947.

DC —LIBRARY OF CONGRESS, Motion Pictures, Broadcasting and Recorded Sound Div, Washington, 20540.
Notes: Over 5600 papers and broadcast recordings of Raymond Swing (1887-1968).

IL —CENTER FOR RESEARCH LIBRARIES, 6050 S Kenwood Ave, Chicago, 60637. Donald B Simpson, Dir; Esther Smith, Collection Development Librn
Holdings: Microforms
Notes: Microfilms of: *Daily Report of Foreign Radio Broadcasts,* 1941-1974, *Foreign Broadcast Information Service,* area editions, 1974-, *Voice of America* scripts, 1953-, *BBC Home Service News,* 1939-1945, foreign broadcasts as monitored by CBS, Aug 1939-March 1945 and BBC monitoring service reports, 1974-.

IN —INDIANA UNIVERSITY, Lilly Library, Seventh St, Bloomington, 47405. William R Cagle, Librn
Holdings: Cat Mss
Notes: Extensive holdings of BBC scripts; some others. Mss incl papers of television writer John McGreevey, 1922- , who began as a radio writer for radio station KTAR in Phoenix, Arizona, 1944-52. He also produced scripts for Armstrong Circle Theatre of Today, Cavalcade of America, Dr Christian, and Suspense, the original scripts of which are in his collection. 1645 items.
See also entry under Welles, Orson.

†MA —BOSTON UNIVERSITY, Mugar Memorial Library, Special Collections Dept, 771 Commonwealth Avenue, Boston, 02215. Howard B Gotlieb, Dir
Notes: Extensive papers of mystery and science fiction writers, and film, radio and TV writers, performers, etc. 14 years of original Little Orphan Annie art. Collections built around papers of individuals are supplemented by their printed works.

NY —CITY UNIVERSITY OF NEW YORK, City College, Morris R Cohen Library, North Academic Center, Convent Ave & 137th St, New York, 10031. Barbara J Dunlap, Archivist
Holdings: // Mss Pix Phonorecords
Notes: Ira Marion (Ira Silberstein), a 1930 graduate of City College, was a voluminous writer of radio scripts for WJZ, The Blue Network, and ABC. The Collection consists of over 2000 scripts for such programs as "Milton Cross Presents," "Crime Doesn't Pay," "The Black Museum," etc. There is also some personal correspondence and correspondence with the networks. Collection is partially inventoried.

NY —NEW YORK PUBLIC LIBRARY, Performing Arts Research Center, Billy Rose Theatre Collection, 111 Amsterdam Ave, New York, 10023. Dorothy L Swerdlove, Cur
Holdings: Cat

NY —NEW YORK PUBLIC LIBRARY, General Library of the Performing Arts, 111 Amsterdam Ave, New York, 10023. Larry Cioppa, Drama Specialist
Holdings: Vols (40,000) Cat Phonorecords
Notes: Drama material on all aspects of the theater. Film, radio, television and related performing arts. Incl 5000 drama recordings.

†NY —SYRACUSE UNIVERSITY LIBRARIES, E S Bird Library, George Arents Research Library, Rm 600, Syracuse, 13210. Mr Sidney Huttner, Librn
Notes: Radio Scripts, especially The Shadow and Nick Carter. Street and Smith Collection.

OH —OHIO STATE UNIVERSITY, William Oxley Thompson Memorial Library, 1858 Neil Ave Mall, Columbus, 43210. Robert A Tibbetts, Cur of Special Collections
Holdings: Vols (475) Cat Mss

OR —UNIVERSITY OF OREGON LIBRARY, Special Collections Div, Eugene, 97403. Kenneth W Duckett, Curator
Holdings: Cat Mss
Notes: Nearly 20 mss collections containing radio scripts from such series as "Death Valley Days," "Ethel and Albert," "The

RADIO SCRIPTS (cont.)

Couple Next Door," "Famous Jury Trials," and "Gang Busters." Publication: Martin Schmitt, comp, *Catalogue of Manuscripts in the University of Oregon Library* (Eugene: University of Oregon Books, 1971).
See also entry under Television Scripts

PA —TEMPLE UNIVERSITY LIBRARIES, Special Collections Dept, Rare Books & Mss Section, Philadelphia, 19122. Thomas M Whitehead, Cur
Holdings: Cat
Notes: Developing collection of 91 linear feet (June 1972) of American and British radio and television rehearsal and camera scripts. Incl Lux Radio Theatre (US, 1934-1955); scripts of Carlton E Morse-*One Man's Family, I Love A Mystery,* etc; BBC scripts of Terence Tiller; et al Guide and description of the Lux Radio Theatre collections issued as a masters thesis (Temple University, 1967).

TX —ABILENE CHRISTIAN UNIVERSITY, Margaret & Herman Brown Library, ACU Sta, Abilene, 79601. Callie Faye Milliken, Assoc Dir
Holdings: Mss Audiotapes Videotapes 16mm Films
Notes: Extensive collection of films, audiotapes, and scripts used in developing the religious radio-television program "Herald of Truth," which has been aired by Members of Churches of Christ since 1952.

VA —GEORGE MASON UNIVERSITY, Fenwick Library, Special Collections Dept, 4400 University Drive, Fairfax, 22030. Ruth Kerns, Public Services Librn
Notes: The Federal Theatre Project Collection includes 5000 playscripts, 2500 radio scripts, 25,000 photographs, 40 blueprints, 1000 posters, over 1600 costume designs, 350 scene designs, 750 production notebooks, 1700 programs and heralds, 26 musical scores and 18 cubic feet of research materials and play readers reports.

WA —GONZAGA UNIVERSITY, Crosby Library, East 502 Boone Ave, Spokane, 99258. Robert Burr, Dir
Notes: Books, records, memorabilia and papers, incl Jack Benny Radio Show scripts.

WY —UNIVERSITY OF WYOMING, William Robertson Coe Library, 13 & Ivinson, Laramie, 82071.
Notes: The papers of Morgan Beatty (1902-1975), an eminent newsman in print and broadcast journalism. Contains several thousand letters, many from prominent personalities, extensive background files of his "News of the World" and other broadcasts, and several thousand radio scripts and feature news stories.

AB —UNIVERSITY OF CALGARY, Libraries, Special Collections Div, 2500 University Dr, Calgary, T2N 1N4, Can.
Holdings: Vols (5000) Cat Mss
Notes: The Division has extensive collections of the papers of modern Canadian authors (qv individuals), incl Hugh MacLennan, Mordecai Richler, Brian Moore, W O Mitchell, Cliff Faulknor, Christie Harris, Robert Kroetsch, Rudy Wiebe, Claude Peloquin, George Ryga, Andre Langevin, Malcolm Ross, Bruce Hutchison, John Mellor, Grant MacEwan, James Gray, Ernest Watkins, Len Peterson, Michael Cook, & Joanna Glass. The papers of musician Morris Surdin contain hundreds of Canadian Broadcasting Corporation scripts, and constitute a valuable addition to the purely literary manyscript collections. The Division also houses small collections of letters and manuscripts of Canadian poets such as Earle Birney, George Bowering, Mary Pickthall, Grace Leroy Aitkens, Helen Ball, Marion Kathleen Henry, Helen Geddes, Agnes Aston Hill, Edith Catherine Slater, and Gilbert E Murray, as well asthe archives of the literary periodicals *Tish, Imago,* and *Ariel.* The manuscript collections are complemented by a book collection of some 5000 volumes.

PQ —CONCORDIA UNIVERSITY LIBRARIES, Norris Library, 1435 Drummond, Montreal, H3G 1M8, Can. N

Robins, Special Collections Librn
Holdings: Cat Mss
Notes: Collection of 14,000 English language radio drama scripts broadcast over the Canadian Broadcasting Corp from 1930s to date. Presently being accessed by computer. Contains two sections: the main collection is the Esse W Ljungh Collection: besides plays, incl CBC memos, correspondence, etc; the second is the T Frank Willis Collection and consists of the scripts, letters and memos of the late producer.

RADIO SERVICING see
Radio—Repairing

RADIO STATION WQXR, NEW YORK

†NY —COLUMBIA UNIVERSITY LIBRARIES, Butler Library, Rare Book and Manuscript Library, 535 W 114 St, New York, 10027.
Notes: Papers of Elliot M Sanger, co-founder, executive vice-president and general manager of radio station WQXR in New York City. Also incl his bound file of the complete WQXR *Program Guide* from June 1936 through Dec 1963.

RADIO WORKERS UNION see United Electrical, Radio, and Machine Workers

RADIO WRITERS' GUILD OF AMERICA

NY —NEW YORK PUBLIC LIBRARY, Performing Arts Research Center, Billy Rose Theatre Collection, 111 Amsterdam Ave, New York, 10023. Dorothy L Swerdlove, Cur
Holdings: Cat

RADIOACTIVE FALLOUT

NM —UNIVERSITY OF CALIFORNIA, Los Alamos National Laboratory, Libraries, PO Box 1663, MSP 362, Los Alamos, 87545. J Arthur Freed, Head Librn
Holdings: Vols (800,000) Cat Films Microforms
Budget: ($700,000)
Notes: Incl 500,000 classified and unclassified reports. There are 25 branch libraries and a central collection. The Medical Library contains about 40,000 vols in the areas of biomedical research.

RADIOACTIVE WASTE

ID —EG&G, INEL Technical Library, 1776 Science Center, Idaho Falls, 83401. Brent Jacobsen, Head Librn; Heather Redding, Ref Librn
Holdings: Vols (33,000) Cat Microforms
Notes: Energy research and development included in libraries collection. Incl over 500,000 AEC, ERDA, NRC, and foreign reports. Unclassified materials may be used by the public in the library by appointment or borrowed by interlibrary loan. Incl 12,000 bound documents, 520,000 microfiche, 400 periodical subscriptions.

NM —UNIVERSITY OF CALIFORNIA, Los Alamos National Laboratory, Libraries, PO Box 1663, MSP 362, Los Alamos, 87545. J Arthur Freed, Head Librn
Holdings: Vols (800,000) Cat Films Microforms
Budget: ($700,000)
Notes: Incl 500,000 classified and unclassified reports. There are 25 branch libraries and a central collection. The Medical Library contains about 40,000 vols in the areas of biomedical research.

RADIOACTIVITY

ON —ATOMIC ENERGY OF CANADA LIMITED, Main Library, Technical Information Branch, Chalk River Nuclear Laboratories, Chalk River, K0J 1J0, Can. Harry Greenshields, Chief Librn
Holdings: Vols (128,700) Microforms
Budget: ($662,400)
Notes: The Main Library, Atomic Energy of

Canada Limited, is the Canadian repository for the literature of nuclear science and technology. Its collections reflect both fundamental and nuclear aspects of biology, chemistry, electronics, engineering, mathematics, computers, metallurgy, physics and other specific areas of science involving nuclear technology with special emphasis on heavy water reactor systems. 512,000 research reports are available in paper copy and microfiche form. Incl US DOE, INIS and other offshore nuclear research reports. 386,000 microforms.

RADIOACTIVITY, ENVIRONMENTAL
see Radioecology

RADIOBIOLOGY

IL —ARGONNE NATIONAL LABORATORY, Biological and Medical Research Branch Library, 9700 S Cass Ave, Argonne, 60439. Rebecca Smith, Librn
Notes: Incl 14,000 vols monographs, 250 current journals. Materials may be used by the public in the library by prior arrangement. Photocopies may be supplied for interlibrary loan, for which a processing and handling charge is made.

MD —US ARMED FORCES RADIOBIOLOGY RESEARCH INSTITUTE, Naval Medical Command, Bethesda, 20014. Nannette M Pope, Head, Library Division
Holdings: Vols (50,000)
Budget: ($150,000)
Notes: Collection consists of monographs, technical reports, serials, and microfiche related to radiation effects on human and animal biology.

OH —OHIO STATE UNIVERSITY, Biological Sciences Library, 1735 Neil Ave, Columbus, 43210. Victoria Welborn, Librn
Holdings: Vols (85,000) Cat Mss Maps Microforms

RADIOBIOLOGY—HISTORY

TN —UNIVERSITY OF TENNESSEE, KNOXVILLE, Library, Knoxville, 37996. John Dobson, Special Collections Librn
Holdings: Vols (20,000) Cat Mss Maps Pix
Notes: Tennesseana; 19th century American fiction; southern Indians; early Imprints. Separate catalog; holdings also listed in comprehensive public catalog in Main Library. Rare books card catalog with special headings calling attention to unusual features of the books; unpublished registers and calendars to ms collection. *Kefauver* collection, 59,000 pounds of political papers and memorabilia, reconstructed Senate office; *Radiation Biology Archives* (ca 60,000 pieces), papers of scientists from several countries dealing with the development of radiation biology. Also, 18 vols of extremely rare Southwest Territory and *Tennessee Official Journals,* printed in Knoxville, 1794-1796. The rare *Acts and Journals* are described in *The Lost Roulstone Imprints,* by John Dobson (Knoxville: Univ of Tennessee Libraries, 1975), 70 pp.

RADIOCARBON see Carbon

RADIOCHEMISTRY

IL —ARGONNE NATIONAL LABORATORY, Chemistry Branch Library, 9700 S Cass Ave, Argonne, 60439. Betty Guttman, Librn
Notes: Incl 20,000 vols monographs, 190 current journals. Materials may be used by the public in the library by prior arrangement. Photocopies may be supplied for interlibrary loan, for which a processing and handling charge is made.

RADIOECOLOGY

NC —NATIONAL MARINE FISHERIES SERVICE, SOUTHEAST FISHERIES CENTER, Beaufort Laboratory, Library, Beaufort, 28516. Ann Bowman Hall, Librn
Holdings: Vols (15,000) Cat

RADIOECOLOGY, MARINE see Marine Radioecology

RADIOLOGICAL PHYSICS see Radiology

RADIOLOGY

AL —UNIVERSITY OF ALABAMA, BIRMINGHAM, Lister Hill Library of the Health Sciences, University Sta, Birmingham, 35294. Richard B Fredericksen, Dir

CT —YALE MEDICAL LIBRARY, 333 Cedar St, New Haven, 06510.
Holdings: Vols (334,215) Cat Mss Pix Slides Microforms
Budget: ($361,650)
Notes: Incl films, audiotapes, artifacts, etc.

MD —JOHNS HOPKINS HOSPITAL, John W Pierson Memorial Library, Dept of Radiology, 601 N Broadway, Baltimore, 21205. S Elaine Pinkney, Librn
Holdings: Vols (6000) Cat Slides Audiotapes Videotapes
Budget: $4700
Notes: Incl Diagnostic Radiology, Radiotherapy, Ultrasound, and Computed Axial Tomography.

MD —US ARMED FORCES RADIOBIOLOGY RESEARCH INSTITUTE, Naval Medical Command, Bethesda, 20014. Nannette M Pope, Head, Library Division
Holdings: Vols (50,000)
Budget: ($150,000)
Notes: Collection consists of monographs, technical reports, serials, and microfiche related to radiation effects on human biology.

MI —UNIVERSITY OF MICHIGAN, Public Health Library, Ann Arbor, 48109. Mary Townsend, Head
Holdings: Vols (55,000) Cat Maps Pix
Budget: ($24,000)

MN —MAYO MEDICAL LIBRARY, History of Medicine Collection, Rochester, 55905. Nancy R Hensel, Librn
Holdings: Vols (18,000) Cat Mss Maps Pix Slides
Notes: The collection consists of over 18,000 vols, 6500 of which are considered source material (rare or reprint editions of classics). 4308 items from Garrison-Morton are available in the collection. Appropriate bibliographies, biographies and histories of medicine are a part of the collection. Fields of collecting interest are anesthesiology, dermatology, cardiology, neurology, immunology and radiology. Eight medical incunabula.

NJ —BERLEX LABORATORIES, Research & Development Library, 110 E Hanover Ave, Cedar Knolls, 07927. Lorene Lingelbach, Librn
Holdings: Vols (10,000) Cat Microforms
Notes: The library was established in 1972 by consolidating the collections of companies which merged with Berlex Laboratories. 425 periodical titles are received currently.

RI —MIRIAM HOSPITAL MEDICAL LIBRARY, 164 Summit Ave, Providence, 02906. Ann LeClaire, Dir of Library Services
Holdings: Cat Cassettes
Notes: Special collection on the renal system with emphasis on kidney transplantation and dialysis.

SC —BAPTIST MEDICAL CENTER, Amelia White Pitts Memorial Library, Taylor at Marion Sts, Columbia, 29220. Lois W Smith, Medical Librn
Holdings: Vols (3000) Cat

TX —UNIVERSITY OF TEXAS, M D Anderson Hospital and Tumor Institute, Research Medical Library, Texas Medical Center, Houston, 77030. Marie Harvin, Research Medical Librn
Holdings: Vols (48,000) Cat
Notes: Library attempts to collect every publication in all languages related to clinical cancer (or oncology). Aim is an exhaustive collection in this field. Collect heavily

(research level) in pathology, radiology, nuclear medicine, genetics and cell biology.

WA —BATTELLE-PACIFIC NORTHWEST LABORTORIES, Technical Library, PO Box 999, Richland, 99352. Wayne Snyder, Librn
Holdings: Vols (50,000) Cat Microforms
Budget: ($500,000)
Notes: Holdings: 50,000 books; 35,000 bound periodical vols; 200,000 technical reports in microform. Subscriptions: 1800 journals and other serials. Services: interlibrary loans; literature searching; translation; library open to public with restrictions.

RADIOLOGY (MEDICINE) see Radiology

RADIO-METEOROGRAPH see Radiosondes

RADIOSONDES

CA —UNIVERSITY OF CALIFORNIA, LOS ANGELES, Engineering & Mathematical Sciences Library, 405 Hilgard, Los Angeles, 90024. Rosalee I Wright, Librn
Notes: Collection includes WMO publications (comprehensive); IGY data series on surface observations, radiosonde and rawinsonde observations, upper wind observations, and radiation data (mostly in microform); selected government report or data series, eg from NOAA, NCC and AF Geophysics Laboratory.

RAEMAEKERS, LOUIS

CA —HOOVER INSTITUTION ON WAR, REVOLUTION & PEACE, Stanford University, Stanford, 94305. Milorad M Drachkovitch, Archivist
Holdings: // Mss
Notes: Papers, 1903-1939, of Louis Raemaekers, Belgian artist and cartoonist. Correspondence relating to business and art work, World War I sketches, drawings, cartoons, watercolors, ink drawings, clippings, invitations and honors, and photos. 27 ft. Unpublished finding aid in repository.

RAETO-ROMANCE LANGUAGE AND LITERATURE

MA —HARVARD UNIVERSITY LIBRARY, Cambridge, 02138.
Holdings: Cat
Notes: Downs 3167.

RAFFERTY, SCOTT

MA —JOHN F KENNEDY LIBRARY, Columbia Point, Boston, 02125. Henry J Gwiazda II, Cur
Notes: The Burke Marshall papers, 50 archives boxes re civil rights, 1961-1964 and the Bedford-Stuyvesant Development and Restoration Corporations; the Joseph Dolan papers, 1 box; the Thomas Johnston papers, 3 boxes; the James Mc Shane papers, 2 boxes; the Frank Mankiewicz papers, 15 boxes; and the Scott Rafferty papers, 4 boxes.

RAFINESQUE, CONSTANTINE SAMUEL

KS —UNIVERSITY OF KANSAS, Kenneth Spencer Research Library, Special Collections Dept, Lawrence, 66045. Alexandra Mason, Librn
Holdings: Vols 101 Cat Mss
Notes: About 2600 items before 1800. Espec strong in herbals, medical botany, Linnaeus, early American botanists (William Darlington, C S Rafinesque). Incl material from T J Fitzpatrick collection. Noncirculating.

RAGO, HENRY

IN —INDIANA UNIVERSITY, Lilly Library, Seventh St, Bloomington, 47405. William R Cagle, Librn
Holdings: // Cat Mss
Notes: Correspondence and writings, 1930-

1969, of poet, editor, Henry Rago, 1915-1969. (ca 3400 items). Also, office files of poetry during years that Rago was editor, 1955-1969.

RAGTIME MUSIC see Jazz

RAGUET, HENRY

TX —UNIVERSITY OF TEXAS LIBRARIES, General Libraries, Barker Texas History Center, PO Box P, Austin, 78712. Don Carleton, Dir

RAGWEED

†CO —NATIONAL JEWISH HOSPITAL AND RESEARCH CENTER-NATIONAL ATHSMA CENTER, Gerald Tucker Memorial Medical Library, 3800 Colfax Ave, Denver, 80206. Helen-Ann Brown, Librn
Holdings: Vols (8500)
Notes: Allergy, asthma, immunology, research in molecular and cellular biology, medicine, tuberculosis and diseases of the chest.

RAILROAD BRIDGES

MO —WASHINGTON UNIVERSITY, Libraries, Special Collections Dept, Campus Box 1061, St Louis, 63130.
Notes: Terminal Railroad Association Records (1889-date), of more than 450 original tracings of the Eads Bridge (1874-). Drawings show in fine and complete detail all the design features of this internationally known St Louis landmark.

RAILROAD CONSTRUCTION see Railroad Engineering

RAILROAD ENGINEERING

NY —ENGINEERING SOCIETIES LIBRARY, 345 E 47 St, New York, 10017. S Kirk Cabeen, Dir
Holdings: Vols (250,000) Cat Maps 16mm Films Microforms
Notes: One of the largest, most comprehensive engineering libraries in the world. Covers all engineering disciplines; particularly strong in electrical and electronic, mechanical, mining and metallurgical, petroleum, chemical, industrial, air conditioning and refrigeration engineering. Incl Wheeler Collection of early materials on magnetism and electricity. 125, 000 bound periodical vols; 10,000 maps; 5000 serial subscriptions (many foreign-language). Virtually all materials abstracted in Engineering Index (1884-date) are incl in Library. Noncirculating, except to members of professional engineering societies which support the Library. See Engineering Societies Library, New York, Classed Subject Catalog and Index (Boston: G K Hall, 1963); and Supplements, 1-10, 1964-1973.

VA —ENSCO, INC, Technical Library, 5400 Port Royal Rd, Springfield, 22151. Sue E Littlepage, Research Librn
Holdings: Vols (3000) Uncat Mss Maps Slides
Notes: Especially railroad technology and seismology.

RAILROAD PERIODICALS see Periodicals, Railroad

RAILROAD STATIONS see Railroads—Stations

RAILROAD WORKERS see Railroads—Employees

RAILROADS

DE —HAGLEY MUSEUM AND LIBRARY, Eleutherian Mills-Hagley Foundation Inc, PO Box 3630, Greenville, 19807. Richmond D Williams, Dir; Heddy A Richter, Imprints Librn
Notes: Records of the Reading Railroad

RAILROADS (cont.)

(1845-1940; 1000 cubic feet) contain minute books and financial records documenting the history of both the parent and subsidiary companies. Voluminous correspondence files describe all aspects of railroad operations.

IL —AMERICAN RAILWAY CAR INSTITUTE, Library, 303 E Wakcer Dr, Suite 732, Chicago, 60601. Elwyn T Ahnquist, Pres
Notes: Historical and current data on new orders, deliveries and backlogs of railroad cars. Publish for members monthly detailed reports. Also conduct forecasts and special studies. No photocopying.

IL —NORTHWESTERN UNIVERSITY, Transportation Center Library, Evanston, 60201. Mary Roy, Librn
Holdings: Vols (116,000)
Notes: The emphasis in this collection is on current developments in transportation operations and socioeconomics--management, planning, impact and regulation. All modes of transportation and containerization are incl; the geographic scope covers domestic and foreign activity at the urban, intercity and international levels. Publications on new systems developments and the application of analytic techniques to operations are well represented. Incl 19,000 pamphlets; 9000 company reports. *Services are offered on research conducted outside Northwestern. A fee schedule is available on request.* Publications: *Current Literature in Traffic and Transportation* (bi-monthly accessions bulletin citing 625 books, reports and periodical articles per issue).

IL —ILLINOIS STATE UNIVERSITY, Milner Library, Dept of Special Collections, Normal, 61761. Robert Sokan, Librn
Holdings: Vols 1564 // Uncat Maps Pix
Notes: The Price Transportation Collection. The collection spans the years from 1870 to 1960. Emphasis on railroads and steamships. Incl much material from US and foreign transportation companies.

MA —HARVARD UNIVERSITY, Baker Library of the Graduate School of Business Administration, Kress Library of Business and Economics, Soldiers Field, Boston, 02163. Ruth E Rogers, Cur
Holdings: Cat
Notes: Covers the progress of economic thought and the evolution of economic institutions and business life, with special strength in agriculture, banking, commerce, finance, industry, money, railroads, socialism, tariff. Restricted use: noncirculating. Collection available on microfilm: *Goldsmiths'-Kress Library of Economic Literature,* published by Research Publications, Inc. Downs 1477, 2704, 2712, 2719, 2727, Supplement 962, 963.

MA —AMERICAN ANTIQUARIAN SOCIETY LIBRARY, 185 Salisbury St, Worcester, 01609. Marcus A McCorison, Dir & Librn
Holdings: Vols 5200 Cat
Notes: Incl the Thomas Winthrop Streeter Collection on Transportation. The finest and most complete documentation of early American railroads, canals, bridges, turnpikes, and harbors in existence.

MS —UNIVERSITY OF SOUTHERN MISSISSIPPI, William David McCain Graduate Library, Box 5148, Southern Sta, Hattiesburg, 39406.
Holdings: Cat Mss
Notes: Collections incl the 450 cubic feet of records of the Association of American Railroads for the period 1914-1937; 72 cubic feet of records of the Gulf, Mobile, and Ohio Railroad for the period 1869-1965 (bulk dates 1925-1955); 23 cubic feet of records of the Illinois Central Railroad - Vicksburg, Mississippi Division for the period 1913-1961; and 245 cubic feet of records of the Mississippi Central Railroad for the period 1898-1967. A guide to these records is available for loan. See entries under the name of the individual railroad.

NE —NEBRASKA STATE HISTORICAL SOCIETY, Library, 1500 R St, Box 82554, Lincoln, 68501. M Ann Reinert, Library Dept Head
Holdings: Vols (100,000) Cat Maps Pix Microforms
Budget: ($200,000)
Notes: Strong emphasis in Nebraska, Great Plains, and Trans-Missouri history. Incl collection of 400 atlases and 3000 separate maps primarily relating to Nebraska 1854-present.
See also entry under Great Plains

NJ —NEW JERSEY DEPT OF TRANSPORTATION, Library, 1035 Parkway Ave, Trenton, 08625. Margaret L Webb, Librn
Holdings: Vols 2000 Cat Mss Maps Microforms
Notes: Emphasis is on highway, bus, rail, and air transportation. There is a finding-list-index to the department archives, over 1800 items.

NM —THOMAS BRANIGAN MEMORIAL LIBRARY, 200 E Picacho Ave, Las Cruces, 88001. Don Dresp, Dir
Notes: John Sharer Collection (cat).

NY —NEW YORK PUBLIC LIBRARY, Research Libraries, Science and Technology Research Center, Fifth Ave & 42 St, New York, 10018.
Holdings: Vols (1,100,000) Cat Microforms
Budget: ($647,259)

NY —NEW YORK PUBLIC LIBRARY, Research Libraries, Economic & Public Affairs Div, Fifth Ave & 42 St, New York, 10018. Edward DiRoma, Chief
Holdings: Vols (1,500,000) Cat Microforms

OH —ALLEN COUNTY HISTORICAL SOCIETY, Elizabeth M MacDonell Memorial Library, 620 W Market St, Lima, 45801. Raymond F Schuck, Cur, Allen County Museum; Anna B Selfridge, Asst Cur, Manuscripts & Archives
Holdings: Vols (6824) Cat Mss Maps Pix Slides Audiotapes Microforms
Notes: Includes history of Allen County; railroad; railroad labor history; genealogy.

PA —FRANKLIN INSTITUTE LIBRARY, 20 & The Parkway, Philadelphia, 19103. Miriam Padusis, Dir; Charles Wilt, Readers Servs Librn
Holdings: Vols (300,000) Cat Maps Pix Microforms

TX —ABILENE CHRISTIAN UNIVERSITY, Margaret & Herman Brown Library, ACU Sta, Abilene, 79601. Callie Faye Milliken, Assoc Dir
Notes: Walter and Nella Robbins Railroad Collection. 10,000 items, including books, time tables, passes, pictures, promotional, memorabilia.

TX —AMARILLO PUBLIC LIBRARY, 413 E Fourth, Amarillo, 79101. Mary Kay Snell, Librn
Holdings: Vols Cat Mss Maps Pix
Notes: The southwest collections incl materials on the history of Texas, Louisiana, New Mexico, Arkansas, Missouri and Kansas. General subjects covered incl overland journeys, early narratives, early biographies, Indian captivities, outlaws, US government reports, Mississippi and Ohio Rivers, the Mexican War, reports of Catholic missionaries, Niles Register, early publications, fur trade, western trails, Texas Rangers, sheriffs and Texas as a sovereign state, buffalo hunting, Indian wars, cowboys, the arrival of farmers, fences, and towns. Over 1600 items which incl books, documents, maps, mss, pamphlets, unpublished theses, interviews and photographs. The three major collections are the William Henry Bush Collection, the Laurence J Fitzsimon Collection and the Calendar of John L McCarty.

VT —MARTHA CANFIELD MEMORIAL FREE LIBRARY, Russell Vermontiana Collection, Arlington, 05250. D L Thomas, Cur; M L Thomas, Cur
Notes: Russell Collection of Vermontiana. 260 pamphlet boxes (nonbook items). Special railroad collection (unindexed). Also 250 diaries, ledgers, account books and minute books, 1757-1940. Not all briefed. Incl 1000 mss, 100 maps, 300 pictures, Canfield family and Dorothy Canfield Fisher papers.

ON —NATIONAL RESEARCH COUNCIL OF CANADA, Aeronautical/Mechanical Engineering Branch Library, Montreal Rd, Ottawa, K1A 0R6, Can. Louise Fletcher, Head
Notes: This branch library of the Canada Institute for Scientific and Technical Information (CISTI) of the National Research Council of Canada, Ottawa, has a collection strong in aeronautical engineering, automatic control, CAD/CAM, robotics, ocean, wind, and solar energy power, hydraulic and coastal engineering, icing, low temperature research, naval engineering, metals and metallurgy, incl composites, tribology, and air, railroad, marine transportation. Library supported the Council contribution to the development of the remote manipular Canadarm for NASA's Space Shuttle Orbiters and more recently, the Canadian Astronaut Program which will contribute payload specialists to NASA's Space Shuttle Program in 1984. 35,000 monographs, 1200 serials. Report collection: over 500,000 items.

PQ —CANADIAN NATIONAL RAILWAYS, Headquarters Library, 935 Lagauchetiere St W, Montreal, H3C 3N4, Can. Gilda Martinello, System Librn
Holdings: Vols 32,000 Cat Microforms
Notes: History, administration and operation of railways and related civil, mechanical and electrical engineering.

RAILROADS—BRIDGES see Railroad Bridges

RAILROADS—CALIFORNIA

CA —SAN DIEGO PUBLIC LIBRARY, Social Sciences Section, 820 E St, San Diego, 92101. Margaret E Queen, Supvr
Budget: ($36,000)
Notes: Good general collection with emphasis on railroads of California. Good materials on street railways and cable cars of western cities.

RAILROADS—CHICAGO

IL —CENTER FOR RESEARCH LIBRARIES, 6050 S Kenwood Ave, Chicago, 60637. Donald B Simpson, Dir; Esther Smith, Collection Development Librn
Holdings: Vols Uncat
Notes: Large collection of the original reports, studies and drawings of Chicago Railroad Terminal Studies, 1912-1915.

RAILROADS—EMPLOYEES

NY —CORNELL UNIVERSITY, New York State School of Industrial & Labor Relations, Martin P Catherwood Library, Ives Hall, Ithaca, 14853. Shirley F Harper, Dir
Holdings: Cat Mss Pix
Notes: All nonoperating files and memorabilia of the United Transportation Union. Also material on and from other railroad unions, and records of the New York, Ontario, and Western Railway, the New York and Pennsylvania Railway, and the American Shortline Railroad Association.

OH —ALLEN COUNTY HISTORICAL SOCIETY, Elizabeth M MacDonell Memorial Library, 620 W Market St, Lima, 45801. Raymond F Schuck, Cur, Allen County Museum; Anna B Selfridge, Asst Cur, Manuscripts & Archives
Holdings: Vols (6824) Cat Mss Maps Pix Slides Audiotapes Microforms
Notes: Includes history of Allen County; railroad; railroad labor history; genealogy.

RAILROADS—ENGINEERING see Railroad Engineering

RAILROADS—EQUIPMENT AND SUPPLIES

MO —WASHINGTON UNIVERSITY, Libraries, Special Collections Dept, Campus Box 1061, St Louis, 63130.
Holdings: //
Notes: Records of the St Louis Car Company, 1887-1973, incl the transportation

RAILROADS—EQUIPMENT AND SUPPLIES (cont.)

manufacturing enterprise's files of over 20,000 photographs and negatives of the firm's products; over 2000 original tracings of railroad and street car equipment. Also printed material about the firm, and catalogs published by the company from 1904 to 1965.

RAILROADS—GUIDES see Railroads—Timetables

RAILROADS—HISTORY

CA —AZUSA PACIFIC COLLEGE, Marshburn Memorial Library, Citrus & Alosta, Azusa, 91702. Edward Peterman, Librn
Holdings: Vols (6000) Uncat
Budget: ($30,000)
Notes: Significant holdings in the George E Fullerton Library of Californiana and Western Americana.

CA —OCCIDENTAL COLLEGE, Library, 1600 Campus Rd, Los Angeles, 90041. Michael C Sutherland, Special Collections Librn
Holdings: Vols (1500) Uncat Mss Maps Pix
Notes: The John Lloyd-Butler Collection of books covering such subjects as exploration of railroad routes, railroad construction and operation, annual reports and timetables of individual railroads, historical and biographical works, and several runs of railroad journals.

CA —ROSEVILLE PUBLIC LIBRARY, 225 Taylor St, Roseville, 95678. Susan L Nickerson, Dir
Holdings: Cat Mss Maps Pix Slides

CA —SAN BERNARDINO VALLEY COLLEGE, Samuel Andrews Memorial Library, 701 S Mt Vernon, San Bernardino, 92403. Robin Calote, Librn
Holdings: Vols 201 Cat
Budget: $500

CA —SAN DIEGO PUBLIC LIBRARY, Social Sciences Section, 820 E St, San Diego, 92101. Margaret E Queen, Supvr
Budget: ($36,000)
Notes: Good general collection with emphasis on railroads of California. Good materials on street railways and cable cars of western cities.

CA —HOOVER INSTITUTION ON WAR, REVOLUTION & PEACE, Stanford University, Stanford, 94305. Milorad M Drachkovitch, Archivist
Holdings: // Mss
Notes: Records, 1917-1923, 1931-1936, on the US Commission of Railway Experts to Russia. Papers relating to activities of the commission, to the Russian railway service Corps, the Inter-Allied Railway Committee, the Russian political scene, and events in Siberia during the Russian Revolution and civil war. Persons represented incl John Frank Stevens, chairman of the commission. Correspondents incl George H Emerson, H H Fisher, Benjamin O Johnson, and Charles H Smith. 2 boxes.

CA —STANFORD UNIVERSITY LIBRARIES, Cecil H Green Library, Stanford, 94305. Michael T Ryan, Cur
Holdings: Vols (1700) // Cat Mss Maps Pix
Notes: The Timothy Hopkins Transportation Collection. Mss on early railroading in England, India, and US. Construction and operation of Central Pacific. Papers of men connected with Central and Southern Pacific and subsidiaries. United Railroads of San Francisco. Some materials on shipping and aviation.

CA —BAY AREA ELECTRIC RAILROAD ASSOCIATION, California Railway Museum, Star Rte 283, Box 150, Suisun City, 94585. Vernon J Sappers, Librn
Holdings: Vols (5000) Uncat Maps Pix Slides 16mm Films
Notes: Technical journals and publications pertaining to steam and electric railroads. In addition, there are ten cabinets of files of the following railroad companies: Key System, Southern Pacific and Associated Companies,
Western Pacific Railroad, Sacramento Northern Railroad, Pacific Electric Railway, Northern Electric Railway, Oakland Antioch & Eastern Railway. These files deal with the history of each railroad.

CO —COLORADO HISTORICAL SOCIETY, Research Collections, 1300 Broadway, Denver, 80203. Catherine Kane, Head Public Service and Access
Holdings: Cat Mss Pix Microfilms
Notes: Correspondence and business records of cattle companies and cattlemen and railroads gathered as part of the Western Range Cattle Industry Study. Also, correspondence and records of companies, organizations and related materials arranged by state (1850-1945). About 50,000 items.

CO —DENVER PUBLIC LIBRARY, Western History Department, 1357 Broadway, Denver, 80203. Eleanor M Gehres, Head
Holdings: Vols (50,000) Cat Mss Maps Pix Audiotapes Microforms
Notes: Western US History. The department has a separate catalog, published in 1970 in 7 vols by G K Hall Co. First supplement published in 1975 in 1 vol. There is a subject index of some 3 million entries to newspapers and magazines of the Rocky Mountain region, added to daily. The Western Newspaper Microfilm Center contains approx 7000 reels of Western US newspapers. Collection has ca 275,000 negatives and prints of Western life; and ca 2500 maps, cataloged and classified.

CO —FORT LEWIS COLLEGE, Library, Southwest Collection, College Heights, Durango, 81301. Daniel W Lester, Dir
Holdings: Vols (7000) Cat Mss Maps Pix Slides Microforms
Budget: ($3800)
Notes: Also have separate catalog of the special collections concerning the Southwest, Indians, mine records, railroad records, etc.

CO —COLORADO RAILROAD MUSEUM, Golden, 80401. R W Richardson, Exec Dir
Holdings: Vols 1000 Uncat Mss Maps Pix
Notes: Western railroads; mountain narrowgauge. Collections incl, in addition to railroad books, the papers and files of operating lines in Colorado, collected over past 30 years: letter files, records and record books, day to day operations, telegrams and other forms recording the day, week and month.

CT —CONNECTICUT ELECTRIC RAILWAY ASSOCIATION, INC, Southern New England, PO Box 360, East Windsor, 06088. William E Wood, Dir of Museum
Holdings: Vols 1500 Uncat Mss Maps Pix
Notes: Some 1500 items. The collection can be opened only on application.

CT —YALE UNIVERSITY, Box 1603A, Yale Station, New Haven, 06520.

DE —HAGLEY MUSEUM AND LIBRARY, Eleutherian Mills-Hagley Foundation Inc, PO Box 3630, Greenville, 19807. Richmond D Williams, Dir; Heddy A Richter, Imprints Librn
Notes: Records of the Reading Railroad (1845-1940; 1000 cubic feet) contain minute books and financial records documenting the history of both the parent and subsidiary companies. Voluminous correspondence files describe all aspects of railroad operations.

DE —UNIVERSITY OF DELAWARE, Hugh M Morris Library, S College Ave, Newark, 19711. T Stuart Dick, Special Collections
Holdings: // Mss
Notes: Personal and business letters and receipts of the Albertson family, a Quaker lumber and lime merchants (1782-1862) residing in Plymouth, Montgomery Co, Pa. Included are many letters concerning the Plymouth RR and rules and regulations for its administration.

DE —HISTORICAL SOCIETY OF DELAWARE, Library, 505 Market St Mall, Wilmington, 19801. Barbara E Benson, Library Dir
Holdings: Cat Mss Maps Pix
Notes: Collection incl papers and other mss materials.

DC —GEORGETOWN UNIVERSITY, Library, Special Collections Div, 37 & O Sts NW, Washington, 20057. George M Barringer, Special Collections Librn;
Nicholas B Sheetz, Mss Librn
Holdings: Cat Mss
Notes: Chiefly American, incl posters and memorabilia. Major collections include (1) collection of shipping, railroad, and customs receipts which document commerce between Baltimore and Philadelphia. The earliest records are from a company run by John F F Wessels, later associated with Christian Mayer and Frederick Konig. (2) Collection assembled by Jerimiah J O'Connor consisting of a wide assortment of materials pertaining to railroads, principally in the United States. Incl are train schedules and time tables, printed promotional material, published manufacturer's brochures and catalogues, stock certificates, maps, photographs, and a variety of printed and other types of ephemera.

DC —LIBRARY OF CONGRESS, Rare Book & Special Collections Div, Washington, 20540. William Matheson, Chief
Notes: Important holdings relating to subjects such as railroads and canals. Material by and about Robert Fulton is particularly strong. The division contains many pre-Civil War technical manuals.

DC —NATIONAL ARCHIVES AND RECORDS SERVICE, National Archives Library, Pennsylvania Ave & Eighth St NW, Washington, 20408.
Notes: Extensive archival records of defunct American railroads.

IL —CENTER FOR RESEARCH LIBRARIES, 6050 S Kenwood Ave, Chicago, 60637. Donald B Simpson, Dir; Esther Smith, Collection Development Librn
Holdings: Vols 10,000 // Uncat
Notes: Collection of annual and other reports of US and some foreign railroads, late 19th century to 1930s. Timetables and guides. Large collection of the original reports, studies and drawings of Chicago Railroad Terminal Studies, 1912-1915.

IL —LOYOLA UNIVERSITY OF CHICAGO, E M Cudahy Memorial Library, 6525 N Sheridan Rd, Chicago, 60626.
Notes: Dorr E Felt Pamphlet and Clipping Collection. Emphasizes political and economic issues, 1902-35, and documents Illinois Manufacturers Association Conference, September 8-9, 1919; Air Board of Chicago, April 16, 1921-August 1, 1930; Allied Debts to the US, May 15, 1923-September 30, 1926; Bolshevism, Communism, "Red" Russia, 1924-27; Child Labor Bill, March 30, 1915, 1914-20; Labor, March, 1902-March, 1932; Railroad Strike, August 25, 1916-August 7, 1920; The War, August, 1914-October 23, 1930; War Industries Commission, June, 1918-November 23, 1928. A pamphlet list // is available for each topic.

IL —MUSEUM OF SCIENCE AND INDUSTRY, Library, 57th St and Lake Shore Dr, Chicago, 60637. Carla Hayden, Coordinator
Holdings: Vols (15,000) Cat Maps Pix
Budget: ($10,000)
Notes: Occupying the site of the Fine Arts Building of Chicago's Columbian Exposition of 1893, the Museum Library has been the recipient of numerous gifts in this field, not only of materials from Chicago's Columbian Expositions, Century of Progress and Railroad Fairs but also from the New York World's Fair, St Louis, Paris Exposition Universelle, San Francisco's Panama-Pacific etc. Incl blueprints of some buildings and areas. No separate catalog or index to this extensive collection.

IL —NEWBERRY LIBRARY, 60 W Walton St, Chicago, 60610. Diana Haskell, Cur of Modern Mss
Holdings: Vols 250 Uncat
Notes: Annual reports of American railroads from the 1880s until 1960. Reports of the Illinois and Iowa Railroad Commissions, Poor's Manual and histories of the ICC and the railroads themselves also incl.
See also entries under Illinois, Central; Burlington Railroad; Pullman Corporation.

IL —NEWBERRY LIBRARY, 60 W Walton St, Chicago, 60610. Diana Haskell, Cur of Modern Mss
Holdings: // Mss Maps Posters Timetables
Notes: Collection of 350 sq feet of archival

RAILROADS—HISTORY (cont.)

material is particularly valuable for the long series of letters from the President, Stuyvesant Fish, 1887-1906 (80 vols). The richest part of the collection runs from 1880 to 1905. There are no "working papers" dealing with railway operations or personnel for this period, but rather administrative detail at the higher levels. Carolyn Curtis Mohr, comp, *Guide to the Illinois Central Archives in the Newberry Library*, 1851-1906. Chicago: The Newberry Library, 1951.

IL —LAKE FOREST COLLEGE, Donnelley Library, Lake Forest, 60045. Arthur H Miller Jr, College Librn
Holdings: Vols (1500) Cat Mss Maps Pix
Budget: ($1000)
Notes: Elliott Donnelley Collection (received 1976) of mostly mid-20th century books and periodicals on Western railroads and mountain narrow gauge, world narrow gauge and short lines, steam, live steam, model railroading, and some traction. Purchases keep collection emphasis current (50-75 new books per year, 22 periodical subscriptions). Also, the Munson Paddock Colleccton (received 1977) of train illustrations, maps, and timetables, 1850-1950. In addition to American technical and historical books and periodicals, the collection contains books of views, narrations of rail travel (particularly American West), and US local histories--all with illustrations of trains. Most titles are late 19th century Americna. The 1550 volumes are supplemented by related holdings of more than 150 pamphlets, 600 timetables, 2000 unbound periodical issues, 200 maps, 75 diagrams (engines, cars) hundreds of clippings of train illustrations, and 1000 photographs. In progress is a card index of illustrations by wheel type line, and manufacturer. Together, the collections contain about 7000 items.

IL —SCHAUMBURG TOWNSHIP PUBLIC LIBRARY, 32 W Library Lane, Schaumburg, 60194. Michael Madden, Librn
Holdings: Vols (20,000) Cat
Budget: ($60,000)
Notes: Maintained as business and economics subject center under the North Suburban Library System's Coordinated Acquisitions Program.

IN —INDIANA UNIVERSITY, Lilly Library, Seventh St, Bloomington, 47405. William R Cagle, Librn
Holdings: // Mss Pix
Notes: Papers of US Senator and Vice-President Charles Warren Fairbanks, 1819-1939. Contains correspondence with prominent political figures, friends, relatives, etc; speeches; law office papers; photographs. Most of the material is for his early years of practice as a railroad attorney and his senatorial and vice-presidential years. The later papers deal with the settlement of his estate. 150,006 items.

IN —INDIANA STATE UNIVERSITY, EVANSVILLE, Library, 8600 University Blvd, Evansville, 47712. Gina R Walker, Acting Archivist
Holdings: Cat Mss Pix
Notes: Evansville (Indiana) Suburban and Newburgh Railway Company. Minutes, directors' reports, stockholders annual meetings, certificates of shares. Dates 1887-1950. Restricted use: noncirculating.

IN —WILLARD LIBRARY, 21 First Ave, Evansville, 47710. Joan Elliott, Special Collections Librn
Holdings: Vols (525) Cat
Notes: Menus from 1920-1950s, foreign and domestic, with emphasis on menus from famous trains and ships.

IN —INDIANA HISTORICAL SOCIETY, Library, 315 W Ohio St, Indianapolis, 46202. Robert K O'Neill, Dir
Notes: Incl rare books, mss, pictures, maps, and ephemera relating to the history of Indiana and the Old Northwest. Mss dealing with the Old Northwest, incl a large collection of William Henry Harrison materials; papers of leading nineteenth-century Indiana figures; letters of Civil War soldiers; records of twentieth-century social welfare organizations. Rare books collection incl Jesuit *Relations*, early travel accounts, and early Indiana imprints. Pictures incl Indiana small-town life; Monon Railroad Colleciton; Callis Steamboat Collection, dealing with Terre Haute. Maps of Indiana; Sanborn real estate atlases for Indianapolis. Special collections in Indiana black, ethnic, and architectural history.

IN —PURDUE UNIVERSITY LIBRARIES, Graduate School of Management, Krannert Library, West Lafayette, 47907. Gordon Law, Librn
Notes: An important resource at the Krannert Library is its Special Collection of Business and Economics, consisting of some 8000 rare pre-20th century strengths in books, journals, tracts and pamphlets covering primarily the early literature of economic thought and business practices in America and abroad, 1500-1870. A catalog was issued in 1979.

IN —PURDUE UNIVERSITY LIBRARIES, West Lafayette, 47907. Edwin Posey, Librn
Holdings: Vols (6271) Cat Mss Maps Pix Microforms
Budget: $2683
Notes: The William Freeman Myrick Goss Library of the History of Engineering with an emphasis on railroads.

IA —STATE HISTORICAL SOCIETY OF IOWA LIBRARY, 402 Iowa Ave, Iowa City, 52240. Darold J Brown, Librn
Holdings: Vols 1500 Cat Mss Maps Pix
Notes: Incl timetables, pamphlet materials, company records, annual reports, histories, periodicals.

IA —UNIVERSITY OF IOWA, University Libraries, Iowa City, 52242. Frank Paluka, Head, Special Collections Dept
Holdings: // Mss
Notes: Collection especially concerns the Union Pacific and Rock Island Railroads. 45 linear feet of ms material. Described in Richard M Kolbet, "The Levi O Leonard Railroad Collection," *Books at Iowa*, April 1968.

KS —KANSAS STATE UNIVERSITY, Library, Special Collections & University Archives, Manhattan, 66506. Antonia Q Pigno, Coordr; John J Vander Velde, Librn; Anthony R Crawford, Univ Archivist
Holdings: Vols 25 // Cat Mss
Notes: Dan Casement, 1868-1953, was a wealthy Manhattan rancher. He graduated from Princeton in 1890. During the years 1897-1901 he helped his father, Jack build a railroad across Costa Rica. Jack had built the Union Pacific across the US. Dan Casement opposed the New Deal, incl the Agricultural Adjustment Act; he wrote articles and made radio speeches against them. Most of the 2500 letters congratulate him on his stand.

KS —HARVEY COUNTY HISTORICAL SOCIETY, Historical Library & Museum, 203 Main St, Newton, 67114. Mike Smurr, Dir
Holdings: Maps Pix
Notes: Our Library-Museum is limited to literature, pictures, and artifacts of interest to this locality, Harvey County, KS. Newton has been a RR point since the Santa Fe built here in 1871, so we have an unusually good collection of railroad items. Hundreds of pictures, many timetables, passes, and items small enough to be housed in our building. Attention is also given to early-day agriculture in mid-Kansas, especially wheat-raising by early settlers in central Kansas.

ME —BOWDOIN COLLEGE, Library, Brunswick, 04011. Dianne M Gutscher, Cur of Special Collections
Holdings: Cat Mss
Notes: Atlantic and St Lawrence Railroad Papers. This archive of the first international railroad from Portland, Maine, to Montreal contains approx 800 items for the years 1844-1889. It consists of the official records of the railroad, including committee reports, secretary's minutes, copybooks, misc notes, reports, leases, pamphlets and broadsides as well as correspondence.

MD —BALTIMORE STREETCAR MUSEUM, Transit Research Center, 1901 Falls Rd, PO Box 7184, Baltimore, 21218. George F Nixon, Cur
Holdings: Cat Mss Pix Slides 16mm Films
Notes: Transit Research Center is devoted to the collection of memorabilia, photos, drawings, printed matter, etc, pertinent to public rail transportation in Baltimore and Maryland. Incl streetcar systems, interurban lines, and main line railroads in the area. Also incl bus history. Existing collection moved to larger facilities (Feb 1978). Incl materials donated by The Baltimore Transit Co, United Railways and Electric Co, as well as private collections.

MD —MARYLAND HISTORICAL SOCIETY, Library, 201 W Monument St, Baltimore, 21201. William B Keller, Head Librn
Holdings: Cat Mss Maps Pix Slides Microforms
Notes: Espec relating to Maryland and Baltimore. Extensive collection.

MA —HARVARD UNIVERSITY, Baker Library of the Graduate School of Business Administration, Kress Library of Business and Economics, Soldiers Field, Boston, 02163. Ruth E Rogers, Cur
Holdings: Cat
Notes: Corporation Records Division: Active file of annual reports of over 20,000 corporations, US and foreign; SEC reports, and other financial documents. Large collection of older material, especially railroads and canals; financial services. Mainly noncirculating.

MA —HARVARD UNIVERSITY, Graduate School of Business Administration, Baker Library, Soldiers Field, Boston, 02163. Mary V Chatfield, Librn; Florence Bartoshesky, Cur of Manuscripts and Archives
Notes: An extensive collection. Historical emphasis on railroads and canals. Incl Boston and Worcester RR; Western RR; and Boston and Albany RR.

†MA —JOHN F KENNEDY LIBRARY, Columbia Point, Boston, 02125. Dan H Fenn Jr, Dir
Holdings: // Cat Mss
Notes: Records of the Presidential Railraod Commisssion, 1961-1962. 99 linear ft of mss. Holdings are described in "Historical Materials in the John F Kennedy Library." Copies may be obtained by writing the Research Archivist.

MA —SOCIETY FOR THE PRESERVATION OF NEW ENGLAND ANTIQUITIES, Library, 141 Cambridge St, Boston, 02114. Ellie Reichlin, Librn & Cur of Photographic Collections
Notes: Boston and Albany Railroad Archive (1890s-1920s): original negatives with prints of stations, structures along rail lines, views of construction. 1500 pieces. *See also* entry under Transportation - History.

MA —UNIVERSITY OF LOWELL, Library, One University Ave, Lowell, 01854. Martha Mayo, Special Collections Librn
Holdings: Vols 1000 Cat Mss Pix Maps
Notes: The Boston and Maine Railroad Historical Society has located their collection of B&M Railroad archives, books, timetables, photographs and engineering drawings at the University of Lowell. Their rapidly growing collection is primarily concerned with the New England railroads.

MA —AMERICAN ANTIQUARIAN SOCIETY LIBRARY, 185 Salisbury St, Worcester, 01609. Marcus A McCorison, Dir & Librn
Holdings: Cat Mss Maps Pix
Notes: Outstanding collection, especially for early period, primarily to 1840; thereafter for States of the East and Midwest to the Civil War. Over 6000 items. Incl the Thomas Winthrop Streeter Collection of Transportation; much on the history of canals, bridges, turnpikes, and harbors.

MI —UNIVERSITY OF MICHIGAN, Engineering-Transportation Library, 312 Undergraduate Library, Ann Arbor, 48109. Sharon A Balius, Assoc Librn
Holdings: Cat Mss Pix
Notes: Incl annual reports, pamphlets, timetables, charters, laws, surveys and advertising brochures for railroad companies

RAILROADS—HISTORY (cont.)

of the US and Canada. Also incl are the papers of George M Brown and Charles Ellet, Jr, original drawings by Otto Kuhler and a collection of materials on the Shay locomotive, as well as a large collection of prints and photographs.

MI —EDISON INSTITUTE, Greenfield Village and Henry Ford Museum, Archives & Research Library, PO Box 1970, Dearborn, 48121. Steve Hamp, Dir; Joan W Gartland, Librn
Notes: Incl Dunbar collection of prints, broadsides and drawings documenting *History of Travel in America*, 1680-1910 (1741 items) and the Walker Locomotive collection, 1820-1931 (308 items). It also incl 19th century maps and travelers guides and an antique automotive file.

MI —DETROIT PUBLIC LIBRARY, Burton Historical Collection, 5201 Woodward Ave, Detroit, 48202. Alice Dalligan, Chief

MN —JAMES JEROME HILL REFERENCE LIBRARY, Fourth St at Market St, Saint Paul, 55106. Virgil F Massman, Dir
Holdings: Vols (197,000) Mss
Budget: ($170,000)
Notes: Railroad history, and espec about the Great Northern Railway and James Jerome Hill.

MS —UNIVERSITY OF SOUTHERN MISSISSIPPI, William David McCain Graduate Library, Box 5148, Southern Sta, Hattiesburg, 39406.
Holdings: Cat Mss
Notes: Collections incl the 450 cubic feet of records of the Association of American Railroads for the period 1914-1937; 72 cubic feet of records of the Gulf, Mobile, and Ohio Railroad for the period 1869-1965 (bulk dates 1925-1955); 23 cubic feet of records of the Illinois Central Railroad - Vicksburg, Mississippi Division for the period 1913-1961; and 245 cubic feet of records of the Mississippi Central Railroad for the period 1898-1967. A guide to these records is available for loan. See entries under the name of the individual railroad.

MO —UNIVERSITY OF MISSOURI-KANSAS CITY, General Library, Snyder Collection of Americana, 5100 Rockhill Road, Kansas City, 64110. Kenneth J LaBudde, Dir; Robert Paustian, Asst Dir
Holdings: Vols 25,000 Cat
Notes: Nucleus was Robert M Snyder, Jr Americana Collection of some 14,000 items. Contains printed materials on 19th-century American history, especially the Trans-Mississippi West. Strengths include the history of Kansas City and Jackson County, Missouri, Kansas and Missouri county and state histories, American frontier religion (esp the Mormons and Alexander Campbell's Disciples of Christ), the history of railroads and transportation, the cattle trade, 19th-Century biography and autobiography, North American Indians and early Kansas and Missouri imprints.

MO —NATIONAL MUSEUM OF TRANSPORT, Reference Library, 3105 Barrett Station Rd, Saint Louis, 63122. John P Roberts, Secretary
Holdings: Vols (10,000) Cat Mss Maps Pix Slides

MO —WASHINGTON UNIVERSITY, Libraries, Special Collections Dept, Campus Box 1061, St Louis, 63130.
Notes: Collections incl (1) Terminal Railroad Association Records (1889-date), of more than 450 original tracings of the Eads Bridge (1874-date). Drawings show in fine and complete detail all the design features of this internationally known St Louis landmark. (2) Papers of Charles W Bryan Jr, incl correspondence, personal journals, scrapbooks, photographs, and printed material associated with the Federal Shipbuilding Company from 1917 to 1948 and as president of the Pullman Standard Car Manufacturing Company from 1950 to 1958. (3) Records of the St Louis Car Company, 1887-1973, incl the transportation manufacturing enterprise's files of over 20,000 photographs andnegatives of the firm's

products; over 2000 original tracings of railroad and street car equipment. Also printed material about the firm, and catalogs published by the company from 1904 to 1965.

NE —NEBRASKA STATE HISTORICAL SOCIETY, Fort Robinson Museum, Box 304, Crawford, 69339. Vance Nelson, Cur
Holdings: Vols (1500) Cat Mss Maps Pix Slides Phonorecords Audiotapes 16mm Films Microforms

Notes: Materials related to the history of Fort Robinson, and incl the Post Medical Library, reference books on state government, etc, Western Americana: books on ranching, homesteaders, Indian wars, etc; microfilm records for Fort Robinson records, Red Cloud and Spotted Tail Indian Agency records, Crawford and Chadron Nebraska newspapers, diaries and interviews. Library incl the E Kopac Collection of books dealing with Western Americana; particularly Indian wars, transportation, guns and railroads.

NE —KEARNEY STATE COLLEGE, Calvin T Ryan Library, Kearney, 68847. John Mayeski, Dir; Anita Norman, Reference Librn

Holdings: Vols (1700) Cat Mss Maps Pix Slides Microforms
Notes: Collection attempts to cover total historical development of Nebraska. Special strengths incl overland journeys, pony express, sod houses, and the Union Pacific. Special consideration has been given to Indians of Nebraska and the cattle industry. The collection is well supported by the library's general strength of Western Americana.

NE —NEBRASKA STATE HISTORICAL SOCIETY, Archives, 1500 R St, Box 82554, Lincoln, 68501. James E Potter, State Archivist
Holdings: Cat Mss Microforms
Budget: ($290,000)

Notes: Collection estimated 4,000 cu. ft. of personal papers, business records, church records, and organizational records relating to the history of Nebraska and the Great Plains, ca. 1854-present with a particularly strong emphasis in the subject areas of Indians of North America, agriculture, railroad history, 19th century agrarian political movements, irrigation, and settlement of the Great Plains. Public records holdings of an estimated 10,000 cu. ft. of Nebraska state, county and some municipal government agencies include the official files of Nebraska governors, the Nebraska Legislature, and many territorial and state agencies 1854-present; and numerous tax records, court records, marriage records, naturalization records, and school census records for Nebraska counties. Newspaper collection of 20,000 rolls of microfilm, non-circulating but available for purchase, cataloged according to place published so specific titles must be requested.

NV —UNIVERSITY OF NEVADA, RENO, University Library, Special Collections Dept, Reno, 89557. Robert E Blesse, Head
Holdings: Vols (150) Cat Mss Photogs Maps
Notes: Includes 370 cu ft manuscripts, 2000 photographs. Major collection include papers of Nevada railroad companies Virginia and Truckee, Carson and Colorado, Eureka and Palisade, and Nevada Copper Belt. Materials are collected which deal with the history and development of railroads within Nevada and those which have run through the state.

NH —NEW HAMPSHIRE HISTORICAL SOCIETY, Library, 30 Park St, Concord, 03301. William Copeley, Assoc Librn
Holdings: Vols 200 Cat Maps Pix
Budget: ($9000)

Notes: Material relates to all New Hampshire railroads of importance and to several major New England railroads. Incl articles of incorporation, printed copies of leases, annual reports, transcripts of court cases and transcripts of legislative hearings.

NJ —STEVENS INSTITUTE OF TECHNOLOGY, Samuel C Williams Library, Castle Point Sta, Hoboken, 07030. Jane G Hartye, Special Collections Librn
Holdings: Vols (250) Cat Pix Microforms
Budget: ($1500)

Notes: Col John Stevens and his sons Robert Livingston Stevens and Edwin Augustus Stevens. Thet were responsible for the first steam locomotives and railroad; they were involved in shipbuilding, building the "Juliana," the "Phoenix" and ferries. We have a huge amount of uncataloged data on the "Stevens Battery." The Stevens family played an extremely important role in developing the City of Hoboken; Edwin Augustus Stevens established Stevens Institute of Technology. Through the Stevens family, we have much historical data on the City of Hoboken and the State of New Jersey. Our collection includes microfilm of the Stevens Papers and of Hoboken.

NJ —PRINCETON UNIVERSITY, Library, Pliny Fisk Library of Economics and Finance, Princeton, 08544. Louise Tompkins, Librn
Holdings: Vols 5000 Cat
Notes: The American railroad corporations collection is strongest for the period 1865-1915. Incl books, pamphlets, broker's circulars, newspaper clippings, annual reports and mortgages. There is a separate catalog which indexes the material by name of corporation. A good description of the collection is contained in Brayer, Herbert O "The Pliny Fisk Collection of Railroad and Corporation Finance," *The Princeton University Chronicle*, vol 6, no 4 (1944-1945), pp 171-178.

NM —MUSEUM OF NEW MEXICO, Photo Archives, Box 2087, Santa Fe, 87503. Arthur L Olivas, Cur; Richard Rudisill, Photo Historian
Holdings: Cat Pix Slides
Notes: Archives incl 200,000 photographs, cataloged, and 40,000 slides. Primary function of the archives is to preserve significant historical material, and these pictures are mainly for research rather than general browsing. Photographs may be ordered as research copies for set fees. Reproduction or publication requires written permission plus additional required fees. Subject matter covered is extensive, incl Southwest town views, Southwest Indians, military subjects, missions, pioneer life, recreation (indoor and outdoor, toys, games, gambling, camping, etc), disasters, exhibits and expositions, portraits (those identified filed by last name), tools and equipment (agricultural, mechanical, housekeeping, etc), and transportation (railroad, stagecoaches, carriages, wagons, etc).

NY —COLGATE UNIVERSITY, Everett Needham Case Library, Hamilton, 13346. Bruce M Brown, Collections Librn
Notes: New York State railroads. Incl timetables, maps, pictures, clippings, letters and misc materials. Extensive collection on Central New England Railroad.

RAILROADS—HISTORY (cont.)

NY —CORNELL UNIVERSITY, New York State School of Industrial & Labor Relations, Martin P Catherwood Library, Ives Hall, Ithaca, 14853. Shirley F Harper, Dir
Holdings: Cat Mss Pix
Notes: All nonoperating files and memorabilia of the United Transportation Union. Also material on and from other railroad unions, and records of the New York, Ontario, and Western Railway, the New York and Pennsylvania Railway, and the American Shortline Railroad Association.

NY —COLUMBIA UNIVERSITY LIBRARIES, Rare Book & Manuscript Library, 801 Butler Library, 535 W 114 St, New York, 10027. Kenneth A Lohf, Librn
Holdings: Pix
Notes: William Barclay Parsons Collection of Railroad Prints, relating primarily to American and English railroads. Restricted use.

NY —ELECTRIC RAILROADERS ASSOCIATION, Frank J Sprague Memorial Library, 89 E 42nd St, New York, 10018. Hugh A Dunne, First VP
Notes: Private library. Incl all forms of railroads operated by electricity. Forms of electric railroads included: street railways, subways & elevated lines, high-speed interurbans, suburban commuter lines, electrified trunk lines, monorails, mountain climbing inclines, etc. Also railroad timetables.

NY —NEW YORK PUBLIC LIBRARY, Research Libraries, Science and Technology Research Center, Fifth Ave & 42 St, New York, 10018.
Holdings: Vols (1,100,000) Cat Microforms
Budget: ($647,259)

NY —NEW YORK PUBLIC LIBRARY, Research Libraries, Economic & Public Affairs Div, Fifth Ave & 42 St, New York, 10018. Edward DiRoma, Chief
Holdings: Vols (1,500,000) Cat Microforms

NY —JERVIS PUBLIC LIBRARY, 613 N Washington St, Rome, 13440. William A Dillon, Dir
Holdings: Vols (1500) // Cat Mss Maps Slides
Notes: John Bloomfield Jervis Collection contains personal library (1500 vols) and papers (1300 items) of chief engineer of Croton aqueduct and other waterworks, canals, and railroads circa 1825-1860. Papers available on micorfilm; indexes to papers available from Jervis Public Library.

NY —STATE UNIVERSITY OF NEW YORK, STONY BROOK, Melville Library, Dept of Special Collections, Stony Brook, 11794. Evert Volkersz, Head
Holdings: Vols 40 Cat Pix
Notes: Forty albums combining detailed pencil drawings of Long Island Railroad tracks and explanatory notes with more than 5000 identified photographs, 1885-1968; 300 timetables, 1895-date; and related materials, compiled by Robert Emery.

NC —DUKE UNIVERSITY, William R Perkins Library, Durham, 27706. Elvin E Strowd, University Librn
Notes: The Railroad Corporation Reports collection is made up of 8000 items, issued primarily since 1900, though many go back as far as the middle of the 19th century for main trunk lines in the United States.

NC —NORTH CAROLINA STATE UNIVERSITY, D H Hill Library, Box 7111, Raleigh, 27695. I T Littleton, Dir
Holdings: Vols (1700) Cat
Budget: $1500
Notes: Emphasis on the history of railroads. Incl monographs.

OH —ALLEN COUNTY HISTORICAL SOCIETY, Elizabeth M MacDonell Memorial Library, 620 W Market St, Lima, 45801. Raymond F Schuck, Cur, Allen County Museum; Anna B Selfridge, Asst Cur, Manuscripts & Archives
Holdings: Vols (6824) Cat Mss Maps Pix Slides Audiotapes Microforms
Notes: Includes history of Allen County; railroad; railroad labor history; genealogy.

PA —SCRANTON PUBLIC LIBRARY, Local History & Genealogical Section, Vine St & Washington Ave, Scranton, 18503. Bettina Manzo, Librn
Holdings: Vols (2000) Cat Mss Maps Pix Microforms
Notes: Emphasis on northeastern Pennsylvania. Also, historical materials about local churches, schools, businesses, architecture, clubs and organizations, demographics, geography and geology, and biographies.

PA —PENNSYLVANIA STATE UNIVERSITY, Fred Lewis Pattee Library, Special Collections Dept, University Park, 16802. Charles Mann, Chief, Special Collections
Holdings: Vols (1976) Cat Mss Pix Slides
Budget: ($37,000)
Notes: Includes The Beaver Collection (576 vols) in honor of James Beaver, Governor of Pennsylvania, mostly county histories, atlases and Regimental Civil War histories; John M Read Pamphlets (1400 titles), 1830-1890, relating to canals, railroads and civil law. No photocopying.

†SD —SOUTH DAKOTA SCHOOL OF MINES & TECHNOLOGY, Devereaux Library, Rapid City, 57701.
Holdings: Vols (3786) Cat Mss Maps Pix Audiotapes Microforms
Notes: This special collection, in general, relates to the Black Hills area of South Dakota and Wyoming, especially mining and exploration of the area; the West River area of South Dakota, primarily county histories; and South Dakota Territorial and State materials. There are also specialized areas of this collection: (1) *Marion N Bruce Collection.* Documents, correspondence, books and periodicals dealing with weather modification in South Dakota; (2) *Mildred Fielder Collection.* Mss, pictures, books and periodicals from an author whose special area was the Black Hills. Most of her work on railroads, mines, trails, etc, relates to historical aspects. Collection incl research materials, galley proofs and final copies of her various publications; (3) *Cleophas C O'Harra Collection.* Mss, pictures, books and original source materials, primarily related to the Black Hills area andexpeditions thereto. Much of the data was collected for a book on the Black Hills which was never published; and (4) *Caving Collection.* Maps of various caves in Black Hills area, being kept current and updated by members of the Paha Sapa Grotto. Also, some books and periodicals on caving in general.

TX —HARDIN-SIMMONS UNIVERSITY, Richardson Library, Abilene, 79601. Joe F Dahlstrom, Dir
Holdings: Vols (10,000) Cat Mss Maps Pix Microforms
Notes: Special collection name is Richardson Research Center, named in honor of Dr Rupert N Richardson. Collect in the areas of his own research interests, especially that portion of the US that was once a part of Mexico. Emphases on the history of ranching, railroads, discovery and exploration, Texas county histories, etc. Incl 350 items printed and/or designed by El Paso printer Carl Hertzog; the Judge R C Crane collection of Texana and a similar collection of Louise Kelley's; and the Research Publication's Western Americana collection (microfilm).

TX —SOUTHERN METHODIST UNIVERSITY, DeGolyer Library, Box 396, SMU, Dallas, 75275. Clifton H Jones, Dir
Holdings: Vols (15,000) Cat Mss Maps Pix
Notes: One of the largest railroad photograph collections in the world; about 230,000 prints and 70,000 negatives, all countries. Accompanied by a major collection (12,000 vols), of railroadiana; much on locomotives. All languages.

TX —AMON CARTER MUSEUM, Library, 3501 Camp Bowie Blvd, PO Box 2365, Fort Worth, 76101. Milan R Hughston, Microfilm Librn
Holdings: Cat
Notes: Earliest newspaper is from 1787 (Kentucky), and cut-off date is 1900. Trying to get a good coverage of the entire nation and Western Canada for the 19th century. The archivist has prepared a card index of selected stories from the entire runs of *Harper's Weekly and Leslie's Illustrated* Newspaper. This subject index fills 24 catalog drawers. The selections were made on the basis of current and potential research being done by the curatorial staff, with emphasis on the American and Canadian West, Indians, artists, railroads and pictorial matter. The index also incl subject entries for stories from other papers, such as the *Arkansas Gazette, Missouri Republican* and various Texas newspapers. These have not been read systematically, as were the above, but as they are found they are added to the index.

TX —RAILROAD & PIONEER MUSEUM, Library, 710 Jack Baskin St, PO Box 5126, Temple, 76501. Mary Pat McLaughlin, Dir
Holdings: Vols 200 Cat Mss Maps Pix Slides Phonorecords Audiotapes 16mm Films

UT —UNIVERSITY OF UTAH, Marriott Library, Special Collections, Salt Lake City, 84112. Gregory C Thompson, Cur

VA —VIRGINIA POLYTECHNIC INSTITUTE AND STATE UNIVERSITY LIBRARY, Blacksburg, 24061. Glenn L McMullen, Special Collections Librn
Holdings: Vols 1000 Cat Mss Maps
Notes: Collection of ca 300 linear feet of archival records (1830-1940) of the Norfolk and Western Railway, its predecessors, and subsidiaries, and of the defunct predecessors of the Southern Railway. The collection incl minutebooks, correspondence and subject files, and other ms materials for ca 200 railroad companies operating in the Southeast and Midwest, incl the Norfolk and Western; Norfolk and Petersburg; Southside; Atlantic, Mississippi, and Ohio; Virginia and Tennessee; Richmond and Danville; Memphis and Charleston; East Tennessee and Virginia; and South Carolina Canal and Railroad Company. The collection also incl printed materials such as annual reports and other documents for these companies.

WA —TACOMA PUBLIC LIBRARY, 1102 Tacoma Ave S, Tacoma, 98402. Kevin Hegarty, Dir
Holdings: Mss
Notes: 300 ft of mss of Tacoma Division, Northern Pacific Railway and Power and other traction companies.

WI —MILWAUKEE PUBLIC LIBRARY, 814 W Wisconsin Ave, Milwaukee, 53233. Donald J Sager, City Librn
Holdings: Maps Pix Publications Documents Mss
Notes: Incl books, documents, pamphlets, pictures, slides, magazines, maps, timetables. The library is the official depository for the Chicago, Milwaukee and St Paul RR including the drawings of the Milwaukee Rd, which number in the thousands.

WY —UNIVERSITY OF WYOMING, William Robertson Coe Library, 13 & Ivinson, Laramie, 82071.
Notes: The papers of Octave Chanute (1832-1910), pioneer railroad engineer and prominent aeronautic pioneer. Incl several hundred aviation photographs, letters, articles, pamphlets, speeches, and clippings, particularly on early-day gliders, with which Chanute was greatly involved.

AB —PETER WHYTE FOUNDATION, Archives of the Canadian Rockies, Box 160, Banff, T0L 0C0, Can. Mary Andrews, ACR Librn
Holdings: Vols (4247) Cat Mss Maps Pix Slides Phonorecords Audiotapes Videotapes 16mm Films Filmstrips Microforms
Budget: ($1500)
Notes: Collect all available material which touches on the Rocky Mountains of Canada (from the US border to the Peace River in the north; from west of Calgary on the east to the town of Revelstoke, BC on the west). This material incl history (the early explorers, Indians, construction f the railroads, mountaineering, and development of the national parks), natural history (geology, botany, wildlife) and poetry and fiction with the Rockies as a setting.

MB —UNIVERSITY OF MANITOBA, Elizabeth Dafoe Library, Government

RAILROADS—HISTORY (cont.)

Publications Section, Winnipeg, R3T 2N2, Can. June Dutka, Head
Holdings: Vols 1200 // Uncat
Notes: The set consists of material in the field of railway transportation as well as records dealing with telephone and pipeline cases during the time when the board had jurisdiction over these subjects (1904-1967). It also incl useful indexes which the company prepared.

ON —PUBLIC ARCHIVES OF CANADA, Library, 395 Wellington St, Ottawa, K1A 0N3, Can. Dawn E Monroe, Collections Development Officer
Holdings: Vols (80,000) Cat
Notes: Andrew Merrilees Collection (about 1800 items). Documents relating to transportation. His personal wealth, knowledge, business contacts and determination enabled him to obtain material from many sources. The core of the collection concerns railways, a personal interest since his Andrew Merrilees Company bought and sold railroad materials. The collection has some of the best examples of material on the technical aspect of the railway business. Most has some connection to the Canadian rail industry from its early beginning until 1930. Access to the collection is restricted.

PQ —MCGILL UNIVERSITY, McLennan Library, Rare Books and Special Collections Dept, 3459 McTavish St, Montreal, H3A 1Y1, Can.
Notes: 12,680 original prints and posters dating from the 16th century to the present. Prints representing many graphic techniques; special subject areas such as: early railways, Japanese woodblocks, Napoleon, early Canadian portraits.

RAILROADS—HISTORY—LATIN AMERICA

RI —BROWN UNIVERSITY, John Hay Library, 20 Prospect St, Providence, 02912. Mark N Brown, Cur Mss
Holdings: Vols (3500) // Cat Mss Maps
Notes: George Earl Church Collection, formed by a civil engineer, explorer and Fellow of the Royal Geographic Society, who specialized in railroad construction. Although part of the collection is devoted to American Revolutionary and Civil War history, the majority, 2000 vols, pertains to Central and South America. The imprints, which are predominantly 18th century, include Lima, Madrid, Rome, Mexico City, Seville, Barcelona, Lisbon, and Cadiz as well as *Nova orbis regionum ac insularum veteribus incognitarum* (Basle: 1537). Major subject areas are: anthropology, commerce, economics, engineering, ethnology, geography, history, law, mineral resources, railroad surveys, voyages of exploration and dictionaries of the South American Indian langauges. The most significant ms is an historical account of the Bolivian mining town of Potosi from 1545-1737.

RAILROADS—MAPS

NY —ELECTRIC RAILROADERS ASSOCIATION, Frank J Sprague Memorial Library, 89 E 42nd St, New York, 10018. Hugh A Dunne, First VP
Notes: Private library. Incl all forms of railroads operated by electricity. Forms of electric railroads included: street railways, subways & elevated lines, high-speed interurbans, suburban commuter lines, electrified trunk lines, monorails, mountain climbing inclines, etc. Also railroad timetables.

TX —MIDWESTERN STATE UNIVERSITY, Moffett Library, 3400 Taft St, Wichita Falls, 76308.
Holdings: // Uncat Maps
Notes: Land elevation maps of the Missouri-Kansas-Texas Railroad Northwestern Division (Wichita Falls, TX to Forgan, OK). Maps date from 1908; some are updated to 1970. Index or guide to maps prepared by railroad is available.

RAILROADS—NEW ENGLAND

NH —DARTMOUTH COLLEGE, Baker Memorial Library, Hanover, 03755.
Holdings: Cat
Notes: The Chase-Streeter Collection. Chiefly surveys, hearings, reports of New Hampshire railroads. Noncirculating.

RAILROADS—PICTURES, ILLUSTRATIONS, ETC.

IL —LAKE FOREST COLLEGE, Donnelley Library, Lake Forest, 60045. Arthur H Miller Jr, College Librn
Holdings: Vols (1500) Cat Mss Maps Pix
Budget: ($1000)
Notes: Elliott Donnelley Collection (received 1976) of mostly mid-20th century books and periodicals on Western railroads and mountain narrow gauge, world narrow gauge and short lines, steam, live steam, model railroading, and some traction. Purchases keep collection emphasis current (50-75 new books per year, 22 periodical subscriptions). Also, the Munson Paddock Collecction (received 1977) of train illustrations, maps, and timetables, 1850-1950. In addition to American technical and historical books and periodicals, the collection contains books of views, narrations of rail travel (particularly American West), and US local histories--all with illustrations of trains. Most titles are late 19th century Americna. The 1550 volumes are supplemented by related holdings of more than 150 pamphlets, 600 timetables, 2000 unbound periodical issues, 200 maps, 75 diagrams (engines, cars) hundreds of clippings of train illustrations, and 1000 photographs. In progress is a card index of illustrations by wheel type line, and manufacturer. Together, the collections contain about 7000 items.

NY —STATE UNIVERSITY OF NEW YORK, STONY BROOK, Melville Library, Dept of Special Collections, Stony Brook, 11794. Evert Volkersz, Head
Holdings: Vols 40 Cat Pix
Notes: Forty albums combining detailed pencil drawings of Long Island RailRoad tracks and explanatory notes with more than 5000 identified photographs, 1885-1968; 300 timetables, 1895-date; and related materials, compiled by Robert Emery.

TX —SOUTHERN METHODIST UNIVERSITY, DeGolyer Library, Box 396, SMU, Dallas, 75275. Clifton H Jones, Dir
Holdings: Vols (15,000) Cat Mss Maps Pix
Notes: One of the largest railroad photograph collections in the world; about 230,000 prints and 70,000 negatives, all countries. Accompanied by a major collection (12,000 vols) of railroadiana; much on locomotives. All languages.

RAILROADS—RUSSIA

CA —HOOVER INSTITUTION ON WAR, REVOLUTION & PEACE, Stanford University, Stanford, 94305. Milorad M Drachkovitch, Archivist
Holdings: // Mss
Notes: Records, 1917-1923, 1931-1936, on the US Commission of Railway Experts to Russia. Papers relating to activities of the commission, to the Russian railway Service Corps, the Inter-Allied Railway Committee, the Russian political scene, and events in Siberia during the Russian Revolution and civil war. Persons represented incl John Frank Stevens, chairman of the commission. Correspondents incl George H Emerson, H H Fisher, Benjamin O Johnson, and Charles H Smith. 2 boxes.

RAILROADS—SOUTHERN STATES

NC —DUKE UNIVERSITY, William R Perkins Library, Durham, 27706. Elvin E Strowd, University Librn
Notes: The Railroad Corporation Reports collection is made up of 8000 items, issued primarily since 1900, though many go back as far as the middle of the 19th century for main trunk lines in the United States.

RAILROADS—STATIONS

IN —INDIANA HISTORICAL SOCIETY, Library, 315 W Ohio St, Indianapolis, 46202. Robert K O'Neill, Dir
Holdings: Vols Cat Mss Pix Microforms
Notes: Records of Indiana architects, contractors, and engineers, as well as records concerning the structures created by non-Indiana professionals with the state. Types of material collected incl office files, correspondence, drawings, blueprints, photographs, personal papers, specifications, books and pamphlets. The collection incl approximately 14,000 drawings, along with another 10,000 on microfilm, from central Indiana architectural firms. Incl among the drawings are approximately 800 for Union Station, Indianapolis.

RAILROADS—TIMETABLES

IL —LAKE FOREST COLLEGE, Donnelley Library, Lake Forest, 60045. Arthur H Miller Jr, College Librn
Holdings: vols (1500) Cat Mss Maps Pix
Budget: ($1000)
Notes: Elliott Donnelley Collection (received 1976) of mostly mid-20th century books and periodicals on Western railroads and mountain narrow gauge, world narrow gauge and short lines, steam, live steam, model railroading, and some traction. Purchases keep collection emphasis current (50-75 new books per year, 22 periodical subscriptions). Also, the Munson Paddock Collecction (received 1977) of train illustrations, maps, and timetables, 1850-1950. In addition to American technical and historical books and periodicals, the collection contains books of views, narrations of rail travel (particularly American West), and US local histories--all with illustrations of trains. Most titles are late 19th century Americna. The 1550 volumes are supplemented by related holdings of more than 150 pamphlets, 600 timetables, 2000 unbound periodical issues, 200 maps, 75 diagrams (engines, cars) hundreds of clippings of train illustrations, and 1000 photographs. In progress is a card index of illustrations by wheel type line, and manufacturer. Together, the collections contain about 7000 items.

KS —HARVEY COUNTY HISTORICAL SOCIETY, Historical Library & Museum, 203 Main St, Newton, 67114. Mike Smurr, Dir
Holdings: Maps Pix
Notes: Our Library-Museum is limited to literature, pictures, and artifacts of interest to this locality, Harvey County, KS. Newton has been a RR point since the Santa Fe built here in 1871, so we have an unusually good collection of railroad items. Hundreds of pictures, many timetables, passes, and items small enough to be housed in our building. Attention is also given to early-day agriculture in mid-Kansas, especially wheat-raising by early settlers in central Kansas.

NY —ELECTRIC RAILROADERS ASSOCIATION, Frank J Sprague Memorial Library, 89 E 42nd St, New York, 10018. Hugh A Dunne, First VP
Notes: Private library. Incl all forms of railroads operated by electricity. Forms of electric railroads included: street railways, subways & elevated lines, high-speed interurbans, suburban commuter lines, electrified trunk lines, monorails, mountain climbing inclines, etc. Also railroad timetables.

NY —STATE UNIVERSITY OF NEW YORK, STONY BROOK, Melville Library, Dept of Special Collections, Stony Brook, 11794. Evert Volkersz, Head
Holdings: Vols 40 Cat Pix
Notes: Forty albums combining detailed pencil drawings of Long Island RailRoad tracks and explanatory notes with more than 5000 identified photographs, 1885-1968; 300 timetables, 1895-date; and related materials, compiled by Robert Emery.

RAILROADS—THE WEST

CA —SAN BERNARDINO VALLEY
COLLEGE, Samuel Andrews Memorial
Library, 701 S Mt Vernon, San Bernardino,
92403. Robin Calote, Librn
Holdings: Vols 201 Cat
Budget: $500

CA —SAN DIEGO PUBLIC LIBRARY, Social
Sciences Section, 820 E St, San Diego,
92101. Margaret E Queen, Supvr
Budget: ($36,000)
Notes: Good general collection with
emphasis on railroads of California. Good
materials on street railways and cable cars of
western cities.

IL —LAKE FOREST COLLEGE, Donnelley
Library, Lake Forest, 60045. Arthur H
Miller Jr, College Librn
Holdings: Vols (1500) Cat Mss Maps Pix
Budget: ($1000)
Notes: Elliott Donnelley Collection
(received 1976) of mostly mid-20th century
books and periodicals on Western railroads
and mountain narrow gauge, world narrow
gauge and short lines, steam, live steam,
model railroading, and some traction.
Purchases keep collection emphasis current
(50-75 new books per year, 22 periodical
subscriptions). Also, the Munson Paddock
Collecction (received 1977) of train
illustrations, maps, and timetables, 1850-
1950. In addition to American technical and
historical books and periodicals, the
collection contains books of views,
narrations of rail travel (particularly
American West), and US local histories--all
with illustrations of trains. Most titles are
late 19th century Americna. The 1550
volumes are supplemented by related
holdings of more than 150 pamphlets, 600
timetables, 2000 unbound periodical issues,
200 maps, 75 diagrams (engines, cars)
hundreds of clippings of train illustrations,
and 1000 photographs. In progress is a card
index of illustrations by wheel type line, and
manufacturer. Together, the collections
contain about 7000 items.

RAILROADS, AERIAL see Railroads, Elevated

RAILROADS, CABLE CAR

CA —SAN DIEGO PUBLIC LIBRARY, Social
Sciences Section, 820 E St, San Diego,
92101. Margaret E Queen, Supvr
Budget: ($36,000)
Notes: Good general collection with
emphasis on railroads of California. Good
materials on street railways and cable cars of
western cities.

RAILROADS, ELECTRIC see Electric Railroads; Street Railroads

RAILROADS, ELEVATED

NY —ELECTRIC RAILROADERS
ASSOCIATION, Frank J Sprague Memorial
Library, 89 E 42nd St, New York, 10018.
Hugh A Dunne, First VP
Notes: Private library. Incl all forms of
railroads operated by electricity. Forms of
electric railroads included: street railways,
subways & elevated lines, high-speed
interurbans, suburban commuter lines,
electrified trunk lines, monorails, mountain
climbing inclines, etc. Also railroad
timetables.

RAILROADS, EUROPEAN

MA —HARVARD UNIVERSITY, Baker
Library of the Graduate School of Business
Administration, Kress Library of Business
and Economics, Soldiers Field, Boston,
02163. Ruth E Rogers, Cur
Notes: An extensive collection. Historical
emphasis on railroads and canals.

RAILROADS, FUNICULAR see Railroads, Cable Car

RAILROADS, NARROW-GAUGE

IL —LAKE FOREST COLLEGE, Donnelley
Library, Lake Forest, 60045. Arthur H

Miller Jr, College Librn
Holdings: Vols (1500) Cat Mss Maps Pix
Budget: ($1000)
Notes: Elliott Donnelley Collection
(received 1976) of mostly mid-20th century
books and periodicals on Western railroads
and mountain narrow gauge, world narrow
gauge and short lines, steam, live steam,
model railroading, and some traction.
Purchases keep collection emphasis current
(50-75 new books per year, 22 periodical
subscriptions). Also, the Munson Paddock
Collecction (received 1977) of train
illustrations, maps, and timetables, 1850-
1950. In addition to American technical and
historical books and periodicals, the
collection contains books of views,
narrations of rail travel (particularly
American West), and US local histories--all
with illustrations of trains. Most titles are
late 19th century Americna. The 1550
volumes are supplemented by related
holdings of more than 150 pamphlets, 600
timetables, 2000 unbound periodical issues,
200 maps, 75 diagrams (engines, cars)
hundreds of clippings of train illustrations,
and 1000 photographs. In progress is a card
index of illustrations by wheel type line, and
manufacturer. Together, the collections
contain about 7000 items.

RAILROADS, STREET see Street Railroads

RAILROADS, UNDERGROUND see Subways

RAILWAY CONDUCTORS UNION see Order of Railway Conductors

RAINACH, WILLIAM M.

LA —LOUISIANA STATE UNIVERSITY,
SHREVEPORT, Library-Archives, 8515
Youree Dr, Shreveport, 71129. Patricia L
Meador, Archivist & Asst Librn
Notes: The archives collection incl the
papers (1930-1977) of Lousiana legislator
William M Rainach (48 linear ft).

RAINE, NORMAN REILLY, 1895-1971

MA —BOSTON UNIVERSITY, Mugar
Memorial Library, Special Collections Dept,
771 Commonwealth Ave, Boston, 02215.
Howard B Gotlieb, Dir
Holdings: //Cat Mss Correspondence Pix

RAINMAKING

NY —STATE UNIVERSITY OF NEW YORK
AT ALBANY, Library, Special Collections
Dept, 1400 Washington Ave, Albany, 12222.
Marion P Munzer, Coordr
Notes: 28 linear feet of mss; 31 linear feet of
pamphlets and periodicals; and 700 volumes
from Vincent J Schaefer's personal library.
Also, papers, photographs, publications, etc,
dealing with his teaching and research on
cloud seeding and other aspects of
atmospheric science.
See also entries under Schaefer, Vincent J;
Atmosphere

RAINS, CLAUDE

MA —BOSTON UNIVERSITY, Mugar
Memorial Library, Special Collections Dept,
771 Commonwealth Ave, Boston, 02215.
Howard B Gotlieb, Dir
Holdings: // Cat Mss Pix
Notes: Mss, correspondence, etc collected in
depth; incl publications by or about.

RAISIN RIVER, BATTLE OF, 1813

MI —MONROE COUNTY LIBRARY
SYSTEM, Ellis Reference and Information
Center, 3700 S Custer Rd, Monroe, 48161.
Marie D Chulski, Head of Reference
Services
Notes: Historic Monroe County, tracing its
beginnings to 1780, is a definite part of
Michigan's history. Many events of the area
and citizens are part of Michigan's heritage.

The Michigan collection besides general
works contains individual county histories,
atlases, biographies, etc. The Monroe County
history collection contains veteran records,
plat books, oral history tapes, family
histories, church records, cemetery index,
atlases and census records. Genealogy
emphasis is not only Monroe County but
includes surrounding counties and the states
with large migration to the area, such as
Ohio, Kentucky, Tennessee and the New
England states.

RAISINS

CA —CALIFORNIA STATE UNIVERSITY,
FRESNO, Henry Madden Library, Dept of
Special Collections, Fresno, 93740. Ronald J
Mahoney, Head
Holdings: Vols (3400) Cat Maps Pix
Notes: Books and pamphlets relating to the
history and development of viticulture and
enology. Emphasizes pre-1920 worldwide
imprints. Incl 900 merchants' catalogs, 1400
pamphlets, 200 wine lists, 750 periodical
issues, and ephemera. Partially cataloged.

RAKSIN, DAVID

CA —UNIVERSITY OF SOUTHERN
CALIFORNIA, Edward L Doheny
Memorial Library, Archives of Performing
Arts, University Park, Los Angeles, 90089.
Robert Knutson, Librn
Holdings: Mss Pix
Notes: Personal collection of papers,
pictures, etc.

RAMA RAU, SANTHA

MA —BOSTON UNIVERSITY, Mugar
Memorial Library, Special Collections Dept,
771 Commonwealth Ave, Boston, 02215.
Howard B Gotlieb, Dir
Holdings: Cat Mss Pix
Notes: Mss, correspondence, etc collected in
depth; incl publications by or about.

RAMAN EFFECT

NY —AMERICAN INSTITUTE OF
PHYSICS, Center for the History of Physics,
Niels Bohr Library, 335 E 45 St, New York,
10017. John Aubry, Librn
Holdings: Cat Mss Maps Pix Microforms

RAMATI, ALEXANDER

MA —BOSTON UNIVERSITY, Mugar
Memorial Library, Special Collections Dept,
771 Commonwealth Ave, Boston, 02215.
Howard B Gotlieb, Dir
Holdings: Cat Mss
Notes: Mss, correspondence, etc collected in
depth; incl publications by or about.

RAMEE, LOUIS DE LA see Ouida

RAMEY, PAUL

DC —LIBRARY OF CONGRESS, Prints &
Photographs Div, Washington, 20540.
Notes: One of photographers represented in
the American National Red Cross
Collection.

RAMON see Gomez De la Serna, Ramon, 1888-1963

RAMPTON, CALVIN

UT —UNIVERSITY OF UTAH, Marriott
Library, Special Collections, Salt Lake City,
84112. Gregory C Thompson, Cur
Holdings: Cat Mss Microfilm Film Oral
History
Notes: Papers of the Utah Governor.

RAMSEY, FRANK PLUMPTON, 1903-1930

PA —UNIVERSITY OF PITTSBURGH,
Hillman Library, Pittsburgh, 15260.
Notes: Economic and philosophical papers of
the English scholar Frank Plumpton Ramsey

RAMSEY, FRANK PLUMPTON, 1903-1930 (cont.)

(1903-1930), incl mss of published and unpublished writings, reading notes, etc. Significant because of his work in modern mathematics, logic, probability, and economics. Complementary to the Library's holdings of the papers of the logical empiricists, Rudolf Carnap and Hans Reichenback.

RAMUS, PETER

MO —SAINT LOUIS UNIVERSITY, Pius XII Memorial Library, Saint Louis Room Collection, 3655 W Pine Blvd, Saint Louis, 63108. Catherine E Weidle, Rare Books Librn
Holdings: Vols Cat Mss
Notes: Books on early education, Jesuitica and Western Americana. Related collections of works by Peter Ramus (University is center for Ramist studies) and Omer Talon; also collections on the Spiritual Exercises of St Ignatius Loyola and on the Sodality of Our Lady. Mss uncataloged.

MO —SAINT LOUIS UNIVERSITY, Pius XII Memorial Library, 3655 W Pine Blvd, Saint Louis, 63108. Walter J Ong, SJ, Cur
Holdings: 450 Cat Mss Microforms
Notes: Large collection of his writings, incl his own working copy (massive revisions in his own hand) of his *Arithmeticae...Geometriae.* The school is a center for Ramist studies. John F Daly, "Ramus: Recently Discovered Unpublished Edition of His Mathematical Works," *Manuscripta*, 17 (1973), 80-90. Walter J Ong, "Christianus Urstitius and Ramus' New Mathematics," *Bibliotheque d'Humanisme et Renaissance* (Geneva), 36 (1974), 603-610. Walter J Ong, *Ramus and Talon Inventory* (Cambridge, Mass: Harvard University Press, 1958; rpt Folcroft, Pa: Folcroft Press, 1970).

RANCH LIFE

AZ —NORTHERN ARIZONA UNIVERSITY, Special Collection Library, CU Box 6022, Flagstaff, 86011. Peter M Whiteley, Coordr/Archivist; William Mullane, Librn
Notes: Ranching Time Book Collection; time book of an unidentified company, possibly of the employees working on the range, 1878-1879. Also, Rimrock Ranch Collection; account journal, 1938. Verde Valley, Ariz.

CO —COLORADO HISTORICAL SOCIETY, Research Collections, 1300 Broadway, Denver, 80203. Catherine Kane, Head Public Service and Access
Holdings: Cat Mss Pix Microforms
Budget:
Notes: Correspondence and business records of cattle companies and cattlemen and railroads gathered as part of the Western Range Cattle Industry Study. Also, correspondence and records of companies, organizations and related materials arranged by state (1850-1945). About 50,000 items.

DC —LIBRARY OF CONGRESS, Prints & Photographs Div, Washington, 20540.
Notes: The Erwin E Smith Collection of cowboy and ranch life. Gift of 1776 original glass and nitrate film negatives of pictures taken by him. Gift of his sister, Mrs L McC Pettis in 1949.

MT —MONTANA HISTORICAL SOCIETY LIBRARY, 225 N Roberts St, Helena, 59601. Robert M Clark, Librn; Brian Cockhill, State Archivist
Holdings: Vols 3000 Cat
Budget: ($2500)
Notes: The Ames and Margaret Booth Teakel Range Life Memorial Collection (cowboy and cattle range subjects). The scope of this collection includes the entire West, not just Montana and contiguous states. Also, L A Huffman Collection; incl 1100 photographs.

NE —NEBRASKA STATE HISTORICAL SOCIETY, Fort Robinson Museum, Box 304, Crawford, 69339. Vance Nelson, Cur
Holdings: Vols (1500) Cat Mss Maps Pix

Slides Phonorecords Audiotapes 16mm Films Microforms
Notes: Materials related to the history of Fort Robinson, and incl the Post Medical Library, reference books on state government, etc, Western Americana: books on ranching, homesteaders, Indian wars, etc; microfilm reocrds for Fort Robinson records, Red Cloud and Spotted Tail Indian Agency records, Crawford and Chadron Nebraska newspapers, diaries and interviews. Library incl the E Kopac Collection of books dealing with Western Americana; particularly Indian wars, transportation, guns and railroads.

†SD —SOUTH DAKOTA SCHOOL OF MINES & TECHNOLOGY, Devereaux Library, Rapid City, 57701.
Holdings: Vols (3786) Cat Mss Maps Pix Audiotapes Microforms
Notes: This special collection, in general, relates to the Black Hills area of South Dakota and Wyoming, especially mining and exploration of the area; the West River area of South Dakota, primarily county histories; and South Dakota Territorial and State materials. There are also specialized areas of this collection: (1) *Marion N Bruce Collection.* Documents, correspondence, books and periodicals dealing with weather modification in South Dakota; (2) *Mildred Fielder Collection.* Mss, pictures, books and periodicals from an author whose special area was the Black Hills. Most of her work on railroads, mines, trails, etc, relates to historical aspects. Collection incl research materials, galley proofs and final copies of her various publications; (3) *Cleophas C O'Harra Collection.* Mss, pictures, books and original source materials, primarily related to the Black Hills area andexpeditions thereto. Much of the data was collected for a book on the Black Hills which was never published; and (4) *Caving Collection.* Maps of various caves in Black Hills area, being kept current and updated by members of the Paha Sapa Grotto. Also, some books and periodicals on caving in general.

TX —HARDIN-SIMMONS UNIVERSITY, Richardson Library, Abilene, 79601. Joe F Dahlstrom, Dir
Holdings: Vols (10,000) Cat Mss Maps Pix Microforms
Notes: Special collection name is Richardson Research Center, named in honor of Dr Rupert N Richardson. Collect in the areas of his own research interests, especially that portion of the US that was once a part of Mexico. Emphases on the history of ranching, railroads, discovery and exploration, Texas county histories, etc. Incl 350 items printed and/or designed by El Paso printer Cart Hertzog; the Judge R C Crane collection of Texana and a similar collection of Louise Kelley's; and the Research Publication's Western Americana collection (microfilm).

TX —AMARILLO PUBLIC LIBRARY, 413 E Fourth, Amarillo, 79101. Mary Kay Snell, Librn
Holdings: Vols Cat Mss Maps Pix
Notes: The southwest collections incl materials on the history of Texas, Louisiana, New Mexico, Arkansas, Missouri and Kansas. General subjects covered incl overland journeys, early narratives, early biographies, Indian captivities, outlaws, US government reports, Mississippi and Ohio Rivers, the Mexican War, reports of Catholic missionaries, Niles Register, early publications, fur trade, western trails, Texas Rangers, sheriffs and Texas as a sovereign state, buffalo hunting, Indian wars, cowboys, the arrival of farmers, fences, and towns. Over 1600 items which incl books, documents, maps, mss, pamphlets, unpublished theses, interviews and photographs. The three major collections are the William Henry Bush Collection, the Laurence J Fitzsimon Collection and the Calendar of John L McCarty.

TX —PANHANDLE-PLAINS HISTORICAL MUSEUM, Research Center, Box 967, WT Sta, Canyon, 79016. Claire R Kuehn, Archivist-Librn
Holdings: Vols 8000 Cat Mss Maps Pix

Microforms
Budget: $2000
Notes: History of the Texas Panhandle. Incl interviews with early settlers taken over a 50-year period, ranch records, and business records relating to the Texas Panhandle and surrounding states.

TX —TEXAS A&M UNIVERSITY, Sterling C Evans Library, Special Collections Div, College Station, 77843. Donald H Dyal, Librn
Holdings: Vols (16,000) Mss Pix
Notes: Jeff Dykes Range Livestock Collection (incl a 600-item collection of J Frank Dobie works). Part of the Dobie Collection is described in Dykes, Jeff C *My Dobie Collection* (College Station, Tex: Friends of the Texas A&M University Library). The E J Dyksterhuis Collection on American forestry, range science, ecology and botany (compiled by Professor Emeritus E J Dyksterhuis).

TX —NORTH TEXAS STATE UNIVERSITY, Archives, NT Station Box 5188, Denton, 76203. Robert LaForte, University Archivist
Notes: The NTSU Archives houses the patron's copy of oral history interviews that are part of the Oral History Collection, an independent project not part of the Archives. This collection of interviews covers, in part, the following subject areas: World War II Pearl Harbor survivors, World War II prisoners of war, Texas legislators, ex-governors of Texas, Texans employed by the administrations of FDR, Texas businessmen and businesswomen, development of the Coastal Bend area of south Texas, and Mexican-American social action activities. Cataloged. Transcriptions available. See *Oral History Collection,* North Texas State University Bulletin, April 1981.

TX —AMON CARTER MUSEUM, Library, 3510 Camp Bowie Blvd, PO Box 2365, Fort Worth, 76113. Nancy G Wynne, Librn
Holdings: Vols (15,000) Cat Mss Pix
Notes: The book collection, microfilm and photo archives have been built toward the goal of the interpretation of American history through art. At present, the greatest strengths are in Western Americana, Western Canadiana, bibliography and American exhibition catalogs. Building a good collection on Alaskan Indian and Eskimo art. Substantial books and files on American artists of the 19th century, and particularly of Charles M Russell and Frederic Remington. Incl 25,000 pictures; 13,000 slides.
See also entries under Newspapers, American; Pictures - Collections.

TX —TEXAS TECH UNIVERSITY, Library, Lubbock, 79409. David J Murrah, Assoc Dir for Special Collections

UT —UNIVERSITY OF UTAH, Marriott Library, Special Collections, Salt Lake City, 84112. Gregory C Thompson, Cur

RAND, CHRISTOPHER

MA —BOSTON UNIVERSITY, Mugar Memorial Library, Special Collections Dept, 771 Commonwealth Ave, Boston, 02215. Howard B Gotlieb, Dir
Holdings: // Cat Mss Pix
Notes: Mss, correspondence, etc collected in depth; incl publications by or about.

RAND CORPORATION

CA —UNIVERSITY OF CALIFORNIA, BERKELEY, University Library, Government Documents Department, 350 Library Annex, Berkeley, 94720. Suzanne Gold, Collection Dept Librn
Holdings: Vols (314,000) Cat Microforms
Budget: ($85,115)
Notes: General collection of government documents, historical and current, on the federal and state levels; as well as international and foreign documents. The Library's holdings are particularly strong in foreign statistics and censuses, and US Congress. The Government Documents Department serves as a full depository for GPO, NASA, State of California, EEC, GATT, IAEA, United Nations, UNESCO,

RAND CORPORATION (cont.)

Rand Corporation (non-classified), IBRD,
OECD, ILO, UNITAR, ITC, and CE.
Selective depository, PL-480 Programs, or
gift or exchange arrangements obtain for the
states of Michigan and Washington and for
Canada, India, Pakistan and Indonesia. Incl
microfilm and 300,000 fiche, cards, and
prints.

CA —HOOVER INSTITUTION ON WAR,
REVOLUTION & PEACE, Stanford
University, Stanford, 94305. Milorad M
Drachkovitch, Archivist
Notes: Reports (printed copies), 1965-1972,
prepared by the Rand Corporation, relating
to the organization, operations, motivation,
and morale of the Viet Cong and the North
Vietnamese. 3 ms boxes.

RANDALL, DAVID ANTON

IN —INDIANA UNIVERSITY, Lilly Library,
Seventh St, Bloomington, 47405. William R
Cagle, Librn
Holdings: Mss
Notes: The David Anton Randall papers incl
his files while working for Scribner's in New
York, as well as much correspondence, etc
with John Carter concerning the English
scene. 900 items.

RANDALL, FLORENCE ENGEL

MA —BOSTON UNIVERSITY, Mugar
Memorial Library, Special Collections Dept,
771 Commonwealth Ave, Boston, 02215.
Howard B Gotlieb, Dir
Holdings: Cat Mss

RANDALL, JAMES RYDER, 1839-1908

DC —GEORGETOWN UNIVERSITY,
Library, Special Collections Div, 37 & O Sts
NW, Washington, 20057. George M
Barringer, Special Collections Librn;
Nicholas B Sheetz, Mss Librn
Holdings: Mss Cat Pix
Notes: Papers of the poet James Ryder
Randall (1839-1908) who is best
remembered for his poem, "Maryland, My
Maryland." The papers best consists of
correspondnece to and from Randall,
numerous mss of poetry, photographs of the
poet, misc printed material and newspaper
clippings.

RANDOLPH, A. PHILIP

IL —CHICAGO HISTORICAL SOCIETY,
Library, Clark St at North Ave, Chicago,
60614. Archie Motley, Manuscript Librn
Notes: Papers, with the Brotherhood of
Sleepng Car Porters Collection.

RANDOLPH, HARRISON

SC —COLLEGE OF CHARLESTON
LIBRARY, Special Collections Dept,
Charleston, 29401.
Notes: Correspondence within the Lancelot
Minor Harris Papers.

RANDOLPH, JAMES ROBBINS, 1891-1971

†VA —VIRGINIA POLYTECHNIC
INSTITUTE AND STATE UNIVERSITY,
Blacksburg, 24061.

RANDOLPH FAMILY

†WI —SEVENTH DAY BAPTIST
HISTORICAL SOCIETY, Library, 3120
Kennedy St, PO Box 1678, Janesville,
53547.
Holdings: Uncat Mss Maps Pix
Notes: Largely the work of Hector Craig
Fitz Randolph, these five file drawers of
material were gathered over a period of
years to trace some of the lines of the family
in New Jersey and elsewhere. Notes and
books.

RANDOM HOUSE, PUBLISHERS

NY —COLUMBIA UNIVERSITY
LIBRARIES, Rare Book & Manuscript
Library, 801 Butler Library, 535 W 114 St,
New York, 10027. Kenneth A Lohf, Librn
Holdings: Mss
Notes: Files and library of Random House,
publishers, 1925-1976. 753,400 items.
Restricted use.

RANGE RESEARCH

AZ —ARIZONA HERITAGE CENTER,
Library, 949 E Second St, Tucson, 85719.
Michael Weber, Dir
Notes: Espec with reference to Arizona, the
West, and the Southwest.

TX —TEXAS A&M UNIVERSITY, Sterling C
Evans Library, Special Collections Div,
College Station, 77843. Donald H Dyal,
Librn
Holdings: Vols 400 Cat
Notes: The E J Dyksterhuis Collection on
American forestry, range science, ecology
and botany (compiled by Professor Emeritus
E J Dyksterhuis).

RANGES (STOCK) see Stock Ranges

RANK, OTTO

NY —COLUMBIA UNIVERSITY
LIBRARIES, Rare Book & Manuscript
Library, 801 Butler Library, 535 W 114 St,
New York, 10027. Kenneth A Lohf, Librn
Holdings: Mss
Notes: Mss and printed materials. 2000
items. Restricted use.

RANKE, LEOPOLD VON

NY —SYRACUSE UNIVERSITY
LIBRARIES, Ernest S Bird Library, George
Arents Research Library for Special
Collections, Syracuse, 13210. Carolyn A
Davis, Manuscripts Librn; Amy S Doherty,
University Archivist; Mark F Weimer, Rare
Book Librn
Notes: Private library of Leopold von Ranke,
father of modern historical scholarship,
acquired in 1886. More than 17,000
volumes, 4000 pamphlets, and 430 mss, and
private papers and letters. A complete
catalogue of the ms collection published in
1983. Incl more than 100 dispatches
(Relazioni) from Venetian ambassadors,
1500-1800, etc. Much unpublished primary
source material.

RANKIN, ANNIE B.

MS —TOUGALOO COLLEGE, L Zenobia
Coleman Library, Tougaloo, 39174. Virgia
Brocks-Shedd, Acting Dir
Budget: ($142,650)
Notes: Civil rights cases and legal papers;
lawsuits; Mississippi, 1960-1968. Local
attorneys have donated papers of cases they
have handled, espec attorneys of two
government-funded legal services offices.
Individual collections: Papers of Aaron
Henry, Rev Robert L T Smith, Sr, Annie B
Rankin and the Howard Kester Papers. Incl
VF holdings of articles from 1930 and on.

RANKIN, JEANNETTE, 1880-1973

MA —RADCLIFFE COLLEGE, Arthur &
Elizabeth Schlesinger Library on the History
of Women in America, 3 James St,
Cambridge, 02138. Patricia Miller King, Dir;
Eva Moseley, Cur of Mss
Holdings: Cat Mss Audiotapes 16mm Films
Microforms
Notes: Incl papers from Jeannette Rankin's
two terms in Congress (1917-19, 1941-43),
mainly about her votes against US entry into
World Wars I and II, from her (mainly
pacifist) activities in the 1960s and 1970,
and family papers.

RANKIN, KARL LOTT, 1898-

NJ —PRINCETON UNIVERSITY, Seeley G
Mudd Manuscript Library, Public Affairs
Papers Collection, Princeton, 08544. Nancy
Bressler, Cur
Notes: Incl 48 boxes; 4 cartons. The papers
cover the period 1920-73. An unpublished
96p guide is available in the Library.

RANKIN, MCKEE

CA —UNIVERSITY OF CALIFORNIA,
DAVIS, Shields Library, Dept of Special
Collections, Davis, 95616. Donald Kunitz,
Head; C Danial Elliott, Asst Head
Holdings: Vols 150 Cat Mss
Notes: Production and direction material
related to McKee Rankin and his family incl
scripts, programs, prompt books,
correspondence, and photographs.

RANNELLS, WILL

OH —OHIO STATE UNIVERSITY, Library
for Communication and Graphic Arts, 242
W 18th St, Columbus, 43210. Lucy S
Caswell, Curator
Notes: Comic strip artists Hal Foster,
Dudley T Fisher, Jr, Mark Szorady, Edwina
Dumm, Jim Baker have original works in the
library. Also new collections of original
cartoons by Windsor McCay, John T
McCutcheon, Dick Moores, Ned White,
Walter Berndt, Jim Larrick, Carl Rose and
Bill Crawford. Also a large collection of the
work of illustrator Will Rannells. The Shel
Dorf Collection incl historic comic strips and
related materials. A small but growing
collection of comic books, especially those
featuring *Katy Keene*, is available in the
library.

RANSOM, JOHN CROWE

NV —UNIVERSITY OF NEVADA, RENO,
University Library, Special Collections Dept,
Reno, 89557. Robert E Blesse, Head
Holdings: Vols (21) Cat Other appearances
459 Cat
Notes: Includes individual works by author
in all editions including translations; also
prefaces, introductions, published
correspondence, appearances in anthologies,
periodicals, etc. Bibliographical research
collection, part of Modern Authors
Collection.

NC —UNIVERSITY OF NORTH
CAROLINA, GREENSBORO, Walter
Clinton Jackson Library, Special Collections
Dept, 1000 Spring Garden St, Greensboro,
27412. Emilie W Mills, Librn
Holdings: Vols (200) Cat Mss Pix
Phonorecords Audiotapes
Notes: Randall Jarrell taught here from 1947
until his death in 1965. Over 3000 ms items
were the gift of the author and incl various
drafts of poems, translations, critical works
and essays. Books incl first, foreign, and
variant editions, association books and many
other heavily annotated by Jarrell readings,
conversations (tapes) with other poets, incl
John Crowe Ransom and Robert Frost. A
one-hour color film made after the poet's
death incl readings of his poems made from
the earlier tapes, and an interview with the
poet's widow, Mary Jarrell. Jarrell
memorabilia is also included.

TN —VANDERBILT UNIVERSITY, Library,
Nashville, 37240. Marice Wolfe, Special
Collections Librn
Holdings: Vols 1000 Cat Mss Pix
Notes: Collection relating to the Fugitive
poets of the 1920s, the Agrarian writers of
the 1930s and their subsequent careers, as a
complement to extensive mss collections in
this field. Chief figures incl Allen Tate, John
Crowe Ransom, Robert Penn Warren,
Andrew Lytle, Donald Davidson, Merrill
Moore, Laura Riding, et al.

RANSOM, WILL

IL —NEWBERRY LIBRARY, 60 W Walton
St, Chicago, 60610. Diana Haskell, Cur of
Modern Mss
Holdings: Cat Mss
Budget: ($30,000)
Notes: Several thousand vols. Incl in
*Dictionary Catalogue of the John M Wing
Foundation and its supplement* (G K Hall).
Newberry also has Will Ransom's archives,
incl his files for his various books on private
presses.

RANSOME, ARTHUR, 1884-1967

DC —GEORGETOWN UNIVERSITY,
Library, Special Collections Div, 37 & O Sts

RANSOME, ARTHUR, 1884-1967 (cont.)

NW, Washington, 20057. George M
Barringer, Special Collections Librn;
Nicholas B Sheetz, Mss Librn
Holdings: Mss Cat Pix
Notes: A collection of books, mss, letters,
clippings, photographs and tapes by and
about the British author Arthur Ransome
(1884-1967). Ransome is best known for his
children's books and his works on Russia.

RANTERS

PA —TEMPLE UNIVERSITY LIBRARIES,
Special Collections Dept, Rare Books & Mss
Section, Philadelphia, 19122. Thomas M
Whitehead, Cur
Holdings: Vols (600) Cat Mss
Notes: Seventeeth and 18th century books
and pamphlets on political, religious, social
and intellectual life and history of England.
Strong holdings of John Cotton, Gilbert
Burnet, Richard Overton, John Lilburne;
Civil War pamphlets, ranter and levellers.
The Nordell and Simpson Collections.

RANUZZI FAMILY

†TX —UNIVERSITY OF TEXAS
LIBRARIES, Humanities Research Center,
Austin, 78712.
Notes: Incl Mss of the Ranuzzi family of
Italy.

RAPE

CA —WOMEN'S HISTORY RESEARCH
CENTER, Microfilm Library, 2325 Oak St,
Berkeley, 94708. Laura X, Librn
Holdings: Microforms
Notes: Incl 500 subject files of material on
Women and Law (General); Politics;
Employment; Education; Rape/Prison/
Prostitution; Black and Third World women.
Collection at University of Wyoming,
Archive of Contemporary History, PO Box
3334, Laramie, Wyoming 82071, c/o David
Crosson. Reasearch inquiries accepted.
Microfilm of collection (40 reels & reel
guides) available through Women's History
Research Center, 2325 Oak St, Berkeley, CA
94708. No collections housed at this address.
CA —LOS ANGELES PUBLIC LIBRARY,
Social Sciences Dept, 630 W Fifth St, Los
Angeles, 90071. Marilyn C Wherley,
Principal Librn
Holdings: Vols 3000 Cat
Budget: ($150,000)
Notes: Emphasis on minorities; immigration
policies, background and social problems of
ethnic minorities in the US and the
Southwest in particular. Incl periodicals,
government publications and documents,
popular and scholarly works on Blacks,
Hispanics and Asians predominantly.
NY —YWCA NATIONAL BOARD, Library,
726-730 Broadway, New York, 10012.
Elizabeth Norris, Librn
Holdings: Vols (3000) Cat Mss
Budget: ($2400)
Notes: Women and their contemporary
interests.

RAPER, ARTHUR FRANKLIN

NC —UNIVERSITY OF NORTH
CAROLINA, CHAPEL HILL, Louis Round
Wilson Academic Affairs Library, Southern
Historical Collection, Chapel Hill, 27514.
Carolyn Wallace, Librn
Notes: Papers of Arthur Franklin Raper.

RAPID TRANSIT see Local Transit

RARE BOOKS

AR —PUBLIC LIBRARY OF PINE BLUFF
AND JEFFERSON COUNTY, Library
System, 200 E Eighth Ave, Pine Bluff,
71601. Cora M Dorsett, Dir
Holdings: Vols 271 Cat Pix Mss
Notes: Incls pictures (2), manuscripts (2).
CA —UNIVERSITY OF CALIFORNIA, SAN
DIEGO, Central University Library,

Mandeville Dept of Special Collections, La
Jolla, 92093. Lynda Corey Claassen, Head
Notes: A special collection that preseves
special materials for research in the
humanities, the collection presently contains
appoximately 25,000 volumes and includes a
wealth of diverse materials. Incl incunabula;
8000 English-language political pamphlets,
17th to 20th centuries; 2000 vols of 18th
century English literature, with special
emphasis on the works fo Daniel Defoe and
Samuel Johnson; 19th and early 20th
century travel guides; first and/or important
editions of writings of D H Lawrence, Ernest
Hemingway, William Butler Yeats, Virginia
Woolf, Aldous Huxley and Robert Southey;
300 volumes of utopian literature, incl
photographs about the Topolobampo
community established in 1886 on the west
coast of Mexico; 500 editions of *The
Rubaiyat of Omar Khayam*; 1500 vols on
history and culture of California; 5000 Little
Blue Books and relatedmaterials; extensive
holdings in theosophy, many documenting
the religious community at Point Loma,
California in 1897.
CT —YALE UNIVERSITY, Box 1603A, Yale
Station, New Haven, 06520.
Notes: Extensive collections in many fields.
DC —LIBRARY OF CONGRESS, General
Reading Rooms Division, Microform
Reading Room, Washington, 20540.
Notes: Microfilm (378,000 reels and strips):
Msss in St Catherine's Monastery on Mt
Sinai and in the Libraries of the Greek and
Armenian Patriarchates in Jerusalem and
selected monasteries on Mt Athos; Modern
Language Association reproductions of mss
and rare books; ms of American interest
filmed by the American Council of Learned
Societies' British Manuscripts project;
Inventories of Latin ms books from
numerous German, Austrian and Italian
archives and libraries; Pandects of the
Notaries of Genoa to 1300; selected
inventories (relating to American history)
from the Archives Nationales (Paris); books
printed in English before 1640; early English
and American literary periodicals; English
parish registers 16th to 19th centuries
(Challen typescripts); early Latin American
imprints; Mexican provincial andlocal
archives from Jalisco, Oaxaca, Parral, Puebla
and other cities; early editions of Petrarch
and Ronsard; 16th and 17th century Russian
imprints; papers of Simon Bolivar; League of
Nations documents; official gazettes of
Indian and Pakistan and their states and of
certain other countries; press translations
from Mainland China, Indonesia, Japan and
Yugoslavia; underground newspapers;
preservation microfilm of books from the
Library's general collections; doctoral
dissertations and misc items. *Microfiche*
(133,000): US city directories to 1860; US
corporation annual reports; US Office of
Education ERIC reports; State labor reports
1865-1900; British radical periodicals; Black
journals (US and British); social and
economic plans of developing countries;
organization of American States documents,
and misc items. *Microprint* (297,000 cards):
Americanimprints to 1810; English and
American plays 1516-1830; Journals and
Sesional Papers of the British House of
Commons; Index to early American
periodicals; US non-depository documents
and UN documents.
DC —US ARMS CONTROL &
DISARMAMENT AGENCY, Library,
George Washington Univ Special
Collections, Washington, 21 St & Virginia
Ave, NW, Rm 5851, Washington, 20451.
Diane Ferguson, Librn
Notes: Rare law books; British, European,
Roman, Canon, American law; incunabula;
Blackstone collection.
FL —FLORIDA STATE UNIVERSITY,
Robert Manning Strozier Library, Special
Collections Dept, Tallahassee, 32306. Opal
M Free, Head, Special Collections
Holdings: Vols (12,254) Cat Mss Maps
Notes: Noncirculating. No photocopying.
GA —CHEROKEE GARDEN LIBRARY,
3101 Andrews Dr NW, Atlanta, 30305.
Sally Bruce McClatchey, Librn
Holdings: Vols 2700
Notes: Southern history and horticulture.

Emphasis on the historical development of
American horticulture, 1634 to 1900.
IL —NORTHWESTERN UNIVERSITY,
Library, Special Collections Dept, 1937
Sheridan Rd, Evanston, 60201. R Russell
Maylone, Cur
Holdings: Vols 27,000 Cat Mss
Notes: Representative collection with
emphasis on the humanities and 19th
century English and American literature in
first editions. Incl Elzeviers, Aldines, Deism,
German classics, Fichte, Gruntvig, Ibsen,
Kant, Kiekegaard, Mark Twain, Walt
Whitman, economic history, Siege and
Commune of Paris, 1870-1871, etc.
IL —MORTON ARBORETUM, Sterling
Morton Library, Lisle, 60532. Ian MacPhail,
Librn
Holdings: Vols (22,000)
Notes: Emphasis is on Woody plants. Print
collection of 3000 pieces; 2000 botanical and
horticultural rare books; Linnaeana. The Jens
Jensen Archive of letters, photographs,
blueprints, landscape plans.
IA —UNIVERSITY OF IOWA, University
Libraries, Iowa City, 52242. Frank Paluka,
Head, Special Collections Dept
Holdings: Vols (13,170) Cat
Notes: Incl 15th and 16th century books,
early American imprints, North American
travel narratives, Roxburghe Club
publications, Italian Renaissance drama, rare
Latin American periodicals, certain modern
art periodicals and other interests. See
Florindo Cetteta, "Italian Plays of the
Renaissance," *Books at Iowa*, April 1965;
Richard M Kolbet, "Narratives of North
American Exploration," *Books at Iowa*, April
1967; Arthur H Minters, "A Talk on Modern
Art Periodicals," *Books at Iowa*, Nov 1967;
Frederick Lauritsen, "Rare Nineteenth-
Century Latin American Periodicals," *Books
at Iowa*, Nov 1969; Donald F Jackson,
"Sixteenth-Century Greek Editions at Iowa,"
Books at Iowa, April 1970; James
Fitzmaurice, "A Gathering of Emblem
Books," *Books at Iowa*, April 1971; Karl
Kahler, "The Hosso Shiyo Sho: A
Compilation of Traditional Legal Thought in
Japan," *Books at Iowa*, Nov 1971.
KS —EMPORIA STATE UNIVERSITY,
William Allen White Library, Emporia,
66801. Mary E Bogan, Special Collections
Librn
Holdings: Vols 1400
Notes: Rare and Valuable Book Collection.
KS —TOPEKA PUBLIC LIBRARY, Special
Collections & Local History Dept, 1515 W
Tenth, Topeka, 66604. Warren Taylor, Librn
Holdings: Vols 500
Notes: Emphasis on illustrated books adult
and children's.
MA —BOSTON UNIVERSITY, Mugar
Memorial Library, Special Collections Dept,
771 Commonwealth Ave, Boston, 02215.
Howard B Gotlieb, Dir
Holdings: Cat
Notes: Numerous special collections.
MA —MASSACHUSETTS
HORTICULTURAL SOCIETY, 300
Massachusetts Ave, Boston, 02115. Becky
Ellis, Librn
Holdings: Vols (37,000)
Notes: Garden history, pomology, flora,
landscape design. Print collection of many
centuries; nursery catalogues from the mid-
18th century. In storage, remodeling, will be
available in about a year. Open to the public.
MI —UNIVERSITY OF MICHIGAN, Library,
Dept of Rare Books & Special Collections,
Ann Arbor, 48109. Robert J Starring, Head
Holdings: Cat Mss Pix
Notes: Rare materials in all classes of
knowledge with special strength in the
history of mathematics and science; English
and American literature; English drama
before 1850; English history; 19th-century
American drama; early Bibles; imaginary
voyages; military art and science; protest
literature (Labadie Collection); papyri;
Western mss of the medieval and renaissance
periods; and Islamic mss.
MI —SUOMI COLLEGE, Finnish-American
Historical Archives, Hancock, 49930.
Kenneth Niemi, Archives Librn
Notes: Collection incl 8000 vols, 152,000

RARE BOOKS (cont.)

mss, 2000 photographs, 760 audiotapes; microforms and maps; 14,000 holdings are cataloged. Subject interests: coop movement, labor, pioneer library of rare books and church records, socialist and communist movements, temperance societies. Special Collections: Finnish language newspapers (includes 100 titles from 1876-present); Suomi Synod Archives; Finnish-American Oral History.

NM —GALLUP PUBLIC LIBRARY, 115 W Hill Ave, Gallup, 87301. Octavia Fellin, Dir
Holdings: Vols 4000 Cat
Notes: Rare and out of print books on the Southwest as well as Children's books.

NY —NEW YORK BOTANICAL GARDEN LIBRARY, Bronx, 10458. Charles R Long, Asst Vice Pres & Dir
Notes: One of the largest botanical collections in the world. Over 900,000 items. Covers botany (150,000 vols), botanists (3000), horticulture (45,000) plant diseases (25,000), plant physiology (15,000), history of botany (1500), conservation of natural resources (15,000), gardening (13,000), paleobotany (7000), ecology (20,000), forestry (5000) medical botany (3000), agriculture (9000) and biology (20,000). Reference library; materials do not circulate, except for member circulating collection (1200) and standard inter-library loan. About 5000 vols uncataloged. Incl art, books, serials, pamphlets, archives and manuscripts, vertical files, microfiche and microfilm, nursery and seed catalogs, photographs, paintings, prints, drawings and engravings. Covers all areas of botanical sciences. This is an OCLC library with fullresource services incl photocopying and photography.

NY —COLUMBIA UNIVERSITY LIBRARIES, C V Strarr East Asian Library, 300 Kent Hall, New York, 10027. James Reardon-Anderson, Librn
Notes: The Chinese Rare Book Collection comprises 193 titles printed in the Ming dynasty (1368-1644) and some 780 titles printed before 1795. It also incl 1041 titles in 9992 vols of Chinese genealogies of which 43 titles in 126 vols are ms editions. The Collection incl all forms of printing and book formats, i e, ms, moveable type, block printing, butterfly, accordian, stitched and western bindings.

NY —NEW YORK PUBLIC LIBRARY, Slavonic Div, Fifth Ave & 42 St, New York, 10018. Edward Kasinec, Chief
Holdings: Vols 122,000 Cat Microforms
Notes: Russian language materials form the main body (ca 70 percent) of the extensive Slavic and Baltic collections of the Slavonic Division. The strength of the collection is in humanities and social sciences, incl military history and government documents. Periodicals and publications of learned societies form an important part of the collection. Holdings of rare book are considerable. See New York Public Library, *Dictionary Catalog of the Slavonic* Collection (Boston: G K Hall, 1974), 44 vols.

NY —NEW YORK PUBLIC LIBRARY, Rare Books and Manuscripts Div, Fifth Ave & 42 St, New York, 10018. William L Joyce, Asst Dir; Francis O Mattson, Curator
Holdings: Vols 110,000 Cat Maps
Budget: ($7161)
Notes: This is Library's general collection of rare materials, the numbering in excess of 100,000 volumes, the nucleus being the Library of James Lenox. Most subjects are represented but the chief strength is Americana, especially before 1801. The collection is particularly rich in the earliest period, 1493-1550; in English Americana before 1641; and in the period of the American Revolution. Other specialties incl: voyages and travels to all parts of the world, incl one of the most extensive collections of De Bry and Hulsius and one of the finest sets of Canadian Jesuit Relations; early Bibles, incl the first copy of the Gutenberg Bible to be brought to this country (1847); 18th century American newspapers and periodicals; English and American literary first editions with notable collections of Shakespeare, Milton, Walton, Bunyan and Whitman. A very extensivecollection of modern fine printing incl a complete file of Kelmscott Press books and nearly complete runs of the major private and special presses such as Allen, Ashendene, Doves, Golden Cockerel, Grabhorn, Nonesuch, Vale, etc; one of the finest institutional collections of books designed by Bruce Rodgers. Described in *Dictionary Catalog of the Rare Book* Division, The Research Libraries of the New York Public Library. This dictionary catalog contains cards representing some 90,000 books and pamphlets from the beginning of European printing in the 15th century to private and special press books of the present day.

NY —UNIVERSITY CLUB, Library, One W 54 St, New York, 10019. Guy St Clair, Library Dir
Holdings: Vols (100,000) Cat Mss Maps Pix
Notes: A private library for the members of the University Club, their guests, and serious scholars upon written application to the Library Director. Holds the Edward Larocque Tinker Collection of Illustrated Books Between the Two World Wars, A Milton Runyon Collection on the History of Printing and Publishing, the Frederic R Coudert "Les Bibliophiles des Paris" Collection, The University Club Rare Book Collection, and the Frederick G Rudge Collection of Books Designed by William E Rudge and Bruce Rogers.

NY —UNIVERSITY OF ROCHESTER, School of Medicine and Dentistry, Edward G Miner Library, 601 Elmwood Ave, Rochester, 14642. Lucretia McClure, Medical Librn; Janet Brady Berk, History of Medicine Librn
Holdings: Vols (185,000) Cat
Notes: The Edward G Miner Library serves the School of Medicine & Dentistry, the School of Nursing, and Strong Memorial Hospital. The collection encompasses all the biomedical fields, nursing and dental research, and is designed to serve the teaching, patient care and research needs of persons in the Medical Center. The Library subscribes to more than 2900 current journals and serials, has an excellent reference collection and an extensive collection of rare and historical works in medicine and nursing.

NY —US MILITARY ACADEMY LIBRARY, West Point, 10996. Elaine B Eatroff, Rare Book Cur
Holdings: Vols 1500 Cat
Notes: Thayer Collection, incl rare editions of 19th century science.

OH —CLEVELAND PUBLIC LIBRARY, Fine Arts and Special Collections Department, 325 Superior Ave, Cleveland, 44114. Alice N Loranth, Head
Holdings: Cat Mss Maps Microfilms
Notes: Rare Books Collection incl 26,000 vols from the various subject department collections in virtually all Library of Congress classifications. Additional rare materials are also incl in other subject areas of Special Collections, such as, chess and checkers; early descriptions and travel in Europe, in the Americas and in the Orient; material related to folklore, such as medieval romance literature, chapbooks, customs pertaining to tobacco and smoking; classic Oriental literary and religious texts in Western and Oriental languages; European and Oriental manuscripts and the East India Company ms collection; sixteenth century imprints (over 700 vols);Derrydale Press collection; early Cleveland imprints; special collections of early editions and limited editions of selelcted works or authors (*Arabian Nights*, Castiglione, Gesta Romanorum, Huarte de San Juan, Omar Khayyam, Rabelais Tegney, Vergilius Polydorus, etc) incl cuneiform tablets, incunabula, Mazarinades (1731 titles), archival materials, some museum objects. *See also* entries under Chess; Folklore; Oriental Languages and Literatures.

†PA —LIBRARY COMPANY OF PHILADELPHIA, 1314 Locust St, Philadelphia, 19107. Edwin Wolf II, Librn
Holdings: Vols (450,000)

RI —PROVIDENCE ATHENAEUM, 251 Benefit St, Providence, 02903. Sally Duplaix, Dir
Holdings: (152,000) Vols
Notes: Material available on interlibrary loan under certain conditions.

SC —WOFFORD COLLEGE, Sandor Teszler Library, N Church St, Spartanburg, 29301. Frank J Anderson, Librn
Notes: Approx 25 books of 16th century (incl Jopocus Badius and Estienne imprints), a 15th century missal of vellum amd about 150 17th century imprints published by the Folio Society, Heritage Press.

†TX —UNIVERSITY OF TEXAS LIBRARIES, General Libraries, Humanities Research Center, PO Box 7219, Austin, 78712. John Chalmers, Librn

UT —UNIVERSITY OF UTAH, Marriott Library, Special Collections, Salt Lake City, 84112. Gregory C Thompson, Cur
Notes: Approx 12,000 volumes, incunabula, illuminated mss, maps, etc. Photocopying and use restricted. The Rare Books section is especially strong in its holdings on overland travel literature and North American Indians. A majority of the books listed in H R Wagner's *The Plains and Rockies* are found in Rare Books as are the works of George Catlin, Karl Bodmer, Edward Curtis, and McKenny and Hall. Some of these are so rare that they must be used under very restricted conditions.

WA —UNIVERSITY OF WASHINGTON LIBRARIES, Health Sciences Library, SB-55, Seattle, 98195. Gerald J Oppenheimer, Dir
Holdings: Vols (232,000) Cat Slides Audiotapes Microforms
Budget: ($550,000)

PR —UNIVERSITY OF PUERTO RICO, Jose M Lazaro Memorial Library (General Library), Box C, University of Puerto Rico Sta, Rio Piedras, 00931. Denise Perez, Head, Puerto Rican Collection
Holdings: Vols (96,782) Cat
Notes: Seek to collect all materials relating to Puerto Rico or the Puerto Ricans in or out of the island. Materials published in Puerto Rico are also collected. The various formats collected are books, pamphlets, mss, maps, slides, microfilm, periodicals and newspapers, academic thesis, tapes, posters, government documents, leaflets and clippings. Have a rare book collection consisting of about 2741 vols. These are books published in Puerto Rico or relating to Puerto Rico before the 20th century. The aim of the collection is to preserve Puerto Rico's bibliographical heritage and to serve the researchers on Puerto Rican studies.

ON —NATIONAL LIBRARY OF CANADA, 395 Wellington St, Ottawa, K1A 0N4, Can. Andre Preibish, Dir
Holdings: Vols 18,000
Notes: The collection contains 42 incunabula. The core collection consists of early Canadiana (1752-1867) and 16th and 17th century books on Canada. The books printed in native languages are a very valuable part of the collection. Canadian Livres d'Artistes collection of limited editions and Canadian *livres d'artistes* received on legal deposit as well as examples of private press publications from other countries also form part of the Rare Book collection.

PQ —BISHOP'S UNIVERSITY, John Bassett Memorial Library, Laurie Allison Room for Special Collections, Lennoxville, J1M 1Z7, Can. Germain Belisle, Chief Librn
Notes: The Marshall Collection. Books dating from the 16th to the 20th century.

RARE EARTHS see Earths, Rare

RASKIN, ELLEN

WI —UNIVERSITY OF WISCONSIN, MADISON, Cooperative Children's Book Center, Helen C White Hall, Rm 4290, 600 N Park St, Madison, 53706. Ginny Moore Kruse, Dir
Holdings: Vols (25,000) Cat
Notes: Cooperative Children's Book Center

RASKIN, ELLEN (cont.)

collections incl most US trade books published for children in last 24 months; first editions of recommended US children's trade books published since 1965; over 400 alternative press books published for children in US and Canada since 1970; children's books about Wisconsin and by Wisconsin authors and illustrators; representative 19th and early 20th century American children's books; 19th century children's periodicals; first and significant editions of Newbury and Caldecott Medal books; historical and contemporary toybooks; 75 vols of Mother Goose published since 1828; 160 vols of Thorton Burgess books, many first editions; ms and original artwork for Ellen Raskin's *The Westing Game* and *The Mysterious Disappearance of Leon (I Mean Noel)*; juvenile mass market and traderomance fiction.

RATHBONE, BASIL, 1892-1967

MA —BOSTON UNIVERSITY, Mugar Memorial Library, Special Collections Dept, 771 Commonwealth Ave, Boston, 02215. Howard B Gotlieb, Dir
Holdings: Cat Mss Pix
Notes: Mss, correspondence, etc collected in depth; incl publications by or about.

RATHER, DAN

MA —BOSTON UNIVERSITY, Mugar Memorial Library, Special Collections Dept, 771 Commonwealth Ave, Boston, 02215. Howard B Gotlieb, Dir
Holdings: Mss Pix
Notes: Mss, correspondence, etc collected in depth; incl publications by or about.

RATIONALISM

MA —HARVARD UNIVERSITY LIBRARY, Cambridge, 02138.
Holdings: Cat

RATIONING

AZ —NORTHERN ARIZONA UNIVERSITY, Special Collection Library, CU Box 6022, Flagstaff, 86011. Peter M Whiteley, Coordr/Archivist; William Mullane, Librn
Notes: US Office of Price Administration Collection; war ration books, stamps and applications from World War II. Incl ration books for gas, shoes, tires, sugar, etc. Early 1940's. Also incl weekly news bulletins put out by the Phoenix District Office of the Office of Price Administration.
CA —CALIFORNIA STATE UNIVERSITY, FRESNO, Henry Madden Library, Dept of Special Collections, Fresno, 93740. Ronald J Mahoney, Head
Holdings: Cat Mss
Notes: The Joseph A Lowande Collection of Worldwide Rationing contains 20th century ration material from Germany and the United States. Especially strong on local rationing from Stadtamhof, Bavaria, 1915-1923.

RAVEL, MAURICE

†TX —UNIVERSITY OF TEXAS LIBRARIES, Austin, 78712.
Notes: Collection of 89 autographed music manuscripts by five french composers: Gabriel Faure, Maurice Ravel, Claude Debussy, Robert Roussel, Paul Dukas. About 60 percent of Roussel's entire repertory is included, as well as nearly one-half of Ravel's total musical output.

RAWINSONDES

CA —UNIVERSITY OF CALIFORNIA, LOS ANGELES, Engineering & Mathematical Sciences Library, 405 Hilgard, Los Angeles, 90024. Rosalee I Wright, Librn
Notes: Collection includes WMO publications (comprehensive); IGY data series on surface observations, radiosonde and rawinsonde observations, upper wind observations, and radiation data (mostly in microform); selected government report or data series, eg from NOAA, NCC and AF Geophysics Laboratory.

RAWLEY FAMILY

NY —CORNELL UNIVERSITY LIBRARIES, Collection of Regional History, Dept of Manuscripts and Univ Archives, Ithaca, 14853.
Notes: Incl 73 pieces; papers, 1837-1953; mss, essays, photos, printed items, various business documents and miscellanea of Daniel and Hiram Rawley and others.

RAWORTH, TOM

CT —UNIVERSITY OF CONNECTICUT, Library, Storrs, 06268. George F Butterick, Cur of Literary Archives
Holdings: Mss
Notes: Repository for his papers.

RAY, MARIE BEYNON (LYONS)

†NJ —ADELPHI UNIVERSITY, Library, Garden City, 11530.
Notes: Marie Beynon (Lyons) Ray Collection incl mss, correspondence with prominent psychiatrists and others during the years 1937-1958.

RAYBURN, SAM

TX —SAM RAYBURN FOUNDATION LIBRARY, 800 W Sam Rayburn Dr, Box 123, Bonham, 75418.
Holdings: Vols 8000 Cat Mss Pix Microforms
Notes: Historical research library--contains all of Speaker Rayburn's papers. Incl books on American history, biography, politics and government, and the Presidents and their writings.
TX —NORTH TEXAS STATE UNIVERSITY, Archives, NT Station Box 5188, Denton, 76203. Robert LaForte, University Archivist
Notes: Part of Oral History Collection. Interviews with Alla Clary, secretary to Speaker Sam Rayburn.

RAYMOND FAMILY

NY —CORNELL UNIVERSITY LIBRARIES, Collection of Regional History, Dept of Manuscripts and Univ Archives, Ithaca, 14853.
Notes: Incl farm papers, (1855-1926)-1947; miscellaneous accounts of C C Raymond, George W Raymond, and other members of the Raymond and Smith families. Unpublished guide available.

LA RAZA UNIDA PARTY

CA —CALIFORNIA STATE UNIVERSITY, FULLERTON, Library, Box 4150, Fullerton, 92634. Alfredo H Zuniga, Coord
Notes: Some materials on the subject; not maintained as a separate collection.

REACTORS, BREEDER see Breeder Reactors

REACTORS, NUCLEAR see Nuclear Reactors

READE, CHARLES, 1814-1884

NJ —PRINCETON UNIVERSITY, Library, Morris L Parrish Collection, Princeton, 08540. Alexander D Wainwright, Cur
Notes: For particulars refer to: Robert B Martin, "The Reade Collection" in the *Chronicle* XVII, 2 (winter, 1956) pp 77-80. The article describes briefly some of the items in one of the finest Reade collection ever assembled. Almost 200 vols.

READ, GEORGE

DE —HISTORICAL SOCIETY OF DELAWARE, Library, 505 Market St Mall, Wilmington, 19801. Barbara E Benson, Library Dir
Holdings: Cat Mss
Notes: Collection incl papers and other mss materials.

READ, SIR HERBERT EDWARD, 1893-1968

BC —UNIVERSITY OF VICTORIA, McPherson Library, Victoria, V8W 3H5, Can.
Notes: Writer, literary and art critic. Incl 4m, ca 1918-65; mss and correspondence. Finding aids: Gerwing, Howard, "A checklist of the Herbert Read Archive in the McPherson Library of the University of Victoria." In *The Malahat Review*, no 9 (January 1969), 192-258; and *Herbert Read: A Memorial Symposium*, ed by Robin Skelton (London, Methuen, 1970,192-258).

READERS AND SPEAKERS

PA —UNIVERSITY OF PITTSBURGH, Hillman Library, Special Collections Dept, 363 Hillman Library, Pittsburgh, 15260. Charles E Aston Jr, Coordinator
Holdings: Vols (13,480) Cat Mss
Notes: The John A Nietz Textbook Collection of primarily American textbooks in 3 areas; primary school books to 1900, secondary texts to ca 1930, and pedagogical books (1000 vols on the history and theory of education incl writings of the key figures in the field of education). Books are cataloged via an in-house computer printout and are accessible via name, title, subject, place, publisher and date. Late 18th and all of the 19th centuries are well represented. Important titles in each subject are discussed in John A Nietz's *Old Textbooks* (Pittsburgh, 1961) and in his *The Evolution of American Secondary School Textbooks* (Rutland, Vt, 1966). Collection also incl the papers (noncirculating) of Prof John A Nietz.

READING

IL —FIELD MUSEUM OF NATURAL HISTORY, Edward E Ayer Ornithology Library Collection, Roosevelt Rd & Lake Shore Dr, Chicago, 60605. W Peyton Fawcett, Librn
Holdings: Vols 3500 Cat
Notes: Ornithological illustrations.
IL —SCOTT, FORESMAN & CO, Editorial Library, 1900 E Lake Ave, Glenview, 60025. S Donal Robertson, Head Librn
Holdings: Vols (30,000) Phonorecords Audiotapes Microforms
Notes: A general collection, fairly heavy in the areas of education and children's literature. Study and teaching of reading is probably the largest single section of the collection.
NY —HOFSTRA UNIVERSITY, Library, 1000 Fulton Ave, Hempstead, 11550. Charles R Andrews, Dean of Library Services
Notes: Nila Banton Smith Collection. Strong collection. History of the Methodology of Teaching Reading.
NY —GRADUATE CENTER OF THE CITY UNIVERSITY OF NEW YORK, William H and Gwynne K Crouse Library for Publishing Arts, 33 W 42 St, New York, 10036. Alfred H Lane, Dir
Notes: Recently established and still growing, but intended to become the authoritative source of materials in the field, of particular value in research about the publishing industry. Open to staff members of publishing houses, students, scholars, authors, printers, and booksellers. Primarily 20th century materials, and particularly useful for research on technical, financial, and historical matters. Much on the history of individual houses, economics of authorship; marketing and distribution of books; etc.
PA —SCHOOL DISTRICT OF PHILADELPHIA, Pedagogical Library, 21 St & Pkwy, Philadelphia, 19103. Helen E

READING (cont.)

Howe, Librn; Patricia K Buck, Asst Librn
Holdings: Vols (47,000) Cat Pix Microforms
Budget: ($25,000)
Notes: Collection emphasis on public school
education K-12 with the main areas
including Afro-American history and culture,
elementary and early childhood education,
secondary education, educational
administration, educational research, reading,
school law, educational psychology. Special
Collections: ERIC (140,000 documents),
Archives of the School District of
Philadelphia. Approx 500 periodical
subscriptions.

RI —PROVIDENCE PUBLIC LIBRARY, 150
Empire St, Providence, 02903. Lance J
Bauer, Special Collections Librn
Notes: Lippitt Hill Tutorial Shelf
(Rochambeau Branch). A resource library for
tutors and parents, centrally located and
open after school; established in 1973. LHT
is a non-profit school volunteer agency
which provides in-school tutoring services,
contributes money for the acquisition of new
books for the LHT Shelf, and the Providence
Public Library maintains the collection. A
collection of educational materials, wich an
emphasis on math and reading, for the
information and use of the general public,
parents, teachers, and especially, tutors. It is
located near the front door of the
Rochambeau Branch.

MB —UNIVERSITY OF WINNIPEG,
Department of English, 515 Portage Ave,
Winnipeg, R3B 2E9, Can. Perry Nodelman,
Cur
Holdings: Vols 1000 Cat
Notes: This collection represents the kind of
material children read during the 19th and
early 20th century on the Canadian Prairies,
not necessarily "Children's Literature."

READING, CHOICE OF see
Bibliography—Best Books

READING RAILROAD

DE —HAGLEY MUSEUM AND LIBRARY,
Eleutherian Mills-Hagley Foundation Inc,
PO Box 3630, Greenville, 19807. Richmond
D Williams, Dir; Heddy A Richter, Imprints
Librn
Notes: Records of the Reading Railroad
(1845-1940; 1000 cubic feet) contain minute
books and financial records documenting the
history of both the parent and subsidiary
companies. Voluminous correspondence files
describe all aspects of railroad operations.

REAGAN, RONALD

†CA —UNIVERSITY OF SOUTHERN
CALIFORNIA, University Library,
Archives of Performing Arts, Los Angeles,
90089. Robert Knutson, Librn
Holdings: Mss
Notes: Ronald Reagan's personal, moving
picture, and political papers.

REAGAN, THOMAS B.

MA —BOSTON UNIVERSITY, Mugar
Memorial Library, Special Collections Dept,
771 Commonwealth Ave, Boston, 02215.
Howard B Gotlieb, Dir
Holdings: Cat Mss Correspondence

REAL ESTATE

AL —UNIVERSITY OF ALABAMA, Business
Library, Box 2937, University, 35486.
Dorothy Eady Brown, Librn; Linda Suttle
Harris, Ref Librn and Data Base Searcher
Holdings: Vols (105,000) Cat Microforms
Budget: ($60,000)
Notes: Incl 90,000 corporation reports and
38,500 microforms.

CA —UNIVERSITY OF CALIFORNIA, LOS
ANGELES, Graduate School of
Management Library, UCLA Campus, Los
Angeles, 90024. Robert Bellanti, Head Librn
Holdings: Vols (128,000) Cat Mss
Microforms
Notes: The

CA —ALAMEDA COUNTY LIBRARY
SYSTEM, Business & Government Library,
2201 Broadway, Oakland, 94612. David
Lewallen, Manager
Holdings: Vols (10,000) Cat Maps
Microforms
Budget: ($50,000)

CA —CONTRA COSTA COUNTY
LIBRARY, 1750 Oak Park Blvd, Pleasant
Hill, 94523. Lyn Talme, Business Specialist
Holdings: Vols (7000)
Notes: Incl 76 periodicals, 1000 corporate
annual reports, and 316 telephone
directories.

DC —MORTGAGE BANKERS ASSN OF
AMERICA, Library, 1125 15th St NW,
Washington, 20005. Timothy Wolf, Librn
Holdings: Vols (6500) Cat
Notes: Non-circulating; no photocopying.

DC —URBAN LAND INSTITUTE, Library,
1090 Vermont Ave, Washington, 20005.
Ann Benson, Librn
Holdings: Vols (9000) Cat
Budget: ($6000)
Notes: Incl 200 serials.

NY —BROOKLYN PUBLIC LIBRARY,
Business Library, 280 Cadman Plaza W,
Brooklyn, 11201. Sylvia Mechanic, Business
Librn
Holdings: Vols (107,000) Cat
Notes: Library received about 1800
periodicals, 3000 serials, 2700 directories,
1600 telephone books from all over the
world with a complete back file on microfilm
for greater New York. Library is a selective
US Government Documents depository.
Subscribes to microfiche SEC 10K reports
for AMEX, NYSE and OTC from 1976 to
date; annual reports for earlier years.
Transnational annual reports, on fiche from
1982-to date. 78 vertical file trays; Sanborn
maps for Brooklyn, special collection of
corporation histories. Publish monthly
newsletter, *Service to Business and Industry*
with our Science Division.

NY —COLUMBIA UNIVERSITY
LIBRARIES, Rare Book & Manuscript
Library, 801 Butler Library, 535 W 114 St,
New York, 10027. Kenneth A Lohf, Librn
Notes: More than 32,000 items documenting
the rise of William Russell Grace's shipping
business and other materials relating to his
career as mayor of New York. Incl records
and correspondence relating to all aspects of
the shipping business in New York and
South America, mining interest in Peru and
Chile, and transportation in Costa Rica and
Nicaragua. Family memorabilia and
photographs, materials concerning New
York Politics, banking and insurance, real
estate interests and Catholic charities, and
letters from Chester A Arthur, John Jacob
Astor, Andrew Carnegie, Grover Cleveland,
Hamilton Fish, John Hay and J Pierpont
Morgan. Restricted use.

NY —INTERNATIONAL PAPER CO,
Corporate Information Center, 77 W 45 St,
New York, 10036. Elizabeth Skerritt,
Corporate Librn
Holdings: Vols 30 Cat Maps Pix Slides
Microforms
Notes: Extensive statistics and VF on paper
industry.

NY —NEW YORK STATE DIVISION OF
HOUSING & COMMUNITY RENEWAL,
Library, 2 World Trade Center, New York,
10047. Carole Williams, Asst Librn, Special
Reference Room
Holdings: Vols 2100 Cat Pix
Budget: $1500
Notes: No photocopying.

NC —GREENSBORO PUBLIC LIBRARY,
Business Library, 201 Greene St, Drawer
X-4, Greensboro, 27402. Lebby B Lamb,
Business Librn
Holdings: Vols (6000) Cat Microforms
Budget: ($12,000)

OH —CLEVELAND PUBLIC LIBRARY,
Business, Economics and Labor Department,
325 Superior Ave, Cleveland, 44114. Joan
Sorger, Head
Holdings: Cat
Notes: Currently receiving over 1700
periodicals and 1300 serial titles; 1000
individual trade, industrial and professional
directories, worldwide; 324 file drawers

annual reports of old companies, many local;
24 drawers historical information on
Cleveland companies. Annual reports, 10-
K's, Proxy Statements (disclosure SEC
filings on fiche); over 200 loose-leaf services;
1700 current telephone and city directories.
Emphasis on current material. Areas of
special strength are banking, investments,
marketing and management. Also strong
insurance, accounting, real estate and
transportation collections. Computerized
sources available incl Dow Jones News
Service and a variety of Dialog business-
related databases.

TX —ECTOR COUNTY LIBRARY,
Department of Business and Technology,
321 W 5th St, Odessa, 79760. Pat Jones,
Dept Head
Notes: 25,000 Corporate Annual Reports
microfilmed reports are complete from 1978-
1983. 200 vertical files, 30 periodicals.
Collection includes the subjects of Business,
Management, Real Estate Accounting, Land
Economics, Labor Economics, Finance,
Personal Finance and Environmental
Economics. Also included are stock and
dividend reports, commodities and bond
reports as well as business rankings. All
items are referenced and cataloged.

REAL ESTATE INVESTMENT

DC —MORTGAGE BANKERS ASSN OF
AMERICA, Library, 1125 15th St NW,
Washington, 20005. Timothy Wolf, Librn
Holdings: Vols (6500) Cat
Notes: Non-circulating; no photocopying.

DC —URBAN LAND INSTITUTE, Library,
1090 Vermont Ave, Washington, 20005.
Ann Benson, Librn

REAL PROPERTY INVESTMENT see
Real Estate Investment

REAPERS see Harvesting Machines

REBELLIONS see Revolutions

REBER, LOUIS

AZ —NORTHERN ARIZONA
UNIVERSITY, Special Collection Library,
CU Box 6022, Flagstaff, 86011. Peter M
Whiteley, Coordr/Archivist; William
Mullane, Librn
Notes: Collection of Louis Reber, 1890-
1966, first paid geologist of the United
Verde Copper Company. He developed the
concept of aerial photography for ore
identification. Incl correspondence and
records of mining activities in Arizona and
the US, 1912-1950's and mining activities in
South Africa and Rhodesia, 1920's.

REBIRTH see Reincarnation

RECEIPTS see Recipes

RECHY, JOHN

MA —BOSTON UNIVERSITY, Mugar
Memorial Library, Special Collections Dept,
771 Commonwealth Ave, Boston, 02215.
Howard B Gotlieb, Dir
Holdings: Cat Mss Pix Correspondence

RECIFE SCHOOL

WI —UNIVERSITY OF WISCONSIN,
MADISON, Memorial Library, Ibero-
American Studies Collection, 728 State St,
Madison, 53706. Suzanne Hodgman,
Bibliographer
Holdings: Vols (129) // Cat
Notes: An unusual collection of 129 volumes
on Brazilian history, literature, and
philosophy. Strongest in works published by
members of the intellectual group known as
the Escola do Recife, the leader of which
was Tobias Barreto. The collection contains
almost all of his works as well as most of the
works, including many rare pamphlets, of
Silvio Romero, Barreto's most illustrious
disciple. No separate listing.

RECIPES

BC —VANCOUVER PUBLIC LIBRARY,
Science & Technology Div, 750 Burrard St,

RECIPES (cont.)

Vancouver, V6Z 1X5, Can. P Haffenden, Head, Science & Technology Div
Holdings: Cat
Notes: Plus special indexes. Recipes File (20 catalog drawers). Also books, pamphlets and periodicals.

RECITATIONS see Readers and Speakers

RECKNAGEL, ARTHUR BERNARD, 1883-1962

NY —CORNELL UNIVERSITY LIBRARIES, Collection of Regional History, Dept of Manuscripts and Univ Archives, Ithaca, 14853.
Notes: Incl papers, 1948-61; monthly reports, pamphlets, speeches, newspaper clippings, 8 photos and other items mainly relating to the forest products industry.

RECLAMATION OF LAND

CA —UNIVERSITY OF CALIFORNIA, BERKELEY, Water Resources Center Archives, 410 O'Brien Hall, Berkeley, 94720. Gerald J Giefer, Librn
Holdings: Vols (83,000) Cat Mss Maps
Notes: The engineering, economic, social and legal aspects of water: water as a natural resource and its utilization; irrigation and reclamation; flood control; municipal and industrial water uses and problems; water rights; and water development projects. Particular concentration is on California and the West. Much ephemeral material. See *Dictionary Catalog of the Water Resources Center Archives, University of California* (Boston: G K Hall, 5 vols; First Supp, 1971; Second Supp, 1972; Third Supp, 1973; Fourth Supp, 1974; Fifth Supp, 1976; and Sixth Supp, 1978).
NE —NEBRASKA STATE HISTORICAL SOCIETY, Archives, 1500 R St, Box 82554, Lincoln, 68501. James E Potter, State Archivist
Holdings: // Uncat Mss Maps Pix Clippings
Notes: Agriculture, reclamation, and irrigation on the Great Plains from 1910 to 1957. Collection of Val Kuska, agricultural development for CB&O Railroad.
UT —UNIVERSITY OF UTAH, Marriott Library, Special Collections, Salt Lake City, 84112. Gregory C Thompson, Cur

RECLAMATION OF WATER see Water Reuse

RECONSTRUCTION (EUROPE, 1919-1923)

CA —HOOVER INSTITUTION ON WAR, REVOLUTION & PEACE, Stanford University, Stanford, 94305. Milorad M Drachkovitch, Archivist
Holdings: Mss
Notes: Records of the European Technical Advisers, a private American advisory organization created to assist in European reconstruction after World War I, incl correspondence, reports, statistics, and financial records, 1919-1923, relating to railway operation, fuel production, and other aspects of economic reconstruction in Austria, Poland, Czechoslavakia and Yugoslavia. 72 ms boxes.

RECONSTRUCTION (EUROPE, 1945-1951)

CA —HOOVER INSTITUTION ON WAR, REVOLUTION & PEACE, Stanford University, Stanford, 94305. Milorad M Drachkovitch, Archivist
Holdings: Mss
Notes: Papers of Howard Palfrey Jones, 1930-1973, incl mss, correspondence, reports, research files, studies, and printed matter, relating primarily to public finance and post-war reconstruction in Germany, 1945-51, to US foreign relations in East Asia, 1951-73, and to his service as Ambassador to Indonesia, 1958-1965 ca 60 ms boxes.

†VA —GEORGE C MARSHALL RESEARCH FOUNDATION AND LIBRARY, Drawer 920, Lexington, 24450. Royster Lyle Jr, Cur Collections
Holdings: Vols Cat Mss Pix Videotapes Films Filmstrips
Notes: The Harry B Price Collection contains over 650 typed pages of interviews with European and American officials concerning the Marshall Plan. This was in preparation for his book, *The Marshall Plan and Its Meaning*. These interviews incl such people as Averell Harriman, George Kennan, and Marshall himself. 15 countries, OEFC (Organization for European Economic Cooperation), and USRO (US Special Representative in Europe) are represented in these interviews. Also in the collection are papers and materials that Cecilia "Jackie" Martin collected as Picture editor for the Marshall Plan Information Service in Europe, 1950-54.

RECONSTRUCTION (U.S., 1863-1877)

ME —BOWDOIN COLLEGE, Library, Brunswick, 04011. Dianne M Gutscher, Cur of Special Collections
Holdings: Mss
Notes: The Oliver Otis Howard Papers consist of more than 150,000 pieces of correspondence, articles, lectures, and ephemera for the period 1843-1908, covering his services as a Civil War officer, as founder of the Freedmen's Bureau, as president of Howard University, as commander of the Department of the Columbia during the Northwest Indian Wars, and as superintendent of the US Military Academy at West Point.
NY —UNIVERSITY CLUB, Library, One W 54 St, New York, 10019. Guy St Clair, Library Dir
Holdings: Vols (100,000) Cat Mss Maps Pix
Notes: A private library for the members of the University Club, their guests, and serious scholars upon written application to the Library Director. Holds the Southern Society Collection of materials on the South, the Civil War and Reconstruction.
NC —DUKE UNIVERSITY, William R Perkins Library, Manuscript Dept, Durham, 27706. Ellen Gartrell, Cur of Mss
Holdings: Cat Mss
RI —BROWN UNIVERSITY, John Hay Library, 20 Prospect St, Providence, 02912. Mark N Brown, Cur Mss
Holdings: // Mss
Notes: Eli H Canfield mss reflect issues of the day and incl the subjects of missions, religious education, temperance, Prohibition, and Reconstruction. There are also 300 letters from Canfield to his son and grandchildren; letters from Europe and the South during and after the Civil War; and papers relating to Christ Church, Brooklyn. Register available. See "The Rev Eli Canfield (1817-1898): Low-church Yankee Episcopalian," ed by William G McLoughlin, Jr, in *Books at Brown*, vol XXIII (1969), pp 135-68.

RECORDING INDUSTRY

DC —LIBRARY OF CONGRESS, Motion Pictures, Broadcasting and Recorded Sound Div, Washington, 20540.
Notes: Recordings, photographs, correspondence, scrapbooks and other memorabilia concerning the invention of the lateral cut disc gramophone record, basis of the modern recording industry, Emile Berliner (1851-1929). Devised word "Gramophone," and invented acoustic tiling.

RECORDINGS, SOUND see Sound Recordings and Reproductions—Collections

RECORDS MANAGEMENT

NJ —H M BAKER ASSOCIATES, Research Collection, 266 E Dudley Ave, Westfield, 07090. Helen Baker Cushman, Managing Associate
Holdings: Vols 2000 Cat Mss Maps Pix Slides
Notes: Baker Associates publishes *The Business History Letter* The Anniversary Manual, "Remember the Year," business histories and anniversary studies which are based on the contents of the collection. Emphasis of the collection is on industrial and business history.

RECORDS OF BIRTH, ETC. see Registers of Births, Etc.; Vital Statistics

RECREATION

AZ —TUCSON PUBLIC LIBRARY, Governmental Reference Library, PO Box 27210, City Hall, Tucson, 85726. Ann Strickland, Librn
Holdings: Vols (4000) Cat Maps Audiotapes Microforms
Notes: Special emphasis on public administration, including public finance, public personnel management, social services, urban planning, public transportation, public works, water management, solid waste management, public recreation and government of growing southwestern US cities in 200,000 to 500,000 population range.
CA —UNIVERSITY OF CALIFORNIA, BERKELEY, Giannini Foundation of Agricultural Economics, Library, 248 Giannini Hall, Berkeley, 94720. Grace Dote, Librn
Holdings: Vols (18,000) Cat Mss Maps Microforms
Notes: Noncirculating collection. No interlibrary loans. Also about 124,000 unbound vols. Open to graduated students and faculties of universities and colleges, research workers and interested public. Mostly English language materials, primarily 1900 to date. Card catalog published by G K Hall Co *Dictionary Catalog of the Giannini Foundation of Agricultural Economics Library, Univ of California*, 12 vols. (Holdings thru 7/71.)
CA —ESALEN SPORT CENTER, Esalen Institute, Big Sur, 93920.
Notes: Emphasizes integration of mind and body.
CA —CALIFORNIA STATE UNIVERSITY, FULLERTON, Library, Box 4150, Fullerton, 92634. Linda Herman, Special Collections Librn
Holdings: Vols (3530) Cat Mss
Notes: Capt P Markham Kerridge Angling Collection incl materials on angling, entomology, ichthyology, conservation, travel, recreation, and related areas. A computer author printout with title, imprint, and various codes is updated annually. Books and pamphlets are supplemented by 2750 periodical issues, and extensive ephemera.
CA —LOS ANGELES PUBLIC LIBRARY, Art, Music & Recreation Dept, 630 W Fifth St, Los Angeles, 90071. Melvin H Rosenberg, Mgr & Principal Librn
Holdings: Vols 24,000 Cat Pix
Budget: ($102,244)
Notes: Incl 15,000 pictures; *Sports Index* (40,000 entries).
DC —CONSERVATION FOUNDATION, Library, 1717 Massachusetts Ave NW, Washington, 20036. Barbara K Rodes, Librn
Holdings: Vols (8000) Cat Maps
Notes: Collection incl natural resources, ecology, city and regional planning, land use, recreation, energy conservation, environmental economics, pollution control, water resources.
DC —SMITHSONIAN INSTITUTION LIBRARIES, National Museum of American History Branch, Washington, 20560. Rhoda S Ratner, Branch Librn
Notes: Emphasis on history of American sports and recreation. Incl some 2000 baseball cards from cigarette and chewing-gum packets; 103 scrapbooks and other memorabilia about Joe Louis; much on bicycling and skating.
IL —UNIVERSITY OF ILLINOIS, URBANA/CHAMPAIGN, Library, Applied Life Studies Library, 1408 W Gregory Dr,

RECREATION (cont.)

Urbana, 61801.
Holdings: Vols (38,000) Cat Microforms
Notes: Special emphasis on leisure studies, recreation surveys and plans, outdoor education, recreation programs, theories of play, supervision, and therapeutic recreation. *See also* entry under Physical Education and Training.

IN —SOUTHWEST INDIANA MENTAL HEALTH CENTER, Library, 415 Mulberry, Evansville, 47714. Donna Yuschak, Librn
Holdings: Vols 850 Cat Slides Audiotapes 16mm Films
Budget: $4000
Notes: Also about 500 pamphlets on psychotherapy, social work, and therapeutic recreation.

MD —MARYLAND-NATIONAL CAPITAL PARK & PLANNING COMMISSION, Montgomery County Planning Department Library, 8787 Georgia Ave, Silver Spring, 20907. Janice C Holt, Librn
Holdings: Vols (5000) Cat
Notes: Specific subject areas include: community facilities, conservation, economics, flood control, highways, housing, human and natural resources. landscape architecture, open space, parks, pollution, population, recreation, transportation, urban renewal, and zoning. Commission's publications are maintained by Records Management (not Library).

MA —UNIVERSITY OF MASSACHUSETTS AT AMHERST, Library, Amherst, 01002.
Notes: Strong collections in physical education, sports studies, exercise, gymnastics, etc.

MA —HARVARD UNIVERSITY, Harvard Forest Library, Petersham, 01366. Catherine M Danahar, Librn
Notes: Emphasis on National Forest recreation, with related subjects incl wildlife and economics.

MN —MINNEAPOLIS PUBLIC LIBRARY & INFORMATION CENTER, Sociology Dept, 300 Nicollet Mall, Minneapolis, 55401. Eileen Scwartzbauer, Dept Head
Holdings: Vols (90,000) Cat Phonorecords Audiotapes Microforms
Budget: ($69,890)
Notes: Special collections: Foundation Center Regional Collection; college catalogs on fiche; adult basic education collection. Separate department catalog.

NY —ADIRONDACK HISTORICAL ASSOCIATION, Museum Library, Blue Mountain Lake, 12812. Jerold Pepper, Librn
Holdings: Vols (7500) Cat Mss Maps Pix Phonorecords Audiotapes 16mm Films Microforms
Notes: Anything about the Adirondacks-- history, people, economics, places, things. Strong in Adirondack art, outdoor recreation, logging, small boats. Resources incl more than 1000 maps, 40,000 pictures, 1600 microfilm reels, 576 linear ft of ms material, and 12 cabinets of VF ephemera, etc.

NC —NORTH AMERICAN YOUTH SPORT INSTITUTE, 4985 Oak Garden Drive, Kernersville, 27284. Jack Hutslar, Exec Dir
Notes: A private management consulting and training firm for adults who are involved with school age youngsters in community sport, recreation and physical education.

NC —NORTH CAROLINA STATE UNIVERSITY, D H Hill Library, Box 7111, Raleigh, 27695. I T Littleton, Dir
Holdings: Vols 3940 Cat
Budget: $1500
Notes: Covers parks and recreation management. Incl monographs. *See also* entry under Parks.

OR —UNIVERSITY OF OREGON LIBRARY, Education-Psychology Dept, Eugene, 97403. Rose Marie Service, Head Dept Librn
Holdings: Microforms
Budget: ($4000)
Notes: General and research collection in health, physical education, recreation and dance incl serials. An important series is *Microforms Publications*, produced by the College of Health, Physical Education and Recreation, University of Oregon, which is comprised of 3632 microcards or microfiche of unpublished research of national significance.

TN —TENNESSEE VALLEY AUTHORITY (TVA), Technical Library, 400 W Summit Hill Dr, E2 B7, Knoxville, 37902. Jesse C Mills, Chief Librn
Holdings: Vols (106,900) Cat Mss Maps Pix Audiotapes Microforms
Budget: ($2,025,000)
Notes: The Technical Library Headquarters Staff (order, cataloging, information, and administration) is located in Knoxville, Tenn. In addition there are branch libraries in Knoxville, Norris, and Chattanooga, Tennessee, and Muscle Shoals, Alabama.

ON —METROPOLITAN TORONTO LIBRARY, Science & Technology Dept, 789 Yonge St, Toronto, M4W 2G8, Can. Margaret Walshe, Head
Holdings: Vols (120,000) Cat VF
Notes: Selective aspects of technology for the specialist, the student and the general public. The department gives high priority to Canadian material.

ON —ONTARIO MINISTRY OF NATURAL RESOURCES, Natural Resources Library, Whitney Block 4540, Toronto, M5S 1B3, Can. Sandra Louet, Librn
Holdings: Cat

ON —SIRLS, Faculty of Human Kinetics & Leisure Studies, University of Waterloo, Waterloo, N2L 3G1, Can. Betty Smith, Database Mgr
Notes: Information Retrieval System for the Sociology of Leisure and Sport (SIRLS) is a computerized online database of about 13,000 entries (1983). Incl dance as a leisure time activity.

RECREATION AREAS

MA —HARVARD UNIVERSITY, Harvard Forest Library, Petersham, 01366. Catherine M Danahar, Librn
Notes: Emphasis on National Forest recreation, with related subjects incl wildlife and economics.

NJ —SUSSEX COUNTY LIBRARY, Rd 3, Box 76, Newton, 07860. Judith Gessel, Reference Librn
Holdings: Cat Maps Slides 16mm Films Filmstrips
Notes: The Sussex County Area Reference Library is one of several locations which were named repositories for materials related to the restudy of the Tocks Island Lake Project. The items in the repository were distributed by the Delaware River Basin Commission. Collection incl study-related hearing transcripts, public notices, press clippings, correspondence, and reports of concern to the Delaware Water Gap National Recreation Area/Tocks Island Area. The Tocks Island Regional Advisory Council, when disbanded, presented its library to the Sussex County Library in 1974. The collection incl reports, surveys, maps, slides, and other materials collected or produced by TIRAC since 1965.

NY —ADIRONDACK HISTORICAL ASSOCIATION, Museum Library, Blue Mountain Lake, 12812. Jerold Pepper, Librn
Holdings: Vols (7500) Cat Mss Maps Pix Phonorecords Audiotapes 16mm Films Microforms
Notes: Anything about the Adirondacks-- history, people, economics, places, things. Strong in Adirondack art, outdoor recreation, logging, small boats. Resources incl more than 500 maps, 40,000 pictures, 1600 microfilm reels (nearly 18,000 items), 600 linear ft of ms material, and 12 cabinets of VF ephemera, etc.

TN —TENNESSEE VALLEY AUTHORITY (TVA), Norris Branch Library, Norris, 37828. Debra D Mills, Librn
Holdings: Cat Microforms
Budget: ($50,000)

WA —UNIVERSITY OF WASHINGTON LIBRARIES, Forest Resources Library, AQ-15, Seattle, 98195. Barbara B Gordon, Head
Holdings: Vols (43,248) Cat Microforms
Budget: ($41,103)
Notes: Modern imprints only. Mostly in English. Emphasis is on Pacific Northwest National Parks and National Forests.

AB —CANADIAN FORESTRY SERVICE, Northern Forest Research Centre Library, 5320 122nd, Edmonton, T6H 3S5, Can. David J S Robinson, Librn
Holdings: Vols (7000) Cat Microforms
Budget: ($25,000)
Notes: Also 23,000 government documents, 2600 research reports, 3000 pamphlets and reprints.

RECREATION RESOURCES ADMINISTRATION

NC —NORTH CAROLINA STATE UNIVERSITY, D H Hill Library, Box 7111, Raleigh, 27695. I T Littleton, Dir
Notes: Covers parks and recreation management. Incl monographs.

WA —UNIVERSITY OF WASHINGTON LIBRARIES, Forest Resources Library, AQ-15, Seattle, 98195. Barbara B Gordon, Head
Notes: Modern imprints only. Mostly in English. Emphasis is on Pacific Northwest National Parks and National Forests.

RECREATIONAL FISHING see Fishing and Angling

RECREATIONS see Hobbies; Play; Sports

RECREATIONS, MATHEMATICAL see Mathematical Recreations

RECUSANT LITERATURE AND RECUSANTS

CA —UNIVERSITY OF SAN FRANCISCO, Richard A Gleeson Library, The Countess Bernardine Murphy Donohue Rare Book Room, San Francisco, 94117. D Steven Corey, Special Collections Librn
Holdings: Vols 300
Notes: Largely from the Virtue-Cahill library in England, and the collection of Charles A Fracchia. Incl important works of Bayly, Cressy, Sergeant, and Worsley. Incl a contemporary manuscript of the trial of Father Garnet, accused of complicity in the Gunpowder Plot.

IL —NEWBERRY LIBRARY, 60 W Walton St, Chicago, 60610. Diana Haskell, Cur of Modern Mss
Holdings: Vols 10,000 Cat
Notes: History and literature of Catholics in England. Incl 500 ms pieces.

MO —SAINT LOUIS UNIVERSITY, Pius XII Memorial Library, 3655 W Pine Blvd, Saint Louis, 63108. William Cole, Dir
Holdings: Vols 250 Cat Mss Slides //
Notes: Fundamental source material for the study of every aspect of Catholic religious, political, and social thought during nearly five hundred years of English, Scottish, and Irish history (early sixteenth century to modern times). Approximately 2220 volumes do not appear in card catalog, and researchers must write ahead to make arrangements, since these volumes are not readily available for public use.

MO —SAINT LOUIS UNIVERSITY, Pius XII Memorial Library, Saint Louis Room Collection, 3655 W Pine Blvd, Saint Louis, 63108. Catherine E Weidle, Rare Books Librn
Holdings: Vols // Uncat Mss
Notes: The collection of books, pamphlets and mss begins with the break with Rome under Henry VIII, continues through the struggle for emancipation and ends with the centenary of the Hierarchy. Separate index.

ON —UNIVERSITY OF TORONTO, Thomas Fisher Rare Book Library, 120 Saint George St, Toronto, M5S 1A5, Can. Richard G Landon, Head
Holdings: Vols 1600 // Cat Mss
Notes: Forbes Collection created by James Forbes (1629?-1712), English nonconformist minister. Kept as a separate library with few additions until present day. (Toronto, 1968). Also Heyworth, P L "Unfamiliar Libraries XVI: The Forbes Library," *The Book Collector*, Autumn 1970.

RECYCLING (WASTE, ETC.) see Salvage (Waste, Etc.)

RED CLOUD INDIAN AGENCY

NE —NEBRASKA STATE HISTORICAL SOCIETY, Fort Robinson Museum, Box

RED CLOUD INDIAN AGENCY (cont.)

304, Crawford, 69339. Vance Nelson, Cur
Holdings: Vols (15,600) Cat Mss Maps Pix
Slides Phonorecords Audiotapes 16mm
Films Microforms
Notes: Materials related to the history of
Fort Robinson, and incl the Post Medical
Library, reference books on state government,
etc, Western Americana: books on ranching,
homesteaders, Indian wars, etc; microfilm
records for Fort Robinson records, Red
Cloud and Spotted Tail Indian Agency
records, Crawford and Chadron, Nebraska
newspapers, diaries and interviews. Library
incl the E Kopac Collection of books dealing
with Western Americana; particularly Indian
wars, transportation, guns and railroads.

RED CROSS

DC —AMERICAN NATIONAL RED
CROSS, National Headquarters Library,
17th & D St NW, Washington, 20006.
Roberta F Biles, Library Director
Holdings: Vols 1500 Cat
Notes: National and International Red
Cross.
DC —NATIONAL ARCHIVES AND
RECORDS SERVICE, National Archives
Library, Pennsylvania Ave & Eighth St NW,
Washington, 20408.
Notes: American National Red Cross has
transferred its archives, 1881-1946, to
NARS. 900 linear ft.

RED CROSS BUREAU OF PUBLIC HEALTH NURSING

MA —SIMMONS COLLEGE ARCHIVES,
300 The Fenway, Boston, 02115. Megan
Sniffin-Marinoff, College Archivist
Notes: Archives of the Simmons College
School of Public Health Nursing (later
reorganized into the School of Nursing)
cover the years 1902-1970. Important
correspondents in the collection incl M
Adelaide Nutting, Mary Beard, Isabel
Stewart, and Anne Hervey Strong, etc. Incl
Strong's records of activity with regard to
nursing education in the National
Organization for Public Health Nursing,
1918-22. 1000 linear feet in institution, incl
special collections nursing and photographs,
nursing.

RED RIVER

MB —UNIVERSITY OF MANITOBA,
Elizabeth Dafoe Library, Archives and
Special Collections Dept, Winnipeg, R3T
2N2, Can. Richard E Bennett, Dept Head;
Corrado A Santoro, Reference Archivist
Notes: Handwritten notes of George Black,
official representative of the Manitoba
government on board the steamer
"Assiniboine" despatched by the government
to give relief to settlers in distress owing to
high water flooding. April 23, 1897.

RED RIVER SETTLEMENT

ON —UNIVERSITY OF TORONTO, Thomas
Fisher Rare Book Library, 120 Saint George
St, Toronto, M5S 1A5, Can. Richard G
Landon, Head
Holdings: Vols 30,000 Mss Maps Pix
Notes: Great variety of material relating to
early exploration and settlement of Canada,
including the search for the Northwest
Passage and the subsequent exploration of
the Arctic. Manuscript and printed material
pertaining to the overland exploration of
northwestern Canada and the Barren Lands.
Manuscript and printed material
documenting early emigration schemes and
colonization attempts, including Selkirk's
Red River settlement.

RED RIVER VALLEY REGION

LA —LOUISIANA STATE UNIVERSITY,
SHREVEPORT, Library-Archives, 8515
Youree Dr, Shreveport, 71129. Patricia L
Meador, Archivist & Asst Librn
Notes: Archives incl catalogued manuscripts

and records, 500 maps, more than 5000
photographs, 1000 architectural drawings,
slides, audiotapes, microforms. The archives
is the depository for the records of the Red
River Valley Association, 1927-present. The
more than 60 linear ft of these records
include minutes, correspondence, programs,
convention materials, maps, photographs,
hearings, legislation, scrapbooks of
newsclippings concerning projects of the
land and water improvement undertaken by
RRVA.
ND —NORTH DAKOTA STATE
UNIVERSITY, Library, Fargo, 58105. John
E Bye, Archivist
Holdings: Vols (2500) Cat Mss Maps Pix
Budget: ($14,000)
Notes: The Collection is administered by the
North Dakota Institute for Regional Studies.
It contains materials on North Dakota
history, especially the Red River Valley,
with emphasis on bonanza farming, pioneer
life, agriculture, local history, literary figures,
business, Fargo, ND, and some political
collections, particularly of the Nonpartisan
League. Also, there is an extensive
photographic collection covering the pioneer
to post-World War I period and includes the
"Hultstrand 'History in Pictures' Collection"
of sod houses, pioneer life and farming. For
the small collections, there has been
published, *Guide to the Small Collection
Manuscripts of the North Dakota Institute
for Regional Studies*, by John E Bye, 1977.
MB —UNIVERSITY OF MANITOBA,
Elizabeth Dafoe Library, Archives and
Special Collections Dept, Winnipeg, R3T
2N2, Can. Richard E Bennett, Dept Head;
Corrado A Santoro, Reference Archivist
Notes: Papers of soil scientist and professor
Joseph Henry Ellis. Soil and land
inspections, surveys and reports; stream bank
erosion studies; river reclamation projects;
field crop experiments; prairie rehabilitation
activities; fertilizer experiments; land
utilization studies; tree planting.

REDDIE, MILTON

†MD —MARYLAND HISTORICAL
SOCIETY, Library, 201 W Monument St,
Baltimore, 21201.
Notes: Eubie Blake's personal and
professional archive. Incl the Baltimore-born
pianist, composer, and songwriter's
collection of songs and instrumental pieces
in mss, extensive documentation of his
collaboration with Noble Sissle, Flournog
Miller, Milton Reddie, and others. The
Broadway musical comedy, Shuffle Along, is
represented in box office records, programs,
scores and parts, photographs, and sheet
music. Blake's involvement with other
productions is similarly documented.

REDDY, T. J.

NC —UNIVERSITY OF NORTH
CAROLINA, CHARLOTTE, J Murrey
Atkins Library, UNCC Station, Charlotte,
28223. Robert F Brabham Jr, Special
Collections Librn
Notes: Incl pamphlets, newspapers, and
ephemera published by various radical
groups, 1960s and 1970s, based largely in
the Midwest; also papers of T J Reddy, a
member of the Charlotte 3, concerning civil
rights, the Wilmington 10, and prison
reforms.

REDEVELOPMENT, URBAN see Cities and Towns—Planning

REDFORD, ROBERT

MA —BOSTON UNIVERSITY, Mugar
Memorial Library, Special Collections Dept,
771 Commonwealth Ave, Boston, 02215.
Howard B Gotlieb, Dir
Holdings: Cat Mss Pix
Notes: Mss, correspondence, etc collected in
depth; incl publications by or about.

REDI, FRANCESCO

NY —NEW YORK ACADEMY OF
MEDICINE, Library, 2 E 103 St, New

York, 10029. Brett A Kirkpatrick, Librn
Holdings: Vols Cat //
Notes: Large collection on Redi; part of the
Rufus Cole Collection.

REDSHIRTS, ITALIAN

†NY —LIBRARY OF THE ITALIAN
RISORGIMENTO, Garibaldi and Meucci
Memorial Museum, John Jay Homestead,
Box AH, Katonah, 10536.
Notes: History of the Italian Unification
Wars and mementos of Garibaldi.

REDWOOD, FOSSIL

OR —UNIVERSITY OF OREGON, Library,
Eugene, 97403. Kenneth W Duckett,
Curator
Notes: Ralph W Chaney's books; about 12,
000 letters; and mss for books and articles.
Largely concerned with various aspects of
peleontology, paleontology, paleobotany, and
the fossil Redwoods.

REED, DANIEL ALDEN, 1875-1959

NY —CORNELL UNIVERSITY LIBRARIES,
Collection of Regional History, Dept of
Manuscripts and Univ Archives, Ithaca,
14853.
Notes: NY Congressman, 1919-59, lawyer,
football coach. Incl papers, 1914-60;
correspondence, newspaper clippings, diary,
photos, drafts of speeches, scrapbooks,
notebooks, citations, certificates, financial
records, and other personal papers.

REED, DAVID

MA —BOSTON UNIVERSITY, Mugar
Memorial Library, Special Collections Dept,
771 Commonwealth Ave, Boston, 02215.
Howard B Gotlieb, Dir
Holdings: Cat Mss

REED, EARL H.

IL —CHICAGO HISTORICAL SOCIETY,
Library, Clark St at North Ave, Chicago,
60614. Archie Motley, Manuscript Librn
Notes: Chicago Architectural Archive
contains the papers of Chicago architects
Barry Byrne and Earl H Reed, the records of
the Illinois Society of Architects, and the
voluminous files of two leading Chicago
architectural firms, Holabird & Root and
Harry M Weese and Associates. Access to
these collections is by arrangement with
Frank Jewell, The Society's Curator of
Architectural Collections.

REED, ISHMAEL

DE —UNIVERSITY OF DELAWARE, Hugh
M Morris Library, S College Ave, Newark,
19711. T Stuart Dick, Special Collections
Holdings: Cat Mss
Notes: Manuscripts, etc incl literary
correspondence from 1878-1981.

REED, STANLEY FORMAN

KY —UNIVERSITY OF KENTUCKY,
Margaret I King Library, Dept of Special
Collections, Lexington, 40506. William
Marshall, Head
Holdings: Cat Mss Pix Audiotapes
Notes: Incl 378 boxes. The largest portion of
the collection was generated or collected by
Judge Reed when he served as Associate
Justice of the Supreme Court, January, 1938
until his retirement in February, 1957.
Period covered: 1865 (1926) - 1976.
Unpublished inventory.

REED, THOMAS BRACKETT, 1839-1902

ME —BOWDOIN COLLEGE, Library,
Brunswick, 04011. Dianne M Gutscher, Cur
of Special Collections
Holdings: Cat Mss
Notes: The Thomas Brackett Reed Papers
contain 200 pieces of correspondence

REED, THOMAS BRACKETT, 1839-1902 (cont.)

primarily relating to his career in the House of Representatives, incl his terms as Speaker. Two large scrapbooks of newsclippings are also part of the collection.
ME —COLBY COLLEGE, Miller Library, Colby Archives, Waterville, 04901.
Holdings: Mss
Notes: Family papers or other correspondence.

REED, WALTER

VA —UNIVERSITY OF VIRGINIA, Alderman Library, Manuscripts Dept, Charlottesville, 22901. Edmund Berkeley Jr, Cur
Holdings: // Mss
Notes: The Philip S and Mary K Hench Collection.

REEDY, WILLIAM MARION

MO —SAINT LOUIS PUBLIC LIBRARY, Gardner Rare Book Room, 1301 Olive St, Saint Louis, 63103. Julanne M Good, Supervisor; Martha Riley, Rare Books Librn
Holdings: Vols (2300) Cat
Budget: ($5573)
Notes: First editions of authors having some association with William Marion Reedy and *Reedy's Mirror*, such as Sara Teasdale, Zoe Akins, Fannie Hurst, Edgar Lee Masters, Babette Deutsch, Richard LeGallienne, etc. Also first editions of selected St Louis and/or Missouri authors such as T S Eliot, Samuel L Clemens, Theodore Dreiser and Tennessee Williams. Noncirculating.

REEMAN, DOUGLAS

MA —BOSTON UNIVERSITY, Mugar Memorial Library, Special Collections Dept, 771 Commonwealth Ave, Boston, 02215. Howard B Gotlieb, Dir
Holdings: Cat Mss Pix
Notes: Mss, correspondence, etc collected in depth; incl publications by or about.

REESE, LIZETTE WOODWORTH, 1856-1935

MD —JOHNS HOPKINS UNIVERSITY, Milton S Eisenhower Library, Charles & 34 Sts, Baltimore, 21218. Ann S Gwyn, Assistant Dir for Special Collections
Holdings: Vols 30 Cat Mss
Notes: Incl 4 mss, 27 letters plus documents. First editions, some autographed.
MA —BRANDEIS UNIVERSITY, Goldfarb Library, 415 South St, Waltham, 02154. Bessie Hahn, Dir
Notes: Lizette W Reese Collection. 6 linear ft of first editions, ms poetry and correspondence of this American poetess. The collection is unprocessed, spring 1984.

REEVES, DAVID WALLIS

RI —PROVIDENCE PUBLIC LIBRARY, 150 Empire St, Providence, 02903. Lance J Bauer, Special Collections Librn
Holdings: Cat Mss Pix
Notes: The musical compositions of David Wallis Reeves, director of the Rhode Island American Band from 1866-1900, are preserved in this collection of approx 150 mss of band, orchestral and conductor's scores, many in Reeves' hand. Memorabilia incl photographs, letters, and the Band's Minute Book, 1859-1906. There are also a very large holdings of 19th century sheet music, some of it unpublished. Complete inventory of all mss and sheet music. Photocopying on a restricted basis only for educational purposes when condition of this frequently fragile material allows.

REEVES, E. J.

NY —NATIONAL SOARING MUSEUM, Library, Harris Hill, RD #3, Elmira, 14903.

REFERENCE BOOK PUBLISHING

NY —GRADUATE CENTER OF THE CITY UNIVERSITY OF NEW YORK, William H

and Gwynne K Crouse Library for Publishing Arts, 33 W 42 St, New York, 10036. Alfred H Lane, Dir
Notes: Recently established and still growing, but intended to become the authoritative source of materials in the field, of particular value in research about the publishing industry. Open to staff members of publishing houses, students, scholars, authors, printers, and booksellers. Primarily 20th century materials, and particularly useful for research on technical, financial, and historical matters. Much on the history of individual houses, economics of authorship; marketing and distribution of books; etc.

REFORM, SOCIAL see Social Problems

REFORM JUDAISM

OH —HEBREW UNION COLLEGE-JEWISH INSTITUTE OF RELIGION, Klau Library, 3101 Clifton Ave, Cincinnati, 45220. David J Gilner, Reference Librn
Holdings: Cat
Notes: Most extensive collection of Reform Judaica in the world, incl Reform liturgies; synagogue and community center literature; Reform responsa; Biblical criticism, etc.

REFORM OF CRIMINALS see Crime and Criminals; Probation

REFORMATION AND COUNTER-REFORMATION

CA —STANFORD UNIVERSITY LIBRARIES, Cecil H Green Library, Stanford, 94305. Peter R Frank, Cur, CDP-Germanic Collection
Holdings: Vols (47,620) Cat Maps
Notes: Extensive holdings in the field of Reformation and Counter-Reformation. First and early editions by Luther, Melanchthon, Bugenhagen, Cochleus, Eck, Hutten, Reuchlin, and minor figures in Special Collections.
CO —UNIVERSITY OF COLORADO, Libraries, Special Collections, Boulder, 80309. Nora J Quinlan, Head
Holdings: Vols 800
Notes: The Mandell Creighton Library. Renaissance papacy, Protestant reform and the Conciliar movement. Separate catalog.
CT —YALE UNIVERSITY, Box 1603A, Yale Station, New Haven, 06520.
DC —FOLGER SHAKESPEARE LIBRARY, 201 E Capitol St, Washington, 20003. Philip A Knachel, Acting Dir
Budget: $4585
Notes: A major collection.
DC —LIBRARY OF CONGRESS, Rare Book & Special Collections Div, Washington, 20540. William Matheson, Chief
Holdings: Vols 423 Cat
Notes: The Reformation Collection comprises important single tracts printed principally in Germany in the early 16th century. The largest part is by Martin Luther, but other authors, such as Melanchthon, von Hutten, Eck, Cotta, Emser, Zwingli, Reuchlin are represented.
GA —EMORY UNIVERSITY, Candler School of Theology, Pitts Theology Library, Atlanta, 30322. Channing Jeschke, Librn; Anita K Delaries, Curator
Notes: The Hartford Seminary Foundation Library (partial). About 205,000 vols, pamphlets, etc.
IL —JESUIT-KRAUSS-MCCORMICK LIBRARY, 1100 E 55th St, Chicago, 60615. Donald Vorp, Dir; Elvire Hilgert, Librn
Holdings: Vols (375,000)
Notes: Collections contain merger of Jesuit Library, Lutheran School of Theology of Chicago (Krauss Library), and McCormick Theological Seminary. Jesuit: Sermones Thesaurus Novi de Tempore (anonymous, Strassbourg 1486); Opera Omnia (Jean Gerson, Strassbourg 1488), 3 vols; Summa Rosella Casuum (Venice 1495); moral theology (major figures of 16th and 17th century scholasticism); early modern editions of patristics and canon law regarding

procedures and organzation of the Catholic Church, incl treatises and multi-volume commentaries. Krauss: Archives of Lutheran Church in America and its predecessors; Reformation imprints; early printed versions of the Bible (L Franklin Gruber Collection); German and Scandanavian (Swedish, Danish, Finnish) theology; Lutheran Church of America document depository. McCormick: Presbyteriana; historical record of Synod of Illinois, UnitedPresbyterian Church of USA; Church Federation of Chicago archives prior to 1969; USA imprints of the Bible (Simms Collection).
IL —NEWBERRY LIBRARY, 60 W Walton St, Chicago, 60610. Diana Haskell, Cur of Modern Mss
Holdings: Cat
Notes: Protestant and Catholic 16th century scholarship and humanism. Political literature of Calvinism and Huguenots. Restricted use: Noncirculating.
IN —INDIANA UNIVERSITY, Lilly Library, Seventh St, Bloomington, 47405. William R Cagle, Librn
Holdings: Vols 135 // Cat
Notes: First and early editions of Luther's writings.
MD —JOHNS HOPKINS UNIVERSITY, Milton S Eisenhower Library, George Peabody Collection, 17 E Mt Vernon Place, Baltimore, 21201. Lyn Hart, Peabody Librn
Notes: Emphasis on materials published before 1950. Strength is a good collection through the 19th century.
MO —NORTHEAST MISSOURI STATE UNIVERSITY, Pickler Memorial Library, Kirksville, 63501. George N Hartje, Librn
Holdings: Vols 25,950 Cat Microforms
Notes: English Renaissance and Reformation history.
MO —CENTER FOR REFORMATION RESEARCH, 6477 San Bonita Ave, Saint Louis, 63105. William S Meltby, Dir
Holdings: Cat Mss Maps Pix Microforms
NY —COLUMBIA UNIVERSITY LIBRARIES, Rare Book & Manuscript Library, 801 Butler Library, 535 W 114 St, New York, 10027. Kenneth A Lohf, Librn
NY —GENERAL THEOLOGICAL SEMINARY, Saint Marks Library, 175 Ninth Ave, New York, 10011. David Green, Dir
Holdings: Vols (200,000) Cat
Notes: Extensive collection.
NC —DUKE UNIVERSITY, William R Perkins Library, Rare Book Room, Durham, 27706. John L Sharpe, III, Cur
Holdings: Vols 300
Notes: Sixteenth century books and pamphlets reflecting both sides of the Reformation, including extensive Luther and Melanchton holdings. The Liechtenstein collection incl 16th and 17th century German theology and church history.
NC —DUKE UNIVERSITY, Divinity School Library, Durham, 27706. Donn Michael Farris, Librn
Holdings: Vols 225,000
Notes: Special collections and subject emphases in this library include: Archaeology, Egyptian; Archaeology, Middle Eastern; Art, Jewish; Bible; Bible-New Testament; Bible-Symbolism; Church Architecture; Egyptology; Fathers of the Church; Society of Friends; Great Britain-Religion-Methodism and Methodist Church; Hymns and Hymnals; Jansenists and Jansenism; Judaica; Mediaeval Christian Mysticism; Methodism and Methodist Church; Methodist Episcopal Church; Methodist Episcopal Church, South; Reformation; Religion-US-History; Rural Church; Theology-Great Britain-17th Century; Theology-Great Britain-18th Century; United Methodist Church; US-Church History; John Wesley.
NC —SOUTHEASTERN BAPTIST THEOLOGICAL SEMINARY LIBRARY, PO Box 752, Wake Forest, 27587. H Eugene McLeod, Librn
Holdings: Cat Microforms
Notes: Incl University Microfilms collection *English Books, 1475-1640*, based on Pollard and Redgrave's *Short Title Catalogue*.
OH —CLEVELAND PUBLIC LIBRARY, Social Sciences Department, 325 Superior

REFORMATION AND COUNTER-REFORMATION (cont.)

Ave, Cleveland, 44114. Thelma Morris, Head
Notes: Strong collection of important editions of and books about the Bible, the Reformation, and patrology.

OH —OHIO STATE UNIVERSITY, William Oxley Thompson Memorial Library, 1858 Neil Ave Mall, Columbus, 43210. Robert A Tibbetts, Cur of Special Collections
Holdings: Vols 1575 Cat

OR —CONCORDIA COLLEGE, Library, 2811 NE Holman St, Portland, 97211. Alma Dobberfuhl, Librn
Holdings: Vols 400 Cat
Budget: $500
Notes: Luther and Reformation Research Collection.

PA —LUTHERAN THEOLOGICAL SEMINARY, Krauth Memorial Library, 7301 Germantown Ave, Philadelphia, 19119. Rev David J Wartluft, Dir Libr
Holdings: Vols (7500) Cat Maps Pix
Notes: Materials by and about the reformers and the history of the Reformation. Incl approx 2000 16th century imprints. Also the critical editions of all major and many minor reformation figures.
See also entry under Numismatics.

ON —TORONTO SCHOOL OF THEOLOGY, Consortium of Libraries, University of Toronto, Toronto, M5S 1A5, Can. R Grane Bracewell, Library Coordr
Holdings: Cat
Notes: A consortium of 7 theological college and faculty libraries at the University of Toronto.

ON —VICTORIA UNIVERSITY, Library, Centre for Reformation and Renaissance Studies, 71 Queen's Park Crescent, Toronto, M5S 1K7, Can. Robert C Brandeis, Chief Librn; James Estes, Dir
Holdings: Vols (15,000) Cat Slides
Notes: The CRRS concentrates on the northern European countries and France; its chief strengths are Erasmus, 650 vols; early printed books, especially 16th century editions of Latin classics; bibliography and the history of printing. The Erasmus holdings are cataloged in W T McCready et al, "The Erasmus Collection in the Centre for Reformation and Renaissance Studies...A Catalogue"...*Reformation and Renaissance* 7 (1971), 32-76 and "A Supplementary List"...*Reformation and Renaissance,* 10 (1974), 116-119. Published catalogs. Humanist Editions of the Classics at CRRS, Toronto, 1979; Humanist Editions of Statutes and History at CRRS, Toronto, 1980; Bibles, Theological Treatises and Other Religious Literature 1491-1700 at CRRS, Toronto, 1981.

ON —WYCLIFFE COLLEGE, Leonard Library, 5 Hoskin Ave, Toronto, M5S 1H7, Can. Adrienne Taylor, Librn; Gayle Ford, Library Technician
Holdings: Vols (47,000) Cat Microforms
Budget: ($11,000)
Notes: Collection of early and rare books of prayer books, sermons, Bibles. Basic reference collection of standard theological dictionaries, encyclopedias, commentaries. Homiletics collection including 19th century works. Strong in church history, Evangelical Anglicanism, English Reformation, Wycliffe studies.

PQ —BISHOP'S UNIVERSITY, John Bassett Memorial Library, Laurie Allison Room for Special Collections, Lennoxville, J1M 1Z7, Can. Germain Belisle, Chief Librn
Holdings: Vols 10,000
Notes: Partially cataloged. Relates to ecclesiastical subjects, dating from as early as the 16th century, largely concerned with the history of the Church of England in Canada and elsewhere.

REFORMATION LITERATURE

CA —STANFORD UNIVERSITY LIBRARIES, Cecil H Green Library, Stanford, 94305. Peter R Frank, Cur, CDP-Germanic Collection
Notes: Library of Prof Rudolf Hildebran,

Leipzig, the first large collection acquired by Stanford in 1895/1896, laid the foundation for an extensive German collection. Hildebrand's library is especially strong in German and Austrian philology (rare dictionaries, etc.), but also in literary works. The collection is now especially strong for the period of the Reformation and Baroque, up to the present, with many rare editions, journals, almanacs, and the like. Sizable collections of women's working class and popular literature, dissertations and Schulschriften. Rare and valuable items in the Stanford Collection of German, Austrian and Swiss Culture, Special Collections. Catalog: *Katalog der Bibliothek des Herrn Prof Dr Rudolf Hildebrand.* Description: *The German Area Collection: A Stanford Tradition* by Peter R Frank.

REFORMED CHURCH

MO —EDEN-WEBSTER LIBRARIES, Eden Theological Seminary, Webster University, 475 E Lockwood, Saint Louis, 63119. Karen M Luebbert, Dir
Notes: History and catechisms.

REFORMED CHURCH, DUTCH see Dutch Reformed Church—History

REFORMED CHURCHES OF THE WORLD

NC —HISTORICAL FOUNDATION OF THE PRESBYTERIAN & REFORMED CHURCHES, Library, Box 847, Montreat, 28757. Jerrold Lee Brooks, Exec Dir
Holdings: Vols (90,000) Cat Mss Maps Pix Slides Phonorecords Audiotapes Videotapes 16mm Films Filmstrips Microforms Archives
Budget: ($350,000)
Notes: Presbyterian and Reformed Churches of the World. History, archives, etc.

REFORMED PRESBYTERIAN CHURCH

NC —HISTORICAL FOUNDATION OF THE PRESBYTERIAN & REFORMED CHURCHES, Library, Box 847, Montreat, 28757. Jerrold Lee Brooks, Exec Dir
Holdings: Vols (90,000) Cat Mss Maps Pix Slides Phonorecords Audiotapes Videotapes 16mm Films Filmstrips Microforms Archives
Budget: ($350,000)
Notes: Presbyterian and Reformed Churches of the World. History, archives, etc.

REFORMERS

CA —HOOVER INSTITUTION ON WAR, REVOLUTION & PEACE, Stanford University, Stanford, 94305. Milorad M Drachkovitch, Archivist
Holdings: Mss
Notes: Papers of Alice Park, 1882-1957, incl diaries, correspondence, pamphlets, clippings, and leaflets, relating to Pacifism and the peace movement, the Ford Peace Ship Expedition of 1915-1916, feminism, socialism, the labor movement, prison reform, child labor legislation, civil liberties, and a variety of other reform movements in the US 30 ms boxes, 3 envelopes.

CT —YALE UNIVERSITY, Box 1603A, Yale Station, New Haven, 06520.
Holdings: Audiotapes Videotapes Microforms
Notes: About 25,000 linear ft of mss and 150,000 photographs are contained in the Division. These are historical mss and Yale Archives, primarily nonliterary American papers from the 18th century to the present.

IL —SOUTHERN ILLINOIS UNIVERSITY, CARBONDALE, Delyte W Morris Library, Special Collections Dept, Carbondale, 62901. David V Koch, Cur of Special Collections; Louisa Bowen, Cur of Manuscripts
Holdings: Cat Mss
Notes: Papers and correspondence of Theodore A Schroeder, constitutional lawyer and founder, with Lincoln Steffens, of the Free Speech League, a forerunner of the American Civil Liberties Union. Contains

extensive correspondence with Comstock, Gompers, Debs, H Ellis, Sanger, Sinclair, John Dewey, Darrow, Mencken, A G Hays, Emma Goldman, W E B Dubois, etc. Incl several thousand letters; notes and mss, records of legal cases and extensive files relating to the early history of psychiatry.

MA —RADCLIFFE COLLEGE, Arthur & Elizabeth Schlesinger Library on the History of Women in America, 3 James St, Cambridge, 02138. Patricia Miller King, Dir; Eva Moseley, Cur of Mss
Notes: Papers of many individual women and organizations concerned with abolition of slavery, woman's rights, temperance, child labor, and other 19th and 20th century reform issues.

NY —UNIVERSITY OF ROCHESTER, Rush Rhees Library, Department of Rare Books and Special Collections, Rochester, 14627. Peter Dzwonkoski, Librn
Holdings: Mss
Notes: Papers of Isaac and Amy Post and family.

REFRACTORIES see Refractory Materials

REFRACTORY MATERIALS

NY —NEW YORK STATE COLLEGE OF CERAMICS AT ALFRED UNIVERSITY, Scholes Library, Harder Hall, Alfred, 14802. Bruce E Connolly, Library Dir
Holdings: Vols (70,000) Cat Mss Slides Microforms
Budget: ($134,000)
Notes: Very specialized collection incl all phases of the arts and sciences related to ceramics. Incl 1112 subscriptions.

REFRIGERATION AND REFRIGERATING MACHINERY

NY —ENGINEERING SOCIETIES LIBRARY, 345 E 47 St, New York, 10017. S Kirk Cabeen, Dir
Holdings: Vols 250,000 Cat Maps 16mm Films Microforms
Notes: One of the largest, most comprehensive engineering liberaries in the world. Covers all engineering disciplines; particularly strong in electrical and electronic, mechanical, mining and metallurgical, petroleum, chemical, industrial, air conditioning and refrigeration engineering. Incl Wheeler Collection of early materials on magnetism and electricity. 125,000 bound periodical volumes; 10,000 maps; 5000 serial subscriptions (many foreign-language). Virtually all materials abstracted in *Engineering Index* (1884-date) are incl in Library. Noncirculating, except to members of professional engineering societies which support the Library. See *Engineering Societies Library, New York, Classed Subject Catalog and Index* (Boston: G K Hall, 1963); and *Supplements,* 1-10, 1964-1973.

NY —CARRIER CORPORATION, Logan Lewis Library, Research Division, Carrier Parkway, Syracuse, 13221. Christine Greene, Librn
Holdings: Vols (5000)
Notes: Emphasis on technical and research and development aspects of the air conditioning, heating and refrigeration industry.

NC —TECHNICAL INSTITUTE OF ALAMANCE, Learning Resources Center, Jimmy Kerr Rd, PO Box 623, Haw River, 27258. Ron Plummer, Coordr
Holdings: Vols (265) Cat Pix Phonorecords Audiotapes 16mm Films Filmstrips Microforms

PA —FRANKLIN INSTITUTE LIBRARY, 20 & The Parkway, Philadelphia, 19103. Miriam Padusis, Dir; Charles Wilt, Readers Servs Librn
Holdings: Vols (300,000) Cat Maps Pix Microforms

SC —HORRY GEORGETOWN TECHNICAL COLLEGE, Library, Hwy 501, Box 1966, Conway, 29526. Barbara Brittain, Librn
Holdings: Vols (20,000) Cat Slides Microforms

REFUGEES, CHINESE

CA —HOOVER INSTITUTION ON WAR, REVOLUTION & PEACE, Stanford University, Stanford, 94305. Milorad M Drachkovitch, Archivist
Holdings: Mss
Notes: Records of Aid Refugee Chinese Intellectuals (ARCI), a private US relief organization, incl correspondence, reports, minutes of meetings, financial records and photographs, 1952-1970, relating to ARCI relief work for Chinese refugees. 44 ms boxes, 3 albums.

REFUGEES, CUBAN

FL —UNIVERSITY OF MIAMI, Otto G Richter Library, PO Box 248214, Coral Gables, 33124. Frank Rodgers, Dir of Libraries
Notes: The Cuban exile periodicals incl 412 titles of which 381 have been published in Miami, Florida. The archival material incl 54 cubic feet of mss, invitations, programs, broadsides, posters, postcards, prints, reports, maps, etc. This collection incl personal and corporate papers of Cubans settled in the US or in other countries. The truth about Cuban Committee Papers: 40 cubic feet. Contains records and correspondence of intellectual and professional Cuban and American leaders in the US dedicated to the course of eliminating Communism from the Western Hemisphere.

REFUGEES, JEWISH

CA —HOOVER INSTITUTION ON WAR, REVOLUTION & PEACE, Stanford University, Stanford, 94305. Milorad M Drachkovitch, Archivist
Notes: Papers of Kurt R Grossman, 1926-73, incl mss of writings, correspondence, clippings, and serial issues, relating to Jewish refugees from Nazi Germany, postwar German and Austrian restitution payments to Jewish war victims, German-Israeli relations, the condition of Jews throughout the world, and civil liberties in the US and Germany. 53 ms boxes, 8 scrapbooks.
NY —YIVO INSTITUTE FOR JEWISH RESEARCH, Library & Archives, 1048 Fifth Ave, New York, 10028. Dina Abramowicz, Librn; Marek Web, Archivist
Notes: Jews in contemporary world. Anti-semitism. Many periodicals and pamphlets.

REFUGEES, RUSSIAN

CA —CLAREMONT COLLEGES, Honnold Library, Ninth & Dartmouth, Claremont, 91711. Tania Rizzo, Special Collections Dept Head
Holdings: Vols 1125 Uncat Mss Pix Microforms
Notes: The combined James Mavor, Raymond Elliott, and Gregory P Tschebotarioff collections incl clippings and periodicals from the Revolutionary period, books and pictorial materials about the royal family, separatist movements, and the emigre experience. Restricted use.
NY —ALEXANDRA TOLSTOY MEMORIAL LIBRARY, Tolstoy Foundation Center, Lake Rd, Valley Cottage, 10989. Tatiana Kalinin, Acting Librn
Holdings: Vols (15,000)
Notes: The Foundation assists political refugees in resettlement throughout the world.

REFUGEES, SOUTHEAST ASIAN

IL —NORTHERN ILLINOIS UNIVERSITY, Founders Memorial Library, Southeast Asia Collection, Normal Rd, De Kalb, 60115. Lee S Dutton Dr, Cur
Holdings: Vols (34,000) Cat Maps Microforms
Notes: An extensive collection of books, periodicals, newspapers, maps, and microforms from or about Southeast Asia. Areas of concentration incl Thailand, Malaysia, Indonesia, Singapore, Brunei, Philippines, Laos, and Burma. Holdings (except rare books, maps, and microforms) are housed in a separate area collection within the Founders Library. A departmental card catalog and specialized reference collection support reference services. A Thai collection of several thousand vols is the largest vernacular component. Extensive Malaysia, Indonesia, Singapore, and Brunei holdings have been acquired through the NPAC program. A collection of Filipino-American newspapers, and a growing collection of children's literature in common and uncommon Southeast Asian languages are available. Resources are accessible to borrowers through OCLC.
†WA —TACOMA COMMUNITY HOUSE MINI LIBRARY, 1311 South M St, Tacoma, 98405.
Notes: A special collection of books, periodicals, and audio-visual materials documents the history of the Vietnamese in America and provides resources for Indochinese educational and social activities.

REFUGEES, SPANISH

MA —BRANDEIS UNIVERSITY, Goldfarb Library, 415 South St, Waltham, 02154. Bessie Hahn, Dir
Notes: Spanish Civil War Collection. Comprising 7000 books and pamphlets in all languages relating to the armed conflict in Spain from 1936-1939. This is a multi-media collection consisting of not only books and pamphlets, but photographs, documentary film footage, newspapers, propaganda leaflets, wall posters, taped interviews, personal memoirs, memorabilia, recordings and some original art work. The collection also includes the archives of American volunteers who served with the Republican forces. There is an author-title card catalog in the Special Collections Card Catalog for the books and pamphlets. There are some finding lists for the other material such as newspapers and periodicals, photographs and wall posters. Some material is restricted from use.

REFUGEES, TIBETAN

CA —HOOVER INSTITUTION ON WAR REVOLUTION & PEACE, Stanford University, Stanford, 94305. Milorad M Drachkovitch, Archivist
Holdings: Mss Pix
Notes: Records of the American Emergency Committee for Tibetan Refugees, incl correspondence, reports, minutes of meetings and photographs, 1959-1970, relating to relief work for Tibetan refugees in Napal and India. 17 ms boxes.

REFUGEES, VIETNAMESE

MI —MICHIGAN STATE UNIVERSITY, International Library, South and Southeast Asia Collection, East Lansing, 48824. Clinton Lockert, Bibliographer
Holdings: Vols (3500) Cat Mss Pix Audiotapes Microforms
Notes: Emphasis is on South Vietnam (1955-1962). The University had a Vietnam Advisory Group headquartered in Saigon during this period. Have complete holdings of *Reports and Documents* Series of the MSU Vietnam Advisory Group. Extensive correspondnece, documents and publications of the American Friends of Vietnam, and of the International Rescue Committee. Very extensive clippings, correspondence, documents, and photographs from the Gilbert Jonas Collection, and the Westley Fishel Collection. Significant unique items. Representative selection of Vietnamese literature.
†NY —STATE UNIVERSITY OF NEW YORK, COLLEGE AT BUFFALO, Vietnamese Immigration Collection, Buffalo, 14260.
Notes: Oral history, interviews, orientation materials, and refugee camp newspapers.

REFUSE AND REFUSE DISPOSAL

AZ —TUCSON PUBLIC LIBRARY, Governmental Reference Library, PO Box 27210, City Hall, Tucson, 85726. Ann Strickland, Librn
Holdings: Vols (4000) Cat Maps Audiotapes Microforms
Notes: Special emphasis on public administration, including public finance, public personnel management, social services, urban planning, public transportation, public works, water management, solid waste management, public recreation and government of growing southwestern US cities in 200,000 to 500,000 population range.
CA —CALIFORNIA DEPT OF TRANSPORTATION, Transportation Library, 5900 Folsom Blvd, PO Box 19128, Sacramento, 95819. Eva Caro, Librn
Holdings: Vols (10,000) Cat Mss Maps Pix Slides Phonorecords Audiotapes Videotapes 16mm Films Filmstrips Microforms
IL —GREELEY & HANSEN ENGINEERS, 222 S Riverside Plaza, Chicago, 60606. Marilyn Cichom, Librn
Holdings: Vols (6000) Cat Maps Slides Microforms
MA —CAMP, DRESSER & MCKEE, Herman G Dresser Library, One Center Plaza, Boston, 02108. Virginia L Carroll, Librn
Holdings: Vols (15,000) Cat Maps Slides Microforms
Notes: Air, land, and water pollution; environmental engineering; hazardous wastes; water resources; solid wastes; resource recycling.
MA —TUFTS UNIVERSITY, Engineering Library, Medford, 02155. Wayne Powell, Science-Engineering Librn
Holdings: Vols (20,000) Cat
Notes: Also 25,000 technical reports. Subject emphases: solid waste management, water pollution control, fluid mechanics.
PA —PENNSYLVANIA DEPT OF ENVIRONMENTAL RESOURCES, Office of Environmental Protection, Technical Reference Library, Fulton Bldg, 17th Floor, Box 2063, Harrisburg, 17120. Wanda R Bell, Librn
Holdings: Vols (2000) Cat Slides Microfilm Microfiche
Notes: 10,000 technical reports; water and wastewater feasibility plans; PA Bulletin, 1970-Present; water pollution; solid waste; mining and reclamation; air quality; acid mine drainage.

REGIMENTAL HISTORIES

NY —NEW YORK PUBLIC LIBRARY, Research Libraries, General Research Division, Fifth Ave & 42 St, New York, 10018. Rodney Phillips, Chief
Holdings: Vols (2,225,000) Cat Maps Pix Microforms
Budget: ($775,718)
Notes: The Strong Collection--US, Great Britain, and Europe.
RI —PROVIDENCE PUBLIC LIBRARY, 150 Empire St, Providence, 02903. Lance J Bauer, Special Collections Librn
Holdings: Vols 5000
Notes: The Harris Collection on the American Civil War and Slavery. Incl 18th and 19th century books, rare pamphlets, and periodicals concerning slavery and the slave trade, and origins, progress and results of the Civil Civil War; also regimental histories; military and naval tactics; personal narratives; women's accounts of the Civil War; works on abolition; sheet music; Union and Confederate broadside ballads; Confederate imprints; *The Liberator* from 1843 through the Civil War; and over 85 editions of *Uncle Tom's Cabin* in 14 languages. Excellent primary and secondary sources for the study of the Civil War and slavery. Material must be used in-house. Photocopying when condition of material allows.
†VA —GEORGE C MARSHALL RESEARCH FOUNDATION AND LIBRARY, Drawer 920, Lexington, 24450. Royster Lyle Jr, Cur Collections
Holdings: Vols Cat Mss Maps Pix Phonorecords Audiotapes Films Filmstrips Microforms
Notes: About 400 posters--American,

REGIMENTAL HISTORIES (cont.)

German, French; complete *Stars and Stipes* for WWII; approx 5000 cataloged photographs, over 5000 uncataloged Office of War information photos, and over 10,000 US Signal Corps photos (uncat). Approx 250 regimental histories, operation reports, and army manuals; published memoirs and letters of Marshall associates; official military histories (American, British); set of 40 books by "Remy" (G Renault-Roulier); over 1200 maps--approx 300 newsmaps, 800 daily situation maps (European Theatre), 37 bound vols of daily situation maps 1944-1945; seven of the *Why We Fight* series (films). Major ms collections incl the papers of generals George C Marshall, Marshall S Carter, William T Sexton, Lucian Truscott, William R Arnold, Paul M Robinett, Frank McCarthy; Forrest C Pogue; colonels Collas Harris, Francis P Miller, William F Friedman; officers of the Women's Army Corp. Hearings and government documents. Agency records copied from NARS. Vertical file arranged by subject.

REGIONAL PLANNING

DC —CONSERVATION FOUNDATION, Library, 1717 Massachusetts Ave NW, Washington, 20036. Barbara K Rodes, Librn
Holdings: Vols (8000) Cat Maps
Notes: Collection incl natural resources, ecology, city and regional planning, land use, recreation, energy conservation, environmental economics, pollution control, water resources.

DC —METROPOLITAN WASHINGTON COUNCIL OF GOVERNMENTS, Map Library, 1875 Eye St NW, Suite 200, Washington, 20006. Susan Kalish, Librn
Holdings: Cat Maps
Notes: 3000 current and retrospective maps covering metropolitan Washington region, incl the District of Columbia; Montgomery and Prince George's counties in Maryland; and Arlington, Fairfax, Prince William and Loudoun counties and the City of Alexandria in Virginia. Maps cover land use, community facilities, transportation, topography, statistical units, and socioeconomic information. Record of holdings on computer printout.

FL —ARCHBOLD BIOLOGICAL STATION, Library, Rt 2, Box 180, Lake Placid, 33852. Fred E Lohrer, Librn
Holdings: Cat Slides
Notes: Florida natural history. Emphasis on south central peninsular Florida. Habitats, plants, vertebrates, land use changes. About 8000 2x2 color transparencies and 35mm films.

GA —UNIVERSITY OF GEORGIA, Libraries, Special Collections Division, Athens, 30602. Vesta Lee Gordon, Asst Dir for Special Collections
Notes: The Arbitron Collection of television and radio program ratings, 1949-date (except past year). In-depth, statistical analyses of the listening public by age, sex, county, some ethnic groups, farm population, listening preferences, etc. 26,302 bound vols. 2 reports, 1949-81. To be added to annually.

IL —LAKE FOREST COLLEGE, Donnelley Library, Lake Forest, 60045. Arthur H Miller Jr, College Librn
Holdings: Vols (500) Cat Maps
Budget: ($1200)
Notes: Focus on development of suburban fringe areas, particularly Lake Co, Ill. and Chicago region: local documents (plans, transit, zoning, maps, etc), US documents, and special studies of suburban issues, such as historic preservation and land use.

IN —INDIANA STATE LIBRARY, Indiana Div, 140 N Senate Ave, Indianapolis, 46204. Robert Logsdon, Acting Head
Holdings: Vols (60,541)
Budget: ($242,431)
Notes: Incl books, pamphlets (50,564), mss (3,000,000), microfilm (1641 reels), photographs (5000), records (37), audiotapes (22), films (107), slides (55 sets), maps (10, 160), VF (37), broadsides (920), newspapers (10,000 bound and wrapped files and 43,000 reels of microfilm). Collects information and materials both current and historical, about Indiana. Separate catalog for printed materials, separate indexes for mss, Indianapolis newspapers and pictures. Other indexes for smaller collections and special subjects.

MD —MARYLAND DEPT OF STATE PLANNING, Library, 301 W Preston St Rm 1101, Baltimore, 21201. Helene W Jeng, Librn; John Somers, Asst Librn
Holdings: Vols (11,100) Cat
Notes: Includes depository of plans relating to Maryland.

MD —MARYLAND-NATIONAL CAPITAL PARK & PLANNING COMMISSION, Montgomery County Planning Department Library, 8787 Georgia Ave, Silver Spring, 20907. Janice C Holt, Librn
Holdings: Vols (5000) Cat Microforms
Notes: Specific subject areas include: community facilities, conservation, economics, flood control, highways, housing, human and natural resources. landscape architecture, open space, parks, pollution, population, recreation, transportation, urban renewal, and zoning. Commission's publications are maintained by Records Management (not Library).

MA —HARVARD UNIVERSITY, Graduate School of Design, Frances Loeb Library, Gund Hall, Cambridge, 02138. James Hodgson, Librn
Holdings: Vols (225,000) Mss Maps Pix Slides Microforms
Budget: ($500,000)
Notes: Covers architecture, landscape architecture, city and regional planning, and urban design. Catalog, in 44 volumes, published in 1968, with 2-volume supplement in 1970, 5-volume supplement in 1974, and 3-volume supplement in 1979. It also analyzes periodical articles. Architecture collection described in *Harvard Library Bulletin*, VI (1952): pp 263-269. Noteworthy holdings incl those on Abbey of Cluny, Le Corbusier, amd Henry Hobson Richardson. Regional Planning collection described in *Harvard Library Bulletin*, VII (1953), 188-195.

MI —MICHIGAN STATE UNIVERSITY, Urban Policy & Planning Library, East Lansing, 48824. Dale E Casper, Librn
Holdings: Vols (12,800) Cat
Budget: ($35,000)
Notes: Serves the curricular and research needs of faculty and students involved in urban and regional policy analysis and community planning.

NJ —MIDDLESEX COUNTY PLANNING BOARD, Library, 40 Livingston Ave, New Brunswick, 08901. Lou Mattei, Planning Supervisor, Data Mgt
Holdings: Vols (3500) Cat
Budget: ($500)

NJ —RUTGERS, THE STATE UNIVERSITY OF NEW JERSEY, Center for Urban Policy Research Library, Bldg 4051-Kilmer, New Brunswick, 08903. Edward E Duensing, Jr
Holdings: Vols 3500 Cat Periodicals VF
Budget: ($4000)
Notes: Collection focuses on the subjects of housing, municipal finance, and planning in American cities. The emphasis is on current material. Incl 5000 cataloged vertical files, 157 periodical subscriptions.

NJ —SUSSEX COUNTY LIBRARY, Rd 3, Box 76, Newton, 07860. Judith Gessel, Reference Librn
Holdings: Cat Maps Slides 16mm Films Filmstrips
Notes: The Sussex Area Reference Library is one of several locations which were named repositories for materials related to the restudy of the Tocks Island Lake Project. The items in the repository were distributed by the Delaware River Basin Commission. Collection incl study-related hearing transcripts, public notices, press clippings, correspondence, and reports of concern to the Delaware Water Gap National Recreation Area/Tocks Island Area. The Tocks Island Regional Advisory Council, when disbanded, presented its library to the Sussex County Library in 1974. The collection incl reports, surveys, maps, slides, and other materials collected or produced by TIRAC since 1965.

NY —NEW YORK STATE DEPT OF STATE, Community Affairs Library, 162 Washington Ave, Albany, 12231. M L Johnson, Librn
Holdings: Vols (14,640) Cat
Notes: Local government. Serves as research arm for official activities. 16,000 items in vertical files; 150 periodicals. Unique Community File collection of about 1600 local governments arranged by counties in the state.

NY —CORNELL UNIVERSITY LIBRARIES, Fine Arts Library, Sibley Hall, Ithaca, 14853. Judith Holliday, Librn
Holdings: Vols (115,000) Cat Maps Pix

OH —OHIO DEPT DEVELOPMENT, Library, 30 E Broad St, PO Box 1001, Columbus, 43216. Jean Fisher, Librn
Holdings: Vols (5000)
Notes: Ohio County Comprehensive Planning Reports. Economic data and census data.

OH —OHIO STATE UNIVERSITY, Engineering Library, 2024 Neil Ave, Columbus, 43210. Mary Jo V Arnold, Librn
Holdings: Vols (132,000) Cat Microforms
Budget: ($110,000)

OR —UNIVERSITY OF OREGON, Bureau of Governmental Research Library, Box 3177, Eugene, 97403. Katherine G Eaton, Head Librn
Holdings: Vols (25,000) Cat Microforms
Budget: ($5000)
Notes: Separate catalog and classification system.

PA —MONTGOMERY COUNTY PLANNING COMMISSION, Library, Court House, Norristown, 19404. Robin McLean, Librn
Holdings: Vols (5000) Cat Slides Microfilms
Notes: Emphasis on Montgomery County land use, transportation, and planning.

PA —UNIVERSITY OF PITTSBURGH, Library, Graduate School of Public and International Affairs, Forbes Quadrangle, 1st floor West, Pittsburgh, 15260. Nicholas C Caruso, Librn
Holdings: Vols (80,000) Cat
Budget: ($150,000)
Notes: The library attempts to collect as many national economic and social development plans as possible from the developing countries of the world. It also holds city, regional and state plans for Pennsylvania, particularly the 9 southwestern counties of Pennsylvania.

PA —UNIVERSITY OF PITTSBURGH, Economics/Center for Regional Economics Studies Library, 4956 Forbes Quad, Pittsburgh, 15260. Patricia Suozzi-Crehan, Librn
Holdings: Vols 20,000
Budget: ($25,724)
Notes: Card catalog for collection. Cards for Economics Collection are in Hillman Library catalog. Collections are working collections reflecting the research and teaching interests of the Dept of Economics faculty and graduate students. The collection covers all aspects of the field of economics and demography.

TN —TENNESSEE VALLEY AUTHORITY (TVA), Technical Library, 400 W Summit Hill Dr, E2 B7, Knoxville, 37902. Jesse C Mills, Chief Librn
Holdings: Vols (106,900) Cat Mss Maps Pix Audiotapes Microforms
Budget: ($2,025,000)
Notes: The Technical Library Headquarters Staff (order, cataloging, information, and administration) is located in Knoxville, Tenn. In addition there are branch libraries in Knoxville, Norris, and Chattanooga, Tennessee, and Muscle Shoals, Alabama.

TN —TENNESSEE STATE PLANNING OFFICE, Library, 301 Seventh Ave N, Nashville, 37219. Eleanor J Burt, Librn
Holdings: Vols (19,616) Cat Maps Slides 16mm Films Microforms
Budget: ($8500)
Notes: Comprehensive planning reference materials; materials about Tennessee for planning at local, regional, and state levels. Incl 200 maps and 1350 slides.

REGIONAL PLANNING (cont.)

AB —ALBERTA DEPT OF THE
ENVIRONMENT, Library, Oxbridge Place,
9820 106th St, Edmonton, T5K 2J6, Can.
Marilyn Corbett, Head, Library Services
Branch
Holdings: Vols (20,000) Cat Microforms
MB —UNIVERSITY OF MANITOBA,
Architecture & Fine Arts Library, Winnipeg,
R3T 2N2, Can. Peter Anthony, Head
Holdings: Vols (50,000) Maps Microforms
Notes: Incl government publications.
ON —UNIVERSITY OF TORONTO, Faculty
of Architecture, Landscape Architecture
Library, 230 College St, Toronto, M5S 1A1,
Can. Pamela Manson-Smith, Librn
Holdings: Vols (14,401) Cat Slides
Notes: Incl architecture and landscape
architecture.

REGISTERS OF BIRTHS, ETC.

CT —NEW HAVEN COLONY HISTORICAL
SOCIETY, Whitney Library, 114 Whitney
Ave, New Haven, 06510. M Ottilia Koel,
Librn & Cur of Mss
Holdings: Cat
Notes: 25,000 printed books and pamphlets;
ca 15,000 linear feet of manuscript material
including historic manuscripts, records of
education, maritime and harbor industry,
private papers, business and family records;
40,000 photographic images; maps and
microforms relating to the early settlement
and subsequent history of New Haven and
vicinity.
IL —NEWBERRY LIBRARY, 60 W Walton
St, Chicago, 60610. Diana Haskell, Cur of
Modern Mss
Notes: Incl many published vital records.
TX —TEXAS STATE LIBRARY, Genealogy
Collection, PO Box 12927, Capitol Station,
Austin, 78711. Robin Rader, Supervisor,
Genealogy Services
Holdings: Vols (9000) Cat Microforms
Budget: ($108,129)
Notes: Emphasis on Texas and southern
states. Census schedules (1790-1910), family
histories, county data. Texas tax rolls. Index
to Texas births and deaths, 1903-1973.
Microfilms of municipal archives of Nuevo
Leon, Mexico. Noncirculating.

REGISTERS OF DEATHS see Registers of Births, Etc.

REGISTRATION OF SHIPS see Ships—Registration and Transfer

REGISTRATION OF TRADEMARKS see Trademarks

REGISTRATION OF VOTERS see Voters, Registration of

REGLA, COUNTS OF

†WA —WASHINGTON STATE
UNIVERSITY, Library, Manuscripts,
Archives & Special Collections, Pullman,
99164. John F Guido, Head
Holdings: // Cat Mss Maps
Notes: Regla, Counts of: The papers of the
Romero de Terreros family, to whom were
granted the titles of Regla, San Cristoval,
and San Francisco, include wills, deed, titles,
property maps, litigation over such things as
sheep walks, water rights, and the titles
themselves. Incl also is much detailed
correspondence between hacienda
adminitrators and the family concerning
weather, crops, and commodity prices.
Several large vols, bound in 1783, document
the history of land acquisitions by the Jesuit
Colegio Maximo de San Pedro y San Pablo
of Mexico City, especially the hacienda of
Santa Lucia, from 1576 to the time of the
Expulsion. Other early papers deal with the
holdings and genealogy of the Marquisates
of Salinas, Salvatierra, and Santiago.
Described by J Horace Nunemaker in the
Hispanic American Historical Review
(August 1945) 25:409; and by Jacquelyn

MGaines in Three Centuries of Mexican
Documents: A Partial Calendar of the Regla
Papers (Pullman, Washington, 1963).

REGULATORS (VIGILANTE GROUPS)
see Vigilance Committees and Vigilantes

REHABILITATION

IL —UNIVERSITY OF ILLINOIS,
URBANA/CHAMPAIGN, Library, Applied
Life Studies Library, 1408 W Gregory Dr,
Urbana, 61801.
Holdings: Vols (38,000) Cat Pix Microforms
See also entry under Physical Education and
Training.
IN —LOGANSPORT STATE HOSPITAL,
Staff Library, Logansport, 46947. Terra
Newton, Librn
Holdings: Vols (3000) Cat
MA —MASSACHUSETTS
REHABILITATION COMMISSION,
Library, 20 Park Plaza, Boston, 02116. June
C Holt, Librn
Holdings: Vols (15,000) Cat Audiotapes
16mm Films Microforms
Budget: ($18,000)
Notes: For staff and community interested in
rehabilitation literature, defined as
publications which deal with impairments
resulting in disabling conditions; mental and
behavioral disorders; employment of the
handicapped; counseling techniques with
handicapped populations; sheltered
workshops, rehabilitation facilities; halfway
houses and independent living arrangements;
psychological aspects of disability; attitudes
toward the handicapped; and other material
on services for the handicapped. Library
subscribes to 70 journals relating to disability
and rehabilitation.
MI —REHABILITATION INSTITUTE,
Learning Resources Center, 261 Mack Blvd,
Detroit, 48201. Daria Drobny, Medical
Librn
Holdings: Vols (2600) Cat Slides
Notes: Physical medicine and rehabilitation.
OH —SAINT ELIZABETH MEDICAL
CENTER, Health Sciences Library, 601
Miami Blvd W, Dayton, 45408. Ann Lewis,
Librn
Holdings: Vols (13,000) Cat Slides
Audiotapes Filmstrips
†ON —METROPOLITAN TORONTO
LIBRARY, Social Sciences Dept, 789 Yonge
St, Toronto, M4W 2G8, Can. Abdus Salam,
Head
Holdings: Vols Cat Maps Phonorecords
Audiotapes 16mm Films Microforms
Notes: Historical and contemporary
Canadian material covering federal and
provincial policies and programs in the fields
of health care, geriatrics, child welfare,
corrections, and care and rehabilitation of
the physically and mentally handicapped.
ON —ONTARIO MINISTRY OF
COMMUNITY & SOCIAL SERVICES,
Library, 880 Bay St, Rm 663, Toronto, M7A
1E9, Can. Sandra Walsh, Chief Librn
Holdings: Vols (30,000) Cat Videotapes
16mm Films Microforms

REHABILITATION, RURAL

IA —IOWA STATE UNIVERSITY, Library,
Ames, 50011. Warren B Kuhn, Dean of
Library Services
Holdings: Cat Mss
Notes: Incl agriculture finance and policy,
agricultural marketing, farm management,
land valuation, and rural development.
Extensive serial holdings.

REHABILITATION, VOCATIONAL see Vocational Rehabilitation

REHABILITATION OF CRIMINALS

DC —FEDERAL BUREAU OF PRISONS,
Library, 320 First St NW, Washington,
20001. Lloyd W Hooker, Librn
Holdings: Vols (2500) Cat
Budget: ($20,000)

NJ —RUTGERS, THE STATE UNIVERSITY
OF NEW JERSEY, John Cotton Dana
Library, 185 University Ave, Newark,
07102. Phyllis Schultze, Librn
Holdings: Vols 40,000 Cat
Notes: National Council on Crime and
Delinquency. Criminology, as applied, means
all phases of crime and delinquency
prevention, control and treatment, ie, the
whole "criminal justice" gamut: police,
courts, probation and parole, prisons,
community rehabilitation centers, etc. In
short, everything except police laboratory
materials. Collection completely cataloged;
all criminological and correctional journals
indexed. Incl many reports of correctional
agencies, research reports, unpublished
monographs, publications in the field by all
government agencies, federal, state, county
and local. Information file contains over 40,
000 such items, as well as about 10,000
uncataloged clippings and other pieces of
information stored by specific subjects.
†ON —METROPOLITAN TORONTO
LIBRARY, Social Sciences Dept, 789 Yonge
St, Toronto, M4W 2G8, Can. Abdus Salam,
Head
Holdings: Vols Cat Maps Phonorecords
Audiotapes 16mm Films Microforms
Notes: The crinimology collection includes
contemporary and historical material on
theories of crinimality, police work, crinimal
law, corrections, and the rehabilitation of
offenders.

REICH, MAX I.

IL —WHEATON COLLEGE, Buswell
Memorial Library, Wheaton, 60187. Paul
Snezek, Library Dir
Holdings: Mss
Notes: Collection includes publications of
pamphlets and articles. Related Topics:
Hebrew Christian Alliance of America.

REICH, STEVE

TX —NORTH TEXAS STATE UNIVERSITY,
Audio Center, Box 5188, NT Station,
Denton, 76203. Morris Martin, Music Librn
Notes: Emphasis on Contemporary and
Avant Garde music. More than 450 musical
compositions (mostly manuscript, many
multi-media). This is an archive of materials
published in, or submitted for publication to,
the contemporary music magazine Source,
the Music of the Avant Garde which
appeared from 1967-1977 (although bearing
dates only through 1973). Composers
represented are the editors (Larry Austin
and Stanley Lunetta), John Cage, Steve
Reich, Pauline Oliveros, Harry Partch,
Morton Feldman, Lukas Foss, Barney
Childs, David Cope, Peter Garland, Philip
Glass, Ben Johnston, Alcides Lanza, Alvin
Lucier, David Rosenboom, Dane Rudhyar,
and Nicolas Slonimsky.

REICHE, FRITZ

NY —AMERICAN INSTITUTE OF
PHYSICS, Center for the History of Physics,
Niels Bohr Library, 335 E 45 St, New York,
10017. John Aubry, Librn
Holdings: Cat Mss Maps Pix Microforms
Notes: Papers and records.

REICHENBACH, HANS

PA —UNIVERSITY OF PITTSBURGH,
Hillman Library, Pittsburgh, 15260.
Notes: Economic and philosophical papers of
the English scholar Frank Plumpton Ramsey
(1903-1930), incl mss of published and
unpublished writings, reading notes, etc.
Significant because of his work in modern
mathematics, logic, probability, and
economics. Complementary to the Library's
holdings of the papers of the logical
empiricists, Rudolf Carnap and Hans
Reichenback.

REICHL, ERNST

†NY —COLUMBIA UNIVERSITY
LIBRARIES, Butler Library, Rare Book and

REICHL, ERNST (cont.)

Manuscript Library, 535 W 114 St, New York, 10027.
Notes: More than 1,000 examples of the books designed by Ernst Reichl from the 1930s to the 1970s. Each volume incl his handwritten notes giving details on the binding and design and the problems he encountered. Also copies of Reichl's own writings, two early diaries and two scrapbooks.

REID, ALBERT T.

†KS —UNIVERSITY OF KANSAS, Spencer Research Library, Lawrence, 66045. Sheryl K Williams, Asst Librn
Notes: Original art by Albert T Reid and 600 other cartoonists, in the Kansas Collection.

REID, CHARLES

MA —BOSTON UNIVERSITY, Mugar Memorial Library, Special Collections Dept, 771 Commonwealth Ave, Boston, 02215. Howard B Gotlieb, Dir
Holdings: Cat Mss
Notes: Mss, correspondence, etc collected in depth; incl publications by or about.

REID, FORREST

PA —BRYN MAWR COLLEGE, Canaday Library, Bryn Mawr, 19010. James Tanis, Dir
Notes: Rare books in the Adelman Collection.

REID, MAYNE, 1818-1883

CA —UNIVERSITY OF CALIFORNIA, LOS ANGELES, Research Library, Dept of Special Collections, 405 Hilgard Ave, Los Angeles, 90024. Edward Shreeves, Chairman, Bibliographers Group; David S Zeidberg, Head
Holdings: Vols 100
Notes: 100 first and other editions of his books; 28 letters.

REID, SAMUEL CHESTER, 1783-1861

DC —LIBRARY OF CONGRESS, Manuscript Division, Washington, 20540. John C Broderick, Chief
Notes: The Samuel Chester Reid Family papers, etc. approx 2000 items.

REID, WHITELAW

MD —JOHNS HOPKINS UNIVERSITY, Milton S Eisenhower Library, Charles & 34 Sts, Baltimore, 21218. Ann S Gwyn, Assistant Dir for Special Collections
Holdings: Cat Mss

REIGN OF TERROR see
France—History—Revolution, 1789-1799

REINCARNATION

IL —UNIVERSITY OF ILLINOIS, URBANA/CHAMPAIGN, Library, University Archives, 19 Library, 1408 W Gregory Drive, Urbana, 61801. Maynard Brichford, University Archivist
Holdings: Vols (5000) Cat
Budget: ($7000)
Notes: The Mandeville Collection in Parapsychology and Occult Sciences. Titles in the Merten J Mandeville Collection are purchased by funds from an endowment provided specifically for the collection on its establishment in 1966 by Merten J Mandeville, Professor Emeritus of Management, who donated 400 vols from his personal library as the nucleus of the collection. There are currently about 5000 titles in the collection, supplemented by related materials in the general collection. Topics include astrology, extrasensory perception, yoga, magic, satanism, faith healing, hypnosis, Eastern religions, witchcraft, fortune telling, reincarnation, flying saucers, ghosts, dreams, numerology, graphology, and mysticism. Biographies and reference books are a part of the collection as are journals devoted to the scientific study of parapsychology.

NY —PARAPSYCHOLOGY FOUNDATION, Eileen J Garrett Library, 228 E 71st St, New York, 10021. Wayne Norman, Librn
Holdings: Vols (9300) Cat
Notes: One of the largest libraries on parapsychology. Main emphasis is on the literature of contemporary parapsychology; also a strong collection on the history of parapsychology (early spiritualism, mysticism, relevant philosophical works, etc). Rare book collection incl early rare books and periodicals on psychical research and psychical phenomena. Receives about 100 titles of periodicals and binds the more significant titles. The library maintains its own periodicals index to parapsychological literature, dating from 1966. Main emphasis literature is on experimental parapsychology, or those publications that approach the subject with an objective and/or analytic point of view.

NY —UNITED LODGE OF THEOSOPHISTS LIBRARY, 347 E 72 St, New York, 10021.
Notes: Ancient and modern philosophy and psychology; comparative religion and mythology; parapsychology; reincarnation research in science and religion.

VA —ASSOCIATION FOR RESEARCH & ENLIGHTENMENT, Library, 67 & Atlantic Avenue, PO Box 595, Virginia Beach, 23451. Stephen Jordan, Library Mgr
Holdings: Vols (1800) Cat
Notes: A R E Library Booklist incl 6000 items in 24 subject categories. This special collection is especially strong in the following subjects: astrology, spiritualism, reincarnation, healing arts, Theosophy, Atlantis, parapsychology and transpersonal psychology.

REINHARDT, MAX

NY —STATE UNIVERSITY OF NEW YORK, BINGHAMTON, Glenn G Bartle Library, Binghamton, 13901. Marion Hanscom, Special Collections Librn
Holdings: Cat
Budget: ($8000)
Notes: Max Reinhardt Archive. Library has extensive (approx 250,000 items) archival material relating to Max Reinhardt, as well as his personal library. This personal library is not a subject collection per se, but contains much information about German theater in the 20th century. The archival material contains letters, prompt books, photographs, playbills, etc.

REINHART, CHARLES STANLEY

NY —COLUMBIA UNIVERSITY LIBRARIES, Rare Book & Manuscript Library, 801 Butler Library, 535 W 114 St, New York, 10027. Kenneth A Lohf, Librn
Holdings: Mss Pix
Notes: Correspondence and drawings. 250 items. Restricted use.

REISS, LIONEL

†MA —HARVARD UNIVERSITY LIBRARY, Widener Library, Judaica Collection, Room M, Cambridge, 02138. Charles Berlin, Bibliographer
Holdings: Cat Pix
Notes: Collection of Jewish portrait studies by Lionel Reiss.

REJUVINATION (SURGICAL)

CT —YALE MEDICAL LIBRARY, 333 Cedar St, New Haven, 06510.
Notes: A special subject emphasis.

REKHTA LANGUAGE see Urdu Language and Literature

REKHTI LANGUAGE see Urdu Language and Literature

RELAPSING FEVER

OH —MIAMI UNIVERSITY, Science Library, Oxford, 45056.
Notes: Zoonoses and related diseases.

Collection partially transferred from Parker-Davis Memorial Library, Hamilton, Mont.

RELIEF (AID) see International Relief; Public Welfare

RELIEF, INTERNATIONAL see International Relief

RELIEF, WAR see War Relief

RELIGION

AZ —COOK CHRISTIAN TRAINING SCHOOL, Mary M McCarthy Library, 708 S Lindon Lane, Tempe, 85281. Mark E Thomas, Librn
Holdings: Vols 2500 Cat Audiotapes Videotapes Filmstrips

CA —UNIVERSITY OF CALIFORNIA, DAVIS, Shields Library, Dept of Special Collections, Davis, 95616. Donald Kunitz, Head; C Danial Elliott, Asst Head
Holdings: Vols 1700 Cat
Notes: A selection of Bibles in various formats and languages, incl New Testament, Gospels, Greek, 12th and 14th centuries; the earliest Latin Bible produced by Koburger, 1478; Tyndale's New Testament, 1525, the first New Testament printed in English; Tremellius Latin Bible, London, 1585; the first Geneva Bible without the Apocryphia, 1599; the London Polyglot Bible, 1657, and others.

†CA —HEBREW UNION COLLEGE, Jewish Institute of Religion, 3077 University Ave, Los Angeles, 90007.
Notes: Bible, Talmud, Rabbinics, Jewish history, philosophy, art and communal science, Hebrew literature, religion, Zionism.

CA —LOS ANGELES PUBLIC LIBRARY, Philosophy & Religion Dept, 630 W Fifth St, Los Angeles, 90071. Marilyn C Wherley, Librn
Holdings: Vols 2500 Cat
Budget: ($60,000)
Notes: Historical, theological and biographical works on all major world religions including materials on leading cults and sects, especially in California. Particular strengths in Christianity, oriental religions and comparative religions. Includes many serials, periodicals, and special indexes.

CA —WHITE MEMORIAL MEDICAL CENTER, Courville-Abbott Memorial Library, 1720 Brooklyn Ave, Los Angeles, 90033. Joyce Marson, Librn

CA —PEPPERDINE UNIVERSITY, Payson Library, Malibu, 90265. Virginia Randolph, Special Collections Librn
Holdings: Vols 1000 Cat Audiotapes Microforms
Notes: Religious history of the Church of Christ. A substantial part of collection is rare and its use is restricted.

CA —THEOSOPHICAL BOOK ASSOCIATION FOR THE BLIND, Baker Memorial Library, Route 2 Krotona 54, Ojai, 93023. Dennis Gotsehalk, Dir
Holdings: Vols 1200
Notes: Free lending library for the blind; Braille books, tapes, cassettes concerning philosophy, religion and theosophical.

CA —MARYMOUNT PALOS VERDES COLLEGE, Library, 30800 Palos Verdes Dr E, Rancho Palos Verdes, 90274. Benita Campbell, Librn
Holdings: Vols 5151 Cat

CA —CALIFORNIA INSTITUTE OF INTEGRAL STUDIES, Library, 3494 21st St, San Francisco, 94110. Vern Haddick, Library Dir
Holdings: Vols (23,000) Cat Maps Phonorecords Audiotapes
Budget: ($10,000)
Notes: Comparative philosophy, psychology and counseling and comparative religions of East and West. Incl 550 audiotapes.

CA —WESTMONT COLLEGE, Roger John Voskuyl Library, Santa Barbara, 93108. John D Murray, Librn
Holdings: Cat Microforms
Notes: The Christ and Culture Collection contains materials which express and illustrate the interaction between the

RELIGION (cont.)

Christian faith (as both faith and life, doctrine and practice) and the liberal arts and sciences.

CA —UNIVERSITY OF CALIFORNIA, SANTA CRUZ, University Library, Special Collections, Santa Cruz, 95064. Rita Bottoms, Special Collections Librn; Margaret Felts, South Pacific Collection Bibliographer

CT —YALE UNIVERSITY, Divinity School Library, 409 Prospect St, New Haven, 06520. John Bollier, Librarian
Holdings: Vols (340,000)
Notes: Collection incl 340,000 vols, 1452 periodical subscriptions, 8500 microforms and 3500 films.

DC —CATHOLIC UNIVERSITY OF AMERICA, Mullen Library, 620 Michigan Ave NE, Washington, 20064. B Gutekunst, Humanities Librn
Holdings: Vols (20,000) Cat

DC —LIBRARY OF CONGRESS, Manuscript Division, Washington, 20540. John C Broderick, Chief
Holdings: 357,000 Items
Notes: The records of Moral Re-Armament, incl the personal papers of its founder, Frank N D Buchman.

GA —EMORY UNIVERSITY, Candler School of Theology, Pitts Theology Library, Atlanta, 30322. Channing Jeschke, Librn; Anita K Delaries, Curator
Holdings: Cat Mss
Notes: Incl records (85 vols) of the Methodist Church in Georgia: 1614 mss and ms volumes dating from 1830. Also, the Hartford Seminary Foundation Library (205,000 vols).

IL —JESUIT-KRAUSS-MCCORMICK LIBRARY, 1100 E 55th St, Chicago, 60615. Donald Vorp, Dir; Elvire Hilgert, Librn
Holdings: Vols (375,000)
Notes: Collections contain merger of Jesuit Library, Lutheran School of Theology of Chicago (Krauss Library), and McCormick Theological Seminary. Jesuit: Sermones Thesaurus Novi de Tempore (anonymous, Strassbourg 1486); Opera Omnia (Jean Gerson, Strassbourg 1488), 3 vols; Summa Rosella Casuum (Venice 1495); moral theology (major figures of 16th and 17th century scholasticism); early modern editions of patristics and canon law regarding procedures and organzation of the Catholic Church, incl treatises and multi-volume commentaries. Krauss: Archives of Lutheran Church in America and its predecessors; Reformation imprints; early printed versions of the Bible (L Franklin Gruber Collection); German and Scandanavian (Swedish, Danish, Finnish) theology; Lutheran Church of America document depository.
McCormick: Presbyteriana; historical record of Synod of Illinois, UnitedPresbyterian Church of USA; Church Federation of Chicago archives prior to 1969; USA imprints of the Bible (Simms Collection). See also entries under Catholic Church; Lutheran Church; Presbyterian Church

IL —LUTHERAN GENERAL HOSPITAL LIBRARY, 1775 Dempster St, Park Ridge, 60068. Joanne Crispen, Dir of Library Services
Holdings: Vols (21,298) Cat Slides Audiotapes Videotapes 16mm Films Filmstrips
Budget: ($52,600)

IL —WHEATON COLLEGE, Library, Marion E Wade Collection, Irving & Franklin Sts, Wheaton, 60187. Lyle Dorsett, Cur; Marjorie Mead, Associate Cur
Notes: Literary papers of Frederic Buechner, author of eleven novels and nine nonfiction on works dealing with religious topics. Also, the CS Lewis papers, in the Wade Collection.

MA —BOSTON COLLEGE LIBRARIES, Chestnut Hill, 02167.

MA —HISTORIC DEERFIELD-POCUMTUCK VALLEY MEMORIAL ASSOCIATION, Libraries, Memorial St, Box 53, Deerfield, 01342. David R Proper, Librn
Holdings: Vols (17,000) Cat Mss Maps Pix Microforms
Notes: Local and regional history, especially western Massachusetts. Also, remnants of several collection of books available to early Deerfield and Greenfield residents. Strong ms collection dealing with the region's families, businesses, etc. These consist of sermons, diaries, town and church records, voluntary societies' archives, etc. Extensive collection of photographs of the people and buildings of Deerfield and its environs, and travels in Maine, California, and England (1880s to 1920s). Also, large collection of glassplate negatives. Houses the Connecticut Valley Bibliography, a comprehensive card file on the history and culture of the Connecticut Valley of Massachusetts.

MA —NEW ENGLAND QUAKER RESEARCH LIBRARY, PO Box 655, North Amherst, 01059. Francis W Holmes, Librn
Holdings: Vols (6000) Cat Mss Pix Slides Phonorecords Audiotapes Microforms
Budget: ($300)
Notes: No photocopying on premises. Subject emphases: Quakers and Quaker concerns; Pacifism; Racism; Feminism; Religion; Bible; Poverty.

MA —AMERICAN ANTIQUARIAN SOCIETY LIBRARY, 185 Salisbury St, Worcester, 01609. Marcus A McCorison, Dir & Librn

MN —MINNEAPOLIS PUBLIC LIBRARY & INFORMATION CENTER, Sociology Dept, 300 Nicollet Mall, Minneapolis, 55401. Eileen Scwartzbauer, Dept Head
Holdings: Vols (90,000) Cat Phonorecords Audiotapes Microforms
Budget: ($69,890)
Notes: Special collections: Foundation Center Regional Collection; college catalogs on fiche; adult basic education collection. Separate department catalog.

MO —UNIVERSITY OF MISSOURI-KANSAS CITY, General Library, 5100 Rockhill Road, Kansas City, 64110. Kenneth J LaBudde, Dir; Gordon Hendrickson, Assoc Dir; Marilyn Carbonell, Ref Librn
Holdings: Vols 8300 Cat
Notes: Primarily Christian, includes former Kansas City Ecumenical Library.

MO —UNIVERSITY OF MISSOURI-SAINT LOUIS, Thomas Jefferson Library, Manuscript and Historical Society Collection, 8001 Natural Bridge Rd, Saint Louis, 63121.
Holdings: Mss Pix Tapes
Notes: ca

NE —CREIGHTON UNIVERSITY, Reinert/Alumni Library, California at 24th St, Omaha, 68178. Raymond B Means, Dir
Holdings: Vols (19,175) Cat Mss
Budget: ($14,100)
Notes: In addition to English, Latin and Greek predominate in the collection. Emphasis on Catholic religion, history and saints.

NY —NEW YORK STATE LIBRARY, General Reference Library, Albany, 12224. Christian Beauregard, Librn
Holdings: Vols 32,500 Cat
Notes: Although purchases in this field are highly selective, the library has received gift collections, such as the Bishop Doane collection.

NY —ALFRED UNIVERSITY, Herrick Memorial Library, Alfred, 14802. June E Brown, Head Librn
Holdings: Vols (1200) // Cat Mss
Notes: The Bergren Collection. A comprehensive collection on Biblical Studies in the Old and New Testaments. Incudes material on the Dead Sea Scrolls, Eastern religions, and Hebrew and Aramaic languages.

NY —CANISIUS COLLEGE, Andrew L Bouwhuis Library, 2001 Main St, Buffalo, 14208. Peter J Laux, Dir
Holdings: Vols 16,865 Cat
Budget: $4000
Notes: Have also a complete set of the Jesuit "Relations."

NY —AMERICAN SOCIETY FOR PSYCHICAL RESEARCH LIBRARY, 5 W 73 St, New York, 10023. Rhea A White, Consultant to the Library
Holdings: Vols (7000) Cat Mss Pix
Budget: ($1500)
Notes: Incl books on spiritualism, as well as works in psychology, religion, philosophy, physics, anthropology, etc which have a possible bearing on parapsychology. An attempt is made to obtain all serious books on parapsychology in English.

NY —GENERAL THEOLOGICAL SEMINARY, Saint Marks Library, 175 Ninth Ave, New York, 10011. David Green, Dir
Holdings: Vols (200,000) Cat
Notes: Extensive collection.

NY —NEW YORK PUBLIC LIBRARY, Jewish Division, Fifth Ave & 42 St, New York, 10018. Leonard S Gold, Chief
Holdings: Vols (200,000) Cat Mss Microforms
Budget: ($33,383)
Notes: A collection of material in all languages on Judaism, Jewish history, literature and traditions from the earliest times to date and works in the Hebrew alphabet (mainly Hebrew and Yiddish) on a variety of subjects. The division has extensive files of Jewish periodicals and newspapers. The collection of rare Hebraica incl medieval texts, cabalistic works, ethical and philosophical tracts in book form. See Dictionary Catalog of the Jewish Collection (Boston: G K Hall, 1960), 14 vols. First Supplement (Boston: G K Hall, 1975), 8 vols.

NY —UNION THEOLOGICAL SEMINARY, Library, 3041 Broadway at Reinhold Niebuhr Place, New York, 10027. Richard D Spoor, Dir
Holdings: Vols (580,000) Cat Mss Microforms
Budget: ($750,000)

NY —US MILITARY ACADEMY LIBRARY, West Point, 10996. Elaine B Eatroff, Rare Book Cur
Holdings: Vols 1500 Cat
Notes: Thayer Collection, incl rare editions of 19th century science.

NC —SAINT MARY'S COLLEGE, Sarah Graham Kenan Library, 900 Hillsborough St, Ralcigh, 27611.

NC —SOUTHEASTERN BAPTIST THEOLOGICAL SEMINARY LIBRARY, PO Box 752, Wake Forest, 27587. H Eugene McLeod, Librn
Holdings: Cat Slides Audiotapes Videotapes Microforms

OH —PUBLIC LIBRARY OF CINCINNATI & HAMILTON COUNTY, Education & Religion Dept, 800 Vine St, Cincinnati, 45202. Susan F Hettinger, Head
Holdings: Vols (45,000) Cat
Budget: ($10,000)
Notes: Theological and religious collection: religion, church history, theology, 18th and 19th century Protestant writings and sermons.

OH —CLEVELAND PUBLIC LIBRARY, Social Sciences Department, 325 Superior Ave, Cleveland, 44114. Thelma Morris, Head
Notes: Strong collection of important editions of and books about the Bible, the Reformation, and patrology.

PA —JANKOLA LIBRARY AND SLOVAK ARCHIVES, Danville, 17821.
Holdings: Vols 900

PA —LUTHERAN THEOLOGICAL SEMINARY, Krauth Memorial Library, 7301 Germantown Ave, Philadelphia, 19119. Rev David J Wartluft, Dir Libr

PA —TEMPLE UNIVERSITY LIBRARIES, Special Collections Dept, Conwellana-Templana Collection, 13 & Berks St, Philadelphia, 19122. Miriam I Crawford, Cur
Holdings: Vols (2200) Cat Mss Pix Slides Phonorecords Audiotapes 16mm Films VF
Budget: ($30,000)
Notes: The Conwellana Collection is a memorial to Dr Russell H Conwell, founder of Temple University and pastor of the Baptist Temple (Grace Baptists Church) of Philadelphia from 1882 to his death in 1925. The Collection contains almost all of his published works; his personal library of almost 2000 books, emphasizing Biblical and religious thoughts; mss both by Conwell and about his development of the institutional church; letters, including a large number written to his assistant pastor, Arthur E

RELIGION (cont.)

Harris; a near-complete bound set of his sermons and of the *Temple Review* of the Baptist Temple in which they appeared over a 36-year period; and an extensive file of articles, photographs and information on his activities. Card catalog of the Conwellana-Templana Collection incl books by and about Russell Conwell. Separate card files index his sermons, quotationsfrom his sermons, and items in the *Temple Review*. *Russell Herman Conwell, 1843-1925, A Bibliography,* by Maurice F Tauber (Philadelphia Temple University Library, 1935. 40 leaves mimeographed). *Russell Herman Conwell: The Individual and His Influence: Catalog of an Exhibition,* by Miriam I Crawford (Temple University General Alumni Association, 1977; unpaged).

PA —UNIVERSITY OF PITTSBURGH, Hillman Library, Pittsburgh, 15260. Glenora E Rossell, Head
Holdings: Vols (22,950) Cat
Notes: The collection is strong in the history, theory and methodology of religious studies and religion in relation to the arts, culture and history and nature of religion particularly in Christianity (medieval, Reformation, contemporary movement), in Religion in South and East Asia, in Religion in North America, in Religion in Latin America and in Judaism.

TN —LEE COLLEGE, Library, Ocoee St, Cleveland, 37311. Frances Arrington, Head Librn; JoAnne Sparks, Religion Librn
Holdings: Vols 28,204 Cat Slides Phonorecords Audiotapes Filmstrips
Budget: $27,000
Notes: General religion collection which supports undergraduate and graduate level curriculum. The Pentecostal Research Center houses two special collections: the Church of God (Cleveland, Tennessee) collection and the Pentecostal collection. The latter includes works about the movement and its history, works by Pentecostal authors, and specific subject areas (Holy Spirit, glossolalia, divine healing).

TN —HISTORICAL COMMISSION-SUNDAY SCHOOL BOARD, Southern Baptist Convention, Dargan-Carver Library, 127 Ninth Ave N, Nashville, 37234. Howard Gallimore, Supvr
Holdings: Vols (10,000) Cat Mss Maps Pix Slides Phonorecords Audiotapes Videotapes 16mm Films Filmstrips Microforms
Budget: ($38,734)
Notes: Extensive holdings in proceedings and minutes of organized Baptist bodies; state conventions and associations, Baptist journals, and documentation of major Southern Baptist controversies. Material on Black, Russian, and other Baptists. Much on religious education and American religion. Large collection of Sunday School literature. Incl thousands of mss, pictures, slides, records, etc, and 12,000,000 pages on microforms.

TX —ABILENE CHRISTIAN UNIVERSITY, Margaret & Herman Brown Library, ACU Sta, Abilene, 79601. Callie Faye Milliken, Assoc Dir
Holdings: Vols (30,000) Cat Mss Slides Audiotapes Filmstrips Microforms

TX —SOUTHWESTERN BAPTIST THEOLOGICAL SEMINARY, Roberts Library, 2001 W Seminary Dr, PO Box 22000-2E, Fort Worth, 76122. Keith C Wills, Dir
Holdings: Vols 56,000 Cat Mss Slides Audiotapes Videotapes 16mm Films Filmstrips Microforms
Budget: $34,000

TX —OBLATE SCHOOL OF THEOLOGY, Library, 285 Oblate Dr, San Antonio, 78216. James Maney, Libr Dir
Holdings: Vols (22,000) Cat
Budget: ($15,500)

TX —TRINITY UNIVERSITY, Elizabeth Coates Maddux Library, 715 Stadium Dr, San Antonio, 78284. Richard Hume Werking, Library Dir; Craig Likness, Head Bibliographer
Notes: General reference.

TX —P C NELSON MEMORIAL LIBRARY, Southwestern Assemblies of God College, 1200 Sycamore, Waxahachie, 75165. Murl M Winters, Dir
Holdings: Vols (21,877) Cat
Budget: ($11,358)
Notes: Incl William Burton McCafferty Pentecostal Periodical Collection (mostly before 1950; while several titles have moderate runs, many titles are represented by only one or two issues). Holdings: one 4-drawer filing cabinet. Index to the following Pentecostal periodicals: "Pentecostal Evangel," "Church of God Evangel," "Pentecost" (published by Donald Gree), "Christ's Ambassadors Herald," and "Missionary Challenge." Format: card catalog. Entries to date: 60,872.

VA —ASSOCIATION FOR RESEARCH & ENLIGHTENMENT, Library, 67 & Atlantic Avenue, PO Box 595, Virginia Beach, 23451. Stephen Jordan, Library Mgr
Holdings: Vols (3000) Cat
Notes: Emphasis on Christian, Buddhist, Hindu religions, mysticism, comparative religion, psychological approach to biofeedback, autogenics, etc.

WA —SEATTLE PUBLIC LIBRARY, 1000 Fourth Ave, Seattle, 98104. Ronald A Dubberly, City Librn
Holdings: Cat

WA —UNIVERSITY OF WASHINGTON LIBRARIES, Philosophy Library, 331 Savery, DK-50, Seattle, 98195. Carolyn Mateer, Acting Selector
Holdings: Vols (18,302) Cat
Budget: ($27,516)
Notes: Collection includes materials in philosophy of language, law, mind, ethics, logic, mataphysics, religion, science, epistemology, social and political philosophy and the history of philosophy.

WI —SEVENTH DAY BAPTIST HISTORICAL SOCIETY, Library, 3120 Kennedy Rd, PO Box 1678, Janesville, 53547. D Scott Smith, Historian
Holdings: Vols (500) Cat Mss
Notes: US Seventh Day Baptists Collection, incl records, letters. Established at Newport, Rhode Island, in 1671, this denomination is a part of the Free-Church evangelical movement in America. The General Conference was organized in 1801. The national and international headquarters of the Seventh Day Baptist denomination is located at Janesville, Wisconsin. Also have records, publications, etc of the denomination's mission in Shanghai, 1846-1950; further, materials (6 boxes) on the Church's work in Nyasaland (Malawi), 1895-1914, and then at a later period.

AB —CANADIAN UNION COLLEGE, Library, Box 460, College Heights, T0C 0Z0, Can. Keith Clouten, Library Services Dir
Holdings: Vols (5000) Cat Audiotapes 16mm Films Microforms
Notes: Largely theology, comparative religion, church history, especially of Seventh-day Adventists.

MB —UNIVERSITY OF MANITOBA, Saint Paul's College Library, Winnipeg, R3T 2M6, Can. Rev H J Drake, SJ, Head
Holdings: Vols 5865 Cat
Budget: $2400

ON —HURON COLLEGE, Silcox Memorial Library, 1349 Western Rd, London, N6G 1H3, Can. Pamela MacKay, Chief Librn
Holdings: Vols (28,000) Cat
Budget: ($24,710)
Notes: Covers Bible, church history, church music, liturgics, pastoralia, religious studies, systematics. 95 periodical subscriptions including foreign language materials. Rare books collection of 750 volumes, including collections of sermons, commentaries, particularly rare bibles, many in foreign languages.

ON —NATIONAL LIBRARY OF CANADA, 395 Wellington St, Ottawa, K1A 0N4, Can. Andre Preibish, Dir
Holdings: Vols 10,000
Notes: Includes 130 serial titles, theses, pamphlets, government publications relating to family and marriage. The following disciplines covered: anthropology, psychology and psychiatry, law, economics, religion, sociology, demography, education, political science and biology. Earliest title 1630.

ON —UNIVERSITY OF OTTAWA, Morisset Library, 65 Hastey St, Ottawa, K1N 9A5, Can. Yvon Richer, University Chief Librn
Holdings: Vols (30,000) Cat Maps Slides Microforms
Notes: Only a small portion of this material is housed in Special Collections, but it is one of the strongest elements of our regular collection. Incl 336 cataloged periodical sets. Additional support, particulary in archaeology, philosophy and religion is also available at the affiliated St Paul University, 223 Main Street, Ottawa.

†ON —METROPOLITAN TORONTO LIBRARY, Social Sciences Dept, 789 Yonge St, Toronto, M4W 2G8, Can. Abdus Salam, Head
Holdings: Vols Cat Maps Phonorecords Audiotapes 16mm Films Microforms
Notes: The collection is strong in the history and philosophy of religion and comparative religions; literature of all the major religions of the world; works on the devotional and practical aspects of religion; and books on such sacred scripture as the Bible. In addition, our holdings contain many denominational studies on religion in Canada, as well as more than 300 congregational histories, particularly Ontario churches and synagogues.

ON —TORONTO SCHOOL OF THEOLOGY, Consortium of Libraries, University of Toronto, Toronto, M5S 1A5, Can. R Grane Bracewell, Library Coordr
Holdings: Cat
Notes: A consortium of 7 theological college and faculty libraries at the University of Toronto.

ON —WILFRID LAURIER UNIVERSITY, Waterloo Lutheran Seminary Library, (formerly Waterloo Lutheran University), 75 University Ave W, Waterloo, N2L 3C5, Can. Erich R W Schultz, University Librn
Holdings: Vols (30,000) Cat Microforms
Budget: ($22,500)
Notes: One of the largest Lutheran collections in Canada.

PQ —CONCORDIA UNIVERSITY LIBRARIES, 1455 de Maisonneuve Blvd W, Montreal, H3G 1M8, Can. Martin Cohen, Special Collections Librn
Holdings: Vols 60// Cat Mss
Notes: The Maximilien Bibaud Collection contains the author's memoirs and correspondence as well as his writing on diverse subjects such as religion, theology, Canadian, European and ancient history, and the French language. 51 vols of ms materials.

PQ —CONCORDIA UNIVERSITY LIBRARIES, 1455 de Maisonneuve Blvd W, Montreal, H3G 1M8, Can. Dorothy Cameron, Reference Librn
Notes: Collection incl Judaism History, Talmudie Period (17 titles), Medieval and early modern 1750- (9 titles); modern 1750- (9 titles); Philosophy - Jewish (38 titles); Ethics (2000 titles); Christianity modern period 1453- (278 titles).

SK —UNIVERSITY OF REGINA, Campion College, Library, Regina, S4S 0A2, Can. Myfanwy Truscott, Librn
Holdings: Vols (50,000) Cat
Budget: ($100,000)

RELIGION—ECONOMIC ASPECTS see Economics in Religion

RELIGION—HISTORY

CA —UNIVERSITY OF CALIFORNIA, LOS ANGELES, Research Library, Western European Collection, Los Angeles, 90024. Edward Shreeves, Chairman, Bibliographers Group; Mary E Greco, Western European Bibliographer
Holdings: Mss Maps Pix Microforms
Notes: Good general coverage. Special strengths in the religious history of the 17th and 18th centuries.

†CA —ATMANIKETAN ASHRAM LIBRARY, 1291 Weber St, Pomona, 91768. Notes: Sri Aurobindo, Indian spirituality,

RELIGION—HISTORY (cont.)

Vedanta, Sanskrit studies, Vedic-Upanishadic texts, education.

CT —YALE UNIVERSITY, Box 1603A, Yale Station, New Haven, 06520.

DC —HARVARD UNIVERSITY, Dumbarton Oaks, Research Library, 1703 32nd St NW, Washington, 20007. Irene Vaslef, Librn
Holdings: Vols (91,000) Cat Maps Pix Slides Microforms
Budget: ($219,000)
Notes: Byzantine civilization (including art, archaeology, literature, history, religion, law, music, etc). Extensive supplemental material on Classical, Hellenistic, Medieval, Islamic, Medieval Slavic cultures. 62,000 b/w photographs, 25,000 slides and transparencies, 1000 microfilms of books and manuscripts. Printed description of collection in *Harvard Library Bulletin*, vol 19, no 1 (Jan 1971), pp 25-35 and vol 19, no 2 (April 1971), pp 204-214, pp 25-35 and vol 19, no 2 (April 1971), pp 204-214.

IN —FREE METHODIST CHURCH OF NORTH AMERICA, Marston Memorial Historical Center Library, 901 College Ave, Winona Lake, 46590. Evelyn L Mottweiler, Librn
Holdings: Vols (6000) Cat Mss
Budget: ($16,000)
Notes: Denominational headquarters of the Free Methodist Church in North America. Specializing in history and doctrine of Methodism and related subjects. Outstanding Wesley collection. Methodist and Free Methodist holdings of the Library are included in the Methodist Union Catalog: *Pre-1976 Imprints*, ed by Kenneth E Rowe. *See also* entry under Wesley, John.

MA —OLD STURBRIDGE VILLAGE, Research Library, Sturbridge, 01566. Theresa Rini Percy, Librn
Holdings: Cat Mss
Notes: New England, 1790-1850: basic secondary works and representative sampling of sermons, tracts and other source materials.

MA —BRANDEIS UNIVERSITY, Goldfarb Library, 415 South St, Waltham, 02154. Bessie Hahn, Dir
Holdings: Vols
Notes: Perry Miller Collection on the Colonial Religious Experience in America: Consists of 18 linear ft of books dating from the 17th and 18th century relating to the religious experience in the American colonies. Access to the collection is through the Main Card Catalog and Special Collections Card Catalog.

NY —HOFSTRA UNIVERSITY, Library, 1000 Fulton Ave, Hempstead, 11550. Charles R Andrews, Dean of Library Services
Notes: The personal library of Paul Radin. See description of the American Philosophical Society Library's collection of his anthropological papers under this entry (Pa).

NY —UNIVERSITY OF ROCHESTER, Rush Rhees Library, Department of Rare Books and Special Collections, Rochester, 14627. Peter Dzwonkoski, Librn
Holdings: Vols 300 Cat
Notes: A most unusual collection in size and scope of material by and about William Sherlock, Dean of St Paul's, 1691-1707, and other nonjuring writers.

NC —DUKE UNIVERSITY, Divinity School Library, Durham, 27706. Donn Michael Farris, Librn

PA —AMERICAN PHILOSOPHICAL SOCIETY, Library, 105 S Fifth St, Philadelphia, 19106. Edward C Carter II, Librn
Notes: The anthropological papers of Paul Radin in fields of ethnology, social organization, primitive religion, linguistics, and mythology. He worked mostly among the Winnebago, Ojibwa, Fox, Zapotec, Wappo, Wintun, and Huave Indian tribes; also Italian and other ethnic minorities of San Francisco.

PA —FRIENDS HISTORICAL LIBRARY OF SWARTHMORE COLLEGE, Swarthmore,

1908I. J William Frost, Dir
Holdings: Vols (35,000) Cat Mss Pix Slides Films Microforms
Notes: Library's collection contain information on the history and doctrine of the Society of Friends, Quaker contributions to literature, science, business, education, and government, plus their reform efforts in peace, Indian rights, women's rights, and abolition of slavery. As an official depository of the records of the records of Philadelphia and Baltimore Yearly Meetings, the library holds, either in the original manuscript or on microfilm, the largest collection in the world of Quaker meeting archives, incl some records of Ohio and Illinois Yearly Meetings (Hicksite), and microfilm copies of minutes and registers of many meetings in New England, New York, North Carolina, Indiana, and Great Britain. Among the more than 250 mss collections, described in *Guide to the Manuscript Collections of Friends Historical Library of Swarthmore College* (1982), are papersof individual Quaker leaders, families, and organizations.

RI —BROWN UNIVERSITY, John Hay Library, 20 Prospect St, Providence, 02912. Mark N Brown, Cur Mss
Holdings: Mss
Notes: Several collections, incl the Isaac Backus (qv), the Francis Wayland (qv), and the Asa Messer (qv), involve the history of religion in America.
See also entry under Baptists - History

VA —LYNCHBURG COLLEGE, Knight-Capron Library, Lynchburg, 24501. Mary C Scudder, Dir
Holdings: Vols (8847) Cat Maps
Notes: Religious works and history, 15th-19th century. Part of the Capron Collection.

†ON —METROPOLITAN TORONTO LIBRARY, Social Sciences Dept, 789 Yonge St, Toronto, M4W 2G8, Can. Abdus Salam, Head
Holdings: Vols Cat Maps Phonorecords Audiotapes 16mm Films Microforms
Notes: The collection is strong in the history and philosophy of religion and comparative religions; literature of all the major religions of the world; works on the devotional and practical aspects of religion; and books on such sacred scripture as the Bible. In addition, our holdings contain many denominational studies on religion in Canada, as well as more than 300 congregational histories, particularly Ontario churches and synagogues.

ON —VICTORIA UNIVERSITY, Library, Centre for Reformation and Renaissance Studies, 71 Queen's Park Crescent, Toronto, M5S 1K7, Can. Robert C Brandeis, Chief Librn; James Estes, Dir
Holdings: Vols (15,000) Cat Slides
Notes: The CRRS concentrates on the northern European countries and France; its chief strengths are Erasmus, 650 vols; early printed books, especially 16th century editions of Latin classics; bibliography and the history of printing. The Erasmus holdings are cataloged in W T McCready et al, "The Erasmus Collection in the Centre for Reformation and Renaissance Studies...A Catalogue"...*Reformation and Renaissance* 7 (1971), 32-76 and "A Supplementary List"...*Reformation and Renaissance*, 10 (1974), 116-119. Published catalogs. Humanist Editions of the Classics at CRRS, Toronto, 1979; Humanist Editions of Statutes and History at CRRS, Toronto, 1980; Bibles, Theological Treatises and Other Religious Literature 1491-1700 at CRRS, Toronto, 1981.

RELIGION—PSYCHOLOGY see Psychology, Religious

RELIGION, COMPARATIVE

CA —LOS ANGELES PUBLIC LIBRARY, Philosophy & Religion Dept, 630 W Fifth St, Los Angeles, 90071. Marilyn C Wherley, Librn
Holdings: Vols 2500 Cat
Budget: ($60,000)
Notes: Historical, theological and

biographical works on all major world religions including materials on leading cults and sects, especially in California. Particular strengths in Christianity, oriental religions and comparative religions. Includes many serials, periodicals, and special indexes.

NY —UNITED LODGE OF THEOSOPHISTS LIBRARY, 347 E 72 St, New York, 10021.
Notes: Ancient and modern philosophy and psychology; comparative religion and mythology; parapsychology; reincarnation research in science and religion.

WI —UNIVERSITY OF WISCONSIN, MADISON, Memorial Library, Western European Humanities Collection, 728 State St, Madison, 53706. Charles Szabo, Bibliographer
Notes: The George B Wild Collection of Classical and Nineteenth Century German Literature. An extensive collection emphasizing history, biography, criticism, philosophy, literature, and comparitive religion. Supplements the Library's great German language and literature holdings.

†ON —METROPOLITAN TORONTO LIBRARY, Social Sciences Dept, 789 Yonge St, Toronto, M4W 2G8, Can. Abdus Salam, Head
Holdings: Vols Cat Mss Phonorecords Audiotapes 16mm Films Microforms
Notes: The collection is strong in the history and philosophy of religion and comparative religions; literature of all the major religions of the world; works on the devotional and practical aspects of religion; and books on such sacred scripture as the Bible. In addition, our holdings contain many denominational studies on religion in Canada, as well as more than 300 congregational histories, particularly Ontario churches and synagogues.

RELIGION, GREAT BRITAIN see Great Britain—Religion

RELIGION, ICELANDIC see Iceland—Religion

RELIGION, ORIENTAL

CA —LOS ANGELES PUBLIC LIBRARY, Philosophy & Religion Dept, 630 W Fifth St, Los Angeles, 90071. Marilyn C Wherley, Librn
Holdings: Vols 2500 Cat
Budget: ($60,000)
Notes: Historical, theological and biographical works on all major world religions including materials on leading cults and sects, especially in California. Particular strengths in Christianity, oriental religions and comparative religions. Includes many serials, periodicals, and special indexes.

CA —CALIFORNIA INSTITUTE OF INTEGRAL STUDIES, Library, 3494 21st St, San Francisco, 94110. Vern Haddick, Library Dir
Holdings: Vols (23,000) Cat Maps Phonorecords Audiotapes
Budget: ($10,000)
Notes: Comparative philosophy, psychology and counseling and comparative religions of East and West. Incl 550 audiotapes.

IL —UNIVERSITY OF ILLINOIS, URBANA/CHAMPAIGN, Library, University Archives, 19 Library, 1408 W Gregory Drive, Urbana, 61801. Maynard Brichford, University Archivist
Holdings: Vols (5000) Cat
Budget: ($7000)
Notes: The Mandeville Collection in Parapsychology and Occult Sciences. Titles in the Merten J Mandeville Collection are purchased by funds from an endowment provided specifically for the collection on its establishment in 1966 by Merten J Mandeville, Professor Emeritus of Management, who donated 400 vols from his personal library as the nucleus of the collection. There are currently about 5000 titles in the collection, supplemented by related materials in the general collection. Topics include astrology, extrasensory perception, yoga, magic, satanism, faith

RELIGION, ORIENTAL (cont.)

healing, hypnosis, Eastern religions, witchcraft, fortune telling, reincarnation, flying saucers, ghosts, dreams, numerology, graphology, and mysticism. Biographies and reference books are a part of the collection as are journals devoted to the scientific study of parapsychology.

NY —ALFRED UNIVERSITY, Herrick Memorial Library, Alfred, 14802. June E Brown, Head Librn
Holdings: Vols (1200) // Cat Mss
Notes: The Bergren Collection. A comprehensive collection on Biblical Studies in the Old and New Testaments. Includes material on the Dead Sea Scrolls, Eastern religions, and Hebrew and Aramaic languages.

NY —INSTITUTE FOR ADVANCED STUDIES OF WORLD RELIGIONS (IASWR), Melville Memorial Library, State University of New York, Stony Brook, 11794. C T Shen, Dir
Holdings: Vols 45,000 Periodicals Mss Maps Microforms
Notes: Incl extensive reference and research facilities in about 30 languages for the study of Buddhism, Shinto, Hinduism, Taoism, Sikhism, Islam, etc; their thought, history, culture, art and societal role; works on the comparative study of religions. Microforms: 3400 Indic mss in microform, 80 percent Hinduism, 20 percent Buddhism; catalog available. Xylographs in Tibetan and Chinese editions of Tibetan collected works. Refer inquiries to L L Yang and H G Robinson. See also entries under Buddha and Buddhism; Hinduism; China-Religion; Japan-Religion

OH —CLEVELAND PUBLIC LIBRARY, Fine Arts and Special Collections Department, 325 Superior Ave, Cleveland, 44114. Alice N Loranth, Head
Holdings: Vols 7100 Cat Mss
Notes: Emphasis is on religious texts in their original languages and Western translation. Treatises on religious beliefs and practices are also incl. Strong holdings in Buddhism, Egyptian religion, Hinduism, Judaica, Lamaistic texts, Islam, Sikhism and Zoroastrianism. Works on primitive religion cover aspects of animism, totemism, fetishism. Special emphasis on Islam in China. See also entries under Islam; Judaica.

VA —ASSOCIATION FOR RESEARCH & ENLIGHTENMENT, Library, 67 & Atlantic Avenue, PO Box 595, Virginia Beach, 23451. Stephen Jordan, Library Mgr
Holdings: Vols (3000) Cat
Notes: Emphasis on Christian, Buddhist, Hindu religions, mysticism, comparative religion, psychological approach to biofeedback, autogenics, etc.

RELIGION, PRIMITIVE

MA —COLLEGE OF THE HOLY CROSS, Dinand Library, College St, Worcester, 01610. James M Mahoney, Cur of Special Collection
Holdings: // Mss
Notes: The Joseph J Williams, SJ Collection contains 107 mss and 865 letters concerning religious practices of tribes in Africa. Collection is indexed, restricted use.

NY —HOFSTRA UNIVERSITY, Library, 1000 Fulton Ave, Hempstead, 11550. Charles R Andrews, Dean of Library Services
Notes: The personal library of Paul Radin. See description of the American Philosophical Society Library's collection of his anthropological papers under this entry (Pa).

OH —CLEVELAND PUBLIC LIBRARY, Fine Arts and Special Collections Department, 325 Superior Ave, Cleveland, 44114. Alice N Loranth, Head
Holdings: Vols (7100) Cat Mss
Notes: Part of the Oriental Religion Collection. Emphasis is on religious texts in their original languages and Western translations. Treatises on religious beliefs and

practices are also incl. Strong holdings in Buddhism, Egyptian religion, Hinduism, Judaica, Lamaistic texts, Islam, Sikhism and Zoroastrianism. Works on primitive religion cover aspects of animism, totemism, fetishism, etc. Special emphasis on Islam in China.
See also entry under Folklore; Religion, Oriental

PA —AMERICAN PHILOSOPHICAL SOCIETY, Library, 105 S Fifth St, Philadelphia, 19106. Edward C Carter II, Librn
Notes: The anthropological papers of Paul Radin in fields of ethnology, social organization, primitive religion, linguistics, and mythology. He worked mostly among the Winnebago, Ojibwa, Fox, Zapotec, Wappo, Wintun, and Huave Indian tribes; also Italian and other ethnic minorities of San Francisco.

RELIGION, SCANDINAVIAN see Scandinavia—Religion

RELIGION AND BIRTH CONTROL

NY —PLANNED PARENTHOOD FEDERATION OF AMERICA, Katharine Dexter McCormick Library, 810 Seventh Ave, New York, 10019. Gloria A Roberts, Head Librn
Holdings: Vols (4000) Cat
Notes: Birth control, teenagers, contraception and contraceptive research, family planning, religion and birth control.

RELIGION AND PSYCHOLOGY see Psychology, Religious

RELIGION AND SLAVERY

GA —AGNES SCOTT COLLEGE, McCain Library, E College Ave, Decatur, 30030. Judith Bourgeois Jensen, Librn
Holdings: Vols (945) Uncat
Budget: $300
Notes: The Frontier Religion Collection, which was given by Prof Walter Brownlow Posey, traces the effects of slavery on religion in the Old South Frontier prior to 1860. A catalog file (by author entry only) accompanies the collection at present. Noncirculating.

NC —BELMONT ABBEY COLLEGE, Abbot Vincent Taylor Library, Belmont, 28012. Marjorie McDermott, Dir
Holdings: Vols (1000) Cat
Notes: Consists of books dealing with the history of North and South Carolina from colonial times to the present. Incl are several county histories, some early newspapers, and a strong section on the history of religion (especially the Roman Catholic Church) in the two states.

OH —MASSILLON PUBLIC LIBRARY, 208 Lincoln Way E, Massillon, 44646. Camille Leslie, Dir
Holdings: // Mss Maps
Notes: 22 linear ft. Correspondence and business papers of Thomas Rotch and Arvine Wales who migrated in 1811 from New England to Ohio; and of Arvine C Wales, his son, lawyer and civic leader in Massillon, Ohio. Covers period ca 1780-1880; contains much Quaker and anti-slavery material, as well as material on early Ohio. Index in preparation.

RELIGION AND SOCIAL PROBLEMS see Church and Social Problems

RELIGIONS, MODERN see Sects

RELIGIONS, NEW

CA —LOS ANGELES PUBLIC LIBRARY, Philosophy & Religion Dept, 630 W Fifth St, Los Angeles, 90071. Marilyn C Wherley, Librn
Holdings: Vols 100 Cat
Budget: ($60,000)
Notes: Comprehensive collection of materials on cults and sects with emphasis on those active in the Southern California

area. Includes special files, indexes and pamphlets.

PA —TEMPLE UNIVERSITY LIBRARIES, Special Collections Dept, Contemporary Culture Collection, Philadelphia, 19122. Patricia J Case, Cur
Notes: The Contemporary Culture Collection. See full entry under US-Social Life and Customs.

WI —UNIVERSITY OF WISCONSIN, MADISON, Memorial Library, Ibero-American Studies Collection, 728 State St, Madison, 53706. Suzanne Hodgman, Bibliographer
Holdings: Vols (394) Uncat
Notes: Brazilian Positivist Collection. The collection consists of a nearly complete set of the official publications of the Positivist Church of Brazil. It includes first editions of pamphlets and booklets from the late 19th century, in addition to later reprints. A typescript listing of the collection is available. Collection is housed in the Rare Book Department.

RELIGIOUS ART see Christian Art and Symbolism; Church Architecture

RELIGIOUS BOOK PUBLISHING

NY —GRADUATE CENTER OF THE CITY UNIVERSITY OF NEW YORK, William H and Gwynne K Crouse Library for Publishing Arts, 33 W 42 St, New York, 10036. Alfred H Lane, Dir
Notes: Recently established and still growing, but intended to become the authoritative source of materials in the field, of particular value in research about the publishing industry. Open to staff members of publishing houses, students, scholars, authors, printers, and booksellers. Primarily 20th century materials, and particularly useful for research on technical, financial, and historical matters. Much on the history of individual houses, economics of authorship; marketing and distribution of books; etc.

RELIGIOUS BRASSES see Brass Religious Objects

RELIGIOUS DENOMINATIONS see Religion; Sects

RELIGIOUS DISPUTATIONS see Disputations, Religious

RELIGIOUS EDUCATION

CT —YALE UNIVERSITY, Divinity School Library, 409 Prospect St, New Haven, 06520. John Bollier, Librarian
Holdings: Vols (340,000)
Notes: Collection incl 340,000 vols, 1452 periodical subscriptions, 8500 microforms and 3500 films.

MO —EDEN-WEBSTER LIBRARIES, Eden Theological Seminary, Webster University, 475 E Lockwood, Saint Louis, 63119. Karen M Luebbert, Dir
Notes: History and catechisms.

NY —UNION THEOLOGICAL SEMINARY, Library, 3041 Broadway at Reinhold Niebuhr Place, New York, 10027. Richard D Spoor, Dir
Holdings: Vols (580,000) Cat Mss Microforms
Budget: ($750,000)

NC —SOUTHEASTERN BAPTIST THEOLOGICAL SEMINARY LIBRARY, PO Box 752, Wake Forest, 27587. H Eugene McLeod, Librn
Holdings: Cat Slides Audiotapes Videotapes Microforms

OR —MULTNOMAH SCHOOL OF THE BIBLE, Library, 8435 NE Gilsan St, Portland, 97220. James F Scott, Dir of Library; Susan Johnson, Asst Librn
Holdings: Vols (40,686) Cat Slides Phonorecords Audiotapes Filmstrips
Budget: ($33,950)
Notes: Multnomah School of the Bible is an evangelical school that educates students through a program of instruction having the

RELIGIOUS EDUCATION (cont.)

Bible as its center. It supports this centralized Bible major with several ancillary, pertinent supporting minors, ie, Christian education, pastoral, missions and New Testament Greek.

RI —BROWN UNIVERSITY, John Hay Library, 20 Prospect St, Providence, 02912. Mark N Brown, Cur Mss
Holdings: // Mss
Notes: Eli H Canfield mss reflect issues of the day and incl the subjects of missions, religious education, temperance, Prohibition and Reconstruction. There are also 300 letters from Canfield to his son and grandchildren; letters from Europe and the South during and after the Civil War; and papers relating to Christ Church, Brooklyn. Register available. See "The Rev Eli Canfield (1817-1898): Low-church Yankee Episcopalian," ed by William G McLoughlin, Jr, in *Books at Brown, vol XXIII* (1969), pp. 135-68.

TN —HISTORICAL COMMISSION-SUNDAY SCHOOL BOARD, Southern Baptist Convention, Dargan-Carver Library, 127 Ninth Ave N, Nashville, 37234. Howard Gallimore, Supvr
Holdings: Vols (10,000) Cat Mss Maps Pix Slides Phonorecords Audiotapes Videotapes 16mm Films Filmstrips Microforms
Budget: ($38,734)
Notes: Extensive holdings in proceedings and minutes of organized Baptist bodies; state conventions and associations, Baptist journals, and documentation of major Southern Baptist controversies. Material on Black, Russian, and other Baptists. Much on religious education and American religion. Large collection of Sunday School literature. Incl thousands of mss, pictures, slides, records, etc, and 12,000,000 pages on microforms.

TX —ABILENE CHRISTIAN UNIVERSITY, Margaret & Herman Brown Library, ACU Sta, Abilene, 79601. Callie Faye Milliken, Assoc Dir
Holdings: Vols (3000) Cat
Notes: Sewell Bible Library. This collection is strong in general reference books in religion, 19th and 20th century church history, and religious education. The personal library of ACU's fourth president Jesse P Sewell, has been augmented by gifts from friends and purchases by the Library.

TX —SOUTHWESTERN BAPTIST THEOLOGICAL SEMINARY, Roberts Library, 2001 W Seminary Dr, PO Box 22000-2E, Fort Worth, 76122. Keith C Wills, Dir
Holdings: Vols 110,000 Cat Mss Maps Pix Slides Audiotapes Videotapes 16mm Films Filmstrips Microforms
Budget: $50,000

ON —HURON COLLEGE, Silcox Memorial Library, 1349 Western Rd, London, N6G 1H3, Can. Pamela MacKay, Chief Librn
Holdings: Vols (28,000) Cat
Budget: ($24,710)
Notes: Covers Bible, church history, church music, liturgics, pastoralia, religious education, philosophy of religion, religious studies, systematics. 95 periodical subscriptions including foreign lanuage materials. Rare books collection of 750 volumes, including collections of sermons, commentaries, particularly rare bibles, many in foreign languages.

ON —TORONTO SCHOOL OF THEOLOGY, Consortium of Libraries, University of Toronto, Toronto, M5S 1A5, Can. R Grane Bracewell, Library Coordr
Holdings: Cat
Notes: A consortium of 7 theological college and faculty libraries at the University of Toronto.

RELIGIOUS FOUNDATIONS

MD —SOVEREIGN HOSPITALLER ORDER OF SAINT JOHN, Villa Anneslie, 529 Dunkirk Road, Baltimore, 21212.
Notes: The Sovereign Hospitaller Order of Saint John is an ecumenical Christian religious Order founded in the 11th century; successor Order to the Knights of Rhodes and the Knights of Malta.

RELIGIOUS GROUPS

CT —YALE UNIVERSITY, Box 1603A, Yale Station, New Haven, 06520.

OH —MASSILLON PUBLIC LIBRARY, 208 Lincoln Way E, Massillon, 44646. Camille Leslie, Dir
Holdings: Vols 73 Cat Mss
Budget: $100
Notes: Collection is limited to historical studies; nothing on modern communes. Special emphasis on Shakers and Zoarites. No separate catalog.

UT —UNIVERSITY OF UTAH, Marriott Library, Special Collections, Salt Lake City, 84112. Gregory C Thompson, Cur
Notes: Papers, correspondence, and manuscripts, of Sonia Johnson, excommunicated Mormon feminist. Part of the collection has a time seal on it.

RELIGIOUS HISTORY see Church History

RELIGIOUS LIBERTY

IL —SOUTHERN ILLINOIS UNIVERSITY, CARBONDALE, Delyte W Morris Library, Special Collections Dept, Carbondale, 62901. David V Koch, Cur of Special Collections; Louisa Bowen, Cur of Manuscripts
Holdings: Vols 430 Cat Mss Pix
Notes: Personal papers (78 linear feet) of Theodore Schroeder, 1873-1957, founder of the Free Speech League, incl archives of the League. Thousands of letters, mss, and notes, with letters from Anthony Comstock, Samuel Gompers, Eugene V Debs, Havelock Ellis, Margaret Sanger, Upton Sinclair, H L Mencken, and Emma Goldman. The archives reflect Schroeder's crusades in the areas of free speech, sex expression, religion, and psychoanalysis. Inventory and name index available at the Library. Described by Ralph E McCoy, *Theodore Schroeder, the Cold Enthusiast,* Carbondale: Southern Illinois University Libraries, 1973. (Bibliographic Contributions, No 8).

IN —INDIANA UNIVERSITY, Lilly Library, Seventh St, Bloomington, 47405. William R Cagle, Librn
Holdings: Vols (1000) // Cat Mss
Notes: 1000 vols of contemporary printings (largely British) relating to Anglo-American relations leading to the American Revolution.

MA —HARVARD UNIVERSITY LIBRARY, Cambridge, 02138.
Holdings: Cat

NC —SOUTHEASTERN BAPTIST THEOLOGICAL SEMINARY LIBRARY, PO Box 752, Wake Forest, 27587. H Eugene McLeod, Librn
Holdings: Cat Microforms

PA —FRIENDS HISTORICAL LIBRARY OF SWARTHMORE COLLEGE, Swarthmore, 19081. J William Frost, Dir
Holdings: Vols (35,000) Cat Mss Microforms
Notes: Library's collections contain information on the history and doctrine of the Society of Friends, Quaker contributions to literature, science, business, education, and government, plus their reform efforts in peace, Indian rights, women's rights, and abolition of slavery. Incl works reflecting Friends' concern for religious liberty in Great Britain and the US, with accounts of persecution for concientious objection to war, refusal to pay tithes, etc.

UT —UNIVERSITY OF UTAH, Marriott Library, Special Collections, Salt Lake City, 84112. Gregory C Thompson, Cur
Notes: Papers, correspondence, and manuscripts, of Sonia Johnson, excommunicated Mormon feminist. Part of the collection has a time seal on it.

RELIGIOUS MUSIC see Church Music

RELIGIOUS NEWSPAPERS see Newspapers, Religious

RELIGIOUS ORDERS see Military Religious Orders; Monasticism and Religious Orders

RELIGIOUS PAINTING see Christian Art and Symbolism

RELIGIOUS PSYCHOLOGY see Psychology, Religious

RELIGIOUS SCULPTURE see Christian Art and Symbolism

RELOCATION OF JAPANESE (WORLD WAR II) see Japanese in the U.S.

REMARQUE, ERICH MARIA

NY —NEW YORK UNIVERSITY, Elmer Holmes Bobst Library, Div of Special Collections, Washington Sq S, New York, 10012. Frank Walker, Librn; Patrick McGuire, Asst Librn
Notes: His mss, published books, personal library, etc, incl his diaries, 1918, 1935-54, and 1964-65.

REMEY, CHARLES MASON, 1874-1974

NY —CORNELL UNIVERSITY LIBRARIES, Collection of Regional History, Dept of Manuscripts and Univ Archives, Ithaca, 14853.
Notes: Papers, 1940-49; 6 ft. Architect, Baha'i.

REMINGTON TYPEWRITER CO.

DE —HAGLEY MUSEUM AND LIBRARY, Eleutherian Mills-Hagley Foundation Inc, PO Box 3630, Greenville, 19807. Richmond D Williams, Dir; Heddy A Richter, Imprints Librn
Notes: Sperry Univac has deposited a large amount of historical records. Approximately 2000 cubic feet of records, files and photographs that document the invention and development of computers and the rapid growth of the industry were officially released by Sperry Corporation to the Library. The collection includes technical and legal documents relating to the ENIAC and UNIVAC computers as well as records of the founding of the E Remington Typewriter Company and other predecessor companies of the Sperry organization, such as The Library Bureau, Kardex, Rodic Rubber and the Powers Accounting Machinery Company. Thus our knowledge of the Sperry predecessors dates back in this collection to 1902.

REMINGTON, FREDERIC

CO —DENVER PUBLIC LIBRARY, 1357 Broadway, Denver, 80203.
Notes: Correspondence, papers, pictures, diaries, etc.

LA —R W NORTON ART GALLERY, Library, 4747 Creswell Ave, Shreveport, 71106. Jerry M Bloomer, Librn
Holdings: Cat Mss Pix
Notes: Extensive collection of all known books, pamphlets, catalogs, etc published about Remington as well as books written and/or illustrated by him. Also incl prints of his paintings, as well as original paintings, sculpture, watercolors, drawings, etc, by Remington (the latter housed in the Gallery collection).

NY —SAINT LAWRENCE UNIVERSITY, Owen D Young Library, Canton, 13617. Mahlon Peterson, Librn
Holdings: Cat Mss Pix
Notes: Frederic Remington's correspondence with Poultney Bigelow and others is the most important part of this collection. Also incl is an extensive collection of magazines in which articles written and/or illustrated by Remington first appeared, a collection of prints of Remington paintings, and many books by and about Remington. There are restrictions on use of this material. Over 400 items.

TX —TEXAS A&M UNIVERSITY, Sterling C Evans Library, Special Collections Div, College Station, 77843. Donald H Dyal, Librn
Notes: The Western Illustrators Collection is comprised of approximately 3500 illustrated books, pamphlets, and other items. The collection incl illustrated works by Charles Marion Russell, Frederic Sackrider Remington, and other artists of the American West. Numerous other artists of the West and Southwest are represented, many of them contemporary moderns. Quite a lot of the books have additional unique original drawings by the artists.

TX —AMON CARTER MUSEUM, Library, 3510 Camp Bowie Blvd, PO Box 2365, Fort Worth, 76113. Nancy G Wynne, Librn
Holdings: Vols (25,000) Cat Mss Pix
Notes: The book collection, microfilm and photo archives have been built toward the goal of the interpretation of American

REMINGTON, FREDERIC (cont.)

history through art. At present, the greatest strengths are in Americana, Western Canadiana, bibliography, American exhibition catalogs and history of photography. Substantial books and files on American artists of the 19th and early 20th century, and particularly of Charles M Russell and Frederic Remington. Incl 25,000 pictures; 13,000 slides.
See also entries under Newspapers, American; Pictures - Collections.

REMOTE FACSIMILE DUPLICATOR
see Facsimile Transmission

REMOTE SENSING

CA —NASA, Ames Research Center, Libraries, Library Br 202-3, Moffett Field, 94035. Sarah Dueker, Chief, Library Branch
Holdings: Cat Audiotapes Microforms
Notes: Main library collections cover physical sciences, engineering and mathematical fields related to research programs in aeronautics-space research. Life sciences library collections cover medical, physiological, behavioral and biological sciences related to research programs. Also emphases on remote sensing of earth resources and the search for extraterrestrial life. 950 journal titles and 85,000 monographs. Reports collection includes 60,000 hard copy reports and 900,000 microfiche.

CA —UNIVERSITY OF CALIFORNIA, SANTA BARBARA, Map and Imagery Laboratory, Santa Barbara, 93106. Larry Carver, Dept Head
Notes: Remote sensing/cartographic interpretation and information transfer laboratory and training available to all patrons.

ME —BIGELOW LABORATORY FOR OCEAN SCIENCES & MAINE DEPT OF MARINE RESOURCES, Library, McKown Point, West Boothbay Harbor, 04575. Pamela Shephard-Lupo, Librn
Holdings: Vols Cat
Budget: ($55,000)
Notes: This library presently serves two institutions. The Maine Dept of Marine Resources has maintained the library since 1957 and thus the majority of our holdings are geared to their needs, ie fish biology and stock assessment on a local, national and international level. In 1973 Bigelow Laboratory for Ocean Sciences came to West Boothbay Harbor and began to contribute to the library with a very specialized collection on the Gulf of Maine marine chemistry, phytoplankton and nutrient cycles.

NM —UNIVERSITY OF NEW MEXICO, Technology Application Center, 2500 Central SE, Albuquerque, 87131. Amy Budge, Photo Search Service
Holdings: Cat Maps Pix Slides Audiotapes Microforms
Notes: Remote sensing; energy information; all earth-oriented photography.

OH —PREFORMED LINE PRODUCTS CO, Research & Engineering Library, 660 Beta Drive, Mayfield Village, (Mailing add: PO Box 91129, Cleveland, 44101). Edwina T Barron, Librn
Holdings: Vols (11,500) Cat Mss Microfiche Pix VF
Budget: ($30,500)
Notes: Library covering research and engineering fields emphasizing this subject. Aerodynamic characteristics and electrical characteristics of power cables, communication cables (including fiber optics), cable support systems, as well as associated fittings and hardware; in service behavior of manufactured products and materials as it relates to its static and dynamic forces and environmental conditions; oceanographic cable fittings and terminations.

TN —UNIVERSITY OF TENNESSEE, Space Institute Library, Tullahoma, 37388. Helen B Mason, Librn
Holdings: Vols (14,000) Cat Microforms
Budget: ($50,000)
Notes: Incl NASA and other series of technical reports.

REMY see Renault-Roulier, G.

RENAISSANCE

†CA —CLAREMONT COLLEGES, Honnold Library, Claremont, 91711.
Notes: Florentine Renaissance, particularly 1450-1500. Angelo Poliziano (1454-1494), the humanist scholars and writers of the Medici circle, and the Platonic Academy.

CA —UNIVERSITY OF CALIFORNIA, SAN DIEGO, Central University Library, Mandeville Dept of Special Collections, La Jolla, 92093. Lynda Corey Claassen, Head
Holdings: Vols (4100) Cat Mss Maps Pix Slides
Notes: The Renaissance Collection is composed of the Library of Don Cameron Allen and the Whitfield Baldwin Collection. Much of classical authors in 16th and 17th century editions. Incl 3000 monographs dating from 1475 to 1750, which illuminate history, literature, politics, church history, philosophy and travel.

CA —UNIVERSITY OF CALIFORNIA, LOS ANGELES, Art Library, Elmer Belt Library of Vinciana, 405 Hilgard Ave, Los Angeles, 90024. Joyce Pellerano Ludmer, Art Librn
Holdings: Vols (10,000) Cat Pix Microforms VF
Notes: The Renaissance, with emphasis on Leonardo da Vinci.

CA —STANFORD UNIVERSITY LIBRARIES, Cecil H Green Library, Stanford, 94305. Michael T Ryan, Cur
Holdings: Vols Cat Maps
Notes: An emphasis in the Rare Book Collection.

CO —UNIVERSITY OF COLORADO, Libraries, Special Collections, Boulder, 80309. Nora J Quinlan, Head
Holdings: Vols 800
Notes: The Mandell Creighton Library. Renaissance papacy, Protestant reform and the Conciliar movement. Separate catalog.

CT —LEE ASH, (personal collection), 66 Humiston Dr, Bethany, 06525.
Holdings: Mss Maps Pix

DC —FOLGER SHAKESPEARE LIBRARY, 201 E Capitol St, Washington, 20003. Philip A Knachel, Acting Dir
Holdings: Vols (223,571) Cat Mss Pix Periodicals Microfilms
Notes: Collections described in *Catalog of Printed Books of the Folger Shakespeare Library*, 28 vols; *First Supplement*, 3 vols (Boston: G K Hall, 1970, 1976); *Second Supplement* in 2 vols (Boston: G K Hall, 1981); *Catalog of Manuscripts of the Folger Shakespeare Library*, 3 vols (Boston: G K Hall, 1971); and *The Widening Circle: The Story of the Folger Library and Its Collections* (Washington, DC: Folger Shakespeare Library, 1976). Collections incl 39 vols of plays with ms annotations and stage directions by John Philip Kemble. Library use restricted to advanced research scholars.

IL —NEWBERRY LIBRARY, 60 W Walton St, Chicago, 60610. Diana Haskell, Cur of Modern Mss
Holdings: Cat Mss Maps
Notes: Heaviest in-depth collecting for European history and literature occurs within the period 1300-1600, making the so-called Renaissance period the richest area for original research at this library.

KS —UNIVERSITY OF KANSAS, Kenneth Spencer Research Library, Special Collections Dept, Lawrence, 66045. Alexandra Mason, Librn
Holdings: Vols 10,000 Cat Mss Maps Pix
Notes: Summerfield Collection of Renaissance and Early Modern Printed Books. Renaissance mss. Noncirculating. Strong in French, Spanish, Italian political, economic and natural history; voyages and travels; law; humanists; some literature; good in emblem books, dictionaries, bibliography. Mss particularly good for economic history. Printed books include Leon Dorez' library and the historical portions of Sir William Stirling-Maxwell's library (strong in Spain and Charles V).

MI —UNIVERSITY OF MICHIGAN, Fine Arts Library, Tappan Hall, Ann Arbor, 48109. Margaret Jensen, Fine Arts Librn; Joy Alexander, Cur Slide Collection
Holdings: Vols (50,000) Cat Slides Microforms
Notes: The slide collection (250,000 slides) is owned and seviced by the History of Art Department; it is not part of the University of Michigan library system, but is used in conjunction with the library material, and housed in the same building.

MN —SAINT JOHN'S ABBEY & UNIVERSITY, Hill Monastic Manuscript Library, Collegeville, 56321. Julian G Plante, Dir
Holdings: Vols (61,000) Cat Mss Pix Slides Microforms
Notes: Films of 61,000 mss. The total number of codices or bound handwritten mss represents the holdings of several hundred libraries in Europe, mostly Austria, Spain, Ethiopia, West Germany, Portugal, and also Italy, Hungary, Poland, Great Britain, Belgium, Yugoslavia, France, Switzerland, and the Netherlands.

MO —NORTHEAST MISSOURI STATE UNIVERSITY, Pickler Memorial Library, Kirksville, 63501. George N Hartje, Librn
Holdings: Vols 25,950 Cat Microforms
Notes: English Renaissance and Reformation history.

MO —CENTER FOR REFORMATION RESEARCH, 6477 San Bonita Ave, Saint Louis, 63105. William S Meltby, Dir
Holdings: Cat Mss Maps Pix Microforms

MO —SAINT LOUIS UNIVERSITY, Pius XII Memorial Library, 3655 W Pine Blvd, Saint Louis, 63108. William Cole, Dir
Holdings: Slides Microforms
Notes: Collection covers all areas of learning and European history from Classical Antiquity to early modern period. Researchers using collection receive assistance in paleography, bibliography and reference search. Approx 10,000 1000-foot reels of microfilm (not counting master negatives) reproducing Vatican Library's Latin, Greek, Hebrew, Arabic and Ethiopic mss. Some 8000 100-foot reels of microfilm (again not counting master negative) reproducing rare and out of print books relating to subject areas in the mss. Over 50,000 color slides of medieval and Renaissance mss illuminations. A reference collection of modern materials relating to ms research.

NJ —PRINCETON UNIVERSITY, Library, Manuscript Collection, Nassau St, Princeton, 08540. Jean F Preston, Cur
Holdings: Mss Pix
Notes: The collection of Medieval and Renaissance manuscripts, totaling 350 book manuscripts, incl items collected by Robert Garrett and Grenville Kane. The collection is supplemented by several single leaves. See *Princeton University Library Chronicle*, v 3, p 123-35; v 11, p 37-44. Ricci, Seymour de *Census of Medieval and Renaissance Manuscripts in the United States and Canada* (New York: H W Wilson Co, 1935-40); and *Supplement*, ed by W H Bond, 1962.

NY —COLUMBIA UNIVERSITY LIBRARIES, Rare Book & Manuscript Library, 801 Butler Library, 535 W 114 St, New York, 10027. Kenneth A Lohf, Librn

NC —DUKE UNIVERSITY, William R Perkins Library, Rare Book Room, Durham, 27706. John L Sharpe, III, Cur
Notes: Manuscript collection of more than 150 items.

PA —HAVERFORD COLLEGE, Magill Library, Quaker Collection, Haverford, 19041. Edwin B Bonner, Librn & Cur
Holdings: Vols 105 Cat
Notes: Rare books and mss of the English Renaissance period, especially contemporaries of Shakespeare.

UT —BRIGHAM YOUNG UNIVERSITY, Harold B Lee Library, Unversity Hill, Provo, 84602. Sterling Albrecht, Dir
Holdings: Vols 1600 Cat Mss

ON —VICTORIA UNIVERSITY, Library, Centre for Reformation and Renaissance Studies, 71 Queen's Park Crescent, Toronto, M5S 1K7, Can. Robert C Brandeis, Chief Librn; James Estes, Dir
Holdings: Vols (15,000) Cat Slides
Notes: The CRRS concentrates on the

RENAISSANCE (cont.)

northern European countries and France; its chief strengths are Erasmus, 650 vols; early printed books, especially 16th century editions of Latin classics; bibliography and the history of printing. The Erasmus holdings are cataloged in W T McCready et al, "The Erasmus Collection in the Centre for Reformation and Renaissance Studies...A Catalogue"...*Reformation and Renaissance* 7 (1971), 32-76 and "A Supplementary List"...*Reformation and Renaissance*, 10 (1974), 116-119. Published catalogs. Humanist Editions of the Classics at CRRS, Toronto, 1979; Humanist Editions of Statutes and History at CRRS, Toronto, 1980; Bibles, Theological Treatises and Other Religious Literature 1491-1700 at CRRS, Toronto, 1981.

RENAISSANCE ART see Art, Renaissance

RENAISSANCE CIVILIZATION see Civilization, Renaissance

RENAISSANCE LAW see Law, Renaissance

RENAISSANCE MANUSCRIPTS see Manuscripts, Renaissance

RENAISSANCE MUSIC see Music, Renaissance

RENAL SYSTEM

RI —MIRIAM HOSPITAL MEDICAL LIBRARY, 164 Summit Ave, Providence, 02906. Ann LeClaire, Dir of Library Services
Holdings: Cat Cassettes
Notes: Special collection on the renal system with emphasis on kidney transplantation and dialysis.

RENAULT-ROULIER, G.

†VA —GEORGE C MARSHALL RESEARCH FOUNDATION AND LIBRARY, Drawer 920, Lexington, 24450. Royster Lyle Jr, Cur Collections
Holdings: Vols Cat Mss Maps Pix Phonorecords Audiotapes Films Filmstrips Microforms
Notes: About 400 posters-American, German, French; complete *Stars and Stripes* for WWII; approx 5000 cataloged photographs, over 5000 uncataloged Office of War information photos, and over 10,000 US Signal Corps photos (uncat). Approx 250 regimental histories, operation reports, and army manuals; published memoirs and letters of Marshall associates; official military histories (American, British); over 1200 maps-approx 300 newsmaps, 800 daily situation maps (European Theatre), 37 bound vols of daily situation maps 1944-1945; seven of the *Why We Fight* series (films). Major ms collections incl the papers of generals George C Marshall, Marshall S Carter, William T Sexton, Lucian Truscott, William R Arnold, Paul M Robinett, Frank McCarthy; colonels Collas Harris, Francis P Miller, William F Friedman; officers of the Women's Army Corps. Hearingsand government documents. Agency records copied from NARS. Vertical file arranged by subject.

RENDEZVOUS OF MOUNTAIN MEN see Mountain Men; Trapping and Trappers

RENEWABLE ENERGY SOURCES

CA —UNIVERSITY OF CALIFORNIA, RIVERSIDE, Physical Sciences Library, Riverside, 92517. Richard W Vierich, Librn
Holdings: Vols (89,000) Cat Microforms
Budget: ($347,700)
NY —CARY ARBORETUM OF THE NEW YORK BOTANICAL GARDEN, Institute of Ecosystem Studies, Library, Box AB,

Millbrook, 12545. Betsy Calvin, Librn
Holdings: Vols 10,000

RENO, MILO

IA —UNIVERSITY OF IOWA, University Libraries, Iowa City, 52242. Robert A McCown, Mss Librn
Holdings: Mss
Notes: Speeches, correspondence, news clippings, and other papers of the farm leader (Milo Reno) relating to the Iowa Division of the Farmers' Educational and Co-operative Union of America and the National Farmers' Holiday Association. 3 ft of mss.

REPAIR MANUALS

MI —MICHIGAN STATE UNIVERSITY, Libraries, Special Collections Div, East Lansing, 48824. Jannette Fiore, Librn
Notes: The Russel B Nye Popular Culture Collection in the Michigan State Univ Libraries incl over (45,000) items. Most of the collection is organized into 4 categories: comic art, popular fiction, popular information materials and materials relating to the popular performing arts. About 3900 items. Almanacs, Blue Books, and works popularizing knowledge or offering self-help and how-to advice. There are ca 350 issues of 100 19th and 20th century almanacs. The Blue Books incl ca 2000 Little Blue Books, over 600 Big Blue Books and a good number of issues of the various Haldeman-Julius magazines. In addition to almanacs and Blue Books, Popular Information incl books of advice on etiquette, life and love, how-to-succeed books, popular history, science and biography, and several hundred public schooltextbooks from the 19th and early 20th centuries.
NC —WILSON COUNTY TECHNICAL INSTITUTE, Library, 902 Herring Ave, PO Box 4305, Wilson, 27893. Shirley Gregory, Librn
Holdings: Vols (150) Cat Slides Phonorecords Audiotapes 16mm Films Filmstrips
Notes: Emphasis on operation, maintenance, and safety for operator's of earthmoving equipment and cranes. Incl 50 operator's manuals and 80 audiovisual programs.
PA —CARNEGIE LIBRARY OF PITTSBURGH, Science & Technology Dept, 4400 Forbes Ave, Pittsburgh, 15213. Catherine M Brosky, Dept Head
Notes: Collection of installation, maintenance and repair manuals, parts lists, some company reports and othe materials.
ON —METROPOLITAN TORONTO LIBRARY, Science & Technology Dept, 789 Yonge St, Toronto, M4W 2G8, Can. Margaret Walshe, Head
Holdings: Vols (120,000) Cat Microforms
Notes: Repair manual collection incl automobile shop manuals, truck, tractor, motorcycle, snowmobile, bicycle, outboard motors, and household appliance repair manuals and/or parts manuals. Also, television, radio, and hi-fi equipment schematic diagrams. Service information available for auto radios, CB radios, communication equipment, tape recorders.

REPATRIATION

CA —HOOVER INSTITUTION ON WAR, REVOLUTION & PEACE, Stanford University, Stanford, 94305. Milorad M Drachkovitch, Archivist
Holdings: Mss Pix
Notes: Two collections: (1) Papers of Julius Epstein, journalist, research associate at the Hoover Institution, and author of *Operation Keelhaul: The Story of Forced Repatriation*, incl correspondence, speeches and writings, clippings, photographs, and printed matter, 1939-72, relating to his research on the events of World War II, communism, forced repatriation of Russian prisoners of the Soviet Union following World War II, Katyn forest massacres, and unreported deaths of Soviet Cosmonauts, as well as his efforts to obtain restricted government documents on

these subjects. 180 ms boxes. (2) Three handwritten diaries, July 10, 1951-May 22, 1952, by Admiral Charles Turner Joy, Chief United Nations negotiator at the Korean military armistice negotiations at Panmunjom, 1951-53, mainly concerning prisoner of war issues and repatriation questions. 3 volsin 1/2 ms box.

REPERTORY THEATRE OF LINCOLN CENTER

NY —NEW YORK PUBLIC LIBRARY, Performing Arts Research Center, Billy Rose Theatre Collection, 111 Amsterdam Ave, New York, 10023. Dorothy L Swerdlove, Cur
Notes: Office and production files incl all activities at the Vivian Beaumont Theatre and The Forum Theatre under the management of Jules Irving, 1965-1973. Incl 183 cartons of material, much of which is still unprocessed, but which can be made available to researchers.

REPETTI, REV. WILLIAM C.

DC —GEORGETOWN UNIVERSITY, Library, Special Collections Div, 37 & O Sts NW, Washington, 20057. George M Barringer, Special Collections Librn; Nicholas B Sheetz, Mss Librn
Holdings: Mss Cat
Notes: Principally a collection of typescripts containing Fr Repetti's unpublished history of the Society of Jesus in the Philippines, 1589-1615; with other mss material and correspondence dealing with Fr Repetti's researches in Philippine Jesuit and seismological history and on the life of Pye Neale.

THE REPORTER (MAGAZINE)

NC —WAKE FOREST UNIVERSITY, Z Smith Reynolds Library, Artom Collection, Box 7777, Reynolds Station, Winston-Salem, 27109. Elen Knott, Archivist
Holdings: Cat Pix
Notes: World history, from 1949. Incl newspaper clippings, periodical tearsheets, press releases, research studies, documents, and pamphlets, covering domestic and foreign politics, government, economics, health, housing, civil rights, education, conservation, business, finance, the arts and humanities. Biographical file of over 1000 names. The collection was the news morgue of *The Reporter*, 1949-1968. Separate book catalog.

REPORTS, SCIENTIFIC AND TECHNICAL see Technical Reports

REPPLIER, AGNES

PA —FREE LIBRARY OF PHILADELPHIA, Rare Book Dept, Logan Sq, Philadelphia, 19103. Marie E Korey, Rare Book Librn
Holdings: Cat Mss
Notes: The Anne von Moschzisker Memorial Collection of 30 first editions and autograph letters.

REPRODUCTION

DC —CENTER FOR BIOETHICS, Library, Kennedy Institute, Georgetown University, 3520 Prospect St NW, Washington, 20057. Doris Goldstein, Dir; Judith Mistichelli, Senior Librn
Holdings: Vols (8200)
Notes: Largest library of its kind. Incl 31, 000 journal articles on applied ethics. Produces computer database *Bioethicsline*, available through MEDLARS; and the printed annual *Bibliography of Bioethics*. Other library publications are: *New Titles in Bioethics* (monthly); *Scope Notes* series on current topics.
MA —UNIVERSITY OF MASSACHUSETTS AT AMHERST, Library, Amherst, 01003. Siegfried Feller, Assoc Dir for Collection Development
Holdings: Cat
Notes: Veterinary medicine and animal

REPRODUCTION (cont.)

sciences. Special emphases; reproductive physiology, poultry genetics, animal nutrition.

TX —SOUTHWEST FOUNDATION FOR RESEARCH AND EDUCATION LIBRARY, Preston C Northrup Memorial Library, Baboon Information Center, W Loop 410 at Military Dr, PO Box 28147, San Antonio, 78284. Dorothy M Brooks, Baboon
Notes: Principle field of research: Birth defects, atherosclerosis, reproductive physiology, cancer, genetics, organic chemistry, parasitology, primatology and behavioral sciences and their application to problems of drug abuse, alcoholism and ecology. Maintains the largest baboon colony in the world.

REPTILES AND AMPHIBIANS

CA —CALIFORNIA ACADEMY OF SCIENCES, J W Mailliard Jr Library, Golden Gate Park, San Francisco, 94118. Ray Brian, Librn
Notes: Downs No 2160.

DC —SMITHSONIAN INSTITUTION LIBRARIES, Natural History Branch, Washington, 20560. Sylvia Churgin, Chief Librn
Holdings: Vols 1400 Cat Mss Maps Pix Slides Microforms

FL —ARCHBOLD BIOLOGICAL STATION, Library, Rt 2, Box 180, Lake Placid, 33852. Fred E Lohrer, Librn
Holdings: Vols (2000) Cat Periodicals

IL —FIELD MUSEUM OF NATURAL HISTORY, Library, Roosevelt Rd & Lake Shore Dr, Chicago, 60605. W Peyton Fawcett, Librn; Benjamin W Williams, Assoc Librn
Holdings: Vols (210,000) Cat
Budget: ($100,000)
Notes: Extensive collections--publications of learned societies and institutions and monographic works--in all fields of natural history, with emphasis on taxonomy and evolutionary biology; and on museum publications, American and foreign: anthropology, especially archaeology and ethnology of the Americas, Africa, East Asia, and Oceania; botany, particularly strong for the Americas; geology, chiefly paleontology and meteoritic studies; and zoology, worldwide (birds, fishes, insects, mammals, mollusks, reptiles and amphibians).

MI —UNIVERSITY OF MICHIGAN, Museums Library, Ann Arbor, 48109. Patricia B Yocum, Librn
Holdings: Vols 2500 Cat

NY —AMERICAN MUSEUM OF NATURAL HISTORY, Library Services Dept, Central Park W & 79th St, New York, 10024. Nina J Root, Chairwoman; Mary Genett, Asst Librn for Reference Services
Holdings: Vols (385,000) Cat Mss Maps Pix Slides Microforms
Notes: Nearly all collections are outstanding for depth of coverage and international range. Early and historic works, rare books, colored illustrations, and relevant serial publications necessary to the researches of the scientific staff and the work of the educational division. Open to the public.

PA —ZOOLOGICAL SOCIETY OF PHILADELPHIA, Library, 34 & Girard Ave, Philadelphia, 19104. Alyssa N Scheuermann, Librn
Holdings: Vols (500) Cat
Notes: Photocopying with permission.

PA —CARNEGIE LIBRARY OF PITTSBURGH, Science & Technology Dept, 4400 Forbes Ave, Pittsburgh, 15213. Catherine M Brosky, Dept Head
Notes: Subject of secondary interest with emphasis on North America. Covers paleobotany, vertebrates and invertebrates, foraminifera, mollusks, fish, reptiles, mammals. Abstracts, indexes, catalogs, bibliographies, journals, continuations, federal, state and society publications available.

WI —MILWAUKEE PUBLIC MUSEUM, Reference Library, 800 W Wells St, Milwaukee, 53233. Judith Campbell Turner, Museum Librn
Holdings: Vols (90,000) Cat Maps Microforms

REPTON, HUMPHREY, 1752-1818

MI —MICHIGAN STATE UNIVERSITY, Libraries, Special Collections Div, East Lansing, 48824. Jannette Fiore, Librn
Notes: The published works of Humphrey Repton renowned British landscape designer.

REPUBLIC OF TEXAS see
Texas—History

REPUBLIC STUDIOS CORPORATION

CA —UNIVERSITY OF CALIFORNIA, LOS ANGELES, Research Library, Dept of Special Collections, 405 Hilgard Ave, Los Angeles, 90024. Edward Shreeves, Chairman, Bibliographers Group; David S Zeidberg, Head
Notes: 69 linear feet of continuity scripts and shooting scripts.

REPUBLICAN NATIONAL COMMITTEE

NY —CORNELL UNIVERSITY LIBRARIES, Collection of Regional History, Dept of Manuscripts and Univ Archives, Ithaca, 14853.
Notes: Incl records, 1918-66, of some of the highest offices; microfilms, phonograph records, tape recordings, transcriptions of campaign speeches, one-minute television spots, newspaper clippings, cartoons, press releases, photos, minutes of meetings, and many other items.

REPUBLICAN PARTY

AZ —NORTHERN ARIZONA UNIVERSITY, Special Collection Library, CU Box 6022, Flagstaff, 86011. Peter M Whiteley, Coordr/Archivist; William Mullane, Librn
Notes: Republican Party of Arizona, Coconino County Committee Collection; records, 1952-1967. Also incl materials of the Flagstaff Republican Women's Club.

CA —UNIVERSITY OF CALIFORNIA, LOS ANGELES, Research Library, Dept of Special Collections, 405 Hilgard Ave, Los Angeles, 90024. Edward Shreeves, Chairman, Bibliographers Group; David S Zeidberg, Head
Notes: 8 linear feet of correspondence, pamphlets, and clippings concerning women's suffrage, the Progressive and Republican parties, minimum wage laws, etc.

DC —REPUBLICAN NATIONAL COMMITTEE LIBRARY, 310 First St SE, Washington, 20003. Joanna Evans, Librn
Holdings: Vols 5000 Cat Maps Microforms

IA —UNIVERSITY OF IOWA, University Libraries, Iowa City, 52242. Robert A McCown, Mss Librn
Holdings: Mss
Notes: Correspondence, subject files, speeches, trip files, photographs, tape recordings, notebooks, and other materials of the Chairman of the Republican National Committee, 1974-77. 45 ft of mss.

OH —RUTHERFORD B HAYES LIBRARY, 1337 Hayes Ave, Fremont, 43420. Watt P Marchman, Dir
Holdings: Cat Mss
Notes: Personal, business and political correspondence; receipts and other papers. Letterbooks of A L Conger and business papers of the Zanesville Street Railway.

REQUIEMS

NC —UNIVERSITY OF NORTH CAROLINA, CHAPEL HILL, Music Library, Hill Hall, Chapel Hill, 27514.
Holdings: Vols (90,000) Cat Mss Pix Slides Phonorecords Audiotapes Microforms
Budget: ($60,000)
Notes: Extensive holdings of early

theoretical treatises; complete editions; performing scores; music periodicals; reference works.

RESEARCH, MEDICAL see Medical Research

RESEARCH, MUSICAL see Musicology

RESEARCH, VETERINARY see Veterinary Research

RESEARCH TRIANGLE PARK, NORTH CAROLINA

NC —DUKE UNIVERSITY, William R Perkins Library, Manuscript Dept, Durham, 27706. Ellen Gartrell, Cur of Mss
Holdings: Cat Mss
Notes: Strongest for textile and tobacco industries in Southeastern US, 19th-20th centuries. Incl papers of B N Duke, Richard H Wright, British-American Tobacco Co; business records of textile mills and several lumber companies, Romeo Guest papers on development of Research Triangle Park, North Carolina.

RESETTLEMENT see Rehabilitation, Rural

RESIDENCES see Architecture, Domestic

RESISTANCE OF MATERIALS see Strength of Materials

RESISTANCE WELDING see Welding

RESORTS see Health Resorts, Watering Places, Etc.

RESOURCE MANAGEMENT see Conservation of Natural Resources

RESOURCES, MARINE see Marine Resources

RESOURCES, NATURAL see Natural Resources

RESPIRATION

MA —INSTRUMENTATION LABORATORY, Library, 113 Hartwell Ave, Lexington, 02173. Jacqueline R Kates, Librn
Holdings: Vols (6000) Cat Microforms Reprints

RESPIRATORY ORGANS—DISEASES

RI —MIRIAM HOSPITAL MEDICAL LIBRARY, 164 Summit Ave, Providence, 02906. Ann LeClaire, Dir of Library Services
Holdings: Cat Cassettes
Notes: Special collection on the renal system with emphasis on kidney transplantation and dialysis.

WV —US VETERANS ADMINISTRATION HOSPITAL, Library, 1540 Spring Valley Dr, Huntington, 25704. Evelyn J Schaffer, Librn
Holdings: Vols (3700) Cat Slides Phonorecords Audiotapes Videotapes 16mm Films Filmstrips Microforms

RESPONSA

DC —LIBRARY OF CONGRESS, African and Middle Eastern Division, Washington, 20540.
Holdings: Cat Mss Microforms
Notes: Hebraica: about 109,000 vols in Hebrew, Yiddish, Judeo-Arabic, Judeo-Persian, Ladino, Syriac, Ethiopic; espec strong in Biblical subjects, responsa literature, and socio-political aspects.

FL —UNIVERSITY OF FLORIDA LIBRARY, Isser and Rae Price Library of Judaica, 18 Libr East, Gainesville, 32611. Robert Singerman, Head Librn
Budget: ($30,000)
Notes: Total holdings estimated at 55,000

RESPONSA (cont.)

vols dealing with the political, social, economic and intellectual history of the Jews in the ancient, medieval and modern periods and in all geographic areas. The following areas are especially well represented by printed matter in all relevant languages: Bibliography, Festschriften, History, Bible, Judaism and Jewish theology, liturgy, responsa, rabbinical literature, Jewish law, Hebrew language and literature, Yiddish language and literature, anti-semitism, Zionism, Palestine and the *Yishuv*, and the State of Israel. German and American Judaica form a collecting emphasis with holdings for all the standard histories as well as histories of individual synagogues, institutions and local communities. Works in Hebrew and Yiddish comprise about 60 percent of the collection (estimated 30,000 vols). With few exceptions, holdingsare limited to nineteenth and twentieth century imprints, with complete sets of journals and thousands of ephemeral pamphlets, many of them commemorating anniversaries, enhancing the research value of the collection, the largest Judaica research library in the southeastern United States. Only about half of the collection is cataloged; the collection is a circulating one and vols may be borrowed on interlibrary loan. Incl the Leonard C Mishkin Collection (40,000 vols), the largest personal Judaica collection in the United States, the Shlomo Marenof Collection (3500 vols), and the inventory of Bernard Morgenstern's Lower East Side Book Store (8000 vols). Scholars should inquire in advance of their visit. *The Isser and Rae Price Library of Judaica* Report (circulation 2900 copies) is mailed gratis twice a year to all interested parties. Special catalogs:Pre-1881 Hebrew imprints recorded in a chronological card file.

MA —HEBREW COLLEGE, Jacob & Rose Grossman Library and Lawrence Jay & Anne Cable Rubenstein Library, 43 Hawes St, Brookline, 02146. Maurice Tuchman, Librn
Holdings: Vols 700 Cat Mss
Notes: Responsa literature.

NY —YESHIVA UNIVERSITY, Library, 500 West 185th Street, New York, 10033. Pearl Berger
Holdings: Cat

OH —HEBREW UNION COLLEGE-JEWISH INSTITUTE OF RELIGION, Klau Library, 3101 Clifton Ave, Cincinnati, 45220. David J Gilner, Reference Librn
Holdings: Cat
Notes: Contains half of the Freehof collection of responsa literature. Strongest in Jewish civil law.

RESTAURANT MANAGEMENT see Hotel and Restaurant Management

RESTAURANTS, LUNCH ROOMS, BARS, ETC.

CA —UNIVERSITY OF CALIFORNIA, LOS ANGELES, Research Library, Dept of Special Collections, 405 Hilgard Ave, Los Angeles, 90024. Edward Shreeves, Chairman, Bibliographers Group; David S Zeidberg, Head
Holdings: // Uncat Mss
Notes: The Clifford E Clinton Collection: 3 linear feet of mss and clippings from the collection of the owner of Clinton's Cafeteria, Los Angeles.

DE —WIDENER UNIVERSITY, Delaware Campus Library, Box 7139, Concord Pike, Wilmington, 19803. Jane E Hukill, Library Dir
Holdings: Vols (48,000) Microforms
Notes: Incl food service, restaurants, motels, volume feeding, cookery.

NY —CORNELL UNIVERSITY LIBRARIES, Hotel Administration Library, Statler Hall, Ithaca, 14853. Margaret J Oaksford, Librn
Holdings: Vols (25,000) Cat Mss Maps
Budget: ($60,000)
Notes: Extensive collections on management, travel, hotels, food and beverage, wine, real estate and tourism. Incl menu collection.

RESTAURANTS, LUNCH ROOMS, ETC. —MANAGEMENT see Hotel and Restaurant Management

RESTORATION MOVEMENT (CHRISTIAN) see Restoration of the Church (Movement)

RESTORATION OF ART OBJECTS see Art Objects—Conservation and Restoration

RESTORATION OF BOOKS see Books—Conservation and Restoration

RESTORATION OF BUILDINGS see Architecture—Conservation and Restoration

RESTORATION OF MANUSCRIPTS see Manuscripts—Conservation and Restoration

RESTORATION OF THE CHURCH (MOVEMENT)

OK —MIDWEST CHRISTIAN COLLEGE, Library, 6600 N Kelley Ave, Oklahoma City, 73111. Jean Cavett, Dir
Holdings: Vols (7000) Cat Pix Phonorecords Audiotapes Filmstrips Microforms
Notes: The Restoration Movement (to restore the Church to its New Testament form). Incl churches called "Christian Churches," Churches of Christ, "Disciples of Christ," and a few called just "Christ's Church."

RESTRAINT OF ANIMALS see Animals, Treatment of

RETAIL ADVERTISING see Advertising

RETAIL TRADE

IL —UNIVERSITY OF ILLINOIS, URBANA/CHAMPAIGN, Library, Home Economics Library, 314 Bevier Hall, Champaign, 61820. Barbara C Swain, Librn
Holdings: Vols Cat
Notes: Textiles, clothing, and interior design.

IL —CHICAGO HISTORICAL SOCIETY, Library, Clark St at North Ave, Chicago, 60614. Robert L Brubaker, Librn
Holdings: Vols (150,000) Cat
Notes: Catalogs of major mail order houses and many special industries and stores in Chicago (and some firms elsewhere) since the late 19th century.

IL —MONTGOMERY WARD CORPORATE LIBRARY, One Montgomery Ward Plaza, Chicago, 60671. Barbara J Burnett, Librn
Holdings: Vols (1300) Cat Mss Pix

IL —SEARS, ROEBUCK & CO, Merchandise Development & Testing Laboratory Library, Sears Tower, Dept 817, Chicago, 60684. Mary M McCarron, Librn
Holdings: Cat Pix Microforms
Notes: Microfilmed sets of Sears, Roebuck catalogs have been placed in more than 100 libraries in key geographic locations. Contain catalogs from 1888 to date.

IN —PURDUE UNIVERSITY LIBRARIES, Consumer & Family Sciences Library, Stone Hall W, West Lafayette, 47907. Emily Alward, Librn
Holdings: Vols (14,000) Cat

MI —OAKLAND COMMUNITY COLLEGE, Auburn Hills Campus, Learning Resources Center, 2900 Featherstone Rd, Auburn Hills, 48057. Eugene F Larson, Dept Chairman
Holdings: Vols 500 Cat Slides Audiotapes Videotapes 16mm Films Filmstrips

OR —BASSIST COLLEGE LIBRARY, 2000 SW Fifth Ave, Portland, 97201. Norma Bassist, Librn
Holdings: Vols 575 Cat Mss Pix Slides

RETAIL TRADE AS A PROFESSION

NY —ELIZABETH SETON COLLEGE LIBRARY, Yonkers, 10701. Sr Margaret Sullivan, Librn

SC —HORRY GEORGETOWN TECHNICAL COLLEGE, Library, Hwy 501, Box 1966, Conway, 29526. Barbara Brittain, Librn
Holdings: Vols (20,000) Cat Maps Slides Microforms

RETAILING—VOCATIONAL GUIDANCE see Retail Trade As a Profession

RETARDED CHILDREN see Mentally Handicapped Children; Slow-Learning Children

RETI, RUDOLPH, 1885-1957

DC —LIBRARY OF CONGRESS, Music Division, Washington, 20540.
Notes: Music mss and papers of Rudolph Reti.

RETIREMENT

DC —AMERICAN ASSOCIATION OF RETIRED PERSONS (AARP), National Gerontology Resource Center, 1909 K St NW, Washington, 20049. Paula M Lovas, Librn; Mary F Power, Coordr, Reference Service
Holdings: Vols (15,000) Cat Microforms
Budget: ($60,000)
Notes: Retirement, retirement planning and social gerontology. Incl government documents and reports, journals, and bibliographies.

DC —US DEPT OF LABOR, Library, 200 Constitution Ave NW, Washington, 20210. Sabina Jacobson, Dir
Holdings: Vols (550,000) Cat

MI —INSTITUTE OF GERONTOLOGY, Gerontology Library, University of Michigan, 300 N Ingalls St, Ann Arbor, 48109. Willie M Edwards, Librn
Holdings: Vols (10,000) Cat Pix Audiotapes 16mm Films
Notes: All subjects concerning the aged and aging in the US, Western Europe and strong emphasis on Great Britain. On VF (24) unpublished research papers, newsletters from elderly association, centers on aging.

OR —UNIVERSITY OF OREGON LIBRARY, 1607 Agate St, Eugene, 97403. Ruth M Brewer, Resource Librn
Notes: Social and psychological aspects of aging.

ON —CANADA DEPT OF LABOUR, Library, Ottawa, K1A 0J2, Can. Monique Marchand, Chief Librn
Holdings: Vols (100,000) Cat Microforms

RETIREMENT PENSIONS see Old Age Pensions

RETRIBUTION see Future Life

RETTIE, JAMES C.

OR —UNIVERSITY OF OREGON, Library, Eugene, 97403. Kenneth W Duckett, Curator
Notes: Papers of James C Rettie, Senior Economist of the Department of the Interior.

REUBEN, WILLIAM A.

MI —UNIVERSITY OF MICHIGAN, Dept of Rare Books & Special Collections, Ann Arbor, 48109. Edward C Weber, Head, Labadie Collection
Notes: The Labadie Collection of radical materials, containing papers, tracts, handbills, and publications of minority political and social reform organizations from the mid-1800s to the present, incl 8000 serial titles and 20,000 uncataloged pamphlets. Also ms collections of the papers of William A Reuben.

REUCHLIN, JOHANN

CA —STANFORD UNIVERSITY LIBRARIES, Cecil H Green Library,

REUCHLIN, JOHANN (cont.)

Stanford, 94305. Peter R Frank, Cur, CDP-Germanic Collection
Notes: Extensive holdings in the field of Reformation and Counter-Reformation. First and early editions by Luther, Melanchthon, Bugenhagen, Cochleus, Eck, Hutten, Reuchlin, and minor figures in Special Collections.

REUSE OF WATER see Water Reuse

REUTHER, WALTER

†MA —JOHN F KENNEDY LIBRARY, Columbia Point, Boston, 02125. Dan H Fenn Jr, Dir
Holdings: // Cat Mss Audiotapes
Notes: Tapes, notes, and transcripts of interviews conducted by Frank Cormier and William Eaton in preparation for their book *Reuther,* the biography of Walter Reuther, 1967-1970. 1 linear ft of mss. Holdings are described in "Historical Materials in the John F Kennedy Library." Copies may be obtained by writing the Research Archivist.
MI —WAYNE STATE UNIVERSITY, Walter P Reuther Library, Archives of Labor & Urban Affairs, Detroit, 48202. Philip Mason, Dir
Holdings: Vols (4000) Cat Mss Pix Slides Phonorecords Audiotapes Videotapes 16mm Films Filmstrips Microforms
Budget: ($450,000)
Notes: See Warner Pflug, *A Guide to the Archives of Labor History and Urban Affairs* (Wayne State University Press, 1974).

REVELATION

SC —UNIVERSITY OF SOUTH CAROLINA, Thomas Cooper Library, Columbia, 29208. Kenneth E Toombs, Dir of Libraries; Roger Mortimer, Rare Book Librn
Holdings: Vols 45 Cat
Notes: One of the few very strong collections of Muggletonian theology.

REVERE, ANNE

MA —BOSTON UNIVERSITY, Mugar Memorial Library, Special Collections Dept, 771 Commonwealth Ave, Boston, 02215. Howard B Gotlieb, Dir
Holdings: Cat Mss Pix Scrapbooks

REVERE, PAUL

MA —AMERICAN ANTIQUARIAN SOCIETY LIBRARY, 185 Salisbury St, Worcester, 01609. Marcus A McCorison, Dir & Librn
Notes: A rare collection relating to the beginnings of the art among Anglo-Americans. Incl copies of all of Paul Revere's engravings, and nearly all of Peter Pelhams's mezzotints, as well as most of the works by other early American engravers. Examples of about half the works in Stauffer and Fielding subject and engraver catalogs.

REVERSE OSMOSIS TECHNOLOGY

MA —ABCOR, INC, Library, 850 Main St, Wilmington, 01887. Eileen Smith, Librn
Holdings: Vols (2000) Cat
Budget: ($10,000)
Notes: Reverse osmosis technology. Particularly strong in government technical reports.

REVIVAL (RELIGION) see Evangelistic Work

REVOLUTION, AMERICAN see U.s. —History—Revolution

REVOLUTION, FRENCH see France—History—Revolution, 1789-1799

REVOLUTION OF 1848 IN FRANCE see France—History—February Revolution, 1848

REVOLUTIONS

CA —HOOVER INSTITUTION ON WAR, REVOLUTION & PEACE, Stanford

University, Stanford, 94305. Milorad M Drachkovitch, Archivist
Holdings: Cat Mss Maps Pix Slides Microforms
Notes: One of the nation's most extensive collections in many specialized areas. Described in *Archival and Manuscript Materials at the Hoover Institution...A Checklist of Major Collections* (July 1977).
PA —UNIVERSITY OF PITTSBURGH, Hillman Library, Pittsburgh, 15260. Glenora E Rossell, Head
Holdings: Vols 3000 Cat Microforms
Notes: Social and political history of Latin America in the 20th century with emphasis on revolutionary and radical movements, and social change.

REXROTH, KENNETH, 1905-1982

CA —UNIVERSITY OF CALIFORNIA, LOS ANGELES, Research Library, Dept of Special Collections, 405 Hilgard Ave, Los Angeles, 90024. Edward Shreeves, Chairman, Bibliographers Group; David S Zeidberg, Head
Holdings: Vols 50 Mss
Notes: 50 first and other editions of his books; 21 linear feet of mss, correspondence and ephemera. No photocopying.
NV —UNIVERSITY OF NEVADA, RENO, University Library, Special Collections Dept, Reno, 89557. Robert E Blesse, Head
Holdings: // Vols (99) Cat
Notes: Includes individual works by author in all editions including translations; also prefaces, introductions, published correspondence, appearances in anthologies, periodicals, etc. Bibliographical research collection, part of Modern Authors Collection.

REYNARD THE FOX

OH —CLEVELAND PUBLIC LIBRARY, Fine Arts and Special Collections Department, 325 Superior Ave, Cleveland, 44114. Alice N Loranth, Head
Holdings: Vols (700) Cat Mss
Notes: Part of the Fables Collection, which is strong in Medieval European and Oriental works. Numerous rare and early editions of Reynard the Fox (200 vols), Panchatantra, Bidpai, Hitopadesa, etc, are incl. Aesop and the modern fabulists are incl only by representative editions.
See also entry under Fables

REYNOLDS, DYER MARION ICHABOD

TN —MEMPHIS STATE UNIVERSITY, John Willard Brister Library, Memphis, 38152. John Terreo, Special Collections Librn
Notes: Dyer Marion "Ichabod" Reynolds Circus Collection, 1878-1980. A multi-formated collection of photographic negatives and prints, letters, newspaper and periodical clippings, scrapbooks, albums, handbills, posters, route cards, couriers, lithographs, and small artifacts documenting in general details the zenith and gradual decline of the American Circus as the dominant form of entertainment in the US. Correspondence incl letters from the Reynolds family to Reynolds and from Reynolds to circus performers and employees concerning various topics about the circus. Unpublished finding aid to the collection can be found in the Mississippi Valley Collection.

REYNOLDS, GENE

CA —UNIVERSITY OF CALIFORNIA, LOS ANGELES, Theater Arts Library, Los Angeles, 90024. Edward Shreeves, Chairman, Bibliographers Group; Audree Malkin, Head, Theater Arts Library
Notes: Gene Reynolds (producer) Collection: complete files for the *Lou Grant* and *M*A*S*H* television series, incl various versions of the scripts, research materials, and production materials.

REZNIKOFF, CHARLES

AZ —UNIVERSITY OF ARIZONA, University Library, Special Collections,

Tucson, 85721. Louis A Hieb, Head
Holdings: Vols (7000) Cat Mss Microforms
Budget: ($30,000)
Notes: In the 20th century, the major emphasis is Bukowski, Wakoski, Wilder, Reznikoff, Ginzberg, Ferlinghetti, Snyder, Whalen, Everson, Joyce Carol Oates, and Kurt Vonnegut.
CA —UNIVERSITY OF CALIFORNIA, SAN DIEGO, Central University Library, Mandeville Dept of Special Collections, La Jolla, 92093. Lynda Corey Claassen, Head; Michael Davidson, Cur, Archive for New Poetry
Notes: An extensive collection of modern English-language poetry published since World War II, the Archive contains over 28,000 books, over 1000 magazine titles, and some 900 tapes and records. The Archive maintains substantial collections of papers from Paul Blackburn, Charles Reznikoff, Lew Welch, Jerome Rothenberg, Louis Zukofsky, and other major contemporary American poets.
SC —COLLEGE OF CHARLESTON LIBRARY, Special Collections Dept, Charleston, 29401.
Notes: Typescript of the first section of Reznikoff's book, The Jews of Charleston.

RHAEDER, HAROLD A.

DC —SMITHSONIAN INSTITUTION, Archives Div, Washington, 20560. William W Moss, Archivist
Holdings: Cat Mss Maps Pix Slides
Notes: The archives have accessioned, processed and described the records of the US National Museum's Division of Mollusks, 1885-1951, principally outgoing correspondence from Honorary Curator William H Dall (q v), Curator Paul Bartsch and Assistant Curator Harold A Rhaeder covering the period 1885-1937.

RHATICUS

MN —UNIVERSITY OF MINNESOTA, O Meredith Wilson Library, 309 19 Ave S, Minneapolis, 55455. Austin J McLean, Chief, Special Collections
Holdings: Vols (103) // Cat Mss
Notes: Basically mathematical astronomy with emphasis on eclipses. Particular strengths are the works of such authors as Delambre, Euclid, Newton, Ptolemy, and Rhaticus. Important in this respect are 6 of the 10 known printed editions of the Alphonsine Astronomical Tables.

RHAETO-ROMANIC LANGUAGE see Raeto-Romance Language and Literature

RHETORIC

MI —NORTHERN MICHIGAN UNIVERSITY, Lydia M Olson Library, Elizabeth L Harden Drive, Marquette, 49855. Stephen H Peters, Cataloger
Notes: A section of the personal library of Moses Coit Tyler containing a large number of books on the foundations of language and rhetoric.

RHEUMATIC DISEASES see Rheumatism

RHEUMATISM

CT —YALE UNIVERSITY, Medical Historical Library, Klebs Collection, 333 Cedar St, New Haven, 06520. Ferenc A Gyorgyey, Librn
Notes: The Arnold Carl Klebs Medical Collection of books, pamphlets, etc, incl the library of his father, Edwin T A Klebs, pathologist. Strong in bibliography of early printed medical books, herbals, plague tracts, inoculation, vaccination and tubercular diseases.
NY —HOSPITAL FOR SPECIAL SURGERY, Kim Barrett Memorial Library, 535 E 70 St, New York, 10021. Munir U Din, Librn
Holdings: Vols 2520 Cat Slides Audiotapes Videotapes 16mm Films
Budget: $12,000
Notes: Incl 2520 books, 2493 bound

RHEUMATISM (cont.)

journals, 98 videotapes, 117 sound slide programs, 7 motion pictures, 22 audiotapes. No photocopying.
See also entry under Diseases - Rheumatic
TX —HOUSTON ACADEMY OF MEDICINE-TEXAS MEDICAL CENTER, Library, Jesse H Jones Library Bldg, Houston, 77030. Elizabeth Borst White, Special Collections Librn
Holdings: Vols (1300) Mss Pix
Notes: Burbank Collection on Arthritis, Rheumatism and Gout. An exhaustive collection on arthritis and gout before 1957. Largely from the 16th-19th centuries (also a medical manuscript dated about 1450). Bound volumes of German, French and American offprints complement the monograph collection. In 1983 the Kevin Fraser Addition to this Collection included 130 titles published before 1900.

RHEUMATOID ARTHRITIS IN CHILDREN

MD —NATIONAL LIBRARY OF MEDICINE, 8600 Rockville Pike, Bethesda, 20209. Harold M Schoolinam, Actg Dir
Budget: ($46,400)

RHINE, J. B.

NC —DUKE UNIVERSITY, William R Perkins Library, Manuscript Dept, Durham, 27706. Ellen Gartrell, Cur of Mss
Holdings: Mss
Notes: Correspondence, research notes, financial records, reprints of J B Rhine and Parapsychology Laboratory at Duke (ca 200,000 items, 1934-62).

RHOADS, J. E., AND SONS

DE —HAGLEY MUSEUM AND LIBRARY, Eleutherian Mills-Hagley Foundation Inc, PO Box 3630, Greenville, 19807. Richmond D Williams, Dir; Heddy A Richter, Imprints Librn
Notes: Records of J E Rhoads & Sons (1727-1962; 550 cubic feet), leather manufacturers of Wilmington, Delaware. The archive incl administrative, financial, production and sales records. There is also a good deal of printed and photographic material.

RHODE ISLAND

RI —PROVIDENCE JOURNAL CO, News Library, 75 Fountain St, Providence, 02902. Joseph O Mehr, Librn
Holdings: Maps Pix Microforms Clippings
Notes: News clippings, primarily concerning Rhode Island and Rhode Islanders. Compiles Journal-Bulletin Almanac, (A Rhode Island Reference Book).

RHODE ISLAND—GENEALOGY

RI —PROVIDENCE PUBLIC LIBRARY, 150 Empire St, Providence, 02903. Lance J Bauer, Special Collections Librn
Notes: The Arnold Collection (Knight Memorial Library) consists of tombstone records, family notes, probate records, newspaper clippings, and books relating to Rhode Island genealogy and history. The core of the collection consists of the tombstone records and family notes. The greater part of this material has been typed from mss information that was gathered by James Arnold. The tombstone records are arranged in loose-leaf folders by cities and towns of Rhode Island. The family notes are also arranged in loose-leaf folders, but alphabetically by family name. All this material has been indexed. Because of its uniqueness, the core collection is invaluable to anyone searching for local genealogical information.
RI —RHODE ISLAND HISTORICAL SOCIETY, Library, 121 Hope St, Providence, 02906. Paul R Campbell, Library Dir
Holdings: Vols (150,000) Cat Mss Maps Pix

Films Microforms
Notes: Books do not circulate. No interlibrary loan.
RI —WESTERLY PUBLIC LIBRARY, Broad St, Westerly, 02891. David J Panciera, Library Dir
Holdings: Vols (3000) Cat Mss Maps Pix Audiotapes Microforms
Notes: Extensive coverage of history of Westerly and surrounding area; also general material on Rhode Island and Connecticut. Books, clippings, mss, etc. Many unique family genealogies; local photographs; postcards. Special materials on Seventh-Day Baptist Church; Westerly granite industry; Wilcox Park; Watch Hill. Separate catalog.

RHODE ISLAND—HISTORY

MA —OLD STURBRIDGE VILLAGE, Research Library, Sturbridge, 01566. Theresa Rini Percy, Librn
Holdings: Cat Microforms
Notes: To 1900.
†NY —UNIVERSITY OF ROCHESTER, Rush Rhees Library, History of Medicine Section, Rochester, 14627.
Notes: A collection of some 400 items, mostly letters and mss, relating to the Bartlett family of Rhode Island. Incl items concerning the medical career of Elisha Bartlett from 1832-1855; also correspondence with contemporary physicians and surgeons.
RI —UNIVERSITY OF RHODE ISLAND, Library, Special Collections, Kingston, 02881. David Maslyn, Head
Notes: Extensive collections.
RI —US NAVAL WAR COLLEGE, Historical Collection & Museum, Newport, 02841. Anthony S Nicolosi, Dir; Evelyn Cherpak, Cur
Holdings: Mss
Notes: Collections incl over 200,000 separate pieces; chiefly papers of naval officers and records of organizations associated with the US Navy, the Naval War College, the college's major study areas, and the Navy in the Narragansett Bay region; oral history collection; Naval War College Archives, 1884-present; records of conferences held at the College; newspaper collections dealing with naval themes and military conflicts.
RI —BROWN UNIVERSITY, John Hay Library, 20 Prospect St, Providence, 02912. Mark N Brown, Cur Mss
Holdings: Vols 15,000 Cat Mss Maps Pix
Notes: Numerous collections involving the history of Rhode Island. Of particular importance are the Rhode Island Collection; The Sydney S Rider Collection (qv); The Dorr Collection (qv); and The Charles Warren Lippitt Collection (qv). 150,000 ms pieces. Rhode Island Manuscripts, 1638-1912. Letters, mss, and documents (ca three thousand items) pertaining to Rhode Island, the bulk of which date from 1638 to 1840. Subjects incl Colonial, Revolutionary, and Federal history; trade; shipping; government; and politics. There are eight letters and documents by Roger Williams, a letter signed by George Washington, and large groups of papers for Benjamin Bourne, Benjamin and Henry Fry, the Providence-Norwich Turnpike Society, the Washington Insurance Company, and Greene and Turner families. Solomon Drowne papers. He was a physician and Professor of Botany atBrown, Class of 1773. Mss incl accounts, invoices, receipts; originals and copies of prose and poetry; notes of Dr Drowne; sketches and valentines; political, legal and military documents; and ships' papers. Subjects incl Colonial and Revolutionary history of Rhode Island and Brown University; medicine and botany 1770-1834; the early history of Morgantown, Virginia; Union, Pennsylvania; and Marietta, Ohio; business and trade in the Colonial period; and the Continental Congress. Correspondence with most persons of importance in his time.
RI —PROVIDENCE PUBLIC LIBRARY, 150 Empire St, Providence, 02903. Lance J Bauer, Special Collections Librn
Notes: The Arnold Collection (Knight

Memorial Library) consists of tombstone records, family notes, probate records, newspaper clippings, and books relating to Rhode Island genealogy and history. The core of the collection consists of the tombstone records and family notes. The greater part of this material has been typed from mss information that was gathered by James Arnold. The tombstone records are arranged in loose-leaf folders by cities and towns. The family notes are also arranged in loose-leaf folders, but alphabetically by family name. All this material has been indexed. Because of its uniqueness, the core collection is invaluable to anyone searching for local genealogical information.
See also entry under Photographs - Collections
RI —RHODE ISLAND HISTORICAL SOCIETY, Library, 121 Hope St, Providence, 02906. Paul R Campbell, Library Dir
Holdings: Vols (150,000) Cat Mss Maps Pix Films Microforms
Notes: Books do not circulate. No interlibrary loan.
†RI —RHODE ISLAND JEWISH HISTORICAL ASSOCIATION, 130 Sessions St, Providence, 02906.
Notes: History of Rhode Island Jews and Jews in the US.
RI —RHODE ISLAND STATE ARCHIVES, Library, Room 43, State House, Smith St, Providence, 02903. Phyllis Silva, Dir
Holdings: Cat Mss Maps Microforms
Notes: All original mss, 1638-1860, Colony Records, census, Petition to Gen Assembly, Letters to and from governors, Revolutionary War Records, etc. We are primarily a General Assembly Archives.
RI —WESTERLY PUBLIC LIBRARY, Broad St, Westerly, 02891. David J Panciera, Library Dir
Holdings: Vols (3000) Cat Mss Maps Pix Audiotapes Microforms
Notes: Extensive coverage of history of Westerly and surrounding area; also general material on Rhode Island and Connecticut. Books, clippings, mss, etc. Many unique family genealogies; local photographs; postcards. Special materials on Seventh-Day Baptist Church; Westerly granite industry; Wilcox Park; Watch Hill. Separate catalog.

RHODE ISLAND—INDUSTRIES

RI —RHODE ISLAND HISTORICAL SOCIETY, Library, 121 Hope St, Providence, 02906. Paul R Campbell, Library Dir
Holdings: Mss
Budget: ($200,000)
Notes: The Brown and Ives collection of manufacturing records. Incl the records of the Brown and Ives firm; their principal management agency, the firm of Goddard Brothers; and cotton mills owned by Brown and Ives. Collection incl 1000 mss.

RHODE ISLAND—MAPS

RI —PROVIDENCE PUBLIC LIBRARY, Rhode Island Collection, 150 Empire St, Providence, 02903. Jeanne L Richardson, Librn
Notes: Rhode Island Collection is divided into five categories: books; maps; pictures and pamphlets; plus the Rhode Island Index: 4 catalog cases (total of 185 drawers) containing index to material on Rhode Island. This is primarily a subject index. Author cards made only for books and articles by Rhode Island authors; title cards for periodicals in collection. *Providence Journal* and *Evening Bulletin* are indexed daily for all pertinent articles about the state and its people. Incl are cards for pertinent articles in books and periodicals in other parts of the library.

RHODE ISLAND—POLITICS AND GOVERNMENT

RI —PROVIDENCE PUBLIC LIBRARY, 150 Empire St, Providence, 02903. Lance J

RHODE ISLAND—POLITICS AND GOVERNMENT (cont.)

Bauer, Special Collections Librn
Notes: The Daniel Berkeley Updike Autograph Collection of 800 ms letters and historical documents, primarily New England, from late 17th to mid-19th century with emphasis on Rhode Island politics; American Revolution; French military figures; naval heroes of the Revolution, Tripolitan War and War of 1812; Civil War figures and US Presidents. Illustrious personages represented incl: Henry David Thoreau, Daniel Webster, John Hay, Marquis de Lafayette, Henry Wadsworth Longfellow, and other notables. Material must be used in-house. Limited photocopying for educational purposes only.

RHODE ISLAND—THEATRES

IA —UNIVERSITY OF IOWA, University Libraries, Iowa City, 52242. Robert A McCown, Mss Librn
Holdings: Mss
Notes: Keith/Albee Vaudeville Collection. Records of a vaudeville, theatre, and moving-pictures business established by Benjamin Franklin Keith, 1846-1914, and Edward Franklin Albee, 1857-1930. The collection includes clipping books, report books, cash books, subject files, signs and posters. Theatres in the following cities are represented in the collection: Providence, RI, Pawtucket, RI, Woonsocket, RI, and Webster, Mass. The business was later part of RKO Pictures, Inc. Unpublished register in the library. 50 ft of mss.

RHODES, CECIL

CT —YALE UNIVERSITY, Box 1603A, Yale Station, New Haven, 06520.

RHODES, EUGENE MANLOVE

NM —NEW MEXICO STATE UNIVERSITY, Library, Box 3475, Las Cruces, 88003. James Dyke, Dir
Holdings: Vols 91 Cat
Notes: Books, manuscripts, etc by and about Eugene Manlove Rhodes, New Mexico author.

RHODES, JOHN J.

AZ —ARIZONA STATE UNIVERSITY, Library, Arizona Collection, Tempe, 85281. Edward C Oetting, Head
Holdings: Cat Mss
Notes: Papers, etc.

RHODESIA

CA —HOOVER INSTITUTION ON WAR, REVOLUTION & PEACE, Stanford University, Stanford, 94305. Milorad M Drachkovitch, Archivist
Notes: Collection of leaflets, newsletters, pamphlets, and other ephemera of various political action groups and other organizations, 1969-1974, relating to political and economic developments in southern African countries, incl Angola, Mozambique, Rhodesia (Zimbabwe), Union of South Africa, and South West Africa (Namibia). 5 ms boxes.
CT —YALE UNIVERSITY, Box 1603A, Yale Station, New Haven, 06520.
Holdings: Mss Pix
DC —HOWARD UNIVERSITY, Moorland-Spingarn Research Center, 500 Howard Place NW, Washington, 20059. Clifford L Muse, Jr, Acting Dir
MI —MICHIGAN STATE UNIVERSITY, International Library, Africana Collection, East Lansing, 48824. Eugene de Benko, Librn; Onuma Ezera, Bibliographer for Africana
Holdings: Vols (82,700) Cat Mss Maps Pix Slides Phonorecords Audiotapes Videotapes Filmstrips Microforms
Budget: ($78,000)
See also entry under Africa for full description.

RHODESIA, SOUTHERN see Rhodesia

RHODODENDRON

WA —RHODODENDRON SPECIES FOUNDATION, PO Box 3798, Federal Way, 98003. Karen Gunderson, Mgr
Holdings: Vols 1000
Notes: Species of rhododendron. Rhododendron reference library.

RHOPALOCERA see Butterflies and Moths

RHYMES see Riddles

RHYNCHOTA see Hemiptera

RHYS, KEIDRYCH

BC —UNIVERSITY OF VICTORIA, McPherson Library, Victoria, V8W 3H5, Can.

RHYTHM (MUSIC)

TN —COUNTRY MUSIC FOUNDATION, Library & Media Center, 4 Music Sq E, Nashville, 37203. Charlie Seemann, Dir
Holdings: Vols (6000) Mss Pix Slides Phonorecords Audiotapes Videotapes 16mm Films Microforms
Notes: The largest collection in the world dealing with American country music. Related subject areas are also included-- Anglo-American folksong, popular music in general (soul, jazz, rock and roll, rhythm and blues, etc), recorded sound technology, music law.

RIBALOW, HAROLD U.

MA —BOSTON UNIVERSITY, Mugar Memorial Library, Special Collections Dept, 771 Commonwealth Ave, Boston, 02215. Howard B Gotlieb, Dir
Holdings: Cat Mss Correspondence

RIBICOFF, ABRAHAM, 1910-

†CT —CONNECTICUT STATE LIBRARY, Hartford, 06106.
Notes: Papers of many Connecticut governors, senators and congressmen, incl John Dempsey, Abraham Ribicoff, and Thomas J Dodd.
DC —LIBRARY OF CONGRESS, Manuscript Division, Washington, 20540. John C Broderick, Chief
Notes: Senatorial and other papers of Abraham Ribicoff.
DC —LIBRARY OF CONGRESS, Washington, 20540.
Notes: Papers of Senator Abraham Ribicoff. His gubernatorial and some other papers are at the Connecticut State Library.

RICE

CA —UNIVERSITY OF CALIFORNIA, BERKELEY, Science Libraries, Natural Resources Library, 40 Giannini Hall, Berkeley, 94720. Norma Kobzina, Head Librn
Holdings: Vols (100,000) Cat Maps Microforms
Budget: ($40,000)
Notes: Subject empahsis is on basic agricultural and pest management research, particularly in the areas of tropical and subtropical agriculture and plantation crops, ie, cotton, rice, tobacco, and sugar. Materials in agricultural engineering, farm machinery, and veterinary medicine are not acquired for the Berkeley campus. Serials, especially the extensive holdings of foreign titles, constitute the collection's major strength. Over 5700 serials are being received currently.
LA —UNIVERSITY OF SOUTHERN LOUISIANA, Dupre Library, Jefferson Caffery Louisiana Room, 302 East St Mary Blvd, Lafayette, 70504. Cynthia J Rice, Louisiana Room Ref Librn
Notes: Rice industry.

SC —COLLEGE OF CHARLESTON LIBRARY, Special Collections Dept, Charleston, 29401.
Notes: Papers, 1873-1925, incl correspondence, ledgers, and other financial papers of two Charleston-based rice mills, West Point and Chisolm Rice Mill Companies.
SC —FRANCIS MARION COLLEGE, James A Rogers Library, Florence, 29501. H Paul Dove, Dir; Roger K Hux, Special Collections Librn
Holdings: Vols (600) Cat Maps Audiotapes Microforms
Notes: The Pee Dee Region of South Carolina. Emphasis on Colonial and Revolutionary periods, rice and indigo culture, plantations. Includes old rural church library with children's books.

RICE, MSGR. CHARLES OWEN

PA —UNIVERSITY OF PITTSBURGH, Hillman Library, Archives of Industrial Society, 363 Hillman Library, Pittsburgh, 15260. Frank A Zabrosky, Cur
Holdings: Documents Mss Pix Newspapers Audiotapes Microforms
Notes: Records of trade unions, service employee unions, teacher unions in the 20th century; personal papers of individuals involved in the labor union movement. Unique collection: Msgr Charles Owen Rice Papers, 1935-.
PA —PENNSYLVANIA STATE UNIVERSITY, Fred Lewis Pattee Library, Labor History Collection, University Park, 16802. Peter Gottlieb, Archivist
Holdings: Cat Mss Pix
Notes: Personal papers.

RICE, ELIZABETH

MA —SIMMONS COLLEGE ARCHIVES, 300 The Fenway, Boston, 02115. Megan Sniffin-Marinoff, College Archivist
Notes: Archives of the Simmons College School of Public Health Nursing (later reorganized into the School of Nursing) cover the years 1902-1970. Important correspondents in the collection incl M Adelaide Nutting, Mary Beard, Isabel Stewart, and Anne Hervey Strong, etc. Incl Strong's records of activity with regard to nursing education in the National Organization for Public Health Nursing, 1918-22. 1000 linear feet in institution, incl special collections nursing and photographs, nursing.

RICE, JAMES HENRY, 1868-1935

SC —COLLEGE OF CHARLESTON LIBRARY, Special Collections Dept, Charleston, 29401.
Notes: Papers incl correspondence regarding literary, social, and political activities.

RICE FAMILY

OH —RUTHERFORD B HAYES LIBRARY, 1337 Hayes Ave, Fremont, 43420. Watt P Marchman, Dir
Holdings: Vols 500 Cat Mss Maps Pix
Notes: Drs John B and Robert H Rice of Fremont, Ohio. Incl 300 linear ft of mss, 25 boxes of pictures. Index in collection. Listed in Guide to Manuscripts of the Ohio Historical Society, 401.

RICH, LORIMER

NY —SYRACUSE UNIVERSITY LIBRARIES, Ernest S Bird Library, George Arents Research Library for Special Collections, Syracuse, 13210. Carolyn A Davis, Manuscripts Librn; Amy S Doherty, University Archivist; Mark F Weimer, Rare Book Librn
Notes: The George Arents Research Library for Special Collections at Syracuse University contains the papers of Harley James McKee, Lorimer Rich, Frederick Lear, Max Abramovitz, James I Arnold, Pietro Bulluschi, Claude Bragdon, Marcel Breuer, William Lescaze, Skidmore Owings

RICH, LORIMER (cont.)

 & Merrill, Ralph Walker, Eric Fisher Wood, Minoru Yamasaki, Joseph Louis Young, and Archimedes Russell.

RICHARD III, 1452-1485

 NY —RICHARD III SOCIETY, American Branch Library, 288 College Avenue, Staten Island, 10314. Julie Lord, Librn
 Holdings: Vols 200 Uncat Mss Pix Audiotapes
 Notes: Recent fiction on Richard III, early works, standard biographies, student papers, unpublished playscripts, prints, photos, tapes of lectures. Period of interest 1450-1500, centered on Richard III, his life and character. Collection also contains city chronicles, banquets and coronation rolls, and privy purse accounts.

RICHARDS, ELLEN HENRIETTA SWALLOW

 MA —MASSACHUSETTS INSTITUTE OF TECHNOLOGY, Institute Archives, Special Collections, Cambridge, 02139.
 Notes: Papers of William Barton Rogers, geologist, founder and first President of the Massachusetts Institute of Technology (1862-1870, 1878-1881). Major correspondents incl Louis Agassiz, Joseph Henry, Thomas Sterry Hunt, and Ellen Swallow Richards. Unpublished finding aid, incl correspondent index, available in Archives.

RICHARDS, GRANT

 DC —GEORGETOWN UNIVERSITY, Library, Special Collections Div, 37 & O Sts NW, Washington, 20057. George M Barringer, Special Collections Librn; Nicholas B Sheetz, Mss Librn
 Holdings: Mss Cat Pix
 Notes: A portion of the archives of the English publisher Grant Ricards (1872-1948), containing manuscripts, correspondence, photographs, clippings, and printed ephemera. Incl is extensive correspondence from such artists and authors as Neville Cardus; Frank Harris; Sir Hugh Lane; Lady Augusta Gregory; David Low; T Sturge Moore; and C R W Nevinson.
 DC —LIBRARY OF CONGRESS, Washington, 20540.
 Notes: Three collections are pertinent to Housman: (1) The AE Housman Collection, with most of the surviving fragments of the poetry notebooks, along with some of the letters AEH received on publication of *Last Poems*; (2) The Laurence Housman Collection, Chiefly of correspondence LH had with Maude M Hawkins, one of AEH's biographers; (3) The Grant Richards Collection preserves over a hundred autograph letters from AEH, and several hundred typescript copies of his letters; copies of to AEH from Grant Richards; letters to GR about AEH; and drafts and proofs of Richard's memoir. Scattered in other LC collections (Cyril Clemens; Van Doren, etc) are other letters from AEH. LC has only a few books from Housman's library.
 IL —UNIVERSITY OF ILLINOIS, URBANA/CHAMPAIGN, Library, 1408 W Gregory Drive, Urbana, 61801. Norman B Brown, Asst Dir for Special Collections
 Notes: The Rare Book collection of the records of Richards' publishing career includes 45 volumes of his letters to authors, printers, etc, and over 15,000 letters from authors, literary agents, etc. Including approximately 110 of A E Housman.

RICHARDS, JANET E.

 DC —GEORGETOWN UNIVERSITY, Library, Special Collections Div, 37 & O Sts NW, Washington, 20057. George M Barringer, Special Collections Librn; Nicholas B Sheetz, Mss Librn
 Holdings: Mss
 Notes: The papers of Miss Janet E Richards,

lecturer and columnist, consisting of correspondence, family records, and photographs; incl material on women's suffrage and the Oberammergau Passion Play.

RICHARDS, JOHNNY

 TX —NORTH TEXAS STATE UNIVERSITY, Audio Center, Box 5188, NT Station, Denton, 76203. Morris Martin, Music Librn
 Notes: More than 1600 manuscript jazz compositions, (incl scores and parts, alternate versions, expanded arrangements) by Stan Kenton, Johnny Richards, Joe Coccia, Lennie Niehaus, Pete Rugolo, Willie Maiden, Bob Curnow, Ken Hanna, Gene Rowland, Bob Graettinger and others, used by the Stan Kenton Band and given to North Texas State University in 1962 and at Kenton's death in 1979. Unpublished catalog: Breeden, Leon, *Stan Kenton Music in the NTSU Jazz Studies Library and the NTSU Music Library*, Denton, 1983 (99 pages).

RICHARDS, LINDA, 1841-1930

 MA —BOSTON UNIVERSITY, Mugar Memorial Library, Special Collections Dept, 771 Commonwealth Ave, Boston, 02215. Howard B Gotlieb, Dir
 Holdings: // Pix
 Notes: Correspondence, memorabilia and photographs of New England Hospital for Women and Children.
 MA —SIMMONS COLLEGE ARCHIVES, 300 The Fenway, Boston, 02115. Megan Sniffin-Marinoff, College Archivist
 Notes: Archives of the Simmons College School of Public Health Nursing (later reorganized into the School of Nursing) cover the years 1902-1970. Important correspondents in the collection incl M Adelaide Nutting, Mary Beard, Isabel Stewart, and Anne Hervey Strong, etc. Incl Strong's records of activity with regard to nursing education in the National Organization for Public Health Nursing, 1918-22. 1000 linear feet in institution, incl special collections nursing and photographs, nursing.

RICHARDSON, ELIOT

 DC —LIBRARY OF CONGRESS, Manuscript Division, Washington, 20540. John C Broderick, Chief
 Notes: Papers; over 15,000 items.

RICHARDSON, HENRY HOBSON

 MA —HARVARD UNIVERSITY, Graduate School of Design, Frances Loeb Library, Gund Hall, Cambridge, 02138. James Hodgson, Librn
 Holdings: Cat Mss Pix
 Notes: Books of the architect. Drawings are in Houghton Library, Harvard University.

RICHARDSON, HOLDEN CHESTER

 DC —LIBRARY OF CONGRESS, Manuscript Division, Washington, 20540. John C Broderick, Chief
 Notes: His papers; Naval Historical Foundation Collection.

RICHARDSON, TONY

 AZ —NORTHERN ARIZONA UNIVERSITY, Special Collection Library, CU Box 6022, Flagstaff, 86011. Peter M Whiteley, Coordr/Archivist; William Mullane, Librn
 Notes: Articles by Richardson appearing in western pulp magazines, 1960's. Richardson has numerous pseudonyms, and was from Flagstaff, Ariz. See also the cataloged Richardson book collection.

RICHLER, MORDECAI, 1931-

 AB —UNIVERSITY OF CALGARY, Libraries, Special Collections Div, 2500 University Dr, Calgary, T2N 1N4, Can.
 Holdings: Cat Mss
 Notes: The papers of Mordecai Richler

include correspondence, 1954-1972, manuscripts, including early drafts, notes, and corrections of novels, essays, stories, television plays, radio plays, screen plays, files of published material from journals and magazines, film, television and book reviews from major world newspapers, interviews, critical articles, proofs and other materials related to *Canadian Writing Today*, publisher's royalty statements, contracts, film contracts.

RICHMAN, HARRY

 MA —BOSTON UNIVERSITY, Mugar Memorial Library, Special Collections Dept, 771 Commonwealth Ave, Boston, 02215. Howard B Gotlieb, Dir
 Holdings: Cat Mss Pix
 Notes: Mss, correspondence, etc collected in depth; incl publications by or about.

RICHMOND, GRACE

 NY —STATE UNIVERSITY OF NEW YORK, COLLEGE AT FREDONIA, Daniel A Reed Library, Fredonia, 14063. John P Saulitis, Dir of Library Services; Joanne L Schweik, Supv of Special Collections; Joseph Chouinard, Music Librn
 Holdings: Vols 68 Cat Mss Pix Audiotapes
 Budget: $150
 Notes: Grace Richmond was a popular novelist who wrote from 1890-1930. Her books sold more than 150,000 copies and most were published in popular magazines prior to book publication. Reed Library has her family correspondence (covering years from 1882-1930), materials relevant to her writing (notebooks, review clippings, tear sheets, and many photographs), the medical records of Dr Nelson Richmond, Grace's husband, and oral interview tapes (cassettes) done in preparation to writing a biography of Mrs Richmond. Collection also incl the descriptive bibliography of her writings, done as a Master's Thesis.

RICHMOND, JUDAH L., 1807-1868

 NY —CORNELL UNIVERSITY LIBRARIES, Collection of Regional History, Dept of Manuscripts and Univ Archives, Ithaca, 14853.
 Notes: Baptist clergyman. Incl family papers, 1844-62; one reel of microfilm, one diary, and five personal letters.

RICHTER, CHARLES

 †CA —CALIFORNIA INSTITUTE OF TECHNOLOGY, Robert A Millikan Memorial Library, Archives, 1201 E California Blvd, Pasadena, 91125.
 Notes: Geophysicist Charles Richter's lecture notes and oral history interview. Incl notes from courses at Caltech taught by physicist Paul Epstein (1883-1966), such as higher dynamics, 1925; thermodynamics, 1925/26; quantum theory, 1926-28, 1940.

RICHTER, CONRAD

 MA —BOSTON UNIVERSITY, Mugar Memorial Library, Special Collections Dept, 771 Commonwealth Ave, Boston, 02215. Howard B Gotlieb, Dir
 Holdings: // Cat Mss
 Notes: Mss, correspondence, etc collected in depth; incl publications by or about.

RICHTER, MAX CLEMENS

 CA —UNIVERSITY OF CALIFORNIA, DAVIS, Shields Library, Dept of Special Collections, Davis, 95616. Donald Kunitz, Head; C Danial Elliott, Asst Head
 Holdings: Cat Mss Pix Slides
 Notes: Clippings and photographs of Max Clemens Richter, California beekeeper; miscellaneous articles and clippings on all aspects of beekeeping. 350 items. Described in: USDA Agricultural Research Service, *Beekeeping in the United States* (Agricultural Handbook, no 335, rev ed 1977); and Johansson, Tag Sigvard Kjell,

RICHTER, MAX CLEMENS (cont.)

Apicultural Literature Published in Canada and the United States (New York, 1972).

RICKER, NATHAN

IL —UNIVERSITY OF ILLINOIS, URBANA/CHAMPAIGN, Library, University Archives, 19 Library, 1408 W Gregory Drive, Urbana, 61801. Maynard Brichford, University Archivist
Holdings: Cat Mss Maps Pix Slides Microforms
Notes: Papers, archival records, etc.

RICKEY, GEORGE

NY —STATE UNIVERSITY OF NEW YORK, COLLEGE AT PURCHASE, Library, Lincoln Ave, Purchase, 10577. Robert W Evans, Dir
Holdings: Uncat Mss Pix
Notes: Gift of the artist, George Rickey, and his wife, whose collection of constructivist art works has also been given to the Neuberger Museum at the College at Purchase. The collection consists largely of over 1000 announcements and catalogs of exhibitions of constructivist works and materials about the artists.

RIDDELL, CHARLOTTE ELIZA LAWSON (COWAN), 1832-1906

CA —UNIVERSITY OF CALIFORNIA, LOS ANGELES, Research Library, Dept of Special Collections, 405 Hilgard Ave, Los Angeles, 90024. Edward Shreeves, Chairman, Bibliographers Group; David S Zeidberg, Head
Holdings: Vols 50
Notes: 50 first and other editions of her books; 23 letters.

RIDDELL, ISAAC

SC —COLLEGE OF CHARLESTON LIBRARY, Special Collections Dept, Charleston, 29401.
Notes: Papers, 1849.

RIDDLES

KS —WICHITA PUBLIC LIBRARY, Art & Music Division, 223 S Main, Wichita, 67202. Leonard Messineo, Jr, Head, Art & Music Division; Deborah Hamilton, Special Collections Librn
Notes: Joan O'Bryant Kansas Folklore Collection. Contains approximately 200 hours of folkmusic and oral histories on tape; over 27,000 note cards covering topics such as anecdotes, beliefs, customs, games, jokes, medicines and cures, proverbs, recipes, rhymes, riddles, sayings, songs, speech and dialect, etc; 102 research papers covering family histories, town and area histories, biographies, tales, recipes, etc; and well over 70 mounted quilt blocks-covering the folk history of Kansas. This material was collected by Joan O'Bryant and her students from 1947-1964, the period in which she taught Folklore and English at Wichita State University.
OH —CLEVELAND PUBLIC LIBRARY, Fine Arts and Special Collections Department, 325 Superior Ave, Cleveland, 44114. Alice N Loranth, Head
Holdings: Vols (41,050) Cat Mss Microforms
Notes: Part of the Folklore Collection. One of the large folklore collections in the US. Comprehensive in scope, incl folk tales, riddles, proverbs, folk songs, ballads, fables, chapbooks, medieval romances, works on superstition, magic, witchcraft, and studies of folk habits, beliefs, manners and customs. Described in Cleveland, Public Library, White Collection of Folklore and Orientalia; *Catalog of Folklore, Folklife, and Folk Songs* 2nd ed (Boston: G K Hall, 1978), 3 vols; introduction by Alice N Loranth.
See also entry under Folklore

RIDENOUR, NINA, 1904-

KS —MENNINGER FOUNDATION, Archives, 5600 W Sixth St, Box 829, Topeka, 66601. Alice Brand, Librn; Mark West, Archivist
Notes: 7 boxes, 1926-76. Consists of mss, correspondence, publications, and material related to the American Theatre Wing Community Plays.

RIDER, SYDNEY S., 1833-1917

RI —BROWN UNIVERSITY, John Hay Library, 20 Prospect St, Providence, 02912. Mark N Brown, Cur Mss
Holdings: // Cat Mss
Notes: The Sidney S Rider Papers collection-miscellaneous mss and about 15,000 items relating to Rhode Island history for the period 1678-1883 gathered by the Providence bookseller (1833-1917). Incl letters, documents, and business papers, many of which relate to shipping and trade; and an offical ms copy of the Acts and Resolves of the General Assembly for the period 1678-1747. See also the Dorr Papers, the Thomas A Jenckes Papers, the Samuel Mowry Papers, the Jonah Titus Papers, the Augustus Woodbury Papers, and Rhode Island Manuscripts.

RIDGWAY, MATTHEW

PA —US ARMY MILITARY HISTORY INSTITUTE, Carlisle Barracks, 17013. Richard J Sommers, Chief Archivist-Historian
Holdings: Mss Cat
Notes: TheKorean War collection, personal correspondence, daily logs, recollections, and official papers of US officers and soldiers serving in the Korean War, incl Generals Edward Almond, George Barth Bruce Clarke, Matthew Ridgway, and Arthur Trudeau.

THE RIDICULOUS see Wit and Humor

RIDING see Horse Breeding

RIDING, LAURA

IL —NORTHWESTERN UNIVERSITY, Library, Special Collections Dept, 1937 Sheridan Rd, Evanston, 60201. R Russell Maylone, Cur
Holdings: Vols 25 Cat Mss
Notes: Correspondence; proof copies of books.
OK —UNIVERSITY OF TULSA, McFarlin Library, Dept of Rare Books and Special Collections, 600 S College, Tulsa, 74104. David Farmer, Dir; Toby Murray, Archivist; Caroline Swinson, Cur of Manuscripts & Art
Holdings: Mss Pix Phonorecords
Notes: The Ellsworth Mason Graves/Riding Collection, incl first editions, typescripts, photographs, recordings and ephemera. The Library also has the library (8000 vols) of Cyril Connolly. Mostly modern literature; many presentation copies.
TN —VANDERBILT UNIVERSITY, Library, Nashville, 37240. Marice Wolfe, Special Collections Librn
Holdings: Vols 1000 Cat Mss Pix
Notes: Collection relating to the Fugitive poets of the 1920s, the Agrarian writers of the 1930s and their subsequent careers, as a complement to extensive mss collections in this field. Chief figures incl Allen Tate, John Crowe Ransom, Robert Penn Warren, Andrew Lytle, Donald Davidson, Merrill Moore, Laura Riding, et al.
WI —UNIVERSITY OF WISCONSIN, MADISON, Memorial Library, British & American Language & Literature Collection, 728 State St, Madison, 53706. Yvonne Schofer, Bibliographer
Notes: First editions; an archive of some 127 letters and associated material, to publishers and scholars, some typescripts, of considerable research interest. Uncataloged. Stocks holdings (books) cataloged. Part of 20th Century Collection.
BC —UNIVERSITY OF VICTORIA, McPherson Library, Victoria, V8W 3H5, Can.
Notes: Incl 276 pages; photocopies: 38 pages, ca 1960-73; mss and copy of essays, sections of books and letter to the TLS; mostly unpublished with brief descriptions by the author; copy of Alan Clark's comments on Laura Riding's On 'the Fable of the Dice.'

RIEGGER, WALLINGFORD

DC —LIBRARY OF CONGRESS, Music Division, Washington, 20540.
Notes: Mss in Koussevitzky Archives.

RIENOW, ROBERT, 1907-

NY —STATE UNIVERSITY OF NEW YORK AT ALBANY, Library, Special Collections Dept, 1400 Washington Ave, Albany, 12222. Marion P Munzer, Coordr
Notes: Correspondence, lecture notes, speeches, mss, clippings dealing with work by Robert Rienow and his wife, Leona Train, on wildlife conservation, anti-nuclear movement, and population control (15 linear feet).
See also entries under Natural Resources; Wildlife Conservation; Population

RIFKIN, SHEPARD

MA —BOSTON UNIVERSITY, Mugar Memorial Library, Special Collections Dept, 771 Commonwealth Ave, Boston, 02215. Howard B Gotlieb, Dir
Holdings: Mss

RIFLES

DC —NATIONAL RIFLE ASSOCIATION OF AMERICA, Reference Library, 1600 Rhode Island Ave, 7th Floor, Washington, 20036. Maureen Booth, Librn
Notes: Coll on rifles and hand guns; inter-library loan limited to members and libraries.
MA —LUCIUS BEEBE MEMORIAL LIBRARY, Main St, Wakefield, 01880.
Holdings: Vols (350) Cat
Notes: Target shooting.
NY —REMINGTON ARMS CO, Remington Gun Museum, Catherine St, Ilion, 13357. Laurence Goodstal, Cur
Notes: Museum displays sporting and military firearms built by Remington Arms Co, ca 1825 to modern firearms of today.
†WA —WASHINGTON STATE UNIVERSITY, Library, Manuscripts, Archives & Special Collections, Pullman, 99164. John F Guido, Head
Holdings: Cat Mss Maps Pix
Notes: The Carl Parcher Russell papers, a vast resource (24,916 items; 45 linear feet) on American Indian and Western pioneer activities and artifacts. Much on the fur trade; pioneer life; mountain men and trapping; wildlife; primitive life in detail. Also the National Park Service, parks, monuments, etc. Described in *Carl Parcher Russell: An Indexed Register of His Scholarly and Professional Papers, 1920-1967, in the Washington State University Library* (Pullman, 1970), 149 pp.

RIGBY, RAY

MA —BOSTON UNIVERSITY, Mugar Memorial Library, Special Collections Dept, 771 Commonwealth Ave, Boston, 02215. Howard B Gotlieb, Dir
Holdings: Cat Mss

RIGHT AND LEFT (POLITICAL SCIENCE)

AZ —NORTHERN ARIZONA UNIVERSITY, Special Collection Library, CU Box 6022, Flagstaff, 86011. Peter M Whiteley, Coordr/Archivist; William Mullane, Librn
Holdings: Vols 9000 Cat Mss Phonorecords Microforms
Notes: The large Allderdice Collection of thousands of books, pamphlets, periodicals, and organizational files reflects the conservative, communist, socialist, facist, anarchist, and other viewpoints, etc, during the 20th century.

RIGHT AND LEFT (POLITICAL SCIENCE) (cont.)

CA —UNIVERSITY OF CALIFORNIA, DAVIS, Shields Library, Dept of Special Collections, Davis, 95616. Donald Kunitz, Head; C Danial Elliott, Asst Head
Notes: Overview of American political movements from the 1890s to the present: socialism, communism, labor, to ecology and women's liberation.

CA —CALIFORNIA STATE UNIVERSITY, FULLERTON, Library, 800 N State College Blvd, Fullerton, 92634. Lynn M Coppel, Librn
Holdings: Pamphlets Serials Ephemera
Notes: Freedom Center of Polemic Political Ephemera incl 8000 pamphlets and over 4000 periodical titles. Strongest in right wing American politics and British socialism. Separate card catalogs for the pamphlets and folders. Periodicals are listed in the CSUF periodicals printout and the *California State University and Colleges Union List of Periodicals.*

CT —UNIVERSITY OF CONNECTICUT, Library, Storrs, 06268. Ellen Embardo, Cur Special Collections
Holdings: Cat
Notes: Alternative Press Collection. Primarily periodicals and newspapers from the 1960s to today of an alternative or underground nature. Books and pamphlets are incl, representing both the left and the right-wing viewpoints. A catalog is available. Also have archives of the First Casualty Press, which was deeply involved with Vietnam veterans' experiences in Vietnam.

HI —HAWAII PACIFIC COLLEGE, Meader Library, 1060 Bishop St, Honolulu, 96813. Barbara Burton Hoefler, Head Librn
Holdings: Vols 900 Cat
Notes: Un-American activities represented by history, biography, political science, and fiction.

IL —NORTHERN ILLINOIS UNIVERSITY, Founders Memorial Library, Rare Books and Special Collections Dept, De Kalb, 60115. William R DuBois, Dept Head
Holdings: Vols (1350) // Cat
Notes: American, British and Soviet pamphlet publications, ca 1860-1955 by or the radical labor movement, socialists, communists and the radical labor movement, socialists, communists and the radicl right. Some Nazi/anti-Nazi material. Collection is computer-indexed by author, title, series, publisher and date.

IL —NORTHWESTERN UNIVERSITY, Library, Special Collections Dept, 1937 Sheridan Rd, Evanston, 60201. R Russell Maylone, Cur
Holdings: Vols (14,000) Cat
Notes: Periodicals and pamphlets concerning many social and political movements in the 20th century, with emphasis on anarchism, struggles of the working class, women's rights, and student protest of the 1960s. Foreign material incl. An additional 10,000 pieces arranged by subject.

LA —TULANE UNIVERSITY, Howard-Tilton Memorial Library, Special Collections Div, 7001 Freret St, New Orleans, 70118. Wilbur E Meneray, Librn
Holdings: Cat Audiotapes Microforms
Notes: Books, pamphlets, serial publications and circulars from over 2000 individuals and organizations representing the fringe of 20th century US political opinion.

MD —UNIVERSITY OF MARYLAND, BALTIMORE COUNTY, Albin O Kuhn Library and Gallery, 5401 Wilkens Ave, Baltimore, 21228. Ann Copeland, Special Collections Librn
Holdings: // Uncat
Notes: The collection incl more than 1000 pamphlets and broadsides on communism, fascism, Trotskyism, socialism, etc.

MA —BRANDEIS UNIVERSITY, Goldfarb Library, 415 South St, Waltham, 02154. Bessie Hahn, Dir
Notes: Hall-Hoag Archives on Extremism in the U.S. Approx 5000 pieces of Extremist literature, both Right and Left, dealing with various social, religious and political aspects

of the US from the 1960s, 1970s and 1980s. A finding list is in Special Collections. Material is arranged by the name of the sponsoring organization in alphabetical order.

MI —MICHIGAN STATE UNIVERSITY, Libraries, Special Collections Div, East Lansing, 48824. Jannette Fiore, Librn
Holdings: Vols (10,500) Cat Mss
Notes: Published and unpublished material generated by (1) American left and right, 1900, (2) the New Left, 1969-1970, and (3) current left, right, and alternate life-style groups. (Supported by appropriate secondary material in the Research Library). Also have in microform radical pamphlet literature from the Tamiment Library (New York University), the Right Wing Collection of the University of Iowa, et al.

NJ —PRINCETON UNIVERSITY, Library, Rare Books Dept, Princeton, 08544. Stephen Ferguson, Cur
Holdings: Vols 100 Cat
Notes: Right Wing literature, incl material on organizations.

NC —DUKE UNIVERSITY, William R Perkins Library, Manuscript Dept, Durham, 27706. Ellen Gartrell, Cur of Mss
Holdings: Cat Mss
Notes: Diverse holdings include Socialist Party of America Papers, 1900-1976 (240,000 items); J B Matthews's extensive files on liberals and radicals, 1930s-1960s; papers of mainly conservative southern politicians; Ku Klux Klan papers.

TX —ABILENE CHRISTIAN UNIVERSITY, Margaret & Herman Brown Library, ACU Sta, Abilene, 79601. Callie Faye Milliken, Assoc Dir
Holdings: Vols 5000 // Cat
Notes: Donner Library of Americanism Books, pamphlets, documents, and periodical materials dealing with American politics of the far right collected by Robert Donner during and after World War II. Also incl materials on Jews and Freemasonry.

WI —UNIVERSITY OF WISCONSIN, MILWAUKEE, Library, Box 604, Milwaukee, 53201. William C Roselle, Dir
Holdings: Vols 2500 Cat Mss Pix
Notes: Fromkin Memorial Collection, emphasizing third party forces in American politics. Restricted use: noncirculating. Special subject catalog of pamphlet material.

RIGHT TO LIFE

DC —CENTER FOR BIOETHICS, Library, Kennedy Institute, Georgetown University, 3520 Prospect St NW, Washington, 20057. Doris Goldstein, Dir; Judith Mistichelli, Senior Librn
Holdings: Vols (8200)
Notes: Largest library of its kind. Incl 31,000 journal articles on applied ethics. Produces computer database *Bioethicsline,* available through MEDLARS; and the printed annual *Bibliography of Bioethics.* Other library publications are: *New Titles in Bioethics* (monthly); *Scope Notes* series on current topics.

RIGHTS, CIVIL see Civil Rights

RIGHTS, WATER see Water Rights

RIGHTS OF WOMEN see Women—Civil Rights

RIIS, JACOB AUGUST

NY —CITY UNIVERSITY OF NEW YORK, City College, Morris R Cohen Library, North Academic Center, Convent Ave & 137th St, New York, 10031. Barbara J Dunlap, Archivist
Holdings: Cat Mss Pix
Notes: The Jacob Riis papers. Four file drawers. Restricted use.

NY —MUSEUM OF THE CITY OF NEW YORK, Library, Fifth Ave & 103 St, New York, 10025.
Notes: The Jacob A Riis Collection of New York City photographs, especially of slum life at about the turn of the century.

NY —NEW YORK PUBLIC LIBRARY, Rare Books and Manuscripts Div, Fifth Ave & 42 St, New York, 10018. William L Joyce, Asst Dir; Susan E Davis, Cur of Mss
Budget: ($7161)
Notes: The papers of Jacob A Riis, incl diaries, mss, etc.

RILEY, JAMES WHITCOMB

IN —INDIANA UNIVERSITY, Lilly Library, Seventh St, Bloomington, 47405. William R Cagle, Librn
Holdings: Vols (400) // Cat Mss
Notes: Some 400 first and later printings of Riley's works, plus books from Riley's library. Extensive mss and correspondence. Incl his forgery of "Leonainie."

IN —INDIANAPOLIS-MARION COUNTY PUBLIC LIBRARY, 40 E Saint Clair St, Indianapolis, 46204. Raymond E Gnat, Dir
Holdings: Vols 270 Uncat Mss Pix
Notes: Incl correspondence and scrapbooks, published editions. Restricted use.

VA —UNIVERSITY OF VIRGINIA, Alderman Library, Clifton Waller Barrett Collection, Charlottesville, 22901. Joan St C Crane, Cur of American Literature Collections
Notes: Papers.

VA —UNIVERSITY OF VIRGINIA, Alderman Library, Rare Book Dept, Charlottesville, 22901. Julius P Barclay, Cur
Holdings: Vols 178 Cat Mss

RILKE, RAINER MARIA

CT —YALE UNIVERSITY, Beinecke Rare Book & Manuscript Library, German Literature Collection, Box 1603A, Yale Sta, New Haven, 06520. Christa Sammons, Cur
Holdings: Vols 150 Cat Mss
Notes: A collection of all the first editions of Rilke's works, special and limited printings, and English translations. No photocopying.

KS —UNIVERSITY OF KANSAS, Kenneth Spencer Research Library, Special Collections Dept, Lawrence, 66045. Alexandra Mason, Librn
Holdings: Vols 1800 Cat
Notes: Based on Henry Sagan collection. Particularly strong in periodicals, ephemeral publications, various states of first editions. Noncirculating.

MA —HARVARD UNIVERSITY LIBRARY, Houghton Library, Cambridge, 02138. F Thomas Noonan, Cur, Reading Room; Lawrence Dowler, Associate Librn
Holdings: Cat Mss
Notes: Catalog published by Insel-Verlag, Frankfurt AM, 1966.

PA —BIBLIOGRAPHICAL CENTER OF GERMAN LITERATURE, University of Pittsburgh, Dept of Germanic Languages & Literatures, 102 Loeffler Bldg, Pittsburgh, 15260. Klaus W Jonas, Dir
Holdings: Cat Mss Pix Microforms
Notes: Center for the development of collections and bibliographical control of the record of publications, mss, correspondence, etc, by or relating to modern German authors. Special sections have been developed for Mann, Rilke, Hauptmann, Hesse, Broch, Sachs and others. Described by Professor Klaus W Jonas's "The German Literature Center in Pittsburgh," *Stechert-Hafner Book News,* vol 24, no 8, April 1970; "Documentation in Modern German Literature: A Progress Report," *Jahrbuch fuer Internationale Germanistik,* vol 4, no 2, 1972, and in *German and Austrian Contributions to World Literature* (1890-1970). Department of Germanic Languages and Literatures, University of Pittsburgh, 1983. 96 pp.

RILLA, WOLF

MA —BOSTON UNIVERSITY, Mugar Memorial Library, Special Collections Dept, 771 Commonwealth Ave, Boston, 02215. Howard B Gotlieb, Dir
Holdings: Cat Mss Correspondence Pix

RIMBAUD, JEAN ARTHUR, 1854-1891

CA —UNIVERSITY OF CALIFORNIA, LOS ANGELES, Research Library, Dept of

RIMBAUD, JEAN ARTHUR, 1854-1891 (cont.)

Special Collections, 405 Hilgard Ave, Los Angeles, 90024. Edward Shreeves, Chairman, Bibliographers Group; David S Zeidberg, Head
Holdings: Vols 200
Notes: 200 books by and about him.

MO —SOUTHWEST MISSOURI STATE UNIVERSITY, Duane G Meyer Library, 901 S National, Box 175, Springfield, 65804. Robert D Harvey, Dir
Holdings: Vols 1520 Cat Pix
Notes: The William J Jones Rimbaud Collection contains material by and about Rimbaud. Translations of Rimbaud's works incl six languages: English, German, Italian, Japanese, Spanish and Swedish. Incl articles, clippings, miscellaneous items. Catalog: F C St Aubyn, *The William J Jones Rimbaud Collection*, with a foreword by Henri Peyre. Springfield, MO: Southwest Missouri State College Library, 1965. (Lists items 1-659 only).

RIME

ON —UNIVERSITY OF TORONTO, Thomas Fisher Rare Book Library, 120 Saint George St, Toronto, M5S 1A5, Can. Richard G Landon, Head
Holdings: Vols 700
Notes: Rime Collection comprises anthologies of Italian poetry and collections of early "rime" by one author. Emphasis on 16th and 17th centuries. Holdings partially described in Molinaro, Julius A, *A Bibliography of Sixteenth-Century Italian Verse Collections in the University of Toronto Library* (Toronto, 1969).

RIMMER, ROBERT H.

MA —BOSTON UNIVERSITY, Mugar Memorial Library, Special Collections Dept, 771 Commonwealth Ave, Boston, 02215. Howard B Gotlieb, Dir
Holdings: Cat Mss Pix Correspondence

RIMMER, WILLIAM

MA —FRANCIS A COUNTWAY LIBRARY OF MEDICINE, Boston Medical Library/Harvard Medical Library, 10 Shattuck St, Boston, 02115. C Robin LeSueur, Librn; Richard J Wolfe, Cur, Rare Books & Manuscripts
Holdings: Mss
Notes: Manuscript collection.

RIMSKY-KORSAKOV, NICHOLAS

MO —UNIVERSITY OF MISSOURI-COLUMBIA, Ellis Library, Art, Archaeology and Music Dept, Columbia, 65201. Bonnie MacEwan, Librn
Holdings: Vols Cat
Notes: Russian editions of complete works of Glinka, Tchaikowsky and Rimsky-Korsakov.

RINEHART, MARY ROBERTS

PA —UNIVERSITY OF PITTSBURGH, Hillman Library, Special Collections Dept, Mary Roberts Rinehart Collection, 363 Hillman Library, Pittsburgh, 15260. Charles E Aston, Jr, Coordr
Holdings: Vols 416 Cat Mss Pix Memorabilia
Notes: Mrs Rinehart was a native Pittsburgher. The collection consists of books and 22 ft of mss written by her, interviews, and biographical material.

RINGLING, JOHN

FL —RINGLING MUSEUM OF THE CIRCUS, Library, PO Box 1838, Sarasota, 33578. Nan Fisher, Visitor Services Specialist
Holdings: Vols (350) Cat
Notes: Collection also incl long runs (and indexes) of circus periodicals.

RINGWOOD, GWEN PHARIS, 1910-

AB —UNIVERSITY OF CALGARY, Libraries, Special Collections Div, 2500 University Dr, Calgary, T2N 1N4, Can.
Holdings: Mss
Notes: Correspondence, newsclippings, photographs, reviews and mss (3.5 meters) for drama, fiction, poetry and non-fiction, 1935-81.

RIO GRANDE RIVER

TX —UNIVERSITY OF TEXAS, EL PASO, Library, Special Collections Dept, El Paso, 79968. Cesar Caballero, Dept Head
Budget: ($6000)
Notes: Border Studies Manuscript Collection. Incl 20 linear ft, unpublished conference papers, research reports, articles and other ephemera. This collection was established to support the development of a Border Studies Program at U T El Paso. The collection is currently in the process of being indexed.

RIOTS AND RIOTERS

CA —UNIVERSITY OF CALIFORNIA, LOS ANGELES, Research Library, Dept of Special Collections, 405 Hilgard Ave, Los Angeles, 90024. Edward Shreeves, Chairman, Bibliographers Group; David S Zeidberg, Head
Holdings: // Uncat Mss
Notes: The Carey McWilliams Collection of personal papers, clippings and reports. Incl material on the problems of the Mexican American, 1930-1940, and on the Zoot-Suit Riots.

CA —UNIVERSITY OF CALIFORNIA, LOS ANGELES, Research Library, Western European Collection, Los Angeles, 90024. Edward Shreeves, Chairman, Bibliographers Group; Mary E Greco, Western European Bibliographer
Holdings: Mss Maps Pix Microforms
Budget: ($5000)
Notes: Early modern and modern France. Special strengths in intellectual and religious history of the seventeenth and eighteenth centuries, Jansenism in particular, and popular culture of the nineteenth and twentieth centuries. Good coverage.

CA —HOOVER INSTITUTION ON WAR, REVOLUTION & PEACE, Stanford University, Stanford, 94305. Milorad M Drachkovitch, Archivist
Notes: The New Left Politics Collection consists of monographs and serials on the New Left that are cataloged. In addition, the collection subscribes to numerous underground newspapers and has obtained special subject collections such as the Free Speech Movement at Berkeley 1964-1965, SNCC and Mississippi Summer 1964, and the insurrection at San Francisco State College in 1968-1969. There is also a good collection on the French student revolts of 1968. The collection is a supervised one and not open to browsers. Interested students and scholars are welcome. Only limited photocopying is permitted.

MI —DETROIT PUBLIC LIBRARY, Burton Historical Collection, 5201 Woodward Ave, Detroit, 48202. Alice Dalligan, Chief
Holdings: Vols Cat Pix VF
Notes: Collection on the race riots of the week of 23 July 1967.

OH —KENT STATE UNIVERSITY, University Archives, Kent, 44242. Stephen C Morton, University Archivist
Holdings: Cat Mss Maps Pix Microforms
Notes: The May 4, 1970 incident; 50 linear ft. Separate catalog. Partial description in *Cleveland State Law Review*, Winter, 1973.

RIPLEY, GEORGE

IL —UNIVERSITY OF ILLINOIS, URBANA/CHAMPAIGN, Library, Illinois Historical Survey Library, 1408 W Gregory Dr, 1A Library, Urbana, 61801.
Holdings: Vols 50 Cat Mss Maps Pix Microforms
Notes: Communitarianism in America. The ms material, contained in 30 separate collections (10 cubic feet), concentrates on the period 1840-70. It incl correspondence, records, minutes, ledgers and diaries.

Communal societies such as Biship Hill, Brook Farm, New Harmony, the North American Phalanx and the Sodus Bay Phalanx are represented. Among the correspondents are Albert Brisbane, Parke Godwin, Sarah Grimke, Richard Owen, Robert Owen, Robert Dale Owen, and George Ripley. Numerous pictures. Guide to the collections published in 1976.

RISING, WILLARD B.

CA —UNIVERSITY OF CALIFORNIA, BERKELEY, Bancroft Library, Manuscripts Division, Berkeley, 94720. James D Hart, Dir
Notes: Correspondence and papers relative to the history of modern chemistry.

RISK (INSURANCE)

ON —REED STENHOUSE, Research Dept, PO Box 250, T-D Centre, Toronto, M5K 1J6, Can. G R E Bromwich, VP & Mgr Research Dept
Notes: All types of insurance covered incl unusual ones. Considerable quantity of material on law related to insurance. Extensive clipping and pamphlet files.

RISORGIMENTO (ITALIAN HISTORY) see Italy—History—Risorgimento, 1830-1870

RITES AND CEREMONIES—JEWS see Jews—Rites and Ceremonies

RITTER, WILLIAM E.

CA —UNIVERSITY OF CALIFORNIA, BERKELEY, Bancroft Library, Manuscripts Division, Berkeley, 94720. James D Hart, Dir
Holdings: Cat Mss Maps Pix Microforms
Notes: Papers, correspondence, etc.

RIVER BASIN DEVELOPMENT

OR —UNIVERSITY OF OREGON, Library, Eugene, 97403. Kenneth W Duckett, Curator
Notes: Papers of James C Rettie, Senior Economist of the Department of the Interior.

RIVER CHANNELIZATION see Stream Channelization

RIVER ENGINEERING

MS —US ARMY ENGINEER WATERWAYS EXPERIMENT STATION, Library Branch, PO Box 631, Vicksburg, 39180. Bernice Black, Chief Librn
Holdings: Cat Mss Maps Microforms

RIVERBOATS

IN —INDIANA UNIVERSITY, Lilly Library, Seventh St, Bloomington, 47405. William R Cagle, Librn
Holdings: // Mss Pix
Notes: Business papers and correspondence of Howard Ship Yards & Dock Co, Jeffersonville, Ind, 1834-1942. Incl correspondence with captains, ship owners, Howard family members, etc; some photos of Howard-built ships during construction; ca 10,000 blueprints, drawings and scale specifications for riverboat constructions; business ledgers and cash books; general office files. 265,000 items.

LA —TULANE UNIVERSITY, Howard-Tilton Memorial Library, Special Collections Div, 7001 Freret St, New Orleans, 70118. Wilbur E Meneray, Librn
Holdings: Vols 950 Mss Pix
Notes: Incl 30,000 photographs of river vessels, published works about river transportation, correspondence and mementos of riverboat captains and papers of the Mississippi Valley Association and the Gulf Intracoastal Canal Association.

LA —LOUISIANA STATE UNIVERSITY, SHREVEPORT, Library-Archives, 8515

RIVERBOATS (cont.)

Youree Dr, Shreveport, 71129. Patricia L Meador, Archivist & Asst Librn
Notes: Archives incl catalogued manuscripts and records, 500 maps, more than 5000 photographs, 1000 architectural drawings, slides. The collection's primary emphasis is the history of North Louisiana, particularly Northwest Louisiana. The 1500 linear ft incl area plantation records and ledgers; personal papers of area pioneers, planters, legislators, politicians, educators, businessmen, and architects; papers and records of longtime (1919-1961) Caddo Parish Coroner, Willis P Butler; the Samuel G Wiener, Sr architectual records (1921-1976) with drawings and photographs; the Ted Flaxman architectual records (1919-1968); the papers (1860-1921) of architect Nathaniel S Allen; the collection of Dewey A Somdal,Shreveport architect, historian and collector, with emphasis on steamboats, travel on the Red River and Louisiana history, 1780-1972.

MO —SAINT LOUIS PUBLIC LIBRARY, Gardner Rare Book Room, 1301 Olive St, Saint Louis, 63103. Julanne M Good, Supervisor; Martha Riley, Rare Books Librn
Holdings: Vols 100 Cat Maps
Budget: ($5573)
Notes: Small growing collection of travels incl St Louis or Missouri, largely transferred from the general stacks, although an occasional purchase is made. Incl early business directories of St Louis, river pilots' handbooks and maps. Noncirculating.

SD —W H OVER MUSEUM, 414 E Clark, University of South Dakota, Vermillion, 57069. Julia Vodicka, Dir
Holdings: Cat Pix
Notes: The Stanley J Morrow Collection of Stereographs: frontier military posts, Indians, riverboats, pioneer life in Dakota Territory. The 440 stereographs of this collection were made in Dakota Territory and the Upper Missouri region between 1868 and 1883 by Stanley J Morrow, Yankton, D T. Copy photographs may be ordered. The collection is described in Wesley Hurt's *Stanley J Morrow: Pioneer Photographer.*

WI —UNIVERSITY OF WISCONSIN, LA CROSSE, Murphy Library, 1631 Pine St, La Crosse, 54601. Edwin L Hill, Special Collections Librn
Holdings: Vols 50 Cat Pix
Budget: $9000
Notes: The steamboat project undertakes to collect photographs, sketches, and basic information on upper Mississippi River steamboats. Collection now incl about 20,000 photographs and sketches, with data file. Most photos are copy prints; some are protected by copyright and may not be used for commercial purposes. Most photos are unpublished. Collecting and data searching actively pursued. Boats from tributary rivers included. Collection is supplemented by primary and secondary sources and active field research. Overall arrangement is alphabetical by boat name, with notation of special categories of boats.

RIVERS

MS —US ARMY ENGINEER WATERWAYS EXPERIMENT STATION, Library Branch, PO Box 631, Vicksburg, 39180. Bernice Black, Chief Librn
Holdings: Vols (350,000) Cat Mss Maps Microforms

OH —PUBLIC LIBRARY OF CINCINNATI & HAMILTON COUNTY, Dept of Rare Books & Special Collections, 800 Vine St, Library Square, Cincinnati, 45202. Yeatman Anderson III, Cur
Holdings: Cat Mss Maps Pix Slides Microforms
Notes: Inland River Collection. Incl logbooks, account books, personal correspondence, diaries, etc. Also, a picture collection of 14,000 items (steamboats, towboats, river views, crews, construction, barges, etc).

PA —PHILADELPHIA MARITIME MUSEUM, Library, 321 Chestnut St,

Philadelphia, 19106. Dorothy H Mueller, Librn
Holdings: Vols (8000) Cat Mss Maps Pix Slides 16mm Films
Notes: Maritime history of Bay and River Delaware and of the port of Philadelphia. Includes shipbuilding and shipbuilders on the Delaware River, mercantile activity, recreational activity, maritime-related organizations, institutions and people, development of Philadelphia as a port, vessel registers 1878-1970s. Artifacts & prints.

MB —UNIVERSITY OF MANITOBA, Elizabeth Dafoe Library, Archives and Special Collections Dept, Winnipeg, R3T 2N2, Can. Richard E Bennett, Dept Head; Corrado A Santoro, Reference Archivist
Notes: Papers of soil scientist and professor Joseph Henry Ellis. Soil and land inspections, surveys and reports; stream bank erosion studies; river reclamation projects; field crop experiments; prairie rehabilitation activities; fertilizer experiments; land utilization studies; tree planting.

RIVERS—POLLUTION see Oil Pollution of Rivers, Harbors, Etc.; Water—Pollution and Control

RIVERS, LUCIUS MENDEL, 1905-1970

†DC —LIBRARY OF CONGRESS, Manuscript Division, Washington, 20540.
Notes: The papers, etc, of Lucius Mendel Rivers.

RIVES, AMELIE (PRINCESS TROUBETZSKOY)

†AL —MUSEUMS OF THE CITY OF MOBILE, Reference Library, 355 Government St, Mobile, 36602. Caldwell Delaney, Adminr

VA —UNIVERSITY OF VIRGINIA, Alderman Library, Manuscripts Dept, Charlottesville, 22901. Edmund Berkeley Jr, Cur
Holdings: Cat Mss Pix
Notes: Extensive collection of mss and printed materials.

RIVES, WILLIAM CABELL

VA —UNIVERSITY OF VIRGINIA, Alderman Library, Manuscripts Dept, Charlottesville, 22901. Edmund Berkeley Jr, Cur
Holdings: Cat Mss Pix
Notes: Papers, personal and political, etc.

RKO STUDIOS

CA —ACADEMY OF MOTION PICTURE ARTS & SCIENCES, Margaret Herrick Library, 8949 Wilshire Blvd, Beverly Hills, 90211. Linda Harris Mehr, Library Administrator
Notes: Stills archive.
See also entry under Moving Pictures.

CA —UNIVERSITY OF CALIFORNIA, LOS ANGELES, Theater Arts Library, Los Angeles, 90024. Edward Shreeves, Chairman, Bibliographers Group; Audree Malkin, Head, Theater Arts Library
Notes: John Mansbridge (art director) Collection: approx 5000 set stills and photographs of sketches of productions made at RKO Studios, 1932-1957; photographs from a variety of other studios; personal research photographs.

ROAD ACCIDENTS see Traffic Accidents

ROAD BUILDING see Road Construction

ROAD CONSTRUCTION

CA —CALIFORNIA DEPT OF TRANSPORTATION, Transportation Library, 5900 Folsom Blvd, PO Box 19128, Sacramento, 95819. Eva Caro, Librn
Holdings: Vols (10,000) Cat Mss Maps Pix Slides Phonorecords Audiotapes Videotapes 16mm Films Filmstrips Microforms

DC —NATIONAL RESEARCH COUNCIL, Transportation Research Board Library,

2101 Constitution Ave NW, Washington, 20418. Lisbeth L Luke, Librn
Holdings: Vols (17,000) Cat Microforms VF
Notes: Photocopying available.

MN —MINNESOTA DEPARTMENT OF TRANSPORTATION, Library, Information Services Section, B-10 Transportation Bldg, Saint Paul, 55155. Jerome C Baldwin, Librn
Holdings: Vols (7500) Reports Microfiche Periodicals
Budget: ($26,000)
Notes: Incl books and reports, 10,000 microfiche, (400) periodicals.

ON —ROADS & TRANSPORTATION ASSOCIATION OF CANADA, Library, 1765 St Laurent Blvd, Ottawa, K1G 3V4, Can. Charles James, Librn
Holdings: Vols (18,000) Cat
Budget: ($8000)
Notes: All areas of ground transportation and road construction.

PQ —WARNOCK HERSEY PROFESSIONAL SERVICES, 128 Elmslie St, La Salle, H8R 1V8, Can.
Holdings: Vols (3090) Cat
Budget: ($6000)

ROAD DESIGN see Roads—Design

ROAD MARKINGS AND SIGNS see Signs and Signboards

ROAD TRAFFIC see Traffic Engineering

ROAD TRANSPORTATION see Transportation

ROADS

CA —ASSOCIATION OF BAY AREA GOVERNMENTS, MTC/ABAG Library, 101 Eighth St, Oakland, 94607. Diane Gillman, Information Coord
Notes: Concentrates heavily on the nine-county Bay Area region. About 10,000 monographs and serials. Title catalog, OCLC/ATS. Central collection of documents for six transit properties in Bay Area.

MD —MARYLAND-NATIONAL CAPITAL PARK & PLANNING COMMISSION, Montgomery County Planning Department Library, 8787 Georgia Ave, Silver Spring, 20907. Janice C Holt, Librn
Holdings: Vols (5000) Cat Microforms
Notes: Specific subject areas include: community facilities, conservation, economics, flood control, highways, housing, human and natural resources. landscape architecture, open space, parks, pollution, population, recreation, transportation, urban renewal, and zoning. Commission's publications are maintained in Records Management (not Library).

NJ —HAMMOND, Editorial Department Library, 515 Valley St, Maplewood, 07040. Ernest J Dupuy, Librn
Holdings: Vols (10,000) Cat Maps Pix
Notes: Also about 15,000 maps; 50 vertical file drawers of administrative, census, national parks, highway, and related materials. No photocopying.

NJ —NEW JERSEY DEPT OF TRANSPORTATION, Library, 1035 Parkway Ave, Trenton, 08625. Margaret L Webb, Librn
Holdings: Vols 2000 Cat Mss Maps Microforms
Notes: Emphasis is on highway, bus, rail, and air transportation. There is a finding-list-index to the department archives, over 1800 items.

NY —ENGINEERING SOCIETIES LIBRARY, 345 E 47 St, New York, 10017. S Kirk Cabeen, Dir
Holdings: Vols 250,000 Cat Maps 16mm Films Microforms
Notes: One of the largest, most comprehensive engineering libraries in the world. Covers all engineering disciplines; particulary strong in electrical and electronic, mechanical, mining and metallurgical, petroleum, chemical, industrial, air conditioning and refrigeration engineering. Incl Wheeler Collection of early

ROADS (cont.)

materials on magnetism and electricity. 125,000 bound periodical volumes; 10,000 maps; 5000 serial subscriptions (many foreign-language). Virtually all materials abstracted in *Engineering Index* (1884-date) are incl in Library. Noncirculating, except to members of professional engineering societies which support the Library. See *Engineering Societies Library, New York, Classed Subject Catalog and Index* (Boston: G K Hall, 1963); and *Supplements*, 1-10, 1964-1973.

NY —NEW YORK PUBLIC LIBRARY, Research Libraries, Science and Technology Research Center, Fifth Ave & 42 St, New York, 10018.
Holdings: Vols (1,100,000) Cat Microforms
Budget: ($647,259)

PA —FRANKLIN INSTITUTE LIBRARY, 20 & The Parkway, Philadelphia, 19103. Miriam Padusis, Dir; Charles Wilt, Readers Servs Librn
Holdings: Vols (300,000) Cat Maps Pix Microforms

PQ —WARNOCK HERSEY PROFESSIONAL SERVICES, 128 Elmslie St, La Salle, H8R 1V8, Can.
Holdings: Vols (3090) Cat
Budget: ($6000)

ROADS—CONSTRUCTION see Road Construction

ROADS—DESIGN

DC —NATIONAL RESEARCH COUNCIL, Transportation Research Board Library, 2101 Constitution Ave NW, Washington, 20418. Lisbeth L Luke, Librn
Holdings: Vols (17,000) Cat Microforms VF
Notes: Photocopying available.

MI —UNIVERSITY OF MICHIGAN, Transportation Research Institute, Library, 2901 Baxter Rd, Ann Arbor, 48109. Ann C Grimm, Librn
Holdings: Vols (57,000) Cat Mss Maps Pix Slides Microforms
Budget: ($25,000)

ROADS—HISTORY

IN —PURDUE UNIVERSITY LIBRARIES, Graduate School of Management, Krannert Library, West Lafayette, 47907. Gordon Law, Librn
Notes: An important resource at the Krannert Library is its Special Collection of Business and Economics, consisting of some 8000 rare pre-20th century strengths in books, journals, tracts and pamphlets covering primarily the early literature of economic thought and business practices in America and abroad, 1500-1870. A catalog was issued in 1979.

MI —UNIVERSITY OF MICHIGAN, Engineering-Transportation Library, 312 Undergraduate Library, Ann Arbor, 48109. Sharon A Balius, Assoc Librn
Holdings: Mss Pix
Budget:
Notes: Incl the papers of Frank F Rogers, Michigan State Highway Commissioner, and the papers of the Lincoln Highway Association.

ROADS—MAINTENANCE AND REPAIR

DC —NATIONAL RESEARCH COUNCIL, Transportation Research Board Library, 2101 Constitution Ave NW, Washington, 20418. Lisbeth L Luke, Librn
Holdings: Vols (17,000) Cat Microforms VF
Notes: Photocopying available.

ON —ROADS & TRANSPORTATION ASSOCIATION OF CANADA, Library, 1765 St Laurent Blvd, Ottawa, K1G 3V4, Can. Charles James, Librn
Holdings: Vols (18,000) Cat
Budget: ($8000)
Notes: All areas of ground transportation and road construction.

ROADS—TOLLS see Toll Roads

ROBB, JOHN DONALD

NM —UNIVERSITY OF NEW MEXICO, Fine Arts Library, Fine Art Bldg, Albuquerque, 87131. James B Wright, Librn
Notes: The John Donald Robb Archives of Southwestern Music, incl 22,000 titles on Native American music, Hispanic music and cowboy music.

ROBBERS see Brigands and Robbers

ROBBINS, HAROLD

MA —BOSTON UNIVERSITY, Mugar Memorial Library, Special Collections Dept, 771 Commonwealth Ave, Boston, 02215. Howard B Gotlieb, Dir
Holdings: Cat Mss Correspondence

ROBBINS, JEROME, 1918-

NY —NEW YORK PUBLIC LIBRARY, Performing Arts Research Center, Dance Collection, 111 Amsterdam Ave, New York, 10023. Genevieve Oswald, Cur
Notes: Clippings, programs, photographs, and films. The Jerome Robbins Film Archive contains 2,600,000 feet of motion picture film representing 2230 individual film titles, and 1650 videotape titles. Every type of dance is included. For description, see Moving Pictures - Collections.

ROBBINS, JOHN ALBERT, 1914-

NC —DUKE UNIVERSITY, William R Perkins Library, Jay B Hubbell Center for American Literary Historiography, Durham, 27706. Erma Whittington, Librn
Notes: 77,312 items, including manuscripts, pictures, clippings, and correspondence. "The objective of the Center is to gather the papers and materials of significant scholars and critics in American literary history." The Center is a part of the Perkins Library Manuscripts Department.

ROBERT, THOMAS

SC —COLLEGE OF CHARLESTON LIBRARY, Special Collections Dept, Charleston, 29401.
Notes: Papers, 1776-79, 1792, incl Robert's plantation journal of receipts, list of slaves, expenses, and "recipe for a consumption."

ROBERTS, BENJAMIN, AND FAMILY

NY —ROBERTS WESLEYAN COLLEGE, Kenneth B Keating Library, 2301 Westside Dr, Rochester, 14624. Charles H Canon
Holdings: Vols (500) Cat Mss Pix
Notes: This is not a large or comprehensive collection, but it does contain some unique mss and pictorial material, particularly material pertaining to the Roberts family. Benjamin Titus Roberts, the founder of this institution, was a principal founder of the Free Methodist Church.

ROBERTS, BRIGHAM H.

†UT —UNIVERSITY OF UTAH, Marriott Library, Salt Lake City, 84112.
Notes: His papers.

ROBERTS, KENNETH

CT —TRINITY COLLEGE LIBRARY, Watkinson Library, 300 Summit St, Hartford, 06106. Jeffrey Kaimowitz, Cur
Holdings: Cat
Notes: First editions, etc.

NH —DARTMOUTH COLLEGE, Baker Memorial Library, Hanover, 03755.
Holdings: Cat Mss Maps Pix Slides
Notes: Papers, working library, incl all of his personal diaries from 1913 to 1957. The diaries from 1936 to 1957 are closed until 2006 AD. This is the last of 2 series of gifts of Robert's papers, etc, given by his niece and secretary Marjorie Mosser Ellis. In addition, MIT has given its collection of the manuscripts, research papers, galleys, etc. concerning *Arundel* to the Dartmouth collection. Noncirculating.

ROBERTS, LYDIA J.

TN —VANDERBILT UNIVERSITY, Medical Center Library, Nashville, 37232. Mary H Teloh, Special Collections Librn
Holdings: Uncat Mss Pix Videotapes
Notes: The nucleus of the developing nutrition collection at Vanderbilt is the papers of medical researcher Joseph Goldberger, MD, and his associate W Henry Sebrell, Jr, MD. The collection consists of first editions and translations of classic books on pellagra, and the letters, mss, and notebooks compiled by Dr Goldberger and Dr Sebrell during their years of research on pellagra. See *Nutrition Reviews*, 33(10):310-312, Oct 1975. 10 linear ft of mss. Library also has the archives of the American Institute of Nutrition and manuscripts representing the work of Karl Mason, PhD, Helen S Mitchell, PhD, Lydia J Roberts, PhD, and John B Youmans, MD.

ROBERTS, R. ELLIS

CA —UNIVERSITY OF CALIFORNIA, SAN DIEGO, Central University Library, Mandeville Dept of Special Collections, La Jolla, 92093. Lynda Corey Claassen, Head
Holdings: Cat Mss
Notes: Complete set of Cuala Press books. Many manuscript letters between Elizabeth Yeats and R Ellis Roberts.

ROBERTS, URSULA (SUSAN MILES)

NY —ALFRED UNIVERSITY, Herrick Memorial Library, Alfred, 14802. June E Brown, Head Librn
Notes: The Evelyn Tennyson Openhym Collection of modern British literature and social history. Correspondence addressed to Ursula Roberts ("Susan Miles"), many pieces concerning the British peace movement of the 1930s.

ROBERTS, WALTER ORR, 1915-

CO —UNIVERSITY OF COLORADO, Libraries, Western Historical Collections, Boulder, 80309.
Holdings: Mss Slides Films
Notes: Papers of the world renowned space scientist and recipient of many honors, Walter Orr Roberts (1915-), who is currently associated with the University of Colorado as a professor of astro-geophysics. He has written extensively on solar activity and its effects on earth. The collection is comprised of correspondence with individuals and business and research organizations, reports, proposals, and conference data, speeches, committee papers, studies, research notes, lectures and student papers plus a few personal papers, printed matter, films and slides. Also there are personal items which belonged to M Sydney Chapman and were given to Roberts. 60 boxes, 1940s-1970s. A typescript inventory is available.

ROBERTS, WILLA MAE

MO —HARRY S TRUMAN LIBRARY, Independence, 64050. Benedict K Zobrist, Dir
Holdings: Mss
Notes: Papers of Harry S Truman's administration; also papers of Edwin G Arnold, James P Aylword, Willa Mae Roberts. Approx 13,000,000 pages on hand.

ROBERTSON, A. WILLIS, 1890-1971

VA —COLLEGE OF WILLIAM AND MARY, Earl Gregg Swem Library, Williamsburg, 23185. Margaret C Cook, Cur of Manuscripts & Rare Books
Holdings: // Cat Mss
Notes: Professional papers, chiefly senatorial files (1933-1966) of A Willis Robertson, US Senator 1946-1966 and chairman of Senate Committee on Banking and Commerce. 150,000 items.

ROBERTSON, BENJAMIN FRANKLIN, JR., 1903-1943

SC —CLEMSON UNIVERSITY, Libraries, Clemson, 29631. Michael F Kohl, Head of

ROBERTSON, BENJAMIN FRANKLIN, JR., 1903-1943 (cont.)

Special Collections
Holdings: Cat Mss Pix
Notes: Papers of Ben Robertson, a newsman and war correspondent for *PM*, the *New York Herald Tribune*, and the Associated Press. Collection incl news-clippings, incl reviews of his books, magazine travel articles and news stories; and notes by him; 2 log books and pictures. Partial inventory, unpublished.

ROBERTSON, H. P.

CA —CALIFORNIA INSTITUTE OF TECHNOLOGY, Robert A Millikan Memorial Library, Archives, 1201 E California Blvd, Pasadena, 91125. Judith R Goodstein, Archivist
Holdings: Vols (3000) Cat Mss Maps Pix Slides Phonorecords Audiotapes Videotapes 16mm Films Microforms
Notes: Ms sources for the history of astrophysics, cosmology, mathematical physics, experimental physics, radio astronomy, geophysics and biophysics. Collections incl the papers of: George Ellery Hale, Jesse Greenstein, H P Robertson, Richard Feynman, Paul Epstein, Max Delbruck, and Beno Gutenberg. Candid photos of physicists at meetings; etchings and photographs of Einstein; scientific medals; selected pieces of scientific apparatus (including the oil-drop machine constructed by Millikan at Caltech in the early 1920s); the reprint collection of Paul Epstein; over 3000 landmark books in the history of 20th century physics and mathematics. Printed publications include: Daniel Kevles, *Guide to the Microfilm Edition of the George Ellery Hale Papers* (Pasadena, Carnegie Institute of Washington and Caltech), 1968; Judith R Goodstein, *The Robert Andrews Millikan Collection at the California Institute of Technology: Guide to a Microfilm Edition* (Pasadena, Caltech), 1977; Judith R Goodstein and Carolyn Kopp, *The Theodore von Karman Collections at the California Institute of Technology* (Pasadena, Archives), 1981.

ROBERTSON, HEATHER

MB —UNIVERSITY OF MANITOBA, Elizabeth Dafoe Library, Archives and Special Collections Dept, Winnipeg, R3T 2N2, Can. Richard E Bennett, Dept Head; Corrado A Santoro, Reference Archivist
Holdings: Pix
Notes: Photographs of western prairie Canada as collected by Heather Robertson from archives and museums across Canada for use in her book *Salt from the Earth*. Pictures are between 1880-1915, showing such things as immigrant families, farms, towns and city life on the prairies, churches, schools, railroads, homestead residences and other aspects of life in the developing Canadian West.

ROBERTSON, JOHN HENRY (JOHN CONNELL), 1909-1965

ON —MCMASTER UNIVERSITY, Mills Memorial Library, Div of Archives & Research Collections, Hamilton, L8S 4L6, Can. G R Hill, Univ Librn
Holdings: // Mss
Notes: Mss and typescripts of his published and unpublished novels, correspondence, personal papers, and clippings. Collection described in *McMaster University Library Research News*, vol 1, no 2, Spring 1969.

ROBESON, PAUL

NY —COLUMBIA UNIVERSITY LIBRARIES, Rare Book & Manuscript Library, 801 Butler Library, 535 W 114 St, New York, 10027. Kenneth A Lohf, Librn
Notes: The L S Alexander Gumby Collection, which incl much on Paul Robeson. Restricted use.

ROBIN HOOD

OH —CLEVELAND PUBLIC LIBRARY, Fine Arts and Special Collections Department, 325 Superior Ave, Cleveland, 44114. Alice N Loranth, Head
Holdings: Vols 550 Cat
Notes: One of the outstanding Robin Hood collections in the world. Incl the comprehensive collection of Robin Hood material, formed by J H Gable in Nebraska. Forms part of the Folklore Collection.
See also entry under Folklore

ROBINETT, GEN. PAUL M.

†VA —GEORGE C MARSHALL RESEARCH FOUNDATION AND LIBRARY, Drawer 920, Lexington, 24450. Royster Lyle Jr, Cur Collections
Holdings: Cat Mss Maps Pix
Notes: Papers, incl personal correspondence, etc, especially with regard to service during World War II.

ROBINS, ELIZABETH

NY —NEW YORK UNIVERSITY, Elmer Holmes Bobst Library, 70 Washington Sq S, New York, 10012.
Holdings: Vols Mss Pix
Notes: An extensive archive, incl important theatrical material as well as material on the early feminist movement. Literary mss, diaries, letters and photographs.
†WA —WASHINGTON STATE UNIVERSITY, Library, Manuscripts, Archives & Special Collections, Pullman, 99164. John F Guido, Head
Holdings: Vols Mss Pix
Notes: The library of Virginia and Leonard Woolf (from Monk's House and Victoria Sq) forms the nucleus of the collection. Incl works by Virginia and Leonard Woolf, the Bloombsbury Group, as well as by other friends eg, Elizabeth Robins, Victoria Sackville-West, Harold Nicholson, etc. Partially cataloged.

ROBINSON, BUDD

MA —BOSTON UNIVERSITY, Mugar Memorial Library, Special Collections Dept, 771 Commonwealth Ave, Boston, 02215. Howard B Gotlieb, Dir
Holdings: Cat Mss

ROBINSON, CHARLES MULFORD

MA —HARVARD UNIVERSITY, Graduate School of Design, Frances Loeb Library, Gund Hall, Cambridge, 02138. James Hodgson, Librn
Notes: See *Harvard Library Bulletin*, XV (1967), 281-286.

ROBINSON, EDWARD G.

CA —UNIVERSITY OF SOUTHERN CALIFORNIA, Edward L Doheny Memorial Library, Archives of Performing Arts, University Park, Los Angeles, 90089. Robert Knutson, Librn
Holdings: Mss Pix
Notes: Personal collection of papers, pictures, etc.

ROBINSON, EDWIN ARLINGTON

CT —TRINITY COLLEGE LIBRARY, Watkinson Library, 300 Summit St, Hartford, 06106. Jeffrey Kaimowitz, Cur
Holdings: Cat Mss Pix
Notes: Incl H Bacon Collamore Collection. See *Edwin Arlington Robinson, A Bio-Bibliography* (Hartford: Watkinson Library, 1971).
ME —COLBY COLLEGE, Miller Library, Alfred King Champman Room, Waterville, 04901.
Holdings: Mss
Notes: Papers, etc.
MA —HARVARD UNIVERSITY LIBRARY, Houghton Library, Cambridge, 02138. Rodney G Dennis, Cur of Manuscripts
Holdings: Cat Mss

MA —WILLIAMS COLLEGE, Sawyer Library, Williamstown, 01267. Phyllis L Cutler, Dir
Holdings: Vols 300 Cat Mss
Budget: $175
NV —UNIVERSITY OF NEVADA, RENO, University Library, Special Collections Dept, Reno, 89557. Robert E Blesse, Head
Holdings: // Vols 39 Cat Other appearances 585 Cat
Notes: Includes individual works by author in all editions including translations; also prefaces, introductions, published correspondence, appearances in anthologies, periodicals, etc. Bibliographical research collection, part of Modern Authors Collection.
NH —UNIVERSITY OF NEW HAMPSHIRE, Dimond Library, Durham, 03824. Barbara A White, Special Collections Librn
Holdings: Vols 100 Cat Mss
Budget: $500
Notes: Strong collection. Incl some mss.
NY —HOFSTRA UNIVERSITY, Library, 1000 Fulton Ave, Hempstead, 11550. Charles R Andrews, Dean of Library Services
NY —NEW YORK PUBLIC LIBRARY, Rare Books and Manuscripts Div, Fifth Ave & 42 St, New York, 10018. William L Joyce, Asst Dir; Susan E Davis, Cur of Mss
Holdings: Mss
Budget: ($7161)
Notes: Incl personal and literary mss, papers, etc.
NY —SYRACUSE UNIVERSITY LIBRARIES, Ernest S Bird Library, George Arents Research Library for Special Collections, Syracuse, 13210. Carolyn A Davis, Manuscripts Librn; Amy S Doherty, University Archivist; Mark F Weimer, Rare Book Librn
Notes: Original mss and correspondence.
OH —OBERLIN COLLEGE LIBRARY, Oberlin, 44074. William A Moffett, Dir of Libraries
Holdings: Uncat Mss
Notes: First editions, etc.
RI —UNIVERSITY OF RHODE ISLAND, Library, Special Collections, Kingston, 02881. David Maslyn, Head
Notes: Extensive collections.
VA —UNIVERSITY OF VIRGINIA, Alderman Library, Clifton Waller Barrett Collection, Charlottesville, 22901. Joan St C Crane, Cur of American Literature Collections
Notes: Papers.

ROBINSON, EMMETT

SC —COLLEGE OF CHARLESTON LIBRARY, Special Collections Dept, Charleston, 29401.
Notes: Papers, 1935-1941, incl typescript of his "Source history of the drama in ante-bellum Charleston, SC (1800-1861)". Incl playbills of performances involving Robinson.

ROBINSON, IRENE see Robinson, William Wilcox and Irene

ROBINSON, JACKIE

NY —COLUMBIA UNIVERSITY LIBRARIES, Rare Book & Manuscript Library, 801 Butler Library, 535 W 114 St, New York, 10027. Kenneth A Lohf, Librn
Notes: Restricted use. The Paul Magriel Boxing Collection on the history and literature of pugilism. The L S Alexander Gumby Collection, which incl much on Jackie Robinson.

ROBINSON, JAMES H.

LA —AMISTAD RESEARCH CENTER, 400 Esplanade Ave, New Orleans, 70116. Clifton H Johnson, Exec Dir; Florence E Borders, Senior Archivist
Holdings: Vols (10,000) Cat Mss Pix Audiotapes Microforms
Budget: ($315,000)
Notes: In addition, 8,000,000 ms pieces, 10,

ROBINSON, JAMES H. (cont.)

000 pictures, 3500 microforms, and 500 audiotapes. Amistad Research Center is an historical research library devoted to the collection and use of primary source materials on the history of America's ethnic minorities, with particular emphasis on Afro-Americans, American Indians, and immigrant groups. Among the larger institutional collections held are the archives and records of the American Missionary Association, the American Home Missionary Society, the Race Relations Dept of the Anti-Defamation League, the Catholic Committee of the South, and the National Association of Human Rights Workers, (formerly NAIRO, National Association of Intergroup Related Officials). Also, private papers of the Harlem Renaissance poet, Countee Cullen; educator and civil rights leader, Mary McLeod Bethune; 20th century civil rights lawyer, Alexander P Tureaud; 19th century Black attorney and judge, George Ruffin; founder and director of Operation Crossroads Africa, Dr James H Robinson; and over 70 others.

ROBINSON, JEROME, 1910-1976

CA —UNIVERSITY OF CALIFORNIA, LOS ANGELES, Research Library, Dept of Special Collections, 405 Hilgard Ave, Los Angeles, 90024. Edward Shreeves, Chairman, Bibliographers Group; David S Zeidberg, Head
Notes: More than 10,000 photographs and 20,000 negatives of live-action shots of theatrical productions in New York and Los Angeles, ca 1930 to mid-1950s.

ROBINSON, JILL

MA —BOSTON UNIVERSITY, Mugar Memorial Library, Special Collections Dept, 771 Commonwealth Ave, Boston, 02215. Howard B Gotlieb, Dir
Holdings: Mss Correspondence

ROBINSON, LENNOX

IL —SOUTHERN ILLINOIS UNIVERSITY, CARBONDALE, Delyte W Morris Library, Special Collections Dept, Carbondale, 62901. David V Koch, Cur of Special Collections; Louisa Bowen, Cur of Manuscripts
Holdings: Vols 215 Cat Mss Pix
Notes: Personal papers of Lennox Robinson, with books from his collections 1910-1954, incl play and other fiction mss; correspondence incl 174 letters from Lady Augusta Gregory and 99 from William Butler Yeats. 12 linear feet. Inventory and name index available in library.

ROBINSON, SUGAR RAY

NY —COLUMBIA UNIVERSITY LIBRARIES, Rare Book & Manuscript Library, 801 Butler Library, 535 W 114 St, New York, 10027. Kenneth A Lohf, Librn
Notes: Restricted use. The Paul Magriel Boxing Collection on the history and literature of pugilism. The L S Alexander Gumby Collection, which incl much on Sugar Ray Robinson.

ROBINSON, VICTOR

IL —SOUTHERN ILLINOIS UNIVERSITY, CARBONDALE, Delyte W Morris Library, Carbondale, 62901.
Holdings: Cat Mss Pix
Notes: Incl the papers of Drs William Josephus and Victor Robinson; with the papers of Theodore A Schroeder. Much on sex instruction and birth control.

ROBINSON, WILLIAM WILCOX AND IRENE

CA —CLAREMONT COLLEGES, Ella Strong Denison Library, Scripps College, Claremont, 91711. Judy Harvey Sahak, Librn
Holdings: // Cat Mss
Notes: In addition to books, includes the manuscripts, correspondence, and original drawings by Irene Robinson of 11 children's books.
CA —UNIVERSITY OF CALIFORNIA, LOS ANGELES, Research Library, Dept of Special Collections, 405 Hilgard Ave, Los Angeles, 90024. Edward Shreeves, Chairman, Bibliographers Group; David S Zeidberg, Head
Holdings: Mss Pix
Notes: 60 linear feet of correspondence, mss, research materials, photographs, and ephemera, ca 1843-1972.

ROBINSON FAMILY

NY —CORNELL UNIVERSITY LIBRARIES, Collection of Regional History, Dept of Manuscripts and Univ Archives, Ithaca, 14853.
Notes: Incl papers, 1868-1950; correspondence, legal documents, and related papers dealing with the law practice of James Richards Robinson (1885-1953), letters and miscellaneous items relating to his service as a NY assemblyman (1923-36); pamphlets, broadsides, trade cards, photos, mss orations and essays, and personal and household accounts.

ROBISON, HOWARD W., 1916-

NY —CORNELL UNIVERSITY LIBRARIES, Collection of Regional History, Dept of Manuscripts and Univ Archives, Ithaca, 14853.
Notes: Attorney, Congressman. Papers, 1957-74; 250 ft., ca 137 transcripts. Restricted.

ROBOTICS see Automation

ROBOTS see Automation

ROBSON, DAME FLORA

DC —GEORGETOWN UNIVERSITY, Library, Special Collections Div, 37 & O Sts NW, Washington, 20057. George M Barringer, Special Collections Librn; Nicholas B Sheetz, Mss Librn
Holdings: Mss Pix
Notes: The papers of Christopher Sykes, biographer, journalist, and novelist; containing mss, letters, photographs, and drawings. With extensive correspondence from Harold Acton; Angela, Countess of Antrim; Sir John Betjeman; Ivy Compton-Burnett; Alick Dru; T S Eliot; Max Beerbohm; Graham Greene; John Hayward; Lord Patrick Kinross; Compton Mackenzie; Nancy Mitford; Anthony Powell; Dame Flora Robson; Cecil Roth; Sir John Russell; Osbert Sitwell; John Sparrow; Freya Stark; James Stern; and Evelyn Waugh, among others. Also, considerable research material about Evelyn Waugh, Adam von Trott, Robert Byron, Lady Nancy Astor; and the foundation of the state of Israel.

ROBSON, J. N.

SC —COLLEGE OF CHARLESTON LIBRARY, Special Collections Dept, Charleston, 29401.
Notes: Papers, 1861-1902, contains business ledgers (1861-1874), balance ledger (1871-1875), receipt book and letter (1898-1902), copy books (1873-1874, 1890-1895).

ROBSON, MARK

CA —UNIVERSITY OF CALIFORNIA, LOS ANGELES, Theater Arts Library, Los Angeles, 90024. Edward Shreeves, Chairman, Bibliographers Group; Audree Malkin, Head, Theater Arts Library
Notes: Mark Robson (Director) Collection. Scripts in various versions, and voluminous production material such as budgets, legal papers, cast and crew information, shooting schedules, post-production files, publicity, storyboards, photographs, posters, set designs and correspondence. Incl such films as *Inn of Sixth Happiness, From the Terrace, Von Ryan's Express, Valley of the Dolls,* and *Earthquake.*

ROCHAMBEAU, JEAN BAPTISTE DONATIEN DE VIMEUR, COMTE DE, 1725-1807

DC —LIBRARY OF CONGRESS, Manuscript Division, Washington, 20540. John C Broderick, Chief
Notes: Papers and revolutionary war maps of the Comte de Rochambeau.

ROCHE, JOSEPHINE

CO —UNIVERSITY OF COLORADO, Libraries, Western Historical Collections, Boulder, 80309.
Holdings: Cat Mss Pix
Notes: The Josephine Roche Papers (1910-1971). Miss Roche, at various times, as the head of the Rocky Mountain Fuel Company, trustee of the UMWA Welfare Fund, assistant secreaty of the US Treasury (1934-1937), and chairman of an interdepartmental committee to coordinate the health and welfare activities of the federal government; she also served in the girls' department of the Denver Juvenile Court (1915-1918, 1925- 1927). The collection consists of 28 boxes of correspondence, published materials, and speeches relating to her various positions and activities. A detailed guide is available.

ROCHE, THOMAS C.

DC —LIBRARY OF CONGRESS, Prints & Photographs Div, Washington, 20540.
Notes: Civil War Photograph Collection incl photographs commissioned by Mathew Brady and others. Brady employed 20 photographers at the height of his operations. His staff incl Alexander and James Gardner, James F Gibson, and Thomas C Roche.

ROCHESTER LYCEUM THEATRE

NY —CORNELL UNIVERSITY LIBRARIES, Collection of Regional History, Dept of Manuscripts and Univ Archives, Ithaca, 14853.
Notes: Incl records, 1888-1934; ca 300 photos, many signed, of stage and screen stars; scrapbooks of press releases and clippings, box office statements and correspondence.

ROCK ENGINEERING see Rock Mechanics

ROCK ISLAND RAILROAD

IA —UNIVERSITY OF IOWA, University Libraries, Iowa City, 52242. Frank Paluka, Head, Special Collections Dept
Holdings: // Mss
Notes: Collection especially concerns the Union Pacific and Rock Island Railroads. 45 linear feet of ms material. Described in Richard M Kolbet, "The Levi O Leonard Railroad Collection," *Books at Iowa,* April 1968.

ROCK MECHANICS

MS —US ARMY ENGINEER WATERWAYS EXPERIMENT STATION, Library Branch, PO Box 631, Vicksburg, 39180. Bernice Black, Chief Librn
Holdings: Vols (350,000) Cat Mss Maps Microforms

ROCK MUSIC see Music, Rock

ROCKEFELLER, WINTHROP

NY —ROCKEFELLER UNIVERSITY, Rockefeller Archive Center, Hillcrest, Pocantico Hills, North Tarrytown, 10591. Joseph W Ernst, Dir; J William Hess, Assoc Dir
Notes: Papers relative to the Rockefeller Family, Foundations, University, and other specific enterprises and contributions to particular areas of social, physical,

ROCKEFELLER, WINTHROP (cont.)

educational, and historic reform,
preservation, conservation, or development.
Extensive records of administrative,
financial, physical, or intellectual
relationships.

ROCKEFELLER ARCHIVES

NY —ROCKEFELLER UNIVERSITY,
Rockefeller Archive Center, Hillcrest,
Pocantico Hills, North Tarrytown, 10591.
Joseph W Ernst, Dir; J William Hess, Assoc
Dir
Notes: Depository for the archives of
Rockefeller University, the Rockefeller
Foundation, the Rockefeller Brothers Fund
and the Rockefeller family.

ROCKEFELLER ENTERPRISES

NY —STATE UNIVERSITY OF NEW
YORK, BINGHAMTON, Glenn G Bartle
Library, Binghamton, 13901. Marion
Hanscom, Special Collections Librn
Notes: Papers, correspondence, etc of the
former aide to the Rockefeller enterprises.
Incl much on the Colorado mine strikes.

ROCKEFELLER FAMILY

NY —ROCKEFELLER UNIVERSITY,
Rockefeller Archive Center, Hillcrest,
Pocantico Hills, North Tarrytown, 10591.
Joseph W Ernst, Dir; J William Hess, Assoc
Dir
Notes: Papers relative to the Rockefeller
Family, Foundations, University, and other
specific enterprises and contributions to
particular areas of social, physical,
educational, and historic reform,
preservation, conservation, or development.
Extensive records of administrative,
financial, physical, or intellectual
relationships.

ROCKEFELLER SANITARY
COMMISSION (RSC)

NY —ROCKEFELLER UNIVERSITY,
Rockefeller Archive Center, Hillcrest,
Pocantico Hills, North Tarrytown, 10591.
Joseph W Ernst, Dir; J William Hess, Assoc
Dir
Notes: Papers relative to the Rockefeller
Family, Foundations, University, and other
specific enterprises and contributions to
particular areas of social, physical,
educational, and historic refrom,
preservation, conservation, or development.
Extensive records of administrative,
financial, physical, or intellectual
relationships.

ROCKET ENGINES

MD —US NAVAL ACADEMY, Nimitz
Library, Annapolis, 21402. Alice S
Creighton, Assistant Librn for Special
Collections
Notes: Typescript of Goddard's research
notes, 1921-1943. Incl numerous
photographs of experimental equipment and
tests.
†MA —CLARK UNIVERSITY, Robert
Hutchings Goddard Library, Worcester,
01610. Dorothy Mosa Kowski, Rare Books
Librn
Notes: The collection of the papers,
correspondence, diaries, experiment notes,
etc, of Dr Robert Hutchings Goddard,
"Father of American Rocketry."

ROCKET FLIGHT see Space Flight and
Technology

ROCKET MOTORS see Rocket Engines

ROCKET RESEARCH

AL —UNIVERSITY OF ALABAMA,
HUNTSVILLE, Library, Box 2600,
Huntsville, 35807. John Warren, Dir
Holdings: Vols (4500)
Notes: The Willy Ley Collection of
Rocketry and Space Travel.

MD —US NAVAL ACADEMY, Nimitz
Library, Annapolis, 21402. Alice S
Creighton, Assistant Librn for Special
Collections
Holdings: Vols 23 Cat Pix
Notes: Typescript of Goddard's research
notes, 1921-1943. Incl numerous
photographs of experimental equipment and
tests.
†MA —CLARK UNIVERSITY, Robert
Hutchings Goddard Library, Worcester,
01610. Dorothy Mosa Kowski, Rare Books
Librn
Holdings: Cat Mss Maps Pix Slides
Notes: The collection of the papers,
correspondence, diaries, experiment notes,
etc, of Dr Robert Hutchings Goddard,
"Father of American Rocketry."

ROCKETS—MOTORS see Rocket
Engines

ROCKETS—RESEARCH see Rocket
Research

ROCKETS AND
ROCKETRY—HISTORY

AL —UNIVERSITY OF ALABAMA,
HUNTSVILLE, Library, Box 2600,
Huntsville, 35807. John Warren, Dir
Holdings: Vols (4500)
Notes: The Willy Ley Collection of
Rocketry and Space Travel.
DC —SMITHSONIAN INSTITUTION
LIBRARIES, National Air & Space Museum
Branch, NASM Bldg, Sixth & Independence
Ave SW, Washington, 20560. Frank A
Pietropaoli, Branch Chief
Holdings: Vols (39,000) Cat Mss Maps Pix
Slides Microforms
Notes: History of flight and aerospace
development, incl biographical material on
aviation pioneers, balloons and ballooning.
Extensive photographic collection (600,000
pictures). Incl the Sherman Fairchild
Collection of aeronautical photographs
(transferred from the American Institute of
Aeronautics and Astronautics). Also incl the
Bella Landauer Aeronautical Sheet Music
Collection (1500 pieces). 2000 films; 800,000
microforms; 9000 volumes bound.
MD —US NAVAL ACADEMY, Nimitz
Library, Annapolis, 21402. Alice S
Creighton, Assistant Librn for Special
Collections
Holdings: Vols 23 Cat Pix
Notes: Typescript of Goddard's research
notes, 1921-1943. Incl numerous
photographs of experimental equipment and
tests.
†MA —CLARK UNIVERSITY, Robert
Hutchings Goddard Library, Worcester,
01610. Dorothy Mosa Kowski, Rare Books
Librn
Holdings: Cat Mss Maps Pix Slides
Notes: The collection of the papers,
correspondence, diaries, experiment notes,
etc, of Dr Robert Hutchings Goddard,
"Father of American Rocketry."
NJ —PRINCETON UNIVERSITY, Library,
Manuscript Collection, Nassau St, Princeton,
08540. Jean F Preston, Cur
Holdings: Cat Mss Maps Pix
Notes: Incl the collection of G Edward
Pendray detailing the entry of the United
States into the space age; much on early
rocketry and the work of Richard H
Goddard. Incl 7 boxes, 17 file drawers.
PA —FRANKLIN INSTITUTE LIBRARY, 20
& The Parkway, Philadelphia, 19103.
Miriam Padusis, Dir; Charles Wilt, Readers
Servs Librn
Holdings: Vols (300,000) Cat Maps Pix
Microforms

ROCKEY, KENNETH HENRY, 1895-

NJ —PRINCETON UNIVERSITY, Library,
Manuscript Collection, Nassau St, Princeton,
08540. Jean F Preston, Cur
Holdings: Cat Mss
Notes: Incl 8 cartons of papers.

ROCKS

MA —HARVARD UNIVERSITY LIBRARY,
Geological Sciences Library, 24 Oxford St,
Cambridge, 02138. Constance Wick, Librn
Holdings: Vols (51,000) Cat Mss Maps Pix
16mm Films Microforms
Notes: The Geological Sciences Library
supports the research efforts of faculty,
graduate students, and upper-level
undergraduate and graduate instruction in
the geological sciences. Subjects collected
deal with the earth sciences in general,
mineralogy, petrology, geochemistry,
geophysics, crystallography, structural
geology, regional geology, economic geology,
some geomorphology, and some gemology.
The collection incl 850 serial publications
and 15,000 maps.

ROCKS (ENGINEERING) see Rock
Mechanics

ROCKS—AGE see Geological Time

ROCKS—MECHANICS see Rock
Mechanics

ROCKY MOUNTAIN REGION

†CO —DENVER BOTANIC GARDENS,
Helen Fowler Library, 909 York St, Denver,
80206. Solange G Gignac, Librn
Notes: Emphasis on Bromeliada Literature;
horticulture; Colorado, Oregon, and Rocky
Mountains Region botany; landscape
architecture; juvenile horticultural and
botanical literature. Incl over 5000
pamphlets on botany and horticulture; also,
197 watercolors of Colorado wildflowers by
Emma Irvine, and 250 of Oregon by Lillian
Hallock.
CO —DENVER PUBLIC LIBRARY, Western
History Department, 1357 Broadway,
Denver, 80203. Eleanor M Gehres, Head
Holdings: Vols (50,000) Cat Mss Maps Pix
Audiotapes Microforms
Notes: Western US History. The department
has a separate catalog, published in 1970 in
7 vols by G K Hall Co. First supplement
published in 1975 in 1 vol. There is a subject
index of some 3 million entries to
newspapers and magazines of the Rocky
Mountain region, added to daily. The
Western Newspaper Microfilm Center
contains approx 7000 reels of Western US
newspapers. Collection has ca 275,000
negatives and prints of Western life; and ca
2500 maps, cataloged and classified.
CO —COLORADO STATE UNIVERSITY,
Libraries, Fort Collins, 80523. John
Newman, Special Collections Librn
Holdings: Vols (11,000) Cat Mss Pix
Notes: The Western American Literature
Collection incl fiction, poetry, pictures, art,
and other works of the imagination set in the
American Frontier West and modern rural
West, especially the Rocky Mountain Area.
CO —VAIL PUBLIC LIBRARY, 292 W
Meadow Dr, Vail, 81657. Charlyn M C
Canada, Librn
Holdings: Vols (500) Cat Maps
Budget: ($5300)
Notes: The alpine environment.
ID —IDAHO STATE UNIVERSITY, Library,
Pocatello, 83209. Gary Domitz, Social
Science Librn
Holdings: Cat Mss Maps Pix
Notes: Extensive collection.
IN —INDIANA UNIVERSITY, Lilly Library,
Seventh St, Bloomington, 47405. William R
Cagle, Librn
Holdings: // Cat Mss Maps
Notes: Description and travel of the US
Plains and Rockies; overland accounts; issues
of California newspapers of the gold rush
era, etc.
PA —UNIVERSITY OF PENNSYLVANIA,
Van Pelt Library, Rare Books Collection, 34
& Walnut Sts, Philadelphia, 19104. Daniel
Traister, Special Collections Librn
Holdings: Vols 2500 //
Notes: Robert Dechert Collection: early
exploration, 17th and 18th centuries; western
Americana, 19th century; Canadiana, incl
Jesuit relations.
UT —UNIVERSITY OF UTAH, Marriott
Library, Special Collections, Salt Lake City,
84112. Gregory C Thompson, Cur
Notes: Includes: Utah, Idaho, Montana,

ROCKY MOUNTAIN REGION (cont.)

Wyoming, Colordo, Arizona, Nevada, New Mexico. Subject emphasis include: Mormons, Reclamation, Conservation, Railroad Development, Explorations and Overland Travel, Range Cattle and Sheep Industries, Native Americans, Fur Trade, Mining, Military. Topics of interest include: history, literature, geography, anthropology, economics, language, architecture, art.

AB —ALPINE CLUB OF CANADA LIBRARY, Archives of the Canadian Rockies, Box 160, Banff, T0L 0C0, Can. E J Hart, Head Archivist
Holdings: Vols (2429) Cat Mss Maps Pix Slides Audiotapes
Budget: ($1000)
Notes: The Archives of the Canadian Rockies is the custodian of the library and archival collection of the Alpine Club of Canada. The materials cover mountaineering technique and attempts worldwide, incl the Alps, Rockies, Himalayas, Andes, etc. Subject areas incl history, personal records, mountain rescue and medicine, alpine flora and fauna, guide books, manuals and handbooks. A large part of the archival collection is concentrated on the Canadian Rocky Mountains, as the headquarters of The Alpine Club of Canada is in Banff, Alberta.

AB —PETER WHYTE FOUNDATION, Archives of the Canadian Rockies, Box 160, Banff, T0L 0C0, Can. Mary Andrews, ACR Librn
Holdings: Vols (4247) Cat Mss Maps Pix Slides Phonorecords Audiotapes Videotapes 16mm Films Filmstrips Microforms
Budget: ($1500)
Notes: Collect all available material which touches on the Rocky Mountains of Canada (from the US border to the Peace River in the north; from the west of Calgary on the east to the town of Revelstoke, BC on the west). This material incl history (the early explorers, Indians, construction of the railroads, mountaineering, and development of the national parks), natural history (geology, botany, wildlife) and poetry and fiction with the Rockies as a setting. Collect maps of the area, photographs, tape recordings of the pioneers. We also house on our premises the Alpine Club of Canada's library, which is one of the most comprehensive collections on the subject of mountaineering worldwide. Noncirculating.

ROCKY MOUNTAIN SPOTTED FEVER

OH —MIAMI UNIVERSITY, Science Library, Oxford, 45056.
Notes: Zoonoses and related diseases. Collection partially transferred from Parker-Davis Memorial Library, Hamilton, Mont.

RODEOS

OK —NATIONAL COWBOY HALL OF FAME AND WESTERN HERITAGE, Library, 1700 NE 63 St, Oklahoma City, 73111. Esther Long, Librn
Holdings: Vols (8000) Uncat
Notes: Art of the American West. Covers western art and artists; rodeo and its history; cowboys; the cattle industry; and biographies on prominent westerners. Personal collection of Walter Brennen; collections of artists, Carl Link and James Earl Frazier.

WV —SALEM COLLEGE, Library, Salem, 26426. Myron J Smith, Jr, Librn
Notes: Collection supports "the most complete equestrian studies program available anywhere". *Myron J Smith, Equestrian Studies:* the Salem College [Bibliographical] Guide to Sources in English, 1950-1980. Metuchen, NJ: Scarecrow Press, 1981; 4645 entries.

RODGERS, RICHARD, 1902-1979

DC —LIBRARY OF CONGRESS, Music Division, Washington, 20540.
Notes: Autograph piano-vocal scores for many popular musical comedies written with Lorenz Hart; mss scores produced during Rodgers' long association with Oscar Hammerstein II; mss for later musicals, films, the television series *Victory at Sea;* orchestrations prepared by Robert Russell Bennett for 8 Rodgers and Hammerstein musicals and other arrangements and original compositions by Bennett.

RODGERS AND HAMMERSTEIN ARCHIVES OF RECORDED SOUND

NY —NEW YORK PUBLIC LIBRARY, Performing Arts Research Center, Rodgers & Hammerstein Archives of Recorded Sound, 111 Amsterdam Ave, New York, 10023.
Holdings: Cat Phonorecords Audiotapes
Notes: 400,000 sound recordings on disc, tape, wire, and cylinder; classical and popular music, jazz, speech, etc. Printed materials related to recordings and the recording industry. Major collection of manufacturers' catalogs.

RODIC RUBBER CO.

DE —HAGLEY MUSEUM AND LIBRARY, Eleutherian Mills-Hagley Foundation Inc, PO Box 3630, Greenville, 19807. Richmond D Williams, Dir; Heddy A Richter, Imprints Librn
Notes: Sperry Univac has deposited a large amount of historical records. Approximately 2000 cubic feet of records, files and photographs that document the invention and development of computers and the rapid growth of the industry were officially released by Sperry Corporation to the Library. The collection includes technical and legal documents relating to the ENIAC and UNIVAC computers as well as records of the founding of the E Remington Typewriter Company and other predecessor companies of the Sperry organization, such as The Library Bureau, Kardex, Rodic Rubber and the Powers Accounting Machinery Company. Thus our knowledge of the Sperry predecessors dates back in this collection to 1902.

RODIN, AUGUSTE

IN —INDIANA UNIVERSITY, Lilly Library, Seventh St, Bloomington, 47405. William R Cagle, Librn
Holdings: // Mss Pix
Notes: Literary papers and correspondence of French writer Judith Jeanne Cladel, 1869-1967. Much of the collection relates to French sculptor Auguste Rodin, who Cladel much admired and about whom she wrote several articles. Also incl copies of Rodin's correspondence, ca 1879-1917, and several photographs of Rodin and his studio. 1589 items.

RODITI, EDOUARD, 1910-

CA —UNIVERSITY OF CALIFORNIA, LOS ANGELES, Research Library, Dept of Special Collections, 405 Hilgard Ave, Los Angeles, 90024. Edward Shreeves, Chairman, Bibliographers Group; David S Zeidberg, Head
Holdings: Vols 50 Mss
Notes: Incl 30 linear feet of mss, correspondence, and memorabilia. No photocopying.

RODNEY, THOMAS, 1744-1811

RI —BROWN UNIVERSITY, John Hay Library, 20 Prospect St, Providence, 02912. Mark N Brown, Cur Mss
Holdings: // Mss
Notes: Some papers of Thomas Rodney, farmer, Revolutionary War officer, member of the Continental Congress, Judge of the Delaware Supreme Court, and US Judge for the Mississippi Territory. 73 letters, essays, poems, documents, notes on court cases in Mississippi and Delaware for the period 1791-1810, and a journal for 1792-1800 about personal matters and Delaware politics. Register available.

RODNEY FAMILY

DE —HISTORICAL SOCIETY OF DELAWARE, Library, 505 Market St Mall, Wilmington, 19801. Barbara E Benson, Library Dir
Holdings: Cat Mss
Notes: Collection incl papers and other mss materials.

RODRIGUEZ ALCALA, HUGO

CA —UNIVERSITY OF CALIFORNIA, RIVERSIDE, University Library, 4045 Canyon Crest Dr, Box 5900, Riverside, 92517.
Holdings: Vols (1,000) Cat Mss Maps Pix
Notes: General research collection in the humanities and social sciences, with special strengths in history (mainly 19th and 20th centuries), literature, folklore and economic conditions, many books from the library of Julio Cesar Chaves. The Special Collections contains the papers of Juan Silvano Godoi, statesman and historian, his diaries (1897-1903, 1905-1921), the papers and correspondence of the historians Nicolas Diaz Perez, Viriato Diaz Perez, and of Hugo Rodriguez Alcala. See Thomas L Whigham and Jerry W Cooney, *Paraguayan History: Manuscript Sources in the United States,* in *Latin American Review,* vol 18 (1983) no 1: p 104-108.

ROE, FRANK GILBERT, 1878-1973

BC —UNIVERSITY OF VICTORIA, McPherson Library, Victoria, V8W 3H5, Can.
Notes: Railway engineer; writer. Incl unpublished nonfiction mss; poetry mss; articles; correspondence; certificates; notebooks; photographs; railroad time books; maps.

ROEBLING FAMILY

NJ —RUTGERS, THE STATE UNIVERSITY OF NEW JERSEY, Alexander Library, Special Collections and Archives, College Ave & Huntington St, New Brunswick, 08903. Ronald L Becker, Cur of Manuscripts and Rare Books
Notes: Roebling Family (1823-) incl the papers of John A Roebling, Washington A Roebling, and Ferdinand W Roebling and the John A Roebling's Son Company incl materials relating to the Brooklyn Bridge and other bridge construction.

ROEBURT, JOHN

MA —BOSTON UNIVERSITY, Mugar Memorial Library, Special Collections Dept, 771 Commonwealth Ave, Boston, 02215. Howard B Gotlieb, Dir
Holdings: // Cat Mss Pix
Notes: Mss, correspondence, etc collected in depth; incl publications by or about.

ROENTGENOGRAPHY, MEDICAL see Tomography

ROERICH, NICHOLAS K., 1874-1947

NC —UNIVERSITY OF NORTH CAROLINA, CHARLOTTE, J Murrey Atkins Library, UNCC Station, Charlotte, 28223. Robert F Brabham Jr, Special Collections Librn
Holdings: Cat
Notes: Part of the Suzuki Collection of books on Mahayana Buddhism. It incl 10 vols and 25 paintings and sketches of Himalayan scenes. Cataloged.

ROETHKE, THEODORE

MO —WASHINGTON UNIVERSITY, John M Olin Library, Campus Box 1061, St Louis, 63130.
Notes: Extensive collection of printed material.

NV —UNIVERSITY OF NEVADA, RENO, University Library, Special Collections Dept,

ROETHKE, THEODORE (cont.)

Reno, 89557. Robert E Blesse, Head
Holdings: Vols (33) Cat Other appearances
690 Cat
Notes: Includes individual works by author
in all editions including translations; also
prefaces, introductions, published
correspondence, appearances in anthologies,
periodicals, etc. Bibliographical research
collection, part of Modern Authors
Collection.
WA —UNIVERSITY OF WASHINGTON
LIBRARIES, Suzzallo Library, Special
Collections Division, Rare Book Collection,
FM-25, Seattle, 98195. Gary Menges,
Coordinator for Special Collections
Notes: Extensive collection; includes first
editions.

ROGERS, BRUCE

CA —SAN DIEGO STATE UNIVERSITY,
Malcolm A Love Library, 5300 Campanile
Dr, San Diego, 92182. D Dickinson, Univ
Librn; Don L Bosseau, Dir
Notes: Collected publications of certain fine
presses and illustrators as: Golden Cockerel,
Black Sparrow, Roycroft, Mosher, Bruce
Rogers, Janus Press.
CT —CONNECTICUT COLLEGE, Library,
Mohegan Ave, New London, 06320. Brian
Rogers, College Librn
Holdings: Vols 100 Cat
Notes: Incl several volumes given by the
Carl and Lily Pforzheimer Foundation with
bookplate designed by Rogers.
DC —LIBRARY OF CONGRESS, Rare Book
& Special Collections Div, Washington,
20540. William Matheson, Chief
Notes: Incl 226 vols and 790 ms pieces of
trade books designed by Rogers,
correspondence, and other ms material.
IL —NEWBERRY LIBRARY, John M Wing
Foundation on the History of Printing, 60 W
Walton St, Chicago, 60610. Diana Haskell,
Cur of Modern Mss
Holdings: Vols (30,000) Cat Mss
Budget: ($50,000)
Notes: The collection covers printing and
printing history of Western Europe and the
Americas from its invention to the present.
It is particularly rich in incunabula (about
2000); the works of the great printers,
among others Aldus, Bodoni, Baskerville,
and Rogers. Printed catalog: A Dictionary
Catalogue. (Boston: G K Hall, 1961);
Supplements (1981). Brief descriptions:
James M Wells, "The John M Wing
Foundation of the Newberry Library," The
Book Collector, VIII, 2 (Summer 1959), pp
157-162; Lawrece W Towner, An
Uncommon Collection of Uncommon
Collections (Chicago: The Newberry Library,
1977), pp 25-26.
IL —NORTHWESTERN UNIVERSITY,
Library, Special Collections Dept, 1937
Sheridan Rd, Evanston, 60201. R Russell
Maylone, Cur
Holdings: Vols 2000 Cat Mss Drawings
Layouts
Notes: The John J Louis Memorial
Collection: works dealing with the
typographic arts and extensive collections of
the major typographers, especially Rogers,
Dwiggins, Goudy, Clelland and Kittredge.
5000 representative examples of the work of
the modern private press from Strawberry
Hill to the current small printers. Additional
material in the general collection.
IN —PURDUE UNIVERSITY LIBRARIES,
Special Collections Dept, West Lafayette,
47907. Keith Dowden, Asst Dir, Special
Collections
Holdings: Vols 925 Cat Mss Pix
Notes: Bruce Rogers Collection. Incl book
design examples and books about fine
printing. The nucleus of the collection is
Bruce Rogers' own collection left to his alma
mater, Purdue University. Some unique
material.
ME —BOWDOIN COLLEGE, Library,
Brunswick, 04011. Dianne M Gutscher, Cur
of Special Collections
Holdings: Vols
Notes: The Frederic Wilson Main Collection

contains several hundred books, pamphlets,
and clippings relating to the art of printing
and bookmaking. Most major contemporary
presses are represented, and it incl examples
of the typographic work of Bruce Rogers,
Frederic W Goudy, Daniel Berkeley Updike,
and Rudolph Ruzicka, to mention only a
few.
MA —WHEATON COLLEGE, Library,
Norton, 02766. Sherrie S Bergman, College
Librn
Holdings: Vols (300) Cat
Notes: The Paul H Smart Collection of
Private Press Books. Espec strong in Bruce
Rogers and Doves Press.
NJ —NEWARK PUBLIC LIBRARY, Art &
Music Dept, 5 Washington St, Newark,
07101. William J Dane, Supv
Holdings: Vols (3500) Cat
Notes: R C Jenkinson Collection of Finely
Printed Books. Shows the physical form of
the book and its development through the
centuries. There is always a related exhibit in
this section of the library covering such
subjects as letter forms, printing, individual
pressess and publishers, papermaking, etc.
Extensive Bruce Rogers collection.
NY —BUFFALO & ERIE COUNTY PUBLIC
LIBRARY, Rare Book Room, Lafayette Sq,
Buffalo, 14203. William H Loos, Cur
Holdings: Vols 275 Cat
NY —CARL H PFORZHEIMER LIBRARY,
41 E 42 St, New York, 10017. Mihai H
Handrea, Librn
Holdings: Cat Mss Pix
Notes: English Literature from Caxton to
1700; first editions of 18th and 19th
centuries, incl mss material on Shelley and
his circle; fine presses (Bruce Rogers);
George Gissing; women writers 1790-1840,
(Mary Wollstonecraft, Mary Hays, Lady
Blessington).
NY —GROLIER CLUB OF NEW YORK
LIBRARY, 47 E 60 St, New York, 10022.
Robert Nikirk, Librn
Notes: Large collection of books and
ephemera designed by him, with many
drawings and book dummies; unpublished
personal archives, etc.
NY —NEW YORK PUBLIC LIBRARY, Rare
Books and Manuscripts Div, Fifth Ave & 42
St, New York, 10018. William L Joyce, Asst
Dir; Francis O Mattson, Curator
Holdings: Cat
Budget: ($7161)
Notes: One of the finest institutional
collections of books designed by Bruce
Rogers.
NY —UNIVERSITY CLUB, Library, One W
54 St, New York, 10019. Guy St Clair,
Library Dir
Holdings: Vols (100,000) Cat Mss Maps Pix
Notes: A private library for the members of
the University Club, their guests, and serious
scholars upon written application to the
Library Director. Holds the Edward
Larocque Tinker Collection of Illustrated
Books Between the Two World Wars, A
Milton Runyon Collection on the History of
Printing and Publishing, the Frederic R
Coudert "Les Bibliophiles des Paris"
Collection, The University Club Rare Book
Collection, and the Frederick G Rudge
Collection of Books Designed by William E
Rudge and Bruce Rogers.
NY —ROCHESTER INSTITUTE OF
TECHNOLOGY, Melbert B Cary Jr
Graphic Arts Collection, School of Printing,
One Lomb Memorial Drive, Rochester,
14623. David Pankow, Cur
Holdings: Vols (11,000) Cat Mss Pix
NC —DAVIDSON COLLEGE, E H Little
Library, Davidson, 28036. Leland M Park,
Dir; Chalmers G Davidson, Dir
Holdings: Vols 150 Cat
PA —EASTERN COLLEGE, Frank Warner
Memorial Library, Saint Davids, 19087.
James L Sauer, Librn
Holdings: Uncat Mss Pix
Notes: The Harry C Goebel Collection. Incl
Bruce Rogers printings (over 460); press
books (about 350); oriental art (over 250);
bookplates (with a separate collection of an
almost complete set of bookplates designed
by Edwin Davis French); Christmas Books;
art and graphic arts (incl the French Graphic

Arts Collection of Adolph DeMilly); first
editions of Christopher Morley; Print
Collection (1315 prints); Oriental art realia
and artifacts.

ROGERS, EDITH NOURSE

MA —RADCLIFFE COLLEGE, Arthur &
Elizabeth Schlesinger Library on the History
of Women in America, 3 James St,
Cambridge, 02138. Patricia Miller King, Dir;
Eva Moseley, Cur of Mss
Notes: Incl the audiotapes and transcripts of
the Women in the Federal Government Oral
History Project, also papers of Clara M
Beyer, Martha May Eliot, MD, Elizabeth
Holtzman, Jeannette Rankin, Edith Nourse
Rogers, and Mary Elizabeth Switzer.

ROGERS, ELIZA NEWKIRK, 1877-1966

MA —MASSACHUSETTS INSTITUTE OF
TECHNOLOGY, Institute Archives, Special
Collections, Cambridge, 02139.
Notes: Papers of Howe, Manning and Almy,
an architectural firm that started in 1913 as
Lois Lilley Howe and Manning, was an
unusual and successful partnership of women
architects. The collection incl
correspondence, financial data, reports,
specifications, photographs, blueprints,
drawings, and research material from the
firm. Housing projects incl Mariemont,
Ohio, as well as designs and renovations for
New England especially in the Colonial
Revival style.

ROGERS, FRANK

MI —UNIVERSITY OF MICHIGAN,
Engineering-Transportation Library, 312
Undergraduate Library, Ann Arbor, 48109.
Sharon A Balius, Assoc Librn
Holdings: Mss Pix
Budget:
Notes: Rogers was Michigan State Highway
Commissioner from 1913-1928. The
collection contains correspondence,
photographs and scrapbooks as well as
volumes from Rogers' personal library.

ROGERS, FRED TERRY, 1914-1956

TX —RICE UNIVERSITY, Fondren Library,
6100 S Main St, PO Box 1892, Houston,
77251. Dr Samuel M Carrington, Jr,
University Librn
Holdings: // Cat Mss Pix
Notes: Papers of Fred Terry Rogers (1931-
1956; 9 linear ft); incl researches in Beta ray
spectrography.

ROGERS, JAMES HARRIS, 1850-1929

DC —GEORGETOWN UNIVERSITY,
Library, Special Collections Div, 37 & O Sts
NW, Washington, 20057. George M
Barringer, Special Collections Librn;
Nicholas B Sheetz, Mss Librn
Holdings: Cat
Notes: Papers of James Harris Rogers (1850-
1929) consisting of newspaper clippings,
photographs, and correspondence about his
work and reputation as an inventor. Incl are
several photographs of General John J
Pershing's visit to Roger's lab when the
latter was honored for his invention of the
underground and subsea wireless and its
contribution to the war effort.

ROGERS, SAMUEL

OH —OHIO UNIVERSITY, Vernon R Alden
Library, Department of Archives and Special
Collections, Athens, 45701. Gary A Hunt,
Head
Holdings: Vols 78 Cat
Notes: Rogers' published works in first and
later editions, incl many variants.

ROGERS, W. S.

KS —WICHITA PUBLIC LIBRARY, Local
History Dept, 223 S Main, Wichita, 67202.
William Clark Ellington, Jr, Dept Head &
City Historian
Notes: The Local History collection consists

ROGERS, W. S. (cont.)

of a photographic archive of Wichita and Sedgwick county subjects and views. Many early Wichita and Sedgwick county town builders are represented in this extensive collection. The photographic archive also includes the prints and glass plates of pioneer photographers, W S Rogers of Wichita and John R Salmon of Mount Hope, Ks. Manuscripts, diaries and a general file of historical information covering Wichita and Sedgwick county history are maintained for public use. Rare early editions of the Wichita Beacon are also part of the Local History section.

ROGERS, WILL

OK —WILL ROGERS MEMORIAL LIBRARY, W Will Rogers Blvd, Box 157, Claremore, 74017. Reba N Collins, Dir
Holdings: Vols (2800) Cat Slides Phonorecords Audiotapes Videotapes 16mm Films Microforms
Notes: Thousands of original manuscripts, letters, photographs, plus many other personal items, all by or about Will Rogers. Library is available by appointment or special permission.
OK —OKLAHOMA STATE UNIVERSITY, Library, Stillwater, 74708. Roscoe Rouse, Dir
Holdings: Cat
Notes: Books by and about him.

ROGERS, WILLIAM BARTON, 1804-1882

MA —MASSACHUSETTS INSTITUTE OF TECHNOLOGY, Institute Archives, Special Collections, Cambridge, 02139.
Notes: Papers of William Barton Rogers, geologist, founder and first President of the Massachusetts Institute of Technology (1862-1870, 1878-1881). Major correspondents incl Louis Agassiz, Joseph Henry, Thomas Sterry Hunt, and Ellen Swallow Richards. Unpublished finding aid, incl correspondent index, available in Archives.

ROGERS, WILLIAM KING

OH —RUTHERFORD B HAYES LIBRARY, 1337 Hayes Ave, Fremont, 43420. Watt P Marchman, Dir
Holdings: Cat Mss Maps Pix
Notes: Papers of William K Rogers who was private secretary to President Rutherford B Hayes. (6 linear feet of ms material). Incl correspondence, diary, business papers, documents, legal papers, clippings, etc (3000 pieces). Index and description in *Guide to Manuscripts of the Ohio Historical Society*, 405.

ROGET, ELIZABETH

MA —BOSTON UNIVERSITY, Mugar Memorial Library, Special Collections Dept, 771 Commonwealth Ave, Boston, 02215. Howard B Gotlieb, Dir
Holdings: Cat Mss

ROLFE, FREDERICK WILLIAM (BARON CORVO)

CT —LEE ASH, (personal collection), 66 Humiston Dr, Bethany, 06525.
Notes: A large collection of Baron Corvo's 1st editions, English and American, incl *Tarcissus*, and what is probably the only signed Corvo painting in the Western Hemisphere. Much ephemeral material and books, etc relating to Corvo. No mss materials.
DC —GEORGETOWN UNIVERSITY, Library, Special Collections Div, 37 & O Sts NW, Washington, 20057. George M Barringer, Special Collections Librn; Nicholas B Sheetz, Mss Librn
Holdings: Mss Cat Pix
Notes: The papers of the Irish man-of-letters

Sir Shane Leslie (1885-1971) containing letters, mss, diaries, notebooks, clippings, and photographs. Extensive correspondence by Margot Asquith, countess of Oxford and Asquith; Lady Violet Bonham-Carter; Burke Cochran; Lord Alfred Douglas; Moreton Frewen; Cardinal Gasquet; Vyvyan Holland; Lady Leonie Leslie; Sir Wilfrid Meynell; Sir Horace Plunkett; John Quinn; Frederick Rolfe (Baron Corvo); and Elizabeth Russell, among others. Also incl research files on Sir Winston Churchill (Leslie's first cousin); Leonard Jerome; Maria Anne Fitzherbet (wife of King George IV); Ghosts and Ghost stories; and Eton College.
†NC —WAKE FOREST UNIVERSITY, Z Smith Reynolds Library, Box 7777, Reynold Sta, Winston-Salem, 27109. Richard J Murdoch, Rare Book Librn
Holdings: Vols 78 Cat

ROLL SEALS see Cylinder Seals

ROLLAND, ROMAIN

IN —INDIANA UNIVERSITY, Lilly Library, Seventh St, Bloomington, 47405. William R Cagle, Librn
Holdings: Cat Mss
Notes: Letters, 1906-1918, of Romain Rolland, 1866-1944 (119 items). All published in Cahiers Romain Rolland, 14.
MA —HARVARD UNIVERSITY LIBRARY, Houghton Library, Cambridge, 02138. Rodney G Dennis, Cur of Manuscripts
Holdings: Cat Mss Microforms
Notes: Incl extensive microfilm collection of correspondence.

ROLLINS, CARL PURLINGTON

CT —YALE UNIVERSITY, Sterling Memorial Library, Arts of the Book Collection, New Haven, 06520. Gay Walker, Cur
Holdings: Vols 1200
Notes: 1200 vols of private printing library, incl many designed and printed by him, correspondence, note books, posters, ephemera. *Works by Carl P Rollins* (bibliography).
NY —ROCHESTER INSTITUTE OF TECHNOLOGY, Melbert B Cary Jr Graphic Arts Collection, School of Printing, One Lomb Memorial Drive, Rochester, 14623. David Pankow, Cur
Holdings: Vols (11,000) Cat Mss Pix

ROLLO BOOKS

ME —PORTLAND PUBLIC LIBRARY, 5 Monument Sq, Portland, 04101. Edward V Chenevert, Library Dir
Holdings: Vols 159 // Cat Pix
Notes: This collection contains mostly fiction and some history written by a Congregational clergyman, educator and Maine author of children's books. Of the 28 titles in the Rollo series, Portland Public Library has 22.

ROMAIC LANGUAGE AND LITERATURE see Greek Language and Literature, Modern

ROMAN ANTIQUITIES see Classical Antiquities

ROMAN ART see Art, Roman

ROMAN CATHOLIC CHURCH see Catholic Church

ROMAN LAW

CA —UNIVERSITY OF CALIFORNIA, BERKELEY, School of Law, Library, Berkeley, 94720. Stephan G Kuttner, Dir, Canon Law Collection
Holdings: Vols (23,000) Cat Mss Microforms
Notes: Entirely supported by the R D and S M Robbins Endowment, the Robbins Canon Law Collection emphasizes particularly Roman Catholic, Eastern and Anglican canon law. Additional subject areas being developed are ecclesiastical history and

institutions, historical and contemporary church and state relations, and ecumenical studies. Library is in process of obtaining complete microfilms of all medieval canon and Roman law mss held by the Vatican Library.
CT —YALE UNIVERSITY, Law Library, 127 Wall St, New Haven, 06520. Morris L Cohen, Librn
Holdings: cat
DC —LIBRARY OF CONGRESS, Law Library, 101 Independence Ave, SE, Washington, 20540. Carleton W Kenyon, Dir
Notes: Publications and mss on Roman law.
IL —NORTHWESTERN UNIVERSTIY, School of Law, Library, 357 E Chicago Ave, Chicago, 60611. George S Grossman, Dir
Holdings: Cat Mss
Notes: Comprehensive collections of Anglo-American and foreign (especially European) law; Roman and Canon law (selective); international law; European Common Market; Williams Collection of Legal Instruments (AD 1300-1700); George W Shaw Collection of Early European Law. Incl 500 ms legal documents.
†LA —LOUISIANA STATE UNIVERSITY, Law Library, Baton Rouge, 70803.
Notes: Strong in civil law and French code materials. An extensive collection of German and Roman materials which were part of the Otto Lenel Collection.
MA —HARVARD UNIVERSITY LIBRARY, Law School Library, Langdell Hall, Cambridge, 02138. Harry S Martin III, Librn
Holdings: Cat Mss
MO —SAINT LOUIS UNIVERSITY, Pius XII Memorial Library, 3655 W Pine Blvd, Saint Louis, 63108. William Cole, Dir
Holdings: Slides Microforms
Notes: Collection covers all areas of learning and European history from Classical Antiquity to early modern period. Researchers using collection receive assistance in paleography, bibliography and reference search. Approx 10,000 1000-foot reels of microfilm (not counting master negatives) reproducing Vatican Library's Latin, Greek, Hebrew, Arabic and Ethiopic mss. Some 8000 100-foot reels of microfilm (again not counting master negative) reproducing rare and out of print books relating to subject areas in the mss. Over 50,000 color slides of medieval and Renaissance mss illuminations. A reference collection of modern materials relating to ms research.
NY —COLUMBIA UNIVERSITY LIBRARIES, Law School Library, Law Building, 435 W 116 St, New York, 10027. James L Hoover, Librn
Holdings: Vols (735,000) Cat
Notes: Incl substantial special collections in foreign and international law; also copyright law, ecclesiastical and medieval law; Roman law.
NY —UNIVERSITY OF ROCHESTER, Rush Rhees Library, Department of Rare Books and Special Collections, Rochester, 14627. Peter Dzwonkoski, Librn
Holdings: Vols 450 Cat
Notes: Collection of materials on 16th and 17th century European law and political theory with special emphasis on works emanating from the French Civil Wars of the late 16th century. Particularly notable are the editions of the works of Francois Hotman and the editions of the Corpus Juris Civils printed in Lyon. No photocopying.
OH —HEBREW UNION COLLEGE-JEWISH INSTITUTE OF RELIGION, Klau Library, 3101 Clifton Ave, Cincinnati, 45220. David J Gilner, Reference Librn
Holdings: Cat

ROMANCE LANGUAGES AND LITERATURES

CA —SAN JOSE PUBLIC LIBRARY, 180 W San Carlos St, San Jose, 95113. Homer Fletcher, Dir
Holdings: Vols 8300 Uncat
Notes: Especially strong in Spanish Literature. Also includes Guglielmo, Marconi Memorial Collection (Italian), as well as holdings in French, Portugese and Latin.

ROMANCE LANGUAGES AND LITERATURES (cont.)

LA —LOUISIANA STATE UNIVERSITY, Library, Baton Rouge, 70803. Anna H Perrault, Humanities Bibliographer
Holdings: Vols (35,000) Cat Microforms
Budget: ($30,000)
Notes: Espec strong in philology, French language, and literature.

MA —HARVARD UNIVERSITY LIBRARY, Widener Library, Cambridge, 02138.
Holdings: Cat
Notes: See *Harvard Library Bulletin*, IV (1950), 271-276.

MI —UNIVERSITY OF MICHIGAN, Library, Dept of Rare Books & Special Collections, Ann Arbor, 48109. Robert J Starring, Head
Holdings: Cat

MO —SAINT LOUIS UNIVERSITY, Pius XII Memorial Library, 3655 W Pine Blvd, Saint Louis, 63108. William Cole, Dir
Holdings: Slides Microforms
Notes: Collection covers all areas of learning and European history from Classical Antiquity to early modern period. Researchers using collection receive assistance in paleography, bibliography and reference search. Approx 10,000 1000-foot reels of microfilm (not counting master negatives) reproducing Vatican Library's Latin, Greek, Hebrew, Arabic and Ethiopic mss. Some 8000 100-foot reels of microfilm (again not counting master negative) reproducing rare and out of print books relating to subject areas in the mss. Over 50,000 color slides of medieval and Renaissance mss illuminations. A reference collection of modern materials relating to ms research.

MO —WASHINGTON UNIVERSITY, John M Olin Library, Campus Box 1061, St Louis, 63130.

NY —NEW YORK PUBLIC LIBRARY, Oriental Div, Fifth Ave & 42 St, New York, 10018. E Christian Filstrup, Chief
Holdings: Cat Mss Microforms
Budget: ($56,455)
Notes: Published catalog of holdings.

ROMANCE LITERATURE

KY —UNIVERSITY OF KENTUCKY, Margaret I King Library, Dept of Special Collections, Lexington, 40506. William Marshall, Head
Holdings: Vols (8000) Cat Mss
Notes: W Hugh Peal Collection of mss and books chiefly relating to British and American literature. Particularly strong in Lamb, Wordsworth, Coleridge and Southey. Incl 4 cubic feet of mss. Incl 16th-20th centuries.

ROMANCES

MA —HARVARD UNIVERSITY LIBRARY, Widener Library, Cambridge, 02138.
Holdings: Cat
Notes: Downs 3643. Medieval romances.

OH —CLEVELAND PUBLIC LIBRARY, Fine Arts and Special Collections Department, 325 Superior Ave, Cleveland, 44114. Alice N Loranth, Head
Holdings: Vols 3000 Cat Mss
Notes: Critical studies, translations, original medieval mss, facsimile reproductions of mss, early printed editions are well represented. The Arthurian and Charlemagne cycles, the *Nibelungenlied* and other Germanic titles, Amadis de Gaula and his numerous progeny, Alexander the Great, Barlaam and Joasaph, and the Seven Wise Masters of Rome are some of the strengths of the collection. Material in the Dewey/Brett Collection is classified by related cycles and their versions in various languages.
See also entry under Folklore; Literature, Medieval; Rare Books

PA —UNIVERSITY OF PENNSYLVANIA, Van Pelt Library, Rare Books Collection, 34 & Walnut Sts, Philadelphia, 19104. Daniel Traister, Special Collections Librn

ROMANCES, FRENCH see Romances

ROMANESQUE SCULPTURE see Sculpture, Romanesque

ROMANIA see Rumania

ROMANOVSKII, NIKOLAI MAKSIMILIANOVICH

WI —UNIVERSITY OF WISCONSIN, MADISON, Memorial Library, Slavic Studies Collection, 728 State St, Madison, 53706. Aleksander Rolich, Bibliographer for Slavic Studies; Robert P Gakovich, Slavic Cataloger; Valdis J Zeps, Baltic Studies Center
Holdings: Vols 1000 // Cat
Notes: The Prince Romanovskii private library reflects his various professional and public interests as a member of the Suite of Tsar Alexander II, as President of the Mineralogical Society and as General of the Cavalry and General-Adjutant. Books on protocol, religion, science, technology, military science, transportation and mining are among the 1000 volumes in his library, as well as an unusual array of maps.

ROMANSH LANGUAGE see Raeto-Romance Language and Literature

ROMANTICISM

KY —UNIVERSITY OF KENTUCKY, Margaret I King Library, Dept of Special Collections, Lexington, 40506. William Marshall, Head
Holdings: Vols 1500 Cat
Notes: French romantic literature.

ROMBERG, SIGMUND, 1887-1951

DC —LIBRARY OF CONGRESS, Music Division, Washington, 20540.
Notes: Collection incl mss, librettos, and film scripts. Romberg's personal collection of 543 phonodiscs is housed in the Motion Picture, Broadcasting, and Recorded Sound Division.

ROME—ANTIQUITIES

MA —HARVARD UNIVERSITY LIBRARY, Widener Library, Cambridge, 02138.
Holdings: Cat
Notes: John Harvey Treat collection on Christian Antiquities of Rome comprises more than 1000 vols.

NY —BROOKLYN MUSEUM, Wilbour Library of Egyptology, Eastern Parkway, Brooklyn, 11238. Diane Guzman, Librn
Holdings: Vols (30,000) Cat Maps
Notes: The Wilbour Library of Egyptology ranks as one of the world's finest, most complete collections of works on all aspects of the culture of Ancient Egypt (down to the Islamic conquest). A card catalog records authors, subjects, series and titles of all books, periodicals and and 12,000 pamphlets. A description of the collection, as of 1924, may be found in: William Burt Cook, Jr, *Catalogue of the Egyptological Library and other Books from the Collection of the Late Charles Edwin Wilbour* (Brooklyn, NY: Brooklyn Museum, 1924). Middle Eastern art formerly included, now transferred to the Brooklyn Museum.

ROME—HISTORY

PA —UNIVERSITY OF PITTSBURGH, Hillman Library, Pittsburgh, 15260. Glenora E Rossell, Head
Holdings: Vols (11,550) Cat
Notes: The classics collection is particularly strong in Greek and Latin literature, Greek and Roman history, Greek philosophy, Greek and Latin language, and Greek epigraphy. In combination with the Frick Fine Arts collection has a good collection in Greek and Roman art and archaeology. The collection of journals is also quite strong in these areas. There has been an emphasis in collecting books by and about Homer, Aristotles, Euripides, Vergil, Cicero and Petronius. It has a unique collection of unpublished PhD dissertations and Master's theses on Petronius. It has a basic collection on Greek and Latin paleography and papyrology.

ROME, HAROLD

DC —LIBRARY OF CONGRESS, Music Division, Washington, 20540.
Notes: Music mss.

ROME, SEVEN WISE MASTERS OF see Seven Wise Masters of Rome

ROMEO GUEST

NC —DUKE UNIVERSITY, William R Perkins Library, Manuscript Dept, Durham, 27706. Ellen Gartrell, Cur of Mss
Holdings: Cat Mss
Notes: Strongest for textile and tobacco industries in Southeastern US, 19th-20th centuries. Incl papers of B N Duke, Richard H Wright, British-American Tobacco Co; business records of textile mills and several lumber companies, Romeo Guest papers on development of Research Triangle Park, North Carolina.

ROMER, TADEUSZ

CA —HOOVER INSTITUTION ON WAR, REVOLUTION & PEACE, Stanford University, Stanford, 94305. Milorad M Drachkovitch, Archivist
Notes: Papers of Tadeusz Romer (microfilm), Polish statesman, diplomat and professor; Polish Ambassador to the USSR, 1942-43; and Polish Minister of Foreign Affairs in the Polish Government-in-Exile (London), 1943-44; incl correspondence, memoranda, speeches and writings, reports, telegrams, minutes of meetings, clippings, printed matter and other materials, 1913-1975, relating to his government service in Poland and abroad, his subsequent years after emigration, political events in Poland, and Polish foreign relations. Originals located at the Public Archives of Canada.

ROMERO DE TERREROS FAMILY

†WA —WASHINGTON STATE UNIVERSITY, Library, Manuscripts, Archives & Special Collections, Pullman, 99164. John F Guido, Head
Holdings: // Cat Mss Maps
Notes: Regla, Counts of: The papers of the Romero de Terreros family, to whom were granted the titles of Regla, San Cristoval, and San Francisco, include wills, deeds, titles, property maps, litigation over such things as sheep walks, water rights, and the titles themselves. Incl also is much detailed correspondence between hacienda administrators and the family concerning weather, crops, and commodity prices. Several large vols, bound in 1783, document the history of land acquisitions by the Jesuit Colegio Maximo de San Pedro y San Pablo of Mexico City, especially the hacienda of Santa Lucia, from 1576 to the time of the Expulsion. Other early papers deal with the holdings and genealogy of the Marquisates of Salinas, Salvatierra, and Santiago. Described by J Horace Nunemaker in *theHispanic American Historical Review - Three Centuries of Mexican Documents: A Partial Calendar of the Regla Papers* (Pullman, Washington, 1963).

ROMMEN, HEINRICH A., 1897-1967

DC —GEORGETOWN UNIVERSITY, Library, Special Collections Div, 37 & O Sts NW, Washington, 20057. George M Barringer, Special Collections Librn; Nicholas B Sheetz, Mss Librn
Holdings: Mss Cat
Notes: The papers of Heinrich A Rommen (1897-1967), educator and authority on political philosphy and international law, consisting of correspondence, mss, clippings, photographs, and printed material. Incl material on religious opposition, in particular Catholic opposition, within Germany to the Hitler regime.

RONIN see Outlaws

RONSARD, PIERRE DE

CA —UNIVERSITY OF CALIFORNIA, LOS ANGELES, William Andrews Clark Memorial Library, 2520 Cimarron St, Los Angeles, 90018.
Holdings: Cat
Notes: Original editions.

CT —UNIVERSITY OF CONNECTICUT, Library, Storrs, 06268. R H Schimmelpfeng, Dir of Special Collections
Notes: First editions and critical works.

DC —LIBRARY OF CONGRESS, Washington, 20540.
Holdings: Cat
Notes: Microfilms of early editions.

RONSARD, PIERRE DE (cont.)

MO —WASHINGTON UNIVERSITY, John M Olin Library, Campus Box 1061, St Louis, 63130.
Notes: A collection of 16th century books pertaining to Ronsard and his circle (particularly titles which Ronsard might have had occasion to consult). Consisting in general of working texts, not rarities, the collection is highlighted by three early editions of the collected works of Ronsard. Also mss related to the work of Paul Laumonier, particularly his critical edition of the works of Ronsard, completed by Professor Isidore Silver and Professor Raymond Lebegue. Printed works and selected archival materials.

ROOD-LOFTS see Church Architecture

ROOFING

MI —CONSTRUCTION CONSULTANTS, 900 Pallister, Detroit, 48202. Joan M Boram, Librn
Holdings: Vols (500) Cat Microforms
Notes: The only library in the country devoted entirely to the subject of roofing and waterproofing. Incl books and vinyl binders containing articles culled from various journals, papers from manufacturers and independent testing and laboratory facilities pertinent government documents, and in-house papers, arranged according to subject matter and indexed. When necessary, papers are cross-referenced. Also, an extensive collection of legal materials relating to roofing and waterproofing failures. Lawyers from all parts of the country avail themselves of these materials.

ROOMING HOUSES see Hotels, Taverns, Etc.

ROOS, WILLIAM AND AUDREY

MA —BOSTON UNIVERSITY, Mugar Memorial Library, Special Collections Dept, 771 Commonwealth Ave, Boston, 02215. Howard B Gotlieb, Dir
Holdings: Cat Mss Pix
Notes: Mss, correspondence, etc collected in depth; incl publications by or about.

ROOSEVELT, ELEANOR, 1884-1962

MA —BRANDEIS UNIVERSITY, Goldfarb Library, 415 South St, Waltham, 02154. Bessie Hahn, Dir
Notes: Approx 125 letters to and from Eleanor Roosevelt dating from 1929 through 1962. There is a finding list to the correspondence in Special Collections.
MI —NORTHWOOD INSTITUTE, Strosacker Library, 3225 Cook Rd, Midland, 48640. Catherine Chen, Head Librn
Notes: The Margaret Chase Smith collection of all her papers, speeches, and broadcast interviews. Incl a tape of a debate Smith once had with Eleanor Roosevelt.

ROOSEVELT, FRANKLIN DELANO

CA —HOOVER INSTITUTION ON WAR, REVOLUTION & PEACE, Stanford University, Stanford, 94305. Milorad M Drachkovitch, Archivist
Holdings: Mss
Notes: Papers, 1900-1967, of Raymond Moley, political adviser to Franklin D Roosevelt and political columnist. Correspondence, reports, memoranda, speeches and writings, notes, and printed matter. The most prominent part of the collection consists of ms drafts of 81 Roosevelt speeches with annotations by both Moley and Roosevelt. 220 ms boxes. Unpublished register is available in repository.
DC —GEORGETOWN UNIVERSITY, Library, Special Collections Div, 37 & O Sts NW, Washington, 20057. George M Barringer, Special Collections Librn; Nicholas B Sheetz, Mss Librn
Holdings: // Cat Mss Pix
Notes: Papers of Fulton Oursler, editor of

Liberty and, later, *Reader's Digest*, including substantial correspondences with Upton Sinclair, H L Mencken, and President Franklin D Roosevelt.
IL —NORTHWESTERN UNIVERSITY, Library, Special Collections Dept, 1937 Sheridan Rd, Evanston, 60201. R Russell Maylone, Cur
Holdings: Vols 740 Cat Mss Pix
Notes: The Hunt H Unger Collection. Incl books published about Franklin D Roosevelt to 1960, letters, magazine articles, pamphlets, ephemera, memorabilia.
†MA —JOHN F KENNEDY LIBRARY, Columbia Point, Boston, 02125. Dan H Fenn Jr, Dir
Holdings: // Cat
Notes: Louis Brownlow's papers relating to government reorganization during the Roosevelt administration and James P Warburg's personal papers and general files relating to the New Deal and his role as advisor to FDR. 23 linear ft of mss. Holdings are described in "Historical Materials in the John F Kennedy Library." Copies may be obtained by writing the Research Archivist.
MN —UNIVERSITY OF MINNESOTA, O Meredith Wilson Library, 309 19 Ave S, Minneapolis, 55455. Austin J McLean, Chief, Special Collections
Holdings: Vols (879) Uncat Mss Pix 16mm Films
Notes: Publications by FDR and works written about him and his political career. Included is a large collection of memorabilia, such as commemorative china, campaign buttons, posters, etc. A complete listing is available in the Division.
NY —NEW YORK STATE LIBRARY, State Education Bldg Annex, Washington Ave, Albany, 12224.
Notes: Books, pamphlets, clippings and manuscript materials on and by him.
NY —SAINT LAWRENCE UNIVERSITY, Owen D Young Library, Canton, 13617. Mahlon Peterson, Librn
Holdings: Vols 400 Cat Pix
Notes: The Hyman Collection.
NY —CORNELL UNIVERSITY LIBRARIES, Collection of Regional History, Dept of Manuscripts and Univ Archives, Ithaca, 14853.
Notes: One letter, dated April 1, 1929, to a Cornell University student.
NY —COLUMBIA UNIVERSITY LIBRARIES, Rare Book & Manuscript Library, 801 Butler Library, 535 W 114 St, New York, 10027. Kenneth A Lohf, Librn
Holdings: Vols 59 Uncat
Notes: The Jacob J Padell Collection. Letters and books from Franklin Delano Roosevelt's personal library. 89 items. Restricted use.
OH —BOWLING GREEN STATE UNIVERSITY, Jerome Library, Center for Archival Collections, Bowling Green, 43403. Paul D Yon, Dir; Elaine R Ezell, Reference Archivist; Nancy Steen, Rare Books Librn
Holdings: Vols Cat Pix Charts Periodicals Pamphlets
Budget: ($3000)
Notes: The Eugene Ockuly extensive collection of materials relating to Roosevelt's life and times, incl books, periodicals, pamphlets, letters, photographs, and press releases.
†PA —CABRINI COLLEGE, Holy Spirit Library, Eagle & King of Prussia Rds, Radnor, 19087.
VA —UNIVERSITY OF VIRGINIA, Alderman Library, Manuscripts Dept, Charlottesville, 22901. Edmund Berkeley Jr, Cur
Notes: The papers of Major General Edwin M Watson (President Franklin D Roosevelt's military aide in the years before and during World War II). Incl some 16,000 documents and other articles, reflect both the full scope of Watson's duties as an aide to Roosevelt and his personal associations with the president and other national leaders during his years of service.
WI —BELOIT COLLEGE LIBRARIES, Beloit, 53511. Dennis W Dickinson, Dir
Holdings: Vols 1000 Cat Pix
Notes: The Joseph C Rheingold Collection

on FDR covers roughly the period, 1930-1950, and incl books pro and con, with some first editions. Incl books written by Roosevelt associates, cabinet members, etc, and deals with the entire Roosevelt period in US history. Many periodical articles from contemporary magazines of the period have been collected. Also books by members of the Roosevelt family.

ROOSEVELT, THEODORE

AZ —PHOENIX PUBLIC LIBRARY, Arizona Room, 12 E McDowell, Phoenix, 85004. Jeannette Brush, Librn
Holdings: Vols (30,000) Cat Maps Pix
Budget: ($12,000)
See also entry under Arizona - History.
DC —LIBRARY OF CONGRESS, Rare Book & Special Collections Div, Washington, 20540. William Matheson, Chief
Notes: President Theodore Roosevelt's library of late 19th and early 20th century works on hunting, exploration, and natural history, with a few earlier classics in these fields.
DC —LIBRARY OF CONGRESS, Manuscript Division, Washington, 20540. John C Broderick, Chief
Notes: The Presidential Papers collection incl the papers, etc, of numerous Presidents.
DC —LIBRARY OF CONGRESS, Motion Pictures, Broadcasting and Recorded Sound Div, Washington, 20540.
Notes: The Theodore Roosevelt Association Collection of news films of Roosevelt.
MA —BOSTON UNIVERSITY, Mugar Memorial Library, Special Collections Dept, 771 Commonwealth Ave, Boston, 02215. Howard B Gotlieb, Dir
Holdings: Vols 300 Mss Maps Pix
Notes: Mss, correspondence, etc collected in depth; incl publications by or about.
MA —HARVARD UNIVERSITY, Harvard College Library, Theodore Roosevelt Collection, Cambridge, 02138. Wallace F Dailey, Cur
Holdings: Vols 12,000 Cat Mss Pix Microforms
Notes: Catalog, 5 vols, published by the Library in 1970. See also *Harvard Library Bulletin*, V (1951), 376-378; Manuscripts, XXIX (1977), 147-154. Supplement to catalog and mss index available on-site; publication pending.
†MA —WILLIAMS COLLEGE, Chapin Library of Rare Books, PO Box 426, Williamstown, 01267. Robert L Volz, Custodian
Holdings: Vols 160 Cat Mss
Notes: No material available on interlibrary loan.
NY —NEW YORK STATE LIBRARY, State Education Bldg Annex, Washington Ave, Albany, 12224.
Notes: Books, pamphlets and manuscripts on and by him. Some "Bull Moose" posters, etc. Incl manuscript of the "Rough Riders."
NY —C W POST CENTER OF LONG ISLAND UNIVERSITY, B Davis Schwartz Memorial Library, Greenvale, 11548. Jean Goldberg, Special Collections Librn
Notes: Primarily naval and US history. Incl almost all his writings.
NY —SAGAMORE HILL NATIONAL HISTORIC SITE, Library, 304 Cove Neck Rd, Oyster Bay, 11771.
Holdings: Vols 250 Pix Videotapes 16mm Films Filmstrips
Notes: Life and times of Theodore Roosevelt. Cataloged.
ND —DICKINSON STATE COLLEGE, Stoxen Library, Dickinson, 58601. James Martz, Acquisitions Librn
Holdings: Vols 229 Cat Mss Pix Microforms
ND —THEODORE ROOSEVELT NATIONAL PARK, Library, PO Box 7, Medora, 58645. Susan Snow, Librn; Miki Hellickson, Chief Naturalist
Holdings: Vols (1500) Cat Mss Maps Pix Slides Audiotapes 16mm Films
Budget: ($5000)
Notes: Theodore Roosevelt, cattle country history, natural history. Also 2400 pictures and 2200 slides.
†OH —OHIO NORTHERN UNIVERSITY, Heterick Memorial Library, 525 S Main St, Ada, 45810.

ROOSTERS see Poultry

ROOT, ELIHU

CA —HOOVER INSTITUTION ON WAR,
REVOLUTION & PEACE, Stanford
University, Stanford, 94305. Milorad M
Drachkovitch, Archivist
Holdings: // Mss
Notes: Papers, 1916-1932, of Hugh
Anderson Moran, clergyman.
Correspondence, photos, memoranda, ms
articles and other papers relating to Moran's
work as director of prisoner-of-war relief in
Siberia, 1916-1917, as special aid to the
Elihu Root diplomatic mission to Russia,
1917, and as secretary to the Young Men's
Christian Association in Manchuria, 1918,
and to his later interests in Russian affairs. 2
ft.

DC —GEORGETOWN UNIVERSITY,
Library, Special Collections Div, 37 & O Sts
NW, Washington, 20057. George M
Barringer, Special Collections Librn;
Nicholas B Sheetz, Mss Librn
Holdings: Cat Mss
Notes: Correspondence written to Edythe
Patten Corbin, prominent Washington
socialite and wife of General Henry Clark
Corbin. Extensive correspondence, spanning
numerous years, is incl from William
Howard Taft, Philip Bunau-Varilla, Myron T
Herrick, General John Pershing, and Elihu
Root, among others. The correspondence
contains extensive discussions of national
and international affairs.

ROPE, WIRE see Wire Rope and Wire

ROPER, DANIEL C.

NC —DUKE UNIVERSITY, William R
Perkins Library, Manuscript Dept, Durham,
27706. Ellen Gartrell, Cur of Mss
Holdings: Cat Mss
Notes: Papers, etc.

ROPES, JOHN CODMAN, 1836-1899

MA —BOSTON UNIVERSITY, Mugar
Memorial Library, Special Collections Dept,
771 Commonwealth Ave, Boston, 02215.
Howard B Gotlieb, Dir
Holdings: // Cat Mss
Notes: Part of Military Historical Society of
Massachusetts Collection.

ROSE see Roses

ROSE, ALEXANDER

SC —COLLEGE OF CHARLESTON
LIBRARY, Special Collections Dept,
Charleston, 29401.
Notes: Correspondence between John
Forraws and Alexander Rose regarding the
purchase of a vessel and the use of slaves as
collateral.

ROSE, BEN

AZ —UNIVERSITY OF ARIZONA, Center
for Creative Photography, 843 E University
Blvd, Tucson, 85721. James Enyeart, Dir;
Terence Pitts, Cur and Librn
Notes: Center has significant collections
consisting of more than 25 photographs plus
other archival material such as negatives,
contact sheets, work prints, correspondence,
financial records, diaries, project files, etc.
Inventories of the collections are available to
researchers. Published guides available for
some collections.

ROSE, CARL

OH —OHIO STATE UNIVERSITY, Library
for Communication and Graphic Arts, 242
W 18th St, Columbus, 43210. Lucy S
Caswell, Curator
Notes: Original cartoons by Winsor McCay,
John T McCutcheon, Dick Moores, Ned
White, Walter Berndt, Jim Larrick, Carl
Rose and Bill Crawford.

ROSE, FLORENCE

CA —UNIVERSITY OF CALIFORNIA, LOS
ANGELES, Research Library, Dept of

Special Collections, 405 Hilgard Ave, Los
Angeles, 90024. Edward Shreeves,
Chairman, Bibliographers Group; David S
Zeidberg, Head
Notes: Personal files of Florence Rose,
executive secretary for the Meals for
Millions Foundation.

ROSE, JOSEPH NELSON

DC —SMITHSONIAN INSTITUTION,
Archives Div, Washington, 20560. William
W Moss, Archivist
Holdings: Cat Mss Pix
Notes: The Archives holds the records of the
National Museum of Natural History's
Division of Plants and the Department of
Botany, 1870-1970, as well as
correspondence of botanists incl Joseph
Nelson Rose and William Ralph Maxon.

ROSE FEVER see Hay Fever

ROSECRANS, WILLIAM STARKE,
1819-1898

CA —UNIVERSITY OF CALIFORNIA, LOS
ANGELES, Research Library, Dept of
Special Collections, 405 Hilgard Ave, Los
Angeles, 90024. Edward Shreeves,
Chairman, Bibliographers Group; David S
Zeidberg, Head
Notes: 55 linear feet of correspondence,
accounts, and family papers.

ROSEN, JACK

MA —BOSTON UNIVERSITY, Mugar
Memorial Library, Special Collections Dept,
771 Commonwealth Ave, Boston, 02215.
Howard B Gotlieb, Dir
Holdings: Caricatures

ROSENBERG, ISAAC

NY —HOFSTRA UNIVERSITY, Library,
1000 Fulton Ave, Hempstead, 11550.
Charles R Andrews, Dean of Library
Services

ROSENBERG, JULIUS

CA —UNIVERSITY OF CALIFORNIA, SAN
DIEGO, Central University Library,
Mandeville Dept of Special Collections, La
Jolla, 92093. Lynda Corey Claassen, Head
Notes: Papers of Harold Clayton Urey
(1893-1981), winner of the 1934 Nobel Prize
in chemistry for his discovery of Deuterium.
Incl files concerning the Emergency
Committee of Atomic Scientists, 1946-49;
also some material on the Rosenberg/Sobell
spy cases; also on his works as science
advisor to John F Kennedy (president-elect).

ROSENFELD, PAUL

CT —YALE UNIVERSITY, Box 1603A, Yale
Station, New Haven, 06520.
Holdings: Cat Mss

ROSENFIELD, JOHN

TX —DALLAS PUBLIC LIBRARY, Fine Arts
Div, 1515 Young St, Dallas, 75201. Richard
L Waters, Acting Dir; Jane Holahan,
Manager
Notes: On-line index of 41 years of critical
writings from the *Dallas Morning News*.
Some letters, papers, ephemera also.

ROSENMAN, SAMUEL I.

NY —COLUMBIA UNIVERSITY
LIBRARIES, Rare Book & Manuscript
Library, 801 Butler Library, 535 W 114 St,
New York, 10027. Kenneth A Lohf, Librn
Holdings: Mss Pix
Notes: Papers, mss, archives, etc. 100 items.
Restricted use.

ROSENTHAL, JEAN, 1912-1969

WI —UNIVERSITY OF WISCONSIN,
MADISON, Memorial Library, Theatre

Collection, 728 State St, Madison, 53706.
Notes: Broadway production records, etc, of
the state lighting authority, Jean Rosenthal.

ROSENWALD, LESSING JULIUS, 1891-
1979

DC —LIBRARY OF CONGRESS, Rare Book
& Special Collections Div, Washington,
20540. William Matheson, Chief
Notes: See description of collection in this
division under Blockbooks; Illustrated Books;
Incunabula. Some of his papers are in the
Manuscript Division.

ROSES

†CA —HUNTINGTON BOTANICAL
GARDENS LIBRARY, 1151 Oxford Rd,
San Marino, 91108. Ann Ravenscroft,
Secretary
Holdings: Vols (8000)
Notes: Emphases on history of botanical
science; papers and notes of American
botanists and naturalists of The West;
botanical illustration, etc. Subtropical
horticulture, incl cacti and succulents of
Australia, South Africa, and Mexico.

OR —LIBRARY ASSOCIATION OF
PORTLAND, Social Science Dept, 801 SW
Tenth Ave, Portland, 97205. James
Burghardt, Dir
Holdings: Vols 306 Cat
Notes: The Thomas Newton Cook Rose
Library and the Jesse Currey Memorial Rose
Collection.

ROSICRUCIANS

AZ —WORLD UNIVERSITY, Library, 711 E
Blacklidge Dr, Tucson, 85719. Howard John
Zitko, Cur
Holdings: Vols (15,000) Cat Mss Maps
Audiotapes
Notes: Collection concerns what are
generally called the "frontier sciences." No
interlibrary loan.

CA —FRANCIS BACON LIBRARY, 655 N
Dartmouth Ave, Claremont, 91711.
Elizabeth S Wrigley, Dir
Holdings: Vols 550 Cat Mss Maps Pix
Notes: Incl the first published manifestos
(17th century) as well as current vols and
periodicals. Many clippings, articles, etc.

CA —ROSICRUCIAN ORDER, AMORC,
Research Library, Rosicrucian Park, San
Jose, 95191. Clara Campbell, Librn
Holdings: Cat
Notes: Collection incl materials on
Rosicrucians, ancient Egyptian history,
parapsychology and mysticism. No
interlibrary loans.

ROSKOLENKO, HARRY

MA —BOSTON UNIVERSITY, Mugar
Memorial Library, Special Collections Dept,
771 Commonwealth Ave, Boston, 02215.
Howard B Gotlieb, Dir
Holdings: Cat Mss
Notes: Mss, correspondence, etc collected in
depth; incl publications by or about.

ROSS, DARRELL

CA —UNIVERSITY OF CALIFORNIA, LOS
ANGELES, Theater Arts Library, Los
Angeles, 90024. Edward Shreeves,
Chairman, Bibliographers Group; Audree
Malkin, Head, Theater Arts Library
Notes: Darrell Ross, professor emeritus of
UCLA Dept of Theater Arts, Collection:
covers the history of television programming
and production from the 1940's to 1980, and
complements the film and videotape
holdings of the UCLA Film/TV Archives.
Incl television books, scripts, photographs,
periodicals, clippings, bibliographies, and
research material dating from the 1930's.

ROSS, EARLE D.

IA —IOWA STATE UNIVERSITY, Library,
Dept of Special Collections, Ames, 50011.
Stanley M Yates, Head
Notes: Earle D Ross papers. Ross was an
early researcher in agricultural history.

ROSS, HAROLD

NY —NEW YORK UNIVERSITY, Elmer Holmes Bobst Library, Div of Special Collections, Washington Sq S, New York, 10012. Frank Walker, Librn; Patrick McGuire, Asst Librn
Notes: Extensive Geoffrey T Hellman collection of articles, letters and memorabilia; much material concerning Harold Ross; a great deal on New York City.

ROSS, HERBERT AND NORA KAYE

MA —BOSTON UNIVERSITY, Mugar Memorial Library, Special Collections Dept, 771 Commonwealth Ave, Boston, 02215. Howard B Gotlieb, Dir
Holdings: Cat Mss Correspondence Pix

ROSS, HOLT E.

MS —MISSISSIPPI STATE UNIVERSITY, Mitchell Memorial Library, Box 5408, Mississippi State, 39762. Frances N Coleman, Head, Special Collections
Holdings: Cat Mss
Notes: The Holt E Ross papers, a collection dealing with labor organization in Mississippi, incl correspondence, speeches, poems, legal papers, published materials and newspaper clippings collected by Mr Ross during his career as a labor leader, the collection also pertains to the state, national and international labor scene.

ROSS, MALCOLM MACKENZIE, 1911-

AB —UNIVERSITY OF CALGARY, Libraries, Special Collections Div, 2500 University Dr, Calgary, T2N 1N4, Can.
Holdings: Cat Mss
Notes: The Malcolm Ross Papers include correspondence about Ross's academic career from 1934 to the present and his correspondence with other scholars. There is an important collection of correspondence with Canadian writers and poets. The major part of the papers consists of Malcolm Ross's editorial correspondence about the New Canadian Library reprint series from 1962-1976.

ROSS, W.E. DAN

MA —BOSTON UNIVERSITY, Mugar Memorial Library, Special Collections Dept, 771 Commonwealth Ave, Boston, 02215. Howard B Gotlieb, Dir
Holdings: Cat Mss Pix
Notes: Mss, correspondence, etc collected in depth; incl publications by or about.

ROSSA, JEREMIAH O'DONOVAN

MA —BOSTON COLLEGE LIBRARIES, Thomas P O'Neill Library, Irish Collection, Chestnut Hill, 02167. Ralph Coffman, Cur
Holdings: Vols (10,000) Cat Mss Maps Pix
Notes: Nearly every aspect of Irish history and literature are covered in this collection. Items of special interest are the many papers of Patrick Andrew Collins, president of the Irish Land League, and letters of Jeremiah O'Donovan Rossa, poet, editor and leader in the Fenian and related organizations. Holdings also incl a facsimile of the famous illuminated ms of the Gospels, the *Book of Kells*; a complete vol of *Malton's Views of Dublin, 1799; The Ordinance Surveys;* a complete set of the *Irish Bulletin;* and Colgan's *Acta Sanctorum Hiberniae* describing the lives of the Irish saints.

ROSSEEL, JOSEPH

NY —SAINT LAWRENCE UNIVERSITY, Owen D Young Library, Canton, 13617. Mahlon Peterson, Librn
Holdings: Cat Mss Maps Pix
Notes: The Parish-Rosseel Papers. The bulk of the material falls within the period 1807-1816 and consists of the correspondence of David Parish and Joseph Rosseel. Very valuable source of information on the settlement of the North Country and the War of 1812 as well as the general social and economic conditions of the time. Approx 1600 items.

ROSSEN, ROBERT

CA —UNIVERSITY OF CALIFORNIA, LOS ANGELES, Theater Arts Library, Los Angeles, 90024. Edward Shreeves, Chairman, Bibliographers Group; Audree Malkin, Head, Theater Arts Library
Notes: Robert Rossen (director) Collection: screenplays, photographs, production material, scrapbooks, clippings, and personal notes.

ROSSER, THOMAS L.

VA —UNIVERSITY OF VIRGINIA, Alderman Library, Manuscripts Dept, Charlottesville, 22901. Edmund Berkeley Jr, Cur
Holdings: Cat Mss Maps Pix
Notes: About 1500 collections have material pertaining to the Civil War and particularly to the Army of Northern Virginia and campaigns and battles in Virginia. There are letters, diaries, reminiscences, maps, and pictorial material of Confederate soldiers and civilians, as well as papers of Robert E Lee, J E B Stuart, Thomas L Rosser, Jubal A Early, John Daniel Imboden, William "Extra Billy" Smith, Henry Alexander Wise, Eppa Hunton, and John S Mosby.

ROSSETTI, DANTE GABRIEL

NJ —PRINCETON UNIVERSITY, Library, Rare Books Dept, Princeton, 08544. Stephen Ferguson, Cur
Holdings: Cat
Notes: The Janet Troxell Collection of documents relating to the Pre-Raphaelite Movement, the Rossetti family, William Bell Scott, etc.
See also entry under Pre-Raphaelites and Pre-Raphaelitism.

ROSSETTI FAMILY

NJ —PRINCETON UNIVERSITY, Library, Rare Books Dept, Princeton, 08544. Stephen Ferguson, Cur
Holdings: Cat
Notes: The Janet Troxell Collection of documents relating to the Pre-Raphaelite Movement, the Rossetti family, William Bell Scott, etc.

ROSSINI, GIOACCHINO ANTONIO

BC —UNIVERSITY OF VICTORIA, McPherson Library, Victoria, V8W 3H5, Can.
Notes: Incl transcripts: 218 pages, ca 1825; ms; Spanish album containing copies of a selection from *Italian in Algiers, Othello,* etc.

ROSSMAN, ELEANOR

CA —UNIVERSITY OF CALIFORNIA, LOS ANGELES, Theater Arts Library, Los Angeles, 90024. Edward Shreeves, Chairman, Bibliographers Group; Audree Malkin, Head, Theater Arts Library
Notes: Eleanor Rossman Collection: 900 photographs, 1940-1965, consisting of motion picture and theater stills, portraits of motion picture and stage personalities, theater programs, and clippings related to stage productions.

ROSSNER, JUDITH

MA —BOSTON UNIVERSITY, Mugar Memorial Library, Special Collections Dept, 771 Commonwealth Ave, Boston, 02215. Howard B Gotlieb, Dir
Holdings: Cat Mss Correspondence

ROSTEN, LEO CALVIN, 1908-

MA —BRANDEIS UNIVERSITY, Goldfarb Library, 415 South St, Waltham, 02154. Bessie Hahn, Dir
Notes: 9 linear ft of first and signed editions of Leo Rosten and 39 linear ft of mss, book reviews, and promotional material. The collection has not been processed as yet, spring 1984.

ROTH, CECIL

DC —GEORGETOWN UNIVERSITY, Library, Special Collections Div, 37 & O Sts NW, Washington, 20057. George M Barringer, Special Collections Librn; Nicholas B Sheetz, Mss Librn
Holdings: Mss Pix
Notes: The papers of Christopher Sykes, biographer, journalist, and novelist; containing mss, letters, photographs, and drawings. With extensive correspondence from Harold Acton; Angela, Countess of Antrim; Sir John Betjeman; Ivy Compton-Burnett; Alick Dru; T S Eliot; Max Beerbohm; Graham Greene; John Hayward; Lord Patrick Kinross; Compton Mackenzie; Nancy Mitford; Anthony Powell; Dame Flora Robson; Cecil Roth; Sir John Russell; Osbert Sitwell; John Sparrow; Freya Stark; James Stern; and Evelyn Waugh, among others. Also, considerable research material about Evelyn Waugh, Adam von Trott, Robert Byron, Lady Nancy Astor; and the foundation of the state of Israel.

ROTH, HENRY

MA —BOSTON UNIVERSITY, Mugar Memorial Library, Special Collections Dept, 771 Commonwealth Ave, Boston, 02215. Howard B Gotlieb, Dir
Holdings: Cat Mss Pix
Notes: Mss, correspondence, etc collected in depth; incl publications by or about.

ROTH, HERRICK

CO —UNIVERSITY OF COLORADO, Libraries, Western Historical Collections, Boulder, 80309.
Holdings: Mss
Notes: Papers of Herrick Roth (b 1916), who was one of the founders in 1946 of the American Federation of Teachers local in Denver. In 1951 he left teaching to devote himself full-time to the labor movement. From 1962 until his ouster by George Meany in 1973 he served as President of the Colorado Labor Council. Since then he has taught at Denver University, run unsuccessfully for the US Senate and served as head of the State Employment Service. The collection contains correspondence, pamphlets, clippings and other material on Roth's labor union, political and social interests. The largest portion of the material deals with the Colorado Labor Council and the American Federation of Teachers. 25 boxes, 1950s-1970s. Typescript inventory is available.

ROTH, PHILIP

DC —LIBRARY OF CONGRESS, Manuscript Division, Washington, 20540. John C Broderick, Chief
Notes: His papers, incl mss of his books.
NV —UNIVERSITY OF NEVADA, RENO, University Library, Special Collections Dept, Reno, 89557. Robert E Blesse, Head
Holdings: Vols (76) Cat Other appearances 120 Cat
Notes: Includes individual works by author in all editions including translations; also prefaces, introductions, published correspondence, appearances in anthologies, periodicals, etc. Bibliographical research collection, part of Modern Authors Collection.

ROTHA, PAUL, 1907-

CA —UNIVERSITY OF CALIFORNIA, LOS ANGELES, Research Library, Dept of Special Collections, 405 Hilgard Ave, Los Angeles, 90024. Edward Shreeves, Chairman, Bibliographers Group; David S Zeidberg, Head
Holdings: Vols Cat Mss Pix
Notes: 21 linear feet of typescripts, books, drawings, and diaries.

ROTHCHILD, SYLVIA

MA —BOSTON UNIVERSITY, Mugar
Memorial Library, Special Collections Dept,
771 Commonwealth Ave, Boston, 02215.
Howard B Gotlieb, Dir
Holdings: Cat Mss Correspondence

ROTHENBERG, JEROME, 1931-

CA —UNIVERSITY OF CALIFORNIA, SAN
DIEGO, Central University Library,
Mandeville Dept of Special Collections, La
Jolla, 92093. Lynda Corey Claassen, Head;
Michael Davidson, Cur, Archive for New
Poetry
Notes: An extensive collection of modern
English-language poetry published since
World War II, the Archive contains over 28,
000 books, over 1000 magazine titles, and
some 900 tapes and records. The Archive
maintains substantial collections of papers
from Paul Blackburn, Charles Reznikoff,
Lew Welch, Jerome Rothenberg, Louis
Zukofsky, and other major contemporary
American poets.
FL —UNIVERSITY OF MIAMI, Otto G
Richter Library, PO Box 248214, Coral
Gables, 33124. Frank Rodgers, Dir of
Libraries
Notes: Innovative and experimental writing
of the 1960s and 1970s. Incl generous
proportion of press books: Black Sparrow,
Auerhahn, and many others; also other
private publications ranging from the best to
the least attractive. Format incl postcards
and broadsides as well as periodical and
book form. Writers incl Charles Bukowski,
Diane Wakoski, Jerome Rothenberg, Clayton
Eshleman, and many of their
contemporaries. 2400 items.
See also entry under Poetry, Modern.

ROTHKO, MARK

DC —NATIONAL GALLERY OF ART,
Library, Sixth & Constitution Ave NW,
Washington, 20565. J M Edelstein, Chief
Librn
Notes: 285 pictures by abstract artist given
by the Mark Rothko Foundation.

ROTHSTEIN, DAVID

IL —CHICAGO HISTORICAL SOCIETY,
Library, Clark St at North Ave, Chicago,
60614. Archie Motley, Manuscript Librn
Notes: Papers of labor union counsel.
See also entry under Labor-History.

ROTHENSTEIN, SIR WILLIAM

IN —INDIANA UNIVERSITY, Lilly Library,
Seventh St, Bloomington, 47405. William R
Cagle, Librn
Notes: Contemporary with and depicting
Lincoln; the War of 1812 and other periods.
Incl significant mss of the modern
cartoonists and caricaturists Ardizzone,
Beerbohm, Fontane Fox, Kin Hubbard,
Charles Bacon Jackson, McCutcheon,
Messick, Nast, Rothenstein, Sendak, and
many miscellaneous items.
MA —HARVARD UNIVERSITY LIBRARY,
Houghton Library, Cambridge, 02138.
Rodney G Dennis, Cur of Manuscripts
Holdings: Mss

ROTHERMERE, LORD

CA —HOOVER INSTITUTION ON WAR,
REVOLUTION & PEACE, Stanford
University, Stanford, 94305. Milorad M
Drachkovitch, Archivist
Notes: Papers of Princess Stephanis zu
Hohenlohe, confidant and intermediary of
Lord Rothermere, owner of the Daily Mail,
London, and Adolf Hitler, incl
correspondence, memoranda, telegrams,
clippings, and printed matter, 1914-1972,
relating to improvement of German-English
relations in the 1930s, political developments
in Hungary, and Princess Hohenlohe's
personal life in Europe and the US, as well
as her associations with various publishing
houses. 4 ms boxes.

ROTOGRAVURES

MN —3M COMPANY, Mertle Library, 3M
Center, Bldg 235-1D, Saint Paul, 55101.
Holdings: Vols (4000) // Cat Mss Pix
Notes: The collection of Joseph S Mertle,
includes patents, portraits, a clipping file,
and other historical graphic arts books and
periodicals.

ROTTLANDER, BERNHARD

BC —UNIVERSITY OF VICTORIA,
McPherson Library, Victoria, V8W 3H5,
Can.
Notes: Notebook titled on cover "Kant
Kommentar Dritter Band," on
"Ausarbeitungen zur Kritik der reinen
Vernunft, zur Kritik der praktischen
Vernunft, zu den Prolegomenen und zur
Metaphysik der Sitten, auch zu Reinholds
Briefen. Item: Zur Kritik der Urteilskraft
Dritter Band;" holograph in ink, pages, 268-
403.

ROUCEK, JOSEPH

†PA —BALCH INSTITUTE FOR ETHNIC
STUDIES, Library, 18 S Seventh St,
Philadelphia, 19106.
Notes: His papers.

ROUGH RIDERS

AZ —PHOENIX PUBLIC LIBRARY, Arizona
Room, 12 E McDowell, Phoenix, 85004.
Jeannette Brush, Librn
Holdings: Vols (30,000) Cat Maps Pix
Budget: ($12,000)
See also entry under Arizona - History.

ROUGHEAD, WILLIAM

IN —INDIANA UNIVERSITY, Lilly Library,
Seventh St, Bloomington, 47405. William R
Cagle, Librn
Holdings: Vols 21 Cat Mss
Notes: A complete collection of Pearson's
works, including many with the author's
annotations. Manuscripts include extensive
correspondence between Pearson and two
British crime enthusiasts, William Roughead
and Marie Belloc-Lowndes.

ROUNDS see Glees, Catches, Rounds, Etc.

ROUS, PEYTON

PA —AMERICAN PHILOSOPHICAL
SOCIETY, Library, 105 S Fifth St,
Philadelphia, 19106. Edward C Carter II,
Librn
Holdings: Cat Mss
Notes: Medical research.

ROUSSEL, ROBERT

†TX —UNIVERSITY OF TEXAS
LIBRARIES, Austin, 78712.
Notes: Collection of 89 autographed music
manuscripts by five french composers:
Gabriel Faure, Maurice Ravel, Claude
Debussy, Robert Roussel, Paul Dukas. About
60 percent of Roussel's entire repertory is
included, as well as nearly one-half of
Ravel's total musical output.

ROUSSEAU, JEAN JACQUES

CA —UNIVERSITY OF CALIFORNIA, LOS
ANGELES, William Andrews Clark
Memorial Library, 2520 Cimarron St, Los
Angeles, 90018.
Holdings: Cat
Notes: Original editions.
MA —HARVARD UNIVERSITY LIBRARY,
Houghton Library, Cambridge, 02138.
Rodney G Dennis, Cur of Manuscripts
Holdings: Cat Mss
Notes: For mss, see Romanic Review, XX
(1929), 209-221.
WI —UNIVERSITY OF WISCONSIN,
MADISON, Memorial Library, Western
European Humanities Collection, 728 State
St, Madison, 53706. Charles Szabo,
Bibliographer
Notes: Rousseau Collection. This collection
is noted for its range of materials by and
about Rousseau and his impact on 18th
century thought. Includes many rare
ephemeral pieces, some 37 first or early
editions of Rousseau, contemporary
pamphlets, books, and extracts both for and
against Rousseau, and a few 19th century
judgments.
ON —UNIVERSITY OF TORONTO, Thomas
Fisher Rare Book Library, 120 Saint George
St, Toronto, M5S 1A5, Can. Richard G
Landon, Head
Holdings: Vols 700 Mss Pix
Notes: Rousseau Collection contains first
and early editions of Rousseau's works and
editions of contemporary critics of his work.
Specially bound deluxe editions of works
with specially commissioned illustrations;
some original drawings by C F Chauvet and
C N Cochin; two books from Rousseau's
library; engraved portraits, medallions struck
in Rousseau's honour, and small statuettes
and busts. Manuscript material includes
some letters and other documents and
voluminous research notes taken at the
request of a patron who planned to write a
history of women.

ROWAN, STEPHEN C.

DC —LIBRARY OF CONGRESS,
Washington, 20540.
Holdings: Mss
Notes: His papers, 1808-1890; incl private
journals, letterbook, etc. Deposited by the
Naval Historical Foundation.

ROWELL, CHESTER HARVEY, 1867-1948

CA —CALIFORNIA STATE UNIVERSITY,
FRESNO, Henry Madden Library, Dept of
Special Collections, Fresno, 93740. Ronald J
Mahoney, Head
Holdings: Vols 4 Cat Mss
Notes: Approx 300 letters, 1882-1938.

ROWELL, MILO E.

CA —HOOVER INSTITUTION ON WAR,
REVOLUTION & PEACE, Stanford
University, Stanford, 94305. Milorad M
Drachkovitch, Archivist
Holdings: Mss
Notes: Papers of Milo E Rowell, Lt Col, US
Army, and lawyer in the Government
Section of General Headquarters, Supreme
Commander for the Allied Powers, incl
reports, drafts, and memoranda, December
1945-March 1946, relating to the writing of
the revised Japanese constitution, as required
in the Potsdam Declaration of 1945. 1/2 ms
box.

ROWING

CA —UNIVERSITY OF CALIFORNIA,
BERKELEY, Bancroft Library, Manuscripts
Division, Berkeley, 94720. James D Hart,
Dir
Notes: Wide scope but emphasis on the
University's teams.
CT —YALE UNIVERSITY, Box 1603A, Yale
Station, New Haven, 06520.
Notes: Papers of Walter Camp, father of
American football and foremost authority on
sports and physical fitness. 48 microfilm
reels; incl also over 20,000 clippings, etc on
sports, providing virtual history, 1866-1925.
Published guide to the collection for sale.

ROWLAND, GENE

TX —NORTH TEXAS STATE UNIVERSITY,
Audio Center, Box 5188, NT Station,
Denton, 76203. Morris Martin, Music Librn
Notes: More than 1600 manuscript jazz
compositions, (incl scores and parts,
alternate versions, expanded arrangements)
by Stan Kenton, Johnny Richards, Joe
Coccia, Lennie Niehaus, Pete Rugolo, Willie
Maiden, Bob Curnow, Ken Hanna, Gene
Rowland, Bob Graettinger and others, used

ROWLAND, GENE (cont.)

by the Stan Kenton Band and given to North Texas State University in 1962 and at Kenton's death in 1979. Unpublished catalog: Breeden, Leon, *Stan Kenton Music in the NTSU Jazz Studies Library and the NTSU Music Library*, Denton, 1983 (99 pages).

ROWLAND, HENRY A.

MD —JOHNS HOPKINS UNIVERSITY, Milton S Eisenhower Library, Charles & 34 Sts, Baltimore, 21218. Ann S Gwyn, Assistant Dir for Special Collections
Holdings: Vols 13 Cat Mss
Notes: Cataloged in manuscript room; incl 3852 ms items.

ROWLANDSON, THOMAS, 1756-1827

DC —LIBRARY OF CONGRESS, Prints & Photographs Div, Washington, 20540.
Notes: The British Cartoon collection contains 10,000 British political caricatures and satires dating from the 17th through mid 19th centuries. Incl the work of Henry Bunbury, George Cruikshank, Issac Cruikshank, Matthew Darly, James Gillray, and Thomas Rowlandson.

MD —UNIVERSITY OF MARYLAND, BALTIMORE COUNTY, Albin O Kuhn Library and Gallery, 5401 Wilkens Ave, Baltimore, 21228. Ann Copeland, Special Collections Librn
Holdings: Vols (800) // Cat Pix
Notes: The Edgar and Kathleen Merkle Collection of 19th-century English graphic satire centers around the work of George E Cruikshank. Other artists represented incl Rowlandson, Gillray, Hogarth, and "Phiz." Rare items incl Cruikshank's lavish hand-colored film *Scraps and Sketches* (1828).

MA —BOSTON PUBLIC LIBRARY, Print Collection, Dartmouth St at Copley Sq, Boston, 02117. Sinclair H Hitchings, Keeper of Prints
Holdings: Cat
Notes: The caricature collection incl 300 American prints (colonial period to 1900), 65 of these are by Thomas Nast; 400 English prints (mostly 18th century) many by Thomas Rowlandson and James Gillray; and several thousand 19th century French items, large numbers of them by Daumier. Items are cataloged by artist when known; or else by publisher or country. In addition, the American caricatures are arranged chronologically.

NJ —PRINCETON UNIVERSITY, Library, Rare Books Dept, Princeton, 08544. Stephen Ferguson, Cur
Holdings: Cat
Notes: Dickson Q Brown Collection of Thomas Rowlandson. About 920 vols with Rowlandson illustrations, incl over 100 vols about Rowlandson. These consist substantially of all the books for which Rowlandson executed illustration (incl many items not listed in Joseph Grego's standard bibliography of the artist's work). Also incl are almost all vols in which a drawing by Rowlandson was reproduced (photomechanically) or any mention was made of his name. Finally, works of importance on the artistic and social history of the period. Also incl a file of the *Repository of Arts* form 1809-1827, 55 miscellaneous vols, and 96 prints. For further details consult: E D H Johnson, "Special Collections at Princeton. V. The Works of Thomas Rowlandson" in the *Princeton University Library Chronicle* II, 1 (November, 1940) pp 7-20, and Joseph Grego. *Rowlandson the Caricaturist. A Selection from his Works with Anecdotal Descriptions of his Famous Caricatures.* (London, 1880). (2 vols in Graphic Arts; this copy is annotated, presumably by D Q Brown, to indicate material in the collection.)

NY —NEW YORK PUBLIC LIBRARY, Rare Books and Manuscripts Div, Fifth Ave & 42 St, New York, 10018. William L Joyce, Asst Dir; Bernard McTigue, Cur, Arents Collection
Holdings: Cat Mss Pix

RI —BROWN UNIVERSITY, John Hay Library, 20 Prospect St, Providence, 02912. Mark N Brown, Cur Mss
Holdings: Vols Uncat Mss Pix
Notes: Paul Revere Bullard Collection of 185 19th century caricatures by English, French, German, Russian, and Spanish cartoonists who lampooned Napoleon throughout his career, plus 220 similar caricatures from other sources. The major English artists represented are: James Gillray, George and Isaac Cruikshank, Thomas Rowlandson, and George Woodward. Some items also part of the Anne S. K. Brown Military Collection at Brown Univ.

ROWSON, SUSANNA

VA —UNIVERSITY OF VIRGINIA, Alderman Library, Clifton Waller Barrett Collection, Charlottesville, 22901. Joan St C Crane, Cur of American Literature Collections
Notes: Papers.

ROY, GABRIELLE, 1909-1983

ON —NATIONAL LIBRARY OF CANADA, 395 Wellington St, Ottawa, K1A 0N4, Can. Andre Preibish, Dir
Notes: Papers of Gabrielle Roy, major Canadian author. Incl mss, unpublished versions of books, letters, memorabilia, etc.

ROY, R. O.

LA —LOUISIANA STATE UNIVERSITY, SHREVEPORT, Library-Archives, 8515 Youree Dr, Shreveport, 71129. Patricia L Meador, Archivist & Asst Librn
Notes: The archives collection incl the papers (1899-1965) of oil man R O Roy.

ROY, REGINALD HERBERT

BC —UNIVERSITY OF VICTORIA, McPherson Library, Victoria, V8W 3H5, Can.
Notes: 1 mss, notes, correspondence, proofs; company diaries: Comp C Seaforth Company (Highlanders) of Canada (Dec 1944-July 1945); individual diary: Major J S Gooch (Oct 1917-Nov 1918); intelligence logs: 2nd Canadian Infantry Brigade, 1st Canadian Infantry Division (July-May 1945); 5th Canadian Armoured Division (April-May 1945); war diaries: 5th Canadian Mounted Rifles.

ROYAL, WILLIAM

IL —ILLINOIS STATE HISTORICAL SOCIETY, Library, Old State Capitol, Springfield, 62706. Roger D Bridges, Head Librn
Notes: Papers, 55 items, 1827-1857. Methodist pioneer circuit-rider.

ROYAL AFRICAN COMPANY

WI —UNIVERSITY OF WISCONSIN, MADISON, Memorial Library, 728 State St, Madison, 53706. David Henige, Librn
Holdings: Cat Microforms
Notes: Collection consists of 90 microfilm reels of extant records of the Royal African Company (T70 series in the Public Record Office, London) together with several smaller collections of materials relating to the English presence on the Gold Coast in the 17th and 18th centuries. *En ensemble,* it is the most complete collection of its kind in the US. Various parts are described in David Henige, "Some Materials on the Early Guinea Coast in the United Kingdon," *Africal Research and Documentation,* no 11 (1976), pp 25-28.

ROYAL ARCHITECTURAL INSTITUTE OF CANADA

AB —UNIVERSITY OF CALGARY, Libraries, Special Collections Div, 2500 University Dr, Calgary, T2N 1N4, Can.
Holdings: Cat Mss
Notes: Files of the Alberta Association of Architects from its foundation in 1906 onwards: Acts and By-Laws; Correspondence; Membership and Temporary Licence Applications; Ledgers; Minutes; Yearbooks and Newsletters. Also contains files of correspondence with the Royal Architectural Institute of Canada and provincial Architectural Associations. An inventory is on hand 9000 document boxes.

ROYAL ASTRONOMICAL SOCIETY OF CANADA

†ON —PUBLIC ARCHIVES OF CANADA, Library, 395 Wellington St, Ottawa, K1A 0N3, Can. Dawn E Monroe, Collections Dept Officer
Holdings: 4 Feet
Notes: Records of the Royal Astronomical Society of Canada, 1868-1968.

ROYAL CANADIAN NORTHWEST MOUNTED POLICE

NY —ALFRED UNIVERSITY, Herrick Memorial Library, Alfred, 14802. June E Brown, Head Librn
Notes: The Howells/Frechette Collection. Family documents, 7000 letters of William Cooper Howells (American consul to Quebec, later to Toronto), William Dean Howells, his sister Annie Frechette, Achille Frechette (official translator, Canadian House of Commons), and Louis Frechette (poet laureate of Canada).

ON —ROYAL CANADIAN MOUNTED POLICE HEADQUARTERS, Library, 1200 Alta Vista Dr, Ottawa, K1A 0R2, Can. G Wyatt, Librn
Holdings: Vols (58,000) Mss Microforms
Notes: Founded in 1936. Police science and management criminology, internal inter-library loans. Incl in 58,000 volumes, 1200 essays, 40,000 microforms, 34,000 subscriptions, and other serials. Open with permission from RCMP commissioner. Plan to affiliate with the Canadian Police.

ROYAL SOCIETY, LONDON

CT —YALE UNIVERSITY, Box 1603A, Yale Station, New Haven, 06520.
Holdings: Cat Mss
Notes: The papers of Sir Charles Blagden, ca 1777-1820, many of them relating to his secretaryship of the Royal Society.

ROYAL SOCIETY, LONDON—PUBLICATIONS

NY —NEW YORK PUBLIC LIBRARY, Research Libraries, General Research Division, Fifth Ave & 42 St, New York, 10018. Rodney Phillips, Chief
Holdings: Vols (2,225,000) Cat Maps Pix Microforms
Budget: ($775,718)

ROYALE GENDARMERIE

ON —ROYAL CANADIAN MOUNTED POLICE HEADQUARTERS, Library, 1200 Alta Vista Dr, Ottawa, K1A 0R2, Can. G Wyatt, Librn
Holdings: Vols (58,000) Mss Microforms
Notes: Plan to Affiliate with the Canadian Police. Open with permission from RCMP commissioner, founded in 1936. Police science and management criminology, internal inter-library loans. Incl in 58,000 volumes, 1200 essays, 40,000 microforms, 34,000 subscriptions, and other serials.

ROYCE, JOSIAH, 1855-1916

CA —UNIVERSITY OF CALIFORNIA, LOS ANGELES, Research Library, Dept of Special Collections, 405 Hilgard Ave, Los Angeles, 90024. Edward Shreeves, Chairman, Bibliographers Group; David S Zeidberg, Head
Notes: 10 linear feet of writings by and about Royce.

ROYCE, JOSIAH, 1855-1916 (cont.)

MD —JOHNS HOPKINS UNIVERSITY, Milton S Eisenhower Library, Charles & 34 Sts, Baltimore, 21218. Ann S Gwyn, Assistant Dir for Special Collections
Holdings: Vols 70 Cat Mss
Notes: Some first editions. 57 letters, his dissertation ms. Cataloged in manuscript room.

ROYBAL, EDWARD R., 1916-

CA —UNIVERSITY OF CALIFORNIA, LOS ANGELES, Research Library, Dept of Special Collections, 405 Hilgard Ave, Los Angeles, 90024. Edward Shreeves, Chairman, Bibliographers Group; David S Zeidberg, Head
Holdings: Mss Pix
Notes: 25 linear feet of mss, correspondence, and photographs concerning his activities as a Los Angeles City Councilman.

RUANDA

DC —HOWARD UNIVERSITY, Moorland-Spingarn Research Center, 500 Howard Place NW, Washington, 20059. Clifford L Muse, Jr, Acting Dir

RUBBER

OH —AKRON-SUMMIT COUNTY PUBLIC LIBRARY, Business, Labor & Government Div, 55 S Main St, Akron, 44326. William G Johnson, Head
Holdings: Vols 650 Cat
Budget: ($12,000)
Notes: Akron rubber companies: Goodyear, Goodrich, Firestone, General--annual reports, 1930 to date. Corporation file of clippings for Akron corporations. History and technology of rubber and synthetic rubber.
OH —MONSANTO CO, Library, Polymer Products Division, 260 Springside Dr, Akron, 44313. J P Ferrin, Librn
Holdings: Vols 500 Cat Microforms
Notes: Literature on rubber chemicals
PA —FRANKLIN INSTITUTE LIBRARY, 20 & The Parkway, Philadelphia, 19103. Miriam Padusis, Dir; Charles Wilt, Readers Servs Librn
Holdings: Vols (300,000) Cat Maps Pix Microforms
PA —CARNEGIE LIBRARY OF PITTSBURGH, Science & Technology Dept, 4400 Forbes Ave, Pittsburgh, 15213. Catherine M Brosky, Dept Head
Holdings: Vols (380,000) Cat Maps Microforms
Budget: ($240,000)
Notes: Incl many journals. Encyclopedias, general reference books, abstracts, indexes and bibliographies.
ON —DUNLOP RESEARCH CENTRE, Sheridan Park Research Community, Mississauga, L5K 1Z8, Can. Shirley A Morrison, Librn
Holdings: Vols 2000 Cat
Budget: ($4000)
Notes: Mainly current materials. Not open to the public except by appointment.

RUBBER—ANALYSIS

CA —UNIVERSITY OF SOUTHERN CALIFORNIA, Seaver Science Library, University Park, Los Angeles, 90089. A Albert Baker, Head
Holdings: Cat Microforms
Notes: The David K Spence Rubber Technology Collection. Also rubber formulary on punched cards.

RUBBER, ARTIFICIAL

IL —UNIVERSITY OF ILLINOIS, URBANA/CHAMPAIGN, Chemistry Library, 255 Noyes Laboratory, Urbana, 61801. Lucille M Wert, Chemistry Librn; Susan Eilering, Asst Chemistry Librn
Holdings: Vols (150,000) Cat Microforms
Notes: Collection incl monographs, treatises and serials covering all the fields of chemistry.

OH —AKRON-SUMMIT COUNTY PUBLIC LIBRARY, Business, Labor & Government Div, 55 S Main St, Akron, 44326. William G Johnson, Head
Holdings: Vols 650 Cat
Budget: ($12,000)
Notes: Akron rubber companies: Goodyear, Goodrich, Firestone, General--annual reports, 1930 to date. Corporation file of clippings for Akron corporations. History and technology of rubber and synthetic rubber.

RUBBER, SYNTHETIC see Rubber, Artificial

RUBBER INDUSTRY AND TRADE

CA —UNIVERSITY OF SOUTHERN CALIFORNIA, Seaver Science Library, University Park, Los Angeles, 90089. A Albert Baker, Head
Holdings: Cat Microforms
Notes: The David K Spence Rubber Technology Collection. Also rubber formulary on punched cards.
DE —HAGLEY MUSEUM AND LIBRARY, Eleutherian Mills-Hagley Foundation Inc, PO Box 3630, Greenville, 19807. Richmond D Williams, Dir; Heddy A Richter, Imprints Librn
Notes: Sperry Univac has deposited a large amount of historical records. Approximately 2000 cubic feet of records, files and photographs that document the invention and development of computers and the rapid growth of the industry were officially released by Sperry Corporation to the Library. The collection includes technical and legal documents relating to the ENIAC and UNIVAC computers as well as records of the founding of the E Remington Typewriter Company and other predecessor companies of the Sperry organization, such as The Library Bureau, Kardex, Rodic Rubber and the Powers Accounting Machinery Company. Thus our knowledge of the Sperry predecessors dates back in this collection to 1902.
OH —AKRON-SUMMIT COUNTY PUBLIC LIBRARY, Business, Labor & Government Div, 55 S Main St, Akron, 44326. William G Johnson, Head
Holdings: Vols 650 Cat
Budget: ($12,000)
Notes: Akron rubber companies: Goodyear, Goodrich, Firestone, General--annual reports, 1930 to date. Corporation file of clippings for Akron corporations. History and technology of rubber and synthetic rubber.
OH —UNIVERSITY OF AKRON, American History Research Center, Akron, 44325.
Notes: Corporate archives of the B F Goodrich Co, 1868-1969. Also, partial archive of the General Tire and Rubber Co.
PA —CARNEGIE LIBRARY OF PITTSBURGH, Science & Technology Dept, 4400 Forbes Ave, Pittsburgh, 15213. Catherine M Brosky, Dept Head
Holdings: Vols (380,000) Cat Maps Microforms
Budget: ($240,000)
Notes: General information. Manufactuers directories, including old editions, standards and specifications, trade catalogs, basic periodicals, indexes, and bibliographies.

RUBEN, SAMUEL

CA —UNIVERSITY OF CALIFORNIA, BERKELEY, Bancroft Library, Manuscripts Division, Berkeley, 94720. James D Hart, Dir
Notes: Papers and research notes relative to the history of modern chemistry.

RUBENS, PETER PAUL

NC —UNIVERSITY OF NORTH CAROLINA, CHAPEL HILL, Art Library, Art Classroom Studio Bldg, 079A, Chapel Hill, 27514. Philip A Rees, Art Librn
Holdings: Vols (47,000) Cat Microforms
Budget: ($52,000)
Notes: Emphasis on European and American art and architecture, ancient to modern. Special strengths: Rubens and 19th century French painting.

RUBIN, MICHAEL

MA —BOSTON UNIVERSITY, Mugar Memorial Library, Special Collections Dept, 771 Commonwealth Ave, Boston, 02215. Howard B Gotlieb, Dir
Holdings: Cat Mss

RUBIN, THEODORE ISAAC

MA —BOSTON UNIVERSITY, Mugar Memorial Library, Special Collections Dept, 771 Commonwealth Ave, Boston, 02215. Howard B Gotlieb, Dir
Holdings: Cat Mss
Notes: Mss, correspondence, etc collected in depth; incl publications by or about.

RUBRICATION OF BOOKS AND MANUSCRIPTS see Illuminated Books and Manuscripts

RUDER, WILLIAM E.

NY —UNION COLLEGE, Schaffer Library, Archives of Science and Technology, Schenectady, 12308. Ellen Fladger, Archivist
Notes: Papers etc.

RUDGE, WILLIAM E.

NY —UNIVERSITY CLUB, Library, One W 54 St, New York, 10019. Guy St Clair, Library Dir
Notes: A private library for the members of the University Club, their guests, and serious scholars upon written application to the Library Director. Holds the Edward Larocque Tinker Collection of Illustrated Books Between the Two World Wars, A Milton Runyon Collection on the History of Printing and Publishing, the Frederic R Coudert "Les Bibliophiles des Paris" Collection, The University Club Rare Book Collection, and the Frederick G Rudge Collection of Books Designed by William E Rudge and Bruce Rogers.

RUDOLPH, THE RED-NOSED REINDEER

PA —FREE LIBRARY OF PHILADELPHIA, Rare Book Dept, Logan Sq, Philadelphia, 19103. Marie E Korey, Rare Book Librn
Holdings: Uncat Mss Phonorecords
Notes: The Colonel Richard Gimble Collection of Robert L May's "Rudolph, the Red-Nosed Reindeer": 200 books and periodicals, manuscripts, musical scores, newspaper clippings, and records.

RUFFIN, GEORGE

LA —AMISTAD RESEARCH CENTER, 400 Esplanade Ave, New Orleans, 70116. Clifton H Johnson, Exec Dir; Florence E Borders, Senior Archivist
Holdings: Vols (10,000) Cat Mss Pix Audiotapes Microforms
Budget: ($315,000)
Notes: In addition, 8,000,000 ms pieces, 10, 000 pictures, 3500 microforms, and 500 audiotapes. Amistad Research Center is an historical research library devoted to the collection and use of primary source materials on the history of America's ethnic minorities, with particular emphasis on Afro-Americans, American Indians, and immigrant groups. Among the larger institutional collections held are the archives and records of the American Missionary Association, the American Home Missionary Society, the Race Relations Dept of the Anti-Defamation League, the Catholic Committee of the South, and the National Association of Human Rights Workers, (formerly NAIRO, National Association of Intergroup Related Officials). Also, private papers of the Harlem Renaissance poet, Countee Cullen; educator and civil rights leader, Mary McLeod Bethune;20th century

RUFFIN, GEORGE (cont.)

civil rights lawyer, Alexander P Tureaud; 19th century Black attorney and judge, George Ruffin; founder and director of Operation Crossroads Africa, Dr James H Robinson; and over 70 others.

RUG MANUFACTURE see Weaving

RUGGLES, CARL

CT —YALE UNIVERSITY, Music Library, 98 Wall St, New Haven, 06520. Harold E Samuel, Librn
Holdings: Vols (118,000) Cat Mss Pix Phonorecords Audiotapes
Notes: Personal papers and musical mss.
See also entry under Music, American

RUGGLES, WESLEY

CA —UNIVERSITY OF CALIFORNIA, LOS ANGELES, Theater Arts Library, Los Angeles, 90024. Edward Shreeves, Chairman, Bibliographers Group; Audree Malkin, Head, Theater Arts Library
Notes: Wesley Ruggles (director) Collection: screenplays, stories, treatments, production material, and correspondence for his feature films, short subjects, and television productions; clippings relating to his career.

RUGOLO, PETE

TX —NORTH TEXAS STATE UNIVERSITY, Audio Center, Box 5188, NT Station, Denton, 76203. Morris Martin, Music Librn
Notes: More than 1600 manuscript jazz compositions, (incl scores and parts, alternate versions, expanded arrangements) by Stan Kenton, Johnny Richards, Joe Coccia, Lennie Niehaus, Pete Rugolo, Willie Maiden, Bob Curnow, Ken Hanna, Gene Rowland, Bob Graettinger and others, used by the Stan Kenton Band and given to North Texas State University in 1962 and at Kenton's death in 1979. Unpublished catalog: Breeden, Leon, *Stan Kenton Music in the NTSU Jazz Studies Library and the NTSU Music Library*, Denton, 1983 (99 pages).

RUGS—PATTERNS

NY —FASHION INSTITUTE OF TECHNOLOGY, Edward C Blum Design Laboratory, 227 W 27 St, New York, 10001. Laura Sinderbrand, Dir
Holdings: Cat Pix Slides
Notes: The largest resource of it kind consisting of 4 million indexed swatches and 300 swatch books, jacquard point paper, croquis, quilts, rug samples, laces, embroideries, and color swatch cards. A collection of international scope incl antique and contemporary textiles; woven and printed patterns created for apparel and home furnishings which may be adapted to china, giftware, floor covering, wallpaper, and package design. A comprehensive research facility comprised of over one million articles of dress dating from the 17th Century to the present, incl men's, women's, children's clothes, furs, foundation garments and lingerie, as well as an outstanding grouping of 19th and 20th century designer clothing. Accessories as diverse as hats, handbags, gloves, hosiery, shoes, shawls, and costume jewelry offer an additonal resource to this international collection.

RUGS, ORIENTAL

WI —MILWAUKEE PUBLIC LIBRARY, 814 W Wisconsin Ave, Milwaukee, 53233. Donald J Sager, City Librn
Holdings: Vols Cat
Notes: Special strength.
See also entry under Art, Decorative.

RUINS see Archaeology

RUIZ, MANUEL, JR.

CA —STANFORD UNIVERSITY LIBRARIES, Cecil H Green Library, Stanford, 94305. Michael T Ryan, Cur
Notes: Papers of Ernesto Galarza, Bert Corona, Manuel Ruiz, Jr, Eduardo Queredo, Edward Valenzuela.

RUKEYSER, MURIEL

NV —UNIVERSITY OF NEVADA, RENO, University Library, Special Collections Dept, Reno, 89557. Robert E Blesse, Head
Holdings: Vols (55) Cat
Notes: Includes individual works by author in all editions including translations; also prefaces, introductions, published correspondence, appearances in anthologies, periodicals, etc. Bibliographical research collection, part of Modern Authors Collection. Other appearances 400 cataloged.

RULE OF THE ROAD (IN TRAFFIC) see Traffic Regulations

RULE WYNN AND RULE, CALGARY

AB —UNIVERSITY OF CALGARY, Libraries, Special Collections Div, 2500 University Dr, Calgary, T2N 1N4, Can.
Holdings: Cat Mss Pix
Notes: 15,000 pictures; 9 meters mss. The Edmonton architectural firm of Rule Wynn & Rule established a second office in Calgary in 1949. In 1967, this branch became known as Rule Wynn & Hames and, in 1972, as W G Hames Associates, from which time onwards it developed independently from the Edmonton office. The collection consists of original working drawings (1949-69) and supporting file material (1959-73) of buildings in Calgary and Southern Alberta. Major contracts incl Elveden House, the Calgary Petroleum Club and Glencoe Club, and numerous schools in and around Calgary. Inventories will be available shortly.
See also entry under Rule Wynn and Rule, Edmonton.

RULE WYNN AND RULE, EDMONTON

AB —UNIVERSITY OF CALGARY, Libraries, Special Collections Div, 2500 University Dr, Calgary, T2N 1N4, Can.
Holdings: Cat Mss Pix
Notes: Collection consists of 9041 architectural drawings, some photographs, and some specifications of the Alberta architectural firm of Rule Wynn & Rule, of Edmonton. Projects of the years between 1937 and 1959 cover churches, schools, hospitals, stores, factories, warehouses, movie theatres and private residences. Major contracts were: Library at the University of Alberta, edmonton; the Colonel Belcher Hospital, Calgary; Elveden House, Calgary; Calgary Petroleum Club. Project lists are on hand. 7.5 meters of documents.

RULERS (KINGS, QUEENS, ETC.)

CA —STANFORD UNIVERSITY LIBRARIES, Cecil H Green Library, Stanford, 94305. Michael T Ryan, Cur
Holdings: Cat Pix
Notes: The Dr and Mrs Leon Kolb Portrait Collection. Over 1600 portraits (engravings, etchings, mezzotints, lithographs) of rulers, statesmen, authors, scholars and other famous personages from ancient times to the 19th century. A catalog of the collection, compiled by Dr Susan Lenkey, was published in 1972.

MO —UNIVERSITY OF MISSOURI-SAINT LOUIS, Thomas Jefferson Library, 8001 Natural Bridge Rd, Saint Louis, 63121.
Holdings: Vols 800 Cat
Notes: Ernest Augustine Collection: From the family of Ernest Augustus, Duke of Cumberland, King of Hanover (1771-1851). The collection of about 800 vols contains books printed and from the family's collections from the 18th century through the end of World War I. Many of the books contain dedications from the crowned heads of Europe. The last additions to this portion of the collection apparently come from the time of Ernst August Christian Georg, who married Viktoria Luise Adelheid Mathilde Charlotte, who was the only daughter of Wilhelm II, German Emporer and King of Prussia. Languages represented: German, English, French. The original owner, Ernest Augustus, Duke of Cumberland, was son of George III and became King of Hanover (present day section of Germany) on the accession of his niece Victoria to the throne ofEngland.

OH —CLEVELAND PUBLIC LIBRARY, History and Geography Department, 325 Superior Ave, Cleveland, 44114. JoAnn Petrello, Head
Holdings: Cat
Notes: This biography, reference, and circulating collection incl many fine first editions mostly in English; however, other languages are also represented. Strong on biographies of rulers and statesmen, travellers' journals, etc.

RUMAKER, MICHAEL

CT —UNIVERSITY OF CONNECTICUT, Library, Storrs, 06268. George F Butterick, Cur of Literary Archives
Holdings: Mss Pix Audiotapes
Notes: Repository for the writer's papers.

BC —SIMON FRASER UNIVERSITY, Library, Burnaby, V5A 1S6, Can. Percilla Groves, Special Collections Librn
Holdings: Cat Mss
Notes: Letters written to Eshleman by Allen Ginsberg (8 pp), William Carlos Williams and Florence Williams (5 pp), Robert Duncan (4 pp), and Edward Dorn (5 pp), while Eshleman was editor of *Folio* (1959-1961). Tss from Gregory Corso (2 pp), Louis Zukofsky (8 pp), Michael Rumaker (3 pp).

RUMANIA

IL —UNIVERSITY OF ILLINOIS, URBANA/CHAMPAIGN, Slavic and East European Library, Urbana, 61801. Marianna Tax Choldin, Head
Holdings: Vols (12,000) Cat
Notes: Extensive coverage.

PA —UNIVERSITY OF PITTSBURGH, Hillman Library, Pittsburgh, 15260.
Holdings: Vols 500
Notes: A Rumanian collection, which deals with the country's history; racial, ethnic and religious minorities; folklore; art; literature; customs; agriculture; politics.

WI —UNIVERSITY OF WISCONSIN, MADISON, Memorial Library, Slavic Studies Collection, 728 State St, Madison, 53706. Aleksander Rolich, Bibliographer for Slavic Studies; Robert P Gakovich, Slavic Cataloger; Valdis J Zeps, Baltic Studies Center
Holdings: Vols (25,000) Cat
Notes: The Balcanica collection in Memorial Library exceeds 25,000 volumes and active collecting continues at over 2000 titles per year in Bulgarian, Rumanian, Turkish and the languages of Yugoslavia. Many rare and unique titles are to be found in this collection, including serial titles, such as *Nova Vreme* (1897-1923, 1947-to date), *Nova Europa* (1920-1939), and unique Turkish Salnameh. The emphasis is on historical materials, but there is considerable strength in South Slavic literatures and linguistics. The Rumanian materials are of more recent vintage.

RUMANIA—HISTORY

CA —UNIVERSITY OF CALIFORNIA, LOS ANGELES, Library, Slavic Collection, 405 Hilgard Ave, Los Angeles, 90024. Edward Shreeves, Chairman, Bibliographers Group; Leon Ferder, Slavic Bibliographer
Holdings: Vols (250,000) Cat Maps Microforms
Notes: The entire range of humanities, social sciences, and the arts. One of the most comprehensive US collections for material not only on Russia and the Soviet Union, but also on Bulgaria, Czechoslovakia, Poland, Yugoslavia, the non-Slavic countries

RUMANIA—HISTORY (cont.)

of Eastern Europe (Romania, Hungary, Albania) and Soviet Central Asia. Holdings in Russian and Slavic linguistics, Russian literature, and Russian history are particularly strong, covering all periods. The collections are described in some detail in Paul Horecky's book on US Slavic collections.

CA —HOOVER INSTITUTION ON WAR, REVOLUTION & PEACE, Stanford University, Stanford, 94305. Milorad M Drachkovitch, Archivist
Holdings: Mss Pix
Notes: Two collections: (1) Papers of Radu Inimescu, Rumanian Minister of Air and Navy, 1932-38, and Rumanian Ambassador to the United States, 1938-40, incl correspondence, reports, dispatches, memoranda, clippings, photos, and other material, 1918-40, relating to his service in the Rumanian government and to the development of aviation in Rumania. Prinarily in Rumanian. 5 ms boxes. (2) Papers of N Titulescu, Rumanian Minister of Foreign Affairs and Minister of Finance, consisting of diaries, correspondence, memoranda, reports, manuscripts, clippings, printed matter and other materials relating to Titulescu's career as statesman and diplomat, 1923-1938. Incl is documentation on Rumania's negotiations with the USSR 1931-32. 15 1/2 ms boxes.

†DC —LIBRARY OF CONGRESS, Washington, 20540.

IN —INDIANA UNIVERSITY, University Libraries, Bloomington, 47401. Murlin Croucher, Librn for Slavic Studies
Holdings: Vols (300,000) Cat Maps Microforms
Budget: ($63,000)
Notes: The collection, established after World War II, covers material of, and on, the Soviet Union (55 percent) and Eastern Europe (45 percent) in the languages of the area and in western European languages as well. Material is chiefly in the fields of humanities and social sciences. Many other Slavic and East European books are located in the Lilly Library (rare book library).

OH —OHIO STATE UNIVERSITY, William Oxley Thompson Memorial Library, Hilander Room, 1858 Neil Ave Mall, Columbus, 43210. Predrag Matejic, Cur; G Koolemans Beynen, Slavic Bibliographer
Holdings: Vols (200,000) Cat Maps Microforms
Budget: ($45,000)
Notes: Area studies of Central, Southeastern and Eastern Europe. Emphasis on on Slavic literatures, languages and history. At present economics, sociology, law (Russian only) have been added. Within this framework the following priorities have been established: Material in Russian problems; then Medieval Slavic (Cyrillic); then Polish, then Serbo-Croatian, then Bulgarian, and now Rumanian. Special attention is paid to serials, bibliographies, ms descriptions and dictionaries (incl biographical and encyclopedias). Apart from materials in native languages, materials in the following languages are acquired: Old Church Slavonic, Greek, English, French, German, Italian, a few in Scandinavian languages, incl Finnish, and a few in Baltic languages. The Hillandar Room holds approx 2000 Slavic mss, 1050 from Hilandar Monastery, Mount Athos, on microform and a related referencecollection.

OH —KENT STATE UNIVERSITY, Libraries, Dept of Special Collections, Kent, 44242. Dean H Keller, Cur
Holdings: Vols 175 Cat Mss Pix
Notes: The collection relates espec to Queen Marie.

RUMANIAN ACADEMY AND INSTITUTES—PUBLICATIONS

IL —UNIVERSITY OF ILLINOIS, URBANA/CHAMPAIGN, Slavic and East European Library, Urbana, 61801. Marianna Tax Choldin, Head
Holdings: Vols (12,000) Cat
Notes: Extensive coverage.

RUMANIAN LANGUAGE AND LITERATURE

IL —UNIVERSITY OF ILLINOIS, URBANA/CHAMPAIGN, Slavic and East European Library, Urbana, 61801. Marianna Tax Choldin, Head
Holdings: Vols (13,000) Cat
Notes: Extensive coverage.

MA —HARVARD UNIVERSITY LIBRARY, Cambridge, 02138.
Holdings: Cat

MA —BOSTON COLLEGE LIBRARIES, Chestnut Hill, 02167.

NY —NEW YORK PUBLIC LIBRARY, Donnell Foreign Language Library, 20 W 53 St, New York, 10019. Bosiljka Stevanovic, Supvr Librn
Holdings: Vols 300 Cat
Notes: Rumanian collection incl Rumanian authors of Rumanian expression. No separate catalog.

OH —CLEVELAND PUBLIC LIBRARY, Foreign Literature Dept, 325 Superior Ave, Cleveland, 44114. Natalia Bezugloff, Head
Holdings: Vols 2450 Cat
Notes: Romanian language and literature. A popular circulating collection containing classics and the standard works with emphasis on belles lettres, history and biography. A variety of other subjects such as learning languages, hobbies, how to do books, art, children's books, spoken phonodiscs and cassettes, periodcials, etc.
See also entry under Foreign Language Collections

OH —OHIO STATE UNIVERSITY, William Oxley Thompson Memorial Library, Hilander Room, 1858 Neil Ave Mall, Columbus, 43210. Predrag Matejic, Cur; G Koolemans Beynen, Slavic Bibliographer
Holdings: Vols (200,000) Cat Maps Microforms
Budget: ($45,000)
Notes: Area studies of Central, Southeastern and Eastern Europe. Emphasis on on Slavic literatures, languages and history. At present economics, sociology, law (Russian only) have been added. Within this framework the following priorities have been established: Material in Russian Russian problems; then Medieval Slavic (Cyrillic); then Polish, then Serbo-Croatian, then Bulgarian and now Romanian. Special attention is paid to serials, bibliographies, ms descriptions and dictionaries (incl biographical and encyclopedias). Apart from materials in native languages, materials in the following languages are acquired: Old Church Slavonic, Greek, English, French, German, Italian, a few in Scandinavian languages, incl Finnish, and a few in Baltic languages. The Hillandar Room holds approx 2000 Slavic mss, 1050 from Hilandar Monastery, Mount Athos, on microform and a related referencecollection.

OH —KENT STATE UNIVERSITY, Libraries, Ethnic Collections, Kent, 44242.
Holdings: Vols 950 Cat
See also entry under Foreign Language Collections

WI —UNIVERSITY OF WISCONSIN, MADISON, Memorial Library, Slavic Studies Collection, 728 State St, Madison, 53706. Aleksander Rolich, Bibliographer for Slavic Studies; Robert P Gakovich, Slavic Cataloger; Valdis J Zeps, Baltic Studies Center
Holdings: Vols (25,000) Cat
Notes: The Balcanica collection in Memorial Library exceeds 25,000 volumes and active collecting continues at over 2000 titles per year in Bulgarian, Rumanian, Turkish and the languages of Yugoslavia. Many rare and unique titles are to be found in this collection, including serial titles, such as Nova Vreme (1897-1923, 1947-to date), Nova Europa (1920-1939), and unique Turkish Salnameh. The emphasis is on historical materials, but there is considerable strength in South Slavic literatures and linguistics. The Rumanian materials are of more recent vintage.

RUMANIAN LAW see Law, Rumanian

RUMANIAN PERIODICALS see Periodicals, Rumanian

RUMANIANS IN THE U.S.

MN —UNIVERSITY OF MINNESOTA, Immigration History Research Center, 826

Berry St, Saint Paul, 55114. Susan Griegs, Cur
Holdings: Vols (35,000) Mss Maps Pix Phonorecords Audiotapes 16mm Films Microforms
See also entry under US - Emigration and Immigration

RUMANISH LANGUAGE see Raeto-Romance Language and Literature

RUMELY, EDWARD A.

IN —INDIANA UNIVERSITY, Lilly Library, Seventh St, Bloomington, 47405. William R Cagle, Librn
Holdings: // Mss Pix
Notes: Papers of Edward A Rumely, 1892-1964, founder of Interlaken School in Indiana and apostle of the New School Movement in the US. 10,000 items in this nearly 100,000 item collection relate to Interlaken and to such college preparatory training as represented by Interlaken.

RUMFORD, BENJAMIN VON GRAF, 1753-1814

NH —DARTMOUTH COLLEGE, Baker Memorial Library, Hanover, 03755.
Holdings: Vols 400 Cat Mss
Notes: Incl 15 linear ft of mss; concerns Rumford and his scientific research.

RUMFORD SCIENTIFIC DRAWINGS

MA —HARVARD UNIVERSITY LIBRARY, Houghton Library, Cambridge, 02138. Rodney G Dennis, Cur of Manuscripts
Holdings: Cat Mss Pix
Notes: See Harvard Library Bulletin, IX (1955), 350-364.

RUMSHINSKY, JOSEPH

CA —UNIVERSITY OF CALIFORNIA, LOS ANGELES, Music Library, Schonberg Hall, Los Angeles, 90024. Stephen M Fry, Music Librn
Notes: Mss.

RUNES AND RUNOLOGY

MD —JOHNS HOPKINS UNIVERSITY, Milton S Eisenhower Library, Charles & 34 Sts, Baltimore, 21218. Ann S Gwyn, Assistant Dir for Special Collections
Holdings: Vols 3250 Cat
Notes: Incl 2000 reprints. Chiefly modern Scandinavian scholarship and literature, especially Danish. Also runology, Old Scandinavian, history, linguistics, and archaeology. (Incl Lis Jacobsen collection).

NY —CORNELL UNIVERSITY LIBRARIES, John M Olin Library, Fiske Icelandic Collection, Ithaca, 14853. Louis A Pitschmann, Librn
Holdings: Vols (34,000) Cat Mss Maps Pix Microforms
Budget: ($3000)
Notes: Collection aims at comprehensive coverage of Iceland in all aspects with major emphasis on the literature and language (both old and modern). Such subjects as runology, Scandinavian and Germanic mythology, early Norwegian history and history of the Viking period and of the Norse explorations of Greenland and North America are also well represented. For printed catalogs of the Collection's holdings see Downs 3608, 3609. Records for approximately 40 percent of the collection have been entered into OCLC and RLIN.

SD —AUGUSTANA COLLEGE, Mikkelsen Library & Learning Resource Center, Center for Western Studies, Sioux Falls, 57197. Ronelle Thompson, Dir Library
Holdings: Vols (40,000) Cat Mss Maps Pix Slides Microforms
Budget: ($130,000)
Notes: The Center for Western Studies, located in the Mikkelsen Library, is an archival and research agency of Augustana College. Dedicated to the history and culture of the Great Plains and the Trans-Mississippi

RUNES AND RUNOLOGY (cont.)

West, the Center collects and preserves materials relating to Plains Indians, immigrant settlers, Norwegiana, Western Americana, Herbert Krause, Frederick Manfred, Donald Parker, Richard F Pettigrew, Augustana College, the Episcopal Diocese of South Dakota, the South Dakota District of the American Lutheran Church, the South Dakota Penitentiary and Minnehaha County.

RUNIC ALPHABETS see Runes and Runology

RUNNELS, REP. HAROLD

NM —EASTERN NEW MEXICO UNIVERSITY, Golden Library, Special Collections, Portales, 88130. Mary Jo Walker, Special Collections Librn
Notes: Papers and files of the late Congressman Harold Runnels (D NMex).

RURAL ARCHITECTURE see Architecture, Domestic

RURAL COMMUNITY DEVELOPMENT see Rural Development

RURAL CONDITIONS

DC —INTERNATIONAL LABOR ORGANIZATION, International Labor Office, Washington Branch Library, 1750 New York Ave NW, Rm 330, Washington, 20006. Karen J Mark, Librn
Holdings: Vols (13,500) Cat Pix 16mm Films Monographs
Notes: Wide range of titles dealing with worldwide labor and social matters. The library contains ILO publications and documentation only, dating back to 1919. Also, a collection of ILO films and photos. See *Subject Guide to Publications of the ILO, 1919-1964* and *ILO Catalogue of Publications in Print, 1982* (ILO).

IL —MCLEAN COUNTY HISTORICAL SOCIETY LIBRARY & MUSEUM, 201 E Grove, Bloomington, 61701. Barbara Dunbar, Dir; Greg Koos, Archivist
Holdings: Vols (3000) Cat Mss Maps Pix
Notes: Collection also strong in social history, educational history (one room schools and rural education), womens history.

IA —IOWA STATE UNIVERSITY, Library, Ames, 50011. Warren B Kuhn, Dean of Library Services
Holdings: Cat Mss
Notes: Incl agriculture finance and policy, agricultural marketing, farm management, land valuation, and rural development. Extensive serial holdings.

KY —UNIVERSITY OF KENTUCKY, Agricultural Library, Agricultural Science Center North, Lexington, 40506. Antoinette Paris Powell, Librn
Holdings: Vols (90,000) Cat Microforms
Budget: ($110,385)

KY —UNIVERSITY OF LOUISVILLE, Ekstrom Library, Photographic Archives, Louisville, 40292. J C Anderson, Cur; David G Horvath, Asst Cur
Holdings: Vols (750,000) Cat Pix Slides
Budget: ($60,000)
Notes: Photographs in three broad areas: works of outstanding photographers; examples of major developments in the art and technology of photography; photographs important as sociological, historical, or behavioral documents. Actors and actresses, Louisville's Macauley Theatre. Standard Oil of New Jersey Collection, 85,000 pictures of oil industry's effect on life in the 20th century (1943-1950, directed by Roy Stryker); Stryker's collection from Farm Security Administration series on rural conditions, 1935-1942; Jones and Laughlin Steel Corp Picture Library, by Stryker. Stryker manuscripts, 1934-1972. Caufield and Shook commercial photographs, Louisville area, 1920-1949. Jean Thomas "The Traipsin' Woman" photographs of Kentucky mountain folkways. Kate Matthews' (1870-1956) photographs incl prototypes for "Little Colonel" Series. Other collections described in unpublishedbrochure. Print duplication service.

MI —MICHIGAN STATE UNIVERSITY, International Library, Sahel Documentation Center, East Lansing, 48824. Eugene deBenko, Librn; Learthen Dorsey, Librn
Holdings: Vols (5100) Cat Mss Maps Pix Slides Phonorecords Audiotapes Videotapes Microforms
Budget: ($8000)
Notes: See description under The Sahel.

MI —MICHIGAN STATE UNIVERSITY, International Library, South and Southeast Asia Collection, East Lansing, 48824. Clinton Lockert, Bibliographer
Holdings: Vols 55,700 Cat Mss Maps Audiotapes Microforms
Notes: Serials and monographs of South Asia received on PL 480 for India, Pakistan, Sri Lanka, and Nepal since 1968. Emphasis is upon Social Sciences, Humanities, and Science. Areas of strength are Anthropology and rural development.

NY —CORNELL UNIVERSITY LIBRARIES, Collection of Regional History, Dept of Manuscripts and Univ Archives, Ithaca, 14853.
Notes: The noncurrent records, letters, records of meetings and other historic data dating back to Dec 4, 1867, the date of organization of the National Grange. Also the papers of Louis I Taber, National Master of the Grange from 1923 to 1941.

NY —COLUMBIA UNIVERSITY LIBRARIES, Rare Book & Manuscript Library, 801 Butler Library, 535 W 114 St, New York, 10027. Kenneth A Lohf, Librn
Holdings: Mss
Notes: The papers of Professor Frank Tannenbaum, approx 28,000 items of correspondence and mss relating to Latin American and Mexican history, also the US Farm Security Program, 1934-1937. Professor Tannenbaum also bequeathed his research library of more than 3000 vols on all phases of Latin American history and literature to Columbia. Restricted use.

NC —UNIVERSITY OF NORTH CAROLINA, CHAPEL HILL, Wilson Library, Rare Book Collection, Chapel Hill, 27514. Paul S Koda, Cur of Rare Books
Holdings: Cat Mss
Notes: 160 letterfile boxes of the extensive correspondence of Eugene Cunningham Branson, Professor of Rural Economics at the University of North Carolina from 1914 to 1933.

NC —DUKE UNIVERSITY, William R Perkins Library, Manuscript Dept, Durham, 27706. Ellen Gartrell, Cur of Mss
Holdings: Cat Mss
Notes: Alliance for the Guidance of Rural Youth Papers (24,000 items, 1920- 1963) and related papers of Amber (Arthun) Warburton (31,400 items 1917-1976) plus North Carolinan Congressmen's papers; Robert W Hudgens papers, etc.

PA —PENNSYLVANIA STATE UNIVERSITY, Fred Lewis Pattee Library, Life Sciences Library, University Park, 16802. Keith Roe, Head
Notes: This collection is strong in periodical runs, particularly European learned societies and agriculture. It contains extensive collections of Experiment Station publications and has developed specialties in Mycology and Fusaria. There is also a special collection of 1105 glass slides on early Pennsylvania lumbering.

ON —UNIVERSITY OF GUELPH, Library, Guelph, N1G 2W1, Can. Margaret Beckman, Chief Librn; Ellen Pearson, Ref Librn
Notes: 15,000 monographs, 350 periodical subscriptions, 5000 documents, also maps, mss, audio/videotapes, 16mm films. Supports research activities related to planning theory, public administration, rural sociology, rural planning and development, rural and urban community studies, regional analysis, rural environment and resource use, policy design.

RURAL CREDIT see Agricultural Credit

RURAL DEVELOPMENT

DC —INTERNATIONAL LABOR ORGANIZATION, International Labor Office, Washington Branch Library, 1750 New York Ave NW, Rm 330, Washington, 20006. Karen J Mark, Librn
Holdings: Vols (13,500) Cat Pix 16mm Films Monographs
Notes: Wide range of titles dealing with worldwide labor and social matters. The library contains ILO publications and documentation only, dating back to 1919. Also, a collection of ILO films and photos. See *Subject Guide to Publications of the ILO, 1919-1964* and *ILO Catalogue of Publications in Print, 1982* (ILO).

MA —HARVARD UNIVERSITY, Institute for International Development, Library, Coolidge Hall, 1737 Cambridge St, Cambridge, 02138. Barbara Mitchell, Librn
Holdings: Vols (17,000) Periodicals
Notes: Economic development, rural development, statistical material on selected underdeveloped countries. Incl 75 periodical titles.

PA —UNIVERSITY OF PITTSBURGH, Library, Graduate School of Public and International Affairs, Forbes Quadrangle, 1st floor West, Pittsburgh, 15260. Nicholas C Caruso, Librn
Holdings: Vols (80,000) Cat
Budget: ($150,000)
Notes: The library attempts to collect as many national economic and social development plans as possible from the developing countries of the world. It also holds city, regional and state plans for Pennsylvania, particularly, the 9 southwestern counties of Pennsylvania.

ON —UNIVERSITY OF GUELPH, Library, Guelph, N1G 2W1, Can. Margaret Beckman, Chief Librn; Ellen Pearson, Ref Librn
Notes: 15,000 monographs, 350 periodical subscriptions, 5000 documents, also maps, mss, audio/videotapes, 16mm films. Supports research activities related to planning theory, public administration, rural sociology, rural planning and development, rural and urban community studies, regional analysis, rural environment and resource use, policy design.

RURAL ECONOMIC DEVELOPMENT see Rural Development

RURAL ELECTRIFICATION

WA —WESTERN WASHINGTON UNIVERSITY, Center for Pacific Northwest Studies, High St, Bellingham, 98225. James W Scott, Dir
Holdings: Mss Maps Pix
Notes: The Vaughan Brown Collection. Vaughan Brown, a retired attorney, is a former Postmaster of Bellingham and a former member of the house and senate of Washington State, retiring from the latter in the 1950s. This voluminous collection consists of political papers and materials in large part, covering state and local matters. Rural electrification is one of the major topics covered, and there is much illustrative campaign literature, largely Democratic, but incl some Republican. Personal, financial and legal papers are also included. Mainly Pacific Northwest--especially Washington and, in particular Whatcom County, but also some of whose papers are included. Partially cataloged.

RURAL LIFE see Farm Life; Outdoor Life

RURAL REHABILITATION see Rehabilitation, Rural

RURAL SOCIOLOGY see Sociology, Rural

RUSH, BENJAMIN, 1745-1813

KS —MENNINGER FOUNDATION, Archives, 5600 W Sixth St, Box 829, Topeka, 66601. Alice Brand, Librn; Mark West, Archivist
Notes: 1 box, 1791-1812. Contains correspondence and miscellaneous materials.

PA —LIBRARY COMPANY OF PHILADELPHIA, 1314 Locust St,

RUSH, BENJAMIN, 1745-1813 (cont.)

Philadelphia, 19107. Edwin Wolf II, Librn; Kenneth Finkel, Cur of Prints
Holdings: Vols 1000 Cat Mss Maps
Notes: Early American books, pamphlets and broadsides concerning popular and professional medicine, to 1820. Of major importance are books owned by Benjamin Rush, Revolutionary-era doctor. Many of his mss, though housed in the Historical Society of Pennsylvania, remain the property of the Library Company.

RUSH FAMILY

NJ —PRINCETON UNIVERSITY, Library, Manuscript Collection, Nassau St, Princeton, 08540. Jean F Preston, Cur
Holdings: Mss Pix
Notes: The collection, which deals mainly with the period 1745-1877, occupies 57 ms boxes. An unpublished typescript guide (200 p) is available in the Library.

RUSK, RALPH LESLIE

NC —DUKE UNIVERSITY, William R Perkins Library, Jay B Hubbell Center for American Literary Historiography, Durham, 27706. Erma Whittington, Librn
Notes: 77,312 items, including manuscripts, pictures, clippings, and correspondence. "The objective of the Center is to gather the papers and materials of significant scholars and critics in American literary history." The Center is a part of the Perkins Library Manuscripts Department.

RUSK, THOMAS J.

TX —STEPHEN F AUSTIN STATE UNIVERSITY, Ralph W Steen Library, Special Collections Dept, Box 13055, SFA Sta, Nacogdoches, 75962. Linda Cheves Nicklas, Special Collections Librn
Holdings: Mss Maps Pix
Budget: ($5000)
Notes: Incl personal and business papers, letters, diaries, and other records of East Texans and East Texas institutions and businesses. Major collections incl papers of Karl Wilson Baker, George L Crocket, Bennett Blake, McFarland-Russell family, Orton family, Samuel E Asbury; and records of Nacogdoches University, East Texas Historical Association, Kelly Plow Company and many local organizations; 60 Thomas J Rusk letters. Indexes, calendars and inventories are available. Description: SFASU, A Guide to Special Collections, 1980.

RUSKIN, JOHN

AL —SAMFORD UNIVERSITY, Special Collections Library, 800 Lakeshore Dr, Birmingham, 35229. Annie Ford Wheeler, Acting Head Librn
Holdings: Vols 550 Cat Mss Pix
Notes: Incl most first editions, a few autographs, a few mss. Substantial collection of secondary works.
CA —SAN DIEGO PUBLIC LIBRARY, Wangenheim Rm, 820 E St, San Diego, 92101. Eileen Boyle, Librn
Holdings: Vols 250 Cat Mss
Notes: Primarily first editions.
CT —YALE UNIVERSITY, Box 1603A, Yale Station, New Haven, 06520.
Holdings: Cat Mss
Notes: Over 1800 letters.
MA —HARVARD UNIVERSITY LIBRARY, Houghton Library, Cambridge, 02138. Rodney G Dennis, Cur of Manuscripts
Holdings: Cat Mss
NY —UNIVERSITY OF ROCHESTER, Rush Rhees Library, Department of Rare Books and Special Collections, Rochester, 14627. Peter Dzwonkoski, Librn
Holdings: Vols 400 Cat Letters Drawings
Notes: Described in exhibition catalogue: "The Sydney Ross Collection of John Ruskin," University of Rochester Library, 15 February-15 May 1981.

OH —OHIO UNIVERSITY, Vernon R Alden Library, Department of Archives and Special Collections, Athens, 45701. Gary A Hunt, Head
Holdings: Vols 94 Cat
Notes: Mostly first editions.
†PA —HUNT INSTITUTE FOR BOTANICAL DOCUMENTATION, Hunt Botanical Library, Carnegie-Mellon University, Pittsburgh, 15213.
Notes: Nearly 500 letters, nearly half sent to John Ruskin.
BC —UNIVERSITY OF VICTORIA, McPherson Library, Victoria, V8W 3H5, Can.

RUSSELL, ANDREW J.

MA —BOSTON UNIVERSITY, Mugar Memorial Library, Special Collections Dept, 771 Commonwealth Ave, Boston, 02215. Howard B Gotlieb, Dir
Holdings: Mss

RUSSELL, ARCHIMEDES

NY —SYRACUSE UNIVERSITY LIBRARIES, Ernest S Bird Library, George Arents Research Library for Special Collections, Syracuse, 13210. Carolyn A Davis, Manuscripts Librn; Amy S Doherty, University Archivist; Mark F Weimer, Rare Book Librn
Notes: The George Arents Research Library for Special Collections at Syracuse University contains the papers of Harley James McKee, Lorimer Rich, Frederick Lear, Max Abramovitz, James I Arnold, Pietro Bulluschi, Claude Bragdon, Marcel Breuer, William Lescaze, Skidmore Owings & Merrill, Ralph Walker, Eric Fisher Wood, Minoru Yamasaki, Joseph Louis Young, and Archimedes Russell.

RUSSELL, ARTHUR

BC —UNIVERSITY OF VICTORIA, McPherson Library, Victoria, V8W 3H5, Can.
Notes: Incl mss of Ruth Pitter: Homage to a Poet, tributes from thirty admirers of her work; correspondence to Russell; proofs.

RUSSELL, BENJAMIN, 1810-1895

NY —CORNELL UNIVERSITY LIBRARIES, Collection of Regional History, Dept of Manuscripts and Univ Archives, Ithaca, 14853.
Notes: Presbyterian clergyman. Incl papers, 1833-1891; one mss volume containing autobiographical material and diary entries; sermons, notes and correspondence.

RUSSELL, BERTRAND

ON —MCMASTER UNIVERSITY, Mills Memorial Library, Div of Archives & Research Collections, Hamilton, L8S 4L6, Can. G R Hill, Univ Librn
Holdings: Cat Mss Pix
Notes: About 250,000 items of his letters, manuscripts and library.

RUSSELL, BRUCE ALEXANDER, 1903-1963

CA —UNIVERSITY OF CALIFORNIA, LOS ANGELES, Research Library, Dept of Special Collections, 405 Hilgard Ave, Los Angeles, 90024. Edward Shreeves, Chairman, Bibliographers Group; David S Zeidberg, Head
Notes: 72 linear feet of editorial cartoons published in the Los Angeles Times.

RUSSELL, CARL PARCHER

†WA —WASHINGTON STATE UNIVERSITY, Library, Manuscripts, Archives & Special Collections, Pullman, 99164. John F Guido, Head
Holdings: Cat Mss Maps Pix
Notes: The Carl Parcher Russell papers, a vast resource (24,916 items; 45 linear feet) on American Indian and Western pioneer activities and artifacts. Much on the fur trade; pioneer life; mountain men and trapping; wildlife; primitive life in detail. Also the National Park Service, parks, monuments, etc Described in Carl Parcher Russell: An Indexed Register of His Scholarly and Professional Papers, 1920-1967, in the Washington State University Library (Pullman, 1970), 149 pp.

RUSSELL, CHARLES MARION

LA —R W NORTON ART GALLERY, Library, 4747 Creswell Ave, Shreveport, 71106. Jerry M Bloomer, Librn
Holdings: Cat Pix
Notes: Extensive collection of books, pamphlets, catalogs, etc published about Russell as well as books written and/or illustrated by him. Also incl prints of his paintings, as well as original paintings, sculpture, watercolors, drawings, etc, by Russell (the latter housed in the Gallery collection).
NE —UNIVERSITY OF NEBRASKA-LINCOLN, Don L Love Library, University Archives and Special Collections, Lincoln, 68588. Joseph G Svoboda, University Archivist
Holdings: Pix Slides
Notes: R D Warden Collection of Charles Marion Russell. "Largest private collection of literature on Russell, 'The Cowboy Artist.'" 7000 items, incl first editions of every book and pamphlet by Russell and over 1000 periodical appearances of his art; 900 color prints; 142 drawings; color slides; scrapbooks about Russell and his family, from 1889.
TX —TEXAS A&M UNIVERSITY, Sterling C Evans Library, Special Collections Div, College Station, 77843. Donald H Dyal, Librn
Notes: The Western Illustrators Collection is comprised of approximately 3500 illustrated books, pamphlets, and other items. The collection incl illustrated works by Charles Marion Russell, Frederic Sackrider Remington, and other artists of the American West. Numerous other artists of the West and Southwest are represented, many of them contemporary moderns. Quite a lot of the books have additional unique original drawings by the artists.
TX —AMON CARTER MUSEUM, Library, 3510 Camp Bowie Blvd, PO Box 2365, Fort Worth, 76113. Nancy G Wynne, Librn
Holdings: Vols (25,000) Cat Mss Pix
Notes: The book collection, microfilm and photo archives have been built toward the goal of the interpretation of American history through art. At present, the greatest strengths are in Americana, Western Canadiana, bibliography, American exhibition catalogs and history of photography. Substantial books and files on American artists of the 19th and early 20th century, and particularly of Charles M Russell and Frederic Remington. Incl 25,000 pictures; 13,000 slides.
See also entries under Newspapers, American; Pictures - Collections.

RUSSELL, ELIZABETH

DC —GEORGETOWN UNIVERSITY, Library, Special Collections Div, 37 & O Sts NW, Washington, 20057. George M Barringer, Special Collections Librn; Nicholas B Sheetz, Mss Librn
Holdings: Mss Cat Pix
Notes: The papers of the Irish man-of-letters Sir Shane Leslie (1885-1971) containing letters, mss, diaries, notebooks, clippings, and photographs. Extensive correspondence by Margot Asquith, countess of Oxford and Asquith; Lady Violet Bonham-Carter; Burke Cochran; Lord Alfred Douglas; Moreton Frewen; Cardinal Gasquet; Vyvyan Holland; Lady Leonie Leslie; Sir Wilfrid Meynell; Sir Horace Plunkett; John Quinn; Frederick Rolfe (Baron Corvo); and Elizabeth Russell, among others. Also incl research files on Sir Winston Churchill (Leslie's first cousin); Leonard Jerome; Maria Anne Fitzherbet (wife of King George IV); Ghosts and Ghost stories; and Eton College.

RUSSELL, FRANCIS, 1910-

MA —BOSTON UNIVERSITY, Mugar
Memorial Library, Special Collections Dept,
771 Commonwealth Ave, Boston, 02215.
Howard B Gotlieb, Dir
Holdings: Mss

MA —BRANDEIS UNIVERSITY, Goldfarb
Library, 415 South St, Waltham, 02154.
Bessie Hahn, Dir
Notes: Sacco and Vanzetti Case Collection.
Consists of 23 linear ft of material collected
by both Tom O'Connor and Francis Russell
relating to this celebrated American trial.
This collection is unprocessed.

RUSSELL, HENRY NORRIS

NY —AMERICAN INSTITUTE OF
PHYSICS, Center for the History of Physics,
Niels Bohr Library, 335 E 45 St, New York,
10017. John Aubry, Librn
Notes: The Sources for History of Modern
Astrophysics documents the history of 20th-
century astrophysics. Incl some 400 hours of
oral history interviews with astronomers,
such as Bart Bok, S Chandrasekhar, Martin
Schwarzschild, and A E Whitford. The
project also organized and cataloged the
papers of Henry Norris Russell, Frank
Schlesinger, Otto Struve, Ejnar Hertzsprung,
Harlow Shapley, Charles Young, Robert
Atkinson, Seth Chandler, Theodore
Dunham, Jr, and G C McVittie.

RUSSELL, JAMES

VA —UNIVERSITY OF VIRGINIA,
Alderman Library, Clifton Waller Barrett
Collection, Charlottesville, 22901. Joan St C
Crane, Cur of American Literature
Collections
Notes: Papers.

RUSSELL, SIR JOHN

DC —GEORGETOWN UNIVERSITY,
Library, Special Collections Div, 37 & O Sts
NW, Washington, 20057. George M
Barringer, Special Collections Librn;
Nicholas B Sheetz, Mss Librn
Holdings: Mss Pix
Notes: The papers of Christopher Sykes,
biographer, journalist, and novelist;
containing mss, letters, photographs, and
drawings. With extensive correspondence
from Harold Acton; Angela, Countess of
Antrim; Sir John Betjeman; Ivy Compton-
Burnett; Alick Dru; T S Eliot; Max
Beerbohm; Graham Greene; John Hayward;
Lord Patrick Kinross; Compton Mackenzie;
Nancy Mitford; Anthony Powell; Dame
Flora Robson; Cecil Roth; Sir John Russell;
Osbert Sitwell; John Sparrow; Freya Stark;
James Stern; and Evelyn Waugh, among
others. Also, considerable research material
about Evelyn Waugh, Adam von Trott,
Robert Byron, Lady Nancy Astor; and the
foundation of the state of Israel.

RUSSELL, JONATHAN, 1771-1832

RI —BROWN UNIVERSITY, John Hay
Library, 20 Prospect St, Providence, 02912.
Mark N Brown, Cur Mss
Holdings: // Mss
Notes: Papers of Jonathan Russell,
merchant, diplomat, and Massachusetts
Congressman, Brown Class of 1791. A
collection of 7000 items containing a diary
and a letterbook (1809-1813); records of US
Commissioners at Ghent (1813-1814) and of
the American Legation at Stockholm (1814-
1816); correspondence and documents for
the period 1795-1830; and notes, largely
official, when Russell was Charge d'Affaires
at Paris (1810) and for 1814-1818 when he
was Minister to Sweden and Norway and a
member of the US Congress.

RUSSELL, LAWRENCE

BC —UNIVERSITY OF VICTORIA,
McPherson Library, Victoria, V8W 3H5,
Can.
Notes: Incl mss of "The Man from Aran: A

Study of Liam O'Flaherty" published in the
British Columbia Library Quarterly, vol 31,
no 1, 1968.

RUSSELL, LILLIAN

NY —UNIVERSITY OF ROCHESTER, Rush
Rhees Library, Department of Rare Books
and Special Collections, Rochester, 14627.
Peter Dzwonkoski, Librn
Holdings: Cat Mss Pix
Notes: Lillian Russell's papers, etc.

RUSSELL, PETER

BC —UNIVERSITY OF VICTORIA,
McPherson Library, Victoria, V8W 3H5,
Can.

RUSSELL, SEN. RICHARD B.

GA —UNIVERSITY OF GEORGIA,
Libraries, Special Collections Division,
Athens, 30602. Vesta Lee Gordon, Asst Dir
for Special Collections
Notes: Collection contains 1394.8 linear feet
of mss: papers of US Senator Richard B
Russell; US Congressmen John W Davis,
Maston O'Neal, Robert G Stephens Jr, John
L Pilcher, Dudley M Hughes; Governors
Hoke Smith, Lester Maddox, Carl Sanders.

RUSSELL, ROSALIND

CA —UNIVERSITY OF CALIFORNIA, LOS
ANGELES, Theater Arts Library, Los
Angeles, 90024. Edward Shreeves,
Chairman, Bibliographers Group; Audree
Malkin, Head, Theater Arts Library
Notes: Russell/Brisson Collection (Rosalind
Russell, actress and her husband, Frederick
Brisson, producer): screenplays and
television scripts in various versions,
treatments, production material, programs,
business records, personal and business
correspondence, accounting records, awards,
certificates, scrapbooks, press clippings,
magazine interviews, posters, playbills,
portraits, production stills, fashion and
publicity stills, tapes and 35mm films.

RUSSELL, WILLIAM CLARK, 1844-1911

CA —UNIVERSITY OF CALIFORNIA, LOS
ANGELES, Research Library, Dept of
Special Collections, 405 Hilgard Ave, Los
Angeles, 90024. Edward Shreeves,
Chairman, Bibliographers Group; David S
Zeidberg, Head
Holdings: Vols 50
Notes: 50 first and other editions of his
books; 23 letters.

RUSSIA

CA —UNIVERSITY OF CALIFORNIA,
BERKELEY, University Library, Slavic
Collections, Berkeley, 94720. Edward
Kasinec, Librn
Holdings: Vols (210,000) Cat Maps
Microforms
Budget: ($40,000)
Notes: Strong research collections for
Bulgaria, Czechoslovakia, Poland, Russia-
USSR, and Yugoslavia. Holdings are
excellent in economics, folklore, history,
linguistics, and literature. Publications issued
by academies, major universities, and
principal scholarly institutions are well
represented. Extensive periodical holdings
have been built up, largely as a result of
early exchange arrangements. More than
4000 Slavic-language serials are currently
being received. Farmington Plan and PL480
commitments have augmented Yugoslav
resources. Sizable Slavic-language collections
are to be found in Branch Libraries as well,
in such subjects as agriculture, biology, earth
sciences, forestry, and mathematics.

CA —UNIVERSITY OF CALIFORNIA,
BERKELEY, University Library, Slavic
Collections, Berkeley, 94720. Edward
Kasinec, Librn
Notes: Russian Pacifica collection, the best
on the West coast, incl materials in the
folowing areas: Russian exploration and

settlement of the North American continent;
Russian exploration and settlement and
colonization of Siberia; Russian exploration
of the Pacific; Russian communities in
Manchuria and other parts of the Far East.
While many items pertaining to the
geographical area are found in the Main
Library's stack collection, the bulk of
Russian Pacifica holdings is concentrated in
the Bancroft Library. The Bancroft
collections contain the greater number of
items listed in the two major bibliographies
of Russian Pacifica: Valentin Lada-
Macarski's *Bibliography of Books on Alaska
Published before 1868* (Yale Univ Press,
1969), and V I Mezhov's *Sibirskaia
bibliografiia* (S Petersburg: Semenov, 1903).
During 1983-84, with the assistanceof Title
II-C funding, a major project of collection
evaluation and development was undertaken
in the area of Russian Racifica, resulting in
the acquisition on microfilm of several
hundred items, incl a part of the holdings of
the Museum of Russian Culture in San
Francisco relating to Siberia and Russian
communities in China.

CA —UNIVERSITY OF CALIFORNIA, LOS
ANGELES, Research Library, Dept of
Special Collections, 405 Hilgard Ave, Los
Angeles, 90024. Edward Shreeves,
Chairman, Bibliographers Group; David S
Zeidberg, Head
Notes: 90 linear feet in various collections
pertaining to political and social activities in
the US, Europe, Latin America, and the
USSR.

CA —UNIVERSITY OF CALIFORNIA, LOS
ANGELES, Library, Slavic Collection, 405
Hilgard Ave, Los Angeles, 90024. Edward
Shreeves, Chairman, Bibliographers Group;
Leon Ferder, Slavic Bibliographer
Holdings: Vols (250,000) Cat Mss Maps
Notes: The entire range of humanities, social
sciences, and the arts. One of the most
comprehensive US collections for material
not only on Russia and the Soviet Union,
but also on Bulgaria, Czechoslovakia,
Poland, Yugoslavia, the non-Slavic countries
of Eastern Europe (Romania, Hungary,
Albania) and Soviet Central Asia. Holdings
in Russian and Slavic linguistics, Russian
literature, and Russian history are
particularly strong, covering all periods. The
collections are described in some detail in
Paul Horecky's book on US Slavic
collections.

CA —HOOVER INSTITUTION ON WAR,
REVOLUTION & PEACE, Stanford
University, Stanford, 94305. Milorad M
Drachkovitch, Archivist
Holdings: Mss Pix
Notes: Records of *National Republic*
magazine, incl newspaper clippings, printed
matter, pamphlets, reports, indices, notes,
bulletins, lettergrams, weekly letters, and
photographs, 1905-1960, relating to pacifist,
communist, facist, and other radical
movements as well as political developments
in the US and Soviet Russia. 826 ms boxes.

CT —YALE UNIVERSITY, Box 1603A, Yale
Station, New Haven, 06520.

DC —LIBRARY OF CONGRESS, Rare Book
& Special Collections Div, Washington,
20540. William Matheson, Chief
Notes: Books accumulated in the Russian
imperial family palace prior to 1917 on
politics, administration, history, travel, law,
military affairs, etc. Chiefly from the 19th
century.

IL —NATIONAL COUNCIL OF THE
YMCAS, YMCA Historical Library, 6400
Shafer Ct, Rosemont, 60018. Eleanor R
Murphy, Librn
Holdings: Vols (15,000) Cat Mss Pix
Notes: YMCA work in Russia and with
Russian emigres in Europe. See Edward
Kasinec, "The YMCA National Board
Historical Library," *Slavic Bibliographic and
Documentation Center Newsletter*,
Washington, DC, November 1971, no 5,
page 9. No separate catalog. Collection incl
virtually complete files of Russian language
publications of the YMCA Press (Prague-
Berlin, and Paris, after 1925), and the
Chekhov Publishing House (NY, 1951-56),
along with its archives, correspondence, etc.

RUSSIA (cont.)

Some primary material is restricted. Application should be made to librarian for permission.

IL —UNIVERSITY OF ILLINOIS, URBANA/CHAMPAIGN, Slavic and East European Library, Urbana, 61801. Marianna Tax Choldin, Head
Holdings: Vols (420,000) Cat
Notes: One of the largest Slavic and East European collections. Strong in Russian and Soviet materials-humanities, sciences, and social sciences; languages and literatures; periodicals, newspapers, and microforms. Ca 260,000 volumes in languages of the Soviet Union plus 20,000 Russian and Ukrainian titles on microform. Extensive coverage of Czechoslovakia (35,000 vols); Yugoslavia (31,000 vols); Bulgaria (9200 vols); Poland (34,600 vols); Romania (13,000 vols); and Hungary (18,000 vols) and the languages, literatures, and history of these countries.

MA —HARVARD UNIVERSITY, Russian Research Center, Library, 1737 Cambridge St, Cambridge, 02138. Susan Jo Gardos, Librn
Holdings: Vols 14,000 Cat Microforms
Budget: $8000
Notes: A working library for the Center; research collections in this field are provided by other Harvard libraries.

NE —UNIVERSITY OF NEBRASKA-LINCOLN, Don L Love Library, Lincoln, 68588. Joseph G Svoboda, University Archivist
Holdings: Vols 5000 Cat
Notes: The main subject area is Russian and Soviet history, but related to other aspects of Russian and Soviet society: art, literature, politics, communist party, Soviet imperialism, etc. About one half of the collection is in Russian, the other half in English, French and German.

NH —DARTMOUTH COLLEGE, Baker Memorial Library, Hanover, 03755.
Holdings: Cat Mss Maps
Notes: 1200 atlases and 90,000 maps. Areas of special interest: historical cartography, polar regions, USSR.

NY —COLUMBIA UNIVERSITY LIBRARIES, Lehman Library, Slavic and East Central European Collection, 420 W 118 St, New York, 10027. Nina Lencek, Bibliographer
Holdings: // Uncat
Notes: The Soviet Nationalities Collection consists of published materials in the Indo-European, Uralic, Altaic, Transcaucasian, and Paleo-Siberian languages of the Soviet Union and contains more than 14,000 volumes as well as current and discontinued periodical literature. The author/title catalog for this collection is in Russian translation except for Armenian books, which are cataloged in the original. The collection is circulating and available through interlibrary loan.

NY —NEW YORK PUBLIC LIBRARY, Slavonic Div, Fifth Ave & 42 St, New York, 10018. Edward Kasinec, Chief
Holdings: Vols 122,000 Cat Microforms
Notes: Russian language materials form the main body (ca 70 percent) of the extensive Slavic and Baltic collections of the Slavonic Division. The strength of the collection is in humanities and social sciences, incl military history and government documents. Periodicals and publications of learned societies form an important part of the collection. Holdings of rare books are considerable. See New York Public Library, *Dictionary Catalog of the Slavonic Collection* (Boston: G K Hall, 1974), 44 vols.

†OH —OHIO NORTHERN UNIVERSITY, Heterick Memorial Library, 525 S Main St, Ada, 45810.

WA —UNIVERSITY OF WASHINGTON LIBRARIES, Suzzallo Library, Slavic & East European Section, FM-25, Seattle, 98195. Barbara A Galik, Head
Holdings: Vols (250,000) Cat Mss Maps Pix Phonorecords Audiotapes Microforms
Budget: ($85,000)
Notes: Strong research collections for Russia--USSR, including Central Asia. Holdings are excellent in historical source materials, language, literature, geography, economics, the fine ares, and folklore. There are extensive holdings of the publcations of academies, major universities, and principal scholarly institutions, especially of long serial runs. Sizeable Slavic language collections are also to be found in the sciences among the branch libraries of the university.

WI —BELOIT COLLEGE LIBRARIES, Beloit, 53511. Dennis W Dickinson, Dir
Holdings: Cat
Notes: This small collection incl most of the Stalin Prize novels, many works published "behind the Iron Curtain," and some titles in English translation. Also incl complete sets of distinguished Russian authors in Russian editions. Books purchased in history, geography, economics, etc to supplement the Winkelman Collection of Russian Literature.

PQ —CONCORDIA UNIVERSITY LIBRARIES, 1435 Drummond St, Montreal, H3G 1M8, Can. P E Filion, University Librn
Notes: A collection of 5000 Russian works covering a wide range of time and subjects. Incl are many historical works published since 1945, vols on modern Soviet economics, collected works of classic Russian literary figures, a number of important bibliographies, technical dictionaries and art books.

PQ —MCGILL UNIVERSITY, McLennan Library, Rare Books and Special Collections Dept, 3459 McTavish St, Montreal, H3A 1Y1, Can.
Holdings: Vols 2275
Notes: Yiddish poetry of the 20th century of worldwide publication, incl rare Soviet Union imprints, in the Fishstein Collection.

RUSSIA—CIVILIZATION AND CULTURE

AK —ALASKA STATE LIBRARY, Alaska Historical Library Collection, Pouch G, Juneau, 99811. Phyllis Demuth, Readers Services Librn
Notes: Russian history collection, especially strong in Russian military history.

CA —MUSEUM OF RUSSIAN CULTURE, 2450 Sutter St, San Francisco, 94115. Nicholas Slobodchikoff, Dir
Holdings: Vols (15,000) Pix
Notes: Incl 10,000 periodicals. Much on Imperial Russia and Russian immigration to the US. Also incl 12,000 Russian newspapers.

DC —WOODROW WILSON INTERNATIONAL CENTER FOR SCHOLARS, Kennan Institute for Advanced Russian Studies, 1000 Jefferson Dr SW, Washington, 20560. V David Zdenek, Librn
Holdings: Vols 5000
Notes: Incl materials on Russians, Ukrainians, Byelorussians, and on other Soviet republics.

KS —UNIVERSITY OF KANSAS, Watson Library, Lawrence, 66045. George Jerkovich, Cur Slavic Collections
Notes: Strong in literature, language, linguistics, history, politics, economy, geography, philosophy, religion and law. Russian collection is very strong in pre and post-revolutionary rare serial and monographic titles. Also incl complete works of Russian authors of the 18th, 19th and 20th centuries. Emigre literature and current Soviet literature are maintained at teaching and research levels.

MA —BOSTON COLLEGE LIBRARIES, Chestnut Hill, 02167.

NE —UNIVERSITY OF NEBRASKA-LINCOLN, Don L Love Library, Lincoln, 68588. Joseph G Svoboda, University Archivist
Holdings: Vols 5000 Cat
Notes: The main subject area is Russian and Soviet history, but related to other aspects of Russian and Soviet society: art, literature, politics, communist party, Soviet imperialism, etc. About one half of the collection is in Russian, the other half in English, French and German. Incl are periodicals.

NY —NEW YORK PUBLIC LIBRARY, Slavonic Div, Fifth Ave & 42 St, New York, 10018. Edward Kasinec, Chief
Holdings: Cat Microforms
Notes: See: New York Public Library, Slavonic Div, *Dictionary Catalog of the Slavonic Collection*, 2nd ed, rev and enl (Boston: G K Hall, 1974), 44 vols; and New York Public Library, *Dictionary Catalog of the Research Libraries* (New York, 1972-).

OH —HEBREW UNION COLLEGE-JEWISH INSTITUTE OF RELIGION, Klau Library, 3101 Clifton Ave, Cincinnati, 45220. David J Gilner, Reference Librn
Holdings: Cat
Notes: Excellent collection of pre-revolutionary monographs and periodicals; recent "exile" literature.

PA —KUTZTOWN UNIVERSITY, Rohrbach Library, Kutztown, 19530.
Holdings: Vols 12,000 Cat

WA —UNIVERSITY OF WASHINGTON LIBRARIES, Suzzallo Library, Slavic & East European Section, FM-25, Seattle, 98195. Barbara A Galik, Head
Holdings: Vols (250,000) Cat Mss Maps Pix Phonorecords Audiotapes Microforms
Budget: ($85,000)
Notes: Strong research collections for Russia--USSR, including Central Asia. Holdings are excellent in historical source materials, language, literature, geography, economics, the fine ares, and folklore. There are extensive holdings of the publcations of academies, major universities, and principal scholarly institutions, especially of long serial runs. Sizeable Slavic language collections are also to be found in the sciences among the branch libraries of the university.

RUSSIA—DESCRIPTION AND TRAVEL

CA —CALIFORNIA STATE UNIVERSITY, FRESNO, Henry Madden Library, Dept of Special Collections, Fresno, 93740. Ronald J Mahoney, Head
Holdings: Uncat
Notes: The Alexander Pronin Collection of Russian Postcards of approx 1500 Russian postcards, 1890-1920, illustrating Russian art, architecture and life. Approx 150 are partially used, incl various World War I censors' marks.

IN —INDIANA UNIVERSITY, Lilly Library, Seventh St, Bloomington, 47405. William R Cagle, Librn
Holdings: // Cat Mss
Notes: Emphasis on travel. Incl Russo-Turkish relations; Georgia and the Caucasus.

ON —METROPOLITAN TORONTO LIBRARY, History Dept, 789 Yonge St, Toronto, M4W 2G8, Can. Michael Pearson, Head
Holdings: Vols (2500) Cat
Notes: The collection includes reports, diaries and personal narratives of travels and voyages of exploration and discovery from the Renaissance to the present day. Areas of emphasis are the exploration of the interior of North America, early oceanic voyages of discovery and accounts of travellers to Russia. The collection also includes a number of early editions, standard collected works such as the publications of the Hakluyt Society, accounts of shipwrecks as well as a representative collection of guide books from the 18th century to the present.

RUSSIA—ECONOMIC POLICY

CA —CLAREMONT COLLEGES, Honnold Library, Ninth & Dartmouth, Claremont, 91711. Tania Rizzo, Special Collections Dept Head
Holdings: Vols 1000 Uncat Pix Periodicals
Notes: Collection of James Mavor (1859-1925) who published histories of the Russian Revolution and economy. Mostly in Russian. Indexed. Restricted use.

CA —RAND CORP, Library, 1700 Main St, Santa Monica, 90406. Vivian J Arterbery, Library Mgr
Holdings: Vols 5000 // Cat
Notes: Russian economic conditions. All material in Russian.

RUSSIA—ECONOMIC POLICY (cont.)

IA —IOWA STATE UNIVERSITY, Library, Dept of Special Collections, Ames, 50011. Stanley M Yates, Head
Holdings: Mss Pix
Notes: Lauren K Soth was editor of Des Moines Register and Tribune from 1954-75, winning a Pulitzer Prize for Editorial Writing in 1956 for his editorials which helped establish agricultural exchanges with the Soviet Union. 20 linear ft, finding aid available.

NY —NEW YORK PUBLIC LIBRARY, Slavonic Div, Fifth Ave & 42 St, New York, 10018. Edward Kasinec, Chief
Holdings: Cat Microforms
Notes: See: New York Public Library, Slavonic Div, *Dictionary Catalog of the Slavonic Collection*, 2nd ed, rev and enl (Boston: G K Hall, 1974), 44 vols; and New York Public Library, *Dictionary Catalog of the Research Libraries* (New York, 1972-).

†NY —US ARMY RUSSIAN INSTITUTE (USARI), APO, New York, 09053.
Holdings: Vols (24,841)
Notes: A research and language facility of the Army Foreign Affairs Officers Speciality (USSR), located in Garmisch, West Germany. 65 percent of the collection is in Russian; 35 percent in English and other languages. Contains most representative Soviet Newspapers and periodicals, as well as American and other English language publications.

RUSSIA—FOREIGN RELATIONS

IA —IOWA STATE UNIVERSITY, Library, Dept of Special Collections, Ames, 50011. Stanley M Yates, Head
Holdings: Mss Pix
Notes: Lauren K Soth was editor of Des Moines Register and Tribune from 1954-75, winning a Pulitzer Prize for Editorial Writing in 1956 for his editorials which helped establish agricultural exchanges with the Soviet Union. 20 linear ft, finding aid available.

NY —NEW YORK PUBLIC LIBRARY, Slavonic Div, Fifth Ave & 42 St, New York, 10018. Edward Kasinec, Chief
Holdings: Cat Microforms
Notes: See: New York Public Library, Slavonic Div, *Dictionary Catalog of the Slavonic Collection*, 2nd ed, rev and enl (Boston: G K Hall, 1974), 44 vols; and New York Public Library, *Dictionary Catalog of the Research Libraries* (New York, 1972-).

†NY —US ARMY RUSSIAN INSTITUTE (USARI), APO, New York, 09053.
Holdings: Vols (24,841)
Notes: A research and language facility of the Army Foreign Affairs Officers Speciality (USSR), located in Garmisch, West Germany. 65 percent of the collection is in Russian; 35 percent in English and other languages. Contains most representative Soviet Newspapers and periodicals, as well as American and other English language publications.

RUSSIA—HISTORY

AK —ALASKA STATE LIBRARY, Alaska Historical Library Collection, Pouch G, Juneau, 99811. Phyllis Demuth, Readers Services Librn
Holdings: Vols 3000
Notes: Strong in Russian military history.

AZ —NORTHERN ARIZONA UNIVERSITY, Special Collection Library, CU Box 6022, Flagstaff, 86011. Peter M Whiteley, Coordr/Archivist; William Mullane, Librn
Holdings: Vols 9000 Cat Mss Phonorecords Microforms
Notes: The large Allderdice Collection of thousands of books, pamphlets, periodicals, and organizational files reflects the conservative, communist, socialist, facist, anarchist, and other viewpoints, etc, during the 20th century.

†CA —UNIVERSITY OF CALIFORNIA, BERKELEY, LIBRARIES, Berkeley, 94720.
Notes: Comprehensive collection of indexes to more than 40 provincial Russian periodicals dealing with the Russians Orthodox Church during the Imperial period. More than 200 photocopies of letters, telegrams, sketches, and photographs from the collection of the Grand Duchess Mariia Alexandrovna, daughter of Emperor Alexander II of Russia. Dating from last third of the 19th century. Incl correspondence from her parents, court, and other friends. Copies made available by the Executive Committee of the Museum of Russian Culture in San Francisco.

CA —CLAREMONT COLLEGES, Honnold Library, Ninth & Dartmouth, Claremont, 91711. Tania Rizzo, Special Collections Dept Head
Holdings: Vols 1125 Uncat Mss Pix Microfilms
Notes: The combined James Mavor, Raymond Elliott, and Gregory P Tschebotarioff collections incl clippings and periodicals from the Revolutionary period, books and pictorial materials about the royal family, separatist movements, and the emigre experience. Restricted use.

CA —CALIFORNIA STATE UNIVERSITY, FULLERTON, Library, Box 4150, Fullerton, 92634. Linda Herman, Special Collections Librn
Holdings: Uncat Microforms
Notes: 121 microfilm reels of British Foreign Office records: *Russia: Correspondence 1914-1918. Guide to collection in British Foreign Office. Russia: Correspondence 1906-1945* (Wilmington: Scholarly Resources, 1976).

CA —UNIVERSITY OF CALIFORNIA, LOS ANGELES, Library, Slavic Collection, 405 Hilgard Ave, Los Angeles, 90024. Edward Shreeves, Chairman, Bibliographers Group; Leon Ferder, Slavic Bibliographer
Holdings: Vols (250,000) Cat Mss Maps
Notes: The Slavic Collection at UCLA consists of materials from and relating to Russia and the Soviet Union, Poland, Czechoslovakia, Yugoslavia, Bulgaria, the Sorbians in East Germany, and works by Slavic emigres. The collection contains nearly 250,000 vols, and is particularly strong in linguistics, literature, history and social sciences, and reference materials. Slavic materials are collected in hard copy and microform, and incl monographs, serials (incl newspapers), reference works, proceedings of Slavistic congresses and symposia, and also *Festschriften* and dissertations.

CA —CALIFORNIA INSTITUTE OF TECHNOLOGY, Robert A Millikan Memorial Library, Archives, 1201 E California Blvd, Pasadena, 91125. Judith R Goodstein, Archivist
Holdings: Vols (3000) Uncat Mss Maps Pix Slides Phonorecords Audiotapes Videotapes 16mm Films Microforms
Notes: Over 70 collections (1830s-present) relating to history of 19th-20th centuries science and technology and the history of the Institute. Included are personal and professional papers of Caltech scientists and administrative officers; divisional records and faculty committees; over 5000 photographs of American and European scientists. Mss collections documents more than a century of American political, social, and intellectual history; the development of the physical sciences, aeronautics, molecular biology, and seismology in the US and abroad; and social and political conditions in Europe between the two World Wars. There are also family letters relating to 19th century American life before and during the Civil War (the Morley and A G Throop papers); to 19th century social conditions in Russia and Hungary (the Paul Epstein papers and Theodore von Karman papers); andto the development of 20th century Italian mathematics.

CA —MUSEUM OF RUSSIAN CULTURE, 2450 Sutter St, San Francisco, 94115. Nicholas Slobodchikoff, Dir
Holdings: Vols (15,000) Pix
Notes: Incl 10,000 periodicals. Much on Imperial Russia and Russian immigration to the US. Also incl 12,000 Russian newspapers.

CA —HOOVER INSTITUTION ON WAR, REVOLUTION & PEACE, Stanford University, Stanford, 94305. Milorad M Drachkovitch, Archivist
Holdings: // Mss
Notes: Two collections: (1) Records of the Imperial Russian Secret Police (Okhrana) headquarters in Paris, 1883-1917. Materials incl reports of agents in the field, Paris office reports, dispatches, circulars, studies, correspondence, and other material. 203 ms boxes, 10 clipping volumes, 163,802 biographical and reference cards, and 16 boxes of photographs. Unpublished register is available in repository. (2) Letters (handwritten in Russian), 1914-18, of Grand Duke Georgii Mikhailovich, son of Grand Duke Mikhail Nikolaevich (son of Tsar Nicholas I), nephew of Tsar Alexander II, and special representative of Tsar Nicholas II at various fronts during World War I, to his daughter Princess Kseniia dealing with his official functions; events before, during and after the Revolution; and family matters. 2 ms boxes.

CA —STANFORD UNIVERSITY LIBRARIES, Cecil H Green Library, Stanford, 94305. Wojciech Zalewski, Cur, Russian & East European Collection
Holdings: Vols (200,000) Cat Maps Microforms
Budget: ($90,000)
Notes: Strong collection prior to 20th century, but Stanford University Libraries' collecting effort is coordinated with Hoover Institution, Stanford, and holdings are not duplicated. Collection descriptions: Wojciech Zalewski, *Russian Materials in the Main Library of Stanford University, A Collection Survey* (Stanford: Stanford University Libraries, 1974). Wojciech Zalerski, "Stanford University" in P L Horecky, ed, *East Central and Southeast Europe, A Handbook of Library and Archival Resources in North America* (Santa Barbara: Clio Press, 1976).

CO —GREELEY PUBLIC LIBRARY, City Complex Bldg, Greeley, 80631. Esther Fromm, Librn

CT —YALE UNIVERSITY, Box 1603A, Yale Station, New Haven, 06520.
Notes: Books by and about Lenin and mss by many emigre authors.

DC —GEORGETOWN UNIVERSITY, Library, Special Collections Div, 37 & O Sts NW, Washington, 20057. George M Barringer, Special Collections Librn; Nicholas B Sheetz, Mss Librn
Holdings: Mss Cat Pix
Notes: Correspondence, memoranda, reports, mss of articles and addresses, pamphlets, and newspaper clippings constituting the papers of Robert F Kelley (1894-1975). Kelley served as US Military Attache to the Baltic Provinces from 1920-22, before entering the foreign service in 1922. From 1926-37 he served as Chief of the Division of Eastern European Affairs in the State Department. In 1937 he was transferred to Ankara, Turkey where he remained until his retirement from foreign service in 1945. The papers most directly concern USSR internal affairs as well as US - USSR relations from the years immediately prior to recognition in 1933 through the cold war years of the early 1960's. Apart from State Department material, additional material is incl from Kelley's involvement in the American Committee for Liberation from Bolshevism and the establishment of Radio Liberty.

DC —LIBRARY OF CONGRESS, Washington, 20540.
Notes: Project of a consortium to microfilm about 200,000 pp of material on Great Britain, France, Russia and Prussia, for the period 1848-1918 in the ms and documentary collections of the Austrian State Archives. The collection will incl, among others, documents on the Austro-Prussian War of 1866, the treaty negotiations between France and Italy in 1868-1870, the Orient Question of 1877-1878, the persecution of Jews in Russia in 1882, the Congo Conference in Berlin, 1884-1887 and the British-Portuguese conflict in East Africa, 1889-1891. Copies are available

RUSSIA—HISTORY (cont.)

at LC, the Center for Research Libraries, the Hampshire Inter-Library Center, and the libraries of Boston College, Yale, Harvard, Duke, Stanford and the University of Virginia.

DC —WOODROW WILSON INTERNATIONAL CENTER FOR SCHOLARS, Kennan Institute for Advanced Russian Studies, 1000 Jefferson Dr SW, Washington, 20560. V David Zdenek, Librn
Holdings: Vols 5000
Notes: Incl materials on Russians, Ukrainians, Byelorussians, and on other Soviet republics.

IL —UNIVERSITY OF ILLINOIS, URBANA/CHAMPAIGN, Slavic and East European Library, Urbana, 61801. Marianna Tax Choldin, Head
Holdings: Vols (420,000) Cat Microforms
Notes: One of the largest Slavic and East European collections. Strong in Russian and Soviet materials-humanities, sciences, and social sciences; languages and literatures; periodicals, newspapers, and microforms. Ca 260,000 volumes in languages of the Soviet Union plus 20,000 Russian and Ukrainian titles on microform. Extensive coverage of Czechoslovakia (35,000 vols); Yugoslavia (31,000 vols); Bulgaria (9200 vols); Poland (34,600 vols); Romania (13,000 vols); and Hungary (18,000 vols) and the languages, literatures, and history of these countries.

IN —INDIANA UNIVERSITY, Lilly Library, Seventh St, Bloomington, 47405. William R Cagle, Librn
Holdings: // Cat Mss
Notes: Emphasis on travel. Incl Russo-Turkish relations; Georgia and the Caucasus.

IN —INDIANA UNIVERSITY, University Libraries, Bloomington, 47401. Murlin Croucher, Librn for Slavic Studies
Holdings: Vols (300,000) Cat Maps Microforms
Budget: ($63,000)
Notes: The collection, established after World War II, covers material of, and on, the Soviet Union (55 percent) and Eastern Europe (45 percent) in the languages of the area and in western European languages as well. Material is chiefly in the fields of humanities and social sciences. Many other Slavic and East European books are located in the Lilly Library (rare book library).

KS —UNIVERSITY OF KANSAS, Kenneth Spencer Research Library, Special Collections Dept, Lawrence, 66045. Alexandra Mason, Librn
Holdings: Cat Mss Maps
Notes: Strong in 17th-19th centuries. Noncirculating.

KS —UNIVERSITY OF KANSAS, Watson Library, Lawrence, 66045. George Jerkovich, Cur Slavic Collections
Notes: Strong in literature, language, linguistics, history, politics, economy, geography, philosophy, religion and law. Russian collection is very strong in pre and post-revolutionary rare serial and monographic titles. Also incl complete works of Russian authors of the 18th, 19th and 20th centuries. Emigre literature and current Soviet literature are maintained at teaching and research levels.

MA —HARVARD UNIVERSITY LIBRARY, Widener Library, Slavic Collections, Cambridge, 02138. Hugh M Olmsted, Slavic Dept Head
Holdings: Vols Cat Mss
Notes: Russian history shelflist through June, 1976 lists 39,379 titles, excluding White Russian and the Ukraine (earlier version was incl in *Widener Library Shelflist*, volumes 28-31, 1971). The collections continue to be developed actively, and are strong both in current and in antiquarian materials. Materials on the Revolution incl Aleksinskii, Smolensk, John Reed, and Trotsky archives. See *Harvard Library Bulletin XVII* (1969), pp 425-433. For summary of ms and archival materials, see Steven A Grant and John H Brown, *The Russian Empire and Soviet Union; A Guide to Manuscripts and Archival Materials in the United States*, 1981, pp 218-219, 224-233.

MO —WASHINGTON UNIVERSITY, John M Olin Library, Campus Box 1061, St Louis, 63130.
Holdings: Vols 10,000 Cat Microforms
Notes: Incl the Edna Fischel Gelhorn Collection on the history of the Russian revolutionary movement and the Soviet Union.

NE —AMERICAN HISTORICAL SOCIETY OF GERMANS FROM RUSSIA (AHSGR), 615 Twelfth St, Lincoln, 68502. Mary Lynn Tuck, Librn
Holdings: Vols (1900) Mss Maps Pix Phonorecords Videotapes Audiotapes Microforms VF
Notes: History of German people from Russia and history of people of German-Russian ancestry. Including times in Russia, Germany, US, Canada, Mexico, Argentina, Brazil, Paraguay, Korea, and Japan. This Society has fifty-six chapters in the United States. 1900 volumes, 100 maps; 500 mss; 1200 vertical files; 2000 pictures; 40,000 obituary files, 40,000 family group charts, 50 phonorecords, 20 videotapes, 50 audiotapes, 15 reel-to-reel tapes, 150 periodicals, 250 microforms, 250 family histories-published and unpublished.

NE —UNIVERSITY OF NEBRASKA-LINCOLN, Don L Love Library, Lincoln, 68588. Joseph G Svoboda, University Archivist
Holdings: Vols 5000 Cat
Notes: The main subject area is Russian and Soviet history, but related to other aspects of Russian and Soviet society: art, literature, politics, communist party, Soviet imperialism, etc. About one half of the collection is in Russian, the other half in English, French and German. Incl are periodicals.

NJ —PRINCETON UNIVERSITY, Library, Rare Books Dept, Princeton, 08544. Stephen Ferguson, Cur
Holdings: Mss
Notes: Papers of Louis Fischer, journalist and authority on the Soviet Union.

NM —NEW MEXICO STATE UNIVERSITY, Library, Box 3475, Las Cruces, 88003. James Dyke, Dir
Holdings: Vols 184 // Cat
Notes: The Mashbir Collection deals with 18th and 19th century Russian history.

NY —CORNELL UNIVERSITY LIBRARIES, John M Olin Library, Ithaca, 14853. Marilyn B Kann, Slavic Studies Librn
Holdings: Vols 14,000 Cat Microforms

NY —NEW YORK PUBLIC LIBRARY, Slavonic Div, Fifth Ave & 42 St, New York, 10018. Edward Kasinec, Chief
Holdings: Vols 122,000 Cat Microforms
Notes: Russian language materials form the main body (ca 70 percent) of the extensive Slavic and Baltic collections of the Slavonic Division. The strength of the collection is in humanities and social sciences, incl military history and government documents. Periodicals and publications of learned societies form an important part of the collection. Holdings of rare books are considerable. See New York Public Library, *Dictionary Catalog of the Slavonic Collection* (Boston: G K Hall, 1974), 44 vols.

NY —SHEVCHENKO SCIENTIFIC SOCIETY INC, 63 Fourth Ave, New York, 10003. Svitlana Andrushkiw, Librn
Notes: Ukrainian history, literature, art. Slavic studies. Ukrainians in the US and foreign countries. Support graduate level research.

†NY —US ARMY RUSSIAN INSTITUTE (USARI), APO, New York, 09053.
Holdings: Vols (24,841)
Notes: A research and language facility of the Army Foreign Affairs Officers Speciality (USSR), located in Garmisch, West Germany. 65 percent of the collection is in Russian; 35 percent in English and other languages. Contains most representative Soviet Newspapers and periodicals, as well as American and other English language publications.

NY —ALEXANDRA TOLSTOY MEMORIAL LIBRARY, Tolstoy Foundation Center, Lake Rd, Valley Cottage, 10989. Tatiana Kalinin, Acting Librn
Holdings: Vols (15,000)
Notes: The Foundation assists political refugees in resettlement throughout the world.

OH —HEBREW UNION COLLEGE-JEWISH INSTITUTE OF RELIGION, Klau Library, 3101 Clifton Ave, Cincinnati, 45220. David J Gilner, Reference Librn
Holdings: Cat
Notes: Excellent collection of pre-revolutionary monographs and periodicals; recent "exile" literature.

OH —OHIO STATE UNIVERSITY, William Oxley Thompson Memorial Library, Hilander Room, 1858 Neil Ave Mall, Columbus, 43210. Predrag Matejic, Cur; G Koolemans Beynen, Slavic Bibliographer
Holdings: Vols (200,000) Cat Maps Microforms
Budget: ($45,000)
Notes: Area studies of Central, Southeastern and Eastern Europe. Emphasis on on Slavic literatures, languages and history. At present economics, sociology, law (Russian only) have been added. Within this framework the following priorities have been established: Material in Russian problems; then Medieval Slavic (Cyrillic); then Polish, then Serbo-Croatian, then Bulgarian, and now Romanian. Special attention is paid to serials, bibliographies, ms descriptions and dictionaries (incl biographical and encyclopedias). Apart from materials in native languages, materials in the following languages are acquired: Old Church Slavonic, Greek, English, French, German, Italian, a few in Scandinavian languages, incl Finnish, and a few in Baltic languages. The Hillandar Room holds approx 2000 Slavic mss, 1050 from Hilandar Monastery, Mount Athos, on microform and a related referencecollection.

OH —MIAMI UNIVERSITY, King Library, Walter Havighurst Special Collections Library, Oxford, 45056. Helen Ball, Cur of Special Collections
Holdings: Vols 2500
Notes: Collection concerns 19th century Russia on political, military and cultural issues, incl periodicals.

OR —UNIVERSITY OF OREGON LIBRARY, Social Science Dept, Eugene, 97403. Holway R Jones, Head Dept Librn
Holdings: Cat
Notes: Primary strength lies in the period prior to 1800.

PA —KUTZTOWN UNIVERSITY, Rohrbach Library, Kutztown, 19530.
Holdings: Vols 12,000 Cat

TX —SOUTHERN METHODIST UNIVERSITY, DeGolyer Library, Box 396, SMU, Dallas, 75275. Clifton H Jones, Dir
Notes: Small collection of first editions of prominent authors.

WA —UNIVERSITY OF WASHINGTON LIBRARIES, Suzzallo Library, Slavic & East European Section, FM-25, Seattle, 98195. Barbara A Galik, Head
Holdings: Vols (250,000) Cat Mss maps Pix Phonorecords Audiotapes Microforms
Budget: ($85,000)
Notes: Strong research collections for Russia--USSR, including Central Asia. Holdings are excellent in historical source materials. There are extensive holdings of the publications of academies, major universities, and principal scholarly institutions, especially of long serial runs.

WI —UNIVERSITY OF WISCONSIN, GREEN BAY, Library/Learning Center, Green Bay, 54301. Marian A Gould, Acting Dir, Special Collections/University Archives
Holdings: Vols 700 // Cat
Notes: This represents the collection of Leon Kramer, "idealist, philosophical anarchist and bookseller." Much of the material concerns radical literature and small socialist and communist parties in the US, although there is a considerable amount of books, booklets, and pamphlets published in Germany, Italy, and other parts of Europe. Incl uncounted pamphlets.

WI —UNIVERSITY OF WISCONSIN, MADISON, Memorial Library, 728 State St,

RUSSIA—HISTORY (cont.)

Madison, 53706. Erwin K Welsch, Social Studies Bibliographer
Notes: Incl Romanovskii Library: approx 1000 vols from the library of Prince Nikolai Romanovskii, grandson of Tsar Nicholas I. A general collection of Slavic books, with emphasis on history, law, royalty, local government, economics and geology. Also, and extensive collection of brochures, pamphlets, newspapers, broadsheets and broadsides, propaganda materials for the Russian Revolutionary Movement that culminated in the 1917 uprising, printed between 1825 and 1925.

WI —UNIVERSITY OF WISCONSIN, MADISON, Memorial Library, Slavic Studies Collection, 728 State St, Madison, 53706. Aleksander Rolich, Bibliographer for Slavic Studies; Robert P Gakovich, Slavic Cataloger; Valdis J Zeps, Baltic Studies Center
Holdings: Cat
Notes: Russian Underground Collection. Materials in the Russian Underground Collection embrace the Russian Revolutionary Movement from 1825 to 1917, including a considerable number of Free Press publications. Among the 1500 titles are included about 100 journals, many political tracts, leaflets, broadsides and brochures of various political groups, largely socialist, religious nonconformists (L Tolstoi) and a large number of the satirical journals that appeared between 1905-1907. Restricted use: Rare Book Department.

AB —UNIVERSITY OF ALBERTA, Cameron Library, The Bruce Peel Special Collections Room, Edmonton, T6G 2J8, Can. John Charles, Special Collections Librn
Holdings: Vols (8420)
Notes: Ukranian language, literature, history and economics. Special catalogs of Soviet and European books and periodicals.

RUSSIA—HISTORY—REVOLUTION, 1917-1921

CA —CALIFORNIA STATE UNIVERSITY, FULLERTON, Library, Box 4150, Fullerton, 92634. Linda Herman, Special Collections Librn
Holdings: Uncat Microforms
Notes: 121 microfilm reels of British Foreign Office records: *Russia: Correspondence 1914-1918.* Guide to collection in *British Foreign Office. Russia: Correspondence 1906-1945* (Wilmington Scholarly Resources, 1976).

CA —HOOVER INSTITUTION ON WAR, REVOLUTION & PEACE, Stanford University, Stanford, 94305. Milorad M Drachkovitch, Archivist
Notes: Three collections: (1) Papers of David D Grimm, Professor of Law and Rector of Petersburg University, 1899-1910, Assistant Minister of Education in the Russian Provisional Government, 1917, and an emigre political activist and journalist, incl correspondence, memoranda, press reports, printed and other material, 1919-1934, relating to his service to the Russian emigre community in Finland and other parts of Europe and to the Russian Civil War, 4 ms boxes. (2) Letters (handwritten in Russian), 1914-18, of Grand Duke Georgii Mikhailovich, son of Grand Duke Mikhaii Nikolaevich (son of Tsar Nicholas I), nephew of Tsar Alexander II, and special representative of Tsar Nicholas II at various fronts during World War I, to his daughter Princess Kseniia dealing with his official functions; events before, during and after the Revolution; and family matters. 2 ms boxes. (3) Records of the Russian Embassy in France, incl correspondence, reports, memoranda, and notes, 1917-24, relating to relations between France and the Russian Provisional Government, the Russian Revolution, counter-revolutionary movements, the Paris Peace Conference, and Russian emigres after the revolution. In Russian and French. 36 1/2 ms boxes.

CA —HOOVER INSTITUTION ON WAR, REVOLUTION & PEACE, Stanford

University, Stanford, 94305. Milorad M Drachkovitch, Archivist
Notes: The Herman Axelbank Film Collection on Russian history. Much footage dating from about 1901-1921. Subjects incl Royal Family, Moscow and St Petersburg scenes, the Revolution and Civil War, espec good coverage of Leon Trotsky's role, Siberia, and the Far East. The first 28 of 266 reels have been received (April 1983).

IL —UNIVERSITY OF ILLINOIS, URBANA/CHAMPAIGN, Slavic and East European Library, Urbana, 61801. Marianna Tax Choldin, Head
Holdings: Vols (420,000) Cat Microforms
Notes: One of the largest Slavic and East European collections. Strong in Russian and Soviet materials-humanities, sciences, and social sciences; languages and literatures; periodicals, newspapers, and microforms. Ca 260,000 volumes in languages of the Soviet Union plus 20,000 Russian and Ukrainian titles on microform. Extensive coverage of Czechoslovakia (35,000 vols); Yugoslavia (31,000 vols); Bulgaria (9200 vols); Poland (34,600 vols); Romania (13,000 vols); and Hungary (18,000 vols) and the languages, literatures, and history of these countries.

IN —INDIANA UNIVERSITY, Lilly Library, Seventh St, Bloomington, 47405. William R Cagle, Librn
Holdings: // Cat Mss
Notes: Correspondence and writings of Max Eastman, 1892-1968. Major portion of correspondence is concerned with Eastman's writings and the responses of various people to his articles, essays, etc. There is very little in the collection relating to *The Masses* or to *The Liberator*, or to his sister Crystal Eastman. 4096 items. Related collections incl Eastman's correspondence with Trotsky, 1922-1933; papers of Anstice Ford Eastman, Max Eastman's physician brother; and the correspondence and writings of Eliena Vassilyenva (Krylenko) Eastman, 1895-1946 (the second Mrs Eastman). Holdings also incl fairly complete file of Eastman's publications in first edition or first printed appearance.

†NY —COLUMBIA UNIVERSITY LIBRARIES, Butler Library, Rare Book and Manuscript Library, 535 W 114 St, New York, 10027.
Notes: Papers of the US Solicitor General, 1930-33, relating to the American Red Cross Mission to Russia, 1917-18.

NY —HUNTER COLLEGE LIBRARY, Bernstein Collection, 695 Park Ave, New York, 10021. William Omeichenko, Cur of Special Collection
Holdings: Vols (8000) Cat Pamphlets
Notes: The Bernstein Collection deals with the development of the Russian revolutionary movement, in particular, the rise and growth of the Russian Social Democratic Party. In addition to this specialized source material, there are works on history, economics, religion and theology, and, finally, various editions of works of the great Russian writers and an impressive array of works devoted to the history of art, culture, and linguistics.

UT —UNIVERSITY OF UTAH, Marriott Library, Special Collections, Salt Lake City, 84112. Gregory C Thompson, Cur
Holdings: Vols 300
Notes: Russian Emigre Publications 1917-1921.

RUSSIA—IMPRINTS

DC —LIBRARY OF CONGRESS, Rare Book & Special Collections Div, Washington, 20540. William Matheson, Chief
Notes: Important and rare Russian imprints of the 17th, 18th, and early 19th centuries in literature, history, bibliography, largely selected from the 80,000-volume Gennadii Yudin Collection. QJLC vol 3, Feb 1946.

RUSSIA—PICTURES, ILLUSTRATIONS

DC —LIBRARY OF CONGRESS, Prints & Photographs Div, Washington, 20540.
Notes: The Sergei Mikhailovich Prokudin-Gorskii Collection of photographs of Imperial Russia, early 20th century.

RUSSIA—RELIGION

NY —NEW YORK PUBLIC LIBRARY, Slavonic Div, Fifth Ave & 42 St, New York, 10018. Edward Kasinec, Chief
Holdings: Cat Microforms
Notes: See: New York Public Library, Slavonic Div, *Dictionary Catalog of the Slavonic Collection*, 2nd ed, rev and enl (Boston: G K Hall, 1974), 44 vols; and New York Public Library, *Dictionary Catalog of the Research Libraries* (New York, 1972-).

RUSSIAN ACADEMY OF SCIENCES

IL —CENTER FOR RESEARCH LIBRARIES, 6050 S Kenwood Ave, Chicago, 60637. Donald B Simpson, Dir; Esther Smith, Collection Development Librn
Holdings: Vols 36,000 Cat Maps
Budget: $5000
Notes: In 1958 the Russian Academy of Science supplied as complete a set of its publications as it could assemble, incl publications of branches. Approx 60 percent complete 1725-1957. Nearly complete for printed publications 1958 to date.

RUSSIAN ALASKA

AK —ALASKA STATE LIBRARY, Alaska Historical Library Collection, Pouch G, Juneau, 99811. Phyllis Demuth, Readers Services Librn
Holdings: Vols (24,000) Cat Mss Maps Pix Slides Phonorecords Audiotapes Videotapes 16mm Films Microforms

CA —UNIVERSITY OF CALIFORNIA, BERKELEY, University Library, Slavic Collections, Berkeley, 94720. Edward Kasinec, Librn
Notes: Russian Pacifica collection, the best on the West coast, incl materials in the folowing areas: Russian exploration and settlement of the North American continent; Russian exploration and settlement and colonization of Siberia; Russian exploration of the Pacific; Russian communities in Manchuria and other parts of the Far East. While many items pertaining to the geographical area are found in the Main Library's stack collection, the bulk of Russian Pacifica holdings is concentrated in the Bancroft Library. The Bancroft collections contain the greater number of items listed in the two major bibliographies of Russian Pacifica: Valentin Lada-Macarski's *Bibliography of Books on Alaska Published before 1868* (Yale Univ Press, 1969), and V I Mezhov's *Sibirskaia bibliografiia* (S Petersburg: Semenov, 1903). During 1983-84, with the assistanceof Title II-C funding, a major project of collection evaluation and development was undertaken in the area of Russian Racifica, resulting in the acquisition on microfilm of several hundred items, incl a part of the holdings of the Museum of Russian Culture in San Francisco relating to Siberia and Russian communities in China.

RUSSIAN AMERICAN NEWSPAPERS
see Newspapers, Russian American

RUSSIAN ART see Art, Russian

RUSSIAN AUTHORS see Authors, Russian

RUSSIAN CHILDREN'S LITERATURE
see Children's Literature, Russian

RUSSIAN CHURCH RECORDS FROM ALASKA

DC —LIBRARY OF CONGRESS, Manuscript Division, Washington, 20540. John C Broderick, Chief
Holdings: Cat Mss Pix
Notes: Mss, papers, records, etc.

RUSSIAN GERMANS

†CO —COLORADO STATE UNIVERSITY, Germans from Russia Project, History Dept, Fort Collins, 80523.

RUSSIAN GERMANS (cont.)

CO —GREELEY PUBLIC LIBRARY, City Complex Bldg, Greeley, 80631. Esther Fromm, Librn
Holdings: Vols 679 Cat Maps Pix Phonorecords Microforms
Notes: American Historical Society of Germans from Russia, the history of people of German-Russian ancestry. Also, incl 105 maps, 4 phonorecords.

NE —AMERICAN HISTORICAL SOCIETY OF GERMANS FROM RUSSIA (AHSGR), 615 Twelfth St, Lincoln, 68502. Mary Lynn Tuck, Librn
Holdings: Vols (1900) Mss Maps Pix Phonorecords Videotapes Audiotapes Microforms VF
Notes: History of German people from Russia and history of people of German-Russian ancestry. Including times in Russia, Germany, US, Canada, Mexico, Argentina, Brazil, Paraguay, Korea, and Japan. This Society has fifty-six chapters in the United States. 1900 volumes, 100 maps; 500 mss; 1200 vertical files; 2000 pictures; 40,000 obituary files, 40,000 family group charts, 50 phonorecords, 20 videotapes, 50 audiotapes, 15 reel-to-reel tapes, 150 periodicals, 250 microforms; 250 family histories-published and unpublished.

†NY —US ARMY RUSSIAN INSTITUTE (USARI), APO, New York, 09053.
Holdings: Vols (24,841)
Notes: A research and language facility of the Army Foreign Affairs Officers Speciality (USSR), located in Garmisch, West Germany. 65 percent of the collection is in Russian; 35 percent in English and other languages. Contains most representative Soviet Newspapers and periodicals, as well as American and other English language publications.

ND —NORTH DAKOTA INSTITUTE FOR REGIONAL STUDIES, North Dakota State University, Fargo, 58105. Michael M Miller, Archivist
Holdings: Vols 300 Cat
Notes: Incl family, community and county histories, maps, cassette tapes, sound recordings, video tapes, photographs, and slides. Emphasis on the Black Sea Germans from Russia; official repository of the Germans from Russia Heritage Society. For the "Germans from Russia Heritage Collection" there has been published, *Researching the Germans from Russia* (1984), compiled by Michael M Miller.

ND —NORTH DAKOTA STATE UNIVERSITY, Library, Fargo, 58105. John E Bye, Archivist
Notes: Books, newspapers, other printed materials and audio-visual records, both in English and German. The collection documents the migration of Germans to Russia, especially the Black Sea region, in the early 19th century and their later immigration to the United States.

ND —UNIVERSITY OF NORTH DAKOTA, Chester Fritz Library, Dept of Special Collections, Grand Forks, 58202. Daniel F Rylance, Special Collections Coordr
Holdings: Vols (5500) Uncat Mss Maps Pix Microforms
Budget: ($2500)
Notes: Also the Orin G Libby Manuscript Collection (900 collections), and the Aandahl Collection of Western History on North Dakota and the Northern Great Plains. Emphasis on agriculture, politics, pioneering, Germans from Russia, etc. Guides to the collections available from the Coordinator of Special Collections.

RUSSIAN GERMANS IN THE U.S.

KS —FORT HAYS STATE UNIVERSITY, Forsyth Library, Ethnic Heritage Studies Collection, 600 Park St, Hays, 67601. Esta Lou Riley, Archivist/Special Collections Librn
Holdings: Vols 335 Microforms Pix Phonorecords Videotapes Maps
Notes: Emphasis on ethnic groups in Kansas, especially Germans from Russia. Does not circulate. Incl 1 linear foot vertical file material.

ND —NORTH DAKOTA INSTITUTE FOR REGIONAL STUDIES, North Dakota State University, Fargo, 58105. Michael M Miller, Archivist
Notes: Incl family, community and county histories, maps, cassette tapes, sound recordings, video tapes, photographs, and slides. Emphasis on the Black Sea Germans from Russia; official repository of the Germans from Russia Heritage Society. For the "Germans from Russia Heritage Collection" there has been published, *Researching the Germans from Russia* (1984), compiled by Michael M Miller.

ND —UNIVERSITY OF NORTH DAKOTA, Chester Fritz Library, Dept of Special Collections, Grand Forks, 58202. Daniel F Rylance, Special Collections Coordr
Holdings: Vols (5500) Uncat Mss Maps Pix Microforms
Budget: ($2500)
Notes: Also the Orin G Libby Manuscript Collection (900 collections), and the Aandahl Collection of Western History on North Dakota and the Northern Great Plains. Emphasis on agriculture, politics, pioneering, Germans from Russia, etc. Guides to the collections available from the Coordinator of Special Collections.

RUSSIAN JEWS see Jews, Russian

RUSSIAN LANGUAGE AND LITERATURE

CA —LOS ANGELES PUBLIC LIBRARY, Foreign Languages Dept, 630 W Fifth St, Los Angeles, 90071. Sylva Manoogian, Principal Librn
Holdings: Vols 11,862 Cat
Budget: ($41,500)

CA —UNIVERSITY OF CALIFORNIA, LOS ANGELES, Library, Slavic Collection, 405 Hilgard Ave, Los Angeles, 90024. Edward Shreeves, Chairman, Bibliographers Group; Leon Ferder, Slavic Bibliographer
Holdings: Vols (250,000) Cat Mss Maps
Notes: The Slavic Collection at UCLA consists of materials from and relating to Russia and the Soviet Union, Poland, Czechoslovakia, Yugoslavia, Bulgaria, the Sorbians in East Germany, and works by Slavic emigres. The collection contains nearly 250,000 vols, and is particularly strong in linguistics, literature, history and social sciences, and reference materials. Slavic materials are collected in hard copy and microform, and incl monographs, serials (incl newspapers), reference works, proceedings of Slavistic congresses and symposia, and also *Festschriften* and dissertations.

CA —CALIFORNIA STATE UNIVERSITY, NORTHRIDGE, Delmar T Oviatt & South Libraries, 1811 Nordhoff St, Northridge, 91330. Donald L Read, Special Collections Dept

CA —STANFORD UNIVERSITY LIBRARIES, Cecil H Green Library, Stanford, 94305. Wojciech Zalewski, Cur, Russian & East European Collection
Holdings: Vols (200,000) Cat Maps Microforms
Budget: ($90,000)
Notes: Strong collection prior to 20th century, but Stanford University Libraries' collecting effort is coordinated with Hoover Institution, Stanford, and holdings are not duplicated. Collection descriptions: Wojciech Zalewski, *Russian Materials in the Main Library of Stanford University, A Collection Survey* (Stanford: Stanford University Libraries, 1974). Wojciech Zalerski, "Stanford University" in P L Horecky, ed, *East Central and Southeast Europe, A Handbook of Library and Archival Resources in North America* (Santa Barbara: Clio Press, 1976).

CT —YALE UNIVERSITY, Box 1603A, Yale Station, New Haven, 06520.

IL —UNIVERSITY OF ILLINOIS, URBANA/CHAMPAIGN, Slavic and East European Library, Urbana, 61801. Marianna Tax Choldin, Head
Holdings: Vols (420,000) Cat Microforms
Notes: One of the largest Slavic and East European collections. Strong in Russian and Soviet materials-humanities, sciences, and social sciences; languages and literatures; periodicals, newspapers, and microforms. Ca 260,000 volumes in languages of the Soviet Union plus 20,000 Russian and Ukrainian titles on microform. Extensive coverage of Czechoslovakia (35,000 vols); Yugoslavia (31,000 vols); Bulgaria (9200 vols); Poland (34,600 vols); Romania (13,000 vols); and Hungary (18,000 vols) and the languages, literatures, and history of these countries.

IN —INDIANA UNIVERSITY, Lilly Library, Seventh St, Bloomington, 47405. William R Cagle, Librn
Holdings: // Cat
Notes: Major 19th and 20th century Russian literature.

MA —HARVARD UNIVERSITY LIBRARY, Widener Library, Slavic Collections, Cambridge, 02138. Hugh M Olmsted, Slavic Dept Head
Holdings: Cat Mss Microforms
Notes: Russian literature shelflist through June, 1976 lists 31,368 titles (earlier version was incl in *Widener Library Shelflist*, volumes 28-31, 1971). The language and literature collections continue to be developed actively, and are strong both in current and in antiquarian materials. See also *Harvard Library Bulletin* XVII (1969), pp 425-433, and *Catalog of Kilgour Collection of Russian Literature, 1750-1920*, published by Library in 1959. Collection incl Church Slavonic and literary mss, correspondence and autographs of literary figures. Strong collection of theatre materials in Theatre Collection. For general survey of Harvard's archival and ms holdings, see Steven A Grant and John H Brown, *The Russian Empire and Soviet Union; A Guide to Manuscripts and Archival Materials in the United States*, 1981, pp 218-219, 224-223.

MI —UNIVERSITY OF MICHIGAN, Graduate Library, Ann Arbor, 48109. Janet White, Reference Librn
Holdings: Cat Microforms

NY —CORNELL UNIVERSITY LIBRARIES, John M Olin Library, Ithaca, 14853. Marilyn B Kann, Slavic Studies Librn
Holdings: Vols 30,000 Cat Microforms

NY —NEW YORK PUBLIC LIBRARY, Donnell Foreign Language Library, 20 W 53 St, New York, 10019. Bosiljka Stevanovic, Supvr Librn
Holdings: Vols 8817 Cat
Notes: Russian collection incl Russian authors of Russian expression. No separate catalog.

NY —NEW YORK PUBLIC LIBRARY, Slavonic Div, Fifth Ave & 42 St, New York, 10018. Edward Kasinec, Chief
Holdings: Vols 122,000 Cat Microforms
Notes: Russian language materials form the main body (ca 70 percent) of the extensive Slavic and Baltic collections of the Slavonic Division. The strength of the collection is in humanities and social sciences, incl military history and government documents. Periodicals and publications of learned societies form an important part of the collection. Holdings of rare books are considerable. See New York Public Library, *Dictionary Catalog of the Slavonic Collection* (Boston: G K Hall, 1974), 44 vols.

†NY —US ARMY RUSSIAN INSTITUTE (USARI), APO, New York, 09053.
Holdings: Vols (24,841)
Notes: A research and language facility of the Army Foreign Affairs Officers Speciality (USSR), located in Garmisch, West Germany. 65 percent of the collection is in Russian; 35 percent in English and other languages. Contains most representative Soviet Newspapers and periodicals, as well as American and other English language publications.

NY —ALEXANDRA TOLSTOY MEMORIAL LIBRARY, Tolstoy Foundation Center, Lake Rd, Valley Cottage, 10989. Tatiana Kalinin, Acting Librn
Holdings: Vols (15,000)
Notes: The Foundation assists political refugees in resettlement throughout the world.

RUSSIAN LANGUAGE AND LITERATURE (cont.)

NC —CUMBERLAND COUNTY PUBLIC LIBRARY, North Carolina Foreign Language Center, 328 Gillespie St, Fayetteville, 28301. Patrick M Valentine, Coordinator
Holdings: Vols 750 Cat
Budget: $500
Notes: The largest book collections are, in descending order of size, German Spanish, French, Japanese, Korean and Vietnamese, with fair sized collections in Italian, Russian, Chinese, Arabic, Greek, Hungarian, Polish, Hebrew, Thai, and Hindi. The Center has several shelves each of books in Bengali, Dutch, Marathi, Portuguese, Urdu, and Yiddish. Smaller collections of one to three shelves each incl Catalan, Croatian, Czech, Danish, Finnish, Gujarati, Icelandic, Kannada, Latin, Lithuanian, Malayalam, Norwegian, Panjabi, Persian (Farsi), Romanian, Slovak, Swedish, Tagalog, Tamil, Telegu, and Ukrianian. The Center has grammars, dictionaries and occasionally other readings in languages from Afrikaans and Albanian to Welsh, Yoruba and Zulu.

OH —CLEVELAND PUBLIC LIBRARY, Foreign Literature Dept, 325 Superior Ave, Cleveland, 44114. Natalia Bezugloff, Head
Holdings: Vols 15,590 Cat
Notes: A popular circulating collection containing classics and the standard works with emphasis on belles lettres, history and biography. A variety of other subjects such as learning languages, how to do books, art, children's books, spoken phonodiscs and cassettes, periodicals, etc. Incl 1020 ephemera.
See also entry under Foreign Language Collections

OH —OHIO STATE UNIVERSITY, William Oxley Thompson Memorial Library, 1858 Neil Ave, Columbus, 43210. A Robert Thorson, Head, Circulation Dept
Holdings: Cat Mss Microforms
Notes: This collection presently contains films of 2000 mss from the Hilandar Monastery, Mt Athos. Expansion will add Byzantine, Bulgarian, Russian and Valachian mss on film.

PA —PENNSYLVANIA STATE UNIVERSITY, Fred Lewis Pattee Library, Slavic Library Program, University Park, 16802. Wasyl O Luciw, Head
Holdings: Vols (75,000) Cat Mss Pix
Budget: ($18,000)
Notes: The collection covers a wide range of languages Slavic and East European but its principal strengths are in Russian and Ukrainian. A special collection of 1576 volumes includes pre-revolutionary Russian, fine press publications, in our rare collection and children's literature. Besides book volumes, we have quite a large collection of manuscripts, documents, photographs and many periodicals, also including out of print books on microforms.

WA —UNIVERSITY OF WASHINGTON LIBRARIES, Suzzallo Library, Slavic & East European Section, FM-25, Seattle, 98195. Barbara A Galik, Head
Holdings: Vols (250,000) Cat Mss Maps Pix Phonorecords Audiotapes Microforms
Budget: ($8500)
Notes: Strong research collections for Russia--USSR, including Central Asia. Holdings are excellent in language and literature, including Old Russian literature. There are extensive holdings of the publications of academies, major universities, and principal scholarly institutions, especially of long serial runs.

WI —BELOIT COLLEGE LIBRARIES, Beloit, 53511. Dennis W Dickinson, Dir
Holdings: Cat
Notes: This small collection incl most of the Stalin Prize novels, many works published "behind the Iron Curtain," and some titles in English translation. Also incl complete sets of distinguished Russian authors in Russian editions. Books purchased in history, geography, economics, etc to supplement the Winkelman Collection of Russian Literature.

MB —UNIVERSITY OF MANITOBA, Elizabeth Dafoe Library, Slavic Collection, Winnipeg, R3T 2N2, Can. John S Muchin, Librn
Holdings: Vols (33,000) Cat Mss Microforms
Budget: ($5000)
Notes: Material in all Slavic languages, mostly in Russian (approx 15,000 vols), Ukrainian (approx 15,000 vols), Polish, Old Church Slavic; mainly literature, language, history, art, geography, economics, statistics, political science; newspapers and periodicals; over 20,000 vols of microforms. Cited in Slavic Collection of the University of Manitoba Libraries, John S Muchin (Winnipeg: University of Manitoba Libraries and UVAN, 1970).

PQ —CONCORDIA UNIVERSITY LIBRARIES, 1435 Drummond St, Montreal, H3G 1M8, Can. P E Filion, University Librn
Notes: A collection of 5000 Russian works covering a wide range of time and subjects. Incl are many historical works published since 1945, vols on modern Soviet economics, collected works of classic Russian literary figures, a number of important bibliographies, technical dictionaries and art books.

RUSSIAN LAW see Law, Soviet

RUSSIAN MEDICINE see Medicine, Russian

RUSSIAN MUSIC see Music, Russian

RUSSIAN NEWSPAPERS see Newspapers, Russian

RUSSIAN NOBILITY

†CA —UNIVERSITY OF CALIFORNIA, BERKELEY, LIBRARIES, Berkeley, 94720.
Notes: Comprehensive collection of indexes to more than 40 provincial Russian periodicals dealing with the Russians Orthodox Church during the Imperial period. More than 200 photocopies of letters, telegrams, sketches, and photographs from the collection of the Grand Duchess Mariia Alexandrovna, daughter of Emperor Alexander II of Russia. Dating from last third of the 19th century. Incl correspondence from her parents, court, and other friends. Copies made available by the Executive Committee of the Museum of Russian Culture in San Francisco.

CA —CLAREMONT COLLEGES, Honnold Library, Ninth & Dartmouth, Claremont, 91711. Tania Rizzo, Special Collections Dept Head
Holdings: Vols 1125 Uncat Mss Pix Microforms
Notes: The combined James Mavor, Raymond Elliott, and Gregory P Tschebotarioff collections incl clippings and periodicals from the Revolutionary period, books and pictorial materials about the royal family, separatist movements, and the emigre experience. Restricted use.

CA —HOOVER INSTITUTION ON WAR, REVOLUTION & PEACE, Stanford University, Stanford, 94305. Milorad M Drachkovitch, Archivist
Holdings: Mss
Notes: Letters (handwritten in Russian), 1914-18, of Grand Duke Georgii Mikhailovich, son of Grand Duke Mikhail Nikolaevich (son of Tsar Nicholas I), nephew of Tsar Alexander II, and special representative of Tsar Nicholas II at various fronts during World War I, to his daughter Princess Ksenila dealing with his official functions; events before, during and after the Revolution; and family matters. 2 ms boxes.

RUSSIAN ORTHODOX EASTERN CHURCH see Orthodox Eastern Church, Russian

RUSSIAN PERIODICALS see Periodicals, Russian

RUSSIAN PHILOSOPHY see Philosophy, Russian

RUSSIAN REFUGEES see Refugees, Russian

RUSSIAN SATIRE see Satire, Russian

RUSSIAN SCIENCE see Science, Russian

RUSSIAN SOCIAL DEMOCRATIC PARTY

MA —HARVARD UNIVERSITY LIBRARY, Houghton Library, Cambridge, 02138.

Rodney G Dennis, Cur of Manuscripts
Holdings: Mss
Notes: Archives dealing with the Zemstvo and Russian Social Democratic Workers' party.

NY —HUNTER COLLEGE LIBRARY, Bernstein Collection, 695 Park Ave, New York, 10021. William Omeichenko, Cur of Special Collection
Holdings: Vols (8000) Cat Pamphlets
Notes: The Bernstein Collection deals with the development of the Russian revolutionary movement, in particular, the rise and growth of the Russian Social Democratic Party. In addition to this specialized source material, there are works on history, economics, religion and theology, and, finally, various editions of works of the great Russian writers and an impressive array of works devoted to the history of art, culture, and linguistics.

RUSSIAN SOCIAL DEMOCRATIC WORKERS' PARTY see Russian Social Democratic Party

RUSSIANS IN CANADA

PA —BALCH INSTITUTE FOR ETHNIC STUDIES, Library, 18 S Seventh St, Philadelphia, 19106. R Joseph Anderson, Library Dir

RUSSIANS IN THE U.S.

CA —MUSEUM OF RUSSIAN CULTURE, 2450 Sutter St, San Francisco, 94115. Nicholas Slobodchikoff, Dir
Holdings: Vols (15,000) Pix
Notes: Incl 10,000 periodicals. Much on Imperial Russia and Russian immigration to the US. Also incl 12,000 Russian newspapers.

MN —UNIVERSITY OF MINNESOTA, Immigration History Research Center, 826 Berry St, Saint Paul, 55114. Susan Griegs, Cur
Holdings: Vols (35,000) Mss Maps Pix Phonorecords Audiotapes 16mm Films Microforms
See also entry under US - Emigration and Immigration

NY —NEW YORK PUBLIC LIBRARY, Slavonic Div, Fifth Ave & 42 St, New York, 10018. Edward Kasinec, Chief
Holdings: Cat Microforms
Notes: See: New York Public Library, Slavonic Div, Dictionary Catalog of the Slavonic Collection, 2nd ed, rev and enl (Boston: G K Hall, 1974), 44 vols; and New York Public Library, Dictionary Catalog of the Research Libraries (New York, 1972-).

NY —ARCHIVES OF THE ORTHODOX CHURCH IN AMERICA, PO Box 675, Syosset, 11791. Dennis Rhodes, Archivist
Notes: Incl material on Orthodox Churches in the Western Hemisphere espec in North America.

NY —ALEXANDRA TOLSTOY MEMORIAL LIBRARY, Tolstoy Foundation Center, Lake Rd, Valley Cottage, 10989. Tatiana Kalinin, Acting Librn
Holdings: Vols (15,000)
Notes: The Foundation assists political refugees in resettlement throughout the world.

NY —SAINT VLADIMIRS' ORTHODOX THEOLOGICAL SEMINARY, 575 Scarsdale Rd, Yonkers, 10707. Paul D Garrett, Librn
Holdings: Vols (36,000) Pix
Notes: Incl 250 periodicals. A major source of materials on Orthodox Church theology. Much on works of art.

PA —BALCH INSTITUTE FOR ETHNIC STUDIES, Library, 18 S Seventh St, Philadelphia, 19106. R Joseph Anderson, Library Dir
Holdings: Vols 280 Cat Mss Pix Microforms

RUSSO-TURKISH WAR, 1853-1856 see Crimean War, 1853-1856

RUST see Corrosion and Anticorrosives

RUSTLESS COATINGS see Corrosion and Anticorrosives

RUTH, GEORGE HERMAN (BABE)

KS —SAINT MARY COLLEGE, Library, Leavenworth, 66048. Therese Deplazes,

RUTH, GEORGE HERMAN (BABE)
(cont.)

Special Collections Librn
Notes: Holographs of American
personalities, mostly of Colonial,
Revolutionary, Confederacy periods, and
19th Century. Incl ms letters, deeds,
petitions, wills, slave papers. Holographs of
Col Philip Marsteller (one of George
Washington's pall bearers), family papers of
Richard, Mary and Edward Cutts; love
letters to Mary "Polly" Carter, Frank Ellery
(grandson of William Ellery, signer of the
Declaration of Independence), letters of
Connie Mack and Babe Ruth, of some
American authors.

RUTHENBERG, CHARLES E.

OH —OHIO HISTORICAL SOCIETY,
Archives Library Division, 1982 Velma Ave,
Columbus, 43211. Dennis East, Division
Chief
Notes: His papers.

RUTHENIAN LANGUAGE AND
LITERATURE see Ukrainian Language
and Literature

RUTLEDGE FAMILY

SC —COLLEGE OF CHARLESTON
LIBRARY, Special Collections Dept,
Charleston, 29401.
Notes: Papers, 1883-1889, incl the Rutledge
family ledger recording annuity payments
made to servants during the years 1883-
1889.

RUTTENBERG, HAROLD J.

PA —PENNSYLVANIA STATE
UNIVERSITY, Fred Lewis Pattee Library,
Labor History Collection, University Park,
16802. Peter Gottlieb, Archivist
Holdings: Cat Mss Pix
Notes: Personal papers.

RUTTERS OF THE SEA

CT —YALE UNIVERSITY, Box 1603A, Yale
Station, New Haven, 06520.
Holdings: Cat Maps
Notes: "The best collection of printed rutters
in America is that of Henry C Taylor at Yale
University Library," S E Morison, *The
European Discovery of America*, 1971, p
150.

RUZICKA, RUDOLPH

ME —BOWDOIN COLLEGE, Library,
Brunswick, 04011. Dianne M Gutscher, Cur
of Special Collections
Holdings: Vols
Notes: The Frederic Wilson Main Collection
contains several hundred books, pamphlets,
and clippings relating to the art of printing
and bookmaking. Most major contemporary
presses are represented, and it incl examples
of the typographic work of Bruce Rogers,
Frederic W Goudy, Daniel Berkeley Updike,
and Rudolph Ruzicka, to mention only a
few.

RYAN, CORNELIUS, 1920-1974

OH —OHIO UNIVERSITY, Vernon R Alden
Library, Department of Archives and Special
Collections, Athens, 45701. Gary A Hunt,
Head
Holdings: Vols 674 Cat Mss Maps Pix
Audiotapes
Notes: The Cornelius Ryan Memorial
Collection of World War II Papers,
containing the research files, correspondence
and working library assembled by Ryan in
the course of writing his three major books
on World War II. The research papers incl
some 3,072 files for individual participants in
the Normandy invasion, the battle for Berlin,
and the Market-Garden operation. Also incl
are 166 audio recordings of interviews
conducted by Ryan, many with leading

figures associated with the war, such as
Eisenhower, Chuikov, Gavin, Montgomery,
and Prince Bernhard of the Netherlands.

RYAN, JOHN

NY —NATIONAL SOARING MUSEUM,
Library, Harris Hill, RD #3, Elmira, 14903.

RYCK, MAURICE MARTIN DE

WI —UNIVERSITY OF WISCONSIN,
MADISON, Memorial Library, 728 State St,
Madison, 53706. David Henige, Librn
Holdings: // Cat Mss Maps Microforms
Notes: These 5 microfilm reels of archival
materials relate to the career of Maurice
Martin de Ryck, who served as Governor of
Equateur Province, Belgian Congo, as well as
other miscellaneous data relating to
Equateur Province. In addition to the
microforms, the originals of these
microforms are housed in the Rare Book
Department of the Memorial Library.

RYE SMUT see Ergot

RYGA, GEORGE, 1932-

AB —UNIVERSITY OF CALGARY,
Libraries, Special Collections Div, 2500
University Dr, Calgary, T2N 1N4, Can.
Holdings: Cat Mss
Notes: The papers include manuscripts for
George Ryga's poetry, short stories, novels,
feature film screenplays, radio and television
scripts, stage plays, musicals, essays, and
public addresses. The correspondence covers
the years 1960-1975, and includes a set of
files of Ryga's literary agent, Renee Paris,
for the years 1963-1976.

RYUKYU ISLANDS

HI —UNIVERSITY OF HAWAII, Library,
2550 The Mall, Honolulu, 96822. Joyce
Wright, Head, Asia Collection; Masato
Matsu, Head, East Asia Vernacular
Collection
Holdings: Vols 64,481 Cat Microforms
Notes: The Asia Collection includes
materials from and relating to Japan in all
languages. In addition to the cataloged
Japanese language volumes (above), there
are an estimated 15,000 not yet processed.
No figures are available for western language
volumes about Japan, which are
supplemented by retrospective materials in
the main library collection. Scope: social
sciences and humanities. Subject strengths:
Japanese history, especially Tokugawa
period, Buddhism, Ryukyus and Satsuma
(Sakamaki Collection), Hokkaido. *Catalog of
the Glenn Shaw Collection at the East West
Center Library,* by H Arai & M Gibu,
Honolulu, 1967 (East West Center Library
Occasional Paper No 8); *Research Resources
on Hokkaido, Sakhalen and the Kuriles at
the East-West Center Library,* by M Matsui
and K Shimanaka, Honolulu, 1967 (East-
West Center Library Occasional Paper No
9);*Ryukyuan Research Resources at the
University of Hawaii,* by Shunzo Sakamaki,
Honolulu, 1965 (Ryukyuan Research Center.
Research Series No 1).
NY —SYRACUSE UNIVERSITY
LIBRARIES, Ernest S Bird Library, George
Arents Research Library for Special
Collections, Syracuse, 13210. Carolyn A
Davis, Manuscripts Librn; Amy S Doherty,
University Archivist; Mark F Weimer, Rare
Book Librn
Holdings: Vols 2000 Cat Pix Microforms
Notes: Collection of material relating to
Okinawa and the Southern Ryukyus, largely
in Japanese. Library has published *Catalog of
the Ryukyu Research Collection*, compiled
by Douglas G Haring, 1969.

S

SABBATARIANS

WI —SEVENTH DAY BAPTIST
HISTORICAL SOCIETY, Library, 3120
Kennedy Rd, PO Box 1678, Janesville,
53547. D Scott Smith, Historian
Notes: US Seventh Day Baptists Collection,
incl records, letters. Established at Newport,
Rhode Island, in 1671, this denomination is
a part of the Free-Church evangelical
movement in America. The General
Conference was organized in 1801. The
national and international headquarters of
the Seventh Day Baptist denomination is
located at Janesville, Wisconsin. Also have
records, publications, etc of the
denomination's mission in Shanghai, 1846-
1950; further, materials (6 boxes) on the
Church's work in Nyasaland (Malawi),
1895-1914, and then at a later period.

SABBATHARIANS see Sabbatarians

SABIR

MA —HARVARD UNIVERSITY LIBRARY,
Cambridge, 02138.
Holdings: Cat

SABOTAGE

CA —HARVEY G WOLFE LIBRARY, PO
Box 3514, Grand Central Sta, Glendale,
91201. Douglas L Evans, Librn
Holdings: Vols (6580) Mss Maps Pix
Budget: ($4500)
Notes: Main emphasis on espionage, military
intelligence, and sabotage.
MD —INTERNATIONAL ASSOCIATION
OF CHIEFS OF POLICE, 13 Firstfield Rd,
PO Box 6010, Gaithersburg, 20760.
Holdings: Vols (6000) Cat Mss
Notes: Collection heavy in criminal
investigation, crime prevention, police
administration and management. Collecting
in public sector labor relations, family
violence, terrorism.

SAC INDIANS see Sauk Indians

SACAJAWEA

MO —MISSOURI HISTORICAL SOCIETY,
Library, Jefferson Memorial Bldg, Saint
Louis, 63112. Stephanie Klein, Librn-
Archivist; Peter Michel, Cur of Manuscripts
Notes: A collection of material on 119
women who lived or worked in St Louis and
Missouri as educators, artists, and
homemakers, or played significant roles in
US politics and social reform. Incl
Sacajawea, Susan B Anthony, Fannie Hurst,
Carry Nation, Patience Worth, etc.

SACCO, NICOLA, 1891-1927

IN —INDIANA STATE UNIVERSITY,
Cunningham Memorial Library, Dept of
Rare Books & Special Collections, Terre
Haute, 47809. Lawrence J McCrank, Head
Notes: The Debs Collection consists of
aprox 7000 pieces of correspondence
between Theodore Debs (brother of E V)
and other persons, such as Sinclair Lewis,
Upton Sinclair, Ethel Barrymore, Emma
Goldman, Robert G Ingersoll, Carl
Sandburg, Norman Thomas, Sacco and
Vanzetti and many others. Many of the
letters are from E V Debs to his brother; a
good portion of these are from the federal
penitentiary at Atlanta. Entire
correspondence file has been microfilmed.
750 pamphlets cover all aspects of the labor
movement, socialism and radical thought
from the 19th century to appprox 1950. A
collection ca 200 related books is also
housed in the collection. See: J Robert
Constantine and Gail Malmgreen, eds, The
Papers of Eugene V Debs, 1834-1945. A
Guide to the Microfilm Edition. NY:
Microfilming Corp of America, 1983
(University Microfilms is the new
distributer).

MA —HARVARD UNIVERSITY LIBRARY,
Law School Library, Langdell Hall,
Cambridge, 02138. Erika S Chadbourn, Cur
of Mss
Notes: Legal documents, pictorial material,
microfilms. Incl holograph letters of Sacco
and Vanzetti, 1920-1928. Typed
chronological list in repository.
MA —BRANDEIS UNIVERSITY, Goldfarb
Library, 415 South St, Waltham, 02154.
Bessie Hahn, Dir
Notes: Sacco and Vanzetti Case Collection.
Consists of 23 linear ft of material collected
by both Tom O'Connor and Francis Russell
relating to this celebrated American trial.
This collection is unprocessed.

SACCO AND VANZETTI CASE, 1920-1928

MA —HARVARD UNIVERSITY LIBRARY,
Law School Library, Langdell Hall,
Cambridge, 02138. Erika S Chadbourn, Cur
of Mss
Holdings: Cat Mss Microforms
Notes: Legal documents, pictorial material,
microfilms. Incl holograph letters of Sacco
and Vanzetti, 1920-1928. Typed
chronological list in repository.
MA —BRANDEIS UNIVERSITY, Goldfarb
Library, 415 South St, Waltham, 02154.
Bessie Hahn, Dir
Notes: Sacco and Vanzetti Case Collection.
Incl 23 linear feet of material collected by
both Tom O'Connor and Francis Russell
relating to this celebrated American trial.
This collection is unprocessed, spring 1984.

SACHS, NELLY

PA —BIBLIOGRAPHICAL CENTER OF
GERMAN LITERATURE, University of
Pittsburgh, Dept of Germanic Languages &
Literatures, 102 Loeffler Bldg, Pittsburgh,
15260. Klaus W Jonas, Dir
Holdings: Cat Mss Pix Microforms
Notes: Center for the development of
collections and bibliographical control of the
record of publications, mss, correspondence,
etc, by or relating to modern German
authors. Special sections have been
developed for Mann, Rilke, Hauptmann,
Hesse, Broch, Sachs and others. Described
by Professor Klaus W Jonas's "The German
Literature Center in Pittsburgh,"
Stechert-Hafner Book News, vol 24, no 8,
April 1970; "Documentation in Modern
German Literature: A Progress Report,"
Jahrbuch fuer Internationale Germanistik,
vol 4, no 2, 1972, and in German and
Austrian Contributions to World Literature
(1890-1970). Department of Germanic
Languages and Literatures, University of
Pittsburgh, 1983. 96 pp.

SACK, JOHN

MA —BOSTON UNIVERSITY, Mugar
Memorial Library, Special Collections Dept,
771 Commonwealth Ave, Boston, 02215.
Howard B Gotlieb, Dir
Holdings: Mss Pix
Notes: Mss, correspondence, etc collected in
depth; incl publications by or about.

SACKVILLE-WEST, LADY VICTORIA, 1892-1962

IL —ILLINOIS STATE UNIVERSITY, Milner
Library, Dept of Special Collections,
Normal, 61761. Robert Sokan, Librn
Notes: First editions, limited editions,
ephemera, etc.
IN —INDIANA UNIVERSITY, Lilly Library,
Seventh St, Bloomington, 47405. William R
Cagle, Librn
Notes: Letters of Sir Harold Nicolson,
(1886-1968), and his wife, Lady Victoria
Sackville-West (1892-1962). About 10,500
letters exchanged between 1910 and 1962.
ON —VICTORIA UNIVERSITY, Library, 71
Queen's Park Crescent, Toronto, M5S 1K7,
Can. Robert C Brandeis, Chief Librn
Holdings: Vols Cat
Notes: A collection of first editions and

others of Virginia Woolf and Bloomsbury
writers: Clive Bell, Roger Fry, E M Forster,
V Sackville-West, K Mansfield, etc. Contains
a significant collection of Hogarth Press
books, and many of those handprinted by
the Woolfs.

SACRAMENTO, CALIFORNIA—HISTORY

CA —UNIVERSITY OF CALIFORNIA,
DAVIS, Shields Library, Dept of Special
Collections, Davis, 95616. Donald Kunitz,
Head; C Danial Elliott, Asst Head
Holdings: Uncat Mss Pix
Notes: Correspondence, family papers,
photographs, and memorabilia of the Lindley
Family, early Sacramento, California,
merchants, document life in Sacramento
during the second half of the 19th century.
400 items.
CA —SACRAMENTO PUBLIC LIBRARY,
828 I St, Sacramento, 95814. Dorothy
Harvey, Librn, Special Collections
Holdings: Vols 270 Cat
Notes: Incl reports, studies, histories,
yearbooks, guidebooks. Sacramento Bee and
Sacramento Union are indexed 1905 to 1937
and 1974 to date; clipping file contains
selected clippings and ephemera; picture file
contains black and white photos of
Sacramento buildings, streets, and events. A
depository for city and county documents
was established in 1975; the collection now
contains 4000 documents.

SACRED ART see Christian Art and Symbolism

SACRED CHORUSES see Choruses, Sacred

SACRED MUSIC see Church Music

SACRED NUMBERS see Symbolism of Numbers

SACRED SONGS

CA —SAN DIEGO PUBLIC LIBRARY, Art,
Music & Recreation Sect, 820 E St, San
Diego, 92101. Barbara A Tuhill, Supvr
Holdings: Vols 132 Cat
Notes: A collection of gift sheet music has
been organized into bound volumes by date
of copyright covering popular songs from the
1800s through the 1950s. Each volume is
arranged with a table of contents by title,
and is also indexed in a special Song Title
Index. Special volumes also cover the hits of
World War I, ballads, religious songs and
other subjects. Reference use only.
NJ —NEWARK PUBLIC LIBRARY, Art &
Music Dept, 5 Washington St, Newark,
07101. William J Dane, Supv
Holdings: Vols Uncat
Notes: 2500 song sheets of popular music,
with emphasis on late 19th and 20th century
titles. General collection of art songs, sacred
songs, folk songs, Tune Dex and standard
song collections incl all of Sears. Special
song indexes supplement printed indexes.
OH —CLEVELAND PUBLIC LIBRARY, Fine
Arts and Special Collections Department,
325 Superior Ave, Cleveland, 44114. Alice
N Loranth, Head
Holdings: Vols 1500 Cat
Notes: Mostly in English, representing
various denominations. Department
maintains its own index by first line and/or
tune name.
PA —LUTHERAN THEOLOGICAL
SEMINARY, Krauth Memorial Library,
7301 Germantown Ave, Philadelphia, 19119.
Rev David J Wartluft, Dir Libr
Holdings: Vols (2800) Cat
Notes: Lutheran, of all countries. American
publications of many denominations also
represented. Incl the Luther D Reed
collection of Lutheran hymnals.
RI —BROWN UNIVERSITY, John Hay
Library, Harris Collection, Prospect St,
Providence, 02912. Rosemary L Cullen, Cur
Holdings: Vols (200,000) Cat Mss Pix
Phonorecords Microforms
Budget: ($15,000)
Notes: The Harris Collection of American

SACRED SONGS (cont.)

Poetry and Plays is principally composed of American and Canadian poetry and plays from the 17th century to the present. Extensive holdings in hymnals of the 17th to the 20th centuries, incl a number of Pennsylvania German hymnals, and sheet music from the 18th - 20th centuries. Collection incl the MacDougall Collection of Psalters and Hymnals. See *Dictionary Catalog of The Harris Collection of American Poetry and Plays* (Boston: G K Hall, 1972), 13 vols; Supplement (1977), 3 vols. Separate catalog.

TX —SOUTHWESTERN BAPTIST THEOLOGICAL SEMINARY, Music Library, Fort Worth, 76122. Phillip W Sims, Librn
Holdings: Vols (19,000) Cat
Budget: ($30,000)
Notes: Incl in the Treasure Section are approx 250 tune books, plus many very old hymnals and other antiquarian items. Incl 97,000 pieces of sheet music, 24,000 scores, 7500 phonograph records and 3500 audiocassettes. The entire collection is cataloged except the periodicals and about one fourth of the sheet music.

SADDLEMYER, ANN

BC —UNIVERSITY OF VICTORIA, McPherson Library, Victoria, V8W 3H5, Can.
Notes: Incl transcripts; typescripts, galleys (missing 20 pages), and page proofs of *Letters to Molly; John Millington Synge to Maire O'Neill.* Corrected page proofs of *Lady Gregory, Collected Plays,* 1970, Coole edition. Anglo-Irish Miscellany of photocopied articles.

SADDLERY

†WA —WASHINGTON STATE UNIVERSITY, Library, Manuscripts, Archives & Special Collections, Pullman, 99164. John F Guido, Head
Holdings: Cat Mss Maps Pix
Notes: The Carl Parcher Russell papers, a vast resource (24,916 items; 45 linear feet) on American Indian and Western pioneer activities and artifacts. Much on the fur trade; pioneer life; mountain men and trapping; wildlife; primitive life in detail. Also the National Park Service, parks, monuments, etc. Described in *Carl Parcher Russell: An Indexed Register of His Scholarly and Professional Papers, 1920-1967, in the Washington State University Library* (Pullman, 1970), 149 pp.

SADDLES AND SADDLEMAKING see Saddlery

SADISM

CA —UNIVERSITY OF CALIFORNIA, LOS ANGELES, Research Library, Dept of Special Collections, 405 Hilgard Ave, Los Angeles, 90024. Edward Shreeves, Chairman, Bibliographers Group; David S Zeidberg, Head
Notes: 27 linear feet of books, photographs, clippings, and notebooks relating to sado-masochism.

IN —INDIANA UNIVERSITY, Institute for Sex Research Library, 416 Morrison Hall, Bloomington, 47401. Douglas Freeman, Collections and Services Librn; Joan Brewer, Information Services Librn
Holdings: Vols (62,000) Cat Mss Pix Microforms
See also entry under Sex.

SADLEIR, MICHAEL, 1888-1957

CA —UNIVERSITY OF CALIFORNIA, LOS ANGELES, Research Library, Dept of Special Collections, 405 Hilgard Ave, Los Angeles, 90024. Edward Shreeves, Chairman, Bibliographers Group; David S Zeidberg, Head
Holdings: Vols 150
Notes: 150 books; Also Michael Sadleir

Collection of 19th century fiction (10,000 books); 25 letters.

SADO-MASOCHISM see Masochism; Sadism

SAFETY, INDUSTRIAL see Industrial Safety

SAFETY, THEATRE

MA —MASSACHUSETTS INSTITUTE OF TECHNOLOGY, Institute Archives, Special Collections, Cambridge, 02139.
Notes: Papers of John Ripley Freeman, a hydraulic engineer, President of Associated Factory Mutual Fire Insurance Companies, and a consulting engineer. Collection primarily documents his activities as a consultant on hydraulics projects in the United States, Canada, China, Columbia, Mexico and Panama. Also, his work on the hydraulics of fire prevention, safety precautions for theaters, and seismology; his promotion of the National Hydraulics Laboratory and of European engineering practices; his involvement with the Engineering Foundation, the National Bureau of Standards, and the National Research Council; and his investments in mining, manufacturing, and land speculation. Unpublished finding aid available in Archives.

SAFETY, TRAFFIC see Traffic Safety

SAFETY APPLIANCES

MI —UNIVERSITY OF MICHIGAN, Transportation Research Institute, Library, 2901 Baxter Rd, Ann Arbor, 48109. Ann C Grimm, Librn
Holdings: Vols (57,000) Cat Mss Maps Pix Slides Microforms
Budget: ($25,000)
Notes: All aspects of highway safety. All items are cataloged and indexed using a thesaurus developed in-house. Incl engineering medical, biomechanical, psychological, legal, economic and social aspects of highway, vehicle and traffic safety.

MO —CENTRAL MISSOURI STATE UNIVERSITY, Ward Edwards Library, Warrensburg, 64093. Lonnie Lawson, Science and Technology Librn
Holdings: Vols (3200) Cat Slides Microforms
Budget: ($3000)
Notes: Safety materials (plus 5200 vertical file pieces) cover traffic safety, industrial hygiene, school safety, farm and home safety.

PA —FREE LIBRARY OF PHILADELPHIA, Automobile Reference Collection, Logan Sq, Philadelphia, 19103. Louis G Helverson, Jr, Librn in Charge
Holdings: Vols (14,000) Cat Pix Slides
Notes: Collection is concerned with all aspects of automotive industry and its history. Includes shop manuals, instruction books, parts books, and periodicals dealing with all types of bicycles, tricycles and motor vehicles. Industry statistics, corporate annual reports, environmental problems, safety. Incl 18,000 pictures, 1700 slides, 648 microfilm reels, 23,000 sales catalogs, 5000 pieces of ephemera.

SAFETY BELTS, AUTOMOBILE see Automobile Seat Belts

SAFETY EDUCATION

IL —NATIONAL SAFETY COUNCIL, Library, 444 N Michigan Ave, Chicago, 60611. Ruth K Hammersmith, Mgr, Library
Holdings: Cat Microforms
Budget: ($22,000)
Notes: NSC Library has a comprehensive collection of accident prevention, occupational and industrial safety and health material. The Safety Research Information Section (SRIS) begun in 1968 has a collection of over 12,000 indexed and cataloged research documents. The Library also has a collection of over 5000 safety-

related books, 12,000 Research Reports, 60,000 general information items, a collection of historically valuable safety-related information. The Library data is part of an inhouse computer system.

IL —UNIVERSITY OF ILLINOIS, URBANA/CHAMPAIGN, Library, Applied Life Studies Library, 1408 W Gregory Dr, Urbana, 61801.
Holdings: Vols (38,000) Cat Pix Microforms
See also entry under Physical Education and Training.

MI —UNIVERSITY OF MICHIGAN, Transportation Research Information Institute, Public Information Materials Center, 2901 Baxter Rd, Ann Arbor, 48109. Ann Grimm, Librn
Holdings: Vols (5000) Cat Print Materials Slides Phonorecords Audiotapes 16mm Films
Budget: ($200)
Notes: Collection of materials (mostly available free from originators) produced for public information campaigns on alcohol and highway safety, and adult and child restraint systems. Book catalogs to collection available (mailing list): *Alcohol/Safety Public Information Materials Catalog,* no 7. A C Grimm (UMTRI, June 1983); and *Restraint System Public Information Materials Catalog,* no 5, A C Grimm (UMTRI, June 1983).

MO —CENTRAL MISSOURI STATE UNIVERSITY, Ward Edwards Library, Warrensburg, 64093. Lonnie Lawson, Science and Technology Librn
Holdings: Vols (3200) Cat Slides Microforms
Budget: ($3000)
Notes: Safety materials (plus 5200 vertical file pieces) cover traffic safety, industrial hygiene, school safety, farm and home safety.

NC —WILSON COUNTY TECHNICAL INSTITUTE, Library, 902 Herring Ave, PO Box 4305, Wilson, 27893. Shirley Gregory, Librn
Holdings: Vols (150) Cat Slides Phonorecords Audiotapes 16mm Films Filmstrips
Notes: Emphasis on operator's manuals and 80 audiovisual programs.

PA —FREE LIBRARY OF PHILADELPHIA, Automobile Reference Collection, Logan Sq, Philadelphia, 19103. Louis G Helverson, Jr, Librn in Charge
Holdings: Vols (14,000) Cat Pix Slides
Notes: Collection is concerned with all aspects of automotive industry and its history. Includes shop manuals, instruction books, parts books, and periodicals dealing with all types of bicycles, tricycles and motor vehicles. Industry statistics, corporate annual reports, environmental problems, safety. Incl 18,000 pictures, 1700 slides, 648 microfilm reels, 23,000 sales catalogs, 5000 pieces of ephemera.

SAFETY EDUCATION, INDUSTRIAL

DC —US DEPT OF LABOR, Library, 200 Constitution Ave NW, Washington, 20210. Sabina Jacobson, Dir
Holdings: (550,000) Cat

MO —CENTRAL MISSOURI STATE UNIVERSITY, Ward Edwards Library, Warrensburg, 64093. Lonnie Lawson, Science and Technology Librn
Holdings: Vols (3200) Cat Slides Microforms
Budget: ($3000)
Notes: Safety materials (plus 5200 vertical file pieces) cover traffic safety, industrial hygiene, school safety, farm and home safety.

ON —CANADA DEPT OF LABOUR, Library, Ottawa, K1A 0J2, Can. Monique Marchand, Chief Librn
Holdings: Vols (100,000) Cat Microforms

PQ —NORANDA RESEARCH CENTRE, Library, 240 Hymus Blvd, Pointe-Claire, H9R 1G5, Can. Shirley Courtis, Librn
Holdings: Vols (7000)

SAFETY MEASURES see Industrial Safety

SAGAS

MA —HARVARD UNIVERSITY LIBRARY, Widener Library, Cambridge, 02138.
Holdings: Cat Mss
Notes: Strong points are the Icelandic

SAGAS (cont.)

collection (with strong holdings of sagas and eddas). See also *Distributable Union Catalog* (Harvard).

NY —CORNELL UNIVERSITY LIBRARIES, John M Olin Library, Fiske Icelandic Collection, Ithaca, 14853. Louis A Pitschmann, Librn
Holdings: Vols (34,000) Cat Mss Maps Pix Microforms
Budget: ($3000)
Notes: Collection aims at comprehensive coverage of Iceland in all aspects with major emphasis on the literature and language (both old and modern). Such subjects as runology, Scandinavian and Germanic mythology, early Norwegian history and history of the Viking period and of the Norse explorations of Greenland and North America are also well represented. For printed catalogs of the Collection's holdings see Downs 3608, 3609. Records for approximately 40 percent of the collection have been entered into OCLC and RLIN.

OH —CLEVELAND PUBLIC LIBRARY, Fine Arts and Special Collections Department, 325 Superior Ave, Cleveland, 44114. Alice N Loranth, Head
Holdings: Vols 1100 Cat
Notes: Part of the Icelandic and Old Norse Languages and Literatures Collection. Sagas and philological studies are emphasized. One of the notable collections is Tegner's Frithjof's saga which alone is represented by about 225 editions.
See also entries under Folklore; Rare Books.

WI —UNIVERSITY OF WISCONSIN, MADISON, Memorial Library, Rare Books Collection, 728 State St, Madison, 53706. Gretchen Lagana, Cur
Holdings: // Cat Mss
Notes: The core of this extensive collection consists of books from the libraries of Chester H Thordarson and Rasmus B Anderson. Very strong in Old Norse language and literature, incl important editions of saga literature and manuscript series in facsimile. Also incl works on modern Icelandic, important works in Icelandic history, and a good collection of Icelandic literature through the mid-twentieth century. Some of the early and rare material is kept in the Dept of Rare Books and Special Collections.

SAGE, GEORGE BYRON

CA —AMERICAN FILM INSTITUTE, Louis B Mayer Library, 2021 N Western Ave, PO Box 27999, Los Angeles, 90027. Anne G Schlosser, Dir
Notes: George Byron Sage Story Analyst Collection contains 4,000 synopses and reader reports written by Sage during period at 20th Century Fox (1941-1973).

SAGINAW AND MANISTEE LUMBER COMPANY

AZ —NORTHERN ARIZONA UNIVERSITY, Special Collection Library, CU Box 6022, Flagstaff, 86011. Peter M Whiteley, Coordr/Archivist; William Mullane, Librn
Notes: The lumber company was located in Williams and Flagstaff, Ariz. Records, 1902-1954, incl correspondence, bills of sale, time sheets, contracts and agreements. Also incl some records of Saginaw Power Company (19 feet).

SAGUENAY REGION

PQ —SPECIAL LIBRARY FOR LA SOCIETE HISTORIQUE DU SAGUENAY, 930 est, Jacques-Cartier, PO Box 456, Chicoutimi, G7H 5C8, Can. Roland Belanger, Archivist
Holdings: Vols 850 Uncat Mss Maps Pix
Notes: All concerning the history and geography of the Saguenay Region Incl about 50,000 pictures.

SAHAPTIN INDIANS see Nez Perce Indians

THE SAHEL

MI —UNIVERSITY OF MICHIGAN, Center for Research on Economic Development, Library, 240 Lorch Hall, Ann Arbor, 48109. Carol Wilson, Information/Resources Coordinator
Holdings: Vols (21,000) Cat 16mm Films Microforms
Budget: ($7000)
Notes: Publications that list library and its collection: *Directory of Third World Studies in the US* (African Studies Assn, 1981), *National Reference Center Directory* 1983 (NRC), *World Guide to Libraries* 1983 (Saur Verlag), *Research Centers Directory 1983* (Gale Research), and *A Directory of Information Resources in US* (Library of Congress, 1978). Collection's focus is Third World economic development. Other areas of interest are economic planning, developing countries, Africa (specifically francophone Africa), the Sahel, African agricultural economics, commodities production, financial statistics, development plans from less developed countries (LDC), and international development. Each part of the library's collection (working papers/reports, periodicals and government documents) has its own catalog and cataloging system.

MI —MICHIGAN STATE UNIVERSITY, International Library, Sahel Documentation Center, East Lansing, 48824. Eugene deBenko, Librn; Learthen Dorsey, Librn
Holdings: Vols (5100) Cat Mss Maps Pix Slides Phonorecords Audiotapes Videotapes Microforms
Budget: ($8000)
Notes: Sahel Documentation Center was established in September 1976 in support of research on the development of the drought-stricken Sahelian countries (Chad, Niger, Senegal, Mauritania, Mali, Upper Volta, The Gambia and Cape Verde). Emphasis on the socio-economic conditions and rural development of the area. Collection contains primary and secondary sources: books, mss, maps, reports, journals and microforms. Description of the collection: *Sahel-Bibliographic Bulletin/Bulletin* Bibliographique, a bilingual quarterly (v 1 nos 1-4, 1977); and *Documentation for Development in the Sahel* 1977, (37 pp).

PA —DUQUESNE UNIVERSITY, Library, 600 Forbes Ave, Pittsburgh, 15219. Holdings: Vols (7407) Cat Maps Slides Microforms
Notes: Mostly concerned with Africa south of the Sahara. CIDESA file (Centre International de Documentation Economique et Social Africaine) contains material dealing with economic and social problems of the African continent. Collection strong in materials on economics and Hausa and Swahili languages.

SAIL SHIP PERIODICALS see Periodicals, Sailship

SAILING AND SAILING SHIPS

FL —MARTIN COUNTY PUBLIC LIBRARY, 701 E Ocean Blvd, Stuart, 33494. LeRoy Hennings Jr, Dir
Holdings: Vols 173 Cat
Notes: Selim Walker McArthur collection on sailing. The heart of the collection deals with the building of sailing ship models and dates from the 1920s. This material is unique.

NY —STATE UNIVERSITY OF NEW YORK, Maritime College, Stephen B Luce Library, Fort Schuyler, Bronx, 10465. Richard H Corson, Librn
Holdings: Vols (68,000) Cat Slides Phonorecords Audiotapes Videotapes 16mm Films Microforms
Budget: ($90,000)
Notes: Incl history of ships with special emphasis on US sailing ships of the 19th century. Extensive holdings in periodical literature with long and complete runs of many titles. Mainly English language.

RI —BROWN UNIVERSITY, John Carter Brown Library, Providence, 02912. Norman Fiering, Librn; Everett C Wilkie Jr, Bibliographer; Susan Danforth, Cur Maps & Prints
Notes: Extensive collection, incl works on navigation, shipbuilding, mariners' health, and explorations accomplished by ship.

MB —AQUATIC HALL OF FAME & MUSEUM OF CANADA, Library, 25 Poseidon Bay, Winnipeg, R3M 3E4, Can. Notes: Aquatic sports, incl swimming, diving, water polo and synchronized swimming. Aquatic memorabilia; records covering Olympics, World Games, Pan-American Games, Commonwealth Games and Canadian Championships; coaching; record books. Collections on sailing and sailing ships, and yachts and yachting, incl books from the Cutty Sark Club of Winnipeg, covering sailing of the past.

NS —CANADIAN COAST GUARD COLLEGE, Library, PO Box 4500, Sydney, B1P 6L1, Can. David MacSween, Librn
Holdings: Vols 500 Cat 16mm Films

SAILING VESSELS see Sailing and Sailing Ships

SAILORS

MD —SEAFARER'S HARRY LUNDEBERG SCHOOL OF SEAMANSHIP, Paul Hall Library and Maritime Museum, Piney Point, 20674. Janice McAteer Smolek, Librn
Holdings: Mss Pix Slides Audiotapes Videotapes 16mm Films Filmstrips Microforms
Notes: Special collection on maritime studies incl books, mss, periodicals, audiovisuals, and archival materials pertaining to maritime history and vocational skills required by the maritime industry. Incl some rare books.

RI —BROWN UNIVERSITY, John Carter Brown Library, Providence, 02912. Norman Fiering, Librn; Everett C Wilkie Jr, Bibliographer; Susan Danforth, Cur Maps & Prints
Notes: Extensive collection, incl works on navigation, shipbuilding, mariners' health, and explorations accomplished by ship.

RI —BROWN UNIVERSITY, John Hay Library, Anne S K Brown Military Collection, 20 Prospect St, Providence, 02912. Richard B Harrington, Cur
Notes: The Anne S K Brown Military Collection has been formed over the past forty or more years by Mrs John Nicholas Brown, now of Newport, and contains approximately 40,000 volumes and 60,000 prints, drawings and watercolors as well as a number of oil paintings and about 5000 miniature model soldiers. At its beginning (and still today) the emphasis or focus of this collection has been upon the history of, and the accurate contemporary illustration of, military and naval uniforms of all nations from the early XVII century to the present. In the course of time, however, the collection has come to incl also a vast and related amount of material on military and naval history, military and naval arts and tactics, wars, campaigns, ceremonies, biography, portraits and caricatures of this and earlier periods. It has been probably the largest private collection of such a nature inthe world, and it contains much ms and graphic documentation which is unique. It has been useful to numerous scholars and historians, editors, filmmakers and publishers for research and for illustrative material and has also contributed to many museum exhibitions. In 1982 the entire collection, with its complete card catalog and subject index, has been presented to Brown University, where it is located in the John Hay Library. Special requests are taken care of by phone, mail and appointments with the curator.

SAILORS, MERCHANT

MD —SEAFARER'S HARRY LUNDEBERG SCHOOL OF SEAMANSHIP, Paul Hall Library and Maritime Museum, Piney Point, 20674. Janice McAteer Smolek, Librn
Holdings: Mss Pix Slides Audiotapes Videotapes 16mm Films Filmstrips Microforms
Notes: Special collection on maritime studies incl books, mss, periodicals, audiovisuals,

SAILORS, MERCHANT (cont.)

and archival materials pertaining to maritime history and maritime labor union history and vocational skills required by the maritime industry. Incl some rare books.

NY —STATE UNIVERSITY OF NEW YORK, Maritime College, Stephen B Luce Library, Fort Schuyler, Bronx, 10465. Richard H Corson, Librn
Holdings: Vols (68,000) Cat Maps Pix Slides Phonorecords Audiotapes Videotapes 16mm Films Filmstrips Microforms
Budget: ($90,000)
Notes: Incl full runs of newspapers of the major maritime unions on microfilm.

NY —SEAMEN'S CHURCH INSTITUTE OF NEW YORK, Joseph Conrad Library, 15 State St, New York, 10004. Bonnie Golightly, Librn
Holdings: Vols (23,500)
Budget: ($8500)
Notes: Merchant seamen, merchant ships, voyages, navigation, marine engineering, shipbuilding. Large collection of ship registers: *Lloyd's Register of Shipping*, a partial coverage of the years 1764-1865 in reprints, complete coverage for the years 1877 to date; *American Bureau of Shipping*, 1916 to date; *Merchant Vessels of the US*, 1891 to date. *Society of Naval Architects and Marine Engineers Transactions*, vol 1, 1893 to date. The picture file consists mostly of photographs of merchant ships. This is supplemented by scrapbooks. The index to the pictures, scrapbooks, books and vertical file are in one subject catalog. We subscribe to and keep for several years numerous maritime periodicals. The maritime history collection incl sailing ships as well as steamships.

SAILORS, TIN see Military Miniatures

SAILPLANES (AERONAUTICS) see Gliders (Aeronautics)

ST. CATHERINE'S MONASTERY MANUSCRIPTS

DC —LIBRARY OF CONGRESS, General Reading Rooms Division, Microform Reading Room, Washington, 20540.
Holdings: Cat Mss Maps Pix Microforms
Notes: Microform materials only in this LC Division. Works of individual authors; holdings of collections; archival records, etc, press releases and translations, etc.

SAINT CLAIR COAL COMPANY

DE —HAGLEY MUSEUM AND LIBRARY, Eleutherian Mills-Hagley Foundation Inc, PO Box 3630, Greenville, 19807. Richmond D Williams, Dir; Heddy A Richter, Imprints Librn
Notes: Westmoreland Coal Company records (1854-1982; 350 cubic feet) document the history of the nation's oldest bituminous coal mining company which operated in the Connellsville, Pa area (1880-89) and southern West Virginia (1906-56). Penn Virginia Corporation records (1864-1970; 120 cubic feet) document the history of one of Virginia's most significant coal mining companies. Also, Saint Clair Coal Company (1895-1930; 15 cubic feet). Records document the history of an important Schuylkill County, Pa anthracite coal producer. The colleciton incl minute books, financial records and photographs.

ST. DENIS, RUTH, 1880-1968

CA —LOS ANGELES PUBLIC LIBRARY, Frances Howard Goldwyn Hollywood Regional Library, 1623 Ivar Ave, Los Angeles, 90028. Sally Dumaux, Librn
Holdings: Vols (100,000) Uncat Pix VF
Budget: ($60,000)
Notes: There is both a general and reference collection covering the history of dance, mainly Europe and the US. Special Collections: Gladys Littell-Ruth St Denis, 1880-1968, covering circa 1941-1957 incl

photographs, programs, flyers, and brochures; Dance Programs, over 400 programs and playbills, mainly Los Angeles and New York from the 1930s to the present.

CA —UNIVERSITY OF CALIFORNIA, LOS ANGELES, Research Library, Dept of Special Collections, 405 Hilgard Ave, Los Angeles, 90024. Edward Shreeves, Chairman, Bibliographers Group; David S Zeidberg, Head
Holdings: Mss Pix Microfilm
Notes: 80 linear feet of handwritten journals, scrapbooks, memorabilia and music for her dances. Additional material in the Maude Emily Glass papers.

NY —NEW YORK PUBLIC LIBRARY, Performing Arts Research Center, Dance Collection, 111 Amsterdam Ave, New York, 10023. Genevieve Oswald, Cur
Notes: Comprehensive collection of biographical and visual materials, much of it also relating to Ted Shawn and the Denishawn Dancers. Includes 5000 photographs, clippings and programs, scrapbooks, 50 motion picture films, tape-recorded interviews, and ten cartons of manuscript materials.

ST. DOMINIC, ORDER OF see Dominicans

SAINT-EXUPERY, ANTOINE DE

†NY —COLUMBIA UNIVERSITY LIBRARIES, Butler Library, Rare Book and Manuscript Library, 535 W 114 St, New York, 10027.
Notes: Lewis Galantiere's papers, etc, with much on Antoine de Saint-Exupery, French language and literature, modern French authors and their works, etc. Considerable correspondence with many of the latter as well as with American and British authors.

ST. FRANCIS, ORDER OF see Franciscans

SAINT-GAUDENS, AUGUSTUS

NH —DARTMOUTH COLLEGE, Baker Memorial Library, Hanover, 03755.
Holdings: Cat Mss Pix
Notes: Family papers.

NY —NEW YORK HISTORICAL SOCIETY, Library, 170 Central Park W, New York, 10024. James Gregory, Librn
Notes: 4 linear ft of correspondence and papers, 1842-1920, of Stanford White (architect). Incl a great many letters from American artists and sculptors such as Augustus Saint-Gaudens and John La Farge.

ST. GEORGE, KATHARINE PRICE COLLIER

NY —CORNELL UNIVERSITY LIBRARIES, Collection of Regional History, Dept of Manuscripts and Univ Archives, Ithaca, 14853.
Notes: US Congresswoman. Incl papers, 1939-(1947-64); scrapbooks of clippings, copies of speeches, newsletters, press releases, photos, guestbooks, films, phonograph records, tape recordings, itineraries, bills she introduced, memoranda, and other items. Unpublished guide available. Restricted.

ST. JOAN see Joan of Arc, St.

ST. JOHN, ROBERT

MA —BOSTON UNIVERSITY, Mugar Memorial Library, Special Collections Dept, 771 Commonwealth Ave, Boston, 02215. Howard B Gotlieb, Dir
Holdings: Cat Mss Pix
Notes: Mss, correspondence, etc collected in depth; incl publications by or about.

ST. JOHN, SOVEREIGN HOSPITALLER ORDER OF

MD —SOVEREIGN HOSPITALLER ORDER OF SAINT JOHN, Villa Anneslie, 529

Dunkirk Road, Baltimore, 21212.
Holdings: Vols 15
Notes: An ecumenical Christian religious Order founded in the 11th century; successor Order to the Knights of Rhodes and the Knights of Malta.

ST. JOHN D'EL REY MINING COMPANY

TX —UNIVERSITY OF TEXAS LIBRARIES, Nettie Lee Benson Latin American Collection, Sid Richardson Hall 1.109, Austin, 78712. Laura Gutierrez-Witt, Head Librn
Holdings: Mss
Notes: Over 1,000,000 ms pages containing the business records, 1830-1960, of the St. John d'el Rey Mining Company, which operates gold and iron ore mines in Brazil.

ST. LAWRENCE RIVER AREA

NY —SAINT LAWRENCE UNIVERSITY, Owen D Young Library, Canton, 13617. Mahlon Peterson, Librn
Holdings: Cat Mss Maps Pix
Notes: Collection consists of pamphlets, speeches, maps, newspaper clippings, photographs, and government reports relating to the decision to build the Seaway and its subsequent construction. Over 1200 items.

OH —CLEVELAND PUBLIC LIBRARY, Science & Technology Dept, 325 Superior Ave, Cleveland, 44114. Jean Z Piety, Head
Holdings: Cat Pix
Notes: Special collection covers the environmental sciences concerned with the Great Lakes-St Lawrence drainage basins. Emphasis is on limnology, ecology, meteorology, hydraulics, biology, pollution of air and water, natural history and general research. Most of the material indexed has been donated by numerous agencies around the Great Lakes.

ST. LOUIS, MISSOURI

MO —MISSOURI BOTANICAL GARDEN LIBRARY, PO Box 299, Saint Louis, 63166. M R Crosby, Dir of Research
Holdings: Uncat Mss Maps Pix
Notes: Papers of Henry Shaw relating to St. Louis business and economic history and founding of the Missouri Botanical Garden. About 40 vols and 60 boxes of files containing 40,000 ms pieces.

MO —MISSOURI HISTORICAL SOCIETY, Library, Jefferson Memorial Bldg, Saint Louis, 63112. Stephanie Klein, Librn-Archivist; Peter Michel, Cur of Manuscripts
Holdings: Vols (500) Cat
Notes: Five hundred volumes of sheet music. In additions, over 5000 pieces of individual sheet music. Most of this music was published in St Louis, and many have St Louis themes. Collection will remain in storage until 1986.

MO —SAINT LOUIS PUBLIC LIBRARY, Gardner Rare Book Room, 1301 Olive St, Saint Louis, 63103. Julanne M Good, Supervisor; Martha Riley, Rare Books Librn
Holdings: Vols 100 Cat Maps
Budget: ($5573)
Notes: Small growing collection of travels incl St Louis or Missouri, largely transferred from the general stacks, although an occasional purchase is made. Incl early business directories of St Louis, river pilots' handbooks and maps. Noncirculating.

MO —SAINT LOUIS PUBLIC LIBRARY, Documents Dept, 1301 Olive St, Saint Louis, 63103. Anne Watts, Librn
Notes: Depository for documents of the US, Missouri, and St Louis, Missouri. Incl 20,000 items.

MO —WASHINGTON UNIVERSITY, John M Olin Library, Saint Louis, 63130. B J Johnston, Urban and Regional Studies Bibliographer
Holdings: Vols 53,000 Cat Microforms
Notes: 19,000 Microforms; publications, reports, documents.

MO —WASHINGTON UNIVERSITY, John M Olin Library, Lindell & Skinker Blvd,

ST. LOUIS, MISSOURI (cont.)

Saint Louis, 63130. Beryl H Manne, Archivist
Holdings: Mss Pix Audiotapes 16mm Films Filmstrips Microforms
Notes: The University Archives and Research Collection at the John M Olin Library of Washington University is a growing ms archives collecting original source material pertaining to 20th century political, business, and social welfare history of the St Louis metropolitan area. Incl the personal papers of prominent St Louis politicians, businessmen, engineers, educators, scientists, architects. Holdings especially strong in municipal and county governmental affairs.

MO —WASHINGTON UNIVERSITY, Libraries, Special Collections Dept, Campus Box 1061, St Louis, 63130.
Notes: Terminal Railroad Association Records (1889-date), of more than 450 original tracings fo the Eads Bridge (1874-date). Drawings show in fine and complete detail all the design features of this internationally known St Louis landmark.

ST. LOUIS, MISSOURI—HISTORY

MO —SAINT LOUIS PUBLIC LIBRARY, History & Genealogy Dept, 1301 Olive Blvd, Saint Louis, 63103. Noel C Holobeck, Librn
Holdings: Cat Maps Microforms
Notes: Extensive collection. See also *Genealogical Materials and Local Histories in the St Louis Public Library*, by Georgia Gambrill, 1966; first supplement, 1971. Local history index (card file). Vertical file material.

MO —UNIVERSITY OF MISSOURI-SAINT LOUIS, Thomas Jefferson Library, Manuscript and Historical Society Collection, 8001 Natural Bridge Rd, Saint Louis, 63121.
Holdings: Mss Pix Tapes
Notes: ca

MO —WASHINGTON UNIVERSITY, School of Medicine, Archives, 660 S Euclid Ave, Saint Louis, 63110. Paul G Anderson, Archivist
Holdings: Mss Pix Audiotapes
Budget: ($38,000)
Notes: Institutional records and papers of faculty of Washington University School of Medicine and its predecessors and associated hospitals. Contains records of St Louis Medical College, Missouri Medical Barnard Free Skin and Cancer Hospital, Barnes Hospital, St Louis Children's Hospital and Jewish Hospital of St Louis. Incl papers of William Beaumont, Joseph Erlanger, Leo Loeb, Evarts Graham, Edmund V Cowdry, Helen Graham, Carl V Moore, Margaret Smith and others. Oral history program. See also: Anderson, Paul G and Hoolihan, Christopher, eds. *Special Collections* (St Louis: Washington University School of Medicine, 1981). 960 linear feet.

MO —WASHINGTON UNIVERSITY, John M Olin Library, Lindell & Skinker Blvd, Saint Louis, 63130. Beryl H Manne, Archivist
Holdings: Mss Pix Audiotapes 16mm Films Filmstrips Microforms
Notes: The University Archives and Research Collection at the John M Olin Library of Washington University is a growing ms archives collecting original source material pertaining to 20th century political, business, and social welfare history of the St Louis metropolitan area. Incl the personal papers of prominent St Louis politicians, businessmen, engineers, educators, scientists, architects. Holdings especially strong in municipal and county governmental affairs.

MO —WASHINGTON UNIVERSITY, Libraries, Special Collections Dept, Campus Box 1061, St Louis, 63130.
Notes: The Spanish Archive of St Louis Collection.

ST. LOUIS, MISSOURI—POLITICS AND GOVERNMENT

MO —SAINT LOUIS PUBLIC LIBRARY, Documents Dept, 1301 Olive St, Saint Louis, 63103. Anne Watts, Librn
Notes: Depository for documents of the US, Missouri, and St Louis, Missouri. Incl 20,000 items.

MO —WASHINGTON UNIVERSITY, John M Olin Library, Lindell & Skinker Blvd, Saint Louis, 63130. Beryl H Manne, Archivist
Holdings: Mss Pix Audiotapes 16mm Films Filmstrips Microforms
Notes: The University Archives and Research Collection at the John M Olin Library of Washington University is a growing ms archives collecting original source material pertaining to 20th century political, business, and social welfare history of the St Louis metropolitan area. Incl the personal papers of prominent St Louis politicians, businessmen, engineers, educators, scientists, architects. Holdings especially strong in municipal and county governmental affairs.

MO —WASHINGTON UNIVERSITY, Libraries, Special Collections Dept, Campus Box 1061, St Louis, 63130.
Notes: Incl the St Louis Mayoral Papers Collection: Papers of Aloys P Kaufmann, 1944-49; Raymond R Tucker, 1953-65; Alphonso J Cervantes, 1965-73; John H Poelker, 1973-77; James F Conway, 1977-81. Also, the papers of Joseph R Badarraco, espec files from his term as president of St Louis Board of Aldermen, 1972-75. Rich in City Planning Commission reports, etc, particularly redevelopment proposals and projects. Other records incl those of Harland Bartholomew and Associates, early city planning firm active in St Louis and other cities.

ST. LOUIS CAR COMPANY, 1887-1973

MO —WASHINGTON UNIVERSITY, Libraries, Special Collections Dept, Campus Box 1061, St Louis, 63130.
Holdings: //
Notes: Records of the St Louis Car Company, 1887-1973, incl the transportation manufacturing enterprise's files of over 20,000 photographs and negatives of the firm's products; over 2000 original tracings of railroad and street car equipment. Also printed material about the firm, and catalogs published by the company from 1904 to 1965.

ST. MARK'S POETRY PROJECT

CA —UNIVERSITY OF CALIFORNIA, LOS ANGELES, Research Library, Dept of Special Collections, 405 Hilgard Ave, Los Angeles, 90024. Edward Shreeves, Chairman, Bibliographers Group; David S Zeidberg, Head
Holdings: Mss
Notes: 1 linear foot of mss, correspondence, and ephemera.

ST. PIERRE AND MIQUELON

NF —MEMORIAL UNIVERSITY OF NEWFOUNDLAND, University Library, Centre for Newfoundland Studies, Elizabeth Ave, Saint John's, A1C 5S7, Can. Anne Hart, Head
Holdings: Vols (48,000) Cat Maps Microforms
Budget: ($50,000)
Notes: Materials about Newfoundland, by Newfoundlanders, or published in Newfoundland, incl Labrador. Also, St Pierre and Miquelon. Bibliography of Newfoundland materials is being compiled (now over 7,000 items).

SAINT-SAENS, CAMILLE

IL —NORTHWESTERN UNIVERSITY, Music Library, 1937 Sheridan Rd, Evanston, 60201. Don L Roberts, Head Music Librn
Holdings: Uncat Mss Pix
Notes: Incl materials in the NU Music Library Special Collections and in the Moldenhouer Archive. Most of the materials uncataloged at this time. 450 letters; music mss; documents; photographs.

SAINT-SIMON, CLAUDE HENRI

WI —UNIVERSITY OF WISCONSIN, MADISON, Memorial Library, Rare Books Collection, 728 State St, Madison, 53706. Gretchen Lagana, Cur
Holdings: Vols 175 Cat Microforms
Notes: A collection of first editions and related materials concerning the 19th century French political and social theorist Claude Henri Saint-Simon and his followers. Includes all of his important works and most of those of his disciples in France as well as a collection of pamphlets (on microfiche) showing his influence throughout France and of periodicals for which he wrote or edited (partly in the original and partly on microfilm). *UW Library News,* vol 12 (Feb 1967), pp 1-6 contains a partial description of the collection.

ST. THOMAS AQUINAS see Thomas Aquinas, St.

SAINTS

DC —DOMINICAN HOUSE OF STUDIES, Dominican College Library, 487 Michigan Ave NE, Washington, 20017. J Raymond Vandegrift, OP, Librn
Holdings: Vols (5000) Cat
Budget: ($1350)
Notes: The Dominican Order (its history, spirituality, government, liturgy), its members (directories, biographies, bibliographies, lives of saints) and works written by Dominicans: incunabula, rare books, dissertations, periodicals (2300 vols), monographs. Incl periodicals either about the Order or edited by Dominicans. Does not incl titles about the congregations of Dominican Sisters. The Library's catalog contains analytics for Dominican contributors to monographs.

DC —GEORGETOWN UNIVERSITY, Library, Special Collections Div, 37 & O Sts NW, Washington, 20057. George M Barringer, Special Collections Librn; Nicholas B Sheetz, Mss Librn
Holdings: Cat

MD —UNIVERSITY OF MARYLAND, BALTIMORE, Health Sciences Library, 111 S Greene St, Baltimore, 21201. Cyril C H Feng, Dir
Holdings: Vols (1000) Cat Mss Pix VF
Notes: The Clarence J Grieves Dental Historical Collection is one of the strongest collections of its kind in the United States. It includes some of the most significant early dental imprints; early records of the Maryland State Dental Association; and an excellent collection of prints on early dentistry and St Apollonia.

NE —CREIGHTON UNIVERSITY, Reinert/Alumni Library, California at 24th St, Omaha, 68178. Raymond B Means, Dir
Holdings: Vols (19,175) Cat Mss
Budget: ($14,100)
Notes: In addition to English, Latin and Greek predominate in the collection. Emphasis on Catholic religion, history and saints.

OH —CLEVELAND PUBLIC LIBRARY, Fine Arts and Special Collections Department, 325 Superior Ave, Cleveland, 44114. Alice N Loranth, Head
Holdings: Vols 1000 Cat Mss
Notes: Part of the Literature, Medieval and Folklore Collections. Medieval texts, translations, facsimile reproductions, bibliographies and catalogs of mss, romances, epics, early chronicles and histories, Icelandic sagas, fabliaux (tales), legends, lives of the Saints are well represented. Monographs, scholarly journals and serials on philology, linguistics, and literature with special emphasis on Middle English, Old French, Middle High German, Middle Dutch and early Irish texts.
See also entries under Folklore; Literature, Medieval.

SALANDINI, REV. FR. VICTOR

CA —STANFORD UNIVERSITY LIBRARIES, Cecil H Green Library,

SALANDINI, REV. FR. VICTOR (cont.)

Stanford, 94305. Michael T Ryan, Cur
Notes: Correspondence, papers, and material
on farm labor and migrant workers of recent
years. Incl papers of Ernesto Galarza and
the National Agricultural Workers Union
(NAWU), Fr Victor Salandini and Fr James
L Vizzard.

SALEM, MASSACHUSETTS—HISTORY

MA —PEABODY INSTITUTE LIBRARY,
Danvers Archival Center, 15 Sylvan St,
Danvers, 01923. Richard B Trask, Archivist,
Rare Books & Special Collections
Holdings: Vols 5000 Cat Mss
Notes: The Ellerton J Brehaut Collection on
New England witchcraft, especially Salem
witchcraft. (Danvers, where the library is
located, was part of Salem at the time of the
witchcraft trials.) 17th and 18th century
English and American books on witchcraft;
transcripts of all known trial records.
Manuscript records of the First Church of
Salem Village. Special catalog to collection.
Danvers History Collection consists of 5000
volumes, 250,000 mss, numerous photos,
newspaper clippings, maps, audiotapes, and
visual tapes.
†MA —OLD STURBRIDGE VILLAGE,
Research Library, Sturbridge, 01566.
Notes: Danvers history and Salem village
history. Incl mss, pictures and material on
Salem witchcraft trials.

SALES

NY —SALES & MARKETING
MANAGEMENT, Library, 633 Third Ave,
New York, 10017. John D Roberts, Librn
Holdings: Vols (500) Uncat

SALESMEN AND SALESMANSHIP see Salespersons and Selling

SALESPERSONS AND SELLING

IN —INDIANA UNIVERSITY, Lilly Library,
Seventh St, Bloomington, 47405. William R
Cagle, Librn
Holdings: Vols 335 // Cat Mss Pix
Notes: Street cries, chiefly from the Virginia
Warren Collection. Limited photocopying.
NY —SALES & MARKETING EXECUTIVES
INTERNATIONAL, Marketing Information
Center, 330 W 42nd St, New York, 10036.
Alayne J Ambrogio, Dir
Holdings: Vols (600) Cat
Budget: ($1500)
Notes: Extensive collection incl many
textbooks. For members only.
NY —SALES & MARKETING
MANAGEMENT, Library, 633 Third Ave,
New York, 10017. John D Roberts, Librn
Holdings: Vols (500) Uncat
NC —GREENSBORO PUBLIC LIBRARY,
Business Library, 201 Greene St, Drawer
X-4, Greensboro, 27402. Lebby B Lamb,
Business Librn
Holdings: Vols (6000) Cat Microforms
Budget: ($12,000)

SALINGER, JEROME DAVID

NV —UNIVERSITY OF NEVADA, RENO,
University Library, Special Collections Dept,
Reno, 89557. Robert E Blesse, Head
Holdings: Vols (35) Cat
Notes: Includes individual works by author
in all editions including translations; also
prefaces, introductions, published
correspondence, appearances in anthologies,
periodicals, etc. Bibliographical research
collection, part of Modern Authors
Collection. Other appearances 75 cataloged.

SALISBURY, LAURENCE E., 1891-1976

CA —HOOVER INSTITUTION ON WAR,
REVOLUTION & PEACE, Stanford
University, Stanford, 94305. Milorad M
Drachkovitch, Archivist
Holdings: Mss
Notes: Papers of Laurence E Salisbury, US

foreign service officer, 1920-44, and editor of
American Istitute of Pacific Relations'
publication, *Far Easters Survey*,, 1944-48,
incl correspondence, writings, reports,
memoranda and other material, 1916-73,
relating to his government service in China,
Japan, and the Philippines, American foreign
relations with these countries, and political
developments in the US 4 ms boxes.

SALISBURY, LEAH

NY —COLUMBIA UNIVERSITY
LIBRARIES, Rare Book & Manuscript
Library, 801 Butler Library, 535 W 114 St,
New York, 10027. Kenneth A Lohf, Librn
Holdings: Mss Pix
Notes: Papers, mss, archives, etc. 185,000
items. Restricted use.

SALISHAN INDIANS

†WA —WASHINGTON STATE
UNIVERSITY, Library, Manuscripts,
Archives & Special Collections, Pullman,
99164. John F Guido, Head
Holdings: Cat Mss Maps Pix
Notes: The collection is especially rich in
documents relating to the exploration,
settlement and development of the Palouse
Country, the Inland Empire, the Columbia
Basin and the Pacific Northwest. Described
in *Selected Manuscript Resources in the
Washington State University Library*
(Pullman, 1974); and other published and
unpublished inventories and registers.

SALMON, JOHN R.

KS —WICHITA PUBLIC LIBRARY, Local
History Dept, 223 S Main, Wichita, 67202.
William Clark Ellington, Jr, Dept Head &
City Historian
Notes: The Local History collection consists
of a photographic archive of Wichita and
Sedgwick county subjects and views. Many
early Wichita and Sedgwick county town
builders are represented in this extensive
collection. The photographic archive also
includes the prints and glass plates of
pioneer photographers, W S Rogers of
Wichita and John R Salmon of Mount Hope,
Ks. Manuscripts, diaries and a general file of
historical information covering Wichita and
Sedgwick county history are maintained for
public use. Rare early editions of the Wichita
Beacon are also part of the Local History
section.

SALMON FISHERIES

†WA —WASHINGTON STATE
UNIVERSITY, Library, Manuscripts,
Archives & Special Collections, Pullman,
99164. John F Guido, Head
Holdings: Cat Mss Maps Pix
Notes: The manuscript collection incl
business and financial records of banks,
breweries, fisheries, insurance, land, lumber
and livestock companies, trade and
commodity associations; as well as the
personal and professional papers of authors,
aviators, educators, engineers, farmers,
historians, pioneers, politicians and scientists;
especially rich in documents relating to the
exploration, settlement and development of
the Palouse Country, the Inland Empire, the
Columbia Basin and the Pacific Northwest.
Described in *Selected Manuscript Resources
in the Washington State University Library*
(Pullman, 1974); and other published and
unpublished inventories and registers.

SALMON FISHING

NH —UNIVERSITY OF NEW HAMPSHIRE,
Dimond Library, Durham, 03824. Barbara A
White, Special Collections Librn
Holdings: Vols 2000 Cat
Notes: Special emphasis on fly-tying and
trout and salmon fishing.
PA —LAFAYETTE COLLEGE, David Bishop
Skillman Library, Easton, 18042. Dorothy
Cieslicki, Librn
Holdings: Vols (825) Cat
Notes: Robert Tinsman Angling Collection.

Incl 58 editions of Walton, *Compleat Angler*.
Also, the Robert S Conahay, Jr, Atlantic
Salmon Collection, which incl over 1000
hand-tied salmon and trout flies, many
mounted and framed.

SALMON FISHING, ATLANTIC see Atlantic Salmon—Fishing

SALNAMEH

WA —UNIVERSITY OF WASHINGTON
LIBRARIES, Suzzallo Library, Near East
Section, FM-25, Seattle, 98195. Fawzi W
Khoury, Head
Holdings: Vols (49,000) Cat Mss Maps
Slides Phonorecords 16mm Films Filmstrips
Microforms
Budget: ($26,396)
Notes: Incl a 2000 vol collection in Ottoman
Turkish in the fields of language and
literature and 55 volumes of the original 62
volumes of *Devlet Salnameh* series of official
manuyals published in the Ottoman Empire.
WI —UNIVERSITY OF WISCONSIN,
MADISON, Memorial Library, Slavic
Studies Collection, 728 State St, Madison,
53706. Aleksander Rolich, Bibliographer for
Slavic Studies; Robert P Gakovich, Slavic
Cataloger; Valdis J Zeps, Baltic Studies
Center

SALOONS see Hotels, Taverns, Etc.

SALT INDUSTRY AND TRADE

NY —ONONDAGA COUNTY DEPT OF
PARKS AND RECREATION, Office of
Museums and Historical Sites, PO Box 146,
Liverpool, 13088. Elaine Wisowaty, Asst
Cur; Dennis Connors, Cur
Holdings: Vols 50 Cat Mss Maps Pix Slides
Audiotapes
Budget: ($3500)
Notes: History of the NY State Salt Industry
in Onondaga County.

SALT RIVER PROJECT

AZ —NORTHERN ARIZONA
UNIVERSITY, Special Collection Library,
CU Box 6022, Flagstaff, 86011. Peter M
Whiteley, Coordr/Archivist; William
Mullane, Librn
Notes: Jay Price Collection; correspondence,
files, and reports pertaining to *Forestry*
Topics, 1950's. Incl information on
watershed and forest management for the
Salt River and Central Arizona Projects as
part of the Arizona Water Resource
Committee files, 1956-1960; and files of the
Soil Conservation Society, Arizona Chapter,
1956-1957 (2 feet).

SALTEAUX INDIANS see Chippewa Indians

SALTER, GEORGE

IL —NEWBERRY LIBRARY, 60 W Walton
St, Chicago, 60610. Diana Haskell, Cur of
Modern Mss
Holdings: // Uncat Mss Pix
Notes: Primary repository. Original drawings,
book and dust jacket designs, lecture notes,
Magazine covers. Noncirculating.

SALTUS, EDGAR EVERTON

CT —YALE UNIVERSITY, Box 1603A, Yale
Station, New Haven, 06520.
Holdings: Cat Mss

SALTZMANN-STEVENS, MINNIE

IL —ILLINOIS STATE UNIVERSITY, Milner
Library, Dept of Special Collections,
Normal, 61761. Robert Sokan, Librn
Holdings: Mss Pix
Notes: Opera singer in the US and Europe.
Letters, autographs, autobiography,
biographical sketch, photos of Madame
Saltzmann-Stevens and other opera stars,
programs, news clippings, contracts and
scrapbook. Incl letters written by Florence

SALTZMANN-STEVENS, MINNIE (cont.)

Fifer Bohrer, member of the Illinois State Senate and Jean De Reszke, Madame Saltzmann-Stevens' voice instructor. Incl 568 items, some musical scores.

EL SALVADOR

CT —YALE UNIVERSITY, Sterling Memorial Library, Latin American Collections, New Haven, 06520. Lee H Williams Jr, Cur
Holdings: Vols (300,000) Cat Maps Pix Slides Phonorecords 16mm Films Filmstrips
See also entry under Latin America

KS —UNIVERSITY OF KANSAS, Watson Library, Lawrence, 66045. George Jerkovich, Cur Slavic Collections
Notes: Over 6000 valuable Central American titles, of which fewer than half in a random sample are presently located in OCLC, and over half not incl in published holdings of the University of Texas or Tulane University. A special grant is supporting cataloging of the collection.

MA —PAN AMERICAN SOCIETY OF NEW ENGLAND, Shattuck Library, 152 North Street, Boston, 02109. Vivian Ingrao, Dir
Holdings: Vols (10,000) Cat Slides Phonorecords
Notes: Books on art, literature, history, and economy of Pan American countries.

SALVADOR, FRANCIS

SC —COLLEGE OF CHARLESTON LIBRARY, Special Collections Dept, Charleston, 29401.
Notes: Coat of arms granted by the English College of Heralds, in 1745, to Francis Salvador, the grandfather of the Francis Salvador who brought it from England to South Carolina.

SALVAGE (WASTE, ETC.)

IL —GREELEY & HANSEN ENGINEERS, 222 S Riverside Plaza, Chicago, 60606. Marilyn Cichom, Librn
Holdings: Vols (6000) Cat Maps Slides Microforms

MA —CAMP, DRESSER & MCKEE, Herman G Dresser Library, One Center Plaza, Boston, 02108. Virginia L Carroll, Librn
Holdings: Vols (15,000) Cat Maps Slides Microforms
Notes: Air, land, and water pollution; environmental engineering; hazardous wastes; water resources; solid wastes; resource recycling.

MA —TUFTS UNIVERSITY, Engineering Library, Medford, 02155. Wayne Powell, Science-Engineering Librn
Holdings: Vols (20,000) Cat
Notes: Also 25,000 technical reports. Subject emphases: solid waste management, water pollution control, fluid mechanics.

NY —US ENVIRONMENTAL PROTECTION AGENCY, Region II, Technical Library, 26 Federal Plaza, New York, 10278. Audrey Thomas, Regional Librn
Holdings: Vols 4200 Cat
Notes: Incl 16,000 reports, 225,000 microfiche, 100 current subscriptions.

UT —EIMCO TECHNOLOGY & RESEARCH CENTER, Process Machinery Div, Technical Library, 414 W 300 S, Salt Lake City, 84110.
Holdings: Vols (1450) Cat

SALVATION ARMY

NY —SALVATION ARMY ARCHIVES AND RESEARCH CENTER, 145 West 15th St, New York, 10011. Thomas Wilstead, Archivist/Administrator; Judith Johnson, Archivist
Holdings: Vols Pix Audiotapes Microforms VF
Notes: Official files and records, minutes, correspondence and photographs. Papers of Salvation Army officers. Material published by or about the Salvation Army. Incl 2300

books and pamplets, 300 serials, 40 VF, 685 microfilm reels, 300 sound recordings, 280 sound tapes, 445 films, 14,000 photoprints and negatives, 250 slides and 1050 cubic ft of archives.

SALVERSON, LAURA GOODMAN, 1890-1970

ON —NATIONAL LIBRARY OF CANADA, 395 Wellington St, Ottawa, K1A 0N4, Can. Andre Preibish, Dir
Notes: Literary Manuscripts collection contains papers of several important Canadian authors writing in English and/or French eg Clare Bice (1909-1976), noted author and illustrator of children's books; Andre Giroux, novelist, writer for television and broadcaster; Roger Lemelin, well-known author of Au pied de la pente douce, Les Plouffe, and Pierre le magnifique; Gabrielle Roy (1909-1983), author of many novels, including Bonheur d'occasion, La Petite Poule d'Eau and Rue Deschambault; Laura Goodman Salverson (1890-1970), writer, public speaker and teacher; Phyllis Webb, poet.

SAMARITANS

OH —HEBREW UNION COLLEGE-JEWISH INSTITUTE OF RELIGION, Klau Library, 3101 Clifton Ave, Cincinnati, 45220. David J Gilner, Reference Librn
Holdings: Cat Mss
Notes: Incl various Samaritan liturgies.

SAMOA

DE —UNIVERSITY OF DELAWARE, Hugh M Morris Library, S College Ave, Newark, 19711. T Stuart Dick, Special Collections
Holdings: Cat Mss Pix
Notes: The George Handy Bates Samoan Papers (about 400 items). Calendared mss. Berlin Samoan Conference Papers. Downs 5382.

DC —GEORGETOWN UNIVERSITY, Library, Special Collections Div, 37 & O Sts NW, Washington, 20057. George M Barringer, Special Collections Librn; Nicholas B Sheetz, Mss Librn
Holdings: Cat
Notes: Papers of Chauncey Brewster Chapman, Jr (1919-1980), attorney, from his early legal career in private practice and his years in the Department of Interior where he served as solicitor for territories from 1967-1979. The bulk of the papers concerns judicial and legal matters in regard to territories outside the United States, as well as internal departmental affairs. Of particular interest is material concerning Samoa from 1969-1980.

SAMPLEY, ARTHUR

TX —NORTH TEXAS STATE UNIVERSITY, Archives, NT Station Box 5188, Denton, 76203. Robert LaForte, University Archivist
Notes: Part of Oral History Collection. Interviews with former poet laureate of Texas.

SAMUEL READY SCHOOL

MD —UNIVERSITY OF BALTIMORE, Langsdale Library, 1420 Maryland Ave, Baltimore, 21201. Gerry Watkins, Head of Special Collections Dept
Notes: Student records, historical files, financial records, deeds, pictures pertaining to Samuel Ready School (1880-1978); 65 cubic feet.

SAMUELSON, AGNES

IA —STATE HISTORICAL SOCIETY OF IOWA LIBRARY, 402 Iowa Ave, Iowa City, 52240. Darold J Brown, Librn
Holdings: Cat
Notes: Thousands of individual items and smaller collections. Two hundred larger collections incl the papers of Cyrus C Carpenter, Jonathan P Dolliver, Gilbert

Haugen, W W Waymack, Ephraim Adams, A C Dodge, Dorothy Houghton, Jesse Macy, Agnes Samuelson, Donald Johnson, Jack Miller, Ruth Sayre, Samuel Kirkwood, Thomas McKnight, Robert Lucas, Dwight McCarty, William Larrabee. Includes church, school, company and organization records, Civil War materials.

SANBORN, FRANKLIN B.

MA —CONCORD FREE PUBLIC LIBRARY, 129 Main St, Concord, 01742. Rose Marie Mitten, Dir
Holdings: Cat Mss Letters Pix
Notes: Mr Sanborn knew Concord and the Concord Authors well.

SAN DIEGO, CALIFORNIA

CA —UNIVERSITY OF CALIFORNIA, SAN DIEGO, Central University Library, Mandeville Dept of Special Collections, La Jolla, 92093. Lynda Corey Claassen, Head
Notes: Several rare and extremely valuable books dealing with the discovery and early history of the San Diego region.

CA —SAN DIEGO HISTORICAL SOCIETY, Research Archives, Casa de Balboa 1649 El Prado, Balboa Park PO Box 81825, San Diego, 92138. Sylvia Arden, Head Librn & Archivist
Holdings: Cat Mss Maps Pix Audiotapes
Notes: Emphasis on San Diego County and early materials of Riverside and Imperial counties. Over 10,000 photographs also.

CA —SAN DIEGO PUBLIC LIBRARY, 820 E St, San Diego, 92101. Rhoda E Kruse, Sr Librn
Notes: Also 450 bound periodicals. Incl extensive local history; papers of Foss and Kelly families; some material on John D Spreckels; papers of Southern California Exposition, San Diego 200th Anniversary Committee; Census microfilms; registers of voters 1866-1909; *San Diego Union* Index, which also incl material on Baja Califorina; records of Little Landers Colony, a 1910 Utopian group founded in the Tia Juana River Valley.

SAN FRANCISCO, CALIFORNIA

CA —NATIONAL MARITIME MUSEUM, SAN FRANCISCO, J Porter Shaw Library, Golden Gate National Recreation Area, Fort Mason, San Francisco, 94123. David A Hull, Librn; Herbert Beckwith, Catalog Librn; Irene Stachura, Ref Librn; John Maounis, Photo Librn
Holdings: Vols (12,000) Mss Maps Pix Slides Microforms Periodicals VF
Budget: ($4000)
Notes: Pacific Coast maritime history. The photo collection of 160,000 is partly cataloged and classified. The library has complete runs of *Merchant Vessels of US* and *Lloyd's Register of Shipping* to 1970. The collection is particularly strong on Pacific Coast and San Francisco maritime history. About 250 log books; scrapbooks. Oral history interviews, vertical files. 60 percent of books are cataloged.

PA —AMERICAN PHILOSOPHICAL SOCIETY, Library, 105 S Fifth St, Philadelphia, 19106. Edward C Carter II, Librn
Notes: The anthropological papers of Paul Radin in fields of ethnology, social organization, primitive religion, linguistics, and mythology. He worked mostly among the Winnebago, Ojibwa, Fox, Zapotec, Wappo, Wintun, and Huave Indian tribes; also Italian and other ethnic minorities of San Francisco.

SAN FRANCISCO BAY AREA

CA —AZUSA PACIFIC COLLEGE, Marshburn Memorial Library, Citrus & Alosta, Azusa, 91702. Edward Peterman, Librn
Holdings: Vols (6000) Uncat
Budget: ($30,000)
Notes: Significant holdings in the George E Fullerton Library of Californiana and Western Americana.

SAN FRANCISCO BAY AREA (cont.)

CA —GRADUATE THEOLOGICAL UNION
LIBRARY, New Religious Movements
Research Collection, Public Services and
Special Collections Dept, 2400 Ridge Road,
Berkeley, 94709. Diane Choquette, Dept
Head
Holdings: Vols (3000) Mss Pix
Notes: Begun in 1977, the collection focuses
on religious movements new to America
since 1960, and unorthodox religious
movements resurgent since 1960. American
forms of Hinduism, Buddhism, Sikhism, and
Sufism are included along with occultism,
Neo-Paganism, esoteric and alternative
forms of Christianity, feminist spirituality,
and human potential movements having a
spiritual aspect. Legal issues, such as
deprogramming, and the question of church/
state relations are an important part of the
collection. The Library is a depository for
publications of the Unification Church in
America, the Church of Scientology, and the
International Society for Krishna
Consciousness (America). The responses of
mainstream religions and concerned citizens
groups are also included. Besides 3000
monographs, the library has 400 periodical
titles, 200 posters from the San
FranciscoBay Area, 1965-77, 300 research
papers, and 31 linear feet of ephemera.
CA —OAKLAND PUBLIC LIBRARY,
Oakland History Room, 125 14th St,
Oakland, 94612. William W Sturm, Librn
Holdings: Vols 20,000 Cat Mss Maps Pix
Microforms
Notes: The Oakland History Room
Collection is a reference collection of books,
pamphlets, periodicals, pictures, and
newspaper clippings. California items incl as
much biographical material as possible
clipped from the *Oakland Tribune, Oakland
Post, California Voice,* the *Montclarion,* and
Alameda Times-Star. (Library no longer
clips *San Francisco Chronicle* or *Examiner*).
These clippings are filed by subjects. An
index of all the subjects with many cross
references are made. An index of articles
from about 75 magazines dealing with
California subjects is kept up to date. The
log books of the Coast Guard Cutter *Bear*
from 1889 to 1932 are in the collection. The
Jack London collection is listed separately.
Ms pages and letters from Joaquin Miller
and a fewmiscellaneous letters from other
authors are also incl. A set of George
Sterling, both inscribed and not inscribed, is
owned by the Room.
CA —SOCIETY OF CALIFORNIA
PIONEERS, Library, 456 McAllister St, San
Francisco, 94102. Grace E Baker, Librn
Holdings: Vols (12,000) Cat Mss Maps Pix
Microforms
Notes: California history, especially the gold
rush and the San Francisco earthquake,
Sherman collection of early California music,
business letterheads of early California firms,
San Francisco City Directories 1850-1944,
records of California Battalion 1846-47, ms
material on overland diaries, ships' logs and
passenger lists. Also, large photograph
collection.
†CA —UNIVERSITY OF SAN FRANCISCO,
Richard A Gleeson Library, The Countess
Bernardine Murphy Donohue Rare Book
Room, San Francisco, 94117. D Steven
Corey, Special Collections Librn
Holdings: Vols 400 Pix
Notes: Emphasis is on fine printing, chiefly
American, but all aspects of Christmas are
covered. The entire collection is about 1500
items; much ephemera, and many pieces
relating to San Francisco.
NY —HOFSTRA UNIVERSITY, Library,
1000 Fulton Ave, Hempstead, 11550.
Charles R Andrews, Dean of Library
Services
Notes: The personal library of Paul Radin.
See description of the American
Philosophical Society Library's collection of
his anthropological papers under this entry
(Pa).
PA —DREXEL UNIVERSITY LIBRARIES,
Engineering Library, 32 & Chestnut Sts,

Philadelphia, 19104. Charlotte T Duvally,
Librn
Holdings: Vols 18,545 Uncat Microforms
Notes: The only library in Philadelphia area
holding the Bay Area (San Francisco) air
pollution control microfilm library. Access
via uniterm subject cards (manual retrieval
system) index, accession card file index,
author card file index.

SAN FRANCISCO BAY AREA—DESCRIPTION—VIEWS

NY —VISUAL STUDIES WORKSHOP,
Research Center, 31 Prince St, Rochester,
14607. Linn Underhill, Coordr; Robert
Bretz, Librn
Holdings: Vols (8000) Cat Pix Slides
Audiotapes Videotapes
Notes: Strong emphasis on photography
(over 1,000,000 pictures) and the
photographic arts in many subject areas incl
in this volume. Heavy emphasis on early
photographic processes and collections of
examples of them. Also collections of
individual photographers' works.

SAN FRANCISCO MIME TROUPE

CA —UNIVERSITY OF CALIFORNIA,
DAVIS, Shields Library, Dept of Special
Collections, Davis, 95616. Donald Kunitz,
Head; C Danial Elliott, Asst Head
Holdings: Mss Pix
Notes: Scripts, promptbooks, photographs,
correspondence and business archives of
radical San Francisco theatre groups of the
1960s: San Francisco Mime Troupe,
Firehouse Theatre, Universal Movement
Theatre Repertory (UMTR), and the Living
Theatre.

SANBORN FIRE INSURANCE MAPS

AL —UNIVERSITY OF ALABAMA, W S
Hoole Special Collections Library, Amelia
Gayle Goorgas Library, PO Box S,
University, 35486. Joyce H Lamont, Cur
Holdings: Cat Maps
Notes: 3500 maps, primarily early maps of
Alabama and the Southeast, but also 16th
and 17th century maps of Europe. Also 6000
Sanborn Fire Insurance Maps for every
Alabama county (1888-1925).
DC —LIBRARY OF CONGRESS, Geography
and Map Division, Washington, 20540. John
A Wolter, Chief
Holdings: Cat Mss Maps Pix Slides
Microforms
Notes: Sanborn Fire Insurance Map
collection of insurance maps of US cities,
late 19th and 20th centuries.
See also entry under Maps and Atlases -
Collections
GA —UNIVERSITY OF GEORGIA,
Libraries, Map Collection, Athens, 30602.
John Sutherland, Cur of Maps
Notes: Collection contains 291,165 cataloged
maps and 192,068 aerial photographs,
specializing in Georgia, Southeast US,
Central and South America, and Europe.
Major subject specializations are topography,
geology, soils and vegetation. Special
cartographic collection of Sanborn Fire
Insurance Maps (7000 sheets).
IN —INDIANA HISTORICAL SOCIETY,
Library, 315 W Ohio St, Indianapolis,
46202. Robert K O'Neill, Dir
Holdings: Vols Mss Maps Pix
Notes: Incl Indianapolis city directories;
Sanborn real estate atlases; city histories;
photographs, most notable the Bretzman
Collection; personal papers of local
individuals, mostly 19th century; records of
various Indianapolis social welfare
organizations; the Shortridge High School
Collection.
KY —UNIVERSITY OF KENTUCKY,
Margaret I King Library, Map Collection,
Lexington, 40506. Gwen Curtis, Head
Holdings: Maps Microforms
Notes: Collection of Sanborn Insurance
Maps of Kentucky cities, 99 percent
complete.
PA —PENNSYLVANIA STATE
UNIVERSITY, Fred Lewis Pattee Library,

Maps Section, University Park, 16802. Karl
Proehl, Head
Notes: Depositories for US Geological
Survey topographic maps; Defense mapping
agency topographic maps and nautical
charts; National Ocean Survey nautical and
aeronautical charts; Canadian topographic
maps. Sanborn Fire Insurance maps for
Pennsylvania villages and towns. 1970 and
1980 census maps for Pennsylvania counties,
townships, and cities. General coverage for
foreign countries-topographic and thematic
maps. Map catalog by area and subdivided
by subject; atlas catalog by author-title and
area-subject; shelf list catalogs for maps and
atlases. See *Pennsylvania Maps and Atlases
in The Pennsylvania State University
Libraries,* by Ruby M Miller (Pennsylvania
State University Libraries, 1971. 682 pp).
UT —UNIVERSITY OF UTAH, Marriott
Library, Special Collections, Salt Lake City,
84112. Gregory C Thompson, Cur
Holdings: Maps
Notes: Approx 1000 maps, historical of
Utah, incl Sanborn Maps.

SANDAGE, ALLAN

NY —AMERICAN INSTITUTE OF
PHYSICS, Center for the History of Physics,
Niels Bohr Library, 335 E 45 St, New York,
10017. John Aubry, Librn
Notes: The Sources for History of Modern
Astrophysics documents the history of 20th-
century astrophysics. Incl some 400 hours of
oral history interviews with astronomers,
such as Bart Bok, S Chandrasekhar, Martin
Schwarzschild, and A E Whitford. The
project also organized and cataloged the
papers of Henry Norris Russell, Frank
Schlesinger, Otto Struve, Ejnar Hertzsprung,
Harlow Shapley, Charles Young, Robert
Atkinson, Seth Chandler, Theodore
Dunham, Jr, and G C McVittie.

SANDBURG, CARL

DE —UNIVERSITY OF DELAWARE, Hugh
M Morris Library, S College Ave, Newark,
19711. T Stuart Dick, Special Collections
Holdings: Cat Mss Pix
Notes: Manuscripts, etc, incl literary
correspondence.
IL —NEWBERRY LIBRARY, 60 W Walton
St, Chicago, 60610. Diana Haskell, Cur of
Modern Mss
Holdings: Cat Mss Pix
Notes: Includes the Oliver R Barrett
collection.
IL —UNIVERSITY OF ILLINOIS,
URBANA/CHAMPAIGN, Library, Rare
Book Room, 346 Library, 61801.
Norman B Brown, Asst Dir for Special
Collections; N Frederick Nash, Librn
Holdings: Vols 6349 Cat Mss Pix
Notes: Extensive collection, described in:
Catalog of the Rare Book Room, (Boston: G
K Hall, 1972). Supplement (1978). Incl Carl
Sandburg's papers, mss, pictures,
memorabilia, etc. Much on Abraham
Lincoln, Approximately 50,000 mss (90
linear ft).
IN —INDIANA UNIVERSITY, Lilly Library,
Seventh St, Bloomington, 47405. William R
Cagle, Librn
Notes: Writings by author Carl Sandburg.
IN —INDIANA STATE UNIVERSITY,
Cunningham Memorial Library, Dept of
Rare Books & Special Collections, Terre
Haute, 47809. Lawrence J McCrank, Head
Notes: The Debs Collection consists of
aprox 7000 pieces of correspondence
between Theodore Debs (brother of E V)
and other persons, such as Sinclair Lewis,
Upton Sinclair, Ethel Barrymore, Emma
Goldman, Robert G Ingersoll, Carl
Sandburg, Norman Thomas, Sacco and
Vanzetti and many others. Many of the
letters are from E V Debs to his brother; a
good portion of these are from the federal
penitentiary at Atlanta. Entire
correspondence file has been microfilmed.
750 pamphlets cover all aspects of the labor
movement, socialism and radical thought
from the 19th century to appprox 1950. A
collection ca 200 related books is also

SANDBURG, CARL (cont.)

housed in the collection. See: J Robert Constantine and Gail Malmgreen, eds, *The Papers of Eugene V Debs, 1834-1945. A Guide to the Microfilm Edition.* NY: Microfilming Corp of America, 1983 (University Microfilms is the new distributer).

NV —UNIVERSITY OF NEVADA, RENO, University Library, Special Collections Dept, Reno, 89557. Robert E Blesse, Head
Holdings: // Vols (87) Cat Other appearances 685 Cat
Notes: Includes individual works by author in all editions including translations; also prefaces, introductions, published correspondence, appearances in anthologies, periodicals, etc. Bibliographical research collection, part of Modern Authors Collection.

NC —UNIVERSITY OF NORTH CAROLINA, CHARLOTTE, J Murrey Atkins Library, UNCC Station, Charlotte, 28223. Robert F Brabham Jr, Special Collections Librn
Holdings: Cat Mss Pix
Notes: Part of the Harry Golden Papers which incl correspondence, speeches, clippings, criticism, etc, much of it collected by Golden in writing his 1961 biography of his friend.

PA —DICKINSON COLLEGE, Boyd Lee Spahr Library, W High St, Carlisle, 17013. Yates M Forbis, Dir
Holdings: Mss Pix Audiotapes
Notes: The Sandburg-Champlain collection of mss, letters, books, photographs, and memorabilia. Inc. some 200 vols with references to Sandburg or his friends, or contain pieces written by Sandburg. Memorabilia incl eye-shade, audiotapes, etc by Sandburg and Miss Chanplain.

VA —UNIVERSITY OF VIRGINIA, Alderman Library, Manuscripts Dept, Charlottesville, 22901. Edmund Berkeley Jr, Cur
Notes: Incl works, mss, unpublished poems and letters. The Quincy Wright Sandburg Collection.

VA —UNIVERSITY OF VIRGINIA, Alderman Library, Clifton Waller Barrett Collection, Charlottesville, 22901. Joan St C Crane, Cur of American Literature Collections
Holdings: Vols 150 Cat Mss Pix
Notes: Works by and about him. Includes important early mss, letters. Published description: *Carl Sandburg, Philip Green Wright, and the Asgard Press, 1900-1910--A Descriptive Catalogue of Early Books, Manuscripts, and Letters in the Clifton Waller Barrett Library,* comp by Joan St C Crane (Charlottesville: Published for the Associates of the University of Virginia Library by the University Press of Virginia, [1975]).

SANDBURG, HELGA

MA —BOSTON UNIVERSITY, Mugar Memorial Library, Special Collections Dept, 771 Commonwealth Ave, Boston, 02215. Howard B Gotlieb, Dir
Holdings: Cat Mss Pix
Notes: Mss, correspondence, etc collected in depth; incl publications by or about.

SANDERFORD, GHENT

TX —NORTH TEXAS STATE UNIVERSITY, Archives, NT Station Box 5188, Denton, 76203. Robert LaForte, University Archivist
Notes: Part of Oral History Collection. Interviews and documents. Sanderford was secretary to Governor Miriam A "Ma" Ferguson. Some material concerning impeachment of James E "Pa" Ferguson.

SANDERS, GOV. CARL

GA —UNIVERSITY OF GEORGIA, Libraries, Special Collections Division, Athens, 30602. Vesta Lee Gordon, Asst Dir for Special Collections
Notes: Collection contains 1394.8 linear feet

of mss: papers of US Senator Richard B Russell; US Congressmen John W Davis, Maston O'Neal, Robert G Stephens Jr, John L Pilcher, Dudley M Hughes; Governors Hoke Smith, Lester Maddox, Carl Sanders.

SANDERS, ED

CT —UNIVERSITY OF CONNECTICUT, Library, Storrs, 06268. George F Butterick, Cur of Literary Archives
Holdings: Mss Audiotapes
Notes: Repository for his papers.

SANDERS, WHITEY

NE —UNIVERSITY OF NEBRASKA-LINCOLN, Don L Love Library, University Archives and Special Collections, Lincoln, 68588. Joseph G Svoboda, University Archivist
Holdings: Vols (1000) // Cat Mss Maps Pix Audiotapes 16mm Films

KY —WESTERN KENTUCKY UNIVERSITY, Kentucky Library, Bowling Green, 42101. Riley Handy, Head, Special Collections; Connie Mills, Maps & Music Librn; Nancy Baird, Photographs Librn; Nancy Solley, Conservation Librn
Holdings: Vols (25,000) Cat Mss Maps Pix Microforms
Notes: Besides Kentucky history, other strengths are Mammoth Cave, South Union Shakers, Kentucky religion; and steamboat photos (3300 cataloged pictures); 8000 Kentucky postal cards, etc.

SANDOZ, MARI

Notes: The Mari Sandoz Collection consists of four basic parts. The first contains correspondence files, 25,000 letters in all, including letters received from 1925 on and carbon copies of letters sent. The correspondence files are a rich source of information about the author's life and career, creative writing, and Plains Indian and western American history. The second portion of the collection is the author's personal library of books and periodicals, many annotated. Part three contains the author's published works, including most of the editions, foreign and domestic and some unpublished manuscripts as well. Many of the early drafts of books, copy-edited manuscripts, and galley and proofs are also contained in this portion of the collection. The final part of the collections consists of the author's resource files, research and reading notes, clippings, and related materials. These materials fill over fifty standard letter boxes. In addition, the prepared 45,000 index cards refering to information contained both in and out of the collection.

TX —SOUTHERN METHODIST UNIVERSITY, DeGolyer Library, Box 396, SMU, Dallas, 75275. Clifton H Jones, Dir
Holdings: Vols (80,000) Cat Mss Maps Pix Slides Microforms
Notes: First editions of prominent authors; also of books in subject emphasis collections. All subjects listed in this vol are strong. Numerous collections of personal papers relating to subjects also.

SANDUSKY VALLEY

OH —RUTHERFORD B HAYES LIBRARY, 1337 Hayes Ave, Fremont, 43420. Watt P Marchman, Dir
Holdings: Vols 450 Cat Mss Maps Pix Slides Microforms
Notes: Especially the Sandusky Valley area.

SANE see Committee for a Sane Nuclear Policy (Sane)

SANGER, ELLIOT M.

†NY —COLUMBIA UNIVERSITY LIBRARIES, Butler Library, Rare Book and Manuscript Library, 535 W 114 St, New York, 10027.
Notes: Papers of Elliot M Sanger, co-founder, executive vice-president and general manager of radio station WQXR in New York City. Also incl his bound file of the complete WQXR *Program Guide* from June 1936 through Dec 1963.

SANGER, MARGARET

DC —LIBRARY OF CONGRESS, Manuscript Division, Washington, 20540. John C Broderick, Chief
Notes: Papers of Margaret (Higgins) Sanger.

IL —SOUTHERN ILLINOIS UNIVERSITY, CARBONDALE, Delyte W Morris Library, Special Collections Dept, Carbondale, 62901. David V Koch, Cur of Special Collections; Louisa Bowen, Cur of Manuscripts
Holdings: Cat Mss
Notes: Papers and correspondence of Theodore A Schroeder, constitutional lawyer and founder, with Lincoln Steffens, of the Free Speech League, a forerunner of the American Civil Liberties Union. Contains extensive correspondence with Comstock, Gompers, Debs, H Ellis, Sanger, Sinclair, John Dewey, Darrow, Mencken, A G Hays, Emma Goldman, W E B Dubois, etc. Incl several thousand letters; notes and mss; records of legal cases and extensive files relating to the early history of psychiatry.

NY —UNIVERSITY OF ROCHESTER, Rush Rhees Library, Department of Rare Books and Special Collections, Rochester, 14627. Peter Dzwonkoski, Librn
Holdings: Cat Mss
Notes: Correspondence, reports, articles written by Wile on birth control (including many letters from Margaret Sanger), left and right handedness, sex education, child development, and mental hygiene.

SANGER, MARJORY BARTLETT

SC —COLLEGE OF CHARLESTON LIBRARY, Special Collections Dept, Charleston, 29401.
Notes: Contains 42 illustrations by John Henry Dick for Marjory Bartlett Sanger's *World of the Great White Heron* (1967).

SANITARY AFFAIRS see Public Health

SANITARY ENGINEERING

KY —UNIVERSITY OF KENTUCKY, Robert E Shaver Library of Engineering, 355 Anderson Hall, Lexington, 40506. Russell H Powell, Engineering Librn
Holdings: Vols (48,000) Cat Microforms

MD —NATIONAL LIBRARY OF MEDICINE, 8600 Rockville Pike, Bethesda, 20209. Harold M Schoolinam, Actg Dir
Budget: ($46,400)
Notes: Correspondence of George E Waring, pioneering American sanitary engineer of the 19th century.

NY —ENGINEERING SOCIETIES LIBRARY, 345 E 47 St, New York, 10017. S Kirk Cabeen, Dir
Holdings: Vols 250,000 Cat Maps 16mm Films Microforms
Notes: One of the largest, most comprehensive engineering libraries in the world. Covers all engineering disciplines; particularly strong in electrical and electronic, mechanical, mining and metallurgical, petroleum, chemical, industrial, air conditioning and refrigeration engineering. Incl Wheeler Collection of early materials on magnetism and electricity. 125, 000 bound periodical volumes; 10,000 maps; 5000 serial subscriptions (many foreign-language). Virtually all materials abstracted in *Engineering Index* (1884-date) are incl in

SANITARY ENGINEERING (cont.)

Library. Noncirculating, except to members of professional engineering societies Library, New York, *Classed Subject Catalog and Index* (Boston: G K Hall, 1963); and *Supplements*, 1-10, 1964-1973.

PA —FRANKLIN INSTITUTE LIBRARY, 20 & The Parkway, Philadelphia, 19103. Miriam Padusis, Dir; Charles Wilt, Readers Servs Librn
Holdings: Vols (300,000) Cat Maps Pix Microforms

SANITATION

CA —STANFORD UNIVERSITY LIBRARIES, Lane Medical Library, Stanford University, Medical Center, Stanford, 94305. Peter Stangl, Librn
Notes: Papers of Adelaide Brown, sanitation and prenatal care.

TX —HOUSTON ACADEMY OF MEDICINE-TEXAS MEDICAL CENTER, Library, Jesse H Jones Library Bldg, Houston, 77030. Elizabeth Borst White, Special Collections Librn
Holdings: Vols (900) Cat
Notes: Mading Collection on Public Health. English-language materials dealing with American public health conditions before 1925. Emphasis is on epidemiology and infectious diseases (excluding venereal disease), incl material on sanitation and climatology. Federal, state or municipal reports on health, mortality and sanitation are included. Also 500 pamphlets.

SANSKRIT LANGUAGE AND LITERATURE

CA —UNIVERSITY OF CALIFORNIA, LOS ANGELES, Research Library, Indo/Pacific Collection, 405 Hilgard Ave, Los Angeles, 90024. Edward Shreeves, Chairman, Bibliographers Group; Charlotte Spence, Indo/Pacific Bibliographer
Holdings: Vols Cat Mss Maps Pix Microforms
Notes: The South Asian collection has been developed on two levels. On the research level it focuses on (1) the cultural, economic, political and social history of India from about 1859 to 1947; (2) linguistic and literary studies, with particular emphasis given to Sanskrit and Pali; and (3) the history of the Portuguese experience in South Asia. On the teaching level, materials are collected which relate to India before 1859, and from 1947 to date, as well as materials relating to the other political entities of South Asia. A description of the South Asian collection is included in the May, 1977 issue of *The Librarian*, and in *South Asian Library Resources in North America* (1975).

CT —YALE UNIVERSITY, Box 1603A, Yale Station, New Haven, 06520.

HI —UNIVERSITY OF HAWAII, Library, 2550 The Mall, Honolulu, 96822. Joyce Wright, Head, Asia Collection; Masato Matsu, Head, East Asia Vernacular Collection
Holdings: Vols 75,215 Cat Microforms
Notes: The Asia Collection holds material from and relating to Bangladesh, India, Nepal, Pakistan, and Sri Lanka in western and Asian languages. South Asian languages currently acquired: Bengali, Hindi, Marathi, Nepali, Pali, Prakrit, Sanskrit, Tamil. Period emphasis: social sciences and the humanities (literature, economics, history, religion/philosophy). Holdings are supplemented by a large uncataloged backlog, much of it accessible through the Library of Congress Accessions Lists for the area and by over 7000 cataloged titles in the main library collection. South *Asian Library Resources in North America: A Survey Prepared for the Boston Conference, 1974*, ed by M L P Patterson (Zug, Switzerland: Tutes Documentation Company, 1975). (Bibliotheca Asiatica 12-), "University of Hawaii," pp 103-114.

MD —JOHNS HOPKINS UNIVERSITY, Milton S Eisenhower Library, Charles & 34

Sts, Baltimore, 21218. Ann S Gwyn, Assistant Dir for Special Collections
Holdings: Vols 3000// Cat Mss
Notes: Very complete collection, but not up-to-date.

MA —HARVARD UNIVERSITY LIBRARY, Widener Library, Cambridge, 02138.
Holdings: Cat Mss
Notes: Research collection supplemented by Seminar Library (2584 vols) in Widener building.

MI —UNIVERSITY OF MICHIGAN, Graduate Library, South Asian Dept, Ann Arbor, 48109. Om P Sharma, Librn
Holdings: Vols (365,000) Cat Maps Slides Microforms
Notes: The major emphasis is on social sciences and humanities. Besides materials in classical languages, South Asian vernaculars being retained are Hindi, Bengali, Urdu, Marathi and Tamil; strong in classical languages, especially Sanskrit, Pali, and Prakrit.

MI —MICHIGAN STATE UNIVERSITY, International Library, South and Southeast Asia Collection, East Lansing, 48824. Clinton Lockert, Bibliographer
Holdings: Vols 55,700 // Cat Mss Maps Audiotapes Microforms
Notes: Serials and monographs of South Asia received on PL 480 for India, Pakistan, Sri Lanka, and Nepal since 1968. Emphasis is upon social sciences, humanities, and science. Areas of strength are anthropology and rural development. This subject has been de-emphasized, additions are not being made.

MO —UNIVERSITY OF MISSOURI-COLUMBIA, Ellis Library, Ninth and Lowry, Columbia, 65201. Murari Lal Nagar, Librn
Holdings: Vols 100,000 Maps Microforms
Notes: The South Asia Studies Program at the University of Missouri-Columbia, is an interdepartmental, multi-disciplinary area studies program on India, Pakistan, Bangladesh, Sri Lanka and Nepal. Depository for the PL480 Program of the Library of Congress in many languages from South Asia. There are library resources in Sanskrit, Hindi, Bengali, Panjabi, and Malayalam. The library is particularly strong in Baroda, Bengal and the Punjab.

NY —NEW YORK PUBLIC LIBRARY, Oriental Div, Fifth Ave & 42 St, New York, 10018. E Christian Filstrup, Chief
Holdings: Cat Mss Microforms
Budget: ($56,455)
Notes: Published catalog of holdings.

NY —UNIVERSITY OF ROCHESTER, Rush Rhees Library, Rochester, 14627. Datta S Kharbas, Head
Holdings: Vols 100,000 Cat Maps Microforms
Notes: Area studies collection on East Asia and South Asia. Major emphasis is on social sciences and humanities. Over 57,000 volumes on East Asia, out of which 29,000 volumes are in Chinese and 15,000 in Japanese. Extensive holdings on Chinese and Japanese histories. Catalog of East Asian collection consisting of Chinese and Japanese language holdings published in 1968, with two subsequent supplements. Over 33,000 volumes on South Asia. Considerable depth in social sciences, history, politics and anthropology. Extensive holdings in Sanskrit, Hindi, and Marathi.

OH —CLEVELAND PUBLIC LIBRARY, Fine Arts and Special Collections Department, 325 Superior Ave, Cleveland, 44114. Alice N Loranth, Head
Holdings: Vols 3200 Cat Mss
Notes: One of the largest Sanskrit collections in the United States, emphasizing linguistics, classic text editions and their translations. Separate catalog of main entries for titles in Sanskrit (2810 vols) is maintained.
See also entries under India; Indic Languages and Literatures; Oriental Languages and Literatures.

TX —UNIVERSITY OF TEXAS LIBRARIES, Asian Collection, PO Box P, Austin, 78712. Kevin Lin, Asian Librn; Merry Burlingham, South Asian Librn
Holdings: Vols (58,000) Cat Microforms
Notes: Materials in Hindi, Sanskrit, Urdu,

Prakrit, and Pali (acquired chiefly through the Special Foreign Acquisitions Program) and selected English-language materials, incl Indian censuses and district gazetters and Pakistani censuses.

WA —UNIVERSITY OF WASHINGTON LIBRARIES, Suzzallo Library, South Asian Section, Seattle, 98195. Irene M Joshi, Librn
Holdings: Vols (127,000) Maps Microforms Audiotapes
Notes: A nationally important collection of 127,000 vols incl approx 45,000 vols in South Asian languages and 22,000 uncataloged titles. The collection is especially strong in anthropology, classical Sanskrit literature, economic history, economics, history, linguistics, philosophy and political science. The microform holdings incl the Indian census from 1881, newspapers from 1838, legislative debates from 1854, development plans and serial titles. Twenty-eight newspapers and nearly 5000 serial titles are received from history, politics and government, Near Eastern and East Asian studies which also support South Asian studies. The Law Library has a collection of South Asian legal materials.

SANSOME, WILLIAM

NV —UNIVERSITY OF NEVADA, RENO, University Library, Special Collections Dept, Reno, 89557. Robert E Blesse, Head
Holdings: Vols (59) Cat
Notes: Includes individual works by author in all editions including translations; also prefaces, introductions, published correspondence, appearances in anthologies, periodicals, etc. Bibliographical research collection, part of Modern Authors Collection. Other appearances 150 cataloged.

SANTA ANNA, ANTONIO LOPEZ DE

DC —GEORGETOWN UNIVERSITY, Library, Special Collections Div, 37 & O Sts NW, Washington, 20057. George M Barringer, Special Collections Librn; Nicholas B Sheetz, Mss Librn
Holdings: Vols (100) Cat Mss Pix
Notes: Includes papers of Mexican Emperor Iturbide; President and General Santa Anna; and of Revs Richard Tierney, SJ, Edmund A Walsh, SJ, and Wilfrid Parsons, SJ.

IN —INDIANA UNIVERSITY, Lilly Library, Seventh St, Bloomington, 47405. William R Cagle, Librn
Holdings: Vols (10,000) // Cat Mss
Notes: Historical pronouncements and documents by the leaders of the movement of Mexican independence. Partially cataloged.
See also entry under Mexico - History

KS —SANTA FE TRAIL CENTER, Library, Rte 3, Larned, 67550. Kim Keiswetter, Archivist/Education Dir
Holdings: Uncat Mss Maps Pix Slides
Budget: ($2500)
Notes: Archives and history of Pawnee County, Kansas and the Santa Fe Trail. Strong slide and picture collections.
See also entry under Santa Fe Trail

SANTA FE TRAIL

KS —SANTA FE TRAIL CENTER, Library, Rte 3, Larned, 67550. Kim Keiswetter, Archivist/Education Dir
Notes: Archives and history of Pawnee County, Kansas, and the Santa Fe Trail. Strong slide and picture collections.

SANTAYANA, GEORGE

†IL —SOUTHERN ILLINOIS UNIVERSITY, CARBONDALE, Library, Special Collections Dept, Carbondale, 62901.
Notes: Archives of the Library of Living Philosophers, a publishing project founded by Paul Arthur Schilpp in 1938 to provide a forum for contemporary philosophers to reply to their critics. Incl correspondence from John Dewey, George Santayana, Alfred North Whitehead, G E Moore, and Albert Einstein.

MA —HARVARD UNIVERSITY LIBRARY, Houghton Library, Cambridge, 02138.

SANTAYANA, GEORGE (cont.)

Rodney G Dennis, Cur of Manuscripts
Holdings: Cat Mss
NY —COLUMBIA UNIVERSITY
LIBRARIES, Rare Book & Manuscript
Library, 801 Butler Library, 535 W 114 St,
New York, 10027. Kenneth A Lohf, Librn
Holdings: Mss
Notes: Extensive collection of mss, papers,
publications, etc. 870 items. Restricted use.
ON —UNIVERSITY OF WATERLOO,
Library, Waterloo, N2L 3G1, Can. Susan
Bellingham, Special Collections Librn
Holdings: Vols 350
Notes: Collection consists of Santayana's
personal library. Most books contain
extensive annotations. Also contains copies
of books by and about Santayana. Collection
described in *A Catalogue of the Library of
George Santayana in the University of
Waterloo Library.* University of Waterloo
Library Bibliography #8, 1980.

SANTEE, ROSS

CA —AZUSA PACIFIC COLLEGE,
Marshburn Memorial Library, Citrus &
Alosta, Azusa, 91702. Edward Peterman,
Librn
Holdings: Vols (150) Uncat
Notes: The Odo B Stade Collection of
First Editions. No photocopying.

SANTERRE FAMILY

TX —UNIVERSITY OF TEXAS,
ARLINGTON, Library, PO Box 19497,
Arlington, 76019. Chas Colley, Dir Special
Collections
Holdings: // Mss
Notes: Santerre Collection. This is the
library of the Santerre family who emigrated
from France, Belgium, and Switzerland in
1855 to join the Utopian Socialist colony of
Victor Prosper Considerant in what is now
Dallas, Texas. Typical selection of books of a
middle-class, well-educated family of the
period. Some title deeds, legal papers, family
letters, first Paris editions of works of
Considerant, Charles Fourier; French
translations of English classics, devotional
works. See George H Santerre, *White Cliffs
of Dallas* (Dallas, Texas: Book Craft, 1955).

SARCOMA see Tumors

SARDI'S RESTAURANT

NY —NEW YORK PUBLIC LIBRARY,
Performing Arts Research Center, Billy Rose
Theatre Collection, 111 Amsterdam Ave,
New York, 10023. Dorothy L Swerdlove,
Cur
Holdings: Cat
Notes: Incl approx 270 original theatre
caricatures by Alex Gard from the
restaurant.

SARGEANT, WINTHROP

MA —BOSTON UNIVERSITY, Mugar
Memorial Library, Special Collections Dept,
771 Commonwealth Ave, Boston, 02215.
Howard B Gotlieb, Dir
Holdings: Cat Mss
Notes: Mss, correspondence, etc collected in
depth; incl publications by or about.

SARGENT, FRANCES HERRIOT

RI —BROWN UNIVERSITY, John Hay
Library, 20 Prospect St, Providence, 02912.
Mark N Brown, Cur Mss
Holdings: Mss
Notes: Papers of William O Fuller (1828-
1910), music teacher of Providence,
comprising letters 1848 from Europe, incl a
letter from Franz Liszt; papers of Johann
Christian Gottlieb Graupner (1767-1836)
and John Rowe Parker (fl 1820s) collected
by Horace Mason Reynolds, relating to the
music-publishing business in Boston, 1802-
1838; papers of the American folklorist

Mellinger Edward Henry (1873-1946)
relating to his research and publications on
American folk-songs 1910-1942; papers,
1912-1948, of Providence composer Hugh
Frederick MacColl (1885-1953); papers of
Frances Herriot Sargent, stage manager for
"Porgy" and "Porgy and Bess", relating to
productions of these, 1928-1942.

SARGENT, HELEN D., 1904-1959

KS —MENNINGER FOUNDATION,
Archives, 5600 W Sixth St, Box 829,
Topeka, 66601. Alice Brand, Librn; Mark
West, Archivist
Notes: 9 boxes, 1934-1959. Incl in her
papers are mss, research notes, and
correspondence.

SARGENT, PAMELA

†PA —TEMPLE UNIVERSITY LIBRARY,
Philadelphia, 19122. Thomas M Whitehead,
Librn
Notes: More than 100 cubic ft of mss, incl
papers of Michael Bishop, Ben Bova, Jack
Dann, Gardner Dozois, Lloyd Eshback, Tom
Purdom, Pamela Sargent, John Varley, and
George Zebrowski.

SARNOFF, DAVID

NJ —RCA CORP, David Sarnoff Research
Center, Library, PO Box 432, Princeton,
08540. Wendy Chu, Librn
Holdings: Vols (800) Cat Mss Pix
Phonorecords Audiotapes 16mm Films
Microforms
Notes: Memorabilia and papers.

SAROYAN, ARAM, 1943-

CA —UNIVERSITY OF CALIFORNIA, LOS
ANGELES, Research Library, Dept of
Special Collections, 405 Hilgard Ave, Los
Angeles, 90024. Edward Shreeves,
Chairman, Bibliographers Group; David S
Zeidberg, Head
Holdings: Vols 30 Mss
Notes: Incl 12 linear feet of mss and letters.
No photocopying.
BC —UNIVERSITY OF VICTORIA,
McPherson Library, Victoria, V8W 3H5,
Can.

SAROYAN, WILLIAM

CA —CALIFORNIA STATE UNIVERSITY,
FRESNO, Henry Madden Library, Dept of
Special Collections, Fresno, 93740. Ronald J
Mahoney, Head
Holdings: Vols 500 Cat
Notes: All editions and languages by and
about Saroyan. Partially cataloged. Incl
clippings, periodical articles and playbills.
CA —FRESNO COUNTY FREE LIBRARY,
2420 Mariposa St, Fresno, 93721. Linda J
Goff, Local History Librn
Holdings: Vols 783 Cat Mss Pix
Notes: Books by and about him. Also
holograph, ephemera (such as newspaper
clippings, periodical articles, transcript of a
radio interview, play programs, portraits,
dust jackets, broadsides), musical scores,
phonorecords, and an unpublished typescript
of three plays. The library maintains a
separate catalog and a separate shelf list for
the Saroyan Collection, in the Reference
Department. There is, in addition, a printed
annotated catalog of the collection as it was
when acquired by the library.
CA —UNIVERSITY OF CALIFORNIA, LOS
ANGELES, Research Library, Dept of
Special Collections, 405 Hilgard Ave, Los
Angeles, 90024. Edward Shreeves,
Chairman, Bibliographers Group; David S
Zeidberg, Head
NV —UNIVERSITY OF NEVADA, RENO,
University Library, Special Collections Dept,
Reno, 89557. Robert E Blesse, Head
Holdings: // Vols 146 Cat Other
appearances 375 Cat
Notes: Includes individual works by author
in all editions including translations; also
prefaces, introductions, published
correspondence, appearances in anthologies,

periodicals, etc. Bibliographical research
collection, part of Modern Authors
Collection.
NY —COLUMBIA UNIVERSITY
LIBRARIES, Rare Book & Manuscript
Library, 801 Butler Library, 535 W 114 St,
New York, 10027. Kenneth A Lohf, Librn
Notes: Forty years of literary
correspondence between the Harold Matson
Literary Agency and numerous notable
authors. Restricted use.
PA —BALCH INSTITUTE FOR ETHNIC
STUDIES, Library, 18 S Seventh St,
Philadelphia, 19106. R Joseph Anderson,
Library Dir

SASKATCHEWAN—HISTORY

SK —MOOSE JAW PUBLIC LIBRARY,
Archives, 461 Langdon Crescent, Moose
Jaw, S6H 0X6, Can. Fay Hutchinson
Holdings: Vols 2760 Cat 3500 Mss Maps Pix
Slides Microforms VF
Budget: $2400
Notes: Emphasis on Moose Jaw and
surrounding area.
SK —SASKATCHEWAN ARCHIVES
BOARD, University of Regina, Regina, S4S
0A2, Can. Ian E Wilson, Provincial
Archivist
Holdings: Mss Maps Pix Audiotapes
Videotapes 16mm Films Microforms
Budget: $900,000
Notes: The Saskatchewan Archives Board
attempts to document the history of the area
now the Province of Saskatchewan and its
communities through all archival media.
Collection incl 5800 meters of mss, 4800
maps, 250,000 pictures, 10,000 architectural
drawings, 4400 audiotapes, 1648 16mm films
and 9400 microfilm reels. Individual
collections are listed in *The Union List of
Manuscripts in Canadian Repositories*
(Ottawa, 1975 & 1976). Detailed catalogs,
indexes and inventories are available in two
offices. (Second office is located at
University of Saskatchewan, Saskatoon, Sask
S7N 0W0 Canada.)
SK —SASKATCHEWAN LEGISLATIVE
LIBRARY, 234 Legislative Bldg, Regina,
S4S 0B3, Can. Marian Powell, Librn
Holdings: Vols 300 Cat
Notes: Western Canadiana and Canadian
history.

SASS, HERBERT RAVENEL

SC —COLLEGE OF CHARLESTON
LIBRARY, Special Collections Dept,
Charleston, 29401.
Notes: Correspondence within the Lancelot
Minor Harris Papers.

SASSOON, SIEGFRIED

NV —UNIVERSITY OF NEVADA, RENO,
University Library, Special Collections Dept,
Reno, 89557. Robert E Blesse, Head
Holdings: // Vols (90) Cat Other
appearances 360 Cat
Notes: Includes individual works by author
in all editions including translations; also
prefaces, introductions, published
correspondence, appearances in anthologies,
periodicals, etc. Bibliographical research
collection, part of Modern Authors
Collection.
NY —ALFRED UNIVERSITY, Herrick
Memorial Library, Alfred, 14802. June E
Brown, Head Librn
Notes: The Evelyn Tennyson Openhym
Collection of modern British literature and
social history.
NY —HOFSTRA UNIVERSITY, Library,
1000 Fulton Ave, Hempstead, 11550.
Charles R Andrews, Dean of Library
Services
OK —UNIVERSITY OF TULSA, McFarlin
Library, Dept of Rare Books and Special
Collections, 600 S College, Tulsa, 74104.
David Farmer, Dir; Toby Murray, Archivist;
Caroline Swinson, Cur of Manuscripts & Art
Notes: The Len Weaver Collection of
Siegfried Sassoon, incl all the published
writings, and some very rare early
publications. A number of books came from

SASSOON, SIEGFRIED (cont.)

Sassoon's own library, while others are inscribed to such friends as Edmund Gosse, Edward Marsh, Edith Sitwell, and E M Forster.

ON —MCMASTER UNIVERSITY, Mills Memorial Library, Div of Archives & Research Collections, Hamilton, L8S 4L6, Can. G R Hill, Univ Librn
Holdings: // Cat Mss
Notes: H G Wells' correspondence with Siegfried Sassoon, 1916-1942, incomplete ms drafts of "The Mind of the Race," "Mr Britting Sees It Through," "The Two Ways." Annotated typescripts of "The Two Ways," "The Mind of the Race," "Scientific War," "Civilians in Warfare" and carbon typescript of "The Problem of the Troublesome Collaborator," as well as large book and serial collection of Wells' writings.

SATAN see Devil Worship; Satanism

SATANISM

CA —GRADUATE THEOLOGICAL UNION LIBRARY, New Religious Movements Research Collection, Public Services and Special Collections Dept, 2400 Ridge Road, Berkeley, 94709. Diane Choquette, Dept Head
Holdings: Vols (3000) Mss Pix
Notes: Begun in 1977, the collection focuses on religious movements new to America since 1960, and unorthodox religious movements resurgent since 1960. American forms of Hinduism, Buddhism, Sikhism, and Sufism are included along with occultism, Neo-Paganism, esoteric and alternative forms of Christianity, feminist spirituality, and human potential movements having a spiritual aspect. Legal issues, such as deprogramming, and the question of church/state relations are an important part of the collection. The Library is a depository for publications of the Unification Church in America, the Church of Scientology, and the International Society for Krishna Consciousness (America). The responses of mainstream religions and concerned citizens groups are also included. Besides 3000 monographs, the library has 400 periodical titles, 200 posters from the San FranciscoBay Area, 1965-77, 300 research papers, and 31 linear feet of ephemera.

CA —LOS ANGELES PUBLIC LIBRARY, Philosophy & Religion Dept, 630 W Fifth St, Los Angeles, 90071. Marilyn C Wherley, Librn
Holdings: Vols 700 Cat
Budget: ($60,000)
Notes: Comprehensive coverage of popular and scholarly works on all aspects of the occult including black magic, witchcraft, demonology, paranormal occurances, psychical research and metaphysics. Includes many serials, periodicals and special indexes.

CT —LEE ASH, (personal collection), 66 Humiston Dr, Bethany, 06525.
Holdings: Mss Maps Pix

IL —UNIVERSITY OF ILLINOIS, URBANA/CHAMPAIGN, Library, University Archives, 19 Library, 1408 W Gregory Drive, Urbana, 61801. Maynard Brichford, University Archivist
Holdings: Vols (5000) Cat
Budget: ($7000)
Notes: The Mandeville Collection in Parapsychology and Occult Sciences. Titles in the Merten J Mandeville Collection are purchased by funds from an endowment provided specifically for the collection on its establishment in 1966 by Merten J Mandeville, Professor Emeritus of Management, who donated 400 vols from his personal library as the nucleus of the collection. There are currently about 5000 titles in the collection, supplemented by related materials in the general collection. Topics include astrology, extrasensory perception, yoga, magic, satanism, faith healing, hypnosis, Eastern religions, witchcraft, fortune telling, reincarnation, flying saucers, ghosts, dreams, numerology,

graphology, and mysticism. Biographies and reference books are a part of the collection as are journals devoted to the scientific study of parapsychology.

IN —INDIANAPOLIS-MARION COUNTY PUBLIC LIBRARY, Social Sciences Div, PO Box 211, Indianapolis, 46206. Lois R Laube, Head
Holdings: Vols 358 Cat
Notes: Restricted use. No photocopying.

MI —MICHIGAN STATE UNIVERSITY, Libraries, Special Collections Div, East Lansing, 48824. Jannette Fiore, Librn
Holdings: Vols 1440// Uncat Mss
Notes: Works from 15th to 19th centuries on crinimology, criminal law and jurisprudence, including witchcraft, demonology, et al, chiefly in German and Latin.

SATELLITE BROADCASTING

IL —UNIVERSITY OF ILLINOIS, URBANA/CHAMPAIGN, Library, Communications Library, 122 Gregory Hall, Urbana, 61801. Nancy Allen, Librn
Holdings: Vols (18,000) Cat
Budget: ($27,000)
Notes: Studies of telephone, teletext, videotex, cable and satellite systems, and other electronic media.

NJ —AT&T BELL LABORATORIES, Libraries and Information Systems Center, 600 Mountain Ave, Murray Hill, 07974. W D Penniman, Dir
Holdings: Vols (273,100) Cat Mss Audiotapes Videotapes Microforms
Budget: ($670,000)
Notes: Restricted use to AT&T employees. Catalogs/Indexes: Bell Laboratories Library Network and Book Serial Catalogs; Bell Laboratories Translations. Bell Laboratories Library Network with New Jersey libraries located in Holmdel, Murray Hill, Piscataway, Whippany, Princeton, Short Hills, Summit, West Long Branch, Crawford Hill; libraries also in Allentown, Pennsylvania; Reading, Pennsylvania; New York, New York; Atlanta, Georgia; Columbus, Ohio; Naperville, Illinois; Indianapolis, Indiana; North Andover, Massachusetts.

SATELLITE IMAGERY

†AZ —UNIVERSITY OF ARIZONA, Space Imagery Center, Lunar & Planetary Laboratory, Tucson, 85721. Gail G Georgenson, Librn
Notes: Planetary science. Interests incl Space Probs - Gemini; Apollo; Lunar Orbiter; Mariner 6, 7 9, 10; Pioneer 10 & 11; Viking 1 & 2. Regional Planetary Image Facilities are in Flagstaff, Ariz; Pasadena, Calif; Saint Louis, MO; Ithaca, NY; Providence, RI; Houston, Tex; Rome, Italy; London, England.

CA —UNIVERSITY OF CALIFORNIA, SANTA BARBARA, Map and Imagery Laboratory, Santa Barbara, 93106. Larry Carver, Dept Head
Notes: Worldwide coverage of Landsat imagery donated by US Dept of Agriculture Aerial Photography Field Office. Consists of 153,000 scenes, covering most of the earth's surface between the years 1975 and 1980. Incl 300,000 maps, 1800 atlases, 9 globes, 300 relief models, 1,500,000 satellite imagery and aerial photographs, 700 reference books and gazetteers, 25 serials (titles received), and 21,000 microforms.

SATELLITES, ARTIFICIAL see Artificial Satellites

SATIRE

†CT —UNIVERSITY OF CONNECTICUT LIBRARY, Special Collections Dept, Storrs, 06268. Richard H Schimmelpfeng, Dir of Special Collections
Notes: Good and unusual collection.

SATIRE, ENGLISH

KS —UNIVERSITY OF KANSAS, Kenneth Spencer Research Library, Special

Collections Dept, Lawrence, 66045. Alexandra Mason, Librn
Holdings: Vols 300 Cat Mss
Notes: In addition to Marlborough holdings throughout the 18th century collections, the department has particular strength in satire and panegyric on John Churchill, Duke of Marlborough, in the Robert Horn Collection (over 150 vols). See Hyde, Ann, The Queen's General: John Churchill, First Duke of Marlborough, 1650-1722, an exhibition... in the Kenneth Spencer Research Library (Lawrence: Univsersity of Kansas Libraries) 1972. Noncirculating.

SATIRE, POLITICAL see Political Satire

SATIRE, RUSSIAN

WI —UNIVERSITY OF WISCONSIN, MADISON, Memorial Library, Slavic Studies Collection, 728 State St, Madison, 53706. Aleksander Rolich, Bibliographer for Slavic Studies; Robert P Gakovich, Slavic Cataloger; Valdis J Zeps, Baltic Studies Center
Holdings: Cat
Notes: Russian Underground Collection. Materials in the Russian Underground Collection embrace the Russian Revolutionary Movement from 1825 to 1917. including a considerable number of Free Press publications. Among the 1500 titles are included about 100 journals, many political tracts, leaflets, broadsides and brochures of various political groups, largely socialist, religious nonconformists (L Tolstoi) and a large number of the satirical journals that appeared between 1905-1907. Restricted use: Rare Book Department.

SATSUMA

HI —UNIVERSITY OF HAWAII, Library, 2550 The Mall, Honolulu, 96822. Joyce Wright, Head, Asia Collection; Masato Matsu, Head, East Asia Vernacular Collection
Holdings: Vols 64,481 Cat Microforms
Notes: The Asia Collection includes materials from and relating to Japan in all languages. In addition to the cataloged Japanese language volumes (above), there are an estimated 15,000 not yet processed. No figures are available for western language volumes about Japan, which are supplemented by retrospective materials in the main library collection. Scope: social sciences and humanities. Subject strengths: Japanese history, especially Tokugawa period, Buddhism, Ryukyus and Satsuma (Sakamiaki Collection), Hokkaido. Catalog of the Glenn Shaw Collection at the East West Center Library, by H Arai & M Gibu, Honolulu, 1967 (East West Center Library Occasional Paper No 8); Research Resources on Hokkaido, Sakhalen and the Kuriles at the East-West Center Library, by M Matsui and K Shimanaka, Honolulu, 1967(East West Center Library Occasional Paper No 9); Ryukyuan Research Resources at the University of Hawaii, by Shunzo Sakamaki, Honolulu, 1965 (Ryukyuan Research Center. Research Series No 1).

SATURDAY EVENING POST (MAGAZINE)

VA —GEORGE MASON UNIVERSITY, Fenwick Library, Special Collections Dept, 4400 University Drive, Fairfax, 22030. Ruth Kerns, Public Services Librn
Notes: The Ollie Atkins Photographic Collection. Atkins, award-winning photographer with the Saturday Evening Post, was also White House photographer under several administrations. The collection incl more than 15,000 prints, negatives, contact sheets, slides and 4000 images covering subjects of historical, artistic and social significance from 1948 to 1968.

SAUDI ARABIA

CA —HOOVER INSTITUTION ON WAR, REVOLUTION & PEACE, Stanford

SAUDI ARABIA (cont.)

University, Stanford, 94305. Peter Duignan, Cur; Karen Fung, Deputy Cur
Holdings: Vols (100,000)
Notes: For full description of collection, see Hoover Institution entry under Near East.
VA —UNIVERSITY OF VIRGINIA, Alderman Library, Manuscripts Dept, Charlottesville, 22901. Edmund Berkeley Jr, Cur
Holdings: Cat Mss Pix
Notes: Papers of J Rives Childs, foreign sevice officer in Saudi Arabia, Yemen, Ethiopia, and Morocco, and Casanova scholar.

SAUER, CHRISTOPHER

PA —JUNIATA COLLEGE LIBRARY, Huntingdon, 16652. David Eyman, Dir
Holdings: Vols 5000// Cat Mss
Notes: Early Pennsylvania imprints, many in German. Large collection of imprints from Christopher Sauer's press. Early Brethren and other German sectarian (Schwenkfelders, Anabaptists) tracts from Pennsylvania and Europe. Several of the collections have been described in *American German Review* (1941), *Pennsylvania History* (1940, 1959), and *Pennsylvania Magazine* (1943).
PA —FREE LIBRARY OF PHILADELPHIA, Rare Book Dept, Logan Sq, Philadelphia, 19103. Marie E Korey, Rare Book Librn
Holdings: Uncat
Notes: 2400 books, pamphlets and broadsides in the German Language printed in the US and Canada from 1732 to 1850 for the use of the Pennsylvania Germans and their descendants. Numerous Christopher Sauer imprints.
SC —WOFFORD COLLEGE, Sandor Teszler Library, N Church St, Spartanburg, 29301. Frank J Anderson, Librn
Holdings: Vols 1247 Uncat
Notes: Haynes-Brown Hymnal Collection consists of all denominations of rare items and colonial imprints, incl Christopher Saur and Isaiah Thomas imprints. Collection is being augmented by Pierce Gault of Washington, DC.

SAUK INDIANS

IL —AUGUSTANA COLLEGE, Library, Rock Island, 61201. Marjorie M Miller, Special Collections Librn
Holdings: Vols 2000 Cat Mss
Notes: The John Hauberg Upper Mississippi Valley Collection. Incl strong collection of immigrant guide books for the Midwestern states. Fine collection relative to the Sauk and Fox tribes and Black Hawk in particular.
KS —UNIVERSITY OF KANSAS, Kenneth Spencer Research Library, Kansas Collection, Lawrence, 66045. Sheryl K Williams, Cur
Holdings: Vols (45,000) Cat Mss Pix
Notes: Several photographic collections devoted exclusively to American Indian subjects, collections of personal papers, contemporary American Indian periodicals, 19th century tracts and treatises. Wars, missionary contracts, reservation life, etc in Kansas, Oklahoma and Nebraska. Good holdings treating Potawatomie Indians (Prairie Band), Sauk, Fox, Osage.

SAULSBURY, WILLARD

DE —UNIVERSITY OF DELAWARE, Hugh M Morris Library, S College Ave, Newark, 19711. T Stuart Dick, Special Collections
Holdings: // Cat Mss
Notes: Incl business, legal, personal and political papers of Willard Saulsbury, spanning 1850-1927. Saulsbury was a US Senator from Delaware. Incl letters and telegrams from Woodrow Wilson relating to the work of the Democratic National Committee, party politics, etc. (1912-1918).

SAULTEAUX INDIANS see Chippewa Indians

SAUNDERS, HENRY SCHOLEY, 1864-1951

RI —BROWN UNIVERSITY, John Hay Library, 20 Prospect St, Providence, 02912.

Mark N Brown, Cur Mss
Notes: The Henry Scholey Saunders Collection of Whitman and Whitmaniana, collected 1915-1940, which contains very few original items by Whitman and consists mainly of about 15,000 of Saunders' bibliographical and topical notes, as well as essays and lectures by himself and other Whitmanites.

SAUNDERS, MARGARET MARSHALL, 1861-1947

†ON —MCMASTER UNIVERSITY, Library, Hamilton, L8S 4L6, Can.
Notes: Margaret Saunders' typescripts and carbon typescripts of "Poor Phobe" and "Fight and Forget."

SAUTEUX INDIANS see Chippewa Indians

SAVAGE, HENRY

MA —BOSTON UNIVERSITY, Mugar Memorial Library, Special Collections Dept, 771 Commonwealth Ave, Boston, 02215. Howard B Gotlieb, Dir
Holdings: Cat Mss Pix
Notes: Mss, correspondence, etc collected in depth; incl publications by or about.

SAVAGE, J. GUTHERIE

AZ —NORTHERN ARIZONA UNIVERSITY, Special Collection Library, CU Box 6022, Flagstaff, 86011. Peter M Whiteley, Coordr/Archivist; William Mullane, Librn
Notes: Collection of Cline Platt, president of the *Arizona Daily Sun*, Flagstaff, local historian. Historical files concerning Flagstaff and Coconino County, Incl pioneer reminiscences of Black Family, Babbitt Brothers Trading Company records, correspondence and business papers of J Gutherie Savage, 1880's-1890's, Flagstaff attorney; and Ammon Hennacy, correspondence and subject files, 1950's-1960's. Hennacy (Phoenix, Arizona, and Salt Lake City, Utah) was a noted Christian anarchist.

SAVAGE, SARAH

SC —COLLEGE OF CHARLESTON LIBRARY, Special Collections Dept, Charleston, 29401.
Notes: Papers, 1843.

SAVAGES see Man, Primitive

SAVANNAH, GEORGIA—HISTORY

GA —CHATHAM-EFFINGHAM-LIBERTY REGIONAL, 2002 Bull St, Savannah, 31499. Irma Harlan, Dir; Alice Driscoll, Head Ref Dept
Holdings: Vols 4800 Cat Maps Pix Microforms
Notes: Scrapbooks incl newspaper clippings, letters, photographs, pamphlets, programs of special events, postcards, typewritten mss. Emphasis on Georgia and Savannah history. Extensive microfilm collections of newspapers, censuses of Georgia counties; local and state history dissertations, etc. Incl 2100 microfilms.

SAVATE see Boxing

SAVINGS BANKS

DE —HAGLEY MUSEUM AND LIBRARY, Eleutherian Mills-Hagley Foundation Inc, PO Box 3630, Greenville, 19807. Richmond D Williams, Dir; Heddy A Richter, Imprints Librn
Notes: Incl collections: Artisans' Savings Bank of Wilmington, Delaware (1861-1967; 150 cubic feet).

SAVOIE FAMILY see Savoy (Savoie) Family

SAVONAROLA, GIROLAMO

NY —COLUMBIA UNIVERSITY LIBRARIES, Rare Book & Manuscript

Library, 801 Butler Library, 535 W 114 St, New York, 10027. Kenneth A Lohf, Librn
Holdings: Cat
Notes: Incl 34 15th century editions. Restricted use.

SAVOY

MD —UNIVERSITY OF MARYLAND, Library, Rare Book Collection, College Park, 20742. Donald Farren, Assoc Dir for Special Collections
Holdings: Vols (10,000) Cat
Notes: Ranging from incunabula to modern first editions, the Rare Book Collection is particularly strong in materials relating to the history of France and in *exempla* of interest to students of bibliography. Related collections include sizable groups of books and other items relating to the Savoy, to *Expressionismus*, and to Pompeii. Pamphlet collections include many Mazarinades, many pamphlets relating to slavery and abolition, numerous French plays, and press books.

SAVOY (SAVOIE) FAMILY

LA —NICHOLLS STATE UNIVERSITY, Ellender Memorial Library, Thibodaux, 70310. Randall A Detro, Dir; Philip D Uzee, Archivist
Holdings: Uncat Mss Maps Pix Microforms
Notes: Louisiana and local history; family papers of the period, etc.

SAWMILLS—HISTORY

OR —GEORGIA-PACIFIC HISTORICAL MUSEUM, Library, 900 SW Fifth, Portland, 97204. Richard Thompson, Museum Dir
Holdings: Vols (300) Uncat Videotapes 16mm Films Pix
Notes: Use of collection is by written request for specific information or materials.

SAWYER, CHARLES B., 1894-1964

OH —CASE WESTERN RESERVE UNIVERSITY, Sears Library, Archive of Science and Technology, 11161 East Blvd, Cleveland, 44106.
Notes: Papers.

SAWYER, RALPH A.

MI —UNIVERSITY OF MICHIGAN, Libraries, Michigan Historical Collections, Ann Arbor, 48109. Mary Jo Pugh, Reference Archivist
Notes: Ralph A Sawyer's papers (1918-78). Incl material relating to his work as consultant at the test of the hydrogen bomb at the Naval Proving Grounds, Bikini Atoll.

SAWYER, RUTH

MN —COLLEGE OF SAINT CATHERINE, Library, 2004 Randolph Ave, Saint Paul, 55105. Sister Elizabeth Delmore, Library Dir
Holdings: Vols 2100 Cat Mss Pix Phonorecords Audiotapes
Budget: $500
Notes: The Ruth Sawyer Collection. Also personal letters, medals.

SAXOPHONE MUSIC

IN —BALL STATE UNIVERSITY, Alexander M Bracken Library, Muncie, 47306. Nyal Williams, Music Librn
Holdings: Vols (30,000) Cat Mss
Budget: ($20,000)
Notes: Incl archives of International Horn Society, Tubists Universal Brotherhood Association Library, Cecil Leeson Archival Saxophone Collection, and Archives of Buescher Music Instrument Manufacturing Company.

SAYEN, CLARENCE

MI —WAYNE STATE UNIVERSITY, Walter P Reuther Library, Archives of Labor & Urban Affairs, Detroit, 48202. Philip Mason, Dir
Notes: In 1968, the Air Line Pilots

SAYEN, CLARENCE (cont.)

Association placed their important historical records in the Archives. The personal papers of former ALPA President Clarence Sayen and other pilot leaders form an important part of this collection.

SAYERS, DOROTHY L.

CA —UNIVERSITY OF CALIFORNIA, SAN DIEGO, Central University Library, Mandeville Dept of Special Collections, La Jolla, 92093. Lynda Corey Claassen, Head
Notes: The Ira Wolff Collection numbers some 6000 volumes and emphasizes English-language detective fiction from the mid-19th century to the present, containing important or first editions of the works of Agatha Christie, Dorothy Sayers, Raymond Chandler, Dashiell Hammett, and Wilkie Collins.

DC —GEORGETOWN UNIVERSITY, Library, Special Collections Div, 37 & O Sts NW, Washington, 20057. George M Barringer, Special Collections Librn; Nicholas B Sheetz, Mss Librn
Holdings: Mss Cat
Notes: The literary papers of author and art curator, James Laver (1899-1975), and those of his wife, the actress Veronica Turleigh; consisting of letters, with a considerable number written by Lady Cnythia Asquith; Clifford Box; Enid Bagnold; Nicholas Bentley; Violet Clifton; Desmond MacCarthy; Sir Edward Marsh; Sir Francis Meynell; Kate O'Brien; Dorothy L Sayers; Andre Simon; Enid Starkie; A J A Symons; Angela Thirkell; and Alec Waugh.

IL —WHEATON COLLEGE, Library, Marion E Wade Collection, Irving & Franklin Sts, Wheaton, 60187. Lyle Dorsett, Cur; Marjorie Mead, Associate Cur
Holdings: Vols (6500) Mss Pix Audiotapes Videotapes
Notes: Extensive Marion E Wade Collection of seven British authors contains virtually all of Sayers' published and unpublished manuscripts. A solid library of detection studies is also available for the researcher.

SAYINGS see Aphorisms, Apothegms, Epigrams, Maxims, and Proverbs

SAYRE, RUTH

IA —STATE HISTORICAL SOCIETY OF IOWA LIBRARY, 402 Iowa Ave, Iowa City, 52240. Darold J Brown, Librn
Holdings: Cat
Notes: Thousands of individual items and smaller collections. Two hundred larger collections incl the papers of Cyrus C Carpenter, Jonathan P Dolliver, Gilbert Haugen, W W Waymack, Ephraim Adams, A C Dodge, Dorothy Houghton, Jesse Macy, Agnes Samuelson, Donald Johnson, Jack Miller, Ruth Sayre, Samuel Kirkwood, Thomas McKnight, Robert Lucas, Dwight McCarty, William Larrabee. Includes church, school, company and organization records, Civil War materials.

SCALA, FRANCIS MARIA

DC —LIBRARY OF CONGRESS, Music Division, Washington, 20540.
Holdings: Pix
Notes: The Francis Maria Scala Collection. Scala led the US Marine Band, 1855-1871. Incl music, correspondence, clippings, programs, and photographs.

SCALING, PSYCHOLOGICAL see Psychometrics

SCANDINAVIA

CA —CLAREMONT COLLEGES, Honnold Library, Ninth & Dartmouth, Claremont, 91711. Franklin D Scott, Cur, Nordic Collection; Penelope Garris, Librn
Holdings: Vols (25,000) Cat Maps Pix Slides Audiotapes Videotapes Periodicals
Notes: Nordic Collections are broadly inclusive, but emphasize history of Scandinavia, Baltic countries, and Hanseatic cities. Nucleus of collections from gifts and endowment of Waldemar Westergaard, supplemented with relevant collections of David Bjork, John H Wuorinen, Ingolf Olsen, Henry Steele Commager, Franklin Scott (incl Scandinavian migration to America), Eric Bellquist, and other gifts and purchases. Eight vertical file drawers of news bulletins in English or vernaculars, 1941-. See: Franklin D Scott, "The Westergaard-Bjork Collection at the Honnold Library, the Claremont Colleges," *Scandinavian Studies,* 41 (1969), 346-354. Collection incl complete publications of Nordic Council.

CT —YALE UNIVERSITY, Box 1603A, Yale Station, New Haven, 06520.
Holdings: Cat Mss
Notes: Incl dissertations.

MN —HERITAGE RESEARCH CENTER, Box 26305, Minneapolis, 55426.
Holdings: Vols 5000 Cat Mss
Notes: Fiction and nonfiction related to Scandinavia.

SCANDINAVIA—ANTIQUITIES

SD —AUGUSTANA COLLEGE, Mikkelsen Library & Learning Resource Center, Center for Western Studies, Sioux Falls, 57197. Ronelle Thompson, Dir Library
Holdings: Vols (40,000) Cat Mss Maps Pix Slides Microforms
Budget: ($130,000)
Notes: The Maurice Dunlap Collection. Mr Dunlap was US Consul to Norway in the late 1930s. The books principally are on the subject of Runes and Scandinavian antiquities.

SCANDINAVIA—DESCRIPTION AND TRAVEL

MN —UNIVERSITY OF MINNESOTA, O Meredith Wilson Library, 309 19 Ave S, Minneapolis, 55455. Austin J McLean, Chief, Special Collections
Holdings: Cat
Notes: Predominantly 19th century accounts of travelers in the Scandinavian countries.

SCANDINAVIA—EMIGRATION AND IMMIGRATION

CA —CLAREMONT COLLEGES, Honnold Library, Ninth & Dartmouth, Claremont, 91711. Franklin D Scott, Cur, Nordic Collection; Penelope Garris, Librn
Holdings: Vols (25,000) Cat Maps Pix Slides Audiotapes Videotapes Periodicals
Notes: Nordic Collections are broadly inclusive, but emphasize history of Scandinavia, Baltic countries, and Hanseatic cities. Nucleus of collections from gifts and endowment of Waldemar Westergaard, supplemented with relevant collections of David Bjork, John H Wuorinen, Ingolf Olsen, Henry Steele Commager, Franklin Scott and other gifts and purchases. Eight vertical file drawers of news bulletins in English or vernaculars, 1941-. See: Franklin D Scott, "The Westergaard-Bjork Collection at the Honnold Library, the Claremont Colleges," *Scandinavian Studies,* 41 (1969), 346-354.

SCANDINAVIA—HISTORY

CA —CLAREMONT COLLEGES, Honnold Library, Ninth & Dartmouth, Claremont, 91711. Franklin D Scott, Cur, Nordic Collection; Penelope Garris, Librn
Holdings: Vols (25,000) Cat Maps Pix Slides Audiotapes Videotapes Periodicals
Notes: Nordic Collections are broadly inclusive, but emphasize history of Scandinavia, Baltic countries, and Hanseatic cities. Nucleus of collections from gifts and endowment of Waldemar Westergaard, supplemented with relevant collections of David Bjork, John H Wuorinen, Ingolf Olsen, Henry Steele Commager, Franklin Scott and other gifts and purchases. Eight vertical file drawers of news bulletins in

English or vernaculars, 1941-. See: Franklin D Scott, "The Westergaard-Bjork Collection at the Honnold Library, the Claremont Colleges," *Scandinavian Studies,* 41 (1969), 346-354. Collection incl complete publications of Nordic Council.

IL —NORTH PARK COLLEGE LIBRARY, 5125 N Spaulding Ave, Chicago, 60625. Dorothy-Ellen Gross, Dir
Holdings: Vols (4500) Cat
Notes: Scandinavian Collection, with materials mostly Swedish, but some titles in Norwegian, Danish, Finnish and Icelandic. Separate shelf list, but also incl in union catalog. General collection with emphasis on literature and history. Other Swedish books in the field of religion available through Mellander Library on same campus.

SCANDINAVIA—RELIGION

MB —UNIVERSITY OF MANITOBA, Elizabeth Dafoe Library, Icelandic Collection, Winnipeg, R3T 2N2, Can. Sigrid Johnson, Librn
Holdings: Vols (22,500) Cat Mss Maps Pix Audiotapes Microforms
Budget: ($4200)
Notes: Material mostly in Icelandic, some in other Scandinavian languages. All subject areas incl with primary emphasis placed on language, literature and history of Icelanders in Canada, especially Manitoba (incl mss); early publications of sagas and religious literature; numerous periodicals and newspapers, incl Islandske Maanedstidender, 1773, the first Icelandic periodical, and Framfari, 1877, the first Icelandic newspaper in North America; collections of Icelandic music, such as S K Hall Collection (published and mss); Guttormur J Guttormsson and Stephan G Stephansson Memorial Collections; Vilhjalmur Stefansson publications. Cited in, Saunderson, H H, *The Chair of Icelandic Language and Literature at the University of Manitoba.* Winnipeg: University of Manitoba, 1961.

SCANDINAVIAN AUTHORS see Authors, Scandinavian

SCANDINAVIAN LANGUAGES AND LITERATURES

CA —UNIVERSITY OF CALIFORNIA, BERKELEY, University Library, Scandinavian Collections, Berkeley, 94720. Helvi M Bessenyei, Librn
Holdings: VOLS 20,000
Budget: $15,530
Notes: Research collections covering the full range of Scandinavian languages and literatures, with extensive periodical holdings. Particular strengths are Old Norse and Swedish. Moreover, special emphasis is on the late 19th century Scandinavian authors from Kierkegaard to Strinberg. The language and literature collections are supplemented by substantial resources in related disciplines. Some rare book materials are housed in the Bancroft Library.

CA —CLAREMONT COLLEGES, Honnold Library, Ninth & Dartmouth, Claremont, 91711. Franklin D Scott, Cur, Nordic Collection; Penelope Garris, Librn
Holdings: Vols (25,000) Cat Maps Pix Slides Audiotapes Videotapes
Notes: Nordic Collections are broadly inclusive, but emphasize history of Scandinavia, Baltic countries, and Hanseatic cities. Nucleus of collections from gifts and endowment of Waldemar Westergaard, supplemented with relevant collections of David Bjork, John H Wuorinen, Ingolf Olsen, Henry Steele Commager, Franklin Scott, Jens Nyholm, and other gifts and purchases. Eight vertical file drawers of news bulletins in English or vernaculars, 1941-. See: Franklin D Scott, "The Westergaard-Bjork Collection at the Honnold Library, the Claremont Colleges," *Scandinavian Studies,* 41 (1969), 346-354.

IL —NORTH PARK COLLEGE LIBRARY, 5125 N Spaulding Ave, Chicago, 60625. Dorothy-Ellen Gross, Dir
Holdings: Vols (4500) Cat
Notes: Scandinavian Collection, with

SCANDINAVIAN LANGUAGES AND LITERATURES (cont.)

materials mostly Swedish, but some titles in Norwegian, Danish, Finnish and Icelandic. Separate shelf list, but also incl in union catalog. General collection with emphasis on literature and history. Other Swedish books in the field of religion available through Mellander Library on same campus.

MD —JOHNS HOPKINS UNIVERSITY, Milton S Eisenhower Library, Charles & 34 Sts, Baltimore, 21218. Ann S Gwyn, Assistant Dir for Special Collections
Holdings: Vols 3250 Cat
Notes: Incl 2000 reprints. Chiefly modern Scandinavian scholarship and literature, especially Danish. Also runology, Old Scandinavian, history, linguistics, and archaeology. (Incl Lis Jacobsen collection).

MA —HARVARD UNIVERSITY LIBRARY, Widener Library, Cambridge, 02138.
Holdings: Cat Mss
Notes: Strong points are the Icelandic collection (with strong holdings of sagas and eddas) and Strindberg. See also *Distributable Union Catalog* (Harvard).

MN —HERITAGE RESEARCH CENTER, Box 26305, Minneapolis, 55426.
Holdings: Vols 5000 Cat Pix
Notes: Fiction and nonfiction related to Scandinavia.

MN —MINNEAPOLIS PUBLIC LIBRARY & INFORMATION CENTER, Literature & Language Dept, 300 Nicollet Mall, Minneapolis, 55401. Dorothy D Thews, Head
Holdings: Vols (210,000) Cat Microforms Phonorecords Audiotapes
Budget: ($49,124)
Notes: Foreign language collection: 30,000 vols, separate catalog. Theatre collection: 9 vertical file drawers. Books integrated with department collection.

NE —DANA COLLEGE, C A Dana-Life Library, Blair, 68008. Ronald D Johnson, Head Librn
Holdings: Vols (10,000) Cat Audiotapes
Notes: Strong emphasis on Danish literature although we include other Scandinavian countries. Have an oral history tape collection with recordings of Danish emigrants to the midwest. Our book collection is strongest in the literature area with history a close second.

NC —DUKE UNIVERSITY, William R Perkins Library, Durham, 27706. Elvin E Strowd, University Librn
Notes: The Scandinavian collection of 3000 items is a collection of Scandinavian literature, primarily representing the latter half of the 18th century and early 19th century.

SD —AUGUSTANA COLLEGE, Mikkelsen Library & Learning Resource Center, Center for Western Studies, Sioux Falls, 57197. Ronelle Thompson, Dir Library
Holdings: Vols (40,000) Cat Mss Maps Pix Slides Microforms
Budget: ($130,000)
Notes: The Center for Western Studies, located in the Mikkelsen Library, is an archival and research agency of Augustana College. Dedicated to the history and culture of the Great Plains and the Trans-Mississippi West, the Center collects and preserves materials relating to Plains Indians, immigrant settlers, Norwegiana, Western Americana, Herbert Krause, Frederick Manfred, Donald Parker, Richard F Pettigrew, Augustana College, the Episcopal Diocese of South Dakota, the South Dakota District of the American Lutheran Church, the South Dakota Penitentiary and Minnehaha County.

WA —UNIVERSITY OF WASHINGTON LIBRARIES, Suzzallo Library, Scandinavian Collections, FM-25, Seattle, 98195. A Gerald Anderson, Librn
Holdings: Vols (50,000) Cat Mss Pix
Budget: ($15,546)
Notes: Research collections with emphasis on languages and literatures, and auxiliary strengths in history, political science, social science. Archival and other special materials relating to Scandinavian-Americans in the Pacific Northwest are located in other appropriate collections.

WI —UNIVERSITY OF WISCONSIN, MADISON, Memorial Library, 728 State St, Madison, 53706. Erwin K Welsch, Social Studies Bibliographer
Holdings: Vols (50,000) Cat Mss Phonorecords
Notes: Strongest in 19th-century and 20th-century Danish, Norwegian and Swedish literatures, incl literary periodicals and critical works. Special collections incl the "Mimer's Collection," consisting of 1000 vols collected by Rasmus B Anderson, founder of the UW Scandinavian Studies Department, with the aid of the Norwegian violinist Ole Bull and which consists largely of Old Norse materials, and the "Olson Collection," about 400 vols of Scandinavian literary classics from the 19th century. The holdings in Icelandic and Old Norse are substantial (although the modern Icelandic collection is not) with some unique manuscript materials from the 17th and 18th centuries collected by Chester Thordarson. There is also a collection of experimental literature, particularly Danish poetry, from the 1960s.

MB —UNIVERSITY OF MANITOBA, Elizabeth Dafoe Library, Icelandic Collection, Winnipeg, R3T 2N2, Can. Sigrid Johnson, Librn
Holdings: Vols (22,500) Cat Mss Maps Pix Audiotapes Microforms
Notes: Material mostly in Icelandic, some in other Scandinavian languages. All subject areas incl with primary emphasis placed on language, literature and history of Icelanders in Canada, especially Manitoba (incl mss); early publications of sagas and religious literature; numerous periodicals and newspapers, incl Islandske Maanedstidender, 1773, the first Icelandic periodical, and Framfari, 1877, the first Icelandic newspaper in North America; collections of Icelandic music, such as S K Hall Collection (published and mss); Guttormur J Guttormsson and Stephan G Stephansson Memorial Collections; Vilhjalmur Stefansson publications. Cited in, Saunderson, H H, *The Chair of Icelandic Language and Literature at the University of Manitoba.* Winnipeg: University of Manitoba, 1961.

SCANDINAVIAN MYTHOLOGY see Mythology, Norse

SCANDINAVIAN PERIODICALS see Periodicals, Scandinavian

SCANDINAVIANS IN THE U.S.

CA —CLAREMONT COLLEGES, Honnold Library, Ninth & Dartmouth, Claremont, 91711. Franklin D Scott, Cur, Nordic Collection; Penelope Garris, Librn
Holdings: Vols (25,000) Cat Maps Pix Slides Audiotapes Videotapes Periodicals
Notes: Nordic Collections are broadly inclusive, but emphasize history of Scandinavia, Baltic countries, and Hanseatic cities. Nucleus of collections from gifts and endowment of Waldemar Westergaard, supplemented with relevant collections of David Bjork, John H Wuorinen, Ingolf Olsen, Henry Steele Commager, Franklin Scott (incl Scandinavian migration to America), and other gifts and purchases. Eight vertical file drawers of news bulletins in English or vernaculars, 1941-. See: Franklin D Scott, "The Westergaard-Bjork Collection at the Honnold Library, the Claremont Colleges," *Scandinavian Studies,* 41 (1969), 346-354. Collection incl complete publications of Nordic Council.

PA —BALCH INSTITUTE FOR ETHNIC STUDIES, Library, 18 S Seventh St, Philadelphia, 19106. R Joseph Anderson, Library Dir
Holdings: Vols 900 Cat Mss Pix

SD —AUGUSTANA COLLEGE, Mikkelsen Library & Learning Resource Center, Center for Western Studies, Sioux Falls, 57197. Ronelle Thompson, Dir Library
Notes: The Center for Western Studies, located in the Mikkelsen Library, is an archival and research agency of Augustana College. Dedicated to the history and culture of the Great Plains and the Trans-Mississippi West, the Center collects and preserves materials relating to Plains Indians, immigrant settlers, Norwegiana, Western Americana, Herbert Krause, Frederick Manfred, Donald Parker, Richard F Pettigrew, Augustana College, the Episcopal Diocese of South Dakota, the South Dakota District of the American Lutheran Church, the South Dakota Penitentiary and Minnehaha County.

WA —UNIVERSITY OF WASHINGTON LIBRARIES, Suzzallo Library, Scandinavian Collections, FM-25, Seattle, 98195. A Gerald Anderson, Librn
Holdings: Vols (50,000) Cat Mss Pix
Budget: ($15,546)
Notes: Research collections with emphasis on languages and literatures, and auxiliary strengths in history, political science, social science. Archival and other special materials relating to Scandinavian-Americans in the Pacific Northwest are located in other appropriate collections.

SCANDRETT, RICHARD BROWN, JR., 1891-1969

NY —CORNELL UNIVERSITY LIBRARIES, Collection of Regional History, Dept of Manuscripts and Univ Archives, Ithaca, 14853.
Notes: Attorney, politician. Incl papers, (1907-51)-1966; microfilms, tape recordings, speeches, magazine articles, postcards, 2 interviews, and many other items. Unpublished guide available.

SCARFE, FRANCIS

MA —BOSTON UNIVERSITY, Mugar Memorial Library, Special Collections Dept, 771 Commonwealth Ave, Boston, 02215. Howard B Gotlieb, Dir
Holdings: Cat Mss
Notes: Mss, correspondence, etc collected in depth; incl publications by or about.

SCHAEFER, VINCENT J., 1906-

NY —STATE UNIVERSITY OF NEW YORK AT ALBANY, Library, Special Collections Dept, 1400 Washington Ave, Albany, 12222. Marion P Munzer, Coordr
Notes: 28 linear feet of mss; 31 linear feet of pamphlets and periodicals; and 700 volumes from Vincent J Schaefer's personal library. Also, papers, photographs, publications, etc, dealing with his teaching and research on cloud seeding and other aspects of atmospheric science.
See also entries under Atmosphere; Rainmaking

SCHAFER, R. MURRAY, 1933-

AB —UNIVERSITY OF CALGARY, Libraries, Special Collections Div, 2500 University Dr, Calgary, T2N 1N4, Can.
Holdings: Mss
Notes: Mss (50 cm) incl sketches and musical scores, 1956-71.
See also entry under Musicians, Canadian.

SCHAFFNER, FRANKLIN J.

PA —FRANKLIN & MARSHALL COLLEGE, Library, Lancaster, 17604. Kathleen J Moretto, Library Dir
Holdings: Mss Pix
Notes: The Franklin J Schaffner Film Library consists of shooting scripts in various drafts, still photos, posters and other memorabilia of all the motion picture films directed by Mr Schaffner. Actual prints of all the films incl, but not circulated.

SCHAUINGER, J. HERMAN

DC —GEORGETOWN UNIVERSITY, Library, Special Collections Div, 37 & O Sts NW, Washington, 20057. George M

SCHAUINGER, J. HERMAN (cont.)

Barringer, Special Collections Librn;
Nicholas B Sheetz, Mss Librn
Holdings: Mss Cat
Notes: Correspondence, mss, reviews, and
clippings, comprising the papers of J.
Herman Schauinger, historian of early
United States Catholic history. Incl is
Xeroxed and transcribed research material
on Fr Stephen Badin, Bishop Benoit J Flaget,
Bishop Jean B M David, Orestes Brownson,
and William Gaston.

SCHENCK, HUBERT G.

CA —HOOVER INSTITUTION ON WAR,
REVOLUTION & PEACE, Stanford
University, Stanford, 94305. Milorad M
Drachkovitch, Archivist
Holdings: Mss
Notes: Correspondence, diary,
mimeographed reports, newspaper and
magazine clippings, photographs, etc dealing
with Colonel H G Schenck's activities as
Chief, Natural Resources Section, General
Headquarters, Supreme Commander of the
Allied Powers, Tokyo, 1945-1951; as Chief,
Mutual Security Mission to China, 1951-
1954; and as Consultant, US Foreign
Operations Administration, 1954-55. Also
incl is sundry material on economic affairs in
Japan and Taiwan, 1943-1959. 21 ms boxes,
34 envelopes.

SCHENCK, ROBERT C.

CA —UNIVERSITY OF CALIFORNIA,
RIVERSIDE, University Library, 4045
Canyon Crest Dr, Box 5900, Riverside,
92517.
Notes: The Oswald Jonas Memorial
Collection holds the musicological mss,
letters, biographical materials, and notebooks
of Heinrich Schenker and also the papers of
the late Oswald Jonas, musicologist and
leading authority on the life and work of
Schenker. Incl Schenker's diary;
correspondence with Anthony van Hoboken,
Reinhard Oppel, Moriz Violin, Eugen
d'Albert, and Oswald Jonas; the proofs and
mss of his published works; printed editions
from his library with notes, marginalia, and
critical annotations; *Urlinie* tables; and
miscellanea. A guide to the collection will be
published by the library.
OH —MIAMI UNIVERSITY, King Library,
Walter Havighurst Special Collections
Library, Oxford, 45056. Helen Ball, Cur of
Special Collections

SCHEPELER, GERTRUT ELIZABETH

SC —COLLEGE OF CHARLESTON
LIBRARY, Special Collections Dept,
Charleston, 29401.
Notes: Papers incl a petition with, affidavit
of residency, for citizenship of Gertrut
Schepeler, immigrant from Germany, Feb 1,
1805.

SCHERMAN, HARRY

NY —COLUMBIA UNIVERSITY
LIBRARIES, Rare Book & Manuscript
Library, 801 Butler Library, 535 W 114 St,
New York, 10027. Kenneth A Lohf, Librn
Holdings: Mss
Notes: Papers, incl mss, letters, reviews, etc.
19,500 items. Restricted use.

SCHEUCH, FREDERICK C.

DC —GEORGETOWN UNIVERSITY,
Library, Special Collections Div, 37 & O Sts
NW, Washington, 20057. George M
Barringer, Special Collections Librn;
Nicholas B Sheetz, Mss Librn
Holdings: Mss Cat
Notes: A collection of 242 medieval Latin
and Catalan charters previously belonging to
Frederick C Scheuch, ranging in date from
1261 to 1690. The documents comprise the
archives of the Sala family who owned the
castle of Montorroell in Catalonia, Spain.

See Joseph J Gwara, Jr's *The Sala Family
Archives: A Handlist of Medieval and Early
Modern Catalonian Manuscripts.*

SCHEVENELS, WALTER, 1894-1966

CA —HOOVER INSTITUTION ON WAR,
REVOLUTION & PEACE, Stanford
University, Stanford, 94305. Milorad M
Drachkovitch, Archivist
Holdings: Mss
Notes: Papers of Walter Schevenels, Belgian
syndicalist and international trade union
official, General Secretary of the
International Federation of Trade Unions,
1929-1945, and General Secretary for the
European Regional Organization of the
International Confederation of Free Trade
Unions, 1951-1966, incl correspondence,
reports, speeches, writings, telegrams,
bulletins, interviews, pamphlets, clippings,
and printed materials, 1930-1966, relating to
syndicalism and free European trade unions,
labor and laboring classes in Europe, and
international labor problems. 13 ms boxes.

SCHIDDEL, EDMUND

MA —BOSTON UNIVERSITY, Mugar
Memorial Library, Special Collections Dept,
771 Commonwealth Ave, Boston, 02215.
Howard B Gotlieb, Dir
Holdings: // Cat Mss Pix
Notes: Mss, correspondence, etc collected in
depth; incl publications by or about.

SCHILD, ALFRED, 1921-1977

†TX —UNIVERSITY OF TEXAS
LIBRARIES, General Libraries, Humanities
Research Center, PO Box 7219, Austin,
78712. John Chalmers, Librn
Notes: The papers of Alfred Schild (1921-
1977), incl letters from P A M Dirac. Schild
was a physicist. Collection especially strong
in documenting the formation and activities
of the "Texas Group" of relativists.

SCHILLER, ALBERT

NY —ROCHESTER INSTITUTE OF
TECHNOLOGY, Melbert B Cary Jr
Graphic Arts Collection, School of Printing,
One Lomb Memorial Drive, Rochester,
14623. David Pankow, Cur
Holdings: Vols (11,000) Cat
Notes: An extensive collection of the work
of typographic artist Albert Schiller. Incl
type pictures, their type forms,
correspondence, sketches, books, proofs, and
ephemera.

SCHILLER, FERDINAND CANNING SCOTT, 1864-1937

CA —UNIVERSITY OF CALIFORNIA, LOS
ANGELES, Research Library, Dept of
Special Collections, 405 Hilgard Ave, Los
Angeles, 90024. Edward Shreeves,
Chairman, Bibliographers Group; David S
Zeidberg, Head
Holdings: Mss
Notes: 9 linear feet of books, mss,
correspondence, ephemera, etc.

SCHILLER, JOHANN CHRISTOPH FRIEDRICH VON

MA —HARVARD UNIVERSITY LIBRARY,
Cambridge, 02138.
Holdings: Cat

SCHILPP, PAUL ARTHUR

†IL —SOUTHERN ILLINOIS UNIVERSITY,
CARBONDALE, Library, Special
Collections Dept, Carbondale, 62901.
Notes: Archives of the Library of Living
Philosophers, a publishing project founded
by Paul Arthur Schilpp in 1938 to provide a
forum for contemporary philosophers to
reply to their critics. Incl correspondence
from John Dewey, George Santayana, Alfred
North Whitehead, G E Moore, and Albert
Einstein.

SCHIZOPHRENIA AND SCHIZOPHRENICS

MA —MCLEAN HOSPITAL MEDICAL
LIBRARY, 115 Mill St, Belmont, 02178.
Hector Bossange, Dir
Holdings: Vols 25,611 Cat
Notes: Extensive collection.
RI —BROWN UNIVERSITY, John Hay
Library, 20 Prospect St, Providence, 02912.
Mark N Brown, Cur Mss
Notes: Papers of Earl F Zinn, American
psychiatrist, comprising medical records of
350 hours of analytical interviews with a
schizophrenic patient for a period of about
four years in the 1930s; also a portfolio of
art work by the same patient and a letter
from Freud.

SCHLESINGER, ARTHUR M., JR.

†MA —JOHN F KENNEDY LIBRARY,
Columbia Point, Boston, 02125. Dan H Fenn
Jr, Dir
Holdings: // Cat Mss
Notes: His personal papers and White House
files, 1948-1965. 65 linear ft of mss.
Holdings are described in "Historical
Materials in the John F Kennedy Library."
Copies may be obtained by writing the
Research Archivist.

SCHLESINGER, FRANK

NY —AMERICAN INSTITUTE OF
PHYSICS, Center for the History of Physics,
Niels Bohr Library, 335 E 45 St, New York,
10017. John Aubry, Librn
Notes: The Sources for History of Modern
Astrophysics documents the history of 20th-
century astrophysics. Incl some 400 hours of
oral history interviews with astronomers,
such as Bart Bok, S Chandrasekhar, Martin
Schwarzschild, and A E Whitford. The
project also organized and cataloged the
papers of Henry Norris Russell, Frank
Schlesinger, Otto Struve, Ejnar Hertzsprung,
Harlow Shapley, Charles Young, Robert
Atkinson, Seth Chandler, Theodore
Dunham, Jr, and G C McVittie.

SCHMIDT, ARTHUR P., COMPANY

DC —LIBRARY OF CONGRESS, Music
Division, Washington, 20540.
Notes: The business papers and music mss of
the Arthur P Schmidt Company. Numerous
works by important composers.

SCHMIDT, HENRY A.

NM —MUSEUM OF NEW MEXICO, Photo
Archives, Box 2087, Santa Fe, 87503.
Arthur L Olivas, Cur; Richard Rudisill,
Photo Historian
Holdings: Cat Pix Slides
Notes: Extensive collection of his work.

SCHMIDT, MAARTEN

NY —AMERICAN INSTITUTE OF
PHYSICS, Center for the History of Physics,
Niels Bohr Library, 335 E 45 St, New York,
10017. John Aubry, Librn
Notes: The Sources for History of Modern
Astrophysics documents the history of 20th-
century astrophysics. Incl some 400 hours of
oral history interviews with astronomers,
such as Bart Bok, S Chandrasekhar, Martin
Schwarzschild, and A E Whitford. The
project also organized and cataloged the
papers of Henry Norris Russell, Frank
Schlesinger, Otto Struve, Ejnar Hertzsprung,
Harlow Shapley, Charles Young, Robert
Atkinson, Seth Chandler, Theodore
Dunham, Jr, and G C McVittie.

SCHMIDT, OTTO L.

IL —CHICAGO HISTORICAL SOCIETY,
Library, Clark St at North Ave, Chicago,
60614. Archie Motley, Manuscript Librn
Notes: Papers of: Emmet Dedmon,
newspaper editor; Richard J Finnegan,

SCHMIDT, OTTO L. (cont.)

newspaper editor; Rev Andres M Greeley, sociologist and author; attorney and civil liberties activist Pearl Hart; Robert J Havighurst, educator; social activist John Kearney; Kenesaw Mountain Landis, Federal Judge and first Commissioner of Baseball; Judge David F Matchett; Ivan Molek, Slovenian language publisher in Chicago; Max R Naiman, Communist Party activist; Ralph G Newman, book and autograph dealer and manuscript appraiser; Otto L Schmidt, physician and President of the Chicago and Illinois State Historical Societites; and Dempsey Travis, black mortgage banker.

SCHMITT, FLORENT, 1870-1958

BC —UNIVERSITY OF VICTORIA, McPherson Library, Victoria, V8W 3H5, Can.

SCHNEBLY, ELLSWORTH

AZ —NORTHERN ARIZONA UNIVERSITY, Special Collection Library, CU Box 6022, Flagstaff, 86011. Peter M Whiteley, Coordr/Archivist; William Mullane, Librn
Notes: Personal records, 1940's-1970's. Incl files on the Schnebly Hill Road, early 1950's and photographs of Sedona and Oak Creek Canyon, early 1900's. Also incl educational materials from the 1930's-1950's. (8 feet).

SCHNEIDER, ISIDOR

NY —COLUMBIA UNIVERSITY LIBRARIES, Rare Book & Manuscript Library, 801 Butler Library, 535 W 114 St, New York, 10027. Kenneth A Lohf, Librn
Holdings: Mss
Notes: Publications and papers, by and about. 5000 items. Restricted use.

SCHNEIR, WALTER AND MIRIAM

MA —BOSTON UNIVERSITY, Mugar Memorial Library, Special Collections Dept, 771 Commonwealth Ave, Boston, 02215. Howard B Gotlieb, Dir
Holdings: Cat Mss Pix
Notes: Mss, correspondence, etc collected in depth; incl publications by or about.

SCHNITZLER, ARTHUR, 1862-1931

CA —UNIVERSITY OF CALIFORNIA, LOS ANGELES, Research Library, Dept of Special Collections, 405 Hilgard Ave, Los Angeles, 90024. Edward Shreeves, Chairman, Bibliographers Group; David S Zeidberg, Head
Holdings: Vols 25
Notes: 25 books; 38 reels of microfilm of material being kept at University Library, Cambridge. No photocopying.

SCHOENBERG, ARNOLD

CA —CALIFORNIA STATE UNIVERSITY, LONG BEACH, Library, Dept of Special Collections & Archives, 1250 Bellflower Blvd, Long Beach, 90840. John Ahouse, Special Collections Librn
Holdings: Mss Phonorecords Audiotapes
Notes: Almost all of the papers, recordings, etc, published and unpublished, of Gerald V Strang.
DC —LIBRARY OF CONGRESS, Music Division, Washington, 20540.
Notes: Mss in Koussevitzky Archives. Papers and recordings of composer Arnold Schoenberg. Extensive correspondence with other composers, writers, etc.
TX —NORTH TEXAS STATE UNIVERSITY, Audio Center, Box 5188, NT Station, Denton, 76203. Morris Martin, Music Librn
Notes: Arnold Schoenberg manuscripts (compositions, sketches, exercises, arrangements) and correspondence with Hans Nachod covering almost 50 years. See Newlin Dika, "The Schoenberg-Nachod

Collection: a Preliminary Report," in *Musical Quarterly*, vol 54 (1968), pp. 31-46; Kimmey, John A, Jr *The Arnold Schoenberg-Hans Nachod Collection* (Detroit Studies in Music Bibliography, No. 41) Detroit: Information Coordinators, 1979.

SCHOICHET, NATHAN L.

CA —UNIVERSITY OF CALIFORNIA, LOS ANGELES, Research Library, Dept of Special Collections, 405 Hilgard Ave, Los Angeles, 90024. Edward Shreeves, Chairman, Bibliographers Group; David S Zeidberg, Head
Notes: 7.5 linear feet of correspondence and legal papers concerning cases in which he was involved as an attorney for the ACLU.

SCHOLARS

CA —STANFORD UNIVERSITY LIBRARIES, Cecil H Green Library, Stanford, 94305. Michael T Ryan, Cur
Holdings: Cat Pix
Notes: The Dr and Mrs Leon Kolb Portrait Collection. Over 1600 portraits (engravings, etchings, mezzotints, lithographs) of rulers, statesmen, authors, scholars and other famous personages from ancient times to the 19th century. A catalog of the collection, compiled by Dr Susan Lenkey, was published in 1972.

SCHOLARLY PUBLISHING

NY —GRADUATE CENTER OF THE CITY UNIVERSITY OF NEW YORK, William H and Gwynne K Crouse Library for Publishing Arts, 33 W 42 St, New York, 10036. Alfred H Lane, Dir
Notes: Recently established and still growing, but intended to become the authoritative source of materials in the field, of particular value in research about the publishing industry. Open to staff members of publishing houses, students, scholars, authors, printers, and booksellers. Primarily 20th century materials, and particularly useful for research on technical, financial, and historical matters. Much on the history of individual houses, economics of authorship; marketing and distribution of books; etc.

SCHOLARSHIP see Learning and Scholarship

SCHOLASTICISM

DC —DOMINICAN HOUSE OF STUDIES, Dominican College Library, 487 Michigan Ave NE, Washington, 20017. J Raymond Vandegrift, OP, Librn
Holdings: Vols (3700) Cat
Budget: $650
Notes: Incl works about Thomas Aquinas--commentaries, *festschriften,* biographies--and works both by and about his followers, the Thomists--histories, biographies, periodicals, monograph series, manuals, incunabula, rare books, and the papers presented at Thomistic congresses.
See also entry under Thomas Aquinas, St.
IL —JESUIT-KRAUSS-MCCORMICK LIBRARY, 1100 E 55th St, Chicago, 60615. Donald Vorp, Dir; Elvire Hilgert, Librn
Notes: Collection contains merger of Jesuit Library, Lutheran School of Theology of Chicago (Krauss Library), and McCormick Theological Seminary. Jesuit: Sermones Thesaurus Novi de Tempore (anonymous, Strassbourg 1486); Opera Omnia (Jean Gerson, Strassbourg 1488), 3 vols; Summa Rosella Casuum (Venice 1495); moral theology (major figures of 16th and 17th century scholasticism); early modern editions of patristics and canon law regarding procedures and organzation of the Catholic Church, incl treatises and multi-volume commentaries.
See also entries under Religion; Lutheran Church; Presbyterian Church
MO —SAINT LOUIS UNIVERSITY, Pius XII Memorial Library, 3655 W Pine Blvd, Saint

Louis, 63108. William Cole, Dir
Holdings: Slides Microforms
Notes: Collection covers all areas of learning and European history from Classical Antiquity to early modern period. Researchers using collection receive assistance in paleography, bibliography and reference search. Approx 10,000 1000-foot reels of microfilm (not counting master negatives) reproducing Vatican Library's Latin, Greek, Hebrew, Arabic and Ethiopic mss. Some 8000 100-foot reels of microfilm (again not counting master negative) reproducing rare and out of print books relating to subject areas in the mss. Over 50,000 color slides of medieval and Renaissance mss illuminations. A reference collection of modern materials relating to ms research.

SCHOLLE, AUGUST

MI —WAYNE STATE UNIVERSITY, Walter P Reuther Library, Archives of Labor & Urban Affairs, Detroit, 48202. Philip Mason, Dir
Notes: The history of the labor movement in Detroit and Michigan. The records of the Wayne County and Michigan AFL-CIO, Association of Catholic Trade Unionists, and the Detroit Industrial Mission are housed in the Archives. The official files of August Scholle, as President of the Michigan AFL-CIO, complement the organizational records in the Archives.

SCHOLZ, JANOS

NC —UNIVERSITY OF NORTH CAROLINA, GREENSBORO, Walter Clinton Jackson Library, Special Collections Dept, 1000 Spring Garden St, Greensboro, 27412. Emilie W Mills, Librn
Notes: Randall Jarrell taught at the University from 1947 until his death in 1965. Over 3000 ms items were the gift of the author and incl various drafts of poems, translations, critical works and essays. Books incl first, foreign, and variant editions, association books and many other heavily annotated by Jarrell readings, conversations (tapes) with other poets, incl John Crowe Ransom and Robert Frost. A one-hour color film made after the poet's death incl readings of his poems made from the earlier tapes, and an interview with the poet's widow, Mary Jarrell. Jarrell memorablilia is also included.

SCHONBERG, HAROLD C.

MA —BOSTON UNIVERSITY, Mugar Memorial Library, Special Collections Dept, 771 Commonwealth Ave, Boston, 02215. Howard B Gotlieb, Dir
Holdings: Cat Mss Pix
Notes: Mss, correspondence, etc collected in depth; incl publications by or about.

SCHONFIELD, HUGH

MA —BOSTON UNIVERSITY, Mugar Memorial Library, Special Collections Dept, 771 Commonwealth Ave, Boston, 02215. Howard B Gotlieb, Dir
Holdings: Cat Mss Pix
Notes: Mss, correspondence, etc collected in depth; incl publications by or about.

SCHOOL ADMINISTRATION see School Management and Organization

SCHOOL ARCHITECTURE see School Buildings

SCHOOL BUILDINGS

CA —ESHERICK, HOMSEY, DODGE & DAVIS, Library, 2789 25th St, San Francisco, 94110. Elizabeth Walton, Librn
Holdings: Vols (2500) Cat Maps Pix Slides
Notes: General history of architecture; solar energy applications to architecture; handbooks, codes, and standards; school and university architecture. Also incl is a large collection of product literature catalogs and samples (uncataloged).

SCHOOL BUILDINGS—COMMUNITY USE see Community Centers

SCHOOL ENDOWMENTS see Endowments

SCHOOL FINANCE see Education—Finance

SCHOOL HYGIENE

CT —YALE MEDICAL LIBRARY, 333 Cedar St, New Haven, 06510.
Notes: A special subject emphasis.

SCHOOL INSPECTION see School Management and Organization

SCHOOL LAW see Education—Law and Legislation

SCHOOL LIBRARIES

†PA —UNIVERSITY OF PITTSBURGH, Graduate School of Library & Information Sciences Library, L I S Bldg, Third Fl, Pittsburgh, 15260. Jean Kindlin, Librn
Notes: Extensive collection on the historical development of school libraries, media services, and evaluation of materials for use in all types of schools. Incl 54,800 vols, 7524 bound periodicals, 630 periodical subscriptions.

SCHOOL LIFE see Students

SCHOOL MANAGEMENT AND ORGANIZATION

MA —HARVARD UNIVERSITY, Graduate School of Education, Monroe C Gutman Library, 6 Appian Way, Cambridge, 02138. Susan S Baughman, Associate Librn
Holdings: Vols (150,000) Cat Mss Microforms
Budget: ($95,000)
Notes: A comprehensive research collection that seeks to acquire all scholarly works published in the English language in the fields of education, educational administration, educational psychology, and human development. Selective coverage in the related areas of counseling and psychology, business administration, finance, forecasting, statistical analysis and survey design, public and social policy, linguistics, demographics, and international and economic development. Incl 4000 educational and psychological tests.
MA —BOSTON COLLEGE LIBRARIES, Chestnut Hill, 02167.
Notes: The archives of the Citywide Coordinating Council of Boston, Mass, established in 1975 to monitor the desegregation of the Boston school system and to foster public awareness in the implementation of the court's desegregation orders. Incl the collection of transcripts of School Committee meetings; the central files, reflecting the functioning of the council office; and the files of the senior staff, containing the key administrative records of the Council.
PA —SCHOOL DISTRICT OF PHILADELPHIA, Pedagogical Library, 21 St & Pkwy, Philadelphia, 19103. Helen E Howe, Librn; Patricia K Buck, Asst Librn
Holdings: Vols (47,000) Cat Pix Microforms
Budget: ($25,000)
Notes: Collection emphasis on public school education K-12 with the main areas including Afro-American history and culture, elementary and early childhood education, secondary education, educational administration, educational research, reading, school law, educational psychology. Special Collections: ERIC (140,000 documents), Archives of the School District of Philadelphia. Approx 500 periodical subscriptions.

SCHOOL ORGANIZATION see School Management and Organization

SCHOOL REPORTS see Schulschriften and Schulprogramme

SCHOOL TAXES see Education—Finance

SCHOOL YEARBOOKS see Yearbooks

SCHOOLHOUSES see School Buildings

SCHOOLS—CURRICULA see Education—Curricula

SCHOOLS—FINANCE see Education—Finance

SCHOOLS—LAW AND LEGISLATION see Education—Law and Legislation

SCHOOLS—SANITARY AFFAIRS see School Hygiene

SCHOOLS, COMMERCIAL see Business Education

SCHOOLS AS SOCIAL CENTERS see Community Centers

SCHOONOVER, FRANK E.

DE —DELAWARE ART MUSEUM, Library, 2301 Kentmere Pkwy, Wilmington, 19806.
Anne Hoslam, Librn
Holdings: Cat Mss Pix
Notes: The Frank E Schoonover and other collections. Archives, letters, sketches, photographs, memorabilia, clippings.
PA —FREE LIBRARY OF PHILADELPHIA, Rare Book Dept, Logan Sq, Philadelphia, 19103. Marie E Korey, Rare Book Librn
Holdings: Vols (1000) Cat Mss Pix
Notes: The Thornton Oakley Collection containing 1000 pieces of original art, autograph letters, and books and periodicals, illustrated by Howard Pyle and his students, incl Maxfield Parish, Frank Schoonover, Jessie Wilcox Smith, and N C Wyeth.

SCHOTT, WEBSTER

MA —BOSTON UNIVERSITY, Mugar Memorial Library, Special Collections Dept, 771 Commonwealth Ave, Boston, 02215. Howard B Gotlieb, Dir
Holdings: Cat Mss
Notes: Mss, correspondence, etc collected in depth; incl publications by or about.

SCHROEDER, THEODORE A.

IL —SOUTHERN ILLINOIS UNIVERSITY, CARBONDALE, Delyte W Morris Library, Special Collections Dept, Carbondale, 62901. David V Koch, Cur of Special Collections; Louisa Bowen, Cur of Manuscripts
Holdings: Cat Mss
Notes: Papers and correspondence of Theodore A Schroeder, constitutional lawyer and founder, with Lincoln Steffens, of the Free Speech League, a forerunner of the American Civil Liberties Union. Contains extensive correspondence with Comstock, Gompers, Debs, H Ellis, Sanger, Sinclair, John Dewey, Darrow, Mencken, A G Hays, Emma Goldman, W E B Dubois, etc. Incl several thousand letters; notes and mss, records of legal cases and extensive files relating to the early history of psychiatry. The archives reflect Schroeder's crusades in the areas of free speech, sex expression, religion, and psychoanalysis. Inventory and name index available at the Library. Described by Ralph E McCoy, *Theodore Schroeder, the Cold Enthusiast*, Carbondale: Southern Illinois University Libraries, 1973. (Bibliographic Contributions, No 8).

SCHULSCHRIFTEN AND SCHULPROGRAMME

CA —STANFORD UNIVERSITY LIBRARIES, Cecil H Green Library, Stanford, 94305. Peter R Frank, Cur, CDP-Germanic Collection
Holdings: 3500 // Cat
Notes: In the 19th century, professors in high schools and colleges (gymnasien) in German-speaking countries were supposed to do scholarly work, in addition to their teaching. The results of the research were usually published in the annual school reports (Schulschriften, Schulprogramme), covering such fields as classics, language, literature, history, etc. Stanford's holdings incl long runs of Schulschriften from Austria and Germany, from colleges from Memel to Aschen, Kiel to Klausenburg and Triest. These sets are mainly in the period 1850-1940.

SCHUMAN, WILLIAM

DC —LIBRARY OF CONGRESS, Music Division, Washington, 20540.
Notes: Mss in Koussevitzky Archives.

SCHUMANN, PETER

CA —UNIVERSITY OF CALIFORNIA, DAVIS, Shields Library, Dept of Special Collections, Davis, 95616. Donald Kunitz, Head; C Danial Elliott, Asst Head
Holdings: Cat Mss Pix Videotapes 16mm Films
Notes: A collection of correspondence, reviews, programs, posters, and newsletters document the performance of the Bread and
Puppet Theatre formed in 1962 by Peter Schumann. 260 items.

SCHUMANN-HEINK, ERNESTINE, 1861-1936

CA —CLAREMONT COLLEGES, Honnold Library, Ninth & Dartmouth, Claremont, 91711. Tania Rizzo, Special Collections Dept Head
Holdings: Vols (7000) Uncat Music Mss Pix Ephemera
Notes: The Schumann-Heink Bequest made to Pomona College in 1938. Collection consists of music and professional and personal memorabilia, 1885-1936. Nearly 10,000 items total, mostly music, some in manuscript (printed scores partly catalogued among general library holdings); 350 letters and cards; journals, diaries, and day books; 175 photographs; and clippings, programs, awards, and other items. Complete inventory in preparation. Restricted use.

SCHUSTER, A. AND B., COMPANY

AZ —NORTHERN ARIZONA UNIVERSITY, Special Collection Library, CU Box 6022, Flagstaff, 86011. Peter M Whiteley, Coordr/Archivist; William Mullane, Librn
Notes: Correspondence and financial records of the A and B Schuster Company, mercantile company in Holbrook, Ariz, 1890's-1950's (scattered, 53 feet).

SCHUSTER, M. LINCOLN

†NY —COLUMBIA UNIVERSITY LIBRARIES, Butler Library, Rare Book and Manuscript Library, 535 W 114 St, New York, 10027.
Notes: Over 30,000 papers relating to M Lincoln Schuster and the publishing firm, Simon & Schuster. Incl file of letters written by Simon to Schuster from 1921-53, author and subject files of notes and clippings, advertising notebooks, files relating to the books written and edited by Schuster, galley and page proofs, photographs and memorabilia, and other correspondence.

SCHUYLER, PHILIP

NY —NEW YORK PUBLIC LIBRARY, Rare Books and Manuscripts Div, Fifth Ave & 42 St, New York, 10018. William L Joyce, Asst Dir; Susan E Davis, Cur of Mss
Holdings: Mss
Budget: ($7161)
Notes: Incl personal and lterary mss, papers, etc.

SCHWAB, MARTIN F.

AZ —NORTHERN ARIZONA UNIVERSITY, Special Collection Library, CU Box 6022, Flagstaff, 86011. Peter M Whiteley, Coordr/Archivist; William Mullane, Librn
Notes: Collection of Frank Gold, lawyer. File on Martin F Schwab/Harry H Nash sensational murder trial, Flagstaff, 1920-1921. Also incl photographs of biographical material on Gold.

SCHWABACH LANGUAGE AND LITERATURE

IL —CZECHOSLOVAK HERITAGE MUSEUM AND LIBRARY, 2701 S Harlem Ave, Berwyn, 60402.
Holdings: Vols 150
Notes: Incl 50 periodicals.

SCHWABE, GEORGE BLAINE

OK —UNIVERSITY OF OKLAHOMA, Bizzell Memorial Library, Western History Collections, 401 W Brooks, Norman, 73069. John Ezell, Cur
Holdings: Mss Pix Documents Maps
Notes: US Representative. His papers. Guide available.

SCHWARTZ, CHARLES

IL —CHICAGO HISTORICAL SOCIETY, Library, Clark St at North Ave, Chicago,

SCHWARTZ, CHARLES (cont.)

60614. Archie Motley, Manuscript Librn
Notes: Papers of Gottlieb and Schwartz, Chicago law firm.

SCHWARTZ, DELMORE, 1913-1966

CA —UNIVERSITY OF CALIFORNIA, LOS ANGELES, Research Library, Dept of Special Collections, 405 Hilgard Ave, Los Angeles, 90024. Edward Shreeves, Chairman, Bibliographers Group; David S Zeidberg, Head
Holdings: Vols 943
Notes: 943 books from his library, many heavily annotated; 9 holograph notebooks.
NV —UNIVERSITY OF NEVADA, RENO, University Library, Special Collections Dept, Reno, 89557. Robert E Blesse, Head
Holdings: Vols (19) Cat
Notes: Includes individual works by author in all editions including translations; also prefaces, introductions, published correspondence, appearances in anthologies, periodicals, etc. Bibliographical research collection, part of Modern Authors Collection. Other appearances 360 cataloged.

SCHWARTZ, MAURICE

NY —YIVO INSTITUTE FOR JEWISH RESEARCH, Library & Archives, 1048 Fifth Ave, New York, 10028. Dina Abramowicz, Librn; Marek Web, Archivist
Holdings: Cat Mss Pix Slides
Notes: Yiddish drama in the original and in English translation from its 19th-century beginnings to the present; the Yiddish theatre in the Soviet Union and the theatrical activities in the ghettos during the Nazi regime; special collections of Sholem Perelmuter, Mendel Elkin, Maurice Schwartz, Abraham Goldfaden, Jacob Gordin, and Mark Schweid; records of the Union of Jewish Actors in Poland between the two world wars; the Vilna YIVO Collection of posters, playbills, and Photographs; recordings.

SCHWARZ, FRANZ XAVER

DC —LIBRARY OF CONGRESS, Rare Book & Special Collections Div, Washington, 20540. William Matheson, Chief
Notes: The Third Reich Collection incl materials from the libraries of Hermann Goring, Heinrich Himmler, Franz Xaver Schwarz, and other Nazi leaders.

SCHWARZ, LEO W.

IA —UNIVERSITY OF IOWA, University Libraries, Iowa City, 52242.
Holdings: Vols 1850 Mss
Notes: The Leo W Schwarz Collection, a valuable and rare group of books dealing with Hasidic literature, a portion on Old Testament studies and works on Jewish history, philosophy and culture, the Jews in Nazi Germany, Jewish folklore and the history of the Jews in the US. Incl about 850 books in Hebrew and 1000 in other languages, mss of several of Schwarz's books and articles, correspondence, notes, and background research relating to his publications.

SCHWARZ, TED

AZ —ARIZONA STATE UNIVERSITY, Library, Tempe, 85287. Marilyn Wurzburger, Special Collections Librn
Notes: Reflecting his roles of reporter, photographer and novelist, Ted Schwarz's papers cover subject areas such as investigative journalism, psychology, criminal justice, law, numismatics, visual communication, photography and writing as a career. Collection incl extensive research materials from the author's study and reporting of the "Hillside Strangler" case which deals with multiple personalities. Partially cataloged and indexed, the collection consists of 140 linear feet of multi-media materials: vols, magazines, newspaper articles, galley proofs, interviews and correspondence, reel-to-reel tapes, audiotapes and videotapes.

SCHWARZSCHILD, MARTIN

NY —AMERICAN INSTITUTE OF PHYSICS, Center for the History of Physics, Niels Bohr Library, 335 E 45 St, New York, 10017. John Aubry, Librn
Notes: The Sources for History of Modern Astrophysics documents the history of 20th-century astrophysics. Incl some 400 hours of oral history interviews with astronomers, such as Bart Bok, S Chandrasekhar, Martin Schwarzschild, and A E Whitford. The project also organized and cataloged the papers of Henry Norris Russell, Frank Schlesinger, Otto Struve, Ejnar Hertzsprung, Harlow Shapley, Charles Young, Robert Atkinson, Seth Chandler, Theodore Dunham, Jr, and G C McVittie.

SCHWEID, MARK

NY —YIVO INSTITUTE FOR JEWISH RESEARCH, Library & Archives, 1048 Fifth Ave, New York, 10028. Dina Abramowicz, Librn; Marek Web, Archivist
Holdings: Cat Mss Pix Slides
Notes: Yiddish drama in the original and in English translation from its 19th-century beginnings to the present; the Yiddish theatre in the Soviet Union and the theatrical activities in the ghettos during the Nazi regime; special collections of Sholem Perelmuter, Mendl Elkin, Maurice Schwartz, Abraham Goldfaden, Jacob Gordin, and Mark Schweid; records of the Union of Jewish Actors in Poland between the two world wars; the Vilna YIVO Collection of posters, playbills, and photographs; recordings.

SCHWEIKHER, PAUL

AZ —NORTHERN ARIZONA UNIVERSITY, Special Collection Library, CU Box 6022, Flagstaff, 86011. Peter M Whiteley, Coordr/Archivist; William Mullane, Librn
Notes: Paul Schweikher Collection of original renderings and working drawings, from one of the most well-known of the Chicago architects. Schweikher was formerly head of the Architecture Departments at Yale and Carnegie-Mellon Universities. The collection is extensive and features most of his architectural drawings ever executed.

SCHWEITZER, ALBERT, 1875-1965

MA —BRANDEIS UNIVERSITY, Goldfarb Library, 415 South St, Waltham, 02154. Bessie Hahn, Dir
Notes: Albert Schweitzer Collection consists of 255 letters of correspondence to and from Dr Albert Schweitzer and other staff members of the Lambarene Hospital, Gabon, Africa. Also included in the collection are some artifacts, memorabilia and two commemorative Albert Schweitzer volumes. A guide to the collection was published in *Guide to Albert Schweitzer Collections in the United States.* New York, 1981.

SCHWENKFELDER RELIGIOUS MOVEMENT

PA —JUNIATA COLLEGE LIBRARY, Huntingdon, 16652. David Eyman, Dir
Holdings: Vols 5000// Cat Mss
Notes: Early Pennsylvania imprints, many in German. Large collection of imprints from Christopher Sauer's press. Early Brethren and other German sectarian (Schwenkfelders, Anabaptists) tracts from Pennsylvania and Europe. Several of the collections have been described in *American German Review* (1941), *Pennsylvania History* (1940, 1959), and *Pennsylvania Magazine* (1943).

SCHWIMMER, ROSIKA

CA —HOOVER INSTITUTION ON WAR, REVOLUTION & PEACE, Stanford University, Stanford, 94305. Milorad M Drachkovitch, Archivist
Holdings: // Mss
Notes: Papers, 1914-1933, of Rosika Schwimmer, feminist, pacifist, lecturer and Hungarian minister to Switzerland during the Karolyi regime, 1918-1919. Correspondence, monographs, newspaper and magazine clippings relating to Mme Schwimmer's career, particularly her organization of , and affiliation with, the Henry Ford Peace Expedition, 1915-1916, her participation in the Neutral Conference for Continuous Mediation, 1916, and her subsequent career in Hungary and the United States. 2 ft.

SCHWOB, MARCEL

UT —BRIGHAM YOUNG UNIVERSITY, Harold B Lee Library, Unversity Hill, Provo, 84602. Sterling Albrecht, Dir
Notes: Incl memorabilia.

SCIENCE

AZ —UNIVERSITY OF ARIZONA, University Library, Special Collections, Tucson, 85721. Louis A Hieb, Head
Holdings: Vols 2000 Cat Mss
Budget: ($30,000)
Notes: Early printed source materials in the history of sceince. Specializing in the areas of chemistry, physics, mathematics, astronomy, ornithology and the natural sciences.
CA —UNIVERSITY OF CALIFORNIA, BERKELEY, Bancroft Library, Manuscripts Division, Berkeley, 94720. James D Hart, Dir
Holdings: Vols Cat Mss Maps Pix Slides Microforms
Notes: Collection of early and rare editions, supported by related holdings in the Biology and Main libraries. Mss (230,000) consisting primarily of sceintists' private papers, constitute the most significant part of the collection. Major emphasis is on scientific developments centered in Berkeley since the inception of the Lawrence Radiation Laboratory, and on the growth of the electronics industry located in the Palo Alto area, in the Vicinity of Stanford University. Incl are the private papers of Ernest Lawrence and Emil Fischer. A series of oral histories complements these holdings.
CA —CLAREMONT COLLEGES, Norman F Sprague Memorial Library, 12 & Dartmouth, Claremont, 91711. David Kuhner, Librn
Holdings: Vols 1000 Cat Mss Maps Pix
Notes: The reference library collected by Herbert Clark Hoover and Lou Henry Hoover in the preparation of their 1912 translation of *De re metallica.* Incl 24 incunabula, 6 mss, titles of 16th to 19th centuries, with emphasis on mining, metallurgy, early science, and travel. Hoover's correspondence (approx 600 pieces) with British & European booksellers, period 1907-1914. Printed catalog, "Bibliotheca de Re Metallica," published in 1980. Restricted use.
CA —UNIVERSITY OF CALIFORNIA, DAVIS, Physical Sciences Library, Davis, 95616. Scott Kennedy, Head
Holdings: Vols 3725 Cat
Budget: ($4000)
Notes: Incl areas of astronomy, chemistry, engineering, geology, mathematics, and physics. Strong in journal runs and reference materials. See individual subject headings for collection details.
CA —UNIVERSITY OF SOUTHERN CALIFORNIA, Seaver Science Library, University Park, Los Angeles, 90089. A Albert Baker, Head
Holdings: Vols (200,000) Microforms
Budget: ($700,000)
Notes: Includes technical reports (12,000), serial and periodical titles (3600).
CA —CALIFORNIA INSTITUTE OF TECHNOLOGY, Robert A Millikan Memorial Library, Archives, 1201 E California Blvd, Pasadena, 91125. Judith R Goodstein, Archivist
Holdings: Vols (3000) Uncat Mss Maps Pix

SCIENCE (cont.)

Slides Phonorecords Audiotapes Videotapes 16mm Films Microforms

Notes: Over 70 collections (1830s-present) relating to history of 19th-20th centuries science and technology and the history of the Institute. Included are personal and professional papers of Caltech scientists and administrative officers; divisional records and faculty committees; over 5000 photographs of American and European scientists. Mss collections documents more than a century of American political, social, and intellectual history; the development of the physical sciences, aeronautics, molecular biology, and seismology in the US and abroad; and social and political conditions in Europe between the two World Wars. There are also family letters relating to 19th century American life before and during the Civil War (the Morley and A G Throop papers); to 19th century social conditions in Russia and Hungary (the Paul Epstein papers and Theodore von Karman papers); andto the development of 20th century Italian mathematics.

CA —CALIFORNIA INSTITUTE OF TECHNOLOGY, Robert A Millikan Memorial Library, 1201 E California Blvd, Pasadena, 91125. Judith R Goodstein, Archivist
Holdings: Vols (2300) Cat
Notes: Emphasis on the period of Galileo and Kepler. Incl the Watson History of Science Collection and the Rocco Collection. Catalogs.

CA —CONTRA COSTA COUNTY LIBRARY, 1750 Oak Park Blvd, Pleasant Hill, 94523. Barbara Potter, Librn
Holdings: Vols (18,000)

CA —SAN DIEGO STATE UNIVERSITY, Malcolm A Love Library, 5300 Campanile Dr, San Diego, 92182. D Dickinson, Univ Librn; Don L Bosseau, Dir
Holdings: Vols (1500) Cat Mss Maps Pix Slides 4200 Other Items
Notes: The Ernst Zinner Collection, incl 2 incunables, autographs of scientists, portraits, pictures of sundials, 31 ms letters.

CA —UNIVERSITY OF CALIFORNIA, SANTA CRUZ, University Library, Special Collections, Santa Cruz, 95064. Rita Bottoms, Special Collections Librn; Margaret Felts, South Pacific Collection Bibliographer
Notes: General circulation.

CA —STANFORD UNIVERSITY LIBRARIES, Cecil H Green Library, Stanford, 94305. Michael T Ryan, Cur
Holdings: Vols 9000 Mss Pix
Notes: The Frederick E Brasch Collection (4000 vols cat). History of science, with emphasis on Newton, his precursors, contemporaries and successors. The Samuel I and Cecile M Barchas Collection in the History of Science and Ideas. Rare books in the history of science with emphasis on physics and astronomy, and rare landmark books in all history of science subjects and time periods.

CT —YALE UNIVERSITY, Box 1603A, Yale Station, New Haven, 06520.

CT —YALE UNIVERSITY, Kline Science Library, Kline Biology Tower Rm C-8, PO Box 6666, New Haven, 06511. Richard J Dionne, Head
Holdings: Vols (175,480) Cat 16mm Film Microforms
Budget: ($340,000)
Notes: Comprehensive collection on biological sciences, physics, and chemistry. Incl Evans Collection of Bryology and Lichenology (with catalog cards in both Kline Science Library and Sterling Memorial Library). Also incl AEC reports (hardcopy and microform) to 1970.

CT —YALE UNIVERSITY, Medical Historical Library, Klebs Collection, 333 Cedar St, New Haven, 06520. Ferenc A Gyorgyey, Librn
Notes: Incl the collection of Harvey Cushing, John Fulton and Arnold C Klebs, and historical collections of the Yale Medical Library.

DC —CENTER FOR BIOETHICS, Library, Kennedy Institute, Georgetown University, 3520 Prospect St NW, Washington, 20057. Doris Goldstein, Dir; Judith Mistichelli, Senior Librn
Holdings: Vols 8200
Notes: Largest library of its kind. Incl 31, 000 journal articles. Collects in the following subject areas: applied ethics; medical ethics; philosophy of medicine; science, technology and society; sociology of medicine; patient-physician care; sexuality; contraception; abortion; population policy; reproductive technologies; in vitro fertilization; genetic counseling and screening; genetic engineering; mental organ transplantation; death and dying; "baby doe" issues; euthanasia; suicide; use of chemical and biological weapons. Produces computer database *Bioethicsline*, available through MEDLARS; and the printed annual *Bibliography of Bioethics*. Other library publications are: *New Titles in Bioethics* (monthly); *Scope Notes* series on current topics.

DC —GEORGETOWN UNIVERSITY, Medical Center, John Vinton Dahlgren Memorial Library, 3900 Reservoir Rd NW, Washington, 20057. Clementine Pellegrino, Librn
Holdings: Vols (1000) Cat Mss Pix Slides
Notes: The Alexis Carrel Collection. Medical research of man and society. Biological specimens and numerous unpublished mss. The Alexis Carrel Collection incl: a complete set of Dr Carrel's scientific notebooks starting in 1906; Col Charles Lindbergh's notebooks from 1935-1939 and those of De Ebeling, Dr Carrel's collaborator for 25 years; the ms of *Man the Unknown*, numerous specimens of Dr Carrel's work in transplantation of blood vessels, kidney, thyroid and other organs; considerable data on tissue cultivation. Correspondence from 1906 until his death to his wife, brother, cousins, nieces, etc; correspondence to many of the great scientists of the era, as well as all correspondence relating to his book *Man the Unknown*. There is a separate index to the collection.

DC —LIBRARY OF CONGRESS, African and Middle Eastern Division, Washington, 20540.
Holdings: Cat Mss Microforms
Notes: Orientalia: the Orientalia Division contains 1,400,000 vols in Oriental languages. Chinese: more than 422,000 vols, espec strong in local histories and Ch'ing (1644-1911) period material. Japanese: over 574,000 vols, espec strong in economics, statistics, history literature; 12,000 government, learned society, and university periodical titles, particularly science, technology, and social sciences. Korean: 56, 000 vols, espec strong in social sciences and modern history.

DC —LIBRARY OF CONGRESS, Science & Technology Div, Washington, 20540.
Holdings: Cat Pix Microforms
Notes: One of the world's major collections of technical report literature, comprising nearly 3 million documents (1.7 Million on microform) currently increasing by about 100,000 annually. Receives reports in all fields of scientific research and development supported by or of interest to government agencies, incl Dept of Energy, Dept of Defense, National Aeronautics and Space Administration, Office of Education, and the National Technical Information Service, as well as many industrial and foreign reports. Also some 30,000 OSRD reports on World War II research and development and current Soviet state standards (GOST). Reports are available for consultation in the Science and Technology Division's Science Reading Room and for purchase ofphotoduplicates. Subject access is provided through the various indexing media issued by the report supplying agencies, and in some instances through in-house finding aids.

DC —NATIONAL GEOGRAPHIC SOCIETY, Library, 1146 16th St NW, Washington, 20036. Susan Fifer Canby, Dir
Holdings: Vols (63,000) Cat Mss Maps Pix
Notes: Material concerning land, sea, and space exploration--past and present. All fields of anthropology, natural history, geography, etc.

DC —NATIONAL SCIENCE FOUNDATION, Library, 1800 G St NW, Room 1242, Washington, 20550. Florence E Heckman, Ref Librn
Holdings: Vols 15,000 Cat Microforms
Budget: $184,000

DC —SMITHSONIAN INSTITUTION LIBRARIES, National Museum of American History Branch, Washington, 20560. Rhoda S Ratner, Branch Librn
Holdings: Vols (369,650) Cat Mss Maps Pix Slides Microforms

DC —SMITHSONIAN INSTITUTION LIBRARIES, General Library, Washington, 20560. Mary Claire Grey, Chief Cent Ref & Loan Servs
Holdings: Vols (79,000) Cat Mss Maps Pix Slides Microforms

FL —MIAMI-DADE PUBLIC LIBRARY SYSTEM, One Biscayne Blvd, Miami, 33132. Theresa L Liangi, Science & Technical Librn
Holdings: Vols 8000 Cat
Notes: Incl 240 journals and on-line reference searching.

GA —FERNBANK SCIENCE CENTER LIBRARY, 156 Heaton Park Dr NE, Atlanta, 30307. Mary Larsen, Librn; Janice MacLeod, Bibliographic Instructor
Holdings: Vols (12,000) Cat Maps Pix Slides Microforms
Budget: ($35,000)
Notes: Science with emphasis on astronomy, biology, outdoor education. Incl 5500 color slides; periodicals on microfilm.

GA —GEORGIA INSTITUTE OF TECHNOLOGY, Price Gilbert Memorial Library, 225 North Ave, Atlanta, 30332. Edward Graham Roberts, Dir
Holdings: Vols (1,661,559) Cat Maps Slides Microforms
Budget: ($1,383,302)
Notes: Incl (4,307,996) patents and (568, 490) government documents.

IL —ARGONNE NATIONAL LABORATORY, Library, Technical Information Services Dept, 9700 Cass Ave, Argonne, 60439. Hillis L Griffin, Dir
Notes: The ANL library system consists of eight branch libraries with centralized processing services. The entire collection numbers 70,000 monographic titles, 3700 journal titles, and over 1 million scientific and technical reports. Materials may be used by the public in the library by prior arrangement. Photocopies may be supplied for interlibrary loan, for which a processing and handling charge is made.

IL —CENTER FOR RESEARCH LIBRARIES, 6050 S Kenwood Ave, Chicago, 60637. Donald B Simpson, Dir; Esther Smith, Collection Development Librn

IL —MUSEUM OF SCIENCE AND INDUSTRY, Library, 57th St and Lake Shore Dr, Chicago, 60637. Carla Hayden, Coordinator
Holdings: Vols (15,000) Cat Pix Slides
Budget: ($10,000)
Notes: Children's non-fiction collection; science education materials, incl filmstrips, films, software, kits, and textbooks.

IL —UNIVERSITY OF CHICAGO LIBRARIES, John Crerar Library Collections, 1100 E 57th St, Chicago, 60637. Robert Rosenthal, Special Collections Librn
Notes: The John Crerar Library's extensive science, medicine, and engineering collections have been transferred in trust to the University of Chicago Libraries. Incl rare books and special collections as listed here.

IL —NORTHBROOK PUBLIC LIBRARY, 1201 Cedar Lane, Northbrook, 60062. Carole Klein-Alexander, Head of Reference Service
Holdings: Vols (4688) Cat
Budget: ($6800)
Notes: Maintained as technology subject center for North Suburban Library System's Coordinated Acquistions Program through 1979. Library will attempt to maintain collection through its own budget.

IL —UNIVERSITY OF ILLINOIS, URBANA/CHAMPAIGN, Library, Rare

SCIENCE (cont.)

Book Room, 346 Library, Urbana, 61801.
Norman B Brown, Asst Dir for Special
Collections; N Frederick Nash, Librn
Holdings: Cat Mss Maps Pix Slides
Microforms
Notes: Extensive collection, described in:
Catalog of the Rare Book Room, (Boston: G
K Hall, 1972). Supplement (1978).

IL —UNIVERSITY OF ILLINOIS,
URBANA/CHAMPAIGN, Slavic and East
European Library, Urbana, 61801. Marianna
Tax Choldin, Head
Holdings: Vols (420,000) Cat Microforms
Notes: One of the largest Slavic and East
European collections. Strong in Russian and
Soviet materials-humanities, sciences, and
social sciences; languages and literatures;
periodicals, newspapers, and microforms. Ca
260,000 volumes in languages of the Soviet
Union plus 20,000 Russian and Ukrainian
titles on microform. Extensive coverage of
Czechoslovakia (35,000 vols); Yugoslavia
(31,000 vols); Bulgaria (9200 vols); Poland
(34,600 vols); Romania (13,000 vols); and
Hungary (18,000 vols) and the languages,
literatures, and history of these countries.

IN —INDIANA UNIVERSITY, Lilly Library,
Seventh St, Bloomington, 47405. William R
Cagle, Librn
Holdings: Cat Mss
Notes: First appearances in print of great
scientific discoveries. Mss incl papers of
many scientists, particularly the biological
sciences; also of some inventors.

IN —INDIANA STATE UNIVERSITY,
Science Library, Terre Haute, 47809. Susan
J Thompson, Science Librn
Holdings: Vols (40,000) Cat Microforms
Budget: ($160,846)

IA —IOWA STATE UNIVERSITY, Library,
Dept of Special Collections, Ames, 50011.
Stanley M Yates, Head
Holdings: Mss
Notes: Papers of Iowa Academy of Science.
The Academy was organized in 1875 and
has endeavored to develop interest in
science, strengthen the bonds between
scientists and stimulate scientific research
and work in Iowa. 18 linear ft, finding aid
available.

KS —UNIVERSITY OF KANSAS, Kenneth
Spencer Research Library, Special
Collections Dept, Lawrence, 66045.
Alexandra Mason, Librn
Holdings: Cat Mss Maps Pix
Notes: Ellis Collection of Ornithology,
natural history and voyages and travels;
botanical literature from Fitzpatrick
collection (especially medical botany, early
American Botanists, renaissance herbals,
Metthioli); some early chemistry and
mathematics; scientific voyages and travels;
De Beer collection of offprints in
embryology, endocrinology, and systematic
zoology; D'Arcy Wentworth Thompson
collection of separates in natural history and
classics; Herrick, Coghill and Roofe
collections in neurology. Noncirculating.

KY —NAVAL ORDNANCE SYSTEMS
COMMAND, Technical Library, Code
50122, Louisville, 40214. Libby Miles, Librn
Holdings: Vols 5500 Cat Maps Microforms
Notes: Excel in Government specifications,
ordnance pamphlets, and all types of other
Government documents. Large service in
Industry Standard on film, some volumes.

ME —COLLEGE OF THE ATLANTIC,
Thorndike Library, Bar Harbor, 04609.
Marcie L Dworak, Libr Dir
Notes: A rebuilding, fire-destroyed library
(1983).

MD —JOHNS HOPKINS UNIVERSITY,
Milton S Eisenhower Library, Charles & 34
Sts, Baltimore, 21218. Ann S Gwyn,
Assistant Dir for Special Collections
Notes: Foreign and American doctoral
dissertations and reprints to 1964. Largest
number in history of science, 85,000. Also
biology, chemistry, geology, meteorology,
psychology, physics and mathematics. Johns
Hopkins not included. Incl 100,000 Western
European doctoral dissertations, espec
French and German; some Scandinavian.

Collection is located in Gillman Storage
Area accessible through Special Collection
Division.

MD —JOHNS HOPKINS UNIVERSITY,
Milton S Eisenhower Library, Charles & 34
Sts, Baltimore, 21218. Ann S Gwyn,
Assistant Dir for Special Collections
Holdings: Cat Mss
Notes: Chiefly important for the history of
universities in the US, and for the history of
science. Correspondence of academic leaders
such as Andrew White, Daniel Colt Gilman
and Charles W Eliot; scientific figures:
Rowland and Osler. State Department
correspondence of Isaiah Bowman in World
War II. American statesmen from
Washington to Wilson; literary figures,
chiefly American and German; many
Hopkins professors and Maryland civic
leaders. Housed in the Frieda C Thies
Manuscript Room. About 75,000 mss.

MD —JOHNS HOPKINS UNIVERSITY,
Milton S Eisenhower Library, Charles & 34
Sts, Baltimore, 21218. Ann S Gwyn,
Assistant Dir for Special Collections
Holdings: Vols 21,000 Cat Slides
Microforms
Notes: Particularly good in serials. Long
runs, some back to 18th century, in all
languages.

MD —MARYLAND ACADEMY OF
SCIENCES, Maryland Science Center, 601
Light Street, Baltimore, 21230.
Notes: Planetarium and exhibits.

MD —UNIVERSITY OF BALTIMORE,
Langsdale Library, 1420 Maryland Ave,
Baltimore, 21201. Gerry Watkins, Head of
Special Collections Dept
Holdings: Cat Mss Maps
Notes: Incl the entire stock (10,000 vols) of
Peter Decker, New York antiquarian
bookdealer (acquired in 1970); incl Peter
Decker's mss of his published works and his
records as a dealer in Americana.

†MA —BOSTON PUBLIC LIBRARY, Copley
Sq, Boston, 02117.
Holdings: Cat Microforms
Notes: Microform Publication by Readex
Microprint Corp Landmarks of Science.

MA —CHILDREN'S MUSEUM, Resource
Center, Museum Wharf, 300 Congress St,
Boston, 02210. Marie Ariel, Librn; Maria
Russell, Resource Services Mgr
Holdings: Vols 300 Cat Mss Filmstrips
Notes: Curriculum materials and materials
for children and adults. Available for
reference use by the public; borrowing
privileges for Museum members; activity and
curriculum kits available to public, schools
and community groups for rental fee.
Subject-related programs and services offered
by Museum staff.

MA —MUSEUM OF SCIENCE, Library,
Science Park, Boston, 02114. Edward D
Pearce, Librn
Holdings: Vols 33,000 Cat

MA —HARVARD UNIVERSITY LIBRARY,
History of Science Library, Widener Library
91, Cambridge, 02138. Erwin N Hiebert,
Chairman
Holdings: Vols 23,480 Cat Microforms
Budget: $2100
Notes: Major research collection in this
subject is in general collection of Harvard
Library, but this library contains George
Sarton collection described in *Harvard
Library Bulletin,* IV (1950), 276-277.

MA —MASSACHUSETTS INSTITUTE OF
TECHNOLOGY, Institute Archives, Special
Collections, Cambridge, 02139.
Notes: Derr and I Austin Kelly collections
contain significant monuments of science,
technology and printing.

MA —BOSTON COLLEGE LIBRARIES,
Science Library, Devlin Hall, Chestnut Hill,
02167. F Clifford McElroy, Science Librn
Holdings: Vols (54,508) Cat Maps
Microforms
Budget: ($94,270)
Notes: Library is being absorbed into the
general collection.

MA —SMITH COLLEGE, Library,
Northampton, 01063. Ruth Mortimer, Cur
of Rare Books
Holdings: Vols 600 Cat
Notes: No photocopying.

†MA —WILLIAMS COLLEGE, Chapin
Library of Rare Books, PO Box 426,
Williamstown, 01267. Robert L Volz,
Custodian
Holdings: Vols 375 Cat
Notes: No material available on interlibrary
loan.

MI —UNIVERSITY OF MICHIGAN, Library,
Dept of Rare Books & Special Collections,
Ann Arbor, 48109. Robert J Starring, Head
Holdings: Cat Msss Pix
Notes: Chiefly pre-1800 imprints.

MI —UNIVERSITY OF MICHIGAN,
Museums Library, Ann Arbor, 48109.
Patricia B Yocum, Librn
Holdings: Vols (100,000) Cat Maps
Microforms

MN —MINNEAPOLIS PUBLIC LIBRARY &
INFORMATION CENTER, Science &
Technology Dept, 300 Nicollet Mall,
Minneapolis, 55401. Edythe Abrahamson,
Librn
Notes: Separate card catalog, telephone
reference service, and directory service. Incl
periodicals; large file of corporation annual
reports; VF local company histories and
annual reports; domestic and foreign
telephone directories; trade and industrial
directories; historical US stock quotations,
1891-date; local OTC quotations, 1933-date;
indexes and abstracting services; looseleaf
reference services.

MN —SAINT PAUL PUBLIC LIBRARY,
Science and Industry Room, 90 W Fourth
St, Saint Paul, 55102. Virginia B Stavn,
Supvr
Holdings: Vols 19,000 Cat
Budget: ($79,500)

MO —LINDA HALL LIBRARY, 5109 Cherry
St, Kansas City, 64110. Larry X Besant, Dir;
Wilma L Hartman, Librn for Public Services;
Siegfried Ruschin, Librn for Collection
Development
Holdings: Cat Maps Microforms
Budget: $1,000,000
Notes: Over 600,000 vols, 870,000
microforms, over 100,000 engineering
standards and specifications. Also, patents,
technical reports, specifications, and
conference proceedings. Receives 16,400
serial publications in some 40 languages, in
science and technology, and 36,000 total
serial titles. Academy publications, back to
the 17th century, and some 3000 books of
historical significance in science and
technology (History of Science Collection)
are among the strongest areas in the library
collection. Downs number-2169 and in
Supplement many references 1031, 1105,
1106, 1123-24, etc. It would be difficult to
break down strengths in the individual areas
of the sciences and technology. Collection is
comprehensive throughout these subject
areas (except for clinical medicine and
surgery, which are out of scope). Open to
the public.

MO —SAINT LOUIS UNIVERSITY, Pius XII
Memorial Library, 3655 W Pine Blvd, Saint
Louis, 63108. William Cole, Dir
Holdings: Vols 4500 Cat

NH —US ARMY COLD REGIONS
RESEARCH AND ENGINEERING
LABORATORY, 72 Lyme Road, Hanover,
03755. Nancy Liston, Librn
Holdings: Cat Maps Microforms
Notes: The primary material consists of
reports, documents, journal articles, cited in
the library's "Bibliography on Cold Regions
Science and Technology." About one third of
the items cited in vols 1-22 are on microfilm
or in report or reprint form; beginning with
vol 23, all items are microfiched and sent to
the library, which now has over 55,000 items
on microfiche. These are indexed by author
and subject in the annual volume of the
Bibliography.

NJ —RUTGERS, THE STATE UNIVERSITY
OF NEW JERSEY, Library of Science &
Medicine, PO Box 1029, Piscataway, 08854.
Frank Polach, Dir
Holdings: Vols (275,000) Cat Maps

NJ —PRINCETON UNIVERSITY, Library,
Rare Books Dept, Princeton, 08544. Stephen
Ferguson, Cur
Holdings: Cat

NJ —BECTON, DICKINSON & CO,
Corporate Library/Information Center,

SCIENCE (cont.)

Rutherford, 07070. Lynda M Wiseman,
Corporate Librn
Holdings: Vols (3500) Cat Microforms
Notes: Open to the public by appointment
and ILL.

NY —NEW YORK STATE LIBRARY, State
Education Bldg Annex, Washington Ave,
Albany, 12224.
Notes: Augmented and now important
collection of books and journals, foreign and
domestic. Incl all journals translated from
the Russian.

NY —PRATT INSTITUTE LIBRARY, 200
Willoughby Ave, Brooklyn, 11205.

NY —BUFFALO & ERIE COUNTY PUBLIC
LIBRARY, Rare Book Room, Lafayette Sq,
Buffalo, 14203. William H Loos, Cur
Holdings: Vols 700 Cat

NY —BUFFALO MUSEUM OF SCIENCE,
Buffalo Society of Natural Sciences,
Research Library, Humboldt Park, Buffalo,
14211. Marcia T Morrison, Chief Librn
Notes: Subject emphases: natural sciences,
anthropology, archaeology; vols 37,000
cataloged. Also, first and rare editions of
books in the history of science; vols 291.
Milestones of Science describes epochal
books in the history of science as
represented in the library of the Buffalo
Society of Natural Sciences. Catalog
compiled by Ruth A Sparrow, Buffalo
Society of Natural Sciences. Collection
Catalog no 1 Buffalo Museum of Science,
Buffalo, New York, 1972. Colored
frontispiece, 308 pages (of which 207 are
plates). 100 limited numbered edition; 2000
regular edition. See especially no 68
Audubonia-letters, mss, autographs.

NY —CORNELL UNIVERSITY LIBRARIES,
John M Olin Library, History of Science
Collections, Ithaca, 14853. Lillian A Clark,
Administrative Supervisor; David W Corson,
History of Science Librn
Notes: Very extensive collection of history,
biography and bibliography.
See also entry under Science - History

NY —COLUMBIA UNIVERSITY
LIBRARIES, Engineering Library, 422
Mudd Bldg, New York, 10027.
Holdings: Microforms
Notes: Over 1,000,000 technical reports,
mostly on microfiche, incl virtually complete
sets of unclassified AEC and NASA
documents; also strong in AD & PB series.
For all users, with no restrictions as to
affiliation.

NY —INTERNATIONAL PAPER CO,
Corporate Information Center, 77 W 45 St,
New York, 10036. Elizabeth Skerritt,
Corporate Librn
Holdings: Vols 1000

NY —NEW YORK PUBLIC LIBRARY,
Research Libraries, Science and Technology
Research Center, Fifth Ave & 42 St, New
York, 10018.
Holdings: Vols (1,100,000) Cat Microforms
Budget: ($647,259)
Notes: Covers all the pure and applied
sciences except the biological sciences.
Particularly strong in aeronautics,
biochemistry, chemical engineering,
chemistry, communications, electricity,
electronics, engineering, geology,
mathematics, metallurgy, meteorology,
mining, navigation, paper, petroleum,
physics, shipbuilding, and textiles.

NY —NEW YORK PUBLIC LIBRARY, Mid-
Manhattan Library, Science & Business
Dept, 455 Fifth Ave, New York, 10016.
Frederick E Dusold, Sr Principal Librn
Holdings: Vols (110,000) Cat Microforms
Budget: ($134,000)
Notes: With rare exceptions all works in
English. Current material; policy precludes
archival collecting. Collection geared toward
the undergraduate college student, with
consideration given to the professional, the
lay reader and the beginning graduate
student. A collection of monographs, texts,
treatises, standard reference works and
periodicals in the philosophy, history and
theory of science. Special strength in
mathematics and life sciences. Circulating

books are available in addition to an
extensive reference collection.

NY —UNIVERSITY OF ROCHESTER,
Carlson Library, Hutchison Hall, River
Campus, Rochester, 14627. Michael W
Poulin, Librn
Holdings: Vols (48,720) Cat Microforms
Notes: Strong collection in the field and
related areas.

NY —UNION COLLEGE, Schaffer Library,
Archives of Science and Technology,
Schenectady, 12308. Ellen Fladger, Archivist
Notes: Research and development. Papers of
Ernst Fredrik Werner Alexanderson, Philip
L Alger, Howard I Becker, Ernst Julius Berg,
Gabriel Kron, Samuel P Nixdorff, Birger W
Nordlander, William E Ruder, George
Westinghouse, and William Comings White.

NY —US MILITARY ACADEMY LIBRARY,
West Point, 10996. Elaine B Eatroff, Rare
Book Cur
Holdings: Vols 1500 Cat
Notes: Thayer Collection, incl rare editions
of 19th century science. An emphasis on
astronomy; earliest imprints 1476.

NC —DUKE UNIVERSITY, William R
Perkins Library, Durham, 27706. Elvin E
Strowd, University Librn
Notes: The James Ray Newman collection
of several thousand books and more than
8000 manuscripts is broad in scope and
particularly strong in mathematics,
philosophy, logic and history and philosophy
of science.

NC —WAKE TECHNICAL COLLEGE,
Library, Audio-Visual Dept, 9101
Fayetteville Road, Raleigh, 27603. James
Gray, Librn; Horst Garloff, Audio-Visual
Specialist
Holdings: Vols (32,332) Cat Maps Slides
Phonorecords Audiotapes Videotapes 16mm
Films Filmstrips Microforms

OH —PUBLIC LIBRARY OF CINCINNATI
& HAMILTON COUNTY, Science &
Technology Dept, 800 Vine St, Cincinnati,
45202. Rosemary Gaiser, Head
Holdings: Vols (250,000) Cat
Notes: Pure and applied science. Incl over
1600 periodicals and serial titles and more
than 100 abstracting and indexing services in
major fields of science and technology.

OH —CLEVELAND PUBLIC LIBRARY,
Science & Technology Dept, 325 Superior
Ave, Cleveland, 44114. Jean Z Piety, Head
Holdings: Cat
Notes: Primarily an engineering collection
with basic sciences; strong in 19th and 20th
century American, British, and Canadian
technical societies' publications;
comprehensive bibliography, standards and
specifications; Rand Corp; 4400 periodicals
and serial; extensive collections in chemistry,
pamphlets (60,000). Incl collections on
geology, aeronautics and agriculture.

OR —OREGON STATE UNIVERSITY,
Library, Corvallis, 97331. Melvin George,
Dir
Holdings: Vols (980,000) Cat
Notes: Incl 7800 serial publications currently
received in science, technology and
agriculture.

OR —UNIVERSITY OF OREGON
LIBRARY, Science Library, Eugene, 97403.
George Shipman, Head Librn; Terry
Morrison, Reference Librn; Isabel A Stirling,
Head Science Librn
Holdings: Vols 200,000 Cat Microforms
Budget: $548,000
Notes: General collection for the physical
and life sciences. 3,000 current journal
subscriptions. Separate Mathematics library.
Incl general collection of pure science, "from
astronomy to zoology." Incl 1850 mss
(unpublished theses and dissertations) and
18,000 microforms.

PA —ALLEGHENY COLLEGE, Lawrence
Lee Pelletier Library, Meadville, 16335.
Margaret L Moser, Librn
Holdings: Vols (3000) Cat
Notes: James Winthrop's original collection.
History, science, language among principal
subject fields. Part of original gift to this
library, 1819-23. Listed in Timothy Alden,
*Catalogus Bibliothecae Collegii
Alleghaniensis*, 1823. Downs 180.

PA —FRANKLIN INSTITUTE LIBRARY, 20
& The Parkway, Philadelphia, 19103.

Miriam Padusis, Dir; Charles Wilt, Readers
Servs Librn
Holdings: Vols (300,000) Cat Maps Pix
Microforms

PA —LIBRARY COMPANY OF
PHILADELPHIA, 1314 Locust St,
Philadelphia, 19107. Edwin Wolf II, Librn;
Kenneth Finkel, Cur of Prints
Holdings: Vols (400,000) Cat Maps Pix
Budget: ($25,000)
Notes: American science and industry before
1860. Books, pamphlets, etc on science incl
math, pysics, astronomy, and industry, incl
business and engineering. Incl many 18th
century books printed in England and
France but used by American colonials in
their study and research. Impossible to
estimate the exact size of collection since it
is not separated from general collection.

PA —CARNEGIE LIBRARY OF
PITTSBURGH, Science & Technology Dept,
4400 Forbes Ave, Pittsburgh, 15213.
Catherine M Brosky, Dept Head
Holdings: Vols (380,000) Cat Maps
Microforms
Budget: ($240,000)
Notes: Long runs of periodicals,
monographs, serials, handbooks, abstracts,
indexes, bibliographies, tables of data,
society publications. Modern and classic
materials.

†RI —UNIVERSITY OF RHODE ISLAND,
Library, Kingston, 02881.
Notes: Extensive collections.

RI —BROWN UNIVERSITY, John Carter
Brown Library, Providence, 02912. Norman
Fiering, Librn; Everett C Wilkie Jr,
Bibliographer; Susan Danforth, Cur Maps &
Prints
Notes: Incl pre-Columbian materials; general
works of a scientific nature, incl science of
navigation, that formed background
knowledge of European scientific inquiry
until 1800.
See also entry under Medicine - History and
Historic

†SD —SOUTH DAKOTA SCHOOL OF
MINES & TECHNOLOGY, Devereaux
Library, Rapid City, 57701.
Holdings: Vols (166,200) Cat Maps
Audiotapes Filmstrips Microforms
Notes: Supportive collection incl periodicals
and technical reports (NASA, ACRL, JPL,
etc); and extensive government document
materials (NBS, Dept of Commerce, HEW,
etc).

TX —SOUTHERN METHODIST
UNIVERSITY, Science/Engineering
Library, Dallas, 75275. Devertt D Bickston,
Librn
Holdings: Vols (166,000) Cat Maps Pix
Microforms
Notes: Incl 65,000 bound periodicals, 236,
000 government documents, 178,000 maps,
112,000 microforms, and 1416 periodical
subscriptions.

TX —FORT WORTH PUBLIC LIBRARY, 300
Taylor St, Fort Worth, 76102. John R
McCracken, Manager
Holdings: Vols (12,500) Cat
Budget: ($21,000)

VA —US PATENT OFFICE, Science Library,
2021 Jefferson Davis Hwy, Arlington,
22202. Henry Rosicky, Chief Librn
Holdings: Vols 250,000 Cat Pix Microforms
Notes: Strengths are in applied sciences and
technology. Public card catalog in Reading
Room listing books by author, title, and
subject, and periodicals by title and subject.
Over 77,000 additional volumes of
periodicals.

WA —SEATTLE PUBLIC LIBRARY, 1000
Fourth Ave, Seattle, 98104. Ronald A
Dubberly, City Librn
Holdings: Cat Maps Microforms

WA —UNIVERSITY OF WASHINGTON
LIBRARIES, Suzzallo Library, Natural
Sciences Library, FM-25, Seattle, 98195.
Nancy G Blase, Head
Holdings: Vols (192,353)
Budget: ($219,809)

WI —MILWAUKEE PUBLIC LIBRARY, 814
W Wisconsin Ave, Milwaukee, 53233.
Donald J Sager, City Librn
Holdings: Vols (30,000) Cat
Notes: Strong collection acquired to support

SCIENCE (cont.)

state interlibrary loan. Covers all the pure and applied sciences. Incl over (1600) periodicals and serial titles and more than (100) abstracting and indexing services in major fields of science and technology. Strong general reference service.

BC —VANCOUVER PUBLIC LIBRARY, Science & Technology Div, 750 Burrard St, Vancouver, V6Z 1X5, Can. P Haffenden, Head, Science & Technology Div
Holdings: Cat
Notes: Plus special indexes, incl Organization and Association File (primarily local, British Columbian, and Canadian), begun in 1950s, expanded since 1960s; Government Documents File; Chart File; Standards File and Index.

MB —UNIVERSITY OF MANITOBA, Science Library, Machray Hall, Winnipeg, R3T 2N2, Can. V Simosko, Head
Holdings: Vols 113,500 Cat
Notes: 113,500 volumes, 1550 serials, 10,750 government publications, 1100 microfiche, all cataloged.

ON —ONTARIO SCIENCE CENTRE LIBRARY, 770 Don Mills Rd, Don Mills, M3C 1T3, Can. Jeanne DuPerrault, Librn
Holdings: Pix Slides 16mm Films Videotapes
Notes: 500 films, 30,000 slides and photographs, 50 videotapes, 100 periodicals.

ON —CANADA INSTITUTE FOR SCIENTIFIC & TECHNICAL INFORMATION, Montreal Rd, Ottawa, K1A 0S2, Can. Elmer V Smith, Dir
Holdings: Vols Microforms
Budget: ($17,000,000)
Notes: National collection for science in Canada. Excellent collection of serials and technical reports. Journals do not circulate. 14 Branch Libraries maintain subject collections in aeronautical engineering, astronomy, biotechnology, building and construction, biology, chemistry, electrical engineering, energy, industrial materials, physics, marine biology, ocean engineering. Access to these collections is available via the central library. 2,300,000 reports, books, serials and conference proceedings; 1,600,000 of these are on microfiche.

ON —UNIVERSITY OF OTTAWA, Vanier Library, 11 Somerset St East, Ottawa, K1N 9A4, Can. J David Holmes, Librn
Holdings: Vols (140,000) Cat
Budget: $570,700
Notes: This collection contains teaching and research level material to support all branches of the pure sciences and engineering. Incl periodicals (3000), cataloged.

ON —METROPOLITAN TORONTO LIBRARY, Science & Technology Dept, 789 Yonge St, Toronto, M4W 2G8, Can. Margaret Walshe, Head
Holdings: Vols (120,000) Cat Maps VF
Notes: All aspects of science for the specialist, the student, and the general public. The department gives high priority to Canadian materials.

PQ —ECOLE POLYTECHNIQUE BIBLIOTHEQUE, Campus de l'Universite de Montreal, PO Box 6079, Station "A", Montreal, H3C 3A7, Can. Josee Schepper, Chief of Public Services
Holdings: Vols (111,000) Cat Maps Microforms
Budget: ($330,000)
Notes: Catalog available on microfiche.

PQ —TROIS-RIVIERES COLLEGE LIBRARY, CEGEP de Trois-Rivieres-Bibliotheque, 3500 de Courval, Trois-Rivieres, G9A 5E6, Can. Denis Simard, Librn
Holdings: Vols (95,000) Cat Maps Pix Slides Phonorecords Audiotapes Viedotapes 16mm Films Filmstrips Microforms

SCIENCE—AUTHORSHIP see Technical Writing

SCIENCE—EARLY WORKS TO 1800

MA —BRANDEIS UNIVERSITY, Goldfarb Library, 415 South St, Waltham, 02154.

Bessie Hahn, Dir
Notes: Vito Volterra Collection on the History of Science and Mathematics. A collection of more than 5000 vols containing the major works in Volterra. Inclusive dates are the 16th through the 20th century. The collection also contains over 16,000 offprints and pamphlets, most of which are dedication copies from the author to Volterra. No catalog of the books extant, but an author-title finding list for the 16,000 offprintsand pamphlets is available in Special Collections.

SCIENCE—FICTION see Science Fiction

SCIENCE—HISTORY

CA —STANFORD UNIVERSITY LIBRARIES, Cecil H Green Library, Stanford, 94305. Michael T Ryan, Cur
Holdings: Vols 9000 Mss Pix
Notes: The Frederick E Brasch Collection (4000 vols cat). History of science, with emphasis on Newton, his precursors, contemporaries and successors. The Samuel I and Cecile M Barchas Collection in the History of Science and Ideas. Rare books in the history of science with emphasis on physics and astronomy, and rare landmark books in all history of science subjects and time periods.

†CT —TRINITY COLLEGE LIBRARY, Hartford, 06106.
Notes: Incl the Ostrom Enders Collection (6000 vols), primarily of ornithology. Also rich in rare color plate books, scientific texts and periodicals from the early 17th century to the present.

CT —BURNDY LIBRARY, Electra Square, Norwalk, 06856. Philip J Weimerskirch, Asst Dir
Holdings: Vols 18,000
Notes: 3000 portraits of scientists and a small collection of early scientific instruments.

DC —SMITHSONIAN INSTITUTION, Archives Div, Washington, 20560. William W Moss, Archivist
Holdings: Cat Mss Pix
Notes: The Archives holds the records of the Smithsonian's National Museum of Natural History, National Museum of American History, Smithsonian Astrophysical Observatory, National Air and Space Museum, National Zoological Park, Smithsonian Tropical Research Institute, and Chesapeake Bay Center for Environmental Studies.

IL —NEWBERRY LIBRARY, 60 W Walton St, Chicago, 60610. Diana Haskell, Cur of Modern Mss
Holdings: Vols 1500 Cat
Notes: Only titles to 1650 identified. Strong in mathematics, geography, the occult sciences, natural history and philosophy, and medicine.

IA —IOWA STATE UNIVERSITY, Library, Ames, 50011. Warren B Kuhn, Dean of Library Services
Holdings: Cat
Notes: Extensive holdings of serial backfiles, especially in chemistry, physics, mathematics, biological sciences.

MD —JOHNS HOPKINS UNIVERSITY, Milton S Eisenhower Library, Charles & 34 Sts, Baltimore, 21218. Ann S Gwyn, Assistant Dir for Special Collections
Notes: Particularly good in serials. Long runs, some back to 18th century, in all languages.

MD —MARYLAND ACADEMY OF SCIENCES, Maryland Science Center, 601 Light Street, Baltimore, 21230.
Notes: Planetarium and exhibits.

MA —HARVARD UNIVERSITY LIBRARY, Gray Herbarium Library, 22 Divinity Ave, Cambridge, 02138. Barbara A Callahan, Librn
Notes: Arnold Arboretum and Gray Herbarium Libraries hold one of the nation's largest collections (149,000 items).

MA —BRANDEIS UNIVERSITY, Goldfarb Library, 415 South St, Waltham, 02154. Bessie Hahn, Dir
Notes: Vito Volterra Collection on the History of Science and Mathematics. A

collection of more than 5000 vols containing the major works in Volterra. Inclusive dates are the 16th through the 20th century. The collection also contains over 16,000 offprints and pamphlets, most of which are dedication copies from the author to Volterra. No catalog of the books extant, but an author-title finding list for the 16,000 offprints and pamphlets is available in Special Collections.

MO —LINDA HALL LIBRARY, 5109 Cherry St, Kansas City, 64110. Larry X Besant, Dir; Wilma L Hartman, Librn for Public Services; Siegfried Ruschin, Librn for Collection Development
Holdings: Cat Maps Microforms
Budget: $1,000,000
Notes: Over 600,000 vols, 870,000 microforms, over 100,000 engineering standards and specifications. Also, patents, technical reports, specifications, and conference proceedings. Receives 16,400 serial publications in some 40 languages, in science and technology, and 36,000 total serial titles. Academy publications, back to the 17th century, and some 3000 books of historical significance in science and technology (History of Science Collection) are among the strongest areas in the library collection. Downs number-2169 and in Supplement many references 1031, 1105, 1106, 1123-24, etc. It would be difficult to break down strengths in the individual areas of the sciences and technology. Collection is comprehensive throughout these subject areas (except for clinical medicine and surgery, which are out of scope). Open to the public.

MO —SAINT LOUIS UNIVERSITY, Pius XII Memorial Library, 3655 W Pine Blvd, Saint Louis, 63108. William Cole, Dir
Holdings: Slides Microforms
Notes: Collection covers all areas of learning and European history from Classical Antiquity to early modern period. Researchers using collection receive assistance in paleography, bibliography and reference search. Approx 10,000 1000-foot reels of microfilm (not counting master negatives) reproducing Vatican Library's Latin, Greek, Hebrew, Arabic and Ethiopic mss. Some 8000 100-foot reels of microfilm (again not counting master negative) reproducing rare and out of print books relating to subject areas in the mss. Over 50,000 color slides of medieval and Renaissance mss illuminations. A reference collection of modern materials relating to ms research.

NY —NEW YORK BOTANICAL GARDEN LIBRARY, Bronx, 10458. Charles R Long, Asst Vice Pres & Dir
Holdings: Vols 2000 Cat VF
Budget: ($356,000)
Notes: Over 900,000 items, incl books, serials, pamphlets, archives and manuscripts, vertical files, microfiche and microfilm, nursery and seed catalogs, photographs, paintings, prints, drawings and engravings. Covering all areas of botanical sciences.

NY —BUFFALO MUSEUM OF SCIENCE, Buffalo Society of Natural Sciences, Research Library, Humboldt Park, Buffalo, 14211. Marcia T Morrison, Chief Librn
Notes: First and rare editions of books in the history of science. *Milestones of Science* describes epochal books in the history of science as represented in the library of the Buffalo Society of Natural Sciences. Catalog compiled by Ruth A Sparrow, Buffalo Society of Natural Sciences. Collection Catalog no 1 Buffalo Museum of Science, Buffalo, New York, 1972. Colored frontispiece, 308 pages (of which 207 are plates). 100 limited numbered edition; 2000 regular edition. See especially no 68 Audubonia-letters, mss, autographs.

NY —CORNELL UNIVERSITY LIBRARIES, Collection of Regional History, Dept of Manuscripts and Univ Archives, Ithaca, 14853.
Notes: Incl records, 1959-64; 18 reels of tape recordings, programs, lists of participants, copies of the Congress bulletins, memoranda, press releases, minutes, final report and other items concerning the International Congress of the History of Science held at Cornell University, NY, and Philadelphia in August and September, 1962.

SCIENCE—HISTORY (cont.)

NY —CORNELL UNIVERSITY LIBRARIES, John M Olin Library, History of Science Collections, Ithaca, 14853. Lillian A Clark, Administrative Supervisor; David W Corson, History of Science Librn
Holdings: Vols 33,000 Cat
Notes: Early printed source materials reflecting the development of all the sciences, medicine, and technology from the Renaissance through the first half of the 19th century. Approximately 25,000 pre-1800 imprints. Special strengths incl Adelmann Collection in the history of anatomy and embryology (6,000 vols), Robison Collection of the works of Robert Boyle (175 vols), Lavoisier Collection in latter 18th century chemistry (2,000 vols, 500 mss), Hill Collection in history of North American ornithology, Hollister Collection in the history of engineering, early European medical dissertations (6,500 titles), the Boncompagni archives, and the La Forte archives. For descriptions see: Cornell University Libraries. *The History of Science Collections,* Ithaca, NY, 1973, 10 pp, illus (Its *Special Collections,* no 3). All materials noncirculating; reading room open to public. Referenceand photocopy services.

NY —AMERICAN INSTITUTE OF PHYSICS, Center for the History of Physics, Niels Bohr Library, 335 E 45 St, New York, 10017. John Aubry, Librn
Holdings: Vols (16,000) Cat Mss Pix Slides Phonorecords Audiotapes 16mm Films Microforms
Notes: The Library contains an extensive collection of published works relating to the history of modern physics and astronomy. Its archives incl letter, notebooks and other papers of physicists, as well as the records of leading American physics societies and institutions. Its collections of ms autobiographies, oral history interviews, and other tape recordings, and pictorial materials (incl unpublished film footage) are unrivaled in the field of history of science. It maintains the International Catalog of Sources for History of Physics and and Astronomy.

NY —COLUMBIA UNIVERSITY LIBRARIES, Science Library, 303 Mathematics Bldg, New York, 10027. Suzanne Fedunok, Head of Reference/ Collection Development
Holdings: Vols 4000
Notes: Collection comprises over 70,000 volumes, mainly of serials and superseded monographs from learned academics and societies.

†NY —COLUMBIA UNIVERSITY LIBRARIES, Butler Library, Rare Book and Manuscript Library, 535 W 114 St, New York, 10027.
Notes: 76 vols of diaries of Lynn Thorndike, 1902-63. A record of his daily reading, progress in research and writing, European travels, relations with scholars and librarians, and other personal matters.

NY —NEW YORK PUBLIC LIBRARY, Research Libraries, Science and Technology Research Center, Fifth Ave & 42 St, New York, 10018.
Holdings: Vols (1,100,000) Cat Microforms
Budget: ($647,259)

NY —UNIVERSITY OF ROCHESTER, Rush Rhees Library, Rochester, 14627. Datta S Kharbas, Head
Holdings: Vols 100,000 Cat Maps Microforms
Notes: Area studies collection on East Asia and South Asia. Major emphasis is on social sciences and humanities. Over 57,000 volumes on East Asia, out of which 29,000 volumes are in Chinese and 15,000 in Japanese. Extensive holdings on Chinese and Japanese histories. Catalog of East Asian collection consisting of Chinese and Japanese language holdings published in 1968, with two subsequent supplements. Over 33,000 volumes on South Asia. Considerable depth in social sciences, history, politics and anthropology. Extensive holdings in Sanskrit, Hindi, and Marathi.

NY —STATE UNIVERSITY OF NEW YORK, STONY BROOK, Biology Library, Stony Brook, 11794. Doris Williams, Biology Librn
Holdings: Vols 625 // Uncat
Notes: Raymond Pearl Collection. The collection contains reprints collected by Raymond Pearl, founder of the *Quarterly Review of Biology.* The reprints are indexed by author and arranged by twenty subjects relating to biology and the history of science.

NY —US MILITARY ACADEMY LIBRARY, West Point, 10996. Elaine B Eatroff, Rare Book Cur
Notes: Thayer Collection, incl rare editions of 19th century science. An emphasis on astronomy; earliest imprints 1476.

NC —DUKE UNIVERSITY, William R Perkins Library, Durham, 27706. Elvin E Strowd, University Librn
Notes: The James Ray Newman collection of several thousand books and more than 8000 manuscripts is broad in scope and particularly strong in mathematics, philosophy, logic and history and philosophy of science.

OH —OHIO UNIVERSITY, Vernon R Alden Library, Department of Archives and Special Collections, Athens, 45701. Gary A Hunt, Head
Holdings: Vols 1737 Uncat Pix
Notes: The J W Morgan Collection in the History of Chemistry and Science. The emphasis is upon chemistry. Rangers from 16th to 20th centuries, with greatest strength in 18th and 19th centuries, and in American and British imprints. See Moss, Roger W, Jr *The Morgan Collection in the History of Chemistry: A Checklist* (Athens, Ohio University Library, 1965).

OH —CASE WESTERN RESERVE UNIVERSITY LIBRARIES, Cleveland, 44106. Susie Hanson, Special Collections Librn
Holdings: Cat Maps Pix Microforms
Notes: Concentrates on 18th, 19th and early 20th century science and technology.

OH —CLEVELAND PUBLIC LIBRARY, Science & Technology Dept, 325 Superior Ave, Cleveland, 44114. Jean Z Piety, Head
Holdings: Cat
Notes: Many early volumes.

OK —UNIVERSITY OF OKLAHOMA, University Libraries, 401 W Brooks, Norman, 73019. Duane Roller, Cur
Holdings: Vols (61,000)
Notes: The History of Science Collections hold more than 61,000 vols. Incl the first printed editions of most major scientific works, all editions of many works; several thousand vols of early scientific journals; biographies of scientists; histories of science and of the sciences; encyclopedias and dictionaries; all the scholarly resources needed for the study of the history of science.

PA —BRYN MAWR COLLEGE, Canaday Library, Bryn Mawr, 19010. James Tanis, Dir
Notes: Rare books: Michaelis, Zirkle (Botany) and Castle (Ornithology and Botanical Illustration) Collections.

PA —HAVERFORD COLLEGE, Magill Library, Special Collections Dept, Haverford, 19041. Diana Alteu, Manuscripts Librn; E Rotau Sargent, Cricket Collection Librn
Notes: The Charles Roberts autograph letters collection of some 20,000 pieces, incl many of scientists and literary and political figures.

PA —AMERICAN PHILOSOPHICAL SOCIETY, Library, 105 S Fifth St, Philadelphia, 19106. Edward C Carter II, Librn
Holdings: Cat Mss Microforms
Notes: The society's archives are an important part of this collection. Especially strong for 18th-20th centuries.

PA —FRANKLIN INSTITUTE LIBRARY, 20 & The Parkway, Philadelphia, 19103. Miriam Padusis, Dir; Charles Wilt, Readers Servs Librn
Holdings: Vols (300,000) Cat Maps Pix Microforms

PA —LIBRARY COMPANY OF PHILADELPHIA, 1314 Locust St, Philadelphia, 19107. Edwin Wolf II, Librn; Kenneth Finkel, Cur of Prints
Holdings: Vols (400,000) Cat Maps Pix
Budget: ($25,000)
Notes: American science and industry before 1860. Books, pamphlets, etc on science incl math, pysics, astronomy, and industry, incl business and engineering. Incl many 18th century books printed in England and France but used by American colonials in their study and research. Impossible to estimate the exact size of collection since it is not separated from general collection.

PA —BUHL PLANETARIUM & INSTITUTE OF POPULAR SCIENCE, Staff Library, Allegheny Sq, Pittsburgh, 15212. Al DeSena, Dir
Holdings: Vols 1000 Cat Mss Maps Pix Slides Films
Notes: Science-oriented vols with several texts of historical value dating back to the 19th century.

PA —CARNEGIE LIBRARY OF PITTSBURGH, Science & Technology Dept, 4400 Forbes Ave, Pittsburgh, 15213. Catherine M Brosky, Dept Head
Holdings: Vols (380,000) Cat Maps Microforms
Budget: ($240,000)
Notes: Current works, incl standard journals acquired; some old and rare items in collection; source books and reference sets. Complete runs of the publications of numerous scientific societies and academies.

PA —UNIVERSITY OF PITTSBURGH, Hillman Library, Pittsburgh, 15260. Glenora E Rossell, Head
Holdings: Vols (6100) Cat Microforms
Notes: This History and Philosophy of Science collection is rapidly growing to support research interests in a very new synoptic approach in the integration of history of science, philosophy of science, and history of philosophy, and the intensive new program of instruction. The trend of collection is to include works in philosophical foundations of contemporary physics and cosmology, the philosophical problems of the social sciences, science and theology in the 17th century, the relation between science and epistemology in the 18th and 19th centuries; problems of microphysics, history of molecular biology, theories of scientific explanation, and relation between science and metaphysics.

RI —BROWN UNIVERSITY, John Hay Library, 20 Prospect St, Providence, 02912. Mark N Brown, Cur Mss
Holdings: Vols 17,000 Cat Mss
Notes: History of Science Collections incl resources from several specific named collections of volumes printed from the 15th to 20th centuries incl the Albert E Lownes Collection of Significant Books in in the History of Science. Works published before 1700 are unusually rich in Mathematica, Astronomy and Astrology. Publications of the various scientific academies are well represented and incl the *Philosophical Transactions of the Royal Society of London* (beginning in 1665) and *The American Journal of Science.* Also incl are the personal libraries of two 18th century American physicians: Dr Solomon Drowne, Brown class of 1773 (370 vols), and Dr William Hunter, Brown class of 1791 (73 vols).

SC —COLLEGE OF CHARLESTON LIBRARY, Special Collections Dept, Charleston, 29401.
Notes: (1) Lewis Reeves Gibbes Papers incl material relating to his study of medicine in Paris (1836-1837), correspondence, astronomical calculations, zoological observations, printed copies of his publications, scrapbooks and newsclippings regarding his scientific work. (2) Materials from the Elliott Society of Natural History. (3) Frank R Fisher Papers which record the scientific and technological studies covering a wide range of areas, particularly astronomical observations (often accompanied by drawings or photos) made in Charleston in the 1880s, at times in consultation with Lewis R Gibbes. An inventor of scientific instruments, Fisher's work incl a "Machine for Ruling Diffraction Plates" for which a detailed description and photograph are provided. Incl in-depth record of Fisher's experiences, scientific and personal, of the 1886Earthquake, accompanied by diagrams.

SCIENCE—HISTORY (cont.)

SC —CLEMSON UNIVERSITY, Libraries, Clemson, 29631. Michael F Kohl, Head of Special Collections
Holdings: Vols 1500 //
Notes: Book collection initiated with gifts from Mrs Bernard Behrend. Incl early editions by Galileo, Newton, Priestly, and other great scientists. Collecting emphasis has been upon engineering.
See also entry under Behrend, Bernard A.

TX —UNIVERSITY OF TEXAS, DALLAS, Health Science Center, Reference Dept & History of Health Sciences Dept, 5323 Harry Hines Blvd, Dallas, 75235. Helen Mayo, Head
Holdings: Vols (10,000) Cat Pix Slides Audiotapes Videotapes Microforms
Notes: History of Medicine collection contains ca 10,000 vols. This total is comprised of pre-1900 journals, primary materials in the History of Medicine and the History of Science, and secondary studies in these two areas. The major strengths of this collection are in the areas of epidemics and plagues, military medicine, and collected works of famous medical pioneers. Incl in this collection are the medical journals published by the county medical societies in Texas, local publications by Dallas County medical organizations, and ephemeral material in a similar vein. The university archives contain all theses and dissertations form UTHSCD and miscellaneous institutional documents circulated by the school's administration.

UT —UNIVERSITY OF UTAH, Middle East Library, Salt Lake City, 84112. Ragai N Makar, Librn
Holdings: Vols 3000 Cat Mss Pix Microforms
Budget: ($40,000)
Notes: The Martin Levey Collection, one of the finest on Arabic science in the country. Incl books and mss on all the sciences and medicine through the 14th century: 3000 books; 5000 offprints; 1000 microfilmed mss in German, Arabic, and French.

WA —UNIVERSITY OF WASHINGTON LIBRARIES, Suzzallo Library, Natural Sciences Library, FM-25, Seattle, 98195. Nancy G Blase, Head
Holdings: Vols (192,353)
Budget: ($219,809)

WI —UNIVERSITY OF WISCONSIN, MADISON, Memorial Library, History of Science Collection, 728 State St, Madison, 53706. John Neu, Bibliographer
Holdings: Cat Mss
Budget: ($15,000)
Notes: Major research collection of primary and secondary materials in all fields of the history of science and technology. Special collections in this area include the Dennis I Duveen Collection on the History of Chemistry; William A Cole Collection in the History of Chemistry; Chester H Thordarson Collection, notable for its wide variety of books in the history of early English science as well as books that illustrate and record the development of the various branches of natural history; Joseph Priestley Collection, Robert Boyle Collection, Carl von Linne Collection. See John Neu, ed, Chemical, Medical and Pharmaceutical Books Printed before 1800 in the Collections of the University of Wisconsin Libraries (Madison and Milwaukee: University of Wisconsin Press, 1965); Dennis I Duveen, Bibliotheca Alchemica et Chemica: An Annotated Catalogue of Printed Books on Alchemy, Chemistry and Cognate Subjects in the Library of Dennis I Duveen (London: Dawsons of Paul Mall, 1965). Restricted use: Rare Book Department.

WI —UNIVERSITY OF WISCONSIN, MADISON, Memorial Library, 728 State St, Madison, 53706. Erwin K Welsch, Social Studies Bibliographer
Notes: Thordarson Collection. Chester H Thordarson, who came to the United States as an immigrant from Iceland and became a noted electrical engineer, built up this remarkable collection on the history and development of English science: over 10,000 vols in fine condition. Particularly strong in ornithology and botany, its rarities have been described in the Papers of the Bibliogrphical Society of America, vols 23 (1930) and 44 (1950). Purchased from his widow. The nucleus of the Library's Rare Book Collection.

WI —UNIVERSITY OF WISCONSIN, MADISON, Memorial Library, 728 State St, Madison, 53706. Erwin K Welsch, Social Studies Bibliographer
Notes: Incl William Lilly Collection, works by the 17th century astrologer; William Stanley Marshall Collection, some 30 first and early editions from a former UW professor of zoology; Isaac Newton Library, 10 vols.

MB —UNIVERSITY OF MANITOBA, Science Library, Machray Hall, Winnipeg, R3T 2N2, Can. V Simosko, Head
Holdings: Vols (90,000) Cat Microforms

ON —QUEEN'S UNIVERSITY, Douglas Library, Kingston, K7L 5C4, Can. William F E Morley, Cur, Special Collections
Holdings: Vols 6980 Cat Mss Pix
Notes: Subject strength of the collections.

ON —METROPOLITAN TORONTO LIBRARY, Science & Technology Dept, 789 Yonge St, Toronto, M4W 2G8, Can. Margaret Walshe, Head
Holdings: Vols (120,000) Cat Maps VF
Notes: All aspects of science for the specialist, the student, and the general public. The department gives high priority to Canadian materials.

ON —UNIVERSITY OF TORONTO, Thomas Fisher Rare Book Library, 120 Saint George St, Toronto, M5S 1A5, Can. Richard G Landon, Head
Holdings: Vols 4000
Notes: The Science Collection is especially rich in works on Renaissance astronomy, physics and mechanics and has noteworthy holdings of works of English experimental scientists in the 17th and 18th centuries with excellent collections of the works of Robert Boyle, Robert Hooke, and Sir Isaac Newton. Includes virtually all important early editions of Euclid; alchemical works of the 16th and 17th centuries together with the works of 18th century chemists like Lavoisier and Priestly; works on agriculture with special emphasis on British agriculture in the 18th century; and a variety of other works important in the history of science in all its branches. In addition the Fisher Library has many other specialized scientific collections which are listed separately.

SCIENCE—JAPAN

MI —GENERAL MOTORS, Research Laboratories Library, General Motors Technical Center, Warren, 48090. Robert W Gibson, Librn

SCIENCE—POLAND

NY —STATE UNIVERSITY OF NEW YORK, COLLEGE AT BUFFALO, Lockwood Memorial Library, Polish Collection, Buffalo, 14260. William Borodacz, Cur
Holdings: Vols 10,000 Cat
Notes: Incl theses and dissertations. Exchange with Polish Academy of Science, Warsaw. Poles and Polish-Americans are largest Buffalo ethnic group. Slides and films also. Bibliography: Polish Collections at the State University of New York at Buffalo, 2 vols, Sept 83, $150.

SCIENCE—SOCIAL ASPECTS

CA —UNIVERSITY OF CALIFORNIA, SAN DIEGO, Central University Library, Mandeville Dept of Special Collections, La Jolla, 92093. Lynda Corey Claassen, Head
Notes: Papers of Harold Clayton Urey (1893-1981), winner of the 1934 Nobel Prize in chemistry for his discovery of Deuterium. Incl files concerning the Emergency Committee of Atomic Scientists, 1946-49; also some material on the Rosenberg/Sobell spy cases; also on his works as science advisor to John F Kennedy (president-elect).

NY —AMERICAN INSTITUTE OF PHYSICS, Center for the History of Physics, Niels Bohr Library, 335 E 45 St, New York, 10017. John Aubry, Librn
Holdings: Vols (16,000) Cat Mss Pix Slides Phonorecords Audiotapes 16mm Films Microforms
Notes: The Library contains an extensive collection of published works relating to the history of modern physics and astronomy. Its archives incl letter, notebooks and other papers of physicists, as well as the records of leading American physics societies and institutions. Its collections of ms autobiographies, oral history interviews, and other tape recordings, and pictorial materials (incl unpublished film footage) are unrivaled in the field of history of science. It maintains the International Catalog of Sources for History of Physics and and Astronomy.

SCIENCE—STUDY AND TEACHING

CA —UNIVERSITY OF CALIFORNIA, BERKELEY, Science Education Library, Lawrence Hall of Science, Berkeley, 94720. Ann M Jensen, Librn
Holdings: Vols (6000)
Notes: Emphasis on innovative materials in the field of science, mathematics, and environmental education.

NY —AMERICAN MUSEUM OF NATURAL HISTORY, Library Services Dept, Central Park W & 79th St, New York, 10024. Nina J Root, Chairwoman; Mary Genett, Asst Librn for Reference Services
Holdings: Vols (385,000) Cat Mss Maps Pix Slides Microforms
Notes: Nearly all collections are outstanding for depth of coverage and international range. Early and historic works, rare books, colored illustrations, and relevant serial publications supplement the modern scientific publications necessary to the researches of the scientific staff and the work of the educational division. Open to the public.

†NY —COLUMBIA UNIVERSITY LIBRARIES, Butler Library, Rare Book and Manuscript Library, 535 W 114 St, New York, 10027.
Notes: 76 vols of diaries of Lynn Thorndike, 1902-63. A record of his daily reading, progress in research and writing, European travels, relations with scholars and librarians, and other personal matters.

WA —PACIFIC SCIENCE CENTER FOUNDATION, Library, 200 Second Ave N, Seattle, 98109. Sally Luttrel-Monten, Mgr
Holdings: Vols (3000) Cat
Notes: A resource center for science teachers and museum education staff. It is not a technical or reserarch science library. Materials in general science, science education, and math education.

SCIENCE, AMERICAN see Science; Science—History

SCIENCE, APPLIED see Technology

SCIENCE, ARABIC

UT —UNIVERSITY OF UTAH, Middle East Library, Salt Lake City, 84112. Ragai N Makar, Librn
Holdings: Vols 3000 Cat Mss Pix Microforms
Budget: ($40,000)
Notes: The Martin Levey Collection, one of the finest on Arabic science in the country. Incl books and mss on all the sciences and medicine through the 14th century; 3000 books. 5000 offprints; 1000 microfilmed mss in German, Arabic, and French.

SCIENCE, EXPERIMENTAL

†NY —COLUMBIA UNIVERSITY LIBRARIES, Butler Library, Rare Book and Manuscript Library, 535 W 114 St, New York, 10027.
Notes: 76 vols of diaries of Lynn Thorndike, 1902-63. A record of his daily reading,

SCIENCE, EXPERIMENTAL (cont.)

progress in research and writing, European travels, relations with scholars and librarians, and other personal matters.

SCIENCE, MENTAL see Psychology

SCIENCE, MORAL see Ethics

SCIENCE, POLITICAL see Political Science

SCIENCE, RUSSIAN

IL —CENTER FOR RESEARCH LIBRARIES, 6050 S Kenwood Ave, Chicago, 60637. Donald B Simpson, Dir; Esther Smith, Collection Development Librn
Holdings: Vols 36,000 Cat Maps
Budget: $5000
Notes: Receive about 1200 current serials in science and technology, and all monographs published by Akademiia Nauk SSR. have extensive backfiles of Akademiia Nauk SSSR monographic and serial publications.

MA —BOSTON COLLEGE LIBRARIES, Chestnut Hill, 02167.

OH —BATTELLE MEMORIAL INSTITUTE LIBRARY, 505 King Ave, Columbus, 43201. Carol Young, Librn
Holdings: Vols (150,000) Cat Maps Microforms
Notes: Large collection of Russian and Eastern European science and technology. Over 1600 current journal titles and extensive monography and serial holdings in Slavic languages.

SCIENCE AND SOCIETY see Science—Social Aspects

SCIENCE AND SPACE see Space Sciences

SCIENCE FICTION

AZ —UNIVERSITY OF ARIZONA, University Library, Special Collections, Tucson, 85721. Louis A Hieb, Head
Holdings: Vols 13,000 Mss Pix Phonorecords Filmstrips
Budget: ($30,000)
Notes: Emphasis is on American and British science fiction from the 1930s to date. Sixty authors are collected exhaustively. Extension selections are made also from the comtemporary science fiction market. Fantasy and sword and sorcery are not emphasized. The collection is very strong in pulp magazine holdings. All cataloged items are fully represented in the University Library main card catalog. In addition, Special Collections maintains separate files for all science fiction holdings, cataloged and uncataloged.

CA —CALIFORNIA STATE UNIVERSITY, FULLERTON, Library, Box 4150, Fullerton, 92634. Linda Herman, Special Collections Librn
Holdings: Cat Mss
Notes: The university general library houses the fully cataloged books of science and speculative fiction; the Record Library maintains the records and tapes; the Reserve Room services the 8000 paperbacks; and Special Collections handles the 303 document boxes of mss of over 30 authors, and 4850 periodical issues, 150 folders of ephemera, and the support reference materials. There are also 450 volumes in the Science Fiction Writers of America regional depository in Special Collections. A major collection of science fiction magazines dating from the 1930s. Incl a complete run from 1926 to 1940 of *Amazing,* the first major science fiction magazine. Also incl are short-span publications and runs of British s/f publications.

†CA —FULLERTON COLLEGE, William T Boyce Library, 321 E Chapman Ave, Fullerton, 92634.
Notes: Books, mss, correspondence of Philip K. Dick, science fiction writer, author of the classic *Do Androids Dream of Electric Sheep* (which was made into a movie as *Blade Runner*).

CA —UNIVERSITY OF CALIFORNIA, LOS ANGELES, Research Library, Dept of Special Collections, 405 Hilgard Ave, Los Angeles, 90024. Edward Shreeves, Chairman, Bibliographers Group; David S Zeidberg, Head
Holdings: Vols 7000 Cat
Notes: 7000 books; 6500 pulp magazines; 3500 more recent paperbacks.

CA —UNIVERSITY OF CALIFORNIA, RIVERSIDE, University Library, 4045 Canyon Crest Dr, Box 5900, Riverside, 92517.
Holdings: Vols (30,000)
Notes: The Eaton Collection of science fiction and fantasy materials, incl 5,600 pulp magazines; also horror, supernatural, and Gothic mystery fiction; boys' books; utopian and dystopian fiction, imaginary voyages, future war and lost race fiction; large holdings in French language science fiction and fantasy; critical and scholarly works pertaining to these genres; videotapes of science fiction/fantasy films and shooting scripts. Collection covers science fiction/fantasy literature from the 16th-17th centuries to the present. Strong individual author collections of Jules Verne, H Rider Haggard, H G Wells, Edgar Rice Burroughs, and Philip K Dick. For a complete description of the collection see: George Slusser, "The J Lloyd Eaton Collection," *Special Collections*, II, 1/2, 25-38 (1983), and *Dictionary Catalog of the J Lloyd Eaton Collection of Science Fiction and Fantasy Literature* (Boston: G K Hall) 1982.

CA —SAN DIEGO PUBLIC LIBRARY, Literature & Language Sect, 820 E St, San Diego, 92101. Alyce Archuleta, Senior Librn
Holdings: Vols 202 // Uncat
Notes: Incl mystery series from 1930s and 1940s, and early fantasy and science fiction in paperback form (will circulate). Some first editions; collections has separate author-title index (will not circulate).

CA —SAN DIEGO STATE UNIVERSITY, Malcolm A Love Library, 5300 Campanile Dr, San Diego, 92182. D Dickinson, Univ Librn; Don L Bosseau, Dir
Holdings: Mss Audiotapes
Notes: Elizabeth Chater Collection in Science Fiction. Includes Tolkien Collection, fantasy, folklore, Gothic novels, mostly autographed first editions, some rare and scarce, includes manuscripts, graphics, cassette tapes. Examples: authors included, Isaac Asimov, Ray Bradbury, Joan Vinge, Greg Baer, Frederick Pohl, Andre Norton, etc. Examples of periodicals; Amazing Stories, Famous Fantastic Mysteries of the 1940s, The Black Cat, 1895. (3000 items)

CA —SAN FRANCISCO ACADEMY OF COMIC ART, Library, 2850 Ulloa, San Francisco, 94116.
Notes: Incl largest collection of pulp magazines in US. Paper copies of all major American newspapers, emphasis on Hearst papers. Extensive collection of Sherlockiana and a member of the National Sherlockiana Society. Also extensive collection of early motion picture tapes, books, magazines and posters. 19th and early 20th century children's books also in the holdings. Collection incl 1,000,000 comic strips, 22,000 comic books, 12,500 hard cover mystery books, 8000 hard cover science fiction books and copies of all science fiction pulp magazines.

CA —SAN FRANCISCO PUBLIC LIBRARY, Civic Center, San Francisco, 94102. Dennis L Maness, Cur
Holdings: Vols 2000 Cat
Notes: McComas Collection of Fantasy and Science Fiction. In addition to the 2000 vols of fiction, there is incl a complete run (vol 1, no 1) of 92 fantasy and science fiction magazines, starting with *Amazing* in 1926.

CT —YALE UNIVERSITY, Box 1603A, Yale Station, New Haven, 06520.
Notes: Incl the Gimbel Collection of Science Fiction Dime Novels, the Frank Reade and Jack Wright "boy inventor" dime novels published before 1900, and the Bryher Collection of boys' books.

DC —LIBRARY OF CONGRESS, Rare Book & Special Collections Div, Washington, 20540. William Matheson, Chief
Notes: Late 19th and early 20th century English and American editions of Jules Verne, many with distinctive illustrations and bindings.

†GA —UNIVERSITY OF GEORGIA, Libraries, Athens, 30602.
Notes: Science fiction, 4000 vols, mostly circulating.

IL —NORTHERN ILLINOIS UNIVERSITY, Founders Memorial Library, Rare Books and Special Collections Dept, De Kalb, 60115. William R DuBois, Dept Head
Holdings: Cat
Notes: American science fiction. Incl 2600 magazines. Noncirculating. Limited photocopying.

IN —INDIANA UNIVERSITY, Lilly Library, Seventh St, Bloomington, 47405. William R Cagle, Librn
Holdings: Cat Mss
Notes: Extensive holdings of first editions and pulps. An exhibition catalog, Science Fiction and Fantasy (Bloomington, Lilly Library, 1975), describes the collection.

KS —UNIVERSITY OF KANSAS, Kenneth Spencer Research Library, Special Collections Dept, Lawrence, 66045. Alexandra Mason, Librn
Holdings: Vols 4000 Cat Mss
Notes: US and foreign science fiction incl periodicals, 1920s to date, North American repository for World SF. Mss of science fiction writers and Science Fiction Research Association, some owned, some on deposit. Incl fan literature (uncat). Noncirculating.

KY —UNIVERSITY OF KENTUCKY, Margaret I King Library, Dept of Special Collections, Lexington, 40506. William Marshall, Head
Holdings: Vols 1650 Cat
Notes: Most of the collection is in paperback form.

†LA —TULANE UNIVERSITY, Libraries, Rare Books Dept, New Orleans, 70118. Sylvia V Metzinger, Librn
Notes: Science fiction, 1000 vols and growing. Rosel George Brown and Robert A Heinlein special collections.

MD —UNIVERSITY OF MARYLAND, BALTIMORE COUNTY, Albin O Kuhn Library and Gallery, 5401 Wilkens Ave, Baltimore, 21228. Ann Copeland, Special Collections Librn
Holdings: Vols (4500) Cat Mss Pix Phonorecords
Notes: The Azriel Rosenfeld Science Fiction Research Collection of about 20,000 items, incl over 4000 issues of science fiction periodicals such as *Analog, Galaxy,* and a complete run of *Amazing Stories,* as well as 4500 hard cover and paperback books. A developed section of indexes, reference books and criticisms of science fiction makes this a valuable research collection. Complementing these resources is the Walter Coslet Collection of 10,000 fanzines. The unusual science fiction art collection centers around the work of illustrator Frank Kelly Freas. Unique items incl Freas' designs for NASA's Skylab I patch. Also of interest are mss, galley and page proofs by such major science fiction writers as Isaac Asimov (*The Foundation*), Harry Harrison, Frederick Pohl, Gordon Dickson, etc. The Library provides reference service (by mail or in person) to scholars and other persons interested in the area of research.

†MA —BOSTON UNIVERSITY, Mugar Memorial Library, Special Collections Dept, 771 Commonwealth Avenue, Boston, 02215. Howard B Gotlieb, Dir
Notes: Extensive papers of mystery and science fiction writers, and film, radio and TV writers, performers, etc. 14 years of original Little Orphan Annie art. Collections built around papers of individuals are supplemented by their printed works.

MA —HARVARD UNIVERSITY LIBRARY, Widener Library, Cambridge, 02138.
Holdings: Cat
Notes: See *Harvard Library Bulletin*, IX (1955), 422-423, and *Harvard Alumni Bulletin*, LX (1957), 209-211, 223.

SCIENCE FICTION (cont.)

MI —MICHIGAN STATE UNIVERSITY, Libraries, Special Collections Div, East Lansing, 48824. Jannette Fiore, Librn
Holdings: Vols 4000 Cat
Notes: The Russel B Nye Popular Culture Collection in the Michigan State Univ Libraries incl over (45,000) items. Most of the collection is organized into 4 categories: comic art, popular fiction, popular information materials and materials relating to the popular performing arts. Popular fiction in the collection is organized into juvenile, detective-mystery, and science fiction, westerns and women's fiction. In addition, there is a sample collection of dime novels and story papers (ca 400 issues representing nearly 100 titles). Pulp magazines which fall into none of the separate categories are housed with the dime novels and story papers. Juvenile Fiction: ca 4000 vols. Emphasis is on juvenile series fiction of the 19th and 20th centuries, with nearly 200 girls and 300 boys series represented. 19th-century "Sunday School" books andboth fiction and non-fiction scouting books are also included. Western Fiction: An exceptionally fine institutional collection, with over 3000 novels (most published between 1900 and 1950), almost all hardbound and in dust jackets, and nearly 500 pulp magazine issues representing more than fifty titles. The most important pulp runs are Street and Smith's *Western Story Magazine* and Warner Publications's *Ranch Romances*. Women's Fiction: Over 3000 novels and ca 1000 issues of romance, confession and movie magazines and pulps from the 1920s through the 1970s. Most of the novels are in the romance category, with over 2000 Harlequin novels, a good representation of other modern best-selling romances, and several dozen titles from late 19th-century romance series. Science Fiction: ca 3000 books and periodicals. MSU is a depository for the Science Fiction Writersof America, which contributes review copies of new books. The bulk of the collection is periodicals, with 71 titles represented. Most issues come from the period from the late 1940s to the present. The collection subscribes to most major science fiction magazines and holds a fanzine collection which now numbers over 2500. Detective-Mystery Fiction: ca 3500 novels, in paper and hardback, and pulps representing 28 titles from 1920-1950. Complete runs of *The London Mystery Magazine* and *Ellery Queen's Mystery Magazine* are included, along with a large sample collection of the more sensational detective and crime fiction magazines from the 1930s through the present.

MN —MINNESOTA SCIENCE FICTION SOCIETY, Library, Box 2128, Loop Station, Minneapolis, 55402. Dennis Lien, Librn
Holdings: Vols (1200)
Notes: Not open to the public, members only.

†NM —UNIVERSITY OF NEW MEXICO, Zimmerman Library, Special Collections, Albuquerque, 87106.
Notes: Science fiction magazines almost ocmplete 1926-1950.

NM —EASTERN NEW MEXICO UNIVERSITY, Golden Library, Special Collections, Portales, 88130. Mary Jo Walker, Special Collections Librn
Holdings: Vols 11,940 Cat Mss Pix Audiotapes
Notes: Incl 700 magazine titles (10,318 issues), 11,940 vols, mss and correspondences of the following science fiction writers: Jack Williamson, Edmond Hamilton, Leigh Brackett, Forrest J Ackerman and Piers Anthony (Jacob), plus *Astounding/Analog* ms files (1954-1975). Also serves as a depository for Science Fiction Writers of America. Incl separate catalog for published books and unpublished registers to personal papers. The Williamson Register is being prepared for publication. Collection is described in *Anatomy of Wonder*, by Neil Barron (NY: Bowker,

1981); and *Special Collections, II* (winter, 1982), pp 49-57.

†NY —SARAH LAWRENCE COLLEGE, Esther Raushenbush Library, 1 Meadway, Bronxville, 10708. Rose Ann Burstein, Librn
Notes: 600 vols of science fiction with 60 in the German language.

NY —SYRACUSE UNIVERSITY LIBRARIES, Ernest S Bird Library, George Arents Research Library for Special Collections, Syracuse, 13210. Carolyn A Davis, Manuscripts Librn; Amy S Doherty, University Archivist; Mark F Weimer, Rare Book Librn
Holdings: Vols (5000) Cat Mss
Notes: Manuscript materials relating to Hal Clement, Galaxy Press, Hugo Gernsback, Gnome Press, Mercury Press, Larry Niven, Frederick G Pohl, and Roger Zelazny.

OH —BOWLING GREEN STATE UNIVERSITY, Jerome Library, Institute for Great Lakes Research, Bowling Green, 43403. Richard J Wright, Dir
Notes: Perhaps the most complete collection of Ray Bradbury books, mss, periodicals, pamphlets, records, and memorabilia.

OH —OHIO STATE UNIVERSITY, William Oxley Thompson Memorial Library, 1858 Neil Ave Mall, Columbus, 43210. Robert A Tibbetts, Cur of Special Collections
Holdings: Vols 800 Cat
Notes: Incl science fiction magazines. Also number of fanzines, which are uncataloged.

†OH —UNIVERSITY OF DAYTON, Roesch Library, Dayton, 45469. Linda Hinrichs
Notes: Science fiction collection (SFWA depository).

OH —KENT STATE UNIVERSITY, Libraries, Dept of Special Collections, Kent, 44242. Dean H Keller, Cur
Holdings: Vols (2000) Uncat Mss Pix

†OK —UNIVERSITY OF TULSA, McFarlin Library, Dept of Rare Books and Special Collections, 600 South College Avenue, Tulsa, 74104. Dr David Farmer, Librn
Notes: Non-circulating science fiction collection.

OR —AMERICAN PRIVATE PRESS ASSOCIATION, 112 E Burnett St, Stayton, 97383. Martin M Horvat, Librn
Notes: The collection is divided into two primary segments: the first is the traditional one of Amateur Journalism, the second is science fiction and fantasy oriented. The collection was once at New York University Libraries but moved in 1981.

PA —TEMPLE UNIVERSITY LIBRARIES, Special Collections Dept, Rare Books & Mss Section, Philadelphia, 19122. Thomas M Whitehead, Cur
Holdings: Vols 6000 Cat Mss
Notes: The David Charles Paskow Science Fiction Collection of hardbacks and paperbacks, with additions of printed books and mss, kept as a separate unit of the Department of Special Collections. The collection is particularly good in the period 1950-1970, though dates basically from the late twenties. Books, periodicals and mss. Some fantasy, extensive fanzines. No listing or catalog available at this tims. Manuscript deposits of Ben Bova, Gardner Dozois, Jack Dann, George Zebrowski, Tom Purdom, Pamela Sargent, John Varley, and others.

†PA —UNIVERSITY OF PITTSBURGH, Hillman Library, 363 Hillman Library, Pittsburgh, 15260. Charles E Aston, Jr, Coordr
Notes: 2000 vols.

PA —PENNSYLVANIA STATE UNIVERSITY, Fred Lewis Pattee Library, Special Collections Dept, University Park, 16802. Charles Mann, Chief, Special Collections
Holdings: Vols 3856 Cat
Budget: ($37,000)
Notes: Fantastic Fiction of all genres. Collection also has 607 paperback volumes. There is also a substantial number of science fiction titles in the general stacks.

RI —BROWN UNIVERSITY, John Hay Library, 20 Prospect St, Providence, 02912. Mark N Brown, Cur Mss
Holdings: Vols (600) Cat Mss Pix Phonorecords Audiotapes
Notes: Howard Phillips Lovecraft Collection

of books, amateur and professional magazines, plus mss/typescripts by and about Howard Phillips Lovecraft, incl first and subsequent editions of Lovecraft's work in 12 languages; complete runs of *Weird Tales, Marvel Tales, The Californian, Driftwood, Rainbow, Leaves,* and *Amateur Fantasy Correspondent* plus scattered issues of 50 amateur and professional magazines; 1500 letters written by Lovecraft to more than 200 correspondents, 270 mss/ typescripts of his essays, fiction and poetry plus over 3000 mss/typescripts of essays, fiction, letters, and poetry written by his correspondents. Photocopying of mss is restricted.

TX —TEXAS A&M UNIVERSITY, Sterling C Evans Library, Special Collections Div, College Station, 77843. Donald H Dyal, Librn
Holdings: Vols 7000 Cat
Notes: Computerized printout of author-title list is updated periodically. Now in circulating collection.

TX —DALLAS PUBLIC LIBRARY, Central Library, Humanities Division, 1515 Young St, Dallas, 75201. Richard L Waters, Acting Dir; Ron Boyd, Fiction Librn
Holdings: Vols Cat Microforms
Notes: Cited in Tymn, Marshall, Roger C Schlobin, and L W Currey. *A Research Guide to Science Fiction* New York: Garland, 1977. The science fiction collection now exceeds 8000 circulating vols. In addition, the Library purchased in 1983 the personal library and archives of Brian Aldiss (which will be for reference use only). This collection consists of 350 books by Aldiss, 1900 other books by other science fiction writers, 800 issues of science fiction and fantasy periodicals, 100 vols concerning astronautics and space travel, over 1000 typescript pages of mss(incl 6 corrected mss), several sound recordings (incl BBC tapes), and a considerable amount of correspondence.

†UT —BRIGHAM YOUNG UNIVERSITY, Harold B Lee Library, Provo, 84602. Elizabeth Pope, Librn
Notes: Science Fiction-Fantasy Collection, extensive circulating collection. Arkham House near complete, non-circulating. Mysteries, westerns and gothic romances in general fiction. Edgar Rice Burroughs 1st edition collection does not circulate. Science fiction and fantasy art special collection.

WI —UNIVERSITY OF WISCONSIN, LA CROSSE, Murphy Library, 1631 Pine St, La Crosse, 54601. Edwin L Hill, Special Collections Librn
Holdings: Vols 1000 Cat
Notes: The Paul W Skeeters Collection of science fiction, fantasy, and horror literature. Complements the library's complete collection of Arkham House books, which contains many titles autographed by August Derleth, and H P Lovecraft's complete fiction and poetic works.

WI —UNIVERSITY OF WISCONSIN, MADISON, Memorial Library, British & American Language & Literature Collection, 728 State St, Madison, 53706. Yvonne Schofer, Bibliographer
Holdings: Vols
Notes: A collection of mystery fiction mostly of the British Golden Age of the 20s and 30s, in original and reprint form; strong holdings for H Adams, J Rhode, A Upfield, and many others. Stacks. Substantial holdings also for fantasy and science fiction, mostly in stacks; Arkham House and A Derleth materials, restricted use only.

†WY —UNIVERSITY OF WYOMING, American Heritage Center, Laramie, 82071. Gene M Gressley, Librn
Notes: Science fiction books, leters, mss and fan material collected by D A Wolheim, J V Shea, F Ackerman and R Bloch.

†BC —UNIVERSITY OF BRITISH COLUMBIA LIBRARY, Special Collections Dept, 1956 Main Mall, University Campus, Vancouver, V6T 1Y3, Can. Anne Yandle, Librn
Notes: Science fiction, pulps, 30 titles (1940s-1950s). Article by John McKinley, "The Science Fiction Collection at the

SCIENCE FICTION (cont.)

University Of British Columbia" (British Columbia Library Quarterly, 34:4, April 1971, p 5-19).

MB —UNIVERSITY OF WINNIPEG, Library, 515 Portage Ave, Winnipeg, R3B 2E9, Can. W R Converse, Chief Librn
Holdings: Vols 1300 Cat Microforms
Notes: Collection incl all major science fiction writers, all science fiction classics, *Amazing Stories Monthly* and *Amazing Stories Quarterly*. Also incl fantasy, eg, Edgar Rice Burroughs' Tarzan stories, as well as his Martian stories. Collection will very soon incl all science fiction periodicals on microfilm.

NB —UNIVERSITY OF NEW BRUNSWICK, Ward Chipman Library, PO Box 5050, Saint John, E2L 4L5, Can. Dennis Abblitt, Librn
Notes: Science Fiction and Fantasy Collection, 14,000 books, 9000 magaines. Extensive fanzines. Some comics, posters, records, undergrounds in science fiction genre. Pamphlet and microfiche on magazine collection available.

ON —TORONTO PUBLIC LIBRARY, Spaced Out Library, 40 Saint George St, Toronto, M5S 2E4, Can. Doris Mehegan, Librn
Holdings: Cat
Budget: ($18,000)
Notes: Part of the Toronto Public Library. Science fiction, fantasy and related non-fiction. Incl 25,000 items and 8,000 periodicals. Complete catalog and indexes.

SCIENCE FICTION PERIODICALS see
Periodicals, Science Fiction

SCIENCE FICTION WRITERS OF AMERICA

†MI —MICHIGAN STATE UNIVERSITY, Libraries, East Lansing, 48824. Jannette Flore, Librn
Notes: Good samples of Big-Little Books, foreign comics, dime novels, pulps, TV scripts, underground comics. SFWA and Clarion depository.

SCIENCE STORIES see Science Fiction

SCIENCES, OCCULT see Occult Sciences

SCIENCES, SOCIAL see Social Sciences

SCIENTIFIC AND TECHNICAL PERIODICALS see Periodicals, Scientific and Technical

SCIENTIFIC APPARATUS see Scientific Instruments and Apparatus

SCIENTIFIC EDUCATION see Science—Study and Teaching

SCIENTIFIC EXPEDITIONS

CA —UNIVERSITY OF SOUTHERN CALIFORNIA, Allan Hancock Foundation, Hancock Library of Biology and Oceanography, Los Angeles, 90007. Kimberly Douglas, Librn
Holdings: Vols (16,000) Cat Maps
Notes: Mostly marine, but incl some land expeditions. Covers all geographical areas. Also incl serial collection of 80,000 vols.

DC —NATIONAL GEOGRAPHIC SOCIETY, Library, 1146 16th St NW, Washington, 20036. Susan Fifer Canby, Dir
Holdings: Vols (63,000) Cat Mss Maps Pix
Notes: Material concerning land, sea, and space exploration--past and present. All fields of anthropology, natural history, geography, etc.

DC —SMITHSONIAN INSTITUTION, Archives Div, Washington, 20560. William W Moss, Archivist
Holdings: Mss Maps Pix
Notes: The Archives holds correspondence and records of a number of scientific expeditions with which the Smithsonian was connected, incl the Western Union Telegraph Expedition, the Smithsonian

Roosevelt African Expedition, and the United States Exploring Expedition.

DC —SMITHSONIAN INSTITUTION LIBRARIES, General Library, Washington, 20560. Mary Claire Grey, Chief Cent Ref & Loan Servs
Holdings: Vols (79,000) Cat Mss Maps Pix Slides Microforms

FL —UNIVERSITY OF MIAMI, Otto G Richter Library, PO Box 248214, Coral Gables, 33124. Frank Rodgers, Dir of Libraries
Holdings: Vols Microforms
Notes: The Rosenstiel School of Marine and Atmospheric Sciences Library is one of the major marine science collections in the United States and is especially strong in the literature of tropical oceanography. Special collections in the library incl 200 oceanographic atlases and more than 50 sets of the world's major expedition reports. The library also maintains a nautical chart collection. 3000 microforms; 1000 current subscriptions.

IN —INDIANA UNIVERSITY, Lilly Library, Seventh St, Bloomington, 47405. William R Cagle, Librn
Holdings: Cat
Notes: First and early printings of 15th through 17th century European voyages to the western hemisphere, incl such collections as the *Decades* of Peter Martyr, the *Grands* and *Petits Voyages* gathered by DeBry, and *Hakluyt's Principail Navigations*; travels to the Orient, incl first printed accounts of Marco Polo; the Protuguese in India from the time of the arrival of Vasco da Gama; 18th century voyages by Captain James Cook, Le Comte de Laperouse and others; and the great scientific expeditions of the 18th and 19th centuries. Also, first appearances in print of great scientific discoveries.

KS —UNIVERSITY OF KANSAS, Kenneth Spencer Research Library, Special Collections Dept, Lawrence, 66045. Alexandra Mason, Librn
Holdings: Cat Mss Maps
Notes: Ellis Collection of Ornithology and Natural History contains many accounts of scientific expeditions, mostly concerned with natural history. Noncirculating.

ME —BOWDOIN COLLEGE, Library, Brunswick, 04011. Dianne M Gutscher, Cur of Special Collections
Holdings: Mss
Notes: The papers (about 15,000 items) of Robert A Bartlett, arctic explorer and shipmaster for Admirals Robert E Peary and Donald B MacMillan, contain 10,000 mss, 23,000 photographs, clippings, diaries, 300 maps, logbooks and some printed material relating to Bartlett's arctic voyages. Also, Admiral MacMillan's personal library of about 4000 books relating to arctic exploration, several volumes of clippings, numerous scrapbooks, ms diaries, logbooks, and journals, photographs, maps, and other records.

MI —UNIVERSITY OF MICHIGAN, Library, Dept of Rare Books & Special Collections, Ann Arbor, 48109. Robert J Starring, Head
Holdings: Cat Mss Maps Pix
Notes: Includes over 100 books, mostly autographed presentation copies from polar explorers to donor William H Hobbs, and 62 scrapbooks, notebooks, albums, and made-up volumes of pamphlets, documents and correspondence, 11 relating to Admiral Peary. Also there are such primary records from Professor Hobb's own expeditions as his journals, radio logs, purchase requistions, pilot balloon ascension reports and graphs, and anemoscope records. In addition there are an estimated 3500 items of correspondence with explorers and other notables, 800 photographs, and maps.

MI —OLIVET COLLEGE, Burrage Library, Olivet, 49076. Chris Miko, Dir
Holdings: Vols (2000) Cat
Notes: The collection consists primarily of early printed voyages of the arctic and antarctic from the earliest times to the mid-20th century.

NV —FORESTA INSTITUTE FOR OCEAN AND MOUNTAIN STUDIES, Library,

6205 Franktown Rd, Carson City, 89701. Shannon Porter, Librn
Holdings: Vols 500 Cat Mss Maps Pix Slides
Notes: Collection incl historical and contemporary accounts of Antarctic voyages; special emphasis on ecology, plant and animal life, fish, and whales. Also, about 1500 pamphlets, etc. Bibliography of whales and whaling materials in library published in 1977.

NY —AMERICAN MUSEUM OF NATURAL HISTORY, Library Services Dept, Central Park W & 79th St, New York, 10024. Nina J Root, Chairwoman; Mary Genett, Asst Librn for Reference Services
Holdings: Vols (385,000) Cat Mss Maps Pix Slides Microforms
Notes: Nearly all collections are outstanding for depth of coverage and international range. Early and historic works, rare books, colored illustrations, and relevant serial publications supplement the modern scientific publications necessary to the researches of the scientific staff and the work of the educational division. Open to the public.

NY —COLUMBIA UNIVERSITY LIBRARIES, Rare Book & Manuscript Library, 801 Butler Library, 535 W 114 St, New York, 10027. Kenneth A Lohf, Librn
Holdings: Vols 700 Cat Mss
Notes: First editions, mss, letters and memorabilia relating to the exploration of the North and South Poles. 700 vols, 500 items. Restricted use.

NY —NEW YORK PUBLIC LIBRARY, Research Libraries, General Research Division, Fifth Ave & 42 St, New York, 10018. Rodney Phillips, Chief
Holdings: Vols (2,225,000) Cat Maps Pix Microforms
Budget: ($775,718)

NC —DUKE UNIVERSITY, William R Perkins Library, Rare Book Room, Durham, 27706. John L Sharpe, III, Cur
Holdings: Vols 1000
Notes: Collection of various accounts of voyages and scientific expeditions, primarily in the 18th and 19th centuries.

PA —CARNEGIE LIBRARY OF PITTSBURGH, Science & Technology Dept, 4400 Forbes Ave, Pittsburgh, 15213. Catherine M Brosky, Dept Head
Notes: Of secondary interest in acquistition because of the department's role in cooperating with Pittsburgh institutions and others across the Commonwealth in sharing resources, the cooperative acquisition of materials, and the provision of services and information. However, some aspects of the subject aer emphasized. There are separate entries for each of these specialities in this vol.

PA —PENNSYLVANIA STATE UNIVERSITY, Fred Lewis Pattee Library, University Park, 16802. Stuart Forth, Dean of Libraries
Holdings: Vols Cat Maps
Notes: Based primarily on an interest in Australia and the Pacific Ocean, the Pennsylvania State University Libraries have developed a strong collection of voyages, including manyl 17th and 18th century editions of specific voyages, eg, Cook, La Perouse, Vancouver, collected editions both French and English, together with related publications, eg, De Brosses, Dalrymple. The collections include both exploration and scientific voyages in original editions and reprints.

RI —BROWN UNIVERSITY, John Carter Brown Library, Providence, 02912. Norman Fiering, Librn; Everett C Wilkie Jr, Bibliographer; Susan Danforth, Cur Maps & Prints
Notes: Extensive holdings of European scientific expeditions to the New World (Malaspina, La Perouyse, etc).

VA —UNIVERSITY OF VIRGINIA, Alderman Library, Manuscripts Dept, Charlottesville, 22901. Edmund Berkeley Jr, Cur
Holdings: Cat Mss Maps Pix
Notes: Personal and official papers of Sir Andrew Snape Hamond and Graham Eden Hamond concern British naval operations

SCIENTIFIC EXPEDITIONS (cont.)

during the American Revolution and in the Mediterranean during the Napoleonic Wars. Paul P Hoffman (ed) *Guide to the Naval Papers of Sir Andrew Snape Hamond . . . and Sir Graham Eden Hamond . . .* (Charlottesville, Va: Microfilm Publications, University of Virginia, 1966). Papers of US and Confederate naval officer Samuel Barron; US fleet surgeon and Brooklyn Navy Yard surgeon Gustavus R B Horner; US naval surgeon John S Whittle on a scientific expedition to the Pacific, 1838-1841; and US naval officer William Conway Whittle on West Indies and Mediterranean cruises, 1823-1831.

ON —NATIONAL MUSEUMS OF CANADA, Library Services Directorate, Ottawa, K1A 0M8, Can. Valerie Monkhouse, Director
Holdings: Vols 500 // Maps
Notes: The personal library of RM Anderson, late Curator Emeritus of the Zoology Division, and leader of the Southern Party, Canadian Arctic Expedition, 1913-1918. The collection contains books on zoology (mainly ornithology and mammalogy), expeditions (some early and rare materials), and several runs of ornithological journals and numerous reprints. The collection is only partially cataloged.

SCIENTIFIC INSTRUMENTS AND APPARATUS

CT —BURNDY LIBRARY, Electra Square, Norwalk, 06856. Philip J Weimerskirch, Asst Dir
Holdings: Vols 18,000
Notes: 3000 portraits of scientists and a small collection of early scientific instruments.

MA —WELLESLEY COLLEGE, Whitin Observatory, Astronomy Dept, Wellesley, 02181.
Notes: Sir William Huggins' (1824-1910) diaries, ca 5 inches (1856-1900) plus scientic instruments and apparatus.

NY —AMERICAN MUSEUM-HAYDEN PLANETARIUM, Richard S Perkin Library, 81 St & Central Park W, New York, 10024. Sandra Kitt, Librn
Holdings: Vols (15,000) Cat Maps Pix Slides
Budget: ($8000)
Notes: Considered one of the strongest and most complete astronomy libraries on the east coast. Contains the Bliss Collection of Ancient Astronomical Instruments; also the Mt Wilson/Bloman Sky Survey to the 45 degree declination; the Lick Observatory Survey; *American Emphemeris and Nautical Almanac*, 1855-date.

OH —UNIVERSITY OF AKRON, Archives of the History of American Psychology, Akron, 44325. John A Popplestone, Dir
Holdings: Cat Mss Pix Slides Films
Notes: Nearly 1200 ft of psychologists' personal papers and documents, as well as organizational records, and over 600 items of historic laboratory apparatus. Also, photographs, films, intelligence and aptitude tests, etc from the 19th century to date.

SCIENTIFIC MANAGEMENT see Industrial Management

SCIENTIFIC PERIODICALS see Periodicals, Scientific and Technical

SCIENTIFIC PROPERTY see Patent Laws and Legislation

SCIENTIFIC REPORTS see Technical Reports

SCIENTIFIC VOYAGES see Scientific Expeditions

SCIENTIFIC WRITING see Technical Writing

SCIENTISTS

†AZ —UNIVERSITY OF ARIZONA, Library, Tucson, 85721.
Notes: The Pierre Lecomte du Nouy

Collection incl scarce, original editions of the works of contemporary scientists and thinkers, editions of his own works, his mss, and many volumes inscribed to him.

CA —UNIVERSITY OF CALIFORNIA, BERKELEY, Bancroft Library, Manuscripts Division, Berkeley, 94720. James D Hart, Dir
Holdings: Cat Mss Maps Pix Slides Microforms
Notes: Collection of early and rare editions, supported by related holdings in the Biology and Main libraries. Mss (230,000) consisting primarily of scientists' private papers, constitute the most significant part of the collection. Major emphasis is on scientific developments centered in Berkeley since the inception of the Lawrence Radiation Laboratory, and on the growth of the electronics industry located in the Palo Alto area, in the vicinity of Stanford University. Incl are the private papers of Ernest Lawrence and Emil Fischer, among other individual scientists (some of them listed separately in this book). Extensive collections of papers and archives relative to the history of modern physical, biological, earth, and human sciences.

CA —CLAREMONT COLLEGES, Norman F Sprague Memorial Library, 12 & Dartmouth, Claremont, 91711. David Kuhner, Librn
Notes: The reference library collected by Herbert Clark Hoover and Lou Henry Hoover in the preparation of their 1912 translation of *De re metallica*. Incl 24 incunabula, 6 mss, titles of 16th to 19th centuries, with emphasis on mining, metallurgy, early science, and travel. Hoover's correspondence (approx 600 pieces) with British & European booksellers, period 1907-1914. Printed catalog, "Bibliotheca de Re Metallica," published in 1980. Restricted use.

CA —UNIVERSITY OF CALIFORNIA, SAN DIEGO, Central University Library, Mandeville Dept of Special Collections, La Jolla, 92093. Lynda Corey Claassen, Head
Notes: Papers of Harold Clayton Urey (1893-1981), winner of the 1934 Nobel Prize in chemistry for his discovery of Deuterium. Incl files concerning the Emergency Committee of Atomic Scientists, 1946-49; also some material on the Rosenberg/Sobell spy cases; also on his works as science advisor to John F Kennedy (president-elect).

CA —CALIFORNIA INSTITUTE OF TECHNOLOGY, Robert A Millikan Memorial Library, Archives, 1201 E California Blvd, Pasadena, 91125. Judith R Goodstein, Archivist
Notes: Over 70 collections (1830s-present) relating to history of 19th-20th centuries science and technology and the history of the Institute. Included are personal and professional papers of Caltech scientists and administrative officers; divisional records and faculty committees; over 5000 photographs of American and European scientists. Mss collections documents more than a century of American political, social, and intellectual history; the development of the physical sciences, aeronautics, molecular biology, and seismology in the US and abroad; and social and political conditions in Europe between the two World Wars. There are also family letters relating to 19th century American life before and during the Civil War (the Morley and A G Throop papers); to 19th century social conditions in Russia and Hungary (the Paul Epstein papers and Theodore von Karman papers); andto the development of 20th century Italian mathematics.

CA —SAN DIEGO STATE UNIVERSITY, Malcolm A Love Library, 5300 Campanile Dr, San Diego, 92182. D Dickinson, Univ Librn; Don L Bosseau, Dir
Notes: The Ernest Zinner Collection, incl 2 incunables, autographs of scientists, portraits, pictures of sundials, 31 ms letters.

CA —STANFORD UNIVERSITY LIBRARIES, Cecil H Green Library, Stanford, 94305. Michael T Ryan, Cur
Notes: The Frederick E Brasch Collection (4000 vols cat). History of science, with emphasis on Newton, his precursors, contemporaries and successors. The Samuel I

and Cecile M Barchas Collection in the History of Science and Ideas. Rare books in the history of science with emphasis on physics and astronomy, and rare landmark books in all history of science subjects and time periods.

CT —YALE UNIVERSITY, Medical Historical Library, Klebs Collection, 333 Cedar St, New Haven, 06520. Ferenc A Gyorgyey, Librn
Notes: The Arnold Carl Klebs Medical Collection (15,000 vols, pamphlets, etc), incl the library of his father, Edwin Th A Klebs, pathologist. Strong in bibliography of early printed medical books, herbals, plague tracts, inoculation, vaccination and tubercular diseases.

DC —GEORGETOWN UNIVERSITY, Medical Center, John Vinton Dahlgren Memorial Library, 3900 Reservoir Rd NW, Washington, 20057. Clementine Pellegrino, Librn
Notes: The Alexis Carrel Collection. Medical research of man and society. Biological specimens and numerous unpublished mss. The Alexis Carrel Collection incl: a complete set of Dr Carrel's scientific notebooks starting in 1906; Col Charles Lindbergh's notebooks from 1935-1939 and those of De Ebeling, Dr Carrel's collaborator for 25 years; the ms of *Man the Unknown*, numerous specimens of Dr Carrel's work in transplantation of blood vessels, kidney, thyroid and other organs; considerable data on tissue cultivation. Correspondence from 1906 until his death to his wife, brother, cousins, nieces, etc; correspondence to many of the great scientists of the era, as well as all correspondence relating to his book *Man the Unknown*. There is a separate index to the collection.

IN —INDIANA UNIVERSITY, Lilly Library, Seventh St, Bloomington, 47405. William R Cagle, Librn
Notes: First appearances in print of great scientific discoveries. Mss incl papers of many scientists, particularly the biological sciences; also of some inventors.

IA —HERBERT HOOVER PRESIDENTIAL LIBRARY, West Branch, 52358. Dale C Mayer, Archivist
Notes: Unpublished papers of physicists and astronomers, 1917-1969.

KS —UNIVERSITY OF KANSAS, Kenneth Spencer Research Library, Special Collections Dept, Lawrence, 66045. Alexandra Mason, Librn
Notes: Ellis Collection of Ornithology, natural history and voyages and travels; botanical literature from Fitzpatrick collection (especially medical botany, early American Botanists, renaissance herbals, Metthioli); some early chemistry and mathematics; scientific voyages and travels; De Beer collection of offprints in embryology, endocrinology, and systematic zoology; D'Arcy Wentworth Thompson collection of separates in natural history and classics; Herrick, Coghill and Roofe collections in neurology. Noncirculating.

ME —BOWDOIN COLLEGE, Library, Brunswick, 04011. Dianne M Gutscher, Cur of Special Collections
Holdings: Cat Mss
Notes: The Parker Cleaveland Papers cover the period 1795-1858 and number about 1600 items. They are principally concerned with his tenure as professor of chemistry, mineralogy, and natural philosophy at Bowdoin. They incl personal correspondence, lecture notes, and writings on scientific subjects, incl his mss of the first American work on mineralogy and geology.

MD —JOHNS HOPKINS UNIVERSITY, Milton S Eisenhower Library, Charles & 34 Sts, Baltimore, 21218. Ann S Gwyn, Assistant Dir for Special Collections
Notes: Foreign and American doctoral dissertations and reprints to 1964. Largest number in history of science, 85,000. Also biology, chemistry, geology, meteorology, psychology, physics and mathematics. Johns Hopkins not included. Incl 100,000 Western European doctoral dissertations, espec French and German; some Scandinavian.

SCIENTISTS (cont.)

Collection is located in Gillman Storage Area accessible through Special Collection Division.

MD —JOHNS HOPKINS UNIVERSITY, Milton S Eisenhower Library, Charles & 34 Sts, Baltimore, 21218. Ann S Gwyn, Assistant Dir for Special Collections
Notes: Chiefly important for the history of universities in the US, and for the history of science. Correspondence of academic leaders such as Andrew White, Daniel Colt Gilman and Charles W Eliot; scientific figures: Rowland and Osler. State Department correspondence of Isaiah Bowman in World War II. American statesmen from Washington to Wilson; literary figures, chiefly American and German; many Hopkins professors and Maryland civic leaders. Housed in the Frieda C Thies Manuscript Room. About 75,000 mss.

MA —WELLESLEY COLLEGE, Margaret Clapp Library, College Archives, Wellesley, 02181.
Notes: Records of the Departments of Astronomy, Biological Sciences, Botany, Chemistry, Geology, Physics, Zoology, and individuals connected with these departments at Wellesley College (27 linear feet).

†MO —UNIVERSITY OF MISSOURI-COLUMBIA, Western Historical Manuscripts Collection, Columbia, 65201.
Notes: Papers of the Laws Observatory, 1877-1954.

MO —WASHINGTON UNIVERSITY, School of Medicine, 660 S Euclid Ave, Saint Louis, 63110.

MO —WASHINGTON UNIVERSITY, School of Medicine, Archives, 660 S Euclid Ave, Saint Louis, 63110. Paul G Anderson, Archivist
Notes: Institutional records and papers of faculty of Washington University School of Medicine and its predecessors and associated hospitals. Contains records of St Louis Medical College, Missouri Medical Barnard Free Skin and Cancer Hospital, Barnes Hospital, St Louis Children's Hospital and Jewish Hospital of St Louis. Incl papers of William Beaumont, Joseph Erlanger, Leo Loeb, Evarts Graham, Edmund V Cowdry, Helen Graham, Carl V Moore, Margaret Smith and others. Oral history program. See also: Anderson, Paul G and Hoolihan, Christopher, eds. Special Collections (St Louis: Washington University School of Medicine, 1981). 960 linear feet.

NH —DARTMOUTH COLLEGE, Baker Memorial Library, Hanover, 03755.
Holdings: 50 Boxes
Notes: The papers of George Robert Stibitz (1904-), concerning the invention and development of the digital computer (1937-1963).

NJ —PRINCETON UNIVERSITY, Library, University Archives, Princeton, 08540.
Holdings: 2 Boxes
Notes: Records of Project Matterhorn, 1951-1966.

NM —UNIVERSITY OF CALIFORNIA, Los Alamos National Laboratory, Libraries, PO Box 1663, MSP 362, Los Alamos, 87545. J Arthur Freed, Head Librn
Holdings: Vols (800,000) Cat Films Microforms
Budget: ($700,000)
Notes: Incl 500,000 classified and unclassified reports. There are 25 branch libraries and a central collection. The Medical Library contains about 40,000 vols in the areas of biomedical research.

NY —STATE UNIVERSITY OF NEW YORK AT ALBANY, Library, Special Collections Dept, 1400 Washington Ave, Albany, 12222. Marion P Munzer, Coordr
Notes: Eugene I Rabinowitch's correspondence and administrative files dealing with his academic and publishing career; editorship of the Bulletin of Atomic Scientists, establishment of the Center for Science and the Study of Society at the State University of New York at Albany (16 linear feet).
See also entries under Rabinowitch, Eugene I; Bulletin of Atomic Scientists

NY —CORNELL UNIVERSITY LIBRARIES, Collection of Regional History, Dept of Manuscripts and Univ Archives, Ithaca, 14853.
Notes: French zoologist, Edmond Perrier, director of the Museum National d'Histoire Naturelle of Paris. Letters, 1873-1917, from colleagues, students, the public, and relatives. Also, about 200 drafts from the hand of Perrier, from 1876-1919. In addition, about 1000 mss and letters from 19th century French scientists Louis Guillaume Figuier, Nicolas Flammation, and Edouard Toulouse, and British comparative anatomist Richard Owen.

†NY —COLUMBIA UNIVERSITY LIBRARIES, Butler Library, Rare Book and Manuscript Library, 535 W 114 St, New York, 10027.
Notes: 76 vols of diaries of Lynn Thorndike, 1902-63. A record of his daily reading, progress in research and writing, European travels, relations with scholars and librarians, and other personal matters.

NY —US MILITARY ACADEMY LIBRARY, West Point, 10996. Egon A Weiss, Librn
Holdings: Mss
Notes: Records of the Department of Chemistry, Mechanics, and Physics (1881-1971), of the US Military Academy at West Point. 9.75 ft of mss.

PA —AMERICAN PHILOSOPHICAL SOCIETY, Library, 105 S Fifth St, Philadelphia, 19106. Edward C Carter II, Librn
Holdings: Cat Mss

SC —CLEMSON UNIVERSITY, Libraries, Clemson, 29631. Michael F Kohl, Head of Special Collections
Holdings: Vols 1500 //
Notes: Book collection initiated with gifts from Mrs Bernard Behrend. Incl early editions by Galileo, Newton, Priestly, and other great scientists. Collecting emphasis has been upon engineering.

UT —BRIGHAM YOUNG UNIVERSITY, Harold B Lee Library, Unversity Hill, Provo, 84602. Sterling Albrecht, Dir
Holdings: 40 Boxes
Notes: Papers of Harvey Fletcher, about half consisting of publications of other scientists (ca 1934-ca 1971).

†ON —PUBLIC ARCHIVES OF CANADA, Library, 395 Wellington St, Ottawa, K1A 0N3, Can. Dawn E Monroe, Collections Dept Officer
Holdings: 4 Feet
Notes: Records of the Royal Astronomical Society of Canada, 1868-1968.

PQ —MCGILL UNIVERSITY, McLennan Library, University Archives, 3459 McTavish St, Montreal, H3A 1Y1, Can. Martha Caya, Archivist
Holdings: Vols (7) notebooks
Notes: The papers of the McGill Physical Society, 1897-1959. Original mss and handwritten work available for Scholarly research only. Microfilm available to public.

SCIENTISTS—CARICATURES AND CARTOONS

MN —MAYO MEDICAL LIBRARY, History of Medicine Collection, Rochester, 55905. Nancy R Hensel, Librn
Holdings: Pix
Notes: The Comfort Collection of caricatures of physicians and scientists from Vanity Fair. Description: Mann, Ruth J: "The unheroic representation of heroes." Mayo Clin Proc. 46:197-199, Mar 1971.

SCIENTISTS—PICTURES, ILLUSTRATIONS, ETC.

PA —FRANKLIN INSTITUTE LIBRARY, Dept of Historical Programs, 20th St and Parkway, Philadelphia, 19103.
Holdings: 2500 Items
Notes: Julian P Scott Collection of photographs of scientists (1920-1938).

SCIENTISTS, ATOMIC see Atomic Scientists

SCIENTOLOGY

CA —GRADUATE THEOLOGICAL UNION LIBRARY, New Religious Movements Research Collection, Public Services and Special Collections Dept, 2400 Ridge Road, Berkeley, 94709. Diane Choquette, Dept Head
Holdings: Vols (3000) Mss Pix
Notes: Begun in 1977, the collection focuses on religious movements new to America since 1960, and unorthodox religious movements resurgent since 1960. American forms of Hinduism, Buddhism, Sikhism, and Sufism are included along with occultism, Neo-Paganism, esoteric and alternative forms of Christianity, feminist spirituality, and human potential movements having a spiritual aspect. Legal issues, such as deprogramming, and the question of church/state relations are an important part of the collection. The Library is a depository for publications of the Unification Church in America, the Church of Scientology, and the International Society for Krishna Consciousness (America). The responses of mainstream religions and concerned citizens groups are also included. Besides 3000 monographs, the library has 400 periodical titles, 200 posters from the San FranciscoBay Area, 1965-77, 300 research papers, and 31 linear feet of ephemera.

CA —UNIVERSITY OF CALIFORNIA, LOS ANGELES, Research Library, Dept of Special Collections, 405 Hilgard Ave, Los Angeles, 90024. Edward Shreeves, Chairman, Bibliographers Group; David S Zeidberg, Head
Notes: 4 linear feet of instructional material and other publications.

SCOBEY, FRANK E.

OH —OHIO HISTORICAL SOCIETY, Archives Library Division, 1982 Velma Ave, Columbus, 43211. Dennis East, Division Chief
Notes: His papers.

SCORES, MUSIC see Miniature Scores (Music); Music Scores—Collections

SCOTLAND

CT —LEE ASH, (personal collection), 66 Humiston Dr, Bethany, 06525.
Holdings: Cat Mss Pix
Notes: Incl books, letters, ephemera, etc.

IL —LAKE FOREST COLLEGE, Donnelley Library, Lake Forest, 60045. Arthur H Miller Jr, College Librn
Holdings: Vols 1500 Cat
Notes: The R Douglas Stuart Collection of Scotiana. The collection consists of books dealing with the history, genealogy, and culture of Scotland. Incl basis 18th, 19th and 20th century historical and heraldic works; numerous genealogies and histories of clans; literary works by Scottish writers; travel and settlement by Scotsmen in other areas of the world; paleography; books on Scottish art and artists; and some ephemeral works on non-Scottish subjects but which are by writers of Scottish descent or which have Scottish imprints.

NV —UNIVERSITY OF NEVADA, RENO, University Library, Special Collections Dept,

SCOTLAND (cont.)

Reno, 89557. Robert E Blesse, Head
Holdings: Vols 650 Uncat
Notes: First and early editions, books about
Robert Burns, Scotland, his contemporaries.
Publication: Robert Burns, an exhibition...
University of Nevada Press, Bibliographic
Series no 1, 1962.

SCOTLAND—GENEALOGY

IN —INDIANA UNIVERSITY, Lilly Library,
Seventh St, Bloomington, 47405. William R
Cagle, Librn
Holdings: Cat Mss
Notes: Books and manuscripts on Scottish
history, genealogy, literature, travel,
topography, and natural history to 1707, and
nineteenth century books of travel and
description.

SCOTLAND—HISTORY

FL —FLORIDA STATE UNIVERSITY,
Robert Manning Strozier Library,
Tallahassee, 32306. John Mackay Shaw, Cur
Holdings: Vols 5000 Cat
Notes: The Scottish Collection is a broad
choice of works relating to such areas as
local and national history, politics, social
customs, poetry, fiction, travel, religion,
genealogy and biography. A list, "Books of
Scottish Influence and Significance,"
enumerates the holdings, including books,
periodicals, records and maps. Of special
interest is a gathering of rare Jacobite
pamphlets.
IL —LAKE FOREST COLLEGE, Donnelley
Library, Lake Forest, 60045. Arthur H
Miller Jr, College Librn
Holdings: Vols 1500 Cat
Notes: The R Douglas Stuart Collection of
Scotiana. The collection consists of books
dealing with the history, genealogy, and
culture of Scotland. Incl basic 18th, 19th and
20th century historical and heraldic works;
numerous genealogies and histories of clans;
literary works of Scottish writers; travel and
settlement by Scotsmen in other areas of the
world; paleography; books on Scottish art
and artists; and some ephemeral ut which
are by writers of Scottish descent or which
have Scottish imprints.
IN —INDIANA UNIVERSITY, Lilly Library,
Seventh St, Bloomington, 47405. William R
Cagle, Librn
Holdings: Cat Mss
Notes: Books and manuscripts on Scottish
history, geneology, literature, travel,
topography, and natural history to 1707, and
nineteenth century books of travel and
description.
MO —SAINT LOUIS UNIVERSITY, Pius XII
Memorial Library, 3655 W Pine Blvd, Saint
Louis, 63108. William Cole, Dir
Holdings: Vols 250 Cat Mss Slides //
Notes: Fundamental source material for the
study of every aspect of Catholic religious,
political, and social thought during nearly
five hundred years of English, Scottish, and
Irish history (early sixteenth century to
modern times). Approximately 2220 volumes
do not appear in card catalog, and
researchers must write ahead to make
arrangements, since these volumes are not
readily available for public use.
OH —CLEVELAND PUBLIC LIBRARY,
History and Geography Department, 325
Superior Ave, Cleveland, 44114. JoAnn
Petrello, Head
Holdings: Cat
Notes: Extensive British History Collection
(incl Ireland, Scotland), especially 1660-
1800. Rare books. Collection of British
Learned Society serials; English Political
Pamphlet Collection. No photocopying.
BC —UNIVERSITY OF BRITISH
COLUMBIA, Library, Special Collections
Div, 1956 Main Mall, Vancouver, V6T 1Y3,
Can. Anne Yandle, Head
Holdings: Vols 1500 Cat Mss
Notes: Books by Burns, about Burns and his
works, by and about his contemporaries and
followers, and about contemporary Scotland.

NS —SAINT FRANCIS XAVIER
UNIVERSITY, Angus L MacDonald
Library, Antigonish, B0H 1C0, Can.
Maureen Lonergan, Librn
Holdings: Vols 5298 Cat Mss Maps Pix
Phonorecords Audiotapes
Notes: Books on or about Scotland and
Scottish people; books and pamphlets
dealing with Scottish immigrants to Canada;
books written in Gaelic; complete file of
MacTalla (Gaelic newspaper published in
Cape Brenton); reports and records of
Scottish societies. Separate catalog. See "The
St Francis Xavier University Celtic
Collection," by Calum IN MacLeod in
Special Collections in Canadian Libraries
(Ottawa: Canadian Library Assn, 1963) (
Occasional Paper, 53).
ON —UNIVERSITY OF GUELPH, Library,
Guelph, N1G 2W1, Can. Margaret
Beckman, Chief Librn; Ellen Pearson, Ref
Librn
Holdings: Vols 20,000 Cat Mss Maps Pix
Slides Phonorecords Audiotapes Videotapes
16mm Films Microforms
Budget: ($20,000)
Notes: All aspects and periods of Scottish
Culture, Life, Geography, History Literature,
etc. Extensive archival and rare material,
especially related to emigrants, cities of
Aberdeen and Glasgow, Jacobite Movement.
Special catalogs can be produced for any
part of the collections from automated
library records. (All records for all formats
are in machine readable form.)
ON —QUEEN'S UNIVERSITY, Douglas
Library, Kingston, K7L 5C4, Can. William F
E Morley, Cur, Special Collections
Holdings: Vols 100 Uncat
Notes: The MacGillivray Collection. Scottish
books, especially those dealing with clans,
tartans and heraldry. Also the Buchan
Collection, 5000 vols.

SCOTS IN CANADA

PA —BALCH INSTITUTE FOR ETHNIC
STUDIES, Library, 18 S Seventh St,
Philadelphia, 19106. R Joseph Anderson,
Library Dir
NS —SAINT FRANCIS XAVIER
UNIVERSITY, Angus L MacDonald
Library, Antigonish, B0H 1C0, Can.
Maureen Lonergan, Librn
Holdings: Vols 5298 Cat Mss Maps Pix
Phonorecords Audiotapes
Notes: Books on or about Scotland and
Scottish people; books and pamphlets
dealing with Scottish immigrants to Canada;
books written in Gaelic; complete file of
MacTalla (Gaelic newspaper published in
Cape Breton); reports and records of
Scottish societies. Separate catalog. See "The
St Francis Xavier University Celtic
Collection," by Calum IN MacLeod in
Special Collection in Canadian Libraries
(Ottawa: Canadian Library Assn, 1963)
(Occasional Paper, 53).
ON —PUBLIC ARCHIVES OF CANADA,
Library, 395 Wellington St, Ottawa, K1A
0N3, Can. Dawn E Monroe, Collections
Development Officer
Holdings: Vols (80,000) Cat Mss Maps
Notes: In addition to the Public Archives'
subject strengths and collection, there are
incl positive microfilm copies of the
Hudson's Bay Company records up to 1870;
limited research by staff on behalf of
inquirers. For originals and additional HBC
material, address The Honorary Secretary,
The Hudson's Bay Record Society, Beaver
House, Great Trinity Lane, London, EC 4,
England.

SCOTS IN THE U.S.

FL —FLORIDA STATE UNIVERSITY,
Robert Manning Strozier Library, Special
Collections Dept, Tallahassee, 32306. Opal
M Free, Head, Special Collections
Holdings: Vols 1709
Notes: The John MacKay Shaw Collection
of books of Scottish significance.
PA —BALCH INSTITUTE FOR ETHNIC
STUDIES, Library, 18 S Seventh St,
Philadelphia, 19106. R Joseph Anderson,
Library Dir
Holdings: Vols 100 Cat

SCOTT, AUSTIN WAKEMAN, 1884-1981

MA —HARVARD UNIVERSITY LIBRARY,
Law School Library, Langdell Hall,
Cambridge, 02138. Erika S Chadbourn, Cur
of Mss
Holdings: Cat Mss
Notes: Professional papers. Typed inventory
in repository. Inclusive dates: 1906-1979.

SCOTT, CLEMENT WILLIAM

NY —UNIVERSITY OF ROCHESTER, Rush
Rhees Library, Department of Rare Books
and Special Collections, Rochester, 14627.
Peter Dzwonkoski, Librn
Holdings: Cat Mss Pix
Notes: Papers, etc, incl books by and about,
etc.
BC —UNIVERSITY OF VICTORIA,
McPherson Library, Victoria, V8W 3H5,
Can.

SCOTT, DUNCAN CAMPBELL, 1862-1947

MB —UNIVERSITY OF MANITOBA,
Elizabeth Dafoe Library, Archives and
Special Collections Dept, Winnipeg, R3T
2N2, Can. Richard E Bennett, Dept Head;
Corrado A Santoro, Reference Archivist
Notes: Two handwritten letters and four of
his printed poems.

SCOTT, FRANK AUGUSTUS, 1873-1949

NJ —PRINCETON UNIVERSITY, Library,
Manuscript Collection, Nassau St, Princeton,
08540. Jean F Preston, Cur
Holdings: // Mss
Notes: Incl 3 boxes; 5 cartons of papers.

SCOTT, HUGH

VA —UNIVERSITY OF VIRGINIA,
Alderman Library, Manuscripts Dept,
Charlottesville, 22901. Edmund Berkeley Jr,
Cur
Holdings: Cat Mss Pix Phonorecords
Audiotapes Videotapes 16mm Films
Notes: Papers, personal and political, etc.

SCOTT, HUGH LENOX, 1853-1934

NJ —PRINCETON UNIVERSITY, Library,
Manuscript Collection, Nassau St, Princeton,
08540. Jean F Preston, Cur
Holdings: // Mss
Notes: Incl 1 box of papers.

SCOTT, JAMES BROWN, 1866-1945

DC —GEORGETOWN UNIVERSITY,
Library, Special Collections Div, 37 & O Sts
NW, Washington, 20057. George M
Barringer, Special Collections Librn;
Nicholas B Sheetz, Mss Librn
Holdings: Mss Cat Pix
Notes: The papers of James Brown Scott
(1866-1945), internationalist and authority in
international law, consisting of
correspondence, memoranda, documents,
minutes, printed material, manuscripts of
articles and addresses, photographs, and
newspaper clippings. Incl is material from
Scott's activities as Solicitor (1906-1910)
and Special Advisor (1914-1917) for the
State Department, as delegate to the Second
Hague Conference (1907) and the Paris
Peace Conference (1919), his membership
and offices in the Carnegie Endowment for
International Peace, the American Society of
International Law, and the Institut de Droit
International, as well as Scott's involvement
in numerous courts of international
arbitration. Also incl is material relating to
Pan-American law. Correspondence incl
letters from Charles Evans Hughes, Robert
Bacon, William Jennings Bryam,James
Bryce, Nicholas Murray Bulter, Andrew
Carnegie, Charles Francis Adams, Frank B
Kellogg, Robert Lansing, Franklin Roosevelt,
Elihu Root, and Woodrow Wilson, among
many others.

SCOTT, NATALIE ANDERSON

MA —BOSTON UNIVERSITY, Mugar
Memorial Library, Special Collections Dept,
771 Commonwealth Ave, Boston, 02215.
Howard B Gotlieb, Dir
Holdings: Cat Mss
Notes: Incl publications by.

SCOTT, SIR WALTER

†AL —UNIVERSITY OF ALABAMA, Amelia
Gayle Gorgas Library, PO Box S,
University, 35486.
Holdings: Vols (5425) Cat Mss Maps Pix
Microforms
Notes: Incl a collection of Sir Walter Scott
first editions, 41 vols; Robinson Jeffers
collection of 37 vols and mss; Lafcadio
Hearn Collection of 110 vols and pamphlets.
CA —UNIVERSITY OF CALIFORNIA, LOS
ANGELES, William Andrews Clark
Memorial Library, 2520 Cimarron St, Los
Angeles, 90018.
Holdings: Cat
Notes: Small collection, original editions,
etc.
CT —TRINITY COLLEGE LIBRARY, 300
Summit St, Hartford, 06106. Ralph S
Emerick, Librn
Holdings: Vols 500 Cat
Notes: Incl all first editions, most in the
original boards and associated material.
ID —UNIVERSITY OF IDAHO, Library,
Dept of Special Collections & Archives,
Moscow, 83843.
Holdings: Vols 1200 Cat
Budget: $500
Notes: Incl first editions and other works by
and about Scott. Charles A Webbert, *The
Earl Larrison Collection of Sir Walter Scott*
(University of Idaho Publication No 1).
NJ —PRINCETON UNIVERSITY, Library,
Morris L Parrish Collection, Princeton,
08540. Alexander D Wainwright, Cur
Holdings: Vols 42
Notes: The collection contains over 6500
vols, as well as many theatre programs,
playbills, photographs, clippings and other
miscellanea. Parrish's goal was to assemble
in both the English and the American first
editions, in the original condition as issued,
everything that a given author published. He
was also interested in a high standard of
condition for his books. Many additions
have been acquired since the Parrish
collection came to the Library as a bequest
in 1944. The collection is an assemblage of
author collections, consisting of books by:
William Harrison Ainsworth, James
Matthew Barrie, William Black, The Brontes,
William Wilkie Collins, Dinah Mulock
Craik, Marie de la Ramee ("Ouida"),
Benjamin Disraeli, Charles Dickens, Charles
Dodgson, George du Maurier, George Eliot
(ie Mary Ann Evans), Elizabeth Gaskell,
Thomas Hardy, Thomas Hughes, Charles
Kingsley, Charles Lever, Edward George
Earle Bulwer-Lytton, Mary Maxwell, George
Meredith, Charles Reade, Walter Scott,
Robert Louis Stevenson, William Makepeace
Thackeray, Trollope Family, Ellen Wood,
and Charlotte Yonge.
NY —STATE UNIVERSITY OF NEW
YORK, COLLEGE AT BUFFALO,
Lockwood Memorial Library, Main St,
Buffalo, 14260. Stanton F Biddle, Assoc Dir
Notes: A large collection.
NY —COLUMBIA UNIVERSITY
LIBRARIES, Rare Book & Manuscript
Library, 801 Butler Library, 535 W 114 St,
New York, 10027. Kenneth A Lohf, Librn
Holdings: Cat
NY —NEW YORK UNIVERSITY, Elmer
Holmes Bobst Library, Div of Special
Collections, Washington Sq S, New York,
10012. Frank Walker, Librn; Patrick
McGuire, Asst Librn
Holdings: Vols (100,000) Cat Mss Pix
Notes: The Fales Collection of first (and
other) editions of English and American
novels from about 1750 to date (about 70,
000 titles). Mss (30,000) pieces.
OH —OHIO UNIVERSITY, Vernon R Alden
Library, Department of Archives and Special
Collections, Athens, 45701. Gary A Hunt,
Head
Holdings: Vols 137 Cat

SCOTT, WILLIAM BELL

NJ —PRINCETON UNIVERSITY, Library,
Rare Books Dept, Princeton, 08544. Stephen
Ferguson, Cur
Holdings: Cat
Notes: The Janet Troxell Collection of
documents relating to the Pre-Raphaelite
Movement, the Rossetti family, William Bell
Scott, etc.

SCOTT, WINFIELD TOWNLEY, 1910-1968

MO —WASHINGTON UNIVERSITY,
Libraries, Special Collections Dept, Campus
Box 1061, St Louis, 63130.
Notes: A small but significant collection.
RI —BROWN UNIVERSITY, John Hay
Library, 20 Prospect St, Providence, 02912.
Mark N Brown, Cur Mss
Holdings: // Mss
Notes: Papers of Winfield Townley Scott,
poet, essayist, Literary Editor of the
Providence Journal, and Instructor of
English at Brown. Brown class of 1931, 32
portfolios of mss, typescripts and proofs of
Scott's poetry and prose, and 8 literary
notebooks. About 7000 pieces of
correspondence, chiefly from American
writers and publishers, and incl 700 letters
and copies of letters from Scott, family
correspondence, clippings, photographs, and
tape recordings. Correspondents include
most modern American writers. Register
available.

SCOTTISH CLANS see Clans and Clan
Systems

SCOTTISH FOLK SONGS see Folk
Songs, Scottish

SCOTTISH LANGUAGE AND LITERATURE

CA —SONOMA STATE UNIVERSITY,
Salazar Library, 1801 E Cotati Ave, Rohnert
Park, 94928. Sandra Walton, Librn
Holdings: Vols (650)
Notes: The W W Lyman Collection of Celtic
literature, consisting of Irish, Scottish and
Welsh fiction, poetry and plays.
DE —UNIVERSITY OF DELAWARE, Hugh
M Morris Library, S College Ave, Newark,
19711. T Stuart Dick, Special Collections
Holdings: Mss
Notes: Incl Scottish literary renaissance
drafts, typescripts, articles, book reviews,
sketches, miscellaneous memoranda by
Christopher M Grieve (Hugh Maediarmid),
when he was in London (1931-32). Also incl
are autograph notes, plays, prose, verse, and
correspondence for Sydney Goodsir Smith.
†NY —COLUMBIA UNIVERSITY
LIBRARIES, Butler Library, Rare Book and
Manuscript Library, 535 W 114 St, New
York, 10027.

SCOTTISH TARTANS see Tartans

SCOUTS AND SCOUTING

NM —BOY SCOUTS OF AMERICA, Ernest
Thompson Seton Memorial Library,
Philmont Scout Ranch & Explorer Base,
Cimarron, 87714. Eleanor Pratt, Dir of
Museums
Holdings: Vols (3000) Cat Mss Maps Pix
Notes: Along with Seton's library, his
writings (books, articles, short stories,
Birchbark Roll, Indian Woodbadge work
with young people), approx 3000 study skins
of birds and small animals. Also approx 3000
of his pen and ink, water color and oil
paintings. This collection was given to the
Boy Scouts of America by Seton's widow.
The museum, library, collections room and
laboratory were built for BSA by Mr L O
Crosby of Picayune, Mississippi. (See also
the diaries at the library of the American
Museum of Natural History, New York,
NY.) The 33 volumes of Seton's journals
(diaries) were given to the American
Museum of Natural History by Joseph F
Cullman 3rd; he also had copies made for
the Seton Memorial Library. Our second
museum is the Kit Carson Museum, a living
history museum, open June, July and
August.
TX —BOY SCOUTS OF AMERICA, Library,
1325 Walnut Hill Lane, Irving, 75062. Ann
Lamont McVicar, Librn
Holdings: Vols 3000 Cat Pix Slides
Notes: Early and current books on the Boy
Scouts of America, and on the subjects of
scouts and scouting.
PQ —MCGILL UNIVERSITY, McLennan
Library, Rare Books and Special Collections
Dept, 3459 McTavish St, Montreal, H3A
1Y1, Can.
Holdings: Vols 830
Notes: Incl scouting manuals, especially
those of Sir Robert Baden-Powell, as well as
some items on the history of scouting.

SCRAPBOOKS—COLLECTIONS

CA —LOS ANGELES PUBLIC LIBRARY,
Frances Howard Goldwyn Hollywood
Regional Library, 1623 Ivar Ave, Los
Angeles, 90028. Sally Dumaux, Librn
Holdings: Vols (100,000) Cat Mss Pix VF
Budget: ($60,000)
Notes: A general and a research collection
on theatre history, US and foreign, with
special emphasis on Los Angeles, Chicago,
and New York theatre from the late 1800s
to the present. Other aspects of the
collection include theatre design, make-up,
costume, and acting and directing
techniques. Also includes biographies of
actors and actresses (many signed). The play
collection of over 15,000 titles covers mainly
English and American plays of the 19th and
20th century. There are over 5000 playbills,
scrapbooks, posters, and programs. Special
Collections: "Hellzapoppin," NY, 1938-40.
Includes photographs, clippings, and
programs.
DC —SMITHSONIAN INSTITUTION,
National Museum of American Art & the
National Portrait Gallery Library, Eighth &
F Sts, NW, Washington, 20560. Cecilia
Chin, Librn
Holdings: Vols (47,000) Cat Microforms
Budget: ($60,000)
Notes: Subscribe to 600 foreign and
domestic periodicals on art and American
history. Holdings of older bound periodicals.
Collection emphasizes American art,
contemporary American and European
painting, portraiture, American biography.
Uncataloged material incl: 350 vertical file
drawers of clippings, small catalogs and
other ephemera on artists, art organizations,
museums, etc; mss and archival material on
American artists; the "Ferdinand Perret
Library"--180 scrapbooks with card index on
California art and artists, incl clippings,
catalogs, reproductions, etc; card
bibliography of books and periodical
literature on portraiture--international,
retrospective and current--in progress.
GA —CHATHAM-EFFINGHAM-LIBERTY
REGIONAL, 2002 Bull St, Savannah,
31499. Irma Harlan, Dir; Alice Driscoll,
Head Ref Dept
Holdings: Vols 4800 Cat Maps Pix
Microforms Scrapbooks
Notes: Scrapbooks incl newspaper clippings,
letters, photographs, pamphlets, programs of
special events, postcards, typewritten mss.
Emphasis on Georgia and Savannah history.
Extensive microfilm collections of
newspapers, censuses of Georgia counties;
local and state history dissertations, etc. Incl
2100 microforms.
IL —SOUTHERN ILLINOIS UNIVERSITY,
CARBONDALE, Delyte W Morris Library,
Carbondale, 62901.
Notes: Scrapbook collection (15) on Ulysses
S Grant.
MA —STONEHILL COLLEGE, Cushing-
Martin Library, Washington St, North
Easton, 02356. James J Kenneally, Cur
Holdings: Cat Mss Pix
Notes: About 12,000 letters, speeches and

SCRAPBOOKS—COLLECTIONS (cont.)

photographs; 104 scrapbooks, plus other memorabilia of Representative Martin, of Massachusetts, 1925-1965; Speaker of the House, 1947-1949, 1953-1955.

MI —DETROIT PUBLIC LIBRARY, Burton Historical Collection, 5201 Woodward Ave, Detroit, 48202. Alice Dalligan, Chief

NE —UNIVERSITY OF NEBRASKA-LINCOLN, Don L Love Library, University Archives and Special Collections, Lincoln, 68588. Joseph G Svoboda, University Archivist
Holdings: Pix Slides
Notes: R D Warden Collection of Charles Marion Russell. "Largest private collection of literature on Russell, The Cowboy Artist," 7000 items, incl first editions of every book and pamphlet by Russell and over 1000 periodical appearances of his art; 900 color prints, 142 drawings; color slides; scrapbooks about Russell and his family, from 1889.

NY —MUSEUM OF MODERN ART, Dept of Film, 11 W 53 St, New York, 10019. Eileen Bowser, Cur
Holdings: Mss
Notes: Special collections: D W Griffith: personal papers and scrapbooks (cataloged); Carl Lerner Collection: notebooks, scripts, letters (cataloged); Harry McWilliams Collection: promotional and advertising material; Merritt Crawford Collection: documents and letters on early film history (cataloged). Also, special material relating to Robert Flaherty, Helen Van Dongen, Thomas Ince, Paul Terry, G W Pabst, film censorship. Extensive clipping files and scripts on motion pictures. Partially cataloged.

NY —NEW YORK PUBLIC LIBRARY, Performing Arts Research Center, Billy Rose Theatre Collection, 111 Amsterdam Ave, New York, 10023. Dorothy L Swerdlove, Cur
Holdings: Cat
See also entry under Theatre-History.

NY —NEW YORK PUBLIC LIBRARY, Local History and Genealogy Div, Fifth Ave & 42 St, New York, 10018. Gunther E Pohl, Chief
Holdings: Vols (160,000) Cat Pix
Budget: ($38,548)
Notes: Extensive collection of county, city, town and village histories of the United States and of the British Isles and the Republic of Ireland. For state and national histories of the United States refer to the American History Division. All other local histories are part of the General Research and Humanities Division. Collection includes over 60,000 mounted photophaphs of New York City views arranged by address and/or subject. 20,000 film and glass plate negatives depicting NYC tenement housing conditions (1902-1938). Also the Lloyd L Acker collection of 48,000 film negatives depicting NYC buildings, 1935-1975. Collection of Lewis W Hine photographic prints made by the photographer on immigration, child labor, women at work and men at work. Eugene Armbruster Collection of Long Island views; DB Austin's photographs of Long Island and western Amreicana; scrapbooks, andpostcards of NYC and other US regions (200,000). See United States Local History Catalog (Boston: GK Hall, 1974), 2 vols.

NY —VISUAL STUDIES WORKSHOP, Research Center, 31 Prince St, Rochester, 14607. Linn Underhill, Coordr; Robert Bretz, Librn
Holdings: Vols (8000) Cat Pix Slides Audiotapes Videotapes
Notes: Strong emphasis on photography (over 1,000,000 pictures) and the photographic arts in many subject areas incl in this volume. Heavy emphasis on early photographic processes and collections of examples of them. Also collections of individual photographers' works.

PA —UNIVERSITY OF PITTSBURGH, Special Collections Dept, Curtis Theatre Collection, 363 Hillman Library, Pittsburgh, 15260. Jeanette Blanco, Cur
Holdings: Vols (4000) Cat Mss Pix Slides Microforms VF
Notes: The legitimate theatre of plays, musicals and vaudeville, chiefly of New York City and Pittsburgh, from 1865, and other US, community, summer, college and foreign theatre. Incl 500,000 programs, 12,000 pictures, 300 posters, the Oliver P Merriman Scrapbooks and 300 other scrapbooks, clippings and other ephemera. Vols incl over 3000 acting editions and playscripts. Separate collections: Ralph G Allen Burlesque Skits Collection; Michael Ellis Papers; William P Halstead Theatre Collection; Kenyon Family Papers; Philip Dunning Playscripts Collection; Pittsburgh Playhouse Records; Pittsburgh Savoyards Records. Noncirculating.

VA —UNIVERSITY OF VIRGINIA, Alderman Library, Manuscripts Dept, Charlottesville, 22901. Edmund Berkeley Jr, Cur
Holdings: Cat Mss Pix
Notes: Papers of Edwin Swift Balch, author of The North Pole and Bradley Land, and Antarctica, and authority on the Cook-Peary controversy incl scrapbooks and correspondence.

SCREEN ACTORS GUILD

CA —UNIVERSITY OF CALIFORNIA, LOS ANGELES, Theater Arts Library, Los Angeles, 90024. Edward Shreeves, Chairman, Bibliographers Group; Audree Malkin, Head, Theater Arts Library
Notes: The Charlton Heston Archives, incl correspondence, scripts, movie posters, still photographs, scrapbooks, interviews, awards, etc, covering his forty-year acting career in fifty-four films. He served six terms as President of the Screen Actors Guild, longer than anyone else.

SCRIBNER, CHARLES, AND SON, PUBLISHERS

NJ —PRINCETON UNIVERSITY, Library, Manuscript Collection, Nassau St, Princeton, 08540. Jean F Preston, Cur
Holdings: Mss
Notes: The publisher's archive incl 500 ms boxes and 108 letterbooks. See Princeton University Library Chronicle, v 28, pp 187-89. An unpublished typescript guide (81 p) is available in the Library.

SCRIBNER RARE BOOK SHOP

NY —GROLIER CLUB OF NEW YORK LIBRARY, 47 E 60 St, New York, 10022. Robert Nikirk, Librn
Notes: Catalogs representative of the genre from the earliest times. Also, archive copies of the Scribner Rare Book Shop, NYC.

SCRIP see Securities

SCRIPPS, ELLEN BROWNING

CA —CLAREMONT COLLEGES, Ella Strong Denison Library, Scripps College, Claremont, 91711. Judy Harvey Sahak, Librn
Holdings: Uncat Mss Pix
Notes: Includes biographies. Also financial and business records, personal and business correspondence, diaries.

SCRIPPS-HOWARD NEWSPAPERS

DC —LIBRARY OF CONGRESS, Manuscript Division, Washington, 20540. John C Broderick, Chief
Notes: Papers of Roy W Howard (1883-1964), past president and chairman of the board of Scripps-Howard Newspapers. Some 85,000 items for the years 1923-64, incl business and personal correspondence, maintained under state and city of origin, with separate files in each year for the various Scripps-Howard newspapers, especially for the World Telegram (New York City).

SCRIPTS, MOVING PICTURES see Moving Pictures—Scripts

SCRIPTS, RADIO see Radio Scripts

SCRIPTS, TELEVISION see Television Scripts

SCRIPTURES, HOLY see Bible

SCROLLS, DEAD SEA see Dead Sea Scrolls

SCROLLS, ORIENTAL

NY —BUFFALO MUSEUM OF SCIENCE, Buffalo Society of Natural Sciences, Research Library, Humboldt Park, Buffalo, 14211. Marcia T Morrison, Chief Librn
Holdings: Vols 900 Cat Mss Pix
Notes: The Elizabeth W Hamlin Oriental Library of Art and Archaeology. Incl 75 scrolls.

PA —UNIVERSITY OF PITTSBURGH, Henry Clay Frick Fine Arts Library, Pittsburgh, 15260. Anne W Gordon, Fine Arts Librn
Holdings: Vols (55,000) Cat Pix Slides Microforms
Notes: Emphasis is on the art of the Western World--Architecture, sculpture, painting, minor arts, archaeology, with special strength in the Byzantine, early Christian, medieval, renaissance and modern periods. The Oriental field is represented, incl replicas of scrolls. Studio arts are also covered. Illuminated ms facsimiles. Extensive collections of slides and photographs for study of art history are available in the building but not administered by the art library.

SCRUGGS, PHILIP LIGHTFOOT

VA —UNIVERSITY OF VIRGINIA, Alderman Library, Manuscripts Dept, Charlottesville, 22901. Edmund Berkeley Jr, Cur
Holdings: Cat Mss Pix
Notes: Papers, etc.

SCUBA DIVING

IL —NATIONAL COUNCIL OF THE YMCAS, YMCA Historical Library, 6400 Shafer Ct, Rosemont, 60018. Eleanor R Murphy, Librn
Notes: Large collection, incl historical material, on basketball, wrestling, track and field, swimming, diving, scuba and volleyball.

SCULLING see Rowing

SCULPTORS

IA —IOWA STATE UNIVERSITY, Library, Dept of Special Collections, Ames, 50011. Stanley M Yates, Head
Holdings: // Mss Pix
Notes: The Christian Petersen (1885-1961) Papers. Petersen was on Iowa State University faculty 1937-1961; executed many pieces of sculpture. Collection incl correspondence, articles about Peterson, original sketches and about 400 photographs. Collection is 9 linear ft.

MA —JONES LIBRARY, 43 Amity St, Amherst, 01002. Daniel J Lombardo, Cur of Special Collections
Holdings: Vols 30 Cat Mss Pix
Notes: Incl drawings, photographs, and models of many of Sidney Waugh's sculptures. Unpublished guide available.

MA —RADCLIFFE COLLEGE, Arthur & Elizabeth Schlesinger Library on the History of Women in America, 3 James St, Cambridge, 02138. Patricia Miller King, Dir; Eva Moseley, Cur of Mss
Holdings: // Cat Mss Pix
Notes: Correspondence, writings, etc of the sculptor Harriet Goodhue Hosmer, (1830-1908). Probably largest collection of her papers. Available on microfilm. Inventory published by G K Hall; see Hamilton Family for citation. Also papers of Alma Kline and Cornelia Van Auken Chapin (1893-).

SCULPTURE

CA —J PAUL GETTY MUSEUM, Photo Archives, 17985 Pacific Coast Hwy, Malibu, 90265. William Reeder, Cur
Holdings: Pix
Notes: Incl photographs of works of art at the Museum (180,000 cataloged, 500,000 uncataloged), incl ancient art, western European art (painting, sculpture, graphics) and European decorative arts, medieval and Renaissance to 19th century, and antiquities.

CA —CALIFORNIA COLLEGE OF ARTS & CRAFTS, Meyer Library, Broadway at College, Oakland, 94618. Robert L Harper, Head Librn
Holdings: Vols (29,000) Cat Pix
Budget: ($10,000)
Notes: All fields of arts and crafts.

SCULPTURE (cont.)

CA —PASADENA PUBLIC LIBRARY, Fine
Arts Division, Reference Services, 285 E
Walnut St, Pasadena, 91101. Anne Cain,
Principal Librn
Holdings: Vols (10,000) Cat Pix Films
Notes: Library has 55 vertical drawers of
pictures and clippings, constantly revised
and added to. Incl over 130,000 pictures, 64
films.

CA —SAN DIEGO PUBLIC LIBRARY, Art,
Music & Recreation Sect, 820 E St, San
Diego, 92101. Barbara A Tuhill, Supvr
Holdings: Vols 250 Cat Pix
Notes: Mainly Italian Renaissance and
Oriental, as well as methods and procedures.
From the private library of Donal Hord,
local sculptor. For reference use only.

DC —SMITHSONIAN INSTITUTION,
Hirshhorn Museum & Sculpture Garden
Library, Eighth & Independence Ave SW,
Washington, 20560. Anna Brooke, Librn
Holdings: Vols (12,000) Cat Pix Slides
Microforms Audiotapes 16mm Films VF
Budget: ($79,000)
Notes: Twentieth century painting and
sculpture. Incl 4000 pictures and 3500 slides.

IL —ART INSTITUTE OF CHICAGO,
Ryerson & Burnham Libraries, Michigan
Ave & Adams St, Chicago, 60603. Daphne
C Roloff, Dir
Holdings: Vols (136,000) Cat Mss Slides
Microforms
Budget: ($167,000)
Notes: Total collection incl 300,000 slides.

IN —INDIANA UNIVERSITY, Art Museum
Bldg, Fine Arts Bldg, Bloomington, 47401.
Betty Jo Irvine, Fine Arts Librn
Holdings: Vols (57,000) Cat Pix Microforms
Budget: ($52,000)
Notes: Art forms relevant to the periods and
places involved.

IN —ALLEN COUNTY PUBLIC LIBRARY,
900 Webster St, Fort Wayne, 46802. Paul
Deane, Reader Services Dept Head; Kay
Lynn Isca, Art Music & AV Dept Head
Holdings: Vols 6000 Cat Pix Slides
Phonorecords Audiotapes Films

LA —R W NORTON ART GALLERY,
Library, 4747 Creswell Ave, Shreveport,
71106. Jerry M Bloomer, Librn
Holdings: Cat

MA —ROBBINS LIBRARY, 700
Massachusetts Ave, Arlington, 02174. Peter
L Fenton, Dir
Holdings: Cat Mss Pix
Notes: This extensive special collection is
comprised of material on Cyrus Dallin, a
prominent sculptor of Arlington,
Massachusetts, and his work. Arranged by
subject, files contain pictures, newspapers
and magazine articles on particular
sculptures. Also incl biograhical material,
programs of exhibits, letters, honors and
awards received, photographic portraits of
Dallin and an autograph collection, among
other material. The Smithsonian Institution
has microfilmed the collection.

MA —MELROSE PUBLIC LIBRARY, 69 W
Emerson St, Melrose, 02176. Diane E Shaw,
Art Librn
Holdings: Vols (8500) Cat Pix Slides
Phonorecords
Budget: ($6900)
Notes: Framed and unframed art
reproductions, slides (2773), periodicals,
clippings, recordings (3000). incl the Mary
Livermore Collection of Sacred Art, the
Odlin Collection and the Pierre Gendrot
Collection of Fine Art.

MA —OLD STURBRIDGE VILLAGE,
Research Library, Sturbridge, 01566.
Theresa Rini Percy, Librn
Holdings: Cat
Notes: New England, 1790-1850. Incl
gravestone rubbings.

MI —CRANBROOK ACADEMY OF ART,
500 Lone Pine Rd, Box 801, Bloomfield
Hills, 48013. Diane Gunn, Librn
Holdings: Vols (25,000) Slides

MI —KALAMAZOO INSTITUTE OF ARTS
LIBRARY, 314 S Park St, Kalamazoo,
49006. Marianne Cavanaugh, Librn
Holdings: Vols (5000) Cat Slides
Budget: $2000
Notes: Incl (8000) slides. Vertical file on

artists. Collection is supplemented by 55
current subscriptions to periodicals in visual
arts. Emphasis is on 20th century art and on
American art. Collection supports permanent
collection in prints, paintings, photography,
and sculpture.

MI —MONROE COUNTY LIBRARY
SYSTEM, Bedford Branch, 8575 Jackman
Road, Temperance, 48182. Paula
Kaczmarek, Head, Bedford Branch
Holdings: Vols 6500 Cat Periodicals AV
Budget: $8000
Notes: Circulating general collection of
popular art books, especially Western
European and American painting; also
includes technique, graphic arts,
photography, sculpture, architecture.
Periodicals held five years.

MN —MINNEAPOLIS COLLEGE OF ART
& DESIGN, Library, 200 E 25 St,
Minneapolis, 55404. Richard Kronstedt,
Head Librn
Holdings: Vols 800 Cat Slides
Notes: Incl exhibit catalogs; collection
emphasis on 20th century sculpture and
sculptors.

MN —WALKER ART CENTER, Staff
Reference Library, Vineland Place,
Minneapolis, 55403. Rosemary Furtak, Librn
Holdings: Vols 5000 Cat Pix
Notes: Incl 10,000 catalogs of individual
artists; museum gallery catalogs-10,000
catalogs of major exhibitions from all over
the world dating back to 1940. VF material
and tapes.

MO —THE NELSON-ATKINS MUSEUM OF
ART, Kenneth & Helen Spencer Art
Reference Library, 4525 Oak St, Kansas
City, 64111. Stanley W Hess, Librn
Notes: European sculpture.

NY —BROOKLYN MUSEUM, Art Reference
Library, 188 Eastern Parkway, Brooklyn,
11238.
Holdings: Vols (130,000)

NY —PRATT INSTITUTE LIBRARY, Art &
Architecture Dept, 200 Willoughby Ave,
Brooklyn, 11205. Sydney Star Keaveney,
Prof
Holdings: Vols (30,000) Cat Pix Slides
Budget: ($50,000)
Notes: Art and architecture, incl sculpture,
photography, painting, design, costume, and
commercial art. Incl 60,000 slides. Use
restricted to Pratt faculty and students.

NY —THE CLOISTERS, Metropolitan
Museum of Art (Branch), Fort Tryon Park,
New York, 10040. Suse C Childs, Librn
Holdings: Vols (5000) Cat Mss Pix Slides
Notes: A branch of the Metropolitan
Museum of Art devoted solely to the
literature of medieval art. Incl 16,000 slides
and 5000 photographs with unique strengths
in certain aspects of medieval art.

NY —METROPOLITAN MUSEUM OF ART,
Thomas J Watson Library, Fifth Ave & 82
St, New York, 10028. William B Walker,
Chief Librn
Holdings: Vols (250,000) Cat Mss
Microforms
Notes: All fields of art: 1400 periodicals, incl
bulletins and annual reports, catalogs, etc of
American and foreign art societies,
museums, etc; incl sales catalogs, exhibition
catalogs, clipping file on individual artists
and subjects, autograph letters. See *Library
Catalog of the Metropolitan Museum of Art,
New York,* second ed, rev and enl (Boston,
G K Hall, 1980, 48 v and first supplement,
1982). Since 1980, holdings have been
cataloged in RLIN.

†NY —METROPOLITAN MUSEUM OF
ART, Photograph & Slide Library, 82 St &
Fifth Ave, New York, 10028. Margaret P
Nolan, Chief Librn
Holdings: Cat Slides
Notes: Over 286,000 (125,000 in 2 x 2
color). The slides illustrate the history of
architecture, sculpture, painting and the
decorative arts from prehistoric times to the
present. Incl a representative coverage of the
Metropolitan Museum collections as well as
objects from other museums and private
collections. Slides available for rental to the
public.

NY —NEW YORK PUBLIC LIBRARY, Art,
Prints, and Photographs Div, Fifth Ave & 42

St, New York, 10018. Donald Anderle,
Chief
Holdings: Cat Mss Pix

NC —NORTH CAROLINA STATE
UNIVERSITY, Harry B Lyons Design
Library, P. O. Box 7701, Raleigh, 27607.
Maryellen LoPresti, Librn
Notes: Collection covers architecture,
landscape architecture, design and related
professions. Additional materials maybe
found on art, painting sculpture photography
and solar energy design. The library
presently houses a total of 28,000 books,
periodical and serial volumes to support the
curriculum. A product and trade literature
file and a vertical file of pamplets are also
locally cataloged in the library representing
an additional 3000 items of materials
available for use. A significant collections of
over 50,000 cataloged slides primarily
representing the areas of art and
architectural history are also contained in
the library facility. See *Directory of Special
Libraries and Information Centers.*

OH —CLEVELAND PUBLIC LIBRARY, Fine
Arts and Special Collections Department,
325 Superior Ave, Cleveland, 44114. Alice
N Loranth, Head
Holdings: Vols 2980 Cat
Notes: A good representation of sculptors
and their works from all countries and
periods. Special emphasis on contemporary
American sculpture. Incl books on technical
aspects.

PA —PHILADELPHIA COLLEGE OF ART,
Library, Broad & Spruce Sts, Philadelphia,
19102. Hazel Gustow, Dir
Holdings: Vols 25,000 Cat Periodicals Pix
Slides Microforms VF
Notes: Printed materials on the arts (history,
techniques, aesthetics, etc.). Current buying
incl most significant books coming into print
or being reprinted, mainly in English. Incl
about 22,000 titles, periodicals, 30 cabinets
vertical file materials, etc.

PA —UNIVERSITY OF PITTSBURGH,
Henry Clay Frick Fine Arts Library,
Pittsburgh, 15260. Anne W Gordon, Fine
Arts Librn
Holdings: Vols (55,000) Cat Pix Slides
Microforms
Notes: Emphasis is on the art of the Western
World-architecture, sculpture, painting,
minor arts, archaeology, with special
strength in the Byzantine, early Christian,
medieval, renaissance and modern periods.
The Oriental field is represented, incl
replicas of scrolls. Studio arts are also
covered. Illuminated ms facsimiles.
Extensive collections of slides and
photographs for study of art history are
available in the building but not administered
by the art library.

TX —UNIVERSITY OF TEXAS LIBRARIES,
Fine Arts Library, PO Box P, Austin, 78712.
Carole L Cable, Fine Arts Librn
Holdings: Vols (55,000) Cat Pix
Notes: Emphasis is on historical as well as
practical aspects.

TX —CISCO JUNIOR COLLEGE, Maner
Memorial Library, LRC Rte 3, Cisco, 76437.
Oleta Shirley, Dir
Holdings: Vols 1000 Cat
Notes: Artist, Randy Steffen, wrote about
Army uniforms; Indians; and also displayed
his sculpture.

VA —COLONIAL WILLIAMSBURG
FOUNDATION, Abby Aldrich Rockefeller
Folk Art Center, PO Box C, Williamsburg,
23187. Anne E Watkins, Registrar
Holdings: Vols 1200 Cat Maps Pix Slides
Notes: American folk art emphasis.

WI —UNIVERSITY OF WISCONSIN,
MADISON, Kohler Art Library, 800
University Ave, Madison, 53706. William C
Bunce, Chief; Louise Hunning, Ref Librn
Holdings: Vols (83,000) Cat Microforms
Notes: Incl over 10,000 exhibition and
auction catalogs.

AB —SOUTHERN ALBERTA INSTITUTE
OF TECHNOLOGY, Learning Resources
Centre, 1301 16 Ave NW, Calgary, T2M
0L4, Can. Tom Skinner, Historian
Holdings: Vols (5000) Cat Pix Slides Films
Audiotapes Filmstrips Videotapes
Notes: Serves Alberta College of Art (4-year
professional course).

SCULPTURE (cont.)

ON —NATIONAL GALLERY OF
CANADA, Library, National Museums of
Canada, Ottawa, K1A 0M8, Can. J Hunter,
Chief Librn

ON —METROPOLITAN TORONTO
LIBRARY, Fine Arts Dept, 789 Yonge St,
Toronto, M4W 2G8, Can. Alan Suddon,
Head
Holdings: Vols (42,000) Cat Pix Microforms
Notes: Extensive collection.

SCULPTURE—HISTORY

CA —STANFORD UNIVERSITY
LIBRARIES, Art & Architecture Library,
102 Cummings Art Bldg, Stanford, 94305.
Alexander D Ross, Art Librarian
Holdings: Vols (110,000) Cat
Notes: Incl materials of scholarly interest on
the history of the visual arts: painting,
sculpture, architecture, drawing,
printmaking, etc, for all regions and periods.

NY —FRICK ART REFERENCE LIBRARY,
10 E 71 St, New York, 10021. Helen
Sanger, Librn
Holdings: Vols (154,384) Cat Pix Per
Notes: History of painting, drawing,
sculpture and illuminated mss of US and
western Europe from 4th century AD to
about 1860. 54,862 art auction catalogs; 420,
507 study photographs.

NY —NEW YORK PUBLIC LIBRARY, Art,
Prints, and Photographs Div, Fifth Ave & 42
St, New York, 10018. Donald Anderle,
Chief
Holdings: Vols (150,000) Cat Mss Pix
Microforms
Notes: History and design in the fine and
applied arts. Architecture, painting, drawing,
sculpture, costume, furniture, advertising art,
prints, photography, crafts, and jewelry are
among the subjects covered from ancient
times to the present. See: New York Public
Library *Dictionary Catalog of the Art and
Architecture Division* (Boston, G K Hall,
1975), 30 vols. Holdings after that time are
incl in the *Dictionary Catalog of the
Research Libraries*. African Art and Afro-
American Art are collected by the
Schomburg Center for Research in Black
Culture.

SCULPTURE, AMERICAN

NJ —MONTCLAIR ART MUSEUM
LIBRARY, 3 South Mountain Ave, PO Box
1582, Montclair, 07042. Edith A Rights,
Librn
Holdings: Vols (10,000) Cat Pix Slides
Audiotapes
Budget: ($3500)
Notes: American painting and sculpture. Incl
5000 pictures; 10,000 slides; posters.
Audiotapes on American art and artists.

OH —CLEVELAND PUBLIC LIBRARY, Fine
Arts and Special Collections Department,
325 Superior Ave, Cleveland, 44114. Alice
N Loranth, Head
Holdings: Vols (2980) Cat
Notes: Part of the Sculpture Collection,
which incl a good representation of sculptors
and their works from all countries and
periods. Special emphasis on contemporary
American sculpture. Incl books on technical
aspects.

OK —THOMAS GILCREASE INSTITUTE
OF AMERICAN HISTORY & ART
LIBRARY, 1400 North 25th West Ave,
Tulsa, 74127. Sarah Hirsch, Librn
Holdings: Vols Cat Mss Maps Pix
Notes: Trans-Mississippi West, US, Indian
and Hispanic history. The Gilcrease Library
contains a total of about 40,000 mss; 10,000
imprints; 5000 photographs; 600 maps and
50,000 vols.

SCULPTURE, ITALIAN

CA —SAN DIEGO PUBLIC LIBRARY, Art,
Music & Recreation Sect, 820 E St, San
Diego, 92101. Barbara A Tuhill, Supvr
Holdings: Vols 250 Cat Pix
Notes: Mainly Italian Renaissance and
Oriental, as well as methods and procedures.
From the private library of Donal Hord,
local sculptor. For reference use only.

SCULPTURE, MINIMAL

NY —STATE UNIVERSITY OF NEW
YORK, COLLEGE AT PURCHASE,
Library, Lincoln Ave, Purchase, 10577.
Robert W Evans, Dir
Holdings: Uncat Mss Pix
Notes: Gift of the artist, George Rickey, and
his wife, whose collection of constructivist
art works has also been given to the
Neuberger Museum at the College at
Purchase. The collection consists largely of
over 1000 announcements and catalogs of
exhibitions of constructivist works and
material about the artists.

SCULPTURE, ORIENTAL

CA —SAN DIEGO PUBLIC LIBRARY, Art,
Music & Recreation Sect, 820 E St, San
Diego, 92101. Barbara A Tuhill, Supvr
Holdings: Vols 250 Cat Pix
Notes: Mainly Italian Renaissance and
Oriental, as well as methods and procedures.
From the private library of Donal Hord,
local sculptor. For reference use only.

SCULPTURE, RELIGIOUS see Christian Art and Symbolism

SCULPTURE, RENAISSANCE

CA —SAN DIEGO PUBLIC LIBRARY, Art,
Music & Recreation Sect, 820 E St, San
Diego, 92101. Barbara A Tuhill, Supvr
Holdings: Vols 250 Cat Pix
Notes: Mainly Italian Renaissance and
Oriental, as well as methods and procedures.
From the private library of Donal Hord,
local sculptor. For reference use only.

SCULPTURE, ROMANESQUE

MA —HARVARD UNIVERSITY, Harvard
College Library, Fine Arts Library, Fogg
Museum, 32 Quincy St, Cambridge, 02138.
Wolfgang M Freitag, Librn
Holdings: Vols (202,000) Cat Mss Pix Slides
Budget: ($176,500)
Notes: All areas of art history, with
emphasis on Italian primitives, Italian
Renaissance, master drawings, Romanesque
sculpture, architectural history, ms materials
(particulary American artists'), conservation
and restoration of art objects. Incl the
Berenson repertory of photographs from the
Harvard Center for Italian Renaissance
Studies in Florence, and the Decimal Index
to the Art of the Low Countries. Separate
card catalogs for books, photographs and
lantern slides, registers for ms holdings
which are not incl in *National Union
Catalog of Manuscript Collections.* Slides
total over 230,000; over 745,000 pictures.
Fine Arts Library Catalogue (14 volumes)
and *Catalogue of Auction Sales Catalogues*
(1 volume) (Boston: G K Hall, 1972); *A
Guide to the Fine Arts Library* (Cambridge,
Mass: 1971); *Guide to the Harvard Libraries*,
microfiche edition of holdingscataloged
through 1981 published 1984 (Munich/New
York: Saur).

SEA see Oceans

SEA, DOMINION OF THE see Sea Power

SEA ANIMALS see Marine Fauna

SEA FISHERIES see Fisheries

SEA LOCKS see Locks (Hydraulic Engineering)

SEA POWER

MD —US NAVAL ACADEMY, Nimitz
Library, Annapolis, 21402. Alice S
Creighton, Assistant Librn for Special
Collections
Holdings: Vols (22,000) Cat Mss Pix
Notes: Books and periodicals, with emphasis
on seapower. Incl rare and historically
significant works, naval and general history.
US Naval Academy materials (histories,
class albums, Lucky Bags, student
publications, etc), and copies of transcripts
of the Naval Institute's oral history
interviews with US naval officers.
Manuscripts incl 205 volumes of ships' logs,
letterbooks, order books, and watch, station
and quarter bills, 1796-1938; papers of
various naval officers, incl Vice Admiral
Wilson Brown, Commander George M
Bache, Admiral Harry S Knapp, Lieutenant
Edwin J DeHaven, and others; family
correspondence of Admiral David Dixon
Porter; and several thousand World War II
naval action reports. Approximately 15,000
pictures incl portraits of naval officers,
pictures of US and some foreign ships,
World War II naval news photos and USNA
photographs.

RI —US NAVAL WAR COLLEGE, Historical
Collection & Museum, Newport, 02841.
Anthony S Nicolosi, Dir; Evelyn Cherpak,
Cur
Holdings: Mss
Notes: Collections incl over 200,000
separate pieces; chiefly papers of naval
officers and records of organizations
associated with the US Navy, the Naval War
College, the college's major study areas, and
the Navy in the Narragansett Bay region;
oral history collection; Naval War College
Archives, 1884-present; records of
conferences held at the College; newspaper
collections dealing with naval themes and
military conflicts.

SEABURY, BISHOP SAMUEL

NY —GENERAL THEOLOGICAL
SEMINARY, Saint Marks Library, 175
Ninth Ave, New York, 10011. David Green,
Dir
Holdings: Vols (200,000) Cat
Notes: Extensive collection.

SEACOAST DEFENSES see Coast Defenses

SEACOAST EROSION see Coast Changes

SEACOAST PROTECTION see Shore Protection

SEAGER, ALLAN, 1906-1968

MA —BOSTON UNIVERSITY, Mugar
Memorial Library, Special Collections Dept,
771 Commonwealth Ave, Boston, 02215.
Howard B Gotlieb, Dir
Holdings: // Cat Mss
Notes: Incl publications by.

SEAL HARBOR, MAINE

NY —ROCKEFELLER UNIVERSITY,
Rockefeller Archive Center, Hillcrest,
Pocantico Hills, North Tarrytown, 10591.
Joseph W Ernst, Dir; J William Hess, Assoc
Dir
Notes: Papers relative to the Rockefeller
Family, Foundations, University, and other
specific enterprises and contributions to
particular areas of social, physical,
educational, and historic reform,
preservation, conservation, or development.
Extensive records of administrative, physical,
or intellectual relationships.

SEAL HARBOR ROADS (1911-1961)

NY —ROCKEFELLER UNIVERSITY,
Rockefeller Archive Center, Hillcrest,
Pocantico Hills, North Tarrytown, 10591.
Joseph W Ernst, Dir; J William Hess, Assoc
Dir
Notes: The Rockefeller Archive Center, a
division of The Rockefeller University,
preserves and makes available to scholars the
records of the University, the Rockefeller
Foundation, the Rockefeller Brothers Fund,
members of the family, and those of other
individuals and organizations associated with
their endeavors. Collections at the Center

SEAL HARBOR ROADS (1911-1961) (cont.)

document a century of philanthropy by legions of associated social and scientific pioneers, providing a unique window into the past.

SEALS (ANIMALS) AND SEALING

WA —WESTERN WASHINGTON UNIVERSITY, Center for Pacific Northwest Studies, High St, Bellingham, 98225. James W Scott, Dir
Holdings: // Cat Mss Maps Pix
Notes: The Archie W Shiels Collection. Archie W Shiels, who died in his 95th year in 1974, was formerly Managing Dir of Pacific American Fisheries and an author of some note on Alaskan topics. A few papers of his company are incl in the collection, which is primarily focused on Alaska, particularly its history and its seal and other fisheries. See also entry for Galen A Biery.

SEALS (NUMISMATICS)

CA —LOS ANGELES PUBLIC LIBRARY, Genealogy & Local History Dept, 630 W 5th St, Los Angeles, 90071. Lucile Lipman, Sr Librn
Holdings: Pix
Budget: ($16,000)
Notes: Collection of California city and county seals.
CO —AMERICAN NUMISMATIC ASSOCIATION LIBRARY, 818 N Cascade Ave, Colorado Springs, 80903. Nancy W Green, Librn
Holdings: Vols (20,000) Cat Slides
Notes: One of the largest numismatic libraries, the collection incl books, periodicals and auction catalogs on coins and coin collecting, medals, tokens, military orders and decorations, paper money, primitive money, banks and banking, seals and scarabs. ANA publishes a classified subject catalog of its collection and is open to the public for research and reference services. Only members may check books out.
CT —YALE UNIVERSITY, Box 1603A, Yale Station, New Haven, 06520.
Notes: Part of the Newell Collection of Western Asiatic Seals. Contains 472 cylindrical-shaped roll seals.
CT —YALE UNIVERSITY, Sterling Memorial Library, Babylonian Collection, 120 High St, New Haven, 06520. William W Hallo, Cur
Holdings: Vols (12,000) Cat Mss Pix
Budget: $2500
Notes: 30,000 mss in form of Babylonian tablets; 6000 seals and other art objects from Mesopotamia and the rest of the Ancient Near East.
NY —AMERICAN NUMISMATIC SOCIETY LIBRARY, Broadway between 155 & 156 Sts, New York, 10032. Francis D Campbell Jr, Chief Librn
Holdings: Vols (50,000) Cat Mss Maps Pix Slides 16mm Films Microforms
Budget: ($6000)
Notes: Incl materials devoted to coins, medals, decorations, orders, tokens, paper money, seals, heraldry. Aids materials incl history, economic history, art history, archaeology, inscriptions and a number of encyclopedias and biographical dictionaries. Dictionary card catalog provides access to the materials: *Dictionary Catalogue of the Library of the American Numismatic Society.* (Boston: G K Hall, 1962). 6 vols and vol listing the auction catalogs in our collection; *First Supplement: 1962-1967; Second Supplement: 1968-1972; Third Supplement: 1973-1977* (Boston: G K Hall, 1967, 1973, 1978). Noncirculating.
NY —NEW YORK PUBLIC LIBRARY, Rare Books and Manuscripts Div, Fifth Ave & 42 St, New York, 10018. William L Joyce, Asst Dir; Susan E Davis, Cur of Mss
Holdings: Cat Mss
Budget: ($7161)

SEAMAN, JONATHAN

PA —US ARMY MILITARY HISTORY INSTITUTE, Carlisle Barracks, 17013.

Richard J Sommers, Chief Archivist-Historian
Holdings: Mss Cat
Notes: 2000 boxes mss. The Viet Nam War collection, personal letters, daily logs, memoirs, speeches, and official papers of American officers and soldiers serving in Viet Nam or elsewhere in the world during the era. Almost all these papers are from Generals, incl William DePuy, Harold K Johnson, Bruce Palmer, Jonathan Seaman, and William Westmoreland.

SEAMANSHIP

MD —SEAFARER'S HARRY LUNDEBERG SCHOOL OF SEAMANSHIP, Paul Hall Library and Maritime Museum, Piney Point, 20674. Janice McAteer Smolek, Librn
Holdings: Mss Pix Slides Audiotapes Videotapes 16mm Films Filmstrips Microforms
Notes: Special collection on maritime studies incl books, mss, periodicals, audiovisuals, and archival materials pertaining to maritime history and maritime labor union history and vocational skills required by the maritime industry. Incl some rare books.

SEAMEN, MERCHANT see Sailors, Merchant

SEANCES

MB —UNIVERSITY OF MANITOBA, Elizabeth Dafoe Library, Archives and Special Collections Dept, Winnipeg, R3T 2N2, Can. Richard E Bennett, Dept Head; Corrado A Santoro, Reference Archivist
Notes: Papers of Thomas Glendenning Hamilton, physician and surgeon, member of the Manitoba Legislative Assembly, psychic researcher. Winnipeg, Manitoba. Important collection, emphasis is on psychic research with limited amount of materials regarding his medical and political careers. Seance attendance registers, records and affidavits, lecture notes, correspondence, newspaper clippings, books and journal articles. Photographs, slides and ca 50 boxes of glass plate negatives.

SEAPOWER see Sea Power

SEAPOWER SYMPOSIUM, INTERNATIONAL see International Seapower Symposium, 1970-1973

SEARS, ROEBUCK, AND COMPANY

IL —SEARS, ROEBUCK & CO, Merchandise Development & Testing Laboratory Library, Sears Tower, Dept 817, Chicago, 60684. Mary M McCarron, Librn
Holdings: Cat Pix Microforms
Notes: Microfilmed sets of Sears, Roebuck catalogs have been placed in more than 100 libraries in key geographic locations. Contain catalogs from 1888 to date.
PA —CARNEGIE LIBRARY OF PITTSBURGH, Science & Technology Dept, 4400 Forbes Ave, Pittsburgh, 15213. Catherine M Brosky, Dept Head
Notes: About 25,000 trade catalogs emphasizing American business and industry with a few foreign ones. Also in this collection are installation, maintenance and repair manuals, parts lists, some company reports and other materials. Generally of historical value as current additions were reduced after 1955. Complete set of Sears, Roebuck and Company catalogs from 1888. *Sweets Catalogs* complete except for 1 or 2 years.

SEASHORE

FL —US NAVAL COASTAL SYSTEMS CENTER, Technical Information Service Branch, Panama City, 32407. Myrtle J Rhodes, Librn
Holdings: Vols (30,000) Cat
Notes: Coastal and ocean technology, inshore undersea warfare, mine countermeasures, torpedo defense, underwater sound.

SEASONGOOD, MURRAY

OH —PUBLIC LIBRARY OF CINCINNATI & HAMILTON COUNTY, Government and Business Dept, 800 Vine St, Cincinnati, 45202. Paul T Hudson, Head
Holdings: Vols 2000 Cat
Notes: The Murray Seasongood Collection of Government, Law and Public Administration contains works on local government, city management, public finance and municipal law. The collection also houses the collected works of Murray Seasongood.

SEAT BELTS, AUTOMOBILE see Automobile Seat Belts

SEATTLE, WASHINGTON

WA —SEATTLE PUBLIC LIBRARY, 1000 Fourth Ave, Seattle, 98104. Ronald A Dubberly, City Librn
Holdings: Vols 70,000 Cat Pix
Notes: Incl 28,000 photographs of Seattle and Pacific Northwest architecture and views. Balance of picture collection about 650,000 items.
WA —UNIVERSITY OF WASHINGTON LIBRARIES, Suzzallo Library, Manuscripts Section, FM-25, Seattle, 98195. Karyl Winn, Librn
Notes: Files of locally produced newsfilm from station KOMO-TV in Seattle, from 1954.

SEAWEED

ME —BIGELOW LABORATORY FOR OCEAN SCIENCES & MAINE DEPT OF MARINE RESOURCES, Library, McKown Point, West Boothbay Harbor, 04575. Pamela Shephard-Lupo, Librn
Holdings: Vols Cat VF
Budget: ($55,000)
Notes: This library presently serves two institutions. The Maine Dept of Marine Resources has maintained the library since 1957 and thus the majority of our holdings are geared to their needs, ie fish biology and stock assessment on a local, national and international level. In 1973 Bigelow Laboratory for Ocean Sciences came to West Boothbay Harbor and began to contribute to the library with a very specialized collection of the Gulf of Maine marine chemistry, phytoplankton and nutrient cycles.

SEBRELL, W. HENRY, JR.

TN —VANDERBILT UNIVERSITY, Medical Center Library, Nashville, 37232. Mary H Teloh, Special Collections Librn
Holdings: Uncat Mss Pix Videotapes
Notes: The nucleus of the developing nutrition collection at Vanderbilt is the papers of medical researcher Joseph Goldberger, MD, and his associate W Henry Sebrell, Jr, MD. The collection consists of first editions and translations of classic books on pellagra, and the letters, mss, and notebooks compiled by Dr Goldberger and Dr Sebrell during their years of research on pellagra. See *Nutrition Reviews,* 33 (10):310-312, Oct 1975. 10 linear ft of mss.

SECKER, MARTIN

IN —INDIANA UNIVERSITY, Lilly Library, Seventh St, Bloomington, 47405. William R Cagle, Librn
Holdings: Vols // Cat Mss
Notes: First editions. Ms correspondence of D H Lawrence with publisher Martin Secker, 1911-1930. 200 items.
OK —UNIVERSITY OF TULSA, McFarlin Library, Dept of Rare Books and Special Collections, 600 S College, Tulsa, 74104. David Farmer, Dir; Toby Murray, Archivist; Caroline Swinson, Cur of Manuscripts & Art
Notes: The personal library of Martin Secker's books which he published, including volumes with significant inscriptions or letters from his authors.

SECOND ADVENT

MI —ANDREWS UNIVERSITY, James White
Library, Berrien Springs, 49104. Marley H
Soper, Dir
Holdings: Cat Mss Pix
Notes: Advent Source Collection. Deals with
prophecy of the Bible and the Advent hope
in historical context. About 3700 items.
Materials gathered by Dr L R Froom in the
preparation of his four-volume set entitled
Prophetic Faith of Our Fathers, ca 1946-
1954. Not available by interlibrary loan, but
may be used at this library.

SECOND ADVENTISTS see Advent
Christian Church and Adventist Movement

SECOND INTERNATIONAL see
International, Second

SECOND LANGUAGE LEARNING

CA —UNIVERSITY OF CALIFORNIA, LOS
ANGELES, Education & Psychology
Library, 390 Powell Library Bldg, Los
Angeles, 90024. Barbara Duke, Librn
Holdings: Vols (133,000) Cat Audiotapes
Microforms
Notes: Research collection serving graduate
students and faculty in Education,
Psychology, Kinesiology and Teaching
English as a Second Language. Areas of
emphasis incl higher education, education
and work, comparative education, early
childhood development, reading, second
language acquisition, cognition, perception,
personality, social psychology, motor control
and learning. Library has Univ of Oregon
microfiche collection of unpublished research
in sports, physical education, and recreation
and is a depository for ERIC microfiche.
MI —UNIVERSITY OF MICHIGAN, English
Language Institute/Linguistics Library, 1013
N University Bldg, Ann Arbor, 48109.
Patricia M Aldridge, Librn
Holdings: Vols (4500) Cat Maps VF
Videotapes
Notes: Second language learning, especially
English as a second languge.

SECONDARY EDUCATION see
Education, Secondary

SECONDARY SCHOOLS see Education,
Secondary

SECRET SERVICE

CA —HOOVER INSTITUTION ON WAR,
REVOLUTION & PEACE, Stanford
University, Stanford, 94305. Milorad M
Drachkovitch, Archivist
Notes: Two collections: (1) Papers of Yves
Godard, officer, French Army, 1932-1961;
director of police in Aleria, 1958-60; and
organizer of the Organisaton de l'Armee
Secrete (OAS) 1961-62; incl correspondence
messages, reprots, dossiers, maps, photos,
news clippings, speeches and writings, and
other material, 1929-74, related to military
and resistance operations during World War
II; to military operations during Indochinese
War; and to military, police, and terrorist
activities during the Algerian independence
struggle. Incl records of the Armee Secrete
de Haute-Savoie (Secret Army of Resistance
Fighters of Haute-Savoie). 13 ms boxes; 1
oversize volume; 1 envelope. (2) Ms diaries,
1914-1924, microfilms, photographs and
photostats of documents from the
Personlicher Stab Reichsfuhrer SS,
Schriftgutverwaltung dealing with the life
and career of Himmleras Reichsfuhrer SS
and Chef der Deutschen Polizei, 1934-1945.
6 notebooks (plus 25 loose pages), 5
microfilm reels, 2 photo albums, 14 ms boxes
incl 24 tapes of Himmler speeches, 1940-44.

SECRET SOCIETIES

CA —HARVEY G WOLFE LIBRARY, PO
Box 3514, Grand Central Sta, Glendale,
91201. Douglas L Evans, Librn
Holdings: Vols (6580) Mss Maps Pix
Budget: ($4500)
Notes: Main emphasis on espionage, military
intelligence, and sabotage.

CA —UNIVERSITY OF CALIFORNIA, LOS
ANGELES, Research Library, Dept of
Special Collections, 405 Hilgard Ave, Los
Angeles, 90024. Edward Shreeves,
Chairman, Bibliographers Group; David S
Zeidberg, Head
Holdings: Mss Pix
Notes: Political, economic, financial, press,
diplomatic, espionage, secret societies,
occultism, and comtemporary biographical
archives and documents, 1910-1965,
assembled by the editor of *Les documents
politiques, diplomatiques et financiers*
(Paris), Roger Mennevee. Separate finding
aid for the Archive (ca 1200 linear feet).
IL —WHEATON COLLEGE, Buswell
Memorial Library, Wheaton, 60187. Paul
Snezek, Library Dir
Holdings: Mss Pix
Notes: Blanchard's papers, correspondence,
books and photographs. Also a complete set
of the periodical Christian Cynosure. *Related
Topics*: Anti-slavery, Abolitionists, Secret
Societies, Wheaton College.
MI —MICHIGAN STATE UNIVERSITY,
Libraries, Special Collections Div, East
Lansing, 48824. Jannette Fiore, Librn
Holdings: Vols 1440 // Uncat Mss
Notes: Works from 15th to 19th centuries
on criminology, criminal law and
jurisprudence, including witchcraft,
demonology, et al, chiefly in German and
Latin.

SECRET WRITING see Cryptography

SECRETARIAL PRACTICE see Office
Practice

SECTS

AZ —WORLD UNIVERSITY, Library, 711 E
Blacklidge Dr, Tucson, 85719. Howard John
Zitko, Cur
Holdings: Vols (15,000) Cat Mss Maps
Audiotapes
Notes: Collection concerns the "frontier
sciences." No interlibrary loan.
CA —GRADUATE THEOLOGICAL UNION
LIBRARY, New Religious Movements
Research Collection, Public Services and
Special Collections Dept, 2400 Ridge Road,
Berkeley, 94709. Diane Choquette, Dept
Head
Holdings: Vols (3000) Mss Pix
Notes: Begun in 1977, the collection focuses
on religious movements new to America
since 1960, and unorthodox religious
movements resurgent since 1960. American
forms of Hinduism, Buddhism, Sikhism, and
Sufism are included along with occultism,
Neo-Paganism, esoteric and alternative
forms of Christianity, feminist spirituality,
and human potential movements having a
spiritual aspect.
CA —LOS ANGELES PUBLIC LIBRARY,
Philosophy & Religion Dept, 630 W Fifth St,
Los Angeles, 90071. Marilyn C Wherley,
Librn
Holdings: Vols 200 Cat
Budget: ($60,000)
Notes: Comprehensive collection of
materials on cults and sects with emphasis
on those active in the Southern California
area. Includes special files, indexes and
pamphlets.
OH —HEBREW UNION COLLEGE-JEWISH
INSTITUTE OF RELIGION, Klau Library,
3101 Clifton Ave, Cincinnati, 45220. David
J Gilner, Reference Librn
Holdings: Cat
TN —LEE COLLEGE, Library, Ocoee St,
Cleveland, 37311. Frances Arrington, Head
Librn; JoAnne Sparks, Religion Librn
Holdings: Vols 5086 Cat Slides
Phonorecords Audiotapes Filmstrips
Microforms
Notes: The Pentecostal Research Center
houses two special collections: the Church of
God (Cleveland, Tennessee) collection and
the Pentecostal collection. The latter
includes works about the movement and its
history, works by Pentecostal authors, and
specific subject areas (Holy Spirit,
glossolalia, divine healing).

SECTS, JEWISH see Jewish Sects

SECURITIES

NY —CORNELL UNIVERSITY LIBRARIES,
Graduate School of Management, Malott
Hall, Ithaca, 14853. Betsy Ann Olive, Librn
Holdings: Vols (135,000) Cat Microforms
Budget: ($130,000)

SECURITIES EXCHANGE see Stock
Exchanges

SECURITY, ECONOMIC see Economic
Security

SECURITY, INTERNAL see Internal
Security

SECURITY, INTERNATIONAL

ON —NATIONAL DEFENCE COLLEGE &
CANADIAN LAND FORCES
COMMAND & STAFF COLLEGE, Fort
Frontenac Library and Staff College Library,
Fort Frontenac, Kingston, K7K 2X8, Can. S
K Kamra, Chief Librn
Holdings: Vols 70,000 Cat Maps
Budget: $50,000

SECURITY OFFENSES see Subversive
Activities

SEDAINE FAMILY

BC —UNIVERSITY OF VICTORIA,
McPherson Library, Victoria, V8W 3H5,
Can.
Notes: Brussels civil servants, 1699-1917.
Francois Grenier correspondence; Charles
Cabaille official papers 1777; Jean Francois
Sedaine, 1793-1829; Henri Sedaine, 1804-
1890, official papers, commissions,
certificates, 1831-1871; Robert Sedaine,
1843-1917?, official papers, diary, personal
correspondence, miscellaneous. Sedaine
Genealogy; Dubois Genealogy; Jean Thierry
Genealogy. 2 anonymous comedies:
Harlequin Journaliste and *Dormeur d'avril la
dupe de soimeme*.

SEDGWICK FAMILY

MA —STOCKBRIDGE LIBRARY
ASSOCIATION, Main St, Box H,
Stockbridge, 01262. Rosemary Schmeyer,
Librn
Holdings: Vols (1200) Cat Mss Maps Pix
Notes: The Historical Room contains
approximately 1200 vols of genealogical
reference, ie, Massachusetts Soldiers and
Sailors of the Revolution, Vital Statistics for
towns in Massachusetts, local history, Indian
history, books by and about Stockbridge
residents, and a large collection of family
papers of the Sedgwick and Field families
among many others. These are being
cataloged with the help of a special grant.

SEDIMENTATION AND DEPOSITION

IL —UNIVERSITY OF ILLINOIS,
URBANA/CHAMPAIGN, Library,
Geology Library, 223 Natural History Bldg,
Urbana, 61801. Dederick Ward, Librn
Holdings: Vols (105,186) Cat Maps
Microforms
MA —HARVARD UNIVERSITY, Museum of
Comparative Zoology, Library, 26 Oxford St,
Cambridge, 02138. Eva S Jonas, Librn
Holdings: Cat
NY —UNIVERSITY OF ROCHESTER, Rush
Rhees Library, Geology/Map Library,
Rochester, 14627. Arleen N Somerville,
Librn
Holdings: Vols (12,424) Cat Maps
Notes: Strong collection in the field and
related areas.

SEE, THOMAS JEFFERSON JACKSON, 1866-1962

†CA —UNIVERSITY OF CALIFORNIA,
SANTA CRUZ, Lick Observatory Archives,

SEE, THOMAS JEFFERSON JACKSON, 1866-1962 (cont.)

Santa Cruz, 95064.
Notes: His correspondence (1888-1944).

SEED INDUSTRY AND TRADE—CATALOGS

CA —R MITCHEL BEAUCHAMP
BOTANICAL LIBRARY, 1843 E 16th St,
National City, 92050.
Notes: Native flora. Survey and exploration
reports. American seed and bulb and bulb
catalogs.

TN —THE BOTANICAL GARDENS, Minnie
Ritchie and Joel Owsley Cheek Memorial
Library, Forrest Park Drive, Nashville,
37205. Richard C Page, Dir Botanical
Gardens
Holdings: Vols (3500) Cat Pix Slides
Budget: $2500
Notes: Collection of nursery and seed trade
catalogs.

SEEDING OF CLOUDS see Rainmaking

SEFARDIC JEWS see Sephardim

SEGREGATION AND DESEGREGATION

DC —HOWARD UNIVERSITY, Moorland-
Spingarn Research Center, 500 Howard
Place NW, Washington, 20059. Clifford L
Muse, Jr, Acting Dir
Holdings: Vols (106,086) Mss Maps Pix
Slides Phonorecords Audiotapes 16mm
Films Filmstrips Microforms
Budget: ($854,753)
See also entry under Blacks

MA —BOSTON COLLEGE LIBRARIES,
Chestnut Hill, 02167.
Notes: The archives of the Citywide
Coordinating Council of Boston, Mass. 140
linear ft //. Official records of the group
created by Federal Court order to implement
desegregation of the Boston Public Schools.
The Council was formed in May 1975 and
dissolved in August 1978. Collection incl
minutes of School Committee and Council
meetings, annual and interim Council
reports, correspondence between the Court
and the Council, monitors' reports on
busing, attendance, building maintenance
and teaching staff. For reference use only, by
arrangement with librarian.

MS —UNIVERSITY OF SOUTHERN
MISSISSIPPI, William David McCain
Graduate Library, Box 5148, Southern Sta,
Hattiesburg, 39406.
Holdings: Uncat Mss
Notes: Records (1967-1975; 2 cubic feet) of
the Mississippi Association of Educators
concerning the merger of the predominantly
Black, Mississippi Teachers Association and
the predominantly White, Mississippi
Education Association. The collection incl
correspondence, minutes of meetings,
conference hearings, resolutions, proposals
and constitutions from various state
education associations.

NC —UNIVERSITY OF NORTH
CAROLINA, CHAPEL HILL, Louis Round
Wilson Academic Affairs Library, Southern
Historical Collection, Chapel Hill, 27514.
Carolyn Wallace, Librn
Notes: The papers of Algernon Lee Butler,
former judge of the United States Court for
the Eastern District of North Carolina
(1959-1975).

VA —UNIVERSITY OF VIRGINIA,
Alderman Library, Manuscripts Dept,
Charlottesville, 22901. Edmund Berkeley Jr,
Cur
Holdings: Cat Mss Pix
Notes: Material in over 420 collections
documents the history and culture of Afro-
Americans incl letters and narratives by
slaves and masters, plantation accounts,
letters from Liberian immigrants, folklore,
literature, the desegregation movement in
Virginia in the 1960s and 1970s and the
"massive resistance" of Virginia political
leaders. Michael F Plunkett (ed) A Guide to

Materials on the History, Literature, and
Culture of Afro-Americans in the
Manuscripts Department, University of
Virginia Library.

SEIBEL, FRED O.

†VA —UNIVERSITY OF VIRGINIA, Library,
Charlottesville, 22901.
Notes: Bernard Meeks original cartoons and
drawings collection, 326 items incl some
original comic strip art. Fred O Seibel
collection of ca 6000 original drawings, and
cartoonists' working papers and files.
Additional collection of editorial cartoons by
Oscar Cesare, Jeff MacNelly, Art Wood, etc.
Examples of almost all political and many
comic artists working in he mid-20th
century.

SEIFERT, SHIRLEY

MO —WASHINGTON UNIVERSITY,
Libraries, Special Collections Dept, Campus
Box 1061, St Louis, 63130.
Notes: A small but significant collection.

SEIFFERT, MARJORIE ALLEN, 1885-1970

CO —UNIVERSITY OF COLORADO,
Libraries, Special Collections, Boulder,
80309. Nora J Quinlan, Head
Holdings: Vols 80 Cat Mss
Notes: Incl 1 letter file box of mss and 5
letter file boxes of correspondence.

SEIGNETTE-ELECTRICITY see Ferroelectricity

SEISMIC SEA WAVES see Tsunamis

SEISMIC SURGES see Tsunamis

SEISMOGRAPHY see Seismology

SEISMOLOGY

CA —ASSOCIATION OF BAY AREA
GOVERNMENTS, MTC/ABAG Library,
101 Eighth St, Oakland, 94607. Diane
Gillman, Information Coord
Notes: Concentrates heavily on the nine-
county Bay Area region. About 10,000
monographs and serials. Title catalog,
OCLC/ATS. Central collection of
documents for six transit properties in Bay
Area.

CA —CALIFORNIA INSTITUTE OF
TECHNOLOGY, Robert A Millikan
Memorial Library, Archives, 1201 E
California Blvd, Pasadena, 91125. Judith R
Goodstein, Archivist
Notes: A Guide to the Seismology
Microfiche Collection Publications is
available. Incl Bulletin of the CIT
Seismological Laboratory; Provisional
Readings at Pasadena (1966-74), Airletters
(1974-79); Station Clock Corrections;
International Seismological Summary, 1918-
42; Gutenberg-Richter Notepads, 1904-1958.
In addition, collections relating to history of
19th and 20th century science and
technology and the history of the Institute.
Mss collections document development of
physical sciences, aeronautics, molecular
biology, and seismology in the US and
abroad. Mss collections incl papers of Harry
Oscar Wood, seismologist.

CA —EARTHQUAKE ENGINEERING
RESEARCH CENTER, Library, 1301 S
46th St, Richmond, 94804. Joy Svihra,
Librn; Helen Tseng, Asst Librn
Holdings: Vols (20,000) Cat Maps Pix Slides
16mm Films Microforms
Notes: Unique collection on earthquake
engineering is enriched by foreign
documents received on an exchange basis
that are generally not available elsewhere in
the US. A major part of the collection
circulates. Accessed through dictionary
catalog and the Abstract Journal in
Earthquake Engineering. A printed catalog
was published in May, 1975 as EERC
Report 75-12, listing holdings through 1974.

New holdings are listed in EERRC News
(quarterly) and the Library's Acquisitions
Alert (bimonthly).

DC —GEORGETOWN UNIVERSITY,
Library, Special Collections Div, 37 & O Sts
NW, Washington, 20057. George M
Barringer, Special Collections Librn;
Nicholas B Sheetz, Mss Librn
Holdings: Cat Mss
Notes: Principally a collection of typescripts
containing Fr Repetti's unpublished history
of the Society of Jesus in the Philippines,
1589-1615; with other mss material and
correspondence dealing with Fr Repetti's
researches in Philippine Jesuit and
seismological history and on the life of Pye
Neale. Correspondence, documents, mss,
notebooks, and newspaper clippings,
predominantly of a professional nature. Rev
Francis A Tondorf, SJ (1870-1929) founded
the seismological observatory at Georgetown
University in 1909, serving as director until
his death, in addition to other duties as
professor of physics, biology, geology and
astronomy. An internationally recognized
authority in seismology, Tondorf published
numerous articles and lectures.

MA —MASSACHUSETTS INSTITUTE OF
TECHNOLOGY, Institute Archives, Special
Collections, Cambridge, 02139.
Notes: Papers of John Ripley Freeman, a
hydraulic engineer, President of Associated
Factory Mutual Fire Insurance Companies,
and a consulting engineer. Collection
primarily documents his activities as a
consultant on hydraulics projects in the
United States, Canada, China, Columbia,
Mexico and Panama. Also, his work on the
hydraulics of fire prevention, safety
precautions for theaters, and seismology; his
promotion of the National Hydraulics
Laboratory and of European engineering
practices; his involvement with the
Engineering Foundation, the National
Bureau of Standards, and the National
Research Council; and his investments in
mining, manufacturing, and land speculation.
Unpublished finding aid available in
Archives.

MA —BOSTON COLLEGE LIBRARIES,
Catherine B O'Connor Geophysics Library,
Weston Observatory, Weston, 02193. F
Clifford McElroy, Science Librn
Holdings: Vols (10,231) Cat Maps
Microforms
Budget: ($10,000)
Notes: This collection is being absorbed into
the general collection.

NY —AMERICAN MUSEUM OF
NATURAL HISTORY, Library Services
Dept, Central Park W & 79th St, New York,
10024. Nina J Root, Chairwoman; Mary
Genett, Asst Librn for Reference Services
Notes: Especially strong in periodical
literature.

NY —COLUMBIA UNIVERSITY
LIBRARIES, Geoscience Library, Lamont-
Doherty Geological Observatory, Palisades,
10964. Susan Klimley, Librn
Holdings: Vols (20,000) Cat
Notes: Geosciences, incl geochemistry,
marine geology, seismology and
paleoclimatology.

VA —ENSCO, INC, Technical Library, 5400
Port Royal Rd, Springfield, 22151. Sue E
Littlepage, Research Librn
Holdings: Vols 500

ON —ENERGY, MINES & RESOURCES
CANADA, Earth Physics Branch Library,
Ottawa, K1A 0Y3, Can. W M Tsang, Chief
Librn
Holdings: Vols (6000) Cat Maps Pix Slides
Microforms
Notes: Incl an extensive collection of
references called Seismological Pamphlet
File incl reprints, private reports,
seismograms, etc, all cataloged separately
and being added to continuously.

SEISMOLOGY—MAPS

CA —US GEOLOGICAL SURVEY
LIBRARY, 345 Middlefield Rd, Menlo
Park, 94025.
Holdings: Vols (200,000)

SEITZ, FREDERICK

IL —UNIVERSITY OF ILLINOIS,
URBANA/CHAMPAIGN, Library,

SEITZ, FREDERICK (cont.)

University Archives, 19 Library, 1408 W
Gregory Drive, Urbana, 61801. Maynard
Brichford, University Archivist
Holdings: Cat Mss Maps Pix Slides
Microforms
Notes: Papers, archival records, etc.

MA —BOSTON UNIVERSITY, Mugar
Memorial Library, Special Collections Dept,
771 Commonwealth Ave, Boston, 02215.
Howard B Gotlieb, Dir
Holdings: Mss
Notes: Mss, correspondence, etc collected in
depth; incl publications by or about.

SELECTION, NATURAL see Natural Selection

SELENOLOGY see Moon

SELF-DESTRUCTION see Suicide and Suicide Attempts

SELF-HELP (PSYCHOLOGY)

CA —LOS ANGELES PUBLIC LIBRARY,
Philosophy & Religion Dept, 630 W Fifth St,
Los Angeles, 90071. Marilyn C Wherley,
Librn
Holdings: Vols 550 Cat
Budget: ($60,000)
Notes: Scholarly and popular materials
constitute an important aspect of the
comprehensive general psychology
collection.

CT —YALE MEDICAL LIBRARY, 333 Cedar
St, New Haven, 06510.
Notes: An extensive collection on mental
hygiene.

MI —MICHIGAN STATE UNIVERSITY,
Libraries, Special Collections Div, East
Lansing, 48824. Jannette Fiore, Librn
Notes: The Russel B Nye Popular Culture
Collection in the Michigan State Univ
Libraries incl over (45,000) items. Most of
the collection is organized into 4 categories:
comic art, popular fiction, popular
information materials and materials relating
to the popular performing arts. About 3900
items. Almanacs, Blue Books, and works
popularizing knowledge or offering self-help
and how-to advice. There are ca 350 issues
of 100 19th and 20th century almanacs. The
Blue Books incl ca 2000 Little Blue Books,
over 600 Big Blue Books and a good number
of issues of the various Haldeman-Julius
magazines. In addition to almanacs and Blue
Books, Popular Information incl books of
advice on etiquette, life and love, how-to-
succeed books, popular history, science and
biography, and several hundred public
schooltextbooks from the 19th and early
20th centuries.

MO —UNITY LIBRARY, Unity School of
Christianity, Unity Village, 64065. Alfreda
Williams, Library Dir
Holdings: Vols (50,000) Cat Mss Maps Pix
Slides Microforms
Notes: Incl Archives and Historical
collections of the Unity School of
Christianity, as well as the archives of the
International New Thought Alliance.

VA —ASSOCIATION FOR RESEARCH &
ENLIGHTENMENT, Library, 67 &
Atlantic Avenue, PO Box 595, Virginia
Beach, 23451. Stephen Jordan, Library Mgr
Holdings: Vols (3000) Cat
Notes: Emphasis on Christian, Buddhist,
Hindu religions, mysticism, comparative
religion, psychological approach to
biofeedback, autogenics, etc.

SELF-HYPNOSIS see Autogenic Training; Hypnotism

SELLE, JOE (PHOTOGRAPHER)

NY —VISUAL STUDIES WORKSHOP,
Research Center, 31 Prince St, Rochester,
14607. Linn Underhill, Coordr; Robert
Bretz, Librn
Holdings: Vols (8000) Cat Pix Slides
Audiotapes Videotapes
Notes: Strong emphasis on photography

(over 1,000,000 pictures) and the
photographic arts in many subject areas incl
in this volume. Heavy emphasis on early
photographic processes and collections of
examples of them. Also collections of
individual photographers' works.

SELLERS, CON

MS —UNIVERSITY OF SOUTHERN
MISSISSIPPI, William David McCain
Graduate Library, Box 5148, Southern Sta,
Hattiesburg, 39406.
Holdings: Cat Mss
Notes: 4.3 cubic feet holdings. Literary mss
and related correspondence of Con Sellers, a
best selling author of popular novels and
historical novels. Sellers writes under
numerous pseudonyms and has written such
best sellers as *Dallas* and *Night Shadows*.

SELZNICK, DAVID O.

†TX —UNIVERSITY OF TEXAS
LIBRARIES, Humanities Research Center,
Harry Ransom Center, PO Box 7219,
Austin, 78712.
Notes: The David O Selznick archives, incl
1961 file boxes of correspondence and 38
four-drawer file cases of manuscript
materials, drawings, and paintings.

SELZNICK, IRENE MAYER

MA —BOSTON UNIVERSITY, Mugar
Memorial Library, Special Collections Dept,
771 Commonwealth Ave, Boston, 02215.
Howard B Gotlieb, Dir
Holdings: Cat Mss Pix
Notes: Mss, correspondence, etc collected in
depth; incl publications by or about.

SEMANTICS

MO —WASHINGTON UNIVERSITY, John
M Olin Library, Campus Box 1061, St Louis,
63130.
Holdings: Vols (1300) Cat Mss
Notes: The Philip M Arnold Semeiology
Collection is concerned with the study of
signs and symbols. Topics incl cryptography;
artificial memory; decipherment of unknown
languages; universal languages; early
developments in stenography, telegraphy;
and communication systems for the blind,
the deaf and the mute; and various forms of
nonverbal communication. Limited
photocopying. Noncirculating.

SEMASIOLOGY see Semantics

SEMEIOTIC see Signs and Symbols

SEMICONDUCTORS see Transistors and Semiconductors

SEMINOLE INDIANS

FL —HISTORICAL ASSOCIATION OF
SOUTHERN FLORIDA, Charlton W
Tebeau Library of Florida History, 101 W
Flager St, Miami, 33130. Rebecca A Smith,
Cur of Research Materials
Holdings: Vols (3000) Cat Mss Maps Pix
Slides Audiotapes 16mm Films Microforms
Notes: History of Florida, with emphasis on
southern area. Less extensively, history of
the Caribbean area, especially as related to
Florida. Florida materials incl anthropology,
archaeology, Indians of south Florida, incl
Seminole Indians, Dade County history, and
a complete run of the newspaper *The
American Eagle* (1906-date), printed by
Koreshan Unity, Estero, Florida. Incl 300
feet of mss, 1500 maps, 75,000 pictures,
2000 slides, 125 audiotapes, 25 16mm films,
200 microforms, 50 feet of vertical files, and
7000 postcards. Work in progress on guide
to ms collection and on indexing of
photographs. Also incl books and journals on
museum science: conservation and
preservation of museum materials.

OK —OKLAHOMA HISTORICAL
SOCIETY, Library, Historical Bldg,
Oklahoma City, 73105. Andrea Clark, Dir,

Library Resources Division
Holdings: Vols (43,000) Cat Mss Maps Pix
Microforms
Notes: The Society also has the Indian
Archives Collection of 2,500,000 pieces
(Mary Lee Boyle, Archivist). This is an
extensive collection of records, particularly
of the Five Civilized Tribes. Incl tribal rolls,
agency reports, manuscripts, etc.

OK —THOMAS GILCREASE INSTITUTE
OF AMERICAN HISTORY & ART
LIBRARY, 1400 North 25th West Ave,
Tulsa, 74127. Sarah Hirsch, Librn
Holdings: Vols Cat Mss Maps Pix
Notes: Trans-Mississippi West, US, Indian
and Hispanic history. The Gilcrease Library
contains a total of about 40,000 mss; 10,000
imprints; 5000 photographs; 600 maps and
50,000 vols.

SEMIOTIC see Signs and Symbols

SEMITIC LANGUAGES

NY —NEW YORK PUBLIC LIBRARY,
Oriental Div, Fifth Ave & 42 St, New York,
10018. E Christian Filstrup, Chief
Holdings: Cat Mss Microforms
Budget: ($56,455)
Notes: Published catalog of holdings.

NY —YESHIVA UNIVERSITY, Library, 500
West 185th Street, New York, 10033. Pearl
Berger
Holdings: Cat

†PA —DROPSIE UNIVERSITY, Library,
Broad & York Sts, Philadelphia, 19132.

SEMITICS

CT —YALE UNIVERSITY, Beinecke Rare
Book & Manuscript Library, Osborn
Collection, New Haven, 06520. Stephen R
Parks, Cur
Holdings: Mss

MD —JOHNS HOPKINS UNIVERSITY,
Milton S Eisenhower Library, Charles & 34
Sts, Baltimore, 21218. Ann S Gwyn,
Assistant Dir for Special Collections
Holdings: Cat Mss Maps
Notes: Strong collection, espec in Biblical
studies, Hebraica, and Assyriology, but with
some omissions. Includes Leopold Strouse
Rabbinical Library with Hebrew and
Oriental mss.

NY —COLUMBIA UNIVERSITY
LIBRARIES, Rare Book & Manuscript
Library, 801 Butler Library, 535 W 114 St,
New York, 10027. Kenneth A Lohf, Librn
Holdings: Vols (5000)
Notes: Incl the Arthur Jeffrey Collection.

†PA —DROPSIE UNIVERSITY, Library,
Broad & York Sts, Philadelphia, 19132.

WI —UNIVERSITY OF WISCONSIN,
MADISON, Memorial Library, Western
European Humanities Collection, 728 State
St, Madison, 53706. Charles Szabo,
Bibliographer
Notes: The Joseph L Baron Collection of
Judaica. Includes volumes in Hebrew,
German, and English in the field of Semitic
studies. Supplements the Library's Judaica
holdings.

SEMPLE, ELLEN CHURCHILL

KY —UNIVERSITY OF KENTUCKY,
Margaret I King Library, Dept of Special
Collections, Lexington, 40506. William
Marshall, Head
Holdings: // Cat Mss
Notes: Geopolitics. Ellen Churchill Semple's
correspondence, notes for books and articles.
4 vols, 84 pieces and 74 packages.

SENATORS see Legislators—U.S.

SENDAK, MAURICE

IN —INDIANA UNIVERSITY, Lilly Library,
Seventh St, Bloomington, 47405. William R
Cagle, Librn
Notes: Contemporary with and depicting
Lincoln; the War of 1812 and other periods.
Incl significant mss of the modern
cartoonists and caricaturists Ardizzone,
Beerbohm, Fontane Fox, Kin Hubbard,

SENDAK, MAURICE (cont.)

Charles Bacon Jackson, McCutcheon, Messick, Nast, Rothenstein, Sendak, and many miscellaneous items.

SENECA INDIANS

†NY —STATE UNIVERSITY OF NEW YORK, COLLEGE AT FREDONIA, Daniel A Reed Library, Fredonia, 14063. Holdings: Vols (1100) Cat Mss Maps Pix Slides Audiotapes Videotapes Microforms Budget: ($1000)
Notes: The Reed Library Local History Collection incl materials pertaining to Chautauqua and Cattaraugus Counties in Western New York, and to some extent materials of Allegany County. The collection ranges from rare items (such as early County histories, early survey maps and atlases, and records from the establishment of the school, the Fredonia Academy, in 1827, which is now the State University College at Fredonia) to current publications (County Legislature Proceedings, Health Department reports, directories, etc). Of special note are diaries, a series of oral history tapes on rural education; geological materials incl aerial photographs and some Indian history of the Seneca Nation.
NY —STATE UNIVERSITY OF NEW YORK, COLLEGE OF ARTS & SCIENCE AT GENESEO, Milne Library, Geneseo, 14454. William T Lane, Head of Information Services & Archivist
Holdings: Vols (3700) Cat Mss Maps Slides Budget: ($1000)
Notes: Genesee Valley Historical Collection. County, town, village, family and church histories for the counties of Allegany, Genesee, Livingston, Monroe, Orleans and Wyoming. Materials on the Seneca Indians, Genesee Valley Canal, and the geology of western New York state.
See also entry under Wadsworth Family

SENEFELDER, ALOYS, 1771-1834

PA —TEMPLE UNIVERSITY LIBRARIES, Special Collections Dept, Rare Books & Mss Section, Philadelphia, 19122. Thomas M Whitehead, Cur
Notes: The lithography collection emphasizes the technical process rather than the artistic medium and stresses the years 1800-1835. Significant are the early manuals, the Kubilius Louis Prang Collection and the documentation of early Mexican lithography. Some holdings are listed in the 1972 publication: Aloys Senefelder 1771-1834: A Catalogue of Early Technical Literature and Selected Lithograph. A register of the Mexican documents is available.

SENEGAL

DC —HOWARD UNIVERSITY, Moorland-Spingarn Research Center, 500 Howard Place NW, Washington, 20059. Clifford L Muse, Jr, Acting Dir
MI —MICHIGAN STATE UNIVERSITY, International Library, Sahel Documentation Center, East Lansing, 48824. Eugene deBenko, Librn; Learthen Dorsey, Librn
Holdings: Vols (5100) Cat Mss Maps Pix Slides Phonorecords Audiotapes Videotapes Microforms
Budget: ($8000)
Notes: See description under The Sahel.

SENESCENCE see Aging and Aged

SENIOR CITIZENS see Aging and Aged

SENNETT, MACK

CA —ACADEMY OF MOTION PICTURE ARTS & SCIENCES, Margaret Herrick Library, 8949 Wilshire Blvd, Beverly Hills, 90211. Linda Harris Mehr, Library Administrator
Notes: Papers.
See also entry under Moving Pictures.

SENSATION see Senses and Sensation

SENSES AND SENSATION

CT —YALE MEDICAL LIBRARY, 333 Cedar St, New Haven, 06510.
Notes: A special subject emphasis.

SENSING DEVICES

OH —PREFORMED LINE PRODUCTS CO, Research & Engineering Library, 660 Beta Drive, Mayfield Village, (Mailing add: PO Box 91129, Cleveland, 44101). Edwina T Barron, Librn
Holdings: Vols (11,500) Cat Mss Microfiche Pix VF
Budget: ($30,500)
Notes: Library covering research and engineering fields emphasizing this subject. Aerodynamic characteristics and electrical characteristics of power cables, communication cables (including fiber optics), cable support systems, as well as associated fittings and hardware; in service behavior of manufactured products and materials as it relates to its static and dynamic forces and environmental conditions; oceanographic cable fittings and terminations.

SENSING DEVICES, REMOTE see Remote Sensing

SEPARATION (TECHNOLOGY)

IL —ARGONNE NATIONAL LABORATORY, Chemistry Branch Library, 9700 S Cass Ave, Argonne, 60439. Betty Guttman, Librn
Notes: Separation science. Incl 20,000 vols monographs, 190 current journals. Materials may be used by the public in the library by prior arrangement. Photocopies may be supplied for interlibrary loan, for which a processing and handling charge is made.
UT —EIMCO TECHNOLOGY & RESEARCH CENTER, Process Machinery Div, Technical Library, 414 W 300 S, Salt Lake City, 84110.
Holdings: Vols (1450) Cat

SEPARATION OF CHURCH AND STATE see Church and State

SEPARATISM (RELIGION) see Dissenters, Religious

SEPHARDIC JEWS see Sephardim

SEPHARDIM

CA —UNIVERSITY OF CALIFORNIA, SANTA BARBARA, Library, Dept of Special Collections, Santa Barbara, 93106. Christian F Brun, Head
Holdings: Cat Mss Pix
FL —UNIVERSITY OF FLORIDA LIBRARY, Isser and Rae Price Library of Judaica, 18 Libr East, Gainesville, 32611. Robert Singerman, Head Librn
Budget: ($30,000)
Notes: Total holdings estimated at 55,000 vols dealing with the political, social, economic and intellectual history of the Jews in the ancient, medieval and modern periods and in all geographic areas. The following areas are especially well represented by printed matter in all relevant languages: Bibliography, Festschriften, History, Bible, Judaism and Jewish theology, liturgy, responsa, rabbinical literature, Jewish law, Hebrew language and literature, Yiddish language and literature, anti-semitism, Zionism, Palestine and the Yishuv, and the State of Israel. German and American Judaica form a collecting emphasis with holdings for all the standard histories as well as histories of individual synagogues, institutions and local communities. Works in Hebrew and Yiddish comprise about 60 percent of the collection (estimated 30,000 vols). With few exceptions, holdings are limited to nineteenth and twentieth century imprints, with complete sets of journals and thousands of ephemeral pamphlets, many of them commemorating anniversaries, enhancing the research value of the collection, the largest Judaica research library in the southeastern United States. Only about half of the collection is cataloged; the collection is a circulating one and vols may be borrowed on interlibrary loan. Incl the Leonard C Mishkin Collection (40,000 vols), the largest personal Judaica collection in the United States, the Shlomo Marenof Collection (3500 vols), and the inventory of Bernard Morgenstern's Lower East Side Book Store (8000 vols). Scholars should inquire in advance of their visit. The Isser and Rae Price Library of Judaica Report (circulation 2900 copies) is mailed gratis twice a year to all interested parties. Special catalogs:Pre-1881 Hebrew imprints recorded in a chronological card file.

SEPULCHRAL BRASSES see Brasses

SEPULCHRAL MONUMENTS see Gravestones

SEQUOIA NATIONAL PARK

CA —CALIFORNIA STATE UNIVERSITY, FRESNO, Henry Madden Library, Dept of Special Collections, Fresno, 93740. Ronald J Mahoney, Head
Holdings: Vols 15 Uncat Mss
Notes: Material relating to the history and preservation of Mineral King area of Sequoia National Park. Used by John LeRoy Harper when writing Mineral King: Public Concern with Government Policy (Arcata, Calif, 1982). Incl documents, clippings and pamphlets.

SERBIA

CA —HOOVER INSTITUTION ON WAR, REVOLUTION & PEACE, Stanford University, Stanford, 94305. Milorad M Drachkovitch, Archivist
Holdings: Mss Pix
Notes: Papers of William A Drayton, 1913-1946, incl correspondence, reports, memoranda, speeches and writings, photographs, and other materials, relating to Serbia, during and after World War I, and W A Drayton's activities as an American volunteer in the Serbian Army. member of the Serbian Delegation to Paris Peace Conference,and Inter-Allied Commissioner of Bulgarian Atrocities Commission. 2 ms boxes.

SERBIA—HISTORY

CA —CROATIAN-SERBIAN-SLOVENE GENEALOGICAL SOCIETY, 2527 San Carlos Ave, San Carlos, 94070. Adam S Eterovich, Dir
Holdings: Vols (1000) Mss
Notes: Incl index of names of 130,000 Croatians and Serbs in the United States before 1905. Dir operates Ragusan Press.
CA —STANFORD UNIVERSITY LIBRARIES, Cecil H Green Library, Stanford, 94305. Wojciech Zalewski, Cur, Russian & East European Collection
Holdings: Vols (200,000) Cat Maps Microforms
Budget: ($90,000)
Notes: Strong collection prior to 20th century, but Stanford University Libraries' collecting effort is coordinated with Hoover Institution, Stanford, and holdings are not duplicated. Collection descriptions: Wojciech Zalewski, Russian Materials in the Main Library of Stanford University, A Collection Survey (Stanford: Stanford University Libraries, 1974). Wojciech Zalerski, "Stanford University" in P L Horecky, ed, East Central and Southeast Europe, A Handbook of Library and Archival Resources in North America (Santa Barbara: Clio Press, 1976).
WI —UNIVERSITY OF WISCONSIN, MADISON, Memorial Library, Slavic Studies Collection, 728 State St, Madison, 53706. Aleksander Rolich, Bibliographer for Slavic Studies; Robert P Gakovich, Slavic Cataloger; Valdis J Zeps, Baltic Studies Center
Holdings: Vols (1000) Cat
Notes: The Komadinish Collection in Serbian and Yugoslav social and political history embraces publications and pamphlets

SERBIA—HISTORY (cont.)

of peasant, socialist and other radical movements of the last half of the nineteenth century up to World War II. It consists of some 1000 items, mostly in Serbo-Croatian, and represents only part of the private library acquired from the survivors of Milan Komadinic (1882-1944).

SERBIAN ACADEMY PUBLICATIONS

IL —UNIVERSITY OF ILLINOIS, URBANA/CHAMPAIGN, Slavic and East European Library, Urbana, 61801. Marianna Tax Choldin, Head
Holdings: Vols (31,000) Cat
Notes: Extensive coverage.

SERBIAN CHURCH SLAVIC LANGUAGE see Church Slavic Languages and Literature

SERBIAN LANGUAGE see Serbo-Croatian Language and Literature

SERBIAN LITERATURE

IL —UNIVERSITY OF ILLINOIS, URBANA/CHAMPAIGN, Slavic and East European Library, Urbana, 61801. Marianna Tax Choldin, Head
Holdings: Vols (31,000) Cat
Notes: Extensive coverage.
NY —NEW YORK PUBLIC LIBRARY, Donnell Foreign Language Library, 20 W 53 St, New York, 10019. Bosiljka Stevanovic, Supvr Librn
Holdings: Vol 219 Cat
Notes: Serbian collection incl Serbian authors of Serbian expression. No separate catalog.
OH —OHIO STATE UNIVERSITY, William Oxley Thompson Memorial Library, 1858 Neil Ave, Columbus, 43210. A Robert Thorson, Head, Circulation Dept
Holdings: Cat Mss Microforms
Notes: This collection presently contains films of 2000 mss from the Hilandar Monastery, Mt Athos. Expansion will add Byzantine, Bulgarian, Russian and Valachian mss on film.

SERBIAN MANUSCRIPTS see Manuscripts, Serbian

SERBIAN NEWSPAPERS see Newspapers, Serbian

SERBIAN PERIODICALS see Periodicals, Serbian

SERBIANS see Serbs

SERBO-CROATIAN LANGUAGE AND LITERATURE

CA —LOS ANGELES PUBLIC LIBRARY, Foreign Languages Dept, 630 W Fifth St, Los Angeles, 90071. Sylva Manoogian, Principal Librn
Holdings: Vols 1257 Cat
Budget: ($41,500)
CA —UNIVERSITY OF CALIFORNIA, LOS ANGELES, Library, Slavic Collection, 405 Hilgard Ave, Los Angeles, 90024. Edward Shreeves, Chairman, Bibliographers Group; Leon Ferder, Slavic Bibliographer
Holdings: Vols (250,000) Cat Mss Maps
Notes: The Slavic Collection at UCLA consists of materials from and relating to Russia and the Soviet Union, Poland, Czechoslovakia, Yugoslavia, Bulgaria, the Sorbians in East Germany, and works by Slavic emigres. The collection contains nearly 250,000 vols, and is particularly strong in linguistics, literature, history and social sciences, and reference materials. Slavic materials are collected in hard copy and microform, and incl monographs, serials (incl newspapers), reference works, proceedings of Slavistic congresses and symposia, and also *Festschriften* and dissertations.

CA —STANFORD UNIVERSITY LIBRARIES, Cecil H Green Library, Stanford, 94305. Wojciech Zalewski, Cur, Russian & East European Collection
Holdings: Vols (200,000) Cat Maps Microforms
Budget: ($90,000)
Notes: Strong collection prior to 20th century, but Stanford University Libraries' collecting effort is coordinated with Hoover Institution, Stanford, and holdings are not duplicated. Collection descriptions: Wojciech Zalewski, *Russian Materials in the Main Library of Stanford University, A Collection Survey* (Stanford: Stanford University Libraries, 1974). Wojciech Zalerski, "Stanford University" in P L Horecky, ed, *East Central and Southeast Europe, A Handbook of Library and Archival Resources in North America* (Santa Barbara: Clio Press, 1976).

IL —UNIVERSITY OF ILLINOIS, URBANA/CHAMPAIGN, Slavic and East European Library, Urbana, 61801. Marianna Tax Choldin, Head
Holdings: Vols (420,000) Cat
Notes: One of the largest Slavic and East European collections. Strong in Russian and Soviet materials-humanities, sciences, and social sciences; languages and literatures; periodicals, newspapers, and microforms. Ca 260,000 volumes in languages of the Soviet Union plus 20,000 Russian and Ukrainian titles on microform. Extensive coverage of Czechoslovakia (35,000 vols); Yugoslavia (31,000 vols); Bulgaria (9200 vols); Poland (34,600 vols); Romania (13,000 vols); and Hungary (18,000 vols) and the languages, literatures, and history of these countries.
MA —HARVARD UNIVERSITY LIBRARY, Widener Library, Slavic Collections, Cambridge, 02138. Hugh M Olmsted, Slavic Dept Head
Holdings: Cat Microforms
Notes: Serbian and Croatian literature shelflist through June, 1976 lists 5923 titles (earlier version was incl in *Widener Library Shelflist*, volumes 28-31, 1971). The language and literature collections continue to be developed actively, and are strong both in current and in antiquarian materials. See also *East Central and Southeast Europe; A Handbook of Library and Archival Resources in North America*, edited by P L Horecky and D H Kraus, 1976, pp 149-154.
NY —NEW YORK PUBLIC LIBRARY, Donnell Foreign Language Library, 20 W 53 St, New York, 10019. Bosiljka Stevanovic, Supvr Librn
Holdings: Vols 124 Cat
Notes: Croatian collection incl Croatian authors of Croatian expression. No separate catalog.
NY —NEW YORK PUBLIC LIBRARY, Slavonic Div, Fifth Ave & 42 St, New York, 10018. Edward Kasinec, Chief
Holdings: Cat Microforms
Notes: See New York Public Library, *Dictionary Catalog of the Slavonic Collection* (Boston: G K Hall, 1974), 44 vols.
OH —CLEVELAND PUBLIC LIBRARY, Foreign Literature Dept, 325 Superior Ave, Cleveland, 44114. Natalia Bezugloff, Head
Holdings: Vols 2250 Cat
Notes: Serbian language and literature. A popular circulating collection containing classics and the standard works with emphasis on belles lettres, history and biography. A variety of other subjects such as learning languages, hobbies, how to do books, art, children's books, spoken phonodiscs and cassettes, periodcials, etc. *See also* entry under Foreign Language Collections
OH —KENT STATE UNIVERSITY, Libraries, Ethnic Collections, Kent, 44242.
Holdings: Vols 325 Cat
Notes: Two separate collections: Serbian, 150 vols; Croation, 175 vols.
See also entry under Foreign Language Collections
WI —UNIVERSITY OF WISCONSIN, MADISON, Memorial Library, Slavic Studies Collection, 728 State St, Madison, 53706. Aleksander Rolich, Bibliographer for

Slavic Studies; Robert P Gakovich, Slavic Cataloger; Valdis J Zeps, Baltic Studies Center
Holdings: Vols (25,000) Cat
Notes: The Balcanica collection in Memorial Library exceeds 25,000 volumes and active collecting continues at over 2000 titles per year in Bulgarian, Rumanian, Turkish and the languages of Yugoslavia. Many rare and unique titles are to be found in this collection, including serial titles, such as *Nova Vreme* (1897-1923, 1947-to date), *Nova Europa* (1920-1939), and unique Turkish Salnameh. The emphasis is on historical materials, but there is considerable strength in South Slavic literatures and linguistics. The Rumanian materials are of more recent vintage.
WI —SAINT SAVA SERBIAN ORTHODOX CATHEDRAL LIBRARY, 3201 S 51 St, Milwaukee, 53219. Dijo Radisich, Librn
Holdings: 1500 Vols

SERBO-CROATIANS see Croats; Serbs

SERBS

NY —NEW YORK PUBLIC LIBRARY, Slavonic Div, Fifth Ave & 42 St, New York, 10018. Edward Kasinec, Chief
Holdings: Cat Microforms
Notes: See New York Public Library, Slavonic Div, *Dictionary Catalog of the Slavonic Collection*, 2nd ed, rev and enl (Boston: G K Hall, 1974), 44 vols; and New York Public Library, *Dictionary Catalog of the Research Libraries* (New York, 1972-).
WI —UNIVERSITY OF WISCONSIN, MADISON, Memorial Library, Slavic Studies Collection, 728 State St, Madison, 53706. Aleksander Rolich, Bibliographer for Slavic Studies; Robert P Gakovich, Slavic Cataloger; Valdis J Zeps, Baltic Studies Center
Holdings: Vols (1000) Cat
Notes: The Komadinish Collection in Serbian and Yugoslav social and political history embraces publications and pamphlets of peasant, socialist and other radical movements of the last half of the nineteenth century up to World War II. It consists of some 1000 items, mostly in Serbo-Croatian, and represents only part of the private library acquired from the survivors of Milan Komadinic (1882-1944).
WI —SAINT SAVA SERBIAN ORTHODOX CATHEDRAL LIBRARY, 3201 S 51 St, Milwaukee, 53219. Dijo Radisich, Librn
Holdings: 1500 Vols

SERBS IN THE U.S.

CA —CROATIAN-SERBIAN-SLOVENE GENEALOGICAL SOCIETY, 2527 San Carlos Ave, San Carlos, 94070. Adam S Eterovich, Dir
Holdings: Vols (1000) Mss
Notes: Incl index of names of 130,000 Croatians and Serbs in the United States before 1905. Dir operates Ragusan Press.
MN —UNIVERSITY OF MINNESOTA, Immigration History Research Center, 826 Berry St, Saint Paul, 55114. Susan Griegs, Cur
Holdings: Vols (35,000) Mss Maps Pix Phonorecords Audiotapes 16mm Films Microforms
See also entry under US - Emigration and Immigration
PA —BALCH INSTITUTE FOR ETHNIC STUDIES, Library, 18 S Seventh St, Philadelphia, 19106. R Joseph Anderson, Library Dir
Holdings: Vols Cat
PA —UNIVERSITY OF PITTSBURGH, Hillman Library, Archives of Industrial Society, 363 Hillman Library, Pittsburgh, 15260. Frank A Zabrosky, Cur
Holdings: Mss Maps Pix Audiotapes Documents
WI —SAINT SAVA SERBIAN ORTHODOX CATHEDRAL LIBRARY, 3201 S 51 St, Milwaukee, 53219. Dijo Radisich, Librn
Holdings: 1500 Vols

SERFDOM

NC —DUKE UNIVERSITY, William R Perkins Library, Durham, 27706. Elvin E

SERFDOM (cont.)

Strowd, University Librn
Notes: The Bruno Lasker collection contains
51 portfolios; the Perkins Library general
collection and other collections contain a
significant amount of material on the subject
of slavery and antislavery.

SERGE, VICTOR

NY —COLUMBIA UNIVERSITY
LIBRARIES, Rare Book & Manuscript
Library, 801 Butler Library, 535 W 114 St,
New York, 10027. Kenneth A Lohf, Librn
Holdings: Mss Microforms
Notes: Family papers on 8 reels of
microfilm. Restricted use.

SERGEANT, JOHN

†CA —UNIVERSITY OF SAN FRANCISCO,
Richard A Gleeson Library, Dept of
The Countess
Bernardine Murphy Donohue Rare Book
Room, San Francisco, 94117. D Steven
Corey, Special Collections Librn
Holdings: Vols (300) Cat
Notes: Largely from the Virtue-Cahill library
in England, and the collection of Charles A
Fracchia. Incl important works of Bayly,
Cressy, Sergeant, and Worsley. Incl a
contemporary manuscript of the trial of
Father Garnet, accused of complicity in the
Gunpowder Plot.

SERIAL ART see Minimal Art

SERIALS see Periodicals—Collections

SERICULTURE

MA —UNIVERSITY OF LOWELL, Library,
One University Ave, Lowell, 01854. Martha
Mayo, Special Collections Librn
Holdings: Vols 2500 Cat Mss Pix Slides
Notes: Books and journals on all aspects of
textile technology.

SERIES, JUVENILE see Children's
Literature—Juvenile Series

SERLING, ROD

CA —UNIVERSITY OF CALIFORNIA, LOS
ANGELES, Research Library, Dept of
Special Collections, 405 Hilgard Ave, Los
Angeles, 90024. Edward Shreeves,
Chairman, Bibliographers Group; David S
Zeidberg, Head
Holdings: Mss Pix
Notes: 8.5 linear feet of scripts,
correspondence, and business records. No
photocopying.

SERMONS—COLLECTIONS

CT —CONNECTICUT STATE LIBRARY,
231 Capitol Ave, Hartford, 06106.
Holdings: // Cat
Notes: Contains election sermons.
Particularly strong for Connecticut.
CT —YALE UNIVERSITY, Beinecke Rare
Book & Manuscript Library, Osborn
Collection, New Haven, 06520. Stephen R
Parks, Cur
Holdings: Mss
Notes: 17th and 18th century English
sermons.
DC —GEORGETOWN UNIVERSITY,
Library, Special Collections, 37 & O Sts
NW, Washington, 20057. George M
Barringer, Special Collections Librn;
Nicholas B Sheetz, Mss Librn
Holdings: Mss Cat
Notes: Collection of over 450 Catholic
sermons preached in Maryland and
Pennsylavania during the eighteenth century.
The majority of the sermons appear in
original manuscript form. Forty-two authors
are represented; there are eight unidentified
sermons.
FL —UNIVERSITY OF FLORIDA, Libraries,
Special Collections, W University Ave,
Gainesville, 32611. Sidney Ives, Librn &
Rare Books
Holdings: Vols (8000) Cat Mss
Notes: English tracts and sermons from 17th

and early 18th centuries; also 7000 tracts
from Victorian Era.
GA —EMORY UNIVERSITY, Candler School
of Theology, Pitts Theology Library, Atlanta,
30322. Channing Jeschke, Librn; Anita K
Delaries, Curator
Notes: 10 linear feet of ms and printed
material (1822-92) documenting the life of
Cardinal Henry Edward Manning (1808-92).
The most notable items are his sermons,
sermon notes and speeches; items on
Archdiocese of Westminster. Finding aid
available.
IL —JESUIT-KRAUSS-MCCORMICK
LIBRARY, 1100 E 55th St, Chicago, 60615.
Donald Vorp, Dir; Elvire Hilgert, Librn
Holdings: Vols (375,000)
Notes: Collections contain merger of Jesuit
Library, Lutheran School of Theology of
Chicago (Krauss Library), and McCormick
Theological Seminary. Jesuit: Sermones
Thesaurus Novi de Tempore (anonymous,
Strassbourg 1486); Opera Omnia (Jean
Gerson, Strassbourg 1488), 3 vols; Summa
Rosella Casuum (Venice 1495); moral
theology (major figures of 16th and 17th
century scholasticism); early modern editions
of patristics and canon law regarding
procedures and organzation of the Catholic
Church, incl treatises and multi-volume
commentaries. Krauss: Archives of Lutheran
Church in America and its predecessors;
Reformation imprints; early printed versions
of the Bible (L Franklin Gruber Collection);
German and Scandanavian (Swedish,
Danish, Finnish) theology; Lutheran Church
of America document repository.
McCormick: Presbyteriana; historical record
of Synod of Illinois, UnitedPresbyterian
Church of USA; Church Federation of
Chicago archives prior to 1969; USA
imprints of the Bible (Simms Collection).
IL —NEWBERRY LIBRARY, 60 W Walton
St, Chicago, 60610. Diana Haskell, Cur of
Modern Mss
Holdings: Cat
Notes: English and American through 19th
century.
MA —STURGIS LIBRARY, Rte 6A,
Barnstable, 02630. Susan R Klein, Chief
Librn
Holdings: Vols (1500) Cat Mss Maps
Microforms
Budget: ($1000)
Notes: Lothrop Room Collection of
genealogy and history is considered to be the
finest on Cape Cod. No printed vital records
for the County of Barnstable, but 37 books
of handwritten Genealogical Notes of Cape
Cod Families (1620-1850), also on
microfilm. Also incl is the Stanley W Smith
Collection of books, pamphlets and
manuscript materials (mostly original land
deeds, all Cape Cod oriented, some of them
Indian and dating from the early 1700s). The
Percy F Rex Collection represents a unique
library of Cape Cod literature. Many
rareties, incl early sermons preached on the
Cape and pamphlets on Cape Cod canal, etc.
MA —NEW ENGLAND HISTORIC
GENEALOGICAL SOCIETY, Library, 101
Newbury St, Boston, 02116. Ralph J
Crandell, Dir
Holdings: Vols (250,000) Mss Maps
Microforms Pix
Notes: New England genealogy. Especially
strong Massachusetts, Maine, and New
Hampshire, although all states are well
represented, as are the relevancies of each
subject listed in this volume with regard to
British antecedent and contemporary history.
Special strengths in local history and
biography, obituaries, etc, incl parish
registers, censuses, British and American.
3125 linear ft of mss.
MA —HISTORIC DEERFIELD-
POCUMTUCK VALLEY MEMORIAL
ASSOCIATION, Libraries, Memorial St,
Box 53, Deerfield, 01342. David R Proper,
Librn
Holdings: Vols (17,000) Cat Mss Maps Pix
Microforms
Notes: Local and regional history, especially
western Massachusetts. Also, remnants of
several collection of books available to early
Deerfield and Greenfield residents. Strong

ms collection dealing with the region's
families, businesses, etc. These consist of
sermons, diaries, town and church records,
voluntary societies' archives, etc. Extensive
collection of photographs of the people and
buildings of Deerfield and its environs, and
travels in Maine, California, and England
(1880s to 1920s). Also, large collection of
glassplate negatives. Houses the Connecticut
Valley Bibliography, a comprehensive card
file on the history and culture of the
Connecticut Valley of Massachusetts.
MI —UNIVERSITY OF MICHIGAN, William
L Clements Library, Ann Arbor, 48109.
John C Dann, Dir
Notes: The
NY —NEW YORK STATE LIBRARY, State
Education Bldg Annex, Washington Ave,
Albany, 12224.
Holdings: Vols 173 Cat Microforms
Notes: Good, representative collection. Not
all indexed for retrieval. In addition hold
microfilm collection of Evans, Shaw-
Shoemaker titles.
NY —NEW YORK HISTORICAL SOCIETY,
Library, 170 Central Park W, New York,
10024. James Gregory, Librn
Holdings: Mss
Notes: Incl original mss, illustrative
materials, etc.
NY —NEW YORK PUBLIC LIBRARY,
Research Libraries, General Research
Division, Fifth Ave & 42 St, New York,
10018. Rodney Phillips, Chief
Holdings: Vols (2,225,000) Cat Maps Pix
Microforms
Budget: ($775,718)
NC —SOUTHEASTERN BAPTIST
THEOLOGICAL SEMINARY LIBRARY,
PO Box 752, Wake Forest, 27587. H Eugene
McLeod, Librn
Holdings: Cat Audiotapes Videotapes
Microforms
Notes: Incl many American sermons from
the 17th and 18th centuries.
OH —HEBREW UNION COLLEGE-JEWISH
INSTITUTE OF RELIGION, Klau Library,
3101 Clifton Ave, Cincinnati, 45220. David
J Gilner, Reference Librn
Holdings: Cat Mss
Notes: About 6000 mss in Hebrew
characters representing various languages,
such as Hebrew, Ladino, Yiddish, Spanish,
Italian, German; also mss in Arabic,
Ethiopian, Chinese and Persian alphabets.
Incl literary, archival, sermonic and halakhic
mss.
OH —PUBLIC LIBRARY OF CINCINNATI
& HAMILTON COUNTY, Education &
Religion Dept, 800 Vine St, Cincinnati,
45202. Susan F Hettinger, Head
Holdings: Vols (45,000) Cat
Budget: ($10,000)
Notes: Theological and religious collection:
religion, church history, theology, 18th and
19th century Protestant writings and
sermons.
OR —GEORGE FOX COLLEGE, Shambaugh
Library, Newberg, 97132. F E Walls, Librn
Dir
Holdings: Vols 3000 Cat Mss Pix Slides
PA —JANKOLA LIBRARY AND SLOVAK
ARCHIVES, Danville, 17821.
Holdings: Vols 300
PA —TEMPLE UNIVERSITY LIBRARIES,
Special Collections Dept, Conwellana-
Templana Collection, 13 & Berks St,
Philadelphia, 19122. Miriam I Crawford, Cur
Holdings: Vols (2200) Cat Mss Pix Slides
Phonorecords Audiotapes 16mm Films VF
Budget: ($30,000)
Notes: The Conwellana Collection is a
memorial to Dr Russell H Conwell, founder
of Temple University and pastor of the
Baptist Temple (Grace Baptists Church) of
Philadelphia from 1882 to his death in 1925.
The Collection contains almost all of his
published works; his personal library of
almost 2000 books, emphasizing Biblical and
religious thoughts; mss both by Conwell and
about his development of the institutional
church; letters, including a large number
written to his assistant pastor, Arthur E
Harris; a near-complete bound set of his
sermons and of the Temple Review of the
Baptist Temple in which they appeared over

SERMONS—COLLECTIONS (cont.)

a 36-year period; and an extensive file of articles, photographs and information on his activities. Card catalog of the Conwellana-Templana Collection incl books by and about Russell Conwell. Separate card files index his sermons, quotationstrom his sermons, and items in the *Temple Review*. *Russell Herman Conwell, 1843-1925, A Bibliography*, by Maurice F Tauber (Philadelphia Temple University Library, 1935. 40 leaves mimeographed). *Russell Herman Conwell: The Individual and His Influence: Catalog of an Exhibition*, by Miriam I Crawford (Temple University General Alumni Association, 1977; unpaged).

RI —BROWN UNIVERSITY, John Hay Library, 20 Prospect St, Providence, 02912. Mark N Brown, Cur Mss
Holdings: Mss
Notes: The Brown University Manuscript Collection incl sermons of Jones Very (qv); Isaac Backus (qv); Francis Wayland (qv); Eli Canfield (qv); among others.

SC —COLLEGE OF CHARLESTON LIBRARY, Special Collections Dept, Charleston, 29401.
Notes: Incl in the papers of Nathaniel Russell Middleton and James Warley Miles (1818-1875).

ON —HURON COLLEGE, Silcox Memorial Library, 1349 Western Rd, London, N6G 1H3, Can. Pamela MacKay, Chief Librn
Holdings: Vols (28,000) Cat
Budget: ($24,710)
Notes: Cover Bible, church history, church music, liturgics, pastoralia, religious education, philosophy of religion, religious studies, systematics. 95 periodical subscriptions including foreign langauge materials. Rare books collection of 750 volumes, including collections of sermons, commentaries, particularly rare bibles, many in foreign languages.

ON —WYCLIFFE COLLEGE, Leonard Library, 5 Hoskin Ave, Toronto, M5S 1H7, Can. Adrienne Taylor, Librn; Gayle Ford, Library Technician
Holdings: Vols (47,000) Cat Microforms
Budget: ($11,000)
Notes: Collection of early and rare books, of prayer books, sermons, Bibles. Basic reference collection of standard theological dictionaries, encyclopedias, commentaries. Homiletics collection incl 19th century works. Strong in church history, Evangelical Anglicanism, English Reformation, Wycliffe studies.

SERMONS—INDEXES

OH —CLEVELAND PUBLIC LIBRARY, Social Sciences Department, 325 Superior Ave, Cleveland, 44114. Thelma Morris, Head
Notes: An index by subject and biblical text of 2000 volumes, incl books and periodicals.

SEROLOGY

NY —MILTON HELPERN LIBRARY OF LEGAL MEDICINE, 520 First Ave, New York, 10016. Barry W Seaver, Librn
Holdings: Vols (2480) Cat Pix Slides Microforms
Notes: Forensic (legal) medicine (incl forensic pathology, serology, toxicology and criminalistics).

ON —ONTARIO MINISTRY OF HEALTH, Laboratory Services Branch, Library, Box 9000, Terminal A, Toronto, M5W 1R5, Can. Doris A Standing, Librn
Holdings: Vols (4000) Cat
Budget: ($50,000)
Notes: Medical laboratory technology and related subjects: microbiology; environmental bacteriology (limited to testing of milk, food and water for bacterial quality, etc); biological chemistry (clinical); mycology; parasitology; virology; immunology; serology; automated laboratory techniques; biohazard control.

SERVANTS

DC —HOWARD UNIVERSITY, Moorland-Spingarn Research Center, 500 Howard Place NW, Washington, 20059. Clifford L Muse, Jr, Acting Dir
Holdings: Vols (106,086) Mss Maps Pix Slides Phonorecords Audiotapes 16mm Films Filmstrips Microforms
Budget: ($854,753)
See also entry under Blacks

SERVETUS, MICHAEL, 1509-1553

MD —JOHNS HOPKINS UNIVERSITY, Institute of the History of Medicine, 1900 E Monument St, Baltimore, 21205. Doris Thibodeau, Librn
Holdings: Vols 145 Cat

SERVIANS see Serbs

SERVICE ORGANIZATIONS

KY —ASBURY THEOLOGICAL SEMINARY, B L Fisher Library, Wilmore, 40390. D William Faupel, Dir of Library Services
Holdings: Uncat
Notes: A collection of 35 document boxes of publicity materials on nearly 300 service organizations (Christian, missionary, social, educational), fugitive materials which would serve as primary sources for a study of their history and work--form letters (strictly fund raising letters deleted), brochures, etc.

SERVOMECHANISMS

MA —MASSACHUSETTS INSTITUTE OF TECHNOLOGY, Institute Archives, Special Collections, Cambridge, 02139.

SESSIONS, ROGER

DC —LIBRARY OF CONGRESS, Music Division, Washington, 20540.
Notes: Mss in Koussevitzky Archives.

SETON, ANYA

MA —BOSTON UNIVERSITY, Mugar Memorial Library, Special Collections Dept, 771 Commonwealth Ave, Boston, 02215. Howard B Gotlieb, Dir
Holdings: Cat
Notes: Memorabilia, primarily correspondence incl papers of her mother, Grace Gallatin Seton.

SETON, ERNEST THOMPSON

NM —BOY SCOUTS OF AMERICA, Ernest Thompson Seton Memorial Library, Philmont Scout Ranch & Explorer Base, Cimarron, 87714. Eleanor Pratt, Dir of Museums
Holdings: Vols (3000) Cat Mss Maps Pix
Notes: Along with Seton's library, his writings (books, articles, short stories, Birchbark Roll, Indian Woodbadge work with young people), approx 3000 study skins of birds and small animals. Also approx 3000 of his pen and ink, water color and oil paintings. This collection was given to the Boy Scouts of America by Seton's widow. The museum, library, collections room and laboratory were built for BSA by Mr L O Crosby of Picayune, Mississippi. (See also the diaries at the library of the American Museum of Natural History, New York, NY.) The 33 volumes of Seton's journals (diaries) were given to the American Museum of Natural History by Joseph F Cullman 3rd; he also had copies made for the Seton Memorial Library. Our second museum is the Kit Carson Museum, a living history museum, open June, July and August.

NY —AMERICAN MUSEUM OF NATURAL HISTORY, Library Services Dept, Central Park W & 79th St, New York, 10024. Nina J Root, Chairwoman; Mary Genett, Asst Librn for Reference Services
Holdings: Cat Mss Pix Microforms
Notes: The Ernest Thompson Seton diaries. Thousands of pages of an unpublished 67-year diary record of one of the world's most famous naturalists, the gift of Joseph F Cullman III, a Trustee of the Museum.

Preserved in 35 protective cases, the gift incl unpublished diaries, notebooks, and some other writings. The diary begins 12 June 1879; the last entries were written in hospital, just a month before Seton's death in 1946. Literally hundreds of examples of flora and fauna are pictured in the diaries in original pencil, pen-and-ink, and watercolor sketches, on nearly every page. Research will reveal information on the Indian sign language, the Boy Scouts of America, the Woodcraft League of America, and the wilderness of Canada, Florida, Texas, the West and Southwest, etc.

VA —UNIVERSITY OF VIRGINIA, Alderman Library, Clifton Waller Barrett Collection, Charlottesville, 22901. Joan St C Crane, Cur of American Literature Collections
Notes: Papers.

SETTLE, MARY LEE

MA —BOSTON UNIVERSITY, Mugar Memorial Library, Special Collections Dept, 771 Commonwealth Ave, Boston, 02215. Howard B Gotlieb, Dir
Holdings: Cat Mss
Notes: Mss, correspondence, etc collected in depth; incl publications by or about.

SETTLEMENTS, SOCIAL see Social Settlements

SEUSS, DR. see Geisel, Theodor Seuss (Dr. Seuss)

SEVEN DAYS (NEWSPAPER)

PA —TEMPLE UNIVERSITY, Samuel Paley Library, Berks & 13 Sts, Philadelphia, 19122.
Notes: Archives of the magazine, *Seven Days*, which first appeared in 1975 and was considered the succesor of *Ramparts*. Leading editor was David Dellinger, one of the defendants in the Chicago Conspiracy Trail. Incl office files, correspondence, editorial files, and a selection of Dellinger's papers relating to *Seven Days*.

SEVEN LIBERAL ARTS see Education, Medieval

SEVEN WISE MASTERS OF ROME

OH —CLEVELAND PUBLIC LIBRARY, Fine Arts and Special Collections Department, 325 Superior Ave, Cleveland, 44114. Alice N Loranth, Head
Holdings: Vols (3000) Cat Mss
Notes: Part of the Romances Collection, which incl critical studies, and early printed editions. The Arthurian and Charlemagne cycles, the Nibelungenlied and other Germanic titles, Amadis de Gaula and his numerous progeny, Alexander the Great, Barlaam and Joasaph, and the Seven Wise Masters of Rome are some of the strengths of the collection. Material in the Dewey/Brett Collection is classified by related cycles and their versions in various languages.
See also entry under Romances.

SEVENTH-DAY ADVENTISTS

CA —PACIFIC UNION COLLEGE, Nelson Memorial Library, Angwin, 94508. Taylor D Ruhl, Dir
Holdings: Mss Vols Cat Microforms Photographs VF

CA —LOMA LINDA UNIVERSITY, Dell E Webb Memorial Library, Loma Linda, 92354. James R Nix, Assoc University Archivist
Holdings: Vols 16,000 Cat Mss Maps Pix Slides Audiotapes Microforms
Notes: Incl materials by and about Seventh-day Adventists, as well as University archival materials. Other Seventh-day Adventist materials also in Riverside campus library collection.

MI —ANDREWS UNIVERSITY, James White Library, Berrien Springs, 49104. Marley H Soper, Dir
Holdings: Vols 110 // Cat
Notes: Hymns of the Seventh-Day Adventist

SEVENTH-DAY ADVENTISTS (cont.)

faith. The collection begins with the 1849 edition of the hymnal and continues to the present. Not available by interlibrary loan, but may be used at this library.

OH —KETTERING COLLEGE OF MEDICAL ARTS, Learning Resources Center, 3737 Southern Blvd, Kettering, 45429. Edward Collins, Librn
Holdings: Vols 563 Cat Slides
Budget: $565

†WI —SEVENTH DAY BAPTIST HISTORICAL SOCIETY, Library, 3120 Kennedy St, PO Box 1678, Janesville, 53547.
Holdings: Vols (500) Cat Mss
Notes: Sabbatarianism began in England in the 17th century and was brought to the US by English- and German-speaking Seventh Day Baptists, from whom the Seventh-day Adventist movement emerged after 1844. The doctrine of both denominations and of the Church of God-Seventh Day are set in this collection, 1653 to date.

AB —CANADIAN UNION COLLEGE, Library, Box 460, College Heights, T0C 0Z0, Can. Keith Clouten, Library Services Dir
Holdings: Vols (5000) Cat Audiotapes 16mm Films Microforms
Notes: Largely theology, comparative religion, church history, especially of Seventh-day Adventists.

SEVENTH-DAY BAPTISTS

RI —WESTERLY PUBLIC LIBRARY, Broad St, Westerly, 02891. David J Panciera, Library Dir
Holdings: Vols (3000) Cat Mss Maps Pix Audiotapes Microforms
Notes: Extensive coverage of history of Westerly and surrounding area; also general material on Rhode Island and Connecticut. Books, clippings, mss, etc. Many unique family genealogies; local photographs; postcards. Special materials on Seventh-Day Baptist Church; Westerly granite industry; Wilcox Park; Watch Hill. Separate catalog.

WV —SALEM COLLEGE, Library, Salem, 26426. Myron J Smith, Jr, Librn

WI —SEVENTH DAY BAPTIST HISTORICAL SOCIETY, Library, 3120 Kennedy Rd, PO Box 1678, Janesville, 53547. D Scott Smith, Historian
Holdings: Vols (600) Cat Mss Maps Pix
Notes: US Seventh Day Baptists Collection, incl records, letters. Established at Newport, Rhode Island, in 1671, this denomination is a part of the Free-Church evangelical movement in America. The General Conference was organized in 1801. The national and international headquarters of the Seventh Day Baptist denomination is located at Janesville, Wisconsin. Also have records, publications, etc of the denomination's mission in Shanghai, 1846-1950; further, materials (6 boxes) on the Church's work in Nyasaland (Malawi), 1895-1914, and then at a later period.

SEVENTH-DAY CHURCH OF GOD see Church of God, Seventh Day

SEVILLE, SPAIN

CA —UNIVERSITY OF CALIFORNIA, SAN DIEGO, Central University Library, Mandeville Dept of Special Collections, La Jolla, 92093. Lynda Corey Claassen, Head
Notes: Hispanic Collection: Approx 6000 vols describe cultures of Spain, Portugal, Mexico, Latin America, and South America. Works of literature, history, philosophy and art date from the 15th to the mid-19th century. Highlights of the collection include rare 18th century Spanish provincial dramas and works on the history of Seville and Andalusia.

SEWAGE DISPOSAL AND TREATMENT

IL —GREELEY & HANSEN ENGINEERS, 222 S Riverside Plaza, Chicago, 60606.

Marilyn Cichom, Librn
Holdings: Vols (6000) Cat Maps Slides Microforms

SEWALL, HENRY

ME —BOWDOIN COLLEGE, Library, Brunswick, 04011. Dianne M Gutscher, Cur of Special Collections
Holdings: Mss
Notes: The Mellen Papers contain approx 5000 printed and mss items relating to New England history from the 18th to the 20th centuries. Of primary importance are the Henry Sewall papers, which incl his Revolutionary War correspondence, addresses, genealogical notes, and other documents. The archive also incl papers from the Mellen, Hawkins, Manley, Harward, and other New England families.

SEWARD, WILLIAM, HENRY, 1801-1872

NY —UNIVERSITY OF ROCHESTER, Rush Rhees Library, Department of Rare Books and Special Collections, Rochester, 14627. Peter Dzwonkoski, Librn
Holdings: Mss
Notes: William Henry Seward papers, which contain approximately 150,000 items, relate to American political, social, and diplomatic history, ca 1825-1872. Also a collection of approx 4000 pamphlets of the same time period and subjects, which were owned by him. The latter are fully cataloged. Each letter in the collection has been indexed by name of letter writer. Unpublished register is available in repository. Available on microfilm from Research Publications Inc.

SEWELL, FATHER BROCARD

BC —UNIVERSITY OF VICTORIA, McPherson Library, Victoria, V8W 3H5, Can.
Notes: Editor of *The Aylesford Review,* incl 108 pages, 1924-63; correspondence concerning subjects featured in *The Aylesford Review,* of which Father Sewell was editor; letters from Eleanor Farjean (re Elizabeth Myers and Sarah Jackson), John Betjeman, Arthur Machen, Joseph Delteil, Una, Lady Troubridge (re Radcliffe Hall), Beatrice Warde (re Frederick Rolfe), Stevie Smith, Graham Greene, Shelagh Delaney, John Gawsworth, Father C C Martindale (re John Gray and Aubrey Beardsley), Alyse Gregory (re Theodore Powys), John Cooper Powys and Louis Willkinson (re Hilaire Belloc); letters from Eric Gill to Clare Pepler; notes of G K Chesterton's for a letter to Father Vincent McNabb.

SEWELL, ELIZABETH

MA —BOSTON UNIVERSITY, Mugar Memorial Library, Special Collections Dept, 771 Commonwealth Ave, Boston, 02215. Howard B Gotlieb, Dir
Holdings: Cat Mss Pix
Notes: Mss, correspondence, etc collected in depth; incl publications by or about.

SEX

IN —INDIANA UNIVERSITY, Institute for Sex Research Library, 416 Morrison Hall, Bloomington, 47401. Douglas Freeman, Collections and Services Librn; Joan Brewer, Information Services Librn
Holdings: Vols (62,000) Cat Mss Pix Microforms
Notes: Comprehensive coverage, incl historical works and current research, pictures and photographs, has been attempted in topics related to sex behavior. Available to any qualified researcher with demonstrable research needs.

NY —YWCA NATIONAL BOARD, Library, 726-730 Broadway, New York, 10012. Elizabeth Norris, Librn
Holdings: Vols (3000) Cat Mss
Budget: ($2400)
Notes: Women and their contemporary interests.

OH —CLEVELAND PUBLIC LIBRARY, Social Sciences Department, 325 Superior Ave, Cleveland, 44114. Thelma Morris, Head
Notes: Incl books and periodicals on personal relationships, the family, and sex relations.

SEX—RESEARCH see Sex Research

SEX DISCRIMINATION

DC —US COMMISSION ON CIVIL RIGHTS, National Clearinghouse Library, 1121 Vermont Ave NW, Washington, 20005. Lenora McMillan, Chief Librn
Holdings: Vols (10,200) Cat Slides Microforms
Notes: The National Clearinghouse Library has a special collection of the US Commission on Civil Rights publications from its inception (1957) to present date.

MA —RADCLIFFE COLLEGE, Arthur & Elizabeth Schlesinger Library on the History of Women in America, 3 James St, Cambridge, 02138. Patricia Miller King, Dir; Eva Moseley, Cur of Mss
Notes: The papers of the 1974 class action suit against *The New York Times* that charged the newspaper with "a pattern and practice of discrimination in employment on the basis of sex." The *Times* agreed to an affirmative action plan, and the suit was resolved in 1978.

SEX DYSFUNCTIONS

IN —INDIANA UNIVERSITY, Institute for Sex Research Library, 416 Morrison Hall, Bloomington, 47401. Douglas Freeman, Collections and Services Librn; Joan Brewer, Information Services Librn
Holdings: Vols (62,000) Cat Mss Pix Microforms
See also entry under Sex.

SEX EDUCATION

AZ —WORLD UNIVERSITY, Library, 711 E Blacklidge Dr, Tucson, 85719. Howard John Zitko, Cur
Holdings: Vols (15,000) Cat Mss Maps Audiotapes
Notes: Collection concerns the "frontier sciences." No interlibrary loan.

CA —LOS ANGELES PUBLIC LIBRARY, Social Sciences Dept, 630 W Fifth St, Los Angeles, 90071. Marilyn C Wherley, Principal Librn
Holdings: Vols 3000 Cat
Budget: ($150,000)
Notes: Books, clippings, pamphlets, periodicals, government publications, bibliogrpahies, popular and scholarly works on homosexuality, husband-wife relations, abortion, rape, and sex education.

IL —SOUTHERN ILLINOIS UNIVERSITY, CARBONDALE, Delyte W Morris Library, Carbondale, 62901.
Holdings: Cat Mss Pix
Notes: Incl the papers of Drs William Josephus and Victor Robinson; with the papers of Theodore A Schroeder. Much on sex instruction and birth control.

IL —UNIVERSITY OF ILLINOIS, URBANA/CHAMPAIGN, Library, Applied Life Studies Library, 1408 W Gregory Dr, Urbana, 61801.
Holdings: Vols (38,000) Cat Pix Microforms
See also entry under Physical Education and Training.

IN —INDIANA UNIVERSITY, Institute for Sex Research Library, 416 Morrison Hall, Bloomington, 47401. Douglas Freeman, Collections and Services Librn; Joan Brewer, Information Services Librn
Holdings: Vols (62,000) Cat Mss Pix Microforms
See also entry under Sex.

NY —PLANNED PARENTHOOD FEDERATION OF AMERICA, Katharine Dexter McCormick Library, 810 Seventh Ave, New York, 10019. Gloria A Roberts, Head Librn
Holdings: Vols (4000) Cat
Notes: Birth control, teenagers,

SEX EDUCATION (cont.)

contraception and contraceptive research, family planning, religion and birth control.

NY —UNIVERSITY OF ROCHESTER, Rush Rhees Library, Department of Rare Books and Special Collections, Rochester, 14627. Peter Dzwonkoski, Librn
Holdings: Cat Mss
Notes: Correspondence, reports, articles written by Wile on birth control (including many letters from Margaret Sanger), left and right handedness, sex education, child development, and mental hygiene.

WI —PLANNED PARENTHOOD OF WISCONSIN, Maurice Ritz Resource Library & Bookstore, 1135 W State St, Milwaukee, 53233. Ann McIntyre, Librn
Holdings: Vols (2500) Cat Pix Slides Phonorecords 16mm Films Filmstrips VF
Notes: Special emphasis on family planning and reproductive health, birth control and contraception.

SEX EXPRESSION

CA —WOMEN'S HISTORY RESEARCH CENTER, Microfilm Library, 2325 Oak St, Berkeley, 94708. Laura X, Librn
Holdings: Mss Pix Microforms
Notes: Incl material (150 subject files) on physical and mental health and illnesses; sex roles; biology; women and the life cycle; birth/population control; sex and sexuality; black and Third World women. Collection at University of Wyoming. Archive of Contemporary History, PO Box 3334, Laramie, Wyoming 82701, c/o David Crosson. Research inquiries accepted. Microfilm of collection (14 reels and reel guides) available at many universities and through Women's History Research Center, 2325 Oak St, Berkeley, CA 94708. No collections housed at this address.

CA —LOS ANGELES PUBLIC LIBRARY, Social Sciences Dept, 630 W Fifth St, Los Angeles, 90071. Marilyn C Wherley, Principal Librn
Holdings: Vols 3000 Cat
Budget: ($150,000)
Notes: Books, clippings, pamphlets, periodicals, government publications, bibliogrpahies, popular and scholarly works on homosexuality, husband-wife relations, abortion, rape, and sex education.

IL —SOUTHERN ILLINOIS UNIVERSITY, CARBONDALE, Delyte W Morris Library, Special Collections Dept, Carbondale, 62901. David V Koch, Cur of Special Collections; Louisa Bowen, Cur of Manuscripts
Holdings: Vols 430 Cat Mss Pix
Notes: Personal papers (78 linear feet) of Theodore Schroder, 1873-1957, founder of the Free Speech League, incl archives of the League. Thousands of letters, mss, and notes, with letters from Anthony Comstock, Samuel Gompers, Eugene V Debs, Havelock Ellis, Margaret Sanger, Upton Sinclair, H L Mencken, and Emma Goldman. The archives reflect Schroeder's crusades in the areas of free speech, sex expression, religion, and psychoanalysis. Inventory and name index available at the Library. Described by Ralph E McCoy, *Theodore Schroder, the Cold Enthusiast*, Carbondale: Southern Illinois University Libraries, 1973. (Bibliographic Contributions, No 8).

SEX IN ART see Sex in the Arts

SEX IN THE ARTS

†CA —INSTITUTE FOR THE ADVANCED STUDY OF HUMAN SEXUALITY, 1523 Franklin St, San Francisco, 94109.

CA —INTERNATIONAL MUSEUM OF EROTIC ART, Formerly, San Francisco, 94108.
Notes: Unfortunately this renowned collection has been dispersed and no longer (1984) exists, including the Phyllis and Eberhard Kronhausen collection, according to the information we have been given.

SEX OFFENDERS

IN —INDIANA UNIVERSITY, Institute for Sex Research Library, 416 Morrison Hall,

Bloomington, 47401. Douglas Freeman, Collections and Services Librn; Joan Brewer, Information Services Librn
Holdings: Vols (62,000) Cat Mss Pix Microforms
See also entry under Sex.

SEX RESEARCH

CA —WOMEN'S HISTORY RESEARCH CENTER, Microfilm Library, 2325 Oak St, Berkeley, 94708. Laura X, Librn
Holdings: Mss Pix Microforms
Notes: Incl material (150 subject files) on physical and mental health and illnesses; sex roles; biology; women and the life cycle; birth/population control; sex and sexuality; black and Third World women. Collection at University of Wyoming. Archive of Contemporary History, PO Box 3334, Laramie, Wyoming 82701, c/o David Crosson. Research inquiries accepted. Microfilm of collection (14 reels and reel guides) available at many universities and through Women's History Research Center, 2325 Oak St, Berkeley, CA 94708. No collections housed at this address.

CA —HOMOSEXUAL INFORMATION CENTER, Library, 6758 Hollywood Blvd Rm 208, Los Angeles, 90028. Don Slater, Librn
Holdings: Vols Unpublished Mss Pix Phonorecords
Notes: Contains over 5000 mss, periodicals, and pamphlets on the homosexual movement, from 1948, and records the movements's organizational, social, and political history. Incl are periodicals in Japanese, French, German, Dutch, and other European languages, and newsletters, records, and reports of homosexual organizations probably not to be found in any other archive. The Library publishes bibliographies, selected reading lists, a directory of homosexual movement organizations and publications, and a newsletter. It participates in an ILL network.

†CA —INSTITUTE FOR THE ADVANCED STUDY OF HUMAN SEXUALITY, 1523 Franklin St, San Francisco, 94109.

IN —INDIANA UNIVERSITY, Institute for Sex Research Library, 416 Morrison Hall, Bloomington, 47401. Douglas Freeman, Collections and Services Librn; Joan Brewer, Information Services Librn
Holdings: Vols (62,000) Cat Mss Pix Phonorecords Audiotapes Slides Films Microforms
Budget: ($20,000)
Notes: One of the greatest and most extensive collection on sexual behavior, the library collects materials on all aspects of sex activity, with special emphasis on behavioral and social aspects. Also collects erotic literature and sexual ephemera. Incl 1056 audiotapes, 23 vertical file drawers, 108 phonorecords, 55,000 pictures, 5000 slides, and 1700 films. Rich in French, German and American sources; also much Oriental. Semitraditional erotic poetry and song of 17th-18th century England. Bawdy limericks, double-entendre, puns, slang, erotic literature, graffiti, slang and special dictionaries, proverbs and sayings, epigrams and research materials of the Kinsey Studies, etc. Contact Information Service for: literature searching, preparation of bibliographies, permission to use collection. Limited photocopying.

MA —BOSTON UNIVERSITY, Mugar Memorial Library, Special Collections Dept, 771 Commonwealth Ave, Boston, 02215. Howard B Gotlieb, Dir
Holdings: Mss Pix
Notes: Mss, correspondence, etc collected in depth; incl publications by or about.

MA —FRANCIS A COUNTWAY LIBRARY OF MEDICINE, Boston Medical Library/ Harvard Medical Library, 10 Shattuck St, Boston, 02115. C Robin LeSueur, Librn; Richard J Wolfe, Cur, Rare Books & Manuscripts
Holdings: Vols (500,000) Cat Mss Maps Pix Microforms
Notes: Combines resources of the Harvard Medical School and the Boston Medical

Library. Strong in serials and medical history in all fields of medicine, incl incunabula, non-medical books by doctors, travel books by doctors. 500,000 medical dissertations and theses. Special strength in all medical subjects listed in this volume.

SEXTON, ANNE

†TX —UNIVERSITY OF TEXAS LIBRARIES, General Libraries, Humanities Research Center, PO Box 7219, Austin, 78712. John Chalmers, Librn
Notes: Complete archives of the Pulitzer Prize poet, Anne Sexton (1928-1974). Includes some of her suicide notes; also correspondence with Maxine Kumin, another Pulitzer winner.

SEXTON, GEN. WILLIAM T.

†VA —GEORGE C MARSHALL RESEARCH FOUNDATION AND LIBRARY, Drawer 920, Lexington, 24450. Royster Lyle Jr, Cur Collections
Holdings: Vols Cat Mss Maps Pix Phonorecords Audiotapes Films Filmstrips Microforms
Notes: About 400 posters-American, German, French; complete *Stars and Stripes* for WWII; approx 5000 cataloged photographs, over 5000 uncataloged Office of War information photos, and over 10,000 US Signal Corps photos (uncat). Approx 250 regimental histories, operation reports, and army manuals; published memoirs and letters of Marshall associates; official military histories (American, British); over 1200 maps-approx 300 newsmaps, 800 daily situation maps (European Theatre), 37 bound vols of daily situation maps 1944-1945; seven of the *Why We Fight* series (films). Major ms collections incl the papers of generals George C Marshall, Marshall S Carter, William T Sexton, Lucian Truscott, William R Arnold, Paul M Robinett, Frank McCarthy; Forrest C Pogue; colonels Collas Harris, Francis P Miller, William F Friedman; officers of the Women's Army Corps. Hearingsand government documents. Agency records copied from NARS. Vertical file arranged by subject.

SEXUAL ETHICS

DC —CENTER FOR BIOETHICS, Library, Kennedy Institute, Georgetown University, 3520 Prospect St NW, Washington, 20057. Doris Goldstein, Dir; Judith Mistichelli, Senior Librn
Holdings: Vols (8200)
Notes: Largest library of its kind. Incl 31,000 journal articles on applied ethics. Produces computer database *Bioethicsline*, available through MEDLARS; and the printed annual *Bibliography of Bioethics*. Other library publications are: *New Titles in Bioethics* (monthly); *Scope Notes* series on current topics.

MI —UNIVERSITY OF MICHIGAN, Dept of Rare Books & Special Collections, Ann Arbor, 48109. Edward C Weber, Head, Labadie Collection
Holdings: Vols (40,000) Cat Mss Pix Phonorecords Audiotapes Microforms
Notes: Serials and pamphlets from 19th and early 20th centuries as well as recent materials.

WI —PLANNED PARENTHOOD OF WISCONSIN, Maurice Ritz Resource Library & Bookstore, 1135 W State St, Milwaukee, 53233. Ann McIntyre, Librn
Holdings: Vols (2500) Cat Pix Slides Phonorecords 16mm Films Filmstrips VF
Notes: Special emphasis on family planning and reproductive health, birth control and contraception.

SEXUAL FREEDOM see Sexual Ethics

SEXUALITY

CA —CALIFORNIA STATE UNIVERSITY, NORTHRIDGE, Delmar T Oviatt & South Libraries, 1811 Nordhoff St, Northridge, 91330. Donald L Read, Special Collections

SEXUALITY (cont.)

Dept
Holdings: Vols 1800 Cat
Notes: Books and other materials devoted to all aspects of human sexuality, particularly strong in prostitution and homosexuals and homosexuality.

DC —CENTER FOR BIOETHICS, Library, Kennedy Institute, Georgetown University, 3520 Prospect St NW, Washington, 20057. Doris Goldstein, Dir; Judith Mistichelli, Senior Librn
Holdings: Vols 8200
Notes: Largest library of its kind. Incl 31,000 journal articles. Collects in the following subject areas: applied ethics; medical ethics; philosophy of medicine; science, technology and society; sociology of medicine; patient-physician care; sexuality; contraception; abortion; population policy; reproductive technologies; in vitro fertilization; genetic counseling and screening; genetic engineering; mental organ transplantation; death and dying; "baby doe" issues; euthanasia; suicide; use of chemical and biological weapons. Produces computer database *Bioethicsline*, available through MEDLARS; and the printed annual *Bibliography of Bioethics*. Other library publications are: *New Titles in Bioethics* (monthly); *Scope Notes* series on current topics.

NY —LESBIAN HERSTORY EDUCATIONAL FOUNDATION INC, Lesbian Herstory Archives, PO Box 1258, New York, 10116. Deborah Edel, Treasurer
Notes: Lesbian, feminist, and Gay books and periodicals on all aspects of Lesbian culture, photographs and slides of Lesbians and Lesbian art, records, tapes, graphics and crafts. Also, unpublished materials such as first drafts, term papers from Lesbian and Gay studies courses, diaries, letters, poetry, and conference notes.

NY —PLANNED PARENTHOOD FEDERATION OF AMERICA, Katharine Dexter McCormick Library, 810 Seventh Ave, New York, 10019. Gloria A Roberts, Head Librn
Holdings: Vols (4000) Cat
Notes: Birth control, teenagers, contraception and contraceptive research, family planning, religion and birth control.

SEYMOUR, CHARLES

CT —YALE UNIVERSITY, Box 1603A, Yale Station, New Haven, 06520.
Notes: Papers, diaries, etc.

SEYMOUR, ISAAC

SC —COLLEGE OF CHARLESTON LIBRARY, Special Collections Dept, Charleston, 29401.
Notes: Papers incl warrant for imprisonment of Issac Seymour, ship master, for non-payment of taxes, 1792.

SEYMOUR, JOHN LAWRENCE, 1893-

CA —CLAREMONT COLLEGES, Honnold Library, Ninth & Dartmouth, Claremont, 91711. Tania Rizzo, Special Collections Dept Head
Holdings: Vols 606 Cat Mss
Notes: Opera scores, librettos, books about opera, principally of the 17th and 18th centuries. Gift of John Laurence Seymour. Many librettos (uncataloged) in 2 languages, with programs collected by the donor, 1920s to 60s. Multiple copies of Seymour's compositions and files of his personal papers. Restricted use.

SEYMOUR-SMITH, MARTIN

NY —STATE UNIVERSITY OF NEW YORK, COLLEGE AT BUFFALO, Poetry/Rare Books Collection, 420 Capen Hall, Buffalo, 14260. Robert J Bertholf, Cur
Notes: Extensive holdings of the publications, mss, correspondence, working mss, ephemera of the British poet Martin Seymour-Smith. Incl in collection are the working mss, notes, journal and other papers for the biography of Robert Graves.

SHAD FISHERIES

NJ —GLOUCESTER COUNTY HISTORICAL SOCIETY LIBRARY, 17 Hunter St, PO Box 409, Woodbury, 08096. Edith E Hoelle, Librn
Holdings: Cat Mss
Notes: Cataloged mss pertaining to the Howell Family of Fancy Hill, Gloucester County, NJ from 1739-1890. Incl letters, bills, account books and memorabilia of the Shad Fisheries along the Delaware River and Etna Furnace at Tuckahoe, NJ, a 19th century bog iron furnace; lists of (State of) Delaware suppliers to the Continental Army, Revolutionary War, etc, as well as household memorabilia of Anna Blackwood Howell (1769-1855), ca 3800 items.

SHAFER, ROBERT

OH —SAINT GREGORY SEMINARY, ATHENAEUM OF OHIO, 6616 Beechmont Ave, Cincinnati, 45230. Sister Loretto Driscoll, Librn
Holdings: // Mss
Notes: Letters, literary mss, reviews, reprints, research notes of RS, English scholar, author, professor, active in "New Humanism." The name Robert Shafer is frequently found in literature among that group of men known as the "new humanists" in the late twenties and early thirties. RS is best known as the author of *From Beowulf to Thomas Hardy*, one of the first English literature survey texts, used for many years in college courses. An unpublished biography and guide to the collection is available for users. (A similar collection of materials of RS is owned by the University of Wyoming).

SHAFTESBURY, ANTHONY ASHLEY COOPER, THIRD EARL OF

OH —MIAMI UNIVERSITY, King Library, Walter Havighurst Special Collections Library, Oxford, 45056. Helen Ball, Cur of Special Collections
Holdings: Vols 60 Cat
Notes: Most extensive collection of editions of Shaftesbury's *Characteristicks*.

SHAKERS

CT —CONNECTICUT STATE LIBRARY, 231 Capitol Ave, Hartford, 06106.
Holdings: Cat Mss
Notes: Material received from the Enfield Shaker Community, incl ms diaries, journals, hymn books; also other resources. The Library acquires only new material on the subject today.

DE —HENRY F DUPONT WINTERTHUR MUSEUM LIBRARY, Winterthur, 19735. Frank H Sommer, III, Head
Holdings: Cat Mss
Notes: Extremely rare and early Shaker books and manuscripts. (*Shaker Guide*, 1970).

DC —LIBRARY OF CONGRESS, Rare Book & Special Collections Div, Washington, 20540. William Matheson, Chief
Notes: Most of the collection consists of 19th century books and pamphlets about or written by the Shakers. See Mary Richmond's *Shaker Literature*, (Hancock, Massachusetts: Shaker Community, 1977), which records the Library holdings.

IN —INDIANA UNIVERSITY, Lilly Library, Seventh St, Bloomington, 47405. William R Cagle, Librn
Holdings: // Cat Mss
Notes: First and early printings of the Icarian communities (1840-1880) and of works by Rappites and the Owneites; also New Harmony, Indiana. Mss relating to the Shaker community in Kentucky (1826-1828) in the Charles Willing Byrd collection.

KY —WESTERN KENTUCKY UNIVERSITY, Kentucky Library, Bowling Green, 42101. Riley Handy, Head, Special Collections; Connie Mills, Maps & Music Librn; Nancy Baird, Photographs Librn; Nancy Solley, Conservation Librn
Holdings: Vols (25,000) Cat Mss Maps Pix Microforms
Notes: Besides Kentucky history, other strengths are Mammoth Cave, South Union Shakers, Kentucky religion; and steamboat photos (3300 cataloged pictures); 8000 Kentucky postal cards, etc.

MA —FRUITLANDS MUSEUMS LIBRARY, Prospect Hill, RR 2 Box 87, Harvard, 01451. Richard S Reed, Dir; John L Crispen, Admin Secy
Budget: ($21,900)
Notes: Fruitlands (utopian community), books and mss; New England Transcendentalism; and Shakers' books and mss, primarily the Harvard Shaker Society and Shirley Shaker Society. 97 mss journals from the Harvard Community; 26 mss journals from the Shirley Community; 1 mss journal from Entfield, NH; incl day books, ledgers, and music mss.

MA —BERKSHIRE ATHENAEUM, 1 Wendell Ave, Pittsfield, 01201. Ruth T Degenhardt, Head Local History & Literature
Holdings: Vols 200 Cat Mss
Budget: ($2000)
Notes: Large and representative collection. Specific area of focus in Hancock, Massachusetts, and New Lebanon, New York, Shaker communities. Also contains 500 unbound pamphlets; 20 handwritten hymnals. Published guide to collection: Richmond, Mary L comp, *Shaker Literature: A Bibliography* (Hanover, NH: University Press of New England, 1977).

MA —WILLIAMS COLLEGE, Sawyer Library, Williamstown, 01267. Phyllis L Cutler, Dir
Holdings: Vols 1100 Cat Mss Maps Microforms
Budget: $500
Notes: Incl 1186 microfiche. Particularly strong in Shaker music and imprints. Restricted to serious scholars. Photocopying permissions limited.

MA —AMERICAN ANTIQUARIAN SOCIETY LIBRARY, 185 Salisbury St, Worcester, 01609. Marcus A McCorison, Dir & Librn
Holdings: Cat
Notes: Outstanding collection of Shaker imprints and ancillary materials; manuscript holdings trivial. (*Shaker Guide*, 1970).

NY —NEW YORK STATE LIBRARY, State Education Bldg Annex, Washington Ave, Albany, 12224.
Holdings: Cat Mss Microforms
Notes: Excellent collection of printed material: pamphlets, books. Diaries and journals, religious and business records. 15 linear feet of mss.

NY —BUFFALO & ERIE COUNTY PUBLIC LIBRARY, Rare Book Room, Lafayette Sq, Buffalo, 14203. William H Loos, Cur
Holdings: Vols 305 Cat
Notes: Holdings recorded in *Shaker Literature in the Rare Book Room of the Buffalo and Erie County Public Library, A Bibliography*, comp by Esther C Winter and rev by Joanna S Ellett (Buffalo, 1967).

NY —NEW YORK PUBLIC LIBRARY, Rare Books and Manuscripts Div, Fifth Ave & 42 St, New York, 10018. William L Joyce, Asst Dir; Francis O Mattson, Curator
Holdings: Cat
Budget: ($7161)
Notes: Shaker materials are held in the Manuscript Division.

NY —SHAKER MUSEUM, Emma B King Library, Shaker Museum Rd, Old Chatham, 12136. Viki Sand, Dir; Ann Kelly, Archivist
Holdings: Vols 2500 Cat Mss Maps Pix Slides Phonorecords Audiotapes 16mm Films Filmstrips Microforms
Notes: Incl also about 750 mss of Shaker interest; 150 maps or drawings; 1800 deeds, letters, and indentures; about 5000 pictures. Collection on Society of Shakers includes membership rolls, patents, deeds, diaries and account books.

NY —SYRACUSE UNIVERSITY LIBRARIES, Ernest S Bird Library, George

SHAKERS (cont.)

Arents Research Library for Special
Collections, Syracuse, 13210. Carolyn A
Davis, Manuscripts Librn; Amy S Doherty,
University Archivist; Mark F Weimer, Rare
Book Librn
Holdings: Vols 525 Cat
Notes: Primary and secondary materials
about the sect officially known as the United
Society of Believers in Christ's Second
Appearing.

OH —WESTERN RESERVE HISTORICAL
SOCIETY, History Library, William P
Palmer Civil War Collection, 10825 East
Blvd, Cleveland, 44106. Kermit J Pike, Dir
Holdings: Mss Pix
Notes: "Largest collection of Shakeriana in
the world". Pike, Kermit J, *A Guide to
Shaker Manuscripts...*, Cleveland: The
Western Reserve Historical Society, 1974.
Manuscripts (122 linear feet).

OH —WARREN COUNTY HISTORICAL
SOCIETY, Museum Library, 105 S
Broadway, PO Box 223, Lebanon, 45036.
Victoria Visintainer, Dir
Holdings: Vols (1030) Cat Microforms
Budget: ($3500)
Notes: Warren County, Ohio history and
genealogy. Incl 690 general information files;
879 family files; 21 vols of cemetery,
marriage and birth records; 75,000 index
cards on individuals; 317 microfilm reels of
local newspapers (1807-1976), court and
census records; file of *Ohio Historical
Society Quarterly*; ledgers; diaries; and 4
vols of oral history. Society also holds
Shaker Collection, incl books, periodicals,
pamphlets, maps and pictures (600 pieces).

OH —MASSILLON PUBLIC LIBRARY, 208
Lincoln Way E, Massillon, 44646. Camille
Leslie, Dir
Holdings: Vols 73 Cat Mss
Budget: $100
Notes: Collection is limited to historical
studies; nothing on modern communes.
Special emphasis on Shakers and Zoarites.
No separate catalog.

PA —BALCH INSTITUTE FOR ETHNIC
STUDIES, Library, 18 S Seventh St,
Philadelphia, 19106. R Joseph Anderson,
Library Dir

SHAKESPEARE, WILLIAM, AND
SHAKESPEARIANA

CA —FRANCIS BACON LIBRARY, 655 N
Dartmouth Ave, Claremont, 91711.
Elizabeth S Wrigley, Dir
Holdings: Vols 1600 Cat Mss Maps Pix
Microforms
Notes: Anti-Shakespeareana incl many
pamphlets, magazine articles, newspaper
clippings and reviews. Many unpublished
mss and correspondence with early
Baconians and other anti-Shakespeareans.

CA —SAN DIEGO PUBLIC LIBRARY,
Literature & Language Sect, 820 E St, San
Diego, 92101. Alyce Archuleta, Senior Librn
Holdings: Vols 112 Cat
Notes: Emphasis on late 19th-century works.
Separate author-title index.

CT —LEE ASH, (personal collection), 66
Humiston Dr, Bethany, 06525.
Holdings: Cat Mss Pix
Notes: Incl books, letters, ephemera, etc,
especially concerning the Oxford
controversy.

CT —YALE UNIVERSITY, Box 1603A, Yale
Station, New Haven, 06520.

DC —FOLGER SHAKESPEARE LIBRARY,
201 E Capitol St, Washington, 20003. Philip
A Knachel, Acting Dir
Holdings: Vols (223,571) Cat Mss Pix
Periodicals Microfilms
Notes: Collections described in *Catalog of
Printed Books of the Folger Shakespeare
Library*, 28 vols; *First Supplement*, 3 vols
(Boston: G K Hall, 1970, 1976); *Second
Supplement* in 2 vols (Boston: G K Hall,
1981); *Catalog of Manuscripts of the Folger
Shakespeare Library*, 3 vols (Boston: G K
Hall, 1971); and *The Widening Circle: The
Story of the Folger Library and Its
Collections* (Washington, DC: Folger

Shakespeare Library, 1976). Collections incl
39 vols of plays with ms annotations and
stage directions by John Philip Kemble.
Library use restricted to advanced research
scholars.

DC —LIBRARY OF CONGRESS, Rare Book
& Special Collections Div, Washington,
20540. William Matheson, Chief
Notes: The collection, formed by Col
George Fabyan, consists of 1096 volumes,
269 pamphlets and 33 periodicals, all
devoted, apart from a small number of works
on general subjects, to two major areas of
interest: cryptography and the Bacon-
Shakespeare controversy. The former
includes two copies of the first edition of
Trithemius' *Polygraphia* (1518), plus five
editions of the *Steganographia*. The volumes
of the Bacon-Shakespeare controversy
consist of the original collection of John
Dane of Boston together with Col Fabyan's
additions. No less than 33 of the 69 distinct
editions of Bacon printed before 1640 (as
listed in the STC) are found in the
collection.

IL —UNIVERSITY OF ILLINOIS,
URBANA/CHAMPAIGN, Library, Rare
Book Room, 346 Library, Urbana, 61801.
Norman B Brown, Asst Dir for Special
Collections; N Frederick Nash, Librn
Holdings: Cat Mss Maps Pix Slides
Microforms
Notes: Incl Baldwin, Ingold, and Motley
collections in the Rare Book Room.
Collection described in: *Catalog of the Rare
Book Room*, (Boston: G K Hall, 1972).
Supplement (1978).

IN —INDIANA UNIVERSITY, Lilly Library,
Seventh St, Bloomington, 47405. William R
Cagle, Librn
Holdings: // Mss Pix
Notes: An extensive collection of early
editions of Shakespeare, incl all four Folios.
Photographs, etc, of actors and actresses are
located in 3 ms collections: (1) Johnson,
William Spencer, 1813-1897, printer.
Correspondence and photographs from
actors and actresses, 1846-1894. 129 items;
(2) Stock, Keith Lievesley, 1911- , professor.
Autographs, etc, of people associated with
19th-early 20th century theatre in England.
279 items; and (3) Woodward, Sidney C,
journalist. Correspondence, autographs, and
pictures, 1769-1961, of actors, actresses, and
other theatre people, mostly American and
British. 1235 items. Also, in Printed Books
Division: small pictures (largely engravings
excerpted from books) of Shakespearean
actors and actresses, 18th into 20th century.

KS —SAINT MARY COLLEGE, Library,
Leavenworth, 66048. Therese Deplazes,
Special Collections Librn
Holdings: Vols 675 Cat Pix Tapes Slides
Notes: Incl facsimile of first folio of 1623;
the earliest printing of single work of
Shakespeare, *Coriolanus*, 1734; complete set,
Shakespeare, edited by Samuel Johnson,
George Stevens and F Malone, 1792;
scrapbooks, theatre programs, prints,
memorabilia.

MA —HARVARD UNIVERSITY LIBRARY,
Widener Library, Cambridge, 02138.
Holdings: Cat
Notes: See *Harvard Library Notes*, I (1923),
258-267, and *Wilson Library Bulletin*,
XXXVIII (1963/64), 640-644.

MA —GORDON COLLEGE, Winn Library,
Vining Collection, 255 Grapevine Rd,
Wenham, 01984. John Beauregard, Dir
Holdings: Vols 200 Cat
Notes: The Vining Collection (of rare
books). Incl 2d and 4th folio editions.

MI —UNIVERSITY OF MICHIGAN, Library,
Dept of Rare Books & Special Collections,
Ann Arbor, 48109. Robert J Starring, Head
Holdings: Vols 9383 Cat Mss
Notes: Incl 2nd, 3rd, and 4th folios; rare
17th and 18th century editions and
adaptations of the individual plays;
promptbooks; and Shakespeareana. Almost
half of the collection is made up of the most
important editions of Shakespeare's collected
works published from 1632 to the present.
Collected works are not cataloged.

MN —UNIVERSITY OF MINNESOTA, O
Meredith Wilson Library, 309 19 Ave S,

Minneapolis, 55455. Austin J McLean,
Chief, Special Collections
Notes: Extensive Mss collection incl
numerous plays in varying states of
completion never published and a
voluminous amount of material on
Shakespeare, also unpublished, as well as
correspondence from 20th-century American
and English writers.

NH —DARTMOUTH COLLEGE, Baker
Memorial Library, Hanover, 03755.
Holdings: Uncat
Notes: Allerton C Hickmott collection of
four folios, nearly 40 quartos, almost all of
the adaptations published during the
Restoration; and Shakespeare source books
and early allusions to him. Described in *This
Ivory Pale*. Noncirculating.

NJ —PRINCETON UNIVERSITY, Library,
Manuscript Collection, Nassau St, Princeton,
08540. Jean F Preston, Cur
Holdings: Vols 1615 Cat Mss Pix
Notes: The book collection incl items from
the Shakespeare and Company lending
library in Paris. The mss are housed in about
300 ms boxes. See *Princeton University
Library Chronicle*, v 26, p 7-12. An
unpublished guide (55 p) is available for
consultation. Also incl 11 quartos from the
David and Donald Maggin gift.

NY —NEW YORK PUBLIC LIBRARY,
Performing Arts Research Center, Billy Rose
Theatre Collection, 111 Amsterdam Ave,
New York, 10023. Dorothy L Swerdlove,
Cur
Holdings: Cat
See also entry under Theatre - History.

NY —NEW YORK PUBLIC LIBRARY,
Research Libraries, General Research
Division, Fifth Ave & 42 St, New York,
10018. Rodney Phillips, Chief
Holdings: Vols (2,225,000) Cat Maps Pix
Microforms
Budget: ($775,718)

NY —NEW YORK PUBLIC LIBRARY, Rare
Books and Manuscripts Div, Fifth Ave & 42
St, New York, 10018. William L Joyce, Asst
Dir; Francis O Mattson, Curator
Holdings: Cat
Budget: ($7161)
Notes: Literary first editions. Incl notable
collections of Shakespeare, Milton, Walton,
Bunyan and Whitman (The Oscar Lion
Collection).

NY —STATE UNIVERSITY OF NEW
YORK, COLLEGE AT OSWEGO, Penfield
Library, Oswego, 13126. Anne Commerton,
Dir
Holdings: Vols 1200 Cat

NC —UNIVERSITY OF NORTH
CAROLINA, CHAPEL HILL, Wilson
Library, Rare Book Collection, Chapel Hill,
27514. Paul S Koda, Cur of Rare Books
Holdings: Vols 300 // Cat
Notes: The Tannenbaum Collection of
Shakespeare contains works by and about
Shakespeare collected by one of the great
Shakespeare scholars. Adjunct to the
holdings are the second, third, and fourth
folios donated by William A Whitaker.

NC —SAINT MARY'S COLLEGE, Sarah
Graham Kenan Library, 900 Hillsborough St,
Raleigh, 27611.

OH —CLEVELAND PUBLIC LIBRARY,
Literature Dept, 325 Superior Ave,
Cleveland, 44114. Evelyn Ward, Head
Holdings: Cat Phonorecords
Notes: A well-rounded and comprehensive
collection covering all phases of the subject.
Contains an extensive body of biographical
and critical studies, works on productions
and stage history, pictorial works,
periodicals, yearbooks, and reference tools.
A wide variety of texts incl excellent
specimens of the work of early editors,
facsimiles of quarto and folio editions,
facsimiles of promptbooks, and fine
contemporary editions. There is also
considerable strength in the wider field of
Elizabethan drama and theatre, and the book
material is supplemented by a substantial
collection of theatre programs, reviews and
recordings.

PA —HAVERFORD COLLEGE, Magill
Library, Quaker Collection, Haverford,
19041. Edwin B Bonner, Librn & Cur
Holdings: Vols 105 Cat
Notes: Rare books and mss of the English

SHAKESPEARE, WILLIAM, AND SHAKESPEARIANA (cont.)

Renaissance period, especially contemporaries of Shakespeare.

PA —FREE LIBRARY OF PHILADELPHIA, Rare Book Dept, Logan Sq, Philadelphia, 19103. Marie E Korey, Rare Book Librn
Holdings: // Cat
Notes: Incl the Joseph E Widener gift of the Four Folios of Shakespeare. No photocopying.

PA —UNIVERSITY OF PENNSYLVANIA, Furness Memorial Library, 3420 Walnut St, Philadelphia, 19104. Georgianna Ziegler, Cur
Holdings: Vols (18,000) Cat Mss Pix Microforms
Notes: A scholar's working library. Contains material by or about Shakespeare, and other Elizabethan dramatists. Incl many of the works that served as Shakespeare's sources, and extensive material on the history of the English and American stage. Also a large collection of dissertations on Shakespeare. See Downs 534-5.

RI —BROWN UNIVERSITY, John Hay Library, 20 Prospect St, Providence, 02912. Mark N Brown, Cur Mss
Holdings: Vols (300) // Cat
Notes: Brown-Ives Shakespeare Collection of 18th and early 19th century Shakespeare scholarship incl: biographies; critical works; editions of the plays in English, French, and German; works on sources and characters; and the forgeries of John Payne Collier and William Henry Ireland. The collection is supplemented by the general rare books collection, incl first, second, and fourth folio editions of the comedies, histories and tragedies.

TX —UNIVERSITY OF TEXAS LIBRARIES, General Libraries, PO Box P, Austin, 78713. Carolyn Bucknell, Asst Dir for Collection Development
Holdings: Cat Microforms

†TX —UNIVERSITY OF TEXAS LIBRARIES, Hoblitzelle Theatre Arts Library, Austin, 78712.
Notes: Memorabilia of B Iden Payne, internationally known Shakespearean director.

†VA —GEORGE C MARSHALL RESEARCH FOUNDATION AND LIBRARY, Drawer 920, Lexington, 24450. Royster Lyle Jr, Cur Collections
Holdings: Vols Uncat Mss
Notes: Items on secret writing and signaling, radar, telephony and telegraphy, and the study of the Shakespeare-Bacon authorship controversy.

WI —BELOIT COLLEGE LIBRARIES, Beloit, 53511. Dennis W Dickinson, Dir
Holdings: Cat
Notes: The Montagu Modder Shakespeare Collection of several thousand vols was set up as a memorial to a former English faculty member.

WI —MILWAUKEE PUBLIC LIBRARY, 814 W Wisconsin Ave, Milwaukee, 53233. Donald J Sager, City Librn
Holdings: Vols (2700) Cat
Notes: Incl most of the significant editions of Shakespeare starting with Rowe.

WI —UNIVERSITY OF WISCONSIN, MILWAUKEE, Library, Box 604, Milwaukee, 53201. William C Roselle, Dir
Holdings: Vols (68,000) Cat Mss Phonorecords Audiotapes
Notes: Special strenghts of the literature collection include Shakespeare Research Collection (1800 volumes), 17th Century Collection (600 volumes), William Blake, James Joyce, Howard Fast (English-language editions and unique collection of foreign-language translations), contemporary small press poetry publications, etc.

BC —LEGISLATIVE LIBRARY (PROVINCIAL), Parliament Bldgs, Victoria, V8V 1X4, Can. J H MacEachern, Head, Government Documents Division
Holdings: // Cat

ON —UNIVERSITY OF TORONTO, Thomas Fisher Rare Book Library, 120 Saint George St, Toronto, M5S 1A5, Can. Richard G Landon, Head
Holdings: Vols (3000) Uncat Mss
Notes: Fisher Collection named after donor, Sidney Fisher. Contains the first four folios of Shakespeare and most significant collected works edited during the 18th and 19th centuries. Some early editions of works believed to have been sources for Shakespeare's plays. Biographical and critical works. Works on English topography and antiquities, with special emphasis on London. Manuscript of account of Richard III, originally written by Sir George Buck in 1620, and copied by his great-nephew sometime later in the century.

SHAMBERG, B. D.

CA —UNIVERSITY OF CALIFORNIA, LOS ANGELES, Theater Arts Library, Los Angeles, 90024. Edward Shreeves, Chairman, Bibliographers Group; Audree Malkin, Head, Theater Arts Library
Notes: B D Shamberg (agent) Collection: corporation and client correspondence, contracts, agreements, and portraits. Incl are clients such as Burt Reynolds, Stella and Luther Adler, and Dennis Day.

SHAN LANGUAGE

NY —NEW YORK PUBLIC LIBRARY, Oriental Div, Fifth Ave & 42 St, New York, 10018. E Christian Filstrup, Chief
Holdings: // Cat Mss Microforms
Budget: ($56,455)
Notes: Published catalog of holdings. Currently collected in Western language materials only.

SHANKS, GRAHAM LAWSON, 1889-1977

MB —UNIVERSITY OF MANITOBA, Elizabeth Dafoe Library, Archives and Special Collections Dept, Winnipeg, R3T 2N2, Can. Richard E Bennett, Dept Head; Corrado A Santoro, Reference Archivist
Notes: Daily desk diaries of G L Shanks, Head of the Department of Agricultural Engineering at the University of Manitoba, 1921-1955.

SHANNON, FRED

IL —UNIVERSITY OF ILLINOIS, URBANA/CHAMPAIGN, Library, University Archives, 19 Library, 1408 W Gregory Drive, Urbana, 61801. Maynard Brichford, University Archivist
Holdings: Cat Mss Maps Pix Slides Microforms
Notes: Papers, archival records, etc.

SHANNON, RICHARD

ME —COLBY COLLEGE, Miller Library, Colby Archives, Waterville, 04901.
Holdings: Mss
Notes: Family papers or other correspondence.

SHAPIRO, KARL

MO —WASHINGTON UNIVERSITY, Libraries, Special Collections Dept, Campus Box 1061, St Louis, 63130.
Notes: A small but significant collection.

NV —UNIVERSITY OF NEVADA, RENO, University Library, Special Collections Dept, Reno, 89557. Robert E Blesse, Head
Holdings: Vols (29) Cat Other appearances 545 Cat
Notes: Includes individual works by author in all editions including translations; also prefaces, introductions, published correspondence, appearances in anthologies, periodicals, etc. Bibliographical research collection, part of Modern Authors Collection.

SHAPIRO, VICTOR MANSFIELD

CA —UNIVERSITY OF CALIFORNIA, LOS ANGELES, Research Library, Dept of Special Collections, 405 Hilgard Ave, Los Angeles, 90024. Edward Shreeves, Chairman, Bibliographers Group; David S Zeidberg, Head
Holdings: Mss Pix
Notes: 4 linear feet of public relations and promotional materials relating to the moving picture industry.

SHAPLEIGH, FREDERICK ELISHA, 1884-1968

NY —CORNELL UNIVERSITY LIBRARIES, Collection of Regional History, Dept of Manuscripts and Univ Archives, Ithaca, 14853.
Notes: Rural sociologist, educational researcher, editor. Incl papers, 1908-20; surveys, many with maps, charts and photos; ms editorials, clippings, copies of Shapleigh's articles and other items. Unpublished guide available.

SHAPLEY, HARLOW

IA —HERBERT HOOVER PRESIDENTIAL LIBRARY, West Branch, 52358. Dale C Mayer, Archivist
Notes: Papers.

MA —HARVARD UNIVERSITY LIBRARY, Cambridge, 02138.
Holdings: Cat Mss
Notes: Mss, correspondence, notebooks, diaries, etc from 1905 to date.

NY —AMERICAN INSTITUTE OF PHYSICS, Center for the History of Physics, Niels Bohr Library, 335 E 45 St, New York, 10017. John Aubry, Librn
Notes: The Sources for History of Modern Astrophysics documents the history of 20th-century astrophysics. Incl some 400 hours of oral history interviews with astronomers, such as Bart Bok, S Chandrasekhar, Martin Schwarzschild, and A E Whitford. The project also organized and cataloged the papers of Henry Norris Russell, Frank Schlesinger, Otto Struve, Ejnar Hertzsprung, Harlow Shapley, Charles Young, Robert Atkinson, Seth Chandler, Theodore Dunham, Jr, and G C McVittie.

SHAPOVAL ARCHIVE

NY —NEW YORK PUBLIC LIBRARY, Slavonic Div, Fifth Ave & 42 St, New York, 10018. Edward Kasinec, Chief
Holdings: Vols 180 // Cat Mss
Notes: The Ukrainian archive of Mykyta Shapoval consists mainly of the correspondence of General Mykola Shapoval (Army of the Ukrainian National Republic, 1917-1920) and of his family. Documents, mss, diaries relating to the activities and events of Ukrainians in Czechoslovakia and France are included. The material covers the period of the 1920s through 1950s.

SHARON, CONNECTICUT

CT —LEE ASH, (personal collection), 66 Humiston Dr, Bethany, 06525.
Holdings: Cat Mss Maps Pix Slides Microforms
Notes: Especially history, biography, bibliography (and citations), illus material, association items, ephemera, etc.

SHARP, WALTER BENONA AND ESTELLE BOUGHTON

TX —RICE UNIVERSITY, Fondren Library, Woodson Research Center, 6100 S Main St, PO Box 1892, Houston, 77251. Nancy Parker, Dir Woodson Research Center
Notes: The papers of Walter Benona Sharp and Estelle Boughton Sharp. His papers consist of letters written to his wife and family from 1890 to 1912 as well as papers relating to his involvement in the oil business. Her papers cover a variety of topics, incl United Charities, the peace movement, Rice University, her business and financial affairs, and her efforts to record the history of the oil industry in the Southwest.

SHARP, WILLIAM

ON —UNIVERSITY OF TORONTO, Thomas Fisher Rare Book Library, 120 Saint George

SHARP, WILLIAM (cont.)

St, Toronto, M5S 1A5, Can. Richard G
Landon, Head
Holdings: Vols 5400 Cat Mss
Notes: Three collections. Duncan Collection
is named for donor, Douglas Duncan, art
dealer and collector,, Toronto. Contains first
and subsequent important editions of
Richard Aldington, Max Beerbohm, Norman
Douglas, Aldoux Huxley, and D H
Lawrence. Manuscripts by Beerbohm,
Aldington, Lawrence, William Sharp.
Endicott Collection named in honor of
Norman J Endicott, Professor of English,
University of Toronto, contains first and
significant later editions of over fifty British
writers whose major work falls into the
period from 1880 to 1930. Fisher Collection
named for donor, Charles B Fisher, contains
first and significant editions of Kipling,
Norman Douglas, and Lord Dunsany.

SHARPLES, JAMES

PA —FRIENDS HISTORICAL LIBRARY OF
SWARTHMORE COLLEGE, Swarthmore,
19081. J William Frost, Dir
Holdings: Vols (35,000) Cat Mss Pix Slides
Films Microforms
Notes: Library has an extensive collection of
pictures, largely photographs, of individual
Quakers and Quaker groups, meeting houses,
and other buildings such as residences,
schools, colleges, and institutions. In
addition to photographs, the library has
prints, silhouettes, drawings, and a few
paintings. Highlighting the library's art
works are drawings by Benjamin West, and
paintings by West, Edward Hicks, James
Sharples, and Howard Pyle.

SHAW, ALBERT

NY —NEW YORK PUBLIC LIBRARY, Rare
Books and Manuscripts Div, Fifth Ave & 42
St, New York, 10018. William L Joyce, Asst
Dir; Susan E Davis, Cur of Mss
Holdings: Mss
Budget: ($7161)
Notes: Incl personal and literary mss, papers,
etc.

SHAW, GEORGE BERNARD, 1856-1950

CA —CALIFORNIA STATE UNIVERSITY,
FULLERTON, Library, Box 4150,
Fullerton, 92634. Linda Herman, Special
Collections Librn
Holdings: Vols 500 Mss
Notes: Writings by and about with mss
materials by G B Shaw.
CA —UNIVERSITY OF CALIFORNIA, LOS
ANGELES, Research Library, Dept of
Special Collections, 405 Hilgard Ave, Los
Angeles, 90024. Edward Shreeves,
Chairman, Bibliographers Group; David S
Zeidberg, Head
Holdings: Vols 250 Mss
Notes: Incl 1.5 linear feet of mss,
correspondence, ephemera, and art objects
by or relating to him.
CT —YALE UNIVERSITY, Box 1603A, Yale
Station, New Haven, 06520.
Notes: Incl ms and clipping file.
DE —UNIVERSITY OF DELAWARE, Hugh
M Morris Library, S College Ave, Newark,
19711. T Stuart Dick, Special Collections
Holdings: Cat Mss
Notes: First English, American and variant
editions.
MA —BOSTON UNIVERSITY, Mugar
Memorial Library, Special Collections Dept,
771 Commonwealth Ave, Boston, 02215.
Howard B Gotlieb, Dir
Holdings: Cat Mss Pix
Notes: Correspondence collected in depth;
incl publications by.
MA —HARVARD UNIVERSITY LIBRARY,
Houghton Library, Cambridge, 02138.
Rodney G Dennis, Cur of Manuscripts
Holdings: Mss
NY —HOFSTRA UNIVERSITY, Library,
1000 Fulton Ave, Hempstead, 11550.
Charles R Andrews, Dean of Library

Services
Notes: Strong collection. Incl some mss.
NY —CORNELL UNIVERSITY LIBRARIES,
John M Olin Library, Dept of Rare Books,
Ithaca, 14853. Donald D Eddy, Librn
Holdings: Vols 2641 Cat Mss
Notes: The Bernard F Burgunder Collection
incl materials by and about Shaw. Downs
2119.
NC —UNIVERSITY OF NORTH
CAROLINA, CHAPEL HILL, Wilson
Library, Rare Book Collection, Chapel Hill,
27514. Paul S Koda, Cur of Rare Books
Holdings: Vols 4000 Cat Pix
Notes: The George Bernard Shaw Collection
from the Library of Archibald Henderson
contains almost 4000 books and pamphlets
and 1000 playbills, programs, cartoons, and
pictures of play productions written by or
relating to George Bernard Shaw. It also incl
first and many later editions of the plays,
novels, and essays. There are also rough
proofs and rehearsal copies of plays, foreign
language translations, biographical and
critical material. Over 100 scrapbooks of
clippings from newspapers and periodicals
are included.
PA —BUCKNELL UNIVERSITY, Ellen
Clarke Bertrand Library, Lewisburg, 17837.
Ann de Klerk, Librn
Holdings: Vols 500 Cat Mss Pix
Notes: The William D Chase Collection of
Shawiana.
BC —UNIVERSITY OF VICTORIA,
McPherson Library, Victoria, V8W 3H5,
Can.
Notes: Mss: "An Explanation" - preface to
Shaw's edition of the Shaw-Ellen Terry
correspondence; "Motives of Socialism";
correspondence: with Elbridge Adams, H
Bland, William Archer, William J Pickerell,
Harold Laski; marked proofs: "Shaw Speaks
on War"; ephemera; 2 letters from Janet A
Church to H Bland.
ON —UNIVERSITY OF GUELPH, Library,
Guelph, N1G 2W1, Can. Margaret
Beckman, Chief Librn; Ellen Pearson, Ref
Librn
Holdings: Vols 600 Cat Phonorecords
Audiotapes Videotapes 16mm Films
Microforms
ON —QUEEN'S UNIVERSITY, Douglas
Library, Kingston, K7L 5C4, Can. William F
E Morley, Cur, Special Collections
Holdings: Vols (2850) Cat
Notes: Collection incl all the original
volumes in the Cuala Press series and a
facsimile reprint of each plus about 170
other works by and about W B Yeats, 200 by
and about James Joyce, 240 by and about G
B Shaw.

SHAW, HENRY

MO —MISSOURI BOTANICAL GARDEN
LIBRARY, PO Box 299, Saint Louis, 63166.
M R Crosby, Dir of Research
Holdings: Uncat Mss Maps Pix
Notes: Papers of Henry Shaw relating to St
Louis business and economic history and
founding of the Missouri Botanical Garden.
About 40 vols and 60 boxes of files
containing 40,000 ms pieces.

SHAW, IRWIN

MA —BOSTON UNIVERSITY, Mugar
Memorial Library, Special Collections Dept,
771 Commonwealth Ave, Boston, 02215.
Howard B Gotlieb, Dir
Holdings: Cat Mss Pix
Notes: Mss, correspondence, etc collected in
depth; incl publications by or about.

SHAW, NINEVEH

IL —ILLINOIS STATE HISTORICAL
SOCIETY, Library, Old State Capitol,
Springfield, 62706. Roger D Bridges, Head
Librn
Notes: His papers, 80 items, 1822-1858.
Black Hawk War soldier.

SHAW FAMILY

†MA —UNIVERSITY OF
MASSACHUSETTS AT AMHERST,

Library, Amherst, 01003.
Notes: Microform collections of materials in
other American libraries.

SHAW FESTIVAL THEATRE

†ON —METROPOLITAN TORONTO
LIBRARY, Theatre Collections, 789 Yonge
St, Toronto, M4W 2G8, Can.
Notes: Full photographic records of the
Shaw Festival Theatre, Niagara-on-the-Lake.
Photographs taken at every stage of the
work, 1972-73, by William C Helwig.

SHAW FESTIVAL THEATRE FOUNDATION, ONTARIO

ON —UNIVERSITY OF GUELPH, Library,
Guelph, N1G 2W1, Can. Margaret
Beckman, Chief Librn; Ellen Pearson, Ref
Librn
Notes: 100 boxes of archival material, also
pix, props, models, costumes, prompt books.
Archives of the Shaw Festival Theatre
Foundation, Niagara-on-the-Lake, Ontario.

SHAWN, TED, 1891-1972

NY —NEW YORK PUBLIC LIBRARY,
Performing Arts Research Center, Dance
Collection, 111 Amsterdam Ave, New York,
10023. Genevieve Oswald, Cur
Notes: Comprehensive collection of
biographical and visual materials, much of it
also relating to Ruth St Denis, the
Denishawn Dancers, and the Jacob's Pillow
Dance Festival. Includes 8000 photographs,
15,000 clippings and programs, 100
scrapbooks, 76 motion picture films, 50 tape-
recorded interviews or commentaries, and
about 4000 manuscripts and letters. The Ted
Shawn Collection, 1920-72, comprises 28
drawers of holographs, typescripts, business
records, and correspondence.

SHAY, EPHRAIM

MI —UNIVERSITY OF MICHIGAN,
Engineering-Transportation Library, 312
Undergraduate Library, Ann Arbor, 48109.
Sharon A Balius, Assoc Librn
Holdings: Pix
Notes: This collection consists of 80
photographs of the Shay locomotive, patent
information, sales catalogs and other related
materials.

SHAYON, ROBERT LEWIS

MA —BOSTON UNIVERSITY, Mugar
Memorial Library, Special Collections Dept,
771 Commonwealth Ave, Boston, 02215.
Howard B Gotlieb, Dir
Holdings: Cat Mss Pix
Notes: Mss, correspondence, etc collected in
depth; incl publications by or about.

SHAYS' REBELLION, 1786-1787

MA —JONES LIBRARY, 43 Amity St,
Amherst, 01002. Daniel J Lombardo, Cur of
Special Collections
Holdings: Cat Mss Maps Pix
Notes: Unpublished guide available.
MA —CONCORD FREE PUBLIC LIBRARY,
129 Main St, Concord, 01742. Rose Marie
Mitten, Dir
Holdings: Cat Mss
Notes: Rev Grindall Reynolds, a 19th
century minister in Concord, Massachusetts,
wrote a retrospective 5 vol ms about Shays'
Rebellion, which is incl. In his research, he
collected depositions from various
individuals and towns about the events at
the Concord courthouse and about persons
participating. Also Daniel Wood's (1760-
1843) February 1787 list of men and
payments of Capt Roger Brown's Company
in this rebellion from Concord,
Massachusetts.
MA —PETERSHAM HISTORICAL
SOCIETY, Library, N Main St, Petersham,
01366. Delight G Haines, Librn
Holdings: Vols (900) Cat Mss Maps Pix
Notes: The Petersham area. Genealogical

SHAYS' REBELLION, 1786-1787 (cont.)

files on Petersham families. Incl Daniel
Sharp Rebellion.

SHEA, JOHN GILMARY, 1824-1892

DC —GEORGETOWN UNIVERSITY,
Library, Special Collections Div, 37 & O Sts
NW, Washington, 20057. George M
Barringer, Special Collections Librn;
Nicholas B Sheetz, Mss Librn
Holdings: Cat
Notes: Papers of John Gilmary Shea (1824-
1892), noted Catholic historian and linguist
of Indian languages who published over two
hundred titles during his lifetime. The papers
incl correspondence to Shea, manuscripts
and notes reflecting his research, collected
documents and manuscripts, and various
photographs. Correspondence written to
Shea incl letters from George Bancroft,
Francis Parkman, Jared Sparks, Harriet
Beecher Stowe, E B O'Callahan, Hanry
Schoolcraft, Charles White, D D, Charles
Currier, P T Barnum, Frederick Douglass,
Thomas A Edison, Oliver Wendell Holmes,
as well as noted members of the Church
hierarchy. A long span of correspondence
from Shea to the historian, Edmund Mallet
contains many insights into Shea's life and
work. Photographs incl likenesses of
Elizabeth Seton, Isaac Hecker and George
Bancroft. Also incl in the papers are
numerous documents andmss concerning
Shea's work in the field of Native American
history, language, and culture.

SHEDD, MARGARET

MA —BOSTON UNIVERSITY, Mugar
Memorial Library, Special Collections Dept,
771 Commonwealth Ave, Boston, 02215.
Howard B Gotlieb, Dir
Holdings: Cat Mss
Notes: Mss, correspondence, etc collected in
depth; incl publications by or about.

SHEED, WILFRID

MA —BOSTON UNIVERSITY, Mugar
Memorial Library, Special Collections Dept,
771 Commonwealth Ave, Boston, 02215.
Howard B Gotlieb, Dir
Holdings: Cat Mss
Notes: Mss, correspondence, etc collected in
depth; incl publications by or about.

SHE' ELOTH U-TESHUVOTH see
Responsa

SHEEN, ABP. FULTON JOHN

NY —SAINT BERNARD'S INSTITUTE,
Library, 1100 S Goodman st, Rochester,
14620. Sebastian A Falcone, Dir
Holdings: Mss
Notes: Sheeniana, incl his books, papers,
sermons, etc.

SHEEP, MERINO see Merino Sheep

SHEEP RANCHING

AZ —NORTHERN ARIZONA
UNIVERSITY, Special Collection Library,
CU Box 6022, Flagstaff, 86011. Peter M
Whiteley, Coordr/Archivist; William
Mullane, Librn
Notes: Account journal, 1916-1934, Ariz, of
the White River Sheep Company. This
company appears to have been connected
with T E Pollock, Flagstaff, Ariz.
TX —AMARILLO PUBLIC LIBRARY, 413 E
Fourth, Amarillo, 79101. Mary Kay Snell,
Librn
Holdings: Vols 1210 Cat Maps Filmstrips VF
Notes: The Meat Industry Collection
contains documents, periodicals, pamphlets,
AV materials on the production and
processing and marketing of cattle, swine,
sheep, poultry and rabbits. Most of the
collection circulates except for the
magazines.
UT —UNIVERSITY OF UTAH, Marriott
Library, Special Collections, Salt Lake City,
84112. Gregory C Thompson, Cur

SHEET MUSIC see Music
Scores—Collections

SHEFFIELD, JAMES ROCKWELL

CT —YALE UNIVERSITY, Sterling Memorial
Library, Latin American Collections, New
Haven, 06520. Lee H Williams Jr, Cur
Holdings: Vols (300,000) Cat Maps Pix
Slides Phonorecords 16mm Films Filmstrips
See also entry under Latin America

SHELDON, CHARLES M.

KS —TOPEKA PUBLIC LIBRARY, Special
Collections & Local History Dept, 1515 W
Tenth, Topeka, 66604. Warren Taylor, Librn
Notes: Rex Stout materials; Charles M
Sheldon materials; materials published in
Topeka.

SHELDON, EDWARD AUSTIN

MA —HARVARD UNIVERSITY LIBRARY,
Theatre Collection, Cambridge, 02138.
Jeanne T Newlin, Cur
Notes: One of the largest existing collections
of playbills, programs, prints, photographs,
promptbooks, and other materials relating
to the performing arts, the scope is worldwide;
resources on the English-speaking stage of
the 18th and 19th centuries are unequalled.
Incl materials on ballet and modern dance,
the circus, magic, minstrel shows, cinema,
and pantomime. For description, see
Harvard Library Bulletin, VI (1925): pp 281-
301. Also, papers of Robert E Sherwood
(1896-1955), John Mason Bowers, George
Pierce Baker, Edward Sheldon, Percy
Mackaye; Angus McBean collection of
photographs of the London Stage, 1937-
1965; Alix Jeffry collection of photographs
of the Off-Broadway Theatre; and others.
NY —STATE UNIVERSITY OF NEW
YORK, COLLEGE AT OSWEGO, Penfield
Library, Oswego, 13126. Anne Commerton,
Dir
Holdings: Cat Mss Pix
Notes: Sheldon was an educator and first
president of the Oswego College. Incl about
100 letters. 2 ft. Unpublished guide.

SHELLEY, MARY GODWIN

NC —DUKE UNIVERSITY, William R
Perkins Library, Durham, 27706. Elvin E
Strowd, University Librn
Notes: The Shelley-Goodwin Collection of
Lord Abinger is a microfilm copy of the
Shelley and Godwin collection. Lord
Abinger's entire manuscript collection,
representing the last portion of the papers of
Sir Percy Florence Shelley which is still in
private hands, has been reproduced on 16
reels of film. The Bodleian Library is the
only other location for this film.

SHELLEY, PERCY BYSSHE, 1792-1822

CA —CLAREMONT COLLEGES, Honnold
Library, Ninth & Dartmouth, Claremont,
91711. Tania Rizzo, Special Collections
Dept Head
Holdings: Vols 200 //
Notes: The William W Clary Collection.
First, limited, and special editions of books,
pamphlets, offprints by or about him.
CA —UNIVERSITY OF CALIFORNIA, LOS
ANGELES, William Andrews Clark
Memorial Library, 2520 Cimarron St, Los
Angeles, 90018.
Holdings: Cat
Notes: Small collection, original editions,
etc.
CA —STANFORD UNIVERSITY
LIBRARIES, Cecil H Green Library,
Stanford, 94305. Michael T Ryan, Cur
Holdings: Vols (23,000) Cat
Notes: The Charlotte Ashley Felton
Memorial Library. Incl first editions.
MD —JOHNS HOPKINS UNIVERSITY,
Milton S Eisenhower Library, Charles & 34
Sts, Baltimore, 21218. Ann S Gwyn,
Assistant Dir for Special Collections
Holdings: Vols Cat Mss Microforms
Notes: The Osler Collection (Tudor and

Stuart Club) contains original editions of
Shelley, Milton, Keats, Donne, Defoe,
Thomas Fuller, Golden Book of Marcus
Aurelius (1559). A collection of his articles
made by Walt Whitman. 17th and 18th
century commonplace books in English and
French, in ms. Most English translations of
Jakob Boehme. Cards in main catalog. Also,
not included in the above figure, Pollard and
Redgrave's and Wing's Early English Books
on microfilm.
MA —HARVARD UNIVERSITY LIBRARY,
Houghton Library, Cambridge, 02138.
Rodney G Dennis, Cur of Manuscripts
Holdings: Mss
NY —CARL H PFORZHEIMER LIBRARY,
41 E 42 St, New York, 10017. Mihai H
Handrea, Librn
Holdings: Cat Mss Pix
Notes: English Literature from Caxton to
1700; first editions of 18th and 19th
centuries, incl mss material on Shelley and
his circle; fine presses (Bruce Rogers);
George Gissing; women writers 1790-1840,
(Mary Wollstonecraft, Mary Hays, Lady
Blessington).
NC —DUKE UNIVERSITY, William R
Perkins Library, Durham, 27706. Elvin E
Strowd, University Librn
Notes: The Shelley-Goodwin Collection of
Lord Abinger is a microfilm copy of the
Shelley and Godwin collection. Lord
Abinger's entire manuscript collection,
representing the last portion of the papers of
Sir Percy Florence Shelley which is still in
private hands, has been reproduced on 16
reels of film. The Bodleian Library is the
only other location for this film.

SHELLS

CT —LEE ASH, (personal collection), 66
Humiston Dr, Bethany, 06525.
FL —ROLLINS COLLEGE, Mills Memorial
Library, Winter Park, 32789. Patricia J
Delks, Dir of Libraries
Notes: Special shell museum collection.
Restricted use.
NY —AMERICAN MUSEUM OF
NATURAL HISTORY, Library Services
Dept, Central Park W & 79th St, New York,
10024. Nina J Root, Chairwoman; Mary
Genett, Asst Librn for Reference Services
Notes: Shells of the world, with considerable
on European, Russian, and Asian
conchology.
PA —ACADEMY OF NATURAL SCIENCES
LIBRARY, 19 Benjamin Franklin Parkway,
Philadelphia, 19103.
Holdings: Vols (180,000) Cat Mss Maps Pix
Slides Microforms
Notes: Incl (250,000) mss. Described in
Academy of Natural Sciences of
Philadelphia: Catalog (Boston: G K Hall,
1972); Guide to the Manuscript Collections
in the Academy of Natural Sciences of
Philadelphia, by Venia T Phillips
(Philadelphia: Academy of Natural Sciences,
1963).

SHELTER BELTS see Windbreaks,
Shelterbelts, Etc.

SHENCK, CARL A.

NC —NORTH CAROLINA STATE
UNIVERSITY, Forest Resources Library,
4012 Biltmore Hall, Raleigh, 27650. Pamela
E Puryear, Head
Holdings: Vols (9000) Cat Microforms
Notes: Incl 24 file drawers of mss of Carl A
Shenck, prominent American forester and
founder of the Biltmore Forest School, the
first school of forestry in the Western
Hemisphere.

SHEPARD, EDWARD M.

NY —CITY UNIVERSITY OF NEW YORK,
City College, Morris R Cohen Library,
North Academic Center, Convent Ave &
137th St, New York, 10031. Barbara J
Dunlap, Archivist
Holdings: Cat Mss Pix
Notes: Incl personal papers.

SHEPARD, ODELL

DC —GEORGETOWN UNIVERSITY,
Library, Special Collections Div, 37 & O Sts
NW, Washington, 20057. George M
Barringer, Special Collections Librn;
Nicholas B Sheetz, Mss Librn
Holdings: Mss Cat
Notes: Correspondence between the author
and poet Sister Miriam Gallagher; and
numerous authors such as Theodore
Maynard, Robert Tristram Coffin, and John
Hall Wheelock, among others. Of particular
interest are long runs of correspondence
from H L Mencken (1937-1943, 64 TLS)
and Odell Shepard (1933-1945, 47 TLS and
ALS).

SHEPARD, SAM

MA —BOSTON UNIVERSITY, Mugar
Memorial Library, Special Collections Dept,
771 Commonwealth Ave, Boston, 02215.
Howard B Gotlieb, Dir
Holdings: Cat Mss Pix
Notes: Mss, correspondence, etc collected in
depth; incl publications by or about.

SHEPARD FAMILY

NY —STATE UNIVERSITY OF NEW
YORK, COLLEGE AT OSWEGO, Penfield
Library, Oswego, 13126. Anne Commerton,
Dir
Holdings: Cat Mss Pix
Notes: Correspondence, legal and business
records and writings of members of the
Sidney Shepard family, primarily reflecting
business and personal relations with the
family of Orasmus H Marshall, to which
Shepard family was related by marriage. The
papers cover the years 1838-1936. Incl
records of Sidney Shepard Co and catalog of
Shepard family library. Unpublished guide.

SHEPHERD, ARTHUR

OH —CASE WESTERN RESERVE
UNIVERSITY LIBRARIES, Cleveland,
44106. Susie Hanson, Special Collections
Librn
Holdings: Cat Mss Phonorecords Audiotapes
Notes: The collection, contained in three 4-
drawer vertical files, consists of ms, printed,
taped and recorded compositions by Arthur
Shepard, correspondence with other
personalities in the field of music, concert
programs, teaching materials used in his
classes, and other memorabilia. Application
for use should be made to the Reference
Department.
†UT —UNIVERSITY OF UTAH, Library, Salt
Lake City, 84112.
Notes: Collection transferred from Case
Western Reserve University.

SHEPHERD, SAM

CA —UNIVERSITY OF CALIFORNIA,
DAVIS, Shields Library, Dept of Special
Collections, Davis, 95616. Donald Kunitz,
Head; C Danial Elliott, Asst Head
Holdings: Vols Uncat Mss Pix
Notes: Business papers of off-Broadway
literary and theatrical agent, Toby Cole, for
the years 1957-73. Incl mss by Saul Bellow
and Sam Shepherd, among others. 4000 pix.

SHEPLEY PAPERS

ME —BOWDOIN COLLEGE, Library,
Brunswick, 04011. Dianne M Gutscher, Cur
of Special Collections
Notes: Besides a general collection of 13,000
volumes relating to the State of Maine, there
are also many ms collections touching on the
political, economic and social history of
Maine. These incl Shepley Papers; 1000
items, 1802-1940.

SHERER, LORRAINE MILLER

CA —UNIVERSITY OF CALIFORNIA, LOS
ANGELES, Research Library, Dept of
Special Collections, 405 Hilgard Ave, Los
Angeles, 90024. Edward Shreeves,
Chairman, Bibliographers Group; David S
Zeidberg, Head
Holdings: Mss Pix
Notes: 30 linear feet of mss, correspondence,
photographs, and other material collected by
and used in her research of Mojave Indian
history and culture.

SHERLOCK, JOHN

MA —BOSTON UNIVERSITY, Mugar
Memorial Library, Special Collections Dept,
771 Commonwealth Ave, Boston, 02215.
Howard B Gotlieb, Dir
Holdings: Cat Mss Pix
Notes: Mss, correspondence, etc collected in
depth; incl publications by or about.

SHERLOCK, WILLIAM

NY —UNIVERSITY OF ROCHESTER, Rush
Rhees Library, Department of Rare Books
and Special Collections, Rochester, 14627.
Peter Dzwonkoski, Librn
Holdings: Vols 226 Cat
Notes: A most unusual collection in size and
scope of material by and about William
Sherlock, Dean of St Paul's, 1691-1707. No
photocopying.

SHERMAN, JOHN

OH —RUTHERFORD B HAYES LIBRARY,
1337 Hayes Ave, Fremont, 43420. Watt P
Marchman, Dir
Notes: Correspondence in the Lyman-
Lincoln Collection.
OH —MANSFIELD-RICHLAND COUNTY
PUBLIC LIBRARY, 43 W Third St,
Mansfield, 44902. Jeffrey R Krull, Dir; Boyd
Addlesperger, Sherman Room Librn
Holdings: Vols 600 // Cat Mss
Notes: Personal library of Senator John
Sherman, incl US social and political history,
slavery and abolition, Civil War, and
Western exploration.

SHERMAN, WILLIAM TECUMSEH, 1820-1891

DC —GEORGETOWN UNIVERSITY,
Library, Special Collections Div, 37 & O Sts
NW, Washington, 20057. George M
Barringer, Special Collections Librn;
Nicholas B Sheetz, Mss Librn
Holdings: Mss Cat Pix
Notes: Correspondence, manuscripts, diaries,
documents, ledgers, scrapbooks,
photographs, and printed material
concerning the Ewing and Sherman families.
Incl are 10 ALS (1859-1891) from William
T Sherman to his daughter Minnie Sherman
Fitch and grand-daughter, Eleanor Sherman
Fitch; AMs, "Speech at West Point" (1887),
written and delivered by Sherman; material
from General Charles Ewing, incl leaves
from a letter book (1887-1881), diary (1862,
1864); letter written to Thomas Ewing
referring to the loss of government money in
the retreat from Pilot's Knob; and a Ewing
autograph book (1893-96). Also incl are
numerous genealogical documents and notes.
DC —LIBRARY OF CONGRESS, Manuscript
Division, Washington, 20540. John C
Broderick, Chief
Notes: Papers of General William Tecumseh
Sherman. Also, Civil War maps.
OH —RUTHERFORD B HAYES LIBRARY,
1337 Hayes Ave, Fremont, 43420. Watt P
Marchman, Dir
Notes: A collection of over 75 pieces of
correspondence, mostly outgoing, authored
by the famous Civil War general and
commander of the US Army. Index in
collections. Additional correspondence
available in Rutherford B Hayes Papers.

SHERWIN, SAMUEL B., 1917-

CA —HOOVER INSTITUTION ON WAR,
REVOLUTION & PEACE, Stanford
University, Stanford, 94305. Milorad M
Drachkovitch, Archivist
Holdings: Mss
Notes: Papers of Samuel B Sherwin, US
Deputy Assistant Secretary of Commerce for
Domestic Commerce, 1975-77, incl
transcripts of speeches and Congressional
testimony, studies, and reports, 1975-76,
relating to US commercial policy. 2 ms
boxes.

SHERWOOD, MARY MARTHA (BUTTS), 1775-1851

CA —UNIVERSITY OF CALIFORNIA, LOS
ANGELES, Research Library, Dept of
Special Collections, 405 Hilgard Ave, Los
Angeles, 90024. Edward Shreeves,
Chairman, Bibliographers Group; David S
Zeidberg, Head
Holdings: Vols 400
Notes: 400 first and other editions of her
books; 7 letters.

SHERWOOD, ROBERT EMMET, 1896-1955

MA —HARVARD UNIVERSITY LIBRARY,
Houghton Library, Cambridge, 02138. F
Thomas Noonan, Cur, Reading Room;
Lawrence Dowler, Associate Librn
Holdings: Mss
Notes: Papers of Robert Emmet Sherwood,
1896-1955. Complement materials in other
Harvard libraries.

SHEWRING, WALTER H.

DC —GEORGETOWN UNIVERSITY,
Library, Special Collections Div, 37 & O Sts
NW, Washington, 20057. George M
Barringer, Special Collections Librn;
Nicholas B Sheetz, Mss Librn
Notes: The papers of Walter H Shewring,
author, editor, and translator; containing
correspondence manuscripts.

SHIELDS, PETER J.

CA —UNIVERSITY OF CALIFORNIA,
DAVIS, Shields Library, Dept of Special
Collections, Davis, 95616. Donald Kunitz,
Head; C Danial Elliott, Asst Head
Holdings: Cat Mss Pix
Notes: The Shields Collection documents the
career of California Superior Court Judge
Peter J Shields of Sacramento, his 49 years
on the bench and his relationship with
prominent political figures. 1050 items.

SHIELS, ARCHIE W.

WA —WESTERN WASHINGTON
UNIVERSITY, Center for Pacific Northwest
Studies, High St, Bellingham, 98225. James
W Scott, Dir
Holdings: // Cat Mss Maps Pix
Notes: The Archie W Shiels Collection.
Archie W Shiels, who died in his 95th year
in 1974, was formerly Managing Dir of
Pacific American Fisheries and an author of
some note on Alaskan topics. A few papers
of his company are incl in the collection,
which is primarily focused on Alaska,
particularly its history and its seal and other
fisheries.
See also entry under Galen A Biery

SHIFRIN, SEYMOUR

CT —YALE UNIVERSITY, Music Library, 98
Wall St, New Haven, 06520. Harold E
Samuel, Librn
Notes: Personal papers and musical mss.
See also entry under Music, American.

SHIGA, NAOYA

FL —UNIVERSITY OF FLORIDA, Libraries,
Gainesville, 32611. Ray Jones, Research
Librn; Max Willocks, Librn
Holdings: Vols (2000)
Notes: An extensive collection of modern
and premodern Japanese prose fiction in
English translation and Japanese. Incl
complete works of a number of important
modern Japanese authors such as Yasunari
Kawabata, Naoya Shiga, Junichiro Tanizaki,
and Yukio Mishima.

SHILLABER, BENJAMIN

VA —UNIVERSITY OF VIRGINIA,
Alderman Library, Manuscripts Dept,
Charlottesville, 22901. Edmund Berkeley Jr,
Cur
Holdings: Cat Mss
Notes: First editions, mss, papers, etc.

SHILOH, BATTLE OF, 1862

TN —MEMPHIS PINK PALACE MUSEUM,
Library, 3050 Central Ave, Memphis, 38111.
Coralu D Buddenbahm, Librn
Holdings: Vols (3600) Cat Maps Pix Slides
Phonorecords Audiotapes Videotapes 16mm
Films Filmstrips
Budget: ($4000)
Notes: Museum specializes in the history
and culture of the Mid-South. A number of
books owned by The Shiloh Military Trail,
Inc are on loan to the Museum and are
available for reference.

SHINKARENKO, N. V.

CA —HOOVER INSTITUTION ON WAR,
REVOLUTION & PEACE, Stanford
University, Stanford, 94305. Milorad M
Drachkovitch, Archivist
Holdings: // Mss Pix
Notes: Memoirs, supplemented by letters
and photos, of Nikolai Vsevolodovich, who
used the pseudonym N Belogorskii. Memoirs
deal mainly with the Russian Revolution.

SHINN, EVERETT

DE —DELAWARE ART MUSEUM, Library,
2301 Kentmere Pkwy, Wilmington, 19806.
Anne Hoslam, Librn
Holdings: Vols (25,000) Cat Mss
Notes: The collection is rich in the following
subjects: Howard Pyle and his pupils; John
Sloan and the eight; history of the book and
printing; and English and American
illustrated books. There is also a section on
contemporary photography. Archival
material on Albert Mumford Lindsay,
Jerome Myers, Everett Shinn, Gayle Porter
Hoskins, Frank Schoonover.

SHIP CREW LISTS

MA —BEDFORD FREE PUBLIC LIBRARY,
613 Pleasant St, Bedford, 02740. Paul A
Cyr, Cur of the Melville Room
Holdings: Vols 1020 Cat Mss Pix
Notes: One of the nation's most extensive
collections (72,000 pieces) on American
whaling. Incl all forms of documents used in
the industry, over 40,000 mss. Library has a
printed list of its logbooks and a seamen's
card file of men who sailed from New
Bedford Customs District contains 250,000
names. Library has published an addendum
to "Starbuck" and "Whaling Masters," and
"Birth of a Whaleship," 1964, both by
Reginald B Hegarty.

SHIP MODELS

FL —MARTIN COUNTY PUBLIC
LIBRARY, 701 E Ocean Blvd, Stuart,
33494. LeRoy Hennings Jr, Dir
Holdings: Vols 173 Cat
Notes: Selim Walker McArthur collection on
sailing. The heart of the collection deals with
the building of sailing ship models and dates
from the 1920s. This material is unique.
MA —MASSACHUSETTS INSTITUTE OF
TECHNOLOGY MUSEUM, Hart Nautical
Collections, 77 Massachusetts Ave, Rm 5-
329, Cambridge, 02139. John W
Waterhouse, Cur
Holdings: Vols (800) Cat Maps Pix
Notes: Ship and marine engineering
development. Museum is under jurisdiction
of MIT's Dept of Ocean Engineering.
Collection incl various collections of prints
and photographs of ships and yachts;
working drawings from the Herreshoff
Manufacturing Co, 1870-1945, and of the
George Lawley and Son Corp; working
drawings and models from the Munro,
Owen, and Paine Collections.

RI —PROVIDENCE PUBLIC LIBRARY, 150
Empire St, Providence, 02903. Lance J
Bauer, Special Collections Librn
Holdings: Vols 225 // Uncat Pix
Notes: A fine collection of books, technical
drawings, photographs, pamphlets and other
ephemera concerned with naval architecture
from the library of Alfred S Brownell. An
important highlight of this collection are 11
ship models of Atlantic fishing craft, 9 of
which were built by Brownell; these models
are permanently on display. Incl 550
technical drawings, photographs, indexed.

SHIP PASSENGER LISTS

CA —POMONA PUBLIC LIBRARY, Special
Collections, 625 S Garey Ave, PO Box 2271,
Pomona, 91766. David Streeter, Librn
Holdings: Cat Maps Microforms
Notes: Complete California census through
1900 on microfilm; 1850 California Census
index; reconstructed passenger lists; overland
arrivals. Scattered censuses on microfilm
from other states. All printed indexes to US
Census; general US research collection. Basic
heraldry and coats-of-arms.

SHIP REGISTERS

†CA —UNIVERSITY OF CALIFORNIA,
LOS ANGELES, Library, Dept of Special
Collections, 405 Hilgard Ave, Los Angeles,
90024.
Notes: Books and ephemera relating to
North Atlantic passenger lines. James V
Mink's Collection.
CA —SAN DIEGO PUBLIC LIBRARY, Social
Sciences Section, 820 E St, San Diego,
92101. Margaret E Queen, Supvr
Budget: ($36,000)
Notes: Books on the history of commercial
and naval ships. Almost complete file of
Jane's Fighting Ships, 1898 to present;
Lloyd's Register of Ships, 1764-1900 and
1950 to the present.
ME —PENOBSCOT MARINE MUSEUM,
Library, Church St, Searsport, 04974.
Charles Howard, Librn
Holdings: Vols (4000) Cat Mss Maps Pix
Budget: ($5000)
Notes: Maine maritime history, log books,
journals, diaries, marine charts, ships
registers, photographs, archives & mss, and
books relating to world navigation. The
greatest emphasis is placed on the Penobscot
Bay region.
PA —PHILADELPHIA MARITIME
MUSEUM, Library, 321 Chestnut St,
Philadelphia, 19106. Dorothy H Mueller,
Librn
Holdings: Vols (8000) Cat Mss Maps Pix
Slides 16mm Films
Notes: Maritime history of Bay and River
Delaware and of the port of Philadelphia.
Includes shipbuilding and shipbuilders on the
Delaware River, mercantile activity,
recreational activity, maritime-related
organizations, institutions and people,
development of Philadelphia as a port, vessel
registers 1878-1970s. Also, artifacts and
prints.

SHIPBUILDING

CA —SAN DIEGO PUBLIC LIBRARY,
Science & Industry Section, 820 E St, San
Diego, 92101. Joanne Anderson, Senior
Librn
Holdings: Vols 1000 Cat
CT —MYSTIC SEAPORT, MUSEUM, G W
Blunt White Library, Greenmanville Ave,
Mystic, 06355. Gerald E Morris, Librn
Holdings: Vols (40,000) Imprints
Microforms
Budget: ($100,000)
Notes: American maritime history. The
library is also a government depository for
maritime materials with a subscription to
184 line items. Incl 400,000 mss, 4000 maps
and charts, 30,000 ships' plans. Open to the
public.
IN —INDIANA UNIVERSITY, Lilly Library,
Seventh St, Bloomington, 47405. William R
Cagle, Librn
Holdings: // Mss Pix
Notes: Business papers and correspondence

of Howard Ship Yards & Dock Co,
Jeffersonville, Ind, 1834-1942. Incl
correspondence with captains, ship owners,
Howard family members, etc; some photos
of Howard-built ships during construction; ca
10,000 blueprints, drawings and scale
specifications for riverboat constructions;
business ledgers and cash books; general
office files. 265,600 items.
ME —MAINE MARITIME MUSEUM,
Library and Archives, 963 Washington St,
Bath, 04530. Nathan R Lipfert, Asst Cur
Holdings: Vols (5000) Cat Maps Pix Slides
Notes: The collection is limited primarily to
shipbuilding in Bath, Maine, and to a lesser
extent Maine as a whole. The unique aspects
of the collection are a large collection of
photographs of wooden shipbuilding and
related trades, photographs of the vessels
themselves, and a large collection of papers
of a shipbuilding company in Bath active
throughout the 19th century.
ME —ANTIQUE BOAT SOCIETY, Archives
& Library, Learning Place, Manset, 04656.
Admiral E R Welles, Cur
Holdings: Vols (200) Uncat Maps Pix
Notes: Data relative to mariner items that
have aged 25 years or more, designs of boats
and accessories, charts, pictures, books and
sometimes original items themselves. This is
a research library with no lending.
Researchers should telephone (207) 244-
5015 to make arrangements.
MD —STEAMSHIP HISTORICAL SOCIETY
OF AMERICA (SSHSA), University of
Baltimore Library, 1420 Maryland Ave,
Baltimore, 21201.
Holdings: Vols (3500) Cat Maps Pix Slides
16mm Films
Budget: ($15,000)
Notes: Powered Maritime Transportation
Collection. Photo bank of over 15,000
negatives and 25,000 prints, arranged
alphabetically by vessel name. Extensive
blueprint and tracing collection. Collection
documents history of steam navigation from
the early 19th century to the present.
Emphasis upon East Coast American vessels
of late 19th and early 20th centuries and
upon transatlantic vessels. Some coverage of
Great Lakes and inland river steamboats.
Very little about sailing vessels. No
published catalog. Books listed in OCLC.
Collection located at University of
Baltimore. Address for Society is 414 Pelton
Ave, Staten Island, NY 10310, attention:
Alice S Wilson, Secretary and SSHSA Librn.
MD —CALVERT MARINE MUSEUM,
Library, PO Box 97, Solomons, 20688.
Holdings: Uncat Mss Maps Pix Slides
Audiotapes
Notes: Vessel lists of boats built in the
country; lists of vessels owned in Calvert
County, ships papers, half models, building
plans and blueprints, artifacts, shipyard
papers (correspondence, material lists, etc)
and contracts.
See also entries under Shipwrecks; US -
History - War of 1812.
MA —STURGIS LIBRARY, Rte 6A,
Barnstable, 02630. Susan R Klein, Chief
Librn
Holdings: Vols (1000) Mss Pix
Budget: $500
Notes: Massachusetts maritime history. The
Henry Crocker Kittredge Maritime History
Collection contains vols, mss, documents
and photographs, many of great rarity,
related to the history of maritime life of
Barnstable County incl its shipmasters,
shipbuilding and fishing industries. Major
emphasis of materials is on eighteenth,
nineteenth and early 20th centuries. The
core of the collection was provided through
an estate gift of Henry Crocker Kittredge,
Harvard scholar and maritime historian
(1890-1967).
MA —MASSACHUSETTS INSTITUTE OF
TECHNOLOGY, Institute Archives, Special
Collections, Cambridge, 02139.
Notes: Bryant, Clark, and Forbes collections
on early navigation and shipbuilding.
MA —MASSACHUSETTS INSTITUTE OF
TECHNOLOGY MUSEUM, Hart Nautical
Collections, 77 Massachusetts Ave, Rm 5-
329, Cambridge, 02139. John W

SHIPBUILDING (cont.)

Waterhouse, Cur
Holdings: Vols (800) Cat Maps Pix
Notes: Ship and marine engineering development. Museum is under jurisdiction of MIT's Dept of Ocean Engineering. Collection incl various collections of prints and photographs of ships and yachts; working drawings from the Herreshoff Manufacturing Co, 1870-1945, and of the George Lawley and Son Corp; working drawings and models from the Munro, Owen, and Paine Collections.

MI —UNIVERSITY OF MICHIGAN, Transportation Research Institute, Library, 2901 Baxter Rd, Ann Arbor, 48109. Ann C Grimm, Librn
Holdings: Vols (57,000) Cat Mss Maps
Budget: ($25,000)
Notes: Special emphasis.

NJ —STEVENS INSTITUTE OF TECHNOLOGY, Samuel C Williams Library, Castle Point Sta, Hoboken, 07030. Jane G Hartye, Special Collections Librn
Holdings: // Cat Mss Pix
Notes: Two collections: (1) The US Ironclad Monitor was designed by Capt John Ericsson and launched January 30, 1862. The "Monitor" participated in the historic battle with the "Merrimac" on March 9, 1862. It sank off Cape Hatteras on December 31, 1862. Our collection includes original design drawings of the "Monitor," 38 of which were drawn by Capt Ericsson and 34 by C W McCord. The copies of these drawings are now in the National Archives. No Photocoppying. (2) Stevens and Edwin Augustus Stevens were responsible for the first steam locomotives and railroad; they were involved in shipbuilding, building the "Juliana," the "Phoenix" and ferries. We have a huge amount of uncataloged data on the "Stevens Battery." The Stevens family played an extremely important role in developing the City of Hoboken; Edwin Augustus Stevens established Stevens Institute of Technology. Through theStevens family, we have much historical data on the City of Hoboken and the State of New Jersey. Our collection includes microfilm of the Stevens Papers and of Hoboken.

NY —STATE UNIVERSITY OF NEW YORK, Maritime College, Stephen B Luce Library, Fort Schuyler, Bronx, 10465. Richard H Corson, Librn
Holdings: Vols (68,000) Cat Maps Pix Slides Audiotapes Videotapes 16mm Films Filmstrips Microforms
Budget: ($90,000)
Notes: Incl extensive holdings in periodical literature with long and complete runs of many titles containing diagrams and plans, many of which are fold-outs. Approximately 3500 research reports in paper and microfiche format. Mainly English language.

NY —WEBB INSTITUTE OF NAVAL ARCHITECTURE, Livingston Library, Crescent Beach Rd, Glen Cove, 11542. Fred H Forrest, Librn
Holdings: Vols 600 Cat
Notes: Marine history, emphasizing ship history. Collection of ship plans. Access by appointment only.

NY —US MERCHANT MARINE ACADEMY, Schuyler Otis Bland Memorial Library, Steamboat Rd, Kings Point, 11024. Stephen R Wiist, Acting Chief Librn
Holdings: Vols (130,000) Cat Mss Maps Pix Slides Phonorecords Microforms
Budget: ($75,000)
Notes: All aspects of maritime affairs.

NY —NEW YORK PUBLIC LIBRARY, Research Libraries, Science and Technology Research Center, Fifth Ave & 42 St, New York, 10018.
Holdings: Vols (1,100,000) Cat Microforms
Budget: ($647,259)

NY —SEAMEN'S CHURCH INSTITUTE OF NEW YORK, Joseph Conrad Library, 15 State St, New York, 10004. Bonnie Golightly, Librn
Holdings: Vols (23,500) Cat Pix
Budget: ($8500)
Notes: Merchant seamen, merchant ships,

voyages, navigation, marine engineering, shipbuilding. Large collection of ship registers: *Lloyd's Register of Shipping*, a partial coverge of the years 1764-1865 in reprints, complete coverage for the years 1877 to date; *American Bureau of Shipping*, 1916 to date; *Merchant Vessels of the US*, 1891 to date. *Society of Naval Architects and Marine Engineers Transactions*, vol 1, 1893 to date. The picture file consists mostly of photographs of merchant ships. This is supplemented by scrapbooks. The index to the pictures, scrapbooks, books and vertical file are in one subject catalog. We subscribe to and keep for several years numerous maritime periodicals. The maritime history collection incl sailing ships as well as steamships.

PA —PENN SHIP BUILDING CO, Library, Morton Ave, Chester, 19013. John Del Razo, Librn
Holdings: Vols (16,269) Cat Maps
Notes: Shipbuilding. Incl nautical charts.

PA —FRANKLIN INSTITUTE LIBRARY, 20 & The Parkway, Philadelphia, 19103. Miriam Padusis, Dir; Charles Wilt, Readers Servs Librn
Holdings: Vols (300,000) Cat Maps Pix Microforms

PA —PHILADELPHIA MARITIME MUSEUM, Library, 321 Chestnut St, Philadelphia, 19106. Dorothy H Mueller, Librn
Holdings: Vols (8000) Cat Mss Maps Pix Slides 16mm Films
Notes: Maritime history of Delaware Bay and River and of the port of Philadelphia. Includes shipbuilding and shipbuilders on the Delaware River, mercantile activity, recreational activity, maritime-related organizations, institutions and people, development of Philadelphia as a port, vessel registers 1878-1970s. Also, artifacts and prints.

PA —US NAVY, Philadelphia Naval Shipyard Technical Library, Philadelphia Naval Shipyard, Philadelphia, 19112. Alice R Murray, Dir
Holdings: Vols (12,500) Cat Pix
Notes: The Library also has (70,000) technical manuals, (3500) research and development reports. Over (400) current periodicals.

RI —BROWN UNIVERSITY, John Carter Brown Library, Providence, 02912. Norman Fiering, Librn; Everett C Wilkie Jr, Bibliographer; Susan Danforth, Cur Maps & Prints
Notes: Extensive collection, incl works on navigation, shipbuilding, mariners' health, and explorations accomplished by ship.

RI —PROVIDENCE PUBLIC LIBRARY, 150 Empire St, Providence, 02903. Lance J Bauer, Special Collections Librn
Holdings: Vols 225 // Uncat Pix
Notes: A fine collection of books, technical drawings, photographs, pamphlets and other ephemera concerned with naval architecture from the library of Alfred S Brownell. An important highlight of this collection are 11 ship models of Atlantic fishing craft, 9 of which were built by Brownell; these models are permanently on display. Incl 550 technical drawings, photographs, indexed.

WA —PUGET SOUND NAVAL SHIPYARD, Engineering Library, Code 202.5, Bremerton, 98314. Carol J Swanson, Engineering Librn
Holdings: Vols 2000 Cat

NS —NOVA SCOTIA MUSEUM, Library, 1747 Summer St, Halifax, B3H 3A6, Can. M S Whiteside, Librn
Notes: Emphasis is on social history.

SHIPBUILDING—HISTORY

MO —WASHINGTON UNIVERSITY, Libraries, Special Collections Dept, Campus Box 1061, St Louis, 63130.
Notes: Papers of Charles W Bryan Jr, incl correspondence, personal journals, scrapbooks, photographs, and printed material associated with the Federal Shipbuilding Company from 1917 to 1948, and as president of the Pullman Standard Car Manufacturing Company from 1950 to 1958.

SHIPLEY, MAYNARD

PA —TEMPLE UNIVERSITY LIBRARIES, Special Collections Dept, Conwellana-Templana Collection, 13 & Berks St, Philadelphia, 19122. Miriam I Crawford, Cur
Holdings: Vols 30 Cat Mss Pix
Budget: ($30,000)
Notes: Miriam Allen De Ford was a prolific writer on a variety of topics, including history, biography, social reform and crime stories. Her books, as well as a number of the 25 Little Blue Books, she wrote for J H Haldeman, are in the Collection, along with correspondence, proofs, and clippings related to her writings and typescript, page proof and galleys of her *Stone Walls*. The Socialist activities of her husband, Maynard Shipley, are detailed in *Up Hill All the Way* and in some of the correspondence.

SHIPPING

CA —STANFORD UNIVERSITY LIBRARIES, Cecil H Green Library, Stanford, 94305. Michael T Ryan, Cur
Holdings: Vols (1700) // Cat Mss Maps Pix
Notes: The Timothy Hopkins Transportation Collection. Mss on early railroading in England, India, and US. Construction and operation of Central Pacific. Papers of men connected with Central and Southern Pacific and subsidiaries. United Railroads of San Francisco. Some materials on shipping and aviation.

IL —NORTHWESTERN UNIVERSITY, Transportation Center Library, Evanston, 60201. Mary Roy, Librn
Holdings: Vols (116,000)
Notes: The emphasis in this collection is on current developments in transportation operations and socioeconomics--management, planning, impact and regulation. All modes of transportation and containerization are incl; the geographic scope covers domestic and foreign activity at the urban, intercity and international levels. Publications on new systems developments and the application of analytic techniques to operations are well represented. Incl 19,000 pamphlets; 9000 company reports. *Services are offered on research conducted outside Northwestern. A fee schedule is available on request.* Publications: *Current Literature in Traffic and Transportation* (bi-monthly accessions bulletin citing 625 books, reports and periodical articles per issue). Maritime transportation.

MD —MARYLAND HISTORICAL SOCIETY, Library, 201 W Monument St, Baltimore, 21201. William B Keller, Head Librn
Holdings: Maps Pix Films
Notes: Ships and shipping, description and travel, yachts and yachting, sailing, marine transport, Baltimore, and the Port of Maryland. Incl books, periodicals, maps, charts, pictures, ship plans, log books, films, etc.

MA —HARVARD UNIVERSITY, Graduate School of Business Administration, Baker Library, Soldiers Field, Boston, 02163. Mary V Chatfield, Librn; Florence Bartoshesky, Cur of Manuscripts and Archives
Holdings: Cat Mss
Notes: Incl strong collection on the China trade. See *American Neptune*, XIII (1953), 118-124.

NY —STATE UNIVERSITY OF NEW YORK AT ALBANY, Library, Special Collections Dept, 1400 Washington Ave, Albany, 12222. Marion P Munzer, Coordr
Notes: Correspondence and financial records of Abraham Bell and Son, New York shipping line which exported cotton and brought back British and English immigrants in the 1830s and 1840s. Additional correspondence and papers of James W Bell from 1862-1917; James C Bell from 1864-1899; and Bell Brothers, a money-lending business in Yonkers (22 linear feet). Part of the Library's German Exile Collection. *See also* entries under Exiles, Political; Emigration and Immigration

NY —STATE UNIVERSITY OF NEW YORK, Maritime College, Stephen B Luce

SHIPPING (cont.)

Library, Fort Schuyler, Bronx, 10465.
Richard H Corson, Librn
Holdings: Vols (68,000) Cat Maps Pix Slides
Phonorecords Audiotapes Videotapes 16mm
Films Filmstrips Microforms
Budget: ($90,000)
Notes: Marine transportation, especially
ocean transportation. Incl extensive holdings
in periodical literature with long and
complete runs of many titles. Approximately
3500 recent research reports in paper and
microfiche format. Mainly English language.

NY —US MERCHANT MARINE
ACADEMY, Schuyler Otis Bland Memorial
Library, Steamboat Rd, Kings Point, 11024.
Stephen R Wiist, Acting Chief Librn
Holdings: Vols (130,000) Cat Mss Maps Pix
Slides Phonorecords Microforms
Budget: ($75,000)
Notes: All aspects of maritime affairs.

NY —COLUMBIA UNIVERSITY
LIBRARIES, Rare Book & Manuscript
Library, 801 Butler Library, 535 W 114 St,
New York, 10027. Kenneth A Lohf, Librn
Notes: More than 32,000 items documenting
the rise of William Russell Grace's shipping
business and other materials relating to his
career as mayor of New York. Incl records
and correspondence relating to all aspects of
the shipping business in New York and
South America, mining interest in Peru and
Chile, and transportation in Costa Rica and
Nicaragua. Family memorabilia and
photographs, materials concerning New
York Politics, banking and insurance, real
estate interests and Catholic charities, and
letters from Chester A Arthur, John Jacob
Astor, Andrew Carnegie, Grover Cleveland,
Hamilton Fish, John Hay and J Pierpont
Morgan. Restricted use.

RI —PROVIDENCE PUBLIC LIBRARY, 150
Empire St, Providence, 02903. Lance J
Bauer, Special Collections Librn
Notes: The Nicholson Whaling Collection is
one of the largest and certainly most
distinguished whaling collections in the
world, amassed in the early part of this
century and bequeathed to the Providence
Public Library in 1956. The logbooks,
journals and account books record over 1000
voyages from 1762-1922 and incl many
illustrated logs and a large number of
journals of whaling wives. These are
completely cataloged and microfilmed. Also
incl are 13 boxes of business
correspondence, bills of ladings, ships'
papers, crew records, etc, and over 300
printed books. Many of the printed books
are also quite rare, especially some first
editions of 19th century voyages such as of
the *Essex*. Contains material on Hawaiian
whaling and material printed in Hawaii.
Material must be used in-house.
Photocopying on a restricted basis only for
educational purposes when condition allows.
No complete photocopying of logbooks. The
microfilm of the mss is available for
interlibrary loans.

TX —ROSENBERG LIBRARY, Galveston and
Texas History Center, 2310 Sealy Ave,
Galveston, 77550. Jane Kenamore, Archivist
Holdings: Vols 7368 Cat Mss Maps Pix
Slides Microforms
Budget: $60,000
Notes: Emphasis on upper Texas coast
material; Republic of Texas period; Civil
War period; Shipping; Texas Navy; Jean
Laffite; Texas politics, 19th-20th century;
Railroads; Texas journalism, incl microfilms
of Galveston newspapers, 1838-date.

NS —NOVA SCOTIA MUSEUM, Library,
1747 Summer St, Halifax, B3H 3A6, Can. M
S Whiteside, Librn
Notes: Emphasis is on social history.

ON —NATIONAL RESEARCH COUNCIL
OF CANADA, Aeronautical/Mechanical
Engineering Branch Library, Montreal Rd,
Ottawa, K1A 0R6, Can. Louise Fletcher,
Head
Notes: This branch library of the Canada
Institute for Scientific and Technical
Information (CISTI) of the National
Research Council of Canada, Ottawa, has a
collection strong in aeronautical engineering,
automatic control, CAD/CAM, robotics,
ocean, wind, and solar energy power,
hydraulic and coastal engineering, icing, low
temperature research, naval engineering,
metals and metallurgy, incl composites,
tribology, and air, railroad, marine
transportation. Library supported the
Council contribution to the development of
the remote manipular Canadarm for
NASA's Space Shuttle Orbiters and more
recently, the Canadian Astronaut Program
which will contribute payload specialists to
NASA's Space Shuttle Program in 1984. 35,
000 monographs, 1200 serials. Report
collection: over 500,000 items.

SHIPPING—HISTORY

CA —CLAREMONT COLLEGES, Honnold
Library, Ninth & Dartmouth, Claremont,
91711. Tania Rizzo, Special Collections
Dept Head
Holdings: Vols 353 Mss Maps Pix
Notes: Ms and typescript volumes of
account books, ledgers, log books, journals,
annual reports, cargo lists, correspondence,
etc. Given to Pomona College by the Robert
Dollar Co upon the liquidation of the Pacific
Steamship Co Thompson, R C, comp,
*Calendar of Archives and Records of Certain
Pacific Coast Steamship Companies*
(typescript prepared 1940-1941). Restricted
use.

CA —NATIONAL MARITIME MUSEUM,
SAN FRANCISCO, J Porter Shaw Library,
Golden Gate National Recreation Area, Fort
Mason, San Francisco, 94123. David A Hull,
Librn; Herbert Beckwith, Catalog Librn;
Irene Stachura, Ref Librn; John Maounis,
Photo Librn
Holdings: Vols (12,000) Mss Maps Pix Slides
Microforms Periodicals VF
Budget: ($4000)
Notes: Pacific Coast maritime history. The
photo collection of 160,000 is partly
cataloged and classified. The library has
complete runs of *Merchant Vessels of US*
and *Lloyd's Register of Shipping* to 1970.
The collection is particularly strong on
Pacific Coast and San Francisco maritime
history. About 250 log books; scrapbooks.
Oral history interviews, vertical files. 60
percent of books are cataloged.

DE —UNIVERSITY OF DELAWARE, Hugh
M Morris Library, S College Ave, Newark,
19711. T Stuart Dick, Special Collections
Notes: The personal and business papers of
many prominent Delaware Valley politicians,
merchants, lawyers, engineers. A few of
those represented are the Latimer Shipping
Papers, David Lenox (qv), John Lukens (see
Lukens Family entry), Samuel Meredith
(qv), George Messersmith (qv), and Willard
Saulsbury (qv). Among the literary papers
are collections of personal correspondence,
holograph manuscripts of poetry, short
stories and novels. Those represented
include, among others, John Malsolm
Brinnin, Erskine Caldwell, Waldo Frank,
Elizabeth Jennings, Robert Underwood
Johnson, Donald Justice, Walter Lowenfels,
Howard McCord, Arthur Mizener, Ulrick
O'Connor, Ishmael Reed, Carl Sandburg,
Gilbert Sorrentino, Kurt Vonnegut, Tennesse
Williams, William Carlos Williams, Edmund
Wilson, Louis Untermeyer, William Butler
Yeats, the *Pagany* archives, *Signature*
archives, and Proscenium PressPapers.

DC —GEORGETOWN UNIVERSITY,
Library, Special Collections Div, 37 & O Sts
NW, Washington, 20057. George M
Barringer, Special Collections Librn;
Nicholas B Sheetz, Mss Librn
Holdings: Mss Cat
Notes: Collection of shipping, railroad, and
customs receipts which document commerce
between Baltimore and Philadelphia. The
earliest records are from a company run by
John F F Wessels, later associated with
Christian Mayer and Frederick Konig.

ME —BOWDOIN COLLEGE, Library,
Brunswick, 04011. Dianne M Gutscher, Cur
of Special Collections
Holdings: Mss
Notes: The Dodge Papers contain material
concerning about 30 maritime cases handled
by Boston lawyer, John Calvin Dodge (1810-
1890), whose practice was for the most part
in the departments of admiralty and marine
insurance. A small collection of 24 letters of
Otis Kimball, for the period 1850-64,
concerns Bath, Maine, shipping. The
Magoun and Clapp Papers consist of about
10,000 pieces of mss material about the
vessels owned or operated by this Bath,
Maine, firm from 1846-1864. Incl are letters
from ships' masters, lists of ships' stores,
invoices, insurance policies, etc. The
Patterson Papers contain 125 pieces, 1820-
1874, incl correspondence, bills, shipping
documents, log book, sea journal, and photos
of Actor P Patterson, shipmaster of
Kennebunkport, Maine, and of Benjamin
Patterson, shipmaster of Saco, Maine. The
Stetson Paperscontain about 1000 items,
primarily 1797-1888, of maritime and family
material from Wiscasset, Maine, incl records
of ships owned by Moses Carleton and
Erastus Foote and three ships' logs. The
Maritime Papers contain 50 items of Bibber
and Randall Company material; William G
Randall notebooks; and documents
concerning Portland shipping; Newburyport,
Mass, shipping; the steamers "Huntress" and
"Kearsarge;" and a journal of a voyage on the
ship "Natchez" of Brunswick. The Captain
John Thomas Papers consist of 929 pieces of
correspondence and ships' records, 1807-
1871, of this Bowdoinham, Maine,
shipmaster and his family. The Tucker
Papers contain about 8000 letters and
documents of this Wiscasset, Maine,
shipping family for the period 1813-1860,
incl a thorough documentation of the
construction and voyages of eight ships
belongingto the family enterprise.

MI —MICHIGAN TECHNOLOGICAL
UNIVERSITY, Archives, Copper County
Historical Collections, Houghton, 49931.
Theresa Sanderson Spence, University
Archivist
Holdings: Uncat Mss Maps Pix
Notes: Wide variety of material on mining,
fishing, lumbering and marine activities.
Special interest in Great Lakes shipping.
Collection is accessioned but not indexed.
637 folders (25 file boxes) of material.

NY —US MERCHANT MARINE
ACADEMY, Schuyler Otis Bland Memorial
Library, Steamboat Rd, Kings Point, 11024.
Stephen R Wiist, Acting Chief Librn
Holdings: Vols (130,000) Cat Mss Maps Pix
Slides Phonorecords Microforms
Budget: ($75,000)
Notes: All aspects of maritime affairs.

†NY —COLUMBIA UNIVERSITY
LIBRARIES, Butler Library, Rare Book and
Manuscript Library, 535 W 114 St, New
York, 10027.
Notes: The papers of William Russell Grace,
founder of W R Grace & Co and mayor of
New York City, 1880-82 and 1885-86.
Documents the rise of the Grace shipping
business, mining interests in Peru and Chile,
and transportation in Costa Rica and
Nicaragua. Also materials concerning New
York politics, banking and insurance, real
estate interests and Catholic charities.

OH —RUTHERFORD B HAYES LIBRARY,
1337 Hayes Ave, Fremont, 43420. Watt P
Marchman, Dir
Holdings: Vols 500 Cat Mss Maps Pix Slides
Notes: The Great Lakes Marine Collection,
incl the Capt Frank E Hamilton Collection;
Great Lakes boats and shipping. Incl 300
charts; over 20,000 pictures with 2500
negatives, 30 glass plates). Index and
findings aids with the collection.

SHIPPING—REGISTERS see Ship
Registers

SHIPPING, INLAND WATER see Inland
Water Transportation

SHIPS

CA —LONG BEACH PUBLIC LIBRARY,
Literature & History Dept, 101 Pacific Ave,
Long Beach, 90802. Harriet J Friis, Head
Holdings: Vols Pamphlets Documents Pix

SHIPS (cont.)

Maps Periodicals Audiotapes Microforms
Notes: Collection documents the history and
continuing development of Long Beach.
Publications of the City of Long Beach are
incl, as well as a selective index to the Long
Beach *Independent* and other local
newspapers. Also incl material on the
steamship *Queen Mary*. Items in the
collection do not circulate. Incl city
directories.

†CA —UNIVERSITY OF CALIFORNIA,
Library, Los Angeles, 90024.
Notes: the Neil Arthur Getz Memorial
collection regarding Allied, German, Italian,
and Japanese ships, airplanes, and military
vehicles of all kinds; types of warships,
decognition manuals, spotters' handbooks,
and military dictionaries.

CA —SAN DIEGO PUBLIC LIBRARY,
Science & Industry Section, 820 E St, San
Diego, 92101. Joanne Anderson, Senior
Librn
Holdings: Vols 1000 Cat

CA —NATIONAL MARITIME MUSEUM,
SAN FRANCISCO, J Porter Shaw Library,
Golden Gate National Recreation Area, Fort
Mason, San Francisco, 94123. David A Hull,
Librn; Herbert Beckwith, Catalog Librn;
Irene Stachura, Ref Librn; John Maounis,
Photo Librn
Holdings: Vols (12,000) Mss Maps Pix Slides
Microforms Periodicals VF
Budget: ($4000)
Notes: Pacific Coast maritime history. The
photo collection of 160,000 is partly
cataloged and classified. The library has
complete runs of *Merchant Vessels of US*
and *Lloyd's Register of Shipping* to 1970.
The collection is particularly strong on
Pacific Coast and San Francisco maritime
history. About 250 log books; scrapbooks.
Oral history interviews, vertical files. 60
percent of books are cataloged.

MD —CALVERT MARINE MUSEUM,
Library, PO Box 97, Solomons, 20688.
Holdings: Uncat Mss Maps Pix Slides
Audiotapes
Notes: Vessel lists of boats built in the
county; lists of vessels owned in Calvert
County, ships papers, half models, building
plans and blueprints, artifacts, shipyard
papers (correspondence, material lists, etc)
and contracts.
See also entries under Shipwrecks; US -
History - War of 1812.

MA —STURGIS LIBRARY, Rte 6A,
Barnstable, 02630. Susan R Klein, Chief
Librn
Holdings: Vols (1000) Mss pix
Budget: $500
Notes: Massachusetts maritime history. The
Henry Crocker Kittredge Maritime History
Collection contains vols, mss, documents
and photographs, many of great rarity,
related to the history of maritime life of
Barnstable County incl its shipmasters,
shipbuilding and fishing industries. Major
emphasis of materials is on eighteenth,
nineteenth and early 20th centuries. The
core of the collection was provided through
an estate gift of Henry Crocker Kittredge,
Harvard scholar and maritime historian
(1890-1967).

NY —STATE UNIVERSITY OF NEW
YORK, Maritime College, Stephen B Luce
Library, Fort Schuyler, Bronx, 10465.
Richard H Corson, Librn
Holdings: Vols (68,000) Cat Maps Pix Slides
Phonorecords Audiotapes Videotapes 16mm
Films Filmstrips Microforms
Budget: ($90,000)
Notes: Incl history of ships with special
emphasis on US sailing ships of the 19th
century. Extensive holdings in periodical
literature with long and complete runs of
many titles. Approximately 3500 recent
research reports in paper and microfiche
format. Mainly English language.

NY —US MERCHANT MARINE
ACADEMY, Schuyler Otis Bland Memorial
Library, Steamboat Rd, Kings Point, 11024.
Stephen R Wiist, Acting Chief Librn
Holdings: Vols (130,000) Cat Mss Maps Pix

Slides Phonorecords Microforms
Budget: ($75,000)
Notes: All aspects of maritime affairs.

NY —NEW YORK PUBLIC LIBRARY,
Research Libraries, Science and Technology
Research Center, Fifth Ave & 42 St, New
York, 10018.
Holdings: Vols (1,100,000) Cat Microforms
Budget: ($647,259)

RI —PROVIDENCE PUBLIC LIBRARY, 150
Empire St, Providence, 02903. Lance J
Bauer, Special Collections Librn
Notes: A fine collection of books, technical
drawings, photographs, pamphlets and other
ephemera concerned with naval architecture
from the library of Alfred S Brownell. An
important highlight of this collection are 11
ship models of Atlantic fishing craft, 9 of
which were built by Brownell; these models
are permanently on display. Incl 550
technical drawings, photographs, indexed.
See also entry under Log Books.

VA —MARINERS MUSEUM, Library,
Newport News, 23606. Ardie L Kelly, Librn
Holdings: Vols (60,000) Cat Mss Maps Pix
Slides
Notes: Incl collections of over 150,000
photographs of merchant ships, naval vessels,
sailing ships, lighthouses, portraits of naval
men, harbors, canals, etc, and maps, ships'
papers, and log books. Catalogs of various
parts of the collection published by G K
Hall, Boston.

BC —VANCOUVER PUBLIC LIBRARY,
Science & Technology Div, 750 Burrard St,
Vancouver, V6Z 1X5, Can. P Haffenden,
Head, Science & Technology Div
Holdings: Cat
Notes: Plus special indexes, incl
Organization and Association File (primarily
local, British Columbian, and Canadian),
begun in 1950s, expanded since 1960s; Ship
Index (a source of pictures, historical and
current information; engineering data, plans,
etc); Boat Plans Index.

SHIPS—ACCIDENTS see Marine Accidents

SHIPS—GREAT LAKES

MD —STEAMSHIP HISTORICAL SOCIETY
OF AMERICA (SSHSA), University of
Baltimore Library, 1420 Maryland Ave,
Baltimore, 21201.
Holdings: Vols (3500) Cat Maps Pix Slides
16mm Films
Budget: ($15,000)
Notes: Powered Maritime Transportation
Collection. Photo bank of over 15,000
negatives and 25,000 prints, arranged
alphabetically by vessel name. Extensive
blueprint and tracing collection. Collection
documents history of steam navigation from
the early 19th century to the present.
Emphasis upon East Coast American vessels
of late 19th and early 20th centuries and
upon transatlantic vessels. Some coverage of
Great Lakes and inland river steamboats.
Very little about sailing vessels. No
published catalog. Books listed in OCLC.
Collection located at University of
Baltimore. Address for Society is 414 Pelton
Ave, Staten Island, NY 10310, attention:
Alice S Wilson, Secretary and SSHSA Librn.

MI —MACKINAC ISLAND STATE PARK
COMMISSION, Library, Bos 30028,
Lansing, 48909. Keith R Widder, Cur
Holdings: Vols (1000) Cat Mss Maps Pix
Slides Audiotapes
Budget: ($2500)
Notes: Mackinac area history-research
collection: archaeology, historic preservation,
etc. Great Lakes ships and shippings.

NY —STATE UNIVERSITY OF NEW
YORK, COLLEGE AT OSWEGO, Penfield
Library, Oswego, 13126. Anne Commerton,
Dir
Holdings: Cat Mss
Notes: Collection of data and newspapers,
notes and correspondence for writing a book
on shipwrecks on Lake Ontario and in
particular, Oswego Harbor, by Richard F
Palmer, Syracuse Newspapers reporter.
Photographs accompanied this material but

were removed to be added to our local
history photograph collection. Eight inches
of material.

OH —BOWLING GREEN STATE
UNIVERSITY, Jerome Library, Institute for
Great Lakes Research, Bowling Green,
43403. Richard J Wright, Dir
Holdings: Vols (2500) Cat Mss Maps Pix
Slides Phonorecords Audiotapes Videotapes
16mm Films Microforms
Budget: ($8300)
Notes: About 50 major ms collections, most
of them processed; several thousand minor
ms items, unprocessed. 100,000 pictures, incl
several thousand film and glass plate
negatives. Microforms of government vessel
registries, vessel passages, 1500 maps, some
mss. 6000 naval architectural drawings, 600
vols of scrapbooks. 140 periodical titles,
current and op. Author/title/subject catalog.

OH —RUTHERFORD B HAYES LIBRARY,
1337 Hayes Ave, Fremont, 43420. Watt P
Marchman, Dir
Holdings: Vols 500 Cat Mss Maps Pix Slides
Notes: The Great Lakes Marine Collection,
incl the Capt Frank E Hamilton Collection;
Great Lakes boats and shipping. Incl 300
charts; over 20,000 pictures (with 2500
negatives, 30 glass plates). Index and
findings aids with the collection.

WI —MILWAUKEE PUBLIC LIBRARY, 814
W Wisconsin Ave, Milwaukee, 53233.
Donald J Sager, City Librn
Holdings: Vols 1500 Cat Mss Maps Pix
Slides
Notes: The Great Lakes Marine Collection
consists of Runge Marine Collection, Wilson
Marine Collection, and other collections on
Great Lakes Marine History. Has data on
about 85,000 ships and more than 20,000
pictures of Great Lakes vessels. Complete
runs of reference material such as U S. List
of merchant vessels. Greens, etc. Extensive
collection of lake charts.

SHIPS—HISTORY

CA —LONG BEACH PUBLIC LIBRARY,
Literature & History Dept, 101 Pacific Ave,
Long Beach, 90802. Harriet J Friis, Head
Holdings: Vols Pamphlets Documents Pix
Maps Periodicals Audiotapes Microforms
Notes: Collection documents the history and
continuing development of Long Beach.
Publications of the City of Long Beach are
incl, as well as a selective index to the Long
Beach *Independent* and other local
newspapers. Also incl material on the
steamship *Queen Mary*. Items in the
collection do not circulate. Incl city
directories.

†CA —UNIVERSITY OF CALIFORNIA,
LOS ANGELES, Library, Dept of Special
Collections, 405 Hilgard Ave, Los Angeles,
90024.
Notes: Books and ephemera relating to
North Atlantic passenger lines. James V
Mink's Collection.

CA —SAN DIEGO PUBLIC LIBRARY, Social
Sciences Section, 820 E St, San Diego,
92101. Margaret E Queen, Supvr
Budget: ($36,000)
Notes: Books on the history of commercial
and naval ships. Almost complete file of
Jane's Fighting Ships, 1898 to the present;
Lloyd's Register of Ships, 1764-1900 and
1950 to the present.

CA —FITZ HUGH LUDLOW MEMORIAL
LIBRARY, PO Box 99346, San Francisco,
94109. Michael R Aldrich, Exec Cur
Holdings: Cat Mss Maps Pix Slides
Phonorecords Audiotapes Videotapes
Notes: Collection stored. Important mail
inquiries only. No interlibrary lending or
telephone queries. This collections emphasis
historical and literary works about opium
and its derivatives, mostly in English, going
back to the 17th century but mostly from
the 19th and early 20th centuries. Excellent
collection of De Quincey in different
editions. Many books, pamphlets, and art
relating to the 19th century international
opium trade, the Chinese Opium Wars,
clipper ships, and resulting international
legal action in the early 20th century.
Outstanding collection of the English,

SHIPS—HISTORY (cont.)

French, and American opium-addict confessional literature. Also incl many volumes and offprints relevant to narcotic drug prevention, treatment, and education.

CA —HOOVER INSTITUTION ON WAR, REVOLUTION & PEACE, Stanford University, Stanford, 94305. Milorad M Drachkovitch, Archivist
Holdings: Mss Pix
Notes: Papers of Lloyd M Bucher, Commander, U S Navy, and Commander of the USS *Pueblo,* incl correspondence, newspapers clippings, reports, copies of court inquiries, photographs, plaques, memorabilia, and other materials, 1970-75, relating to the *Pueblo* incident and its aftermath. Incl is a typewritten manuscript of his memoirs, entitled "Bucher, My Story." 68 ms boxes, 1 oversize package.

CT —MYSTIC SEAPORT, MUSEUM, G W Blunt White Library, Greenmanville Ave, Mystic, 06355. Gerald E Morris, Librn
Holdings: Vols (40,000) Imprints Microforms
Budget: ($100,000)
Notes: American maritime history. The library is also a government depository for maritime materials with a subscription to 184 line items. Incl 400,000 mss, 4000 maps and charts, 30,000 ships' plans. Open to the public.

IN —WILLARD LIBRARY, 21 First Ave, Evansville, 47710. Joan Elliott, Special Collections Librn
Holdings: Vols (525) Cat
Notes: Menus from 1920-1950s, foreign and domestic, with emphasis on menus from famous trains and ships.

ME —ANTIQUE BOAT SOCIETY, Archives & Library, Learning Place, Manset, 04656. Admiral E R Welles, Cur
Holdings: Vols (200) Uncat Maps Pix
Notes: Data relative to mariner items that have aged 25 years or more, designs of boats and accessories, charts, pictures, books and sometimes original items themselves. This is a research library with no lending. Researchers should telephone (207) 244-5015 to make arrangements.

MD —STEAMSHIP HISTORICAL SOCIETY OF AMERICA (SSHSA), University of Baltimore Library, 1420 Maryland Ave, Baltimore, 21201.
Holdings: Vols (3500) Cat Maps Pix Slides 16mm Films
Budget: ($15,000)
Notes: Powered Maritime Transportation Collection. Photo bank of over 15,000 negatives and 25,000 prints, arranged alphabetically by vessel name. Extensive blueprint and tracing collection. Collection documents history of steam navigation from the early 19th century to the present. Emphasis upon East Coast American vessels of late 19th and early 20th centuries and upon transatlantic vessels. Some coverage of Great Lakes and inland river steamboats. Very little about sailing vessels. No published catalog. Books listed in OCLC. Collection located at University of Baltimore. Address for Society is 414 Pelton Ave, Staten Island, NY 10310, attention: Alice S Wilson, Secretary and SSHSA Librn.

MA —BEDFORD FREE PUBLIC LIBRARY, 613 Pleasant St, Bedford, 02740. Paul A Cyr, Cur of the Melville Room
Holdings: Vols 1020 Cat Mss Pix
Notes: One of the nation's most extensive collections (72,000 pieces) on American whaling. Incl all forms of documents used in the industry, over 40,000 mss. Library has a printed list of its logbooks and a seamen's card file of men who sailed from New Bedford Customs District contains 250,000 names. Library has published an addendum to "Starbuck" and "Whaling Masters," and "Birth of a Whaleship," 1964, both by Reginald B Hegarty.

MA —OLD DARTMOUTH HISTORICAL SOCIETY, 18 Johnny Cake Hill, New Bedford, 02740. Richard C Kugler, Dir
Holdings: Vols (15,000) Mss Maps Pix Slides Phonorecords Audiotapes 16mm Films Microforms
Budget: ($5000)
Notes: Whaling Museum Library contains one of the most comprehensive collections of printed and manuscript material ever assembled on the history of the whaling industry. Although primary emphasis is on American participation in this industry, foreign works are well-represented. Particularly noteworthy are the 5000 rare books and pamphlets assembled by the distinguished whaling scholar, Charles F Batchelder. Also, material on merchant ships and the natural history of whales. Incl 750 ft mss, 1070 log books, 650 maps, 25,000 pix, and 1800 microforms.

MA —PEABODY MUSEUM OF SALEM, Phillips Library, E India Sq, Salem, 01970. Gregor Trinkaus-Randall, Librn
Holdings: Vols (100,000) Cat Mss Maps Pix
Notes: Maritime history of New England. No published indexes; listed in Hamer's *Guide to Archives...*

MN —UNIVERSITY OF MINNESOTA, James Ford Bell Library, 309 19th Ave S, Minneapolis, 55455. John Parker, Cur
Holdings: Vols (11,000) Cat Mss Maps
Notes: Collection of original materials relating to European expansion, 1400-1800.

NY —STATE UNIVERSITY OF NEW YORK, Maritime College, Stephen B Luce Library, Fort Schuyler, Bronx, 10465. Richard H Corson, Librn
Holdings: Vols (68,000) Cat Maps Pix Slides Phonorecords Audiotapes Videotapes 16mm Films Filmstrips Microforms
Budget: ($60,000)
Notes: Incl history of ships with special emphasis on US sailing ships of the 19th century. Extensive holdings in periodical literature with long and complete runs of many titles. Mainly English language.

NY —WEBB INSTITUTE OF NAVAL ARCHITECTURE, Livingston Library, Crescent Beach Rd, Glen Cove, 11542. Fred H Forrest, Librn
Holdings: Vols 700 Cat
Notes: Marine history, emphasizing ship history. Collection of ship plans. Access by appointment only.

NY —US MERCHANT MARINE ACADEMY, Schuyler Otis Bland Memorial Library, Steamboat Rd, Kings Point, 11024. Stephen R Wiist, Acting Chief Librn
Holdings: Vols (130,000) Cat Mss Maps Pix Slides Phonorecords Microforms
Budget: ($75,000)
Notes: All aspects of maritime affairs.

NY —NEW YORK HISTORICAL SOCIETY, Library, 170 Central Park W, New York, 10024. James Gregory, Librn
Notes: Randall J LeBoeuf Jr's collection of Robert Fulton and related material, 1764-1857, consisting of correspondence, drawings, legal papers, etc, relating to steam engines and boats, canals, and torpedoes. The correspondence incl John Quincy Adams, Henry Clay, De Witt Clinton, Albert Gallatin, Benjamin H Latrobe, James Madison, James Monroe, John Livingston, Robert R Livingston, and William Thornton. Also incl are Fulton's expense and note book, 1803-1808, and Robert R Livingston's receipt book, 1808-1812. Approx 215 items, cataloged.

MB —AQUATIC HALL OF FAME & MUSEUM OF CANADA, Library, 25 Poseidon Bay, Winnipeg, R3M 3E4, Can.
Notes: Aquatic sports, incl swimming, diving, water polo and synchronized swimming. Aquatic memorabilia; records covering Olympics, World Games, Pan-American Games, Commonwealth Games and Canadian Championships; coaching; records books. Collections on sailing and sailing ships, and yachts and yachting, incl books from the Cutty Sark Club of Winnipeg, covering sailing of the past.

SHIPS—PLANS

CA —NATIONAL MARITIME MUSEUM, SAN FRANCISCO, J Porter Shaw Library, Golden Gate National Recreation Area, Fort Mason, San Francisco, 94123. David A Hull, Librn; Herbert Beckwith, Catalog Librn; Irene Stachura, Ref Librn; John Maounis, Photo Librn
Holdings: Vols (12,000) Mss Maps Pix Slides Microforms
Budget: ($4000)
Notes: Ca 50,000 plans including uncataloged Union Iron Works/Bethlehem Shipbuilding plan archive of ca 30,000. Pacific Coast maritime history. The photo collection of 150,000 is partly cataloged and classified. The library has complete runs of *Merchant Vessels of US* and *Lloyd's Register of Shipping.* The collection is particularly strong on Pacific Coast and San Francisco maritime history. About 250 log books; scrapbooks. 60 percent of books are cataloged.

CT —MYSTIC SEAPORT, MUSEUM, G W Blunt White Library, Greenmanville Ave, Mystic, 06355. Gerald E Morris, Librn
Holdings: Vols (40,000) Imprints Microforms
Budget: ($100,000)
Notes: American maritime history. The library is also a government depository for maritime materials with a subscription to 184 line items. Incl 400,000 mss, 4000 maps and charts, 30,000 ships' plans. Open to the public.

IN —INDIANA UNIVERSITY, Lilly Library, Seventh St, Bloomington, 47405. William R Cagle, Librn
Holdings: // Mss Pix
Notes: Business papers and correspondence of Howard Ship Yards & Dock Co, Jeffersonville, Ind, 1834-1942. Incl correspondence with captains, ship owners, Howard family members, etc; some photos of Howard-built ships during construction; ca 10,000 blueprints, drawings and scale specifications for riverboat constructions; business ledgers and cash books; general office files. 265,600 items.

MD —MARYLAND HISTORICAL SOCIETY, Library, 201 W Monument St, Baltimore, 21201. William B Keller, Head Librn
Holdings: Maps Pix Films
Notes: Ships and shipping, description and travel, yachts and yachting, sailing, marine transport, Baltimore, and the Port of Maryland. Incl books, periodicals, maps, charts, pictures, ship plans, log books, films, etc.

MD —STEAMSHIP HISTORICAL SOCIETY OF AMERICA (SSHSA), University of Baltimore Library, 1420 Maryland Ave, Baltimore, 21201.
Holdings: Vols (3500) Cat Maps Pix Slides 16mm Films
Budget: ($15,000)
Notes: Powered Maritime Transportation Collection. Photo bank of over 15,000 negatives and 25,000 prints, arranged alphabetically by vessel name. Extensive blueprint and tracing collection. Collection documents history of steam navigation from the early 19th century to the present. Emphasis upon East Coast American vessels of late 19th and early 20th centuries and upon transatlantic vessels. Some coverage of Great Lakes and inland river steamboats. Very little about sailing vessels. No published catalog. Books listed in OCLC. Collection located at University of Baltimore. Address for Society is 414 Pelton Ave, Staten Island, NY 10310, attention: Alice S Wilson, Secretary and SSHSA Librn.

MD —CALVERT MARINE MUSEUM, Library, PO Box 97, Solomons, 20688.
Holdings: Uncat Mss Maps Pix Slides Audiotapes
Notes: Vessel list of boats built in the county; lists of vessels owned in Calvert County, ships papers, half models, building plans and blueprints, artifacts, shipyards papers (correspondence, material lists, etc) and contracts.
See also entry under Shipwrecks; US - History - War of 1812

MA —MASSACHUSETTS INSTITUTE OF TECHNOLOGY MUSEUM, Hart Nautical Collections, 77 Massachusetts Ave, Rm 5-329, Cambridge, 02139. John W Waterhouse, Cur
Holdings: Vols (800) Cat Maps Pix
Notes: Ship and marine engineering

SHIPS—PLANS (cont.)

development. Museum is under jurisdiction of MIT's Dept of Ocean Engineering. Collection incl various collections of prints and photographs of ships and yachts; working drawings from the Herreshoff Manufacturing Co, 1870-1945, and of the George Lawley and Son Corp; working drawings and models from the Munro, Owen, and Paine Collections.

NJ —STEVENS INSTITUTE OF TECHNOLOGY, Samuel C Williams Library, Castle Point Sta, Hoboken, 07030. Jane G Hartye, Special Collections Librn
Holdings: // Cat Mss Pix
Notes: Known as the US Ironclad Monitor, it was designed by Capt John Ericsson and launched January 30, 1862. The "Monitor" participated in the historic battle with "Merrimac" on March 9, 1862. It sank off Cape Hatteras on December 31, 1862. Our collection includes original design drawings of the "Monitor," 38 of which were drawn by Capt Ericsson and 34 by C W McCord. The copies of these drawings are now in the National Archives. No photocopying.

PA —US NAVY, Philadelphia Naval Shipyard Technical Library, Philadelphia Naval Shipyard, Philadelphia, 19112. Alice R Murray, Dir
Holdings: Vols (12,500) Cat Pix
Notes: The Library also has (70,000) technical manuals. (3500) research and development reports. Over (400) current periodicals.

SHIPS—REGISTERS see Ship Registers

SHIPS—REGISTRATION AND TRANSFER

BC —MARITIME MUSEUM OF BRITISH COLUMBIA, 28 Bastion Sq, Victoria, V8W 1H9, Can. C H Shaw, Dir
Holdings: Vols (2500) Cat Mss Maps Pix Slides Microforms
Budget: ($110,000)
Notes: Also 4000 registration cards; 6000 pictures.

SHIPWRECKS

IL —CHICAGO HISTORICAL SOCIETY, Library, Clark St at North Ave, Chicago, 60614. Robert L Brubaker, Librn
Holdings: Vols (150,000) Cat Mss Maps Pix
Notes: Incl the J Norman Jensen Collection, a file of approximately 8500 cards concerning ships that sank in the Great Lakes area from 1679 to 1947.

MD —STEAMSHIP HISTORICAL SOCIETY OF AMERICA (SSHSA), University of Baltimore Library, 1420 Maryland Ave, Baltimore, 21201.
Holdings: Vols (3500) Cat Maps Pix Slides 16mm Films
Budget: ($15,000)
Notes: Powered Maritime Transportation Collection. Photo bank of over 15,000 negatives and 25,000 prints, arranged alphabetically by vessel name. Extensive blueprint and tracing collection. Collection documents history of steam navigation from the early 19th century to the present. Emphasis upon East Coast American vessels of late 19th and early 20th centuries and upon transatlantic vessels. Some coverage of Great Lakes and inland river steamboats. Very little about sailing vessels. No published catalog. Books listed in OCLC. Collection located at University of Baltimore. Address for Society is 414 Pelton Ave, Staten Island, NY 10310, attention: Alice S Wilson, Secretary and SSHSA Librn.

MD —CALVERT MARINE MUSEUM, Library, PO Box 97, Solomons, 20688.
Holdings: Cat Maps
Notes: Calvert County, Md. Shipwreck Survey. Consists of all known shipwrecks within the Patuxent River and waters adjacent to Calvert County. Some associated artifacts are in the Museum's collections.

NY —NEW YORK PUBLIC LIBRARY, Research Libraries, Science and Technology Research Center, Fifth Ave & 42 St, New York, 10018.
Holdings: Vols (1,100,000) Cat Microforms
Budget: ($647,259)

NY —STATE UNIVERSITY OF NEW YORK, COLLEGE AT OSWEGO, Penfield Library, Oswego, 13126. Anne Commerton, Dir
Holdings: Cat Mss
Notes: Collection of data and newspapers, notes and correspondence for writing a book on shipwrecks on Lake Ontario and in particular, Oswego Harbor, by Richard F Palmer, Syracuse Newspapers reporter. Photographs accompanied this material but were removed to be added to our local history photograph collection. Eight inches of material.

NY —SUFFOLK COUNTY HISTORICAL SOCIETY, Library, 300 W Main St, Riverhead, 11901. Betty Carpenter, Librn
Holdings: Vols (15,000) Cat Mss Maps Pix

NC —NATIONAL PARK SERVICE, Cape Hatteras National Seashore, Reference Library, Rte 1, Box 675, Manteo, 27954.
Holdings: Cat Mss Maps Pix
Notes: US Lifesaving Service, records and annual reports.

OH —BOWLING GREEN STATE UNIVERSITY, Jerome Library, Institute for Great Lakes Research, Bowling Green, 43403. Richard J Wright, Dir
Holdings: Vols (2500) Cat Mss Maps Pix Slides Phonorecords Audiotapes Videotapes 16mm Films Microforms
Budget: ($8300)
Notes: About 50 major ms collections, most of them processed; several thousand minor ms items, unprocessed. 100,000 pictures, incl several thousand film and glass plate negatives. Microforms of government vessel registries, vessel passages, 1500 maps, some mss. 6000 naval architectural drawings, 600 vols of scrapbooks. 140 periodical titles, current and op. Author/title/subject catalog.

OH —RUTHERFORD B HAYES LIBRARY, 1337 Hayes Ave, Fremont, 43420. Watt P Marchman, Dir
Holdings: Vols 500 Cat Mss Maps Pix Slides
Notes: The Great Lakes Marine Collection, incl the Capt Frank E Hamilton Collection; Great Lakes boats and shipping. Incl 300 charts; over 20,000 pictures (with 2500 negatives, 30 glass plates). Index and findings aids with the collection.

WI —MILWAUKEE PUBLIC LIBRARY, 814 W Wisconsin Ave, Milwaukee, 53233. Donald J Sager, City Librn
Holdings: Vols 1500 Cat Mss Maps Pix Slides
Notes: The Great Lakes Marine Collection consists of Runge Marine Collection, Wilson Marine Collection, and other collections on Great Lakes Marine History. Has data on about 85,000 ships and more than 20,000 pictures of Great Lakes vessels. Complete runs of reference material such as US. List of merchant vessels, Greens, etc. Extensive collection of lake charts, special indexes to Great Lakes shipwrecks.

ON —METROPOLITAN TORONTO LIBRARY, History Dept, 789 Yonge St, Toronto, M4W 2G8, Can. Michael Pearson, Head
Holdings: Vols (2500) Cat
Notes: The collection includes reports, diaries and personal narratives of travels and voyages of exploration and discovery from the Renaissance to the present day. Areas of emphasis are the exploration of the interior of North America, early oceanic voyages of discovery and accounts of travellers to Russia. The collection also includes a number of early editions, standard collected works such as the publications of the Hakluyt Society, accounts of shipwrecks as well as a representative collection of guide books from the 18th century to the present.

SHIPYARDS

IN —INDIANA UNIVERSITY, Lilly Library, Seventh St, Bloomington, 47405. William R Cagle, Librn
Holdings: // Mss Pix
Notes: Business papers and correspondence of Howard Ship Yards & Dock Co, Jeffersonville, Ind, 1834-1942. Incl correspondence with captains, ship owners, Howard family members, etc; some photos of Howard-built ships during construction; ca 10,000 blueprints, drawings and scale specifications for riverboat constructions; business ledgers and cash books; general office files. 265,600 items.

ME —MAINE MARITIME MUSEUM, Library and Archives, 963 Washington St, Bath, 04530. Nathan R Lipfert, Asst Cur
Holdings: Vols (5000) Cat Maps Pix Slides
Notes: The collection is limited primarily to shipbuilding in Bath, Maine, and to a lesser extent Marine as a whole. The unique aspects of the collection are a large collection of photographs of wooden shipbuilding and related trades, photographs of the vessels themselves, and a large collection of papers of a shipbuilding company in Bath active throughout the 19th century.

MD —CALVERT MARINE MUSEUM, Library, PO Box 97, Solomons, 20688.
Holdings: Uncat Mss Maps Pix Slides Audiotapes
Notes: Vessels lists of boats built in the county; lists of vessels owned in Calvert County, ships papers, half models, building plans and blueprints, artifacts, shipyard papers (correspondence, material lists, etc) and contracts. See also entries under Shipwrecks and U S-History-War of 1812.

NY —US MERCHANT MARINE ACADEMY, Schuyler Otis Bland Memorial Library, Steamboat Rd, Kings Point, 11024. Stephen R Wiist, Acting Chief Librn
Holdings: Vols (130,000) Cat Mss Maps Pix Slides Phonorecords Microforms
Budget: ($75,000)
Notes: All aspects of maritime affairs.

VA —PORTSMOUTH PUBLIC LIBRARY, 601 Court St, Portsmouth, 23704. Dean Burgess, Library Dir
Holdings: Vols 500 Cat Mss Maps Pix Slides Microforms
Notes: Portsmouth was founded in 1752 and was the headquarters for the British army throughout the Revolution. It has the oldest and now the largest American Navy Shipyard dating to before the Revolution and called the Norfolk Naval Shipyard. It also was the site of the building of the Merimac (which battled the Monitor off Portsmouth's waterfront). Several pre-revolutionary houses remain in the historic downtown area although most are from the Federal period 1800-1830. Portsmouth is often neglected in American history books perhaps because it was a Tory town.

SHIRER, WILLIAM L.

IA —COE COLLEGE, Stewart Memorial Library, Cedar Rapids, 52402. R Doyle, Dir of Library Services
Holdings: // Uncat
Notes: Incl in 5 ms boxes the original ms, supplementary outlines and notes of his best seller, *The Rise and Fall of the Third Reich,* donated by William L Shirer. Also incl some correspondence and a bibliography.

SHIRLEY, JAMES, 1596-1666

†ON —MCMASTER UNIVERSITY, Library, Hamilton, L8S 4L6, Can.
Notes: First editions of some 29 of his plays, some later editions of the plays, a copy of the rare *Grammatica Anglo-Latina* (1651) and an interesting copy of the *Poems* (1646) with ms notes an a ms poem bound in.

SHIRREFFS, GORDON D.

CA —UNIVERSITY OF CALIFORNIA, LOS ANGELES, Research Library, Dept of Special Collections, 405 Hilgard Ave, Los Angeles, 90024. Edward Shreeves, Chairman, Bibliographers Group; David S Zeidberg, Head
Notes: 7.5 linear feet of mss and papers.

SHISHMANIAN, JOHN AMAR

CA —HOOVER INSTITUTION ON WAR, REVOLUTION & PEACE, Stanford

SHISHMANIAN, JOHN AMAR (cont.)

University, Stanford, 94305. Milorad M
Drachkovitch, Archivist
Holdings: // Mss
Notes: Papers, 1914-1945, of John Amar
Shishmanian. Correspondence, reports,
translations of various articles, photo album
mostly of Armenians and personal
memorabilia, relating to Shishmanian's
career as head of the Armenian Volunteers
with the French Foreign Legion (1918), the
war in Cilicia (1918-1921), the treatment of
Armenia at the end of World War I and the
Treaty of Sevres, 1920. 2 boxes. Unpublished
preliminary register in repository.

SHIVERS, ALLAN

TX —NORTH TEXAS STATE UNIVERSITY,
Archives, NT Station Box 5188, Denton,
76203. Robert LaForte, University Archivist
Notes: Part of Oral History Collection.
Interviews 1965-68 with Shivers, former
state senator (1934-45) and governor of
Texas (1950-57). Permission required.

SHLEPPEY, JOHN W.

OK —UNIVERSITY OF TULSA, McFarlin
Library, Dept of Rare Books and Special
Collections, 600 S College, Tulsa, 74104.
David Farmer, Dir; Toby Murray, Archivist;
Caroline Swinson, Cur of Manuscripts & Art
Holdings: Cat
Notes: The Indian collection of John W
Shleppey. Indian materials of some 6000
bibliographic items, excl of mss and
photographs. Emphasis on Indian Territory
imprints, laws, Cherokee and Choctaw tribes,
etc.

SHO DIALECT see Karen Language

SHOE INDUSTRY AND TRADE see
Boots and Shoes—Trade and Manufacture

SHOEMAKER, HENRY W.

PA —PENNSYLVANIA STATE
UNIVERSITY, Fred Lewis Pattee Library,
Special Collections Dept, University Park,
16802. Charles Mann, Chief, Special
Collections
Holdings: Vols (93) Cat Mss
Budget: ($37,000)
Notes: Publications and correspondence of
the Pennsylvania historian and folklorist
Henry W Shoemaker, 1900-1950.

SHOEMAKER, JACK

NY —STATE UNIVERSITY OF NEW
YORK, COLLEGE AT BUFFALO, Poetry/
Rare Books Collection, 420 Capen Hall,
Buffalo, 14260. Robert J Bertholf, Cur
Notes: Extensive archive of Jack Shoemaker,
a prominent bookseller, publisher, and poet.
Incl mss, work sheets, correspondence,
ephemera, and business records of the Sand
Dollar and Unicorn bookshops and the
Maya Press. Also incl mss and letters of
prominent modern poets.

SHOEMAKERS UNION see Boot and
Shoemakers Union

SHOES see Boots and Shoes

SHOFSTALL, WELDON P.

AZ —NORTHERN ARIZONA
UNIVERSITY, Special Collection Library,
CU Box 6022, Flagstaff, 86011. Peter M
Whiteley, Coordr/Archivist; William
Mullane, Librn
Notes: Correspondence, scrapbooks,
speeches, personal files, 1950-1974. Former
Arizona State Superintendent of Public
Instruction, 1969-1975. (7 feet).

SHOOTING

MA —LUCIUS BEEBE MEMORIAL
LIBRARY, Main St, Wakefield, 01880.
Holdings: Vols (350) Cat
Notes: The Keough Collection of guns and
arms and armor.

SHOOTING STARS see Meteors

SHOPPERS' GUIDES see Consumer
Education

SHOPPING BAGS

NJ —NEWARK PUBLIC LIBRARY, Art &
Music Dept, 5 Washington St, Newark,
07101. William J Dane, Supv
Notes: Collection of 400 contemporary
shopping bags (paper) arranged by design
elements such as color, overall pattern,
lettering, foreign sourced, etc.

SHORE EROSION see Coast Changes

SHORE PROTECTION

FL —UNIVERSITY OF FLORIDA, Coastal
Engineering Archives, 433 Weil Hall,
Gainesville, 32611. Lucile Lehmann, Librn
Holdings: Cat Maps Pix Slides
Budget: ($4000)
Notes: 7000 technical reports, in addition to
maps, pictures, aerial photographs, 400
hydrographic surveys, etc. The Archives is
not part of the University library system but
is a special collection of the Coastal and
Oceanographic Engineering Dept.
ON —INTERNATIONAL JOINT
COMMISSION LIBRARY, 100 Ouellette
Ave, Seventh Floor, Windsor, N9A 6T3,
Can. Pat Murrary, Librn
Notes: Emphasis on water resources, water
quality, land use, coastal zones, Great Lakes.
Library includes 40,000 government reports
from federal, provincial and state
governments; 5000 monographs to support
Great Lakes Water Quality Agreement
Community. Collection also includes 243
periodicals, 1700 microfiche, 800 slides &
vertical files.

SHORRIS, EARL

MA —BOSTON UNIVERSITY, Mugar
Memorial Library, Special Collections Dept,
771 Commonwealth Ave, Boston, 02215.
Howard B Gotlieb, Dir
Holdings: Cat Mss
Notes: Incl publications by.

SHORT, WALTER C., 1880-1949

CA —HOOVER INSTITUTION ON WAR,
REVOLUTION & PEACE, Stanford
University, Stanford, 94305. Milorad M
Drachkovitch, Archivist
Notes: Typewritten documentation of events
and conditions leading up to the Japanese
attack on Pearl Harbor, December 7, 1941,
assembled by Lt Gen W C Short,
Commanding General, U S Army, Hawaiian
Department for his defense before the
"Roberts Commission," which investigated
the attack. 1/2 ms box.

SHORT TITLE CATALOGUE BOOKS

CA —FRANCIS BACON LIBRARY, 655 N
Dartmouth Ave, Claremont, 91711.
Elizabeth S Wrigley, Dir
Holdings: Vols 4000 Cat Mss Maps Pix
Microforms
Notes: One of the widest collections of
Bacon and Baconiana extant with secondary
material, histories, chronicles, etc of
contemporary writers of the chronicles, etc,
of contemporary writers of the Elizabethan
and Jacobean periods of English history; also
journal articles, theses, and dissertations.
Over 1000 titles in the STC and Wing
periods; detailed collations of these vols
published. Incl phonotapes. Published
Concordance to the Essays of Francis Bacon
(Detroit: Gale Research Co, 1973).
CA —UNIVERSITY OF CALIFORNIA, LOS
ANGELES, William Andrews Clark
Memorial Library, 2520 Cimarron St, Los
Angeles, 90018.
Holdings: Cat
†MA —BOSTON PUBLIC LIBRARY, Copley
Sq, Boston, 02117.
Holdings: Uncat Microforms
Notes: Microform publication by University

Microfilms. Early English Books, 1475-1640,
based on Pollard and Redgrave *Short-Title
Catalog*. 1927 reels.
MN —UNIVERSITY OF MINNESOTA, O
Meredith Wilson Library, 309 19 Ave S,
Minneapolis, 55455. Austin J McLean,
Chief, Special Collections
Holdings: Vols (9000) Ctat
Notes: Special concentration on volumes
from the Stuart Period. Holdings are cited in
the new revisions of the STC and Wing.
NY —NEW YORK STATE LIBRARY, State
Education Bldg Annex, Washington Ave,
Albany, 12224.
Holdings: Microforms
Notes: English books, 1475-1640. University
Microfilms collection. Access thru Pollard
and Redgrave, *Short-title Catalogue*. English
books, 1641-1700. University Microfilms
collection. Access thru Wing, *Short-title
Catalogue*.
NY —BUFFALO & ERIE COUNTY PUBLIC
LIBRARY, Rare Book Room, Lafayette Sq,
Buffalo, 14203. William H Loos, Cur
Holdings: Vols 900 Cat
Notes: Holdings described in *Pollard and
Redgrave Titles; A Checklist of Items in the
Rare Book Room of the Buffalo and Erie
County Public Library* (Buffalo, 1968); and
*Wing Titles; A Checklist of Items in the
Rare Book Room, Buffalo and Erie County
Public Library* (Buffalo, 1968).
PA —FREE LIBRARY OF PHILADELPHIA,
Rare Book Dept, Logan Sq, Philadelphia,
19103. Marie E Korey, Rare Book Librn
Holdings: Vols (1000) // Uncat
Notes: Wing and Short Title Catalogue
Books; books and pamphlets printed in
Great Britain between 1475 and 1700.
PA —UNIVERSITY OF PENNSYLVANIA,
Van Pelt Library, Rare Books Collection, 34
& Walnut Sts, Philadelphia, 19104. Daniel
Traister, Special Collections Librn
Holdings: Cat Microforms
Notes: The University Library has acquired
approx 20,000 editions of the University
Microfilms Xerox Collection of STC (Pollard
and Redgrave) books. See (University of
Pennsylvania) *Library Chronicle*, vol 34, no
1, winter 1968, Frye, Ronald M "The New
Photocopy Library of British Renaissance
Books at the University of Pennsylvania."
ON —QUEEN'S UNIVERSITY, Douglas
Library, Kingston, K7L 5C4, Can. William F
E Morley, Cur, Special Collections
Holdings: Vols 1000 Cat Mss
Notes: Dated collection (books printed
before 1700).

**SHORTER, RT. REV. MSGR. JOSEPH
A., 1863-1936**

KS —SAINT MARY COLLEGE, Library,
Leavenworth, 66048. Therese Deplazes,
Special Collections Librn
Holdings: Cat Mss
Notes: About 1000 items in the Joseph A
Shorter papers. More than 100 in the
Maurice Colfax Fields Collection.

SHORTHAND

CT —YALE UNIVERSITY, Box 1603A, Yale
Station, New Haven, 06520.
Holdings: Cat Mss
IL —NEWBERRY LIBRARY, 60 W Walton
St, Chicago, 60610. Diana Haskell, Cur of
Modern Mss
Holdings: Vols 2500
Notes: James W Beers Collection. Restricted
use: noncirculating.
MI —UNIVERSITY OF MICHIGAN, Library,
Dept of Rare Books & Special Collections,
Ann Arbor, 48109. Robert J Starring, Head
Holdings: Vols Mss
Notes: 18th-20th centuries.
MO —WASHINGTON UNIVERSITY, John
M Olin Library, Campus Box 1061, St Louis,
63130.
Holdings: Vols (1300) Cat Mss
Notes: The Philip M Arnold Semeiology
Collection is concerned with the study of
signs and symbols. Topics incl cryptography;
artificial memory; decipherment of unknown
languages; universal languages; early

SHORTHAND (cont.)

developments in stenography, telegraphy; and communication systems for the blind, the deaf and the mute; and various forms of nonverbal communication. Limited photocopying. Noncirculating.

NY —NEW YORK STATE LIBRARY, State Education Bldg Annex, Washington Ave, Albany, 12224.
Holdings: Cat
Notes: Historical collection based on 1913 gift collection of New York Shorthand Reporters Association and gifts from its librarian and editor, David O'Keefe, and Spencer Rodgers. Over 1000 vols plus pamphlets.

NY —SAINT JOHN'S UNIVERSITY, Special Collections Dept, Grand Central & Utopia Pkwys, Jamaica, 11439. Szilvia E Szmuk, Librn
Holdings: // Cat
Notes: The Saul Heller Collection consists of 18th and early 19th century volumes on the practical and theoretical aspects of stenography. No photocopying.

NY —NEW YORK PUBLIC LIBRARY, Research Libraries, General Research Division, Fifth Ave & 42 St, New York, 10018. Rodney Phillips, Chief
Holdings: Vols (2,225,000) Cat Maps Pix Microforms
Budget: ($775,718)
Notes: Outstanding collection incl Charles Currier Beale collection covering Pitman and other English systems and Gregg Publishing Co gifts. Coverage is from the 17th century to the present day, comprising all systems: Continental European, British and American systems. See Karl Brown and Daniel C Haskell *Shorthand Books in The New York Public Library* (New York: The Library, 1935).

SHOSHONE INDIANS

NV —UNIVERSITY OF NEVADA, RENO, University Library, Special Collections Dept, Reno, 89557. Robert E Blesse, Head
Holdings: Vols 1100 Mss Pix
Notes: Incl over 5000 photographs, government documents, periodicals, 80 cubic feet, mss, and audiotapes. The Great Basin Indian Collection contains materials on the anthropology, archaeology, and ethnohistory of the Great Basin region. Materials are collected for a defined group of 65 tribes incl Washo, Shoshone, Northern and Southern Paiute, the major tribes of the region. Collection of importance incl the Sven Liljeblad Collection, linguistics and ethnography; papers of US agent Lorenzo D Greel, 1902-22; Robert Leland Collection, Indian water rights.

SHOTGUNS

NY —REMINGTON ARMS CO, Remington Gun Museum, Catherine St, Ilion, 13357. Laurence Goodstal, Cur
Notes: Museum displays sporting and military firearms built by Remington Arms Co, ca 1825 to modern firearms of today.

SHOUP, DAVID MONROE, 1904-

CA —HOOVER INSTITUTION ON WAR, REVOLUTION & PEACE, Stanford University, 94305. Milorad M Drachkovitch, Archivist
Holdings: Mss Pix Phonorecords 16mm Films
Notes: Papers of David M Shoup, Gen, U S Marine Corps, commander of Marine forces at Tarawa, 1943, chief of staff, 2d Marine Division, 1944, and commandant of the Marine Corps, 1960-63, incl correspondence, memoranda, writings, printed matter, photographs, films and sound recordings, 1927-71, relating to the Tarawa campaign, other World War II campaigns in the Pacific Theater, postwar activities of the Marine Corps, and the Vietnam war. 21 ms boxes, 9 linear ft.

SHOVELS

MA —STONEHILL COLLEGE, Donahue Hall, Washington St, North Easton, 02356.

Louise M Kenneally, Archivist & Special Collections Librn
Holdings: //
Notes: The Arnold B Tofias Industrial Archives; 2000 linear feet of records and correspondence of the Ames Shovel Company of North Easton, Mass. About 800 shovels and other artifacts. Covers the period 1774-1956.

SHOW CARDS see Advertising Cards

SHOWMEN see Entertainers

SHREVE, HENRY MILLER, 1785-1851

LA —LOUISIANA STATE UNIVERSITY, SHREVEPORT, Library-Archives, 8515 Youree Dr, Shreveport, 71129. Patricia L Meador, Archivist & Asst Librn
Notes: Archives incl catalogued manuscripts and records, 500 maps, more than 5000 photographs, 1000 architectural drawings, slides. The archives has on microfilm more than 200 letters (1827-1842) of Henry Miller Shreve, relating to the improvement of the Ohio, Mississippi and Red Rivers. Microfilm records also include those of the Shreveport City Council, Caddo and Bossier Parish Police Juries, Caddo Levee Board, the Shreveport Chamber of Commerce, and the Louisiana State Fair. Original and microfilm copies of the *Italia Moderna*, an Italian newspaper published by Frank Fulco in Shreveport, 1929-1946, are available for use in the archives. Other area newspapers are on microfilm and available for use.

SHREVEPORT LITTLE THEATRE

LA —LOUISIANA STATE UNIVERSITY, SHREVEPORT, Library-Archives, 8515 Youree Dr, Shreveport, 71129. Patricia L Meador, Archivist & Asst Librn
Notes: Theatre and music is documented in the John Wray and Margaret Mary Young Theatre Collection, (5 linear ft) (1929-1981), the Joe Gifford Papers (1946-1960) (3 linear ft), the Shreveport Little Theatre Records (6 linear ft), the Nathaniel S Allen Papers (1860-1930), the records of the Shreveport Symphony (1948-1978) and oral history interviews on the topics. The archives collection also incl 60 linear ft of records (1949-1981) of Holiday-In-Dixie, Shreveport-Bossier's spring-time festival.

SHRIMPS

TX —UNIVERSITY OF TEXAS, Marine Science Institute Library, Port Aransas, 78373. Ruth Grundy, Librn
Holdings: Vols (45,000) Cat Maps Pix
Budget: ($70,000)
Notes: Current researches in marine science, especially concerning the Gulf of Mexico, the Texas Coastal Zone, and the Continental Shelf. Incl journals.

SHRINES

CT —YALE UNIVERSITY, Medical Historical Library, 333 Cedar St, New Haven, 06510. Ferenc A Gyorgyey, Librn
OH —UNIVERSITY OF DAYTON, Marian Library, 300 College Park Ave, Dayton, 45469. Rev Theodore Koehler, SM, Dir/Cur
Holdings: Vols (65,000) Cat Mss Pix Slides Phonorecords Audiotapes Filmstrips Microforms
Budget: ($12,000)
Notes: Part of largest and most comprehensive collection in the world of literature on the Virgin Mary. Incl Vloberg collection of pictures, ms notes and offprints on Marian iconography; 10,000 holy cards from 19th and 20th centuries; 2600 postcard views of shrines; 3000 postcards of Marian art; philatelic collection of 1000 stamps and 200 first-day covers; 1000 photographs.

SHRUBS

IL —MORTON ARBORETUM, Sterling Morton Library, Lisle, 60532. Ian MacPhail, Librn
Holdings: Vols (20,000) Cat Maps Pix
Budget: ($10,000)
Notes: The library is especially concerned

with the literature of woody plants (trees and shrubs) of north temperate zones but has substantial holdings in the taxonomy and systematics of plants in general, both wild and cultivated, flora of different parts of the world, and a growing collection on plant monographs. Also about 2000 pictures. Described in *The Morton Arboretum Quarterly*, vol 9, no 4 (Winter 1973), pp 56-61.

MA —MASSACHUSETTS HORTICULTURAL SOCIETY, 300 Massachusetts Ave, Boston, 02115. Becky Ellis, Librn
Holdings: Vols (37,000)
Notes: Garden history, pomology, flora, landscape design. Print collection of many centuries; nursery catalogues from the mid-18th century. In storage, remodeling, will be available in about a year. Open to the public.

MA —HARVARD UNIVERSITY LIBRARY, Arnold Arboretum Library, 22 Divinty Ave, Cambridge, 02138. Barbara A Callahan, Librn
Holdings: Vols (89,239) Cat Mss Maps Pix Slides Microforms
Notes: Specializes in trees (arboriculture and dendrology). Horticultural Library maintained at The Arborway, Jamaica Plain, Mass.

MA —NEW ENGLAND WILD FLOWER SOCIETY, INC, Lawrence Newcomb Library, Hemenway Rd, Framingham, 01701. Mary M Walker, Librn
Holdings: Vols (2500)
Budget: ($1000)
Notes: Incl 15,000 slides (35mm) and 4 vertical files.

OH —THE DAWES ARBORETUM LIBRARY, 7770 Jacksontown Rd SE, Newark, 43055. Alan D Cook, Senior Horticulturist
Holdings: Vols 5000

PA —LONGWOOD GARDENS, INC, Library, Kennett Square, 19348. Enola Jane N Teeter, Librn

SHUBERT BROTHERS

†NY —SHUBERT ARCHIVE, Lyceum Theatre, 149 W 45th St, New York, 10036. Brigitte Kueppers, Archivist
Notes: The vast Shubert Archive, mostly unexplored is the largest collection in the world representative of the "business" of the theatre. It includes almost all of the Shubert empire's correspondence from the turn of the century to the 1950s, road company records, thousands of playscripts (American and European), set and costume designs, music scores for Shubert productions, business, financial, and legal records, actors' contracts, etc.

SHULMAN, MAX

MA —BOSTON UNIVERSITY, Mugar Memorial Library, Special Collections Dept, 771 Commonwealth Ave, Boston, 02215. Howard B Gotlieb, Dir
Holdings: Cat Mss Pix
Notes: Mss, correspondence, etc collected in depth; incl publications by or about.

SHUMARD, BENJAMIN FRANKLIN

MO —SAINT LOUIS PUBLIC LIBRARY, Gardner Rare Book Room, 1301 Olive St, Saint Louis, 63103. Julanne M Good, Supervisor; Martha Riley, Rare Books Librn
Holdings: Vols 600 Cat
Notes: Collection of natural history from the library of Benjamin Franklin Shumard, nineteenth century paleontologist and conchologist, and selected material pre-dating 1870 transferred from St Louis Public Library's general stack area. Noncirculating.

SHURCLIFF, WILLIAM ASAHEL

MA —MASSACHUSETTS INSTITUTE OF TECHNOLOGY, Institute Archives, Special Collections, Cambridge, 02139.
Notes: Correspondence, newsletters, fact-sheets, newspaper and magazine articles, books and reports of the Citizens' League

SHURCLIFF, WILLIAM ASAHEL (cont.)

Against the Sonic Boom, established in 1967 by William Shurcliff to oppose the sonic boom, stop commercial supersonic transport production, and influence public opinion and policy decisions on the SST. Major correspondents incl Bo Lundberg, Richard Wiggs, several US congressmen, and CLASB members.

SHUVAK LANGUAGE see Chuvashian Language

SHYRE, PAUL

MA —BOSTON UNIVERSITY, Mugar Memorial Library, Special Collections Dept, 771 Commonwealth Ave, Boston, 02215. Howard B Gotlieb, Dir
Holdings: Cat Mss Pix
Notes: Mss, correspondence, etc collected in depth; incl publications by or about.

SIAMESE LANGUAGE see Thai Language and Literature

SIBELIUS, JAN

IN —BUTLER UNIVERSITY, Irwin Library, Hugh Thomas Miller Rare Book Room, 4600 Sunset Ave, Indianapolis, 46208. Gisela Terrell, Rare Books Librn
Holdings: Vols Cat Phonorecords Audiotapes
Notes: Sibelius Collection. It contains mostly the lesser-known compositions, and includes scores in print, hectograph, and manuscript, many of them unpublished and unknown in the US. Also rare secondary sources, mostly Finnish and Swedish imprints. Also a collection of mostly historical recordings, probably complete up to 1972. Placed in trust in the Rare Book Room by Dr Harold E Johnson, Sibelius scholar, 1982-1983. A preliminary checklist is available. The recordings include many pieces by lesser-known Finnish composers.
See also entry under Composers, Finnish.

SIBERIA

CA —UNIVERSITY OF CALIFORNIA, BERKELEY, University Library, Slavic Collections, Berkeley, 94720. Edward Kasinec, Librn
Notes: Russian Pacifica collection, the best on the West coast, incl materials in the folowing areas: Russian exploration and settlement of the North American continent; Russian exploration and settlement and colonization of Siberia; Russian exploration of the Pacific; Russian communities in Manchuria and other parts of the Far East. While many items pertaining to the geographical area are found in the Main Library's stack collection, the bulk of Russian Pacifica holdings is concentrated in the Bancroft Library. The Bancroft collections contain the greater number of items listed in the two major bibliographies of Russian Pacifica: Valentin Lada-Macarski's Bibliography of Books on Alaska Published before 1868 (Yale Univ Press, 1969), and V I Mezhov's Sibirskaia bibliografiia (S Petersburg: Semenov, 1903). During 1983-84, with the assistanceof Title II-C funding, a major project of collection evaluation and development was undertaken in the area of Russian Pacifica, resulting in the acquisition on microfilm of several hundred items, incl a part of the holdings of the Museum of Russian Culture in San Francisco relating to Siberia and Russian communities in China.
CA —HOOVER INSTITUTION ON WAR, REVOLUTION & PEACE, Stanford University, Stanford, 94305. Milorad M Drachkovitch, Archivist
Holdings: Mss Pix Slides
Notes: Two collections: (1) Papers, 1914-1932, of William Sidney Graves, Army officer. Correspondence, reports, monographs, photos and other material, relating to the Allied intervention in Russia and to American Expeditionary Forces in Siberia (1918-1919) of which Maj Gen Graves was commander. 3 boxes. Unpublished preliminary inventory in repository. (2) Papers of W H Vatcher, Jr, 1939-65, incl correspondence, mss, pamphlets, leaflets, slides, photographs, and other material, relating to South African political parties; Afrikaner and African nationalism; Afrikaner Broederbond; U S, Japanese, and North Korean propaganda and psychological warfare methods during World War II and the Korean war. Incl "Siberian Sketchbook," a ms with photos by W H Vatcher. 18 ms boxes, 1 box, 4 envelopes.
CA —HOOVER INSTITUTION ON WAR, REVOLUTION & PEACE, Stanford University, Stanford, 94305. Milorad M Drachkovitch, Archivist
Notes: The Herman Axelbank Film Collection on Russian history. Much footage dating from about 1901-1921. Subjects incl Royal Family, Moscow and St Petersburg scenes, the Revolution and Civil War, espec good coverage of Leon Trotsky's role, Siberia, and the Far East. The first 28 of 266 reels have been received (April 1983).
IL —FIELD MUSEUM OF NATURAL HISTORY, The Berthold Laufer Library, Roosevelt Rd & Lake Shore Dr, Chicago, 60605. W Peyton Fawcett, Librn
Holdings: Vols (12,000) // Cat Mss Maps Budget:
Notes: The part of the museum's collection of Berthold Laufer (1874-1934), Curator of Anthropology, dealing with the peoples of the pre-19th century Chinese Empire (incl Manchuria, Mongolia, Sinkiang and Tibet); their anthropology, art and religion; influences upon their cultures by those of India, Siberia, Japan, Indonesia, and Oceania--and vice versa. Incl about 500 books in Tibetan. About 2/3 of the collection is cataloged.
WA —UNIVERSITY OF WASHINGTON LIBRARIES, Rare Books, Special Collections Dept, Seattle, 98195. Sandra Kroupa, Librn
Notes: Part of a set of Siberian primers prepared in the early 1930s by Soviet ethnographers. Some are first attempts to transcribe Siberian languages. All are in Latin phonetic script, not in Cyrillic.

SIBERT, WILLIAM LUTHER

AL —GADSDEN PUBLIC LIBRARY, 254 College St, Gadsden, 35999. Margaret C Rouse, Reference Librn
Holdings: Vols 269// Cat Mss Maps Pix
Notes: Sibert Collection, the papers of William Luther Sibert, director of construction of the Panama Canal. Mr Siebert was an Etowah County native and Gadsden resident, 1860-1935. Collection received from Mrs Mary Papoi (Aug 1976) and John Freeman (Aug 1977). Separate card index.

SIBLEY, U. ERWIN

GA —GEORGIA COLLEGE, Ina Dillard Russell Library, Special Collections Dept, Milledgeville, 31061. Janice C Fennell, Dir of Libraries; Nancy Davis, Special Collections Assoc
Holdings: Uncat Mss
Notes: Personal and official correspondence of Judge U Erwin Sibley, 1912-1978. Incl personal correspondence between Judge Sibley and Congressman Carl Vinson for years 1932-1972 (34 folders).

SICKNESS INSURANCE see Insurance, Health

SIDEROGRAPHY see Engravers, Engraving and Engravings

SIDESHOWS see Amusement Parks

SIDNEY, MARGARET see Lothrop, Harriet Mulford

SIEGE OF PETERSBURG see Petersburg, Virginia—Siege, 1864-1865

SIEGEL, DON

MA —BOSTON UNIVERSITY, Mugar Memorial Library, Special Collections Dept, 771 Commonwealth Ave, Boston, 02215. Howard B Gotlieb, Dir
Holdings: Mss Pix
Notes: Mss, correspondence, etc collected in depth; incl publications by or about.

SIEGEL, ROBERT H.

IL —WHEATON COLLEGE, Buswell Memorial Library, Wheaton, 60187. Paul Snezek, Library Dir
Notes: Mss 15 linear feet of poems, correspondence and manuscripts.

SIEGES

MN —UNIVERSITY OF MINNESOTA, O Meredith Wilson Library, 309 19 Ave S, Minneapolis, 55455. Austin J McLean, Chief, Special Collections
Holdings: Vols (410) Cat
Notes: Fortification from the Renaissance to 1800. Related materials on attack and defense and accounts of famous sieges.

SIERRA CLUB

CA —UNIVERSITY OF CALIFORNIA, LOS ANGELES, Research Library, Dept of Special Collections, 405 Hilgard Ave, Los Angeles, 90024. Edward Shreeves, Chairman, Bibliographers Group; David S Zeidberg, Head
Notes: 6 linear feet of miscellaneous ephemera, membership rosters, activity mailings, etc, of the parent organization and associate chapters. Incl 10 linear feet of correspondence, newsletters, and records of the Angeles Chapter of the Sierra Club.
CA —UNIVERSITY OF THE PACIFIC, Library, Stockton, 95211. Hiram L Davis, Dir of Libraries
Notes: The John Muir papers. Muir was the founder of the Sierra Club, a prime mover in the development of the national park systems, and a major force in the preservationist branch of the conservation movement.
MO —UNIVERSITY OF MISSOURI-SAINT LOUIS, Thomas Jefferson Library, Manuscript and Historical Society Collection, 8001 Natural Bridge Rd, Saint Louis, 63121.
Holdings: Mss Pix Tapes
Notes: ca

SIERRA NEVADA MOUNTAINS

CA —AZUSA PACIFIC COLLEGE, Marshburn Memorial Library, Citrus & Alosta, Azusa, 91702. Edward Peterman, Librn
Holdings: Vols (6000) Uncat
Budget: ($30,000)
Notes: Significant holdings in the George E Fullerton Library of Californiana and Western Americana.
CA —CALIFORNIA STATE UNIVERSITY, FRESNO, Henry Madden Library, Dept of Special Collections, Fresno, 93740. Ronald J Mahoney, Head
Holdings: Vols (6200) Cat Mss Maps Pix
Notes: California history, with emphasis on San Joaquin Valley and Sierra Nevada. Also incl material relating to the history and preservation of Mineral King area of Sequoia National Park. Used by John LeRoy Harper when writing Mineral King: Public Concern with Government Policy (Arcata, Calif, 1982). Incl documents, clippings and pamphlets.
NV —UNIVERSITY OF NEVADA, RENO, University Library, Special Collections Dept, Reno, 89557. Robert E Blesse, Head
Holdings: Vols 25 Uncat Mss Pix
Notes: Papers of James E Church founder and developer of the modern science of snow surveying. Church collection, 180 cubic feet, incl his writings, papers, and over 7000 photographs of Church's snow surveying expeditions in the Sierra Nevada mountains and elsewhere in the world. Papers of the Western Snow Conference, 80 cubic feet.

SIEVEKING, LANCE

IN —INDIANA UNIVERSITY, Lilly Library, Seventh St, Bloomington, 47405. William R

SIEVEKING, LANCE (cont.)

Cagle, Librn
Holdings: Cat Mss Pix
Notes: Papers, 1724-1971, of British writer, radio producer, Lancelot de Giberne Sieveking, 1896-1974, and of his ancestors. Incl correspondence; radio plays; manuscripts for short stories novels, and non-fiction works; diaries; drawings; and photographs. (ca 15,000 items)

SIGHT see Vision

SIGHT-SAVING BOOKS

IN —MORRISSON-REEVES LIBRARY, 80 N Sixth St, Richmond, 47374. Harriet E Bard, Librn
Holdings: Vols 1992 Cat
Notes: Diverse collection of fiction and nonfiction titles.
MN —SAINT PAUL PUBLIC LIBRARY, 90 W Fourth St, Saint Paul, 55102. Ortha Robbins, Supvr of Circulation Room
Holdings: Vols 2000 Cat
Notes: Large type (18 pt) collection for visually handicapped adults.
NY —BUFFALO & ERIE COUNTY PUBLIC LIBRARY, Fiction Dept, Lafayette Sq, Buffalo, 14203. Irene Dwigans, Head
Holdings: Vols 8419 Cat
Notes: Books in 18 point type.
NY —WILLARD PSYCHIATRIC CENTER, Patients Library, Willard, 14588. Helen Bunting, Chief Library Services
Holdings: Vols (23,025) Cat Phonorecords
TX —PHARR MEMORIAL LIBRARY, 200 S Athol, Pharr, 78577. Karen Mier, Asst Librn
Holdings: Vols 360 Cat
Notes: Large print books.
WA —WASHINGTON LIBRARY FOR THE BLIND AND PHYSICALLY HANDICAPPED, 821 Lenora St, Seattle, 98129. Jan Ames, Regional Librn
Holdings: Vols 159,485 Cat Phonorecords Audiotapes
Notes: Serves blind, visually impaired, physically handicapped, and learning disabled. A Regional Library and a Machine Agency for the State of Washington. Incl 19,655 Braille volumes, 59,600 cassette volumes, 99,885 recorded disc volumes, plus collections in large print and ink print reference materials.
BC —UNIVERSITY OF BRITISH COLUMBIA, Charles Crane Memorial Library, 2075 Westbrook Hall, Vancouver, V6T 1W5, Can. Paul E Thiele, Librn
Holdings: Vols (25,000) Cat Maps Phonorecords Audiotapes
Notes: This is a special library serving blind, visually inpaired and physically handicapped college and university students with books and materials in Braille (approx 25,000 vols) phonotape (4000 Vols); various other phono media incl cassette and disc (approx 3000 vols), large type (300 vols) and print materials. We offer recording services and copying of prerecorded material plus transcription of print into Braille or Large Type. Also incl 12 Contour maps. Library uses BRF message service; BIF Communication #TB-18; ENVOY 100; Electronic Mail #CIANE.

SIGILLOGRAPHY see Seals (Numismatics)

SIGN LANGUAGE, INDIAN see Indians—Sign Language

SIGNATURE ARCHIVES

DE —UNIVERSITY OF DELAWARE, Hugh M Morris Library, S College Ave, Newark, 19711. T Stuart Dick, Special Collections
Holdings: Cat Mss Pix
Notes: Manuscripts, etc, incl literary correspondence.

SIGNBOARDS see Signs and Signboards

SIGNETS see Seals (Numismatics)

SIGNIFICANT BOOKS see Bibliography—Best Books

SIGNS (OMENS) see Omens

SIGNS AND SIGNBOARDS

CA —CALIFORNIA DEPT OF TRANSPORTATION, Transportation Library, 5900 Folsom Blvd, PO Box 19128, Sacramento, 95819. Eva Caro, Librn
Holdings: Vols (10,000) Cat Mss Maps Pix Slides Phonorecords Audiotapes Videotapes 16mm Films Filmstrips Microforms
NJ —FAIRLEIGH DICKINSON UNIVERSITY, Friendship Library, 285 Madison Ave, Madison, 07940. James Fraser, Library Dir; Renee Weber, Cur
Holdings: Vols 1200 Cat Mss Pix Slides Phonorecords 16mm Films
Notes: Official depository for the Outdoor Advertising industry. Collection initiated in August 1972. About 100,000 items. It is the concern of the Outdoor Advertising Association of America that this collection become the definitive collection on the industry in this country. Incl 20,000 mss, 10,000 pictures, 30,000 slides. 15 original billboards.
NY —NEW YORK STATE LIBRARY, State Education Bldg Annex, Washington Ave, Albany, 12224.
Holdings: Cat
Notes: World War I (including Benjamin Walworth Arnold collection), World War II (including war industries and civilian cooperation); UN posters; a few theater posters, miscellaneous items.

SIGNS AND SYMBOLS

MN —MINNEAPOLIS COLLEGE OF ART & DESIGN, Library, 200 E 25 St, Minneapolis, 55404. Richard Kronstedt, Head Librn
MN —MAYO MEDICAL LIBRARY, History of Medicine Collection, Rochester, 55905. Nancy R Hensel, Librn
Holdings: Pix
Notes: Over 300 bookplates of physicians and medical institutions. Listed. Collection described: Mann, Ruth J: "Of bookplates, books, and their owners." *Mayo Clin Proc* 46:358-360, May 1971.

SIGOURNEY, LYDIA HOWARD (HUNTLEY)

CT —TRINITY COLLEGE LIBRARY, Watkinson Library, 300 Summit St, Hartford, 06106. Jeffrey Kaimowitz, Cur
Holdings: // Cat
Notes: Cat.
CT —YALE UNIVERSITY, Box 1603A, Yale Station, New Haven, 06520.
CT —CONNECTICUT COLLEGE, Library, Mohegan Ave, New London, 06320. Brian Rogers, College Librn
Holdings: Vols (382,000) Cat Mss
VA —UNIVERSITY OF VIRGINIA, Alderman Library, Manuscripts Dept, Charlottesville, 22901. Edmund Berkeley Jr, Cur
Holdings: Cat Mss
Notes: First editions, mss, papers, etc.

SIHASAPA INDIANS see Blackfoot Indians

SIKHISM see Sikhs—Religion

SIKHS—RELIGION

CA —GRADUATE THEOLOGICAL UNION LIBRARY, New Religious Movements Research Collection, Public Services and Special Collections Dept, 2400 Ridge Road, Berkeley, 94709. Diane Choquette, Dept Head
Holdings: Vols (3000) Mss Pix
Notes: Begun in 1977, the collection focuses on religious movements new to America since 1960, and unorthodox religious movements resurgent since 1960. American forms of Hinduism, Buddhism, Sikhism, and Sufism are included along with occultism, Neo-Paganism, esoteric and alternative forms of Christianity, feminist spirituality, and human potential movements having a spiritual aspect. Legal issues, such as deprogramming, and the question of church/state relations are an important part of the collection. The Library is a depository for publications of the Unification Church in America, the Church of Scientology, and the International Society for Krishna Consciousness (America). The responses of mainstream religions and concerned citizens groups are also included. Besides 3000 monographs, the library has 400 periodical titles, 200 posters from the San FranciscoBay Area, 1965-77, 300 research papers, and 31 linear feet of ephemera.
OH —CLEVELAND PUBLIC LIBRARY, Fine Arts and Special Collections Department, 325 Superior Ave, Cleveland, 44114. Alice N Loranth, Head
Holdings: Vols (7100) Cat Mss
Notes: Part of the Oriental Religion Collection. Emphasis is on religion texts in their original languages and Western translations. Treatises on religious beliefs and practices are also incl. Strong holdings in Buddhism, Egyptian religion, Hinduism, Judaica, Lamaistic texts, Islam, Sikhism and Zoroastrianism. The rarest material on the sikhs comes from the library of Max A Macauliffe.
See also entry under Religion, Oriental.

SIKKIM

CA —UNIVERSITY OF CALIFORNIA, BERKELEY, University Library, 438 Main Library, Berkeley, 94720. Kenneth R Logan, South Asia Librn
Notes: South Asia collection (India, Pakistan, Bangladesh, Nepal, Sri Lanka) contain 150,000-200,000 titles. Covers at research level the social sciences and humanities in western languages and 20 South Asian languages. Subject areas: history, political science, lanuage and literature (especially strong in Hindi, Urdu, Tamil, Sanskrit and Nepali), art and art history, sociology, education, music, environmental design, philosophy and religion, anthropology, geography, national and local government publications. Formats: monographs, periodicals, newspapers, microforms, maps, sound recordings, video-tapes, pamphlets. Special strengths: modern Hindi literature; history of South Asian countries; government publications of India, late 19th and 20th centuries. Member of South Asia Microform Project; Participant in Library of Congress AcquisitionsPrograms for India, Pakistan, Nepal, and Bangladesh.

SILK

MA —UNIVERSITY OF LOWELL, Library, One University Ave, Lowell, 01854. Martha Mayo, Special Collections Librn
Holdings: Vols 2500 Cat Mss Pix Slides
Notes: Books and journals on all aspects of textile technology.

SILK MANUFACTURE AND TRADE—HISTORY

NJ —PASSAIC COUNTY HISTORICAL SOCIETY, Lamhurt Castle, Valley Rd, Paterson, 07503. Helen D Hamilton, Dir
Holdings: Vols (5000) Cat Mss Maps PIx
Notes: Material on the Society for the Establishment of Useful Manufacturing (founded) by Alexander Hamilton, papers relating to John Holland, who developed the submarine, the industrial magnates of the area who were active in the manufacture of locomotives, Colt revolvers, and textiles, especially silk.

SILLIPHANT, STERLING, 1918-

CA —UNIVERSITY OF CALIFORNIA, LOS ANGELES, Research Library, Dept of Special Collections, 405 Hilgard Ave, Los Angeles, 90024. Edward Shreeves, Chairman, Bibliographers Group; David S Zeidberg, Head
Holdings: Mss Pix
Notes: 36 linear feet of television and moving picture scripts. No photocopying.

SILLITOE, ALAN

NV —UNIVERSITY OF NEVADA, RENO, University Library, Special Collections Dept,

SILLITOE, ALAN (cont.)

Reno, 89557. Robert E Blesse, Head
Holdings: Vols (85) Cat
Notes: Includes individual works by author in all editions including translations; also prefaces, introductions, published correspondence, appearances in anthologies, periodicals, etc. Bibliographical research collection, part of Modern Authors Collection. Other appearances 195 cataloged.

SILVA, LUIGI, 1903-1961

NC —UNIVERSITY OF NORTH CAROLINA, GREENSBORO, Walter Clinton Jackson Library, Special Collections Dept, 1000 Spring Garden St, Greensboro, 27412. Emilie W Mills, Librn
Holdings: Vols (2000) Cat Mss Pix Phonorecords Microforms
Notes: The original collection of over 2000 books, mss, music scores, published and unpublished cello compositions, notes, programs, photographs and related items came from the library of Luigi Silva, cellist, teacher, and musicologist. Special strength is in recital pieces for the cello. The cello music dates from the 18th century and incl Silva's own transcriptions and arrangements for his projected editions of all the Boccherini sonatas, left incomplete at the time of his death in 1961. Silva's own history of cello techniques, also unfinished, is in the collection. Several 18th century cello sonatas were added to the collection by Silva's long-time friend and eminent cellist, Janos Scholz. A published catalog is available.

SILVANNEAU, MARIA LOUISA

SC —COLLEGE OF CHARLESTON LIBRARY, Special Collections Dept, Charleston, 29401.
Notes: Papers incl warrant for sheriff's sale of Maria Silvanneau, a free "person of color" for non-payment of capitation tax, June 28, 1849.

SILVER

ON —UNIVERSITY OF TORONTO, Thomas Fisher Rare Book Library, 120 Saint George St, Toronto, M5S 1A5, Can. Richard G Landon, Head
Holdings: Vols 1000 Cat
Notes: Langdon Collection, named for donor, John E Langdon. Contains material on silver and silversmiths around the world with special emphasis on Canada.

SILVER, ISADORE

MO —WASHINGTON UNIVERSITY, Libraries, Special Collections Dept, Campus Box 1061, St Louis, 63130.
Notes: Family and business correspondence.

SILVER, SAMUEL, 1915-1976

CA —UNIVERSITY OF CALIFORNIA, BERKELEY, Bancroft Library, Manuscripts Division, Berkeley, 94720. James D Hart, Dir
Holdings: Mss
Notes: Papers of Samuel Silver, specialist on applied electromagnetic, microwave, and radio astronomical problems. Much on the International Union of Radio Science. 48 linear ft.

SILVER MINES AND MINING

NV —UNIVERSITY OF NEVADA, RENO, University Library, Special Collections Dept, Reno, 89557. Robert E Blesse, Head
Holdings: Vols (400) Cat Pix Mss
Notes: An extensive collection of books, photographs (2000), and manuscripts (100 cu ft), published reports, government publications dealing with mining in Nevada from the mid 19th century to the present. Primary emphasis is on the Comstock Lode, Virginia City, Nevada but material is

available on mining in all geographic areas of the state. The 105 manuscript collections include business papers and records of mining companies, and papers of firms which provided materials and equipment to the mining industry.

SILVER PLATE see Silverware

SILVER QUESTION

CO —UNIVERSITY OF COLORADO, Libraries, Special Collections, Boulder, 80309. Nora J Quinlan, Head
Holdings: Vols Cat
Notes: Dickson H Leavens Collection. Over 750 vols and 500 binders of material (incl clippings and pamphlets) related to the history of silver money. An extensive and all-encompassing collection on the subject.
NE —NEBRASKA STATE HISTORICAL SOCIETY, Archives, 1500 R St, Box 82554, Lincoln, 68501. James E Potter, State Archivist
Holdings: Uncat Mss
Notes: Silver and the money question; also material on the Greenback Party. Printed speeches and tracts relating to the money question, 1890-1895. Many written by prominent political figures of the day. Also, soldiers pensions, railroads, election laws and public lands. Collection of John Davis, Congressman from Kansas, 1891-1895.

SILVERSMITHING

MI —CRANBROOK ACADEMY OF ART, 500 Lone Pine Rd, Box 801, Bloomfield Hills, 48013. Diane Gunn, Librn
Holdings: Vols 25,000
Notes: Incl 20,000 slides.
MO —THE NELSON-ATKINS MUSEUM OF ART, Kenneth & Helen Spencer Art Reference Library, 4525 Oak St, Kansas City, 64111. Stanley W Hess, Librn
NY —COLGATE UNIVERSITY, Everett Needham Case Library, Hamilton, 13346. Bruce M Brown, Collections Librn
Holdings: Vols 106 Cat Mss
Notes: Also about 70 pamphlets, catalogs; exhibit catalogs; some manuscripts of the works of George B Cutten; letters.
PA —ATHENAEUM OF PHILADELPHIA, 219 S Sixth St, Philadelphia, 19106. Roger W Moss Jr, Librn
Holdings: Cat Mss
Notes: 14 boxes of papers relating to the silversmith Thomas Fletcher (1787-1866).
RI —PROVIDENCE PUBLIC LIBRARY, 150 Empire St, Providence, 02903. Lance J Bauer, Special Collections Librn
Holdings: Vols 122 // Cat
Notes: Works dating from 1670 on the history, lore and legends of precious stones, and the history and practice of jewelry and silversmithing. Restricted use.
ON —UNIVERSITY OF TORONTO, Thomas Fisher Rare Book Library, 120 Saint George St, Toronto, M5S 1A5, Can. Richard G Landon, Head
Holdings: Vols 1000 Cat
Notes: Langdon Collection, named for donor, John E Langdon. Contains material on silver and silversmiths around the world with special emphasis on Canada.

SILVERWARE

DC —NATIONAL SOCIETY, DAUGHTERS OF THE AMERICAN REVOLUTION, DAR Museum Reference Library, 1776 D St NW, Washington, 20006. Christine Minter-Dowd, Dir; Michael W Berry, Cur; Jean Martin, Registrar
Holdings: Vols (1600) Cat
Budget: ($500)
Notes: American decorative arts, 1700-1850, especially ceramics (incl British imports and Chinese export porcelain) and silverware.
IL —ART INSTITUTE OF CHICAGO, Ryerson & Burnham Libraries, Michigan Ave & Adams St, Chicago, 60603. Daphne C Roloff, Dir
Holdings: Vols (136,000) Cat Mss Slides Microforms
Budget: ($167,000)
Notes: Total collection incl 300,000 slides.

IN —ALLEN COUNTY PUBLIC LIBRARY, 900 Webster St, Fort Wayne, 46802. Paul Deane, Reader Services Dept Head; Kay Lynn Isca, Art Music & AV Dept Head
Holdings: Vols 1257 Cat Pix
MA —OLD STURBRIDGE VILLAGE, Research Library, Sturbridge, 01566. Theresa Rini Percy, Librn
Holdings: Cat Pix
Notes: New England, 1790-1850.
NY —GENEVA HISTORICAL SOCIETY, James Luckett Memorial Archives, 543 S Main St, Geneva, 14456. Eleanore Clise, Librn
NY —COLGATE UNIVERSITY, Everett Needham Case Library, Hamilton, 13346. Bruce M Brown, Collections Librn
Holdings: Vols 106 Cat Mss
Notes: Also about 70 pamphlets, catalogs; exhibit catalogs; some manuscripts of the works of George B Cutten; letters.
WI —MILWAUKEE PUBLIC LIBRARY, 814 W Wisconsin Ave, Milwaukee, 53233. Donald J Sager, City Librn
Holdings: Vols Cat
Notes: Strength in American and European decorative arts incl ceramics, glassware, jewelry, porcelain, silverware, furniture, interior decoration, textile arts and handicraft.
See also entry under Art, Decorative.

SILVICULTURE see Forests and Forestry

SIMENON, GEORGES, 1903-

OH —OHIO UNIVERSITY, Vernon R Alden Library, Department of Archives and Special Collections, Athens, 45701. Gary A Hunt, Head
Holdings: Vols 118 Cat
Notes: A comprehensive collection of first editions.

SIMMEL, JOHANNES MARIO

MA —BOSTON UNIVERSITY, Mugar Memorial Library, Special Collections Dept, 771 Commonwealth Ave, Boston, 02215. Howard B Gotlieb, Dir
Holdings: Cat Mss Pix
Notes: Mss, correspondence, etc collected in depth; incl publications by or about.

SIMMONS, ALBERT

SC —COLLEGE OF CHARLESTON LIBRARY, Special Collections Dept, Charleston, 29401.
Notes: Correspondence within the Lancelot Minor Harris Papers.

SIMMONS, FURNIFOLD M.

NC —DUKE UNIVERSITY, William R Perkins Library, Manuscript Dept, Durham, 27706. Ellen Gartrell, Cur of Mss
Holdings: Cat Mss
Notes: Papers, etc.

SIMMS, WILLIAM GILMORE

NC —DUKE UNIVERSITY, William R Perkins Library, Durham, 27706. Elvin E Strowd, University Librn
Notes: The Ethel Carr Peacock collection of 7000 volumes is strong in holdings of 19th century American literature.
VA —UNIVERSITY OF VIRGINIA, Alderman Library, Clifton Waller Barrett Collection, Charlottesville, 22901. Joan St C Crane, Cur of American Literature Collections
Notes: Papers.

SIMON, CHARLIE MAY

TN —MEMPHIS STATE UNIVERSITY, John Willard Brister Library, Memphis, 38152. John Terreo, Special Collections Librn
Notes: Charlie May Simon, author of children's books and adult biographies.

SIMON, RALPH, 1917-

OH —OHIO HISTORICAL SOCIETY, Archives Library Division, 1982 Velma Ave,

SIMON, RALPH, 1917- (cont.)

Columbus, 43211. Dennis East, Division Chief
Holdings: 1 linear ft
Notes: His papers (1962-1974).

SIMON AND SCHUSTER

†NY —COLUMBIA UNIVERSITY LIBRARIES, Butler Library, Rare Book and Manuscript Library, 535 W 114 St, New York, 10027.
Notes: Over 30,000 papers relating to M Lincoln Schuster and the publishing firm, Simon & Schuster. Incl file of letters written by Simon to Schuster from 1921-53, author and subject files of notes and clippings, advertising notebooks, files relating to the books written and edited by Schuster, galley and page proofs, photographs and memorabilia, and other correspondence.

SIMONS, HANS, 1893-1972

NY —STATE UNIVERSITY OF NEW YORK AT ALBANY, Library, Special Collections Dept, 1400 Washington Ave, Albany, 12222. Marion P Munzer, Coordr
Notes: Mss, speeches, lectures of Hans Simons (4.5 linear feet). Part of the Library's German Exile Collection.

SIMPSON, CHARLES TORREY

FL —FLORIDA DEPT OF STATE, Florida State Archives, Florida Photographic Collection, R A Gray Bldg, Tallahassee, 32301. Mrs Allen Morris, Archives Supervisor
Notes: Charles A Mosier, Charles Torrey Simpson and J K Small, 500 photographs of Florida flora, made by these famous naturalists, mostly in South Dade county. Added March, 1983, 2200 glass and nitrate negatives by J K Small.

SIMPSON, HERBERT WILLIAM, 1904-1970

IN —INDIANA STATE UNIVERSITY, EVANSVILLE, Library, 8600 University Blvd, Evansville, 47712. Gina R Walker, Acting Archivist
Holdings: Uncat Mss
Notes: Papers, etc of the nationally known graphic arts specialist Herbert William Simpson (1904-1970), advertising man, type designer and calligrapher. Original examples of calligraphy and graphic design executed for commercial ads and occasional pieces for personal interest. Materials of about 1940-1970.

SIMPSON, LOUIS ASTON MARANTZ, 1923-

NY —STATE UNIVERSITY OF NEW YORK, STONY BROOK, Melville Library, Dept of Special Collections, Stony Brook, 11794. Evert Volkersz, Head
Holdings: Cat

SIMPSON, WILLIAM

PA —US ARMY MILITARY HISTORY INSTITUTE, Carlisle Barracks, 17013. Richard J Sommers, Chief Archivist-Historian
Holdings: Mss Cat
Notes: The World War II collection, personal letters, daily logs, reminiscences, speeches, and official papers of American officers and soldiers serving in the European, Mediterranean, Middle Eastern, China-Burma-India, Southwest Pacific, and Central Pacific Theaters and in the Zone of the Interior during the Second World War. Most of these collections are manuscripts of General officers, incl Omar Bradley, Stephen Chamberlin, Lewis Hershey, John Lucas, William Simpson, and Brehon Somervell.

SIMS, MARIAN

NC —UNIVERSITY OF NORTH CAROLINA, CHARLOTTE, J Murrey Atkins Library, UNCC Station, Charlotte, 28223. Robert F Brabham Jr, Special Collections Librn
Holdings: Vols Cat Mss Pix
Notes: Files of Bonnie Ethel Cone as first president of Charlotte College and vice chancellor of the University of North Carolina at Charlotte; papers of Charlotte area women's organizations, eg AAUW and DAR; archives of Charlotte Unitarian Church; papers of novelist and short story writer Marian Sims; collections of family papers from North and South Carolina; and first editions of 18th and early 20th century American women novelists.

SIMULATION METHODS

CO —SOCIAL SCIENCE EDUCATION CONSORTIUM, Resource & Demonstration Center (RDC), 855 Broadway, Boulder, 80302. Regina McCormick, Staff Assoc
Holdings: Vols (16,000) Cat Filmstrips Microforms
Notes: Contains over 15,000 elementary and secondary social studies textbooks, audiovisuals, games and simulations, professional books, and the complete ERIC microfiche collection. Staff available to travel to all parts of the US to consult on curriculum development, instructional methods, materials analysis and selection, evaluation, new materials, teaching strategies, and trends in the social studies.

SINALOA, MEXICO see Mexico—Sinaloa

SINCLAIR, HAROLD

IL —ILLINOIS STATE UNIVERSITY, Milner Library, Dept of Special Collections, Normal, 61761. Robert Sokan, Librn
Holdings: Vols 70 Uncat Mss Pix
Notes: Incl his mss.

SINCLAIR, JO

MA —BOSTON UNIVERSITY, Mugar Memorial Library, Special Collections Dept, 771 Commonwealth Ave, Boston, 02215. Howard B Gotlieb, Dir
Holdings: Cat Mss PIx
Notes: Mss, correspondence, etc collected in depth; incl publications by or about.

SINCLAIR, UPTON, 1878-1968

CA —OCCIDENTAL COLLEGE, Library, 1600 Campus Rd, Los Angeles, 90041. Michael C Sutherland, Special Collections Librn
Holdings: Vols (1000) Cat
Notes: Given by Dr Elmer Belt, this collection is made up of first and foreign editions of nearly all of Sinclair's writings.
CA —UNIVERSITY OF CALIFORNIA, LOS ANGELES, Research Library, Dept of Special Collections, 405 Hilgard Ave, Los Angeles, 90024. Edward Shreeves, Chairman, Bibliographers Group; David S Zeidberg, Head
Holdings: Vols 175
Notes: 175 books by or about him; 20 letters.
†CA —UNIVERSITY OF CALIFORNIA LIBRARY, Santa Cruz, 95064.
Notes: The Robert and Genevieve Hahn Collection of works by and about Sinclair, incl various editions, periodicals, and ephemera relating to the Sinclair Centenary (1978), some oral history tapes from that event and files of the *Upton Sinclair Quarterly.*
DC —GEORGETOWN UNIVERSITY, Library, Special Collections Div, 37 & O Sts NW, Washington, 20057. George M Barringer, Special Collections Librn; Nicholas B Sheetz, Mss Librn
Holdings: // Cat Mss Pix
Notes: Papers of Fulton Oursler, editor of *Liberty* and, later, *Reader's Digest,* including substantial correspondence with Upton Sinclair, H L Mencken, and President Franklin D Roosevelt.
IL —SOUTHERN ILLINOIS UNIVERSITY, CARBONDALE, Delyte W Morris Library, Special Collections Dept, Carbondale, 62901. David V Koch, Cur of Special Collections; Louisa Bowen, Cur of Manuscripts
Holdings: Cat Mss
Notes: Papers and correspondence of Theodore A Schroeder, constitutional lawyer and founder, with Lincoln Steffens, of the Free Speech League, a forerunner of the American Civil Liberties Union. Contains extensive correspondence with Comstock, Gompers, Debs, H Ellis, Sanger, Sinclair, John Dewey, Darrow, Mencken, A G Hays, Emma Goldman, W E B Dubois, etc. Incl several thousand letters; notes and mss, records of legal cases and extensive files relating to the early history of psychiatry.
IN —INDIANA UNIVERSITY, Lilly Library, Seventh St, Bloomington, 47405. William R Cagle, Librn
Holdings: // Cat Mss Pix
Notes: Upton Sinclair's library of books, some clippings and photographs. Extensive ms holdings by and about Upton Sinclair. First and other editions of all his works. Descriptive catalog of an extensive exhibit.
IN —INDIANA STATE UNIVERSITY, Cunningham Memorial Library, Dept of Rare Books & Special Collections, Terre Haute, 47809. Lawrence J McCrank, Head
Notes: The Debs Collection consists of aprox 7000 pieces of correspondence between Theodore Debs (brother of E V) and other persons, such as Sinclair Lewis, Upton Sinclair, Ethel Barrymore, Emma Goldman, Robert G Ingersoll, Carl Sandburg, Norman Thomas, Sacco and Vanzetti and many others. Many of the letters are from E V Debs to his brother; a good portion of these are from the federal penitentiary at Atlanta. Entire correspondence file has been microfilmed. 750 pamphlets cover all aspects of the labor movement, socialism and radical thought from the 19th century to appprox 1950. A collection ca 200 related books is also housed in the collection. See: J Robert Constantine and Gail Malmgreen, eds, *The Papers of Eugene V Debs, 1834-1945. A Guide to the Microfilm Edition.* NY: Microfilming Corp of America, 1983 (University Microfilms is the new distributor).
PA —BALCH INSTITUTE FOR ETHNIC STUDIES, Library, 18 S Seventh St, Philadelphia, 19106. R Joseph Anderson, Library Dir
TX —UNIVERSITY OF HOUSTON, M D Anderson Memorial Library, University Park, Houston, 77004. David Farmer, Cur, Special Collections; Jean Jackson, Assistant Cur
Holdings: Vols 150 Cat
Notes: Emphasis is limited to printed texts, both first editions and reprints.

SINDHI LANGUAGE AND LITERATURE

AZ —UNIVERSITY OF ARIZONA, Library, Oriental Studies Collection, Tucson, 85721. Mary J McWhorter, Actg Head Librn
Holdings: Vols (95,000) Cat Microforms
Budget: ($30,000)
See also entry under Oriental Languages and Literatures
NY —NEW YORK PUBLIC LIBRARY, Oriental Div, Fifth Ave & 42 St, New York, 10018. E Christian Filstrup, Chief
Holdings: Cat Mss Microforms
Budget: ($56,455)
Notes: Published catalog of holdings.

SINEL, JOSEPH

CA —CALIFORNIA COLLEGE OF ARTS & CRAFTS, Meyer Library, Broadway at College, Oakland, 94618. Robert L Harper, Head Librn
Holdings: Vols 100 Cat Mss Pix Slides Audiotapes
Notes: The Sinel Collection was given to Meyer Library after the death of Mr Sinel. It includes mock-ups and sketches for most of his industrial and graphic designs (penny weight scale; Safeway logo; various

SINEL, JOSEPH (cont.)

brochures; typewriters). It includes his correspondence dating from the early 1930s, when he entered the profession, until his death in 1975.

SINGAPORE

CA —UNIVERSITY OF CALIFORNIA, LOS ANGELES, Research Library, Indo/Pacific Collection, 405 Hilgard Ave, Los Angeles, 90024. Edward Shreeves, Chairman, Bibliographers Group; Charlotte Spence, Indo/Pacific Bibliographer
Holdings: Vols Cat Mss Maps Pix Microforms
Notes: The Southeast Asian collection has been developed on a combination of the research and teaching levels; it focuses on the cultural, economic, political and social history of the area from ancient times to the present day. Although all the individual countries of the region are represented, some priority is given to Malaysia, Singapore, Indonesia and the Philippines. The majority of the materials is in Western languages except for a collection of several thousand books in Thai, and a smaller collection of materials in Vietnamese, Indonesian, Malaysian, and the Philippine languages.

HI —UNIVERSITY OF HAWAII, Library, 2550 The Mall, Honolulu, 96822. Joyce Wright, Head, Asia Collection; Masato Matsu, Head, East Asia Vernacular Collection
Holdings: Vols 331,620 Cat Microforms
Notes: The Asia Collection holds materials from and about Southeast Asia: Brunei, Burma, Cambodia (Kampuchea), Indonesia, Laos, Malaysia, Philippines, Singapore, Thailand. Large contemporary Indonesian language collection. Several thousand vols in Thai and in Vietnamese. Minimal holdings in Burmese, Khmer, Lao languages. Social sciences and humanities emphasis for the post-World War II period. Western language coverage supplemented by retrospective holdings in the main library collection.

IL —CENTER FOR RESEARCH LIBRARIES, 6050 S Kenwood Ave, Chicago, 60637. Donald B Simpson, Dir; Esther Smith, Collection Development Librn
Holdings: Uncat
Notes: Selected monographs, serials and government publications received on NPAC 1971 forward.

IL —NORTHERN ILLINOIS UNIVERSITY, Founders Memorial Library, Southeast Asia Collection, Normal Rd, De Kalb, 60115. Lee S Dutton Dr, Cur
Holdings: Vols (34,000) Cat Maps Microforms
Notes: An extensive collection of books, periodicals, newspapers, maps, and microforms from or about Southeast Asia. Areas of concentration incl Thailand, Malaysia, Indonesia, Singapore, Brunei, Philippines, Laos, and Burma. Holdings (except rare books, maps, and microforms) are housed in a separate area collection within the Founders Library. A departmental card catalog and specialized reference collection support reference services. A Thai collection of several thousand vols is the largest vernacular component. Extensive Malaysia, Indonesia, Singapore, and Brunei holdings have been acquired through the NPAC program. A collection of Filipino-American newspapers, and a growing collection of children's literature in common and uncommon Southeast Asian languages are available. Resources are accessible to borrowers through OCLC.

MI —UNIVERSITY OF MICHIGAN, Harlan Hatcher Graduate Library, Ann Arbor, 48109. Susan Go, Librn
Holdings: Vols (250,000) Cat Mss Maps Pix Slides Microforms
Notes: Incl in the Michigan Historical Collections (primarily archival material) are papers of Michiganders in southeast Asia, mostly the Philipines, eg papers of Joseph R Hayden, Frank Murphy and G Mennen Williams, also, on film, the selected papers of Philippines president Manuel Quezon. All aspects of the countries, cultures and peoples of Brunei, Burma, Khymer, Indonesia, Laos, Malaysia, Philippines, Singapore, Thailand, Portuguese Timor and Vietnam. Also the Malayo-Polynesian (Austronesian), Mon-Khmer (Austroasiatic), and Sino-Tibetan language groupings.

NY —CORNELL UNIVERSITY LIBRARIES, John M Olin Library, John M Echols Collection on Southeast Asia, Ithaca, 14853. Giok Po Oey, Curator
Holdings: Vols (167,000) Cat Mss Maps Pix Microforms
Budget: ($90,000)
Notes: Additions published in the collection's monthly accessions list (Ithaca: Cornell University, Southeast Asia Program, 1959-). Holdings through December 1980 listed in Cornell University Libraries Southeast Asia Catalog (Boston: G K Hall, 1976, First supplement, 1983), 10 vols.

OH —OHIO UNIVERSITY, Vernon R Alden Library, Southeast Asia Collection, Athens, 45701. Lian The-Mulliner, Head
Holdings: Vols (68,000) Cat Maps Slides Phonorecords Videotapes 16mm Films Filmstrips Microforms
Budget: ($35,000)
Notes: Emphasis on Indonesia, Malaysia, Singapore, Brunei and the Philippines. Incl language and literature, history, civilization and culture, art, medicine, philosophy and economic conditions. Separate catalog.

SINGAPORE—COMMERCE

†CA —FAR EAST MERCHANTS ASSOCIATION, Femas Trade Library, 1597 Curtis St, Berkeley, 94702.
Notes: Trade with Far Eastern countries, esp China, Japan, Philippine Islands and Singapore.

SINGER, ISAAC BASHEVIS

NY —NEW YORK UNIVERSITY, Fales Library, 70 Washington Sq S, New York, 10012.
Holdings: Cat
Notes: Incl first editions, etc.

SINGERS

CA —UNIVERSITY OF CALIFORNIA, SANTA BARBARA, Library, Dept of Special Collections, Santa Barbara, 93106. Christian F Brun, Head
Holdings: Mss Pix Phonorecords
Notes: Correspondence, mss, photographs, paintings, etc relating to Lotte Lehmann's life and career. 10,000 items.

CA —UNIVERSITY OF CALIFORNIA, SANTA BARBARA, Arts Library, Music Section, Santa Barbara, 93106. Susan Sonnet Bower, Asst Music Librn
Holdings: Cat Phonorecords
Notes: The Archival Sound Recordings Collection: 15,000 78rpm discs, containing representative performances by almost every opera and lieder singer recorded.

DC —LIBRARY OF CONGRESS, Music Division, Washington, 20540.
Notes: The Geraldine Farrar Collection incl correspondence, scripts, contracts, programs, playbills, scrapbooks, posters, and photographs. Also in the Motion Picture, Broadcasting, and Recorded Sound Division are 50 disc recordings of radio broadcast transcriptions and special pressings made by the Gramophone and Typewriter Company, Ltd.

GA —GEORGIA STATE UNIVERSITY, William R Pullen Library, Atlanta, 30303. Leslie S Hough, Dir
Notes: Large collection of the papers of songwriter, singer, composer, and publisher Johnny Mercer. Incl correspondence, music scores, an unpublished autobiography, phono discs, water colors, etc.

ME —NORDICA MEMORIAL ASSOCIATION, Library, RFD 3, Farmington, 04938.
Holdings: Vols 400 Cat Mss Pix

MA —BOSTON UNIVERSITY, Mugar Memorial Library, Special Collections Dept, 771 Commonwealth Ave, Boston, 02215. Howard B Gotlieb, Dir
Holdings: Cat Mss Pix
Notes: Incl personal papers and literary productions of numerous modern actors, actresses, musicians (composers and performance) of all kinds. A complete list is availble.

NY —STATE UNIVERSITY OF NEW YORK, BINGHAMTON, Glenn G Bartle Library, Binghamton, 13901. Marion Hanscom, Special Collections Librn
Notes: Frances R Conole Archive. A collection of 50,000 plus sound recordings devoted to the preservation of 20th century vocal art as recorded over the last ninety years. Emphasis is on opera singers from 1900-1960. Over 3000 singers are represented with an excess of 4000 complete performances of over 400 operas.

SC —COLLEGE OF CHARLESTON LIBRARY, Special Collections Dept, Charleston, 29401.
Notes: Meltzer Music Collection incl autographed leeters and/or photographs of composers and singers; it contains correspondence from C C Chaminade, Alphonse Daudet, Claude Debussy (1907), Emory Elgar (1916), George Gershwin (1928), J Massenet (1888, 1909), Felix Mendelsohn-Bartholdy (1839), Puccini (1911), and C Wolf-Ferrari (1911). Contains also a biography of Charles Henry Meltzer and newsclippings concerning the collection. One box.

SINGHALESE LANGUAGE see Sinhalese Language and Literature

SINGING

CA —UNIVERSITY OF CALIFORNIA, SANTA BARBARA, Arts Library, Music Section, Santa Barbara, 93106. Susan Sonnet Bower, Asst Music Librn
Holdings: Cat Phonorecords
Notes: The Archival Sound Recordings Collection: 15,000 78rpm discs, containing representative performances by almost every opera and lieder singer recorded.

†DC —CATHOLIC UNIVERSITY OF AMERICA, Music Library, Washington, 20064. Betty Libbey, Head Music Library
Holdings: Cat Microforms
Notes: A large collection to support advanced degree study. Emphasis on church music, musicology, history and criticism, instrumental and vocal music, solo music for all voices, instruments, and musical forms.

MI —DETROIT PUBLIC LIBRARY, Music & Performing Arts Dept, 5201 Woodward, Detroit, 48202. Agatha Pfeiffer Kalkanis, Chief
Holdings: Vols 19,000 Cat Mss Pix Microforms
Notes: Also incl (77,000) scores. General collection intended for practical use in performance and for scholarly research. Good working collection of bibliographies, thematic catalogs, dictionaries and encyclopedias, periodical indexes. Many sets of collected works, monumental editions, historical anthologies. Good representation of opera and operetta, art song and folk song, solo instrumental literature and chamber music in practical editions. 2575 titles of choral music, chiefly sacred, for use by choirs. 17,000 titles of popular sheet music, uncataloged but thoroughly indexed. Considerable recent holdings of books and periodicals in foreign languages. Special collections of black and local materials. 25,000 recordings and extensive discographical literature. Collection of publishers' trade catalogs.

NY —NEW YORK PUBLIC LIBRARY, Music Div, 111 Amsterdam Ave, New York, 10023. Frank C Campbell, Dir
Holdings: Vols (300,000) Cat Mss Pix Microforms
Notes: Described in Dictionary Catalog of the Music Collection, The Research Libraries of the New York Public Library, 33 vols (532,000 cards), 1964, $2190; Supplement 1, 1 vol (17,000 cards), 1966,

SINGING (cont.)

$100. Also, *Bibliographic Guide to Music,* 2 vols, 1975-1976, $70 ea. Literature pertaining to virtually all musical subjects, and scores covering the broadest range of musical style and history are represented in this catalog. Special strengths of the collection incl folk songs, 18th and 19th-century librettos, full scores of operas, complete works, historical editions, Beethoven, Americana, American music, periodicals, vocal music, literature on the voice, programs, record catalogs, and mss in detail; sheet music, 355,414; sound recordings, 400,000; clippings and programs, 2 million; broadsides, 1821; songsters, 375; pictures, 51,002; ms, 29,877.

SINGING, CHORAL see Choral Music

SINGLE TAX

MI —UNIVERSITY OF MICHIGAN, Dept of Rare Books & Special Collections, Ann Arbor, 48109. Edward C Weber, Head, Labadie Collection
Holdings: Vols (40,000) Cat
Notes: Mostly 19th-century U S pamphlets.

SINGPHO LANGUAGE see Kachin Language

SINHALESE LANGUAGE AND LITERATURE

NY —NEW YORK PUBLIC LIBRARY, Oriental Div, Fifth Ave & 42 St, New York, 10018. E Christian Filstrup, Chief
Holdings: Cat Mss Microforms
Budget: ($56,455)
Notes: Published catalog of holdings.

SINKIANG

IL —FIELD MUSEUM OF NATURAL HISTORY, The Berthold Laufer Library, Roosevelt Rd & Lake Shore Dr, Chicago, 60605. W Peyton Fawcett, Librn
Holdings: Vols (12,000) // Cat Mss Maps
Notes: The part of the museum's collection of Berthold Laufer (1874-1934), Curator of Anthropology, dealing with the peoples of the pre-19th century Chinese Empire (incl Manchuria, Mongolia, Sinkiang and Tibet); their anthropology, art and religion; influences upon their cultures by those of India, Siberia, Japan, Indonesia, and Oceania--and vice versa. Incl about 500 books in Tibetan. About 2/3 of the collection is cataloged.

SINNOTT, EDMUND

CT —YALE UNIVERSITY, Box 1603A, Yale Station, New Haven, 06520.
Notes: Papers.

SINO-TIBETAN LANGUAGES see Indochinese Languages

SINSHEIMER, ROBERT L.

†CA —CALIFORNIA INSTITUTE OF TECHNOLOGY, Robert A Millikan Memorial Library, Archives, 1201 E California Blvd, Pasadena, 91125.
Notes: Papers of Robert L Sinsheimer (1920-), mainly from the period 1971-1976, some of which relate to the recombinant DNA controversy.

SIODMAK, CURT

MA —BOSTON UNIVERSITY, Mugar Memorial Library, Special Collections Dept, 771 Commonwealth Ave, Boston, 02215. Howard B Gotlieb, Dir
Holdings: Cat Mss
Notes: Mss, correspondence, etc collected in depth; incl publications by or about.

SIOUAN INDIANS

MN —BROWN COUNTY HISTORICAL SOCIETY, Museum and Archives, Center St

and Broadway, Box 116, New Ulm, 56073. Paul Klammer, Dir
Holdings: Vols (250) Mss Maps Pix Slides Phonorecords Audiotapes Videotapes 16mm Films Filmstrips Microforms
Notes: History of Brown County, Minn. Also have *Historical Files,* about 500 pieces in vertical files incl newspaper clippings, advertising, letterheads, etc, pertaining to Brown County businesses, industry, schools, governmental units, etc. *Family Files,* about documents, letters, etc. Also collection of Siouan Uprising of 1862-clippings, copies of treaties, letters, etc. (65 vols, 10 mss, 25 maps, 40 pix, 50 slides).
MN —COLLEGE OF SAINT CATHERINE, Library, 2004 Randolph Ave, Saint Paul, 55105. Sister Elizabeth Delmore, Library Dir
Holdings: Vols (800) Cat Mss Slides Phonorecords Audiotapes Filmstrips Microforms
Budget: ($800)
Notes: Both historical and cultural aspects. Special emphasis on Chippewa and Sioux Indian tribes.
MO —UNIVERSITY OF MISSOURI-COLUMBIA, Ellis Library, Language and Literature Dept, Columbia, 65201. Jeaneice Brewer, Librn
Holdings: Vols (3500) Cat
Notes: Consists of the personal library of John G Neihardt, 1881-1973, poet, literary critic, and lecturer. Lived among Omaha Indians and Ogalala Sioux Indians to study their character and history. Poet laureate of Nebraska. Literary editor of *St Louis Post-Dispatch,* 1926-38. Poet in residence and lecturer in English, U of Missouri, 1949-66. Manuscripts Collection of Ellis Library.
NE —NEIHARDT STUDY CENTER, Library, Bancroft, 68004. John Lindahl, Cur; Ann Reinert, Librn
Notes: The Center will preserve the published works and papers of John G Neihardt, State Poet Laureate and authority on Plains Indians.
SD —SOUTH DAKOTA HISTORICAL RESOURCE CENTER, Library, Soldiers Memorial Bldg, Pierre, 57501. Rosemary Evetts, Librn
†SD —SOUTH DAKOTA SCHOOL OF MINES & TECHNOLOGY, Devereaux Library, Rapid City, 57701.
Holdings: Vols 153 Cat
Notes: Indians of North American with emphasis on the Sioux Indians. Some of the books concern wars and battles with Indians, especially the Custer Massacre.
SD —SIOUXLAND HERITAGE MUSEUMS, Pettigrew Museum Library, 131 N Duluth Ave, Sioux Falls, 57104. Ms Lee N McLaird, Cur of Collections
Holdings: Vols (7500) Cat Mss Maps Pix
Budget: ($900)
Notes: Pettigrew Museum Library is a support service of the Siouxland Heritage Museums. US Senator R F Pettigrew established the core collection in 1926, covering natural history (incl North American Indian anthropology) and state-local history (concentrating on exploration and settlement to about 1900). The collection also incl the Senator's private papers (ca 1870-1926). Additions to the collection since 1926 have emphasized Plains Indian anthropology, state-local history, baseball and museology, supporting the work of the Museum staff. The collection is mostly cataloged and is inter-indexed with Augustana College, Sioux Falls College, and Sioux Falls Public Libraries (as well as having its own catalog). The photograph collection includes prints by D F Barry as well as other photographers' work with native peoples.
WI —DOUGLAS COUNTY HISTORICAL MUSEUM, 906 E Second St, Superior, 54880. James E Lundsted, Dir
Notes: Photographs by David Barry, of Sioux Indians at time of Custer fiasco, 1875-1888.

SIOUX INDIANS see Siouan Indians

SIPLEY, LOUIS WALTON

NY —INTERNATIONAL MUSEUM OF PHOTOGRAPHY AT GEORGE

EASTMAN HOUSE, Archives, 900 East Ave, Rochester, 14607. Rachel Stuhlman, Head Librn
Holdings: Vols (30,000) Cat Mss Microforms
Budget: ($104,000)
Notes: History, aesthetics and technology of photography and cinematography, incl the Gabriel Cromer, Josef Maria Eder, Alden Scott Boyer, Louis Walton Sipley/3M Collections, and the James Card Collection from 1893. Covers photographic, especially cinematographic history; also hundreds of negatives of Edward Muybridge as well as his notebooks. Incl 450,000 pictures and slides. Also the Lewis Hine Collection of social documentary photography.

SIPONATA see Hemiptera

SIPPRELL, CLARA

NY —SYRACUSE UNIVERSITY LIBRARIES, Ernest S Bird Library, George Arents Research Library for Special Collections, Syracuse, 13210. Carolyn A Davis, Manuscripts Librn; Amy S Doherty, University Archivist; Mark F Weimer, Rare Book Librn
Notes: The George Arents Research Library for Special Collections at Syracuse University contains the papers of Margaret Bourke-White, Clara Sipprell, Gerda Peterich, Edward John Wall, Louis Fabian Bachrach, Joseph Costa (National Press Photographers Association), the University Archives Photographic Collection, and other misc photographs.

SIRC

ON —SPORT INFORMATION RESOURCE CENTER (SIRC), 333 River Rd, Ottawa, K1L 8H9, Can. Gilles Chiasson, Director
Notes: International documentation center for sport information. Large collection of sports, with 1200 sports journals and a 6000 piece microfilm collection. Published 1600 page *Sport Bibliography* containing over 70,000 citations. Computer data base of about 100,000 citations. All aspects of all sports, in many languages.

SIRINGO, CHARLES A., 1855-1928

CA —AZUSA PACIFIC COLLEGE, Marshburn Memorial Library, Citrus & Alosta, Azusa, 91702. Edward Peterman, Librn
Holdings: Vols (150) Uncat
Notes: The Odo B Stade Collection of Literary First Editions. No photocopying.

SIRLS (DATA BASE)

ON —SIRLS, Faculty of Human Kinetics & Leisure Studies, University of Waterloo, Waterloo, N2L 3G1, Can. Betty Smith, Database Mgr
Notes: Information Retrieval System for the Sociology of Leisure and Sport (SIRLS) is a computerized online database of about 13,000 entries (1983). Incl dance as a leisure time activity.

SISKIND, AARON

AZ —UNIVERSITY OF ARIZONA, Center for Creative Photography, 843 E University Blvd, Tucson, 85721. James Enyeart, Dir; Terence Pitts, Cur and Librn
Notes: Center has significant collections consisting of more than 25 photographs plus other archival material such as negatives, contact sheets, work prints, correspondence, financial records, diaries, project files, etc. Inventories of the collections are available to researchers. Published guides available for some collections.

SISSLE, NOBLE

†MD —MARYLAND HISTORICAL SOCIETY, Library, 201 W Monument St, Baltimore, 21201.
Notes: Eubie Blake's personal and professional archive. Incl the Baltimore-born

SISSLE, NOBLE (cont.)

pianist, composer, and songwriter's collection of songs and instrumental pieces in mss, extensive documentation of his collaboration with Noble Sissle, Flournog Miller, Milton Reddie, and others. The Broadway musical comedy, Shuffle Along, is represented in box office records, programs, scores and parts, photographs, and sheet music. Blake's involvement with other productions is similarly documented.

SISTERS OF LORETTO

AZ —NORTHERN ARIZONA UNIVERSITY, Special Collection Library, CU Box 6022, Flagstaff, 86011. Peter M Whiteley, Coordr/Archivist; William Mullane, Librn
Notes: Sisters of Loretto Collection; correspondence, class records, photos, publications, 1912-1966. Sisters of Loretto operated the School of Nativity, Flagstaff, 1899-1966. Incl information on Sister Mary Imelda (Lorabel Wallace), Flagstaff native, educator and Pulitzer Prize winning children's author.

SITWELL, EDITH OSBERT AND SACHEVERELL

CA —UNIVERSITY OF CALIFORNIA, BERKELEY, Bancroft Library, Manuscripts Division, Berkeley, 94720. James D Hart, Dir
Notes: Letters from them in various collections.
DC —GEORGETOWN UNIVERSITY, Library, Special Collections Div, 37 & O Sts NW, Washington, 20057. George M Barringer, Special Collections Librn; Nicholas B Sheetz, Mss Librn
Holdings: Mss Pix
Notes: The papers of Christopher Sykes, biographer, journalist, and novelist; containing mss, letters, photographs, and drawings. With extensive correspondence from Harold Acton; Angela, Countess of Antrim; Sir John Betjeman; Ivy Compton-Burnett; Alick Dru; T S Eliot; Max Beerbohm; Graham Greene; John Hayward; Lord Patrick Kinross; Compton Mackenzie; Nancy Mitford; Anthony Powell; Dame Flora Robson; Cecil Roth; Sir John Russell; Osbert Sitwell; John Sparrow; Freya Stark; James Stern; and Evelyn Waugh, among others. Also, considerable research material about Evelyn Waugh, Adam von Trott, Robert Byron, Lady Nancy Astor; and the foundation of the state of Israel.
IL —ILLINOIS STATE UNIVERSITY, Milner Library, Dept of Special Collections, Normal, 61761. Robert Sokan, Librn
Notes: First editions, limited editions, ephemera, etc.
MA —BOSTON UNIVERSITY, Mugar Memorial Library, Special Collections Dept, 771 Commonwealth Ave, Boston, 02215. Howard B Gotlieb, Dir
Holdings: Cat Mss Pix
Notes: Mainly correspondence. Incl some mss, particularly those of Sacheverell.
NV —UNIVERSITY OF NEVADA, RENO, University Library, Special Collections Dept, Reno, 89557. Robert E Blesse, Head
Holdings: // Vols (97) Cat Other appearances 450 Cat
Notes: Includes individual works by author in all editions including translations; also prefaces, introductions, published correspondence, appearances in anthologies, periodicals, etc. Bibliographical research collection, part of Modern Authors Collection.
NY —HOFSTRA UNIVERSITY, Library, 1000 Fulton Ave, Hempstead, 11550. Charles R Andrews, Dean of Library Services
†WA —WASHINGTON STATE UNIVERSITY, Library, Manuscripts, Archives & Special Collections, Pullman, 99164. John F Guido, Head
Holdings: Vols Cat Mss
Notes: Among the significant holdings are

the William George Fretton papers relating to Conventry, England; the Thomas Balston collection of Sitwelliana, which incl correspondence, monographs and first editions, as well as holograph poems of Edith, Osbert and Sacheverell Sitwell; and first editions and correspondence of Elizabeth Robins. A short-title catalog of English books prior to 1700 is cited in Down's American Literary Resources: p 664.

SIWASH INDIANS see Salishan Indians

SIX NATIONS see Iroquois Indians

SIXTEENTH CENTURY

MO —CENTER FOR REFORMATION RESEARCH, 6477 San Bonita Ave, Saint Louis, 63105. William S Meltby, Dir
Holdings: Cat Mss Maps Pix Microforms

SIZEMORE, CHRIS COSTNER

NC —DUKE UNIVERSITY, William R Perkins Library, Manuscript Dept, Durham, 27706. Ellen Gartrell, Cur of Mss
Notes: The personal papers of Chris Costner Sizemore, who is widely known as the subject of the book and movie, "The Three Faces of Eve." Incl poems and other writings, diaries, drawings, photographs, tapes of interviews, and some printed material.

SKATING

CO —UNITED STATES FIGURE SKATING ASSOCIATION, 20 First St, Colorado Springs, 80906.
Notes: Rule books and other publications on figure skating.
DC —SMITHSONIAN INSTITUTION LIBRARIES, National Museum of American History Branch, Washington, 20560. Rhoda S Ratner, Branch Librn
Notes: Emphasis on history of American sports and recreation. Incl some 2000 baseball cards from cigarette and chewing-gum packets; 103 scrapbooks and other memorabilia about Joe Louis; much on bicycling and skating.

SKEES AND SKEE-RUNNING see Skis and Skiing

SKELTON, ROBIN

BC —UNIVERSITY OF VICTORIA, McPherson Library, Victoria, V8W 3H5, Can.
Notes: Poet, professor. Incl mss, proofs and correspondence (incl Malahat Review files).

SKEPTICISM

MA —HARVARD UNIVERSITY LIBRARY, Cambridge, 02138.
Holdings: Cat

SKETCHING see Drawing

SKID ROW

NJ —RUTGERS, THE STATE UNIVERSITY OF NEW JERSEY, Center of Alcohol Studies Library, Smithers Hall, New Brunswick, 08903. Penny Page, Librn
Holdings: Vols (8075) Cat Mss Microforms
Budget: ($110,000)
Notes: See entry for Rutgers University under Alcoholism.

SKIDMORE, OWINGS AND MERRILL

NY —SYRACUSE UNIVERSITY LIBRARIES, Ernest S Bird Library, George Arents Research Library for Special Collections, Syracuse, 13210. Carolyn A Davis, Manuscripts Librn; Amy S Doherty, University Archivist; Mark F Weimer, Rare Book Librn
Notes: The George Arents Research Library for Special Collections at Syracuse

University contains the papers of Harley James McKee, Lorimer Rich, Frederick Lear, Max Abramovitz, James I Arnold, Pietro Bulluschi, Claude Bragdon, Marcel Breuer, William Lescaze, Skidmore Owings & Merrill, Ralph Walker, Eric Fisher Wood, Minoru Yamasaki, Joseph Louis Young, and Archimedes Russell.

SKIING see Skis and Skiing

SKINNER, B. F.

SC —COLLEGE OF CHARLESTON LIBRARY, Special Collections Dept, Charleston, 29401.
Notes: Contains biographical and family history material of Wendell Mitchel Levi; invertebrate anatomy course notes from the College of Charleston; University of Chicago Law School casebooks; correspondence concerning pigeons and camellias; notes, photographs, mss, typescripts, and galleys of published works; and other materials relating to pigeons and camellias. Among the more prominent correspondents are B F Skinner, Madame Chiang Kai-Shek, and Mary Bonner.

SKINNER, CORNELIA OTIS

NY —NEW YORK PUBLIC LIBRARY, Performing Arts Research Center, Billy Rose Theatre Collection, 111 Amsterdam Ave, New York, 10023. Dorothy L Swerdlove, Cur
Holdings: Cat Mss Pix
Notes: Papers, scrapbooks, mss, photographs, memorabilia, etc.

SKINNER FAMILY

NY —STATE UNIVERSITY OF NEW YORK, COLLEGE AT OSWEGO, Penfield Library, Oswego, 13126. Anne Commerton, Dir
Holdings: // Cat Mss
Notes: Avery Skinner was a prominent politician in Oswego County from 1826 to the 1840s. This collection centers on his interests in genealogy, religion, and local history. 5 linear inches.

SKIS AND SKIING

CO —VAIL PUBLIC LIBRARY, 292 W Meadow Dr, Vail, 81657. Charlyn M C Canada, Librn
Holdings: Vols (450) Cat Maps
Budget: ($500)
Notes: The alpine environment.
MA —APPALACHIAN MOUNTAIN CLUB, 5 Joy St, Boston, 02108. Fran Belcher, Librn
Holdings: Vols (6500) Cat Maps Pix Slides
Budget: ($3000)
Notes: Mountaineering, espec the White Mountains. Bound editions of other countries, mountaineering journals.
MI —NATIONAL SKI HALL OF FAME, Research Library, Mather Ave, PO Box 191, Ishpeming, 49849. Russell M Magnaghi, Archivist/Historian
Notes: Approximately 1000 titles, ski-related magazines, newspapers. In house only; no interlibrary loans.
NH —DARTMOUTH COLLEGE, Baker Memorial Library, Hanover, 03755.
Holdings: Cat
NY —RACQUET & TENNIS CLUB, Library, 370 Park Ave, New York, 10022. Gerald Belliveau, Jr, Librn
Holdings: Vols (17,500) Cat
Budget: ($6000)
Notes: Specializes in court tennis, lawn tennis, early American sport. See Dictionary Catalogue of the Library of Sports in the Racquet and Tennis Club (Boston: G K Hall, 1971). Also, Robert W Henderson, Early American Sport, 3rd ed. (Cranbury, NJ: Fairleigh Dickinson University Press, 1977).
WA —MOUNTAINEERS INC, Library, 300 3rd Ave West, Seattle, 98119. Verna M Ness, Library Cur
Holdings: Vols (3000) Cat
Notes: Collection incl some 19th century vols of Alpine information, incl the first

SKIS AND SKIING (cont.)

issue of *The Alpine Journal* (1863). Bound serials of many important American climbing publications. Small sub-collections for American Alpine Club members and for The Mountaineer Foundation, the latter on conservation and ecology. In the main collection backpacking, skiing and natural history are also represented.

AB —ALPINE CLUB OF CANADA, 111 Bear St, PO Box 160, Banff, T0L 0C0, Can. Mary Andrews, Librn
Holdings: Vols (4247) Cat Mss Maps Pix Slides
Budget: ($1300)
Notes: One of the most extensive collections.

BC —UNIVERSITY OF BRITISH COLUMBIA, Library, 1956 Main Mall, Vancouver, V6T 1Y3, Can. Anne Yandle, Special Collections Librn
Notes: British Columbia Mountaineering Club photograph collection covering many years of activities. Incl 420 negatives, 2 albums (photos), 1 book.

ON —CANADIAN SKI MUSEUM, 457A Sussex Dr, Ottawa, K1N 6Z4, Can. Sally Ingels, Librn
Notes: Mainly but not exclusively Canadian material. Artifacts used for displays.

SKLAR, GEORGE

MA —BOSTON UNIVERSITY, Mugar Memorial Library, Special Collections Dept, 771 Commonwealth Ave, Boston, 02215. Howard B Gotlieb, Dir
Holdings: Cat Mss
Notes: Mss, correspondence, etc collected in depth; incl publications by or about.

SKULLS

NY —AMERICAN MUSEUM OF NATURAL HISTORY, Library Services Dept, Central Park W & 79th St, New York, 10024. Nina J Root, Chairwoman; Mary Genett, Asst Librn for Reference Services
Holdings: Uncat
Notes: Incl a large, classified collection of human skulls as phrenological phenomena.

SKYDIVING

IN —THE MICHAEL HORAN PARACHUTING RESOURCES LIBR, 115 N 13 St, Richmond, 47374. Michael Horan, Librn
Holdings: Vols 250 Uncat
Notes: Current, out of print, and rare books on parachuting, incl periodicals from the US, Canada, and Great Britain, 1950-date. Also, material on skydiving. The "largest collection of (parachuting) books in the US."

SLACK, CHARLES WESLEY, 1825-1885

†OH —KENT STATE UNIVERSITY, Libraries, Kent, 44242.
Notes: Papers of the noted editor and publisher, Boston editor, and publisher of the Commonwealth. Prominent in the freesoil and antislavery movements.

SLADE, HARVEY

FL —FLORIDA DEPT OF STATE, Florida State Archives, Florida Photographic Collection, R A Gray Bldg, Tallahassee, 32301. Mrs Allen Morris, Archives Supervisor
Holdings: Maps Pix Slides Films Audiotapes
Notes: Areas of emphasis within the collection: (1) Florida government. There is a complete file of governors' photos, and many photos of legislative sessions and legislators going back to the late 1800s. (2) Stanley J Morrow. Mr Morrow learned his craft under Mathew B Brady. He worked in Florida from 1882-1887. Collection has several hundred of his glass negatives that document a period of southward expansion in Florida. (3) Alvan S Harper, Tallahassee portrait artist; 1700 glass negatives of

Tallahassee people between 1885-1910. (4) W A Fishbaugh. Several thousand photographs of the "boom," Miami and Coral Gables in the 1920s. (5) Charles A Mosier, Charles Torrey Simpson and J K Small; 500 photographs of Florida flora, made by these famous naturalists, mostly in South Dade County. Added March, 1983; 2200 glass and nitrate negatives by J K Small. Collection alsoincl 40,000 negatives (4x5) made by Harvey Slade in Tallahassee, 1946-1975, predominantly portraits; also 15,000 news story negatives (4x5 and 2x2) relative to local and state government, 1957-1969, unprinted, from *The Tallahassee Democrat*.

SLANG

CA —UNIVERSITY OF CALIFORNIA, LOS ANGELES, Research Library, African Studies Collection, 405 Hilgard Ave, Los Angeles, 90024. Edward Shreeves, Chairman, Bibliographers Group; Joseph J Lauer, African Studies Bibliographer
Holdings: Maps Pix Slides Phonorecords Audiotapes Microforms
Notes: General collection mainly in the humanities and social sciences, covering prehistoric times to the present. Particular strengths include: early travel and exploration, mission field, literature, vernacular languages and literatures, Portuguese Africa, slavery (have the British Foreign Office's *General Correspondence. Slave Trade* on microfilm). Extensive holdings of journals, newspapers and government publications. The collection was described in the *Handbook of American Resources for African Studies* (1967).

CA —FITZ HUGH LUDLOW MEMORIAL LIBRARY, PO Box 99346, San Francisco, 94109. Michael R Aldrich, Exec Cur
Holdings: Mss Maps Pix Slides Phonorecords Audiotapes Videotapes
Notes: Collection stored. Important mail inquiries only. No interlibrary lending or telephone queries. The heart of this special collection of psychoactive drug literature is about 400 vols of memoirs or lightly-disguised fiction concerning psychoactive drugs, plus about 600 vols related to Beat writers of the 1950s-60s, plus about 300 vols related to the "Hippie" movement of the 1960s, plus 600 vols (mostly paperback) of drug-related pornography, and several hundred vols related to drug slang, drugs and music, drug art, drug cuisine, etc. In addition we have many boxes of offprints, files of newspaper clippings, complete runs to underground newspapers, and many artifacts related to this area. Much of the 1950s-60s-70s literature is autographed or inscribed.

IN —INDIANA UNIVERSITY, Institute for Sex Research Library, 416 Morrison Hall, Bloomington, 47401. Douglas Freeman, Collections and Services Librn; Joan Brewer, Information Services Librn
Holdings: Vols (62,000) Cat Mss Pix Phonorecords Audiotapes Slides Films Microforms
Budget: ($20,000)
Notes: One of the greatest and most extensive collections on sexual behavior, the library collects materials on all aspects of sex activity, with special emphasis on behavioral and social aspects. Also collects erotic literature and sexual ephemera. Incl 105 audiotapes, 23 vertical file drawers, 108 phonorecords, 55,000 pictures, 5000 slides, and 1700 films. Rich in French, German and American sources; also much Oriental. Semitraditional erotic poetry and song of 17th-18th century England. Bawdy limericks, double-entendre, puns, slang, erotic literature, graffiti, slang and special dictionaries, proverbs and sayings, epigrams and research materials of the Kinsey Studies, etc. Contact Information Service for: literature searching, preparation of bibliographies, permission to use collection. Limited photocopying.

SLATER, SAMUEL AND JOHN, COMPANY

CT —UNIVERSITY OF CONNECTICUT, Historical Manuscripts and Archives

Division, Box U-205, Storrs, 06268. Randall Jimerson, Librn
Holdings: Vols 55
Notes: Business records of pioneer Connecticut textile manufacturers, Samuel and John Slater. Other Slater correspondence and records are in the Baker Library at Harvard and the Rhode Island Historical Society. Most of the records at University of Connecticut relate to the Slater Company's mills and company stores in Jewett City and Hopeville, Conn, 1825-1880. Incl financial records, correspondence and employee account books.

SLATTERY, HARRY A.

NC —DUKE UNIVERSITY, William R Perkins Library, Manuscript Dept, Durham, 27706. Ellen Gartrell, Cur of Mss
Holdings: Cat Mss
Notes: Papers, etc.

SLAUGHTER, FRANK

MA —BOSTON UNIVERSITY, Mugar Memorial Library, Special Collections Dept, 771 Commonwealth Ave, Boston, 02215. Howard B Gotlieb, Dir
Holdings: Cat Mss
Notes: Mss, correspondence, etc collected in depth; incl publication by or about.

NC —DUKE UNIVERSITY, William R Perkins Library, Manuscript Dept, Durham, 27706. Ellen Gartrell, Cur of Mss
Holdings: Cat Mss
Notes: Papers, correspondence, etc.

SLAUSON FAMILY

CA —AZUSA PACIFIC COLLEGE, Marshburn Memorial Library, Citrus & Alosta, Azusa, 91702. Edward Peterman, Librn
Holdings: Vols (1000) // Uncat Maps Pix
Notes: Macneil Family Collection on Local History. These items relate to the Slauson, Macneil and Wilcox families, incl photographs, diaries, letters, maps, books, and finanical and legal documents.

SLAVE TRADE—PERSONAL NARRATIVES

DC —HOWARD UNIVERSITY, Moorland-Spingarn Research Center, 500 Howard Place NW, Washington, 20059. Clifford L Muse, Jr, Acting Dir
Holdings: Vols (94,000) Mss Maps Pix Slides Phonorecords Audiotapes 16mm Films Filmstrips Microforms
Budget: ($854,753)
See also entry under Blacks

SLAVERY AND ANTISLAVERY

CA —CALIFORNIA STATE UNIVERSITY, LONG BEACH, Library, Dept of Special Collections & Archives, 1250 Bellflower Blvd, Long Beach, 90840. John Ahouse, Special Collections Librn
Holdings: Vols 400 Cat
Notes: Incl memoirs, pamphlets, and tracts.

CA —LOS ANGELES PUBLIC LIBRARY, Social Sciences Dept, 630 W Fifth St, Los Angeles, 90071. Marilyn C Wherley, Principal Librn
Holdings: Vols 5000 Cat Microforms
Budget: ($150,000)
Notes: Black Studies Collection. Pamphlets, bibliographies, indexes, periodicals, with some historical runs on microfilm, strong collection on slavery and anti-slavery, abolition, civil rights movements, with emphasis on the black experience in the United States. No spearate catalog.

CA —UNIVERSITY OF CALIFORNIA, SANTA BARBARA, Library, Dept of Special Collections, Santa Barbara, 93106. Christian F Brun, Head
Holdings: Vols 24,500 Cat Mss Maps Pix Microforms
Budget: $7000
Notes: The William Wyles Collection of Americana. Incl American Civil War,

SLAVERY AND ANTISLAVERY (cont.)

Abraham Lincoln, Westward Movement, Americans for the Orient, slavery, abolition movement, etc.

CT —TRINITY COLLEGE LIBRARY, Watkinson Library, 300 Summit St, Hartford, 06106. Jeffrey Kaimowitz, Cur
Holdings: Cat

DC —HOWARD UNIVERSITY, Moorland-Spingarn Research Center, 500 Howard Place NW, Washington, 20059. Clifford L Muse, Jr, Acting Dir
Holdings: Vols (106,086) Mss Maps Pix Slides Phonorecords Audiotapes 16mm Films Filmstrips Microforms
Budget: ($854,753)
See also entry under Blacks

DC —LIBRARY OF CONGRESS, Rare Book & Special Collections Div, Washington, 20540. William Matheson, Chief
Notes: Daniel Murray Pamphlet Collection on Afro-American history, 1850-1920, pertains chiefly to slavery and the abolitionist movement.

FL —UNIVERSITY OF FLORIDA, Libraries, Special Collections, W University Ave, Gainesville, 32611. Sidney Ives, Librn & Rare Books
Holdings: Cat Mss Maps
Notes: This collection, of manuscripts only, deals especially with Haiti, revolutionary period and after. Also a very large group of notaries' papers useful for research in trade and slavery, etc.

IL —NEWBERRY LIBRARY, 60 W Walton St, Chicago, 60610. Diana Haskell, Cur of Modern Mss
Holdings: Cat
Notes: Espec antislavery literature.

IL —WHEATON COLLEGE, Buswell Memorial Library, Wheaton, 60187. Paul Snezek, Library Dir
Holdings: Mss Pix
Notes: Blanchard's papers, correspondence, books and photographs. Also a complete set of the periodical *Christian Cynosure.* *Related Topics:* Anti-slavery, Abolitionists, Secret Societies, Wheaton College.

MD —JOHNS HOPKINS UNIVERSITY, Milton S Eisenhower Library, Charles & 34 Sts, Baltimore, 21218. Ann S Gwyn, Assistant Dir for Special Collections
Holdings: Vols Cat
Notes: Collection begun by James G Birney, candidate for the US presidency in 1840 and 1844. Incl 350 books, pamphlets (bound), histories, biographies, minutes, reports, and newspapers form 1790. Some proslavery works and some rare titles. Most complete file of Benjamin Lundy's *Philanthropist,* 1817-1818. No published catalog.

MD —UNIVERSITY OF MARYLAND, Library, Rare Book Collection, College Park, 20742. Donald Farren, Assoc Dir for Special Collections
Holdings: Vols (10,000) Cat
Notes: Ranging from incunabula to modern first editions, the Rare Book Collection is particularly strong in materials relating to the history of France and in *exempla* of interest to students of bibliography. Related collections include sizable groups of books and other items relating to the Savoy, to *Expressionismus,* and to Pompeii. Pamphlet collections include many Mazarinades, many pamphlets relating to slavery and abolition, numerous French plays, and press books.

MD —PRINCE GEORGE'S COUNTY MEMORIAL LIBRARY SYSTEM, Oxon Hill Branch Library, Sojourner Truth Collection, 6200 Oxon Hill Rd, Oxon Hill, 20745. Cherie Phillips Barnett, Librn
Holdings: Vols (3000) Cat Mss Pix Films Phonorecords Microforms VF
Budget: ($3500)
Notes: The Sojourner Truth Collection on Blacks in America is a representative collection of materials by and about Black Americans, their historical problems and accomplishments. The collection, containing certain unique and rare items, emphasizes the Black woman, the Black family, slavery and anti-slavery, Black literature, Blacks in the military and slave narratives. Also incl

current US government publications concerning the Black American. A supportive collection of films, recordings, paperbacks, and periodicals is available. Programs, displays, and bibliographies are prepared in order to develop interest in the collection.

MA —UNIVERSITY OF MASSACHUSETTS AT AMHERST, Library, Amherst, 01003. Siegfried Feller, Assoc Dir for Collection Development
Holdings: Cat
Notes: Incl 375 pamphlets, mainly abolitionist and oriented to the US publications of antislavery societies, etc, 1725-1911. Indexed calendar.

†MA —BOSTON PUBLIC LIBRARY, Copley Sq, Boston, 02117.
Holdings: Vols 2500 Cat Microforms
Notes: Microform Publication by Lost Cause Press. Antislavery Propaganda in the Oberlin College Library.

MA —BOSTON PUBLIC LIBRARY, Rare Books and Manuscripts, Copley Square, Boston, 02117. Laura V Monti, Keeper of Rare Books
Notes: Significant material, in volume, is devoted to economic and political relationships between New England and the Maritime Provinces in the 18th Century; much on Abolitionists and the antislavery movement. Described in *Canadian Manuscripts in the Boston Public Library* (Boston: G K Hall), 1 vol. Incl about 17,000 items.

MA —HARVARD UNIVERSITY LIBRARY, Widener Library, Cambridge, 02138.
Holdings: Cat Mss

MA —BOSTON COLLEGE LIBRARIES, Thomas P O'Neill Library, Nicholas M Williams Ethnological Collection, Chestnut Hill, 02167. Frank J Seegraber, Special Collections Librn
Holdings: Vols 10,000 // Cat Mss Maps
Notes: Collection emphasizes Caribbeana, especially Jamaica, to 1940. Incl discovery, exploration and natural history of the British, French and Spanish settlements; the slave question; piracy. There are over 6000 mss, 5000 of which are Anansi folk tales recorded by native school children. Also small ancillary sections of Africana and Judaica. For reference use only, by arrangement with librarian.

MA —WILLIAMS COLLEGE, Sawyer Library, Williamstown, 01267. Phyllis L Cutler, Dir
Holdings: Vols 250 // Cat
Notes: The Strickland Kneass Collection on Slavery in the US and the slave trade.

MI —UNIVERSITY OF MICHIGAN, William L Clements Library, Ann Arbor, 48109. John C Dann, Dir
Notes: The William L. Clements Library of Americana is a non-circulating rare book library of original source material, printed and manuscript, dealing with America, from the discovery period into the late nineteenth century. The collection includes approximately 55,000 books and pamphlets, 550 linear feet of manuscripts, 4,100 volumes of newspapers, 36,000 maps, 40,000 pieces of sheet music, and 1,000 prints. The collection is strongest for the period of the American Revolution, and includes the papers of Thomas Gage, Sir Henry Clinton, and the Earl of Shelburne. Other areas of strength include antislavery, cartography and geography, discovery and exploration, American Indians, The Civil War, tune-books, sermons and orations, and the War of 1812. There are selective research collections dealing with Christopher Columbus, Thomas Paine, Benjamin Franklin, George Washington, Thomas Jefferson, and the Federalist Papers. Publications describing the collections of the library are: Author/Title catalog of Americana 1493-1860 in the William L. Clements Library... 7 volumes, Boston, G. K. Hall, 1970; Guide to the

manuscript collections of the William L. Clements Library, by Arlene P. Shy 3d edition, Boston, G. K. Hall, 1978; Guide to the manuscript maps in the William L. Clements Library, compiled by Christian Burn, Ann Arbor, U. of Michigan, 1959; and Research catalog of maps of America, to 1860 in the William L. Clements Library..., edited by Douglas W. Marshall, 4 volumes, Boston, G. K. Hall, 1972.

NY —BUFFALO & ERIE COUNTY PUBLIC LIBRARY, Rare Book Room, Lafayette Sq, Buffalo, 14203. William H Loos, Cur
Holdings: Vols 650 Cat Mss

NY —NEW YORK PUBLIC LIBRARY, Schomburg Center for Research in Black Culture, 515 Lenox Ave, New York, 10037. Catherine J Lenix Hooker, Interim Administrator
Holdings: Vols (85,000) Cat Mss Maps Pix Slides Phonorecords Audiotapes Videotapes 16mm Films Filmstrips Microforms
Notes: Materials in all formats about Black peoples throughout the world. Extensive archival holdings, vertical files, Afro-American and African art. Collections incl 182 groups of mss, 100,000 photographs, 6500 slides, 5600 phonorecords, 2300 audiotapes, and over 30,000 microforms. Described in *The Dictionary Catalog of the Schomburg Collection,* 9 vols, and supplements to 1974, 7 vols (Boston: G K Hall, 1962-1975); and *Bibliographic Guide to Black Studies* (Boston: G K Hall). Since 1972, the Center's holdings have been incl in the *Dictionary Catalog of the Research Libraries, New York Public Library.*

NY —CORNELL UNIVERSITY LIBRARIES, John M Olin Library, Dept of Rare Books, Ithaca, 14853. Donald D Eddy, Librn
Holdings: Vols 7822 Cat Mss

NY —NEW YORK PUBLIC LIBRARY, Research Libraries, Economic & Public Affairs Div, Fifth Ave & 42 St, New York, 10018. Edward DiRoma, Chief
Holdings: Vols (1,500,000) Cat Microforms

NY —NEW YORK PUBLIC LIBRARY, Research Libraries, American History Div, Fifth Ave & 42 St, New York, 10018.
Holdings: Vols (25,000) Maps Microforms
Notes: See *Dictionary Catalog of the History of Americas Collection* (Boston: G K Hall, 1961), 28 vols.

NC —DUKE UNIVERSITY, William R Perkins Library, Durham, 27706. Elvin E Strowd, University Librn
Notes: The Bruno Lasker collection contains 51 portfolios; the Perkins Library general collection and other collections contain a significant amount of material on the subject of slavery and antislavery.

NC —DUKE UNIVERSITY, William R Perkins Library, Manuscript Dept, Durham, 27706. Ellen Gartrell, Cur of Mss
Holdings: Cat Mss
Notes: Especially US South, incl slavery and slave trade, abolition movement, freedmen, civil rights. Notable are papers of black educator Charles N Hunter, many plantation records, and British antislavery papers of William Wilberforce and William Smith.

NC —DUKE UNIVERSITY, William R Perkins Library, Rare Book Room, Durham, 27706. John L Sharpe, III, Cur
Notes: A vast collection composed primarily of pamphlets recording the views of 18th and 19th century America (both northern and southern) and Europe toward slavery.

OH —KENT STATE UNIVERSITY, University Archives, Kent, 44242. Stephen C Morton, University Archivist
Holdings: Uncat Mss
Notes: One cubic foot of manuscripts and

SLAVERY AND ANTISLAVERY (cont.)

printed materials of Betsy Mix Cowles, abolitionist, educator and women's rights advocate. Ms Cowles chaired the Women's Rights Convention at Salem, Ohio in 1850. The collection contains correspondence dating from 1832, diaries, finanical records, anti-slavery tracts, addresses, poems, pamphlets, and materials about Ms Cowles.

OH —MASSILLON PUBLIC LIBRARY, 208 Lincoln Way E, Massillon, 44646. Camille Leslie, Dir
Holdings: // Mss Maps
Notes: 22 linear ft. Correspondence and business papers of Thomas Rotch and Arvin Wales who migrated in 1811 from New England to Ohio; and of Arvin C Wales, his son, lawyer and civic leader in Massillon, Ohio. Covers period ca 1780-1880; contains much Quaker and anti-slavery material, as well as material on early Ohio. Index in preparation.

OH —OBERLIN COLLEGE LIBRARY, Oberlin, 44074. William A Moffett, Dir of Libraries
Holdings: Cat
Notes: Antislavery propaganda material in the Library has been issued in microform publication by the Lost Cause Press, Lexington, Ky.

OH —WILMINGTON COLLEGE, Watson Library, Quaker Collection, Pyle Center, Box #1227, Wilmington, 45177. Audrey Haines, Cur
Holdings: Vols (6000) Cat Mss Maps Pix Microforms
Notes: Collection houses Wilmington College archives, 1870-present, and serves as repository for the records of the Wilmington and Ohio Valley Yearly Meetings of the Religious Society of Friends (Quakers), ca 1800-present. Also incl 120 Quaker periodical and newsletter titles, ca 1828-present; several hundred pamphlets, tracts, and epistles; 220 genealogical works, primarily Quaker families; and 3900 vols on Quaker history, philosophy, thought, and practice, particularly peace, war, slavery, education, and biography, ca 1750-present. Incl some fiction, poetry and children's books. Rare or fragile materials, reference works, pamphlets, and genealogies do not circulate. Please notify prior to visiting.

PA —HAVERFORD COLLEGE, Magill Library, Quaker Collection, Haverford, 19041. Edwin B Bonner, Librn & Cur
Holdings: Vols (32,000) Cat Mss Maps Pix Phonorecords Audiotapes Microforms
Notes: Incl material about Society of Friends from inception in England, 1650, to the present. Formats incl periodicals, diaries, documents of individual Friends, families, Quaker Meetings and institutions, incl archives of Haverford College. Emphases on American Indians, antislavery, women, minorities, the Rufus M Jones Mysticism collection, Quaker fiction, and Delaware Valley, Pennsylvania.

PA —HISTORICAL SOCIETY OF PENNSYLVANIA, Library, 1300 Locust St, Philadelphia, 19107. David Fraser, Librn
Holdings: Vols (230,000) Mss Maps Pix Microforms
Notes: Incl over 14,000,000 ms pieces. The Library Company of Philadelphia mss are on deposit with the Historical Society of Pennsylvania. Many of the Society's rare books are on deposit with the Library Company. The Society maintains the collections of the Genealogical Society of Pennsylvania, incl some 20,000 printed genealogies, original mss, family, church, and civil records.

PA —LIBRARY COMPANY OF PHILADELPHIA, 1314 Locust St, Philadelphia, 19107. Edwin Wolf II, Librn; Kenneth Finkel, Cur of Prints
Holdings: Vols (400,000) Cat Mss Maps Pix
Budget: ($25,000)
Notes: With the collection of The Historical Society of Pennsylvania, one of the richest collections of mss, books and other materials on the slave trade, the abolition movement and other chapters of Blacks in the New World. Incl printed material on the history of Blacks in the US, the West Indies, and Africa, to 1906.

PA —TEMPLE UNIVERSITY LIBRARIES, Special Collections Dept, Rare Books & Mss Section, Philadelphia, 19122. Thomas M Whitehead, Cur
Holdings: Vols (10,000) Mss Pix
Notes: "The Charles Blockson Afro-American Historical Collection". Curated by Charles Blockson. The Private Library of Charles Blockson established as a collection at Temple University. Approximately 25,000 items of Afro-American literature, history of slavery and African and Caribbean history and culture. Selective catalog (exhibition) available.

PA —FRIENDS HISTORICAL LIBRARY OF SWARTHMORE COLLEGE, Swarthmore, 19081. J William Frost, Dir
Holdings: Vols (35,000) Cat Mss Pix Microforms
Notes: Library's collections contain information on the history and doctrine of the Society of Friends, Quaker contributions to literature, science, business, education, and government, plus their reform efforts in peace, Indian rights, women's rights, and abolition of slavery. Among the more than 250 mss collections are papers of several Quaker abolitionists, incl Lucretia Mott and John Greenleaf Whittier.

RI —BROWN UNIVERSITY, John Hay Library, 20 Prospect St, Providence, 02912. Mark N Brown, Cur Mss
Holdings: // Mss
Notes: Three ms boxes and 29 notebooks of George S Burleigh, containing letters for the period 1839 to 1903 reflecting his interests in Transcendentalism; the anti-slavery, temperance, and woman's liberation movements; the Sabbath Question; and the publication of his writing in reform periodicals. Two manuscript boxes and 29 notebooks contain poems by Burleigh.

RI —BROWN UNIVERSITY, John Carter Brown Library, Providence, 02912. Norman Fiering, Librn; Everett C Wilkie Jr, Bibliographer; Susan Danforth, Cur Maps & Prints
Notes: Works documenting slavery and slave trade in European possessions in the New World until 1833. Particular strengths are British and French abolition movements in the early nineteenth century. (Little material on slavery in what became the United States).

RI —PROVIDENCE PUBLIC LIBRARY, 150 Empire St, Providence, 02903. Lance J Bauer, Special Collections Librn
Holdings: Vols 5000 Cat Mss Maps Pix
Notes: The Harris Collection on the American Civil War and Slavery. Incl 18th and 19th century books, rare pamphlets, and periodicals concerning slavery and the slave trade, and origins, progress and results of the Civil Civil War; also regimental histories; military and naval tactics; personal narratives; women's accounts of the Civil War; works on abolition; sheet music; Union and Confederate broadside ballads; Confederate imprints; *The Liberator* from 1843 through the Civil War; and over 85 editions of *Uncle Tom's Cabin* in 14 languages. Excellent primary and secondary sources for the study of the Civil War and slavery. Material must be used in-house. Photocopying when condition of material allows.

TX —UNIVERSITY OF TEXAS LIBRARIES, General Libraries, PO Box P, Austin, 78713. Carolyn Bucknell, Asst Dir for Collection Development
Holdings: Cat Microforms
Notes: Large collection of anti-slavery pamphlets.

TX —WEST TEXAS STATE UNIVERSITY, Cornette Library, PO Box 748 WT Sta, Canyon, 79016. Faye Hendrickson, Special Collections Asst
Holdings: Vols (451,253) Uncat Microforms
Notes: Includes microform collections.

TX —EAST TEXAS STATE UNIVERSITY, James G Gee Library, Special Collections Dept, East Texas Station, Commerce, 75428. James Conrad, Dept Head
Holdings: Vols (3500) Cat Mss Pix Slides
Notes: The books on Black Literature (with the exception of those on Texas folklore) and Slavery in the US have been transferred to the general stack area of the library; however, our collection of county histories of Texas, which is still housed in the Special Collections, continues to grow. In addition, we have acquired sizeable collections of books on Texas folklore and Texas place names; and World War II posters. Another new area is printing arts in Texas. There is a separate dictionary card catalog for the book collection in the Special Collections Department.

VA —VIRGINIA UNION UNIVERSITY, William J Clark Library, 1500 N Lombardy St, Richmond, 23220. Verdelle V Bradley, Librn
Holdings: Vols 9905 Cat Pix Slides Phonorecords Audiotapes Filmstrips Microforms
Notes: Incl 1369 microforms. Special collection on slavery is not cataloged; oral history tapes of Black Virginians, especially in religious contexts.

SLAVERY AND THE CHURCH

GA —AGNES SCOTT COLLEGE, McCain Library, E College Ave, Decatur, 30030. Judith Bourgeois Jensen, Librn
Holdings: Vols (945) Uncat
Budget: $300
Notes: The Frontier Religion Collection, which was given by Prof Walter Brownlow Posey, traces the effects of slavery on religion in the Old South Frontier prior to 1860. A catalog file (by author entry only) accompanies the collection at present. Noncirculating.

SLAVERY IN THE U.S.

CA —UNIVERSITY OF CALIFORNIA, SANTA BARBARA, Library, Dept of Special Collections, Santa Barbara, 93106. Christian F Brun, Head
Holdings: Vols 24,500 Cat Mss Maps Pix Microforms
Budget: $7000
Notes: The William Wyles Collection of Americana. Incl American Civil War, Abraham Lincoln, Westward Movement, Americans for the Orient, slavery, abolition movement, etc.

DC —HOWARD UNIVERSITY, Moorland-Spingarn Research Center, 500 Howard Place NW, Washington, 20059. Clifford L Muse, Jr, Acting Dir
Holdings: Vols (106,086) Mss Maps Pix Slides Phonorecords Audiotapes 16mm Films Filmstrips Microforms
Budget: ($854,753)
See also entry under Blacks

GA —AGNES SCOTT COLLEGE, McCain Library, E College Ave, Decatur, 30030. Judith Bourgeois Jensen, Librn
Holdings: Vols (945) Uncat
Budget: $300
Notes: The Frontier Religion Collection, which was given by Prof Walter Brownlow Posey, traces the effects of slavery on religion in the Old South Frontier prior to 1860. A catalog file (by author entry only) accompanies the collection at present. Noncirculating.

IL —CHICAGO PUBLIC LIBRARY, Special Collections Div, Cultural Center, 78 E Washington St, Chicago, 60602. Laura Linard, Cur
Holdings: Vols (7000) Cat Mss Maps Pix
Notes: The Civil War and American History Research Collection at the Chicago Public Library is our largest collection. It spans the pre-war sectional crisis as well as Reconstruction. Scarce slavery pamphlets; large collection of regimental histories; manuscripts of US Grant, Sherman, Breckinridge; letters and diaries of soldiers and other officers; original photographs of individuals and field shots; Confederate Battle Plan for the Battle of Shiloh (original); swords, rifles, uniforms, flags and other military accessories. A substantial part of this collection has been cataloged. The museum objects are inventoried (Grand Army Hall and Memorial Association of

SLAVERY IN THE U.S. (cont.)

Illinois Collection).See *Treasures of The Chicago Public Library*, comp by Thomas A Oriando and Marie Gecik, 1977, pp 36-79.

IL —NEWBERRY LIBRARY, 60 W Walton St, Chicago, 60610. Diana Haskell, Cur of Modern Mss
Holdings: Cat
Notes: Espec antislavery literature.

IL —ILLINOIS STATE UNIVERSITY, Milner Library, Dept of Special Collections, Normal, 61761. Robert Sokan, Librn
Holdings: Vols 1200 Cat
Notes: The Harold K Sage Lincoln Collection consists of approx 1200 book items, 1500 pamphlets which are uncataloged, and ephemera (ie newspaper clippings, correspondence). The collection incl biographies, collections of his speeches, commemoration ceremony speeches, juvenalia and books dealing with Lincoln's relationship to special subject areas such as religion and slavery. Many of the books are limited editions, presentation or autographed copies with correspondence from authors and/or editors inserted.

IN —WILLARD LIBRARY, 21 First Ave, Evansville, 47710. Joan Elliott, Special Collections Librn
Holdings: Vols (500) Cat Mss
Budget: ($4000)
Notes: Incl books and pamphlets (slave narratives, works by and about abolitionists, accounts of underground railroad activity), some abolitionist newspapers. Incl some reprints, but mostly original 19th century imprints.

LA —TULANE UNIVERSITY, Howard-Tilton Memorial Library, Special Collections Div, 7001 Freret St, New Orleans, 70118. Wilbur E Meneray, Librn
Holdings: Mss
Notes: Correspondence, business papers and legal documents of New Orleans businessman and philanthropist John McDonogh including his interest in the emancipation of slaves.

ME —BOWDOIN COLLEGE, Library, Brunswick, 04011. Dianne M Gutscher, Cur of Special Collections
Holdings: Mss Pix
Notes: The Oliver Otis Howard Papers consist of more than 150,000 pieces of correspondence, articles, lectures, and ephemera for the period 1843-1908, covering his services as a Civil War officer, as founder of the Freedmen's Bureau, as president of Howard University, and as superintendent of the US Military Academy at West Point.

MD —PRINCE GEORGE'S COUNTY MEMORIAL LIBRARY SYSTEM, Oxon Hill Branch Library, Sojourner Truth Collection, 6200 Oxon Hill Rd, Oxon Hill, 20745. Cherie Phillips Barnett, Librn
Holdings: Vols (3000) Cat Mss Pix Films Phonorecords Microforms VF
Budget: ($3500)
Notes: The Sojourner Truth Collection on Blacks in America is a representative collection of materials by and about Black Americans, their historical problems and accomplishments. The collection, containing certain unique and rare items, emphasizes the Black woman, the Black family, slavery and anti-slavery, Black literature, Blacks in the military and slave narratives. Also incl current US government publications concerning the Black American. A supportive collection of films, recordings, paperbacks, and periodicals is available. Programs, displays, and bibliographies are prepared in order to develop interest in the collection.

MA —BOSTON PUBLIC LIBRARY, Rare Books and Manuscripts, Copley Square, Boston, 02117. Laura V Monti, Keeper of Rare Books
Notes: Significant material, in volume, is devoted to economic and political relationships between New England and the Maritime Provinces in the 18th Century; much on Abolitionists and the antisalvery movement. Described in *Canadian Manuscripts in the Boston Public Library*

(Boston: G K Hall), 1 vol. Incl about 17,000 items.

MA —PEABODY INSTITUTE LIBRARY, Danvers Archival Center, 15 Sylvan St, Danvers, 01923. Richard B Trask, Archivist, Rare Books & Special Collections
Holdings: Vols 179 Cat
Notes: The Parker Pillsbury Collection is made up primarily of 19th century antislavery tracts and books owned by abolitionist Parker Pillsbury, 1809-1898.

MA —WILLIAMS COLLEGE, Sawyer Library, Williamstown, 01267. Phyllis L Cutler, Dir
Holdings: Vols 250 // Cat
Notes: The Strickland Kneass Collection on Slavery in the US and the slave trade.

MA —AMERICAN ANTIQUARIAN SOCIETY LIBRARY, 185 Salisbury St, Worcester, 01609. Marcus A McCorison, Dir & Librn
Holdings: Cat Mss Pix
Notes: Rich in early writings of Black authors in poetry, fiction, drama, and essays inspired by them, plus numerous newspapers and magazine files of Black publications. Many rare 18th century tracts on slavery; fine collections which illuminate the Black-White relationships, as well as documents dealing with the Black heritage-soldiers, religion, folklore, music.

MS —UNIVERSITY OF SOUTHERN MISSISSIPPI, William David McCain Graduate Library, Box 5148, Southern Sta, Hattiesburg, 39406.
Holdings: Vols (5000)
Notes: The Ernest A Walen Collection on the history of the Confederate States of America. Incl over 600 Confederate imprints. Catalog in progress.

MO —LINCOLN UNIVERSITY, Page Library, Chestnut St, Jefferson City, 65101.
Holdings: Vols (2000) Cat Phonorecords Filmstrips
Notes: Most books are early Negro writings on slavery and the Black experience. Ethnic Studies Center housed in the Library. It has special collections of books, films, filmstrips and local oral history tapes relating to ethnicity and ethnic studies. A part-time administrator is to be in charge.

NY —NEW YORK STATE LIBRARY, State Education Bldg Annex, Washington Ave, Albany, 12224.
Holdings: Cat
Notes: Printed handbills and posted announcements of historic and everyday events, theater performances; auctions, advertisements; land sales; slave sales, reward posters for runaways; inducements to enlist for military serice. Over 2000 pieces. Also over 1300 poetic broadside ballads.

NY —NEW YORK HISTORICAL SOCIETY, Library, 170 Central Park W, New York, 10024. James Gregory, Librn
Holdings: Mss
Notes: Incl original mss, illustrative materials, etc.

NY —NEW YORK PUBLIC LIBRARY, Slavonic Div, Fifth Ave & 42 St, New York, 10018. Edward Kasinec, Chief
Holdings: Cat Microforms
Notes: Described in *Dictionary Catalog of the Slavonic Collection* (Boston: G K Hall, 1974), 44 vols.

NY —UNIVERSITY OF ROCHESTER, Rush Rhees Library, Department of Rare Books and Special Collections, Rochester, 14627. Peter Dzwonkoski, Librn
Holdings: Mss
Notes: Autograph letters and other mss, incl in the Isaac and Amy Post family papers, Frederick Douglass Papers, and Porter family papers.

NY —JERVIS PUBLIC LIBRARY, 613 N Washington St, Rome, 13440. William A Dillon, Dir
Holdings: // Cat Mss
See also entry under Autograph - Collections

NC —DUKE UNIVERSITY, William R Perkins Library, Manuscript Dept, Durham, 27706. Ellen Gartrell, Cur of Mss
Holdings: Cat Mss
Notes: Especially US South, incl slavery and slave trade, abolition movement, freedmen, civil rights. Notable are papers of black

educator Charles N Hunter, many plantation records, and British antislavery papers of William Wilberforce and William Smith.

NC —DUKE UNIVERSITY, William R Perkins Library, Rare Book Room, Durham, 27706. John L Sharpe, III, Cur
Notes: A vast collection composed primarily of pamphlets recording the views of 18th and 19th century America (both northern and southern) and Europe toward slavery.

OH —OBERLIN COLLEGE LIBRARY, Oberlin, 44074. William A Moffett, Dir of Libraries
Holdings: Cat

PA —GETTYSBURG COLLEGE, Musselman Library, Gettysburg, 17325. Willis M Hubbard, College Librn
Holdings: Vols (4000) Cat Mss Maps Pix Slides Microforms
Budget: ($1200)
Notes: Incl material on slavery.

PA —HISTORICAL SOCIETY OF PENNSYLVANIA, Library, 1300 Locust St, Philadelphia, 19107. David Fraser, Librn
Holdings: Vols (230,000) Mss Mp
Notes: Incl over 14,000,000 ms pieces. The Library Company of Philadelphia mss are on deposit with the Historical Society of Pennsylvania. Many of the Society's rare books are on deposit with the Library Company. The Society maintains the collections of the Genealogical Society of Pennsylvania, incl some 20,000 printed genealogies, original mss, family, church, and civil records.

PA —LIBRARY COMPANY OF PHILADELPHIA, 1314 Locust St, Philadelphia, 19107. Edwin Wolf II, Librn; Kenneth Finkel, Cur of Prints
Holdings: Vols (400,000) Cat Mss Maps Pix
Budget: ($25,000)
Notes: With the collection of The Historical Society of Pennsylvania, one of the richest collections of mss, books and other materials on the slave trade, the abolition movement and other chapters of Blacks in the New World. Incl printed material on the history of Blacks in the US, the West Indies, and Africa, to 1906.

PA —TEMPLE UNIVERSITY LIBRARIES, Special Collections Dept, Rare Books & Mss Section, Philadelphia, 19122. Thomas M Whitehead, Cur
Holdings: Vols (10,000) Mss Pix
Notes: The private library of Charles Blockson established as a collection at Temple University. Approximately 25,000 items of Afro-American literature, history of slavery and African and Carribbean histroy and history and culture. Selective catalog (exhibition) available.

PA —CARLOW COLLEGE, Grace Library, Fifth Ave, Pittsburgh, 15213. Joan M Mitchell, Dir of Library Services
Holdings: Vols (1786) Cat
Budget: ($500)
Notes: No photocopying.

RI —PROVIDENCE PUBLIC LIBRARY, 150 Empire St, Providence, 02903. Lance J Bauer, Special Collections Librn
Holdings: Vols 5000 Cat Mss Maps Pix
Notes: The Harris Collection on the American Civil War and Slavery. Incl 18th and 19th century books, rare pamphlets, and periodicals concerning slavery and the slave trade, and origins, progress and results of the Civil Civil War; also regimental histories; military and naval tactics; personal narratives; women's accounts of the Civil War; works on abolition; sheet music; Union and Confederate broadside ballads; Confederate imprints; *The Liberator* from 1843 through the Civil War; and over 85 editions of *Uncle Tom's Cabin* in 14 languages. Excellent primary and secondary sources for the study of the Civil War and slavery. Material must be used in-house. Photocopying when condition of material allows.

SC —COLLEGE OF CHARLESTON LIBRARY, Special Collections Dept, Charleston, 29401.
Notes: Papers, 1840, incl warrant for sheriff's sale of Hetty Barron, a "free person of color," for non-payment of capitation tax, March 20, 1840; correspondence between

SLAVERY IN THE U.S. (cont.)

John Forraws and Alexander Rose regarding the purchase of a vessel and the use of slaves as collateral; marriage settlement trust deed, involving transfer of ownership of slaves from Samuel and Hannah Motte Prioleau to James Hamilton, Jr; warrant for sheriff's sale of Maria Silvanneau, a free "person of color" for non-payment of capitation tax, June 28, 1849. Also, South Carolina Province Court of Cannon Pleas papers 1748-1760. Incl sheriff's warrant for the appearance of John Bross in court to make payment to Edward Power, plaintiff in a suit against him.

TX —UNIVERSITY OF TEXAS LIBRARIES, General Libraries, PO Box P, Austin, 78713. Carolyn Bucknell, Asst Dir for Collection Development
Holdings: Vols Cat Microforms
Notes: The Littlefield Collection of research materials, incl many rare items, on the history of the Old South.

TX —EAST TEXAS STATE UNIVERSITY, James G Gee Library, Special Collections Dept, East Texas Station, Commerce, 75428. James Conrad, Dept Head
Holdings: Vols (3500) Cat Mss Pix Slides
Notes: The books on Black Literature (with the exception of those on Texas folklore) and Slavery in the US have been transferred to the general stack area of the library; however, our collection of county histories of Texas, which is still housed in the Special Collections, continues to grow. In addition, we have acquired sizeable collections of books on Texas folklore and Texas place names; and World War II posters. Another new area is printing arts in Texas. There is a separate dictionary card catalog for the book collection in the Special Collections Department.

VA —UNIVERSITY OF VIRGINIA, Alderman Library, Manuscripts Dept, Charlottesville, 22901. Edmund Berkeley Jr, Cur
Holdings: Cat Mss Maps Pix
Notes: 19th Century Virginia Family Papers Collections enable a researcher to obtain an excellent picture of the economic and social interactions on large plantations in Virginia during the 19th century. They are invaluable as research sources in the study of slavery, women's history, economic history, agrarian and political history. Among the more notable collections are the papers of John Hartwell Cocke and the Cocke family, Berkeley family, Joseph Carrington Cabell, Watson family, Carter-Smith family, Pocket Plantation, Bruce family, Carter family, Hubard family, and many others. 100 linear ft of mss.

VA —VIRGINIA UNION UNIVERSITY, William J Clark Library, 1500 N Lombardy St, Richmond, 23220. Verdelle V Bradley, Librn
Holdings: Vols 9905 Cat Pix Slides Phonorecords Audiotapes Filmstrips Microforms
Notes: Incl 1369 microforms. Special collection on slavery is not cataloged; oral history tapes of Black Virginians, especially in religious contexts.

†ON —METROPOLITAN TORONTO LIBRARY, Social Sciences Dept, 789 Yonge St, Toronto, M4W 2G8, Can. Abdus Salam, Head
Holdings: Vols Cat Maps Phonorecords Audiotapes 16mm Films Microforms
Notes: Collection is both current and historical. Strong in immigrants' guides, government reports and statistics, analyses, histories and studies of ethnic groups. Strong on the Underground Railroad.

SLAVERY IN THE U.S.—PERSONAL NARRATIVES

DC —LIBRARY OF CONGRESS, Manuscript Division, Washington, 20540. John C Broderick, Chief
Notes: A file of ex-slave narratives, collected by the WPA Federal Writers Project between 1936-41. Approx 15,000 to 20,000 original manuscripts. Narratives of ex-slaves and children of slaves from all the Southern states and border states are thought to be included in the collection.

VA —UNIVERSITY OF VIRGINIA, Alderman Library, Manuscripts Dept, Charlottesville, 22901. Edmund Berkeley Jr, Cur
Holdings: Cat Mss Pix
Notes: Material in over 420 collections documents the history and culture of Afro-Americans incl letters and narratives by slaves and masters, plantation accounts, letters from Liberian immigrants, folklore, literture, the desegregation movement in Virginia in the 1960s and 1970s and the "massive resistance" of Virginia political leaders. Michael F Plunkett (ed) *A Guide to Materials on the History, Literature, and Culture of Afro-Americans in the Manuscripts Department, University of Virginia Library.*

SLAVES, EMANCIPATION OF see Emancipation Proclamation

SLAVES AND SLAVERY see Slavery and Antislavery

SLAVIC ART see Art, Slavic

SLAVIC CIVILIZATION see Civilization, Slavic

SLAVIC (CYRILLIC) MANUSCRIPTS see Manuscripts, Slavic (Cyrillic)

SLAVIC FOLKLORE see Folklore, Slavic

SLAVIC HISTORY

CA —UNIVERSITY OF CALIFORNIA, LOS ANGELES, Library, Slavic Collection, 405 Hilgard Ave, Los Angeles, 90024. Edward Shreeves, Chairman, Bibliographers Group; Leon Ferder, Slavic Bibliographer
Holdings: Vols (250,000) Cat
Notes: The Slavic Collection at UCLA consists of materials from and relating to Russia and the Soviet Union, Poland, Czechoslovakia, Yugoslavia, Bulgaria, the Sorbians in East Germany, and works by Slavic emigres. The collection contains nearly 250,000 vols, and is particularly strong in linguistics, literature, history and social sciences, and reference materials. Slavic materials are collected in hard copy and microform, and incl monographs, serials (incl newspapers), reference works, proceedings of Slavistic congresses and symposia, and also *Festschriften* and dissertations.

CO —UNIVERSITY OF SOUTHERN COLORADO, Library, 2200 Bonforte Blvd, Pueblo, 81001.
Holdings: Vols (4000) Cat Mss Maps Pix Phonorecords Audiotapes Sheet Music
Budget: ($10,000)
Notes: Yugoslavian; especially Slovenian history and culture. The collection was inaugurated in 1969. Besides published titles, 2800 in English, and 900 in Slavic languages, there are memorabilia, organizational records, and newspapers, magazines, and music. There is a separate card catalog of items in the collection. Colorado has had a number of Slavic colonies and this collection attempts to recapture the history of these early settlers. Incl sheet music and phonorecords.

CT —YALE UNIVERSITY, Beinecke Rare Book & Manuscript Library, Osborn Collection, New Haven, 06520. Stephen R Parks, Cur
Holdings: Mss

MA —HARVARD UNIVERSITY LIBRARY, Widener Library, Slavic Collections, Cambridge, 02138. Hugh M Olmsted, Slavic Dept Head
Holdings: Cat Mss Microforms Archives
Notes: History sections of Widener Library's SLAV class shelflist through June, 1976 list 67,222 titles (earlier version was incl in the published *Widener Library Shelflist*, volumes 28-31, 1971). An additional 30,000 Slavic history titles are estimated to have been added in the period 1976-1983. These figures exclude microforms and most serial publications issued by academies of sciences, universities, pedagogical institutes and other such bodies. Slavic microforms are estimated at 30,000 reels of microfilm, 62,000 microfiches. Many other relevant materials are scattered through other sections of the University Library collections. Slavic collections throughout are strong both in current and in antiquarian holdings, and continue to be developed actively. See also *Harvard Library Bulletin*, XVII (1969), pp425-433; *East Central and Southeast Europe; A Handbook of Library and Archival Resources in North America*, edited by P L Horecky and D H Kraus, 1976, pp 113-154; and S A Grant and J H Brown, *The Russian Empire and The Soviet Union; A Guide to Manuscripts and Archival Materials in the United States*, 1981, pp 218-219, 224-233. For more detailed listings, see also in the present volume under individual Slavic headings.

SLAVIC LANGUAGES AND LITERATURES

CA —UNIVERSITY OF CALIFORNIA, LOS ANGELES, Library, Slavic Collection, 405 Hilgard Ave, Los Angeles, 90024. Edward Shreeves, Chairman, Bibliographers Group; Leon Ferder, Slavic Bibliographer
Holdings: Vols (250,000) Cat Mss Maps
Notes: The Slavic Collection at UCLA consists of materials from and relating to Russia and the Soviet Union, Poland, Czechoslovakia, Yugoslavia, Bulgaria, the Sorbians in East Germany, and works by Slavic emigres. The collection contains nearly 250,000 vols, and is particularly strong in linguistics, literature, history and social sciences, and reference materials. Slavic materials are collected in hard copy and microform, and incl monographs, serials (incl newspapers), reference works, proceedings of Slavistic congresses and symposia, and also *Festschriften* and dissertations.

CA —CALIFORNIA STATE UNIVERSITY, NORTHRIDGE, Delmar T Oviatt & South Libraries, 1811 Nordhoff St, Northridge, 91330. Donald L Read, Special Collections Dept

CA —STANFORD UNIVERSITY LIBRARIES, Cecil H Green Library, Stanford, 94305. Wojciech Zalewski, Cur, Russian & East European Collection
Holdings: Vols (200,000) Cat Maps Microforms
Budget: ($90,000)
Notes: Strong collection prior to 20th century, but Stanford University Libraries' collecting effort is coordinated with Hoover Institution, Stanford, and holdings are not duplicated. Collection descriptions: Wojciech Zalewski, *Russian Materials in the Main Library of Stanford University, A Collection Survey* (Stanford: Stanford University Libraries, 1974). Wojciech Zalerski, "Stanford University" in P L Horecky, ed, *East Central and Southeast Europe, A Handbook of Library and Archival Resources in North America* (Santa Barbara: Clio Press, 1976).

CO —UNIVERSITY OF SOUTHERN COLORADO, Library, 2200 Bonforte Blvd, Pueblo, 81001.
Holdings: Vols (4000) Cat Mss Maps Pix Phonorecords Audiotapes Sheet Music
Budget: ($10,000)
Notes: Yugoslavian; especially Slovenian history and culture. The collection was inaugurated in 1969. Besides published titles, 2800 in English, and 900 in Slavic languages, there are memorabilia, organizational records, and newspapers, magazines, and music. There is a separate card catalog of items in the collection. Colorado has had a number of Slavic colonies and this collection attempts to recapture the history of these early settlers. Incl sheet music and phonorecords.

CT —YALE UNIVERSITY, Box 1603A, Yale Station, New Haven, 06520.

SLAVIC LANGUAGES AND LITERATURES (cont.)

IL —UNIVERSITY OF ILLINOIS, URBANA/CHAMPAIGN, Slavic and East European Library, Urbana, 61801. Marianna Tax Choldin, Head
Holdings: Vols (420,000) Cat Microforms
Notes: One of the largest Slavic and East European collections. Strong in Russian and Soviet materials-humanities, sciences, and social sciences; languages and literatures; periodicals, newspapers, and microforms. Ca 260,000 volumes in languages of the Soviet Union plus 20,000 Russian and Ukrainian titles on microform. Extensive coverage of Czechoslovakia (35,000 vols); Yugoslavia (31,000 vols); Bulgaria (9200 vols); Poland (34,600 vols); Romania (13,000 vols); and Hungary (18,000 vols) and the languages, literatures, and history of these countries.

KS —UNIVERSITY OF KANSAS, Watson Library, Lawrence, 66045. George Jerkovich, Cur Slavic Collections
Notes: Strong in South Slavic old periodicals and monographs in literature, language, linguistics and history. For the Slavic collections, the major geographical areas involved are Russia-Soviet Union, Poland and Yugoslavia. Also, sizeable collections on Bulgaria, Czechoslovakia, and the Baltic states. Incl emigre literature. University's holdings of Slavica are the largest in the region between the Mississippi and the Sierra Madres. Total of Slavica in 1983 stands at 158,344 vols in Slavic languages of Central, Southeastern and Eastern Europe and the Soviet Union. In addition, Slavic resources in non-Slavic languages totals 58, 936 vols.

MA —HARVARD UNIVERSITY LIBRARY, Widener Library, Slavic Collections, Cambridge, 02138. Hugh M Olmsted, Slavic Dept Head
Holdings: Vols Cat Microforms Mss
Notes: Literature portions of Widener Library's SLAV class shelflist through June, 1976 list 64,780 titles (earlier version was incl in the published Widener Library Shelflist, volumes 28-31, 1971). This figure excludes microforms; Slavic language and linguistics; most serial publications issued by academies of sciences, universities, pedagogical institutes, and other such bodies; as well as material acquired in the period 1976-1983 (the latter category estimated at 50,000 titles). Slavic microforms are estimated at 30,000 reels of microfilm, 62, 000 microfiches. Many other relevant materials are scattered through relevant sections of the University Library collections. Slavic materials are strong throughout both in current and in antiquarian holdings, and continue to be developed actively. See also Harvard Library Bulletin, XVII (1969), pp425-433; East Central and Southeast Europe; A Handbook of Library and Archival Resources in North America, edited by P L Horecky and D H Kraus, 1976, pp 113-154; and S A Grant and J H Brown, The Russian Empire and The Soviet Union; A Guide to Manuscripts and Archival Materials in the United States, 1981, pp 218-219, 224-233. For more detailed listings, see also in the present volume under individual Slavic headings.

NJ —PRINCETON UNIVERSITY, Library, Rare Books Dept, Princeton, 08544. Stephen Ferguson, Cur
Holdings: Cat

NY —CORNELL UNIVERSITY LIBRARIES, John M Olin Library, Ithaca, 14853. Marilyn B Kann, Slavic Studies Librn
Holdings: Vols 12,500 Cat Microforms

NY —NEW YORK PUBLIC LIBRARY, Slavonic Div, Fifth Ave & 42 St, New York, 10018. Edward Kasinec, Chief
Holdings: Cat Microforms
Notes: Described in Dictionary Catalog of the Slavonic Collection (Boston: G K Hall, 1974), 44 vols.

NY —MANHATTANVILLE COLLEGE, Library, Purchase, 10577.
Holdings: Vols (1000) Cat
Notes: A Slavic book collection. Incl classics of Russian, Polish, Serbo-Croatian and Slovenian literature, both in original languages and in translation. Studies in Slavic philosophy and literature, dictionaries, bibliographies and other reference works, as well as the collected works of major 19th century authors.

OH —OHIO STATE UNIVERSITY, William Oxley Thompson Memorial Library, Hilander Room, 1858 Neil Ave Mall, Columbus, 43210. Predrag Matejic, Cur; G Koolemans Beynen, Slavic Bibliographer
Holdings: Vols (200,000) Cat Maps Microforms
Budget: ($45,000)
Notes: Area studies of Central, Southeastern and Eastern Europe. Emphasis on on Slavic literatures, languages and history. At present economics, sociology, law (Russian only) have been added. Within this framework the following priorities have been established: Material in Russian problems; then Medieval Slavic (Cyrillic); then Polish, then Serbo-Croatian, then Bulgarian, and now Romanian. Special attention is paid to serials, bibliographies, ms descriptions and dictionaries (incl biographical and encyclopedias). Apart from materials in native languages, materials in the following languages are acquired: Old Church Slavonic, Greek, English, French, German, Italian, a few in Scandinavian languages, incl Finnish, and a few in Baltic languages. The Hillandar Room holds approx 2000 Slavic mss, 1050 from Hilandar Monastery, Mount Athos, on microform and a related referencecollection.

PA —ALLIANCE COLLEGE, Washington Hall Library, Fullerton Ave, Cambridge Springs, 16403. Stanley J Kozaczka, Head Librn
Holdings: Vols (23,000) Cat Mss Maps Pix Slides Phonorecords Audiotapes Videotapes 16mm Films Filmstrips Microforms
Notes: Polish and Polish-American history, literature and culture. Current publications of world press in Polish. Collection founded in 1912 under patronage of the Polish National Alliance was lost to fire in 1931, but rebuilding began immediately. Incl 100 maps, 1000 pictures, 1000 slides and 100 phonorecords.

PA —JANKOLA LIBRARY AND SLOVAK ARCHIVES, Danville, 17821.
Holdings: Vols (1500)
Notes: Slovak studies and representation of other Slavic groups.

PA —PENNSYLVANIA STATE UNIVERSITY, Fred Lewis Pattee Library, Slavic Library Program, University Park, 16802. Wasyl O Luciw, Head
Holdings: Vols (75,000) Cat Mss Pix
Budget: ($18,000)
Notes: The collection covers a wide range of languages Slavic and East European but its principal strengths are in Russian and Ukrainian. A special collection of 1576 volumes includes pre-revolutionary Russian, fine press publications, in our rare collection and children's literature. Besides book volumes, we have quite a large collection of manuscripts, documents, photographs and many periodicals, also including out of print books on microforms.

WA —UNIVERSITY OF WASHINGTON LIBRARIES, Suzzallo Library, Slavic & East European Section, FM-25, Seattle, 98195. Barbara A Galik, Head
Holdings: Vols (250,000) Cat Mss Maps Pix Phonorecords Audiotapes Microforms
Budget: ($85,000)
Notes: Strong research collections for Russia-USSR, including Central Asia, Eastern Europe and the Balkans, especially Yugoslavia and Poland. Holdings are excellent in language, literature and folklore. There are extensive holdings of the publications of academies, major universities, and principal scholarly institutions, especially of long serial runs.

MB —UNIVERSITY OF MANITOBA, Elizabeth Dafoe Library, Slavic Collection, Winnipeg, R3T 2N2, Can. John S Muchin, Librn
Holdings: Vols (33,000) Cat Mss Microforms
Budget: ($5000)
Notes: Material in all Slavic languages, mostly in Russian (approx 15,000 vols), Ukrainian (approx 15,000 vols), Polish, Old Church Slavic; mainly literature, language, history, art, geography, economics, statistics, political science; newspapers and periodicals; over 20,000 vols of microforms. Cited in Slavic Collection of the University of Manitoba Libraries, John S Muchin (Winnipeg: University of Manitoba Libraries and UVAN, 1970).

SLAVIC MUSIC see Music, Slavic

SLAVIC NEWSPAPERS see Newspapers, Slavic

SLAVIC PERIODICALS see Periodicals, Slavic

SLAVIC STUDIES

CA —UNIVERSITY OF CALIFORNIA, BERKELEY, University Library, Slavic Collections, Berkeley, 94720. Edward Kasinec, Librn
Holdings: Vols (210,000) Cat Maps Microforms
Budget: ($40,000)
Notes: Strong research collections for Bulgaria, Czechoslovakia, Poland, Russia-USSR, and Yugoslavia. Holdings are excellent in economics, folklore, history, linguistics, and literature. Publications issued by academies, major universities, and principal scholarly institutions are well represented. Extensive periodical holdings have been built up, largely as a result of early exchange arrangements. More than 4000 Slavic-language serials are currently being received. Farmington Plan and PL480 commitments have augmented Yugoslav resources. Sizable Slavic-language collections are to be found in Branch Libraries as well, in such subjects as agriculture, biology, earth sciences, forestry, and mathematics.

CA —UNIVERSITY OF CALIFORNIA, LOS ANGELES, Library, Slavic Collection, 405 Hilgard Ave, Los Angeles, 90024. Edward Shreeves, Chairman, Bibliographers Group; Leon Ferder, Slavic Bibliographer
Holdings: Vols (250,000) Cat Maps Microforms
Notes: The Slavic Collection at UCLA consists of materials from and relating to Russia and the Soviet Union, Poland, Czechoslovakia, Yugoslavia, Bulgaria, the Sorbians in East Germany, and works by Slavic emigres. The collection contains nearly 250,000 vols, and is particularly strong in linguistics, literature, history and social sciences, and reference materials. Slavic materials are collected in hard copy and microform, and incl monographs, serials (incl newspapers), reference works, proceedings of Slavistic congresses and symposia, and also Festschriften and dissertations.

IL —UNIVERSITY OF ILLINOIS, URBANA/CHAMPAIGN, Slavic and East European Library, Urbana, 61801. Marianna Tax Choldin, Head
Holdings: Vols (420,000) Cat Microforms
Notes: One of the largest Slavic and East European collections. Strong in Russian and Soviet materials-humanities, sciences, and social sciences; languages and literatures; periodicals, newspapers, and microforms. Ca 260,000 volumes in languages of the Soviet Union plus 20,000 Russian and Ukrainian titles on microform. Extensive coverage of Czechoslovakia (35,000 vols); Yugoslavia (31,000 vols); Bulgaria (9200 vols); Poland (34,600 vols); Romania (13,000 vols); and Hungary (18,000 vols) and the languages, literatures, and history of these countries.

IN —INDIANA UNIVERSITY, University Libraries, Bloomington, 47401. Murlin Croucher, Librn for Slavic Studies
Holdings: Vols (300,000) Cat Maps Microforms
Budget: ($63,000)
Notes: The collection, established after World War II, covers material of, and on, the Soviet Union (55 percent) and Eastern Europe (45 percent) in the languages of the

SLAVIC STUDIES (cont.)

area and in western European languages as well. Materials is chiefly in the fields of humanities and social sciences. Many other Slavic and East European books are located in the Lilly Library (rare book library).

IN —VOLHYNIAN BIBLIOGRAPHIC CENTER, 307 N Overhill Drive, Bloomington, 47401. Max Boyko, Mgr
Notes: Collect materials on Volhynia in Western Ukraine. Compile and publish bibliographies on the region.

MA —HARVARD UNIVERSITY LIBRARY, Widener Library, Slavic Collections, Cambridge, 02138. Hugh M Olmsted, Slavic Dept Head
Holdings: Cat Mss Microforms
Notes: Widener Library's SLAV class shelflist through June, 1976 list 67,222 titles (earlier version was incl in the published *Widener Library Shelflist*, volumes 28-31, 1971). This figure incl Slavic history and literatures only. It excludes microforms; language and linguistics; most serial publications of academies of sciences, universities, pedagogical institutes, and such bodies; and all new additions to the collection since 1976. Slavic microforms are estimated at 30,000 reels of microfilm, 62, 000 microfiches. Many other relevant materials are scattered through other sections of the University Library collections. (eg, anthropology and archaeology, art and architecture, folklore, law, the social sciences, rare books, and manuscripts). In Slavic history, language and linguistics, and literature, an estimated 80, 000 titles were addedin the period 1976-1983. See also *Harvard Library Bulletin*, XVII (1969), pp 425-433; *East Central and Southeast Europe; A Handbook of Library and Archival Resources in North America,* edited by P L Horecky and D H Kraus, 1976, pp 113-154; and S A Grant and J H Brown, *The Russian Empire and The Soviet Union; A Guide to Manuscripts and Archival Materials in the United States,* 1981, pp 218-219, 224-233. For more detailed listings, see also in the present volume under individual Slavic headings.

NY —SHEVCHENKO SCIENTIFIC SOCIETY INC, 63 Fourth Ave, New York, 10003. Svitlana Andrushkiw, Librn
Holdings: Vols (35,000)
Notes: Incl books, periodicals in Ukrainian, Polish Russian, Byelorussian, as well as in the English language. Also Polish Russian language and and Literature; Byelorussian Language and Literature. The Society has a rare book and archival section which contains rare editions, mss, documents, photographs, some microforms. Society is in the process of establishing vertical files and full cataloging of all holdings. Collection consists of approx 35,000 volumes. Basically a research, non-lending library. Graduate level researchers are welcome. By appointment.

NY —UKRAINIAN ACADEMY OF ARTS AND SCIENCES IN THE UNITED STATES (UAAS), 206 W 100 St, New York, 10025. William Omelchenko, Director
Holdings: 45,000 Vols Mss

OH —SLOVAK INSTITUTE, Saint Andrew's Abbey, 2900 King Dr, Cleveland, 44104. Rev Andrew Pier, Dir
Holdings: Vols (10,000)
Notes: Promotes cultural interests, especially work of Slovak authors, artists, and musicians through its Slovak Writers and Artists Association. Private library. Permission required.

OH —BATTELLE MEMORIAL INSTITUTE LIBRARY, 505 King Ave, Columbus, 43201. Carol Young, Librn
Holdings: Vols (150,000) Cat Maps Microforms
Notes: Large collection of Russian and Eastern European science and technology. Over 1600 current journal titles and extensive monography and serial holdings in Slavic languages.

OH —OHIO STATE UNIVERSITY, William Oxley Thompson Memorial Library,

Hilander Room, 1858 Neil Ave Mall, Columbus, 43210. Predrag Matejic, Cur; G Koolemans Beynen, Slavic Bibliographer
Holdings: Vols (200,000) Cat Maps Microforms
Budget: ($45,000)
Notes: Area studies of Central, Southeastern and Eastern Europe. Emphasis on on Slavic literatures, languages and history. At present economics, sociology, law (Russian only) have been added. Within this framework the following priorities have been established: Material in Russian problems; then Medieval Slavic (Cyrillic); then Polish, then Serbo-Croatian, then Bulgarian, and now Romanian. Special attention is paid to serials, bibliographies, ms descriptions and dictionaries (incl biographical and encyclopedias). Apart from materials in native languages, materials in the following languages are acquired: Old Church Slavonic, Greek, English, French, German, Italian, a few in Scandinavian languages, incl Finnish, and a few in Baltic languages. The Hillandar Room holds approx 2000 Slavic mss, 1050 from Hilandar Monastery, Mount Athos, on microform and a related referencecollection.

PA —ALLIANCE COLLEGE, Washington Hall Library, Fullerton Ave, Cambridge Springs, 16403. Stanley J Kozaczka, Head Librn
Holdings: Vols (23,000) Cat Mss Maps Pix Slides Phonorecords Audiotapes Videotapes 16mm Films Filmstrips Microforms
Notes: Polish and Polish-American history, literature and culture. Current publications of world press in Polish. Collection founded in 1912 under patronage of the Polish National Alliance was lost to fire in 1931, but rebuilding began immediately. Incl 100 maps, 1000 pictures, 1000 slides and 100 phonorecords.

PA —JANKOLA LIBRARY AND SLOVAK ARCHIVES, Danville, 17821.
Holdings: Vols 1000
Notes: Slovak studies and representation of other Slavic groups.

PA —THE SLOVAK MUSEUM AND ARCHIVES AT JEDNOTA ESTATES, Rosedale & Jednota Sts, PO Box 150, Middletown, 17057. Edward A Tuleya, Cur & Archivist
Holdings: Vols 4000 Slides
Notes: Incl periodicals and artifacts; Slovak national costumes; looms and tools; lace, embroidery, ribbons; prayer books; documents; ceramics.

PA —SLAVIA LIBRARY, 418 W Nittany Ave, State College, 16801. W O Luciw, Founder & Dir; Jurij A Luciw, Asst Dir
Holdings: Vols (45,000) Mss Pix
Budget: ($3500)
Notes: Incl 5000 periodicals, 3000 av materials, 4000 artifacts, and 200 art works. Also 16,000 letters, etc from Slavic and other personages.

MB —UNIVERSITY OF MANITOBA, Elizabeth Dafoe Library, Slavic Collection, Winnipeg, R3T 2N2, Can. John S Muchin, Librn
Holdings: Vols (33,000) Cat Mss Microforms
Budget: ($5000)
Notes: Material in all Slavic languages, mostly in Russian (approx 15,000 vols), Ukrainian (approx 15,000 vols), Polish, Old Church Slavic; mainly literature, language, history, art, geography, economics, statistics, political science; newspapers and periodicals; over 20,000 vols of microforms. Cited in *Slavic Collection of the University of Manitoba Libraries,* John S Muchin (Winnipeg: University of Manitoba Libraries and UVAN, 1970).

SLAVIK, JURAJ, 1880-1969

CA —HOOVER INSTITUTION ON WAR, REVOLUTION & PEACE, Stanford University, Stanford, 94305. Milorad M Drachkovitch, Archivist
Holdings: Mss
Notes: Papers of Juraj Slavik, Czechoslaovakian diplomat and government offical with service as Minister and Envoy to Poland, 1936-39, Minister of Interior, 1940-

45, Minister of Foreign Affairs, 1945-46, and Ambassador to the US, 1946-48, incl correspondence, speeches and writings, reports, dispatches, memoranda, telegrams, clippings, and other material, 1934-1966, relating to his diplomatic and governmental career, foreign affairs of and political developments in Czechoslovakia, the Czechoslovakian emigre community, and anti-communist movements in the US. 32 ms boxes.

SLAVIN, ALBERTA

MO —UNIVERSITY OF MISSOURI-SAINT LOUIS, Thomas Jefferson Library, Manuscript and Historical Society Collection, 8001 Natural Bridge Rd, Saint Louis, 63121.

SLAVONIC STUDIES

CA —UNIVERSITY OF CALIFORNIA, LOS ANGELES, Library, Slavic Collection, 405 Hilgard Ave, Los Angeles, 90024. Edward Shreeves, Chairman, Bibliographers Group; Leon Ferder, Slavic Bibliographer
Holdings: Vols (250,000) Cat
Notes: The entire range of humanities, social sciences, and the arts. One of the most comprehensive US collections for material not only on Russia and the Soviet Union, but also on Bulgaria, Czechoslovakia, Poland, Yugoslavia, the non-Slavic countries of Eastern Europe (Romania, Hungary, Albania) and Soviet Central Asia. Holdings in Russian and Slavic linguistics, Russian literature, and Russian history are particularly strong, covering all periods. The collections are described in some detail in Paul Horecky's book on US Slavic collections.

NY —NEW YORK PUBLIC LIBRARY, Slavonic Div, Fifth Ave & 42 St, New York, 10018. Edward Kasinec, Chief
Holdings: Cat Microforms
Notes: Described in *Dictionary Catalog of the Slavonic Collection* (Boston: G K Hall, 1974), 44 vols.

PA —ALLIANCE COLLEGE, Washington Hall Library, Fullerton Ave, Cambridge Springs, 16403. Stanley J Kozaczka, Head Librn
Holdings: Vols (23,000) Cat Mss Maps Pix Slides Phonorecords Audiotapes Videotapes 16mm Films Filmstrips Microforms
Notes: Polish and Polish-American history, literature and culture. Current publications of world press in Polish. Collection founded in 1912 under patronage of the Polish National Alliance was lost to fire in 1931, but rebuilding began immediately. Incl 100 maps, 1000 pictures. 1000 slides and 100 phonorecords.

SLAVS IN THE U.S.

CA —UNIVERSITY OF CALIFORNIA, BERKELEY, University Library, Slavic Collections, Berkeley, 94720. Edward Kasinec, Librn
Holdings: Vols 1917 Cat Pix
Notes: The Masaryk-Benes Library is a rich resource for the study of Czechoslovak and European history, especially for the period 1918-1939. It contains Masaryk's own works in original and later editions, as well as in translation (231 volumes), and books about Thomas and Jan Masaryk and family (573). Benes is represented by his own writings (100) and items about him and his family (69). Miscellaneous titles (335) on Slavic problems, and on the history of Czechoslovakia, complete the monograph collection. The balance consists of periodical articles, reprints, and newpapers clippings. Publication dates range from 1883 to 1945, with the bulk of the material published during 1920-1940.

CA —UNIVERSITY OF CALIFORNIA, LOS ANGELES, Library, Slavic Collection, 405 Hilgard Ave, Los Angeles, 90024. Edward Shreeves, Chairman, Bibliographers Group; Leon Ferder, Slavic Bibliographer
Holdings: Vols (250,000) Cat Mss Maps
Notes: The entire range of humanities, social

SLAVS IN THE U.S. (cont.)

sciences, and the arts. One of the most comprehensive US collections for material not only on Russia and the Soviet Union, but also on Bulgaria, Czechoslovakia, Poland, Yugoslavia, the non-Slavic countries of Eastern Europe (Romania, Hungary, Albania) and Soviet Central Asia. Holdings in Russian and Slavic linguistics, Russian literature, and Russian history are particularly strong, covering all periods. The collections are described in some detail in Paul Horecky's book on US Slavic collections.

CO —UNIVERSITY OF SOUTHERN COLORADO, Library, 2200 Bonforte Blvd, Pueblo, 81001.
Holdings: Vols (4000) Cat Mss Maps Pix Phonorecords Audiotapes Sheet Music
Budget: ($10,000)
Notes: Yugoslavian; especially Slovenian history and culture. The collection was inaugurated in 1969. Besides published titles, 2800 in English, and 900 in Slavic languages, there are memorabilia, organizational records, and newspapers, magazines, and music. There is a separate card catalog of items in the collection. Colorado has had a number of Slavic colonies and this collection attempts to recapture the history of these early settlers. Incl sheet music and phonorecords.

KS —UNIVERSITY OF KANSAS, Watson Library, Lawrence, 66045. George Jerkovich, Cur Slavic Collections
Notes: Strong in South Slavic old periodicals and monographs in literature, language, linguistics and history. For the Slavic collections, the major geographical areas involved are Russia-Soviet Union, Poland and Yugoslavia. Also, sizeable collections on Bulgaria, Czechoslovakia, and the Baltic states. Incl emigre literature.

WA —UNIVERSITY OF WASHINGTON LIBRARIES, Suzzallo Library, Slavic & East European Section, FM-25, Seattle, 98195. Barbara A Galik, Head
Holdings: Vols (250,000) Cat Mss Maps Pix Phonorecords Audiotapes Microforms
Budget: ($85,000)
Notes: Strong research collections for Russia-USSR, including Central Asia, Yugoslavia, Poland and the Balkans generally. Holdings are excellent in historical source materials, language, literature, geography, economics, the fine arts, and folklore. There are extensive holdings of the publications of academies, major universities, and principal scholarly institutions, especially of long serial runs. Sizeable Slavic language collections are also to be found in the sciences among the branch libraries of the university.

SLEEP

TN —VANDERBILT UNIVERSITY, Medical Center Library, Nashville, 37232. Mary H Teloh, Special Collections Librn
Holdings: Vols (900) // Cat
Notes: The Moll Collection contains about 900 items on hypnosis and sleep: books, reprints, inaugural theses, lectures, and newspaper clippings. The collection was accumulated by Dr Albert Moll (1862-1939), a prominent Berlin neurologist. The newspaper clippings date from 1880 through 1906 and are mostly German. The books, lectures, reprints, and theses date from the 16th to the early 20th century. See *Bulletin of the Medical Library Association*, 65(1) :65-66, Jan 1977.

SLEEPER, HAROLD REEVE, 1893-1960

NY —CORNELL UNIVERSITY LIBRARIES, Collection of Regional History, Dept of Manuscripts and Univ Archives, Ithaca, 14853.
Notes: Architect. Incl papers, 1911-1960; correspondence, records, files, sketches, photos and phonograph records dealing mainly with architectural work; scrapbooks, research notes for books, articles and lectures.

SLEIGHT, MORRIS

IL —CHICAGO HISTORICAL SOCIETY, Library, Clark St at North Ave, Chicago, 60614. Archie Motley, Manuscript Librn
Notes: Papers of Morris Sleight of Illinois relative to his experiences in California during the 1850s.

SLEIGHT OF HAND see Magic and Magicians

SLEMP, CAMPBELL BASCOM

VA —UNIVERSITY OF VIRGINIA, Alderman Library, Manuscripts Dept, Charlottesville, 22901. Edmund Berkeley Jr, Cur
Holdings: Cat Mss Pix Maps
Notes: Papers, personal and political, etc.

SLET (PHYSICAL FITNESS FESTIVAL)

IL —AMERICAN SOKOL EDUCATIONAL AND PHYSICAL CULTURE, 6424 W Cermak Road, Berwyn, 60402. Annette Schabowski, Librn
Holdings: Vols 2000 Pix
Notes: Incl theses and dissertations on Czech life, folk dancing, gymnastics, etc.

SLIDES (PHOTOGRAPHY) —COLLECTIONS

AZ —TUCSON MUSEUM OF ART LIBRARY, 140 N Main, Tucson, 85705. Dorcas Worsley, Librn
Holdings: Vols (2000)
Notes: Extensive file of biographical and critical information on Arizona artists which is continually being increased. Subject card index to magazines on Western art and artists in magazines not indexed in *Art Index* 12 drawers in 1984, and continues to grow. Have a collection of 15,000 slides.

DC —LIBRARY OF CONGRESS, Washington, 20540.
Notes: Papers and working materials of Charles Eames (1907-1978), American architect and designer. Incl are original negatives and prints of the 106 educational films he created, business correspondence 1944 to 1978, some 400,000 color slides, 31,000 black and white photographs, production materials for exhibits, and drawings for all his major furniture designs. Acquired on a grant of $500,000 from IBM.

IA —BICKELHAUPT ARBORETUM FREE LENDING LIBRARY, 340 S Fourteenth St, Clinton, 52732. Francie B Hill, Librn
Notes: Strong on indoor plants, horticulture, ecology, energy conservation, plant entomology and pathology, urban tree planting; also curriculum materials. Over 3000 slides available for lending.

MO —MISSOURI BOTANICAL GARDEN LIBRARY, PO Box 299, Saint Louis, 63166. M R Crosby, Dir of Research

NM —GALLUP PUBLIC LIBRARY, 115 W Hill Ave, Gallup, 87301. Octavia Fellin, Dir
Holdings: Vols 2000 Cat
Notes: The Southwest and Southwest Indians.

NY —STATE UNIVERSITY OF NEW YORK, STONY BROOK, Health Sciences Library, PO Box 66, East Setauket, 11733.
Notes: Slide Collection of Historical Medical Photographs is an archive of 3000 slides pertaining to the history of medical care in America--Medical and public health activities from the 1850s to the 1950s. An illustrated catalogue, published by Greenwood Press, is scheduled for 1984.

OH —OHIO STATE UNIVERSITY, Library for Communication and Graphic Arts, 242 W 18th St, Columbus, 43210. Lucy S Caswell, Curator
Notes: Library will receive collection of materials on this subject at a future date.

†OH —KINGWOOD CENTER, Library, 900 Park Ave W, Mansfield, 44906.
Notes: Espec ornamental horticulture, home gardening, landscaping, and floral arrangements. Incl 12,000 35mm slides of plants.

SLIP BALLADS

RI —BROWN UNIVERSITY, John Hay Library, 20 Prospect St, Providence, 02912. Mary T Russo, Cur of Broadsides
Notes: A collection of 5000 separate and 2000 bound slip ballads or slip sheets published from 1830 to 1870 which record all aspects of everyday life and illustrate the manner in which people responded to politics, military, social and economic events. Retrospective pieces added annually. Partial catalog. collections of Carriers' Addresses and Slip Ballads are other areas of concentration, along with smaller collections of greeting cards, postcards, and posters. Historical material is represented by the Lincoln, John Hay, Rider and Drowne Collections. The Koopman Collection is especially strong in examples of fine printing. Partially cataloged.

SLOANE, JOHN

DE —DELAWARE ART MUSEUM, Library, 2301 Kentmere Pkwy, Wilmington, 19806. Anne Hoslam, Librn
Holdings: Cat
Notes: The collection contains Sloan's personal library and other related materials. The John Sloan archives, on deposit at the museum, incl diaries, letters, photographs, clipping files, memorabilia. The curator of the archives is Elizabeth H Hawkes.

SLONIMSKY, NICOLAS

DC —LIBRARY OF CONGRESS, Music Division, Washington, 20540.
Notes: Papers, incl correspondence and mss of Nicolas Slonimsky, composer and musical lexicographer.

SLOVAK ARTISTS see Artists, Slovak

SLOVAK AUTHORS see Authors, Slovak

SLOVAK COSTUME see Costume, Slovak

SLOVAK LANGUAGE AND LITERATURE

CA —UNIVERSITY OF CALIFORNIA, LOS ANGELES, Library, Slavic Collection, 405 Hilgard Ave, Los Angeles, 90024. Edward Shreeves, Chairman, Bibliographers Group; Leon Ferder, Slavic Bibliographer
Holdings: Vols (250,000) Cat
Notes: The Slavic Collection at UCLA consists of materials from and relating to Russia and the Soviet Union, Poland, Czechoslovakia, Yugoslavia, the Sorbians in East Germany, and works by Slavic emigres. The collection contains nearly 250,000 vols, and is particularly strong in linguistics, literature, history and social sciences, and reference materials. Slavic materials are collected in hard copy and microform, and incl monographs, serials (incl newspapers), reference works, proceedings of Slavistic congresses and symposia, and also *Festschriften* and dissertations.

MA —HARVARD UNIVERSITY LIBRARY, Widener Library, Slavic Collections, Cambridge, 02138. Hugh M Olmsted, Slavic Dept Head
Holdings: Cat Microforms
Notes: Czech and Slovak literature shelflist through June, 1976 lists 7632 titles (earlier version was incl in *Widener Library Shelflist*, volumes 28-31, 1971). The Slovak language and literature collections continue to be developed actively, and are strong both in current and in antiquarian materials. See also *East Central and Southeast Europe; A Handbook of Library and Archival Resources in North America*, edited by P L Horecky and D H Kraus, 1976, pp 119-122.

NY —NEW YORK PUBLIC LIBRARY, Slavonic Div, Fifth Ave & 42 St, New York, 10018. Edward Kasinec, Chief
Holdings: Cat Microforms
Notes: See New York Public Library,

SLOVAK LANGUAGE AND LITERATURE (cont.)

Slavonic Div, *Dictionary Catalog of the Slavonic Collection,* 2nd ed, rev and enl. (Boston: G K Hall, 1974), 44 vols. Contains approx 724,000 cards. Both roman and non-roman alphabet language materials published before 1972 are included. See also: New York Public Library, *Dictionary Catalog of the Research Libraries* (New York, 1972-). Incl materials acquired and cataloged after 1971. The catalog is issued as basic vols with cumulative supplements; the basic vols, cumulating all previous vols and supplements, are reissued from time to time.

OH —CLEVELAND PUBLIC LIBRARY, Foreign Literature Dept, 325 Superior Ave, Cleveland, 44114. Natalia Bezugloff, Head
Holdings: Vols 4080 Cat
Notes: A popular circulating collection containing classics and the standard works with emphasis on belles lettres, history and biography. A variety of other subjects such as learning languages, how to do books, art, children's books, spoken phonodiscs and cassettes, periodicals, etc. Incl 50 ephemera.
See also entry under Foreign Language Collections

OH —SLOVAK INSTITUTE, Saint Andrew's Abbey, 2900 King Dr, Cleveland, 44104. Rev Andrew Pier, Dir
Holdings: Vols (10,000)
Notes: Promotes cultural interests, especially work of Slovak authors, artists, and musicians through its Slovak Writers and Artists Association. Private library. Permission required.

OH —KENT STATE UNIVERSITY, Libraries, Ethnic Collections, Kent, 44242.
Holdings: Vols 350 Cat
See also entry under Foreign Language Collections.

PA —JANKOLA LIBRARY AND SLOVAK ARCHIVES, Danville, 17821.
Holdings: Vols 1800
Notes: Slovak studies and representation of other Slavic groups.

PA —THE SLOVAK MUSEUM AND ARCHIVES AT JEDNOTA ESTATES, Rosedale & Jednota Sts, PO Box 150, Middletown, 17057. Edward A Tuleya, Cur & Archivist
Holdings: Vols 300
Notes: Incl periodicals and artifacts.

SLOVAK MUSIC see Music, Slovak

SLOVAK STUDIES

PA —THE SLOVAK MUSEUM AND ARCHIVES AT JEDNOTA ESTATES, Rosedale & Jednota Sts, PO Box 150, Middletown, 17057. Edward A Tuleya, Cur & Archivist
Holdings: Vols 4000
Notes: Incl periodicals and artifacts; Slovak national costumes; looms and tools; lace, embroidery, ribbons; prayer books; documents; ceramics.

SLOVAKIA

†OH —FIRST CATHOLIC SLOVAK UNION OF THE USA AND CANADA, Library, 3289 East 55 St, Cleveland, 44127.
Notes: Slovakia and books by Slovak authors.

†OH —SLOVAK INSTITUTE, Slovak Writers and Artists Association Library, St Andrew's Abbey, 2900 East Blvd, Cleveland, 44104.
Notes: Slovak history, art, literature, cultural achievements of Americans of Slovak ancestry.

SLOVAKS IN THE U.S.

MN —UNIVERSITY OF MINNESOTA, Immigration History Research Center, 826 Berry St, Saint Paul, 55114. Susan Griegs, Cur
Holdings: Vols (35,000) Mss Maps Pix Phonorecords Audiotapes 16mm Films Microforms
Notes: See entry under US-Emigration and Immigration.

OH —SLOVAK INSTITUTE, Saint Andrew's Abbey, 2900 King Dr, Cleveland, 44104. Rev Andrew Pier, Dir
Holdings: Vols (10,000)
Notes: Promotes cultural interests, especially work of Slovak authors, artists, and musicians through its Slovak Writers and Artists Association. Private library. Permission required.

PA —JANKOLA LIBRARY AND SLOVAK ARCHIVES, Danville, 17821.
Holdings: 1500 Vols
Notes: Slovak studies and representation of other Slavic groups.

PA —THE SLOVAK MUSEUM AND ARCHIVES AT JEDNOTA ESTATES, Rosedale & Jednota Sts, PO Box 150, Middletown, 17057. Edward A Tuleya, Cur & Archivist
Holdings: Vols 400 Maps Pix Phonorecords
Notes: Incl periodicals and artifacts; rich collection of the history of the Jednota Fraternal Organization, its branches and districts; pamphlets on convention activities, banners, uniforms, badges. Phonograph recordings; mining equipment; paintings of mining scenes; letters. Photographs of Jednota officers and groups, of Jednota Orphanage and equipment used by children; pictures of classes. Desk used by Father Mathew Jankola, priest, patriot and educator. Confessional, cymbal, and maps.

PA —SLOVAK EASTERN CATHOLIC SYNOD OF AMERICA, 515 W Main, Monongahela, 15063.
Holdings: 1500 Vols
Notes: Promotes use of the Byzantine Rite among Slovak-Americans. Special interest in Sts Cyril and Methodius.

PA —BALCH INSTITUTE FOR ETHNIC STUDIES, Library, 18 S Seventh St, Philadelphia, 19106. R Joseph Anderson, Library Dir
Holdings: Vols 160 Cat Mss Microforms

PA —LUTHERAN THEOLOGICAL SEMINARY, Krauth Memorial Library, 7301 Germantown Ave, Philadelphia, 19119. Rev David J Wartluft, Dir Libr
Holdings: Vols (3500) Cat Mss Microforms
Notes: Incl published minutes of United Lutheran Church in America, Lutheran Church in America, General Council and General Synod affiliated churches. Archives of General Council housed in library, also New Jersey Synod, Northeastern Pennsylvania Synod, Southeastern Pennsylvania Synod, Upper New York Synod and Slovak Zion Synod. Also incl papers of early Lutheran leaders: Muhlenbergs, Henkels, etc.

PA —UNIVERSITY OF PITTSBURGH, Hillman Library, Archives of Industrial Society, 363 Hillman Library, Pittsburgh, 15260. Frank A Zabrosky, Cur
Holdings: Mss Maps Pix Audiotapes Microforms
Notes: Incl documents; newspapers; records of churches, fraternal/beneficial societies; social/cultural organizations.

SLOVENES IN THE U.S.

MN —UNIVERSITY OF MINNESOTA, Immigration History Research Center, 826 Berry St, Saint Paul, 55114. Susan Griegs, Cur
Holdings: Vols (35,000) Mss Maps Pix Phonorecords Audiotapes 16mm Films Microforms
Notes: See entry under US-Emigration and Immigration.

PA —BALCH INSTITUTE FOR ETHNIC STUDIES, Library, 18 S Seventh St, Philadelphia, 19106. R Joseph Anderson, Library Dir
Holdings: Cat Microforms

PA —UNIVERSITY OF PITTSBURGH, Hillman Library, Archives of Industrial Society, 363 Hillman Library, Pittsburgh, 15260. Frank A Zabrosky, Cur
Holdings: Mss Maps Audiotapes Microforms
Notes: Incl documents and newspapers.

SLOVENIA—HISTORY

CO —UNIVERSITY OF SOUTHERN COLORADO, Library, 2200 Bonforte Blvd, Pueblo, 81001.
Holdings: Vols (4000) Cat Mss Maps Pix Phonorecords Audiotapes Sheet Music
Budget: ($10,000)
Notes: Yugoslavian; especially Slovenian history and culture. The collection was inaugurated in 1969. Besides published titles, 2800 in English, and 900 in Slavic languages, there are memorabilia, organizational records, and newspapers, magazines, and music. There is a separate card catalog of items in the collection. Colorado has had a number of Slavic colonies and this collection attempts to recapture the history of these early settlers. Incl sheet music and phonorecords.

IL —CZECHOSLOVAK HERITAGE MUSEUM AND LIBRARY, 2701 S Harlem Ave, Berwyn, 60402.
Holdings: Vols 450
Notes: Incl 1500 periodicals, 250 artifacts, 150 art works. A mjaor resource for American-Czech and Slovak history. Much on Chicago's Czech community. Also collection of books written in "Schwabach."

TX —SLOVANSKA PODPORUJICI JEDNOTA STATU TEXAS, Slavonic Benevolent Order of the State of Texas, SPJST Library, Archives, Museum, 520 N Main St, Temple, 76501. Otto Hanus, Cur-Librn; Thelma Bartosh, Asst Cur-Librn
Holdings: 15,000 Vols Mss Pix
Notes: 2000 periodicals; 1500 artifacts.

SLOVENIAN AMERICAN NEWSPAPERS see Newspapers, Slovenian American

SLOVENIAN LANGUAGE (OLD) see Church Slavic Languages and Literature

SLOVENIAN LANGUAGE AND LITERATURE

IL —UNIVERSITY OF ILLINOIS, URBANA/CHAMPAIGN, Slavic and East European Library, Urbana, 61801. Marianna Tax Choldin, Head
Holdings: Vols (31,000) Cat
Notes: Extensive coverage.

MA —HARVARD UNIVERSITY LIBRARY, Widener Library, Slavic Collections, Cambridge, 02138. Hugh M Olmsted, Slavic Dept Head
Holdings: Cat Microforms
Notes: Yugoslav literature shelflist through June, 1976 lists 5923 titles (earlier version was incl in *Widener Library Shelflist,* volumes 28-31, 1971). The Slovenian language and literature collections continue to be developed actively, and are strong both in in current and in antiquarian materials. See also *East Central and Southeast Europe; A Handbook of Library and Archival Resources in North America,* edited by P L Horecky and D H Kraus, 1976, pp 149-154.

NY —NEW YORK PUBLIC LIBRARY, Slavonic Div, Fifth Ave & 42 St, New York, 10018. Edward Kasinec, Chief
Holdings: Cat Microforms
Notes: See New York Publis Library, *Dictionary Catalog of the Slavonic Collection* (Boston: G K Hall, 1974), 44 vols.

OH —CLEVELAND PUBLIC LIBRARY, Foreign Literature Dept, 325 Superior Ave, Cleveland, 44114. Natalia Bezugloff, Head
Holdings: Vols 3150 Cat
Notes: A popular circulating collection containing classics and the standard works with emphasis on belles lettres, history and biography. A variety of other subjects such as learning languages, how to do books, art, children's books, spoken phonodiscs and cassettes, periodicals, etc. Incl 130 ephemera.
See also entry under Foreign Language Collections

OH —KENT STATE UNIVERSITY, Libraries, Ethnic Collections, Kent, 44242.
Holdings: Vols 100 Cat
See also entry under Foreign Language Collections.

TX —SLOVANSKA PODPORUJICI JEDNOTA STATU TEXAS, Slavonic

SLOVENIAN LANGUAGE AND LITERATURE (cont.)

Benevolent Order of the State of Texas, SPJST Library, Archives, Museum, 520 N Main St, Temple, 76501. Otto Hanus, Cur-Librn; Thelma Bartosh, Asst Cur-Librn
Holdings: 15,00 Vols Mss Pix
Notes: 2000 periodicals; 1500 artifacts.

SLOW-LEARNING CHILDREN

PQ —HOPITAL SAINTE-JUSTINE POUR LES ENFANTS, Centre d'Information sur la Sante de l'Enfant, 3175 Cote Sainte-Catherine, Montreal, H3T 1C5, Can. Louis LucLecompte, Librn
Holdings: Vols (7000) Cat Audiotapes Videotapes 16mm Films Microforms
Budget: ($11,000)
Notes: 40 percent of collection in French.

SLOYD

WI —UNIVERSITY OF WISCONSIN-STOUT, Library Learning Center, Menomonie, 54751. Philip Sawin Jr, Coll Develop Librn
Notes: Industrial Arts collection is a major one, including the Verne C Fryklund Papers. The program was begun in 1883 as an original purpose of the University. The collection contains original editions on sloyd, a 19th century Swedish system of manual training based on wood carving and carpentry.

SLUGS see Tokens

SLUM CLEARANCE see Cities and Towns—Planning; Housing; Slums

SLUMS

NY —MUSEUM OF THE CITY OF NEW YORK, Library, Fifth Ave & 103 St, New York, 10025.
Notes: The Jacob A Riis Collection of New York City photographs, especially of slum life at about the turn of the century.

†PA —TEMPLE UNIVERSITY LIBRARIES, Special Collections Dept, Urban Archives Center, Philadelphia, 19122. Thomas Whitehead, Cur of Mss
Holdings: Cat
Notes: Incl the records of several separate collections which are deposited in the Urban Archives Center. Many collections contain photographs, maps and pamphlets, in addition to manuscripts. All collections in the Urban Archives are separately cataloged.

SMALL, EDWARD

CA —UNIVERSITY OF SOUTHERN CALIFORNIA, Edward L Doheny Memorial Library, Archives of Performing Arts, University Park, Los Angeles, 90089. Robert Knutson, Librn
Holdings: Mss Pix
Notes: Personal collection of papers, pictures, etc.

SMALL, J. K.

FL —FLORIDA DEPT OF STATE, Florida State Archives, Florida Photographic Collection, R A Gray Bldg, Tallahassee, 32301. Mrs Allen Morris, Archives Supervisor
Notes: Charles A Mosier, Charles Torrey Simpson and J K Small, 500 photographs of Florida flora, made by these famous naturalists, mostly in South Dade county. Added March, 1983, 2200 glass and nitrate negatives by J K Small.

SMALL, STRACHAN THOMAS

SC —COLLEGE OF CHARLESTON LIBRARY, Special Collections Dept, Charleston, 29401.
Notes: Papers incl diary on a voyage to China, 1850-51. Manuscript and typescript copies.

SMALL ARMS see Firearms

SMALL BUSINESS—ACCOUNTING see Accounting

SMALL FAMILY

SC —COLLEGE OF CHARLESTON LIBRARY, Special Collections Dept, Charleston, 29401.
Notes: Papers, 1794-1967, contain genealogical reports and historical sketches of the Small and Whaley families, and materials gathered in researching the Small family's history; incl also correspondence of Robert Scott Small and family (1922-1931), and material relating to the death of Robert Scott Small (February 21, 1931).

SMALL LOANS see Loans, Personal

SMALL PRESSES see Little Presses

SMALLPOX—PREVENTION

CT —YALE UNIVERSITY, Medical Historical Library, Klebs Collection, 333 Cedar St, New Haven, 06520. Ferenc A Gyorgyey, Librn
Notes: The Arnold Carl Klebs Medical Collection books, pamphlets, etc, incl the library of his father, Edwin T A Klebs, pathologist. Strong in bibliography of early printed medical books, herbals, plague tracts, inoculation, vaccination and tubercular diseases.

SMALLS FAMILY

SC —COLLEGE OF CHARLESTON LIBRARY, Special Collections Dept, Charleston, 29401.
Notes: Papers, 1945-1964 incl family correspondence and material from Avery Institute, local church papers, the South Carolina Conference of Branches NAACP, and the Victoria Society.

SMEDLEY, AGNES

GA —EMORY UNIVERSITY, Robert W Woodruff Library, Atlanta, 30322. Herbert Johnson, Dir
Holdings: Mss Pix Cat
Notes: The Philip J Jaffe Papers and books about communism and the Communist Party in the US, incl copies of rare magazines, private mss, the papers of such controversial figures as Anna Louise Strong, Agnes Smedley, Norman Bethune and Koji Ariyoshi, and documentation of the growth of Chinese communism. 36 linear ft mss.

SMEKAL-RAMAN EFFECT see Raman Effect

SMELTER WORKERS UNION see International Union of Mine, Mill, and Smelter Workers

SMET, PIERRE-JEAN DE

†WA —WASHINGTON STATE UNIVERSITY, Library, Manuscripts, Archives & Special Collections, Pullman, 99164. John F Guido, Head
Holdings: // Mss Maps Pix
Notes: Papers, 1821-1973, covering Father De Smet's early sojourns at Whitemarsh and St Louis, his founding of the Rocky Mountain Missions, his long service as Procurator and Socius of the Missouri Province, and his many travels. Correspondence with his family in Beligum, mss of his published journals, 2 small maps, sketches and engravings used to illustrate his books. Incl about 100 small pencil sketches by Father Nicholas Point depicting the 1841 journey from Westport to St Mary's Mission in the Bitterroot Valley. Described in The Record, 30 (1969) 6-40; and 32 (1972) 47-63.

SMILEY FAMILY PAPERS

CA —A K SMILEY PUBLIC LIBRARY, 125 W Vine St, Redlands, 92373. Larry E Burgess, Archivist
Holdings: Vols (3500) Mss Maps Pix Phonorecords Microforms
Budget: ($45,000)
Notes: Emphasis on San Bernadino County and the Redlands area. Especially prized is The Citrograph, 1887-1908 (bound vols and microfilm) edited by Scipio Craig, prominent in state, national, and newspaper circles. The ms collection (250,000 pieces) incl the Smiley Family papers, much on water development, and on the citrus industry. The photograph collection (over 5000) covers the history of the area; there are many stereographs and glass slides. The collection on Indians of California and the Southwest was begun from a special gift by Andrew Carnegie honoring his friend. Albert K Smiley.

SMITH (MAGAZINE)

MI —MICHIGAN STATE UNIVERSITY, Libraries, Special Collections Div, East Lansing, 48824. Jannette Fiore, Librn
Holdings: Uncat Mss
Notes: Archive of papers and records, correspondence, publications, production files, etc.

SMITH, A. E.

ON —UNIVERSITY OF TORONTO, Thomas Fisher Rare Book Library, 120 Saint George St, Toronto, M5S 1A5, Can. Richard G Landon, Head
Holdings: Vols 2500 Mss Pix Phonorecords
Notes: Kenny Collection named for original collector, Robert Kenny of Toronto. Chiefly material on and by the Labor Progressive Party and the Communist Party of Canada, including their constitutions, reports of national conventions, leaflets, posters, election material, ephemera. Manuscript material of A E Smith, Tim Buck and other Canadian communists.

SMITH, ADAM

MD —JOHNS HOPKINS UNIVERSITY, Milton S Eisenhower Library, Charles & 34 Sts, Baltimore, 21218. Ann S Gwyn, Assistant Dir for Special Collections
Holdings: Vols Cat Mss
Notes: Chiefly original sources of English economic thought and history since Adam Smith, Chartism, trades unions, the Factory Acts, Luddites, Poor Law, Owenism, early socialism, Nauvoo Colony. Most items are rarities. J S Mill mss letters and correspondence, and original papers on the inception of the Industrial Revolution. 56 titles from library of Adam Smith. Important editions of The Wealth of Nations. Also many pamphlets from 16th century, and the Mercantilists. No published catalog. Cards in main catalog. Collection housed separately in Abram Hutzler Reading Room.

MA —HARVARD UNIVERSITY, Baker Library of the Graduate School of Business Administration, Kress Library of Business and Economics, Soldiers Field, Boston, 02163. Ruth E Rogers, Cur
Notes: Comprehensive collection of editions of Adam Smith.

SMITH, ALFRED E., 1873-1944

DC —GEORGETOWN UNIVERSITY, Library, Special Collections Div, 37 & O Sts NW, Washington, 20057. George M Barringer, Special Collections Librn; Nicholas B Sheetz, Mss Librn
Holdings: Mss Cat Pix
Notes: Papers and memorabilia of the Honorabe Alfred E Smith (1873-1944) former Governor of New York and candidate for President in 1928. Among significant items in the collection are a series of scrapbooks containing newspaper clippings, letters, photographs, and related material documenting the political rise of the "Happy Warrior." The scrapbooks span Smith's political career from 1913, when he was elected Speaker of the New York Assembly, through the twenties, when he

SMITH, ALFRED E., 1873-1944 (cont.)

was the unsuccessful Democratic candidate for the Presidency. Photographs cover many aspects of his family life and political career. The collection incl a small quantity of correspondence with politicians such as Nelson A Rockefeller and Robert F Wagner.

NY —NEW YORK STATE LIBRARY, State Education Bldg Annex, Washington Ave, Albany, 12224.
Holdings: Cat Mss Pix
Notes: Public and private papers; emphasis on years he was governor of New York. 135 linear feet.

SMITH, ASHBEL

TX —UNIVERSITY OF TEXAS LIBRARIES, General Libraries, Barker Texas History Center, PO Box P, Austin, 78712. Don Carleton, Dir
Holdings: Vols (132,000) Cat Mss Maps Pix Slides Phonorecords Audiotapes Microforms
See also entry under Texas-History

SMITH, AUGUSTUS WILLIAM, 1802-1866

RI —BROWN UNIVERSITY, John Hay Library, 20 Prospect St, Providence, 02912. Mark N Brown, Cur Mss
Holdings: // Mss
Notes: Papers of Augustus William Smith, Professor of Astronomy and Mathematics and President of Wesleyan University: Professor of Natural Philosophy, United States Naval Academy. Approx 335 items with inclusive dates 1816-1918. There are letters and autograph mss of scientific import written by Smith while at Hamilton and Wesleyan colleges; a notebook, part of which records Smith's journey to Labrador in 1860 as a member of the US government expedition to observe the solar eclipse; diplomas; civilian commissions, deeds, and photographs.

SMITH, BOB

CA —UNIVERSITY OF CALIFORNIA, LOS ANGELES, Theater Arts Library, Los Angeles, 90024. Edward Shreeves, Chairman, Bibliographers Group; Audree Malkin, Head, Theater Arts Library
Notes: Bob Smith (art director) Collection: extensive collection of blueprints, set design sketches, location photographs, and watercolor sketches for motion pictures.

SMITH, SIR C. AUBREY

ON —RIDLEY COLLEGE LIBRARY, PO Box 3013, Saint Catharines, L2R 7C3, Can.
Notes: The Karl Andre Auty Collection of over 3000 books on cricket, kept current by endowed funds. Incl the scrapbooks of Sir C Aubrey Smith's career in cricket, from the 19th century.

SMITH, CHARD POWERS

CT —YALE UNIVERSITY, Box 1603A, Yale Station, New Haven, 06520.
Holdings: Mss

SMITH, CHARLES ALPHONSO

VA —UNIVERSITY OF VIRGINIA, Alderman Library, Manuscripts Dept, Charlottesville, 22901. Edmund Berkeley Jr, Cur
Holdings: Cat Mss
Notes: Correspondence and other papers.

SMITH, CLARK ASHTON

RI —BROWN UNIVERSITY, John Hay Library, 20 Prospect St, Providence, 02912. Mark N Brown, Cur Mss
Holdings: Mss Pix Vols
Notes: Papers of Clark Ashton Smith (1893-1961), the Californian fantasy author and poet. Correspondents incl George Sterling, Samuel Loveman, H P Lovecraft, and August Derleth.

SMITH, DAVID STANLEY

CT —YALE UNIVERSITY, Music Library, 98 Wall St, New Haven, 06520. Harold E Samuel, Librn
Holdings: Vols (118,000) Cat Mss Pix Phonorecords Audiotapes
Notes: Personal papers and musical mss.
See also entry under Music, American.

SMITH, DUDLEY

†TX —TEXAS A&M UNIVERSITY, Sterling C Evans Library, College Station, 77843.
Notes: Papers of Dudley Smith, advisor of the Association of Sugar Producers of Puerto Rico.

SMITH, EBEN

CO —DENVER PUBLIC LIBRARY, 1357 Broadway, Denver, 80203.
Notes: Correspondence, papers, pictures, diaries, etc.

SMITH, ELDER, AND COMPANY

CA —CLAREMONT COLLEGES, Honnold Library, Ninth & Dartmouth, Claremont, 91711. Tania Rizzo, Special Collections Dept Head
Holdings: 1600 Cat Mss
Notes: 1600 items of correspondence with Mary Augusta Ward, 1885-1919. Restricted use.
See also entry under Ward, Mary Augusta (Arnold)

SMITH, ERIC

DC —GEORGETOWN UNIVERSITY, Library, Special Collections Div, 37 & O Sts NW, Washington, 20057. George M Barringer, Special Collections Librn; Nicholas B Sheetz, Mss Librn
Holdings: Cat Mss Maps Pix Slides Phonorecords Audiotapes
Notes: Includes the papers (1912-49) of Sen Robert F Wagner; the archives (1903-) of the American Political Science Association and of its local Washington chapter; the archives of the Center for Public Financing of Elections; a collection of several hundred political cartoons by Eric Smith; and other smaller collections.

SMITH, F. HOPKINSON

VA —UNIVERSITY OF VIRGINIA, Alderman Library, Clifton Waller Barrett Collection, Charlottesville, 22901. Joan St C Crane, Cur of American Literature Collections
Notes: Papers.

SMITH, FRANK VINING

MA —HINGHAM PUBLIC LIBRARY, 66 Leavitt St, Hingham, 02043. Walter T Dziura, Dir
Holdings: Cat Mss Maps Pix Slides Microforms
Notes: A collection of about 2000 items relating to the history of the town from the 1600's to the present. Incl correspondence, legal documents, diaries and day books, account books, broadsides, pictures. Contains a large portion of four major collections: those of historian George Lincoln, historian Solomon Lincoln, historian Mason Foley and Hinghamiana collector Norman A Hersey. Items of special importance incl papers of town clerk Daniel Cushing, from the 1600's; Revolutionary War troop muster rolls; early land grant maps of the town; papers of artists Frank Vining Smith and Isaac Sprague; correspondence of Massachusetts governor John D Long; steamship history. An unpublished catalog of the collection is available through interlibrary loan. Most of the collection is on microfilm and may be borrowed through interlibrary loan.

SMITH, GEORGE OTIS

ME —COLBY COLLEGE, Miller Library, Alfred King Champman Room, Waterville, 04901.
Holdings: Mss
Notes: Papers, etc.

SMITH, GERALD K.

NC —DUKE UNIVERSITY, William R Perkins Library, Durham, 27706. Elvin E Strowd, University Librn
Notes: The (Quasi)-Nazi collection consists of approximately 7000 items, primarily pamphlets published in the United States by and about Nazi sympathizers Gerald K Smith, Father Coughlin, etc and organizations with Nazi leanings.

SMITH, GERRITT

NY —UNIVERSITY OF ROCHESTER, Rush Rhees Library, Department of Rare Books and Special Collections, Rochester, 14627. Peter Dzwonkoski, Librn
Holdings: Cat Mss
Notes: Letters to Samuel Drummond Porter and Susan Farley Porter from family members, fellow abolitionists Frederick Douglass and Gerritt Smith, and their son while a soldier during the Civil War.

SMITH, H. ALLEN

IL —SOUTHERN ILLINOIS UNIVERSITY, CARBONDALE, Delyte W Morris Library, Special Collections Dept, Carbondale, 62901. David V Koch, Cur of Special Collections; Louisa Bowen, Cur of Manuscripts
Holdings: Vols 60 Cat Mss
Notes: Personal papers, 1944-1968, incl correspondence and mss. 15 linear feet. Inventory available at library.

SMITH, HAMILTON, 1804-1875

IN —INDIANA UNIVERSITY, Lilly Library, Seventh St, Bloomington, 47405. William R Cagle, Librn
Holdings: // Mss
Notes: Business papers and records of Indiana Cotton Mills, 1850-1947. Incl letterpress books, journals, consignment records, financial records, stock ledgers, as well as some records for the Cannelton Cotton Manufacturing Co, 1865-1867, and for D Newcomb & Co, a coal mining firm in Newburgh, Indiana, 1870-1875. 18,360 items. A related collection is that of Hamilton Smith's papers, 1823-1874. Smith (1804-1875) was a Louisville, Kentucky lawyer and businessman involved in the organization and operation of the Cannelton Cotton Mill in 1848 until its sale to Indiana Cotton Mills in 1853.

SMITH, HANNAH WHITHALL

KY —ASBURY THEOLOGICAL SEMINARY, B L Fisher Library, Wilmore, 40390. D William Faupel, Dir of Library Services
Holdings: Uncat
Notes: A collection of letters, papers, and religious papers. Incl holiness-penticostal. 25 document boxes.

SMITH, HENRY HOLMES

AZ —UNIVERSITY OF ARIZONA, Center for Creative Photography, 843 E University Blvd, Tucson, 85721. James Enyeart, Dir; Terence Pitts, Cur and Librn
Notes: Center has significant collections consisting of more than 25 photographs plus other archival material such as negatives, contact sheets, work prints, correspondence, financial records, diaries, project files, etc. Inventories of the collections are available to researchers. Published guides available for some collections.

SMITH, HENRY P., III, 1911-

NY —CORNELL UNIVERSITY LIBRARIES, Collection of Regional History, Dept of Manuscripts and Univ Archives, Ithaca, 14853.
Notes: Attorney, Congressman. Papers, 1965-74; 88 ft. Restricted.

SMITH, GOV. HOKE

GA —UNIVERSITY OF GEORGIA, Libraries, Special Collections Division,

SMITH, GOV. HOKE (cont.)

Athens, 30602. Vesta Lee Gordon, Asst Dir for Special Collections
Notes: Collection contains 1394.8 linear feet of mss: papers of US Senator Richard B Russell; US Congressmen John W Davis, Maston O'Neal, Robert G Stephens Jr, John L Pilcher, Dudley M Hughes; Governors Hoke Smith, Lester Maddox, Carl Sanders.

SMITH, HOWARD ALEXANDER, 1880-1966

NJ —PRINCETON UNIVERSITY, Library, Manuscript Collection, Nassau St, Princeton, 08540. Jean F Preston, Cur
Holdings: // Cat Mss
Notes: Incl 38 volumes; 286 cartons of papers. *Terms of access:* the bulk of the papers may be read by qualified scholars but the volumes of the diary for the years 1927-1935 inclusive will not be made accessible until January 1, 1990, without the approval of a specified committee. An unpublished typescript guide (395p) is available in the Library.

SMITH, HOWARD WORTH

VA —UNIVERSITY OF VIRGINIA, Alderman Library, Manuscripts Dept, Charlottesville, 22901. Edmund Berkeley Jr, Cur

SMITH, HUGH MCCORMICK, 1865-1941

DC —GEORGETOWN UNIVERSITY, Library, Special Collections Div, 37 & O Sts NW, Washington, 20057. George M Barringer, Special Collections Librn; Nicholas B Sheetz, Mss Librn
Holdings: Mss Cat
Notes: Diaries and journals kept by Hugh McCormick Smith (1865-1941) and his wife, Emma, documenting their years in Siam. In 1922 Smith resigned his position as United States Commissioner of Fisheries, accepting an invitiation from the King of Siam to serve as advisor on Siamese fisheries. When the first Siamese Department of Fisheries was created in 1926, Smith was named director, remaining in that office until his return to the United States in 1934. The diaries not only contain accounts of Smith's work in Siam, but also provide vivid descriptions of Siamese life, culture, and topography.

SMITH, JEDEDIAH STRONG, 1799-1831

CA —UNIVERSITY OF THE PACIFIC, Holt-Atherton Pacific Center for Western Studies, Stockton, 95211. Hiram L Davis, Dir of Libraries
Holdings: Mss Maps Pix
Notes: Research material, about 1200 items, related to the activities of the Jedediah Strong Smith Society, with headquarters on this campus. Incl data relating to Smith genealogy plus mss by John Neihardt, Peter Decker, Alson J Smith, and Maurice Sulliivan. Also incl is a negative photocopy of Samuel "Don Pablo" Parkman's transcription of Smith's original journal.

SMITH, JESSIE WILCOX

PA —FREE LIBRARY OF PHILADELPHIA, Rare Book Dept, Logan Sq, Philadelphia, 19103. Marie E Korey, Rare Book Librn
Holdings: Vols (1000) Cat Mss Pix
Notes: The Thornton Oakley Collection containing 1000 pieces of original art, autograph letters, and books and periodicals, illustrated by Howard Pyle and his students, incl Maxfield Parish, Frank Schoonover, Jessie Wilcox Smith, and N C Wyeth.

SMITH, GEN. JOHN, 1750-1836

DC —GEORGETOWN UNIVERSITY, Library, Special Collections Div, 37 & O Sts NW, Washington, 20057. George M

Barringer, Special Collections Librn; Nicholas B Sheetz, Mss Librn
Holdings: Mss Cat
Notes: The Richard X Evans Collection. The family archives of Richard X Evans, incl the papers of General John Smith (1750-1836), a member of Congress; Robert Mills (1781-1855); architect; and Alexander Dimitry (1805-1883), educator and diplomat.

SMITH, LOGAN PEARSALL

CT —LEE ASH, (personal collection), 66 Humiston Dr, Bethany, 06525.
Holdings: Mss Maps Pix
Notes: First editions, mss, ephemera, memorabilia.

OH —KENT STATE UNIVERSITY, Libraries, Dept of Special Collections, Kent, 44242. Dean H Keller, Cur
Holdings: Vols 38 Cat Mss
Notes: Incl 53 ms pieces.

SMITH, MARGARET

MO —WASHINGTON UNIVERSITY, School of Medicine, Archives, 660 S Euclid Ave, Saint Louis, 63110. Paul G Anderson, Archivist
Holdings: Mss Pix Audiotapes
Budget: ($38,000)
Notes: Institutional records and papers of faculty of Washington University School of Medicine and its predecessors and associated hospitals. Contains records of St Louis Medical College, Missouri Medical Barnard Free Skin and Cancer Hospital, Barnes Hospital, St Louis Children's Hospital and Jewish Hospital of St Louis. Incl papers of William Beaumont, Joseph Erlanger, Leo Loeb, Evarts Graham, Edmund V Cowdry, Helen Graham, Carl V Moore, Margaret Smith and others. Oral history program. See also: Anderson, Paul G and Hoolihan, Christopher, eds. *Special Collections* (St Louis: Washington University School of Medicine, 1981). 960 linear feet.

SMITH, MARGARET CHASE

ME —MARGARET CHASE SMITH LIBRARY CENTER, Skowhegan, 04976. James C MacCampbell, Dir
Notes: Senator Margaret Chase Smith's papers, her home and property in Skowhegan, donated by her to Northwood Institute, a business education college headquartered in Midland, Michigan. Also information on Senator Joseph McCarthy.

SMITH, MARY LOUISE

IA —UNIVERSITY OF IOWA, University Libraries, Iowa City, 52242. Robert A McCown, Mss Librn
Holdings: Mss
Notes: Correspondence, subject files, speeches, trip files, photographs, tape recordings, notebooks, and other materials of the Chairman of the Republican National Committee, 1974-77. 45 ft of mss.

SMITH, PAUL JORDAN, 1885-1971

CA —UNIVERSITY OF CALIFORNIA, LOS ANGELES, Research Library, Dept of Special Collections, 405 Hilgard Ave, Los Angeles, 90024. Edward Shreeves, Chairman, Bibliographers Group; David S Zeidberg, Head
Holdings: Mss
Notes: 24 linear feet of papers, mss, and correspondence.

SMITH, PETE

CA —UNIVERSITY OF CALIFORNIA, LOS ANGELES, Theater Arts Library, Los Angeles, 90024. Edward Shreeves, Chairman, Bibliographers Group; Audree Malkin, Head, Theater Arts Library
Holdings: Cat Mss Pix
Notes: Script Collection, Screenplays: a collection of more than 6000 unpublished scripts for American, British and some foreign language films. An important part of

the collection is the Metro-Goldwyn-Mayer Screenplay Collection which covers the period 1924-1947. Incl are the *Andy Hardy*, *Dr Kildare*, and *Maisie* film series which are virtually complete, and a number of short features, such as *Robert Benchley Series*, *Pete Smith Specialties*, and *Our Gang* Comedies.

SMITH, ROBERT L. T., SR.

MS —TOUGALOO COLLEGE, L Zenobia Coleman Library, Tougaloo, 39174. Virgia Brocks-Shedd, Acting Dir
Budget: ($142,650)
Notes: Civil rights cases and legal papers; lawsuits; Mississippi, 1960-1968. Local attorneys have donated papers of cases they have handled, espec attorneys of two government-funded legal services offices. Individual collections: Papers of Aaron Henry, Rev Robert L T Smith, Sr, Annie B Rankin and the Howard Kester Papers. Incl VF holdings of articles from 1930 and on.

SMITH, ROBERT PAUL

MA —BOSTON UNIVERSITY, Mugar Memorial Library, Special Collections Dept, 771 Commonwealth Ave, Boston, 02215. Howard B Gotlieb, Dir
Holdings: Cat Mss
Notes: Mss, correspondence, etc collected in depth; incl publications by or about.

SMITH, SAMUEL, 1721-1776

NJ —RUTGERS, THE STATE UNIVERSITY OF NEW JERSEY, Alexander Library, Special Collections and Archives, College Ave & Huntington St, New Brunswick, 08903. Ronald L Becker, Cur of Manuscripts and Rare Books
Holdings: Mss
Notes: Papers, etc (2 linear feet).

SMITH, SIDNEY LAWTON

WI —UNIVERSITY OF WISCONSIN, MADISON, Memorial Library, Rare Books Collection, 728 State St, Madison, 53706. Gretchen Lagana, Cur
Holdings: //
Notes: Doane-Davidson Bookplate Collection. This collection of approximately 10,000 bookplates is composed of two collections originally belonging to Gilbert H Doane and Flora Davidson. There are extensive separate collections of University of Wisconsin libraries bookplates, medical, animal, and punning plates, as well as the plates of two Boston engravers: Sidney Lawton Smith and Joseph Winfield Spenceley. The collection is indexed. Housed in the Dept of Rare Books and Special Collections.

SMITH, STEVIE

MO —WASHINGTON UNIVERSITY, Libraries, Special Collections Dept, Campus Box 1061, St Louis, 63130.
Notes: A small but significant collection of correspondence.

SMITH, SYDNEY GOODSIR

DE —UNIVERSITY OF DELAWARE, Hugh M Morris Library, S College Ave, Newark, 19711. T Stuart Dick, Special Collections
Holdings: Mss
Notes: Incl Scottish literary renaissancee drafts, typescripts, articles, book reviews, sketches, miscellaneous memoranda by Christopher M Grieve (Hugh Maediarmid), when he was in London (1931-32). Also incl are autogrph notes, plays, prose, verse, and correspondence for Sydney Goodsir Smith.

SMITH, TERRENCE LORE

MA —BOSTON UNIVERSITY, Mugar Memorial Library, Special Collections Dept, 771 Commonwealth Ave, Boston, 02215. Howard B Gotlieb, Dir
Holdings: Mss Audiotapes Microforms
Notes: Mss, correspondence, etc collected in depth; incl publications by or about.

SMITH, VIAN, 1920-1969

MA —BOSTON UNIVERSITY, Mugar
Memorial Library, Special Collections Dept,
771 Commonwealth Ave, Boston, 02215.
Howard B Gotlieb, Dir
Holdings: // Cat Mss Pix
Notes: Mss, correspondence, etc collected in
depth; incl publications by or about.

SMITH, W. EUGENE

AZ —UNIVERSITY OF ARIZONA, Center
for Creative Photography, 843 E University
Blvd, Tucson, 85721. James Enyeart, Dir;
Terence Pitts, Cur and Librn
Notes: Center has significant collections
consisting of more than 25 photographs plus
other archival material such as negatives,
contact sheets, work prints, correspondence,
financial records, diaries, project files, etc.
Inventories of the collections are available to
researchers. Published guides available for
some collections.

SMITH, WILL L.

TX —TEXAS A&M UNIVERSITY, Sterling C
Evans Library, University Archives, College
Station, 77843. Charles R Schultz,
University Archivist
Holdings: Mss
Notes: The Archives of Modern Politics:
Texas Legislator Will L Smith, 1962-1971.

SMITH, WILLIAM

NC —DUKE UNIVERSITY, William R
Perkins Library, Manuscript Dept, Durham,
27706. Ellen Gartrell, Cur of Mss
Holdings: Cat Mss
Notes: Incl 50,000 items, 18th-20th
centuries, representing the political,
diplomatic, military, ecclesiastical, and
economic affairs of Great Britain and the
British Empire. Incl papers of William
Wilberforce, William Smith, John Wilson
Croker, John Backhouse, Malet Family, etc.
See also entry under Slavery and
Antislavery.

SMITH, WILLIAM 'EXTRA BILLY'

VA —UNIVERSITY OF VIRGINIA,
Alderman Library, Manuscripts Dept,
Charlottesville, 22901. Edmund Berkeley Jr,
Cur
Holdings: Cat Mss Maps Pix
Notes: About 1500 collections have material
pertaining to the Civil War and particularly
to the Army of Northern Virginia and
campaigns and battles in Virginia. There are
letters, diaries, reminiscences, maps, and
pictorial material of Confederate soldiers and
civilians, as well as papers of Robert E Lee,
J E B Stuart, Thomas L Rosser, Jubal A
Early, John Daniel Imboden, William "Extra
Billy" Smith, Henry Alexander Wise, Eppa
Hunton, and John S Mosby.

SMITH, WILLIAM JAY

MO —WASHINGTON UNIVERSITY,
Libraries, Special Collections Dept, Campus
Box 1061, St Louis, 63130.
Notes: Literary and professional papers of
the American poet. More than 600 letters
and 500 other pieces, 1924-1968. Also incl
books, photographs, etc. Described in
Special Collections: An Annotated Guide to
the Holdings of the Manuscript Division and
the University Archives and Research
Collection.

SMITH FAMILY

NC —ROWAN PUBLIC LIBRARY, History
and Genealogy Dept, Salisbury, 28144.
Philip Barton, Dir
Holdings: Vols (2800) Cat Mss Maps
Microforms
Budget: ($1500)
Notes: Generally, the History and
Genealogy Collection is composed of
materials relating to local and North
Carolina State history and materials for
genealogical research. Primary emphasis is
on genealogical research materials. The
nucleus of the genealogical collection is the
McCubbins Collection. The Collection
consists primarily of deed abstracts of
Rowan County. Another collection
representing part of the genealogical research
collection is the Smith Collection, consisting
of notes and correspondence collected over a
wide span of years about Smiths of the US.
A recent addition is the Archibald
Henderson Collection of literary works of
North Carolinians, Transylvania materials
and materials dealing with North Carolina
State history and political science.

SMITHSONIAN INSTITUTION

DC —SMITHSONIAN INSTITUTION,
Archives Div, Washington, 20560. William
W Moss, Archivist
Holdings: Cat Mss Pix
Notes: The Archives holds some 2400 linear
meters of records documenting the history of
the Smithsonian, 1846-1980. See Guide to
the Smithsonian Archives for more
information.

SMITHSONIAN ROOSEVELT
AFRICAN EXPEDITION

DC —SMITHSONIAN INSTITUTION,
Archives Div, Washington, 20560. William
W Moss, Archivist
Holdings: Mss Maps Pix
Notes: The Archives holds correspondence
and records of a number of scientific
expeditions with which the Smithsonian was
connected, incl the Western Union
Telegraph Expedition, the Smithsonian
Roosevelt African Expedition, and the
United States Exploring Expedition.

SMOG CONTROL DEVICES (MOTOR
VEHICLES) see Motor Vehicles—Pollution
Control Devices

SMOKING

MD —OFFICE ON SMOKING AND
HEALTH, Park Bldg, Rm 116, 5600 Fishers
Lane, Rockville, 20857. Donald R Shopland,
Technical Information Officer
Notes: Smoking, tobacco and nicotine as
related to health. Approx 40,000 reprints.
The technical information center of the
clearinghouse issues at irregular intervals
(about 6 times per year) the Smoking and
Health Bulletin. The Bulletin contains those
items added to the collection from the
world-wide literature on smoking.
Bibliographic and reference services can be
obtained by writing or calling the
Clearinghouse. Over 10,000 records, 1970- ,
are stored in an automated file and are
capable of search and retrieval. Printout
information corresponds to that found in the
Smoking and Health Bulletin. The
Clearinghouse has been named the
"Collaborating Center for Smoking and
Health" by the World Health Organization.
All items entered into the holdings of the
technical information center have been
processed for computer search and retrieval.
Bibliographic citations and informative
abstracts available from this system
correspond in format to those found in the
Smoking and Health Bulletin.
NY —TOBACCO MERCHANTS
ASSOCIATION OF THE US, Howard S
Cullman Library, Suite 705, 1220 Broadway,
New York, 10001. R Robert Sengstacken,
Dir Information Servs
Notes: Trademark and brand files for
tobacco products and smokers' articles.
OH —CLEVELAND PUBLIC LIBRARY, Fine
Arts and Special Collections Department,
325 Superior Ave, Cleveland, 44114. Alice
N Loranth, Head
Holdings: Vols (1356) Cat Pix
Notes: Part of the Tobacco Collection. Incl
numerous items: 16th century herbals;
official proclamations issued by the English,
French, Portuguese, Dutch governments and
tobacco premium cards, etc. The manners
and customs aspect of smoking is
emphasized. Some museum dictionary
catalog maintained.
OH —KENT STATE UNIVERSITY,
University Archives, Kent, 44242. Stephen C
Morton, University Archivist
Holdings: Uncat Mss Pix
Notes: Books, periodical articles, and
correspondence from various members of the
Fuller Family of Austinburg, Ohio. The
collection includes correspondence of Ira
Fuller (1840s), his son Allen O Fuller, his
wife, and their daughter Jeannette Fuller
(1868-1952), a midwestern temperance
lecturer and union organizer and interested
correspondent in the Non-Tobacco League
of America.

SMOOT, SEN. REED

UT —UNIVERSITY OF UTAH, Marriott
Library, Special Collections, Salt Lake City,
84112. Gregory C Thompson, Cur
Holdings: Cat Mss Microfilm Film Oral
History
Notes: Papers.

SMOTHERS BROTHERS

CA —UNIVERSITY OF CALIFORNIA, LOS
ANGELES, Theater Arts Library, Los
Angeles, 90024. Edward Shreeves,
Chairman, Bibliographers Group; Audree
Malkin, Head, Theater Arts Library
Notes: Smothers Brothers Collection: scripts,
films, tapes and music for their various
television shows, 1967-1975.

SMRTI LITERATURE see Sanskrit
Language and Literature

SMYRL, ELWIN

NH —MANCHESTER HISTORIC
ASSOCIATION, Library, 129 Amherst St,
Manchester, 03104. Elizabeth Lessard, Librn
Holdings: // Cat Mss
Notes: Elwin Smyrl was a local textile
designer who worked from 1906 to 1966 in
both natural and synthetic fibers. His early
work was for the Amoskeag Manufacturing
Co. After 1936, he developed headliners for
cars for General Motors Corp, synthetic
cord for Firestone Tires, etc. Collection incl
14 museum storage boxes; textile samples,
textile graphs.

SMYTH, DAME ETHEL MARY, 1855-
1944

MI —UNIVERSITY OF MICHIGAN, School
of Music, Music Library, Moore Bldg, Ann
Arbor, 48109. Peggy Daub, Head
Holdings: Vols 2000 Cat Mss
Notes: Women's Music Collection. Unusual
collection of music by women composers
published from 1750-1950. Includes some
material closely associated with Dame Ethel
Smyth and a small collection of letters by
women musicians in Hatcher Graduate
Library. Catalog to be published late in
1984.
NC —UNIVERSITY OF NORTH
CAROLINA, GREENSBORO, Walter
Clinton Jackson Library, Special Collections
Dept, 1000 Spring Garden St, Greensboro,
27412. Emilie W Mills, Librn
Holdings: Cat Mss
Notes: 78 letters by the English composer
Dame Ethel Mary Smyth, chiefly to
Emmeline Pankhurst, written from Helouan,
Egypt, 1913-1914. Other letters incl several
from Empress Eugenie and members of her
circle, and several letters to Lady Ponsonby.
This group of letters mainly traces the
composer's interest in the suffrage
movement and the development of her
musical career. No photocopying.

SMYTH, JAMES ADGER

SC —COLLEGE OF CHARLESTON
LIBRARY, Special Collections Dept,
Charleston, 29401.
Notes: Papers, 1857-1858.

SMYTHE, WILLIAM

CA —CALIFORNIA INSTITUTE OF
TECHNOLOGY, Robert A Millikan
Memorial Library, Archives, 1201 E
California Blvd, Pasadena, 91125. Judith R
Goodstein, Archivist
Notes: Interviewed for the Oral History
Program of the Archives.

SNAKES

DC —SMITHSONIAN INSTITUTION
LIBRARIES, Natural History Branch,
Washington, 20560. Sylvia Churgin, Chief
Librn
Holdings: Vols 1400 Cat Mss Maps Pix
Slides Microforms
MI —UNIVERSITY OF MICHIGAN,
Museums Library, Ann Arbor, 48109.
Patricia B Yocum, Librn
Holdings: Vols 2500 Cat
NY —AMERICAN MUSEUM OF
NATURAL HISTORY, Library Services
Dept, Central Park W & 79th St, New York,
10024. Nina J Root, Chairwoman; Mary
Genett, Asst Librn for Reference Services
Holdings: Vols (385,000) Cat Mss Maps Pix
Slides Microforms
Notes: Nearly all collections are outstanding
for depth of coverage and international
range. Early and historic works, rare books,
colored illustrations, and relevant serial
publications supplement the modern
scientific publications necessary to the
researches of the scientific staff and the
work of the educational division. Open to
the public.

SNOW

CO —WORLD DATA CENTER A:
GLACIOLOGY (SNOW AND ICE),
CIRES, University of Colorado, Boulder,
80309. Ann M Brennan, Librn
Holdings: Vols 10,000 Maps Pix Microforms
Budget: $2000
Notes: Glaciology, all forms of snow and ice.
Bibliographic information will be contained
in a data file which will be fully searchable.
Partially cataloged (UDC).
NV —UNIVERSITY OF NEVADA, RENO,
University Library, Special Collections Dept,
Reno, 89557. Robert E Blesse, Head
Holdings: Vols 25 Uncat Mss Pix
Notes: Papers of James E Church founder
and developer of the modern science of
snow surveying. Church collection, 180
cubic feet, incl his writings, papers, and over
7000 photographs of Church's snow
surveying expeditions in the Sierra Nevada
mountains and elsewhere in the world.
Papers of the Western Snow Conference, 80
cubic feet.

SNOW, CHARLES H.

CA —UNIVERSITY OF CALIFORNIA,
SANTA BARBARA, Library, Dept of
Special Collections, Santa Barbara, 93106.
Christian F Brun, Head
Holdings: Vols 536 Cat Mss Pix
Notes: Complete collection of California's
most prolific author. Incl translations, mss,
etc.

SNOW, CHARLES PERCY

NV —UNIVERSITY OF NEVADA, RENO,
University Library, Special Collections Dept,
Reno, 89557. Robert E Blesse, Head
Holdings: Vols (89) Cat
Notes: Includes individual works by author
in all editions including translations; also
prefaces, introductions, published
correspondence, appearances in anthologies,
periodicals, etc. Bibliographical research
collection, part of Modern Authors
Collection. Other appearances 430 cataloged.

SNOW, EDWARD ROWE

MA —BOSTON UNIVERSITY, Mugar
Memorial Library, Special Collections Dept,
771 Commonwealth Ave, Boston, 02215.

Howard B Gotlieb, Dir
Holdings: // Cat Mss Pix
Notes: Mss, correspondence, etc collected in
depth; incl publications by or about.

SNOW, HELEN FOSTER see Wales, Nym (Helen Foster Snow), 1907-

SNOW, ROBERT

MO —WASHINGTON UNIVERSITY,
Libraries, Special Collections Dept, Campus
Box 1061, St Louis, 63130.
Notes: Family and business correspondence.

SNOW HILL COMMUNITY

WI —SEVENTH DAY BAPTIST
HISTORICAL SOCIETY, Library, 3120
Kennedy Rd, PO Box 1678, Janesville,
53547. D Scott Smith, Historian
Holdings: Cat Mss Maps Pix
Notes: Julies Sachse Collection. Ephrata
Community records (1729-1883). Original
music mss, some illuminated; samples of
early printing of Bibles and books form an
important part of this collection. Some
material also on Snow Hill, daughter colony,
et al. About 500 items; incl artifacts. Much
of this collection now in Pennsylvania State
Archives, Pennsylvania Historical and
Museum Commission, Philadelphia.

SNOW SURVEYING

NV —UNIVERSITY OF NEVADA, RENO,
University Library, Special Collections Dept,
Reno, 89557. Robert E Blesse, Head
Holdings: Vols 25 Uncat Mss Pix
Notes: Papers of James E Church founder
and developer of the modern science of
snow surveying. Church collection, 180
cubic feet, incl his writings, papers, and over
7000 photographs of Church's snow
surveying expeditions in the Sierra Nevada
mountains and elsewhere in the world.
Papers of the Western Snow Conference, 80
cubic feet.

SNOWSHOES AND SNOWSHOEING

CO —UNIVERSITY OF COLORADO,
Libraries, Special Collections, Boulder,
80309. Nora J Quinlan, Head
Notes: Over 2500 vols on the history of
mountaineering covering everything from the
Golden Age of mountaineering in the
nineteenth century to accounts of
expeditions undertaken today. In addition
runs of such journals as the Rock and Fell
Club, the Ladies' Alpine Club Journal, etc.
Subjects covered incl history, technique,
medicine, biographies, illustrations, etc. In
addition, approx 15 1/2 feet of ms material.
AB —ALPINE CLUB OF CANADA, 111
Bear St, PO Box 160, Banff, T0L 0C0, Can.
Mary Andrews, Librn

SNYDER, CHARLES M.

NY —STATE UNIVERSITY OF NEW
YORK, COLLEGE AT OSWEGO, Penfield
Library, Oswego, 13126. Anne Commerton,
Dir
Holdings: // Cat Mss Maps
Notes: Collection of Charles M Snyder,
professor of History at Oswego and
Collector of local and regional history.
Collection also incl Snyder's class notes and
materials; and notes and mss of books
Snyder wrote or planned to write. 4 linear ft.
Also, the Bradley Benedict Burt papers, with
much on Oswego County.

SNYDER, GARY

CA —UNIVERSITY OF CALIFORNIA,
DAVIS, Shields Library, Dept of Special
Collections, Davis, 95616. Donald Kunitz,
Head; C Danial Elliott, Asst Head
Holdings: Cat Mss
Notes: The Gary Snyder Papers contains ms
worksheets and notebooks, copies of
publications with works by Snyder, and
correspondence to Snyder by many well-
known poets of his generation: Robert Bly,
Kirby Congdon, Cid Corman, Gregory
Corso, Robert Creeley, Lawrence
Ferlinghetti, Anselm Hollo, Joanne Kyger,
John Montogomery, Philip Whalen, etc.
5500 items.
MO —WASHINGTON UNIVERSITY, John
M Olin Library, Campus Box 1061, St Louis,
63130.
Notes: Extensive collection of printed
material, small amount of correspondence.
BC —SIMON FRASER UNIVERSITY,
Library, Burnaby, V5A 1S6, Can. Percilla
Groves, Special Collections Librn
Holdings: // Cat
Notes: Letters from Gary Snyder to Joanne
Kyger, 1959-1960, and carbon copies of
Kyger's letters to Snyder.

SOARING (AERONAUTICS) see Gliding and Soaring

SOARING SOCIETY OF AMERICA

NY —NATIONAL SOARING MUSEUM,
Library, Harris Hill, RD #3, Elmira, 14903.
Notes: Historical business records.

SOBELL, MORTON

CA —UNIVERSITY OF CALIFORNIA, SAN
DIEGO, Central University Library,
Mandeville Dept of Special Collections, La
Jolla, 92093. Lynda Corey Claassen, Head
Notes: Papers of Harold Clayton Urey
(1893-1981), winner of the 1934 Nobel Prize
in chemistry for his discovery of Deuterium.
Incl files concerning the Emergency
Committee of Atomic Scientists, 1946-49;
also some material on the Rosenberg/Sobell
spy cases; also on his works as science
advisor to John F Kennedy (president-elect).

SOCCER

OK —SOCIETY FOR THE NORTH
AMERICAN CULTURAL SURVEY, Dept
of Geography, Oklahoma State University,
Stillwater, 74078. John Rooney, Dir; Todd
Zdorkowski, Asst
Notes: Producing a cultural survey of North
American sports and games. John Rooney
has published several books on the
geography of sports. SWAC's current project
involves mapping the continent-wide
distributions and the participation patterns
for the major and minor professional, college
and high school sports.

SOCIAL CENTERS see Community Centers

SOCIAL CONDITIONS see Social History

SOCIAL DANCING

NY —NEW YORK PUBLIC LIBRARY,
Performing Arts Research Center, Dance
Collection, 111 Amsterdam Ave, New York,
10023. Genevieve Oswald, Cur
Holdings: Vols (40,000) Cat Mss Pix
Audiotapes Videotapes 16mm Films
Microforms
Budget: ($9,280)
Notes: Multi-media collection, international
in scope. European and American social
dances are fully documented ranging from
16th century dances such as the basse danse,
bourree, and galliarde to the twist and
hustle. Collection includes historical
treatises, manuals of instruction, a unique
15th century Italian manuscript of the
Jewish dancing master Guglielmo Ebreo,
19th century American ballroom dance
handbooks, anti-dance tracts, photographs,
prints, articles and clippings. Motion pictures
include footage of social dance competitions
and exhibition ballroom dancing. Over 15,
000 individual dances have been indexed.
Published catalog: *Dictionary Catalog of the
Dance Collection*, Boston, G K Hall, 1974,
10 vols. Annual supplements: *Bibliographic
Guide to Dance*, also published by G K Hall,
1975-.

SOCIAL DEMOCRACY see Socialism

SOCIAL DEVELOPMENT

CA —SOUTHERN CALIFORNIA LIBRARY
FOR SOCIAL STUDIES & RESEARCH,

SOCIAL DEVELOPMENT (cont.)

6120 S Vermont Ave, Los Angeles, 90044.
Sarah Cooper, Dir
Holdings: Vols (15,000) Mss Maps Pix Slides
Phonorecords Audiotapes 16mm Films News
Clips
Budget: ($30,000)
Notes: Marxist, non-Marxist and anti-
Marxist approaches to social change. Other
important functions of the library: to make
available source materials to those engaged
in the Marxist vs no-Marxist dialog; to aid
historians, economists, sociologists, writers,
students and labor organizations researching
the history of grassroots social movements;
and to preserve primary and secondary
sources on labor, minorities, women and
radicalism. Collection incl 50 mss, 75 maps,
500 pictures, 1000 slides, 100 phonorecords,
2000 audiotapes, 50 16mm films and 150,
000 newspaper clippings.
PA —UNIVERSITY OF PITTSBURGH,
Library, Graduate School of Public and
International Affairs, Forbes Quadrangle, 1st
floor West, Pittsburgh, 15260. Nicholas C
Caruso, Librn
Holdings: Vols (80,000) Cat Microforms
Budget: ($117,900)
Notes: The library attempts to collect as
many national economic and social
development plans as possible from the
developing countries of the world. It also
holds city, regional and state plans for
Pennsylvania, particularly the 9
southwestern counties of Pennsylvania.
ON —DEPT OF REGIONAL INDUSTRIAL
EXPANSION, Ottawa Library, 235 Queen
St, Ottawa, K1A 0H5, Can. Steven Rush,
Librn
Holdings: Vols (100,000) Cat Maps
Microforms
Notes: Pertaining to Manufacturing.
Contains 1500 reports of ARDA projects
(Agricultural Rehabilitation and
Development Agency); also NEWSTART
project reports. There is a published book
catalog and two supplements. 15,000
documents; 3000 periodical subscriptions.

SOCIAL ECOLOGY see Human Ecology

SOCIAL HISTORY

DC —US DEPT OF LABOR, Library, 200
Constitution Ave NW, Washington, 20210.
Sabina Jacobson, Dir
Holdings: Vols (550,000) Cat
IL —MCLEAN COUNTY HISTORICAL
SOCIETY LIBRARY & MUSEUM, 201 E
Grove, Bloomington, 61701. Barbara
Dunbar, Dir; Greg Koos, Archivist
Holdings: Vols (3000) Cat Mss Maps Pix
Notes: Illinois history, emphasis on McLean
County. Strong in military heritage of
Illinois, particularly the 33rd and 94th
regiments (III Vol Inf) in the Civil War. Incl
150 LF archives and 1000 pictures.
Photocopying.
IL —WAUKEGAN PUBLIC LIBRARY, 128
N County St, Waukegan, 60085. Andrew W
Stimson, Librn
Holdings: Vols 4000 Cat
Notes: Maintained as the Current Social
Conditions subject center under the North
Suburban Library System's Coordinated
Acquisitions Program.
IN —PURDUE UNIVERSITY LIBRARIES,
Graduate School of Management, Krannert
Library, West Lafayette, 47907. Gordon
Law, Librn
Notes: An important resource at the
Krannert Library is its Special Collection of
Business and Economics, consisting of some
8000 rare pre-20th century strengths in
books, journals, tracts and pamphlets
covering primarily the early literature of
economic thought and business practices in
America and abroad, 1500-1870. A catalog
was issued in 1979.
NY —NEW YORK PUBLIC LIBRARY, Rare
Books and Manuscripts Div, Fifth Ave & 42
St, New York, 10018. William L Joyce, Asst
Dir; Susan E Davis, Cur of Mss
Notes: A large mass of holdings on this
topic.

NY —VISUAL STUDIES WORKSHOP,
Research Center, 31 Prince St, Rochester,
14607. Linn Underhill, Coordr; Robert
Bretz, Librn
Holdings: Vols (8000) Cat Pix Slides
Audiotapes Videotapes
Notes: Strong emphasis on photography
(over 1,000,000 pictures) and the
photographic arts in many subject areas incl
in this volume. Heavy emphasis on early
photographic processes and collections of
examples of them. Also collections of
individual photographers' works.
NY —STATE UNIVERSITY OF NEW
YORK, STONY BROOK, Melville Library,
Dept of Special Collections, Stony Brook,
11794. Evert Volkersz, Head
Holdings: Cat Mss
Notes: Printed and ms materials relating to
local and regional Long Island history, incl
Brooklyn and Queens. Ms collections focus
on women, environment, social welfare, and
politics. Much on the Long Island Railroad
(qv).
ON —CANADA DEPT OF LABOUR,
Library, Ottawa, K1A 0J2, Can. Monique
Marchand, Chief Librn
Holdings: Vols (100,000) CAt Microforms
ON —DEPT OF REGIONAL INDUSTRIAL
EXPANSION, Ottawa Library, 235 Queen
St, Ottawa, K1A 0H5, Can. Steven Rush,
Librn
Holdings: Vols (100,000) Cat Maps
Microforms
Notes: Social History of the International
Industrial Organization. Contains 1500
reports of ARDA projects (Agricultural
Rehabilitation and Development Agency);
also NEWSTART project reports. There is a
published book catalog and two supplements.
15,000 documents; 3000 periodical
subscriptions.

SOCIAL HYGIENE see Prostitution; Public Health

SOCIAL INDICATORS

DC —US DEPT OF LABOR, Library, 200
Constitution Ave NW, Washington, 20210.
Sabina Jacobson, Dir
Holdings: Vols (550,000) Cat
ON —CANADA DEPT OF LABOUR,
Library, Ottawa, K1A 0J2, Can. Monique
Marchand, Chief Librn
Holdings: Vols (100,000) Cat Microforms

SOCIAL INSURANCE see Insurance, Social

SOCIAL INTEGRATION

DC —HOWARD UNIVERSITY, Moorland-
Spingarn Research Center, 500 Howard
Place NW, Washington, 20059. Clifford L
Muse, Jr, Acting Dir
Holdings: Vols (106,086) Mss Maps Pix
Slides Phonorecords Audiotapes 16mm
Films Filmstrips Microforms
Budget: ($854,753)
See also entry under Blacks

SOCIAL MEDICINE

CA —STANFORD UNIVERSITY
LIBRARIES, Lane Medical Library,
Stanford University, Medical Center,
Stanford, 94305. Peter Stangl, Librn
Notes: Phillip King Brown's papers on
health insurance and socialized medicine.
CT —YALE MEDICAL LIBRARY, 333 Cedar
St, New Haven, 06510.
Notes: A special subject emphasis.
CT —YALE UNIVERSITY, Box 1603A, Yale
Station, New Haven, 06520.
Holdings: Mss Pix
Notes: The Contemporary Medical Care and
Health Policy Collection. Letters, memos,
records, photographs, etc of the principal
strategists of the social medical movement in
the US.
NY —MONTEFIORE HOSPITAL &
MEDICAL CENTER, Karl Cherkasky
Social Medicine Library, 111 E 210 St,
Bronx, 10467. Victor Sidel, Dir
Holdings: Vols (500) Cat
Budget: ($1000)

SOCIAL MOVEMENTS

IN —PURDUE UNIVERSITY LIBRARIES,
Graduate School of Management, Krannert
Library, West Lafayette, 47907. Gordon
Law, Librn
Notes: An important resource at the
Krannert Library is its Special Collection of
Business and Economics, consisting of some
8000 rare pre-20th century strengths in
books, journals, tracts and pamphlets
covering primarily the early literature of
economic thought and business practices in
America and abroad, 1500-1870. A catalog
was issued in 1979.

SOCIAL PLANNING see Social Policy

SOCIAL POLICY

MA —HARVARD UNIVERSITY, Graduate
School of Education, Monroe C Gutman
Library, 6 Appian Way, Cambridge, 02138.
Susan S Baughman, Associate Librn
Holdings: Vols (150,000) Cat Mss
Microforms
Budget: ($95,000)
Notes: A comprehensive research collection
that seeks to acquire all scholarly works
published in the English language in the
fields of education, educational
administration, educational psychology, and
human development. Selective coverage in
the related areas of counseling and
psychology, business administration, finance,
forecasting, statistical analysis and survey
design, public and social policy, linguistics,
demographics, and international and
economic development. Incl 4000
educational and psychological tests.
MA —BOSTON COLLEGE LIBRARIES,
Graduate School of Social Work Library,
McGuinn Hall, Chestnut Hill, 02167.
Harriet J Nemiccolo, Librn
Holdings: Vols 28,300 Cat Audiotapes
Videotapes Microforms
Notes: The colleciton covers specifically all
areas of social work education and all
aspects of social welfare services. Holdings
incl government doucments, doctoral
dissertations. Library is computerized and
offers customized data based literature
searches. There are 385 journal titles.
ON —WILFRID LAURIER UNIVERSITY,
Library, (Formerly Waterloo Lutheran
University), 75 University Ave W, Waterloo,
N2L 3C5, Can. Erich R W Schultz, Librn
Holdings: Vols (20,000) Cat Microforms
Budget: ($27,000)

SOCIAL PROBLEMS

CA —UNIVERSITY OF CALIFORNIA, LOS
ANGELES, Research Library, Public Affairs
Service, 405 Hilgard Ave, Los Angeles,
90024. Edward Shreeves, Chairman,
Bibliographers Group; Eugenia Eaton, Head,
Public Affairs Service
Holdings: Uncat
Notes: Current non-governmental English-
language pamphlets (192,819), broadsides,
leaflets and other ephemera on public affairs,
from 1960, representing a wide spectrum of
political and social opinions. Social welfare
and industrial relations are strong fields.
Legal loose-leaf labor services, such as the
Daily Labor Report, the Government
Employee Relations Report and the Labor
Relations Reporter, as well as labor
pamphlets from the mid-1940s, reflect a
long-standing responsibility to the
University's Institute of Industrial Relations.
CA —UNIVERSITY OF SOUTHERN
CALIFORNIA, Social Work Library,
University Park, Los Angeles, 90007. Ruth
Britton, Librn
Holdings: Vols 25,000 Cat Audiotapes
Videotapes
Notes: Social work and social welfare. Incl
129 journal titles.
CO —UNIVERSITY OF COLORADO,
Libraries, Western Historical Collections,
Boulder, 80309.
Holdings: Mss
Notes: The Colorado WCTU was organized

SOCIAL PROBLEMS (cont.)

in Longmont in 1880, two years after the
formation of the first three locals in Greeley,
Evans and Longmont. The Colorado WCTU
was active in woman's suffrage, prison
reform, homes for unwed mothers, day
nurseries, 8-hour laws, and other reforms in
addition to their primary concern of
prohibition. The collection contains minutes
of the Boulder Chapter (1881-1950) plus
minutes of other Colorado local chapters for
shorter periods of time. In addition there are
state convention proceedings (1882-1969),
state officers' minutes and reports, and many
pamphlets and publications. 13 boxes and 12
oversize folders, 1878-1975. A published
guide is available.

DC —GEORGETOWN UNIVERSITY,
Library, Special Collections Div, 37 & O Sts
NW, Washington, 20057. George M
Barringer, Special Collections Librn;
Nicholas B Sheetz, Mss Librn
Holdings: Cat
Notes: Correspondence, documents,
manuscripts, and newspaper clippings
comprising the personal papers of Ref John
LaFarge, SJ (1880-1963), noted Catholic
social thinker. The bulk of the papers dates
from LaFarge's ministry in Southern
Maryland and from his years as editor
America in New York. Incl is material from
his extensive involvement with the Catholic
Interracial Council, Catholic Layman's
Union, and other interracial and social
organizations. LaFarge, son of artist John
LaFarge, was a member of an unusually
gifted family. Incl among the family
correspondence are letters from Oliver
LaFarge, author and anthropologist, and
from Christopher LaFarge, author.

DC —INTERNATIONAL LABOR
ORGANIZATION, International Labor
Office, Washington Branch Library, 1750
New York Ave NW, Rm 330, Washington,
20006. Karen J Mark, Librn
Holdings: Vols (13,500) Cat Pix 16mm Films
Monographs
Notes: Wide range of titles dealing with
worldwide labor and social matters. The
library contains ILO publications and
documentation only, dating back to 1919.
Also, a collection of ILO films and photos.
See *Subject Guide to Publications of the
ILO, 1919-1964* and *ILO Catalogue of
Publications in Print, 1982* (ILO).

DC —US DEPT OF LABOR, Library, 200
Constitution Ave NW, Washington, 20210.
Sabina Jacobson, Dir
Holdings: Vols (550,000) Cat

MA —JOHN F KENNEDY LIBRARY,
Columbia Point, Boston, 02125. Henry J
Gwiazda II, Cur
Notes: The Burke Marshall papers, 50
archives boxes re civil rights, 1961-1964 and
the Bedford-Stuyvesant Development and
Restoration Corporations; the Joseph Dolan
papers, 1 box; the Thomas Johnston papers,
3 boxes; the James Mc Shane papers, 2
boxes; the Frank Mankiewicz papers, 15
boxes; and the Scott Rafferty papers, 4
boxes. Robert F Kennedy Journalism
Awards Collections: newspaper and
magazine articles, and radio and television
programs on the disadvantaged in American
society, 1969-present; 21 microfilms for the
newsprint and magazine enters, 1969-1977;
50 archives boxes of radio tapes and scripts,
1969-1981.

MA —HARVARD UNIVERSITY LIBRARY,
Social Relations/Sociology Library, William
James Hall, Cambridge, 02138. Annelise
Katz, Librn
Holdings: Vols (16,800) Cat
Notes: Supplements resources of Harvard
Library's central collection.

MI —UNIVERSITY OF MICHIGAN, Social
Work Library, 1548 Frieze Bldg, Ann Arbor,
48109. Christina W Neal, Head
Holdings: Vols (33,000)

MI —MICHIGAN STATE UNIVERSITY,
Urban Policy & Planning Library, East
Lansing, 48824. Dale E Casper, Librn
Holdings: Vols (4900) // Cat
Budget: ($35,000)
Notes: A reference collection in the Urban

Policy and Planning Library consists of
indexes, abstracts, bibliographies, directories
and statistical handbooks. There is a 4000
volume pamphlet collection which covers
topics incl: community development block
grants, redlining, revenue sharing, municipal
finance, land use and many other topics as
well. A topically arranged newspaper
clippings collection provides retrospective
and current newsorthy information on urban
problems, legislation and solutions. A
periodical collection consists of the current
issues of about 120 urban and ethnic studies
journals.

NY —HUDSON INSTITUTE, Library, Quaker
Ridge Rd, Croton-on-Hudson, 10520.
Mildred Schneck, Librn
Holdings: Vols (10,000) Cat
Budget: ($40,000)
Notes: Social sciences and world futures.
About 30 percent of the collection
emphasizes materials useful to our ongoing
program of examining possible world futures:
social and economic indicators, forecasts,
current social problems, arms control and
disarmament.

NY —GENERAL THEOLOGICAL
SEMINARY, Saint Marks Library, 175
Ninth Ave, New York, 10011. David Green,
Dir
Holdings: Vols (200,000) Cat Mss Maps Pix
Slides Microforms

NY —SWEDISH INFORMATION SERVICE,
Library, 825 Third Ave, New York, 10022.
Elisabeth Halvarsson, Librn
Holdings: Vols 8000 Cat Pix Slides
Phonorecords l6mm Films Filmstrips
Notes: Covers history, language, literature,
education, social sciences, and economy of
Sweden, as well as Swedes in US, and
Modern Swedish Society. Films rented on
limited basis.

NY —ROCKEFELLER UNIVERSITY,
Rockefeller Archive Center, Hillcrest,
Pocantico Hills, North Tarrytown, 10591.
Joseph W Ernst, Dir; J William Hess, Assoc
Dir
Notes: The Rockefeller Archive Center, a
division of The Rockefeller University,
preserves and makes available to scholars the
records of the University, the Rockefeller
Foundation, the Rockefeller Brothers Fund,
members of the family, and those of other
individuals and organizations associated with
their endeavors. Collections at the Center
document a century of philanthropy by
legions of associated social and scientific
pioneers, providing a unique window into the
past.

PA —TEMPLE UNIVERSITY LIBRARIES,
Special Collections Dept, Contemporary
Culture Collection, Philadelphia, 19122.
Patricia J Case, Cur
Notes: The Contemporary Culture
Collection. See full entry under US-Social
Life and Customs.

†PA —TEMPLE UNIVERSITY LIBRARIES,
Special Collections Dept, Urban Archives
Center, Philadelphia, 19122. Thomas
Whitehead, Cur of Mss
Holdings: Cat
Notes: Incl the records of several separate
collections which are depostied in the Urban
Archives Center. Many collections contain
photographs, maps and pamphlets, in
addition to manuscripts. All collections in
the Urban Archives are sepertely cataloged.

PA —FRIENDS HISTORICAL LIBRARY OF
SWARTHMORE COLLEGE, Swarthmore,
19081. J William Frost, Dir
Holdings: Vols (35,000) Cat Mss Pix
Microforms
Notes: Library's collections contain
information on the history and doctrine of
the Society of Friends, Quaker contributions
to literature, science, business, education,
and government, plus their reform efforts in
peace, Indian rights, women's rights,
abolition of slavery, and temperance. Among
the more than 250 mss collections are the
papers of many Quaker leaders and records
of numerous Quaker educational and
philanthropic organizations. prisoners.

WI —STATE HISTORICAL SOCIETY OF
WISCONSIN, Archives, 816 State St,
Madison, 53706. Harold L Miller, Reference

Archivist
Holdings: Mss Pix Audiotapes Microforms
Notes: Records and papers of organizations
and individuals engages in social and
political reform activities. Major focus areas
are civil rights, 1950s to the present, and
anti-Vietnam war and other protest
movements of the 1960s to the present. Also
covered are other reform movements,
socialism, and communism from the 1930s
to the present. Collections are described in
*Social Action Collection at the State
Historical Society of Wisconsin: A Guide,*
(1983) and in current accession notes in the
Wisconsin Magazine of History. Major
collections are also listed in Hamer, *Guide
to Manuscripts and Archives in the United
States,* (1961) and in the *National Union
Catalog of Manuscript Collections,* (1959-
date).

ON —CANADA DEPT OF LABOUR,
Library, Ottawa, K1A 0J2, Can. Monique
Marchand, Chief Librn
Holdings: Vols (100,000) Cat Microforms

SOCIAL PROBLEMS AND THE CHURCH see Church and Social Problems

SOCIAL PSYCHOLOGY

MI —LAFAYETTE CLINIC LIBRARY, 951
E Lafayette, Detroit, 48207. Nancy E Ward,
Librn
Holdings: Vols (7000) Cat
Notes: Special emphasis on the biological
aspects, causes and treatment of mental
illness.

NJ —PRINCETON UNIVERSITY,
Psychology Library, Green Hall, Princeton,
08540. Janice D Welburn, Librn
Holdings: Vols (19,839) Cat Microforms
Budget: ($50,000)
Notes: Library receives approx 450 current
serial titles. Primarily serves an experimental
psychology department, with interests in
social, personality, developmental,
physiological and cognitive psychology, as
well as learning and perception. Incl 3886
microforms.

NY —COLUMBIA UNIVERSITY
LIBRARIES, Psychology Library, 409
Schermerhorn, New York, 10027. Barbara A
List, Reference/Collection Development
Librn
Holdings: Vols (25,000) Cat Microforms
Budget: ($23,300)
Notes: Incl material on animal physiology,
cognition, psycholinguistics, learning
theories, memory, perception, personality,
sensation, sensorimotor activities, vision.

SOCIAL PSYCHOTECHNICS see Psychology, Applied

SOCIAL PURITY see Sexual Ethics

SOCIAL REFORM see Social Problems

SOCIAL SCIENCES

CA —LOS ANGELES PUBLIC LIBRARY,
Social Sciences Dept, 630 W Fifth St, Los
Angeles, 90071. Marilyn C Wherley,
Principal Librn
Holdings: Vols 165,000 Cat Microforms
Budget: ($150,000)
Notes: Popular and scholarly works on all
aspects of the subject fields.

CA —UNIVERSITY OF CALIFORNIA, LOS
ANGELES, Library, Slavic Collection, 405
Hilgard Ave, Los Angeles, 90024. Edward
Shreeves, Chairman, Bibliographers Group;
Leon Ferder, Slavic Bibliographer
Holdings: Vols (250,000) Cat Maps
Microforms
Notes: The entire range of humanities, social
sciences, and the arts. One of the most
comprehensive US collections for material
not only on Russia and the Soviet Union,
but also on Bulgaria, Czechoslovakia,
Poland, Yugoslavia, the non-Slavic countries
of Eastern Europe (Romania, Hungary,
Albania) and Soviet Central Asia. Holdings
in Russian and Slavic linguistics, Russian
literature, and Russian history are

SOCIAL SCIENCES (cont.)

particularly strong, covering all periods. The collections are described in some detail in Paul Horecky's book on US Slavic collections.

CA —CALIFORNIA INSTITUTE OF TECHNOLOGY, Humanities and Social Sciences Library, Millikan Library 1-32, Pasadena, 91125. Janet Casebier, Librn
Holdings: Vols (140,000) Cat Microforms
Notes: Incl 57,000 Microforms.

CA —ABC-CLIO, Inge Boehm Library, 2040 Alameda Padre Serra, PO Box 4397, Santa Barbara, 93103. Hope Smith, Librn
Holdings: Vols (2000) Uncat
Budget: ($10,000)
Notes: Current serials (2000) and reference works on history: world history, 1450-present; US and Canadian history, prehistory-present; and history-related social sciences and humanities. Library serves as support unit in the publication of *Historical Abstracts* and *America: History and Life.*

CO —SOCIAL SCIENCE EDUCATION CONSORTIUM, Resource & Demonstration Center (RDC), 855 Broadway, Boulder, 80302. Regina McCormick, Staff Assoc
Holdings: Vols (16,000) Cat Filmstrips Microforms
Notes: Contains over 15,000 elementary and secondary social studies textbooks, audiovisuals, games and simulations, professional books, and the complete ERIC microfiche collection. Staff available to travel to all parts of the US to consult on curriculum development, instructional methods, materials analysis and selection, evaluation, new materials, teaching strategies, and trends in the social studies.

CT —YALE UNIVERSITY, Social Science Library, 140 Prospect St, New Haven, 06520. Billie I Salter, Librn
Holdings: Vols 40,000 Cat Microforms
Notes: Organized in 1972, the Library serves the School of Organization and Management and houses the Economic Growth Center Collection. It is also a core collection for the departments of economics, political science, and sociology. Its Social Science Data Archive of machine-readable computer tapes, related catalogs, and code books contains political, economic, and social data sources.

†DC —CATHOLIC UNIVERSITY OF AMERICA, Social Work/Social Sciences Library, Washington, 20064.
Holdings: Vols 7000 Cat Microforms
Notes: Incl 1875 microfilm reels; pamphlet collection.

DC —GEORGETOWN UNIVERSITY, Library, Special Collections Div, 37 & O Sts NW, Washington, 20057. George M Barringer, Special Collections Librn; Nicholas B Sheetz, Mss Librn
Holdings: Mss Cat
Notes: Papers of Goetz A Briefs (1889-1974), economist and educator, who lived in Germany (1915-1934) and in the United States (1934-1974). In addition to teaching, Briefs held official positions in both governments. The papers incl correspondence and mss, principally in the field of economics and the "ethos problem." The bulk of the material dates from Brief's immigration to the United States in 1934.

DC —LIBRARY OF CONGRESS, African and Middle Eastern Division, Washington, 20540.
Holdings: Cat Mss Microforms
Notes: Orientalia: the Orientalia Division contains 1,400,000 vols in Oriental languages. Chinese: more than 422,000 vols, espec strong in local histories and Ch'ing (1644-1911) period material. Japanese: over 574,000 vols, espec strong in economics, statistics, history, literature; 12,000 government, learned society, and university periodical titles, particularly science, technology, and social sciences. Korean: 56,000 vols, espec strong in social sciences and modern history.

DC —US DEPT OF STATE, Library, Rm 3239 NS, Washington, 20520. Conrad P Eaton, Librn
Holdings: Vols (750,000) Cat Microforms
Notes: Incl 7200 microfilm reels.

DC —US OFFICE OF PERSONNEL MANAGEMENT, Library, 1900 E St NW, Washington, 20415. Betty B Guerin, Supv Librn
Holdings: Vols 75,000 Cat Microforms
Notes: US Civil Service Commission terminated by Act of Congress, 10/78. US Office of Personnel Management created and effective 1/79. Library houses a comprehensive collection of civil service documents, newspaper clippings, legislative histories of all major legislation relating to civil service incl microfilms of dissertations, mss, rare items and a complete collection of agency issuances.

GA —UNIVERSITY OF GEORGIA, Libraries, Special Collections Division, Athens, 30602. Vesta Lee Gordon, Asst Dir for Special Collections
Notes: The Arbitron Collection of television and radio program ratings, 1949-date (except past year). In-depth, statistical analyses of the listening public by age, sex, county, some ethnic groups, farm population, listening preferences, etc. 26,302 bound vols. 2 reports, 1949-81. To be added to annually.

IL —UNIVERSITY OF CHICAGO, National Opinion Research Center, Library, 6030 S Ellis Ave, Chicago, 60637.
Holdings: Vols 2000 Cat Mss Maps
Notes: Collection incl book, periodical and ephemeral materials in public opinion research with an academic approach predominant. Methodology is represented mainly in published works ordinarily available in any research library. Substantive works, ie, applications of the method, reports of findings, are less generally available, especially the poll and survey releases of domestic and foreign organizations; we collect some of these and make them available to scholars. Collection is not exhaustive but reflects current and past staff interests. Incl also about 600 studies conducted by the National Opinion Research Center on a wide variety of subjects.

MA —MCLEAN HOSPITAL MEDICAL LIBRARY, 115 Mill St, Belmont, 02178. Hector Bossange, Dir
Holdings: Vols 25,611 Cat
Notes: Extensive collection.

MA —HARVARD UNIVERSITY LIBRARY, Widener Library, Modern Greek Collection, Cambridge, 02138. Evangelie Flessas, Librn
Holdings: Vols (80,000) Cat Mss Microforms
Notes: Collection in Greek language.

MA —HARVARD UNIVERSITY LIBRARY, Social Relations/Sociology Library, William James Hall, Cambridge, 02138. Annelise Katz, Librn
Holdings: Vols (16,800) Cat
Notes: Supplements resources of Harvard Library's central collection.

MI —INSTITUTE FOR SOCIAL RESEARCH, Library, 426 Thompson, PO Box 1248, Ann Arbor, 48106. Adye Bel Evans, Librn
Holdings: Vols (1150) Uncat

MI —UNIVERSITY OF MICHIGAN, Library, Dept of Rare Books & Special Collections, Ann Arbor, 48109. Robert J Starring, Head
Holdings: Cat
Notes: Incl the library of Professor Karl Heinrich Rau of the University of Heidelberg, acquired in 1871, containing 6076 vols especially rich in works on political economics and European statistics before 1850.

NY —NEW YORK STATE LIBRARY, State Education Bldg Annex, Washington Ave, Albany, 12224.
Holdings: Cat Microforms
Notes: Exceptionally strong collection in the social sciences; incl US and other documents, newspapers, pamphlets. Holdings thru 1956 published in New York State Library, *Checklist in the Social Sciences,* an author listing with abbreviated title. Supplement to 1959.

NY —STATE UNIVERSITY OF NEW YORK, COLLEGE AT BUFFALO, E H Butler Library, 1300 Elmwood Ave, Buffalo, 14222. George C Newman, Dir
Holdings: Vols (465,130) Cat Maps Microforms
Budget: ($466,000)
Notes: Fully cataloged collections in education, incl education of exceptional children, art education, social sciences education, etc, are strong since the College was formerly a college of education and approx 60 percent of current graduates still obtain some degree enabling them to teach. Incl Curriculum Laboratory containing courses of study, elementary and secondary textbooks, and collections for children's literature courses (MA in Children's Literature offered). Collection consists of 465,130 volumes incl 64,255 bound periodical volumes, plus 19,120 microfilm reels and 457,988 microtext pieces other than reels. Subscribe to 2263 periodicals.

NY —HUDSON INSTITUTE, Library, Quaker Ridge Rd, Croton-on-Hudson, 10520. Mildred Schneck, Librn
Holdings: Vols (10,000) Cat
Budget: ($40,000)
Notes: Social sciences and world futures. About 30 percent of the collection enphasizes materials useful to our ongoing program of examining possible world futures; social and economic indicators, forecasts, current social problems, arms control and disarmament.

NY —COLUMBIA UNIVERSITY LIBRARIES, Whitney M Young Jr Memorial Library of Social Work, 420 W 118 St, New York, 10027. Tyrone Cannon, Librn
Holdings: Vols (118,646) Cat
Notes: The collection covers the history and philosophy of social work, social work methodology, and all aspects of social welfare services, especially child welfare, mental hygiene, correction, the aging, social security and medical care, rehabilitation, aspects and problems of civil rights and automation. There is also a substantial representation of literature in psychiatry and the behavioral and social sciences. The reference section includes more than 419 periodicals, publications issued by voluntary agencies, government publications, doctoral dissertations and masters' essays in the field and standard reference works. Reference service is available.

NY —COLUMBIA UNIVERSITY LIBRARIES, Lehman Library, Bureau of Applied Social Research Archive, 420 W 118th St, New York, 10027. David Lewis, Librn
Holdings: // Mss
Notes: Comprised of files relating to projects and studies undertaken by the bureau between its opening in 1935 and its closing in 1977. Files incl proposals, drafts, interim reports, codebooks, final reports, and articles and books which were published as a result of a specific study. The collection does not circulate.

NY —JOINT COUNCIL ON ECONOMIC EDUCATION, Library, 2 Park Ave, New York, 10016.
Holdings: Vols 2000 Cat
Notes: The Edwin G Nourse Library of Economic Education.

NY —NEW YORK PUBLIC LIBRARY, Research Libraries, Economic & Public Affairs Div, Fifth Ave & 42 St, New York, 10018. Edward DiRoma, Chief
Holdings: Vols (1,500,000) Cat Microforms

NY —NEW YORK PUBLIC LIBRARY, Mid-Manhattan Library, History and Social Sciences Dept, 455 Fifth Ave, New York, 10016. Robert Sheehan, Sr Principal Librn
Holdings: Vols (80,000) Cat Phonorecords Audiotapes Microforms
Budget: ($40,000)
Notes: Incl anthropology, women's studies, general law, criminal justice, social work, and social aspects of medicine. Reference and circulating copies. 500 periodicals; 100 vertical file drawers.

NY —RESEARCH INSTITUTE FOR THE STUDY OF MAN, Library, 162 E 78 St, New York, 10021. Judith Selakoff, Librn
Holdings: Vols (14,500) Cat Mss Maps VF
Notes: The non-Hispanic Caribbean. Incl material on all aspects of life in non-Hispanic Caribbean, with primary emphasis on anthropology and the social sciences.

NY —UTICA-MARCY PSYCHIATRIC CENTER, MARCY CAMPUS, Professional

SOCIAL SCIENCES (cont.)

Library, 1213 Court St, Utica, 13502. Janina Strife, Librn
Holdings: Vols (3000) Cat
Budget: ($6000)

NY —US MILITARY ACADEMY LIBRARY, West Point, 10996. Elaine B Eatroff, Rare Book Cur
Holdings: Vols 1500 Cat
Notes: Thayer Collection, incl rare editions of 19th century science.

NC —NORTH CAROLINA DEPT OF HUMAN RESOURCES, Div of Health Services, Public Health Library, PO Box 2091, Raleigh, 27602. Elnora H Turner, Librn
Holdings: Vols (15,000) Cat

OH —CLEVELAND PUBLIC LIBRARY, Social Sciences Department, 325 Superior Ave, Cleveland, 44114. Thelma Morris, Head
Holdings: Cat
Notes: Extensive collection. Full runs of periodicals.

OH —BATTELLE MEMORIAL INSTITUTE LIBRARY, 505 King Ave, Columbus, 43201. Carol Young, Librn
Holdings: Vols (150,000) Cat Maps Microforms
Notes: Large collection of Russian and Eastern European science and technology. Over 1600 current journal titles and extensive monography and serial holdings in Slavic languages.

PR —CARIBBEAN REGIONAL LIBRARY, General Library, University of Puerto Rico, Rio Piedras, (Mailing add: PO Box 21917, University Station, San Juan, 00931). Carmen M Costa de Ramos, Librn
Holdings: Vols (115,605) Cat Maps Pix Microforms
Notes: Collection is specialized in the Caribbean with emphasis in the areas of interest to developing countries: social sciences, politics, economics, labor, education, commerce, tourism, literature, etc. The *Current Caribbean Bibliography* is compiled at the Caribbean Regional Library, with card contributions from all countries of the Caribbean; it also lists all the new additions to the library.

†ON —METROPOLITAN TORONTO LIBRARY, Social Sciences Dept, 789 Yonge St, Toronto, M4W 2G8, Can. Abdus Salam, Head
Holdings: Vols 105,000 Cat Mss Microforms
Notes: This and other sections, incl the largest publicly accessible government document collection in Ontario, formed of laws, statutes, debates and gazettes from Canada, her provinces, Great Britain and the US.

ON —TORONTO SCHOOL OF THEOLOGY, Consortium of Libraries, University of Toronto, Toronto, M5S 1A5, Can. R Grane Bracewell, Library Coordr
Holdings: Cat
Notes: A consortium of 7 theological college and faculty libraries at the University of Toronto.

SK —SASKATCHEWAN LEGISLATIVE LIBRARY, 234 Legislative Bldg, Regina, S4S 0B3, Can. Marian Powell, Librn
Holdings: Vols (29,000) Cat Microforms
Notes: Emphasis on books published in Canada.

SOCIAL SCIENCES—METHODOLOGY

KS —KANSAS NEUROLOGICAL INSTITUTE, Menninger Professional Library, 3107 W 21 St, Topeka, 66604. Richard Gray, Librn
Holdings: Vols 200 Cat
Notes: Incl development disabilities; special education; nursing care for the handicapped; programs for the mentally retarded; behavioral psychology; supervision in mental health/mental retardation; staff training in mental health/mental retardation.

SOCIAL SCIENCES—STUDY AND TEACHING (SECONDARY)

CO —UNIVERSITY OF COLORADO, Libraries, Western Historical Collections,

Boulder, 80309.
Holdings: Cat Mss
Notes: This collection consists of 48 boxes of the Sociological Resources for the Social Studies, a high school curriculum updating and reform project (1964-1973) in sociology, incl correspondence, memoranda, and manuscripts for all facets of the project, which was sponsored by the American Sociological Association and financed by the National Science Foundation.

SOCIAL SECURITY see Insurance, Social

SOCIAL SERVICE see Social Work

SOCIAL SERVICE, MEDICAL see Medical Social Work

SOCIAL SERVICE, PSYCHIATRIC see Psychiatric Social Work

SOCIAL SETTLEMENTS

IL —CHICAGO HISTORICAL SOCIETY, Library, Clark St at North Ave, Chicago, 60614. Archie Motley, Manuscript Librn
Notes: Papers of these Chicago setlement houses: Association House; Chicago Commons; Christopher House; Emerson House; Erie Neighborhood House; Fellowship House; Gads Hill Center; Marillac House; Mary McDownell Settlement (formerly the University of Chicago Settlement); Olivet Community Center; Parkway Community Center.

MA —RADCLIFFE COLLEGE, Arthur & Elizabeth Schlesinger Library on the History of Women in America, 3 James St, Cambridge, 02138. Patricia Miller King, Dir; Eva Moseley, Cur of Mss
Notes: Records of settlement houses, most of them in Boston (eg, Denison House, North Bennett Street Industrial School, Rutland Corner House), and of founders and head workers of settlements, notably Mary (Kingsbury) Simhovitch (1867-1951) of New York's Greenwich House and Eva Whiting White (1885-1974) of Elizabeth Peabody House, Boston.

NY —COLUMBIA UNIVERSITY LIBRARIES, Rare Book & Manuscript Library, 801 Butler Library, 535 W 114 St, New York, 10027. Kenneth A Lohf, Librn
Holdings: Mss
Notes: Papers of Lillian D Wald, relating to the founding and administration of the Henry Street Settlement, and other philanthropic and liberal causes in which she was active. 30,000 items. Restricted use.

†PA —TEMPLE UNIVERSITY LIBRARIES, Special Collections Dept, Urban Archives Center, Philadelphia, 19122. Thomas Whitehead, Cur of Mss
Holdings: Cat
Notes: Incl the records of several separate collections which are deposited in the Urban Archives Center. Many collections contain photographs, maps and pamphlets, in addition to manuscripts. All collections in the Urban Archives are separately cataloged.

SOCIAL STUDIES see Social Sciences

SOCIAL SURVEYS

CT —YALE UNIVERSITY, Social Science Library, 140 Prospect St, New Haven, 06520. Billie I Salter, Librn
Holdings: Vols (40,000) Cat Microforms
See also entry under Social Sciences.

NY —COLUMBIA UNIVERSITY LIBRARIES, Lehman Library, Bureau of Applied Social Research Archive, 420 W 118th St, New York, 10027. David Lewis, Librn
Holdings: // Mss
Notes: Comprised of files relating to projects and studies undertaken by the bureau between its opening in 1935 and its closing in 1977. Files incl proposals, drafts, interim reports, codebooks, final reports, and articles and books which were published as a result of a specific study. The collection does not circulate.

PA —UNIVERSITY OF PITTSBURGH, Library, Graduate School of Public and International Affairs, Forbes Quadrangle, 1st floor West, Pittsburgh, 15260. Nicholas C Caruso, Librn
Holdings: Vols (80,000) Cat
Budget: ($150,000)
Notes: The library attempts to collect as many national economic and social development plans as possible from the developing countries of the world. It also holds city, regional and state plans for Pennsylvania, particularly the 9 southwestern counties of Pennsylvania.

SOCIAL WELFARE see Public Welfare; Social Problems

SOCIAL WORK

AZ —TUCSON PUBLIC LIBRARY, Governmental Reference Library, PO Box 27210, City Hall, Tucson, 85726. Ann Strickland, Librn
Holdings: Vols (4000) Cat Maps Audiotapes Microforms
Notes: Special emphasis on public administration, including public finance, public personnel management, social services, urban planning, public transportation, public works, water management, solid waste management, public recreation and government of growing southwestern US cities in 200,000 to 500,000 population range.

CA —UNIVERSITY OF CALIFORNIA, LOS ANGELES, Research Library, Public Affairs Service, 405 Hilgard Ave, Los Angeles, 90024. Edward Shreeves, Chairman, Bibliographers Group; Eugenia Eaton, Head, Public Affairs Service
Holdings: Uncat
Notes: Current non-governmental English-language pamphlets (192,819), broadsides, leaflets and other ephemera on public affairs, from 1960, representing a wide spectrum of political and social opinions. Social welfare and industrial relations are strong fields. Legal loose-leaf labor services, such as the *Daily Labor Report*, the *Government Employee Relations Report* and the *Labor Relations Reporter*, as well as labor pamphlets from the mid-1940s, reflect a long-standing responsibility to the University's Institute of Industrial Relations.

CA —UNIVERSITY OF SOUTHERN CALIFORNIA, Social Work Library, University Park, Los Angeles, 90007. Ruth Britton, Librn
Holdings: Vols 25,000 Cat Audiotapes Videotapes
Notes: Social work and social welfare. Incl 129 journal titles.

CO —COLORADO STATE DEPARTMENT OF SOCIAL SERVICES LIBRARY, 1575 Sherman St, Denver, 80203. Maynard Chapman, Librn
Holdings: Vols 9924 Cat

†DC —CATHOLIC UNIVERSITY OF AMERICA, Social Work/Social Sciences Library, Washington, 20064.
Holdings: Vols 7000 Cat Microforms
Notes: Incl 1875 microfilm reels; pamphlet collection.

DC —NATIONAL COUNCIL ON THE AGING, Library, 600 Maryland Ave SW, Washington, 20024.
Holdings: Vols 14,000 Cat
Notes: Emphasis on psychosocial, legislative, economic and health aspects. Incl 20 vertical file drawers of Archival materials.

GA —UNIVERSITY OF GEORGIA, Libraries, Special Collections Division, Athens, 30602. Vesta Lee Gordon, Asst Dir for Special Collections
Notes: The Arbitron Collection of television and radio program ratings, 1949-date (except past year). In-depth, statistical analyses of the listening public by age, sex, county, some ethnic groups, farm population, listening preferences, etc. 26,302 bound vols. 2 reports, 1949-81. To be added to annually.

IL —CHICAGO HISTORICAL SOCIETY, Library, Clark St at North Ave, Chicago, 60614. Archie Motley, Manuscript Librn
Notes: Social welfare history collections incl

SOCIAL WORK (cont.)

these papers: Action Committee for Decent Childcare, Chicago; Clifford W Barnes (industrialist, philanthropist, congregational minister, social reformer, founder of the Chicago Community Trust and the Chicago Sunday Evening Club); Louise Hadduck DeKoven Bowen (social worker, President, Juvenile Protective Association and the Hull House Association); Deton Brooks (social research executive, public welfare official); Chapin Hall for Children, formerly the Chicago Nursery and Half-Orphan Asylum (home for children from broken homes); Chicago Area Project (pioneering juvenile delinquency prevention and research project directed by Clifford R Shaw and Henry D McKay); Files of the Institute for Juvenile Research and the Illinois Department of Corrections; Chicago Boys Clubs; Chicago Community Trust; Chicago Lung Association and predecessor organizations; Citizens Committee on the Juvenile Court; Emily Washburn Dean (social worker, President, Juvenile Protective Association, Vice President, Illinois Society for Mental Hygiene, Republican Party activist); Raymond M Hilliard (welfare administrator, Director Cook County Dept of Public Aid, Commissioner of the Department of Welfare of New York City and the Cook County Department of Public Aid); Infant Welfare Society, Chicago; Jewish Community Centers of Chicago; Jewish Community Centers of Chicago-Max Straus Center; Jewish Home for Aged, BMZ (Orthodox), Chicago; John Howard Association, Chicago (penal reform and legislation organization); Hans W Mattick: criminologist, sociologist, Assistant Warden Cook County Jail, Director Chicago Youth Development Project, Director, Center for Sudies in Criminal Justice, University of Chicago; National Association of Social Workers-Chicago Area Chapter; Wilfred Reynolds (social service executive, Executive Director, Welfare Council of Metropolitan Chicago); audio tapes of 73 "Problems of the City" programs broadcast over Chicago Radio Station WAIT; Lea Demarest Taylor (social worker, head resident Chicago Commons, President National Federation of Settlements, daughter of Graham Taylor, founder of Chicago Commons); United Charities of Chicago (a union of the Chicago Relief and Aid Society and the Chicago Bureau of Charities); Visiting Nurse Association of Chicago; Welfare Council of Metropolitan Chicago; Welfare Public Relations Forum, Chicago. Papers of these Chicago settlement houses: Association House; Chicago Commons; Christopher House; Emerson House; Erie Neighborhood House; Fellowship House; Gads Hill Center; Marillac House; Mary McDowell Settlement (formerly the University of Chicago Settlement); Olivet Community Center; Parkway Community Center.

IN —SOUTHWEST INDIANA MENTAL HEALTH CENTER, Library, 415 Mulberry, Evansville, 47714. Donna Yuschak, Librn
Holdings: Vols 850 Cat Slides Audiotapes 16mm Films
Budget: $4000
Notes: Also about 500 pamphlets on psychotherapy, social work, and therapeutic recreation.

IN —LARUE D CARTER MEMORIAL HOSPITAL, Medical Library, 1315 W Tenth St, Indianapolis, 46202. Philip I Enz, Librn
Holdings: Vols (14,600) Audiotapes
Budget: ($15,500)
Notes: Incl 100 audiotapes and 219 journal subscriptions.

IN —WESTVILLE CORRECTIONAL CENTER, Library Services, PO Box 473, Westville, 46391. Catherine M Mohlke, Dir of Library Services
Holdings: Vols 1000 Cat

KS —JOHNSON COUNTY MENTAL HEALTH CENTER, John R Keach Memorial Library, 6000 Lamar Ave, Mission, 66202. Krista Hilton-Ross, Librn
Holdings: Vols (1000) Cat Mss

KS —KANSAS STATE DEPT OF SOCIAL & REHABILITATION SERVICES, SRS-Staff Development Library, Feldman Bldg, 2700 W Sixth St, Topeka, 66606. Jean Barton, Librn
Holdings: Vols 5000 Cat Mss Slides Audiotapes Videotapes 16mm Films
Budget: $1000

LA —TULANE UNIVERSITY, Howard-Tilton Memorial Library, Special Collections Div, 7001 Freret St, New Orleans, 70118. Wilbur E Meneray, Librn
Holdings: Mss
Notes: Correspondence, minute books, financial records and published reports of 25 public and private social agencies in New Orleans from 1815 to the present. Use of the collections is restricted. No photocopying.

LA —CENTRAL LOUISIANA STATE HOSPITAL, Medical & Professional Library, PO Box 31, Pineville, 71360. B Carol McGee, Librn
Holdings: Vols 9400 Cat Audiotapes 16mm Films
Budget: $25,000

MD —UNIVERSITY OF MARYLAND, BALTIMORE, Health Sciences Library, 111 S Greene St, Baltimore, 21201. Cyril C H Feng, Dir
Holdings: Vols (400) Cat VF
Notes: The Social Work Historical Collection contains works from the library collection of Charlotte Marie Stopes and includes numerous publications on contraception and birth control.

MA —SIMMONS COLLEGE, School of Social Work Library, 51 Commonwealth Ave, Boston, 02115. Marilyn Bregoni, Librn
Holdings: Vols (20,000) Cat Mss

MA —HARVARD UNIVERSITY LIBRARY, Cambridge, 02138.
Holdings: Cat
Notes: Social classes and social welfare.

MA —BOSTON COLLEGE LIBRARIES, Graduate School of Social Work Library, McGuinn Hall, Chestnut Hill, 02167. Harriet J Nemiccolo, Librn
Holdings: Vols (28,300) Cat Audiotapes Videotapes Microforms
Notes: The collection covers specifically all areas of social work education and all aspects of social welfare services. Holdings incl government documents, doctoral dissertations. Library is computerized and offers customized data based literature searches. There are 385 journal titles.

MI —UNIVERSITY OF MICHIGAN, Social Work Library, 1548 Frieze Bldg, Ann Arbor, 48109. Christina W Neal, Head
Holdings: Vols (33,000)

NH —NEW HAMPSHIRE COLLEGE, Harry A B and Gertrude C Shapiro Library, 2500 N River Rd, Manchester, 03104. Richard Pantano, Dir
Holdings: Vols (66,000) Cat Mss Maps Slides Audiotapes Videotapes 16mm Films Filmstrips Microforms
Notes: Library is a selective US Government Documents depository, and New Hampshire State Documents depository. Subscribe to microfiche SEC 10K reports to AMEX and NYSE (1975-), as well as AMEX and NYSE company annual reports (1977-); AICPA publications and cassettes. Strong collections in accounting; business; business education; computers; hotel and restaurant management; and social service.

NY —LONG ISLAND JEWISH-HILLSIDE MEDICAL CENTER, Hillside Div, Health Sciences Library, PO Box 38, Glen Oaks, 11004. Joan L Kauff, Librn
Holdings: Vols (9000) Cat

NY —COLUMBIA UNIVERSITY LIBRARIES, Rare Book & Manuscript Library, 801 Butler Library, 535 W 114 St, New York, 10027. Kenneth A Lohf, Librn
Holdings: Mss
Notes: Papers of Lillian D Wald, relating to the founding and administration of the Henry Street Settlement, and other philanthropic and liberal causes in which she was active. 30,000 items. Restricted use. Papers of the Community Service Society of New York. Incl files, books, photographs (1000) and bound volumes of periodicals and conference proceedings. Among the papers

are central and district administrative records, committee correspondence and minutes, and files of programs sponsored by the organization. Also more than 1000 photographs by Jessie Tarbox Beals and Lewis W Hine depicting conditions of the poor.

NY —COLUMBIA UNIVERSITY LIBRARIES, Whitney M Young Jr Memorial Library of Social Work, 420 W 118 St, New York, 10027. Tyrone Cannon, Librn
Holdings: Vols (118,646) Cat
Notes: The collection covers the history and philosophy of social work, social work methodology, and all aspects of social welfare services, especially child welfare, mental hygiene, correction, the aging, social security and medical care, rehabilitation, aspects and problems of civil rights and automation. There is also a substantial representation of literature in psychiatry and the behavioral and social sciences. The reference section includes more than 419 periodicals, publications issued by voluntary agencies, government publications, doctoral dissertations and masters' essays in the field and standard reference works. Reference service is available.

NY —FAMILY SERVICE, America Library, 44 E 23 St, New York, 10010. Joan Fenton, Librn
Holdings: Vols (3600) Cat
Notes: No photocopying.

NY —THE FOUNDATION CENTER, Library, 888 Seventh Ave, New York, 10106. Candace Kuhta, Coordr, Public Services
Holdings: Vols (2500) Cat Microforms
Budget: ($12,000)
Notes: 200,000 Foundation IRS returns on aperture cards; 500 annual reports. All available material on foundations, both current and historical. Private foundation tax returns; annual reports; books, pamphlets, and articles on foundations and philanthropy. Publish *The Foundation Directory, The Foundation Grants Index, Source Book Profiles, National Data Book, Foundation Grants to Individuals, Comsearch Printouts, Corporate Foundation Profiles, America's voluntary spirit.* Washington Library, 1001 Connecticut Ave, NW. Field offices: Foundation Center, Cleveland, 739 National City Bank Bldg, 629 Euclid Ave, Cleveland, Ohio 44114; Foundation Center, San Francisco, 312 Sutter St, San Francisco, Calif 94108. Over 130 regional depositories of foundation information and reports, in all states, Mexico, Puerto Rico, Canada, the Virgin Islands and England.

NY —HUNTER COLLEGE, School of Social Work, Library, 129 E 79 St, New York, 10021. Charles Elder, Head Librn
Holdings: Vols (42,000) Cat Mss Maps Microforms
Notes: Social work and related social science disciplines. Extensive vertical files. Emphasis on family therapy, psychoanalysis and psychotherapy, and psychopoetry.

NY —NEW YORK CITY HUMAN RESOURCES ADMINISTRATION, McMillan Library, 109 E 16 St, New York, 10003. Harold Benson, Librn
Holdings: Vols (13,000) Cat Mss
Budget: ($18,000)
Notes: Public welfare in all aspects; the poor in America, administration, management, child welfare, social services, social work in contemporary society, and urban affairs.

NY —NEW YORK PUBLIC LIBRARY, Rare Books and Manuscripts Div, Fifth Ave & 42 St, New York, 10018. William L Joyce, Asst Dir; Susan E Davis, Cur of Mss
Notes: Many collections pertaining to this topic.

NY —SALVATION ARMY ARCHIVES AND RESEARCH CENTER, 145 West 15th St, New York, 10011. Thomas Wilstead, Archivist/Administrator; Judith Johnson, Archivist
Holdings: Vols Pix Audiotapes Microforms VF
Notes: Official files and records, minutes, correspondence and photographs. Papers of

SOCIAL WORK (cont.)

Salvation Army officers. Material published by or about the Salvation Army. Incl 2300 books and pamplets, 300 serials, 40 VF, 685 microfilm reels, 300 sound recordings, 280 sound tapes, 445 films, 14,000 photoprints and negatives, 250 slides and 1050 cubic ft of archives.

NY —YESHIVA UNIVERSITY, Library, 500 West 185th Street, New York, 10033. Pearl Berger
Holdings: Cat

NY —STATE UNIVERSITY OF NEW YORK, STONY BROOK, Melville Library, Dept of Special Collections, Stony Brook, 11794. Evert Volkersz, Head
Holdings: Cat Mss
Notes: Printed and ms materials relating to local and regional Long Island history. Ms collections focus on women, environment, social welfare, and politics. Much on the Long Island Railroad (qv).

OH —ATHENS MENTAL HEALTH & MENTAL RETARDATION CENTER, Staff Library, Richland Ave, Athens, 45701. Judy McGinn, Librn
Holdings: Vols (3000) Cat Audiotapes

OH —ROLLMAN PSYCHIATRIC INSTITUTE, Clinical Library, 3009 Burnet Ave, Cincinnati, 45219. M Glassmann, Dir
Holdings: Vols (3000) Cat

OH —CLEVELAND PUBLIC LIBRARY, Social Sciences Department, 325 Superior Ave, Cleveland, 44114. Thelma Morris, Head
Holdings: Cat
Notes: Extensive collection. Full runs of periodicals.

OH —OHIO STATE UNIVERSITY, Social Work Library, 1947 N College Rd, Columbus, 43210. Toyo S Kawakami, Librn
Holdings: Vols (46,410) Cat
Budget: ($11,960)
Notes: VF incl approx 4500 pamphlets, arranged by LC subject headings. 278 serial titles on social work, social and public service, crime and delinquency, corrections, criminal justice, marriage and the family, probation, and related topics, are received.

†PA —TEMPLE UNIVERSITY LIBRARIES, Special Collections Dept, Urban Archives Center, Philadelphia, 19122. Thomas Whitehead, Cur of Mss
Holdings: Cat
Notes: Incl the records of several separate collections which are deposited in the Urban Archives Center. Many collections contain photographs, maps and pamphlets, in addition to manuscripts. All collections in the Urban Archives are separately cataloged.

PA —UNIVERSITY OF PENNSYLVANIA, Smalley Library of Social Work, 3701 Locust Walk, Philadelphia, 19104. Evelyn Butler, Social Work Librn
Holdings: Vols 37,000 Cat Maps Pix Microforms
Budget: $10,000

PA —FRIENDS HISTORICAL LIBRARY OF SWARTHMORE COLLEGE, Swarthmore, 19081. J William Frost, Dir
Holdings: Vols (35,000) Cat Mss Pix Microforms
Notes: Library's collection contain information on the history and doctrine of the Society of Friends, Quaker contributions to literature, science, business, education, and government, plus their reform efforts in peace, Indian rights, women's rights, and abolition of slavery. Among the over 250 mss collections are several which contain records of schools and charitable organizations established by Quakers, many of which provided aid to Blacks and Indians.

VA —UNITED WAY OF AMERICA INFORMATION CENTER, 701 North Fairfax St, United Way Plaza, Alexandria, 22314. Henry M Smith, Dir; Barbara L Owen, Librn
Holdings: Vols (1200) Cat Microforms
Notes: Incl 5000 research reports and studies on microfiche; 100 vertical file drawers. Services primarily for United Way organizations: United Funds, Community Chests, Health and Welfare Planning Councils.

WA —UNIVERSITY OF WASHINGTON LIBRARIES, Social Work Library, JH-30, Seattle, 98195. Guela Johnson, Librn
Holdings: Vols (23,000) Cat
Budget: ($25,519)
Notes: Social Work and related social disciplines. Extensive pamphlet collection.

WI —UNIVERSITY OF WISCONSIN, MADISON, School of Social Work, Virginia L Franks Library, 425 Henry Mall, Rm 230, Madison, 53706. Thurston Davini, Librn
Holdings: Vols 12,000 Cat Journals
Budget: $16,000
Notes: Special emphasis on social gerontology, child abuse/foster care, and social work with minorities.

BC —UNIVERSITY OF BRITISH COLUMBIA, School of Social Work, Marjorie Smith Library, Vancouver, V6T 1W5, Can. Judith Frye, Head, Social Work Library
Holdings: Vols 16,000 Cat Microforms Audiotapes
Budget: $12,000

BC —VANCOUVER PUBLIC LIBRARY, Sociology Div, 750 Burrard St, Vancouver, V6Z 1X5, Can.
Holdings: Cat
Notes: Incl special files of pamphlets, clippings, etc.

†MB —UNIVERSITY OF MANITOBA, Library, Winnipeg, R3T 2N2, Can.
Notes: Especially social gerontology.

NF —WATERFORD HOSPITAL, Health Sciences Library, Waterford Bridge Rd, Saint John's, A1E 4J8, Can. Maisie Young, Librn
Holdings: Vols (2000) Cat Pix Phonorecords Audiotapes Videotapes 16mm Films Filmstrips
Notes: Material incl aspects of psychiatry related to medicine, nursing, psychology, social work, etc. Also incl manuscript work on a history of the hospital, which closely parallels a history of psychiatry in Newfoundland. Journals are only kept for ten years.

ON —CANADIAN COUNCIL ON SOCIAL DEVELOPMENT, Information Centre, Box 3505 C, Ottawa, K1Y 4G1, Can. Odette Gosselin, Library Technician
Holdings: Vols 20,000 Cat Pix Audiotapes
Budget: $6000
Notes: Historical as well as current materials on Canadian social policy. Part of on-line information system.

ON —ONTARIO MINISTRY OF COMMUNITY & SOCIAL SERVICES, Library, 880 Bay St, Rm 663, Toronto, M7A 1E9, Can. Sandra Walsh, Chief Librn
Holdings: Vols (30,000) Cat Slides Videotapes 16mm Films Microforms

ON —WILFRID LAURIER UNIVERSITY, Library, (Formerly Waterloo Lutheran University), 75 University Ave W, Waterloo, N2L 3C5, Can. Erich R W Schultz, Librn
Holdings: Vols (20,000) Cat Microforms
Budget: ($27,000)

PQ —MCGILL UNIVERSITY, Nursing/Social Work Library, 3506 University St, Montreal, H3A 1Y1, Can. Wendy Patrick, Librn
Holdings: Vols (35,000) Cat

SOCIAL WORK—NEW YORK (CITY)

NY —COLUMBIA UNIVERSITY LIBRARIES, Rare Book & Manuscript Library, 801 Butler Library, 535 W 114 St, New York, 10027. Kenneth A Lohf, Librn
Notes: Papers of Lillian D Wald, relating to the founding and administration of the Henry Street Settlement, and other philanthropic and liberal causes in which she was active. 30,000 items. Restricted use. Papers of the Community Service Society of New York. Incl files, books, photographs (1000) and bound volumes of periodicals and conference proceedings. Among the papers are central and district administrative records, committee correspondence and minutes, and files of programs sponsored by the organization. Also more than 1000 photographs by Jessie Tarbox Beals and Lewis W Hine depicting conditions of the poor.

†NY —COLUMBIA UNIVERSITY LIBRARIES, Butler Library, Rare Book and Manuscript Library, 535 W 114 St, New York, 10027.
Notes: Papers of Mobilization for Youth, a New York City social service agency. Incl correspondence, minutes, memoranda, reports, project proposals, financial records, and related printed material. Also, papers of the Community Service Society, a New York City social service agency. Incl correspondence, reports, memoranda, case records, photographs, and printed materials.

SOCIALISM

AZ —NORTHERN ARIZONA UNIVERSITY, Special Collection Library, CU Box 6022, Flagstaff, 86011. Peter M Whiteley, Coordr/Archivist; William Mullane, Librn
Holdings: Vols 9000 Cat Mss Phonorecords Microforms
Notes: The large Allderdice Collection of thousands of books, pamphlets, periodicals, and organizational files reflects the conservative, communist, socialist, facist, anarchist, and other viewpoints, etc, during the 20th century.

CA —UNIVERSITY OF CALIFORNIA, DAVIS, Shields Library, Dept of Special Collections, Davis, 95616. Donald Kunitz, Head; C Danial Elliott, Asst Head
Notes: Overview of American political movements from the 1890s to the present: socialism, communism, labor, to ecology and women's liberation.

CA —SOUTHERN CALIFORNIA LIBRARY FOR SOCIAL STUDIES & RESEARCH, 6120 S Vermont Ave, Los Angeles, 90044. Sarah Cooper, Dir
Holdings: Vols (15,000) Mss Maps Pix Slides Phonorecords Audiotapes 16mm Films News Clips
Budget: ($30,000)
Notes: Marxist, non-Marxist and anti-Marxist approaches to social change. Other important functions of the library: to make available source materials to those engaged in the Marxist vs no-Marxist dialog; to aid historians, economists, sociologists, writers, students and labor organizations researching the history of grassroots social movements; and to preserve primary and secondary sources on labor, minorities, women and radicalism. Collection incl 50 mss, 75 maps, 500 pictures, 1000 slides, 100 phonorecords, 2000 audiotapes, 50 16mm films and 150, 000 newspaper clippings.

CA —CALIFORNIA STATE UNIVERSITY, NORTHRIDGE, Delmar T Oviatt & South Libraries, 1811 Nordhoff St, Northridge, 91330. Donald L Read, Special Collections Dept
Holdings: Vols 2000 Uncat
Notes: Partial contents: Liberal Publication Dept, London. Pamphlets and leaflets (1893-1903; 1905-1914), Fabian tracts (1884-1904), Irish Loyal and Patriotic Union. Pamphlets and leaflets (1887). Particularly strong in letters from John Burns' personal correspondence (approx 100). Entire collection, 20 linear feet. Indexed in *Century of Change, 1815-1914; A Collection of Original Pamphlets, Tracts, Posters, Holograph Letters, Manuscripts, etc.* (Guernsey, Channel Islands: Guernsey Books, 1972).

CA —UNIVERSITY OF CALIFORNIA, RIVERSIDE, University Library, 4045 Canyon Crest Dr, Box 5900, Riverside, 92517.
Holdings: Vols 5,000 Cat
Notes: Printed works on Nazism, German history and politics 1918-1945, supported by two closely related collections of contemporary publications on 19th-century European socialism and labor movements; incl many NSDAP publications.

CA —HOOVER INSTITUTION ON WAR, REVOLUTION & PEACE, Stanford University, Stanford, 94305. Milorad M Drachkovitch, Archivist
Holdings: Mss
Notes: Papers of Alice Park, 1883-1957, incl diaries, correspondence, pamphlets, clippings, and leaflets, relating to Pacifism and the peace movement, the Ford Peace

SOCIALISM (cont.)

Ship Expedition of 1915-1916, feminism, socialism, the labor movement, prison reform, child labor legislation, civil liberties, and a variety of other reform movements in the US. 30 ms boxes, 3 envelopes.

IL —NEWBERRY LIBRARY, 60 W Walton St, Chicago, 60610. Diana Haskell, Cur of Modern Mss
Holdings: Cat
Notes: 19th century socialism and communism.

IL —NORTHERN ILLINOIS UNIVERSITY, Founders Memorial Library, Rare Books and Special Collections Dept, De Kalb, 60115. William R DuBois, Dept Head
Holdings: Vols (1350) // Cat
Notes: American, British and Soviet pamphlet publications, ca 1860-1955 by or about the radical labor movement, socialists, communists and the radical right. Some Nazi/anti-Nazi material. Collection is computer-indexed by author, title, series, publisher and date.

IN —INDIANA UNIVERSITY, Lilly Library, Seventh St, Bloomington, 47405. William R Cagle, Librn
Holdings: // Cat Mss
Notes: First and early printings of the Icarian communities (1840-1880) and of works by Rappites and the Owenities; also New Harmony, Indiana. Mss relating to the Shaker community in Kentucky (1826-1828) in the Charles Willing Byrd collection.

IN —INDIANA STATE UNIVERSITY, Cunningham Memorial Library, Dept of Rare Books & Special Collections, Terre Haute, 47809. Lawrence J McCrank, Head
Holdings: Uncat Mss Pix
Budget: ($1350)
Notes: The Debs Collection consists of aprox 7000 pieces of correspondence between Theodore Debs (brother of E V) and other persons, such as Sinclair Lewis, Upton Sinclair, Ethel Barrymore, Emma Goldman, Robert G Ingersoll, Carl Sandburg, Norman Thomas, Sacco and Vanzetti and many others. Many of the letters are from E V Debs to his brother; a good portion of these are from the federal penitentiary at Atlanta. Entire correspondence file has been microfilmed. 750 pamphlets cover all aspects of the labor movement, socialism and radical thought from the 19th century to appprox 1950. A collection ca 200 related books is also housed in the collection. See J Robert Constantine and Gail Malmgreen, eds, *The Papers of Eugene V Debs, 1834-1945. A Guide to the Microfilm Edition.* NY: Microfilming Corp of America, 1983 (University Microfilms is the new distributer).

KS —UNIVERSITY OF KANSAS, Kenneth Spencer Research Library, Special Collections Dept, Lawrence, 66045. Alexandra Mason, Librn
Holdings: Vols 7800 // Cat
Notes: Leon Josephson collection of pamphlets and other ephemera on modern socialism, especially Communist Party of America. Noncirculating.

MD —UNIVERSITY OF MARYLAND, BALTIMORE COUNTY, Albin O Kuhn Library and Gallery, 5401 Wilkens Ave, Baltimore, 21228. Ann Copeland, Special Collections Librn
Holdings: // Uncat
Notes: The collection incl more than 1000 pamphlets and broadsides on communism, fascism, Trotskyism, socialism, etc.

MA —HARVARD UNIVERSITY, Baker Library of the Graduate School of Business Administration, Kress Library of Business and Economics, Soldiers Field, Boston, 02163. Ruth E Rogers, Cur
Holdings: Cat
Notes: Covers the progress of economic thought and the evolution of economic institutions and business life, with special strength in agriculture, banking, commerce, finance, industry, money, railroads, socialism, tariff. Restricted use: noncirculating. Collection available on microfilm: *Goldsmiths'-Kress Library of Economic Literature,* published by Research Publications, Inc. Downs 1477, 2704, 2712, 2719, 2727, Supplement 962, 963.

MI —UNIVERSITY OF MICHIGAN, Dept of Rare Books & Special Collections, Ann Arbor, 48109. Edward C Weber, Head, Labadie Collection
Holdings: Vols (40,000) Cat Mss Pix Phonorecords Audiotapes Microforms
Notes: Strong on publications of the Fourth International.

MI —SUOMI COLLEGE, Finnish-American Historical Archives, Hancock, 49930. Kenneth Niemi, Archives Librn
Notes: Collection incl 8000 vols, 152,000 mss, 2000 photographs, 760 audiotapes; microforms and maps; 14,000 holdings are cataloged. Subject interests: coop movement, labor, pioneer library of rare books and church records, socialist and communist movements, temperance societies. Special Collections: Finnish language newspapers (includes 100 titles from 1876-present); Suomi Synod Archives; Finnish-American Oral History.

NY —NEW YORK PUBLIC LIBRARY, Research Libraries, Economic & Public Affairs Div, Fifth Ave & 42 St, New York, 10018. Edward DiRoma, Chief
Holdings: Vols (1,500,000) Cat Microforms

NY —NEW YORK UNIVERSITY, Elmer Holmes Bobst Library, Div of Special Collections, Tamiment Library of Labor History, Washington Sq, New York, 10012. Dorothy Swanson, Librn
Holdings: Cat Mss Maps Pix Microforms
Notes: Books, pamphlets, newspapers, periodicals and mss. Large microfilm collection. Described in Daniel Bell's *The Tamiment Library* (1969), available free from the Tamiment librarian, and *Elmer Holmes Bobst Library Information Bulletin 8* (updated periodically).

NC —DUKE UNIVERSITY, William R Perkins Library, Durham, 27706. Elvin E Strowd, University Librn

OH —OHIO UNIVERSITY, Vernon R Alden Library, Department of Archives and Special Collections, Athens, 45701. Gary A Hunt, Head
Holdings: Vols 184 Cat
Notes: Incl most of the Left Book Club editions published by that organization in the 1930s and 1940s, with some of the club's flyers and leaflets.

PA —TEMPLE UNIVERSITY LIBRARIES, Special Collections Dept, Conwellana-Templana Collection, 13 & Berks St, Philadelphia, 19122. Miriam I Crawford, Cur
Holdings: Vols 30 Cat Mss Pix
Budget: ($30,000)
Notes: Miriam Allen De Ford was a prolific writer on a variety of topics, including history, biography, social reform and crime stories. Her books, as well as a number of the 25 Little Blue Books she wrote for J H Haldeman, are in the Collection, along with correspondence, proofs, and clippings related to her writings and the typescript, page proof and galleys of her *Stone Walls.* The Socialist activities of her husband, Maynard Shipley, are detailed in *Up Hill All the Way* and in some of the correspondence.

RI —BROWN UNIVERSITY, John Hay Library, 20 Prospect St, Providence, 02912. Mark N Brown, Cur Mss
Holdings: // Cat Mss
Notes: More than 3000 pieces of correspondence of John Brooks Wheelwright, American poet and socialist, dealing with political, social, literary, and personal matters in 45 ms boxes and 3 scrapbooks for the period 1915-1940. Incl architectural notes; literary mss incl a diary, unpublished verse, reviews, early drafts of books and notes for *A Novel about Ideas;* and several hundred mss dealing with socialist theory, ethics and practice, and politics related to his association with the Socialist Workers Party.

TX —UNIVERSITY OF TEXAS LIBRARIES, General Libraries, PO Box P, Austin, 78713. Carolyn Bucknell, Asst Dir for Collection Development
Holdings: Cat Microforms

WI —UNIVERSITY OF WISCONSIN, GREEN BAY, Library/Learning Center, Green Bay, 54301. Marian A Gould, Acting Dir, Special Collections/University Archives
Holdings: Vols 700 // Cat
Notes: This represents the collection of Leon Kramer, "idealist, philosophical anarchist and bookseller." Much of the material concerns radical literature and small socialist and communist parties in the US, although there is a considerable amount of books, booklets, and pamphlets published in Germany, Italy, and other parts of Europe. Incl uncounted pamphlets.

WI —STATE HISTORICAL SOCIETY OF WISCONSIN, Archives, 816 State St, Madison, 53706. Harold L Miller, Reference Archivist
Holdings: Mss Pix Microforms
Notes: Records and papers documenting the history of the labor and Socialist movements in the United States from 1850s to the present. Incl are records of labor and socialist organizations incl American Federation of Labor and the Socialist Labor Party, and papers of individual labor and socialist leaders such as Morris Hillquit and John L Lewis. Collections are described in *A Guide to Labor Papers in the State Historical Society of Wisconsin* (1978) and in current accession notes in the *Wisconsin Magazine of History.* Major collections are also listed in Hamer, *Guide to Manuscripts and Archives in the United States,* (1961) and in the *National Union Catalog of Manuscript Collections,* (1959-date). *See also* entry under Social Problems.

WI —UNIVERSITY OF WISCONSIN, MADISON, Memorial Library, 728 State St, Madison, 53706. Erwin K Welsch, Social Studies Bibliographer
Notes: Incl reports of 81 Socialist Congresses held in France from 1876 to 1914, some in ms, pamphlet or octavo vols, Socialist press, largely in microfilm copy; the Saint-Simon Collection, ca 100 items written by the early 19th century French socio-political philosopher and his followers; Hermann Schlueter Collection, ca 600 titles gathered by the German Socialist; and the William English Walling Collection of Socialistica, 200 works on French and Germ;an labor movements.

ON —UNIVERSITY OF TORONTO, Thomas Fisher Rare Book Library, 120 Saint George St, Toronto, M5S 1A5, Can. Richard G Landon, Head
Holdings: Vols 700 Cat Mss Audiotapes
Notes: Woodsworth Collection of books, pamphlets, and broadsides relating to the history of socialist and labour movements in Canada with particular emphasis on the CCF party in Ontario. Presented by the Ontario Woodsworth Memorial Foundation and designated as part of its official archives. Ms material from the files of the Ontario Woodsworth House in Toronto, and from former party members. Incl some private papers.

SOCIALISM—CANADA

ON —UNIVERSITY OF TORONTO, Thomas Fisher Rare Book Library, 120 Saint George St, Toronto, M5S 1A5, Can. Richard G Landon, Head
Holdings: Vols 700 Cat Mss Audiotapes
Notes: Woodsworth Collection of books, pamphlets, and broadsides relating to the history of socialist and labour movements in Canada with particular emphasis on the CCF party in Ontario. Presented by the Ontario Woodsworth Memorial Foundation and designated as part of its official archives. Ms material from the files of the Ontario Woodsworth House in Toronto, and from former party members. Incl some private papers.

SOCIALISM—FRANCE

WI —UNIVERSITY OF WISCONSIN, MADISON, Memorial Library, 728 State St, Madison, 53706. Erwin K Welsch, Social Studies Bibliographer
Holdings: Vols 3500 Cat Mss Pix

SOCIALISM—FRANCE (cont.)

Microforms
Notes: French Socialism Collection, 1871-
1914. Collection of pamphlets, periodicals,
and monographs on French socialism and
the working-class movement. Incl the reports
of 81 socialist congresses held from 1876 to
1914 (original, manuscript or microfilm),
manuscripts and other materials from the
First International, and a very large
collection (in microform) of periodicals,
together with a substantial number of
volumes in the original. Described in Jack A
Clarke, "French Social Congresses," *Journal
of Modern History*, 31 (June, 1959), pp 124-
129; Robert Brecy, *Le Mouvement syndical
en France 1871-1921* (Paris, 1963) can also
be used as a guide since 90 percent of the
items cited are in the collection.

SOCIALISM—GREAT BRITAIN

CA —CALIFORNIA STATE UNIVERSITY,
FULLERTON, Library, 800 N State College
Blvd, Fullerton, 92634. Lynn M Coppel,
Librn
Holdings: Pamphlets Serials Ephemera
Notes: Freedom Center of Polemic Political
Ephemera incl 8000 pamphlets and over
4000 periodical titles. Strongest in right wing
American politics and British socialism.
Separate card catalogs for the pamphlets and
folders. Periodicals are listed in the CSUF
periodicals printout and the *California State
University and Colleges Union List of
Periodicals.*

IN —PURDUE UNIVERSITY LIBRARIES,
Graduate School of Management, Krannert
Library, West Lafayette, 47907. Gordon
Law, Librn
Holdings: Vols (7000) Cat Mss Maps Pix
Microforms
Notes: The collection consists of books,
journals and pamphlets dating from the early
16th to late 19th century, covering to a large
degree the early literature in economic
thought and business practices both here and
abroad. No photocopying.

MA —BRANDEIS UNIVERSITY, Goldfarb
Library, 415 South St, Waltham, 02154.
Bessie Hahn, Dir
Notes: Radical pamphlet collection. Approx
5000 pamphlets from the 1920s through the
1950s dealing with socialism and
communism in the US and Great Britain.
There is an author-title card catalog to ca
500 of the items in the Special Collections
Card Catalog.

†WA —WASHINGTON STATE
UNIVERSITY, Library, Manuscripts,
Archives & Special Collections, Pullman,
99164. John F Guido, Head
Holdings: Vols Mss Pix
Notes: The library of Virginia and Leonord
Woolf (from Monk's House and Victoria Sq)
forms the nucleus of the collection, which
incorporates the library of Sir Leslie
Stephen, Virginia's father. Leonard's
interests are reflected by works concerning
the Labour Party, the Fabian Society, as well
as Ceylon. Their interest in printing and
publishing works of significance is reflected
by the collection of Hogarth Press
publications (1917-1941). Incl works by
Virginia and Leonard Woolf, the Bloomsbury
Group, as well as by other friends--eg,
Elizabeth Robins, Victoria Sackville-West,
Harold Nicholson, etc. Many of these are
unique copies, ie, of association and textual
interest. Other 20th century English authors
incl the Sitwells, Margaret Sackville, Rose
Macaulay, D H Lawrence, John Masefield,
Rupert Croft-Cooke, and Charles Williams.
Partially cataloged.

SOCIALISM—HISTORY

IN —PURDUE UNIVERSITY LIBRARIES,
Graduate School of Management, Krannert
Library, West Lafayette, 47907. Gordon
Law, Librn
Notes: An important resource at the
Krannert Library is its Special Collection of
Business and Economics, consisting of some

8000 rare pre-20th century strengths in
books, journals, tracts and pamphlets
covering primarily the early literature of
economic thought and business practices in
America and abroad, 1500-1870. A catalog
was issued in 1979.

SOCIALISM—LATIN AMERICA

PA —UNIVERSITY OF PITTSBURGH,
Hillman Library, Pittsburgh, 15260. Glenora
E Rossell, Head
Holdings: Vols (172,000) Cat Microforms
Notes: History and contemporary aspects of
socialism, labor and radical movements in
Latin America.

SOCIALISM—SERBIA

WI —UNIVERSITY OF WISCONSIN,
MADISON, Memorial Library, Slavic
Studies Collection, 728 State St, Madison,
53706. Aleksander Rolich, Bibliographer for
Slavic Studies; Robert P Gakovich, Slavic
Cataloger; Valdis J Zeps, Baltic Studies
Center
Holdings: Vols (1000) Cat
Notes: The Komadinich Collection in
Serbian and Yogoslav social and political
history embraces publications and pamphlets
of peasant, socialist and other radical
movements of the last half of the nineteenth
century up to World War II. It consists of
some 1000 items mostly in Serbo-Croatian,
and represents only part of the private
library acquired from the survivors of Milan
Komadinic (1882-1944).

SOCIALISM—U.S.

CA —CALIFORNIA STATE UNIVERSITY,
LONG BEACH, Library, Dept of Special
Collections & Archives, 1250 Bellflower
Blvd, Long Beach, 90840. John Ahouse,
Special Collections Librn
Holdings: // Cat Pix
Notes: Dorothy Healey Collection of
pamphlets, clippings, books and articles on
radical politics, especially in Southern
California.

CA —UNIVERSITY OF CALIFORNIA, LOS
ANGELES, Research Library, Dept of
Special Collections, 405 Hilgard Ave, Los
Angeles, 90024. Edward Shreeves,
Chairman, Bibliographers Group; David S
Zeidberg, Head
Holdings: Mss
Notes: 14 linear feet of mss and printed
materials of the Socialist Party (US),
collected by Hyman Weintraub, William
Goldberg, and others, incl Minutes of the
National Executive Committee.

MA —BRANDEIS UNIVERSITY, Goldfarb
Library, 415 South St, Waltham, 02154.
Bessie Hahn, Dir
Notes: Radical pamphlet collection. Approx
5000 pamphlets from the 1920s through the
1950s dealing with socialism and
communism in the US and Great Britain.
There is an author-title card catalog to ca
500 of the items in the Special Collections
Card Catalog.

PA —BALCH INSTITUTE FOR ETHNIC
STUDIES, Library, 18 S Seventh St,
Philadelphia, 19106. R Joseph Anderson,
Library Dir
Holdings: Cat Microforms

WI —STATE HISTORICAL SOCIETY OF
WISCONSIN, Archives, 816 State St,
Madison, 53706. Harold L Miller, Reference
Archivist
Holdings: Mss Pix Microforms
Notes: Records and papers documenting the
history of the labor and Socialist movements
in the United States from 1850s to the
present. Incl are records of labor and
socialist organizations incl American
Federation of Labor and the Socialist Labor
Party, and papers of individual labor and
socialist leaders such as Morris Hillquit and
John L Lewis. Collections are described in *A
Guide to Labor Papers in the State
Historical Society of Wisconsin* (1978) and
in current accession notes in the *Wisconsin
Magazine of History*. Major collections are
also listed in Hamer, *Guide to Manuscripts*

and Archives in the United States, (1961)
and in the *National Union Catalog of
Manuscript Collections*, (1959-date).

SOCIALISM—YUGOSLAVIA

WI —UNIVERSITY OF WISCONSIN,
MADISON, Memorial Library, Slavic
Studies Collection, 728 State St, Madison,
53706. Aleksander Rolich, Bibliographer for
Slavic Studies; Robert P Gakovich, Slavic
Cataloger; Valdis J Zeps, Baltic Studies
Center
Holdings: Vols (1000) Cat
Notes: The Komadinich Collection in
Serbian and Yogoslav social and political
history embraces publications and pamphlets
of peasant, socialist and other radical
movements of the last half of the nineteenth
century up to World War II. It consists of
some 1000 items mostly in Serbo-Croatian,
and represents only part of the private
library acquired from the survivors of Milan
Komadinic (1882-1944).

SOCIALIST LABOR PARTY

WI —STATE HISTORICAL SOCIETY OF
WISCONSIN, Archives, 816 State St,
Madison, 53706. Harold L Miller, Reference
Archivist
Holdings: Mss Pix Microforms
Notes: Records and papers documenting the
history of the labor and Socialist movements
in the United States from 1850s to the
present. Incl are records of labor and
socialist organizations incl American
Federation of Labor and the Socialist Labor
Party, and papers of individual labor and
socialist leaders such as Morris Hillquit and
John L Lewis. Collections are described in *A
Guide to Labor Papers in the State
Historical Society of Wisconsin* (1978) and
in current accession notes in the *Wisconsin
Magazine of History*. Major collections are
also listed in Hamer, *Guide to Manuscripts
and Archives in the United States*, (1961)
and in the *National Union Catalog of
Manuscript Collections*, (1959-date).

SOCIALIST PARTY (U.S.)

AZ —NORTHERN ARIZONA
UNIVERSITY, Special Collection Library,
CU Box 6022, Flagstaff, 86011. Peter M
Whiteley, Coordr/Archivist; William
Mullane, Librn
Notes: Papers, 1897-1964 of the Socialist
Party (US). Microfilm collection. Reference
department incl guide and index. Originals
located at Duke University. These papers are
a portion of the Allderdice Collection of
20th century conservative and radical
literature located in Special Collections (142
reels of microfilm).

CA —UNIVERSITY OF CALIFORNIA, LOS
ANGELES, Research Library, Dept of
Special Collections, 405 Hilgard Ave, Los
Angeles, 90024. Edward Shreeves,
Chairman, Bibliographers Group; David S
Zeidberg, Head
Holdings: Mss
Notes: 14 linear feet of mss and printed
materials of the Socialist Party (US),
collected by Hyman Weintraub, William
Goldberg, and others, incl Minutes of the
National Executive Committee.

DC —LIBRARY OF CONGRESS,
Washington, 20540.
Notes: Some 4500 pamphlets and sheets
dealing primarily with subversive and radical
activities in the US from 1900 to 1950. Incl
tracts and campaign literture of the
Communist and Socialist Parties in the US
and works by party leaders; materials on the
economic, political, and human rights issues
of the pre-World War II, World War II, and
early civil rights campaign periods; and
pamphlets by various anti-war and anti-draft
organizations, material on Russia, and
materials on the communist movement in
other countries.

IN —INDIANA STATE UNIVERSITY,
Cunningham Memorial Library, Dept of
Rare Books & Special Collections, Terre
Haute, 47809. Lawrence J McCrank, Head
Notes: Microfilm editions of the Socialist
Party of America and other papers.

SOCIALIST PARTY (U.S.) (cont.)

NY —CORNELL UNIVERSITY LIBRARIES,
Collection of Regional History, Dept of
Manuscripts and Univ Archives, Ithaca,
14853.
Notes: Incl papers, 1907-20; 5 reels
microfilm; financial reports, lists of office
candidates, party resolutions, convention
minutes, strike appeals, debates and a text of
the party platform. Also incl silent film, ca
1940, that denounces Fascism in general and
Benito Mussolini in particular.

NC —DUKE UNIVERSITY, William R
Perkins Library, Manuscript Dept, Durham,
27706. Ellen Gartrell, Cur of Mss
Holdings: Cat Mss
Notes: Incl 240,000 items, 1900-1976. Office
files of the Party, incl correspondence,
speeches, reports, clippings, financial
records, periodicals, pictures, etc. Also a
subject file and material on related
organizations. Most of collection has been
commercially microfilmed.

PA —BALCH INSTITUTE FOR ETHNIC
STUDIES, Library, 18 S Seventh St,
Philadelphia, 19106. R Joseph Anderson,
Library Dir

SOCIALIST PARTY, AMERICAN see
Socialist Party (U.S.)

SOCIALIST PARTY OF AMERICA

MI —MICHIGAN STATE UNIVERSITY,
Labor and Industrial Relations Library, East
Lansing, 48824. Martha Jane Soltow, Librn
Holdings: Cat Microforms
Notes: This material is composed primarily
of special collections of papers on microfilm
or microfiche.

NC —DUKE UNIVERSITY, William R
Perkins Library, Manuscript Dept, Durham,
27706. Ellen Gartrell, Cur of Mss
Holdings: Cat Mss
Notes: Ca 240,000 items, 1900-76. Office
files of the Party, incl correspondence,
speeches, reports, clippings, financial
records, periodicals, pictures, etc. Also, a
subject file and material on related
organizations. Most of collection has been
commercially microfilmed.

SOCIALIST WORKERS PARTY

NY —CORNELL UNIVERSITY LIBRARIES,
Collection of Regional History, Dept of
Manuscripts and Univ Archives, Ithaca,
14853.
Notes: Incl papers, 1907-20; 5 reels
microfilm; financial reports, lists of office
candidates, party resolutions, convention
minutes, strike appeals, debates and a text of
the party platform.

RI —BROWN UNIVERSITY, John Hay
Library, 20 Prospect St, Providence, 02912.
Mark N Brown, Cur Mss
Holdings: // Cat Mss
Notes: More than 3000 pieces of
correspondence of John Brooks Wheelright,
American poet and socialist, dealing with
political, social, literary, and personal
matters in 45 ms boxes and 3 scrapbooks for
the period 1915-40. Incl architectural notes;
literary mss incl a diary, unpublished verse,
reviews, early drafts of books, and notes for
A Novel about Ideas; and several hundred
mss dealing with socialist theory, ethics and
practice, and politics related to his
association with the Socialist Workers Party.

SOCIALIZED MEDICINE see Insurance,
Health; Medical Care, Prepaid; Medicine,
State

SOCIETIES, COOPERATIVE see
Cooperative Societies

SOCIETY, HIGH see Upper Classes

SOCIETY AND ACADEMY
PUBLICATIONS

NC —DUKE UNIVERSITY, William R
Perkins Library, Durham, 27706. Elvin E
Strowd, University Librn

SOCIETY AND LANGUAGE see
Sociolinguistics

SOCIETY FOR RESEARCH IN CHILD
DEVELOPMENT

MD —NATIONAL LIBRARY OF
MEDICINE, 8600 Rockville Pike, Bethesda,
20209. Harold M Schoolinam, Actg Dir
Budget: ($46,400)
Notes: Archives of the Society for Research
in Child Development.

SOCIETY FOR THE ESTABLISHMENT
OF USEFUL MANUFACTURING

NJ —PASSAIC COUNTY HISTORICAL
SOCIETY, Lamhurt Castle, Valley Rd,
Paterson, 07503. Helen D Hamilton, Dir
Holdings: Vols (5000) Cat Mss Maps Pix
Notes: Material on the Society for the
Establishment of Useful Manufacturing
(founded) by Alexander Hamilton, papers
relating to John Holland, who developed the
submarine, the industrial magnates of the
area who were active in the manufacture of
locomotives, Colt revolvers, and textiles,
especially silk.

SOCIETY FOR THE PROPAGATION
OF THE GOSPEL (SPG)

MA —EPISCOPAL DIOCESE OF
MASSACHUSETTS, Diocesan Library, 1
Joy St, Boston, 02108. Mark J Duffy,
Archivist; Margaret A Dempsey, Asst
Archivist
Holdings: Mss Pix
Budget: $37,000
Notes: Official material of the Diocese of
Massachusetts, incl parish histories,
biographies and writings of bishops and
clergymen; prayer books and hymnals of the
American Church; Americana; colonial
Church histories; materials relating to the
Society for the Propagation of the Gospel
(SPG); 18th and 19th century pamphlets.

SOCIETY OF AMERICAN FORESTERS

AZ —NORTHERN ARIZONA
UNIVERSITY, Special Collection Library,
CU Box 6022, Flagstaff, 86011. Peter M
Whiteley, Coordr/Archivist; William
Mullane, Librn
Notes: Southwest Section Collection;
records, correspondence, 1944-1960.

CA —FOREST HISTORY SOCIETY INC,
Library, 109 Coral St, Santa Cruz, 95060.
Mary E Johnson, Librn
Notes: Incl archives of the Society of
American Foresters, the American Forestry
Association, the National Lumber
Manufactures Association, National Forest
Products Association, and the American
Forest Institute.

SOCIETY OF AMERICAN MAGICIANS

NY —NEW YORK PUBLIC LIBRARY,
Performing Arts Research Center, Billy Rose
Theatre Collection, 111 Amsterdam Ave,
New York, 10023. Dorothy L Swerdlove,
Cur
Holdings: Cat
Notes: Approx one-third of the book
collection is a private collection housed by
the Theatre Collection but under the aegis of
the Society of American Magicians. Use of
the material is limited to the membership of
the Society. Permission for use must be
secured from the Secretary of the Society.

SOCIETY OF JESUS see Jesuits

SOCIETY OF MAYFLOWER
DESCENDANTS IN THE STATE OF
NORTH CAROLINA

NC —DUKE UNIVERSITY, William R
Perkins Library, Durham, 27706. Elvin E
Strowd, University Librn
Notes: The Society of Mayflower

Descendants in the State of North Carolina
collection numbers 250 volumes. It is a
collection of family history and genealogy.

SOCIETY OF PRINTERS ARCHIVES

MA —BOSTON UNIVERSITY, Mugar
Memorial Library, Special Collections Dept,
771 Commonwealth Ave, Boston, 02215.
Howard B Gotlieb, Dir
Holdings: Mss Pix
Notes: The archives of The Society of
Printers.

SOCIETY OF THE CINCINNATI

DC —SOCIETY OF THE CINCINNATI,
Library, 2118 Massachusetts Ave NW,
Washington, 20008. John D Kilbourne, Dir
of Museum & Library
Holdings: Vols (12,000) Cat Mss Maps Pix
Slides Microforms
Budget: ($65,000)
Notes: Because of the French connections of
the Society of the Cincinnati, a particular
effort is made to incl information about the
French contribution to the American
Revolution. The collection is also rich in
biographical materials concerning the officer
personnel of the American and French
armies of the American Revolution. There
are two significant sub-sections of this
collection: The George Rogers Clark
Collection concerning the history of the Old
Northwest (to 1820); and the Member-
Author collection, writings of members of
the Society of the Cincinnati in various
fields. It is advisable to make an
appointment for use of the collections.

SC —COLLEGE OF CHARLESTON
LIBRARY, Special Collections Dept,
Charleston, 29401.
Notes: Program booklet and guest list of the
"Dinner given to the General Society of the
Cincinnati by the ... Charleston, South
Carolina," April 8, 1908. Includes colored
engravings of the Revolutionary War attack
upon Fort Moultrie, drawn by one of its
defenders, Lieutenant Henry Gray.

SOCIETY OF THE FRIENDLY SONS
OF ST. PATRICK

NY —AMERICAN IRISH HISTORICAL
SOCIETY, Library, 991 Fifth Ave, New
York, 10028. Lisa M Hottin, Cur; William D
Griffin, Librn
Holdings: Vols (20,000) Cat Maps Pix Slides
Notes: Archives and Manuscripts: The
documents and papers of Friends of Irish
Freedom, The Land League, the Society of
the Friendly Sons of St Patrick, the Catholic
Club, and the Guild of Catholic Lawyers.
The papers of New York State Supreme
Court Justice Daniel F Cohalan. This is the
largest and most complete collection of over
20,000 American Irish and Irish history,
biography and literature in the United States.
Incl American-Irish Newspaper collections
dating from 1811, the most comprehensive
in the US; 1000 rare books and special
editions. Special collections incl regular
exhibits of Irish or American Irish interest
incl mss, letters, books, photographs and
memorabilia. Permanent collection of
representative works of Irish painters.

SOCIETY OF THE TAMMANY see
Tammany Hall

SOCIOLINGUISTICS

MI —UNIVERSITY OF MICHIGAN, English
Language Institute/Linguistics Library, 1013
N University Bldg, Ann Arbor, 48109.
Patricia M Aldridge, Librn
Holdings: Vols (4500) Cat Maps VF
Videotapes
Notes: The collection on teaching English as
a foreign language is fairly complete; in
modern language study it is also quite good.
Supporting subjects are linguistics and
English grammar; psychology, American
culture, education, foreign student
adjustment, and bibliography are covered.

SOCIOLOGISTS

†MA —FRANCIS A COUNTWAY LIBRARY
OF MEDICINE, Boston, 02115.

NY —STATE UNIVERSITY OF NEW YORK
AT ALBANY, Library, Special Collections
Dept, 1400 Washington Ave, Albany, 12222.
Marion P Munzer, Coordr
Notes: Concentration of materials from
1940-1960, relative to the family of Hans
Staudinger and his administrative positions
at the New School for Social Research; to
his interests in the Deutsche Theatre; and to
his work in aiding German exiles. Incl 31.5
linear feet of mss and teaching materials;
personal library of books, periodicals,
pamphlets. Part of the Library's German
Exile Collection.
See also entries under Staudinger, Hans;
New School for Social Research; Exiles,
Political

†NY —COLUMBIA UNIVERSITY
LIBRARIES, Butler Library, Rare Book and
Manuscript Library, 535 W 114 St, New
York, 10027.
Notes: Papers, etc, of Paul F Lazarsfeld.

RI —BROWN UNIVERSITY, John Hay
Library, 20 Prospect St, Providence, 02912.
Mark N Brown, Cur Mss
Holdings: Vols 1200 // Cat Mss Pix
Notes: The Lester Frank Ward Collection is
formed from the library and literary remains
of Lester Frank Ward, a pioneer in the study
of sociology. Books and pamphlets which
reflect his interest in botany, geology,
philosophy and sociology are supplemented
by Ward's working scrapbooks and card
indexes. The mss incl personal papers, notes,
typescripts, proofs of published writings,
diaries for 1860-1890, an unpublished
autobiography and 5800 letters received by
him.

SOCIOLOGY

CT —YALE UNIVERSITY, Social Science
Library, 140 Prospect St, New Haven,
06520. Billie I Salter, Librn
Holdings: Vols (40,000) Cat Microforms
Notes: Incl the Trigant Burrow Manuscript
Collection transferred from the Lifwynn
Foundation.

DC —US COMMISSION ON CIVIL
RIGHTS, National Clearinghouse Library,
1121 Vermont Ave NW, Washington,
20005. Lenora McMillan, Chief Librn
Holdings: Vols (10,200) Cat Slides
Microforms
Notes: The National Clearinghouse Library
has a special collection of the US
Commission on Civil Rights publications
from its inception (1957) to present date.

DC —US DEPT OF JUSTICE, Drug
Enforcement Administration, Library, 1405 I
St NW, Washington, 20537. Morton S
Goren, Librn
Holdings: Vols (10,000) Cat Microforms
Notes: Narcotics and dangerous drugs
control.

IL —LUTHERAN GENERAL HOSPITAL
LIBRARY, 1775 Dempster St, Park Ridge,
60068. Joanne Crispen, Dir of Library
Services
Holdings: Vols (21,298) Cat Slides
Audiotapes Videotapes 16mm Films
Filmstrips
Budget: ($52,600)

IN —INDIANA UNIVERSITY, Institute for
Sex Research Library, 416 Morrison Hall,
Bloomington, 47401. Douglas Freeman,
Collections and Services Librn; Joan Brewer,
Information Services Librn
Holdings: Vols (62,000) Cat Mss Pix
Microforms
See also entry under Sex.

KS —JOHNSON COUNTY MENTAL
HEALTH CENTER, John R Keach
Memorial Library, 6000 Lamar Ave,
Mission, 66202. Krista Hilton-Ross, Librn
Holdings: Vols (1000) Cat Mss

MD —UNION MEMORIAL HOSPITAL,
Nursing Library, 3301 N Calvert St,
Baltimore, 21218. Carolyn Daugherty, Librn
Holdings: Vols (4000) Cat Mss Pix

MA —MCLEAN HOSPITAL MEDICAL
LIBRARY, 115 Mill St, Belmont, 02178.

Hector Bossange, Dir
Holdings: Vols 25,611 Cat
Notes: Extensive collection.

MA —HARVARD UNIVERSITY LIBRARY,
Widener Library, Cambridge, 02138.
Holdings: Cat
Notes: *Widener Library Shelflist* Nos 45-46
(1973) lists some 47,000 volumes on
sociology.

MA —HARVARD UNIVERSITY LIBRARY,
Social Relations/Sociology Library, William
James Hall, Cambridge, 02138. Annelise
Katz, Librn
Holdings: Vols (16,800) Cat
Notes: Supplements resources of Harvard
Library's central collection.

MA —BRANDEIS UNIVERSITY, Goldfarb
Library, 415 South St, Waltham, 02154.
Bessie Hahn, Dir
Notes: 6 linear ft of research and working
papers of American sociologist, Paul
Kecskemeti. This collection is unprocessed,
spring 1984.

MN —MINNEAPOLIS PUBLIC LIBRARY &
INFORMATION CENTER, Sociology
Dept, 300 Nicollet Mall, Minneapolis,
55401. Eileen Scwartzbauer, Dept Head
Holdings: Vols (90,000) Cat Phonorecords
Audiotapes Microforms
Budget: ($69,890)
Notes: Special collections: Foundation
Center Regional Collection; college catalogs
on fiche; adult basic education collection.
Separate department catalog.

MO —SAINT LOUIS POLICE LIBRARY,
315 S Tucker Blvd, Saint Louis, 63102.
Cathy Reilly, Librn
Holdings: Vols (21,000) Cat Mss Pix
Microforms
Budget: ($18,400)
Notes: Library on all subjects of police work
is open to the public for general reference
use.

MO —SAINT LOUIS PSYCHOANALYTIC
INSTITUTE, Betty Golde Smith Memorial
Library, 4524 Forest Park Blvd, Saint Louis,
63108. Rheba Symeonoglou, Librn
Holdings: Vols (5566) Cat
Budget: ($4000)
Notes: Primarily a psychoanalytic library.
Considerable material in the fields of
psychiatry, psychology and sociology.
Special section (about 400 books) for the lay
reader, who is also welcome to read any of
the other material in the library. Library has
incorporated the *Index of the Chicago
Institute for Psychoanalysis*, an index to
periodical articles by author, title and
subject. Collection described in *Reference
Encyclopedia of American Psychology and
Psychiatry*, Barry T Klein, ed 3655 W Pine
Blvd, St Louis, Mo 63108.

NH —FRANKLIN PIERCE COLLEGE,
Frank S DiPietro Library, College Rd,
Rindge, 03461. Robert W Chatfield, Dir
Notes: Human Relations Area Files (New
Haven).

NY —BANK STREET COLLEGE OF
EDUCATION LIBRARY, 610 W 112 St,
New York, 10025. Eleanor Kule Seid,
Library Dir
Holdings: Vols (90,000) Cat Microforms
Notes: Education, guidance, psychology,
educational psychology, curricula, textbooks,
black studies, etc. All subjects are integrated
in one professional collection; in addition
there are two separately cataloged and
shelved collections: Children's and
Elementary Curriculum Materials.

NY —COLUMBIA UNIVERSITY
LIBRARIES, Rare Book & Manuscript
Library, 801 Butler Library, 535 W 114 St,
New York, 10027. Kenneth A Lohf, Librn
Holdings: Mss
Notes: Incl the papers (5000 items) of
Professor Robert Morrison MacIver:
correspondence, notes, drafts of mss, etc on
sociology, political power and juvenile
delinquency, incl his participation on the
City of New York Juvenile Delinquency
Evaluation Project, on which he served after
his retirement from Columbia University.
Restricted use.

NY —GENERAL THEOLOGICAL
SEMINARY, Saint Marks Library, 175
Ninth Ave, New York, 10011. David Green,

Dir
Holdings: Vols (200,000) Cat Mss Maps Pix
Slides Microforms
Notes: Extensive collection.

NY —NEW YORK CITY HUMAN
RESOURCES ADMINISTRATION,
McMillan Library, 109 E 16 St, New York,
10003. Harold Benson, Librn
Holdings: Vols (13,000) Cat Mss
Budget: ($18,000)
Notes: Public welfare in all aspects; the poor
in America, administration, management,
child welfare, social services, social work in
contemporary society, and urban affairs.

NY —NEW YORK PUBLIC LIBRARY,
Research Libraries, Economic & Public
Affairs Div, Fifth Ave & 42 St, New York,
10018. Edward DiRoma, Chief
Holdings: Vols (1,500,000) Cat Microforms

NC —NORTH AMERICAN YOUTH SPORT
INSTITUTE, 4985 Oak Garden Drive,
Kernersville, 27284. Jack Hutslar, Exec Dir
Notes: A private management consulting and
training firm for adults who are involved
with school age youngsters in community
sport, recreation and physical education. Incl
Sport Scene, quarterly publication; resource
list; reference center.

OH —OHIO STATE UNIVERSITY, William
Oxley Thompson Memorial Library,
Hilander Room, 1858 Neil Ave Mall,
Columbus, 43210. Predrag Matejic, Cur; G
Koolemans Beynen, Slavic Bibliographer
Holdings: Vols (200,000) Cat Maps
Microforms
Budget: ($45,000)
Notes: Area studies of Central, Southeastern
and Eastern Europe. Emphasis on on Slavic
literatures, languages and history. At present
economics, sociology, law (Russian only)
have been added. Within this framework the
following priorities have been established:
Material in Russian problems; then Medieval
Slavic (Cyrillic); then Polish, then Serbo-
Croatian, then Bulgarian, and now
Romanian. Special attention is paid to
serials, bibliographies, ms descriptions and
dictionaries (incl biographical and
encyclopedias). Apart from materials in
native languages, materials in the following
languages are acquired: Old Church
Slavonic, Greek, English, French, German,
Italian, a few in Scandinavian languages, incl
Finnish, and a few in Baltic languages. The
Hillander Room holds approx 2000 Slavic
mss, 1050 from Hilandar Monastery, Mount
Athos, on microform and a related
referencecollection.

PA —UNIVERSITY OF PENNSYLVANIA,
Annenberg School of Communications
Library, 3620 Walnut St, Philadelphia,
19104. Sandra B Grilikhes, Head
Holdings: Vols 20,000 Cat Microforms
Notes: Theory and research in
communication, incl visual communication,
via social psychology, anthropology,
ethnography, and sociology. All aspects of
mass media with emphasis on methodology
in research. Utilizes content analysis and
computer operations. Special collections: film
catalogs; collection of Annenberg Faculty
Publications.

PA —UNIVERSITY OF PITTSBURGH,
Hillman Library, Pittsburgh, 15260. Glenora
E Rossell, Head
Holdings: Vols (19,150) Cat
Notes: Especially strong in social theory,
social history, social groups, criminology and
urban sociology. Emphasis is currently being
given to administration of justice, sociology
of the child, sociology of the aged, sociology
of education and sociology of religion. This
collection is strengthened by the US
government publications depository
collection, the partial UN depository
collection, the Canadian government
publications collection and the collection of
the Social Work Library.

WA —SEATTLE PUBLIC LIBRARY, 1000
Fourth Ave, Seattle, 98104. Ronald A
Dubberly, City Librn
Holdings: Cat

WY —US AIR FORCE INSTITUTE OF
TECHNOLOGY, Library, Dept 9 Bldg 831,
FE, Warren AFB, 82001. Patricia A
Johnson, Librn
Holdings: Vols (7000) Cat Microforms
Budget: ($9000)
Notes: The Library supports graduate

SOCIOLOGY (cont.)

programs for students (Air Force Missile-Combat Crewman) seeking a Master of Business Administration Degree. Civilian students and other military personnel are also admitted.

BC —VANCOUVER PUBLIC LIBRARY, Sociology Div, 750 Burrard St, Vancouver, V6Z 1X5, Can.
Holdings: Cat
Notes: Incl special files of pamphlets, clippings, etc.

ON —CANADA PUBLIC SERVICE COMMISSION, Library, Room 930 W Tower, Esplande Laurier, Ottawa, K1A 0M7, Can. A Campbell, Chief Librn
Holdings: Vols 7000 Cat
Budget: $20,000
Notes: Library supports the research, administrative, and instructional needs of the Commission. English and French materials.

ON —NATIONAL LIBRARY OF CANADA, 395 Wellington St, Ottawa, K1A 0N4, Can. Andre Preibish, Dir
Holdings: Vols 10,000
Notes: Includes 130 serial titles, theses, pamphlets, government publications relating to family and marriage. The following disciplines covered: anthropology, psychology and psychiatry, law, economics, religion, sociology, demography, education, political science and biology. Earliest title 1630.

†ON —METROPOLITAN TORONTO LIBRARY, Social Sciences Dept, 789 Yonge St, Toronto, M4W 2G8, Can. Abdus Salam, Head
Holdings: Vols Cat Maps Phonorecords Audiotapes 16mm Films
Notes: A large collection of material covering the origins, organization and development of human society. Includes sociological theory, research methods, use of statistics, etc. Strongest in Canadian, American and British aspects.

ON —SIRLS, Faculty of Human Kinetics & Leisure Studies, University of Waterloo, Waterloo, N2L 3G1, Can. Betty Smith, Database Mgr
Notes: Information Retrieval System for the Sociology of Leisure and Sport (SIRLS) is a computerized online database of about 13,000 entries (1983). Incl dance as a leisure time activity.

SOCIOLOGY—HISTORY

RI —BROWN UNIVERSITY, John Hay Library, 20 Prospect St, Providence, 02912. Mark N Brown, Cur Mss
Holdings: Vols 1200 // Cat Mss Pix
Notes: The Lester Frank Ward Collection is formed from the library and literary remains of Lester Frank Ward, a pioneer in the study of sociology. Books and pamphlets which reflect his interest in botany, geology, philosophy and sociology are supplemented by Ward's working scrapbooks and card indexes. The mss incl personal papers, notes, typescripts, proofs of published writings, diaries for 1860-1890, an unpublished autobiography and 5800 letters received by him.

SOCIOLOGY, DESCRIPTIVE see Social History

SIMONS, ALBERT

SC —COLLEGE OF CHARLESTON LIBRARY, Special Collections Dept, Charleston, 29401.
Notes: Papers, 1915-1976, incl notes, sketchbooks composed in Europe and the United States, newsclippings dealing with Simons' career, and a large collection of art photographs used as instructional material.

SOCIOLOGY, RURAL

IA —IOWA STATE UNIVERSITY, Library, Ames, 50011. Warren B Kuhn, Dean of Library Services
Holdings: Vols 500 Cat
Notes: The private collection of Professor

George Henry Von Tungeln, probably the earilest regular staff member in rural sociology in any land-grant college in the country.

KY —UNIVERSITY OF KENTUCKY, Agricultural Library, Agricultural Science Center North, Lexington, 40506. Antoinette Paris Powell, Librn
Holdings: Vols (90,000) Cat Microforms
Budget: ($110,385)

NC —DUKE UNIVERSITY, Divinity School Library, Durham, 27706. Donn Michael Farris, Librn

WI —UNIVERSITY OF WISCONSIN, MADISON, College of Agricultural & Life Sciences, Steenbock Memorial Library, 550 Babcock Dr, Madison, 53706. Jan Kennedy, Dir
Holdings: Vols (186,312) Cat Docs Microforms

ON —UNIVERSITY OF GUELPH, Library, Guelph, N1G 2W1, Can. Margaret Beckman, Chief Librn; Ellen Pearson, Ref Librn
Notes: 15,000 monographs, 350 periodical subscriptions, 5000 documents, also maps, mss, audio/videotapes, 16mm films. Supports research activities related to planning theory, public administration, rural sociology, rural planning and development, rural and urban community studies, regional analysis, rural environment and resource use, policy design.

SOCIOLOGY, SPORTS see Sports Sociology

SOCIOLOGY, URBAN

AZ —NORTHERN ARIZONA UNIVERSITY, Special Collection Library, CU Box 6022, Flagstaff, 86011. Peter M Whiteley, Coordr/Archivist; William Mullane, Librn
Notes: Roger Kelly Collection; notes and files for book *American Indians in Small Cities: A Survey of Urban Acculturation in Two Northern Arizona Communities* (Flagstaff: Northern Arizona University, 1966).

MN —UNIVERSITY OF MINNESOTA, Architecture Library, 89 Church St, Minneapolis, 55455. A Kristine Johnson, Librn
Holdings: Vols (27,000) Cat Mss
Budget: ($20,000)
Notes: Incl architecture, architectural history, landscape architecture, design methodology, housing, urban sociology, interior design, etc.

NJ —PRINCETON UNIVERSITY, Architecture Library, School of Architecture, Princeton, 08544. Frances Chen, Librn

SOCIOLOGY OF LANGUAGE see Sociolinguistics

SOD HOUSES

NE —KEARNEY STATE COLLEGE, Calvin T Ryan Library, Kearney, 68847. John Mayeski, Dir; Anita Norman, Reference Librn
Holdings: Vols (1700) Cat Mss Maps Pix Slides Microforms
Notes: Collection attempts to cover total historical development of Nebraska. Special strengths incl overland journeys, pony express, sod houses, and the Union Pacific. Special consideration has been given to Indians of Nebraska and the cattle industry. The collection is well supported by the Library's general strength of Western Americana.

ND —NORTH DAKOTA STATE UNIVERSITY, Library, Fargo, 58105. John E Bye, Archivist
Holdings: Vols (2500) Cat Mss Maps Pix
Budget: ($14,000)
Notes: The Collection is administered by the North Dakota Institute for Regional Studies. It contains materials on North Dakota history, especially the Red River Valley, with emphasis on bonanza farming, pioneer life, agriculture, local history, literary figures, business, Fargo, ND, and some political

collections, particularly of the Nonpartisan League. Also, there is an extensive photographic collection covering the pioneer to post-World War I period and includes the "Hultstrand 'History in Pictures' Collection" of sod houses, pioneer life and farming. For the small collections, there has been published, *Guide to the Small Collection Manuscripts of the North Dakota Institute for Regional Studies*, by John E Bye, 1977.

SODA WATER see Carbonated Beverages

SODALITY OF OUR LADY

MO —SAINT LOUIS UNIVERSITY, Pius XII Memorial Library, Saint Louis Room Collection, 3655 W Pine Blvd, Saint Louis, 63108. Catherine E Weidle, Rare Books Librn
Holdings: Vols Cat
Notes: Books on Jesuitica; also collections on the Spiritual Exercises of St Ignatius Loyola and on the Sodality of Our Lady.

SODUS BAY PHALANX

IL —UNIVERSITY OF ILLINOIS, URBANA/CHAMPAIGN, Library, Illinois Historical Survey Library, 1408 W Gregory Dr, 1A Library, Urbana, 61801.
Holdings: Vols 50 Cat Mss Maps Pix Microforms
Notes: Communitarianism in America. The ms material, contained in 30 separate collections (10 cubic feet), concentrates on the period 1840-70. It incl correspondence, records, minutes, ledgers and diaries. Communal societies such as Bishop Hill, Brook Farm, New Harmony, the North American Phalanx and the Sodus Bay Phalanx are represented. Among the corresondents are Albert Brisbane, Parke Godwin, Sarah Grimke, Richard Owen, Robert Owen, Robert Dale Owen, and George Ripley. Numerous pictures. Guide to the collections published in 1976.

SOFISM see Sufism

SOFT COAL see Coal

SOFT DRINK INDUSTRY

IN —HURTY-PECK LIBRARY OF BEVERAGE LITERATURE, 5650 W Raymond Street, PO Box 41167, Indianapolis, 46208. Ben Wilson, Librn
Holdings: Vols (6000) Cat //
Notes: The most comprehensive collection, in English, in the world on beverages of all types. History, manufacture, formulae, customs. Books on beer and brewing; cocoa and chocolate; coffee; liquors and spirits; soft drinks; tea; and wine.

SOFT DRINKS see Carbonated Beverages

SOFTBALL

OK —AMATEUR SOFTBALL ASSOCIATION OF AMERICA, Research Center Library, 2801 NE 50 St, Oklahoma City, 73111. Gail Peck, Research Asst
Notes: Books (about 75), magazine articles (about 70); master's thesis and doctoral dissertations (about 35), videotapes (about 25); newspaper clippings; programs and guidebooks including some foreign ones. All of above cataloged and in process of expansion. Total library holdings approximately 300.

SOGDIAN LANGUAGE

NY —NEW YORK PUBLIC LIBRARY, Oriental Div, Fifth Ave & 42 St, New York, 10018. E Christian Filstrup, Chief
Holdings: Cat Mss Microforms
Budget: ($56,455)
Notes: Published catalog of holdings.

SOGLOW, OTTO

MA —BOSTON UNIVERSITY, Mugar Memorial Library, Special Collections Dept,

SOGLOW, OTTO (cont.)

771 Commonwealth Ave, Boston, 02215.
Howard B Gotlieb, Dir
Holdings: Cat
Notes: Cartoons of "The Little King" and
others for the *New Yorker*, incl publications
by or about.

SOHN, LOUIS BRUNO, 1914-

MA —HARVARD UNIVERSITY LIBRARY,
Law School Library, Langdell Hall,
Cambridge, 02138. Erika S Chadbourn, Cur
of Mss
Holdings: Cat Mss
Notes: Professional papers. Typed inventory
in repository. Inclusive dates: 1936-1979.
Additions expected.

SOIL—POLLUTION

CO —COLORADO STATE UNIVERSITY,
Libraries, Fort Collins, 80523. K Suzanne
Johnson, Biomedical Sciences, Librn
Holdings: Vols (2000) Cat Microforms
Budget: ($2000)

SOIL CONSERVATION

IA —IOWA STATE UNIVERSITY, Library,
Dept of Special Collections, Ames, 50011.
Stanley M Yates, Head
Holdings: // Mss
Notes: Ralph K Bliss was director of the ISU
Extension Service and was active in state
conservation and state agricultural planning.
20 linear ft, finding aid available.
PA —DELAWARE COUNTY PLANNING
DEPT, Library, Third & Orange St, Media,
19063. Jane Taggart Quin, Librn
Holdings: Vols 4800 Cat
Budget: $1500
MB —UNIVERSITY OF MANITOBA,
Elizabeth Dafoe Library, Archives and
Special Collections Dept, Winnipeg, R3T
2N2, Can. Richard E Bennett, Dept Head;
Corrado A Santoro, Reference Archivist
Notes: Papers of soil scientist and professor
Joseph Henry Ellis. Soil and land
inspections, surveys and reports; stream bank
erosion studies; river reclamation projects;
field crop experiments; prairie rehabilitation
activities; fertilizer experiments; land
utilization studies; tree planting.
SK —CANADA PRAIRIE FARM
REHABILITATION ADMINISTRATION
LIBRARY, Motherwell Bldg, Regina, S4P
0R5, Can. C Kosack, Head
Holdings: Vols (10,000) Cat
Budget: ($8000)
Notes: PFRA is a Canadian federal
government agency initiated to alleviate the
effects of drought and water shortages on the
prairies. The collection covers engineering
(dams), agricultural economics, hydrology,
irrigation, community pastures, and soil and
water conservation.

SOIL CULTIVATION see Tillage

SOIL ENGINEERING see Soil Mechanics

SOIL FERTILITY

CO —COLORADO STATE UNIVERSITY,
Libraries, Fort Collins, 80523. Marjorie
Rhoades, Engineering Sciences Librn
Holdings: Vols (6000) Cat
Budget: ($5000)
Notes: Water and Soil in Arid Regions
(WASAR) is an index and guide to books,
conference papers, journal articles,
government documents and technical
reports, mostly in English, with the
appropriate subject areas and held by
Colorado State University Libraries. The
bibliographical citations are of selected items
dealing with soils, water, arid lands, crops,
foods and nutrition with certain economic,
political, ecological and historical parameters
also included. The information needs of
developing countries and of those who serve
them are the prime criteria for inclusion.
BC —CANADIAN FORESTRY SERVICE,
Pacific Forest Research Centre, Library, 506

West Burnside Rd, Victoria, V8Z 1M5, Can.
Alice Solyma, Librn
Holdings: Vols (60,500) Cat Microforms
Notes: Incl soil biology, soil microbiology,
soil ecology, fauna, fertility, moisture.
PE —AGRICULTURE CANADA, Research
Station Library, PO Box 1210,
Charlottetown, C1A 7M8, Can. Barrie
Stanfield, Librn
Holdings: Vols (2300) Cat
Budget: ($5000)

SOIL MACHINERY

AL —US DEPT OF AGRICULTURE,
SCIENCE & EDUCATION
ADMINISTRATION, National Tillage
Machinery Laboratory, Library, PO Box
792, Auburn, 36830. William A Gill,
Collaborator
Holdings: Vols (39,000) Cat Mss Maps Pix
Slides 16mm Films Microforms
Budget: ($20,000)
Notes: The National Tillage Machinery
Laboratory (NTML) has a special technical
library comprised of highly selective
engineering and physical science materials
pertinent to soil-machine relations, such as
tillage, earthmoving, mining, soil
trafficability, and vehicle mobility. A high
percentage of the library material comes
from sources outside the US and outside
agriculture. Particularly strong in Russian-
language literature.

SOIL MECHANICS

AL —US DEPT OF AGRICULTURE,
SCIENCE & EDUCATION
ADMINISTRATION, National Tillage
Machinery Laboratory, Library, PO Box
792, Auburn, 36830. William A Gill,
Collaborator
Holdings: Vols (39,000) Cat Mss Maps Pix
Slides 16mm Films Microforms
Budget: ($20,000)
Notes: The National Tillage Machinery
Laboratory (NTML) has a special technical
library comprised of highly selective
engineering and physical science materials
pertinent to soil-machine relations, such as
tillage, earthmoving, mining, soil
trafficability, and vehicle mobility. A high
percentage of the library material comes
from sources outside the US and outside
agriculture. Particularly strong in Russian-
language literature.
CA —CALIFORNIA DEPT OF
TRANSPORTATION, Transportation
Library, 5900 Folsom Blvd, PO Box 19128,
Sacramento, 95819. Eva Caro, Librn
Holdings: Vols (10,000) Cat Mss Maps Pix
Slides Phonorecords Audiotapes Videotapes
16mm Films Filmstrips Microforms
KY —UNIVERSITY OF KENTUCKY, Robert
E Shaver Library of Engineering, 355
Anderson Hall, Lexington, 40506. Russell H
Powell, Engineering Librn
Holdings: Vols (48,000) Cat Microforms
MS —US ARMY ENGINEER WATERWAYS
EXPERIMENT STATION, Library Branch,
PO Box 631, Vicksburg, 39180. Bernice
Black, Chief Librn
Holdings: Vols (350,000) Cat Mss Maps
Microforms

SOIL SCIENCE

CA —LOS ANGELES PUBLIC LIBRARY,
Science & Technology Dept, 630 W Fifth St,
Los Angeles, 90071. Billie M Connor, Dept
Head
Holdings: Vols (14,000) Cat Maps
Notes: Includes agricultural publications of
the US Department of Agriculture,
California and other state experiment station
publications on all aspects of plant and
animal husbandry, soil science and analysis,
including Soil Surveys. Emphasis is on the
Western states and semi-tropical areas.
CA —CALIFORNIA STATE POLYTECHNIC
UNIVERSITY, POMONA, University
Library, 3801 W Temple Ave, Pomona,
91768. Harold Schleiser, Actg Dir
Notes: General reference materials on
agricultural business management,

agricultural engineering, animal science,
horticulture and plant and soil science.
DE —UNIVERSITY OF DELAWARE,
Agriculture Library, 2 Townsend Hall,
Newark, 19717. Frederick Getze, Assoc
Librn
Holdings: Vols (32,500)
Notes: Strong in entomology and ornamental
horticulture. Extensive collection of state
agriculture documents for each US state and
Puerto Rico. Library subscribes to 500
serials (English and foreign).
FL —UNIVERSITY OF FLORIDA, Institute
of Food & Agricultural Sciences, Hume
Library, Gainesville, 32611. Albert C
Strickland, Librn
Holdings: Vols (135,000) Cat Mss
Microforms
Notes: Including journals and monographs,
this collection is a general agricultural one.
The emphasis is on tropical agriculture,
especially Latin America. Entomology is
very strong. The library offers on-line
information retrieval using Lockheed and
SDC data bases.
IA —IOWA STATE UNIVERSITY, Library,
Ames, 50011. Warren B Kuhn, Dean of
Library Services
Holdings: Cat
Notes: Incl soil conservation. Extensive
serial holdings.
KY —UNIVERSITY OF KENTUCKY,
Agriculture Library, Agricultural Science
Center North, Lexington, 40546. Antoinette
P Powell, Head Librn
Holdings: Vols (90,000) Cat Maps
Microforms
Budget: ($110,582)
MD —NATIONAL AGRICULTURAL
LIBRARY, Rare Books Dept, 10301
Baltimore Blvd, Beltsville, 20705. Alan
Susoni, Librn
Notes: A special collection of soil science
publications, manuscripts, maps, slides, and
unpublished journals from the personal
library of the late Charles E Kellogg. Incl
some rare copies of important works in the
field and journals Kellogg kept on his many
foreign travels.
AB —CANADIAN FORESTRY SERVICE,
Northern Forest Research Centre Library,
5320 122nd, Edmonton, T6H 3S5, Can.
David J S Robinson, Librn
Holdings: Vols (7000) Cat Microforms
Budget: ($25,000)
Notes: Also 23,000 government documents,
2600 research reports, 3000 pamphlets and
reprints.
BC —CANADIAN FORESTRY SERVICE,
Pacific Forest Research Centre, Library, 506
West Burnside Rd, Victoria, V8Z 1M5, Can.
Alice Solyma, Librn
Holdings: Vols (60,500) Cat Microforms
Notes: Incl soil biology, soil microbiology,
soil ecology, fauna, fertility, moisture.
MB —UNIVERSITY OF MANITOBA,
Agriculture Library, Dafoe Rd, Winnipeg,
R3T 2N2, Can. Judy Harper, Head
Holdings: Vols (9000) Cat
ON —AGRICULTURE CANADA, Research
Branch, Neatby Library, Rm 3032, K W
Neatby Bldg, CEF, Ottawa, K1A 0C6, Can.
Marcel Charette, Library Technician
Holdings: Vols 3200 Cat

SOILS

AL —US DEPT OF AGRICULTURE,
SCIENCE & EDUCATION
ADMINISTRATION, National Tillage
Machinery Laboratory, Library, PO Box
792, Auburn, 36830. William A Gill,
Collaborator
Holdings: Vols (39,000) Cat Mss Maps Pix
Slides 16mm Films Microforms
Budget: ($20,000)
Notes: The National Tillage Machinery
Laboratory (NTML) has a special technical
library comprised of highly selective
engineering and physical science materials
pertinent to soil-machine relations, such as
tillage, earthmoving, mining, soil
trafficability, and vehicle mobility. A high
percentage of the library material comes
from sources outside the US and outside
agriculture. Particularly strong in Russian-
language literature.

SOILS (cont.)

CA —UNIVERSITY OF CALIFORNIA, RIVERSIDE, Physical Sciences Library, Riverside, 92517. Richard W Vierich, Librn
Holdings: Vols (89,000) Cat Microforms
Budget: ($347,700)

CO —COLORADO STATE UNIVERSITY, Libraries, Fort Collins, 80523. Marjorie Rhoades, Engineering Sciences Librn
Holdings: Vols (6000) Cat
Budget: ($5000)
Notes: Water and Soil in Arid Regions (WASAR) is an index and guide to books, conference papers, journal articles, government documents and technical reports, mostly in English, within the appropriate subject areas and held by Colorado State University Libraries. The bibliographical citations are of selected items dealing with soils, water, arid lands, crops, foods and nutrition with certain economic, political, ecological and historical parameters also included. The information needs of developing countries and of those who serve them are the prime criteria for inclusion.

DC —NATIONAL RESEARCH COUNCIL, Transportation Research Board Library, 2101 Constitution Ave NW, Washington, 20418. Lisbeth L Luke, Librn
Holdings: Vols (17,000) Cat Microforms VF
Notes: Photocopying available.

GA —UNIVERSITY OF GEORGIA, Libraries, Map Collection, Athens, 30602. John Sutherland, Cur of Maps
Notes: Collection contains 291,165 cataloged maps and 192,068 aerial photographs, specializing in Georgia, Southeast US, Central and South America, and Europe. Major subject specializations are topography, geology, soils and vegetation. Special cartographic collection of Sanborn Fire Insurance Maps (7000 sheets).

IN —PURDUE UNIVERSITY LIBRARIES, Life Sciences Library, Lilly Hall of Life Sciences, West Lafayette, 47907. Martha J Bailey, Librn
Holdings: Vols (73,404) Cat Microforms
Budget: ($223,445)
Notes: Incl materials in agronomy, animal sciences, botany, entomology, forestry, horticulture, biological sciences and agricultural engineering.

IA —IOWA STATE UNIVERSITY, Library, Ames, 50011. Warren B Kuhn, Dean of Library Services
Holdings: Cat
Notes: Incl soil conservation. Extensive serial holdings.

MA —MASSACHUSETTS AUDUBON SOCIETY, Hathaway Environmental Education Institute, Lincoln, 01773. Louise C Maglione, Librn
Notes: Largest and most comprehensive collection in the field of environmental education; especially good in the curriculum area. Extensive sections on animal, behavioral and environmental issues, and quality of environment.

NY —ROCKEFELLER UNIVERSITY, Rockefeller Archive Center, Hillcrest, Pocantico Hills, North Tarrytown, 10591. Joseph W Ernst, Dir; J William Hess, Assoc Dir
Notes: Papers of Nobelist Edward L Tatum (1926-1975), who conducted essential research in the genetics and metabolism of bacteria, yeast, and molds.

WA —UNIVERSITY OF WASHINGTON LIBRARIES, Forest Resources Library, AQ-15, Seattle, 98195. Barbara B Gordon, Head
Holdings: Vols (43,248) Cat Microforms
Budget: ($41,103)
Notes: Modern imprints only. Mostly in English, some Euripean and East Asian languages. International in scope but emphasis is on Pacific Northwest. Incl 1,236 microforms.

WI —UNIVERSITY OF WISCONSIN, MADISON, College of Agricultural & Life Sciences, Steenbock Memorial Library, 550 Babcock Dr, Madison, 53706. Jan Kennedy, Dir
Holdings: Vols (186,312) Cat Microforms
Notes: Extensive general agricultural collection supporting the College of Agricultural and Life Sciences in agronomy, dairy science, agricultural engineering, entomology, botany, natural resources, nutrition, forestry, genetics, veterinary science, meat and animal science, poultry science, and soils. Collection includes USDA, USDI, experiment station and state documents.

MB —UNIVERSITY OF MANITOBA, Elizabeth Dafoe Library, Archives and Special Collections Dept, Winnipeg, R3T 2N2, Can. Richard E Bennett, Dept Head; Corrado A Santoro, Reference Archivist
Notes: Papers of soil scientist and professor Joseph Henry Ellis. Soil and land inspections, surveys and reports; stream bank erosion studies; river reclamation projects; field crop experiments; prairie rehabilitation activities; fertilizer experiments; land utilization studies; tree planting.

ON —ROADS & TRANSPORTATION ASSOCIATION OF CANADA, Library, 1765 St Laurent Blvd, Ottawa, K1G 3V4, Can. Charles James, Librn
Holdings: Vols (18,000) Cat
Budget: ($8000)
Notes: All areas of ground transportation and road construction.

SOILS (ENGINEERING) see Soil Mechanics

SOILS—MAPS

CA —UNIVERSITY OF CALIFORNIA, DAVIS, Agricultural Economics Library, Davis, 95616. Susan Casement, Head
Holdings: Vols 6200 Maps
Budget: $10,000
Notes: Agricultural business; Land economics and development; soil survey maps. 170,000 pamphlets.

DC —LIBRARY OF CONGRESS, Geography and Map Division, Washington, 20540. John A Wolter, Chief
Holdings: Cat Mss Maps Pix Slides Microforms
See also entry under Maps and Atlases - Collections

SOILS—MECHANICS see Soil Mechanics

SOJA BEAN see Soybean

SOJA MAX see Soybean

SOKOL

IL —AMERICAN SOKOL EDUCATIONAL AND PHYSICAL CULTURE, 6424 W Cermak Road, Berwyn, 60402. Annette Schabowski, Librn
Holdings: Vols 2000 Pix
Notes: Incl theses and dissertations on Czech life, folk dancing, gymnastics, etc.

SOLANO, SOLITA, 1888-1975

DC —LIBRARY OF CONGRESS, Manuscript Division, Washington, 20540. John C Broderick, Chief
Notes: The Janet Flanner-Solita Solano Papers, containing correspondence, literary mss, printed material, photographs, and mementoes.

SOLAR ENERGY

AZ —ARIZONA STATE UNIVERSITY, Daniel E Noble Science & Engineering Library, Solar Energy Collection, Tempe, 85287. George Machovec, Science Reference & Solar Energy Librn
Holdings: Vols 5000 Cat Mss Pix Microforms
Notes: In 1970 the International Energy Society officially donated its research collection to the Arizona State University Library. Since that time ASU has continued to acquire new materials in the field so that it now houses one of the largest solar energy collections in existence. The emphasis of the collection is on terrestrial solar thermal and photovoltaic applicatons of solar energy. Also incl are wind energy, ocean thermal energy conversion and space applications of solar energy. Books, journals and bound conference proceedings may be located through the general card catalog and public serials list in the library. US Government Documents Department. Technical reports, patents, unbound archival material are located in the separate solar energy room of the Noble Library. Access to these important unbound papers is provided through our computer-based Solar Energy Index (updated biennially). The Index is available for purchase from Pergamon Press.

CA —ESHERICK, HOMSEY, DODGE & DAVIS, Library, 2789 25th St, San Francisco, 94110. Elizabeth Walton, Librn
Holdings: Vols (2500) Cat Maps Pix Slides
Notes: General history of architecture; solar energy applications to architecture; residential architecture; zoo architecture; handbooks, codes, and standards; school and university architecture. Also incl is a large collection of product literature catalogs and samples (uncataloged).

KS —WICHITA PUBLIC LIBRARY, 223 S Main, Wichita, 67202. Larry DePiesse, Head, Business & Technology Dept; Jayne F Young, Business & Technology Dept
Holdings: Vols 800 Cat
Budget: $700
Notes: 456 of our holdings are circulating books. The remaining 344 books are in a special non-circulating collection, the "Energy Collection." Includes solar, wind, nuclear, etc.

NH —TOTAL ENVIRONMENTAL ACTION, INC. (TEA), Library of Conservation, Environmental Studies, and Renewable Energy, 7 Church Hill, Harrisville, 03450. Bruce Anderson, Pres
Holdings: 10,000 Vols
Notes: Available for sale. Library in temporary storage, summer 1983. One of the most extensive private collections. Reports, surveys, monographs, technical papers, bibliographies, and indexes to highly specialized studies.

NM —UNIVERSITY OF CALIFORNIA, Los Alamos National Laboratory, Libraries, PO Box 1663, MSP 362, Los Alamos, 87545. J Arthur Freed, Head Librn
Holdings: Vols (800,000) Cat Films Microforms
Budget: ($700,000)
Notes: Incl 500,000 classified and unclassified reports. There are 25 branch libraries and a central collection. The Medical Library contains about 40,000 vols in the areas of biomedical research.

NY —CARY ARBORETUM OF THE NEW YORK BOTANICAL GARDEN, Library, Box AB, Millbrook, 12545. Fred Strum, Librn
Notes: This collection of alternative energy sources consists of publications concerned with solar energy, wind power, biofuel, methanol, small hydroelectric projects, and wood power.

NC —NORTH CAROLINA STATE UNIVERSITY, Harry B Lyons Design Library, P. O. Box 7701, Raleigh, 27607. Maryellen LoPresti, Librn
Notes: Collection covers architecture, landscape architecture, design and related professions. Additional materials maybe found on art, painting sculpture photography and solar energy design. The library presently houses a total of 28,000 books, periodical and serial volumes to support the curriculum. A product and trade literature file and a vertical file of pamplets are also locally cataloged in the library representing an additional 3000 items of materials available for use. A significant collections of over 50,000 cataloged slides primarily representing the areas of art and architectural history are also contained in the library facility. See Directory of Special Libraries and Information Centers.

TN —TENNESSEE VALLEY AUTHORITY (TVA), Technical Library, 400 W Summit Hill Dr, E2 B7, Knoxville, 37902. Jesse C Mills, Chief Librn
Holdings: Vols (106,900) Cat Mss Maps Pix Audiotapes Microforms
Budget: ($2,025,000)
Notes: The Technical Library Headquarters

SOLAR ENERGY (cont.)

Staff (order, cataloging, information, and administration) is located in Knoxville Tenn. In addition there are branch libraries in Knoxville, Norris, and Chattanooga, Tennessee, and Muscle Shoals, Alabama.

TX —MCDERMOTT HUDSON ENGINEERING, Library, 5900 Hillcroft, Houston, 77036. Chris Ramirez, Librn
Holdings: Vols (750) Uncat Microforms
Notes: Emphasis is on all forms of alternative energy sources and energy conversion.

ON —NATIONAL RESEARCH COUNCIL OF CANADA, Aeronautical/Mechanical Engineering Branch Library, Montreal Rd, Ottawa, K1A 0R6, Can. Louise Fletcher, Head
Notes: This branch library of the Canada Institute for Scientific and Technical Information (CISTI) of the National Research Council of Canada, Ottawa, has a collection strong in aeronautical engineering, automatic control, CAD/CAM, robotics, ocean, wind, and solar energy power, hydraulic and coastal engineering, icing, low temperature research, naval engineering, metals and metallurgy, incl composites, tribology, and air, railroad, marine transportation. Library supported the Council contribution to the development of the remote manipular Canadarm for NASA's Space Shuttle Orbiters and more recently, the Canadian Astronaut Program which will contribute payload specialists to NASA's Space Shuttle Program in 1984. 35,000 monographs, 1200 serials. Report collection: over 500,000 items.

SOLAR HEAT see Solar Heating and Cooling

SOLAR-HEATED HOUSES see Solar Houses

SOLAR HOUSES

CA —ESHERICK, HOMSEY, DODGE & DAVIS, Library, 2789 25th St, San Francisco, 94110. Elizabeth Walton, Librn
Holdings: Vols (2500) Cat Maps Pix Slides
Notes: General history of architecture; solar energy applications to architecture; zoo architecture; handbooks, codes, and standards; school and university architecture. Also incl is a large collection of product literature catalogs and samples (uncataloged).

SOLAR POWER see Solar Energy

SOLAR RADIATION

CO —COLORADO STATE UNIVERSITY, Libraries, Fort Collins, 80523. Marjorie Rhoades, Engineering Sciences Librn
Holdings: Vols (8000) Cat
Budget: ?($6000)
Notes: Atmosphere; upper atmosphere; atmospheric chemistry; atmospheric circulation; atmospheric radiation; atmospheric research; atmospheric thermodynamics; cloud physics; and clouds.

MD —SMITHSONIAN ENVIRONMENTAL RESEARCH CENTER, Branch Library, 12441 Parklawn Dr, Rockville, 20852. Angela N Haggins, Chief
Holdings: Vols (3300) Cat Maps Pix Slides

WA —UNIVERSITY OF WASHINGTON LIBRARIES, Suzzallo Library, Natural Sciences Library, FM-25, Seattle, 98195. Nancy G Blase, Head

ON —QUEEN'S UNIVERSITY, Douglas Library, Kingston, K7L 5C4, Can. William F E Morley, Cur, Special Collections
Holdings: Vols (802) Uncat
Notes: Riche-Covington Collection supports McNichol Collection (history of telecommunications), brings it up to date; also astrophysics, astronomy, solar radiation. Bibliography available.

SOLAR WIND

ON —NATIONAL RESEARCH COUNCIL OF CANADA, Aeronautical/Mechanical Engineering Branch Library, Montreal Rd, Ottawa, K1A 0R6, Can. Louise Fletcher, Head
Notes: This branch library of the Canada Institute for Scientific and Technical Information (CISTI) of the National Research Council of Canada, Ottawa, has a collection strong in aeronautical engineering, automatic control, CAD/CAM, robotics, ocean, wind, and solar energy power, hydraulic and coastal engineering, icing, low temperature research, naval engineering, metals and metallurgy, incl composites, tribology, and air, railroad, marine transportation. Library supported the Council contribution to the development of the remote manipular Canadarm for NASA's Space Shuttle Orbiters and more recently, the Canadian Astronaut Program which will contribute payload specialists to NASA's Space Shuttle Program in 1984. 35,000 monographs, 1200 serials. Report collection: over 500,000 items.

SOLBERG, ERLING D., 1902-

NY —CORNELL UNIVERSITY LIBRARIES, Collection of Regional History, Dept of Manuscripts and Univ Archives, Ithaca, 14853.
Notes: Land economist. Papers, 1942-70; 6 ft.

SOLDIERS

NY —US MILITARY ACADEMY LIBRARY, West Point, 10996. Marie T Capps, Maps & Mss Librn
Holdings: Maps Pix
Notes: Emphasis on the history of the Academy and its graduates. 180 collections; 8500 items. Partially cataloged.

RI —BROWN UNIVERSITY, John Hay Library, Anne S K Brown Military Collection, 20 Prospect St, Providence, 02912. Richard B Harrington, Cur
Notes: The Anne S K Brown Military Collection has been formed over the past forty or more years by Mrs John Nicholas Brown, now of Newport, and contains approximately 40,000 volumes and 60,000 prints, drawings and watercolors as well as a number of oil paintings and about 5000 miniature model soldiers. At its beginning (and still today) the emphasis or focus of this collection has been upon the history of, and the accurate contemporary illustration of, military and naval uniforms of all nations from the early XVII century to the present. In the course of time, however, the collection has come to incl also a vast and related amount of material on military and naval history, military and naval arts and tactics, wars, campaigns, ceremonies, biography, portraits and caricatures of this and earlier periods. It has been probably the largest private collection of such a nature inthe world, and it contains much ms and graphic documentation which is unique. It has been useful to numerous scholars and historians, editors, filmmakers and publishers for research and for illustrative material and has also contributed to many museum exhibitions. In 1982 the entire collection, with its complete card catalog and subject index, has been presented to Brown University, where it is located in the John Hay Library. Special requests are taken care of by phone, mail and appointments with the curator.

SOLDIERS, TIN see Military Miniatures

SOLDIERS' LIFE

PA —TEMPLE UNIVERSITY LIBRARIES, Special Collections Dept, Conwellana-Templana Collection, 13 & Berks St, Philadelphia, 19122. Miriam I Crawford, Cur
Holdings: // Mss
Budget: ($30,000)
Notes: The University archives contains two groups of letters written by former students in the armed forces to the University President and to the Dean, during World War I, recounting their experiences, another larger group of letters written by such students in World War II to the Director of Athletics, the letters of condolence written by the University President in the latter war to bereaved parents, and a file of brief autobiographical accounts of their war experiences written by the student soldiers after World War I.

ON —FORT MALDEN NATIONAL HISTORIC PARK, Library, 100 Laird Ave, Box 38, Amherstburg, N9V 2Z2, Can. Sally E Snyder, Librn
Holdings: Vols (400) Cat Mss Pix Slides
Notes: British and Canadian military life, weaponry, uniforms, from about 1760 to 1860.

SOLDIERS' NEWSPAPERS see Newspapers, Soldiers'

SOLDIERS' PERIODICALS see Periodicals, Soldiers'

SOLDIERS' SONGS see War Songs

SOLDIERS' UNIFORMS see Uniforms, Military and Naval

SOLERI, PAOLO

AZ —ARIZONA STATE UNIVERSITY, Home Architecture Library, Paolo Soleri Archive, Tempe, 85287.
Holdings: Vols 1500 Cat Mss Pix Slides Phonorecords Audiotapes Videotapes Films Filmstrips
Notes: Archive tries to collect everything about Soleri (1919-), incl drawings, correspondence, posters, mss, speeches, etc. See "Paolo Soleri Archive" in Man-Environment Systems, vol 5, no 5, 1975, pp 277-279.

SOLID-LIQUID SEPARATION

UT —EIMCO TECHNOLOGY & RESEARCH CENTER, Process Machinery Div, Technical Library, 414 W 300 S, Salt Lake City, 84110.
Holdings: Vols (1450) Cat

SOLID STATE ELECTRONICS

KY —UNIVERSITY OF KENTUCKY, Robert E Shaver Library of Engineering, 355 Anderson Hall, Lexington, 40506. Russell H Powell, Engineering Librn
Holdings: Vols (48,000) Cat Microforms

MA —RAYTHEON CO, Research Div, Library, 131 Spring St, Lerington, 02193. Martha C Adamson, Head Librn
Holdings: Vols (5000) Cat
Notes: 6000 technical reports, 125 journal subscriptions.

SOLID STATE PHYSICS

CA —UNIVERSITY OF CALIFORNIA, LOS ANGELES, Physics Library, 213 Kinsey Hall, Los Angeles, 90024. J Wally Pegram, Librn
Holdings: Vols (37,000) Cat
Notes: UCLA physics theses; current SLAC preprints in high-energy physics. (592) current serials subscriptions.

IL —ARGONNE NATIONAL LABORATORY, Library, Technical Information Services Dept, 9700 Cass Ave, Argonne, 60439. Hillis L Griffin, Dir
Notes: The ANL library system consists of eight branch libraries with centralized processing services. The entire collection numbers 70,000 monographic titles, 3700 journal titles, and over 1 million scientific and technical reports. Materials may be used by the public in the library by prior arrangement. Photocopies may be supplied for interlibrary loan, for which a processing and handling charge is made. The branch libraries are: Biological and Medical Research; Chemical Engineering; Chemistry; Mathematics/Physics/Computer Science; Reactor Science/Engineering; Materials Science; Solid State Physics; High-Energy Physics/Environmental Sciences.

SOLID STATE PHYSICS (cont.)

IL —ARGONNE NATIONAL
LABORATORY, Solid State Physics Branch
Library, 9700 S Cass Ave, Argonne, 60439.
Yvette Woell, Librn
Notes: Incl 5000 vols monographs, 101
current journals. Materials may be used by
the public in the library by prior
arrangement. Photocopies may be supplied
for interlibrary loan, for which a processing
and handling charge is made.

IL —UNIVERSITY OF ILLINOIS,
URBANA/CHAMPAIGN, Library,
Physics/Astronomy Library, 204 Loomis
Laboratory, 1110 West Green St, Urbana,
61801. Bernice Lord Hulsizer, Librn
Holdings: Vols (34,000) Cat
Budget: ($130,000)
Notes: Solid state physics is our prime
collecting area, and we represent in our
collection very close to complete coverage
both in books and journals.

MA —RAYTHEON CO, Research Div,
Library, 131 Spring St, Lerington, 02193.
Martha C Adamson, Head Librn
Holdings: Vols (5000) Cat
Notes: 6000 technical reports, 200 journal
subscriptions.

MA —MASSACHUSETTS INSTITUTE OF
TECHNOLOGY, Lincoln Laboratory,
Library, 244 Wood St, Lexington, 02173.
Jane H Katayama, Library Mgr
Holdings: Vols (70,000) Cat
See also entry under Communications
Research

NY —CORNELL UNIVERSITY LIBRARIES,
Manuscript and Archives Division, Ithaca,
14853. H Thomas Hickerson, Special
Collections Librn
Notes: Raymond Bowers' papers, 1950-78.

NY —AMERICAN INSTITUTE OF
PHYSICS, Center for the History of Physics,
Niels Bohr Library, 335 E 45 St, New York,
10017. John Aubry, Librn
Notes: Primarily professional
correspondence from the 1920s to the 1970s
of Prof John Hasbrouck Van Vleck, first
American awarded a PhD in theoretical
physics (1922). Won the Nobel Prize for his
work in quantum physics theory and on solid
state physics. Other of his papers are
deposited in the Harvard University
Archives.

NY —UNIVERSITY OF ROCHESTER,
Physics-Optics-Astronomy Library, Bausch
& Lomb Bldg, River Campus, Rochester,
14627. Loretta Caren, Librn
Holdings: Vols (20,000) Cat
Notes: Strong research level collection in the
field and related areas.

PA —PENNSYLVANIA STATE
UNIVERSITY, Earth & Mineral Sciences
Library, 105 Deike Bldg, University Park,
16802. Emilie McWilliams, Head Librn
Holdings: Vols (58,000) Cat Maps
Microforms
Budget: ($49,750)
Notes: This collection includes substantial
numbers of geological maps, and strong
periodical holdings including microform.

TX —RICE UNIVERSITY, Fondren Library,
6100 S Main St, PO Box 1892, Houston,
77251. Dr Samuel M Carrington, Jr,
University Librn
Holdings: // Cat Mss Pix
Notes: Papers of William V Houston, incl his
research papers in spectroscopy, theory of
solid state, quantum mechanics and
superconductivity (15 linear ft).

SOLID WASTE MANAGEMENT see
Refuse and Refuse Disposal; Salvage
(Waste, Etc.)

SOLID WASTES see Factory and Trade
Waste; Waste Products

SOLIDARITY (POLAND)

DC —LIBRARY OF CONGRESS, European
Division, Washington, 20540.
Notes: The Library of Congress collection of
"Solidarity" and other uncensored Polish
materials incl books, periodicals, documents,
bulletins, cartoons, and posters, most of
which are photocopies of originals held by
other libraries.

SOLOW, HERBERT, 1903-1964

CA —HOOVER INSTITUTION ON WAR,
REVOLUTION & PEACE, Stanford
University, Stanford, 94305. Milorad M
Drachkovitch, Archivist
Holdings: Mss
Notes: Papers of Herbert Solow, American
journalist, and editor of Fortune, 1945-1964,
incl correspondence, speeches, drafts of
writings, memoranda, depositions, clippings
and other printed matter, 1924-76, relating
to the communist movement in the US, the
Non-Partisan Defense League, the
Commision of Inquiry into the Charges
Made Against Leon Trotsky in the Moscow
Trials, Soviet espionage in the US, Zionism,
and post-World War II international business
enterprises. Incl some papers of Mrs Herbert
Solow, 1964-76 8 ms boxes.

SOLUBLE FERMENTS see Enzymes

SOMALIA

DC —HOWARD UNIVERSITY, Moorland-
Spingarn Research Center, 500 Howard
Place NW, Washington, 20059. Clifford L
Muse, Jr, Acting Dir

SOMAN, FLORENCE JANE

MA —BOSTON UNIVERSITY, Mugar
Memorial Library, Special Collections Dept,
771 Commonwealth Ave, Boston, 02215.
Howard B Gotlieb, Dir
Holdings: Cat Mss
Notes: Mss, correspondence, etc collected in
depth; incl publications by or about.

SOMATOLOGY

CA —UNIVERSITY OF CALIFORNIA,
BERKELEY, Humanities-Social Sciences
Libraries, Anthropology Library, 230
Kroeber Hall, Berkeley, 94720. Dorothy A
Koenig, Librn
Holdings: Vols (55,000) Cat Microforms
Notes: The library maintains general
research collections covering all aspects of
social and physical anthropology,
anthropological linguistics and archaeology
(excluding classical archaeology). Serials
constitute the collection's special strength.

DC —SMITHSONIAN INSTITUTION
LIBRARIES, Anthropology Branch,
Washington, 20560. Jean C Smith, Asst Dir
for Bureau Services
Holdings: Vols (54,000) Cat Mss Maps Pix
Slides Microforms
Notes: Physical anthropology, archaeology,
ethnology, language and languages; Indians
of both continents.

SOMDAL, DEWEY A.

LA —LOUISIANA STATE UNIVERSITY,
SHREVEPORT, Library-Archives, 8515
Youree Dr, Shreveport, 71129. Patricia L
Meador, Archivist & Asst Librn
Notes: Archives incl catalogued manuscripts
and records, 500 maps, more than 5000
photographs, 1000 architectural drawings,
slides. The collection's primary emphasis is
the history of North Louisiana, particularly
Northwest Louisiana. The 1500 linear ft incl
area plantation records and ledgers; personal
papers of area pioneers, planters, legislators,
politicians, educators, businessmen, and
architects; papers and records of longtime
(1919-1961) Caddo Parish Coroner, Willis P
Butler; the Samuel G Wiener, Sr architectual
records (1921-1976) with drawings and
photographs; the Ted Flaxman architectual
records (1919-1968); the papers (1860-1921)
of architect Nathaniel S Allen; the collection
of Dewey A Somdal,Shreveport architect,
historian and collector, with emphasis on
steamboats, travel on the Red River and
Louisiana history, 1780-1972.

SOMERS, RICHARD, 1778-1804

NJ —GLOUCESTER COUNTY
HISTORICAL SOCIETY LIBRARY, 17
Hunter St, PO Box 409, Woodbury, 08096.
Edith E Hoelle, Librn
Holdings: Cat Mss
Notes: Richard Somers was in the US Navy
during the War with France and the War
with Tripoli. This collection incl lists of
ships' stores, letters to and from Somers
regarding his command, orders, lists of his
crews, receipts for supplies, his Oath of
Allegiance as Midshipman (May 8, 1798),
memoranda, deeds, etc.

SOMERS FAMILY

NJ —GLASSBORO STATE COLLEGE,
Savitz Library, Stewart Room, Glassboro,
08028. Clara Kirner, Special Collection
Librn
Notes: Papers.

SOMERVELL, BREHON

PA —US ARMY MILITARY HISTORY
INSTITUTE, Carlisle Barracks, 17013.
Richard J Sommers, Chief Archivist-
Historian
Holdings: Mss Cat
Notes: The World War II collection,
personal letters, daily logs, reminiscences,
speeches, and official papers of American
officers and soldiers serving in the European,
Mediterranean, Middle Eastern, China-
Burma-India, Southwest Pacific, and Central
Pacific Theaters and in the Zone of the
Interior during the Second World War. Most
of these collections are manuscripts of
General officers, incl Omar Bradley, Stephen
Chamberlin, Lewis Hershey, John Lucas,
William Simpson, and Brehon Somervell.

SOMMER, FREDERICK

AZ —UNIVERSITY OF ARIZONA, Center
for Creative Photography, 843 E University
Blvd, Tucson, 85721. James Enyeart, Dir;
Terence Pitts, Cur and Librn
Notes: Center has significant collections
consisting of more than 25 photographs plus
other archival material such as negatives,
contact sheets, work prints, correspondence,
financial records, diaries, project files, etc.
Inventories of the collections are available to
researchers. Published guides available for
some collections.

SOMMERS FAMILY

PA —PHILADELPHIA MARITIME
MUSEUM, Library, 321 Chestnut St,
Philadelphia, 19106. Dorothy H Mueller,
Librn
Holdings: // Mss
Notes: Hepburn Collection. Consists of the
family papers of John Barry, Patrick Hayes,
and the Sommers and Keene families of
Philadelphia. Includes personal
correspondence, financial and business
papers, and diaries and journals. Dates range
from 1723-1876. 300 ms pieces.

SONAR

FL —US NAVAL COASTAL SYSTEMS
CENTER, Technical Information Service
Branch, Panama City, 32407. Myrtle J
Rhodes, Librn
Holdings: Vols (30,000) Cat
Notes: Costal and ocean technology, inshore
undersea warfare, mine countermeasures,
torpedo defense, underwater sound.

MA —HARVARD UNIVERSITY LIBRARY,
Cambridge, 02138.
Notes: The papers of George Washington
Pierce (1898-1955).

OH —PREFORMED LINE PRODUCTS CO,
Research & Engineering Library, 660 Beta
Drive, Mayfield Village, (Mailing add: PO
Box 91129, Cleveland, 44101). Edwina T
Barron, Librn
Holdings: Vols (10,000) Cat Mss Maps Pix
Slides
Budget: ($30,000)
Notes: Library covering research and
engineering fields emphasizing this subject.
Also aerodynamic and electrical
characteristics of power and communications

SONAR (cont.)

cables and their associated fittings; oceanographic cable fittings and terminations; environmental sensing and monitoring devices. Includes 140 circulating periodicals; 10 bound. Many unpublished reports from organizations all over the world.

SONATAS

NC —UNIVERSITY OF NORTH CAROLINA, CHAPEL HILL, Music Library, Hill Hall, Chapel Hill, 27514. Holdings: Vols (90,000) Cat Mss Pix Slides Phonorecords Audiotapes Microforms Budget: ($60,000)
Notes: Extensive holdings of early theoretical treatises; complete editions; performing scores; music periodicals; reference works.

SONG BELLS see Xylophone

SONG BOOKS—COLLECTIONS

CA —UNIVERSITY OF CALIFORNIA, LOS ANGELES, Research Library, Dept of Special Collections, 405 Hilgard Ave, Los Angeles, 90024. Edward Shreeves, Chairman, Bibliographers Group; David S Zeidberg, Head
Holdings: Vols 950
Notes: 450 books; 500 books of hymns and hymnals; 1800 British and American popular songs and broadside ballads, ca 1770-1865.

DC —LIBRARY OF CONGRESS, Music Division, Washington, 20540.
Notes: Musical aspects of the revolutionary workers' movement represented in the Workers Music League's publications and activities; also, the Composers' Collective, etc.

DC —LIBRARY OF CONGRESS, American Folklife Center, Archive of Folk Culture, Washington, 20540.
Notes: Georgia vernacular architecture, food customs, storytelling, and gospel singing traditions, in local black and white communities. Thousands of color transparencies, etc.

IL —DE PAUL UNIVERSITY, Library, 2323 N Seminary, Chicago, 60614. Kathryn De Graff, Special Collections Librn
Holdings: Vols (900) // Uncat
Notes: The Anita Peabody Sports Collection of approx 900 volumes, incl about 250 periodical volumes, covering such topics as foxhunting, gambling, horse racing, and breeding, along with rule books and song books. Materials cover the middle to late 19th century. A complete run of *The Sporting Magazine*, begun in 1792, is also part of the collection.

IL —NEWBERRY LIBRARY, 60 W Walton St, Chicago, 60610. Diana Haskell, Cur of Modern Mss
Holdings: Cat Mss
Notes: 18th and 19th century secular songbooks, hymnody and psalmody. Small selection of ms song books. Noncirculating.

ME —PORTLAND PUBLIC LIBRARY, 5 Monument Sq, Portland, 04101. Edward V Chenevert, Library Dir
Notes: Collection incl 5000 phonorecords, 400 cassettes. Other collections within the department include sheet music, songbooks, picture file, periodicals, and choral music.

MA —AMERICAN ANTIQUARIAN SOCIETY LIBRARY, 185 Salisbury St, Worcester, 01609. Marcus A McCorison, Dir & Librn
Holdings: Cat Pix
Notes: Secular songs (2000 pieces); American sheet music collection (about 60,000 pieces) is the largest to 1800 and the third largest to 1825. Also the most extensive collection of American psalmody (over 5000 vols before 1880).

MI —ANDREWS UNIVERSITY, James White Library, Berrien Springs, 49104. Marley H Soper, Dir
Holdings: Vols 110// Cat
Notes: Hymms of the Seventh-Day

Adventist faith. The collection begins with the 1849 edition of the hymnal and continues to the present. Not available by interlibrary loan, but may be used at this library.

NY —BUFFALO & ERIE COUNTY PUBLIC LIBRARY, Music Dept, Lafayette Sq, Buffalo, 14203. Norma Jean Lamb, Head
Notes: 103,000 song sheets (80,000 loose; 23,000 in bound volumes). Unique items of 18th century American music publications. Large collection of 19th century broadsides and songsters. Some mss of contemporary American composers.

NY —BARNARD A & MORRIS N YOUNG LIBRARY OF EARLY AMERICAN POPULAR MUSIC, 270 Riverside Dr, New York, 10025. Morris N Young, Cur
Holdings: Cat Mss Pix Phonorecords Audiotapes Microforms
Notes: 48,000 items of American popular music, mostly 1790-1910. Incl books, serials, sheet music, broadsides, anthologies, air checks, broadcasting and music business memorabilia, and correspondence.

PA —FREE LIBRARY OF PHILADELPHIA, Music Dept, Logan Sq, Philadelphia, 19103. Frederick James Kent, Head
Holdings: Vols 400 Cat
Notes: The Songster Collection contains songbooks of all types, campaign songsters, union songbooks and patriotic song collections, covering most of American music history. There is also a collection of 400 slip sheet and broadside ballads dating from the Civil War period.

PA —PENNSYLVANIA STATE UNIVERSITY, Arts Library, 405 E Pattee Library, University Park, 16802. Daniel Zager, Music Librn
Holdings: Vols (14,000) Cat Phonorecords
Notes: The music collection supports a School of Music curriculum which is comprehensive at the undergraduate and masters degree levels. The collection includes scores (collected works and performance editions), books, periodicals, and recordings. The Special Collections area of the library includes the following music collections: the manuscripts, published scores, personal papers, and some recordings of the American composer Charles Wakefield Cadman; 18th and 19th century American tunebooks and 18th and 19th century Pennsylvania German hymnbooks and songbooks; and the Doyle Guntharp collection of field recordings of fiddler's performances and interviews from Central Pennsylvania.

RI —BROWN UNIVERSITY, John Hay Library, Harris Collection, Prospect St, Providence, 02912. Rosemary L Cullen, Cur
Holdings: Vols (200,000) Cat Mss Pix Phonorecords Microforms
Budget: ($15,000)
Notes: The Harris Collection of American Poetry and Plays is principally composed of American and Canadian poetry and plays from the 17th century to the present. Extensive holdings in songsters, hymnals, secular music, musical scores, and sheet music with lyrics (170,000 pieces). Incl large collection of Stephen Foster sheet music and music by Rhode Island composers and lyricists. See *Dictionary Catalog of The Harris Collection of American Poetry and Plays* (Boston: G K Hall, 1972), 13 vols; Supplement (1977), 3 vols. Separate catalog.

SONGS—COLLECTIONS

CA —OAKLAND PUBLIC LIBRARY, Art, Music and Recreation Section, 125 14 St, Oakland, 94612. Richard Colvig, Senior Librn
Holdings: Vols (5000) Cat Phonorecords Audiotapes
Budget: ($6700)
Notes: 10,000 scores, incl chamber music (piano and organ collections especially strong), miniature scores, opera scores, songs and song collections; 30,000 octavos (anthems and choral music of all kinds); 5000 books about music; 8000 phonorecords; and audiocassettes.

CA —PASADENA PUBLIC LIBRARY, Alice Coleman Batchelder Music Library,

Reference Services, 285 E Walnut, Pasadena, 91101. Anne Cain, Principal Librn
Holdings: Vols (8012) Cat Pix
Notes: Separate record catalog of over 10,000 phonorecords; over 4400 music scores. Special index of songs in collection. Over 150,000 pictures.

CA —SAN DIEGO PUBLIC LIBRARY, Art, Music & Recreation Sect, 820 E St, San Diego, 92101. Barbara A Tuhill, Supvr
Holdings: Vols 132 Cat
Notes: A collection of gift sheet music has been organized into bound volumes by date of copyright covering popular songs from the 1800s through the 1950s. Each volume is arranged with a table of contents by title, and is also indexed in a special Song Title Index. Special volumes also cover the hits of World War I, ballads, religious songs and other subjects. Reference use only.

CA —UNIVERSITY OF CALIFORNIA, SANTA BARBARA, Arts Library, Music Section, Santa Barbara, 93106. Susan Sonnet Bower, Asst Music Librn
Holdings: Cat Phonorecords
Notes: The Archive of Recorded Vocal Music: 20,000 78 rpm discs, containing representative performances by almost every opera and lieder singer recorded.

CA —SANTA CRUZ PUBLIC LIBRARY, Art, Music, Film Dept, 224 Church St, Santa Cruz, 95060. Alma Westberg, Librn
Holdings: Vols (1500) Cat Mss
Budget: ($750)
Notes: The music collection is in a catalog separate from the general one. It consists of approx 1700 cataloged books about music; 2100 bound, cataloged books of music incl opera and musical comedy scores; 2700 pieces of sheet music which incl sacred, art and popular songs, and instrumental solos. Good collection of chamber music from baroque to contemporary composers. Also a special collection of 10,000 pieces of American popular sheet music of the period from the 1860s to 1970s incl songs of California. The record collection, primarily classical, consists of about 5500 records.

DC —LIBRARY OF CONGRESS, American Folklife Center, Archive of Folk Culture, Washington, 20540.
Notes: Georgia vernacular architecture, food customs, storytelling, and gospel singing traditions, in local black and white communities. Thousands of color transparencies, etc.

FL —MIAMI-DADE PUBLIC LIBRARY SYSTEM, One Biscayne Blvd, Miami, 33132. Don Chauncey, AV Librn; Barbara Young, Art & Music Dept Libra
Holdings: Vols 9,000 Cat Phonorecords
Notes: Incl 8250 pieces of popular sheet music; 650 song books (mostly popular music).

IL —CHICAGO PUBLIC LIBRARY, Special Collections Div, Cultural Center, 78 E Washington St, Chicago, 60602. Laura Linard, Cur
Holdings: Vols (7000) Cat Mss Maps Pix
Notes: The Civil War and American History Research Collection at the Chicago Public Library is our largest collection. It spans the pre-war sectional crisis as well as Reconstruction. Scarce slavery pamphlets; large collection of regimental histories; manuscripts of US Grant, Sherman, Breckinridge; letters and diaries of soldiers and other officers; original photographs of individuals and field shots; Confederate Battle Plan for the Battle of Shiloh (original); swords, rifles, uniforms, flags and other military accessories. A substantial part of this collection has been cataloged. The museum objects are inventoried (Grand Army Hall and Memorial Association of Illinois Collection). See *Treasures of The Chicago Public Library*, comp by Thomas A Oriando and Marie Gecik, 1977, pp 36-79.

IL —UNIVERSITY OF ILLINOIS, URBANA/CHAMPAIGN, Library, Music Library, Urbana, 61801. William M McClellan, Librn
Holdings: Vols (200,000) Cat Mss Slides Sound Recordings Microforms Books Scores
Budget: ($65,000)
Notes: Introductory, instructive, research

SONGS—COLLECTIONS (cont.)

and reference materials to support work at graduate level in ethnomusicology,, musicology, music education, performance areas. Special areas incl about 2500 pre-1800 music mss and editions of music on microfilm, 2400 graduate music theses on microfilm, a special collection of 30,000 titles of American vocal sheet music covering the period 1790-1970, the Rafael Joseffy Collection of about 2000 pieces of 19th century piano music (incl performer markings), the Joseph Szigeti Collection (700 items: published music, mss, recordings), mainly violin and piano music by various composers. Also incl a special collection of 45,000 78 rpm sound recordings (uncat) of classical music and jazz; a collection of 2900 titles from Chicago radio station WGN. Incl orchestrations, a collection of 500,000 items (uncat) from stock of Hunleth Music Store, St Louis, Missouri, mainly early 20th century imprints of songs, wind music, string music, piano, sets of theatre orchestra parts, dance band orchestrations. A separate collection of choral octavos and instrumental parts is maintained, incl 135,000 pieces of choral music, 30,500 orchestral parts, and 5500 wind ensemble parts. Also, music publishers' catalogues (mainly European and American), ca 126 cubic feet, 1860s-1950s.

MD —TOWSON STATE UNIVERSITY, Fine Arts Bldg, Room 457, Towson, 21204. Edwin L Gerhardt, Curator
Notes: The Gerhardt Library of Musical Information is a segregated representative collection of music literature, phonograph and tape recordings, pictures and artifacts. It incl special sections on Thomas Alva Edison and the phonograph, John Philip Sousa and bands, old popular songs and percussion. Most of the material is out of print and hard to find. It is *not* a collection of scores or manuscripts. A detailed outline is available upon request. Direct all correspondence to the curator, Edwin L Gerhardt, 4926 Leeds Ave, Baltimore, MD 21227, (301) 242-0328.

MA —BOSTON PUBLIC LIBRARY, Music Division, 666 Boylston St, Box 286, Boston, 02117. Ruth Bleecker, Cur of Music
Holdings: Vols (100,000) Cat Mss Pix Microforms
Notes: The Allen A Brown Music Library is the nucleus of the collection. There is a *Dictionary Catalog of the Music Collection* (Boston: G K Hall, 1976; 24 vols). Incl music scores.

MA —BRANDEIS UNIVERSITY, Goldfarb Library, 415 South St, Waltham, 02154. Bessie Hahn, Dir
Notes: Early American Sheet Music Collection. Consists of 30 linear ft of early American song sheets of the 20th century. This collection is unprocessed, spring 1984.

MA —AMERICAN ANTIQUARIAN SOCIETY LIBRARY, 185 Salisbury St, Worcester, 01609. Marcus A McCorison, Dir & Librn
Holdings: Cat Pix
Notes: Secular songs-2000 pieces; American sheet music (about 60,000) collection is the largest to 1800 and the third largest to 1825. Also the most extensive collection of American psalmody (over 5000 volumes before 1880).

MI —DETROIT PUBLIC LIBRARY, Music & Performing Arts Dept, 5201 Woodward, Detroit, 48202. Agatha Pfeiffer Kalkanis, Chief
Holdings: Cat
Notes: Collection of 5000 song collections of all types, as well as individual sacred and secular songs and folk songs. Incl all collections in standard indexes (Sears, DeCharms & Breed, Leigh, etc). Printed indexes supplemented by song index on cards in department, which incorporates title entries for more than 17,000 titles of 19th and 20th century popular sheet music, otherwise uncataloged. Popular music collection rich in show tunes, added on current basis, and in songs by Detriot writers and printed by publishing houses once active in Detroit (Remick, Whitney, etc). Much on Black's music and songs.

MN —SAINT PAUL PUBLIC LIBRARY, Arts & Audiovisual Services, 90 W Fourth St, Saint Paul, 55102. Delores Sundbye, Supervising Librn
Holdings: Vols (30,000)
Notes: The Field Collection of 15,000 pieces of sheet music of 19th and 20th century popular songs. Indexed but not cataloged.

NJ —NEWARK PUBLIC LIBRARY, Art & Music Dept, 5 Washington St, Newark, 07101. William J Dane, Supv
Holdings: Vols Uncat
Notes: 2500 song sheets of popular music, with emphasis on late 19th and 20th century titles. General collection of art songs, sacred songs, folk songs, Tune Dex and standard song collections incl all of Sears. Special song indexes supplement printed indexes.

NJ —PRINCETON UNIVERSITY, Library, William Seymour Theatre Collection, Princeton, 08544. Mary Ann Jensen, Cur
Notes: Orchestral parts and conductor's scores for several thousand popular songs and special musical effects used in movie houses to the end of the silent picture era.

NY —BROOKLYN PUBLIC LIBRARY, Art & Music Div, Grand Army Plaza, Brooklyn, 11238. Sue H Sharma, Chief
Holdings: Vols (4500) Cat Mss
Notes: Over 50,000 items, most of which circulate to the public. The collection contains some reference materials, incl the complete works of many composers; over 3500 popular song folios with our own in-house index for locating individual songs; some rare editions and mss of local composers; and a small collection of rare sheet music beginning with the 18th century. The circulating collection incl standard vocal scores, methods, piano music, etc, and is one of the largest public library collections in the country.

NY —BUFFALO & ERIE COUNTY PUBLIC LIBRARY, Music Dept, Lafayette Sq, Buffalo, 14203. Norma Jean Lamb, Head
Notes: 103,000 song sheets (80,000 loose; 23,000 in bound volumes). Unique items of 18th century American music publications. Large collection of 19th century broadsides and songsters. Some mss of contemporary American composers.

NC —APPALACHIAN STATE UNIVERSITY, Belk Library, Appalachian Collection, Boone, 28608. Eric J Olson, Librn
Holdings: Vols (12,000) Cat Mss Maps Pix Slides Phonorecords Audiotapes
Budget: ($4000)
Notes: The Appalachian Collection incl the Fry Collectin of handmade quilts and coverlets; the York Collection of folk songs and ballads, plus tapes; the I G Greer Collection of Folk Songs and Ballads; the Amos Abrams ballad collection; artifacts, incl the Tatum Collection of household items, furniture, and farm implements; Daniel Boone loom; oral history tapes; the Jack Guy Collection of tapes of area music and photographs; and regional genealogy. This is a very comprehensive study on the Southern Appalachian Region. Separate catalog for the collection.

OH —HEBREW UNION COLLEGE-JEWISH INSTITUTE OF RELIGION, Klau Library, 3101 Clifton Ave, Cincinnati, 45220. David J Gilner, Reference Librn
Holdings: Vols 5000 Cat Mss
Notes: Incl the Birnbaum Jewish Music Collection of 3000 mss; Jewish song index of recordings in the Hebrew Union College collection.

OH —CLEVELAND PUBLIC LIBRARY, Fine Arts and Special Collections Department, 325 Superior Ave, Cleveland, 44114. Alice N Loranth, Head
Holdings: Vols 6720 Sheet Music Cat
Notes: Incl collections by individual composers, miscellaneous collections, nationality, periods of music, style, and general song collections. 20,430 sheet music. Cataloged.

PA —FREE LIBRARY OF PHILADELPHIA, Music Dept, Logan Sq, Philadelphia, 19103. Frederick James Kent, Head
Holdings: Vols 400 Cat
Notes: The Songster Collection contains songbooks of all types, campaign songsters, union songbooks and patriotic song collections, covering most of American music history. There is also a collection of 40 slip sheet and broadside ballads dating from the Civil War period.

RI —BROWN UNIVERSITY, John Hay Library, McLellan Lincoln Collection, 20 Prospect St, Providence, 02912. Jennifer B Lee, Special Collections Librn
Notes: Sheet music collection has almost every piece of Lincoln sheet music known to exist from minstrel songs to funeral marches, memorial songs and campaign songs. Statuary is well represented and incl two Rogers groups, an original Truman Bartlett plaster statuette of Lincoln, and replicas of Leonard Volk's work.

VT —MIDDLEBURY COLLEGE, Starr Library, Flanders Ballad Collection, Middlebury, 05753. Jennifer Post Quinn, Cur
Holdings: Vols (3000) Cat Mss Pix Phonorecords Audiotapes
Notes: Begun as Helen Hartness Flanders' private collection in 1930, given to Middlebury College, 1941. Incl over 9000 New England items recorded or transcribed since 1930: ballads and folk songs of British, American, French-Canadian, and Russian origin; religious songs; fiddle tunes; dance music. Incl research collection of folklore and folksong monographs, scores, tunebooks, journals. Reference: Quinn, Jennifer Post. *An Index to the Field Recordings in the Flanders Ballad Collection at Middlebury College, Middlebury, Vermont* Middlebury, VT, Middlebury College, 1983.

VA —SWEET BRIAR COLLEGE, Library, Sweet Briar, 24595. John Jaffe, Librn
Holdings: Vols 175 // Cat Phonorecords
Notes: Sigred Onegin Collection. Incl 18th and 19th century opera scores; 4000 songs; and phonorecords.

†WA —SEATTLE PUBLIC LIBRARY, Music Dept, Fourth & Madison, Seattle, 98104. Carolyn Holmquist, Head
Holdings: Vols 22,300 Cat
Notes: Books 11,00, music 10,000, dance 1300 vols, 14,000 phonorecords, 28,000 pieces of sheet music. Special indexes: symphony orchestra program notes. World, National and local premiere dates. Song titles in collections, 60,000 cards. Music literature, printed music and sheet music, and phonograph record collections all have separate catalogs.

BC —VANCOUVER PUBLIC LIBRARY, Art Div, 750 Burrard St, Vancouver, V6Z 1X5, Can.
Holdings: Cat Pix
Notes: Book and pamphlet collection. Also, (1) Newspaper Clippings File: 31 drawers of relevant clippings from major newspapers, incl the *Sun, Province, Toronto Globe and Mail, Christian Science Monitor, New York Times,* etc on arts, music, architecture; incl biographical material (16 drawers). (2) Picture File about 500,000 pictures in 150 cabinet drawers, strong in architecture, costume, interior decoration, painting, sculpture, also portraits. (3) Exhibition Catalogs File: British Columbia and elsewhere. (4) Association and Organization File: organizations in the Lower Mainland in arts, music, city planning, etc, begun in 1940s; (5) Canadian Artists Index: begun in 1964, alphabetically by artist, with about 300,000 citationsto reproductions of work and biographical material on Canadian artist from the division's books and other sources; (6) Miscellaneous Index: material not covered in other special or published indexes, primarily of Canadian and local cultural events, hard-to-find informations, etc. Local newspapers, special Canadian publications and British film journals are the most regularly indexed items. (7) Song Index started in the 1930s. (8) Title Index to song collections and sheet music in the VPL collection, approx 100,000 entries.

†BC —VANCOUVER PUBLIC LIBRARY, Vancouver, V6Z 1X5, Can.
Notes: Indexes to folk dances; children's songs; children's plays. No longer updated.

SONGS—INDEXES

CA —SAN DIEGO PUBLIC LIBRARY, Art, Music & Recreation Sect, 820 E St, San

SONGS—INDEXES (cont.)

Diego, 92101. Barbara A Tuhill, Supvr
Holdings: Vols 132 Cat
Notes: A collection of gift sheet music has
been organized into bound volumes by date
of copyright covering popular songs from the
1800s through the 1950s. Each volume is
arranged with a table of contents by title,
and is also indexed in a special Song Title
Index. Special volumes also cover the hits of
World War I, ballads, religious songs and
other subjects. Reference use only.

NY —NEW YORK PUBLIC LIBRARY, Music
Div, 111 Amsterdam Ave, New York,
10023. Frank C Campbell, Chief
Notes: 576-drawer index of songs published
separately and in collections.

OH —HEBREW UNION COLLEGE-JEWISH
INSTITUTE OF RELIGION, Klau Library,
3101 Clifton Ave, Cincinnati, 45220. David
J Gilner, Reference Librn
Holdings: Vols 5000 Cat Mss
Notes: Incl the Birnbaum Jewish Music
Collection of 3000 mss; Jewish song index of
recordings in the Hebrew Union College
collection.

OH —CLEVELAND PUBLIC LIBRARY, Fine
Arts and Special Collections Department,
325 Superior Ave, Cleveland, 44114. Alice
N Loranth, Head
Notes: 71 drawers of index cards, incl 37
drawers of songs, 31 drawers of hymns and 3
drawers of Christmas carols. A "Spanish
Ballad Index" on cards is in the Special
Collections were extensive indexes for
French, Provencal and Italian songs are also
maintained.

SONGS, AMERICAN

IN —INDIANA UNIVERSITY, Lilly Library,
Seventh St, Bloomington, 47405. William R
Cagle, Librn
Holdings: Vols 100,000 // Cat
Notes: 100,000 pieces in the Starr American
Sheet Music Collection, 1800s to ca 1950.

KY —UNIVERSITY OF LOUISVILLE, School
of Music, Dwight Anderson Memorial Music
Library, 2301 S Third St, Louisville, 40292.
Marion Korda, Librn
Notes: Early American sheet music;
emphasis on Louisville imprints. A collection
of songs and piano music. 192 vols of early
music, plus 1000 single items; 82 vols of
Louisville music programs; information file;
additional 85 vols of songsters. Incl "Traipsin
Women" (Jean Thomas) Collection; archives.
No photocopying.

MD —TOWSON STATE UNIVERSITY, Fine
Arts Bldg, Room 457, Towson, 21204.
Edwin L Gerhardt, Curator

MA —BRANDEIS UNIVERSITY, Goldfarb
Library, 415 South St, Waltham, 02154.
Bessie Hahn, Dir
Notes: Early American Sheet Music.
Consists of 30 linear feet of early American
song sheets of the 19th century. This
collection is unprocessed.

NY —BARNARD A & MORRIS N YOUNG
LIBRARY OF EARLY AMERICAN
POPULAR MUSIC, 270 Riverside Dr, New
York, 10025. Morris N Young, Cur
Holdings: Cat Mss Pix Phonorecords
Audiotapes Microforms
Notes: 48,000 items of American popular
music, mostly 1790-1910. Incl books serials,
sheet music, broadsides, anthologies, air
checks, broadcasting and music business
memorabilia, and correspondence.

PA —FREE LIBRARY OF PHILADELPHIA,
Music Dept, Logan Sq, Philadelphia, 19103.
Frederick James Kent, Head
Holdings: Vols 400 Cat
Notes: The Songster Collection contains
songbooks of all types, campaign songsters,
union songbooks and patriotic song
collections, covering most of American
music history. There is also a collection of
400 slip sheet and broadside ballads dating
from the Civil War period.

PA —UNIVERSITY OF PITTSBURGH,
Stephen Foster Memorial, Foster Hall
Collection, Pittsburgh, 15260. Deane L
Root, Cur
Holdings: Vols (1000) Cat Mss Pix

Phonorecords VF //
Budget: ($50,000)
Notes: Collection comprises more than 10,
000 separate American items: original mss
and letters; first editions, and early modern
editions of Foster's music; personal
possessions of the composer; books;
magazine and newspaper articles; pictures
and portraits; phonograph records;
broadsides; and other material.

RI —BROWN UNIVERSITY, John Hay
Library, 20 Prospect St, Providence, 02912.
Mark N Brown, Cur Mss
Notes: The Sheet Music Collection
concentrates on music of American imprint,
incl 170,000 vocal pieces filed by title, plus
80,000 instrumental pieces filed by
composer. Major strengths are in 19th
century music, especially prior to 1830; Civil
War music, both Union and Confederate;
lithographic covers; World War I songs;
political campaign music; and band music.
An additional 100,000 pieces of American
and European imprint remain unprocessed.
See also entries under US - History - Civil
War; American Ballads and Songs.

WI —MILWAUKEE PUBLIC LIBRARY, 814
W Wisconsin Ave, Milwaukee, 53233.
Donald J Sager, City Librn
Holdings: Vols 20,000 Cat
Notes: Good collection of folios of American
popular songs, mainly of the 50s and 60s,
separately indexed. Also sheet music of
American popular songs from 1890-1950.
See also entry under Music.

SONGS, ART see Art Song

SONGS, CAMPAIGN see Campaign Songs

SONGS, CHINESE

CA —UNIVERSITY OF CALIFORNIA, LOS
ANGELES, Music Dept, Ethnomusicology
Archive, 405 Hilgard Ave, Los Angeles,
90024. Ann Briegleb, Ethnomusicology
Librn
Notes: Minimal collection of recordings,
uncataloged.

SONGS, COLLEGE see Students' Songs

SONGS, POPULAR see Music, Popular

SONGS, WAR see War Songs

SONGSTERS see Song Books—Collections

SONGWRITERS see Music, Popular—Writing and Publishing

SONNEBORN, TRACY MORTON

IN —INDIANA UNIVERSITY, Lilly Library,
Seventh St, Bloomington, 47405. William R
Cagle, Librn
Notes: Collections incl papers of geneticists
and biologists, most notably those of Nobel
Prize winner Hermann Joseph Muller, 1890-
1967 and Tracy Morton Sonneborn, 1905-
1981. Also papers of plant geneticists Ralph
Cleland, 1892-1971, and Paul Weatherwax,
1888-1976.

SONNECK, OSCAR GEORGE THEODORE, 1873-1928

DC —LIBRARY OF CONGRESS, Music
Division, Washington, 20540.
Notes: The collections of Oscar George
Theodore Sonneck, first chief of the Music
Division, Library of Congress.

SONNET SEQUENCES (MAGAZINE)

DC —GEORGETOWN UNIVERSITY,
Library, Special Collections Div, 37 & O Sts
NW, Washington, 20057. George M
Barringer, Special Collections Librn;
Nicholas B Sheetz, Mss Librn
Holdings: Vols (3000) Uncat Mss
Notes: The Murray L Marshall Collection,
including several thousand issues of
American poetry magazines; a complete run

of Sonnet Sequences, 1929-58; and Mr
Marshall's editorial files for Sonnet
Sequences.

SONIC BOOM

MA —MASSACHUSETTS INSTITUTE OF
TECHNOLOGY, Institute Archives, Special
Collections, Cambridge, 02139.
Notes: Correspondence, newsletters, fact-
sheets, newspaper and magazine articles,
books and reports of the Citizens League
Against the Sonic Boom, established in 1967
by William Shurcliff to oppose the sonic
boom, stop commercial supersonic transport
production, and influence public opinion and
policy decisions on the SST. Major
correspondents incl Bo Lundberg, Richard
Wiggs, several US congressmen, and CLASB
members.

SONORAN DESERT

AZ —ARIZONA-SONORA DESERT
MUSEUM, Library, Rte 9, Box 900, Tucson,
85743. Janice Hunter, Librn
Holdings: Vols (3000) Cat Pix Slides
Videotapes 16mm Films
Notes: Ecology and natural history of the
Southwest. Carr Collection on beavers. Incl
200 pictures, 5000 slides, 40 videotapes, and
6 films. Separate index of slides.

SOPHOCLES

NC —DUKE UNIVERSITY, William R
Perkins Library, Durham, 27706. Elvin E
Strowd, University Librn
Notes: The Spranger Collection of classical
studies contains 2500 items. The principal
dramatists, Euripides, Aeschylus,
Aristophanes and Sophocles are fairly
comprehensively covered by way of critical
texts and studies up to 1968. Practically all
the texts are represented by Loeb and Bude
translations, and also Didot's 19th century
series. Reference books includes a complete
Pauly-Wissowa, Briquet, long runs of the
Classical Review and Quarterly, the O E D
and some 30 to 40 volumes of codex
facsimiles of Euripides and others.

SOPORIFICS see Drugs

SORBIAN LANGUAGE see Wendic Language and Literature

SORBIAN-LUSATIAN STUDIES

CA —STANFORD UNIVERSITY
LIBRARIES, Cecil H Green Library,
Stanford, 94305. Wojciech Zalewski, Cur,
Russian & East European Collection
Notes: Beginning research collection.

DC —LIBRARY OF CONGRESS,
Washington, 20540.

MA —HARVARD UNIVERSITY LIBRARY,
Cambridge, 02138.

SORBIC LANGUAGE see Wendic Language and Literature

SORCERY see Magic and Magicians; Witchcraft

SOREL, EDWARD

DC —LIBRARY OF CONGRESS, Prints &
Photographs Div, Washington, 20540.
Notes: Swann Collection is strong in the
work of contemporary cartoonists. Among
the 400 artists represented are Peter Arno,
Bil Canfield, Al Capp, Miguel Covarrubias,
Louis Dalrymple, Whitney Darrow, Rube
Goldberg, Thomas Nast, Jose Guadalupe
Posada, Edward Sorel, and John Tenniel.

SORENSON, THEODORE C.

†MA —JOHN F KENNEDY LIBRARY,
Columbia Point, Boston, 02125. Dan H Fenn
Jr, Dir
Holdings: // Cat Mss
Notes: His files and papers from his service
as an aide to JFK, 1953-1964. 45 linear ft of

SORENSON, THEODORE C. (cont.)

mss. Holdings are described in "Historical Materials in the John F Kennedy Library." Copies may be obtained by writing the Research Archivist.

SOROKIN, PITIRIM A.

SK —UNIVERSITY OF SASKATCHEWAN, Library, Saskatoon, S7N 0W0, Can. S Perkins, Librn
Holdings: Vols 1000 // Cat Mss
Notes: The personal library of Pitirim A Sorokin (Russian-American sociologist). The books incl a complete collection of his own writings, notebooks, mss (9 meters), and correspondence, as well as numerous clippings and reprints and extensive journal files. Bibliography of his works available.

SORRENTINO, ANTHONY M.

IL —CHICAGO HISTORICAL SOCIETY, Library, Clark St at North Ave, Chicago, 60614. Archie Motley, Manuscript Librn
Notes: Papers.

SORRENTINO, GILBERT

DE —UNIVERSITY OF DELAWARE, Hugh M Morris Library, S College Ave, Newark, 19711. T Stuart Dick, Special Collections
Holdings: Cat Mss Pix
Notes: Manuscripts etc, incl literary correspondence.

SORROW see Grief

SOTH, LAUREN K.

IA —IOWA STATE UNIVERSITY, Library, Dept of Special Collections, Ames, 50011. Stanley M Yates, Head
Holdings: Mss Pix
Notes: Soth was editor of Des Moines Register and Tribune from 1954-75, winning a Pulitzer Prize for Editorial Writing in 1956 for his editorials which helped establish agricultural exchanges with the Soviet Union. 20 linear ft, finding aid available.

SOTHERN, E. H.

CA —UNIVERSITY OF CALIFORNIA, DAVIS, Shields Library, Dept of Special Collections, Davis, 95616. Donald Kunitz, Head; C Danial Elliott, Asst Head
Holdings: Uncat Mss Pix
Notes: Photographs, clippings, and coresspondence of personalities of American and British theatre in the 19th and 20th centuries, such as Edwin Booth, Joseph Jefferson, Julia Marlowe, E H Sothern, Ellen Terry, Henry Irving, McKee Rankin, and Fanny Davenport.

SOUL

MD —JOHNS HOPKINS UNIVERSITY, Milton S Eisenhower Library, George Peabody Collection, 17 E Mt Vernon Place, Baltimore, 21201. Lyn Hart, Peabody Librn
Notes: Noncirculating.
MI —ANDREWS UNIVERSITY, James White Library, Berrien Springs, 49104. Marley H Soper, Dir
Holdings: Cat Microforms
Notes: Advent Source Collection. Deals with prophecy of the Bible and the Advent hope in historical context. About 3700 items. Materials gathered by Dr L R Froom in the preparation of his four-volume set entitled *Prophetic Faith of Our Fathers*, ca 1946-1954. Not available by interlibrary loan, but may be used at this library.

SOUL MUSIC see Music, Soul

SOULCRAFT

AZ —WORLD UNIVERSITY, Library, 711 E Blacklidge Dr, Tucson, 85719. Howard John Zitko, Cur
Holdings: Vols (15,000) Cat Mss Maps

Audiotapes
Notes: Collection concerns the "frontier sciences." No interlibrary loan.

SOULE ART PHOTO COMPANY

MA —SOCIETY FOR THE PRESERVATION OF NEW ENGLAND ANTIQUITIES, Library, 141 Cambridge St, Boston, 02114. Ellie Reichlin, Librn & Cur of Photographic Collections
Notes: Commercial, institutional and residential buildings, many interiors by prominent architects in Boston and suburbs. Some copy negatives. 1200 pieces; indexed by architect and style.

SOUND see Acoustics

SOUND EFFECTS

MD —UNIVERSITY OF MARYLAND, BALTIMORE COUNTY, Albin O Kuhn Library and Gallery, 5401 Wilkens Ave, Baltimore, 21228. Ann Copeland, Special Collections Librn
Holdings: Cat 1500
Notes: Collection incl Billy "Crash" Gould's sound effects archive; contents incl taped effects and artifacts such as "telephones," "squeaking doors," "chimes," "train whistles," etc.

SOUND MOVING PICTURES see Moving Pictures, Talking

SOUND NAVIGATION AND RANGING see Sonar

SOUND RECORDINGS AND REPRODUCTIONS—COLLECTIONS

CA —BERKELEY PUBLIC LIBRARY, Art and Music Div, 2090 Kittredge St, Berkeley, 97404. Diane Davenport, Reference
Holdings: Vols (20,000) Cat Pix Phonorecords Slides Audiotapes
CA —UNIVERSITY OF CALIFORNIA, BERKELEY, Humanities-Social Sciences Libraries, Music Library, 24 Morrison Hall, Berkeley, 94720. Michael A Keller, Head Librn
Holdings: Vols 80,000 Cat Mss Phonorecords Slides Microforms
Notes: The Library maintains an outstanding music reference collection. It is rich in primary source materials for research, particularly in the areas of opera, 18th-century instrumental music, music theory. Incl 30,000 sound recordings. See the following: Vincent Dukles and Minnie Elmer, *Thematic Catalogue of a Collection of 18th-Century Italian Instrumental Music in the Music Library of the University of California, Berkeley* (Univ of California Press, 1963); Alan Curtis, Musique classique francaise a Berkeley, in *Revue de Musicologie*, 56 (1970) pp 123-164. Minnie Elmer, *Autograph Manuscripts of Ernest Bloch at the University of California; Cum Notis Variorum, the Newsletter of the Music Library of the University of California* (Published 10 times annually since April 1976).
CA —CALIFORNIA STATE UNIVERSITY, HAYWARD, Library, Hayward, 94542. Melissa Rose, Dir
Holdings: Vols (15,986) Cat Phonorecords
Budget: ($21,000)
Notes: The score collection covers the entire range of instrumental and vocal concert music, incl collected works of various composers, and representative collections of hymnals, folk music, musical comedy, and some popular music. Sound recordings range from ethnomusicological collections to electronic music. Emphasis is on concert music, but there is a large collection of jazz and a selective collection of popular music. Separate catalog.
CA —INSTITUTE OF THE AMERICAN MUSICAL, Library, 121 N Detroit St, Los Angeles, 90036. Miles Kreuger, Cur
Holdings: Cat Mss Maps Pix Slides Phonorecords
Notes: Reference materials on the American

musical theatre and motion pictures incl 40,000 phonograph records, sound tapes, and cylinders dating back to the 1890s; record catalogs to 1900; thousands of theatre and film programs, periodicals, sheet music and vocal scores as early as 1830; thousands of motion picture press books and over 200,000 stills from 1914 to the present; every musical comedy script published in America and dozens in ms form, original or photocopy materials from the archives of movie palaces, films and record companies, incl discographies of many major Broadway and Hollywood stars; and thousands of books on theatre, film, broadcasting, world's fairs and other allied areas of showmanship.
CA —LOS ANGELES PUBLIC LIBRARY, Science & Technology Dept, 630 W Fifth St, Los Angeles, 90071. Billie M Connor, Dept Head
Holdings: Vols (12,000) Cat
Notes: Materials on the application of electronic devices, circuits and systems in various fields such as computers, automatic control, sound productions and reproduction, radio and telecommunications. Extensive holdings of materials on computers, peripherals, and software including many texts pertaining to specific programming languages. Complete collection of Howard Sams schematics for radio, television, and other electronic equipment repair as well as historical sets of Rider's Radio and Television schematics.
CA —LOS ANGELES PUBLIC LIBRARY, Central Library, Audio Visual Dept, 630 W Fifth St, Los Angeles, 90071. Richard V Partlow, Principal Librn
Budget: ($71,989)
Notes: Includes 16mm film (4300), VHS video (300), audio recordings (20,000), audio cassettes (5500), picture file (220,000 estimated clippings), filmstrips (60), periodicals (65). Material on all subject areas are included.
CA —UNIVERSITY OF CALIFORNIA, LOS ANGELES, Music Library, Schonberg Hall, Los Angeles, 90024. Stephen M Fry, Music Librn
Holdings: Vols Phonorecords
Notes: Incl 35,000 musical recordings (disc and tapes) of classical repertoire.
CA —UNIVERSITY OF CALIFORNIA, LOS ANGELES, Music Dept, Ethnomusicology Archive, 405 Hilgard Ave, Los Angeles, 90024. Ann Briegleb, Ethnomusicology Librn
Holdings: Cat Mss Maps Pix Slides Audiotapes Phonorecords
Notes: Ethnomusicology of the non-Western world. Incl 7769 tapes and 8957 phonodisc recordings.
CA —PASADENA PUBLIC LIBRARY, Alice Coleman Batchelder Music Library, Reference Services, 285 E Walnut, Pasadena, 91101. Anne Cain, Principal Librn
Holdings: Vols (8012) Cat Pix Phonorecords
Notes: Separate record catalog of over 10,000 phonorecords; over 4400 music scores. Special index of songs in collection. Over 150,000 pictures.
CA —SACRAMENTO PUBLIC LIBRARY, 828 I St, Sacramento, 95814. Dorothy Harvey, Librn, Special Collections
Holdings: Vols 26,000 Cat
Notes: Scores, sheet music, phonorecords and card indexes.
CA —SAN DIEGO PUBLIC LIBRARY, Art, Music & Recreation Sect, 820 E St, San Diego, 92101. Barbara A Tuhill, Supvr
Holdings: Cat Phonorecords
Budget: $4500
Notes: A total of 6817 discs for reference listening in the library and 15,631 discs for circulation, both monaural and stereo. Covers audio and talking books, spoken word, literature, language instruction, sound effects as well as music.
CA —FITZ HUGH LUDLOW MEMORIAL LIBRARY, PO Box 99346, San Francisco, 94109. Michael R Aldrich, Exec Cur
Holdings: Phonorecords
Notes: Collection stored. Important mail inquiries. No interlibrary lending or telephone inquiries. Collection emphasizes books, songbooks, discographies, and

SOUND RECORDINGS AND REPRODUCTIONS—COLLECTIONS (cont.)

phonograph records relative to psychoactive drug-using musicians and their art. Incl many pictures, sheet music, and some autographed or inscribed materials, mostly from the 20th century of works by or about Milton "Mezz" Mezzrow, Billie Holiday, the Beatles, Bob Dylan, and recent drug-related rock music. About 600 record albums.

CA —SAN FRANCISCO STATE UNIVERSITY, Frank V de Bellis Collection, 1630 Holloway Ave, San Francisco, 94132. Serena de Bellis, Cur
Holdings: Uncat Mss Phonorecords Audiotapes Microforms
Notes: Rare and current materials. Music by Italian composers, medieval through contemporary (10,000 scores). Phonorecords, cylinders, tapes, etc (20,000); primarily vocal (all nationalities).

CA —SAN FRANCISCO STATE UNIVERSITY, J Paul Leonard Library, 1630 Holloway Ave, San Francisco, 94132. Susan Quinlan, Curriculum Librn
Holdings: Vols (49,246) Cat Phonorecords Audiotapes 8mm Films Microforms
Budget: ($8500)
Notes: The young people's collection or children's literature collection of 17,843 vols incl books with reading and interest levels ranging from preschool through senior high school. The Marguerite Archer collection of historical children's books contains an additional 3000 vols. Have 19,755 textbooks, 5150 curriculum guides, 1970 pamphlets. Collection emphasizes instructional materials that can be utilized in the school classroom. Professional books and journals and other media relating to educational history, philosophy, research, theories of teaching, etc are in the main collection.

CA —MARISKA ALDRICH MEMORIAL FOUNDATION, Library of Rare Music, PO Box 369, 8451-8491 Swarthout Canyon Rd, Wrightwood, 92397. Anna Mary Anderson, Pres
Holdings: Vols (6000) Uncat Pix Slides Phonorecords Audiotapes
Notes: Collection incl 35,000 recordings, 52,000 phonorecords, 11,000 LPs, 2000 piano rolls (for Amtico, Dew Art, Art Echo), 22,000 tapes, scores and sheet music. All dating back to 1900, all in mint condition. Starting a new collection of videotapes. Reference use only.

CT —YALE UNIVERSITY, Sterling Memorial Library, Yale Collection of Historical Sound Recordings, 120 High St, New Haven, 06520. Richard Warren Jr, Cur
Holdings: Vols Mss Pix Phonorecords Audiotapes
Notes: Incl "classical music" ("concert music") of all types from Western culture, jazz, the American Musical Theatre, spoken material (literary, dramatic, documentary). The aim of the Collection is to document performance practice in the fields collected. See the article by Karol Berger in the *Journal of the Association for Recorded Sound Collection*, vol VI, no 1, pp 13-25. Partially cataloged.

CT —CONNECTICUT COLLEGE, Greer Music Library, New London, 06320. Philip Youngholm, Music Librn
Holdings: Vols (6000) Cat Mss Phonorecords Audiotapes Microforms
Budget: ($12,000)
Notes: Incl 9000 music scores, 11,000 phonodiscs, 100 audiotapes and 40 microforms.

CT —UNIVERSITY OF CONNECTICUT, University Library, Music Library, U-Box 12, Storrs, 06268. Dorothy Bognar, Librn
Holdings: Phonorecords
Notes: 15,000 sound recordings.

CT —UNIVERSITY OF HARTFORD, Hartt School of Music, Allen Memorial Library, 200 Bloomfield Ave, West Hartford, 06117. Ethel Bacon, Music Librn
Holdings: Vols (56,806) Cat Slides Phonorecords Audiotapes Filmstrips Microforms
Budget: ($14,500)
Notes: Cataloged materials incl 12,000 books

on music, 66 slides, 17,000 phonorecords, 1000 audiotapes, 57 filmstrips, 683 microforms, and 26,000 music scores. Also, the Kalmen Opperman Collection: 350 vols of clarinet music, solo through ensemble. Also, the Robert E Smith Collections of 34,000 phonorecords, 150 audiotapes with 80 vols of transcripts from his two radio programs: Your Box At The Opera; Theater of Melody (uncataloged).

†DC —CATHOLIC UNIVERSITY OF AMERICA, Music Library, Washington, 20064. Betty Libbey, Head Music Library
Holdings: Cat Phonorecords Microforms
Notes: A large collection to support advanced degree study. Emphasis on church music, musicology, history and criticism, instrumental and vocal music, solo music for all voices, instruments, and musical forms.

DC —HOWARD UNIVERSITY, Moorland-Spingarn Research Center, 500 Howard Place NW, Washington, 20059. Clifford L Muse, Jr, Acting Dir
Holdings: Vols (106,086) Cat Mss Maps Pix Slides Phonorecords Audiotapes 16mm Films Filmstrips Microforms
Budget: ($854,753)
Notes: *The Glenn Carrington Collection: A Guide to the Books, Manuscripts, Music and Recordings* (DC MSRC, 1977). *Dictionary Catalog of the Jesse E Moorland Collection of Negro Life and History*, 9 vols and Supplement, 3 vols (Boston: G K Hall, 1970, 1977). *Dictionary Catalog of the Arthur Spingarn Collection of Negro Authors*, 2 vols (Boston: G K Hall, 1970). Guide to Processed Collections in the Manuscript Division of the Moorland-Spingarn Research Center (DC, MSRC, 1983). The Moorland-Spingarn Research Center is recognized as one of the largest and most comprehensive repositories in the world for the collection, preservation and dissemination of historical materials documenting from antiquity to the present the history and culture of Black people in Africa, Europe, the Caribbean and the US. Since 1973, the Research Center has greatly expanded its facilities and resources and currently provides research services in all aspects of library and archival research, including manuscripts, oral history, music, prints and photographs and general library materials. The Research Center also maintains professional xerographic, micrographic, photographic and similar reproduction laboratories.

DC —LIBRARY OF CONGRESS, Motion Pictures, Broadcasting and Recorded Sound Div, Washington, 20540.
Holdings: Cat Mss Maps Pix Slides Phonorecords Microforms
Notes: The division's 1.2 million music and speech recordings (6.25 million titles as of 1979) date from the earliest years of the recording industry to the present. Noncommercial material comprises approx 60 per cent of the collection—American radio broadcasts (late 1920s to the present), original field recordings of ethnographic interest, recordings of the Library's music and literary programs, material transferred from government agencies, and unpublished voice transcriptions and popular, folk, and classical music performances acquired from private collectors. Although international in scope, the collection of commercial sound recordings is predominantly American and incl an outstanding selection of pre-1900 releases and extensive 20th century holdings, particularly of material published since 1972. The collections contain sound recordings in such forms as waxcylinder, instantaneous disc, pressed disc, magnetic wire, and tape. Several specialized inventories, indexes, and catalogs have been prepared for portions of the collection.
See also entries under Folk Songs; Poetry - Collections; and Berliner Gramophone Records.

DC —LIBRARY OF CONGRESS, Motion Pictures, Broadcasting and Recorded Sound Div, Washington, 20540.
Notes: The Walsh Collection of early recordings incl an estimated 40,000 discs and 500 cylinders of mostly pre-1926 material. Also incl related items such as

autographed posters, playbills, sheet music, programs, photographs and advertisements.

FL —UNIVERSITY OF MIAMI, Music Library, PO Box 248165, Coral Gables, 33124. Nancy Kobialke, Librn
Holdings: Vols Cat Phonorecords
Budget: ($25,000)
Notes: Emphasis on research editions and performing editions with parts for 2-8 players. Nearly 24,000 musical scores. Recordings are mostly classical, but incl 1200 jazz LPs and 1200 ethnic LPs from all parts of world. *Inter-American Music Archive* is special catalog of Latin American holdings. Collection incl 15,500 cataloged phonorecords.

FL —ORLANDO PUBLIC LIBRARY, 100 Block of Central Ave, Orlando, 32806. Helen M Struthers, AV Librn
Holdings: Cat Phonorecords Audiotapes
Budget: ($5500)
Notes: 7155 LP recordings with emphasis on classical music; also jazz, country-western, easy-listening, spoken arts, foreign language study, dictation. Young Adult Dept has additional 850 contemporary and rock records. Library serves as subregional talking book library for the blind and physically handicapped, maintaining 7858 titles. Also, 681 audiotapes on all subjects. All materials circulate for 3 weeks.

FL —FLORIDA STATE UNIVERSITY, Warren D Allen Music Library, Tallahassee, 32306. Dale L Hudson, Music Librn
Holdings: // Uncat Phonorecords
Notes: General music collection serving the School of Music. Incl 40,000 music scores, 19,000 phonorecords, 1500 audiotapes and 2000 microforms. Special Collection: The Carl Helwig Hungarian-Slavic-Americana Recorded Sound Collection is in accessible storage, with 6000 discs and 1400 tapes arranged as nearly as possible according to Helwig's plan. Tapes dated, but not yet shelved in any visible order. Special equipment would be required to do any transcription; hence study of the contents needs to be made before attempt to rerecord. Some materials are deteriorating. Mr Helwig made radio transcriptions, recorded speeches and celebrations, choral concerts and many other perhaps unique performances. Some commercial recordings, but the great bulk of collection produced by Mr Helwig himself. Also some correspondence, espec concerning recording contracts.

IL —CHICAGO PUBLIC LIBRARY, Music Section, Fine Arts Division, 78 E Washington St, Chicago, 60602. Rosalinda I Hack, Fine Arts Division Chief; Richard C Schwegel, Head, Music Section
Holdings: Vols 50,000 Cat
Notes: Reference and circulating collection of primarily LPs in all areas of music. Strong contemporary popular collection including material by local artists. Limited number of 78s. Growing collection of videocassettes. Listening facilities available.

IL —ROOSEVELT UNIVERSITY, Murray-Green Library, 430 S Michigan Ave, Chicago, 60605. Donald Draganski, Music Librn
Holdings: Vols (28,000) Uncat Mss Pix Phonorecords Microforms
Notes: Subscribe to over 92 music periodicals; record collection of more than 10,000 albums; 8000 pieces of sheet music; pamphlet file; music theses on microfilm; complete file of music publishers catalogs; scores; tapes of old 78 recordings; music education; and electronic music.

IL —NORTHWESTERN UNIVERSITY, Melville J Herskovits Library of African Studies, Evanston, 60201. Hans E Panofsky, Cur
Holdings: Phonorecords
Notes: Complete set of recordings by and on African authors assembled by the Transcription Centre, London. Incl 2391 books and pamphlets on African languages.

IL —NORTHWESTERN UNIVERSITY, Music Library, 1937 Sheridan Rd, Evanston, 60201. Don L Roberts, Head Music Librn
Holdings: Cat Phonorecords Audiotapes
Notes: Materials in the Moldenhauer Archive. Have 31,000 LPs; and 4500 reels of

SOUND RECORDINGS AND REPRODUCTIONS—COLLECTIONS (cont.)

tape. Emphasis on recordings of 20th century music.

IL —UNIVERSITY OF ILLINOIS, URBANA/CHAMPAIGN, Library, Music Library, Urbana, 61801. William M McClellan, Librn
Holdings: Vols (200,000) Cat Mss Slides Phonorecords Microforms
Budget: ($65,000)
Notes: Introductory, instructive, research and reference materials to support work at graduate level in ethnomusicology,, musicology, music education, performance areas. Special areas incl about 2500 pre-1800 music mss and editions of music on microfilm, 2400 graduate music theses on microfilm, a special collection of 30,000 titles of American vocal sheet music covering the period 1790-1970, the Rafael Joseffy Collection of about 2000 pieces of 19th century piano music (incl performer markings), the Joseph Szigeti Collection (700 items: published music, mss, recordings), mainly violin and piano music by various composers. Also incl a special collection of 45,000 78 rpm sound recordings (uncat) of classical music and jazz; a collection of 2900 titles from Chicago radio station WGN. Incl orchestrations, a collection of 500,000 items (uncat) from stock of Hunleth Music Store, St Louis, Missouri, mainly early 20th century imprints of songs, wind music, string music, piano, sets of theatre orchestra parts, dance band orchestrations. A separate collection of choral octavos and instrumental parts is maintained, incl 135,000 pieces of choral music, 30,500 orchestral parts, and 5500 wind ensemble parts. Also, music publishers' catalogues (mainly European and American), ca 126 cubic feet, 1860s-1950s.

IN —INDIANA UNIVERSITY, Music Library, Bloomington, 47401. David E Fenske, Head
Holdings: Cat Phonorecords Audiotapes
Budget:
Notes: Over 33,0000 phonorecords and 37,000 audiotapes. Also a collection of Latin American music, funded by the Rockefeller Foundation as part of the activities of the Latin-American Music Center. Interlibrary loan encouraged. Incl 1000 phonorecords. See Juan Orrego-Salas, *Music from Latin America available at Indiana University: scores, tapes, and records* (Bloomington: Latin-American Music Center, 1971), 412 pp.

IN —BUTLER UNIVERSITY, Irwin Library, Hugh Thomas Miller Rare Book Room, 4600 Sunset Ave, Indianapolis, 46208. Gisela Terrell, Rare Books Librn
Holdings: Cat
Notes: Sibelius Collection. It contains mostly the lesser-known compositions, and includes scores in print, hectograph, and manuscript, many of them unpublished and unknown in the US. Also rare secondary sources, mostly Finnish and Swedish imprints. Also a collection of mostly historical recordings, probably complete up to 1972. Placed in trust in the Rare Book Room by Dr Harold E Johnson, Sibelius scholar, 1982-1983. A preliminary checklist is available. The recordings include many pieces by lesser-known Finnish composers.

IN —BUTLER UNIVERSITY, Jordan College of Music, Library, 4600 Sunset, Indianapolis, 46208. Phyllis J Schoonover, Librn
Holdings: Vols (5383) Cat Phonorecords Audiotapes
Budget: ($16,500)
Notes: There is a separate card catalog for 3800 scores, 4673 phonorecords, and books.

IN —MORRISSON-REEVES LIBRARY, 80 N Sixth St, Richmond, 47374. Harriet E Bard, Librn
Holdings: Cat Phonorecords
Notes: All recordings circulate and are long-playing, monaural and stereo: 4527 adult and 799 juvenile discs. Mainly classical music but incl spoken records, musicals, folk music, rock music and jazz. Popular music titles are indexed by song title.

IN —INDIANA UNIVERSITY, SOUTH BEND, Library, 1700 Mishawaka Ave, South Bend, 46615. James L Mullins, Dir
Holdings: Vols (1490) Cat Mss Maps Pix Phonorecords
Notes: Incl design materials, scripts, theatre music, rare editions, theatre programs, playbills, clippings and periodicals from the 1850s to the 1940s.

KS —SAINT MARY COLLEGE, Library, Leavenworth, 66048. Therese Deplazes, Special Collections Librn
Holdings: Cat Phonorecords

KS —KANSAS STATE UNIVERSITY, Library, Special Collections & University Archives, Manhattan, 66506. Antonia Q Pigno, Coordr; John J Vander Velde, Librn; Anthony R Crawford, Univ Archivist
Holdings: Vols 1000 Cat
Notes: Eclectic collection of scores and books from the library of Prof Charles Stratton. Sound recordings and additional scores from this collection are located in the library's Audio Visual Department.

KY —LOUISVILLE FREE PUBLIC LIBRARY, Fourth & York Sts, Louisville, 40203. Barbara L Pickett, Mgr Reference & Adult Servs
Holdings: Cat Phonorecords
Notes: The 30,000 records are in a closed collection for listening within system only. Records are purchased first for use on one of the two library FM noncommercial educational stations and then placed in the archive collection. No photocopying.

LA —LOUISIANA STATE MUSEUM, Louisiana Historical Center, 400 Esplanade Ave, (Mailing add: 751 Chartres St, New Orleans, 70116). Edward F Haas, Chief Cur
Holdings: Vols 2000 Cat Pix Slides Phonorecords Audiotapes
Notes: New Orleans Jazz Museum and Archives Collection. Donated to the Louisiana State Museum by the New Orleans Jazz Club in 1977. It was formerly a private museum sponsored by the Jazz Club and housed at 833 Conti St, New Orleans, La 70130. Emphasis is New Orleans jazz, incl 8000 pieces of sheet music; 12,000 phonorecords; 15,000 pictures; 1000 slides; and 1000 audiotapes. A guide to the collection is in preparation.

LA —NEW ORLEANS PUBLIC LIBRARY, Art & Music Div, 219 Loyola Ave, New Orleans, 70140. Marilyn Wilkins, Head
Holdings: Cat Phonorecords
Budget: $3500
Notes: 25,000 circulating long-playing records. Also the Fischer collection of golden age singers. Catalogs. The Souchon Jazz Collection has been transferred to Tulane University.

MD —PEABODY CONSERVATORY LIBRARY, 21 E Mt Vernon Place, Baltimore, 21202. Edwin A Quist, Librn
Holdings: Vols 70,000 Cat Mss Pix Phonorecords Audiotapes Videotapes Microforms
Budget: $30,000
Notes: The Peabody Conservatory Library, formerly a part of the Peabody Institute Library (now the George Peabody Library of the Johns Hopkins University) supplies the library needs of the faculty and student body of the Peabody Conservatory of Music. While the collection has numerous research capabilities, it is basically a collection of musical scores. The entire history of Western music is represented through collected editions, monumental anthologies, study scores, performing editions and a large collection of books and music periodicals. This collection is supplemented by a listening facility containing 14,000 discs and an ensembles library containing scores and parts of orchestral, band and chorus works.

MD —UNIVERSITY OF MARYLAND, BALTIMORE COUNTY, Albin O Kuhn Library and Gallery, 5401 Wilkens Ave, Baltimore, 21228. Ann Copeland, Special Collections Librn
Holdings: Cat 16,500 Phonorecords Audiotapes Videotapes
Notes: Phonorecord collection incl classical, popular and ethnic music, as well as spoken word (documentary, literary and

instructional spanning every academic discipline). Classical collection contains an extensive selection of opera. Popular collection is strong in current top 40, jazz, country and synthesized/electronic music. Videocassettes incl language instruction, photography, early television collections and video as an art form. Multi-media sets incl language instruction and photography.

MD —UNIVERSITY OF MARYLAND, Music Library, International Piano Archives at Maryland, College Park, 20742. Neil Ratliff, Head Librn; Morgan Cundiff, Piano Archives Librn
Holdings: Cat Mss Pix Phonorecords Audiotapes VF
Notes: A collection centered around the performance of piano music. Incl 90 percent of all disc and cylinder recordings of serious piano music ever issued. (16,000 phonorecords, 1200 audiotapes, 4000 music scores, 2300 piano rolls, all cataloged.) *Catalog of the Reproducing Piano Rolls in the International Piano Archives at Maryland.* College Park: University of Maryland Music Library, 1983. 280 p. (Publications of the Music Library. University of Maryland College Park, 2) *Microfiche Catalog of the Disc Recordings in the International Piano Archives at Maryland.* College Park: University of Maryland Music Library, 1984. 1031 microfiche. (Publications of the Music Library, University of Maryland College Park, 3).

MA —BOSTON UNIVERSITY, Mugar Memorial Library, Special Collections Dept, 771 Commonwealth Ave, Boston, 02215. Howard B Gotlieb, Dir
Notes: Personal collection of Arthur Fiedler, incl 6000 scores and sound recordings, manuscripts, photographs, memorabilia, library, and test pressings of Fiedler's performances.

MA —NEW ENGLAND CONSERVATORY OF MUSIC, Harriet M Spaulding Library, 33 Gainsborough St, Boston, 02115.
Notes: Incl 55,000 books and music scores of New England composers; the Preston Collection of Musicians' Letters; Firestone Hour Collection of Music; and Vaughn Monroe Collection of Camel Caravan.

MA —HARVARD UNIVERSITY LIBRARY, Widener Library, Milman Parry Collection of Oral Literature & the James A Notopoulos Collection, Cambridge, 02138. Albert B Lord, Cur
Holdings: Cat Mss Phonorecords

MA —HARVARD UNIVERSITY LIBRARY, Eda Kuhn Loeb Music Library, Harvard University Music Library Bldg, Cambridge, 02138. Michael Ochs, Librn
Holdings: Cat Phonorecords
Notes: Contains 34,000 titles (disks, reels and cassettes).

MA —HARVARD UNIVERSITY LIBRARY, Hilles Library, Susan A E Morse Music Collection, 59 Shepard St, Cambridge, 02138. Cathy Balshone-Becze, Music Librn
Holdings: Cat Phonorecords
Notes: Incl more than 8000 phonograph records and 6500 scores.

MA —HARVARD UNIVERSITY LIBRARY, Lamont Library, Woodberry Poetry Rm, Cambridge, 02138. Stratis Haviaras, Cur
Holdings: Cat Phonorecords Audiotapes
Notes: Incl 2300 phonorecords and 3050 audiotapes. For recordings of poets, see *Harvard Library Bulletin*, III (1949), 441-445, and VIII (1954), 65-73.

MA —MELROSE PUBLIC LIBRARY, 69 W Emerson St, Melrose, 02176. Diane E Shaw, Art Librn
Holdings: Vols (8500) Cat Pix Slides Phonorecords
Budget: ($6900)
Notes: Framed and unframed art reproductions (110), slides (2773), periodicals, clippings, sound recordings (3000). Incl the Mary Livermore Collection of Sacred Art, the Odlin Collection, and the Pierre Gendrot Collection of Fine Art.

MA —SMITH COLLEGE, Werner Josten Library for the Performing Arts, Northampton, 01063. Marlene M Wong, Librn
Notes: Special collection: Einstein Collection

SOUND RECORDINGS AND REPRODUCTIONS—COLLECTIONS (cont.)

of Music of the 16th-18th centuries copied in score by Alfred Einstein; 25,982 books, also 34,131 music scores, 42,405 phonorecords, 150 microforms. No photocopying.

MI —UNIVERSITY OF MICHIGAN, School of Music, Music Library, Moore Bldg, Ann Arbor, 48109. Peggy Daub, Head
Holdings: Vols 19,000 Cat Phonorecords
Notes: A collection of current recordings intended primarily to support curricular needs. Also includes 1500 volumes deposited by Radio Canada International.

MI —DETROIT PUBLIC LIBRARY, Music & Performing Arts Dept, 5201 Woodward, Detroit, 48202. Agatha Pfeiffer Kalkanis, Chief
Holdings: Cat Phonorecords
Notes: One of the oldest record collections in a public library (established 1921). Consists of circulating rental collection (all LPs, 19,000) and reference and archive collections (LPs and 78s, 6000). Emphasis is on broad range of concert music in all mediums and from all periods. Also folk music, literary, documentary recordings, and instructional recordings. Main library collection supplemented by independent collections in 15 branch libraries and by a collection in the Children's Library. No tapes or taping facilities. No taping or other copying permitted.

MI —WAYNE STATE UNIVERSITY, Walter P Reuther Library, Archives of Labor & Urban Affairs, Detroit, 48202. Philip Mason, Dir
Notes: An inconographic collection, containing more than 12,000 photographs, closely parallels the events and people described in the labor collections. Tapes, films, and phonograph records pertaining to a myriad of labor topics are also available. Interested researchers are invited to utilize these audio-visual materials in their studies.

MI —MICHIGAN STATE UNIVERSITY, Music Library, East Lansing, 48824. Roseann Hammill, Librn
Holdings: Phonorecords
Notes: 17,987 scores; 5,851 recordings.

MI —WESTERN MICHIGAN UNIVERSITY, Harper C Maybee Music and Dance Library, Dalton Center, Kalamazoo, 49008. Gregory Fitzgerald, Librn
Holdings: Vols 10,000 Cat Phonorecords Audiotapes
Notes: Incl 12,000 musical scores; 10,000 books on music. Collection has separate catalog.

MN —MINNEAPOLIS PUBLIC LIBRARY & INFORMATION CENTER, Art, Music & Films Dept, 300 Nicollet Mall, Minneapolis, 55401. Mary Alice Walker, Music Specialist
Holdings: Vols (94,200) Cat Phonorecords Audiotapes
Budget: ($111,642)
Notes: Collection incl phonorecords (15,000 78 rpm's; 31,732 LP's); audiotapes (1450); and sheet music (60,540).

MS —UNIVERSITY OF MISSISSIPPI, John Davis Williams Library, University, 38677.
Notes: The folklore library of Professor Kenneth S Goldstein comprises more than 12,000 vols and 4500 phonodiscs. Incl a comprehensive 3000 vol collection of editions of collected folksongs and works about the evolution of the Anglo-American folksong, as well as works treating the folklore and folk life of Britain, Ireland, Canada, and Australia. The collection contains specialized holdings on children's lore and games, Afro-American folklore, and folklore theory. The phonodisc collection is rich in examples of American, English, Scottish, and Irish revival.

MO —SAINT LOUIS PUBLIC LIBRARY, Popular Library, 1301 Olive Blvd, Saint Louis, 63103. Mary Lou Allen, Librn
Holdings: Vols (54,255) Cat
Budget: ($10,253)
Notes: Incl music books (7,000); scores (24,000); recordings (discs & tapes, 23,200); music periodicals (55).

MO —WASHINGTON UNIVERSITY, Gaylord Music Library, Saint Louis, 63130. Suzanne Bell, Music Librn
Holdings: Cat Phonorecords Audiotapes Microforms
Notes: Music books, scores, bound periodicals (65,294); recordings (discs and and tapes, 16,114); sheet music, (50,000); choral music (8000). 345 microfilm; 390 microcards.

NJ —ELIZABETH PUBLIC LIBRARY, Art & Music Dept, 11 S Broad St, Elizabeth, 07202. Roman Sawycky, Head
Holdings: Vols (20,000) Cat Pix Phonorecords 16mm Films Filmstrips
Budget: ($10,000)
Notes: Incl 200,000 pictures, 12,000 phonorecords and 700 films and filmstrips.

NJ —FAIRLEIGH DICKINSON UNIVERSITY, Friendship Library, 285 Madison Ave, Madison, 07940. James Fraser, Library Dir; Renee Weber, Cur
Notes: Incl 5000 phonorecords; cylinders; 1500 pieces of sheet music; publishers catalogs; victrolas. The George H Moss Collection traces the history of music and theatre from 1890-1950 through publisher's catalogs; sheet music; cylinders and phonorecords. A published list of the sheet music is available.

NJ —RUTGERS, THE STATE UNIVERSITY OF NEW JERSEY, Institute of Jazz Studies, 135 Bradley Hall, Newark, 07102. Dan Morgenstern, Dir; Edward Berger, Cur; Maxie Griffin, Librn
Holdings: Vols 2500 Cat Mss Pix Phonorecords
Notes: Original collection from Marshall Stearns who founded the Institute. Incl archives of George Hoefer, Charles Edward Smith, Walter C Allen, and other jazz scholars. 60,000 phonorecords. Oral history project.

NJ —WESTMINSTER CHOIR COLLEGE, Talbott Library, Hamilton Ave at Walnut Lane, Princeton, 08540. Sherry L Vellucci, Acting Dir
Holdings: Cat Phonorecords Audiotapes Videotapes
Budget: ($30,000)
Notes: Talbott Library supports the curriculum of a music college which grants undergraduate and graduate degrees in church music, music education and music performance (voice, piano, organ and choral conducting), with an emphasis on choral music. Incl 7000 phonorecords, 3500 titles in quantity of choral music, 30,000 single copies of choral music.

NY —STATE UNIVERSITY OF NEW YORK, BUFFALO, Baird Music Library, Baird Hall, Amherst, 14260. James B Coover, Dir
Holdings: Vols (104,000) Cat Mss Pix Slides Phonorecords Microforms
Notes: Nearly complete collections of *Denkmaeler and Gesamtausgaben* and other historical sets. Strong collection of dictionaries, bibliographies, biographies, facsimiles, works on organology and ethnomusicology. Special emphasis on operas, scores of the avant-garde and urban popular music and music librarianship. Good collection of medieval and Renaissance anthologies, contemporary and avant-garde recordings. Houses Archives of the Center of the Creative and Performing Arts. Collections incl 1000 slides, 14,000 phonorecords, and 33,000 scores and parts. Computerized record catalog in process.

NY —STATE UNIVERSITY OF NEW YORK, BINGHAMTON, Glenn G Bartle Library, Binghamton, 13901. Marion Hanscom, Special Collections Librn
Notes: Frances R Conole Archive. A collection of 50,000-plus sound recordings devoted to the preservation of 20th century vocal art as recorded over the last ninety years. Emphasis is on opera singers from 1900-1960. Over 3000 singers are represented with an excess of 4000 complete performances of over 400 operas.

NY —BUFFALO & ERIE COUNTY PUBLIC LIBRARY, Music Dept, Lafayette Sq, Buffalo, 14203. Norma Jean Lamb, Head
Holdings: Phonorecords Audiotapes
Notes: 64,000 records and 4000 audiocassettes for reference and circulation.

NY —NATIONAL BASEBALL HALL OF FAME AND MUSEUM, National Baseball Library, Cooperstown, 13326. Thomas R Heitz, Librn
Notes: An extensive collection of phonograph and tape recordings of baseball music, interviews, season highlights and game play-by-play descriptions. Note: Restrictions may apply to certain tape recordings.

†NY —STATE UNIVERSITY OF NEW YORK, COLLEGE AT FREDONIA, Daniel A Reed Library, Fredonia, 14063.
Holdings: Vols (8000) Cat Phonorecords Audiotapes
Budget: ($12,500)
Notes: The Music Library supports the curricular needs of a large department of music which now has programs in both music education and performance. Separate card catalogs are maintained for 26,000 scores and more than 12,000 recordings and tape cassettes. The library has a small collection of 19th century American tunebooks, some Lowell Mason materials and a collection of sheet music and dance band arrangements numbering more than 3200 pieces and covering the period from 1850 through the big band era.

NY —QUEENS BOROUGH PUBLIC LIBRARY, Art & Music Div, 89-11 Merrick Blvd, Jamaica, 11432. Dorothea Wu, Head
Holdings: Vols (85,000) Cat Maps Pix Phonorecords Audiotapes Microforms
Budget: ($44,000)
Notes: The Picture Collection, covering all subjects, consists of approximately 1,500,000 pictures, mainly reproductions and clippings from books and magazines, photographs, and postcards on all subjects; The Framed Picture Collection, approx 180 framed pictures, mostly reproductions of paintings from various periods; and The Phonorecord and Cassette Collection consists of approx 3500 reference phonorecords and 6500 circulating records as well, as 1000 reference cassettes and 1500 circulating cassettes.

NY —CITY UNIVERSITY OF NEW YORK, City College, Morris R Cohen Library, North Academic Center, Convent Ave & 137th St, New York, 10031. Barbara J Dunlap, Archivist
Holdings: Vols 75 // Phonorecords Audiotapes
Notes: Kimball Flaccus Collection of Recordings made at City College between 1938 and 1941 under the direction of faculty member Flaccus, himself a poet. Incl are recordings by Edgar Lee Masters, Richard Aldington, Marianne Moore, Robinson Jeffers, Allen Tate, John Peale Bishop, and W H Auden. In some cases these were the first recordings made by the poets reading from their own works. In addition to the recordings, the collection comprises some seventy-five volumes of poetry from the period, many of them signed first editions. The original 99 discs (some of aluminum) have been transcribed onto cassette tape so patrons may hear them without damage to the originals.

NY —COLUMBIA UNIVERSITY LIBRARIES, Music Library, 701 Dodge, Broadway & 116 St, New York, 10027. M Haefliger, Librn
Holdings: Vols (55,020) Cat Audiotapes Phonorecords Microforms
Notes: Incl record collection of early pre-electric vocal 78 rpm recordings. Restricted use. Many rare music items and collections are also found within the Columbia Libraries Rare Books and Mss Division.

NY —HISPANIC SOCIETY OF AMERICA, Library, 613 W 155 St, New York, 10032. Martha M de Narvaez, Cur of Mss; Irene S Frye, Asst Librn
Holdings: Vols (150,000) Cat Mss Maps Pix Slides Phonorecords Microforms
Notes: History, art, literature and general culture of the Hispanic countries (where Spanish or Portuguese is spoken). Incl (18,000) vols printed before 1701, incl (250) incunabula; over (100,000) later vols, plus thousands of periodicals. About (200,000) mss incl ms maps. Printed atlases are in the Book Collection. Some microfilms, chiefly of

SOUND RECORDINGS AND REPRODUCTIONS—COLLECTIONS
(cont.)

our early books. Engraved and printed separate maps; reference collection of over 100,000 photographs; slides: all in Department of Iconography, not in library. Catalogs: *Catalogue of the Hispanic Society of America* (Boston: G K Hall, 1962), 10 vols; *First Supplement* (Boston, 1970), 4 vols. Early books: *Printed Books 1468-1700;* Mss: *Catalogo de los Manuscritos Poeticos Castellanos* (15th-17th centuries; 3 vols); *Medieval Manuscripts in the Library; Golden Age Drama Manuscripts*(the latter in press). Recordings are not entered in the card catalog.
See also entry under Spain

NY —NEW YORK PUBLIC LIBRARY, Schomburg Center for Research in Black Culture, 515 Lenox Ave, New York, 10037. Catherine J Lenix Hooker, Interim Administrator
Notes: A repository for 10,000 phonodiscs and 2000 tapes covering African and West Indian folk music, early blues, and jazz.

NY —NEW YORK PUBLIC LIBRARY, Performing Arts Research Center, Rodgers & Hammerstein Archives of Recorded Sound, 111 Amsterdam Ave, New York, 10023.
Holdings: Vols Cat Phonorecords Audiotapes Microforms Videotapes
Notes: Sound

NY —NEW YORK PUBLIC LIBRARY, Music Div, 111 Amsterdam Ave, New York, 10023. Frank C Campbell, Chief
Holdings: Vols (300,000) Cat Mss Pix Phonorecords Audiotapes Microforms
Notes: Described in *Dictionary Catalog of the Music Collection, The Research Libraries of the New York Public Library,* 33 vols (532,000 cards), 1964, $2190; Supplement 1, 1 vol (17,000 cards), 1966, $100. Also, *Bibliographic Guide to Music,* 2 vols, 1975-1976, $70 ea. Literature pertaining to virtually all musical subjects, and scores covering the broadest range of musical style and history are represented in this catalog. Special strengths of the collection incl folk songs, 18th and 19th-century librettos, full scores of operas, complete works, historical editions, Beethoven, Americana, American music, periodicals, vocal music, literature on the voice, programs, record catalogs, and mss in detail; sheet music, 355,414; sound recordings, 400,000; clippings and programs, 2 million; broadsides, 1821; songsters, 375; pictures, 51,002; ms, 29,877.

NY —NEW YORK PUBLIC LIBRARY, General Library of the Performing Arts, 111 Amsterdam Ave, New York, 10023. John Hildreth, Recorded Music Specialist; Janice Frank, Librn
Holdings: Cat Phonorecords Audiotapes
Budget: $42,660
Notes: Listening facilities are available in the building. 28,000 circulating music records; 4200 spoken records, incl collection of dance instruction records.

NY —US COMMITTEE FOR UNICEF, Information Center on Children's Cultures, 331 E 38 St, New York, 10016. Melinda Greenblatt, Chief Librn
Holdings: Vols (17,500) Cat Pix Slides Phonorecords Films Filmstrips
Notes: Social and cultural aspects of lives of children from developing countries. Especially strong in the area of school textbooks from Near Eastern Asian, African, Latin American, Caribbean, and Pacific Area countries; holidays and celebrations related to children all over the world; children's books in English which describe child life in other countries. Especially strong collection of folklore, and folklore of children, from all regions mentioned above.

NY —STATE UNIVERSITY OF NEW YORK, COLLEGE AT PLATTSBURGH, Feinberg Library, Special Collections, 153 Hawkins Hall, Plattsburgh, 12901. Joseph G Swinyer, Librn
Notes: 100 discs.
See also entry under New York (State) - History.

NY —EASTMAN SCHOOL OF MUSIC, Sibley Music Library, 44 Swan St, Rochester, 14604. Ruth Watanabe, Librn
Holdings: Vols (360,000) Cat Mss Pix Phonorecords Microforms
Notes: Research material for music theory, history, and performance. Incl an additional uncataloged collection of 300,000 pieces. The Sibley Music Library is a full-service branch of the University of Rochester Library System. Bibliographical lists of journals prepared twice annually. Historical items described in *University of Rochester Library Bulletin*. List of new reference work compiled quarterly. Also incl music scores.

NY —ROCHESTER MUSEUM & SCIENCE CENTER, Strasenburgh Planetarium, Todd Library, 663 East Ave, Rochester, 14607. Donald Hall, Dir
Holdings: Vols 500 Cat Maps Slides Phonorecords
Notes: Also, 8300 slides of astronomical and aeronautical subjects; 400 recordings; 150 celestial charts.

NY —YONKERS PUBLIC LIBRARY, Grinton I Will Library, 1500 Central Park Ave, Yonkers, 10701. Joan W Stevenson, Head of Fine Arts Dept
Holdings: Vols (13,000) Cat Phonorecords
Budget: ($36,000)
Notes: Incl periodicals, 70 titles (ca 15 yr back issues); 27 vertical file drawers (18 on artists & musicians); 1230 slides; 2200 music scores; cat; sheet music, ca 1200 titles; 140 libretti; 13,000 phonograph albums; cat; 1000 cassettes. Books, scores, phonograph albums, cassettes are cataloged. Rare collection of 57 test pressings of Geraldine Farrar, some of which have never been issued.

NC —APPALACHIAN STATE UNIVERSITY, Music Library, Broyhill Music Center, Boone, 28608. Joan O Falconer, Librn
Holdings: Vols 1800 Phonorecords
Budget: ($9500)
Notes: A collection of music scores, chamber music, and 7000 recordings, supported by basic reference books. Former emphasis on music education materials now being expanded to include extensive performance materials and titles appropriate to a liberal arts curriculum through the master's degree level. The University Library (Belk Library) houses the main collection of book materials in music. Incl 12,000 music scores and parts and 7000 phonorecords.

NC —UNIVERSITY OF NORTH CAROLINA, CHAPEL HILL, Music Library, Hill Hall, Chapel Hill, 27514.
Holdings: Vols (90,000) Cat Mss Pix Slides Phonorecords Audiotapes Microforms
Budget: ($60,000)

NC —DUKE UNIVERSITY, William R Perkins Library, Durham, 27706. Elvin E Strowd, University Librn
Notes: Books, serials and pamphlets (2,820, 527); music scores (31,551); motion pictures (285); microforms (1,055,627); tapes, cassettes and phonorecords, the library is a depository for Radio Canada International recordings, (2289); and manuscripts, US Government publications, maps, and broadsides, additions in all formats are ongoing.

NC —CUMBERLAND COUNTY PUBLIC LIBRARY, North Carolina Foreign Language Center, 328 Gillespie St, Fayetteville, 28301. Patrick M Valentine, Coordinator
Notes: The larger music record collections are in Arabic, French, German, Hungarian, Korean, Japanese, Russian, Spanish and Swedish. The records often incl poetry and prose readings as well as folk, dance and popular music. The Center also carries educational sound filmstrips in French, German, Italian, and Spanish. The North Carolina Foreign Language Center offers records and cassette tapes with instruction booklets for learning or maintaining proficiency in the languages. Languages available are Afrikaan, Albanian, Amharic, Arabic, Armenian, Baluchi, Bulgarian, Burmese, Cambodian, Chinese (Cantonese and Mandarin), Czech, Danish, Dutch,

Finnish, French, German, Greek (ancient and modern), Hausa, Hebrew, Hindi, Hungarian, Indonesian, Irish-Gaelic, Italian, Japanese, Kirundi, Korean, Latin, Lithuanian, Luganda, Malay, More, Norwegian, Persian, Polish, Portuguese, Romanian, Russian, Scottish-Gaelic, Serbo-Croatian, Shona, Sinhalese, Slovak, Spanish, Swahili, Swedish, Tagalog, Taiwanese, Telugu, Thai, Turkish, Twi, Ukrainian, Urdu, Vietnamese, Yiddish, and Yoruba.

NC —MARS HILL COLLEGE, Music Dept, Music Library, Mars Hill, 28754. Pat McManus, Music Librn
Holdings: Vols 8000 Cat Phonorecords
Budget: $3500

OH —HEBREW UNION COLLEGE-JEWISH INSTITUTE OF RELIGION, Klau Library, 3101 Clifton Ave, Cincinnati, 45220. David J Gilner, Reference Librn
Holdings: Vols 5000 Cat Mss Phonorecords
Notes: Incl the Birnbaum Jewish Music Collection of 3000 mss; Jewish song index of recordings in the Hebrew Union College collection.

OH —PUBLIC LIBRARY OF CINCINNATI & HAMILTON COUNTY, Films and Recordings Center, 800 Vine St, Cincinnati, 45202. Robert Hudzik, Head
Holdings: Cat
Notes: Emphasis is upon classical and spoken arts, with strong holdings in jazz, folk, children's and local artists. The Films and Recordings Center also circulates 5269 (cataloged) audiotapes in a similar subject range, and incl motivational, old radio and contemporary issues programming.

OH —CASE WESTERN RESERVE UNIVERSITY, Kulas Music Library, 11118 Bellflower Rd, Cleveland, 44106. Timothy Robson, Music Librn
Notes: Containing deposit of a collection of some 800 records of music and the spoken word in French, English, and Spanish presented by Radio Canada International in Montreal.

OH —CLEVELAND PUBLIC LIBRARY, Fine Arts and Special Collections Department, 325 Superior Ave, Cleveland, 44114. Alice N Loranth, Head
Holdings: Cat Phonorecords Audiotapes
Notes: Library collection in the subject departments incl: classical, modern, jazz and popular musical recordings. Drama, poetry and prose readings. Language learning records are available in several modern languages. Also cassettes.

OR —UNIVERSITY OF OREGON LIBRARY, Music Dept, Eugene, 97403. Leslie K Greer, Music Librn
Holdings: Cat Phonorecords Audiotapes
Budget: $8,000
Notes: Incl 25,500 sound recordings.

OR —LIBRARY ASSOCIATION OF PORTLAND, Art & Music Dept, 801 S W Tenth Ave, Portland, 97205. Barbara K Padden, Librn
Holdings: Vols Cat Pix Slides Phonorecords
Notes: Art book titles: 21,325; music book titles (incl dance books): 10,800; sheet music titles: 19,550; slides on art subjects: about 12,000; phonorecord albums: 27,000; picture clippings: about 2 million; color reproductions of old and modern masters: about 640.

PA —FREE LIBRARY OF PHILADELPHIA, Music Dept, Drinker Library of Choral Music, Logan Sq, Philadelphia, 19103. Frederick James Kent, Head
Holdings: Cat Phonorecords
Budget: $7000
Notes: Musical recordings in every area. 19, 000 33rpms; 21,000 78rpms. Archival collection of 78s, primarily Victor Red Seals, 1927-1945. Use restricted to on-site listening only. Special circulating collection of records (over 3000) for loan to local residents only.

PA —CARNEGIE LIBRARY OF PITTSBURGH, Music and Art Dept, 4400 Forbes Ave, Pittsburgh, 15213. Ida Reed, Dept Head
Holdings: Vols 96,000 Cat Mss Pix Phonorecords
Notes: Emphasis in lending collection on practical editions of music since 1600. Reference collection incl early and first

SOUND RECORDINGS AND REPRODUCTIONS—COLLECTIONS (cont.)

editions, monumental sets, historical anthologies, bibliographies. Thematic catalogs, dictionaries, encyclopedias, etc. Files of periodicals begin with year 1722 and incl notable collection of 19th century American music journals. Also, 30,000 phonorecords. Library compiles indexes of orchestral performances, piano, song, organ, and violin materials.

PA —UNIVERSITY OF PITTSBURGH, Music Library, B-31 Music Bldg, Pittsburgh, 15260. Norris L Stephens, Music Librn
Holdings: Vols 35,000 Cat Mss Maps Pix Slides Phonorecords Microforms
Notes: Over 20,000 phonorecords. Emphasis on opera, classical western art forms, jazz, ethnomusicology and electronic music.

PA —PENNSYLVANIA STATE UNIVERSITY, Rare Book Room, University Park, 16802. Charles Mann, Chief, Rare Books and Special Collections
Holdings: Vols (13,000) Cat Mss Pix Phonorecords
Budget: ($24,000)
Notes: The Allison-Shelley Collection of translations of German literature, history, science, medicine, biography, children's literature, and other cultural manifestations into English. Incl 3000 letters and mss of British and American translations of German writings. Also phonograph records of German art songs. Further, the collection contains a large collection of Bayard Taylor's works, letters, and mss. An annotated exhibition catalog of selected items is available from the Office of the Dean of Libraries.

PA —PENNSYLVANIA STATE UNIVERSITY, Arts Library, 405 E Pattee Library, University Park, 16802. Daniel Zager, Music Librn
Holdings: Vols 13,000 Cat Phonorecords
Notes: The Special Collections area of the library holds ca 1000 uncataloged recordings of lieder.
See also entry under Music.

PA —WEST CHESTER UNIVERSITY, Music Library, Swope Hall, University Ave, West Chester, 19383. Ruth I Weidner, Music Librn
Budget: ($26,000)
Notes: Large basic music collection (scores, sheet music, and 21,000 phonorecords) which is especially strong in collected works, historical editions, opera, keyboard music, and miniature scores. Incl 24,000 music scores. All music is fully cataloged. Scope of collection is broad and excludes only music education and curriculum materials. Collection does not include books about music or periodicals but does have about 500 reference books. For the most part collection is music published during or available within the past twenty years.

SC —COLLEGE OF CHARLESTON LIBRARY, Special Collections Dept, Charleston, 29401.
Notes: The Kenneth Hanson Archives of Sound Recordings chronicling the growth of the recording industry through the 1940s. Over 400 cylinder records of marches, popular songs, vaudeville acts, and speeches.

SC —CONVERSE COLLEGE, Gwathmey Library, Spartanburg, 29301. Darlene E Fawver, Music Librn
Holdings: Phonorecords
Notes: Incl 10,000 phonorecords.

SD —UNIVERSITY OF SOUTH DAKOTA, Shrine to Music Museum, USD Box 194, Vermillion, 57069. Andre P Larson, Dir
Holdings: Phonorecords
Budget: ($205,036)
Notes: The Shrine to Music Museum is one of America's major collections of musical resource materials, incl more than 4000 antique musical instruments from all over the world, plus an extensive supporting library of several thousand books, music, periodicals, recordings, photographs, and related musical memorabilia. The collection of 19th and early 20th-century sheet music

and music for wind instruments is probably the most extensive in the country. Inquiries and visits are welcomed.

TN —COUNTRY MUSIC FOUNDATION, Library & Media Center, 4 Music Sq E, Nashville, 37203. Charlie Seemann, Dir
Holdings: Vols (6000) Mss Pix Slides Phonorecords Audiotapes Videotapes 16mm Films Microforms
Notes: The largest collection in the world dealing with American country music. Related subject areas are also included; Anglo-American folksong, popular music in general (soul, jazz, rock and roll, rhythm and blues, etc), recorded sound technology, music law.

TN —VANDERBILT UNIVERSITY, Music Library, 419 21st Ave South, Nashville, 37203. Shirley Marie Watts, Librn
Holdings: Vols (23,000) Cat Phonorecords Audiotapes Microforms
Budget: ($10,600)
Notes: Tapes of lectures, master classes and recitals incl in seminars in piano teaching held at George Peabody College for Teachers, 1970-76. Also, Francis Robinson Collection of Sound Recordings. 23,000 books and musical scores, 10,000 phonorecords, 350 audiotapes, 1650 microforms. All materials cataloged.

TX —DALLAS PUBLIC LIBRARY, Central Library, Humanities Division, 1515 Young St, Dallas, 75201. Richard L Waters, Acting Dir; Ron Boyd, Fiction Librn
Holdings: Vols Cat Microforms
Notes: Cited in Tymn, Marshall, Roger C Schlobin, and L W Currey. A Research Guide to Science Fiction New York: Garland, 1977. The science fiction collection now exceeds 8000 circulating vols. In addition, the Library purchased in 1983 the personal library and archives of Brian Aldiss (which will be for reference use only). This collection consists of 350 books by Aldiss, 1900 other books by other science fiction writers, 800 issues of science fiction and fantasy periodicals, 100 vols concerning astronautics and space travel, over 1000 typescript pages of mss (incl 6 corrected mss), several sound recordings (incl BBC tapes), and a considerable amount of correspondence.

TX —NORTH TEXAS STATE UNIVERSITY, Audio Center, Box 5188, NT Station, Denton, 76203. Morris Martin, Music Librn
Holdings: Cat Pix Phonorecords Audiotapes
Notes: Collection of approximately 35,000 recordings (disc, tape, cassette) of a broad range of music (classical, popular, jazz, ethnic, historical, and current). Archival collections of Duke Ellington, Arturo Toscanini, Don Gillis, jazz (incl the famed One O'Clock Lab Band), others in the NTSU School of Music, including performing groups, ensembles, student and faculty recitals.

TX —SOUTHWESTERN BAPTIST THEOLOGICAL SEMINARY, Music Library, Fort Worth, 76122. Phillip W Sims, Librn
Holdings: Vols (19,000) Cat
Budget: ($30,000)
Notes: Incl in the Treasure Section are approx 250 tune books, plus many very old hymnals and other antiquarian items. Incl 97,000 pieces of sheet music, 24,000 scores, 7500 phonograph records and 3500 audiocassettes. The entire collection is cataloged except the periodicals and about one fourth of the sheet music.

TX —BAYLOR UNIVERSITY, Moody Memorial Library, Crouch Music Library, 1312 S Third St, PO Box 6307, Waco, 76706. Avery T Sharp, Librn
Holdings: Vols (75,000) Cat Phonorecords Audiotapes Microforms
Budget: ($48,000)
Notes: Areas of strength: The Frances G Spencer Collection of American Printed Music, 30,000 items of popular sheet music of the 19th and 20th centuries, completely cataloged; complete collection of Denkmaler, Gesamtausgeben and other historical sets, periodicals, dictionaries, library catalogs, thematic indexes, etc; 55,000 volumes of music scores and music literature; 20,000

phonorecords, tapes and microfilm; 400 early American hymn books. Collection has separate catalog.

UT —UTAH STATE UNIVERSITY, Merrill Library, Department of Special Collections & Archives, Logan, 84322. A J Simmonds, Curator; Jeanie F Simmonds, Archivist; Bradford R Cole, Mss Librn
Holdings: Vols 1100 Uncat Mss Pix Slides Phonorecords
Notes: The Austin E and Alla S Fife folklore archive of western, cowboy, and folksong materials. Over 300 pictures; 4200 slides; 800 field recordings; 75 ft of ms items. Complete card index to folklore themes in the collection. See Catalog of recordings in "A Bibliography of the Archives of the Utah Humanities Research Foundation," Bulletin of the University of Utah, vol XXXVIII, no 9 (Dec 1947): pp 26-35; description of Fife Mormon collection in Western Folklore Quarterly, vol VII, no 3 (July 1948): pp 299-301; description of "Fife Collection of Western American Folksong and Folklore" in The Folklore and Folk Music Archivist, vol VII, no 2 (Spring 1964): pp 41-44.

UT —UTAH STATE UNIVERSITY, Merrill Library, Department of Special Collections & Archives, Logan, 84322. A J Simmonds, Curator; Jeanie F Simmonds, Archivist; Bradford R Cole, Mss Librn
Notes: 3000 Edison cylinders and diamond disc recordings, 1904-1925. Special author, title, and music-type registers available in the library.

VT —MIDDLEBURY COLLEGE, Starr Library, Flanders Ballad Collection, Middlebury, 05753. Jennifer Post Quinn, Cur
Holdings: Vols (3000) Cat Mss Pix Phonorecords Audiotapes
Notes: Begun as Helen Hartness Flanders' private collection in 1930, given to Middlebury College, 1941. Incl over 9000 New England items recorded or transcribed since 1930: ballads and folk songs of British, American, French-Canadian, and Russian origin; religious songs; fiddle tunes; dance music. Incl research collection of folklore and folksong monographs, scores, tunebooks, journals. Reference: Quinn, Jennifer Post. An Index to the Field Recordings in the Flanders Ballad Collection at Middlebury College, Middlebury, Vermont Middlebury College, 1983.

VA —UNIVERSITY OF VIRGINIA, Alderman Library, Manuscripts Dept, Charlottesville, 22901. Edmund Berkeley Jr, Cur
Holdings: Cat Mss Pix Phonorecords
Notes: Virginia Folklore Collection (23,000 items) incl the following collection: Virginia WPA Folklore Files, compiled ca 1936-1943, under US Works Project Administration, ca 8000 items. Black and white folklore and folk music collected by field workers from informants throughout Virginia. Incl ms reports, phonorecords. Described in Rosenberg, Bruce A (comp) The Folksongs of Virginia: A Checklist of the WPA Holdings in the Alderman Library, University of Virginia (Charlottesville: University Press of Virginia, 1969); also, typescript and computer printed guides-Charles L Perdue Jr, and others (comps), The White Folklore of the Virginia WPA Files: A Checklist... (Charlottesville, 1973); Thomas Barden and others (comps), Afro-American Folklore of the WPA Folklore Files in the Alderman Library... (Charlottesville, 1973).

VA —UNIVERSITY OF VIRGINIA, Alderman Library, Music Collection, Charlottesville, 22901. Evan Bonds, Music Librn
Holdings: Vols (38,000) Cat Mss Phonorecords Microforms
Budget: ($50,000)
Notes: Sizeable amount of rare book material: extensive ms collections, principally of traditional music; extensive collection of miscellaneous imprints of performing editions; valuable collection of 18th-century imprints incl rare tutors, etc in the Alexander MacKay-Smith Collection; the Monticello Music Collection; printed and ms

SOUND RECORDINGS AND REPRODUCTIONS—COLLECTIONS (cont.)

collection of the music of John Powell; extensive collections, ms and typescript, and discs of traditional music; some Randall Thompson mss; 250 tapes; 9000 phonorecords.

VA —SWEET BRIAR COLLEGE, Library, Sweet Briar, 24595. John Jaffe, Librn
Holdings: Vols 175 // Cat Phonorecords
Notes: Sigred Onegin Collection. Incl 18th and 19th century opera scores; 4000 songs; and phonorecords.

†WA —SEATTLE PUBLIC LIBRARY, Music Dept, Fourth & Madison, Seattle, 98104. Carolyn Holmquist, Head
Notes: 30,362 phonorecords. Separate catalog.

WA —UNIVERSITY OF WASHINGTON LIBRARIES, Music Library, DN-10, Seattle, 98195. David A Wood, Music Librn
Holdings: Vols 36,697 Cat Phonorecords Audiotapes
Budget: ($7373)
Notes: Incl 28,874 phonorecords and 7,823 audiotapes.

WI —MILWAUKEE PUBLIC LIBRARY, 814 W Wisconsin Ave, Milwaukee, 53233. Donald J Sager, City Librn
Holdings: Vols 113,058 Cat Phonorecords
Budget: $10,904
Notes: Collection of recordings of all types from 1900 to present; 66,350 78rpm discs, arranged by label and producer, incl examples of over 400 labels; 6800 LP discs partially cataloged; 850 transcriptions discs of the 1940s and 1950s of local and international events and speeches; circulating collection of 40,000.

PR —UNIVERSITY OF PUERTO RICO, Jose M Lazaro Memorial Library, Music Room, Box C, University of Puerto Rico Sta, Rio Piedras, 00931. Ramon Arollo, Librn
Holdings: Vols (42,550) Cat Mss Slides Phonorecords Audiotapes Microforms
Notes: Incl over 9142 scores, 19,000 phonorecords, 7488 music books, 5191 newspapers, and 134 audiotapes.

BC —UNIVERSITY OF BRITISH COLUMBIA, Charles Crane Memorial Library, 2075 Westbrook Hall, Vancouver, V6T 1W5, Can. Paul E Thiele, Librn
Holdings: Vols (25,000) Cat Phonorecords Audiotapes
Notes: This is a special library serving blind, visually impaired and physically handicapped college and university students with books and materials in Braille (approx 25,000 vols) phonotape (4000 Vols); various other phono media incl cassette and disc (approx 3000 vols), large type (300 vols) and print materials. We offer recording services and copying of prerecorded material plus transcription of print into Braille or Large Type. Also incl 12 contour maps.

MB —UNIVERSITY OF MANITOBA, Music Library, 223 Music Bldg, Winnipeg, R3T 2N2, Can. Vladimir Simosko, Head
Holdings: Vols 15,000 Cat
Notes: Incl performance music (27,750 items); 4200 phonorecords.

ON —NATIONAL FILM, TELEVISION AND SOUND ARCHIVES, Documentation & Public Service, 395 Wellington St, Ottawa, K1A 0N3, Can. Jana Vosikovska, Chief; Gloria Grant, Librn; Sylvie Robitaille, Stills and Posters Librn
Notes: Several collections supporting the documentation on film, television and recorded sound: 1060 periodical titles (450 current), some on microfilm. Picture-stills, 265,000; moving picture posters, 6000; cataloged microfiche, 33,000 (vertical file material put on microfilm, then into a fiche format). Index cards (periodical references, credits): 334,000 cards (Film Title Index: 250,000 cards; Personalities Index: 84,000 cards).

ON —NATIONAL LIBRARY OF CANADA, 395 Wellington St, Ottawa, K1A 0N4, Can. Andre Preibish, Dir
Holdings: Vols 35,000
Notes: Includes 2000 pieces of Canadian

sheet music (mostly 19th century imprints), 40,000 cylinders, discs, tapes; over 600 serials titles devoted to music; 200 archival collections of composers, musicians and conductors, eg papers of Healy Willan, eminent composer; Glen Gould, well-known pianist; Sir Ernest MacMillan, conductor, director and composer. Since 1950 the Canadian imprints have been received on legal deposit. Intensive purchases aim at a comprehensive collection of Canadian music.

ON —UNIVERSITY OF OTTAWA, Morisset Library, 65 Hastey St, Ottawa, K1N 9A5, Can. Yvon Richer, University Chief Librn
Holdings: Vols (12,000)
Notes: Incl 100 periodicals, 16,000 scores and 5150 sound recordings. Scores and recordings are housed in the music department, and monographs and periodicals in the Morisset Library. The collection is particularly strong in sixteenth to nineteenth century continental European music and musicology.

ON —METROPOLITAN TORONTO LIBRARY, Languages Centre, 789 Yonge St, Toronto, M4W 2G8, Can. Barbara Gunther, Head
Holdings: Vols (90,000) Cat Phonorecords Audiotapes
Notes: Original literature in over 80 languages; books, records, cassettes, microfilm on language studies; newspapers and periodicals from 50 counties. Language study materials. Issue quarterly additions lists by language. Collect North American Indian and Eskimo language materials. Occasional bibliographies.

ON —METROPOLITAN TORONTO LIBRARY, Music Dept, 789 Yonge St, Toronto, M4W 2G8, Can. Isabel Rose, Head
Holdings: Cat
Budget: ($54,000)
Notes: 14,800 books, 40,000 scores; 1900 pieces of retrospective Canadian sheet music; 500 pieces of American and British sheet music, pre-1980; 17,000 phonorecords; 180 current periodical titles; 2800 bound peiodicals; 340 reels of microfilmed periodicals; 16,000 concert programs, chiefly Toronto city; 8850 newspaper clipping files; music picture files integrated with Fine Art Dept picture collection.

PQ —UNIVERSITY OF MONTREAL, Bibliotheque de Musique, 200 Vincent d'Indy, bp 6128, succursale "A", Montreal, H3C 3J7, Can. Claude Soulard, Librn
Notes: Special emphasis on the classical period and contemporary music. Incl 11,895 music scores, 11,857 records and tapes and 6250 microforms.

SOURIAN, PETER

MA —BOSTON UNIVERSITY, Mugar Memorial Library, Special Collections Dept, 771 Commonwealth Ave, Boston, 02215. Howard B Gotlieb, Dir
Holdings: Cat Mss
Notes: Incl publications by.

SOUSA, JOHN PHILIP, 1854-1932

IL —UNIVERSITY OF ILLINOIS, URBANA/CHAMPAIGN, Library, Bands & Busch Instrument Collection, 1103 S Sixth St, Champaign, 61820. John Cranford, Librn
Holdings: Vols (8600) Cat Mss
Notes: Printed music, about 8400; plus the Sousa Library, 1900 vols, printed music about 1500; also the Clarke Library, 400 vols, printed music, approximately 375. No photocopying.

MD —TOWSON STATE UNIVERSITY, Fine Arts Bldg, Room 457, Towson, 21204. Edwin L Gerhardt, Curator
Notes: The Gerhardt Library of Musical Information is a segregated representative collection of music literature, phonograph and tape recordings, pictures and artifacts. It incl special sections on Thomas Alva Edison and the phonograph, John Philip Sousa and bands, old popular songs and percussion. Most of the material is out of print and hard to find. It is not a collection of scores or manuscripts. A detailed outline is available upon request. Direct all correspondence to

the curator, Edwin L Gerhardt, 4926 Leeds Ave, Baltimore, MD 21227, (301) 242-0328. See also entry under Band Music

WI —UNIVERSITY OF WISCONSIN, MADISON, Mills Music Library, 728 State St, Madison, 53706. Arne Arneson, Music Librn
Holdings: // Uncat Mss
Notes: Tams-Witmark Collection formed part of the rental collection of the firm bearing that name. Includes piano-conductor scores (some in mss); ca 65 sets of orchestral parts for operas; 70 vocal scores of works by American composers including Herbert, Sousa, Edwards and De Koven; ca 100 sets of orchestral parts of comic operas; ca 4000 vocal scores of European operas. Restricted use.

SOUTAR, WILLIAM

BC —UNIVERSITY OF VICTORIA, McPherson Library, Victoria, V8W 3H5, Can.

THE SOUTH (U.S.) see Southern States

SOUTH AFRICA see Africa, South

SOUTH AMERICA

CA —UNIVERSITY OF CALIFORNIA, SAN DIEGO, Central University Library, Mandeville Dept of Special Collections, La Jolla, 92093. Lynda Corey Claassen, Head
Notes: Hispanic Collection: Approx 6000 vols describe cultures of Spain, Portugal, Mexico, Latin America, and South America. Works of literature, history, philosophy and art date from the 15th to the mid-19th century. Highlights of the collection include rare 18th century Spanish provincial dramas and works on the history of Seville and Andalusia.

NY —CORNELL UNIVERSITY LIBRARIES, John M Olin Library, Ithaca, 14853.
Holdings: Vols 190,000 Mss Maps 16mm Films Microforms
Budget: $40,000
Notes: Latin American materials in the Cornell University Libraries may be found in all of the campus libraries. The largest single collection is located in the John M Olin Library, and the holdings and budget statements above refer only to this collection. The Olin Library collection incl both materials published in Latin America as well as those published anywhere in the world dealing with Latin America. Its central focus is on social science materials for South America, particularly the central Andes (Ecuador, Peru, Bolivia), Brazil, and the River Plate countries. Although the collection is historical in scope, with materials dating back to the "Columbus letter" of 1493, the greatest collecting effort is directed toward materials on contemporary Latin America: its culture, society, politics, etc. The materials are fully integrated into the general collections of the libraries, and there is no separate catalog of the collection. Deborah A Wood's Directed Cultural Change in Peru: A Guide to the Vicos Collection (1975) describes this archival collection, located in the Library's Dept of Manuscripts and University Archives.

NY —AMERICAN MUSEUM OF NATURAL HISTORY, Library Services Dept, Central Park W & 79th St, New York, 10024. Nina J Root, Chairwoman; Mary Genett, Asst Librn for Reference Services

RI —BROWN UNIVERSITY, John Hay Library, 20 Prospect St, Providence, 02912. Mark N Brown, Cur Mss
Holdings: Vols (3500) // Cat Mss Maps
Notes: George Earl Church Collection, formed by a civil engineer, explorer and Fellow of the Royal Geographic Society, who specialized in railroad construction. Although part of the collection is devoted to American Revolutionary and Civil War history, the majority, over 2000 volumes, pertains to Central and South America. The imprints, which are predominantly 18th century, include Lima, Madrid, Rome,

SOUTH AMERICA (cont.)

Mexico City, Seville, Barcelona, Lisbon, and Cadiz as well as *Nova orbis regionum ac insularum veteribus incognitarum* (Basle:1573). Major subject areas are: anthropology, commerce, economics, engineering, ethnology, geography, history, law, mineral resources, railroad surveys, voyages of exploration and dictionaries of the South American Indian languages. The most significant ms is an historical account of the Bolivian mining town of Potosi from 1545-1737.

TX —UNIVERSITY OF TEXAS LIBRARIES, Nettie Lee Benson Latin American Collection, Sid Richardson Hall 1.109, Austin, 78712. Laura Gutierrez-Witt, Head Librn
Holdings: Vols (450,000) Cat Mss Maps Pix Phonorecords Filmstrips Microforms
See also entry under Latin America.

SOUTH AMERICA—COMMERCE

NY —COLUMBIA UNIVERSITY LIBRARIES, Rare Book & Manuscript Library, 801 Butler Library, 535 W 114 St, New York, 10027. Kenneth A Lohf, Librn
Notes: More than 32,000 items documenting the rise of William Russell Grace's shipping business and other materials relating to his career as mayor of New York. Incl records and correspondence relating to all aspects of the shipping business in New York and South America, mining interest in Peru and Chile, and transportation in Costa Rica and Nicaragua. Family memorabilia and photographs, materials concerning New York Politics, banking and insurance, real estate interests and Catholic charities, and letters from Chester A Arthur, John Jacob Astor, Andrew Carnegie, Grover Cleveland, Hamilton Fish, John Hay and J Pierpont Morgan. Restricted use.

SOUTH AMERICA—DESCRIPTION AND TRAVEL

MN —UNIVERSITY OF MINNESOTA, James Ford Bell Library, 309 19th Ave S, Minneapolis, 55455. John Parker, Cur
Holdings: Vols (11,000) Cat Mss Maps
Notes: Collection of original materials relating to European expansion, 1400-1800.

SOUTH AMERICA—GAZETTES

NY —NEW YORK PUBLIC LIBRARY, Research Libraries, Economic & Public Affairs Div, Fifth Ave & 42 St, New York, 10018. Edward DiRoma, Chief
Holdings: Vols (1,500,000) Cat Microforms

SOUTH AMERICA—HISTORY

DC —LIBRARY OF CONGRESS, Manuscript Division, Washington, 20540. John C Broderick, Chief
Notes: The Harkness Collection contains documents relating to the first 200 years of Spanish rule in Mexico and Peru.

NY —HISPANIC SOCIETY OF AMERICA, Library, 613 W 155 St, New York, 10032. Martha M de Narvaez, Cur of Mss; Irene S Frye, Asst Librn
Holdings: Vols (150,000) Cat Mss Maps Pix Slides Phonorecords Micorforms
Notes: History, art, literature and general culture of the Hispanic countries (where Spanish or Portuguese is spoken). Incl (18,000) vols printed before 1701, incl (250) incunabula; over (100,000) later vols, plus thousands of periodicals. About (200,000) mss incl ms maps. Printed atlases are in the Book Collection. Some microfilms, chiefly of our early books. Engraved and printed separate maps; reference collection of over 100,000 photographs; slides: all in Department of Iconography, not in library.
Catalogs: *Catalogue of the Hispanic Society of America* (Boston: G K Hall, 1962), 10 vols; *First Supplement* (Boston, 1970), 4 vols. Early books: *Printed Books 1468-1700; Mss: Catalogo de los Manuscritos Poeticos*

Castellanos (15th-17th centuries; 3 vols); *Medieval Manuscripts in the Library; Golden Age Drama Manuscripts*(the latter in press).

SOUTH ASIA see Asia, South

SOUTH CAROLINA

NC —DUKE UNIVERSITY, William R Perkins Library, Durham, 27706. Elvin E Strowd, University Librn
Notes: The Flowers Collection of Southern Americana currently consists of 4,300,500 items. Additions are ongoing. Included in this collection are several types of materials, which are housed in appropriate sections of the library. The various types of materials are: manuscripts, books, pamphlets, maps, music, broadsides, newspapers, photographs, engravings, prints and memorabilia.

†NC —WAKE FOREST UNIVERSITY, Z Smith Reynolds Library, Box 7777, Reynolds Sta, Winston-Salem, 27109. Richard J Murdoch, Rare Book Librn
Holdings: Vols 9500 Cat

SC —CLEMSON UNIVERSITY, Libraries, Clemson, 29631. Michael F Kohl, Head of Special Collections
Holdings: Vols 10,000 Cat Mss Maps
Notes: South Carolina material with particular emphasis on the Northwestern section of the state, Clemson University related collections, 20th century politics, agriculture, and textiles.

SC —PRESBYTERIAN COLLEGE, Library, Clinton, 29325. Lennart Pearson, Librn
Holdings: Vols 2000 Cat Maps Pix
Notes: Separate catalog.

SC —UNIVERSITY OF SOUTH CAROLINA, South Caroliniana Library, Columbia, 29208. Allen Stokes, Librn
Holdings: Vols 55,000 Cat Mss Maps Pix Microforms
Notes: All forms of South Caroliniana, printed and ms, of private, business or institutional nature, except the official unpublished records of state agencies. Many ms holdings have been reported to the National Union Catalog of Manuscript Collections. An abbreviated but comprehensive description of our mss and newspaper holdings can be found in John Hammond Moore's *Research Materials in South Carolina: A Guide* (Columbia, 1967), pp 65-145 and Allen Stokes and E L Inabinett, *A Guide to the Manuscript Collection of the South Caroliniana Library* (Columbia, 1982).

SOUTH CAROLINA—GENEALOGY

FL —ORLANDO PUBLIC LIBRARY, Local History & Genealogy Dept, 100 Block of Central Ave, Orlando, 32806. Eileen B Willis, Librn
Holdings: Vols 11,000 Cat Maps Microforms
Budget: $8000
Notes: Genealogy collection on Md, Del, W Va, NC, SC, Ala, Miss, La, Texas, Ark, Ky, Ohio, Ill, Ind, and Mich are well represented. Most other states are covered by smaller collections.
See also entry under Genealogy - Collections.

NC —PUBLIC LIBRARY OF CHARLOTTE & MECKLENBURG COUNTY, Local History and Genealogy Dept, 310 N Tryon St, Charlotte, 28202. Mary L Phillips, Librn
Holdings: Vols (2153) Cat Mss Microforms
Notes: Special interest in North Carolina, South Carolina, and Southern genealogy.

SC —SOUTH CAROLINA HISTORICAL SOCIETY LIBRARY, Fireproof Bldg, 100 Meeting St, Charleston, 29401. Gene Widdell, Dir
Holdings: Vols (50,000) Cat Mss Maps Pix Microforms
Notes: In addition to material dealing exclusively with South Carolina, the society also has holdings in the field of regional history which incl South Carolina, and books relating to other neighboring states.

SC —GREENVILLE COUNTY LIBRARY, 300 College St, Greenville, 29601. Joan Sorensen, Asst Dir of Public Servs
Holdings: Vols 4000 Cat Maps Microforms
Notes: A Family Index and Vistors Register

are maintained. The major emphasis is on the southeastern US but not restricted to this area.

SC —GREENWOOD COUNTY LIBRARY, Star Fort Chapter, DAR Collection, N Main St, Greenwood, 29646. Mary McCord, Dir
Holdings: Vols 170 Cat Mss
Notes: Genealogical and regional history of upper South Carolina.

SOUTH CAROLINA—HISTORY

NC —BELMONT ABBEY COLLEGE, Abbot Vincent Taylor Library, Belmont, 28012. Marjorie McDermott, Dir
Holdings: Vols (1000) Cat
Notes: Consists of books dealing with the history of North and South Carolina from colonial times to the present. Incl are several county histories, some early newspapers, and a strong section on the history of religion (especially the Roman Catholic Church) in the two states.

NC —UNIVERSITY OF NORTH CAROLINA, CHARLOTTE, J Murrey Atkins Library, UNCC Station, Charlotte, 28223. Robert F Brabham Jr, Special Collections Librn
Holdings: Vols Cat Maps Mss Pix Microforms
Notes: Papers of individuals and organizations which document the history, culture, and civiliation of North and South Carolina. Emphasis is on the Metrolina region of the two states with particular attention on the social, political, and architectural history of Charlotte and Mecklenburg County, NC.

NC —DUKE UNIVERSITY, William R Perkins Library, Manuscript Dept, Durham, 27706. Ellen Gartrell, Cur of Mss
Holdings: Cat Mss
Notes: Especially strong for North Carolina, South Carolina, Virginia, Georgia, and Alabama. 18th-20th centuries. See *Guide to the Cataloged Collections of the Manuscript Department of the William R Perkins Library* (1980, ed by Richard C Davis and Linda A Miller).

SC —CHARLESTON LIBRARY SOCIETY, Library, 164 King St, Charleston, 29401. Catherine Sadler, Librn
Holdings: Vols 20,000 Cat Mss Maps Pix Microforms
Notes: South Caroliniana. Also, more than 500 bound pamphlet vols; 2000 rolls of microfilm.

SC —CHARLESTON MUSEUM LIBRARY, 360 Meeting St, Charleston, 29403. John Brumgardt, Museum Dir
Holdings: Vols 30,000 Cat Mss Maps Pix

SC —COLLEGE OF CHARLESTON LIBRARY, Special Collections Dept, Charleston, 29401.
Notes: (1) Papers of the Charleston High School 1843-1976, (for white boys until recently), one of the nation's oldest public institutions of secondary education, dating from 1839. Also papers of The Memminger School (for white girls until recently); two black schools: Avery Institute (1866-1940) and Laing School (1866-1980). (2) South Carolina Court of Common Pleas Papers, 1948-1760, 1810. (3) Charleston history papers incl papers of Charleston County's Citizen's Council, Office of County Clerk, 1700-1936, Charleston Daily Courier, 1864; Charleston Library Society, 1762; Charleston, SC, Appeals Court, 1849; Chamber of Commerce, 1823-1839 and 1858; City Council, 1832-1859 and 1867; and Voter Registration Notice, 1815.

SC —MEDICAL UNIVERSITY OF SOUTH CAROLINA, Waring Historical Library, 171 Ashley Ave, Charleston, 29425. W Curtis Worthington, Jr, Dir; Anne K Donato, Cur
Holdings: Vols 6000 Cat Mss Pix Slides Microforms
Budget: ($3000)
Notes: The nucleus of our collections are the rare medical books that belonged to the Library of the Medical Society of South Carolina (a Charleston society founded in 1789, which started our college of medicine in 1824). Our special interest is the collection of South Carolina medical material

SOUTH CAROLINA—HISTORY (cont.)

and anything connected with the Medical University of South Carolina. we have old medical instruments and equipment, also.

SC —SOUTH CAROLINA HISTORICAL SOCIETY LIBRARY, Fireproof Bldg, 100 Meeting St, Charleston, 29401. Gene Widdell, Dir
Holdings: Vols (50,000) Cat Mss Maps Pix Microforms
Notes: In addition to material dealing exclusively with South Carolina, the society also has holdings in the field of regional history which incl South Carolina, and books relating to other neighboring states.

SC —CLEMSON UNIVERSITY, Libraries, Clemson, 29631. Michael F Kohl, Head of Special Collections
Notes: South Carolina material with particular emphasis on the Northwestern section of the state, Clemson University related collections, 20th century politics, agriculture, and textiles.

SC —UNIVERSITY OF SOUTH CAROLINA, Institute of Archaeology and Anthropology, Research Report Library, Maxcy College, Columbia, 29208. Kenn Pinson, Ms Archivist
Holdings: Mss Maps Pix Slides
Notes: Reports of research performed by the Institute of Archeology and Anthropology. Incl four series: the *Institute of Archeology and Anthropology Notebook; Research Manuscript Series;* and *Anthropological Studies, Popular Series.* Partially cataloged.

SC —UNIVERSITY OF SOUTH CAROLINA, South Caroliniana Library, Columbia, 29208. Allen Stokes, Librn
Holdings: Vols 60,000 Cat Mss Maps Pix Microforms
Notes: Incl 2,000,000 ms items. An abbreviated listing of manuscript and newspaper holdings can be found in John Hammond Moore. *Research Materials in South Carolina: A Guide,* Columbia, 1967 and Allen Stokes and E L Inabinett, *A Guide to the Manuscript Collection of the South Caroliniana Library* (Columbia, 1982).

SC —FRANCIS MARION COLLEGE, James A Rogers Library, Florence, 29501. H Paul Dove, Dir; Roger K Hux, Special Collections Librn
Holdings: Vols (600) Cat Maps Audiotapes Microforms
Notes: The Pee Dee Region of South Carolina. Emphasis on Colonial and Revolutionary periods, rice and indigo culture, plantations. Includes old rural church library with children's books.

SC —FURMAN UNIVERSITY, Library, James Buchanan Duke Bldg, Greenville, 29613. J Glenwood Clayton, Special Collection Librn
Holdings: Vols 1200 Cat Mss Maps Pix Microforms
Notes: Special Collection incl the Furman University archives and a very small amount of South Carolina material. Approx 85 percent of material is South Carolina Baptist records.

SC —GREENVILLE COUNTY LIBRARY, 300 College St, Greenville, 29601. Joan Sorensen, Asst Dir of Public Servs
Holdings: Vols 6500 Cat Mss Maps Pix Microforms
Notes: An index to local South Carolina newspapers is maintained; also a picture collection.

SC —GREENWOOD COUNTY LIBRARY, Star Fort Chapter, DAR Collection, N Main St, Greenwood, 29646. Mary McCord, Dir
Holdings: Vols 170 Cat Mss
Notes: Genealogical and regional history of upper South Carolina.

SC —WINTHROP COLLEGE, Ida Jane Dacus Library, Rock Hill, 29733. Ron J Chepesiuk, Special Collections Librn
Holdings: Cat Mss Maps Slides Videotapes 16mm Films Microforms
Budget: ($30,000)
Notes: Concentrates on women's history in South Carolina; local history Winthrop College archives and records. 200,000 ms pieces.

SC —WOFFORD COLLEGE, Sandor Teszler Library, N Church St, Spartanburg, 29301.

Frank J Anderson, Librn
Holdings: Vols 1000 Cat Mss Maps Pix

SOUTH CAROLINA—HISTORY—COLONIAL PERIOD

DC —LIBRARY OF CONGRESS, Geography and Map Division, Washington, 20540. John A Wolter, Chief
Notes: The American Map Collection incl 167 works produced between 1750 and 1790 incl copies of *A Map of the Most Inhabited Part of Virginia* by Joshua Fry and Peter Jefferson (1755 and 1775 editions), John Montresor's *A Map of the Province of New York* (1777), William Gerard De Brahm's *A Map of South Carolina and a Part of Georgia* (1757), and *A Plan of the City of Philadelphia* (1776) by Benjamin Easburn.

SC —COLLEGE OF CHARLESTON LIBRARY, Special Collections Dept, Charleston, 29401.
Notes: Papers, 1667, incl a receipt for money paid to a diocese in England, and an order by Ashley Cooper to pay a pension to the Duke of York; indenture for the sale of a tract of land in Prince Willliam Parish, Granville County, SC, granted to Hugh Bryan by King George II and given to Rev George Whitefield and then by Rev Whitefield to Mary Bryan, Nov 24, 1752 and a plat of the tract dated Dec 29, 1747; account book of the John Cordes estate, 1764-1798; with a family history for the years 1695-1728; papers, incl correspondence (October 19, 1700) of Edward Hyrne to his wife in England, detailing his experiences in the colony of Charles Town (photocopy of typescript, original to be found in the Taurus Gallery, London);Henry Laurens' Ledger, a business account book, 1766-1773.

SOUTH CAROLINA—POLITICS AND GOVERNMENT

SC —COLLEGE OF CHARLESTON LIBRARY, Special Collections Dept, Charleston, 29401.
Notes: Incl papers of Charleston County Citizen's Council; Office of County Clerk, 1700-1936; Charleston Daily Courier, 1864; Charleston Library Society, 1762; Charleston, SC, Appeals Court, 1849; Chamber of Commerce, 1823-1839 and 1858; City Council, 1832-1859 and 1867; and Voter Registration Notice, 1815.

SC —CLEMSON UNIVERSITY, Libraries, Clemson, 29631. Michael F Kohl, Head of Special Collections
Holdings: Uncat Mss Pix Audiotapes Videotapes
Notes: The Senator Strom Thurmond Collection. The papers of this South Carolina Governor and US Senator pertain to all aspects of his career. Approximately 1700 cubic feet of material.

†SC —STROM THURMOND CENTER FOR EXCELLENCE IN GOVERNMENT AND PUBLIC SERVICE, Clemson University Library, Clemson, 29631.

SOUTH CAROLINA—RELIGIOUS LIFE AND CUSTOMS

SC —COLLEGE OF CHARLESTON LIBRARY, Special Collections Dept, Charleston, 29401.
Notes: St John's German Lutheran Church, Charleston, SC, papers, 1786-1931 incl birth, baptism, confirmation, marriage and death records (1743-1917); lists of pewholders (1812-1844). Also St Andrews Society, Charleston, SC, papers, 1730-1939.

SOUTH CAROLINA—SOCIAL LIFE AND CUSTOMS

SC —COLLEGE OF CHARLESTON LIBRARY, Special Collections Dept, Charleston, 29401.
Notes: Account book of the John Cordes

estate, 1764-1798, with a family history for the years 1695-1728; Rutledge family papers.

SOUTH CAROLINA ASSOCIATION OF COLLEGES

SC —COLLEGE OF CHARLESTON LIBRARY, Special Collections Dept, Charleston, 29401.
Notes: Papers, 1945-1965.

SOUTH CAROLINA AUTHORS see Authors, South Carolina

SOUTH CAROLINA COASTAL COUNCIL

SC —COLLEGE OF CHARLESTON LIBRARY, Special Collections Dept, Charleston, 29401.
Notes: Papers, 1978- .

SOUTH CAROLINA COMMITTEE OF CONFERENCE ON INDIAN AFFAIRS

SC —COLLEGE OF CHARLESTON LIBRARY, Special Collections Dept, Charleston, 29401.
Notes: Papers incl report of the committee regarding sending Catawba Indian officials to New York "to make a peace with the Six Nations" of Indians, May 17, 1758.

SOUTH CAROLINA FARMERS' ALLIANCE

SC —CLEMSON UNIVERSITY, Libraries, Clemson, 29631. Michael F Kohl, Head of Special Collections
Holdings: // Cat Mss
Notes: Scrapbooks, ledgers, books, magazines of the Pendleton Farmers' Association; 3954 ms pieces from the South Carolina State Grange, 1872-1895 (Patrons of Husbandry).

SOUTH CAROLINA SOCIETY

SC —COLLEGE OF CHARLESTON LIBRARY, Special Collections Dept, Charleston, 29401.
Notes: Papers, 1827-1888.

SOUTH CAROLINA STATE GRANGE

SC —CLEMSON UNIVERSITY, Libraries, Clemson, 29631. Michael F Kohl, Head of Special Collections
Holdings: // Cat Mss
Notes: Scrapbooks, ledgers, books, magazines of the Pendleton Farmers' Association; 3954 ms pieces from the South Carolina Farmers' Alliance; 1800 items from the South Carolina State Grange, 1872-895 (Patrons of Husbandry).

SOUTH DAKOTA—HISTORY

DC —LIBRARY OF CONGRESS, Prints & Photographs Div, Washington, 20540.
Notes: The John C H Grabill collection of photographs of frontier life in Colorado, South Dakota, and Wyoming, late 19th century, incl views of hunters, prospectors, cowboys, Chinese immigrants, and US Army personnel.

KS —UNIVERSITY OF KANSAS, Kenneth Spencer Research Library, Kansas Collection, Lawrence, 66045. Sheryl K Williams, Cur
Holdings: Vols (90,000) Cat Mss Maps Pix
Notes: All aspects of the American West and trans-Mississippi history, especially northern and central regions. Overland diaries, catographic history, Indians, emigration and immigration, printing history, cattle industry, agriculture and farm life, conservation are some special interests, in addition to the usual political, economic, military and social interests.

SD —NORTHERN STATE COLLEGE, Beulah Williams Library, Documents & Reference Dept, Aberdeen, 57401. Keith W Warne, Librn
Holdings: Vols 7000 Cat Maps Pix

SOUTH DAKOTA—HISTORY (cont.)

Audiotapes Microforms
Budget: $1000
Notes: Incl state documents, materials about South Dakota and the surrounding area and works by South Dakota residents. Also incl the South Dakota National Guard Oral History Project with collection of South Dakota history.

SD —SOUTH DAKOTA HISTORICAL RESOURCE CENTER, Library, Soldiers Memorial Bldg, Pierre, 57501. Rosemary Evetts, Librn
Holdings: Vols 1020 Cat Mss Maps Pix
Budget: $2000
Notes: South Dakota state and territorial materials. Picture collection has been cataloged and numbers approximately 20,000 items, of which we have negatives for about half. South Dakota materials include items on general state and territorial history, biographical, autobiographical, political, geological, economic and county and town materials.

†SD —SOUTH DAKOTA SCHOOL OF MINES & TECHNOLOGY, Devereaux Library, Rapid City, 57701.
Holdings: Vols (3786) Cat Mss Maps Pix Audiotapes Microforms
Notes: This special collection, in general, relates to the Black Hills area of South Dakota and Wyoming, especially mining and exploration of the area; the West River area of South Dakota Territorial and State materials. There are also specialized areas of the collection: (1) Marion N Bruce Collection. Documents, correspondence books and periodicals dealing with weather modification in South Dakota; (2) Mildred Fielder Collection. Mss, pictures, books and periodicals from an author whose special area was the Black Hills. Most of her work on railroads, mines, trails, etc, relates to historical aspects. Collection incl research materials, galley proofs and final copies of her various publications; (3) Cleophas C O'Harra Collection. Mss, pictures, books and original source materials, primarily related to the date was collected for a book on the Black Hills which was neverpublished; and (4)Caving Collection. Maps of various caves in Black Hills area, being kept current and updated by members of the Paha Sapa Grotto. Also, some books and periodicals on caving in general.

SD —AUGUSTANA COLLEGE, Mikkelsen Library & Learning Resource Center, Center for Western Studies, Sioux Falls, 57197. Ronelle Thompson, Dir Library
Holdings: Vols (40,000) Cat Mss Maps Pix Slides Microforms
Budget: ($130,000)
Notes: Personal collection of Dr Herbert Krause, author in residence and Professor of Literature, Augustana College. Collection principally of his mss, correspondence, and materials concerning the upper midwest and Dakotas literature and history. There are some materials concerning ornithology also. This collection is the basic collection of the contributor's Center for Western Studies, Augustana College. No photocopying.

SD —SIOUXLAND HERITAGE MUSEUMS, Pettigrew Museum Library, 131 N Duluth Ave, Sioux Falls, 57104. Ms Lee N McLaird, Cur of Collections
Holdings: Vols (7500) Cat Mss Maps Pix
Budget: ($900)
Notes: Pettigrew Museum Library is a support service of the Siouxland Heritage Museums. US Senator R F Pettigrew established the core collection in 1926, covering natural history (incl North American Indian anthropology) and state-local history (concentrating on exploration and settlement to about 1900). The collection also incl the Senator's private papers (ca 1870-1926). Additions to the collection since 1926 have emphasized Plains Indian anthropology, state-local history, baseball and museology, supporting the work of the Museum staff. The collection is mostly cataloged and is inter-indexed with Augustana College, Sioux Falls College, and

Sioux Falls Public Libraries (as well as having its own catalog). The photograph collection includes prints by D F Barry as well as other photographers' work with native peoples.

SOUTH DAKOTA—MAPS

OK —TULSA CITY-COUNTY LIBRARY, Business & Technology Dept, 400 Civic Center, Tulsa, 74103. Craig Buthod, Head
Notes: Original General Land Office survey maps for the states of Arizona, Arkansas, Colorado, Illinois, Indiana, Idaho, Kansas, Michigan, Missouri, Montana, Nebraska, Nevada, New Mexico, North Dakota, Ohio, Oklahoma, South Dakota, Utah and Wyoming. Incomplete coverage of each state.

SOUTH DAKOTA—SOCIAL LIFE AND CUSTOMS

IA —DRAKE UNIVERSITY, Cowles Library, 28 St & University Ave, Des Moines, 50311.
Notes: Nearly 3000 musical works used by orchestras and musicians to accompany silent films, donated by Dorman Hundling who had played in orchestras in theatres owned by his family in South Dakota and Iowa.

SOUTH DAKOTA AUTHORS see Authors, South Dakota

SOUTH DAKOTA BADLANDS see Badlands of South Dakota

SOUTH PACIFIC

CA —UNIVERSITY OF CALIFORNIA, SAN DIEGO, Central University Library, Mandeville Dept of Special Collections, La Jolla, 92093. Lynda Corey Claassen, Head
Notes: Pacific Collection: Various cultures of the Pacific rim and Pacific islands are described in these works. The Kingdom of Tonga is a special focus of the collection. The Melanesian Archive preserves published and unpublished research materials documenting the culture of this archipelago.

CA —PACIFIC GROVE PUBLIC LIBRARY, 550 Central Ave, Pacific Grove, 93950. Margaret McBride, Library Dir
Holdings: Vols (1200) // Cat
Notes: Alvin Seale South Seas Collection, incl rare and unusual items, accounts of early voyages, ships' logs and artifacts. Separate catalog. Gift of Alvin Seale, curator of Steinhart Aquarium, San Francisco, 1937.

SOUTH PACIFIC COMMISSION

CA —UNIVERSITY OF CALIFORNIA, SANTA CRUZ, University Library, Special Collections, Santa Cruz, 95064. Rita Bottoms, Special Collections Librn; Margaret Felts, South Pacific Collection Bibliographer
Holdings: Vols (10,000) Cat
Notes: South Pacific Collection. Monographs, rare books, serials, documents and atlases which treat of the Pacific areas of Polynesia, Melanesia, Micronesia, Australia and New Zealand, but excluding western New Guinea (Irian Jaya), the Philippines and Southeast Asia. Approximately 10 percent of the titles are multi-volume documents such as parliamentary papers, legislative journals, official yearbooks, statistical sourcebooks, laws and statutes. The collection includes an exhaustive selection of current journals and monographic series from and about the Pacific: early serials, South Pacific Commission publications, US Government and US Trust Territory publications, serials from museums, universities and scholarly societies. Chief emphasis has been placed on acquisition of the literature of history, description and travel, ethnology andanthropology, literature and literary criticism, political and constitutional histories. Other extensive holdings are in the fields of geography and maps, voyages, mission histories, mythology and folklore,

art, linguistics, and science fields of natural history, environmental studies, biology, zoology, botany, geology and astronomy. Printed catalog is available. This is an ongoing, growing collection.

SOUTH POLE

DC —NATIONAL GEOGRAPHIC SOCIETY, Library, 1146 16th St NW, Washington, 20036. Susan Fifer Canby, Dir
Holdings: Vols (63,000) Cat Mss Maps Pix
Notes: Material concerning land, sea, and space exploration--past and present. All fields of anthropology, natural history, geography, etc.

NY —COLUMBIA UNIVERSITY LIBRARIES, Rare Book & Manuscript Library, 801 Butler Library, 535 W 114 St, New York, 10027. Kenneth A Lohf, Librn
Holdings: Vols 700 Cat
Notes: First editions, mss, letters and memorabilia relating to the exploration of the North and South Poles. 700 vols, 500 ms items. Restricted use.

NY —EXPLORERS CLUB, James B Ford Memorial Library, 46 E 70 St, New York, 10021. Janet Baldwin, Librn
Holdings: Vols (24,000) Cat Maps
Notes: Additions to the collection depend upon gifts. Access by appointment only.

NY —NEW YORK PUBLIC LIBRARY, Research Libraries, General Research Division, Fifth Ave & 42 St, New York, 10018. Rodney Phillips, Chief
Holdings: Vols (2,225,000) Cat Maps Pix Microforms
Budget: ($775,718)

SOUTH SEA BUBBLE

MA —HARVARD UNIVERSITY, Graduate School of Business Administration, Baker Library, Soldiers Field, Boston, 02163. Mary V Chatfield, Librn; Florence Bartoshesky, Cur of Manuscripts and Archives
Holdings: Cat
Notes: Bancroft Collection on the South Sea Company. See Business Historical Society Bulletin, IX (1935), 93-96.

SOUTH SEAS see Islands of the Pacific

SOUTH YEMEN see Yemen, South

SOUTHARD, ELMER ERNEST, 1876-1920

CA —FRANCIS BACON LIBRARY, 655 N Dartmouth Ave, Claremont, 91711. Elizabeth S Wrigley, Dir
Holdings: Mss Pix
Notes: Correspondence of Walter Arensberg with artists John Covert, Marcel Duchamp, Francis Picabia and his wife Gabrielle Buffet Picabia, and psychiatrist Elmer Ernest Southard, 1876-1920.

KS —MENNINGER FOUNDATION, Archives, 5600 W Sixth St, Box 829, Topeka, 66601. Alice Brand, Librn; Mark West, Archivist
Notes: 2 boxes, 1905-20. Incl correspondence, publications, miscellaneous materials.

SOUTHARD, SAMUEL LEWIS, 1787-1842

NJ —PRINCETON UNIVERSITY, Library, Manuscript Collection, Nassau St, Princeton, 08540. Jean F Preston, Cur
Holdings: Mss
Notes: The collection fills 163 ms boxes. See Princeton University Library Chronicle, v 20 p 45-47. An unpublished typescript guide (xviii, 789 p), is available in the Library.

SOUTHCOTT, JOHANNA

†TX —UNIVERSITY OF TEXAS LIBRARIES, General Libraries, Humanities Research Center, PO Box 7219, Austin, 78712. John Chalmers, Librn

SOUTHEAST ASIA see Asia, Southeast

SOUTHEAST ASIAN ART see Art, Southeast Asian

SOUTHERN ASSOCIATION OF PHYSICAL EDUCATION FOR COLLEGE WOMEN

NC —UNIVERSITY OF NORTH CAROLINA, GREENSBORO, Walter

SOUTHERN ASSOCIATION OF PHYSICAL EDUCATION FOR COLLEGE WOMEN (cont.)

Clinton Jackson Library, Special Collections Dept, 1000 Spring Garden St, Greensboro, 27412. Emilie W Mills, Librn
Notes: Archive incl histories and other records of the organization for 1920-1970. Collection incl 1000 items.

SOUTHERN BORNEO see Indonesia

SOUTHERN CALIFORNIA FOLKDANCE FEDERATION

CA —UNIVERSITY OF CALIFORNIA, LOS ANGELES, Research Library, Dept of Special Collections, 405 Hilgard Ave, Los Angeles, 90024. Edward Shreeves, Chairman, Bibliographers Group; David S Zeidberg, Head
Notes: 9 linear feet of records: minutes, correspondence, programs, etc.

SOUTHERN CHRISTIAN LEADERSHIP CONFERENCE

SC —COLLEGE OF CHARLESTON LIBRARY, Special Collections Dept, Charleston, 29401.
Notes: Septima Poinsette Clark Collection contains personal papers, recorded interviews and discussions, numerous writings for speeches and/or publication, various honorary degrees and awards, and materials reflecting Septima Poinsette Clark's activities as educator and civil rights activist, among them papers from the National Association for the Advancement of Colored People and the Southern Christian Leadership Conference.

SOUTHERN FOREST DISEASE AND INSECT COUNCIL

GA —UNIVERSITY OF GEORGIA, Libraries, Athens, 30602. Arlene E Luchsinger, Asst Dir Branch Libraries
Notes: Collection of over 1000 photographs on Southern forestry and the Southern logging industry, 1939-46. This gift, from the Southern Forest Institute, includes the records and files of four groups formed to solve specific problems of Southern forests.

SOUTHERN FOREST RESOURCE COUNCIL

GA —UNIVERSITY OF GEORGIA, Libraries, Athens, 30602. Arlene E Luchsinger, Asst Dir Branch Libraries
Notes: Collection of over 1000 photographs on Southern forestry and the Southern logging industry, 1939-46. This gift, from the Southern Forest Institute, includes the records and files of four groups formed to solve specific problems of Southern forests.

SOUTHERN INTERCOLLEGIATE ATHLETIC CONFERENCE

AL —TUSKEGEE INSTITUTE, Hallis Burke Frissel Library, Tuskegee Institute, 36088. Daniel Williams, Librn
Notes: The Robert Stewart Darnaby Collection on Blacks in American sports. Much on the Southern Intercollegiate Athletic Conference, incl historical materials. Large resources on Tuskegee athletics.

SOUTHERN MUSIC see Music, Southern

SOUTHERN PACIFIC RAILROAD

CA —ROSEVILLE PUBLIC LIBRARY, 225 Taylor St, Roseville, 95678. Susan L Nickerson, Dir
Holdings: Cat Mss Maps Pix Slides

SOUTHERN PINE BEETLE ACTION COMMITTEE

GA —UNIVERSITY OF GEORGIA, Libraries, Athens, 30602. Arlene E

Luchsinger, Asst Dir Branch Libraries
Notes: Collection of over 1000 photographs on Southern forestry and the Southern logging industry, 1939-46. This gift, from the Southern Forest Institute, includes the records and files of four groups formed to solve specific problems of Southern forests.

SOUTHERN RHODESIA see Rhodesia

SOUTHERN SKY SURVEY

CT —YALE UNIVERSITY, Dept of Astronomy Library, 260 Whitney Ave, Box 6666, New Haven, 06511.
Notes: A collection of about 3000 (17 x 17 inch) plates taken with the 20-inch double astrograph at El Leoncito, Argentina. These plates record stars and galaxies as faint as the 19th magnitude south of -15 degrees declination.

SOUTHERN STATES

AL —BIRMINGHAM PUBLIC LIBRARY, Dept of Archives & Mss, 2020 Seventh Ave N, Birmingham, 35203. Marvin Y Whiting, Archivist & Cur
Holdings: Cat Docs Mss //
Notes: Business and personal papers of Harry Welles Coffin covering the period from 1878 to 1938 in Birmingham, Alabama. Coffin was a vice president of The Alabama Company, a coal mining and iron products manufacturing firm. The business records incl correspondence, reports, financial records, and other documents relating to iron, steel, and coal industries in North Central Alabama. The personal papers mainly consist of love letters from Coffin to Minnie Everist Smith. These and other letters describe life on Birmingham's Southside area from 1885-1938.
AL —SAMFORD UNIVERSITY, Special Collections Library, 800 Lakeshore Dr, Birmingham, 35229. Annie Ford Wheeler, Acting Head Librn
Holdings: Uncat Mss Maps Pix Microforms
Notes: The William H Brantely Collection is in superb condition, consisting of early works on travels, Indians, and law in the southeast, plus scarce imprints of Alabama.
†AL —UNIVERSITY OF ALABAMA, Amelia Gayle Gorgas Library, PO Box S, University, 35486.
Notes: Incl the T P Thompson Collection on the Southern States; Shelby Iron Works Collection, Papers 1862-1923. Unpubluished guide in the library for ms collections.
DC —HOWARD UNIVERSITY, Moorland-Spingarn Research Center, 500 Howard Place NW, Washington, 20059. Clifford L Muse, Jr, Acting Dir
Holdings: Vols (106,086) Mss Maps Pix Slides Phonorecords Audiotapes 16mm Films Filmstrips Microforms
Budget: ($854,753)
See also entry under Blacks
DC —LIBRARY OF CONGRESS, Manuscript Division, Washington, 20540. John C Broderick, Chief
Notes: A file of ex-slave narratives, collected by the WPA Federal Writers Project between 1936-41. Approx 15,000 to 20,000 original manuscripts. Narratives of ex-slaves and children of slaves from all the Southern states and border states are thought to be included in the collection.
DC —LIBRARY OF CONGRESS, American Folklife Center, Archive of Folk Culture, Washington, 20540.
Notes: Georgia vernacular architecture, food customs, storytelling, and gospel singing traditions, in local black and white communities. Thousands of color transparencies, etc.
FL —ARCHBOLD BIOLOGICAL STATION, Library, Rt 2, Box 180, Lake Placid, 33852. Fred E Lohrer, Librn
Holdings: Vols (2000) Cat Periodicals
GA —UNIVERSITY OF GEORGIA, Libraries, Athens, 30602. Arlene E Luchsinger, Asst Dir Branch Libraries
Notes: Collection of over 1000 photographs on Southern forestry and the Southern logging industry, 1939-46. This gift, from the

Southern Forest Institute, includes the records and files of four groups formed to solve specific problems of Southern forests.
GA —UNIVERSITY OF GEORGIA, Libraries, Map Collection, Athens, 30602. John Sutherland, Cur of Maps
Holdings: Cat Maps
Budget: ($20,000)
Notes: Holdings as of Jan 1984 were: sheet maps, 285,000; aerial photographs, 186,000; three-dimensional maps, 40; atlases, 800 (note: the Libraries contain other atlases; these are part of the map collection as such). The collection contains maps from all countries and in all languages, although the area of specialization is the US, with particular emphasis on the southeastern sector. The collection is a depository for maps from the US Geological Survey, DMATC, NOAA, and Georgia's Dept of Transportation. Collection has 7100 sheets of Sanborn maps for Georgia. Bibliographies available for atlases, Sanborn sheets, and air photo holdings.
GA —EMORY UNIVERSITY, Robert W Woodruff Library, Special Collections Dept, Atlanta, 30322. Linda M Matthews, Head Special Collections; Virginia J H Cain, Processing Archivist; Richard H F Lindemann, Reference Archivist
Holdings: Vols (16,000) Cat Mss Maps Pix Microforms
GA —SOUTHERN REGIONAL EDUCATION BOARD LIBRARY, 1340 Spring St NW, Atlanta, 30309. Ann H Carter, Research Asst/Librn
Holdings: Vols (5000) Cat Microforms
Budget: ($2000)
Notes: Particularly higher education in the South. No photocopying.
LA —LOUISIANA STATE UNIVERSITY, Middleton Library, Dept of Archives & Manuscripts, Room 202, Baton Rouge, 70803. M Stone Miller Jr, Head
Holdings: Cat Mss Pix Microforms
Notes: History of Louisiana and lower Mississippi Valley, colonial through 20th century. Scope: political, social and literary history; economic history, incl forestry, banking, agriculture, transportation and trade; national, regional, and Louisiana history; military history. About 4,500,000 items.
LA —AMISTAD RESEARCH CENTER, 400 Esplanade Ave, New Orleans, 70116. Clifton H Johnson, Exec Dir; Florence E Borders, Senior Archivist
Budget: ($315,000)
Notes: Originally established at Fisk University, in Nashville, by the American Missionary Association (AMA), this research center on Black American History consists of mss, photographs, clippings, books, pamphlets, taped speeches and interviews; also, the papers of such leaders as W E B DuBois, Countee Cullen, and Mary McLeod Bethune. Also materials on other American minorities, such as Native Americans, Asian Americans, Hispanics, etc.
MD —MARYLAND HISTORICAL SOCIETY, Library, 201 W Monument St, Baltimore, 21201. William B Keller, Head Librn
Holdings: Vols (65,000) Cat Mss Maps Pix Slides
Budget: $8000
Notes: Large collection of Maryland State Colonization Papers; Maryland and Baltimore business records; Baltimore & Ohio Railroad Papers; Baltimore Theatre records and programs (late 18th, early 19th century); Maryland lottery tickets; Benjamin H Latrobe (architectural) Papers; Maryland maps, plats, prints, newspapers; Baltimore history large collection (30,000 items Maryland local history and genealogy, 100,000 mss); iron industry papers; Maryland currency; sheet music (8000 pieces, largely Baltimore publishers); Lester S Levy "Star-Spangled Banner" collection (probably the largest in the world--over 250 pieces).
MS —UNIVERSITY OF SOUTHERN MISSISSIPPI, William David McCain Graduate Library, Box 5148, Southern Sta, Hattiesburg, 39406.
Holdings: Vols 12,000 Cat Mss Maps Pix

SOUTHERN STATES (cont.)

Microforms
Notes: Mississippiana Collection incl government publications, newspapers, works on geography, literature, history, politics and travel. Also incl papers of Theodore G Bilbo, William M Colmer, Paul B Johnson, Sr and Paul B Johnson, Jr, Con Sellers, the University of Southern Mississippi Archives, an oral history collection, and a genealogy collection. See also entries under individual names and subjects.

NY —ROCKEFELLER UNIVERSITY, Rockefeller Archive Center, Hillcrest, Pocantico Hills, North Tarrytown, 10591. Joseph W Ernst, Dir; J William Hess, Assoc Dir
Notes: Papers relative to the Rockefeller Family, Foundations, University, and other specific enterprises and contributions to particular areas of social, physical, educational, and historic reform, preservation, conservation, or development. Extensive records of administrative, financial, physical, or intellectual relationships.

NC —DUKE UNIVERSITY, William R Perkins Library, Durham, 27706. Elvin E Strowd, University Librn
Notes: The Flowers Collection of Southern Americana currently consists of 4,300,500 items. Additions are ongoing. Included in this collection are several types of materials, which are housed in appropriate sections of the library. The various types of materials are: manuscripts, books, pamphlets, maps, music, broadsides, newspapers, photographs, engravings, prints and memorabilia.

NC —DUKE UNIVERSITY, William R Perkins Library, Manuscript Dept, Durham, 27706. Ellen Gartrell, Cur of Mss
Holdings: Cat Mss
Notes: Especially strong for North Carolina, South Carolina, Virginia, Georgia, and Alabama. 18th-20th centuries. See *Guide to the Cataloged Collections of the Manuscript Department of the William R Perkins Library.*

NC —UNIVERSITY OF NORTH CAROLINA, GREENSBORO, Walter Clinton Jackson Library, Special Collections Dept, 1000 Spring Garden St, Greensboro, 27412. Emilie W Mills, Librn
Holdings: Vols 1000 Cat Mss Pix
Notes: Selection of special or limited editions, collected works and anthologies, southern writers from the 1920s, who taught part-time or participated in arts forums on this campus during the 1950s and 1960s. Count incl works in special and general collections.

NC —MOUNT OLIVE COLLEGE, Moye Library, Free Will Baptist Historical Collection, Mount Olive, 28365. Gary Fenton Barefoot, Librn
Holdings: Vols 800 Cat Mss Pix Audiotapes 8mm Films Microforms
Notes: Free Will Baptists history in general, with concentration in North Carolina and the South. The collection was begun in 1954 by joint action of the college and the Historical Commission of the North Carolina State Convention of Original Free Will Baptists. Collection is perhaps the best on the Free Will Baptist denomination in existence. Particular strength lies in the 225 vols of mss and printed minutes of associations, etc. Over 5000 clipings and pamphlets. The collection is housed and cataloged separately from the main library collection. Various special indexes (obituaries, churches, etc) are also maintained. Quite a number of vols and materials of associational value related to the General Baptists, Baptists, etc, are also a part of the collection. The cataloged vols are represented in the North Carolina Union Catalog and in Starr's Baptist Bibliography. In thecase of Starr, however, holdings are only incl in the more recent vols.

TN —UNIVERSITY OF TENNESSEE, CHATTANOOGA, Library, Chattanooga, 37401. Joseph A Jackson, Dir of Libraries
Holdings: Vols 6000 Cat Maps
Notes: The Civil War Collection, a gift of

about 3500 vols for the Charles R and Anne Bachman Hyde Collection from Mrs Hyde, who spent a lifetime collecting Southern Americana with particular emphasis on the Confederate viewpoint. Also incl the Wilder Collection, from the Federal point of view. Established as a memorial to Gen John T Wilder. restricted use: reference only.

TN —CHUCALISSA MUSEUM, 1987 Indian Village Dr, Memphis, 38109. Gerald P Smith, Cur
Holdings: Vols (1100) Cat Mss
Budget: ($200)
Notes: Collection emphasizes midsouth archaeology, but incl some regional ethnographic and geological titles. Noncirculating.

TN —MEMPHIS PINK PALACE MUSEUM, Library, 3050 Central Ave, Memphis, 38111. Coralu D Buddenbahm, Librn
Holdings: Vols (3600) Cat Maps Pix Slides Phonorecords Audiotapes Videotapes 16mm Films Filmstrips
Budget: ($4,000)
Notes: Museum specializes in the history and culture of the Mid-South. A number of books owned by The Shiloh Military Trail, Inc are on loan to the Museum and are available for reference.

TN —TENNESSEE STATE LIBRARY & ARCHIVES, 403 Seventh Ave N, Nashville, 37219. Olivia K Young, State Librn & Archivist
Holdings: Uncat Pix
Notes: Mainly picture postcards of Tennessee and southern scenes, but largest part of the collection is the Mrs. Joseph H Thompson Collection incl cards from Europe, Africa, Asia and North and South America.

TX —UNIVERSITY OF TEXAS LIBRARIES, General Libraries, PO Box P, Austin, 78713. Carolyn Bucknell, Asst Dir for Collection Development
Holdings: Vols Cat Microforms
Notes: The Littlefield Collection of research materials, incl many rare items, on the history of the Old South.

TX —UNIVERSITY OF MARY HARDIN-BAYLOR, Townsend Memorial Library, Ninth & Wells, Belton, 76513. Izoro Daphane Kerley, Asst Librn
Holdings: Vols Cat

VA —UNIVERSITY OF VIRGINIA, Alderman Library, Tracy W McGregor Collection, Charlottesville, 22901. William H Runge, Cur
Holdings: Vols 18,000 Cat Mss Maps Pix Microforms
Notes: Library spans 15th-20th century, concentrating on Southeastern American history. Rare collection of books on early exploration and travel; foundation of the Virginia Colony; Civil War. Books in foreign languages. Collection cataloged by date of publiction. Special shelflist. Published descriptions: William H Runge, "The Tracy W McGregor Library and Its Founder," *The Univeristy of Virginia News Letter* vol 39, no 11, July 15, 1963; *Description of the Tracy W McGregor Library, University of Virginia, With Rules for Its Use and a Biographical Sketch of Its Founder* (Charlottesville: Tracy W McGregor Library, 1951).

VA —WASHINGTON AND LEE UNIVERSITY, Library, Lexington, 24450. Maurice Leach, Dir; Richard Oram, Asst Special Collections Librn
Holdings: Vols (25,000) Cat Mss Maps Pix
Notes: Incl over 10,000 ms pieces, the collection emphasizes the life of General Robert E Lee, Virginia, and the Civil War, etc. Pictures from 1870-1930; 8000 glass photographs by Miley.

SOUTHERN STATES—ECONOMIC CONDITIONS

NC —DUKE UNIVERSITY, William R Perkins Library, Durham, 27706. Elvin E Strowd, University Librn

SOUTHERN STATES—GENEALOGY

AL —BIRMINGHAM PUBLIC LIBRARY, Southern History Dept, 2020 Seventh Ave

N, Birmingham, 35203. Virginia K Scott, Head
Holdings: Vols (50,000) Cat Microforms
Notes: History and social conditions of the southeastern US. Significant holdings on border areas such as Texas, Pennsylvania, Maryland. Strong genealogical collection with emphasis on the southeastern area of the US. Very strong Civil War Collection and early southern travel accounts. See George Ray Stewart, *The Special Collections in the Birmingham Public Library.* MA Thesis, Emory University, 1971.

AL —SAMFORD UNIVERSITY, Special Collections Library, 800 Lakeshore Dr, Birmingham, 35229. Annie Ford Wheeler, Acting Head Librn
Holdings: Vols 2500 Cat Mss Microforms
Notes: Chiefly southeast US and Ireland. Incl abstracts, printed genealogies, and census indexes (microfilm). Substantial amounts of material in the Bledsoe-Kelly mss. Incl 100,000 ms pieces.

AL —WHEELER BASIN REGIONAL LIBRARY, 504 Cherry St NE, PO Box 1766, Decatur, 35602. Margarete Lange, Reference Librn
Holdings: Vols 300 Cat Mss Microforms
Notes: Primary emphasis on Alabama and Southern genealogy, although other areas are incl.

FL —TAMPA-HILLSBOROUGH COUNTY PUBLIC LIBRARY, 900 N Ashley St, Tampa, 33602. Joseph Hipp, Dir

MS —UNIVERSITY OF SOUTHERN MISSISSIPPI, William David McCain Graduate Library, Box 5148, Southern Sta, Hattiesburg, 39406.
Holdings: Vols 1200 Mss
Notes: Southern States legal records; military records; hereditary societies' lineages; specialized indices; 1790-1900 censuses on microfilm; Huguenot collection; miscellaneous records on microfiche. Also Mississippiana Collection: government publications, newspapers, works of Theodore G Bilbo, William M Colmer, Paul B Johnson and Paul B Johnson, Jr, Con Sellers, the University of Southern Mississippi Archives, an oral history collection, and a genealogy collection.

NC —PUBLIC LIBRARY OF CHARLOTTE & MECKLENBURG COUNTY, Local History and Genealogy Dept, 310 N Tryon St, Charlotte, 28202. Mary L Phillips, Librn
Holdings: Vols (2153) Cat Mss Microforms
Notes: Special interest in North Carolina, South Carolina, and Southern genealogy.

NC —DUKE UNIVERSITY, William R Perkins Library, Durham, 27706. Elvin E Strowd, University Librn
Notes: The Flowers Collection of Southern Americana currently consists of 4,300,500 items. Additions are ongoing. Included in this collection are several types of materials, which are housed in appropriate sections of the library. The various types of materials are: manuscripts, books, pamphlets, maps, music, broadsides, newspapers, photographs, engravings, prints and memorabilia. Also Society of Mayflower Descendants in the State of North Carolina collection numbers 250 volumes. It is a collection of family history and genealogy.

TN —CHATTANOOGA-HAMILTON COUNTY, Bicentennial Library, Local History and Genealogy Dept, 1001 Broad St, Chattanooga, 37402. Clara W Swann, Librn
Holdings: Vols (24,561) Cat Mss Maps Pix Microforms
Budget: ($7000)
Notes: Emphasis on southern states, and eastern Tennessee counties, with considerable material on New England, Pennsylvania, and Maryland genealogy and history. Census records on microfilm. Special indexes and clipping files. Noncirculating.

TX —FORT WORTH PUBLIC LIBRARY, 300 Taylor St, Fort Worth, 76102. Patricia Chadwell, Social Sciences Librn; Paul Campbell, Librn, History Section
Holdings: Vols (25,000) Cat Mss Maps Microforms
Budget: $7600
Notes: Collection emphasizes southern states, but is national in scope. Substantial

SOUTHERN STATES—GENEALOGY (cont.)

group of British material, and material on Huguenots.

TX —LUBBOCK CITY-COUNTY LIBRARY, 1306 Ninth St, Lubbock, 79401. Marlene M Harp, Dir, Adult Services
Holdings: Vols (10,000) Mss Microforms
Notes: Books on southern history and genealogy, Florida map collection.

SOUTHERN STATES—HISTORY

AL —BIRMINGHAM PUBLIC LIBRARY, Southern History Dept, 2020 Seventh Ave N, Birmingham, 35203. Virginia K Scott, Head
Holdings: Vols (40,000) Cat Microforms
Notes: History and social conditions of the southeastern US. Significant holdings on border areas such as Texas, Pennsylvania, Maryland. Strong genealogical collection with emphasis on the southeastern area of the US. Very strong Civil War Collection and early southern travel accounts. See George Ray Stewart, *The Special Collections in the Birmingham Public Library*. MA Thesis, Emory University, 1971.

CT —YALE UNIVERSITY, Box 1603A, Yale Station, New Haven, 06520.
Holdings: Vols Cat Mss
Notes: Particular strength in the antebellum period.

FL —TAMPA-HILLSBOROUGH COUNTY PUBLIC LIBRARY, 900 N Ashley St, Tampa, 33602. Joseph Hipp, Dir

GA —CHEROKEE GARDEN LIBRARY, 3101 Andrews Dr NW, Atlanta, 30305. Sally Bruce McClatchey, Librn
Holdings: Vols 2700
Notes: Southern history and horticulture. Emphasis on the historical development of American horticulture, 1634 to 1900.

GA —AGNES SCOTT COLLEGE, McCain Library, E College Ave, Decatur, 30030. Judith Bourgeois Jensen, Librn
Holdings: Vols (945) Uncat
Budget: $300
Notes: The Frontier Religion Collection, which was given by Prof Walter Brownlow Posey, traces the effects of slavery on religion in the Old South Frontier prior to 1860. A catalog file (by author entry only) accompanies the collection at present. Noncirculating.

LA —LOUISIANA STATE UNIVERSITY, Troy H Middleton Library, Louisiana Room, Baton Rouge, 70803. Evangeline Mills Lynch, Head Librn; Ruth Murray, Associate Librn
Holdings: Vols (33,500) Cat Maps VF
Notes: Louisiana Collection of history, description and travel, biography, agriculture, literature, politics and government, folklore, anthropology, geography, geology, education, language, music and natural history. Especially large subject collections may be found on Louisiana, the history of the lower Mississippi Valley, Abraham Lincoln, Romance languages and literatures, sugar culture and technology, Southern history, petroleum engineering, plant pathology, micropaleontology, ornithology, and various aspects of crawfish life, biology and culture. Complete depository of Louisiana State Documents; extensive newspapers clipping files; separate card catalog; items listed in Louisiana Union Catalog; restricted use (research and reference). Incl both materials about Louisiana and by Louisianians without regard to subject. LSU Press Collection(preservation copy of each title kept for exhibit purposes only). LSU theses and dissertations from 1900-date. LSU Faculty Collection. Also, 1300 maps, 104 VF drawers, 250 boxes of uncataloged pamphlets.

MD —JOHNS HOPKINS UNIVERSITY, Milton S Eisenhower Library, Charles & 34 Sts, Baltimore, 21218. Ann S Gwyn, Assistant Dir for Special Collections

MD —UNIVERSITY OF MARYLAND, BALTIMORE COUNTY, Albin O Kuhn Library and Gallery, 5401 Wilkens Ave, Baltimore, 21228. Ann Copeland, Special Collections Librn
Holdings: Vols 600 // Uncat Mss
Notes: Major items in the Hugh Davis Graham papers on southern history include *Southern School News*, Southern Regional Council publications, and reports on civil rights and intergration in the 1950s and 1960s.

MS —UNIVERSITY OF SOUTHERN MISSISSIPPI, William David McCain Graduate Library, Box 5148, Southern Sta, Hattiesburg, 39406.
Holdings: Vols 12,000 Cat Mss Maps Pix Microforms
Notes: Mississippiana Collection incl government publications, newspapers, works on geography, literature, history, politics and travel. Also incl are the papers of Theodore G Bilbo, William M Colmer, Paul B Johnson and Paul B Johnson, Jr, Con Sellers, the University of Southern Mississippi Archives, an oral history collection, and a genealogy collection. In addition, Southern States legal records; military records; hereditary societies' lineages; specialized indices; 1790-1900 censuses on microfilm; Huguenot collection; miscellaneous records on microfiche.

MS —MISSISSIPPI STATE UNIVERSITY, Mitchell Memorial Library, Box 5408, Mississippi State, 39762. Frances N Coleman, Head, Special Collections
Holdings: Vols (15,000) Cat Mss Maps Pix Microforms
Notes: Social and political history of Mississippi, incl University Archives (now separate branch). Microfilms of Protestant Church records. There are strong collections on history of the Southern States, Mississippi authors (especially Faulkner, Williams, Carter, Welty, and Young); also the John C Stennis Collection of over 2 million items, his books, papers, photographs, etc. Incl 400 collections of mss; papers of US Rep David R Bowen 1973-1983; papers of US Rep G V Montgomery 1967-.

NY —UNIVERSITY CLUB, Library, One W 54 St, New York, 10019. Guy St Clair, Library Dir
Holdings: Vols (100,000) Cat Mss Maps Pix
Notes: A private library for the members of the University Club, their guests, and serious scholars upon written application to the Library Director. Holds the Southern Society Collection of materials on the South, the Civil War and Reconstruction.

NC —UNIVERSITY OF NORTH CAROLINA, CHAPEL HILL, Wilson Library, Rare Book Collection, Chapel Hill, 27514. Paul S Koda, Cur of Rare Books
Holdings: Vols 8300 Cat
Notes: Over 8300 pamphlets printed in and/or concerning the South; they cover the period from 1820 to the present and include a wide range of subjects.

NC —DUKE UNIVERSITY, William R Perkins Library, Durham, 27706. Elvin E Strowd, University Librn
Notes: The Flowers Collection of Southern Americana currently consists of 4,300,500 items. Additions are ongoing. Included in this collection are several types of materials, which are housed in appropriate sections of the library. The various types of materials are: manuscripts, books, pamphlets, maps, music, broadsides, newspapers, photographs, engravings, prints and memorabilia.

NC —DUKE UNIVERSITY, William R Perkins Library, Manuscript Dept, Durham, 27706. Ellen Gartrell, Cur of Mss
Holdings: Cat Mss
Notes: Especially strong for North Carolina, South Carolina, Virginia, Georgia, and Alabama. 18th-20th centuries. See *Guide to the Cataloged Collections of the Manuscript Department of the William R Perkins Library*.

SC —SOUTH CAROLINA HISTORICAL SOCIETY LIBRARY, Fireproof Bldg, 100 Meeting St, Charleston, 29401. Gene Widdell, Dir
Holdings: Vols (50,000) Cat Mss Maps Pix Microforms
Notes: In addition to material dealing exclusively with South Carolina, the society also has holdings in the field of regional history which incl South Carolina, and books relating to other neighboring states.

TN —MEMPHIS STATE UNIVERSITY, John Willard Brister Library, Memphis, 38152. John Terreo, Special Collections Librn
Notes: Jefferson Davis-Joel Addison Family papers, 1864-1889. President of the Confederacy. Personal and business correspondence, receipts, notes, cancelled checks, and other papers, of Davis, following the Civil War (primarily 1877-1889) and his son-in-law, Joel Addison Hayes (1848-1919), banker of Memphis, TN, relating chiefly to management of Davis' plantation, Brierfield, near Vicksburg, MS, stocks and mining investments, and land sales. Incl correspondence between Davis' wife Varina (Howell) Davis and her daughter Margaret Howell (Davis) (1848-1908), and between Addison Hayes and members of his family.

TN —MEMPHIS/SHELBY COUNTY PUBLIC LIBRARY & INFORMATION CENTER, History & Travel Dept, 1850 Peabody Ave, Memphis, 38104. James R Johnson, Head
Holdings: Vols (9700) Cat Mss Maps Pix Microforms
Notes: Tennessee history, especially Memphis and Shelby County.

TX —UNIVERSITY OF TEXAS LIBRARIES, General Libraries, PO Box P, Austin, 78713. Carolyn Bucknell, Asst Dir for Collection Development
Holdings: Vols Cat Microforms
Notes: The Littlefield Collection of research materials, incl many rare items, on the history of the Old South.

VA —RANDOLPH-MACON COLLEGE, Walter Hines Page Library, Ashland, 23005. Flavia Reed Owen, Librn
Holdings: Vols 5000 Serials
Budget: $6000
Notes: Bibliographical listing of collection in Intellectual Life in The Colonial South, 1585-1763/by Richard Beale Davis. (Knoxville: University of Tennessee Press, c 1978) 3 v.

VA —VIRGINIA POLYTECHNIC INSTITUTE AND STATE UNIVERSITY LIBRARY, Blacksburg, 24061. Glenn L McMullen, Special Collections Librn
Holdings: Vols (1000) Cat Mss Maps
Notes: Collection of ca 300 linear feet of archival records (1830-1940) of the Norfolk and Western Railway, its predecessors, and subsidiaries, and of the defunct predecessors of the Southern Railway. The collection incl minutebooks, correspondence and subject files, and other ms materials for ca 200 railroad companies operating in the Southeast and Midwest, incl the Norfolk and Western; Norfolk and Petersburg; Southside; Atlantic, Mississippi, and Ohio; Virginia and Tennessee; Richmond and Danville; Memphis and Charleston; East Tennessee and Virginia; and South Carolina Canal and Railroad Company. The collection also incl printed materials such as annual reports and other documents for these companies.

VA —VIRGINIA STATE LIBRARY, 12 & Capitol Sts, Richmond, 23219.
Holdings: Vols 38,000 Cat Mss Maps Pix
Notes: Books on southern history and genealogy, Florida map collection.

SOUTHERN STATES—HISTORY—CIVIL WAR see U.S.—History — Civil War

SOUTHERN STATES—POLITICS AND GOVERNMENT

NC —DUKE UNIVERSITY, William R Perkins Library, Durham, 27706. Elvin E Strowd, University Librn

SOUTHERN STATES—RELIGION

NC —DUKE UNIVERSITY, William R Perkins Library, Durham, 27706. Elvin E Strowd, University Librn

SOUTHERN STATES—SOCIAL LIFE AND CUSTOMS

NC —DUKE UNIVERSITY, William R Perkins Library, Durham, 27706. Elvin E

SOUTHERN STATES—SOCIAL LIFE AND CUSTOMS (cont.)

Strowd, University Librn
Notes: The Flowers Collection of Southern Americana currently consists of 4,300,500 items. Additions are ongoing. Included in this collection are several types of materials, which are housed in appropriate sections of the library. The various types of materials are: manuscripts, books, pamphlets, maps, music, broadsides, newspapers, photographs, engravings, prints and memorabilia.

VA —RANDOLPH-MACON COLLEGE, Walter Hines Page Library, Ashland, 23005. Flavia Reed Owen, Librn
Holdings: Vols 5000 Serials
Budget: $6000
Notes: Bibliographical listing of collection in Intellectual Life in The Colonial South, 1585-1763/by Richard Beale Davis. (Knoxville: University of Tennessee Press, c 1978) 3 v.

SOUTHEY, ROBERT

CA —UNIVERSITY OF CALIFORNIA, SAN DIEGO, Central University Library, Mandeville Dept of Special Collections, La Jolla, 92093. Lynda Corey Claassen, Head
Holdings: Vols 350 Cat
Notes: Literary and historical output.

KY —UNIVERSITY OF KENTUCKY, Margaret I King Library, Dept of Special Collections, Lexington, 40506. William Marshall, Head
Holdings: Vols (8000) Cat Mss
Notes: W Hugh Peal Collection of mss and books chiefly relating to British and American literature. Particularly strong in Lamb, Wordsworth, Coleridge and Southey. Incl 4 cubic feet of mss. Incl 16th-20th centuries.

LA —TULANE UNIVERSITY, Howard-Tilton Memorial Library, Special Collections Div, 7001 Freret St, New Orleans, 70118. Wilbur E Meneray, Librn
Holdings: Vols 245 Cat
Notes: Published works by and about Robert Stendhal.

MD —JOHNS HOPKINS UNIVERSITY, Milton S Eisenhower Library, Charles & 34 Sts, Baltimore, 21218. Ann S Gwyn, Assistant Dir for Special Collections
Holdings: Vols 250 Cat Mss
Notes: Very strong Raymond Dexter Havens Collection, incl original and rare editions, and some of Southey's own books and memorabilia; a few letters.

MA —HARVARD UNIVERSITY LIBRARY, Houghton Library, Cambridge, 02138. Rodney G Dennis, Cur of Manuscripts
Holdings: Mss

NY —UNIVERSITY OF ROCHESTER, Rush Rhees Library, Department of Rare Books and Special Collections, Rochester, 14627. Peter Dzwonkoski, Librn
Holdings: Vols 300 Cat Mss Pix
Notes: Incl aprox 250 letters; manuscripts of poems incl the first complete draft of parts 1-7 of "The Curse of Kehama," and the fair-copy of the first version of "Joan of Arc"; also 17 autobiographical epistles to John May written between 1820-1826. The collection is described in: Volz, Robert and James Rieger, "The Rochester Southey Collection," the Wordsworth Circle, vol 5, no 2 (Spring, 1974), pp 89-91.

ON —VICTORIA UNIVERSITY, Library, 71 Queen's Park Crescent, Toronto, M5S 1K7, Can. Robert C Brandeis, Chief Librn
Holdings: Vols 1100 Cat Mss
Notes: A significant collection (second only to the British Museum) of books, mss, notebooks, correspondence, etc of Samuel Taylor Coleridge and his circle and family, including letters and mss of Wordsworth, Lamb and Southey, Catalog of collection by H O Dendurent in The Wordsworth Circle (Temple University, Philadelphia, Pa) 5:4 (Autumn 1974).

ON —UNIVERSITY OF WATERLOO, Library, Waterloo, N2L 3G1, Can. Susan Bellingham, Special Collections Librn
Holdings: Vols 800
Notes: Collection of works by and about

Robert Southey is a part of the Bertram R Davis Collection. Original and rare editions, some of Southey's own books, some manuscript pieces held in trust.

SOUTHWEST

AZ —FULTON-HAYDEN MEMORIAL LIBRARY, Dragoon, 85609. Mario Nick Klimiades, Librn
Holdings: Vols 17,000 Cat Mss Maps Pix Microforms
Budget: $3500
Notes: The Fulton-Hayden Memorial Library is a special collection of books about archaeology and ethnology specifically as they pertain to the western hemisphere and particularly to Mexico and the greater American Southwest.

AZ —FORT HUACHUCA HISTORICAL ASSOCIATION, Fort Huachuca, 85705. James P Finley, Dir
Holdings: Cat Mss Maps Pix Slides Microforms
Notes: Voluminous collection of documents concering Fort Huachuca, southeastern Arizona, Indians, poineer settlements, and military history. About 50,000 manuscript pieces and documents.

AZ —HUBBELL TRADING POST NATIONAL HISTORIC SITE, Library, PO Box 150, Ganado, 86505. L Edward Gastellum, Supt
Holdings: Vols (500) Cat Mss Maps Pix Slides Audiotapes
Notes: Incl copies of the Hubbell Trading Post Manuscripts and archives. Much on Navajo Indian life.

AZ —COLORADO RIVER INDIAN TRIBES MUSEUM/LIBRARY, Rte One, Box 23-B, Parker, 85344. Priscilla Johnson, Librn
Holdings: Cat Mss Maps Pix Slides Audiotapes Microforms
Notes: Library deals with the four tribes of the Colorado River Indian Reservation: Mojave, Chemehuevi, Navajo, and Hopi. Emphasis is also given to the prehistoric cultures of this area; Patayan and Hohokam. Library collections include original manuscripts and other documents, photographs, oral history tape recordings, cultural items and artifacts. Copies of many documents relating to the reservation are in bound volumes, microfilm, and photocopies. Photos relative to the reservation from various other collections are copied in our collection. Of particular interest is the museum baskets-the largest Chemehuevi basket collection. Other artifacts give special emphasis to the Mohave culture.

AZ —TOMBSTONE CITY LIBRARY, Box 218, Tombstone, 85638.

AZ —ARIZONA HERITAGE CENTER, Library, 949 E Second St, Tucson, 85719. Michael Weber, Dir
Notes: Espec with reference to Arizona, the West, and the Southwest.

AZ —ARIZONA STATE MUSEUM, Library, University of Arizona, Tucson, 85721. Hans R Bart, Museum Librn
Holdings: Vols (35,000) Cat Mss Maps Pix Slides Phonorecords Microforms
Budget: ($2000)

AZ —TUCSON PUBLIC LIBRARY, Governmental Reference Library, PO Box 27210, City Hall, Tucson, 85726. Ann Strickland, Librn
Holdings: Vols (4000) Cat Maps Audiotapes Microforms
Notes: Special emphasis on public administration, including public finance, public personnel management, social services, urban planning, public transportation, public works, water management, public recreation and government of growing southwestern US ccities in 200,000 to 500,000 population range.

AZ —YUMA CITY-COUNTY LIBRARY, 350 Third Ave, Yuma, 85364. Nancy R Cummings, Library Dir
Holdings: Vols 2500 Cat Microforms
Notes: The Southwest Collection incl Yuma, Arizona, surrounding states and Northern Mexico.

CA —CARLSBAD CITY LIBRARY, 1250 Elm Ave, Carlsbad, 92008. Clifford E Lange, Library Dir
Holdings: Vols 1300 Cat //

CA —LOS ANGELES PUBLIC LIBRARY, Social Sciences Dept, 630 W Fifth St, Los Angeles, 90071. Marilyn C Wherley, Principal Librn
Holdings: Vols 400 Microforms
Budget: ($150,000)
Notes: Emphasis on minorities; immigration policies, background and social problems of ethnic minorities in the US and the Southwest in particular. Incl periodicals, government publications and documents, popular and scholarly works on Blacks, Hispanics and Asians predominantly.

CO —COLORADO SPRINGS FINE ARTS CENTER LIBRARY, 30 W Dale St, Colorado Springs, 80903. Roderick Dew, Librn
Holdings: Vols (20,000) Cat
Budget: ($4000)
Notes: Specialize in fine arts and anthropology of the Southwest. Incl auction and exhibition catalogs.

DC —LIBRARY OF CONGRESS, Prints & Photographs Div, Washington, 20540.
Notes: The Erwin E Smith Collection of cowboy and ranch life. Gift of 1776 original glass and nitrate film negatives of pictures taken by him. Gift of his sister, Mrs L McC Pettis in 1949.

NM —UNIVERSITY OF NEW MEXICO, Zimmerman Library, Albuquerque, 87131.
Holdings: Mss Pix
Notes: Entire professional library and archives of John Gaw Meen, architect of the Southwest. Incl pictures of many buildings taken by noted photographers.

†NM —UNIVERSITY OF NEW MEXICO, Medical Center Library, Albuquerque, 87131. Beatrice Kovacs, Chief, Collections and Resource Development
Notes: Concern is health care and health services in New Mexico; medicine and medicine men of Indian tribes of the Southwest; and history of medicine and health in the Southwest.

NM —NEW MEXICO HIGHLANDS UNIVERSITY, Donnelly Library, National Ave, Las Vegas, 87701. Karen Jaggers, Assoc Librn
Holdings: Vols (5000) Cat Mss Maps Pix Microforms
Notes: The outstanding collection is the Arrott Collection on Fort Union, New Mexico, 1851-1891. Other collection incl Spanish Archives, Mexican Archives, Archdiocese of Santa Fe, Archivo del Parral; New Mexico Land Grants.

NM —MUSEUM OF NEW MEXICO, Laboratory of Anthropology Library, PO Box 2087, Santa Fe, 87503. Laura Holt, Librn
Holdings: Vols (16,000) Cat Mss Maps
Notes: Southwestern archaeology, anthropology, ethnology. Noncirculating. Also incl the personal Library (2000 vols) of Sylvanus Morley, Meso-American archaeologist and historian. Some materials on Indians of Middle America.

NY —STATE UNIVERSITY OF NEW YORK, COLLEGE OF ARTS & SCIENCE AT GENESEO, Milne Library, Geneseo, 14454. William T Lane, Head of Information Services & Archivist
Holdings: // Pix
Notes: The Martha Blow Wadsworth Collection. Photographs taken or collected by Mrs Wadsworth from the 1890s to around 1910. There are 33 albums containing 4561 mounted photographs, and 3 boxes containing 345 hand-tinted lantern slides. Subjects include horseback rides from Washington, DC to Avon, NY (1905-1909); US Army packtrain trips in the southwestern US (1907-1910); Hopi, Navajo, and Zuni Indians (1910); motor trip through France and England (1909); Panama Canal construction; Alaskan boundary survey trip; and the Wadsworth family of Livingston County, NY. There are no negatives. Inventory in repository. Open to qualified investigators with permission of archivist. Gift of Michael Moukhanoff, Ashantee, NY, 1976.

NY —AMERICAN MUSEUM OF NATURAL HISTORY, Library Services Dept, Central Park W & 79th St, New York,

SOUTHWEST (cont.)

10024. Nina J Root, Chairwoman; Mary Genett, Asst Librn for Reference Services
Holdings: Cat Mss Pix Microforms
Notes: The Ernest Thompson Seton diaries. Thousands of pages of an unpublished 67-year diary record of one of the world's most famous naturalists, the gift of Joseph F Cullman III, a Trustee of the Museum. Preserved in 35 protective cases, the gift incl unpublished diaries, notebooks, and some other writings. The diary begins 12 June 1879; the last entries were written in hospital, just a month before Seton's death in 1946. Literally hundreds of examples of flora and fauna are pictured in the diaries in original pencil, pen-and-ink, and watercolor sketches, on nearly every page. Research will reveal information on the Indian sign language, the Boy Scouts of America, the Woodcraft League of America, and the wilderness of Canada, Florida, Texas, the West and Southwest, etc.

TX —AMARILLO PUBLIC LIBRARY, 413 E Fourth, Amarillo, 79101. Mary Kay Snell, Librn
Notes: Collections

TX —UNIVERSITY OF TEXAS LIBRARIES, General Libraries, Barker Texas History Center, PO Box P, Austin, 78712. Don Carleton, Dir
Holdings: Vols (132,000) Cat Mss Maps Pix Slides Phonorecords Audiotapes Microforms
Notes: Materials pertaining to the historical, social, economic, scientific, humanistic and literary development of Texas. Rich in early state imprints, as well as the period of the Republic. Archival and ms holdings number over 18,000,000 items. Texas history prior to the Republic is covered by the Bexar Archives.

TX —WEST TEXAS STATE UNIVERSITY, Cornette Library, PO Box 748 WT Sta, Canyon, 79016. Faye Hendrickson, Special Collections Asst
Holdings: Vols (1850) Uncat Micoroforms
Notes: Includes microform collection.

TX —TEXAS A&M UNIVERSITY, Sterling C Evans Library, Special Collections Div, College Station, 77843. Donald H Dyal, Librn
Holdings: Vols (16,000) Mss Pix
Notes: Jeff Dykes Range Livestock Collection (incl a 600-item collection of J Frank Dobie works). Part of the Dobie Collection is described in Dykes, Jeff C *My Dobie Collection* (College Station, Tex: Friends of the Texas A & M University Library).

TX —BISHOP COLLEGE, Southwest Research Center Library, 3837 Simpson-Stuart Rd, Dallas, 75241.
Holdings: Vols 3,000
Notes: History and current status of blacks in the Southwestern US.

TX —TEXAS CHRISTIAN UNIVERSITY, Mary Couts Burnett Library, Fort Worth, 76129.
Notes: Assimilated into main collection of the University Library, adding special strengths but no longer maintained as a separate collection.

TX —TEXAS TECH UNIVERSITY, Library, Lubbock, 79409. David J Murrah, Assoc Dir for Special Collections

TX —KEMP PUBLIC LIBRARY, 1300 Lamar St, Wichita Falls, 76301. Jeannine Humphris, Libr Admin
Holdings: Vols (1775) Cat Mss Maps

SOUTHWEST—GENEALOGY

AZ —CHURCH OF JESUS CHRIST OF LATTER DAY SAINTS, Arizona Branch Genealogical Library, 464 E First Ave, Mesa, 85204. Joseph Lindbloom, Dir
Holdings: Vols (14,000) Cat Mss Maps Pix Microforms
Notes: Incl 25,000 microfilms with access to 1,300,000 rolls of microfilm available on loan.

CA —UNIVERSITY OF CALIFORNIA, BERKELEY, Bancroft Library, Manuscripts Division, Berkeley, 94720. James D Hart, Dir
Holdings: Vols Mss Maps Pix Slides Microforms
Notes: Approxi. twelve million pieces, with primary emphasis on California, with a lesser emphasis on the other Pacific States, incl. Alaska and the Province of British Columbia. In general, the Bancroft Library seeks to acquire historical and biographical works and primary source materials, documenting: the development of a geographic area or political unit; man and his activities, and his impact on the land and on his institutions. Methodological and theoretical work and texts in the physical and biological sciences are not collected, as a rule; exceptions here are publications essential to the study of an area's historical development and those providing general background information. Hubert Howe Bancroft's own distinguished holdings, assembled 1860-1880, constitute the core of the collection. The Bancroft Library's collections are noncirculating. A. G. K. Hall catalog has been published. The Bolton Collection (146,000 pages of archival material) contains ms. materials for the history of the Pacific Coast and the Southwest, gathered by Herbert Eugene Bolton. There is a comprehensive key to the arrangement of the collection.

OK —OKLAHOMA HISTORICAL SOCIETY, Library, Historical Bldg, Oklahoma City, 73105. Andrea Clark, Dir, Library Resources Division
Holdings: Vols (43,000) Cat Mss Maps Pix Microforms
Notes: The Society also has the Indian Archives Collection of 2,500,000 pieces (Mary Lee Boyle, Archivist). This is an extensive collection of records, particularly of the Five Civilized Tribes. Incl tribal rolls, agency reports, manuscripts, etc.

TX —DALLAS PUBLIC LIBRARY, Texas/ Dallas History and Archives Division, 1515 Young St, Dallas, 75201. Richard L Waters, Acting Dir; Wayne Gray, Manager
Notes: Dallas and Texas history.

TX —ECTOR COUNTY LIBRARY, Texas-Southwest History & Genealogy Dept, 321 W 5th St, Odessa, 79761. Jan Carter, Head
Holdings: Vols (6968) Cat Phonorecords Microforms
Budget: ($4000)
Notes: The genealogy collection is non-circulating. The materials are arranged by state and all periodicals for that state are shelved with the books. National Archives Census Microfilm is held, mainly, for Southern States and migratory routes into Texas.

TX —SAN ANTONIO COLLEGE, Library, 1001 Howard St, San Antonio, 78284. James O Wallace, Dir
Holdings: Vols 439 Cat Mss
Notes: Southwest Genealogical Society Collection. See: San Antonio College Library, *The Southwest Genealogical Society, A Catalogue of Holdings on Deposit in the Library.* San Antonio, Texas; San Antonio College, 1967.

SOUTHWEST—HISTORY

AZ —NORTHERN ARIZONA UNIVERSITY, Special Collection Library, CU Box 6022, Flagstaff, 86011. Peter M Whiteley, Coordr/Archivist; William Mullane, Librn
Holdings: Cat Mss Pix
Notes: Various collections, incl (1) Battle of Big Dry Wash; letters concerning placement of monument at the Battle of Big Dry Wash, last major Indian battle in Arizona, 1882, located near the Mogollon Rim. Incl letters written by W C Barnes, author of *Arizona Place Names*, and E G Miller, former Coconino National Forest supervisor, 1929-1934. (2) Henry William Bigler Collection. He was a Mormon pioneer with the Mormon Battalion, and was present at the Sutter gold discovery in Calif; journal, 1846-1853. (3) J Francisca Chavez Collection; photocopied report and journal by Chavez of his march while in command of the escort to the civil officers of the Arizona Territory from Santa Fe, New Mexico to Fort Whipple, Ariz, 1864.
See also entry under Arizona-History

AZ —PHOENIX PUBLIC LIBRARY, Arizona Room, 12 E McDowell, Phoenix, 85004. Jeannette Brush, Librn
Holdings: Vols (30,000) Cat Maps Pix
Budget: $12,000
Notes: The Arizona Room incl the following collections: James McClintock Collection on Arizona history--books, pamphlets, clippings, letters, scrapbooks and photos, notably of the Rough Riders and their training in the Prescott area; Indians of the Southwest, VF of clippings and pamphlets covering biography, local history, organizations, law and politics in Phoenix, Maricopa County and Arizona; US, Arizona and Phoenix government documents; 2500 maps, National Forest maps, historical, climatological, geological, vegetation and flood plain maps, as well as a few old, rare or unique items; and a comprehensive collection of materials relating to the Superstition Mountains and the search for the Lost Dutchman Gold Mine and others.

AZ —SIERRA VISTA LIBRARY, 2950 E Tacoma St, Sierra Vista, 85635. Catherine Helmick, Acting Library Administrator
Holdings: Vols (350) Cat
Notes: Arizona and the Southwest: primarily history; some natural history, social life and customs, desert living biography, and regional fiction.

AZ —ARIZONA STATE MUSEUM, Library, University of Arizona, Tucson, 85721. Hans R Bart, Museum Librn
Holdings: Vols 1000 Cat Mss
Notes: Books on Spanish missions in Arizona, New Mexico, Texas, California and particularly northern Mexico (Sonora). A private collection given to the library; it is not kept separate.

CA —ARCADIA PUBLIC LIBRARY, 20 W Duarte Rd, Arcadia, 91006. James M Domney, City Librn
Notes: California history.

CA —AZUSA PACIFIC COLLEGE, Marshburn Memorial Library, Citrus & Alosta, Azusa, 91702. Edward Peterman, Librn
Holdings: Vols (6000) Uncat
Budget: ($30,000)
Notes: Significant holdings in the George E Fullerton Library of California and Western Americana.

CA —BURBANK PUBLIC LIBRARY, 110 N Glenoaks Blvd, Burbank, 91502. Mary Ann Grasso, Coordr; Barbara Stones, Coordr, Media Project
Holdings: Vols 4000 Cat
Notes: Incl materials on all states west of the Mississippi River. Many good runs of state historical journals and regional periodicals. About half the listings in J Frank Dobie's *Guide to Life and Literature of the Southwest.* See description in *California Librarian,* April 1965, "The Burbank Western History Collection," by Thomas F Parker.

CA —CALIFORNIA STATE UNIVERSITY, FULLERTON, Library, Box 4150, Fullerton, 92634. Alfredo H Zuniga, Coord
Notes: Some materials on the subject; not maintained as a separate collection.

CO —FORT LEWIS COLLEGE, Library, Southwest Collection, College Heights, Durango, 81301. Daniel W Lester, Dir
Holdings: Vols (7000) Cat Mss Maps Pix Slides Microforms
Budget: ($3800)
Notes: Also have separate catalog of the

SOUTHWEST—HISTORY (cont.)

special collections concerning the Southwest, Indians, mine records, railroad, etc.

CT —YALE UNIVERSITY, Beincke Rare Book & Manuscript Library, Western Americana Collection, Wall & High St, New Haven, 06520. George Miles, Cur
Holdings: Cat Mss Maps Pix
Notes: Incl much historical ephemeral material.

NM —NEW MEXICO HIGHLANDS UNIVERSITY, Donnelly Library, National Ave, Las Vegas, 87701. Karen Jaggers, Assoc Librn
Holdings: Vols 2650
Notes: The outstanding collection is the Arrott Collection on Fort Union, New Mexico, 1851-1891. Other collection incl Spanish Archives, Mexican Archives, Archdiocese of Santa Fe, Archivo del Parral; New Mexico Land Grants.

NM —EASTERN NEW MEXICO UNIVERSITY, Golden Library, Special Collections, Portales, 88130. Mary Jo Walker, Special Collections Librn
Holdings: Vols Cat Mss Pix Audiotapes
Notes: Incl 176 cataloged books by F Stanley (pseudonym of Catholic priest and historian Stanley Francis Louis Crocchiola), plus his collection of periodicals and books by other writers pertaining to southwestern history (particularly New Mexico and the Texas panhandle); 22.25 cubic ft of mss, correspondence files, photographs of F Stanley and others, and two oral history interviews with F Stanley. Unpublished register of collection available. Bio/bibliography of F Stanley in preparation.

NM —ROSWELL PUBLIC LIBRARY, 301 N Pennsylvania Ave, Roswell, 88201. Sarah Beth Galloway, Library Dir
Holdings: Vols (2000) Cat Maps
Budget: $1500
Notes: Covers literature (fiction and nonfiction), history, biography, geography, of Oklahoma, Texas, Colorado, New Mexico and Arizona.

NM —MUSEUM OF NEW MEXICO, History Library, PO Box 2087, Santa Fe, 87503. Orlando Romero
Holdings: Vols 10,000 Cat Mss Maps Microforms
Notes: History of the Southwest, emphasis on history of New Mexico, incl New Mexican newspapers. Restricted use; noncirculating. 2500 maps; 700 microforms.

OK —OKLAHOMA HISTORICAL SOCIETY, Library, Historical Bldg, Oklahoma City, 73105. Andrea Clark, Dir, Library Resources Division
Holdings: Vols (43,000) Cat Mss Maps Pix Microforms
Notes: The Society also has the Indian Archives Collection of 2,500,000 pieces (Mary Lee Boyle, Archivist). This is an extensive collection of records, particularly of the Five Civilized Tribes. Incl tribal rolls, agency reports, manuscripts, etc.

TX —HARDIN-SIMMONS UNIVERSITY, Richardson Library, Abilene, 79601. Joe F Dahlstrom, Dir
Holdings: Vols (10,000) Cat Mss Maps Microforms
Notes: Special collection name is Richardson Research Center, named in honor of Dr Rupert N Richardson. Collect in the areas of his own research interests, especially that portion of the US that was once a part of Mexico. Emphases on the history of ranching, railroads, discovery and exploration, Texas county histories, etc. Incl 350 items printed and-or designed by El Paso printer Carl Hertzog; the Judge R C Crane collection of Texana and a similar collection of Louise Kelley's; and the Research Publication's Western American collection (microfilm).

TX —PANHANDLE-PLAINS HISTORICAL MUSEUM, Research Center, Box 967, WT Sta, Canyon, 79016. Claire R Kuehn, Archivist-Librn
Notes: History of the Spanish Southwest Collection. 23 reels of microfilm (100 ft each). Microfilm copies of correspondence,

reports and miscellaneous documents and maps from the Archivo General de Indias, Seville, Spain, Museo Naval, Madrid, archives in Mexico and other Latin American countries, dealing with the expedition of Francisco Vazquez de Coronado.

TX —CISCO JUNIOR COLLEGE, Maner Memorial Library, LRC Rte 3, Cisco, 76437. Oleta Shirley, Dir
Holdings: Vols 3000 Cat
Notes: Texana and history of the Southwest.

TX —DALLAS PUBLIC LIBRARY, Texas/Dallas History and Archives Division, 1515 Young St, Dallas, 75201. Richard L Waters, Acting Dir; Wayne Gray, Manager
Holdings: Vols (152,442) Cat Maps Pix Slides Microforms
Budget: ($38,540)
Notes: Dallas and Texas history.

TX —UNIVERSITY OF TEXAS, DALLAS, Health Science Center, Reference Dept & History of Health Sciences Dept, 5323 Harry Hines Blvd, Dallas, 75235. Helen Mayo, Head
Holdings: Vols (10,000) Cat Pix Slides Audiotapes Videotapes Microforms
Notes: History of Medicine collection contains ca 10,000 vols. This total is comprised of pre-1900 journals, primary materials in the History of Medicine and the History of Science, and secondary studies in these two areas. The major strengths of this collection are in the areas of epidemics and plagues, military medicine, and collected works of famous medical pioneers. Incl in this collection are the medical journals published by the county medical societies in Texas, local publications by Dallas County medical organizations, and ephemeral material in a similar vein. The university archives contain all theses and dissertations form UTHSCD and miscellaneous institutional documents circulated by the school's administration.

TX —EL PASO PUBLIC LIBRARY, Southwest Collection, 501 N Oregon, El Paso, 79901. Mary A Sarber, Head
Holdings: Vols (12,000) Cat Mss Maps Pix
Budget: ($11,000)
Notes: Research collection includes rare books and mss journals, vertical files, index to El Paso newspapers, microfilmed newspapers, photographs, and architectural plans. Separate catalog. Limited to materials on Texas, New Mexico, Arizona and Mexico. Special collections of material by and about Tom Lea Jr, and Carl Hertzog. Aultman Collection of photographs includes 3500 on El Paso Southwest and 2500 on Mexican Revolution. Cited in Lovelace, Lisa, "The Southwest Collection of the El Paso Public Library". *Great Plains Journal*, vol 2, no 2, pp 161-166; Aultman, Otis A *Photographs from the Border: The Otis A Aultman Collection*, El Paso Public Library Association, 1977.

TX —UNIVERSITY OF TEXAS, EL PASO, Library, Special Collections Dept, El Paso, 79968. Cesar Caballero, Dept Head
Holdings: Vols 8440 Cat
Budget: ($5000)
Notes: Southwest and Border Studies Collection. This collection contains books on the history of Texas, New Mexico and other Southwestern States. It also contains a growing number of books on Border Studies.

TX —ECTOR COUNTY LIBRARY, Texas-Southwest History & Genealogy Dept, 321 W 5th St, Odessa, 79761. Jan Carter, Head
Holdings: Vols (8500) Cat Maps Pix
Budget: ($4000)
Notes: A card catalog of Texas-History; Southwest, New-History; Oklahoma-History is located in the Texas-Southwest History Dept. A card file by subject is a guide to vertical file materials and Texas, New Mexico, Oklahoma, Arizona periodicals. The Texas-History collection has reference, closed shelf, and circulating books.

TX —KEMP PUBLIC LIBRARY, 1300 Lamar St, Wichita Falls, 76301. Jeannine Humphris, Libr Admin
Holdings: Vols (1775) Cat Mss Maps

UT —UTAH STATE UNIVERSITY, Merrill Library, Department of Special Collections

& Archives, Logan, 84322. A J Simmonds, Curator; Jeanie F Simmonds, Archivist; Bradford R Cole, Mss Librn
Holdings: Vols 4000 Cat
Notes: Books pamphlets, manuscripts on the history of Arizona and New Mexico. Complete holding of the Wallace bibliography citations. All books Cat.

SOUTHWEST—MAPS

AZ —ARIZONA STATE UNIVERSITY, University Library, Map Service, Tempe, 85281.
Holdings: Maps
Notes: 150,000 maps which cover the world, some concentration on Arizona and Southwest. Also some historical maps.

AZ —ARIZONA HISTORICAL SOCIETY, Research Library, Maps Section, 949 E Second St, Tucson, 85710.
Holdings: Maps
Notes: Historical maps of Arizona and the southwest. Ninety percent of collection is pre-1900. 1500 maps in the collection.

AZ —UNIVERSITY OF ARIZONA, Library, Map Collection, Tucson, 85721. Mary L Blakely, Map Librn
Holdings: Maps
Notes: 180,000 for world special concentration of Arizona and Southwest maps.

SOUTHWEST—POLITICS AND GOVERNMENT

TX —RICE UNIVERSITY, Fondren Library, Woodson Research Center, 6100 S Main St, PO Box 1892, Houston, 77251. Nancy Parker, Dir Woodson Research Center
Notes: The papers of Walter Benona Sharp and Estelle Boughton Sharp. His papers consist of letters written to his wife and family from 1890 to 1912 as well as papers relating to his involvement in the oil business. Her papers cover a variety of topics, incl United Charities, the peace movement, Rice University, her business and financial affairs, and her efforts to record the history of the oil industry in the Southwest.

SOUTHWEST, NEW see Southwest

SOUTHWEST, OLD

MO —WASHINGTON UNIVERSITY, John M Olin Library, Campus Box 1061, St Louis, 63130.
Holdings: Vols (1800) Cat Mss
Notes: Incl material from the Arthur C Hoskins, Richard S Hawes, Ernst C Krohn, George N Meissner, Strafford Lee Morton, and Edgar M Queeny collections; strong in early travel liteature of the US and Latin America; accounts of exploration in the Mississippi Valley and Trans-Mississippi West; miscellaneous accounts of history, pioneer life, and travel in the Ohio Valley, Old Southwest, and California; material on the American Indian; 18th century American music; early American imprints.

TN —UNIVERSITY OF TENNESSEE, KNOXVILLE, Library, Knoxville, 37996. John Dobson, Special Collections Librn
Holdings: Vols (20,000) Cat Mss Maps Pix
Notes: Tennesseana; 19th century American fiction; southern Indians; early Imprints. Separate catalog; holdings also listed in comprehensive public catalog in Main Library. Rare books card catalog with special headings calling attention to unusual features of the books; unpublished registers and calendars to ms collection. *Kefauver* collection, 59,000 pounds of political papers and memorabilia, reconstructed Senate office; *Radiation Biology Archives* (ca 60,000 pieces), papers of scientists from several countries dealing with the development of radiation biology. Also, 18 vols of extremely rare Southwest Territory and *Tennessee Official Journals*, printed in Knoxville, 1794-1796. The rare *Acts and Journals* are described in *The Lost Roullstone Imprints*, by John Dobson (Knoxville: Univ of Tennessee Libraries, 1975), 70 pp.

SOUTH-WEST AFRICA see Namibia

SOUTHWESTERN ARCHITECTURE see Architecture, Southwestern

SOUTHWESTERN ART see Art, Southwestern

SOUTHWESTERN INDIANS see Indians of North America and Mexico—Southwest

SOUTHWORTH, E. D. E. N.

NC —DUKE UNIVERSITY, William R Perkins Library, Manuscript Dept, Durham, 27706. Ellen Gartrell, Cur of Mss
Holdings: Cat Mss
Notes: Papers, correspondence, etc.

SOUTHWORTH-ANTHOENSEN PRESS

ME —UNIVERSITY OF MAINE AT PORTLAND-GORHAM, Portland Campus Library, 96 Falmouth St, Portland, 04103. Albert A Howard, Special Collections Librn
Holdings: Vols 900 Cat
Notes: Collection incl broadsides, prospectuses and other printed ephemera (not cataloged). Also some imprints of Southworth-Anthoensen. Collection is comprehensive. Collection is in main catalog and there is a separte shelf list.

SOUTHWORTH PRESS

ME —PORTLAND PUBLIC LIBRARY, 5 Monument Sq, Portland, 04101. Edward V Chenevert, Library Dir
Holdings: Vols 427 Cat
Notes: Originated as the Southworth Printing Company and was concerned with producing religious tracts. The scope of the press broadened under the later ownership (ca 1923) of Fred Anthoensen; it is still publishing.

SOUVARINE, BORIS K.

CA —HOOVER INSTITUTION ON WAR, REVOLUTION & PEACE, Stanford University, Stanford, 94305. Milorad M Drachkovitch, Archivist
Holdings: Mss
Notes: Papers of Boris K Souvarine, Russian-born French communist, incl correspondence, writings, clippings, printed matter and other material, 1925-1971, relating to the French Communist Party, the Communist International, Marxism, Soviet agricultural and economic policies, and political events in 20th century Russia. The papers consist primarily of correspondence with Ekaterina Kuskova, Sergei Prokopovich, Nikolai V Vilsky and the Marx-Engels Institute (Moscow).

SOVIET LAW see Law, Soviet

SOVIET UNION see Russia

SOY-BEAN see Soybean

SOYA BEAN see Soybean

SOYBEAN

IL —ILLINOIS FARM BUREAU LIBRARY, 1701 Towanda Ave, PO Box 1901, Bloomington, 61701. Rue E Olson, Librn
Holdings: Vols (24,000) Cat Microforms
Budget: ($25,000)
Notes: Emphasis on Illinois.

SOYER, MOSES

DC —SMITHSONIAN INSTITUTION, National Museum of American Art & the National Portrait Gallery Library, Eighth & F Sts, NW, Washington, 20560. Cecilia Chin, Librn

SOYOT LANGUAGE

NY —NEW YORK PUBLIC LIBRARY, Oriental Div, Fifth Ave & 42 St, New York,

10018. E Christian Filstrup, Chief
Holdings: Cat Mss Microforms
Budget: ($56,455)
Notes: Published catalog of holdings.

SPACE EXPLORATION (ASTRONAUTICS) see Outer Space Exploration

SPACE FLIGHT AND TECHNOLOGY

AL —UNIVERSITY OF ALABAMA, HUNTSVILLE, Library, Box 2600, Huntsville, 35807. John Warren, Dir
Holdings: Vols (4500)
Notes: The Willy Ley Collection of Rocketry and Space Travel.

CA —HOOVER INSTITUTION ON WAR, REVOLUTION & PEACE, Stanford University, Stanford, 94305. Milorad M Drachkovitch, Archivist
Holdings: Mss
Notes: Papers of Charles E Weakley, Vice Admiral US Navy, commander, Antisubmarine Warfare Force, Atlantic Fleet, 1963-67, and assistant administrator for management development, National Aeronautics and Space Administration, 1968-72, incl correspondence, order, drafts of speeches, printed matter, photographs, and sound recordings, 1945-72, relating to post-World War II US antisubmarine force operations and to NASA activities 4 ms boxes.

CO —DENVER PUBLIC LIBRARY, 1357 Broadway, Denver, 80203.
Holdings: Cat Maps Pix
Notes: The Ross-Barrett Historical Aeronautics Collection, incl ballooning. Also early "man in space" technical material.

MA —SMITHSONIAN INSTITUTION LIBRARIES, Astrophysical Observatory Branch, 60 Garden St, Cambridge, 02138. Joyce Rey, Librn
Holdings: Vols (10,000) Cat Maps Pix Microforms

NJ —PRINCETON UNIVERSITY, Library, Manuscript Collection, Nassau St, Princeton, 08540. Jean F Preston, Cur
Holdings: Cat Mss Maps Pix
Notes: Incl the collection of G Edward Pendray detailing the entry of the United States into the space age; much on early rocketry and the work of Richard H Goddard. Incl 71 boxes, 17 file drawers.

NY —IBM CORP, Information Retrieval and Library Services, Owego, 13827. Richard Duffy, Librn
Holdings: Vols (12,000) Cat Pix Microforms
Notes: Computer technology for military and space use. Also 45,000 reports, 7500 bound period vols.

PA —ALLIANCE COLLEGE, Washington Hall Library, Fullerton Ave, Cambridge Springs, 16403. Stanley J Kozaczka, Head Librn
Notes: A NASA depository of declassified documents.

AB —CENTENNIAL PLANETARIUM, Library, PO Box 2100, 701 Eleventh St, Calgary, T2P 2M5, Can. Sig Wieser, Librn
Holdings: Vols (400) Uncat Pix Audiotapes 16mm Films
Notes: Also western Canadian aviation history with bias towards technology; and history of space technology; and history of space technology.

SPACE LAW

OK —UNIVERSITY OF OKLAHOMA, Law Library, 300 Timberdell Rd, Norman, 73019. Laura N Gasaway, Dir
Holdings: Vols 2500 Cat 16mm Films Microforms
Notes: Legal and non-legal materials; American and foreign; treatises and periodicals. There has been only limited development of this collection since 1970.

SPACE MEDICINE see Aerospace Medicine

SPACE PHYSICS

IA —UNIVERSITY OF IOWA, Physics Library, Iowa City, 52242. Jack W Dickey,

Physics Librn
Holdings: Vols (36,199) Cat
Budget: ($79,000)
Notes: General physics and space physics.

NJ —AT&T BELL LABORATORIES, Libraries and Information Systems Center, 600 Mountain Ave, Murray Hill, 07974. W D Penniman, Dir
Holdings: Vols (273,100) Cat Mss Audiotapes Videotapes Microforms
Budget: ($670,000)
Notes: Use restricted to BTL Employees. Catalogs/Indexes: Bell Laboratories Library Network Book Catalog; Bell Laboratories Bibliographies; Bell Laboratories Translations. Bell Laboratories Library Networks.

SPACE RADIATION see Aerospace Medicine

SPACE SCIENCES

†AZ —UNIVERSITY OF ARIZONA, Space Imagery Center, Lunar & Planetary Laboratory, Tucson, 85721. Gail G Georgenson, Librn
Notes: Planetary science. Interests incl Space Probs - Gemini; Apollo; Lunar Orbiter; Mariner 6, 7 9, 10; Pioneer 10 & 11; Viking 1 & 2. Regional Planetary Image Facilities are in Flagstaff, Ariz; Pasadena, Calif; Saint Louis, MO; Ithaca, NY; Providence, RI; Houston, Tex; Rome, Italy; London, England.

CA —UNIVERSITY OF CALIFORNIA, BERKELEY, Bancroft Library, Manuscripts Division, Berkeley, 94720. James D Hart, Dir
Holdings: Mss
Notes: Papers of Samuel Silver, specialist on applied electromagnetic, microwave, and radio astronomical problems. Much on the International Union of Radio Science. 48 linear ft.

CA —GRIFFITH OBSERVATORY, Library, 2800 E Observatory Rd, Los Angeles, 90027. E C Krupp, Dir
Holdings: Vols (2200) Cat Pix Slides Phonorecords
Budget: ($1000)
Notes: No separate catalog. No photocopying.

CA —UNIVERSITY OF CALIFORNIA, LOS ANGELES, Engineering & Mathematical Sciences Library, 405 Hilgard, Los Angeles, 90024. Rosalee I Wright, Librn
Holdings: Vols (180,000) Cat Microforms
See also entry under Engineering

CA —UNIVERSITY OF CALIFORNIA, LOS ANGELES, Geology-Geophysics Library, 4697 Geology Bldg, Los Angeles, 90024. Sarah E How, Geology-Geophysics Librn
Holdings: Vols (85,000) Cat Maps Microforms
Notes: Incl theses and dissertations of UCLA Dept of Earth and Space Sciences; and (2000) serial titles.

CA —NASA, Ames Research Center, Libraries, Library Br 202-3, Moffett Field, 94035. Sarah Dueker, Chief, Library Branch
Holdings: Cat Audiotapes Microforms
Notes: Main library collections cover physical sciences, engineering and mathematical fields related to research programs in aeronautics-space research. Life sciences library collections cover medical, physiological, behavioral and biological sciences related to research programs. Also emphasis on remote sensing of earth resources and the search for extraterrestrial life. 950 journal titles and 85,000 monographs. Reports collection includes 60, 000 hard copy reports and 900,000 microfiche.

CO —UNIVERSITY OF COLORADO, Libraries, Western Historical Collections, Boulder, 80309.
Holdings: Mss Slides Films
Notes: Papers of the world renowned space scientist and recipient of many honors, Walter Orr Roberts (1915-), who is currently associated with the University of Colorado as a professor of astro-geophysics. He has written extensively on solar activity

SPACE SCIENCES (cont.)

and its effects on earth. The collection is comprised of correspondence with individuals and business and research organizations, reports, proposals and conference data, speeches, committee papers, studies, research notes, lectures and student papers plus a few personal papers, printed matter, films and slides. Also there are personal items which belonged to M Sydney Chapman and were given to Roberts. 60 boxes, 1940s-1970s. Typescript inventory is available.

FL —FLORIDA INSTITUTE OF TECHNOLOGY, Library, 150 W University Blvd, PO Box 1150, Melbourne, 32901. L L Henson, Dir of Libraries
Holdings: Vols 800 Cat Maps Pix

IA —UNIVERSITY OF IOWA, Physics Library, Iowa City, 52242. Jack W Dickey, Physics Librn
Holdings: Vols (36,199) Cat
Budget: ($79,000)
Notes: General physics and space physics.

MA —UNIVERSITY OF MASSACHUSETTS AT AMHERST, Physical Sciences Library, Amherst, 01003. Siegfried Feller, Assoc Dir for Collection Development
Holdings: Vols Cat Microforms
Notes: Incl extensive holdings of journals, NACA and NASA publications, and AEC documents (microfiche).

NJ —AT&T BELL LABORATORIES, Libraries and Information Systems Center, 600 Mountain Ave, Murray Hill, 07974. W D Penniman, Dir
Holdings: Vols (273,100) Cat Mss Audiotapes videotapes Microforms
Budget: ($670,000)
Notes: Restricted use to AT&T employees. Catalogs/Indexes: Bell Laboratories Library Network and Book Serial Catalogs; Bell Laboratories Translations. Bell Laboratories Library Network with New Jersey libraries located in Holmdel, Murray Hill, Piscataway, Whippany, Princeton, Short Hills, Summit, West Long Branch, Crawford Hill; libraries also in Allentown, Pennsylvania; Reading, Pennsylvania; New York, New York; Atlanta, Georgia; Columbus, Ohio; Naperville, Illinois; Indianapolis, Indiana; North Andover, Massachusetts.

NY —POLYTECHNIC INSTITUTE OF NEW YORK, Long Island Center Library, Route 110, Farmingdale, 11735. Lorraine Schein, Branch Librn
Notes: Wood Memorial Collection (reference); NACA/NASA documents.

NY —AMERICAN INSTITUTE OF AERONAUTICS & ASTRONAUTICS, Technical Information Service, 555 West 57th St, New York, 10019. Patricia Marshall, Dir, Library Resources
Holdings: Vols (57,000) Cat Microforms
Notes: Basis of published literature input to NASA Information System: Special index-- Semimonthly issues of *International Aerospace Abstracts* with cumulated annual indexes.

NY —AMERICAN MUSEUM-HAYDEN PLANETARIUM, Richard S Perkin Library, 81 St & Central Park W, New York, 10024. Sandra Kitt, Librn
Holdings: Vols (15,000) Cat Maps Pix Slides
Notes: Considered one of the strongest and most complete astronomy libraries on the east coast. Contains the Bliss Collection of Ancient Astronomical Instruments; also the Mt Wilson/Bloman Sky Survey to the 45 degree declination; the Lick Observatory Survey; *American Ephemeris and Nautical Almanac*, 1855-date.

NY —IBM CORP, Information Retrieval and Library Services, Owego, 13827. Richard Duffy, Librn
Holdings: Vols (12,000) Cat Pix Microforms
Notes: Computer technology for military and space use. Also 45,000 reports, 7500 bound period vols.

PA —ENSANIAN PHYSICOCHEMICAL INSTITUTE, Library, PO Box 98, Eldred, 16731. Elisabeth Anahid Ensanian, Chief Librn
Holdings: Vols 200 Cat Mss Slides Films

Microforms
Budget: $3800
Notes: The institute has pioneered the field of Gravitation Chemistry (term coined at the institute) and has original date and reports on this pheomenon, generated from its own research, that cannot be found elsewhere in the world. Also publishes own technical journal. This special collection, which also incl the biological effects of weightlessness, is continually being increased.

PA —FRANKLIN INSTITUTE LIBRARY, 20 & The Parkway, Philadelphia, 19103. Miriam Padusis, Dir; Charles Wilt, Readers Servs Librn
Holdings: Vols (300,000) Cat Maps Pix Microforms

PA —BUHL PLANETARIUM & INSTITUTE OF POPULAR SCIENCE, Staff Library, Allegheny Sq, Pittsburgh, 15212. Al DeSena, Dir
Holdings: Vols 1000 Cat Mss Maps Pix Slides Films
Notes: Science-oriented vols with several texts of historical value dating back to the 19th century.

PA —UNIVERSITY OF PITTSBURGH, Physics Library, 208 Engineering Hall, Pittsburgh, 15260. Paul J Kobulnicky, Physical Sciences Librn
Holdings: Vols (25,000) Cat Microforms
Budget: ($100,000)
Notes: The Physics Library collection is both a graduate student research-level collection in basic experimental and theoretical physics with emphasis on solid-state, nuclear, upper-atmosphere, space, and crystallography, and also a collection in the earth and planetary sciences, serving both graduate and undergraduate students. The collection is cataloged in both the University of Pittsburgh, Hillman Library union catalog and in a seperate catalog in the Physics Library.

†SD —SOUTH DAKOTA SCHOOL OF MINES & TECHNOLOGY, Devereaux Library, Rapid City, 57701.
Holdings: Vols 400 Cat
Notes: Also, about 7400 hard copies of NASA Technical Reports. Have a Lunar Orbiter Photograph Collection.

TN —UNIVERSITY OF TENNESSEE, Space Institute Library, Tullahoma, 37388. Helen B Mason, Librn
Holdings: Vols (14,000) Cat Microforms
Budget: ($50,000)
Notes: Incl NASA and other series of technical reports.

UT —HANSEN PLANETARIUM LIBRARY, 15 S State St, Salt Lake City, 84101. Randall A Curtis, Librn; Sharon Johnston, Children's Librn
Holdings: Vols 1500 Cat Maps Pix Audiotapes
Budget: $1800

AB —CENTENNIAL PLANETARIUM, Library, PO Box 2100, 701 Eleventh St, Calgary, T2P 2M5, Can. Sig Wieser, Librn
Holdings: Vols (400) Uncat Pix Audiotapes 16mm Films
Notes: Also western Canadian aviation history with bias towards technology; and history of space technology.

SPACE SHIPS—PILOTS see Astronauts

SPACE TRAVEL see Space Flight and Technology

SPACE VEHICLES—INSTRUMENTS see Astronautical Instruments

SPAIN

CA —UNIVERSITY OF CALIFORNIA, SAN DIEGO, Central University Library, Mandeville Dept of Special Collections, La Jolla, 92093. Lynda Corey Claassen, Head
Notes: Hispanic Collection: Approx 6000 vols describe cultures of Spain, Portugal, Mexico, Latin America, and South America. Works of literature, history, philosophy and art date from the 15th to the mid-19th century. Highlights of the collection include rare 18th century Spanish provincial dramas and works on the history of Seville and Andalusia.

MO —WASHINGTON UNIVERSITY, John M Olin Library, Campus Box 1061, St Louis, 63130.
Holdings: Vols (15,000) Cat Microforms
Notes: Major subject concentraion.

NY —HISPANIC SOCIETY OF AMERICA, Library, 613 W 155 St, New York, 10032. Martha M de Narvaez, Cur of Mss; Irene S Frye, Asst Librn
Holdings: Vols (150,000) Cat Mss Maps Pix Slides Phonorecords Microforms
Notes: History, art, literature and general culture of the Hispanic countries (where Spanish or Portuguese is spoken). Incl (18,000) vols printed before 1701, incl (250) incunabula; over (100,000) later vols, plus thousands of periodicals. About (200,000) mss incl ms maps. Printed atlases are in the Book Collection. Some microfilms, chiefly of our early books. Engraved and printed separate maps; reference collection of over 100,000 photographs; slides: all in Department of Iconography, not in library. Catalogs: *Catalogue of the Hispanic Society of America* (Boston: G K Hall, 1962), 10 vols; *First Supplement* (Boston, 1970), 4 vols. Early books: *Printed Books 1468-1700*; Mss: *Catalogo de los Manuscritos Poeticos Castellanos* (15th-17th centuries; 3 vols); *Medieval Manuscripts in the Library*; *Golden Age Drama Manuscripts* (the latter in press).

SPAIN—CIVILIZATION AND CULTURE

CT —UNIVERSITY OF CONNECTICUT, Library, Storrs, 06268. R H Schimmelpfeng, Dir of Special Collections
Holdings: Vols (1650) Cat Mss Maps Pix
Notes: Collection incl all aspects of the history, social life, politics, economics, etc, of Madrid. Core of collection was property of Jose Luis Oliva Escribano.

WI —UNIVERSITY OF WISCONSIN, MADISON, Seminary of Medieval Spanish Studies, 1130 Van Hise Hall, Madison, 53706. Lloyd A Kasten, Emeritus Prof of Spanish
Notes: Spanish medieval materials forming a part of the Seminary of Medieval Spanish Studies, 100 reels of microfilm, 2500 pamphlets and reprints, photostats, and over 600,000 vocabulary cards.

SPAIN—EXPLORING EXPEDITIONS

NY —STATE UNIVERSITY OF NEW YORK, STONY BROOK, Melville Library, Dept of Special Collections, Stony Brook, 11794. Evert Volkersz, Head
Holdings: Uncat
Notes: Spanish-American colonial trade. 101 documents of the 16th and 17th centuries presenting information about trade and administration of the Spanish-American colonies and important for linking political and financial connection. A listing of the materials is available.

SPAIN—HISTORY

CA —UNIVERSITY OF CALIFORNIA, BERKELEY, Bancroft Library, Manuscripts Division, Berkeley, 94720. James D Hart, Dir
Holdings: Mss Microforms
Notes: In addition to numerous mss relating to the history of western North America (westen plains to the Pacific Coast, Alaska to Panama), The Bancroft Library has many ms collections of significance in other areas. The following collections are large enough to justify the attention of serious researchers; most are analyzed in unpublished keys to arrangement. History collections incl Archives of California (1757-1822), Archives of Mexico and Spain (microcopies); Herbert Eugene Bolton; British West Indies Documents, Danish West Indies Documents, Dutch West Indies Documents; John Charles Fremont; Japanese American Evacuation and Resettlement. Scientific and technological collections incl the papers of many important modern scientists (some individually listed in this volume).

SPAIN—HISTORY (cont.)

CA —UNIVERSITY OF CALIFORNIA, SAN DIEGO, Central University Library, Mandeville Dept of Special Collections, La Jolla, 92093. Lynda Corey Claassen, Head
Notes: Hispanic Collection: Approx 6000 vols describe cultures of Spain, Portugal, Mexico, Latin America, and South America. Works of literature, history, philosophy and art date from the 15th to the mid-19th century. Highlights of the collection include rare 18th century Spanish provincial dramas and works on the history of Seville and Andalusia. Also, Southworth Collection: Focusing on the founding of Spain's Second Republic and the Spanish Civil War of 1936-1939, the collection numbers approximately 13,000 monographs, pamphlets, and newspapers. Works by both Republicans and Falangists are included, as are works by non-Spanish writers working during that period.

†CT —PHILIPPINE-AMERICAN RESEARCH CENTER, Library, PO Box507, Sharoni, 06069. John Silva, Dir
Holdings: Vols 200 Maps Pix
Notes: Philippine history and culture from pre-colonial times to the present, as well as under Spanish, Japanese, and American regimes, and post-independence. Mostly rare works of the late 19th and early 20th century; history and anthropology. Over 2, 500 photographs. Incl maps, posters, memorabilia. Limited copying. Visits by appointment.

CT —UNIVERSITY OF CONNECTICUT, Library, Storrs, 06268. R H Schimmelpfeng, Dir of Special Collections
Holdings: Cat Maps Pix
Notes: Three collections: (1) Manuscript material relating to activities in the Philippines and Spain of Valeriano Weyler y Nicolau, Duque de Rubi ("Butcher Weyler"). Uncataloged. (2) Collection of newspapers and periodicals formerly belonging to the Duque de T'Serclaes. Ranging from the 17th century through the 20th, the bulk of titles are from 1800-1840, covering the Napoleonic period and the Latin American wars of independence. (3) All aspects of the history, social life, politics, economics, etc, of Madrid. Core of collection was property of Jose Luis Oliva Escribano.

DC —AMERICAN HISTORICAL COLLECTION, US Embassy, Manilla, Philippines, c/o US Dept of State, Washington, 20525. Aurora P Galvez, Librn; Lewis E Gleeck Jr, Cur
Notes: The American Historical Collection is located at 1201 Roxas Blvd, Metro Manilla, Philippines. Incl the William Cameron Forbes, Eugene A Perkins Memorial Library, Leonard Dawson, and Sternberg Collections. Some Spanish Period materials, much on later history, espec American period.

DC —GEORGETOWN UNIVERSITY, Library, Special Collections Div, 37 & O Sts NW, Washington, 20057. George M Barringer, Special Collections Librn; Nicholas B Sheetz, Mss Librn
Holdings: Mss Cat
Notes: A collection of 242 medieval Latin and Catalan charters previously belonging to Frederick C Scheuch, ranging in date from 1261 to 1690. The documents comprise the archives of the Sala family who owned the castle of Montorroell in Catalonia, Spain. See Joseph J Gwara, Jr's *The Sala Family Archives: A Handlist of Medieval and Early Modern Catalonian Manuscripts.*

IN —INDIANA UNIVERSITY, Lilly Library, Seventh St, Bloomington, 47405. William R Cagle, Librn
Holdings: Vols 10,000 // Cat Mss
Notes: Begins with the conquest of Mexico by Cortes and his letters to Charles V, in first and subsequent editions and translations, through the Revolution of 1910. Incl. the most important reforms of the Enlightenment concerning the economy, commerce, mining, science, and the expulsion of the Jesuits. The period of independence, the best represented aspects of which are the effect of the Napoleonic invasion of Spain in 1808, the constitutional crisis in Spain and the colonies provoked by the capture of the Spanish royal family by Napoleon, the policy of Ferdinand VII and the most important decisions by all the viceroys, bishops and archbishops. From the revolutionary side, the historical pronouncements and documents by the leaders of the movement of independence, such as Hidalgo, Morelos, Guerrero, and Iturbide, and the legal and political documents that gave structure to the Revolution. The empire with Iturbide and the period of political instability and strife that followed the independence, the reforms of Juarez, Maximillian's Empire, and its corollary, the dictatorial regime of Porfirio Diaz through the Revolution of 1910, are also well documented.

KS —UNIVERSITY OF KANSAS, Kenneth Spencer Research Library, Special Collections Dept, Lawrence, 66045. Alexandra Mason, Librn
Holdings: Cat Mss Maps
Notes: Great Britian, Italy, France, Spain, Eastern Europe (especially Poland), mediaeval to late 18th century. Noncirculating.

MA —HARVARD UNIVERSITY LIBRARY, Widener Library, Cambridge, 02138. Ellen H Brow, Specialist in Book Selection
Notes: *Widener Library Shelflist* No 41 (1972) lists some 13,000 vols on Spanish history. Intensive collecting for the Civil War of 1936-1939 is emphasized.

MO —WASHINGTON UNIVERSITY, John M Olin Library, Campus Box 1061, St Louis, 63130.
Holdings: Vols (15,000) Cat Microforms
Notes: Major subject concentration.

NY —HISPANIC SOCIETY OF AMERICA, Library, 613 W 155 St, New York, 10032. Martha M de Narvaez, Cur of Mss; Irene S Frye, Asst Librn
Holdings: Vols (150,000) Cat Mss Maps Pix Slides Phonorecords Microforms
Notes: History, art, literature and general culture of the Hispanic countries (where Spanish or Portuguese is spoken). Incl (18, 000) vols printed before 1701, incl (250) incunabula; over (100,000) later vols, plus thousands of periodicals. About (200,000) mss incl ms maps. Printed atlases are in the Book Collection. Some microfilms, chiefly of our early books. Engraved and printed separate maps; reference collection of over 100,000 photographs; slides: all in Department of Iconography, not in library. Catalogs: *Catalogue of the Hispanic Society of America* (Boston: G K Hall, 1962), 10 vols; *First Supplement* (Boston, 1970), 4 vols. Early books: *Printed Books 1468-1700;* Mss: *Catalogo de los Manuscritos Poeticos Castellanos* (15th-17th centuries; 3 vols); *Medieval Manuscripts in the Library; Golden Age Drama Manuscripts* (the latter in press).

NY —NEW YORK PUBLIC LIBRARY, Research Libraries, General Research Division, Fifth Ave & 42 St, New York, 10018. Rodney Phillips, Chief
Holdings: Vols (2,225,000) Cat Maps Pix Microforms
Budget: ($775,718)

OK —THOMAS GILCREASE INSTITUTE OF AMERICAN HISTORY & ART LIBRARY, 1400 North 25th West Ave, Tulsa, 74127. Sarah Hirsch, Librn
Holdings: Vols Cat Mss Maps Pix
Notes: Trans-Mississippi West, US, Indian and Hispanic history. The Gilcrease Library contains a total of about 40,000 mss; 10,000 imprints; 5000 photographs; 600 maps and 50,000 vols.

TX —STEPHEN F AUSTIN STATE UNIVERSITY, Ralph W Steen Library, Special Collections Dept, Box 13055, SFA Sta, Nacogdoches, 75962. Linda Cheves Nicklas, Special Collections Librn
Holdings: Vols (93)// Cat
Notes: The Robert Bruce Blake Collection. Volumes contain the official and private documents and proceedings of the 18th and 19th century Spanish and Mexican governments in Texas, translations of the Bexar and Nacogdoches Archives, biographies of East Texas families, general historical essays on Texas topics and other materials relating to Texas and East Texas. A description of contents and a partial name index are available. Description: SFASU, *A Guide to Special Collections,* 1980.

WI —UNIVERSITY OF WISCONSIN, MADISON, Seminary of Medieval Spanish Studies, 1130 Van Hise Hall, Madison, 53706. Lloyd A Kasten, Emeritus Prof of Spanish
Holdings: Vols (7500) // Cat Mss Pix Slides Microforms
Notes: Vocabulary cards totalling 625,000, plus 1700 printed volumes, scattered photostats, 100 microfilms, 2500 pamphlets and reprints on medieval Spanish law, language and literature. The nucleus of the collection is photostats of the mss of unpublished works of Alfonso X. Restricted circulation.

WI —UNIVERSITY OF WISCONSIN, MADISON, Memorial Library, 728 State St, Madison, 53706. Erwin K Welsch, Social Studies Bibliographer
Notes: Biblioteca de Obras Anormales: 2700 items containing vols, broadsides, leaflets, pamphlets, cartoons and mss on history, science, philosophy, religion, politics, literature and art from the 14th century to the present in French, Italian, English, Latin, Portuguese and Catalan, but chiefly in Spanish, acquired in 1960.

WI —UNIVERSITY OF WISCONSIN, MADISON, Memorial Library, Ibero-American Studies Collection, 728 State St, Madison, 53706. Suzanne Hodgman, Bibliographer
Notes: Materials on Latin America, Spain and Portugal may be found in all campus libraries. Strongest holdings are in language and literature, and in history, although many other disciplines in the humanities and social sciences are well represented: political science, sociology, economics, anthropology, statistics, etc. Incl the Porter "Curiosae" Collection (2711 items): Primarily covers 18th century Spanish literature. Approximately 500 of the 2711 items are uncataloged and housed in a special collection in the Rare Book Department. These range in date from the 14th century and include papal bulls, royal decrees, copies of royal decrees proclaimed by local authorities, government of Manresa edicts, manuscripts, broadsides, and pamphlets, as well as facsimiles of early Catalanpoetry. A typescript checklist of the entire collection is available. Hispanic history, language and literature. Restricted use for items held in the Rare Book Dept.

WI —UNIVERSITY OF WISCONSIN, MADISON, Memorial Library, 728 State St, Madison, 53706. Sandra Pfahler, Librn
Notes: Spanish medieval materials forming a part of the Seminary of Medieval Spanish Studies, 100 reels of microfilm, 2500 pamphlets and reprints, photostats, and over 600,000 vocabulary cards.

ON —QUEEN'S UNIVERSITY, Douglas Library, Kingston, K7L 5C4, Can. William F E Morley, Cur, Special Collections
Notes: Incl the W C Atkinson (of Galsgow) Collection.

SPAIN—HISTORY—WAR OF 1898 see U.s.—History—War of 1898

SPAIN—HISTORY—CIVIL WAR, 1936-1939

CA —UNIVERSITY OF CALIFORNIA, DAVIS, Shields Library, Dept of Special

SPAIN—HISTORY—CIVIL WAR, 1936-1939 (cont.)

Collections, Davis, 95616. Donald Kunitz, Head; C Danial Elliott, Asst Head
Holdings: Vols 850 Uncat
Notes: Pamphlets (over 800), both pro- and anti-Franco cover the immediate causes of the Spanish Civil War, its furation and aftermath. Most are in Spanish. Also 15 posters (reproductions) from the war.
CA —UNIVERSITY OF CALIFORNIA, SAN DIEGO, Central University Library, Mandeville Dept of Special Collections, La Jolla, 92093. Lynda Corey Claassen, Head
Holdings: Vols 12,500 Cat Mss Maps Pix
Notes: Southworth Collection: Focusing on the founding of Spain's Second Republic and the Spanish Civil War of 1936-1939, the collection numbers approximately 13,000 monographs, pamphlets, and newspapers. Works by both Republicans and Falangists are included, as are works by non-Spanish writers during that period.
CA —HOOVER INSTITUTION ON WAR, REVOLUTION & PEACE, Stanford University, Stanford, 94305. Milorad M Drachkovitch, Archivist
Holdings: Mss Pix
Notes: Papers of Joaquin Maurin, Spanish political activistm journalist, and author, incl correspondence, writings, newspaper and magazine clippings, photographs, printed matter, and other material, 1920-1973, relating to his political and literary careers, communism and socialism in Spain, the Spanish Civil War, and the American Literary Agency. 23 ms boxes, 1 oversize box.
IL —NORTHWESTERN UNIVERSITY, Library, Special Collections Dept, 1937 Sheridan Rd, Evanston, 60201. R Russell Maylone, Cur
Holdings: Vols 1500 Cat Maps Pix
Notes: Newspapes, magazines, books, pamphlets, mineographed and printed government documents and journals, 1200 photographs, 50 posters, 30 scrapbooks of clippings from Dutch newspapers concening the war. Complete set of non-intervention conference proceedings.
IN —INDIANA UNIVERSITY, Lilly Library, Seventh St, Bloomington, 47405. William R Cagle, Librn
Holdings: // Mss Pix
Notes: Papers of Claude G Browners, newspaperman, author ambassador to Spain, 1933-1936, and ambassador to Chile, 1939-1953. Collection incl diaries, materials relating to both ambassadorships, particularly important for spanish Civil War period; speeches; some original political cartoons; awards, medals, etc; newspaper clippings, etc, 1868-1972. 18,386 items.
MA —HARVARD UNIVERSITY LIBRARY, Widener Library, Cambridge, 02138. Ellen H Brow, Specialist in Book Selection
Holdings: Cat
Notes: Inclusive collection, listed in *Widener Library Shelflist* No 41 (1972).
MA —BRANDEIS UNIVERSITY, Goldfarb Library, 415 South St, Waltham, 02154. Bessie Hahn, Dir
Notes: Comprising
MI —UNIVERSITY OF MICHIGAN, Dept of Rare Books & Special Collections, Ann Arbor, 48109. Edward C Weber, Head, Labadie Collection
Holdings: Vols (40,000) Cat Mss Pix Microforms
Notes: Noteworthy for Anarchists and Trotskyist coverage.
MO —WASHINGTON UNIVERSITY, John M Olin Library, Campus Box 1061, St Louis, 63130.
Holdings: Vols (15,000) Cat Microforms
Notes: Major subject concentration.
NY —ADELPHI UNIVERSITY, Library, Garden City, 11530. Jerome Yavarkovsky, Dean of Libraries
Holdings: Vols 100 // Cat Mss Maps Pix
Notes: Correspondence, drawings, cartoons, miltiary report leaflets and photographs of medical facilities in the Spanish Civil War; Gladnick papers containing rosters of volunteers.

ON —UNIVERSITY OF TORONTO, Thomas Fisher Rare Book Library, 120 Saint George St, Toronto, M5S 1A5, Can. Richard G Landon, Head
Holdings: Vols 650 Uncat Mss
Notes: Spanish Civil War Collection consists of books and pamphlets about Spain in the 1930's, both contemporary publications and later works; includes some fiction set in Spain in the 1930's; posters. Partially a gift from the Canadian Committee for a Democratic Spain.

SPAIN—IMPRINTS

NY —HISPANIC SOCIETY OF AMERICA, Library, 613 W 155 St, New York, 10032. Martha M de Narvaez, Cur of Mss; Irene S Frye, Asst Librn
Holdings: Vols (150,000) Cat Mss Maps Pix Slides Phonorecords Microforms
Notes: History, art, literature and general culture of the Hispanic countries (where Spanish or Portuguese is spoken). Incl (18,000) vols printed before 1701, incl (250) incunabula; over (100,000) later vols, plus thousands of periodicals. About (200,000) mss incl ms maps. Printed atlases are in the Book Collection. Some microfilms, chiefly of our early books. Engraved and printed separate maps; reference collection of over 100,000 photographs; slides: all in Department of Iconography, not in library. Catalogs: *Catalogue of the Hispanic Society of America* (Boston: G K Hall, 1962), 10 vols; *First Supplement* (Boston, 1970), 4 vols. Early books: *Printed Books 1468-1700;* Mss: *Catalogo de los Manuscritos Poeticos Castellanos* (15th-17th centuries; 3 vols); *Medieval Manuscripts in the Library; Golden Age Drama Manuscripts*(the latter in press).

SPAIN—LIBRARIES

MN —SAINT JOHN'S ABBEY & UNIVERSITY, Hill Monastic Manuscript Library, Collegeville, 56321. Julian G Plante, Dir
Notes: Films of 61,000 mss. The total number of codices (bound handwritten mss) represents the holdings of several hundred libraries in Europe and elsewhere: Austria, Spain, Malta, Ethiopia, West Germany, Portugal, England, but also with concentrations of holdings from Italy, Hungary, Poland, Great Britain, Belgium, Yugoslavia, France, Switzerland and the Netherlands, and Vatican City. Also incl 70,000 exposures.

SPAIN—POLITICS AND GOVERNMENT

MA —BRANDEIS UNIVERSITY, Goldfarb Library, 415 South St, Waltham, 02154. Bessie Hahn, Dir
Notes: Spanish Civil War Collection. Comprising 7000 books and pamphlets in all languages relating to the armed conflict in Spain from 1936-1939. This is a multi-media collection consisting of not only books and pamphlets, but photographs, documentary film footage, newspapers, propaganda leaflets, wall posters, taped interviews, personal memoirs, memorabilia, recordings and some original art work. The collection also includes the archives of American volunteers who served with the Republican forces. There is an author-title card catalog in the Special Collections Card Catalog for the books and pamphlets. There are some finding lists for the other material such as newspapers and periodicals, photographs and wall posters. Some material is restricted from use.

SPAIN—SOCIAL LIFE AND CUSTOMS

NY —HISPANIC SOCIETY OF AMERICA, Library, 613 W 155 St, New York, 10032. Martha M de Narvaez, Cur of Mss; Irene S Frye, Asst Librn
Holdings: Vols (150,000) Cat Mss Maps Pix Slides Phonorecords Microforms
Notes: History, art, literature and general culture of the Hispanic countries (where Spanish or Portuguese is spoken). Incl (18,000) vols printed before 1701, incl (250) incunabula; over (100,000) later vols, plus thousands of periodicals. About (200,000) mss incl ms maps. Printed atlases are in the Book Collection. Some microfilms, chiefly of our early books. Engraved and printed separate maps; reference collection of over 100,000 photographs; slides: all in Department of Iconography, not in library. Catalogs: *Catalogue of the Hispanic Society of America* (Boston: G K Hall, 1962), 10 vols; *First Supplement* (Boston, 1970), 4 vols. Early books: *Printed Books 1468-1700;* Mss: *Catalogo de los Manuscritos Poeticos Castellanos* (15th-17th centuries; 3 vols); *Medieval Manuscripts in the Library; Golden Age Drama Manuscripts*(the latter in press).

SPALDING, ALBERT

MA —BOSTON UNIVERSITY, Mugar Memorial Library, Special Collections Dept, 771 Commonwealth Ave, Boston, 02215. Howard B Gotlieb, Dir
Holdings: // Cat Mss Pix
Notes: Mss, correspondence, scores, etc collected in depth; incl publications by or about.

SPALDING, HENRY HARMON

†WA —WASHINGTON STATE UNIVERSITY, Library, Manuscripts, Archives & Special Collections, Pullman, 99164. John F Guido, Head
Holdings: Vols Cat Mss Maps Pix Microforms
Notes: Ms resources for the study of Pacific Northwest Indians incl the papers of historians William Compton Brown, Carl Parcher Russell, and Lucullus Virgil McWhorter; and missionaries Henry Harmon Spalding, Elkanah Walker and Marcus Whitman. A few of these resources have been described in the following publications: *William Compton Brown: A Calendar of His Papers in the Washington State University Library* (Pullman, 1966); *Carl Parcher Russell: An Indexed Register of His Scholarly and Professional Papers, 1920-1967, in the Washington State University Library* (Pullman, 1970); *The Papers of Lucullus Virgil McWhorter*, compiled by Nelson A Ault (Pullman, 1959).

SPALDING FAMILIES

NY —SYRACUSE UNIVERSITY LIBRARIES, Ernest S Bird Library, George Arents Research Library for Special Collections, Syracuse, 13210. Carolyn A Davis, Manuscripts Librn; Amy S Doherty, University Archivist; Mark F Weimer, Rare Book Librn
Notes: Papers and memorabilia, incl ms writings. Papers 1796-1901 (1.5 linear feet).

SPANIARDS IN THE U.S.

DC —LIBRARY OF CONGRESS, Manuscript Division, Washington, 20540. John C Broderick, Chief
Notes: The Harkness Collection contains documents relating to the first 200 years of Spanish rule in Mexico and Peru.
PA —BALCH INSTITUTE FOR ETHNIC STUDIES, Library, 18 S Seventh St, Philadelphia, 19106. R Joseph Anderson, Library Dir

SPANIOL LANGUAGE see Ladino Language and Literature

SPANISH AMERICA

†CA —ANAHEIM PUBLIC LIBRARY, 500 W Broadway, Anaheim, 92805.
TX —STEPHEN F AUSTIN STATE UNIVERSITY, Ralph W Steen Library, Special Collections Dept, Box 13055, SFA Sta, Nacogdoches, 75962. Linda Cheves Nicklas, Special Collections Librn
Holdings: Vols (93)// Cat
Notes: The Robert Bruce Blake Collection.

SPANISH AMERICA (cont.)

Volumes contain the official and private documents and proceedings of the 18th and 19th century Spanish and Mexican governments in Texas, translations of the Bexar and Nacogdoches Archives, biographies of East Texas families, general historical essays on Texas topics and other materials relating to Texas and East Texas. A description of contents and a partial name index are available. Description: SFASU, *A Guide to Special Collections*, 1980.

SPANISH AMERICA—DISCOVERY AND EXPLORATION see
America—Discovery and Exploration

SPANISH AMERICA—HISTORY

IL —QUINCY COLLEGE LIBRARY, Quincy, 62301. Victor Kingery, OFM, Librn
Holdings: Vols 5000 // Maps
Notes: Books in Spanish as well as English. This is the library of the late historian Rev Francis Borgia Steck, OFM. Incl 300 maps.
NY —HISPANIC SOCIETY OF AMERICA, Library, 613 W 155 St, New York, 10032. Martha M de Narvaez, Cur of Mss; Irene S Frye, Asst Librn
Holdings: Vols (150,000) Cat Mss Maps Pix Slides Phonorecords Microforms
Notes: History, art, literature and general culture of the Hispanic countries (where Spanish or Portuguese is spoken). Incl (18,000) vols printed before 1701, incl (250) incunabula; over (100,000) later vols, plus thousands of periodicals. About (200,000) mss incl ms maps. Printed atlases are in the Book Collection. Some microfilms, chiefly of our early books. Engraved and printed separate maps; reference collection of over 100,000 photographs; slides: all in Department of Iconography, not in library. Catalogs: *Catalogue of the Hispanic Society of America* (Boston: G K Hall, 1962), 10 vols; *First Supplement* (Boston, 1970), 4 vols. Early books: *Printed Books 1468-1700*; Mss: *Catalogo de los Manuscritos Poeticos Castellanos* (15th-17th centuries; 3 vols); *Medieval Manuscripts in the Library*; *Golden Age Drama Manuscripts* (the latter in press).
NY —STATE UNIVERSITY OF NEW YORK, STONY BROOK, Melville Library, Dept of Special Collections, Stony Brook, 11794. Evert Volkersz, Head
Holdings: Uncat
Notes: Spanish-American colonial trade. 101 documents of the 16th and 17th centuries presenting information about trade and administration of the Spanish-American colonies and important for linking political and financial connection. A listing of the materials is available.
RI —BROWN UNIVERSITY, John Carter Brown Library, Providence, 02912. Norman Fiering, Librn; Everett C Wilkie Jr, Bibliographer; Susan Danforth, Cur Maps & Prints
Holdings: Vols (40,000) Cat Mss Maps Pix
Notes: History of the Americas during the Colonial Period.
TX —UNIVERSITY OF TEXAS, ARLINGTON, Library, PO Box 19497, Arlington, 76019. Chas Colley, Dir Special Collections
Holdings: // Uncat Microforms
Notes: The Yucatan Archives. The University of Texas at Arlington Library has microfilmed the pre-1900 holdings of the Archivo Notarial de Yucatan, a small part of the Archivo General del Estado (the Documentos Coloniales and Sesiones del Congreso, 1823-1933), about half of the Archivo del Arzobispado, and most of the newspapers held by the Hemeroteca del Estado de Yucatan. The collection contains 1052 rolls of 35mm microfilm copies. A preliminary guide is available upon request.
TX —UNIVERSITY OF TEXAS, EL PASO, Special Collections, Mexican Archives, El Paso, 79968. Cesar Caballero, Special Collections Librn; Bud Newman, Special Collections Librn
Budget: $5000
Notes: Incl 24 archival collections on over

2000 microform reels. Made up of church and civil archives in several cities of Texas, New Mexico, Chihuahua and Durango, the collection covers both the Spanish and Mexican epochs of the region. A holdings list and guide to the collection is available for purchase.

SPANISH AMERICA—IMPRINTS

DC —LIBRARY OF CONGRESS, Rare Book & Special Collections Div, Washington, 20540. William Matheson, Chief
Notes: Publications of the Spanish colonies in America, 1543-1820, mostly Mexican, Peruvian, and Guatemalan, with a few titles from other countries.

SPANISH AMERICAN LITERATURE

AZ —UNIVERSITY OF ARIZONA, Library, Tucson, 85721. W David Laird, Librn
CT —YALE UNIVERSITY, Box 1603A, Yale Station, New Haven, 06520.
IL —SOUTHERN ILLINOIS UNIVERSITY, CARBONDALE, Delyte W Morris Library, Carbondale, 62901.
Holdings: Vols (19,000) Cat
Notes: Especially strong in Ecuadorean and Mexican literature; complete or almost complete files of many important literary journals published in Spanish America. Described in Woodbridge, Hensley C, "Faculty and library collaboration in developing the Latin American collection for area studies programs at Southern Illinois University," Twelfth Seminar on the Acquisition of Latin American Library Materials, Final Report and Working Papers, vol 2, pp 99-108 (1967).
MA —HARVARD UNIVERSITY LIBRARY, Widener Library, Cambridge, 02138. Ellen H Brow, Specialist in Book Selection
Holdings: Cat Mss Microforms
Notes: Shelflist published in 1969 (*Widener Library Shelflist*, No 21) lists 17,851 vols. For manuscript, see *Hispanic American Historical Review*, XVII (1937), 259-277.
MO —WASHINGTON UNIVERSITY, John M Olin Library, Campus Box 1061, St Louis, 63130.
Holdings: Vols (50,000) Cat
Notes: Strong collection. Much unusual material.
PA —UNIVERSITY OF PITTSBURGH, Hillman Library, Pittsburgh, 15260. Glenora E Rossell, Head
Holdings: Vols 30,000 Cat Microforms
Notes: A general collection of Latin American literature, with emphasis on Cuba, Mexico, Chile, Guatemala, Ecuador, Peru, Bolivia, and Cuban literature are extremely good. Very strong in contemporary literature of the whole area.
PR —UNIVERSITY OF PUERTO RICO, Jose M Lazaro Memorial Library, Sala Zenobia y Juan Ramon Jimenez, Rio Piedras, 00931. Raquel Sarraga, Librn
Holdings: Vols (8000) Cat Mss Phonorecords Audiotapes Filmstrips
Notes: This special collection was created because Juan Ramon Jimenez, Nobel Prize for Literature, and one of the leading Spanish poets of this century, donated his personal library and papers to the University of Pureto Rico. Its main importance is that its contents represent the best Spanish literature of this century and the biobliographical data on the "Modernismo" period is very rich. The papers bring the opportunity to study the creative process of Juan Ramon Jimenez as well as they were written. The collection incl rare books, first editions autographed by their authors, magazines (some are rare collections), thousands of Juan Ramon's originals and manuscripts, letters of some of the top literary writers of this century, photographs (3061), paper clippings (32,000), paintings, furniture and personal belongings.

SPANISH AMERICAN NEWSPAPERS
see Newspapers, Spanish American

SPANISH-AMERICAN WAR, 1898 see
U.S.—History—War of 1898

SPANISH AMERICANS

MO —WASHINGTON UNIVERSITY, Libraries, Special Collections Dept, Campus

Box 1061, St Louis, 63130.
Notes: The Spanish Archive of St Louis Collection.
TX —UNIVERSITY OF TEXAS, EL PASO, Library, Special Collections Dept, El Paso, 79968. Cesar Caballero, Dept Head
Notes: Oral History Collection. A product of the Oral History Institute at U T El Paso, this collection consists of tapes and transcripts of interviews with prominent and not so prominent persons of the community of El Paso, Juarez and other parts of the Border region.

SPANISH AMERICANS IN THE U.S.

GA —UNIVERSITY OF GEORGIA, Libraries, Special Collections Division, Athens, 30602. Vesta Lee Gordon, Asst Dir for Special Collections
Notes: The Arbitron Collection of television and radio program ratings, 1949-date (except past year). In-depth, statistical analyses of the listening public by age, sex, county, some ethnic groups, farm population, listening preferences, etc. 26,302 bound vols. 2 reports, 1949-81. To be added to annually.

SPANISH ARCHITECTURE see
Architecture, Spanish

SPANISH ARMADA, 1588

MA —HARVARD UNIVERSITY LIBRARY, Widener Library, Cambridge, 02138.
Holdings: Cat
Notes: See *Harvard Library Notes*, III (1940), 303-307. Downs 4293.

SPANISH ART see Art, Spanish

SPANISH AUTHORS see Authors, Spanish

SPANISH CIVILIZATION see
Civilization, Hispanic; Spain—Civilization and Culture

SPANISH DANCE

IL —CHICAGO PUBLIC LIBRARY, Art Section, Fine Arts Division, 78 E Washington St, Chicago, 60602. Rosalinda I Hack, Fine Arts Division Chief; Yvonne S Brown, Head, Art Section
Holdings: Vols 2500
Notes: Reference and circulating collection of books, periodicals, pamphlets, and videotapes on all aspects of the dance eg ballet, social dance, square dance, jazz and folkdance. Focus of the collection is on ballet, history, biographies of dancers, and dance instruction. Subject is supplemented by a dance videotape collection, the *Folk Dance Index* a comprehensive index to descriptions of folkdances of all nations. Special Collections: Eliza Stigler Dance Collection of 200 dance books on ballet and dance history with particular emphasis on Spanish Dance. Ruth Page Archives: small collection of memorabilia documents the career of Ms Page. Reference collection of 85 dance videotapes that document notable dance performances, from the past and present by well known dancers and dance groups. Subject concentration is that of ballet, with some examples of ethnic dance. There is alsoa collection of tapes that document Chicago area dance groups, dancers, and choreographers. A file to the contents of the tapes is available.

SPANISH DRAMA

CA —UNIVERSITY OF CALIFORNIA, SAN DIEGO, Central University Library, Mandeville Dept of Special Collections, La Jolla, 92093. Lynda Corey Claassen, Head
Notes: Hispanic Collection: Approx 6000 vols describe cultures of Spain, Portugal, Mexico, Latin America, and South America. Works of literature, history, philosophy and art date from the 15th to the mid-19th century. Highlights of the collection include rare 18th century Spanish provincial dramas and works on the history of Seville and Andalusia.

SPANISH DRAMA (cont.)

IL —NORTHWESTERN UNIVERSITY, Library, Special Collections Dept, 1937 Sheridan Rd, Evanston, 60201. R Russell Maylone, Cur
Holdings: Vols (15,000) Cat
Notes: Spanish drama from the 18th to 20th centuries, incl Castilian, Catalan, Valencian, and Mexican. 12,000 plays.

KY —UNIVERSITY OF KENTUCKY, Margaret I King Library, Dept of Special Collections, Lexington, 40506. William Marshall, Head
Holdings: Cat
Notes: 2000 French and approximately 2000 Spanish and German plays. 18th-19th centuries.

MI —UNIVERSITY OF MICHIGAN, Library, Dept of Rare Books & Special Collections, Ann Arbor, 48109. Robert J Starring, Head
Holdings: Cat
Notes: Strong collections of American, English, French and Spanish dramatic works before 1900.

MO —UNIVERSITY OF MISSOURI-COLUMBIA, Ellis Library, Language and Literature Dept, Columbia, 65201. Jeaneice Brewer, Librn
Holdings: Vols Cat Microforms
Notes: Strong collection of 19th century Spanish drama. Copies of manuscript and printed 17th century (Golden Age) Spanish drama from two large commercially prepared microform collections plus hundreds of microfilm copies of plays acquired from libraries all over the world. Also strong in critical materials covering the same period.

NH —DARTMOUTH COLLEGE, Baker Memorial Library, Hanover, 03755.
Holdings: Vols 16,000 Cat
Notes: Largely 1860-1930.

NY —CENTER FOR INTER-AMERICAN RELATIONS, Library, 680 Park Ave, New York, 10021.
Notes: Most, but not all, of the 1000 plays and reference books are in Spanish and Portuguese.

NY —HISPANIC SOCIETY OF AMERICA, Library, 613 W 155 St, New York, 10032. Martha M de Narvaez, Cur of Mss; Irene S Frye, Asst Librn
Holdings: Cat Mss Maps Pix Slides Phonorecords Microforms
Notes: Mss of the Golden Age of Spanish Drama. Hundreds of mss (some with stage business, notes and annotations); numerous titles of rare 17th-century and later printed books on the drama and the stage; English translations of Spanish plays and Spanish translations of international drama; letters and documents of the major and minor dramatists and performers from 1904 to the present day. Catalogs: *Catalogue of the Hispanic Society of America* (Boston: G K Hall, 1962), 10 vols; *First Supplement* (Boston, 1970), 4 vols. Early books: *Printed Books 1468-1700*; Mss: *Catalogo de los Manuscritos Poeticos Castellanos* (15th-17th centuries; 3 vols); *Medieval Manuscripts in the Library; Golden Age Drama Manuscripts* (the latter in press).

NY —NEW YORK PUBLIC LIBRARY, Performing Arts Research Center, Billy Rose Theatre Collection, 111 Amsterdam Ave, New York, 10023. Dorothy L Swerdlove, Cur
Holdings: Cat
Notes: Described in *Catalog of the Theatre and Drama Collections*, The Research Libraries of The New York Public Library. 1967. To be Supplemented. Part 1, *Drama Collection: Listing by Cultural Origin*, 6 vols (120,000 cards), $585; Part II, *Drama Collection: Author Listing*, 6 vols (115,000 cards), $790. This catalog represents the major portion of the Research Libraries' Drama Collection. Incl are more than 120,000 plays written in Western languages. Translations of plays published in the Cyrillic, Hebrew and Oriental alphabets are also listed. Excluded are children's plays, Christmas plays, and moralities. The catalog is in two parts: a listing by author (or title, in the case of anonymous plays); and a listing

by cultural origin. An analysis of this latter section reveals the Research Libraries' interest in collecting widely from the literatures of the world: American, 20,000 entries; English, 21,000; French, 22,000; Spanish, 16,000; German, 14,000; and a strong representation of plays written in minor languages.

OH —OHIO STATE UNIVERSITY, William Oxley Thompson Memorial Library, 1858 Neil Ave Mall, Columbus, 43210. Robert A Tibbetts, Cur of Special Collections
Holdings: Vols 2200 Cat
Notes: Espec 17th century. Incl the Claude Anibal Collection.

OH —OBERLIN COLLEGE LIBRARY, Oberlin, 44074. William A Moffett, Dir of Libraries
Holdings: Cat
Notes: 7530 plays in 400 vols.

PA —UNIVERSITY OF PENNSYLVANIA, Van Pelt Library, Rare Books Collection, 34 & Walnut Sts, Philadelphia, 19104. Daniel Traister, Special Collections Librn
Holdings: Cat
Notes: About 1200 plays in 17th century editions.

SPANISH FLORIDA CLAIMS

FL —UNIVERSITY OF MIAMI, Otto G Richter Library, PO Box 248214, Coral Gables, 33124. Frank Rodgers, Dir of Libraries
Notes: The rare Floridiana collection incl a great variety of primary source materials such as mss, maps, photographs, scrapbooks, correspondence, clippings, etc. Particular subject strengths in this collection incl: Spanish exploration and colonialization of Florida, the Florida Indians, wildlife conservation, landscaping, corporate records, etc. The rare Floridiana collection is complemented by a collection of titles ranging from the oldest to the very latest published books on Florida subjects.

FL —SAINT PETERSBURG PUBLIC LIBRARY, 3745 Ninth Ave N, Saint Petersburg, 33713. Luccille Bostforff, Reference Supvr
Holdings: Vols 2240 Cat Maps Pix Microfroms
Notes: Florida document depository. Spanish land grants on micorfilm. Local newspapers on microfilm. Approximately 196,000 cards indexing local newspapers and Florida magazines by subject. Incl 125 pictures, 2474 microfilm reels; 30,943 pamphlets and documents.

SPANISH IN THE U.S. see Spaniards in the U.S.; Spanish Americans in the U.S.

SPANISH INQUISITION see Inquisition—Spain

SPANISH LANGUAGE AND LITERATURE

CA —UNIVERSITY OF CALIFORNIA, BERKELEY, University Library, Hispanic Collections, Berkeley, 94720. Gaston Somoshegyi-Szokol, Librn
Holdings: Vols (50,000)
Notes: Strong research collection. The Golden Age of Spanish Literature is especially well represented: numerous variant textual editions are available for many authors, along with related literary criticism; moreover, these holdings are supplemented in the Bancroft Library by first editions and other rare imprints of works by such authors as Lope de Vega, Calderon de la Barca, Tirso de Molina, and Cervantes. The collection of Spanish literary journals ranks as one of the finest outside Spain, and is rich in 19th and 20th century publications.

CA —UNIVERSITY OF CALIFORNIA, SAN DIEGO, Central University Library, Mandeville Dept of Special Collections, La Jolla, 92093. Lynda Corey Claassen, Head
Notes: The Romero collection of classical printers. Spanish history, literature, and culture; local history of Seville and Andalusia.

CA —LOS ANGELES PUBLIC LIBRARY, Foreign Languages Dept, 630 W Fifth St, Los Angeles, 90071. Sylva Manoogian, Principal Librn
Holdings: Vols 49,447
Budget: ($41,500)

CA —UNIVERSITY OF THE PACIFIC, Library, Stockton, 95211. Hiram L Davis, Dir of Libraries
Notes: An excellent condition.

DC —CATHOLIC UNIVERSITY OF AMERICA, Mullen Library, 620 Michigan Ave NE, Washington, 20064. B Gutekunst, Humanities Librn
Holdings: Vols 9000 Cat

DC —GEORGETOWN UNIVERSITY, Library, Special Collections Div, 37 & O Sts NW, Washington, 20057. George M Barringer, Special Collections Librn; Nicholas B Sheetz, Mss Librn
Holdings: Cat
Notes: The Isla Collection. Four 18th century mss dealing with the satire on bad preaching, *Historia del Famoso predicador Fray Gerundio de Campazas alias Zotes*, by the Jesuit priest Jose Francisco de Isla (1703-1781).

DC —LIBRARY OF CONGRESS, Hispanic Division, Washington, 20540.
Notes: The Archive of Hispanic Literature on Tape is a repository of recorded poetry and prose from the Spanish- and Portuguese-speaking world. Most of the outstanding Hispanic literary figures of the last 30 years are included.

IL —SOUTHERN ILLINOIS UNIVERSITY, CARBONDALE, Delyte W Morris Library, Carbondale, 62901.
Holdings: Vols (19,000) Cat
Notes: Especially strong in Ecuadorean and Mexican literature; complete or almost complete files of many important literary journals published in Spanish America. Described in Woodbridge, Hensley C, "Faculty and library collaboration in developing the Latin American collection for area studies programs at Southern Illinois University," Twelfth Seminar on the Acquisition of Latin American Library Materials, Final Report and Working Papers, vol 2, pp 99-108 (1967).

KS —UNIVERSITY OF KANSAS, Kenneth Spencer Research Library, Special Collections Dept, Lawrence, 66045. Alexandra Mason, Librn
Holdings: Cat Mss
Notes: 16th and 17th century Spanish-language imprints in Summerfiled Collection; Cervantes collections; a few Spansih mss. Noncirculating.

KY —UNIVERSITY OF KENTUCKY, Margaret I King Library, Dept of Special Collections, Lexington, 40506. William Marshall, Head
Holdings: Cat Mss
Notes: Incl 921 pieces of ecclesiastical, political, legal and personal letters and documents, many in Medieval Latin. Period covered: 12th-18th centuries.

MA —BOSTON PUBLIC LIBRARY, South End Branch, Multilingual Library, 685 Tremont St, Boston, 02118. Laura H Reyes, Librn
Holdings: Cat

MA —HARVARD UNIVERSITY LIBRARY, Widener Library, Cambridge, 02138. Ellen H Brow, Specialist in Book Selection
Holdings: Cat
Notes: *Widener Library Shelflist* No 41 (1972) lists some 20,000 volumes on Spanish literature; the Cervantes collection is outstanding, and there is a collection of 10,000 gozos and goigs.

MI —WAYNE STATE UNIVERSITY, G Flint Purdy Library, Detroit, 48202. K L Kaul, Asst Dir & Head
Notes: Materials noted in *A Descriptive Catalogue of the Spanish Comedias Suelta and the Private Library of Professor B B Ashcom* (1965).

MO —WASHINGTON UNIVERSITY, John M Olin Library, Campus Box 1061, St Louis, 63130.
Holdings: Vols (15,000) Cat Microforms
Notes: Major subject concentration.

NY —HEMPSTEAD PUBLIC LIBRARY, Foreign Language Collection, 115 Nichols

SPANISH LANGUAGE AND LITERATURE (cont.)

Court, Hempstead, 11550. Irene A Duszkiewicz, Dir
Notes: Mainly French, German, Italian, Spanish, Polish, Yiddish, Hebrew. Holdings in other languages, including Asian.

NY —HISPANIC SOCIETY OF AMERICA, Library, 613 W 155 St, New York, 10032. Martha M de Narvaez, Cur of Mss; Irene S Frye, Asst Librn
Holdings: Vols (150,000) CAt Mss Maps Pix Slides Phonorecords Microforms
Notes: History, art, literature and general culture of the Hispanic countries (where Spanish or Portuguese is spoken). Incl (18,000) vols printed before 1701, incl (250) incunabula; over (100,000) later vols, plus thousands of periodicals. About (200,000) mss incl ms maps. Printed atlases are in the Book Collection. Some microfilms, chiefly of our early books. Engraved and printed separate maps; reference collection of over 100,000 photographs; slides: all in Department of Iconography, not in library. Catalogs: *Catalogue of the Hispanic Society of America* (Boston: G K Hall, 1962), 10 vols; *First Supplement* (Boston, 1970), 4 vols. Early books: *Printed Books 1468-1700*; Mss: *Catalogo de los Manuscritos Poeticos Castellanos* (15th-17th centuries; 3 vols); *Medieval Manuscripts in the Library*; *Golden Age Drama Manuscripts* (the latter in press).

NY —NEW YORK PUBLIC LIBRARY, Research Libraries, General Research Division, Fifth Ave & 42 St, New York, 10018. Rodney Phillips, Chief
Holdings: Vols (2,225,000) Cat Maps Pix Microforms
Budget: ($775,718)

NY —NEW YORK PUBLIC LIBRARY, Donnell Foreign Language Library, 20 W 53 St, New York, 10019. Bosiljka Stevanovic, Supvr Librn
Holdings: Vols 9959 Cat
Notes: Books of interest by and about the Dominican Republic, Puerto Rico and Cuba.

NY —NEW YORK PUBLIC LIBRARY, Mid-Manhattan Library, Literature and Language Dept, 455 Fifth Ave, New York, 10016. Eric Steele, Sr Principal Librn
Holdings: Vols (160,000) Cat Phonorecords Microforms Audiotapes
Budget: ($92,000)
Notes: College-oriented collection. Standard editions of all major authors. Emphasis on criticism in Spanish and English. Extensive runs of most important journals in the field.

NC —CUMBERLAND COUNTY PUBLIC LIBRARY, North Carolina Foreign Language Center, 328 Gillespie St, Fayetteville, 28301. Patrick M Valentine, Coordinator
Holdings: Vols 2800 Cat
Budget: $1500
Notes: The largest book collections are, in descending order of size, German Spanish, French, Japanese, Korean and Vietnamese, with fair sized collections in Italian, Russian, Chinese, Arabic, Greek, Hungarian, Polish, Hebrew, Thai, and Hindi. The Center has several shelves each of books in Bengali, Dutch, Marathi, Portuguese, Urdu, and Yiddish. Smaller collections of one to three shelves each incl Catalan, Croatian, Czech, Danish, Finnish, Gujarati, Icelandic, Kannada, Latin, Lithuanian, Malayalam, Norwegian, Panjabi, Persian (Farsi), Romanian, Slovak, Swedish, Tagalog, Tamil, Telegu, and Ukrianian. The Center has grammars, dictionaries and occasionally other readings in languages from Afrikaans and Albanian to Welsh, Yoruba and Zulu.

OH —CLEVELAND PUBLIC LIBRARY, Foreign Literature Dept, 325 Superior Ave, Cleveland, 44114. Natalia Bezugloff, Head
Holdings: Vols 18,200 Cat
Notes: A popular circulating collection containing classics and the standard works with emphasis on belles lettres, history and biography. A variety of other subjects such as learning languages, how to do books, art, children's books, spoken phonodiscs and cassettes, periodicals, etc. Incl 280 ephemera.
See also entry under Foreign Language Collections

†OH —KENT STATE UNIVERSITY LIBRARY, Special Collections, Kent, 44242. Dean H Keller, Librn
Notes: 125 comics, golden age and Spanish language, original art by Chuck Ayers, Rog Bollen and Tom Wilson.

OR —UNIVERSITY OF PORTLAND, Wilson W Clark Memorial Library, 5000 N Willamette Blvd, PO Box 03017, Portland, 97203. Rev Joseph P Browne, CSC, Dir
Holdings: Vols 1900 Cat
Notes: Includes the Salvador Macias Memorial Collection.

PA —UNIVERSITY OF PENNSYLVANIA, Van Pelt Library, Rare Books Collection, 34 & Walnut Sts, Philadelphia, 19104. Daniel Traister, Special Collections Librn
Holdings: Cat
Notes: Especially Golden Age and linguistics. About 1200 plays in 17th century editions.

PA —UNIVERSITY OF PITTSBURGH, Hillman Library, Pittsburgh, 15260. Glenora E Rossell, Head
Holdings: Vols 30,000 Cat Microforms
Notes: A general collection of Latin American literature, with emphasis on Cuba, Mexico, Chile, Guatemala, Ecuador, Peru, Bolivia, and Argentina. The holdings on Bolivian, Ecuadorian, and Cuban literature are extremely good. Very strong in contemporary literature of the whole area.

PA —UNIVERSITY OF PITTSBURGH, Hillman Library, Special Collections Dept, Ramon Gomez de la Serna Collection, Pittsburgh, 15260. Charles Aston Jr, Coordinator
Holdings: Vols 129 Uncat Mss Pix
Notes: Ramon Gomez de la Serna's published and unpublished ms and correspondence material, 60,000 pieces, relating to *greguerias* and other works. Incl the auth's subject clipping file. Books are first editions of the author's works, his copies. Partial inventory to the collection exists in the department. 17 ft mss.

PA —PENNSYLVANIA STATE UNIVERSITY, Fred Lewis Pattee Library, Library Hispanic Program, University Park, 16802. Donald C Henderson, Head
Holdings: Vols (50,000) Cat Mss
Budget: ($21,000)
Notes: Fine general holdings cover all periods, with special collections on Gongora and Valle-Inclan; supports doctoral programs.

TX —UNIVERSITY OF TEXAS LIBRARIES, General Libraries, PO Box P, Austin, 78713. Carolyn Bucknell, Asst Dir for Collection Development
Holdings: Cat Microforms

TX —FORT WORTH PUBLIC LIBRARY, North Branch, 601 Park St, Fort Worth, 76106. Betty M Hennington, Branch Head
Holdings: Vols (1630) Cat Phonorecords Audiotapes Videotapes Filmstrips
Budget: ($4000)
Notes: There is a separate catalog in North Branch for Spanish-language materials. The collection incl books in all areas.

TX —PHARR MEMORIAL LIBRARY, 200 S Athol, Pharr, 78577. Karen Mier, Asst Librn
Holdings: Vols 709 Cat

WI —UNIVERSITY OF WISCONSIN, MADISON, Seminary of Medieval Spanish Studies, 1130 Van Hise Hall, Madison, 53706. Lloyd A Kasten, Emeritus Prof of Spanish
Holdings: Vols (7500)// Cat Mss Pix Slides Microforms
Notes: Medieval materials and subjects. 100 reels of microfilm, 2500 pamphlets and reprints. Incl a 300-volume collection on 13th century Spanish law. Other emphases: language studies (incl 616,247 vocabulary cards), dictionaries, bibliographies, periodicals. The nucleus of the collection is photostats of the mss of unpublished works of Alfonso X. Restricted circulation.

WI —UNIVERSITY OF WISCONSIN, MADISON, Memorial Library, Ibero-American Studies Collection, 728 State St, Madison, 53706. Suzanne Hodgman, Bibliographer
Holdings: Vols 2711// Mss
Notes: Porter "Curiosae" Collection. Primarily covers 18th century Spanish literature. Approximately 500 of the 2711 items are uncataloged and housed in a special collection in the Rare Book Department. These range in date from the 14th century and include papal bulls, royal decrees, copies of royal decrees proclaimed by local authorities, government of Manresa edicts, manuscripts, broadsides, and pamphlets, as well as facsimiles of early Catalan poetry. A typescript checklist of the entire collection is available. This collection is part of the Library's extensive holdings in Hispanic history, language and literature. Restricted use for materials housed in the Rare Book Department.

PR —UNIVERSITY OF PUERTO RICO, Jose M Lazaro Memorial Library, Sala Zenobia y Juan Ramon Jimenez, Rio Piedras, 00931. Raquel Sarraga, Librn
Holdings: Vols (8000) Cat Mss Phonorecords Audiotapes Filmstrips
Notes: This special collection was created because Juan Ramon Jimenez, Nobel Prize for Literature, and one of the leading Spanish poets of this century, donated his personal library papers to the University of Puerto Rico. Its main importance is that its contents represent the best Spanish literature of this century and the bibliographical data on the "Modernismo" period is very rich. The papers bring the opportunity to study the creative process of Juan Ramon Jimenez as well as the historical literary period in which they were written. The collection incl rare books, first editions autographed by their authors, magazines (some are rare collections), thousands of Juan Ramon's originals and manuscripts, letters of some of the top literary writers of this century, photographs (3061), paper clippings (32,000), paintings, furniture and personal belongings.

ON —QUEEN'S UNIVERSITY, Douglas Library, Kingston, K7L 5C4, Can. William F E Morley, Cur, Special Collections
Notes: Incl the W C Atkinson (of Glasgow) Collection. Special strengths in works by and about Cervantes.

ON —UNIVERSITY OF TORONTO, Thomas Fisher Rare Book Library, 120 Saint George St, Toronto, M5S 1A5, Can. Richard G Landon, Head
Holdings: Vols 1700 Cat
Notes: Buchanan Collection named for its donor M A Buchanan, Prof of Italian and Spanish, University of Toronto. Includes a large group of Spanish plays. Holdings partially listed in Molinaro, J A, *A Bibliography of Comedias Sueltas in the University of Toronto Library* (Toronto, 1959).

SPANISH LITERATURE—PHILIPPINE ISLANDS see Philippine Languages and Literature

SPANISH NEWSPAPERS see Newspapers, Spanish

SPANISH PERIODICALS see Periodicals, Spanish

SPARGO, JOHN

VT —UNIVERSITY OF VERMONT, Guy W Bailey/David W Howe Library, Burlington, 05405. John Buehler, Asst Dir for Special Collections

SPARK, MURIEL

MO —WASHINGTON UNIVERSITY, Libraries, Special Collections Dept, Campus Box 1061, St Louis, 63130.
Notes: A major collection, incl mss, correspondence, literary papers, photographs, etc. Described in *Special Collections: an Annotated Guide to the Holdings of the Manuscript Division and the University Archives and Research Collection*.

SPARK, MURIEL (cont.)

OK —UNIVERSITY OF TULSA, McFarlin
Library, Dept of Rare Books and Special
Collections, 600 S College, Tulsa, 74104.
David Farmer, Dir; Toby Murray, Archivist;
Caroline Swinson, Cur of Manuscripts & Art
Holdings: Mss
Notes: A comprehensive collection of the
writings of Muriel Spark.

BC —UNIVERSITY OF VICTORIA,
McPherson Library, Victoria, V8W 3H5,
Can.
Notes: Incl mss notebook containing 32
childhood poems; 2 small sketches; ms of
poem, The Miners; letter, May 18, 1958, to
Derek Stanford.

SPARK PLUGS

MI —GENERAL MOTORS CORP, AC Spark
Plug Div, Engineering Library, 1300 N Dort
Hwy, Flint, 48556. Eileen L Lane, Librn
Holdings: Vols (150) Uncat Microforms
Notes: Incl Thomas Register microfiche
catalogs (over 100); Society of Automotive
Engineers Transactions. Over 150
automotive service manuals, allied and
competitive; some foreign. Also 100
cartridges of microfilm on military
specifications.

SPARKS, JARED

MA —HARVARD UNIVERSITY LIBRARY,
Houghton Library, Cambridge, 02138.
Rodney G Dennis, Cur of Manuscripts
Holdings: Cat Mss

SPARKS, NED

ON —METROPOLITAN TORONTO
LIBRARY, Theatre Dept, 789 Yonge St,
Toronto, M4W 2G8, Can. Heather
McCallum, Head
Holdings: Vols (30,500) Mss Pix Slides
Phonorecords Microforms
Notes: The collection incl clippings,
photographs and personal correspondence of
the Canadian-born film comedian.
See also entry under Actors and Actresses.

SPARRING see Boxing

SPARROW, JOHN

DC —GEORGETOWN UNIVERSITY,
Library, Special Collections Div, 37 & O Sts
NW, Washington, 20057. George M
Barringer, Special Collections Librn;
Nicholas B Sheetz, Mss Librn
Holdings: Mss Pix
Notes: The papers of Christopher Sykes,
biographer, journalist, and novelist;
containing mss, letters, photographs, and
drawings. With extensive correspondence
from Harold Acton; Angela, Countess of
Antrim; Sir John Betjeman; Ivy Compton-
Burnett; Alick Dru; T S Eliot; Max
Beerbohm; Graham Greene; John Hayward;
Lord Patrick Kinross; Compton Mackenzie;
Nancy Mitford; Anthony Powell; Dame
Flora Robson; Cecil Roth; Sir John Russell;
Osbert Sitwell; John Sparrow; Freya Stark;
James Stern; and Evelyn Waugh, among
others. Also, considerable research material
about Evelyn Waugh, Adam von Trott,
Robert Byron, Lady Nancy Astor; and the
foundation of the state of Israel.

SPAS see Health Resorts, Watering Places, Etc.

SPEAIGHT, ROBERT

MA —BOSTON UNIVERSITY, Mugar
Memorial Library, Special Collections Dept,
771 Commonwealth Ave, Boston, 02215.
Howard B Gotlieb, Dir
Holdings: Cat Mss Pix
Notes: Mss, correspondence, etc collected in
depth; incl publications by or about.

SPEAKERS (RECITATION BOOKS) see Readers and Speakers

SPEAKING see Preaching; Rhetoric

SPEAKING IN TONGUES see Glossolalia

SPECIAL COLLECTIONS IN LIBRARIES see Libraries—Special Collections

SPECIALIZED AGENCIES OF THE UNITED NATIONS see International Agencies

SPECIE see Money

SPECIES, CLASSIFICATION OF see Biology—Classification; Botany—Classification; Taxonomy

SPECIFICATIONS see Standards and Specifications

SPECK, FRANK G.

PA —AMERICAN PHILOSOPHICAL
SOCIETY, Library, 105 S Fifth St,
Philadelphia, 19106. Edward C Carter II,
Librn
Notes: Papers, incl American Indian
anthropological studies.

SPECTACLES see Eyeglasses

SPECTERS see Apparitions; Ghosts

SPECTRA see Spectrum Analysis and Spectroscopy

SPECTROCHEMICAL ANALYSIS see Spectrochemistry

SPECTROCHEMISTRY

PA —UNIVERSITY OF PITTSBURGH,
Chemistry Library, 200 Alumni Hall,
Pittsburgh, 15260. Paul J Kobulnicky,
Physical Sciences Librn
Holdings: Vols (20,000) Cat Microforms
Budget: ($100,000)
Notes: This library has traditionally limited
its collection to pure chemistry. Complete
spectral files with index.

SPECTROGRAPH AND SPECTROGRAPHY

TX —RICE UNIVERSITY, Fondren Library,
6100 S Main St, PO Box 1892, Houston,
77251. Dr Samuel M Carrington, Jr,
University Librn
Holdings: // Cat Mss Pix
Notes: Papers of Fred Terry Rogers (1931-
1956; 9 linear ft); incl researches in Beta ray
spectrography.

SPECTROSCOPY see Spectrum Analysis and Spectroscopy

SPECTRUM, MOLECULAR see Molecular Spectra

SPECTRUM ANALYSIS AND SPECTROSCOPY

CA —BECKMAN INSTRUMENTS, Research
Library, 2500 Harbor Blvd, Fullerton, 92634.
Jean R Miller, Librn
Holdings: Vols (7000) Cat Slides Audiotapes
Videotapes Microforms
Budget: ($9000)
Notes: Strong collections in scientific and
analytic instrumentation, electrochemistry,
analytical chemistry, optics and spectroscopy
chromatography, clinical chemistry and
biochemistry.

CA —UNIVERSITY OF CALIFORNIA, LOS
ANGELES, Physics Library, 213 Kinsey
Hall, Los Angeles, 90024. J Wally Pegram,
Librn
Holdings: Vols (37,000) Cat
See also entry under Physics.

CA —INTERNATIONAL BUSINESS
MACHINES RESEARCH LIBRARY, 5600
Cottle Rd, San Jose, 95193. Phil Grincewich,
Mgr Technical Information
Holdings: Vols (13,500) Cat
Notes: Collection includes emphasis on laser
spectroscopy, organic photomaterial and
chemical dynamics. Incl 21,000 vols of 770
journals. On-line search facility. Vols are
divided into three libraries, Technical
Research, Technical Information, and
Programing. Not open to public.

IL —ARGONNE NATIONAL
LABORATORY, Chemistry Branch Library,
9700 S Cass Ave, Argonne, 60439. Betty
Guttman, Librn
Notes: Incl 20,000 vols monographs, 190
current journals. Materials may be used by
the public in the library by prior
arrangement. Photocopies may be supplied
for interlibrary loan, for which a processing
and handling charge is made.

MI —UNIVERSITY OF MICHIGAN,
Chemistry-Pharmacy Library, 2000
Chemistry Bldg, Ann Arbor, 48109. Stephen
C Lucchetti, Librn
Holdings: Vols (50,000) Cat Microforms
Budget: ($130,000)
Notes: Incl 15,000 edge-notched cards of
spectra.

NY —AMERICAN INSTITUTE OF
PHYSICS, Center for the History of Physics,
Niels Bohr Library, 335 E 45 St, New York,
10017. John Aubry, Librn
Notes: Papers and records.

PA —UNIVERSITY OF PITTSBURGH,
Chemistry Library, 200 Alumni Hall,
Pittsburgh, 15260. Paul J Kobulnicky,
Physical Sciences Librn
Holdings: Vols (20,000) Cat Microforms
Budget: ($100,000)
Notes: This library has traditionally limited
its collection to pure chemistry. Complete
spectral files with index.

TX —RICE UNIVERSITY, Fondren Library,
6100 S Main St, PO Box 1892, Houston,
77251. Dr Samuel M Carrington, Jr,
University Librn
Holdings: // Cat Mss Pix
Notes: Papers of William V Houston, incl his
research papers in spectroscopy, theory of
solid state, quantum mechanics and
superconductivity (15 linear ft).

SPECTRUM OF THE STARS see Stars—Spectra

SPECULATION

IL —CHICAGO BOARD OF TRADE,
Library, 141 W Jackson Blvd, Chicago,
60604. Darlene Appleman, Librn
Holdings: Vols (4000) Cat Microforms
Notes: Incl materials on commodity
exchanges, commodities that are traded on
futures exchanges, finance, and agriculture
economics. Commodity Futures Trading, A
Bibliography is published annually. The
archives of the Chicago Board of Trade are
located in the Manuscript Collection at the
University of Illinois at Chicago Circle
Campus. A published catalog, The Archives
of the Chicago Board of Trade, 1959-1925,
is available from the Chicago Board of
Trade.

NY —HUDSON INSTITUTE, Library, Quaker
Ridge Rd, Croton-on-Hudson, 10520.
Mildred Schneck, Librn
Holdings: Vols (10,000) Cat
Budget: ($40,000)
Notes: Social sciences and world futures.
About 30 percent of the collection
emphasizes materials useful to our ongoing
program of examining possible world futures:
social and economic indicators, forecasts,
current social problems, arms control and
disarmament.

SPEECH, DISORDERS OF

CA —LOS ANGELES PUBLIC LIBRARY,
Science & Technology Dept, 630 W Fifth St,
Los Angeles, 90071. Billie M Connor, Dept
Head
Holdings: Vols (7500)
Notes: A well-rounded collection of
materials related to consumer health,
medicine and drugs as well as materials for
the allied health and medical professions.
Includes a sound representative selection of
basic texts covering various aspects of
medical treatment, drugs, diseases and
syndromes. Indexes are collected as well as a
basic collection of journals. The directories
collection is strong. The broadest possible
collection of books oriented toward
consumer health, medicine, diets and
nutrition is maintained, both traditional and
alternative. Texts and examination study
books are collected for nurses, laboratory
technicians, physcial therapists, speech
therapists, paramedics and other allied health
professions.

DC —ALEXANDER GRAHAM BELL
ASSOCIATION FOR THE DEAF, Volta
Bureau Library, 3417 Volta Place, NW,
Washington, 20007.
Holdings: Vols (30,000) Cat Mss Pix Slides
Audiotapes Videotapes Microforms
Budget: $16,000
Notes: Incl 350 ms pieces, 500 pictures, 150
slides, 200 audiotapes, 25 videotapes and
500 microforms. Not open to public.

MO —WASHINGTON UNIVERSITY, School
of Medicine, Library, 660 South Euclid Ave,

SPEECH, DISORDERS OF (cont.)

Saint Louis, 63110. Christopher Hoolihan,
Rare Book Librn
Holdings: Vols 850
Budget: $3000
Notes: The CID/Max A Goldstein
Collection in Speech and Hearing. Incl some
of the earliest and most of the classic books.
Also materials of the Central Institute for
the Deaf (CID). Collection being cataloged.
All items cataloged are in OCLC data base.

OK —PHILLIPS UNIVERSITY, Zollars
Memorial Library, University Sta, Enid,
73701. John L Sayre, Dir of University
Libraries
Holdings: Vols 2050 Cat Pix Slides
Microforms Games
Notes: Works on speech and hearing
disorders, research, and therapy.

PA —EYE & EAR HOSPITAL OF
PITTSBURGH, Blair-Lippincott Library,
230 Lothrop St, Pittsburgh, 15213. Bruce A
Johnston, Medical Librn
Holdings: Vols (6000) Cat
Notes: Special emphasis on ophthalmology,
otorhinolaryngology, audiology, and speech
pathology.

WI —MARQUETTE UNIVERSITY, Memorial
Library, 1415 W Wisconsin Ave, Milwaukee,
53233. Jay Kirk, Health Sciences Librn
Notes: Supports curriculum and research.

SPEECH, FREE see Free Speech

SPEECH ANATOMY

†CT —YALE UNIVERSITY, Medical Library,
333 Cedar St, New Haven, 06520.

SPEECH DEFECTS see Speech, Disorders of

SPEECHES—COLLECTIONS

DC —LIBRARY OF CONGRESS, Motion
Pictures, Broadcasting and Recorded Sound
Div, Washington, 20540.
Notes: Recordings of speeches given at the
National Press Club, Washington, D.C.,
1952-present.

MA —JOHN F KENNEDY LIBRARY,
Columbia Point, Boston, 02125. Henry J
Gwiazda II, Cur
Notes: The Robert F Kennedy Papers cover
the period from 1937-1968 and are divided
into four subcollections: the Pre-
Administration, Attorney General's, Senate,
and 1968 Presidential Campaign Papers. In
the Pre-Administration Papers, over 140
archives boxes or 70 percent of the materials
are open to research. The Personal and
Political Papers of this subcollection are
almost entirely open. Most of the
unprocessed mss are in the Working Files
and involve investigative work on labor
racketeering. Seventy five percent or 185
archives boxes of the Attorney General's
Papers are open, incl the correspondence,
the John F Kennedy Library File, the
Speech and Trip Files for 1961-1964. For
the Senate Papers, 200 boxes are open for
the 1964 Senate Campaign, the Legislative
Subject File, and the Speech and Trip Files
for 1964-1968. The speeches and press
releases(incl in the Senate subcollection
Speech File) and "The Black Books" (16
boxes) on state and delegate information are
open for the 1968 campaign. Each
subcollection has its own finding aid. The
Library also has available for research about
100 audiotapes of Robert F Kennedy's
public addresses from 1962-1966 and some
50 oral history interviews on RFK and one
(1000 pages) by RFK. There are also
available the major documentaries on RFK
and a number of films donated by the major
networks for research use in the Library.

SPELEOLOGY AND SPELEOLOGISTS

NY —AMERICAN MUSEUM OF
NATURAL HISTORY, Library Services
Dept, Central Park W & 79th St, New York,
10024. Nina J Root, Chairwoman; Mary
Genett, Asst Librn for Reference Services

†SD —SOUTH DAKOTA SCHOOL OF
MINES & TECHNOLOGY, Devereaux
Library, Rapid City, 57701.
Holdings: Vols (3786) Cat Mss Maps Pix
Audiotapes Microforms
Notes: This special collection, in general,
relates to the Black Hills area of South
Dakota and Wyoming, especially mining and
exploration of the area; the West River area
of South Dakota, primarily county histories;
and South Dakota Territorial and State
materials. There are also specialized areas of
this collection: (1) Marion N Bruce
Collection. Documents, correspondence,
books and periodicals dealing with weather
modification in South Dakota; (2) Mildred
Fielder Collection. Mss, pictures, books and
periodicals from an author whose special
area was the Black Hills. Most of her work
on railroads, mines, trails, etc, relates to
historical aspects. Collection incl research
materials, galley proofs and final copies of
her various publications; (3) Cleophas C
O'Harra Collection. Mss, pictures, books
and original source materials, primarily
related to the Black Hills area
andexpeditions thereto. Much of the data
was collected for a book on the Black Hills
which was never published; and (4) Caving
Collection. Maps of various caves in Black
Hills area, being kept current and updated
by members of the Paha Sapa Grotto. Also,
some books and periodicals on caving in
general.

SPELLERS

PA —UNIVERSITY OF PITTSBURGH,
Hillman Library, Special Collections Dept,
John A Nietz Textbook Collection, 363
Hillman Library, Pittsburgh, 15260. Charles
E Aston, Jr, Coordr
Holdings: Vols 13,480 Cat Vols 3000 Uncat
Mss
Notes: The John A Nietz Textbook
Collection of primarily American textbooks
in 3 areas; primary school books to 1900,
secondary texts to ca 1930 and pedagogical
books (1000 vols on the history and theory
of education incl writings of the key figures
in the field of education). Books are
cataloged via an inhouse computer printout,
and are accessible via name, title, subject,
place, publisher and date. Late 18th and all
of the 19th century are well represented.
Important titles in each subject are discussed
in John A Nietz's *Old Textbooks*
(Pittsburgh, 1961) and in his *The Evolution
of American Secondary School Textbooks*
(Rutland, Vt, 1966). Collection also incl the
papers (noncirculating) of Prof John A
Nietz.

SPELLS

OH —CLEVELAND PUBLIC LIBRARY, Fine
Arts and Special Collections Department,
325 Superior Ave, Cleveland, 44114. Alice
N Loranth, Head
Holdings: Vols (1600) Cat
Notes: Part of the Witchcraft Collection,
which incl witchcraft, magic, sorcery,
magical manuals, devil worship, incantations,
charms, talismans, amulets and spells.
Contemporary urban practices are almost
entirely omitted.
See also entries under Folklore; Witchcraft.

SPELMAN FUND

VA —UNIVERSITY OF VIRGINIA,
Alderman Library, Manuscripts Dept,
Charlottesville, 22901. Edmund Berkeley Jr,
Cur
Notes: Papers of Guy Moffett, Executive of
the Spelman Fund; about 1500 items, 1920-
1963.

SPENCELEY, JOSEPH WINFIELD

WI —UNIVERSITY OF WISCONSIN,
MADISON, Memorial Library, Rare Books
Collection, 728 State St, Madison, 53706.
Gretchen Lagana, Cur
Holdings: //
Notes: Doane-Davidson Bookplate

Collection. This collection of approximately
10,000 bookplates is composed of two
collections originally belonging to Gilbert H
Doane and Flora Davidson. There are
extensive separate collections of University
of Wisconsin libraries bookplates, medical,
animal, and punning plates, as well as the
plates of two Boston engravers: Sidney
Lawton Smith and Joseph Winfield
Spenceley. The collection is indexed. Housed
in the Dept of Rare Books and Special
Collections.

SPENCER, HERBERT

IL —NORTHWESTERN UNIVERSITY,
Library, Special Collections Dept, 1937
Sheridan Rd, Evanston, 60201. R Russell
Maylone, Cur
Holdings: Mss
Notes: 24 letters to J S Mill from Herbert
Spencer.

SPENCER, LESTER

CA —UNIVERSITY OF CALIFORNIA, LOS
ANGELES, Music Library, Schonberg Hall,
Los Angeles, 90024. Stephen M Fry, Music
Librn
Notes: Mss.

SPENCER, PLATT R.

IL —NEWBERRY LIBRARY, 60 W Walton
St, Chicago, 60610. Diana Haskell, Cur of
Modern Mss
Holdings: Cat Mss Pix
Budget: $800
Notes: Incl writing specimen books and
about 7000 ms pieces on American
handwriting, espec the Spencerian hand,
and the history of business schools.

SPENCER, SARA

AZ —ARIZONA STATE UNIVERSITY,
Library, Tempe, 85287. Marilyn
Wurzburger, Special Collections Librn
Holdings: Vols (108) Pix
Notes: Collection covers various aspects of
Children's Theatre from 1944 through the
present. Areas of emphasis incl International
and National Child Drama Associations,
award-winning theatres, educational
programs, regional groups and prominent
figures in Children's Theatre incl: Irene
Vickers Baker, Isabel Burger, Virginia Lee
Comer, Rita Criste, Moses Goldberg,
Kenneth Graham, Aurand Harris, Paul
Kozelka, George Latshaw, Rosemary Musil,
Sara Spencer, Winifred Ward, Susan Zeder
and Lin Wright. Publications incl
newsletters, research papers, bibliographies
and records of the proceedings of the
Children's Theatre Association of America.
80 linear feet of scripts, documents,
publications, films, tapes (oral history)
programs, correspondence, photographs,
working papers and clippings. Partially
indexed; finding guides available.

SPENDER, STEPHEN

CA —UNIVERSITY OF CALIFORNIA,
BERKELEY, Bancroft Library, Manuscripts
Division, Berkeley, 94720. James D Hart,
Dir
Holdings: Uncat Mss
Notes: Collection of notebooks containing
drafts of poems; letters to Spender from TS
Eliot, EM Forester, Allen Ginsberg, Aldous
Huxley, Ezra Pound, Edith Sitwell, Boris
Pasternak and others. Personal journals also.

IL —NORTHWESTERN UNIVERSITY,
Library, Special Collections Dept, 1937
Sheridan Rd, Evanston, 60201. R Russell
Maylone, Cur
Holdings: Vols 450 Cat Mss
Notes: Incl 137 letters from T S Eliot to
Stephen Spender, and 70 letters from Eliot
to John Middleton Murray.

NV —UNIVERSITY OF NEVADA, RENO,
University Library, Special Collections Dept,
Reno, 89557. Robert E Blesse, Head
Holdings: Vols (127) Cat Other appearances
1070 Cat
Notes: Includes individual works by author

SPENDER, STEPHEN (cont.)

in all editions including translations; also prefaces, introductions, published correspondence, appearances in anthologies, periodicals, etc. Bibliographical research collection, part of Modern Authors Collection.
BC —UNIVERSITY OF VICTORIA, McPherson Library, Victoria, V8W 3H5, Can.
Notes: Incl 2 letters from Spender to M Wollman; portrait etching of Spender by Edgar Holloway.

SPENSER, EDMUND

IL —NEWBERRY LIBRARY, 60 W Walton St, Chicago, 60610. Diana Haskell, Cur of Modern Mss
Holdings: Vols 500 Cat
Budget: $1000
Notes: Spenser and Spenseriana.
MD —JOHNS HOPKINS UNIVERSITY, Milton S Eisenhower Library, Charles & 34 Sts, Baltimore, 21218. Ann S Gwyn, Assistant Dir for Special Collections
Holdings: Vols 450 Cat
Notes: Probably best working collection of Spenseriana. Every edition of scholarly significance plus critical and bibliographic material. Most rare and first editions. Photocopies of those not owned. Downs (1951-) 3548.
WA —UNIVERSITY OF WASHINGTON LIBRARIES, Suzzallo Library, Special Collections Division, Rare Book Collection, FM-25, Seattle, 98195. Gary Menges, Coordinator for Special Collections
Notes: Extensive collection; includes first editions.

SPERRY CORPORATION

DE —HAGLEY MUSEUM AND LIBRARY, Eleutherian Mills-Hagley Foundation Inc, PO Box 3630, Greenville, 19807. Richmond D Williams, Dir; Heddy A Richter, Imprints Librn
Notes: Records of the Sperry-Univac Company (1940-1975; 400 cubic feet) document the early development and rapid growth of the computer industry. The collection incl technical and administrative documents relating to the ENIAC, BINAC and UNIVAC computers.

SPERRY-UNIVAC COMPANY (1940-1975)

DE —HAGLEY MUSEUM AND LIBRARY, Eleutherian Mills-Hagley Foundation Inc, PO Box 3630, Greenville, 19807. Richmond D Williams, Dir; Heddy A Richter, Imprints Librn
Notes: Records of the Sperry-Univac Company (1940-1975; 400 cubic feet) document the early development and rapid growth of the computer industry. The collection incl technical and administrative documents relating to the ENIAC, BINAC and UNIVAC computers.

SPG see Society for the Propagation of the Gospel (SPG)

SPHRAGISTICS see Seals (Numismatics)

SPICE TRADE

MN —UNIVERSITY OF MINNESOTA, James Ford Bell Library, 309 19th Ave S, Minneapolis, 55455. John Parker, Cur
Holdings: Vols (11,000) Cat Mss Maps
Notes: Collection of original materials relating to European expansion, 1400-1800.

SPICER, JACK

BC —SIMON FRASER UNIVERSITY, Library, Burnaby, V5A 1S6, Can. Percilla Groves, Special Collections Librn
Holdings: Cat Mss
Notes: Mss of poems, handwritten, in pencil, for two books of poems: *Language* and *The*

Book of Magazine Verse, 88 pages, plus holograph of *Imaginary Elegies*, 33 pp and holograph poem, "A redwood forest...", one page.

SPIDERS

CA —UNIVERSITY OF CALIFORNIA, BERKELEY, Life Sciences Library, Entomology Library, 201 Wellman Hall, Berkeley, 94720. Nancy Axelrod, Librn
Holdings: Vols (12,000) Cat Microforms
Notes: A highly specialized collection limited to materials on insects, arachnida and animal parasites. Special emphasis is given to works on pest control, particularly on biological methods of control. The library's holdings in the field of parasitology emphasize medical parasitology. Incl over (17,000) pamphlets.
DC —SMITHSONIAN INSTITUTION LIBRARIES, Entomology Branch, Washington, 20560. Jean C Smith, Asst Dir for Bureau Services
Holdings: Vols (17,000) Cat Maps Pix
HI —BERNICE P BISHOP MUSEUM, Library, PO Box 19000-A, Honolulu, 96819. Cynthia Timberlake, Librn
Holdings: Vols (90,000) Cat Mss Maps Pix Slides Microforms
Budget: ($30,000)
Notes: Only American library devoted exclusively to the Pacific region. Collection reflects historical and contemporary research emphases of Bishop Museum; ie the natural and cultural history of the Pacific. Areas of concentration incl archaeology, ethnology, linguistics, voyages and explorations, history, vertebrate and invertebrate zoology, botany and museology. Strong special collections incl photographs, mss and archives, maps and art. Publications: Quarterly "Additions to the Catalog," *Dictionary Catalog of the Library* (9 vols and 2 suppl; Boston: G K Hall, 1964-69).
NY —CORNELL UNIVERSITY LIBRARIES, Comstock Memorial Library of Entomology, Ithaca, 14853. Edwin Spragg, Librn
Holdings: Vols (30,000) Cat Maps Pix Audiotapes Microforms
Budget: ($13,500)
Notes: Major topics: general and applied entomology. Minor topics: parasitology, medical entomology, ecology, zoological nomenclature and allied orders of arthropods. Separate catalog to the collection, also extensive collection of reprints. Apiculture material kept at nearby A R Mann Library.
NY —AMERICAN MUSEUM OF NATURAL HISTORY, Library Services Dept, Central Park W & 79th St, New York, 10024. Nina J Root, Chairwoman; Mary Genett, Asst Librn for Reference Services
Holdings: Vols (385,000) Cat Mss Maps Pix Slides Microforms
Notes: Nearly all collections are outstanding for depth of coverage and international range. Early and historic works, rare books, colored illustrations, and relevant serial publications supplement the modern scientific publications necessary to the researches of the scientific staff and the work of the educational division. Open to the public.

SPIES

CA —UNIVERSITY OF CALIFORNIA, SAN DIEGO, Central University Library, Mandeville Dept of Special Collections, La Jolla, 92093. Lynda Corey Claassen, Head
Notes: Papers of Howard Clayton Urey (1893-1981), winner of the 1934 Nobel Prize in chemistry for his discovery of Deuterium. Incl files concerning the Emergency Committee of Atomic Scientists, 1946-49; also some material on the Rosenberg/Sobell spy cases; also on his works as science advisor to John F Kennedy (president-elect).
CA —HOOVER INSTITUTION ON WAR, REVOLUTION & PEACE, Stanford University, Stanford, 94305. Milorad M Drachkovitch, Archivist
Holdings: Mss Pix
Notes: Two collections: (1) Papers of Lloyd

M Bucher, Commander, US Navy, and Commander of the USS *Pueblo*, incl correspondence, newspaper clippings, reports, copies of court inquiries, photographs, plaques, memorabilia, and other materials, 1970-75, relating to the *Pueblo* incident and its aftermath. Incl is a typewritten manuscript of his memoirs, entitled "Bucher, My Story." 68 boxes, 1 oversize package. (2) Papers of Yves Godard, officer, French Army, 1932-1961; director of police in Algeria, 1958-60; and organizer of the Organisation de l'Armee Secrete (OAS) 1961-62; incl correspondence, messages, reports, dossiers, maps, photos, news clippings, speeches and writings, and other material, 1929-74, related to military and resistance operations during World War II; to military, police, and terrorist activities during the Algerian independence struggle. Incl records of the ArmeeSecrete de Haute-Savoie (Secret Army of Resistance Fighters of Haute-Savoie). 13 ms boxes; 1 oversize volume; 1 envelope.

NY —COLUMBIA UNIVERSITY LIBRARIES, Rare Book & Manuscript Library, 801 Butler Library, 535 W 114 St, New York, 10027. Kenneth A Lohf, Librn
Holdings: Mss
Notes: Major General William H Donovan's papers, on research materials on espionage during the American Revolution. 15,000 items.

†VA —GEORGE C MARSHALL RESEARCH FOUNDATION AND LIBRARY, Drawer 920, Lexington, 24450. Royster Lyle Jr, Cur Collections
Holdings: Vols Uncat Mss Slides Microforms
Notes: The William F. Friedman Collection. Separate catalog. Incl. papers and correspondence relating to William and Elizabeth S. Friedman's personal interests and U.S. government assignments: books, pamphlets, technical papers, periodicals, microfilm, slides and newspaper clippings dealing with cryptology. Items on secret writing and signaling, radar, telephony and telegraphy, and the study of the Shakespeare-Bacon authorship controversy, Vols. of fiction relating to spies and codes, cryptographic game books for children, Civil War code items. Examples of ancient writings of Europe, Crete, and Easter Island, and material on the Aztecs, Incas, and particularly the Mayans. Also a copy of the Voynich mss., an undeciphered work, and other rare vols. on the subject dating from the 17th century. The library also has a separate collection of diaries kept by Gilbert Sandford Vernam, cryptographer and inventor. The diary is an almost day-by-day record, 1918-1926, of Vernam's inventions and development of his outstanding contributions to cryptography including techniques widely adopted by the armed forces for enciphering and deciphering coded messages. There is a typed index to this collection. No photocopying.

SPIGELGASS, LEONARD

MA —BOSTON UNIVERSITY, Mugar Memorial Library, Special Collections Dept, 771 Commonwealth Ave, Boston, 02215. Howard B Gotlieb, Dir
Holdings: Cat Mss Pix
Notes: Mss, correspondence, etc collected in depth; incl publications by or about.

SPILLER, ROBERT ERNEST

NC —DUKE UNIVERSITY, William R Perkins Library, Jay B Hubbell Center for

SPILLER, ROBERT ERNEST (cont.)

American Literary Historiography, Durham, 27706. Erma Whittington, Librn
Notes: 77,312 items, including manuscripts, pictures, clippings, and correspondence. "The objective of the Center is to gather the papers and materials of significant scholars and critics in American literary history." The Center is a part of the Perkins Library Manuscripts Department.

SPILMAN, LOUIS

VA —UNIVERSITY OF VIRGINIA, Alderman Library, Manuscripts Dept, Charlottesville, 22901. Edmund Berkeley Jr, Cur
Holdings: Cat Mss Pix
Notes: Papers, etc.

SPINAL CORD INJURIES

MA —MASSACHUSETTS REHABILITATION COMMISSION, Library, 20 Park Plaza, Boston, 02116. June C Holt, Librn
Holdings: Vols Cat
Notes: For staff and community interested in rehabilitation literature, defined as publications which deal with impairments resulting in disabling conditions; mental and behavioral disorders; employment of the handicapped; counseling techniques with handicapped populations; sheltered workshops, rehabilitation facilities; halfway houses and independent living arrangements; psychological aspects of disability; attitudes toward the handicapped; and other material on services for the handicapped. Library subscribes to 70 journals relating to disability and rehabilitation.

SPINELLI, MARCOS, 1904-1970

MA —BOSTON UNIVERSITY, Mugar Memorial Library, Special Collections Dept, 771 Commonwealth Ave, Boston, 02215. Howard B Gotlieb, Dir
Holdings: // Cat Mss
Notes: Correspondence.

SPINGARN, ARTHUR B., 1878-1971

DC —HOWARD UNIVERSITY, Moorland-Spingarn Research Center, 500 Howard Place NW, Washington, 20059. Clifford L Muse, Jr, Acting Dir

SPINNING

MI —PORTAGE LAKE DISTRICT LIBRARY, 105 Huron, Houghton, 49931. Bethany Patterson, Dir
Holdings: Vols 100 Cat Pix
Notes: Weaving and related crafts, spinning, etc. Some foreign language materials.

SPINOZA, BENEDICT

CA —UNIVERSITY OF CALIFORNIA, LOS ANGELES, Research Library, Dept of Special Collections, 405 Hilgard Ave, Los Angeles, 90024. Edward Shreeves, Chairman, Bibliographers Group; David S Zeidberg, Head
Holdings: Vols 1900
Notes: 1900 books by or about him; portrait.
NY —COLUMBIA UNIVERSITY LIBRARIES, Rare Book & Manuscript Library, 801 Butler Library, 535 W 114 St, New York, 10027. Kenneth A Lohf, Librn
Holdings: Vols 4000 Cat
Notes: Restricted use: noncirculating.
NY —NEW YORK PUBLIC LIBRARY, Research Libraries, General Research Division, Fifth Ave & 42 St, New York, 10018. Rodney Phillips, Chief
Holdings: Vols (2,225,000) Cat Maps Pix Microforms
Budget: ($775,718)
OH —HEBREW UNION COLLEGE-JEWISH INSTITUTE OF RELIGION, Klau Library, 3101 Clifton Ave, Cincinnati, 45220. David J Gilner, Reference Librn
Holdings: Cat Mss Pix
Notes: Many early editions and languages.

Described in Berg, Fanny K, "The Spinoza Collection in the Hebrew Union College Library," *Studies in Bibliography and Booklore* (1953-54), pp 167-182.

SPIRIT, HOLY see Holy Spirit

SPIRITISM see Spiritualism

SPIRITS see Demonology; Spiritualism; Witchcraft

SPIRITS, ALCOHOLIC see Liquors

SPIRITUAL HEALING see Faith Cure

SPIRITUAL LIFE

CA —GRADUATE THEOLOGICAL UNION LIBRARY, New Religious Movements Research Collection, Public Services and Special Collections Dept, 2400 Ridge Road, Berkeley, 94709. Diane Choquette, Dept Head
Holdings: Vols (3000) Mss Pix
Notes: Begun in 1977, the collection focuses on religious movements new to America since 1960, and unorthodox religious movements resurgent since 1960. American forms of Hinduism, Buddhism, Sikhism, and Sufism are included along with occultism, Neo-Paganism, esoteric and alternative forms of Christianity, feminist spirituality, and human potential movements having a spiritual aspect.
CA —SAINT MARY'S COLLEGE, Library, Moraga, 94575. Brother Casimir Reichlin, Dir of the Library; Brother Richard Lemberg FSC, Asst Librn
DC —GEORGETOWN UNIVERSITY, Woodstock Theological Center Library, Box 37445, Washington, 20013. Thomas a Marshall, SJ, Librn
Holdings: Vols (165,000)
Notes: On Catholic spirituality.
WI —DERANCE FOUNDATION, 7700 W Blue Mound Rd, Milwaukee, 53213. Harry John, Pres
Holdings: Vols (5200)
Notes: On Catholic spirituality. Private non-circulating collection.

SPIRITUAL LIFE—CATHOLIC AUTHORS

DC —GEORGETOWN UNIVERSITY, Woodstock Theological Center Library, Box 37445, Washington, 20013. Thomas a Marshall, SJ, Librn
Holdings: Vols (165,000)
Notes: On Catholic spirituality.
WI —DERANCE FOUNDATION, 7700 W Blue Mound Rd, Milwaukee, 53213. Harry John, Pres
Holdings: Vols (5200)
Notes: On Catholic spirituality. Private non-circulating collection.

SPIRITUALISM

AZ —WORLD UNIVERSITY, Library, 711 E Blacklidge Dr, Tucson, 85719. Howard John Zitko, Cur
Holdings: Vols (15,000) Cat Mss Maps Audiotapes
Notes: Collection concerns what are generally called the "frontier sciences." No interlibrary loan.
CT —YALE UNIVERSITY, Box 1603A, Yale Station, New Haven, 06520.
Holdings: Cat Mss
Notes: Incl 165 letters of Andrew Jackson Davis to William Green, Jr, concerning personal, family, and financial matters, as well as Davis's works with Spiritualism and healing, 1848-1881.
DC —LIBRARY OF CONGRESS, Rare Book & Special Collections Div, Washington, 20540. William Matheson, Chief
Holdings: Cat
Notes: The Houdini Collection of Magic and Spiritism consists of over 4000 vols of printed works and a large number of scrapbooks containing clippings, programs, catalogs, posters, etc. The McManus-Young

collection of 1076 vols, as well as mss, prints, and organized scrapbooks on Houdini, the history of magic, and related fields.
See also entry under Houdini, Harry
MD —JOHNS HOPKINS UNIVERSITY, Milton S Eisenhower Library, George Peabody Collection, 17 E Mt Vernon Place, Baltimore, 21201. Lyn Hart, Peabody Librn
Notes: Noncirculating.
NY —AMERICAN SOCIETY FOR PSYCHICAL RESEARCH LIBRARY, 5 W 73 St, New York, 10023. Rhea A White, Consultant to the Library
Holdings: Vols (7000) Cat Mss Pix
Budget: ($1500)
Notes: Incl books on spiritulism, as well as works in psychology, religion, philosophy, physics, anthropology, etc which have a possible bearing on parapsychology. An attempt is made to obtain all serious books on parapsychology in English.
NY —PARAPSYCHOLOGY FOUNDATION, Eileen J Garrett Library, 228 E 71st St, New York, 10021. Wayne Norman, Librn
Holdings: Vols 8200 Cat
Notes: One of the largest libraries on parapsychology. Main emphasis is on the literature of contemporary parapsychology; also a strong collection on the history of parapsychology (early spiritualism, mysticism, reevant philosophical works, etc). Rare book collection incl early rare books and periodicals on psychical research and psychical phenomena. Receives about 100 titles. There is no index to periodical parapsychological literature but the library maintains its own periodicals index. Main emphasis in on the experimental parapsychology, or those publications that approach the subject with an objective and analytic point of view.
NY —UNIVERSITY OF ROCHESTER, Rush Rhees Library, Department of Rare Books and Special Collections, Rochester, 14627. Peter Dzwonkoski, Librn
Holdings: Vols 3000 Cat
Notes: Principal strength is late eighteenth and early nineteenth century American imprints.
RI —BROWN UNIVERSITY, John Hay Library, 20 Prospect St, Providence, 02912. Mark N Brown, Cur Mss
Holdings: // Mss
Notes: Sarah Helen Whitman, 1803-1898, an American poet and friend of Edgar Allan Poe. A group of about 500 ms for the period 1835-1922, chiefly correspondence, notes, and articles by Mrs Whitman. Subjects include: Poe, English and American literature, spiritualism, and personal matters. Also incl correspondence and copies of letters, mss, and reminiscences of Mrs Whitman gathered by her literary heirs; letters to and from James Albert Harrison (1848-1911) regarding his books on Poe; and letters from Maria Clemm Poe to Mrs Whitman about Poe.
VA —ASSOCIATION FOR RESEARCH & ENLIGHTENMENT, Library, 67 & Atlantic Avenue, PO Box 595, Virginia Beach, 23451. Stephen Jordan, Library Mgr
Holdings: Vols (1800) Cat
Notes: A R E Library Booklist incl 6000 items in 24 subject categories. This special collection is especially strong in the following subjects: astrology, spiritualism, reincarnation, healing arts, Theosophy, Atlantis, parapsychology and transpersonal psychology.
MB —UNIVERSITY OF MANITOBA, Elizabeth Dafoe Library, Archives and Special Collections Dept, Winnipeg, R3T 2N2, Can. Richard E Bennett, Dept Head; Corrado A Santoro, Reference Archivist
Notes: Papers of Thomas Glendenning Hamilton, physician and surgeon, member of the Manitoba Legislative Assembly, psychic researcher. Winnipeg, Manitoba. Important collection, emphasis is on psychic research with limited amount of materials regarding his medical and political careers. Seance attendance registers, records and affidavits, lecture notes, correspondence, newspaper clippings, books and journal articles. Photographs, slides and ca 50 boxes of glass plate negatives.

SPIRITOUS LIQUORS see Liquors

SPITSBERGEN

MI —MICHIGAN TECHNOLOGICAL UNIVERSITY, Archives, Copper Country Historical Collections, Houghton, 49931. Theresa Sanderson Spence, University Archivist
Holdings: Vols 100 Cat Mss Maps Pix
Notes: Miscellaneous materials relating to the island. Additional material was acquired with the Scott Turner Collection (former Director, US Bureau of Mines). Contents of 3 file boxes are related primarily to mining activities on the island. A gift list consititutes the index to the original Spitsbergen Collection. Accession list for the Turner acquistiton.

SPIVAK, LAWRENCE E.

DC —LIBRARY OF CONGRESS, Washington, 20540.
Notes: His newspaper clippings, recordings, 500 kinescope films of his weekly television series (1949-1965), early tapes and recordings of radio programs.
DC —LIBRARY OF CONGRESS, Motion Pictures, Broadcasting and Recorded Sound Div, Washington, 20540.
Notes: Recordings, videotapes, and films of *Meet the Press,* papers of its producer Lawrence E Spivak, and related pictorial material.

SPOCK, BENJAMIN, 1903-

NY —SYRACUSE UNIVERSITY LIBRARIES, Ernest S Bird Library, George Arents Research Library for Special Collections, Syracuse, 13210. Carolyn A Davis, Manuscripts Librn; Amy S Doherty, University Archivist; Mark F Weimer, Rare Book Librn
Notes: Incl correspondence of Dr Benjamin Spock (1903-) on medical subjects. Vietnam peace movement, nuclear disarmament, state and national politics, and civil rights. Papers 1904-76 (112 linear feet).

SPORT FISHERY RESEARCH see Fisheries—Research

SPORT FISHING see Fishing and Angling

SPORTING BOOKS

CT —TRINITY COLLEGE LIBRARY, 300 Summit St, Hartford, 06106. Ralph S Emerick, Librn
Holdings: Cat
Notes: Incl Sherman Parker Collection of Izaak Walton.
CT —YALE UNIVERSITY, Box 1603A, Yale Station, New Haven, 06520.
NJ —PRINCETON UNIVERSITY, Library, Rare Books Dept, Princeton, 08544. Stephen Ferguson, Cur
Holdings: Cat
Notes: Laurence Roberts Carton Hunting Collection. Consists of over 1000 vols, comprising a portion of the Library's sizable Sporting Books Collection. See: William Dix, "The Hunting Library of Laurence Roberts Carton" in the *Princeton University Library Chronicle* XV, 1 (Autumn, 1953) pp 43-45. The books are a discriminating and representative collection of the literature of fox hunting and related subjects, particularly in England and America. Works from the 15th century are represented by facsimiles and other modern printed versions. There are a number of first editions of notable 16th, 17th and 18th century books, especially in English. The verse and fiction of sport are extensively represented, and biographies of dozens of notable figures and histories of scores of individual packs and hunting territories can be found. Incidental to the collection is thefine collection of illustrated hunting books. It is rich in examples of the work of the major illustrators of the period who helped make,

and in turn were made by, the popularity of the sporting book. Especially notable are the works of Henry Alken.
See also entry under Fishing and Angling.
NY —C W POST CENTER OF LONG ISLAND UNIVERSITY, B Davis Schwartz Memorial Library, Greenvale, 11548. Jean Goldberg, Special Collections Librn
Holdings: Vols 750
Notes: The Franklin B Lord Collection.
NY —AMERICAN MUSEUM OF NATURAL HISTORY, Library Services Dept, Central Park W & 79th St, New York, 10024. Nina J Root, Chairwoman; Mary Genett, Asst Librn for Reference Services
Holdings: Vols (385,000) Cat Mss Maps Pix Slides Microforms
Notes: Nearly all collections are outstanding for depth of coverage and international range. Early and historic works, rare books, colored illustrations, and relevant serial publications supplement the modern scientific publications necessary to the researches of the scientific staff and the work of the educational division. Open to the public.
SC —FRANCIS MARION COLLEGE, James A Rogers Library, Florence, 29501. H Paul Dove, Dir; Roger K Hux, Special Collections Librn
Holdings: Vols (400) Cat
Notes: Includes publications of the Small Arms Technical Pub Co, emphasis on hunting and fishing.

SPORTING DOGS see Hunting Dogs

SPORTING PRINTS

CA —HUNTINGTON LIBRARY, Art Gallery & Botanical Gardens, 1151 Oxford Rd, San Marino, 91108. Robert L Middlekauff, Dir; Daniel H Woodward, Librn
Notes: Some 1500 scarce books on English and American sports from the Renaissance to modern times. Many English and American sporting prints.
CT —YALE UNIVERSITY, Box 1603A, Yale Station, New Haven, 06520.
NJ —PRINCETON UNIVERSITY, Library, Rare Books Dept, Princeton, 08544. Stephen Ferguson, Cur
Holdings: Cat

SPORTS

AL —AUBURN UNIVERSITY, Ralph Brown Draughon Library, Mell St, Auburn, 36830. Gene Geiger, Special Collections Librn
Notes: Streit Collection.
AL —MOBILE PUBLIC LIBRARY, Special Collections Div, 701 Government St, Mobile, 36602.
Notes: The Mobile area; incl papers of the Forbes Trading Co, 1795-1840; Bank of Mobile papers, 1820-.
AL —TUSKEGEE INSTITUTE, Hallis Burke Frissel Library, Tuskegee Institute, 36088. Daniel Williams, Librn
Notes: The Robert Stewart Darnaby Collection on Blacks in American sports. Much on the Southern Intercollegiate Athletic Conference, incl historical materials. Large resources on Tuskegee athletics.
CA —UNIVERSITY OF CALIFORNIA, BERKELEY, Bancroft Library, Manuscripts Division, Berkeley, 94720. James D Hart, Dir
Notes: Wide scope but emphasis on the University's teams.
CA —FIRST INTERSTATE BANK, Athletic Foundation, 2141 W Adams, Los Angeles, 90018. W R Schroeder, Managing Dir
Notes: One of the most extensive library and museum collections relating to sports, the Olympic Games, etc. Bound vols of sports sections from several newspapers. Large collection of college and university annuals and yearbooks; souvenir publications from amateur, college, and professional sporting events. Also, large museum collection of sports memorabilia, ledger of halls of fame with thousands of names of outstanding athletes in all sports. Repository for the Association of Sports Museums and Halls of Fame. Noncirculating.

CA —LOS ANGELES PUBLIC LIBRARY, Art, Music & Recreation Dept, 630 W Fifth St, Los Angeles, 90071. Melvin H Rosenberg, Mgr & Principal Librn
Holdings: Vols 24,000 Cat Pix
Budget: ($102,244)
Notes: Incl 15,000 pictures; *Sports Index* (40,000 entries).
CA —UNIVERSITY OF CALIFORNIA, LOS ANGELES, Education & Psychology Library, 390 Powell Library Bldg, Los Angeles, 90024. Barbara Duke, Librn
Holdings: Vols (133,000) Cat Microforms
Notes: Library has University of Oregon microfiche collection of unpublished research in sports, physical education, and recreation.
CO —UNITED STATES FIGURE SKATING ASSOCIATION, 20 First St, Colorado Springs, 80906.
Notes: Rule books and other publications on figure skating.
CT —TRINITY COLLEGE LIBRARY, 300 Summit St, Hartford, 06106. Ralph S Emerick, Librn
CT —YALE UNIVERSITY, Box 1603A, Yale Station, New Haven, 06520.
Notes: Papers of Walter Camp, father of American football and foremost authority on sports and physical fitness. 48 microfilm reels; incl also over 20,000 clippings, etc on sports, providing virtual history, 1866-1925. Published guide to the collection for sale.
DC —NATIONAL RIFLE ASSOCIATION OF AMERICA, Reference Library, 1600 Rhode Island Ave, 7th Floor, Washington, 20036. Maureen Booth, Librn
Notes: Shooting sports, trap and sheet; interlibrary loan limited to members and libraries.
FL —INTERNATIONAL GAME FISH ASSOCIATION, Fort Lauderdale, 33316. E K Harry, President
Notes: Large library on freshwater and saltwater recreational angling, game fish species and related subjects. Reference library only. No books are removed from premises.
IL —AMERICAN FISHING TACKLE MANUFACTURERS ASSOCIATION, 2625 Clearhook Dr, Arlington Heights, 60005.
Notes: A newly begun library, 1983. Emphasis on fishing tackle of all kinds.
IL —AMERICAN SOKOL EDUCATIONAL AND PHYSICAL CULTURE, 6424 W Cermak Road, Berwyn, 60402. Annette Schabowski, Librn
Holdings: Vols 2000 Pix
Notes: Incl theses and dissertations on Czech life, folk dancing, gymnastics, etc.
IL —DE PAUL UNIVERSITY, Library, 2323 N Seminary, Chicago, 60614. Kathryn De Graff, Special Collections Librn
Holdings: Vols (900) // Uncat
Notes: The Anita Peabody Sports Collection of approx 900 volumes, incl about 250 periodical volumes, covering such topics as foxhunting, gambling, horse racing, and breeding, along with rule books and song books. Materials cover the middle to late 19th century. A complete run of *The Sporting Magazine,* begun in 1792, is also part of the collection.
IL —NATIONAL COUNCIL OF THE YMCAS, YMCA Historical Library, 6400 Shafer Ct, Rosemont, 60018. Eleanor R Murphy, Librn
Notes: Large collection, incl historical material, on basketball, wrestling, track and field, swimming, diving, scuba and volleyball.
IL —UNIVERSITY OF ILLINOIS, URBANA/CHAMPAIGN, Library, Applied Life Studies Library, 1408 W Gregory Dr, Urbana, 61801.
Holdings: Vols (38,000) Cat Pix Microforms
Notes: Library has own card catalog and shelf list for this collection; it is also represented in the main card catalog and shelf list of the University of Illinois Library. Card indexes to games and sports are incl in books in the collection, also to folk and national dances. Try to have fairly complete coverage of books published in all aspects of the field of physical education which would be of interest to students, as well as a lot of more general books on sports. Coverage of health education and recreation is also quite

SPORTS (cont.)

complete. This is one of the few (if not only) departmental libraries in the US devoted to this field. Published catalog: *Dictionary Catalog of the Applied Life Studies Library* (formerly Physical Education Library) *University of Illinois at Urbana-Champaign* v 1-4 (Boston: G K Hall, 1977) and *First Supplement* v 1-2 (Boston: G K Hall, 1982).

IN —UNITED STATES TRACK AND FIELD HALL OF FAME, Angola, 46703.

IN —NATIONAL TRACK AND FIELD HALL OF FAME, USA National Office Athletics Congress, 155 W Washington, Indianapolis, 46204. Berny Wagner, National Coach/Coordr; Ollan Cassel, Exec Dir
Notes: Collection will be located in Hoosier Dome (South Capital Ave, Indianapolis) after its completion. Incl books, film, tapes, and memorabilia.

IN —UNIVERSITY OF NOTRE DAME, University Libraries, Notre Dame, 46556.
Notes: Very likely the largest collection of sporting materials in the world. Over 500 sports and games are represented in a half-million documents. All physical forms of records are included, and there is no geographical restriction. Major center for research into all aspects of games and sports.

KS —GREYHOUND HALL OF FAME, 407 South Buckeye, Abilene, 67410. Edward Scheele, Dir
Holdings: Vols Cat Pix
Notes: Dog racing as a sport. Incl programs, magazines, memorabilia.

KY —UNIVERSITY OF KENTUCKY, Margaret I King Library, Dept of Special Collections, Lexington, 40506. William Marshall, Head
Holdings: Vols (400) Uncat
Notes: Early physical education manuals and textbooks to 1925; 18th and 19th century sports, games.

LA —NEW ORLEANS PUBLIC LIBRARY, Art & Music Div, 219 Loyola Ave, New Orleans, 70140. Marilyn Wilkins, Head
Holdings: Cat Pix
Budget: $23,500

MD —LACROSSE FOUNDATION HALL OF FAME AND LIBRARY, Newton H White Jr, Athletic Center, Homeswood, Baltimore, 21218. Ann Gwyn, Librn
Holdings: Microforms
Notes: Large collection of books and memorabilia.

MA —UNIVERSITY OF MASSACHUSETTS AT AMHERST, Library, Amherst, 01002.
Notes: Strong collections in physical education, sports studies, exercise, gymnastics, etc.

MA —HARVARD UNIVERSITY LIBRARY, Widener Library, Cambridge, 02138.
Notes: Extensive collection of all phases of sports. Incl the Fearing Collection on Angling and Fishing containing over 15,000 books, mss, photographs, etc.

MI —UNIVERSITY OF MICHIGAN, Bentley Historical Library, Michigan Historical Collections, 1150 Beal Ave, Ann Arbor, 48109. Francis X Blovin Jr, Dir
Notes: Substantial holdings relating to the University's Sports activities. Also, 93 scrapbooks on Joe Louis.

MI —DETROIT PUBLIC LIBRARY, Burton Historical Collection, 5201 Woodward Ave, Detroit, 48202. Alice Dalligan, Chief
Notes: The extensive Ernie Harwell Collection on sports, incl baseball strength, espec the Detroit Tigers.

MI —FRANKFORT LIBRARY, 630 Main St, Frankfort, 49635. Elsie Gilbert, Librn
Notes: Some emphasis on hang-gliding.

MN —MINNEAPOLIS PUBLIC LIBRARY & INFORMATION CENTER, Sociology Dept, 300 Nicollet Mall, Minneapolis, 55401. Eileen Scwartzbauer, Dept Head
Holdings: Vols (90,000) Cat Phonorecords Audiotapes Microforms
Budget: ($69,890)
Notes: Special collections: Foundation Center Regional Collection; college catalogs on fiche; adult basic education collection. Separate department catalog.

NJ —US GOLF ASSOCIATION, Library and Museum, Golf House, Route 512, PO Box

Golf, Far Hills, 07936. Janet Seagle, Librn
Notes: Believed to be one of the largest collections, over 7000 vols, on golf, golfers, and golfing.

NJ —MONTCLAIR STATE COLLEGE, Harry A Sprague Library, Upper Montclair, 07043.
Holdings: // Cat
Notes: Collection of over 150 physical education textbooks; 19th to early 20th century.

NY —NATIONAL BASEBALL HALL OF FAME AND MUSEUM, National Baseball Library, Cooperstown, 13326. Thomas R Heitz, Librn
Budget: ($6000)
Notes: The National Baseball Library incl the folowing special collections: Literature, a comprehensive collection of vols incl biographies, general histories, team and league histories, encyclopedias, directories, dictionaries, general reference materials, fiction, poetry, and children's books. Complete runs of *Baseball Digest, Baseball Magazine, Sport Magazine, Sports Illustrated,* team publications, and numerous other journals of interest to baseball researchers. A comprehensive collection of the public official documents of organized baseball for the major and minor leagues. Extensive runs of *The Sporting News, New York Clipper, Sporting Life* and other 19th and 20th century news publications. Current newspaper files are also available. A comprehensive collection of Spalding, Reach and other guides dating back to the 1870s. A comprehensivecollection of major league team publications, media guides, yearbooks and press releases. Biographical files: personal and career data on all major league players, past and present, as well as biographical data on managers, coaches, scouts, umpires, executives, broadcasters, sportswriters, authors and baseball personalities. The files contain an estimated 2,500,000 documents, questionnaires and news clippings. A file of minor league player record cards useful for tracing the careers of former baseball players, and several other collections of baseball-related items.

NY —C W POST CENTER OF LONG ISLAND UNIVERSITY, B Davis Schwartz Memorial Library, Greenvale, 11548. Manju Prasad-Rao, Media Librn
Notes: The Franklin B Lord Collection of some 600 vols on hunting and fishing. Many 19th century.

NY —REMINGTON ARMS CO, Remington Gun Museum, Catherine St, Ilion, 13357. Laurence Goodstal, Cur
Notes: Museum displays sporting and military firearms built by Remington Arms Co, ca 1825 to modern firearms of today.

NY —QUEENS BOROUGH PUBLIC LIBRARY, Art & Music Div, 89-11 Merrick Blvd, Jamaica, 11432. Dorothea Wu, Head
Holdings: Vols (85,000) Cat Maps Pix Phonorecords Audiotapes Microforms
Budget: ($44,000)
Notes: The Picture Collection, covering all subjects, consists of approximately 1,500,000 pictures, mainly reproductions and clippings from books and magazines, photographs, and postcards on all subjects; The Framed Picture Collection, approx 180 framed pictures, mostly reproductions of paintings from various periods; and The Phonorecord and Cassette Collection consists of approx 3500 reference phonorecords and 6500 circulating records as well as 1000 reference cassettes and 1500 circulating cassettes.

NY —COLUMBIA UNIVERSITY LIBRARIES, Rare Book & Manuscript Library, 801 Butler Library, 535 W 114 St, New York, 10027. Kenneth A Lohf, Librn
Notes: The Elliot V Bell Collection of over 500 books on fishing and angling, from the 17th to 20th centuries; more than 20 early editions of Izaak Walton. Also, the Paul Magriel Boxing Collection on the history and literature of pugilism. The L S Alexander Gumby Collection, which incl 9 Joe Louis scrapbooks, and much on Jack Johnson, Sugar Ray Robinson, Jackie Robinson. Much on Columbia sports and athletics. Good strengths in material on

Columbia's sports figures, incl Lou Gehrig, Lou Little, etc. Restricted use.

NY —NEW YORK PUBLIC LIBRARY, Research Libraries, General Research Division, Fifth Ave & 42 St, New York, 10018. Rodney Phillips, Chief
Holdings: Vols (2,225,000) Cat Maps Pix Microforms
Budget: ($775,718)

NY —RACQUET & TENNIS CLUB, Library, 370 Park Ave, New York, 10022. Gerald Belliveau, Jr, Librn
Holdings: Vols (17,500) Cat
Budget: ($6000)
Notes: Specializes in court tennis, lawn tennis, early American sport. See *Dictionary Catalogue of the Library of Sports in the Racquet and Tennis Club* (Boston: G K Hall, 1971). Also, Robert W Henderson, *Early American Sport,* 3rd ed. (Cranbury, NJ: Fairleigh Dickinson University Press, 1977).

NY —NATIONAL MUSEUM OF RACING, The Thoroughbred Racing Hall of Fame, Union Ave, Saratoga Springs, 12866. Elaine E Mann, Dir
Notes: Founded in 1950 to collect materials on the origin, history, and development of breeding and racing thoroughbred horses.

NY —GLADDING INTERNATIONAL SPORT FISHING MUSEUM, Octagon House, South Otselic, 13155.
Notes: Important collection of old and new books on angling and related subjects.

†NY —SYRACUSE UNIVERSITY LIBRARIES, Ernest S Bird Library, Syracuse, 13210.
Notes: A few choice rare books in the George Arents Collection.

NC —NORTH AMERICAN YOUTH SPORT INSTITUTE, 4985 Oak Garden Drive, Kernersville, 27284. Jack Hutslar, Exec Dir
Notes: A private management consulting and training firm for adults who are involved with school age youngsters in community sport, recreation and physical education.

OH —PRO FOOTBALL HALL OF FAME, Library, 2121 Harrison Ave NW, Canton, 44708. Anne Mangus, Librn; Joe Horrigan, Cur
Notes: Incl materials on all aspects of professional football, with special emphasis on the 119 men enshrined in the Hall of Fame. Mainly a research library. Incl periodicals and a vast array of historical material and mementos. Incl 17,000 pictures, 1500 slides, 50 audiotapes, 1300 16mm films, 3000 game programs and and 500 team media guides.

OH —PUBLIC LIBRARY OF CINCINNATI & HAMILTON COUNTY, Dept of Rare Books & Special Collections, 800 Vine St, Library Square, Cincinnati, 45202. Yeatman Anderson III, Cur
Notes: Large hunting and fishing collection, and a nearly complete set of Derrydale Press publications.

OH —COLLEGE FOOTBALL HALL OF FAME, Library, PO Box 300, Kings Mills, 45034. Don Schumacher, Cur
Notes: College of Football History, tourist attraction. Museum of football memorabilia and publications. Library not open to public.

OH —NATIONAL FOOTBALL HALL OF FAME, Kings Island Dr, Kings Mills, 45034. Don Schumacher, Librn in Charge

OK —NATIONAL WRESTLING HALL OF FAME, 405 West Hall of Fame Ave, Stillwater, 74075.
Notes: Collection built around collegiate and amateur wrestling, incl Olympic competition, from the late 1890s to the present.

OK —SOCIETY FOR THE NORTH AMERICAN CULTURAL SURVEY, Dept of Geography, Oklahoma State University, Stillwater, 74078. John Rooney, Dir; Todd Zdorkowski, Asst
Notes: Producing a cultural survey of North American sports and games. John Rooney has published several books on the geography of sports. SWAC's current project involves mapping the continent-wide distributions and the participation patterns for the major and minor professional, college and high school sports.

PA —HAVERFORD COLLEGE, Magill Library, Special Collections Dept,

SPORTS (cont.)

Haverford, 19041. Diana Alteu, Manuscripts Librn; E Rotau Sargent, Cricket Collection Librn
Notes: The C C Morris Cricket Library Association Collection. Perhaps the largest cricket collection in the Western Hemisphere. Incl books, periodicals, photographs, both foreign and American. Much on cricket in the Philadelphia area.

PA —UNIVERSITY OF PENNSYLVANIA, Archives and Records Center, North Facade - Franklin Field, Philadelphia, 19104. Mark Frazier Lloyd, Archivist
Notes: R Tait McKenzie's personal papers, and the J William White Collection of personal papers--sealed until 2016. Incl materials relating to McKenzie's sculpting and the sports medallions and medals which he sculpted. Biographical and reserved materials for two books about him. Incl 39 cu ft.

PA —UNIVERSITY OF PITTSBURGH, Hillman Library, Special Collections Dept, 363 Hillman Library, Pittsburgh, 15260. Charles E Aston Jr, Coordinator
Notes: The Bernard S Horne Memorial Collection of over 230 editions of Walton's *The Complete Angler;* also of Robert Smith Surtees' books.

PA —PENNSYLVANIA STATE UNIVERSITY, Fred Lewis Pattee Library, University Park, 16802.
Notes: Numerous and large collections on many sports. Also, materials supporting every aspect of the program of the Center for Women and Sport, incl research into kinetics, endocrinology, physiology, psychology, etc.

TX —UNIVERSITY OF TEXAS LIBRARIES, General Libraries, PO Box P, Austin, 78713. Carolyn Bucknell, Asst Dir for Collection Development
Notes: Much on Texas' and the University's athletic programs and athletes.

VT —THE AMERICAN MUSEUM OF FLY FISHING, PO Box 42, Manchester, 05254.
Holdings: Vols (1500)
Notes: Large collection for conservation of all fishing equipment, rods, reels, and flies.

VA —NATIONAL SPORTING LIBRARY, Chronicle of the Horse Bldg Publishing Offices, PO Box 1335, Middleburg, 22117. Judith Ozment, Librn
Holdings: Vols (11,000) Cat Mss Pix
Notes: Horse sports.

VA —JAMES RIVER GOLF MUSEUM AND LIBRARY, James River Country Club, 1500 Country Club Rd, Newport News, 23606. Weymouth Crumbler, Librn
Holdings: Vols (800)
Notes: About 900 volumes on old and modern golf; 450 gold clubs 1780-present, 150 gold balls 1820-1830.

WI —UNIVERSITY OF WISCONSIN, MADISON, Memorial Library, Rare Books Collection, 728 State St, Madison, 53706. Gretchen Lagana, Cur
Notes: Nearly 20,000 vols of books and serials.

WI —MILWAUKEE PUBLIC LIBRARY, 814 W Wisconsin Ave, Milwaukee, 53233. Donald J Sager, City Librn
Holdings: Vols 50,200 Cat
Budget: $15,317
Notes: The major sports resource collection in the area. Emphasis on the local area, incl newspaper clippings on local sports, organizations and individuals; archival materials and publications from major local sports organizations; a collection of material on Olympic Games; important works on boxing from the turn of the century; all major sports record books holding for 20-70 years, as well as most volumes in Spalding's Athletic Library Series and the NCAA.

BC —CANADIAN LACROSSE HALL OF FAME AND LIBRARY, Box 308, New Westminster, V3L 4Y6, Can. Archie W Miller, Cur
Notes: Incl a large collection of memorabilia, archival material and a small library of lacrosse around the world, particularly in Canada.

BC —BRITISH COLUMBIA SPORTS HALL OF FAME AND LIBRARY, BC Pavilion, Vancouver, V5K 4W3, Can.
Notes: Sports in British Columbia. Incl sports film collection.

BC —UNIVERSITY OF BRITISH COLUMBIA, Library, 1956 Main Mall, Vancouver, V6T 1Y3, Can. Anne Yandle, Special Collections Librn
Notes: British Columbia Mountaineering Club photograph collection covering many years of activities. Incl 420 negatives, 2 albums (photos), 1 book.

BC —VANCOUVER PUBLIC LIBRARY, Sociology Div, 750 Burrard St, Vancouver, V6Z 1X5, Can.
Holdings: Cat
Notes: Incl special files of pamphlets, clippings, etc.

ON —CANADIAN FOOTBALL HALL OF FAME, 58 Jackson St, West, Hamilton, L8P 1L4, Can. William McBride, Dir
Holdings: Vols Cat
Notes: History of Canadian football for 115 years. Incl programs, memorabilia, 200 16mm films of all Canadian championship games since 1950's. Also a museum and archives of Canadian Rugby Football Union with original minutes of meetings and photographs and artifacts.

ON —INTERNATIONAL HOCKEY HALL OF FAME AND MUSEUM, PO Box 82, York and Alfred Sts, Kingston, K7L 4V6, Can. Doug Nichols, Pres
Notes: Hockey books from 1886; scrapbooks, programs, guides, and magazines.

ON —UNIVERSITY OF WESTERN ONTARIO, Dept of Special Collections, London, N6A 5B9, Can. Beth Miller, Librn
Notes: Large and important collection on Canadian participation in pre-Olympic and other Game series. Incl minutes of annual meetings of the Athletic Union of Canada, 1884-1898, 1908-1954.

ON —CANADIAN SKI MUSEUM, 457A Sussex Dr, Ottawa, K1N 6Z4, Can. Sally Ingels, Librn
Notes: Mainly but not exclusively Canadian material. Artifacts used for displays.

ON —SPORT INFORMATION RESOURCE CENTER (SIRC), 333 River Rd, Ottawa, K1L 8H9, Can. Gilles Chiasson, Director
Notes: The database "SPORT" created by this institution is available for searching on SDC Search Services. Incl 20,000 monographs, 1400 current periodical subscriptions and 130,000 bibliographical references.

ON —RIDLEY COLLEGE LIBRARY, PO Box 3013, Saint Catharines, L2R 7C3, Can.
Notes: The Karl Andre Auty Collection of over 3000 books on cricket, kept current by endowed funds. Incl the scrapbooks of Sir C Aubrey Smith's career in cricket, from the 19th century.

ON —CANADA SPORTS HALL OF FAME, Exhibition Place, Toronto, M6K 3C3, Can. Cheryl Rielly, Librn
Notes: Incl sports library of John W Davies, supporter of Commonwealth Games in Canada.

†ON —METROPOLITAN TORONTO LIBRARY, 789 Yonge St, Toronto, M4W 2G8, Can.
Notes: Good subject strengths.

ON —SIRLS, Faculty of Human Kinetics & Leisure Studies, University of Waterloo, Waterloo, N2L 3G1, Can. Betty Smith, Database Mgr
Notes: Information Retrieval System for the Sociology of Leisure and Sport (SIRLS) is a computerized online database of about 13,000 entries (1983). Incl dance as a leisure time activity.

ON —UNIVERSITY OF WINDSOR, Leddy Library, Windsor, N9B 3P4, Can. P Jerome Malone, Librn
Notes: Human kinetics, with emphasis on the history, psychology, sociology, philosophy, and administration of sports and their organization. Also hold archival records, etc of numerous Canadian sports organizations: Canadian Intercollegiate Athletic Union (CIAU), Ontario-Quebec AA, Ontario Universities AA, etc. Local and Regional history. 40 feet of materials.

PQ —UNIVERSITY OF MONTREAL, Physical Education Library, Montreal, H3C 3J7, Can. Lisa Mayrand, Dir
Holdings: Vols 15,000
Notes: Perhaps Canada's largest university library sports collection. Collection is bilingual (in English and French). 441 periodical subscriptions, 890 periodical titles, 4000 microfiche and 317 microfilms. On line with Ottawa's SIRC data base (qv).

SPORTS—ALABAMA

AL —TUSKEGEE INSTITUTE, Hallis Burke Frissel Library, Tuskegee Institute, 36088. Daniel Williams, Librn
Notes: The Robert Stewart Darnaby Collection on Blacks in American sports. Much on the Southern Intercollegiate Athletic Conference, incl historical materials. Large resources on Tuskegee athletics.

SPORTS—BRITISH COLUMBIA

BC —UNIVERSITY OF BRITISH COLUMBIA, Library, 1956 Main Mall, Vancouver, V6T 1Y3, Can. Anne Yandle, Special Collections Librn
Notes: British Columbia Mountaineering Club photograph collection covering many years of activities. Incl 420 negatives, 2 albums (photos), 1 book.

SPORTS—CALIFORNIA

CA —UNIVERSITY OF CALIFORNIA, BERKELEY, Bancroft Library, Manuscripts Division, Berkeley, 94720. James D Hart, Dir
Notes: Wide scope but emphasis on the University's teams.

SPORTS—CANADA

ON —UNIVERSITY OF WESTERN ONTARIO, Dept of Special Collections, London, N6A 5B9, Can. Beth Miller, Librn
Notes: Large and important collection on Canadian participation in pre-Olympic and other Game series. Incl minutes of annual meetings of the Athletic Union of Canada, 1884-1898, 1908-1954.

†ON —PUBLIC ARCHIVES OF CANADA, Library, 395 Wellington St, Ottawa, K1A 0N3, Can.
Notes: The historical papers of the Montreal Amateur Athletic Association. Incl minute books, annual reports, correspondence, posters, and souvenir programs from 1861 to 1934.

ON —RIDLEY COLLEGE LIBRARY, PO Box 3013, Saint Catharines, L2R 7C3, Can.
Notes: The Karl Andre Auty Collection of over 3000 books on cricket, kept current by endowed funds. Incl the scrapbooks of Sir C Aubrey Smith's career in cricket, from the 19th century.

ON —METROPOLITAN TORONTO LIBRARY, Science & Technology Dept, 789 Yonge St, Toronto, M4W 2G8, Can. Margaret Walshe, Head
Holdings: Vols (120,000) Cat Microforms VF
Notes: Emphasis on sports history and statistics as well as performance and coaching techniques. Extensive file system of news clippings, magazine tearsheets, and pamphlets. Collection incl around 900 files in a subject arrangement and over 1200 biographical files on Canadian sports figures, past and present.

ON —UNIVERSITY OF WINDSOR, Leddy Library, Windsor, N9B 3P4, Can. P Jerome Malone, Librn
Notes: Human kinetics, with emphasis on the history, psychology, sociology, philosophy, and administration of sports and their organization. Also hold archival records, etc of numerous Canadian sports organizations: Canadian Intercollegiate Athletic Union (CIAU), Ontario-Quebec AA, Ontario Universities AA, etc. Local and Regional history. 40 feet of materials.

SPORTS—HISTORY

CA —FIRST INTERSTATE BANK, Athletic Foundation, 2141 W Adams, Los Angeles,

SPORTS—HISTORY (cont.)

90018. W R Schroeder, Managing Dir
Notes: One of the most extensive library and museum collections relating to sports, the Olympic Games, etc. Bound vols of sports sections from several newspapers. Large collection of college and university annuals and yearbooks; souvenir publications from amateur, college, and professional sporting events. Also, large museum collection of sports memorabilia, ledger of halls of fame with thousands of names of outstanding athletes in all sports. Repository for the Association of Sports Museums and Halls of Fame. Noncirculating.

CA —HUNTINGTON LIBRARY, Art Gallery & Botanical Gardens, 1151 Oxford Rd, San Marino, 91108. Robert L Middlekauff, Dir; Daniel H Woodward, Librn
Notes: Some 1500 scarce books on English and American sports from the Renaissance to modern times. Many English and American sporting prints.

CT —YALE UNIVERSITY, Box 1603A, Yale Station, New Haven, 06520.

†DC —LIBRARY OF CONGRESS, Washington, 20540.
Notes: Library of Congress and other governmental libraries contain considerable material on sports, international competition, agency or department involvement with national and international events, etc. Researchers should not overlook such resources; the National Archives' holdings are remarkably extensive for they include agency foreign documentation, eg in the United States Information Service.

DC —SMITHSONIAN INSTITUTION LIBRARIES, National Museum of American History Branch, Washington, 20560. Rhoda S Ratner, Branch Librn
Notes: Emphasis on history of American sports and recreation. Incl some 2000 baseball cards from cigarette and chewing-gum packets; 103 scrapbooks and other memorabilia about Joe Louis; much on bicycling and skating.

IL —NATIONAL COUNCIL OF THE YMCAS, YMCA Historical Library, 6400 Shafer Ct, Rosemont, 60018. Eleanor R Murphy, Librn
Notes: Large collection, incl historical material, on basketball, wrestling, track and field, swimming, diving, scuba and volleyball.

IL —UNIVERSITY OF ILLINOIS, URBANA/CHAMPAIGN, Library, University Archives, 19 Library, 1408 W Gregory Drive, Urbana, 61801. Maynard Brichford, University Archivist
Holdings: Vols (1663) // Cat Mss Pix
Notes: The Avery Brundage Collection. Incl his papers and material on amateur athletics, Olympic games, and sports. Published guide is available: *Avery Brundage Collection, 1908-1957* (Cologne: Karl Hofmann Schorndorf, 1977). 517,000 ms pieces. There is also a collection on Olympic sports and other aspects of sports kept in the Brundage Room.

IN —UNIVERSITY OF NOTRE DAME, University Libraries, Notre Dame, 46556.
Notes: Very likely the largest collection of sporting materials in the world. Over 500 sports and games are represented in a half-million documents. All physical forms of records are included, and there is no geographical restriction. Major center for research into all aspects of games and sports.

MA —HARVARD UNIVERSITY LIBRARY, Widener Library, Cambridge, 02138.
Notes: Extensive collection of all phases of sports. Incl the Fearing Collection on Angling and Fishing containing over 15,000 books, mss, photographs, etc.

MI —UNIVERSITY OF MICHIGAN, William L Clements Library, Ann Arbor, 48109. John C Dann, Dir
Notes: Good collection of early American sports.

PA —CUMBERLAND COUNTY HISTORICAL SOCIETY, The Hamilton Library, 21 N Pitt St, PO Box 626, Carlisle, 17013. Cordelia M Neitz, Librn
Holdings: Vols 60 Mss Pix
Notes: Containing most of the magazines

and journals published by the school, incl also yearbooks, commencement and other programs, illustrated brochures of the school, and several hundred photographs of classes, buildings, teaching facilities, school activities, athletes (Jim Thorpe being one) and athletic teams; one of the most complete collections of its kind in the US.

WI —MILWAUKEE PUBLIC LIBRARY, 814 W Wisconsin Ave, Milwaukee, 53233. Donald J Sager, City Librn
Holdings: Vols Cat
Notes: The major sports resource collection in the area. Emphasis on the local area, incl newspaper clippings on local sports, organizations and individuals; archival materials and publications from major local sports organizations; a collection of material on Olympic Games; important works on boxing from the turn of the century; all major sports record books holding for 20-70 years, as well as most volumes in Spalding's Athletic Library Series and the NCAA.

†ON —PUBLIC ARCHIVES OF CANADA, Library, 395 Wellington St, Ottawa, K1A 0N3, Can.
Notes: The historical papers of the Montreal Amateur Athletic Association. Incl minute books, annual reports, correspondence, posters, and souvenir programs from 1861 to 1934.

ON —METROPOLITAN TORONTO LIBRARY, Science & Technology Dept, 789 Yonge St, Toronto, M4W 2G8, Can. Margaret Walshe, Head
Holdings: Vols (120,000) Cat Microforms VF
Notes: Emphasis on sports history and statistics as well as performance and coaching techniques. Extensive file system of news clippings, magazine tearsheets, and pamphlets. Collection incl around 900 files in a subject arrangement and over 1200 biographical files on Canadian sports figures, past and present.

ON —UNIVERSITY OF WINDSOR, Leddy Library, Windsor, N9B 3P4, Can. P Jerome Malone, Librn
Notes: Human kinetics, with emphasis on the history, psychology, sociology, philosophy, and administration of sports and their organization. Also hold archival records, etc of numerous Canadian sports organizations: Canadian Intercollegiate Athletic Union (CIAU), Ontario-Quebec AA, Ontario Universities AA, etc. Local and Regional history. 40 feet of materials.

PQ —UNIVERSITY OF MONTREAL, Physical Education Library, Montreal, H3C 3J7, Can. Lisa Mayrand, Dir
Holdings: Vols 15,000
Notes: Perhaps Canada's largest university library sports collection. Collection is bilingual (in English and French). 441 periodical subscriptions, 890 periodical titles, 4000 microfiche and 317 microfilms. On line with Ottawa's SIRC data base (qv).

SPORTS—MEDICAL ASPECTS see Sports Medicine

SPORTS—MICHIGAN

MI —UNIVERSITY OF MICHIGAN, Bentley Historical Library, Michigan Historical Collections, 1150 Beal Ave, Ann Arbor, 48109. Francis X Blovin Jr, Dir
Notes: Substantial holdings relating to the University's Sports activities. Also, 93 scrapbooks on Joe Louis.

SPORTS—PHILADELPHIA

PA —HAVERFORD COLLEGE, Magill Library, Special Collections Dept, Haverford, 19041. Diana Alteu, Manuscripts Librn; E Rotau Sargent, Cricket Collection Librn
Notes: The C C Morris Cricket Library Association Collection. Perhaps the largest cricket collection in the Western Hemisphere. Incl books, periodicals, photographs, both foreign and American. Much on cricket in the Philadelphia area.

SPORTS—PHYSIOLOGICAL ASPECTS

PA —UNIVERSITY OF PENNSYLVANIA, Archives and Records Center, North Facade

- Franklin Field, Philadelphia, 19104. Mark Frazier Lloyd, Archivist
Notes: R Tait McKenzie's personal papers, and the J William White Collection of personal papers--sealed until 2016. Incl materials relating to McKenzie's sculpting and the sports medallions and medals which he sculpted. Biographical and reserved materials for two books about him. Incl 39 cu ft.

ON —UNIVERSITY OF WINDSOR, Leddy Library, Windsor, N9B 3P4, Can. P Jerome Malone, Librn
Notes: Human kinetics, with emphasis on the history, psychology, sociology, philosophy, and administration of sports and their organization. Also hold archival records, etc of numerous Canadian sports organizations: Canadian Intercollegiate Athletic Union (CIAU), Ontario-Quebec AA, Ontario Universities AA, etc. Local and Regional history. 40 feet of materials.

SPORTS—PSYCHOLOGICAL ASPECTS

IL —UNIVERSITY OF ILLINOIS, URBANA/CHAMPAIGN, Library, Applied Life Studies Library, 1408 W Gregory Dr, Urbana, 61801.
Holdings: Vols (38,000) Cat Microforms
See also entry under Physical Education and Training.

MA —UNIVERSITY OF MASSACHUSETTS AT AMHERST, Library, Amherst, 01002.
Notes: Strong collections in physical education, sports studies, exercise, gymnastics, etc.

NC —NORTH AMERICAN YOUTH SPORT INSTITUTE, 4985 Oak Garden Drive, Kernersville, 27284. Jack Hutslar, Exec Dir
Notes: A private management consulting and training firm for adults who are involved with school age youngsters in community sport, recreation and physical education.

PA —PENNSYLVANIA STATE UNIVERSITY, Fred Lewis Pattee Library, University Park, 16802.
Notes: Numerous and large collections on many sports. Also, materials supporting every aspect of the program of the Center for Women and Sport, incl research into kinetics, endocrinology, physiology, psychology, etc.

PQ —UNIVERSITY OF MONTREAL, Physical Education Library, Montreal, H3C 3J7, Can. Lisa Mayrand, Dir

SPORTS—TEXAS

TX —UNIVERSITY OF TEXAS LIBRARIES, General Libraries, PO Box P, Austin, 78713. Carolyn Bucknell, Asst Dir for Collection Development
Notes: Much on Texas' and the University's athletic programs and athletes.

SPORTS, AMATEUR

CA —FIRST INTERSTATE BANK, Athletic Foundation, 2141 W Adams, Los Angeles, 90018. W R Schroeder, Managing Dir
Notes: One of the most extensive library and museum collections relating to sports, the Olympic Games, etc. Bound vols of sports sections from several newspapers. Large collection of college and university annuals and yearbooks; souvenir publications from amateur, college, and professional sporting events. Also, large museum collection of sports memorabilia, ledger of halls of fame with thousands of names of outstanding athletes in all sports. Repository for the Association of Sports Museums and Halls of Fame. Noncirculating.

SPORTS, AQUATIC see Aquatic Sports

SPORTS MEDICINE

OH —SAINT ELIZABETH MEDICAL CENTER, Health Sciences Library, 601 Miami Blvd W, Dayton, 45408. Ann Lewis, Librn
Holdings: Vols (13,000) Cat Slides Audiotapes Filmstrips

ON —SPORT INFORMATION RESOURCE CENTER (SIRC), 333 River Rd, Ottawa,

SPORTS MEDICINE (cont.)

K1L 8H9, Can. Gilles Chiasson, Director
Notes: The database "SPORT" created by
this institution is available for searching on
SDC Search Services. Incl 20,000
monographs, 1400 current periodical
subscriptions and 130,000 bibliographical
references.
ON —UNIVERSITY OF WINDSOR, Leddy
Library, Windsor, N9B 3P4, Can. P Jerome
Malone, Librn
Notes: Human kinetics, with emphasis on
the history, psychology, sociology,
philosophy, and administration of sports and
their organization. Also hold archival
records, etc of numerous Canadian sports
organizations: Canadian Intercollegiate
Athletic Union (CIAU), Ontario-Quebec
AA, Ontario Universities AA, etc. Local and
Regional history. 40 feet of materials.
PQ —UNIVERSITY OF MONTREAL,
Physical Education Library, Montreal, H3C
3J7, Can. Lisa Mayrand, Dir

SPORTS PSYCHOLOGY

ON —UNIVERSITY OF WINDSOR, Leddy
Library, Windsor, N9B 3P4, Can. P Jerome
Malone, Librn
Notes: Human kinetics, with emphasis on
the history, psychology, sociology,
philosophy, and administration of sports and
their organization. Also hold archival
records, etc of numerous Canadian sports
organizations: Canadian Intercollegiate
Athletic Union (CIAU), Ontario-Quebec
AA, Ontario Universities AA, etc. Local and
Regional history. 40 feet of materials.

SPORTS SOCIOLOGY

ON —UNIVERSITY OF WINDSOR, Leddy
Library, Windsor, N9B 3P4, Can. P Jerome
Malone, Librn
Notes: Human kinetics, with emphasis on
the history, psychology, sociology,
philosophy, and administration of sports and
their organization. Also hold archival
records, etc of numerous Canadian sports
organizations: Canadian Intercollegiate
Athletic Union (CIAU), Ontario-Quebec
AA, Ontario Universities AA, etc. Local and
Regional history. 40 feet of materials.

SPORTSMANSHIP

CA —FIRST INTERSTATE BANK, Athletic
Foundation, 2141 W Adams, Los Angeles,
90018. W R Schroeder, Managing Dir
Notes: One of the most extensive library and
museum collections relating to sports, the
Olympic Games, etc. Bound vols of sports
sections from several newspapers. Large
collection of college and university annuals
and yearbooks; souvenir publications from
amateur, college, and professional sporting
events. Also, large museum collection of
sports memorabilia, ledger of halls of fame
with thousands of names of outstanding
athletes in all sports. Repository for the
Association of Sports Museums and Halls of
Fame. Noncirculating.
CT —YALE UNIVERSITY, Box 1603A, Yale
Station, New Haven, 06520.
IL —UNIVERSITY OF ILLINOIS,
URBANA/CHAMPAIGN, Library, Applied
Life Studies Library, 1408 W Gregory Dr,
Urbana, 61801.
Holdings: Vols (38,000) Cat Microforms
See also entry under Physical Education and
Training.
IN —UNIVERSITY OF NOTRE DAME,
University Libraries, Notre Dame, 46556.
Notes: Very likely the largest collection of
sporting materials in the world. Over 500
sports and games are represented in a half-
million documents. All physical forms of
records are included, and there is no
geographical restriction. Major center for
research into all aspects of games and sports.

SPOTTED FEVER OF THE ROCKY MOUNTAINS see Rocky Mountain Spotted Fever

SPOTTED TAIL INDIAN AGENCY

NE —NEBRASKA STATE HISTORICAL
SOCIETY, Fort Robinson Museum, Box

304, Crawford, 69339. Vance Nelson, Cur
Holdings: Vols (1500) Cat Mss Maps Pix
Slides Phonorecords Audiotapes 16mm
Films Microforms
Notes: Materials related to the history of
Fort Robinson, and incl the Post Medical
Library, reference books on state
government, etc. Western Americana: books
on ranching, homesteaders, Indian wars, etc;
microfilm records for Fort Robinson records,
Red Cloud and Spotted Tail Indian Agency
records, Crawford and Chadron, Nebraska
newspapers, diaries and interviews. Library
incl the E Kopac Collection of books dealing
with Western Americana; particularly Indian
wars, transportation, guns and railroads.

SPOTTSWOOD, GORDON, AND SON

FL —FLORIDA DEPT OF STATE, Florida
State Archives, Florida Photographic
Collection, R A Gray Bldg, Tallahassee,
32301. Mrs Allen Morris, Archives
Supervisor
Notes: 25,000 (8x10, 4x5 & 35mm)
negatives by Jacksonville commercial
photographer Gordon Spottswood & Son,
1916-1967. Subjects incl Jacksonville people
(individuals and groups), street scenes,
commercial buildings, Atlantic Coast Line &
Seaboard Airline Railroads, and Boy Scout
Activities.

SPRAGUE, FRANK J.

NY —NEW YORK PUBLIC LIBRARY, Rare
Books and Manuscripts Div, Fifth Ave & 42
St, New York, 10018. William L Joyce, Asst
Dir; Susan E Davis, Cur of Mss
Holdings: Mss
Budget: ($7161)
Notes: Incl personal and literary mss, paprs,
etc.

SPRAGUE, ISAAC

MA —HINGHAM PUBLIC LIBRARY, 66
Leavitt St, Hingham, 02043. Walter T
Dziura, Dir
Holdings: Cat Mss Maps Pix Slides
Microforms
Notes: A collection of about 2000 items
relating to the history of the town from the
1600's to the present. Incl correspondence,
legal documents, diaries and day books,
account books, broadsides, pictures. Contains
a large portion of four major collections:
those of historian George Lincoln, historian
Soloman Lincoln, historian Mason Foley and
Hinghamiana collector Norman A Hersey.
Items of special importance incl papers of
town clerk Daniel Cushing, from the 1600's;
Revolutionary War troop muster rolls; early
land grant maps of the town; papers of
artists Frank Vining Smith and Isaac
Sprague; correspondence of Massachusetts
governor John D Long; steamship history.
An unpublished catalog of the collection is
available through interlibrary loan. Most of
the collection is on microfilm and may be
borrowed through interlibrary loan.

SPRAGUE, STEPHEN

AZ —UNIVERSITY OF ARIZONA, Center
for Creative Photography, 843 E University
Blvd, Tucson, 85721. James Enyeart, Dir;
Terence Pitts, Cur and Librn
Notes: Center has significant collections
consisting of more than 25 photographs plus
other archival material such as negatives,
contact sheets, work prints, correspondence,
financial records, diaries, project files, etc.
Inventories of the collections are available to
researchers. Published guides available for
some collections.

SPRAY TECHNOLOGY

IA —DELEVAN DIVISION OF COLT
INDUSTRIES INC, Engineering Library,
811 Fourth St, PO Box 100, West Des
Moines, 50265. G A Hartman, Librn
Holdings: Vols 2000 Cat Mss Slides
Microforms
Budget: $400
Notes: Incl liquid atomization, droplet size

measurement and representation, fuel
nozzles for combustors, and spray nozzles
for industrial and agricultural applications.

SPRINGS (THERMAL)

†NY —MEDICAL RESEARCH LIBRARY
OF BROOKLYN, Academy of Medicine of
Brooklyn & The State University of New
York Downstate Medical Center, 450
Clarkson St, Brooklyn, 11203. Kenneth E
Moody, Dir
Notes: Extensive collection of 18th-19th
century material.
See also entry under Medicine.

SPROUSE, PHILIP D., 1906-

CA —HOOVER INSTITUTION ON WAR,
REVOLUTION & PEACE, Stanford
University, Stanford, 94305. Milorad M
Drachkovitch, Archivist
Holdings: Maps Pix
Notes: Papers of Ambassador Philip D
Sprouse, incl printed matter, news clippings,
maps, invitations, programs of various
events, diplomatic list, and photographs
relating to the George C Marshall Mission
to China, 1945-1946, activities to Philip D
Sprouse as US Ambassador to Cambodia,
1962-1964, cultural and political aspects of
recent Cambodia history. 2 ms boxes.

SPRUANCE, RAYMOND AMES

RI —US NAVAL WAR COLLEGE, Historical
Collection & Museum, Newport, 02841.
Anthony S Nicolosi, Dir; Evelyn Cherpak,
Cur
Holdings: Mss
Notes: A collection of official
correspondence, and orders, much of which
deals with his command of the 5th Fleet,
Pacific, during WW II and the Battle of
Midway. Miscellaneous items incl clippings,
mementos, speeches and photographs. The
research materials of Thomas Buell for his
biography of Spruance, The Quiet Warrior,
also contains valuable Spruance career and
personal material. Adm Spruance was
President of the Naval War College, 1946-
1948 and Ambassador to the Philippines,
1952-1955.

SPRUCE TREES

BC —CANADIAN FORESTRY SERVICE,
Pacific Forest Research Centre, Library, 506
West Burnside Rd, Victoria, V8Z 1M5, Can.
Alice Solyma, Librn
Holdings: Vols (60,500) Cat Microforms
Notes: Incl rearing, biological control,
identification, dispersal, insect pest
management, comprehensive collection re
Mountain Pine Beetle, Western Spruce
Budworm, Douglas Fir Tussack Moth.

SPURRED RYE see Ergot

SPY see Ward, Leslie (Spy)

SPY PRINTS

MN —MAYO MEDICAL LIBRARY, History
of Medicine Collection, Rochester, 55905.
Nancy R Hensel, Librn
Holdings: Pix
Notes: The Comfort Collection of caricatures
of physicians and scientists from Vanity Fair.
Description: Mann, Ruth J: "The unheroic
representation of heroes." Mayo Clin Proc.
46:197-199, Mar 1971.

SPYING see Espionage; Spies

SPYRI, JOHANNA

TX —NORTH TEXAS STATE UNIVERSITY,
Rare Book and Texana Collections, NT
Station Box 5188, Denton, 76203. Kenneth
Lavender, University Bibliographer
Notes: 59 editions of Heidi and memorabilia.

SQUARE DANCING

IL —CHICAGO PUBLIC LIBRARY, Art
Section, Fine Arts Division, 78 E

SQUARE DANCING (cont.)

Washington St, Chicago, 60602. Rosalinda I Hack, Fine Arts Division Chief; Yvonne S Brown, Head, Art Section
Holdings: Vols 2500
Notes: Reference and circulating collection of books, periodicals, pamphlets, and videotapes on all aspects of the dance eg ballet, social dance, square dance, jazz and folkdance. Focus of the collection is on ballet, history, biographies of dancers, and dance instruction. Subject is supplemented by a dance videotape collection, the *Folk Dance Index* a comprehensive index to descriptions of folkdances of all nations. Special Collections: Eliza Stigler Dance Collection of 200 dance books on ballet and dance history with particular emphasis on Spanish Dance. Ruth Page Archives: small collection of memorabilia documents the career of Ms Page. Reference collection of 85 dance videotapes that document notable dance performances, from the past and present by well known dancers and dance groups. Subject concentration is that of ballet, with some examples of ethnic dance. There is alsoa collection of tapes that document Chicago area dance groups, dancers, and choreographers. A file to the contents of the tapes is available.

SQUARES see Magic Squares

SQUARES, MAGIC see Magic Squares

SQUAT THEATRE

CA —UNIVERSITY OF CALIFORNIA, DAVIS, Shields Library, Dept of Special Collections, Davis, 95616. Donald Kunitz, Head; C Danial Elliott, Asst Head
Holdings: Uncat Mss Pix Film
Notes: Archives of an experimental theatre group, documenting years, 1969-81, with productions in Hungary and New York. 1500 items.

SQUIER, EPHRAIM GEORGE

DC —LIBRARY OF CONGRESS, Manuscript Division, Washington, 20540. John C Broderick, Chief
Notes: Ephraim George Squier's papers and maps of Central America. Maps are located in the Geography and Maps Division; mss in the Manuscript Division.

SQUIRE, SIR JOHN COLLINGS

NY —HOFSTRA UNIVERSITY, Library, 1000 Fulton Ave, Hempstead, 11550. Charles R Andrews, Dean of Library Services
BC —UNIVERSITY OF VICTORIA, McPherson Library, Victoria, V8W 3H5, Can.

SQUIRE, JOSEPH

AL —BIRMINGHAM PUBLIC LIBRARY, Dept of Archives & Mss, 2020 Seventh Ave N, Birmingham, 35203. Marvin Y Whiting, Archivist & Cur
Holdings: Cat Docs Mss //
Notes: Papers of Joseph Squire, a mining engineer and geologist active in Shelby and Jefferson counties in Alabama from 1859 until his death in 1911. Though the collection spans the years 1873-1898, its bulk is business correspondence, 1888-1889, concerning purchase of coal lands for businessmen in Shelby County.

SRI AUROBINDO

†CA —ATMANIKETAN ASHRAM LIBRARY, 1291 Weber St, Pomona, 91768.
Notes: Sri Aurobindo, Indian spirituality, Vedanta, Sanskrit studies, Vedic-Upanishadic texts, education.

SRI LANKA

CA —UNIVERSITY OF CALIFORNIA, BERKELEY, University Library, 438 Main Library, Berkeley, 94720. Kenneth R Logan, South Asia Librn
Notes: South Asia collection (India, Pakistan, Bangladesh, Nepal, Sri Lanka) contain 150,000-200,000 titles. Covers at research level the social sciences and humanities in western languages and 20 South Asian languages. Subject areas: history, political science, lanugage and literature (especially strong in Hindi, Urdu, Tamil, Sanskrit and Nepali), art and art history, sociology, education, music, environmental design, philosophy and religion, anthropology, geography, national and local government publications. Formats: monographs, periodicals, newspapers, microforms, maps, sound recordings, video-tapes, pamphlets. Special strengths: modern Hindi literature; history of South Asian countries; government publications of India, late 19th and 20th centuries. Member of South Asia Microform Project; Participant in Library of Congress AcquisitionsPrograms for India, Pakistan, Nepal, and Bangladesh.
HI —UNIVERSITY OF HAWAII, Library, 2550 The Mall, Honolulu, 96822. Joyce Wright, Head, Asia Collection; Masato Matsu, Head, East Asia Vernacular Collection
Holdings: Vols (400,000)
Notes: The Asia Collection holds material from and relating to Bangladesh, India, Nepal, Pakistan, and Sri Lanka in western and Asian languages. South Asian languages currently acquired: Bengali, Hindi, Marathi, Nepali, Pali, Prakrit, Sanskrit, Tamil. Period emphasis is post-World War II. Subject emphases: social sciences and the humanities (literature, economics, history, religion/ philosophy). Holdings are supplemented by a large uncataloged backlog, much of it accessible through the Library of Congress Accessions Lists for the area and by over 7000 cataloged titles in the main library collection. *South Asian Resources in North America: A Survey Prepared for the Boston Conference, 1974*, ed by M L P Patterson (Zug, Switzerland: Tutes Documentation Company, 1975). (Bibliotheca Asiatica 12-), "University of Hawaii," pp 103-114.
IL —CENTER FOR RESEARCH LIBRARIES, 6050 S Kenwood Ave, Chicago, 60637. Donald B Simpson, Dir; Esther Smith, Collection Development Librn
Holdings: Uncat Microforms
Notes: Monographs, serials and government documents from 1969, received on PL 480. Six newspapers on microfilm, from 1967.
MA —HARVARD UNIVERSITY LIBRARY, Cambridge, 02138.
Holdings: Cat
MI —UNIVERSITY OF MICHIGAN, Graduate Library, South Asian Dept, Ann Arbor, 48109. Om P Sharma, Librn
Holdings: Vols (365,000) Cat Maps Slides Microforms
Notes: The major emphasis is on social sciences and humanities. Besides materials in classical languages, South Asian vernaculars being retained are Hindi, Bengali, Urdu, Marathi and Tamil; strong in classical languages, especially Sanskrit, Pali, and Prakrit.
MI —MICHIGAN STATE UNIVERSITY, International Library, South and Southeast Asia Collection, East Lansing, 48824. Clinton Lockert, Bibliographer
Holdings: Vols 55,700 Cat Mss Maps Audiotapes Microforms
Notes: Serials and monographs of South Asia recieved on PL 480 for India, Pakistan, Sri Lanka, and Nepal since 1968. Emphasis is upon Social Sciences, Humanities, and Science. Areas of stength are Anthropology and rural development.
MO —UNIVERSITY OF MISSOURI-COLUMBIA, Ellis Library, Ninth and Lowry, Columbia, 65201. Murari Lal Nagar, Librn
Holdings: Vols 100,000 Maps Slides Phonorecords 16mm Films Filmstrips Microforms
Notes: The South Asia Studies Program at the University of Missouri-Columbia, is an interdepartmental, multi-disciplinary area studies program on India, Pakistan, Bangladesh, Sri Lanka and Nepal. Depository for the PL480 Program of the Library of Congress in many languages from South Asia. There are library resources in Sanskrit, Hindi, Bengali, Punjabi, and Malayalam. The library is particularly strong in Baroda, Bengal and the Punjab.
NY —NEW YORK PUBLIC LIBRARY, Oriental Div, Fifth Ave & 42 St, New York, 10018. E Christian Filstrup, Chief
Holdings: Cat Mss Microforms
Budget: ($56,455)
Notes: Described in *Dictionary Catalog of the Oriental Collection*, The Research Libraries of the New York Public Library, 1960, 16 vols, and *First Supplement*, 1976, 8 vols (144,000 cards). This catalog incl 318, 000 entries for works in about 100 languages of the East, and all works in Western languages on Oriental subjects. The Oriental Collection numbers about 120,000 vols; its Arabic and Indic holdings and those on ancient Egypt and the ancient Near East are among the largest in the US. There is also a collection of 30,000 vols of PL 480 material from Egypt, Pakistan, and India to which there is main entry access, but which is not incorporated into the dictionary catalog. Other outstanding features of the Oriental Collection incl extensive holdings of Japanese technical and scientific periodicals; a unique collection of linguistic works, grammars, anddictionaries; and unusually good coverage of the field of Oriental religions and philosophies. The catalog contains numerous subject references to periodical articles in all languages. All entries are arranged alphabetically according to the Roman alphabet.
TX —UNIVERSITY OF TEXAS LIBRARIES, General Libraries, PO Box P, Austin, 78713. Carolyn Bucknell, Asst Dir for Collection Development
Holdings: Cat Microforms
†WA —WASHINGTON STATE UNIVERSITY, Library, Manuscripts, Archives & Special Collections, Pullman, 99164. John F Guido, Head
Holdings: Vols Mss Pix
Notes: The library of Virginia and Leonard Woolf (from Monk's House and Victoria Sq) forms the nucleus of the collection. Leonard's interests are reflected by works concerning the Labour Party, the Fabian Society, as well as Ceylon. Their interest in printing and publishing works on significance is reflected by the collection of Hogarth Press publications (1917-1941).

STAFFORD, JEAN

CO —UNIVERSITY OF COLORADO, Libraries, Special Collections, Boulder, 80309. Nora J Quinlan, Head
Notes: Mss, correspondence, tear sheets and printed works of Jean Stafford, winner of the Pulitzer Prize for her short stories in 1970. In all, 16.6 feet of ms material. In addition, 270 vols form Jean Stafford's own library incl works which she reviewed. Partially cataloged.

STAGE see Actors and Actresses; Drama; Theatre; Theatre—History

STAGE DESIGN

IL —SOUTHERN ILLINOIS UNIVERSITY, CARBONDALE, Delyte W Morris Library, Special Collections Dept, Carbondale, 62901. David V Koch, Cur of Special Collections; Louisa Bowen, Cur of Manuscripts
Holdings: Vols 110 Uncat Mss Pix
Notes: The personal papers (75 linear feet) and art work of Mordecai Gorelik, stage designer, director, and playwright, incl a large volume of correspondence with persons of the theater, in the US and abroad, scripts of plays, and thousands of sketches, drawings, and photographs of stage settings.
IL —NORTHWESTERN UNIVERSITY, Library, Special Collections Dept, 1937 Sheridan Rd, Evanston, 60201. R Russell Maylone, Cur
Holdings: Vols 210 Cat Mss Pix

STAGE DESIGN (cont.)

Phonorecords
Notes: Collection is being cataloged according to the Craig bibliography of Fletcher & Rood. Collection incl material about Ellen Terry and Henry Irving, as well as original art work by Craig, stage designs and other ephemera. Collection created J Wesley Swanson and given to Northwestern Unversity Library by his sister.

MI —UNIVERSITY OF MICHIGAN, Library, Dept of Rare Books & Special Collections, Ann Arbor, 48109. Robert J Starring, Head
Holdings: Cat Mss Pix
Notes: Extensive holdings of books on the theatre. Also, in the Charles Sanders Collection, about 14,000 British and American playbills and programs mostly of the 19th century, as well as scrapbooks, posters, and about 750 photographs and prints of actors and actresses. In the Ellen Van Volkenburg-Maurice Browne Collection, about 4000 photographs of stage productions and friends and associates, as well as programs, posters, scrapbooks of mounted clippings, about 200 original stage and costume designs, promptbooks, and play manuscripts, representing the American and British careers of this husband-wife team from 1912 to about 1940. The Chicago Little Theatre, 1912-1917, is well represented. Also contains more than 6000 items of correspondence with theatrical and literary figures. Another collection contains 143 Alfred Lunt letters, mainly from 1909-1915.

MN —MINNEAPOLIS COLLEGE OF ART & DESIGN, Library, 200 E 25 St, Minneapolis, 55404. Richard Kronstedt, Head Librn

NJ —HADDON HEIGHTS PUBLIC LIBRARY, 608 Station Ave, Haddon Heights, 08035. Robert J Hunter, Librn
Holdings: Vols (1900) Cat Phonorecords

NY —NEW YORK PUBLIC LIBRARY, Performing Arts Research Center, Billy Rose Theatre Collection, 111 Amsterdam Ave, New York, 10023. Dorothy L Swerdlove, Cur
Holdings: Cat Pix Videotapes 16mm Films
Notes: See entries under Theatre; Jo Mielziner.

NY —NEW YORK PUBLIC LIBRARY, Performing Arts Research Center, Dance Collection, 111 Amsterdam Ave, New York, 10023. Genevieve Oswald, Cur
Notes: Approximately 2000 original stage and costume designs chiefly from the first three decades of the 20th century. Particularly strong representation of the works of Russian artists such as Benois, Berman, Dobuzhinskii, Gontcharova, Larionov, Soudeikine, Tchelitchew, and Bakst. Also well-represented are Rouben Ter-Arutunian and Isamu Noguchi. The Ruth Page Collection contains 750 original designs by Antoni Clave, Andre Delfau, Georges Wakhevitch, Isamu Noguchi, Bernard Dayde, Robert Fletcher, Nicholas Remisoff, and Sviatoslav Roerich. Descriptions of individual designs listed in *Dictionary Catalog of the Dance Collection*, published by GK Hall, Boston, 1974, in 10 vols, and in annual supplements: *Bibliographic Guide to Dance*.

†UT —BRIGHAM YOUNG UNIVERSITY, Harold B Lee Library, University Hill, Provo, 84602.
Notes: The Theodore Fuchs Collection of material relating to modern stage lighting and design. Incl books, theses, seminar reports, theatre brochures, commercial catalogs, class notebooks, professional publications, course material, files, slides, photographs, programs, blueprints, technical correspondence and recording discs.

VA —GEORGE MASON UNIVERSITY, Fenwick Library, Special Collections Dept, 4400 University Drive, Fairfax, 22030. Ruth Kerns, Public Services Librn
Notes: The Federal Theatre Project Collection includes 5000 playscripts, 2500 radio scripts, 25,000 photographs, 40 blueprints, 1000 posters, over 1600 costume designs, 350 scene designs, 750 production notebooks, 1700 programs and heralds, 26 musical scores and 18 cubic feet of research materials and play readers reports.

WA —UNIVERSITY OF WASHINGTON LIBRARIES, Drama Library, BH-20, Seattle, 98195. Liz Fugate, Drama Librn
Holdings: Vols
Budget: ($13,182)
Notes: Collection incl history; criticism; costume; make-up; scene design; lighting; creative dramatics; children's theatre; directing; playwriting; acting. Special Collections include 19th century acting editions, contemporary acting editions and local theatre posters. 17,731 items cataloged, 24,255 uncataloged.

ON —NATIONAL LIBRARY OF CANADA, 395 Wellington St, Ottawa, K1A 0N4, Can. Andre Preibish, Dir
Holdings: Vols 8000
Notes: Includes 100 serial titles, also programs, play bills etc on microfilm. Performing arts collection consists of Canadian titles received on legal deposit and purchased. Areas of concentration: Canadian theatre and dance; European and American performing arts tradition; theatre architecture; stage craft; costume history, dance history and notation etc.

ON —METROPOLITAN TORONTO LIBRARY, Theatre Dept, 789 Yonge St, Toronto, M4W 2G8, Can. Heather McCallum, Head
Holdings: Vols (30,500) Mss Pix Slides Phonorecords Microforms
Notes: Over 2400 original stage designs record work done for theatre and dance productions in festival and regional theatres across Canada.

STAGE LIGHTING

NY —NANANNE PORCHER OSPREY DESIGNS, Library, 49 W 96 St, New York, 10028.
Notes: Lighting records for Lyric Opera of Chicago, 1961-1966; Dallas Civic Opera, 1959-1964; American Ballet Theatre, 1965-1966, 1971-1977; etc.

PA —PENNSYLVANIA STATE UNIVERSITY, Fred Lewis Pattee Library, Special Collections Dept, University Park, 16802. Charles Mann, Chief, Special Collections
Holdings: Slides
Notes: Equipment and manufacturers' records of American theatre lighting-drawings, lab notes, correspondence, books, catalogs, slides, layouts, and schedules.

†UT —BRIGHAM YOUNG UNIVERSITY, Harold B Lee Library, University Hill, Provo, 84602.
Notes: The Theodore Fuchs Collection of material relating to modern stage lighting and design. Incl books, theses, seminar reports, theatre brochures, commercial catalogs, class notebooks, professional publications, course material, files, slides, photographs, programs, blueprints, technical correspondence and recording discs.

WA —UNIVERSITY OF WASHINGTON LIBRARIES, Drama Library, BH-20, Seattle, 98195. Liz Fugate, Drama Librn
Holdings: Vols
Budget: ($13,182)
Notes: Collection incl history; criticism; costume; make-up; scene design; lighting; creative dramatics; children's theatre; directing; playwriting; acting. Special Collections include 19th century acting editions, contemporary acting editions and local theatre posters. 17,731 items cataloged, 24,255 uncataloged.

WI —UNIVERSITY OF WISCONSIN, MADISON, Memorial Library, Theatre Collection, 728 State St, Madison, 53706.
Notes: Broadway production records, etc, of the stage lighting authority, Jean Rosenthal.

STAGE MONEY

NY —HAMPDEN-BOOTH THEATRE LIBRARY AT THE PLAYERS, 16 Gramercy Park, New York, 10003. Louis A Rachow, Librn/Cur
Holdings: Mss Pix
Notes: Nearly 300 burlesque scripts and vaudeville skits, music in ms, 25 photographs in character, two song books of the period, a notebook of stage gags and repartee, typescript of biography of Chuck Callahan (30 pages), and a number of ephemeral pieces, stage money, programs, etc. 4 boxes of indexed material. Described in *The Players Bulletin*, Spring 1966, pp 20-21; and *Performing Arts Resources* vol 3 (New York: Theatre Library Association, 1976), pp 143-150. Described in *Theatre & Performing Arts Collections* (New York: Haworth Press, 1981).

STAGG, AMOS ALONZO

CA —UNIVERSITY OF THE PACIFIC, Holt-Atherton Pacific Center for Western Studies, Stockton, 95211. Hiram L Davis, Dir of Libraries
Holdings: Cat Mss
Notes: Primarily correspondence and newspaper clippings from the papers of Amos Alonzo Stagg, football coach and athletic director at the University of Chicago and later at the College of the Pacific. 1 linear ft (2 document boxes).

STAGG, JERRY

MA —BOSTON UNIVERSITY, Mugar Memorial Library, Special Collections Dept, 771 Commonwealth Ave, Boston, 02215. Howard B Gotlieb, Dir
Holdings: Cat Mss
Notes: Mss, correspondence, etc collected in depth; incl publications by or about.

STAINED GLASS see Glass Painting and Staining

STALIN PRIZE NOVELS

WI —BELOIT COLLEGE LIBRARIES, Beloit, 53511. Dennis W Dickinson, Dir
Holdings: Cat
Notes: This small collection incl most of the Stalin Prize novels, many works published "behind the Iron Curtain," and some titles in English translation. Also incl complete sets of distinguished Russian authors in Russian editions. Books purchased in history, geography, economics, etc to supplement the Winkelman Collection of Russian Literature.

STALLINGS, CARL W.

WY —UNIVERSITY OF WYOMING, William Robertson Coe Library, Archives - American Heritage Center, PO Box 3412, Laramie, 82071.
Notes: Music manuscripts of Carl W Stalling, writer of music for such cartoons as "Mickey Mouse," "Silly Symphonies," "Three Little Pigs," "Bugs Bunny," "Looney Tunes," and other productions of Walt Disney and Warner Brothers. Incl 1300 complete original scores, more than 2000 sheets of other music, and many other materials.

STAMP ACT, 1765

NJ —GLASSBORO STATE COLLEGE, Savitz Library, Stewart Room, Glassboro, 08028. Clara Kirner, Special Collection Librn
Holdings: Cat Mss
Notes: Only known copy of mss of the *Stamp Act Congress Journal, 1765*, which belonged to Caesar Rodney.

STAMP CATALOGS see Catalogs, Postage Stamp

STAMP COLLECTING AND STAMP COLLECTORS see Postage Stamps—Collections

STAMPS, POSTAGE see Postage Stamps

STANDARD OF VALUE see Money

STANDARDS AND SPECIFICATIONS

CA —NORTHROP CORPORATION, Aircraft Group, Library Services Dept, 3360/82, One

STANDARDS AND SPECIFICATIONS (cont.)

Northrop Ave, Hawthorne, 90250. J E Reynolds, Manager
Holdings: Vols (15,000) Cat Microforms
Notes: Incl file of military specifications and standards, Air Force Technical Orders, and other military manuals, handbooks, regulations, instructions, etc. Also 400,000 microfiche; 60,000 reports. Library use restricted to employees; others by interlibrary loan.

CA —LOS ANGELES PUBLIC LIBRARY, Science & Technology Dept, 630 W Fifth St, Los Angeles, 90071. Billie M Connor, Dept Head
Holdings: Vols 125,000 Microforms
Budget: $30,000
Notes: Current standards, specifications, test methods, and recommended practices issued by the US National Bureau of Standards, British Standards Institution, ANSI, ASTM, IEEE, SAE, API, UL and other leading national standardization organizations. Limited backfiles. Current and historical (1967). Military and Federal Standards and Specifications. Partially cataloged.

CA —UNIVERSITY OF CALIFORNIA, LOS ANGELES, Engineering & Mathematical Sciences Library, 405 Hilgard, Los Angeles, 90024. Rosalee I Wright, Librn
Holdings: Vols (180,000) Cat Microforms
Notes: Incl engineering handbooks and material data compilations; ASTM, ESDU, CCITT, and IEEE standards, DIN (English translation only), SAE Aerospace Standards and selected ASME Codes.
See also entry under Engineering

CA —CALIFORNIA DEPT OF TRANSPORTATION, Transportation Library, 5900 Folsom Blvd, PO Box 19128, Sacramento, 95819. Eva Caro, Librn
Holdings: Vols (10,000) Cat Mss Maps Pix Slides Phonorecords Audiotapes Videotapes 16mm Films Filmstrips Microforms

CA —GARRETT CORPORATION, AiResearch Manufacturing Company, Technical Library, 2525 W 190 St, Torrance, 90509. Joanna M Sutton, Head Librn
Holdings: Vols 15,000 Cat Microforms
Notes: Incl 250,000 microforms, 130,000 reports (hard copy), 100,000 military specifications and standards, 30,000 NACA reports (hard copy).

IL —CHICAGO PUBLIC LIBRARY, Business/Science/Technology Div, Science/Technology Information Center, 425 North Michigan Ave, Chicago, 60611. Lynda Sanford, Head; John R Moore, Environment Collection Coordinator & Engineering Librn
Holdings: Vols 250 Cat 16mm Films
Budget: $36,000
Notes: Collection incl current ACI, ANS, ANSI, API, ASHRAE, ASME, ASTM, AWS, AWWA, DIN (fasteners only), EIA, IEEE, ISO, NEMA, NFPA, SAE, and UL industrial standards in complete sets. Also held are all active Military Specifications and Standards, Federal Specifications and Standards, Federal Test Methods, Joint Army-Navy Specifications, CIDs, DIDs, QPLs, MS-Drwings, Military Handbooks, and H-Series Handbooks. The Chicago Building Code, BOC Codes, National Building Code, and Uniform Building Code vols for recent years only are available. 1100 cartridges of 16mm film, depository for government standards documents.

IL —CHICAGO BRIDGE & IRON CO, Technical Library, 800 Jorie Blvd, Oak Brook, 60521. Susan Beatty, Librn
Holdings: Vols (7500) Cat
Budget: ($39,500)
Notes: Industrial Standards Collection.

IA —ROCKWELL INTERNATIONAL, Collins Division, Cedar Rapids Information Center, 500 Collins Rd, Cedar Rapids, 52498. Judith A Leavitt, Supvr
Holdings: Vols 10,000 Cat
Notes: Also 8000 technical reports; 10,000 military, Federal, and industrial specifications; 3000 bound periodicals (400 periodical subsriptions). Restricted use: for company use only and interlibrary loan.

KY —NAVAL ORDNANCE SYSTEMS COMMAND, Technical Library, Code 50122, Louisville, 40214. Libby Miles, Librn
Holdings: Vols 5500 Cat Maps Microforms
Notes: Excel in Government specifications, ordnance pamphlets, and all types of other Government documents. Large service in Industry Standard on film, some volumes.

MN —MTS SYSTEMS CORP, Information Services, PO Box 24012, Minneapolis, 55424. Kathleen Werner, Technical Librn
Holdings: Cat Mss Pix Slides Phonorecords Audiotapes Videotapes 16mm Films Microforms
Notes: Material testing machines. Incl 2000 ms reports, 10,000 pictures, 6000 slides.

MN —JAMES JEROME HILL REFERENCE LIBRARY, Fourth St at Market St, Saint Paul, 55106. Virgil F Massman, Dir
Holdings: Vols (197,000) Cat
Budget: ($8000)
Notes: Engineering standards incl American National Standards Institute, ASTM, NFPA, NEMA, TAPPI, SAE, and others.

MO —LINDA HALL LIBRARY, 5109 Cherry St, Kansas City, 64110. Larry X Besant, Dir; Wilma L Hartman, Librn for Public Services; Siegfried Ruschin, Librn for Collection Development
Holdings: Cat Maps Microforms
Budget: $1,000,000
Notes: Over 600,000 vols, 870,000 microforms, over 100,000 engineering standards and specifications. Also, patents, technical reports, specifications, and conference proceedings. Receives 16,400 serial publications in some 40 languages, in science and technology, and 36,000 total serial titles. Academy publications, back to the 17th century, and some 3000 books of historical significance in science and technology (History of Science Collection) are among the strongest areas in the library collection. Downs number-2169 and in Supplement many references 1031, 1105, 1106, 1123-24, etc. It would be difficult to break down strengths in the individual areas of the sciences and technology. Collection is comprehensive throughout these subject areas (except for clinical medicine and surgery, which are out of scope). Open to the public.

MO —SAINT LOUIS PUBLIC LIBRARY, 1301 Olive St, Saint Louis, 63103. Therese F Dawson, Librn, Applied Science Dept
Holdings: Vols 150,000 Cat Maps Pamphlets Microforms
Notes: Incl industrial standards and specifications.

NY —NEW YORK STATE LIBRARY, State Education Bldg Annex, Washington Ave, Albany, 12224.
Holdings: Cat Maps Microforms
Notes: Strong collection acquired to supports state interlibrary loan. Holdings to 1960 published in New York State Library, Checklist in Sceince and Technology, an author listing and abbreviated title. Incl extensive microforms holdings of technical reports: AEC, NASA, NTIS, SAE Transactions. Strong holdings related to standard and specifications: military and federal, commercial, National Bureau of Standards, American National Standards Institute, etc.

NY —NEW YORK STATE LIBRARY, General Reference Library, Albany, 12224. Christian Beauregard, Librn

NY —ENGINEERING SOCIETIES LIBRARY, 345 E 47 St, New York, 10017. S Kirk Cabeen, Dir
Holdings: Vols 250,000 Cat Maps 16mm Films Microforms
Notes: One of the largest, most comprehensive engineering libraries in the world. Covers all engineering disciplines; particularly strong in electrical and electronic, mechanical, mining and metallurgical, petroleum, chemical, industrial, air conditioning and refrigeration engineering. Incl Wheeler Collection of early materials on magnetisn and electricity. 125,000 bound periodical volumes; 10,000 maps; 5000 serial subscriptions (many foreign-language). Virtually all materials abstracted in Engineering Index (1884-date) are incl in

Library. Noncirculating, except to members of professional engineering societies which support the Library. See Engineering Societies Library, New York, Classed Subject Catalog and Index (Boston: G K Hall, 1963); and Supplements, 1-10, 1964-1973.

NY —EASTMAN KODAK COMPANY, Kodak Park Div, Engineering Library, Bldg 23, Rochester, 14650. Raymond Curtin, Librn
Holdings: Vols (14,000) Uncat Microforms
Notes: The library is not open to the public. Use of the library for reference purposes may be requested and appointments may be obtained through the librarian.

NY —HARRIS CORP, Government Support Systems Division, Information Center, 6801 Jericho Tpke, Syosset, 11791. Eleanor Pienitz, Librn
Notes: Incl 7000 defense reports, 4600 government documents.

OH —PUBLIC LIBRARY OF CINCINNATI & HAMILTON COUNTY, Science & Technology Dept, 800 Vine St, Cincinnati, 45202. Rosemary Gaiser, Head
Notes: Engineering standards and specifications. An extensive collection of American publications in this field, incl the standards of ASTM and ANSI; and standards and specifications of the federal government incl federal and military specifications and standards. Noncirculating.

OH —CLEVELAND PUBLIC LIBRARY, Science & Technology Dept, 325 Superior Ave, Cleveland, 44114. Jean Z Piety, Head
Holdings: Cat
Notes: Collection incl: (1) American, Canadian and British Standards; (2) standards of the International Electrotechnical Commission and the International Organization for Standardization (ISO Recommendations); (3) selected DINs (Deutsche Industrie Normen); and (4) the standards of all major technical societies. Special card Index File facilitates use of the collection, providing access by sponsoring agency and abbreviation.

PA —DREXEL UNIVERSITY LIBRARIES, Science-Technology Div, 32 & Chestnut Sts, Philadelphia, 19104. Charlotte T Duvally, Engineering Librn
Holdings: Cat
Budget: ($500)
Notes: Almost complete sets of standards of the American National Standards Institute, IEEE, ASTM, National Electrical Manufacturer's Association, US National Bureau of Standards and TAPPI. Selective sets of Underwriters Laboratory standards and British standards.

PA —CARNEGIE LIBRARY OF PITTSBURGH, Science & Technology Dept, 4400 Forbes Ave, Pittsburgh, 15213. Catherine M Brosky, Dept Head
Holdings: Vols (380,000) Cat Maps Microforms
Budget: ($240,000)
Notes: An area of primary interest. Complete sets of US Federal Specifications and Standards, US Department of Defense (Military) Specifications and Standards, US National Bureau of Standards publications, etc; those specifications and standards prepared by the American National Standards Institute (ANSI), British Standards Institution (BS). Also, as examples, the Aerospace Material Specifications (AMS), and those issued by the American Society for Testing and Materials (ASTM), American Society of Mechanical Engineers (ASME), American Welding Society (AWS), Society of Automotive Engineers (SAE), National Electrical Manufactures Association (NEMA), Institution of Electrical Engineers (IEE), Institute of Electrical and Electronic Engineers (IEEE), American Gear Manufacturers Association (AGMA), and many others are maintained and added tocurrently. Building codes, journals, indexes, reference works.

TX —FLUOR ENGINEERS INC, Houston Library, 4620 N Braeswood, PO Box 35000, Houston, 77235. R S Holab-Abelman, Librn
Holdings: Vols (2500) Cat Maps
Budget: ($10,000)
Notes: Construction, environmental and

STANDARDS AND SPECIFICATIONS (cont.)

chemical engineering, coal technology. Incl 2000 job books covering all areas of company interests.

WA —UNIVERSITY OF WASHINGTON LIBRARIES, Engineering Library, FH-15, Seattle, 98195. Harold N Wiren, Engineering Librn
Holdings: Vols (108,313) Cat Microforms
Budget: ($314,409)
Notes: About a million technical reports and the US patent specifications on microfilm are strong adjuncts to the collection which covers all fields of engineering.

WI —MILWAUKEE PUBLIC LIBRARY, 814 W Wisconsin Ave, Milwaukee, 53233. Donald J Sager, City Librn
Holdings: Cat
Notes: Hardcopies incl American Concrete Institute; American National Standards Institute (ANSI); American Petroleum Institute (irreg); ASTM standards; American Water Works Assoc; Electronic Industries Assoc; International Organization for Standardization; National Electrical Manufacturers Assoc (NEMA); Society of Automotive Engineers; Underwriters Laboratories (irreg); National Fire Protection Assoc (codes); US Federal Specifications and Standards; IEEE standards (irreg); International Electrotechnical Commission (irreg); American Society for Mechanical Engineers (superseded copies are retained).

BC —VANCOUVER PUBLIC LIBRARY, Science & Technology Div, 750 Burrard St, Vancouver, V6Z 1X5, Can. P Haffenden, Head, Science & Technology Div
Holdings: Cat
Notes: Plus special indexes, incl Organization and Association File (primarily local, British Columbian, and Canadian), begun in 1950s, expanded since 1960s; Government Documents File; Standards File and Index.

ON —CANADA DEPT OF PUBLIC WORKS, Library, Sir Charles Tupper Bldg, Ottawa, K1A 0M2, Can. A I S Sinclair, Librn
Holdings: Vols 2500 Uncat
Budget: $7500
Notes: Collection comprises all current Standards of Canadian Government Specifications Board, Canadian Standards Association and Standards Council of Canada. In addition, ASTM annual book of standards since 1974, Agrement Board certificates, information sheets and papers, as well as other selected ISO and American standards comprise the collection.

ON —CANADIAN STANDARDS ASSOCIATION, Information Centre, 178 Rexdale Blvd, Rexdale, M9W 1R3, Can. Cameron D Mcdonald, Head Librn
Holdings: Vols 2000 Cat Slides
Notes: 50,000 engineering and product standards; national and international. A supporting collection of books, periodicals and technical information files supports the standards collection. No photocopying.

ON —METROPOLITAN TORONTO LIBRARY, Science & Technology Dept, 789 Yonge St, Toronto, M4W 2G8, Can. Margaret Walshe, Head
Holdings: Vols (120,000) Cat VF
Notes: Complete files for Canadian Standards Association; Canadian Government Specifications Board; ANSI. ASTM, ASME and IEEE standards are also collected. Canadian coverage is emphasized.

STANDISH, BURT L. (PSEUD.)

CT —YALE UNIVERSITY, Box 1603A, Yale Station, New Haven, 06520.
Notes: The Merriwell Series, by "Burt L Standish."

STANFORD LISTENING POST, 1940-1945

CA —HOOVER INSTITUTION ON WAR, REVOLUTION & PEACE, Stanford University, Stanford, 94305. Milorad M Drachkovitch, Archivist
Holdings: Mss
Notes: The records of the Stanford Listening Post, 1940-1945, incl correspondence, transcripts of radio broadcasts, study papers, notes, and card indexes relating to a project to record and study radio broadcasts from East Asis. 29 ms boxes.

STANLEY, F. see Crocchiola, Stanley Francis Louis

STANLEY, LEO L.

CA —STANFORD UNIVERSITY LIBRARIES, Lane Medical Library, Stanford University, Medical Center, Stanford, 94305. Peter Stangl, Librn
Notes: Leo L Stanley's records of his years as resident physician at San Quentin prison. Volumes from 1916-23 and 1931-50.

STANLEY AND STANLEY

AB —UNIVERSITY OF CALGARY, Libraries, Special Collections Div, 2500 University Dr, Calgary, T2N 1N4, Can.
Holdings: Cat // Pix
Notes: 4630 pictures. Consists of original working drawings of the Edmonton architectural firm of Stanley & Stanley, and its successive partnerships of Dewar Stevenson & Stanley, K C Stanley & Company, and Ross M Stanley. Through Dewar Stevenson & Stanley, the collection provides a link to the Calgary firm of Stevenson Raines Barrett Christie Hutton Seton & Partners (qv). Although providing a fair cross-section through building types, the projects consist mainly of residences, churches, cinemas, and Canada Safeway and Loblaw's Stores. Major projects are the Edmonton City Hall (1954), Concordia College (1958), St John's Ambulance Brigade Headquarters(1953), and shortly. The collection is completed.

STANS, MAURICE H.

MN —MINNESOTA HISTORICAL SOCIETY LIBRARY, 690 Cedar St, Saint Paul, 55101. Patricia C Harpole, Chief of Reference Library; Bonnie G Wilson, Head of Special Libraries
Notes: Materials by such well-known figures as Hubert H. Humphrey, Eugene J. McCarthy, Orville L Freeman, Maurice H. Stans, Donald M Fraser, Albert H Quie, Clark MacGregor and John A Blatnik. A list of these holdings is on file in the Audio-Visual Library, the tapes are housed in the MHS Research Center, 1500 Mississippi Street, St Paul, Minn.

STANSBURY, HOWARD

†UT —UNIVERSITY OF UTAH, Marriott Library, Salt Lake City, 84112.
Notes: Original drawings and personal papers of John Hudson, a gold rush Forty-Niner who helped chart the Great Salt Lake with Captain Howard Stansbury.

STANTON, EDWIN M.

DC —LIBRARY OF CONGRESS, Manuscript Division, Washington, 20540. John C Broderick, Chief
Notes: Papers; additions, 1977- .

STANTON, ELIZABETH CADY, 1815-1902

DC —LIBRARY OF CONGRESS, Manuscript Division, Washington, 20540. John C Broderick, Chief
Notes: Papers; additions, 1977- .

NY —CORNELL UNIVERSITY LIBRARIES, Collection of Regional History, Dept of Manuscripts and Univ Archives, Ithaca, 14853.
Notes: Suffragist. Papers, 1861-68, (photocopies and microfilm, 35mm, 1 neg., 1 pos.); .1 ft.

NY —VASSAR COLLEGE, Library, Rare Books & Manuscripts Collection, Box 20, Poughkeepsie, 12601. Lisa Browar, Cur
Holdings: Mss Pix
Notes: Emphasis is on women in the US, women's rights, suffrage and Equal Rights Amendment. Manuscript collections incl papers of Elizabeth Cady Stanton, Paulina Wright Davis, Maria Mitchell and Alma Lutz.

NY —UNIVERSITY OF ROCHESTER, Rush Rhees Library, Department of Rare Books and Special Collections, Rochester, 14627. Peter Dzwonkoski, Librn
Holdings: Cat Mss Pix
Notes: Approximately 300 letters including correspondence with Rachel Foster Avery (178 letters); Harriet Taylor Upton, Amy Post, Elizabeth Cady Stanton, and others. Also includes photographs, printed ephemera, and museum pieces.

STANTON, PATRICK, 1907-1976

†PA —BALCH INSTITUTE FOR ETHNIC STUDIES, Library, 18 S Seventh St, Philadelphia, 19106.
Notes: Papers of Patrick Stanton (1907-1976), an activist in Irish-American cultural and social programs. Incl in the collection is a unique manuscript volume of poetry by Donal O'Herlihy, Fenian activist of the 1860s.

STAR CATALOGS see Stars—Catalogs

STAR-SPANGLED BANNER

IN —INDIANA UNIVERSITY, Lilly Library, Seventh St, Bloomington, 47405. William R Cagle, Librn
Holdings: // Cat
Notes: 19th century printings with and without music. Some in the Starr American Sheet Music Collection.

MD —MARYLAND HISTORICAL SOCIETY, Library, 201 W Monument St, Baltimore, 21201. William B Keller, Head Librn
Holdings: Cat Mss Maps Pix
Notes: The Lester S Levy "Star Spangled Banner" Collection, probably the largest in the world--over 250 pieces.

PA —FREE LIBRARY OF PHILADELPHIA, Sheet Music Collection, Logan Sq, Philadelphia, 19103. Connie Jessum, Librn
Budget: ($2000)
Notes: Covers entire span of American popular expression in song and instrumental music (piano) from colonial times to the present. Incl Newland-Zeuner and Edward I Keffer Collections on loan from the Musical Fund Society. Items printed before 1825 indexed in Sonneck-Upton and Wolfe. Checklists for cover illustrations, musical shows or films and special subjects. Songs are filed by title; piano music by composer. Examples of special materials not filed in regular collection incl early Philadelphia composers and publications, national (centennial and state), patriotic ("Star-Spangled Banner"), political (Presidents), and war (1861; 1914; 1939) songs. Most of the ms materials are anonymous. Collection contains 138,360 pieces of sheet music.

STAR TREK ARCHIVE

CA —UNIVERSITY OF CALIFORNIA, LOS ANGELES, Theater Arts Library, Los Angeles, 90024. Edward Shreeves, Chairman, Bibliographers Group; Audree Malkin, Head, Theater Arts Library
Holdings: Cat Mss Pix Slides
Notes: Archival collections-Star Trek Archive: Gene Roddenberry's complete files of 3 years production of the Star Trek television series. Incl are scripts, business records and correspondence, and production materials.

STARK, FREYA

DC —GEORGETOWN UNIVERSITY, Library, Special Collections Div, 37 & O Sts NW, Washington, 20057. George M Barringer, Special Collections Librn; Nicholas B Sheetz, Mss Librn
Holdings: Mss Pix
Notes: The papers of Christopher Sykes, biographer, journalist, and novelist;

STARK, FREYA (cont.)

containing mss, letters, photographs, and drawings. With extensive correspondence from Harold Acton; Angela, Countess of Antrim; Sir John Betjeman; Ivy Compton-Burnett; Alick Dru; T S Eliot; Max Beerbohm; Graham Greene; John Hayward; Lord Patrick Kinross; Compton Mackenzie; Nancy Mitford; Anthony Powell; Dame Flora Robson; Cecil Roth; Sir John Russell; Osbert Sitwell; John Sparrow; Freya Stark; James Stern; and Evelyn Waugh, among others. Also, considerable research material about Evelyn Waugh, Adam von Trott, Robert Byron, Lady Nancy Astor; and the foundation of the state of Israel.

STARK, JOHN

NH —NEW HAMPSHIRE HISTORICAL SOCIETY, Manuscripts Library, 30 Park St, Concord, 03301. Thomas E Camden, Cur
Holdings: Cat Mss
Notes: John Stark (1728-1822) pioneer, farmer and Revolutionary general from New Hampshire. Papers span the period, 1743-1814, and incl correspondence, accounts and receipts for personal business, receipts for military provisioning, and military returns for companies under Stark's command. The correspondence is primarily from the period, 1776-1783, and relates to Stark's activities during the Revolution. There is an index to the collection at the New Hampshire Historical Society. About 500 items.

STARK MANUFACTURING COMPANY (1838-1922)

NH —MANCHESTER HISTORIC ASSOCIATION, Library, 129 Amherst St, Manchester, 03104. Elizabeth Lessard, Librn
Notes: Stark Manufacturing Company (1838-1922) corporate records: Ledgers (2 volumes), payrolls (1 folder), contracts of indentured servants (1 document).

STARR, JAMES HARPER

TX —UNIVERSITY OF TEXAS LIBRARIES, General Libraries, Barker Texas History Center, PO Box P, Austin, 78712. Don Carleton, Dir

STARR, JIMMY

AZ —ARIZONA STATE UNIVERSITY, Library, Tempe, 85287. Marilyn Wurzburger, Special Collections Librn
Notes: The Jimmy Starr Film History Collection contains the personal library and working materials of Jimmy Starr, Hollywood movie columnist from the 1920s-1960s. In addition to working as a press agent, Mr Starr was a columnist for the now defunct *Los Angeles Record* and the *Los Angeles Herald & Express*, and his columnswere widely syndicated; he also wrote silent comedies for Mack Sennett, scripts for the talkies, as well as several mystery novels. The collection incl over 2100 biographical files of entertainers containing well over 20,000 contemporary newspaper and periodical clippings; over 3000 stills; reviews, premiere invitations and other ephemera for over 6000 films; and other writers. Also, there are reference books, selected film periodicals and scrapbooks which round out the collection. The material is partially cataloged; finding guides are available.

STARRETT, VINCENT

CA —UNIVERSITY OF SAN FRANCISCO, Richard A Gleeson Library, The Countess Bernardine Murphy Donohue Rare Book Room, San Francisco, 94117. D Steven Corey, Special Collections Librn
Holdings: Vols 125
Notes: Incl a number of rarities and inscribed copies.
IL —NORTHERN ILLINOIS UNIVERSITY, Founders Memorial Library, Rare Books and Special Collections Dept, De Kalb, 60115. William R DuBois, Dept Head
Holdings: Vols 75 Cat
IN —INDIANA UNIVERSITY, Lilly Library, Seventh St, Bloomington, 47405. William R Cagle, Librn
Holdings: // Cat Mss Pix
Notes: Books from the library of Vincent Starrett. Papers and correspondence of Starrett, 1803-1959 (377 items).

STARS

CA —GRIFFITH OBSERVATORY, Library, 2800 E Observatory Rd, Los Angeles, 90027. E C Krupp, Dir
Holdings: Vols Cat Pix Slides Phonorecords
Budget: ($1000)
Notes: No separate catalog. No photocopying.
CA —UNIVERSITY OF CALIFORNIA, SANTA CRUZ, University Library, Special Collections, Santa Cruz, 95064. Rita Bottoms, Special Collections Librn; Margaret Felts, South Pacific Collection Bibliographer
Holdings: Cat
Notes: Astronomy Library. Incl all major astronomical and astrophysical journals and an extensive collection of domestic and foreign observatory publications. The book collection is particularly strong in stellar structure and evolution, stellar spectroscopy, the interstellar medium, galactic structure, external galaxies, general ralativity and gravitational radiation, and high-energy astrophysics.
CT —YALE UNIVERSITY, Dept of Astronomy Library, 260 Whitney Ave, Box 6666, New Haven, 06511.
Holdings: Cat Pix Slides
Notes: Over 3000 plates of asteroids, pictures taken with Yale telescopes in the Northern and Southern Hemispheres. Also about 65,000 stellar parallax plates and about 1000 (17 x 17 in) zone catalog plates recording some 200,000 star positions. There is also a collection of about 500 plates recording the location of the north celestial pole among the stars. Of this latter, only one other similar collection exists, at the Pulkova Observatory, near Leningrad.

STARS—ATLASES

CA —UNIVERSITY OF CALIFORNIA, BERKELEY, Science Libraries, Astronomy-Mathematics-Statistics-Computer Science Library, 100 Evans Hall, Berkeley, 94720. Kimiyo Hom, Head
Holdings: Vols (53,000) Cat Maps Microforms
Budget: ($117,301)
Notes: A research collection in the fields of astronomy, mathematics, statistics and computer science. In the field of astronomy, emphasis is given to star charts, atlases and catalogs. In mathematics, the collection's strengths are in pure mathematics, mathematical statistics and probability theory. The computer science holdings emphasize the mathematics and theory of the field. The Library's serial holdings are particularly rich in foreign-language materials. Some 1300 serial titles are currently being received; over 4000 pamphlets. (Holdings in the AMSCS Library are complemented by approx 15,000 additional vols in the Main Library, as well are rare book materials in The Bancroft Library.)
NY —ROCHESTER MUSEUM & SCIENCE CENTER, Strasenburgh Planetarium, Todd Library, 663 East Ave, Rochester, 14607. Donald Hall, Dir
Holdings: Vols 500 Cat Maps Slides
Notes: Also 8050 slides of astronomical and aeronautical subjects; 400 recordings; 150 celestial charts.

STARS—CATALOGS

CA —UNIVERSITY OF CALIFORNIA, BERKELEY, Science Libraries, Astronomy-Mathematics-Statistics-Computer Science Library, 100 Evans Hall, Berkeley, 94720. Kimiyo Hom, Head
Holdings: Vols (52,000) Cat Maps Microforms
Budget: ($117,301)
Notes: A research collection in the fields of astronomy, mathematics, statistics and computer science. In the field of astronomy, emphasis is given to star charts, atlases and catalogs. In mathematics, the collection's strengths are in pure mathematics, mathematical statistics and probability theory. The computer science holdings emphasize the mathematics and theory of the field. The Library's serial holdings are particulary rich in foreign-language materials. Some 1300 serial titles are currently being received; over 4000 pamphlets. (Holdings in the AMSCS Library are complemented by approx 15,000 additional vols in the Main Library, as well as rare book materials in The Bancroft Library.)

STARS—PHOTOGRAPHIC MEASUREMENTS

CA —UNIVERSITY OF CALIFORNIA, SANTA CRUZ, University Library, Special Collections, Santa Cruz, 95064. Rita Bottoms, Special Collections Librn; Margaret Felts, South Pacific Collection Bibliographer
Holdings: Cat
Notes: Astronomy Library. Incl all major astronomical and astrophysical journals and an extensive collection of domestic and foreign observatory publications. The book collection is particularly strong in stellar structure and evolution, stellar spectroscopy, the interstellar medium, galactic structure, external galaxies, general relativity and gravitational radiation, and high-energy astrophysics.

STARS—SPECTRA

CA —UNIVERSITY OF CALIFORNIA, SANTA CRUZ, University Library, Special Collections, Santa Cruz, 95064. Rita Bottoms, Special Collections Librn; Margaret Felts, South Pacific Collection Bibliographer
Holdings: Cat
Notes: Astronomy Library. Incl all major astronomical and astrophysical journals and an extensive collection of domestic and foreign observatory publications. The book collection is particularly strong in stellar structure and evolution, stellar spectroscopy, the interstellar medium, galactic stucture, external galaxies, general relativity and gravitational radiation, high-energy astrophysics.

STARS, FALLING see Meteors

STARVATION see Famines

STATE AND CHURCH see Church and State

STATE AND INSURANCE see Insurance, Social

STATE AND MEDICINE see Medical Policy

STATE CONSTITUTIONS see Constitutions, State

STATE DOCUMENTS

CA —LOS ANGELES PUBLIC LIBRARY, Social Sciences Dept, 630 W Fifth St, Los Angeles, 90071. Marilyn C Wherley, Principal Librn
Holdings: Vols 1550 Cat
Budget: ($150,000)
Notes: Serials, including state legislative manuals and rosters of public officials. Complete depository for California legislative materials dating from 1850 to present. 10,000 uncataloged pieces.
CA —UNIVERSITY OF CALIFORNIA, LOS ANGELES, Research Library, Public Affairs Service, 405 Hilgard Ave, Los Angeles, 90024. Edward Shreeves, Chairman, Bibliographers Group; Eugenia Eaton, Head,

STATE DOCUMENTS (cont.)

Public Affairs Service
Holdings: Microforms
Notes: Depository for the official publications of California cities and counties, the state of California, the United States government, the United Nations and some of its specialized agencies (including the Food and Agricultural Organization and UNESCO), and such regional organizations as the European Communities and Organization of American States. Selected publications of other American cities and counties, of the other states and possessions of the United States, of interstate organizations, and of foreign governments (with emphasis on major world powers, Africa, Latin America and the Near and Middle East) and intergovernmental organizations.

CO —COLORADO STATE LIBRARY, State Publications Depository & Distribution Center, 1362 Lincoln St, Denver, 80203. Tom Reynolds, Consultant
Holdings: Vols 15,000 Microforms
Notes: Publications are cataloged on OCLC, Center produces on index.

DC —LIBRARY OF CONGRESS, Serial and Government Publications Division, Washington, 20540.
Notes: Serials. One of the largest and most extensive collections in the world, incl periodicals; scientific and learned journals in all languages and in all fields except agriculture and medicine; US Government serials (Federal, State, County, and Municipal); national foreign government serials from all countries; provincial serials from provinces possessing autonomy; municipal serials from prinicipal cities; newspapers (850,000 unbound isssues, 75,000 bound vols, 270,000 microfilm reels), 12,000 microprint cards of early American newspapers, 1704-1820, incl 1500 titles currently received, 500 of these being representative titles from all States of the Union and 1000 from all foreign countries.

DC —US BUREAU OF THE CENSUS, Library, Federal Office Bldg 3, Rm 2451, Washington, 20233. Betty Baxtresser, Chief, ASD Library Branch
Holdings: Vols (64,000) Cat
Notes: Periodic reports from the governments of the states, counties, cities with populations of over 10,000 and selected special districts of the US. Emphasis is on the financial aspects of governments. Reports are listed in a computer print-out comprising a volume of the printed *Catalogs of the Bureau of the Census Library.*

FL —FLORIDA STATE UNIVERSITY, Robert Manning Strozier Library, Tallahassee, 32306. Judith Depew, Head, Documents-Maps Dept
Holdings: Vols (680,000) Uncat Microforms
Notes: A depository for Florida, GPO, NASA, UN, and UNESCO documents, with standing orders for British, ILO, OAS, IMF; selected documents are purchased from various government levels. The collection incl historical as well as current material, especially Florida, US, Great Britain. The Library's holdings are strong in congressional bills and hearings, decennial censuses, and British Sessional papers. Number of volumes incl microprint and microfiche, but not cataloged documents and microfilm.

ID —IDAHO STATE UNIVERSITY, Library, Pocatello, 83209. Joseph K W Lu, Librn
Holdings: Uncat Maps Microforms
Budget: ($10,000)
Notes: Over a million items. Partial depository for US Government publications (893,229 items); incl ERIC microfiche and unclassified AEC and Dept of Energy publications in microform; depository for Idaho State Government publications (1600 items); other state government publications (31,005 items); and foreign and international government bodies (24,504 items).

IL —CENTER FOR RESEARCH LIBRARIES, 6050 S Kenwood Ave, Chicago, 60637. Donald B Simpson, Dir;

Esther Smith, Collection Development Librn
Holdings: Vols 700,000 Uncat Microforms
Budget: $6000
Notes: An attempt is being made to collect all official publications of all 50 states, from 1952. Also have very extensive backfiles of older material and *Microfilm Collection of Early State Records.*

KY —UNIVERSITY OF KENTUCKY, Margaret I King Library, Government Publications Dept, Lexington, 40506. Sandra McAninch, Head
Holdings: Cat 16mm Films
Notes: All Kentucky State publications and selectively, other state publications. Incl papers.

LA —LOUISIANA STATE UNIVERSITY, Troy H Middleton Library, Louisiana Room, Baton Rouge, 70803. Evangeline Mills Lynch, Head Librn; Ruth Murray, Associate Librn
Holdings: Vols (33,500) Cat Maps VF
Notes: Louisiana Collection of history, description and travel, biography, agriculture, literature, politics and government, folklore, anthropology, geography, geology, education, language, music and natural history. Especially large subject collections may be found on Louisiana, the history of the lower Mississippi Valley, Abraham Lincoln, Romance languages and literatures, sugar culture and technology, Southern history, petroleum engineering, plant pathology, micropaleontology, ornithology, and various aspects of crawfish life, biology and culture. Complete depository of Louisiana State Documents; extensive newspapers clipping files; separate card catalog; items listed in Louisiana Union Catalog; restricted use (research and reference). Incl both materials about Louisiana and by Louisianians without regard to subject. LSU Press Collection(preservation copy of each title kept for exhibit purposes only). LSU theses and dissertations from 1900-date. LSU Faculty Collection. Also, 1300 maps, 104 VF drawers, 250 boxes of uncataloged pamphlets.

†MA —BOSTON PUBLIC LIBRARY, Copley Sq, Boston, 02117.
Holdings: Cat Microforms
Notes: Microform Publication by General Microfilm Co. State Documents on Microfiche, based on the *Legislative Research Checklist.*

MI —MONROE COUNTY LIBRARY SYSTEM, Ellis Reference and Information Center, 3700 S Custer Rd, Monroe, 48161. Marie D Chulski, Head of Reference Services
Holdings: Vols Periodicals Microforms Pamphlets
Notes: Depository for documents of the US Michigan, Southeast Michigan region and Monroe County, Michigan.

MO —MISSOURI WESTERN STATE COLLEGE, Hearnes Learning Resources Center, 4525 Downs Dr, Saint Joseph, 64507. Susan Bushhammer, Librn
Holdings: Vols (1200) Cat Maps
Notes: Became a state document depository in 1976.

NE —NEBRASKA LIBRARY COMMISSION, Publications Clearinghouse, 1420 P St, Lincoln, 68508. Patricia Sloan, Federal Documents Librn; Vern Buis, State Documents Librn
Holdings: Vols 36,500
Notes: Depository for all Nebraska state government publications since July 1972. State publications are indexed in *Nebraska State Publications Checklist*, published by the Publications Clearinghouse and issued bimonthly in microfiche format.

NY —NEW YORK STATE LIBRARY, State Education Bldg Annex, Washington Ave, Albany, 12224.
Notes: Large and important collection from the 50 states. Official depository for New York State documents.

NC —DUKE UNIVERSITY, William R Perkins Library, Public Documents and Maps Department, Durham, 27706. Jaia Barrett, Head
Holdings: Vols Maps Pamphlets Microforms
Notes: A selective depository for US

Government publications since 1890, the Department currently holds well over 500,000 items, plus publications of the European Community (a depository collection), the League of Nations, the UN and UN-affiliated agencies. Other international organizations, publications are acquired also, as are state government publications, especially from the Southeast, California, New York and Illinois. The Documents Department holds services the major map collections of Perkins Library. These collections include topographic, geologic, and special subject maps which are worldwide in coverage. The department is a depository for the US Defense Mapping Agency and the US Geological Survey. In addition, there are many other maps of general and specific interest, including US and foreign road maps. As appropriate, maps are also held in the Perkins Library's Rare BookRoom and Manuscript Department. Atlases are shelved in the Reference Department and in the bookstacks of Perkins Library.

OK —OKLAHOMA DEPT OF LIBRARIES, Law Library, 109 State Capital, Oklahoma City, 73105. Robert Clark, Dir; Betty Brown, Okla Collection Librn; Virginia Collier, US Documents; Jan Blakely, State Documents; Blane Dessy, Library Science
Holdings: Cat
Notes: Oklahoma state documents. Incl 3200 titles.

TX —TEXAS STATE LIBRARY, US Documents Collection, 1200 Brazos, PO Box 12927 Capitol Sta, Austin, 78711. Bonnie Grobar, Librn
Holdings: Vols 30,000 Microforms
Notes: The Texas State Library has been the state depository for Texas state publications since 1974. The library contains the most complete collection of current and retrospective state publications in the state. Most of the items circulate, and all can be purchased in microfiche on demand.

TX —NORTH TEXAS STATE UNIVERSITY, Government Documents Dept, NT Station Box 5188, Denton, 76203. Melody Kelley, Librn
Notes: Depository: 350,156 paper; 95,692 fiche. Congressional hearings 1823-1956. NTSU Libraries are also a depository for Texas State documents. Separate card catalogs for US documents.

WA —WASHINGTON STATE LIBRARY, Olympia, 98504. Ann Bregent, Librn
Holdings: 110,676 Documents
Notes: Regional deposetory for US documents. Incl documents from the Western States and Washington State.

STATE GOVERNMENT

KY —COUNCIL OF STATE GOVERNMENTS, States Information Center, Iron Works Pike, PO Box 11910, Lexington, 40578. Sue Stoltz, Dir
Holdings: Vols 18,000 Cat
Notes: State government administration and procedures. Major portion of collection is research reports of state legislatures, other state government agencies, and current affairs topics of interest to state governments. Incl 200 current journals.

LA —PUBLIC AFFAIRS RESEARCH COUNCIL OF LOUISIANA, Library, 300 Louisiana Ave, PO Box 3118, Baton Rouge, 70821. Jan Brashear, Research Librn
Holdings: Vols (7000) Cat Mss
Notes: State and local government problems with emphasis on Louisiana. Strong in the areas of education and public finance.

OR —UNIVERSITY OF OREGON, Bureau of Governmental Research Library, Box 3177, Eugene, 97403. Katherine G Eaton, Head Librn
Holdings: Vols (25,000) Cat Microforms
Budget: ($5000)
Notes: Separate catalog and classification system.

PA —UNIVERSITY OF PENNSYLVANIA, Fels Center of Government, 39 & Walnut St, Philadelphia, 19104. Nancy K Smith, Librn
Holdings: Vols (18,180) Cat Maps
Notes: Restricted use: Staff, students and government officials.

STATE GOVERNMENT (cont.)

PA —SCRANTON PUBLIC LIBRARY, Vine
& N Washington Sts, Scranton, 18503.
Thomas McHale, Dir
Holdings: Vols (975) Cat
Budget: ($6000)

STATE MEDICINE see Medical Policy

STATE MUNICIPAL LEAGUES

DC —NATIONAL LEAGUE OF CITIES,
Municipal Reference Service, 1301
Pennsylvania Ave NW, Washington, 20004.
Olivia Kredel, Mgr
Holdings: Vols (20,000)
Notes: Collection of publications of state
municipal leagues. Archives of National
League of Cities.

STATE PLANNING see Economic Policy;
Regional Planning

STATEN ISLAND, NEW YORK—HISTORY

NY —STATEN ISLAND HISTORICAL
SOCIETY LIBRARY, Centre St, Staten
Island, 10306. Stephen Barto, Librn
Holdings: Vols (9000) Uncat Periodicals Mss
Maps Pix Microforms VF
Notes: Holdings incl 550 cubic ft mss, 36
drawers of vertical files. Visitors by
appointment only.

STATES, IDEAL see Utopias

STATESMEN AND STATESWOMEN

CA —STANFORD UNIVERSITY
LIBRARIES, Cecil H Green Library,
Stanford, 94305. Michael T Ryan, Cur
Holdings: Cat Pix
Notes: The Dr and Mrs Leon Kolb Portrait
Collection. Over 1600 portraits (engravings,
etchings, mezzotints, lithographs) of rulers,
statesmen, authors, scholars and other
famous personages from ancient times to the
19th century. A catalog of the collection,
compiled by Dr Susan Lenkey, was
published in 1972.

OH —CLEVELAND PUBLIC LIBRARY,
History and Geography Department, 325
Superior Ave, Cleveland, 44114. JoAnn
Petrello, Head
Holdings: Cat
Notes: This biography, reference, and
circulating collection incl many fine first
editions mostly in English; however, other
languages are also represented. Strong on
biographies of rulers and statesmen,
travellers' journals, etc.

STATIC TENSIONS see Tensions, Static
and Dynamic

STATIONS, RAILROAD see
Railroads—Stations

STATISTICAL INFERENCE see
Mathematical Statistics; Probabilities
(Statistics)

STATISTICAL PHYSICS

CA —INTERNATIONAL BUSINESS
MACHINES RESEARCH LIBRARY, 5600
Cottle Rd, San Jose, 95193. Phil Grincewich,
Mgr Technical Information
Holdings: Vols (13,500) Cat
Notes: Incl 21,000 vols of 770 journals. On-
line search facility. Vols are divided into
three libraries, Technical Research,
Technical Information, and Programing. Not
open to public.

STATISTICS

AL —UNIVERSITY OF ALABAMA, Business
Library, Box 2937, University, 35486.
Dorothy Eady Brown, Librn; Linda Suttle
Harris, Ref Librn and Data Base Searcher
Holdings: Vols (105,000) Cat Microforms
Budget: ($60,000)
Notes: Incl 90,000 corporation reports and
38,500 microforms.

CA —UNIVERSITY OF CALIFORNIA,
BERKELEY, Science Libraries, Astronomy-
Mathematics-Statistics-Computer Science
Library, 100 Evans Hall, Berkeley, 94720.
Kimiyo Hom, Head
Holdings: Vols (53,000) Cat Maps
Microforms
Budget: ($117,301)
Notes: A research collection in the fields of
astronomy, mathematics, statistics and
computer science. In the field of astronomy,
emphasis is given to star charts, atlases and
catalogs. In mathematics, the collection's
strengths are in pure mathematics,
mathematical statistics and probability
theory. The computer science holdings
emphasize the mathematics and theory of
the field. The Library's serial holdings are
particularly rich in foreign-language
materials. Some 1300 serial titles are
currently being received; over 4000
pamphlets. (Holdings in the AMSCS Library
are complemented by approx 15,000
additional vols in The Bancroft Library.)

CA —UNIVERSITY OF CALIFORNIA,
BERKELEY, University Library,
Government Documents Department, 350
Library Annex, Berkeley, 94720. Suzanne
Gold, Collection Dept Librn
Holdings: Vols (314,000) Cat Microforms
Budget: ($85,115)
Notes: General collection of government
documents, historical and current, on the
federal and state levels; as well as
international and foreign documents. The
Library's holdings are particularly strong in
foreign statistics and censuses, and US
Congress. The Government Documents
Department serves as a full depository for
GPO, NASA, State of California, EEC,
GATT, IAEA, United Nations, UNESCO,
Rand Corporation (non-classified), IBRD,
OECD, ILO, UNITAR, ITC, and CE.
Selective depository, PL-480 Programs, or
gift or exchange arrangements obtain for the
states of Michigan and Washington and for
Canada, India, Pakistan and Indonesia. Incl
microfilm and 300,000 fiche, cards, and
prints.

CA —STANFORD UNIVERSITY
LIBRARIES, Mathematical & Computer
Sciences Library, Stanford, 94305. Harry
Llull, Branch Librn
Holdings: Vols (42,000) Cat

CT —YALE UNIVERSITY, Statistics Library,
Dana House, 24 Hillhouse Ave, New Haven,
06520. Billie I Salter, Librn
Holdings: Vols 3695 Cat
Budget: $5130

DC —EDISON ELECTRIC INSTITUTE,
Library-8th Floor, 1111 19th St NW,
Washington, 20036. Ethel Tiberg, Mgr,
Library Services
Holdings: Vols (13,321) Cat Maps Pix
Microforms

DC —EXPORT-IMPORT BANK OF THE
UNITED STATES, EXIMBANK Library,
811 Vermont Ave NW, Washington, 20571.
Theodora McGill, Librn; John Posniak, Asst
Librn
Holdings: Vols (15,000) Maps Audiotapes
Notes: The library has almost a complete set
of the Economist Intelligence unit of
London's *Quarterly Economic Reviews*;
various types of materials with general,
economic and statistical data on virtually
every country of the world; incl foreign
government publications, publications of
various international organizations, and US
Government documents.

DC —INTERNATIONAL MONETARY
FUND AND WORLD BANK, Joint Bank-
Fund Library, Washington, 20431. Maureen
M Moore, Librn
Holdings: Vols Cat Films Microforms
Notes: Incl foreign trade and statistical
bulletins and yearbooks, central bank reports
and bulletins, budget papers, security
yearbooks, economic development plans and
reports on economic conditions from the 132
member countries. An index of periodical
material compiled by the Library staff has
been published as: *Economics and Finance;
Index to Periodical Articles, 1947-1971*;
First Supplement, 1972, 1973, 1974 (Second
Supplement, 1975, 1976, 1977, in

preparation), 5 vols. (Boston: G K Hall,
1972, 1975). Also, The Developing Areas: *A
Classed Bibliography of the Joint Bank-Fund
Library*, Vol 1: *Latin America and the
Caribbean*; Vol 2: *Africa and the Middle
East*; Vol 3: *Asia and Oceania* (Boston: G K
Hall, 1976).

DC —POPULATION REFERENCE
BUREAU, Joseph Sunnen Library, 1337
Connecticut Ave NW, Washington, 20037.
Janice Beattie, Dir, Library & Information
Servs
Holdings: Vols 10,000 Documents Journals
Notes: Data search-Popline, Dialog. Incl 460
journals.

DC —US BUREAU OF THE CENSUS,
Library, Federal Office Bldg 3, Rm 2451,
Washington, 20233. Betty Baxtresser, Chief,
ASD Library Branch
Holdings: Cat Microforms
Notes: Emphasis on statistics of agriculture,
business, construction, economics, foreign
trade, governments, housing, industry,
population, transportation, statistical
methodology, and data processing. Library
holdings are largely current materials
covering the Bureau's programs. Outdated
materials are withdrawn regularly.

GA —UNIVERSITY OF GEORGIA,
Libraries, Special Collections Division,
Athens, 30602. Vesta Lee Gordon, Asst Dir
for Special Collections
Notes: The Arbitron Collection of television
and radio program ratings, 1949-date (except
past year). In-depth, statistical analyses of
the listening public by age, sex, county, some
ethnic groups, farm population, listening
preferences, etc. 26,302 bound vols. 2
reports, 1949-81. To be added to annually.

IL —ENCYCLOPAEDIA BRITANNICA,
Editorial Library, 310 S Michigan Ave,
Chicago, 60604. Terry Miller, Editorial
Librn
Holdings: Vols (25,000) Cat Maps
Microforms
Budget: ($80,000)
Notes: This collection is not open to the
general public, but photocopies of materials
will be made. Collection contains all major
and most minor encyclopedias and
dictionaries. A large collection of atlases and
statistical data on all foreign countries is
maintained.

IL —FEDERAL RESERVE BANK OF
CHICAGO, Library, 230 S La Salle St, PO
Box 834, Chicago, 60690. Dorothy Phillips,
Librn
Holdings: Vols (19,000) Cat
Notes: Restricted use: noncirculating. No
photocopying.

IN —PURDUE UNIVERSITY LIBRARIES,
Mathematical Sciences Library, West
Lafayette, 47907. Richard Funkhouser, Librn
Holdings: Vols (44,005) Cat Microforms
Budget: ($67,985)

IA —IOWA STATE UNIVERSITY, Library,
Ames, 50011. Warren B Kuhn, Dean of
Library Services
Holdings: Cat
Notes: Extensive international serial
holdings.

MA —UNIVERSITY OF MASSACHUSETTS
AT AMHERST, Physical Sciences Library,
Amherst, 01003. Siegfried Feller, Assoc Dir
for Collection Development
Holdings: Cat
Notes: Extensive journal holdings, incl
mathematical statistics.

MA —BOSTON PUBLIC LIBRARY,
Government Documents Department,
Boston, 02117. V Lloyd Jameson, Cur
Holdings: Maps Microforms
Notes: Foreign statistical documents,
especially population, trade, and yearbooks.

MI —UNIVERSITY OF MICHIGAN, Library,
Dept of Rare Books & Special Collections,
Ann Arbor, 48109. Robert J Starring, Head
Holdings: Cat Microforms
Notes: Incl the library of Professor Karl
Heinrich Rau of the University of
Heidelberg, acquired in 1871, containing
6076 vols especially rich in works on
political economics and European statistics
before 1850.

MI —UNIVERSITY OF MICHIGAN,
Mathematics Library, 3027 Angell Hall, Ann

STATISTICS (cont.)

Arbor, 48109. John W Weigel II, Physical
Sciences Librn
Holdings: Vols 44,000 Cat Microforms
Budget: $68,000

NJ —BERLEX LABORATORIES, Research &
Development Library, 110 E Hanover Ave,
Cedar Knolls, 07927. Lorene Lingelbach,
Librn
Holdings: Vols (10,000) Cat Microforms
Notes: The library was established in 1972
by consolidating the collections of
companies which merged with Berlex
Laboratories. 425 periodical titles are
received currently.

NJ —AT&T BELL LABORATORIES,
Libraries and Information Systems Center,
600 Mountain Ave, Murray Hill, 07974. W
D Penniman, Dir
Holdings: Vols (346,000) Cat Microforms
Notes: Restricted use to AT&T employees.
Catalogs/Indexes: Bell Laboratories Library
Network and Book Serial Catalogs; Bell
Laboratories Translations. Bell Laboratories
Library Network with New Jersey libraries
located in Holmdel, Murray Hill,
Piscataway, Whippany, Princeton, Short
Hills, Summit, West Long Branch, Crawford
Hill; libraries also in Allentown,
Pennsylvania; Reading, Pennsylvania; New
York, New York; Atlanta, Georgia;
Columbus, Ohio; Naperville, Illinois;
Indianapolis, Indiana; North Andover,
Massachusetts.

NJ —PRINCETON UNIVERSITY, Fine Hall
Library of Mathematics, Physics & Statistics,
Princeton, 08540. Peter Cziffra, Librn
Holdings: Vols (82,000) Cat Microforms
Budget: ($155,000)
Notes: All aspects of pure mathematics;
applied mathematics, numerical methods,
linear programming, etc are collected
selectively. Emphasis on pure, as opposed to
applied, physics; few acquisitions in plasma
physics. Also, mathematical statistics.
Separate catalog; most titles also in main
catalog of Firestone Library.

NY —CORNELL UNIVERSITY LIBRARIES,
Mathematics Library, White Hall, Ithaca,
14853. Steven W Rockey, Librn
Holdings: Vols 28,000 Cat Microforms

NY —NEW YORK PUBLIC LIBRARY,
Research Libraries, Economic & Public
Affairs Div, Fifth Ave & 42 St, New York,
10018. Edward DiRoma, Chief
Holdings: Vols (1,500,000) Cat Microforms
Notes: Especially statistical yearbooks and
reports; business statistics; official censuses.

NY —NEW YORK UNIVERSITY, Courant
Institute of Mathematical Sciences Library,
251 Mercer St, New York, 10012. Nancy
Gubman, Librn
Holdings: Vols (52,000) Cat Audiotapes
Microforms
Notes: Collection covers all aspects of
mathematics, theoretical computer science,
and mathematical physics on the level of
graduate research. Catalog is located in
Courant Institute Library.

NY —UNITED NATIONS, Dag
Hammarskjold Library, Rm L382, New
York, 10017. Vladimir Orlov, Librn
Holdings: Cat

NY —UNIVERSITY OF ROCHESTER,
Carlson Library, Hutchison Hall, River
Campus, Rochester, 14627. Michael W
Poulin, Librn
Holdings: Vols (48,720) Cat Microforms
Notes: Strong collection in the field and
related areas.

NC —NORTH CAROLINA STATE
UNIVERSITY, D H Hill Library, Box 7111,
Raleigh, 27695. I T Littleton, Dir
Holdings: Vols 4125 Cat
Budget: $1500
Notes: Incl monographs.

PA —UNIVERSITY OF PENNSYLVANIA,
Lippincott Library of the Wharton School,
Philadelphia, 19104. Michael Halperin, Librn
Holdings: Cat Microforms
Notes: Espec source material and statistical
data.

PA —PENNSYLVANIA STATE
UNIVERSITY, Mathematics Library, 109

McAllister Bldg, University Park, 16802.
Miriam D Pierce, Librn
Holdings: Vols (29,101) Cat
Budget: ($35,000)

TX —SOUTHERN METHODIST
UNIVERSITY, Fondren Library, Dallas,
75275. Curt Holleman, Librn for Collection
Development

WA —UNIVERSITY OF WASHINGTON
LIBRARIES, Mathematics Research
Library, GN-50, Seattle, 98195. Martha
Tucker Murdoch, Head
Holdings: Vols (25,388) Cat
Budget: ($68,364)
Notes: Pure and theoretical statistics.
See also entry under Mathematics.

MB —UNIVERSITY OF MANITOBA,
Science Library, Machray Hall, Winnipeg,
R3T 2N2, Can. V Simosko, Head
Holdings: Vols (90,000) Cat Microforms

ON —STATISTICS CANADA LIBRARY, R
H Coats Bldg, Tunney's Pasture, Ottawa,
K1A 0T6, Can. G Ellis, Chief Librn
Holdings: Vols 100,000 Cat Microforms
Notes: Statistics--Canadian and foreign.

STATISTICS—HISTORY

PA —UNIVERSITY OF PITTSBURGH,
Hillman Library, Pittsburgh, 15260.
Notes: Economic and philosophical papers of
the English scholar Frank Plumpton Ramsey
(1903-1930), incl mss of published and
unpublished writings, reading notes, etc.
Significant because of his work in modern
mathematics, logic, probability, and
economics. Complementary to the Library's
holdings of the papers of the logical
empiricists, Rudolf Carnap and Hans
Reichenback.

STATISTICS, AGRICULTURAL see Agriculture—Statistics

STATISTICS, FOREIGN AND INTERNATIONAL

DC —US BUREAU OF THE CENSUS,
Library, Federal Office Bldg 3, Rm 2451,
Washington, 20233. Betty Baxtresser, Chief,
ASD Library Branch
Holdings: Cat Microforms
Notes: Incl censuses, statistical yearbooks,
and statistical bulletins from about 100
foreign countries printed in nearly 40
languages. The span of coverage varies,
depending upon the publication program of
each country and on publications exchange
arrangements. Materials in this collection are
arranged by geographic unit, then by subject.
Publications of the international
organizations are arranged by organizational
unit, then by subject.

STATISTICS, MATHEMATICAL see Mathematical Statistics

STATUES see Monuments and Statues

STATUETTES see Bronzes

STAUDINGER, HANS, 1910-1980

NY —STATE UNIVERSITY OF NEW YORK
AT ALBANY, Library, Special Collections
Dept, 1400 Washington Ave, Albany, 12222.
Marion P Munzer, Coordr
Notes: Concentration of materials from
1940-1960, relative to the family of Hans
Staudinger and his administrative positions
at the New School for Social Research; to
his interests in the Deutsche Theatre; and to
his work in aiding German exiles. Incl 31.5
linear feet of mss and teaching materials;
personal library of books, periodicals,
pamphlets. Part of the Library's German
Exile Collection.
See also entries under Economists;
Sociologists; New School for Social Research

STAVRIANOS, L. S.

CA —HOOVER INSTITUTION ON WAR,
REVOLUTION & PEACE, Stanford
University, Stanford, 94305. Milorad M

Drachkovitch, Archivist
Notes: Research files of Professor L S
Stavrianos, incl reports, press releases,
newspaper clippings, pamphlets, and other
ephemeral publications relating to political
developments in Greece and Cyprus, 1946-
1960. 3 ms boxes.

STC BOOKS see Short Title Catalogue Books

STEACIE, EDGAR W. B., 1900-1962

†ON —PUBLIC ARCHIVES OF CANADA,
Library, 395 Wellington St, Ottawa, K1A
0N3, Can. Dawn E Monroe, Collections
Dept Officer
Holdings: 7 Feet
Notes: His papers (1925-1963).

STEAD, CHRISTINA

MA —BOSTON UNIVERSITY, Mugar
Memorial Library, Special Collections Dept,
771 Commonwealth Ave, Boston, 02215.
Howard B Gotlieb, Dir
Holdings: Cat Mss
Notes: Mss, correspondence, incl
publications by.

STEAM—HISTORY

PA —NEWCOMEN SOCIETY OF THE
UNITED STATES, Thomas Newcomen
Library of Steam Technology and Industrial
History, 412 Newcomen Rd, Exton, 19341.
Holdings: Vols 3500 Cat Mss Pix Slides
Microforms
Notes: Steam history and technology. Also,
over 1100 trade catalogs.

STEAM ENGINES

IN —PURDUE UNIVERSITY LIBRARIES,
Graduate School of Management, Krannert
Library, West Lafayette, 47907. Gordon
Law, Librn
Notes: An important resource at the
Krannert Library is its Special Collection of
Business and Economics, consisting of some
8000 rare pre-20th century strengths in
books, journals, tracts and pamphlets
covering primarily the early literature of
economic thought and business practices in
America and abroad, 1500-1870. A catalog
was issued in 1979.

RI —BROWN UNIVERSITY, John Hay
Library, 20 Prospect St, Providence, 02912.
Mark N Brown, Cur Mss
Holdings: // Mss
Notes: 500 mss and typescripts, 1838 to
1880, of George Henry Corliss, mechanical
engineer, inventor, and manufacturer of the
Corliss Steam Engine. Incl professional and
business correspondence, patent
specifications, and contracts relating to the
engineering firms with which he was
associated. The original collection was a gift
of Mr K Brooke Anderson in 1946 and was
supplemented by a deposit from the Baker
Library, Harvard University.

STEAM ENGINES—HISTORY

PA —SWARTHMORE COLLEGE, Library,
Swarthmore, 19081. Michael J Durkan,
Librn
Holdings: Vols 959 Cat Mss
Notes: This was the collection belonging to
Greville Bathe. It is comprised of books on
machines and steam engines published from
the 16th-20th century. Also works on
military engineering.

STEAMBOATS AND STEAMSHIPS

†AL —MUSEUMS OF THE CITY OF
MOBILE, Reference Library, 355
Government St, Mobile, 36602. Caldwell
Delaney, Adminr

IL —ILLINOIS STATE UNIVERSITY, Milner
Library, Dept of Special Collections,
Normal, 61761. Robert Sokan, Librn
Holdings: Vols 1564 // Uncat Maps Pix
Notes: The Price Transportation Collection.

STEAMBOATS AND STEAMSHIPS (cont.)

The collection spans the years from 1870 to 1960. Emphasis on railroads and steamships. Incl much material from US and foreign transportation companies.

IN —INDIANA UNIVERSITY, Lilly Library, Seventh St, Bloomington, 47405. William R Cagle, Librn
Holdings: // Mss Pix
Notes: Business papers and correspondence of Howard Ship Yards & Dock Co, Jeffersonville, Ind, 1834-1942. Incl correspondence with captains, ship owners, Howard family members, etc; some photos of Howard-built ships during construction; ca 10,000 blueprints, drawings and scale specifications for riverboat constructions; business ledgers and cash books; general office files. 265,600 items.

IN —INDIANA HISTORICAL SOCIETY, Library, 315 W Ohio St, Indianapolis, 46202. Robert K O'Neill, Dir
Notes: Callis Steamboat Collection.

KY —WESTERN KENTUCKY UNIVERSITY, Kentucky Library, Bowling Green, 42101. Riley Handy, Head, Special Collections; Connie Mills, Maps & Music Librn; Nancy Baird, Photographs Librn; Nancy Solley, Conservation Librn
Holdings: Vols (25,000) Cat Mss Maps Pix Microforms
Notes: Besides Kentucky history, other strengths are Mammoth Cave, South Union Shakers, Kentucky religion; and steamboat photos (3300 cataloged pictures); 8000 Kentucky postal cards, etc.

OH —PUBLIC LIBRARY OF CINCINNATI & HAMILTON COUNTY, Dept of Rare Books & Special Collections, 800 Vine St, Library Square, Cincinnati, 45202. Yeatman Anderson III, Cur
Holdings: Cat Mss Maps Pix Slides Microforms
Notes: Inland River Collection. Incl logbooks, account books, personal correspondence, diaries, etc. Also, a picture collection of 14,000 items (steamboats, towboats, river views, crews, construction, barges, etc).

WI —UNIVERSITY OF WISCONSIN, LA CROSSE, Murphy Library, 1631 Pine St, La Crosse, 54601. Edwin L Hill, Special Collections Librn
Holdings: Vols 50 Cat Pix
Budget: $9000
Notes: The steamboat project undertakes to collect photographs, sketches, and basic information on upper Mississippi River steamboats. Collection now incl about 20,000 photographs and sketches, with data file. Most photos are copy prints; some are protected by copyright and may not be used for commercial purposes. Most photos are unpublished. Collecting and data searching actively pursued. Boats from tributary rivers included. Collection is supplemented by primary and secondary sources and active field research. Overall arrangement is alphabetical by boat name, with notation of special categories of boats.

STEAMBOATS AND STEAMSHIPS—DISASTERS

IL —CHICAGO HISTORICAL SOCIETY, Library, Clark St at North Ave, Chicago, 60614. Robert L Brubaker, Librn
Holdings: Vols (150,000) Cat Mss Maps Pix
Notes: Incl the J Norman Jensen Collection, a file of approximately 8500 cards concerning ships that sank in the Great Lakes area from 1679 to 1947.

STEAMBOATS AND STEAMSHIPS—HISTORY

AL —MOBILE PUBLIC LIBRARY, Special Collections Div, 701 Government St, Mobile, 36602.
Holdings: Cat Mss Pix
Notes: Papers of the John B Waterman Steamship Company.

KY —FILSON CLUB, 118 W Breckinridge St, Louisville, 40203. Dorothy C Rush, Librn
Holdings: Vols (40,000) Cat Mss Maps Pix Microforms
Notes: Maintain a card catalog for books, pamphlets, maps and broadsides; separate catalog for newspapers incl a chronological file; and mss incl a chronological file. Collect anything about Kentucky, including Kentucky authors. Has file on Kentucky families.

LA —LOUISIANA STATE UNIVERSITY, SHREVEPORT, Library-Archives, 8515 Youree Dr, Shreveport, 71129. Patricia L Meador, Archivist & Asst Librn
Notes: Archives incl catalogued manuscripts and records, 500 maps, more than 5000 photographs, 1000 architectural drawings, slides. The collection's primary emphasis is the history of North Louisiana, particularly Northwest Louisiana. The 1500 linear ft incl area plantation records and ledgers; personal papers of area pioneers, planters, legislators, politicians, educators, businessmen, and architects; papers and records of longtime (1919-1961) Caddo Parish Coroner, Willis P Butler; the Samuel G Wiener, Sr architectual records (1921-1976) with drawings and photographs; the Ted Flaxman architectual records (1919-1968); the papers (1860-1921) of architect Nathaniel S Allen; the collection of Dewey A Somdal, Shreveport architect, historian and collector, with emphasis on steamboats, travel on the Red River and Louisiana history, 1780-1972.

MD —STEAMSHIP HISTORICAL SOCIETY OF AMERICA (SSHSA), University of Baltimore Library, 1420 Maryland Ave, Baltimore, 21201.
Holdings: Vols (3500) Cat Maps Pix Slides 16mm Films
Budget: ($15,000)
Notes: Powered Maritime Transportation Collection. Photo bank of over 15,000 negatives and 25,000 prints, arranged alphabetically by vessel name. Extensive blueprint and tracing collection. Collection documents history of steam navigation from the early 19th century to the present. Emphasis upon East Coast American vessels of late 19th and early 20th centuries and upon transatlantic vessels. Some coverage of Great Lakes and inland river steamboats. Very little about sailing vessels. No published catalog. Books listed in OCLC. Collection located at University of Baltimore. Address for Society is 414 Pelton Ave, Staten Island, NY 10310, attention: Alice S Wilson, Secretary and SSHSA Librn.

MA —HINGHAM PUBLIC LIBRARY, 66 Leavitt St, Hingham, 02043. Walter T Dziura, Dir
Holdings: Cat Mss Maps Pix Slides Microforms
Notes: A collection of about 2000 items relating to the history of the town from the 1600s to the present. Incl steamship history. An unpublished catalog of the collection is available through interlibrary loan. Most of the collection is on microfilm and may be borrowed through interlibrary loan.

NJ —MONMOUTH COUNTY HISTORICAL ASSOCIATION, Library, 70 Court St, Freehold, 07728. Loretta M Zwolak, Archivist & Librn
Holdings: Vols (6500) Cat Mss Maps Pix Slides Microforms
Budget: ($15,800)
Notes: Especially Monmouth County area. See Monmouth County Historical Association Bulletin, vol 1, no 2 July 1948, p 23-48. Allaire Papers (Howell Works); Battle of Monmouth; Mott Family Papers; North American Phalanx; Philip Freneau; Steamship Coll.

NY —NEW YORK STATE OFFICE OF PARKS & RECREATION, TACONIC REGION, Clermont State Historic Park, Library, RR 1, Box 215, Germantown, 12526. Bruce E Naramore, Historic Site Manager
Holdings: Vols 200 Cat Mss Maps
Notes: Primarily correspondence from Robert Fulton to the Chancellor Robert R Livingston. Covers most aspects of the planning and building of the "Clermont," the first successful steamboat; also its navigation. Maps and diagrams of construction of the original vessel. Interesting highlights into the lives of the two partners, and their success. It is interesting to note here that the Chancellor and Robert Fulton never called the vessel the "Clermont," rather, simply the "steamboat" and the "North River Steamboat, of Clermont" (as the ship was registered). No photocopying. Includes passenger ticket receipt books of the "North River Steam-Boat, of Clermont."

NY —NEW YORK HISTORICAL SOCIETY, Library, 170 Central Park W, New York, 10024. James Gregory, Librn

TX —SOUTHERN METHODIST UNIVERSITY, DeGolyer Library, Box 396, SMU, Dallas, 75275. Clifton H Jones, Dir
Holdings: Cat Mss Maps Pix
Notes: Transportation, especially railroads and trans-Atlantic steamboats.

WI —OSHKOSH PUBLIC MUSEUM, Library, 1331 Algoma Blvd, Oshkosh, 54901. Kitty A Hobson, Archivist
Holdings: Cat Mss Maps Pix Slides Audiotapes 16mm Films
Notes: Books, mss, photographs, etc, dealing with the history of Oshkosh and Winnebago County, Wisconsin, with special emphasis on lumbering and steamboating.

STEAMBOATS AND STEAMSHIPS—REGISTERS see Ship Registers

STEAMSHIPS see Steamboats and Steamships

STEARS, FRANK W., 1856-1939

MA —COLLEGE OF THE HOLY CROSS, Dinand Library, College St, Worcester, 01610. James M Mahoney, Cur of Special Collection
Notes: Boston merchant, political advisor to Calvin Coolidge. Collection contains correspondence (282 letters), during period 1919-1923. Also (36) letters from Calvin Coolidge to him; scrapbooks. Restricted use; noncirculating.

STEBBINS, JOEL, 1878-1966

WI —UNIVERSITY OF WISCONSIN, MADISON, Memorial Library, Division of Archives, 728 State St, Madison, 53706. Jay Frank Cook, Librn
Holdings: Mss
Notes: Personal and professional correspondence, papers from 1902-1948. 1.3 cu ft of records.

STEBBINS, N.L.

MA —SOCIETY FOR THE PRESERVATION OF NEW ENGLAND ANTIQUITIES, Library, 141 Cambridge St, Boston, 02114. Ellie Reichlin, Librn & Cur of Photographic Collections
Holdings: Vols (3000) Cat Pix Microforms
Budget: ($75,000)
Notes: Photograph collections, all media (incl daguerreotypes, ambrotypes, etc, stereographic views, carte de visite) depicting New England buildings; interiors; street and town views; occupations; pastimes; transport and personalities. Covers 1840s-1930s, with some more recent additons. Amateur and professional photographers represented. Cataloged in part, otherwise arranged by localities, subject, personal name. Special collections incl: marine photographs by N L Stebbins and Henry Peabody (1880s-1920s); Boston and Albany railroad photographic archive, early 1900s; Quabbin Valley views; historic American Buildings Survey photographs (17th to early 19th century architecture) by Arthur Haskell; Baldwin Coolidge collection, and many others. Size: 500,000 prints, ca 75,000 negatives (glass plates and copy negs). These are cataloged. Some special indexes incllandscape design (arbors, conservatories, flower beds, bandstands etc); photographers represented; architects represented (partial), and pending, interiors (specific features of); occupations.

STEDMAN, EDMUND CLARENCE

NY —COLUMBIA UNIVERSITY LIBRARIES, Rare Book & Manuscript

STEDMAN, EDMUND CLARENCE (cont.)

Library, 801 Butler Library, 535 W 114 St, New York, 10027. Kenneth A Lohf, Librn
Holdings: Mss
Notes: Incl mss and letters of literary figures of late 19th and early 20th centuries. 75,000 items. Restricted use.

STEDMAN, FORT, BATTLE OF, 1865
see Petersburg, Virginia—Siege, 1864-1865

STEED, THOMAS JEFFERSON

OK —UNIVERSITY OF OKLAHOMA, Bizzell Memorial Library, Western History Collections, 401 W Brooks, Norman, 73069. John Ezell, Cur
Holdings: Mss Documents Pix
Notes: US Representative. His papers.

STEEL

DE —HAGLEY MUSEUM AND LIBRARY, Eleutherian Mills-Hagley Foundation Inc, PO Box 3630, Greenville, 19807. Richmond D Williams, Dir; Heddy A Richter, Imprints Librn
Notes: Records of the Lukens Steel Co of Coatsville, Pa (1798-1944; 750 cubic feet) incl administrative, accounting, payroll, production and sales records documenting the history of one of America's oldest iron and steel companies. Records of the Phoenix Steel Corporation (1827-1962; 335 cubic feet) incl minute books, financial records, payroll and production records documenting the history of this important Delaware Valley steel producer. Also, Alan Wood Steel Company of Conshohocken, Pa (1728-1937; 250 cubic feet).

DC —COMMISSION OF THE EUROPEAN COMMUNITIES, European Community Information Service Library, 2100 M St NW Suite 707, Washington, 20037. Barbara Sloan, Head of Public Inquiries
Holdings: Vols (35,000) Cat Maps Pix Microforms Exhibits
Notes: Library contains all of the official documents and occasional publications of the Institutions of the European Communities, ie, European Economic Community (Common Market), European Atomic Energy Community (Euratom), European Coal and Steel Community (ECSC). It collects non-Community publications about European integration, international trade and monetary affairs. Also has the publications of the General Agreements for Tariffs and Trade (GATT), Western European Union, and Council of Europe. Also, 1000 vertical files.

IN —INLAND STEEL RESEARCH LABORATORIES, Research Library, 3001 E Columbus Dr, East Chicago, 46312. Barbara Minne Banek, Librn
Holdings: Vols (4500) Cat 16mm Films Filmstrips Microforms
Notes: Emphasis on metallurgy and steel. Also 7000 bound periodical vols; 3500 government publications, 47 vertical file drawers of translations, 15 vertical file drawers of patents.

PA —UNITED STATES STEEL CORP, Research Laboratory, Technical Information Center, MS 88, Monroeville, 15146. Angela R Pollis, Staff Supvr of Technical Information Services
Holdings: Vols (30,000) Cat Mss Microforms

PA —FRANKLIN INSTITUTE LIBRARY, 20 & The Parkway, Philadelphia, 19103. Miriam Padusis, Dir; Charles Wilt, Readers Servs Librn
Holdings: Vols (300,000) Cat Maps Pix Microforms

PA —CARNEGIE LIBRARY OF PITTSBURGH, Science & Technology Dept, 4400 Forbes Ave, Pittsburgh, 15213. Catherine M Brosky, Dept Head
Holdings: Vols (380,000) Cat Maps Microforms
Budget: ($240,000)
Notes: Of primary interest. Chemistry, metallurgy, manufacture, history. Long runs

of periodicals, serials, monographs, trade publication, Society publications, standards, specifications.

PA —COLT INDUSTRIES, Crucible Research Center Library, Box 88, Pittsburgh, 15230. Patricia J Aducci, Technical Librn

STEEL ENGRAVING see Engravers, Engraving and Engravings

STEEL INDUSTRY AND TRADE

AL —BIRMINGHAM PUBLIC LIBRARY, Dept of Archives & Mss, 2020 Seventh Ave N, Birmingham, 35203. Marvin Y Whiting, Archivist & Cur
Holdings: Cat Docs Mss //
Notes: Business and personal papers of Harry Welles Coffin covering the period from 1878 to 1938 in Birmingham, Alabama. Coffin was a vice president of The Alabama Company, a coal mining and iron products manufacturing firm. The business records incl correspondence, reports, financial records, and other documents relating to iron, steel, and coal industries in North Central Alabama. The personal papers mainly consist of love letters from Coffin to Minnie Everist Smith. These and other letters describe life on Birmingham's Southside area from 1885-1938.

AL —UNITED STATES PIPE & FOUNDRY CO, Technical Services Library, PO Box 10406, Birmingham, 35202. Phil McGrath, Mgr
Holdings: Vols (3100) Cat
Notes: Books and periodicals on ferrous metallurgy and allied subjects. Restricted use: company personnel and interlibrary loan only.

DE —HAGLEY MUSEUM AND LIBRARY, Eleutherian Mills-Hagley Foundation Inc, PO Box 3630, Greenville, 19807. Richmond D Williams, Dir; Heddy A Richter, Imprints Librn
Notes: Records of the Lukens Steel Co of Coatsville, Pa (1798-1944; 750 cubic feet) incl administrative, accounting, payroll, production and sales records documenting the history of one of America's oldest iron and steel companies. Records of the Phoenix Steel Corporation (1827-1962; 335 cubic feet) incl minute books, financial records, payroll and production records documenting the history of this important Delaware Valley steel producer. Also, Alan Wood Steel Company of Conshohocken, Pa (1728-1937; 250 cubic feet).

MI —LE SAULTE DE SAINTE MARIE HISTORIC SITES, PO Box 1668, Sault Sainte Marie, 49783. Thomas Nance, Curator
Notes: 300 Great Lakes logbooks cover more than 100 years of freighter history of the local Wilson Marine Transit Company. Incl Marine News, 59 vols, 1900-1968, plus related reports, directoies, and yearbooks of steel industry.

OH —TIMKEN CO, Timken Research Library, 1835 Dueber Ave SW, Canton, 44706. Joellen A Hadbavny, Librn
Holdings: Vols (20,000) Cat Mss Slides
Notes: Incl (7500) translations, reports, etc.

PA —BETHLEHEM STEEL CORP, Schwab Information Center, Eighth & Eaton Aves, Bethlehem, 18016. Darla L Wagner, Dir of Library Services
Holdings: Vols 15,000 Cat
Notes: Technical and economic information on steelmaking and the steel industry.

PA —UNITED STATES STEEL CORP, Research Laboratory, Technical Information Center, MS 88, Monroeville, 15146. Angela R Pollis, Staff Supvr of Technical Information Services
Holdings: Vols 30,000 Cat Mss Microforms
Notes: Ferrous metallurgy.

PA —FRANKLIN INSTITUTE LIBRARY, 20 & The Parkway, Philadelphia, 19103. Miriam Padusis, Dir; Charles Wilt, Readers Servs Librn
Holdings: Vols (300,000) Cat Maps Pix Microforms
Budget: ($18,000)

PA —CARNEGIE LIBRARY OF PITTSBURGH, Science & Technology Dept,

4400 Forbes Ave, Pittsburgh, 15213. Catherine M Brosky, Dept Head
Holdings: Vols (380,000) Cat Maps Microforms
Budget: ($240,000)
Notes: General information acquired in subject areas relating to iron and steel and other metals. Manufacturers directories, including old editions, standards and specifications, trade catalogs, basic periodicals, indexes, and bibliographies. See also entry under Technology.

PA —COLT INDUSTRIES, Crucible Research Center Library, Box 88, Pittsburgh, 15230. Patricia J Aducci, Technical Librn

PA —PENNSYLVANIA STATE UNIVERSITY, Fred Lewis Pattee Library, Labor History Collection, University Park, 16802. Peter Gottlieb, Archivist
Holdings: Cat Mss Pix
Notes: Penn State is "provisional repository" for papers and records of the United Steel Workers of America, incl records from the USWA international headquarters in Pittsburgh and from 29 district offices. A comprehensive oral history program with union members is underway.

ON —MCMASTER UNIVERSITY, Mills Memorial Library, Div of Archives & Research Collections, Hamilton, L8S 4L6, Can. G R Hill, Univ Librn
Holdings: Mss
Notes: Archvies and records of several constituents of the steel industry and trade: General Steel Wares (42 linear ft); US Steel Workers of America, Local 1005, 1937-1972 (55 linear ft) and District 6, 1953-1972 (273 linear ft).

STEEL WORKERS UNION see United Steel Workers of America (USWA)

STEELE, A. T.

AZ —ARIZONA STATE UNIVERSITY, Library, Tempe, 85287. Marilyn Wurzburger, Special Collections Librn
Notes: The A T Steele Collection is a unique compilation of articles and documents dealing with events in China from 1932-1949. The collection is divided into five parts: dispatches, newspaper clippings, pamphlets and books, original documents of the Communist Party (circa 1945) and memorabilia, written and/or collected by American journalist A T Steele. Dispatches cover events in China from 1940-1949 and are mostly first-hand experiences of Steele. These dispatches, not all of which were published, often contain details absent in the final copy. Post-war topics incl truce negotiations between the Nationalists and Chinese Communists and the "Manchurian Question." Incl 12 linear feet of materials. Index available.

STEELE, GEN. FREDERICK

CA —STANFORD UNIVERSITY LIBRARIES, Cecil H Green Library, Stanford, 94305. Michael T Ryan, Cur
Holdings: Mss
Notes: Papers of Frederick Steele, US Civil War general.

STEERE, WILLIAM CAMPBELL

MO —MISSOURI BOTANICAL GARDEN LIBRARY, PO Box 299, Saint Louis, 63166. M R Crosby, Dir of Research
Notes: The William Campbell Steere Collection of over 1000 volumes and 5000 pamphlets on bryology. Especially strong in the 19th century literature and from 1750 to the present.

STEER-WEBSTER, V. C.

ON —MCMASTER UNIVERSITY, Mills Memorial Library, Div of Archives & Research Collections, Hamilton, L8S 4L6, Can. G R Hill, Univ Librn
Holdings: // Mss Maps Pix
Notes: Colonel Steer-Webster played a leading part in the invention, design, and

STEER-WEBSTER, V. C. (cont.)

development of the "Mulberry" artificial harbor installations used for the invasion of Europe in WW II. The collection comprises memoranda, drawings, photographs, and maps.

STEFANSSON, VILHJALMUR

CA —CLAREMONT COLLEGES, Honnold Library, Ninth & Dartmouth, Claremont, 91711. Tania Rizzo, Special Collections Dept Head
Holdings: Vols 250 // Uncat Mss
Notes: Papers of Elbert A Wickes, 1884-1975, theatrical and lecture tour manager. Among his clients were Winston Churchill, William Butler Yeats, Houdini, Lowell Thomas, Vilhjalmur Stefansson, and Roy Chapman Andrews.

NH —DARTMOUTH COLLEGE, Baker Memorial Library, Hanover, 03755.
Holdings: Cat Mss Maps Pix Audiotapes Microforms
Notes: The Vilhjalmur Stefansson Collection. First editions, mss, and his own working library. Noncirculating.

MB —UNIVERSITY OF MANITOBA, Elizabeth Dafoe Library, Icelandic Collection, Winnipeg, R3T 2N2, Can. Sigrid Johnson, Librn
Holdings: Vols (23,000) Cat
Notes: Material mostly in Icelandic, some in other Scandinavian languages. All subject areas incl with primary emphasis placed on language, literature and history of Icelanders in Canada, especially Manitoba (incl mss); early publications of sagas and religious literature; numerous periodicals and newspapers, incl Islandske Maanedstidender, 1773, the first Icelandic periodical, and Framfari, 1877, the first Icelandic newspaper in North America; collections of Icelandic music, such as S K Hall Collection (published and mss); Guttormur J Guttormsson and Stephan G Stephansson Memorial Collections; Vilhjalmur Stefansson publications. Cited in, Saunderson, H H, *The Chair of Icelandic Language and Literature at the University of Manitoba.* Winnipeg: University of Manitoba, 1961.

STEFFEN, RANDY

TX —CISCO JUNIOR COLLEGE, Maner Memorial Library, LRC Rte 3, Cisco, 76437. Oleta Shirley, Dir
Holdings: Vols (1000)
Notes: Artist who wrote about army uniforms, Indians, and sculpture.

STEFFENS, LINCOLN

IL —SOUTHERN ILLINOIS UNIVERSITY, CARBONDALE, Delyte W Morris Library, Special Collections Dept, Carbondale, 62901. David V Koch, Cur of Special Collections; Louisa Bowen, Cur of Manuscripts
Holdings: Cat Mss
Notes: Papers and correspondence of Theodore A Schroeder, constitutional lawyer and founder, with Lincoln Steffens, of the Free Speech League, a forerunner of the American Civil Liberties Union. Contains extensive correspondence with Comstock, Gompers, Debs, H Ellis, Sanger, Sinclair, John Dewey, Darrow, Mencken, A G Hays, Emma Goldman, W E B Dubois, etc. Incl several thousand letters; notes and mss, records of legal cases and extensive files relating to the early history of psychiatry.

NY —COLUMBIA UNIVERSITY LIBRARIES, Rare Book & Manuscript Library, 801 Butler Library, 535 W 114 St, New York, 10027. Kenneth A Lohf, Librn
Holdings: Mss
Notes: Correspondence and mss. 37,000 items. Restricted use.

STEGANOGRAPHY see Cryptography

STEGNER, WALLACE

CA —STANFORD UNIVERSITY LIBRARIES, Cecil H Green Library, Stanford, 94305. Michael T Ryan, Cur
Holdings: Vols Cat
Notes: Also incl correspondence and literary mss.

NV —UNIVERSITY OF NEVADA, RENO, University Library, Special Collections Dept, Reno, 89557. Robert E Blesse, Head
Holdings: Vols (70) Cat Other appearances 190 Cat
Notes: Includes individual works by author in all editions including translations; also prefaces, introductions, published correspondence, appearances in anthologies, periodicals, etc. Bibliographical research collection, part of Modern Authors Collection.

STEICHEN, EDWARD

AZ —UNIVERSITY OF ARIZONA, Center for Creative Photography, 843 E University Blvd, Tucson, 85721. James Enyeart, Dir; Terence Pitts, Cur and Librn
Notes: Center has significant collections consisting of more than 25 photographs plus other archival material such as negatives, contact sheets, work prints, correspondence, financial records, diaries, project files, etc. Inventories of the collections are available to researchers. Published guides available for some collections.

STEIGER, SAM

AZ —NORTHERN ARIZONA UNIVERSITY, Special Collection Library, CU Box 6022, Flagstaff, 86011. Peter M Whiteley, Coordr/Archivist; William Mullane, Librn
Notes: Washington Office correspondence and files, 1970-1976. US Representative from Ariz, Third District, 1967-1976. (67 feet).

STEIN, CLARENCE S., 1882-1975

NY —CORNELL UNIVERSITY LIBRARIES, Collection of Regional History, Dept of Manuscripts and Univ Archives, Ithaca, 14853.
Notes: Architect, planner. Papers, 1905-73; 26.2 ft.

STEIN, GERTRUDE, 1874-1946

CA —CLAREMONT COLLEGES, Ella Strong Denison Library, Scripps College, Claremont, 91711. Judy Harvey Sahak, Librn
Holdings: Vols 100 Cat Mss Pix
Notes: The Addison M Metcalf Collection is still being expanded.

CA —UNIVERSITY OF CALIFORNIA, LOS ANGELES, Research Library, Dept of Special Collections, 405 Hilgard Ave, Los Angeles, 90024. Edward Shreeves, Chairman, Bibliographers Group; David S Zeidberg, Head
Holdings: Vols 350 Cat Mss
Notes: Based on the Gilbert A Harrison Collection: 350 first and other editions of her books; 3 linear feet of mss, correspondence, galley and page proofs, photographs and art objects.

CT —YALE UNIVERSITY, Box 1603A, Yale Station, New Haven, 06520.
Holdings: Cat Mss
Notes: Incl mss, clippings, and pictures.

CT —CONNECTICUT COLLEGE, Library, Mohegan Ave, New London, 06320. Brian Rogers, College Librn
Holdings: Vols (382,000) Cat
Notes: Primarily first editions.

DE —UNIVERSITY OF DELAWARE, Hugh M Morris Library, S College Ave, Newark, 19711. T Stuart Dick, Special Collections
Holdings: Cat Mss Pix
Notes: Manuscripts, etc, incl literary correspondence.

IL —NORTHWESTERN UNIVERSITY, Library, Special Collections Dept, 1937 Sheridan Rd, Evanston, 60201. R Russell Maylone, Cur
Holdings: Vols 20,000 Cat
Notes: First, limited, special editions, works about and ephemera of the major authors of the 20th century as well as representative minor writers. Incl English, American, French and German authors and to a lesser extent Italian, Spanish and other European writers. Extensive collections of Lawrence Durrell, T S Eliot, William Faulkner, Robert Graves, Ernest Hemingway, James Joyce, Karl Kraus, D H Lawrence, Hugh MacDiarmid, Henry Miller, Anais Nin, Ezra Pound, Gertrude Stein, H G Wells, W B Yeats. 15,000 "little magazines" titles (exclusive of runs in the general library collections).

NY —ADELPHI UNIVERSITY, Library, Garden City, 11530. Jerome Yavarkovsky, Dean of Libraries
Holdings: Vols 160 Cat Mss
Notes: Expatriate American writers of the 1920s and 1930s, with primary emphasis on the works of Gertrude Stein and Laura Riding Jackson.

†NC —WAKE FOREST UNIVERSITY, Z Smith Reynolds Library, Box 7777, Reynold Sta, Winston-Salem, 27109. Richard J Murdoch, Rare Book Librn
Holdings: Vols 160 Cat Mss Microforms
Notes: Incl typescript, galleys, page proofs and other material related to the publication of *What Are Masterpieces?*

PA —BRYN MAWR COLLEGE, Canaday Library, Bryn Mawr, 19010. James Tanis, Dir
Notes: Rare books and manuscripts.

STEINBECK, JOHN

CA —AZUSA PACIFIC COLLEGE, Marshburn Memorial Library, Citrus & Alosta, Azusa, 91702. Edward Peterman, Librn
Holdings: Vols (150) Uncat
Notes: The Odo B Stade Collection of Literary First Editions. No photocopying.

CA —UNIVERSITY OF CALIFORNIA, BERKELEY, Bancroft Library, Manuscripts Division, Berkeley, 94720. James D Hart, Dir
Holdings: Cat Mss
Notes: Letters and papers are arranged in several groups. Among the more important items are the full ms of *The Red Pony*; scenario for the film, *The Red Pony*; and galley proofs for *The Wayward Bus*. A good collection of published works by and about Steinbeck complements these ms holdings.

CA —BIBLIOGRAPHIC RESEARCH LIBRARY, 964 Chapel Hill Way, San Jose, 95122. Robert B Harmon, Bibliographer
Holdings: Vols (759) Uncat Microforms
Budget: ($500)
Notes: Private research library emphasizing bibliography, political science, John Steinbeck and Ernest Hemingway.

CA —STANFORD UNIVERSITY LIBRARIES, Cecil H Green Library, Stanford, 94305. Michael T Ryan, Cur
Holdings: Vols (23,000) Cat Mss Pix
Notes: The Charlotte Ashley Felton Memorial Library. Incl first editions, correspondence, and literary mss.

IN —BALL STATE UNIVERSITY, University Libraries, Special Collections Dept, University Ave, Muncie, 47306. David C Tambo, Head of Special Collections
Holdings: Vols 750 Cat Mss Pix Phonorecords Audiotapes 16mm Films Filmstrips Microforms
Notes: Incl typescripts of some works about him, autographed first editions, Armed Service Editions, foreign editions, nonbook materials. Described in *The Special Steinbeck Collection of the Ball State University Library: A Bibliographical Handbook*, comp by Tetsumaro Hayashi and Donald L Siefker (Muncie, Ind; The John Steinbeck Society of America, 1972), 30 pp. Also: Juanita Smith, "The Steinbeck Collection in Honor of Elizabeth R Otis at The Alexander M Bracken Library," *Steinbeck Quarterly* II (Summer-Fall 1978): 103-5.

MN —UNIVERSITY OF MINNESOTA, O Meredith Wilson Library, 309 19 Ave S, Minneapolis, 55455. Austin J McLean, Chief, Special Collections
Holdings: Vols 969 Uncat Mss Pix

STEINBECK, JOHN (cont.)

Audiotapes
Notes: First and later editions of all published works, including periodical contributions and critical and biographical works about him. Complete listing available in the Division.

NV —UNIVERSITY OF NEVADA, RENO, University Library, Special Collections Dept, Reno, 89557. Robert E Blesse, Head
Holdings: // Vols (211) Cat Other appearances 260 Cat
Notes: Includes individual works by author in all editions including translations; also prefaces, introductions, published correspondence, appearances in anthologies, periodicals, etc. Bibliographical research collection, part of Modern Authors Collection.

NY —COLUMBIA UNIVERSITY LIBRARIES, Rare Book & Manuscript Library, 801 Butler Library, 535 W 114 St, New York, 10027. Kenneth A Lohf, Librn
Holdings: Vols Mss
Notes: Publications and papers, by and about. Restricted use.

NY —HAMPDEN-BOOTH THEATRE LIBRARY AT THE PLAYERS, 16 Gramercy Park, New York, 10003. Louis A Rachow, Librn/Cur
Holdings: Mss Pix
Notes: The Franklin Heller Collection, incl correspondence, photographs; playscripts by Moss Hart and George S Kaufman, John Steinbeck, Thomas Wolfe, and others. (110 items). Described in *Theatre & Performing Arts Collections* (New York: Haworth Press, 1981).

VA —UNIVERSITY OF VIRGINIA, Alderman Library, Manuscripts Dept, Charlottesville, 22901. Edmund Berkeley Jr, Cur
Holdings: Cat Mss Pix Phonorecords
Notes: First editions; mss, incl *Grapes of Wrath*; papers; etc.

STEINBERG, WILLIAM

PA —UNIVERSITY OF PITTSBURGH, Music Library, B-31 Music Bldg, Pittsburgh, 15260. Norris L Stephens, Music Librn

STEINER, RUDOLF

CA —SAN DIEGO PUBLIC LIBRARY, Literature & Language Sect, 820 E St, San Diego, 92101. Alyce Archuleta, Senior Librn
Holdings: Cat
Notes: Old and current reference and circulating works on the subject. Incl complete works by Blavatsky, much by Rudolf Steiner, and C Zain. Strong in astrology, witchcraft, parapsychology.

STEINHAUS, ARTHUR H., 1897-1974

TN —UNIVERSITY OF TENNESSEE, KNOXVILLE, Library, Knoxville, 37996. John Dobson, Special Collections Librn
Holdings: Mss
Notes: Papers of the eminent physiologist Arthur H Steinhaus (1897-1974).

STEINMETZ, CHARLES PROTEUS

†NY —NEW YORK STATE LIBRARY, State Education Bldg, Annex, Washington Ave, Albany, 12224. John A Humphrey, Asst Commissioner for Libraries & State Librn
Holdings: Cat Mss
Notes: His library collection.

STELLMAN, LOUIS JOHN, 1877-1961

CA —UNIVERSITY OF CALIFORNIA, LOS ANGELES, Research Library, Dept of Special Collections, 405 Hilgard Ave, Los Angeles, 90024. Edward Shreeves, ◄ Chairman, Bibliographers Group; David S Zeidberg, Head
Notes: 150 images of San Francisco Chinatown and the Mother Lode country.

STELOFF, FRANCES

NY —SKIDMORE COLLEGE, Lucy Scribner Library, Saratoga Springs, 12866. David Eyman, Librn
Holdings: Cat
Notes: Incl Frances Steloff's personal collection of modern first editions acquired as proprietor of the Gotham Book Mart, New York City. Incl clippings, photographs.

STEMMER, CHARLIE

AZ —NORTHERN ARIZONA UNIVERSITY, Special Collection Library, CU Box 6022, Flagstaff, 86011. Peter M Whiteley, Coordr/Archivist; William Mullane, Librn
Notes: Personal effects, books, letters, photographs of him, 1900's-1960's. Schoolbooks, report cards, ephemera from the Arizona Normal School. Also incl a carbon copy of typewritten ms of Stemmer's autobiography: *A Brand for the Burning.*

STENCIL WORK

NY —HISTORICAL SOCIETY OF EARLY AMERICAN DECORATION, 19 Dove St, Albany, 12210. Doris Fry, Dir; Laura Olf, Librn
Holdings: Cat Pix Slides
Notes: The Library is housed with the Museum Collection of the Society. Incl examples of 19th century American country painting on tin, stenciling on wood and tin, bronzing decoration on wood, English stenciled tin and wood, bronzed items, painted objects, reverse painting on glass and examples of other decorating techniques of the period. Also included is a large collection of painted recordings of designs from early articles. Many of these were done by Esther Stevens Brazer in the 1930s. Another large collection has been added since that time. The library material is related to this interest. See *The Decorator*, official publication of the Historical Society of Early American Decoration. Other publications: *The Ornamented Chair* and *The Ornamented Tray* (both ed by Zilla Rider Lea), *Antique Decorations* by Brazer.

STENDHAL (MARIE HENRI BEYLE)

LA —TULANE UNIVERSITY, Howard-Tilton Memorial Library, Special Collections Div, 7001 Freret St, New Orleans, 70118. Wilbur E Meneray, Librn
Holdings: Vols 1738 Cat Mss 553
Notes: Published works by and about Marie Beyle (Stendhal) and manuscripts of the Beyle family, but not including Stendhal.

STENNETT, JOSEPH

WI —SEVENTH DAY BAPTIST HISTORICAL SOCIETY, Library, 3120 Kennedy Rd, PO Box 1678, Janesville, 53547. D Scott Smith, Historian
Holdings: Vols 200 Uncat Mss Pix
Notes: English Seventh Day Baptists Collection. These materials have to do with early and middle years of Baptist movement (1662-1920) in England, incl work of John James, Joseph Stennett, Peter Chamberlen, et al, Sabbatarians or Seventh Day Baptists. About 300 items incl record books, tracts, correspondence.

STENNIS, JOHN C.

MS —MISSISSIPPI STATE UNIVERSITY, Mitchell Memorial Library, Box 5408, Mississippi State, 39762. Frances N Coleman, Head, Special Collections
Holdings: Vols (15,000) Cat Mss Maps Pix Microforms
Notes: Social and political history of Mississippi, incl University Archives (now separate branch). Microfilms of Protestant Church records. There are strong collections on history of the Southern States, Mississippi authors (especially Faulkner, Williams, Carter, Welty, and Young); also the John C Stennis Collection of over 2 million items, his books, papers, photographs, etc. Incl 400 collections of mss; papers of US Rep David R Bowen 1973-1983; papers of US Rep G V Montgomery 1967-.

STENOGRAPHY see Shorthand

STEPHEN, SIR LESLIE

†WA —WASHINGTON STATE UNIVERSITY, Library, Manuscripts, Archives & Special Collections, Pullman, 99164. John F Guido, Head
Holdings: Vols Mss Pix
Notes: The library of Virginia and Leonard Woolf (from Monk's House and Victoria Sq) forms the nucleus of the collection which incorporates the library of Sir Leslie Stephen, Virginia's father. Partially cataloged.

STEPHEN, WILLIAM

SC —COLLEGE OF CHARLESTON LIBRARY, Special Collections Dept, Charleston, 29401.
Notes: Papers, 1793, incl a letter to Stephen from Frederick Garrissen requesting shipment of goods (itemized, priced list accompanying) to be sold on consignment, May 3, 1793; Garrissen complains of privateers and unsettled shipping conditions due to wars.

STEPHENS, CHARLES ASBURY, 1844-1931

ME —BOWDOIN COLLEGE, Library, Brunswick, 04011. Dianne M Gutscher, Cur of Special Collections
Holdings: Vols 50 Cat Mss
Notes: This collection consists of approximately 50 volumes of Stephens' writings and 2350 manuscripts of his books, correspondence, speeches and other related items.

STEPHENS, ELVIS

TX —NORTH TEXAS STATE UNIVERSITY, Archives, NT Station Box 5188, Denton, 76203. Robert LaForte, University Archivist
Notes: Labor arbitration manuscript collections incl papers of arbitrators Byron R Abernethy, J D Dunn, and Elvis Stephens. These arbitration papers cover the years 1960-1980 and emphasize cases in the southwestern United States and Puerto Rico. Published Description: J D Dunn and Elvis Stephens Collections, *The National Union Catalog of Manuscript Collections: Catalog 1979* Washington: Library of Congress, 1980.

STEPHENS, JAMES

IL —ILLINOIS STATE UNIVERSITY, Milner Library, Dept of Special Collections, Normal, 61761. Robert Sokan, Librn
Notes: First editions, limited editions, ephemera, etc.

OH —KENT STATE UNIVERSITY, Libraries, Dept of Special Collections, Kent, 44242. Dean H Keller, Cur
Holdings: Vols 75 Cat Mss

PA —BUCKNELL UNIVERSITY, Ellen Clarke Bertrand Library, Lewisburg, 17837. Ann de Klerk, Librn
Holdings: Cat Mss

STEPHENS, REP. ROBERT G., JR.

GA —UNIVERSITY OF GEORGIA, Libraries, Special Collections Division, Athens, 30602. Vesta Lee Gordon, Asst Dir for Special Collections
Notes: Collection contains 1394.8 linear feet of mss: papers of US Senator Richard B Russell; US Congressmen John W Davis, Maston O'Neal, Robert G Stephens Jr, John L Pilcher, Dudley M Hughes; Governors Hoke Smith, Lester Maddox, Carl Sanders.

STEPHENSON, NATHANIEL WRIGHT, 1867-1935

SC —COLLEGE OF CHARLESTON LIBRARY, Special Collections Dept, Charleston, 29401.
Notes: Correspondence within the Lancelot Minor Harris Papers.

STEREOMETRY see Mensuration

STEREOPHOTOGRAMMETRY see Photogrammetry

STEREOPHOTOGRAPHS—COLLECTIONS

CA —POMONA PUBLIC LIBRARY, Special Collections, 625 S Garey Ave, PO Box 2271, Pomona, 91766. David Streeter, Librn
Holdings: Uncat Slides
Notes: Contains 550 lantern slides (mostly of California) and 4200 color 35mm transparencies of world travel, 1960s. Also, the Burton Frasher Postal Card Collection of 60,000 negatives and prints of California, Arizona, Colorado, New Mexico, Nevada, and Utah; 30,000 world views, 8000 California views. There are also world views in nearly 1000 stereophotographs.

KY —UNIVERSITY OF LOUISVILLE, Ekstrom Library, Photographic Archives, Louisville, 40292. J C Anderson, Cur; David G Horvath, Asst Cur
Holdings: Vols (750,000) Cat Pix Slides
Budget: ($60,000)
Notes: Collections described in unpublished brochure. Print duplication service.
See also entry under Photographs - Collections

ME —MAINE HISTORICAL SOCIETY, Library, 485 Congress St, Portland, 04101.
Holdings: Vols (60,000) Cat Mss Maps Pix
Notes: The Society's holdings cover all of Maine in its scope, with special emphasis on the Portland region.

MA —BOSTON PUBLIC LIBRARY, Print Collection, Dartmouth St at Copley Sq, Boston, 02117. Sinclair H Hitchings, Keeper of Prints
Notes: The photographs are chiefly American. They deal especially with the exploratory surveys of the American West, with the transcontinental railroad project, and with American Indians. The works of Bell, O'Sullivan. W H Jackson and others are represented. The collection also contains early photos-in-the round of Boston and circa 11 daguerrotypes, ambrotypes and tintprints in a few examples, about 200 stereopitcons and a viewer. The total number of photographs is circa 5000; many are cataloged in the Boston Archives of the Print Department. A survey of the collection, written by Rachel Homer in 1970, is *Photographs from the Boston Public Library*. Now out of print, the book illustrates 27 items that demonstrate the wide variety of techniques and subject matter in the collection. No photocopying.

MA —CONCORD FREE PUBLIC LIBRARY, 129 Main St, Concord, 01742. Rose Marie Mitten, Dir
Holdings: Cat Mss Maps Pix Slides
Notes: Extensive collection.

MA —AMERICAN ANTIQUARIAN SOCIETY LIBRARY, 185 Salisbury St, Worcester, 01609. Marcus A McCorison, Dir & Librn
Holdings: Cat Maps Pix Slides
Notes: About 90,000 postal cards and 60,000 stereophotographs. Arranged geographically or by subject. Postal cards date from 1893; stereos 1860-1890. Also some rare copybook covers of views, 1794-1860. Extensive slide collection.

NY —NEW YORK PUBLIC LIBRARY, Research Libraries, American History Div, Fifth Ave & 42 St, New York, 10018.
Holdings: // Cat
Notes: Stereophotograph collection (18,000 items), housed in the Art, Prints, and Photographs Division, is worldwide in scope of subjects. Stereoscopes are available for viewing purposes.

NY —STATE UNIVERSITY OF NEW YORK, COLLEGE AT PURCHASE, Library, Lincoln Ave, Purchase, 10577. Robert W Evans, Dir
Holdings: Vols (1400) Mss Pix Slides
Notes: The Gerald D McDonald Collection. Over 1400 books on moving pictures and all aspects of the industry: production, directing, acting. Thousands of pictures of actors and actresses, directors, etc. Also about 2000 slides picturing movie personalities, etc; stereoptican pictures, buttons, bottle caps, playing cards, etc.

NY —MARGARET WOODBURY STRONG MUSEUM, 1 Manhattan Square, Rochester, 14607.
Holdings: Vols (20,000) Periodicals
Notes: The Margaret Woodbury Strong Museum Library contains a collection of approx 20,000 books, periodicals and ephemera of and concerning the 19th and early 20th centuries. A large part of the library's holdings reflect the interests of Margaret Strong and her family: domestic life and literature of the 19th century and world travel, with particular emphasis on the Orient. The library's resources are available to all visitors for research. Book stacks and rare book storage are not open for browsing and do not circulate, but facilities are provided in reading room for study.

NY —VISUAL STUDIES WORKSHOP, Research Center, 31 Prince St, Rochester, 14607. Linn Underhill, Coordr; Robert Bretz, Librn
Holdings: Vols (8000) Cat Pix Slides Audiotapes Videotapes
Notes: Strong emphasis on photography (over 1,000,000 pictures) and the photographic arts in many subject areas incl in this volume. Heavy emphasis on early photographic processes and collections of examples of them. Also collections of individual photographer's works.

SD —W H OVER MUSEUM, 414 E Clark, University of South Dakota, Vermillion, 57069. Julia Vodicka, Dir
Holdings: Cat Pix
Notes: The Stanley J Morrow Collection of Stereographs: frontier military posts, Indians, riverboats, pioneer life in Dakota Territory. The 440 stereographs of this collection were made in Dakota Territory and the Upper Missouri region between 1868 and 1883 by Stanley J Morrow, Yankton, DT. Copy photographs may be ordered. The collection is described in Wesley Hurt's *Stanley J Morrow: Pioneer Photographer*.

STERLING, GEORGE

CA —UNIVERSITY OF SAN FRANCISCO, Richard A Gleeson Library, The Countess Bernardine Murphy Donohue Rare Book Room, San Francisco, 94117. D Steven Corey, Special Collections Librn
Holdings: Vols 100 Mss
Notes: Incl inscribed copies, periodical appearances, ephemera.

STERN, CHARLES FRANK, 1880-1960

CA —UNIVERSITY OF CALIFORNIA, LOS ANGELES, Research Library, Dept of Special Collections, 405 Hilgard Ave, Los Angeles, 90024. Edward Shreeves, Chairman, Bibliographers Group; David S Zeidberg, Head
Holdings: Mss
Notes: 4 linear feet of mss, correspondence, and clippings relating to his career as California Superintendent of Banks, Vice President of the First National Bank of Los Angeles, and co-owner of the Cuyamaca Water Company, San Diego.

STERN, DANIEL

MA —BOSTON UNIVERSITY, Mugar Memorial Library, Special Collections Dept, 771 Commonwealth Ave, Boston, 02215. Howard B Gotlieb, Dir
Holdings: Cat Mss
Notes: Mss, correspondence, etc collected in depth; incl publications by or about.

STERN, GLADYS BRONWYN, 1890-1973

MA —BOSTON UNIVERSITY, Mugar Memorial Library, Special Collections Dept, 771 Commonwealth Ave, Boston, 02215. Howard B Gotlieb, Dir
Holdings: // Cat Mss Pix
Notes: Mss, correspondence, etc collected in depth; incl publications by or about.

STERN, JAMES

DC —GEORGETOWN UNIVERSITY, Library, Special Collections Div, 37 & O Sts NW, Washington, 20057. George M Barringer, Special Collections Librn; Nicholas B Sheetz, Mss Librn
Holdings: Mss Pix
Notes: The papers of Christopher Sykes, biographer, journalist, and novelist; containing mss, letters, photographs, and drawings. With extensive correspondence from Harold Acton; Angela, Countess of Antrim; Sir John Betjeman; Ivy Compton-Burnett; Alick Dru; T S Eliot; Max Beerbohm; Graham Greene; John Hayward; Lord Patrick Kinross; Compton Mackenzie; Nancy Mitford; Anthony Powell; Dame Flora Robson; Cecil Roth; Sir John Russell; Osbert Sitwell; John Sparrow; Freya Stark; James Stern; and Evelyn Waugh, among others. Also, considerable research material about Evelyn Waugh, Adam von Trott, Robert Byron, Lady Nancy Astor; and the foundation of the state of Israel.

STERN, RICHARD MARTIN

MA —BOSTON UNIVERSITY, Mugar Memorial Library, Special Collections Dept, 771 Commonwealth Ave, Boston, 02215. Howard B Gotlieb, Dir
Holdings: Cat Mss
Notes: Mss, correspondence, etc collected in depth; incl publications by or about.

STERN, STEWART

CA —AMERICAN FILM INSTITUTE, Louis B Mayer Library, 2021 N Western Ave, PO Box 27999, Los Angeles, 90027. Anne G Schlosser, Dir
Notes: Stewart Stern Collection contains scripts and related working materials from all his films and TV shows.

STERNE, LAURENCE

IN —INDIANA UNIVERSITY, Lilly Library, Seventh St, Bloomington, 47405. William R Cagle, Librn
Holdings: Vols 300 // Cat
Notes: First editions and other related 18th century printings.

MA —HARVARD UNIVERSITY LIBRARY, Widener Library, Cambridge, 02138.
Holdings: Cat
Notes: See *Harvard Library Bulletin*, XVI (1968), 400-401.

STETTINIUS, EDWARD R., JR.

VA —UNIVERSITY OF VIRGINIA, Alderman Library, Manuscripts Dept, Charlottesville, 22901. Edmund Berkeley Jr, Cur
Holdings: Cat Mss Pix Phonorecords Audiotapes
Notes: Personal, political, and business papers.

STEUBEN, BARON FRIEDRICH W. VON

DC —GEORGETOWN UNIVERSITY, Library, Special Collections Div, 37 & O Sts NW, Washington, 20057. George M Barringer, Special Collections Librn; Nicholas B Sheetz, Mss Librn
Holdings: Mss Cat Pix
Notes: Collection of correspondence, journals, documents, photographs, and newspaper clippings concerning the family of Mimika Farish Frith. Incl is correspondence (9 ALS, 1779-1781) from Baron von Steuben to his aide-de-campe Pierre Etienne Du Ponceau and two letters (ALS, 1781) from Du Ponceau to von Steuben. Also incl is a bound journal kept by Du Ponceau from 1794-1820 which served as a family register, diary and account book. Also incl is correspondence and documents from the Bauduy, Farish and Sassenay families spanning the period from 1782-1932. Of

STEUBEN, BARON FRIEDRICH W. VON (cont.)

particular interest is a bound volume of photographs from the Suez Canal, Ceylon, Colombo, Java, Borneo and New Guinea, taken by Frederick G Farish in 1907.

STEVENS, ERNEST J.

IL —CHICAGO HISTORICAL SOCIETY, Library, Clark St at North Ave, Chicago, 60614. Archie Motley, Manuscript Librn
Notes: Business history acquisitions incl the records of the Illinois Manufacturers' Association; customer complaint files of the Better Business Bureau of Metropolitan Chicago; Chicago Board of Underwriters; papers of George S Bowen, Illinois capitalist; and Ernest J Stevens.

STEVENS, GEORGE

CA —ACADEMY OF MOTION PICTURE ARTS & SCIENCES, Margaret Herrick Library, 8949 Wilshire Blvd, Beverly Hills, 90211. Linda Harris Mehr, Library Administrator
Notes: Papers.
See also entry under Moving Pictures.

STEVENS, HON. HENRY HERBERT, 1878-1973

BC —UNIVERSITY OF VICTORIA, McPherson Library, Victoria, V8W 3H5, Can.

STEVENS, HENRY, OF VERMONT, 1819-1886

CA —UNIVERSITY OF CALIFORNIA, LOS ANGELES, Research Library, Dept of Special Collections, 405 Hilgard Ave, Los Angeles, 90024. Edward Shreeves, Chairman, Bibliographers Group; David S Zeidberg, Head
Holdings: Cat Mss Pix
Notes: 31 linear feet of correspondence and business records of this London bookseller.
VT —UNIVERSITY OF VERMONT, Guy W Bailey/David W Howe Library, Burlington, 05405. John Buehler, Asst Dir for Special Collections
Notes: Manuscripts and printed material on Henry Stevens of Vermont.

STEVENS, RISE

MA —BOSTON UNIVERSITY, Mugar Memorial Library, Special Collections Dept, 771 Commonwealth Ave, Boston, 02215. Howard B Gotlieb, Dir
Holdings: Cat Mss Pix
Notes: Mss, correspondence, etc collected in depth; incl publications by or about.

STEVENS, THOMAS WOOD

AZ —UNIVERSITY OF ARIZONA, Library, Tucson, 85721. W David Laird, Librn
Notes: Drama collection incl works by and about Thomas Wood Stevens and the theater in Chicago and Pittsburgh. Programs, scrapbooks, prompt books, private press imprints, personal correspondence.

STEVENS, WALLACE

CA —HUNTINGTON LIBRARY, Art Gallery & Botanical Gardens, 1151 Oxford Rd, San Marino, 91108. Robert L Middlekauff, Dir; Daniel H Woodward, Librn
Holdings: Vols 200 Cat Mss Pix
Notes: His literary archives. Incl 184 literary mss, 2,381 letters, 30 photographs and ephemera
CT —TRINITY COLLEGE LIBRARY, Watkinson Library, 300 Summit St, Hartford, 06106. Jeffrey Kaimowitz, Cur
Holdings: Cat
Notes: First editions, etc.
CT —YALE UNIVERSITY, Box 1603A, Yale Station, New Haven, 06520.
Holdings: Cat Mss

FL —UNIVERSITY OF MIAMI, Otto G Richter Library, PO Box 248214, Coral Gables, 33124. Frank Rodgers, Dir of Libraries
Notes: 300 books, journals, cards, partly in a special collection; noncirculating.
MO —WASHINGTON UNIVERSITY, John M Olin Library, Campus Box 1061, St Louis, 63130.
Notes: Extensive collection of printed material.
NV —UNIVERSITY OF NEVADA, RENO, University Library, Special Collections Dept, Reno, 89557. Robert E Blesse, Head
Holdings: // Vols (40) Cat Other appearances 1035 Cat
Notes: Includes individual works by author in all editions including translations; also prefaces, introductions, published correspondence, appearances in anthologies, periodicals, etc. Bibliographical research collection, part of Modern Authors Collection.
NH —DARTMOUTH COLLEGE, Baker Memorial Library, Hanover, 03755.
Holdings: Cat Mss
Notes: First editions, mss, etc. Noncirculating.
RI —BROWN UNIVERSITY, John Hay Library, Harris Collection, Prospect St, Providence, 02912. Rosemary L Cullen, Cur
Holdings: Vols (200,000) Cat Mss Pix Phonorecords Microforms
Budget: ($15,000)
Notes: The Harris Collection of American Poetry and Plays is principally composed of American and Canadian poetry and plays, 17th century-date. Extensive holdings in songsters, gift books and annuals, hymnals, pageants, broadside verse, carriers' addresses, women poets, juvenile poetry, (incl Mother Goose and The Night Before Christmas), sheet music with lyrics, small press publications, fine printing, black poets, "little magazines," Yiddish-American literature. All movements or schools of American poetry are represented. Incl first editions of most American poets and playwrights, notably Whitman, Poe, Wallace Stevens, Eugene O'Neill, Edward Albee, Ezra Pound, T S Eliot, William Carlos Williams, Amy Lowell, Phyllis Wheatley, Robert Frost, Allen Ginsberg, Bliss Carman, and Stephen Foster sheet music. Also incl the Saunders Walt Whitman Collection (1300 vols); the LangdonCollection of Pageants (250 vols); the Asa Cushman Collection of plays in ms and prompt copies; the MacDougall Collection of Psalters and Hymnals; 4000 plays issued by Walter H Baker Co, Boston (1890-1957); the Vaxer Collection of Yiddish Poetry, Plays and Music (1700 vols). Collections incl 200,000 vols, 30,000 broadsides, 55,000 mss, 170,000 pieces of sheet music, 450 phonorecords, and 375 microfilm reels. See Dictionary Catalog of the Harris Collection of American Poetry and Plays (Boston: G K Hall, 1972), 13 vols; Supplement (1977), 3 vols. See also, American Poetry, 1609-1900, A Collection on Microfilm, Segment I (1609-1820); Segment II (1821-1850); Segment III (1851-1870) (Woodbridge, Conn: Research Publications). Separate catalog.

STEVENS FAMILY

NJ —STEVENS INSTITUTE OF TECHNOLOGY, Samuel C Williams Library, Castle Point Sta, Hoboken, 07030. Jane G Hartye, Special Collections Librn
Holdings: Vols (250) Cat Pix Microforms
Budget: ($1500)
Notes: Col John Stevens and his sons Robert Livingston Stevens and Edwin Augustus Stevens. They were responsible for the first steam locomotives and railroad; they were involved in shipbuilding, building the "Juliana," the "Phoenix" and ferries. We have a huge amount of uncataloged data on the "Stevens Battery." The Stevens family played an extremely important role in developing the City of Hoboken; Edwin Augustus Stevens established Stevens Institute of Technology. Through the Stevens family, we have much historical data on the City of

Hoboken and the State of New Jersey. Our collectin includes microfilm of the Stevens Papers of of Hoboken.

STEVENSON, ADLAI EWING, 1900-1965

NJ —PRINCETON UNIVERSITY, Library, Manuscript Collection, Nassau St, Princeton, 08540. Jean F Preston, Cur
Holdings: // Cat Mss Pix
Notes: The Adlai Stevenson Collection of personal papers is contained in 1569 boxes. Terms of Access: The bulk of the personal papers may be read by qualified scholars. See Princeton University Library Chronicle, v 26, p 15. An unpublished typescript guide (456 p) is available in the Library.

STEVENSON, COKE R.

TX —NORTH TEXAS STATE UNIVERSITY, Archives, NT Station Box 5188, Denton, 76203. Robert LaForte, University Archivist
Notes: Part of Oral History Collection. Interviews with former Texas Speaker of the House and Governor (1941-46).

STEVENSON, D. E.

MA —BOSTON UNIVERSITY, Mugar Memorial Library, Special Collections Dept, 771 Commonwealth Ave, Boston, 02215. Howard B Gotlieb, Dir
Holdings: Cat Mss Pix
Notes: Mss, correspondence, etc collected in depth; incl publications by or about.

STEVENSON, ROBERT LOUIS, 1850-1894

CA —UNIVERSITY OF CALIFORNIA, LOS ANGELES, William Andrews Clark Memorial Library, 2520 Cimarron St, Los Angeles, 90018.
Holdings: Cat
Notes: Small collection, original editions, etc.
CA —SILVERADO MUSEUM, Library, Saint Helena, 94574. Ellen Shaffer, Cur
Holdings: Vols 3000 Cat Mss Pix
Notes: The museum is devoted to the life and works of Robert Louis Stevenson. Incl 1000 letters, 125 mss, 1000 photos, 100 paintings, prints, etc, 8 sculptures, memorabilia. Total collection: 7600 items.
CT —TRINITY COLLEGE LIBRARY, Watkinson Library, 300 Summit St, Hartford, 06106. Jeffrey Kaimowitz, Cur
Holdings: Cat
Notes: See McKay, George L, A Stevenson Library: Catalogue of a Collection of Writings by and about Robert Louis Stevenson, formed by Edwin J Beinecke (New Haven: Yale University Library, 1951-1964), 6 vols.
CT —YALE UNIVERSITY, Box 1603A, Yale Station, New Haven, 06520.
Holdings: Cat Mss Pix
Notes: Published catalog.
MA —HARVARD UNIVERSITY LIBRARY, Widener Library, Harry Elkins Widener Collection, Cambridge, 02138. F Thomas Noonan, Cur
Holdings: Cat Mss
Notes: Catalog privately printed in 1913.
NJ —PRINCETON UNIVERSITY, Library, Morris L Parrish Collection, Princeton, 08540. Alexander D Wainwright, Cur
Notes: Almost 700 vols total. For particulars refer to: Alexander Wainwright. Robert Louis Stevenson A Catalogue of the Henry E Gerstley Stevenson Collection, of the Stevenson Section of the Morris L Parrish Collection of Victorian Novelists and Items from Other Collections of the Department of Rare Books and Special Collections in the Princeton University Library Princeton, 1971. 3944.3.073 and (ExB)Z8843.P95.
†NC —WAKE FOREST UNIVERSITY, Z Smith Reynolds Library, Box 7777, Reynold Sta, Winston-Salem, 27109.
Notes: A significant collection.
PA —TEMPLE UNIVERSITY LIBRARIES, Special Collections Dept, Rare Books & Mss

STEVENSON, ROBERT LOUIS, 1850-1894 (cont.)

Section, Philadelphia, 19122. Thomas M Whitehead, Cur
Holdings: Vols 200 Cat
Notes: The collection of the Rev Dr Frederick E Maser with additions. First, forged, and limited editions. Incl correspondence.

STEVENSON RAINES (ET AL.) ARCHITECTS

AB —UNIVERSITY OF CALGARY, Libraries, Special Collections Div, 2500 University Dr, Calgary, T2N 1N4, Can.
Holdings: Cat Mss Pix Audiotapes 35mm Films Microforms
Notes: Collection consists of 38,031 architectural drawings of the Calgary firm of Stevenson Raines Barrett Hutton Seton & Partners who, under various names and partnerships, have been established since 1906. The projects represent a true cross-section of building activity of a growing Western city and complement the collections of Rule Wynn & Rule, Cawston, Long and McMillan, the firm that merged with that of Beatson Finlayson Howatt in 1982, (qv). Outstanding projects are: MacEwan Hall and Earth Sciences Building at the University of Calgary; Mount Royal College, Calgary; Red Deer College, Red Deer, etc. An inventory and project list are on hand. 266 meters of documents. Also incl are reels of microfilm, aperture cards, models and one oral history interview.
See also entry under Beatson Finlayson Howatt & Partners.

STEWART, DAVID ALEXANDER, 1847-1937

MB —UNIVERSITY OF MANITOBA, Elizabeth Dafoe Library, Archives and Special Collections Dept, Winnipeg, R3T 2N2, Can. Richard E Bennett, Dept Head; Corrado A Santoro, Reference Archivist
Notes: A letter from Dr Stewart to R Douglas of the Geographic Board of Canada regarding the origins of two Manitoba place names: "Ninette" and "Overend's Lake".

STEWART, EDWIN CROWELL, 1864-1921

NY —CORNELL UNIVERSITY LIBRARIES, Collection of Regional History, Dept of Manuscripts and Univ Archives, Ithaca, 14853.
Notes: NY State Senator and Assemblyman. Incl scrapbooks, (1894-1904)-1921; newspaper clippings and cartoons, invitations, programs, telegrams and correspondence.

STEWART, GEORGE RIPPEY

NV —UNIVERSITY OF NEVADA, RENO, University Library, Special Collections Dept, Reno, 89557. Robert E Blesse, Head
Holdings: Vols 194 Cat
Notes: Includes individual works by author in all editions including translations; also prefaces, introductions, published correspondence, appearances in anthologies, periodicals, etc. Bibliographical research collection, part of Modern Authors Collection.

STEWART, ISABEL

MA —SIMMONS COLLEGE ARCHIVES, 300 The Fenway, Boston, 02115. Megan Sniffin-Marinoff, College Archivist
Notes: Archives of the Simmons College School of Public Health Nursing (later reorganized into the School of Nursing) cover the years 1902-1970. Important correspondents in the collection incl M Adelaide Nutting, Mary Beard, Isabel Stewart, and Anne Hervey Strong, etc. Incl Strong's records of activity with regard to nursing education in the National Organization for Public Health Nursing, 1918-22. 1000 linear feet in institution, incl special collections nursing and photographs, nursing.

STEWART, PAUL

OK —UNIVERSITY OF OKLAHOMA, Bizzell Memorial Library, Western History Collections, 401 W Brooks, Norman, 73069. John Ezell, Cur
Holdings: Mss Documents
Notes: US Representative. His papers. Guide available.

STEWART, RAMONA

MA —BOSTON UNIVERSITY, Mugar Memorial Library, Special Collections Dept, 771 Commonwealth Ave, Boston, 02215. Howard B Gotlieb, Dir
Holdings: Cat Mss
Notes: Mss, correspondence, etc collected in depth; incl publications by or about.

STIBITZ, GEORGE ROBERT, 1904-

NH —DARTMOUTH COLLEGE, Baker Memorial Library, Hanover, 03755.
Holdings: 50 Boxes
Notes: The papers of George Robert Stibitz (1904-), concerning the invention and development of the digital computer (1937-1963).

STIEGLITZ, ALFRED, 1864-1946

CT —YALE UNIVERSITY, Box 1603A, Yale Station, New Haven, 06520.
Holdings: Mss Pix
Notes: Mss, clippings and pictures.
DC —NATIONAL GALLERY OF ART, Library, Sixth & Constitution Ave NW, Washington, 20565. J M Edelstein, Chief Librn
Notes: Collection constists of "master set" of 1600 Stieglitz images donated by his widow, Georgia O'Keefe, in 1949.
MD —UNIVERSITY OF MARYLAND, BALTIMORE COUNTY, Albin O Kuhn Library and Gallery, Edward L Bafford Photography Collection, 5401 Wilkens Ave, Baltimore, 21228. Tom Beck, Cur
Holdings: Vols (3000) Cat Pix Slides
Notes: The Edward L Bafford Photography Collection contains 200,000 images, negatives, cameras, and books representing the entire history and aesthetics of photography. The theme of the collection is photography as a social force, as represented by the 5000 photographs and negatives by Lewis Hine and by William Henry Jackson's *Photographs of the Yellowstone National Park and Views of Montana and Wyoming* Territories. Another important historical document is the rare *Photographic Sketchbook of the Civil War* by Alexander Gardner. There are also a large number of photographs by both 19th and 20th century photographers, such as Edward Curtis, Eadweard Muybridge, Alfred Stieglitz, Diane Arbus, Lotte Jacobi, and many others. In addition, UMBC has been awarded the photographic archives of the *News American*.

STIFLER, WILLIAM W.

†MA —SUFFOLK UNIVERSITY, Library, Boston, 02114.
Notes: Papers.

STIGLER, WILLIAM GRADY

OK —UNIVERSITY OF OKLAHOMA, Bizzell Memorial Library, Western History Collections, 401 W Brooks, Norman, 73069. John Ezell, Cur
Holdings: Mss Documents Maps
Notes: US Representative. His papers. Guide available.

STILES, EZRA

CT —YALE UNIVERSITY, Box 1603A, Yale Station, New Haven, 06520.
Holdings: Cat Mss

STILLMAN, WILLIAM JAMES

NY —UNION COLLEGE, Schaffer Library, Schenectady, 12308. Ann Seemann, Librn; Ellen Fladger, Archivist
Holdings: // Mss Pix
Notes: Letters to and from him. About 450 letters. Indexed.

STILL'S DISEASE see Rheumatoid Arthritis in Children

STILLWELL, JERRY E. AND NORMA J.

NY —CORNELL UNIVERSITY LIBRARIES, Collection of Regional History, Dept of Manuscripts and Univ Archives, Ithaca, 14853.
Notes: Ornithologists, authors. Incl papers, 1948-64; diaries, notes, extensive correspondence, notebooks, journals, newspaper clippings, 3 phonograph records concerning birdcalls, typescripts and other items. Unpublished guide available.

STILWELL, JOSEPH WARREN

CA —HOOVER INSTITUTION ON WAR, REVOLUTION & PEACE, Stanford University, Stanford, 94305. Milorad M Drachkovitch, Archivist
Holdings: // Mss
Notes: Papers, 1941-1945, of Joseph Warren Stilwell, Army officer who commanded US forces in the China-Burma-India Theater, 1942-1944, and the 10th Army, Pacific Theater, 1945. Diary (1941-1944), "black-book" (reflections and analyses of the day's events, 1943-1944), other personal papers and miscellaneous documents on military operations. 6 ft.

STIMSON, HENRY L.

CT —YALE UNIVERSITY, Box 1603A, Yale Station, New Haven, 06520.
Holdings: Mss
Notes: 50,000 items. Mss, personal papers. Materials to 4 March 1933 available.
CT —YALE UNIVERSITY, Sterling Memorial Library, Latin American Collections, New Haven, 06520. Lee H Williams Jr, Cur
Holdings: Vols (300,000) Cat Maps Pix Slides Phonorecords 16mm Films Filmstrips
See also entry under Latin America

STINEHOUR PRESS

NC —UNIVERSITY OF NORTH CAROLINA, GREENSBORO, Walter Clinton Jackson Library, Special Collections Dept, 1000 Spring Garden St, Greensboro, 27412. Emilie W Mills, Librn
Notes: Emphasis is on American small publishers since late 19th century attention to fine printing, sound production and textual content are exemplary. Significant holdings of books published by The Typophiles, Stinehour Press, David R Godine, Jargon Society and Way and Williams are included with selective holdings of other small commercial publishers and printers, incl R H Russell, Copeland and Day, Stone and Kimball.

STITES, RAYMOND S., 1899-1975

KS —MENNINGER FOUNDATION, Archives, 5600 W Sixth St, Box 829, Topeka, 66601. Alice Brand, Librn; Mark West, Archivist
Notes: 20 boxes, 1924-74. Incl are mss, journals, correspondence, and publications.

STOBIE, MARGARET R.

MB —UNIVERSITY OF MANITOBA, Elizabeth Dafoe Library, Archives and Special Collections Dept, Winnipeg, R3T 2N2, Can. Richard E Bennett, Dept Head; Corrado A Santoro, Reference Archivist
Notes: Research materials used by Margaret R Stobie in her book *Frederick Philip Grove*

STOBIE, MARGARET R. (cont.)

(1973) and which emphasize Grove's life and career in rural Manitoba. Also 15 cassette tapes of 88 interviews on Grove conducted by Prof Stobie.

STOCK, KEITH LIEVESLEY, 1911-

IN —INDIANA UNIVERSITY, Lilly Library, Seventh St, Bloomington, 47405. William R Cagle, Librn
Holdings: // Mss Pix
Notes: Photographs, etc, of actors and actresses are located in 3 ms collections: (1) Johnson, William Spencer, 1813-1897, printer. Correspondence and photographs from actors and actresses, 1846-1894. 129 items; (2) Stock, Keith Lievesley, 1911- , professor. Autographs, etc of people associated with 19th-early 20th century theatre in England. 279 items; and (3) Woodward, Sidney C, journalist. Correspondence, autographs, and pictures, 1769-1961, of actors, actresses, and other theatre people, mostly American and British. 1235 items. Also, in Printed Books Division: small pictures (largely engravings excerpted from books) of Shakespearean actors and actresses, 18th into 20th century.

STOCK AND STOCKBREEDING

NY —NEW YORK STATE OFFICE OF PARKS & RECREATION, TACONIC REGION, Clermont State Historic Park, Library, RR 1, Box 215, Germantown, 12526. Bruce E Naramore, Historic Site Manager
Holdings: Vols (5000) Cat Mss Maps
Notes: Period editions of pre - and post-American Revolutionary War agricultural technology. Many belonged to the Chancellor Robert R Livingston (1746-1813). Incl land drainage, hybrids, fertilizers, and the introduction of Merino sheep.
TX —TEXAS A&M UNIVERSITY, Sterling C Evans Library, Special Collections Div, College Station, 77843. Donald H Dyal, Librn
Holdings: Vols (16,000) Mss Pix
Notes: Jeff Dykes Range Livestock Collection (incl a 600-item collection of J Frank Dobie works). Part of the Dobie Collection is described in Dykes, Jeff C *My Dobie Collection* (College Station, Tex: Friends of the Texas A & M University Library).

STOCK AND STOCKBREEDING—EQUIPMENT AND SUPPLIES

CA —UNIVERSITY OF CALIFORNIA, DAVIS, Shields Library, Dept of Special Collections, Davis, 95616. Donald Kunitz, Head; C Danial Elliott, Asst Head
Notes: Manufacturers' catalogs, manuals, part lists, photos, ephemera pertaining to historical and current data on tractors, engines, combines, hay equipment, etc.

STOCK BREEDING see Stock and Stockbreeding

STOCK CORPORATIONS see Corporations

STOCK EXCHANGES

NY —AMERICAN STOCK EXCHANGE, Martin J Keena Memorial Library, 86 Trinity Place, New York, 10006. Margaret A Balogh, Supvr
Holdings: Vols 500 Microforms
Notes: Incl over 13,000 microfilm reels and microfiche; and bound periodicals.

STOCK MARKET see Stock Exchanges

STOCK RANGES

AZ —NORTHERN ARIZONA UNIVERSITY, Special Collection Library,

CU Box 6022, Flagstaff, 86011. Peter M Whiteley, Coordr/Archivist; William Mullane, Librn
Notes: Diary of A F Potter, apparently a government official, written while touring the cattle and sheep ranges of Texas, New Mexico, and Arizona, 1904. Also, Ranching Time Book Collection; time book of an unidentified company, possibly of the employees working on the range, 1878-1879.
MT —MONTANA HISTORICAL SOCIETY LIBRARY, 225 N Roberts St, Helena, 59601. Robert M Clark, Librn; Brian Cockhill, State Archivist
Holdings: Vols 3000 Cat
Budget: ($2500)
Notes: The Ames and Margaret Booth Teakel Range Life Memorial Collection (cowboy and cattle range subjects). The scope of this collection includes the entire West, not just Montana and contiguous states. Also, L A Huffman Collection; incl 1100 photographs.
TX —TEXAS A&M UNIVERSITY, Sterling C Evans Library, Special Collections Div, College Station, 77843. Donald H Dyal, Librn
Holdings: Vols (16,000) Mss Pix
Notes: Jeff Dykes Range Livestock Collection (incl a 600-item collection of J Frank Dobie works). Part of the Dobie Collection is described in Dykes, Jeff C *My Dobie Collection* (College Station, Tex: Friends of the Texas A & M University Library).
TX —TEXAS TECH UNIVERSITY, Library, Lubbock, 79409. David J Murrah, Assoc Dir for Special Collections

STOCK YARDS see Stockyards

STOCKBREEDING   see Stock and Stockbreeding

STOCKHAUSEN, KARLHEINZ

DC —LIBRARY OF CONGRESS, Music Division, Washington, 20540.
Notes: Mss in Koussevitzky Archives.

STOCKINGS see Hosiery

STOCKTON, CHARLES H.

RI —US NAVAL WAR COLLEGE, Historical Collection & Museum, Newport, 02841. Anthony S Nicolosi, Dir; Evelyn Cherpak, Cur
Holdings: Mss
Notes: The Charles H Stockton Papers incl correspondence regarding his naval career and Naval War College presidency, 1896-1908; his unpublished autobiography; journals of cruises to the Asiatic, Arctic and other locations. Stockton was also president of George Washington University and professor of international law, 1910-1918.

STOCKTON, GILCHRIST BAKER, 1890-1973

CA —HOOVER INSTITUTION ON WAR, REVOLUTION & PEACE, Stanford University, Stanford, 94305. Milorad M Drachkovitch, Archivist
Holdings: Mss Pix
Notes: Papers of G B Stockton, 1911-59, incl correspondence, dispatches, reports, clippings, and photographs, relating to activities of the Commission for Relief in Belgium, 1915-16, and of the American Relief Administration in Austria, 1919-20; to US and Florida politics, 1924-28; to US-Austrian relations, 1930-33; and to the establishment of the Jacksonville, Florida, Naval Air Base. 11 ms boxes.

STOCKYARDS

CO —COLORADO HISTORICAL SOCIETY, Research Collections, 1300 Broadway, Denver, 80203. Catherine Kane, Head Public Service and Access
Holdings: Cat Mss Pix Microforms
Budget:
Notes: Correspondence and business records

of cattle companies and cattlemen and railroads gathered as part of the Western Range Cattle Industry Study. Also, correspondence and records of companies, organizations and related materials arranged by state (1850-1945). About 50,000 items.

STOECKEL, GUSTAVE

CT —YALE UNIVERSITY, Music Library, 98 Wall St, New Haven, 06520. Harold E Samuel, Librn
Notes: Personal papers and musical mss. *See also* entry under Music, American.

STOEVING, (CARL HEINRICH) PAUL

NE —UNIVERSITY OF NEBRASKA-LINCOLN, Don L Love Library, University Archives and Special Collections, Lincoln, 68588. Joseph G Svoboda, University Archivist
Holdings: Vols 25 // Cat
Notes: Collection consists of mss of 6 novels, 6 plays, one essay, and 12 musical works. No photocopying.

STOICHIOMETRY see Chemistry, Physical and Theoretical

STOKES, HAROLD PHELPS

CT —YALE UNIVERSITY, Box 1603A, Yale Station, New Haven, 06520.
Notes: His papers (2000 items); incl Asian diary.

STOKOWSKI, LEOPOLD

DC —LIBRARY OF CONGRESS, Music Division, Washington, 20540.
Notes: A collection of 120 historic high-fidelity and stereophonic recordings of Leopold Stokowski conducting the Philadelphia Orchestra made in 1931 and 1932.

STOMATOLOGY see Mouth

STONE, EDWARD C.

MA —BOSTON UNIVERSITY, Mugar Memorial Library, Special Collections Dept, 771 Commonwealth Ave, Boston, 02215. Howard B Gotlieb, Dir
Holdings: // Mss
Notes: Correspondence.

STONE, HARLAN FISKE

MA —JONES LIBRARY, 43 Amity St, Amherst, 01002. Daniel J Lombardo, Cur of Special Collections
Holdings: Cat Pix Mss 16mm Films
Notes: Unpublished guide available.

STONE, IRVING, 1903-

CA —AZUSA PACIFIC COLLEGE, Marshburn Memorial Library, Citrus & Alosta, Azusa, 91702. Edward Peterman, Librn
Holdings: Vols (331) // Uncat
Notes: The Irving Stone Collection of Lincolniana. Books used by Irving Stone in the preparation of his bestselling novel *Love is Eternal* (Lincoln). The books are signed by Stone; many contain his editorial comments. Also, his collection for *Those Who Love* (John and Abigail Adams). No photocopying.
CA —FRANCIS BACON LIBRARY, 655 N Dartmouth Ave, Claremont, 91711. Elizabeth S Wrigley, Dir
Holdings: Mss Pix
Notes: Arensberg's miscellaneous correspondence with American literary figures (1920's-50's) including Bruce Bliven, Catherine Drinker Bowen, Kay Boyle, Witter Bynner, Edwin Corle, Helen A Keller, Lysander Kemp, Kenneth Macgowan, John Macy, Henry Miller, Lewis Mumford, Clifford Odets, Kenneth Patchen, Irving Stone, and William Carlos Williams.
CA —UNIVERSITY OF CALIFORNIA, LOS ANGELES, Research Library, Dept of

STONE, IRVING, 1903- (cont.)

Special Collections, 405 Hilgard Ave, Los Angeles, 90024. Edward Shreeves, Chairman, Bibliographers Group; David S Zeidberg, Head
Holdings: Mss
Notes: 113 linear feet of mss, correspondence, and papers. Mr Stone's permission is required to consult this material.

STONE, LUCY, 1818-1893

DC —LIBRARY OF CONGRESS, Manuscript Division, Washington, 20540. John C Broderick, Chief
Notes: Susan B Anthony's papers in the Manuscript Division incl scrapbooks, correspondence, speeches, and related material. Diaries from the years 1865-1906 contain brief comments regarding her lecture tours on behalf of woman suffrage and referrences to such associates as Amelia Bloomer, Lucretia Mott, and Lucy Stone.
MA —RADCLIFFE COLLEGE, Arthur & Elizabeth Schlesinger Library on the History of Women in America, 3 James St, Cambridge, 02138. Patricia Miller King, Dir; Eva Moseley, Cur of Mss
Holdings: Cat Mss
Notes: Personal papers and mss.

STONE, NORMAN

IL —WHEATON COLLEGE, Buswell Memorial Library, Wheaton, 60187. Paul Snezek, Library Dir
Holdings: Mss
Notes: A collection of over 200 films and 30 sound recordings. *Related Topics:* BBC.

STONE, PHILOSOPHERS' see Alchemy

STONE, WILBUR MACEY

NC —UNIVERSITY OF NORTH CAROLINA, CHARLOTTE, J Murrey Atkins Library, UNCC Station, Charlotte, 28223. Robert F Brabham Jr, Special Collections Librn
Holdings: Vols 500 Cat Mss
Notes: Principally American and English. Strength of the collection is US, 1800-1850. Incl 200 vols from the collection of Elizabeth Botteme Lewis. Also incl first editions of Andrew Lang's fairy books, several series of books for boys (early 20th century), and 1960s comic books. Also incl small collection of papers of and ephemera collected by Wilbur Macey Stone, collector and writer about historical children's books.

STONE CARVING see Sculpture

STONEWARE see Pottery

STONEWORK, DECORATIVE see Sculpture

STONG, PHILIP DUFFIELD

IA —DRAKE UNIVERSITY, Cowles Library, 28 St & University Ave, Des Moines, 50311.
Notes: 1200 pieces of correspondence of the Iowa novelist Philip Duffield Stong (1899-1957), mostly to and from his mother.

STONY INDIANS see Assiniboin Indians

STOPES, MARIE CHARLOTTE CARMICHAEL, 1880-1958

CA —UNIVERSITY OF CALIFORNIA, SANTA BARBARA, Library, Dept of Special Collections, Santa Barbara, 93106. Christian F Brun, Head
Holdings: Vols 1550 Cat Mss
Notes: The Marie Stopes Collection.
NY —STATE UNIVERSITY OF NEW YORK, STONY BROOK, Melville Library, Dept of Special Collections, Stony Brook, 11794. Evert Volkersz, Head
Holdings: Cat Mss Maps Pix

STOPPARD, TOM

CA —SAN DIEGO STATE UNIVERSITY, Malcolm A Love Library, 5300 Campanile Dr, San Diego, 92182. D Dickinson, Univ Librn; Don L Bosseau, Dir
Notes: Collected works in first edition of certain prominent authors, as H G Wells, Somerset Maugham, William Dean Howells, Gertrude Atherton, Tom Stoppard, James Clavell, G A Henty, Henry Raup Wagner.

STORAGE, OPTICAL see Optical Storage

STORAGE DEVICES, COMPUTER see Computer Storage Devices

STORAGE ELEMENTS (CALCULATING MACHINES) see Magnetic Memory (Electronic Computers)

STORES, COOPERATIVE see Cooperative Societies

STORES, DEPARTMENT see Department Stores

STORM, THEODOR, 1817-1888

IN —INDIANA UNIVERSITY, Lilly Library, Seventh St, Bloomington, 47405. William R Cagle, Librn
Holdings: Vols 250 // Cat Mss
Notes: First editions, critical works, etc. Also, a small collection of correspondence and articles pertaining to Theodor Storm collected by Professor Elmer Otto Wooley, 1883-1964.

STORM AND STRESS see Sturm und Drang Movement

STORM PUBLISHERS

NY —STATE UNIVERSITY OF NEW YORK AT ALBANY, Library, Special Collections Dept, 1400 Washington Ave, Albany, 12222. Marion P Munzer, Coordr
Notes: Correspondence with authors; mss; reviews and publicity of works published by Storm Publishers (5.4 linear feet). Part of the Library's German Exile Collection. *See also* entry under Publishers and Publishing

STORMS

HI —INTERNATIONAL TSUNAMI INFORMATION CENTER, PO Box 50027, Honolulu, 96850. Bonnie Dong, Librn
Notes: Large collection on tsunamis, their causes, oceanographic organization and mareographic records, forecasting, mapping, etc.
IL —CHICAGO HISTORICAL SOCIETY, Library, Clark St at North Ave, Chicago, 60614. Robert L Brubaker, Librn
Holdings: Cat
Notes: The J Norman Jensen Collection of Lake and River Disasters, 1679-1947. 8500 card entries.

STORY (MAGAZINE)

NJ —PRINCETON UNIVERSITY, Library, Manuscript Collection, Nassau St, Princeton, 08540. Jean F Preston, Cur
Holdings: Mss
Notes: The Whit Burnett Collection, which deals in large part with *Story: The Magazine of the Short Story*, fills 163 boxes and 9 cartons. See *Princeton University Library Chronicle*, v 27, p 107-12. Unpublished checklist available.

STORYTELLING

IN —INDIANAPOLIS-MARION COUNTY PUBLIC LIBRARY, Riley Room for Young People, PO Box 211, Indianapolis, 46206. Margaret Barks, Head
Holdings: Vols 1110 Cat
Notes: The Harding Memorial Collection. This is a resource collection of folk and fairy tales as well as other suitable materials for telling.
MN —COLLEGE OF SAINT CATHERINE, Library, 2004 Randolph Ave, Saint Paul, 55105. Sister Elizabeth Delmore, Library Dir
Holdings: Vols 2100 Cat Mss Pix Phonorecords Audiotapes
Budget: $500
Notes: The Ruth Sawyer Collection. Also personal letters, medals.
NY —CHILDREN'S BOOK COUNCIL, Library, 67 Irving Place, New York, 10003.
Holdings: Vols (750) Cat
Notes: Besides award-winning books, the Children's Book Council maintains a noncirculating examination collection of children's books published by CBC members during the past year, adding books of the current year as they are published. Collection also incl critical and historical studies of children's books; bibliographies, selection aids and other reference books; biographies of authors and illustrators; facsimile editions and catalogs of collections and exhibitions; and books about publishing, writing, and storytelling. There is an author/ title card catalog and a separate illustrator card catalog for this collection. No photocopying.
OH —CLEVELAND PUBLIC LIBRARY, Children's Literature Dept, 325 Superior Ave, Cleveland, 44114. Ruth M Hadlow, Head
Notes: Department has a general collection with special attention to the demands of adults working with children.

STOTT, RAYMOND TOOLE

CA —UNIVERSITY OF CALIFORNIA, SANTA BARBARA, Library, Dept of Special Collections, Santa Barbara, 93106. Christian F Brun, Head
Notes: Most comprehensive Maugham collection on the west coast. Assembled and donated by Raymond Toole Stott, Maugham's official bibliographer and friend. Incl nearly all early rare books, first editions, unusual variants, and a series of letters from Maugham to Stott.

STOUGHTON, ARTHUR A.

MB —UNIVERSITY OF MANITOBA, Elizabeth Dafoe Library, Archives and Special Collections Dept, Winnipeg, R3T 2N2, Can. Richard E Bennett, Dept Head; Corrado A Santoro, Reference Archivist
Notes: A collection of papers of and about Prof Arthur A Stoughton, founder of the Dept of Architecture at the University of Manitoba, and of his wife. Incl are 45 letters and a unpublished biography.

STOUT, REX

KS —TOPEKA PUBLIC LIBRARY, Special Collections & Local History Dept, 1515 W Tenth, Topeka, 66604. Warren Taylor, Librn
Notes: Rex Stout materials; Charles M Sheldon materials; materials published in Topeka.
MA —BOSTON COLLEGE LIBRARIES, Chestnut Hill, 02167.
Holdings: Vols 2400 Mss
Notes: The library and personal papers of Rex Stout, 1886-1975, creator of the Nero Wolfe detective stories. Mss incl a number of adaptations for radio and television; correspondence covers Stout's years as President of the Authors' Guild, also as Chairman of the Writers' War Board. For reference use only by arrangement with librarian. Incl 125 literary mss; 21 cubic ft correspondence.

STOUT, SAMUEL HOLLINGSWORTH

TX —UNIVERSITY OF TEXAS LIBRARIES, General Libraries, Barker Texas History Center, PO Box P, Austin, 78712. Don Carleton, Dir

STOWE, CALVIN ELLIS, 1802-1886

CT —STOWE-DAY LIBRARY, 77 Forest St, Hartford, 06105. Diana J Royce, Librn
Holdings: Vols (15,000) Cat Mss Pix
Notes: 150,000 cataloged mss and

STOWE, CALVIN ELLIS, 1802-1886 (cont.)

publications concerning architecture, decorative arts, history and literature of the period 1840-1900, with emphasis on Nook Farm, Mark Twain, Harriet Beecher Stowe, Calvin E Stowe, Charles Dudley Warner, William Hooker Gillette, Isabella Beecher Hooker. Incl 5000 pictures.
ME —BOWDOIN COLLEGE, Library, Brunswick, 04011. Dianne M Gutscher, Cur of Special Collections
Holdings: Vols Cat Mss
Notes: The Stowe Collection consists of a small number of items, primarily letters, of Calvin and Harriet Stowe, as well as a collection of volumes by Harriet, incl first editions of most of her works.

STOWE, HARRIET ELIZABETH BEECHER, 1811-1896

CT —STOWE-DAY LIBRARY, 77 Forest St, Hartford, 06105. Diana J Royce, Librn
Holdings: Vols (15,000) Cat Mss Pix
Notes: 150,000 cataloged mss and publications concerning architecture, decorative arts, history and literature of the period 1840-1900, with emphasis on Nook Farm, Mark Twain, Harriet Beecher Stowe, Calvin E Stowe, Charles Dudley Warner, William Hooker Gillette, Isabella Beecher Hooker. Incl 5000 pictures.
ME —BOWDOIN COLLEGE, Library, Brunswick, 04011. Dianne M Gutscher, Cur of Special Collections
Holdings: Vols Cat Mss
Notes: The Stowe Collection consists of a small number of items, primarily letters, of Calvin and Harriet Stowe, as well as a collection of volumes by Harriet, incl first editions of most of her works.
MA —RADCLIFFE COLLEGE, Arthur & Elizabeth Schlesinger Library on the History of Women in America, 3 James St, Cambridge, 02138. Patricia Miller King, Dir; Eva Moseley, Cur of Mss
Holdings: Cat Mss
Notes: Personal papers and mss.
RI —PROVIDENCE PUBLIC LIBRARY, 150 Empire St, Providence, 02903. Lance J Bauer, Special Collections Librn
Holdings: Vols 5000 Cat Mss Maps Pix
Notes: The Harris Collection on the American Civil War and Slavery. Incl 18th and 19th century books, rare pamphlets, and periodicals concerning slavery and the slave trade, and origins, progress and results of the Civil War; also regimental histories; military and naval tactics; personal narratives; women's accounts of the Civil War; works on abolition; sheet music; Union and Confederate broadside ballads; Confederate imprints; *The Liberator* from 1843 through the Civil War; and over 85 editions of *Uncle Tom's Cabin* in 14 languages. Excellent primary and secondary sources for the study of the Civil War and slavery. Material must be used in-house. Photocopying when condition of material allows.
VA —UNIVERSITY OF VIRGINIA, Alderman Library, Clifton Waller Barrett Collection, Charlottesville, 22901. Joan St C Crane, Cur of American Literature Collections
Holdings: Vols 125 Cat Mss
Notes: 150 letters and manuscripts.
WA —UNIVERSITY OF WASHINGTON LIBRARIES, Suzzallo Library, Special Collections Division, Rare Book Collection, FM-25, Seattle, 98195. Gary Menges, Coordinator for Special Collections
Notes: Printing history, including early printed books and modern fine printing; book arts, including papermaking, decorated papers, bookbinding, book design, and artist's books; American literature, 19th century includes: Stephen Crane, Ralph Waldo Emerson, Nathaniel Hawthorne, Henry James, Henry Wadsworth Longfellow, Herman Melville, Frank Norris, Harriet Beecher Stowe and Walt Whitman and 20th century includes: Theodore Roethke; illustrated books, including emblem books,

historical children's illustration, books illustrated with prints, and artist's books; costume history; voyages and travels; preservation of library materials.
WI —UNIVERSITY OF WISCONSIN, MADISON, Memorial Library, British & American Language & Literature Collection, 728 State St, Madison, 53706. Yvonne Schofer, Bibliographer
Holdings: Vols 2200 Mss Microforms Documents Periodicals
Notes: A collection of primary and secondary materials for nine major American women writers: Anne Bradstreet; Louisa May Alcott, Emily Dickinson, Kate Chopin, Mary Williams Freeman, Margaret Fuller, Sarah Orne Jewett, Charlotte Perkins Gilman, Harriet Beecher Stowe. Primary materials also collected for a list of less well known authors together with manuscripts and archives of letters of special research interest. Variety of holdings: fiction, poetry, drama, biography and autobiography, letters, memoirs, diaries, travel, domestic economy and other kinds of writings by women mostly of the 19th century. Held in Dept of Rare Books and Special Collections.

STRACHEY, GILES LYTTON

CT —LEE ASH, (personal collection), 66 Humiston Dr, Bethany, 06525.
Holdings: Mss Maps Pix
Notes: Strong collection. Incl some mss.
NY —HOFSTRA UNIVERSITY, Library, 1000 Fulton Ave, Hempstead, 11550. Charles R Andrews, Dean of Library Services

STRAINS AND STRESSES

CA —UNIVERSITY OF CALIFORNIA, LOS ANGELES, Engineering & Mathematical Sciences Library, 405 Hilgard, Los Angeles, 90024. Rosalee I Wright, Librn
Holdings: Vols (180,000) Cat Microforms
See also entry under Engineering
IL —CHICAGO BRIDGE & IRON CO, Technical Library, 800 Jorie Blvd, Oak Brook, 60521. Susan Beatty, Librn
Holdings: Vols (7500) Cat
Budget: ($39,500)
KY —UNIVERSITY OF KENTUCKY, Robert E Shaver Library of Engineering, 355 Anderson Hall, Lexington, 40506. Russell H Powell, Engineering Librn
Holdings: Vols (48,000) Cat Microforms
MN —MTS SYSTEMS CORP, Information Services, PO Box 24012, Minneapolis, 55424. Kathleen Werner, Technical Librn
Holdings: Cat Mss Pix Slides Phonorecords Audiotapes Videotapes 16mm Films Microforms
Notes: Material testing machines. Incl 2000 ms reports, 10,000 pictures, 6000 slides.
OH —PREFORMED LINE PRODUCTS CO, Research & Engineering Library, 660 Beta Drive, Mayfield Village, (Mailing add: PO Box 91129, Cleveland, 44101). Edwina T Barron, Librn
Holdings: Vols (11,500) Cat Mss Microfiche Pix VF
Budget: ($30,500)
Notes: Library covering research and engineering fields emphasizing this subject. Aerodynamic characteristics and electrical characteristics of power cables, communication cables (including fiber optics), cable support systems, as well as associated fittings and hardware; in service behavior of manufactured products and materials as it relates to its static and dynamic forces and environmental conditions; oceanographic cable fittings and terminations.
PA —ENSANIAN PHYSICOCHEMICAL INSTITUTE, Electrotopography Library, PO Box 98, Eldred, 16731. Elisabeth Anahid Ensanian, Chief Librn
Holdings: Cat Maps Slides
Budget: ($45,000)
Notes: Electrotopography is a new science (the Institute has pioneered the field and has coined the terms "electrotopograph" and "electrotopography") concerned with the mapping of electrical fields associated with

metals, alloys, semiconductors, and living organisms. These fields may be natural and/ or induced, and are converted into mappings which exhibit certain systems characteristics for both normal and stress states.

STRAND, PAUL

AZ —UNIVERSITY OF ARIZONA, Center for Creative Photography, 843 E University Blvd, Tucson, 85721. James Enyeart, Dir; Terence Pitts, Cur and Librn
Notes: Center has significant collections consisting of more than 25 photographs plus other archival material such as negatives, contact sheets, work prints, correspondence, financial records, diaries, project files, etc. Inventories of the collections are available to researchers. Published guides available for some collections.

STRANG, GERALD V.

CA —CALIFORNIA STATE UNIVERSITY, LONG BEACH, Library, Dept of Special Collections & Archives, 1250 Bellflower Blvd, Long Beach, 90840. John Ahouse, Special Collections Librn
Holdings: Mss Phonorecords
Notes: Almost all of the papers, recordings, etc, published and unpublished, of Gerald V Strang.

STRANG, SAMUEL A.

SC —COLLEGE OF CHARLESTON LIBRARY, Special Collections Dept, Charleston, 29401.
Notes: Papers, 1844.

STRANGER, JOYCE

MA —BOSTON UNIVERSITY, Mugar Memorial Library, Special Collections Dept, 771 Commonwealth Ave, Boston, 02215. Howard B Gotlieb, Dir
Holdings: Cat Mss
Notes: Mss, correspondence, etc collected in depth; incl publications by or about.

STRATEGY (MILITARY)

NM —UNIVERSITY OF CALIFORNIA, Los Alamos National Laboratory, Libraries, PO Box 1663, MSP 362, Los Alamos, 87545. J Arthur Freed, Head Librn
Holdings: Vols (800,000) Cat Films Microforms
Budget: ($700,000)
Notes: Incl 500,000 classified and unclassified reports. There are 25 branch libraries and a central collection. The Medical Library contains about 40,000 vols in the areas of biomedical research.
OK —US ARMY FIELD ARTILLERY SCHOOL LIBRARY, Morris Swett Library, Snow Hall, Fort Sill, 73503. Lester L Miller Jr, Chief Librn
Notes: Field artillery; artillery; ordnance; military history; military science; weapons and weapons systems; ammunition; ballistics; missiles; Field Artillery unit histories; military periodicals analytical index file (VF). Incl US and foreign artillery; survey data; photographs on army subjects.
PA —US ARMY WAR COLLEGE LIBRARY, Carlisle Barracks, 17013. Barbara E Stevens, Dir
Holdings: Vols (125,000) Cat Maps Microforms Audiotapes
Budget: ($251,000)
Notes: Physical access to the collection is limited. Individual items available on interlibrary loan. Older historical material is in the US Army Military History Institute, Carlisle Barracks, Pennsylvania, 17013.
RI —US NAVAL WAR COLLEGE, Historical Collection & Museum, Newport, 02841. Anthony S Nicolosi, Dir; Evelyn Cherpak, Cur
Holdings: Mss
Notes: Collections incl over 200,000 separate pieces; chiefly papers of naval officers and records of organizations associated with the US Navy, the Naval War College, the college's major study areas, and

STRATEGY (MILITARY) (cont.)

the Navy in the Narragansett Bay region;
oral history collection; Naval War College
Archives, 1884-present; records of
conferences held at the College; newspaper
collections treating with naval themes and
military conflicts.

RI —BROWN UNIVERSITY, John Hay
Library, Anne S K Brown Military
Collection, 20 Prospect St, Providence,
02912. Richard B Harrington, Cur
Holdings: Vols (40,000) Cat Mss Pix
Notes: The Anne S K Brown Military
Collection has been formed over the past
forty or more years by Mrs John Nicholas
Brown, now of Newport, and contains
approximately 40,000 volumes and 60,000
prints, drawings and water-colours as well as
a number of oil paintings and about 5000
miniature model soldiers. At its beginning
(and still today) the emphasis or focus of this
collection has been upon the history of - and
the accurate contemporary illustration of -
military and naval uniforms of all nations
from the early XVII century to the present.
In the course of time, however, the
collection has come to incl also a vast and
related amount of material on military and
naval history, military and naval arts and
tactics, wars, campaigns, ceremonies,
biography, portraits and caricatures of this
and earlier periods. It has been probably the
largest private collection of such a nature
inthe world, and it contains much ms and
graphic documentation which is unique. It
has been useful to numerous scholars and
historians, editors, film-makers and
publishers for research and for illustrative
material and has also contributed to many
museum exhibitions. In 1982 the entire
collection, with its complete card-catalogue
and subject index, has been presented to
Brown University, where it is located in the
John Hay Library. Special requests are taken
care of by phone, mail and appointments
with the curator.

RI —PROVIDENCE PUBLIC LIBRARY, 150
Empire St, Providence, 02903. Lance J
Bauer, Special Collections Librn
Notes: The Daniel Berkeley Updike
Autograph Collection of 800 ms letters and
historical documents, primarily New
England, from late 17th to mid-19th century
with emphasis on Rhode Island politics;
American Revolution; French military
figures; naval heroes of the Revolution,
Tripolitan War and War of 1812; Civil War
figures and US presidents. Illustrious
personages represented incl: Henry David
Thoreau, Daniel Webster, John Hay,
Marquis de Lafayette, Henry Wadsworth
Longfellow, and other notables. Material
must be used in-house. Limited
photocopying for educational purposes only.

STRATEMEYER, EDWARD

MS —UNIVERSITY OF SOUTHERN
MISSISSIPPI, William David McCain
Graduate Library, Box 5148, Southern Sta,
Hattiesburg, 39406.
Holdings: Vols 132
Notes: The Lena Y de Grummond
Collection of Children's Literature. Incl the
Robert L Dartt Collection of over 1800
books for boys from the late 19th and early
20th centuries. Extensive Henty (over 550
vols), Alger, Brereton, Castlemon, Fenn,
Kingston, Optic, and Stratemeyer holdings.
Catalog in progress.

STRATFORD FESTIVAL, ONTARIO

†ON —METROPOLITAN TORONTO
LIBRARY, Theatre Dept, Toronto, M4W
2G8, Can.
Notes: Papers of Jack Karr, Canadian film
and theatre critic, and public relations
director for Stratford Festival and O'Keefe
Centre.

STRATFORD-UPON-AVON FESTIVAL

NY —NEW YORK PUBLIC LIBRARY,
Performing Arts Research Center, Billy Rose
Theatre Collection, 111 Amsterdam Ave,
New York, 10023. Dorothy L Swerdlove,
Cur
Holdings: Cat
See also entry under Theatre - History.

AB —UNIVERSITY OF CALGARY, Library,
Calgary, T2N 1N4, Can. Apollonia Steele,
Special Collections Librn
Holdings: Cat Mss Pix
Notes: Incl the books and papers of W
Bridges Adams, Shakespearian actor,
director and historian. Mr Bridges Adams
was Director of the Stratford-upon-Avon
Festival from 1919 to 1934 and was the
author of two major works, The British
Theatre and The Irresistible Theatre.
Extensive correspondence with well-known
literary and musical figures.

STRATTON-PORTER, GENE

IN —WABASH CARNEGIE PUBLIC
LIBRARY, 188 W Hill St, Wabash, 46992.
Linda Robertson, Librn
Holdings: Vols 43 Cat Pix
Notes: Incl nearly a full set of first editions,
plus many newspaper and magazine clippings
and nature photos and descriptions by the
author. Members of author's family are
buried in this country and genealogical
information can be obtained from cemetery
records.

STRAUS, RALPH, 1882-1950

ON —MCMASTER UNIVERSITY, Mills
Memorial Library, Div of Archives &
Research Collections, Hamilton, L8S 4L6,
Can. G R Hill, Univ Librn
Holdings: // Mss
Notes: Mss of "Suicide by Order,"
"Nathaniel Winkle," "This Wretched Book,"
"Society," and "A Sonnet," correspondence
with publishers, and news clippings.

STRAUSS, FRANCES

MA —BOSTON UNIVERSITY, Mugar
Memorial Library, Special Collections Dept,
771 Commonwealth Ave, Boston, 02215.
Howard B Gotlieb, Dir
Holdings: Mss

STRAUSS, LEWIS LICHTENSTEIN

IA —HERBERT HOOVER PRESIDENTIAL
LIBRARY, West Branch, 52358. Dale C
Mayer, Archivist
Notes: Papers.

STRAVINSKY, IGOR

DC —LIBRARY OF CONGRESS, Music
Division, Washington, 20540.
Notes: Mss in Koussevitzky Archives.

NY —NEW YORK PUBLIC LIBRARY, Music
Div, 111 Amsterdam Ave, New York,
10023. Frank C Campbell, Chief

STRAW FIDDLE see Xylophone

STRAW VOTES see Public Opinion Polls

STREAM CHANNELIZATION

MO —US FISH & WILDLIFE SERVICE,
Columbia National Fisheries Research
Laboratory, Rte One, Columbia, 65201. Axie
Hindman, Librn
Holdings: Vols (2000) Cat Microforms
Budget: ($7000)
Notes: Pesticides in aquatic biota; fisheries
research; fresh-water ecology. Also incl
collection in water pollution, acid rain,
aquatic invertebrets, environment and 10,000
reprints.

STREAM ECOLOGY

MO —US FISH & WILDLIFE SERVICE,
Columbia National Fisheries Research
Laboratory, Rte One, Columbia, 65201. Axie
Hindman, Librn
Holdings: Vols (2000) Cat Microforms
Budget: ($7000)
Notes: Pesticides in aquatic biota; fisheries
research; fresh-water ecology. Also incl
collection in water pollution, acid rain,
aquatic invertebrets, environment and 10,000
reprints.

STREAM POLLUTION see
Water—Pollution and Control

STREAMLINING see Aerodynamics

STREET AND SMITH COLLECTION

†NY —SYRACUSE UNIVERSITY
LIBRARIES, E S Bird Library, George
Arents Research Library, Rm 600, Syracuse,
13210. Mr Sidney Huttner, Librn
Notes: Radio Scripts, especially The Shadow
and Nick Carter. Street and Smith
Collection.

STREET CARS see Electric
Railroads—Cars

STREET CRIES

IN —INDIANA UNIVERSITY, Lilly Library,
Seventh St, Bloomington, 47405. William R
Cagle, Librn
Holdings: Vols 335 // Cat Mss Pix
Notes: Street cries, chiefly from the Virginia
Warren Collection. Limited photocopying.

STREET RAILROADS

CA —SAN DIEGO PUBLIC LIBRARY, Social
Sciences Section, 820 E St, San Diego,
92101. Margaret E Queen, Supvr
Budget: ($36,000)
Notes: Good general collection with
emphasis on railroads of California. Good
materials on street railways and cable cars of
western cities.

CA —BAY AREA ELECTRIC RAILROAD
ASSOCIATION, California Railway
Museum, Star Rte 283, Box 150, Suisun
City, 94585. Vernon J Sappers, Librn
Holdings: Vols (5000) Uncat Maps Pix
Slides 16mm Films
Notes: Technical journals and publications
pertaining to steam and electric railroads. In
addition, there are ten cabinets of files of the
following railroad companies: Key System,
Southern Pacific and Associated Companies,
Western Pacific Railroad, Sacramento
Northern Railroad, Pacific Electric Railway,
Northern Electric Railway, Oakland Antioch
& Eastern Railway. These files deal with the
history of each railroad.

CT —CONNECTICUT ELECTRIC
RAILWAY ASSOCIATION, INC, Southern
New England, PO Box 360, East Windsor,
06088. William E Wood, Dir of Museum
Holdings: Vols 1500 Uncat Mss Maps Pix
Notes: Some 1500 items. The collection can
be opened only on application.

IL —CHICAGO TRANSIT AUTHORITY,
Anthon Memorial Library, Merchandise
Mart Plaza, PO Box 3555, Chicago, 60654.
Joseph Benson, Dir
Holdings: Vols (10,000) Cat Maps Slides
Microforms
Budget: ($27,200)
Notes: Urban transportation. Use of
collection by appointment with Librarian.

MD —BALTIMORE STREETCAR
MUSEUM, Transit Research Center, 1901
Falls Rd, PO Box 7184, Baltimore, 21218.
George F Nixon, Cur
Holdings: Cat Mss Pix Slides 16mm Films
Notes: Transit Research Center is devoted to
the collection of memorabilia, photos,
drawings, printed matter, etc pertinent to
public rail transportation in Baltimore and
Maryland. Incl streetcar systems, interurban
lines, and main line railroads in the area.
Also incl bus history. Incl materials donated
by The Baltimore Transit
Co, United Railways and Electric Co, as well
as private collections.

MA —HARVARD UNIVERSITY, Baker
Library of the Graduate School of Business
Administration, Kress Library of Business
and Economics, Soldiers Field, Boston,
02163. Ruth E Rogers, Cur
Notes: An extensive collection. Historical
emphasis on railroads and canals.

STREET RAILROADS (cont.)

MN —MINNESOTA HISTORICAL
SOCIETY LIBRARY, 690 Cedar St, Saint
Paul, 55101. Patricia C Harpole, Chief of
Reference Library; Bonnie G Wilson, Head
of Special Libraries

MO —NATIONAL MUSEUM OF
TRANSPORT, Reference Library, 3105
Barrett Station Rd, Saint Louis, 63122. John
P Roberts, Secretary
Holdings: Vols (10,000) Cat Mss Maps Pix
Slides

NY —ELECTRIC RAILROADERS
ASSOCIATION, Frank J Sprague Memorial
Library, 89 E 42nd St, New York, 10018.
Hugh A Dunne, First VP
Notes: Private library. Incl all forms of
railroads operated by electricity. Forms of
electric railroads included: street railways,
subways & elevated lines, high-speed
interurbans, suburban commuter lines,
electrified trunk lines, monorails, mountain
climbing inclines, etc. Also railroad
timetables.

OR —OREGON ELECTRIC RAILWAY
HISTORICAL SOCIETY, Library, HCR 71,
Box 1318, Forest Grove, 97116. Paul V
Class, Cur
Holdings: Vols (125) Uncat Pix Slides 16mm
Films

PA —ERIE COUNTY HISTORICAL
SOCIETY LIBRARY, 417 State St, Erie,
16501. Helen Andrews, Librn
Notes: Original research materials in 16 legal
size drawers, including Pennsylvania
Population Company papers, Old Erie
Academy papers, Erie Street railway papers,
Harry Burleigh (black singer & composer)
transcripts and research papers; also four
letter size drawers with old account books.

WA —WESTERN WASHINGTON
UNIVERSITY, Center for Pacific Northwest
Studies, High St, Bellingham, 98225. James
W Scott, Dir
Holdings: Vols 400 // Cat Mss
Notes: Puget Sound Power and Light
Company Records Collection consists of the
complete company records of 41 former
companies, which were bought out,
amalgamated with or in other ways came
under the control of Puget Sound Power and
Light Company. Most of the companies were
concerned with transportation or the
production of power--both gas and
electricity. Among the companies
represented are street railways, interurban
railways, traction companies and gas
companies, all of which operated in the
region west of the Cascades, especially in the
Puget Sound area but with a few as far south
as Vancouver, Washington. The collection
has been placed in the Center for Pacific
Northwest Studies by the Puget Sound
Power and Light Company on a permanent
loan basis.

STREET RAILROADS—CARS see
Electric Railroads—Cars; Trolley Cars

STREET TRAFFIC see Traffic Engineering

STREET TRAFFIC REGULATIONS see
Traffic Regulations

STREETCARS   see Electric
Railroads—Cars; Trolley Cars

STREETER, THOMAS W.

MA —AMERICAN ANTIQUARIAN
SOCIETY LIBRARY, 185 Salisbury St,
Worcester, 01609. Marcus A McCorison,
Dir & Librn
Notes: Extensive bibliographic notes
concerning Thomas W Streeter's collection
of Americana.

STRENGTH OF MATERIALS

CA —UNIVERSITY OF CALIFORNIA, LOS
ANGELES, Engineering & Mathematical
Sciences Library, 405 Hilgard, Los Angeles,
90024. Rosalee I Wright, Librn
Holdings: Vols (180,000) Cat Microforms
See also entry under Engineering

CA —CALIFORNIA DEPT OF
TRANSPORTATION, Transportation
Library, 5900 Folsom Blvd, PO Box 19128,
Sacramento, 95819. Eva Caro, Librn
Holdings: Vols (10,000) Cat Mss Maps Pix
Slides Phonorecords Audiotapes Videotapes
16mm Films Filmstrips Microforms

PA —FRANKLIN INSTITUTE LIBRARY, 20
& The Parkway, Philadelphia, 19103.
Miriam Padusis, Dir; Charles Wilt, Readers
Servs Librn
Holdings: Vols (300,000) Cat Maps Pix
Microforms

TX —UNIVERSITY OF TEXAS LIBRARIES,
Richard W McKinney Engineering Library,
1.3 ECJ, Austin, 78712. Susan B Ardis,
Librn
Holdings: Vols (83,548) Cat Microforms

STRESSES see Strains and Stresses

STRIBLING, FRANCIS T., 1810-1874

KS —MENNINGER FOUNDATION,
Archives, 5600 W Sixth St, Box 829,
Topeka, 66601. Alice Brand, Librn; Mark
West, Archivist
Notes: 1 box, 1817-1868. Consists of letters
written to Stribling.

STRICKLAND, LILY

SC —CONVERSE COLLEGE, Gwathmey
Library, Spartanburg, 29301. Darlene E
Fawver, Music Librn
Notes: Incl 7,000 music book titles, 10,000
scores and 10,000 phonorecords; Lily
Strickland Collection (manuscripts, printed
music, memorabilia); Radiana Pazmor
Collection (personal correspondence with
Aaron Copland, Charles Ives, Darius
Milhaud, Maurice Ravel, Virgil Thomson
and others); autographed books, scores,
manuscripts, and facsimiles of former Deans
of the School of Music (R H Peters, Ernst
Bacon, Edwin Gerschefski) and such
notables as Henry Cowell and Carlisle Floyd.

STRINDBERG, JOHANN AUGUST

CA —UNIVERSITY OF CALIFORNIA,
BERKELEY, University Library,
Scandinavian Collections, Berkeley, 94720.
Helvi M Bessenyei, Librn
Holdings: Vols 20,000
Budget: $15,530
Notes: Research collections covering the full
range of Scandinavian languages and
literatures, with extensive periodical
holdings. Particular strengths are Old Norse
and Swedish. Moreover, special emphasis is
on the late 19th century Scandinavian
authors from Kierkegaard to Strinberg. The
language and literature collections are
supplemented by substantial resources in
related disciplines. Some rare book materials
are housed in the Bancroft Library.

MA —HARVARD UNIVERSITY LIBRARY,
Widener Library, Cambridge, 02138.
Holdings: Cat
Notes: See Distributable Union Catalog
(Harvard).

MN —UNIVERSITY OF MINNESOTA, O
Meredith Wilson Library, 309 19 Ave S,
Minneapolis, 55455. Austin J McLean,
Chief, Special Collections
Holdings: Vols 841 Uncat Pix
Notes: The life, work, and influences of
August Strindberg. First and later editions,
translations, critical works, and an extensive
collection of theater programs, periodical
articles and newspaper clippings of reviews
of his plays. Facsimiles of Strindberg's
manuscripts in the Swedish Royal Library. A
complete listing is available in the Division.

STRING ORCHESTRA MUSIC—COLLECTIONS

MI —DETROIT PUBLIC LIBRARY, Music &
Performing Arts Dept, 5201 Woodward,
Detroit, 48202. Agatha Pfeiffer Kalkanis,
Chief
Holdings: Cat
Notes: One of the oldest record collections

in a public library (established 1921).
Consists of ciruculating rental collection (all
LPs, 19,000) and reference and archive
collections (LPs and 78s, 6000). Emphasis is
on broad range of concert music in all
mediums and from all periods. Also Folk
music, literary, documentary recordings, and
instructional recordings. Main library
collection supplemented by independent
collections in 15 branch libraries and by a
collection in the Children's Library. No
tapes or taping facilities. No taping or other
copying permitted.

STRINGED INSTRUMENTS

DC —LIBRARY OF CONGRESS, Music
Division, Washington, 20540.
Holdings: Cat Mss Maps Pix Slides
Microforms
Notes: Incl the Whittall Foundation of
Stradivari instruments (3 violins, viola,
cello).

IL —NEWBERRY LIBRARY, 60 W Walton
St, Chicago, 60610. Diana Haskell, Cur of
Modern Mss
Holdings: Cat Mss Microforms
Notes: Incl the library of Count Pio Resse
and a portion of Alfred Cortot library.
Particularly strong in Italian theoretical
treatises, vocal music and music for fretted
instruments. Restricted use: noncirculating.

STRIP MINING

TN —TENNESSEE VALLEY AUTHORITY
(TVA), Technical Library, 400 W Summit
Hill Dr, E2 B7, Knoxville, 37902. Jesse C
Mills, Chief Librn
Holdings: Vols (106,900) Cat Mss Maps Pix
Audiotapes Microforms
Budget: ($2,025,000)
Notes: The Technical Library Headquarters
Staff (order, cataloging, information, and
administration) is located in Knoxville,
Tenn. In addition there are branch libraries
in Knoxville, Norris, and Chattanooga,
Tennessee, and Muscle Shoals, Alabama.

STROKE

KS —KANSAS NEUROLOGICAL
INSTITUTE, Menninger Professional
Library, 3107 W 21 St, Topeka, 66604.
Richard Gray, Librn

TX —AMERICAN HEART ASSOCIATION,
Library, 7320 Greenville Ave, Dallas, 75231.
Katie Trickey, Librn; Barbara Lightfoot, Info
Spec
Holdings: Vols (4000) Cat
Budget: ($20,000)

STRONG, ANNA LOUISE

GA —EMORY UNIVERSITY, Robert W
Woodruff Library, Atlanta, 30322. Herbert
Johnson, Dir
Holdings: Mss Pix Cat
Notes: The Philip J Jaffe Papers and books
about communism and the Communist Party
in the US, incl copies of rare magazines,
private mss, the papers of such controversial
figures as Anna Louise Strong, Agnes
Smedley, Norman Bethune and Koji
Ariyoshi, and documentation of the growth
of Chinese communism. 36 linear ft mss.

STRONG, ANNE HERVEY

MA —SIMMONS COLLEGE ARCHIVES,
300 The Fenway, Boston, 02115. Megan
Sniffin-Marinoff, College Archivist
Notes: Archives of the Simmons College
School of Public Health Nursing (later
reorganized into the School of Nursing)
cover the years 1902-1970. Important
correspondents in the collection incl M
Adelaide Nutting, Mary Beard, Isabel
Stewart, and Anne Hervey Strong, etc. Incl
Strong's records of activity with regard to
nursing education in the National
Organization for Public Health Nursing,
1918-22. 1000 linear feet in institution, incl
special collections nursing and photographs,
nursing.

STRONG, AUSTIN

NY —COLUMBIA UNIVERSITY
LIBRARIES, Rare Book & Manuscript

STRONG, AUSTIN (cont.)

Library, 801 Butler Library, 535 W 114 St, New York, 10027. Kenneth A Lohf, Librn
Holdings: Mss
Notes: Papers, mss, archives, etc. 3500 items. Restricted use.

STRONG, LEONARD ALFRED GEORGE

MI —UNIVERSITY OF MICHIGAN, Library, Dept of Rare Books & Special Collections, Ann Arbor, 48109. Robert J Starring, Head
Holdings: Cat Mss
BC —UNIVERSITY OF VICTORIA, McPherson Library, Victoria, V8W 3H5, Can.

STRONG, PHILIP GRANDIN, 1901-1971

NJ —PRINCETON UNIVERSITY, Library, Manuscript Collection, Nassau St, Princeton, 08540. Jean F Preston, Cur
Holdings: // Mss
Notes: Incl 17 boxes of papers. The collection includes material dating back to 1776.

STROZZI FAMILY

IL —NEWBERRY LIBRARY, 60 W Walton St, Chicago, 60610. Diana Haskell, Cur of Modern Mss
Holdings: Cat Mss
Notes: Collection of mss, largely literary in character. Incl writings of G B Strozzi, il vecchio, and G B Strozzi, il giovane. Primarily 17th century.

STRUCTURAL ENGINEERING see Strains and Stresses; Strength of Materials; Structures, Theory of

STRUCTURAL GEOLOGY see Geomorphology

STRUCTURAL MATERIALS see Building Materials

STRUCTURES, THEORY OF

CA —UNIVERSITY OF CALIFORNIA, LOS ANGELES, Engineering & Mathematical Sciences Library, 405 Hilgard, Los Angeles, 90024. Rosalee I Wright, Librn
Holdings: Vols (180,000) Cat Microforms
See also entry under Engineering
CA —COGSWELL COLLEGE, Library, 600 Stockton St, San Francisco, 94108. Judith Carson-Croes, Dir
Holdings: Vols (12,000) Cat
IL —CHICAGO BRIDGE & IRON CO, Technical Library, 800 Jorie Blvd, Oak Brook, 60521. Susan Beatty, Librn
Holdings: Vols (7500) Cat
Budget: ($39,500)
KY —UNIVERSITY OF KENTUCKY, Robert E Shaver Library of Engineering, 355 Anderson Hall, Lexington, 40506. Russell H Powell, Engineering Librn
Holdings: Vols (48,000) Cat Microforms
NY —EASTMAN KODAK COMPANY, Kodak Park Div, Engineering Library, Bldg 23, Rochester, 14650. Raymond Curtin, Librn
Holdings: Vols (14,000) Uncat Microforms
Notes: The library is not open to the public. Use of the library for reference purposes may be requested and appointments may be obtained through the librarian.
NC —DUKE UNIVERSITY, School of Engineering, Library, Durham, 27706. Eric J Smith, Librn
Holdings: Vols (72,000) Cat Microforms
Budget: ($110,000)
PA —FRANKLIN INSTITUTE LIBRARY, 20 & The Parkway, Philadelphia, 19103. Miriam Padusis, Dir; Charles Wilt, Readers Servs Librn
Holdings: Vols (300,000) Cat Maps Pix Microforms
PA —UNIVERSITY OF PENNSYLVANIA, Towne Scientific Library, 220 S 33 St, Philadelphia, 19104. Charles Meyers, Librn
Holdings: Vols (65,000) Cat

STRUIK, DIRK J.

MA —MASSACHUSETTS INSTITUTE OF TECHNOLOGY, Institute Archives, Special Collections, Cambridge, 02139.
Notes: Papers.

STRUVE, OTTO, 1897-1963

†CA —UNIVERSITY OF CALIFORNIA, SANTA CRUZ, Lick Observatory Archives, Santa Cruz, 95064.
Notes: Astronomer. His correspondence (1926-44).
NY —AMERICAN INSTITUTE OF PHYSICS, Center for the History of Physics, Niels Bohr Library, 335 E 45 St, New York, 10017. John Aubry, Librn
Notes: The Sources for History of Modern Astrophysics documents the history of 20th-century astrophysics. Incl some 400 hours of oral history interviews with astronomers, such as Bart Bok, S Chandrasekhar, Martin Schwarzschild, and A E Whitford. The project also organized and cataloged the papers of Henry Norris Russell, Frank Schlesinger, Otto Struve, Ejnar Hertzsprung, Harlow Shapley, Charles Young, Robert Atkinson, Seth Chandler, Theodore Dunham, Jr, and G C McVittie.

STRYK, LUCIEN

MA —BOSTON UNIVERSITY, Mugar Memorial Library, Special Collections Dept, 771 Commonwealth Ave, Boston, 02215. Howard B Gotlieb, Dir
Holdings: Cat Mss Pix
Notes: Mss, correspondence, etc collected in depth; incl publications by or about.

STRYKER, ROY

KY —UNIVERSITY OF LOUISVILLE, Ekstrom Library, Photographic Archives, Louisville, 40292. J C Anderson, Cur; David G Horvath, Asst Cur
Holdings: Vols (750,000) Cat Pix Slides
Budget: ($60,000)
Notes: Photographs in three broad areas: works of outstanding photographers; examples of major developments in the art and technology of photography; photographs important as sociological, historical, or behavioral documents. Actors and actresses, Louisville's Macauley Theatre. Standard Oil of New Jersey Collection, 85,000 pictures of oil industry's effect on life in the 20th century (1943-1950, directed by Roy Stryker); Stryker's collection from Farm Security Administration series on rural conditions, 1935-1942; Jones and Laughlin Steel Corp. Picture Library, by Stryker. Stryker manuscripts, 1934-1972. Caufield and Shook commercial photographs, Louisville area, 1920-1949. Jean Thomas "The Traipsin' Woman" photographs of Kentucky mountain folkways. Kate Matthews' (1870-1956) photographs incl prototypes for "Little Colonel" Series. Other collection described in unpublished brochure Print duplication service.

STUART, J. E. B. (JAMES EWELL BROWN), 1833-1864

VA —UNIVERSITY OF VIRGINIA, Alderman Library, Manuscripts Dept, Charlottesville, 22901. Edmund Berkeley Jr, Cur
Holdings: Cat Mss Maps Pix
Notes: About 1500 collections have material pertaining to the Civil War and particularly to the Army of Northern Virginia and campaigns and battles in Virginia. There are letters, diaries, reminiscences, maps, and pictorial material of Confederate soldiers and civilians, as well as papers of Robert E Lee, J E B Stuart, Thomas L Rosser, Jubal A Early, John Daniel Imboden, William "Extra Billy" Smith, Henry Alexander Wise, Eppa Hunton, and John S Mosby.

STUART, JESSE

IN —INDIANA STATE UNIVERSITY, Cunningham Memorial Library, Dept of Rare Books & Special Collections, Terre Haute, 47809. Lawrence J McCrank, Head
Holdings: Vols 50 Cat
Notes: First editions of almost all of Stuart's books. Most vols are autographed. Also incl biographies and criticisms.
KY —BOYD COUNTY PUBLIC LIBRARY, 1740 Central Ave, Ashland, 41101. Juliette Bryson, Dir
Holdings: Vols 264 Cat
Notes: Kentucky authors, with emphasis on books by and about Jesse Stuart.
KY —UNIVERSITY OF KENTUCKY, Margaret I King Library, Dept of Special Collections, Lexington, 40506. William Marshall, Head
Holdings: Vols 56 Cat Mss
Notes: First editions, etc.

STUART, REGINALD RAY

†CA —UNIVERSITY OF THE PACIFIC, Library, Stockton, 95211.
Notes: Papers.

STUART DE ROTHESAY, BARON CHARLES STUART, 1779-1845

CA —UNIVERSITY OF CALIFORNIA, LOS ANGELES, Research Library, Dept of Special Collections, 405 Hilgard Ave, Los Angeles, 90024. Edward Shreeves, Chairman, Bibliographers Group; David S Zeidberg, Head
Holdings: Maps
Notes: 11 linear feet of unprocessed papers; his collection of 530 continental maps.

STUD-BOOKS see Horses—Stud-Books

STUDEBAKER FAMILY AND PLANT

IN —SOUTH BEND PUBLIC LIBRARY, Local History Dept, 122 W Wayne, South Bend, 46624.
Holdings: Vols (5900) Cat Maps Pix Microforms
Notes: Indiana, with emphasis on St Joseph County and South Bend. Collection incl material on the Studebaker family and plant.

STUDENT EXCHANGE

CO —WESTERN INTERSTATE COMMISSION FOR HIGHER EDUCATION, Wiche Library, PO Drawer P, Boulder, 80302. Karon M Kelly, Dir Library Services
Holdings: Vols (10,000) Cat Microforms
Notes: Incl medical and nursing education, student exchange programs, minority involvement in education, management systems in higher education.

STUDENT GUIDANCE see Vocational Guidance

STUDENT LIFE AND CUSTOMS see Students

STUDENT MOVEMENT see Youth Movement

STUDENT NEWSPAPERS see Newspapers, Student

STUDENT RELOCATION (JAPANESE)

CA —HOOVER INSTITUTION ON WAR, REVOLUTION & PEACE, Stanford University, Stanford, 94305. Milorad M Drachkovitch, Archivist
Holdings: Mss
Notes: Correspondence, questionnaires, student education records, and other miscellaneous items pertaining to the National Japanese American Student Relocation Council, 1942-1946. 101 cartons and 17 drawers of index cards.

STUDENT STRIKES

CA —UNIVERSITY OF CALIFORNIA, LOS ANGELES, Research Library, Dept of Special Collections, 405 Hilgard Ave, Los Angeles, 90024. Edward Shreeves, Chairman, Bibliographers Group; David S Zeidberg, Head
Notes: 7 linear feet of correspondence, ephemera, and broadsides produced by US and European protest movements.

IL —NORTHWESTERN UNIVERSITY, Library, Special Collections Dept, 1937 Sheridan Rd, Evanston, 60201. R Russell Maylone, Cur
Holdings: Vols 1000 Cat
Notes: Very large collection of original journals from the 1960s and 1970s, mostly American and Canadian, but also several English and French. Also high school papers. Subjects incl left-wing politics, American Indian ecology, drug culture, anti-war and environmental issues. Women's collection of serial holdings largest in country. All hard copy with exception of some of the Women's collection.

MD —UNIVERSITY OF MARYLAND, BALTIMORE COUNTY, Albin O Kuhn Library and Gallery, 5401 Wilkens Ave, Baltimore, 21228. Ann Copeland, Special Collections Librn
Holdings: Vols 1000 // Uncat
Notes: The Hugh Davis Graham papers relate to Dr Graham's work as Co-Director of the Task Force on the History of Violence in America (for the National Commission on the Causes and Prevention of Violence). The Collection consists of materials dealing with all aspects of violence as well as movements specifically related to the 1960s ("Ban the Bomb," etc). The collection is topically arranged and available for research use.

MI —MICHIGAN STATE UNIVERSITY, Libraries, Special Collections Div, East Lansing, 48824. Jannette Fiore, Librn
Holdings: Vols (10,500) Cat Mss
Notes: Published and unpublished material generated by (1) American left and right, 1900, (2) the New Left, 1969-1970, and (3) current left, right, and alternate life-style groups. (Supported by appropriate secondary material in the Research Library). Also have in microform radical pamphlet literature from the Tamiment Library (New York University), the Right Wing Collection of the University of Iowa, et al.

OH —KENT STATE UNIVERSITY, University Archives, Kent, 44242. Stephen C Morton, University Archivist
Holdings: Cat Mss Maps Pix Microforms
Notes: The May 4, 1970 incident; 50 linear ft. Separate catalog. Partial description in Cleveland State Law Review, Winter, 1973.

WI —UNIVERSITY OF WISCONSIN, MADISON, Memorial Library, Rare Books Collection, 728 State St, Madison, 53706. Gretchen Lagana, Cur
Holdings: Uncat Pix Microforms
Notes: A collection of pamphlets, posters, and miscellaneous materials produced by students and other left-wing groups in France during the revolt of May-June 1968. Also included are books on the event and pictures taken by a UW student in Paris at the time. Collection partly described in UW Library News, vol 13 (Dec 1968), pp 1-8. Housed in the Dept of Rare Books and Special Collections.

ON —MCMASTER UNIVERSITY, Mills Memorial Library, Div of Archives & Research Collections, Hamilton, L8S 4L6, Can. G R Hill, Univ Librn
Holdings: Mss
Notes: Office files of the Combined Universities Campaign for Nuclear Disarmament (1959-1964) and its successor, The Student Union for Peace Action (1964-1967). Correspondence between branches and with others.

STUDENT UNION FOR PEACE ACTION

ON —MCMASTER UNIVERSITY, Mills Memorial Library, Div of Archives &

Research Collections, Hamilton, L8S 4L6, Can. G R Hill, Univ Librn
Holdings: Mss
Notes: Office files of the Combined Universities Campaign for Nuclear Disarmament (1959-1964) and its successor, The Student Union for Peace Action (1964-1967). Correspondence between branches and with others.

STUDENTS

CA —UNIVERSITY OF CALIFORNIA, LOS ANGELES, Research Library, Social Sciences Collection, 405 Hilgard Ave, Los Angeles, 90024. Edward Shreeves, Chairman, Bibliographers Group; Oscar L Sims, Social Sciences Bibliographer
Notes: A collection of over 200 underground newspapers on 26 reels of microfilm. Among the titles included are: The Tribe, The Berkeley Barb, New York Roach, Rat, and Win.

CA —UNIVERSITY OF CALIFORNIA, LOS ANGELES, Research Library, Western European Collection, Los Angeles, 90024. Edward Shreeves, Chairman, Bibliographers Group; Mary E Greco, Western European Bibliographer
Holdings: Mss Maps Pix Microforms
Budget: ($5000)
Notes: Early modern and modern France. Special strengths in intellectual and religious history of the seventeenth and eighteenth centuries. Jansenism in particular, and popular culture of the nineteenth and twentieth centuries. Good coverage.

CA —HOOVER INSTITUTION ON WAR, REVOLUTION & PEACE, Stanford University, Stanford, 94305. Milorad M Drachkovitch, Archivist
Holdings: Mss Pix
Notes: Records of the International Commission of the US National Student Association, a confederation of student bodies at American colleges and universities, incl correspondence, reports, memoranda, minutes of meetings, bulletins, circulars, questionnaires, notes, lists, financial records, printed matter, and photographs, 1946-1967, relating to the international activities of the association, such as delegation and scholarship exchanges with other nations, American representation at annual International Student Conferences, and relations with analogous student organizations abroad as well as to the effects of world politics on education. 313 ms boxes and 7 envelopes.

IL —NORTHWESTERN UNIVERSITY, Library, Special Collections Dept, 1937 Sheridan Rd, Evanston, 60201. R Russell Maylone, Cur
Holdings: Vols (14,000) Cat
Notes: Periodicals and pamphlets concerning many social and political movements in the 20th century, with emphasis on anarchism, struggles of the working class, women's rights, and student protest of the 1960s. Foreign material incl. An additional 10,000 pieces arranged by subject.

IA —AMERICAN COLLEGE TESTING PROGRAM, Library, Box 168, Iowa City, 52243. Lois Renter, Head Librn
Holdings: Vols (22,000) Cat Microforms
Budget: ($36,000)
Notes: Emphasis on students, educational testing, educational psychology, post-secondary education, psychometrics. Excludes educational history and philosophy, curricula and teaching.

NY —CORNELL UNIVERSITY LIBRARIES, Collection of Regional History, Dept of Manuscripts and Univ Archives, Ithaca, 14853.
Notes: Records, 1876-1915, 1925-1932, 1959. of several student clubs at Cornell University. Also, records, ca 1946-ca 1961, of activities of various political, social, recreational, cultural, religious, and charitable clubs and organizations at Cornell University.

OH —BOWLING GREEN STATE UNIVERSITY, Jerome Library, Center for Archival Collections, Bowling Green, 43403. Paul D Yon, Dir; Elaine R Ezell, Reference

Archivist; Nancy Steen, Rare Books Librn
Holdings: Vols (4000) Cat Mss Pix Slides Maps Microforms
Budget: ($25,000)
Notes: Incl pamphlets. The archives of four national professional associations have been donated to the CAC, creating a special collecting area concerning student affairs in higher education. The National Association for Women Deans, Counselors and Administrators (NAWDAC), the National Association of Student Personnel Administrators (NASPA), the American College Personnel Association (ACPA), and the Association of Fraternity Advisors (AFA), to date, have designated the CAC as the repository for their archives. These collections document the issues, professional education and activities of those employed within the student affairs area in colleges and universities in the US.

ON —MCMASTER UNIVERSITY, Mills Memorial Library, Div of Archives & Research Collections, Hamilton, L8S 4L6, Can. G R Hill, Univ Librn
Holdings: // Mss
Notes: Office files, correspondence, financial records, briefs, and reports of the Ontario Union of Students, Canadian Union of Students and its predecessor the National Federation of Canadian University Students.

STUDENTS, FOREIGN

CO —WESTERN INTERSTATE COMMISSION FOR HIGHER EDUCATION, Wiche Library, PO Drawer P, Boulder, 80302. Karon M Kelly, Dir Library Services
Holdings: Vols (10,000) Cat Microforms
Notes: Incl medical and nursing education, student exchange programs, minority involvement in education, management systems in higher education.

MI —UNIVERSITY OF MICHIGAN, English Language Institute/Linguistics Library, 1013 N University Bldg, Ann Arbor, 48109. Patricia M Aldridge, Librn
Holdings: Vols (4500) Cat Maps VF Videotapes
Notes: The collection on teaching English as a foreign language is fairly complete; in modern language study it is also quite good. Supporting subjects are linguistics and English grammar; psychology, American culture, education, foreign student adjustment, and bibliography are covered.

STUDENTS' SONGS

NY —BARNARD A & MORRIS N YOUNG LIBRARY OF EARLY AMERICAN POPULAR MUSIC, 270 Riverside Dr, New York, 10025. Morris N Young, Cur
Holdings: Cat Mss Pix Phonorecords Audiotapes Microforms
Notes: 48,000 items of American popular music, mostly 1790-1910. Incl books, serials, sheet music, broadsides, anthologies, air checks, broadcasting and music business memorabilia, and correspondence.

STUDIO ART see Art, Studio

STUDIO ONE TELEVISION PROGRAM

NY —NEW YORK PUBLIC LIBRARY, Performing Arts Research Center, Billy Rose Theatre Collection, 111 Amsterdam Ave, New York, 10023. Dorothy L Swerdlove, Cur
Holdings: // Uncat
Notes: Incl master scripts of Studio One productions from November 1948 to April 1952.

STUDY, COURSES OF see Education—Curricula

STURGES, PRESTON

CA —UNIVERSITY OF CALIFORNIA, LOS ANGELES, Research Library, Dept of Special Collections, 405 Hilgard Ave, Los Angeles, 90024. Edward Shreeves,

STURGES, PRESTON (cont.)

Chairman, Bibliographers Group; David S Zeidberg, Head
Holdings: Mss Pix
Notes: 50 linear feet of correspondence, production material, and moving picture scripts. No photocopying. Theater Arts Library collection contains his unpublished autobiography, correspondence, scripts with notes and revisions for such films as *If I Were King, The Great McGinty, The Palm Beach Story, Sullivan's Travels, The Miracle of Morgan's Creek, Hail the Conquering Hero,* and *Unfaithfully Yours.*

STURGIS, SAMUEL BOOTH

PA —BALCH INSTITUTE FOR ETHNIC STUDIES, Library, 18 S Seventh St, Philadelphia, 19106. R Joseph Anderson, Library Dir

STURM UND DRANG MOVEMENT

MA —HARVARD UNIVERSITY LIBRARY, Cambridge, 02138.
Holdings: Cat
NY —NEW YORK PUBLIC LIBRARY, Research Libraries, General Research Division, Fifth Ave & 42 St, New York, 10018. Rodney Phillips, Chief
Holdings: Vols (2,225,000) Cat Maps Pix Microforms
Budget: ($775,718)

STYRON, WILLIAM

NV —UNIVERSITY OF NEVADA, RENO, University Library, Special Collections Dept, Reno, 89557. Robert E Blesse, Head
Holdings: Vols 35 Cat
Notes: Includes individual works by author in all editions including translations; also prefaces, introductions, published correspondence, appearances in anthologies, periodicals, etc. Bibliographical research collection, part of Modern Authors Collection.
NC —DUKE UNIVERSITY, William R Perkins Library, Manuscript Dept, Durham, 27706. Ellen Gartrell, Cur of Mss
Holdings: Cat Mss
Notes: Papers, correspondence, etc.
NC —DUKE UNIVERSITY, William R Perkins Library, Rare Book Room, Durham, 27706. John L Sharpe, III, Cur
Notes: A collection of Duke University authors, established around 1963, with the writings of the students of William Blackburn and greatly enhanced by the gift of Professor Blackburn's collection. Represented are James Applewhite, Fred Chappell, Guy Davenport, Reynolds Price, William Styron, Frances Gray Patton, and Anne Tyler. Printed works are in the Rare Book Room and manuscripts are in the Manuscript Department.

STYLE IN DRESS see Costume; Fashion

SUAHELI LANGUAGE see Swahili Language

SUBARIAN LANGUAGE see Mittanian Language

SUBGRAVITY STATE—PHYSIOLOGICAL EFFECT see Weightlessness

SUBJECT HEADINGS

ON —UNIVERSITY OF TORONTO, Faculty of Library and Information Science Library, Subject Analysis Systems, Room 404, 140 St George St, Toronto, M5S 1A1, Can. Diane Henderson, Librn
Holdings: Vols (2000) Cat Microforms
Notes: The Subject Analysis Systems Collection is the major North American collection of classification schemes, thesauri, and subject heading lists, and it is the major world collection in the English language.

SUBMARINE BOATS

AL —MOBILE PUBLIC LIBRARY, Special Collections Div, 701 Government St, Mobile, 36602.
Notes: Hunley Collection-Papers, illustrations, etc concerning the building and history of CSS Hunley, first submarine, 1861-1865.
HI —PACIFIC SUBMARINE MUSEUM, Library, Naval Submarine Base, Pearl Harbor, 96860. Ray W de Yarmin, Cur
Holdings: Vols (1500) Cat Mss Maps Pix Slides Phonorecords 16mm Films
Budget: ($600)
Notes: Incl 3000 pictures. Extensive missile and torpedo collection; submarine models; salvage/deep-sea diver exhibit; Arctic exploration by submarines Worl War II submarine components. Research program for students, authors, lecturers, etc.
NJ —PASSAIC COUNTY HISTORICAL SOCIETY, Lamhurt Castle, Valley Rd, Paterson, 07503. Helen D Hamilton, Dir
Holdings: Vols (5000) Cat Mss Maps Pix
Notes: Material on the Society for the Establishment of Useful Manufacturing (founded) by Alexander Hamilton, papers relating to John Holland, who developed the submarine, the industrial magnates of the area who were active in the manufacture of locomotives, Colt revolvers, and textiles, especially silk.
NY —NEW YORK PUBLIC LIBRARY, Research Libraries, Science and Technology Research Center, Fifth Ave & 42 St, New York, 10018.
Holdings: Vols (1,100,000) Cat Microforms
Budget: ($647,259)

SUBMARINE GEOLOGY

NC —UNIVERSITY OF NORTH CAROLINA, CHAPEL HILL, Geology Library, Mitchell Hall 029A, Chapel Hill, 27514. Miriam L Sheaves, Librn
Holdings: Vols (41,000) Cat Maps
Notes: Earth sciences, paleontology, oceanography, geology, geophysics. Incl theses and dissertations; 103,000 map sheets.

SUBMARINE MINES see Mines, Military and Submarine

SUBMARINE WARFARE

CA —HOOVER INSTITUTION ON WAR, REVOLUTION & PEACE, Stanford University, Stanford, 94305. Milorad M Drachkovitch, Archivist
Holdings: Mss Pix
Notes: Two collections: (1) Papers of Elton W Grenfell, Vice Admiral, US Navy; commander, Submarine Force, Pacific Fleet, 1956-59; and commander, Submarine Force, Atlantic Fleet, 1960-64; incl correspondence, orders, drafts of speeches and photographs, 1926-69, relating to US submarine operations during World War II and in the postwar period. 11 1/2 ms boxes, 5 binders. (2) Papers of Charles E Weakley, Vice Admiral, US Navy, commander, Antisubmarine Warefare Force, Atlantic Fleet, 1963-67, and assistant administrator for management development, National Aeronautics and Space Administration, 1968-72, incl correspondence, orders, drafts of speeches, printed matter, photographs, and sound recordings, 1945-72, relating to post-World War II US antisubmarine force operations and to NASA activities. 4 ms boxes.
FL —US NAVAL COASTAL SYSTEMS CENTER, Technical Information Service Branch, Panama City, 32407. Myrtle J Rhodes, Librn
Holdings: Vols (30,000) Cat
Notes: Coastal and ocean technology, inshore undersea warfare, mine countermeasures, torpedo defense, underwater sound.

SUBMARINES see Submarine Boats

SUBSCRIPTION LIBRARIES see Libraries, Subscription

SUBSISTENCE STORES see Military Supplies

SUBSONIC AERODYNAMICS see Aerodynamics

SUBTERRANEAN WATER see Water, Underground

SUBURBS

IL —LAKE FOREST COLLEGE, Donnelley Library, Lake Forest, 60045. Arthur H Miller Jr, College Librn
Holdings: Vols (500) Cat Maps
Budget: ($1200)
Notes: Focus on development of suburban fringe areas, particularly Lake Co, Ill, and Chicago region: local documents (plans, transit, zoning maps, etc), US documents, and special studies of suburban issues, such as historic preservation and land use.
NY —ELECTRIC RAILROADERS ASSOCIATION, Frank J Sprague Memorial Library, 89 E 42nd St, New York, 10018. Hugh A Dunne, First VP
Notes: Private library. Incl all forms of railroads operated by electricity. Forms of electric railroads included: street railways, subways & elevated lines, high-speed interurbans, suburban commuter lines, electrified trunk lines, monorails, mountain climbing inclines, etc. Also railroad timetables.
ON —CANADIAN HOUSING INFORMATION CENTER, Canada Mortgage and Housing Corp, CMHC Annex Bldg Ground Floor, Montreal Rd, Ottawa, K1A 0P7, Can. Leslie Jones, Mgr
Holdings: Cat
Notes: Residential rehabiliatation.

SUBVERSIVE ACTIVITIES

CA —HARVEY G WOLFE LIBRARY, PO Box 3514, Grand Central Sta, Glendale, 91201. Douglas L Evans, Librn
Holdings: Vols (6580) Mss Maps Pix
Budget: ($4500)
Notes: Main emphasis on espionage, military intelligence, and sabotage.
CA —HOOVER INSTITUTION ON WAR, REVOLUTION & PEACE, Stanford University, Stanford, 94305. Milorad M Drachkovitch, Archivist
Holdings: Mss
Notes: Reports and transcripts of hearings (printed, mimeogaphed and typewritten), of the US Subversive Activities Control Board, a quasi-judicial US government agency, 1950-72, relating to communist and communist-front activities in the US. 70 ms boxes, 6 cu ft boxes.
DC —LIBRARY OF CONGRESS, Washington, 20540.
Notes: Some 4500 pamphlets and sheets dealing primarily with subversive and radical activities in the US from 1900 to 1950. Incl tracts and campaign literature of the Communist and Socialist Parties in the US and works by party leaders; materials on the economic, political, and human rights issues of the pre-World War II, World War II, and early civil rights campaign periods; and pamphlets by various anti-war and anti-draft organizations, material on Russia, and materials on the communist movement in other countries.
MA —BRANDEIS UNIVERSITY, Goldfarb Library, 415 South St, Waltham, 02154. Bessie Hahn, Dir
Notes: Hall-Hoag Archives on Extremism in the US. Approx 5000 pieces of Extremist literature, both Right and Left, dealing with various social, religious and political aspects of the US from the 1960s, 1970s and 1980s. A finding list is in Special Collections. Material is arranged by the name of the sponsoring organization in alphabetical order.
NC —DUKE UNIVERSITY, William R Perkins Library, Durham, 27706. Elvin E Strowd, University Librn
Notes: The (Quasi)-Nazi collection consists of approximately 7000 items, primarily pamphlets published in the United States by and about Nazi sympathizers Gerald K Smith, Father Coughlin, etc and organizations with Nazi leanings.
WI —STATE HISTORICAL SOCIETY OF WISCONSIN, Archives, 816 State St, Madison, 53706. Harold L Miller, Reference Archivist
Notes: Papers of Eugene and Peggy Dennis, Communist Party activists, 1926 - date. He was national head, CP, USA. Papers trace development of CIO in '30s, Farmer-Labor-Progressive Federation, and other Wisconsin and national political groups. Much on Senator Joseph McCarthy.

SUBVERSIVE ACTIVITIES (cont.)

MB —UNIVERSITY OF MANITOBA, Elizabeth Dafoe Library, Archives and Special Collections Dept, Winnipeg, R3T 2N2, Can. Richard E Bennett, Dept Head; Corrado A Santoro, Reference Archivist
Notes: Murray S Donnelly Papers, 1925-1961. Incl correspondence and reports dealing with foreign elements (fifth columns) in Canada during WW II working to sabotage the Canadian war effort, 1944. 1925 train pass to Imperial Conference held in Australia. Material relating to the life and times of J W Dafoe of the *Manitoba Free Press* from various individuals who knew him, for the purpose of writing a biography on Dafoe.

SUBWAYS

NY —ELECTRIC RAILROADERS ASSOCIATION, Frank J Sprague Memorial Library, 89 E 42nd St, New York, 10018. Hugh A Dunne, First VP
Notes: Private library. Incl all forms of railroads operated by electricity. Forms of electric railroads included: street railways, subways & elevated lines, high-speed interurbans, suburban commuter lines, electrified trunk lines, monorails, mountain climbing inclines, etc. Also railroad timetables.

SUCROSE CHEMISTRY

DC —SUGAR ASSOCIATION LIBRARY, 1511 K Street, NW, Washington, 20005. Holdings: Vols 1000 Cat Mss Maps Pix Microforms
Budget: $8000
Notes: Sugar utilization and research, public health, food technology, and sucrose chemistry.

SUDAN

CA —HOOVER INSTITUTION ON WAR, REVOLUTION & PEACE, Stanford University, Stanford, 94305. Peter Duignan, Cur; Karen Fung, Deputy Cur
Holdings: Vols (100,000)
Notes: For full description of collection, see Hoover Instition entry under Near East.

SUFFRAGE

†AL —MUSEUMS OF THE CITY OF MOBILE, Reference Library, 355 Government St, Mobile, 36602. Caldwell Delaney, Adminr
Notes: Mobile Equal Suffrage Assoc Coll.
CA —LOS ANGELES PUBLIC LIBRARY, Social Sciences Dept, 630 W Fifth St, Los Angeles, 90071. Marilyn C Wherley, Principal Librn
Holdings: Vols 2000 Microforms
Budget: ($150,000)
Notes: Books, pamphlets, periodicals, national convention proceedings, biographies of leading suffragettes in Great Britain and the United States. No separate catalog. Popular and scholarly works on the course and significance of the movement. Incl current women's liberation movement.
DC —LIBRARY OF CONGRESS, Manuscript Division, Washington, 20540. John C Broderick, Chief
Notes: Papers of Maud Wood Park (1871-1955), first president of the League of Women Voters. 3500 items, incl personal and professional correspondence, family papers, speeches and lectures, reports, photographs, and an autograph collection, documenting the women's rights movement in the US, particularly in the first half of the 20th century. The papers of Carrie Chapman Catt date chiefly from 1890-1920 and pertain to her efforts to secure voting rights for women. Material from after 1920 relates to her world peace movement activities. Also, many materials related to Susan B Anthony.
NY —VASSAR COLLEGE, Library, Rare Books & Manuscripts Collection, Box 20, Poughkeepsie, 12601. Lisa Browar, Cur
Holdings: Mss Pix
Notes: Emphasis is on women in the US, women's rights, suffrage and Equal Rights Amendment. Manuscript collections incl papers of Elizabeth Cady Stanton, Paulina Wright Davis, Maria Mitchell and Alma Lutz.
NY —UNIVERSITY OF ROCHESTER, Rush Rhees Library, Department of Rare Books and Special Collections, Rochester, 14627. Peter Dzwonkoski, Librn
Holdings: Mss
Notes: Autograph letters and other mss incl in the Amy and Isaac Post family papers, Susan B Anthony Papers, and other collections.
See also entry under Anthony, Susan Brownell, 1820-1906.
RI —BROWN UNIVERSITY, John Hay Library, 20 Prospect St, Providence, 02912. Mark N Brown, Cur Mss
Holdings: Vols (15,000) // Cat Mss Maps Pix
Notes: Sidney S Rider Collection of 5000 books, 10,000 pamphlets and 8000 mss formed in the 19th century by a Providence antiquarian bookseller. The primary focus is on all aspects of Rhode Island: social, political, and economic history from the 17th to the mid-19th century, with some attention given to general New England history. The most significant group of primary materials within the collection relates to Thomas Wilson Dorr and the political movements in Rhode Island ca 1840-1850, especially the Dorr Rebellion over the issue of suffrage.

SUFISM

CA —GRADUATE THEOLOGICAL UNION LIBRARY, New Religious Movements Research Collection, Public Services and Special Collections Dept, 2400 Ridge Road, Berkeley, 94709. Diane Choquette, Dept Head
Holdings: Vols (3000) Mss Pix
Notes: Begun in 1977, the collection focuses on religious movements new to America since 1960, and unorthodox religious movements resurgent since 1960. American forms of Hinduism, Buddhism, Sikhism, and Sufism are included along with occultism, Neo-Paganism, esoteric and alternative forms of Christianity, feminist spirituality, and human potential movements having a spiritual aspect. Legal issues, such as deprogramming, and the question of church/state relations are an important part of the collection. The Library is a depository for publications of the Unification Church in America, the Church of Scientology, and the International Society for Krishna Consciousness (America). The responses of mainstream religions and concerned citizens groups are also included. Besides 3000 monographs, the library has 400 periodical titles, 200 posters from the San FranciscoBay Area, 1965-77, 300 research papers, and 31 linear feet of ephemera.

SUGAR AND SUGARCANE

CA —UNIVERSITY OF CALIFORNIA, BERKELEY, Science Libraries, Natural Resources Library, 40 Giannini Hall, Berkeley, 94720. Norma Kobzina, Head Librn
Holdings: Vols (100,000) Cat Maps Microforms
Budget: ($40,000)
Notes: Subject emphasis is on basic agricultural and pest management research, particularly in the areas of tropical and subtropical agriculture and plantation crops, ie, cotton, rice, tobacco, and sugar. Materials in agricultural engineering, farm machinery, and veterinary medicine are not acquired for the Berkeley campus. Serials, especially the extensive holdings of foreign titles, constitute the collection's major strength. Over 5700 serials are being received currently.
CO —GREAT WESTERN SUGAR COMPANY, Library, PO Box 5308, Terminal Annex, Denver, 80217.
Holdings: Vols 2000 Cat Maps Pix
Notes: Incl specialized foreign language periodicals from 1800s to date.

DC —SUGAR ASSOCIATION LIBRARY, 1511 K Street, NW, Washington, 20005. Holdings: Vols 1000 Cat Mss Maps Pix Slides Microforms
Budget: $8000
Notes: Sugar utilization and research, public health, food technology, and source chemistry.
LA —LOUISIANA STATE UNIVERSITY, Troy H Middleton Library, Baton Rouge, 70803. Lance E Dickson, Acting Dir
Holdings: Vols 1200 Cat Mss
Notes: Extensive holdings on all aspects of sugar cane growing and cane sugar production, especially in Louisiana and the Southern States. Some archival material from Cuba, Puerto Rico, Trinidad, and other areas of the world.
LA —NICHOLLS STATE UNIVERSITY, Ellender Memorial Library, Thibodaux, 70310. Randall A Detro, Dir; Philip D Uzee, Archivist
Holdings: Uncat Mss Maps Pix Microforms
Notes: Louisiana and local history; family papers of the period, etc.
PA —FRANKLIN INSTITUTE LIBRARY, 20 & The Parkway, Philadelphia, 19103. Miriam Padusis, Dir; Charles Wilt, Readers Servs Librn
Holdings: Vols (300,000) Cat Maps Pix Microforms

SUGAR AND SUGARCANE—MANUFACTURE AND REFINING

CO —COLORADO HISTORICAL SOCIETY, Research Collections, 1300 Broadway, Denver, 80203. Catherine Kane, Head Public Service and Access
Budget: ($100,000)
Notes: Strong ms holdings in western and Colorado business history in such areas as mining, water, transportation, sugar industry.
CO —GREAT WESTERN SUGAR COMPANY, Library, PO Box 5308, Terminal Annex, Denver, 80217.
Holdings: Vols 2000 Cat Maps Pix
Notes: Incl specialized foreign language periodicals from 1880s to date.
DC —SUGAR ASSOCIATION LIBRARY, 1511 K Street, NW, Washington, 20005. Holdings: Vols 1000 Cat Mss Maps Pix Slides Microforms
Budget: $8000
Notes: Sugar utilization and research, public health, food technology, and sucrose chemistry.
LA —LOUISIANA STATE UNIVERSITY, Troy H Middleton Library, Baton Rouge, 70803. Lance E Dickson, Acting Dir
Holdings: Vols 1200 Cat Mss
Notes: Extensive holdings on all aspects of sugar cane growing and cane sugar production, especially in Louisiana and the Southern States. Some archival material from Cuba, Puerto Rico, Trinidad, and other areas of the world.
LA —LOUISIANA STATE UNIVERSITY, Troy H Middleton Library, Louisiana Room, Baton Rouge, 70803. Evangeline Mills Lynch, Head Librn; Ruth Murray, Associate Librn
Holdings: Vols (33,500) Cat Maps VF
Notes: Louisiana Collection of history, description and travel, biography, agriculture, literature, politics and government, folklore, anthropology, geography, geology, education, language, music and natural history. Especially large subject collections may be found on Louisiana, the history of the lower Mississippi Valley, Abraham Lincoln, Romance languages and literatures, sugar culture and technology, Southern history, petroleum engineering, plant pathology, micropaleontology, ornithology, and various aspects of crawfish life, biology and culture. Complete depository of Louisiana State Documents; extensive newspapers clipping files; separate card catalog; items listed in Louisiana Union Catalog; restricted use (research and reference). Incl both materials about Louisiana and by Louisianians without regard to subject. LSU Press

SUGAR AND SUGARCANE—MANUFACTURE AND REFINING (cont.)

Collection(preservation copy of each title kept for exhibit purposes only). LSU theses and dissertations from 1900-date. LSU Faculty Collection. Also, 1300 maps, 104 VF drawers, 250 boxes of uncataloged pamphlets.

NY —CORNELL UNIVERSITY LIBRARIES, Collection of Regional History, Dept of Manuscripts and Univ Archives, Ithaca, 14853.
Notes: Oral history interviews, 1965-66, concerning the planning, establishment, and operation of a sugar beet industry in a 13-county area of NY from 1961-66.

SUGAR PERIODICALS see Periodicals, Sugar

SUGAR PINE TREES

CA —CALIFORNIA STATE UNIVERSITY, FRESNO, Henry Madden Library, Dept of Special Collections, Fresno, 93740. Ronald J Mahoney, Head
Holdings: // Uncat Pix
Notes: The Harry Pidgeon Collection of photographs of logging in the Sugar Pine area of the Sierra Nevada mountains, Madera County, California. About 600 photos, 1913-1925.

SUGAR REFINING see Sugar and Sugarcane—Manufacture and Refining

SUGARMON, RUSSELL B. JR.

TN —MEMPHIS STATE UNIVERSITY, John Willard Brister Library, Memphis, 38152. John Terreo, Special Collections Librn
Notes: Memphis attorney and civil rights leader Russell B Sugarmon, Jr, 1959-1976.

SUGGESTION, MENTAL see Mental Suggestion

SUGGESTIVE THERAPEUTICS see Therapeutics, Suggestive

SUICIDE AND SUICIDE ATTEMPTS

DC —CENTER FOR BIOETHICS, Library, Kennedy Institute, Georgetown University, 3520 Prospect St NW, Washington, 20057. Doris Goldstein, Dir; Judith Mistichelli, Senior Librn
Holdings: Vols 8200
Notes: Largest library of its kind. Incl 31,000 journal articles. Collects in the following subject areas: applied ethics; medical ethics; philosophy of medicine; science, technology and society; sociology of medicine; patient-physician care; sexuality; contraception; abortion; population policy; reproductive technologies; in vitro fertilization; genetic counseling and screening; genetic engineering; mental organ transplantation; death and dying; "baby doe" issues; euthanasia; suicide; use of chemical and biological weapons. Produces computer database *Bioethicsline*, available through MEDLARS; and the printed annual *Bibliography of Bioethics*. Other library publications are: *New Titles in Bioethics* (monthly); *Scope Notes* series on current topics.

NY —CREEDMOOR PSYCHIATRIC CENTER, Health Sciences Library, Bldg 51, 80-45 Winchester Blvd, Queens Village, 11427. Susan Taubman, Dir of Library; Pushpa Bhati, Sr Librn
Holdings: Vols (12,000) Cat Slides Phonorecords Audiotapes Filmstrips Microfiche
Budget: ($50,000)
Notes: Particularly strong in the areas of neurology, pharmacology, psychoanalysis, and psychopharmacology.

SULKY RACING see Harness Racing

SULLIVAN, ANNE see Macy, Anne Sullivan

SULLIVAN, ARTHUR see Gilbert and Sullivan

SULLIVAN, ED, 1902-1974

†WI —STATE HISTORICAL SOCIETY OF WISCONSIN, Library, 816 State St, Madison, 53706.
Notes: Papers, correspondence, production records, radio programs, columns, and other writings. Also films and other documentation of the Ed Sullivan Show.

SULLIVAN, JOHN

IL —WHEATON COLLEGE, Library, Marion E Wade Collection, Irving & Franklin Sts, Wheaton, 60187. Lyle Dorsett, Cur; Marjorie Mead, Associate Cur
Holdings: Vols (6500)
Notes: Extensive Marion E Wade Collection contains the personal library of John Sullivan, Gilbert Keith Chesterton's bibliographer.

NH —NEW HAMPSHIRE HISTORICAL SOCIETY, Manuscripts Library, 30 Park St, Concord, 03301. Thomas E Camden, Cur
Holdings: Cat Mss
Notes: John Sullivan (1740-1795), major general during the American Revolution, later, a politician and judge of the US district court in New Hampshire, from Durham, New Hampshire. Papers are primarily correspondence and cover the period 1772-1791. Papers relate to Sullivan's activities as a general during the Revolution, and to his political and judicial activity during the 1780s. About 500 items.

SULLIVAN, LEONOR K.

DC —GEORGETOWN UNIVERSITY, Library, Special Collections Div, 37 & O Sts NW, Washington, 20057. George M Barringer, Special Collections Librn; Nicholas B Sheetz, Mss Librn
Holdings: Cat Mss Pix
Notes: Panama Canal, and papers of Tomas Herran, Earl Harding, Thomas E Martin, William McCan, Clark Thompson, Leonor K Sullivan, and Capt Miles Duval.

SULLIVAN, LOUIS

NY —COLUMBIA UNIVERSITY LIBRARIES, Avery Architectural and Fine Arts Library, 201 Avery Hall, New York, 10027. Angela Giral, Librn
Holdings: Cat Mss Pix
Notes: Incl large collection of his drawings.

SULLIVAN, MARK, 1874-1952

CA —HOOVER INSTITUTION ON WAR, REVOLUTION & PEACE, Stanford University, Stanford, 94305. Milorad M Drachkovitch, Archivist
Holdings: Mss
Notes: Papers of Mark Sullivan, editor of *Collier's Weeley*, 1912-19, and newspaper columnist for the *New York Herald-Tribune*, 1923-52, incl correspondence, diaries, speeches and writings, memoranda, and printed matter, 1883-1952, relating to the career of Mark Sullivan; journalism in the US; and social, political, and economic developments in the US from 1900 to 1952. 62 ms boxes, 10 scrapbooks, 3 envelopes.

SULZER, WILLIAM, 1863-1941

NY —CORNELL UNIVERSITY LIBRARIES, Collection of Regional History, Dept of Manuscripts and Univ Archives, Ithaca, 14853.
Notes: Governor of NY, Congressman, assemblyman. Incl papers, 1894-1932; letters, microfilm, and printed material pertaining to the American Party.

SUMATRA see Indonesia

SUMERIAN LANGUAGE AND LITERATURE

NY —NEW YORK PUBLIC LIBRARY, Oriental Div, Fifth Ave & 42 St, New York, 10018. E Christian Filstrup, Chief
Holdings: Cat Mss Microforms
Budget: ($56,455)
Notes: Published catalog of holdings.

SUMERIAN SYLLABARIES see Cuneiform Writing

SUMEROLOGY

PA —UNIVERSITY OF PENNSYLVANIA, University Museum Library, 33 & Spruce Sts, Philadelphia, 19104. Jean S Adelman, Librn
Holdings: Vols (80,000) Cat
Notes: World archaeology, with special emphasis on North and Central America, Egyptology, Sumerology, and the classical world. All holdings are listed in museum library catalog and are also listed in University of Pennsylvania main library (union) catalog.

SUMNER, CHARLES

MA —HARVARD UNIVERSITY LIBRARY, Houghton Library, Cambridge, 02138. Rodney G Dennis, Cur of Manuscripts
Holdings: Cat Mss
MI —NORTHERN MICHIGAN UNIVERSITY, Lydia M Olson Library, Elizabeth L Harden Drive, Marquette, 49855. Stephen H Peters, Cataloger
Notes: A major section of the personal library of Moses Coit Tyler. Strong in the Colonial and Early National periods. Includes biographies and published letters and writings of such figures as Benjamin Franklin, John Adams, John Jay, Thomas Jefferson, Charles Sumner.

SUMNER, WILLIAM GRAHAM

CT —YALE UNIVERSITY, Box 1603A, Yale Station, New Haven, 06520.
Holdings: Cat Mss

SUN—RADIATION see Solar Radiation

SUN DIALS

CA —SAN DIEGO STATE UNIVERSITY, Malcolm A Love Library, 5300 Campanile Dr, San Diego, 92182. D Dickinson, Univ Librn; Don L Bosseau, Dir
Holdings: Vols 2700 Cat Mss Maps Pix Slides
Notes: The Ernst Zinner Collection, incl 2 incunables, autographs of scientists, portraits, pictures of sundials, 31 ms letters.
PA —FRANKLIN INSTITUTE LIBRARY, 20 & The Parkway, Philadelphia, 19103. Miriam Padusis, Dir; Charles Wilt, Readers Servs Librn
Holdings: Vols 2400 Cat Mss
Notes: One of the finest collections of horology in the world.

SUN-HEATED HOUSES see Solar Houses

SUN OIL COMPANY

DE —HAGLEY MUSEUM AND LIBRARY, Eleutherian Mills-Hagley Foundation Inc, PO Box 3630, Greenville, 19807. Richmond D Williams, Dir; Heddy A Richter, Imprints Librn
Notes: Records of Sun Oil Company (1889-1966; 750 cubic feet) contain both administrative and operating records as well as papers of key executive officers: Joseph N Pew, Joseph N Pew, Jr and Arthur Pew.

SUN YAT-SEN

CA —HOOVER INSTITUTION ON WAR, REVOLUTION & PEACE, Stanford University, Stanford, 94305. Milorad M Drachkovitch, Archivist
Holdings: // Mss
Notes: Letters, copies of telegrams and misc newspaper clippings relating to the Chinese Revolution and especially to an American conceived plan for financing a revolution to overthrow the Ch'ing Dynasty. Principal correspondents incl Boothe, Homer Lea, a friend of Boothe and military adviser to Sun Yat-sen, W W Allen, a friend of Boothe and a New York consulting engineer, Yung Wing, a well-known Chinese-American of Hartford, Conn, Charles B Hill and Sun Yat-sen. Unpublished inventory at repository.

SUNDANESE LANGUAGE

NY —NEW YORK PUBLIC LIBRARY, Oriental Div, Fifth Ave & 42 St, New York, 10018. E Christian Filstrup, Chief
Holdings: // Cat Mss Microforms
Budget: ($56,455)
Notes: Published catalog of holdings.

SUNDAY, BILLY

TX —LE TOURNEAU COLLEGE, Margaret
Estes Library, 2100 S Mobberly Ave, PO
Box 7001, Longview, 75601. Rachel Miley,
Acting Dir of Library Services
Holdings: Vols (178,846) Cat Mss Maps Pix
Slides Microforms
Budget: ($40,000)

SUNDAY SCHOOL LITERATURE

PA —FREE LIBRARY OF PHILADELPHIA,
Rare Book Dept, Logan Sq, Philadelphia,
19103. Marie E Korey, Rare Book Librn
Holdings: Vols (10,000) Cat
Notes: The American Sunday-School Union
Collection of its publications issued from
1824 until about 1900.

RI —BROWN UNIVERSITY, John Hay
Library, 20 Prospect St, Providence, 02912.
Mark N Brown, Cur Mss
Holdings: Vols (2000) Cat Mss
Notes: Several collections of religious history
strong in material on Baptist,
Congregational, and Unitarian Churches in
the 19th century, incl the ms records some
Rhode Island congregations plus the papers
of Isaac Backus, Brown University presidents
and faculty, Jones Very, Mary Ann Atwood,
Thomas Ustick, and Charles King Newcomb;
incl numerous ephemeral and pamphlet
publications that relate to Baptist Church
history, creed, biography, Sunday School
literature and missions.
See also entry under Sacred Songs

TN —HISTORICAL COMMISSION-
SUNDAY SCHOOL BOARD, Southern
Baptist Convention, Dargan-Carver Library,
127 Ninth Ave N, Nashville, 37234. Howard
Gallimore, Supvr
Holdings: Vols (10,000) Cat Mss Maps Pix
Slides Phonorecords Audiotapes Videotapes
16mm Films Filmstrips Microforms
Budget: ($38,734)
Notes: Extensive holdings in proceedings
and minutes of organized Baptist bodies;
state conventions and associations, Baptist
journals, and documentation of major
Southern Baptist controversies. Material on
Black, Russian, and other Baptists. Much on
religious education and American religion.
Large collection of Sunday School literature.
Incl thousands of mss, pictures, slides,
records, etc, and 12,000,000 pages on
microforms.

SUNDAY-SCHOOL UNION, AMERICAN see American Sunday-School Union

SUPAI INDIANS see Havasupai Indians

SUPERCONDUCTIVITY

MA —AVCO EVERETT RESEARCH
LABORATORY, INC, Library, 2385 Revere
Beach Parkway, Everett, 02149. Lorraine T
Nazzaro, Librn
Holdings: Vols (24,000) Cat Maps
Microforms
Budget: ($150,000)
Notes: Incl 50,000 reports.

TX —RICE UNIVERSITY, Fondren Library,
6100 S Main St, PO Box 1892, Houston,
77251. Dr Samuel M Carrington, Jr,
University Librn
Holdings: // Cat Mss Pix
Notes: Papers of William V Houston, incl his
research papers in spectroscopy, theory of
solid state, quantum mechanics and
superconductivity (15 linear ft).

SUPERIOR CHILDREN see Gifted Children

SUPERNATURAL IN LITERATURE

CA —UNIVERSITY OF CALIFORNIA,
RIVERSIDE, University Library, 4045
Canyon Crest Dr, Box 5900, Riverside,
92517.
Holdings: Vols (30,000)
Notes: The Eaton Collection of science

fiction and fantasy materials, incl 5,600 pulp
magazines; also horror, supernatural, and
Gothic mystery fiction; boys' books; utopian
and dystopian fiction, imaginary voyages,
future war and lost race fiction; large
holdings in French language science fiction
and fantasy; critical and scholarly works
pertaining to these genres; videotapes of
science fiction/fantasy films and shooting
scripts. Collection covers science fiction/
fantasy literature from the 16th-17th
centuries to the present. Strong individual
author collections of Jules Verne, H Rider
Haggard, H G Wells, Edgar Rice Burroughs,
and Philip K Dick. For a complete
description of the collection see: George
Slusser, "The J Lloyd Eaton Collection,"
Special Collections, II, 1/2, 25-38 (1983),
andDictionary Catalog of the J Lloyd Eaton
Collection of Science Fiction and Fantasy
Literature (Boston: G K Hall) 1982.

MD —JOHNS HOPKINS UNIVERSITY,
Milton S Eisenhower Library, George
Peabody Collection, 17 E Mt Vernon Place,
Baltimore, 21201. Lyn Hart, Peabody Librn
Notes: Noncirculating.

OH —BOWLING GREEN STATE
UNIVERSITY, Jerome Library, Center for
Archival Collections, Bowling Green, 43403.
Paul D Yon, Dir; Elaine R Ezell, Reference
Archivist; Nancy Steen, Rare Books Librn
Holdings: Vols 1600 Cat Mss Pix
Budget: ($3000)
Notes: The Robert Aickman Collection
contains about 40 of Aickman's manuscripts
of both published and unpublished works as
well as the late author's personal library
which is strong in the areas of English
literature and theatre of the 19th and 20th
centuries and in the area of the supernatural.

PA —TEMPLE UNIVERSITY LIBRARIES,
Special Collections Dept, Rare Books & Mss
Section, Philadelphia, 19122. Thomas M
Whitehead, Cur
Holdings: Vols (200) Cat
Notes: Holdings include contemporary
printed books, first and later editions, of
18th and early 19th century gothic fiction.
Significant strength in Matthew Gregory
"Monk" Lewis books.

ON —QUEEN'S UNIVERSITY, Douglas
Library, Kingston, K7L 5C4, Can. William F
E Morley, Cur, Special Collections
Holdings: Vols (2050) Cat
Notes: The library has purchased the H P
Lovecraft collection (225 vols) and has built
up a most interesting collection in Gothic
Fantasy and tales of the occult. Also, 6500
pulp magazines, uncat. (List available).

SUPERSONIC AIR TRANSPORTS see Supersonic Transport Planes

SUPERSONIC AIRLINERS see Supersonic Transport Planes

SUPERSONIC THERAPY see Ultrasonic Waves—Therapeutic Use

SUPERSONIC TRANSPORT PLANES

MA —MASSACHUSETTS INSTITUTE OF
TECHNOLOGY, Institute Archives, Special
Collections, Cambridge, 02139.
Notes: Correspondence, newsletters, fact-
sheets, newspaper and magazine articles,
books and reports of the Citizens' League
Against the Sonic Boom, established in 1967
by William Shurcliff to oppose the sonic
boom, stop commercial supersonic transport
production, and influence public opinion and
policy decisions on the SST. Major
correspondents incl Bo Lundberg, Richard
Wiggs, several US congressmen, and CLASB
members.

SUPERSTITION

CA —LOS ANGELES PUBLIC LIBRARY,
Philosophy & Religion Dept, 630 W Fifth St,
Los Angeles, 90071. Marilyn C Wherley,
Librn
Holdings: Vols 500 Cat
Budget: ($60,000)
Notes: Comprehensive coverage of popular

and scholarly works on myths, legends,
superstitions and primitive religions.

†CA —UNIVERSITY OF CALIFORNIA LOS
ANGELES, Center for the Study of
Comparative Folklore and Mythology, Los
Angeles, 90024.
Notes: Archive, consisting of nearly 500,000
entries and cross-references, developed by
Prof Wayland D Hand over the past 40
years as part of his monumental Dictionary
of American Popular Beliefs and
Superstitions. Entries have been drawn from
both field collections and from printed and
published sources. Analytical data stress
both the historical component and the
comparative approach. Of special interest is
the emphasis on magical medicine, although
natural and botanical medicine are also well
represented.

OH —CLEVELAND PUBLIC LIBRARY, Fine
Arts and Special Collections Department,
325 Superior Ave, Cleveland, 44114. Alice
N Loranth, Head
Holdings: Vols (41,050) Cat Mss Pix
Microforms
Notes: Part of the Folklore Collection. One
of the large folklore collections in the US.
Comprehensive in scope, incl folk tales,
riddles, proverbs, folk songs, ballads, fables,
chapbooks, medieval romances, works on
superstition, magic, witchcraft and studies of
folk habits beliefs, manners and customs.
Archival holdings incl the "Newbell Niles
Puckett Archives on Popular Beliefs and
Superstitions" (19 linear ft); "Black Names in
America" (10 linear ft); miscellaneous
folklore papers (10 linear ft); "Religious Life
of the Southern Black" (6 linear ft);
"Canadian Lumberjack Songs" (20 tapes);
and the "M A Klipple African Folktales" (19
linear ft). Described in Cleveland Library,
White collection of folklore and Orientalia.
Catalog of Folklore, Folklife and Folk Songs
2nd edition (Boston: G K Hall, 1978). 3
vols; introduction byAlice N Loranth.
Puckett, N N, Popular Beliefs and
Superstitions: a Collection of Newbell Niles
Puckett. Edited by Wayland D Hand, et al.
(Boston: G K Hall, 1981) 3 vols.
See also entry under Folklore

SUPPLIES, MILITARY see Military Supplies

SUPREME COURT see U.s. Supreme Court

SURDIN, MORRIS, 1914-

AB —UNIVERSITY OF CALGARY,
Libraries, Special Collections Div, 2500
University Dr, Calgary, T2N 1N4, Can.
Holdings: Mss
Notes: The Morris Surdin collection is made
up of scripts, scores and related materials for
some 2500 dramatic works, produced on
radio, television, or the stage, for which
Surdin has composed the musical
accompaniment.

SURFACE, FRANK MACY

CA —HOOVER INSTITUTION ON WAR,
REVOLUTION & PEACE, Stanford
University, Stanford, 94305. Milorad M
Drachkovitch, Archivist
Holdings: // Mss
Notes: Papers, 1920-1931, of Frank Macy
Surface, economist and statistician.
Correspondence and reports relating to the
American Relief Administration, US Food
Administration and European relief
following World War I. Persons represented
incl Herbert Hoover and Alonzo E Taylor. 8
ft. Finding aid in repository.

SURFACE, WILLIAM

MA —BOSTON UNIVERSITY, Mugar
Memorial Library, Special Collections Dept,
771 Commonwealth Ave, Boston, 02215.
Howard B Gotlieb, Dir
Holdings: Cat Mss
Notes: Mss, correspondence, etc collected in
depth; incl publications by.

SURFACE COATINGS see Coatings

SURFACE SCIENCE

IL —UNIVERSITY OF ILLINOIS,
URBANA/CHAMPAIGN, Library,
Physics/Astronomy Library, 204 Loomis
Laboratory, 1110 West Green St, Urbana,
61801. Bernice Lord Hulsizer, Librn
Holdings: Vols (34,000) Cat
Budget: ($130,000)
Notes: A relatively new field in which we
are collecting research materials, books and
journals, as rapidly as possible.

SURFACES (TECHNOLOGY)

IL —UNIVERSITY OF ILLINOIS,
URBANA/CHAMPAIGN, Library,
Physics/Astronomy Library, 204 Loomis
Laboratory, 1110 West Green St, Urbana,
61801. Bernice Lord Hulsizer, Librn
Holdings: Vols (34,000) Cat
Budget: ($130,000)
Notes: A relatively new field in which we
are collecting research materials, books and
journals, as rapidly as possible.
NJ —WITCO CHEMICAL CORP, Corporate
Research Center Library, 100 Bauer Dr,
Oakland, 07436. Jo Therese Smith, Mgr,
Information Services
Holdings: Vols (9000) Cat
Budget: ($52,000)

SURGERY

CA —WESTERN MEDICAL CENTER,
Medical Library, 1025 S Anaheim Blvd,
Anaheim, 92805. Evelyn Simpson, Dir
Holdings: Vols 400 Cat Audiotapes
Videotapes
Notes: Incl 400 audiotapes, 200 bound
journals. Photocopying.
CA —LONG BEACH COMMUNITY
HOSPITAL, Medical Library, 1720 Termino
Ave, PO Box 2587, Long Beach, 90801. Lois
O Clark, Librn
Holdings: Vols (3800) Cat Audiotapes
Videotapes 16mm Films Filmstrips
Budget: ($3000)
Notes: Incl 2800 audiotapes and 280
videotapes.
CT —YALE MEDICAL LIBRARY, 333 Cedar
St, New Haven, 06510.
Holdings: Vols (334,215) Cat Mss Pix Slides
Microforms
Budget: ($361,650)
Notes: Incl films, audiotapes, artifacts, etc.
DE —SAINT FRANCIS HOSPITAL
MEDICAL LIBRARY, Seventh & Clayton
Sts, Wilmington, 19805. Sister Joan Ignatius
McCleary, Librn
Holdings: Vols (3000) Cat Audiotapes
DE —US VETERANS ADMINISTRATION
CENTER, Medical Library, Wilmington,
19805. Mrs Donald Passidoma, Chief Librn
Holdings: Vols (5000) Cat
Notes: Staff only.
GA —CENTRAL STATE HOSPITAL,
Medical Library, Medical/Surgical Center,
Milledgeville, 31062. Aurelia S Spence,
Librn
Holdings: Vols (2000) Cat Audiotapes
Videotapes
Budget: ($6000)
MD —MEDICAL & CHIRURGICAL
FACULTY OF THE STATE OF
MARYLAND, Library, 1211 Cathedral St,
Baltimore, 21201. Joseph E Jensen, Librn
Holdings: Vols (110,000) Cat Mss Maps Pix
Slides Audiotapes Videotapes Microforms
Budget: ($250,000)
Notes: Library for the state medical society.
Open to the public, but circulation is
restricted to members. The current
acquisitions policy emphasizes English
language monographs and periodicals on all
aspects of clinical medicine, and on the
social, economic, legal and administrative
aspects of medical practice in the United
States. The library subscribes to all state
medical society journals in the United States.
Holdings include a very fine history of
medicine and rare medical book collection,
and a strong collection of medical
monographs and serials prior to 1900.

MD —NATIONAL LIBRARY OF
MEDICINE, 8600 Rockville Pike, Bethesda,
20209. Harold M Schoolinam, Actg Dir
Holdings: Vols (3,150,000) Cat Mss
Audiotapes Videotapes 16mm Films
Filmstrips Microforms
Budget: ($46,400)
Notes: The world's largest medical library.
Materials are collected exhaustively in some
40 biomedical areas and, to a lesser degree,
in related subject areas such as general
chemistry, physics, zoology, botany, and
instrumentation. Holdings include 82,000
monographic volumes, pre-1871; 438,000
monographic volumes, 1871-present; 714,000
bound serial volumes; 281,000 theses; 172,
000 pamphlets; 1,207,000 manuscripts; 156,
000 microforms; 12,000 audiovisuals; and 75,
000 prints and photographs. Pre-1871
material is in a separate historical collection.
Approximately 24,000 serial titles are
currently received.
MA —NEW ENGLAND COLLEGE OF
OPTOMETRY, Library, 420 Beacon St,
Boston, 02115. F Eleanor Warner, Librn
Holdings: Vols (7500) Cat Mss Slides
Phonorecords Audiotapes Videotapes 16mm
Films Microforms
Budget: ($30,000)
Notes: Acquisitions in optometry and
ophthalmology are comprehensive; they are
selective in areas of surgery and the
therapeutic use of drugs. Collection incl 75
slide/tape programs; 75 videotapes; 11 VF
drawers of pamphlets and reprints; 16 units
of realia; 275 periodical subscriptions.
Publishes periodicals holdings list,
audiovisual holdings list and an acquisitions
list. Open to the public for reference use.
MA —US VETERANS ADMINISTRATION
MEDICAL CENTER, Medical Library, 150
S Huntington Ave, Jamaica Plain, Boston,
02130. Patricia J McGrath, Chief Librn
Holdings: Vols (5702) Cat
Notes: Incl health care, surgery, neurology.
400 journal subscriptions, 5000 bound
volumes.
NY —ALBERT EINSTEIN COLLEGE OF
MEDICINE, D Samuel Gottesman Library,
1300 Morris Park Ave, Bronx, 10461.
Charlotte K Lindner, Dir
NY —BAPTIST MEDICAL CENTER OF
NEW YORK, Alyn M Steinhardt Library,
2749 Linden Blvd, Brooklyn, 11208. Ana
McBean, Librn
Holdings: Vols (150) Cat Slides
Phonorecords Audiotapes 16mm Films
Filmstrips
†NY —MEDICAL RESEARCH LIBRARY
OF BROOKLYN, Academy of Medicine of
Brooklyn & The State University of New
York Downstate Medical Center, 450
Clarkson St, Brooklyn, 11203. Kenneth E
Moody, Dir
NY —ERIE COUNTY MEDICAL CENTER,
Medical Library, 462 Grider St, Buffalo,
14215. Anthony Ciko, Sr Medical Librn
Holdings: Vols (13,000) Cat Slides
Audiotapes Videotapes
Budget: ($42,000)
NY —MARY IMOGENE BASSETT
HOSPITAL, Medical Library, Copperstown,
13326. Wendy Rice, Librn
Holdings: Vols (30,000) Cat
NY —BOOTH MEMORIAL MEDICAL
CENTER, Health Education Library, Main
St at Booth Memorial Ave, Flushing, 11355.
Rita Maier, Library Dir
Holdings: Vols (3000) Cat Audiotapes
Notes: Computer assisted instruction
program for surgery. Incl 7000 bound
journals; software slide tape programs.
NY —FLUSHING HOSPITAL & MEDICAL
CENTER, Medical Library, Parsons Blvd &
45 Ave, Flushing, 11355. Maria Czechowicz,
Dir
Holdings: Vols (5741) Cat Audiotapes
Budget: ($8000)
NY —HOSPITAL FOR SPECIAL SURGERY,
Kim Barrett Memorial Library, 535 E 70 St,
New York, 10021. Munir U Din, Librn
Holdings: Vols 2520 Cat Slides Audiotapes
Videotapes 16mm Films
Budget: $12,000
Notes: Incl 2520 Books, 2493 Bound
Journals, 98 Videotapes, 117 Sound Slide

Programs, 7 Motion Pictures, 22 Audiotapes.
No photocopying.
NY —SAINT CLARE'S HOSPITAL &
HEALTH CENTER, Medical Library, 415
W 51 St, New York, 10019. James H Kirk,
Librn
Holdings: Vols (1500) Cat Slides Audiotapes
Microforms
Budget: ($16,000)
Notes: Clinical medicine and surgery. Also
5600 bound journals and 650 audiotapes.
Shelf list; separate catalog in progress.
NY —SOUTH NASSAU COMMUNITIES
HOSPITAL, Jules Redish Memorial Medical
Library, 2445 Oceanside Rd, Oceanside,
11572. Claire Joseph, Dir
Holdings: Vols (750) Cat
Budget:
Notes: Incl (6500) bound journals.
OK —UNIVERSITY OF OKLAHOMA,
Health Sciences Center, Department of
Surgery Library, Oklahoma Memorial
Hospital, PO Box 26307, Oklahoma City,
73126. Linda O'Rourke, Librn
RI —MIRIAM HOSPITAL MEDICAL
LIBRARY, 164 Summit Ave, Providence,
02906. Ann LeClaire, Dir of Library
Services
Holdings: Cat Cassettes
Notes: Special collection on the renal system
with emphasis on kidney transplantation and
dialysis.
VT —PUTNAM MEMORIAL HOSPITAL,
Medical Library, 100 Hospital Dr,
Bennington, 05201. Lynn Crandall, Library
Coordinator
Holdings: Vols (1000) Cat Audiotapes
Notes: Incl 10,000 journals (earliest 1975)
and 8 titles in audiotapes.
WA —SWEDISH HOSPITAL MEDICAL
CENTER, Medical Library, 747 Summit
Ave, Seattle, 98104.
Holdings: Vols (2072) Cat
WV —US VETERANS ADMINISTRATION
HOSPITAL, Library, 1540 Spring Valley Dr,
Huntington, 25704. Evelyn J Schaffer, Librn
Holdings: Vols (3700) Cat Slides
Phonorecords Audiotapes Videotapes 16mm
Films Filmstrips Microforms
PQ —CENTRE HOSPITALIER, HOSPITAL
SAINT FRANCOIS D'ASSISSE, Medical
and Administrative Library, SFA 10, Rue de
l'Espinay, Quebec, G1L 3L5, Can. Ulric
Lefebvre, Bibliotechnicienne
Holdings: Vols 7219 Cat Slides Audiotapes
16mm Films Filmstrips

SURGERY—HISTORY

GA —MEDICAL COLLEGE OF GEORGIA,
Library, Laney Walker Blvd, Augusta,
30902. Dorothy H Mims, Librn for Special
Collections
Holdings: Vols (2500) // Cat
Notes: Special collection of late 18th and
early 19th century medical books;
particularly strong in the surgical classics of
the period.
IA —UNIVERSITY OF IOWA, Health
Sciences Library, John Martin Rare Book
Room, Iowa City, 52242. Richard Eimas,
Librn
Holdings: Vols (2200) Cat Slides
Notes: Catalog: Iowa, University, Health
Sciences Library. *Heirs of Hippocrates* (Iowa
City, IA, Friends of the University of Iowa
Libraries, 1980). Collection is particularly
strong in areas of anatomy and surgery. It
also contains 300 books and reprints by and
about Sir William Osler as well as over 80
letters written by Osler.
MD —MEDICAL & CHIRURGICAL
FACULTY OF THE STATE OF
MARYLAND, Library, 1211 Cathedral St,
Baltimore, 21201. Joseph E Jensen, Librn
Holdings: Vols (10,000) // Cat Mss Maps
Pix
See also entry under Medicine - History and
Historic
MN —UNIVERSITY OF MINNESOTA,
Owen H Wangensteen Historical Library of
Biology & Medicine, Diehl Hall,
Minneapolis, 55455. Judith Overmier, Cur
Holdings: Vols (35,000) Cat Mss
Budget: ($80,000)
Notes: Strength in anesthesia, sepsis and

SURGERY—HISTORY (cont.)

antisepsis, obstetrics, especially puerperal fever and caesarian section.

NY —NEW YORK ACADEMY OF MEDICINE, Library, 2 E 103 St, New York, 10029. Brett A Kirkpatrick, Librn
Holdings: Vols Cat Mss
Notes: Samuel W Lambert, Jr, Collection on anatomy, surgery and history of medicine. Also incl the Edwin Smith surgical papyrus (ca 1800 BC).

OH —CLEVELAND MEDICAL LIBRARY ASSOCIATION/CASE WESTERN RESERVE UNIVERSITY, Cleveland Health Sciences Library, Historical Division, Allen Memorial Medical Library, 11000 Euclid Ave, Cleveland, 44106. Glen Jenkins, Rare Book Librarian & Archivist
Notes: Incl 15,000 historical vols, 6000 in the supporting collection. Incl about 1000 16th-18th century titles. Strength of collection: diseases, epidemiology, anatomy, surgery, medicine, obstetrics, gynecology, pediatrics and yellow fever. Incl also medical Americana, listed in Robert B Austin *Early American Medical Imprints,* 1668-1820 (Washington, DC, HEW, Public Health Service, 1961) and ca 7000 19th century works. Our total medical Americana collection also incl journals (not counted), mss and archives (900 linear ft) and 5000 pictures, especially of the Western Reserve. Anatomical works discussed in I Ebner and G Jenkins *Skeletons in Our Closet* (Cleveland, Cleveland Health Sciences Library, 1983)

PA —TEMPLE UNIVERSITY LIBRARIES, Special Collections Dept, Conwellana-Templana Collection, 13 & Berks St, Philadelphia, 19122. Miriam I Crawford, Cur
Holdings: Vols 10 Cat Mss Pix Audiotapes
Budget: ($30,000)
Notes: W Wayne Babcock (1872-1963) was a surgeon and medical educator of international reputation. The introduction of spinal anesthesia and of steel wire sutures were among his innovations. His personal papers (unprocessed) include manuscripts, correspondence, journal articles, documents, and news clippings, chiefly on medical topics and experiences spanning the first half of the 20th century. 10 linear ft.

RI —BROWN UNIVERSITY, John Hay Library, 20 Prospect St, Providence, 02912. Mark N Brown, Cur Mss
Holdings: // Mss
Notes: Papers of William Williams Keen, American surgeon, Brown Class of 1859. Of the 13,700 items in this collection, 13,200 consist of correspondence for the period 1858 to 1932 with noted scientists, physicians, and public figures. Also diaries, mss, and typescripts of articles, addresses, and lectures. A source for the history of medicine and surgery in the US, 1860-1930. Register available.

TN —VANDERBILT UNIVERSITY, Medical Center Library, Nashville, 37232. Mary H Teloh, Special Collections Librn
Holdings: Vols 3000 Cat Mss Pix Slides
Notes: The rare books collection incl works by Auenbrugger, Beaumont, Elyot, Jenner, Laennec, Vesalius, and Vigo. The working collection for the history of medicine is particularly strong in American imprints of the late 18th and 19th century. These emphases are supported in the general collection by some notable runs of the 18th and 19th century European and American medical journals. Strong subject collections include: military medicine, nutrition, surgery and urology. There is also under development a collection of the scientific writings of medical educators connected with Vanderbilt.

SURGERY, PLASTIC

MA —FRANCIS A COUNTWAY LIBRARY OF MEDICINE, Boston Medical Library/ Harvard Medical Library, 10 Shattuck St, Boston, 02115. C Robin LeSueur, Librn; Richard J Wolfe, Cur, Rare Books & Manuscripts
Holdings: Vols (500,000) Cat Mss Maps Pix Microforms
Notes: Combines resources of the Harvard Medical School and the Boston Medical Library. Strong in serials and medical history in all fields of medicine, incl incunabula, non-medical books by doctors, travel books by doctors. 500,000 medical dissertations and theses. Special strength in all medical subjects listed in this volume.

NY —COLUMBIA UNIVERSITY LIBRARIES, Health Sciences Library, 701 W 168 St, New York, 10032. Rachael K Goldstein, Librn
Holdings: Vols 1105 Cat
Notes: Landmark works, incl those from the Jerome P Webster Library of Plastic Surgery. Support materials for this collection incl 4000 books, 8000 theses, ca 50,000 black and white photographs, ca 10,000 Kodachrome slides, 71 vols of original drawings of surgical procedures. Restricted to members of the medical profession.

SURGERY, PSYCHIC see Medicine, Psychic

SURGICAL ATLASES

CT —YALE MEDICAL LIBRARY, 333 Cedar St, New Haven, 06510.

SURGICAL TECHNICIANS see Operating Room Technicians

SURINAM

CT —YALE UNIVERSITY, Sterling Memorial Library, Latin American Collections, New Haven, 06520. Lee H Williams Jr, Cur
Holdings: Vols (300,000) Cat Maps Pix Slides Phonorecords 16mm Films Filmstrips
See also entry under Latin America

NY —AMERICAN MUSEUM OF NATURAL HISTORY, Library Services Dept, Central Park W & 79th St, New York, 10024. Nina J Root, Chairwoman; Mary Genett, Asst Librn for Reference Services

SURNAMES see Names, Personal

SURREALISM see Art, Surrealistic

SURTEES, ROBERT SMITH

PA —UNIVERSITY OF PITTSBURGH, Hillman Library, Special Collections Dept, 363 Hillman Library, Pittsburgh, 15260. Charles E Aston Jr, Coordinator
Notes: The Bernard S Horne Memorial Collection of over 230 editions of Walton's *The Complete Angler;* also of Robert Smith Surtees' books.

SURTZ, FR. EDWARD, S. J., 1909-1973

IL —LOYOLA UNIVERSITY OF CHICAGO, E M Cudahy Memorial Library, 6525 N Sheridan Rd, Chicago, 60626.
Notes: Thomas Cranmer's working library and papers, incl ms of a critical edition of Thomas Cranmer's *Censurae* that Fr Surtz was working on at the time of his death.

SURVEY OF RACE RELATIONS, STANFORD UNIVERSITY

CA —HOOVER INSTITUTION ON WAR, REVOLUTION & PEACE, Stanford University, Stanford, 94305. Milorad M Drachkovitch, Archivist
Holdings: // Mss
Notes: Records, 1923-1935, on the Survey of Race Relations at Stanford University, California. Materials relating to studies on acculturization patterns of minority groups on the Pacific coast. The survey attempted a complete investigation of the economc, religious, educational, civic, biological, and social conditions and tendencies prevailing among the Chinese, Japanese, and other nonwhite residents of the Pacific coast area of the US and Canada. 37 boxes.
Unpublished preliminary inventory in the repository.

SURVEYING

MI —UNIVERSITY OF MICHIGAN, Harlan Hatcher Graduate Library, Map Room, Ann Arbor, 48109. James O Minton, Map Librn
Notes: The collection consists of approx 300,000 sheet maps incl maps and charts received on deposit from the US Geological Survey, Defense Mapping Agency, and the National Ocean Service. The collection also incl approx 5000 reference volumes related to cartography, surveying, and mapping, with emphasis on place-name literature (gazetteers, dictionaries), books on how to use and interpret maps, carto-bibliographies, and state (provincial, etc), regional, national, and international atlases. The collection is strongest geographically in materials of Michigan, Midwest, Anglo-America, and Europe; chronologically, 1850-date; and thematically, in topographic and geologic maps, although all subjects are collected. The collection maintains a separate catalog of holdings. Reference volumes are fully cataloged and classified.

NV —UNIVERSITY OF NEVADA, RENO, University Library, Special Collections Dept, Reno, 89557. Robert E Blesse, Head
Holdings: Vols (25) Uncat Photogs Mss
Notes: Papers of James E Church founder and developer of the modern science of snow surveying. Church collection, 180 cu ft, includes his writings, papers, and over 7000 photographs of Church's snow surveying expeditions in the Sierra Nevada mountains and elsewhere in the world. Papers of the Western Snow Conference, 80 cu ft.

NY —PAUL SMITHS COLLEGE, Frank L Cubley Library, Paul Smiths, 12970. Theodore Mack, Librn
Holdings: Vols 100 Cat Slides Audiotapes Filmstrips

OK —US ARMY FIELD ARTILLERY SCHOOL LIBRARY, Morris Swett Library, Snow Hall, Fort Sill, 73503. Lester L Miller Jr, Chief Librn
Notes: Field artillery; artillery; ordnance; military history; military science; weapons and weapons systems; ammunition; ballistics; missiles; Field Artillery unit histories; military periodicals analytical index file (VF). Incl US and foreign artillery; survey data; photographs on army subjects.

VT —VERMONT TECHNICAL COLLEGE, Hartness Library, Randolph Center, 05061. Dewey Patterson, Library Dir
Holdings: Vols 3550 Cat

WI —MADISON AREA TECHNICAL COLLEGE, Technical Center Library, 2125 Commercial Ave, Madison, 53704. J B Jeffcott, Librn
Holdings: Vols 350 Cat Slides Phonorecords Audiotapes 16mm Films Filmstrips Microforms

PQ —SERVICE DE LA DOCUMENTATION ET DES RENSEIGNEMENTS MINISTERE DE L'ENERGIE ET DES RESSOURCES, 2000B, chemin Sainte-Foy, 7th floor, Quebec, G1R 4X7, Can. Normand Guerette, Dir
Holdings: Vols (114,800) Slides Videotapes
Notes: In 1979, the Bibliotheque du ministere des Richesses naturelles du Quebec merged with the Bibliotheque du ministere des Terres et Forets. The result of this merger was the creation of the service de la Documentation et des Renseignements du ministere de l'Energie et des Ressources. Publications: Info-Biblio Terres et Forets; Mines; Energy.

SURVEYING—HISTORY

IL —ADLER PLANETARIUM, History of Astronomy Collection, 1300 S Lake Shore Dr, Chicago, 60605. Roderick Webster, Cur; Marjorie Webster, Cur; Sara Schechner Genuth, Asst Cur
Holdings: Vols (430) Uncat Mss Maps Pix
Notes: Historical surveying instruments. Price Photographic Archives (2800) containing prints of instruments. Incl (1000) scientific instruments. Noncirculating.
See also entries under Astronomy - History; Navigation - History; Horology.

SURVEYS, LIBRARY see Library Surveys

SURVEYS, SOCIAL see Social Surveys

SURVEYS, TRAFFIC see Traffic Surveys

SURVIVORS' BENEFITS (OLD AGE PENSIONS) see Old Age Pensions

SUSIAN LANGUAGE see Elamite Language

SUSPENDED ANIMATION see Trance

SUSPENDED SENTENCE see Probation

SUSTAINED-RELEASE DRUGS see Delayed-Action Preparations

SUTHERLAND, ARTHUR EUGENE, 1902-1973

MA —HARVARD UNIVERSITY LIBRARY, Law School Library, Langdell Hall,

SUTHERLAND, ARTHUR EUGENE, 1902-1973 (cont.)

Cambridge, 02138. Erika S Chadbourn, Cur of Mss
Holdings: Cat Mss
Notes: Professional papers. Typed inventory in repository. Inclusive dates: 1923-1972.

SUTHERLAND, DONALD

NE —UNIVERSITY OF NEBRASKA-LINCOLN, Don L Love Library, University Archives and Special Collections, Lincoln, 68588. Joseph G Svoboda, University Archivist
Notes: Virginia Faulkner was recognized as one of Nebraska's most distinguished writers and scholars. The Virginia Faulkner Collection, containing over 2000 titles, is housed in the Special Collections Department of Love Library. It is especially strong in twentieth century writers and in University of Nebraska Press publications. Of especial value to scholars are her extensive holdings of Willa Cather, Wright Morris and John Neihardt. Her correspondence with S N Behrman, E B White, Edward Wagenknecht, Donald Sutherland, Wright Morris, Louise Pound, Mari Sandoz, Hazel Barnes, Alfred A and Blanche Knopf, and others provide insight into the literary development of these figures, as well as chronicle the intellectual thought of the period. Amassed in a separate file, these letters are available to interested scholars.

SUTRO, ADOLPH

CA —UNIVERSITY OF SAN FRANCISCO, Richard A Gleeson Library, The Countess Bernardine Murphy Donohue Rare Book Room, San Francisco, 94117. D Steven Corey, Special Collections Librn
Notes: Engineer of the Sutro Tunnel in Nevada and San Francisco mayor. One box of personal papers, 8 boxes of archives of Sutro Baths in San Francisco, one box of photographs, three boxes of source material for the biography by R E Jr and M F Stewart.

SWAHILI LANGUAGE

OH —CLEVELAND PUBLIC LIBRARY, Foreign Literature Dept, 325 Superior Ave, Cleveland, 44114. Natalia Bezugloff, Head
Holdings: Vols 100 Cat
Notes: Language and literature. A popular circulating collection with emphasis on language learning; spoken phonodiscs and cassettes.
See also entry under Foreign Language Collections

PA —DUQUESNE UNIVERSITY, Library, 600 Forbes Ave, Pittsburgh, 15219.
Holdings: Vols (7407) Cat Maps Slides Microforms
Notes: Mostly concerned with Africa south of the Sahara. CIDESA file (Centre International de Documentation Economique et Social Africaine) contains material dealing with economic and social problems of the African continent. Collection strong in materials on economics and Hausa and Swahili languages.

SWAIM, E. H.

DC —GEORGETOWN UNIVERSITY, Library, Special Collections Div, 37 & O Sts NW, Washington, 20057. George M Barringer, Special Collections Librn; Nicholas B Sheetz, Mss Librn
Holdings: Mss Cat
Notes: The E H Swaim Collection. A collection of letters, affidavits, and photographs relating to the assassination of Abraham Lincoln and the subsequent career of John Wilkes Booth. Much of this material was gathered by Finis L Bates, Clarence True Wilson, and W P Campbell (whose research files were brought together by Swaim) and is for the most part by people who were involved in the events surrounding the assassination; members of the Booth family and their acquaintances; and individuals who claimed to have known Booth later in Texas and Oklahoma.

SWALLOW, ALAN, 1915-1967

CA —UNIVERSITY OF CALIFORNIA, LOS ANGELES, Research Library, Dept of Special Collections, 405 Hilgard Ave, Los Angeles, 90024. Edward Shreeves, Chairman, Bibliographers Group; David S Zeidberg, Head
Notes: 14 linear feet of papers, largely unsorted, mostly concerning his publishing activities.

SWAN, ALFRED J.

VA —UNIVERSITY OF VIRGINIA, Alderman Library, Music Collection, Charlottesville, 22901. Evan Bonds, Music Librn
Holdings: Cat Mss Pix
Notes: Scores, books, correspondence of the Russian music historian Alfred J Swan, related to his study of Soviet music (particularly Russian church music and folk songs) and musicians. Published description: Velimirovic, Milos, "The Swan Music Collection," *Chapter & Verse* (Journal of the Associates of the Univ of Va Library), Nov 1977, pp 20-21.

SWANSON, CLAUDE

VA —UNIVERSITY OF VIRGINIA, Alderman Library, Manuscripts Dept, Charlottesville, 22901. Edmund Berkeley Jr, Cur
Holdings: Cat Mss Pix
Notes: Papers, personal and political, etc.

SWANSON, GLORIA

†TX —UNIVERSITY OF TEXAS LIBRARIES, Hoblitzelle Theatre Arts Library, Austin, 78712.
Notes: A 100,000-item collection of correspondence and documents related to the career and personal life of Gloria Swanson, one of the largest archives from 1913 to 1983. Correspondence with Mary Pickford, William Faulkner, and the Kennedy Family, the latter to remain sealed until the year 2000.

SWANSON, ROBERT STERLING

WI —UNIVERSITY OF WISCONSIN-STOUT, Library Learning Center, Menomonie, 54751. Philip Sawin Jr, Coll Develop Librn
Notes: Papers. Swanson was the fifth head of the University of Wisconsin-Stout. Not yet cataloged.

SWARD, ROBERT

MO —WASHINGTON UNIVERSITY, Libraries, Special Collections Dept, Campus Box 1061, St Louis, 63130.
Notes: A major collection, incl books, mss, correspondence, literary papers, photographs, etc. Described in *Special Collections: an Annotated Guide to the Holdings of the Manuscript Division and the University Archives and Research Collection.*
BC —UNIVERSITY OF VICTORIA, McPherson Library, Victoria, V8W 3H5, Can.
Notes: Incl 8 cm, 1967-71; mss.

SWAZILAND

DC —HOWARD UNIVERSITY, Moorland-Spingarn Research Center, 500 Howard Place NW, Washington, 20059. Clifford L Muse, Jr, Acting Dir
OH —OHIO UNIVERSITY, Vernon R Alden Library, Athens, 45701. Kent Mulliner, Africana Specialist
Holdings: Vols (30,000) Cat Maps Microforms
Notes: Major emphasis on South Africa, East Africa, and Nigeria. Incl extensive collection of government reports and newspapers on microfilm.

SWEDEN

NY —SWEDISH INFORMATION SERVICE, Library, 825 Third Ave, New York, 10022. Elisabeth Halvarsson, Librn
Holdings: Vols 8000 Cat Pix Slides Phonorecords 16mm Films Filmstrips
Notes: Covers history, language, literature, education, social sciences and economy of Sweden, as well as Swedes in US, and Modern Swedish Society. Films rented on limited basis.

SWEDEN—FOREIGN RELATIONS

RI —BROWN UNIVERSITY, John Hay Library, 20 Prospect St, Providence, 02912. Mark N Brown, Cur Mss
Holdings: // Mss
Notes: Papers of Jonathan Russell, merchant, diplomat, and Massachusetts Congressman. Brown Class of 1791. A collection of 7000 items containing a diary and a letterbook (1809-1813); records of US Commissioners at Ghent (1813-1814) and of the American Legation at Stockholm (1814-1816); correspondence and documents for the period 1795-1830; and notes, largely official, when Russell was Charge d'Affaires at Paris (1810) and for 1814-1818 when he was Minister to Sweden and Norway and a member of the US Congress.

SWEDEN—HISTORY

CA —CLAREMONT COLLEGES, Honnold Library, Ninth & Dartmouth, Claremont, 91711. Franklin D Scott, Cur, Nordic Collection; Penelope Garris, Librn
Holdings: Vols (25,000) Cat Maps Pix Slides Audiotapes Videotapes Periodicals
Notes: Nordic Collections are broadly inclusive, but emphasize history of Scandinavia, Baltic countries, and Hanseatic cities. Nucleus of collections from gifts and endowment of Waldemar Westergaard, supplemented with relevant collections of David Bjork, John H Wuorinen, Ingolf Olsen, Henry Steele Commager, Franklin Scott (incl Scandinavian migration to America), Eric Bellquist, and other gifts and purchases. Eight vertical file drawers of news bulletins in English or vernaculars, 1941-.
See: Franklin D Scott, "The Westergaard-Bjork Collection at the Honnold Library, the Claremont Colleges," *Scandinavian Studies*, 41 (1969), 346-354. Collection incl complete publications of Nordic Council.
†DC —LIBRARY OF CONGRESS, Rare Book Division, Washington, 20540.
Notes: A collection of considerable strength.
IL —NORTH PARK COLLEGE LIBRARY, 5125 N Spaulding Ave, Chicago, 60625. Dorothy-Ellen Gross, Dir
Holdings: Vols (4500) Cat
Notes: Scandinavian Collection, with materials mostly Swedish, but some titles in Norwegian, Danish, Finnish and Icelandic. Separate shelf list, but also incl in union catalog. General collection with emphasis on literature and history. Other Swedish books in the field of religion available through Mellander Library on same campus.
IL —AUGUSTANA COLLEGE, Library, Rock Island, 61201. Marjorie M Miller, Special Collections Librn
Holdings: Vols 5000 Cat Mss Maps Pix Microforms
Notes: The largest collection of Swedish-Americana in this country. Many rare books relative to the Delaware Swedes (latter half of 17th century). Most of the valuable (rare) materials are gifts. The unique Swedish-American newspaper collection (with the cooperation of the Royal Library, Stockholm) has been microfilmed. Letters and papers of pioneer pastors are especially significant. The Lars Esbjorn, Eric Norelius, T N Hasselquist and Olof Olsson (all clergymen) letters are of foremost importance. (Listed in *N U C of Manuscript Collections*).

SWEDEN—HISTORY (cont.)

MN —UNIVERSITY OF MINNESOTA, O
Meredith Wilson Library, 309 19 Ave S,
Minneapolis, 55455. Austin J McLean,
Chief, Special Collections
Holdings: Vols 2655 // Uncat
Notes: A collection of Swedish royal decrees
(Arstrycket), which span the years 1640-
1824.

NY —SWEDISH INFORMATION SERVICE,
Library, 825 Third Ave, New York, 10022.
Elisabeth Halvarsson, Librn
Holdings: Vols 8000 Cat Pix Slides
Phonorecords 16mm Films Filmstrips
Notes: Covers history, language, literature,
education, social sciences and economy of
Sweden, as well as Swedes in US, and
Modern Swedish society. Films rented on
limited basis.

WA —UNIVERSITY OF WASHINGTON
LIBRARIES, Suzzallo Library, Scandinavian
Collections, FM-25, Seattle, 98195. A
Gerald Anderson, Librn
Holdings: Vols (50,000) Cat Mss Pix
Budget: ($15,546)
Notes: Research collections with emphasis
on languages and literatures, and auxiliary
strengths in history, political science, social
science. Archival and other special materials
relating to Scandinavian- Americans in the
Pacific Northwest are located in other
appropriate collections.

SWEDEN—RELIGION

IL —EVANGELICAL COVENANT
CHURCH, Archives and Historical Library,
North Park College, 5125 N Spaulding Ave,
Chicago, 60625. Sigurd F Westberg,
Archivist
Holdings: Vols 4000 Cat Mss Pix Audiotapes
16mm Films Microforms
Budget: $7000
Notes: The church archives of the
Evangelical Covenant Church. This is a
denominational archive though we do have a
great deal of background material from
Sweden. We also have some materials from
closely related churches. Hold both official
and unofficial publications. Also, letters,
diaries, sermons and photographs of pastors,
missionaries, teachers, and lay leaders.

SWEDENBORGIANISM see New Jerusalem Church

SWEDES IN THE U.S.

IL —AUGUSTANA COLLEGE, Swenson
Swedish Immigration Research Center, Rock
Island, 61201. Kermit Westerberg, Archivist
Holdings: Vols 5000 Cat Mss Maps Pix
Microforms
Notes: The largest collection of Swedish-
Americana in this country. Many rare books
relative to the Delaware Swedes (latter half
of 17th century). Most of the valuable (rare)
materials are gifts. The unique Swedish-
American newspaper collection (with the
cooperation of the Royal Library,
Stockholm) has been microfilmed. Letters
and papers of pioneer pastors are especially
significant. The Lars Esbjorn, Eric Norelius,
T N Hasselquist and Olof Olsson (all
clergymen) letters are of foremost
importance. (Listed in NUC of Manuscript
Collections).

†MN —CARVER COUNTY HISTORICAL
SOCIETY LIBRARY, 119 South Cherry St,
Waconia, 55387.
Notes: Early 1860 library of Swedes and
Germans in the locality.

NY —SWEDISH INFORMATION SERVICE,
Library, 825 Third Ave, New York, 10022.
Elisabeth Halvarsson, Librn
Holdings: Vols 8000 Cat Pix Slides
Phonorecords 16mm Films Filmstrips
Notes: Covers history, language, literature,
education, social sciences and economy of
Sweden, as well as Swedes in US, and
Modern Swedish Society. Films rented on
limited basis.

PA —BALCH INSTITUTE FOR ETHNIC
STUDIES, Library, 18 S Seventh St,
Philadelphia, 19106. R Joseph Anderson,
Library Dir
Holdings: Vols 400 Cat Mss Pix
Notes: The Amandus Johnson Collection of
his papers, incl biographical material on 20th
century Swedish-Americans, much of
records from the American Swedish
Historical Museum in South Philadelphia,
and source documents on the early Swedish
settlement of the Delaware Valley.
See also entry under Johnson, Amandus,
1877-1974.

WA —UNIVERSITY OF WASHINGTON
LIBRARIES, Suzzallo Library, Scandinavian
Collections, FM-25, Seattle, 98195. A
Gerald Anderson, Librn
Holdings: Vols (50,000) Cat Mss Pix
Budget: ($15,546)
Notes: Research collections with emphasis
on languages and literatures, and auxiliary
strengths in history, political science, social
science. Archival and other special materials
relating to Scandanavian-Americans in the
Pacific Northwest are located in other
appropriate collections.

SWEDISH AMERICAN NEWSPAPERS see Newspapers, Swedish American

SWEDISH ART see Art, Swedish

SWEDISH LANGUAGE AND LITERATURE

CA —UNIVERSITY OF CALIFORNIA,
BERKELEY, University Library,
Scandinavian Collections, Berkeley, 94720.
Helvi M Bessenyei, Librn
Holdings: Vols 20,000
Budget: $15,530
Notes: Research collections covering the full
range of Scandinavian languages and
literatures, with extensive periodical
holdings. Particular strengths are Old Norse
and Swedish. Moreover, special emphasis is
on the late 19th century Scandinavian
authors from Kierkegaard to Strinberg. The
language and literature collections are
supplemented by substantial resources in
related disciplines. Some rare book materials
are housed in the Bancroft Library.

CA —LOS ANGELES PUBLIC LIBRARY,
Foreign Languages Dept, 630 W Fifth St,
Los Angeles, 90071. Sylva Manoogian,
Principal Librn
Holdings: Vols 3214 Cat
Budget: ($41,500)

†DC —LIBRARY OF CONGRESS, Rare Book
Division, Washington, 20540.
Notes: A collection of considerable strength.

IL —NORTH PARK COLLEGE LIBRARY,
5125 N Spaulding Ave, Chicago, 60625.
Dorothy-Ellen Gross, Dir
Holdings: Vols (4500) Cat
Notes: Scandinavian Collection, with
materials mostly Swedish, but some titles in
Norwegian, Danish, Finnish and Icelandic.
Separate shelf list, but also incl in union
catalog. General collection with emphasis on
literature and history. Other Swedish books
in the field of religion available through
Mellander Library on same campus.

NY —NEW YORK PUBLIC LIBRARY,
Donnell Foreign Language Library, 20 W 53
St, New York, 10019. Bosiljka Stevanovic,
Supvr Librn
Holdings: Vols 356 Cat
Notes: Swedish collection incl Swedish
authors of Swedish expression. No separate
catalog.

NY —SWEDISH INFORMATION SERVICE,
Library, 825 Third Ave, New York, 10022.
Elisabeth Halvarsson, Librn
Holdings: Vols 8000 Cat Pix Slides
Phonorecords 16mm Films Filmstrips
Notes: Covers history, language, literature,
education, social sciences and economy of
Sweden, as well as Swedes in US, and
Modern Swedish Society. Films rented on
limited basis.

NC —DUKE UNIVERSITY, William R
Perkins Library, Durham, 27706. Elvin E
Strowd, University Librn
Notes: The Scandinavian collection of 3000
items is a collection of Scandinavian
literature, primarily representing the latter
half of the 18th century and early 19th
century.

OH —CLEVELAND PUBLIC LIBRARY,
Foreign Literature Dept, 325 Superior Ave,
Cleveland, 44114. Natalia Bezugloff, Head
Holdings: Vols 3110 Cat
Notes: A popular circulating collection
containing classics and the standard works
with emphasis on belles lettres, history and
biography. A variety of other subjects such
as learning languages, how to do books, art,
children's books, spoken phonodiscs and
cassettes, periodicals, etc.
See also entry under Foreign Language
Collections

OH —KENT STATE UNIVERSITY, Libraries,
Ethnic Collections, Kent, 44242.
Holdings: Vols 50 Cat
See also entry under Foreign Language
Collections

WA —UNIVERSITY OF WASHINGTON
LIBRARIES, Suzzallo Library, Scandinavian
Collections, FM-25, Seattle, 98195. A
Gerald Anderson, Librn
Holdings: Vols (50,000) Cat Mss Pix
Budget: ($15,546)
Notes: Research collections with emphasis
on languages and literatures, and auxiliary
strengths in history, political science, social
science. Archival and other special materials
relating to Scandinavian- Americans in the
Pacific Northwest are located in other
appropriate collections.

SWEDISH MYTHOLOGY see Mythology, Norse

SWEITZER, PAUL

AZ —NORTHERN ARIZONA
UNIVERSITY, Special Collection Library,
CU Box 6022, Flagstaff, 86011. Peter M
Whiteley, Coordr/Archivist; William
Mullane, Librn
Notes: Paul Sweitzer Collection; subject files
and mss relating to Flagstaff area stories of
the Arizona Daily Sun, Flagstaff, 1960's-
1977. Sweitzer was a Flagstaff journalist.

SWENSON, MAY

MO —WASHINGTON UNIVERSITY,
Libraries, Special Collections Dept, Campus
Box 1061, St Louis, 63130.
Notes: A major collection, incl books, mss,
correspondence, literary papers, photographs,
etc. Described in Special Collections: an
Annotated Guide to the Holdings of the
Manuscript Division and the University
Archives and Research Collection.

SWIDLER, JOSEPH CHARLES, 1907-

DC —LIBRARY OF CONGRESS, Manuscript
Division, Washington, 20540. John C
Broderick, Chief
Notes: Papers of Joseph C Swidler,
Chairman, Federal Power Commission,
Kennedy Administration.

SWIFT, JONATHAN

CA —UNIVERSITY OF CALIFORNIA, LOS
ANGELES, William Andrews Clark
Memorial Library, 2520 Cimarron St, Los
Angeles, 90018.
Holdings: Cat
Notes: Extensive collection, first editions,
etc.

†CA —STANFORD UNIVERSITY
LIBRARIES, Stanford, 94305.
Notes: In collection of English and
American Literature.

MI —UNIVERSITY OF MICHIGAN, Library,
Dept of Rare Books & Special Collections,
Ann Arbor, 48109. Robert J Starring, Head
Holdings: Vols 950 Cat
Notes: Chiefly editions, translations and
adaptations of Gulliver's Travels in collected
works and separate editions, and forming
part of the Hubbard Imaginary Voyages
Collection.

NY —CORNELL UNIVERSITY LIBRARIES,
John M Olin Library, Dept of Rare Books,

SWIFT, JONATHAN (cont.)

Ithaca, 14853. Donald D Eddy, Librn
Notes: A collection of Jonathan Swift
material, incl mss.

PA —UNIVERSITY OF PENNSYLVANIA,
Van Pelt Library, Rare Books Collection, 34
& Walnut Sts, Philadelphia, 19104. Daniel
Traister, Special Collections Librn
Holdings: Vols 1750 Cat
Notes: Incl 18th and early 19th century
editions of collected works and individual
titles, in English and foreign languages.

PA —CARLOW COLLEGE, Grace Library,
Fifth Ave, Pittsburgh, 15213. Joan M
Mitchell, Dir of Library Services
Holdings: Vols 543 // Cat Phonorecords
Audiotapes
Notes: The Gladys Wholey Curran
Collection, which consists primarily of titles
in the area of Irish Literature, specifically
those titles concerned with the study of the
Irish playwrights and poets. The collection is
particularly strong in volumes related to the
study of Jonathan Swift, John M Synge, and
William B Yeats. In addition, there is
notable focus upon Irish history of the 17th
and 18th centuries. No photocopying.

WI —UNIVERSITY OF WISCONSIN,
MADISON, Memorial Library, British &
American Language & Literature Collection,
728 State St, Madison, 53706. Yvonne
Schofer, Bibliographer
Holdings: Vols 100 Cat
Notes: Teerink Swift Collection. Consists of
100 volumes on and about Jonathan Swift
and other literary and historical figures of his
age, from the collection of Dr H Teerink, the
Dutch bibliographer of Swift. Included are
some 20 editions of Gulliver's Travels in
English, French, German, and Dutch;
numerous editions of *A Tale of a Tub;* first
editions, such as John Bull pamphlets and
*The History of the Four Last Years of the
Queen;* and many scholarly editions, with
commentaries. Supplements other Swift and
the English novel, there are contemporary
editions of Mandeville, Pope, Woodes
Rogers, and others. Held in Dept of Rare
Books and Special Collections and in stacks.

SWIFT, WILLIAM K.

IL —CHICAGO HISTORICAL SOCIETY,
Library, Clark St at North Ave, Chicago,
60614. Archie Motley, Manuscript Librn
Notes: Papers of William K Swift on the
Illinois and Michigan Canal.

SWIMMING AND DIVING

FL —INTERNATIONAL SWIMMING HALL
OF FAME LIBRARY, 1 Hall of Fame Dr,
Fort Lauderdale, 33316. Marion Washburn,
Librn
Holdings: Vols (3000) Cat Mss Audiotapes
Videotapes 16mm Films
Notes: All aspects of swimming: history,
instruction, competition. Incl rare and out of
print editions, complete set of *NCAA
Swimming Guides* (1915-date), numerous
periodicals (eg, *Swimming World,* 1951-
date), and small collection of materials on
related aquatic sports: diving, synchronized
swimming, etc. Also have materials on
Olympic Games, 1896-date, covering
history, results, pictorial essays, programs,
etc

IL —NATIONAL COUNCIL OF THE
YMCAS, YMCA Historical Library, 6400
Shafer Ct, Rosemont, 60018. Eleanor R
Murphy, Librn
Notes: Large collection, incl historical
material, on basketball, wrestling, track and
field, swimming, diving, scuba and volleyball.

MB —AQUATIC HALL OF FAME &
MUSEUM OF CANADA, Library, 25
Poseidon Bay, Winnipeg, R3M 3E4, Can.
Notes: Aquatic sports, incl swimming,
diving, water polo and synchronized
swimming. Aquatic memorabilia; records
covering Olympics, World Games, Pan-
American Games, Commonwealth Games
and Canadian Championships; coaching;
record books. Collections on sailing ships,

and yachts and yachting, incl books from the
Cutty Sark Club of Winnipeg, covering
sailing of the past.

SWINBURNE, ALGERNON CHARLES

CT —TRINITY COLLEGE LIBRARY,
Watkinson Library, 300 Summit St,
Hartford, 06106. Jeffrey Kaimowitz, Cur
Holdings: Cat
Notes: First editions, etc.

DC —GEORGETOWN UNIVERSITY,
Library, Special Collections Div, 37 & O Sts
NW, Washington, 20057. George M
Barringer, Special Collections Librn;
Nicholas B Sheetz, Mss Librn
Holdings: Mss
Notes: Extensive collection of books, mss,
and letters by and about the poet Algernon
Charles Swinburne and his circle.

MA —HARVARD UNIVERSITY LIBRARY,
Houghton Library, Cambridge, 02138.
Rodney G Dennis, Cur of Manuscripts
Holdings: Mss

MI —UNIVERSITY OF MICHIGAN, Library,
Dept of Rare Books & Special Collections,
Ann Arbor, 48109. Robert J Starring, Head
Holdings: Vols (390) Cat Mss Pix
Notes: Includes many first editions and
association copies. In addition there are 235
manuscript items, over 70 in Swinburne's
holograph, and including as a special series
65 items of correspondence of major donor
Lowell Kerr with Swinburne scholars; also
photographs and Swinburneana.

NY —SYRACUSE UNIVERSITY
LIBRARIES, Ernest S Bird Library, George
Arents Research Library for Special
Collections, Syracuse, 13210. Carolyn A
Davis, Manuscripts Librn; Amy S Doherty,
University Archivist; Mark F Weimer, Rare
Book Librn
Holdings: Cat Mss Pix Slides Microforms
Notes: The extensive Swinburne collection
of John Simon Mayfield Syracuse, NY
13210.

WI —UNIVERSITY OF WISCONSIN,
MADISON, Memorial Library, British &
American Language & Literature Collection,
728 State St, Madison, 53706. Yvonne
Schofer, Bibliographer
Holdings: Vols (1000)// Cat
Notes: Arthur Beatty Collection. Consists of
over 1000 volumes, principally in the
English poetry of the Romantic period,
strong in Coleridge, Tennyson, Swinburne,
the prose of De Quincy and the folk poetry
and balladry of Great Britain and Europe.
Outstanding for its first and other editions of
Wordsworth. About 200 titles in the
Department of Rare Books and Special
Collections; the rest is in stacks.

SWINE

TX —AMARILLO PUBLIC LIBRARY, 413 E
Fourth, Amarillo, 79101. Mary Kay Snell,
Librn
Holdings: Vols 1210 Cat Maps Filmstrips VF
Notes: The Meat Industry Collection
contains documents, periodicals, pamphlets,
AV materials on the production of
processing and marketing of cattle, swine,
sheep, poultry and rabbits. Most of the
collection circulates except for the
magazines.

SWINE FEVER

NY —US DEPT OF AGRICULTURE,
Agriculture Research Service, Plum Island
Animal Disease Laboratory, PO Box 848,
Greenport, 11944. Stephen Perlman, Librn
Holdings: Vols 15,000 Cat Pix Slides
Microforms
Budget: $30,000

SWING, PHILIP DAVID, 1883-1963

CA —UNIVERSITY OF CALIFORNIA, LOS
ANGELES, Research Library, Dept of
Special Collections, 405 Hilgard Ave, Los
Angeles, 90024. Edward Shreeves,
Chairman, Bibliographers Group; David S
Zeidberg, Head
Notes: 75 linear feet of correspondence and

photographs recording his career as a
congressman, State official, and private
attorney.

SWING, RAYMOND, 1887-1968

DC —LIBRARY OF CONGRESS, Motion
Pictures, Broadcasting and Recorded Sound
Div, Washington, 20540.
Notes: Over 5600 papers and broadcast
recordings of Raymond Swing (1887-1968).

SWING MUSIC see Jazz

SWINNERTON, FRANK

CT —YALE UNIVERSITY, Box 1603A, Yale
Station, New Haven, 06520.

PA —BRYN MAWR COLLEGE, Canaday
Library, Bryn Mawr, 19010. James Tanis,
Dir
Notes: Rare books in the Adelman
Collection.

SWISS IN THE U.S.

PA —BALCH INSTITUTE FOR ETHNIC
STUDIES, Library, 18 S Seventh St,
Philadelphia, 19106. R Joseph Anderson,
Library Dir
Holdings: Vols 75 Cat Mss Microforms

SWISS LANGUAGES AND
LITERATURE

CA —STANFORD UNIVERSITY
LIBRARIES, Cecil H Green Library,
Stanford, 94305. Peter R Frank, Cur, CDP-
German Collection; Mary Jane Parrine, Cur,
CDP-Romance Collection
Notes: Strong collection of German-Swiss
and Romance-Swiss literature, with emphsis
from the Enlightenment to the present. Rare
items in the Stanford Collection of German,
Austrian and Swiss Culture and Special
Collections.

WI —UNIVERSITY OF WISCONSIN,
MADISON, Memorial Library, Western
European Humanities Collection, 728 State
St, Madison, 53706. Charles Szabo,
Bibliographer
Notes: Swiss Literature Romande Collection.
An extensive collection of the literature of
the French-speaking portion of Switzerland
of the 19th and 20th centuries, representing
some 738 authors. Originally the private
libraries of Leon Savary and Rene Morax.
Includes the major Romand writers, as well
as many works by lesser-known and ordinary
writers of the period. No photocopying.

SWITZER, MARY ELIZABETH

MA —RADCLIFFE COLLEGE, Arthur &
Elizabeth Schlesinger Library on the History
of Women in America, 3 James St,
Cambridge, 02138. Patricia Miller King, Dir;
Eva Moseley, Cur of Mss
Notes: Incl the audiotapes and transcripts of
the Women in the Federal Government Oral
History Project, also papers of Clara M
Beyer, Martha May Eliot, MD, Elizabeth
Holtzman, Jeannette Rankin, Edith Nourse
Rogers, and Mary Elizabeth Switzer.

SWITZER, ROBERT E., 1918-

KS —MENNINGER FOUNDATION,
Archives, 5600 W Sixth St, Box 829,
Topeka, 66601. Alice Brand, Librn; Mark
West, Archivist
Notes: 9 boxes, 1956-75. His papers consist
of correspondence and mss.

SWITZERLAND—HISTORY

CA —STANFORD UNIVERSITY
LIBRARIES, Cecil H Green Library,
Stanford, 94305. Peter R Frank, Cur, CDP-
German Collection; Mary Jane Parrine, Cur,
CDP-Romance Collection
Holdings: Cat
Notes: The Swiss collection covers a broad
range of Swiss history, civilization and
culture of both the German- and Romance-

SWITZERLAND—HISTORY (cont.)

Swiss part. Strong holdings of Kanton and city histories, yearbooks and periodicals. Rare items in the Stanford Collection of German, Austrian and Swiss Culture, Special Collections.

†CT —YALE UNIVERSITY, Library, Box 1603A, Yale Station, New Haven, 06520.

†NY —NEW YORK PUBLIC LIBRARY, 455 Fifth Ave, New York, 10016.

SWOPE, HENRIETTA H., 1902-1980

†MA —RADCLIFFE COLLEGE, Arthur & Elizabeth Schlesinger Library on History of Women in America, 3 James St, Cambridge, 02138.
Notes: Papers, etc.

SWOPE, HERBERT BAYARD

MA —BOSTON UNIVERSITY, Mugar Memorial Library, Special Collections Dept, 771 Commonwealth Ave, Boston, 02215. Howard B Gotlieb, Dir
Holdings: Mss Pix
Notes: Mss, correspondence, etc collected in depth; incl publications by or about.

SYKES, CHRISTOPHER

DC —GEORGETOWN UNIVERSITY, Library, Special Collections Div, 37 & O Sts NW, Washington, 20057. George M Barringer, Special Collections Librn; Nicholas B Sheetz, Mss Librn
Holdings: Mss Pix
Notes: The papers of Christopher Sykes, biographer, journalist, and novelist; containing mss, letters, photographs, and drawings. With extensive correspondence from Harold Acton; Angela, Countess of Antrim; Sir John Betjeman; Ivy Compton-Burnett; Alick Dru; T S Eliot; Max Beerbohm; Graham Greene; John Hayward; Lord Patrick Kinross; Compton Mackenzie; Nancy Mitford; Anthony Powell; Dame Flora Robson; Cecil Roth; Sir John Russell; Osbert Sitwell; John Sparrow; Freya Stark; James Stern; and Evelyn Waugh, among others. Also, considerable research material about Evelyn Waugh, Adam von Trott, Robert Byron, Lady Nancy Astor; and the foundation of the state of Israel.

SYKES, SIR MARK

DC —GEORGETOWN UNIVERSITY, Library, Special Collections Div, 37 & O Sts NW, Washington, 20057. George M Barringer, Special Collections Librn; Nicholas B Sheetz, Mss Librn
Holdings: Mss Pix
Notes: The papers of Christopher Sykes, biographer, journalist, and novelist; containing mss, letters, photographs, and drawings. With extensive correspondence from Harold Acton; Angela, Countess of Antrim; Sir John Betjeman; Ivy Compton-Burnett; Alick Dru; T S Eliot; Max Beerbohm; Graham Greene; John Hayward; Lord Patrick Kinross; Compton Mackenzie; Nancy Mitford; Anthony Powell; Dame Flora Robson; Cecil Roth; Sir John Russell; Osbert Sitwell; John Sparrow; Freya Stark; James Stern; and Evelyn Waugh, among others. Also, considerable research material about Evelyn Waugh, Adam von Trott, Robert Byron, Lady Nancy Astor; and the foundation of the state of Israel.

SYLLABARIES, ASSYRO-BABYLONIAN AND SUMERIAN see Cuneiform Writing

SYLVESTER, JAMES JOSEPH, 1814-1897

RI —BROWN UNIVERSITY, John Hay Library, 20 Prospect St, Providence, 02912. Mark N Brown, Cur Mss
Holdings: // Mss Microforms
Notes: Correspondence of James Joseph Sylvester, English mathematician and professor at Oxford and John Hopkins, with English and American mathematicians containing 107 letters and 2 reels of microfilm for the period 1842-1897. Correspondents incl Raymond C Archibald, Augustus De Morgan, John Simon Newcomb, Sir William Thomson, John Tyndall, and others.

SYMBOLISM

IL —UNIVERSITY OF ILLINOIS, URBANA/CHAMPAIGN, Slavic and East European Library, Urbana, 61801. Marianna Tax Choldin, Head
Holdings: Cat Microforms
Notes: IDC microfiche collection. (959) titles of symbolism, futurism, constructivism, acmeism, imagism, and zemstvo publications.

MD —JOHNS HOPKINS UNIVERSITY, Milton S Eisenhower Library, George Peabody Collection, 17 E Mt Vernon Place, Baltimore, 21201. Lyn Hart, Peabody Librn
Notes: Noncirculating.

MN —MINNEAPOLIS COLLEGE OF ART & DESIGN, Library, 200 E 25 St, Minneapolis, 55404. Richard Kronstedt, Head Librn

NY —VISUAL STUDIES WORKSHOP, Research Center, 31 Prince St, Rochester, 14607. Linn Underhill, Coordr; Robert Bretz, Librn

NC —DUKE UNIVERSITY, William R Perkins Library, Rare Book Room, Durham, .7706. John L Sharpe, III, Cur
Notes: The Kanof collection of Judaic art contains more than 950 items on Jewish art, archaeology and symbolism.

NC —DUKE UNIVERSITY, Divinity School Library, Durham, 27706. Donn Michael Farris, Librn
Holdings: Vols (225,000)
Notes: Special collections and subject emphases in this library include: Archaeology, Egyptian; Archaeology, Middle Eastern; Art, Jewish; Bible; Bible-New Testament; Bible-Symbolism; Church Architecture; Egyptology; Fathers of the Church; Society of Friends; Great Britain-Religion-Methodism and Methodist Church; Hymns and Hymnals; Jansenists and Jansenism; Judaica; Mediaeval Christian Mysticism; Methodism and Methodist Church; Methodist Episcopal Church; Methodist Episcopal Church, South; Reformation; Religion-US-History; Rural Church; Theology-Great Britain-17th Century; Theology-Great Britain-18th Century; United Methodist Church; US-Church History; John Wesley.

OH —HEBREW UNION COLLEGE-JEWISH INSTITUTE OF RELIGION, Klau Library, 3101 Clifton Ave, Cincinnati, 45220. David J Gilner, Reference Librn
Holdings: Cat
Notes: Extensive collection of Jewish artists, primarily in the US and Israel; Jewish religious art, etc.

SYMBOLISM IN THE BIBLE

NC —DUKE UNIVERSITY, Divinity School Library, Durham, 27706. Donn Michael Farris, Librn
Holdings: Vols (225,000)
Notes: Special collections and subject emphases in this library include: Archaeology, Egyptian; Archaeology, Middle Eastern; Art, Jewish; Bible; Bible-New Testament; Bible-Symbolism; Church Architecture; Egyptology; Fathers of the Church; Society of Friends; Great Britain-Religion-Methodism and Methodist Church; Hymns and Hymnals; Jansenists and Jansenism; Judaica; Mediaeval Christian Mysticism; Methodism and Methodist Church; Methodist Episcopal Church; Methodist Episcopal Church, South; Reformation; Religion-US-History; Rural Church; Theology-Great Britain-17th Century; Theology-Great Britain-18th Century; United Methodist Church; US-Church History; John Wesley.

SYMBOLISM OF NUMBERS

IL —UNIVERSITY OF ILLINOIS, URBANA/CHAMPAIGN, Library, University Archives, 19 Library, 1408 W Gregory Drive, Urbana, 61801. Maynard Brichford, University Archivist
Holdings: Vols (5000) Cat
Budget: ($7000)
Notes: The Mandeville Collection in Parapsychology and Occult Sciences. Titles in the Merten J Mandeville Collection are purchased by funds from an endowment provided specifically for the collection on its establishment in 1966 by Merten J Mandeville, Professor Emeritus of Management, who donated 400 vols from his personal library as the nucleus of the collection. There are currently about 5000 titles in the collection, supplemented by related materials in the general collection. Topics include astrology, extrasensory perception, yoga, magic, satanism, faith healing, hypnosis, Eastern religions, witchcraft, fortune telling, reincarnation, flying saucers, ghosts, dreams, numerology, graphology, and mysticism. Biographies and reference books are a part of the collection as are journals devoted to the scientific study of parapsychology.

SYMBOLIST LITERATURE

MN —CARLETON COLLEGE LIBRARY, Northfield, 55057.
Holdings: Vols 7000 Cat
Notes: Books and periodicals relating to French literature of the second half of the 19th century, incl the French symbolist and decadent writers and critical works about them. Major writers are well represented as are some of the relatively minor figures, such as Paul Adam, Rene Boylesve, Abel Hermant, Pierre Louys, and others. The collection incl 69 plays written and produced in the period.

PA —TEMPLE UNIVERSITY LIBRARIES, Special Collections Dept, Rare Books & Mss Section, Philadelphia, 19122. Thomas M Whitehead, Cur
Holdings: Vols 100 Uncat Mss Pix
Notes: Collection of French symbolist poets bases on the personal papers of Charles Morice, French poet and critic; first editions and inscribed copies of Morice, Vertaine, Mallame et al; supportive titles: *La Plume*, etc. Incl correspondence.

ON —METROPOLITAN TORONTO LIBRARY, Literature Dept, 789 Yonge St, Toronto, M4W 2G8, Can. Katherine McCook, Head
Holdings: Vols (200) Cat
Notes: Symbolist books, periodicals, pamphlets, especially on French literature. Part of a collection on other international avant-garde literary movements.

SYMBOLIST POETRY

MA —PINE MANOR COLLEGE, Library, 310 Heath St, Chestnut Hill, 02167. Linda Denners, Head Librn
Holdings: Vols (500) Cat
Notes: French symbolist poets.

SYMBOLS see Signs and Symbols

SYMINGTON, JAMES

MO —UNIVERSITY OF MISSOURI-SAINT LOUIS, Thomas Jefferson Library, Manuscript and Historical Society Collection, 8001 Natural Bridge Rd, Saint Louis, 63121.

SYMONS, A. J. A.

DC —GEORGETOWN UNIVERSITY, Library, Special Collections Div, 37 & O Sts NW, Washington, 20057. George M Barringer, Special Collections Librn; Nicholas B Sheetz, Mss Librn
Holdings: Mss Cat
Notes: The literary papers of author and art curator, James Laver (1899-1975), and those of his wife, the actress Veronica Turleigh; consisting of letters, with a considerable number written by Lady Cnythia Asquith; Clifford Box; Enid Bagnold; Nicholas Bentley; Violet Clifton; Desmond

SYMONS, A. J. A. (cont.)

MacCarthy; Sir Edward Marsh; Sir Francis Meynell; Kate O'Brien; Dorothy L Sayers; Andre Simon; Enid Starkie; A J A Symons; Angela Thirkell; and Alec Waugh.

SYMONS, ARTHUR

CA —UNIVERSITY OF SAN FRANCISCO, Richard A Gleeson Library, The Countess Bernardine Murphy Donohue Rare Book Room, San Francisco, 94117. D Steven Corey, Special Collections Librn
Holdings: Vols 102
NJ —PRINCETON UNIVERSITY, Library, Manuscript Collection, Nassau St, Princeton, 08540. Jean F Preston, Cur
Holdings: Mss
Notes: The manuscript section of the collection fills 28 ms boxes. An unpublished typescript guide (44p) is available in the Library.
BC —UNIVERSITY OF VICTORIA, McPherson Library, Victoria, V8W 3H5, Can.

SYMPHONIES—COLLECTIONS

IN —INDIANA UNIVERSITY, Lilly Library, Seventh St, Bloomington, 47405. William R Cagle, Librn
Holdings: Cat
Notes: Extensive holdings of American sheet music; first editions of works by great composers (operas, symphonies, chamber music, etc); scores annotated for performances conducted by Fritz Busch.
OH —CLEVELAND PUBLIC LIBRARY, Fine Arts and Special Collections Department, 325 Superior Ave, Cleveland, 44114. Alice N Loranth, Head
Holdings: Vols (1750) Cat
Notes: Part of the Orchestral Music Collection, which incl scores and parts ranging in size from theatre to symphony orchestra. Incl symphonies, concertos, incidental music and light classical. Indexed. Available for circulation in Cuyahoga County area.

SYNAGOGUE ARCHITECTURE

NY —YIVO INSTITUTE FOR JEWISH RESEARCH, Library & Archives, 1048 Fifth Ave, New York, 10028. Dina Abramowicz, Librn; Marek Web, Archivist
Holdings: Cat Mss Pix Slides
Notes: Original works and reference materials, incl reproductions of 1500 objects; 500 slides. Separate catalog.

SYNAGOGUE ART

†NY —SYNAGOGUE ARCHITECTURAL AND ART LIBRARY, 838 Fifth Ave, New York, 10021.

SYNDICALISM

CA —HOOVER INSTITUTION ON WAR, REVOLUTION & PEACE, Stanford University, Stanford, 94305. Milorad M Drachkovitch, Archivist
Holdings: Mss
Notes: Papers of Walter Schevenels, Belgian syndicalist and international trade union official, General Secretary of the International Federation of Trade Unions, 1929-1945, and General Secretary for the European Regional Organization of the International Confederation of Free Trade Unions, 1951-1966, incl correspondence, reports, speeches, writings, telegrams, bulletins, interviews, pamphlets, clippings, and printed materials, 1930-1966, relating to syndicalism and free European trade unions, labor and laboring classes in Europe, and international labor problems. 13 ms boxes.
MI —UNIVERSITY OF MICHIGAN, Dept of Rare Books & Special Collections, Ann Arbor, 48109. Edward C Weber, Head, Labadie Collection
Holdings: Vols (40,000) Cat Mss Pix Microforms
Notes: International in scope. Mostly 19th century pamphlets.

WI —UNIVERSITY OF WISCONSIN, MADISON, Memorial Library, 728 State St, Madison, 53706. Erwin K Welsch, Social Studies Bibliographer
Holdings: Vols 2500 Cat Microforms
Notes: Espec strong in the publications of French trade unions and syndicalist groups for the period 1870-1940. Incl microforms of some syndicalist and trade union periodicals rarely held in the US, eg *Le Batiment* (1907-1921), *Bulletin federale des dessinateurs de France* (1906-1912), *La Bataille Syndicaliste* (1911-1915), as well as numerous others in their original format; also memoirs of trade union leaders and secondary supporting sources.

SYNGE, JOHN MILLINGTON

PA —CARLOW COLLEGE, Grace Library, Fifth Ave, Pittsburgh, 15213. Joan M Mitchell, Dir of Library Services
Holdings: Vols 543 // Cat Phonorecords Audiotapes
Notes: The Gladys Wholey Curran Collection, which consists primarily of titles in the area of Irish Literature, specifically those titles in the area of Irish Literature, specifically those titles concerned with the study of the Irish playwrights and poets. The collection is particularly strong in volumes related to the study of Jonathan Swift, John M Synge, and William B Yeats. In addition, there is notable focus upon Irish history of the 17th and 18th centuries. No photocopying.
ON —UNIVERSITY OF TORONTO, Thomas Fisher Rare Book Library, 120 Saint George St, Toronto, M5S 1A5, Can. Richard G Landon, Head
Holdings: Vols 5200 Cat
Notes: DeLury Collection named for original donor, Alfred DeLury, Dean of Arts, University of Toronto. Centered on works of W B Yeats and his circle. Especially good holdings of the Yeats family. A E, Lady Gregory, and J M Synge. Incl extensive holdings of many of the minor writers.

SYNODS see Councils and Synods

SYNTHESIZER MUSIC see Electronic Music

SYNTHETIC CHEMISTRY see Chemistry, Organic—Synthesis

SYNTHETIC RUBBER see Rubber, Artificial

SYPHILIS—HISTORY

MD —MEDICAL & CHIRURGICAL FACULTY OF THE STATE OF MARYLAND, Library, 1211 Cathedral St, Baltimore, 21201. Joseph E Jensen, Librn
Holdings: Vols (10,000) Cat Mss Maps Pix

See also entry under Medicine - History and Historic
OH —CLEVELAND MEDICAL LIBRARY ASSOCIATION/CASE WESTERN RESERVE UNIVERSITY, Cleveland Health Sciences Library, Historical Division, Allen Memorial Medical Library, 11000 Euclid Ave, Cleveland, 44106. Glen Jenkins, Rare Book Librarian & Archivist
Holdings: Vols 235 Cat
Notes: Described in "The Cole Collection of Venereals," *Bulletin of the Cleveland Medical Library*, 1954, vol 1, pp 4-6.

SYRIA

CA —PACIFIC SCHOOL OF RELIGION, Bade Institute of Biblical Archeology, 1798 Scenic Ave, Berkeley, 94709. Kay Schellhase, Cur
Holdings: Vols (2500) Cat
Budget: ($700)
Notes: Syro-Palestinian archaeology.
CA —HOOVER INSTITUTION ON WAR, REVOLUTION & PEACE, Stanford University, Stanford, 94305. Peter Duignan, Cur; Karen Fung, Deputy Cur
Holdings: Vols (100,000)
Notes: For full description of collection, see Hoover Institution entry under Near East.

SYRIAC LANGUAGE AND LITERATURE

DC —LIBRARY OF CONGRESS, African and Middle Eastern Division, Washington, 20540.
Holdings: Cat Mss Microforms
Notes: Hebraica: about 109,000 vols in Hebrew, Yiddish, Judeo-Arabic, Judeo-Persian, Ladino, Syriac, Ethiopic; espec strong in Biblical subjects, responsa literature, and socio-political aspects.
MD —JOHNS HOPKINS UNIVERSITY, Milton S Eisenhower Library, George Peabody Collection, 17 E Mt Vernon Place, Baltimore, 21201. Lyn Hart, Peabody Librn
Notes: Noncirculating.
NY —NEW YORK PUBLIC LIBRARY, Oriental Div, Fifth Ave & 42 St, New York, 10018. E Christian Filstrup, Chief
Holdings: Cat Mss Microforms
Budget: ($56,455)
Notes: Published catalog of holdings.

SYRIAC LANGUAGE AND LITERATURE, MODERN

CA —CALIFORNIA STATE COLLEGE, STANISLAUS, Library, 801 W Monte Vista Ave, Turlock, 95380. J Carlyle Parker, Actg Library Dir
Holdings: Vols 100 // Uncat
Notes: The Sayad Collection of Assyriana consists of books in the Syriac dialect of the modern Assyrians, often called Nestorians, who are natives of northwestern Iran. Other books in English relating to the modern Assyrians are also in the collection. Also books on Mesopotamian civilization.

SYRIAC MANUSCRIPTS see Manuscripts, Syriac

SYRIAN AMERICAN NEWSPAPERS see Newspapers, Syrian American

SYRJENIAN LANGUAGE see Syryenian Language and Literature

SYRYENIAN LANGUAGE AND LITERATURE

NY —NEW YORK PUBLIC LIBRARY, Slavonic Div, Fifth Ave & 42 St, New York, 10018. Edward Kasinec, Chief
Holdings: Cat Microforms
Notes: See New York Public Library, *Dictionary Catalog of the Slavonic Collection* (Boston: G K Hall, 1974), 44 vols.

SYSTEM SIMULATION see Simulation Methods

SYSTEMATIC PAINTING see Minimal Art

SYSTEMS ENGINEERING

CA —UNIVERSITY OF CALIFORNIA, LOS ANGELES, Engineering & Mathematical Sciences Library, 405 Hilgard, Los Angeles, 90024. Rosalee I Wright, Librn
Holdings: Vols (180,000) Cat Microforms
See also entry under Engineering
CA —LOGICON INC, Strategic & Information Systems Division, Information Center, 255 W Fifth St, Box 471, San Pedro, 90731. Constance B Davenport, Supervisor
Holdings: Vols (3000) Cat Mss Microforms
Notes: Incl about 3000 books, 250 periocial titles, 5000 technical reports, 10,000 microfiche, 750 standards and specifications. Catalog is computerized. Interactive search capability with Dialog, Orbit, DMS on-line, NASA Recon. Material on computer programming, systems analysis, military systems and operations research.
GA —GEORGIA INSTITUTE OF TECHNOLOGY, Price Gilbert Memorial Library, 225 North Ave, Atlanta, 30332. Edward Graham Roberts, Dir
Holdings: Vols (1,661,559) Cat Maps Slides

SYSTEMS ENGINEERING (cont.)

Microforms
Budget: ($1,383,302)
Notes: Incl (4,307,996) patents and (568,
490) government documents.

IL —LESTER B KNIGHT & ASSOCIATES,
Library, 549 W Randolph St, Chicago,
60606. Clarita M Generao, Librn
Holdings: Vols (10,000) Cat Maps Slides
Notes: Collection is both technical and
nontechnical; incl reports of the studies for
our client companies, which incl European
firms.

NJ —AT&T BELL LABORATORIES,
Libraries and Information Systems Center,
600 Mountain Ave, Murray Hill, 07974. W
D Penniman, Dir
Holdings: Vols (346,000) Cat Microforms
Notes: Restricted use to AT&T employees.
Catalogs/*Indexes*: Bell Laboratories Library
Network and Book Serial Catalogs; Bell
Laboratories Translations. Bell Laboratories
Library Network with New Jersey libraries
located in Holmdel, Murray Hill,
Piscataway, Whippany, Princeton, Short
Hills, Summit, West Long Branch, Crawford
Hill; libraries also in Allentown,
Pennsylvania; Reading, Pennsylvania; New
York, New York; Atlanta, Georgia;
Columbus, Ohio; Naperville, Illinois;
Indianapolis, Indiana; North Andover,
Massachusetts.

TX —UNIVERSITY OF TEXAS LIBRARIES,
Richard W McKinney Engineering Library,
1.3 ECJ, Austin, 78712. Susan B Ardis,
Librn
Holdings: Vols (83,548) Cat Microforms

VA —MITRE CORPORATION, Information
Services, 1820 Dolley Madison Blvd,
McLean, 22102. Paula M Strain, Mgr
Holdings: Vols (10,000) Cat Microforms
Budget: ($142,000)
Notes: Collection incl current and back files
of periodicals in bound and microfilm form,
approx 70,000 technical reports mostly in
microfiche format and 10,000 vols, all of
which are cataloged and indexed. Collection
deals with systems engineering as a
methodology with special emphasis on its
applications in these areas: civil systems;
communication systems; energy; incl
alternate energy sources; environmental
problems; mass and urban transportation;
and aviation operation incl collision
avoidance, landing systems, and traffic
scheduling.

ON —INSTITUTE OF CHARTERED
ACCOUNTANTS OF ONTARIO, The
Merrilees Library, 69 Bloor St E, Toronto,
M4W 1B3, Can. Theresa Wolak, Librn
Holdings: Vols 153 Cat

SZILARD, LEO

CA —UNIVERSITY OF CALIFORNIA, SAN
DIEGO, Central University Library,
Mandeville Dept of Special Collections, La
Jolla, 92093. Lynda Corey Claassen, Head
Notes: Manuscript collection incl papers of
Nobel scientists Harold Urey and Maria
Goeppert Mayer. Papers of physicist Leo
Szilard are located in the department; special
arrangements are required for use.

DC —LIBRARY OF CONGRESS, Manuscript
Division, Washington, 20540. John C
Broderick, Chief
Notes: Correspondence in the J Robert
Oppenheimer Collection.

SZORADY, MARK

OH —OHIO STATE UNIVERSITY, Library
for Communication and Graphic Arts, 242
W 18th St, Columbus, 43210. Lucy S
Caswell, Curator
Notes: Comic strip artists Hal Foster,
Dudley T Fisher, Jr, Mark Szorady, Edwina
Dumm, Jim Baker have original works in the
library. Also new collections of original
cartoons by Windsor McCay, John T
McCutcheon, Dick Moores, Ned White,
Walter Berndt, Jim Larrick, Carl Rose and
Bill Crawford. Also a large collection of the
work of illustrator Will Rannells. The Shel

Dorf Collection incl historic comic strips and
related materials. A small but growing
collection of comic books, especially those
featuring *Katy Keene,* is available in the
library.

SZULC, TAD

MA —BOSTON UNIVERSITY, Mugar
Memorial Library, Special Collections Dept,
771 Commonwealth Ave, Boston, 02215.
Howard B Gotlieb, Dir
Holdings: Cat Mss Pix
Notes: Mss, correspondence, etc collected in
depth; incl publications by or about.

T

TAAFFE, THEOBALD

CT —YALE UNIVERSITY, Art Library, 180 York St, New Haven, 06520. Nancy S Lambert, Art Librn
Holdings: Cat Mss
Notes: "24 letters written by the youthful Charles II before his ascent to the British throne in 1660. . .addressed to Theobald Taaffe." See *New York Times*, 15 May 1971.

TAAL see Afrikaans Language and Literature

TABB, JOHN BANISTER, 1845-1909

MD —JOHNS HOPKINS UNIVERSITY, Milton S Eisenhower Library, Charles & 34 Sts, Baltimore, 21218. Ann S Gwyn, Assistant Dir for Special Collections
Holdings: Cat Mss
Notes: Mss and 70 letters, cataloged in manuscript room.
NC —DUKE UNIVERSITY, William R Perkins Library, Durham, 27706. Elvin E Strowd, University Librn
Holdings: Mss
Notes: Correspondence and drafts of several of Tabb's poems, 1901-1936. 16 items.

TABER, GLADYS

MA —BOSTON UNIVERSITY, Mugar Memorial Library, Special Collections Dept, 771 Commonwealth Ave, Boston, 02215. Howard B Gotlieb, Dir
Holdings: // Cat Mss Pix
Notes: Mss, correspondence, etc collected in depth; incl publications by or about.

TABER, JOHN, 1880-1965

NY —CORNELL UNIVERSITY LIBRARIES, Collection of Regional History, Dept of Manuscripts and Univ Archives, Ithaca, 14853.
Notes: Lawyer, judge, congressman. Incl papers, 1931-59; letters from constituents, amendments to bills, correspondence and material relating to governmental affairs.

TABER, LOUIS I.

NY —CORNELL UNIVERSITY LIBRARIES, Collection of Regional History, Dept of Manuscripts and Univ Archives, Ithaca, 14853.
Notes: The noncurrent records, letters, records of meetings and other historic data dating back to Dec 4, 1867, the date of organization of the National Grange. Also the papers of Louis I Taber, National Master of the Grange from 1923 to 1941.

TABER, LOUIS JOHN, 1878-1960

NY —CORNELL UNIVERSITY LIBRARIES, Collection of Regional History, Dept of Manuscripts and Univ Archives, Ithaca, 14853.
Notes: Agriculturist. Incl papers, 1844-(1897-1959); speeches, reports, diaries, photos, personal correspondence, and family papers and ms and printed material concerning the Taber-Pickett-Bailey family genealogy (1844-1901). Unpublished guide available.

TABLET

DC —GEORGETOWN UNIVERSITY, Library, Special Collections Div, 37 & O Sts NW, Washington, 20057. George M Barringer, Special Collections Librn; Nicholas B Sheetz, Mss Librn
Holdings: Cat Mss
Notes: The papers of the English author, journalist, and historian Douglas Woodruff (1897-1978), containing correspondence, mss, and photographs. Incl is considerable material concerning his years at Oxford University; his editorship for many years of The "Tablet"; English Catholic society in general and English Catholic literature in particular. Also present are research files on the Tichborne Claimant, one of the most famous cases of impersonation in English legal history. There is extensive correspondence from such figures as: Hilaire Belloc; Tom Burns; Rev Martin D'Arcy, SJ; Christopher Dawson; Sir Roy Harrod; Christopher Hollis; Msgr Ronald Knox; Sir Shane Leslie; Sir Arnold Lunn; Rebecca West; and Evelyn Waugh.

TABLEWARE, SILVER see Silverware

TABOR, AUGUSTA

CO —DENVER PUBLIC LIBRARY, 1357 Broadway, Denver, 80203.
Notes: Correspondence, papers, pictures, diaries, etc.

TACHYGRAPHY see Shorthand

TACITUS

CT —YALE UNIVERSITY, Box 1603A, Yale Station, New Haven, 06520.
Holdings: Cat Mss

TADD, JOHN B.

VA —UNIVERSITY OF VIRGINIA, Alderman Library, Clifton Waller Barrett Collection, Charlottesville, 22901. Joan St C Crane, Cur of American Literature Collections
Notes: Papers.

TADJIK LANGUAGE see Tajik Language and Literature

TADZHIK LANGUAGE see Tajik Language and Literature

TAFT, WILLIAM HOWARD

DC —GEORGETOWN UNIVERSITY, Library, Special Collections Div, 37 & O Sts NW, Washington, 20057. George M Barringer, Special Collections Librn; Nicholas B Sheetz, Mss Librn
Holdings: Mss Cat
Notes: Correspondence written to Edythe Patten Corbin, prominent Washington socialite and wife of General Henry Clark Corbin. Extensive correspondence, spanning numerous years, is incl from William Howard Taft, Philip Bunau-Varilla, Myron T Herrick, General John Pershing, and Elihu Root, among others. The correspondence contains extensive discussions of national and international affairs.
DC —LIBRARY OF CONGRESS, Manuscript Division, Washington, 20540. John C Broderick, Chief
Notes: The Presidential Papers collection incl the papers, etc, of numerous Presidents.

TAFT, LORADO

IL —UNIVERSITY OF ILLINOIS, URBANA/CHAMPAIGN, Library, University Archives, 19 Library, 1408 W Gregory Drive, Urbana, 61801. Maynard Brichford, University Archivist
Holdings: Cat Mss Maps Pix Slides Microforms
Notes: Papers, archival records, etc.

TAFT, ROBERT, JR.

DC —LIBRARY OF CONGRESS, Manuscript Division, Washington, 20540. John C Broderick, Chief
Notes: Papers of Robert Taft, Jr.

TAGALOG LANGUAGE AND LITERATURE

NY —NEW YORK PUBLIC LIBRARY, Oriental Div, Fifth Ave & 42 St, New York, 10018. E Christian Filstrup, Chief
Holdings: // Cat Mss Microforms
Budget: ($56,455)
Notes: Published catalog of holdings.

TAGGARD, GENEVIEVE

NH —DARTMOUTH COLLEGE, Baker Memorial Library, Hanover, 03755.
Holdings: Cat Mss Pix
Notes: First editions, mss, etc. Noncirculating. Microfilm of periodical publications available.

TAI LANGUAGE AND LITERATURE see Thai Language and Literature

TAILORING—PATTERN DESIGN

CA —CARLSBAD CITY LIBRARY, 1250 Elm Ave, Carlsbad, 92008. Clifford E Lange, Library Dir
Holdings: Vols (2297) Cat
Notes: Collection of sewing patterns. Catalogs of the patterns have been made up with complete information on size, etc, and have been divided into subject areas, such as gift ideas, toys, dolls, women's clothes, men's clothes, children's clothes, etc. Also patterns for knitted and crocheted wearing apparel. Incl patterns for children's costumes, historical fashions and antique dolls.

TAIWAN

HI —UNIVERSITY OF HAWAII, Library, 2550 The Mall, Honolulu, 96822. Joyce Wright, Head, Asia Collection; Masato Matsu, Head, East Asia Vernacular Collection
Holdings: Vols 60,394 Cat Microforms
Notes: The Asia Collection includes materials from and about China (People's Republic, Taiwan, Hong Kong) in all languages. No figures are available for western language materials relating to China, which are supplemented by retrospective materials in the main library collection. Scope: social sciences and the humanities, traditional and contemporary.

TAJIK LANGUAGE AND LITERATURE

NY —NEW YORK PUBLIC LIBRARY, Oriental Div, Fifth Ave & 42 St, New York, 10018. E Christian Filstrup, Chief
Holdings: Cat Mss Microforms
Budget: ($56,455)
Notes: Published catalog of holdings.

TALBOT, REV. FRANCIS A., S.J., 1889-1955

DC —GEORGETOWN UNIVERSITY, Library, Special Collections Div, 37 & O Sts NW, Washington, 20057. George M Barringer, Special Collections Librn; Nicholas B Sheetz, Mss Librn
Holdings: Mss
Notes: The papers of Rev Francis Talbot, SJ (1889-1955), author and editor who served on the staff of *America* from 1922-1944, as literary editor and then as editor-in-chief. The papers consist of mss of writings and related correspondence and documents, as well as correspondence from noted author such as Willa Cather, G K Chesterton, Oliver St John Gogarty, Shane Leslie, Jacques Maritain, Theodore Maynard, George Putnam and Evelyn Waugh, among others.

TALBOT, MICHAEL

MA —BOSTON UNIVERSITY, Mugar Memorial Library, Special Collections Dept, 771 Commonwealth Ave, Boston, 02215. Howard B Gotlieb, Dir
Holdings: Mss
Notes: Mss, correspondence.

TALENTED CHILDREN see Gifted Children

TALENTED STUDENTS

CO —UNIVERSITY OF COLORADO, Libraries, Western Historical Collections,

TALENTED STUDENTS (cont.)

Boulder, 80309.
Holdings: Cat Mss
Notes: Papers of the Inter-University Committee on the Superior Student, which was organized before the launching of Sputnik, when a conference of 48 American educators meeting at the University of Colorado in June of 1957 called for greater utilization of talented scholars and a central clearing house for honors programs. Funded by a grant from Carnegie Corporation, ICSS was headed by Joseph Cohen. It collected and disseminated information and conducted conferences and consultations from 1958 to 1965. The collection contains administrative files, and surveys, research findings and publications dealing with honors programs. It covers the period 1957-1965 and consists of 62 boxes. A typescript inventory is available.

TALES

CA —LOS ANGELES PUBLIC LIBRARY, Children's Literature Dept, 630 W 5th St, Los Angeles, 90071. Serenna Day, Sr Librn
Holdings: Vols (2120) Cat Phonorecords Filmstrips
Notes: Also includes reference collection, covering some 50 years of published folklore and modern fairy tales. Includes extensive Mother Goose collection, examples of the work of such outstanding illustrators as Edmund Dulac and Arthur Rackham. Many volumes out of print. Index to titles of stories in collections.

DC —HOWARD UNIVERSITY, Moorland-Spingarn Research Center, 500 Howard Place NW, Washington, 20059. Clifford L Muse, Jr, Acting Dir
Holdings: Vols (106,086) Mss Maps Pix Slides Phonorecords Audiotapes 16mm Films Filmstrips Microforms
Budget: ($854,753)
See also entry under Blacks

MA —BOSTON COLLEGE LIBRARIES, Thomas P O'Neill Library, Nicholas M Williams Ethnological Collection, Chestnut Hill, 02167. Frank J Seegraber, Special Collections Librn
Holdings: Vols 10,000 // Cat Mss Maps
Notes: Collection emphasizes Caribbeana, especially Jamaica, to 1940. Incl discovery, exploration, and natural history of the British, French, and Spanish settlements; the slave question; piracy. There are over 6000 manuscripts, 5000 of which are Anansi folk tales recorded by native school children. Also small ancillary sections of Africana and Judaica. For reference use only, by arrangement with librarian.

NE —UNIVERSITY OF NEBRASKA-LINCOLN, Don L Love Library, Lincoln, 68588. Joseph G Svoboda, University Archivist
Holdings: Vols (8000) // Uncat Mss Pix Slides Phonorecords Audiotapes Microforms
Notes: This is an extensive collection belonging to the folklorist Benjamin A Bolkin, about 500 linear ft, consisting of various types of materials. Main emphasis is American folklore, although folklore of all nations is included.

PA —CARNEGIE LIBRARY OF PITTSBURGH, Children's Dept, 4400 Forbes Ave, Pittsburgh, 15213. Amy Kellman, Head
Holdings: Vols 2000 Cat
Notes: Historical children's books. Strong in folk tales.

ON —VICTORIA UNIVERSITY, Library, 71 Queen's Park Crescent, Toronto, M5S 1K7, Can. Robert C Brandeis, Chief Librn
Holdings: Vols 350 // Cat

TALISMANS

OH —CLEVELAND PUBLIC LIBRARY, Fine Arts and Special Collections Department, 325 Superior Ave, Cleveland, 44114. Alice N Loranth, Head
Holdings: Vols (1600) Cat
Notes: Part of the Witchcraft Collection, which incl witchcraft, magic, sorcery, magical manuals, devil worship, incantations, charms, talismans, amulets and spells. Contemporary urban practices are almost entirely omitted.
See also entry under Folklore; Witchcraft

RI —BROWN UNIVERSITY, John Hay Library, 20 Prospect St, Providence, 02912. Mark N Brown, Cur Mss
Notes: The Royal Vale Heath Collection of about 200 of his designs, drawings, models, ocular, and verbal descriptions of simultaneous solutions to linear Diophantine equations in such examples as magic squares, Platonic solids, etc. These curious designs often were devised as talismans in ancient India and were first developed as mathematical problems by the Chinese.

TALKING BOOKS

DC —LIBRARY OF CONGRESS, National Library Service for Blind Physically Handicapped, 1291 Taylor St NW, Washington, 20542. Frank Kunt Cylke, Director; Hylda Kamisar, Head Reference Section
Holdings: Cat
Budget: $35,099,000
Notes: The Library of Congress National Library Service for the Blind and Physically Handicapped administers a free national library service to provide reading materials for persons who cannot read or use conventional print because of visual or physical handicapping conditions. The materials are distributed through a cooperating network of 56 regional and more than 100 subregional (local) libraries. Titles issued in multiple copies under this program total 5100 in braille, 11,200 on disc recordings, and 9700 on cassettes. Additional titles in braille and on tape are made available through a national volunteer program. Other special materials incl books in foreign languages in both braille and recorded form. Other special collections incl a musiccollection for the blind and physically handicapped and a print reference collection on blindness and physical handicapping conditions. The following publications describe the program: *Reading is for Everyone, Fact Sheet; Books for Blind and Physically Handicapped Individuals*, and *A Music Library for Blind and Physically Handicapped Individuals.*

FL —ORLANDO PUBLIC LIBRARY, 100 Block of Central Ave, Orlando, 32806. Helen M Struthers, AV Librn
Holdings: Cat Phonorecords Audiotapes
Budget: ($5500)
Notes: 7155 LP recordings with emphasis on classical music; also jazz, country-western, easy-listening, spoken arts, foreign language study, dictation. Young Adult Dept has additional 850 contemporary and rock records. Library serves as subregional talking book library for the blind and physically handicapped, maintaining 7858 titles. Also, 681 audiotapes on all subjects. All materials circulate for 3 weeks.

NY —WILLARD PSYCHIATRIC CENTER, Patients Library, Willard, 14588. Helen Bunting, Chief Library Services
Holdings: Vols (23,025) Cat Phonorecords

ON —CANADIAN NATIONAL INSTITUTE FOR THE BLIND, National Library, 1929 Bayview Ave, Toronto, M4G 3E8, Can. Francoise Herbert, Dir, Library Services
Holdings: Vols 10,500 Cat
Notes: Separate catalog for both the Talking Book Circulation Library and the Transcription (students and others) Library; Circulation books are on six-track (Clarke and Smith tapes). Transcription titles are available on open reel or two-track or four-track cassettes. Talking books and transcription services are for registered blind readers, students, and others across Canada.

TALKING IN TONGUES see Glossolalia

TALKING PICTURES see Moving Pictures, Talking

TALLANT, ROBERT

LA —NEW ORLEANS PUBLIC LIBRARY, Louisiana Div, 219 Loyola Ave, New Orleans, 70140. Collin B Hamer Jr, Head; Brenda M Osbey, Library Associate
Holdings: Cat Maps Pix
Notes: Louisiana and New Orleans Picture File Collection ranges from the late 19th century-date and incl the following separate collections: Alexander Allison (ca 1898-1951, 337 pieces); Charles Franck (ca 1920-50, 170 pieces); Leda Plauche (ca 1935-53, 220 pieces); C Milo Williams (ca 1910, 85 pieces); Wilson S Howell (ca 1890, 49 pieces); Grauman Marks (ca 1960, 268 pieces); Robert Tallant (ca 1940-50, 70 pieces); Robert E Tracy (1959, 87 pieces); Anthony J Flaherty (ca 1970-84, 83 pieces); George F Mugnier (1880-1920, 186 pieces); Color Slides (ca 1945-date, 500 pieces); 30,000 photographs incl 500 color slides and 104 negatives. Use of the material is restricted to on-site research. Publication must be accompanied by credit cut line. Also, Tallant mss collection, 3 cubic ft.

TALMUD

†CA —HEBREW UNION COLLEGE, Jewish Institute of Religion, 3077 University Ave, Los Angeles, 90007.
Notes: Bible, Talmud, Rabbinics, Jewish history, philosophy, art and communal science, Hebrew literature, religion, Zionism.

IL —HEBREW THEOLOGICAL COLLEGE, Saul Silber Memorial Library, 7135 N Carpenter Rd, Skokie, 60077. Leah Mishkin, Head Librn/Cur
Holdings: Vols (58,000) Cat Mss Microforms
Notes: Main subject is rabbinics (Halachic literature). We also have a very large and important Holocaust Collection.

NY —YESHIVA UNIVERSITY, Library, 500 West 185th Street, New York, 10033. Pearl Berger
Holdings: Cat

OH —HEBREW UNION COLLEGE-JEWISH INSTITUTE OF RELIGION, Klau Library, 3101 Clifton Ave, Cincinnati, 45220. David J Gilner, Reference Librn
Holdings: Cat

PA —DUQUESNE UNIVERSITY, Library, Pittsburgh, 15282. Dena F Jacobson, Music and Reference Librn
Holdings: Vols 3000 Cat
Notes: Main emphasis of collection is on history of Jewish philosophy in the Middle Ages and relationship between Jewish and Christian scholars; collection incl works by 14th century writer Nicolas de Lyra and general Judaica, history of the Jews, theology, Bible texts and commentaries, literature, grammatical works and dictionaries, etc.

PQ —CONCORDIA UNIVERSITY LIBRARIES, 1455 de Maisonneuve Blvd W, Montreal, H3G 1M8, Can. Dorothy Cameron, Reference Librn
Notes: Collection incl Judaism History, Talmudie Period (17 titles), Medieval and early modern (106 titles), modern 1750- (9 titles); Philosophy - Jewish (38 titles); Ethics (2000 titles); Christianity modern period 1453- (278 titles).

TALMUD—FOLKLORE see Folklore, Jewish

TALON, OMER

MO —SAINT LOUIS UNIVERSITY, Pius XII Memorial Library, Saint Louis Room Collection, 3655 W Pine Blvd, Saint Louis, 63108. Catherine E Weidle, Rare Books Librn
Holdings: Vols Cat Mss
Notes: Books on early education, Jesuitica and Western Americana. Related collections of works by Peter Ramus (University is center for Ramist studies) and Omer Talon.

TALONBOOK ARCHIVE

BC —SIMON FRASER UNIVERSITY, Library, Burnaby, V5A 1S6, Can. Percilla Groves, Special Collections Librn
Holdings: // Cat Mss Pix
Notes: Talonbook Archive incl

TALONBOOK ARCHIVE (cont.)

correspondence, mss, photographs, proofs, and business records of this local publisher, 1966-1978.

TAMIL LANGUAGE AND LITERATURE

HI —UNIVERSITY OF HAWAII, Library, 2550 The Mall, Honolulu, 96822. Joyce Wright, Head, Asia Collection; Masato Matsu, Head, East Asia Vernacular Collection
Holdings: Vol 75,215 Cat Microforms
Notes: The Asia Collection holds material from and relating to Bangladesh, India, Nepal, Pakistan, and Sri Lanka in western and Asian languages. South Asian languages currently acquired: Bengali, Hindi, Marathi, Nepali, Pali, Prakrit, Sanskrit, Tamil. Period emphasis is post-World War II. Subject emphases: social sciences and the humanities (literature, economics, history, religion/ philosophy). Holdings are supplemented by a large uncataloged backlog, much of it accessible through the Library of Congress Accessions Lists for the area and by over 7000 cataloged titles in the main library collection. *South Asian Library Resources in North America: A Survey Prepared for the Boston Conference,* 1974, ed by M L P Patterson (Zug, Switzerland: Tutes Documentation Compnay, 1975).(Bibliotheca Asiatica 12-), "University of Hawaii," pp 103-114.

MI —UNIVERSITY OF MICHIGAN, Graduate Library, South Asian Dept, Ann Arbor, 48109. Om P Sharma, Librn
Holdings: Vols (365,000) Cat Maps Slides Microforms
Notes: The major emphasis is on social sciences and humanities. Besides materials in classical languages, South Asian vernaculars being retained are Hindi, Bengali, Urdu, Marathi and Tamil; strong in classical languages, especially Sanskrit, Pali, and Prakrit.

NY —NEW YORK PUBLIC LIBRARY, Oriental Div, Fifth Ave & 42 St, New York, 10018. E Christian Filstrup, Chief
Holdings: Cat Mss Microforms
Budget: ($56,455)
Notes: Published catalog of holdings.

NY —NEW YORK PUBLIC LIBRARY, Donnell Foreign Language Library, 20 W 53 St, New York, 10019. Bosiljka Stevanovic, Supvr Librn
Holdings: Vols 205 Cat
Notes: Tamil collection incl Tamil authors of Tamil expression. No separate catalog.

PA —UNIVERSITY OF PENNSYLVANIA, Van Pelt Library, South Asia Collection, 34 and Walnut Sts, Philadelphia, 19104. Kanta Bhatia, Bibliographer
Holdings: Vols 160,000 Cat
Notes: Incl South Asia social sciences, history, politics, economics and anthroplogy. Extensive holdings in vernacular languages, especially Hindi, Tamil and Sanskrit. Incl 3400 mss.

TAMIRIS, HELEN, 1905-1966

NY —NEW YORK PUBLIC LIBRARY, Performing Arts Research Center, Dance Collection, 111 Amsterdam Ave, New York, 10023. Genevieve Oswald, Cur
Notes: Extensive biographical and visual material. Includes photographs, motion pictures, tape-recorded interviews. The Helen Tamiris Collection, 1926-66, ca 3000 items, comprises correspondence, business records, clippings and scrapbooks, programs, and musical scores.

TAMMANY HALL

NY —COLUMBIA UNIVERSITY LIBRARIES, Rare Book & Manuscript Library, 801 Butler Library, 535 W 114 St, New York, 10027. Kenneth A Lohf, Librn
Holdings: Vols 3000 Cat Mss
Notes: Books, letters, mss and memorabilia relating to the society of Tammany and New York Democratic politics. Collection formed by Edwin P Kilroe. 15,000 items. Restricted use.

TANGANYIKA see Tanzania

TANIZAKI, JUNICHERO

FL —UNIVERSITY OF FLORIDA, Libraries, Gainesville, 32611. Ray Jones, Research Librn; Max Willocks, Librn
Holdings: Vols (2000)
Notes: An extensive collection of modern and premodern Japanese prose fiction in English translation and Japanese. Incl complete works of a number of important modern Japanese authors such as Yasunari Kawabata, Naoya Shiga, Junichiro Tanizaki, and Yukio Mishima.

TANJUR

MA —HARVARD UNIVERSITY LIBRARY, Harvard-Yenching Library, 2 Divinity Ave, Cambridge, 02138. Eugene W Wu, Librn
Notes: See *Harvard Library Bulletin,* IV (1950); p 286. Contains the three rare editions of the *Tripitaka:* The Narthang edition (1732) of both the Kanjur and the Tanjur, the Peking edition of the Kanjur, and the Lhasa edition (1933?) of the Kanjur; also Tibetan-language publications received under the PL480 program.

NY —INSTITUTE FOR ADVANCED STUDIES OF WORLD RELIGIONS (IASWR), Melville Memorial Library, State University of New York, Stony Brook, 11794. C T Shen, Dir
Holdings: Vols 400 Mss Microforms
Notes: Incl, in hard cover, Japanese reduced-size reprint of Peking edition of Kanjur and Tanjur, 168 vols containing 6439 titles and detailed catalog. Kanjur also in Derge, Tog Palace editions and in Mongolian translation. Tanjur in Derge edition arriving in stages. Various catalogs available. In microform: Lhasa ed of Kanjur (Bka-gyur), Cone ed of Tanjur (Bstan-gyur). Refer inquiries to H Robinson.
See also entry under Kanjur

TANKAS

DC —LIBRARY OF CONGRESS, Asian Division, Washington, 20540.
Notes: Chinese and Korean Section. William Woodville Rockhill Collection of Tibetan religious books and mss.

TANKS (MILITARY SCIENCE)

VA —US ARMY TRANSPORTATION MUSEUM, Library, Bldg 300, Fort Eustis, 23604. Dennis P Mroczkowski, Museum Cur
Holdings: Vols (1254) Uncat Maps Pix 16mm Films
Budget: ($150)
Notes: Mainly US Army transportation from WW II on.

TANNENBAUM, FRANK

NY —COLUMBIA UNIVERSITY LIBRARIES, Rare Book & Manuscript Library, 801 Butler Library, 535 W 114 St, New York, 10027. Kenneth A Lohf, Librn
Holdings: Mss
Notes: The papers of Professor Frank Tannenbaum, approx 28,000 items of correspondence and mss relating to Latin American and Mexican history, also the US Farm Security Program, 1934-1937. Professor Tannenbaum also bequeathed his research library of more than 3000 vols on all phases of Latin American history and literature to Columbia. Restricted use.

TANNER, GEORGE S.

AZ —NORTHERN ARIZONA UNIVERSITY, Special Collection Library, CU Box 6022, Flagstaff, 86011. Peter M Whiteley, Coordr/Archivist; William Mullane, Librn
Notes: George S Tanner Collection; records of the Mormon settlement of Northern Arizona. Incl copies of numerous diaries, journals, correspondence, church records, pioneer reminiscences, and other research data. The bulk of the collection incl documents from 1876 through the early 1900's, with continuous materials through the 1970's. See *Register of the Records of the Mormon Settlement in Arizona,* Register 8, Salt Lake City, Special Collections, University of Utah Library, 1974. Also incl drafts of George S Tanner's book, *Colonization on the Little Colorado: The Joseph City Region* (7 feet).

TANNU-TUVA LANGUAGE see Soyot Language

TANTRISM, BUDDHIST

AZ —WORLD UNIVERSITY, Library, 711 E Blacklidge Dr, Tucson, 85719. Howard John Zitko, Cur
Holdings: Vols (15,000) Cat Mss Maps Audiotapes
Notes: Collection concerns the "frontier sciences." No interlibrary loan.

CA —UNIVERSITY OF CALIFORNIA, BERKELEY, University Library, East Asiatic Library, Room 208, Durant Hall, Berkeley, 94720. Donald Shively, Head
Holdings: Vols (500,000) Cat Pix Microforms
Notes: Small but important collection of Tibetan-language research materials in the fields of Buddhist Studies, and Tibetan historical/social conditions. Holdings incl a rare collection of writings from the oldest surviving school of Tibetan Buddhism (The Rin-Chen-Gter-Mdzod Collection), consisting of a monumental corpus of Tantric literature spanning ten centuries of composition. The collections are complemented by related holdings in the Main Library and in the South/Southeast Asia Library Service.

NY —INSTITUTE FOR ADVANCED STUDIES OF WORLD RELIGIONS (IASWR), Melville Memorial Library, State University of New York, Stony Brook, 11794. C T Shen, Dir
Holdings: Vols 5000 Cat Periodicals
Notes: Incl Tantra sections of the Tibetan and Chinese Canons; as well as rich collection of post-canonical tantric meditation cycles in Tibetan together with related iconographic works and limited translations into English and other European languages. Incl some 100 works on Japanese Buddhist Tantrism (Shingon).

TANZANIA

DC —HOWARD UNIVERSITY, Moorland-Spingarn Research Center, 500 Howard Place NW, Washington, 20059. Clifford L Muse, Jr, Acting Dir

MI —MICHIGAN STATE UNIVERSITY, International Library, Africana Collection, East Lansing, 48824. Eugene de Benko, Librn; Onuma Ezera, Bibliographer for Africana
Holdings: Vols (82,700) Cat Mss Maps Pix Slides Phonorecords Audiotapes Videotapes Filmstrips Microforms
Budget: ($78,000)
See also entry under Africa for full description.

TAOISM

CA —LOS ANGELES PUBLIC LIBRARY, Philosophy & Religion Dept, 630 W Fifth St, Los Angeles, 90071. Marilyn C Wherley, Librn
Holdings: Vols 50 Cat
Budget: ($60,000)
Notes: Historical, theological, and biographical works relating to the religion and philosophy of Taoism. Many English translations of sacred works with revelent criticism. Includes scholarly and popular materials on comparative religions.

NY —NEW YORK PUBLIC LIBRARY, Oriental Div, Fifth Ave & 42 St, New York, 10018. E Christian Filstrup, Chief
Holdings: Cat Mss Microforms
Budget: ($56,455)
Notes: Described in *Dictionary Catalog of*

TAOISM (cont.)

the Oriental Collection, The Research Libraries of the New York Public Library, 1960, 16 vols, and *First Supplement*, 1976, 8 vols (144,000 cards). This catalog incl 318,000 entries for works in about 100 languages of the East, and all works in Western languages on Oriental subjects. The Oriental Collection numbers about 120,000 vols; its Arabic and Indic holdings and those on ancient Egypt and the ancient Near East are among the largest in the US. There is also a collection of 30,000 vols of PL 480 material from Egypt, Pakistan, and India to which there is main entry access, but which is not incorporated into the dictionary catalog. Other outstanding features of the Oriental Collection incl extensive holdings of Japanese technical and scientific periodicals; a unique collection of linguistic works, grammars, anddictionaries; and unusually good coverage of the field of Oriental religions and philosophies. The catalog contains numerous subject references to periodical articles in all languages. All entries are arranged alphabetically according to the Roman alphabet.

TAOL LANGUAGE see Afrikaans Language and Literature

TAPE RECORDER MUSIC see Electronic Music

TAPESTRY

MO —THE NELSON-ATKINS MUSEUM OF ART, Kenneth & Helen Spencer Art Reference Library, 4525 Oak St, Kansas City, 64111. Stanley W Hess, Librn
NY —THE CLOISTERS, Metropolitan Museum of Art (Branch), Fort Tryon Park, New York, 10040. Suse C Childs, Librn
Holdings: Vols (5000) Cat Mss Pix Slides
Notes: A branch of the Metropolitan Museum of Art devoted solely to the literature of medieval art. Incl 16,000 slides and 5000 photographs with unique strengths in certain aspects of medieval art.

TAPPAN, ELI TODD

OH —OHIO HISTORICAL SOCIETY, Archives Library Division, 1982 Velma Ave, Columbus, 43211. Dennis East, Division Chief
Notes: His papers.

TARBELL, IDA M.

PA —ALLEGHENY COLLEGE, Lawrence Lee Pelletier Library, Meadville, 16335. Margaret L Moser, Librn
Holdings: Vols 1650 Uncat Mss Pix
Notes: The Lincoln Library of Ida M Tarbell. Much of collection indexed, primarily by personal names. Incl letters concerning Lincoln, his life and times. Also incl pamphlets, clippings, pictures and 10,000 ms pieces.

TARGETS (SHOOTING)

MA —LUCIUS BEEBE MEMORIAL LIBRARY, Main St, Wakefield, 01880.
Holdings: Vols (350) Cat
Notes: The Keough Collection of guns and arms and armor.

TARIFF

MA —HARVARD UNIVERSITY, Baker Library of the Graduate School of Business Administration, Kress Library of Business and Economics, Soldiers Field, Boston, 02163. Ruth E Rogers, Cur
Holdings: Cat
Notes: Covers the progress of economic thought and the evolution of economic institutions and business life, with special strength in agriculture, banking, commerce, finance, industry, money, railroads, socialism, tariff. Restricted use: noncirculating. Collection available on microfilm: *Goldsmiths'-Kress Library of Economic Literature*, published by Research Publications, Inc. Downs 1477, 2704, 2712, 2719, 2727, Supplement 962, 963.
NE —NEBRASKA STATE HISTORICAL SOCIETY, Archives, 1500 R St, Box 82554, Lincoln, 68501. James E Potter, State Archivist
Holdings: Uncat Mss
Notes: Silver and the money question; also material on the Greenback Party. Printed speeches and tracts relating to the money question, 1890-1895. Many written by prominent political figures of the day. Also, pamphlets which relate to income tax, tariffs, free trade, soldiers' pensions, railroads, election laws and public lands. Collection of John Davis, Congressman from Kansas, 1891-1895.

TARKINGTON, BOOTH

IN —INDIANA HISTORICAL SOCIETY, Library, 315 W Ohio St, Indianapolis, 46202. Robert K O'Neill, Dir
Holdings: Vols 75 Cat Mss Pix
Notes: 200 letters and other mss items. First and foreign-language editions of his works.
†MA —WILLIAMS COLLEGE, Chapin Library of Rare Books, PO Box 426, Williamstown, 01267. Robert L Volz, Custodian
Holdings: Vols 60 Cat
Notes: No material available on interlibrary loan.
NJ —PRINCETON UNIVERSITY, Library, Manuscript Collection, Nassau St, Princeton, 08540. Jean F Preston, Cur
Holdings: Mss Pix Cat
Notes: The manuscript section of the collection fills 270 boxes. See *Princeton University Library Chronicle*, v 16, p 45-53. Unpublished checklist available.
VA —UNIVERSITY OF VIRGINIA, Alderman Library, Clifton Waller Barrett Collection, Charlottesville, 22901. Joan St C Crane, Cur of American Literature Collections
Notes: Papers.

TARTANS

ON —QUEEN'S UNIVERSITY, Douglas Library, Kingston, K7L 5C4, Can. William F E Morley, Cur, Special Collections
Holdings: Vols 100 Uncat
Notes: The MacGillivray Collection. Scottish books, especially those dealing with clans, tartans and heraldry. Also the Buchan Collection, 5000 vols.

TARTINI, GIUSEPPE

CA —UNIVERSITY OF CALIFORNIA, BERKELEY, Humanities-Social Sciences Libraries, Music Library, 24 Morrison Hall, Berkeley, 94720. Michael A Keller, Head Librn
Holdings: Vols // Cat Microforms
Notes: A special collection of about 1000 mss originating in Padua during the 2nd half of the 18th century, devoted to the music of Tartini and his school. A catalog has been published: Duckles, Vincent and Minnie Elmer, *Thematic Catalog of a Manuscript Collection of 18th-century Italian instrumental Music in the University of Calif, Berkeley, Music Library* (Berkeley and Los Angeles: Univ of Calif Press, 1963).

TASSO, TORQUATO

CA —UNIVERSITY OF CALIFORNIA, BERKELEY, University Library, French and Italian Collections, Berkeley, 94720. Donald G Williams, Librn
Notes: Research collection with special strengths in early Italian literature (to 1400), and Italian literature of the Renaissance. Strong holdings for such authors as Dante, Petrarch, Boccaccio, Ariosto, Machiavelli, Tasso, and many others. The collections in the Main Library are complemented by significant incunabula, rare books and ms holdings in the Bancroft Library.
MA —HARVARD UNIVERSITY LIBRARY, Widener Library, Cambridge, 02138.
Holdings: Cat

PA —UNIVERSITY OF PENNSYLVANIA, Van Pelt Library, Rare Books Collection, 34 & Walnut Sts, Philadelphia, 19104. Daniel Traister, Special Collections Librn
Holdings: Cat
Notes: Strong collections of 15th and 16th century imprints, especially Boccaccio and Tasso.

TASTE

CT —YALE MEDICAL LIBRARY, 333 Cedar St, New Haven, 06510.
Notes: A special subject emphasis.

TASTE (AESTHETICS) see Aesthetics

TASTING (PHYSIOLOGY) see Taste

TATAR LANGUAGE AND LITERATURE

NY —NEW YORK PUBLIC LIBRARY, Oriental Div, Fifth Ave & 42 St, New York, 10018. E Christian Filstrup, Chief
Holdings: Cat Mss Microforms
Budget: ($56,455)
Notes: Published catalog of holdings.

TATE, ALLEN

MO —WASHINGTON UNIVERSITY, Libraries, Campus Box 1061, Saint Louis, 63130.
Notes: A collection of primary material.
NV —UNIVERSITY OF NEVADA, RENO, University Library, Special Collections Dept, Reno, 89557. Robert E Blesse, Head
Holdings: Vols 54 // Cat
Notes: Includes individual works by author in all editions including translations; also prefaces, introductions, published correspondence, appearances in anthologies, periodicals, etc. Bibliographical research collection, part of Modern Authors Collection.
NJ —PRINCETON UNIVERSITY, Library, Manuscript Collection, Nassau St, Princeton, 08540. Jean F Preston, Cur
Holdings: Mss
Notes: The manuscript section fills 63 ms boxes. An unpublished typescript guide (117 p) is available in the Library.
NY —COLUMBIA UNIVERSITY LIBRARIES, Rare Book & Manuscript Library, 801 Butler Library, 535 W 114 St, New York, 10027. Kenneth A Lohf, Librn
Notes: Over 200 letters; mss, etc. Restricted use.
TN —VANDERBILT UNIVERSITY, Library, Nashville, 37240. Marice Wolfe, Special Collections Librn
Holdings: Vols 1000 Cat Mss Pix
Notes: Collection relating to the Fugitive poets of the 1920s, the Agrarian writers of the 1930s and their subsequent careers, as a complement to extensive mss collections in this field. Chief figures incl Allen Tate, John Crowe Ransom, Robert Penn Warren, Andrew Lytle, Donald Davidson, Merrill Moore, Laura Riding, et al.

TATUM, BROOKING

CA —POMONA PUBLIC LIBRARY, Special Collections, 625 S Garey Ave, PO Box 2271, Pomona, 91766. David Streeter, Librn
Holdings: Cat
Notes: Together, about 100,000 photographs. Burton Frasher collection, 60,000 negatives and prints of California, Arizona, New Mexico, Colorado, Utah, and Nevada, 1920-1940; Loyd Cooper collection, 20,000 negatives and prints of California, 1920-1940; Brooking Tatum, 125 color prints, 50 color 35mm transparencies of California flora; Percy Everett, 4000 color 35mm transparencies of world travels, 1960s.

TATUM, EDWARD L., 1926-1975

NY —ROCKEFELLER UNIVERSITY, Rockefeller Archive Center, Hillcrest, Pocantico Hills, North Tarrytown, 10591. Joseph W Ernst, Dir; J William Hess, Assoc

TATUM, EDWARD L., 1926-1975 (cont.)

Dir
Notes: Papers of Edward L Tatum, Rockefeller University professor. Conducted research in the genetics and metabolism of bacteria, yeasts, and molds. In 1958, he was joint recipient, with Joshua Lederberg and George Beadle, of the Nobel Prize in medicine and physiology.

TAUCHNITZ PUBLICATIONS

CA —UNIVERSITY OF CALIFORNIA, LOS ANGELES, Research Library, Dept of Special Collections, 405 Hilgard Ave, Los Angeles, 90024. Edward Shreeves, Chairman, Bibliographers Group; David S Zeidberg, Head
Holdings: Vols 1400

NY —UNIVERSITY OF ROCHESTER, Rush Rhees Library, Department of Rare Books and Special Collections, Rochester, 14627. Peter Dzwonkoski, Librn
Holdings: Vols 1200 // Cat
Notes: Collection of British authors published by the Leipzig firm of Bernhard Tauchnitz from 1840-1908. Much of the collection was originally in the library of the Kings of Hanover, and those volumes are bound in cloth with the arms of the Royal Family. No photocopying permitted.

†ON —UNIVERSITY OF WESTERN ONTARIO, School of Library and Information Science, Special Collections Room, London, N6A 5B9, Can.
Holdings: Vols 1292
Notes: Collection of British and American authors, many copyright editions. The items range from Number 3 to Number 5294, published between 1842 and 1937. The emphasis is on the paperback editions and also incl dated Bookmarks.

TAVEL, RONALD

MA —BOSTON UNIVERSITY, Mugar Memorial Library, Special Collections Dept, 771 Commonwealth Ave, Boston, 02215. Howard B Gotlieb, Dir
Holdings: Mss Pix
Notes: Mss, correspondence, etc collected in depth; incl publications by or about.

TAVERNER, ALBERT, 1854-1919

ON —METROPOLITAN TORONTO LIBRARY, Theatre Dept, 789 Yonge St, Toronto, M4W 2G8, Can. Heather McCallum, Head
Notes: Records of the Taverner touring company (scripts, prompt books, music correspondence, account books, photographs, clippings and programs) document the career of Albert Taverner and Ida van Courtland who toured Canada and the eastern United States in the late 19th century.
See also entry under Actors and Actresses.

TAVERNS see Hotels, Taverns, Etc.

TAX SHARING see Intergovernmental Relations

TAXATION

CA —UNIVERSITY OF CALIFORNIA, BERKELEY, Institute of Governmental Studies Library, 109 Moses Hall, Berkeley, 94720. Jack Leister, Head Librn
Holdings: Vols (350,000) Cat Mss Maps Microforms
Budget: ($160,000)
Notes: The library collects primarily pamphlets. Incl in the library's holdings are documents from all levels of government, as well as publications issued by professional associations and special interest groups. A G K Hall catalog covering the Institute's Library holdings is available. Since 1937, Library has been depository for all California local documents (city, county & special

district). Formerly: Bureau of Public Administration.
CA —UNIVERSITY OF SOUTHERN CALIFORNIA, Crocker Business Library, Hoffman Hall, University Park, Los Angeles, 90007. Judith A Truelson, Head Librn
Holdings: Vols (100,000) Cat Microforms
Notes: The Roy P Crocker Library of Business Administration, located in Hoffman Hall, houses more than 100,000 volumes and regularly receives approximately 1500 trade, financial, economics, labor, and general business periodicals and newspapers. The areas of subject concentration include business economics, finance and investments, general management/management theory, international business, finance and management, marketing/food marketing, and quantitative business analysis.
CA —HELLER, EHRMAN, WHITE & MCAULIFFE, Library, 44 Montgomery St, San Francisco, 94104. Loretta Mak, Librn
Holdings: Vols (22,500) Cat Audiotapes
Notes: A private library serving 150 attorneys. Emphasis on the areas of taxation, trial practice and corporation laws.
DC —AMERICAN SOCIETY OF ASSOCIATION EXECUTIVES, Information Central, 1575 Eye St NW, Washington, 20005. Cathy L Lalush, Mgr of Research and Info
Notes: Information regarding association management. Resources are designed to provide the association executive with the background knowledge for management decisions through case studies, research and statistical reports, bibliographies and articles.
DC —US TREASURY DEPT, Library, 15 & Pennsylvania Ave NW-Room 5030, Washington, 20220. Elisabeth S Knauff, Mgr Information Services Division
Holdings: Vols (30,000) Cat Microforms
Notes: Tax notes, microfiche, database 1978 to date included, as well as numerous legislative histories.
GA —ATLANTA PUBLIC LIBRARY, Ivan Allen Jr Dept of Science, Industry & Government, One Margaret Mitchell Square, Atlanta, 30303. William D Munro, Head
Holdings: Vols (15,000) Cat Microforms
Budget: ($180,000)
Notes: This collection incl on microform annual reports and Securities Exchange Commission 10-K reports for some 11,000 companies from 1976 to date; current and retrospective stock quotations, stock reports, corporate and industry records and directories and supporting looseleaf services; information file on Atlanta's largest 15,000 with annual updates; and current plat maps for the five county Metro-Atlanta area. Atlanta and Georgia business history sections are being developed. Most material on this collection is noncirculating.
IL —FEDERAL RESERVE BANK OF CHICAGO, Library, 230 S La Salle St, PO Box 834, Chicago, 60690. Dorothy Phillips, Librn
Holdings: Vols (19,000) Cat
Notes: Restricted use: noncirculating. No photocopying.
NY —NEW YORK STATE LIBRARY, State Education Bldg Annex, Washington Ave, Albany, 12224.
Holdings: Vols 2000 Cat
Notes: Also pamphlets, documents and several thousand clippings. Incl 15,000 cards indexing tax material in New York State documents, proceedings of the National Tax Association, and current tax literature. Incl materials on theory and practices in the 50 states.
NY —STATE UNIVERSITY OF NEW YORK AT ALBANY, Library, Special Collections Dept, 1400 Washington Ave, Albany, 12222. Marion P Munzer, Coordr
Notes: Personal and family records of Howard Palfrey Jones (12 linear feet); correspondence, articles, and texts of speeches relating to municipal reform; proposals on tax reforms.
See also entries under Municipal Government; Jones, Howard Palfrey
NY —BROOKLYN PUBLIC LIBRARY, Business Library, 280 Cadman Plaza W, Brooklyn, 11201. Sylvia Mechanic, Business

Librn
Holdings: Vols (107,000) Cat
Notes: Library received about 1800 periodicals, 3000 serials, 2700 directories, 1600 telephone books from all over the world with a complete back file on microfilm for greater New York. Library is a selective US Government Documents depository. Subscribes to microfiche SEC 10K reports for AMEX, NYSE and OTC from 1976 to date; annual reports for earlier years. Transnational annual reports, on fiche from 1982-to date. 78 vertical file trays; Sanborn maps for Brooklyn, special collection of corporation histories. Publish monthly newsletter, Service to Business and Industry with our Science Division.
NY —NEW YORK PUBLIC LIBRARY, Research Libraries, Economic & Public Affairs Div, Fifth Ave & 42 St, New York, 10018. Edward DiRoma, Chief
Holdings: Vols (1,500,000) Cat Microforms
NC —GREENSBORO PUBLIC LIBRARY, Business Library, 201 Greene St, Drawer X-4, Greensboro, 27402. Lebby B Lamb, Business Librn
Holdings: Vols (6000) Cat Microforms
Budget: ($12,000)
PA —UNIVERSITY OF PENNSYLVANIA, Lippincott Library of the Wharton School, Philadelphia, 19104. Michael Halperin, Librn
Holdings: Cat
Notes: Long files of statistical data on the foreign trade of the US and many foreign countries. Extensive materials on foreign taxation and regulation of US enterprises abroad.
ON —CANADIAN TAX FOUNDATION LIBRARY, 130 Adelaide St W, Toronto, M5H 3P5, Can. Marjorie Robinson, Librn
Holdings: Vols (16,500) Cat
Notes: Worldwide scope; emphasis on Canada
ON —ONTARIO MINISTRY OF TREASURY & ECONOMICS, Library Services, Frost Bldg N, Queen's Park, Toronto, M7A 1Y8, Can. Barbara Weatherhead, Head Librn
Holdings: Vols (100,000) Cat Microforms
Budget: ($76,500)
Notes: Index to Ontario regulations.

TAXATION—CANADA

ON —CANADIAN TAX FOUNDATION LIBRARY, 130 Adelaide St W, Toronto, M5H 3P5, Can. Marjorie Robinson, Librn
Holdings: Vols (16,500) Cat
Notes: Worldwide scope; emphasis on Canada.
ON —INSTITUTE OF CHARTERED ACCOUNTANTS OF ONTARIO, The Merrilees Library, 69 Bloor St E, Toronto, M4W 1B3, Can. Theresa Wolak, Librn
Holdings: Vols 301 Cat

TAXATION—HISTORY

IN —PURDUE UNIVERSITY LIBRARIES, Graduate School of Management, Krannert Library, West Lafayette, 47907. Gordon Law, Librn
Holdings: Vols (7000) Cat Mss Maps Pix Microforms
Notes: The collection consists of books, journals and pamphlets dating from the early 16th to late 19th century, covering to a large degree the early literature in economic thought and business practices both here and abroad. No photocopying.

TAXES see Taxation

TAXES, SCHOOL see Education—Finance

TAXONOMY

CA —LOS ANGELES STATE & COUNTY ARBORETUM, Plant Science Library, 301 N Baldwin Ave, Arcadia, 91006. Joan DeFato, Librn
Holdings: Vols (24,000) Cat 16mm Films
Budget: ($6000)
Notes: Emphasis on woody plants, particularly of Australia and South Africa. Botany is weighted toward taxonomy rather than plant physiology.

TAXONOMY (cont.)

CA —RANCHO SANTA ANA BOTANIC
GARDEN LIBRARY, 1500 N College Ave,
Claremont, 91711. Beatrice M Beck, Librn
Notes: Incl emphasis on California flora,
floras of the world, evolutionary biology and
ethnobotany.

CA —CALIFORNIA ACADEMY OF
SCIENCES, J W Mailliard Jr Library,
Golden Gate Park, San Francisco, 94118.
Ray Brian, Librn
Notes: Downs No 2160.

DC —SMITHSONIAN INSTITUTION
LIBRARIES, Botany Branch, Washington,
20560. Ruth Schallert, Branch Librn
Holdings: Vols (21,000) Cat Mss Maps Pix
Microforms
Notes: Taxonomic botany; with the J D
Smith Collection of general botany, the
Dawson Collection on algae, and the
Hitchcock-Chase Collection on grasses.

DC —SMITHSONIAN INSTITUTION
LIBRARIES, Natural History Branch,
Washington, 20560. Sylvia Churgin, Chief
Librn
Holdings: Cat Mss Maps Pix Slides
Microforms
Notes: Invertebrate zoology, Systematics.
Incl crustacea, echinoderms, mollusks,
worms, Cushman collection of foraminifera;
Springer collection on crinoids; Wilson
collection on copepoda.

IL —FIELD MUSEUM OF NATURAL
HISTORY, Library, Roosevelt Rd & Lake
Shore Dr, Chicago, 60605. W Peyton
Fawcett, Librn; Benjamin W Williams, Assoc
Librn
Holdings: Vols (210,000) Cat
Budget: ($100,000)
Notes: Extensive collections--publications of
learned societies and institutions and
monographic works--in all fields of natural
history, with emphasis on taxonomy and
evolutionary biology; and on museum
publications, American and foreign:
anthropology, especially archaeology and
ethnology of the Americas, Africa, East
Asia, and Oceania; botany, particularly
strong for the Americas; geology, chiefly
paleontology and meteoritic studies; and
zoology, worldwide (birds, fishes, insects,
mammals, mollusks, reptiles and
amphibians).

IL —MORTON ARBORETUM, Sterling
Morton Library, Lisle, 60532. Ian MacPhail,
Librn
Holdings: Vols (20,000) Cat Maps Pix
Budget: ($10,000)
Notes: The library is especially concerned
with the literature of woody plants (trees
and shrubs) of north temperate zones but has
substantial holdings in the taxonomy and
systematics of plants in general, both wild
and cultivated, flora of different parts of the
world, and a growing collection on plant
monographs. Also about 2000 pictures.
Described in *The Morton Arboretum
Quarterly*, vol 9, no 4 (Winter 1973), pp 56-
61.

MD —US DEPT OF AGRICULTURE,
National Agricultural Library, 10301
Baltimore Blvd, Beltsville, 20705. Joseph H
Howard, Director
Notes: Worldwide coverage of all aspects of
agriculture and related fields. Crop ecology,
agro-climatic analogs; air pollution effects.
Agronomy: agricultural and tropical and
desert agriculture. For use by the staff of the
USDA. Incl in the former collections of
American Institute of Crop Ecology.

MA —HARVARD UNIVERSITY LIBRARY,
Gray Herbarium Library, 22 Divinity Ave,
Cambridge, 02138. Barbara A Callahan,
Librn
Notes: Arnold Arboretum and Gray
Herbarium Libraries hold one of the nation's
largest collections (149,000 items).

MI —UNIVERSITY OF MICHIGAN,
Museums Library, Ann Arbor, 48109.
Patricia B Yocum, Librn
Holdings: Vols (100,000) Cat Pix
Microforms

MO —MISSOURI BOTANICAL GARDEN
LIBRARY, PO Box 299, Saint Louis, 63166.
M R Crosby, Dir of Research

NY —NEW YORK BOTANICAL GARDEN
LIBRARY, Bronx, 10458. Charles R Long,
Asst Vice Pres & Dir
Holdings: Vols 5000 Cat VF
Budget: ($356,000)
Notes: Over 900,000 items, incl books,
serials, pamphlets, archives and manuscripts,
vertical files, microfiche and microfilm,
nursery and seed catalogs, photographs,
paintings, prints, drawings and engravings.
Covering all areas of botanical sciences.

NY —CORNELL UNIVERSITY LIBRARIES,
Comstock Memorial Library of Entomology,
Ithaca, 14853. Edwin Spragg, Librn
Holdings: Vols (30,000) Cat Maps Pix
Audiotapes Microforms
Budget: ($13,500)
Notes: Major topics: general and applied
entomology. Minor topics: parasitology,
medical entomology, ecology, zoological
nomenclature and allied orders of
arthropods. Separate catalog to the
collection, also extensive collection of
reprints. Apiculture material kept at nearby
A R Mann Library.

NY —AMERICAN MUSEUM OF
NATURAL HISTORY, Library Services
Dept, Central Park W & 79th St, New York,
10024. Nina J Root, Chairwoman; Mary
Genett, Asst Librn for Reference Services
Holdings: Vols (385,000) Cat Mss Maps Pix
Slides Microforms
Notes: Nearly all collections are outstanding
for depth of coverage and international
range. Early and historic works, rare books,
colored illustrations, and relevant serial
publications supplement the modern
scientific publications necessary to the
researches of the scientific staff and the
work of the educational division. Open to
the public.

OH —LLOYD LIBRARY & MUSEUM, 917
Plum St, Cincinnati, 45202. John B Griggs,
Librn
Notes: Botanical taxonomy.

OR —OREGON STATE UNIVERSITY,
Library, Corvallis, 97331. Melvin George,
Dir
Holdings: Vols (980,000) Cat Maps Pix

PA —CARNEGIE LIBRARY OF
PITTSBURGH, Science & Technology Dept,
4400 Forbes Ave, Pittsburgh, 15213.
Catherine M Brosky, Dept Head
Notes: Except for certain special areas, such
as entomology and ornithology and a few
others that are emphasized, this general
subject is of secondary interest. Incl both
modern and classic works. Kept up to date
in cooperation with the Library in Carnegie
Museum of Natural History. Materials
available on the various phyla, classes, orders
and species. Abstracts, indexes,
bibliographies, taxonomic manuals and
standard reference books. Many journals and
society publications complete from the
beginning.

PA —HUNT INSTITUTE FOR BOTANICAL
DOCUMENTATION, Hunt Botanical
Library, Carnegie-Mellon University,
Pittsburgh, 15213. Bernadette G Callery,
Librn
Holdings: Vols (23,000) Cat Pix
Notes: Collection of primarily historical
botany and plant taxonomy, especially 1730-
1840. Includes approximately 500 15th
through 17th century herbals, extensive
collection of 18th and 19th century color-
plate works, floras and monographic works,
and other works on natural history, early
gardening and horticulture, and travel,
particularly that dealing with plant
exploration and introduction. Extensive
biographical materials, on people in plant
sciences. Reference collection and extensive
documentation in botanical bibliography,
especially concerning books published before
1850. Includes as separate collections, the
Strandell Collection of Linnaeana and the
Michel Adanson Library. Over 800 items
described in *Catalogue of Botanical Books in
the Collection of Rachel McMasters Miller
Hunt, 1477-1800* (Pittsburgh, 1958-1960).

TX —UNIVERSITY OF TEXAS, Marine
Science Institute Library, Port Aransas,
78373. Ruth Grundy, Librn
Holdings: Vols (45,000) Cat Maps Pix
Budget: ($70,000)
Notes: Current researches in marine science,
especially concerning the Gulf of Mexico,
the Texas Coastal Zone, and the Continental
Shelf. Incl journals.

ON —AGRICULTURE CANADA, Plant
Research Library, Research Branch, Central
Experimental Farm 49, Ottawa, K1A 0C6,
Can. Mrs E Gavora, Librn
Holdings: Vols (10,500) Cat Maps
Microforms
Notes: One of the most extensive botanical
collections in Canada, especially in the
taxonomy of higher plants and fungi.
Contains many of the basic works from the
starting point of botany in 1753 to date.
Major botanical works of Linnaeus and
others, covering flora of land areas of most
parts of the world.

ON —AGRICULTURE CANADA, Library
Division, Plant Research Library, 49 Central
Experimental Farm Bldg, Ottawa, K1A 0C6,
Can. Eva Gavora, Plant Research Librn
Holdings: (15,000) Items
Notes: Emphasis on flora of North America.

TAYLOR, BAYARD

PA —PENNSYLVANIA STATE
UNIVERSITY, Rare Book Room, University
Park, 16802. Charles Mann, Chief, Rare
Books and Special Collections
Holdings: Vols (13,000) Cat Mss Pix
Budget: ($24,000)
Notes: The Allison-Shelley Collection of
translations of German literature, history,
science, medicine, biography, children's
literature, and other cultural manifestations
into English. Incl 3000 letters and mss of
British and American translations of German
writings. Also phonograph records of
German art songs. Further, the collection
contains a large collection of Bayard
Taylor's works, letters, and mss. An
annotated exhibition catalog of selected
items is available from the Office of the
Dean of Libraries.

TAYLOR, CARL CLEVELAND, 1884-1975

NY —CORNELL UNIVERSITY LIBRARIES,
Collection of Regional History, Dept of
Manuscripts and Univ Archives, Ithaca,
14853.
Notes: Agricultural economist, US Secretary
of Agriculture. Papers, 1920-69; 47 ft.

TAYLOR, EDWARD R., 1844-1919

CT —YALE UNIVERSITY, Box 1603A, Yale
Station, New Haven, 06520.
Holdings: Cat Mss

NY —CORNELL UNIVERSITY LIBRARIES,
Collection of Regional History, Dept of
Manuscripts and Univ Archives, Ithaca,
14853.
Notes: Chemical manufacturer. Corporate
records and family papers, 1812-1925; 10 ft.

TAYLOR, FREDERICK WINSLOW, 1856-1915

NJ —STEVENS INSTITUTE OF
TECHNOLOGY, Samuel C Williams
Library, Castle Point Sta, Hoboken, 07030.
Jane G Hartye, Special Collections Librn
Holdings: Vols (180) Cat Pix Slides
Budget: ($1500)
Notes: Frederick Winslow Taylor is known
as the "father of scientific management," and
we have in our collection volumes of
correspondence relating to the introduction
of this system into industry, government, the
army and navy, etc. This collection also
includes many personal items belonging to
and used by Mr Taylor. Our collection is the
most complete one on the subject of
scientific management.

TAYLOR, GRAHAM

IL —NEWBERRY LIBRARY, 60 W Walton
St, Chicago, 60610. Diana Haskell, Cur of
Modern Mss
Holdings: Cat Mss Pix Microforms
Notes: Primary repository; over 10,000

TAYLOR, GRAHAM (cont.)

pieces. Cataloged mss. Restricted use: noncirculating.

TAYLOR, HARRY BAYLOR

VA —UNIVERSITY OF VIRGINIA, Alderman Library, Manuscripts Dept, Charlottesville, 22901. Edmund Berkeley Jr, Cur
Holdings: Cat Mss
Notes: Papers, 1906-1951, of Harry Baylor Taylor. Episcopal Medical Missionary in Anking.

TAYLOR, JEREMY

IL —NORTHERN ILLINOIS UNIVERSITY, Founders Memorial Library, Rare Books and Special Collections Dept, De Kalb, 60115. William R DuBois, Dept Head
Holdings: Vols 250 Cat Mss Pix
Notes: Contains 5 holograph letters by Jeremy Taylor, a water color portrait of Taylor and a pencil sketch of *The Golden Grove*, a unique copy. Noncirculating.

BC —UNIVERSITY OF VICTORIA, McPherson Library, Victoria, V8W 3H5, Can.
Notes: Incl transcripts: 109 pages, 1677; a holograph compendium of various prayers from Jeremy Taylor's *Worthy Communicant* and his *Holy Living.*

TAYLOR, JOSEPH HENRY

FL —BETHUNE-COOKMAN COLLEGE LIBRARY, Daytona Beach, 32015. Albert M Bethune, Jr, College Archivist
Notes: Papers and private library of the historian, Joseph Henry Taylor.

TAYLOR, KENNETH

IL —WHEATON COLLEGE, Buswell Memorial Library, Wheaton, 60187. Paul Snezek, Library Dir
Holdings: Vols 50 Mss
Notes: 12 linear feet of mss material related to the *Living Bible* translation, *The Bible Story Book. Related Topics:* Bible-Translations.

TAYLOR, LEA D.

IL —CHICAGO HISTORICAL SOCIETY, Library, Clark St at North Ave, Chicago, 60614. Archie Motley, Manuscript Librn
Notes: Papers of Lea Demarest Taylor. *See also* entry under Public Welfare-History.

TAYLOR, PETER

VA —UNIVERSITY OF VIRGINIA, Alderman Library, Manuscripts Dept, Charlottesville, 22901. Edmund Berkeley Jr, Cur
Notes: Letters of many other Virginia authors, such as Sherwood Anderson, Hawthorne Daniel, Murrell Edmunds, George Cary Eggleston, John Fox, John Pendleton Kennedy, Katie Letcher Lyle, Julian Rutherfoord Meade, Thomas Nelson Page, Virginius Dabney, Clifford Dowdey, Jane McClary, Peter Taylor, and others.

TAYLOR, PHOEBE ATWOOD

MA —BOSTON UNIVERSITY, Mugar Memorial Library, Special Collections Dept, 771 Commonwealth Ave, Boston, 02215. Howard B Gotlieb, Dir
Holdings: Cat Mss
Notes: Mss, correspondence, etc collected in depth; incl publications by or about.

TAYLOR, THOMAS, THE PLATONIST

IL —NORTHWESTERN UNIVERSITY, Library, Special Collections Dept, 1937 Sheridan Rd, Evanston, 60201. R Russell Maylone, Cur
Holdings: Vols 65 Cat
Notes: No published description of the

collection, which incl many articles by Taylor extracted from journals.

TAYLOR, ZACHARY

DC —LIBRARY OF CONGRESS, Manuscript Division, Washington, 20540. John C Broderick, Chief
Notes: The Presidential Papers collection incl the papers, etc, of numerous Presidents.

TAYLOR AND TAYLOR, PRINTERS AND PUBLISHERS

CA —CALIFORNIA HISTORICAL SOCIETY, Schubert Hall Library, 2099 Pacific Ave, San Francisco, 94109. Bruce L Johnson, Library Dir
Holdings: Vols 4400 Cat Mss Pix Microforms
Notes: The Edward C Kemble Collections. Not collections of fine printing, but of the history of printing and publishing with emphasis on the Pacific Coast, although the full scope of the collection is not limited to this area. In addition to bibliographic tools and reference works, it contains type specimen books and several long runs of trade periodicals and house organs of San Francisco typefounders. The Taylor & Taylor Archives, a part of this collection, contain the working record of a major San Francisco printing firm. The *Kemble Occasional*, published three times a year from the Kemble Collections, presents scholarly articles on the history of printing. Edward C Kemble was the first historian of printing in California.

TCHAIKOWSKY, PETER ILICH

MO —UNIVERSITY OF MISSOURI-COLUMBIA, Ellis Library, Art, Archaeology and Music Dept, Columbia, 65201. Bonnie MacEwan, Librn
Holdings: Vols Cat
Notes: Russian editions of complete works of Glinka, Tchaikowsky and Rimsky-Korsakov.

TCHUVAK LANGUAGE see Chuvashian Language

TCHUVASHIAN LANGUAGE see Chuvashian Language

TEA

IN —HURTY-PECK LIBRARY OF BEVERAGE LITERATURE, 5650 W Raymond Street, PO Box 41167, Indianapolis, 46208. Ben Wilson, Librn
Holdings: Vols (6000) Cat
Notes: The most comprehensive collection, in English, in the world on beverages of all types. History, manufacture, formulae, customs. Books on beer and brewing; cocoa and chocolate; coffee; liquors and spirits; soft drinks; tea; and wine.

TEA ROOMS see Restaurants, Lunch Rooms, Bars, Etc.

TEACHERS

CO —UNIVERSITY OF COLORADO, Libraries, Western Historical Collections, Boulder, 80309.
Holdings: Mss
Notes: Papers of Herrick Roth (b 1916), who was one of the founders in 1946 of the American Federation of Teachers local in Denver. In 1951 he left teaching to devote himself full-time to the labor movement. From 1962 until his ouster by George Meany in 1973 he served as President of the Colorado Labor Council. Since then he has taught at Denver University, run unsuccessfully for the US Senate and served as head of the State Employment Service. The collection contains correspondence, pamphlets, clippings and other material on Roth's labor union, political and social interests. The largest portion of the material deals with the Colorado Labor Council and the American Federation of Teachers. 25

boxes, 1950s-1970s. Typescript inventory is available.

DC —LIBRARY OF CONGRESS, Manuscript Division, Washington, 20540. John C Broderick, Chief
Holdings: 135,200 Items
Notes: Correspondence, reports, student and financial records, subject files, scrapbooks, clippings, photographs, printed matter, and other memorabilia of Nannie Helen Burroughs (1878-1961).

MS —UNIVERSITY OF SOUTHERN MISSISSIPPI, William David McCain Graduate Library, Box 5148, Southern Sta, Hattiesburg, 39406.
Holdings: Uncat Mss
Notes: Records (1967-1975; 2 cubic feet) of the Mississippi Association of Educators concerning the merger of the predominantly Black, Mississippi Teachers Association and the predominantly White, Mississippi Education Association. The collection incl correspondence, minutes of meetings, conference hearings, resolutions, proposals and constitutions from various state education associations.

PA —KING'S COLLEGE, D Leonard Corgan Library, 14 W Jackson St, Wilkes-Barre, 18711. Judith Tierney, Special Collections Librn
Holdings: Uncat Mss Pix Audiotapes
Notes: Personal papers of Lillian Rifkin Blumenfeld, educator in the early progressive schools in the US, including correspondence, diaries, articles, poems, clippings, photographs and tapes, 1937-1981.

BC —BRITISH COLUMBIA TEACHERS' FEDERATION, Resources Center, 2235 Burrand St, Vancouver, V6J 3H9, Can. T M Murphy, Librn
Holdings: Vols (9900) Cat Audiotapes Videotapes 16mm Films
Budget: $15,500
Notes: Emphasis on teachers' professional in-service training. Curriculum material excluded; audiovisual material lent to BCTF members province- wide.

TEACHERS—EDUCATION AND TRAINING see Teachers—In-Service Training; Teachers, Training of

TEACHERS—EXAMINATIONS see Examinations

TEACHERS—IN-SERVICE TRAINING

BC —BRITISH COLUMBIA TEACHERS' FEDERATION, Resources Center, 2235 Burrand St, Vancouver, V6J 3H9, Can. T M Murphy, Librn
Holdings: Vols (9900) Cat Audiotapes Videotapes 16mm Films
Budget: $15,500
Notes: Emphasis on teachers' professional in-service training. Curriculum material excluded; audiovisual material lent to BCTF members province- wide.

TEACHERS, BUSINESS see Business Teachers

TEACHERS, COMMERCIAL see Business Teachers

TEACHERS, RETIRED

DC —AMERICAN ASSOCIATION OF RETIRED PERSONS (AARP), National Gerontology Resource Center, 1909 K St NW, Washington, 20049. Paula M Lovas, Librn; Mary F Power, Coordr, Reference Service
Holdings: Vols (15,000) Cat Microforms
Budget: ($60,000)
Notes: Retirement, retirement planning and social gerontology. Incl government documents and reports, journals, and bibliographies. Formerly the National Retired Teachers Association/American Association of Retired Persons (NRTA/AARP).

TEACHERS, TRAINING OF

BC —BRITISH COLUMBIA TEACHERS' FEDERATION, Resources Center, 2235

TEACHERS, TRAINING OF (cont.)

Burrand St, Vancouver, V6J 3H9, Can. T M Murphy, Librn
Holdings: Vols 8000 Cat Mss Maps Pix Slides Audiotapes Films Microforms
Notes: Emphasis is on teacher's professional in-service training. Borrowing privileges to BCTF members and Affiliation Library and Institution. Subject bibliographies of the collection are available. Data-Bases, searching available.
SK —SASKATCHEWAN TEACHERS' FEDERATION, Stewart Resources Centre, 2317 Arlington Ave, Saskatoon, S7K 3N3, Can. Susan Dyer, Librn
Holdings: Vols (18,000) Cat Slides Phonorecords Audiotapes Videotapes 16mm Film Filmstrips
Budget: ($15,000)
Notes: Professional teacher-education collection; curriculum materials; and Mary Ellen Burgess Drama Library.

TEACHERS' OATHS see Loyalty Oaths

TEACHING see Education

TEAGUE, OLIN E.

TX —TEXAS A&M UNIVERSITY, Sterling C Evans Library, University Archives, College Station, 77843. Charles R Schultz, University Archivist
Holdings: Mss
Notes: The Archives of Modern Politics: the papers of Texas Congressmen Olin E Teague, 1946-1975.

TEALE, EDWIN WAY

†CT —UNIVERSITY OF CONNECTICUT LIBRARY, Special Collections Dept, Storrs, 06268. Richard H Schimmelpfeng, Dir of Special Collections
Notes: Papers, incl mss, etc. of the naturalist Edwin Way Teale.

TEASDALE, SARA

CT —YALE UNIVERSITY, Box 1603A, Yale Station, New Haven, 06520.
Holdings: Mss
IN —INDIANA UNIVERSITY, Lilly Library, Seventh St, Bloomington, 47405. William R Cagle, Librn
Notes: Writings by author Sara Teasdale.
MO —SAINT LOUIS PUBLIC LIBRARY, Gardner Rare Book Room, 1301 Olive St, Saint Louis, 63103. Julanne M Good, Supervisor; Martha Riley, Rare Books Librn
Holdings: Vols (2300) Cat
Budget: ($5573)
Notes: First editions of authors having some association with William Marion Reedy and *Reedy's Mirror*, such as Sara Teasdale, Zoe Akins, Fannie Hurst, Edgar Lee Masters, Babette Deutsch, Richard LeGallienne, etc. Also first editions of selected St Louis and/or Missouri authors such as T S Eliot, Samuel L Clemens, Theodore Dreiser and Tennessee Williams. Noncirculating.

TECHNICAL ASSISTANCE

DC —ACTION, Photo Library, 806 Connecticut Ave NW, Washington, 20525.
Holdings: Pix Slides
Notes: Volunteer photos for ACTION, VISTA, and older Americans programs. 15,000 photographs.
DC —PEACE CORPS, Information Services Division, 806 Connecticut Ave NW, Room M407, Washington, 20526. Rita C Warpeha, Chief Librn
Holdings: Vols (35,000) Cat
Budget: ($10,000)
WI —UNIVERSITY OF WISCONSIN, MADISON, Land Tenure Center Library, 434 Steenbock Memorial Library, 550 Babcock Dr, Madison, 53706. Teresa J Anderson, Librn
Holdings: Vols (60,000) Cat Mss Maps Microforms
Budget: ($65,000)
Notes: Socio-economic aspects of

agricultural development in the Third World. All materials in the collection are cataloged and classified. The library has its own catalog.
ON —DEPT OF REGIONAL INDUSTRIAL EXPANSION, Ottawa Library, 235 Queen St, Ottawa, K1A 0H5, Can. Steven Rush, Librn
Holdings: Vols (100,000) Cat Maps Microforms
Notes: Contains 1500 reports of ARDA projects (Agricultural Rehabilitation and Development Agency); also NEWSTART project reports. There is a published book catalog and two supplements. 15,000 documents; 3000 periodical subscriptions.

TECHNICAL CHEMISTRY see Chemistry, Technical

TECHNICAL DRAWING see Mechanical Drawing

TECHNICAL EDUCATION

NY —STATE UNIVERSITY OF NEW YORK, COLLEGE AT BUFFALO, E H Butler Library, 1300 Elmwood Ave, Buffalo, 14222. George C Newman, Dir
Holdings: Vols (465,130) Cat Maps Microforms
Budget: ($466,000)
Notes: Fully cataloged collections in education, incl education of exceptional children, art education, social sciences education, etc, are strong since the College was formerly a college of education and approx 60 percent of current graduates still obtain some degree enabling them to teach. Incl Curriculum Laboratory containing courses of study, elementary and secondary textbooks, and collections for children's literature courses (MA in Children's Literature offered). Collection consists of 465,130 volumes incl 64,255 bound periodical volumes, plus 19,120 microfilm reels and 457,988 microtext pieces other than reels. Subscribe to 2263 periodicals.
BC —VANCOUVER COMMUNITY COLLEGE, Vancouver Vocational Institute Library, 250 W Pender St, Vancouver, V6B 1S9, Can. Ross Henderson, Librn
Holdings: Vols (16,000) Cat Audiotapes Videotapes Films Slides
Budget: ($211,000)
Notes: Curriculum support for technical programs, service programs, industrial programs, and business and health programs.

TECHNICAL ILLUSTRATION see Illustration, Technical

TECHNICAL INNOVATIONS see Technological Innovations

TECHNICAL INSTITUTES see Technical Education

TECHNICAL PERIODICALS see Periodicals, Scientific and Technical

TECHNICAL REPORTS

DC —LIBRARY OF CONGRESS, Science & Technology Div, Washington, 20540.
Holdings: Cat Pix Microforms
Notes: One of the world's major collections of technical report literature, comprising nearly 3 million documents (1.7 Million on microform) currently increasing by about 100,000 annually. Receives reports in all fields of scientific research and development supported by or of interest to government agencies, incl Dept of Energy, Dept of Defense, National Aeronautics and Space Administration, Office of Education, and the National Technical Information Service, as well as many industrial and foreign reports. Also some 30,000 OSRD reports on World War II research and development and current Soviet state standards (GOST). Reports are available for consultation in the Science and Technology Division's Science Reading Room and for purchase

ofphotoduplicates. Subject access is provided through the various indexing media issued by the report supplying agencies, and in some instances through in-house finding aids.
MA —HARVARD UNIVERSITY LIBRARY, Gordon McKay Library, Division of Applied Sciences, Pierce Hall, Oxford St, Cambridge, 02138. Julie Sandall Barlas, Librn
Holdings: Cat Microforms
WA —UNIVERSITY OF WASHINGTON LIBRARIES, Engineering Library, FH-15, Seattle, 98195. Harold N Wiren, Engineering Librn
Holdings: Vols (108,313) Cat Microforms
Budget: ($314,409)
Notes: About a million technical reports and the US patent specifications on microfilm are strong adjuncts to the collection which covers all fields of engineering.

TECHNICAL SCHOOLS see Technical Education

TECHNICAL SECRETARIES

SC —HORRY GEORGETOWN TECHNICAL COLLEGE, Library, Hwy 501, Box 1966, Conway, 29526. Barbara Brittain, Librn
Holdings: Vols (20,000) Cat Slides Microforms

TECHNOLOGICAL CHANGE see Technological Innovations

TECHNOLOGICAL INNOVATIONS

DC —US DEPT OF LABOR, Library, 200 Constitution Ave NW, Washington, 20210. Sabina Jacobson, Dir
Holdings: Vols (550,000) Cat
WI —UNIVERSITY OF WISCONSIN, MADISON, Land Tenure Center Library, 434 Steenbock Memorial Library, 550 Babcock Dr, Madison, 53706. Teresa J Anderson, Librn
Holdings: Vols (60,000) Cat Mss Maps Microforms
Budget: ($65,000)
Notes: Socio-economic aspects of agricultural development in the Third World. All materials in the collection are cataloged and classified. The library has its own catalog.
ON —CANADA DEPT OF LABOUR, Library, Ottawa, K1A 0J2, Can. Monique Marchand, Chief Librn
Holdings: Vols (100,000) Cat Microforms

TECHNOLOGY

CA —UNIVERSITY OF CALIFORNIA, DAVIS, Physical Sciences Library, Davis, 95616. Scott Kennedy, Head
Holdings: Vols 125,889 Cat Maps Microforms
Notes: Incl areas of astronomy, chemistry, engineering, geology, mathematics, and physics. Strong in journal runs and reference materials. See individual subject headings for collection details.
CA —CONTRA COSTA COUNTY LIBRARY, 1750 Oak Park Blvd, Pleasant Hill, 94523. Barbara Potter, Librn
Holdings: Vols (18,000)
CA —COGSWELL COLLEGE, Library, 600 Stockton St, San Francisco, 94108. Judith Carson-Croes, Dir
Holdings: Vols (12,000) Cat
CA —UNIVERSITY OF CALIFORNIA, SANTA CRUZ, University Library, Special Collections, Santa Cruz, 95064. Rita Bottoms, Special Collections Librn; Margaret Felts, South Pacific Collection Bibliographer
Notes: General circulation.
CT —YALE UNIVERSITY, Engineering & Applied Science Library, 15 Prospect St, New Haven, 06520. Elizabeth B Hayes, Librn
Holdings: Vols (31,808) Cat Maps Pix Microforms
Notes: Comprehensive holdings. The Library also has NASA depository materials.
DC —CENTER FOR BIOETHICS, Library, Kennedy Institute, Georgetown University,

TECHNOLOGY (cont.)

3520 Prospect St NW, Washington, 20057.
Doris Goldstein, Dir; Judith Mistichelli,
Senior Librn
Holdings: Vols 8200
Notes: Largest library of its kind. Incl 31,
000 journal articles. Collects in the following
subject areas: applied ethics; medical ethics;
philosophy of medicine; science, technology
and society; sociology of medicine; patient-
physician care; sexuality; contraception;
abortion; population policy; reproductive
technologies; in vitro fertilization; genetic
counseling and screening; genetic
engineering; mental organ transplantation;
death and dying; "baby doe" issues;
euthanasia; suicide; use of chemical and
biological weapons. Produces computer
database *Bioethicsline,* available through
MEDLARS; and the printed annual
Bibliography of Bioethics. Other library
publications are: *New Titles in Bioethics*
(monthly); *Scope Notes* series on current
topics.

DC —LIBRARY OF CONGRESS, African and
Middle Eastern Division, Washington,
20540.
Holdings: Cat Mss Microforms
Notes: Orientalia: the Orientalia Division
contains 1,400,000 vols in Oriental languages.
Chinese: more than 422,000 vols, espec
strong in local histories and Ch'ing (1644-
1911) period material. Japanese: over 574,
000 vols, espec strong in economics,
statistics, history, literature; 12,000
government, learned society, and university
periodical titles, particularly science,
technology, and social sciences. Korean: 56,
000 vols, espec strong in social sciences and
modern history.

DC —LIBRARY OF CONGRESS, Science &
Technology Div, Washington, 20540.
Holdings: Cat Pix Microforms
Notes: One of the world's major collections
of technical report literature, comprising
nearly 3 million documents (1.7 Million on
microform) currently increasing by about
100,000 annually. Receives reports in all
fields of scientific research and development
supported by or of interest to government
agencies, incl Dept of Energy, Dept of
Defense, National Aeronautics and Space
Administration, Office of Education, and the
National Technical Information Service, as
well as many industrial and foreign reports.
Also some 30,000 OSRD reports on World
War II research and development and
current Soviet state standards (GOST).
Reports are available for consultation in the
Science and Technology Division's Science
Reading Room and for purchase
ofphotoduplicates. Subject access is provided
through the various indexing media issued
by the report supplying agencies, and in
some instances through in-house finding
aids.

DC —NATIONAL SCIENCE
FOUNDATION, Library, 1800 G St NW,
Room 1242, Washington, 20550. Florence E
Heckman, Ref Librn
Holdings: Vols 15,000 Cat Microforms
Budget: $184,000

DC —SMITHSONIAN INSTITUTION
LIBRARIES, National Museum of American
History Branch, Washington, 20560. Rhoda
S Ratner, Branch Librn
Holdings: Vols (369,650) Cat Mss Maps Pix
Slides Microforms

FL —MIAMI-DADE PUBLIC LIBRARY
SYSTEM, One Biscayne Blvd, Miami,
33132. Theresa L Liangi, Science &
Technical Librn
Holdings: Vols 16,000 Cat
Notes: Incl 260 journals, on-line reference
searching, index of patents and official
gazette.

IL —ARGONNE NATIONAL
LABORATORY, Library, Technical
Information Services Dept, 9700 Cass Ave,
Argonne, 60439. Hillis L Griffin, Dir
Notes: The ANL library system consists of
eight branch libraries with centralized
processing services. The entire collection
numbers 70,000 monographic titles, 3700

journal titles, and over 1 million scientific
and technical reports. Materials may be used
by the public in the library by prior
arrangement. Photocopies may be supplied
for interlibrary loan, for which a processing
and handling charge is made. The branch
libraries are: Biological and Medical
Research; Chemical Engineering; Chemistry;
Mathematics/Physics/Computer Science;
Reactor Science/Engineering; Materials
Science; Solid State Physics; High-Energy
Physics/Environmental Sciences.

IL —CENTER FOR RESEARCH
LIBRARIES, 6050 S Kenwood Ave,
Chicago, 60637. Donald B Simpson, Dir;
Esther Smith, Collection Development Librn
Holdings: Vols 190.000 Cat
Notes: About 5000 current subscriptions to
infrequently held scientific and technical
serials, incl many Russian and Japanese.
Very extensive collection of older scientific
and technical journals, especially medical.

IL —MUSEUM OF SCIENCE AND
INDUSTRY, Library, 57th St and Lake
Shore Dr, Chicago, 60637. Carla Hayden,
Coordinator
Holdings: Vols (15,000) Cat Pix Slides
Budget: ($10,000)
Notes: Incl filmstrips, films, software, kits,
and textbooks.

IL —ELGIN COMMUNITY COLLEGE,
Renner Learning Resource Center, 1700
Spartan Dr, Elgin, 60120. Ethel Apple, Librn
Holdings: Vols (50,000) Cat Microforms

IL —NORTHWESTERN UNIVERSITY,
Seeley G Mudd Library for Science &
Engineering, 2233 Sheridan Rd, Evanston,
60201. Robert C Michaelson, Head
Holdings: Vols (200,000) Cat Microforms
Notes: Collection emphasizes graduate and
research level material.

IL —NORTHBROOK PUBLIC LIBRARY,
1201 Cedar Lane, Northbrook, 60062.
Carole Klein-Alexander, Head of Reference
Service
Holdings: Vols (4688) Cat
Budget: ($6800)
Notes: Maintained as technology subject
center for North Suburban Library System's
Coordinated Acquistions Program through
1979. Library will attempt to maintain
collection through its own budget.

MD —UNIVERSITY OF BALTIMORE,
Langsdale Library, 1420 Maryland Ave,
Baltimore, 21201. Gerry Watkins, Head of
Special Collections Dept
Holdings: Cat Mss Maps
Notes: Incl the entire stock (10,000 vols) of
Peter Decker, New York antiquarian
bookdealer (aquired in 1970); incl Peter
Decker's mss of his published works and his
records as a dealer in Americana.

MD —CAPITOL INSTITUTE OF
TECHNOLOGY, Library, 11301 Springfield
Rd, Laurel, 20708. Pat Wissinger, Librn
Holdings: Vols (10,000) Cat Slides
Phonorecords Microforms
Notes: Electronics, computers,
telecommunications undergraduate academy.

MA —CHILDREN'S MUSEUM, Resource
Center, Museum Wharf, 300 Congress St,
Boston, 02210. Marie Ariel, Librn; Maria
Russell, Resource Services Mgr
Holdings: Vols 300 Cat Mss Filmstrips
Notes: Curriculum materials and materials
for children and adults. Available for
reference use by the public; borrowing
privileges for Museum members; activity and
curriculum kits available to public, schools
and community groups for rental fee.
Subject-related programs and services offered
by Museum staff.

MA —MUSEUM OF SCIENCE, Library,
Science Park, Boston, 02114. Edward D
Pearce, Librn
Holdings: Vols 33,000 Cat

MA —WENTWORTH INSTITUTE OF
TECHNOLOGY, Alumni Library, 550
Huntington Ave, Boston, 02115. Ann
Montgomery Smith, Dir of Libraries
Holdings: Vols (55,00) Cat Microforms
Budget: ($68,500)

MA —MASSACHUSETTS INSTITUTE OF
TECHNOLOGY, Institute Archives, Special
Collections, Cambridge, 02139.
Notes: Derr and I Austin Kelly collections

contain significant monuments of science,
technology and printing.

MI —WASHTENAW COMMUNITY
COLLEGE, Learning Resource Center, P.O.
Box D-1, Ann Arbor, 48106. Adella Scott,
Dir

MI —EDISON INSTITUTE, Greenfield
Village and Henry Ford Museum, Archives
& Research Library, PO Box 1970,
Dearborn, 48121. Steve Hamp, Dir; Joan W
Gartland, Librn
Holdings: Vols 400,000 Cat Mss Maps
Microforms
Notes: 400,000 vols incl pamphlets. The
Archives and research library supports the
program of Greenfield Village and the Henry
Ford Museum. Special collections incl:
automotive literature, ephemera, McGuffey
Readers, trade catalogs, photographs and
graphics.

MI —GENERAL MOTORS, Research
Laboratories Library, General Motors
Technical Center, Warren, 48090. Robert W
Gibson, Librn

MN —MINNEAPOLIS PUBLIC LIBRARY &
INFORMATION CENTER, Science &
Technology Dept, 300 Nicollet Mall,
Minneapolis, 55401. Edythe Abrahamson,
Librn
Notes: Separate card catalog, telephone
reference service, and directory service. Incl
periodicals; large file of corporation annual
reports; VF local company histories and
annual reports; domestic and foreign
telephone directories; trade and industrial
directories; historical US stock quotations,
1891-date; local OTC quotations, 1933-date;
indexes and abstracting services; looseleaf
reference services.

MN —SAINT PAUL PUBLIC LIBRARY,
Science and Industry Room, 90 W Fourth
St, Saint Paul, 55102. Virginia B Stavn,
Supvr
Holdings: Vols 25,000 Cat
Budget: ($79,500)
Notes: Schematics 1920's-date. National
service data 1938-date.

MO —LINDA HALL LIBRARY, 5109 Cherry
St, Kansas City, 64110. Larry X Besant, Dir;
Wilma L Hartman, Librn for Public Services;
Siegfried Ruschin, Librn for Collection
Development
Holdings: Cat Maps Microforms
Budget: $1,000,000
Notes: Over 600,000 vols, 870,000
microforms, over 100,000 engineering
standards and specifications. Also, patents,
technical reports, specifications, and
conference proceedings. Receives 16,400
serial publications in some 40 languages, in
science and technology, and 36,000 total
serial titles. Academy publications, back to
the 17th century, and some 3000 books of
historical significance in science and
technology (History of Science Collection)
are among the strongest areas in the library
collection. Downs number-2169 and in
Supplement many references 1031, 1105,
1106, 1123-24, etc. It would be difficult to
break down strengths in the individual areas
of the sciences and technology. Collection is
comprehensive throughout these subject
areas (except for clinical medicine and
surgery, which are out of scope). Open to
the public.

MO —SAINT LOUIS PUBLIC LIBRARY,
1301 Olive St, Saint Louis, 63103. Therese F
Dawson, Librn, Applied Science Dept
Holdings: Vols 150,000 Cat Maps Pamphlets
Microforms
Notes: Incl industrial standards and
specifications.

NJ —BECTON, DICKINSON & CO,
Corporate Library/Information Center,
Rutherford, 07070. Lynda M Wiseman,
Corporate Librn
Holdings: Vols (3500) Cat Microforms
Notes: Open to the public by appointment
and ILL.

NJ —TRENTON FREE PUBLIC LIBRARY,
Business & Technology Dept, 120 Academy
St, Trenton, 08608. Richard D Rebecca,
Principal Librn
Holdings: Vols (9000) Cat Microforms
Notes: Patent gazette on microfilm.
Chemical abstracts 1907-1979. Incl 400

TECHNOLOGY (cont.)

telephone directories. Interlibrary Loan (photocopies) available.

NY —NEW YORK STATE LIBRARY, State Education Bldg Annex, Washington Ave, Albany, 12224.
Holdings: Cat Maps Microforms
Notes: Strong collection acquired to support state interlibrary loan. Holdings to 1960 published in New York State Library, Checklist in Science and Technology, an author listing with abbreviated title, Incl extensive microform holdings of technical reports: AEC, NASA, NTIS, SAE Transactions. Strong holdings related to standards and specifications: military and federal, commercial, National Bureau of Standards, American National Standards Institute, etc.

NY —BROOME COMMUNITY COLLEGE, Cecil C Tyrrell Learning Resources Center, PO Box 1017, Binghamton, 13902. James D Baker, Dir
Holdings: Vols 69,000 Cat Maps Slides Phonorecords Audiotapes Filmstrips Microforms
Budget: $92,000
Notes: State-of-the-art working materials for the technician. Incl 300 maps, 2000 slides, 1000 phonorecords, 500 audiotapes and 100 filmstrips.

NY —AMERICAN INSTITUTE OF PHYSICS, Center for the History of Physics, Niels Bohr Library, 335 E 45 St, New York, 10017. John Aubry, Librn
Holdings: Vols (16,000) Cat Mss Pix Slides Phonorecords Audiotapes 16mm Films Microforms
Notes: The Library contains an extensive collection of published works relating to the history of modern physics and astronomy. Its archives incl letter, notebooks and other papers of physicists, as well as the records of leading American physics societies and institutions. Its collections of ms autobiographies, oral history interviews, and other tape recordings, and pictorial materials (incl unpublished film footage) are unrivaled in the field of history of science. It maintains the International Catalog of Sources for History of Physics and and Astronomy.

NY —ENGINEERING SOCIETIES LIBRARY, 345 E 47 St, New York, 10017. S Kirk Cabeen, Dir
Holdings: Vols 250,000 Cat Maps 16mm Films Microforms
Notes: One of the largest, most comprehensive engineering libraries in the world. Covers all engineering disciplines; particularly strong in electrical and electronic, mechanical, mining and metallurgical, petroleum, chemical, industrial, air conditioning and refrigeration engineering. Incl Wheeler Collection of early materials on magnetism and electricity. 125,000 bound periodical volumes; 10,000 maps; 5000 serial subscriptions (many foreign-language). Virtually all materials abstracted in Engineering Index (1884-date) are incl in Library. Noncirculating, except to members of professional engineering societies which support the Library. See Engineering Societies Library, New York, Classed Subject Catalog and Index (Boston: G K Hall, 1963); and Supplements, 1-10, 1964-1973.

NY —INTERNATIONAL PAPER CO, Corporate Information Center, 77 W 45 St, New York, 10036. Elizabeth Skerritt, Corporate Librn
Holdings: Vols 1000

NY —NEW YORK PUBLIC LIBRARY, Research Libraries, Science and Technology Research Center, Fifth Ave & 42 St, New York, 10018.
Holdings: Vols (1,100,000) Cat Microforms
Budget: ($647,259)
Notes: Covers all the pure and applied sciences except the biological sciences. Particularly strong in aeronautics, biochemistry, chemical engineering, chemistry, communications, electricity, electronics, engineering, geology, mathematics, metallurgy, meteorology,

mining, navigation, paper, petroleum, physics, shipbuilding, and textiles.

NY —NEW YORK PUBLIC LIBRARY, Mid-Manhattan Library, Science & Business Dept, 455 Fifth Ave, New York, 10016. Frederick E Dusold, Sr Principal Librn
Holdings: Vols (110,000) Cat Microforms
Budget: ($134,000)
Notes: All works are in English. Material is current; policy precludes archival collecting. Collection is geared toward the undergraduate college student, with consideration given to the professional, the lay reader and the beginning graduate student. Collection incl monographs, texts, treatises, standard reference works and periodicals in agriculture, horticulture, home economics, crafts, engineering, industrial chemistry, construction and other technologies. Books are available for circulation in addition to an extensive reference collection.

NY —UNIVERSITY OF ROCHESTER, Carlson Library, Hutchison Hall, River Campus, Rochester, 14627. Michael W Poulin, Librn
Holdings: Vols (48,720) Cat Microforms
Notes: Strong collection in the field and related areas.

NY —UNION COLLEGE, Schaffer Library, Archives of Science and Technology, Schenectady, 12308. Ellen Fladger, Archivist
Notes: Research and development. Papers of Ernst Fredrik Werner Alexanderson, Philip L Alger, Howard I Becker, Ernst Julius Berg, Gabriel Kron, Samuel P Nixdorff, Birger W Nordlander, William E Ruder, George Westinghouse, and William Comings White.

NC —WAKE TECHNICAL COLLEGE, Library, Audio-Visual Dept, 9101 Fayetteville Road, Raleigh, 27603. James Gray, Librn; Horst Garloff, Audio-Visual Specialist
Holdings: Vols (32,332) Cat Maps Slides Phonorecords Audiotapes Videotapes 16mm Films Filmstrips Microforms

OH —PUBLIC LIBRARY OF CINCINNATI & HAMILTON COUNTY, Science & Technology Dept, 800 Vine St, Cincinnati, 45202. Rosemary Gaiser, Head
Holdings: Vols (250,000) Cat
Notes: Pure and applied science. Incl over 1600 periodicals and serial titles and more than 100 abstracting and indexing services in major fields of science and technology.

OH —CLEVELAND PUBLIC LIBRARY, Science & Technology Dept, 325 Superior Ave, Cleveland, 44114. Jean Z Piety, Head
Holdings: Cat
Notes: Primarily an engineering collection with basic sciences; strong in 19th and 20th century American, British, and Canadian technical societies' publications; comprehensive bibliography, standards and specifications; Rand Corp; 4400 periodicals and serial; extensive collections in chemistry, pamphlets (60,000). Incl collections on geology, aeronautics and agriculture.

PA —FRANKLIN INSTITUTE LIBRARY, 20 & The Parkway, Philadelphia, 19103. Miriam Padusis, Dir; Charles Wilt, Readers Servs Librn
Holdings: Vols (300,000) Cat Maps Pix Microforms

PA —TEMPLE UNIVERSITY, Engineering and Architecture Library, 12 & Norris Sts, Philadelphia, 19122. Raelaine Ballou, Librn
Holdings: Vols (12,000) Cat Microforms
Budget: ($13,500)

PA —CARNEGIE LIBRARY OF PITTSBURGH, Science & Technology Dept, 4400 Forbes Ave, Pittsburgh, 15213. Catherine M Brosky, Dept Head
Holdings: Vols (380,000) Cat Maps Microforms
Budget: ($240,000)
Notes: Monographs, handbooks, serials, long runs of periodicals, technical reports, state and federal government documents, patents, standards, specifications, directories, abstracts, indexes, bibliographies, society publications. Modern and classic.

†RI —UNIVERSITY OF RHODE ISLAND, Library, Kingston, 02881.
Notes: Extensive collections.

SC —HORRY GEORGETOWN TECHNICAL COLLEGE, Library, Hwy

501, Box 1966, Conway, 29526. Barbara Brittain, Librn
Holdings: Vols (20,000) Cat Mss Slides Microforms

TN —CHATTANOOGA STATE TECHNICAL COMMUNITY COLLEGE, Augusta R Kolwyk Library, 4601 Amnicola Highway, Chattanooga, 37406. Victoria Leather, Dir

TX —TEXAS A&M UNIVERSITY, Sterling C Evans Library, University Archives, College Station, 77843. Charles R Schultz, University Archivist
Notes: The Archives of Southwestern Technology: papers of nuclear physicist Paul C Aebersold, 1933-1965; papers of geologist and independent oil producer Michel T Halbouty, ca 1930-1983; records of the Texas Section of the American Society of Civil Engineers, ca 1914-1980; and records of the Texas Engineering Experiment Station, ca 1914-1970.

TX —FORT WORTH PUBLIC LIBRARY, 300 Taylor St, Fort Worth, 76102. John R McCracken, Manager
Holdings: Vols (20,000) Cat
Budget: ($21,000)

VA —US PATENT OFFICE, Science Library, 2021 Jefferson Davis Hwy, Arlington, 22202. Henry Rosicky, Chief Librn
Holdings: Vols 250,000 Cat Pix Microforms
Notes: Strengths are in applied sciences and technology. Public card catalog in Reading Room listing books by author, title, and subject, and periodicals by title and subject. Over 77,000 additional volumes of periodicals.

WI —BLACKHAWK TECHNICAL INSTITUTE, PO Box 5009, 6004 Prairie Rd, Janesville, 53547. Grace M Sweeney, Libn
Holdings: Vols 10,000 Cat
Budget: $3000

WI —UNIVERSITY OF WISCONSIN, MADISON, Kurt F Wendt Library, 215 N Randall Ave, Madison, 53706. LeRoy G Zweifel, Librn
Holdings: Vols (95,000) Cat Videotapes Microforms
Notes: Incl LANDSAT Remote Imagery; also, complete US patent collection.

WI —MILWAUKEE PUBLIC LIBRARY, 814 W Wisconsin Ave, Milwaukee, 53233. Donald J Sager, City Librn
Holdings: Vols (30,000) Cat
Notes: Strong collection acquired to support state interlibrary loan. Covers all the pure and applied sciences. Incl over (1600) periodicals and serial titles and more than (100) abstracting and indexing services in major fields of science and technology. Strong general reference service.

AB —SOUTHERN ALBERTA INSTITUTE OF TECHNOLOGY, Learning Resources Centre, 1301 16 Ave NW, Calgary, T2M 0L4, Can. Tom Skinner, Historian
Holdings: Vols (26,000) Cat Maps Pix Slides Films Videotapes Microforms
Budget: ($50,000)
Notes: Wide range of current technical information about electronics and engineering (mechanical, electrical, chemical); emphasis on vocational-technical material. Incl (50,000) slides, (300) videotapes, and (500) films.

BC —VANCOUVER PUBLIC LIBRARY, Science & Technology Div, 750 Burrard St, Vancouver, V6Z 1X5, Can. P Haffenden, Head, Science & Technology Div
Holdings: Cat
Notes: Plus special indexes, incl Organization and Association File (primarily local, British Columbian, and Canadian), begun in 1950s, expanded since 1960s; Government Documents File; Chart File; Standards File and Index; Ship Index (a source of pictures, historical and current information; engineering data, plans, etc); Boat Plans Index; Project Index (to how-to-do-it questions from handicrafts to amateur workshop projects); Recipes File (20 catalog drawers).

ON —ONTARIO SCIENCE CENTRE LIBRARY, 770 Don Mills Rd, Don Mills, M3C 1T3, Can. Jeanne DuPerrault, Librn
Holdings: Pix Slides 16mm Films Videotapes

TECHNOLOGY (cont.)

Budget: ($10,000)
Notes: 500 films, 30,000 slides and photographs, 50 videotapes, 100 periodicals.

ON —CANADA INSTITUTE FOR SCIENTIFIC & TECHNICAL INFORMATION, Montreal Rd, Ottawa, K1A 0S2, Can. Elmer V Smith, Dir
Holdings: Vols Microforms
Budget: ($17,000,000)
Notes: National collection for science in Canada. Excellent collection of serials and technical reports. Journals do not circulate. 14 Branch Libraries maintain subject collections in aeronautical engineering, astronomy, biotechnology, building and construction, biology, chemistry, electrical engineering, energy, industrial materials, physics, marine biology, ocean engineering. Access to these collections is available via the central library. 2,300,000 reports, books, serials and conference proceedings; 1,600,000 of these are on microfiche.

ON —NATIONAL MUSEUMS OF CANADA, Library Services Directorate, Ottawa, K1A 0M8, Can. Valerie Monkhouse, Director
Holdings: Vols 15,500
Budget: $25,000
Notes: History and technology of agriculture, astronomy, aviation, chemistry, communications, computers, electrical engineering, exploration and surveying, fire prevention, forestry, industrial technology, mathematics, medicine, mining, photography, physics, printing, space and transportation. research collection, interlibrary loans available, public may use on the premises.

ON —METROPOLITAN TORONTO LIBRARY, Science & Technology Dept, 789 Yonge St, Toronto, M4W 2G8, Can. Margaret Walshe, Head
Holdings: Vols (120,000) Cat VF
Notes: All aspects of technology for the specialist, the student and the general public. The department gives high priority to Canadian material. Incl books, patents, periodicals, standards, and Geological Survey of Canada publications.

ON —UNIVERSITY OF TORONTO, Thomas Fisher Rare Book Library, 120 Saint George St, Toronto, M5S 1A5, Can. Richard G Landon, Head
Holdings: Vols 4000
Notes: The Science Collection is especially rich in works on Renaissance astronomy, physics and mechanics and has noteworthy holdings of works of English experimental scientists in the 17th and 18th centuries with excellent collections of the works of Robert Boyle, Robert Hooke, and Sir Isaac Newton. Includes virtually all important early editions of Euclid; alchemical works of the 16th and 17th centuries together with the works of 18th century chemists like Lavoisier and Priestly; works on agriculture with special emphasis on British agriculture in the 18th century; and a variety of other works important in the history of science in all its branches. In addition the Fisher Library has many other specialized scientific collections which are listed separately.

PQ —ECOLE POLYTECHNIQUE BIBLIOTHEQUE, Campus de l'Universite de Montreal, PO Box 6079, Station "A", Montreal, H3C 3A7, Can. Josee Schepper, Chief of Public Services
Holdings: Vols (111,000) Cat Maps Microforms
Budget: ($330,000)
Notes: Catalog available on microfiche.

TECHNOLOGY—EARLY WORKS

PA —LIBRARY COMPANY OF PHILADELPHIA, 1314 Locust St, Philadelphia, 19107. Edwin Wolf II, Librn; Kenneth Finkel, Cur of Prints
Holdings: Vols (400,000) Cat Maps Pix
Budget: ($25,000)
Notes: American science and industry before 1860. Books, pamphlets, etc on science incl math, pyics, astronomy, and industry, incl business and engineering. Incl many 18th century books printed in England and France but used by American colonials in their study and research. Impossible to estimate the exact size of collection since it is not separated from general collection.

TECHNOLOGY—EXHIBITIONS see Exhibitions and Expositions

TECHNOLOGY—HISTORY

AZ —ARIZONA STATE MUSEUM, Library, University of Arizona, Tucson, 85721. Hans R Bart, Museum Librn
Holdings: Vols (35,000) Cat Mss Maps Pix Slides Phonorecords Microforms

CA —UNIVERSITY OF CALIFORNIA, BERKELEY, Bancroft Library, Manuscripts Division, Berkeley, 94720. James D Hart, Dir
Holdings: Cat Mss Maps Pix Slides Microforms
Notes: Collection of early and rare editions, supported by related holdings in the Biology and Main libraries. Mss (230,000) consisting primarily of scientists' private papers, constitute the most significant part of the collection. Major emphasis is on scientific developments centered in Berkeley since the inception of the Lawrence Radiation Laboratory, and on the growth of the electronics industry located in the Palo Alto area, in the vicinity of Stanford University. Incl are the private papers of Ernest Lawrence and Emil Fischer. A series of oral histories complements these holdings.

CA —CALIFORNIA INSTITUTE OF TECHNOLOGY, Robert A Millikan Memorial Library, Archives, 1201 E California Blvd, Pasadena, 91125. Judith R Goodstein, Archivist
Holdings: Vols (3000) Uncat Mss Maps Pix Slides
Notes: Over 70 collections (1830s-present) relating to history of 19th-20th centuries science and technology and the history of the Institute. Included are personal and professional papers of Caltech scientists and administrative officers; divisional records and faculty committees; over 5000 photographs of American and European scientists. Mss collections documents more than a century of American political, social, and intellectual history; the development of the physical sciences, aeronautics, molecular biology, and seismology in the US and abroad; and social and political conditions in Europe between the two World Wars. There are also family letters relating to 19th century American life before and during the Civil War (the Morley and A G Throop papers); to 19th century social conditions in Russia and Hungary (the Paul Epstein papers and Theodore von Karman papers); andto the development of 20th century Italian mathematics.

CT —BURNDY LIBRARY, Electra Square, Norwalk, 06856. Philip J Weimerskirch, Asst Dir
Holdings: Vols 2000

DE —HAGLEY MUSEUM AND LIBRARY, Eleutherian Mills-Hagley Foundation Inc, PO Box 3630, Greenville, 19807. Richmond D Williams, Dir; Heddy A Richter, Imprints Librn
Holdings: Vols 14,000 Pamphlets Serials
Notes: Our collection documents the history of American technology, especially the period in which mass production replaced the American system. Our holdings are strong in the chemical technology, transportaion, explosives and pyrotechnics, metallurgy and engineering.

DC —LIBRARY OF CONGRESS, Rare Book & Special Collections Div, Washington, 20540. William Matheson, Chief
Notes: Important holdings relating to subjects such as railroads and canals. Material by and about Robert Fulton is particularly strong. The division contains many pre-Civil War technical manuals.

DC —SMITHSONIAN INSTITUTION LIBRARIES, National Museum of American History Branch, Washington, 20560. Rhoda S Ratner, Branch Librn
Holdings: Vols (369, 650) Cat Mss Maps Pix Slides Microforms

IN —INDIANA UNIVERSITY, Lilly Library, Seventh St, Bloomington, 47405. William R Cagle, Librn
Holdings: // Cat Mss
Notes: First appearances in print of 19th and 20th century technological inventions.

IN —PURDUE UNIVERSITY LIBRARIES, Graduate School of Management, Krannert Library, West Lafayette, 47907. Gordon Law, Librn
Notes: An important resource at the Krannert Library is its Special Collection of Business and Economics, consisting of some 8000 rare pre-20th century strengths in books, journals, tracts and pamphlets covering primarily the early literature of economic thought and business practices in America and abroad, 1500-1870. A catalog was issued in 1979.

IA —IOWA STATE UNIVERSITY, Library, Ames, 50011. Warren B Kuhn, Dean of Library Services
Holdings: Cat
Notes: Extensive holdings of serial backfiles.

MD —MARYLAND ACADEMY OF SCIENCES, Maryland Science Center, 601 Light Street, Baltimore, 21230.
Notes: Planetarium and exhibits.

MA —OLD STURBRIDGE VILLAGE, Research Library, Sturbridge, 01566. Theresa Rini Percy, Librn
Holdings: Cat Slides
Notes: Mainly American technology before 1850, incl building, engineering, lighting, mills, printing, inventions.

MO —LINDA HALL LIBRARY, 5109 Cherry St, Kansas City, 64110. Larry X Besant, Dir; Wilma L Hartman, Librn for Public Services; Siegfried Ruschin, Librn for Collection Development
Holdings: Cat Maps Microforms
Budget: ($1,000,000)
Notes: 500,000 pieces, plus 400,000 microforms. Receives 15,000 serial publications in some 35 languages, in science and technology. Academy publications, back to the 17th century, and some 3000 books of historical significance in science and technology are among the strongest areas in the library collection. Downs number--2169 and in Supplement many references 1031, 1105, 1106, 1123-24, etc. It would be difficult to break down strengths in the individual areas of the sciences and technology. Collects comprehensively throughout these subjects areas (except for clinical medicine and surgery, which is out of scope).

NY —NEW YORK STATE HISTORICAL ASSOCIATION, Library, Lake Rd, Cooperstown, 13326. Amy Barnum, Librn
Holdings: Vols (55,000) Cat Mss Pix
Notes: Mainly pre-Civil War American. Noncirculating.

NY —NEW YORK STATE OFFICE OF PARKS & RECREATION, TACONIC REGION, Clermont State Historic Park, Library, RR 1, Box 215, Germantown, 12526. Bruce E Naramore, Historic Site Manager
Holdings: Vols (5000) Cat Mss Maps
Notes: Collection incl period works concerning technology before and after the American Revolution. Many first editions belonging originally to the Chancellor Robert R Livingston (1746-1813). No photocopying.

NY —CORNELL UNIVERSITY LIBRARIES, John M Olin Library, History of Science Collections, Ithaca, 14853. Lillian A Clark, Administrative Supervisor; David W Corson, History of Science Librn
Holdings: Vols (33,000) Cat
Notes: Early printed source materials in all branches of technology, with special emphasis on civil engineering. Noncirculating.
See also entry under Science - History

NY —NEW YORK HISTORICAL SOCIETY, Library, 170 Central Park W, New York, 10024. James Gregory, Librn
Notes: Randall J LeBoeuf Jr's collection of

TECHNOLOGY—HISTORY (cont.)

Robert Fulton and related material, 1764-1857, consisting of correspondence, drawings, legal papers, etc, relating to steam engines and boats, canals, and torpedoes. The correspondents incl John Quincy Adams, Henry Clay, De Witt Clinton, Albert Gallatin, Benjamin H Latrobe, James Madison, James Monroe, John Livingston, Robert R Livingston, and William Thornton, Also incl are Fulton's expense and note book, 1803-1808, and Robert R Livingston's receipt book, 1808-1812. Approx 215 items, cataloged.

OH —CASE WESTERN RESERVE UNIVERSITY LIBRARIES, Cleveland, 44106. Susie Hanson, Special Collections Librn
Holdings: Cat Maps Pix Microforms
Notes: Concentrates on 18th, 19th and early 20th century science and technology.

OH —CLEVELAND PUBLIC LIBRARY, Science & Technology Dept, 325 Superior Ave, Cleveland, 44114. Jean Z Piety, Head
Holdings: Cat
Notes: Collection contains much on history and many early and rare volumes.

PA —BUCKS COUNTY HISTORICAL SOCIETY, Spruance Library, Pine & Ashland Sts, Doylestown, 18901. Terry A McNealy, Librn
Holdings: Vols (18,000) Cat

PA —FRANKLIN INSTITUTE LIBRARY, 20 & The Parkway, Philadelphia, 19103. Miriam Padusis, Dir; Charles Wilt, Readers Servs Librn
Holdings: Vols (300,000) Cat Maps Pix Microforms

PA —SWARTHMORE COLLEGE, Library, Swarthmore, 19081. Michael J Durkan, Librn
Holdings: Vols 959 Cat Mss
Notes: This was the collection belonging to Greville Bathe. It is comprised of books on machines and steam engines published from the 16th-20th century. Also works on military engineering.

VA —VIRGINIA POLYTECHNIC INSTITUTE AND STATE UNIVERSITY LIBRARY, Blacksburg, 24061. Glenn L McMullen, Special Collections Librn
Holdings: Vols (1500)
Notes: Collection of primarily nineteenth century imprints on transportation, communications, and agricultural technology; technological encyclopedias and compendia; books on inventions and inventors; and travel accounts dealing with industrial and technological change.

WI —UNIVERSITY OF WISCONSIN, MADISON, Memorial Library, History of Science Collection, 728 State St, Madison, 53706. John Neu, Bibliographer
Holdings: Cat Mss
Budget: ($15,000)
Notes: Major research collection of primary and secondary materials in all fields of the history of science and technology. Special collections in this area include the Dennis I Duveen Collection on the History of Chemistry; William A Cole Collection in the History of Chemistry; Chester H Thordarson Collection, notable for its wide variety of books in the history of early English science as well as books that illustrate and record the development of the various branches of natural history; Joseph Priestly Collection, Robert Boyle Collection, Carl Von Linne Collection. See John Neu, ed, *Chemical, Medical and phamaceutical Books Printed before 1800 in the Collections of the University of Wisconsin Libraries* (Madison and Milwaukee: University of Wisconsin Press, 1965); Dennis I Duveen, *Bibliotheca Alchemica et Chemica: An Annotated Catalogue of Printed Books on Alchemy, Chemistry and Cognate Subjects in the Library of Dennis I Duveen* (London: Dawsons of Pall Mall, 1965). Restricted use: Rare Book Department.

TECHNOLOGY, RADIOLOGICAL see Radiology

TECHNOLOGY, RUSSIAN

OH —BATTELLE MEMORIAL INSTITUTE LIBRARY, 505 King Ave, Columbus, 43201. Carol Young, Librn
Holdings: Vols (150,000) Cat Maps Microforms
Notes: Large collection of Russian and Eastern European science and technology. Over 1600 current journal titles and extensive monography and serial holdings in Slavic languages.

TECHNOLOGY AND THE ARTS

CA —CRAFT AND FOLK ART MUSEUM, Library, 5814 Wilshire Blvd, Los Angeles, 90036. Joan M Benedetti, Museum Librn
Holdings: Vols (2000) Slides VF
Notes: Incl 2000 books; 70 journal subscriptions; artists' biographical files: 6 file drawers; clipping files: 8 file drawers; 20,000 slides. Representation of the material culture of all people, traditional and contemporary expressions. Incl visual and printed information on ethnic, traditional, popular, decorative, idiosyncratic, and contemporary crafts as well as vernacular architecture, handmade houses, and design. Information about and for professional artists on health hazards, conservation, and career management. Anthropological and art historical works; exhibition catalogues; slides, photographs, audiocassettes; clipping and pamphlet files. Contemporary Slide Registry of Craftspeople and extensive biographical files of contemporary craft artists. Information and referral files of craft related galleries, shops, festivals, organizations, etc.

CA —CALIFORNIA INSTITUTE OF THE ARTS, Library, 24700 McBean Pkwy, Valencia, 91355. James Elrod, Dir
Holdings: Vols (61,000) Cat Phonorecords Audiotapes
Budget: ($79,568)
Notes: Incl 11,656 audiotapes. Cataloged.

TECUMSEH

OH —GREENE COUNTY DISTRICT LIBRARY, 76 E Market St, PO Box 520, Xenia, 45385. Julie M Overton, Local History Coordr
Holdings: // Uncat
Notes: Galloway Collection of Ohio history is housed in a five-drawer filing cabinet, incl material about Tecumseh and some other Indians and their traditions.

TEENAGE see Adolescence

TEENAGE PREGNANCY

NY —MATERNITY CENTER ASSOCIATION, Library, 48 E 92 St, New York, 10028. Esther Hanchett, Acting Librn
Holdings: Vols 2000 Cat
Notes: No photocopying.

NY —PLANNED PARENTHOOD FEDERATION OF AMERICA, Katharine Dexter McCormick Library, 810 Seventh Ave, New York, 10019. Gloria A Roberts, Head Librn
Holdings: Vols (4000) Cat
Notes: Birth control, teenagers, contraception and contraceptive research, family planning, religion and birth control.

TEENAGE WOMEN—PREGNANCY see Teenage Pregnancy

TEETERS, NEGLEY KING

PA —TEMPLE UNIVERSITY LIBRARIES, Special Collections Dept, Conwellana-Templana Collection, 13 & Berks St, Philadelphia, 19122. Miriam I Crawford, Cur
Holdings: Vols (22) // Cat Mss Pix
Notes: Personal papers of Negley K Teeters. The published writings, manuscripts, correspondence, and research materials of Teeters, criminologist and faculty member of Temple University, covering the years 1927-1971. Contains extended correspondence with his co-author, Harry Elmer Barnes, from 1940 to 1968, and materials dealing with their investigation of the murder trial of Caryl Chessman, which failed to halt his execution in California in 1960. Incl copies of letters from Teeters to Barnes, originals of which are in the Western History Research Center of the University of Wyoming, and incl the Index to the Barnes Papers in that collection. *Descriptive Inventory of the Personal Papers of Negley K Teeters (1896-1971)*, (Conwellana-Templana Collection, Temple University, 1971, addenda 1972 and 1974; 6 leaves; unpublished typescript).

WY —UNIVERSITY OF WYOMING, William Robertson Coe Library, Archives - American Heritage Center, PO Box 3412, Laramie, 82071.

TEETH—DISEASES

IL —AMERICAN DENTAL ASSOCIATION, Bureau of Library Services, 211 E Chicago Ave, Chicago, 60611. Aletha Kowitz, Librn & Dir
Notes: Publish *Index to Dental Literature*.

MD —UNIVERSITY OF MARYLAND, BALTIMORE, Health Sciences Library, 111 S Greene St, Baltimore, 21201. Cyril C H Feng, Dir
Notes: The Clarence J Grieves Dental Historical Collection is one of the strongest collections of its kind in the United States. It includes some of the most significant early dental imprints; early records of the Maryland State Dental Association; and an excellent collection of prints on early dentistry and St Apollonia.

TEFFT, HENRY D.

NM —MUSEUM OF NEW MEXICO, Photo Archives, Box 2087, Santa Fe, 87503. Arthur L Olivas, Cur; Richard Rudisill, Photo Historian
Holdings: Cat Pix Slides
Notes: Extensive collection of his work.

TEGNER, ESAIAS

OH —CLEVELAND PUBLIC LIBRARY, Fine Arts and Special Collections Department, 325 Superior Ave, Cleveland, 44114. Alice N Loranth, Head
Holdings: Vols 225 Cat
Notes: Special strength. Scarce 19th Century editions, translations and versions. Separate "edition" catalog is maintained.
See also entry under Rare Books.

TEILHARD DE CHARDIN, PIERRE

NY —AMERICAN TEILHARD ASSOCIATION FOR THE FUTURE OF MAN, Dept of Religious Studies, Manhattan College, Bronx, 10471. Donald P Gray, Librn
Holdings: 450 Cat Slides
Notes: Material by and about Teilhard de Chardin, philosopher and paleontologist.

TELECOMMUNICATIONS

CA —LOS ANGELES PUBLIC LIBRARY, Science & Technology Dept, 630 W Fifth St, Los Angeles, 90071. Billie M Connor, Dept Head
Holdings: Vols (12,000) Cat
Notes: Materials on the application of electronic devices, circuits and systems in various fields such as computers, automatic control, sound productions and reproduction, radio and telecommunications. Extensive holdings of materials on computers, peripherals, and software including many texts pertaining to specific programming languages. Complete collection of Howard Sams schematics for radio television, and other electronic equipment repair as well as historical sets of Rider's Radio and Television schematics.

CA —CUBIC CORP, Technical Library, 9333 Balboa Ave, PO Box 85587, San Diego, 92138. Maxine Moser, Mgr Tech Librn; Ann Viera, Librn
Holdings: Vols (2500) Cat Maps Microforms
Budget: ($60,000)
Notes: Incl about 20,000 microforms and 1000 bound periodicals, technical reports, technical memoranda. On-line search service

TELECOMMUNICATIONS (cont.)

for employees, including DIALOG, BRS, SDC, DTIC/DROLS, NASA/RECON, RLIN, DMS.

CA —ESL, SUBSIDIARY OF TRW, Research Library, 495 Java Dr, PO Box 3510, Sunnyvale, 94086. Verna Van Valzer, Head Librn
Holdings: Vols 500 Cat
Budget: $7000
Notes: Electronic Communication Systems.

DC —GEORGE WASHINGTON UNIVERSITY, Gelman Library, Telecommunications Information Center, Washington, 20052. Cathy Haworth, Librn
Holdings: Vols (1500) Periodicals
Notes: Incl

IL —UNIVERSITY OF ILLINOIS, URBANA/CHAMPAIGN, Library, Communications Library, 122 Gregory Hall, Urbana, 61801. Nancy Allen, Librn
Holdings: Vols (18,000) Cat
Budget: ($27,000)
Notes: Studies of telephone, teletext, videotex, cable and satellite systems, and other electronic media.

MA —MASSACHUSETTS INSTITUTE OF TECHNOLOGY, Institute Archives, Special Collections, Cambridge, 02139.
Notes: Vail collection incl many early works on telecommunications, electricity, ballooning, aeronautics, and animal magnetism.

MA —MASSACHUSETTS INSTITUTE OF TECHNOLOGY, Lincoln Laboratory, Library, 244 Wood St, Lexington, 02173. Jane H Katayama, Library Mgr
Holdings: Vols (70,000) Cat
See also entry under Communications Research

NJ —AT&T BELL LABORATORIES, Libraries and Information Systems Center, 600 Mountain Ave, Murray Hill, 07974. W D Penniman, Dir
Holdings: Vols (145,000) Cat Microforms
Notes: Restricted use to AT&T employees. Catalogs/Indexes: Bell Laboratories Library Network and Book Serial Catalogs; Bell Laboratories Translations. Bell Laboratories Library Network with New Jersey libraries located in Holmdel, Murray Hill, Piscataway, Whippany, Princeton, Short Hills, Summit, West Long Branch, Crawford Hill; libraries also in Allentown, Pennsylvania; Reading, Pennsylvania; New York, New York; Atlanta, Georgia; Columbus, Ohio; Naperville, Illinois; Indianapolis, Indiana; North Andover, Massachusetts.

NY —AMERICAN TELEPHONE & TELEGRAPH CO, Corporate Research Center, 550 Madison Ave, Fifth floor, New York, 10022. Marianne Benjamin, Chief Librn
Holdings: Vols (8000) Cat Microforms
Notes: Collection incl complete sets of AT&T periodicals and incomplete sets of other periodicals in the field of telephony; complete sets of AT&T companies' annual reports; telephone industry directories; monographs on history and economic aspects of telephony. Member of AT&T Bell Laboratories Library Network.

OH —PREFORMED LINE PRODUCTS CO, Research & Engineering Library, 660 Beta Drive, Mayfield Village, (Mailing add: PO Box 91129, Cleveland, 44101). Edwina T Barron, Librn
Holdings: Vols (11,500) Cat Mss Microfiche Pix VF
Budget: ($30,500)
Notes: Library covering research and engineering fields emphasizing this subject. Aerodynamic characteristics and electrical characteristics of power cables, communication cables (including fiber optics), cable support systems, as well as associated fittings and hardware; in service behavior of manufactured products and materials as it relates to its static and dynamic forces and environmental conditions; oceanographic cable fittings and terminations.

PA —FRANKLIN INSTITUTE LIBRARY, 20 & The Parkway, Philadelphia, 19103.

Miriam Padusis, Dir; Charles Wilt, Readers Servs Librn
Holdings: Vols (300,000) Cat Maps Pix Microforms

WY —UNIVERSITY OF WYOMING, William Robertson Coe Library, Archives - American Heritage Center, PO Box 3412, Laramie, 82071.
Notes: Papers of Knox Charlton Black, incl those of a 12-year period when he worked on a cable important to television.

ON —QUEEN'S UNIVERSITY, Douglas Library, Kingston, K7L 5C4, Can. William F E Morley, Cur, Special Collections
Holdings: Vols (1200) Cat Mss Pix
Notes: McNichol Collection. Books, pamphlets, journals and ephemera. radio sciences. There is a printed catalog of this collection as originally acquired: Catalogue of the McNichol Collection of books on telegraphy, telephony and radio contained in the Douglas Library, comp by Janet S Porteous and edited by Marjorie Sherlock Kingston, 1942.

PQ —BELL CANADA, Information Resource Centre, 1050 Beaver Hall Hill, Montreal, H2Z 1S4, Can.
Holdings: Vols (12,000) Cat
Notes: Restricted use to Bell Canada employees. Incl 650 periodical titles and comprehensive collection of IEE and IEEE publications. Collection in French and English. An Information Resource Center also in Toronto, Ontario, Canada.

TELECOMMUNICATIONS—HISTORY

ON —UNIVERSITY OF GUELPH, Library, Guelph, N1G 2W1, Can. Margaret Beckman, Chief Librn; Ellen Pearson, Ref Librn
Notes: Unique resource pertaining to world-wide telecommunication, largely the proceedings of the World Administrative Radio Conferences (WARC) and other International Telecommunications Union material.

ON —QUEEN'S UNIVERSITY, Douglas Library, Kingston, K7L 5C4, Can. William F E Morley, Cur, Special Collections
Notes: Riche-Covington Collection supports McNichol Collection (history of telecommunications), brings it up to date; also astrophysics, astronomy, solar radiation. Bibliography available.

TELEFAX see Facsimile Transmission

TELEGRAPH—HISTORY

MA —AMERICAN ANTIQUARIAN SOCIETY LIBRARY, 185 Salisbury St, Worcester, 01609. Marcus A McCorison, Dir & Librn
Holdings: Cat Mss Pix
Notes: Incl several hundred forms representing 32 companies established before 1870. Other collections of telegraph forms are also held by the New-York Historical Society and the Western Union Telegraph Company, NYC, as well as by other libraries listed in this volume.

†VA —GEORGE C MARSHALL RESEARCH FOUNDATION AND LIBRARY, Drawer 920, Lexington, 24450. Royster Lyle Jr, Cur Collections
Holdings: Vols Uncat Mss
Notes: Items on secret writing and signaling, radar, telephony and telegraphy, and the study of the Shakespeare-Bacon authorship controversy.

ON —QUEEN'S UNIVERSITY, Douglas Library, Kingston, K7L 5C4, Can. William F E Morley, Cur, Special Collections
Holdings: Vols (1200) Cat Mss Pix
Notes: McNichol Collection. Books, pamphlets, journals and ephemera. Origin and growth to World War II of the telegraphic, telephonic and radio sciences. There is a printed catalog of this collection as originally acquired: Catalogue of the NcNichol Collection of Books on Telephony and Radio Contained in the Douglas Library, comp by Janet S Porteous and edited by Marjorie Sherlock Kingston, 1942.

TELEGRAPH, WIRELESS

†CA —SOCIETY OF WIRELESS PIONEERS (COMMUNICATIONS), PO Box 530,

Santa Rosa, 95402.
Holdings: Vols (2500)
Notes: Museum of early communication memorabilia and equiptment. Compiles statistics on shipwrecks where wireless/radio was involved.

DC —BROADCAST PIONEERS LIBRARY, 1771 N St NW, Washington, 20036. Catharine Heinz, Dir
Holdings: Mss
Notes: Incl the papers of Elmo Neale Pickerill, pioneer in wireless telegraphy and air-to-ground radio communications. Open to public by appointment.

IL —UNIVERSITY OF ILLINOIS, URBANA/CHAMPAIGN, Library, 1408 W Gregory Drive, Urbana, 61801. Norman B Brown, Asst Dir for Special Collections
Holdings: Cat Mss Pix Tapes
Notes: The papers of Joseph T Tykociner (a pioneer in the field of wireless, electronics, sound movies and zetetics). Incl correspondence, notes, books, articles and reprints, photographs and negatives, biographical materials and sound tapes.

MA —HARVARD UNIVERSITY LIBRARY, Cambridge, 02138.
Notes: The papers of George Washington Pierce (1898-1955).

†NY —ANTIQUE WIRELESS ASSOCIATION, Electronic Communication Museum, Main St, Holcomb, 14469. Bruce Kelley, Curator
Holdings: Vols (2000)
Notes: Books on radio and electrical material available for research for members of association. 15,000 radio, television, and electrical artifacts.

TELEGRAPH FORMS

MA —AMERICAN ANTIQUARIAN SOCIETY LIBRARY, 185 Salisbury St, Worcester, 01609. Marcus A McCorison, Dir & Librn
Holdings: Cat Mss Pix
Notes: Incl several hundred forms representing 32 companies established before 1870. Other collections of telegraph forms are also held by the New-York Historical Society and the Western Union Telegraph Company, NYC, as well as by other libraries listed in this volume.

TELEGU LANGUAGE see Telugu Language and Literature

TELEKINESIS see Psychokinesis

TELEOSTEI

TX —UNIVERSITY OF TEXAS, Marine Science Institute Library, Port Aransas, 78373. Ruth Grundy, Librn
Holdings: Vols (45,000) Cat Maps Pix
Budget: ($70,000)
Notes: Current researches in marine science, especially concerning the Gulf of Mexico, the Texas Coastal Zone, and the Continental Shelf. Incl journals.

TELEPATHY see Thought Transference

TELEPHONE

IL —ILLINOIS BELL TELEPHONE CO, Library, 225 W Randolph St, Chicago, 60606. Marguerite J Krynicki, Head Librn
Holdings: Vols (11,000) Cat

NJ —AT&T BELL LABORATORIES, Libraries and Information Systems Center, 600 Mountain Ave, Murray Hill, 07974. W D Penniman, Dir
Holdings: Vols (145,000) Cat Microforosm
Notes: Restricted use to AT&T employees. Catalogs/Indexes: Bell Laboratories Library Network and Book Serial Catalogs; Bell Laboratories Translations. Bell Laboratories Library Network with New Jersey libraries located in Holmdel, Murray Hill, Piscataway, Whippany, Princeton, Short Hills, Summit, West Long Branch, Crawford Hill; libraries also in Allentown, Pennsylvania; Reading, Pennsylvania; New York, New York; Atlanta, Georgia;

TELEPHONE (cont.)

Columbus, Ohio; Naperville, Illinois;
Indianapolis, Indiana; North Andover,
Massachusetts.

PQ —BELL CANADA, Information Resource
Centre, 1050 Beaver Hall Hill, Montreal,
H2Z 1S4, Can.
Holdings: Vols (12,000) Cat
Notes: Restricted use to Bell Canada
employees. Incl 650 periodical titles and
comprehensive collection of IEE and IEEE
publications. Collection in French and
English. An Information Resource Centre
also in Toronto, Ontario, Canada.

TELEPHONE—HISTORY

DC —LIBRARY OF CONGRESS, Manuscript
Division, Washington, 20540. John C
Broderick, Chief
Holdings: 140,000 Items
Notes: The papers of Alexander Graham
Bell and his family. Incl Bell's diaries,
correspondence, printed matter, financial
and legal records, and several hundred vols
of laboratory notebooks which record his
daily work from 1865 to 1922. Also,
materials of Alexander Melville Bell, Mabel
Hubbard Bell, and Gilbert H Grosvenor.

DC —LIBRARY OF CONGRESS, Motion
Pictures, Broadcasting and Recorded Sound
Div, Washington, 20540.
Notes: Recordings, photographs,
correspondence, scrapbooks and other
memorabilia concerning the invention of the
lateral cut disc gramophone record, basis of
the modern recording industry, Emile
Berliner (1851-1929). Devised word
"Gramophone," and invented acoustic tiling.

NM —TELEPHONE PIONEERS OF
AMERICA, Telephone Pioneer Museum,
1209 Mountain Rd Place NE, Albuquerque,
87110. Bob Blade, Cur
Holdings: Vols 900 Cat Maps Pix Slides
Audiotapes 16mm Films
Budget: $1000
Notes: History of telephony in Southwestern
US, from 1870s to the present.

NY —AMERICAN TELEPHONE &
TELEGRAPH CO, Corporate Research
Center, 550 Madison Ave, Fifth floor, New
York, 10022. Marianne Benjamin, Chief
Librn
Holdings: Vols (8000) Cat Microforms
Notes: Collection incl complete sets of
AT&T periodicals and incomplete sets of
other periodicals in the field of telephony;
complete sets of AT&T companies' annual
reports; telephone industry directories;
monographs on history and economic
aspects of telephony. Member of AT&T Bell
Laboratories Library Network.

†VA —GEORGE C MARSHALL
RESEARCH FOUNDATION AND
LIBRARY, Drawer 920, Lexington, 24450.
Royster Lyle Jr, Cur Collections
Holdings: Vols Uncat Mss
Notes: Items on secret writing and signaling,
radar, telephony and telegraphy, and the
study of the Shakespeare-Bacon authorship
controversy.

ON —QUEEN'S UNIVERSITY, Douglas
Library, Kingston, K7L 5C4, Can. William F
E Morley, Cur, Special Collections
Holdings: Vols (1200) Cat Mss Pix
Notes: McNichol Collection. Books,
pamphlets, journals and ephemera. Origin
and growth to World War II of the
telegraphic, telephonic and radio sciences.
There is a printed catalog of this collection
as originally acquired: *Catalogue of the
McNichol Collection of Books on
Telegraphy, Telephony and Radio Contained
in the Douglas Library,* comp by Janet S
Porteous and edited by Marjorie Sherlock
Kingston, 1942.

TELEPHONE, WIRELESS

†CA —SOCIETY OF WIRELESS PIONEERS
(COMMUNICATIONS), PO Box 530,
Santa Rosa, 95402.
Holdings: Vols (2500)
Notes: Museum of early communication

memorabilia and equiptment. Compiles
statistics on shipwrecks where wireless/radio
was involved.

IL —UNIVERSITY OF ILLINOIS,
URBANA/CHAMPAIGN, Library, 1408 W
Gregory Drive, Urbana, 61801. Norman B
Brown, Asst Dir for Special Collections
Holdings: Cat Mss Pix Tapes
Notes: The papers of Joseph T Tykociner (a
pioneer in the field of wireless, electronics,
sound movies and zetetics). Incl
correspondence, notes, books, articles and
reprints, photographs and negatives,
biographical materials and sound tapes.

†NY —ANTIQUE WIRELESS
ASSOCIATION, Electronic Communication
Museum, Main St, Holcomb, 14469. Bruce
Kelley, Curator
Holdings: Vols 2000
Notes: Books on radio and electrical material
available for research for members of
association. 15,000 radio, television, and
electrical artifacts.

TELEPHONE DIRECTORIES

AZ —ARIZONA DAILY STAR, Library, 4850
S Park Ave, PO Box 26807, Tucson, 85726.
Elaine Y Raines, Librn; Michele R Canney,
Asst Librn
Holdings: Cat Maps Pix Microforms
Budget: ($110,000)
Notes: Main resource is 1,800,000 piece
clipping collection of Tucson and Arizona,
from 1939. Holdings incl Tucson telephone
books, from 1940; Tucson city directories,
from 1918; 1500 books on Tucson and
Arizona; daily newspaper (microfilm), from
1877. Index prepared by Univ of Arizona,
1953-1965 and 1979, with plans to index
missing years. Picture collection (150,000)
and VF of ephemera (5000 pieces) are
valuable historical sources.

CA —LOS ANGELES PUBLIC LIBRARY,
Business & Economic Dept, 630 W 5th St,
Los Angeles, 90071. Joan Bartel, Principal
Librn
Holdings: Vols 10,000 Microforms
Notes: Telephone directories for all US cities
10,000 or larger (and many smaller); some
kept retrospectively. Selected collection of
foreign telephone directories 1873-1942,
many western cities and older for major
cities. Ones from cities throughout the US
(approx 2700 volumes). Social registers for
southern California and some other areas.
Trade and industrial directories covering the
US and many foreign countries (estimated
5000 volumes). Many specialized directories
for product lines, etc. Retrospective and
current holdings of most standard
directories. Partially cataloged.

CA —CONTRA COSTA COUNTY
LIBRARY, 1750 Oak Park Blvd, Pleasant
Hill, 94523. Lyn Talme, Business Specialist
Holdings: Vols (7000)
Notes: Incl 76 periodicals, 1000 corporate
annual reports, and 316 telephone
directories.

GA —ATLANTA PUBLIC LIBRARY, Ivan
Allen Jr Dept of Science, Industry &
Government, One Margaret Mitchell Square,
Atlanta, 30303. William D Munro, Head
Holdings: (1600) Cat Microforms
Budget: ($75,000)
Notes: This separately housed collection incl
1100 domestic and foreign telephone
directories, 175 city directories, primarily
from Georgia and the Southeast, and 450
corporate, international, foreign, product,
service, association, and professional
directories. All materials in this collection
are noncirculating. Telephone ready
reference service is provided.

IL —CHICAGO PUBLIC LIBRARY,
Information Center, 425 N Michigan Ave,
Chicago, 60611. Marilyn Boria, Chief Librn
Holdings: Vols (2000) Uncat
Notes: Current editions of US and foreign
directories.

IA —CEDAR RAPIDS PUBLIC LIBRARY,
428 Third Ave SE, Cedar Rapids, 52401.
Ruth Richardson, Asst Dir
Holdings: Uncat
Notes: Current directories for most Iowa
communities, all other US cities of at least

19,000 population, and major foreign cities.
Collection is indexed.

KS —WICHITA PUBLIC LIBRARY, 223 S
Main, Wichita, 67202. Larry DePiesse,
Head, Business & Technology Dept; Jayne F
Young, Business & Technology Dept
Holdings: Vols 1223 Uncat
Notes: Current telephone directories for all
Kansas communities, and for all US cities of
20,000 population (and many smaller). City
directories for Kansas communities. Wichita
city directories, 1877 to present.

KY —BOYD COUNTY PUBLIC LIBRARY,
1740 Central Ave, Ashland, 41101. Juliette
Bryson, Dir
Holdings: Cat Periodicals
Notes: Over 60 city directories and
telephone books relating to the Middle
Atlantic states and southern states primarily,
with some materials from the northeastern
states. Collection will expand to incl more
areas of the US.

MI —DETROIT PUBLIC LIBRARY, Burton
Historical Collection, 5201 Woodward Ave,
Detroit, 48202. Alice Dalligan, Chief

MN —MINNEAPOLIS PUBLIC LIBRARY &
INFORMATION CENTER, Business &
Economics Dept, 300 Nicollet Mall,
Minneapolis, 55401. Mary Lawson, Librn
Notes: Separate card catalog, telephone
reference service, and directory service. Incl
periodical titles; large files of corporation
annual reports; VF of local company
histories and annual reports; domestic and
foreign telephone directories; historical US
stock quotations, 1891-date; local OTC
quotations, 1933-date; indexes and
abstracting services; looseleaf reference
services.

MN —MINNEAPOLIS PUBLIC LIBRARY &
INFORMATION CENTER, Science &
Technology Dept, 300 Nicollet Mall,
Minneapolis, 55401. Edythe Abrahamson,
Librn
Notes: Separate card catalog, telephone
reference service, and directory service. Incl
periodicals; large file of corporation annual
reports; VF local company histories and
annual reports; domestic and foreign
telephone directories; trade and industrial
directories; historical US stock quotations,
1891-date; local OTC quotations, 1933-date;
indexes and abstracting services; looseleaf
reference services.

NJ —TRENTON FREE PUBLIC LIBRARY,
Business & Technology Dept, 120 Academy
St, Trenton, 08608. Richard D Rebecca,
Principal Librn
Holdings: Vols (9000) Cat Microforms
Notes: Incl 400 telephone directories, and
criss cross for county library is in.
Interlibrary loan (photocopies) available.

NY —NEW YORK STATE LIBRARY, State
Education Bldg Annex, Washington Ave,
Albany, 12224.
Holdings: Vols 15,000 Uncat Microforms
Notes: City and telephone directories.
Emphasis in city directories on New York
State and New England. Many 18th century
and early American items. Bulk current.
Telephone directories for New York State
and major cities outside New York.
Microfilm holdings: entries in Spear's
Bibliography of American Directories to
1860. Currently receiving directories of
major cities, 1861-1881.

NY —AMERICAN TELEPHONE &
TELEGRAPH CO, Corporate Research
Center, 550 Madison Ave, Fifth floor, New
York, 10022. Marianne Benjamin, Chief
Librn
Notes: Collection incl complete sets of
AT&T periodicals and incomplete sets of
other periodicals in the field of telephony;
complete sets of AT&T companies' annual
reports; telephone industry directories;
monographs on history and economic
aspects of telephony. Member of AT&T Bell
Laboratories Library Network.

NY —NEW YORK PUBLIC LIBRARY,
Research Libraries, General Research
Division, Fifth Ave & 42 St, New York,
10018. Rodney Phillips, Chief
Holdings: Vols (2,225,000) Cat Maps Pix
Microforms
Budget: ($775,718)
Notes: Directories from all US cities and
towns and those of major foreign cities.

TELEPHONE DIRECTORIES (cont.)

OH —AKRON-SUMMIT COUNTY PUBLIC
LIBRARY, Business, Labor & Government
Div, 55 S Main St, Akron, 44326. William G
Johnson, Head
Holdings: Uncat
Notes: 1600 directories covering
approximately 32,000 cities and towns.

OH —PUBLIC LIBRARY OF CINCINNATI
& HAMILTON COUNTY, Government
and Business Dept, 800 Vine St, Cincinnati,
45202. Paul T Hudson, Head
Holdings: Vols 120,000 Cat
Notes: Department receives over 1200
periodical and loose-leaf service titles, 1500
serial titles and over 1500 telephone
directories. Subjects include political science,
especially foreign relations, economics, law,
public administration and business
management. Dept houses Murray
Seasongood collection of local government.
Dept has extensive census material from
1790. Library is a full depository for US
Government Publications, 1884 to date.

OH —CLEVELAND PUBLIC LIBRARY,
History and Geography Department, 325
Superior Ave, Cleveland, 44114. JoAnn
Petrello, Head
Holdings: Cat
Notes: Cleveland city directories, 1837-date;
local telephone directories, 1920-date.

ON —PUBLIC ARCHIVES OF CANADA,
Library, 395 Wellington St, Ottawa, K1A
0N3, Can. Dawn E Monroe, Collections
Development Officer
Notes: Bell Canada Collection. About 3500
directories. The collection spans everything
from the first listing of Canadian telephone
subscribers in 1878 to all current directories
published by Bell Canada. In the 1900s Bell
directories listed other Canadian companies
and their points of connection as well as lists
of places connected to long distance lines.

ON —METROPOLITAN TORONTO
LIBRARY, Canadian History Dept, 789
Yonge St, Toronto, M4W 2G8, Can.
Notes: Bell Canada Telephone Historical
Collection of 448 reels of microfilm of
Ontario and Quebec telephone books from
1878 to 1979. The collection will be
updated. Toronto city directories from 1868-
1949 are available also.

TELEPHONE EQUIPMENT

NJ —AT&T BELL LABORATORIES,
Libraries and Information Systems Center,
600 Mountain Ave, Murray Hill, 07974. W
D Penniman, Dir
Holdings: Vols (273,100) Cat Mss
Audiotapes Videotapes Microforms
Budget: ($670,000)
Notes: Restricted use to AT&T employees.
Catalogs/Indexes: Bell Laboratories Library
Network and Book Serial Catalogs; Bell
Laboratories Translations. Bell Laboratories
Library Network with New Jersey libraries
located in Holmdel, Murray Hill,
Piscataway, Whippany, Princeton, Short
Hills, Summit, West Long Branch, Crawford
Hill; libraries also in Allentown,
Pennsylvania; Reading, Pennsylvania; New
York, New York; Atlanta, Georgia;
Columbus, Ohio; Naperville, Illinois;
Indianapolis, Indiana; North Andover,
Massachusetts.

OH —PREFORMED LINE PRODUCTS CO,
Research & Engineering Library, 660 Beta
Drive, Mayfield Village, (Mailing add: PO
Box 91129, Cleveland, 44101). Edwina T
Barron, Librn
Holdings: Vols (11,500) Cat Mss Microfiche
Pix VF
Budget: ($30,500)
Notes: Library covering research and
engineering fields emphasizing this subject.
Aerodynamic characteristics and electrical
characteristics of power cables,
communication cables (including fiber
optics), cable support systems, as well as
associated fittings and hardware; in service
behavior of manufactured products and
materials as it relates to its static and
dynamic forces and environmental

conditions; oceanographic cable fittings and
terminations.

TELEPHONY

NJ —AT&T BELL LABORATORIES,
Libraries and Information Systems Center,
600 Mountain Ave, Murray Hill, 07974. W
D Penniman, Dir
Notes: Restricted use to AT&T employees.
Catalogs/Indexes: Bell Laboratories Library
Network and Book Serial Catalogs; Bell
Laboratories Translations. Bell Laboratories
Library Network with New Jersey libraries
located in Holmdel, Murray Hill,
Piscataway, Whippany, Princeton, Short
Hills, Summit, West Long Branch, Crawford
Hill; libraries also in Allentown,
Pennsylvania; Reading, Pennsylvania; New
York, New York; Atlanta, Georgia;
Columbus, Ohio; Naperville, Illinois;
Indianapolis, Indiana; North Andover,
Massachusetts.

NY —AMERICAN TELEPHONE &
TELEGRAPH CO, Corporate Research
Center, 550 Madison Ave, Fifth floor, New
York, 10022. Marianne Benjamin, Chief
Librn
Holdings: Vols (8000) Cat Microforms
Notes: Collection incl complete sets of
AT&T periodicals and incomplete sets of
other periodicals in the field of telephony;
complete sets of AT&T companies' annual
reports; telephone industry directories;
monographs on history and economic
aspects of telephony. Member of AT&T Bell
Laboratories Library Network.

TELESCOPES AND TELESCOPY

CA —CALIFORNIA INSTITUTE OF
TECHNOLOGY, Robert A Millikan
Memorial Library, Archives, 1201 E
California Blvd, Pasadena, 91125. Judith R
Goodstein, Archivist
Notes: About 2000 items from the Palomar
Collection and the Ted Watterson
Collection, 1936-48; a photographic history
of the construction of the telescopes on
Palomar Mountain. Many other Palomar and
Mt Wilson pictures are in the Archive's
central files.

WI —UNIVERSITY OF CHICAGO, Yerkes
Observatory Library, Yerkes Observatory,
PO Box 258, Williams Bay, 53191. J Lola,
Librn
Holdings: Vols 20,000 Cat

TELESCOPES, REFRACTING see
Telescopes and Telescopy

TELEVISION

CA —BURBANK PUBLIC LIBRARY, 110 N
Glenoaks Blvd, Burbank, 91502. Mary Ann
Grasso, Coordr; Barbara Stones, Coordr,
Media Project
Holdings: Vols (32,000) Cat Clippings Pix
VF
Notes: The Warner Research Collection is a full
service research division designed to serve the
production needs of the motion picture, television,
theatrical, and creative arts communities. This is a
see-based service available by appointment only.
Subject specialties include costumes, U.S.
military, crime and criminals, transportation,
license plates, and Sears catalogues.

CA —UNIVERSITY OF CALIFORNIA, LOS
ANGELES, Theater Arts Library, Los
Angeles, 90024. Edward Shreeves,
Chairman, Bibliographers Group; Audree
Malkin, Head, Theater Arts Library
Holdings: Vols (12,500)
Notes: Major research collections covering
the historical, critical, aesthetic, biographical
and technical aspects of film, television and
radio, and the non-book and primary source
material in these fields. Also 166,000
pamphlets, photographs, microforms and

sound recordings. Incl over 4,000,000
moving picture stills, over 32,636
screenplays, and scripts from American and
British Films. Incl 1740 radio scripts and a
collection of 3000 television scripts. Also
incl portraits, clippings files, film festival
programs, motion picture programs, lobby
cards, original sketches and production
materials; the personal and business papers,
records and correspondence of actors,
directors, producers, art directors and screen
and television writers. Incl 100,000 mss.
Extensive poster collection (over 7000, 1915
to date), many forPolish and Czech
productions. Limited photocopying.

CA —CALIFORNIA INSTITUTE OF THE
ARTS, Library, 24700 McBean Pkwy,
Valencia, 91355. James Elrod, Dir
Holdings: Vols (61,000) Cat Phonorecords
Audiotapes
Budget: ($79,568)
Notes: Incl 320 videotapes and 776 16mm
films.

DC —GEORGE WASHINGTON
UNIVERSITY, Gelman Library,
Telecommunications Information Center,
Washington, 20052. Cathy Haworth, Librn
Holdings: Vols (1500) Periodicals
Notes: Incl

IN —BUTLER UNIVERSITY, Jordan College
of Music, Library, 4600 Sunset, Indianapolis,
46208. Phyllis J Schoonover, Librn
Holdings: Vols (5383) Cat
Budget: ($16,500)

IA —UNIVERSITY OF IOWA, University
Libraries, Iowa City, 52242. Robert A
McCown, Mss Librn
Holdings: Mss Pix
Notes: Five collections: Robert Blees collection of
motion picture and television material, 1925-65,
inc, including stories, still production photos, and
motion picture and television scripts of a motion
picture and television script writer; David Swift
collection of motion picture and television
material, 1951-65, including scripts, posters,
photos, drawings, and blueprints for final set
construction of a motion picture and television
producer and writer; the Albert Jay Cohen
collection of motion picture and television
production material, 1948-58, including
correspondence, film scripts, stories, photos,
financial and production papers, and censorship
records; the Arthur A. Ross collection of motion
picture and television material, 1943-65, including
correspondence, scripts, photos, production
records, and artists' sketches of a motion picture
and television script writer; and the Norman Felton
Papers, 1937-1978, including correspondence,
notes, notebooks, subject files, budgets, other
financial records, photographs, and scripts relating
to such television series as The Eleventh Hour,
The Lieutenant, The Man From U.N.C.L.E.,
Jericho, The Strange Report, The Psychiatrist,
Hawkins, and Dr. Kildare, produced by Felton,
124 ft. of mss.

MI —MICHIGAN STATE UNIVERSITY,
Libraries, Special Collections Div, East
Lansing, 48824. Jannette Fiore, Librn
Notes: The Russel B Nye Popular Culture
Collection in the Michigan State Univ
Libraries incl over (45,000) items. Most of
the collection is organized in 4 categories:
comic art, popular fiction, popular
information materials and materials relating
to the popular performing arts. Materials
relating to popular theatre, music, television,

TELEVISION (cont.)

radio, and film. Theatre is best represented. A significant collection of primary materials relating to the tent show incl photographs, financial and other records of the Henderson Stock Company, correspondence, leaflets, handbills and other ephemera from many of the companies playing in the upper midwest in the 1920s and 1930s, and photocopies of 250 tent show scripts.

NY —NEW YORK PUBLIC LIBRARY, Performing Arts Research Center, Billy Rose Theatre Collection, 111 Amsterdam Ave, New York, 10023. Dorothy L Swerdlove, Cur
Holdings: Cat Pix
Notes: As early as 1941 the American Television Society appointed the Theatre Collection the official repository of their archives and urged its members to deposit materials in the Collection. The Collection maintains clipping files on radio and television programs, and on the personnel of these programs. It collects photographs of these individuals, of television and radio studios, equipment, etc. There is a collection of television production scripts, with most of the "Hallmark Hall of Fame" specials and "Studio One" scripts, 1948-1952. The collection of radio scripts incl. material regarding the Radio Writers Guild of America and also runs of several serials written by Elaine Carrington. The book material incl. the standard works on the history of broadcasting and telecasting, vols. on the techniques of the industry.

NY —TELEVISION INFORMATION OFFICE, 745 Fifth Ave, New York, 10022. Leslie Slocum, Librn
Holdings: Vols 5000 Cat Mss
Notes: Social and cultural aspects of television. Research studies; serials; clipping and pamphlet files; books; government documents; special subject heading list. Does not incl technical aspects of TV.

NY —ELIZABETH SETON COLLEGE LIBRARY, Yonkers, 10701. Sr Margaret Sullivan, Librn

NY —YONKERS PUBLIC LIBRARY, Information Services, 7 Main St, Yonkers, 10701. Martita Schwarz, Dept Head
Holdings: Vols (21,500) Cat Maps Microforms
Budget: ($30,000)

OH —PUBLIC LIBRARY OF CINCINNATI & HAMILTON COUNTY, Art & Music Dept, 800 Vine St, Cincinnati, 45202. R Jayne Craven, Head
Holdings: Vols (122,185) Cat Pix
Budget: ($56,100)
Notes: Special collections: Eda Kuhn Loeb, "Artist and the Book, 1875-Date" (now shelved in Rare Book Room); music librettos (2345); exhibition catalogs (5474); large prints and posters (5051); Cincinnati artists vertical files; picture collection (673,906 clippings).

TX —SOUTHERN METHODIST UNIVERSITY, Fondren Library, McCord Theater Collection, Room 301, Dallas, 75275. Edyth Renshaw, Cur; Linda Sellers, Pub Serv
Holdings: Vols (2000) Uncat Mss Pix Slides Phonorecords
Notes: See *Theatre Collections in Libraries and Museums*, Gilder and Freedley (Theatre Arts, 1936). The McCord Theatre Collection encompasses the entire spectrum of the performing arts. The central purpose is to gather records of our regional theater before

such ephemeral material is lost. Records of over two hundred early Texas theaters, some fragmentary and some relatively complete, are in the files. These records incl photographs of buildings, stagehands, orchestras, and performers. Local theatre history incl the once famous Dallas Little Theatre and the Margo Jones Theatre. The national theatre, opera, ballet, and circus archives incl pictures (some autographed), programs, posters, throw-aways, tear sheets, clippings, and letters. Our international archives are small, but we have some excellent material, eg, artifacts from Max Reinhardt's production of "The Miracle" which happened to go bankrupt in Dallas. After a few years the items were given to us. There are posters, tear sheets, souvenir programs, and other colorful items from Morris Gest and the Artef Collection. We have about 200 19th century English playbills and a few from the 18th century. There is a collection of modern English, French, and other European programs, many of them illustrated souvenir programs. Also, magazines on theater, cinema, and television (1800). Scrapbooks covering both southwest and Dallas theater, 1890s-1950s. Special Collections: artifacts and documents on puppets; masks; costume design; circus; and ballet and dance. The Harriet Bacon MacDonald Collection of over 200 photographs of musicians appearing in Dallas during the first three decades of the 20th century. Many autographed. Affiliated with Meadow Theatre of the Arts.

WA —WESTERN WASHINGTON UNIVERSITY, Center for Pacific Northwest Studies, High St, Bellingham, 98225. James W Scott, Dir
Holdings: Mss Pix Phonorecords
Notes: The L Rogan Jones Collection: Broadcasting executive and community leader, Rogan Jones died in 1972. Owner, operator and sr executive of various radio, television and cable transmitting companies, Jones was involved during the 1930s in a famous lawsuit brought by various Washington newspapers and Associated Press against Station KVOS, which he then operated. In a case of changing fortunes, first for, then against KVOS, the case was argued before the US Supreme Court in 1936. A unanimous verdict was finally handed down in favor of the station. It is regarded as a landmark verdict in the history of public broadcasting. Papers on this and other radio and television issues are included in the collection. An *Informational Paper* is presently being prepared on this collection. Partially cataloged.

WI —STATE HISTORICAL SOCIETY OF WISCONSIN, Archives, 816 State St, Madison, 53706. Harold L Miller, Reference Archivist
Holdings: Mss Pix Films Microforms
Notes: Areas represented in collection incl radio, television, the press, public relations and advertising. Emphasis is on development of media in the 20th century; materials are mainly professional papers of individuals or organization or organizational records of firms or associations in the media. Collections are described in *Sources for Mass Communications, Film and Theater Research: A Guide,* (1982) and in current accession notes in the *Wisconsin Magazine of History.* Major collections are also listed in Hamer, *Guide to Manuscripts and Archives in the United States,* (1961) and in the *National Union Catalog of Manuscripts Collections,* (1959-date). Also incl, disc recordings and tape recordings.

†WI —STATE HISTORICAL SOCIETY OF WISCONSIN, Library, 816 State St, Madison, 53706.
Notes: Scripts, notes, correspondence and other items concerning the collaboration of Howard Lindsay and Russel Crouse for the theater, motion pictures and television, as well as the work of each with other collaborators and individually.

ON —NATIONAL FILM, TELEVISION AND SOUND ARCHIVES, Documentation & Public Service, 395 Wellington St, Ottawa, K1A 0N3, Can. Jana Vosikovska, Chief;

Gloria Grant, Librn; Sylvie Robitaille, Stills and Posters Librn
Notes: Several collections supporting the documentation on film, television and recorded sound: 1060 periodical titles (450 current), some on microfilm. Picture-stills, 265,000; moving picture posters, 6000; cataloged microfiche, 33,000 (vertical file material put on microfilm, then into a fiche format). Index cards (periodical references, credits): 334,000 cards (Film Title Index: 250,000 cards; Personalities Index: 84,000 cards).

ON —METROPOLITAN TORONTO LIBRARY, Theatre Dept, 789 Yonge St, Toronto, M4W 2G8, Can. Heather McCallum, Head
Holdings: Vols (30,500) Mss Pix Slides Phonorecords Microforms
Notes: Book and nonbook materials in all areas of the performing arts except music: theatre and drama, moving pictures, dance, television and radio programming, and varieties of popular entertainment such as circus, music hall, vaudeville, puppetry and pantomime. Special collections relating to the history of the performing arts in Canada. Access to the book and periodical collection is provided through a divided dictionary COM catalog on microfiche. In addition, extensive card indexes are available. Published descriptions of the collection: Heather McCallum. Research Collections in Canadian Libraries, Part II. Special Studies no I. *Theatre resources in Canadian collections* (Ottawa: National Library of Canada, 1973); Heather McCallum. "The Theatre Department of the Metropolitan Toronto Library" in *Special Collections,* vol 1 (1), fall 1981.

TELEVISION—BROADCASTING see Television Broadcasting

TELEVISION—HISTORY

CA —AMERICAN FILM INSTITUTE, Louis B Mayer Library, 2021 N Western Ave, PO Box 27999, Los Angeles, 90027. Anne G Schlosser, Dir
Notes: The AFI/Louis B Mayer Oral History Program Collection includes over 40 interviews with pioneers of the film industry. Also included in the collection are transcripts of seminars (1969-1981) and tapes (1981-) containing interviews with professionals from the film and television industry on how films and TV shows are produced. Include directors, writers, cinimatographers, editors, art directors, agents, lawyers, producers, etc. A film production and file index provides original documentation on nearly all US films from 1930-1969; tracks a film from first trade announcement regarding film production to final release.

CA —UNIVERSITY OF CALIFORNIA, LOS ANGELES, Theater Arts Library, Los Angeles, 90024. Edward Shreeves, Chairman, Bibliographers Group; Audree Malkin, Head, Theater Arts Library
Holdings: Vols (12,500)
Notes: Major research collections covering the historical, critical, aesthetic, biographical and technical aspects of film, television and radio, and the non-book and primary source material in these fields. Also 166,000 pamphlets, photographs, microforms and sound recordings. Incl over 4,000,000 moving picture stills, over 32,636 screenplays, and scripts from American and British Films. Incl 1740 radio scripts and a collection of 3000 television scripts. Also incl portraits, clippings files, film festival programs, motion picture programs, lobby cards, original sketches and production materials; the personal and business papers, records and correspondence of actors, directors, producers, art directors and screen and television writers. Incl 100,000 mss. Extensive poster collection (over 7000, 1915 to date), many for Polish and Czech productions. Limited photocopying.

DC —BROADCAST PIONEERS LIBRARY, 1771 N St NW, Washington, 20036.

TELEVISION—HISTORY (cont.)

Catharine Heinz, Dir
Holdings: Vols (6500) Uncat Pix
Phonorecords Audiotapes
Notes: Special collections: Oral History
(750); Havrilla (photos, radio performers);
William S Hedges Collection; Elmo Neale
Pickerill Collection; Joseph E Baudino
Collection; Archive of Federal
Communications Bar Association. Incl 20,
000 pictures, 1450 phonorecords and 1200
audiotapes.

†WI —STATE HISTORICAL SOCIETY OF
WISCONSIN, Library, 816 State St,
Madison, 53706.
Notes: Papers, correspondence, production
records, radio programs, columns, and other
writings. Also films and other documentation
of the Ed Sullivan Show.

TELEVISION—REPAIRING

CA —LOS ANGELES PUBLIC LIBRARY,
Science & Technology Dept, 630 W Fifth St,
Los Angeles, 90071. Billie M Connor, Dept
Head
Holdings: Vols (12,000) Cat
Notes: Materials on the application of
electronic devices, circuits and systems in
various fields such as computers, automatic
control, sound productions and reproduction,
radio and telecommunications. Extensive
holdings of materials on computers,
peripherals, and software including many
texts pertaining to specific programming
languages. Complete collection of Howard
Sams schematics for radio television, and
other electronic equipment repair as well as
historical sets of Rider's Radio and
Television schematics.

KS —WICHITA PUBLIC LIBRARY, 223 S
Main, Wichita, 67202. Larry DePiesse,
Head, Business & Technology Dept; Jayne F
Young, Business & Technology Dept
Holdings: Vols 220 Uncat
Budget: $900
Notes: Sams Photofact Schematics. All
service data publications printed since April
11, 1946. Contains listings on over 138,000
chassis and models of home entertainment
equipment: auto radios, CB radios, modular
hi-fis, scanner-monitors, tape recorders,
transistor radios, videocassette recorders,
and videodisc players. No interlibrary loan.

OH —AKRON-SUMMIT COUNTY PUBLIC
LIBRARY, Science & Technology Div, 55 S
Main St, Akron, 44326. Joyce McKnight,
Head
Holdings: Vols 2250 Cat
Budget: ($24,000)
Notes: Incl Howard Sams and John Rider
schematics.

PA —CARNEGIE LIBRARY OF
PITTSBURGH, Science & Technology Dept,
4400 Forbes Ave, Pittsburgh, 15213.
Catherine M Brosky, Dept Head
Notes: Radio and television schematics and
repair manuals.

SC —HORRY GEORGETOWN
TECHNICAL COLLEGE, Library, Hwy
501, Box 1966, Conway, 29526. Barbara
Brittain, Librn
Holdings: Vols (20,000) Cat Slides
Microforms

WI —MILWAUKEE PUBLIC LIBRARY, 814
W Wisconsin Ave, Milwaukee, 53233.
Donald J Sager, City Librn
Holdings: Vols Cat
Notes: Incl schematics and pamphlets. No
photocopying.

ON —METROPOLITAN TORONTO
LIBRARY, Science & Technology Dept, 789
Yonge St, Toronto, M4W 2G8, Can.
Margaret Walshe, Head
Holdings: Vols (120,000) Cat
Notes: Schematics available for Canadian
television from 1950 to date.

TELEVISION—STAGE LIGHTING see Stage Lighting

TELEVISION—TRANSMITTERS AND TRANSMISSION

WY —UNIVERSITY OF WYOMING,
William Robertson Coe Library, Archives -

American Heritage Center, PO Box 3412,
Laramie, 82071.
Notes: Papers of Knox Charlton Black, incl
those of a 12-year period when he worked
on a cable important to television.

TELEVISION ADVERTISING

GA —UNIVERSITY OF GEORGIA,
Libraries, Special Collections Division,
Athens, 30602. Vesta Lee Gordon, Asst Dir
for Special Collections
Notes: The Arbitron Collection of television
and radio program ratings, 1949-date (except
past year). In-depth, statistical analyses of
the listening public by age, sex, county, some
ethnic groups, farm population, listening
preferences, etc. 26,302 bound vols. 2
reports, 1949-81. To be added to annually.

TELEVISION BROADCASTING

DC —GEORGE WASHINGTON
UNIVERSITY, Gelman Library,
Telecommunications Information Center,
Washington, 20052. Cathy Haworth, Librn
Holdings: Vols (1500) Periodicals
Notes: Incl

GA —UNIVERSITY OF GEORGIA,
Libraries, Special Collections Division,
Athens, 30602. Vesta Lee Gordon, Asst Dir
for Special Collections
Notes: The Arbitron Collection of television
and radio program ratings, 1949-date (except
past year). In-depth, statistical analyses of
the listening public by age, sex, county, some
ethnic groups, farm population, listening
preferences, etc. 26,302 bound vols. 2
reports, 1949-81. To be added to annually.

IL —UNIVERSITY OF ILLINOIS,
URBANA/CHAMPAIGN, Library,
Communications Library, 122 Gregory Hall,
Urbana, 61801. Nancy Allen, Librn
Holdings: Vols (18,000) Cat
Budget: ($27,000)
Notes: Television systems and programs;
history, theory and effects; and skills.

MI —DETROIT PUBLIC LIBRARY, Music &
Performing Arts Dept, 5201 Woodward,
Detroit, 48202. Jean Currie Church, Cur
Holdings: Vols (1375) Cat Mss Pix
Notes: The E Azalia Hackley Collections
document achievements of Blacks in the
fields of music, dance, theatre, motion
pictures, and broadcasting. World-wide in
scope. Extensive clipping files arranged by
personal names, titles and subjects. Incl
musical scores (1500), recordings, and plays.
No taping or other copying of recordings
permitted.

NY —NATIONAL BROADCASTING CO,
Reference Library, 30 Rockefeller Plaza, Rm
1426, New York, 10020. Vera Mayer, Vice-
President Info & Archives
Holdings: Vols (4000) Cat Microforms
Notes: Historical and current material,
periodicals, subject files, clippings, etc. Total
collection: 13,000 vols incl other subjects
such as business, politics and social issues.

NY —NEW YORK PUBLIC LIBRARY,
Performing Arts Research Center, Billy Rose
Theatre Collection, 111 Amsterdam Ave,
New York, 10023. Dorothy L Swerdlove,
Cur
Holdings: Cat
See also entry under Television.

RI —RHODE ISLAND HISTORICAL
SOCIETY, Library, 121 Hope St,
Providence, 02906. Paul R Campbell,
Library Dir
Notes: Rhode Island Film Archive. 3,000,
000 feet of documentary and television
newsfilm.

TX —ABILENE CHRISTIAN UNIVERSITY,
Margaret & Herman Brown Library, ACU
Sta, Abilene, 79601. Callie Faye Milliken,
Assoc Dir
Holdings: Mss Audiotapes Videotapes 16mm
Films
Notes: Extensive collection of films,
audiotapes, and scripts used in developing
the religious radio-television program
"Herald of Truth," which has been aired by
Members of Churches of Christ since 1952.

ON —CANADIAN BROADCASTING
CORP, Head Office Library, 1500 Bronson

Ave, PO Box 8478, Ottawa, K1G 3J5, Can.
Normand Deschamps, Librn
Holdings: Vols (6400) Cat
Budget: ($18,000)
Notes: Emphasis on radio and television
broadcasting. No holdings on technical
aspects.

TELEVISION BROADCASTING—HISTORY

CA —LOS ANGELES PUBLIC LIBRARY,
Frances Howard Goldwyn Hollywood
Regional Library, 1623 Ivar Ave, Los
Angeles, 90028. Sally Dumaux, Librn
Holdings: Vols (100,000) Cat Mss Pix VF
Budget: ($60,000)
Notes: A general and a research collection
covering motion pictures, radio broadcasting,
and television. Over 2000 motion picture
and television scripts. Biographical
information on actors and actresses. Casts,
credits, and other production information on
over 1500 motion pictures from the 1920s to
the present. Collections also include posters,
lobby cards, souvenir programs, scrapbooks,
vertical files, and over 3000 publicity stills.
Including the following Special Collections:
Fred Archer Collection, photographs,
including the Hunchback of Notre Dame
(1923), and personalities of the stage and
screen, 1907-1930; Gilbert A Adrian,
designer, sketches and photographs; Hazel
Flynn, publicist, correspondence and
photographs.

MA —TUFTS UNIVERSITY, Fletcher School
of Law & Diplomacy, Murrow Center of
Public Diplomacy, Medford, 02155. Natalie
Schatz, Cur of Special Collections
Holdings: Vols (1500)// Cat Mss Pix
Phonorecords Audiotapes 16mm Films
Notes: Professional correspondence, reports,
speeches, scripts and interviews relating to
Edward R Murrow's career in broadcasting:
reports, hearings and speeches from his years
as Director of USIA, as well as personal
correspondence, memorabilia, books, some
films and audiotapes. 43,300 pieces.

NY —MUSEUM OF BROADCASTING,
Library, 1 E 53rd St, New York, 10022.
Douglas Gibbons, Dir
Notes: A museum dedicated to the study
and preservation of the history of radio and
television broadcasting. Maintains a
collection of significant radio and television
programs from the 1920s to the present. Incl
10,000 TV programs, 10,000 radio programs,
2000 vols, 2550 original scripts.

NY —NEW YORK PUBLIC LIBRARY,
Performing Arts Research Center, Billy Rose
Theatre Collection, 111 Amsterdam Ave,
New York, 10023. Dorothy L Swerdlove,
Cur
Holdings: Cat
See also entry under Television.

WY —UNIVERSITY OF WYOMING,
William Robertson Coe Library, Performing
Arts Collections, Laramie, 82071. Gene M
Gressley, Dir
Holdings: Mss
Notes: Collections in the Performing Arts
area incl some 300 collections of outstanding
music composers, arrangers, film industry
directors, writers, performers, and
individuals prominent in all aspects of music,
theatre, radio, television and film industry.

TELEVISION COMMERCIALS see Television Advertising

TELEVISION FILMS

CA —AMERICAN FILM INSTITUTE, Louis
B Mayer Library, 2021 N Western Ave, PO
Box 27999, Los Angeles, 90027. Anne G
Schlosser, Dir
Notes: Script Collection includes 2500
motion picture scripts, 1000 television
scripts. Film scripts include annotated
working scripts for directors, writers, editors,
and script supervisors. Television collection
includes series and TV movies. Also MGM
Script Collection of 400 scripts from the
silent period up to the mid-1950's.

CA —UNIVERSITY OF CALIFORNIA,
RIVERSIDE, University Library, 4045

TELEVISION FILMS (cont.)

Canyon Crest Dr, Box 5900, Riverside, 92517.
Holdings: Vols (30,000)
Notes: The Eaton Collection of science fiction and fantasy materials; incl 5,600 pulp magazines; also horror, supernatural, and Gothic mystery fiction; boys' books; utopian and dystopian fiction, imaginary voyages, future war and lost race fiction; large holdings in French language science fiction and fantasy; critical and scholarly works pertaining to these genres; videotapes of science fiction/fantasy films and shooting scripts. Collection covers science fiction/ fantasy literature from the 16th-17th centuries to the present. Strong individual author collections of Jules Verne, H Rider Haggard, H G Wells, Edgar Rice Burroughs, and Philip K Dick. For a complete description of the collection see: George Slusser, "The J Lloyd Eaton Collection," *Special Collections*, II, 1/2, 25-38 (1983), and *Dictionary Catalog of the J Lloyd Eaton Collection of Science Fiction and Fantasy Literature* (Boston: G K Hall) 1982.

CA —CALIFORNIA INSTITUTE OF THE ARTS, Library, 24700 McBean Pkwy, Valencia, 91355. James Elrod, Dir
Holdings: Vols (61,000) Cat Videotapes 16mm Films
Budget: ($7500)
Notes: Incl 320 videotapes and 776 16mm films.

PA —TEMPLE UNIVERSITY LIBRARIES, Special Collections Dept, Rare Books & Mss Section, Philadelphia, 19122. Thomas M Whitehead, Cur
Holdings: Vols (10,000) Mss Pix
Notes: The private library of Charles Blockson established as a collection at Temple University. Approximately 25,000 items of Afro-American literature, history of slavery and African and Carribbean histroy and history and culture. Selective catalog (exhibition) available.

TELEVISION IN EDUCATION

NY —TELEVISION INFORMATION OFFICE, 745 Fifth Ave, New York, 10022. Leslie Slocum, Librn
Holdings: Vols 5000 Cat Mss
Notes: Social and cultural aspects of television. Research studies; serials; clipping and pamphlet files; books; government documents; special subject heading list. Does not incl technical aspects of TV.

TELEVISION INDUSTRY

DC —GEORGE WASHINGTON UNIVERSITY, Gelman Library, Telecommunications Information Center, Washington, 20052. Cathy Haworth, Librn
Holdings: Vols (1500) Periodicals
Notes: Incl

TELEVISION JOURNALISM

WA —UNIVERSITY OF WASHINGTON LIBRARIES, Suzzallo Library, Manuscripts Section, FM-25, Seattle, 98195. Karyl Winn, Librn
Notes: Files of locally produced newsfilm from station KOMO-TV in Seattle, from 1954.

TELEVISION JOURNALISTS see Journalists

TELEVISION NEWS—COLLECTIONS

WA —UNIVERSITY OF WASHINGTON LIBRARIES, Suzzallo Library, Manuscripts Section, FM-25, Seattle, 98195. Karyl Winn, Librn
Notes: Files of locally produced newsfilm from station KOMO-TV in Seattle, from 1954.

TELEVISION PERIODICALS see Periodicals, Television

TELEVISION PROGRAMS

CA —UNIVERSITY OF CALIFORNIA, LOS ANGELES, Theater Arts Library, Los Angeles, 90024. Edward Shreeves, Chairman, Bibliographers Group; Audree Malkin, Head, Theater Arts Library
Holdings: Vols (12,500)
Notes: Major research collections covering the historical, critical, aesthetic, biographical and technical aspects of film, television and radio, and the non-book and primary source material in these fields. Also 166,000 pamphlets, photographs, microforms and sound recordings. Incl over 4,000,000 moving picture stills, over 32,636 screenplays, and scripts from American and British Films. Incl 1740 radio scripts and a collection of 3000 television scripts. Also incl portraits, clippings files, film festival programs, motion picture programs, lobby cards, original sketches and production materials; the personal and business papers, records and correspondence of actors, directors, producers, art directors and screen and television writers. Incl 100,000 mss. Extensive poster collection (over 7000, 1915 to date), many for Polish and Czech productions. Limited photocopying.

CA —DEFENSE LANGUAGE INSTITUTE FOREIGN LANGUAGE CENTER, Academic Library, Presidio of Monterey, Monterey, 93944. Gary D Walter, Librn
Holdings: Videotapes
Budget: $40,000
Notes: Foreign-language commercial television programming.

CA —SAN DIEGO STATE UNIVERSITY, Malcolm A Love Library, 5300 Campanile Dr, San Diego, 92182. D Dickinson, Univ Librn; Don L Bosseau, Dir
Notes: Desi Arnaz Collection of Film and Television Production Material. Includes films, television tapes, out-takes, scripts, correspondence, publicity material. (350 linear ft.)

DC —BROADCAST PIONEERS LIBRARY, 1771 N St NW, Washington, 20036. Catharine Heinz, Dir
Holdings: Vols (6500) Uncat Pix Phonorecords Audiotapes
Notes: Special collections: Oral History (750); Havrilla (photos, radio performers); William S Hedges Collection; Elmo Neale Pickerill Collection; Joseph E Baudino Collection; Archive of Federal Communications Bar Association. Incl 20, 000 pictures, 1450 phonorecords and 1200 audiotapes.

DC —LIBRARY OF CONGRESS, Motion Pictures, Broadcasting and Recorded Sound Div, Washington, 20540.
Notes: The *Amateur Hour* Collection consists of original radio recordings of the Major Bowes series (1935-1944) and disc, tape, and television coverage of the Ted Mack series (1948-1968). Incl applications to appear on the program and accompanying correspondence and news clippings. The *Arthur Godfrey Time* collection is comprised of recordings of the television and radio programs from the years 1949-57 and recordings of several rehearsals and warm-ups.

NY —MUSEUM OF BROADCASTING, Library, 1 E 53rd St, New York, 10022. Douglas Gibbons, Dir
Notes: A museum dedicated to the study and preservation of the history of radio and television broadcasting. Maintains a collection of significant radio and television programs from the 1920s to the present. Incl 10,000 TV programs, 10,000 radio programs, 2000 vols, 2550 original scripts.

OH —CLEVELAND PUBLIC LIBRARY, Literature Dept, 325 Superior Ave, Cleveland, 44114. Evelyn Ward, Head
Holdings: Vols Cat Pix Phonorecords Microforms VF
Notes: Large collection of stills and photographs from cinema and television.

PA —FREE LIBRARY OF PHILADELPHIA, Theatre Collection, Logan Sq, Philadelphia, 19103. Geraldine Duclow, Librn-in-Charge
Holdings: Vols (1,250,000) Uncat Pix
Notes: The Theatre Collection contains books, magazines, playbills, broadsides, posters, photographs, and other memorabilia covering theatre, motion pictures, minstrels, vaudeville, circus, radio and television. The Library's Philadelphia Theatre Index lists the major productions here since 1855, and partially indexes the collection of local playbills which date back to 1803. There are also programs from many other cities, incl New York; some from London date back to 1800. Early film companies as well as the present movie industry are represented by advertising materials and over 30,000 film stills. The Lubin Film Co (1910-1916) Archive has been established with over 600 photographs and related items. Circus programs and route books date back to 1900. There are minstrel programs as early as 1865. Most significant are the mss from Philadelphia's Dumont Minstrels. Various files contain autographs, photographs, newspaper articles and reviews in all pertinent subject areas. Noncirculating.

WA —WESTERN WASHINGTON UNIVERSITY, Center for Pacific Northwest Studies, High St, Bellingham, 98225. James W Scott, Dir
Holdings: // Cat 16mm Films
Notes: KVOS Television Company Film Collection. Incl black and white documentary films produced by KVOS television (1961-1975) covering Canada, the Pacific Northwest, the State of Washington, major world news events, Alaska, Australia and other areas. Topics of academic, scientific, political, cultural, religious, sociological and other sports are included.

WA —UNIVERSITY OF WASHINGTON LIBRARIES, Suzzallo Library, Manuscripts Section, FM-25, Seattle, 98195. Karyl Winn, Librn
Notes: Files of locally produced newsfilm from station KOMO-TV in Seattle, from 1954.

ON —METROPOLITAN TORONTO LIBRARY, Theatre Dept, 789 Yonge St, Toronto, M4W 2G8, Can. Heather McCallum, Head
Holdings: Vols (30,500) Mss Pix Slides Phonorecords Microforms
Notes: Book and nonbook materials in all areas of the performing arts except music: theatre and drama, moving pictures, dance, television and radio programming, and varieties of popular entertainment such as circus, music hall, vaudeville, puppetry and pantomime. Special collections relating to the history of the performing arts in Canada. Access to the book and periodical collection is provided through a divided dictionary COM catalog on microfiche. In addition, extensive card indexes are available. Published descriptions of the collection: Heather McCallum. Research Collections in Canadian Libraries, Part II. Special Studies no I. *Theatre resources in Canadian collections* (Ottawa: National Library of Canada, 1973); Heather McCallum. "The Theatre Department of the Metropolitan Toronto Library" in *Special Collections*, vol 1 (1), fall 1981.

TELEVISION SCRIPTS

CA —BURBANK PUBLIC LIBRARY, 110 N Glenoaks Blvd, Burbank, 91502. Mary Ann Grasso, Coordr; Barbara Stones, Coordr, Media Project
Holdings: Vols (500) Manuals Videocassettes Audiocassettes
Notes: This collection (including technical manuals, production directories, scripts, production lectures, seminars, and university classes), is a free public clearinghouse of industry trends, job skills information, technical advances and management practices required for film and video production. Information covers such technical categories as cinematography, editing, sound recording, lighting, and special effects. Craft areas include directing, scriptwriting, art direction and costume design. Management information covers producing, programming, financing, budgets and distribution for theatrical, broadcast, and non-broadcast markets. Bulk of collection circulates. Reference texts and some other restricted material available for in-library study only. List of holdings available on request.
See also entries under Moving Pictures - Production and Direction; Television

TELEVISION SCRIPTS (cont.)

CA —AMERICAN FILM INSTITUTE, Louis
B Mayer Library, 2021 N Western Ave, PO
Box 27999, Los Angeles, 90027. Anne G
Schlosser, Dir
Notes: Script Collection includes 2500
motion picture scripts, 1000 television
scripts. Film scripts include annotated
working scripts for directors, writers, editors,
and script supervisors. Television collection
includes series and TV movies. Also MGM
Script Collection of 400 scripts from the
silent period up to the mid-1950's.

CA —LOS ANGELES PUBLIC LIBRARY,
Frances Howard Goldwyn Hollywood
Regional Library, 1623 Ivar Ave, Los
Angeles, 90028. Sally Dumaux, Librn
Holdings: Vols (100,000) Cat Mss Pix VF
Budget: ($60,000)
Notes: A general and a research collection
covering motion pictures, radio broadcasting,
and television. Over 2000 motion picture
and television scripts. Biographical
information on actors and actresses. Casts,
credits, and other production information on
over 1500 motion pictures from the 1920s to
the present. Collections also include posters,
lobby cards, souvenir programs, scrapbooks,
vertical files, and over 3000 publicity stills.
Including the following Special Collections:
Fred Archer Collection, photographs,
including the Hunchback of Notre Dame
(1923), and personalities of the stage and
screen, 1907-1930; Gilbert A Adrian,
designer, sketches and photographs; Hazel
Flynn, publicist, correspondence and
photographs.

CA —UNIVERSITY OF CALIFORNIA, LOS
ANGELES, Research Library, Dept of
Special Collections, 405 Hilgard Ave, Los
Angeles, 90024. Edward Shreeves,
Chairman, Bibliographers Group; David S
Zeidberg, Head
Holdings: Pix
Notes: In various collections, incl the
Stanley Chase, Mort Fine, Ernie Kovacs,
Elizabeth Meehan, Ralph Nelson, Rod
Serling, Sterling Silliphant, Wolper
Productions, and William Read Woodfield
collections. No photocopying.

CA —UNIVERSITY OF CALIFORNIA, LOS
ANGELES, Theater Arts Library, Los
Angeles, 90024. Edward Shreeves,
Chairman, Bibliographers Group; Audree
Malkin, Head, Theater Arts Library
Holdings: Vols (12,500)
Notes: Major research collections covering
the historical, critical, aesthetic, biographical
and technical aspects of film, television and
radio, and the non-book and primary source
material in these fields. Also 166,000
pamphlets, photographs, microforms and
sound recordings. Incl over 4,000,000
moving picture stills, over 32,636
screenplays, and scripts from American and
British Films. Incl 1740 radio scripts and a
collection of 3000 television scripts. Also
incl portraits, clippings files, film festival
programs, motion picture programs, lobby
cards, original sketches and production
materials; the personal and business papers,
records and correspondence of actors,
directors, producers, art directors and screen
and television writers. Incl 100,000 mss.
Extensive poster collection (over 7000, 1915
to date), many for Polish and Czech
productions. Limited photocopying.

CA —UNIVERSITY OF CALIFORNIA, LOS
ANGELES, Theater Arts Library, Los
Angeles, 90024. Edward Shreeves,
Chairman, Bibliographers Group; Audree
Malkin, Head, Theater Arts Library
Holdings: Cat Mss Pix
Notes: Television Scripts: approximately
3500 scripts incl such television series as
Mission Impossible, all episodes for the years
1966-1970; *The Real McCoys,* 78 episodes,
1959-1961; *My Friend Irma,* 1965-1959; *My
Mother the Car,* 30 episodes, 1965-1966.
Also, scripts, etc of documentary TV series
Biography, produced by David Wolper.

CA —UNIVERSITY OF CALIFORNIA,
RIVERSIDE, University Library, 4045
Canyon Crest Dr, Box 5900, Riverside,

92517.
Holdings: Vols (30,000)
Notes: The Eaton Collection of science
fiction and fantasy materials, incl 5,600 pulp
magazines; also horror, supernatural, and
Gothic mystery fiction; boys' books; utopian
and dystopian fiction, imaginary voyages,
future war and lost race fiction; large
holdings in French language science fiction
and fantasy; critical and scholarly works
pertaining to these genres; videotapes of
science fiction/fantasy films and shooting
scripts. Collection covers science fiction/
fantasy literature from the 16th-17th
centuries to the present. Strong individual
author collections of Jules Verne, H Rider
Haggard, H G Wells, Edgar Rice Burroughs,
and Philip K Dick. For a complete
description of the collection see: George
Slusser, "The J Lloyd Eaton Collection,"
Special Collections, II, 1/2, 25-38 (1983),
and*Dictionary Catalog of the J Lloyd Eaton
Collection of Science Fiction and Fantasy
Literature* (Boston: G K Hall) 1982.

CA —SAN DIEGO STATE UNIVERSITY,
Malcolm A Love Library, 5300 Campanile
Dr, San Diego, 92182. D Dickinson, Univ
Librn; Don L Bosseau, Dir
Notes: Desi Arnaz Collection of Film and
Television Production Material. Includes
films, television tapes, out-takes, scripts,
correspondence, publicity material. (350
linear ft.)

CT —YALE UNIVERSITY, Box 1603A, Yale
Station, New Haven, 06520.
Holdings: Mss
Notes: 74 television scripts by William A
Graham.

DC —LIBRARY OF CONGRESS, Motion
Pictures, Broadcasting and Recorded Sound
Div, Washington, 20540.
Holdings: Cat Mss Pix
Notes: American Copyright Collection of
films (incl television shows) selected from
those registered for copyright from 1942 to
the present.

GA —UNIVERSITY OF GEORGIA,
Libraries, Special Collections Division,
Athens, 30602. Vesta Lee Gordon, Asst Dir
for Special Collections
Notes: Theater Collection contains the Paris
Music Hall set and costume designs with
original drawings by Erte, Barbier, Zig and
others; British Music Hall Papers; European
toy theater collection; Charles Coburn
papers; television script collection; Tennessee
Williams papers. Collection contains 16,000
pieces.

†IL —UNIVERSITY OF ILLINOIS,
URBANA/CHAMPAIGN, Library, Wright
St, 230 Library UIUC, Urbana, 61801.

IN —INDIANA UNIVERSITY, Lilly Library,
Seventh St, Bloomington, 47405. William R
Cagle, Librn
Holdings: Cat Mss
Notes: Ms holdings incl the papers of
television writer John McGreevey, 1922- ,
containing correspondence and scripts from
preliminary draft to final shooting script for
such programs as *The Waltons, Black
Saddle, The Farmer's Daughter, The
Scottsboro Boys,* etc. 1645 items.

IA —UNIVERSITY OF IOWA, University
Libraries, Iowa City, 52242. Robert A
McCown, Mss Librn
Holdings: Mss Pix

Notes: Five collections: Robert Blees collection of
motion picture and television material, 1925-65,
inc, including stories, still production photos, and
motion picture and television scripts of a motion
picture and television script writer; David Swift
collection of motion picture and television
material, 1951-65, including scripts, posters,
photos, drawings, and blueprints for final set
construction of a motion picture and television
producer and writer; the Albert Jay Cohen
collection of motion picture and television
production material, 1948-58, including
correspondence, film scripts, stories, photos,
financial and production papers, and censorship
records; the Arthur A. Ross collection of motion
picture and television material, 1943-65, including
correspondence, scripts, photos, production
records, and artists' sketches of a motion picture
and television script writer; and the Norman Felton

Papers, 1937-1978, including correspondence,
notes, notebooks, subject files, budgets, other
financial records, photographs, and scripts relating
to such television series as The Eleventh Hour,
The Lieutenant, The Man From U.N.C.L.E.,
Jericho, The Strange Report, The Psychiatrist,
Hawkins, and Dr. Kildare, produced by Felton,
124 ft. of mss.

MD —UNIVERSITY OF MARYLAND,
BALTIMORE COUNTY, Albin O Kuhn
Library and Gallery, 5401 Wilkens Ave,
Baltimore, 21228. Ann Copeland, Special
Collections Librn
Holdings: // Uncat
Notes: Television scripts (576) from a wide
range of shows from the 1960s and early
1970s.

†MA —BOSTON UNIVERSITY, Mugar
Memorial Library, Special Collections Dept,
771 Commonwealth Avenue, Boston, 02215.
Howard B Gotlieb, Dir
Notes: Extensive papers of mystery and
science fiction writers, and film, radio and
TV writers, performers, etc. 14 years of
original Little Orphan Annie art. Collections
built around papers of individuals are
supplemented by their printed works.

†MI —MICHIGAN STATE UNIVERSITY,
Libraries, East Lansing, 48824. Jannette
Flore, Librn
Notes: Good samples of Big-Little Books,
foreign comics, dime novels, pulps, TV
scripts, underground comics. SFWA and
Clarion depository.

NY —NEW YORK PUBLIC LIBRARY,
Performing Arts Research Center, Billy Rose
Theatre Collection, 111 Amsterdam Ave,
New York, 10023. Dorothy L Swerdlove,
Cur
Holdings: Cat
See also entry under Television

NY —NEW YORK PUBLIC LIBRARY,
General Library of the Performing Arts, 111
Amsterdam Ave, New York, 10023. Larry
Cioppa, Drama Specialist
Holdings: Vols (40,000) Cat Phonorecords
Notes: Drama material on all aspects of the
theater. Film, radio, television and related
performing arts. Incl 5000 drama recordings.

OH —OHIO STATE UNIVERSITY, William
Oxley Thompson Memorial Library, 1858
Neil Ave Mall, Columbus, 43210. Robert A
Tibbetts, Cur of Special Collections
Holdings: Vols (475) Cat Mss

OR —UNIVERSITY OF OREGON
LIBRARY, Special Collections Div, Eugene,
97403. Kenneth W Duckett, Curator
Holdings: Cat Mss
Notes: Over 20 mss collections containing
television scripts and some production
materials for primarily westerns such as
"Gunsmoke," "Bonanza," and "Wagon Train,"
but also some mystery and adventure shows.
Publication: Martin Schmitt, comp,
*Catalogue of Manuscripts in the University
of Oregon Library* (Eugene: University of
Oregon Books, 1971).
See also entry under Fiction, Western; Radio
Scripts

PA —TEMPLE UNIVERSITY LIBRARIES,
Special Collections Dept, Rare Books & Mss
Section, Philadelphia, 19122. Thomas M
Whitehead, Cur
Holdings: Cat
Notes: Developing collection of 91 linear
feet (June 1972) of American and British
radio and television rehearsal and camera

TELEVISION SCRIPTS (cont.)

scripts. Incl Lux Radio Theatre (US, 1934-1955); scripts of Carlton E Morse-*One Man's Family, I Love A Mystery,* etc; BBC scripts of Terence Tiller; et al Guide and description of the Lux Radio Theatre collections issued as a masters thesis (Temple University, 1967).

TX —ABILENE CHRISTIAN UNIVERSITY, Margaret & Herman Brown Library, ACU Sta, Abilene, 79601. Callie Faye Milliken, Assoc Dir
Holdings: Mss Audiotapes Videotapes 16mm Films
Notes: Extensive collection of films, audiotapes, and scripts used in developing the religious radio--television program "Herald of Truth," which has been aired by Members of Churches of Christ since 1952.

TELEVISION SERVICING see Television—Repairing

TELEVISION TRANSMISSION see Television—Transmitters and Transmission

TELINGA LANGUAGE see Telugu Language and Literature

TELLER, EDWARD

IA —HERBERT HOOVER PRESIDENTIAL LIBRARY, West Branch, 52358. Dale C Mayer, Archivist
Notes: Papers.

TELLER, WALTER

MA —BOSTON UNIVERSITY, Mugar Memorial Library, Special Collections Dept, 771 Commonwealth Ave, Boston, 02215. Howard B Gotlieb, Dir
Holdings: Cat Mss
Notes: Mss, correspondence, etc collected in depth; incl publications by or about.

TELOOGOO LANGUAGE see Telugu Language and Literature

TELUGU LANGUAGE AND LITERATURE

NY —NEW YORK PUBLIC LIBRARY, Oriental Div, Fifth Ave & 42 St, New York, 10018. E Christian Filstrup, Chief
Holdings: Cat Mss Microforms
Budget: ($56,455)
Notes: Published catalog of holdings.
NY —NEW YORK PUBLIC LIBRARY, Donnell Foreign Language Library, 20 W 53 St, New York, 10019. Bosiljka Stevanovic, Supvr Librn
Holdings: Vols 140 Cat
Notes: Telugu collection incl Telugu authors of Telugu expression. No separate catalog.

TEMIANKA, HENRY

CA —UNIVERSITY OF CALIFORNIA, LOS ANGELES, Music Library, Schonberg Hall, Los Angeles, 90024. Stephen M Fry, Music Librn
Notes: Mss.

TEMPERAMENT TESTS see Character Tests

TEMPERANCE

CO —UNIVERSITY OF COLORADO, Libraries, Western Historical Collections, Boulder, 80309.
Holdings: Mss
Notes: The Colorado WCTU was organized in Longmont in 1880, two years after the formation of the first three locals in Greeley, Evans and Longmont. The Colorado WCTU was active in woman's suffrage, prison reform, homes for unwed mothers, day nurseries, 8-hour laws, and other reforms in addition to their primary concern of prohibition. The collection contains minutes of the Boulder Chapter (1881-1950) plus

minutes of other Colorado local chapters for shorter periods of time. In addition there are state convention proceedings (1882-1969), state officers' minutes and reports, and many pamphlets and publications. 13 boxes and 12 oversize folders, 1878-1975. A published guide is available.
IN —HURTY-PECK LIBRARY OF BEVERAGE LITERATURE, 5650 W Raymond Street, PO Box 41167, Indianapolis, 46208. Ben Wilson, Librn
Holdings: Vols (6000) Cat //
Notes: The most comprehensive collection, in English, in the world on beverages of all types. History, manufacture, formulae, customs. Books on beer and brewing; cocoa and chocolate; coffee; liquors and spirits; soft drinks; tea; and wine.
†MA —UNIVERSITY OF MASSACHUSETTS AT AMHERST, Library, Amherst, 01003.
Notes: The history of the temperance and prohibition movement in the US.
MI —SUOMI COLLEGE, Finnish-American Historical Archives, Hancock, 49930. Kenneth Niemi, Archives Librn
Notes: Collection incl 8000 vols, 152,000 mss, 2000 photographs, 760 audiotapes; microforms and maps; 14,000 holdings are cataloged. Subject interests: coop movement, labor, pioneer library of rare books and church records, socialist and communist movements, temperance societies. Special Collections: Finnish language newspapers (includes 100 titles from 1876-present); Suomi Synod Archives; Finnish-American Oral History.
NJ —RUTGERS, THE STATE UNIVERSITY OF NEW JERSEY, Center of Alcohol Studies Library, Smithers Hall, New Brunswick, 08903. Penny Page, Librn
Holdings: Vols (8075) Cat Mss Microforms
Budget: ($110,000)
See also entry under Alcoholism
NY —NEW YORK PUBLIC LIBRARY, Research Libraries, General Research Division, Fifth Ave & 42 St, New York, 10018. Rodney Phillips, Chief
Holdings: Vols (2,225,000) Cat Maps Pix Microforms
Budget: ($775,718)
Notes: Incl James Black Temperance Collection.
OH —KENT STATE UNIVERSITY, University Archives, Kent, 44242. Stephen C Morton, University Archivist
Holdings: Uncat Mss Pix
Notes: Books, periodicals, and correspondence by Allen O Fuller, and correspondence of Cornelia Cowles Fuller and Jeannette Fuller, a 19th Century temperance advocate. Jeannette was a WCTU lecturer and organizer in Ohio, Pa, Wis, WVa, KY, and Mich. Jeannette was also interested in the Non-Tobacco League of America. A O Fuller was a physician and Baptist minister in Northeastern, Ohio. Correspondence is also included for Ira Fuller (1840s), and Myra Cowles.
OH —GREENE COUNTY DISTRICT LIBRARY, 76 E Market St, PO Box 520, Xenia, 45385. Julie M Overton, Local History Coordr
Holdings: Vols 2 Uncat
Notes: Handwritten WCTU scrapbooks; compiled by Carrie Dodds Geyer, Xenia, Ohio, 1874-1945. Much other material, incl a letter from John G Whittier, 1883.
PA —FRIENDS HISTORICAL LIBRARY OF SWARTHMORE COLLEGE, Swarthmore, 19081. J William Frost, Dir
Holdings: Vols (35,000) Cat Mss
Notes: Library's collections contain information on the history and doctrine of the Society of Friends, Quaker contributions to literature, science, business, education, and government, plus their reform efforts in peace, Indian rights, women's rights, abolition of slavery, and temperance. Among the more than 250 mss collections are the personal papers of several Quaker temperance advocates, of whom observed prison conditions and provided assistance to prisoners.
RI —BROWN UNIVERSITY, John Hay Library, 20 Prospect St, Providence, 02912.

Mark N Brown, Cur Mss
Holdings: // Mss
Notes: Two collections: (1) Eli H Canfield mss reflect issues of the day and incl the subjects of missions, religious education, temperance, Prohibition, and Reconstruction. There are also 300 letters from Canfield to his son and grandchildren; letters from Europe and the South during and after the Civil War; and papers relating to Christ Church, Brooklyn. Register available. See "The Rev Eli Canfield (1817-1898): Low-church Yankee Episcopalian," ed by William G McLoughlin, Jr, in *Books at Brown,* vol XXII (1969), pp 135-68. (2) Three ms boxes and 29 notebooks of George S Burleigh, containing letters for the period 1839 to 1903 reflecting his interests in Transcendentalism; the anti-slavery, temperance, and woman's liberation movements; the Sabbath Question; and the publication of his writing in reformperiodicals. Two manuscript boxes and 29 notebooks contain poems by Burleigh.
WI —UNIVERSITY OF WISCONSIN, MADISON, Memorial Library, 728 State St, Madison, 53706. Erwin K Welsch, Social Studies Bibliographer
Holdings: Vols 1500 // Cat Mss Pix Microforms
Notes: A collection of property of Guy Hayler, an active member of many British temperance groups in the latter part of the 19th and early 20th centuries. Many items contain ms annotations by Hayler concerning individualsor organizations as well as clippings from contemporary sources which have been added. A number of the periodicals are recorded neither in the ULS or BUCOP; particularly notable are periodicals of local British temperance organizations.
NS —DALHOUSIE UNIVERSITY LIBRARY, Halifax, B3H 4H8, Can.
Holdings: Vols (2000)
Notes: Nova Scotia history pamphlets. Compiled by a Nova Scotia newspaper editor, J J Stewart, the pamphlet collection provides a comprehensive view of Nova Scotia society in the 19th century, religious, political, educational, economic, and moral issues are all hotly debated in the collection's pamphlets. Many unique items are to be found in the collection.

TEMPERATURES, LOW see Materials at Low Temperatures

TEMPLETON, ALEC

CT —YALE UNIVERSITY, Music Library, 98 Wall St, New Haven, 06520. Harold E Samuel, Librn
Notes: Personal papers and musical mss.
See also entry under Music, American.

TEN COMMANDMENTS (MOTION PICTURE)

CA —UNIVERSITY OF CALIFORNIA, LOS ANGELES, Theater Arts Library, Los Angeles, 90024. Edward Shreeves, Chairman, Bibliographers Group; Audree Malkin, Head, Theater Arts Library
Notes: The screenplay for the Ten Commandments, revised July 6, 1956, and approx 3000 production stills.
OH —CLEVELAND PUBLIC LIBRARY, Literature Dept, 325 Superior Ave, Cleveland, 44114. Evelyn Ward, Head
Notes: Incl in the W Ward Marsh Cinema Archives is a specially bound copy of the shooting script (accompanied by color transparencies) for Cecil B deMille's remake of *The Ten Commandments.*

TENAMENT HOUSES

NY —MUSEUM OF THE CITY OF NEW YORK, Library, Fifth Ave & 103 St, New York, 10025.
Notes: The Jacob A Riis Collection of New York City photographs, especially of slum life at about the turn of the century.

TENNANT, JOHN A., 1868-1957

NC —UNIVERSITY OF NORTH
CAROLINA, CHARLOTTE, J Murrey
Atkins Library, UNCC Station, Charlotte,
28223. Robert F Brabham Jr, Special
Collections Librn
Notes: Papers of John A Tennant, 1868-
1957, publisher of *The Photo-Miniature,* and
early photographic journal. Incl Tennant's
marked copy of the journal, 1899-1904.

TENNENT, REV. WILLIAM L., JR., AND FAMILY

NJ —PRINCETON UNIVERSITY, Library,
Rare Books Dept, Princeton, 08544. Stephen
Ferguson, Cur

TENNESSEE

TN —CHUCALISSA MUSEUM, 1987 Indian
Village Dr, Memphis, 38109. Gerald P
Smith, Cur
Holdings: Vols (1100) Cat Mss
Budget: ($200)
Notes: Collection emphasizes midsouth
archaeology, but incl some regional
ethnographic and geological titles.
Noncirculating.
TN —MIDDLE TENNESSEE STATE
UNIVERSITY, Andrew L Todd Library,
MTSU Box 13, Murfreesboro, 37132. John
David Marshall, Head, Reference Dept
Holdings: Vols 6500 Cat
Notes: Tennesseeana and books by
Tennessee authors.
TN —TENNESSEE STATE PLANNING
OFFICE, Library, 301 Seventh Ave N,
Nashville, 37219. Eleanor J Burt, Librn
Holdings: Vols (19,616) Cat Maps Slides
Films Microforms
Budget: ($8500)
Notes: Comprehensive planning reference
materials; materials about Tennessee for
planning at local, regional, and state levels.
Incl 200 maps and 1350 slides.

TENNESSEE—GENEALOGY

MI —MONROE COUNTY LIBRARY
SYSTEM, Ellis Reference and Information
Center, 3700 S Custer Rd, Monroe, 48161.
Marie D Chulski, Head of Reference
Services
Notes: Incl individual county histories,
atlases, biographies, etc. The Monroe County
history collection contains veteran records,
plat books, oral history tapes, family
histories, church records, cemetery index,
atlases and census records. Genealogy
emphasis is not only Monroe County but
incl surrounding counties and the states with
large migration to the area, such as Ohio,
Kentucky, Tennessee and the New England
states.
TN —CHATTANOOGA-HAMILTON
COUNTY, Bicentennial Library, Local
History and Genealogy Dept, 1001 Broad St,
Chattanooga, 37402. Clara W Swann, Librn
Holdings: Vols (24,561) Cat Mss Maps Pix
Microforms
Budget: ($7000)
Notes: Emphasis on southern states, and
eastern Tennessee counties, with
considerable material on New England,
Pennsylvania, and Maryland genealogy and
history. Census records on microfilm. Special
indexes and clipping files. Noncirculating.
TN —MEMPHIS/SHELBY COUNTY
PUBLIC LIBRARY & INFORMATION
CENTER, History & Travel Dept, 1850
Peabody Ave, Memphis, 38104. James R
Johnson, Head
Holdings: (5100) Cat Microforms
Budget:
Notes: Covers Memphis and Shelby County,
all subject areas. Features special materials
and mss, groups of Memphis persons. Incl
newspaper clipping file, 1930-date, of local
subjects. Various indexes incl photo,
biography, occupation, first facts (incl
genealogy). Partial index to early Memphis
newspapers in progress.

TN —PUBLIC LIBRARY OF NASHVILLE &
DAVIDSON COUNTY, Nashville Room,
Eighth Ave N & Union, Nashville, 37203.
David Marshall Stewart, Chief Librn
Holdings: Vols Cat Mss Maps Pix Slides
Microforms
Notes: Tennessee genealogy. Nashville
Room has separate catalog. Tennessee
census records are on microfilm. All
materials noncirculating. genealogy.
Nashville Room has separate catalog. The
Naff Collection of programs, autographed
photographs, posters etc tells the story of
professional theatre in Nashville between
1900 and 1960. Tennessee census records
are on microfilm. All materials
noncirculating.

TENNESSEE—HISTORY

†DC —GEORGETOWN UNIVERSITY
LIBRARY, Washington, 20057.
Notes: The papers of David Rankin Barbee,
Washington Post journalist and historian
who devoted 30 years to the study of
Abraham Lincoln, Rose O'Neal Greenhow,
and the history of Tennessee. Extensive
correspondence with Albert J Beveridge,
Henry Steele Commager, and Paul M Angle,
and all of Barbee's research files and
manuscripts.
DC —LIBRARY OF CONGRESS, Manuscript
Division, Washington, 20540. John C
Broderick, Chief
Holdings: Cat Mss
TN —CHATTANOOGA-HAMILTON
COUNTY, Bicentennial Library, Local
History and Genealogy Dept, 1001 Broad St,
Chattanooga, 37402. Clara W Swann, Librn
Holdings: Vols (24,561) Cat Mss Maps Pix
Microforms
Budget: ($7000)
Notes: General emphasis on Tennessee
history, with special attention to collection
of items pertaining to Chattanooga (incl
history, authors, artists, etc). Special indexes
and clipping files supplement book
collection. Tennessee census records on
microfilm. Newspapers and county records
on microfilm. All materials are
noncirculating.
TN —UNIVERSITY OF TENNESSEE,
KNOXVILLE, Library, Knoxville, 37996.
John Dobson, Special Collections Librn
Holdings: Vols (20,000) Cat Mss Maps Pix
Notes: Tennesseana; 19th century American
fiction; southern Indians; early Imprints.
Separate catalog; holdings also listed in
comprehensive public catalog in Main
Library. Rare books card catalog with special
headings calling attention to unusual features
of the books; unpublished registers and
calendars to ms collection. *Kefauver*
collection, 59,000 pounds of political papers
and memorabilia, reconstructed Senate
office; *Radiation Biology Archives* (ca 60,
000 pieces), papers of scientists from several
countries dealing with the development of
radiation biology. Also, 18 vols of extremely
rare Southwest Territory and *Tennessee
Official Journals,* printed in Knoxville, 1794-
1796. The rare *Acts and Journals* are
described in *The Lost Roulstone Imprints,*
by John Dobson (Knoxville: Univ of
Tennessee Libraries, 1975), 70 pp.
TN —UNIVERSITY OF TENNESSEE,
MARTIN, Paul Meek Library, Martin,
38238. Joel A Stowers, Dir
Holdings: Vols (1000) Cat
TN —MEMPHIS STATE UNIVERSITY, John
Willard Brister Library, Memphis, 38152.
John Terreo, Special Collections Librn
Notes: 1968 Memphis Sanitation Workers
Strike. A collection of audiotape interviews
with Memphis governmental officals and
administrators, strikers, union leaders,
religious leaders, and other significant
persons involved in the strike, during which
civil rights leader Dr Martin Luther King, Jr
was assassinated. Also incl are photographic
prints and negatives and the news outakes
from the news departments of the three
Memphis television stations as well as
clippings from newspapers and periodicals.
Published finding aid can be found in the
Mississippi Valley Collection.

TN —MEMPHIS/SHELBY COUNTY
PUBLIC LIBRARY & INFORMATION
CENTER, History & Travel Dept, 1850
Peabody Ave, Memphis, 38104. James R
Johnson, Head
Holdings: Vols (9700) Cat Mss Maps Pix
Microforms
Notes: Covers Memphis and Shelby County,
all subject areas. Features special materials
and mss, groups of Memphis persons. Incl
newspaper clipping file, 1930-date, of local
subjects. Various indexes incl photo,
biography, occupation, first facts (incl
genealogy). Partial index to early Memphis
newspapers in progress.
TN —PUBLIC LIBRARY OF NASHVILLE &
DAVIDSON COUNTY, Nashville Room,
Eighth Ave N & Union, Nashville, 37203.
David Marshall Stewart, Chief Librn
Holdings: Vols (8300) Cat Maps Pix Slides
Microforms
Notes: General emphasis on Tennessee
history with special attention to items
pertaining to Nashville. Books by Nashville
authors and Tennessee genealogy. Nashville
Room has separate catalog. Also, the
Stahlman Collection made up of books and
periodicals of the South, especially
Tennessee, collected mainly during 1920s
and 1930s, but also many earlier rare
imprints. Named for former Nashville
Banner publisher, James G Stahlman, and
donated by the then-current publisher,
Wayne Sargent. Partially cataloged. *The
Stahlman Collection* (Nashville: Public
Library of Nashville and Davidson County,
1975). All materials noncirculating.
TX —UNIVERSITY OF TEXAS LIBRARIES,
General Libraries, PO Box P, Austin, 78713.
Carolyn Bucknell, Asst Dir for Collection
Development
Holdings: Cat Microforms

TENNESSEE—MAPS

TN —UNIVERSITY OF THE SOUTH
ARCHIVES, Jessie Ball DuPont Library,
Sewanee, 37375. Gertrude French Mignery,
Archivist
Notes: Ca 100 of Sewanee and Franklin
County.

TENNESSEE AUTHORS see Authors, Tennessee

TENNESSEE RIVER VALLEY

TN —TENNESSEE VALLEY AUTHORITY
(TVA), Technical Library, 400 W Summit
Hill Dr, E2 B7, Knoxville, 37902. Jesse C
Mills, Chief Librn
Holdings: Vols (106,900) Cat Mss Maps Pix
Audiotapes Microforms
Budget: ($2,025,000)
Notes: The Technical Library Headquarters
Staff (order, cataloging, information, and
administration) is located in Knoxville,
Tenn. In addition there are branch libraries
in Knoxville, Norris, and Chattanooga,
Tennessee, and Muscle Shoals, Alabama.

TENNESSEE VALLEY AUTHORITY (TVA)

AL —UNIVERSITY OF ALABAMA,
HUNTSVILLE, Library, Box 2600,
Huntsville, 35807. John Warren, Dir
Notes: Congressional papers and related
materials of Congressman Robert E Jones,
constant supporter of the TVA.
†MA —JOHN F KENNEDY LIBRARY,
Columbia Point, Boston, 02125. Dan H Fenn
Jr, Dir
Holdings: Cat
Notes: Copies of records and publications of
the Tennessee Valley Authority. 4 linear ft
of mss. Holdings are described in "Historical
Materials in the John F Kennedy Library."
Copies may be obtained by writing the
Research Archivist.
OH —ANTIOCH COLLEGE, Olive Kettering
Library, Livermore St, Yellow Springs,
45387. Nina Myatt, Cur
Holdings: Mss Pix Microfilm
Notes: Personal papers and correspondence

TENNESSEE VALLEY AUTHORITY (TVA) (cont.)

(1920-1975) of Arthur E Morgan former President of Antioch (1920-1936), first director of Ohio's Miami Valley Conservancy District, and first Chairman of the Tennessee Valley Authority (TVA). Mss, film, out-takes, much on the engineering of over 50 water-control projects in this country, Africa, and India. Materials on Edward Bellamy (Morgan wrote biography of Bellamy). Incl family papers. About 175 file boxes. Most TVA material on microfilm. Originals sent to National Archives.

TN —TENNESSEE VALLEY AUTHORITY (TVA), Technical Library, 400 W Summit Hill Dr, E2 B7, Knoxville, 37902. Jesse C Mills, Chief Librn
Holdings: Vols (106,900) Cat Mss Maps Pix Audiotapes Microforms
Budget: ($2,025,000)
Notes: The Technical Library Headquarters Staff (order, cataloging, information, and administration) is located in Knoxville, Tenn. In addition there are branch libraries in Knoxville, Norris, and Chattanooga, Tennessee, and Muscle Shoals, Alabama.

TN —TENNESSEE VALLEY AUTHORITY (TVA), Norris Branch Library, Norris, 37828. Debra D Mills, Librn
Holdings: Vols (8000) Cat Microforms
Budget: ($35,000)

TENNIEL, JOHN

DC —LIBRARY OF CONGRESS, Prints & Photographs Div, Washington, 20540.
Notes: Swann Collection is strong in the work of contemporary cartoonists. Among the 400 artists represented are Peter Arno, Bil Canfield, Al Capp, Miguel Covarrubias, Louis Dalrymple, Whitney Darrow, Rube Goldberg, Thomas Nast, Jose Guadalupe Posada, Edward Sorel, and John Tenniel.

TENNIS

NY —SAINT JOHN'S UNIVERSITY, Special Collections Dept, Grand Central & Utopia Pkwys, Jamaica, 11439. Szilvia E Szmuk, Librn
Holdings: Vols 1600 // Cat
Notes: The William M Fischer Lawn Tennis Library (formerly at New York University) consists of books, periodical, yearbooks, newspaper clippings, photographs, souvenir programs, and memorabilia concerning lawn tennis and other related games. The scope of the collection is historical, covering the years 1887 to 1960. No photocopying.

NY —RACQUET & TENNIS CLUB, Library, 370 Park Ave, New York, 10022. Gerald Belliveau, Jr, Librn
Holdings: Vols (17,500) Cat
Budget: ($6000)
Notes: Specializes in court tennis, lawn tennis, early American sport. See Dictionary Catalogue of the Library of Sports in the Racquet and Tennis Club (Boston: G K Hall, 1971). Also, Robert W Henderson, Early American Sport, 3rd ed. (Cranbury, NJ: Fairleigh Dickinson University Press, 1977).

RI —INTERNATIONAL TENNIS HALL OF FAME & TENNIS MUSEUM, Dwight F Davis Library, 194 Bellevue Ave, Newport, 02840. Mark L Stenning, Cur
Holdings: Vols 1250 Cat Mss Pix Slides Audiotapes 16mm Films
Budget: $10,000
Notes: Computerized collection.

TENNYSON, ALFRED LORD

AL —SAMFORD UNIVERSITY, Special Collections Library, 800 Lakeshore Dr, Birmingham, 35229. Annie Ford Wheeler, Acting Head Librn
Holdings: Vols 400 Cat Mss Pix
Notes: Incl most first editions. Now adding secondary works.

AZ —UNIVERSITY OF ARIZONA, University Library, Special Collections, Tucson, 85721. Louis A Hieb, Head
Holdings: Vols (7000) Cat Mss Microforms
Budget: ($30,000)
Notes: The major collection of 19th century

authors are Byron, Dickens, Scott, Thackeray, Trollope, the Brownings, Stevens, Tennyson, and Wordsworth.

CT —YALE UNIVERSITY, Box 1603A, Yale Station, New Haven, 06520.
Holdings: Cat Mss

KS —UNIVERSITY OF KANSAS, Kenneth Spencer Research Library, Special Collections Dept, Lawrence, 66045. Alexandra Mason, Librn
Holdings: Vols 372 Cat Mss
Notes: Based on W D Paden Collection. Mostly by Tennyson but some about. Many variant editions, etc. Noncirculating.

MA —HARVARD UNIVERSITY LIBRARY, Houghton Library, Cambridge, 02138. Rodney G Dennis, Cur of Manuscripts
Holdings: Cat Mss
Notes: Manuscripts described in Harvard Library Bulletin, X (1956): pp 254-274.

MI —UNIVERSITY OF MICHIGAN, Library, Dept of Rare Books & Special Collections, Ann Arbor, 48109. Robert J Starring, Head
Holdings: Cat Mss

NC —DUKE UNIVERSITY, William R Perkins Library, Durham, 27706. Elvin E Strowd, University Librn
Notes: The Thomas M Owen collection complements other material in the library on English poets and poetry.

OH —OHIO UNIVERSITY, Vernon R Alden Library, Department of Archives and Special Collections, Athens, 45701. Gary A Hunt, Head
Holdings: Vols 372 Cat Mss Audiotapes
Notes: A comprehensive collection of Tennyson's published works, in first and later editions, incl a few mss and related material. Incl 22 different sets (1870-1908) of collected editions; some 30 editions (1878-1913) of the one-volume Works; many editions of each of the individual titles; and the ms journal (1870-1872) of Tennyson's neighbor, J H Mangles, recording or summarizing many conversations with the poet. All editions of all titles are collected, except those published posthumously.

WI —UNIVERSITY OF WISCONSIN, MADISON, Memorial Library, British & American Language & Literature Collection, 728 State St, Madison, 53706. Yvonne Schofer, Bibliographer
Holdings: Vols (1000)// Cat
Notes: Arthur Beatty Collection. Consists of over 1000 volumes, principally in the English poetry of the Romantic period, strong in Coleridge, Tennyson, Swinburne, the prose of De Quincy and the folk poetry and balladry of Great Britain and Europe. Outstanding for its first and other editions of Wordsworth. About 200 titles in the Department of Rare Books and Special Collections; the rest is in stacks.

ON —VICTORIA UNIVERSITY, Library, 71 Queen's Park Crescent, Toronto, M5S 1K7, Can. Robert C Brandeis, Chief Librn
Holdings: Vols (931) // Cat
Notes: A very good general collection of Tennysoniana before 1900 rich in first editions and strong in both British and American editions. Described in: Sinclair, David, "The Tennyson Collection in Victoria University Library," Victorian Studies Association Newsletter 6 (October 1970), 12-14.

TENSIONS, STATIC AND DYNAMIC

OH —PREFORMED LINE PRODUCTS CO, Research & Engineering Library, 660 Beta Drive, Mayfield Village, (Mailing add: PO Box 91129, Cleveland, 44101). Edwina T Barron, Librn
Holdings: Vols (11,500) Cat Mss Microfiche Pix VF
Budget: ($30,500)
Notes: Library covering research and engineering fields emphasizing this subject. Aerodynamic characteristics and electrical characteristics of power cables, communication cables (including fiber optics), cable support systems, as well as associated fittings and hardware; in service behavior of manufactured products and materials as it relates to its static and dynamic forces and environmental

conditions; oceanographic cable fittings and terminations.

TENT SHOWS

MI —MICHIGAN STATE UNIVERSITY, Libraries, Special Collections Div, East Lansing, 48824. Jannette Fiore, Librn
Holdings: Uncat Mss Pix
Notes: The Russel B Nye Popular Culture Collection in the Michigan State Univ Libraries incl over (45,000) items. Most of the collection is organized into 4 categories: comic art, popular fiction, popular information materials and materials relating to the popular performing arts. Materials relating to popular theatre, music, television, radio, and film. Theatre is best represented. A significant collection of primary materials relating to the tent show incl photographs, financial and other records of the Henderson Stock Company, correspondence, leaflets, handbills and other ephemera from many of the companies playing in the upper midwest in the 1920s and 1930s, and photocopies of 250 tent show scripts.

TX —TEXAS TECH UNIVERSITY, Library, Lubbock, 79409. David J Murrah, Assoc Dir for Special Collections

TENURE OF LAND see Land Tenure

TENURE OF OFFICE see Civil Service

TERATOLOGY

AR —NATIONAL CENTER FOR TOXICOLOGICAL RESEARCH, Library, Jefferson, 72079. Susan Laney-Sheehan, Supvr Librn
Holdings: Microforms
Notes: Incl (860) journal titles, (230) current subscriptions.

MD —JOHNS HOPKINS UNIVERSITY, Institute of the History of Medicine, 1900 E Monument St, Baltimore, 21205. Doris Thibodeau, Librn
Holdings: Vols 936 Cat

†NY —MEDICAL RESEARCH LIBRARY OF BROOKLYN, Academy of Medicine of Brooklyn & The State University of New York Downstate Medical Center, 450 Clarkson St, Brooklyn, 11203. Kenneth E Moody, Dir
Notes: Extensive collection of 18th-19th century material.
See also entry under Medicine.

TEREZIN

MA —BRANDEIS UNIVERSITY, Goldfarb Library, 415 South St, Waltham, 02154. Bessie Hahn, Dir
Notes: Theresienstadt Concentration Camp Documents. Consists of over 200 "daily order" bulletins issued by the German command. Many of them incl arrival and departure lists of internees. A finding list to the documents is located in Special Collections. No photocopying of the documents is permitted.

TERMINAL CARE FACILITIES

MA —NATIONAL CENTER FOR DEATH EDUCATION, New England Resource Center for Thanatology & Funeral Service, 656 Beacon St, Boston, 02215. Gail Gruner, Librn
Notes: Hospice care.

NY —CREEDMOOR PSYCHIATRIC CENTER, Health Sciences Library, Bldg 51, 80-45 Winchester Blvd, Queens Village, 11427. Susan Taubman, Dir of Library; Pushpa Bhati, Sr Librn
Holdings: Vols (12,000) Cat Slides Phonorecords Audiotapes Filmstrips Microfiche
Budget: ($50,000)
Notes: Particularly strong in the areas on neurology, pharmacology, psychoanalysis, and psychopharmacology.

TERMINAL RAILROAD ASSOCIATION

MO —WASHINGTON UNIVERSITY, Libraries, Special Collections Dept, Campus

TERMINAL RAILROAD ASSOCIATION (cont.)

Box 1061, St Louis, 63130.
Notes: Terminal Railroad Association Records (1889-date), of more than 450 original tracings of the Eads Bridge (1874-date). Drawings show in fine and complete detail all the design features of this internationally known St Louis landmark.

TERMITES

NY —AMERICAN MUSEUM OF NATURAL HISTORY, Library Services Dept, Central Park W & 79th St, New York, 10024. Nina J Root, Chairwoman; Mary Genett, Asst Librn for Reference Services
Notes: A major literature collection supplements the museum's entomology collections; perhaps the largest in the world.

TERNETTE, NICK

MB —UNIVERSITY OF MANITOBA, Elizabeth Dafoe Library, Archives and Special Collections Dept, Winnipeg, R3T 2N2, Can. Richard E Bennett, Dept Head; Corrado A Santoro, Reference Archivist
Notes: Correspondence, papers, briefs, convention proceedings, election results, resource files, etc. concerning Winipeg politics, emphasis on left wing activities. 2 linear ft, 4 boxes.

TERRAPINS see Turtles and Tortoises

TERRESTRIAL GLOBES see Globes—Collections

TERRESTRIAL MAGNETISM see Magnetism, Terrestrial

TERRESTRIAL PHYSICS see Geophysics

TERROR, REIGN OF see France—History – Revolution, 1789-1799

TERROR TALES see Horror Tales

TERRORISM AND TERRORISTS

MD —INTERNATIONAL ASSOCIATION OF CHIEFS OF POLICE, 13 Firstfield Rd, PO Box 6010, Gaithersburg, 20760.
Holdings: Vols (6000) Cat Mss
Notes: Collection heavy in criminal investigation, crime prevention, police administration and management. Collecting in public sector labor relations, family violence, terrorism.

MO —SAINT LOUIS POLICE LIBRARY, 315 S Tucker Blvd, Saint Louis, 63102. Cathy Reilly, Librn
Holdings: Vols (21,000) Cat Mss Pix Microforms
Budget: ($18,400)
Notes: Library on all subjects of police work is open to public for general reference use.

TERRY, DAME ELLEN, 1848-1928

CA —UNIVERSITY OF CALIFORNIA, DAVIS, Shields Library, Dept of Special Collections, Davis, 95616. Donald Kunitz, Head; C Danial Elliott, Asst Head
Holdings: Uncat Mss Pix
Notes: Photographs, clippings, and correspondence of personalities of American and British theatre in the 19th and 20th centuries, such as Edwin Booth, Joseph Jefferson, Julia Marlowe, E H Sothern, Ellen Terry, Henry Irving, McKee Rankin, Fanny Davenport, and Zero Mostel.

CA —UNIVERSITY OF CALIFORNIA, LOS ANGELES, Research Library, Dept of Special Collections, 405 Hilgard Ave, Los Angeles, 90024. Edward Shreeves, Chairman, Bibliographers Group; David S Zeidberg, Head
Holdings: Vols Cat Mss
Notes: 5 books; 2 linear feet of correspondence of Dame Ellen Terry, 1848-1928.

IL —NORTHWESTERN UNIVERSITY, Library, Special Collections Dept, 1937 Sheridan Rd, Evanston, 60201. R Russell Maylone, Cur
Holdings: Vols 210 Cat Mss Pix Phonorecords
Notes: Collection is being cataloged according to the Craig bibliography of Fletcher & Road. Collecton incl material about Ellen Terry and Henry Irving, as well as original art work by Craig, stage designs and other ephemera. Collection created by J Wesley Swanson and given to Northwestern University Library by his sister.

TN —MEMPHIS STATE UNIVERSITY, John Willard Brister Library, Memphis, 38152. John Terreo, Special Collections Librn
Notes: Theatre Collection, 1789-1972. Correspondence, scripts, programs, handbills, musical scores, clippings, drawings, sketches, and photographs, documenting careers of artists, production of plays, ballett and theatre companies, and theaters and opera houses centering in New York and London, England. Incl drawings, prints, publications, and other personal papers of British producer and designer Edward Gordon Craig (1872-1966), relating to his career, radio talks (1951-1961) for the BBC, acting school in Florence, Italy, and his mother, actress Ellen Terry; and correspondence, scripts, programs, reviews, scrapbooks, photos, and other materials, of American producer Jed Harris (?)-1979, relating to his stage productions (1926-1945).

TERRY, PAUL

NY —MUSEUM OF MODERN ART, Dept of Film, 11 W 53 St, New York, 10019. Eileen Bowser, Cur
Holdings: Mss Pix
Notes: Papers, correspondence, scrapbooks, pictures, etc. Partially cataloged.

TESTACEA see Mollusks

TESTING

IL —CHICAGO BRIDGE & IRON CO, Technical Library, 800 Jorie Blvd, Oak Brook, 60521. Susan Beatty, Librn
Holdings: Vols (7500) Cat
Budget: ($39,500)
Notes: Quality control and nondestructive testing.

NJ —EDUCATIONAL TESTING SERVICE, Carl Campbell Brigham Library, Princeton, 08540. Janet Williams, Librn
Notes: Complete works and papers of Louis L Thurstone, a leading psychometrician of the 20th century.

NY —STATE UNIVERSITY OF NEW YORK, COLLEGE AT BUFFALO, E H Butler Library, 1300 Elmwood Ave, Buffalo, 14222. Jerome Earley, Librn
Notes: The work of J P Guilford, on microfilm, relating to his research on the Structure of the Intellect (SOI) model. 200 reels of microfilm contain the tests, answer sheets, and supporting data for his SOI theory. Corresponds to the Psychological Laboratory Reports at UCLA.

TESTS see Examinations

TESTS, CHARACTER see Character Tests

TESTS, MENTAL see Mental Tests

TESTS AND MEASUREMENTS IN EDUCATION see Educational Tests and Measurements

TETRACHLORODIBENZODIOXIN

MD —NATIONAL LIBRARY OF MEDICINE, 8600 Rockville Pike, Bethesda, 20209. Harold M Schoolinam, Actg Dir
Budget: ($46,400)

TEUTONIC LANGUAGES AND LITERATURES see Germanic Languages and Literatures

TEUTONIC MYTHOLOGY see Mythology, Germanic

TEXAS

CT —YALE UNIVERSITY, Box 1603A, Yale Station, New Haven, 06520.
Holdings: Cat Mss Maps Pix

NY —AMERICAN MUSEUM OF NATURAL HISTORY, Library Services Dept, Central Park W & 79th St, New York, 10024. Nina J Root, Chairwoman; Mary Genett, Asst Librn for Reference Services
Holdings: Cat Mss Pix Microforms
Notes: The Ernest Thompson Seton diaries. Thousands of pages of an unpublished 67-year diary record of one of the world's most famous naturalists, the gift of Joseph F Cullman III, a Trustee of the Museum. Preserved in 35 protective cases, the gift incl unpublished diaries, notebooks, and some other writings. The diary begins 12 June 1879; the last entries were written in hospital, just a month before Seton's death in 1946. Literally hundreds of examples of flora and fauna are pictured in the diaries in original pencil, pen-and-ink, and watercolor sketches, on nearly every page. Research will reveal information on the Indian sign language, the Boy Scouts of America, the Woodcraft League of America, and the wilderness of Canada, Florida, Texas, the West and Southwest, etc.

TX —UNIVERSITY OF TEXAS LIBRARIES, General Libraries, Barker Texas History Center, PO Box P, Austin, 78712. Don Carleton, Dir
Holdings: Vols (132,000) Cat Mss Maps Pix Slides Phonorecords Audiotapes Microforms
Notes: Materials pertaining to the historical, social, economic, scientific, humanistic and literary development of Texas and the American Southwest. Rich in early state imprints, as well as the period of the Republic. Archival and ms holdings measure over 22,000 linear feet. Texas history prior to the Republic is covered by the Bexar Archives. Collection also contains 3000 phonorecords, 750 audiotapes, 20,000 maps, and 8335 microfilm reels.

TX —BEAUMONT PUBLIC LIBRARY SYSTEM, Tyrrell Historical Library, 695 Pearl St, Beaumont, 77701. Mabel Leyda, Librn; Maurine Gray, Dir of Libraries
Holdings: vols 3658 Cat Mss Maps Pix
Budget: $8000
Notes: Emphasis on southeast Texas.

TX —UNIVERSITY OF MARY HARDIN-BAYLOR, Townsend Memorial Library, Ninth & Wells, Belton, 76513. Izoro Daphane Kerley, Asst Librn
Holdings: Vols Cat

TX —ROSENBERG LIBRARY, Galveston and Texas History Center, 2310 Sealy Ave, Galveston, 77550. Jane Kenamore, Archivist
Holdings: Vols 7500 Cat Mss Maps Pix Microforms
Notes: The 7500 vols cited do not incl over 15,000 linear ft of mss. Espec strong on the period of the Texas Republic and earlier. Much on Galveston area history and the Texas Navy.

TX —LE TOURNEAU COLLEGE, Margaret Estes Library, 2100 S Mobberly Ave, PO Box 7001, Longview, 75601. Rachel Miley, Acting Dir of Library Services
Holdings: Vols (178,846) Cat Mss Maps Pix Slides Microforms
Budget: ($40,000)

TX —TEXAS TECH UNIVERSITY, Library, Lubbock, 79409. David J Murrah, Assoc Dir for Special Collections

TX —STEPHEN F AUSTIN STATE UNIVERSITY, Ralph W Steen Library, Special Collections Dept, Box 13055, SFA Sta, Nacogdoches, 75962. Linda Cheves Nicklas, Special Collections Librn
Holdings: Vols (13,500) Cat Mss Maps Pix
Budget: ($5000)
Notes: Emphasis on local and university-related subjects, especially people, culture, events, buildings of Texas, East Texas, and historic Nacogdoches. Extensive ms collection (1200 linear ft); 344 maps; 1600 pictures. Published description: SFASU, *A Guide to Special Collections*, 1980.

TX —ECTOR COUNTY LIBRARY, Texas-Southwest History & Genealogy Dept, 321 W 5th St, Odessa, 79761. Jan Carter, Head
Holdings: Vols (10,000)
Budget: ($4000)
Notes: The Ector County Library is a Texas State Documents Depository. The documents are non-circulating and are not

TEXAS (cont.)

cataloged. Department, subject, and title access is provided.

TX —PHARR MEMORIAL LIBRARY, 200 S Athol, Pharr, 78577. Karen Mier, Asst Librn
Holdings: Vols 601 Cat

TX —UNIVERSITY OF TEXAS, Marine Science Institute Library, Port Aransas, 78373. Ruth Grundy, Librn
Holdings: Vols (45,000) Cat Maps Pix
Budget: ($70,000)
Notes: Current researches in marine science, especially concerning the Gulf of Mexico, the Texas Coastal Zone, and the Continental Shelf. Incl journals.

TX —BAYLOR UNIVERSITY, Moody Memorial Library, Texas History Collection, Waco, 76706. Kent Keeth, Librn
Holdings: Vols (80,000) Cat Mss Maps Pix Slides Phonorecords Audiotapes Microforms
Notes: The Texas Collection gathers materials which relate to life in Texas in all aspects, from earliest days to the present. Incl Baylor University Archives.

TEXAS—COMMERCE AND TRADE

TX —UNIVERSITY OF TEXAS LIBRARIES, General Libraries, PO Box P, Austin, 78713. Carolyn Bucknell, Asst Dir for Collection Development
Notes: Papers of retail grocers, Heidenheimer Brothers, of Galveston, being travelling salesmen's correspondence and other papers, bound by month and year, measuring 35 linear feet.

TEXAS—GENEALOGY

FL —ORLANDO PUBLIC LIBRARY, Local History & Genealogy Dept, 100 Block of Central Ave, Orlando, 32806. Eileen B Willis, Librn
Holdings: Vols 11,000 Cat Maps Microforms
Budget: $8000
Notes: Genealogy collection on Md, Del, W Va, NC, SC, Ala, Miss, La, Texas, Ark, Ky, Ohio, Ill, Ind, and Mich are well represented. Most other states are covered by smaller collections.
See also entry under Genealogy - Collections.

TX —AMARILLO PUBLIC LIBRARY, 413 E Fourth, Amarillo, 79101. Mary Kay Snell, Librn
Holdings: Vols 2194 Cat Microforms
Notes: Publication: Catalog of Genealogical Material in the Amarillo Public Library, 2nd ed (Amarillo: Amarillo Public Library, 1975).

TX —TEXAS STATE LIBRARY, Genealogy Collection, PO Box 12927, Capitol Station, Austin, 78711. Robin Rader, Supervisor, Genealogy Services
Holdings: Vols 9,000 Cat Microforms
Budget: $108,129
Notes: Emphasis on Texas and southern states. Census schedules (1790-1910), family histories, county data. Texas tax rolls. Index to Texas births and deaths, 1903-1973. Microfilms of municipal archives of Nuevo Leon, Mexico. Noncirculating.

TX —BEAUMONT PUBLIC LIBRARY SYSTEM, Tyrrell Historical Library, 695 Pearl St, Beaumont, 77701. Mabel Leyda, Librn; Maurine Gray, Dir of Libraries
Holdings: Microforms
Notes: Incl census records (1305 rolls microfilm).

TX —EAST TEXAS GENEALOGICAL ASSOCIATION, Library, 412A West College St, Carthage, 75633. L R Bagwell, Librn
Holdings: Vols (1200) Cat Mss Maps Pix Slides Microforms
Notes: Local history and genealogy; not confined to Texas.

TX —DALLAS PUBLIC LIBRARY, Texas/ Dallas History and Archives Division, 1515 Young St, Dallas, 75201. Richard L Waters, Acting Dir; Wayne Gray, Manager
Notes: Dallas and Texas history.

TX —LUBBOCK CITY-COUNTY LIBRARY, 1306 Ninth St, Lubbock, 79401. Marlene M

Harp, Dir, Adult Services
Holdings: Vols (10,000) Mss Microforms
Notes: Emphasis on the South and the various immigration routes used by settlers or their descendents from the Virginia-Georgia coast to west Texas. Very few periodical holdings prior to 1955. Material is not available for circulation of interlibrary loan.

TX —ECTOR COUNTY LIBRARY, Texas-Southwest History & Genealogy Dept, 321 W 5th St, Odessa, 79761. Jan Carter, Head
Holdings: Vols (6968) Cat Phonorecords Microforms
Budget: ($4000)
Notes: The genealogy collection is non-circulating. The materials are arranged by state and all periodicals for that state are shelved with the books. National Archives Census Microfilm is held, mainly, for Southern States and migratory routes into Texas.

TEXAS—GOVERNMENT PUBLICATIONS

TX —WEST TEXAS STATE UNIVERSITY, Cornette Library, PO Box 748 WT Sta, Canyon, 79016. Annette F Nall, Documents Librn
Holdings: Vols (20,000) Uncat Microforms
Notes: 515,805 US and State of Texas government documents (with a volume-equivalent of 91,011 volumes), classified by Superintendent of Documents numbers. Largest such collection in State of Texas Depository Library since the 1920s.

TX —BAYLOR UNIVERSITY, Moody Memorial Library, Texas History Collection, Waco, 76706. Kent Keeth, Librn
Holdings: Vols (80,000) Cat Mss Maps Pix Slides Phonorecords Audiotapes Microforms
Notes: The Texas Collection gathers materials which relate to life in Texas in all its aspects, from earliest days to the present. Incl Baylor University Archives.

TEXAS—HISTORY

AL —BIRMINGHAM PUBLIC LIBRARY, Southern History Dept, 2020 Seventh Ave N, Birmingham, 35203. Virginia K Scott, Head
Holdings: Vols (50,000) Cat Microforms
Notes: History and social conditions of the southeastern US. Significant holdings on border areas such as Texas, Pennsylvania, Maryland. Strong genealogical collection with emphasis on the southeastern area of the US. Very strong Civil War Collection and early southern travel accounts. See George Ray Stewart, The Special Collections in the Birmingham Public Library. MA Thesis, Emory University, 1971.

DC —GEORGETOWN UNIVERSITY, Library, Special Collections Div, 37 & O Sts NW, Washington, 20057. George M Barringer, Special Collections Librn; Nicholas B Sheetz, Mss Librn
Holdings: Mss Cat Pix Phonorecords
Notes: Papers of the Honorable Earle Bradford Mayfield (1881-1964), concerning his business, legal and political careers. The papers are particularly useful in the study of Texas politics on the state and national levels. Mayfield served in the Texas State Senate from 1906-1912 and in the United States Senate from 1923-1929. Also incl are the papers of his wife Ora Limpkin Mayfield.

LA —LOUISIANA STATE UNIVERSITY, SHREVEPORT, Library-Archives, 8515 Youree Dr, Shreveport, 71129. Patricia L Meador, Archivist & Asst Librn
Notes: The collection's primary emphasis is the history of North Louisiana, particulary Northwest Louisiana.

MS —UNIVERSITY OF SOUTHERN MISSISSIPPI, William David McCain Graduate Library, Box 5148, Southern Sta, Hattiesburg, 39406.
Holdings: Cat Mss Pix
Notes: Correspondence and records (1847-1892) relating to Alexander Melvorne Jackson's participation in the Mexican War, his service as Secretary of the State of the

New Mexico Territory (1857-1861), and his participation in the Civil War on the side of the Confederacy. Among his correspondents were Albert Gallatin Brown, Reuben Davis, Miguel A Otero, Jacob Thompson, and John Ireland. Incl are photographs of Austin, Texas, ca 1890. 1.1 cubic feet holdings.

NM —EASTERN NEW MEXICO UNIVERSITY, Golden Library, Special Collections, Portales, 88130. Mary Jo Walker, Special Collections Librn
Holdings: Vols Cat Mss Pix Audiotapes
Notes: Incl 176 cataloged books by F Stanley (pseudonym of Catholic priest and historian Stanley Francis Louis Crocchiola), plus his collection of periodicals and books by other writers pertaining to southwestern history (particularly New Mexico and the Texas panhandle); 22.25 cubic ft of mss, correspondence files, photographs of F Stanley and others, and two oral history interviews with F Stanley. Unpublished register of collection available. Bio/bibliography of F Stanley in preparation.

NM —ROSWELL PUBLIC LIBRARY, 301 N Pennsylvania Ave, Roswell, 88201. Sarah Beth Galloway, Library Dir
Holdings: Vols (2000) Cat Maps
Budget: $1000
Notes: Covers literature (fiction and nonfiction), history, biography, geography, of Oklahoma, Texas, Colorado, New Mexico and Arizona.

OK —THOMAS GILCREASE INSTITUTE OF AMERICAN HISTORY & ART LIBRARY, 1400 North 25th West Ave, Tulsa, 74127. Sarah Hirsch, Librn
Holdings: Vols Cat Mss Maps Pix
Notes: Trans-Mississippi West, US, Indian and Hispanic history. The Gilcrease Library contains a total of about 40,000 mss; 10,000 imprints; 5000 photographs; 600 maps and 50,000 vols.

TX —ABILENE CHRISTIAN UNIVERSITY, Margaret & Herman Brown Library, ACU Sta, Abilene, 79601. Callie Faye Milliken, Assoc Dir
Holdings: Vols 1250
Notes: The Marshall Jackson Texas Collection.

TX —HARDIN-SIMMONS UNIVERSITY, Richardson Library, Abilene, 79601. Joe F Dahlstrom, Dir
Holdings: Vols (10,000) Cat Mss Maps Pix Microforms
Notes: Special collection name is Richardson Research Center, named in honor of Dr Rupert N Richardson. Collect in the areas of his own research interests, especially that portion of the US that was once a part of Mexico. Emphases on the history of ranching, railroads, discovery and exploration, Texas county histories, etc. Incl 350 items printed and/or designed by El Paso printer Cart Hertzog; the Judge R C Crane collection of Texana and a similar collection of Louise Kelley's; and the Research Publication's Western Americana collection (microfilm).

TX —AMARILLO PUBLIC LIBRARY, 413 E Fourth, Amarillo, 79101. Mary Kay Snell, Librn
Holdings: Vols Cat Mss Maps Pix
Notes: Collections

TX —UNIVERSITY OF TEXAS, ARLINGTON, Library, PO Box 19497, Arlington, 76019. Chas Colley, Dir Special Collections
Holdings: Vols (8000) Cat Mss Maps Pix Microforms
Notes: Research collection documenting the history and culture of Texas and the American Southwest. Contains a wide range of Texana, especially pre-statehood Texas. Incl one of the most important collections relating to the US-Mexican War, incl all of the items from the Eberstadt Collection relevant to the war. Much rare 19th century Texana. Library routinely acquires all monographs and serial secondary publications of research importance. Separate catalog.

TX —AUSTIN PUBLIC LIBRARY, Austin History Center, 810 Guadalupe Street, PO Box 2287, Austin, 78768. Audray Bateman, Cur
Holdings: Vols 3235 Cat Mss Maps Pix

TEXAS—HISTORY (cont.)

Slides Microforms
Budget: $155,000
Notes: The Austin History Center collection incl approx 370 periodical titles; 69,678 printed items (programs, pamphlets, etc); 2800 scrapbooks and journals; 340 taped interviews, 92,000 mss; 752 maps; 80,000 pictures; 5000 slides; 94,000 clippings. All materials are cataloged. Books are cataloged with library's general collection, but all other materials are cataloged separately. A local newspaper, started in 1871, is in the process of being indexed from the beginning and the current newspaper index is kept up-to-date. A publication program under the name of the Waterloo Press has been sponsored by the Austin History Center Association. To date, 7 books have been produced from original material in the collection. 7 paperback compilations of articles on local history appearing weekly in the local newspaper have beenpublished.

TX —TEXAS STATE LIBRARY, Archives Div, 1201 Brazos, PO Box 12927, Capitol Sta, Austin, 78711. David B Gracy II, State Archivist
Holdings: Vols 30,000 Cat Mss Maps Pix Microforms
Notes: Collections are limited to Texas history, primarily archives of the Texas state government. Mss, 25,000 cubic ft; 3000 maps; 35,000 pictures; 5000 microfilms.

TX —UNIVERSITY OF TEXAS LIBRARIES, General Libraries, Barker Texas History Center, PO Box P, Austin, 78712. Don Carleton, Dir
Holdings: Vols (132,000) Cat Mss Maps Pix Slides Phonorecords Audiotapes Microforms
Notes: Materials pertaining to the historical, social, economic, scientific, humanistic and literary development of Texas and the American Southwest. Rich in early state imprints, as well as the period of the Republic of Texas. Archival and ms holdings measure over 22,000 linear feet. Texas history prior to the Republic is covered by the Bexar Archives; records kept by Spanish and Mexican officials in San Antonio, 1717-1836. The collection was transferred to the University of Texas by the Commissioner's Court of Bexar County in 1899. Incl records relating to government administration and to all aspects of military, ecclesiastical and civil life in Spanish and Mexican Texas. Over 250,000 ms pages and 400 printed pages; also, a microfilm edition (172 reels) published by the University of Texas Library, 1967-1971.

TX —UNIVERSITY OF TEXAS LIBRARIES, General Libraries, Barker Texas History Center, PO Box P, Austin, 78712. Don Carleton, Dir
Notes: Papers of Dr Joseph Henry Barnard (1804-1861), surgeon in the 1836 Texas Revolution. Incl names and statistics relative to the Battle of Coleto, 19 March 1836; also other professional and financial papers.

TX —LEE COLLEGE, Library, PO Box 818, Baytown, 77522. William K Peace, Librn
Notes: Oral history tapes covering the area of east Harris County, Texas. Early history of Baytown, Goose Creek, and Pelly, with some relating to the early development of Humble Oil and Refining Company as remembered by early residents of the area. Also in the western area of Chambers County, Texas, known as Barbers Hill. The original tapes are housed in the Lee College Library, with copies located in the Sterling Municipal Library of Baytown. Incl 75 tapes; 50 transcripts.

TX —PANHANDLE-PLAINS HISTORICAL MUSEUM, Research Center, Box 967, WT Sta, Canyon, 79016. Claire R Kuehn, Archivist-Librn
Holdings: Vols 8000 Cat Mss Maps Pix Microforms
Budget: $2000
Notes: History of the Texas Panhandle. Incl interviews with early settlers taken over a 50-year period, ranch records, and business records relating to the Texas Panhandle and surrounding states.

TX —WEST TEXAS STATE UNIVERSITY, Cornette Library, PO Box 748 WT Sta, Canyon, 79016. Faye Hendrickson, Special Collections Asst
Holdings: Vols (1850) Uncat Microforms
Notes: Includes microfilm collection.

TX —EAST TEXAS GENEALOGICAL ASSOCIATION, Library, 412A West College St, Carthage, 75633. L R Bagwell, Librn
Holdings: Vols (1200) Cat Mss Maps Pix Slides Microforms
Notes: Local history and genealogy; not confined to Texas.

TX —CISCO JUNIOR COLLEGE, Maner Memorial Library, LRC Rte 3, Cisco, 76437. Oleta Shirley, Dir
Holdings: Vols 3000 Cat
Notes: Texana and history of the Southwest.

TX —EAST TEXAS STATE UNIVERSITY, James G Gee Library, Special Collections Dept, East Texas Station, Commerce, 75428. James Conrad, Dept Head
Holdings: Vols (3500) Cat Mss Pix Slides
Budget: ($3000)
Notes: Extensive collection of county histories of Texas. In the process of classifying and preparing catalog cards for archival materials (photographs, non-photographic materials such as deeds, commencement programs, business records, etc and various items relating to the East Texas State University from its beginning as a private school in 1894 as East Texas Normal College). Photographs and mss have been processed and findings aids prepared.

TX —DALLAS PUBLIC LIBRARY, Texas/ Dallas History and Archives Division, 1515 Young St, Dallas, 75201. Richard L Waters, Acting Dir; Wayne Gray, Manager
Holdings: Vols (152,442) Cat Maps Pix Slides Microforms
Budget: ($38,540)
Notes: Dallas and Texas history.

TX —UNIVERSITY OF TEXAS, DALLAS, Health Science Center, Reference Dept & History of Health Sciences Dept, 5323 Harry Hines Blvd, Dallas, 75235. Helen Mayo, Head
Holdings: Vols (10,000) Cat Pix Slides Audiotapes Videotapes Microforms
Notes: History of Medicine collection contains ca 10,000 vols. This total is comprised of pre-1900 journals, primary materials in the History of Medicine and the History of Science, and secondary studies in these two areas. The major strengths of this collection are in the areas of epidemics and plagues, military medicine, and collected works of famous medical pioneers. Incl in this collection are the medical journals published by the county medical societies in Texas, local publications by Dallas County medical organizations, and ephemeral material in a similar vein. The university archives contain all theses and dissertations form UTHSCD and miscellaneous institutional documents circulated by the school's administration.

TX —NORTH TEXAS STATE UNIVERSITY, Archives, NT Station Box 5188, Denton, 76203. Robert LaForte, University Archivist
Notes: Depository for the Texas Regional Historical Resource Depositories Program. Retired county records for Cooke, Denton, Montague, and Wise counties. 186 linear feet. Published Description: *Finding Guide for Microfilm Holdings of the Regional Historical Resource Depositories and Local Records Division.* Austin: Texas State Library, ca 1981. Also, collections on industry, agriculture, politics and government.
See also entries under Agriculture - Texas; Oral History - Collections; Texas - Politics and Government.

TX —NORTH TEXAS STATE UNIVERSITY, Rare Book and Texana Collections, NT Station Box 5188, Denton, 76203. Kenneth Lavender, University Bibliographer
Holdings: Vols 325 Cat
Notes: Texas County histories. Also, city histories of Texas. Separate card catalog.

TX —TEXAS WOMAN'S UNIVERSITY, Bralley Memorial Library, Box 23715, TWU Sta, Denton, 76204. Metta Nicewarner, Spec

Collections Libn
Holdings: Vols Uncat Mss Pix
Notes: The exhibit, "Texas Women: A Celebration of History," prepared by Texas Foundation for Women's Resources, for the Texas Women's History Project, and all resource material used in its completion. Includes books, pamphlets, oral histories, photographs, correspondence and manuscripts.

TX —EL PASO PUBLIC LIBRARY, Southwest Collection, 501 N Oregon, El Paso, 79901. Mary A Sarber, Head
Holdings: Vols (12,000) Cat Mss Maps Pix
Budget: ($11,000)
Notes: Research collection includes rare books and mss journals, vertical files, index to El Paso newspapers, microfilmed newspapers, photographs, and architectural plans. Separate catalog. Limited to materials on Texas, New Mexico, Arizona and Mexico. Special collections of material by and about Tom Lea Jr, and Carl Hertzog. Aultman Collection of photographs includes 3500 on El Paso Southwest and 2500 on Mexican Revolution. Cited in Lovelace, Lisa, "The Southwest Collection of the El Paso Public Library". *Great Plains Journal*, vol 2, no 2, pp 161-166; Aultman, Otis A *Photographs from the Border: The Otis A Aultman Collection,* El Paso Public Library Association, 1977.

TX —UNIVERSITY OF TEXAS, EL PASO, Library, El Paso, 79968. Fred W Hanes, Dir
Holdings: Vols (8440) Cat
Budget: ($5000)

TX —AMON CARTER MUSEUM, Library, 3510 Camp Bowie Blvd, PO Box 2365, Fort Worth, 76113. Nancy G Wynne, Librn
Holdings: Vols (25,000) Cat Mss Pix
Notes: The book collection, microfilm and photo archives have been built toward the goal of the interpretation of American history through art. At present, the greatest strengths are in Americana, Western Canadiana, bibliography, American exhibition catalogs and history of photography. Substantial books and files on American artists of the 19th and early 20th century, and particularly of Charles M Russell and Frederic Remington. Incl 25,000 pictures; 13,000 slides.
See also entries under Newspapers, American; Pictures - Collections.

TX —SOUTHWESTERN BAPTIST THEOLOGICAL SEMINARY, Roberts Library, 2001 W Seminary Dr, PO Box 22000-2E, Fort Worth, 76122. Keith C Wills, Dir
Holdings: Vols 475 Cat Mss Pix Microforms
Budget: $2500

TX —COOKE COUNTY COLLEGE, Mary Josephine Cox Memorial Library, PO Box 815, Gainesville, 76240. Patsy L Wilson, Dir
Holdings: Uncat
Notes: Emphasis on Cooke County College and county history.

TX —ROSENBERG LIBRARY, Galveston and Texas History Center, 2310 Sealy Ave, Galveston, 77550. Jane Kenamore, Archivist
Holdings: Vols 7368 Cat Mss Maps Pix Slides Microforms
Budget: $60,000
Notes: Emphasis on upper Texas coast material; Republic of Texas period; Civil War period; Shipping; Texas Navy; Jean Laffite; Texas politics, 19th-20th century; Railroads; Texas journalism, incl microfilms of Galveston newspapers, 1838-date.

TX —HOUSTON ACADEMY OF MEDICINE-TEXAS MEDICAL CENTER, Library, Jesse H Jones Library Bldg, Houston, 77030. Elizabeth Borst White, Special Collections Librn
Holdings: Uncat Mss Pix Videotapes
Notes: This collection documents the history of medical practice, education and research in Houston and Harris County, Texas. The archives concern institutions or hospitals within the Texas Medical Center, and the careers of local physicians, nurses and biomedical researchers. 450 linear ft of mss, 6000 photographs.

TX —HOUSTON POST LIBRARY, 4747 Southwest Freeway, Houston, 77001. Kathy Foley, Librn
Holdings: Cat Maps Pix Microforms
Notes: Incl 5,000,000 clippings and 3,000, 000 pictures.

TEXAS—HISTORY (cont.)

TX —RICE UNIVERSITY, Fondren Library, Woodson Research Center, 6100 S Main St, PO Box 1892, Houston, 77251. Nancy Parker, Dir Woodson Research Center
Holdings: Mss Maps Pix
Notes: Incl Texas family papers, letters, diaries, business records in several collections.

TX —UNIVERSITY OF HOUSTON, M D Anderson Memorial Library, University Park, Houston, 77004. David Farmer, Cur, Special Collections; Jean Jackson, Assistant Cur
Holdings: Vols 650 Cat Mss Maps Pix
Notes: Emphasis is on 20th century Houston and Harris County, with other local, county, and church histories. Some company histories and family histories are also purchased for this collection. Gulf Coast Area is another subject emphasis. Bulk of the collection is printed vols and several hundred pamphlets incl some of the oldest Texas almanacs. Basis were the collections of Major Richard Burgess of El Paso and the William B Bates Collection of Texana and Western Americana. The Bates Collection is described in two exhibit catalogs. *The William B Bates Collection,* by Lorene Pouncey, Houston, 1965, and *The William B Bates Collection* by Marian Orgain, Houston, 1971. Stress is upon the annexation of Texas and the Mexican War.

TX —SAM HOUSTON STATE UNIVERSITY, Library, PO Box 2179, Huntsville, 77340. Chas Dwyer, Librn
Holdings: Vols 2880 Cat Mss Pix Microforms
Notes: The Porter Confederate Collection is particularly rich in rare material relating to Texas in the Confederacy.

TX —SAN JACINTO MUSEUM OF HISTORY ASSOCIATION, Library, 3800 Park Rd 1836, La Porte, 77571. Winston Atkins, Librn
Holdings: Vols 10,000 Cat Mss Maps Pix
Budget: $5000
Notes: Texas and regional history, incl the exploration and settlement of Texas and Mexico by the Spanish and the Anglo-Texans. Manuscript collection covers period from early 16th century through early 20th century. Primary languages represented: Spanish and English. 200 linear feet.

TX —STEPHEN F AUSTIN STATE UNIVERSITY, Ralph W Steen Library, Special Collections Dept, Box 13055, SFA Sta, Nacogdoches, 75962. Linda Cheves Nicklas, Special Collections Librn
Holdings: Vols (13,500) Cat Mss Maps Pix
Budget: ($5000)
Notes: Emphasis on local and university-related subjects, especially people, culture, events, buildings of Texas, East Texas, and historic Nacogdoches. Extensive ms collection (1200 linear ft); 344 maps; 1600 pictures. Published description: SFASU, *A Guide to Special Collections,* 1980.

TX —ECTOR COUNTY LIBRARY, Texas-Southwest History & Genealogy Dept, 321 W 5th St, Odessa, 79761. Jan Carter, Head
Holdings: Vols (8500) Cat Maps Pix
Budget: ($4000)
Notes: A card catalog of Texas-History; Southwest, New-History; Oklahoma-History is located in the Texas-Southwest History Dept. A card file by subject is a guide to vertical file materials and Texas, New Mexico, Oklahoma, Arizona periodicals. The Texas-History collection has reference, closed shelf, and circulating books.

TX —INSTITUTE OF TEXAN CULTURES, Library, 801 S Bowie Street, PO Box 1226, San Antonio, 78294. Deborah Large, Dir of Library Services
Holdings: Vols (4500) Cat Pix Slides
Budget: ($5200)
Notes: Incl 88,000 pictures and 7000 slides.

TX —SAINT MARY'S UNIVERSITY, Library, 2700 Cincinnati Ave, San Antonio, 78284. Anita C Saxine, Special Collections Librn
Notes: Spanish Colonial History of the Texas Borderlands incl the Spanish archives of

Laredo, 1749-1850. Two bibliographical guides to materials in Special Collections were compiled by Anita C Saxine in 1983: *Reference Sources in Spanish Colonial History of Texas* (Academic Library Guide, no 12, 27 pp); *Penisular War, 1807-1814 by Contemporary Observers* (Academic Library Guide, no 13, 18 pp).

TX —SAN ANTONIO COLLEGE, Library, 1001 Howard St, San Antonio, 78284. James O Wallace, Dir
Holdings: Vols 3500 Cat
Notes: Especially strong for San Antonio and Southwest Texas.

TX —SAN ANTONIO CONSERVATION SOCIETY, Library & Archives, Foundation Library, 107 King William St, San Antonio, 78204. Roland T Jones, Librn
Holdings: Vols 2500 Cat Mss Maps Pix Slides VF
Budget: ($1000)
Notes: San Antonio historic structures and their preservation. SACS Library is staffed entirely by volunteer members of the Society. Architectural plans with vertical files; 750 clippings. Limited hours.

TX —TRINITY UNIVERSITY, Elizabeth Coates Maddux Library, 715 Stadium Dr, San Antonio, 78284. Richard Hume Werking, Library Dir; Craig Likness, Head Bibliographer
Holdings: Vols 1600
Notes: Materials from the collections of Pat Ireland Nixon, Paul Adams and Joe Nicholson.

TX —AUSTIN COLLEGE, Arthur Hopkins Library, 900 N Grand Ave, Sherman, 75090. Gene Gibson, College Librn
Holdings: Vols 595 Cat

TX —BAYLOR UNIVERSITY, Moody Memorial Library, Texas History Collection, Waco, 76706. Kent Keeth, Librn
Holdings: Vols (80,000) Cat Mss Maps Pix Slides Phonorecords Audiotapes Microforms
Notes: The Texas Collection gathers materials which relate to life in Texas in all aspects, from earliest days to the present. Incl Baylor University Archives.

TX —GRAND LODGE OF TEXAS, AF & AM Library & Museum, 715 Columbus Ave, Box 446, Waco, 76702. Janet M Melton, Librn; Emery Stewart, Cur
Holdings: Vols 3500 Cat Mss Maps Pix
Budget: $1500

TX —STAR OF THE REPUBLIC MUSEUM, Library, PO Box 317, Washington, 77880. D Ryan Smith Dir
Holdings: Vols Cat Mss Maps Slides
Notes: Books, maps, mss, etc dealing with the Texas republic; scope incl Spanish Colonial period and Mexican War (1690-1848).

TX —KEMP PUBLIC LIBRARY, 1300 Lamar St, Wichita Falls, 76301. Jeannine Humphris, Libr Admin
Holdings: Vols (1775) Cat Mss Maps

TX —MIDWESTERN STATE UNIVERSITY, Moffett Library, 3400 Taft St, Wichita Falls, 76308.
Holdings: Vols 250 Cat

VA —VIRGINIA POLYTECHNIC INSTITUTE AND STATE UNIVERSITY LIBRARY, Blacksburg, 24061. Glenn L McMullen, Special Collections Librn
Holdings: Vols (4000)
Notes: Collection largely consists of nineteenth century and early twentieth century imprints, emphasizing the role of native Virginians in the development of the trans-Mississippi West, particularly Texas; cowboys and the cattle industry; outlaws and lawlessness; and emigrants' guidebooks to states, cities, and regions in the West.

TEXAS—IMPRINTS

TX —UNIVERSITY OF TEXAS LIBRARIES, General Libraries, Barker Texas History Center, PO Box P, Austin, 78712. Don Carleton, Dir
Holdings: Vols (132,000) Cat Mss Maps Pix Slides Phonorecords Audiotapes Microforms
Notes: See description of collection under Texas-History.

TX —UNIVERSITY OF HOUSTON, M D Anderson Memorial Library, University

Park, Houston, 77004. David Farmer, Cur, Special Collections; Jean Jackson, Assistant Cur
Holdings: Vols 300 Cat
Notes: The collection concentrates on printed materials after the period covered in the Streeter bibliography. Emphasis is on productions of small publishers and nongovernmental publications. Houston imprints collection incl work of job printers as well as commercially produced books, 1845-1920.

TEXAS—LABOR

TX —UNIVERSITY OF TEXAS, ARLINGTON, Library, PO Box 19497, Arlington, 76019. Chas Colley, Dir Special Collections
Holdings: Mss Pix Microforms
Notes: The Texas Labor Archives is a major depository of primary source materials documenting the history of the labor movement in Texas. The The Archives houses records representing local unions and labor councils, statewide labor organizations, union political groups, and district and regional offices of international unions. In addition, many individuals who have been active in unions have donated their personal files and granted tapes interviews concerning their activities in the labor movement. Persons and organizations desiring to retain their original records have allowed the Archives to make copies.

TX —NORTH TEXAS STATE UNIVERSITY, Archives, NT Station Box 5188, Denton, 76203. Robert LaForte, University Archivist
Notes: Labor arbitration manuscript collections incl the papers of arbitrators Byron R Abernathy, J D Dunn, and Elvis Stephens. These arbitration papers cover the years 1960-1980 and emphasize cases in the southwestern United States and Puerto Rico. Published Description: J D Dunn and Elvis Stephens Collections, *The National Union Catalog of Manuscript Collections: Catalog 1979* Washington: Library of Congress, 1980. Page 214.

TEXAS—LIBRARIES

TX —TEXAS STATE LIBRARY, Library Development Division, Library Science Collection, PO Box 12927, 1201 Brazos, Austin, 78711. Anne Ramos, Librn
Holdings: Vols (5837) Cat Audiotapes Videotapes VF
Budget: ($47,851)

TEXAS—MAPS

TX —TEXAS A&M UNIVERSITY, Sterling C Evans Library, College Station, 77843. Judith Rieke, Map Librn; Irene B Hoadley, Dir of Libraries
Notes: Maps of all areas of the world with geographic emphasis on the US and Texas. Subject emphasis on geology, petroleum, soils, highways and streets. Depository for NOS coastal and bathymetric charts, DMA maps, and USGS topographic and geologic maps. An extensive file of publisher's catalogs is available to the public. Collection incls aerial photographs (1100), atlases and gazetteers (1500), maps (82,600).

TX —NORTH TEXAS STATE UNIVERSITY, Government Documents Dept, NT Station Box 5188, Denton, 76203. Melody Kelley, Librn
Notes: 9000 maps, mostly Texas topographic maps.

TX —ROSENBERG LIBRARY, Galveston and Texas History Center, 2310 Sealy Ave, Galveston, 77550. Jane Kenamore, Archivist
Notes: Galveston and Texas maps incl many rarities. US Geological Survey depository.

TEXAS—NATURAL RESOURCES

†TX —UNIVERSITY OF TEXAS, EL PASO, Library, El Paso, 79968.
Notes: Significant collections of water resources information about Texas and California.

TEXAS—POLITICS AND GOVERNMENT

TX —UNIVERSITY OF TEXAS, ARLINGTON, Library, PO Box 19497,

TEXAS—POLITICS AND GOVERNMENT (cont.)

Arlington, 76019. Chas Colley, Dir Special Collections
Holdings: Cat Mss Pix Phonorecords Audiotapes
Notes: The Texas Political History Collection at the University of Texas at Arlington Library is one of the state's leading depositories of 20th century political records. The collection contains the papers of former and current elected officials, of political groups, and of private citizens who have influenced the course of Texas politics and government. Materials in the collection include correspondence, photographs, leaflets, scrapbooks, minutes, and financial records.

TX —UNIVERSITY OF TEXAS LIBRARIES, General Libraries, Barker Texas History Center, PO Box P, Austin, 78712. Don Carleton, Dir

TX —TEXAS A&M UNIVERSITY, Sterling C Evans Library, University Archives, College Station, 77843. Charles R Schultz, University Archivist
Notes: The Archives of Modern Politics: the papers of Texas Congressman Olin E Teague, 1946-1975; Graham Purcell, 1961-1971; Robert R Casey, 1958-1976; and John Young, 1963-1976; Texas Legislators Will L Smith, 1962-1971; Tom Creighton, 1961-1980; Bill Presnal 1974-1983, and Bill Clayton, 1961-1983; Washington DC journalist Bascom N Timmons, ca 1920-1970; and political candidate and religious zealot Jonnie Mae Hackworth, ca 1945-1980.

TX —NORTH TEXAS STATE UNIVERSITY, Archives, NT Station Box 5188, Denton, 76203. Robert LaForte, University Archivist
Notes: Fred H Minor Collection (former Texas Speaker of the House), the Alvin M Owsley Collection (former US diplomat from Texas), the Hermine Tobolowsky Equal Legal Rights Collection (leader of women's equal legal rights in Texas), and the Bullock Hyder Collection (former representative to Texas House from Lewisville). The collections cover Texas politics from the 1920s to the 1970s. Published Description: Fred H Minor Collection, *The National Union Catalog of Manuscript Collections: Catalog 1979* Washington: Library of Congress, 1980. Page 214. Alvin M Owsley Collection, Ibid, p 215. Hermine Tobolowsky Equal Legal Rights Collection, Ibid.

TX —TEXAS WOMAN'S UNIVERSITY, Bralley Memorial Library, Box 23715, TWU Sta, Denton, 76204. Metta Nicewarner, Spec Collections Librn
Holdings: Vols Uncat Mss Audiotapes
Notes: The Hermine Tobolowsky Collection includes material on the Texas lawyer called the "Mother of the Equal Legal Rights Amendment in Texas". Items include correspondence, congressional bills and resolutions, court cases, campaign and platform congressional pledges of support.

TX —UNIVERSITY OF HOUSTON, M D Anderson Memorial Library, University Park, Houston, 77004. David Farmer, Cur, Special Collections; Jean Jackson, Assistant Cur
Holdings: Cat Mss Pix Audiotapes
Notes: This collection consists of 360 document boxes of the personal and public papers of Gov James V Allred, 1920-1960, and family material from 1960 to present date. Some material restricted.

TX —MIDWESTERN STATE UNIVERSITY, Moffett Library, 3400 Taft St, Wichita Falls, 76308.
Holdings: // Uncat Mss
Notes: Papers and correspondence of State Senator George Moffett (Texas) from 1931 to 1964. No separate catalog or index to the collection.

TEXAS—SOCIAL LIFE AND CUSTOMS

TX —NORTH TEXAS STATE UNIVERSITY, Archives, NT Station Box 5188, Denton, 76203. Robert LaForte, University Archivist
Notes: The NTSU Archives houses the patron's copy of oral history interviews that are part of the Oral History Collection, an independent project not part of the Archives. This collection of interviews covers, in part, the following subject areas: World War II Pearl Harbor survivors, World War II prisoners of war, Texas legislators, ex-governors of Texas, Texans employed by the administrations of FDR, Texas businessmen and businesswomen, development of the Coastal Bend area of south Texas, and Mexican-American social action activities. Cataloged. Transcriptions available. See *Oral History Collection,* North Texas State University Bulletin, April 1981.

TX —INSTITUTE OF TEXAN CULTURES, Library, 801 S Bowie Street, PO Box 1226, San Antonio, 78294. Deborah Large, Dir of Library Services
Holdings: Vols (4500) Cat Pix Slides
Budget: ($60,000)
Notes: Incl 88,000 pictures and 7000 slides.

TEXAS ARCHITECTURE see Architecture, Texas

TEXAS AUTHORS see Authors, Texas

TEXAS COMPOSERS see Composers, Texas

TEXAS ENGINEERING EXPERIMENT STATION

TX —TEXAS A&M UNIVERSITY, Sterling C Evans Library, University Archives, College Station, 77843. Charles R Schultz, University Archivist
Notes: The Archives of Southwestern Technology: Records of the Texas Engineering Experiment Station, ca 1914-1970.

TEXAS INSTRUMENTS CORPORATION

TX —TEXAS INSTRUMENTS INC, Library, PO Box 1443, Houston, 77001. Helen Manning, Librn
Holdings: Vols (800) Cat Microforms
Notes: Systems, design, and marketing of microprocessors and electronic semiconductors. Not open to the public.

TEXAS MUSIC see Music, Texas

TEXAS NEWSPAPERS see Newspapers, Texas

TEXTBOOKS—COLLECTIONS

CA —CLAREMONT COLLEGES, Honnold Library, Ninth & Dartmouth, Claremont, 91711. Tania Rizzo, Special Collections Dept Head
Holdings: Vols 200 Uncat
Notes: Early American textbooks, 1713-1881, but chiefly 1800-1850; 3 Confederate imprints, checklisted. See Mauger, Rosa Cage (donor), *Early American School Books Bibliography,* typescript 1957. Restricted use.

CA —CALIFORNIA STATE UNIVERSITY, LONG BEACH, Reference Center, 1250 Bellflower Blvd, Long Beach, 90840.
Holdings: Vols 18,010
Notes: 18,010 textbooks, 14,565 curriculum guides, 1075 teaching aids.

CA —UNIVERSITY OF CALIFORNIA, LOS ANGELES, Research Library, Dept of Special Collections, 405 Hilgard Ave, Los Angeles, 90024. Edward Shreeves, Chairman, Bibliographers Group; David S Zeidberg, Head
Notes: Various collections, incl books, pamphlets, and ephemera by and about Georg Michael Kerschensteiner; modern pre-primers from various countries; 19th century elementary and secondary school textbooks, chiefly American; 20th century California school directories; William Nicholas Hailmann Collection on kindergarten education.

CA —SAN FRANCISCO STATE UNIVERSITY, J Paul Leonard Library, 1630 Holloway Ave, San Francisco, 94132. Susan Quinlan, Curriculum Librn
Holdings: Vols (49,246) Cat Phonorecords Audiotapes 8mm Films Microforms
Budget: ($8500)
Notes: The young people's collection or children's literature collection of 17,843 vols incl books with reading and interest levels ranging from preschool through senior high school. The Marguerite Archer collection of historical children's books contains an additional 3000 vols. Have 19,755 textbooks, 5150 curriculum guides, 1970 pamphlets. Collection emphasizes instructional materials that can be utitlized in the school classroom. Professional books and journals and other media relating to educational history, philosophy, research, theories of teaching, etc are in the main collection.

CO —SOCIAL SCIENCE EDUCATION CONSORTIUM, Resource & Demonstration Center (RDC), 855 Broadway, Boulder, 80302. Regina McCormick, Staff Assoc
Holdings: Vols (16,000) Cat Filmstrips Microforms
Notes: Contains over 15,000 elementary and secondary social studies textbooks, audiovisuals, games and simulations, professional books, and the complete ERIC microfiche collection. Staff available to travel to all parts of the US to consult on curriculum development, instructional methods, materials analysis and selction, evaluation, new materials, teaching strategies, and trends in the social studies.

CT —TRINITY COLLEGE LIBRARY, Watkinson Library, 300 Summit St, Hartford, 06106. Jeffrey Kaimowitz, Cur
Holdings: Vols 7000 Cat
Notes: The Henry Barnard Collection of early American textbooks.

FL —UNIVERSITY OF SOUTH FLORIDA, Library, Tampa, 33620. J B Dobkin, Special Collections Librn
Holdings: Vols 1000 Cat Msss
Budget: ($7500)
Notes: Early American Textbook Collection is limited to books published for use in American primary and secondary schools during the period 1800-1865, regardless of edition. With few exceptions, only works written by American authors are collected. Specimens of American textbooks published before 1800 are collected when encountered, but are not systematically acquired. Textbooks dealing with any subject taught in American schools during the period of interest are suitable for inclusion.

IL —CENTER FOR RESEARCH LIBRARIES, 6050 S Kenwood Ave, Chicago, 60637. Donald B Simpson, Dir; Esther Smith, Collection Development Librn
Holdings: Vols 85,000 Uncat
Notes: US elementary and secondary school textbooks 1850-, shelf arranged by author within broad subject classes.

IL —UNIVERSITY OF CHICAGO LIBRARY, Dept of Special Collections, 1100 E 57 St, Chicago, 60637.
Notes: Littlefield Collection of Early American School Books.

IL —ILLINOIS STATE UNIVERSITY, Milner Library, Dept of Special Collections, Normal, 61761. Robert Sokan, Librn
Holdings: Vols 4150 Uncat
Notes: Cutoff date is 1900. Incl an elementary and secondary textbooks collection.

IN —INDIANA UNIVERSITY, School of Education, Library, Bloomington, 47401. Adele Dendy, Head Librn
Holdings: Vols (35,000) Cat Pix Slides Phonorecords Audiotapes 16mm Films Filmstrips Microforms
Budget:
Notes: Library has complete ERIC collection of microfiche (277,308). 2098 non-ERIC items, 226 serials, and 22,823 nonprint items (housed in educational materials center). Emphasis on recent materials; the historic collections in education are located in the Main Library. The collection is geared to graduate level studies and research. A separate Teaching Materials Center includes 10,000 elementary and secondary textbooks. The Center also includes curriculum guides,

TEXTBOOKS—COLLECTIONS (cont.)

supplementary materials and 17,823 nonprint teaching aids.

IN —INDIANAPOLIS-MARION COUNTY PUBLIC LIBRARY, Social Sciences Div, PO Box 211, Indianapolis, 46206. Lois R Laube, Head
Holdings: Vols 327 Uncat
Notes: Restricted use.

IN —BALL STATE UNIVERSITY, University Libraries, Muncie, 47306. Michael B Wood, Dean
Holdings: Vols 18,000 Cat Pix
Notes: Incl standardized tests; historical collection of textbooks, 1787-1945.

IN —INDIANA STATE UNIVERSITY, Cunningham Memorial Library, Dept of Rare Books & Special Collections, Terre Haute, 47809. Lawrence J McCrank, Head
Holdings: Vols 750 Uncat
Budget: $350
Notes: The private collections of B Walker and W Floyd provided the core of a collection of American textbooks (and European imprints known to have been used in America) primarily of the 1800s (pre WWI), with a special emphasis on titles used in Indiana and the Old Northwest. Collection strengths include readers of all types, geographics, and elementary mathematics. See also the Cunningham Collection of the classics in American education.

KY —UNIVERSITY OF KENTUCKY, Margaret I King Library, Dept of Special Collections, Lexington, 40506. William Marshall, Head
Holdings: Vols (400) Uncat
Notes: Early physical education manuals and textbooks to 1925; 18th and 19th century sports, games.

†MD —UNIVERSITY OF MARYLAND, Library, Music Educators National Conference Historical Center, College Park, 20742. Bruce Wilson, Cur
Holdings: Cat Mss Pix Audiotapes
Notes: The official archive of the Music Educators National Conference (MENC) and a repository for the documentation of music education. Incl the papers of the MENC, state units, and associated organizations and committees; personal papers and association items (notably, relating to Frances Elliott Clark, Lowell Mason, and Luther Whiting Mason); published proceedings of MENC and other groups; oral histories, numerous school music textbooks, and the archive of the Contemporary Music Project.

MA —JONES LIBRARY, 43 Amity St, Amherst, 01002. Daniel J Lombardo, Cur of Special Collections
Holdings: Vols (583) Cat
Notes: The Clifton Johnson Collection of textbooks and children's literature. Books of the 18th and 19th centuries, for use within the library. Does not circulate.

MA —HARVARD UNIVERSITY, Graduate School of Education, Monroe C Gutman Library, 6 Appian Way, Cambridge, 02138. Susan S Baughman, Associate Librn
Holdings: Vols (150,000) Cat Mss Microforms
Budget: ($95,000)
Notes: Incl historical textbook collection of 35,000 volumes, primarily 19th century, and 4000 educational and psychological tests.

MA —HARVARD UNIVERSITY LIBRARY, Cambridge, 02138.
Holdings: Cat
Notes: Downs: 1951, 1953, 1960. Especially early history and textbooks.

MA —HISTORIC DEERFIELD-POCUMTUCK VALLEY MEMORIAL ASSOCIATION, Libraries, Memorial St, Box 53, Deerfield, 01342. David R Proper, Librn
Holdings: Vols (17,000) Cat Mss Maps Pix Microforms
Notes: Local and regional history, especially western Massachusetts. Also, remnants of several collection of books available to early Deerfield and Greenfield residents. Strong ms collection dealing with the region's

families, businesses, etc. These consist of sermons, diaries, town and church records, voluntary societies' archives, etc. Extensive collection of photographs of the people and buildings of Deerfield and its environs, and travels in Maine, California, and England (1880s to 1920s). Also, large collection of glassplate negatives. Houses the Connecticut Valley Bibliography, a comprehensive card file on the history and culture of the Connecticut Valley of Massachusetts.

MA —OLD STURBRIDGE VILLAGE, Research Library, Sturbridge, 01566. Theresa Rini Percy, Librn
Holdings: Cat
Notes: Northeastern US, to 1860.

MA —AMERICAN ANTIQUARIAN SOCIETY LIBRARY, 185 Salisbury St, Worcester, 01609. Marcus A McCorison, Dir & Librn
Notes: Probably the most complete collection of American school texts published before 1821; sparse for later years.

MA —WORCESTER STATE COLLEGE, Learning Resources Center, 486 Chandler St, Worcester, 01602. William G Piekarski, Special Collections Librn
Holdings: Vols (9000) Cat Pix Microforms
Budget: ($12,000)
Notes: Collection contains 9000 elementary and secondary textbooks, 1000 curriculum guides covering the entire US, 800 samples of professional tests, kits, games software. Separate catalog.

MI —MICHIGAN STATE UNIVERSITY, Libraries, Special Collections Div, East Lansing, 48824. Jannette Fiore, Librn
Notes: The Russel B Nye Popular Culture Collection in the Michigan State Univ Libraries incl over (45,000) items. Most of the collection is organized into 4 categories: comic art, popular fiction, popular information materials and materials relating to the popular performing arts. About 3900 items. Almanacs, Blue Books, and works popularizing knowledge or offering self-help and how-to advice. There are ca 350 issues of 100 19th and 20th century almanacs. The Blue Books incl ca 2000 Little Blue Books, over 600 Big Blue Books and a good number of issues of the various Haldeman-Julius magazines. In addition to almanacs and Blue Books, Popular Information incl books of advice on etiquette, life and love, how-to-succeed books, popular history, science and biography, and several hundred public schooltextbooks from the 19th and early 20th centuries.

MO —SAINT LOUIS UNIVERSITY, Pius XII Memorial Library, Saint Louis Room Collection, 3655 W Pine Blvd, Saint Louis, 63108. Catherine E Weidle, Rare Books Librn
Holdings: Vols Cat Mss
Notes: Books on early education, Jesuitica and Western Americana. Related collections of works by Peter Ramus (University is center for Ramist studies) and Omer Talon; also collections on the Spiritual Exercises of St Ignatius Loyola and on the Sodality of Our Lady. Mss uncataloged.

NH —PLYMOUTH STATE COLLEGE, Lamson Library, Plymouth, 03264. Phillip Wei, Dir of Library Services
Holdings: Cat Pix Microforms Films
Budget: ($30,000)
Notes: Incl 30,000 print and 87,000 nonprint items.

NJ —GLASSBORO STATE COLLEGE, Savitz Library, Stewart Room, Glassboro, 08028. Clara Kirner, Special Collection Librn
Holdings: Vols 164 Cat
Notes: Early 19th-century textbooks.

NJ —RUTGERS, THE STATE UNIVERSITY OF NEW JERSEY, Alexander Library, Special Collections and Archives, College Ave & Huntington St, New Brunswick, 08903. Ronald L Becker, Cur of Manuscripts and Rare Books
Notes: Large collection of textbooks in Special Collections and in Alexander Library. Primarily American and English material of the 18th and 19th centuries. Partially cataloged.

NJ —TRENTON STATE COLLEGE, Roscoe L West Library, Pennington Rd, PO Box

940, Trenton, 08625. Paul A DuBois, Dir
Holdings: Vols 675 // Cat
Notes: Primarily 19th-century American school textbooks (spellers, readers, etc) many of which were published before the Civil War.

NJ —MONTCLAIR STATE COLLEGE, Harry A Sprague Library, Upper Montclair, 07043.
Holdings: Vols 10,000 Cat Microforms
Notes: The library holds the complete ERIC collection of microfiche. The Curriculum Laboratory contains some 5000 textbooks and 2500 courses of study in addition to the main collection.

NY —EASTCHESTER HISTORICAL SOCIETY LIBRARY, Box 37, Eastchester, 10709. Madeline D Schaeffer, Librn
Holdings: Vols (6000) Cat Mss Maps Pix Slides
Notes: New York State history with emphasis on Westchester County and local area. Also children's literture, 1750-1910, and juvenile textbooks, 1790-1910. No photocopying.

NY —C W POST CENTER OF LONG ISLAND UNIVERSITY, B Davis Schwartz Memorial Library, Greenvale, 11548. Manju Prasad-Rao, Media Librn
Holdings: Pix Slides Phonorecords Audiotapes Videotapes 16mm Films Filmstrips
Budget: ($12,500)
Notes: The Center, while originally established for schools of Education and Library Science with a k-12 text and trade book collection and media, now incl a circulating non-print collection for the entire campus. (8000) Separate card catalog. Incl children's trade books (17,000); k-12 textbooks (1562 series); and k-12 curriculum guides (3053).

NY —HEMPSTEAD PUBLIC LIBRARY, 115 Nichols Court, Hempstead, 11550. Irene A Duszkiewicz, Dir
Holdings: Vols 366 Cat Mss Maps
Notes: Early American textbooks.

NY —BANK STREET COLLEGE OF EDUCATION LIBRARY, 610 W 112 St, New York, 10025. Eleanor Kule Seid, Library Dir
Holdings: Vols (90,000) Cat Microforms
Notes: Education, guidance, psychology, educational psychology, curricula, textbooks, Black Studies, etc. All subjects are integrated in one professional collection; in addition there are two separate cataloged and shelved collections: Children's and Elementary Curriculum Materials.

NY —CITY UNIVERSITY OF NEW YORK, City College, Library, 138 St & Convent Ave, New York, 10031. Vira C Hinds, Assoc Prof
Holdings: Vols (35,000) Cat
Budget: ($9173)
Notes: Education, incl juveniles (10,437), textbooks, and ERIC collection. Separate author catalog.

NY —COLUMBIA UNIVERSITY LIBRARIES, Teachers College, Milbank Memorial Library, 525 W 120 St, New York, 10027. Jane P Franck, Dir
Notes: Elementary and secondary current US textbooks, 19,000 volumes cataloged. Also, textbooks, historical US, before 1900, 2400 volumes cataloged in main library card catalog. In addition, international and foreign textbooks are chiefly of the 1920-1930 period, at the college and professional level; 19,000 volumes accessible through Special Collections Dept; 12,000 volumes cataloged in main library catalog.

NY —US COMMITTEE FOR UNICEF, Information Center on Children's Cultures, 331 E 38 St, New York, 10016. Melinda Greenblatt, Chief Librn
Holdings: Vols (17,500) Cat Pix Slides Films Filmstrips
Notes: Social and cultural aspects of lives of children from developing countries. Especially strong in the area of school textbooks from Near Eastern Asian, African, Latin American, Caribbean, and Pacific Area countries; holidays and celebrations related to children all over the world; children's books in English strong collection of

TEXTBOOKS—COLLECTIONS (cont.)

folklore, and folklore of children, from all regions mentioned above.

NY —STATE UNIVERSITY OF NEW YORK, COLLEGE AT ONEONTA, James M Milne Library, Oneonta, 13820. Richard D Johnson, Librn
Holdings: Vols (427,646) Cat Mss Maps Pix Slides Phonorecords Audiotapes 16mm Films Filmstrips Microforms
Budget: ($338,299)
Notes: New York State Collection; 19th & early 20th century popular fiction; New York State Verse Collection; Early Textbooks & Early Educational Theory Collection.

NY —UNIVERSITY OF ROCHESTER, Rush Rhees Library, Department of Rare Books and Special Collections, Rochester, 14627. Peter Dzwonkoski, Librn
Holdings: Vols 450
Notes: School textbooks published before 1850.

NY —STATE UNIVERSITY OF NEW YORK, STONY BROOK, Melville Library, Dept of Special Collections, Stony Brook, 11794. Evert Volkersz, Head
Holdings: Uncat
Notes: American and English elementary and secondary textbooks, ca 1790-date.

NC —DUKE UNIVERSITY, William R Perkins Library, Durham, 27706. Elvin E Strowd, University Librn
Notes: The Martin Rowan Chaffin collection of textbooks contains more than 1000 public school textbooks used in North Carolina before the Civil War and used in the state in the late 19th and early twentieth centuries.

NC —UNIVERSITY OF NORTH CAROLINA, GREENSBORO, Walter Clinton Jackson Library, Special Collections Dept, 1000 Spring Garden St, Greensboro, 27412. Emilie W Mills, Librn
Holdings: Vols 300 Cat
Notes: From the late 1700s to 1850, emphasis on American textbooks also incl some Civil War imprints.

OH —HIRAM COLLEGE, Teachout-Price Memorial Library, Hiram, 44234. Joanne M Sawyer, Archivist; Marjorie M Adams, Music Librn
Holdings: Vols 500 Cat
Notes: There is a separate catalog for this collection. Earliest edition is 1770.

OH —MIAMI UNIVERSITY, King Library, Walter Havighurst Special Collections Library, Oxford, 45056. Helen Ball, Cur of Special Collections
Holdings: Vols (3500)
Notes: Collection includes many editions of various McGuffey Readers. A related collection of 3500 volumes of 19th century American textbooks includes history, geography, spelling, rhetoric, elocution, and music books.

OR —UNIVERSITY OF OREGON LIBRARY, Education-Psychology Dept, Eugene, 97403. Rose Marie Service, Head Dept Librn
Holdings: Vols 15,000 Cat Maps Pix Phonorecords Audiotapes Filmstrips Microforms
Notes: The textbooks in the Curriculum Collection are for elementary and secondary levels, special education, and a few for adult basic education. A historical collection of approximately 3000 volumes incl many 19th century textbooks from elementary to college levels.

PA —SCHOOL DISTRICT OF PHILADELPHIA, Pedagogical Library, 21 St & Pkwy, Philadelphia, 19103. Helen E Howe, Librn; Patricia K Buck, Asst Librn
Holdings: Vols (47,000) Cat Pix Microforms
Budget: ($25,000)
Notes: Collection emphasis on public school education K-12 with the main areas including Afro-American history and culture, elementary and early childhood education, secondary education, educational administration, educational research, reading, school law, educational psychology. Special Collections: ERIC (140,000 documents), Archives of the School District of Philadelphia. Approx 500 periodical subscriptions.

PA —UNIVERSITY OF PITTSBURGH, Hillman Library, Special Collections Dept, 363 Hillman Library, Pittsburgh, 15260. Charles E Aston Jr, Coordinator
Holdings: Vols (13,480) Cat Mss
Notes: The John A Nietz Textbook Collection of primarily American textbooks in 3 areas; primary school books to 1900, secondary texts to ca 1930, and pedagogical books (1000 vols on the history and theory of education incl writings of the key figures in the field of education). Books are cataloged via an in-house computer printout and are accessible via name, title, subject, place, publisher and date. Late 18th and all of the 19th centuries are well represented. Important titles in each subject are discussed in John A Nietz's *Old Textbooks* (Pittsburgh, 1961) and in his *The Evolution of American Secondary School Textbooks* (Rutland, Vt, 1966). Collection also incl the papers (noncirculating) of Prof John A Nietz.

PA —PENNSYLVANIA STATE UNIVERSITY, Fred Lewis Pattee Library, Special Collections Dept, University Park, 16802. Charles Mann, Chief, Special Collections
Holdings: Vols 521 Cat
Budget: ($37,000)
Notes: 521 volumes, mostly American, early and mid-19th century.

RI —BROWN UNIVERSITY, John Hay Library, 20 Prospect St, Providence, 02912. Mark N Brown, Cur Mss
Holdings: Vols 4000 // Cat
Notes: Nineteenth century textbooks for secondary schools and colleges predominantly American in imprint.

SD —NORTHERN STATE COLLEGE, Beulah Williams Library, Aberdeen, 57401. Tedine Roos, Curriculum Librn
Notes: 3970 elementary and secondary school textbooks and Pitman-Fearon Microfiche guide collection. Separate catalog.

TN —VANDERBILT UNIVERSITY, George Peabody College for Teachers, Education Library, Box 325, Nashville, 37203. Mary Beth Blalock, Librn
Holdings: Vols (192,541) Cat Pix Slides Filmstrips Microforms
Budget: ($59,000)
Notes: The Education Library (192,541 vols) collects in all areas relating to education with special emphasis on Child Study and Exceptional Children. Special funds are available for continuing purchases in these areas. The collection is strong in curriculum materials, physical education, applied art, psychology related to education and all areas of education. Amoung special papers are over 300 papers by and about Jean Piaget and an extensive author and subject file referring to the location of these papers and books and journal articles by and about Piaget in the rest of the Education Library collection. The Education Library is a Division of the Vanderbilt University Library.

TX —ABILENE CHRISTIAN UNIVERSITY, Margaret & Herman Brown Library, ACU Sta, Abilene, 79601. Callie Faye Milliken, Assoc Dir
Notes: Early Day School Books. Pre-1900 Public School textbooks.

TX —UNIVERSITY OF TEXAS LIBRARIES, General Libraries, PO Box P, Austin, 78713. Carolyn Bucknell, Asst Dir for Collection Development
Holdings: Cat
Notes: Incl textbooks published prior to 1900 and textbooks submitted for adoption by the state of Texas.

TX —SOUTHWEST TEXAS STATE UNIVERSITY, Library, San Marcos, 78666. Bob Harris, Special Collections Librn
Holdings: // Uncat
Notes: American textbooks to 1918. Liberal arts, education, business.

WA —UNIVERSITY OF WASHINGTON LIBRARIES, Suzzallo Library, Curriculum Materials Section, FM-25, Seattle, 98195. Jean Belch, Head
Holdings: Vols 16,000 Cat

ON —QUEEN'S UNIVERSITY, Douglas Library, Kingston, K7L 5C4, Can. William F

E Morley, Cur, Special Collections
Holdings: Vols 2024 Uncat Maps Pix
Notes: World classics and little known titles in English (mostly). Small reference collection. Incl school books, mainly Canadian.

TEXTBOOKS—COLLECTIONS—EARLY WORKS BEFORE 1820

IN —INDIANAPOLIS-MARION COUNTY PUBLIC LIBRARY, Social Sciences Div, PO Box 211, Indianapolis, 46206. Lois R Laube, Head

TEXTBOOKS—PUBLICATION AND DISTRIBUTION

NY —GRADUATE CENTER OF THE CITY UNIVERSITY OF NEW YORK, William H and Gwynne K Crouse Library for Publishing Arts, 33 W 42 St, New York, 10036. Alfred H Lane, Dir
Notes: Recently established and still growing, but intended to become the authoritative source of materials in the field, of particular value in research about the publishing industry. Open to staff members of publishing houses, students, scholars, authors, printers, and booksellers. Primarily 20th century materials, and particularly useful for research on technical, financial, and historical matters. Much on the history of individual houses, economics of authorship; marketing and distribution of books; etc.

TEXTILE CHEMISTRY

CT —BELDING HEMINWAY CO, Belding Corticelli Research Center Library, Grosvenordale, PO Drawer 28, Putnam, 06260.
Holdings: Vols 5000
Notes: Restricted access.

†DE —E I DUPONT DE NEMOURS & CO, Textile Fabrics Library, Experimental Station, Wilmington, 19898.

MD —GILLETTE MEDICAL EVALUATION LABORATORIES, Information Center, 1413 Reasearch Blvd, Rockville, 20034. Patrick Dexter, Librn
Holdings: Cat Microforms

MA —UNIVERSITY OF LOWELL, Library, One University Ave, Lowell, 01854. Martha Mayo, Special Collections Librn
Holdings: Vols (24,000) Cat Mss Maps Pix
Notes: The Olney Collections contain books and journals on all aspects of textile technology particularly textile chemistry and textile engineering. The Flather Collection of the Boott Mill company papers 1835-1954. Photographic collections with emphasis on Lowell's textile industry.

NC —PUBLIC LIBRARY OF CHARLOTTE & MECKLENBURG COUNTY, 310 N Tyron St, Charlotte, 28202. Mae S Tucker, Asst Dir
Holdings: Vols (3950) Cat Slides 16mm Films Filmstrips
Notes: Weaving, chemistry, dyes and dyeing, and color are emphasized. Also hosiery, knitting, machinery, manufacturing, directories and statistics. Have specialized dictionaries in the subject field in both English and other languages. 110 periodical titles.

NC —NORTH CAROLINA STATE UNIVERSITY, Burlington Textile Library, Box 8301 NCSU, Raleigh, 27695. Georgia H Rodeffer, Librn
Holdings: Vols (20,000) Cat Microforms
Notes: Specially housed library covering all phases of the textile industry incl textile chemistry, machinery, weaving, management, apparel manufacture, etc.

TEXTILE DESIGN

CA —CALIFORNIA COLLEGE OF ARTS & CRAFTS, Meyer Library, Broadway at College, Oakland, 94618. Robert L Harper, Head Librn
Holdings: Vols (29,000) Cat Pix
Budget: ($10,000)
Notes: All fields of arts and crafts.

TEXTILE DESIGN (cont.)

NH —MANCHESTER HISTORIC
ASSOCIATION, Library, 129 Amherst St,
Manchester, 03104. Elizabeth Lessard, Librn
Holdings: // Cat Mss
Notes: Elwin Smyrl was a local textile
designer who worked from 1906 to 1966 in
both natural and synthetic fibers. His early
work was for the Amoskeag Manufacturing
Co. After 1936, he developed headliners for
cars for General Motors Corp, synthetic
cord for Firestone Tires, etc. Collection incl
14 museum storage boxes; textile samples,
textile graphs.

NY —FASHION INSTITUTE OF
TECHNOLOGY, Special Collections
Library, 227 W 27 St, New York, 10001.
Barbara Jones, Dir; Janette Rozene, Librn
Holdings: Vols (4900) Cat Periodicals
Audiotapes
Budget: ($7500)
Notes: Incl 61 uncataloged collections of
designer sketches, 30 uncataloged collections
fashion designer or firm scrapbooks, 245
volumes WPA scrapbooks, and 50 oral
history transcripts. Highlights: 19th century
fashion plate periodicals; original fashion
sketches from late 1800s, incl designs by
Lady Duff Gordon, Muriel King, Berley
Studios; scrapbooks compiled by Claire
McCardell, Mainbocher.

NY —NEW YORK PUBLIC LIBRARY, Art,
Prints, and Photographs Div, Fifth Ave & 42
St, New York, 10018. Donald Anderle,
Chief
Holdings: Cat Mss Pix
Notes: Incl volumes on patterning for
weaving and knitting, printing techniques,
and costume and costume design, as well as
all phases of the textile industry.

NC —NORTH CAROLINA STATE
UNIVERSITY, Burlington Textile Library,
Box 8301 NCSU, Raleigh, 27695. Georgia H
Rodeffer, Librn
Holdings: Vols (15,200) Cat Microforms
Notes: Specially housed library covering all
phases of the textile industry incl textile
chemistry, machinery, weaving,
management, apparel manufacturing, etc.

OH —CLEVELAND PUBLIC LIBRARY,
Science & Technology Dept, 325 Superior
Ave, Cleveland, 44114. Jean Z Piety, Head
Holdings: Cat
Notes: Part of the Handicrafts Collection,
which incl crafts of many ethnic groups in
Cleveland.

RI —RHODE ISLAND SCHOOL OF
DESIGN, Library, Two College St,
Providence, 02903. James A Findlay, Dir
Holdings: Vols (70,000) Cat
Budget: ($50,000)

WA —UNIVERSITY OF WASHINGTON
LIBRARIES, Costume and Textile
Collection, FM-25, Seattle, 98195. Krista
Jensen Turnbull, Cur
Holdings: Vols (1500) Cat Pix Slides
Notes: Incl the Elizabeth Bayley Willis
Collection of more than 1000 textiles from
India, and the Seattle Weavers' Guild
Collection of Guatemalan textiles. Coptic
textiles are on loan from Yale University,
and the Boston Museum of Fine Arts gave
the Choate Collection of lace. There are also
good collections of ecclasiastical vestments
and embroideries from many nations,
ranging from 1500 BC to the present.

TEXTILE ENGINEERING

AL —WEST POINT-PEPPERELL INC,
Research Center Information Services, PO
Boc 398, Shawmut, 36876. Philip D
Lawrence, Jr, Supvr
Holdings: Vols 3000 Cat Mss Slides
Microforms
Budget: $34,000

GA —GEORGIA INSTITUTE OF
TECHNOLOGY, Price Gilbert Memorial
Library, 225 North Ave, Atlanta, 30332.
Edward Graham Roberts, Dir
Holdings: Vols (1,661,559) Cat Maps Slides
Microforms
Budget: ($1,383,302)
Notes: Incl (4,307,996) patents and (568,
490) government documents.

MA —MERRIMACK VALLEY TEXTILE
MUSEUM, Library, 800 Massachusetts Ave,
North Andover, 01845. Clare Sheridan,
Librn; Laurence Gross, Cur
Holdings: Vols (35,000) Cat Mss Maps Pix
Slides
Notes: *Checklist of Prints, Drawings and
Painting in the Merrimack Valley Textile
Museum*, Helena E Wright, 1972; *Checklist
of Finished Textiles*, Katherine R Koob,
1980; *New City on the Merrimack: Prints of
Lawrence 1845-1876*, Helena Wright, 1974;
*Homespun to Factory Made: Woolen
Textiles in America 1776-1876* (exhibit
catalog) 1978; *Textile Technology Prints: A
Checklist of Prints, Drawings and Paintings
in the Merrimack Valley Textile Museum*,
Helena E Wright, 1980; *All Sorts of Good
Sufficient Cloth: Linen-making in New
England, 1640-1860*, (exhibit catalogue)
1980; *The Merrimack Valley Textile
Museum: A Guide to the Manuscript
Collections* Helena E Wright, Garland Press
1983.

NC —NORTH CAROLINA STATE
UNIVERSITY, Burlington Textile Library,
Box 8301 NCSU, Raleigh, 27695. Georgia H
Rodeffer, Librn
Holdings: Vols (15,200) Cat Microfilms
Notes: Specially housed library covering all
phases of the textile industry incl textile
chemistry, machinery, weaving,
management, apparel manufacture, etc.

SC —SONOCO PRODUCTS CO, Research
Laboratory, Technical Information Center,
One N Second St, Hartsville, 29550. Ken
Chavis, Dir
Holdings: Vols (4000) Cat Mss Slides
Microforms
Notes: Resstricted to Sonoco employees. No
photocopying.

TEXTILE FABRICS see Textile Industry and Fabrics

TEXTILE FIBERS

†DE —E I DUPONT DE NEMOURS & CO,
Textile Fabrics Library, Experimental
Station, Wilmington, 19898.

MA —UNIVERSITY OF LOWELL, Library,
One University Ave, Lowell, 01854. Martha
Mayo, Special Collections Librn
Holdings: Vols 2500 Cat Mss Pix Slides
Notes: One of the most comprehensive
collections of books and periodical on all
phases of the textile industry and fabrics; all
fibers and processes, dyess and dyeing,
strong in historical materials also. Approx
200 vols, mostly in French, on sericulture
and silk.

NC —NORTH CAROLINA STATE
UNIVERSITY, Burlington Textile Library,
Box 8301 NCSU, Raleigh, 27695. Georgia H
Rodeffer, Librn
Holdings: Vols (15,200) Cat Microforms
Notes: Specially housed library covering all
phases of the textile industry incl textile
chemistry, machinery, weaving,
management, apparel manufacture, etc.

TEXTILE INDUSTRY AND FABRICS

AL —WEST POINT-PEPPERELL INC,
Research Center Information Services, PO
Boc 398, Shawmut, 36876. Philip D
Lawrence, Jr, Supvr
Holdings: Vols 3000 Cat Mss Slides
Microforms
Budget: $34,000

CT —BELDING HEMINWAY CO, Belding
Corticelli Research Center Library,
Grosvenordale, PO Drawer 28, Putnam,
06260.
Holdings: Vols 5000
Notes: Restricted access.

DE —HAGLEY MUSEUM AND LIBRARY,
Eleutherian Mills-Hagley Foundation Inc,
PO Box 3630, Greenville, 19807. Richmond
D Williams, Dir; Heddy A Richter, Imprints
Librn
Notes: Records of the Bancroft, Simpson
and Eddystone Textile Firms in Delaware
and Pennsylvania (1830-1961; 650 cubic
feet). The archive incl administrative,

accounting, purchasing, production, and
personnel records documenting the history
of this important Delaware Valley textile
manufacturer.

DE —WIDENER UNIVERSITY, Delaware
Campus Library, Box 7139, Concord Pike,
Wilmington, 19803. Jane E Hukill, Library
Dir
Holdings: Vols (48,000) Audiotapes
Videotapes Microforms
Notes: Incl fashion design, history of
costume, textiles.

DC —NATIONAL SOCIETY, DAUGHTERS
OF THE AMERICAN REVOLUTION,
DAR Museum Reference Library, 1776 D St
NW, Washington, 20006. Christine Minter-
Dowd, Dir; Michael W Berry, Cur; Jean
Martin, Registrar
Holdings: Vols (1600) Cat
Budget: ($500)

DC —SMITHSONIAN INSTITUTION
LIBRARIES, National Museum of American
History Branch, Washington, 20560. Rhoda
S Ratner, Branch Librn
Holdings: Vols (4500) Cat Pix

IL —UNIVERSITY OF ILLINOIS,
URBANA/CHAMPAIGN, Library, Home
Economics Library, 314 Bevier Hall,
Champaign, 61820. Barbara C Swain, Librn
Holdings: Vols Cat Microforms
Budget: $20,283
Notes: Textiles, apparel and interior design.

IL —UNIVERSITY OF ILLINOIS,
URBANA/CHAMPAIGN, Library, 1408 W
Gregory Drive, Urbana, 61801. Norman B
Brown, Asst Dir for Special Collections
Notes: More than 3000 costume sketches
from Motley, designers, of New York and
London, a firm whose influence covered 50
years of the London and New York stages,
particularly Shakespeare productions. Incl
story boards and fabric swatches from 160
productions. Part of the Rare Book Room.

IN —PURDUE UNIVERSITY LIBRARIES,
Consumer & Family Sciences Library, Stone
Hall W, West Lafayette, 47907. Emily
Alward, Librn
Holdings: Vols (14,000) Cat

MD —GILLETTE MEDICAL EVALUATION
LABORATORIES, Information Center,
1413 Reasearch Blvd, Rockville, 20034.
Patrick Dexter, Librn
Holdings: Cat Microforms

MA —UNIVERSITY OF LOWELL, Library,
One University Ave, Lowell, 01854. Martha
Mayo, Special Collections Librn
Holdings: Vols (24,000) Cat Mss Maps Pix
Notes: The Olney Collections contain books
and journals on all aspects of textile
technology particularly textile chemistry and
textile engineering. The Flather Collection of
the Boott Mill company papers 1835-1954.
Photographic collections with emphasis on
Lowell's textile industry.

MI —PORTAGE LAKE DISTRICT
LIBRARY, 105 Huron, Houghton, 49931.
Bethany Patterson, Dir
Holdings: Vols 100 Cat Pix
Notes: Weaving and related crafts, spinning,
etc. Some foreign language materials.

NH —MANCHESTER HISTORIC
ASSOCIATION, Library, 129 Amherst St,
Manchester, 03104. Elizabeth Lessard, Librn
Holdings: // Cat Mss
Notes: Elwin Smyrl was a local textile
designer who worked from 1906 to 1966 in
both natural and synthetic fibers. His early
work was for the Amoskeag Manufacturing
Co. After 1936, he developed headliners for
cars for General Motors Corp, synthetic
cord for Firestone Tires, etc. Collection incl
14 museum storage boxes; textile samples,
textile graphs.

NM —MUSEUM OF NEW MEXICO,
Museum of International Folk Art Library,
706 Camino Lejo, Santa Fe, 87501. Judith
Sellars, Librn
Holdings: Vols (8000) Cat
Notes: Folk art of all countries, incl such
subjects as costume, ceramics, textiles,
furniture. Restricted use: noncirculating.

NY —BROOKLYN MUSEUM, Art Reference
Library, 188 Eastern Parkway, Brooklyn,
11238.
Holdings: Vols (130,000)

NY —AMALGAMATED CLOTHING &
TEXTILE WORKERS UNION, Research

TEXTILE INDUSTRY AND FABRICS
(cont.)

Dept Library, 15 Union Sq, New York, 10003. Mohammad Homayon Pour, Librn
Holdings: Vols (3200) Cat Pix
Notes: Collective bargaining and economic conditions in the men's and boys' apparel industries and the textile industry.

NY —FASHION INSTITUTE OF TECHNOLOGY, Edward C Blum Design Laboratory, 227 W 27 St, New York, 10001. Laura Sinderbrand, Dir
Holdings: Cat Pix Slides
Notes: 3,500,000 textile swatches. Collection available by appointment for academic research. Fee of $50.00 per year for industrial research.

NY —NEW YORK PUBLIC LIBRARY, Research Libraries, Science and Technology Research Center, Fifth Ave & 42 St, New York, 10018.
Holdings: Vols (1,100,000) Cat Microforms
Budget: ($647,259)

NC —PUBLIC LIBRARY OF CHARLOTTE & MECKLENBURG COUNTY, 310 N Tyron St, Charlotte, 28202. Mae S Tucker, Asst Dir
Holdings: Vols (3950) Cat Slides 16mm Films Filmstrips
Notes: Weaving, chemistry, dyes and dyeing, and color are emphasized. Also hosiery, knitting, machinery, manufacturing, directories and statistics. Have specialized dictionaries in the subject field in both English and other languages. 110 periodical titles.

NC —NORTH CAROLINA STATE UNIVERSITY, Burlington Textile Library, Box 8301 NCSU, Raleigh, 27695. Georgia H Rodeffer, Librn
Holdings: Vols (15,200) Cat Microforms
Notes: Specially housed library covering all phases of the textile industry incl textile chemistry, machinery, weaving, management, apparel manufacture, etc.

OH —OHIO STATE UNIVERSITY, Home Economics Library, Campbell Hall Rm 325, 1787 Neil Ave, Columbus, 43210. Neosha Mackey, Librn
Holdings: Vols (14,000) Cat Microforms
Notes: Separate catalog. Also, book catalog: *Catalog of the Home Economics Library* (Boston: GK Hall, 1976), 3 vols.

OR —OREGON STATE UNIVERSITY, Library, Corvallis, 97331. Melvin George, Dir
Holdings: Vols (980,000) Cat Pix

OR —BASSIST COLLEGE LIBRARY, 2000 SW Fifth Ave, Portland, 97201. Norma Bassist, Librn
Holdings: Vols 20 Cat Mss Pix Slides

PA —FRANKLIN INSTITUTE LIBRARY, 20 & The Parkway, Philadelphia, 19103. Miriam Padusis, Dir; Charles Wilt, Readers Servs Librn
Holdings: Vols (300,000) Cat Maps Pix Microforms

PA —CARNEGIE LIBRARY OF PITTSBURGH, Science & Technology Dept, 4400 Forbes Ave, Pittsburgh, 15213. Catherine M Brosky, Dept Head
Holdings: Vols (380,000) Cat Maps Microforms
Budget: ($240,000)
Notes: General information acquired. Manufacturers directories, including old editions, standards and specifications, trade catalogs, basic periodicals, indexes, and bibliographies.

TX —TEXAS TECH UNIVERSITY, Library, Lubbock, 79409. David J Murrah, Assoc Dir for Special Collections

VT —SHELBURNE MUSEUM, Library, Shelburne, 05482. Barbara Reenstierna, Librn
Holdings: Vols (275) Cat Slides

VA —INSTITUTE OF TEXTILE TECHNOLOGY, Roger Milliken Textile Library, Box 391, Charlottesville, 22902. Linda Justus Cahill, Librn
Holdings: Vols (30,000) Cat Microforms

VA —COLONIAL WILLIAMSBURG FOUNDATION, Abby Aldrich Rockefeller Folk Art Center, PO Box C, Williamsburg,

23187. Anne E Watkins, Registrar
Holdings: Vols (5000) Cat
Notes: American folk arts and crafts. Periodicals of current art, antiques, and history. Researchers wishing to use the library are requested to call the museum for an appointment.

WA —UNIVERSITY OF WASHINGTON LIBRARIES, Suzzallo Library, Natural Sciences Library, FM-25, Seattle, 98195. Nancy G Blase, Head
Holdings: Vols (192,353) Cat
Budget: ($219,809)

WI —UNIVERSITY OF WISCONSIN, MADISON, College of Agricultural & Life Sciences, Steenbock Memorial Library, 550 Babcock Dr, Madison, 53706. Jan Kennedy, Dir
Holdings: Vols (186,312) Cat Docs
Notes: Collection supports the School of Family Resources and Consumer Sciences in areas of textiles and fashion design, interior decorating, consumer science, and nutrition; USDA documents and experiment station publications.

ON —ONTARIO RESEARCH FOUNDATION, Library, Sheridan Park, Mississauga, L5K 1B3, Can. Carl K Wei, Librn
Holdings: Vols (13,000) Cat
Budget: ($14,000)

ON —ROYAL ONTARIO MUSEUM, Main Library and Archives, 100 Queen's Park, Toronto, M5S 2C6, Can. Julia Matthews, Head Librn
Holdings: Vols (85,000) Cat
Notes: Since January 1977, acquisitions have been entered in UTLAS.

TEXTILE INDUSTRY AND FABRICS—CHEMISTRY see Textile Chemistry

TEXTILE INDUSTRY AND FABRICS—HISTORY

CT —UNIVERSITY OF CONNECTICUT, Historical Manuscripts and Archives Division, Box U-205, Storrs, 06268. Randall Jimerson, Librn
Notes: Business records of pioneer Connecticut textile manufacturers, Samuel and John Slater. Other Slater correspondence and records are in the Baker Library at Harvard and the Rhode Island Historical Society. Most of the records at University of Connecticut relate to the Slater Company's mills and company stores in Jewett City and Hopeville, Conn, 1825-1880. Incl financial records, correspondence and employee account books.

MA —HARVARD UNIVERSITY, Graduate School of Business Administration, Baker Library, Soldiers Field, Boston, 02163. Mary V Chatfield, Librn; Florence Bartoshesky, Cur of Manuscripts and Archives
Holdings: Cat Mss
Notes: Extensive holdings of New England textile company original records, 1790-1920. See Robert W Lovett and Eleanor C Bishop, compilers, *Manuscripts in Baker Library*, (Boston: The Library, 1978), 382 pp.

MA —MERRIMACK VALLEY TEXTILE MUSEUM, Library, 800 Massachusetts Ave, North Andover, 01845. Clare Sheridan, Librn; Laurence Gross, Cur
Holdings: Vols (35,000) Cat Mss Maps Pix Slides
Notes: *Checklist of Prints, Drawings and Painting in the Merrimack Valley Textile Museum*, Helena E Wright, 1972; *Checklist of Finished Textiles*, Katherine R Koob, 1980; *New City on the Merrimack: Prints of Lawrence 1845-1876*, Helena Wright, 1974; *Homespun to Factory Made: Woolen Textiles in America 1776-1876* (exhibit catalog) 1978; *Textile Technology Prints: A Checklist of Prints, Drawings and Paintings in the Merrimack Valley Textile Museum*, Helena E Wright, 1980; *All Sorts of Good Sufficient Cloth: Linen-making in New England, 1640-1860*, (exhibit catalogue) 1980; *The Merrimack Valley Textile Museum: A Guide to the Manuscript Collections* Helena E Wright, Garland Press 1983.

MA —OLD STURBRIDGE VILLAGE, Research Library, Sturbridge, 01566. Theresa Rini Percy, Librn
Holdings: Cat Mss Pix
Notes: Hand and industrial methods in New England, 1790-1850, incl dyeing; American and imported fabrics used in New England, to 1850.

NH —MANCHESTER HISTORIC ASSOCIATION, Library, 129 Amherst St, Manchester, 03104. Elizabeth Lessard, Librn
Holdings: Vols 705 Cat Mss Pix
Notes: Part of the archives of the Amoskeag Manufacturing Co (AmCo), one of the early New England textile industries (1828-1936). It was the world's largest producer of cotton goods in the early 20th century. It was established by Boston capital and set up on the same plan as Lowell and Lawrence, Mass, Mills. The remainder of the collection (mainly 20th century) is at the Harvard Business School, Baker Library. Also, the Stark Manufacturing Company (1832-1922) corporate records, ledgers, payrolls, contracts of indentured servants.

NJ —PASSAIC COUNTY HISTORICAL SOCIETY, Lamhurt Castle, Valley Rd, Paterson, 07503. Helen D Hamilton, Dir
Holdings: Vols (5000) Cat Mss Maps Pix
Notes: Material on the Society for the Establishment of Useful Manufacturing (founded) by Alexander Hamilton, papers relating to John Holland, who developed the submarine, the industrial magnates of the area who were active in the manufacture of locomotives, Colt revolvers, and textiles, especially silk.

NY —STATE UNIVERSITY OF NEW YORK, COLLEGE AT OSWEGO, Penfield Library, Oswego, 13126. Anne Commerton, Dir
Holdings: Cat Mss Maps Pix
Notes: Hayes Textile Co papers, 1913 to 1929. The company was founded in 1911 by Thomas Hayes. The papers contain the business records of the company incl ledgers of administration, general accounts, sales and purchases, etc. Unpublished guide.

NC —DUKE UNIVERSITY, William R Perkins Library, Manuscript Dept, Durham, 27706. Ellen Gartrell, Cur of Mss
Holdings: Cat Mss
Notes: Papers of various southern textile mills, especially North Carolina, 19th-20th centuries, incl material on unions and strikes; Sir Thomas Wardle Papers (93 letters of William Morris).

RI —SLATER MILL HISTORIC SITE, SMHS Library, Roosevelt Ave, Pawtucket, 02962. TE Leary, Cur
Holdings: Vols 500 Mss Maps Pix
Budget: $500
Notes: Lewis Hine photos of child labor in RI (1909-1912). Oral history.

RI —PROVIDENCE PUBLIC LIBRARY, 150 Empire St, Providence, 02903. Lance J Bauer, Special Collections Librn
Holdings: Vols 1013 // Cat Pix
Notes: Historical collection. Covers history and technical aspects of the industry.

TX —PANHANDLE-PLAINS HISTORICAL MUSEUM, Research Center, Box 967, WT Sta, Canyon, 79016. Claire R Kuehn, Archivist-Librn
Holdings: Vols 50 Cat
Budget: $500
Notes: Collection supplements historic costume and textile collection of the Museum. Scope: 1850-1950. This is a new collection and is building rapidly. Incl periodicals and catalogs.

WA —UNIVERSITY OF WASHINGTON LIBRARIES, Costume and Textile Collection, FM-25, Seattle, 98195. Krista Jensen Turnbull, Cur
Holdings: Vols (1500) Cat Pix Slides
Notes: Incl the Elizabeth Bayley Willis Collection of more than 1000 textiles from India, and the Seattle Weavers' Guild Collection of Guatemalan textiles. Coptic textiles are on loan from Yale University, and the Boston Museum of Fine Arts gave the Choate Collection of lace. There are also good collections of ecclasiastical vestments and embroideries from many nations, ranging from 1500 BC to the present.

TEXTILE INDUSTRY AND FABRICS—RHODE ISLAND

RI —RHODE ISLAND HISTORICAL
SOCIETY, Library, 121 Hope St,
Providence, 02906. Paul R Campbell,
Library Dir
Holdings: Mss
Budget: ($200,000)
Notes: The Brown and Ives collection of
manufacturing records. Incl the records of
the Brown and Ives firm; their principal
management agency, the firm of Goddard
Brothers; and cotton mills owned by Brown
and Ives. Collection incl 1000 mss.

TEXTILE MACHINERY

MA —MERRIMACK VALLEY TEXTILE
MUSEUM, Library, 800 Massachusetts Ave,
North Andover, 01845. Clare Sheridan,
Librn; Laurence Gross, Cur
Holdings: Vols (35,000) Cat Mss Maps Pix
Slides
Notes: *Checklist of Prints, Drawings and
Painting in the Merrimack Valley Textile
Museum*, Helena E Wright, 1972; *Checklist
of Finished Textiles*, Katherine R Koob,
1980; *New City on the Merrimack: Prints of
Lawrence 1845-1876*, Helena Wright, 1974;
*Homespun to Factory Made: Woolen
Textiles in America 1776-1876* (exhibit
catalog) 1978; *Textile Technology Prints: A
Checklist of Prints, Drawings and Paintings
in the Merrimack Valley Textile Museum*,
Helena E Wright, 1980; *All Sorts of Good
Sufficient Cloth: Linen-making in New
England, 1640-1860*, (exhibit catalogue)
1980; *The Merrimack Valley Textile
Museum: A Guide to the Manuscript
Collections* Helena E Wright, Garland Press
1983.

NC —PUBLIC LIBRARY OF CHARLOTTE
& MECKLENBURG COUNTY, 310 N
Tyron St, Charlotte, 28202. Mae S Tucker,
Asst Dir
Holdings: Vols (3950) Cat Slides 16mm
Films Filmstrips
Notes: Weaving, chemistry, dyes and dyeing,
and color are emphasized. Also, hosiery,
knitting, machinery, manufacturing,
directories and statistics. Have specialized
dictionaries in the subject field in both
English and other languages. 110 periodical
titles.

NC —NORTH CAROLINA STATE
UNIVERSITY, Burlington Textile Library,
Box 8301 NCSU, Raleigh, 27695. Georgia H
Rodeffer, Librn
Holdings: Vols (15,200) Cat Microforms
Notes: Specially housed library covering all
phases of the textile industry incl textile
chemistry, machinery, weaving,
management, apparel manufacuturing, etc.

VA —INSTITUTE OF TEXTILE
TECHNOLOGY, Roger Milliken Textile
Library, Box 391, Charlottesville, 22902.
Linda Justus Cahill, Librn
Holdings: Vols (30,000) Cat Microforms

TEXTILE MILLS

MA —UNIVERSITY OF LOWELL, Library,
One University Ave, Lowell, 01854. Martha
Mayo, Special Collections Librn
Holdings: Vols (24,000) Cat Mss Maps Pix
Notes: The Olney Collections contain books
and journals on all aspects of textile
technology particularly textile chemistry and
textile engineering. The Flather Collection of
the Boott Mill company papers 1835-1954.
Photographic collections with emphasis on
Lowell's textile industry.

MA —MERRIMACK VALLEY TEXTILE
MUSEUM, Library, 800 Massachusetts Ave,
North Andover, 01845. Clare Sheridan,
Librn; Laurence Gross, Cur
Holdings: Vols (35,000) Cat Mss Maps Pix
Slides
Notes: *Checklist of Prints, Drawings and
Painting in the Merrimack Valley Textile
Museum*, Helena E Wright, 1972; *Checklist
of Finished Textiles*, Katherine R Koob,
1980; *New City on the Merrimack: Prints of

Lawrence 1845-1876*, Helena Wright, 1974;
*Homespun to Factory Made: Woolen
Textiles in America 1776-1876* (exhibit
catalog) 1978; *Textile Technology Prints: A
Checklist of Prints, Drawings and Paintings
in the Merrimack Valley Textile Museum*,
Helena E Wright, 1980; *All Sorts of Good
Sufficient Cloth: Linen-making in New
England, 1640-1860*, (exhibit catalogue)
1980; *The Merrimack Valley Textile
Museum: A Guide to the Manuscript
Collections* Helena E Wright, Garland Press
1983.

TEXTILE PLANTS see Textile Fibers

TEXTILES see Textile Industry and Fabrics

THACHER, JOHN BOYD

DC —LIBRARY OF CONGRESS, Rare Book
& Special Collections Div, Washington,
20540. William Matheson, Chief
Notes: See description of collection under
Incunabula.

THACHER, THOMAS DAY

†NY —COLUMBIA UNIVERSITY
LIBRARIES, Butler Library, Rare Book and
Manuscript Library, 535 W 114 St, New
York, 10027.
Notes: Papers of the US Solicitor General,
1930-33, relating to the American Red Cross
Mission to Russia, 1917-18.

THACHER FAMILY

ME —BOWDOIN COLLEGE, Library,
Brunswick, 04011. Dianne M Gutscher, Cur
of Special Collections
Notes: Besides a general collection of 13,000
volumes relating to the State of Maine, there
are also many ms collections touching on the
political, economic and social history of
Maine. These incl Thacher Family Papers;
400 letters, 1782-1892.

THACKERAY, WILLIAM MAKEPEACE, 1811-1863

AZ —UNIVERSITY OF ARIZONA,
University Library, Special Collections,
Tucson, 85721. Louis A Hieb, Head
Holdings: Vols (7000) Cat Mss Microforms
Budget: ($30,000)
Notes: The major collection of 19th century
authors are Byron, Dickens, Scott,
Thackeray, Trollope, the Brownings, Stevens,
Tennyson, and Wordsworth.

CA —UNIVERSITY OF CALIFORNIA, LOS
ANGELES, William Andrews Clark
Memorial Library, 2520 Cimarron St, Los
Angeles, 90018.
Holdings: Cat
Notes: Small collection, original editions,
etc.

CT —TRINITY COLLEGE LIBRARY,
Watkinson Library, 300 Summit St,
Hartford, 06106. Jeffrey Kaimowitz, Cur
Holdings: Cat
Notes: Incl the Sherman P Haight
Collection.

CT —YALE UNIVERSITY, Box 1603A, Yale
Station, New Haven, 06520.

IL —ILLINOIS STATE UNIVERSITY, Milner
Library, Dept of Special Collections,
Normal, 61761. Robert Sokan, Librn
Notes: First editions, limited editions,
ephemera, etc.

MA —HARVARD UNIVERSITY LIBRARY,
Widener Library, Harry Elkins Widener
Collection, Cambridge, 02138. F Thomas
Noonan, Cur
Holdings: // Cat Mss

NJ —PRINCETON UNIVERSITY, Library,
Morris L Parrish Collection, Princeton,
08540. Alexander D Wainwright, Cur
Notes: The Library Company of Philadelphia
exhibited a selection of the Parrish material
in 1940, at which time a privately printed
catalog was compiled. Over 3000 vols in the
collection. The importance of the Parrish
Thackeray collection lies in its depth. Refer

to: Robert F Metzdorf, "M L Parrish and
William Makepeace Thackeray" in the
Chronicle XVII, 2 (winter, 1956) pp 68-70.

NY —NEW YORK PUBLIC LIBRARY, Rare
Books and Manuscripts Div, Fifth Ave & 42
St, New York, 10018. William L Joyce, Asst
Dir; Bernard McTigue, Cur, Arents
Collection
Holdings: Cat Mss Pix

NC —UNIVERSITY OF NORTH
CAROLINA, CHAPEL HILL, Wilson
Library, Rare Book Collection, Chapel Hill,
27514. Paul S Koda, Cur of Rare Books
Holdings: Vols 125 Cat
Notes: The Witaker Collection of William
Makepeace Thackeray incl first editions of
all of Thackeray's major works and many of
his less well-known writings, as well as
original monthly installments of *The
Newcomes, Pendennis*, and *The Virginian*;
also contained are the periodicals *The Snob*
(1829), *The Gownsman* (1829-1830), and
Fraser's Magazine (1837-1847).

THAI LANGUAGE AND LITERATURE

CA —UNIVERSITY OF CALIFORNIA, LOS
ANGELES, Research Library, Indo/Pacific
Collection, 405 Hilgard Ave, Los Angeles,
90024. Edward Shreeves, Chairman,
Bibliographers Group; Charlotte Spence,
Indo/Pacific Bibliographer
Holdings: Vols Cat Mss Maps Pix
Microforms
Notes: The Southeast Asian collection has
been developed on a combination of the
research and teaching levels; it focuses on
the cultural, economic, political and social
history of the area from ancient times to the
present day. Although all the individual
countries of the region are represented, some
priority is given to Malaysia, Singapore,
Indonesia and the Philippines. The majority
of the materials is in Western languages
except for a collection of several thousand
books in Thai, and a smaller collection of
materials in Vietnamese, Indonesian,
Malaysian, and the Philippine languages.

CT —YALE UNIVERSITY, Box 1603A, Yale
Station, New Haven, 06520.

DC —LIBRARY OF CONGRESS, African and
Middle Eastern Division, Washington,
20540.
Holdings: Cat Mss Microforms
Notes: Southern Asian: over 137,000 vols of
literature of the area from Pakistan to the
Philippines.

HI —UNIVERSITY OF HAWAII, Library,
2550 The Mall, Honolulu, 96822. Joyce
Wright, Head, Asia Collection; Masato
Matsu, Head, East Asia Vernacular
Collection
Holdings: Vols 331,620 Cat Microforms
Notes: The Asia Collection holds materials
from and about Southeast Asia: Brunei,
Burma, Cambodia (Kampuchea), Indonesia,
Laos, Malaysia, Philippines, Singapore,
Thailand. Large contemporary Indonesian
language collection. Several thousand vols in
Thai and in Vietnamese. Minimal holdings in
Burmese, Khmer, Lao languages. Social
sciences and humanities emphasis for the
post-World War II period. Western language
coverage supplemented by retrospective
holdings in the main library collection.

IL —NORTHERN ILLINOIS UNIVERSITY,
Founders Memorial Library, Southeast Asia
Collection, Normal Rd, De Kalb, 60115. Lee
S Dutton Dr, Cur
Holdings: Vols (34,000) Cat Maps
Microforms
Notes: An extensive collection of books,
periodicals, newspapers, maps, and
microforms from or about Southeast Asia.
Areas of concentration incl Thailand,
Malaysia, Indonesia, Singapore, Brunei,
Philippines, Laos, and Burma. Holdings
(except rare books, maps, and microforms)
are housed in a separate area collection
within the Founders Library. A departmental
card catalog and specialized reference
collection support reference services. A Thai
collection of several thousand vols is the
largest vernacular component. Extensive
Malaysia, Indonesia, Singapore, and Brunei
holdings have been acquired through the

THAI LANGUAGE AND LITERATURE (cont.)

NPAC program. A collection of Filipino-American newspapers, and a growing collection of children's literature in common and uncommon Southeast Asian languages are available. Resources are accessible to borrowers through OCLC.

NY —NEW YORK PUBLIC LIBRARY, Oriental Div, Fifth Ave & 42 St, New York, 10018. E Christian Filstrup, Chief
Holdings: / / Cat Mss Microforms
Budget: ($56,455)
Notes: Published catalog of holdings. Currently collected in Western language materials only.

NY —NEW YORK PUBLIC LIBRARY, Donnell Foreign Language Library, 20 W 53 St, New York, 10019. Bosiljka Stevanovic, Supvr Librn
Holdings: Vols 581 Cat
Notes: Thai collection incl Thai authors of Thai expression. No separate catalog.

NC —CUMBERLAND COUNTY PUBLIC LIBRARY, North Carolina Foreign Language Center, 328 Gillespie St, Fayetteville, 28301. Patrick M Valentine, Coordinator
Holdings: Vols 250 Cat
Budget: $500
Notes: The largest book collections are, in descending order of size, German Spanish, French, Japanese, Korean and Vietnamese, with fair sized collections in Italian, Russian, Chinese, Arabic, Greek, Hungarian, Polish, Hebrew, Thai, and Hindi. The Center has several shelves each of books in Bengali, Dutch, Marathi, Portuguese, Urdu, and Yiddish. Smaller collections of one to three shelves each incl Catalan, Croatian, Czech, Danish, Finnish, Gujarati, Icelandic, Kannada, Latin, Lithuanian, Malayalam, Norwegian, Panjabi, Persian (Farsi), Romanian, Slovak, Swedish, Tagalog, Tamil, Telegu, and Ukrianian. The Center has grammars, dictionaries and occasionally other readings in languages from Afrikaans and Albanian to Welsh, Yoruba and Zulu.

OH —CLEVELAND PUBLIC LIBRARY, Fine Arts and Special Collections Department, 325 Superior Ave, Cleveland, 44114. Alice N Loranth, Head
Holdings: Vols (2070) Cat Mss
Notes: Emphasis is on language, linguistics, inscriptions, literature and religion. The most important titles refer to Pali texts in Thai. Western translations of classic texts; incl also 370 vols in Thai. Separate catalog of author entries for titles in Thai is maintained.

THAILAND

DC —GEORGETOWN UNIVERSITY, Library, Special Collections Div, 37 & O Sts NW, Washington, 20057. George M Barringer, Special Collections Librn; Nicholas B Sheetz, Mss Librn
Holdings: Mss Cat Pix
Notes: The papers of Hamilton King (1852-1912), American Minister to Siam from 1898-1912. The papers contain correspondence, letter books, diary (1903), mss of articles, reports, and addresses, and newspaper clippings dealing specifically with King's years as ambassador. Correspondence incl letters from George Dewey, Douglas MacArthur, William Alden Smith, J C Burrows, Frank Seward, and members of the Siamese royal family and ministry, incl King Chulalongkorn, Crown Prince Vajiravudh, Prince Dwanwongse, and Prince Damron, among others. Apart from material concerning official diplomatic matters, the papers provide detailed accounts of life in Siam. Of patricular interest is a series of diaries kept by Mrs Hamilton King for the years, 1885, 1898-1915.

DC —GEORGETOWN UNIVERSITY, Library, Special Collections Div, 37 & O Sts NW, Washington, 20057. George M Barringer, Special Collections Librn; Nicholas B Sheetz, Mss Librn
Holdings: Mss Cat
Notes: Diaries and journals kept by Hugh

McCormick Smith (1865-1941) and his wife, Emma, documenting their years in Siam. In 1922 Smith resigned his position as United States Commissioner of Fisheries, accepting an invitiation from the King of Siam to serve as advisor on Siamese fisheries. When the first Siamese Department of Fisheries was created in 1926, Smith was named director, remaining in that office until his return to the United States in 1934. The diaries not only contain accounts of Smith's work in Siam, but also provide vivid descriptions of Siamese life, culture, and topography.

HI —UNIVERSITY OF HAWAII, Library, 2550 The Mall, Honolulu, 96822. Joyce Wright, Head, Asia Collection; Masato Matsu, Head, East Asia Vernacular Collection
Holdings: Vols 331,620 Cat Microforms
Notes: The Asia Collection holds materials from and about Southeast Asia: Brunei, Burma, Cambodia (Kampuchea), Indonesia, Laos, Malaysia, Philippines, Singapore, Thailand. Large contemporary Indonesian language collection. Several thousand vols in Thai and in Vietnamese. Minimal holdings in Burmese, Khmer, Lao languages. Social sciences and humanities emphasis for the post-World War II period. Western language coverage supplemented by retrospective holdings in the main library collection.

IL —NORTHERN ILLINOIS UNIVERSITY, Founders Memorial Library, Southeast Asia Collection, Normal Rd, De Kalb, 60115. Lee S Dutton Dr, Cur
Holdings: Vols (34,000) Cat Maps Microforms
Notes: An extensive collection of books, periodicals, newspapers, maps, and microforms from or about Southeast Asia. Areas of concentration incl Thailand, Malaysia, Indonesia, Singapore, Brunei, Philippines, Laos, and Burma. Holdings (except rare books, maps, and microforms) are housed in a separate area collection within the Founders Library. A departmental card catalog and specialized reference collection support reference services. A Thai collection of several thousand vols is the largest vernacular component. Extensive Malaysia, Indonesia, Singapore, and Brunei holdings have been acquired through the NPAC program. A collection of Filipino-American newspapers, and a growing collection of children's literature in common and uncommon Southeast Asian languages are available. Resources are accessible to borrowers through OCLC.

MA —HARVARD UNIVERSITY LIBRARY, Widener Library, Cambridge, 02138.
Holdings: Cat

MI —UNIVERSITY OF MICHIGAN, Harlan Hatcher Graduate Library, Ann Arbor, 48109. Susan Go, Librn
Holdings: Vols (250,000) Cat Mss Maps Pix Slides Microforms
Notes: Incl in the Michigan Historical Collections (primarily archival material) are papers of Michiganders in southeast Asia, mostly the Philipines, eg papers of Joseph R Hayden, Frank Murphy and G Mennen Williams, also, on film, the selected papers of Philippines president Manuel Quezon. All aspects of the countries, cultures and peoples of Brunei, Burma, Khymer, Indonesia, Laos, Malaysia, Philippines, Singapore, Thailand, Portuguese Timor and Vietnam. Also the Malayo-Polynesian (Austronesian), Mon-Khmer (Austroasiatic), and Sino-Tibetan language groupings.

MI —MICHIGAN STATE UNIVERSITY, International Library, South and Southeast Asia Collection, East Lansing, 48824. Clinton Lockert, Bibliographer
Holdings: Vols (13,500) Cat Mss Maps Pix Audiotapes Microforms
Notes: Emphasis is upon South Vietnam (1955-1962), Thailand (1964-1968) and the Philippines (1898-). Complete holdings of MSU Vietnam Advisory Group, *Reports and Documents*. Extensive materials related to Thailand Project in Education Planning, 1964-1968. Extensive holdings of the Institute of Pacific Relations.

NY —CORNELL UNIVERSITY LIBRARIES, John M Olin Library, John M Echols

Collection on Southeast Asia, Ithaca, 14853. Giok Po Oey, Curator
Holdings: Vols (167,000) Cat Mss Maps Pix Microforms
Budget: ($90,000)
Notes: Additions published in the collection's monthly accessions list (Ithaca: Cornell University, Southeast Asia Program, 1959-). Holdings through December 1980 listed in *Cornell University Libraries Southeast Asia Catalog* (Boston: G K Hall, 1976, First supplement, 1983), 10 vols.

OH —CLEVELAND PUBLIC LIBRARY, Fine Arts and Special Collections Department, 325 Superior Ave, Cleveland, 44114. Alice N Loranth, Head
Holdings: Vols 2070 Cat Mss
Notes: Emphasis is on language, linguistics, inscriptions, literature and religion. The most important titles refer to Pali texts in Thai. Western translations of classic texts also. 370 vols in Thai. Separate catalog of main entries for titles in Thai is maintained.

THAILAND—POPULATION

NC —CAROLINA POPULATION CENTER, Library, University Sq E, Chapel Hill, 27514. Patricia Shipman, Head Librn
Holdings: Vols (20,000) Cat
Budget: ($10,500)
Notes: Try to acquire everything published in English on population, with particular emphasis on the US and developing countries. Also acquire conference proceedings, seminar papers. These and journal articles are indexed and the analytics are incl in the catalog. Incl 13,000 reprints and other pieces of ephemera. Most extensive area files are on India, Africa, Thailand, Iran, Korea, and Latin America. Holdings are recorded on an automated data base. A microfiche catalog is available for use in the Library and for purchase. Access by subject & geographic area are available through the Library's own thesaurus-based indexing systems.

THALAMOPHORA see Foraminifera

THALASSOGRAPHY see Oceanography

THANATOLOGY

MA —NATIONAL CENTER FOR DEATH EDUCATION, New England Resource Center for Thanatology & Funeral Service, 656 Beacon St, Boston, 02215. Gail Gruner, Librn

THANE, ELSWYTH

MA —BOSTON UNIVERSITY, Mugar Memorial Library, Special Collections Dept, 771 Commonwealth Ave, Boston, 02215. Howard B Gotlieb, Dir
Holdings: Cat Mss Maps Pix
Notes: Mss, correspondence, etc collected in depth; incl publications by or about.

THAXTER, CELIA

ME —WESTBROOK COLLEGE, Library, 716 Stevens Ave, Portland, 04103. Dorothy M Healy, Special Collections Librn
Holdings: Vols (3000) Cat Mss Pix
Notes: Collection incl work of Maine women writers. Many mss and scrapbooks are incl. Memorabilia of Mrs Robert E Peary, Mary Ellen Chase, Florence B Jacobs, Celia Thaxter, and Edna St Vincent Millay are notable items. Some rare books, ie Madame Wood novels, are part of the collection.

THAXTER, R.

MA —HARVARD UNIVERSITY LIBRARY, Farlow Reference Library, 20 Divinity Ave, Cambridge, 02138. Geraldine C Kaye, Librn
Holdings: Vols (60,000)
Notes: The Farlow Reference Library provides complete coverage of the systematic literature on algae, bryophytes, fungi, and lichens. Established by bequest of Professor William G Farlow, it is one of the most extensive cryptogamic botany libraries

THAXTER, R. (cont.)

in the US. Incl ms and archival collections of W G Farlow and R Thaxter. Books do not circulate.

THAYER, ELI, 1819-1899

RI —BROWN UNIVERSITY, John Hay Library, 20 Prospect St, Providence, 02912. Mark N Brown, Cur Mss
Notes: Papers of Eli Thayer, educator, US Congressman from Massachusetts, and organizer of the New England Emigrant Aid Company. Brown class of 1845. About 1000 letters, speeches, and articles on political subjects for the period 1841-1898; also Thayer's journal from 1853-1857.

THAYER, EZRA RIPLEY, 1866-1915

MA —HARVARD UNIVERSITY LIBRARY, Law School Library, Langdell Hall, Cambridge, 02138. Erika S Chadbourn, Cur of Mss
Holdings: Cat Mss
Notes: Professional papers. Typed inventory in repository. Inclusive dates: 1882-1915.

THAYER, JAMES BRADLEY, 1831-1902

MA —HARVARD UNIVERSITY LIBRARY, Law School Library, Langdell Hall, Cambridge, 02138. Erika S Chadbourn, Cur of Mss
Holdings: Cat Mss
Notes: Professional papers. Typed inventory in repository. Inclusive dates: 1850-1902.

THAYER, ROBERT H.

DC —LIBRARY OF CONGRESS, Manuscript Division, Washington, 20540. John C Broderick, Chief
Notes: Papers of Robert H Thayer, lawyer and foreign service officer.

THEATRE

AZ —UNIVERSITY OF ARIZONA, University Library, Special Collections, Tucson, 85721. Louis A Hieb, Head
Notes: Specializes in areas of Restoration Drama, 18th, 19th and 20th century English and American authors.

CA —POMONA PUBLIC LIBRARY, Special Collections, 625 S Garey Ave, PO Box 2271, Pomona, 91766. David Streeter, Librn
Holdings: Uncat Mss
Notes: Padua Theater. 14 linear feet of theater archives including original play scripts, original music compositions, tape recordings of play performances, theater advertising, photographs of players, play bills, etc. Theatrical group was also known as The Mexican Players. Period covered: 1930's-1960's.

DC —HOWARD UNIVERSITY, Founders Library, Channing Pollock Theatre Collection, 500 Howard Place NW, Washington, 20059. Marilyn Mahanand, Librn
Holdings: Vols (16,440) Cat Mss Maps Pix Slides Microforms

DC —NATIONAL ENDOWMENT FOR THE ARTS, Library, 1100 Pen Ave NW, Rm 213, Washington, 20506. Christine Morrison, Arts Librn
Holdings: Vols (6000) Cat
Notes: Incl arts and education and public policy in the arts.

IL —CHICAGO PUBLIC LIBRARY, Art Section, Fine Arts Division, 78 E Washington St, Chicago, 60602. Rosalinda I Hack, Fine Arts Division Chief; Yvonne S Brown, Head, Art Section
Holdings: Vols 8000
Notes: Reference and circulating collection of books, periodicals, pamphlets, pictures, and microform. Special emphasis on general theatre history, theatre of the United States, biographies of actors and actresses, and acting techniques. Collection is supplemented by Chicago stagebills and reviews of area theater productions, a pamphlet and curio file on Chicago theater. Much additional materials can be found in our Special Collections Department.

KY —UNIVERSITY OF KENTUCKY, Art Library, 4 Margaret I King Library, Lexington, 40506. Meg Shaw, Art Librn
Holdings: Vols 26,338

LA —LOUISIANA STATE UNIVERSITY, SHREVEPORT, Library-Archives, 8515 Youree Dr, Shreveport, 71129. Patricia L Meador, Archivist & Asst Librn
Notes: Theatre and music is documented in the John Wray and Margaret Mary Young Theatre Collection, (5 linear ft), (1929-1981), the Joe Gifford Papers (1946-1960) (3 linear ft), the Shreveport Little Theatre Records (6 linear ft), the Nathaniel S Allen Papers (1860-1930), the records of the Shreveport Symphony (1948-1978) and oral history interviews on the topics. The archives collection also incl 60 linear ft of records (1949-1981) of Holiday-In-Dixie, Shreveport-Bossier's spring-time festival.

MI —MICHIGAN STATE UNIVERSITY, Libraries, Special Collections Div, East Lansing, 48824. Jannette Fiore, Librn
Notes: The Russel B Nye Popular Culture Collection in the Michigan State Univ Libraries incl over (45,000) items. Most of the collection is organized into 4 categories: comic art, popular fiction, popular information materials and materials relating to the popular performing arts. Materials relating to popular theatre, music, television, radio, and film. Theatre is best represented. A significant collection of primary materials relating to the tent show incl photographs, financial and other records of the Henderson Stock Company, correspondence, leaflets, handbills and other ephemera from many of the companies playing in the upper midwest in the 1920s and 1930s, and photocopies of 250 tent show scripts.

NM —THOMAS BRANIGAN MEMORIAL LIBRARY, 200 E Picacho Ave, Las Cruces, 88001. Don Dresp, Dir
Notes: Max Freudenthal Collection (cat).

NY —STATE UNIVERSITY OF NEW YORK AT ALBANY, Library, Special Collections Dept, 1400 Washington Ave, Albany, 12222. Marion P Munzer, Coordr
Notes: Correspondence of Richard Plant (0.5 linear feet); incl mss, reviews of moving pictures and plays. Part of the Library's German Exile Collection.
See also entry under Plant, Richard

PA —UNIVERSITY OF PITTSBURGH, Special Collections Dept, Curtis Theatre Collection, 363 Hillman Library, Pittsburgh, 15260. Jeanette Blanco, Cur
Holdings: Vols (4000) Cat Mss Pix Slides Microforms VF
Notes: The legitimate theatre of plays, musicals and vaudeville, chiefly of New York City and Pittsburgh, from 1865, and other US, community, summer, college and foreign theatre. Incl 500,000 programs, 12,000 pictures, 300 posters, the Oliver P Merriman Scrapbooks and 300 other scrapbooks, clippings and other ephemera. Vols incl over 3000 acting editions and playscripts. Separate collections: Ralph G Allen Burlesque Skits Collection; Michael Ellis Papers; William P Halstead Theatre Collection; Kenyon Family Papers; Philip Dunning Playscripts Collection; Pittsburgh Playhouse Records; Pittsburgh Savoyards Records. Noncirculating.

RI —BROWN UNIVERSITY, John Hay Library, 20 Prospect St, Providence, 02912. Mark N Brown, Cur Mss
Holdings: Vols (4000) Mss Pix
Notes: Papers of William Chauncey Langdon (1871-1947), incl over 300 pageants, some written and directed by him, 1911-1921.
See also entry under American Drama.

†WI —STATE HISTORICAL SOCIETY OF WISCONSIN, Library, 816 State St, Madison, 53706.
Notes: Scripts, notes, correspondence and other items concerning the collaboration of Howard Lindsay and Russel Crouse for the theater, motion pictures and television, as well as the work of each with other collaborators and individually.

THEATRE—BIBLIOGRAPHY

NY —THEATRE RESEARCH DATA CENTER, Brooklyn College, City University of New York, Brooklyn, 11210. Irving M Brown, Dir; Rosabel A Wang, Systs Coordr; Benito Ortolani, Bibliographer
Notes: Theatre Research Data Center of Brooklyn College in collaboration with the American Society for Theatre Research, is compiling an extensive data base, with the cooperation of other US and international theatre-related scholars and institutions, indexing a broad list of theatre publications: periodicals, books, catalogs, films, discs, tapes, etc, containing material of interest to theatre researchers. Will publish American Society/Theatre Research annual international bibliography starting '84-'85. Database service for online research 1985. Coverage began 1982; retrospective coverage later.

THEATRE—BOSTON

MA —BRANDEIS UNIVERSITY, Goldfarb Library, 415 South St, Waltham, 02154. Bessie Hahn, Dir
Notes: American Theater Programs Collection. Consists of 14 linear ft of American theater and stage programs of the late 19th and early 20th century with particular emphasis on the Boston dramatic scene. This collection is unprocessed, spring 1984.

THEATRE—CALIFORNIA

CA —UNIVERSITY OF CALIFORNIA, DAVIS, Shields Library, Dept of Special Collections, Davis, 95616. Donald Kunitz, Head; C Danial Elliott, Asst Head
Notes: Programs, playbills, posters, designs, and scripts from 19th and 20th century American and British theatre. American materials incl the eastern United States (NYC) and California. Production groupings center in Sir Henry Irving, McKee Rankin, Sir John Martin-Harvey, E L Davenport. Clippings, photographs, and correspondence of theatre personalities; records of the Bread and Puppet Theatre, San Francisco Mime Troupe, Living Theatre, Firehouse Theatre, Squat Theatre, papers of Toby Cole. Described in: Sarlos, Robert K, "The Theatre Collection at Davis," American Society for Theatre Research Newsletter, vol 3, no 1, fall 1974, pp 2-3, 9-10.

CA —UNIVERSITY OF THE PACIFIC, Library, Stockton, 95211. Hiram L Davis, Dir of Libraries
Holdings: // Uncat Mss Pix
Notes: Papers of Vena Woods, 1880-1925, dramatic actress and author. Incl drafts of novels and plays, notes and photos relating to California theatre. Twelve document boxes.

CA —CALIFORNIA INSTITUTE OF THE ARTS, Library, 24700 McBean Pkwy, Valencia, 91355. James Elrod, Dir
Holdings: Vols (61,000) Cat
Budget: ($4500)

THEATRE—CALIFORNIA—PICTURES, ILLUSTRATIONS, ETC.

CA —UNIVERSITY OF CALIFORNIA, LOS ANGELES, Research Library, Dept of Special Collections, 405 Hilgard Ave, Los Angeles, 90024. Edward Shreeves, Chairman, Bibliographers Group; David S Zeidberg, Head
Notes: Various collections, incl the Community Playhouse of Pasadena, George P Johnson Negro Film, Jerome Robinson, theatrical programs, and turn-of-the-century cabinet cards collections.

THEATRE—CANADA

MB —UNIVERSITY OF MANITOBA, Elizabeth Dafoe Library, Archives and Special Collections Dept, Winnipeg, R3T 2N2, Can. Richard E Bennett, Dept Head; Corrado A Santoro, Reference Archivist
Notes: Five folders of records and printed materials by and about the Community Players of Winnipeg. Incl programs, photographs and reports.

THEATRE—CANADA (cont.)

ON —YORK UNIVERSITY, Scott Library,
Downsview, M3J 2R2, Can. Hartwell
Bowsfield, University Archivist
Notes: Literary and political papers of
Canadian playwright, theatre director, and
teacher Herman Voaden, leading exponent
of Canadian national drama, and the concept
of "Symphonic theatre," encompassing all the
living arts, collection covers 1897-1975, incl
personal papers, diaries, etc. Over 700
playbills, 1926-1945, etc.

ON —UNIVERSITY OF GUELPH, Library,
Guelph, N1G 2W1, Can. Margaret
Beckman, Chief Librn; Ellen Pearson, Ref
Librn
Notes: 160 boxes of archival materials, also
props, models, prompt books and pix.
Archives of the Shaw Festival Theatre
Foundation, Niagara-on-the-Lake, Ontario;
the Tarragon Theatre, Toronto, Ontario;
Open Circle, Toronto, Ontario; Young
Peoples Theatre, Toronto, Ontario; Guelph
Spring Festival, Guelph, Ontario.
See also entry under Shaw Festival Theatre
Foundation, Ontario

ON —NATIONAL LIBRARY OF CANADA,
395 Wellington St, Ottawa, K1A 0N4, Can.
Andre Preibish, Dir
Holdings: Vols 8000
Notes: Includes 100 serial titles, also
programs, play bills etc on microfilm.
Performing arts collection consists of
Canadian titles received on legal deposit and
purchased. Areas of concentration: Canadian
theatre and dance; European and American
performing arts tradition; theatre
architecture; stage craft; costume history,
dance history and notation etc.

ON —METROPOLITAN TORONTO
LIBRARY, Theatre Dept, 789 Yonge St,
Toronto, M4W 2G8, Can. Heather
McCallum, Head
Holdings: Vols (30,500) Mss Pix Slides
Phonorecrods Microforms
Notes: The Theatre Department is one of eleven
subject departments of the Metropolitan Toronto
Library, which is generally acknowledged to be the
most comprehensive of Canadian public library
collections. The department balances book and non
book materials in all areas of the performing arts
except music: theatre and drama, moving pictures,
dance, television and radio programming, and
varieties of popular entertainment such as circus,
music hall, vaudeville, puppetry and pantomime.
The department's substantial holdings of rare
books include over 75 court festival books. The
collection is international in scope and is
particularly strong in materials relating to Canadian
theatre history and drama. Non-book holdings
include extensive files of newspaper clippings,
playbills, programs, production and publicity
photographs, posters, and original stage designs,
all of which document for the most part the history
of Canadian theatre and dance companies, a large
collection of British and American theatre portrait
engravings, and a representative selection of 19th
century, Japanese woodblock prints. Special
collections relating to the history of the performing
arts in Canada include the records of the Taverner
Company which played Eastern Canada and the
United States in the late 19th century, Toronto's
Grand Opera House, the Marks Brothers touring
company, film actor Ned Sparks, the Canadian-
born actress Judith Evelyn, Toronto's Crest
Theatre, the Canadian Players, Montreal Repertory
Theatre, dancer/teacher Boris Volkoff, the
Dumbells, the Canadian all-soldier concert party
which originated in France in 1917, and vaudeville
performer Charles Manny.

THEATRE—CHARLESTON, SOUTH CAROLINA

SC —COLLEGE OF CHARLESTON
LIBRARY, Special Collections Dept,
Charleston, 29401.
Notes: (1) Several histories of the Footlight
Players, scrapbooks (1932-1964), programs
(1931-1958), footnotes (1937-1970), scripts
(many adapted from well known works by
Emmett Robinson), photographs, and
posters. Also included is material dealing
with the Dock Street Theatre's history, its
theatre school, and non-Footlight Player
performances. (2) Emmett Robinson papers
incl typescript of his "Source history of the
drama in ante-bellum Charleston, SC (1800-
1861)." Incl playbills of performances
involving Robinson.

THEATRE—CHICAGO

CA —LOS ANGELES PUBLIC LIBRARY,
Frances Howard Goldwyn Hollywood
Regional Library, 1623 Ivar Ave, Los
Angeles, 90028. Sally Dumaux, Librn
Holdings: Vols (100,000) Cat Mss Pix VF
Budget: ($60,000)
Notes: A general and a research collection
on theatre history, US and foreign, with
special emphasis on Los Angeles, Chicago,
and New York theatre from the late 1800s
to the present. Other aspects of the
collection include theatre design, make-up,
costume, and acting and directing
techniques. Also includes biographies of
actors and actresses (many signed). The play
collection of over 15,000 titles covers mainly
English and American plays of the 19th and
20th century. There are over 5000 playbills,
scrapbooks, posters, and programs. Special
Collections: "Hellzapoppin," NY, 1938-40.
Includes photographs, clippings, and
programs.
IL —CHICAGO HISTORICAL SOCIETY,
Library, Clark St at North Ave, Chicago,
60614. Robert L Brubaker, Librn
Holdings: Vols (150,000) Cat Mss Pix
Notes: Chicago theatre programs (5000);
scrapbooks containing reviews and other
clippings; a few letters, reminiscences,
account books, and other records of theatres,
actors and actresses, and managers; theatre
posters. Thomas Conolly Collection of
Theatrical Portraits; other photographs of
theatres, productions, and casts.
IL —CHICAGO PUBLIC LIBRARY, Special
Collections Div, Cultural Center, 78 E
Washington St, Chicago, 60602. Laura
Linard, Cur
Holdings: Mss Pix
Notes: Special Collections maintains a scarce
collection of theatre broadsides, playbills,
programs and other ephemera for Chicago
productions, 1880-1930 as well as a recently
acquired collection of contemporary material
(1971-1981). These are described in
Treasures of The Chicago Public Library,
compiled by Thomas A Orlando and Marie
Gecik, 1977, pp 121-33. The Archives of the
Publicity Department of the Goodman
Theatre (formerly of the Art Institute of
Chicago) are maintained by Special
Collections at The Chicago Public Library.
We also have a nearly complete collection of
the plays of Kenneth Sawyer Goodman, after
whom the Goodman Theatre is named.
Some unique pre-fire material is also to be
found in these collections. A finding aid to
these collections has been prepared.

THEATRE—CHILE

NY —STATE UNIVERSITY OF NEW
YORK, STONY BROOK, Melville Library,
Dept of Special Collections, Stony Brook,
11794. Evert Volkersz, Head
Holdings: // Uncat
Notes: Nineteenth century Chilean playbills,
plays and libretti. A list of holdings is
available. About 570 pamphlets bound in 57
vols.

THEATRE—COSTUME see Costume

THEATRE—DETROIT

MI —DETROIT PUBLIC LIBRARY, Music &
Performing Arts Dept, 5201 Woodward,
Detroit, 48202. Agatha Pfeiffer Kalkanis,
Chief
Holdings: Mss Pix
Notes: Extensive bound files of programs for
Detroit theatres, 1890 to present, partially
indexed by names and titles. Supplemented
by manuscript history of Detroit theatre
1811-1908, and Bonstelle theatre 1910-1929.
Also clipping files.

THEATRE—FOREIGN see International Theatre

THEATRE—GERMANY

NY —STATE UNIVERSITY OF NEW
YORK, BINGHAMTON, Glenn G Bartle
Library, Binghamton, 13901. Marion
Hanscom, Special Collections Librn
Holdings: Cat
Budget: ($8000)
Notes: Max Reinhardt Archive. Library has
extensive (approx 250,000 items) archival
material relating to Max Reinhardt, as well
as his personal library. This personal library
is not a subject collection per se, but
contains much information about German
theater in the 20th century. The archival
material contains letters, prompt books,
photograhs, playbills, etc.

THEATRE—GREAT BRITAIN

TN —MEMPHIS STATE UNIVERSITY, John
Willard Brister Library, Memphis, 38152.
John Terreo, Special Collections Librn
Notes: Theatre Collection, 1789-1972.
Correspondence, scripts, programs, handbills,
musical scores, clippings, drawings, sketches,
and photographs, documenting careers of
artists, production of plays, ballet and
theatre companies, and theaters and opera
houses centering in New York and London,
England. Incl drawings, prints, publications,
and other personal papers of British
producer and designer Edward Gordon Craig
(1872-1966), relating to his career, radio
talks (1951-1961) for the BBC, acting school
in Florence, Italy, and his mother, actress
Ellen Terry; and correspondence, scripts,
programs, reviews, scrapbooks, photos, and
other materials, of American producer Jed
Harris (?-1979), relating to his stage
productions (1926-1945).

THEATRE—HISTORY

†AL —MUSEUMS OF THE CITY OF
MOBILE, Reference Library, 355
Government St, Mobile, 36602. Caldwell
Delaney, Adminr
Notes: Little Theatre of Mobile Coll.
AZ —UNIVERSITY OF ARIZONA, Library,
Tucson, 85721. W David Laird, Librn
Notes: Theatre collection incl works by and
about Thomas Wood Stevens and the theatre
in Pittsburgh and Chicago. Mss of pageants,
programs, scrapbooks, prompt books, private
press imprints, personal correspondence.
CA —CLAREMONT COLLEGES, Honnold
Library, Ninth & Dartmouth, Claremont,
91711. Tania Rizzo, Special Collections
Dept Head
Holdings: Vols 250 // Uncat Mss
Notes: Papers of Elbert A Wickes, 1884-
1975, theatrical and lecture tour manager.

THEATRE—HISTORY (cont.)

Among his clients were Winston Churchill, William Butler Yeats, Houdini, Lowell Thomas, Vilhjalmur Stefansson, and Roy Chapman Andrews. He managed three American tours for the Abbey Players during the 1930s, was partner and producer of Fritz Leiber Shakespeare plays, the Water Follies of 1937, and the Affiliated Lyceum and Chautauquas Association. The collection is rich in autograph and photographic materials. There are 750 items relative to the Abbey Players. Card file and inventory available. Restricted use.

CA —UNIVERSITY OF CALIFORNIA, DAVIS, Shields Library, Dept of Special Collections, Davis, 95616. Donald Kunitz, Head; C Danial Elliott, Asst Head
Holdings: Uncat Mss Pix Slides Audiotapes Videotapes 16mm Films
Notes: Programs, playbills, posters, designs, and scripts from 19th and 20th century American and British theatre. American materials incl the eastern United States (NYC) and California. Production groupings center in Sir Henry Irving, McKee Rankin, Sir John Martin-Harvey, E L Davenport. Clippings, photographs, and correspondence of theatre personalities; records of the Bread and Puppet Theatre, San Francisco Mime Troupe, Living Theatre, Firehouse Theatre, Squat Theatre, papers of Toby Cole. Described in: Sarlos, Robert K, "The Theatre Collection at Davis," *American Society for Theatre Research Newsletter,* vol 3, no 1, fall 1974, pp 2-3, 9-10.

CA —CALIFORNIA STATE UNIVERSITY, LONG BEACH, Library, Dept of Special Collections & Archives, 1250 Bellflower Blvd, Long Beach, 90840. John Ahouse, Special Collections Librn
Holdings: Vols (5000) Cat Pix
Notes: Incl playbills, scripts, scrapbooks from the former Pasadena Playhouse, together with the former Hildebrand Collection of English and American Drama before 1830.

CA —INSTITUTE OF THE AMERICAN MUSICAL, Library, 121 N Detroit St, Los Angeles, 90036. Miles Kreuger, Cur
Holdings: Cat Mss Maps Pix Slides Phonorecords
Notes: Reference materials on the American musical theatre and motion pictures incl 40,000 phonograph records, sound tapes, and cylinders dating back to the 1890s; record catalogs to 1900; thousands of theatre and film programs, periodicals, sheet music and vocal scores as early as 1830; thousands of motion picture press books and over 200,000 stills from 1914 to the present; every musical comedy script published in America and dozens in ms form, original or photocopy materials from the archives of movie palaces, films and record companies, incl discographies of many major Broadway and Hollywood stars; and thousands of books on theatre, film, broadcasting, world's fairs and other allied areas of showmanship.

CA —LOS ANGELES PUBLIC LIBRARY, Literature and Philology Dept, 630 W Fifth St, Los Angeles, 90071. Helene G Mochedlover, Dept Librn
Holdings: Vols (50,000) Cat Pix Slides Microforms
Notes: Incl theatre programs, playbills, clippings, play reviews on 19th and 20th century plays produced in or near Los Angeles. Play collection of over 30,000 vols is particularly strong in 19th and 20th centuries. Annotated subject index to plays is kept up-to-date. A file of local as well as New York and London play reviews is kept. Collection incl microprints and microcards. There are a number of long files of important dramatic periodicals.

CA —LOS ANGELES PUBLIC LIBRARY, Frances Howard Goldwyn Hollywood Regional Library, 1623 Ivar Ave, Los Angeles, 90028. Sally Dumaux, Librn
Holdings: Vols (100,000) Cat Mss Pix VF
Budget: ($60,000)
Notes: A general and a research collection on theatre history, US and foreign, with special emphasis on Los Angeles, Chicago, and New York theatre from the late 1800s to the present. Other aspects of the collection include theatre design, make-up, costume, and acting and directing techniques. Also includes biographies of actors and actresses. The play collection of over 15,000 titles covers mainly English and American plays of the 19th and 20th century. There are over 5000 playbills, scrapbooks, posters, and programs. Special Collections: "Hellzapoppin," NY, 1938-40. Includes photographs, clippings, and programs.

CA —UNIVERSITY OF CALIFORNIA, LOS ANGELES, Research Library, Dept of Special Collections, 405 Hilgard Ave, Los Angeles, 90024. Edward Shreeves, Chairman, Bibliographers Group; David S Zeidberg, Head
Notes: Various collections, incl the Community Playhouse of Pasadena, George P Johnson Negro Film, Jerome Robinson, theatrical programs, and turn-of-the-century cabinet cards collections.

CA —UNIVERSITY OF SOUTHERN CALIFORNIA, Edward L Doheny Memorial Library, Archives of Performing Arts, University Park, Los Angeles, 90089. Robert Knutson, Librn
Holdings: Mss
Notes: Approx 15,000 vols of books and serials about film, incl a large collection of foreign language books and periodicals. Current subscriptions to over 200 serials. Large collection of clippings about motion pictures and television. Warner Brothers Films Collection (1920-1968) incl 700,000 stills and negatives; 3,000 titles of feature, short subject and television screenplays, script materials, set designs, engineering drawings, production records, patent records, music and legal files. Over 1000 bound vols describing the inventory and 100 bound vols of index to the inventory. Universal Pictures Corporation Collection incl 600 boxes of production and publicity department records, incl 1,500 screenplays. Metro-Goldwyn-Mayer Collection incl screenplays from 1919-1958. Twentieth Century-Fox Collection incl screenplays and story department notes from 1919-1967. Hal Roach Studio Collection contains studio records from 1916-mid fifties. More than 150 personal collections from actors, directors, producers, writers, etc. Also have 2,000 additional screenplays; 1,000 posters, 110,000 photographs; 750 recorded soundtracks; 1,500 interview tapes; 400 David Wolper videotapes. A collection of feature films on videotape is being created. There is also a historical collection of motion picture cameras, projectors and other equipment from the earliest times to present.

CA —SAN DIEGO PUBLIC LIBRARY, Art, Music & Recreation Sect, 820 E St, San Diego, 92101. Barbara A Tuhill, Supvr
Holdings: Vols 500 Cat
Notes: The gift of Elwyn B Gould, the collection consists of many first editions of biographies of famous actors and actresses and histories of the American, London and European stages. Theatre program scrapbooks dating from 1890 to 1928, some of local events. For reference use only.

CA —CALIFORNIA HISTORICAL SOCIETY, Schubert Hall Library, 2099 Pacific Ave, San Francisco, 94109. Bruce L Johnson, Library Dir
Holdings: Vols (50,000) Cat Mss Maps Pix
Notes: Strong theatre collection.
See also entry under California - History.

CA —UNIVERSITY OF SAN FRANCISCO, Richard A Gleeson Library, The Countess Bernardine Murphy Donohue Rare Book Room, San Francisco, 94117. D Steven Corey, Special Collections Librn
Holdings: Vols 273
Notes: Typescript plays comprising the George W Poultney Theatre Collection spanning the period 1868-1915, many rare.

CA —UNIVERSITY OF CALIFORNIA, SANTA BARBARA, Library, Dept of Special Collections, Santa Barbara, 93106. Christian F Brun, Head
Holdings: Cat Mss Pix

CA —UNIVERSITY OF CALIFORNIA, SANTA CRUZ, University Library, Special Collections, Santa Cruz, 95064. Rita Bottoms, Special Collections Librn; Margaret Felts, South Pacific Collection Bibliographer
Holdings: Cat Mss Pix
Notes: The Robert McNulty Collection of books by Sir Henry Irving, also photographs, hand-written letters, biographies, prompt books and programs.

CA —CALIFORNIA INSTITUTE OF THE ARTS, Library, 24700 McBean Pkwy, Valencia, 91355. James Elrod, Dir
Holdings: Vols (61,000) Cat
Budget: ($4500)

CO —DENVER PUBLIC LIBRARY, Western History Department, 1357 Broadway, Denver, 80203. Eleanor M Gehres, Head
Holdings: Vols (50,000) Cat Mss Maps Pix Audiotapes Microforms
Notes: Western US History. The department has a separate catalog, published in 1970 in 7 vols by G K Hall Co. First supplement published in 1975 in 1 vol. There is a subject index of some 3 million entries to newspapers and magazines of the Rocky Mountain region, added to daily. The Western Newspaper Microfilm Center contains approx 7000 reels of Western US newspapers. Collection has ca 275,000 negatives and prints of Western life; and ca 2500 maps, cataloged and classified.

CT —YALE UNIVERSITY, Drama Library, 222 York St, Box 1903A, Yale Station, New Haven, 06520. Pamela C Jordan, Librn
Holdings: Vols (24,000) Cat Pix Slides Audiotapes
Budget: ($6000)
Notes: Book collection covers all phases of the dramatic arts: theatre, film, opera, dance, etc, with an emphasis on 20th century theatre. Incl audiotapes of Yale Drama School and Repertory Theatre productions, other plays and dramatic readings, and dialect tapes. Incl 1200 slides on costume design and 2000 slides on architecture, interiors, and furniture. Also incl more than 80,000 pictures on set and costume design.

DC —FOLGER SHAKESPEARE LIBRARY, 201 E Capitol St, Washington, 20003. Philip A Knachel, Acting Dir
Holdings: Vols (223,571) Cat Mss Pix Periodicals Microfilms
Notes: Collections described in *Catalog of Printed Books of the Folger Shakespeare Library,* 28 vols; *First Supplement,* 3 vols (Boston: G K Hall, 1970, 1976); *Second Supplement* in 2 vols (Boston: G K Hall, 1981); *Catalog of Manuscripts of the Folger Shakespeare Library,* 3 vols (Boston: G K Hall, 1971); and *The Widening Circle: The Story of the Folger Library and Its Collections* (Washington, DC: Folger Shakespeare Library, 1976). Collections incl 39 vols of plays with ms annotations and stage directions by John Philip Kemble. Library use restricted to advanced research scholars.

DC —HOWARD UNIVERSITY, Founders Library, Channing Pollock Theatre Collection, 500 Howard Place NW, Washington, 20059. Marilyn Mahanand, Librn
Holdings: Vols (16,440) Cat Mss Maps Pix Slides Microforms
Notes: Much on the Black Theatre.

DC —LIBRARY OF CONGRESS, Rare Book & Special Collections Div, Washington, 20540. William Matheson, Chief
Holdings: Cat
Notes: The Theatre Playbill Collection consists of 7500 playbills relating to performances in Washington (largely), New York, Boston, Philadelphia, Cincinnati, Buffalo, Charlestown, etc between 1823 and 1930, with a concentration in late 19th and early 20th century performances. Incl a large number of theatre playbills for productions in London, Birmingham, Liverpool, Newcastle, Manchester, etc between 1810 and 1880 (especially Shakespearean performances).

DC —LIBRARY OF CONGRESS, Manuscript Division, Washington, 20540. John C Broderick, Chief
Holdings: Cat Mss Pix
Notes: Incl correspondence, literary mss,

THEATRE—HISTORY (cont.)

reports, notes, scrapbooks, photographs, etc. About 10,000 items.

FL —RINGLING MUSEUM OF ART, Art Research Library, PO Box 1838, Sarasota, 33578. Lynell A Morr, Librn
Holdings: Vols (40,000) Cat
Budget: ($24,000)
Notes: Incl an additional 30,000 art auction catalogs, indexed 1970-date.

FL —UNIVERSITY OF SOUTH FLORIDA, Library, Tampa, 33620. J B Dobkin, Special Collections Librn
Holdings: Cat Mss
Notes: The theatre of Dion Boucicault; almost exclusively manuscript materials (a major collection) but with a very few published plays or works by or about Boucicault.

FL —ROLLINS COLLEGE, Mills Memorial Library, Winter Park, 32789. Patricia J Delks, Dir of Libraries
Holdings: Vols 494 // Cat
Notes: Annie Russell (1864-1936) Theatre Collection. Also 97 pamphlets. Noncirculating.

GA —UNIVERSITY OF GEORGIA, Libraries, Special Collections Division, Athens, 30602. Vesta Lee Gordon, Asst Dir for Special Collections
Notes: Theater Collection contains the Paris Music Hall set and costume designs with original drawings by Erte, Barbier, Zig and others; British Music Hall Papers; European toy theater collection; Charles Coburn papers; television script collection; Tennessee Williams papers. Collection contains 16,000 pieces.

IL —SOUTHERN ILLINOIS UNIVERSITY, CARBONDALE, Delyte W Morris Library, Special Collections Dept, Carbondale, 62901. David V Koch, Cur of Special Collections; Louisa Bowen, Cur of Manuscripts
Holdings: Vols 160 Cat Mss Pix
Notes: The personal papers and business records of Erwin Piscator, internationally known producer, director and playwright, associated with the epic theater. This extensive collection consists of scripts, playbills, photographs, business records of various productions abroad, correspondence with actors, directors and playwrights (incl Bertold Brecht), both in America and Europe, and family papers. Also the papers of his widow, Dr Maria Piscator, ballerina, playwright, director and novelist. (Akademie der Kunte, Berlin, *Erwin Piscator,* 1893-1966, 1971.) Detailed inventory and name index available at the Library. Also, the personal papers (75 linear feet) and art work of Mordecai Gorelik, stage designer, director, and playwright, incl a large volume of correspondence with persons of the theatre, in the US and abroad, scripts of plays, and thousands of sketches, drawings, and photographs of stage settings.

IL —CHICAGO PUBLIC LIBRARY, Art Section, Fine Arts Division, 78 E Washington St, Chicago, 60602. Rosalinda I Hack, Fine Arts Division Chief; Yvonne S Brown, Head, Art Section
Holdings: Vols 8000
Notes: Reference and circulating collection of books, periodicals, pamphlets, pictures, and microform. Special emphasis on general theatre history, theatre of the United States, biographies of actors and actresses, and acting techniques. Collection is supplemented by Chicago stagebills and reviews of area theater productions, a pamphlet and curio file on Chicago theater. Much additional materials can be found in our Special Collections Department.

IL. —CHICAGO PUBLIC LIBRARY, Special Collections Div, Cultural Center, 78 E Washington St, Chicago, 60602. Laura Linard, Cur
Holdings: Mss Pix
Notes: Special Collections maintains a scarce collection of theatre broadsides, playbills, programs and other ephemera for Chicago productions, 1880-1930 as well as a recently acquired collection of contemporary material (1971-1981). These are described in

Treasures of The Chicago Public Library, compiled by Thomas A Orlando and Marie Gecik, 1977, pp 121-33. The Archives of the Publicity Department of the Goodman Theatre (formerly of the Art Institute of Chicago) are maintained by Special Collections at The Chicago Public Library. We also have a nearly complete collection of the plays of Kenneth Sawyer Goodman, after whom the Goodman Theatre is named. Some unique pre-fire material is also to be found in these collections. A finding aid to these collections has been prepared.

IL —NORTHERN ILLINOIS UNIVERSITY, Founders Memorial Library, Rare Books and Special Collections Dept, De Kalb, 60115. William R DuBois, Dept Head
Holdings: Vols 2000 // Cat
Notes: Nisbet-Snyder Drama Collection. Contains over 2000 prompt books and prompters' editions of plays, mostly published in England and the US from the last quarter of the 18th century to the end of the 19th century. Noncirculating.

IL —NORTHWESTERN UNIVERSITY, Library, Special Collections Dept, 1937 Sheridan Rd, Evanston, 60201. R Russell Maylone, Cur
Holdings: Vols 210 Cat Mss Pix Phonorecords
Notes: Collection is being cataloged according to the Craig bibliography of Fletcher & Rood. Collection incl material about Ellen Terry and Henry Irving, as well as original art work by E G Craig, stage designs and other ephemera. Collection created by J Wesley Swanson and given to Northwestern University Library by his sister.

IL —LAKE FOREST COLLEGE, Donnelley Library, Lake Forest, 60045. Arthur H Miller Jr, College Librn
Holdings: Cat Mss
Notes: Coverage from 17th century to the present about 5000 pieces, particularly American and English Garrett Leverton Memorial Theatre Library emphasizes the American drama renaissance of the early 20th century. It includes, though, more than 1000 published playscripts, of which a significant number are 19th century.

IL —ILLINOIS STATE UNIVERSITY, Milner Library, Dept of Special Collections, Normal, 61761. Robert Sokan, Librn
Holdings: Vols (6200) Cat Mss Pix Slides
Notes: Circus and related arts collection consists of approx 6200 book items and approx 250,000 nonbook items. The books date from the 16th century to the present, and incl vols specifically concerned with the circus past and present, vaudeville, music halls and variety theaters, theatrical and animal history, biographies, autobiographies and memoirs, novels, poetry, drama, juvenalia and other subjects relating to the circus. Many of the books are limited editions, presentation copies or autographed copies. Incl archives of the Dobritch International Circus (20,000 items).

IN —INDIANA UNIVERSITY, Lilly Library, Seventh St, Bloomington, 47405. William R Cagle, Librn
Holdings: // Mss Pix
Notes: Files of the National Theatre Conference, 1932-1965. Incl the papers of past presidents, executive secretary, and treasurer of the NTC (17,596 items). Also ms of individual plays, eg, Synge's *Playboy of the Western World,* Printer's *The Caretaker,* Barrie's *Peter Pan,* John Whiting's *The Gates of Summer.* Archibald MacLeish's *JB,* LeRoi Jones' *The Baptism* and *Dutchman,* etc.

IN —INDIANA UNIVERSITY, SOUTH BEND, Library, 1700 Mishawaka Ave, South Bend, 46615. James L Mullins, Dir
Holdings: Vols (1490) Cat Mss Maps Pix Phonorecords
Notes: Incl design materials, scripts, theatre music, rare editions, theatre programs, playbills, clippings and periodicals from the 1850s to the 1940s.

IA —UNIVERSITY OF IOWA, University Libraries, Iowa City, 52242. Robert A McCown, Mss Librn
Holdings: Mss
Notes: Keith/Albee Vaudeville Collection.

Records of a vaudeville, theatre, and moving-picture business established by Benjamin Franklin Keith, 1846-1930. The collection includes clippings books, report books, cash books, subject files, signs and posters. Theatres in the following cities are represented in the collection: Providence, RI, Pawtucket, RI, Woonsocket, RI, and Webster, Mass. The business was later part of RKO Pictures, Inc. Unpublished register in the library 50 ft of mss.

KY —HOPKINSVILLE COMMUNITY COLLEGE, Library, North Dr, Hopkinsville, 42240. Marjanna J Frising, Librn
Holdings: Vols (500) Cat Phonorecords Audiotapes Filmstrips
Notes: Incl most notable Broadway plays, both musical and non-musical, with soundtracks available for most. Also a large collection of children's and one-act plays as well as non-musical but best known 3-act plays, incl comedy and mystery plays.

KY —UNIVERSITY OF LOUISVILLE, Ekstrom Library, Photographic Archives, Louisville, 40292. J C Anderson, Cur; David G Horvath, Asst Cur
Holdings: Vols (750,000) Cat Pix Slides
Budget: ($60,000)
Notes: Photographs of actors and actresses, Louisville's Macauley Theatre.

LA —NEW ORLEANS PUBLIC LIBRARY, Art & Music Div, 219 Loyola Ave, New Orleans, 70140. Marilyn Wilkins, Head
Holdings: Cat Pix
Budget: $23,500

ME —BOOTHBAY THEATRE MUSEUM, Library, Corey Lane, Boothbay, 04537. Franklyn Lenthall, Cur
Holdings: Vols 6000 Cat Mss Pix Slides Phonrecords Audiotapes
Notes: The only Theatre Museum, as such, in America. Very extensive photo collection.

MD —MARYLAND HISTORICAL SOCIETY, Library, 201 W Monument St, Baltimore, 21201. William B Keller, Head Librn
Holdings: Cat Mss Maps Pix Slides Microforms
Notes: Espec relating to Maryland and Baltimore. Extensive collection.

†MD —MARYLAND HISTORICAL SOCIETY, Library, 201 W Monument St, Baltimore, 21201.
Notes: Eubie Blake's personal and professional archive. Incl the Baltimore-born pianist, composer, and songwriter's collection of songs and instrumental pieces in mss, extensive documentation of his collaboration with Noble Sissle, Flournog Miller, Milton Reddie, and others. The Broadway musical comedy, Shuffle Along, is represented in box office records, programs, scores and parts, photographs, and sheet music. Blake's involvement with other productions is similarly documented.

MA —BOSTON UNIVERSITY, Mugar Memorial Library, Special Collections Dept, 771 Commonwealth Ave, Boston, 02215. Howard B Gotlieb, Dir
Holdings: Cat Mss Pix
Notes: Incl personal papers and literary productions of numerous modern actors, actresses, musicians (composers and performers) of all kinds. A complete list is available.

MA —HARVARD UNIVERSITY LIBRARY, Theatre Collection, Cambridge, 02138. Jeanne T Newlin, Cur
Holdings: Cat Mss Pix Slides Microforms
Notes: One of the largest existing collections of playbills, programs, prints, photographs, promptbooks, and other materials relating to the performing arts, the scope is worldwide; resources on the English-speaking stage of the 18th and 19th centuries are unequalled. Incl materials on ballet and modern dance, the circus, magic, minstrel shows, cinema, and pantomime. For description, see *Harvard Library Bulletin,* VI (1925): pp 281-301. Also, papers of Robert E Sherwood (1896-1955), John Mason Bowers, George Pierce Baker, Edward Sheldon, Percy Mackaye; Angus McBean collection of photographs of the London Stage, 1937-1965; Alix Jeffry collection of photographs of the Off-Broadway Theatre; and others.

THEATRE—HISTORY (cont.)

MA —LENOX LIBRARY ASSOCIATION,
Main St, Lenox, 01240. Denis J Lesieur, Dir
Holdings: Mss Pix
Notes: Frances Anne "Fanny" Kemble (Mrs
Pierce M Butler), the English actress who
lived in Lenox. Some of her books.

MA —SMITH COLLEGE, Werner Josten
Library for the Performing Arts,
Northampton, 01063. Marlene M Wong,
Librn

MA —AMERICAN JEWISH HISTORICAL
SOCIETY, Library, 2 Thornton Rd,
Waltham, 02154. Nathan M Kaganoff,
Librn-Editor
Holdings: Vols 78,000 Cat Mss Pix
Microforms
Budget: ($9000)
Notes: American Jewish history; incl
paintings (100), theatre posters (500), sheet
music (3500), mss (4 million). Calendar to
individual collection published (2 vols).

MA —AMERICAN ANTIQUARIAN
SOCIETY LIBRARY, 185 Salisbury St,
Worcester, 01609. Marcus A McCorison,
Dir & Librn
Holdings: Pix
Notes: About 1300 theatre posters, from the
late 1870s to the mid-90s.

MI —UNIVERSITY OF MICHIGAN, Library,
Dept of Rare Books & Special Collections,
Ann Arbor, 48109. Robert J Starring, Head
Holdings: Cat Mss Pix
Notes: Extensiveholdings of books on the
theatre. Also, in the Charles Sanders
Collection, about 14,000 British and
American playbills and programs mostly of
the 19th century, as well as scrapbooks,
posters, and about 750 photographs and
prints of actors and actresses. In the Ellen
Van Volkenburg-Maurice Browne Collection,
about 4000 photographs of stage productions
and friends and associates, as well as
programs, posters, scrapbooks of mounted
clippings, about 200 original stage and
costume designs, promptbooks, and play
manuscripts, representing the American and
British careers of this husband-wife team
from 1912 to about 1940. The Chicago Little
Theatre, 1912-1917, is well represented.
Also contains more than 6000 items of
correspondence with theatrical and literary
figures. Another collection contains 143
Alfred Lunt letters, mainly from 1901-1915.

MI —DETROIT PUBLIC LIBRARY, Music &
Performing Arts Dept, 5201 Woodward,
Detroit, 48202. Jean Currie Church, Cur
Holdings: Vols (1375) Cat Mss Pix
Notes: The E Azalia Hackley Collections
document achievements of Blacks in the
fields of music, dance, theatre, motion
pictures, and broadcasting. World-wide in
scope. Extensive clipping files arranged by
personal names, titles and subjects. Incl
musical scores (1500), recordings, and plays.
No taping or other copying of recordings
permitted.

MI —DETROIT PUBLIC LIBRARY, Music &
Performing Arts Dept, 5201 Woodward,
Detroit, 48202. Agatha Pfeiffer Kalkanis,
Chief
Holdings: Mss Pix
Notes: Extensive bound files of programs for
Detroit theatres, 1890 to present, partially
indexed by names and titles. Supplemented
by manuscript history of Detroit theatre
1811-1908, and Bonstelle theatre 1910-1929.
Also clipping files.

MI —MICHIGAN STATE UNIVERSITY,
Libraries, Special Collections Div, East
Lansing, 48824. Jannette Fiore, Librn
Holdings: Uncat Mss Pix
Notes: Photocopies of 250 scripts, with
primary material from the Henderson Stock
Company, including account books, 1900-
1935, approximately 200 photographs of
performers, sets, etc, miscellaneous leaflets,
handbills, and correspondence. Several
additional folders of correspondence, leaflets,
handbills, etc, relating to many tent-show
companies.

MN —MINNEAPOLIS PUBLIC LIBRARY &
INFORMATION CENTER, Literature &
Language Dept, 300 Nicollet Mall,
Minneapolis, 55401. Dorothy D Thews,
Head
Holdings: Vols (210,000) Cat Microforms
Phonorecords Audiotapes
Budget: ($49,124)
Notes: Foreign language collection: 30,000
vols, separate catalog. Theatre collection: 9
vertical file drawers. Books integrated with
department collection. Scrapbooks
containing newspaper clippings re Guthrie
and Cricket Theatres.

MO —WASHINGTON UNIVERSITY,
Libraries, Campus Box 1061, Saint Louis,
63130.
Holdings: 4500 Vols
Notes: The private library of the late Gert
von Gontard. Incl works on art, literature
(especially German), music, and theater.
Contains 1200 vols Goetheana, with first
editions, autographed letters and original
drawings by Goethe. Also material on the
Austrian writer Karl Kraus and the Belgian
artist Frans Masereel.

NE —UNIVERSITY OF NEBRASKA,
OMAHA, Library, 60 & Dodge Sts, Omaha,
68132. Mel Bohn, Librn
Notes: Archives of people's theatre groups
from across the country. Mss 15 linear ft.

NJ —ENGLEWOOD LIBRARY, 31 Engle St,
Englewood, 07631. N E Rhoades, Reference
Librn
Holdings: Vols (8200) Cat

NJ —HADDON HEIGHTS PUBLIC
LIBRARY, 608 Station Ave, Haddon
Heights, 08035. Robert J Hunter, Librn
Holdings: Vols (1900) Cat Phonorecords

NJ —FAIRLEIGH DICKINSON
UNIVERSITY, Friendship Library, 285
Madison Ave, Madison, 07940. James
Fraser, Library Dir; Renee Weber, Cur
Notes: Incl 5000 phonorecords (all 78 rpm);
cylinders; 1500 pieces of sheet music;
publishers catalogs; victrolas. The George H
Moss Collection traces the history of music
and theatre from 1890-1950 through
publisher's catalogs, sheet music, cylinders
and phonorecordings. A published list of the
sheet music is available.

NJ —PRINCETON UNIVERSITY, Library,
Rare Books Dept, Princeton, 08544. Stephen
Ferguson, Cur
Notes: The Valva Collection (gift of the
Worcester, Massachusetts Public Library).
Orchestral parts and conductors' scores for
several thousand popular songs and musical
effects used in movie houses and vaudeville
from the turn of the century to the end of
the silent movie era.

NJ —PRINCETON UNIVERSITY, Library,
William Seymour Theatre Collection,
Princeton, 08544. Mary Ann Jensen, Cur
Holdings: Vols (7000) Cat
Budget: ($9000)
Notes: Plus scrapbooks, playbills, posters.

NM —EASTERN NEW MEXICO
UNIVERSITY, Golden Library, Special
Collections, Portales, 88130. Mary Jo
Walker, Special Collections Librn
Holdings: Vols Phonorecords Pix
Notes: Gift from Hope Sheridan. The Lyric
Theatre and Dance Collection, incl books
(281), periodicals, programs, brochures, as
well as photographs, phonorecordings,
clippings, and memorabilia pertaining to
theatres and touring companies in the US
and abroad.

NY —NEW YORK STATE LIBRARY, State
Education Bldg Annex, Washington Ave,
Albany, 12224.
Holdings: Cat

NY —STATE UNIVERSITY OF NEW
YORK, BINGHAMTON, Glenn G Bartle
Library, Binghamton, 13901. Marion
Hanscom, Special Collections Librn
Holdings: Cat
Budget: ($8000)
Notes: Max Reinhardt Archive. Library has
extensive (approx 250,000 items) archival
material relating to Max Reinhardt, as well
as his personal library. This personal library
is not a subject collection per se, but
contains much information about German
theater in the 20th century. The archival
material contains letters, prompt books,
photograhs, playbills, etc.

†NY —STATE UNIVERSITY OF NEW
YORK, COLLEGE AT BROCKPORT,
Brockport, 14420.
Notes: Microfilm copy of the Lord
Chamberlain's Daybooks, registers of plays
licensed for presentation in London from
1824-1903. Originals in British Museum.
Some other miscellaneous material is incl
from the Lord Chamberlain's office.

NY —THEATRE RESEARCH DATA
CENTER, Brooklyn College, City University
of New York, Brooklyn, 11210. Irving M
Brown, Dir; Rosabel A Wang, Systs Coordr;
Benito Ortolani, Bibliographer
Notes: Theatre Research Data Center of
Brooklyn College in collaboration with the
American Society for Theatre Research, is
compiling an extensive data base, with the
cooperation of other US and international
theatre-related scholars and institutions,
indexing a broad list of theatre publications:
periodicals, books, catalogs, films, discs,
tapes, etc, containing material of interest to
theatre researchers. Will publish American
Society/Theatre Research annual
international bibliography starting '84-'85.
Database service for online research 1985.
Coverage began 1982; retrospective coverage
later.

NY —QUEENS BOROUGH PUBLIC
LIBRARY, Art & Music Div, 89-11 Merrick
Blvd, Jamaica, 11432. Dorothea Wu, Head
Holdings: Vols (85,000) Cat Maps Pix
Phonorecords Audiotapes Microforms
Budget: ($44,000)
Notes: The Picture Collection, covering all
subjects, consists of approximately 1,500,000
pictures, mainly reproductions and clippings
from books and magazines, photographs, and
postcards on all subjects; The Framed
Picture Collection, approx 180 framed
pictures, mostly reproductions of paintings
from various periods; and The Phonorecord
and Cassette Collection consists of approx
3500 reference phonorecords and 6500
circulating records as well as 1000 reference
cassettes and 1500 circulating cassettes.

NY —NEW ROCHELLE PUBLIC LIBRARY,
Fine Arts Dept, Library Plaza, New
Rochelle, 10801. Eugene L Mittelgluck,
Library Dir
Holdings: Vols (13,000) Cat Pix Slides
Budget: ($10,000)
Notes: Incl (430,000) pictures and (6300)
slides.
See also entries under Art; Ballet and the
Dance; Costume; Music.

†NY —COLUMBIA UNIVERSITY
LIBRARIES, Butler Library, Rare Book and
Manuscript Library, 535 W 114 St, New
York, 10027.
Notes: The papers, etc, of Ira A Hards,
American theatre producer and his actress
wife Ina Hammer Hards.

NY —HAMPDEN-BOOTH THEATRE
LIBRARY AT THE PLAYERS, 16
Gramercy Park, New York, 10003. Louis A
Rachow, Librn/Cur
Holdings: Vols 12,000 Cat Mss Pix Slides
Phonotapes
Notes: A strong collection on theatre
history, with special emphasis on 19th and
20th century English and American stage.
Large collection of English playbills of the
18th and 19th centuries; important collection
of prompt books (mainly 19th century);
Edwin Booth, incl memorabilia, rare books,
association items, his 2nd, 3rd, and 4th
Shakespeare Folios, etc. Large collection of
English and American biographies and
pictures of actors and actresses; the John
Mulholland Magic Collection (qv Magic);
the Chuck Callahan Burlesque Collection (qv
Burlesque); and other specialties described
elsewhere in this volume. La Mama
Experimental Theatre Club. The holdings
include printed, typescript and manuscript
material and relate chiefly to the period
when La Mama, under guidance of Ellen
Stewart, was located at 122 Second Avenue-
a symbol of the Off-Off Broadway
movement of the 1960s.The collection is
divided into three sections: (1) Chronological
records of production containing
approximately 140 manuscript and typescript
leaves as well as some additional eighty
pages of source material and worksheets, (2)
Clippings and press coverage including 123

THEATRE—HISTORY (cont.)

clippings from Scottish, English, German and American newspapers and periodicals, and (3) Playbills and programs consisting of 143 broadsides and handbills together with miscellaneous bills of productions and lectures by La Mama artists. Each section has its own calendar and the holdings as a whole are considered to be the most complete in existence for the years 1965-68, since no systematic archives were maintained until after La Mama's move from Second Avenue in 1968. The collection has been designated the Paul F Cranefield Collection of the La Mama Experimental Theatre Club.Described in *Theatre & Performing Arts Collections* (New York: Haworth Press, 1981).

NY —HISPANIC SOCIETY OF AMERICA, Library, 613 W 155 St, New York, 10032. Martha M de Narvaez, Cur of Mss; Irene S Frye, Asst Librn
Holdings: Vols (150,000) Cat Mss Maps Pix Slides Phonorecords Microforms
Notes: Mss of the Golden Age of Spanish Drama. Hundreds of mss (some with stage business, notes and annotations); numerous titles of rare 17th-century and later printed books on the drama and the stage; English translations of Spanish plays and Spanish translations of international drama; letters and documents of the major and minor dramatists and performers from 1904 to the present day. Catalogs: *Catalogue of the Hispanic Society of America* (Boston: G K Hall, 1962), 10 vols; *First Supplement* (Boston, 1970), 4 vols. Early books: *Printed Books 1468-1700*; Mss: *Catalogo de los Manuscritos Poeticos Castellanos* (15th-17th centuries; 3 vols); *Medieval Manuscripts in the Library; Golden Age Drama Manuscripts* (the latter in press).

†NY —NEIGHBORHOOD PLAYHOUSE SCHOOL OF THE THEATRE, Irene Lewisohn Library, 340 E 54 St, New York, 10022. Alice G Owen, Librn
Holdings: Vols 100 Cat Mss Pix
Notes: Theatre and drama are the primary emphases, but incl books on costume, dance, film, poetry, and general literature. Collection supports the school program and class work. 9 VF drawers of scenes, Neighborhood Playhouse-iana, pictures, music boxes, sheet music, etc. A few rare vols. Scenes are indexed; music scores are cataloged.

NY —NEW YORK PUBLIC LIBRARY, Performing Arts Research Center, Billy Rose Theatre Collection, 111 Amsterdam Ave, New York, 10023. Dorothy L Swerdlove, Cur
Holdings: Cat
Notes: Described in *Theatre Collection: Books on the Theatre*, 9 vols (121,800 cards). The word "theatre" is interpreted in its broadest sense to incl the stage, cinema, radio, television, carnivals, nightclub performances, the circus, magic, puppetry, etc. Holdings relating to the stage encompass stage history, production techniques, acting, theatre criticism, biography and material on individual theatres. Although published plays are not incl at the present time, typescripts of plays, prompt books, and scripts of motion pictures, TV, and radio make up an important segment of the collection's holdings. Also large collections of newspapers and periodicals of the industry. This dictionary catalog represents over 23,500 vols and incl index citations for selected articles in various periodicals. Entries are found under author, subject, title, and other secondaryheadings. The larger part of the collection is nonbook materials: clippings, programs, iconography, autographs, letters, scrapbooks, etc, about theatre production. The archives of David Belasco, R H Burnside, Richard Barstow, Theodore Liebler, Winthrop Ames; the memorabilia of such performing artists as Katherine Cornell, Helen Hayes, Maurice Evans, Burl Ives, Paul Muni, Sophie Tucker. In addition to the records of producing offices listed above, the Theatre Collection has the archives of John

Golden, Alexander H Cohen, Leland Hayward, the Chamberlain and Lyman Brown Theatrical Agency, as well as the papers of various press agents, eg, Karl Bernstein, Bill Doll, and Richard Maney. Also the Robinson Locke Collection of several hundred scrapbooks covering the American theatre from ca 1880-1930; theStead Collection of the 18-19th centuries British Theatre; the Henin Collection of the 19th century French theatre; the working papers and memorabilia of Jerome Lawrence and Robert E Lee; typescripts and promptbooks, mainly American theatre 1875-date; Shakespeare production, American and British, 19th-20 century; Becks Collection- 19th century English and American theatre; working scripts of Edward Albee. The Theatre Collection currently clips, catalogs and files new material about stage production-universally. We add typescripts and promptbooks of new plays, programs and photographs of production, etc. A collection of scrapbooks of the New York reviews of all productions done in the New York Theatre (by season) from the season of 1917/18-date; earlier reviews are also available.

NY —NEW YORK PUBLIC LIBRARY, General Library of the Performing Arts, 111 Amsterdam Ave, New York, 10023. Larry Cioppa, Drama Specialist
Holdings: Vols (40,000) Cat Phonorecords
Notes: Drama material on all aspects of the theater. Film, radio, television and related performing arts. Incl 5000 drama recordings.

†NY —SHUBERT ARCHIVE, Lyceum Theatre, 149 W 45th St, New York, 10036. Brigitte Kueppers, Archivist
Notes: The vast Shubert Archive, mostly unexplored is the largest collection in the world representative of the "business" of the theatre. It includes almost all of the Shubert empire's correspondence from the turn of the century to the 1950s, road company records, thousands of playscripts (American and European), set and costume designs, music scores for Shubert productions, business, financial, and legal records, actors' contracts, etc.

NY —THEATRE COLLECTION OF THE INTERNATIONAL THEATRE INSTITUTE OF THE UNITED STATES, INC, Library, Suite 1510, 1860 Broadway, New York, 10023. Elizabeth B Burdick, Dir
Holdings: Vols (4525) Cat Mss Pix
Budget: ($35,000)
Notes: The International Theatre Institute was founded by UNESCO to "promote the exchange of knowledge and practice in the theatre arts." In 1948, eleven nations, incl the United States, became charter members of the international organization, which today has national centers or affiliates in 64 countries. The American center is the International Theatre Institute of the United States (ITI/US). In 1970, as one of its programs to strengthen communication among theatre people, ITI/US opened a library devoted to international theatre since World War II. The Collection's main holdings have been amassed over the 35-year operation of ITI/US through its world-wide exchange of information, publications, and people. Holdings document theatre activity in 140 countries. The 4525 vols on American and foreign theatre(covering history, management, design, stagecraft, theory, criticism, biography, playscripts) represent only a small part of the total collection. Focus is on foreign theatre companies, directors, playwrights, designers, managers, actors. The emphasis is on the acquisition of material which is generally unavailable in this country: foreign yearbooks, house organs, newsletters, programs, press releases, production schedules, brochures, periodicals, monographs, articles, newspaper clippings. While these fugitive items have never been counted, they have been cataloged by country, then indexed by title, subject, or name of theatre. The library receives regularly 250 periodicals on the performing arts (cataloged by country, then indexed by title). It now owns 6417 foreign plays from

80 countries in ms or publishedmss or published editions, in collections and anthologies, and in periodicals. Each play is cataloged by author, title, and country of origin. The section on American theatre incl books, programs, reviews, over 60 periodicals, 2061 American plays. The activities of approx 700 theatres across the country are documented by annual files containing production schedules, press releases, programs, brochures for each theatrical season.

NY —MOUNT PLEASANT PUBLIC LIBRARY, 350 Bedford Rd, Pleasantville, 10570. Charlotte Miller, Dir
Holdings: Vols 3000 Cat Mss Pix
Notes: The Deane Winthrop Pratt collection of acting editions of mostly 19th-20th century British plays. Incl some 200 prompt books, most of them comprehensively marked with production notes. The collection was the product of a 19th-early 20th century proessional actor who turned to direction of suburban amateur acting groups and the prompt books reflect that activity. There are several ms plays by Mr Pratt in the collection. Theatre memorabilia mainly tipped into the various vols. The collection of John W Frost is especially strong in 17th and 18th century drama.

NY —STATE UNIVERSITY OF NEW YORK, COLLEGE AT PURCHASE, Library, Lincoln Ave, Purchase, 10577. Robert W Evans, Dir
Holdings: Vols (1400) Mss Pix Slides
Notes: The Gerald D McDonald Collection. Over 1400 books on moving pictures and all aspects of the industry; production, directing, acting. Thousands of pictures of actors and actresses, directors, etc. Also about 2000 slides picturing movie personalities, etc; stereopticon pictures, buttons, bottle caps, playing cards, etc.

NY —UNIVERSITY OF ROCHESTER, Rush Rhees Library, Department of Rare Books and Special Collections, Rochester, 14627. Peter Dzwonkoski, Librn
Holdings: Vols (300) Cat Mss Pix
Notes: 18th and 19th century English and 19th century American plays and works on theatre. Also includes manuscript collections on theatre, and papers of Clement William Scott, John Lawrence Toole, Authur Wing Pinero, Charles Kean, Lillian Russell and Leon Marks Lion, collection of 130 lithographic theatre posters, and collection of programs and playbills, chiefly Rochester, NY and New York City, 1900-1950. Unpublished guides to ms collections available in repository.

NC —UNIVERSITY OF NORTH CAROLINA, CHAPEL HILL, Wilson Library, Rare Book Collection, Chapel Hill, 27514. Paul S Koda, Cur of Rare Books
Holdings: // Uncat Pix
Notes: The Roland Holt Collection of American Theater. Memorabilia incl 15,000 clippings, programs, pictures, photographs, and articles on the American theatre, 1881-1931. Thirteen scrapbooks arranged chronologically, 19 letter files, 250 photographs in albums, 100 opera libretti. Sixty miscellaneous books on drama, chiefly biograhical.

NC —DUKE UNIVERSITY, William R Perkins Library, Durham, 27706. Elvin E Strowd, University Librn
Holdings: Cat Mss Pix
Notes: Montrose J Moses' collection of books, mss, and papers, mostly concerned with men and women of the theatre, and creative writers of the first third of the century. 3000 books; 22,000 mss.

NC —NORTH CAROLINA SCHOOL OF THE ARTS, Semans Library, PO Box 12189, Winston-Salem, 27107. William D VanHoven, Head Librn
Holdings: Vols (98,000) Cat Slides Microforms Phonorecords Films
Budget: ($105,000)
Notes: Incl clippings, pictures and programs.

OH —BOWLING GREEN STATE UNIVERSITY, Jerome Library, Center for Archival Collections, Bowling Green, 43403. Paul D Yon, Dir; Elaine R Ezell, Reference Archivist; Nancy Steen, Rare Books Librn
Holdings: Vols 1600 Cat Mss Letters Pix
Budget: ($3000)
Notes: The Robert Aickman Collection

THEATRE—HISTORY (cont.)

contains about 40 of Aickman's manuscripts of both published and unpublished works as well as the late author's personal library which is strong in the areas of English literature and theatre of the 19th and 20th centuries and in the area of the supernatural.

OH —HEBREW UNION COLLEGE-JEWISH INSTITUTE OF RELIGION, Klau Library, 3101 Clifton Ave, Cincinnati, 45220. David J Gilner, Reference Librn
Holdings: Vols (4000) Cat
Notes: Photos, posters, playbills, ms music, scenarios and ephemera dealing with the Yiddish theater, 20th century Israel, US, and other countries.

OH —CLEVELAND PUBLIC LIBRARY, Literature Dept, 325 Superior Ave, Cleveland, 44114. Evelyn Ward, Head
Holdings: Cat Mss Pix
Notes: Personal library and other collections of W Ward Marsh, former film critic of the Cleveland *Plain Dealer*. The major categories of the bequest are: production stills which begin with the films of the Thirties and concentrate on those of the Forties and Fifties; an actor/actress file of folders for individual personalities containing studio and agent biographies, clippings and publicity photos; "pressbooks"--kits of advertising materials used for promoting a specific movie; a review file numbering over 20,000 critiques clipped from *Boxoffice, Variety*, and miscellaneous trade journals, incl Marsh's own reviews; and his correspondence. Also incl are a specially bound copy of the shooting script (accompanied by color transparencies) for Cecil B deMille's remake of *The Ten Commandments*; and a collection of more than 70046g X 56g glass slides--dating from the silent era--which were used by theatre owners to promote their upcoming attractions.

OH —CLEVELAND PUBLIC LIBRARY, Literature Dept, 325 Superior Ave, Cleveland, 44114. Evelyn Ward, Head
Holdings: Vols Cat Pix Phonorecords Microforms VF
Notes: History, criticism, biographies of playwrights. Texts of classical, English, American, Continental, European and Oriental plays. Incl Barrett H Clark collection of acting editions, William F McDermont Memorial Collection. Microprint, incl "Three Centuries of English and American Plays." Noteworthy Shakespeare collection: editions, commentary, biography. Recordings: plays, speeches, sound effects. Theatre programs, clippings, play reviews, photographs, typescripts, etc. Reference aids: indexes to plays, theatres, and actors in Cleveland, subject files.

OH —OHIO STATE UNIVERSITY, William Oxley Thompson Memorial Library, 1858 Neil Ave Mall, Columbus, 43210. Robert A Tibbetts, Cur of Special Collections
Holdings: Uncat Mss
Notes: American Playwright' Theatre papers, incl business records and scripts of plays produced or considered for production.

OH —RUTHERFORD B HAYES LIBRARY, 1337 Hayes Ave, Fremont, 43420. Watt P Marchman, Dir
Holdings: Vols 800 Cat Mss Maps Pix Microforms
Notes: American history; northern Ohio; theatre. The collections are housed in a special study room of the Hayes Library. Index in the collections (69 linear feet).

OH —KENT STATE UNIVERSITY, Libraries, Dept of Special Collections, Kent, 44242. Dean H Keller, Cur
Holdings: Vols 25 Cat Mss Pix
Notes: The archive of The Open Theatre group, incl notebooks, correspondence, business papers, publicity material, and clippings.

OK —UNIVERSITY OF OKLAHOMA, Drama Library, 550 Parrington Oval, Norman, 73019. Jan Seifert, Dir
Holdings: Vols (6683) Mss Pix Phonorecords
Notes: Incl VF material, newspaper clippings

and magazine cut-outs covering the theatre and dance. Material dates from 1900. Collection of nearly 6000 plays.

PA —FRANKLIN & MARSHALL COLLEGE, Library, Lancaster, 17604. Kathleen J Moretto, Library Dir
Holdings: Vols Uncat Mss Pix
Notes: The Alexander Corbett Collection of Theatre Memorabilia consists of 650 letters and photographs of actors and actresses during the Victorian era in America.

PA —FREE LIBRARY OF PHILADELPHIA, Theatre Collection, Logan Sq, Philadelphia, 19103. Geraldine Duclow, Librn-in-Charge
Holdings: Vols (1,250,000) Uncat Pix
Notes: The Theatre Collection contains books, magazines, playbills, broadsides, posters, photographs, and other memorabilia covering theatre, motion pictures, minstrels, vaudeville, circus, radio and television. The Library's Philadelphia Theatre Index lists the major productions here since 1855, and partially indexes the collection of local playbills which date back to 1803. There are also programs from many other cities, incl New York; some from London date back to 1800. Early film companies as well as the present movie industry are represented by advertising materials and over 30,000 film stills. The Lubin Film Co (1910-1916) Archive has been established with over 600 photographs and related items. Circus programs and route books date back to 1900. There are minstrel programs as early as 1865. Most significant are the mss from Philadelphia's Dumont Minstrels. Variousfiles contain autographs, photographs, newspaper articles and reviews in all pertinent subject areas. Noncirculating.

PA —TEMPLE UNIVERSITY LIBRARIES, Special Collections Dept, Conwellana-Templana Collection, 13 & Berks St, Philadelphia, 19122. Miriam I Crawford, Cur
Holdings: Mss Pix Audiotapes 16mm Films
Budget: ($30,000)
Notes: Chiefly photographs, both negative and prints, scrapbooks and play programs, plus a few scripts, stage designs and promptbooks, the bulk of which document the productions of the Temple University Theatre, 1930-1969, under the direction of Paul Randall. A small supplementary collection of miscellaneous theatrical programs given at the school, and a continuing collection of play programs and publicity materials of the University Theater since Randall's departure.

PA —UNIVERSITY OF PENNSYLVANIA, Furness Memorial Library, 3420 Walnut St, Philadelphia, 19104. Georgianna Ziegler, Cur
Holdings: Vols (18,000) Cat
Notes: A scholar's working library. Contains material by or about Shakespeare, and other Elizabethan dramatists. Incl many of the works that served as Shakespeare's sources, and extensive material on the history of the English and American stage. Also a large collection of dissertations on Shakespeare. See Downs 534-5.

PA —UNIVERSITY OF PITTSBURGH, Special Collections Dept, Curtis Theatre Collection, 363 Hillman Library, Pittsburgh, 15260. Jeanette Blanco, Cur
Holdings: Mss Pix
Notes: William P Halstead Theatre Collection. Incl clippings, programs, photographs, etc, 1928-1976. Partially cataloged.

RI —BROWN UNIVERSITY, John Hay Library, Harris Collection, Prospect St, Providence, 02912. Rosemary L Cullen, Cur
Holdings: Vols (200,000) Cat Mss Pix Phonorecords Microforms
Budget: ($15,000)
Notes: The Harris Collection of American Poetry and Plays is principally composed of American and Canadian poetry and plays, 17th century-date. Extensive holdings in songsters, gift books and annuals, hymnals, pageants, broadside verse, carriers' addresses, women poets, juvenile poetry, (incl Mother Goose and *The Night Before Christmas*), sheet music with lyrics, small press publications, fine printing, black poets, "little magazines," Yiddish-American literature. All movements or schools of

American poetry are represented. Incl first editions of most American poets and playwrights, notably Whitman, Poe, Wallace Stevens, Eugene O'Neill, Edward Albee, Ezra Pound, T S Eliot, William Carlos Williams, Amy Lowell, Phyllis Wheatley, Robert Frost, Allen Ginsberg, Bliss Carman, and Stephen Foster sheet music. Also incl the Saunders Walt Whitman Collection (1300 vols); the LangdonCollection of Pageants (250 vols); the Asa Cushman Collection of plays in ms and prompt copies; the MacDougall Collection of Psalters and Hymnals; 4000 plays issued by Walter H Baker Co, Boston (1890-1957); the Vaxer Collection of Yiddish Poetry, Plays and Music (1700 vols). Collections incl 200,000 vols, 30,000 broadsides, 55,000 mss, 170,000 pieces of sheet music, 450 phonorecords, and 375 microfilm reels. See *Dictionary Catalog of the Harris Collection of American Poetry and Plays* (Boston: G K Hall, 1972), 13 vols; *Supplement* (1977), 3 vols. See also, *American Poetry, 1609-1900, A Collection on Microfilm, Segment I* (1609-1820); *Segment II* (1821-1850); *Segment III* (1851-1870) (Woodbridge, Conn: Research Publications). Separate catalog.

SC —COLLEGE OF CHARLESTON LIBRARY, Special Collections Dept, Charleston, 29401.
Notes: (1) Several histories of the Footlight Players, scrapbooks (1932-1964), programs (1931-1958), footnotes (1937-1970), scripts (many adapted from well known works by Emmett Robinson), photographs, and posters. Also included is material dealing with the Dock Street Theatre's history, its theatre school, and non-Footlight Player performances. (2) Emmett Robinson papers incl typescript of his "Source history of the drama in ante-bellum Charleston, SC (1800-1861)." Incl playbills of performances involving Robinson.

TN —UNIVERSITY OF TENNESSEE, KNOXVILLE, Library, Knoxville, 37996. John Dobson, Special Collections Librn
Holdings: Cat
Notes: The John C Hodges Collection, incl about 150 original editions of Congreve's works and a large collection of books about him, English drama, and the theater of the 16th and 17th centuries; also material by and about other dramatists of the period. Described in *The John C Hodges Collection of William Congreve in the University of Tennessee Library: A Bibliographical Catalog*, by Albert M Lyles and John Dobson (Knoxville: Univ of Tennessee Libraries, 1970), 135pp.

TN —MEMPHIS STATE UNIVERSITY, John Willard Brister Library, Memphis, 38152. John Terreo, Special Collections Librn
Notes: Theatre Collection, 1789-1972. Correspondence, scripts, programs, handbills, musical scores, clippings, drawings, sketches, and photographs, documenting careers of artists, production of plays, ballett and theatre companies, and theaters and opera houses centering in New York and London, England. Incl drawings, prints, publications, and other personal papers of British producer and designer Edward Gordon Craig (1872-1966), relating to his career, radio talks (1951-1961) for the BBC, acting school in Florence, Italy, and his mother, actress Ellen Terry; and correspondence, scripts, programs, reviews, scrapbooks, photos, and other materials, of American producer Jed Harris (?)-1979, relating to his stage productions (1926-1945).

TN —PUBLIC LIBRARY OF NASHVILLE & DAVIDSON COUNTY, Nashville Room, Eighth Ave N & Union, Nashville, 37203. David Marshall Stewart, Chief Librn
Holdings: Vols Cat Pix
Notes: The Naff Collection of programs, autographed photographs, posters, etc tells the story of professional theatre in Nashville between 1900 and 1960. All materials noncirculating. Theses on Nashville theatre.

†TX —UNIVERSITY OF TEXAS LIBRARIES, Hoblitzelle Theatre Arts Library, Austin, 78712.
Notes: Memorabilia of B Iden Payne, internationally known Shakespearean director.

THEATRE—HISTORY (cont.)

TX —DALLAS PUBLIC LIBRARY, Fine Arts Div, 1515 Young St, Dallas, 75201. Richard L Waters, Acting Dir; Jane Holahan, Manager
Holdings: // Uncat Mss Pix
Notes: The Margo Jones Theatre Collection (75 linear ft) contains the office papers of this theatre: financial, business, legal records, scripts, programs, photos of productions, reviews and clippings, personal correspondence; organizational records. Gift of Dallas Civic Theatre, Inc, 1962 after theatre ceased operation. Described in LC card catalog MS 66-1622. Also The W E Hill Theatre Collection, 18th-20th centuries, ca 75,000 items. Contains letters, portraits, and photos of leading American, British, and European dramatists, actors, managers, and other persons associated with the stage or the performing arts, particularly music; playbills, posters of stage plays, minstrel shows, and circuses; and newspaper and magazine clippings. The bulk of the collection consists of 19th and 20th century items. Described in LC card catalog MS 66-1621. Partiallydescribed in the "Fine Arts Department of the Dallas Public Library presents an exhibit of selected material from the W E Hill theatre collection on the occasion of the opening of the collection..." (1966). Gift of estate of William Ely Hill, 1963. Also The John Rosenfield Collection consisting of ca 2000 playbills assembled by this Amusements Critic of the *Dallas Morning News,* from both his travels and local productions. Also correspondence with various important artists in the theatre. There are also photographs, telegrams, etc of these people. The Dallas Little Theatre Collection consists of printed programs of this group which won the Belasco Cup three consecutive years in New York City; many clippings, photographs and other related newspaper articles. Oral histories are being assembled from persons connected with the theatre during its lifetimefrom 1922-1944.

TX —SOUTHERN METHODIST UNIVERSITY, Fondren Library, McCord Theater Collection, Room 301, Dallas, 75275. Edyth Renshaw, Cur; Linda Sellers, Pub Serv
Holdings: Vols (2000) Uncat Mss Pix Slides Phonorecords
Notes: See *Theatre Collections in Libraries and Museums,* Gilder and Freedley (Theatre Arts, 1936). The McCord Theatre Collection encompasses the entire spectrum of the performing arts. The central purpose is to gather records of our regional theater before such ephemeral material is lost. Records of over two hundred early Texas theaters, some fragmentary and some relatively complete, are in the files. These records incl photographs of buildings, stagehands, orchestras, and performers. Local theatre history incl the once famous Dallas Little Theatre and the Margo Jones Theatre. The national theatre, opera, ballet, and circus archives incl pictures (some autographed), programs, posters, throw-aways, tear sheets, clippings, and letters. Our international archives are small, but we have some excellent material, eg, artifacts from Max Reinhardt's production of"The Miracle" which happened to go bankrupt in Dallas. After a few years the items were given to us. There are posters, tear-sheets, souvenir programs, and other colorful items from Morris Gest and the Artef Collection. We have about 200 19th century English playbills and a few from the 18th century. There is a collection of modern English, French, and other European programs, many of them illustrated souvenir programs. Also, magazines on theater, cinema, and television (1800). Scrapbooks covering both southwest and Dallas theater, 1890s-1950s. Special Collections: artifacts and documents on puppets; masks; costume design; circus; and ballet and dance. The Harriet Bacon MacDonald Collection of over 200 photographs of musicians appearing in Dallas during the first three decades of the 20th century. Many autographed. Affiliated with Meadow Theatre of the Arts.

TX —UNIVERSITY OF HOUSTON, M D Anderson Memorial Library, University Park, Houston, 77004. David Farmer, Cur, Special Collections; Jean Jackson, Assistant Cur
Notes: Cheryl Crawford Collection of theater books, posters, correspondence, original cast show recordings, tapes of discussions by noted theater artists, sheet music, playbills, first drafts of scripts and documents from the Actors Studio.

†TX —MCNAY ART INSTITUTE LIBRARY, San Antonio Museum Association, San Antonio, 78209.
Notes: The Robert L B Tobin Collections.

TX —TRINITY UNIVERSITY, Elizabeth Coates Maddux Library, 715 Stadium Dr, San Antonio, 78284. Richard Hume Werking, Library Dir; Craig Likness, Head Bibliographer
Notes: Considerable collection under an NEH challenge grant.

UT —UNIVERSITY OF UTAH, Marriott Library, Special Collections, Salt Lake City, 84112. Gregory C Thompson, Cur

VA —GEORGE MASON UNIVERSITY, Fenwick Library, Special Collections Dept, 4400 University Drive, Fairfax, 22030. Ruth Kerns, Public Services Librn
Notes: The Federal Theatre Project (FTP) was established in August 1935 as a part of the arts program of the Works Progress Administration (renamed Work Projects Administration in 1939). Supporting 150 separate units throughout the United States, the FTP produced over 830 major stage plays, 6000 radio programs, and innumerable marionette plays, vaudeville shows, outdoor pageants, and circuses. At the conclusion of the project in June 1939, the "product materials" generated by the FTP were sent to the Library of Congress, and the administrative records to the National Archives. The Library's Federal Theatre Project collection was placed on deposit at George Mason University in Fairfax, Virginia, in 1974. Occupying over eight hundred cubic feet of shelf space, the collection is the largest single gathering of original FTP materials and containsdocumentation for many FTP productions, particularly those which originated in the New York City, San Francisco, and Los Angeles areas. Included are 5000 playscripts, 2500 radio scripts, 25,000 photographs, 40 blueprints, 1000 posters, over 1600 costume designs, 350 scene designs, 750 production notebooks, 1700 programs and heralds, 26 musical scores and 18 cubic feet of research materials and play readers' reports.

†WA —WASHINGTON STATE UNIVERSITY, Library, Manuscripts, Archives & Special Collections, Pullman, 99164. John F Guido, Head
Holdings: // Cat Mss Pix
Notes: The Robert Cushman Butler Collection of Theatrical Illustrations contains: approx 1600 illustrations, sheet music covers, programs and playbills; approx 100 mss of actors, actresses and playwrights; and approx 200 volumes of theatrical history and reminiscences, several extra-illustrated, concentrating on 18th-19th century British and American drama. A guide to the collection is in preparation.

WA —UNIVERSITY OF WASHINGTON LIBRARIES, Drama Library, BH-20, Seattle, 98195. Liz Fugate, Drama Librn
Holdings: Vols
Budget: ($13,182)
Notes: Collection incl history; criticism; costume; make-up; scene design; lighting; creative dramatics; children's theatre; directing; playwriting; acting. Special Collections include 19th century acting editions, contemporary acting editions and local theatre posters. 17,731 items cataloged, 24,255 uncataloged.

WI —STATE HISTORICAL SOCIETY OF WISCONSIN, Archives, 816 State St, Madison, 53706. Harold L Miller, Reference Archivist
Holdings: Mss Pix Microforms
Notes: Holdings incl records and papers of prominent organizations and individuals in the theater and motion picture industry, motion picture and television films, scripts, and still photographs, incl the archives of the United Artists Corporation. Collections are described in *Sources for Mass Communications, Film and Theater Research: A Guide,* (1982) and in current accession notes in the *Wisconsin Magazine of History.* Major collections are also in Hamer, *Guide to Manuscripts and Archives in the United States,* (1961) and in the *National Union Catalog of Manuscripts Collections,* (1959-date).

WI —UNIVERSITY OF WISCONSIN, MADISON, Memorial Library, British & American Language & Literature Collection, 728 State St, Madison, 53706. Yvonne Schofer, Bibliographer
Holdings: // Cat Mss Pix
Notes: Thomas H Dickinson Collection. An extensive collection of special interest to scholars and students of the American and European theatre. Includes books, photographs, diaries, memorabilia, individual author collections, prints, sketches, playbills, ephemera concerning the drama and theatre of the US, England, France, Spain, Germany, Italy, Czechoslovakia, Poland, Russia, Rumania, Yugoslavia, Austria, and Japan. Books held by Library: other materials housed in Communication Arts Dept, 6117 Vilas Communication Hall, UW-Madison.

WI —MILWAUKEE PUBLIC LIBRARY, 814 W Wisconsin Ave, Milwaukee, 53233. Donald J Sager, City Librn
Holdings: Vols Cat
Notes: Collection incl programs from old local area theatres from 1850s incl early German theatre to the present; also current programs of all local theatre events.

WY —UNIVERSITY OF WYOMING, William Robertson Coe Library, Performing Arts Collections, Laramie, 82071. Gene M Gressley, Dir
Holdings: Mss
Notes: Collections in the Performing Arts area incl some 300 collections of outstanding music composers, arrangers, film industry directors, writers, performers, and individuals prominent in all aspects of music, theatre, radio, television and film industry.

AB —UNIVERSITY OF CALGARY, Library, Calgary, T2N 1N4, Can. Apollonia Steele, Special Collections Librn
Holdings: Cat Mss Pix
Notes: Incl the books and papers of W Bridges Adams, Shakespearian actor, director and historian. Mr Bridges Adams was Director of the Stratford-upon-Avon Festival from 1919 to 1934 and was the author of two major works, *The British Theatre* and *The Irresistable Theatre.* Extensive correspondence with well-known literary and musical figures.

AB —UNIVERSITY OF ALBERTA, Cameron Library, The Bruce Peel Special Collections Room, Edmonton, T6G 2J8, Can. John Charles, Special Collections Librn
Holdings: Cat
Notes: Incl several hundred posters and playbills.

BC —VANCOUVER PUBLIC LIBRARY, Language & Literature Div, 750 Burrard St, Vancouver, V6Z 1X5, Can. B Kinnear, Head
Notes: Good general collection of plays and dramatic criticism, supplemented by biographical clippings and indexed critical periodical material, compiled by the staff. Also, good general collection of theatre production and history in Fine Arts Division.

ON —MCMASTER UNIVERSITY, Mills Memorial Library, Div of Archives & Research Collections, Hamilton, L8S 4L6, Can. G R Hill, Univ Librn
Holdings: // Mss
Notes: Correspondence between Jacques Copeau and Andre Obey concerning the French theatre, 1924-1945. John Coulter Archive contains extensive correspondence with theatrical figures, such as Tyrone Guthrie and Jean Gascon, authors' scripts for stage plays, television, and radio work, prose works, and research notes on creative

THEATRE—HISTORY (cont.)

interests, and also on Artists Brief to Turgeon Committee which led to Canada Council.

ON —METROPOLITAN TORONTO LIBRARY, Theatre Dept, 789 Yonge St, Toronto, M4W 2G8, Can. Heather McCallum, Head
Holdings: Vols (30,500) Mss Pix Slides Phonorecords Microforms
Notes: The Theatre Department is one of eleven subject departments of the Metropolitan Toronto Library, which is generally acknowledged to be the most comprehensive of Canadian public library collections. The department balances book and non book materials in all areas of the performing arts except music: theatre and drama, moving pictures, dance, television and radio programming, and varieties of popular entertainment such as circus, music hall, vaudeville, puppetry and pantomime. The department's substantial holdings of rare books include over 75 court festival books. The collection is international in scope and is particularly strong in materials relating to Canadian theatre history and drama. Non-book holdings include extensive files of newspaper clippings, playbills, programs, production and publicity photographs, posters, and original stage designs, all of which document for the most part the history of Canadian theatre and dance companies, a large collection of British and American theatre portrait engravings, and a representative selection of 19th century, Japanese woodblock prints. Special collections relating to the history of the performing arts in Canada include the records of the Taverner Company which played Eastern Canada and the United States in the late 19th century, Toronto's Grand Opera House, the Marks Brothers touring company, film actor Ned Sparks, the Canadian-born actress Judith Evelyn, Toronto's Crest Theatre, the Canadian Players, Montreal Repertory Theatre, dancer/teacher Boris Volkoff, the Dumbells, the Canadian all-soldier concert party which originated in France in 1917, and vaudeville performer Charles Manny.

PQ —MCGILL UNIVERSITY, McLennan Library, Rare Books and Special Collections Dept, 3459 McTavish St, Montreal, H3A 1Y1, Can.
Holdings: Vols 2680
Notes: Incl books on the puppet theatre, puppets, toy theatres and their theatrical portraits, pantins, prints and posters, located in the Rosalynde Stearn Puppet Collection. A catalogue is available: The Rosalynde Stearn Puppet Collection, Montreal, 1961. Incl 171 puppets.

THEATRE—IRELAND

IL —NORTHWESTERN UNIVERSITY, Library, Special Collections Dept, 1937 Sheridan Rd, Evanston, 60201. R Russell Maylone, Cur
Holdings: Mss Pix
Notes: Dublin Gate Theatre Archive, incl the complete correspondence files, plays in mss, original production books and directors' notebooks, files of stage design, photographs, press releases, and photographs of many of the theater's productions. Described in Guide to the Archives of the Dublin Gate Theatre, Tine Howe (Evanston, 1978.) Abbey Theatre Materials incl Marie Nic Schubelaigh material: 100 mss and 75 presentation copies.

THEATRE—JEWS

NY —NEW YORK PUBLIC LIBRARY, Performing Arts Research Center, Rodgers & Hammerstein Archives of Recorded Sound, 111 Amsterdam Ave, New York, 10023.
Holdings: Phonorecords
Notes: Collection given by Helen Stambler Latner in memory of her husband, Benedict Stambler, comprises some 4000 phonodiscs, LPs and 78s covering the entire range of Jewish music represented on commercial sound recordings, 1900-1970. Basic areas are cantorial (synagogue music), Yiddish Theatre, folk and popular music, Israeli material, religious instructional material. Virtually all major cantors and theatrical persons who made commercial recordings are represented, with much of the material being rare European original discs. Catalog access presently limited to inventory list with performer index. Large collection of broadcast tapes from Israeli Broadcasting Service.

NY —YIVO INSTITUTE FOR JEWISH RESEARCH, Library & Archives, 1048 Fifth Ave, New York, 10028. Dina Abramowicz, Librn; Marek Web, Archivist
Holdings: Cat Mss Pix Slides
Notes: Yiddish drama in the original and in English translation from its 19th-century beginnings to the present; the Yiddish theatre in the Soviet Union and the theatrical activities in the ghettos during the Nazi regime; special collections of Sholem Perelmuter, Mendl Elkin, Maurice Schwartz, Abraham Goldfaden, Jacob Gordin, and Mark Schweid; records of the Union of Jewish Actors in Poland between the two world wars; the Vilna YIVO Collection of posters, playbills, and photographs; recordings.

OH —HEBREW UNION COLLEGE-JEWISH INSTITUTE OF RELIGION, Klau Library, 3101 Clifton Ave, Cincinnati, 45220. David J Gilner, Reference Librn
Holdings: Vols (4000) Cat
Notes: Photos, posters, playbills, ms music, scenarios and ephemera dealing with the Yiddish theater, 20th century Israel, US, and other countries.

RI —BROWN UNIVERSITY, John Hay Library, Harris Collection, Prospect St, Providence, 02912. Rosemary L Cullen, Cur
Holdings: Vols (200,000) Cat Mss Pix Phonorecords Microforms
Budget: ($15,000)
Notes: The Harris Colleton of American Poetry and Plays is principally composed of American and Canadian poetry and plays from the 17th century to the present. Extensive holdings in Yiddish-American literature, particularly in the late 19th and early 20th centuries. Incl the Vaxer Collection of Yiddish Poetry, Plays and Music (1700 vols). See Dictionary Catalog of the Harris Collection of American Poetry and Plays (Boston: GK Hall, 1972), 13 vols; Supplement (1977), 3 vols. Separate catalog.

THEATRE—LATIN AMERICA

CA —CLAREMONT COLLEGES, Ella Strong Denison Library, Scripps College, Claremont, 91711. Judy Harvey Sahak, Librn
Holdings: Vols 2700 Cat
Notes: Ruth S Lamb Collection of Latin American imprints, predominantly on theatre and drama.

NY —CENTER FOR INTER-AMERICAN RELATIONS, Library, 680 Park Ave, New York, 10021.
Notes: Most, but not all, of the 1000 plays and reference books are in Spanish or Portuguese.

THEATRE—LONDON

DC —LIBRARY OF CONGRESS, Rare Book & Special Collections Div, Washington, 20540. William Matheson, Chief
Notes: Francis Longe Collection of published theatrical works in English, 1607-1812.

MA —HARVARD UNIVERSITY LIBRARY, Theatre Collection, Cambridge, 02138. Jeanne T Newlin, Cur
Notes: One of the largest existing collections of playbills, programs, prints, photographs, promptbooks, and other materials relating to the performing arts, the scope is worldwide; resources on the English-speaking stage of the 18th and 19th centuries are unequalled. Incl materials on ballet and modern dance, the circus, magic, minstrel shows, cinema, and pantomime. For description, see Harvard Library Bulletin, VI (1925): pp 281-301. Also, papers of Robert E Sherwood (1896-1955), John Mason Bowers, George Pierce Baker, Edward Sheldon, Percy Mackaye; Angus McBean collection of photographs of the London Stage, 1937-1965; Alix Jeffry collection of photographs of the Off-Broadway Theatre; and others.

†NY —STATE UNIVERSITY OF NEW YORK, COLLEGE AT BROCKPORT, Brockport, 14420.
Notes: Microfilm copy of the Lord Chamberlain's Daybooks, registers of plays licensed for presentation in London from 1824-1903. Originals in British Museum. Some other miscellaneous material is incl from the Lord Chamberlain's office.

TN —MEMPHIS STATE UNIVERSITY, John Willard Brister Library, Memphis, 38152. John Terreo, Special Collections Librn
Notes: Theatre Collection, 1789-1972. Correspondence, scripts, programs, handbills, musical scores, clippings, drawings, sketches, and photographs, documenting careers of artists, production of plays, ballett and theatre companies, and theaters and opera houses centering in New York and London, England. Incl drawings, prints, publications, and other personal papers of British producer and designer Edward Gordon Craig (1872-1966), relating to his career, radio talks (1951-1961) for the BBC, acting school in Florence, Italy, and his mother, actress Ellen Terry; and correspondence, scripts, programs, reviews, scrapbooks, photos, and other materials, of American producer Jed Harris (?)-1979, relating to his stage productions (1926-1945).

THEATRE—LOS ANGELES

CA —LOS ANGELES PUBLIC LIBRARY, Literature and Philology Dept, 630 W Fifth St, Los Angeles, 90071. Helene G Mochedlover, Dept Librn
Holdings: Vols (50,000) Cat Pix Slides Microforms
Notes: Incl theatre programs, playbills, clippings, play reviews on 19th and 20th century plays produced in or near Los Angeles. Play collection of over 30,000 vols is particularly strong in 19th and 20th centuries. Annotated subject index to plays is kept up-to-date. A file of local as well as New York and London play reviews is kept. Collection incl microprints and microcards. There are a number of long files of important dramatic periodicals.

CA —LOS ANGELES PUBLIC LIBRARY, Frances Howard Goldwyn Hollywood Regional Library, 1623 Ivar Ave, Los Angeles, 90028. Sally Dumaux, Librn
Holdings: Vols (100,000) Cat Pix VF
Budget: ($60,000)
Notes: Over 2000 playbills, photographs, posters, and programs of Los Angeles area theatre from the 1920s to the present. Collection includes Turnabout Theatre Monthly Bulletin, 1942-48, souvenir programs and flyers. Also Pilgrimage Theatre and Hollywood Bowl programs, 1922 to present.

THEATRE—MOBILE, ALABAMA

†AL —MUSEUMS OF THE CITY OF MOBILE, Reference Library, 355

THEATRE—MOBILE, ALABAMA (cont.)

Government St, Mobile, 36602. Caldwell
Delaney, Adminr
Notes: Little Theatre of Mobile Coll.

THEATRE—MONTREAL

ON —METROPOLITAN TORONTO
LIBRARY, Theatre Dept, 789 Yonge St,
Toronto, M4W 2G8, Can. Heather
McCallum, Head
Holdings: Vols (30,500) Mss Pix Slides
Microforms
Notes: The Theatre Department is one of eleven
subject departments of the Metropolitan Toronto
Library, which is generally acknowledged to be the
most comprehensive of Canadian public library
collections. The department balances book and non
book materials in all areas of the performing arts
except music: theatre and drama, moving pictures,
dance, television and radio programming, and
varieties of popular entertainment such as circus,
music hall, vaudeville, puppetry and pantomime.
The department's substantial holdings of rare
books include over 75 court festival books. The
collection is international in scope and is
particularly strong in materials relating to Canadian
theatre history and drama. Non-book holdings
include extensive files of newspaper clippings,
playbills, programs, production and publicity
photographs, posters, and original stage designs,
all of which document for the most part the history
of Canadian theatre and dance companies, a large
collection of British and American theatre portrait
engravings, and a representative selection of 19th
century, Japanese woodblock prints. Special
collections relating to the history of the performing
arts in Canada include the records of the Taverner
Company which played Eastern Canada and the
United States in the late 19th century, Toronto's
Grand Opera House, the Marks Brothers touring
company, film actor Ned Sparks, the Canadian-
born actress Judith Evelyn, Toronto's Crest
Theatre, the Canadian Players, Montreal Repertory
Theatre, dancer/teacher Boris Volkoff, the
Dumbells, the Canadian all-soldier concert party
which originated in France in 1917, and vaudeville
performer Charles Manny.

THEATRE—NASHVILLE

TN —PUBLIC LIBRARY OF NASHVILLE &
DAVIDSON COUNTY, Nashville Room,
Eighth Ave N & Union, Nashville, 37203.
David Marshall Stewart, Chief Librn
Holdings: Vols Cat Pix
Notes: The Naff Collection of programs,
autographed photographs, posters, etc tells
the story of professional theatre in Nashville
between 1900 and 1960. All materials
noncirculating.

THEATRE—NEW YORK

PA —UNIVERSITY OF PITTSBURGH,
Special Collections Dept, Curtis Theatre

Collection, 363 Hillman Library, Pittsburgh,
15260. Jeanette Blanco, Cur
Holdings: Mss Documents Pix
Notes: Production records of Bucks County
Playhouse and New York City; memorabilia.
Catalog in process.

THEATRE—PHILADELPHIA

PA —FREE LIBRARY OF PHILADELPHIA,
Theatre Collection, Logan Sq, Philadelphia,
19103. Geraldine Duclow, Librn-in-Charge
Holdings: Vols (1,250,000) Uncat Pix
Notes: The Theatre Collection contains
books, magazines, playbills, broadsides,
posters, photographs, and other memorabilia
covering theatre, motion pictures, minstrels,
vaudeville, circus, radio and television. The
Library's Philadelphia Theatre Index lists
the major productions here since 1855, and
partially indexes the collection of local
playbills which date back to 1803. There are
also programs from many other cities, incl
New York; some from London date back to
1800. Early film companies as well as the
present movie industry are represented by
advertising materials and over 30,000 film
stills. The Lubin Film Co (1910-1916)
Archive has been established with over 600
photographs and related items. Circus
programs and route books date back to 1900.
There are minstrel programs as early as
1865. Most significant are the mss from
Philadelphia's Dumont Minstrels.
Variousfiles contain autographs, photographs,
newspaper articles and reviews in all
pertinent subject areas. Noncirculating.

PA —TEMPLE UNIVERSITY LIBRARIES,
Special Collections Dept, Conwellana-
Templana Collection, 13 & Berks St,
Philadelphia, 19122. Miriam I Crawford, Cur
Holdings: Mss Pix Audiotapes 16mm Films
Budget: ($30,000)
Notes: Chiefly photographs, both negatives
and prints, scrapbooks and play programs,
plus a few scripts, stage designs and
promptbooks, the bulk of which document
the productions of the Temple University
Theatre, 1930-1969, under the direction of
Paul Randall. A small supplementary
collection of miscellaneous theatrical
programs given at the school, and a
continuing collection of play programs and
publicity materials of the University Theater
since Randall's departure.

THEATRE—NEW YORK—PICTURES, ILLUSTRATIONS, ETC.

CA —UNIVERSITY OF CALIFORNIA, LOS
ANGELES, Research Library, Dept of
Special Collections, 405 Hilgard Ave, Los
Angeles, 90024. Edward Shreeves,
Chairman, Bibliographers Group; David S
Zeidberg, Head
Notes: More than 10,000 photographs and
20,000 negatives of live-action shots of
theatrical productions in New York and Los
Angeles, ca 1930 to mid-1950s.
See also entry under Programs, Theatre-
Collections

THEATRE—PICTURES, ILLUSTRATIONS, ETC.

CA —UNIVERSITY OF CALIFORNIA, LOS
ANGELES, Research Library, Dept of
Special Collections, 405 Hilgard Ave, Los
Angeles, 90024. Edward Shreeves,
Chairman, Bibliographers Group; David S
Zeidberg, Head
Notes: Various collections, incl the
Community Playhouse of Pasadena, George
P Johnson Negro Film, Jerome Robinson,
theatrical programs, and turn-of-the-century
cabinet cards collections.

THEATRE—PITTSBURGH

PA —UNIVERSITY OF PITTSBURGH,
Special Collections Dept, Curtis Theatre
Collection, 363 Hillman Library, Pittsburgh,
15260. Jeanette Blanco, Cur
Holdings: Vols (4000) Cat Mss Documents
Microforms Pix Slides VF
Notes: The legitimate theatre of plays,

musicals and vaudeville, chiefly of New
York City and Pittsburgh, from 1865, and
other US, community, summer, college and
foreign theatre. Incl 500,000 programs, 12,
000 pictures, 300 posters, the Oliver P
Merriman Scrapbooks and 300 other
scrapbooks, clippings and other ephemera.
Vols incl over 3000 acting editions and
playscripts. Separate collections: Ralph G
Allen Burlesque Skits Collection; Michael
Ellis Papers; William P Halstead Theatre
Collection; Kenyon Family Papers; Philip
Dunning Playscripts Collection; Pittsburgh
Playhouse Records; Pittsburgh Savoyards
Records. Noncirculating.

THEATRE—POLAND

CA —UNIVERSITY OF CALIFORNIA, LOS
ANGELES, Library, Slavic Collection, 405
Hilgard Ave, Los Angeles, 90024. Edward
Shreeves, Chairman, Bibliographers Group;
Leon Ferder, Slavic Bibliographer
Holdings: Vols (250,000) Cat
Notes: The Slavic Collection at UCLA
consists of materials from and relating to
Russia and the Soviet Union, Poland,
Czechoslovakia, Yugoslavia, Bulgaria, the
Sorbians in East Germany, and works by
Slavic emigres. The collection contains
nearly 250,000 vols, and is particularly
strong in linguistics, literature, history and
social sciences, and reference materials.
Slavic materials are collected in hard copy
and microform, and incl monographs, serials
(incl newspapers), reference works,
proceedings of Slavistic congresses and
symposia, and also *Festschriften* and
dissertations.

THEATRE—PROGRAMS see Programs, Theatre—Collections

THEATRE—SAN FRANCISCO

CA —UNIVERSITY OF CALIFORNIA,
DAVIS, Shields Library, Dept of Special
Collections, Davis, 95616. Donald Kunitz,
Head; C Danial Elliott, Asst Head
Notes: Scripts, promptbooks, photographs,
correspondence and business archives of
radical San Francisco theatre groups of the
1960s: San Francisco Mime Troupe,
Firehouse Theatre, Universal Movement
Theatre Repertory (UMTR), and the Living
Theatre.
See also entries under Firehouse Theatre;
Theatre - History.

NY —NEW YORK PUBLIC LIBRARY,
Performing Arts Research Center, Billy Rose
Theatre Collection, 111 Amsterdam Ave,
New York, 10023. Dorothy L Swerdlove,
Cur
Holdings: Cat Mss Pix
Notes: The Actors Repertory Theatre
Collection incl scripts, photographs, posters,
scrapbooks, office files, other papers, and
memorabilia relating to this company under
the management of Herbert Blau and Jules
Irving.

VA —GEORGE MASON UNIVERSITY,
Fenwick Library, Special Collections Dept,
4400 University Drive, Fairfax, 22030. Ruth
Kerns, Public Services Librn
Notes: The Federal Theatre Project (WPA)
Collection is on permanent loan from the
Library of Congress and includes
documentation for many FTP productions,
particularly those which originated in the
New York City, San Francisco and Los
Angeles areas.

THEATRE—SPAIN

IL —NORTHWESTERN UNIVERSITY,
Library, Special Collections Dept, 1937
Sheridan Rd, Evanston, 60201. R Russell
Maylone, Cur
Holdings: Cat
Notes: Spanish drama from the 18th to 20th
centuries, incl Castilian, Catalan, Valencian,
and Mexican. 12,000 plays.

THEATRE—STAGE LIGHTING see Stage Lighting

THEATRE—TEXAS

†TX —UNIVERSITY OF TEXAS
LIBRARIES, Hoblitzelle Theatre Arts

THEATRE—TEXAS (cont.)

Library, Austin, 78712.
Notes: Memorabilia of B Iden Payne, internationally known Shakespearean director.

TX —SOUTHERN METHODIST UNIVERSITY, Fondren Library, McCord Theater Collection, Room 301, Dallas, 75275. Edyth Renshaw, Cur; Linda Sellers, Pub Serv
Holdings: Vols (2000) Uncat Mss Pix Slides Phonorecords
Notes: See *Theatre Collections in Libraries and Museums*, Gilder and Freedley (Theatre Arts, 1936). The McCord Theatre Collection encompasses the entire spectrum of the performing arts. The central purpose is to gather records of our regional theater before such ephemeral material is lost. Records of over two hundred early Texas theaters, some fragmentary and some relatively complete, are in the files. These records incl photographs of buildings, stagehands, orchestras, and performers. Local theatre history incl the once famous Dallas Little Theatre and the Margo Jones Theatre. The national theatre, opera, ballet, and circus archives incl pictures (some autographed), programs, posters, throw-aways, tear sheets, clippings, and letters. Our international archives are small, but we have some excellent material, eg, artifacts from Max Reinhardt's production of"The Miracle" which happened to go bankrupt in Dallas. After a few years the items were given to us. There are posters, tear sheets, souvenir programs, and other colorful items from Morris Gest and the Artef Collection. We have about 200 19th century English playbills and a few from the 18th century. There is a collection of modern English, French, and other European programs, many of them illustrated souvenir programs. Also, magazines on theater, cinema, and television (1800). Scrapbooks covering both southwest and Dallas theater, 1890s-1950s. Special Collections: artifacts and documents on puppets; masks; costume design; circus; and ballet and dance. The Harriet Bacon MacDonald Collection of over 200 photographs of musicians appearing in Dallas during the first three decades of the 20th century. Many autographed. Affiliated with Meadow Theatre of the Arts.

THEATRE—TORONTO

ON —METROPOLITAN TORONTO LIBRARY, Theatre Dept, 789 Yonge St, Toronto, M4W 2G8, Can. Heather McCallum, Head
Holdings: Vols (30,500) Mss Pix Slides Microforms

Notes: The Theatre Department is one of eleven subject departments of the Metropolitan Toronto Library, which is generally acknowledged to be the most comprehensive of Canadian public library collections. The department balances book and non book materials in all areas of the performing arts except music: theatre and drama, moving pictures, dance, television and radio programming, and varieties of popular entertainment such as circus, music hall, vaudeville, puppetry and pantomime. The department's substantial holdings of rare books include over 75 court festival books. The collection is international in scope and is particularly strong in materials relating to Canadian theatre history and drama. Non-book holdings include extensive files of newspaper clippings, playbills, programs, production and publicity photographs, posters, and original stage designs, all of which document for the most part the history of Canadian theatre and dance companies, a large collection of British and American theatre portrait engravings, and a representative selection of 19th century, Japanese woodblock prints. Special collections relating to the history of the performing arts in Canada include the records of the Taverner Company which played Eastern Canada and the United States in the late 19th century, Toronto's Grand Opera House, the Marks Brothers touring company, film actor Ned Sparks, the Canadian-born actress Judith Evelyn, Toronto's Crest Theatre, the Canadian Players, Montreal Repertory Theatre, dancer/teacher Boris Volkoff, the Dumbells, the Canadian all-soldier concert party which originated in France in 1917, and vaudeville performer Charles Manny.

THEATRE—VERMONT

VT —UNIVERSITY OF VERMONT, Guy W Bailey/David W Howe Library, Burlington, 05405. John Buehler, Asst Dir for Special Collections
Notes: The papers of the Bread and Puppet Theatre of Glover, Vermont for the years 1962-1972.

THEATRE, ABBEY see Abbey Theatre

THEATRE, ACTORS' REPERTORY see Actors' Repertory Theatre, San Francisco

THEATRE, BREAD AND PUPPET see Bread and Puppet Theatre

THEATRE, CHILDREN'S see Children'S Theatre

THEATRE, EQUITY LIBRARY see Equity Library Theatre

THEATRE, EXPERIMENTAL see Experimental Theatre

THEATRE, FOREIGN see International Theatre

THEATRE, INTERNATIONAL see International Theatre

THEATRE, JEWISH see Theatre—Jews

THEATRE, LIVING see Living Theatre

THEATRE, MODERN—20TH CENTURY

CA —CALIFORNIA INSTITUTE OF THE ARTS, Library, 24700 McBean Pkwy, Valencia, 91355. James Elrod, Dir
Holdings: Vols (61,000) Cat
Budget: ($4500)

THEATRE, OFF AND OFF-OFF BROADWAY see off and off-Off Broadway Theatre

THEATRE, OPEN see Open Theatre

THEATRE, REPERTORY

NY —NEW YORK PUBLIC LIBRARY, Performing Arts Research Center, Billy Rose Theatre Collection, 111 Amsterdam Ave, New York, 10023. Dorothy L Swerdlove, Cur
Holdings: Cat
Notes: Actors Repertory Theatre, San Francisco and Repertory Theatre at Lincoln Center.

THEATRE, SAFETY see Safety, Theatre

THEATRE, TOY see Toy Theatres

THEATRE, YIDDISH see Theatre—Jews

THEATRE ASSOCIATION, AMERICAN see American Theatre Association

THEATRE COMPANY, PHOENIX see Phoenix Theatre Company

THEATRE CONFERENCE, NATIONAL see National Theatre Conference

THEATRE GUILD

CT —YALE UNIVERSITY, Box 1603A, Yale Station, New Haven, 06520.
Holdings: Mss Pix
Notes: The complete archives of The Guild, incl memorabilia, etc.

NY —NEW YORK PUBLIC LIBRARY, Performing Arts Research Center, Billy Rose Theatre Collection, 111 Amsterdam Ave, New York, 10023. Dorothy L Swerdlove, Cur
Holdings: Cat Mss Pix
Notes: Papers, scrapbooks, mss, photographs, memorabilia, etc. Incl ground plans, light plots, costume and property plots for various Theatre Guild productions.

THEATRE LIGHTING see Stage Lighting

THEATRE MUSIC

IA —DRAKE UNIVERSITY, Cowles Library, 28 St & University Ave, Des Moines, 50311.
Notes: Nearly 3000 musical works used by orchestras and musicians to accompany silent films, donated by Dorman Hundling who had played in orchestras in theatres owned by his family in South Dakota and Iowa.

THEATRE NEWSPAPERS see Newspapers, Theatre

THEATRE OF LINCOLN CENTER, REPERTORY see Repertory Theatre of Lincoln Center

THEATRE PERIODICALS see Periodicals, Theatre

THEATRE PROJECT, FEDERAL see Federal Theatre Project (Wpa)

THEATRE REPERTORY, UNIVERSAL MOVEMENT see Universal Movement Theatre Repertory

THEATRICAL AGENCIES

NY —NEW YORK PUBLIC LIBRARY, Performing Arts Research Center, Billy Rose Theatre Collection, 111 Amsterdam Ave, New York, 10023. Dorothy L Swerdlove, Cur
Holdings: Cat Mss Pix
Notes: Papers, scrapbooks, mss, photographs, memorabilia, etc.

THEATRICAL COSTUME see Costume

THEATRICAL MUSIC see Music, Incidental; Music in Theatres; Opera

THEATRICAL SHEETS see Toy Theatres

THEMATIC CUE SHEETS

CA —UNIVERSITY OF CALIFORNIA, LOS ANGELES, Theater Arts Library, Los Angeles, 90024. Edward Shreeves, Chairman, Bibliographers Group; Audree Malkin, Head, Theater Arts Library
Notes: Collection of thematic cue sheets for the musical accompaniment of silent films, 1920-1930.

THEOBALD, ROBERT A., 1884-1957

CA —HOOVER INSTITUTION ON WAR, REVOLUTION & PEACE, Stanford

THEOBALD, ROBERT A., 1884-1957 (cont.)

University, Stanford, 94305. Milorad M Drachkovitch, Archivist
Holdings: Mss
Notes: Papers of Robert A Theobald, Rear Admiral, US Navy; Destroyer Commander, Pacific Fleet, 1940-41; and Commander, Northern Pacific Force in Alaskan Operations, May 1942-January 1943; incl correspondence, speeches and writings, war diaries, dispatches, operations plans and orders, manuals, service lists, memoranda, reports, and war estimates, 1908-59, relating to his career in the US Navy; naval operations in Alaska, May 1942-January 1943, incl the Japanese invasion of the Aleutians, June 1942; and the Japanese attack on Pearl Harbor. 12 ms boxes.

THEOLOGICAL DISPUTATIONS see Disputations, Religious

THEOLOGICAL EDUCATION see Religious Education

THEOLOGICAL SEMINARIES, CATHOLIC

CT —SACRED HEART UNIVERSITY, Library, 5229 Park Ave, PO Box 6460, Bridgeport, 06606. Roch-Josef di Lisio, Actg Dir
Holdings: Vols 1200 Cat
Notes: The John A Rycenga Memorial Collection on American Catholic Higher Education.

THEOLOGY

AZ —COOK CHRISTIAN TRAINING SCHOOL, Mary M McCarthy Library, 708 S Lindon Lane, Tempe, 85281. Mark E Thomas, Librn
Holdings: Vols 2500 Cat Audiotapes Videotapes Filmstrips
CA —AZUSA PACIFIC COLLEGE, Marshburn Memorial Library, Citrus & Alosta, Azusa, 91702. Edward Peterman, Librn
Holdings: Vols 1500 Uncat
Notes: The Monsignor Francis J Weber Collection on American Catholic Church History incl biographies, reference works, theological studies, scholarly journals, monograph series, and the complete works of some Catholic historians. No photocopying.
CA —GRADUATE THEOLOGICAL UNION LIBRARY, New Religious Movements Research Collection, Public Services and Special Collections Dept, 2400 Ridge Road, Berkeley, 94709. Diane Choquette, Dept Head
Holdings: Vols (3000) Mss Pix
Notes: Begun in 1977, the collection focuses on religious movements new to America since 1960, and unorthodox religious movements resurgent since 1960. American forms of Hinduism, Buddhism, Sikhism, and Sufism are included along with occultism, Neo-Paganism, esoteric and alternative forms of Christianity, feminist spirituality, and human potential movements having a spiritual aspect. Legal issues, such as deprogramming, and the question of church/state relations are an important part of the collection. The Library is a depository for publications of the Unification Church in America, the Church of Scientology, and the International Society for Krishna Consciousness (America). The responses of mainstream religions and concerned citizens groups are also included. Besides 3000 monographs, the library has 400 periodical titles, 200 posters from the San Francisco Bay Area, 1965-77, 300 research papers, and 31 linear feet of ephemera.
CA —UNIVERSITY OF CALIFORNIA, DAVIS, Shields Library, Dept of Special Collections, Davis, 95616. Donald Kunitz, Head; C Danial Elliott, Asst Head
Holdings: Vols 1700 Cat
Notes: A selection of Bibles in various

formats and languages, incl New Testament, Gospels, Greek, 12th and 14th centuries; the earliest Latin Bible produced by Koburger, 1478; Tyndale's New Testament, 1525, the first New Testament printed in English; Tremellius Latin Bible, London, 1585; the first Geneva Bible without the Apocryphia, 1599; the London Polyglot Bible, 1657, and others.
CA —BIOLA UNIVERSITY, Rose Memorial Library, 13800 Biola Ave, La Mirada, 90639. A Lawrence Marshburn
Holdings: Vols (178,000) Cat Maps Pix Microforms
Budget: ($430,000)
Notes: Biblical and evangelical materials.
CA —LOS ANGELES PUBLIC LIBRARY, Philosophy & Religion Dept, 630 W Fifth St, Los Angeles, 90071. Marilyn C Wherley, Librn
Holdings: Vols 1400 Cat
Budget: ($60,000)
Notes: Part of the comprehensive holdings on world religions, i.e., Christianity, Judaism, Islam, Hinduism etc.
CA —UNIVERSITY OF CALIFORNIA, LOS ANGELES, William Andrews Clark Memorial Library, 2520 Cimarron St, Los Angeles, 90018.
Holdings: Cat Mss
Notes: Original editions.
CA —SAINT MARY'S COLLEGE, Library, Moraga, 94575. Brother Casimir Reichlin, Dir of the Library; Brother Richard Lemberg FSC, Asst Librn
CA —POINT LOMA NAZARENE COLLEGE, Ryan Library, 3900 Lomaland Dr, San Diego, 92106. Esther Schandorff, Librn
Notes: Arminian-Wesleyan Theological Collection.
†CA —UNIVERSITY OF SAN FRANCISCO, Richard A Gleeson Library, The Countess Bernardine Murphy Donohue Rare Book Room, San Francisco, 94117. D Steven Corey, Special Collections Librn
Holdings: Vols 1200 Uncat Pix
Notes: Modernism in the Catholic Church. Incl extensive holdings concerning George Tyrrell, Alfred Loisy, and Baron Friedrich von Hugel.
CA —STANFORD UNIVERSITY LIBRARIES, Cecil H Green Library, Stanford, 94305. Michael T Ryan, Cur
Holdings: Vols Cat
Notes: An emphasis in the Rare Book Collection.
CT —YALE UNIVERSITY, Divinity School Library, 409 Prospect St, New Haven, 06520. John Bollier, Librarian
Holdings: Vols (340,000)
Notes: Collection incl 340,000 vols, 1452 periodical subscriptions, 8500 microforms and 3500 films.
DC —CATHOLIC UNIVERSITY OF AMERICA, Mullen Library, 620 Michigan Ave NE, Washington, 20064. B Gutekunst, Humanities Librn
Holdings: Vols (20,000) Cat
DC —DOMINICAN HOUSE OF STUDIES, Dominican College Library, 487 Michigan Ave NE, Washington, 20017. J Raymond Vandegrift, OP, Librn
Holdings: Vols (3700) Cat
Budget: $650
Notes: Incl works about Thomas Aquinas-- commentaries, festschiften, biographies--and works both by and about his followers, the Thomists-- histories, biographies, periodicals, monograph series, manuals, incunabula, rare books, and the papers presented at Thomistic congresses.
See also entry under Thomas Aquinas, St.
DC —GEORGETOWN UNIVERSITY, Woodstock Theological Center Library, Box 37445, Washington, 20013. Thomas a Marshall, SJ, Librn
Holdings: Vols (165,000)
Notes: Works by Jesuit authors, from the 16th century on.
FL —UNIVERSITY OF FLORIDA LIBRARY, Isser and Rae Price Library of Judaica, 18 Libr East, Gainesville, 32611. Robert Singerman, Head Librn
Budget: ($30,000)
Notes: Total holdings estimated at 55,000

vols dealing with the political, social, economic and intellectual history of the Jews in the ancient, medieval and modern periods and in all geographic areas. The following areas are especially well represented by printed matter in all relevant languages: Bibliography, Festschriften, History, Bible, Judaism and Jewish theology, liturgy, responsa, rabbinical literature, Jewish law, Hebrew language and literature, Yiddish language and literature, anti-semitism, Zionism, Palestine and the *Yishuv*, and the State of Israel. German and American Judaica form a collecting emphasis with holdings for all the standard histories as well as histories of individual synagogues, institutions and local communities. Works in Hebrew and Yiddish comprise about 60 percent of the collection (estimated 30,000 vols). With few exceptions, holdings are limited to nineteenth and twentieth century imprints, with complete sets of journals and thousands of ephemeral pamphlets, many of them commemorating anniversaries, enhancing the research value of the collection, the largest Judaica research library in the southeastern United States. Only about half of the collection is cataloged; the collection is a circulating one and vols may be borrowed on interlibrary loan. Incl the Leonard C Mishkin Collection (40,000 vols), the largest personal Judaica collection in the United States, the Shlomo Marenof Collection (3500 vols), and the inventory of Bernard Morgenstern's Lower East Side Book Store (8000 vols). Scholars should inquire in advance of their visit. *The Isser and Rae Price Library of Judaica* Report (circulation 2900 copies) is mailed gratis twice a year to all interested parties. Special catalogs: Pre-1881 Hebrew imprints recorded in a chronological card file.
GA —EMORY UNIVERSITY, Candler School of Theology, Pitts Theology Library, Atlanta, 30322. Channing Jeschke, Librn; Anita K Delaries, Curator
Notes: Incl records (85 vols) of the Methodist Church in Georgia; 1614 mss and ms volumes dating from 1830. Also 9.5 linear feet of mss and printed materials documenting the history of the independent African Orthodox Church (1880-1974), and the role of Archbishop Daniel William Alexander (1882-1970), sent to the Library for fear of its possible destruction if kept in South Africa. Finding aid available.
IL —SOUTHERN ILLINOIS UNIVERSITY, CARBONDALE, Delyte W Morris Library, Special Collections Dept, Carbondale, 62901. David V Koch, Cur of Special Collections; Louisa Bowen, Cur of Manuscripts
Holdings: Vols 30 Cat Mss Pix
Notes: Twenty Collections relating to 20th century American philosophy incl the archives of Henry Nelson Wieman, American theologian and philosopher consist of some 30 vols which Wieman authored or co-authored, together with mss (published and unpublished), autobiographical materials, letters, lecture notes, and other papers. See Martin Luther King, *A Comparison of the Conception of God in the Thinking of Paul Tillich and Henry Nelson Wieman*, 1955. Inventory and name index available at the library.
IL —JESUIT-KRAUSS-MCCORMICK LIBRARY, 1100 E 55th St, Chicago, 60615. Donald Vorp, Dir; Elvire Hilgert, Librn
Holdings: Vols (375,000)
Notes: Collections contain merger of Jesuit Library, Lutheran School of Theology of Chicago (Krauss Library), and McCormick Theological Seminary. Jesuit: Sermones Thesaurus Novi de Tempore (anonymous, Strassbourg 1486); Opera Omnia (Jean Gerson, Strassbourg 1488), 3 vols; Summa Rosella Casuum (Venice 1495); moral theology (major figures of 16th and 17th century scholasticism); early modern editions of patristics and canon law regarding procedures and organzation of the Catholic Church, incl treatises and multi-volume commentaries. Krauss: Archives of Lutheran Church in America and its predecessors; Reformation imprints; early printed versions of the Bible (L Franklin Gruber Collection);

THEOLOGY (cont.)

German and Scandanavian (Swedish, Danish, Finnish) theology; Lutheran Church of America document depository. McCormick: Presbyteriana; historical record of Synod of Illinois, UnitedPresbyterian Church of USA; Church Federation of Chicago archives prior to 1969; USA imprints of the Bible (Simms Collection).

IL —GOOD SAMARITAN HOSPITAL, Medical Library, 3815 Highland Ave, Downers Grove, 60695. Karen Ambrose, Librn
Holdings: Vols (50,000) Cat
Budget: ($100,000)

†IN —UNIVERSITY OF NOTRE DAME, Library, 221 Memorial Library, Notre Dame, 46556.
Notes: The Astrik L Gabriel Collection of incunabula.

MD —SAINT MARY'S SEMINARY & UNIVERSITY, School of Theology Library, 5400 Roland Ave, Baltimore, 21210. David Siemen, Dir
Holdings: Vols (170,000) Cat Mss Maps Pix Audiotapes Microforms

MD —MOUNT SAINT MARY'S COLLEGE, Hugh J Phillips Library, Emmitsburg, 21727. Stephen Rockwood, Librn
Holdings: Vols (140,000) Cat Mss Maps Pix
Notes: Early Catholic Americana, especially for western Maryland.

MA —HARVARD UNIVERSITY, Harvard Divinity School, Andover-Harvard Theological Library, 45 Francis Ave, Cambridge, 02138. Maria Grossmann, Librn
Holdings: Vols (370,000) Cat
Notes: For description see *Harvard Library Bulletin*, V (1951): pp 159-180. The collection is particularly strong in biblical studies, Unitarianism and the liberal movement in theology in America, and in European Protestantism, especially German and Dutch controversial theology of the 16th through 18th century.

MA —BOSTON COLLEGE LIBRARIES, Thomas P O'Neill Library, Chestnut Hill, 02167. John D J Slinn, Librn of the Central Library

MI —NORTHERN MICHIGAN UNIVERSITY, Lydia M Olson Library, Elizabeth L Harden Drive, Marquette, 49855. Stephen H Peters, Cataloger
Notes: A section of the personal library of Moses Coit Tyler, including works by Thomas Hooker, John Cotton, Cotton Mather, and Jonathan Edwards.

MI —SAINT MARY'S COLLEGE, Alumni Memorial Library, Orchard Lake, 48033. Sister Mary Ellen Lampe, Librn

MN —SAINT JOHN'S ABBEY & UNIVERSITY, Hill Monastic Manuscript Library, Collegeville, 56321. Julian G Plante, Dir
Holdings: Vols (61,000) Microfilms
Notes: Films of 61,000 mss. The total number of codices or bound handwritten mss represents the holdings of several hundred libraries in Europe, mostly Austria, Spain, Ethiopia, West Germany, Portugal, and also Italy, Hungary, Poland, Great Britain, Belgium, Yugoslavia, France, Switzerland, and the Netherlands.

MO —CONCEPTION ABBEY, Library, Conception, 64433.
Holdings: Vols (2425) // Uncat Mss Microforms
Budget: ($20,000)
Notes: Rare Roman Catholic theological books and mss, mostly 16-19th centuries. A partial catalog of the collection exists. Basically this is a donation received in the last quarter of the 19th century from a 900-year-old Swiss abbey, Engelberg Abbey. Most of our mss are listed in De Ricci census. The incunabula are for the most part listed in Goff's census. No photocopying.

MO —CONCORDIA HISTORICAL INSTITUTE, 801 DeMun Ave, Saint Louis, 63105. Aug R Suelflow, Dir
Holdings: Vols (58,000) Mss Maps Pix Slides Films Microforms
Budget: ($100,000)
Notes: A centralized collection of all information media pertaining to the history and theology of Lutheranism in North America; also German-Americana; indexes and finding aids are available; extensive microfilm collection of mss, books, periodicals, church records; the ms collection exceeds 2,500,000 pages.

MO —SAINT LOUIS UNIVERSITY, Pius XII Memorial Library, 3655 W Pine Blvd, Saint Louis, 63108. William Cole, Dir
Notes: Collection covers all areas of learning and European history from Classical Antiquity to early modern period. Researchers using collection receive assistance in paleography, bibliography and reference search. Approx 10,000 1000-foot reels of microfilm (not counting master negatives) reproducing Vatican Library's Latin, Greek, Hebrew, Arabic and Ethiopic mss. Some 8000 100-foot reels of microfilm (again not counting master negative) reproducing rare and out of print books relating to subject areas in the mss. Over 50,000 color slides of medieval and Renaissance mss illuminations. A reference collection of modern materials relating to ms research.

MO —CENTRAL BIBLE COLLEGE LIBRARY, 3000 N Grant, Springfield, 65802. G J Flokstra Jr, Librn
Holdings: Vols 1975 Cat Mss Audiotapes Microforms
Notes: Holy Spirit theology.

NJ —SAINT SOPHIA UKRAINIAN ORTHODOX THEOLOGICAL SEMINARY, PO Box 240, South Bound Brook, 08880. Iwan Korowytzky, Dir; Fr Wasyl Iwashchuk, Librn
Holdings: 4000 Vols Cat Mss
Budget: ($10,000)
Notes: Open to all.

NY —GENERAL THEOLOGICAL SEMINARY, Saint Marks Library, 175 Ninth Ave, New York, 10011. David Green, Dir
Holdings: Vols (200,000) Cat
Notes: Extensive collection.

NY —UNION THEOLOGICAL SEMINARY, Library, 3041 Broadway at Reinhold Niebuhr Place, New York, 10027. Richard D Spoor, Dir
Holdings: Vols (580,000) Cat Mss Microforms
Budget: ($750,000)

NY —AMERICAN BAPTIST HISTORICAL SOCIETY, Samuel Colgate Baptist Historical Library, 1106 S Goodman St, Rochester, 14620.
Holdings: Vols 65,000 Mss Pix Microforms
Notes: Baptist history, theology, and authors. Annual reports (250,000), 6000 mss, 300 journal subscriptions; clippings. Incl especially, the Henry Sweetser Burrage Collection of 17th and 18th century English Baptist materials; also the Danish Baptist Conference of America Archives. Publish *Baptist Bibliography*, 24 vols.

†NY —COLGATE ROCHESTER DIVINITY SCHOOL, Ambrose Swasey Library, 1100 S Goodman St, Rochester, 14620.
Notes: Ranges through the traditional themes of Christian theology.

†NY —INSTITUTE FOR ADVANCED STUDIES OF WORLD RELIGIONS (IASWR), Library, State University of New York at Stony Brook, Stony Brook, 11794. C T Shen, Librn
Holdings: Vols 45,000 Mss Maps Microforms

NY —SAINT VLADIMIRS' ORTHODOX THEOLOGICAL SEMINARY, 575 Scarsdale Rd, Yonkers, 10707. Paul D Garrett, Librn
Holdings: Vols (36,000) Pix
Notes: Incl 250 periodicals. A major source of materials on Orthodox Church theology. Much on works of art.

NC —DUKE UNIVERSITY, William R Perkins Library, Rare Book Room, Durham, 27706. John L Sharpe, III, Cur
Notes: Liechtenstein collection. Sixteenth and 17th century German theology and church history.

NC —DUKE UNIVERSITY, Divinity School Library, Durham, 27706. Donn Michael Farris, Librn
Holdings: Vols (225,000)
Notes: Special collections and subject emphases in this library include: Archaeology, Egyptian; Archaeology, Middle Eastern; Art, Jewish; Bible; Bible-New Testament; Bible-Symbolism; Church Architecture; Egyptology; Fathers of the Church; Society of Friends; Great Britain-Religion-Methodism and Methodist Church; Hymns and Hymnals; Jansenists and Jansenism; Judaica; Mediaeval Christian Mysticism; Methodism and Methodist Church; Methodist Episcopal Church; Methodist Episcopal Church, South; Reformation; Religion-US-History; Rural Church; Theology-Great Britain-17th Century; Theology-Great Britain-18th Century; United Methodist Church; US-Church History; John Wesley.

NC —SOUTHEASTERN BAPTIST THEOLOGICAL SEMINARY LIBRARY, PO Box 752, Wake Forest, 27587. H Eugene McLeod, Librn
Holdings: Cat Audiotapes Microforms

OH —PUBLIC LIBRARY OF CINCINNATI & HAMILTON COUNTY, Education & Religion Dept, 800 Vine St, Cincinnati, 45202. Susan F Hettinger, Head
Holdings: Vols (45,000) Cat
Budget: ($10,000)
Notes: Theological and religious collection: religion, church history, theology, 18th and 19th century Protestant writings and sermons.

†OH —UNIVERSITY OF DAYTON LIBRARY, Dayton, 45469.
Notes: Major part of the library of the former St Leonard's Franciscan Seminary in Centerville, Ohio. Incl some 1600 rare books, 2500 reference books, 5500 journal volumes, and about 33,000 books of theology and philosophy.

OH —OBERLIN COLLEGE LIBRARY, Oberlin, 44074. William A Moffett, Dir of Libraries
Holdings: Cat
Notes: Of special interest are sermons, hymn books, and hymnals of the late 18th and early 19th centuries.

OR —MULTNOMAH SCHOOL OF THE BIBLE, Library, 8435 NE Gilsan St, Portland, 97220. James F Scott, Dir of Library; Susan Johnson, Asst Librn
Holdings: Vols (40,686) Cat Slides Phonorecords Audiotapes Filmstrips
Budget: ($33,950)
Notes: Multnomah School of the Bible is an evangelical school that educates students through a program of instruction having the Bible as its center. It supports this centralized Bible major with several ancillary, pertinent supporting minors, ie, Christian education, pastoral, missions and New Testament Greek.

OR —UNIVERSITY OF PORTLAND, Wilson W Clark Memorial Library, 5000 N Willamette Blvd, PO Box 03017, Portland, 97203. Rev Joseph P Browne, CSC, Dir
Holdings: Vols (12,000) Cat
Budget: $6000
Notes: Emphasis on Catholic theology.

PA —LANCASTER MENNONITE CONFERENCE HISTORICAL SOCIETY LIBRARY, 2215 Millstream Rd, Lancaster, 17602. Lloyd Zeager, Librn; David J Smucker, Genealogist
Holdings: Vols (55,000) Cat Mss
Budget: ($3186)
Notes: Large collection of Mennonite archival material.

PA —LUTHERAN THEOLOGICAL SEMINARY, Krauth Memorial Library, 7301 Germantown Ave, Philadelphia, 19119. Rev David J Wartluft, Dir Libr

SC —UNIVERSITY OF SOUTH CAROLINA, Thomas Cooper Library, Columbia, 29208. Kenneth E Toombs, Dir of Libraries; Roger Mortimer, Rare Book Librn
Holdings: Vols 45 Cat
Notes: One of the few very strong collections of Muggletonian theology.

TX —SOUTHWESTERN BAPTIST THEOLOGICAL SEMINARY, Roberts Library, 2001 W Seminary Dr, PO Box 22000-2E, Fort Worth, 76122. Keith C Wills, Dir
Holdings: Vols 56,000 Cat Mss Pix Slides Audiotapes Videotapes 16mm Films Filmstrips Microforms
Budget: $34,000

THEOLOGY (cont.)

TX —UNIVERSITY OF SAINT THOMAS, Saint Mary's Seminary, Cardinal Beran Library, 9845 Memorial Dr, Houston, 77024. Constance Walker, Librn
Holdings: Vols 37,500 Cat Phonorecords Audiotapes Microforms
Budget: $60,000
Notes: Library for the Graduate School of Theology.

TX —OBLATE SCHOOL OF THEOLOGY, Library, 285 Oblate Dr, San Antonio, 78216. James Maney, Libr Dir
Holdings: Vols (22,000) Cat
Budget: ($15,500)

WA —SEATTLE UNIVERSITY, A A Lemieux Library, Seattle, 98122.
Notes: A major theology collection comprised of approx 50,000 vols of the former St Thomas Seminary Library, incl an outstanding periodicals section.

†WI —SEVENTH DAY BAPTIST HISTORICAL SOCIETY, Library, 3120 Kennedy St, PO Box 1678, Janesville, 53547.
Holdings: Vols (500) Cat Mss
Notes: Sabbatarianism began in England in the 17th century and was brought to the US by English- and German-speaking Seventh Day Baptists, from whom the Seventh-day Adventist movement emerged after 1844. The doctrine of both denominations and of the Church of God-Seventh Day are set in this collection, 1653 to date.

WI —UNIVERSITY OF WISCONSIN, MADISON, Memorial Library, Western European Humanities Collection, 728 State St, Madison, 53706. Charles Szabo, Bibliographer
Notes: Chwalibog Collection. Contemporary editions of the principal European theologians of the 17th and 18th centuries. The bulk of the collection consists of standard sets of Roman Catholic writers such as Bossuet, Fenelon, and Cardinal Fleury. There are also a number of rare and unusual items dealing with other Christian denominations. There is also a good representation of titles by the philosophers of the 18th century enlightenment.
Supplements the Tank Collection (Calvinism) and the Montauban Collection (French Protestantism).

WI —MARQUETTE UNIVERSITY, Memorial Library, 1415 W Wisconsin Ave, Milwaukee, 53233. Jay Kirk, Health Sciences Librn
Notes: The Philosophy/Theology Collection has particular strengths in the areas of ancient, patristic and medieval thought and in scholastic philosophy and theology after the Middle Ages. This Collection also has an added dimension in its classification arrangement, which brings together into one unified grouping both the works and the criticisms of an individual philosopher or theologian.

WI —SAINT FRANCIS SEMINARY, SCHOOL OF PASTOR MINISTRY, Salzmann Library, 3257 S Lake Dr, Milwaukee, 53207. Lawrence Miech, Librn
Holdings: Vols (65,000) Cat
Budget: ($27,000)

AB —CANADIAN UNION COLLEGE, Library, Box 460, College Heights, T0C 0Z0, Can. Keith Clouten, Library Services Dir
Holdings: Vols (5000) Cat Audiotapes 16mm Films Microforms
Notes: Largely theology, comparative religion, church history, especially of Seventh-day Adventists.

MB —UNIVERSITY OF MANITOBA, Saint John's College, Library, 400 Dysart Rd, Winnipeg, R3T 2M5, Can. Patrick D Wright, Head
Holdings: Vols (45,600) Cat
Notes: Special emphasis on history, literature, and theology of the Anglican church.

MB —UNIVERSITY OF MANITOBA, Saint Paul's College Library, Winnipeg, R3T 2M6, Can. Rev H J Drake, SJ, Head
Holdings: Vols (60,500) Cat

MB —UNIVERSITY OF WINNIPEG, Library, 515 Portage Ave, Winnipeg, R3B 2E9, Can.

W R Converse, Chief Librn
Holdings: Vols (30,000) Cat Microforms
Budget: $11,000
Notes: The University of Winnipeg was a theological college before it became a university in 1967, and so has a strong theological collection. Incl 800 microforms. Also incl materials received for Religious Studies Program.

ON —HURON COLLEGE, Silcox Memorial Library, 1349 Western Rd, London, N6G 1H3, Can. Pamela MacKay, Chief Librn
Holdings: Vols (28,000) Cat
Budget: ($24,710)
Notes: Covers Bible, church history, church music, liturgics, pastoralia, religious education, philosophy of religion, religious studies, systematics. 95 periodical subscriptions including foreign language materials. Rare books collection of 750 volumes, including collections of sermons, commentaries, particularly rare bibles, many in foreign languages.

ON —TORONTO SCHOOL OF THEOLOGY, Consortium of Libraries, University of Toronto, Toronto, M5S 1A5, Can. R Grane Bracewell, Library Coordr
Holdings: Cat
Notes: A consortium of 7 theological college and faculty libraries at the University of Toronto.

ON —UNIVERSITY OF TORONTO, Thomas Fisher Rare Book Library, 120 Saint George St, Toronto, M5S 1A5, Can. Richard G Landon, Head
Holdings: Vols 1600 // Cat Mss
Notes: Forbes Collection created by James Forbes (1629?-1712), English nonconformist minister. Kept as a separate library with few additions until present day. (Toronto, 1968). Also Heyworth, P L "Unfamiliar Libraries XVI: The Forbes Library," The Book Collector, Autumn 1970.

ON —WYCLIFFE COLLEGE, Leonard Library, 5 Hoskin Ave, Toronto, M5S 1H7, Can. Adrienne Taylor, Librn; Gayle Ford, Library Technician
Holdings: Vols (47,000) Cat Microforms
Budget: ($11,000)
Notes: Collection of early and rare books of prayer books, sermons, Bibles. Basic reference collection of standard theological dictionaries, encyclopedias, commentaries. Homiletics collection including 19th century works. Strong in church history, Evangelical Anglicanism, English Reformation, Wycliffe studies.

ON —WILFRID LAURIER UNIVERSITY, Waterloo Lutheran Seminary Library, (formerly Waterloo Lutheran University), 75 University Ave W, Waterloo, N2L 3C5, Can. Erich R W Schultz, University Librn
Holdings: Vols (31,000) Cat Microforms
Budget: ($18,000)
Notes: One of the largest Lutheran collections in Canada.

PQ —BISHOP'S UNIVERSITY, John Bassett Memorial Library, Laurie Allison Room for Special Collections, Lennoxville, J1M 1Z7, Can. Germain Belisle, Chief Librn
Holdings: Vols 10,000
Notes: Partially cataloged. Relates to ecclesiastical subjects, dating from as early as the 16th century, largely concerned with the history of the Church of England in Canada and elsewhere.

PQ —CONCORDIA UNIVERSITY LIBRARIES, 1455 de Maisonneuve Blvd W, Montreal, H3G 1M8, Can. Martin Cohen, Special Collections Librn
Holdings: Vols 60 // Cat Mss
Notes: The Maximilien Bibaud Collection contains the author's memoirs and correspondence as well as his writing on diverse subjects such as religion, theology, Canadian, European and ancient history, and the French language. 51 vols of ms materials.

SK —UNIVERSITY OF REGINA, Campion College, Library, Regina, S4S 0A2, Can. Myfanwy Truscott, Librn
Holdings: Vols (50,000) Cat
Budget: ($100,000)

THEOLOGY—DISPUTATIONS see Disputations, Religious

THEOLOGY—HISTORY

FL —UNIVERSITY OF FLORIDA LIBRARY, Isser and Rae Price Library of

Judaica, 18 Libr East, Gainesville, 32611. Robert Singerman, Head Librn
Budget: ($30,000)
Notes: Total holdings estimated at 55,000 vols dealing with the political, social, economic and intellectual history of the Jews in the ancient, medieval and modern periods and in all geographic areas. The following areas are especially well represented by printed matter in all relevant languages: Bibliography, Festschriften, History, Bible, Judaism and Jewish theology, liturgy, responsa, rabbinical literature, Jewish law, Hebrew language and literature, Yiddish language and literature, anti-semitism, Zionism, Palestine and the Yishuv, and the State of Israel. German and American Judaica form a collecting emphasis with holdings for all the standard histories as well as histories of individual synagogues, institutions and local communities. Works in Hebrew and Yiddish comprise about 60 percent of the collection (estimated 30,000 vols). With few exceptions, holdingsare limited to nineteenth and twentieth century imprints, with complete sets of journals and thousands of ephemeral pamphlets, many of them commemorating anniversaries, enhancing the research value of the collection, the largest Judaica research library in the southeastern United States. Only about half of the collection is cataloged; the collection is a circulating one and vols may be borrowed on interlibrary loan. Incl the Leonard C Mishkin Collection (40,000 vols), the largest personal Judaica collection in the United States, the Shlomo Marenof Collection (3500 vols), and the inventory of Bernard Morgenstern's Lower East Side Book Store (8000 vols). Scholars should inquire in advance of their visit. The Isser and Rae Price Library of Judaica Report (circulation 2900 copies) is mailed gratis twice a year to all interested parties. Special catalogs:Pre-1881 Hebrew imprints recorded in a chronological card file.

IL —UNIVERSITY OF CHICAGO LIBRARY, Dept of Special Collections, 1100 E 57 St, Chicago, 60637.
Notes: American Bible Union and Hengstenberg Collections of Early Theology and Biblical Criticism.

ON —VICTORIA UNIVERSITY, Library, Centre for Reformation and Renaissance Studies, 71 Queen's Park Crescent, Toronto, M5S 1K7, Can. Robert C Brandeis, Chief Librn; James Estes, Dir
Holdings: Vols (15,000) Cat Slides
Notes: The CRRS concentrates on the northern European countries and France; its chief strengths are Erasmus, 650 vols; early printed books, especially 16th century editions of Latin classics; bibliography and the history of printing. The Erasmus holdings are cataloged in W T McCready et al, "The Erasmus Collection in the Centre for Reformation and Renaissance Studies...A Catalogue..." Renaissance and Reformation, 7 (1971), 32-76; D Swift Sewell, "The Erasmus Collection...A Supplementary List..." Renaissance and Reformation, 10 (1974), 116-19. A catalog of the Centre's holdings of Renaissance editions of classical authors is in preparation.

THEOLOGY, ASCETICAL see Asceticism

THEOLOGY, ETHICAL see Christian Ethics

THEOLOGY, MORAL see Christian Ethics

THEOLOGY, MYSTICAL see Mysticism

THEOLOGY, PASTORAL see Pastoral Theology

THEOPHANIES

RI —BROWN UNIVERSITY, John Hay Library, 20 Prospect St, Providence, 02912. Mark N Brown, Cur Mss
Holdings: Vols (900) // Mss
Notes: John William Graham Collection of

THEOPHANIES (cont.)

Literature of Psychic Science--350 predominantly late 19th and early 20th century books dealing with alchemy, black magic, dreams, demonology, church history, mysticism, mediumship, physical and somatic types of psychic experience. Collection described in *Index to Psychic Science* compiled by S R Morgan (Swathmore, 1950). Also, the Damon Collection of Occult and Visionary Literature--550 vols devoted to the development of western mysticism with particular emphasis on American and British thought, incl texts on alchemy, black magic, esoteric church history, dream interpretations, mysticism, witchcraft, the Kabbalah, and visionary testaments and manifestations of all types printed during the 16th to 20th centuries; and the Samuel Wyllys Papers--125 mss, transcripts, and photocopies of legal and government papers relating to Indianaffairs, colonial wars, civil and criminal cases, and the witchcraft trials of 1692-1693. Partially cataloged.

THEOPHRASTUS

PA —PENNSYLVANIA STATE UNIVERSITY, Fred Lewis Pattee Library, Special Collections Dept, University Park, 16802. Charles Mann, Chief, Special Collections
Holdings: Vols 89 Uncat
Budget: ($37,000)
Notes: Gift of Robert E Dengler, it includes early editions of the work of the Greek botanist, beginning with the *editio princeps* of 1483.

THEORETICAL CHEMISTRY see Chemistry, Physical and Theoretical

THEORY OF STRUCTURES see Structures, Theory of

THEOSOPHY

AZ —WORLD UNIVERSITY, Library, 711 E Blacklidge Dr, Tucson, 85719. Howard John Zitko, Cur
Holdings: Vols (15,000) Cat Mss Maps Audiotapes
Notes: Collection concerns what are generally called the "frontier sciences." No interlibrary loan.

CA —UNIVERSITY OF CALIFORNIA, SAN DIEGO, Central University Library, Mandeville Dept of Special Collections, La Jolla, 92093. Lynda Corey Claassen, Head
Holdings: Vols 3500 Uncat Mss Pix
Notes: Consists of two large collections: the Harris and Geiger Collections. History and imprints of Theosophical Society from 1875 to date. Bibliography of collections: Brown, Lauren R, *The Point Loma Theosophical Society: A List of Publications, 1898-1942* (La Jolla, 1977).

CA —THEOSOPHICAL BOOK ASSOCIATION FOR THE BLIND, Baker Memorial Library, Route 2 Krotona 54, Ojai, 93023. Dennis Gotsehalk, Dir
Holdings: Vols 1200
Notes: Free lending library for the blind; Braille books, tapes, cassettes concerning philosophy, religion and theosophical.

CA —SAN DIEGO PUBLIC LIBRARY, Literature & Language Sect, 820 E St, San Diego, 92101. Alyce Archuleta, Senior Librn
Holdings: Vols (140) Cat
Notes: Old and current reference and circulating works on the subject. Incl complete works by Blavatsky, much by Rudolf Steiner, and C Zain. Strong in astrology, witchcraft, parapsychology.

MA —HARVARD UNIVERSITY LIBRARY, Cambridge, 02138.
Holdings: Cat

NY —UNITED LODGE OF THEOSOPHISTS LIBRARY, 347 E 72 St, New York, 10021.
Holdings: Vols 853 Cat
Notes: Original theosophical literature of the 19th century, incl books and magazines; also current periodical literature.

RI —BROWN UNIVERSITY, John Hay Library, 20 Prospect St, Providence, 02912. Mark N Brown, Cur Mss
Holdings: Mss
Notes: Two collections relating to magic (the occult); The Mary Ann Smith Atwood Collection--English theosophist and writer (700 items); and the S Foster Damon, 1893-1971, Collection--poet, dramatist and Professor of English at Brown University (more than 15,000 items), unprocessed.

VA —ASSOCIATION FOR RESEARCH & ENLIGHTENMENT, Library, 67 & Atlantic Avenue, PO Box 595, Virginia Beach, 23451. Stephen Jordan, Library Mgr
Holdings: Vols (1800) Cat
Notes: A R E Library Booklist incl 6000 items in 24 subject categories. This special collection is especially strong in the following subjects: astrology, spiritualism, reincarnation, healing arts, Theosophy, Atlantis, parapsychology and transpersonal psychology.

THERAPEUTICS

MD —MEDICAL & CHIRURGICAL FACULTY OF THE STATE OF MARYLAND, Library, 1211 Cathedral St, Baltimore, 21201. Joseph E Jensen, Librn
Holdings: Vols (10,000) // Cat Mss Maps Pix
See also entry under Medicine - History and Historic

MI —WARNER-LAMBERT/PARKE-DAVIS, Research Library, 2800 Plymouth Rd, Ann Arbor, 48106. Katherine C Owen, Mgr, Library Services
Holdings: Vols (27,977) Cat

†NY —MEDICAL RESEARCH LIBRARY OF BROOKLYN, Academy of Medicine of Brooklyn & The State University of New York Downstate Medical Center, 450 Clarkson St, Brooklyn, 11203. Kenneth E Moody, Dir
Notes: Extensive collection of 18th-19th century material.
See also entry under Medicine.

THERAPEUTICS, SUGGESTIVE

MO —UNITY LIBRARY, Unity School of Christianity, Unity Village, 64065. Alfreda Williams, Library Dir
Holdings: Vols (50,000) Cat Mss Maps Pix Slides Microforms
Notes: Incl Archives and Historical collections of the Unity School of Christianity, as well as the archives of the International New Thought Alliance.

THERAPY, MUSIC see Music Therapy

THERMAL ENERGY

TX —MCDERMOTT HUDSON ENGINEERING, Library, 5900 Hillcroft, Houston, 77036. Chris Ramirez, Librn
Holdings: Vols (750) Uncat Microforms
Notes: Emphasis is on all forms of alternative energy sources and energy conversion.

THERMAL ENERGY, OCEAN see Ocean Thermal Energy

THERMAL EQUILIBRIUM see Thermodynamics

THERMAL WATERS see Geothermal Resources; Springs (Thermal)

THERMODYNAMICS

CA —UNIVERSITY OF CALIFORNIA, BERKELEY, Bancroft Library, Manuscripts Division, Berkeley, 94720. James D Hart, Dir
Notes: Extensive collections of papers and archives relative to the history of modern chemistry.

†CA —CALIFORNIA INSTITUTE OF TECHNOLOGY, Robert A Millikan Memorial Library, Archives, 1201 E California Blvd, Pasadena, 91125.
Notes: Geophysicist Charles Richter's

lecture notes and oral history interview. Incl notes from courses at Caltech taught by physicist Paul Epstein (1883-1966), such as higher dynamics, 1925; thermodynamics, 1925/26; quantum theory, 1926-28, 1940.

CO —COLORADO STATE UNIVERSITY, Libraries, Fort Collins, 80523. Marjorie Rhoades, Engineering Sciences Librn
Holdings: Vols 8000 Cat
Budget: ($6000)

IL —ARGONNE NATIONAL LABORATORY, Reactor Science/ Engineering Branch Library, 9700 S Cass Ave, Argonne, 60439. Marion Benson, Librn
Notes: Incl 10,000 vols monographs, 200 current journals, a comprehensive collection of AEC, ERDA, DOE, and NRC scientific and technical reports. Materials may be used by the public in the library by prior arrangement. Photocopies may be supplied for interlibrary loan, for which a processing and handling charge is made.

KY —UNIVERSITY OF KENTUCKY, Robert E Shaver Library of Engineering, 355 Anderson Hall, Lexington, 40506. Russell H Powell, Engineering Librn
Holdings: Vols (48,000) Cat Microforms

NY —UNIVERSITY OF ROCHESTER, Physics-Optics-Astronomy Library, Bausch & Lomb Bldg, River Campus, Rochester, 14627. Loretta Caren, Librn
Holdings: Vols (20,000) Cat
Notes: Strong research level collection in the field and related areas.

PA —FRANKLIN INSTITUTE LIBRARY, 20 & The Parkway, Philadelphia, 19103. Miriam Padusis, Dir; Charles Wilt, Readers Servs Librn
Holdings: Vols (300,000) Cat Maps Pix Microforms

THERMOFLUIDS

†MA —NORTHEASTERN UNIVERSITY LIBRARIES, Boston, 02115.

THERMONUCLEAR POWER

NM —UNIVERSITY OF CALIFORNIA, Los Alamos National Laboratory, Libraries, PO Box 1663, MSP 362, Los Alamos, 87545. J Arthur Freed, Head Librn
Holdings: Vols (800,000) Cat Films Microforms
Budget: ($700,000)
Notes: Incl 500,000 classified and unclassified reports. There are 25 branch libraries and a central collection. The Medical Library contains about 40,000 vols in the areas of biomedical research.

THERMONUCLEAR WEAPONS

DC —US ARMS CONTROL & DISARMAMENT AGENCY, Library, George Washington Univ Special Collections, Washington, 21 St & Virginia Ave, NW, Rm 5851, Washington, 20451. Diane Ferguson, Librn
Holdings: Vols 4500 // Cat
Notes: Arms control, disarmament and related topics.

NM —UNIVERSITY OF CALIFORNIA, Los Alamos National Laboratory, Libraries, PO Box 1663, MSP 362, Los Alamos, 87545. J Arthur Freed, Head Librn
Holdings: Vols (800,000) Cat Films Microforms
Budget: ($700,000)
Notes: Incl 500,000 classified and unclassified reports. There are 25 branch libraries and a central collection. The Medical Library contains about 40,000 vols in the areas of biomedical research.

THESAURI, COMPUTER

ON —UNIVERSITY OF TORONTO, Faculty of Library and Information Science Library, Subject Analysis Systems, Room 404, 140 St George St, Toronto, M5S 1A1, Can. Diane Henderson, Librn
Notes: The Subject Analysis Systems Collection is the major North American collection of classification schemes, thesauri, and subject heading lists, and it is the major world collection in the English language.

THIAMINE see Vitamin B1

THIOKOL see Rubber, Artificial

THIRD PARTY FORCES (U.S. —POLITICS AND GOVERNMENT)

WI —UNIVERSITY OF WISCONSIN,
MILWAUKEE, Library, Box 604,
Milwaukee, 53201. William C Roselle, Dir
Holdings: Vols 2500 Cat Mss Pix
Notes: Fromkin Memorial Collection,
emphasizing third party forces in American
politics. Restricted use: noncirculating.
Special subject catalog of pamphlet material.

THIRD WORLD

CA —WOMEN'S HISTORY RESEARCH
CENTER, Microfilm Library, 2325 Oak St,
Berkeley, 94708. Laura X, Librn
Holdings: Mss Pix Microforms
Notes: Incl material (150 subject files) on
physical and mental health and illnesses; sex
roles; biology; women and the life cycle;
birth/population control; sex and sexuality;
black and Third World women. Collection at
University of Wyoming. Archive of
Contemporary History, PO Box 3334,
Laramie, Wyoming 82701, c/o David
Crosson. Research inquiries accepted.
Microfilm of collection (14 reels and reel
guides) available at many universities and
through Women's History Research Center,
2325 Oak St, Berkeley, CA 94708. No
collections housed at this address.
MI —UNIVERSITY OF MICHIGAN, Center
for Research on Economic Development,
Library, 240 Lorch Hall, Ann Arbor, 48109.
Carol Wilson, Information/Resources
Coordinator
Holdings: Vols (21,000) Cat 16mm Films
Microforms
Budget: ($7000)
Notes: Publications that list library and its
collection: *Directory of Third World Studies
in the US* (African Studies Assn, 1981),
National Reference Center Directory 1983
(NRC), *World Guide to Libraries* 1983 (Saur
Verlag), *Research Centers Directory 1983*
(Gale Research), and *A Directory of
Information Resources in US* (Library of
Congress, 1978). Collection's focus is Third
World economic development. Other areas
of interest are economic planning,
developing countries, Africa (specifically
francophone Africa), the Sahel, African
agricultural economics, commodities
production, financial statistics, development
plans from less developed countries (LDC),
and international development. Each part of
the library's collection (working papers/
reports, periodicals and government
documents) has its own catalog and
cataloging system.
NY —YWCA NATIONAL BOARD, Library,
726-730 Broadway, New York, 10012.
Elizabeth Norris, Librn
Holdings: Vols (3000) Cat Mss
Budget: ($2400)
Notes: Women and their contemporary
interests.
PA —TEMPLE UNIVERSITY LIBRARIES,
Special Collections Dept, Contemporary
Culture Collection, Philadelphia, 19122.
Patricia J Case, Cur
Notes: The Contemporary Culture
Collection. See full entry under US-Social
Life and Customs.
WI —UNIVERSITY OF WISCONSIN,
MADISON, Land Tenure Center Library,
434 Steenbock Memorial Library, 550
Babcock Dr, Madison, 53706. Teresa J
Anderson, Librn
Holdings: Vols (60,000) Cat Mss Maps
Microforms
Budget: ($65,000)
Notes: Socio-economic aspects of
agricultural development in the Third World.
All materials in the collection are cataloged
and classified. The library has its own
catalog.

THIRTY YEARS' WAR, 1618-1648

MA —HARVARD UNIVERSITY LIBRARY,
Widener Library, Cambridge, 02138.
Holdings: Cat
Notes: See *Harvard Library Bulletin*, XIV

(1960), 191-200 for account of 2600-vol.
Rodolphe Reuss collection.

THISTLE, RALPH

BC —UNIVERSITY OF VICTORIA,
McPherson Library, Victoria, V8W 3H5,
Can.
Notes: Army officer, Canadian Scottish 16th
Battalion. Incl 78 pages, December 7, 1941-
June 30, 1942; diary by an Area Intelligence
Officer of Prince Rupert Defences; also
copies. Finding aids: article based on the
diary by R H Roy, *BC Studies*, no 31,
autumn 1976.

THOM PARTNERSHIP

AB —UNIVERSITY OF CALGARY,
Libraries, Special Collections Div, 2500
University Dr, Calgary, T2N 1N4, Can.
Holdings: Cat Mss Pix
Notes: Collection of 11,500 architectural
drawings, mounted photographs, artists's
renderings, specifications, design notes,
correspondence, office and project files to
some 90 projects by well known architect
Ron Thom. Major contracts: the Trent
University Campuses; Massey College; Shaw
Festival Theatre, etc. Project list and
inventory are on hand. 39 meters of
documents.

THOMAS, ALBERT

TX —RICE UNIVERSITY, Fondren Library,
6100 S Main St, PO Box 1892, Houston,
77251. Dr Samuel M Carrington, Jr,
University Librn
Holdings: Mss Pix
Notes: Papers of the prominent Texas
Congressman.

THOMAS, BOB

CA —UNIVERSITY OF CALIFORNIA, LOS
ANGELES, Theater Arts Library, Los
Angeles, 90024. Edward Shreeves,
Chairman, Bibliographers Group; Audree
Malkin, Head, Theater Arts Library
Holdings: Mss Pix Phonorecords
Notes: Bob Thomas (author and Hollywood
correspondent for the Associated Press)
Collection. Incl mss for his books on Marlon
Brando, Harry Cohn, Irving Thalberg, Walt
Disney, Abbott and Costello, and David O
Selznick; also incl notes, clippings, research
and interviews, eg, John Ford, Cary Grant,
Bill Holden, Rock Hudson, Danny Kaye,
Gene Kelly, Glen Ford, Frank Capra, John
Roselli; all photos collected whether or not
used in the books. Sound track albums.

THOMAS, DYLAN, 1914-1953

CA —CALIFORNIA STATE UNIVERSITY,
FULLERTON, Library, Box 4150,
Fullerton, 92634. Linda Herman, Special
Collections Librn
Holdings: Vols 240
Notes: Writings by and about.
CA —UNIVERSITY OF CALIFORNIA, LOS
ANGELES, Research Library, Dept of
Special Collections, 405 Hilgard Ave, Los
Angeles, 90024. Edward Shreeves,
Chairman, Bibliographers Group; David S
Zeidberg, Head
Holdings: Vols 175 Mss
Notes: 175 first and other editions of his
books; 2 mss; one 65-minute taped reading
(1950).
MA —AMHERST COLLEGE, Library,
Amherst, 01002. John Lancaster, Special
Collections Librn
Holdings: Vols 350 Uncat Mss
Notes: Contains also 9 file feet of periodical
appearances.
MA —HARVARD UNIVERSITY LIBRARY,
Houghton Library, Cambridge, 02138.
Rodney G Dennis, Cur of Manuscripts
Holdings: Mss
NV —UNIVERSITY OF NEVADA, RENO,
University Library, Special Collections Dept,
Reno, 89557. Robert E Blesse, Head
Holdings: Vols 112 // Cat
Notes: Includes individual works by author

in all editions including translations; also
prefaces, introductions, published
correspondence, appearances in anthologies,
periodicals, etc. Bibliographical research
collection, part of Modern Authors
Collection.
NY —VASSAR COLLEGE, Library, Rare
Books & Manuscripts Collection, Box 20,
Poughkeepsie, 12601. Lisa Browar, Cur
Notes: An extensive collection of Elizabeth
Bishop's papers, incl notebooks, mss, drafts,
galleys, etc, as well as correspondence and
business files, with files of letters from
Cummings, Toklas, Dylan Thomas, and
Eudora Welty.
†NC —WAKE FOREST UNIVERSITY, Z
Smith Reynolds Library, Box 7777, Reynold
Sta, Winston-Salem, 27109. Richard J
Murdoch, Rare Book Librn
Holdings: Vols 62 Cat
OH —OHIO STATE UNIVERSITY, William
Oxley Thompson Memorial Library, 1858
Neil Ave Mall, Columbus, 43210. Robert A
Tibbetts, Cur of Special Collections
Holdings: Vols 45 Cat Mss
BC —UNIVERSITY OF VICTORIA,
McPherson Library, Victoria, V8W 3H5,
Can.
Notes: Incl letters from Dylan Thomas to
Clifford Dayment, John Lehmann and G V
Roberts; letters from Daniel Jones to
Roberts; clipping of Thomas' obituary from
The Tenby Observer.

THOMAS, EDWARD

MA —AMHERST COLLEGE, Library,
Amherst, 01002. John Lancaster, Special
Collections Librn
Holdings: Vols (500)
Notes: Strong collection.
NY —HOFSTRA UNIVERSITY, Library,
1000 Fulton Ave, Hempstead, 11550.
Charles R Andrews, Dean of Library
Services

THOMAS, ISAIAH—IMPRINTS

MA —AMERICAN ANTIQUARIAN
SOCIETY LIBRARY, 185 Salisbury St,
Worcester, 01609. Marcus A McCorison,
Dir & Librn
Holdings: Cat Mss
Notes: US printing is remarkably represented
by some 60,000 volumes, about 60 percent
of the number known to have been printed
before 1821. Incl the Isaiah Thomas Papers,
his imprinted books, and his printing press.
The Library is also especially strong in early
English type-specimen books, and American
examples to 1860.
PA —ALLEGHENY COLLEGE, Lawrence
Lee Pelletier Library, Meadville, 16335.
Margaret L Moser, Librn
Holdings: Vols 300 Cat
Notes: Not all books in the collection are
imprints, but all were given to the college
before 1823. Listed in Timothy Alden,
*Catalogus Bibliothecae Collegii
Alleghaniensis*, 1823. Downs 180.
SC —WOFFORD COLLEGE, Sandor Teszler
Library, N Church St, Spartanburg, 29301.
Frank J Anderson, Librn
Holdings: Vols 1247 Uncat
Notes: Haynes-Brown Hymnal Collection
consists of all denominations of rare items
and colonial imprints, incl Christopher Saur
and Isaiah Thomas imprints. Collection is
being augmented by Pierce Gault of
Washington, DC.

THOMAS, JAMES A.

NC —DUKE UNIVERSITY, William R
Perkins Library, Manuscript Dept, Durham,
27706. Ellen Gartrell, Cur of Mss
Holdings: Cat Mss
Notes: Tobacco culture, marketing, trade,
especially US South, 19th-20th century, incl
papers of Duke Family, Richard H Wright,
British-American Tobacco Co, James A
Thomas, Edward J Parrish, United Cigarette
Machine Co; also tobacco advertising (trade
cards, etc).

THOMAS, JEAN

KY —UNIVERSITY OF LOUISVILLE,
Ekstrom Library, Photographic Archives,

THOMAS, JEAN (cont.)

Louisville, 40292. J C Anderson, Cur; David G Horvath, Asst Cur
Notes: "The Traipsin' Woman" photographs of Kentucky mountain folkways.
KY —UNIVERSITY OF LOUISVILLE, School of Music, Dwight Anderson Memorial Music Library, 2301 S Third St, Louisville, 40292. Marion Korda, Librn
Notes: "Traipsin Woman" Collection. Archival; research material. 100 items includes 29 unique items; 25 files of clippings, correspondence; 46 audiovisual items.

THOMAS, JOHN WILLIAM ELMER

OK —UNIVERSITY OF OKLAHOMA, Bizzell Memorial Library, Western History Collections, 401 W Brooks, Norman, 73069. John Ezell, Cur
Holdings: Vols Mss Documents Newspapers Maps Pix
Notes: US Representative; US Senator. His papers.

THOMAS, LOWELL

CA —CLAREMONT COLLEGES, Honnold Library, Ninth & Dartmouth, Claremont, 91711. Tania Rizzo, Special Collections Dept Head
Holdings: Vols 250// Uncat Mss
Notes: Papers of Elbert A Wickes, 1884-1975, theatrical and lecture tour manager. Among his clients were Winston Churchill, William Butler Yeats, Houdini, Lowell Thomas, Vilhjalmur Stefansson, and Roy Chapman Andrews.

THOMAS, M. CAREY

PA —BRYN MAWR COLLEGE, Canaday Library, Bryn Mawr, 19010. James Tanis, Dir
Notes: College Archives, incl M Carey Thomas papers; Research Publications' microfilm collection on women's history.

THOMAS, NORMAN

IN —INDIANA STATE UNIVERSITY, Cunningham Memorial Library, Dept of Rare Books & Special Collections, Terre Haute, 47809. Lawrence J McCrank, Head
Notes: The Debs Collection consists of aprox 7000 pieces of correspondence between Theodore Debs (brother of E V) and other persons, such as Sinclair Lewis, Upton Sinclair, Ethel Barrymore, Emma Goldman, Robert G Ingersoll, Carl Sandburg, Norman Thomas, Sacco and Vanzetti and many others. Many of the letters are from E V Debs to his brother; a good portion of these are from the federal penitentiary at Atlanta. Entire correspondence file has been microfilmed. 750 pamphlets cover all aspects of the labor movement, socialism and radical thought from the 19th century to appprox 1950. A collection ca 200 related books is also housed in the collection. See: J Robert Constantine and Gail Malmgreen, eds, *The Papers of Eugene V Debs, 1834-1945. A Guide to the Microfilm Edition.* NY: Microfilming Corp of America, 1983 (University Microfilms is the new distributer).
NY —NEW YORK PUBLIC LIBRARY, Rare Books and Manuscripts Div, Fifth Ave & 42 St, New York, 10018. William L Joyce, Asst Dir; Susan E Davis, Cur of Mss
Holdings: Mss
Budget: ($7161)
Notes: Incl personal and literary mss, papers, etc.

THOMAS, PIRI

NY —NEW YORK PUBLIC LIBRARY, Schomburg Center for Research in Black Culture, 515 Lenox Ave, New York, 10037. Catherine J Lenix Hooker, Interim Administrator
Notes: Papers, mss, correspondence, etc of the Puerto Rican writer and rehabilitated criminal.

THOMAS, ROSEMARY

NY —COLUMBIA UNIVERSITY LIBRARIES, Rare Book & Manuscript Library, 801 Butler Library, 535 W 114 St, New York, 10027. Kenneth A Lohf, Librn
Notes: Poems and letters. Restricted use.

THOMAS, THEODORE

IL —NEWBERRY LIBRARY, 60 W Walton St, Chicago, 60610. Diana Haskell, Cur of Modern Mss
Holdings: Cat Mss Pix
Notes: Ms and printed scores; letters and photographs; scrapbooks. Noncirculating.

THOMAS A KEMPIS

DC —GEORGETOWN UNIVERSITY, Library, Special Collections Div, 37 & O Sts NW, Washington, 20057. George M Barringer, Special Collections Librn; Nicholas B Sheetz, Mss Librn
Holdings: Cat
MD —JOHNS HOPKINS UNIVERSITY, Milton S Eisenhower Library, George Peabody Collection, 17 E Mt Vernon Place, Baltimore, 21201. Lyn Hart, Peabody Librn
Notes: Noncirculating.
MA —HARVARD UNIVERSITY LIBRARY, Houghton Library, Cambridge, 02138. F Thomas Noonan, Cur, Reading Room; Lawrence Dowler, Associate Librn
Holdings: Cat
Notes: Walter A Copinger's *Hand List* of 1500 editions of the *Imitatio Christi* privately printed in 1908.

THOMAS AQUINAS, ST.

DC —DOMINICAN HOUSE OF STUDIES, Dominican College Library, 487 Michigan Ave NE, Washington, 20017. J Raymond Vandegrift, OP, Librn
Holdings: Vols 1400 Cat
Notes: The collection principally contains both early and contemporary editions of the works of Thomas Aquinas in the original language and in translation. Different editions of the *opera omnia* (including the Leonine edition), the *Index Thomisticus,* bibliographies, rare books and incunabula are included.
See also entry under Thomist Philosophy
†RI —UNIVERSITY OF RHODE ISLAND, Library, Kingston, 02881.
Notes: Strong collection

THOMASON, JOHN W., JR., 1893-1944

DC —GEORGETOWN UNIVERSITY, Library, Special Collections Div, 37 & O Sts NW, Washington, 20057. George M Barringer, Special Collections Librn; Nicholas B Sheetz, Mss Librn
Holdings: Mss
Notes: A collection of letters, documents, original artwork, and books by and about John W Thomason, Jr (1893-1944), a Colonel in the Marines as well as an author and illustrator.

THOMIST PHILOSOPHY

DC —DOMINICAN HOUSE OF STUDIES, Dominican College Library, 487 Michigan Ave NE, Washington, 20017. J Raymond Vandegrift, OP, Librn
Holdings: Vols (3700) Cat Microforms
Budget: $650
Notes: Incl works about Thomas Aquinas--commentaries, *festschriften,* biographies--and works both by and about his followers, the Thomists-- histories, biographies, periodicals, monograph series, manuals, incunabula, rare books, and the papers presented at Thomistic congresses.
See also entry under Thomas Aquinas, St.
†RI —UNIVERSITY OF RHODE ISLAND, Library, Kingston, 02881.
Notes: Strong collection.

THOMPSON, CHARLES WILLIS, 1871-1946

NJ —PRINCETON UNIVERSITY, Library, Manuscript Collection, Nassau St, Princeton, 08540. Jean F Preston, Cur
Holdings: // Mss
Notes: Incl 44 scrapbook volumes; 5 boxes of papers.

THOMPSON, CLARK

DC —GEORGETOWN UNIVERSITY, Library, Special Collections Div, 37 & O Sts NW, Washington, 20057. George M Barringer, Special Collections Librn; Nicholas B Sheetz, Mss Librn
Holdings: Cat Mss Pix
Notes: Panama Canal, and papers of Tomas Herran, Earl Harding, Thomas E Martin, William McCan, Clark Thompson, Leonor K Sullivan, and Capt Miles Duval.

THOMPSON, ERNEST SETON see Seton, Ernest Thompson

THOMPSON, FRANCIS

MA —BOSTON COLLEGE LIBRARIES, Thomas P O'Neill Library, Chestnut Hill, 02167. Frank J Seegraber, Special Collections Librn
Holdings: Vols 1300 Mss Pix Phonorecords Audiotapes Microforms
Notes: This, the most commmplete collection of Thompsoniana in existence, incl incl notebooks, mss, letters, and rare editions, and collateral material relating to poet, his times and his work. The notebooks are the chief source of clues to the identification of 300 of Thompson's unsigned contributions to periodicals. *An Account of the Books and Manuscripts of Francis Thompson,* ed by Rev Terence L Connolly (Boston College, 1937). Works of Wilfrid and Alice Meynell and their children, Viola, Sir Francis, and Everard, are incl in this collection. The items give a well-rounded view of this remarkable family as poets, fiction writers, essayists, biographers, prefacers, and editors. This collection incl mss, poems, correspondence, articles, and book reviews by Coventry Patmore, an English poet, essayist, and critic, and a good friend of Francis Thompson. Among thecorrespondents are Robert Browning, Alfred Tennyson, Matthew Arnold, Ralph Waldo Emerson, Nathaniel Hawthorne, Thomas Carlyle, and William Makepeace Thackeray. For reference use only, by arrangement with librarian.
OH —OHIO UNIVERSITY, Vernon R Alden Library, Department of Archives and Special Collections, Athens, 45701. Gary A Hunt, Head
Holdings: Vols (10,191) Uncat Mss
Notes: The Edmund Blunden Collection of Romantic and Modern Literature, being the private library assembled by Blunden during 6 decades of active collecting. The bulk of the collection (6,264 titles) consists of English imprints from the period 1750-1850, concentrating on literature but also incl contemporary works on art, natural history, philosophy and other subjects important for understanding the background of English Romanticism. Among the authors most heavily represented by first and other early editions are: Allington, Barnes, Bloomfield, Byron, Clare, Coleridge, Cowper, Dyer, Edgeworth, Goldsmith, Hazlitt, Hunt, Lamb, Landor, Scott, Thompson and Wordsworth. Books written by Blunden himself, together with his Georgian contemporaries (particularly W H Davies, Walter De la Mare, and Sigfried Sassoon) form a second major area of strength. Many ofthe modern books are inscribed to Blunden, and nearly all the volumes in the collection bear his annotations.

THOMPSON, FRANK, JR., 1918-

NJ —PRINCETON UNIVERSITY, Library, Manuscript Collection, Nassau St, Princeton, 08540. Jean F Preston, Cur
Holdings: Mss
Notes: 374 cartons of papers. Materials date from 1955.

THOMPSON, JACOB

MS —UNIVERSITY OF SOUTHERN MISSISSIPPI, William David McCain

THOMPSON, JACOB (cont.)

Graduate Library, Box 5148, Southern Sta, Hattiesburg, 39406.
Holdings: Cat Mss Pix
Notes: Correspondence and records (1847-1892) relating to Alexander Melvorne Jackson's participation in the Mexican War, his service as Secretary of the State of the New Mexico Territory (1857-1861), and his participation in the Civil War on the side of the Confederacy. Among his correspondents were Albert Gallatin Brown, Reuben Davis, Miguel A Otero, Jacob Thompson, and John Ireland. Incl are photographs of Austin, Texas, ca 1890. 1.1 cubic feet holdings.

THOMPSON, JOHN REUBEN

VA —UNIVERSITY OF VIRGINIA, Alderman Library, Manuscripts Dept, Charlottesville, 22901. Edmund Berkeley Jr, Cur
Holdings: Cat Mss Pix
Notes: Extensive collection of mss and printed materials.

THOMPSON, PETER (FORGER)

ON —UNIVERSITY OF TORONTO, Thomas Fisher Rare Book Library, 120 Saint George St, Toronto, M5S 1A5, Can. Richard G Landon, Head
Holdings: Vols 100 Maps Pix
Notes: Fisher Collection of etchings by Wenceslaus Hollar. Collection named for donor Sidney T Fisher. Collection includes copies of most books in which Hollar's plates were published. About 3500 loose prints include various states of many etchings; some proofs; group of 19th century forgeries by Peter Thompson; original chalk and wash sketch for Hollar's etching of John the Baptist. See: Pennington, Richard, *A Descriptive Catalogue of the Etched Work of Wenceslaus Hollar, 1607-1677*. Cambridge: 1982. Based in part on Fisher holdings.

THOMPSON, RANDALL

VA —UNIVERSITY OF VIRGINIA, Alderman Library, Music Collection, Charlottesville, 22901. Evan Bonds, Music Librn
Holdings: Vols (38,000) Cat Mss Microforms
Budget: ($22,000)
Notes: Sizeable amount of rare book material: extensive ms collections, principally of traditional music; extensive collection of miscellaneous imprints of performing editions; valuable collection of 18th-century imprints incl rare tutors, etc in the Alexander MacKay-Smith Collection; the Monticello Music Collection; printed and ms collection of the music of John Powell; extensive collections, ms and typescript, and discs of traditional music; some Randall Thompson mss; 250 tapes; 9000 phonorecords.

THOMPSON, RICHARD

IN —LOUIS A WARREN LINCOLN LIBRARY AND MUSEUM, 1300 S Clinton St, Fort Wayne, 46801. Mark E Neely Jr, Dir
Holdings: Vols (17,000) Cat Mss Maps Pix
Notes: Acquire all books on Abraham Lincoln, most on his contemporaries, as many as possible on his times, and historical journals. Constantly acquiring unpublished mss of Lincoln, Lincoln's associates, correspondents, and collateral figures. Have some Kentucky Court Records, Richard Thompson Papers. Publish a monthly bulletin of historical research on Lincoln's life and times called *Lincoln Lore*, which includes an annually updated bibliography of Lincolniana.
OH —RUTHERFORD B HAYES LIBRARY, 1337 Hayes Ave, Fremont, 43420. Watt P Marchman, Dir
Holdings: Cat Mss Pix
Notes: Papers of the Secretary of the Navy

under President R B Hayes; much on American history; religion; Chiriqui Investment Company (5 linear feet). Index in collection; listed in *Guide to Manuscripts of the Ohio Historical Society*, 474.

THOMPSON, STITH

IN —INDIANA UNIVERSITY, Lilly Library, Seventh St, Bloomington, 47405. William R Cagle, Librn
Holdings: // Cat Mss
Notes: Papers, 1911-1964, of folklorist and Indiana University professor, Stith Thompson, 1885-1976.

THOMPSON, WILLIAM TAPPAN, 1812-1882

GA —GEORGIA COLLEGE, Ina Dillard Russell Library, Special Collections Dept, Milledgeville, 31061. Janice C Fennell, Dir of Libraries; Nancy Davis, Special Collections Assoc
Holdings: Uncat Mss
Notes: One scrapbook, one photo album, 9 copies of books by "Major Jones," one pocket diary, original manuscript of *Major Jones' Courtship*, 2 letters, 2 journal articles.

THOMPSON BERWICK PRATT AND PARTNERS

AB —UNIVERSITY OF CALGARY, Libraries, Special Collections Div, 2500 University Dr, Calgary, T2N 1N4, Can.
Holdings: Mss Cat Pix
Notes: Collection consists mainly of 9142 architectural drawings to bank and school buildings of the firm of Thompson Berwick Pratt & Partners in British Columbia. Some office files for the school projects are included, as well as oral history taped interviews. Dates of projects range from 1908 to 1968 (at present) and incl designs for alterations and additions to the Chateau Frontenac, Quebec City (1908); and the MacAuley Nicholls Office Building in Vancouver (1927). 22 meters of documents. Inventories are at hand.

THOMSON, HUGH

CT —YALE UNIVERSITY, Box 1603A, Yale Station, New Haven, 06520.
Holdings: Cat Mss
ME —PORTLAND PUBLIC LIBRARY, 5 Monument Sq, Portland, 04101. Edward V Chenevert, Library Dir
Holdings: Vols 71 // Cat Pix
MA —MOUNT HOLYOKE COLLEGE, Williston Memorial Library, South Hadley, 01075. Anne C Edmonds, Librn
Holdings: (100) Cat
Notes: Books by and about him, incl first editions and original drawings.

THOMSON, JAMES

MA —HARVARD UNIVERSITY LIBRARY, Houghton Library, Cambridge, 02138. Rodney G Dennis, Cur of Manuscripts
Holdings: Mss
NY —COLUMBIA UNIVERSITY LIBRARIES, Rare Book & Manuscript Library, 801 Butler Library, 535 W 114 St, New York, 10027. Kenneth A Lohf, Librn
Notes: Editions of *The Seasons*.
PA —SWARTHMORE COLLEGE, Library, Swarthmore, 19081. Michael J Durkan, Librn
Holdings: Vols 185 // Cat Mss
Notes: This was the collection of John Edwin Wells. Publications before 1750 and each later first printing. Separate (unpublished) catalog. Described briefly by Charles B Shaw in "Special Collections in the College Library," *College and Research Libraries*, November 1957, vol 18, no 6, pp 479-84, 517.

THOMSON, JAMES C., JR.

†MA —JOHN F KENNEDY LIBRARY, Columbia Point, Boston, 02125. Dan H Fenn

Jr, Dir
Holdings: // Cat Mss
Notes: His papers as Assistant to the Assistant Secretary of State for Far Eastern Affairs, 1960-1966. 15 linear ft of mss. Holdings are described in "Historical Materials in the John F Kennedy Library." Copies may be obtained by writing the Research Archivist.

THOMSON, MARGARET COOK, 1889-1975

†MA —RADCLIFFE COLLEGE, Arthur & Elizabeth Schlesinger Library on History of Women in America, 3 James St, Cambridge, 02138.
Notes: Papers, etc.

THOMSON, POLLY

NY —AMERICAN FOUNDATION FOR THE BLIND, M C Migel Memorial Library and Information Center, 15 W 16 St, New York, 10011. Diane Wolfe, Head Librn & Info Ctr Coordr; Marguerite Levine, Supvr Archives
Holdings: Mss Pix Slides Audiotapes 16mm Film
Notes: Helen Keller's papers in Helen Keller Archives. A collection relating to Helen Adams Keller. Incl are correspondence with friends and admirers, speeches, literary mss, legal and genealogical material, photographs, sound recordings, and one film: about Helen Keller, her teacher Anne Sullivan Macy, her companion Polly Thomson, and John Albert Macy, husband of Anne Sullivan Macy. Among the subjects represented are work on behalf of the blind, deaf-blind, and deaf; children and women in factories; planned parenthood; labor movements; peace; and suffrage.

THOMSON, VIRGIL

CT —YALE UNIVERSITY, Box 1603A, Yale Station, New Haven, 06520.
Holdings: Cat Mss
CT —YALE UNIVERSITY, Music Library, 98 Wall St, New Haven, 06520. Harold E Samuel, Librn
Notes: Personal papers and musical mss. *See also* entry under Music, American.
MO —UNIVERSITY OF MISSOURI-KANSAS CITY, General Library, Conservatory of Music Library, 5100 Rockhill Road, Kansas City, 64110. Kenneth J LaBudde, Dir; Richard Belanger, Librn
Holdings: Vols 46,337 Cat
Notes: 276 current serial subscriptions, 7462 microforms, 16,702 sound recordings, some 70,000 other items with specialists in American Music, Virgil Thomson and hymnology.

THOMSONIANISM see Medicine, Botanic

THOREAU, HENRY DAVID

CA —UNIVERSITY OF CALIFORNIA, SANTA BARBARA, Library, Dept of Special Collections, Santa Barbara, 93106. Christian F Brun, Head
Holdings: Mss
Notes: Many first editions. Collection of books by Thoreau and others in Transcendental Movement.
FL —UNIVERSITY OF MIAMI, Otto G Richter Library, PO Box 248214, Coral Gables, 33124. Frank Rodgers, Dir of Libraries
Notes: 3500 items. Nineteenth century well represented by Longfellow and Thoreau collections organized by Thomas DeValcourt at Longfellow House. Additional Thoreau items were purchased later. Innovative and experimental writing of 1960s and 1970s, incl press books from Black Sparrow, Unicorn, Kayak and other small presses, as well as privately published works and many small magazines. Format ranges from postcard and poster to fine limited editions of codex form.

THOREAU, HENRY DAVID (cont.)

MA —HARVARD UNIVERSITY LIBRARY, Houghton Library, Cambridge, 02138. Rodney G Dennis, Cur of Manuscripts
Holdings: Cat Mss
Notes: See lists of manuscripts in Thoreau Society *Bulletin*, 43 (spring 1953): pp 2-4, and 53 (fall 1955): pp 1-2.

MA —CONCORD FREE PUBLIC LIBRARY, 129 Main St, Concord, 01742. Rose Marie Mitten, Dir
Holdings: Cat Mss Maps Pix Slides
Notes: Extensive collection.

MA —CARY MEMORIAL LIBRARY, 1874 Massachusetts Ave, Lexington, 02173. Robert C Hilton, Dir
Holdings: Vols 250
Notes: Books and magazines about and by Thoreau (Piper Collection). Collection does not incl anything rare, but it incl many first editions in excellent condition.

MA —ESSEX INSTITUTE, James Duncan Phillips Library, 132-34 Essex St, Salem, 01970. Prudence K Backman, Manuscript Librn
Notes: The Frazer Clark Collection of over 8000 Hawthorne pieces, incl over 300 editions of *The Scarlet Letter*. The Institute is now said to have the world's most comprehensive collection of Hawthorne, with much correspondence from Melville, Thoreau, etc.

RI —BROWN UNIVERSITY, John Hay Library, 20 Prospect St, Providence, 02912. Mark N Brown, Cur Mss
Holdings: Vols 450 // Cat Mss Maps Pix
Notes: The collection consists of more than one thousand items, incl most printed editions of Thoreau's writings, except those intended primarily for use as textbooks, biographical and critical material, seventeen autograph letters, seventy pages of mss from his nature notes and journals, broadsides, photographs, books from Thoreau's library, and other association items. Also available is the file of correspondence between the collector and various booksellers and scholars generated during the forty years (1920-1960) that the collection was being formed. See "Thoreau Comes to Brown," by Barton L St Armand, in *Books At Brown*, Vol XXII, 1968.

VA —UNIVERSITY OF VIRGINIA, Alderman Library, Clifton Waller Barrett Collection, Charlottesville, 22901. Joan St C Crane, Cur of American Literature Collections
Holdings: Vols 150

WI —BELOIT COLLEGE LIBRARIES, Beloit, 53511. Dennis W Dickinson, Dir
Holdings: Vols 700 Cat
Notes: The Martin Luther King Jr Collection on Nonviolence. This small collection was given by H Vail Deale, Director, at the time of the assassination of Dr King in 1968. Comprises books by and about: M K Gandhi, H D Thoreau, M L King, world peace, pacifism, nonviolence, etc. Contains a 35-year bound file of *Fellowship*, the magazine of US pacifism. At present time there is only a local card index of the collection, though items are fully cataloged in the Public Card Catalog. A specially designed bookplate by local artist, O Vernon Shaffer, is used for books in this collection.

THORNDIKE, LYNN

†NY —COLUMBIA UNIVERSITY LIBRARIES, Butler Library, Rare Book and Manuscript Library, 535 W 114 St, New York, 10027.
Notes: 76 vols of diaries of Lynn Thorndike, 1902-63. A record of his daily reading, progress in research and writing, European travels, relations with scholars and librarians, and other personal matters.

THOROUGHFARES see Roads

THORPE, JIM

PA —CUMBERLAND COUNTY HISTORICAL SOCIETY, The Hamilton Library, 21 N Pitt St, PO Box 626, Carlisle, 17013. Cordelia M Neitz, Librn
Holdings: Vols 60 Mss Pix
Notes: Contains most of the magazines and journals published by the Carlisle Indian School, incl also yearbooks, commencement and other programs, illustrated brochures of the school, and several hundred photographs of classes, buildings, teaching facilities, school activities, athletes (Jim Thorpe being one) and athletic teams; one of the most complete collections of its kind in the US.

THOUGHT, FREE see Free Thought

THOUGHT TRANSFERENCE

MD —JOHNS HOPKINS UNIVERSITY, Milton S Eisenhower Library, George Peabody Collection, 17 E Mt Vernon Place, Baltimore, 21201. Lyn Hart, Peabody Librn
Notes: Noncirculating.

THOUSAND-AND-ONE NIGHTS see Arabian Nights

THREE MILE ISLAND

DC —NATIONAL ARCHIVES AND RECORDS SERVICE, Civil Archives Division, Washington, 20408.
Notes: Records of the President's Commission on the Accident at Three Mile Island (May-December 1979).

THRESHING MACHINES

CA —UNIVERSITY OF CALIFORNIA, DAVIS, Shields Library, Dept of Special Collections, Davis, 95616. Donald Kunitz, Head; C Danial Elliott, Asst Head
Notes: Farming equipment: Manufacturer's catalogs, manuals, parts lists, ephemera, and literature pertaining to historical as well as current data on such items as tractors, engines, combines, hay equipment, etc. Described in "The Higgins Library: A Source for the Study of Agricultural History," Don Kunitz, *Agricultural History*, vol 49, 1975, pp 89-91.

THROOP FAMILY

NJ —PRINCETON UNIVERSITY, Library, Manuscript Collection, Nassau St, Princeton, 08540. Jean F Preston, Cur
Holdings: // Mss Pix
Notes: The collection, which fills 11 ms boxes, also includes some material on the Martin family. An unpublished typescript guide (111p) is available in the Library.

NY —CORNELL UNIVERSITY LIBRARIES, Collection of Regional History, Dept of Manuscripts and Univ Archives, Ithaca, 14853.
Notes: One letter from F W Throop to his brother, A T Throop, describing the Auburn sophomore banquet of 1890.

THURBER, JAMES

NV —UNIVERSITY OF NEVADA, RENO, University Library, Special Collections Dept, Reno, 89557. Robert E Blesse, Head
Holdings: Vols 65 // Cat
Notes: Includes individual works by author in all editions including translations; also prefaces, introductions, published correspondence, appearances in anthologies, periodicals, etc. Bibliographical research collection, part of Modern Authors Collection.

OH —OHIO STATE UNIVERSITY, William Oxley Thompson Memorial Library, 1858 Neil Ave Mall, Columbus, 43210. Robert A Tibbetts, Cur of Special Collections
Holdings: Vols 425 Cat Mss Pix
Notes: Also his mss and papers, etc.

TX —UNIVERSITY OF HOUSTON, M D Anderson Memorial Library, University Park, Houston, 77004. David Farmer, Cur, Special Collections; Jean Jackson, Assistant Cur
Holdings: Vols 250 Cat Mss Pix
Notes: The emphasis of this collection is on textual studies. No published catalog.

THURMOND, SEN. STROM

SC —CLEMSON UNIVERSITY, Libraries, Clemson, 29631. Michael F Kohl, Head of Special Collections
Notes: Senator Strom Thurmond Collection. Papers of SC governor and US senator pertain to all aspects of his career. Approx 1700 cu ft.

THURSTONE, LOUIS L.

MO —WASHINGTON UNIVERSITY, Libraries, Special Collections Dept, Campus Box 1061, St Louis, 63130.
Notes: A small but significant collection.

NJ —EDUCATIONAL TESTING SERVICE, Carl Campbell Brigham Library, Princeton, 08540. Janet Williams, Librn
Notes: Complete works and papers of Louis L Thurstone, a leading psychometrician of the 20th century.

TIAO-YU-T'AI MOVEMENT

WA —UNIVERSITY OF WASHINGTON LIBRARIES, East Asia Library, DO-27, Seattle, 98195. Karl Lo, Head
Holdings: Vols (300,000) Cat Microforms
Budget: ($200,000)
Notes: Southwest China: Joseph Rock Collection, ca 2000 vols; modern Chinese poetry, 1919 to date: ca 700 titles; Asian art, esp Japanese painting: 4097 vols; Tiao-ya-t'ai movement in the US: ca 400 items of periodicals and pamphlets; modern Korean poetry, ancient and modern: ca 1000 titles; Mu-yu-shu folk literature: ca 1000 items.

TIBET

CA —UNIVERSITY OF CALIFORNIA, BERKELEY, University Library, East Asiatic Library, Room 208, Durant Hall, Berkeley, 94720. Donald Shively, Head
Holdings: Vols (500,000) Cat Pix Microforms
Notes: Small but important collection of Tibetan-language research materials in the fields of Buddhist Studies, and Tibetan historical/social conditions. Holdings incl a rare collection of writings from the oldest surviving school of Tibetan Buddhism (The Rin-Chen-Gter-Mdzod Collection), consisting of a monumental corpus of Tantric literature spanning ten centuries of composition. The collections are complemented by related holdings in the Main Library and in the South/Southeast Asia Library Service.

CT —TRINITY COLLEGE LIBRARY, 300 Summit St, Hartford, 06106. Ralph S Emerick, Librn
Holdings: Cat

CT —YALE UNIVERSITY, Box 1603A, Yale Station, New Haven, 06520.
Holdings: Cat Mss

IL —FIELD MUSEUM OF NATURAL HISTORY, The Berthold Laufer Library, Roosevelt Rd & Lake Shore Dr, Chicago, 60605. W Peyton Fawcett, Librn
Holdings: Vols (12,000) // Cat Mss Maps
Notes: The part of the museum's collection of Berthold Laufer (1874-1934), Curator of Anthropology, dealing with the peoples of the pre-19th century Chinese Empire (incl Manchuria, Mongolia, Sinkiang and Tibet); their anthropology, art and religion; influences upon their cultures by those of India, Siberia, Japan, Indonesia, and Oceania--and vice versa. Incl about 500 books in Tibetan. About 2/3 of the collection is cataloged.

MA —HARVARD UNIVERSITY LIBRARY, Harvard-Yenching Library, 2 Divinity Ave, Cambridge, 02138. Eugene W Wu, Librn
Notes: See *Harvard Library Bulletin*, IV (1950); p 286. Contains the three rare editions of the *Tripitaka:* The Narthang edition (1732) of both the Kanjur and the Tanjur, the Peking edition of the Kanjur, and the Lhasa edition (1933?) of the Kanjur; also Tibetan-language publications received under the PL480 program.

NJ —NEWARK MUSEUM LIBRARY, 49 Washington St, PO Box 540, Newark,

TIBET (cont.)

07101. Margaret DiSalvi, Librn
Holdings: Vols 325 Cat Mss Maps Pix Slides
Notes: The Newark Museum has an outstanding collection of Tibetan religious books which are considered part of the museum's collections rather than the library's. The library's collections incl published books, pamphlets, etc, over 1000 photographs of Tibet and Tibetans, and many slides of Tibet and of the museum's collections. Have published a catalog of our Tibetan collections. See, *Catalogue of the Tibetan Collection and other Lamaist Articles*, 5-vols (Newark Museum, Newark, NJ), prepared by Eleanor Olson, Curator Emeritus of the Oriental Collections, 1950-1971.

NY —AMERICAN MUSEUM OF NATURAL HISTORY, Library Services Dept, Central Park W & 79th St, New York, 10024. Nina J Root, Chairwoman; Mary Genett, Asst Librn for Reference Services

NC —UNIVERSITY OF NORTH CAROLINA, CHARLOTTE, J Murrey Atkins Library, UNCC Station, Charlotte, 28223. Robert F Brabham Jr, Special Collections Librn
Notes: Part of the Suzuki Collection of books on Mahayana Buddhism. It incl 10 vols and 25 paintings and sketches of Himalayan scenes. Cataloged.

OH —CLEVELAND PUBLIC LIBRARY, Fine Arts and Special Collections Department, 325 Superior Ave, Cleveland, 44114. Alice N Loranth, Head
Holdings: Vols 1400 Cat Mss
Notes: Emphasis is on literary and religious texts and translations. Numerous facsimile editions of mss. 800 vols in Tibetan. Separate catalog of author entries for titles in Tibetan is maintained.
See also entry under Oriental Languages and Literatures.

TIBET—HISTORY

CT —YALE UNIVERSITY, Box 1603A, Yale Station, New Haven, 06520.

NJ —PRINCETON UNIVERSITY, Library, Gest Oriental Library & East Asian Collections, 317 Palmer Hall, Princeton, 08544. D E Perushek, Cur
Holdings: Cat Mss
See also entry under China.

TIBET—RELIGION

DC —LIBRARY OF CONGRESS, Asian Division, Washington, 20540.
Notes: Chinese and Korean Section. William Woodville Rockhill Collection of Tibetan religious books and mss.

TIBETAN ART see Art, Tibetan

TIBETAN BUDDHISM

NY —INSTITUTE FOR ADVANCED STUDIES OF WORLD RELIGIONS (IASWR), Melville Memorial Library, State University of New York, Stony Brook, 11794. C T Shen, Dir
Holdings: Vols 4400 Periodicals Mss Microforms
Notes: Incl, in hard cover, Japanese reduced-size reprint of Peking edition of Kanjur and Tanjur, 168 vols containing 6439 titles; a 5000 volume modern and growing reprint collection of post-canonical works, obtained through the PL 480, SFC program administered by the Library of Congress; some vols obtained from other sources; 10 rare mss texts; about 250 xylograph volumes. Translations and studies in Japanese, Chinese, English and other European languages. In microform: Microfiche editions; Lhasa ed of Kanjur (Bka-gyur); Cone ed of Tanjur (Bstan-gyur); Yab sras gsuns bum (collected works of Tsong-kha-pa and his two disciples); PL 480 collection: about 2800 titles of native literature on Buddhism, the Bon religion, poetry, epic tales, drama, grammar, lexicography,

medicine, practical manuals, education and modern writings on Tibet's contact with 20thcentury world culture. Some cataloged. Refer inquiries to H G Robinson.

TIBETAN LANGUAGE AND LITERATURE

CA —UNIVERSITY OF CALIFORNIA, BERKELEY, University Library, East Asiatic Library, Room 208, Durant Hall, Berkeley, 94720. Donald Shively, Head
Holdings: Vols (500,000) Cat Pix Microforms
Notes: Small but important collection of Tibetan-language research materials in the fields of Buddhist Studies, and Tibetan historical/social conditions. Holdings incl a rare collection of writings from the oldest surviving school of Tibetan Buddhism (The Rin-Chen-Gter-Mdzod Collection), consisting of a monumental corpus of Tantric literature spanning ten centuries of composition. The collections are complemented by related holdings in the Main Library and in the South/Southeast Asia Library Service.

CT —YALE UNIVERSITY, Box 1603A, Yale Station, New Haven, 06520.

HI —UNIVERSITY OF HAWAII, Library, 2550 The Mall, Honolulu, 96822. Joyce Wright, Head, Asia Collection; Masato Matsu, Head, East Asia Vernacular Collection
Holdings: Vols 3474
Notes: Tibetan language holdings in the Asia Collection acquired through PL480. No figure is available for the number of cataloged volumes. The uncataloged titles are accessible through the Library of Congress Accessions Lists for India.

IL —FIELD MUSEUM OF NATURAL HISTORY, The Berthold Laufer Library, Roosevelt Rd & Lake Shore Dr, Chicago, 60605. W Peyton Fawcett, Librn
Holdings: Vols (12,000) // Cat Mss Maps
Notes: The part of the museum's collection of Berthold Laufer (1874-1934), Curator of Anthropology, dealing with the peoples of the pre-19th century Chinese Empire (incl Manchuria, Mongolia, Sinkiang and Tibet); their anthropology, art and religion; influences upon their cultures by those of India, Siberia, Japan, Indonesia, and Oceania--and vice versa. Incl about 500 books in Tibetan. About 2/3 of the collection is cataloged.

MA —HARVARD UNIVERSITY LIBRARY, Harvard-Yenching Library, 2 Divinity Ave, Cambridge, 02138. Eugene W Wu, Librn
Notes: See *Harvard Library Bulletin*, IV (1950); p 286. Contains the three rare editions of the *Tripitaka*: The Narthang edition (1732) of both the Kanjur and the Tanjur, the Peking edition of the Kanjur, and the Lhasa edition (1933?) of the Kanjur; also Tibetan-language publications received under the PL480 program.

MI —UNIVERSITY OF MICHIGAN, Graduate Library, South Asian Dept, Ann Arbor, 48109. Om P Sharma, Librn
Holdings: Vols (365,000) Cat Maps Slides Microforms
Notes: The major emphasis is on social sciences and humanities. Besides materials in classical languages, South Asian vernaculars being retained are Hindi, Bengali, Urdu, Marathi and Tamil; Strong in classical languages, especially Sanskrit, Pali, and Prakrit.

NJ —PRINCETON UNIVERSITY, Library, Gest Oriental Library & East Asian Collections, 317 Palmer Hall, Princeton, 08544. D E Perushek, Cur
Holdings: Cat Mss
See also entry under China.

NY —COLUMBIA UNIVERSITY LIBRARIES, C V Strarr East Asian Library, 300 Kent Hall, New York, 10027. James Reardon-Anderson, Librn
Holdings: Vols 1000
Notes: Incl 3 editions of the Tripitaka. Tibetan Version (Kanjur); Narthang ed.; Derge ed.; and Top Palace ed. Also incl the Nartang ed. of the Tanjur (Commentaries).

NY —NEW YORK PUBLIC LIBRARY, Oriental Div, Fifth Ave & 42 St, New York, 10018. E Christian Filstrup, Chief
Holdings: Cat Mss Microforms
Budget: ($56,455)
Notes: Published catalog of holdings.

NY —INSTITUTE FOR ADVANCED STUDIES OF WORLD RELIGIONS (IASWR), Melville Memorial Library, State University of New York, Stony Brook, 11794. C T Shen, Dir
Holdings: Vols 5000 Periodicals Mss Maps Microforms
Notes: Incl, in hard cover, Japanese reduced-size reprint of Peking edition of Kanjur and Tanjur, 168 vols containing 6439 titles; a 4400 vol modern and growing reprint collection of post-canonical works, obtained through the PL 480 program administered by the Library of Congress; some vols obtained from other sources; 3 rare ms copies of canonical texts; about 200 xylograph vols. In microform: Snar-thang, and Sde-dge, Lhasa ed of Kanjur (Bka-gyur); Cone ed of Tanjur (Bstan-gyur); Yab Sras Gsungs Bum, works of Tsong-kha-pa and his two disciples; Rin Chen Gter Mdzod Chen Mo; PL 480 collection: about 3000 titles of native literature on Buddhism, the Bon religion, poetry, epic tales, drama, grammar, lexicography, medicine, practical manuals, education and modern writings on Tibet's contact with 20th century world culture. Partically cataloged. Refer inquirieto H G Robinson or J Abritis.

OH —CLEVELAND PUBLIC LIBRARY, Fine Arts and Special Collections Department, 325 Superior Ave, Cleveland, 44114. Alice N Loranth, Head
Holdings: Vols 1000 Cat Mss
Notes: Emphasis is on literary and religious texts and translations. Numerous facsimile editions of mss. 400 vols in Tibetan. Separate catalog of main entries for titles in Tibetan is maintained.

TIBETANS IN NEPAL AND INDIA

CA —HOOVER INSTITUTION ON WAR, REVOLUTION & PEACE, Stanford University, Stanford, 94305. Milorad M Drachkovitch, Archivist
Holdings: Mss Pix
Notes: Records of the American Emergency Committee for Tibetan Refugees, incl correspondence, reports, minutes of meetings and photographs, 1959-1970, relating to relief work for Tibetan refugees in Nepal and India. 17 ms boxes.

TIBETO-BURMAN LANGUAGES AND LITERATURES

NY —NEW YORK PUBLIC LIBRARY, Oriental Div, Fifth Ave & 42 St, New York, 10018. E Christian Filstrup, Chief
Holdings: Cat Mss Microforms
Budget: ($56,455)
Notes: Published catalog of holdings. Currently collected in Western language materials only.

†NY —INSTITUTE FOR ADVANCED STUDIES OF WORLD RELIGIONS (IASWR), Library, State University of New York at Stony Brook, Stony Brook, 11794. C T Shen, Librn
Holdings: Vols 4400 Mss Microforms

TIBETO-CHINESE LANGUAGES see Indochinese Languages

TICKS

HI —BERNICE P BISHOP MUSEUM, Library, PO Box 19000-A, Honolulu, 96819. Cynthia Timberlake, Librn
Holdings: Vols (90,000) Cat Mss Maps Pix Slides Microforms
Budget: ($30,000)
Notes: Only American library devoted exclusively to the Pacific region. Collection reflects historical and contemporary research emphases of Bishop Museum; ie the natural and cultural history of the Pacific. Areas of concentration incl archaeology, ethnology,

TICKS (cont.)

linguistics, voyages and explorations, history, vertebrate and invertebrate zoology, botany and museology. Strong special collections incl photographs, mss and archives, maps and art. Publications: Quarterly "Additions to the Catalog," *Dictionary Catalog of the Library* (9 vols and 2 suppl; Boston: G K Hall, 1964-69).
IA —IOWA STATE UNIVERSITY, Library, Ames, 50011. Warren B Kuhn, Dean of Library Services
Holdings: Cat
Notes: Specific strengths: files, mosquitoes and ticks.

TIDAL WAVES see Tsunamis

TIEDE, TOM

MA —BOSTON UNIVERSITY, Mugar Memorial Library, Special Collections Dept, 771 Commonwealth Ave, Boston, 02215. Howard B Gotlieb, Dir
Holdings: Cat Mss Pix
Notes: Mss, correspondence, etc collected in depth; incl publications by or about.

TIETJENS, EUNICE (HAMMOND)

IL —NEWBERRY LIBRARY, 60 W Walton St, Chicago, 60610. Diana Haskell, Cur of Modern Mss
Holdings: Cat Mss Pix
Notes: Primary repository; 4263 pieces. Restricted use: noncirculating.

TIFFANY, ORIN AND KATHERINE

IL —WHEATON COLLEGE, Buswell Memorial Library, Wheaton, 60187. Paul Snezek, Library Dir
Holdings: Mss
Notes: The collection includes mss, correspondence, lecture tapes, (40), (25 linear feet). 1945 UN conference on International Organization, Canadian Rebellion, 1837-1838, Wheaton Scholastic Society.

TILDEN FAMILY

MA —NEW ENGLAND HISTORIC GENEALOGICAL SOCIETY, Library, 101 Newbury St, Boston, 02116. Ralph J Crandell, Dir
Notes: Family papers, likely to incl personal correspondence, diaries, business records, etc.

TILLAGE

AL —US DEPT OF AGRICULTURE, SCIENCE & EDUCATION ADMINISTRATION, National Tillage Machinery Laboratory, Library, PO Box 792, Auburn, 36830. William A Gill, Collaborator
Holdings: Vols (39,000) Cat Mss Maps Pix Slides 16mm Films Microforms
Budget: ($20,000)
Notes: The National Tillage Machinery Laboratory (NTML) has a special technical library comprised of highly selective engineering and physical science materials pertinent to soil-machine relations, such as tillage, earthmoving, mining, soil trafficability, and vehicle mobility. A high percentage of the library material comes from sources outside the US and outside agriculture. Particularly strong in Russian-language literature.

TILLETT, PAUL D., JR., 1923-1966

NJ —PRINCETON UNIVERSITY, Seeley G Mudd Manuscript Library, Public Affairs Papers Collection, Princeton, 08544. Nancy Bressler, Cur
Notes: Incl 9 boxes. The papers cover the period 1962-66. An unpublished 7p checklist is available in the Library.

TILLICH, PAUL

MA —HARVARD UNIVERSITY, Harvard Divinity School, Andover-Harvard

Theological Library, 45 Francis Ave, Cambridge, 02138. Maria Grossmann, Librn
Holdings: Vols (370,000) Cat Mss
Notes: Personal archives.

TILLMAN, BENJAMIN R., 1847-1918

SC —CLEMSON UNIVERSITY, Libraries, Clemson, 29631. Michael F Kohl, Head of Special Collections
Holdings: // Cat Mss Pix
Notes: Benjamin R Tillman, South Carolina Governor and US Senator. 70 cubic feet of manuscripts arranged chronologically in document boxes. Incl 15 scrapbooks. Name index to incoming letters.

TILTON, THEODORE

NY —SYRACUSE UNIVERSITY LIBRARIES, Ernest S Bird Library, George Arents Research Library for Special Collections, Syracuse, 13210. Carolyn A Davis, Manuscripts Librn; Amy S Doherty, University Archivist; Mark F Weimer, Rare Book Librn
Notes: Mss of abolitionist editor Theodore Tilton; 4 letters.

TIME

DC —US NAVAL OBSERVATORY LIBRARY, 30th & Massachusetts Ave, NW, Washington, 20016. Brenda G Corbin, Librn
Holdings: Vols (75,000) Cat Mss Maps Pix Slides Microforms
Notes: Incl 1000 journals, with monograph and serial publications in the fields of celestial mechanics, fundamental astronomy, time determination, photographic astrometry and astrophysics, data processing, mathematics.
MI —APPLE TREE PRESS, Library, Box 1012, Flint, 48501. W D Chase, Editor/ Librn
Holdings: Vols (1200) Uncat Mss Maps Pix Microforms

TIME—MANAGEMENT see Time Allocation

TIME—ORGANIZATION see Time Allocation

TIME, GEOLOGICAL see Geological Time

TIME, USE OF see Time Allocation

TIME ALLOCATION

ON —SIRLS, Faculty of Human Kinetics & Leisure Studies, University of Waterloo, Waterloo, N2L 3G1, Can. Betty Smith, Database Mgr
Notes: Information Retrieval System for the Sociology of Leisure and Sport (SIRLS) is a computerized online database of about 13,000 entries (1983). Incl dance as a leisure time activity.

TIME AND MOTION STUDIES

IN —PURDUE UNIVERSITY LIBRARIES, Special Collections Dept, West Lafayette, 47907. Keith Dowden, Asst Dir, Special Collections
Holdings: Vols (500) // Cat Slides
Notes: The Gilbreth Collection. Incl motion study equipment and personal working papers and photographs of Frank B and Lillian Gilbreth's work in the development of the field of industrial management. Also, correspondence, certificates, diplomas, memorabilia, published and nonprint material.
NJ —STEVENS INSTITUTE OF TECHNOLOGY, Samuel C Williams Library, Castle Point Sta, Hoboken, 07030. Jane G Hartye, Special Collections Librn
Holdings: Vols (180) Cat Pix Slides
Budget: ($1500)
Notes: Frederick Winslow Taylor is known as the "father of scientific management," and we have in our collection volumes of

correspondence relating to the introduction of this system into industry, government, the army and navy, etc. This collection also includes many personal items belonging to and used by Mr Taylor. Our collection is the most complete one on the subject of scientifc management.

TIME BUDGETS see Time Allocation

TIME CLOCKS

PA —FRANKLIN INSTITUTE LIBRARY, 20 & The Parkway, Philadelphia, 19103. Miriam Padusis, Dir; Charles Wilt, Readers Servs Librn
Holdings: Vols 2400 Cat Mss
Notes: One of the finest collections of horology in the world.

TIME ESTIMATION see Time Allocation

TIME MEASUREMENTS

PA —FRANKLIN INSTITUTE LIBRARY, 20 & The Parkway, Philadelphia, 19103. Miriam Padusis, Dir; Charles Wilt, Readers Servs Librn
Holdings: Vols 2400 Cat Mss
Notes: One of the finest collections of horology in the world.

TIME PERCEPTION

NY —PARAPSYCHOLOGY FOUNDATION, Eileen J Garrett Library, 228 E 71st St, New York, 10021. Wayne Norman, Librn
Holdings: Vols (9300) Cat
Notes: Books, periodicals, pamphlets on parapsychology, its history, and books in other subjects that relate to parapsychology, eg, altered states of consciousness, hypnosis, dreams, time theories, etc.

TIMES PUBLISHING CO.

FL —UNIVERSITY OF SOUTH FLORIDA, Library, Tampa, 33620. J B Dobkin, Special Collections Librn
Notes: Public and private papers of Nelson Poynter, Chairman of the board of Times Publishing Company. Incl political correspondence, photographs, and Pulitzer Prize commendation records.

TIMETABLES, RAILROAD see Railroads—Timetables

TIMME, WALTER

†NY —NEW YORK ACADEMY OF MEDICINE, Library, 2 E 103 ST, New York, 10029.
Notes: Papers of Walter Timme, MD (1874-1956). Timme was a pioneer endocrinologist; described pluriglandular disease, "Timme's Syndrome." Incl correspondence from Harvey Cushing, Paul Dudley White, Charles A Elsberg, Louis I Dublin, Ely Smith Jelliffe, John F Fulton, Edna St Vincent Millay, Eva Le Gallienne, and Irving Ramsey Wiles.

TIMMONS, BASCOM

TX —TEXAS A&M UNIVERSITY, Sterling C Evans Library, University Archives, College Station, 77843. Charles R Schultz, University Archivist
Holdings: Mss
Notes: The Archives of Modern Politics: the papers of Texas Congressmen Washington journalist Bascom Timmons, ca 1920-1970.

TIMOR, EAST see Indonesia

TIMOR, PORTUGUESE

MI —UNIVERSITY OF MICHIGAN, Harlan Hatcher Graduate Library, Ann Arbor, 48109. Susan Go, Librn
Holdings: Vols (250,000) Cat Mss Maps Pix Slides Microforms
Notes: Incl in the Michigan Historical Collections (primarily archival material) are

TIMOR, PORTUGUESE (cont.)

papers of Michiganders in southeast Asia, mostly the Philipines, eg papers of Joseph R Hayden, Frank Murphy and G Mennen Williams, also, on film, the selected papers of Philippines president Manuel Quezon. All aspects of the countries, cultures and peoples of Brunei, Burma, Khmer, Indonesia, Laos, Malaysia, Philippines, Singapore, Thailand, Portuguese Timor and Vietnam. Also the Malayo-Polynesian (Austronesian), Mon-Khmer (Austroasiatic), and Sino-Tibetan language groupings.

NY —CORNELL UNIVERSITY LIBRARIES, John M Olin Library, John M Echols Collection on Southeast Asia, Ithaca, 14853. Giok Po Oey, Curator
Holdings: Vols (167,000) Cat Mss Maps Pix Microforms
Budget: ($90,000)
Notes: Additions published in the collection's monthly accessions list (Ithaca: Cornell University, Southeast Asia Program, 1959-). Holdings through December 1980 listed in *Cornell University Libraries Southeast Asia Catalog* (Boston: G K Hall, 1976, First supplement, 1983), 10 vols.

TIMROD, HENRY

NC —DUKE UNIVERSITY, William R Perkins Library, Durham, 27706. Elvin E Strowd, University Librn
Notes: The Ethel Carr Peacock collection of 7000 volumes is strong in holdings of 19th century American literature.

TIN

ON —RIO ALGOM LIMITED, Library, 120 Adelaide St W, Toronto, M5H 1W5, Can. Penny Lipman, Librn
Holdings: Vols (1500) Cat
Budget: ($7000)
Notes: Espec mining of uranium and copper; geology; mining methods; nuclear energy.

TIN SOLDIERS AND SAILORS see Military Miniatures

TINCTORIAL SUBSTANCES see Dyes and Dyeing

TINKER, EDWARD LAROCQUE

NY —UNIVERSITY CLUB, Library, One W 54 St, New York, 10019. Guy St Clair, Library Dir
Notes: A private library for the members of the University Club, their guests, and serious scholars upon written application to the Library Director. Holds the Edward Larocque Tinker Collection of Illustrated Books Between the Two World Wars, A Milton Runyon Collection on the History of Printing and Publishing, the Frederic R Coudert "Les Bibliophiles des Paris" Collection, The University Club Rare Book Collection, and the Frederick G Rudge Collection of Books Designed by William E Rudge and Bruce Rogers.

TINTYPES

KY —UNIVERSITY OF LOUISVILLE, Ekstrom Library, Photographic Archives, Louisville, 40292. J C Anderson, Cur; David G Horvath, Asst Cur
Holdings: Vols (750,000) Cat Pix Slides
Budget: ($60,000)
Notes: Photographs in three broad areas: works of outstanding photographers; examples of major developments in the art and technology of photography; photographs important as sociological, historical, or behavioral documents. Actors and actresses, Louisville's Macauley Theatre. Standard Oil of New Jersey Collection, 85,000 pictures of oil industry's effect on life in the 20th century (1943-1950, directed by Roy Stryker); Stryker's collection from Farm Security Administration series on rural conditions, 1935-1942; Jones and Laughlin Steel Corp. Picture Library, by Stryker.

Stryker manuscripts, 1934-1972. Caufield and Shook commercial photographs, Louisville area, 1920-1949. Jean Thomas "The Traipsin' Women" photographs of Kentucky mountain folkways. Kate Matthews' (1870-1956) photographs incl prototypes for "Little Colonel" Series. Other collections described in unpublishedbrochure. Print duplication service.

NE —WESTERN HERITAGE MUSEUM, 801 S Tenth St, Omaha, 68108. Jane G Murray, Photo-Archivist
Notes: Tintype pictures from a former art studio.

TINWARE, AMERICAN

MA —OLD STURBRIDGE VILLAGE, Research Library, Sturbridge, 01566. Theresa Rini Percy, Librn
Holdings: Cat Pix
Notes: New England, 1790-1850.

NY —HISTORICAL SOCIETY OF EARLY AMERICAN DECORATION, 19 Dove St, Albany, 12210. Doris Fry, Dir; Laura Olf, Librn
Holdings: Cat Pix Slides
Notes: The Library is housed with the Museum Collection of the Society. Incl examples of 19th century American country painting on tin, stenciling on wood and tin, bronzing decoration on wood, English stencilled tin and wood, bronzed items, painted objects, reverse painting on glass and examples of other decorating techniques of the period. Also included is a large collection of painted recordings of designs from early articles. Many of these were done by Esther Stevens Brazer in the 1930s. Another large collection has been added since that time. The library material is related to this interest. See *The Decorator*, official publication of the Historical Society of Early American Decoration. Other publications: *The Ornamented Chair* and *The Ornamented Tray* (both ed by Zilla Rider Lea), *Antique Decorations* by Brazer.

TIOMKIN, DIMITRI

CA —UNIVERSITY OF SOUTHERN CALIFORNIA, Edward L Doheny Memorial Library, Archives of Performing Arts, University Park, Los Angeles, 90089. Robert Knutson, Librn
Holdings: Mss Pix
Notes: Personal collection of papers, pictures, etc.

TIPPETT, MICHAEL

DC —LIBRARY OF CONGRESS, Music Division, Washington, 20540.
Notes: Mss in Koussevitzky Archives.

TISCHLER, HANS, 1915-

NY —STATE UNIVERSITY OF NEW YORK AT ALBANY, Library, Special Collections Dept, 1400 Washington Ave, Albany, 12222. Marion P Munzer, Coordr
Notes: Correspondence of Hans Tischler; music scores; mss (4 linear feet). Part of the Library's German Exile Collection.
See also entry under Musicology

TISH (PERIODICAL)

AB —UNIVERSITY OF CALGARY, Libraries, Special Collections Div, 2500 University Dr, Calgary, T2N 1N4, Can.
Notes: Archives of the literary periodicals: *Tish, Imago, Ariel, Descant, Canadian Review Magazine* and *Canadian Short Story Magazine*.

TISSUE TRANSPLANTS see Transplantation of Organs, Tissues, Etc.

TISSUES—PRESERVATION

CT —YALE UNIVERSITY, Dept of Human Genetics, 310 Cedar St, PO Box 3333, New Haven, 06510. Barbara J Bachmann, Cur
Holdings: Cat
Notes: Collection of *Escherichia coli K-12*,

containing ampules of 6000 mutant strains of lyophilized (freeze-dried) bacteria, with explanatory cards for each.

TITANIUM AND TITANIUM ALLOYS

PA —COLT INDUSTRIES, Crucible Research Center Library, Box 88, Pittsburgh, 15230. Patricia J Aducci, Technical Librn

TITLE PAGES

PA —FREE LIBRARY OF PHILADELPHIA, Rare Book Dept, Logan Sq, Philadelphia, 19103. Marie E Korey, Rare Book Librn
Holdings: // Uncat
Notes: The John Ashhurst Collection of 5500 printers' marks and title-pages.

TITULESCU, NICHOLAS, 1883-1941

CA —HOOVER INSTITUTION ON WAR, REVOLUTION & PEACE, Stanford University, Stanford, 94305. Milorad M Drachkovitch, Archivist
Holdings: Mss
Notes: Papers of N Titulescu, Rumanian Minister of Foreign Affairs and Minister of Finance, consisting of diaries, correspondence, memoranda, reports, manuscripts, clippings, printed matter and other materials relating to Titulescu's career as statesman and diplomat, 1923-1938. Incl is documentation on Rumania's negotiations with the USSR, 1931-32. 15 1/2 ms boxes.

TOADSTOOLS see Mushrooms

TOBACCO

CA —UNIVERSITY OF CALIFORNIA, BERKELEY, Science Libraries, Natural Resources Library, 40 Giannini Hall, Berkeley, 94720. Norma Kobzina, Head Librn
Holdings: Vols (100,000) Cat Maps Microforms
Budget: ($40,000)
Notes: Subject emphasis is on basic agricultural and pest management research, particularly in the areas of tropical and subtropical agriculture and plantation crops, ie, cotton, rice, tobacco, and sugar. Materials in agricultural engineering, farm machinery, and veterinary medicine are not acquired for the Berkeley campus. Serials, especially the extensive holdings of foreign titles, constitute the collection's major strength. Over 5700 serials are being received currently.

DC —LIBRARY OF CONGRESS, Prints & Photographs Div, Washington, 20540.
Notes: Packaging for American tobacco products, 1840s-1880s. Approx 1000 tobacco labels, arranged by subject.

KY —UNIVERSITY OF KENTUCKY, Margaret I King Library, Dept of Special Collections, Lexington, 40506. William Marshall, Head
Holdings: Vols 125 Cat Mss
Notes: Mss concerning manufacture and trade.

LA —NICHOLLS STATE UNIVERSITY, Ellender Memorial Library, Thibodaux, 70310. Randall A Detro, Dir; Philip D Uzee, Archivist
Holdings: Uncat Mss Maps Pix Microforms
Notes: Louisiana and local history; family papers of the period, etc.

MA —HARVARD UNIVERSITY LIBRARY, Widener Library, Cambridge, 02138.
Holdings: Cat
Notes: See *Harvard Library Notes*, III (1936): pp 101-118.

NY —NEW YORK PUBLIC LIBRARY, Rare Books and Manuscripts Div, Fifth Ave & 42 St, New York, 10018. William L Joyce, Asst Dir; Bernard McTigue, Cur, Arents Collection
Holdings: Cat
Notes: Arents Tobacco Collection: Over 14,000 items in 28 languages, incl books, pamphlets, mss, original drawings, prints and music relating to tobacco. Rare early works in Spanish, Italian, Latin, French, German and English; 16th century herbals; over 81,000 cigarette cards. Publications: Arents,

TOBACCO (cont.)

George, *Tobacco, Its History; Illustrated by the Books, Manuscripts, and Engravings in the Library of George Arents, Jr,* (New York: The Rosenbach Co, 1937-1952), 5 vols: supplemented by *Tobacco: A Catalogue of the Books, Manuscripts and Engravings Acquired since 1942 in the Arents Tobacco Collection at the New York Public Library* (New York, 1958-date).

NY —TOBACCO MERCHANTS ASSOCIATION OF THE US, Howard S Cullman Library, Suite 705, 1220 Broadway, New York, 10001. R Robert Sengstacken, Dir Information Servs
Holdings: Vols (3000)
Notes: Tobacco Industry. Trademark and brand files for tobacco products and smoker's articles. Incl 150 subscriptions, 30 VF.

NC —DUKE UNIVERSITY, William R Perkins Library, Manuscript Dept, Durham, 27706. Ellen Gartrell, Cur of Mss
Holdings: Cat Mss
Notes: Tobacco culture, marketing, trade, especially US South, 19th-20th century, incl papers of Duke Family, Richard H Wright, British-American Tobacco Co, James A Thomas, Edward J Parrish, United Cigarette Machine Co; also tobacco advertising (trade cards, etc).

NC —DUKE UNIVERSITY, William R Perkins Library, Rare Book Room, Durham, 27706. John L Sharpe, III, Cur
Notes: George Arents tobacco collection of several hundred books and pamphlets. Rare and unique material relating to the culture and production of tobacco and the manufacture and distribution of tobacco products.

NC —NORTH CAROLINA STATE UNIVERSITY, Tobacco Literature Service, 2314 D H Hill Library, Box 7111, Raleigh, 27695. Carmen M Marin, Dir
Holdings: Vols 27 Cat
Notes: The D H Hill Library in cooperation with the Agricultural Research Service operates a Tobacco Literature service. The service publishes bimonthly *Tobacco Abstracts: Citations and Abstracts on World Literature on Nicotiana.* Collection incl 73,000 abstracts.

NC —R J REYNOLDS TOBACCO CO, Marketing Intelligence Div, 203 Reynolds Bldg, Winston-Salem, 27102. Anita Scism, Sr Information Center Adminr
Holdings: Vols 1900 Cat Maps Slides Audiotapes Videotapes Microforms
Notes: Emphasis on tobacco and marketing.

NC —R J REYNOLDS TOBACCO CO, Scientific Information Services Library, Bowman Gray Technical Center, BGTC 611-12/205, Winston-Salem, 27102. Nellie W Sizemore, Librn
Holdings: Vols 5000 Cat Microforms

OH —CLEVELAND PUBLIC LIBRARY, Fine Arts and Special Collections Department, 325 Superior Ave, Cleveland, 44114. Alice N Loranth, Head
Holdings: Vols (1356) Cat Pix
Notes: Incl numerous rare items: 16th century herbals: official proclamations issued by the English, French, Portuguese, Dutch governments, and tobacco premium cards, etc. The manners and customs aspect of smoking is emphasized. Some museum objects. Separate shelf list and separate dictionary catalog maintained.

†WA —WASHINGTON STATE UNIVERSITY, Library, Manuscripts, Archives & Special Collections, Pullman, 99164. John F Guido, Head
Holdings: Cat Mss Maps Pix
Notes: The Carl Parcher Russell papers, a vast resource (24,916 items; 45 linear feet) on American Indian and Western pioneer activities and artifacts. Much on the fur trade; pioneer life; mountain men and trapping; wildlife; primitive life in detail. Also the National Park Service, parks, monuments, etc. Described in *Carl Parcher Russell: An Indexed Register of His Scholarly and Professional Papers, 1920-1967, in the Washington State University Library* (Pullman, 1970), 149 pp.

PE —AGRICULTURE CANADA, Research Station Library, PO Box 1210, Charlottetown, C1A 7M8, Can. Barrie Stanfield, Librn
Holdings: Vols (2300) Ct
Budget: ($5000)

PQ —IMPERIAL TOBACCO LIMITED, Corporate Library, 3810 Saint-Antoine St, Montreal, H4C 1B5, Can. Y Mukherjee, Librn
Holdings: Vols 300 Cat Slides Filmstrips
Budget: $10,000
Notes: Incl books, periodicals and ephemera.

TOBACCO—PHYSIOLOGICAL EFFECTS

MD —OFFICE ON SMOKING AND HEALTH, Park Bldg, Rm 116, 5600 Fishers Lane, Rockville, 20857. Donald R Shopland, Technical Information Officer
Notes: Smoking, tobacco and nicotine as related to health. Approx 40,000 reprints. The technical information center of the clearinghouse issues at irregular intervals (about 6 times per year) the *Smoking and Health Bulletin.* The *Bulletin* contains those items added to the collection from the world-wide literature on smoking. Bibliographic and reference services can be obtained by writing or calling the Clearinghouse. Over 10,000 records, 1970- , are stored in an automated file and are capable of search and retrieval. Printout information corresponds to that found in the *Smoking and Health Bulletin.* The Clearinghouse has been named the "Collaborating Center for Smoking and Health" by the World Health Organization.

TOBACCO HABIT

MD —OFFICE ON SMOKING AND HEALTH, Park Bldg, Rm 116, 5600 Fishers Lane, Rockville, 20857. Donald R Shopland, Technical Information Officer
Notes: Smoking, tobacco and nicotine as related to health. Approx 40,000 reprints. The technical information center of the clearinghouse issues at irregular intervals (about 6 times per year) the *Smoking and Health Bulletin.* The *Bulletin* contains those items added to the collection from the world-wide literature on smoking. Bibliographic and reference services can be obtained by writing or calling the Clearinghouse. Over 10,000 records, 1970- , are stored in an automated file and are capable of search and retrieval. Printout information corresponds to that found in the *Smoking and Health Bulletin.* The Clearinghouse has been named the "Collaborating Center for Smoking and Health" by the World Health Organization.

TOBACCO PIPES

†WA —WASHINGTON STATE UNIVERSITY, Library, Manuscripts, Archives & Special Collections, Pullman, 99164. John F Guido, Head
Holdings: Cat Mss Maps Pix
Notes: The Carl Parcher Russell papers, a vast resource (24,916 items; 45 linear feet) on American Indian and Western pioneer activities and artifacts. Much on the fur trade; pioneer life; mountain men and trapping; wildlife; primitive life in detail. Also the National Park Service, parks, monuments, etc. Described in *Carl Parcher Russell: An Indexed Register of His Scholarly and Professional Papers, 1920-1967, in the Washington State University Library* (Pullman, 1970), 149 pp.

TOBAGO see Trinidad and Tobago

TOBEY, CHARLES W.

NH —DARTMOUTH COLLEGE, Baker Memorial Library, Hanover, 03755.
Holdings: Cat Mss
Notes: Personal papers.

TOBIAS, THOMAS

SC —COLLEGE OF CHARLESTON LIBRARY, Special Collections Dept,

Charleston, 29401.
Notes: Correspondence within the Lancelot Minor Harris Papers.

TOBOLOWSKY, HERMINE

TX —NORTH TEXAS STATE UNIVERSITY, Archives, NT Station Box 5188, Denton, 76203. Robert LaForte, University Archivist
Notes: 6 linear feet. Texas political manuscript collections housed in the NTSU Archives incl the Fred H Minor Collection (former Texas Speaker of the House), the Alvin M Owsley Collection (former US diplomat from Texas), and the Bullock Hyder Collection (former representative to Texas House from Lewisville). The collections cover Texas politics from the 1920's to the 1970's. Published Description: Fred H Minor Collection, *The National Union Catalog of Manuscript Collections: Catalog 1979* Washington: Library of Congress, 1980. Alvin M Owsley Collection, Ibid, Hermine Tobolowsky Equal Legal Rights Collection, Ibid.

TX —TEXAS WOMAN'S UNIVERSITY, Bralley Memorial Library, Box 23715, TWU Sta, Denton, 76204. Metta Nicewarner, Spec Collections Libn
Holdings: Vols Uncat Mss Audiotapes
Notes: The Hermine Tobolowsky Collection includes material on the Texas lawyer called the "Mother of the Equal Legal Rights Amendment in Texas". Items include correspondence, congressional bills and resolutions, court cases, campaign and platform congressional pledges of support.

TOCANTINS, LEANDRO M.

PA —CARDEZA FOUNDATION, Tocantins Memorial Library, 1015 Walnut St, Philadelphia, 19107. Doris Riso, Librn
Holdings: Vols 1800 Cat Mss Pix
Notes: Extensive collection of hematology. Mss of the late hematologist, Leandro M Tocantins, renowned for his work in coagulation. Part of the Jefferson University. Currently 39 periodicals in the field of hematology and related biochemistry and immunology are received.

TOCCATAS AND FUGUES see Canons, Fugues, Etc.

TOCH, ERNST

CA —UNIVERSITY OF CALIFORNIA, LOS ANGELES, Music Library, Schonberg Hall, Los Angeles, 90024. Stephen M Fry, Music Librn
Holdings: Cat Mss Pix
Notes: The Ernst Toch Archive of his mss, published works, recordings, correspondence, memorabilia, etc. Described in *UCLA Librarian,* January 1968.

TOCHARISH LANGUAGE see Tokharian Languages

TOCKS ISLAND LAKE PROJECT

NJ —SUSSEX COUNTY LIBRARY, Rd 3, Box 76, Newton, 07860. Judith Gessel, Reference Librn
Holdings: Cat Maps Slides 16mm Films Filmstrips
Notes: The Sussex County Area Reference Library is one of several locations which were named repositories for materials related to the restudy of the Tocks Island Lake Project. The items in the repository were distributed by the Delaware River Basin Commission. Collection incl study-related hearing transcripts, public notices, press clippings, correspondence, and reports of concern to the Delaware Water Gap National Recreation Area/Tocks Island Area. The Tocks Island Regional Advisory Council, when disbanded, presented its library to the Sussex County Library in 1974. The collection incl reports, surveys, maps, slides, and other materials collected or produced by TIRAC since 1965.

TODA LANGUAGE

NY —NEW YORK PUBLIC LIBRARY, Oriental Div, Fifth Ave & 42 St, New York,

TODA LANGUAGE (cont.)

10018. E Christian Filstrup, Chief
Holdings: Cat Mss Microforms
Budget: ($56,455)
Notes: Published catalog of holdings.

TODD, ARTHUR

CA —UNIVERSITY OF CALIFORNIA, LOS
ANGELES, Research Library, Dept of
Special Collections, 405 Hilgard Ave, Los
Angeles, 90024. Edward Shreeves,
Chairman, Bibliographers Group; David S
Zeidberg, Head
Notes: 18 linear feet of mss, correspondence,
memorabilia, and ephemera relating to dance
in the 20th century.

TODD, DAVID PECK, 1855-1939

CT —YALE UNIVERSITY, Box 1603A, Yale
Station, New Haven, 06520.
Holdings: Mss
Notes: His papers, 1862-1939.

TODD, ELI

CT —INSTITUTE OF LIVING, Medical
Library, 400 Washington St, Hartford,
06106. Helen Lansberg, Librn
Holdings: Vols (30,000) Cat Mss Maps Pix
Notes: Three special collections in
psychiatry, neurology and related subjects.
See also entry under Psychiatry

TODD, OLIVER J.

CA —HOOVER INSTITUTION ON WAR,
REVOLUTION & PEACE, Stanford
University, Stanford, 94305. Milorad M
Drachkovitch, Archivist
Holdings: Mss Pix
Notes: Papers of Oliver J Todd, incl diaries,
correspondence, reports, memoranda,
photographs, and other material, relating to
his service as an engineer for the
International Famine Commission in China
and the United Nations Relief and
Rehabilitation Agency as well as to social,
economic, and political conditions in China,
1919-1949. 40 ms boxes.

TOGO

DC —HOWARD UNIVERSITY, Moorland-
Spingarn Research Center, 500 Howard
Place NW, Washington, 20059. Clifford L
Muse, Jr, Acting Dir

TOILET AND TOILETRIES

IL —J WALTER THOMPSON CO,
Information Center, 875 N Michigan Ave,
Chicago, 60611. Edward G Strable, Dir
Holdings: Vols 75 Cat Microforms
Notes: Basis of collection is fugitive
materials (reports, studies, clippings, articles,
releases) on consumer markets and use
patterns of health and beauty aids-about 20
file drawers. Indexing and organization make
for immediate access.

TOKENS

CO —AMERICAN NUMISMATIC
ASSOCIATION LIBRARY, 818 N Cascade
Ave, Colorado Springs, 80903. Nancy W
Green, Librn
Holdings: Vols (20,000) Cat Slides
Notes: One of the largest numismatic
libraries, the collection incl books,
periodicals and auction catalogs on coins and
coin collecting, medals, tokens, military
orders and decorations, paper money,
primitive money, banks and banking, seals
and scarabs. ANA publishes a classified
subject catalog of its collection and is open
to the public for research and reference
services. Only members may check books
out.
NY —AMERICAN NUMISMATIC SOCIETY
LIBRARY, Broadway between 155 & 156
Sts, New York, 10032. Francis D Campbell
Jr, Chief Librn
Holdings: Vols (50,000) Cat Mss Maps Pix

Slides 16mm Films Microforms
Budget: ($6000)
Notes: Incl materials devoted to coins,
medals, decorations, orders, tokens, paper
money, seals, heraldry. Aids materials incl
history, economic history, art history,
archaeology, inscriptions and a number of
encyclopedias and biographical dictionaries.
Dictionary card catalog provides access to
the materials: *Dictionary Catalogue of the
Library of the American Numismatic
Society.* (Boston: G K Hall, 1962). 6 vols
and vol listing the auction catalogs in our
collection; *First Supplement: 1962-1967;
Second Supplement: 1968-1972; Third
Supplement: 1973-1977* (Boston: G K Hall,
1967, 1973, 1978). Noncirculating.

TOKHARIAN LANGUAGES

NY —NEW YORK PUBLIC LIBRARY,
Oriental Div, Fifth Ave & 42 St, New York,
10018. E Christian Filstrup, Chief
Holdings: Cat Mss Microforms
Budget: ($56,455)
Notes: Published catalog of holdings.

TOKLAS, ALICE B.

CT —YALE UNIVERSITY, Box 1603A, Yale
Station, New Haven, 06520.
Holdings: Cat
Notes: Papers, correspondence, etc.
NY —VASSAR COLLEGE, Library, Rare
Books & Manuscripts Collection, Box 20,
Poughkeepsie, 12601. Lisa Browar, Cur
Notes: An extensive collection of Elizabeth
Bishop's papers, incl notebooks, mss, drafts,
galleys, etc, as well as correspondence and
business files, with files of letters from
Cummings, Toklas, Dylan Thomas, and
Eudora Welty.

TOKUGAWA DOCUMENTS

IL —CENTER FOR RESEARCH
LIBRARIES, 6050 S Kenwood Ave,
Chicago, 60637. Donald B Simpson, Dir;
Esther Smith, Collection Development Librn
Holdings: Cat Microforms
Notes: Japanese foreign ministry archives
1868-1945, archives of army, navy, and
other government agencies 1868-1945,
Cabinet archives, Tokugawa docuemnts,
Okuma papers, other archival materials.
Descriptive pamphlet available.

TOLKIEN, J. R. R.

CA —SAN DIEGO STATE UNIVERSITY,
Malcolm A Love Library, 5300 Campanile
Dr, San Diego, 92182. D Dickinson, Univ
Librn; Don L Bosseau, Dir
Holdings: Mss Cassettes
Notes: Elizabeth Chater Collection in
Science Fiction. Includes Tolkien Collection,
fantasy, folklore, Gothic novels, mostly
autographed first editions, some rare and
scarce, includes manuscripts, graphics,
cassette tapes. Examples: authors included,
Isaac Asimov, Ray Bradbury, Joan Vinge,
Greg Baer, Frederick Pohl, Andre Norton,
etc. Examples of periodicals: Amazing
Stories, Famous Fantastic Mysteries of the
1940s, The Black Cat, 1895. (3000 items)
IL —WHEATON COLLEGE, Library, Marion
E Wade Collection, Irving & Franklin Sts,
Wheaton, 60187. Lyle Dorsett, Cur;
Marjorie Mead, Associate Cur
Holdings: Vols (6500) Audiotapes
Videotapes
Notes: Extensive Marion E Wade Collection
(over 6500 vols) of seven British authors incl
an excellent library of works both by and
about J R R Tolkien. Of special interest to
scholars is the collection of secondary source
material on fantasy.
NV —UNIVERSITY OF NEVADA, RENO,
University Library, Special Collections Dept,
Reno, 89557. Robert E Blesse, Head
Holdings: Vols 81 Cat
Notes: Includes individual works by author
in all editions including translations; also
prefaces, introductions, published
correspondence, appearances in anthologies,
periodicals, etc. Bibliographical research
collection, part of Modern Authors
Collection.

WI —MARQUETTE UNIVERSITY, Memorial
Library, 1415 W Wisconsin Ave, Milwaukee,
53233. Jay Kirk, Health Sciences Librn
Notes: Mss, etc.

TOLL ROADS

MA —AMERICAN ANTIQUARIAN
SOCIETY LIBRARY, 185 Salisbury St,
Worcester, 01609. Marcus A McCorison,
Dir & Librn
Holdings: Vols 5200 Cat
Notes: Incl the Thomas Winthrop Streeter
Collection on Transportation. The finest and
most complete documentation of early
American railroads, canals, bridges,
turnpikes, and harbors in existence.

TOLLEFSON, THOR

WA —UNIVERSITY OF WASHINGTON
LIBRARIES, Suzzallo Library, Manuscripts
Section, FM-25, Seattle, 98195. Karyl Winn,
Librn
Notes: Incl 76 linear feet, circa 1947-1964.

TOLSTOI, ILIA L'VOVICH, 1866-1933

MA —BRANDEIS UNIVERSITY, Goldfarb
Library, 415 South St, Waltham, 02154.
Bessie Hahn, Dir
Notes: Eight linear feet of correspondence
by and to Count Ilya and Countess Nadine
Tolstoi. Much of the material is in Russian
script. This collection is unprocessed, spring
1984.

TOLSTOI, LEO

WI —UNIVERSITY OF WISCONSIN,
MADISON, Memorial Library, Slavic
Studies Collection, 728 State St, Madison,
53706. Aleksander Rolich, Bibliographer for
Slavic Studies; Robert P Gakovich, Slavic
Cataloger; Valdis J Zeps, Baltic Studies
Center
Holdings: Cat
Notes: Russian Underground Collection.
Materials in the Russian Underground
Collection embrace the Russian
Revolutionary Movement from 1825 to
1917, including a considerable number of
Free Press publications. Among the 1500
titles are included about 100 journals, many
political tracts, leaflets, broadsides and
brochures of various political groups, largely
socialist, religious nonconformists (L Tolstoi)
and a large number of the satirical journals
that appeared between 1905-1907. Restricted
use: Rare Book Department.

TOMAHAWKS

†WA —WASHINGTON STATE
UNIVERSITY, Library, Manuscripts,
Archives & Special Collections, Pullman,
99164. John F Guido, Head
Holdings: Cat Mss Maps Pix
Notes: The Carl Parcher Russell papers, a
vast resource (24,916 items, 45 linear feet)
on American Indian and Western pioneer
activities and artifacts. Much on the fur
trade; pioneer life; mountain men and
trapping; wildlife; primitive life in detail.
Also the National Park Service, parks,
monuments, etc. Described in *Carl Parcher
Russell: An Indexed Register of His
Scholarly and Professional Papers, 1920-
1967, in the Washington State University
Library* (Pullman, 1970), 149 pp.

TOMBSTONE, ARIZONA

AZ —TOMBSTONE CITY LIBRARY, Box
218, Tombstone, 85638.
Holdings: Cat
Budget: ($1000)

TOMLINSON, CHARLES

NV —UNIVERSITY OF NEVADA, RENO,
University Library, Special Collections Dept,
Reno, 89557. Robert E Blesse, Head
Holdings: Vols 25 Cat
Notes: Includes individual works by author
in all editions including translations; also

TOMLINSON, CHARLES (cont.)

prefaces, introductions, published correspondence, appearances in anthologies, periodicals, etc. Bibliographical research collection, part of Modern Authors Collection.

TOMLINSON, HENRY MAJOR, 1873-1958

CA —CLAREMONT COLLEGES, Honnold Library, Ninth & Dartmouth, Claremont, 91711. Tania Rizzo, Special Collections Dept Head
Holdings: Vols 51 // Cat Mss
Notes: 5 ALsS. First and special editions.

CA —UNIVERSITY OF SAN FRANCISCO, Richard A Gleeson Library, The Countess Bernardine Murphy Donohue Rare Book Room, San Francisco, 94117. D Steven Corey, Special Collections Librn
Holdings: Vols 57
Notes: Comprehensive collection.

CT —YALE UNIVERSITY, Box 1603A, Yale Station, New Haven, 06520.
Holdings: Cat Mss

IL —ILLINOIS STATE UNIVERSITY, Milner Library, Dept of Special Collections, Normal, 61761. Robert Sokan, Librn
Notes: First editions, limited editions, ephemera, etc.

†NC —WAKE FOREST UNIVERSITY, Z Smith Reynolds Library, Box 7777, Reynold Sta, Winston-Salem, 27109. Richard J Murdoch, Rare Book Librn
Holdings: Cat
Notes: A signiciant collection.

TOMOGRAPHY

MD —JOHNS HOPKINS HOSPITAL, John W Pierson Memorial Library, Dept of Radiology, 601 N Broadway, Baltimore, 21205. S Elaine Pinkney, Librn
Holdings: Vols (6000) Cat Slides Audiotapes Videotapes
Budget: $4700
Notes: Incl Diagnostic Radiology, Radiotherapy, Ultrasound, and Computed Axial Tomography.

PA —ENSANIAN PHYSICOCHEMICAL INSTITUTE, Electrotopography Library, PO Box 98, Eldred, 16731. Elisabeth Anahid Ensanian, Chief Librn
Holdings: Vols 7 Cat Maps Slides
Budget: ($45,000)
Notes: Electrotopography is a new science (the Institute has pioneered the field and has coined the terms "electrotopograph" and "electrotopography") concerned with the mapping of electrical fields associated with metals, alloys, semiconductors, and living organisms. These fields may be natural and/or induced and are converted into mappings which exhibit certain systems characteristics for both normal and stress states. In the field of the materials sciences electrotopography permits the mapping of the mechanical properties of metals nondestructively and in the field of diagnostic medicine it permits both the location and quantization of certain types of physical pain without the cooperation of the subject. Three publications are associated with these revolutionary developments and are available at cost:*New Standards in Steel and Metals Technologies; Electrotopographic Sciences & Technology Newsletter;* and *The Journal of Medical Electrotopography.*

TONDORF, REV. FRANCIS A., S.J., 1870-1929

DC —GEORGETOWN UNIVERSITY, Library, Special Collections Div, 37 & O Sts NW, Washington, 20057. George M Barringer, Special Collections Librn; Nicholas B Sheetz, Mss Librn
Holdings: Mss
Notes: Correspondence, document, mss, notebooks, and newspaper clippings, predominantly of a professional nature. Rev Francis A Tondorf, SJ (1870-1929) founded the seismological obervatory at Georgetown University in 1909, serving as director until his death, in addition to other duties as professor of physics, biology, geology and astronomy. As internationally recognized authority in seismology, Tondorf published numerous articles and lectures.

TONER, JOSEPH MEREDITH, 1825-1896

DC —LIBRARY OF CONGRESS, Rare Book & Special Collections Div, Washington, 20540. William Matheson, Chief
Notes: The Joseph Meredith Toner Collection of American Medicine of the 18th and 19th centuries. Also, Toner's personal papers, correspondence, etc.

TONGA ISLANDS

CA —UNIVERSITY OF CALIFORNIA, SAN DIEGO, Central University Library, Mandeville Dept of Special Collections, La Jolla, 92093. Lynda Corey Claassen, Head
Holdings: Vols 607 Cat Mss Maps Pix

TONGUES, GIFT OF see Glossolalia

TOOLE, JOHN LAWRENCE

NY —UNIVERSITY OF ROCHESTER, Rush Rhees Library, Department of Rare Books and Special Collections, Rochester, 14627. Peter Dzwonkoski, Librn
Holdings: Cat Mss Pix
Notes: Papers, etc, incl books by and about, etc.

TOOLS

PA —COLT INDUSTRIES, Crucible Research Center Library, Box 88, Pittsburgh, 15230. Patricia J Aducci, Technical Librn
Notes: Tool steels.

TOOLS—HISTORY

MA —OLD STURBRIDGE VILLAGE, Research Library, Sturbridge, 01566. Theresa Rini Percy, Librn
Holdings: Vols (23,000) Cat Mss Microforms
Notes: New England to 1850. Incl trade catalogs.

MO —SCHOOL OF THE OZARKS, Lois Brownell Research Library, Ralph Foster Museum, Point Lookout, 65726. Robert Esworthy, Librn
Holdings: Vols (1300) Cat

TOOTH DECAY RESEARCH see Dental Caries Research

TOPIARY WORK

MA —HARVARD UNIVERSITY LIBRARY, Arnold Arboretum Library, 22 Divinty Ave, Cambridge, 02138. Barbara A Callahan, Librn
Holdings: Vols (89,239) Cat Mss Maps Pix Slides Microforms
Notes: Specializes in trees (arboriculture and dendrology). Horticultural Library maintained at The Arborway, Jamaica Plain, Mass.

TOPOGRAPHIC MAPS

CA —CALIFORNIA STATE UNIVERSITY, LONG BEACH, Reference Center, 1250 Bellflower Blvd, Long Beach, 90840.
Notes: Incl 22,544 maps and 550 atlases. The map collection is especially strong in California topographical maps.

CA —LOS ANGELES PUBLIC LIBRARY, History Dept, 630 W Fifth St, Los Angeles, 90071. Dorothy Mewshaw, Librn, Map Rm
Holdings: Vols (3000) Cat Maps
Budget: ($85,000)
Notes: The Mary Helen Peterson Collection of Maps and Atlases. World wide coverage, including topographic, political and special purpose maps. Depository for US Geologic Survey topographical maps, Defense Mapping Agency, and National Ocean Survey. Maps of Los Angeles City and County.

CA —POMONA PUBLIC LIBRARY, Special Collections, 625 S Garey Ave, PO Box 2271, Pomona, 91766. David Streeter, Librn
Holdings: Cat Mss Maps
Notes: Some 4000 maps. Strong for Pomona Valley area: tract maps, water company maps; depository for USGS California topographic maps; California earthquake fault maps.

CA —UNIVERSITY OF CALIFORNIA, SANTA BARBARA, Map and Imagery Laboratory, Santa Barbara, 93106. Larry Carver, Dept Head
Notes: Worldwide coverage of Landsat imagery donated by US Dept of Agriculture Aerial Photography Field Office. Consists of 153,000 scenes, covering most of the earth's surface between the years 1975 and 1980. Incl 300,000 maps, 1800 atlases, 9 globes, 300 relief models, 1,500,000 satellite imagery and aerial photographs, 700 reference books and gazetteers, 25 serials (titles received), and 21,000 microforms.

DC —LIBRARY OF CONGRESS, Geography and Map Division, Washington, 20540. John A Wolter, Chief
Holdings: Cat Mss Maps Pix Slides Microforms
See also entry under Maps and Atlases - Collections

FL —FLORIDA STATE UNIVERSITY, Robert Manning Strozier Library, Maps Dept, Tallahassee, 32306. Marianne Donnell, Map Librn
Holdings: Vols (3314) Cat Maps Microforms
Notes: Emphasis on Florida and Florida history. Also a depository for USGS topographic maps of the entire US, National Ocean Survey nautical charts of all American waters, Defense Mapping Agency maps, and various special sets issued by National Ocean Survey. Incl 1140 vols of books, bibliographies, and periodicals; 2070 atlases; 136,000 sheet maps; 104 microfilm reels.

GA —UNIVERSITY OF GEORGIA, Libraries, Map Collection, Athens, 30602. John Sutherland, Cur of Maps
Notes: Collection contains 291,165 cataloged maps and 192,068 aerial photographs, specializing in Georgia, Southeast US, Central and South America, and Europe. Major subject specializations are topography, geology, soils and vegetation. Special cartographic collection of Sanborn Fire Insurance Maps (7000 sheets).

ID —IDAHO STATE UNIVERSITY, Library, Pocatello, 83209. Gary Domitz, Social Science Librn
Holdings: Uncat Maps
Notes: Depository for USGS, 11 western states; depository for Defense Mapping Agency Topographic Center; Idaho county maps.

MA —HARVARD UNIVERSITY, Harvard College Library, Map Collection, Cambridge, 02138. Frank E Trout, Cur
Holdings: Cat Mss Maps
Notes: Harvard Map Collection is comprehensive in global coverage and historical depth. Incl books on history and science of cartography, gazetteers, topographic maps, urban plans, and thematic atlases.

MI —UNIVERSITY OF MICHIGAN, Harlan Hatcher Graduate Library, Map Room, Ann Arbor, 48109. James O Minton, Map Librn
Notes: The collection consists of approx 300,000 sheet maps incl maps and charts received on deposit from the US Geological Survey, Defense Mapping Agency, and the National Ocean Service. The collection also incl approx 5000 reference volumes related to cartography, surveying, and mapping, with emphasis on place-name literature (gazetteers, dictionaries), books on how to use and interpret maps, carto-bibliographies, and state (provincial, etc), regional, national, and international atlases. The collection is strongest geographically in materials of Michigan, Midwest, Anglo-America, and Europe; chronologically, 1850-date; and thematically, in topographic and geologic maps, although all subjects are collected. The collection maintains a separate catalog of holdings. Reference volumes are fully cataloged and classified.

TOPOGRAPHIC MAPS (cont.)

NY —BUFFALO & ERIE COUNTY PUBLIC
LIBRARY, History, Travel & Government
Dept, Lafayette Sq, Buffalo, 14203. Ruth
Willet, Head
Holdings: Cat
Notes: Depository for US Geological Survey
Topographic and Geological Quadrangle
Maps; US Army Service Maps; other
uncataloged maps and charts.

OK —OKLAHOMA STATE UNIVERSITY,
Library, Stillwater, 74708. Roscoe Rouse,
Dir
Holdings: Maps Uncat
Notes: Depository for USGS (full);
Depository for Defense Mapping Agency;
Oklahoma. 160,000 maps.

OR —UNIVERSITY OF OREGON, Map
Library, Eugene, 97403. Peter L Stark, Map
Librarian
Holdings: Maps
Budget: ($4000)
Notes: Incl 105,000 maps. Specializations for
topographic maps incl the US, Canada,
Mexico, Central America, and Europe,
produced by national mapping agencies of
each country, the US Defense Mapping
Agency, and Great Britain's Directorate of
Overseas Survey.

PA —PENNSYLVANIA STATE
UNIVERSITY, Fred Lewis Pattee Library,
Maps Section, University Park, 16802. Karl
Proehl, Head
Holdings: Vols (274,000) Maps
Budget: ($3000)
Notes: Depositories for US Geological
Survey topographic maps; Defense mapping
agency topographic maps and nautical
charts; National Ocean Survey nautical and
aeronautical charts; Canadian topographic
maps. Sanborn Fire Insurance maps for
Pennsylvania villages and towns. General
coverage for foreign countries--topographic
and thematic maps. Map catalog by area and
subdivided by subject; atlas catalog by
author-title and area-subject; shelf list
catalogs for maps and atlases. See
*Pennsylvania Maps and Atlases in the
Pennsylvania State University Libraries*, by
Ruby M Miller (Pennsylvania State
University Libraries, 1972. 682 pp).

ON —METROPOLITAN TORONTO
LIBRARY, History Dept, 789 Yonge St,
Toronto, M4W 2G8, Can. Michael Pearson,
Head
Holdings: Maps
Notes: The collection comprises 40,000
maps: current topographic and thematic
maps; depository for the Canadian National
Topographic series; extensive historical
collection specializing in Toronto and
Ontario, incl insurance plans. 700 atlases:
major world atlases, national and regional
atlases; facsimiles of important early atlases,
some originals. 400 current and retrospective
gazetteers.

PQ —MCGILL UNIVERSITY, McLennan
Library, Rare Books and Special Collections
Dept, 3459 McTavish St, Montreal, H3A
1Y1, Can.
Notes: 5524 sheet maps, 370 atlases, 571
folded maps, 629 guide books, 248 reference
books. The coverage is worldwide,
specializing in North America, Canada,
Quebec, Montreal. Includes a collection of
guide books from the 1800s to the present
day, as well as a reference collection; there is
also a large collection of modern
topographical literature with worldwide
coverage, and an important collection of
postcards particularly of Montreal and the
Province of Quebec. A finding list is
available for 19th century guide books on
Canada: *A Preliminary Guide to Nineteenth
Century Canadian Guide Books: a Survey of
the Holdings of the McLennan Library with
an Historical Introduction*. Montreal, 1982.

TOPOLOBAMPO, SINALOA, MEXICO

CA —CALIFORNIA STATE UNIVERSITY,
FRESNO, Henry Madden Library, Dept of
Special Collections, Fresno, 93740. Ronald J
Mahoney, Head
Holdings: Vols 130 Cat Mss Maps Pix
Notes: Archives of Albert Kinsey Owen,

founder of the utopian colony at
Topolobampo, Sinaloa, Mexico. Over 10,000
letters, maps, documents, pictures,
newspapers, pamphlets, and plans, relating to
the colony and the Credit Foncier Company
already represented in the Library by the
Viola Gabriel Collection of about 800 similar
items and nearly 400 photographs. See *Cat's
Paw Utopia*, by Ray Reynolds (El Cajon,
Calif, 1971). Incl 20 linear feet of ms
material. Partially cataloged.

CA —UNIVERSITY OF CALIFORNIA, SAN
DIEGO, Central University Library,
Mandeville Dept of Special Collections, La
Jolla, 92093. Lynda Corey Claassen, Head
Holdings: Vols 15 // Uncat Mss Maps Pix
Notes: Largely manuscript materials,
pamphlets, newspapers.

CA —UNIVERSITY OF CALIFORNIA,
RIVERSIDE, University Library, 4045
Canyon Crest Dr, Box 5900, Riverside,
92517.
Holdings: Vols Cat Mss Maps
Notes: Pamphlets, ms materials, scrapbook
of newspaper articles relating to
establishment of utopian colony, Credit
Foncier of Sinaloa, and a railroad connection
with the US.

TOPONOMY see Names, Geographical

TORIES, AMERICAN see American Loyalists

TORNADOES

OH —GREENE COUNTY DISTRICT
LIBRARY, 76 E Market St, PO Box 520,
Xenia, 45385. Julie M Overton, Local
History Coordr
Holdings: Uncat
Notes: 8 notebooks concerning the killer
tornado which hit Xenia, Ohio on April 3,
1974, which is said to be the worst in US
history. This material consists of 2 vols of
photos, 2 of personal stories, 3 of newspaper
clippings arranged according to subject
matter, 1 of miscellaneous material from
other publications, some national. Also, 10
notebooks called *Xenia Rebuilds*, clippings
concerning all facets of rebuilding from June
1, 1974 to the present, arranged by subject.

TX —TEXAS TECH UNIVERSITY, Library,
Lubbock, 79409. David J Murrah, Assoc Dir
for Special Collections

TORONTO, CANADA

AB —UNIVERSITY OF CALGARY,
Libraries, Special Collections Div, 2500
University Dr, Calgary, T2N 1N4, Can.
Holdings: Cat Mss Pix Audiotapes 16mm
Films Filmstrips
Notes: Collection consists of about 10,000
architectural drawings, office files, records,
correspondence, design notes, etc, from 1938
onwards, of the architectural firm of John B
Parkin, and its successor firms. 35mm
microfilm of early project drawings, as well
as an extensive photographic record of
buildings in progress and completed, and
oral history taped interviews are included.
Projects: Toronto City Hall; Toronto
International Airport; Sunlife Office
Building, Toronto: Simpsons Tower,
Toronto, etc. Project lists and inventories are
on hand 98,000 documents.

ON —METROPOLITAN TORONTO
LIBRARY, Canadian History Dept, Baldwin
Room Section, 789 Yonge St, Toronto,
M4W 2G8, Can. David B Kotin, Head
Holdings: Vols (52,000) Mss Pix
Notes: This collection consists of material on
Canadian history, geography, travel,
archaeology, genealogy, retrospective city
and telephone directories, collective
biographies, native peoples (excluding
customs, rights and social conditions), Arctic
regions, military history and theory. It is an
extremely strong collection of both current
and retrospective material. Particular
strengths are national and local history
(especially Ontario), Arctic regions, native
peoples, travel (especially Ontario), and
military history. Incl 78,000 historical

pictures, 235 linear meters mss, 14,000
broadsides and 3800 bound newspapers.

ON —METROPOLITAN TORONTO
LIBRARY, Canadian History Dept, 789
Yonge St, Toronto, M4W 2G8, Can.
Notes: Bell Canada Telephone Historical
Collection of 448 reels of microfilm of
Ontario and Quebec telephone books from
1878 to 1979. The collection will be
updated. Toronto city directories from 1868-
1949 are available also.

†ON —METROPOLITAN TORONTO
LIBRARY, 789 Yonge St, Toronto, M4W
2G8, Can.
Notes: Over 15,000 drawings, prints, and
paintings, and over 50,000 photographs of
Canadian scenes, as well as portraits from
the 18th century on. Particularly strong in
material relating to the Toronto area from
the founding in 1793.

ON —UNIVERSITY OF TORONTO, Thomas
Fisher Rare Book Library, 120 Saint George
St, Toronto, M5S 1A5, Can. Richard G
Landon, Head
Holdings: Vols 30,000 Mss
Notes: All currently published and most
earlier major works on the fine and applied
arts in Canada; Canadian art exhibition
catalogues; limited editions illustrated by
Canadian artists; 19th and 20th century
architectural plans for buildings in Toronto
and southern Ontario vicinity (ca 1700).

TORONTO GRAND OPERA HOUSE

ON —METROPOLITAN TORONTO
LIBRARY, Theatre Dept, 789 Yonge St,
Toronto, M4W 2G8, Can. Heather
McCallum, Head
Notes: Special collections relating to the
history of the performing arts in Canada incl
the records of the Taverner Company which
played Eastern Canada and the United
States in the late 19th century, Toronto's
Grand Opera House, the Marks Brothers
touring company, film actor Ned Sparks, the
Canadian-born actress Judith Evelyn, Crest
Theatre (Toronto), the Canadian Players,
Montreal Repertory Theatre, dancer/teacher
Boris Volkoff, The Dumbells, the Canadian
all-soldier concert party which originated in
France in 1917, and vaudeville performer
Charles Manny.

TORPEDOES

FL —US NAVAL COASTAL SYSTEMS
CENTER, Technical Information Service
Branch, Panama City, 32407. Myrtle J
Rhodes, Librn
Holdings: Vols (30,000) Cat
Notes: Coastal and ocean technology,
inshore undersea warfare, mine
countermeasures, torpedo defense,
underwater sound.

HI —PACIFIC SUBMARINE MUSEUM,
Library, Naval Submarine Base, Pearl
Harbor, 96860. Ray W de Yarmin, Cur
Holdings: Vols (1500) Cat Mss Maps Pix
Slides Phonorecords 16mm Films
Budget: ($600)
Notes: Incl 3000 pictures. Extensive missile
and torpedo collection; submarine models;
salvage/deep-sea diver exhibit; Arctic
exploration by submarines Worl War II
submarine components. Research program
for students, authors, lecturers, etc.

NY —NEW YORK HISTORICAL SOCIETY,
Library, 170 Central Park W, New York,
10024. James Gregory, Librn
Notes: Randall J LeBoeuf Jr's collection of
Robert Fulton and related material, 1764-
1857, consisting of correspondence,
drawings, legal papers, etc, relating to steam
engines and boats, canals, and torpedoes.
The correspondents incl John Quincy
Adams, Henry Clay, De Witt Clinton, Albert
Gallatin, Benjamin H Latrobe, James
Monroe, John Livingston, Robert R
Livingston, and William Thornton. Also incl
are Fulton's expense and note book, 1802-
1808, and Robert R Livingston's receipt
book, 1808-1812. Approx 215 items,
cataloged.

RI —US NAVAL WAR COLLEGE, Historical
Collection & Museum, Newport, 02841.

TORPEDOES (cont.)

Anthony S Nicolosi, Dir; Evelyn Cherpak, Cur
Holdings: Mss
Notes: Collections incl over 200,000 separate pieces; chiefly papers of naval officers and records of organizations associated with the US Navy, the Naval War College, the college's major study areas, and the Navy in the Narragansett Bay region; oral history collection; Naval War College Archives, 1884-present; records of conferences held at the College; newspaper collections treating with naval themes and military conflicts.

TORRE, THOMAS DELLA

SC —COLLEGE OF CHARLESTON LIBRARY, Special Collections Dept, Charleston, 29401.
Notes: Correspondence within the Lancelot Minor Harris Papers.

TORRENCE, FREDERICK RIDGLEY, 1875-1950

NJ —PRINCETON UNIVERSITY, Library, Manuscript Collection, Nassau St, Princeton, 08540. Jean F Preston, Cur
Holdings: Mss Pix
Notes: The papers fill 120 ms boxes. See *Princeton University Library Chronicle*, v 15, p 213-14.

TORREY, JOHN

NY —NEW YORK BOTANICAL GARDEN LIBRARY, Bronx, 10458. Charles R Long, Asst Vice Pres & Dir
Holdings: Vols 50 Cat
Budget: ($356,000)
Notes: Over 350,000 mss items in botanical history, individuals, societies, and institutions.

TORTOISES see Turtles and Tortoises

TOSCANINI, ARTURO

TX —NORTH TEXAS STATE UNIVERSITY, Audio Center, Box 5188, NT Station, Denton, 76203. Morris Martin, Music Librn
Notes: Tape recordings of all of Don Gillis's compositions, some out of print or never commercially issued (50 reels) performances by Toscanini, Edward Vito, David Guilet, Doc Severinson; papers (correspondence, artifacts, scrapbooks, program notes); mss (incl scores and unpublished autobiography); tape recordings of performances and interviews with/about conductor Arturo Toscanini: NBC Radio series "Toscanini, the Man Behind the Legend" (171 reels).

TOSCANINI, WALTER, 1898-1971

NY —NEW YORK PUBLIC LIBRARY, Performing Arts Research Center, Dance Collection, 111 Amsterdam Ave, New York, 10023. Genevieve Oswald, Cur
Notes: Extensive research materials in dance were donated in 1955-1971 by Dr. Toscanini as a memorial to his wife, ballerina Cia Fornaroli. The Cia Fornaroli Collection now forms an integral part of the Dance Collection and contains many rare and unique items. For a description see Fornaroli, Cia, 1888-1954.

TOSCANINI MEMORIAL ARCHIVES

NY —NEW YORK PUBLIC LIBRARY, Music Div, 111 Amsterdam Ave, New York, 10023. Frank C Campbell, Chief
Notes: Composers' autographs on microfilm. Works of 17-20th century composers. Major holdings: Bach, Handel, Beethoven. Incl mss.

TOTAL ABSTINENCE see Temperance

TOUCH

CT —YALE MEDICAL LIBRARY, 333 Cedar St, New Haven, 06510.
Notes: A special subject emphasis.

TOULOUSE, EDOUARD

NY —CORNELL UNIVERSITY LIBRARIES, Collection of Regional History, Dept of Manuscripts and Univ Archives, Ithaca, 14853.
Notes: 19th century French scientist. Incl mss and letters from Toulouse.

TOURGEE, ALBION W.

OH —RUTHERFORD B HAYES LIBRARY, 1337 Hayes Ave, Fremont, 43420. Watt P Marchman, Dir
Holdings: Vols 35 Cat Mss

TOURISM see Tourist Trade

TOURIST CAMPS, HOTELS, ETC.

DE —WIDENER UNIVERSITY, Delaware Campus Library, Box 7139, Concord Pike, Wilmington, 19803. Jane E Hukill, Library Dir
Holdings: Vols (48,000) Microforms
Notes: Incl food service, restaurants, motels, volume feeding, cookery.

IA —IOWA FALLS PUBLIC LIBRARY, 520 Rocksylvania, Iowa Falls, 50126. Deanne Keller, Librn
Holdings: Vols 707 Cat Maps Filmstrips
Notes: Regional collection includes modes of travel, various kinds of vacations in the US and world-wide. Information on hotels, as well. An additional (150) travel books in the Children's collection.

NH —NEW HAMPSHIRE COLLEGE, Harry A B and Gertrude C Shapiro Library, 2500 N River Rd, Manchester, 03104. Richard Pantano, Dir
Notes: Hotel and restaurant management. Library is a selective US Government Documents depository, and New Hampshire State Documents depository. Subscribe to microfiche SEC 10K reports to AMEX and NYSE (1975-), as well as AMEX and NYSE company annual reports (1977-); AICPA publications and cassettes. Strong collections in accounting; business; business education; computers; hotel and restaurant management; and social service.

TOURIST COURTS see Tourist Camps, Hotels, Etc.

TOURIST TRADE

CO —UNIVERSITY OF COLORADO, Business Research Div, Travel Reference Center, Boulder, 80309. C R Goeldner, Librn; Karen Duea, Librn
Holdings: Vols (8000) Uncat
Budget: ($7000)
Notes: This collection of travel research studies is maintained by the Business Research Division, University of Colorado, and The Travel and Tourism Research Association. Attempts are made to house all studies dealing with travel research.

FL —FLORIDA DEPT OF COMMERCE, Research Library, 408 Fletcher Bldg, Tallahassee, 32301. Dennis Hitchens, Librn
Holdings: Vols (3000) Cat Mss Maps VF
Budget: ($6000)
Notes: Collect materials related to the 2 divisions of the Florida Dept of Commerce: Economic Development and Tourism, incl titles on Florida (historical and current), international trade, transportation, education, employment, management, industrial development and business. The Florida and US documents collection covers population, manufacturing, employment, agriculture, retail trade, wholesale trade and labor. VF incl files on every city and county, especially local economic data, SIC coded material, out-of-state information, county files, Florida specific material and general subject material. 100 VF drawers.

HI —BANK OF HAWAII, Information Ctr, PO Box 2900, Honolulu, 96846. Sally Campbell, Information Mgr
Holdings: Vols 4000 Cat Maps
Notes: Economics research in developing areas of Hawaii, US Pacific Islands, Asian and other foreign countries. Emphasis on economics, business statistics, demography, finance, banking tourist industry, construction, domestic and foreign trade.

IA —IOWA FALLS PUBLIC LIBRARY, 520 Rocksylvania, Iowa Falls, 50126. Deanne Keller, Librn
Holdings: Vols 707 Cat Maps Filmstrips
Notes: Regional collection includes modes of travel, various kinds of vacations in the US and world-wide. Information on hotels, as well. An additional (150) travel books in the Children's collection.

NY —CORNELL UNIVERSITY LIBRARIES, Hotel Administration Library, Statler Hall, Ithaca, 14853. Margaret J Oaksford, Librn
Holdings: Vols (25,000) Cat Mss Maps
Budget: ($60,000)
Notes: Extensive collections on management, travel, hotels, food and beverage, wine, real estate and tourism. Incl menu collection.

WI —UNIVERSITY OF WISCONSIN-STOUT, Library Learning Center, Menomonie, 54751. Philip Sawin Jr, Coll Develop Librn
Notes: Collection emphasis on theory of tourism as well as statistical data.

PR —CARIBBEAN REGIONAL LIBRARY, General Library, University of Puerto Rico, Rio Piedras, (Mailing add: PO Box 21917, University Station, San Juan, 00931). Carmen M Costa de Ramos, Librn
Holdings: Vols (115,605) Cat Maps Pix Microforms
Notes: Collection is specialized in the Caribbean with emphasis in the areas of interest to developing countries: social sciences, politics, economics, labor, education, commerce, tourism, literature, etc. The *Current Caribbean Bibliography* is compiled at the Caribbean Regional Library, with card contributions from all countries of the Caribbean; it also lists all the new additions to the library.

TOURISTS see Tourist Trade

TOURS AROUND THE WORLD see Voyages and Travels

TOWBOATS see Tugboats

TOWN MEETINGS see Local Government

TOWN PLANNING see Cities and Towns—Planning

TOWNS see Cities and Towns

TOWNSEND, SAMUEL

†AL —UNIVERSITY OF ALABAMA, Amelia Gayle Gorgas Library, PO Box S, University, 35486.
Notes: The Alabama collection contains books about Alabama or by Alabama authors; scrapbooks, pamphlets, newspapers. Such ms collections as the Manly Family Papers, 1819-1930; Samuel Townsend, estate papers, 1827-90; Harry Mell Ayers, 1885-1964; and the Gorgas Family Papers, 1821-1920.

TOWNSEND PLAN

CA —UNIVERSITY OF CALIFORNIA, LOS ANGELES, Research Library, Dept of Special Collections, 405 Hilgard Ave, Los Angeles, 90024. Edward Shreeves, Chairman, Bibliographers Group; David S Zeidberg, Head
Notes: Records of the Townsend National Recovery Plan, Inc: 63 linear feet of correspondence, papers, and accounts for the 12th Regional District (Arizona, California, Colorado and Nevada).

TOWNSHIP GOVERNMENT see Local Government

TOXIC SHOCK SYNDROME

MD —NATIONAL LIBRARY OF MEDICINE, 8600 Rockville Pike, Bethesda,

TOXIC SHOCK SYNDROME (cont.)

20209. Harold M Schoolinam, Actg Dir
Budget: ($46,400)

TOXIC SUBSTANCES see Hazardous Substances

TOXICOLOGY

AR —NATIONAL CENTER FOR
TOXICOLOGICAL RESEARCH, Library,
Jefferson, 72079. Susan Laney-Sheehan,
Supvr Librn
Holdings: Vols (15,000) Cat Mss Slides
Audiotapes 16mm Films Microforms
Notes: Incl (860) journal titles, (230) current
subscriptions.

CA —UNIVERSITY OF CALIFORNIA,
BERKELEY, Life Sciences Libraries, Public
Health Library, 42 Earl Warren Hall,
Berkeley, 94720. Thomas J Alexander, Librn
Holdings: Vols (75,000) Cat Microforms
Notes: Research collection covering all
aspects of public health. Health Department
annual reports from all 50 states are
acquired, as well as such reports from all
California health units and from major US
cities. Serial publications issued by Health
Departments in the 13 western states are
being received.

CA —UNIVERSITY OF CALIFORNIA,
DAVIS, Environmental Toxicology Library,
Davis, 95616. Ming-yu Li, Documentation
Specialist
Holdings: Vols (5000) Cat
Notes: Library is open to the public for
reference only in addition to the cataloged
holdings, the library also maintains a
pamphlet collection of 50 file drawers on
agricultural chemicals, environmental
pollution, heavy metals, food toxicants,
toxicology, pesticides and trace elements.

CA —FITZ HUGH LUDLOW MEMORIAL
LIBRARY, PO Box 99346, San Francisco,
94109. Michael R Aldrich, Exec Cur
Holdings: Vols (500) Cat Pix Slides
Phonorecords Videotapes
Notes: We collect many old pharmacopoeias,
dispensatories, formularies, medical history
books and records, old Pharmaceutical
bottles and labels, etc. Valuable for
researching the history of psychoactive drug
use. Incl a small but valuable collection of
works on anesthesia and toxicology.

DE —E I DUPONT DE NEMOURS & CO,
Haskell Laboratory for Toxicology &
Industrial Medicine, Library, Elkton Rd,
Newark, 19711. Nancy S Selzer, Librn
Holdings: Vols (19,000) Cat Microforms

IA —IOWA STATE UNIVERSITY, College of
Veterinary Medicine, Veterinary Medical
Library, Ames, 50011. Sara R Peterson,
Librn
Holdings: Vols (17,000) Cat Microforms
Notes: Incl comparative and veterinary
medicine with emphasis in the fields of
mammalian anatomy and physiology,
laboratory animal medicine, pathology,
toxicology, biomedical engineering and
clinical veterinary medicine. Incl 2000
uncataloged German theses.

MD —NATIONAL LIBRARY OF
MEDICINE, 8600 Rockville Pike, Bethesda,
20209. Harold M Schoolinam, Actg Dir
Budget: ($46,400)

MD —GILLETTE MEDICAL EVALUATION
LABORATORIES, Information Center,
1413 Reasearch Blvd, Rockville, 20034.
Patrick Dexter, Librn
Notes: Incl 12,000 reprints.

MI —WARNER-LAMBERT/PARKE-DAVIS,
Research Library, 2800 Plymouth Rd, Ann
Arbor, 48106. Katherine C Owen, Mgr,
Library Services
Holdings: Vols (27,977) Cat

MI —MICHIGAN STATE UNIVERSITY,
Science Library, East Lansing, 48824. Carole
S Armstrong, Head
Holdings: Vols 700 Cat
Notes: Both books and journals include titles
in English, French, German and Russian,
with a few in other languages. The scope
includes general toxicology, industrial
toxicology, veterinary toxicology, the
toxicology of metals and insecticides, and
poisons as studied in experimental
pharmacology.

MI —THE UPJOHN COMPANY, Corporate
Technical Library, 301 Henrietta St,
Kalamazoo, 49001. Lorraine Schulte,
Manager
Holdings: Cat Microforms Books Journals

NY —MILTON HELPERN LIBRARY OF
LEGAL MEDICINE, 520 First Ave, New
York, 10016. Barry W Seaver, Librn
Holdings: Vols (2480) Cat Pix Slides
Microforms
Notes: Forsensic (legal) medicine (incl
forensic pathology, serology, toxicology and
criminalistics).

NC —NORTH CAROLINA DEPT OF
HUMAN RESOURCES, Div of Health
Services, Public Health Library, PO Box
2091, Raleigh, 27602. Elnora H Turner,
Librn
Holdings: Vols (15,000) Cat

NC —NATIONAL INSTITUTE OF
ENVIRONMENTAL HEALTH
SCIENCES, Library, PO Box 12233,
Research Triangle Park, 27709. W
Davenport Robertson, Head Librn
Holdings: Vols (9000) Cat Mss Audiotapes
Microforms
Notes: The subject, "environmental health,"
incl toxicology, carcinogenesis,
pharmacology, genetics, biophysics, and
biochemistry. Special emphasis is placed on
cell biology. The collection does not incl
works on pollution control or law. In
addition to the collection there are some
2500 vols in the laboratories. The library has
an automated catalog.

OK —CIVIL AERO MEDICAL INSTITUTE
LIBRARY (CAMI), PO Box 25082, AAC
64D1, Oklahoma City, 73125. Darrell R
Goulden, Medical Librn
Holdings: Vols 8500 Cat Mss
Notes: Aviation and aerospace medicine.
About 175 current periodicals.

PA —PHILADELPHIA COLLEGE OF
PHARMACY & SCIENCE, Joseph W
England Library, 42 St & Woodland Ave,
Philadelphia, 19104. Carol H Fenichel, Dir
of Library Services
Holdings: Vols (53,000) Cat Slides
Phonorecords Audiotapes Videotapes 16mm
Films Filmstrips Microforms
Budget: ($132,000)
Notes: Pharmacy and related subjects, incl
pharmacology, international drug
information history of pharmacy and
toxicology. Incl 320 periodical titles, vertical
files.

WI —UNIVERSITY OF WISCONSIN,
MADISON, School of Pharmacy, F B
Power Pharmaceutical Library, 425 N
Charter St, Madison, 53706. Dolores
Nemec, Librn
Holdings: Vols 33,290 Cat Microforms
Notes: Library incl and administers the
unique national historical pharmaceutical
collection known as the Kremers Reference
Files, and various special historical
collections--historical drug catalogs,
historical college catalogs (pharmacy); the
Kremers manuscript encyclopedia of
historical pharmacy; pharmaceutical
corporation reports; representative
prescription books of pharmacies; and the
pharmaco-literary collection. These
collections are regularly supplemented with
new materials, but are not incl in the
library's holdings statement. The special
collections contain about 800 volumes in
book form; the Kremers Reference Files
presently consist of 350 legal-size file
drawers; and the Kremers manuscript
encyclopedia comprises 145 file boxes. The
Kremers Reference Files--which contain
materials from 1850 to date in the form of
letters, laboratoryrecords, minute books of
organizations, biographical sketches,
prescriptions, pictures, panphlets, circulars,
reprints, broadsides, and other printed
matter--provide detailed historical
information mainly relating to
pharmaceutical subjects. Published catalog:
*Catalog of the F B Power Pharmaceutical
Library, School of Pharmacy, University of
Wisconsin, Madison, Wisconsin* (Boston: G
K Hall, 1976), 4 vols.

TOXICOLOGY, ENVIRONMENTAL

MD —NATIONAL LIBRARY OF
MEDICINE, 8600 Rockville Pike, Bethesda,
20209. Harold M Schoolinam, Actg Dir
Budget: ($46,400)

TOXICOLOGY, INDUSTRIAL see Industrial Toxicology

TOY BOOKS

IN —INDIANA UNIVERSITY, Lilly Library,
Seventh St, Bloomington, 47405. William R
Cagle, Librn
Holdings: Uncat Mss
Notes: The Elisabeth Ball Collection consists
of more than 7,000 books and many
manuscripts from the late seventeenth to the
early twentieth centuries. Strengths include
Newbery and other early imprints,
chapbooks, toy books, horn books,
harlequinades, street cries, and miniature
books.

NY —NEW YORK HISTORICAL SOCIETY,
Library, 170 Central Park W, New York,
10024. James Gregory, Librn
Holdings: Mss
Notes: Incl original mss, illustrative
materials, etc.

WI —UNIVERSITY OF WISCONSIN,
MADISON, Cooperative Children's Book
Center, Helen C White Hall, Rm 4290, 600
N Park St, Madison, 53706. Ginny Moore
Kruse, Dir
Holdings: Vols (25,000) Cat
Notes: Cooperative Children's Book Center
collections incl most US trade books
published for children in last 24 months; first
editions of recommended US children's
trade books published since 1965; over 400
alternative press books published for children
in US and Canada since 1970; children's
books about Wisconsin and by Wisconsin
authors and illustrators; representative 19th
and early 20th century American children's
books; 19th century children's periodicals;
first and significant editions of Newbury and
Caldecott Medal books; historical and
contemporary toybooks; 75 vols of Mother
Goose published since 1828; 160 vols of
Thorton Burgess books, many first editions;
ms and original artwork for Ellen Raskin's
The Westing Game and *The Mysterious
Disappearance of Leon (I Mean Noel)*;
juvenile mass market and traderomance
fiction.

ON —TORONTO PUBLIC LIBRARY,
Osborne Collection of Early Children's
Books, 40 St George St, Toronto, M5S 2E4,
Can. Margaret Crawford Maloney, Special
Collections Librn
Holdings: Vols 21,500 Cat Mss Pix Slides
Notes: *Osborne Collection of Early
Children's Books: A Catalogue*, 2 vols,
published by the Toronto Public Library,
1958; 1975. The Osborne collection is
chiefly books published in England from the
fourteenth century through 1910, with first
or early editions in the original languages of
books adopted by English-speaking children.
The Lillian H Smith Collection comprises
distinguished children's books in English
published since 1910, selected for both
literary and artistic qualities. The Canadiana
Collection consists of 3500 children's books
in English by Canadians, about Canada or
published in Canada. Friends of the Osborne
and Lillian H Smith Collections organized in
1966. Worldwide membership (over 600 in
1983). Publishes an annual gift-book for
members (16 titles to date).

ON —UNIVERSITY OF TORONTO, Thomas
Fisher Rare Book Library, 120 Saint George
St, Toronto, M5S 1A5, Can. Richard G
Landon, Head
Notes: Juvenile Drama Collection of
engravings and lithographs of costumed
characters and sets for juvenile dramas to be
cut out and mounted for use in children's
toy theatre productions. Play booklets.
Model stages. Primarily English. Some
European material. Covers period from 1810
to 1940. Basis of the collection formed by

TOY BOOKS (cont.)

Mr Seaton Reid. Includes 6000 sheets and 150 pamphlets.

TOY SOLDIERS AND SAILORS see Military Miniatures

TOY THEATRES

CA —CALIFORNIA POLYTECHNIC STATE UNIVERSITY LIBRARY, Special Collections and University Archives, San Luis Obispo, 93407. Nancy E Loe, Head Librn
Holdings: Vols (100) Cat
Notes: The Puppetry Collection incl many rare European and American imprints in the puppetry field from the 1900s to the 1940s. 2 cubic feet of puppetry journals all from early 1900s to the 1940s.

GA —UNIVERSITY OF GEORGIA, Libraries, Special Collections Division, Athens, 30602. Vesta Lee Gordon, Asst Dir for Special Collections
Notes: Theater Collection contains the Paris Music Hall set and costume designs with original drawings by Erte, Barbier, Zig and others; British Music Hall Papers; European toy theater collection; Charles Coburn papers; television script collection; Tennessee Williams papers. Collection contains 16,000 pieces.

ON —UNIVERSITY OF TORONTO, Thomas Fisher Rare Book Library, 120 Saint George St, Toronto, M5S 1A5, Can. Richard G Landon, Head
Notes: Juvenile Drama Collection of engravings and lithographs of costumed characters and sets for juvenile dramas to be cut out and mounted for use in children's toy theatre productions. Play booklets. Model stages. Primarily English. Some European material. Covers period from 1810 to 1940. Basis of the collection formed by Mr Seaton Reid. Includes 6000 sheets and 150 pamphlets.

PQ —MCGILL UNIVERSITY, McLennan Library, Rare Books and Special Collections Dept, 3459 McTavish St, Montreal, H3A 1Y1, Can.
Holdings: Vols 2680
Notes: Incl books on the puppet theatre, puppets, toy theatres and their theatrical portraits, pantins, prints and posters, located in the Rosalynde Stearn Puppet Collection. A catalogue is available: The Rosalynde Stearn Puppet Collection. Montreal, 1961. Incl 171 puppets.

TOYS

IL —ILLINOIS STATE UNIVERSITY, Milner Library, Dept of Special Collections, Normal, 61761. Robert Sokan, Librn
Holdings: Vols 170 Uncat Mss Pix Tapes
Notes: Correspondence (1935-1957) to Lois Lenski concerning her doll and toy collection and her books for children; correspondence (1956-1970) from Lois Lenski to Milner Library concerning additions to the collections; bookmarks and Christmas cards designed by Miss Lenski; photograph albums; sketchbooks; scrapbooks (contain photographs, correspondence and sketches); original illustrations; handwritten mss (Houseboat Girl, 1957, and Corn Farm Boy, 1953); typewritten mss (Coal Camp Girl, 1959); articles, plays and speeches written by Miss Lenski, newspaper and magazine clippings; and a tape recording entitled A Talk with Lois Lenski.

NY —MARGARET WOODBURY STRONG MUSEUM, 1 Manhattan Square, Rochester, 14607.
Holdings: Vols (20,000) Periodicals
Notes: The Margaret Woodbury Strong Museum Library contains a collection of approx 20,000 books, periodicals and ephemera of and concerning the 19th and early 20th centuries. A large part of the library's holdings reflect the interests of Margaret Strong and her family: domestic life and literature of the 19th century and world travel, with particular emphasis on the

Orient. The library's resources are available to all visitors for research. Book stacks and rare book storage are not open for browsing and do not circulate, but facilities are provided in reading room for study.

PA —CHESTER COUNTY HISTORICAL SOCIETY, 225 N High St, West Chester, 19380. Rosemary B Philips, Librn; Jack McCarthy, Archivist; Laurie Rofini, Asst Archivist
Notes: Books, photographs, mss on early art, architecture, material culture of Chester County. Espec large collection of paper dolls and paper toys (not limited to Chester County, PA).

TRACE ELEMENTS

AR —NATIONAL CENTER FOR TOXICOLOGICAL RESEARCH, Library, Jefferson, 72079. Susan Laney-Sheehan, Supvr Librn
Holdings: Vols (15,000) Cat Mss Slides Audiotapes 16mm Films Microforms
Notes: Incl (860) journal titles, (230) current subscriptions.

CA —UNIVERSITY OF CALIFORNIA, DAVIS, Environmental Toxicology Library, Davis, 95616. Ming-yu Li, Documentation Specialist
Holdings: Vols (5000) Cat
Notes: Library is open to the public for reference only. In addition to the cataloged holdings, the library also maintains a pamphlet collection of 50 file drawers on agricultural chemicals, environmental pollution, heavy metals, food toxicants, toxicology, pesticides and trace elements.

NH —DARTMOUTH COLLEGE, Dartmouth-Hitchcock Medical Center, Dana Biomedical Library, Hanover, 03756. Shirley J Grainger, Librn
Holdings: Vols (6000) Cat Mss
Notes: Collection incl the Henry Schroeder Collection of Papers on Trace Elements.

TRACK AND FIELD SPORTS

CA —UNIVERSITY OF CALIFORNIA, BERKELEY, Bancroft Library, Manuscripts Division, Berkeley, 94720. James D Hart, Dir
Notes: Wide scope but emphasis on the University's teams.

CT —YALE UNIVERSITY, Box 1603A, Yale Station, New Haven, 06520.
Notes: Papers of Walter Camp, father of American football and foremost authority on sports and physical fitness. 48 microfilm reels; incl also over 20,000 clippings, etc on sports, providing virtual history, 1866-1925. Published guide to the collection for sale.

IL —DE PAUL UNIVERSITY, Library, 2323 N Seminary, Chicago, 60614. Kathryn De Graff, Special Collections Librn
Notes: About 1000 vols on British field sports. Also, 20 hand-colored sets of prints by Edward Troye (1808-1874) of American thoroughbred horses.

IL —NATIONAL COUNCIL OF THE YMCAS, YMCA Historical Library, 6400 Shafer Ct, Rosemont, 60018. Eleanor R Murphy, Librn
Notes: Large collection, incl historical material, on basketball, wrestling, track and field, swimming, diving, scuba and volleyball.

IN —UNITED STATES TRACK AND FIELD HALL OF FAME, Angola, 46703.

IN —NATIONAL TRACK AND FIELD HALL OF FAME, USA National Office Athletics Congress, 155 W Washington, Indianapolis, 46204. Berny Wagner, National Coach/Coordr; Ollan Cassel, Exec Dir
Notes: Collection will be located in Hoosier Dome (South Capital Ave, Indianapolis) after its completion. Incl books, film, tapes, and memorabilia.

IN —UNIVERSITY OF NOTRE DAME, University Libraries, Notre Dame, 46556.
Notes: Very likely the largest collection of sporting materials in the world. Over 500 sports and games are represented in a half-million documents. All physical forms of records are included, and there is no geographical restriction. Major center for research into all aspects of games and sports.

TRACTARIANISM see Oxford Movement

TRACTORS

CA —UNIVERSITY OF CALIFORNIA, DAVIS, Shields Library, Dept of Special Collections, Davis, 95616. Donald Kunitz, Head; C Danial Elliott, Asst Head
Notes: Farming equipment: Manufacturer's catalogs, manuals, parts lists, ephemera, and literature pertaining to historical as well as current data on such items as tractors, engines, combines, hay equipment, etc. Described in "The Higgins Library: A Source for the Study of Agricultural History," Don Kunitz, Agricultural History, vol 49, 1975, pp 89-91.

CA —LOS ANGELES PUBLIC LIBRARY, Science & Technology Dept, 630 W Fifth St, Los Angeles, 90071. Billie M Connor, Dept Head
Holdings: Vols 8000 Cat Microforms
Notes: Shop manuals for American and foreign made cars, trucks, motorcycles, and tractors. Specialized manuals on transmissions, air conditioning, air pollution control devices, electrical components, restoration prices, etc. Parts Lists Directories including flat rate and parts price manuals. Indexes include car and other motor vehicles repair manuals by make and model, road tests for specific models appearing in popular automotive periodicals, and an automobile illustration index.

IL —NORTHERN ILLINOIS REGIONAL HISTORY CENTER, Sven Parson Hall, Northern Illinois University, De Kalb, 60115. Glen Gildemeister, Dir
Holdings: Cat Mss Maps Pix Slides Phonorecords Audiotapes 16mm Films Microforms
Notes: "A research center for advanced research in the humanities. This northern area of Illinois (excluding Cook County) has been virtually untouched by collecting agencies and we hope to fill that void. We will be strong in agribusiness, agricultural implement business, and hybrid farming mechanics....Will be primarily a ms repository, but [have] already taken responsibility for many artifacts and books, some rare."

TRACTS

CA —UNIVERSITY OF CALIFORNIA, SAN DIEGO, Central University Library, Mandeville Dept of Special Collections, La Jolla, 92093. Lynda Corey Claassen, Head
Holdings: Vols 7000 Cat
Notes: British tracts. Printed catalog: Political Pamphlets 1640-1968 (Guernsey, Channel Islands, 1968).

FL —UNIVERSITY OF FLORIDA, Libraries, Special Collections, W University Ave, Gainesville, 32611. Sidney Ives, Librn & Rare Books
Holdings: Vols (8000) Cat Mss
Notes: English tracts and sermons from 17th and early 18th centuries.

MO —UNIVERSITY OF MISSOURI-COLUMBIA, Ellis Library, Special Collections Dept, Ninth & Lowry, Columbia, 65201. Margaret A Howell, Head, Special Collections
Holdings: Vols 20,000 // Cat
Notes: 17th, 18th and 19th century English tracts-religious, political and historical. Also British tracts.

NC —DUKE UNIVERSITY, William R Perkins Library, Rare Book Room, Durham, 27706. John L Sharpe, III, Cur
Notes: English pamphlet collection of about 10,000 items. In the main, 17th and 18th century "political history and international relations of Great Britain." French pamphlet collection. Relating to the political, economic and social life of France from the early 18th century down to 1830.

PQ —MCGILL UNIVERSITY, Libraries, Montreal, H3A 1Y1, Can. Marianne Scott, Dir
Notes: The great Redpath Tracts collection containing 17th and 18th century British tracts.

TRACTS (cont.)

PQ —MCGILL UNIVERSITY, McLennan Library, Rare Books and Special Collections Dept, 3459 McTavish St, Montreal, H3A 1Y1, Can.
Notes: British historical, religious, and political pamphlets (20,090 items) dating mainly from the 17th and 18th centuries, are housed in the Redpath Tracts Collection. Also the mss of Carlyon Wilfory Bellairs on early 20th century British politics and those of Henry Hardinge, 1st Viscount Hardinge of Lahore, are housed in the Manuscript Collection.

TRACY, BENJAMIN F.

RI —US NAVAL WAR COLLEGE, Historical Collection & Museum, Newport, 02841. Anthony S Nicolosi, Dir; Evelyn Cherpak, Cur
Holdings: Mss
Notes: Copies of research source materials relating to the life and career of B F Tracy, Secretary of the Navy, 1889-1893, for the work, *Benjamin F Tracy, Father of the American Fighting Navy* by B F Cooling.

TRACY, ROBERT E.

LA —NEW ORLEANS PUBLIC LIBRARY, Louisiana Div, 219 Loyola Ave, New Orleans, 70140. Collin B Hamer Jr, Head; Brenda M Osbey, Library Associate
Holdings: Cat Maps Pix
Notes: Louisiana and New Orleans Picture File Collection ranges from the late 19th century-date and incl the following separate collections: Alexander Allison (ca 1898-1951, 337 pieces); Charles Franck (ca 1920-50, 170 pieces); Leda Plauche (ca 1935-53, 220 pieces); C Milo Williams (ca 1910, 85 pieces); Wilson S Howell (ca 1890, 49 pieces); Grauman Marks (ca 1960, 268 pieces); Robert Tallant (ca 1940-50, 70 pieces); Robert E Tracy (1959, 87 pieces); Anthony J Flaherty (ca 1970-84, 83 pieces); George F Mugnier (1880-1920, 186 pieces); Color Slides (ca 1945-date, 500 pieces); 30,000 photographs incl 500 color slides and 104 negatives. Use of the material is restricted to on-site research. Publication must be accompanied by credit cut line.

TRADE see Business; Commerce

TRADE, INTERNATIONAL see International Trade

TRADE CARDS

CA —UNIVERSITY OF CALIFORNIA, LOS ANGELES, Research Library, Dept of Special Collections, 405 Hilgard Ave, Los Angeles, 90024. Edward Shreeves, Chairman, Bibliographers Group; David S Zeidberg, Head
Notes: 3000 trade and advertising cards, incl cigarette cards, loose and in albums.
CT —YALE UNIVERSITY, Box 1603A, Yale Station, New Haven, 06520.
Holdings: Cat Mss Pix
Notes: A collection of 19th century advertising art, incl trade cards, cards of special interest, books and miscellaneous maps; also vols on the history of 18th and 19th century trade cards and scrapbooks filled with mounted cards.
CT —YALE UNIVERSITY, Sterling Memorial Library, Arts of the Book Collection, New Haven, 06520. Gay Walker, Cur
Notes: 1000 trade cards and American chromolithographs; other turn-of-the-century printed ephemera.
IL —CHICAGO HISTORICAL SOCIETY, Library, Clark St at North Ave, Chicago, 60614. Robert L Brubaker, Librn
Notes: Over 6000 cards, mostly for Chicago firms, arranged by type of firm or subject. Most are illustrated, many in color.
MA —MERRIMACK VALLEY TEXTILE MUSEUM, Library, 800 Massachusetts Ave, North Andover, 01845. Clare Sheridan, Librn; Laurence Gross, Cur
Holdings: Vols (35,000) Cat Mss Maps Pix

Slides
Notes: *Checklist of Prints, Drawings and Painting in the Merrimack Valley Textile Museum*, Helena E Wright, 1972; *Checklist of Finished Textiles*, Katherine R Koob, 1980; *New City on the Merrimack: Prints of Lawrence 1845-1876*, Helena Wright, 1974; *Homespun to Factory Made: Wollen Textiles in America 1776-1876* (exhibit catalog) 1978; *Textile Technology Prints: A Checklist of Prints, Drawings and Paintings in the Merrimack Valley Textile Museum*, Helena E Wright, 1980; *All Sorts of Good Sufficient Cloth: Linen-making in New England, 1640-1860*, (exhibit catalogue) 1980; *The Merrimack Valley Textile Museum: A Guide to the Manuscript Collections* Helena E Wright, Garland Press 1983.
NJ —NEWARK PUBLIC LIBRARY, Art & Music Dept, 5 Washington St, Newark, 07101. William J Dane, Supv
Holdings: Vols (15,000) Cat
Notes: Original prints and fine facsimiles in all major media from 16th century to contemporary times. Study and special exhibition collection of the traditional and current techniques of graphic art with emphasis on late 19th and 20th century artists; ancillary collections of Japanese prints and printed books, trade cards, music covers, greeting cards, bank notes and historic maps.
NJ —RUTGERS, THE STATE UNIVERSITY OF NEW JERSEY, Alexander Library, Special Collections and Archives, College Ave & Huntington St, New Brunswick, 08903. Ronald L Becker, Cur of Manuscripts and Rare Books
Holdings: Uncat
Notes: Trade cards. About 2000 items.
NY —NEW YORK HISTORICAL SOCIETY, Library, 170 Central Park W, New York, 10024. James Gregory, Librn
Holdings: Mss
Notes: Incl original mss, illustrative materials, etc.
NY —MARGARET WOODBURY STRONG MUSEUM, 1 Manhattan Square, Rochester, 14607.
Holdings: Vols (20,000) Periodicals
Notes: The Margaret Woodbury Strong Museum Library contains a collection of approx 20,000 books, periodicals and ephemera of and concerning the 19th and early 20th centuries. A large part of the library's holdings reflect the interests of Margaret Strong and her family: domestic life and literature of the 19th century and world travel, with particular emphasis on the Orient. The library's resources are available to all visitors for research. Book stacks and rare book storage are not open for browsing and do not circulate, but facilities are provided in reading room for study.
NC —DUKE UNIVERSITY, William R Perkins Library, Manuscript Dept, Durham, 27706. Ellen Gartrell, Cur of Mss
Notes: History of advertising. Over 6000 printed items, incl trade cards, pamphlets, leaflets, broadsides, etc, mainly from US 19th-20th centuries. Also hundreds of tobacco premiums and advertising devices, 1880s.
OH —BOWLING GREEN STATE UNIVERSITY, Library, Popular Culture Library, Bowling Green, 43403.
Notes: Extensive holdings of Big-Little books, comic books, matchbook covers, picture postcards, personal scrapbooks, trading cards, posters, magazines, film pressbooks, juvenile series novels and popular literature.

TRADE CATALOGS—COLLECTIONS

AZ —NORTHERN ARIZONA UNIVERSITY, Special Collection Library, CU Box 6022, Flagstaff, 86011. Peter M Whiteley, Coordr/Archivist; William Mullane, Librn
Notes: Old Miner and Hardware Dealer Catalog Collection; contains mining equipment and hardware catalogs from all over the US, representing many different companies. Types of catalogs incl log

machinery, mining, furniture, plumbing goods, explosives, tolls, and all types of machinery, 1900's-1970's.
CA —UNIVERSITY OF CALIFORNIA, DAVIS, Shields Library, Dept of Special Collections, Davis, 95616. Donald Kunitz, Head; C Danial Elliott, Asst Head
Holdings: Uncat Mss Pix Slides
Notes: Manufacturer's catalogs, manuals, parts lists, ephemera, and literature pertaining to histroical as well as current data on such items as tractors, engines, combines, hay equipment, etc. Described in "The Higgins Library: A Source for the Study of Agricultural History," Don Kunitz, *Agricultural History*, vol 49, 1975, pp 89-91. 13,000 vertical files, cataloged.
CA —LOS ANGELES PUBLIC LIBRARY, Science & Technology Dept, 630 W Fifth St, Los Angeles, 90071. Billie M Connor, Dept Head
Holdings: Vols Cat Microforms
Notes: Current trade catalogs in microform of US companies. Selective representative collection in paper copy concentrating on Southern California and others of lasting importance.
CA —CALIFORNIA HISTORICAL SOCIETY, Schubert Hall Library, 2099 Pacific Ave, San Francisco, 94109. Bruce L Johnson, Library Dir
Holdings: Vols (50,000) Cat Mss Maps Pix
See also entry under California--History
CA —UNIVERSITY OF CALIFORNIA, SANTA BARBARA, Library, Dept of Special Collections, Santa Barbara, 93106. Christian F Brun, Head
Notes: Lawrence B Romaine Collection of over 100,000 American trade catalogs, flyers and posters, 1900-1940s; many subjects. Also, his private correspondence.
DE —HAGLEY MUSEUM AND LIBRARY, Eleutherian Mills-Hagley Foundation Inc, PO Box 3630, Greenville, 19807. Richmond D Williams, Dir; Heddy A Richter, Imprints Librn
Holdings: Vols 25,000
Notes: The Library's large collection of trade catalogs are fully accessible through our card catalog with further access provided by a chronological file. The collection emphasizes the products of Delaware Valley and Chesapeake area manufacturers and distributors in the chemical, iron and steel, leather, railway and petroleum industries from 1880 to 1920.
DC —SMITHSONIAN INSTITUTION LIBRARIES, National Museum of American History Branch, Washington, 20560. Rhoda S Ratner, Branch Librn
Holdings: Vols 225,000 Cat Pix
IL —CHICAGO HISTORICAL SOCIETY, Library, Clark St at North Ave, Chicago, 60614. Robert L Brubaker, Librn
Holdings: Vols (150,000) Cat
Notes: Catalogs of major mail order houses and many special industries and stores in Chicago (and some firms elsewhere) since the late 19th century.
IL —MUSEUM OF SCIENCE AND INDUSTRY, Library, 57th St and Lake Shore Dr, Chicago, 60637. Carla Hayden, Coordinator
Holdings: // Cat
Budget: ($10,000)
Notes: Vertical file collection consists largely of industrial trade catalogs, separately indexed by subject (product) and company name.
MA —HARVARD UNIVERSITY, Graduate School of Business Administration, Baker Library, Soldiers Field, Boston, 02163. Mary V Chatfield, Librn; Florence Bartoshesky, Cur of Manuscripts and Archives
Holdings: Cat
Notes: List of *Trade Catalogs* published by Library, 1960.
MA —SOCIETY FOR THE PRESERVATION OF NEW ENGLAND ANTIQUITIES, Library, 141 Cambridge St, Boston, 02114. Ellie Reichlin, Librn & Cur of Photographic Collections
Holdings: Vols (3000) Cat Pix Microforms
Budget: ($75,000)
Notes: Ephemera and trade catalogs illustrating architectural products,

TRADE CATALOGS—COLLECTIONS (cont.)

furnishings, material culture associated with domestic life, Northeast 18th-19th century, some 20th century additions. Cataloged, ca 5000 items.

MA —OLD STURBRIDGE VILLAGE, Research Library, Sturbridge, 01566. Theresa Rini Percy, Librn
Holdings: Vols (23,000) Cat Mss Microforms
Notes: New England to 1850. Incl trade catalogs.

NY —NEW YORK STATE HISTORICAL ASSOCIATION, Library, Lake Rd, Cooperstown, 13326. Amy Barnum, Librn
Holdings: Vols 1600 Cat
Notes: At the present time a marked copy of L B Romaine's Guide to American Trade Catalogs (1960), with additions, serves as a finding aide. Emphasis on New York State industries of the 19th century. Noncirculating.

NY —COLUMBIA UNIVERSITY LIBRARIES, Avery Architectural and Fine Arts Library, 201 Avery Hall, New York, 10027. Angela Giral, Librn
Notes: Trade catalogs from companies manufacturing building materials and architectural elements before 1960. These incl catalogs of paint, neon signs, millwork, houses, tiles, terra cotta, etc.

NY —NEW YORK HISTORICAL SOCIETY, Library, 170 Central Park W, New York, 10024. James Gregory, Librn
Holdings: Mss
Notes: Incl original mss, illustrative materials, etc.

NY —NEW YORK PUBLIC LIBRARY, Performing Arts Research Center, Rodgers & Hammerstein Archives of Recorded Sound, 111 Amsterdam Ave, New York, 10023.
Holdings: Cat Phonorecords Audiotapes
Notes: Major collection of record manufacturers' catalogs from the 1890's to the present.

NY —MARGARET WOODBURY STRONG MUSEUM, 1 Manhattan Square, Rochester, 14607.
Holdings: Vols (20,000) Periodicals
Notes: The Margaret Woodbury Strong Museum Library contains a collection of approx 20,000 books, periodicals and ephemera of and concerning the 19th and early 20th centuries. A large part of the library's holdings reflect the interests of Margaret Strong and her family: domestic life and literature of the 19th century and world travel, with particular emphasis on the Orient. The library's resources are available to all visitors for research. Book stacks and rare book storage are not open for browsing and do not circulate, but facilities are provided in reading room for study. One of the most rapidly growing research tools of the library is the collection of trade catalogs and advertising pieces.

NY —UNIVERSITY OF ROCHESTER, Rush Rhees Library, Department of Rare Books and Special Collections, Rochester, 14627. Peter Dzwonkoski, Librn
Notes: A large collection of American, Canadian, English, French and German trade catalogs of companies producing and dealing in lenses, optical instruments, surveying equipment, microscopes, binoculars, and similar optical and scientific equipment, ca 1890-1950. Also 200 nursery catalogs, mid 19th century to early 20th century.

OH —OHIO HISTORICAL SOCIETY, Archives Library Division, 1982 Velma Ave, Columbus, 43211. Dennis East, Division Chief
Holdings: Vols 1300 Cat
Notes: The collection incl primarily Ohio firms ca 1850-1920; many products.

PA —NEWCOMEN SOCIETY OF THE UNITED STATES, Thomas Newcomen Library of Steam Technology and Industrial History, 412 Newcomen Rd, Exton, 19341.
Holdings: Vols 3500 Cat Mss Pix Slides Microforms
Notes: Steam history and technology. Also, over 1100 trade catalogs.

PA —COLLEGE OF PHYSICIANS OF PHILADELPHIA, Library, 19 S 22 St, Philadelphia, 19103. Christine Ruggere, Cur, Historical Collections
Holdings: Vols (316,223) Cat Mss
Budget: ($1,096,557)
Notes: Very strong collection.
See also entry under Medicine

PA —FRANKLIN INSTITUTE LIBRARY, 20 & The Parkway, Philadelphia, 19103. Miriam Padusis, Dir; Charles Wilt, Readers Servs Librn
Holdings: Vols 50,000 Cat

PA —CARNEGIE LIBRARY OF PITTSBURGH, Science & Technology Dept, 4400 Forbes Ave, Pittsburgh, 15213. Catherine M Brosky, Dept Head
Holdings: Vols (380,000) Cat Maps Microforms
Budget: ($240,000)
Notes: Generally of historical value as current additions were reduced after 1955. Complete set of Sears, Roebuck and Company catalogs from 1888, Sweets Catalogs complete except for 1 or 2 years.

SK —WESTERN DEVELOPMENT MUSEUM, George Shepherd Library, 2935 Melville St, PO Box 1910, Saskatoon, S7K 3S5, Can. Warren Clubb, Research Coordr
Holdings: Vols Pix Audiotapes Film Maps
Notes: Staff reference library. Open to the public although not a lending library. Extensive holdings of agricultural machinery catalogs, from Canadian and American manufacturers and distributors. Other holdings incl automobiles, aviation, museology and Western Canadian history. Partially cataloged.

TRADE FAIRS see Fairs

TRADE NAMES see Business Names; Trademarks

TRADE PERIODICALS see Periodicals, Trade

TRADE UNION LABELS see Labels, Including Trade Union Labels

TRADE UNIONS

CA   UNIVERSITY OF CALIFORNIA, BERKELEY, University Library, Social Science Library, 30 Stephens Hall, Berkeley, 94720. Bette Erskine, Librn
Holdings: Vols 11,000 Cat Mss Microforms
Notes: The Labor Union Collection consists primarily of labor union journals, newspapers, proceedings and constitutions. Holdings are largely national in scope, with emphasis on Northern California. Approximately 850 current serials are being received. This collection is complemented by labor union materials in the Institute of Industrial Relations Library and in The Bancroft Library, and by holdings in Labor History in the Main Library. Incl 1683 microfilm reels.

CA —UNIVERSITY OF CALIFORNIA, BERKELEY, Institute of Industrial Relations Library, 2521 Channing Way Room 110, Berkeley, 94720. Nanette Sand, Librn
Holdings: Vols 50,000 Cat
Notes: Industrial relations, labor, organizational behavior and related subjects. Institute of Industrial Relations Library has separate card catalog (author, title, subject interfiled) but there is no published catalog. Library has a selective collection of books, periodicals, government documents, union and employer publications, publications of university industrial relations institutes and similar research organizations, pamphlets (50,000), etc. It does not incl archival and manuscript materials, or much material published prior to 1950.

CA —CALIFORNIA STATE UNIVERSITY, FULLERTON, Library, Box 4150, Fullerton, 92634. Linda Herman, Special Collections Librn
Holdings: Cat
Notes: Mostly American (some British) newspapers and journals of labor organizations, late 1800s to present. Incl offical labor association publications as well as early Marxist newspapers and bulletins. Approx 800 labor and labor-related publications.

CA —SOUTHERN CALIFORNIA LIBRARY FOR SOCIAL STUDIES & RESEARCH, 6120 S Vermont Ave, Los Angeles, 90044. Sarah Cooper, Dir
Holdings: Vols (15,000) Mss Maps Pix Slides Phonorecords Audiotapes 16mm Films
Budget: ($30,000)
Notes: Marxist, non-Marxist and anti-Marxist approaches to social change. Other important functions of the library: to make available source materials to those engaged in the Marxist vs no-Marxist dialog; to aid historians, economists, sociologists, writers, students and labor organizations researching the history of grassroots social movements; and to preserve primary and secondary sources on labor, minorities, women and radicalism. Collection incl 50 mss, 75 maps, 500 pictures, 1000 slides, 100 phonorecords, 2000 audiotapes, 50 16mm films and 150,000 newspaper clippings.

CO —UNIVERSITY OF COLORADO, Libraries, Western Historical Collections, Boulder, 80309.
Holdings: Mss Pix
Notes: Two collections: (1) Papers of James G Patton (b 1902), a native of Nucla, Colorado, who spent most of his early life in western Colorado. He became interested in the organization of farmers while promoting farmers' cooperative insurance during the early 1930s. He was successively secretary (1932) and president (1937) of the Colorado Farmers Union and an executive board member (1937) and president (1940-1966) of the National Farmers Union. After his retirement he served as an aide to the Pennsylvania Secretary of Agriculture. Throughout his life he has been deeply involved in agriculture in developing countries. The collection contains correspondence, published materials, and typical files on Patton's wide-ranging agricultural, political and social interests. 30 boxes, 85 vols, 1940s-1970s. (2) The Western Federation of Miners was a radicalhard-rock miners' union that began in Montana and spread to Idaho, Washington, Utah, Colorado, Arizona, New Mexico, Nevada, and California. Its successor, Mine-Mill, resurged during the New Deal years. It merged with the United Steelworkers in 1967. This collection consists of 700 boxes of files, correspondence, and publications; 500 bound vols of minutes, ledgers, magazines, and court proceedings; the library of the Research Department, consisting of approx 360 linear feet of books, pamphlets, and periodicals; a number of artifacts and curios incl union banners and seals, convention delegates' ribbons, photographs and membership cards. Most of the materials are for the period 1936-1937. Typescript inventories are available for both collections.

DC —AMERICAN FEDERATION OF LABOR-CONGRESS OF INDUSTRIAL ORGANIZATIONS, Library, 815 16th St NW, Washington, 20006.
Holdings: Vols (20,000) Cat Pix Microforms
Notes: Labor, labor unions, and related subjects. Incl letters of Samuel Gompers (microfilm); constitutions and conference proceedings of international unions.

IN —INDIANA STATE UNIVERSITY, EVANSVILLE, Library, 8600 University Blvd, Evansville, 47712. Gina R Walker, Acting Archivist
Holdings: Vols 50 Cat Mss Pix Slides Audiotapes
Notes: Daily radio programs broadcast (1949-1954) over several Evansville, Indiana, stations concerning activities of the local United Electrical and Radio and Machine Workers of America union; other local union news; state, national, and international events; editorial commentary. Prepared and presented by Sadelle Berger, community leader. 4 document cases. Also materials collected during year-long Indiana Labor History Project. Oral history interviews, photographs, slides, brochures, newspaper clippings.

TRADE UNIONS (cont.)

IN —BALL STATE UNIVERSITY, Alexander
M Bracken Library, Muncie, 47306. Nyal
Williams, Music Librn
Holdings: Vols (30,000) Cat Mss
Budget: ($12,000)
Notes: Incl archives of International Horn
Society, Tubists Universal Brotherhood
Association Library, Cecil Leeson Archival
Saxophone Collection, and Archives of
Buescher Music Instrument Manufacturing
Company.

IN —INDIANA STATE UNIVERSITY,
Cunningham Memorial Library, Dept of
Rare Books & Special Collections, Terre
Haute, 47809. Lawrence J McCrank, Head
Holdings: Uncat Mss Pix
Budget: ($1350)
Notes: The Debs Collection consists of
aprox 7000 pieces of correspondence
between Theodore Debs (brother of E V)
and other persons, such as Sinclair Lewis,
Upton Sinclair, Ethel Barrymore, Emma
Goldman, Robert G Ingersoll, Carl
Sandburg, Norman Thomas, Sacco and
Vanzetti and many others. Many of the
letters are from E V Debs to his brother; a
good portion of these are from the federal
penitentiary at Atlanta. Entire
correspondence file has been microfilmed.
750 pamphlets cover all aspects of the labor
movement, socialism and radical thought
from the 19th century to appprox 1950. A
collection ca 200 related books is also
housed in the collection. See: J Robert
Constantine and Gail Malmgreen, eds, *The
Papers of Eugene V Debs, 1834-1945. A
Guide to the Microfilm Edition.* NY:
Microfilming Corp of America, 1983
(University Microfilms is the new
distributer).

LA —LOUISIANA STATE UNIVERSITY,
SHREVEPORT, Library-Archives, 8515
Youree Dr, Shreveport, 71129. Patricia L
Meador, Archivist & Asst Librn
Notes: Archives incl cataloged manuscripts
and records, 500 maps, more than 5000
photographs, 1000 architectural drawings,
slides, audiotapes, microforms. The
collection includes 25 linear ft of records of
the United Brotherhood of Carpenters and
Joiners of America, Local No 764, (1900-
1980), two reels of the Louisiana State
Council of Carpenters (1941-1980) and two
linear feet of records of the Woman's Union
Label League (1907-1940).

MD —JOHNS HOPKINS UNIVERSITY,
Milton S Eisenhower Library, Charles & 34
Sts, Baltimore, 21218. Ann S Gwyn,
Assistant Dir for Special Collections
Holdings: Vols 8000 Cat
Notes: Begun in 1902, a nearly complete
collection of convention proceedings, official
journals, constitutions, etc, of national
unions and federations (not incl local
unions). Strongest before 1940, *A Trial
Bibliography of American Trade Union
Publications,* was published by Johns
Hopkins University in 1904, 2nd ed in 1907
(Downs 1645, 67). Unique collection.

MD —UNIVERSITY OF MARYLAND,
Library, Archives & Manuscripts Dept,
College Park, 20742. Mary A Boccaccio,
Head
Holdings: Mss Pix
Notes: University of Maryland publications
and archives; collections of organizational
papers (eg, Baltimore & Ohio Railroad;
various organizations concerned with the
Chesapeake Bay and environs; various labor
unions, particularly those involving the
tobacco industry), mostly associated with
Maryland; collections of papers and mss
associated with literary and public figures
(eg, the late Senator Millard Tydings); oral
histories relating to the archival and mss
collections; associated memorabilia;
photographs, mainly associated with
Maryland. A guide to collections of personal,
family, and organizational papers relating to
Maryland is being prepared.

†MA —JOHN F KENNEDY LIBRARY,
Columbia Point, Boston, 02125. Dan H Fenn
Jr, Dir
Holdings: // Cat Microforms
Notes: Copies of AFL-CIO press releases

and records relating to legislation, relations
with the Federal government, and
international affairs, 1955-1968. 9 rolls of
microfilm. Holdings are described in
"Historical Materials in the John F Kennedy
Library." Copies may be obtained by writing
the Research Archivist.

MA —HARVARD UNIVERSITY LIBRARY,
John F Kennedy School of Government
Library, Manpower and Industrial Relations
Collection, Littauer Library, Cambridge,
02138. James C Damaskos, Librn
Holdings: Vols (120,000) Cat
Notes: Major strength is in publications of
labor unions and government documents
relating to labor.

MI —UNIVERSITY OF MICHIGAN,
Graduate School of Business Administration,
Business Administration Library, Institute
for International Commerce Reading Rm,
Ann Arbor, 48109. Carol Holbrook, Dir
Notes: The collection contains historical and
current materials published by business,
government, US labor unions and
associations on employer-employee
relationship, absenteeism, employee benefits,
executive compensation, fair employment
practices, job satisfaction, management
development and performance appraisal.
Labor union publications incl convention
proceedings, constitutions, histories, manuals
for officers and stewards, newspapers, and
research reports. Incl approx (61,000)
cataloged vertical file items.

NY —CORNELL UNIVERSITY, New York
State School of Industrial & Labor Relations,
Martin P Catherwood Library, Ives Hall,
Ithaca, 14853. Shirley F Harper, Dir

NY —CENTER FOR LABOR STUDIES,
SUNY, Empire State College, Labor College
Library, 330 W 42nd St, New York, 10036.
Jayne Adler, Librn
Holdings: Vols (3000) Cat Videotapes VF
Budget: ($4000)
Notes: Areas being emphasized in
development of the library are: Women and
Labor, Occupational Health and Safety, and
Trade Union Leadership.

NY —NEW YORK PUBLIC LIBRARY,
Research Libraries, General Research Div,
Fifth Ave & 42 St, New York, 10018. Keith
McKinney, Assistant Div Chief
Holdings: Cat
Notes: Current periodicals. Subjects incl
advertising, business and professional
periodicals, international affairs, labor and
trade unions, political and social sciences,
humanities in general. Division holds 10,000
titles.

NY —ROCKEFELLER UNIVERSITY,
Rockefeller Archive Center, Hillcrest,
Pocantico Hills, North Tarrytown, 10591.
Joseph W Ernst, Dir; J William Hess, Assoc
Dir
Notes: Papers relative to the Rockefeller
Family, Foundations, University, and other
specific enterprises and contributions to
particular areas of social, physical,
educational, and historic reform,
preservation, conservation, or development.
Extensive records of administrative,
financial, physical, or intellectual
relationships.

OH —BOWLING GREEN STATE
UNIVERSITY, Jerome Library, Center for
Archival Collections, Bowling Green, 43403.
Paul D Yon, Dir; Elaine R Ezell, Reference
Archivist; Nancy Steen, Rare Books Librn
Holdings: Vols (4000) Cat Mss Pix Slides
Maps Microforms
Budget: ($25,000)
Notes: Incl pamphlets; records of 25 major
labor unions document labor history in
northwest Ohio. Complemented also by the
papers of Edward Lamb, a noted Toledo
lawyer active in labor affairs.

PA —UNIVERSITY OF PENNSYLVANIA,
Lippincott Library of the Wharton School,
Philadelphia, 19104. Michael Halperin, Librn
Holdings: Cat Microforms
Notes: Long files of approx 60 titles of labor
union periodicals. Proceedings of annual
conventions of labor unions. An uncataloged
collection of non-current labor union
contracts in pamphlet file drawers.

PA —UNIVERSITY OF PITTSBURGH,
Hillman Library, Archives of Industrial

Society, 363 Hillman Library, Pittsburgh,
15260. Frank A Zabrosky, Cur
Holdings: Documents Mss Pix Newpapers
Audiotapes Microforms
Notes: Records of trade unions, service
employee unions, teacher unions in the 20th
century; personal papers of individuals
involved in the labor union movement.
Unique collection: Msgr Charles Owen Rice
Papers, 1935-.
See also entry under United Electrical,
Radio and Machine Workers.

PA —PENNSYLVANIA STATE
UNIVERSITY, Fred Lewis Pattee Library,
Labor History Collection, University Park,
16802. Peter Gottlieb, Archivist
Holdings: Cat Mss Pix
Notes: Penn State is "provisional repository"
for papers and records of the United Steel
Workers of America, incl records from the
USWA international headquarters in
Pittsburgh and from 29 district offices. A
comprehensive oral history program with
union members is underway. Also, archives
of the now defunct Printing Crafts Union.

BC —UNIVERSITY OF VICTORIA,
McPherson Library, Victoria, V8W 3H5,
Can.
Notes: Incl 60 cm, 1909-56; minute books of
Victoria and District Trades and Labor
Council: mss: 1909-22, 1930-39, typescripts:
1928-56; minute books of Vancouver Island
Joint Labor Conference: typescript, 1942-45;
minute books of Victoria Labor Council of
the Canadian Congress of Labor: mss: 1942-
56; ephemera: Canadian Congress of Labor;
restrictions: by permission of the Victoria
Labor Council.

TRADE UNIONS—EUROPE

DC —LIBRARY OF CONGRESS, European
Division, Washington, 20540.
Notes: The Library of Congress collection of
"Solidarity" and other uncensored Polish
materials incl books, periodicals, documents,
bulletins, cartoons, and posters, most of
which are photocopies of originals held by
other libraries.

PA —UNIVERSITY OF PITTSBURGH,
Hillman Library, Pittsburgh, 15260. Glenora
E Rossell, Head
Holdings: Vols 700 Cat Pix Microforms
Notes: Advanced industrial societies of
Europe. At Hillman Library are cataloged
the publications of political parties and
interest organizations of Austria (7), Belgium
(5), Denmark (8), Finland (6), France (12),
Germany (9), Great Britain (6), Italy (6),
Netherlands (12), Norway (4), Switzerland
(10), Sweden (6). Supplementing this
collection is the general political science
collection which incl OECD publications,
statistics, parliamentary records and
government documents of these countries.
This collection was developed in cooperation
with the 8 university Council on European
Studies.

TRADE UNIONS—FRANCE

WI —UNIVERSITY OF WISCONSIN,
MADISON, Memorial Library, 728 State St,
Madison, 53706. Erwin K Welsch, Social
Studies Bibliographer
Holdings: Vols 2500 Cat Microforms
Notes: Espec strong in the publications of
French trade unions and syndicalist groups
for the period 1870-1940. Incl microfilms of
some syndicalist and trade union periodicals
rarely held in the US, eg *Le Batiment* (1907-
1921), *Bulletin federale des dessinateurs de
France* (1906-1912), *La Bataille Syndicaliste*
(1911-1915), as well as numerous others in
their original format; also memoirs of trade
union leaders and secondary supporting
sources.

TRADE UNIONS—GERMANY

WI —UNIVERSITY OF WISCONSIN,
MADISON, Memorial Library, 728 State St,
Madison, 53706. Erwin K Welsch, Social
Studies Bibliographer
Holdings: Vols 4000 Microforms
Notes: German trade unionism; espec strong

TRADE UNIONS—GERMANY (cont.)

holdings of German trade union periodicals, congress proceedings and protocols, and annual reports for the Weimar Republic Period (1919-1923). Also strong for German labor in the pre-1914 period. Incl memoirs of trade union leaders and secondary supporting sources. Also, microfilms. A typed list of serial holdings is available (and has been microfilmed).

TRADE UNIONS—HISTORY

IL —CHICAGO HISTORICAL SOCIETY, Library, Clark St at North Ave, Chicago, 60614. Archie Motley, Manuscript Librn
Notes: Labor history collections incl these papers: Chicago Newspaper Guild (labor union); Ernest DeMaio (President of District Council 11 United Electrical, Radio & Machine Workers of American UE, leading activist of the political left, international trade unionist); John Fitzpatrick (labor leader, President Chicago Federation of Labor, member Chicago Journeymen Horse Shoers Union); minutes of the Chicago Federation of Labor; Ben Meyers (labor union counsel, particularly those of the politcial left); Irving Meyers (brother of Ben) and his law partner David Rothstein (labor union counsel, particularly those of the politcal left); Agnes Nestor (labor leader, President International Glove Workers Union and the Women's Trade Union League of Chicago); Victor A Olander(Secretary-Treasurer, Illinois State Federation of Labor and the International Seaman's Union of America; member of the Illinois Emergency Relief Commmission); United Scenic Artists Union Local 350; Chicago Typographical Union No 16.
MA —JOHN F KENNEDY LIBRARY, Columbia Point, Boston, 02125. Henry J Gwiazda II, Cur
Notes: The Robert F Kennedy Papers cover the period from 1937-1968 and are divided into four subcollections: the Pre-Administration, Attorney General's, Senate, and 1968 Presidential Campaign Papers. In the Pre-Administration Papers, over 140 archives boxes or 70 percent of the materials are open to research. The Personal and Political Papers of this subcollection are almost entirely open. Most of the unprocessed mss are in the Working Files and involve investigative work on labor racketeering. Seventy five percent or 185 archives boxes of the Attorney General's Papers are open, incl the correspondence, the John F Kennedy Library File, the Speech and Trip Files for 1961-1964. For the Senate Papers, 200 boxes are open for the 1964 Senate Campaign, the Legislative Subject File, and the Speech and Trip Files for 1964-1968. The speeches and press releases(incl in the Senate subcollection Speech File) and "The Black Books" (16 boxes) on state and delegate information are open for the 1968 campaign. Each subcollection has its own finding aid. The Library also has available for research about 100 audiotapes of Robert F Kennedy's public addresses from 1962-1966 and some 50 oral history interviews on RFK and one (1000 pages) by RFK. There are also available the major documentaries on RFK and a number of films donated by the major networks for research use in the Library.
NY —CORNELL UNIVERSITY, New York State School of Industrial & Labor Relations, Martin P Catherwood Library, Ives Hall, Ithaca, 14853. Shirley F Harper, Dir
NY —NEW YORK UNIVERSITY, Elmer Holmes Bobst Library, Div of Special Collections, Tamiment Library of Labor History, Washington Sq, New York, 10012. Dorothy Swanson, Librn
Holdings: Cat Mss Maps Pix Microforms
Notes: Books, pamphlets, newspapers, periodicals and mss. Large microfilm collection. Described in Daniel Bell's *The Tamiment Library* (1969), available free from the Tamiment librarian, and *Elmer Holmes Bobst Library Information Bulletin 8* (updated periodically).

NY —ROCKEFELLER UNIVERSITY, Rockefeller Archive Center, Hillcrest, Pocantico Hills, North Tarrytown, 10591. Joseph W Ernst, Dir; J William Hess, Assoc Dir
Notes: The Rockefeller Archive Center, a division of The Rockefeller University, preserves and makes available to scholars the records of the University, the Rockefeller Foundation, the Rockefeller Brothers Fund, members of the family, and those of other individuals and organizations associated with their endeavors. Collections at the Center document a century of philanthropy by legions of associated social and scientific pioneers, providing a unique window into the past.
OH —BOWLING GREEN STATE UNIVERSITY, Jerome Library, Center for Archival Collections, Bowling Green, 43403. Paul D Yon, Dir; Elaine R Ezell, Reference Archivist; Nancy Steen, Rare Books Librn
Holdings: Vols (4000) Cat Mss Pix Slides Maps Microforms
Budget: ($25,000)
Notes: Incl pamphlets; records of 25 major labor unions document labor history in northwest Ohio. Complemented also by the papers of Edward Lamb, a noted Toledo lawyer active in labor affairs.
FA —BALCH INSTITUTE FOR ETHNIC STUDIES, Library, 18 S Seventh St, Philadelphia, 19106. R Joseph Anderson, Library Dir
TN —MEMPHIS STATE UNIVERSITY, John Willard Brister Library, Memphis, 38152. John Terreno, Special Collections Librn
Notes: 1968 Memphis Sanitation Workers Strike. A collection of audiotape interviews with Memphis governmental officals and administrators, strikers, union leaders, religious leaders, and other significant persons involved in the strike, during which civil rights leader Dr Martin Luther King, Jr was assassinated. Also incl are photographic prints and negatives and the news outakes from the news departments of the three Memphis television stations as well as clippings from newspapers and periodicals. Published finding aid can be found in the Mississippi Valley Collection.

TRADEMARKS

CA —UNIVERSITY OF CALIFORNIA, DAVIS, Shields Library, Dept of Special Collections, Davis, 95616. Donald Kunitz, Head; C Danial Elliott, Asst Head
Notes: Graphic collection of 2500 fruit box labels used by California citrus growers in marketing their produce. Also a collection of 1500 wine labels from various parts of the world. Federal wine label records contain 20,000 label specimens.
MN —MINNEAPOLIS COLLEGE OF ART & DESIGN, Library, 200 E 25 St, Minneapolis, 55404. Richard Kronstedt, Head Librn
†NY —COLUMBIA UNIVERSITY LIBRARIES, Butler Library, Rare Book and Manuscript Library, 535 W 114 St, New York, 10027.
Notes: Prof Milton Handler's papers, correspondence, etc, largely on antitrust and trademark law.
NY —TOBACCO MERCHANTS ASSOCIATION OF THE US, Howard S Cullman Library, Suite 705, 1220 Broadway, New York, 10001. R Robert Sengstacken, Dir Information Servs
Notes: Trademark and brand files for tobacco products and smokers' articles.
NY —UNITED STATES TRADEMARK ASSOCIATION, 6 E 45 St, New York, 10017. Charlotte Jones, Librn
Holdings: Vols 2100 Cat Pix
WI —MILWAUKEE PUBLIC LIBRARY, 814 W Wisconsin Ave, Milwaukee, 53233. Donald J Sager, City Librn
Holdings: Vols Cat
Notes: Complete US Specification and Drawing Collection. Incl British patents. *US Patent and Trademark Gazette,* 1872 to date, *Canadian Patent Office Record and Register of Copyrights and Trademarks,* 1873 to date. The library is a depository for the US Patent and Trademarks Office publications.

TRADES see Building Trades; Industrial Arts; Occupations

TRADES—WASTE see Waste Products

TRADESMEN'S CARDS see Advertising Cards

TRADING POSTS (NORTH AMERICAN INDIAN) see Indians of North America and Mexico—Trading Posts

TRADITION, ORAL see Oral Tradition and Literature

TRADITIONS see Folklore; Legends; Superstition

TRAFFIC, CITY see Traffic Engineering

TRAFFIC ACCIDENTS

MI —UNIVERSITY OF MICHIGAN, Transportation Research Institute, Library, 2901 Baxter Rd, Ann Arbor, 48109. Ann C Grimm, Librn
Holdings: Vols (57,000) Cat Mss Maps Pix Slides Microforms
Budget: ($25,000)
Notes: All aspects of highway safety. All items are cataloged and indexed using a thesaurus developed in-house. Incl engineering medical, biomechanical, psychological, legal, economic and social aspects of highway, vehicle and traffic safety.
MO —SAINT LOUIS POLICE LIBRARY, 315 S Tucker Blvd, Saint Louis, 63102. Cathy Reilly, Librn
Holdings: Vols (21,000) Cat Mss Pix Microforms
Budget: ($18,400)
Notes: Library on all subjects of police work is open to the public for general reference use.

TRAFFIC ACCIDENTS AND ALCOHOLISM see Drinking and Traffic Accidents

TRAFFIC CENSUS see Traffic Surveys

TRAFFIC CONTROL see Traffic Engineering; Traffic Regulations

TRAFFIC ENGINEERING

CA —UNIVERSITY OF CALIFORNIA, BERKELEY, Institute of Transportation Studies Library, Library, 412 McLaughlin Hall, Berkeley, 94720.
Holdings: Vols (82,000)
Budget: ($215,000)
Notes: US Department of Transportation depository through NTIS.
CA —JHK & ASSOCIATES, Technical Library (West), 5801 Christie Ave, Suite 220, Emeryville, 94608. Richard Presby, Librn
Holdings: Vols 55,000 Cat Mss Maps Pix Slides 16mm Films Filmstrips Microforms
Notes: JHK & Associates has 3 branches in a developing library system specializing in traffic and transportation engineering. The Technical Library (West) contains 30,000 vols, 10,000 mss, 500 maps, 1000 pictures, 1000 slides, 400 16mm films, 600 filmstrips, 2500 microforms and 260 feet of VF. The Technical Library (East), 4660 Kenmore Ave, Alexandria, Va 22304, contains some 15,000 vols, 1500 mss, 1000 slides and 20,000 items in VF. The Technical Library in Atlanta has 500 specialized items pertaining to computerized traffic signal systems.
CA —CALIFORNIA DEPT OF TRANSPORTATION, Transportation Library, 5900 Folsom Blvd, PO Box 19128, Sacramento, 95819. Eva Caro, Librn
Holdings: Vols (10,000) Cat Mss Maps Pix Slides Phonorecords Videotapes 16mm Films Filmstrips Microforms
DC —NATIONAL RESEARCH COUNCIL, Transportation Research Board Library, 2101 Constitution Ave NW, Washington,

TRAFFIC ENGINEERING (cont.)

20418. Lisbeth L Luke, Librn
Holdings: Vols (17,000) Cat Microforms VF
Notes: Photocopying available.

IL —BARTON-ASCHMAN ASSOCIATES,
Library, 820 Davis St, Evanston, 60204.
Holdings: Vols (9000) Cat Mss Microforms

IL —NORTHWESTERN UNIVERSITY,
Transportation Center Library, Evanston,
60201. Mary Roy, Librn
Holdings: Vols (116,000)
Notes: The emphasis in this collection is on
current developments in transportation
operations and socioeconomics--
management, planning, impact and
regulation. All modes of transportation and
containerization are incl; the geographic
scope covers domestic and foreign activity at
the urban, intercity and international levels.
Publications on new systems developments
and the application of analytic techniques to
operations are well represented. Incl 19,000
pamphlets; 9000 company reports. *Services
are offered on research conducted outside
Northwestern. A fee schedule is available on
request.* Publications: *Current Literature in
Traffic and Transportation* (bi-monthly
accessions bulletin citing 625 books, reports
and periodical articles per issue).

KY —UNIVERSITY OF KENTUCKY, Robert
E Shaver Library of Engineering, 355
Anderson Hall, Lexington, 40506. Russell H
Powell, Engineering Librn
Holdings: Vols (48,000) Cat Microforms

MI —UNIVERSITY OF MICHIGAN,
Transportation Research Institute, Library,
2901 Baxter Rd, Ann Arbor, 48109. Ann C
Grimm, Librn
Holdings: Vols (57,000) Cat Mss Maps Pix
Slides Microforms
Budget: ($25,000)
Notes: All aspects of highway safety. All
items are cataloged and indexed using a
thesaurus developed in-house. Incl
engineering medical, biomechanical,
psychological, legal, economic and social
aspects of highway, vehicle and traffic safety.

NY —ENGINEERING SOCIETIES
LIBRARY, 345 E 47 St, New York, 10017.
S Kirk Cabeen, Dir
Holdings: Vols 250,000 Cat Maps 16mm
Films Microforms
Notes: One of the largest, most
comprehensive engineering libraries in the
world. Covers all engineering disciplines;
particularly strong in electrical and
electronic, mechanical, mining and
metallurgical, petroleum, chemical,
industrial, air conditioning and refrigeration
engineering. Incl Wheeler Collection of early
materials on magnetism and electricity. 125,
000 bound periodical volumes; 10,000 maps;
5000 serial subscriptions (many foreign-
language). Virtually all materials abstracted
in *Engineering Index* (1884-to date) are incl
in Library. Noncirculating, except to
members of professional engineering
societies which support the Library. See
*Engineering Societies Library, New York,
Classed Subject Catalog and Index* (Boston:
G K Hall, 1963); and *Supplements*, 1-10,
1964-1973.

TRAFFIC REGULATIONS

IL —NORTHWESTERN UNIVERSITY,
Transportation Center Library, Evanston,
60201. Mary Roy, Librn
Notes: Emphasizing police operations
administration and training, traffic law
enforcement, police traffic operations.

TRAFFIC SAFETY

DC —NATIONAL RESEARCH COUNCIL,
Transportation Research Board Library,
2101 Constitution Ave NW, Washington,
20418. Lisbeth L Luke, Librn
Holdings: Vols (17,000) Cat Microforms VF
Notes: Photocopying available.

IL —UNIVERSITY OF ILLINOIS,
URBANA/CHAMPAIGN, Library, Applied
Life Studies Library, 1408 W Gregory Dr,
Urbana, 61801.
Holdings: Vols (38,000) Cat Microforms
See also entry under Physical Education and
Training

MI —UNIVERSITY OF MICHIGAN,
Transportation Research Institute, Library,
2901 Baxter Rd, Ann Arbor, 48109. Ann C
Grimm, Librn
Holdings: Vols (57,000) Cat Mss Maps
Budget: ($25,000)
Notes: Special emphasis on accident
investigation and data analysis, vehicle
dynamics, biomechanical aspects of trauma,
vision and visibility, alcohol and driving.

MO —CENTRAL MISSOURI STATE
UNIVERSITY, Ward Edwards Library,
Warrensburg, 64093. Lonnie Lawson,
Science and Technology Librn
Holdings: Vols (3200) Cat Slides Microforms
Budget: ($3000)
Notes: Safety materials (plus 5200 vertical
file pieces) cover traffic safety, industrial
hygiene, school safety, farm and home
safety.

ON —ROADS & TRANSPORTATION
ASSOCIATION OF CANADA, Library,
1765 St Laurent Blvd, Ottawa, K1G 3V4,
Can. Charles James, Librn
Holdings: Vols (18,000) Cat
Budget: ($8000)
Notes: All areas of ground transportation
and road construction.

TRAFFIC SURVEYS

DC —NATIONAL RESEARCH COUNCIL,
Transportation Research Board Library,
2101 Constitution Ave NW, Washington,
20418. Lisbeth L Luke, Librn
Holdings: Vols (17,000) Cat Microforms VF
Notes: Photocopying available.

MI —UNIVERSITY OF MICHIGAN,
Transportation Research Institute, Library,
2901 Baxter Rd, Ann Arbor, 48109. Ann C
Grimm, Librn
Holdings: Vols (57,000) Cat Mss Maps Pix
Slides Microforms
Budget: ($25,000)
Notes: All aspects of highway safety. All
items are cataloged and indexed using a
thesaurus developed in-house. Incl
engineering medical biomechanical,
psychological, legal, economic and social
aspects of highway, vehicle and traffic safety.

TRAIN, LEONA

NY —STATE UNIVERSITY OF NEW YORK
AT ALBANY, Library, Special Collections
Dept, 1400 Washington Ave, Albany, 12222.
Marion P Munzer, Coordr
Notes: Correspondence, lecture notes,
speeches, mss, clippings dealing with work
by Robert Rienow and his wife, Leona Train,
on wildlife conservation, anti-nuclear
movement, and population control (15 linear
feet).
See also entries under Rienow, Robert;
Population; Wildlife Conservation.

TRAINED NURSES see Nurses and Nursing

TRAINING, PHYSICAL see Physical Education and Training

TRAINING OF ANIMALS see Animals, Training of

TRAINING OF CHILDREN see Children—Management

TRAINING OF EMPLOYEES see Employees, Training of

TRAINING OF THE MEMORY see Mnemonics

TRAMPING see Hiking

TRAMWAYS see Street Railroads

TRANCE

VA —ASSOCIATION FOR RESEARCH &
ENLIGHTENMENT, Library, 67 &
Atlantic Avenue, PO Box 595, Virginia
Beach, 23451. Stephen Jordan, Library Mgr
Holdings: Vols (250) Cat Audiotapes
Notes: Book collection plus Edgar Cayce
Collection of Readings--384 looseleaf binders
with typescripts of 14,250 discourses and
answers given by him in response to
questions while in a trance state. Readings
cover period 1903 to September 1944.
Subjects range from "Attitudes and
Emotions" through "World Affairs" and
"Yoga." Medical files cover common
ailments from "Acne" and "Arthritis"
through "Whooping Cough."

TRANSCAUCASIA see Armenia; Georgia (Transcaucasia)

TRANSCENDENTALISM

MA —FRUITLANDS MUSEUMS LIBRARY,
Prospect Hill, RR 2 Box 87, Harvard, 01451.
Richard S Reed, Dir; John L Crispen,
Admin Secy
Budget: ($21,900)
Notes: Fruitlands (utopian community),
books and manuscripts; New England
Transcendentalism; and Shakers' books and
mss, primarily the Harvard Shaker Society
and Shirley Shaker Society. Secondary
works, general utopia reference.

NC —DUKE UNIVERSITY, William R
Perkins Library, Rare Book Room, Durham,
27706. John L Sharpe, III, Cur
Notes: Carroll Wilson Collection of
Emersoniana. Complete set of first editions,
a number of autograph letters and other
manuscripts, several periodical issues and
association items.

RI —BROWN UNIVERSITY, John Hay
Library, 20 Prospect St, Providence, 02912.
Mark N Brown, Cur Mss
Holdings: Mss
Notes: Several collections relate in whole or
part to New England Transcendentalism.
See, in particular, the George Shepherd
Burleigh, 1821-1903, Collection; the Charles
King Newcomb, 1820-1894, Collection (200
items or more); the Henry David Thoreau,
1817-1862, Collection; the Jones Very
Collection (150 items).

TRANSDUCERS, PIEZOELECTRIC see Piezoelectric Transducers

TRANSIENT LABOR see Migrant Labor

TRANSISTORS AND SEMICONDUCTORS

AZ —MOTOROLA INC, Technical Library,
2200 W Broadway, Mesa, 85202. Denise
Ashford, Managing Sr Librn
Holdings: Vols (5500) Cat Maps

CA —HUGHES AIRCRAFT CO, Solid State
Products Library, 500 Superior Ave,
Newport Beach, 92663. Barbara Squyres,
Librn
Holdings: Vols (4500)
Budget: ($17,000)
Notes: Incl 2600 journal vols and 500
microforms.

PA —ENSANIAN PHYSICOCHEMICAL
INSTITUTE, Electrotopography Library, PO
Box 98, Eldred, 16731. Elisabeth Anahid
Ensanian, Chief Librn
Holdings: Cat Maps Slides
Budget: ($45,000)
Notes: Electrotopography is a new science
(the Institute has pioneered the field and has
coined the terms "electrotopograph" and
"electrotopography") concerned with the
mapping of electrical fields associated with
metals, alloys, semiconductors, and living
organisms. These fields may be natural and/
or induced, and are converted into mappings
which exhibit certain systems characteristics
for both normal and stress states.

PA —FRANKLIN INSTITUTE LIBRARY, 20
& The Parkway, Philadelphia, 19103.
Miriam Padusis, Dir; Charles Wilt, Readers
Servs Librn
Holdings: Vols (300,000) Cat Maps Pix
Microforms

TRANSIT SYSTEMS see Local Transit

TRANSLATIONS

DC —LIBRARY OF CONGRESS, Rare Book
& Special Collections Div, Washington,

TRANSLATIONS (cont.)

20540. William Matheson, Chief
Notes: An archival set of translations sponsored by the Franklin Book Programs (1952-1978), incl 3000 titles translated into Arabic, Persian, Bengali and other languages.

†MA —CLARK UNIVERSITY, Robert Hutchings Goddard Library, Worcester, 01610. Dorothy Mosa Kowski, Rare Books Librn
Holdings: Cat
Notes: Hundreds of vols of Greek and Latin classics in English translation (the Haven Darling Brackett Collection).

OH —PUBLIC LIBRARY OF CINCINNATI & HAMILTON COUNTY, Fiction Dept, 800 Vine St, Cincinnati, 45202. Janet C Wiehe, Head
Holdings: Vols 110,000 Cat
Notes: Circulating collection of approx 58,000 titles; classic and contemporary fiction with emphasis on 19th and 20th century American novels and short stories, and incl a widely representative selection of fiction translated from foreign languages.

PA —PENNSYLVANIA STATE UNIVERSITY, Rare Book Room, University Park, 16802. Charles Mann, Chief, Rare Books and Special Collections
Holdings: Vols (13,000) Cat Mss Pix
Budget: ($24,000)
Notes: The Allison-Shelley Collection of translations of German literature, history, science, medicine, biography, children's literature, and other cultural manifestations into English. Incl 3000 letters and mss of British and American translations of German writings. Also phonograph records of German art songs. Further, the collection contains a large collection of Bayard Taylor's works, letters, and mss. An annotated exhibition catalog of selected items is available from the Office of the Dean of Libraries.

TRANSMISSION OF HEAT see Heat—Transmission

TRANSMUTATION OF METALS see Alchemy

TRANSPERSONAL PSYCHOLOGY

VA —ASSOCIATION FOR RESEARCH & ENLIGHTENMENT, Library, 67 & Atlantic Avenue, PO Box 595, Virginia Beach, 23451. Stephen Jordan, Library Mgr
Holdings: Vols (1800) Cat
Notes: ARE Library Booklist incl 6000 items in 24 subject categories. This special collection is especially strong in the following subjects: astrology, spiritualism, reincarnation, healing arts, Theosophy, Atlantis, parapsychology and transpersonal psychology.

TRANSPLANTATION OF ORGANS, TISSUES, ETC.

CT —YALE MEDICAL LIBRARY, 333 Cedar St, New Haven, 06510.
Notes: A special subject emphasis.

DC —CENTER FOR BIOETHICS, Library, Kennedy Institute, Georgetown University, 3520 Prospect St NW, Washington, 20057. Doris Goldstein, Dir; Judith Mistichelli, Senior Librn
Holdings: Vols 8200
Notes: Largest library of its kind. Incl 31,000 journal articles. Collects in the following subject areas: applied ethics; medical ethics; philosophy of medicine; science, technology and society; sociology of medicine; patient-physician care; sexuality; contraception; abortion; population policy; reproductive technologies; in vitro fertilization; genetic counseling and screening; genetic engineering; mental organ transplantation; death and dying; "baby doe" issues; euthanasia; suicide; use of chemical and biological weapons. Produces computer database Bioethicsline, available through MEDLARS; and the printed annual Bibliography of Bioethics. Other library

publications are: New Titles in Bioethics (monthly); Scope Notes series on current topics.

DC —GEORGETOWN UNIVERSITY, Medical Center, John Vinton Dahlgren Memorial Library, 3900 Reservoir Rd NW, Washington, 20057. Clementine Pellegrino, Librn
Holdings: Vols (1000) Cat Mss Pix Slides
Notes: The Alexis Carrel Collection. Medical research of man and society. Biological specimens and numerous unpublished mss. The Alexis Carrel Collection incl: a complete set of Dr Carrel's scientific notebooks starting in 1906; Col Charles Lindbergh's notebooks from 1935-1939 and those of De Ebeling, Dr Carrel's collaborator for 25 years; the ms of Man the Unknown, numerous specimens of Dr Carrel's work in transplantation of blood vessels, kidney, thyroid and other organs; considerable data on tissue cultivation. Correspondence from 1906 until his death to his wife, brother, cousins, nieces, etc; correspondence to many of the great scientists of the era, as well as all correspondence relating to his book Man the Unknown. There is a separate index to the collection.

ME —JACKSON LABORATORY, Research Laboratory, Bar Harbor, 04609.
Notes: "Subject: Strain Bibliography of inbred strains of mice, transplantable tumors, and named genes in mice ..." Mouse News Letter. Database discontinued 1984, and has become an archival record.

RI —MIRIAM HOSPITAL MEDICAL LIBRARY, 164 Summit Ave, Providence, 02906. Ann LeClaire, Dir of Library Services
Holdings: Cat Cassettes
Notes: Special collection on the renal system with emphasis on kidney transplantation and dialysis.

TX —HOUSTON ACADEMY OF MEDICINE-TEXAS MEDICAL CENTER, Library, Jesse H Jones Library Bldg, Houston, 77030. Elizabeth Borst White, Special Collections Librn
Holdings: Vols (250) Cat
Notes: Historic texts and classic works are collected with emphasis on surgical intervention in cardiovascular disorders and on replacement with artificial materials or transplantation. About 55 of the titles are 19th century works on hematology.

TRANSPORTATION

AL —UNIVERSITY OF ALABAMA, Business Library, Box 2937, University, 35486. Dorothy Eady Brown, Librn; Linda Suttle Harris, Ref Librn and Data Base Searcher
Holdings: Vols (105,000) Cat Microforms
Budget: ($60,000)
Notes: Incl 90,000 corporation reports and 38,500 microforms.

AZ —TUCSON PUBLIC LIBRARY, Governmental Reference Library, PO Box 27210, City Hall, Tucson, 85726. Ann Strickland, Librn
Holdings: Vols (4000) Cat Maps Audiotapes Microforms
Notes: Special emphasis on public administration, including public finance, public personnel management, social services, urban planning, public transportation, public works, water management, solid waste management, public recreation and government of growing southwestern US cities in 200,000 to 500,000 population range.

CA —UNIVERSITY OF CALIFORNIA, BERKELEY, Institute of Transportation Studies Library, Library, 412 McLaughlin Hall, Berkeley, 94720.
Holdings: Vols (82,000)
Budget: ($215,000)
Notes: The ITS Library is an intermodal and interdisciplinary transportation collection containing 105,000 books, reports, pamphlets, and bound serials, and an additional 25,000 reports in microfiche. The library receives 2350 serial titles. Since 1974, almost all federally sponsored reports on transportation have been acquired in

microfiche or paper copy as part of the library's role as a US Department of Transportation depository or through standing orders with the National Technical Information Service.

CA —JHK & ASSOCIATES, Technical Library (West), 5801 Christie Ave, Suite 220, Emeryville, 94608. Richard Presby, Librn
Holdings: Vols 40,000 Cat Mss Maps Pix Slides 16mm Films Filmstrips Microforms
Notes: JHK & Associates has 3 brances in a developing library system specializing in traffic and transportation engineering. The Technical Library (West) contains 30,000 vols, 10,000 mss, 500 maps, 1000 pictures, 1000 slides, 400 16mm films, 600 filmstrips, 2500 microforms and 260 feet of VF. The Technical Library (East), 4660 Kenmore Ave, Alexandria, Va 22304, contains some 15,000 vols, 1500 mss, 1000 slides and 20,000 items in VF. The Technical Library in Atlanta has 500 specialized items pertaining to computerized traffic signal systems.

CA —BURBANK PUBLIC LIBRARY, 110 N Glenoaks Blvd, Burbank, 91502. Mary Ann Grasso, Coordr; Barbara Stones, Coordr, Media Project
Holdings: Vols (32,000) Cat Clippings Pix VF
Notes: The Warner Research Collection is a full service research division designed to serve the production needs of the motion picture, television, theatrical, and creative arts communities. This is a see-based service available by appointment only. Subject specialties include costumes, U.S. military, crime and criminals, transportation, license plates, and Sears catalogues.

CA —ASSOCIATION OF BAY AREA GOVERNMENTS, MTC/ABAG Library, 101 Eighth St, Oakland, 94607. Diane Gillman, Information Coord
Notes: Concentrates heavily on the nine-county Bay Area region. About 10,000 monographs and serials. Title catalog, OCLC/ATS. Central collection of documents for six transit properties in Bay Area.

CA —CALIFORNIA DEPT OF TRANSPORTATION, Transportation Library, 5900 Folsom Blvd, PO Box 19128, Sacramento, 95819. Eva Caro, Librn
Holdings: Vols (10,000) Cat Mss Maps Pix Slides Phonorecords Audiotapes Videotapes 16mm Films Filmstrips Microforms

CO —COLORADO HISTORICAL SOCIETY, Research Collections, 1300 Broadway, Denver, 80203. Catherine Kane, Head Public Service and Access
Holdings: Mss
Notes: Strong ms holdings in western and Colorado business history in such areas as mining, water, transportation, sugar industry.

CO —REGIONAL TRANSPORTATION DISTRICT, Library, 1600 Blake St, Denver, 80202. Dee Harwood, Librn; Debra Martinez, Information Specialist
Notes: Collection is small; the emphasis is local; selective rather than comprehensive.

DC —AIR TRANSPORT ASSOCIATION OF AMERICA, Library, 1709 New York Ave NW, Washington, 20006. Nellis Gysin, Adm Asst
Holdings: Vols 14,000 Cat Maps Pix Microfilm
Budget: $6000
Notes: Emphasis of collection is air transport, its history and economics. Incl standard transportation texts, official administrative and statistical reports of the regulatory agencies, Congressional documents, annual reports of US scheduled airlines, and a limited number of technical reports.

DC —METROPOLITAN WASHINGTON COUNCIL OF GOVERNMENTS, Map Library, 1875 Eye St NW, Suite 200, Washington, 20006. Susan Kalish, Librn
Holdings: Cat Maps
Notes: 3000 current and retrospective maps covering metropolitan Washington region,

TRANSPORTATION (cont.)

incl the District of Columbia; Montgomery and Prince George's counties in Maryland; and Arlington, Fairfax, Prince William and Doudown counties and the City of Alexandria in Virginia. Maps cover land use, community facilities, transportation, topography, statistical units, and socioeconomic information. Record of holdings on computer printout.

DC —NATIONAL RESEARCH COUNCIL, Transportation Research Board Library, 2101 Constitution Ave NW, Washington, 20418. Lisbeth L Luke, Librn
Holdings: Vols (17,000) Cat Microforms VF
Notes: Photocopying available.

DC —SMITHSONIAN INSTITUTION LIBRARIES, National Museum of American History Branch, Washington, 20560. Rhoda S Ratner, Branch Librn
Holdings: Vols (3900) Cat Maps Pix Slides

IL —CHICAGO HISTORICAL SOCIETY, Library, Clark St at North Ave, Chicago, 60614. Robert L Brubaker, Librn
Holdings: Vols (150,000) Cat Mss Maps Pix
Notes: Substantial holdings for the area east of the Mississippi, especially the Midwest, but little on the trans-Mississippi West. Early printed and ms journals and accounts by explorers and by foreign and domestic travelers; emigrants' guides; prints and photographs; 590 atlases; and about 10,000 maps (especially strong for Chicago, Illinois, the Midwest, US transportation, general maps of the US for the period to 1900, and general maps of the Americas from the 16th century to 1850).

IL —CHICAGO TRANSIT AUTHORITY, Anthon Memorial Library, Merchandise Mart Plaza, PO Box 3555, Chicago, 60654. Joseph Benson, Dir
Holdings: Vols (10,000) Cat Maps Slides Microforms
Budget: ($29,200)
Notes: Urban transportation. Use of collection by appointment with Librarian.

IL —BARTON-ASCHMAN ASSOCIATES, Library, 820 Davis St, Evanston, 60204.
Holdings: Vols (9000) Cat Mss Microforms

IL —NORTHWESTERN UNIVERSITY, Transportation Center Library, Evanston, 60201. Mary Roy, Librn
Holdings: Vols (116,000)
Notes: The emphasis in this collection is on current developments in transportation operations and socioeconomics-- management, planning, impact and regulation. All modes of transportation and containerization are incl; the geographic scope covers domestic and foreign activity at the urban, intercity and international levels. Publications on new systems developments and the application of analytic techniques to operations are well represented. Incl 19,000 pamphlets; 9000 company reports. *Services are offered on research conducted outside Northwestern. A fee schedule is available on request.* Publications: *Current Literature in Traffic and Transportation* (bi-monthly accessions bulletin citing 625 books, reports and periodical articles per issue).

IL —ILLINOIS STATE UNIVERSITY, Milner Library, Dept of Special Collections, Normal, 61761. Robert Sokan, Librn
Holdings: Vols 1564 // Uncat Maps Pix
Notes: The Price Transportation Collection. The collection spans the years from 1870 to 1960. Emphasis on railroads and steamships, Incl much material from US and foreign transportation companies.

KY —UNIVERSITY OF KENTUCKY, Robert E Shaver Library of Engineering, 355 Anderson Hall, Lexington, 40506. Russell H Powell, Engineering Librn
Holdings: Vols (48,000) Cat Microforms

KY —KENTUCKY WESLEYAN COLLEGE LIBRARY, 3000 Frederica, Owensboro, 42301. Stuart Stiffler, Dir
Notes: The Dr and Mrs M David Orrahood Collection.

LA —LOUISIANA STATE UNIVERSITY, Middleton Library, Dept of Archives & Manuscripts, Room 202, Baton Rouge, 70803. M Stone Miller Jr, Head
Holdings: Cat Mss Maps Pix Microforms
Notes: History of Louisiana and lower

Mississippi Valley, colonial through 20th century. Scope: political, social and literary history; economic history, incl forestry, banking, agriculture, transportation and trade; national, regional, and Louisiana history; military history. About 4,500,000 items.

MD —MARYLAND-NATIONAL CAPITAL PARK & PLANNING COMMISSION, Montgomery County Planning Department Library, 8787 Georgia Ave, Silver Spring, 20907. Janice C Holt, Librn
Holdings: Vols (5000) Cat Microforms
Notes: Specific subject areas include: community facilities, conservation, economics, flood control, highways, housing, human and natural resources. landscape architecture, open space, parks, pollution, population, recreation, transportation, urban renewal, and zoning. Commission's publications are maintained by Records Management (not Library).

MA —HARVARD UNIVERSITY, Graduate School of Business Administration, Baker Library, Soldiers Field, Boston, 02163. Mary V Chatfield, Librn; Florence Bartoshesky, Cur of Manuscripts and Archives
Notes: An extensive collection. Historical emphasis on railroads and canals.

MA —US DEPT OF TRANSPORTATION, Transportation Systems Center, Technical Reference Center, Kendall Square, Cambridge, 02141. Hadassah Linfield, Dir
Notes: Incl 69,000 books and reports, 36 VF drawers of maps, 250,000 microfiche.

MA —AMERICAN ANTIQUARIAN SOCIETY LIBRARY, 185 Salisbury St, Worcester, 01609. Marcus A McCorison, Dir & Librn
Holdings: Vols 5200 Cat
Notes: Incl the Thomas Winthrop Streeter Collection on Transportation. The finest and most complete documentation of early American railroads, canals, bridges, turnpikes, and harbors in existence.

MI —GREAT LAKES COMMISSION, Institute of Science and Technology Bldg, 2200 Bonisteel Blvd, Ann Arbor, 48109. Michael J Donahue, Natural Resources Specialist
Holdings: Vols (4000)
Notes: Incl directories, reports and related documents covering Great Lakes-related natural resources management, transportation and economic development issues. The library is available for limited public use upon appointment.

MI —UNIVERSITY OF MICHIGAN, Engineering-Transportation Library, 312 Undergraduate Library, Ann Arbor, 48109. Sharon A Balius, Assoc Librn
Holdings: Pix
Budget:
Notes: The print files cover all areas of transportation. The collection contains 12, 000 pieces incl 18th century engravings, lithographs, photographs, reproductions, and originals. Two separate collections of note are the 250 Currier and Ives prints of transportation topics and 100 original drawings by Otto Kuhler, designer of the first streamlined trains.

MI —MICHIGAN STATE UNIVERSITY, Urban Policy & Planning Library, East Lansing, 48824. Dale E Casper, Librn
Holdings: Vols (12,800) Cat
Budget: ($35,000)
Notes: Serves the curricular and research needs of faculty and students involved in urban and regional policy analysis and community planning.

MI —MICHIGAN DEPARTMENT OF TRANSPORTATION, Library, 425 W Ottawa St, Box 30050, Lansing, 48909. Jeanne F Thomas, Librn
Holdings: Vols 25,000 Cat Mss Microforms
Budget: $14,000
Notes: Transportation--engineering and planning. Documentary retrieval system incl selective indexing of 200 journals; Highway Research Board publications and computer service. Separate catalog.

MI —OAKLAND COUNTY REFERENCE LIBRARY, 1200 N Telegraph Rd, Pontiac, 48053. Phyllis Jose, Library Dir
Holdings: Vols (11,000) Cat
Budget: ($34,000)

MN —NORTHEAST MINNESOTA HISTORICAL CENTER, University of Minnesota, Duluth, Library 375, Duluth, 55812. Patricia Maus, Administrator
Notes: The Northeast Minnesota Historical Center is jointly maintained by the University of Minnesota, Duluth, and the St Louis County Historical Society. Local and regional history collections with emphasis on transportation, lumbering, mining. Photograph collection. Photocopy service available.

MN —JAMES JEROME HILL REFERENCE LIBRARY, Fourth St at Market St, Saint Paul, 55106. Virgil F Massman, Dir
Holdings: Vols (197,000) Mss Maps
Budget: ($170,000)
Notes: Railroad history emphasized.

MN —MINNESOTA DEPARTMENT OF TRANSPORTATION, Library, Information Services Section, B-10 Transportation Bldg, Saint Paul, 55155. Jerome C Baldwin, Librn
Notes: Transportation Engineering.

MS —UNIVERSITY OF SOUTHERN MISSISSIPPI, William David McCain Graduate Library, Box 5148, Southern Sta, Hattiesburg, 39406.
Holdings: Cat Mss
Notes: Collections incl the 450 cubic feet of records of the Association of American Railroads for the period 1914-1937; 72 cubic feet of records of the Gulf, Mobile, and Ohio Railroad for the period 1869-1965 (bulk dates 1925-1955); 23 cubic feet of records of the Illinois Central Railroad - Vicksburg, Mississippi Division for the period 1913- 1961; and 245 cubic feet of records of the Mississippi Central Railroad for the period 1898-1967. A guide to these records is available for loan. See entries under the name of the individual railroad.

NE —NEBRASKA STATE HISTORICAL SOCIETY, Fort Robinson Museum, Box 304, Crawford, 69339. Vance Nelson, Cur
Holdings: Vols (1500) Cat Mss Maps Pix Slides Phonorecords Audiotapes 16mm Films Microforms
Notes: Materials related to the history of Fort Robinson, and incl the Post Medical Library, reference books on state goverment, etc, Western Americana: books on ranching, homesteaders, Indian wars, etc; micrifilm records for Fort Robinson records, Red Cloud and Spotted Tail Indian Agency records, Crawford and Chadron Nebraska newspapers, diaries and interviews. Library incl the E Kopac Collection of books dealing with Western Americana; particularly Indian wars, transportation, guns and railroads.

NJ —MIDDLESEX COUNTY PLANNING BOARD, Library, 40 Livingston Ave, New Brunswick, 08901. Lou Mattei, Planning Supervisor, Data Mgt
Holdings: Vols (3500) Cat
Budget: ($500)

NJ —NEW JERSEY DEPT OF TRANSPORTATION, Library, 1035 Parkway Ave, Trenton, 08625. Margaret L Webb, Librn
Holdings: Vols 2000 Cat Mss Maps Microforms
Notes: Emphasis is on highway, bus, rail, and air transportation. There is a finding-list- index to the department archives, over 1800 items.

NY —STATE UNIVERSITY OF NEW YORK, Maritime College, Stephen B Luce Library, Fort Schuyler, Bronx, 10465. Richard H Corson, Librn
Holdings: Vols (68,000) Cat Pix Slides Audiotapes Videotapes 16mm Films Filmstrips Microforms
Budget: ($90,000)
Notes: Incl the *Transportation Masterfile* (1921-1971), comprising a collection of 700, 000 abstracts and annotated entries contained on 140 reels of 35mm microfilm, a subject guide to the microfilm, and a periodicals directory listing in alphabetical arrangement the 2000 current and discontinued international periodicals abstracted and indexed.

NY —COLUMBIA UNIVERSITY LIBRARIES, Rare Book & Manuscript Library, 801 Butler Library, 535 W 114 St, New York, 10027. Kenneth A Lohf, Librn
Notes: More than 32,000 items documenting

TRANSPORTATION (cont.)

the rise of William Russell Grace's shipping business and other materials relating to his career as mayor of New York. Incl records and correspondence relating to all aspects of the shipping business in New York and South America, mining interest in Peru and Chile, and transportation in Costa Rica and Nicaragua. Family memorabilia and photographs, materials concerning New York Politics, banking and insurance, real estate interests and Catholic charities, and letters from Chester A Arthur, John Jacob Astor, Andrew Carnegie, Grover Cleveland, Hamilton Fish, John Hay and J Pierpont Morgan. Restricted use.

NY —NEW YORK PUBLIC LIBRARY, Research Libraries, Science and Technology Research Center, Fifth Ave & 42 St, New York, 10018.
Holdings: Vols (750,000) Cat Microforms
Notes: Incl William B Parsons Collection on Transportation Engineering.

NY —NEW YORK PUBLIC LIBRARY, Research Libraries, Economic & Public Affairs Div, Fifth Ave & 42 St, New York, 10018. Edward DiRoma, Chief
Holdings: Vols (1,500,000) Cat Microforms

OH —CLEVELAND PUBLIC LIBRARY, Business, Economics and Labor Department, 325 Superior Ave, Cleveland, 44114. Joan Sorger, Head
Holdings: Cat
Notes: Currently receiving over 1700 periodicals and 1300 serial titles; 1000 individual trade, industrial and professional directories, worldwide; 324 file drawers annual reports of old companies, many local; 24 drawers historical information on Cleveland companies. Annual reports, 10-K's, Proxy Statements (disclosure SEC filings on fiche); over 200 loose-leaf services; 1700 current telephone and city directories. Emphasis on current material. Areas of special strength are banking, investments, marketing and management. Also strong insurance, accounting, real estate and transportation collections. Computerized sources available incl Dow Jones News Service and a variety of Dialog business-related databases.

PA —DELAWARE COUNTY PLANNING DEPT, Library, Third & Orange St, Media, 19063. Jane Taggart Quin, Librn
Holdings: Vols 4800 Cat
Budget: $1500

PA —MONTGOMERY COUNTY PLANNING COMMISSION, Library, Court House, Norristown, 19404. Robin McLean, Librn
Holdings: Vols (5000) Cat Slides Microfilms
Notes: Emphasis on Montogomery County land use, transportation, and planning.

PA —UNIVERSITY OF PENNSYLVANIA, Towne Scientific Library, 220 S 33 St, Philadelphia, 19104. Charles Meyers, Librn
Holdings: Vols (65,000) Cat

TN —TENNESSEE VALLEY AUTHORITY (TVA), Technical Library, 400 W Summit Hill Dr, E2 B7, Knoxville, 37902. Jesse C Mills, Chief Librn
Holdings: Vols (106,900) Cat Mss Maps Pix Audiotapes Microforms
Budget: ($2,025,000)
Notes: The Technical Library Headquarters Staff (order, cataloging, information, and administration) is located in Knoxville, Tenn. In addition there are branch libraries in Knoxville, Norris, and Chattanooga, Tennessee, and Muscle Shoals, Alabama.

TX —TEXAS A&M UNIVERSITY, Sterling C Evans Library, Documents Div, College Station, 77843. Lisa Abbott, Technical Reports Librn; Jan Swanbeck, Doc Librn
Holdings: Vols Cat Mss Microforms
Notes: Technical Reports Department incl 24,045 state and foreign government reports on water, transportation, and oceanography, as well as servicing the NTIS microfiche collection of 600,000 films.

WI —UNIVERSITY OF WISCONSIN, MADISON, Memorial Library, 728 State St, Madison, 53706. Erwin K Welsch, Social Studies Bibliographer
Notes: James J Hill Transportation Library.

Materials particularly on the history of American and British railroads, among them 5000 vols of company reports most of which have now been sent to the Center for Research Libraries, acquired from 1908 on.

WI —UNIVERSITY OF WISCONSIN, MILWAUKEE, Library, Box 604, Milwaukee, 53201. William C Roselle, Dir
Holdings: Cat Microforms
Notes: Wisconsin Legislative Reference Bureau Clippings File. Special strength in a collection mostly of Wisconsin emphasis. 440 reels of 16mm microfilm. A subject-chronological arrangement (approximately 1200 subjects covering the years from the 1890s through 1970) of pamphlets and a variety of fugitive materials and of clippings from national and Wisconsin newspapers, popular magazines and scholarly journals, and federal, state, and local government documents.

ON —CANADIAN TRANSPORT COMMISSION, Library, Ottawa, K1A 0N9, Can. Marty H Lovelock, Librn
Holdings: Cat Microforms
Budget: ($50,000)
Notes: Books, documents, periodicals. Emphasis on transportation law and economics.

ON —NATIONAL MUSEUMS OF CANADA, Library Services Directorate, Ottawa, K1A 0M8, Can. Valerie Monkhouse, Director
Holdings: Vols 15,500
Budget: $25,000
Notes: History and technology of agriculture, astronomy, aviation, chemistry, communications, computers, electrical engineering, exploration and surveying, fire prevention, forestry, industrial technology, mathematics, medicine, mining, photography, physics, printing, space and transportation. research collection, interlibrary loans available, public may use on the premises.

ON —NATIONAL RESEARCH COUNCIL OF CANADA, Aeronautical/Mechanical Engineering Branch Library, Montreal Rd, Ottawa, K1A 0R6, Can. Louise Fletcher, Head
Notes: This branch library of the Canada Institute for Scientific and Technical Information (CISTI) of the National Research Council of Canada, Ottawa, has a collection strong in aeronautical engineering, automatic control, CAD/CAM, robotics, ocean, wind, and solar energy power, hydraulic and coastal engineering, icing, low temperature research, naval engineering, metals and metallurgy, incl composites, tribology, and air, railroad, marine transportation. Library supported the Council contribution to the development of the remote manipular Canadarm for NASA's Space Shuttle Orbiters and more recently, the Canadian Astronaut Program which will contribute payload specialists to NASA's Space Shuttle Program in 1984. 35,000 monographs, 1200 serials. Report collection: over 500,000 items.

ON —PUBLIC ARCHIVES OF CANADA, Library, 395 Wellington St, Ottawa, K1A 0N3, Can. Dawn E Monroe, Collections Development Officer
Holdings: Vols (80,000) Cat
Notes: The Library has many works, mostly thematic, on the factors which have influenced Canada's economic development. They are largely general works. The Library's collection also contains numerous printed sources on specific sectors such as agriculture, the exploitation of natural resources, commercial trade, financial transactions, industrial production and the development of transportation and communications networks. For those interested in the history of business and financial institutions, there are studies on the major commercial activities involved in fishing, the fur trade, logging and the foreign trde of manufactured goods, raw materials, energy resources and technological products.

ON —ROADS & TRANSPORTATION ASSOCIATION OF CANADA, Library, 1765 St Laurent Blvd, Ottawa, K1G 3V4, Can. Charles James, Librn
Holdings: Vols (18,000) Cat
Budget: ($8000)
Notes: All areas of ground transportation and road construction.

ON —METROPOLITAN TORONTO LIBRARY, Municipal Reference Library, City Hall, Toronto, M5H 2N1, Can. Margot Hewings, Head
Holdings: Vols (60,000) Cat Maps Pix Microforms Slides VF
Budget: ($112,600)
Notes: Community development; municipal finance; local municipal government; housing; urban pollution; urban transportation; urban affairs; urban geography.

TRANSPORTATION—COSTA RICA

†NY —COLUMBIA UNIVERSITY LIBRARIES, Butler Library, Rare Book and Manuscript Library, 535 W 114 St, New York, 10027.
Notes: The papers of William Russell Grace, founder of W R Grace & Co and mayor of New York City, 1880-82 and 1885-86. Documents the rise of the Grace shipping business, mining interests in Peru and Chile, and transportation in Costa Rica and Nicaragua. Also materials concerning New York politics, banking and insurance, real estate interests and Catholic charities.

TRANSPORTATION—FINANCE

DC —INTERNATIONAL MONETARY FUND AND WORLD BANK, Joint Bank-Fund Library, Washington, 20431. Maureen M Moore, Librn
Holdings: Vols Cat Films Microforms
Notes: Incl foreign trade and statistical bulletins and yearbooks, central bank reports and bulletins, budget papers, security yearbooks, economic development plans and reports on economic conditions from the 132 member countries. An index of periodical material compiled by the Library staff has been published as: *Economics and Finance; Index to Periodical Articles, 1947-1971*; First Supplement, 1972, 1973, 1974 (Second Supplement, 1975, 1976, 1977, in preparation), 5 vols. (Boston: G K Hall, 1972, 1975). Also, The Developing Areas: *A Classed Bibliography of the Joint Bank-Fund Library*, Vol 1: *Latin America and the Caribbean*; Vol 2: *Africa and the Middle East*; Vol 3: *Asia and Oceania* (Boston: G K Hall, 1976).

TRANSPORTATION—HISTORY

†AL —MUSEUMS OF THE CITY OF MOBILE, Reference Library, 355 Government St, Mobile, 36602. Caldwell Delaney, Adminr

CA —AZUSA PACIFIC COLLEGE, Marshburn Memorial Library, Citrus & Alosta, Azusa, 91702. Edward Peterman, Librn
Holdings: Vols (6000) Uncat
Budget: ($30,000)
Notes: Significant holdings in the George E Fullerton Library of Californiana and Western Americana.

CA —STANFORD UNIVERSITY LIBRARIES, Cecil H Green Library, Stanford, 94305. Michael T Ryan, Cur
Holdings: Vols (1700) // Cat Mss Maps Pix
Notes: The Timothy Hopkins Transportation Collection. Mss on early railroading in England, India, and US. Construction and operation of Central Pacific. Papers of men connected with Central and Southern Pacific and subsidiaries. United Railroads of San Francisco. Some materials on shipping and aviation.

CA —THE HAGGIN MUSEUM, Petzinger Library of Californiana, 1201 N Pershing Ave, Stockton, 95203. Diane Freggiaro, Librn/Archivist
Holdings: Vols (7000) Cat Mss Maps Pix Slides Audiotapes 16mm Films
Notes: The Petzinger Library is open by appointment only. Special emphasis on Stockton and San Joaquin County and Valley area, local biography, agriculture, agricultural history, industrial history, farm machinery (especially Holt Manufacturing Co, Stockton). There is a photograph collection of 8500 pictures, and extensive manuscript holdings (about 17,000 pieces).

TRANSPORTATION—HISTORY (cont.)

DE —HAGLEY MUSEUM AND LIBRARY,
Eleutherian Mills-Hagley Foundation Inc,
PO Box 3630, Greenville, 19807. Richmond
D Williams, Dir; Heddy A Richter, Imprints
Librn
Holdings: Vols 14,000
Notes: Our collection documents the history
of American technology, especially the
period in which mass production replaced
the American system. Our holdings are
strong in chemical technology,
transportation, explosives, pyrotechnics,
metallurgy and engineering.

DC —NATIONAL RESEARCH COUNCIL,
Transportation Research Board Library,
2101 Constitution Ave NW, Washington,
20418. Lisbeth L Luke, Librn
Holdings: Vols (17,000) Cat Microforms VF
Notes: Photocopying available.

**DC —SMITHSONIAN INSTITUTION
LIBRARIES,** National Museum of American
History Branch, Washington, 20560. Rhoda
S Ratner, Branch Librn
Holdings: Vols (3900) Cat Maps Pix Slides

**IL —MUSEUM OF SCIENCE AND
INDUSTRY,** Library, 57th St and Lake
Shore Dr, Chicago, 60637. Carla Hayden,
Coordinator
Holdings: Vols (15,000) Cat Maps Pix Slides
Budget: ($10,000)
Notes: Occupying the site of the Fine Arts
Building of Chicago's Columbian Exposition
of 1893, the Museum Library has been the
recipient of numerous gifts in this field, not
only of materials from Chicago's Columbian
Expositions, Century of Progress and
Railroad Fairs but also from the New York
World's Fair, St Louis, Paris Exposition
Universelle, San Francisco's Panama-Pacific
etc. Incl blueprints of some buildings and
areas. No separate catalog or index to this
extensive collection.

IN —PURDUE UNIVERSITY LIBRARIES,
Graduate School of Management, Krannert
Library, West Lafayette, 47907. Gordon
Law, Librn
Notes: An important resource at the
Krannert Library is its Special Collection of
Business and Economic, consisting of some
8000 rare pre-20th century strengths in
books, journals, tracts and pamphlets
covering primarily the early literature of
economic thought and business practices in
America and abroad, 1500-1870. A catalog
was issued in 1979.

IA —IOWA FALLS PUBLIC LIBRARY, 520
Rocksylvania, Iowa Falls, 50126. Deanne
Keller, Librn
Holdings: Vols 707 Cat Maps Filmstrips
Notes: Regional collection includes modes of
travel, various kinds of vacations in the US
and world-wide. Information on hotels, as
well. An additional (150) travel books in the
Children's collection.

**MD —BALTIMORE STREETCAR
MUSEUM,** Transit Research Center, 1901
Falls Rd, PO Box 7184, Baltimore, 21218.
George F Nixon, Cur
Holdings: Cat Mss Pix Slides 16mm Films
Notes: Transit Research Center is devoted to
the collection of memorabilia, photos,
drawings, printed matter, etc, pertinent to
public rail transportation in Baltimore and
Maryland. Incl streetcar systems, interurban
lines, and main line railroads in the area.
Also incl bus history. Existing collection
moved to larger facilities (Feb 1978). Incl
materials donated by The Baltimore Transit
Co, United Railways and Electric Co, as well
as private collections.

MD —UNIVERSITY OF BALTIMORE,
Langsdale Library, 1420 Maryland Ave,
Baltimore, 21201. Gerry Watkins, Head of
Special Collections Dept
Holdings: Cat Mss Maps
Notes: Incl the entire stock (10,000 vols) of
Peter Decker, New York antiquarian
bookdealer (acquired in 1970); incl Peter
Decker's mss of his published works and his
records as a dealer in Americana.

MA —HARVARD UNIVERSITY, Graduate
School of Business Administration, Baker
Library, Soldiers Field, Boston, 02163. Mary
V Chatfield, Librn; Florence Bartoshesky,
Cur of Manuscripts and Archives
Notes: An extensive collection. Historical
emphasis on railroads and canals.

**MA —SOCIETY FOR THE PRESERVATION
OF NEW ENGLAND ANTIQUITIES,**
Library, 141 Cambridge St, Boston, 02114.
Ellie Reichlin, Librn & Cur of Photographic
Collections
Holdings: Vols (3000) Cat Pix Microforms
Budget: ($75,000)
Notes: Photograph collections, all media
(incl daguerreotypes, ambrotypes, etc,
stereographic views, carte de visite)
depicting New England buildings; interiors;
street and town views; occupations; pastimes;
transport and personalities. Covers 1840s-
1930s, with some more recent additons.
Amateur and professional photographers
represented. Cataloged in part, otherwise
arranged by localities, subject, personal
name. Special collections incl: marine
photographs by N L Stebbins and Henry
Peabody (1880s-1920s); Boston and Albany
railroad photographic archive, early 1900s;
Quabbin Valley views; historic American
Buildings Survey photographs (17th to early
19th century architecture) by Arthur
Haskell; Baldwin Coolidge collection, and
many others. Size: 500,000 prints, ca 75,000
negatives (glass plates and copy negs). These
are cataloged. Some special indexes
incllandscape design (arbors, conservatories,
flower beds, bandstands etc); photographers
represented; architects represented (partial),
and pending, interiors (specific features of);
occupations.

**MA —AMERICAN ANTIQUARIAN
SOCIETY LIBRARY,** 185 Salisbury St,
Worcester, 01609. Marcus A McCorison,
Dir & Librn
Holdings: Cat Mss Maps Pix
Notes: Outstanding collection, especially for
early period, primarily to 1840; thereafter for
States of the East and Midwest to the Civil
War. Over 6000 items. Incl the Thomas
Winthrop Streeter Collection of
Transportation; much on the history of
canals, bridges, turnpikes, and harbors.

MI —UNIVERSITY OF MICHIGAN,
Engineering-Transportation Library, 312
Undergraduate Library, Ann Arbor, 48109.
Sharon A Balius, Assoc Librn
Holdings: Mss Maps Pix
Budget:
Notes: Incl materials on all phases of
transportation. Especially strong on history
of railroads, canals, roads, and naval
architecture. Incl large collections of prints,
pamphlets, and annual reports and original
materials of Charles Ellet, Jr, Oliver Evans,
Frank Rogers, and Ephraim Shay.

MI —EDISON INSTITUTE, Greenfield
Village and Henry Ford Museum, Archives
& Research Library, PO Box 1970,
Dearborn, 48121. Steve Hamp, Dir; Joan W
Gartland, Librn
Holdings: Vols 400,000 Cat Mss Maps
Microforms
Notes: Incl Dunbar collection of prints,
broadsides and drawings documenting
History of Travel in America, 1680-1910
(1741 items) and the Walker Locomotive
collection, 1820-1931 (308 items). It also
incl 19th century maps and travelers guides
and an antique automotive file.

MI —R E OLDS MUSEUM LIBRARY, 240
Museum Drive, Lansing, 48933.
Notes: Emphasizes the contributions that
Lansing has made to transportation history;
materials on Oldsmobile, Reo, Star, Durant,
and Bates cars. Incl books, manuals,
magazines, advertisements, photographs,
films, slides, audiotapes, videotapes, VF, and
art reproductions.

**MS —UNIVERSITY OF SOUTHERN
MISSISSIPPI,** William David McCain
Graduate Library, Box 5148, Southern Sta,
Hattiesburg, 39406.
Holdings: Cat Mss
Notes: Collections incl the 450 cubic feet of
records of the Association of American
Railroads for the period 1914-1937; 72 cubic
feet of records of the Gulf, Mobile, and Ohio
Railroad for the period 1869-1965 (bulk
dates 1925-1955); 23 cubic feet of records of
the Illinois Central Railroad - Vicksburg,
Mississippi Division for the period 1913-
1961; and 245 cubic feet of records of the
Mississippi Central Railroad for the period
1898-1967. A guide to these records is
available for loan. See entries under the
name of the individual railroad.

**MO —UNIVERSITY OF MISSOURI-
KANSAS CITY,** General Library, Snyder
Collection of Americana, 5100 Rockhill
Road, Kansas City, 64110. Kenneth J
LaBudde, Dir; Robert Paustian, Asst Dir
Holdings: Vols 25,000 Cat
Notes: Nucleus was Robert M Snyder, Jr
Americana Collection of some 14,000 items.
Contains printed materials on 19th-century
American history, especially the Trans-
Mississippi West. Strengths include the
history of Kansas City and Jackson County,
Missouri, Kansas and Missouri county and
state histories, American frontier religion
(esp the Mormons and Alexander
Campbell's Disciples of Christ), the history
of railroads and transportation, the cattle
trade, 19th-Century biography and
autobiography, North American Indians and
early Kansas and Missouri imprints.

**MO —NATIONAL MUSEUM OF
TRANSPORT,** Reference Library, 3105
Barrett Station Rd, Saint Louis, 63122. John
P Roberts, Secretary
Holdings: Vols (10,000) Cat Mss Maps Pix
Slides

MO —WASHINGTON UNIVERSITY,
Libraries, Special Collections Dept, Campus
Box 1061, St Louis, 63130.
Holdings: //
Notes: Records of the St Louis Car
Company, 1887-1973, incl the transportation
manufacturing enterprise's files of over 20,
000 photographs and negatives of the firm's
products; over 2000 original tracings of
railroad and street car equipment. Also
printed material about the firm, and catalogs
published by the company from 1904 to
1965.

**NJ —NEW JERSEY DEPT OF
TRANSPORTATION,** Library, 1035
Parkway Ave, Trenton, 08625. Margaret L
Webb, Librn
Holdings: Vols 2000 Cat Mss Maps
Microforms
Notes: Emphasis is on highway, bus, rail,
and air transportation. There is a finding-list-
index to the department archives, over 1800
items.

NM —MUSEUM OF NEW MEXICO, Photo
Archives, Box 2087, Santa Fe, 87503.
Arthur L Olivas, Cur; Richard Rudisill,
Photo Historian
Holdings: Cat Pix Slides
Notes: Archives incl 200,000 photographs,
cataloged, and 40,000 slides. Primary
function of the archives is to preserve
significant historical material, and these
pictures are mainly for research rather than
general browsing. Photographs may be
ordered as research copies for set fees.
Reproduction or publication requires written
permission plus additional required fees.
Subject matter covered is extensive, incl
Southwest town views, Southwest Indians,
military subjects, missions, pioneer life,
recreation (indoor and outdoor, toys, games,
gambling, camping, etc), disasters, exhibits
and expositions, portraits (those identified
filed by last name), tools and equipment
(agricultural, mechanical, housekeeping, etc),
and transportation (railroad, stagecoaches,
carriages, wagons, etc).

**NY —STATE UNIVERSITY OF NEW
YORK,** Maritime College, Stephen B Luce
Library, Fort Schuyler, Bronx, 10465.
Richard H Corson, Librn
Holdings: Vols (68,000) Cat Maps Pix Slides
Phonorecords Audiotapes Videotapes 16mm
Films Filmstrips
Budget: ($90,000)
Notes: Incl the *Transportation Masterfile*
(1921-1971), comprising a collection of 700,
000 abstracts and annotated entries
contained on 140 reels of 35mm microfilm, a
subject guide to the microfilm, and a
periodicals directory listing in alphabetical
arrangement the 2000 current and
discontinued international periodicals
abstracted and indexed.

TRANSPORTATION—HISTORY (cont.)

NC —NORTH CAROLINA STATE
UNIVERSITY, D H Hill Library, Box 7111,
Raleigh, 27695. I T Littleton, Dir
Holdings: Vols (1500) Cat
Budget: $1500
Notes: Emphasis on the history of railroads.
Incl monographs.
See also entry under Railroads.

TX —PANHANDLE-PLAINS HISTORICAL
MUSEUM, Research Center, Box 967, WT
Sta, Canyon, 79016. Claire R Kuehn,
Archivist-Librn
Holdings: Vols 85 Cat
Budget: $300
Notes: Supplements Museum's wagon and
carriage collections. Incl periodicals and
catalogs.

TX —SOUTHERN METHODIST
UNIVERSITY, DeGolyer Library, Box 396,
SMU, Dallas, 75275. Clifton H Jones, Dir
Holdings: Vols 50,000 Cat Mss Maps Pix
Notes: History of the trans-Mississippi West
and Mexico, from discovery to present.
Original editions of most of the important
early collections of travels.

VA —VIRGINIA POLYTECHNIC
INSTITUTE AND STATE UNIVERSITY
LIBRARY, Blacksburg, 24061. Glenn L
McMullen, Special Collections Librn
Holdings: Vols (1500)
Notes: Collection of primarily nineteenth
century imprints on transportation,
communications, and agricultural
technology; technological encyclopedias and
compendia; books on inventions and
inventors; and travel accounts dealing with
industrial and technological change.

WA —WESTERN WASHINGTON
UNIVERSITY, Center for Pacific Northwest
Studies, High St, Bellingham, 98225. James
W Scott, Dir
Holdings: Vols 400// Cat Mss
Notes: Puget Sound Power and Light
Company Records Collection consists of the
complete company records of 41 former
companies, which were bought out,
amalgamated with or in other ways came
under the control of Puget Sound Power and
light Company. Most of the companies were
concerned with transportation or the
production of power--both gas and
electricity. Among the companies
represented are street railways, interurban
railways, traction companies and gas
companies, all of which operated in the
region west of the Cascades, especially in the
Puget Sound area but with a few as far south
as Vancouver, Washington. The collection
has been placed in the Center for Pacific
Northwest Studies by the Puget Sound
Power and Light Company on a permanent
loan basis.

WY —UNIVERSITY OF WYOMING,
William Robertson Coe Library, Western
History Research Center, Laramie, 82071.
Gene M Gressley, Dir, Asst to Pres
Holdings: Vols (35,000) Cat Mss Maps Pix
Microforms
Notes: The Western History Research
Center of the University of Wyoming's
William Robertson Coe Library has sizable
ms collections in several areas pertaining to
the history and development of the
American West. Principal ms collection
areas incl; cattle industry history, western
literature, mining and petroleum history,
transportation history, and related western
history topics. The collections are
supplemented by a fine Western Americana
book collection cataloged by the main library
but located at the Western History Research
Center.

SK —WESTERN DEVELOPMENT
MUSEUM, George Shepherd Library, 2935
Melville St, PO Box 1910, Saskatoon, S7K
3S5, Can. Warren Clubb, Research Coordr
Holdings: Vols (13,000) Documents Maps
Pix Slides Audiotapes
Notes: Staff reference library. Open to the
public although not a lending library.
Extensive holdings of agricultural machinery
catalogs, from Canadian and American
manufacturers and distributors. Other
holdings incl automobiles, avaition,
museology and Western Canadian history.
Partially cataloged.

TRANSPORTATION—NICARAGUA

†NY —COLUMBIA UNIVERSITY
LIBRARIES, Butler Library, Rare Book and
Manuscript Library, 535 W 114 St, New
York, 10027.
Notes: The papers of William Russell Grace,
founder of W R Grace & Co and mayor of
New York City, 1880-82 and 1885-86.
Documents the rise of the Grace shipping
business, mining interests in Peru and Chile,
and transportation in Costa Rica and
Nicaragua. Also materials concerning New
York politics, banking and insurance, real
estate interests and Catholic charities.

TRANSPORTATION—SAFETY MEASURES

MI —MICHIGAN DEPARTMENT OF
TRANSPORTATION, Library, 425 W
Ottawa St, Box 30050, Lansing, 48909.
Jeanne F Thomas, Librn
Holdings: Vols 25,000 Cat Mss Microforms
Budget: $14,000
Notes: Transportation--engineering and
planning. Documentary retrieval system incl
selective indexing of 200 journals; Highway
Research Board publications and computer
service. Separate catalog.

TRANSPORTATION—STATISTICS

DC —NATIONAL RESEARCH COUNCIL,
Transportation Research Board Library,
2101 Constitution Ave NW, Washington,
20418. Lisbeth L Luke, Librn
Holdings: Vols (17,000) Cat Microforms VF
Notes: Photocopying available.

DC —US BUREAU OF THE CENSUS,
Library, Federal Office Bldg 3, Rm 2451,
Washington, 20233. Betty Baxtresser, Chief,
ASD Library Branch
Holdings: Cat Microforms
Notes: Emphases on statistics of agriculture,
business, construction, economics, foreign
trade, governments, housing, industry,
population, transportation, statistical
methodology, and data processing. Library
holdings are largely current materials
covering the Bureau's programs. Outdated
materials are withdrown regularly.

TRANSPORTATION, AUTOMOTIVE

IL —NORTHWESTERN UNIVERSITY,
Transportation Center Library, Evanston,
60201. Mary Roy, Librn
Holdings: Vols (116,000)
Notes: The emphasis in this collection is on
current developments in transportation
operations and socioeconomics--
management, planning, impact and
regulation. All modes of transportation and
containerization are incl; the geographic
scope covers domestic and foreign activity at
the urban, intercity and international levels.
Publications on new systems developments
and the application of analytic techniques to
operations are well represented. Incl 19,000
pamphlets; 9000 company reports. *Services
are offered on research conducted outside
Northwestern. A fee schedule is available on
request.* Publications: *Current Literature in
Traffic and Transportation* (bi-monthly
accessions bulletin citing 625 books, reports
and periodical articles per issue).

NJ —NEW JERSEY DEPT OF
TRANSPORTATION, Library, 1035
Parkway Ave, Trenton, 08625. Margaret L
Webb, Librn
Holdings: Vols 2000 Cat Mss Maps
Microforms
Notes: Emphasis is on highway, bus, rail,
and air transportation. There is a finding-list-
index to the department archives, over 1800
items.

ON —ROADS & TRANSPORTATION
ASSOCIATION OF CANADA, Library,
1765 St Laurent Blvd, Ottawa, K1G 3V4,
Can. Charles James, Librn
Holdings: Vols (18,000) Cat
Budget: ($8000)
Notes: All areas of ground transportation
and road construction.

TRANSPORTATION, MILITARY

CA —BURBANK PUBLIC LIBRARY, 110 N
Glenoaks Blvd, Burbank, 91502. Mary Ann
Grasso, Coordr; Barbara Stones, Coordr,
Media Project
Holdings: Vols (32,000) Cat Clippings Pix
VF
Notes: The

VA —US ARMY TRANSPORTATION
MUSEUM, Library, Bldg 300, Fort Eustis,
23604. Dennis P Mroczkowski, Museum Cur
Holdings: Vols (1254) Uncat Maps Pix
16mm Films
Budget: ($150)
Notes: Mainly US Army transportation from
WW II on.

ON —NATIONAL MUSEUMS OF
CANADA, Library Services Directorate,
Ottawa, K1A 0M8, Can. Valerie
Monkhouse, Director
Holdings: Vols 12,000 Cat
Budget: ($60,000)
Notes: Collection includes; arms and armour,
military aeronautics, military and naval arts
and sciences, military and naval equipment,
general military and naval history, military
and naval history of Canada. Research
collection, interlibrary loans available, public
may use on the premises.

TRANSPORTATION PERIODICALS see
Periodicals, Transportation

TRANSSEXUALISM AND TRANSSEXUALS

CA —UNIVERSITY OF CALIFORNIA, LOS
ANGELES, Research Library, Dept of
Special Collections, 405 Hilgard Ave, Los
Angeles, 90024. Edward Shreeves,
Chairman, Bibliographers Group; David S
Zeidberg, Head
Notes: 11 linear feet of books, clippings,
audio tapes and ephemera concerning sexual
minorities, collected by Frank E Schreck.

IN —INDIANA UNIVERSITY, Institute for
Sex Research Library, 416 Morrison Hall,
Bloomington, 47401. Douglas Freeman,
Collections and Services Librn; Joan Brewer,
Information Services Librn
Holdings: Vols (62,000) Cat Mss Pix
Microforms
See also entry under Sex

TRANSVESTISM AND TRANSVESTITES

IN —INDIANA UNIVERSITY, Institute for
Sex Research Library, 416 Morrison Hall,
Bloomington, 47401. Douglas Freeman,
Collections and Services Librn; Joan Brewer,
Information Services Librn
Holdings: Vols (62,000) Cat Mss Pix
Microforms
See also entry under Sex.

TRANSYLVANIA (RUMANIA)

IL —UNIVERSITY OF ILLINOIS,
URBANA/CHAMPAIGN, Slavic and East
European Library, Urbana, 61801. Marianna
Tax Choldin, Head
Holdings: Vols (13,000) Cat
Notes: Extensive coverage.

TRAPIER, PAUL

SC —COLLEGE OF CHARLESTON
LIBRARY, Special Collections Dept,
Charleston, 29401.
Notes: Papers, 1860s, incl genealogical
material of the Trapier family and an
account of his family's experiences during
and immediately after the Civil War.

TRAPPING AND TRAPPERS

NY —AMERICAN MUSEUM OF
NATURAL HISTORY, Library Services
Dept, Central Park W & 79th St, New York,
10024. Nina J Root, Chairwoman; Mary
Genett, Asst Librn for Reference Services
Notes: Especially the Ernest Thompson
Seton diaries.

TRAPPING AND TRAPPERS (cont.)

†WA —WASHINGTON STATE
UNIVERSITY, Library, Manuscripts,
Archives & Special Collections, Pullman,
99164. John F Guido, Head
Holdings: Cat Mss Maps Pix
Notes: The Carl Parcher Russell papers, a
vast resource (24,916 items; 45 linear feet)
on American Indian and Western pioneer
activities and artifacts. Much on the fur
trade; pioneer life; mountain men and
trapping; wildlife; primitive life in detail.
Also the National Park Service, parks,
monuments, etc. Described in *Carl Parcher
Russell: An Indexed Register of His
Scholarly and Professional Papers, 1920-
1967, in the Washington State University
Library* (Pullman, 1970), 149 pp.

TRAPS, ANIMAL see Animal Traps; Trapping and Trappers

TRASH see Refuse and Refuse Disposal

TRAUBEL, ANNE MONTGOMERIE

†DC —LIBRARY OF CONGRESS,
Manuscript Division, Washington, 20540.
Notes: The Horace and Anne Montgomerie
Traubel Papers. Horace Traubel was Walt
Whitman's friend and disciple, and one of
his three literary executors.

TRAUBEL, HORACE

†DC —LIBRARY OF CONGRESS,
Manuscript Division, Washington, 20540.
Notes: The Horace and Anne Montgomerie
Traubel Papers. Horace Traubel was Walt
Whitman's friend and disciple, and one of
his three literary executors.

TRAVEL

AL —SAMFORD UNIVERSITY, Special
Collections Library, 800 Lakeshore Dr,
Birmingham, 35229. Annie Ford Wheeler,
Acting Head Librn
Holdings: Uncat Mss Maps Pix Microforms
Notes: The William H Brantley Collection is
in superb condition, consisting of early
works on travels, Indians, and law in the
southeast, plus scarce imprints of Alabama.
CA —CALIFORNIA STATE UNIVERSITY,
FULLERTON, Library, Box 4150,
Fullerton, 92634. Linda Herman, Special
Collections Librn
Holdings: Vols (3530) Cat Mss
Notes: Capt P Markham Kerridge Angling
Collection incl materials on angling,
entomology, ichthyology, conservation,
travel, recreation, and related areas. A
computer author printout with title, imprint,
and various codes is updated annually.
Books and pamphlets are supplemented by
2750 periodical issues, and extensive
ephemera.
†CA —WED ENTERPRISES, Research
Library, 1401 Flower St, Glendale, 91201.
Notes: Popular art and architecture journals,
pictorial material. Library is not open to the
public.
CA —LOS ANGELES PUBLIC LIBRARY,
History Dept, 630 W Fifth St, Los Angeles,
90071. Mary Pratt, Principal Librn
Holdings: Vols 35,000 Cat Maps 16mm
Films Filmstrips Microforms
Notes: Extensive collection of travel books,
designed to cast light on the customs and life
of the people in all countries during all
periods of history. The collection is planned
to provide background materials for writers,
and for the motion picture, radio, and
television industries.
CA —UNIVERSITY OF CALIFORNIA, LOS
ANGELES, Research Library, Dept of
Special Collections, 405 Hilgard Ave, Los
Angeles, 90024. Edward Shreeves,
Chairman, Bibliographers Group; David S
Zeidberg, Head
Holdings: Cat
Notes: 1000 American and foreign posters,
incl dance, exhibitions, student protest
movements, theater, travel, and World Wars
I and II.

CA —POMONA PUBLIC LIBRARY, Special
Collections, 625 S Garey Ave, PO Box 2271,
Pomona, 91766. David Streeter, Librn
Holdings: Uncat Slides
Notes: Contains 550 lantern slides (mostly of
California) and 4200 color 35mm
transparencies of world travel, 1960s. Also,
the Burton Frasher Postal Card Collection of
60,000 negatives and prints of California,
Arizona, Colorado, New Mexico, Nevada,
and Utah; 30,000 world views; 8000
California views. There are also world views
in nearly 1000 stereophotographs.
CO —UNIVERSITY OF COLORADO,
Business Research Div, Travel Reference
Center, Boulder, 80309. C R Goeldner,
Librn; Karen Duea, Librn
Holdings: Vols (8000) Uncat
Budget: ($7000)
Notes: This collection of travel research
studies is maintained by the Business
Research Division, University of Colorado,
and The Travel and Tourism Research
Association. Attempts are made to house all
studies dealing with travel research.
DC —NATIONAL GEOGRAPHIC
SOCIETY, Library, 1146 16th St NW,
Washington, 20036. Susan Fifer Canby, Dir
Holdings: Vols (63,000) Cat Mss Maps Pix
Notes: Material concerning land, sea, and
space exploration--past and present. All
fields of anthropology, natural history,
geography, etc.
HI —BERNICE P BISHOP MUSEUM,
Library, PO Box 19000-A, Honolulu, 96819.
Cynthia Timberlake, Librn
Notes: Early voyages, natural and general
history, archaeology, and ethnology of the
Pacific area. Hawaiian materials incl mss,
maps, 360,000 photographs dating from
1845, and Hawaiian language newspapers.
IN —INDIANA UNIVERSITY, Lilly Library,
Seventh St, Bloomington, 47405. William R
Cagle, Librn
Holdings: Cat Mss
Notes: Books and manuscripts on Scottish
history, genealogy, literature, travel,
topography, and natural history to 1707, and
nineteenth century books of travel and
description.
IA —IOWA FALLS PUBLIC LIBRARY, 520
Rocksylvania, Iowa Falls, 50126. Deanne
Keller, Librn
Holdings: Vols 707 Cat Maps Filmstrips
Notes: Regional collection includes modes of
travel, various kinds of vacations in the US
and world-wide. Information on hotels, as
well. An additional (150) travel books in the
Children's collection.
KY —KENTUCKY WESLEYAN COLLEGE
LIBRARY, 3000 Frederica, Owensboro,
42301. Stuart Stiffler, Dir
Notes: The Dr and Mrs M David Orrahood
Collection.
MA —HISTORIC DEERFIELD-
POCUMTUCK VALLEY MEMORIAL
ASSOCIATION, Libraries, Memorial St,
Box 53, Deerfield, 01342. David R Proper,
Librn
Holdings: Vols (17,000) Cat Mss Maps Pix
Microforms
Notes: Local and regional history, especially
western Massachusetts. Also, remnants of
several collection of books available to early
Deerfield and Greenfield residents. Strong
ms collection dealing within the region's
families, businesses, etc. These consist of
sermons, diaries, town and church records,
voluntary societies' archives, etc. Extensive
collection of photographs of the people and
buildings of Deerfield and its environs, and
travels in Maine, California, and England
(1880s to 1920s). Also, large collection of
glassplate negatives. Houses the Connecticut
Valley Bibliography, a comprehensive card
file on the history and culture of the
Connecticut Valley of Massachusetts.
MI —EDISON INSTITUTE, Greenfield
Village and Henry Ford Museum, Archives
& Research Library, PO Box 1970,
Dearborn, 48121. Steve Hamp, Dir; Joan W
Gartland, Librn
Notes: Incl Dunbar collection of prints,
broadsides and drawings documenting
History of Travel in America, 1680-1910
(1741 items) and the Walker Locomotive

collection, 1820-1931 (308 items). It also
incl 19th century maps and travelers guides
and an antique automotive file.
MN —MINNEAPOLIS PUBLIC LIBRARY &
INFORMATION CENTER, History &
Travel Dept, 300 Nicollet Mall,
Minneapolis, 55401. Robert K Bruce, Head
Holdings: Vols (186,500) Cat Maps
Phonorecords Audiotapes Microforms
MN —UNIVERSITY OF MINNESOTA, O
Meredith Wilson Library, 309 19 Ave S,
Minneapolis, 55455. Austin J McLean,
Chief, Special Collections
Holdings: Cat
Notes: Predominantly 19th century accounts
of travelers in the Scandinavian countries.
MO —WASHINGTON UNIVERSITY, John
M Olin Library, Campus Box 1061, St Louis,
63130.
Holdings: Vols (1800) Cat Mss
Notes: Incl material from the Arthur C
Hoskins, Richard S Hawes, Ernst C Krohn,
George N Meissner, Stratford Lee Morton,
and Edgar M Queeny collections; strong in
early travel literature of the US and Latin
America; accounts of exploration in the
Mississippi Valley and Trans-Mississippi
West; miscellaneous accounts of history,
pioneer life, and travel in the Ohio Valley,
Old Southwest, and California; material on
the American Indian; 18th century
American music; early American imprints.
NY —CORNELL UNIVERSITY LIBRARIES,
Hotel Administration Library, Statler Hall,
Ithaca, 14853. Margaret J Oaksford, Librn
Holdings: Vols (25,000) Cat Mss Maps
Budget: ($60,000)
Notes: Extensive collections on
management, travel, hotels, food and
beverage, wine, real estate and tourism. Incl
menu collection.
NY —NEW YORK PUBLIC LIBRARY,
Research Libraries, General Research
Division, Fifth Ave & 42 St, New York,
10018. Rodney Phillips, Chief
Holdings: Vols (2,225,000) Cat Maps Pix
Microforms
Budget: ($775,718)
NY —NEW YORK SOCIETY LIBRARY, 53
E 79 St, New York, 10021. Mark Piel, Librn
Holdings: 3500 Vols
Notes: Travel and world explorers in 19th
century.
OH —OHIO UNIVERSITY, Vernon R Alden
Library, Department of Archives and Special
Collections, Athens, 45701. Gary A Hunt,
Head
Holdings: Vols 400 Uncat
Notes: Tourist guidebooks, 1850-1950,
mostly British Isles and European countries,
incl 90 Baedekers and 80 Murrays.
OH —OHIO HISTORICAL SOCIETY,
Archives Library Division, 1982 Velma Ave,
Columbus, 43211. Dennis East, Division
Chief
Holdings: Vols 2000// Cat Mss Pix
Notes: Collection is comprised of books by
Grey, magazines in which his writings
appeared, mss & typescripts, and 700 items
from his personal library, incl scarce items
on hunting, big-game fishing, and travel.
Museum objects are at the Zane Grey
Museum, Zanesville, Ohio, operated by the
Ohio Historical Society.
RI —PROVIDENCE ATHENAEUM, 251
Benefit St, Providence, 02903. Sally Duplaix,
Dir
Holdings: Vols 12,500 Cat
Notes: Concentration is on the 18th and
19th centuries, worldwide in coverage. Incl
many scientific expedition accounts. Approx
3000 may be catagorized as rare books/
special collections. The library projects a
Short Title Catalogue of its rarer holdings in
this area within the next few years.
SC —WOFFORD COLLEGE, Sandor Teszler
Library, N Church St, Spartanburg, 29301.
Frank J Anderson, Librn
Holdings: Vols 300 Uncat Maps
Notes: Material from 16th-20th century
atlases. A miscellaneous collection relating
to voyages, travel and description of various
parts of the world. Bulk of titles are 19th
century imprints. Described in: *Geography
and Travels*, compiled and edited by Frank J
Anderson (Wofford College Library. Special

TRAVEL (cont.)

Collections Checklist no 2), Spartanburg, SC: Wofford Library Press, 1970; 54 pp, mimeo with subject index.

WI —UNIVERSITY OF WISCONSIN-STOUT, Library Learning Center, Menomonie, 54751. Philip Sawin Jr, Coll Develop Librn
Notes: Collection emphasis on theory of tourism as well as statistical data.

WI —UNIVERSITY OF WISCONSIN, MILWAUKEE, American Geographical Society Collection, 2311 E Hartford Ave, PO Box 399, Milwaukee, 53201. Roman Drazniowsky, Cur
Holdings: Vols (196,800)
Budget: ($270,000)
Notes: The largest special collection in the field of geography, cartography, and related fields in the Western Hemisphere. Incl 6469 atlases; 385,610 maps; 72 globes; 33,700 pamphlets; 79,000 photographs; 99,000 Landsat Images. Catalog published by G K Hall, Boston.

BC —VANDUSEN GARDENS LIBRARY, 5251 Oak St, Vancouver, V6M 4H1, Can. Mary Nickel, Librn
Holdings: Vols (2100)

ON —METROPOLITAN TORONTO LIBRARY, History Dept, 789 Yonge St, Toronto, M4W 2G8, Can. Michael Pearson, Head
Holdings: Vols (2500) Cat
Notes: The collection includes reports, diaries and personal narratives of travels and voyages of exploration and discovery from the Renaissance to the present day. Areas of emphasis are the exploration of the interior of North America, early oceanic voyages of discovery and accounts of travellers to Russia. The collection also includes a number of early editions, standard collected works such as the publications of the Hakluyt Society, accounts of shipwrecks as well as a representative collection of guide books from the 18th century to the present.

TRAVEL AND TOURISM RESEARCH ASSOCIATION

CO —UNIVERSITY OF COLORADO, Business Research Div, Travel Reference Center, Boulder, 80309. C R Goeldner, Librn; Karen Duea, Librn
Holdings: Vols (8000) Uncat
Budget: ($7000)
Notes: This collection of travel research studies is maintained by the Business Research Division, University of Colorado, and The Travel and Tourism Research Association. Attempts are made to house all studies dealing with travel research.

TRAVEL BOOKS see Voyages and Travels

TRAVELERS

CO —UNIVERSITY OF COLORADO, Business Research Div, Travel Reference Center, Boulder, 80309. C R Goeldner, Librn; Karen Duea, Librn
Holdings: Vols (8000) Uncat
Budget: ($7000)
Notes: This collection of travel research studies is maintained by the Business Research Division, University of Colorado, and The Travel and Tourism Research Association. Attempts are made to house all studies dealing with travel research.

MA —BRANDEIS UNIVERSITY, Goldfarb Library, 415 South St, Waltham, 02154. Bessie Hahn, Dir
Notes: McKew-Parr Collection on Magellan and the Age of Discovery. Approx 4000 books relating to Magellan and Columbus and other voyagers of the 15th and early 16th century. A card catalog to the collection is located in Special Collections.

OH —CLEVELAND PUBLIC LIBRARY, History and Geography Department, 325 Superior Ave, Cleveland, 44114. JoAnn Petrello, Head
Holdings: Cat
Notes: This biography, reference, and

circulating collection incl many fine first editions mostly in English; however, other languages are also represented. Strong on biographies of rulers and statemen, travellers' journals, etc.

TRAVELS see Scientific Expeditions; Travel; Voyages and Travels

TRAVELS, IMAGINARY see Imaginary Voyages

TRAVIS, DEMPSEY

IL —CHICAGO HISTORICAL SOCIETY, Library, Clark St at North Ave, Chicago, 60614. Archie Motley, Manuscript Librn
Notes: Papers of: Emmet Dedmon, newspaper editor; Richard J Finnegan, newspaper editor; Rev Andres M Greeley, sociologist and author; attorney and civil liberties activist Pearl Hart; Robert J Havighurst, educator; social activist John Kearney; Kenesaw Mountain Landis, Federal Judge and first Commissioner of Baseball; Judge David F Matchett; Ivan Molek, Slovenian language publisher in Chicago; Max R Naiman, Communist Party activist; Ralph G Newman, book and autograph dealer and manuscript appraiser; Otto L Schmidt, physician and President of the Chicago and Illinois State Historical Societies; and Dempsey Travis, black mortgage banker.

TRAVIS, WILLIAM B.

TX —UNIVERSITY OF TEXAS LIBRARIES, General Libraries, Barker Texas History Center, PO Box P, Austin, 78712. Don Carleton, Dir

TRAY PAINTING

NY —HISTORICAL SOCIETY OF EARLY AMERICAN DECORATION, 19 Dove St, Albany, 12210. Doris Fry, Dir; Laura Olf, Librn
Holdings: Cat Pix Slides
Notes: The Library is housed with the Museum Collection of the Society. Incl examples of 19th century American country painting on tin, stenciling on wood and tin, bronzing decoration on wood, English stencilled tin and wood, bronzed items, painted objects, reverse painting on glass and examples of other decorating techniques of the period. Also included is a large collection of painted recordings of designs from early articles. Many of these were done by Esther Stevens Brazer in the 1930s. Another large collection has been added since that time. The library material is related to this interest. See The Decorator, official publication of the Historical Society of Early American Decoration. Other publications: The Ornamented Chair and The Ornamented Tray (both ed by Zilla Rider Lea), Antique Decorations by Brazer.

TREANOR, TOM

CA —LOS ANGELES PUBLIC LIBRARY, History Dept, 630 W Fifth St, Los Angeles, 90071. Frank Louch, Sr Librn
Holdings: Vols 9000 Cat Maps
Budget: ($85,000)
Notes: Includes personal narratives, campaigns, diplomatic histories and peace treaties, memoirs of generals and statesmen, official reports and archives of participating countries. Collection of unit histories is particularly strong. There is an emphasis on personal accounts by combatants and noncombatants from all countries. Established as a memorial to Tom Treanor, correspondent for the Los Angeles Times, and includes his World War II writings. See also entry under Military History

TREASURE TROVE AND TREASURE HUNTING

FL —FLORIDA DEPT OF COMMERCE, Research Library, 408 Fletcher Bldg,

Tallahassee, 32301. Dennis Hitchens, Librn
Holdings: Vols (3000) Cat Mss Maps VF
Budget: ($6000)
Notes: Collect materials related to the 4 divisions of the Florida Dept of Commerce: Economic Development, Tourism, Employment Security and Labor, incl titles on Florida (historical and current), management, industrial development and business. The Florida and US documents collection covers population, manufacturing, employment and labor. VF incl files on every city and county, especially local economic data, and subjects unique to Florida, eg, treasure hunting, historical homes and other attractions. 103 VF drawers of Floridiana.

TREATIES

CA —LOS ANGELES PUBLIC LIBRARY, Social Sciences Dept, 630 W Fifth St, Los Angeles, 90071. Marilyn C Wherley, Principal Librn
Holdings: Vols 2079 Cat
Budget: ($150,000)
Notes: Sets of treaties of League of Nations, United Nations, Great Britain, United States, currently in force, as well as historical. Cumulative indexes of world treaties. No separate catalog.

MA —HARVARD UNIVERSITY LIBRARY, Widener Library, Cambridge, 02138.
Holdings: Cat
Notes: Manual of Collections of Treaties by D P Myers, published by Harvard University Press, 1922.

MA —HARVARD UNIVERSITY LIBRARY, Law School Library, Langdell Hall, Cambridge, 02138. Harry S Martin III, Librn
Holdings: Cat Mss Microforms
Notes: Index to Multilateral Treaties, based on holdings, published by Oceana, 1965.

TREATIES—U.S. see U.S.—Foreign Relations—Treaties

TREATMENT, CONSENT TO see Informed Consent (Medical Law)

TREATMENT OF ANIMALS see Animals, Treatment of

TREATY OF GHENT, 1814 see Ghent, Treaty of, 1814

TREATY OF GUADALUPE HIDALGO, 1848 see Guadalupe Hidalgo, Treaty of, 1848

TREE, SIR HERBERT BEERBOHM

BC —UNIVERSITY OF VICTORIA, McPherson Library, Victoria, V8W 3H5, Can.

TREES

CA —UNIVERSITY OF THE PACIFIC, Library, Stockton, 95211. Hiram L Davis, Dir of Libraries
Holdings: Cat Mss Pix
Notes: Papers of John Muir. Incl are correspondence, mss, clippings, pamphlets, drawings and photographs.

CT —YALE UNIVERSITY, Forestry Library, 205 Prospect St, New Haven, 06511. Joseph A Miller, Librn
Holdings: Vols (115,000) Cat Microforms
Notes: The Forestry Library is a unit of the Yale University Library, housed in and serving primarily the School of Forestry and Environmental Studies. Founded in 1900, it has become one of the largest forestry libraries in the world. Forestry is construed broadly to incl underlying or closely related social, physical, and biological sciences. The literature of North American forestry and forest products is most completely covered, though other countries and foreign languages are well represented. Environmental studies and allied fields of natural resources management have been emphasized during the past 10 years. See Dictionary Catalog of

TREES (cont.)

the Yale Forestry Library, 12 vols (Boston: G K Hall, 1962).

HI —PACIFIC TROPICAL BOTANICAL GARDEN, PO Box 340, Lawal, Kavai, 96765. Dr Clark Dalton, Librn

IL —MORTON ARBORETUM, Sterling Morton Library, Lisle, 60532. Ian MacPhail, Librn
Holdings: Vols (20,000) Cat Maps Pix
Notes: The library is especially concerned with the literature of woody plants (trees and shrubs) of north temperate zones but has substantial holdings in the taxonomy and systematics of plants in general, both wild and cultivated, flora of different parts of the world, and a growing collection on plant monographs. Also about 2000 pictures. Described in *The Morton Arboretum Quarterly*, vol 9, no 4 (Winter 1973), pp 56-61.

IA —BICKELHAUPT ARBORETUM FREE LENDING LIBRARY, 340 S Fourteenth St, Clinton, 52732. Francie B Hill, Librn
Notes: Strong on indoor plants, horticulture, ecology, energy conservation, plant entomology and pathology, urban tree planting; also curriculum materials. Over 3000 slides available for lending.

LA —US FOREST SERVICE, Southern Forest Experiment Station Library, T-10210 Postal Service Bldg, 701 Loyola Ave, New Orleans, 70113. Linda A Korb, Librn
Holdings: Vols (50,000) Cat 16mm Films VF
Budget: ($100,000)
Notes: Field library of the National Agricultural Library (USDA), serving research scientists of the Southern Forest Experiment Station at headquarters in New Orleans and in seven states of the Mid-South and Puerto Rico.

MA —MASSACHUSETTS HORTICULTURAL SOCIETY, 300 Massachusetts Ave, Boston, 02115. Becky Ellis, Librn
Holdings: Vols (37,000)
Notes: Garden history, pomology, flora, landscape design. Print collection of many centuries; nursery catalogues from the mid-18th century. In storage, remodeling, will be available in about a year. Open to the public.

MA —HARVARD UNIVERSITY LIBRARY, Arnold Arboretum Library, 22 Divinty Ave, Cambridge, 02138. Barbara A Callahan, Librn
Holdings: Vols (89,239) Cat Mss Maps Pix Slides Microforms
Notes: Specializes in trees (arboriculture and dendrology). Horticultural Library maintained at The Arborway, Jamaica Plain, Mass.

MA —NEW ENGLAND WILD FLOWER SOCIETY, INC, Lawrence Newcomb Library, Hemenway Rd, Framingham, 01701. Mary M Walker, Librn
Holdings: Vols (2500)
Notes: Incl 15,000 slides (35mm) and 4 vertical files.

NY —NEW YORK BOTANICAL GARDEN LIBRARY, Bronx, 10458. Charles R Long, Asst Vice Pres & Dir
Notes: One of the largest botanical collections in the world. Over 900,000 items. Covers botany (150,000 vols), botanists (3000), horticulture (45,000) plant diseases (25,000), plant physiology (15,000), history of botany (1500), conservation of natural resources (15,000), gardening (13,000), paleobotany (7000), ecology (20,000), forestry (5000) medical botany (3000), agriculture (9000) and biology (20,000). Reference library; materials do not circulate, except for member circulating collection (1200) and standard inter-library loan. About 5000 vols uncataloged. Incl art, books, serials, pamphlets, archives and manuscripts, vertical files, microfiche and microfilm, nursery and seed catalogs, photographs, paintings, prints, drawings and engravings. Covers all areas of botanical sciences. This is an OCLC library with fullresource services incl photocopying and photography.

NY —CARY ARBORETUM OF THE NEW YORK BOTANICAL GARDEN, Library,
Box AB, Millbrook, 12545. Fred Strum, Librn
Notes: This collection of alternative energy sources consists of publications concerned with solar energy, wind power, biofuel, methanol, small hydroelectric projects, and wood power.

NY —CARY ARBORETUM OF THE NEW YORK BOTANICAL GARDEN, Institute of Ecosystem Studies, Library, Box AB, Millbrook, 12545. Betsy Calvin, Librn
Holdings: Vols 10,000

NY —MONROE COUNTY PARKS ARBORETUM, Library, 375 Westfall Road, Rochester, 14620. Mr Kelly, Special Collections Librn
Holdings: Vols (1000)

OH —THE DAWES ARBORETUM LIBRARY, 7770 Jacksontown Rd SE, Newark, 43055. Alan D Cook, Senior Horticulturist
Holdings: Vols 5000

OR —OREGON STATE UNIVERSITY, Library, Corvallis, 97331. Melvin George, Dir
Holdings: Cat Mss Maps Pix Microforms

PA —LONGWOOD GARDENS, INC, Library, Kennett Square, 19348. Enola Jane N Teeter, Librn

BC —CANADIAN FORESTRY SERVICE, Pacific Forest Research Centre, Library, 506 West Burnside Rd, Victoria, V8Z 1M5, Can. Alice Solyma, Librn
Holdings: Vols (60,500) Cat Microforms
Notes: Incl forest and plant pathology, entomology, silviculture, meteorology, mensuration, fire research, hydrology, environmental science and ecology, biometrics, land use and classification, soil science, and forest economics. 400 microforms; 40,000 documents and reports.

ON —ROYAL BOTANICAL GARDENS, Library, Box 399, Hamilton, L8N 3H8, Can. Ina Vrugtman, Librn
Holdings: Vols (4200)
Notes: Strengths in ornamental horticulture, botany, ornithology, entomology, natural history.

TREES—CHEMISTRY see Wood—Chemistry

TREES—DISEASES AND PESTS

AB —CANADIAN FORESTRY SERVICE, Northern Forest Research Centre Library, 5320 122nd, Edmonton, T6H 3S5, Can. David J S Robinson, Librn
Holdings: Vols (7000) Cat Microforms
Budget: ($25,000)
Notes: Also 23,000 government documents, 2600 research reports, 3000 pamphlets and reprints.

BC —CANADIAN FORESTRY SERVICE, Pacific Forest Research Centre, Library, 506 West Burnside Rd, Victoria, V8Z 1M5, Can. Alice Solyma, Librn
Holdings: Vols (60,500) Cat Microforms
Notes: Incl general materials related to plant pathology and comprehensive collection on tree diseases.

TREGASKIS, RICHARD

MA —BOSTON UNIVERSITY, Mugar Memorial Library, Special Collections Dept, 771 Commonwealth Ave, Boston, 02215. Howard B Gotlieb, Dir
Holdings: // Cat Mss Maps Pix
Notes: Mss, correspondence, etc collected in depth; incl publications by or about.

TREMAN FAMILY

NY —CORNELL UNIVERSITY LIBRARIES, Collection of Regional History, Dept of Manuscripts and Univ Archives, Ithaca, 14853.
Notes: Incl papers, 1876-1941; clippings, guest lists, other ms and printed matter, cancelled checks, speeches, obituary notices.

TRENT, COUNCIL OF, 1545-1563

CA —STANFORD UNIVERSITY LIBRARIES, Cecil H Green Library,
Stanford, 94305. Michael T Ryan, Cur
Holdings: Vols Cat
Notes: An emphasis in the Rare Book Collection.

TRIAL PRACTICE

CA —HELLER, EHRMAN, WHITE & MCAULIFFE, Library, 44 Montgomery St, San Francisco, 94104. Loretta Mak, Librn
Holdings: Vols (22,500) Cat Audiotapes
Notes: A private library serving 150 attorneys. Emphasis on the areas of taxation, trial practice and corporation laws.

TRIALS (WAR CRIMES) see War Crime Trials

TRIBUNALS, INTERNATIONAL see International Courts

TRICK-TRACK see Backgammon

TRICKLE IRRIGATION

CA —UNIVERSITY OF CALIFORNIA, RIVERSIDE, University Library, Bio-Agricultural Library, Batchelor Hall, Riverside, 92521. Barbara Montanary, Head
Holdings: Vols 2000 Uncat
Notes: Collection attempts to cover all articles, books or periodicals dealing specifically with drip irrigation from 1960-1978 for all geographical areas.

TRICKS

DC —LIBRARY OF CONGRESS, Rare Book & Special Collections Div, Washington, 20540. William Matheson, Chief
Holdings: Cat
Notes: The Houdini Collection of Magic and Spiritism consists of over 4000 vols of printed works and a large number of scrapbooks containing clippings, programs, catalogs, posters, etc. The McManus-Young collection of 1076 vols, as well as mss, prints, and organized scrapbooks on Houdini, the history of magic, and related fields.

TRICYCLES see Bicycles and Tricycles

TRIDENT 2000

SC —COLLEGE OF CHARLESTON LIBRARY, Special Collections Dept, Charleston, 29401.
Notes: Papers, 1978-date.

TRINIDAD AND TOBAGO

CT —YALE UNIVERSITY, Sterling Memorial Library, Latin American Collections, New Haven, 06520. Lee H Williams Jr, Cur
Holdings: Vols (300,000) Cat Maps Pix Slides Phonorecords 16mm Films Filmstrips
See also entry under Latin America

DC —HOWARD UNIVERSITY, Moorland-Spingarn Research Center, 500 Howard Place NW, Washington, 20059. Clifford L Muse, Jr, Acting Dir

TRINIDAD AND TOBAGO—HISTORY

DC —HOWARD UNIVERSITY, Moorland-Spingarn Research Center, 500 Howard Place NW, Washington, 20059. Clifford L Muse, Jr, Acting Dir

TRINIDAD AND TOBAGO—POLITICS AND GOVERNMENT

DC —HOWARD UNIVERSITY, Moorland-Spingarn Research Center, 500 Howard Place NW, Washington, 20059. Clifford L Muse, Jr, Acting Dir

TRINITY DEVELOPMENT COMPANY

WA —WESTERN WASHINGTON UNIVERSITY, Center for Pacific Northwest Studies, High St, Bellingham, 98225. James W Scott, Dir
Holdings: // Mss Maps
Notes: The Trinity Development Company

TRINITY DEVELOPMENT COMPANY (cont.)

was involved in North Cascades mining operations from the 1920s and into the 1930s. These remaining records were recovered from an abandoned mine near Lake Chelan. Incl are numerous maps and blueprints in various stages of deterioration, and a variety of operational financial records. Partially cataloged.

TRIPITAKA

CT —TRINITY COLLEGE LIBRARY, 300 Summit St, Hartford, 06106. Ralph S Emerick, Librn
Holdings: Cat
CT —YALE UNIVERSITY, Box 1603A, Yale Station, New Haven, 06520.

TRIPOLINE WAR see U.S —History— Tripolitan War, 1801-1805

TRIPP, JOHN

ME —COLBY COLLEGE, Miller Library, Colby Archives, Waterville, 04901.
Holdings: Mss
Notes: Family papers or other correspondence.

TRIPS AROUND THE WORLD see Voyages and Travels

TROCCHI, ALEXANDER

MO —WASHINGTON UNIVERSITY, John M Olin Library, Campus Box 1061, St Louis, 63130.
Notes: A major collection of published and unpublished writings (1944-66) of British-born novelist and editor. Incl mss, correspondence, literary papers, photographs, etc. Described in *Special Collections: an Annotated Guide to the Holdings of the Manuscript Division and the University Archives and Research Collection.*

TROILUS AND CRISEYDE

PA —UNIVERSITY OF PENNSYLVANIA, Van Pelt Library, Rare Books Collection, 34 & Walnut Sts, Philadelphia, 19104. Daniel Traister, Special Collections Librn

TROLLEY CARS

MD —BALTIMORE STREETCAR MUSEUM, Transit Research Center, 1901 Falls Rd, PO Box 7184, Baltimore, 21218. George F Nixon, Cur
Holdings: Cat Mss Slides 16mm Films
Notes: Transit Research Center is devoted to the collection of memorbilia, photos, drawings, printed matter, etc, pertinent to public rail transportation in Baltimore and Maryland. Incl streetcar systems, interurban lines, and main line railroads in the area. Also incl bus history. Incl materials donated by the Baltimore Transit Co, as well as private collections.

TROLLEY LINES

MO —NATIONAL MUSEUM OF TRANSPORT, Reference Library, 3105 Barrett Station Rd, Saint Louis, 63122. John P Roberts, Secretary
Holdings: Vols (10,000) Cat Mss Maps Pix Slides
OH —RUTHERFORD B HAYES LIBRARY, 1337 Hayes Ave, Fremont, 43420. Watt P Marchman, Dir
Holdings: Cat Mss
Notes: Personal, business and political correspondence; receipts and other papers. Letterbooks of A L Conger and business papers of the Zanesville Street Railway.
OR —OREGON ELECTRIC RAILWAY HISTORICAL SOCIETY, Library, HCR 71, Box 1318, Forest Grove, 97116. Paul V Class, Cur
Holdings: Vols (125) Uncat Pix Slides 16mm Films

TROLLOPE, ANTHONY, 1815-1882

CT —YALE UNIVERSITY, Box 1603A, Yale Station, New Haven, 06520.
Holdings: Cat Mss
IL —ILLINOIS STATE UNIVERSITY, Milner Library, Dept of Special Collections, Normal, 61761. Robert Sokan, Librn
Notes: First editions, limited editions, ephemera, etc.
MI —UNIVERSITY OF MICHIGAN, Library, Dept of Rare Books & Special Collections, Ann Arbor, 48109. Robert J Starring, Head
Holdings: Vols 436 Cat Mss Pix
Notes: Incl first editions of most of Trollope's novels (7 in parts); mss of *The Fixed Period and Kept in the Dark* (both only partially in Trollope's hand); 6 ALsS by Trollope; and 10 first editions of Mrs Frances Trollope. A description of the basic collection appeared in W R Steinhoff, "The John W Watling Collection of Anthony Trollope," *Michigan Alumnus Q"uarterly* Review, vol 58 (1952) pp 193-202.
NJ —PRINCETON UNIVERSITY, Library, Morris L Parrish Collection, Princeton, 08540. Alexander D Wainwright, Cur
Notes: Collection has virtually every publication; first editions and many variants, English and American. All periodicals that contained stories or articles by Trollope, many of which were never reprinted. More than 400 vols are cataloged. For particulars refer to: Robert H Taylor '30, "The Trollope Collection" in the *Chronicle* VIII, 1 (November, 1946) pp 33-37. An exhibition entitled "A Great Victorian: Anthony Trollope, 1815-1882" was shown in the Gould Gallery of Firestone Library during 1982-83. The gathering of more than 200 items came entirely from the Parrish Collection and that of Robert H Taylor. Checklist of the exhibition was prepared by Richard M Ludwig and Alexander D Wainwright in December, 1982, copy in Dulles Reading Room (ExB)0639.739 no 42.
NY —NEW YORK PUBLIC LIBRARY, Rare Books and Manuscripts Div, Fifth Ave & 42 St, New York, 10018. William L Joyce, Asst Dir; Bernard McTigue, Cur, Arents Collection
Holdings: Cat Mss Pix
NY —NEW YORK UNIVERSITY, Elmer Holmes Bobst Library, Div of Special Collections, Washington Sq S, New York, 10012. Frank Walker, Librn; Patrick McGuire, Asst Librn
Holdings: Vols (100,000) Cat Mss Pix
Notes: The Fales Collection of first (and other) editions of English and American novels from about 1750 to date (about 70, 000 titles). Mss (30,000) pieces.
PA —BRYN MAWR COLLEGE, Canaday Library, Bryn Mawr, 19010. James Tanis, Dir
Notes: Rare books in the Adelman Collection.

TROLLOPE, FRANCES (MILTON), 1780-1863

CA —UNIVERSITY OF CALIFORNIA, LOS ANGELES, Research Library, Dept of Special Collections, 405 Hilgard Ave, Los Angeles, 90024. Edward Shreeves, Chairman, Bibliographers Group; David S Zeidberg, Head
Holdings: Vols 75 Mss
Notes: Incl 175 mss items: correspondence of the Trollope family and some connections, ca 1825-1915.
MI —UNIVERSITY OF MICHIGAN, Library, Dept of Rare Books & Special Collections, Ann Arbor, 48109. Robert J Starring, Head
Holdings: Vols 10 Cat
Notes: First editions.
See also entry under Trollope, Anthony

TROLLOPE FAMILY

CA —UNIVERSITY OF CALIFORNIA, LOS ANGELES, Research Library, Dept of Special Collections, 405 Hilgard Ave, Los Angeles, 90024. Edward Shreeves, Chairman, Bibliographers Group; David S Zeidberg, Head
Holdings: Vols 250 Mss
Notes: Incl 175 mss items: correspondence of the Trollope family and some connections, ca 1825-1915.
NJ —PRINCETON UNIVERSITY, Library, Morris L Parrish Collection, Princeton, 08540. Alexander D Wainwright, Cur
Holdings: Vols 43
Notes: The collection contains over 6500 vols, as well as many theatre programs, playbills, photographs, and other miscellanea. Parrish's goal was to assemble in both the English and the American first editions, in the original condition as issued, everything that a given author published. He was also interested in a high standard of condition for his books. Many additions have been acquired since the Parrish collection came to the Library as a bequest in 1944. The collection is an assemblage of author collections, consisting of books by: William Harrison Ainsworth, James Matthew Barrie, William Black, The Brontes, William Wilkie Collins, Dinah Mulock Craik, Marie de la Ramee ("Ouida"), Benjamin Disraeli, Charles Dickens, Charles Dodgson, George du Maurier, George Eliot (ie Mary Ann Evans), Elizabeth Gaskell, Thomas Hardy, Thomas Hughes,Charles Kingsley, Charles Lever, Edward George Earle Bulwer-Lytton, Mary Maxwell, George Meredith, Charles Reade, Walter Scott, Robert Louis Stevenson, William Makepeace Thackeray, Trollope Family, Ellen Wood, and Charlotte Yonge.

TROPHIES, SPORTS

CA —FIRST INTERSTATE BANK, Athletic Foundation, 2141 W Adams, Los Angeles, 90018. W R Schroeder, Managing Dir
Notes: One of the most extensive library and museum collections relating to sports, the Olympic Games, etc. Bound vols of sports sections from several newspapers. Large collection of college and university annuals and yearbooks; souvenir publications from amateur, college, and professional sporting events. Also, large museum collection of sports memorabilia, ledger of halls of fame with thousands of names of outstanding athletes in all sports. Repository for the Association of Sports Museums and Halls of Fame. Noncirculating.

TROPICAL AGRICULTURE see Agriculture—Tropics

TROPICAL CROPS

CA —UNIVERSITY OF CALIFORNIA, BERKELEY, Science Libraries, Natural Resources Library, 40 Giannini Hall, Berkeley, 94720. Norma Kobzina, Head Librn
Holdings: Vols (100,000) Cat Maps Microforms
Budget: ($40,000)
Notes: Subject emphasis is on basic agriculture and pest management research, particularly in the areas of tropical and subtropical agriculture and plantation crops, ie, cotton, rice, tobacco, and sugar. Materials in agricultural engineering, farm machinery, and veterinary medicine are not acquired for the Berkeley campus. Serials, especially the extensive holdings of foreign titles, constitute the collection's major strength. Over 5700 serials are being received currently.
FL —RARE FRUIT COUNCIL INTERNATIONAL, 13609 Old Cutler Rd, Miami, 33158. Fred Frazer, Pres; Louise Garavatlia, Librn
Holdings: Vols (300)
Notes: Not open to the public.
HI —PACIFIC TROPICAL BOTANICAL GARDEN, PO Box 340, Lawal, Kavai, 96765. Dr Clark Dalton, Librn
MD —US DEPT OF AGRICULTURE, National Agricultural Library, 10301 Baltimore Blvd, Beltsville, 20705. Joseph H Howard, Director
Holdings: Vols (2,000,000) Cat Mss Maps

TROPICAL CROPS (cont.)

Pix Slides Microforms
Notes: Crop ecology, agro-climatic analogs; air pollution effects. Agronomy: agriculture and tropical and desert agriculture. For use by the staff of the Institute. Incl 5000 pamphlet items. Former collection of American Institute of Crop Ecology.
MA —HARVARD UNIVERSITY, Harvard Forest Library, Petersham, 01366. Catherine M Danahar, Librn
Notes: Tropical botany.

TROPICAL FISH

PA —CARNEGIE LIBRARY OF PITTSBURGH, Science & Technology Dept, 4400 Forbes Ave, Pittsburgh, 15213. Catherine M Brosky, Dept Head
Notes: Except for certain special areas, such as entomology and ornithology and a few others that are emphasized, this general subject is of secondary interest. Incl both modern and classic works. Kept up to date in cooperation with the Library in Carnegie Museum of Natural History. Materials available on the various phyla, classes, orders and species. Abstracts, indexes, bibliographies, taxonomic manuals and standard reference books. Many journals and society publications complete from the beginning.

TROPICAL MEDICINE

MD —MEDICAL & CHIRURGICAL FACULTY OF THE STATE OF MARYLAND, Library, 1211 Cathedral St, Baltimore, 21201. Joseph E Jensen, Librn
Holdings: Vols (10,000) // Cat Mss Maps Pix
See also entry under Medicine - History and Historic
RI —BROWN UNIVERSITY, John Carter Brown Library, Providence, 02912. Norman Fiering, Librn; Everett C Wilkie Jr, Bibliographer; Susan Danforth, Cur Maps & Prints
Notes: Works by European and American physicians or scientists before 1835 dealing with diseases of warm climates or the tropics (ie, yellow feaver, yaws, dry belly-ache, etc).

TROPICS

DC —SMITHSONIAN INSTITUTION, Smithsonian Tropical Research Institute, Washington, 20560. Carol Jopling, Chief Librn
Holdings: Vols (22,000) Cat Mss Maps Pix Slides 16mm Films Microforms
Budget: ($70,000)
Notes: Smithsonian Institution, Smithsonian Tropical Research Institute is located in Balboa, Panama.
FL —UNIVERSITY OF MIAMI, Otto G Richter Library, PO Box 248214, Coral Gables, 33124. Frank Rodgers, Dir of Libraries
Holdings: Vols Microforms
Notes: The Rosenstiel School of Marine and Atmospheric Sciences Library is one of the major marine science collections in the United States and is especially strong in the literature of tropical oceanography. Special collections in the library incl 200 oceanographic atlases and more than 50 sets of the world's major expedition reports. The library also maintains a nautical chart collection. 3000 microforms; 1000 current subscriptions.

TROPICS—DISEASES AND HYGIENE

HI —HAWAII MEDICAL LIBRARY, 1221 Punchbowl St, Honolulu, 96813. John A Breinich, Dir
Holdings: Vols (50,000) Cat Pix Audiotapes Videotapes
Budget: ($121,000)
Notes: Medline service available.
NH —DARTMOUTH COLLEGE, Dartmouth-Hitchcock Medical Center, Dana Biomedical Library, Hanover, 03756. Shirley J Grainger,

Librn
Holdings: Vols (6000) Cat Mss
Notes: Collection incl the Henry Kumm Index to Papers on Poliomyelitis and Tropical Medicine.

TROST, HENRY C.

TX —EL PASO PUBLIC LIBRARY, Southwest Collection, 501 N Oregon, El Paso, 79901. Mary A Sarber, Head
Holdings: Vols 12,000 Cat Mss Maps Pix Microforms
Budget: $11,000
Notes: 400 sets of architectural plans by El Paso firms of Trost and Trost, Percy McGhee, Frazer and Benner. Partial catalog of Trost and Trost buildings. See Engelbrecht, Lloyd C, and Engelbrecht, June-Marie F, Henry C Trost: Architect of the Southwest (El Paso Public Library Association, 1981).

TROTSKY, LEON, AND TROTSKYISM

CA —HOOVER INSTITUTION ON WAR, REVOLUTION & PEACE, Stanford University, Stanford, 94305. Milorad M Drachkovitch, Archivist
Holdings: Mss
Notes: Papers of Herbert Solow, American journalist, and editor of Fortune, 1945-1964, incl correspondence, speeches, drafts of writings, memoranda, depositions, clippings and other printed matter, 1924-76, relating to the communist movement in the US, the Non-Partisan Defense League, the Commission of Inquiry into the Charges Made Against Leon Trotsky in the Moscow Trials, Soviet espionage in the US, Zionism, and post-World War II international business enterprises. Incl some papers of Mrs Herbert Solow, 1964-76. 8 ms boxes.
CA —HOOVER INSTITUTION ON WAR, REVOLUTION & PEACE, Stanford University, Stanford, 94305. Milorad M Drachkovitch, Archivist
Notes: The Herman Axelbank Film Collection on Russian history. Much footage dating from about 1901-1921. Subjects incl Royal Family, Moscow and St Petersburg scenes, the Revolution and Civil War, espec good coverage of Leon Trotsky's role, Siberia, and the Far East. The first 28 of 266 reels have been received (April 1983).
IN —INDIANA UNIVERSITY, Lilly Library, Seventh St, Bloomington, 47405. William R Cagle, Librn
Holdings: // Cat Mss
Notes: Ms incl a collection of Max Eastman's correspondence with Trotsky, 1922-1933;
MD —UNIVERSITY OF MARYLAND, BALTIMORE COUNTY, Albin O Kuhn Library and Gallery, 5401 Wilkens Ave, Baltimore, 21228. Ann Copeland, Special Collections Librn
Holdings: // Uncat
Notes: The colleciton incl more than 1000 pamphlets and broadsides on communism, fascism, Trotskyism, socialism, etc.
MA —HARVARD UNIVERSITY LIBRARY, Houghton Library, Cambridge, 02138. Rodney G Dennis, Cur of Manuscripts
Holdings: Cat Mss
Notes: Archives, filling more than 150 boxes, acquired from Trotsky (before his assassination) and from his widow. A typescript guide is available, but papers for 1928-1940 are to remain closed until 1980.
MI —UNIVERSITY OF MICHIGAN, Dept of Rare Books & Special Collections, Ann Arbor, 48109. Edward C Weber, Head, Labadie Collection
Holdings: Vols (40,000) CAt Mss Pix Phonorecord Audiotapes Microforms
Notes: Strong on publications of the Fourth International.

TROTT, ADAM VON

DC —GEORGETOWN UNIVERSITY, Library, Special Collections Div, 37 & O Sts NW, Washington, 20057. George M Barringer, Special Collections Librn; Nicholas B Sheetz, Mss Librn
Holdings: Mss Pix
Notes: The papers of Christopher Sykes,

biographer, journalist, and novelist; containing mss, letters, photographs, and drawings. With extensive correspondence from Harold Acton; Angela, Countess of Antrim; Sir John Betjeman; Ivy Compton-Burnett; Alick Dru; T S Eliot; Max Beerbohm; Graham Greene; John Hayward; Lord Patrick Kinross; Compton Mackenzie; Nancy Mitford; Anthony Powell; Dame Flora Robson; Cecil Roth; Sir John Russell; Osbert Sitwell; John Sparrow; Freya Stark; James Stern; and Evelyn Waugh, among others. Also, considerable research material about Evelyn Waugh, Adam von Trott, Robert Byron, Lady Nancy Astor; and the foundation of the state of Israel.

TROTTING RACES see Harness Racing

TROUBETSKOY, PRINCESS see Rives, Amelie (Princess Troubetzskoy)

TROUT FISHING

IL —NORTHWESTERN UNIVERSITY, Library, Special Collections Dept, 1937 Sheridan Rd, Evanston, 60201. R Russell Maylone, Cur
Holdings: Vols 250 Cat Pix
Notes: History of fly-fishing, 16th-20th centuries.
NH —UNIVERSITY OF NEW HAMPSHIRE, Dimond Library, Durham, 03824. Barbara A White, Special Collections Librn
Holdings: Vols 2000 Cat
Notes: Special emphasis on fly-tying and trout and salmon fishing.
PA —LAFAYETTE COLLEGE, David Bishop Skillman Library, Easton, 18042. Dorothy Cieslicki, Librn
Holdings: Vols (825) Cat
Notes: Robert Tinsman Angling Collection. Inc 58 editions of Walton, Compleat Angler. Also, the Robert S Conahay Jr, Atlantic Salmon Collection, which incl over 1000 hand-tied salmon and trout flies, many mounted and framed.

TROVILLION, HAL W.

IL —SOUTHERN ILLINOIS UNIVERSITY, CARBONDALE, Delyte W Morris Library, Special Collections Dept, Carbondale, 62901. David V Koch, Cur of Special Collections; Louisa Bowen, Cur of Manuscripts
Holdings: Vols 200 Cat Mss Pix
Notes: Incl the archives of the press and Hal W Trovillion's personal papers.

TROWBRIDGE, JOHN TOWNSEND (PAUL CREYTON)

MD —JOHNS HOPKINS UNIVERSITY, Milton S Eisenhower Library, Charles & 34 Sts, Baltimore, 21218. Ann S Gwyn, Assistant Dir for Special Collections
Holdings: // Cat Mss
Notes: 78 letters, cataloged in manuscript room.

TROYE, EDWARD, 1808-1874

IL —DE PAUL UNIVERSITY, Library, 2323 N Seminary, Chicago, 60614. Kathryn De Graff, Special Collections Librn
Notes: About 1000 vols on British field sports. Also, 20 hand-colored sets of prints by Edward Troye (1808-1874) of American thoroughbred horses.

TRUCKS

CA —LOS ANGELES PUBLIC LIBRARY, Science & Technology Dept, 630 W Fifth St, Los Angeles, 90071. Billie M Connor, Dept Head
Holdings: Vols 8000 Cat Microforms
Notes: Shop manuals for American and foreign made cars, trucks, motorcycles, and tractors. Specialized manuals on transmissions, air conditioning, air pollution control devices, electrical components, restoration prices, etc. Parts Lists Directories including flat rate and parts price manuals. Indexes include car and other motor vehicles

TRUCKS (cont.)

repair manuals by make and model, road tests for specific models appearing in popular automotive periodicals, and an automobile illustration index.

NH —NEW HAMPSHIRE HISTORICAL SOCIETY, Manuscripts Library, 30 Park St, Concord, 03301. Thomas E Camden, Cur
Holdings: Cat Mss Pix
Notes: Abbot-Downing Truck and Body Co records 1813-1945. Incl correspondence, account book, journals, ledgers, order books, accounts receivable, records of sales, balance sheet for New York branch, records of material mortgaged to Josiah E Fernald, banker, of Concord, New Hampshire, other financial papers, drawings, catalogs, and photos of vehicles, clippings, advertisements, and other papers of a firm based in Concord, New Hampshire, and manufacturing wagons, coaches, carriages, and motor-trucks. 33 linear feet, about 22,000 items.

OH —AKRON-SUMMIT COUNTY PUBLIC LIBRARY, Business, Labor & Government Div, 55 S Main St, Akron, 44326. William G Johnson, Head
Holdings: Vols 21 Cat Mss Pix
Notes: Trucking History Collection also incl a great deal of archival material which is uncataloged and essentially unlisted at present time. This archival material is not available for public use at the present time.

OR —HYSTER COMPANY, Engineering Library, 2902 E Cloackman, Portland, 97208. Ruth Jahnke, Engineering Librn
Holdings: Vols (8000) Cat Mss Microforms
Budget: $5000
Notes: Design and manufacture of industrial trucks. Consists mostly of books, papers, proceedings, periodicals and vending catalogs devoted to phases of company management and design and manufacture of product.

PA —FREE LIBRARY OF PHILADELPHIA, Automobile Reference Collection, Logan Sq, Philadelphia, 19103. Louis G Helverson, Jr, Librn in Charge
Holdings: Vols (14,000) Cat Pix Slides
Notes: Collection is concerned with all aspects of automotive industry and its history. Includes shop manuals, instruction books, parts books, and periodicals dealing with all types of bicycles, tricylces and motor vehicles. Industry statistics, corporate annual reports, environmental problems, safety. Incl 18,000 pictures, 1700 slides, 648 microfilm reels, 23,000 sales catalogs, 5000 pieces of ephemera.

TRUCKS, MILITARY see Vehicles, Military

TRUDEAU, ARTHUR

PA —US ARMY MILITARY HISTORY INSTITUTE, Carlisle Barracks, 17013. Richard J Sommers, Chief Archivist-Historian
Holdings: Mss Cat
Notes: TheKorean War collection, personal correspondence, daily logs, recollections, and official papers of US officers and soldiers serving in the Korean War, incl Generals Edward Almond, George Barth Bruce Clarke, Matthew Ridgway, and Arthur Trudeau.

TRUEBLOOD, BENJAMIN FRANKLIN

PA —SWARTHMORE COLLEGE, Peace Collection, Swarthmore, 19081. Jean R Soderlund, Cur of Peace Collection
Notes: International arbitration has been one of the central subject emphases of the Peace Collection since its inception in 1930. Materials incl records and memorabilia of 19th and early 20th century peace leaders and organizations, such as American Peace Society and its branches, Jane Addams, the Wisbech Local Peace Association, English and American Friends' Peace Societies, the Universal Peace Union, William Ladd, Elihu Burritt, and Benjamin F Trueblood (1847-1916), American Peace Society Secretary.

TRUEHEART, H. M., 1865-1934

TX —ROSENBERG LIBRARY, Galveston and Texas History Center, 2310 Sealy Ave, Galveston, 77550. Jane Kenamore, Archivist
Holdings: Mss
Notes: Business records which relate to land development in Texas during the late 19th and early 20th centuries.

TRUMAN, HARRY S.

MO —HARRY S TRUMAN LIBRARY, Independence, 64050. Benedict K Zobrist, Dir
Holdings: Mss
Notes: Papers of Harry S Truman's administration; also papers of Edwin G Arnold, James P Aylword, Willa Mae Roberts. Approx 13,000,000 pages on hand.

NY —NEW YORK PUBLIC LIBRARY, Fifth Ave & 42 St, New York, 10018.
Notes: Supported by a special Harry S Truman Memorial Fund, to collect materials relating to his life and work.

TRUMBO, DALTON

WI —UNIVERSITY OF WISCONSIN, MADISON, Memorial Library, British & American Language & Literature Collection, 728 State St, Madison, 53706. Yvonne Schofer, Bibliographer
Notes: Not a separate collection. Trumbo items included in other collections.

TRUMBULL, JOHN

CT —YALE UNIVERSITY, Box 1603A, Yale Station, New Haven, 06520.
Holdings: Cat Mss

TRUMBULL, LYMAN, 1813-1896

†IL —ILLINOIS STATE HISTORICAL SOCIETY, Library, Old State Capitol, Springfield, 62706.
Notes: Papers, incl letters and mss of US Senator Lyman Trumball (1813-1896).

TRUMBULL FAMILY

†IL —ILLINOIS STATE HISTORICAL SOCIETY, Library, Old State Capitol, Springfield, 62706.
Notes: Papers, incl letters and mss of US Senator Lyman Trumball (1813-1896).

TRUSCOTT, GEN. LUCIAN

†VA —GEORGE C MARSHALL RESEARCH FOUNDATION AND LIBRARY, Drawer 920, Lexington, 24450. Royster Lyle Jr, Cur Collections
Holdings: Cat Maps Pix
Notes: Papers, incl personal correspondence, etc, especially with regard to service during World War II.

TRUSTS, CHARITABLE see Charitable Uses, Trusts, and Foundations

TRUTH, SOJOURNER

MD —PRINCE GEORGE'S COUNTY MEMORIAL LIBRARY SYSTEM, Oxon Hill Branch Library, Sojourner Truth Collection, 6200 Oxon Hill Rd, Oxon Hill, 20745. Cherie Phillips Barnett, Librn
Holdings: Vols (3000) Cat Mss Pix Films Phonorecords Microforms VF
Budget: ($3500)
Notes: The Sojourner Truth Collection on Blacks in America is a representative collection of materials by and about Black Americans, their historical problems and accomplishments. The collection, containing certain unique and rare items, emphasizes the Black woman, the Black family, slavery and anti-slavery, Black literature, Blacks in the military and slave narratives. Also incl current US government publications concerning the Black American. A supportive collection of films, recordings, paperbacks, and periodicals is available. Programs, displays, and bibliographies are prepared in order to develop interest in the collection.

NY —UNIVERSITY OF ROCHESTER, Rush Rhees Library, Department of Rare Books and Special Collections, Rochester, 14627. Peter Dzwonkoski, Librn
Holdings: Mss
Notes: Autograph letters and other mss incl in the Isaac and Amy Post family papers.

TRYON, THOMAS

MA —BOSTON UNIVERSITY, Mugar Memorial Library, Special Collections Dept, 771 Commonwealth Ave, Boston, 02215. Howard B Gotlieb, Dir
Holdings: Cat Mss Pix
Notes: Mss, correspondence, etc collected in depth; incl publications by or about.

TRYON PALACE RESTORATION

NC —TRYON PALACE RESTORATION, Library, 613 Pollock St, New Bern, 28560. Grace C Ipock, Registrar
Holdings: Vols 1400 Cat Maps Pix Slides
Notes: Governor Tryon's recreated library at Tryon Palace comprises 517 titles published before 1770. Other shelves at the historic houses in the complex incl vols published until ca 1820. Sixteen percent of Governor Tryon's inventoried library of 1770 is still sought. No photocopying.

TSCHAGATAJ LANGUAGE see Jagataic Language and Literature

TSIMSHIAN INDIANS

BC —TERRACE PUBLIC LIBRARY, 4610 Park Ave, Terrace, V8G 1V6, Can. Ed Curell, Librn; Gillian Campbell, Librn, Terrace Collection
Holdings: Vols (270) Cat
Budget: ($250)
Notes: The collection is limited to books and pamphlets relating to Terrace, Skeena, and Nass River District history and geography. Emphasis on art and sociology of the Niska and Tsimshian and lives of early missionaries.

TSONG-KHA-PA

†NY —INSTITUTE FOR ADVANCED STUDIES OF WORLD RELIGIONS (IASWR), Library, State University of New York at Stony Brook, Stony Brook, 11794. C T Shen, Librn
Holdings: Vols 25,000 Cat Mss Maps Microforms

TSUNAMIS

HI —INTERNATIONAL TSUNAMI INFORMATION CENTER, PO Box 50027, Honolulu, 96850. Bonnie Dong, Librn
Holdings: Vols 3000
Notes: Large collection on tsunamis, their causes, oceanographic organization and mareographic records, forecasting, mapping, etc.

TUBA MUSIC

IN —BALL STATE UNIVERSITY, Alexander M Bracken Library, Muncie, 47306. Nyal Williams, Music Librn
Holdings: Vols (30,000) Cat Mss
Budget: ($20,000)
Notes: Incl archives of International Horn Society, Tubists Universal Brotherhood Association Library, Cecil Leeson Archival Saxophone Collection, and Archives of Buescher Music Instrument Manufacturing Company.

TUBBS, GARDINER STOW

NY —CORNELL UNIVERSITY LIBRARIES, Collection of Regional History, Dept of Manuscripts and Univ Archives, Ithaca,

TUBBS, GARDINER STOW (cont.)

14853.
Notes: Daguerreotypist. Incl papers, 1844-
(1854-83); correspondence and documents
dealing with photographic processes,
formulas for making solutions used in
photographic development, medical
pamphlets, Tubbs' ms and printed poetry
and prose.

TUBERCULOSIS—HISTORY

†CO —NATIONAL JEWISH HOSPITAL
AND RESEARCH CENTER-NATIONAL
ATHSMA CENTER, Gerald Tucker
Memorial Medical Library, 3800 Colfax
Ave, Denver, 80206. Helen-Ann Brown,
Librn
Holdings: Vols (8500)
Notes: Allergy, asthma, immunology,
research in molecular and cellular biology,
medicine, tuberculosis and diseases of the
chest.
CT —YALE UNIVERSITY, Medical Historical
Library, Klebs Collection, 333 Cedar St,
New Haven, 06520. Ferenc A Gyorgyey,
Librn
Notes: The Arnold Carl Klebs Medical
Collection books, pamphlets, etc, incl the
library of his father, Edwin T A Klebs,
pathologist. Strong in bibliography of early
printed medical books, herbals, plague tracts,
inoculation, vaccination and tubercular
diseases.
MD —JOHNS HOPKINS UNIVERSITY,
Institute of the History of Medicine, 1900 E
Monument St, Baltimore, 21205. Doris
Thibodeau, Librn
Holdings: Vols 4400 Cat
MD —MEDICAL & CHIRURGICAL
FACULTY OF THE STATE OF
MARYLAND, Library, 1211 Cathedral St,
Baltimore, 21201. Joseph E Jensen, Librn
Holdings: Vols (10,000) // Cat Mss Maps
Pix
See also entry under Medicine - History and
Historic
PA —COLLEGE OF PHYSICIANS OF
PHILADELPHIA, Library, 19 S 22 St,
Philadelphia, 19103. Christine Ruggere, Cur,
Historical Collections
Holdings: Vols (316,223) Cat Mss
Budget: ($1,096,557)
Notes: Very strong collection.
See also entry under Medicine

TUBISTS UNIVERSAL
BROTHERHOOD ASSOCIATION

IN —BALL STATE UNIVERSITY, Alexander
M Bracken Library, Muncie, 47306. Nyal
Williams, Music Librn
Holdings: Vols (30,000) Cat Mss
Budget: ($20,000)
Notes: Incl archives of International Horn
Society, Tubists Universal Brotherhood
Association Library, Cecil Leeson Archival
Saxophone Collection, and Archives of
Buescher Music Instrument Manufacturing
Company.

TUCCI, NICCOLO

MA —BOSTON UNIVERSITY, Mugar
Memorial Library, Special Collections Dept,
771 Commonwealth Ave, Boston, 02215.
Howard B Gotlieb, Dir
Holdings: Mss Pix
Notes: Mss, correspondence, etc collected in
depth; incl publications by or about.

TUCK, WILLIAM MUNFORD, 1921-
1968

VA —COLLEGE OF WILLIAM AND
MARY, Earl Gregg Swem Library,
Williamsburg, 23185. Margaret C Cook, Cur
of Manuscripts & Rare Books
Holdings: // Cat
Notes: Professional papers of Tuck, Virginia
governor, 1946-1950 and US. Representative
from the 5th Virginia district. 1953-1968.
100,000 items.

TUCKER, GEORGE

VA —UNIVERSITY OF VIRGINIA,
Alderman Library, Manuscripts Dept,
Charlottesville, 22901. Edmund Berkeley Jr,
Cur
Holdings: Cat Mss Pix
Notes: Extensive collection of mss and
printed materials.

TUCKER, RAYMOND R.

MO —WASHINGTON UNIVERSITY,
Libraries, Special Collections Dept, Campus
Box 1061, St Louis, 63130.
Notes: St Louis Mayoral Papers Collection:
Papers of Aloys P Kaufmann, 1944-49;
Raymond R Tucker, 1953-65; Alphonso J
Cervantes, 1965-73; John H Poelker, 1973-
77; James F Conway, 1977-81.

TUCKER, SOPHIE, 1884-1966

NY —NEW YORK PUBLIC LIBRARY,
Performing Arts Research Center, Billy Rose
Theatre Collection, 111 Amsterdam Ave,
New York, 10023. Dorothy L Swerdlove,
Cur
Holdings: Cat Mss Pix
Notes: Papers, scrapbooks, mss, photographs,
memorabilia, etc.
†OH —HEBREW UNION COLLEGE,
American Jewish Archives, 3101 Clifton
Ave, Cincinnati, 45220.
Notes: Papers and correspondence of Sophie
Tucker (1884-1966).

TUCKER, STERLING

MA —BOSTON UNIVERSITY, Mugar
Memorial Library, Special Collections Dept,
771 Commonwealth Ave, Boston, 02215.
Howard B Gotlieb, Dir
Holdings: Cat Mss
Notes: Mss, correspondence, etc collected in
depth; incl publications by or about.

TUCKER FAMILY (1675-1956)

VA —COLLEGE OF WILLIAM AND
MARY, Earl Gregg Swem Library,
Williamsburg, 23185. Margaret C Cook, Cur
of Manuscripts & Rare Books
Holdings: Vols 1500 Cat Mss
Notes: Tucker-Coleman Papers (1675-1956):
Family, literary, and business papers of the
Tucker Family, particularly St George
Tucker (1752-1827) and Nathaniel Beverley
Tucker (1784-1851). This collection, which
incl 600 Jefferson items, is particularly
important for the study of Virginia social,
economic, and political history during the
period 1770-1850. Also, 30,000 ms items.

TUDA LANGUAGE see Toda Language

TUFTS, JAMES H.

IL —SOUTHERN ILLINOIS UNIVERSITY,
CARBONDALE, Delyte W Morris Library,
Special Collections Dept, Carbondale, 62901.
David V Koch, Cur of Special Collections;
Louisa Bowen, Cur of Manuscripts
Holdings: Cat Mss
Notes: Twenty Collections relating to 20th
century American philosophy incl the papers
of John Dewey, Henry Nelson Wieman,
Stephan C Pepper and Toyohiko Kagawa;
the archives of the Library of Living
Philosphers and the Open Court Publishing
Company; and small collections James H
Tufts, Edward Scribner Ames and Sidney
Hook.

TUGBOATS

OH —PUBLIC LIBRARY OF CINCINNATI
& HAMILTON COUNTY, Dept of Rare
Books & Special Collections, 800 Vine St,
Library Square, Cincinnati, 45202. Yeatman
Anderson III, Cur
Holdings: Cat Mss Maps Pix Slides
Microforms
Notes: Inland River Collection, Incl
logbooks, account books, personal
correspondence, diaries, etc. Also, a picture
collection of 14,000 items (steamboats,
towboats, river views, crews, construction,
barges, etc.)

TUITION see Education—Finance

TULANCINGO, PUEBLA, MEXICO

CA —UNIVERSITY OF CALIFORNIA, LOS
ANGELES, Research Library, Dept of
Special Collections, 405 Hilgard Ave, Los
Angeles, 90024. Edward Shreeves,
Chairman, Bibliographers Group; David S
Zeidberg, Head
Notes: 3 linear feet of legal documents and
papers relating to law suits and land
ownership, ca 1540-1875.

TULAREMIA

OH —MIAMI UNIVERSITY, Science Library,
Oxford, 45056.
Notes: Zoonoses and related diseases.
Collection partially transferred from Parker-
Davis Memorial Library, Hamilton, Mont.

TULLE EMBROIDERY see Lace and
Lace Making

TULLY, JIM, 1888-1947

CA —UNIVERSITY OF CALIFORNIA, LOS
ANGELES, Research Library, Dept of
Special Collections, 405 Hilgard Ave, Los
Angeles, 90024. Edward Shreeves,
Chairman, Bibliographers Group; David S
Zeidberg, Head
Holdings: Vols 10 Mss
Notes: Incl 31 boxes of published and
unpublished mss, galley proofs, etc.

TULSA, OKLAHOMA

OK —TULSA METROPOLITAN AREA
PLANNING COMMISSION LIBRARY,
200 Civic Center, Tulsa, 74103. Mary R
Moss, Head Librn
Holdings: Vols 175 Cat
Notes: Present and past reports of TMAPC
on subjects concerning the growth of our
city and metropolitan areas. Newspaper
clippings from 1969 to present of new
developments in Tulsa and metropolitan
area.

TUMORS

AR —NATIONAL CENTER FOR
TOXICOLOGICAL RESEARCH, Library,
Jefferson, 72079. Susan Laney-Sheehan,
Supvr Librn
Holdings: Microforms
Notes: Incl (860) journal titles, (230) current
subscriptions.
CT —YALE UNIVERSITY, School of
Medicine, Section of Neuropathology
Library, Brain Tumor Registry, New Haven,
06520. Dr Elias Manuelidis, Cur
Holdings: Cat Slides
Notes: The Ernest Sachs Collection of about
8000 microscopic slides of brain tumors.
Also the Harvey Cushing Collection of 800
jars of brain tissue in Formalin, and about
2500 microscopic slides. Another collection,
belonging to the Pathology Department,
consists of brain sections from about 100
monkeys, with 30 slides from each brain.
Not cataloged, in boxes and inaccessible.
ME —JACKSON LABORATORY, Research
Laboratory, Bar Harbor, 04609.
Notes: "Subject: Strain Bibliography of
inbred strains of mice, transplantable tumors,
and named genes in mice ..." Mouse News
Letter. Database discontinued 1984, and has
become an archival record.
NY —COLD SPRING HARBOR
LABORATORY, Library, PO Box 100,
Cold Spring Harbor, 11724. Susan Gensel,
Library Dir; Genemary Falvey, Librn
Holdings: Vols (30,000)
Budget: ($103,500)
Notes: The highly technical collection is
comprised of 20,000 serial vols and 10,000
monographs. The library receives 500
current serial titles. Subjects covered incl
molecular and cellular biology, virology,
biochemistry, microbiology, oncology,
neurobiology, biological risk assessment and
genetic engineering/biotechnology. Special
collections in eugenics and genetics are
primarily historical dealing with the
development of genetics in the US which
had its beginnings here.
NY —MEMORIAL SLOAN KETTERING
CANCER CENTER, Lee Coombe

TUMORS (cont.)

Memorial Library, 1275 York Ave, New York, 10021. Angelina Harmon, Dir
Holdings: Vols (25,000) Cat Mss Pix Slides Phonorecords Audiotapes Videotapes 16mm Films Microforms
Budget: ($450,000)
Notes: Incl an developing archives collection, with some rare materials. An extensive bibliography of the institution's professional staff is maintained along with reprints. The main collection is concentrated in cancer and related fields of research and therapy.

RI —MIRIAM HOSPITAL MEDICAL LIBRARY, 164 Summit Ave, Providence, 02906. Ann LeClaire, Dir of Library Services
Holdings: Cat Cassettes
Notes: Special collection on the renal system with emphasis on kidney transplantation and dialysis.

TX —UNIVERSITY OF TEXAS, M D Anderson Hospital and Tumor Institute, Research Medical Library, Texas Medical Center, Houston, 77030. Marie Harvin, Research Medical Librn
Holdings: Vols (48,000) Cat
Notes: Library attempts to collect every publication in all languages related to clinical cancer (or oncology). Aim is an exhaustive collection in this field. Collect heavily (research level) in pathology, radiology, nuclear medicine, genetics and cell biology.

TUNAMIS see Tsunamis

TUNE BOOKS

MI —UNIVERSITY OF MICHIGAN, William L Clements Library, Ann Arbor, 48109. John C Dann, Dir

Notes: The William L. Clements Library of Americana is a non-circulating rare book library of original source material, printed and manuscript, dealing with America, from the discovery period into the late nineteenth century. The collection includes approximately 55,000 books and pamphlets, 550 linear feet of manuscripts, 4,100 volumes of newspapers, 36,000 maps, 40,000 pieces of sheet music, and 1,000 prints. The collection is strongest for the period of the American Revolution, and includes the papers of Thomas Gage, Sir Henry Clinton, and the Earl of Shelburne. Other areas of strength include antislavery, cartography and geography, discovery and exploration, American Indians, The Civil War, tune-books, sermons and orations, and the War of 1812. There are selective research collections dealing with Christopher Columbus, Thomas Paine, Benjamin Franklin, George Washington, Thomas Jefferson, and the Federalist Papers. Publications describing the collections of the library are: Author/Title catalog of Americana 1493-1860 in the William L. Clements Library... 7 volumes, Boston, G. K. Hall, 1970; Guide to the manuscript collections of the William L. Clements Library, by Arlene P. Shy 3d edition, Boston, G. K. Hall, 1978; Guide to the manuscript maps in the William L. Clements Library, compiled by Christian Burn, Ann Arbor, U. of Michigan, 1959; and Research catalog of maps of America, to 1860 in the William L. Clements Library..., edited by Douglas W. Marshall, 4 volumes, Boston, G. K. Hall, 1972.

*WILLIAM *L. *CLEMENTS *LIBRARY ..., EDITED BY *DOUGLAS *W. *MARSHALL, 4 VOLUMES, *BOSTON, *G. *K. *HALL, 1972.
MI —ANDREWS UNIVERSITY, James White Library, Berrien Springs, 49104. Marley H Soper, Dir
Holdings: Vols 110// Cat
Notes: Hymns of the Seventh-Day Adventist faith. The collection begins with the 1849 edition of the hymnal and continues to the present. Not available by interlibrary loan, but may be used at this library.

†NY —STATE UNIVERSITY OF NEW YORK, COLLEGE AT FREDONIA, Daniel A Reed Library, Fredonia, 14063.
Holdings: Vols (8000) Cat Phonorecords Audiotapes
Budget: ($12,500)
Notes: The Music Library supports the curricular needs of a large department of music which now has programs in both music education and performance. Separate card catalogs are maintained for 26,000 scores and more than 12,000 recordings and tape cassettes. The library has a small collection of 19th century American tunebooks, some Lowell Mason materials and a collection of sheet music and dance band arrangements numbering more than 3200 pieces and covering the period from 1850 through the big band era.

PA —PENNSYLVANIA STATE UNIVERSITY, Arts Library, 405 E Pattee Library, University Park, 16802. Daniel Zager, Music Librn
Holdings: Vols (14,000) Cat Phonorecords
Notes: The music collection supports a School of Music curriculum which is comprehensive at the undergraduate and masters degree levels. The collection includes scores (collected works and performance editions), books, periodicals, and recordings. The Special Collections area of the library includes the following music collections: the manuscripts, published scores, personal papers, and some recordings of the American composer Charles Wakefield Cadman; 18th and 19th century American tunebooks and 18th and 19th century Pennsylvania German hymnbooks and songbooks; and the Doyle Guntharp collection of field recordings of fiddler's performances and interviews from Central Pennsylvania.

SC —WOFFORD COLLEGE, Sandor Teszler Library, N Church St, Spartanburg, 29301. Frank J Anderson, Librn
Holdings: Vols 200 Uncat
Notes: Hayens-Brown Hymnal Collection consists of many denominations of rare items and colonial imprints, incl Saur and Isaiah Thomas imprints. Collection is being augmented by Pierce Gault of Washington, DC.

TX —SOUTHWESTERN BAPTIST THEOLOGICAL SEMINARY, Music Library, Fort Worth, 76122. Phillip W Sims, Librn
Holdings: Vols (19,000) Cat
Budget: ($30,000)
Notes: Incl in the Treasure Section are approx 250 tune books, plus many very old hymnals and other antiquarian items. Incl 97,000 pieces of sheet music, 24,000 scores, 7500 phonograph records and 3500 audiocassettes. The entire collection is cataloged except the periodicals and about one fourth of the sheet music.

TUNGELN, GEORGE HENRY VON, 1883-1914

IA —IOWA STATE UNIVERSITY, Library, Dept of Special Collections, Ames, 50011. Stanley M Yates, Head
Holdings: Vols 500 Cat
Notes: The private collection of Professor George Henry Von Tungeln, probably the earliest regular staff member in rural sociology in any land-grant college in the country.

TUNG OIL

MS —UNIVERSITY OF SOUTHERN MISSISSIPPI, William David McCain

Graduate Library, Box 5148, Southern Sta, Hattiesburg, 39406.
Holdings: Mss
Notes: Collection incl the research records (1934-1977; 33 cubic feet) of Dr James S Long and the research records and organizational records (1939-1971) of the American Tung Oil Institute and its predecessor organizations.
See also entries under Long, Dr James S; American Tung Oil Institute.

TUNGUSIC LANGUAGES

NY —NEW YORK PUBLIC LIBRARY, Oriental Div, Fifth Ave & 42 St, New York, 10018. E Christian Filstrup, Chief
Holdings: Cat Mss Microforms
Budget: ($56,455)
Notes: Published catalog of holdings.

TUNIS, EDWIN

OR —UNIVERSITY OF OREGON, Library, Eugene, 97403. Kenneth W Duckett, Curator
Holdings: Mss
Notes: The papers, etc, of Edwin Tunis.

TUNIS, JOHN

MA —BOSTON UNIVERSITY, Mugar Memorial Library, Special Collections Dept, 771 Commonwealth Ave, Boston, 02215. Howard B Gotlieb, Dir
Holdings: Cat Mss Pix
Notes: Mss, correspondence, etc collected in depth; incl publications by or about.

TUNISIA

CA —HOOVER INSTITUTION ON WAR, REVOLUTION & PEACE, Stanford University, Stanford, 94305. Peter Duignan, Cur; Karen Fung, Deputy Cur
Holdings: Vols (100,000)
See also entry under Hoover Institution - Near East

TUNNELS

MA —NORTH ADAMS PUBLIC LIBRARY, Houghton Memorial Bldg, Church & Main Sts, North Adams, 01247. Constance Griffin, Librn
Holdings: Vols (57)// Cat Mss Pix Microforms
Notes: Books on the building of the Hoosac Tunnel; reports made during the construction; ledgers kept by men working on the tunnel; pictures of the constuction (both photographs and lithographs); and a partial collection of the original plans of the tunnel. No separate catalog.

TUPPER, SIR CHARLES

†ON —MCMASTER UNIVERSITY, Library, Hamilton, L8S 4L6, Can.
Notes: Carbon typescript of "The Life of Sir Charles Tupper," by Rev E M Saunders, with his notes and correspondence with Sir Charles Tupper.

TURAUSKAS, EDUARDAS, 1896-1966

CA —HOOVER INSTITUTION ON WAR, REVOLUTION & PEACE, Stanford University, Stanford, 94305. Milorad M Drachkovitch, Archivist
Holdings: Mss Pix
Notes: Papers of Eduardas Turauskas, 1934-1958, consisting of correspondence, memoranda, reports, printed matter, clippings, photographs, and other materials collected during his career as Lithuanian diplomat, journalist, and statesman. Materials incl documentation on the Soviet occupation of Lithuania, 1940-41; and Lithuanian foreign relations in Europe. 1934-1941. 9 ms boxes.

TURBINES

MA —OLD STURBRIDGE VILLAGE, Research Library, Sturbridge, 01566.

TURBINES (cont.)

Theresa Rini Percy, Librn
Holdings: Vols (23,000) // Mss
Notes: Kinne Collection of trade catalogs of turbines and related machinery, material on water-power history, and turbine patents, 1790-1946. Also Clarence E Kinne papers, 1906-1949. 13 boxes (*Kinne Collection Checklist*, October 1977.)

TURBINES, AIR see Air—Turbines

TURBINES, GAS see Gas Turbines

TURCMAN LANGUAGE see Turkoman Language and Literature

TUREAUD, ALEXANDER P.

LA —AMISTAD RESEARCH CENTER, 400 Esplanade Ave, New Orleans, 70116. Clifton H Johnson, Exec Dir; Florence E Borders, Senior Archivist
Holdings: Vols (10,000) Cat Mss Pix Audiotapes Microforms
Budget: ($350,000)
Notes: In addition, 8,000,000 ms pieces, 10,000 pictures, 3500 microforms, and 500 audiotapes. Amistad Research Center is an historical research library devoted to the collection and use of primary source materials on the history of America's ethnic minorities, with particular emphasis on Afro-Americans, American Indians, and immigrant groups. Among the larger institutional collections held are the archives and records of the American Missionary Association, the American Home Missionary Society, the Race Relations Dept of the Anti-Defamation League, the Catholic Committee of the South, and the National Association of Human Rights Workers (formerly National Association of Intergroup Relations Officials, NAIRO). Also, private papers of the Harlem Renaissance poet, Countee Cullen; educator and civil rights leader, Mary McLeod Bethune; 20th century civil rights lawyer, Alexander P Tureaud; 19th century Black attorney and judge, George Ruffin; founder and director of Operation Crossroads Africa, Dr James H Robinson; and over 70 others.

TURECK, ROSALYN

MA —BOSTON UNIVERSITY, Mugar Memorial Library, Special Collections Dept, 771 Commonwealth Ave, Boston, 02215. Howard B Gotlieb, Dir
Holdings: Mss Pix
Notes: Mss, correspondence, etc collected in depth; incl publications by or about, and files of the International Bach Society, 1966-.
NY —NEW YORK PUBLIC LIBRARY, Performing Arts Research Center, Rodgers & Hammerstein Archives of Recorded Sound, 111 Amsterdam Ave, New York, 10023.
Holdings: audiotapes
Notes: Given by Miss Rosalyn Tureck, the collection consists of more than 500 hours on tape of performances by Miss Tureck, lectures and seminars on performance interpretation of Bach's music, and symposia and workshops of the International Bach Society.

TURF GRASSES

IA —IOWA STATE UNIVERSITY, Library, Ames, 50011. Warren B Kuhn, Dean of Library Services
Holdings: Cat
Notes: Extensive serial holdings.
MI —MICHIGAN STATE UNIVERSITY, Science Library, East Lansing, 48824. Carole S Armstrong, Head
Holdings: Vols 900 Cat
Notes: The collection has 100 journal titles with 650 vols, 160 monographs and 90 additional monographs on establishment, management and genetic improvement of grass.

TURF MANAGEMENT

SC —HORRY GEORGETOWN TECHNICAL COLLEGE, Library, Hwy 501, Box 1966, Conway, 29526. Barbara Brittain, Librn
Holdings: Vols (20,000) Cat Maps Slides Microforms

TURF SPORTS see Horse Racing; Track and Field Sports

TURFANISH LANGUAGE see Tokharian Languages

TURKEY

CA —UNIVERSITY OF CALIFORNIA, LOS ANGELES, Research Library, Dept of Special Collections, 405 Hilgard Ave, Los Angeles, 90024. Edward Shreeves, Chairman, Bibliographers Group; David S Zeidberg, Head
Notes: 94 linear feet of unprocessed Turkish mss.
CA —HOOVER INSTITUTION ON WAR, REVOLUTION & PEACE, Stanford University, Stanford, 94305. Milorad M Drachkovitch, Archivist
Holdings: Mss
Notes: Letters, manuscripts, clippings, and unique documents from the library of Mr Hidayet Dagdeviren, Istanbul, Tukey. The collection covers the last years of the Ottoman Empire and the first years of the Republic as well as special problems on social organization and minorities. 28 ms boxes, 22 vols.
See also entry under Near East
†CT —UNIVERSITY OF CONNECTICUT LIBRARY, Special Collections Dept, Storrs, 06268. Richard H Schimmelpfeng, Dir of Special Collections
Notes: Good and unusual collection.
DC —GEORGETOWN UNIVERSITY, Library, Special Collections Div, 37 & O Sts NW, Washington, 20057. George M Barringer, Special Collections Librn; Nicholas B Sheetz, Mss Librn
Holdings: Mss Cat Maps Pix
Notes: The papers of George Crews McGhee (1912), geologist, oil producer, and diplomat. The papers incl files from McGhee's United States ambassadorships to Turkey (1951-1953) and Germany (1963-1968) as well as his extensive involvement in numerous organizations and committees incl the Combined Raw Materials Board, the Bilderberg Group, the Draper Committee, the Committee for Economic Development, and the Business Council for International Understanding, among many others. Also incl are 264 volumes from the 17th to early 20th century relating to Turkey.
DC —LIBRARY OF CONGRESS, African and Middle Eastern Division, Washington, 20540.
Holdings: Cat Mss Microforms
Notes: Near East: Over 75,000 vols, Arabic, Armenian, Turkish, Persian, and related languages. Special subject strengths incl Islamic philosophy, history, and literature.
IN —INDIANA UNIVERSITY, Lilly Library, Seventh St, Bloomington, 47405. William R Cagle, Librn
Holdings: Cat
Notes: Foreign relations with Russia, largely 19th century.
MA —HARVARD UNIVERSITY LIBRARY, Widener Library, Middle Eastern Dept, Cambridge, 02138. David H Partington, Librn
Holdings: Cat Mss Microforms
Budget: ($55,000)
Notes: Vols IV of the library's *Catalog of Arbic, Persian, and Ottoman Turkish Books* (1968) lists 4000 volumes in Ottoman Turkish; later works printed in the Latin alphabet are to be found in the Library's card catalogs. See also *Harvard Library Bulletin*, XVI (1968), 313-325.
NY —COLUMBIA UNIVERSITY LIBRARIES, Rare Book & Manuscript Library, 801 Butler Library, 535 W 114 St, New York, 10027. Kenneth A Lohf, Librn
Holdings: Mss
Notes: Incl the papers of Ernest Jackh, with much on German-Turkish relations. Restricted use.

WA —UNIVERSITY OF WASHINGTON LIBRARIES, Suzzallo Library, Near East Section, FM-25, Seattle, 98195. Fawzi W Khoury, Head
Notes: Includes a collection of 25,000 Turkish and Turkic materials.
WI —UNIVERSITY OF WISCONSIN, MADISON, Memorial Library, Slavic Studies Collection, 728 State St, Madison, 53706. Aleksander Rolich, Bibliographer for Slavic Studies; Robert P Gakovich, Slavic Cataloger; Valdis J Zeps, Baltic Studies Center
Holdings: Vols (25,000) Cat
Notes: The Balcanica collection in Memorial Library exceeds 25,000 volumes and active collecting continues at over 2000 titles per year in Bulgarian, Rumanian, Turkish and the languages of Yugoslavia. Many rare and unique titles are to be found in this collection, including serial titles, such as *Nova Vreme* (1897-1923, 1947-to date), *Nova Europa* (1920-1939), and unique Turkish Salnameh. The emphasis is on historical materials, but there is considerable strength in South Slavic literatures and linguistics. The Rumanian materials are of more recent vintage.

TURKEY—HISTORY

ME —BOWDOIN COLLEGE, Library, Brunswick, 04011. Dianne M Gutscher, Cur of Special Collections
Holdings: Mss
Notes: A small collection of Cyrus Hamlin material is supplemented by about 500 letters in the Abbott Memorial Collection from and to this missionary, founder of Robert College in Bebek, Turkey, and president of Middlebury College (Vermont).
MA —HARVARD UNIVERSITY LIBRARY, Widener Library, Middle Eastern Dept, Cambridge, 02138. David H Partington, Librn
Holdings: Cat Mss Microforms
Budget: ($55,000)
Notes: Vols IV of the library's *Catalogue of Arabic, Persian, and Ottoman Turkish Books* (1968) lists 4000 vols in Ottoman Turkish; later works printed in the Latin alphabet are listed in the library's card catalogs. See also *Harvard Library Bulletin*, XVI (1968): pp 313-325.
TX —TEXAS TECH UNIVERSITY, Library, Lubbock, 79409. David J Murrah, Assoc Dir for Special Collections
Notes: Archive of Turkish Oral Narrative.

TURKEY—IMPRINTS

†CT —UNIVERSITY OF CONNECTICUT LIBRARY, Special Collections Dept, Storrs, 06268. Richard H Schimmelpfeng, Dir of Special Collections
Notes: Good and unusual collection.
IN —INDIANA UNIVERSITY, Lilly Library, Seventh St, Bloomington, 47405. William R Cagle, Librn
Holdings: Vols 28 // Cat
Notes: One example of each of 18 books printed by Ibrahim Muteferrika, the first Turkish printer.

TURKEY—PICTURES, ILLUSTRATIONS, ETC.

DC —LIBRARY OF CONGRESS, Prints & Photographs Div, Washington, 20540.
Holdings: Vols 51
Notes: The Abdul-Hamid II Collection of photographs of Turkey. Formal views of military installations and personnel, naval vessels, schools, hospitals, historic monuments, fire-fighting and lifesaving equipment, major cities, palaces and stables of the Imperial Court, and other subjects of official interest.

TURKISH LANGUAGE AND LITERATURE

AZ —UNIVERSITY OF ARIZONA, Library, Oriental Studies Collection, Tucson, 85721. Mary J McWhorter, Actg Head Librn
Holdings: Vols (95,000) Cat Microforms
Budget: ($30,000)
See also entry under Oriental Languages and Literatures

TURKISH LANGUAGE AND LITERATURE (cont.)

CA —UNIVERSITY OF CALIFORNIA, LOS ANGELES, Research Library, Near Eastern Collection, Los Angeles, 90024. Edward Shreeves, Chairman, Bibliographers Group; Dunning Wilson, Near Eastern Bibliographer
Holdings: Vols (200,000) Cat Mss Maps Microforms
Notes: Incl ancient cultures and history.

CA —HOOVER INSTITUTION ON WAR, REVOLUTION & PEACE, Stanford University, Stanford, 94305. Peter Duignan, Cur; Karen Fung, Deputy Cur
Holdings: Vols (100,000)
See also entry under Near East

CT —YALE UNIVERSITY, Box 1603A, Yale Station, New Haven, 06520.

†CT —UNIVERSITY OF CONNECTICUT LIBRARY, Special Collections Dept, Storrs, 06268. Richard H Schimmelpfeng, Dir of Special Collections
Notes: Good and unusual collection.

DC —LIBRARY OF CONGRESS, African and Middle Eastern Division, Washington, 20540.
Holdings: Cat Mss Microforms
Notes: Near East: Over 75,000 vols, Arabic, Armenian, Turkish, Persian, and related languages. Special subject strengths incl Islamic philosophy, history, and literature.

MA —HARVARD UNIVERSITY LIBRARY, Widener Library, Middle Eastern Dept, Cambridge, 02138. David H Partington, Librn
Holdings: Cat Mss Microforms
Budget: ($55,000)
Notes: Vols IV of the library's *Catalogue of Arabic, Persian, and Ottoman Turkish Books*, 1968, lists 4000 vols in Ottoman Turkish; later works printed in the Latin alphabet are listed in the library's card catalogs. See also *Harvard Library Bulletin*, XVI (1968): pp 313-325.

MI —UNIVERSITY OF MICHIGAN, Graduate Library, Near East Dept, Ann Arbor, 48109. John A Eilts, Bibliographer
Holdings: Vols (150,000) Cat Mss Maps Microforms
Notes: Excludes Islam in the Far East, Judaism in general, though it does incl specifically Near Eastern Judaism. Incl Bahaism and Arab philosophy, fields of study connected with Islamic or Arabic studies, Turkish language and literature.

NY —NEW YORK PUBLIC LIBRARY, Oriental Div, Fifth Ave & 42 St, New York, 10018. E Christian Filstrup, Chief
Holdings: Cat Mss Microforms
Budget: ($56,455)
Notes: Published catalog of holdings.

NY —NEW YORK PUBLIC LIBRARY, Donnell Foreign Language Library, 20 W 53 St, New York, 10019. Bosiljka Stevanovic, Supvr Librn
Holdings: Vols 155 Cat
Notes: Turkish collection incl Turkish authors of Turkish expression. No separate catalog.

OH —OHIO STATE UNIVERSITY, Library, 1858 Neil Mall, Columbus, 43210. Dona Straley, Islamica Librn
Holdings: Vols (25,000) Cat Maps Microforms
Budget: ($30,000)
Notes: The bulk of the Arabic language collection is in the field of language and literature, with large and medium collections in the fields of Islamica and Middle East history. There are approx 2000 Persian language vols and approx 3000 vols in Turkish materials. Also a substantial supporting collection of materials on Arabic language and literature, Islamica, and Middle East history in all of the major European languages. PL 480 recipient since 1975. No ms holdings.

TX —TEXAS TECH UNIVERSITY, Library, Lubbock, 79409. David J Murrah, Assoc Dir for Special Collections

WA —UNIVERSITY OF WASHINGTON LIBRARIES, Suzzallo Library, Near East Section, FM-25, Seattle, 98195. Fawzi W Khoury, Head
Holdings: Vols 25,000 Cat
Budget: ($52,752)
Notes: Includes a collection of 25,000 Turkish and Turkic materials.

WI —UNIVERSITY OF WISCONSIN, MADISON, Memorial Library, Slavic Studies Collection, 728 State St, Madison, 53706. Aleksander Rolich, Bibliographer for Slavic Studies; Robert P Gakovich, Slavic Cataloger; Valdis J Zeps, Baltic Studies Center
Holdings: Vols (25,000) Cat
Notes: The Balcanica collection in Memorial Library exceeds 25,000 volumes and active collecting continues at over 2000 titles per year in Bulgarian, Rumanian, Turkish and the languages of Yugoslavia. Many rare and unique titles are to be found in this collection, including serial titles, such as *Nova Vreme* (1897-1923, 1947-to date), *Nova Europa* (1920-1939), and unique Turkish *Salnameh*. The emphasis is on historical materials, but there is considerable strength in South Slavic literatures and linguistics. The Rumanian materials are of more recent vintage.

TURKISH MANUSCRIPTS see Manuscripts, Turkish

TURKMAN LANGUAGE see Turkoman Language and Literature

TURKOMAN LANGUAGE AND LITERATURE

NY —NEW YORK PUBLIC LIBRARY, Oriental Div, Fifth Ave & 42 St, New York, 10018. E Christian Filstrup, Chief
Holdings: Cat Mss Microforms
Budget: ($56,455)
Notes: Published catalog of holdings.

TURKO-TATARIC LANGUAGES

NY —NEW YORK PUBLIC LIBRARY, Oriental Div, Fifth Ave & 42 St, New York, 10018. E Christian Filstrup, Chief
Holdings: Cat Mss Microforms
Budget: ($56,455)
Notes: Published catalog of holdings.

TURLEIGH, VERONICA

DC —GEORGETOWN UNIVERSITY, Library, Special Collections Div, 37 & O Sts NW, Washington, 20057. George M Barringer, Special Collections Librn; Nicholas B Sheetz, Mss Librn
Holdings: Mss Cat
Notes: The literary papers of author and art curator, James Laver (1899-1975), and those of his wife, the actress Veronica Turleigh; consisting of letters, with a considerable number written by Lady Cnythia Asquith; Clifford Box; Enid Bagnold; Nicholas Bentley; Violet Clifton; Desmond MacCarthy; Sir Edward Marsh; Sir Francis Meynell; Kate O'Brien; Dorothy L Sayers; Andre Simon; Enid Starkie; A J A Symons; Angela Thirkell; and Alec Waugh.

TURMAN, LAWRENCE

CA —UNIVERSITY OF CALIFORNIA, LOS ANGELES, Research Library, Dept of Special Collections, 405 Hilgard Ave, Los Angeles, 90024. Edward Shreeves, Chairman, Bibliographers Group; David S Zeidberg, Head
Holdings: Mss Pix
Notes: 13 linear feet of screenplays and related materials.

TURN-UP BOOKS see Harlequin and Harlequinades

TURNBULL, AGNES SLIGH

MA —BOSTON UNIVERSITY, Mugar Memorial Library, Special Collections Dept, 771 Commonwealth Ave, Boston, 02215. Howard B Gotlieb, Dir
Holdings: Cat Mss Pix
Notes: Mss correspondence, etc collected in depth; incl publications by or about.

TURNBULL, EDWIN LITCHFIELD

MD —JOHNS HOPKINS UNIVERSITY, Milton S Eisenhower Library, Charles & 34 Sts, Baltimore, 21218. Ann S Gwyn, Assistant Dir for Special Collections
Holdings: // Cat Mss
Notes: Ms letters, articles, scrapbooks made by the author.

TURNER, ARLIN

NC —DUKE UNIVERSITY, William R Perkins Library, Jay B Hubbell Center for American Literary Historiography, Durham, 27706. Erma Whittington, Librn
Notes: 77,312 items, including manuscripts, pictures, clippings, and correspondence. "The objective of the Center is to gather the papers and materials of significant scholars and critics in American literary history." The Center is a part of the Perkins Library Manuscripts Department.

TURNER, BAPTIST NOEL

BC —UNIVERSITY OF VICTORIA, McPherson Library, Victoria, V8W 3H5, Can.
Notes: Rector and writer. Incl 34 cm, 1776-1817; microfilm: 2 negative reels; notebooks containing anecdotes, essays, notes, ideas, verse.

TURNER, FREDERICK JACKSON

MA —HARVARD UNIVERSITY LIBRARY, Houghton Library, Cambridge, 02138. Rodney G Dennis, Cur of Manuscripts
Holdings: Cat Mss
Notes: Correspondence, papers, pictures, diaries, etc.

TURNER, GEORGE E.

CO —DENVER PUBLIC LIBRARY, 1357 Broadway, Denver, 80203.
Notes: Correspondence, papers, pictures, diaries, etc.

TURNPIKES see Toll Roads

TURTLES AND TORTOISES

FL —ARCHBOLD BIOLOGICAL STATION, Library, Rt 2, Box 180, Lake Placid, 33852. Fred E Lohrer, Librn
Holdings: Cat
Notes: Biology of North American land tortoises, *Gopherus*. Incl about 250 cataloged reprints; library is not adding to reprint collection.

TUSAYAN INDIANS see Hopi Indians

TUVA LANGUAGE see Soyot Language

TWAIN, MARK

AZ —UNIVERSITY OF ARIZONA, University Library, Special Collections, Tucson, 85721. Louis A Hieb, Head
Holdings: Vols (7000) Cat Mss Microforms
Budget: ($30,000)
Notes: Major authors collected are Twain, Garland, Hart, Irving, Melville and James.

CA —UNIVERSITY OF CALIFORNIA, BERKELEY, Bancroft Library, Manuscripts Division, Berkeley, 94720. James D Hart, Dir
Holdings: Uncat Mss
Notes: The Mark Twain Papers are the outstanding collection of the author's mss, correspondence, and related documentary material. Inquiries should be addressed to Robert H Hirst, Editor, *Mark Twain Papers*.

CO —DENVER PUBLIC LIBRARY, 1357 Broadway, Denver, 80203.
Holdings: Cat
Notes: Incl first editions.

CT —MARK TWAIN MEMORIAL, 351 Farmington Ave, Hartford, 06105. Wynn Lee, Dir
Holdings: Vols 1500 Cat Mss Pix Slides Microforms
Notes: The Samuel L Clemens Family Collection, 1867 to date. Very large collection of photographs of S L Clemens, his family, friends, houses, etc, plus period photographs filed chronologically and

TWAIN, MARK (cont.)

categorically-no catalog; large collection of related clippings filed under subject headings-no catalog; correspondence, literary mss, documents and other papers-over 1000 items. Card catalog for books (many with SLC's marginalia), magazines, periodicals, pamphlets, letters, mss and documents. Published description of the collection in the Library of Congress Union Catalog of Manuscript Collections. Also have memorabilia and audio recordings. No photocopying.

CT —STOWE-DAY LIBRARY, 77 Forest St, Hartford, 06105. Diana J Royce, Librn
Holdings: Vols (15,000) Cat Mss Pix
Notes: 150,000 cataloged mss and publications concerning architecture, decorative arts, history and literature of the period 1840-1900, with emphasis on Nook Farm, Mark Twain, Harriet Beecher Stowe, Calvin E Stowe, Charles Dudley Warner, William Hooker Gillette, Isabella Beecher Hooker. Incl 5000 pictures.

CT —YALE UNIVERSITY, Box 1603A, Yale Station, New Haven, 06520.
Holdings: Mss Pix
Notes: Incl manuscripts, drawings, notebooks.

IL —NORTHWESTERN UNIVERSITY, Library, Special Collections Dept, 1937 Sheridan Rd, Evanston, 60201. R Russell Maylone, Cur
Holdings: Vols 300 Cat Mss
Notes: First editions, serials, ephemera. Additional material in general collection.

IL —UNIVERSITY OF ILLINOIS, URBANA/CHAMPAIGN, Library, 1408 W Gregory Drive, Urbana, 61801. Norman B Brown, Asst Dir for Special Collections
Holdings: Vols Mss Pix
Notes: The Franklin J Meine Collection of over 2100 items in the Rare Book Room includes almost every edition, 230 photographs, statuettes, memorabilia, etc.

IN —INDIANA UNIVERSITY, Lilly Library, Seventh St, Bloomington, 47405. William R Cagle, Librn
Holdings: Vols 270 // Cat Mss
Notes: The Merle Johnson/J K Lilly Collection, incl first editions, etc.

KS —UNIVERSITY OF KANSAS, Kenneth Spencer Research Library, Special Collections Dept, Lawrence, 66045. Alexandra Mason, Librn
Holdings: Vols 150 Cat Mss
Notes: Mostly by Mark Twain but some about. Typescript of *Tom Sawyer, Detective*. Based on Milton F Barlow collection. Noncirculating.

MA —AMHERST COLLEGE, Library, Amherst, 01002. John Lancaster, Special Collections Librn
Holdings: Vols 100 Cat Mss

MA —HARVARD UNIVERSITY LIBRARY, Houghton Library, Cambridge, 02138. Rodney G Dennis, Cur of Manuscripts
Holdings: Cat Mss

MA —MILLICENT LIBRARY, Centre & William Sts, PO Box 30, Fairhaven, 02719. Rita Steele, Librn
Holdings: // Uncat Mss
Notes: Mark Twain letters. No photocopying.

MI —DETROIT PUBLIC LIBRARY, Rare Books Department, 5201 Woodward Ave, Detroit, 48202.
Holdings: Vols 195 Cat Mss Pix
Notes: Incl first editions, mss, letters, and many photographs. Restricted use. Reference collection.

MO —CULVER-STOCKTON COLLEGE, Carl Johann Memorial Library, Canton, 63435. Robert Lin, Librn
Holdings: Vols 1500 Cat
Budget: $1000
Notes: The Johann Collection covers all aspects of Midwest Americana, with special emphasis on Missouri and Mark Twain.

MO —SAINT LOUIS PUBLIC LIBRARY, Gardner Rare Book Room, 1301 Olive St, Saint Louis, 63103. Julanne M Good, Supervisor; Martha Riley, Rare Books Librn
Holdings: Vols (2300) Cat
Budget: ($5573)
Notes: First editions of authors having some

association with William Marion Reedy and *Reedy's Mirror*, such as Sara Teasdale, Zoe Akins, Fannie Hurst, Edgar Lee Masters, Babette Deutsch, Richard LeGallienne, etc. Also first editions of selected St Louis and/or Missouri authors such as T S Eliot, Samuel L Clemens, Theodore Dreiser and Tennessee Williams. Noncirculating.

NJ —PRINCETON UNIVERSITY, Library, Rare Books Dept, Princeton, 08544. Stephen Ferguson, Cur
Holdings: Vols 200 Cat Mss
Notes: The manuscript section incl about 75 letters and a few prose works. See *Princeton University Library Chronicle*, v 12, p 217.

NY —BUFFALO & ERIE COUNTY PUBLIC LIBRARY, Rare Book Room, Lafayette Sq, Buffalo, 14203. William H Loos, Cur
Holdings: Vols 1500 Mss
Notes: First editions, incl a special collection of English and foreign-language editions of *Huckleberry Finn*. The 200 volume collection now incl 79 foreign editions in 28 different languages. Keystone of the collection is the original ms of the novel. Described in *Huckleberry Finn; A Descriptive Bibliography of the Huckleberry Finn Collection at the Buffalo Public Library*, compiled by Lucille Adams (Buffalo, 1950). Also, The Bulkley Southworth Griffin Collection, incl first editions, reprints, periodicals, translations, comic book editions, and books about Twain. This 1250 volume collection is at present only partially cataloged.

NY —ELMIRA COLLEGE, Gannett-Tripp Learning Center, Elmira, 14901. James D Gray, Dir
Holdings: Vols 650 Cat Mss Pix
Notes: Incl mss, books, etc.

NY —HISTORICAL SOCIETY OF THE TARRYTOWNS, Library, One Grove St, Tarrytown, 10591. Ruth Neuendorffer, Librn
Holdings: Vols (3000) Cat Maps Microforms VF
Notes: History of the Tarrytowns and vicinity. Incl newspapers, 1875-1946, on microfilm. Bound volumes of Tarrytown *Daily News*, 1916-1937.

†NC —WAKE FOREST UNIVERSITY, Z Smith Reynolds Library, Box 7777, Reynold Sta, Winston-Salem, 27109. Richard J Murdoch, Rare Book Librn
Holdings: Vols 360 Cat

PA —UNIVERSITY OF PENNSYLVANIA, Van Pelt Library, Rare Books Collection, 34 & Walnut Sts, Philadelphia, 19104. Daniel Traister, Special Collections Librn
Holdings: Vols 600
Notes: First and later editions of his writings with critical and biographical vols.

†TX —UNIVERSITY OF TEXAS LIBRARIES, General Libraries, Humanities Research Center, PO Box 7219, Austin, 78712. John Chalmers, Librn

TX —SOUTHERN METHODIST UNIVERSITY, DeGolyer Library, Box 396, SMU, Dallas, 75275. Clifton H Jones, Dir
Holdings: Vols (80,000) Cat Mss Maps Pix Slides Microforms
Notes: First editions of prominent authors; also of books in subject emphasis collections. All subjects listed in this vol are strong. Numerous collections of personal papers relating to subjects also.

TX —UNIVERSITY OF TEXAS, EL PASO, Library, El Paso, 79968. Fred W Hanes, Dir
Holdings: Vols 64 Cat
Notes: First editions.

VA —UNIVERSITY OF VIRGINIA, Alderman Library, Clifton Waller Barrett Collection, Charlottesville, 22901. Joan St C Crane, Cur of American Literature Collections
Holdings: Vols 550 Cat Mss
Notes: Important collection of Twain's variant issues; especially *Huckleberry Finn*, nearly 2000 mss; letters.

WI —UNIVERSITY OF WISCONSIN, MADISON, Memorial Library, Rare Books Collection, 728 State St, Madison, 53706. Gretchen Lagana, Cur
Holdings: Vols 550 Cat Mss
Notes: Bassett-Brownell Collection, in addition to many first editions and Twainiana, the collection contains rare

magazines, newspapers, photographs, correspondence and 161 holograph letters dated from 1867 to 1910. Also included is an original portrait in oil of Twain by the late F Luis Mora painted in 1909. Housed in the Dept of Rare Books and Special Collections.

TWEEDALE, GEORGE HAY

WI —UNIVERSITY OF WISCONSIN, MADISON, Memorial Library, South Asian Collection, 728 State St, Madison, 53706. Jack C Wells, Bibliographer
Holdings: Cat Microforms
Notes: Public and private papers as Governor of Madras, India.

TWEEDSMUIR, LORD JOHN BUCHAN AND LADY SUSAN see Buchan, John, 1st Baron Tweedsmuir, 1875-1940

TWENTIETH CENTURY FOX

CA —UNIVERSITY OF CALIFORNIA, LOS ANGELES, Theater Arts Library, Los Angeles, 90024. Edward Shreeves, Chairman, Bibliographers Group; Audree Malkin, Head, Theater Arts Library
Notes: The Twentieth Century Fox Archives, covering the period 1915 to the present. The Archive consists of (1) approx 25,000 scripts in various versions, treatments, story outlines, rough drafts, revised drafts, final shooting scripts, post-production continuities, dialogue scripts, master title sheets, and production material; (2) approx 4 million stills and negatives incl scene stills, make-up, wardrobe, publicity, premiere, sets, and special activities for feature film and publicity stills for 49 television series; (3) production files consisting of 1688 linear feet of records for music compositions, call sheets and construction reports, story department synopsis files, contract synopsis for produced and unproduced properties and purchase of literary material, and story department correspondence.

CA —UNIVERSITY OF SOUTHERN CALIFORNIA, Edward L Doheny Memorial Library, Archives of Performing Arts, University Park, Los Angeles, 90089. Robert Knutson, Librn
Holdings: Mss
Notes: Twentieth Century Fox Collection incl screenplays and story department notes from 1919-1967.

†SC —UNIVERSITY OF SOUTH CAROLINA, Libraries, Columbia, 29208.
Notes: Newsreels made from 1919-63 by Twentieth Century Fox.

TWICHELL, JOSEPH HOPKINS

CT —YALE UNIVERSITY, Box 1603A, Yale Station, New Haven, 06520.
Holdings: Cat Mss

TWIN OAKS COMMUNITY

VA —UNIVERSITY OF VIRGINIA, Alderman Library, Manuscripts Dept, Charlottesville, 22901. Edmund Berkeley Jr, Cur
Holdings: Cat Mss
Notes: Papers of the Twin Oaks Community, Louisa County, Va, an intentional community based on Walden Two, 1967- , incl administrative and financial records, correspondence, and files on other alternative communities.

TYDINGS, MILLARD E.

MD —UNIVERSITY OF MARYLAND, Library, Archives & Manuscripts Dept, College Park, 20742. Mary A Boccaccio, Head
Holdings: Mss Pix
Notes: University of Maryland publications and archives; collections of organizational papers (eg, Baltimore & Ohio Railroad; various organizations concerned with the Chesapeake Bay and environs; various labor

TYDINGS, MILLARD E. (cont.)

unions, particularly those involving the tabaccco industry), mostly associated with Maryland; collections of papers and mss associated with literary and public figures (eg, the late Senator Millard Tydings); oral histories relating to the archival and mss collections; associated memorabilia; photographs, mainly associated with Maryland. A guide to collections of personal, family, and organizational papers relating to Maryland is being prepared.

TYKOCINER, JOSEPH

IL —UNIVERSITY OF ILLINOIS, URBANA/CHAMPAIGN, Library, 1408 W Gregory Drive, Urbana, 61801. Norman B Brown, Asst Dir for Special Collections
Holdings: Cat Mss Pix Audiotapes
Notes: The papers of Joseph T Tykociner (a pioneer in the field of wireless, electronics, sound movies and zetetics). Incl correspondence, notes, books, articles and reprints, photographs and negatives, biographical materials and sound tapes.

TYLER, ANNE

NC —DUKE UNIVERSITY, William R Perkins Library, Manuscript Dept, Durham, 27706. Ellen Gartrell, Cur of Mss
Holdings: Cat Mss
Notes: Papers, correspondence, etc.
NC —DUKE UNIVERSITY, William R Perkins Library, Rare Book Room, Durham, 27706. John L Sharpe, III, Cur
Notes: A collection of Duke University authors, established around 1963, with the writings of the students of William Blackburn and greatly enhanced by the gift of Professor Blackburn's collection. Represented are James Applewhite, Fred Chappell, Guy Davenport, Reynolds Price, William Styron, Frances Gray Patton, and Anne Tyler. Printed works are in the Rare Book Room and manuscripts are in the Manuscript Department.

TYLER, J. HOGE

VA —VIRGINIA POLYTECHNIC INSTITUTE AND STATE UNIVERSITY LIBRARY, Blacksburg, 24061. Glenn L McMullen, Special Collections Librn
Holdings: Vols (2000) Cat Mss Maps Pix Audiotapes
Notes: Primarily Southwest Virginia materials. Collection incl ca 200 mss, account books and other archival records of nineteenth century area businesses and other mining operations; the extant archival records of several Southwest Virginia railroads, incl the Virginia and Tennessee Railroad and the Norfolk and Western Railroad; and papers of historically prominent Southwest Virginians, incl John Apperson, Dr Harvy Black, James P Charlton, W Graham Claytor, Henley Fugate, Clement D Johnston, Germanicus Kent, William Preston, J Hoge Tyler, and William C Wampler. Several oral history collections incl material on Appalachian customs and folklore, particularly in Patrick County.

TYLER, JOHN, AND FAMILY (1664-1935)

DC —LIBRARY OF CONGRESS, Manuscript Division, Washington, 20540. John C Broderick, Chief
Notes: The Presidential Papers collection incl the papers, etc, of numerous Presidents.
VA —COLLEGE OF WILLIAM AND MARY, Earl Gregg Swem Library, Williamsburg, 23185. Margaret C Cook, Cur of Manuscripts & Rare Books
Holdings: // Cat Mss
Notes: Family and professional papers of John Tyler, Virginia Governor (1825-1827) and US President (1841-1845), and his children, particularly Lyon G Tyler, historian and president of the College of William and Mary. 55,310 items.

TYLER, MOSES COIT

MI —NORTHERN MICHIGAN UNIVERSITY, Lydia M Olson Library, Elizabeth L Harden Drive, Marquette, 49855. Stephen H Peters, Cataloger
Holdings: Vols (4000)// Uncat
Notes: The personal "working" library of Moses Coit Tyler, American historian and literary scholar. Included are strong sections dealing with theology, biography, education, and the Colonial and Early National periods of American history and literature. Many volumes were annotated by Tyler. Use restricted to the library.

TYNAN, KATHARINE

IL —SOUTHERN ILLINOIS UNIVERSITY, CARBONDALE, Delyte W Morris Library, Special Collections Dept, Carbondale, 62901. David V Koch, Cur of Special Collections; Louisa Bowen, Cur of Manuscripts
Holdings: Vols 50 Cat Mss Pix
Notes: Personal papers, 1882-1949, 5 linear feet, incl letters from J B Yeats, George Russell, James Stephens, Lionel Johnson, Alice Meynell, Padraic Colum and Lady Gregory. Inventory and name index available at library.

TYPE AND TYPEFOUNDING

CA —CLAREMONT COLLEGES, Ella Strong Denison Library, Scripps College, Claremont, 91711. Judy Harvey Sahak, Librn
Holdings: Cat Mss Pix
Notes: In addition to books and ephemera, collection includes original drawings, paper and metal patterns, matrices, and fonts for types that Frederic S Goudy designed for the Scripps College Press.
CA —CALIFORNIA HISTORICAL SOCIETY, Schubert Hall Library, 2099 Pacific Ave, San Francisco, 94109. Bruce L Johnson, Library Dir
Holdings: Vols 4400 Cat Mss Pix Microforms
Notes: The Edward C Kemble Collections. Not collections of fine printing, but of the history of printing and publishing with emphasis on the Pacific Coast, although the full scope of the collection is not limited to this area. In addition to bibliographic tools and reference works, it contains type specimen books and several long runs of trade periodicals and house organs of San Francisco typefounders. The Taylor & Taylor Archives, a part of this collection, contain the working record of a major San Francisco printing firm. The *Kemble Occasional*, published three times a year from the Kemble Collections, presents scholarly articles on the history of printing. Edward C Kemble was the first historian of printing in California.
CA —STANFORD UNIVERSITY LIBRARIES, Cecil H Green Library, Stanford, 94305. Michael T Ryan, Cur
Holdings: Vols (12,000) Cat
Notes: The Morgan A & Aline D Gunst Memorial Library. The book arts in every century with some of the best examples. Strong collection of examples of California printers and graphic artists. Complete or nearly complete collections of works by the Kelmscott, Doves, Ashendene, Colt, Grabhorn, and Grabhorn-Hoyem presses.
DC —LIBRARY OF CONGRESS, Rare Book & Special Collections Div, Washington, 20540. William Matheson, Chief
Holdings: Vols 1791 Cat Mss
Notes: The Frederic and Bertha Goudy Collection incl original type designs, mss, personal correspondence, type specimens, ephemeral material and a small section of typefounding equipment.
See also entry under Goudy, Frederick W.
IL —NEWBERRY LIBRARY, John M Wing Foundation on the History of Printing, 60 W Walton St, Chicago, 60610. Diana Haskell, Cur of Modern Mss
Holdings: Vols (30,000) Cat Mss
Budget: ($50,000)
Notes: The collection covers printing and printing history of Western Europe and the Americas from its invention to the present. It is particularly rich in incunabula (about 2000); the works of the great printers, among others Aldus, Bodoni, Baskerville, and Rogers. Printed catalog: *A Dictionary* Catalogue. (Boston: G K Hall, 1961); *Supplements* (1981). Brief descriptions: James M Wells, "The John M Wing Foundation of the Newberry Library," *The Book Collector,* VIII, 2 (Summer 1959), pp 157-162; Lawrece W Towner, *An Uncommon Collection of Uncommon* Collections (Chicago: The Newberry Library, 1977), pp 25-26.
†MD —UNIVERSITY OF MARYLAND, Library, R D Remley Collection, College Park, 20742. Donald Farren, Cur Rare Books
Holdings: Vols (2000) Cat
Notes: *Exempla* and secondary works in the areas of typography, calligraphy, book design, book illustration, the history of books, and of publishing, etc. Catalog entries for designers, printing types, private presses, etc.
MA —HARVARD UNIVERSITY LIBRARY, Houghton Library, Printing and Graphic Arts Dept, Cambridge, 02138. Eleanor M Garvey, Cur
Notes: Collection incl illustrated books, fine printing, type specimens, illuminated and calligraphic manuscripts, and drawings for book illustration.
NY —TYPOPHILES INC, Typographic Reference Library, 140 Lincoln Rd, Brooklyn, 11225. Robert L Leslie, Dir
Holdings: 4800 Vols
Notes: History of printing in all languages. Special collection of French and German type specimen books since 1888.
NY —COLUMBIA UNIVERSITY LIBRARIES, Rare Book & Manuscript Library, 801 Butler Library, 535 W 114 St, New York, 10027. Kenneth A Lohf, Librn
Holdings: Vols (5000)
Notes: The library of the American Typefounders Company.
See also entry under Books About Books
NY —GRADUATE CENTER OF THE CITY UNIVERSITY OF NEW YORK, William H and Gwynne K Crouse Library for Publishing Arts, 33 W 42 St, New York, 10036. Alfred H Lane, Dir
Notes: Recently established and intended as a source of 20th century materials, in hard form or microfilm, incl books, pamphlets, reprints, translations, dissertations, periodicals, indexing and abstracting services, yearbooks, reports and directories of organizations, publishers' and antiquarian dealers' catalogs (particularly those who deal in books about books), periodicals, legislative materials, and clippings pertaining to the book industry. Sections of the library deal with printing, including typography, specimen books, history of printing and printing techniques, book design and small press and alternative publishing.
NY —ROCHESTER INSTITUTE OF TECHNOLOGY, Melbert B Cary Jr Graphic Arts Collection, School of Printing, One Lomb Memorial Drive, Rochester, 14623. David Pankow, Cur
Holdings: Vols (11,000) Cat
Notes: Also incl specimens.
PA —TEMPLE UNIVERSITY LIBRARIES, Special Collections Dept, Rare Books & Mss Section, Philadelphia, 19122. Thomas M Whitehead, Cur
Holdings: Vols (500) Mss Pix
Notes: The printing and graphic arts collections stress the technological developments within the printing industry and the achievements in fine printing in the 19th and 20th centuries. Selected additions are continually made of examples and secondary works. Holdings include the Library and archives of Richard W Ellis, typographer, archives of Philadelphia printers and photoengravers. Partially cataloged.
VA —UNIVERSITY OF VIRGINIA, Alderman Library, Rare Book Dept, Charlottesville, 22901. Julius P Barclay, Cur
Holdings: Vols (6500) // Mss
Notes: The Oscar Ogg Collection of Book

TYPE AND TYPEFOUNDING (cont.)

Arts covers calligraphy, letterforms, typography, printing, and graphic arts. Contains early writing books and printed works, as well as modern manuals and other works on printing, publishing, and promotion through graphic arts. The Dept also has the Edward L Stone Collection of Printing Specimens, 3000 items. Contains materials tracing the history of printing, inks, binding styles and materials, types. Also the Tompkins Collection (2000 vols), and the Stevens Watts collection (900 vols).

TYPE PICTURES

NY —ROCHESTER INSTITUTE OF TECHNOLOGY, Melbert B Cary Jr Graphic Arts Collection, School of Printing, One Lomb Memorial Drive, Rochester, 14623. David Pankow, Cur
Holdings: Vols (11,000) Cat
Notes: An extensive collection of the work of typographic artist Albert Schiller. Incl type pictures, their type forms, correspondence, sketches, books, proofs, and ephemera.

TYPEWRITERS—HISTORY

DE —HAGLEY MUSEUM AND LIBRARY, Eleutherian Mills-Hagley Foundation Inc, PO Box 3630, Greenville, 19807. Richmond D Williams, Dir; Heddy A Richter, Imprints Librn
Notes: Sperry Univac has deposited a large amount of historical records. Approximately 2000 cubic feet of records, files and photographs that document the invention and development of computers and the rapid growth of the industry were officially released by Sperry Corporation to the Library. The collection includes technical and legal documents relating to the ENIAC and UNIVAC computers as well as records of the founding of the E Remington Typewriter Company and other predecessor companies of the Sperry organization, such as The Library Bureau, Kardex, Rodic Rubber and the Powers Accounting Machinery Company. Thus our knowledge of the Sperry predecessors dates back in this collection to 1902.
WI —MILWAUKEE PUBLIC MUSEUM, Reference Library, 800 W Wells St, Milwaukee, 53233. Judith Campbell Turner, Museum Librn

TYPEWRITING—COPYING PROCESSES see Photocopying Processes

TYPHOID

CT —YALE UNIVERSITY, Medical Historical Library, Klebs Collection, 333 Cedar St, New Haven, 06520. Ferenc A Gyorgyey, Librn
Notes: The Arnold Carl Klebs Medical Collection books, pamphlets, etc, incl the library of his father, Edwin T A Klebs, pathologist. Strong in bibliography of early printed medical books, herbals, plague tracts, inoculation, vaccination and tubercular diseases.

TYPOGRAPHIC ART see Art, Typographic

TYPOGRAPHICAL DEVICES see Printers' Marks

TYPOGRAPHY see Printing

TYRRELL, GEORGE

†CA —UNIVERSITY OF SAN FRANCISCO, Richard A Gleeson Library, The Countess Bernardine Murphy Donohue Rare Book Room, San Francisco, 94117. D Steven Corey, Special Collections Librn
Holdings: Vols 1200 Uncat Pix
Notes: Modernsim in the Catholic Church. Incl; extensive holdings concerning George Tyrrell, Alfred Loisy, and Baron Friedrich von Hugel.

U

UDE LANGUAGE see Udi Language

UDI LANGUAGE

WA —UNIVERSITY OF WASHINGTON
LIBRARIES, Rare Books, Special
Collections Dept, Seattle, 98195. Sandra
Kroupa, Librn
Notes: Part of a set of Siberian primers
prepared in the early 1930s by Soviet
ethnographers. Some are first attempts to
transcribe Siberian languages. All are in
Latin phonetic script, not in Cyrillic.

UDIC LANGUAGE see Udi Language

UDMURT LANGUAGE see Votiak
Language and Literature

UELSMANN, JERRY

AZ —UNIVERSITY OF ARIZONA, Center
for Creative Photography, 843 E University
Blvd, Tucson, 85721. James Enyeart, Dir;
Terence Pitts, Cur and Librn
Notes: Center has significant collections
consisting of more than 25 photographs plus
other archival material such as negatives,
contact sheets, work prints, correspondence,
financial records, diaries, project files, etc.
Inventories of the collections are available to
researchers. Published guides available for
some collections.

UFO see Unidentified Flying Objects (Ufo)

UGANDA

DC —HOWARD UNIVERSITY, Moorland-
Spingarn Research Center, 500 Howard
Place NW, Washington, 20059. Clifford L
Muse, Jr, Acting Dir

UGARITIC LANGUAGE AND LITERATURE

NY —NEW YORK PUBLIC LIBRARY,
Oriental Div, Fifth Ave & 42 St, New York,
10018. E Christian Filstrup, Chief
Holdings: Cat Mss Microforms
Budget: ($56,455)
Notes: Published catalog of holdings.

UIGHUR LANGUAGE AND
LITERATURE see Uigur Language and
Literature

UIGUR LANGUAGE AND LITERATURE

NY —NEW YORK PUBLIC LIBRARY,
Oriental Div, Fifth Ave & 42 St, New York,
10018. E Christian Filstrup, Chief
Holdings: Cat Mss Microforms
Budget: ($56,455)
Notes: Published catalog of holdings.

UKIYOE see Color Prints, Japanese

UKRAINE

IL —UKRAINIAN BIBLIOGRAPHIC-
REFERENCE CENTER, Library, 2453 W
Chicago Ave, Chicago, 60622. Roman
Weres, Head
Notes: Center for referal and reference
concerning Ukrainian history and Ukrainians
in the US and Canada.
NY —NEW YORK PUBLIC LIBRARY,
Slavonic Div, Fifth Ave & 42 St, New York,
10018. Edward Kasinec, Chief
Holdings: Vols (8870) Cat Microforms
Notes: Subject strength is in Ukrainian
literature, language, and folklore. Ethnology
and history are also well represented.
Holdings of periodicals and publications of
learned societies are considerable. See New
York Public Library, Dictionary Catalog of
the Slavonic Collection (Boston: G K Hall,
1974), 44 vols.
AB —UNIVERSITY OF ALBERTA, Cameron
Library, The Bruce Peel Special Collections

Room, Edmonton, T6G 2J8, Can. John
Charles, Special Collections Librn
Holdings: Vols (8420)
Notes: Ukrainian language, literature, history
and economics. Special catalogs of Soviet
and European books and periodicals.

UKRAINE—HISTORY

CO —UKRAINIAN ARCHIVES MUSEUM,
2460 S University, Denver, 80210. George
Moshinsky, Pres
Holdings: Vols (2000) Mss Pix
Notes: Incl 150,000 documents.
CO —UKRAINIAN RESEARCH
FOUNDATION, 6931 S Yosemite St,
Englewood, 80110.
Holdings: Vols 5000 Mss Pix
Notes: Incl 1000 periodicals. Issuing
Bibliographic Guide to Ukraine and
Documents of Ukrainian History.
CT —UKRAINIAN MUSEUM AND
LIBRARY, 161 Glenbrook Rd, Stamford,
06902. Wasyl Lencyk, Dir
Holdings: Vols (20,000)
Notes: Incl 100 periodicals, 1000 artifacts,
maps from the 1800s, photographs of life in
the US, old and new churches. Emphasis on
religion, history and culture.
DC —WOODROW WILSON
INTERNATIONAL CENTER FOR
SCHOLARS, Kennan Institute for Advanced
Russian Studies, 1000 Jefferson Dr SW,
Washington, 20560. V David Zdenek, Librn
Holdings: Vols 100
Notes: Incl materials on Russians,
Ukrainians, Byelorussians, and on other
Soviet republics.
IL —UKRAINIAN BIBLIOGRAPHIC-
REFERENCE CENTER, Library, 2453 W
Chicago Ave, Chicago, 60622. Roman
Weres, Head
Holdings: Vols 250 Cat Mss Pix Microforms
Budget: $300
Notes: Holdings: Bibliographies of Ukrainica
in all languages in bookform, photostats and
on cards. Union catalog of Ukrainica in
North American libraries on cards (present
holdings: approx 20,000 cards) in bookform,
mss and photostats. Bibliography of
Ukrainian bibliography (in bookform and on
cards). Directories and gazetteers concerning
all aspects of Ukrainian problems, espec
concerning Ukrainian community in North
America. Directory of experts of different
aspects of Ukrainian problems. List of
Ukrainian periodicals, libraries and library
collections in houses and book stores.
Catalogs of Ukrainian bookdealers and other
book dealers also with Ukrainian materials.
IL —UKRAINIAN NATIONAL MUSEUM,
Library, 2453 W Chicago Ave, Chicago,
60622. Emil Basiuk, Librn
Holdings: Vols (11,500) Cat Mss Maps Pix
Slides Microforms
Notes: Department has been organized in
collaboration with the Ukrainian Librarians
of America Association, Ukrainian
Bibliographic-Reference Center. Interlibrary
loans. Collection of books and pamphlets
incl material in Ukrainian and other
languages on Ukrainian history, geography,
literature, language, art, social sciences,
religion and Ukrainian fiction. Large
collection of Ukrainian calendars and
almanacs. Around 100 current periodicals.
Collection of serials and monographs of the
Ukrainian scholarly institutions, collection of
publications of the Institute for the Study of
the USSR. There is a large collection of
Ukrainian postcards showing all aspects of
Ukrainian civilization and culture.
IL —UNIVERSITY OF ILLINOIS,
URBANA/CHAMPAIGN, Slavic and East
European Library, Urbana, 61801. Marianna
Tax Choldin, Head
Holdings: Vols (420,000) Cat Microforms
Notes: One of the largest Slavic and East
European collections. Strong in Russian and
Soviet materials-humanities, sciences, and
social sciences; languages and literatures;
periodicals, newspapers, and microforms. Ca
260,000 volumes in languages of the Soviet
Union plus 20,000 Russian and Ukrainian
titles on microform. Extensive coverage of
Czechoslovakia (35,000 vols); Yugoslavia

(31,000 vols); Bulgaria (9200 vols); Poland
(34,600 vols); Romania (13,000 vols); and
Hungary (18,000 vols) and the languages,
literatures, and history of these countries.
IN —INDIANA UNIVERSITY, University
Libraries, Bloomington, 47401. Murlin
Croucher, Librn for Slavic Studies
Holdings: Vols (300,000) Cat Maps
Microforms
Budget: ($63,000)
Notes: The collection, established after
World War II, covers material of, and on,
the Soviet Union (55 percent) and Eastern
Europe (45 percent) in the languages of the
area and in western European languages as
well. Material is chiefly in the fields of
humanities and social sciences. Many other
Slavic and East European books are located
in the Lilly Library (rare book library).
IN —VOLHYNIAN BIBLIOGRAPHIC
CENTER, 307 N Overhill Drive,
Bloomington, 47401. Max Boyko, Mgr
Notes: Collect materials on Volhynia in
Western Ukraine. Compile and publish
bibliographies on the region.
MA —HARVARD UNIVERSITY LIBRARY,
Widener Library, Slavic Collections,
Cambridge, 02138. Hugh M Olmsted, Slavic
Dept Head
Holdings: Cat
Notes: Ukrainian history shelflist through
June, 1976 lists 2940 titles (earlier version
was incl in Widener Library Shelflist,
volumes 28-31, 1971). This figure does not
incl serial publications of academies of
sciences, universities, pedagogical institutes,
and other learned bodies; microforms; or
materials acquired since 1976. The
Ukrainian collections continue to be
developed actively, and are strong both in
current and in antiquarian materials. For a
general survey of Harvard holdings, see
Steven A Grant and John H Brown, The
Russian Empire and Soviet Union; A Guide
to Manuscripts and Archival Materials in the
United States, 1981, pp 218-219, 224-233.
Also, Ukrainian-language books published in
Galicia, Czechoslovakia, Poland, Germany,
and other European centers of Ukrainian
emigrationbetween 1918 and 1950; and
books published in the US and Canada since
the end of the 19th century.
MI —UKRAINIAN-AMERICAN ARCHIVES
AND MUSEUM, 26601 Ryan Rd, Warren,
48091.
Notes: Historical relics, several thousand
books, periodicals, manuscripts, etc.
Christmas and Easter handicrafts.
MN —ARCHIVES OF THE ASSOCIATION
OF AMERICAN YOUTH OF
UKRAINIAN DESCENT-ODUM, INC,
4004 Roanoke Circle, Minneapolis, 55422.
Antol Lysyj, Archivist
Holdings: Vols (1500)
NJ —UKRAINIAN NATIONAL
ASSOCIATION, 30 Montgomery St, Jersey
City, 07303.
Holdings: Vols (9000) Mss Pix
NY —NEW YORK PUBLIC LIBRARY,
Slavonic Div, Fifth Ave & 42 St, New York,
10018. Edward Kasinec, Chief
Holdings: Vols 180 // Cat Mss
Notes: The Ukrainian archive of Mykyta
Shapoval consists mainly of the
correspondence of General Mykola Shapoval
(Army of the Ukrainian National Republic,
1917-1920) and of his family. Documents,
mss, diaries relating to the activities and
events of Ukrainians in Czechoslovakia and
France are included. The material covers the
period of the 1920s through 1950s. See New
York Public Library, Dictionary Catalog of
the Slavonic Collection (Boston: G K Hall,
1974), 44 vols.
NY —SELFRELIANCE ASSOCIATION OF
AMERICAN UKRAINIANS, 98 Second
Ave, New York, 10003. Yurij Kostien, Librn
Holdings: Vols (2000)
NY —SHEVCHENKO SCIENTIFIC
SOCIETY INC, 63 Fourth Ave, New York,
10003. Svitlana Andrushkiw, Librn
Holdings: Vols 5000
Notes: Incl periodicals. Supports graduate
level research. The Society has a rare book
and archival section which contains rare
editions, mss, documents, photographs, some

UKRAINE—HISTORY (cont.)

microforms. Society is in the process of establishing vertical files and full cataloging of all holdings. Collection consists of approx 35,000 volumes. Basically a research, non-lending library. Graduate level researchers are welcome. By appointment.

NY —UKRAINIAN ACADEMY OF ARTS AND SCIENCES IN THE UNITED STATES (UAAS), 206 W 100 St, New York, 10025. William Omelchenko, Director
Holdings: 45,000 Vols Mss

NY —UKRAINIAN MUSUEM, 203 Second Ave, New York, 10003. Maria Shust, Dir
Notes: Also over 1500 folk artifacts and works of art.

†OH —UKRAINIAN MUSEUM-ARCHIVES, INC, 1202 Kenilworth Ave, Cleveland, 44113.

OH —UNIVERSITY OF DAYTON, Marian Library, 300 College Park Ave, Dayton, 45469. Rev Theodore Koehler, SM, Dir/Cur
Holdings: Vols 405 Slides Clippings
Notes: Incl 200 slides, 1000 pictures and Christmas cards. Religious history of the Ukraine. Liturgical materials in Church Slavic. Religious art centered on Virgin Mary. Brief description in article "Z diial'nosti Mariinskoho Tsentru u Deitoni," *Svoboda* (Jersey City, NJ), 26 Nov 1983.

PA —MANOR JUNIOR COLLEGE, Basileiad Library, Fox Chase Manor, Jenkintown, 19046. Sister M Anne, OSBM, Cur
Holdings: Vols 2500 Cat 200 Uncat Maps Slides Phonorecords

PA —UKRAINIAN HERITAGE STUDIES CENTER, Fox Chase Manor, Jenkintown, 19046. Anna N Maksymowych, Librn
Holdings: Vols 1500 Mss Pix
Budget: $1500
Notes: "Cat" L C.

PA —SLAVIA LIBRARY, 418 W Nittany Ave, State College, 16801. W O Luciw, Founder & Dir; Jurij A Luciw, Asst Dir
Holdings: Vols (45,000) Mss Pix
Budget: ($3500)
Notes: Incl 5000 periodicals, 3000 av materials, 4000 artifacts, and 200 art works. Also 16,000 letters, etc from Slavic and other personages.

UKRAINIAN AMERICAN NEWSPAPERS see Newspapers, Ukrainian American

UKRAINIAN ARCHIVES see Archives, Ukrainian

URKAINIAN AUTHORS see Authors, Ukrainian

UKRAINIAN CATHOLIC CHURCH

IL —CENTER OF UKRAINIAN AND RELIGIOUS STUDIES, 2305 W Superior St, Chicago, 60612.
Holdings: Vols (3000)
Notes: Located in Ukrainian National Museum.

UKRAINIAN IMPRINTS

IN —VOLHYNIAN BIBLIOGRAPHIC CENTER, 307 N Overhill Drive, Bloomington, 47401. Max Boyko, Mgr
Notes: Collect materials on Ukraine. Compile and publish bibliographies on the general bibliography of Ukraine.

SK —UNIVERSITY OF SASKATCHEWAN, Library, Saskatoon, S7N 0W0, Can. S Perkins, Librn
Notes: The Maximchuk Collection for which a short-title list (on cards) has been compiled. The Collection is available for use and a printed bibliography is planned for 1985.

UKRAINIAN LANGUAGE AND LITERATURE

CO —UKRAINIAN ARCHIVES MUSEUM, 2460 S University, Denver, 80210. George Moshinsky, Pres
Holdings: Vols (2000) Mss Pix
Notes: Incl 150,000 documents.

CO —UKRAINIAN RESEARCH FOUNDATION, 6931 S Yosemite St, Englewood, 80110.
Holdings: Vols 5000 Mss Pix
Notes: Incl 1000 periodicals. Issuing *Bibliographic Guide to Ukraine* and *Documents of Ukrainian History.*

CT —UKRAINIAN MUSEUM AND LIBRARY, 161 Glenbrook Rd, Stamford, 06902. Wasyl Lencyk, Dir
Holdings: Vols (20,000)
Notes: Incl 100 periodicals, 1000 artifacts, maps from the 1800s, photographs of life in the US, old and new churches. Emphasis on religion, history and culture.

IL —UKRAINIAN NATIONAL MUSEUM, Library, 2453 W Chicago Ave, Chicago, 60622. Emil Basiuk, Librn
Holdings: Vols (11,500) Cat Mss Maps Pix Slides Microforms
See also entry under Ukraine - History

IN —VOLHYNIAN BIBLIOGRAPHIC CENTER, 307 N Overhill Drive, Bloomington, 47401. Max Boyko, Mgr
Notes: Collect materials on Volhynia in Western Ukraine. Compile and publish bibliographies on the region.

MA —HARVARD UNIVERSITY LIBRARY, Widener Library, Slavic Collections, Cambridge, 02138. Hugh M Olmsted, Slavic Dept Head
Holdings: Cat Microforms
Notes: Ukrainian literature shelflist through June, 1976 lists 5620 titles (earlier version was incl in *Widener Library Shelflist,* volumes 28-31, 1971). The language and literature collections continue to be developed actively, and are strong both in current and in antiquarian materials. Also, Ukrainian-language books published in Galicia, Czechoslovakia, Poland, Germany, and other European centers of Ukrainian emigration between 1918 and 1950; and books pulished in the US and Canada since the end of the 19th century.

MI —UKRAINIAN-AMERICAN ARCHIVES AND MUSEUM, 26601 Ryan Rd, Warren, 48091.
Notes: Historical relics, several thousand books, periodicals, manuscripts, etc. Christmas and Easter handicrafts.

NY —NEW YORK PUBLIC LIBRARY, Donnell Foreign Language Library, 20 W 53 St, New York, 10019. Bosiljka Stevanovic, Supvr Librn
Holdings: Vols 862 Cat
Notes: Ukrainian collection incl Ukrainian authors of Ukrainian expression. No separate catalog.

NY —NEW YORK PUBLIC LIBRARY, Slavonic Div, Fifth Ave & 42 St, New York, 10018. Edward Kasinec, Chief
Holdings: Vols (8870) Cat Microforms
Notes: Subject strength is in Ukrainian literature, language, and folklore. Ethnology and history are also well represented. Holdings of periodicals and publications of learned societies are considerable. See New York Public Library, *Dictionary Catalog of the Slavonic Collection* (Boston: G K Hall, 1974), 44 vols.

NY —SELFRELIANCE ASSOCIATION OF AMERICAN UKRAINIANS, 98 Second Ave, New York, 10003. Yurij Kostien, Librn
Holdings: Vols (2000)

NY —SHEVCHENKO SCIENTIFIC SOCIETY INC, 63 Fourth Ave, New York, 10003. Svitlana Andrushkiw, Librn
Holdings: Vols 20,000
Notes: Incl periodicals. Supports graduate level research. The Society has a rare book and archival section which contains rare editions, mss, documents, photographs, some microforms. Society is in the process of establishing vertical files and full cataloging of all holdings. Collection consists of approx 35,000 volumes. Basically a research, non-lending library. Graduate level researchers are welcome. To use library, make appointment by telephoning (212) 254-5130 or (212) 254-5239.

OH —CLEVELAND PUBLIC LIBRARY, Foreign Literature Dept, 325 Superior Ave, Cleveland, 44114. Natalia Bezugloff, Head
Holdings: Vols 5990 Cat
Notes: A popular circulating collection

containing classics and the standard works with emphasis on belles lettres, history and biography. A variety of other subjects such as learning languages, how to do books, art, children's books, spoken phonodiscs and cassettes, periodicals, etc. Incl 60 ephemera.
See also entry under Foreign Language Collections

OH —KENT STATE UNIVERSITY, Libraries, Ethnic Collections, Kent, 44242.
Holdings: Vols 300 Cat
See also entry under Foreign Language Collections

PA —MANOR JUNIOR COLLEGE, Basileiad Library, Fox Chase Manor, Jenkintown, 19046. Sister M Anne, OSBM, Cur
Holdings: Vols 2500 Cat 200 Uncat Maps Slides Phonorecords

PA —UKRAINIAN HERITAGE STUDIES CENTER, Fox Chase Manor, Jenkintown, 19046. Anna N Maksymowych, Librn
Holdings: Vols 1500 Mss Pix
Budget: $1500
Notes: "Cat" L C.

PA —SLAVIA LIBRARY, 418 W Nittany Ave, State College, 16801. W O Luciw, Founder & Dir; Jurij A Luciw, Asst Dir
Holdings: Vols (45,000) Mss Pix
Budget: ($3500)
Notes: Incl 5000 periodicals, 3000 av materials, 4000 artifacts, and 200 art works. Also 16,000 letters, etc from Slavic and other personages.

PA —PENNSYLVANIA STATE UNIVERSITY, Fred Lewis Pattee Library, Slavic Library Program, University Park, 16802. Wasyl O Luciw, Head
Holdings: Vols (75,000) Cat Mss Pix
Budget: ($18,000)
Notes: The collection covers a wide range of languages Slavic and East European but its principal strengths are in Russian and Ukrainian. A special collection of 1576 volumes includes pre-revolutionary Russian, fine press publications, in our rare collection and children's literature. Besides book volumes, we have quite a large collection of manuscripts, documents, photographs and many periodicals, also including out of print books on microforms.

AB —UNIVERSITY OF ALBERTA, Cameron Library, The Bruce Peel Special Collections Room, Edmonton, T6G 2J8, Can. John Charles, Special Collections Librn
Holdings: Vols (8420)
Notes: Ukrainian language, literature, history and economics. Special catalogs of Soviet and European books and periodicals.

BC —GREATER VANCOUVER LIBRARY FEDERATION, 110-6545 Bonsor, Burnaby, Z5H 1H3, Can. Colleen Smith, Coordr
Holdings: Vols (20,350) Cat
Notes: Deposit provided by the National Library's Multilingual Biblioservice on long-term loan to libraries in the Greater Vancouver Library Federation (Burnaby, New Westminster, N Vancouver City Public, N Vancouver District Public, Port Moody, Vancouver, W Vancouver).

MB —UNIVERSITY OF MANITOBA, Elizabeth Dafoe Library, Slavic Collection, Winnipeg, R3T 2N2, Can. John S Muchin, Librn
Holdings: Vols (33,000) Cat Mss Microforms
Budget: ($5000)
Notes: Material in all Slavic languages, mostly in Russian (approx 15,000 vols), Ukrainian (approx 15,000 vols), Polish, Old Church Slavic; mainly literature, language, history, art, geography, economics, statistics, political science; newspapers and periodicals; over 20,000 vols of microforms. Cited in *Slavic Collection of the University of Manitoba Libraries,* John S Muchin (Winnipeg: University of Manitoba Libraries and UVAN, 1970).

SK —UNIVERSITY OF SASKATCHEWAN, Library, Saskatoon, S7N 0W0, Can. S Perkins, Librn
Notes: The Maximchuk Collection for which a short-title list (on cards) has been compiled. The Collection is available for use and a printed bibliography is planned for 1985.

UKRAINIAN MEDICINE see Medicine, Ukrainian

UKRAINIAN ORTHODOX CHURCH

NJ —SAINT SOPHIA UKRAINIAN ORTHODOX THEOLOGICAL

UKRAINIAN ORTHODOX CHURCH
(cont.)

SEMINARY, PO Box 240, South Bound
Brook, 08880. Iwan Korowytzky, Dir; Fr
Wasyl Iwashchuk, Librn
Holdings: 4000 Vols Cat Mss
Budget: ($10,000)
Notes: Open to all.

URKAINIAN POETRY see Poetry,
Ukrainian

UKRAINIANS IN CANADA

IL —UKRAINIAN BIBLIOGRAPHIC-
REFERENCE CENTER, Library, 2453 W
Chicago Ave, Chicago, 60622. Roman
Weres, Head
Notes: Center for referal and reference
concerning Ukrainian history and Ukrainians
in the US and Canada.

IL —UKRAINIAN MEDICAL
ASSOCIATION OF NORTH AMERICA,
2320 W Chicago Ave, Chicago, 60622. Dr
Paul Pundy, Librn
Holdings: Vols (1000) Pix
Notes: History of Ukrainian medicine, and
contributions of Ukrainian medical
practitioners in the US and Canada. Library
located in Ukrainian National Museum.

PA —BALCH INSTITUTE FOR ETHNIC
STUDIES, Library, 18 S Seventh St,
Philadelphia, 19106. R Joseph Anderson,
Library Dir

UKRAINIANS IN FOREIGN
COUNTRIES

NY —SHEVCHENKO SCIENTIFIC
SOCIETY INC, 63 Fourth Ave, New York,
10003. Svitlana Andrushkiw, Librn
Holdings: Vols 500
Notes: The Society has a rare book and
archival section which contains rare editions,
mss, documents, photographs, some
microforms. Society is in the process of
establishing vertical files and full cataloging
of all holdings. Collection consists of approx
35,000 volumes. Basically a research, non-
lending library. Graduate level researchers
are welcome. To use library, make
appointment by telephoning (212) 254-5130
or (212) 254-5239.

UKRAINIANS IN RUSSIA

MN —ARCHIVES OF THE ASSOCIATION
OF AMERICAN YOUTH OF
UKRAINIAN DESCENT-ODUM, INC,
4004 Roanoke Circle, Minneapolis, 55422.
Antol Lysyj, Archivist
Holdings: Vols (1500)
Notes: Ukrainian descent and USSR, incl a
roster of Ukrainian descension in USSR in
prisons.

UKRAINIANS IN THE U.S.

CO —UKRAINIAN ARCHIVES MUSEUM,
2460 S University, Denver, 80210. George
Moshinsky, Pres
Holdings: Vols (2000) Cat Mss Pix
Notes: Incl 150,000 documents.

CT —UKRAINIAN MUSEUM AND
LIBRARY, 161 Glenbrook Rd, Stamford,
06902. Wasyl Lencyk, Dir
Holdings: Vols (20,000)
Notes: Incl 100 periodicals, 1000 artifacts,
maps from the 1800s, photographs of life in
the US, old and new churches. Emphasis on
religion, history and culture.

IL —CENTER OF UKRAINIAN AND
RELIGIOUS STUDIES, 2305 W Superior
St, Chicago, 60612.
Holdings: Vols (3000)
Notes: Located in Ukrainian National
Museum.

IL —UKRAINIAN BIBLIOGRAPHIC-
REFERENCE CENTER, Library, 2453 W
Chicago Ave, Chicago, 60622. Roman
Weres, Head
Notes: Center for referal and reference
concerning Ukrainian history and Ukrainians
in the US and Canada.

IL —UKRAINIAN MEDICAL
ASSOCIATION OF NORTH AMERICA,
2320 W Chicago Ave, Chicago, 60622. Dr
Paul Pundy, Librn
Holdings: Vols (1000) Pix
Notes: History of Ukrainian medicine, and
contributions of Ukrainian medical
practitioners in the US and Canada. Library
located in Ukrainian National Museum.

IL —UKRAINIAN NATIONAL MUSEUM,
Library, 2453 W Chicago Ave, Chicago,
60622. Emil Basiuk, Librn
Holdings: Vols (11,500) Cat Mss Maps Pix
Slides Microforms
See also entry under Ukraine - History

MA —HARVARD UNIVERSITY LIBRARY,
Widener Library, Slavic Collections,
Cambridge, 02138. Hugh M Olmsted, Slavic
Dept Head
Notes: Ukrainian-language books published
in Galicia, Czechoslovakia, Poland,
Germany, and other European centers of
Ukrainian emigration between 1918 and
1950; and books published in the US and
Canada since the end of the 19th century.

MN —ARCHIVES OF THE ASSOCIATION
OF AMERICAN YOUTH OF
UKRAINIAN DESCENT-ODUM, INC,
4004 Roanoke Circle, Minneapolis, 55422.
Antol Lysyj, Archivist
Holdings: Vols (1500)

MN —UNIVERSITY OF MINNESOTA,
Immigration History Research Center, 826
Berry St, Saint Paul, 55114. Susan Griegs,
Cur
Holdings: Vols (35,000) Mss Maps Pix
Phonorecords Audiotapes 16mm Films
Microforms
See also entry under US - Emigration and
Immigration

NJ —UKRAINIAN NATIONAL
ASSOCIATION, 30 Montgomery St, Jersey
City, 07303.
Holdings: Vols (9000) Mss Pix

NJ —SAINT SOPHIA UKRAINIAN
ORTHODOX THEOLOGICAL
SEMINARY, PO Box 240, South Bound
Brook, 08880. Iwan Korowytzky, Dir; Fr
Wasyl Iwashchuk, Librn
Holdings: 4000 Vols Cat Mss
Budget: ($10,000)
Notes: Open to all.

NY —SELFRELIANCE ASSOCIATION OF
AMERICAN UKRAINIANS, 98 Second
Ave, New York, 10003. Yurij Kostien, Librn
Holdings: Vols (2000)

NY —SHEVCHENKO SCIENTIFIC
SOCIETY INC, 63 Fourth Ave, New York,
10003. Svitlana Andrushkiw, Librn
Holdings: Vols 1000
Notes: The Society has a rare book and
archival section which contains rare editions,
mss, documents, photographs, some
microforms. Society is in the process of
establishing vertical files and full cataloging
of all holdings. Collection consists of approx
35,000 volumes. Basically a research, non-
lending library. Graduate level researchers
are welcome. By appointment.

NY —UKRAINIAN ACADEMY OF ARTS
AND SCIENCES IN THE UNITED
STATES (UAAS), 206 W 100 St, New
York, 10025. William Omelchenko, Director
Holdings: 45,000 Vols Mss

†OH —UKRAINIAN MUSEUM-ARCHIVES,
INC, 1202 Kenilworth Ave, Cleveland,
44113.

PA —UKRAINIAN HERITAGE STUDIES
CENTER, Fox Chase Manor, Jenkintown,
19046. Anna N Maksymowych, Librn
Holdings: Vols 1500 Mss Pix
Budget: $1500
Notes: "Cat" L C.

PA —BALCH INSTITUTE FOR ETHNIC
STUDIES, Library, 18 S Seventh St,
Philadelphia, 19106. R Joseph Anderson,
Library Dir
Holdings: Vols 60 Cat

ULLATHORNE, WILLIAM BERNARD,
1806-1889

DC —GEORGETOWN UNIVERSITY,
Library, Special Collections Div, 37 & O Sts
NW, Washington, 20057. George M

Barringer, Special Collections Librn;
Nicholas B Sheetz, Mss Librn
Holdings: Mss Cat
Notes: A portion of the papers of Bishop
William Bernard Ullathorne (1806-1889),
incl correspondence to and from other
English prelates such as Nicholas Cardinal
Wiseman (1802-1865) and Henry Edeward
Cardinal Manning (1808-1892).

ULLMAN, JAMES RAMSEY

NJ —PRINCETON UNIVERSITY, Library,
Rare Books Dept, Princeton, 08544. Stephen
Ferguson, Cur
Holdings: Mss
Notes: A premier collection of
mountaineering literature. The papers and
personal library of James Ramsey Ullman,
incl his correspondence, diaries, memorabilia
and mss of all his works (his published
writings, scripts for his plays, his magazine
articles and travel journals).

ULTRAFILTRATION

MA —ABCOR, INC, Library, 850 Main St,
Wilmington, 01887. Eileen Smith, Librn
Holdings: Vols (2000) Cat
Budget: ($10,000)
Notes: Environmental technology;
ultrafiltration; waste treament processes. Incl
technical reports. Extensive microfiche
collection on air pollution.

ULTRASONIC THERAPY see Ultrasonic
Waves—Therapeutic Use

ULTRASONIC
WAVES—THERAPEUTIC USE

MD —JOHNS HOPKINS HOSPITAL, John
W Pierson Memorial Library, Dept of
Radiology, 601 N Broadway, Baltimore,
21205. S Elaine Pinkney, Librn
Holdings: Vols (6000) Cat Slides Audiotapes
Videotapes
Budget: $4700
Notes: Incl Diagnostic Radiology,
Radiotherapy, Ultrasound, and Computed
Axial Tomography.

†TN —SAINT THOMAS HOSPITAL, Health
Sciences Library, Box 380, Nashville, 37202.
Dee Platt, Dir
Holdings: Vols (2600) Cat Slides

ULTRASOUND IN PREGNANCY

MD —NATIONAL LIBRARY OF
MEDICINE, 8600 Rockville Pike, Bethesda,
20209. Harold M Schoolinam, Actg Dir
Budget: ($46,400)

ULYANOV, VLADIMIR ILYICH see
Lenin (Vladimir Ilyich Ulyanov)

UNBELIEF see Skepticism

UNDERDEVELOPED AREAS—RURAL
DEVELOPMENT see Rural Development

UNDERDEVELOPED AREAS, AID TO
see Technical Assistance

UNDERDEVELOPED NATIONS see
Developing Nations

UNDERGROUND COMICS see Comic
Books, Strips, Etc., Underground

UNDERGROUND LITERATURE

CA —UNIVERSITY OF CALIFORNIA, LOS
ANGELES, Research Library, Social
Sciences Collection, 405 Hilgard Ave, Los
Angeles, 90024. Edward Shreeves,
Chairman, Bibliographers Group; Oscar L
Sims, Social Sciences Bibliographer
Notes: A collection of over 200 underground
newspapers on 26 reels of microfilm. Among
the titles included are: *The Tribe, The*
Berkeley Barb, New York Roach, Rat, and
Win.

CA —HOOVER INSTITUTION ON WAR,
REVOLUTION & PEACE, Stanford

UNDERGROUND LITERATURE (cont.)

University, Stanford, 94305. Milorad M
Drachkovitch, Archivist
Notes: The New Left Politics Collection
consists of monographs and serials on the
New Left that are cataloged. In addition, the
collection subscribes to numerous
underground newspapers and has obtained
special subject collections such as the Free
Speech Movement at Berkeley 1964-1965,
SNCC and Mississippi Summer 1964, and
the insurrection at San Francisco State
College in 1968-1969. There is also a good
collection on the French student revolts of
1968. The collection is a supervised one and
not open to browsers. Interested students
and scholars are welcome. Only limited
photocopying is permitted.

CT —UNIVERSITY OF CONNECTICUT,
Library, Storrs, 06268. Ellen Embardo, Cur
Special Collections
Holdings: Cat
Notes: Alternative Press Collection.
Primarily periodicals and newspapers from
the 1960s to today of an alternative or
underground nature. Books and pamphlets
are incl, representing both the left and the
right-wing viewpoints. A catalog is available.
Also have archives of the First Casualty
Press, which was deeply involved with
Vietnam veterans' experiences in Vietnam.

DC —LIBRARY OF CONGRESS, Rare Book
& Special Collections Div, Washington,
20540. William Matheson, Chief
Notes: World War II Propaganda and
Underground Movement Collection. More
than 10,000 propaganda leaflets, broadsides,
photographs, pamphlets, and other
ephemera, issued in many languages by both
sides during World War II. Incl strong
representation of the underground resistance
to German occupation of the Baltic states.

DC —LIBRARY OF CONGRESS, European
Division, Washington, 20540.
Notes: The Library of Congress collection of
"Solidarity" and other uncensored Polish
materials incl books, periodicals, documents,
bulletins, cartoons, and posters, most of
which are photocopies of originals held by
other libraries.

MI —UNIVERSITY OF MICHIGAN, Dept of
Rare Books & Special Collections, Ann
Arbor, 48109. Edward C Weber, Head,
Labadie Collection
Holdings: Vols (40,000) Cat Phonorecords
Audiotapes Microforms
Notes: Strong in counterculture serials from
the 1960s and 1970s.

NY —MUSEUM OF CARTOON ART
LIBRARY, Comly Avenue, Rye Brook,
10573.
Notes: Original comics and cartoon art, 60,
000 pieces. 800 animated cartoons. Disney
collection extensive. Samples of Big-Little
Books, foreign comics, fanzines, cartoon
related games, posters, pulps, undergrounds.
Hal Foster, Walt Kelly, Gene Byrns, Tad
Dorgan, Chester Gould extensive original art
collections.

†OH —BOWLING GREEN STATE
UNIVERSITY, Libraries, Bowling Green,
43403. Nancy White Lee, Librn
Notes: Extensive miscellaneous incl Sunday
strips, Big-Little Books, fanzines, foreign
comics, pulps, gum cards, undergrounds, and
movie posters.

WI —UNIVERSITY OF WISCONSIN,
MADISON, Memorial Library, Slavic
Studies Collection, 728 State St, Madison,
53706. Aleksander Rolich, Bibliographer for
Slavic Studies; Robert P Gakovich, Slavic
Cataloger; Valdis J Zeps, Baltic Studies
Center
Holdings: Cat
Notes: Russian Underground Collection.
Materials in the Russian Underground
Collection embrace the Russian
Revolutionary Movement from 1825 to
1917, including a considerable number of
Free Press publications. Among the 1500
titles are included about 100 journals, many
political tracts, leaflets, broadsides and
brochures of various politcal groups, largely
socialist, religious nonconformists (L Tolstoi)

and a large number of the satirical journals
that appeared between 1905-1907. Restricted
use: Rare Book Department.

BC —SIMON FRASER UNIVERSITY,
Library, Burnaby, V5A 1S6, Can. Percilla
Groves, Special Collections Librn
Holdings: Vols (12,000) Cat Mss
Notes: This collection concentrates on
avant-garde American poetry since World
War II. Incl some Canadian poetry
(particularly West Coast poets), some British
and certain of the International Concrete
school. It particularly features the Black
Mountain and San Francisco schools and
those American and Canadian poets
influenced by them. There is a relatively
complete collection of works by Ezra Pound
(qv), William Carlos Williams, Charles
Olson, Gertrude Stein and Louis Zukofsky
together with considerable criticism on these
authors. Also incl certain underground
newspapers and 1600 periodical titles.

UNDERGROUND NEWSPAPERS see
Newspapers, Underground

UNDERGROUND PRESS see
Underground Literature

UNDERGROUND RAILROAD

IN —WILLARD LIBRARY, 21 First Ave,
Evansville, 47710. Joan Elliott, Special
Collections Librn
Holdings: Vols (500) Cat Mss
Budget: ($4000)
Notes: Incl books and pamphlets (slave
narratives, works by and about abolitionists,
accounts of underground railroad activity),
some abolitionist newspapers. Incl some
reprints, but mostly original 19th century
imprints.

NY —UNIVERSITY OF ROCHESTER, Rush
Rhees Library, Department of Rare Books
and Special Collections, Rochester, 14627.
Peter Dzwonkoski, Librn
Holdings: Mss
Notes: Papers of Isaac and Amy Post and
the Porter Family papers.

OH —OBERLIN COLLEGE LIBRARY,
Oberlin, 44074. William A Moffett, Dir of
Libraries
Holdings: Cat

ON —CHATHAM PUBLIC LIBRARY, 120
Queen St, Chatham, N7M 2G6, Can. Arlene
Mason, Head of Reference
Holdings: Mss Maps Pix Slides Microforms
Notes: Collection incl books on Black
history, especially the Underground Railroad
pertaining to the Chatham and Windsor
area; many articles, and a few pictures of
these subjects; also Indians of Kent County.
Kent County and Southern Ontario History
is also a subject of this collection, especially
United Empire Loyalists in Southern
Ontario.

†ON —METROPOLITAN TORONTO
LIBRARY, Social Sciences Dept, 789 Yonge
St, Toronto, M4W 2G8, Can. Abdus Salam,
Head
Holdings: Vols Cat Maps Phonorecords
Audiotapes 16mm Films Microforms
Notes: Collection is both current and
historical. Strong in immigrants' guides,
government reports and statistics, analyses,
histories and studies of ethnic groups. Strong
on the Underground Railroad.

UNDERGROUND RAILROADS see
Subways

UNDERGROUND TEST
PHENOMENOLOGY

NM —UNIVERSITY OF CALIFORNIA, Los
Alamos National Laboratory, Libraries, PO
Box 1663, MSP 362, Los Alamos, 87545. J
Arthur Freed, Head Librn
Holdings: Vols (800,000) Cat Films
Microforms
Budget: ($700,000)
Notes: Incl 500,000 classified and
unclassified reports. There are 25 branch
libraries and a central collection. The
Medical Library contains about 40,000 vols
in the areas of biomedical research.

UNDERGROUND WATER see Water,
Underground

UNDERSEA WARFARE INSHORE

FL —US NAVAL COASTAL SYSTEMS
CENTER, Technical Information Service
Branch, Panama City, 32407. Myrtle J
Rhodes, Librn
Holdings: Vols (30,000) Cat
Notes: Coastal and ocean technology,
inshore undersea warfare, mine
countermeasures, torpedo defense,
underwater sound.

UNDERTAKERS AND
UNDERTAKING

MA —NATIONAL CENTER FOR DEATH
EDUCATION, New England Resource
Center for Thanatology & Funeral Service,
656 Beacon St, Boston, 02215. Gail Gruner,
Librn

UNDERWATER ACOUSTICS

FL —US NAVAL COASTAL SYSTEMS
CENTER, Technical Information Service
Branch, Panama City, 32407. Myrtle J
Rhodes, Librn
Holdings: Vols (30,000) Cat
Notes: Coastal and ocean technology,
inshore undersea warfare, mine
countermeasures, torpedo defense,
underwater sound.

UNDERWATER DEMOLITION TEAMS

FL —US NAVAL COASTAL SYSTEMS
CENTER, Technical Information Service
Branch, Panama City, 32407. Myrtle J
Rhodes, Librn
Holdings: Vols (30,000) Cat
Notes: Coastal and ocean technology,
inshore undersea warfare, mine
countermeasures, torpedo defense,
underwater sound.

UNDERWATER SOUND see Underwater
Acoustics

UNDERWOOD, SENATOR OSCAR W.

VA —UNIVERSITY OF VIRGINIA,
Alderman Library, Manuscripts Dept,
Charlottesville, 22901. Edmund Berkeley Jr,
Cur
Holdings: Cat Mss Pix
Notes: Personal papers of the Senator and
his family, about 500 items.

UNDERWRITING see Insurance;
Securities

UNDEVELOPED AREAS, AID TO see
Technical Assistance

UNDSET, SIGRID

DC —GEORGETOWN UNIVERSITY,
Library, Special Collections Div, 37 & O Sts
NW, Washington, 20057. George M
Barringer, Special Collections Librn;
Nicholas B Sheetz, Mss Librn
Holdings: Mss
Notes: The Archives of the Gallery of Living
Catholic Authors was founded in 1932 by
Sister Mary Joseph of the Sisters of Loretto
to focus attention on modern Catholic
literature, and to provide a depository for
manuscripts, letters, photographs, and books
by contemporary Catholic writers. Contains
material by hundreds of writers, incl Hilaire
Belloc, Roy Campbell, Padraic Colum, Eric
Gill, Paul Horgan, Mary Lavin, Marie Belloc
Lowndes, Kathleen Norris, Alred Noyes,
Sheila Kaye-Smith, Sigrid Undset, and
Evelyn Waugh, to name only a few.

UNEMPLOYMENT see Labor Supply

UNEMPLOYMENT COMPENSATION
see Insurance, Unemployment

UNEMPLOYMENT INSURANCE see
Insurance, Unemployment

UNESCO see United Nations Educational,
Scientific, and Cultural Organization
(UNESCO)

UNEXPLAINED PHENOMENA

NJ —SOCIETY FOR THE INVESTIGATION
OF THE UNEXPLAINED, Library, PO

UNEXPLAINED PHENOMENA (cont.)

Box 265, Little Silver, 07739. Robert C
Warth, Pres
Holdings: Mss Maps Pix Slides Videtapes
Notes: Information file of original material,
map collection, and specialized library.

UNGER, NORMAN

IL —NORTHERN ILLINOIS UNIVERSITY,
Founders Memorial Library, Rare Books and
Special Collections Dept, De Kalb, 60115.
William R DuBois, Dept Head
Holdings: Vols (297) Uncat Mss
Notes: Manuscripts and/or typescripts of
several Hanley novels, stories and plays as
well as almost all of his published works in
sequential editions. Some of the manuscripts
are unpublished; Mr Hanley retains all
copyrights. Collection includes Hanley's
correspondence with Norman Unger.

UNICORN IN LITERATURE AND MYTHOLOGY

NY —THE CLOISTERS, Metropolitan
Museum of Art (Branch), Fort Tryon Park,
New York, 10040. Suse C Childs, Librn
Holdings: Vols (5000) Cat Mss Pix Slides
Notes: A branch of the Metropolitan
Museum of Art devoted solely to the
literature of medieval art. Incl 16,000 slides
and 5000 photographs with unique strengths
in certain aspects of medieval art.

UNIDENTIFIED FLYING OBJECTS (UFO)

AZ —AERIAL PHENOMENA RESEARCH
ORGANIZATION (APRO), Library, 3910
E Kleindale Rd, Tucson, 85712. Coral
Lorrezen, Sec-Treas
Holdings: Uncat Mss Maps Pix Slides
Phonorecords Audiotapes Videotapes
Microforms
Notes: The APRO Library is the information
services division of the Aerial Phenomena
Research Organization and it serves as a
major repository in the field of UFO
research, ufology. Collects monographs and
serials in depth. Heart of the collection is
nearly 45,000 UFO reports collected by
APRO since its inception in 1952. Library
open to serious researchers upon written
application.
AZ —WORLD UNIVERSITY, Library, 711 E
Blacklidge Dr, Tucson, 85719. Howard John
Zitko, Cur
Holdings: Vols (15,000) Cat Mss Maps
Audiotapes
Notes: Collection concerns what are
generally called the "frontier sciences." No
interlibrary loan.
CA —UNIVERSITY OF CALIFORNIA, LOS
ANGELES, Research Library, Dept of
Special Collections, 405 Hilgard Ave, Los
Angeles, 90024. Edward Shreeves,
Chairman, Bibliographers Group; David S
Zeidberg, Head
Notes: 72 linear feet of the records of the
US Air Force Project Blue Book, the group
responsible for investigating reported UFO
sightings in the US and around the world.
Incl scripts for the television program,
Project UFO.
CA —SAN DIEGO PUBLIC LIBRARY,
Science & Industry Section, 820 E St, San
Diego, 92101. Joanne Anderson, Senior
Librn
Holdings: //
Budget: ($33,000)
IL —UNIVERSITY OF ILLINOIS,
URBANA/CHAMPAIGN, Library,
University Archives, 19 Library, 1408 W
Gregory Drive, Urbana, 61801. Maynard
Brichford, University Archivist
Holdings: Vols (5000) Cat
Budget: ($7000)
Notes: The Mandeville Collection in
Parapsychology and Occult Sciences. Titles
in the Merten J Mandeville Collection are
purchased by funds from an endowment
provided specifically for the collection on its
establishment in 1966 by Merten J

Mandeville, Professor Emeritus of
Management, who donated 400 vols from his
personal library as the nucleus of the
collection. There are currently about 5000
titles in the collection, supplemented by
related materials in the general collection.
Topics include astrology, extrasensory
perception, yoga, magic, satanism, faith
healing, hypnosis, Eastern religions,
witchcraft, fortune telling, reincarnation,
flying saucers, ghosts, dreams, numerology,
graphology, and mysticism. Biographies and
reference books are a part of the collection
as are journals devoted to the scientific study
of parapsychology.
NJ —SOCIETY FOR THE INVESTIGATION
OF THE UNEXPLAINED, Library, PO
Box 265, Little Silver, 07739. Robert C
Warth, Pres
Holdings: Mss Maps Pix Slides Videotapes
Notes: Information file of original material,
map collection, and specialized library.

UNIFICATION CHURCH IN AMERICA

CA —GRADUATE THEOLOGICAL UNION
LIBRARY, New Religious Movements
Research Collection, Public Services and
Special Collections Dept, 2400 Ridge Road,
Berkeley, 94709. Diane Choquette, Dept
Head
Holdings: Vols (3000) Mss Pix
Notes: Begun in 1977, the collection focuses
on religious movements new to America
since 1960, and unorthodox religious
movements resurgent since 1960. American
forms of Hinduism, Buddhism, Sikhism, and
Sufism are included along with occultism,
Neo-Paganism, esoteric and alternative
forms of Christianity, feminist spirituality,
and human potential movements having a
spiritual aspect. Legal issues, such as
deprogramming, and the question of church/
state relations are an important part of the
collection. The Library is a depository for
publications of the Unification Church in
America, the Church of Scientology, and the
International Society for Krishna
Consciousness (America). The responses of
mainstream religions and concerned citizens
groups are also included. Besides 3000
monographs, the library has 400 periodical
titles, 200 posters from the San
FranciscoBay Area, 1965-77, 300 research
papers, and 31 linear feet of ephemera.

UNIFORMS

CA —WESTERN COSTUME COMPANY,
Research Library, 5335 Melrose Ave,
Hollywood, 90038. Nancy S Kinney, Dir of
Research
Holdings: Vols 1000 Pix VF
Notes: Incl 9 vertical file drawers of
photographs, 65 binders of current police
uniforms, incl sheriffs, state police, etc. Six
periodical subscriptions on police profession.
Card file index on selected uniform pictures
from periodicals holdings. Collection can be
used only by the customers of Western
Costume Company. All other use is on a fee
basis. Collection is non-circulating.
Photocopying available.
IN —ALLEN COUNTY PUBLIC LIBRARY,
900 Webster St, Fort Wayne, 46802. Paul
Deane, Reader Services Dept Head; Kay
Lynn Isca, Art Music & AV Dept Head
Holdings: Vols 858 Cat Pix
Notes: Incl many uniform plates in color.

UNIFORMS, MILITARY AND NAVAL

CA —BURBANK PUBLIC LIBRARY, 110 N
Glenoaks Blvd, Burbank, 91502. Mary Ann
Grasso, Coordr; Barbara Stones, Coordr,
Media Project
Holdings: Vols (32,000) Cat Clippings Pix
VF
Notes: The Warner Research Collection is a full
service research division designed to serve the
production needs of the motion picture, television,
theatrical, and creative arts communities. This is a
see-based service available by appointment only.
Subject specialties include costumes, U.S.
military, crime and criminals, transportation,
license plates, and Sears catalogues.

CA —WESTERN COSTUME COMPANY,
Research Library, 5335 Melrose Ave,
Hollywood, 90038. Nancy S Kinney, Dir of
Research
Holdings: Vols 3000 Pix VF
Notes: Incl 25 vertical file drawers of
photographs, 30 bound periodical volumes,
bound uniform regulations, insignia and
decorations charts, 27 periodical
subscriptions. Card file index on selected
military uniform pictures from periodicals
holdings. Collection can be used only by the
customers of Western Costume Company.
All other use is on a fee basis. Collection is
non-circulating. Photocopying available.

NY —NEW YORK PUBLIC LIBRARY,
Research Libraries, General Research
Division, Fifth Ave & 42 St, New York,
10018. Rodney Phillips, Chief
Holdings: Vols (2,225,000) Cat Maps Pix
Microforms
Budget: ($775,718)

NY —FORT ONTARIO HISTORIC SITE,
Oswego, 13126. Shelley B Weinreb, Historic
Site Mgr
Holdings: Vols (400) Cat Mss Maps Pix
Slides
Notes: Primary focus is upon military
activities at the mouth of the Oswego River
and the utilization of fortifications (Fort
Ontario, Fort Oswego, and Fort George) at
that point which served to control the outlet
of the traditional Mohawk-Oneida-Oswego
route to the Great Lakes. A limited number
of sources on fortification design, weapons,
uniforms, and military equipment are
included. Also incl 4000 slides and 400
pictures.

NY —US MILITARY ACADEMY LIBRARY,
West Point, 10996. Egon A Weiss, Librn
Holdings: Vols (100,000) Cat Mss Maps Pix
Slides Phonorecords Videotapes 16mm Films
Filmstrips Microforms
Notes: Described in Subject Catalog of the
Military Art and Science Collection in the
Library of the US Military Academy
(Greenwood Publishing Corp, 1969).
RI —BROWN UNIVERSITY, John Hay
Library, Anne S K Brown Military
Collection, 20 Prospect St, Providence,
02912. Richard B Harrington, Cur
Holdings: Vols (40,000) Cat Mss Pix
Notes: The Anne S K Brown Military
Collection has been formed over the past
forty or more years by Mrs John Nicholas
Brown, now of Newport, and contains
approximately 40,000 volumes and 60,000
prints, drawings and watercolors as well as a
number of oil paintings and about 5000
miniature model soldiers. At its beginning
(and still today) the emphasis or focus of this
collection has been upon the history of, and
the accurate contemporary illustration of,
military and naval uniforms of all nations
from the early XVII century to the present.
In the course of time, however, the
collection has come to incl also a vast and
related amount of material on military and
naval history, military and naval arts and
tactics, wars, campaigns, ceremonies,
biography, portraits and caricatures of this
and earlier periods. It has been probably the
largest private collection of such a nature
inthe world, and it contains much ms and
graphic documentation which is unique. It
has been useful to numerous scholars and
historians, editors, filmmakers and publishers
for research and for illustrative material and
has also contributed to many museum
exhibitions. In 1982 the entire collection,
with its complete card catalog and subject
index, has been presented to Brown
University, where it is located in the John
Hay Library. Special requests are taken care
of by phone, mail and appointments with the
curator.
ON —FORT MALDEN NATIONAL
HISTORIC PARK, Library, 100 Laird Ave,
Box 38, Amherstburg, N9V 2Z2, Can. Sally
E Snyder, Librn
Holdings: Vols (400) Cat Mss Pix Slides
Notes: British and Canadian military life,
weaponry, uniforms, from about 1760 to
1860.

UNIFORMS, MILITARY AND NAVAL (cont.)

ON —NATIONAL MUSEUMS OF
CANADA, Library Services Directorate,
Ottawa, K1A 0M8, Can. Valerie
Monkhouse, Director
Holdings: Vols 12,000 Cat
Notes: Collection includes: arms and armour,
military aeronautics, military and naval arts
and sciences, military and naval equipment,
general military and naval history, military
and naval history of Canada. Research
collection; interlibrary loans available; public
may use on the premises.

ON —METROPOLITAN TORONTO
LIBRARY, History Dept, 789 Yonge St,
Toronto, M4W 2G8, Can. Michael Pearson,
Head
Holdings: Vols (11,000) Cat Phonorecords
Audiotapes Microforms
Notes: Includes British army and navy lists
and Prussian and French army lists from
18th century on; British regimental histories;
works on military uniforms and insignia,
especially European; Napoleonic and First
and Second World Wars well represented.

UNIFORMS, NAVAL see Uniforms, Military and Naval

UNIFORMS, POLICE

CA —WESTERN COSTUME COMPANY,
Research Library, 5335 Melrose Ave,
Hollywood, 90038. Nancy S Kinney, Dir of
Research
Holdings: Vols 1000
Notes: Incl 9 vertical file drawers of
photographs, 65 binders of current police
uniforms incl sheriffs, state police, etc. 6
periodical subs on police profession. Card
file index on selected uniform pictures from
periodicals holdings. Collection can be used
only by the customers of Western Costume
Company. All other use is on a fee basis.
Collection is non-circulating. Photocopying
available.

UNION CATALOGS see Catalogs, Union

UNION LABELS see Labels, Including Trade Union Labels

UNION OF SOUTH AFRICA see Africa, South

UNION OF SOVIET SOCIALIST REPUBLICS see Russia

UNION PACIFIC RAILROAD

IA —UNIVERSITY OF IOWA, University
Libraries, Iowa City, 52242. Frank Paluka,
Head, Special Collections Dept
Holdings: // Mss
Notes: Collection especially concerns the
Union Pacific and Rock Island Railroads. 45
linear feet of ms material. Described in
Richard M Kolbet, "The Levi O Leonard
Railroad Collection," Books at Iowa, April
1968.

MA —STONEHILL COLLEGE, Donahue
Hall, Washington St, North Easton, 02356.
Louise M Kenneally, Archivist & Special
Collections Librn
Holdings: //
Notes: The Arnold B Tofias Industrial
Archives; 2000 linear feet of records and
correspondence of the Ames Shovel
Company of North Easton, Mass. About 800
shovels and other artifacts. Covers the
period 1774-1956.

NE —KEARNEY STATE COLLEGE, Calvin
T Ryan Library, Kearney, 68847. John
Mayeski, Dir; Anita Norman, Reference
Librn
Holdings: Vols 1700 Cat Mss Maps Pix
Slides Microforms
Notes: Collection attempts to cover total
historical development of Nebraska. Special
strengths of the collection incl overland
journeys, Pony Express, sod houses, and the
Union Pacific. Special consideration has

been given to Indians of Nebraska and the
cattle industry. The collection is well
supported by the library's general strength of
Western Americana.

UNION SQUARE THEATRE

NY —HAMPDEN-BOOTH THEATRE
LIBRARY AT THE PLAYERS, 16
Gramercy Park, New York, 10003. Louis A
Rachow, Librn/Cur
Holdings: Mss Pix
Notes: The Union Square Theatre
Collection, incl correspondence, original
contracts for plays produced, autobiographies
by many actors and actresses who had
performed at The Union Square Theatre,
sheetmusic, photographs, illustrations,
playbills. This collection was made by Albert
Marshman Palmer and covers the years of
his career as Manager of The Union Square
Theatre. Described in Palmer's Catalog of
the Library of Albert M Palmer (published
in 1906), pp 100-109. Described in Theatre
& Performing Arts Collections (New York:
Haworth Press, 1981).

UNIONS, TRADE see Trade Unions

UNITARIANISM

MA —HARVARD UNIVERSITY, Harvard
Divinity School, Andover-Harvard
Theological Library, 45 Francis Ave,
Cambridge, 02138. Maria Grossmann, Librn
Holdings: Vols (370,000) Cat Mss
Microforms

NY —UNIVERSITY OF ROCHESTER, Rush
Rhees Library, Department of Rare Books
and Special Collections, Rochester, 14627.
Peter Dzwonkoski, Librn
Holdings: Cat Mss
Notes: Correspondence, annual reports,
financial records and ephemera of
congregation, 1829-1960. Church attended
by Susan B Anthony and other active social
reformers. Papers of ministers William
Channing Gannett (1840-1923) and David
Rhys Williams (1890-1970).

RI —BROWN UNIVERSITY, John Hay
Library, 20 Prospect St, Providence, 02912.
Mark N Brown, Cur Mss
Holdings: Vols (2000) Cat Mss
Notes: Several collections of religious history
strong in material on Baptist,
Congregational, and Unitarian Churches in
the 19th century, incl the ms records some
Rhode Island congregations plus the papers
of Isaac Backus, Brown University presidents
and faculty, Jones Very, Mary Ann Atwood,
Thomas Ustick, and Charles King Newcomb;
incl numerous ephemeral and pamphlet
publications that relate to Baptist Church
history, creed, biography, Sunday School
literature and missions.

UNITAS FRATRUM see Moravian Church and Moravians

UNITED AMERICAN FREE WILL BAPTISTS

ME —BATES COLLEGE, George & Helen
Ladd Library, Special Collections, Bardwell
St, Lewiston, 04240. Mary Riley, Special
Collections Librn
Holdings: Vols 380 // Cat Mss
Notes: Free Will Baptists. Incl 23 mss.

UNITED ARAB EMIRATES

CA —HOOVER INSTITUTION ON WAR,
REVOLUTION & PEACE, Stanford
University, Stanford, 94305. Peter Duignan,
Cur; Karen Fung, Deputy Cur
Holdings: Vols (100,000)
Notes: For full description of collection, see
Hoover Institution entry under Near East.

UNITED ARAB REPUBLIC see Egypt

UNITED ARTISTS CORPORATION

WI —STATE HISTORICAL SOCIETY OF
WISCONSIN, Archives, 816 State St,

Madison, 53706. Harold L Miller, Reference
Archivist
Holdings: Mss Pix Microforms
Notes: Holdings incl records and papers of
prominent organizations and individuals in
the theater and motion picture industry,
motion picture and television films, scripts,
and still photographs, incl the archives of the
United Artists Corporation. Collections are
described in Sources for Mass
Communications, Film and Theater
Research: A Guide, (1982) and in current
accession notes in the Wisconsin Magazine
of History. Major collections are also in
Hamer, Guide to Manuscripts and Archives
in the United States, (1961) and in the
National Union Catalog of Manuscripts
Collections, (1959-date).

UNITED ARTISTS WARNER BROTHERS FILMS

DC —LIBRARY OF CONGRESS, American
Film Institute Collection, Washington,
20540.
Notes: Original master negatives of the
entire pre-1949 Warner Brothers library of
films.

UNITED AUTOMOBILE, AEROSPACE AND AGRICULTURAL IMPLEMENT WORKERS OF AMERICA (UAW)

MI —WAYNE STATE UNIVERSITY, Walter
P Reuther Library, Archives of Labor &
Urban Affairs, Detroit, 48202. Philip Mason,
Dir
Notes: The Archives of Labor History and
Urban Affairs of Wayne State University has
long been known for its large and extensive
ms collections related to the labor movement
and to the city in 20th century America. As
the official depository for the United
Automobile, Aerospace and Agriculture
Implement Workers, Congress of Industrial
Organizations, United Farm Workers
Organizing Committee, American
Newspaper Guild, Air Line Pilots
Association, and Industrial Workers of the
World, the Archives has established itself as
a distinguished research institution.

UNITED BRETHREN IN CHRIST

IN —INDIANA CENTRAL UNIVERSITY,
Krannert Memorial Library, 1400 E Hanna
Ave, Indianapolis, 46227. Florabelle Wilson,
Librn
Holdings: Vols 561 Cat
Notes: Collection of books and pamphlets
which have been written by members of the
United Brethren (UB), Evangelical United
Bretheren (EUB) and United Methodist
(UM) Church. The collection has conference
yearbooks, proceedings, and annuals, as well
as biographies and historical information
about the origin and development of these
faiths.

NJ —UNITED METHODIST CHURCH,
Commission on Archives and History, 36
Madison Ave, PO Box 127, Madison, 07940.
Charles Yrigoyen, Jr, General Secy
Holdings: Vols 40,000 Cat Mss Maps Pix
Slides Microforms
Budget: $110,000
Notes: The United Methodist Church
Collection includes these churches and dates:
The United Evangelical Church, 1891-1922;
The Evangelical Association, 1800-1922;
The Evangelical Church, 1922-1946; The
United Brethren in Christ, 1800-1946; The
Evangelical United Brethren Church, 1946-
1968; The Methodist Episcopal Church,
1773-1939; The Methodist Episcopal
Church, South, 1844-1939; The Methodist
Church, 1939-1968; The United Methodist
Church, 1968-date. There is no published
catalog. The Depository is a specialized
collection pertaining to manuscript and
published material dealing with the United
Methodist Church and its antecedent bodies.
It is the official church depository for
preservation of records-over 2 million items.

UNITED CHARITIES

TX —RICE UNIVERSITY, Fondren Library,
Woodson Research Center, 6100 S Main St,

UNITED CHARITIES (cont.)

PO Box 1892, Houston, 77251. Nancy
Parker, Dir Woodson Research Center
Notes: The papers of Walter Benona Sharp
and Estelle Boughton Sharp. His papers
consist of letters written to his wife and
family from 1890 to 1912 as well as papers
relating to his involvement in the oil
business. Her papers cover a variety of
topics, incl United Charities, the peace
movement, Rice University, her business and
financial affairs, and her efforts to record the
history of the oil industry in the Southwest.

UNITED CHINA RELIEF, INC.

NJ —PRINCETON UNIVERSITY, Library,
Manuscript Collection, Nassau St, Princeton,
08540. Jean F Preston, Cur
Holdings: // Cat Mss Pix
Notes: Archives of the United China Relief,
Inc, and United Service to China, Inc. Incl
100 boxes of papers, 1941-1966. An
unpublished typescript guide (36 p) is
available.

UNITED CHURCH OF CANADA

ON —TORONTO SCHOOL OF
THEOLOGY, Consortium of Libraries,
University of Toronto, Toronto, M5S 1A5,
Can. R Grane Bracewell, Library Coordr
Holdings: Cat
Notes: A consortium of 7 theological college
and faculty libraries at the University of
Toronto.

UNITED CIGARETTE MACHINE COMPANY

NC —DUKE UNIVERSITY, William R
Perkins Library, Manuscript Dept, Durham,
27706. Ellen Gartrell, Cur of Mss
Holdings: Cat Mss
Notes: Tobacco culture, marketing, trade,
especially US South, 19th-20th century, incl
papers of Duke Family, Richard H Wright,
British-American Tobacco Co, James A
Thomas, Edward J Parrish, United Cigarette
Machine Co; also tobacco advertising (trade
cards, etc).

UNITED ELECTRICAL, RADIO, AND MACHINE WORKERS

IN —INDIANA STATE UNIVERSITY,
EVANSVILLE, Library, 8600 University
Blvd, Evansville, 47712. Gina R Walker,
Acting Archivist
Holdings: Vols 50 Cat Mss Pix Slides
Audiotapes
Notes: Daily radio programs broadcast
(1949-1954) over several Evansville, Indiana,
stations concerning activities of the local
United Electrical and Radio and Machine
Workers of America union; other local union
news; state, national, and international
events; editorial commentary. Prepared and
presented by Sadelle Berger, community
leader. 4 document cases. Also materials
collected during year-long Indiana Labor
History Project. Oral history interviews,
photographs, slides, brochures, newspaper
clippings.
PA —UNIVERSITY OF PITTSBURGH,
Hillman Library, Archives of Industrial
Society, 363 Hillman Library, Pittsburgh,
15260. Frank A Zabrosky, Cur
Holdings: Mss Microforms
Notes: Incl records of districts and some
locals.
PA —PENNSYLVANIA STATE
UNIVERSITY, Fred Lewis Pattee Library,
Labor History Collection, University Park,
16802. Peter Gottlieb, Archivist
Holdings: Cat Mss
Notes: Trade union's archives, etc.

UNITED EMPIRE LOYALISTS

ON —CHATHAM PUBLIC LIBRARY, 120
Queen St, Chatham, N7M 2G6, Can. Arlene
Mason, Head of Reference
Holdings: Mss Maps Pix Slides Microforms
Notes: Collection incl books on Black

history, especially the Underground Railroad
pertaining to the Chatham and Windsor
area; many articles, and a few pictures of
these subjects; also Indians of Kent County.
Kent County and Southern Ontario History
is also a subject of this collection, especially
United Empire Loyalists in Southern
Ontario.

UNITED EVANGELICAL CHURCH

NJ —UNITED METHODIST CHURCH,
Commission on Archives and History, 36
Madison Ave, PO Box 127, Madison, 07940.
Charles Yrigoyen, Jr, General Secy
Holdings: Vols 40,000 Cat Mss Maps Pix
Slides Microforms
Budget: $110,000
Notes: The United Methodist Church
Collection includes these churches and dates:
The United Evangelical Church, 1891-1922;
The Evangelical Association, 1800-1922;
The Evangelical Church, 1922-1946; The
United Brethren in Christ, 1800-1946; The
Evangelical United Brethren Church, 1946-
1968; The Methodist Episcopal Church,
1773-1939; The Methodist Episcopal
Church, South, 1844-1939; The Methodist
Church, 1939-1968; The United Methodist
Church, 1968-date. There is no published
catalog. The Depository is a specialized
collection pertaining to manuscript and
published material dealing with the United
Methodist Church and its antecedent bodies.
It is the official church depository for
preservation of records-over 2 million items.
NY —CORNELL UNIVERSITY LIBRARIES,
Collection of Regional History, Dept of
Manuscripts and Univ Archives, Ithaca,
14853.
Notes: Records, 1800-47; 2 items. Milton
and Scipio, NY.

UNITED FARM WORKERS UNION

CA —CALIFORNIA STATE UNIVERSITY,
FULLERTON, Library, Box 4150,
Fullerton, 92634. Alfredo H Zuniga, Coord
Notes: Some materials on the subject; not
maintained as a separate collection.
MI —WAYNE STATE UNIVERSITY, Walter
P Reuther Library, Archives of Labor &
Urban Affairs, Detroit, 48202. Philip Mason,
Dir
Notes: Insights into national problems of
discrimination and poverty can ve found in
the records and papers of the United Farm
Workers Organizing Committee and its
Director, Cesar Chavez; the California
Migrant Ministry; and the Citizen's Crusade
Against Poverty, now preserved in the
Archives.

UNITED KINGDOM—GOVERNMENT PUBLICATIONS

AB —UNIVERSITY OF ALBERTA, John
Weir Memorial Law Library, Law Centre,
Second Floor, Edmonton, T6G 2H5, Can.
Lillian MacPherson, Law Librn
Holdings: Vols (140,000) Cat Maps
Audiotapes Microforms
Budget: ($400,000)
Notes: Emphases on Canadian Government
Publications, oil and gas, Canadian and US,
UK, Australian, New Zealand primary
materials. Separate catalog.
ON —LIBRARY OF PARLIAMENT,
Parliament Bldgs, Ottawa, K1A 0A9, Can.
Erik J Spicer, Parliamentary Librn
Holdings: Vols 60,000 Uncat
Notes: Noncirculating; interlibrary loan
restricted.

UNITED METHODIST CHURCH

CA —POINT LOMA NAZARENE
COLLEGE, Ryan Library, 3900 Lomaland
Dr, San Diego, 92106. Esther Schandorff,
Librn
Holdings: Vols 1600 Cat Mss Pix
Notes: Historical material from the period of
the Wesleyan revival to the present day.
IN —DEPAUW UNIVERSITY, Roy O West
Library, University Archives, PO Box 137,

Greencastle, 46135. Virginia C Brann, Sr
Archives Asst
Holdings: Vols (2000) Cat Mss Maps Pix
Slides Microforms
Notes: Archives of DePauw University and
Indiana United Methodism. Select
Bibliographic Guide available upon request.
IN —INDIANA CENTRAL UNIVERSITY,
Krannert Memorial Library, 1400 E Hanna
Ave, Indianapolis, 46227. Florabelle Wilson,
Librn
Holdings: Vols 561 Cat
Notes: Collection of books and pamphlets
which have been written by members of the
United Brethren (UB), Evangelical United
Bretheren (EUB) and United Methodist
(UM) Church. The collection has conference
yearbooks, proceedings, and annuals, as well
as biographies and historical information
about the origin and development of these
faiths.
KS —UNITED METHODIST HISTORICAL
COLLECTION AND LIBRARY, Baker
University Library, Lower Floor, Eighth St,
Baldwin City, 66006. Maxine Kreutziger,
Secy; John Forbes, Supvr
Holdings: Cat Mss Maps Pix Microforms
Budget: ($2000)
Notes: United Methodist Church history,
espec in Kansas. Persons desiring to visit the
collection are advised to make an
appointment or phone ahead to Baker
University (913-594-6451 ext 380 or 414) to
assure that collection is open.
LA —CENTENARY COLLEGE OF
LOUISIANA, Magale Library, Shreveport,
71104. Carolyn Garison, Archivist
Holdings: Vols (2000) Cat Mss Pix
Microforms
Budget: ($750)
Notes: Depository for the records of the
Louisiana Conference and materials relating
to all the antecedent bodies of United
Methodism in Louisiana. Also, collections of
personal and family papers relating to
Louisiana Methodist history and church
histories. We are trying to locate church
records for microfilming. Further emphasis
on Northern Louisiana and Shreveport
history. Catalogs and inventories for all
manuscript and archival materials are housed
with the collection in the Cline Room.
Citations on part of this material will be
found in NUCMC MS65-1830 and Hamer's
Guide to Archives and Manuscripts in the
United States.
MA —UNITED METHODIST CHURCH,
SOUTHERN NEW ENGLAND
CONFERENCE, Commission on Archives
& History, New England Methodist
Historical Society Library, 745
Commonwealth Ave, Boston, 02215. William
E Zimpfer, Librn
Holdings: Vols 13,750 Cat Mss
Budget: $800
Notes: Mainly records of New England
Methodist churches and of Methodist
conferences and institutions in New
England. It is the official repository of the
Southern New England Conference of the
United Methodist Church.
MI —ADRIAN COLLEGE, Shipman Library,
Adrian, 49221. Ronald A Brunger, Cur
Holdings: Vols (1500) Cat Mss
Budget: ($400)
Notes: United Methodist Church, Detroit
Conference. Archives. Incl materials on
Evangelical United Brethren, Methodist,
Methodist Episcopal, Methodist Protestant,
and United Methodist churches.
MO —CENTRAL METHODIST COLLEGE,
George M Smiley Memorial Library,
Fayette, 65248. C E Hix, Dir
Holdings: Vols (1300) Cat Mss
Notes: Archives of the Missouri West
Conference of the United Methodist Church.
Incl journals and books.
NE —NEBRASKA WESLEYAN
UNIVERSITY, Cochrane-Woods Library, 50
& St Paul, Lincoln, 68504. Lois W Collings,
Dir
Holdings: Vols 15,000 Cat Mss Maps Pix
Slides Microforms
Notes: Nebraska history of the United
Methodist Church.
NJ —DREW UNIVERSITY, Library, Madison,
07940. Caroline Coughlin, Assoc Dir
Notes: The national archives of the United
Methodist Church.

UNITED METHODIST CHURCH (cont.)

NJ —UNITED METHODIST CHURCH,
Commission on Archives and History, 36
Madison Ave, PO Box 127, Madison, 07940.
Charles Yrigoyen, Jr, General Secy
Holdings: Vols 40,000 Cat Mss Maps Pix
Slides Microforms
Budget: $110,000
Notes: The United Methodist Church
Collection includes these churches and dates:
The United Evangelical Church, 1891-1922;
The Evangelical Association, 1800-1922;
The Evangelical Church, 1922-1946; The
United Brethren in Christ, 1800-1946; The
Evangelical United Brethren Church, 1946-
1968; The Methodist Episcopal Church,
1773-1939; The Methodist Episcopal
Church, South, 1844-1939; The Methodist
Church, 1939-1968; The United Methodist
Church, 1968-date. There is no published
catalog. The Depository is a specialized
collection pertaining to manuscript and
published material dealing with the United
Methodist Church and its antecedent bodies.
It is the official church depository for
preservation of records-over 2 million items.

NC —DUKE UNIVERSITY, Divinity School
Library, Durham, 27706. Donn Michael
Farris, Librn
Holdings: Vols (225,000)
Notes: Special collections and subject
emphases in this library include:
Archaeology, Egyptian; Archaeology,
Middle Eastern; Art, Jewish; Bible; Bible-
New Testament; Bible-Symbolism; Church
Architecture; Egyptology; Fathers of the
Church; Society of Friends; Great Britain-
Religion-Methodism and Methodist Church;
Hymns and Hymnals; Jansenists and
Jansenism; Judaica; Mediaeval Christian
Mysticism; Methodism and Methodist
Church; Methodist Episcopal Church;
Methodist Episcopal Church, South;
Reformation; Religion-US-History; Rural
Church; Theology-Great Britain-17th
Century; Theology-Great Britain-18th
Century; United Methodist Church; US-
Church History; John Wesley.

SC —WOFFORD COLLEGE, Sandor Teszler
Library, N Church St, Spartanburg, 29301.
Frank J Anderson, Librn
Notes: Library has extensive holdings of
college archives and historical materials of
the SC Conference of the United Methodist
Church. These go back to the early 19th
century. Since church and college have been
in the state, and of great influence on its
affairs, this collection if of interest for the
history of South Carolina.

WV —WEST VIRGINIA WESLEYAN
COLLEGE, Annie Merner Pfeiffer Library,
Buckhannon, 26201. Ben Crutchfield, Jr, Dir
Holdings: Vols 5000 Cat Mss Pix
Notes: Depository for the Methodist
Historical Collection of the United
Methodist Church of West Virginia.

UNITED MINE WORKERS

MI —MICHIGAN STATE UNIVERSITY,
Labor and Industrial Relations Library, East
Lansing, 48824. Martha Jane Soltow, Librn
Holdings: Cat Microforms
Notes: This material is composed primarily
of special collections of papers on microfilm
or microfiche.

UNITED NATIONS

CA —UNIVERSITY OF CALIFORNIA,
BERKELEY, University Library,
Government Documents Department, 350
Library Annex, Berkeley, 94720. Suzanne
Gold, Collection Dept Librn
Holdings: Vols (314,000) Cat Microforms
Budget: ($85,115)
Notes: General collection of government
documents, historical and current, on the
federal and state levels; as well as
international and foreign documents. The
Library's holdings are particularly strong in
foreign statistics and censuses, and US
Congress. The Government Documents
Department serves as a full depository for

GPO, NASA, State of California, EEC,
GATT, IAEA, United Nations, UNESCO,
Rand Corporation (non-classified), IBRD,
OECD, ILO, UNITAR, ITC, and CE.
Selective depository, PL-480 Programs, or
gift or exchange arrangements obtain for the
states of Michigan and Washington and for
Canada, India, Pakistan and Indonesia. Incl
microfilm and 300,000 fiche, cards, and
prints.

CA —LOS ANGELES PUBLIC LIBRARY,
Social Sciences Dept, 630 W Fifth St, Los
Angeles, 90071. Marilyn C Wherley,
Principal Librn
Holdings: Vols 3000 Cat Microforms
Budget: ($150,000)
Notes: Over 10,000 documents, incl agency
reports and official records of sessions,
yearbooks, periodicals, pamphlets, and
unbound publications. Complete depository
since founding of organization, 1945. No
separate catalog.

CA —UNIVERSITY OF CALIFORNIA, LOS
ANGELES, Research Library, Dept of
Special Collections, 405 Hilgard Ave, Los
Angeles, 90024. Edward Shreeves,
Chairman, Bibliographers Group; David S
Zeidberg, Head
Holdings: Cat Mss
Notes: 8.5 linear feet of pamphlets, reports,
and news releases pertaining to the United
Nations Relief and Rehabilitation
Administration (UNRRA), collected by
David N Leff, an official with the Mission.

CA —UNIVERSITY OF CALIFORNIA, LOS
ANGELES, Research Library, Public Affairs
Service, 405 Hilgard Ave, Los Angeles,
90024. Edward Shreeves, Chairman,
Bibliographers Group; Eugenia Eaton, Head,
Public Affairs Service
Holdings: Microforms
Notes: Depository for the official
publications of California cities and counties,
the state of California, the United States
government, the United Nations and some of
its specialized agencies (including the Food
and Agricultural Organization and
UNESCO), and such regional organizations
as the European Communities and
Organization of American States. Selected
publications of other American cities and
counties, of the other states and possessions
of the United States, of interstate
organizations, and of foreign governments
(with emphasis on major world powers,
Africa, Latin America and the Near and
Middle East) and intergovernmental
organizations.

CA —HOOVER INSTITUTION ON WAR,
REVOLUTION & PEACE, Stanford
University, Stanford, 94305. Milorad M
Drachkovitch, Archivist
Holdings: Mss Pix
Notes: Papers of Victor Chi-tsai Hoo,
Nationalist Chinese diplomat and statesman,
1919-1945, and United Nations official,
1945-1972, incl diaries, correspondence,
clippings, reports, memoranda, photographs,
and other material, 1930-1972, relating to
his government service for China, Chinese
political events and foreign relations, Sino-
Soviet relations, and his career with the
United Nations. 7 1/2 ms boxes.

CT —YALE UNIVERSITY LIBRARY,
Government Documents Center, 38
Mansfield St, PO Box 2491, Yale Sta, New
Haven, 06520. Sandra K Peterson,
Documents Librn
Holdings: Microforms
Notes: United Stations depository.

DC —LIBRARY OF CONGRESS, General
Reading Rooms Division, Microform
Reading Room, Washington, 20540.
Holdings: Cat Mss Maps Pix Microforms
Notes: Microform materials only in this LC
Division. Works of individual authors;
holdings of collections; archival records, etc,
press releases and translations, etc.

IL —NORTHWESTERN UNIVERSITY,
Library, Government Publications Dept,
Evanston, 60201. Robert W Baumgartner,
Head
Notes: Collection consists of US federal
documents (depository library since 1876);
state documents (emphasis on Illinois);
municipal documents (emphasis on Evanston

and Chicago); documents of international
organizations (emphasis on United Nations,
United Nations specialized agencies,
Organization of American States, European
Communities). Collection consists of
publications of 44 international
organizations. Shelflist maintained in the
Government Publications Department. Most
publications not incl in the library's general
catalog.

IL —WHEATON COLLEGE, Buswell
Memorial Library, Wheaton, 60187. Paul
Snezek, Library Dir
Holdings: Mss
Notes: The collection includes mss,
correspondence, lecture tapes, (40), (25
linear feet). 1945 UN conference on
International Organization, Canadian
Rebellion, 1837-1838, Wheaton Scholastic
Society.

KY —UNIVERSITY OF KENTUCKY,
Margaret I King Library, Government
Publications Dept, Lexington, 40506. Sandra
McAninch, Head
Holdings: Cat Microforms
Notes: Official records of the bodies of the
UN and its major affiliates and all sales
publications. In 1969, the University of
Kentucky became a UN depository. The
library has the Readex microcard edition
complete and continuing. Incl papers.

MD —JOHNS HOPKINS UNIVERSITY,
Milton S Eisenhower Library, Government
Publications Maps/Law Dept, Charles & 34
Sts, Baltimore, 21218. James Gillispie,
Acting Head
Holdings: Vols (326,946) Maps
Notes: Milton S Eisenhower Library is a
depository library for federal documents
since 1882. Selects about 50 percent of the
items. Incls 326,946 documents, 183,301
maps sheets. Nondepository items listed in
Monthly Catalog on microprint from
January 1953-1975. Monthly Catalog listing
of JPRS translations on microprint from
October 1958-1973. Eisenhower Library is
also a partial depository of UN (May 1946-
date); South Pacific Commission (1969-
date). Had a standing order on League of
Nations (1922-45); UN/ICJ, Hague
(October 1947-date); UN/ILO (May 1929-
date); UNESCO (1957-date); Council of
Europe (March 1954-date); European
Communities (1960-date); OECD (1955-
date); OAS (September 1948-date); OEEC
(1950-54); USGS (topographic maps).

MA —BOSTON PUBLIC LIBRARY,
Government Documents Department,
Boston, 02117. V Lloyd Jameson, Cur
Holdings: Maps Microforms
Notes: We are a depository for UN
documents (since 1971). In accepting this
status we acquired the major portion of the
World Peace Foundation collection, a former
UN depository. The collection incl all those
items normally distributed to a UN
depository and, ending in mid-1971, the
collection incl many documents not usually
available to depository libraries. Also,
microforms of UN Documents and Official
Records, 1946-date.

MA —HARVARD UNIVERSITY LIBRARY,
Law School Library, Langdell Hall,
Cambridge, 02138. Harry S Martin III, Librn
Holdings: Cat

NJ —PRINCETON UNIVERSITY, Library,
Manuscript Collection, Nassau St, Princeton,
08540. Jean F Preston, Cur
Holdings: // Cat Mss Pix
Notes: The Adlai Stevenson Collection of
personal papers is contained in 1569 boxes.
Terms of Access: The bulk of the personal
papers may be read by qualified scholars.
See *Princeton University Library Chronicle*,
v 26, p 15. An unpublished typescript guide
(456 p) is available in the Library.

NY —NEW YORK STATE LIBRARY, State
Education Bldg Annex, Washington Ave,
Albany, 12224.
Holdings: Microforms
Notes: Documents of UN and its specialized
agencies. Also microform: documents and
official records, 1946-date.

NY —STATE UNIVERSITY OF NEW YORK
AT ALBANY, Library, Special Collections
Dept, 1400 Washington Ave, Albany, 12222.

UNITED NATIONS (cont.)

Marion P Munzer, Coordr
Notes: Correspondence, mss, lecture notes, and materials of John Herman Herz on the United Nations Commission to study the Organization of Peace, 1972-1974 (8 linear feet). Part of the Library's German Exile Collection.
See also entry under Herz, John Herman
NY —STATE UNIVERSITY OF NEW YORK, COLLEGE AT NEW PALTZ, Sojourner Truth Library, New Paltz, 12561. W E Connors, Dir
Holdings: Cat Microforms
Notes: Readex documents collection, 1946 to 1973.
NY —CARNEGIE ENDOWMENT FOR INTERNATIONAL PEACE, James Thomson Shotwell Library, Formerly, New York, 10017.
Holdings: Vols (8500) Cat
Notes: This important collection has been dispersed (Summer 1983). The United Nations documents collection has gone to the University of the West Indies, St Augustine, Trinidad. The rest of the library has been given to special collections in the New York area or to the USBE.
NY —COLUMBIA UNIVERSITY LIBRARIES, Law School Library, Law Building, 435 W 116 St, New York, 10027. James L Hoover, Librn
Notes: Depository library for United Nations documents.
NY —NEW YORK PUBLIC LIBRARY, Research Libraries, Economic & Public Affairs Div, Fifth Ave & 42 St, New York, 10018. Edward DiRoma, Chief
Holdings: Vols (1,500,000) Cat Microforms
Notes: Full depository for publications.
NY —UNITED NATIONS, Dag Hammarskjold Library, Grand Central, PO Box 20, New York, 10017. J L Fuchs, Chief, Users' Service
Holdings: Microforms Documents
Notes: Complete collection of documents and publications since 1945. United Nations, specialized agencies and affiliated bodies: official documents and publications; books about the work of these organizations. Incl 300,000 microforms. Restricted use: not open to the public.
OH —CLEVELAND PUBLIC LIBRARY, Social Sciences Department, 325 Superior Ave, Cleveland, 44114. Thelma Morris, Head
Holdings: Vols 109,000 Cat Microforms
Notes: Department houses complete UN depository set. Working documents on microprint; official records on microprint and printed forms; Sales Numbers serially bound.
OR —UNIVERSITY OF OREGON LIBRARY, Documents Section, Eugene, 97403. Tom Stave, Section Head; John Shuler, Documents Librn
Holdings: Vols 4000
Notes: Incl 205 file drawers. Comprehensive collection incl UN agencies.
PA —UNIVERSITY OF PENNSYLVANIA, Van Pelt Library, Rare Books Collection, 34 & Walnut Sts, Philadelphia, 19104. Daniel Traister, Special Collections Librn
Holdings: Cat
Notes: Selective depository for UN documents.
PA —UNIVERSITY OF PITTSBURGH, Hillman Library, Pittsburgh, 15260. Mary E Miller, Documents Librn
Notes: Comprehensive League of Nations and United Nations materials.
PA —PENNSYLVANIA STATE UNIVERSITY, Fred Lewis Pattee Library, Documents Section, University Park, 16802. Diane H Smith, Head
Notes: Depository for US Government publications; depository for Pennsylvania documents; collect United Nations and related international and intergovernmental organization publications; selected publications from Australia, Great Britain, including Parliamentary Papers; census materials; a large microform collection, including Department of Energy (formerly ERDA, AEC), Congressional publications, Patents, OAS, UN. Incl 900,000 documents. United Nations books are uncataloged.
VA —MACARTHUR MEMORIAL, Library & Archives, MacArthur Sq, Norfolk, 23510. Ellen E Folkama, Asst Archivist
Holdings: Vols (4000) Cat Maps Pix Slides Phonorecords Audiotapes 16mm Films Microforms
Notes: Everything relating to the life and related activities of MacArthur. The Archives of the collection consist of 600 shelf-feet of documents from Gen MacArthur's official headquarters files over the period 1941-1951. These papers pertain to all matters with which his various commands were involved: military, naval and air matters; international relations; political science; Japanese occupation, peace treaty and Constitution, etc. Each Record Group is indexed. The indexes are retained here since they are being expanded. They are available for researchers.
†ON —METROPOLITAN TORONTO LIBRARY, Social Sciences Dept, 789 Yonge St, Toronto, M4W 2G8, Can. Abdus Salam, Head
Holdings: Vols Cat Maps Phonorecords Audiotapes 16mm Films Microforms
Notes: General collection of documents of international organizations with emphasis on the United Nations and UNESCO. Collection ranges from international relations to social conditions in underdeveloped countries. Selected League of Nations publications. Both current and historical in scope.

UNITED NATIONS—SPECIALIZED AGENCIES see International Agencies

UNITED NATIONS ASSOCIATION

CA —HOOVER INSTITUTION ON WAR, REVOLUTION & PEACE, Stanford University, Stanford, 94305. Milorad M Drachkovitch, Archivist
Holdings: Mss Pix
Notes: Records of the United Nations Association in San Francisco, incl correspondence, memoranda, reports, agreements, minutes, histories, financial records, lists, press summaries, pamphlets, posters, clippings, motion pictures, photographs, printed matter, etc, 1945-1970, relating to the operations of United Nations organizations, world politics, and international human rights. 37 ms boxes, 2 oversize boxes, 74 motion picture reels.

UNITED NATIONS EDUCATIONAL, SCIENTIFIC, AND CULTURAL ORGANIZATION (UNESCO)

CA —HOOVER INSTITUTION ON WAR, REVOLUTION & PEACE, Stanford University, Stanford, 94305. Milorad M Drachkovitch, Archivist
Holdings: // Mss
Notes: The Grayson N Kefauver Collection. Papers documenting the founding, background, and early history of the United Nations Educational, Scientific, and Cultural Organization. Incl memoranda and reports of individuals, press clippings, and minutes of meetings of organizations participating in its founding. 16 ft.
TX —UNIVERSITY OF TEXAS LIBRARIES, General Libraries, Barker Texas History Center, PO Box P, Austin, 78712. Don Carleton, Dir
Notes: Papers, etc, documenting the career of Luther H Evans.
†ON —METROPOLITAN TORONTO LIBRARY, Social Sciences Dept, 789 Yonge St, Toronto, M4W 2G8, Can. Abdus Salam, Head
Holdings: Vols Cat Maps Phonorecords Audiotapes 16mm Films Microforms
Notes: General collection of documents of international organizations with emphasis on the United Nations and UNESCO. Collection ranges from international relations to social conditions in underdeveloped countries. Selected League of Nations publications. Both current and historical in scope.

UNITED NATIONS RELIEF AND REHABILITATION ADMINISTRATION (UNRRA)

NY —COLUMBIA UNIVERSITY LIBRARIES, Rare Book and Manuscript Library, Lehman Suite & Papers, 801 Butler Library, 535 W 114 St, New York, 10027. Kenneth A Lohf, Librn
Holdings: Vols 80,000 Mss Pix
Notes: Incl ca 10 lin ft. The personal papers of Herbert H Lehman during his tenure as Director-General of UNRRA. Mainly correspondence, memoranda, diaries and photos.
See also entry under Scandrett, Richard Brown, Jr., 1891-1969

UNITED RUSSIAN ORTHODOX BROTHERHOOD ASSOCIATION

PA —UNIVERSITY OF PITTSBURGH, Hillman Library, Archives of Industrial Society, 363 Hillman Library, Pittsburgh, 15260. Frank A Zabrosky, Cur
Holdings: Mss Documents Newpapers Audiotapes Microforms
Notes: Unique collections: Carpatho-Ruthenian Microforms Project (200 reels of microfilms containing newspapers, almanacs and other serials); United Russian Orthodox Brotherhood Association, Records, 1915-1973.

UNITED SERVICE ORGANIZATION (USO)

NY —ROCKEFELLER UNIVERSITY, Rockefeller Archive Center, Hillcrest, Pocantico Hills, North Tarrytown, 10591. Joseph W Ernst, Dir; J William Hess, Assoc Dir
Notes: Papers relative to the Rockefeller Family, Foundations, University, and other specific enterprises and contributions to particular areas of social, physical, educational, and historic reform, preservation, conservation or development. Extensive records of administrative, financial, physical, or intellectual relationships.

UNITED SERVICE TO CHINA, INC.

NJ —PRINCETON UNIVERSITY, Library, Manuscript Collection, Nassau St, Princeton, 08540. Jean F Preston, Cur
Holdings: // Cat Mss Pix
Notes: Archives of the United China Relief, Inc, and United Service to China, Inc. Incl 100 boxes of papers, 1941-1966. An unpublished typescript guide (36 p) is available.

UNITED SOCIETY OF BELIEVERS IN CHRIST'S SECOND APPEARING see Shakers

U.S.—ANTIQUITIES

IL —NEWBERRY LIBRARY, 60 W Walton St, Chicago, 60610. Diana Haskell, Cur of Modern Mss
Holdings: Vols (1000) Mss Pix
Notes: North, Middle and South America.
MA —SOCIETY FOR THE PRESERVATION OF NEW ENGLAND ANTIQUITIES, Library, 141 Cambridge St, Boston, 02114. Ellie Reichlin, Librn & Cur of Photographic Collections
Holdings: Vols (3000) Cat Pix Microforms
Budget: ($75,000)
Notes: Photograph collections, all media (incl daguerreotypes, ambrotypes, etc, stereographic views, carte de visite) depicting New England buildings; interiors; street and town views; occupations; pastimes; transport and personalities. Covers 1840s-1930s, with some more recent additons. Amateur and professional photographers represented. Cataloged in part, otherwise

U.S.—ANTIQUITIES (cont.)

arranged by localities, subject, personal name. Special collections incl: marine photographs by N L Stebbins and Henry Peabody (1880s-1920s); Boston and Albany railroad photographic archive, early 1900s; Quabbin Valley views; historic American Buildings Survey photographs (17th to early 19th century architecture) by Arthur Haskell; Baldwin Coolidge collection, and many others. Size: 500,000 prints, ca 75,000 negatives (glass plates and copy negs). These are cataloged. Some special indexes incllandscape design (arbors, conservatories, flower beds, bandstands etc); photographers represented; architects represented (partial), and pending, interiors (specific features of); occupations.

NY —NASSAU COUNTY MUSEUM, Sands Pt Preserve, Middleneck Rd, Sand Points, 11050.
Holdings: Vols (2500)
Notes: Collection contains almost every published reference on Long Island archaeology, ethnology, and geology, and incl most of those pertaining to the coastal New York area. Open by appointment. No photocopying.

OH —CLEVELAND PUBLIC LIBRARY, History and Geography Department, 325 Superior Ave, Cleveland, 44114. JoAnn Petrello, Head
Holdings: Vols 8000 Cat
Notes: Library collection in the subject departments incl early American archeology. Some rare books and first editions on travel among the Indians. Tribal histories; biographies. Indian languages, linguistics, language dictionaries, music, costumes, arts, festivals, names, vital statistics, etc.

†WA —WASHINGTON STATE UNIVERSITY, Library, Manuscripts, Archives & Special Collections, Pullman, 99164. John F Guido, Head
Holdings: Cat Mss Maps Pix
Notes: The Carl Parcher Russell papers, a vast resource (24,916 items; 45 linear feet) on American Indian and Western pioneer activities and artifacts. Much on the fur trade; pioneer life; mountain men and trapping; wildlife; primitive life in detail. Also the National Park Service, parks, monuments, etc. Described in *Carl Parcher Russell: An Indexed Register of His Scholarly and Professional Papers, 1920-1967, in the Washington State University Library* (Pullman, 1970), 149 pp.

U.S.—BICENTENNIAL, 1976 see Bicentennial of the U.S., 1776-1976

U.S.—BIOGRAPHY

DC —SMITHSONIAN INSTITUTION, National Museum of American Art & the National Portrait Gallery Library, Eighth & F Sts, NW, Washington, 20560. Cecilia Chin, Librn
Holdings: Vols (47,000) Cat Microforms
Budget: ($60,000)
Notes: Subscribe to 600 foreign and domestic periodicals on art and American history. Holdings of older bound periodicals. Collection emphasizes American art, contemporary American and European painting, portraiture, American biography. Uncataloged material incl: 350 vertical file drawers of clippings, small catalogs and other ephemera on artists, art organizations, museums, etc; mss and archival material on American artists; the "Ferdinand Perret Library"--180 scrapbooks with card index on California art and artists, incl clippings, catalogs, reproductions, etc; card bibliography of books and periodical literature on portraiture--international, retrospective and current--in progress.

U.S.—CENSUS

IL —CENTER FOR RESEARCH LIBRARIES, 6050 S Kenwood Ave, Chicago, 60637. Donald B Simpson, Dir; Esther Smith, Collection Development Librn
Holdings: Microforms
Notes: Complete set of 6317 positive microfilm rolls of US Federal Population censuses 1st through 10th, 1790-1880. Soundex index to 1880 census. Partial holdings of original schedules for 1900 and 1910. Partial holdings of original schedules of US non-population censuses.

IL —NEWBERRY LIBRARY, 60 W Walton St, Chicago, 60610. Diana Haskell, Cur of Modern Mss
Holdings: Cat
Notes: Many microfilms and processed transcripts.

†MA —BOSTON PUBLIC LIBRARY, Copley Sq, Boston, 02117.
Holdings: Cat Microforms
Notes: Microform Publication by National Archives. US Census-Federal Population Schedules, 1790-1890; New England states only.

TX —UNIVERSITY OF TEXAS LIBRARIES, Population Research Center Library, 1701 Main Bldg Tower, Austin, 78712. Doreen S Goyer, Librn
Holdings: Vols Cat Microforms
Budget: ($3000)
Notes: The complete US decennial censuses of population, 1790-1970, are on microfilm. There are also many of these volumes in print form, especially publications from the censuses of 1790 through 1840, and 1950 through 1980. *Bibliography* (6 vols and 1 supplement) incl the majority of items in the Population Research Center.

WI —STATE HISTORICAL SOCIETY OF WISCONSIN, Library, 816 State St, Madison, 53706. James L Hansen, Reference Librn
Holdings: Cat Mss Microforms
Notes: Ms federal census of Wisconsin, 1850-1880, indexed; 1820-1880 on microfilm. Federal census on microfilm, 1790-1910, for all states available. Restricted use: noncirculating, except Wisconsin, 1850-1900, on microfilm and Wisconsin indexes, 1820-1870, on microfilm.

U.S.—CHURCH HISTORY

IL —NEWBERRY LIBRARY, 60 W Walton St, Chicago, 60610. Diana Haskell, Cur of Modern Mss
Holdings: Cat
Notes: Many histories of individual churches; also diocesan and state histories especially New England, the Midwest and the West.

NC —DUKE UNIVERSITY, Divinity School Library, Durham, 27706. Donn Michael Farris, Librn
Holdings: Vols 225,000
Notes: Special collections and subject emphases in this library include: Archaeology, Egyptian; Archaeology, Middle Eastern; Art, Jewish; Bible; Bible-New Testament; Bible-Symbolism; Church Architecture; Egyptology; Fathers of the Church; Society of Friends; Great Britain-Religion-Methodism and Methodist Church; Hymns and Hymnals; Jansenists and Jansenism; Judaica; Mediaeval Christian Mysticism; Methodism and Methodist Church; Methodist Episcopal Church; Methodist Episcopal Church, South; Reformation; Religion-US-History; Rural Church; Theology-Great Britain-17th Century; Theology-Great Britain-18th Century; United Methodist Church; US-Church History; John Wesley.

NC —SOUTHEASTERN BAPTIST THEOLOGICAL SEMINARY LIBRARY, PO Box 752, Wake Forest, 27587. H Eugene McLeod, Librn
Holdings: Cat Microforms
Notes: Incl early American sources in Readex Microprint edition of materials listed in Evan's *American Bibliography* and in Shaw and Shoemaker's *American Bibliography: a Preliminary Checklist*.

U.S.—CIVILIZATION

CA —LOS ANGELES PUBLIC LIBRARY, Central Library, Audio Visual Dept, 630 W Fifth St, Los Angeles, 90071. Richard V Partlow, Principal Librn
Budget: ($71,989)
Notes: Includes 16mm film (4300), VHS video (300), audio recordings (20,000), audio cassettes (5500), picture file (220,000 estimated clippings), filmstrips (60), periodicals (65). Material on all subject areas are included.

DC —HOWARD UNIVERSITY, Moorland-Spingarn Research Center, 500 Howard Place NW, Washington, 20059. Clifford L Muse, Jr, Acting Dir
Holdings: Vols (106,086) Cat Mss Maps Pix Slides Phonorecords Audiotapes 16mm Films Filmstrips Microforms
Budget: ($854,753)
Notes: *The Glenn Carrington Collection: A Guide to the Books, Manuscripts, Music and Recordings* (DC MSRC, 1977). *Dictionary Catalog of the Jesse E Moorland Collection of Negro Life and History*, 9 vols and Supplement, 3 vols (Boston: G K Hall, 1970, 1977). *Dictionary Catalog of the Arthur Spingarn Collection of Negro Authors*, 2 vols (Boston: G K Hall, 1970). Guide to Processed Collections in the Manuscript Division of the Moorland-Spingarn Research Center (DC, MSRC, 1983). The Moorland-Spingran Research Center is recognized as one of the largest and most comprehensive repositories in the world for the collection, preservation and dissemination of historical materials documenting from antiquity to the present the history and culture of Black people in Africa, Europe, the Caribbean and the US. Since 1973, the Research Center has greatly expanded its facilitiesand resources and currently provides research services in all aspects of library and archival research, including manuscripts, oral history, music, prints and photographs and general library materials. The Research Center also maintains professional zerographic, micrographic, photographic and similar reproduction laboratories.

IN —UNIVERSITY OF EVANSVILLE, Clifford Memorial Library & Learning Resources, 1800 Lincoln Ave, Evansville, 47714. P Grady Morein, University Librn
Holdings: Vols 19,000 // Cat Mss Pix Microforms
Notes: The Library of American Civilization is a collection of research material for American studies on microfiche. Have book catalogs and catalog cards for the collection.

MA —AMERICAN ANTIQUARIAN SOCIETY LIBRARY, 185 Salisbury St, Worcester, 01609. Marcus A McCorison, Dir & Librn
Holdings: Cat Mss Maps Pix Slides Microforms
Notes: Over half a million manuscript pieces; extensive collection of contemporary imprints before 1850 (with supplementary supporting studies); over 10,000 maps (weak for 15th-17th centuries; excellent for 18th, strongest in 19th century, especially maps of local nature). Strongest collection of American newspapers before 1821 (see entry under Newspapers, American). Also a good collection of portraits of early New Englanders; paintings, engravings,and miniatures. Further, the largest collection of regional, state, county, and local histories.

MI —MICHIGAN STATE UNIVERSITY, Libraries, Special Collections Div, East Lansing, 48824. Jannette Fiore, Librn
Holdings: Vols (55,000) Mss Pix
Notes: Collection of 19th/20th century authors, including selected expatriate authors. Popular Culture Collections have four principal categories of materials: Comic Art, ca 23,500 items (comics, aprox 21,000 cataloged issues, big-little books, reprints and anthologies, etc); Popular Fiction, ca 24,000 items (dime novels, story magazines and pulps, juvenile series, detective, science fiction, western and romantic novels); Popular Information, ca 5000 items (over 2000 public school text books, along with almanacs, big and little blue books, "self-education" materials, etc); Popular Performing Arts, ca 2300 items (tent-show materials, including 250 scripts, photographs, handbills, records and correspondence; plays and entertainments for home and popular

U.S.—CIVILIZATION (cont.)

performance and print materials relating to radio-TV-film). Partially cataloged.

NC —DUKE UNIVERSITY, William R Perkins Library, Jay B Hubbell Center for American Literary Historiography, Durham, 27706. Erma Whittington, Librn
Notes: 77,312 items, including manuscripts, pictures, clippings, and correspondence. "The objective of the Center is to gather the papers and materials of significant scholars and critics in American literary history." The Center is a part of the Perkins Library Manuscripts Department.

OK —SOCIETY FOR THE NORTH AMERICAN CULTURAL SURVEY, Dept of Geography, Oklahoma State University, Stillwater, 74078. John Rooney, Dir; Todd Zdorkowski, Asst
Notes: Has produced a cultural atlas of North America. Contents incl sports and games, general cultural and popular regions, settlement patterns, land division patterns, folk and modern architecture, regional variations in social organization and behavior, language and place names, ethnicity, religion, politics, food ways, music and dance, and place perception.

U.S.—COMMERCE

CA —HOOVER INSTITUTION ON WAR, REVOLUTION & PEACE, Stanford University, Stanford, 94305. Milorad M Drachkovitch, Archivist
Holdings: Mss
Notes: Papers of Samuel B Sherwin, US Deputy Assistant Secretary of Commerce for Domestic Commerce, 1975-77, incl transcripts of speeches and Congressional testimony, studies, and reports, 1975-76, relating to US commercial policy. 2 ms boxes.

ME —BOWDOIN COLLEGE, Library, Brunswick, 04011. Dianne M Gutscher, Cur of Special Collections
Holdings: Mss
Notes: The Hubbard Family Papers contain more than 12,000 pieces of correspondence and other mss materials relating to the Hubbard Family, for the period 1794-1915. Of principal interest are extensive files of letters to and from John Hubbard (1794-1869), governor of Maine, who signed the "Maine Law" (prohibition law) in 1851, and was a commissioner under the Reciprocity Treaty with Great Britain.

TX —UNIVERSITY OF TEXAS LIBRARIES, General Libraries, PO Box P, Austin, 78713. Carolyn Bucknell, Asst Dir for Collection Development
Notes: Papers of retail grocers, Heidenheimer Brothers, of Galveston, being travelling salesmen's correspondence and other papers, bound by month and year, measuring 35 linear feet.

U.S.—COMMERCE—CHINA

MA —HARVARD UNIVERSITY, Graduate School of Business Administration, Baker Library, Soldiers Field, Boston, 02163. Mary V Chatfield, Librn; Florence Bartoshesky, Cur of Manuscripts and Archives
Holdings: Vols (75,000) Cat Mss Pix
Notes: Baker Library strong in historical aspects of business and economics incl original company records, company histories, business biographies, histories of industries, etc; 16,000 pictures. Ms collection of more than 75,000 incl original records of business firms from 1400 (Medici Collection) to present; especially strong in 19th century. New England enterprises, textile firms, international trade, China trade, railroads, papers of several Northeast merchant families, 19th century small business. Also incl pictures, trade cards, clipper ship cards, money, trade catalogs, business cartoons, prices current and exhibit items. See Robert W Lovett and Eleanor C Bishop, compilers, *Business Manuscripts in Baker Library* (Boston: The Library, 1978), 382 pp. Mss are described in the *National Union Catlog of Manuscript Collections* and in Hamer's *A Guide to Archives and Manuscripts in the United States*. Restricted use: Manuscripts noncirculating. Downs: 1636, 2122, 2616, 2675, 2677, 2698, 2700, 2701, 2702, 2706, 2708, 2711, 2713-15, 2716, 2717-18, 2721-26, 2734, 2737, 2774, 2814, 4300, 5162: Supplement 964, 965, 968, 998.

MA —CHINA TRADE MUSEUM, Library, 215 Adams St, Milton, 02186. Lisa L Gwirtzman, Librn
Holdings: Uncat Mss Maps Pix
Notes: A museum collection, archive and library devoted to a history of the China Trade to Boston, (1784-1900). Incl 30,000 papers of Captain Robert Bennet Forbes; 75,000 other China Trade documents; and 3500 period photographs.

U.S.—COMMERCE—JAPAN

†DC —JAPAN ECONOMIC INSTITUTE OF AMERICA LIBRARY, 1000 Connecticut Ave, NW, Washington, 20036.
Notes: Japan - United States trade.

U.S.—COURTS see Courts—U.s.

U.S.—CULTURAL INFLUENCES

TN —TUSCULUM COLLEGE LIBRARY, Greenville, 37743.
Notes: The Charles Coffin Book Collection of nearly 2000 volumes, an important source reflecting the development of higher education in post-Revolutionary America and the westward spread of culture. The collection comprised the College's original library between 1794 and 1827.

U.S.—CUSTOMS RECORDS

NH —PORTSMOUTH ATHENAEUM, 9 Market Sq, Box 848, Portsmouth, 03801. Joseph P Copley, Cur
Notes: Port of Piscataqua, Province of New Hampshire (1771-1775). Mss volume of British Colonial Records.

RI —RHODE ISLAND HISTORICAL SOCIETY, Library, 121 Hope St, Providence, 02906. Paul R Campbell, Library Dir
Notes: 270 cubic feet of records, incl records of US Customs House in Providence, Rhode Island. Correspondence, crew lists, alien and passenger lists, manifests, entries and clearances (1790-1900).

SC —COLLEGE OF CHARLESTON LIBRARY, Special Collections Dept, Charleston, 29401.
Notes: Listing of records (1837-1924) in storage at the Customs House, Charleston, South Carolina.

U.S.—DECLARATION OF INDEPENDENCE

DC —LIBRARY OF CONGRESS, Washington, 20540.

IN —INDIANA UNIVERSITY, Lilly Library, Seventh St, Bloomington, 47405. William R Cagle, Librn
Holdings: Mss
Notes: Some first and early printings. Incl ms collection of signers.

MA —AMHERST COLLEGE, Library, Amherst, 01002. John Lancaster, Special Collections Librn
Holdings: Cat Mss
Notes: These Signers of the Declaration of Independence documents are bound in one volume. Each signer is represented by at least one document.

NY —NEW YORK STATE LIBRARY, State Education Bldg Annex, Washington Ave, Albany, 12224.
Notes: Complete set of signatures of the 56 signers of the Declaration of Independence, numbering over 100 separate items.

U.S.—DEFENSES

PA —US ARMY WAR COLLEGE LIBRARY, Carlisle Barracks, 17013. Barbara E Stevens, Dir
Holdings: Vols (125,000) Cat Maps Microphones Audiotapes
Budget: ($251,000)
Notes: Physical access to the collection is limited. Individual items available on interlibrary loan. Older historical material is in the US Army Military History Institute, Carlisle Barracks, Pennsylvania, 17013.

U.S.—DESCRIPTION AND TRAVEL

CA —AZUSA PACIFIC COLLEGE, Marshburn Memorial Library, Citrus & Alosta, Azusa, 91702. Edward Peterman, Librn
Holdings: Vols (6000) Uncat
Budget: ($30,000)
Notes: Significant holdings in the George E Fullerton Library of Californiana and Western Americana.

IL —CHICAGO HISTORICAL SOCIETY, Library, Clark St at North Ave, Chicago, 60614. Robert L Brubaker, Librn
Holdings: Vols (150,000) Cat Mss Maps Pix
Notes: Substantial holdings for the area east of the Mississippi, especially the Midwest, but little on the trans-Mississippi West. Early printed and ms journals and accounts by explorers and by foreign and domestic travelers; emigrants' guides; prints and photographs; 590 atlases; and about 10,000 maps (especially strong for Chicago, Illinois, the Midwest, US transportation, general maps of the US for the period to 1900, and general maps of the Americas from the 16th century to 1850).

IL —NORTHERN ILLINOIS UNIVERSITY, Founders Memorial Library, Rare Books and Special Collections Dept, De Kalb, 60115. William R DuBois, Dept Head
Holdings: Vols (1000) Cat Maps Pix
Notes: Collection deals with all aspects of Colorado: early travel narratives, history, literature, geology, ecology, maps and some bibliography.

IN —INDIANA UNIVERSITY, Lilly Library, Seventh St, Bloomington, 47405. William R Cagle, Librn
Holdings: // Cat Mss Maps
Notes: Description and travel of the US Plains and Rockies; overland accounts; issues of California newspapers of the gold rush era, etc.

MA —AMERICAN ANTIQUARIAN SOCIETY LIBRARY, 185 Salisbury St, Worcester, 01609. Marcus A McCorison, Dir & Librn
Holdings: Vols 1500 Cat
Notes: Narratives especially. Incl the Donald McKay Frost Collection.

MN —MINNEAPOLIS PUBLIC LIBRARY & INFORMATION CENTER, 300 Nicollet Mall, Minneapolis, 55401. Richard J Hofstad, Athenaeum Librn
Holdings: Vols (500) Cat Maps
Budget: ($8000)

MN —UNIVERSITY OF MINNESOTA, James Ford Bell Library, 309 19th Ave S, Minneapolis, 55455. John Parker, Cur
Holdings: Vols (11,000) Cat Mss Maps
Notes: Collection of original materials relating to European expansion, 1400-1800.

MO —SAINT LOUIS PUBLIC LIBRARY, Gardner Rare Book Room, 1301 Olive St, Saint Louis, 63103. Julanne M Good, Supervisor; Martha Riley, Rare Books Librn
Holdings: Vols 100 Cat Maps
Budget: ($5573)
Notes: Small growing collection of travels incl St Louis or Missouri, largely transferred from the general stacks, although an occasional purchase is made. Incl early business directories of St Louis, river pilots' handbooks and maps. Noncirculating.

MO —WASHINGTON UNIVERSITY, John M Olin Library, Campus Box 1061, St Louis, 63130.
Holdings: Vols (1800) Cat Mss
Notes: Incl material from the Arthur C Hoskins, Richard S Hawes, Ernst C Krohn, George N Meissner, Stratford Lee Morton, and Edgar M Queeny collections; strong in early travel literature of the US and Latin America; accounts of exploration in the Mississippi Valley and Trans-Mississippi West; miscellaneous accounts of history, pioneer life, and travel in the Ohio Valley,

U.S.—DESCRIPTION AND TRAVEL (cont.)

Old Southwest, and California; material on the American Indian; 18th century American music; early American imprints.

NY —NEW YORK HISTORICAL SOCIETY, Library, 170 Central Park W, New York, 10024. James Gregory, Librn
Holdings: Mss
Notes: Incl original mss, illustrative materials, etc.

NY —NEW YORK PUBLIC LIBRARY, Research Libraries, American History Div, Fifth Ave & 42 St, New York, 10018.
Holdings: Vols (25,000) Maps Microforms
Notes: See *Dictionary Catalog of the History of Americas Collection* (Boston: G K Hall, 1961), 28 vols.

PA —AMERICAN PHILOSOPHICAL SOCIETY, Library, 105 S Fifth St, Philadelphia, 19106. Edward C Carter II, Librn
Holdings: Cat Mss Maps Pix
Notes: Collection (as it was in 1970) is incl in *Catalog of Books in the American Philosophical Society Library* (Westport, Conn: Greenwood Publishing Corp, 1970) and *Catalog of Manuscripts in the American Philosophical Society Library* (Westport, Conn: Greenwood Publishing Corp, 1970). Both of these catalogs are reproductions of APS Library catalog cards, incl author, subject, and title entries.

PA —BALCH INSTITUTE FOR ETHNIC STUDIES, Library, 18 S Seventh St, Philadelphia, 19106. R Joseph Anderson, Library Dir
Holdings: Vols Cat
Notes: Incl immigrant guides.

PA —UNIVERSITY OF PENNSYLVANIA, Van Pelt Library, Rare Books Collection, 34 & Walnut Sts, Philadelphia, 19104. Daniel Traister, Special Collections Librn
Holdings: Vols 2500 //
Notes: Robert Dechert Collection: early exploration, 17th and 18th centuries; western Americana, 19th century; Canadiana, incl Jesuit relations.

PA —UNIVERSITY OF PITTSBURGH, Darlington Memorial Library, Special Collections, 601 Cathedral of Learning, Pittsburgh, 15260. Dennis Lambert, Darlington Librn
Holdings: Vols (17,000) Cat Mss Maps Pix
Notes: The Darlington Collection is especially rich in American history of the colonial period, the French and Indian War, the Revolution, and the War of 1812 with geographical emphasis on Western Pennsylvania and Ohio Valley history to 1870 and on Pittsburgh history to 1900. Indian treaties, captivity accounts, US and Pennsylvania travel and description, and early American fiction and prose are represented. A partial guide to the Darlington Manuscript Collections is available by writing for *Darlington Memorial Library: A Descriptive Checklist of its Manuscript Collections,* University of Pittsburgh Bibliographic Series 5, 1969. Noncirculating.

TX —HARDIN-SIMMONS UNIVERSITY, Richardson Library, Abilene, 79601. Joe F Dahlstrom, Dir
Holdings: Vols (10,000) Cat Mss Maps Pix Microforms
Notes: Special collection name is Richardson Research Center, named in honor of Dr Rupert N Richardson. Collect in the ares of his own research interests, especially that portion of the US that was once a part of Mexico. Emphases on the history of ranching, railroads, discovery and exploration, Texas county histories, etc. Incl 350 items printed and/or designed by El Paso printer Carl Hertzog; the Judge R C Crane collection of Texana and a similar collection of Louise Kelley's; and the Research Publication's Western Americana collection (microfilm).

TX —UNIVERSITY OF TEXAS, ARLINGTON, Library, PO Box 19497, Arlington, 76019. Chas Colley, Dir Special Collections
Holdings: Uncat Maps Slides
Notes: The collection focuses on the history of cartography in general, specializing in the discovery and exploration of North America, with special emphasis on Texas and the American West. The collection consists of hundreds of rare maps and atlases dating from 1493, coupled with an extensive collection of related reference works and primary works on exploration and discovery.

VA —UNIVERSITY OF VIRGINIA, Alderman Library, Tracy W McGregor Collection, Charlottesville, 22901. William H Runge, Cur
Holdings: Vols 18,000 Cat Mss Maps Pix Microforms
Notes: Library spans 15th-20th century, concentrating on Southeastern American history. Rare collection of books on early exploration and travel; foundation of the Virginia Colony; Civil War. Books in foreign languages. Collection cataloged by date of publication. Special shelflist. Published descriptions: William H Runge, "The Tracy W McGregor Library and Its Founder," *The University of Virginia News Letter* vol 39, no 11, July 15, 1963; *Description of the Tracy W McGregor Library, University of Virginia, With Rules for Its Use and a Biographical Sketch of Its Founder* (Charlottesville: Tracy W McGregor Library, 1951).

VA —LYNCHBURG COLLEGE, Knight-Capron Library, Lynchburg, 24501. Mary C Scudder, Dir
Holdings: Vols (847) Cat Maps
Notes: North America, 17th-19th century. Part of the Capron Collection. Incl over 200 maps.

U.S.—DESCRIPTION AND TRAVEL—BRITISH WRITINGS

PA —SWARTHMORE COLLEGE, Library, Swarthmore, 19081. Michael J Durkan, Librn
Holdings: Vols 1450 Cat Maps Pix
Notes: Accounts of travel in the US by English visitors.

U.S.—DESCRIPTION AND TRAVEL—VIEWS

DC —LIBRARY OF CONGRESS, Prints & Photographs Div, Washington, 20540.
Notes: Detroit Publishing Company, publishers of postcards and souvenir views of buildings, historical sites, natural landmarks, industry, sports activities, and points of interest throughout the US and, to a lesser extent, Europe, Africa, and Asia. Over 22,000 photoprints and nearly 18,500 original glass negatives.

IL —CHICAGO HISTORICAL SOCIETY, Library, Graphics Collection, Clark St at North Ave, Chicago, 60614. Larry A Viskochil, Cur
Notes: About 1,000,000 pieces. Chiefly concern Chicago, but incl many portraits of national leaders and other materials concerning American history. Incl many early daguerreotypes, ambrotypes, tintypes, stereographs; negatives and photographs from Chicago newspaper morgues, 1900-1965 (250,000); photographs from Chicagoland-in-Pictures, a project for historical photography sponsored by the Society and the Chicago Area Camera Clubs Association since 1948 (22,000); and other photographic materials.

MA —BOSTON PUBLIC LIBRARY, Print Collection, Dartmouth St at Copley Sq, Boston, 02117. Sinclair H Hitchings, Keeper of Prints
Holdings: Cat
Notes: The Americana collection is especially strong in the 19th century. Incl 250 prints of American views, tradesmen's calling cards, illustrated diplomas and advertisements. Also in it is the McGreevey Baseball Collection of 225 photos, photoreproductions and paintings from the period 1870 to 1914. The American portrait collection contains 300 engravings, etchings and lithographs of prominent figures of the 18th and 19th century. In addition there are 200 portraits of Benjamin Franklin. Items cataloged by subject. Prints also by artist/ publisher.

MA —AMERICAN ANTIQUARIAN SOCIETY LIBRARY, 185 Salisbury St, Worcester, 01609. Marcus A McCorison, Dir & Librn
Holdings: Cat Maps Pix Slides
Notes: About 90,000 postal cards and 60,000 stereophotographs. Arranged geographically or by subject. Postal cards date from 1893; stereos 1860-1890. Also some rare copybook covers of views, 1794-1860. Extensive slide collection.

TN —TENNESSEE STATE LIBRARY & ARCHIVES, 403 Seventh Ave N, Nashville, 37219. Olivia K Young, State Librn & Archivist
Holdings: Uncat Pix
Notes: Mainly picture postcards of Tennessee and southern scenes, but largest part of the collection is the Mrs Joseph H Thompson Collection incl cards from Europe, Africa, Asia and North and South America.

U.S.—DIPLOMATIC AND CONSULAR SERVICE

CA —CALIFORNIA STATE UNIVERSITY, FULLERTON, Library, Box 4150, Fullerton, 92634. Linda Herman, Special Collections Librn
Holdings: // Microforms
Notes: Espec strong in records of the State Department. Incl all of the Consular Dispatches published on microfilm (covers years to 1906). Has all records from the Decimal File of the Department of State 1910-1929. One of the largest collections of National Archives Microfilm on the West Coast.

U.S.—DISCOVERY AND EXPLORATION see America—Discovery and Exploration; U.S.__Exploring Expeditions

U.S.—EMIGRATION AND IMMIGRATION

CA —LOS ANGELES PUBLIC LIBRARY, Social Sciences Dept, 630 W Fifth St, Los Angeles, 90071. Marilyn C Wherley, Principal Librn
Holdings: Vols 5000 Cat
Budget: ($150,000)
Notes: Emphasis on minorities; immigration policies, background and social problems of ethnic minorities in the US and the Southwest in particular. Incl periodicals, government publications and documents, popular and scholarly works on Blacks, Hispanics and Asians predominantly.

KS —UNIVERSITY OF KANSAS, Kenneth Spencer Research Library, Kansas Collection, Lawrence, 66045. Sheryl K Williams, Cur
Holdings: Vols (90,000) Cat Mss Maps Pix
Notes: All aspects of the American West and trans-Mississippi history, especially northern and central regions. Overland diaries, cartographic history, Indians, emigration and immigration, printing history, cattle industry, agriculture and farm life, conservation are some special interests, in addition to the usual political, economic, military and social interests.

MN —UNIVERSITY OF MINNESOTA, Immigration History Research Center, 826 Berry St, Saint Paul, 55114. Susan Griegs, Cur
Holdings: Vols (35,000) Mss Maps Pix Phonorecords Audiotapes 16mm Films Microforms
Notes: The Archives contain both published and ms material. Presently the imprint collections consist of nearly 25,000 vols of monographs, 3000 periodical titles, and files of more than 900 ethnic newspapers (of which ca 140 are currently received). For the most part, the printed items were published by ethnic presses in North America. Many of the extensive runs of newspapers are to be found in the Archives'

U.S.—EMIGRATION AND IMMIGRATION (cont.)

microfilm collection of approx 5000 reels. The Archives' ms holdings are made up of 450 individual collections of papers, amounting to 2400 linear ft, or approx 3,000, 000 items. Incl are the records of such societies, churches and publishing companies, as well as collections of personal papers of ethnic leaders, clergymen, journalists, labor leaders, writers, poets and politicians. Partially cataloged.

NY —YIVO INSTITUTE FOR JEWISH RESEARCH, Library & Archives, 1048 Fifth Ave, New York, 10028. Dina Abramowicz, Librn; Marek Web, Archivist
Holdings: Cat Mss Pix Slides
Notes: Emphasis is on immigration history. Incl archives of Jewish organizations which served immigrant masses, such as Educational Alliance, Hias, Hicem, Jewish Desertion Bureau and others. Yiddish language general and labor periodicals in originals and on microfilm. The Yiddish school movement in the US is covered, as well as other cultural activities in the field of the Yiddish theater, literature and the arts. Correspondence of outstanding authors with parties in the US and abroad is an important source of information on Yiddish cultural life and communal affairs.

PA —BALCH INSTITUTE FOR ETHNIC STUDIES, Library, 18 S Seventh St, Philadelphia, 19106. R Joseph Anderson, Library Dir
Notes: Historical aspects; also personal narratives.
See also entry under Emmigration and Immigration.

U.S.—EXECUTIVE DEPARTMENTS

CA —HOOVER INSTITUTION ON WAR, REVOLUTION & PEACE, Stanford University, Stanford, 94305. Milorad M Drachkovitch, Archivist
Holdings: Mss
Notes: Records of the US Executive Branch Organization Commissions (Hoover Commissions), 1947-1949 and 1953-1955, incl correspondence, reports, minutes, press releases, and printed matter, relating to the Commissions' efforts to rationalize the organization of the executive branch of the federal government and especially to the work of the Chairman Herber Hoover. 27 ms boxes. Also, records of the National Citizens Committee for the Reorganization of the Executive Branch of the Government and the Citizens Committee for the Hoover Report, 1949-1958. 103 ms boxes.

U.S.—EXPLORING EXPEDITIONS

CA —AZUSA PACIFIC COLLEGE, Marshburn Memorial Library, Citrus & Alosta, Azusa, 91702. Edward Peterman, Librn
Holdings: Vols (6000) Uncat
Budget: ($30,000)
Notes: Significant holdings in the George E Fullerton Library of Californiana and Western Americana.

DC —SMITHSONIAN INSTITUTION, Archives Div, Washington, 20560. William W Moss, Archivist
Holdings: Mss Maps Pix
Notes: The Archives holds correspondence and records of a number of scientific expeditions with which the Smithsonian was connected, incl the Western Union Telegraph Expedition, the Smithsonian Roosevelt African Expedition, and the United States Exploring Expedition.

IL —NEWBERRY LIBRARY, 60 W Walton St, Chicago, 60610. Diana Haskell, Cur of Modern Mss
Holdings: Vols 1550 Cat Mss
Notes: Early Western travel and overland journeys. The E E Ayer Collection.

†OR —LEWIS AND CLARK COLLEGE, Library, 615 SW Palatine Hill Rd, Portland, 97219.
Notes: Lewis and Clark Expedition Collection.

PA —AMERICAN PHILOSOPHICAL SOCIETY, Library, 105 S Fifth St, Philadelphia, 19106. Edward C Carter II, Librn
Holdings: Cat Mss Maps
Notes: Collection (as it was in 1970) is incl in Catalog of Books in the American Philosophical Society Library (Westport, Conn: Greenwood Publishing Corp, 1970). Both of these are reproductions of APS Library catalog cards, incl author, subject, and title entries.

RI —BROWN UNIVERSITY, John Hay Library, 20 Prospect St, Providence, 02912. Mark N Brown, Cur Mss
Holdings: // Mss
Notes: Papers of Augustus William Smith, Professor of Astronomy and Mathematics and President of Wesleyan University; Professor of Natural Philosophy, United States Naval Academy. Approx 335 items with inclusive dates 1816-1918. There are letters and autograph mss of scientific import written by Smith while at Hamilton and Wesleyan colleges; a notebook, part of which records Smith's journey to Labrador in 1860 as a member of the US government expedition to observe the solar eclipse; diplomas; civilian commissions, deeds, and photographs.

TX —HARDIN-SIMMONS UNIVERSITY, Richardson Library, Abilene, 79601. Joe F Dahlstrom, Dir
Holdings: Vols (10,000) Cat Mss Maps Pix Microforms
Notes: Special collection name is Richardson Research Center, named in honor of Dr Rupert N Richardson. Collect in the areas of his own research interests, especially that portion of the US that was once a part of Mexico. Emphases on the history of ranching, railroads, discovery and exploration, Texas county histories, etc. Incl 350 items printed and/or designed by El Paso printer Carl Hertzog; the Judge R C Crane collection of Texana and a similar collection of Louise Kelley's; and the Research Publication's Western Americana collection (microfilm).

U.S.—FOREIGN RELATIONS

CA —COMMONWEALTH CLUB OF CALIFORNIA, Library, 681 Market St, San Francisco, 94105. Virginia Rees, Librn
Holdings: Vols (6500) Cat Maps Pix
Budget: ($2000)

CA —UNIVERSITY OF CALIFORNIA, SANTA BARBARA, Library, Dept of Special Collections, Santa Barbara, 93106. Christian F Brun, Head
Holdings: Vols 220 Cat
Notes: Bernath Memorial Collection.

CA —HOOVER INSTITUTION ON WAR, REVOLUTION & PEACE, Stanford University, Stanford, 94305. Milorad M Drachkovitch, Archivist
Notes: Two collections: (1) Diaries (handwritten), 1909-1938, by Frederick W B Coleman, US diplomat, documenting his service in the US Army, 1917-19, and his diplomatic service as US Minister to Estonia, Latvia, and Lithuania, 1922-1931, and US Minister to Denmark, 1931-33. 1/2 ms box. (2) Papers of Eugene H Dooman, US diplomat, Counsellor of Embassy at Tokyo, 1937-41, and Special Assistant to the Assistant Secretary of State for Far Eastern Affairs, 1944-45, incl mss of writings, transcripts of speeches, correspondence, diaries and printed matter, 1913-1966, relating to US foreign policy in the Far East, US-Japanese relations, the decision to drop the atomic bomb on Japan, and Allied policy regarding the occupation of Japan. 1 1/2 ms boxes.

DE —UNIVERSITY OF DELAWARE, Hugh M Morris Library, S College Ave, Newark, 19711. T Stuart Dick, Special Collections
Holdings: Cat Mss Pix
Notes: Incl letters and confidential diplomatic dispatches written while George Messersmith was American Consul in Berlin, 1930-34; Ambassador to Cuba; Ambassador to Austria, 1934; Ambassador to Mexico, 1941-42; Ambassador to Argentina, 1942-46;

Business correspondence as President of the Mexican Light and Power Co, 1947-60. Calendar and Index available.

DC —LIBRARY OF CONGRESS, Manuscript Division, Washington, 20540. John C Broderick, Chief
Notes: The papers of former Secretary of State Alexander M Haig. Access to the collection is restricted. Also, papers of Henry A Kissinger. Papers of Robert H Thayer, lawyer and foreign service officer.

DC —US ARMS CONTROL & DISARMAMENT AGENCY, Library, George Washington Univ Special Collections, Washington, 21 St & Virginia Ave, NW, Rm 5851, Washington, 20451. Diane Ferguson, Librn
Holdings: Vols 4500 // Cat
Notes: Arms control, disarmament and related topics.

DC —US DEPT OF STATE, Library, Rm 3239 NS, Washington, 20520. Conrad P Eaton, Librn
Holdings: Vols (750,000) Cat Microforms
Notes: Incl 7200 microfilm reels.

IN —INDIANA UNIVERSITY, Lilly Library, Seventh St, Bloomington, 47405. William R Cagle, Librn
Holdings: // Mss Pix
Notes: Papers of Claude G Bowers, newspaperman, author, ambassador to Spain, 1933-1936, and ambassador to Chile, 1939-1953. Collection incl diaries, materials relating to both ambassadorships, particularly important for Spanish Civil War period; speeches; some original political cartoons; awards, medals, etc; newspaper clippings, etc, 1868-1972. 18,386 items.
See also entry under Berry, Burton Yost.

†MA —JOHN F KENNEDY LIBRARY, Columbia Point, Boston, 02125. Dan H Fenn Jr, Dir
Holdings: Cat Mss Pix Audiotapes Videotapes 16mm Films Microforms
Notes: 20,000,000 pages of papers of President John F Kennedy, his staff, his associates, congressmen and ambassadors. Holdings are described in "Historical Materials in the John F Kennedy Library." Copies may be obtained by writing the Research Archivist.

MA —HARVARD UNIVERSITY, Center for International Affairs, Library, Coolidge Hall, 1737 Cambridge St, Cambridge, 02138. Barbara Mitchell, Librn
Holdings: Vols (13,000)
Notes: Collection emphasizes international politics and also contains considerable statistical material on individual countries. Library currently receives 115 periodical titles.

NJ —PRINCETON UNIVERSITY, Library, Manuscript Collection, Nassau St, Princeton, 08540. Jean F Preston, Cur
Holdings: // Cat Mss Pix
Notes: Four collections: (1) Archives of the United China Relief, Inc, and United Service to China, Inc. Incl 100 boxes of papers. The archive covers the period, 1941 to 1966. An unpublished typescript guide (36 p) is available in the Library. (2) The Adlai Stevenson Collection of personal papers is contained in 1569 boxes. Terms of Access: The bulk of the personal papers may be read by qualified scholars. See Princeton University Library Chronicle, v 26 p 15. An unpublished typescript guide (456 p) is available in the Library. Also, 3 cartons of papers relating to the Bricker Amendment and the treaty-making power of the United States, 1952-1957. (3) The George Frost Kennan Collection incl 38 boxes of papers. Reproduction is not permitted. (4) The John Foster Dulles Collection of personal papers, 1907-59, fill 621 boxes. Unpublished typescript guide (938 p) isavailable in library. Also, oral history collection made 1964-67 by Dulles' friends and colleagues. 275 typescripts. Published catalog: Dulles Oral History Collection, A Descriptive Catalogue (Princeton, 1967). Terms of access: each author controls his transcript, most are open, some are closed. Limited photocopying. See published catalog.

†NY —COLUMBIA UNIVERSITY LIBRARIES, Butler Library, Rare Book and

U.S.—FOREIGN RELATIONS (cont.)

Manuscript Library, 535 W 114 St, New York, 10027.
Notes: The papers of Spruille Braden, American diplomat in Latin American affairs and American representative at the Chaco Peace Conference.

NY —UNIVERSITY OF ROCHESTER, Rush Rhees Library, Department of Rare Books and Special Collections, Rochester, 14627. Peter Dzwonkoski, Librn
Holdings: Mss
Notes: William Henry Seward papers, which contain approximately 250,000 items, relate to American political, social and diplomatic history, ca 1825-1872. Also a collection of approx 4000 pamphlets of the same time period and subjects, which were owned by him. The latter are fully cataloged. Each letter in the collection has been indexed by name of letter writer. Unpublished register is available in repository.

PA —US ARMY WAR COLLEGE LIBRARY, Carlisle Barracks, 17013. Barbara E Stevens, Dir

RI —BROWN UNIVERSITY, John Hay Library, 20 Prospect St, Providence, 02912. Mark N Brown, Cur Mss
Holdings: // Mss
Notes: Papers of Jonathan Russell, merchant, diplomat, and Massachusetts Congressman, Brown Class of 1791. A collection of 7000 items containing a diary and a letterbook (1809-1813); records of US Commissioners at Ghent (1813-1814) and of the American Legation at Stockholm (1814-1816); correspondence and documents for the period 1795-1830; and notes, largely official, when Russell was Charege d' Affaires at Paris (1810) and for 1814-1818 when he was Minister to Sweden and Norway and a member of the US Congress. Several ms collections relating to American diplomatic history: The Samuel Sullivan Cox, 1824-1889, Manuscript Collection--Ohio and New York Congressman, minor diplomat, (qv) (1200 items); the John Hay, 1838-1905, Manuscript Collection--Secretary to Lincoln, Secretary of State, (qv) (12,000); the Jonathan Russell, 1771-1832,Manuscript Collection--merchant, Massachusetts Congressman, and diplomat (qv) (8000 items); and the Henry Wheaton, 1784-1848, Manuscript Collection--jurist, and Charge d'Affaires to Denmark and Minister to Prussia, (qv) (275 items).

SD —NATIONAL COLLEGE OF BUSINESS, Thomas Jefferson Learning Resource Center, 321 Kansas City St, Rapid City, 57701. Linda Watson, Library Dir
Holdings: Vols (26,000) Cat
Notes: Analyses (Index) of national and international issues. Published at irregular, frequent intervals, produced by the American Enterprise Institute for Public Policy Research.

†ON —METROPOLITAN TORONTO LIBRARY, Social Sciences Dept, 789 Yonge St, Toronto, M4W 2G8, Can. Abdus Salam, Head
Holdings: Vols Cat Maps Phonorecords Audiotapes 16mm Films Microforms
Notes: Strong collection emphasizing historical and current aspects of Canadian foreign relations. Areas of special emphasis include Canadian-US relations and Canadian-Great Britain relations. Complete holdings of Canadian and British Treaties from 1686.

U.S.—FOREIGN RELATIONS—CHINA

MA —HARVARD UNIVERSITY LIBRARY, Widener Library, Cambridge, 02138.
Holdings: Cat
Notes: Surveys of collections by Robert L Irick and Valentin H Rabe published by Harvard University Press, 1960 (*Research Aids for American Far Eastern Policy Studies, 1 and 3*).

U.S.—FOREIGN RELATIONS—JAPAN

DC —NATIONAL ARCHIVES AND RECORDS SERVICE, National Archives Library, Pennsylvania Ave & Eighth St NW, Washington, 20408.
Notes: Journals kept by Commodore Matthew C Perry (1794-1858) on his expedition to Japan in 1852-1854. The three journals were kept by Perry as his personal account of the trip, undertaken as a diplomatic mission to establish trade relations with Japan. Incl numerous illustrations of rare birds, flowers, fish, animals, and the life and ceremonies of trade ports along Perry's route.

OH —WILMINGTON COLLEGE, Peace Resource Center, Hiroshima/Nagasaki Memorial Collection, Pyle Center Box 1183, Wilmington, 45177. Helen Redding, Librn
Holdings: Vols Pix Slides Audiotapes Videotapes Film Art Reproductions VF
Notes: The Hiroshima/Nagasaki Memorial Collection is nationally known and respected as a major source of information, films, slides and audiotapes about the atomic bombings of Hiroshima and Nagasaki. An especially signifciant part of the Collection is a continually growing library in Japanese currently numbering more than 500 vols. Here are recorded eyewitness account of the atomic bombings, as well as details of what life has been like in the intervening years for the thousands of survivors (*hibakusha*). Also incl are books of poetry, photo books, juvenile literature, and books dealing with medical information, peace research, peace education, nuclear power, etc. All books in the Hiroshima/Nagasaki Memorial Collection are available for interlibrary loan. An *Annotated Bibliography of Japanese A-Bomb Literature* may be purchased or borrowed from the PRC. In it are briefsummaries in English of each book in the Collection.

U.S.—FOREIGN RELATIONS—RUSSIA

IA —IOWA STATE UNIVERSITY, Library, Dept of Special Collections, Ames, 50011. Stanley M Yates, Head
Notes: Papers of Roswell Garst, Iowa's most famous farmer. Initiator of experimental feeding of corncobs to produce beef, use of hybrid seedcorn, and commercial fertilizers. Credited with opening of agricultural sales and exchanges with Russia in the 1950s.

U.S.—FOREIGN RELATIONS—TREATIES

CA —LOS ANGELES PUBLIC LIBRARY, Social Sciences Dept, 630 W Fifth St, Los Angeles, 90071. Marilyn C Wherley, Principal Librn
Holdings: Vols 5000 Cat
Budget: ($150,000)
Notes: Sets of treaties of League of Nations, United Nations, Great Britain, United States, curently in force, as well as historical. Cumulative indexes of world treaties. No separate catalog.

NJ —PRINCETON UNIVERSITY, Library, Manuscript Collection, Nassau St, Princeton, 08540. Jean F Preston, Cur
Holdings: Mss
Notes: 3 cartons of papers. The collection relates to the Bricker Amendment and the treaty-making power of the United States, 1952-57.

†NY —COLUMBIA UNIVERSITY LIBRARIES, Butler Library, Rare Book and Manuscript Library, 535 W 114 St, New York, 10027.
Notes: The papers of Spruille Braden, American diplomat in Latin American affairs and American representative at the Chaco Peace Conference.

RI —BROWN UNIVERSITY, John Hay Library, 20 Prospect St, Providence, 02912. Mark N Brown, Cur Mss
Holdings: // Mss
Notes: Papers of Jonathan Russell, merchant, diplomat, and Massachusetts Congressman. Brown Class of 1791. A collection of 7000 items containing a diary and a letterbook (1809-1813); records of US Commissioners at Ghent (1813-1814) and of the American Legation at Stockholm (1814-1816); correspondence and documents for the period 1795-1830; and notes, largely official, when Russell was Charge d'Affaires at Paris (1810) and for 1814-1818 when he was Minister to Sweden and Norway and a member of the US Congress.

U.S.—GOVERNMENT see U.S.—Politics and Government

U.S.—GOVERNMENT PUBLICATIONS

AZ —PHOENIX PUBLIC LIBRARY, Arizona Room, 12 E McDowell, Phoenix, 85004. Jeannette Brush, Librn
Holdings: Vols (30,000) Cat Maps Pix
Budget: ($12,000)
See also entry under Arizona - History.

CA —LOS ANGELES PUBLIC LIBRARY, Social Sciences Dept, 630 W Fifth St, Los Angeles, 90071. Marilyn C Wherley, Principal Librn
Holdings: Microforms
Budget: ($150,000)
Notes: US Government serials and documents, including long runs of periodicals and agency reports; congressional indexes, hearings on microfiche, US statutes, congressional series, unbound publications. Depository (selective) since 1891.

CA —UNIVERSITY OF CALIFORNIA, LOS ANGELES, Research Library, Public Affairs Service, 405 Hilgard Ave, Los Angeles, 90024. Edward Shreeves, Chairman, Bibliographers Group; Eugenia Eaton, Head, Public Affairs Service
Holdings: Microforms
Notes: Depository for the official publications of California cities and counties, the state of California, the United States government, the United Nations and some of its specialized agencies (including the Food and Agricultural Organization and UNESCO), and such regional organizations as the European Communities and Organization of American States. Selected publications of other American cities and counties, of the other states and possessions of the United States, of interstate organizations, and of foreign governments (with emphasis on major world powers, Africa, Latin America and the Near and Middle East) and intergovernmental organizations.

CA —CONTRA COSTA COUNTY LIBRARY, Documents Section, 1750 Oak Park Blvd, Pleasant Hill, 94523. Carmen Miller, Documents Librn
Holdings: Vols (65,000) Uncat Maps Microforms
Budget: ($5000)
Notes: Depository for documents of California (since 1947) and the US (since 1964).

CT —YALE UNIVERSITY LIBRARY, Government Documents Center, 38 Mansfield St, PO Box 2491, Yale Sta, New Haven, 06520. Sandra K Peterson, Documents Librn
Holdings: Microforms
Notes: Selective United States depository.

FL —FLORIDA STATE UNIVERSITY, Robert Manning Strozier Library, Tallahassee, 32306. Judith Depew, Head, Documents-Maps Dept
Holdings: Vols (680,000) Uncat Microforms
Notes: A depository for Florida, GPO, NASA, UN, and UNESCO documents, with standing orders for British, ILO, OAS, IMF; selected documents are purchased from various government levels. The collection incl historical as well as current material, especially Florida, US, Great Britain. The Library's holdings are strong in congressional bills and hearings, decennial censuses, and British Sessional papers. Number of volumes incl microprint and microfiche, but not cataloged documents and microfilm.

ID —IDAHO STATE UNIVERSITY, Library, Pocatello, 83209. Joseph K W Lu, Librn
Holdings: Uncat Microforms Documents Maps
Budget: ($10,000)
Notes: Over a million items. Partial

U.S.—GOVERNMENT PUBLICATIONS (cont.)

depository for US Government publications (1,053,430 items); incl ERIC microfiche and unclassified AEC and Dept of Energy publications in microform; depository for Idaho State Government publications (16,000 items); international government bodies (11,000 items).

IL —UNIVERSITY OF ILLINOIS, URBANA/CHAMPAIGN, College of Law, Library, Champaign, 61820. Richard Surles, Law Librn
Holdings: Vols (425,000) Cat Mss Microforms
Notes: Plus 800 reels of microfilm; 150,000 microfiches. Research collection covering both Anglo-American and foreign law. Depository for documents of the US Government, Illinois, and European Economic Communities.

IL —CENTER FOR RESEARCH LIBRARIES, 6050 S Kenwood Ave, Chicago, 60637. Donald B Simpson, Dir; Esther Smith, Collection Development Librn
Holdings: Vols 700,000 Uncat Microforms
Budget: $6000
Notes: An attempt is being made to collect all official publications of all 50 states, from 1952. Also have very extensive backfiles of older material and *Microfilm Collection of Early State Records.*

IL —NORTHWESTERN UNIVERSITY, Library, Government Publications Dept, Evanston, 60201. Robert W Baumgartner, Head
Notes: Collection consists of US federal documents (depository library since 1876); state documents (emphasis on Illinois); municipal documents (emphasis on Evanston and Chicago); documents of international organizations (emphasis on United Nations, United Nations specialized agencies, Organization of American States, European Communities). Collection consists of publications of 44 international organizations. Shelflist maintained in the Government Publications Department. Most publications not incl in the library's general catalog.

KY —UNIVERSITY OF KENTUCKY, Margaret I King Library, Government Publications Dept, Lexington, 40506. Sandra McAninch, Head
Holdings: Cat Maps Microforms
Notes: The University has been a US depository since 1907 and the Kentucky Regional Depository since 1967. The library has complete holdings of the major series and the Readex microprint non-depository collection. Incl papers.

MD —JOHNS HOPKINS UNIVERSITY, Milton S Eisenhower Library, Government Publications Maps/Law Dept, Charles & 34 Sts, Baltimore, 21218. James Gillispie, Acting Head
Holdings: Vols (326,946) Maps
Notes: Milton S Eisenhower Library is a depository library for federal documents since 1882. Selects about 50 percent of the items. Incls 326,946 documents, 183,301 maps sheets. Nondepository items listed in *Monthly Catalog* on microprint from January 1953-1975. Monthly Catalog listing of JPRS translations on microprint from October 1958-1973. Eisenhower Library is also a partial depository of UN (May 1946-date); South Pacific Commission (1969-date). Had a standing order on League of Nations (1922-45); UN/ICJ, Hague (October 1947-date); UN/ILO (May 1929-date); UNESCO (1957-date); Council of Europe (March 1954-date); European Communities (1960-date); OECD (1955-date); OAS (September 1948-date); OEEC (1950-54); USGS (topographic maps).

†MA —BOSTON PUBLIC LIBRARY, Copley Sq, Boston, 02117.
Holdings: Cat Micoroforms
Notes: Microform Publication by Readex Microprint Corp. US Government Publications Depository 1956-date; Non-Depository 1953-date. American State Papers, 1789-1838. US Serial Set, 1817-date.

MA —AMERICAN ANTIQUARIAN SOCIETY LIBRARY, 185 Salisbury St, Worcester, 01609. Marcus A McCorison, Dir & Librn
Notes: One of the strongest collections outside the Library of Congress to 1876. After 1876, only those concerning history, bibliography, and other subject fields emphasized by the society. To 1876: 7000 vols; 10,000 pamphlets.

MI —MONROE COUNTY LIBRARY SYSTEM, Ellis Reference and Information Center, 3700 S Custer Rd, Monroe, 48161. Marie D Chulski, Head of Reference Services
Holdings: Vols Periodicals Microforms Pamphlets
Notes: Depository for US government publications since 1974. Incl 1200 feet paper, 40 feet fiche, books, periodicals, microforms, pamphlets, etc.

MO —UNIVERSITY OF MISSOURI-KANSAS CITY, General Library, US Government Depository Library, 5100 Rockhill Road, Kansas City, 64110. Kenneth J LaBudde, Dir; Shirley Mickelson, Government Documents Librn
Notes: In excess of 460,000 items; selects 85 percent of available US documents.

MO —SAINT LOUIS PUBLIC LIBRARY, Documents Dept, 1301 Olive St, Saint Louis, 63103. Anne Watts, Librn
Holdings: Cat Maps Microforms
Notes: Depository for documents of the US, Missouri and St Louis, Missouri. Incl 1,500,000 items.

NE —NEBRASKA LIBRARY COMMISSION, Publications Clearinghouse, 1420 P St, Lincoln, 68508. Patricia Sloan, Federal Documents Librn; Vern Buis, State Documents Librn
Holdings: Vols (316,000) Cat Microforms
Notes: Depository for US government publications since July 1972; regional depository for Nebraska since July 1974; Joint Regional with the University of Nebraska Libraries since September 1977. Non-depository documents acquired on microfiche from Congressional Information Service's ASI collection. Depository for all Nebraska State government publications since July 1972.
See also entries under Nebraska; State Documents.

NY —NEW YORK STATE LIBRARY, State Education Bldg Annex, Washington Ave, Albany, 12224.
Holdings: Cat Microforms
Notes: Official depository of New York State publications; regional depository of US documents, also in microfilm; depository for Canadian government documents; strong collections of state documents, New York City documents; British sessional papers; also League of Nations, United Nations, OAS documents. Extensive holdings of other domestic and foreign publications. Congressional serial set, incl hearings (1946-date).

NY —COLUMBIA UNIVERSITY LIBRARIES, Lehman Library, Documents Service Center, 420 W 118 St, New York, 10027. Bryan May, Head
Holdings: Uncat Microforms
Notes: Columbia's major repository and service point for US federal documents beginning with 1975 imprints. Documents received on US Deposit, Documents Expediting Project, purchase, and gift. Arrangement: Superintendent of Documents classification. Control: shelflist. Subject access: published catalogs (eg *Monthly Catalog, CIS/Index, American Statistics Index*) and on-line catalogs (eg RLIN, GPO tapes). Major microform holdings and starting date: CIS Committee Prints (1970-81), CIS complete Congressional collection (1975-81), ASI non-depository (1977), Readex non-depository collection (1953-76), *Congressional Record* (1873-), Census of population (1790-1970), Foreign Broadcast Information Service daily reports (1974), Joint Publications Research Service reports (1976), GPO microfiche (1977). The Center's records and toolsprovide information on holdings in other Columbia collections, incl its Technical Reports Center.

NY —NEW YORK PUBLIC LIBRARY, Research Libraries, Economic & Public Affairs Div, Fifth Ave & 42 St, New York, 10018. Edward DiRoma, Chief
Holdings: Vols (1,500,000) Cat Microforms
Notes: Full depository collection from 1884. *See also* entry under Government Publications

NC —DUKE UNIVERSITY, William R Perkins Library, Durham, 27706. Elvin E Strowd, University Librn
Notes: Books, serials and pamphlets (2,820,527); music scores (31,551); motion pictures (285); microforms (1,055,627); tapes, cassettes and phonorecords, the library is a depository for Radio Canada International recordings, (2289); and manuscripts, US Government publications, maps, and broadsides, additions in all formats are ongoing.

NC —DUKE UNIVERSITY, William R Perkins Library, Public Documents and Maps Department, Durham, 27706. Jaia Barrett, Head
Holdings: Vols Maps Pamphlets Microforms
Notes: A selective depository for US Government publications since 1890, the Department currently holds well over 500,000 items, plus publications of the European Community (a depository collection), the League of Nations, the UN and UN-affiliated agencies. Other international organizations, publications are acquired also, as are state government publications, especially from the Southeast, California, New York and Illinois. The Documents Department holds services the major map collections of Perkins Library. These collections include topographic, geologic, and special subject maps which are worldwide in coverage. The department is a depository for the US Defense Mapping Agency and the US Geological Survey. In addition, there are many other maps of general and specific interest, including US and foreign road maps. As appropriate, maps are also held in the Perkins Library's Rare BookRoom and Manuscript Department. Atlases are shelved in the Reference Department and in the bookstacks of Perkins Library.

NC —NORTH CAROLINA STATE UNIVERSITY, D H Hill Library, Box 7111, Raleigh, 27695. I T Littleton, Dir
Holdings: Vols 3400 Cat
Budget: $1500
Notes: Incl monographs.

OH —PUBLIC LIBRARY OF CINCINNATI & HAMILTON COUNTY, Government and Business Dept, 800 Vine St, Cincinnati, 45202. Paul T Hudson, Head
Holdings: Vols 120,000 Cat
Notes: Department receives over 1200 periodical and loose-leaf service titles, 1500 serial titles and over 1500 telephone directories. Subjects include political science, especially foreign relations, economics, law, public administration and business management. Dept houses Murray Seasongood collection of local government. Dept has extensive census material from 1790. Library is a full depository for US Government Publications, 1884 to date.

OH —CLEVELAND PUBLIC LIBRARY, Documents Collection, 325 Superior Ave, Cleveland, 44114. Elizabeth L Fannon, Head
Holdings: Microforms
Notes: Official Government Printing Office depository for US Publications since 1886. Retains all but the most ephemeral items. Currently receive approx 98 percent of those items offered for selection. In addition to GPO the library is an official depository for the Arms Control and Disarmament Agency, US Patents and Trademarks and many map-related items such as US Geological Survey, United States Defense Mapping Agency, United States Department of Commerce-National Oceanic and Atmospheric Administration, aeronautic, lake, coastal, recreational and water charts. A major portion of the Census Bureau, Weather Bureau, Department of Energy, National Aeronautics and Space Administration and National Technical Information Services (SRIM) are automatically received. All tools

U.S.—GOVERNMENT PUBLICATIONS (cont.)

for basic specialized research are available. Department subscribes to CIS Index/ Abstracts andaccompanying microfiche 1970-date and American Statistics Index/ Abstracts and accompanying microfiche.

OK —OKLAHOMA DEPT OF LIBRARIES, Law Library, 109 State Capital, Oklahoma City, 73105. Robert Clark, Dir; Betty Brown, Okla Collection Librn; Virginia Collier, US Documents; Jan Blakely, State Documents; Blane Dessy, Library Science
Holdings: Vols 808,458 Cat Microforms
Notes: US document depository. Incl 911, 246 sheets microfiche; 2800 microfilm.

OR —UNIVERSITY OF OREGON LIBRARY, Documents Section, Eugene, 97403. Tom Stave, Section Head; John Shuler, Documents Librn
Holdings: Vols (250,000) Microforms
Notes: Depository for US government publications.

PA —UNIVERSITY OF PITTSBURGH, Hillman Library, Pittsburgh, 15260. Mary E Miller, Documents Librn
Holdings: Vols 212,785
Notes: Contains Depository publications of US government, Canadian Government (1968-), Commonwealth of Pennsylvania (1970-). Comprehensive League of Nations and United Nations collection. Microforms: US Non-Depository Government Publications (1953-).

PA —PENNSYLVANIA STATE UNIVERSITY, Fred Lewis Pattee Library, Documents Section, University Park, 16802. Diane H Smith, Head
Notes: Depository for US Government publications; depository for Pennsylvania documents; collect United Nations and related international and intergovernmental organization publications; selected publications from Australia, Great Britain, including Parliamentary Papers; census materials; a large microform collection, including Department of Energy (formerly ERDA, AEC), Congressional publications, Patents, OAS, UN. Incl 900,000 documents. US Government publications are uncataloged books and microforms.

TX —TEXAS STATE LIBRARY, US Documents Collection, 1200 Brazos, PO Box 12927 Capitol Sta, Austin, 78711. Bonnie Grobar, Librn
Holdings: Vols 900,000 Microforms
Notes: The Texas State Library became a depository for US documents by law when Texas became a state in 1845. It has been a regional depository since 1963. The collection now contains many valuable and rare documents as well as one of the most complete serial sets in the state.

TX —UNIVERSITY OF TEXAS LIBRARIES, General Libraries, PO Box P, Austin, 78713. Carolyn Bucknell, Asst Dir for Collection Development
Holdings: Cat Microforms
Notes: A depository of US government publications since 1884.

TX —WEST TEXAS STATE UNIVERSITY, Cornette Library, PO Box 748 WT Sta, Canyon, 79016. Annette F Nall, Documents Librn
Holdings: Vols (20,000) Uncat Microforms
Notes: 515,805 US and State of Texas government documents (with a volume-equivalent of 91,011 volumes), classified by Superintendent of Documents' numbers. Largest such collection in State of Texas. Depository Library since the 1920s.

TX —TEXAS TECH UNIVERSITY, Library, Lubbock, 79409. David J Murrah, Assoc Dir for Special Collections

WA —WASHINGTON STATE LIBRARY, Olympia, 98504. Ann Bregent, Librn
Holdings: 800,791 Mss 103 Microfiche
Notes: Regional deposetory for US documents. Incl documents from the Western States and Washington State.

MB —UNIVERSITY OF MANITOBA, Elizabeth Dafoe Library, Government Publications Section, Winnipeg, R3T 2N2, Can. June Dutka, Head
Holdings: Vols 300,000 Uncat Mss Maps Microforms
Notes: Concerned mainly with supporting research programs in the arts (especially sociology, political studies, native studies, history, geography and economics), agriculture, home economics and nursing. Collection consists of Canadian federal publications; depository since 1969 (emphasis on Statistics Canada); holdings of pre-confederation documents, early parliamentary publications, and royal commissions for the post-war years are reasonably complete; provincial documents (emphasis on Manitoba); municipal documents (emphasis on Winnipeg); documents from Great Britain, India and the US (emphasis on US State Agricultural Experimental Stations); publications from international organizations (emphasis on the Food and Agricultural Organization depository since 1945), UNESCO, International Labour Organization and Commission of the EuropeanCommunities. Card catalog is maintained in the Government Publications Section. Most publications are not included in the library's general catalog.

†ON —METROPOLITAN TORONTO LIBRARY, Social Sciences Dept, 789 Yonge St, Toronto, M4W 2G8, Can. Abdus Salam, Head
Holdings: Vols Cat Maps Phonorecords Audiotapes 16mm Films Microforms
Notes: The collection is a full depository for Canadian federal and Ontario provincial publications and contains an exhaustive collection of publications from the various Canadian provinces. It includes statutes, gazettes, legislative debates, journals, reports, etc. Also extensive holdings for the US and Great Britain; comprehensive holdings of treaties for Canada, Great Britain and the US; selected publications for other foreign countries. Types of publications emphasized are statutory laws, treaties, legislative proceedings, government directories and manuals, statistical materials and national yearbooks. Large collection of UN materials; full depository for UNESCO publications; selected publications of various international organizations. The collection is cited in Canada, National Library, Resources Survey Section,Research Collections in Canadian Libraries, Volume 5; Collections of Official Publications in Canada (Ottawa: Supply and Services Canada, 1976).

†ON —METROPOLITAN TORONTO LIBRARY, Social Sciences Dept, 789 Yonge St, Toronto, M4W 2G8, Can. Abdus Salam, Head
Holdings: Vols 105,000 Cat Mss Microforms
Notes: This and other sections, incl the largest publicly accessible government document collection in Ontario, formed of laws, statutes, debates and gazettes from Canada, her provinces, Great Britain and the US.

SK —SASKATCHEWAN LEGISLATIVE LIBRARY, 234 Legislative Bldg, Regina, S4S 0B3, Can. Marian Powell, Librn
Holdings: Cat Microforms
Notes: Government publication; of Saskatchewan, Ontario, Canada, and full exchange with the US. This is a Depository Library. Listed in Microlog. 300,000 documents.

U.S.—HISTORY

AL —MILES COLLEGE, C A Kirkendoll Library, Birmingham, 35208. Mattie Jackson, Librn
Holdings: Vols (3000) Cat
Notes: Books from the private library of Dr Clinton Rossiter, well-known political scientist, historian, lecturer, writer and one of the formost authorities on American constitutional history and political theory.

CA —BURBANK PUBLIC LIBRARY, 110 N Glenoaks Blvd, Burbank, 91502. Mary Ann Grasso, Coordr; Barbara Stones, Coordr, Media Project
Holdings: Vols (32,000) Cat Clippings Pix VF
Notes: The

CA —CALIFORNIA STATE UNIVERSITY, FULLERTON, Library, Box 4150, Fullerton, 92634. Linda Herman, Special Collections Librn
Holdings: // Microforms
Notes: Espec strong in records of the State Department. Incl all of the Consular Dispatches published on microfilm (covers years to 1906). Has all records from the Decimal File of the Department of State 1910-1929. One of the largest collections of National Archives Microfilm on the West Coast.

†CA —WED ENTERPRISES, Research Library, 1401 Flower St, Glendale, 91201.
Notes: Popular art and architecture journals, pictorial material. Library is not open to the public.

CA —CALIFORNIA INSTITUTE OF TECHNOLOGY, Robert A Millikan Memorial Library, Archives, 1201 E California Blvd, Pasadena, 91125. Judith R Goodstein, Archivist
Holdings: Vols (3000) Uncat Mss Maps Pix Slides Phonorecords Audiotapes Videotapes 16mm Films Microforms
Notes: Over 70 collections (1830s-present) relating to history of 19th-20th centuries science and technology and the history of the Institute. Included are personal and professional papers of Caltech scientists and administrative officers; divisional records and faculty committees; over 5000 photographs of American and European scientists. Mss collections documents more than a century of American political, social, and intellectual history; the development of the physical sciences, aeronautics, molecular biology, and seismology in the US and abroad; and social and political conditions in Europe between the two World Wars. There are also family letters relating to 19th century American life before and during the Civil War (the Morley and A G Throop papers); to 19th century social conditions in Russia and Hungary (the Paul Epstein papers and Theodore von Karman papers); andto the development of 20th century Italian mathematics.

CA —COMMONWEALTH CLUB OF CALIFORNIA, Library, 681 Market St, San Francisco, 94105. Virginia Rees, Librn
Holdings: Vols (6500) Cat Maps Pix
Budget: ($2000)

CA —HUNTINGTON LIBRARY, Art Gallery & Botanical Gardens, 1151 Oxford Rd, San Marino, 91108. Robert L Middlekauff, Dir; Daniel H Woodward, Librn
Holdings: Mss Maps Pix Slides Microforms
Notes: Approx 350,000 rare books, 250,000 reference books, manuscript collection of nearly 2,500,000 pieces and between 200, 000 and 300,000 prints, rare photographs and other related materials. The fullest available survey is now Guide to Literary Manuscripts in the Huntington Library, a 539-page handlist published by the Library in 1979.

CA —COLLEGE OF SAN MATEO, Library, 1700 W Hillsdale Blvd, San Mateo, 94402. Gregg T Atkins, Coordinator of Library Services
Holdings: Vols (14,000) Cat Microforms
Notes: Library of American Civilization (beginnings to 1915) produced by Encyclopedia Britannica. The entire collection is on microfiche. The fiche as well as portable readers are availabe to students.

CA —STANFORD UNIVERSITY LIBRARIES, Cecil H Green Library, Stanford, 94305. Michael T Ryan, Cur
Holdings: Cat Mss Pix
Notes: The Elmer E Robinson Collection of American History and Government. Incl correspondence of early American statesmen.

CT —YALE UNIVERSITY, Box 1603A, Yale Station, New Haven, 06520.

DC —LIBRARY OF CONGRESS, Rare Book & Special Collections Div, Washington, 20540. William Matheson, Chief
Notes: Public documents of the first 14 Congresses (1789-1817). Contains over 3680 separate titles. Also, printed texts of 3570 speeches delivered by members of Congress between 1825 and 1940. See A W Greely's Public Documents of the First Fourteen Congresses, (New York: Johnson Reprint Corporation, 1973).

U.S.—HISTORY (cont.)

DC —LIBRARY OF CONGRESS, Manuscript
Division, Washington, 20540. John C
Broderick, Chief
Holdings: Cat Mss Pix Slides Microforms
Notes: Collections of the papers of most of
the presidents, from George Washington
through Calvin Coolidge, of many other
statesmen, military, scientific, and literary
leaders of numerous enterprises and over
100 letters in the controversial series of "love
letters" and "love poems" to and from
President Harding and Mrs Hames (Carrie)
Phillips, unpublished (except for some
unauthorized phrases in newspapers) and
under seal until the year 2014. Also,
reproductions of mss in European archives
relating to American history.
See also entry under Chester Alan Arthur

DC —LIBRARY OF CONGRESS, Prints &
Photographs Div, Washington, 20540.
Notes: Effective October 1, the Library's
Prints and Photographs Division has
discontinued reproduction and reference
service on its collection of photographs
which appeared in *Look* magazine from 1937
to 1971. This limitation on service will
remain in effect until questions of rights and
permissions affecting these photographs can
be clarified. The Library acquired the *Look*
archive in 1971 as additional resources for
research in American life by scholars and
other investigators. It was anticipated that
the photographs would serve as a study
collection for researchers in many fields, but
the major use of the collection has been by
publishers, advertisers, and makers of
documentary films. Such picture users
require clear rights to reproduce the images.
The Library has been unable to satisfy these
requests because of the donor's stipulation
precluding such use. Until some
accommodation canbe made with the donor
to free the collection for a wider range of
public use, collection will remain in remote
cold storage to retard deterioration of
sensitive films, especially color films. This
policy will remain in effect until further
notice. LC Information Bulletin, 10 Oct 83.

DC —LIBRARY OF CONGRESS, Motion
Pictures, Broadcasting and Recorded Sound
Div, Washington, 20540.
Notes: The entire radio archive of the
National Broadcasting Company. Incl 175,
000 recordings of radio programs and events
broadcast from 1933-70. Duplicated at the
Museum of Broadcasting in New York City.

DC —UNIVERSITY OF THE DISTRICT OF
COLUMBIA, Mount Vernon Campus,
Library & Media Services Div, 800 Mount
Vernon Pl, NW, Washington, 20001. Lottie
Wright, Librn
Holdings: Vols (2500) // Uncat
Notes: American history, incl literature,
education, politics, and government.

GA —UNIVERSITY OF GEORGIA,
Libraries, Special Collections Division,
Athens, 30602. Vesta Lee Gordon, Asst Dir
for Special Collections
Notes: Collection contains 1394.8 linear feet
of mss: papers of US Senator Richard B
Russell; US Congressmen John W Davis,
Maston O'Neal, Robert G Stephens Jr, John
L Pilcher, Dudley M Hughes; Governors
Hoke Smith, Lester Maddox, Carl Sanders.

GA —EMORY UNIVERSITY, Robert W
Woodruff Library, Special Collections Dept,
Atlanta, 30322. Linda M Matthews, Head
Special Collections; Virginia J H Cain,
Processing Archivist; Richard H F
Lindemann, Reference Archivist
Holdings: Vols (16,000) Cat Mss Maps Pix
Microforms

GA —WESLEYAN COLLEGE, Willet
Memorial Library, 4760 Forsyth Rd, Macon,
31201. Hasseltine Roberts, Librn
Holdings: Vols 4000 Cat Mss Maps Pix
Notes: The Orville A Park and Tracy
McGregor Collection.

IL —CENTER FOR RESEARCH
LIBRARIES, 6050 S Kenwood Ave,
Chicago, 60637. Donald B Simpson, Dir;
Esther Smith, Collection Development Librn
Holdings: Vols Uncat Microforms
Notes: Over 25,000 reels of positive

microfilm of material in the national
Archives, incl federal population census
records, state dept records and records of
other agencies. Numerous newspaper
backfiles, state document backfiles.

IL —CHICAGO HISTORICAL SOCIETY,
Library, Clark St at North Ave, Chicago,
60614. Robert L Brubaker, Librn
Holdings: Vols (150,000) Cat Mss Pix Maps
Microforms
Notes: Subjects: United States history
(specialties: Chicago, Midwest, Lincoln, Civil
War). Special collections: Chicago
directories, trade catalogs, advertising cards
(6000), theatre programs (5000), and sheet
music (4600); personal papers and records of
Chicago leaders and organizations; negatives
and prints from Chicago newspaper morgues,
1900-1965 (250,000); Meserve Americana,
27 vols, mostly of period of Civil War (8000
portraits); American city prints (historic); J
Norman Jensen Collection of Lake and
River Disasters, 1679-1947 (8500 cards).
Holdings: 422,000 books and pamphlets; 16,
000 bound periodical vols; 7300 vols of
newspapers; 14,000 broadsides and posters;
10,000 maps; 640 atlases; 50,000 clippings;
2500 vols of CHS archives; 35,000
miscellaneous printed pieces; 8600 reels of
microfilm,; 4000 linear feet of mss; 500,000
prints and photographs(black-and-white
photographs, daguerreotypes, ambrotypes,
stereographs, negatives, engravings, and
lithographs).

IL —CHICAGO HISTORICAL SOCIETY,
Library, Clark St at North Ave, Chicago,
60614. Archie Motley, Manuscript Librn
Notes: Nineteenth and eighteenth century
collection of papers incl; American
Colonization Society (anti-slavery group);
American Field Service (World War I
European ambulance service); American Fur
Company; Chicago Cubs (National League
baseball team); Chicago Fire of 1871; Will J
Davis (theatre manager); Declaration of
Independence (complete set of autographs of
signers of the Declaration); Finley Peter
Dunne (journalist, satirist); Robert Fergus
(printer and publisher; firearms agents;
French settlers in North America; Melville
Weston Fuller (Chief Justice of the US);
Grand Army of the Republic; Charles J
Guiteau (President Garfield's assassin);
Haymarket Riot, May 4, 1886; Illinois
Central Railroad (1836-1969); Indians of
North America; Leander Hamilton
McCormick (author, inventor); Harold
Fowler McCormick(manufacturer,
philanthropist, son of inventor Cyrus Hall
McCormick); Mormons (chiefly Illinois
materials); Richard Parker (judge at the trial
of abolitionist John Brown); Zebulon Pike
and Zebulon Montgomery Pike (US Army
officers, explorers); George Mortimer
Pullman (inventor, designer of Pullman cars
and the Pullman and Fluhrer families).

IL —CHICAGO HISTORICAL SOCIETY,
Library, Clark St at North Ave, Chicago,
60614. Archie Motley, Manuscript Librn
Notes: Twentieth century collections incl
these papers: Aero Club of Illinois (aviation
promoters); American Legion, Illinois
Branch; Paul M Angle; Business and
Professional People for the Public Interest, a
public interest law firm; Chicago Municipal
Court; Chicago Peace Council; Chicago
Peace Society; Herma Clark (*Chicago
Tribune* columnist); Frances Crane Lillie
(social activist); Frank Rattray Lillie
(zoologist), the Crane Company; Charles R
Crane and other members of the Crane
family; France Forever, Chicago Chapter;
Frances MacBeth Glessner; William Walter
Husband (Commissioner of Immigration);
Irish Fellowship Club of Chicago; Albert E
Jenner, Jr (member of the Warren
Commission, minority counsel during the
Nixon impeachment hearing); materials on
opera in Chicago and elsewhere; Kenesaw
Mountain Landis(US District Judge, first
Commissioner of Baseball); Nathan F
Leopold (convicted murderer); Philip Lord
(actor); Harry A Musham (naval architect);
Military Training Camps Association of the
United States; Ivan Molek; Ruth Moore;
Ralph G Newman; Northeastern Illinois

Planning Commission; Len O'Connor
(television news commentator); Open Lands
Project; Oral History Archives of Chicago
Polonia; Donald R Richberg; letterbooks of
Chicago law firms involving Julius and
Lessing Rosenthal, Charles Hammill, and
George F Wormser; Otto L Schmidt; Studs
Terkel (author, oral historian); Henry A
Voegeli; Jacob J Weinstein; White City
Construction Co; Elmer Lynn Williams;
World Federalists USA Inc.

IL —NEWBERRY LIBRARY, 60 W Walton
St, Chicago, 60610. Diana Haskell, Cur of
Modern Mss
Holdings: Cat Mss Maps Pix
Notes: American history to 1920.

IL —NORTHWESTERN UNIVERSITY,
Library, Special Collections Dept, 1937
Sheridan Rd, Evanston, 60201. R Russell
Maylone, Cur
Holdings: Vols 2500 Cat //
Notes: County histories, record surveys,
visitations, family histories, biographies,
atlases, census records, church histories and
records, civil surveys and microfilms.

LA —R W NORTON ART GALLERY,
Library, 4747 Creswell Ave, Shreveport,
71106. Jerry M Bloomer, Librn
Holdings: Cat

LA —NICHOLLS STATE UNIVERSITY,
Ellender Memorial Library, Thibodaux,
70310. Randall A Detro, Dir; Philip D Uzee,
Archivist
Holdings: Uncat Mss Maps Pix Microforms
Notes: Louisiana and local history; family
papers of the periods, etc.

MD —JOHNS HOPKINS UNIVERSITY,
Milton S Eisenhower Library, Charles & 34
Sts, Baltimore, 21218. Ann S Gwyn,
Assistant Dir for Special Collections
Holdings: Cat Mss

MD —MARYLAND HISTORICAL
SOCIETY, Library, 201 W Monument St,
Baltimore, 21201. William B Keller, Head
Librn
Holdings: Vols (65,000) Cat Mss Maps Pix
Slides
Budget: $8000
Notes: Large collection of Maryland State
Colonization Papers; Maryland and
Baltimore business records; Baltimore &
Ohio Railroad Papers; Baltimore Theatre
records and programs (late 18th, early 19th
century); Maryland lottery tickets; Benjamin
H Latrobe (architectural) Papers; Maryland
maps, plats, prints, newspapers; Baltimore
history large collection (30,000 items
Maryland local history and genealogy, 100,
000 mss); iron industry papers; Maryland
currency; sheet music (8000 pieces, largely
Baltimore publishers); Lester S Levy "Star-
Spangled Banner" collection (probably the
largest in the world--over 250 pieces).

†MA —JOHN F KENNEDY LIBRARY,
Columbia Point, Boston, 02125. Dan H Fenn
Jr, Dir
Holdings: Vols 20,000 Cat Mss Maps Pix
Slides Phonorecords Audiotapes Videotapes
16mm Films Microforms
Notes: *The* major collection about JFK, his
life, family and administration. It contains
personal papers, audiovisual materials, books,
oral history interviews. Collection is
described in "Historical Materials in the
John F Kennedy Library." "The Kennedy
Collection," a subject guide to the book
collection, is available for sale.

MA —NEW ENGLAND HISTORIC
GENEALOGICAL SOCIETY, Library, 101
Newbury St, Boston, 02116. Ralph J
Crandell, Dir
Holdings: Vols (250,000) Mss Maps
Microforms Pix
Notes: New England genealogy. Especially
strong Massachusetts, Maine, and New
Hampshire, although all states are well
represented, as are the relevancies of each
subject listed in this volume with regard to
British antecedent and contemporary history.
Special strengths in local history and
biography, obituaries, etc, incl parish
registers, censuses, British and American.
3125 linear ft of mss.

MA —HARVARD UNIVERSITY LIBRARY,
Widener Library, American History
Collection, Cambridge, 02138. F Nathaniel

U.S.—HISTORY (cont.)

Bunker, Bibliographer; Charles Warren, Bibliographer
Holdings: Cat
Notes: Published shelflist volumes (*Widener Library Shelflist*, Nos 9-13) list 125,591 volumes as of 1967. See *Harvard Library Bulletin*, XV (1967): pp 376-400 for account of the collection, which is strong in nearly all subdivisions except genealogy.

MA —BRANDEIS UNIVERSITY, Goldfarb Library, 415 South St, Waltham, 02154. Bessie Hahn, Dir
Notes: Perry Miller Collection on the Colonial Religious Experience in America: 18 linear ft of books dating from the 17th and 18th century relating to the religious experience in the American colonies. Access to the collection is through the Main Card Catalog and Special Collections Card Catalog. Daniel Webster Collection: Consists of 11 linear ft of correspondence mainly to Daniel Webster. A finding list to the collection is located in Special Collections.

MA —AMERICAN ANTIQUARIAN SOCIETY LIBRARY, 185 Salisbury St, Worcester, 01609. Marcus A McCorison, Dir & Librn
Holdings: Cat Mss Maps Pix Slides Microforms
Notes: Over half a million manuscript pieces; extensive collection of contemporary imprints before 1850 (with supplementary supporting studies); over 10,000 maps (weak for 15th-17th centuries; excellent for 18th, strongest in 19th century, especially maps of local nature). Also a good collection of portraits of early New Englanders; paintings, engravings, and miniatures. Further, the largest collection of regional, state, county, and local histories. Sixty percent of the total of books and pamphlets known to have been printed in the United States before 1821. Source of Readex Microprint Corp project called *Early American Imprints, 1639-1800,* a Microprint edition of every extant book, pamphlet, and broadside printed in what is now the United States. Keyed to Evans *American Bibliography* will bring these Microprint reproductions up to 1820. One of the great strengths of the collection is its broadsides and American newspapers, the best anywhere. From it emerged Clarence Brigham's monumental *History and Bibliography of American Newspapers,* 1690-1820, which locates every surviving copy of every newspaper printed in the United States before 1821. Readex Microprint Corp is also reproducing this collection. The Society's collections extend beyond 1820, in special strengths, to the turn of the century. The collection incl unusual strengths in Amateur Newspapers (about 50,000 issues), and Bolivian, Chilean, and West Indian newspapers. American Antiquarian Society Collections were the basis for *American Manuscripts 1763-1815,* Cripe and Campbell (Wilmington, DE, 1977).

MI —EDISON INSTITUTE, Greenfield Village and Henry Ford Museum, Archives & Research Library, PO Box 1970, Dearborn, 48121. Steve Hamp, Dir; Joan W Gartland, Librn
Holdings: Vols 400,000 Cat Mss Maps Microforms
Notes: 400,000 vols incl pamphlets. The Archives and research library supports the program of Greenfield Village and the Henry Ford Museum. Special collections incl: automotive literature, ephemera, McGuffey Readers, trade catalogs, photographs and graphics.

MI —NATIONAL HAMILTONIAN PARTY, Library, 3314 Dillon Rd, Flushing, 48433.
Holdings: Vols Cat Mss
Notes: The life and writings of Alexander Hamilton. The National Hamiltonian Library is a part of the offices of the Hamiltonian National Committee, the governing body of the National Hamiltonian Party, a Neo-Federalist political movement. Incl 4835 vols. Also the Kelly Collection, a group of over 10,000 pieces of American political

memorabilia covering presidents and presidential hopefuls of major and minor parties as well as special sectons on women, minorities and families in politics.

MI —NORTHERN MICHIGAN UNIVERSITY, Lydia M Olson Library, Elizabeth L Harden Drive, Marquette, 49855. Stephen H Peters, Cataloger
Notes: A major section of the personal library of Moses Coit Tyler. Strong in the Colonial and Early National periods. Includes biographies and published letters and writings of such figures as Benjamin Franklin, John Adams, John Jay, Thomas Jefferson, Charles Sumner.

MN —MINNEAPOLIS PUBLIC LIBRARY & INFORMATION CENTER, 300 Nicollet Mall, Minneapolis, 55401. Richard J Hofstad, Athenaeum Librn
Holdings: Vols (500) Cat Maps

NE —AMERICAN HISTORICAL SOCIETY OF GERMANS FROM RUSSIA (AHSGR), 615 Twelfth St, Lincoln, 68502. Mary Lynn Tuck, Librn
Holdings: Vols (1900) Mss Maps Pix Phonorecords Videotapes Audiotapes Microforms VF
Notes: History of German people from Russia and history of people of German-Russian ancestry. Including times in Russia, Germany, US, Canada, Mexico, Argentina, Brazil, Paraguay, Korea, and Japan. This Society has fifty-six chapters in the United States. 1900 volumes, 100 maps; 500 mss; 1200 vertical files; 2000 pictures; 40,000 obituary files, 40,000 family group charts, 50 phonorecords, 20 videotapes, 50 audiotapes, 15 reel-to-reel tapes, 150 periodicals, 250 microforms, 250 family histories-published and unpublished.

NE —NEBRASKA STATE HISTORICAL SOCIETY, Archives, 1500 R St, Box 82554, Lincoln, 68501. James E Potter, State Archivist
Holdings: Cat Mss Microforms
Budget: ($290,000)
Notes: Collection

NJ —MACCULLOCH HALL HISTORICAL MUSEUM, Morristown, 07960. Alice A Caulkins, Curator
Notes: The W Parsons Todd Collection.

NJ —PRINCETON UNIVERSITY, Library, Manuscript Collection, Nassau St, Princeton, 08540. Jean F Preston, Cur
Holdings: Mss Pix
Notes: The Blair-Lee Families Collection, which deals in large part with American political and naval history of the period 1733 to 1916, fills over 300 ms boxes. It incl the papers of Francis Preston Blair, Sr, Samuel Phillips Lee, Elizabeth Blair Lee, and Blair Lee. An unpublished partial typescript guide (75 p) is available in the Library.

NY —NEW YORK STATE LIBRARY, State Education Bldg Annex, Washington Ave, Albany, 12224.
Holdings: Cat Mss Maps Pix Microforms
Notes: Emphasis on New York State, and American History in general. Have collection of Lincolniana, American Indians, Shakers, etc. Holdings to 1960 in New York State Library, Checklist in American History; an author listing with abbreviated title.

NY —NEW YORK STATE HISTORICAL ASSOCIATION, Library, Lake Rd, Cooperstown, 13326. Amy Barnum, Librn
Holdings: Vols (55,000) Cat Mss Maps Pix Slides Microforms Tapes
Notes: Emphasis on New York State in 19th century. Noncirculating.

NY —NEW YORK STATE OFFICE OF PARKS & RECREATION, TACONIC REGION, Clermont State Historic Park, Library, RR 1, Box 215, Germantown, 12526. Bruce E Naramore, Historic Site Manager
Holdings: Vols (5000) Cat Mss Maps
Notes: Many period editions concerning the formation of the US. Many of these belonged to the Chancellor Robert R Livingston (1746-1813). Subject matter incl acquisition of continental territories, incl the Louisiana Purchase; political and social subjects also. No photocopying.

NY —C W POST CENTER OF LONG ISLAND UNIVERSITY, B Davis Schwartz

Memorial Library, Greenvale, 11548. Jean Goldberg, Special Collections Librn
Notes: Theodore Roosevelt Collection. Primarily naval and US history. Incl almost all his writings.

NY —GENERAL THEOLOGICAL SEMINARY, Saint Marks Library, 175 Ninth Ave, New York, 10011. David Green, Dir
Holdings: Vols (200,000) Cat Mss Maps Pix Slides Microforms

NY —MUSEUM OF BROADCASTING, Library, 1 E 53rd St, New York, 10022. Douglas Gibbons, Dir
Notes: The entire radio archive of the National Broadcasting Company. Incl 175,000 recordings of radio programs and events broadcast from 1933-1970. Duplicated at the Library of Congress.

NY —NEW YORK PUBLIC LIBRARY, Mid-Manhattan Library, History and Social Sciences Dept, 455 Fifth Ave, New York, 10016. Robert Sheehan, Sr Principal Librn
Holdings: Vols (80,000) Cat Phonorecords Audiotapes Microforms
Budget: ($40,000)
Notes: Strong in material on American Indians and US history in general. Incl the *Library of American Civilization* on microfiche.

NY —NEW YORK PUBLIC LIBRARY, Local History and Genealogy Div, Fifth Ave & 42 St, New York, 10018. Gunther E Pohl, Chief
Holdings: Vols (160,000) Cat Pix
Budget: ($38,548)
Notes: Extensive collection of county, city, town and village histories of the United States. All other local, state, and national histories are part of the General Research and Humanities Division. Collection includes over 60,000 mounted photographs of New York City views arranged by address and/or subject. 20,000 film and glass plate negatives depicting NYC tenement housing conditions (1902-1938). Also the Lloyd L Acker collection of 48,000 film negatives depicting NYC buildings, 1935-1975. Collection of Lewis W Hine photographic prints made by the photographer on immigration, child labor, women at work and men at work. Eugene Armbruster Collection of Long Island views; D B Austin's photographs of Long Island and western Americana; scrapbooks, and postcards of NYC and other US localities (200,000). See *United States Local History Catalog* (Boston: GK Hall, 1974), 2 vols.

NY —NEW YORK PUBLIC LIBRARY, Research Libraries, American History Div, Fifth Ave & 42 St, New York, 10018.
Holdings: Vols (45,000) Cat Maps Microforms
Notes: Collection incl publications of national and state historical societies. Comprehensive, particularly when viewed in conjunction with the parent institutions's documents collection and monographs and serials elsewhere in the Library which are available through use of the American History Division catalog or through use of bibliographies within the division. Strong on Colonial and Revolutionary periods, War of 1812, Mexican War, Civil War, Spanish American War, and the Slavery Controversy. Incl collection of the papers of American statesmen. Fine collection of books by European travellers to the United States during the 19th century. See *Dictionary Catalog of the History of Americas* Collection (Boston: G K Hall, 1961), 28 vols.

NY —NEW YORK SOCIETY LIBRARY, 53 E 79 St, New York, 10021. Mark Piel, Librn
Notes: Incl Governor John Winthrop's Collection on chemistry and alchemy (part of which is at the New York Academy of Medicine Library).

†NY —UNION LEAGUE CLUB, Library, 38 E 37th St, New York, 10016. Jane Reed, Librn
Holdings: Vols (30,000)
Notes: American biography, American history, Civil War.

NY —STATE UNIVERSITY OF NEW YORK, COLLEGE AT OSWEGO, Penfield Library, Oswego, 13126. Anne Commerton,

U.S.—HISTORY (cont.)

Dir
Holdings: Mss
Notes: About 10,000 Millard Fillmore letters (by and to him), incl about 80 from Dorothea Dix. See *New York Times*, 24 March 1969.

NY —JERVIS PUBLIC LIBRARY, 613 N Washington St, Rome, 13440. William A Dillon, Dir
Holdings: Vols (1500) // Cat Mss Maps Slides
Notes: John Bloomfield Jervis Collection contains personal library (1500 vols) and papers (1300 items) of chief engineer of Croton aqueduct and other waterworks, canals, and railroads circa 1825-1860. Papers available on microfilm; indexes to papers available from Jervis Public Library. Two autograph collections. (1) The Huntington Autograph Collection of 108 pieces (originals and typescript with index of signatories). 1689-1897, comprised of correspondence, printed documents, leases, deeds, proclamations, papers relating to slavery and apprenticing. Letters incl 24 from 6 signers of the Declaration of Independence (as Samuel Huntington, Roger Sherman, Robert Morris); 14 letters from and 4 proclamations of Governor Jonathan Trumbull; numerous letters to Benjamin Huntington. (2) The Thomas C Bright Autograph Collection of 169 pieces originals andtypescript with index of signatories, 1702-1872, comprised of correspondence, deeds, indentures, leases. Letters written during the Revolutionary era incl 22 letters from 11 signers of the Declaration of Independence; 2 letters from George Washington. Among the items are letters from Lafayette, Henry Clay, Horace Mann; autographs of men such as Charles Lamb, Noah Webster, John Jay. Letters concerning the feasibility of constructing Erie Canal included.

NC —DUKE UNIVERSITY, William R Perkins Library, Manuscript Dept, Durham, 27706. Ellen Gartrell, Cur of Mss
Holdings: Cat Mss
Notes: Incl 7,000,000 items and 25,000 mss vols, especially strong for Southern states, 18th-20th centuries. Politics, business, religion, education, literature, women, social history, the military, are well represented. See *Guide to the Cataloged Collections of the Manuscript Department of the William R Perkins Library*.

OH —OHIO HISTORICAL SOCIETY, Archives Library Division, 1982 Velma Ave, Columbus, 43211. Dennis East, Division Chief
Holdings: Vols (96,000) Cat Mss Maps Pix Slides Microforms
Budget: ($18,000)
Notes: This library is the primary collection for Ohio. Most purchases are on the rare and op market. Collecting area is early American history, esp relating to exploration into the Northwest Territory. Major subject areas are Ohio politics and government (8 presidents) military history (good collection of regimental histories and Ohio narratives of the Civil War), economic and social history, local history, esp county histories & atlases and city directories. Also, Ohio archaeology, natural history, artifacts. Major media collections are books (96,000), newspapers (25,000 vols and 22,000 microfilm), pictures (50,000), maps (2500), manuscripts (1,500,000). Library is noncirculating except through interlibrary loan of microfilm.

OH —FLESH PUBLIC LIBRARY, 124 W Greene St, Piqua, 45356. Wallace White, Librn
Holdings: Vols (1400) // Cat Maps
Notes: The Jerome C Smiley Collection.

OH —OTTERBEIN COLLEGE, Courtright Memorial Library, Main & Grove Sts, Westerville, 43081. John Becker, Librn
Holdings: Vols 1820 Cat
Budget: $400

PA —ATHENAEUM OF PHILADELPHIA, 219 S Sixth St, Philadelphia, 19106. Roger

W Moss Jr, Librn
Holdings: Vols (20,000)
Notes: A century of American history, 1814-1914.

PA —UNION LEAGUE OF PHILADELPHIA, Library, 140 S Broad St, Philadelphia, 19102. James G Mundy Jr, Librn
Holdings: Vols (23,000) Cat Mss Pix
Notes: Emphasis on Covil War, American social and political history, Philadelphia and Pennsylvania history.

PA —UNIVERSITY OF PITTSBURGH, Darlington Memorial Library, Special Collections, 601 Cathedral of Learning, Pittsburgh, 15260. Dennis Lambert, Darlington Librn
Holdings: Vols (17,000) Cat Mss Maps Pix
Notes: The Darlington Collection is especially rich in American history of the colonial period, the French and Indian war, the Revolution and the War of 1812 with geographical emphasis on Western Pennsylvania and Ohio Valley history to 1870 and on Pittsburgh history to 1900. Indian treaties, captivity accounts, US and Pennsylvania travel and description and early American fiction and prose are represented. A partial guide to the Darlington Manuscript Collections is available by writing for *Darlington Memorial Library: A Descriptive Checklist of Its Manuscripts Collections*. University of Pittsburgh Bibliographic Series 5, 1969. Noncirculating.

TN —COVENANT COLLEGE, Anna Emma Kresge Memorial Library, Lookout Mountain, 37350. Gary B Huisman, Librn
Holdings: Microforms

†TX —UNIVERSITY OF TEXAS LIBRARIES, General Libraries, Humanities Research Center, PO Box 7219, Austin, 78712. John Chalmers, Librn
Notes: The John W F Dulles collection of correspondence, diaries, autographs, speeches, and paintings by famous historical figures from the 17th century to the present. Much of the material is related to Mr Dulles' three relatives who served as Secretaries of State: John Foster Dulles, Robert Lansing, and John W Foster.

TX —SAM RAYBURN FOUNDATION LIBRARY, 800 W Sam Rayburn Dr, Box 123, Bonham, 75418.
Holdings: Vols 8000 Cat Mss Pix Microforms
Notes: Historical research library--contains all of Speaker Rayburn's papers. Incl books on American history, biography, politics and government, and the Presidents and their writings.

TX —AMON CARTER MUSEUM, Library, 3510 Camp Bowie Blvd, PO Box 2365, Fort Worth, 76113. Nancy G Wynne, Librn
Holdings: Vols (25,000) Cat Mss Pix
Notes: The book collection, microfilm and photo archives have been built toward the goal of the interpretation of American history through art. At present, the greatest strengths are in Americana, Western Canadiana, bibliography, American exhibition catalogs and history of photography. Substantial books and files on American artists of the 19th and early 20th century, and particularly of Charles M Russell and Frederic Remington. Incl 25,000 pictures; 13,000 slides.
See also entries under Newspapers, American; Pictures - Collections.

TX —HOUSTON POST LIBRARY, 4747 Southwest Freeway, Houston, 77001. Kathy Foley, Librn

VA —UNIVERSITY OF VIRGINIA, Alderman Library, Tracy W McGregor Collection, Charlottesville, 22901. William H Runge, Cur
Holdings: Vols 18,000 Cat Mss Maps Pix Microforms
Notes: Library spans 15th-20th century, concentrating on Southeastern American History. Rare collection of books on early exploration and travel; foundation of the Virginia Colony; Civil War. Books in foreign languages. Collection cataloged by date of publication. Special shellist. Published descriptions: William H Runge, "The Tracy

W McGregor Library and Its Founder," *The University of Virginia News Letter* vol 39, no 11, July 15, 1963; *Description of the Tracy W McGregor Library, University of Virginia, with Rules for Its Use and a Biographical Sketch of Its Founder* (Charlottesville: Tracy W McGregor Library, 1951).

VA —MARY WASHINGTON COLLEGE, E Lee Trinkle Library, Fredericksburg, 22401. Ruby Y Weinbrecht, Librn
Holdings: Vols 16,000 Cat Maps Microforms
Budget: $19,000

VA —CENTRAL VIRGINIA COMMUNITY COLLEGE, Library, 3506 Wards Rd, Lynchburg, 24502. John B St Leger, Dir of Library Servs
Holdings: Vols (6000)

VA —MACARTHUR MEMORIAL, Library & Archives, MacArthur Sq, Norfolk, 23510. Ellen E Folkama, Asst Archivist
Holdings: Vols (4000) Cat Mss Maps Pix Slides Phonorecords Audiotapes 16mm Films Microforms
Notes: Everything relating to the life and related activities of MacArthur. The Archives of the collection consist of 600 shelf-feet of documents from Gen MacArthur's official headquarters files over the period 1941-1951. These papers pertain to all matters with which his various commands were involved: military, naval and air matters; international relations; political science; Japanese occupation; peace treaty and Constitution, etc. Each Record Group is indexed. The indexes are retained here since they are being expanded. They are available for researchers.

VA —VIRGINIA STATE LIBRARY, 12 & Capitol Sts, Richmond, 23219.
Holdings: Vols 80,000 Cat Mss Maps Pix Microforms
Notes: Jeffersonian Americana (on 2000 microfiche). Separate catalog.

WI —STATE HISTORICAL SOCIETY OF WISCONSIN, Library, 816 State St, Madison, 53706. James L Hansen, Reference Librn
Holdings: Vols (1,600,000) Cat Mss Maps Pix Microforms

Notes: Comprehensive collection of materials relating to US History, including pamphlet materials, newspapers, microforms, manuscripts and 19th century federal and state documents.

ON —NATIONAL LIBRARY OF CANADA, 395 Wellington St, Ottawa, K1A 0N4, Can. Andre Preibish, Dir
Holdings: Vols 44,000 Documents
Budget: $50,000
Notes: Includes 400 serials titles. Collection aims to be comprehensive and covers all aspects of Canadian history. The library has received all Canadian titles on legal deposit since 1950; intensive acquisition of earlier works and those published abroad. In addition, the collection is supported by representative resources for American, British and French history.

U.S.—HISTORY—COLONIAL PERIOD

†AL —MUSEUMS OF THE CITY OF MOBILE, Reference Library, 355 Government St, Mobile, 36602. Caldwell Delaney, Adminr

DC —GEORGETOWN UNIVERSITY, Library, Special Collections Div, 37 & O Sts NW, Washington, 20057. George M Barringer, Special Collections Librn; Nicholas B Sheetz, Mss Librn
Holdings: Cat

IL —NEWBERRY LIBRARY, 60 W Walton St, Chicago, 60610. Diana Haskell, Cur of Modern Mss
Holdings: Cat Mss Maps
Notes: Exhaustive collection of first and important editions, with supportive secondary material. Espec strong: discovery and exploration; Indian relations (incl captivities, treaties, and linguistics). Incl the Frank Cutter Deering Collection of over 2100 rare Colonial and Revolutionary Period works.

IL —UNIVERSITY OF ILLINOIS, URBANA/CHAMPAIGN, Library, Illinois

U.S.—HISTORY—COLONIAL PERIOD (cont.)

Historical Survey Library, 1408 W Gregory Dr, 1A Library, Urbana, 61801.
Holdings: Vols 500 Cat Mss Maps Microforms
Notes: Colonial and Revolutionary Periods-- Midwest, particularly Illinois. Important ms collections (75 cubic feet) under this subject incl: Baynton, Wharton and Morgan, papers, 1757-1799, 6 reels of microfilm; British Archives, 1547-1858, 7000 items, 40 reels of microfilm; Cunningham Collection, 1600-1836, 40 cubic feet (typed copies from Archives in Spain and South America); French Archives, 1671-1796, 3500 items; Gage, Thomas, papers, 1759-1773, 1300 items; Morgan, George, papers, 1766-1826, 280 items, 5 reels of microfilm; Randolph County Records, 1720-1853, 91 items, 59 reels of microfilm; St Clair County Records, 1722-1809, 6 items, 5 reels of microfilm. Guide to the collections published: Maynard J Brichford, Robert M Sutton, Dennis F Walle, *Manuscripts Guide to Collections at the University of Illinois at Urbana-Champaign* (Urbana, Chicago, London: University of Illinois Press, 1976).

MA —BOSTON UNIVERSITY, Mugar Memorial Library, Special Collections Dept, 771 Commonwealth Ave, Boston, 02215. Howard B Gotlieb, Dir
Holdings: Cat Mss
Notes: Correspondence and books.
See also entries under Foxcroft family; Mayhew family

MA —MASSACHUSETTS HISTORICAL SOCIETY LIBRARY, 1154 Boylston St, Boston, 02215. John D Cushing, Librn
Holdings: Mss Maps Microforms
Notes: One of more than 5000 individual collections in the Library, this collection incl the Adams Family papers and materials relating to Massachusetts and New England. The Library's collection of mss has been cataloged and issued in nine folio vols by G K Hall & Co of Boston. It is widely distributed throughout the United States and Europe.

MA —NEW ENGLAND HISTORIC GENEALOGICAL SOCIETY, Library, 101 Newbury St, Boston, 02116. Ralph J Crandell, Dir
Notes: Large collection of printed British and American parish registers; some American ms parish records. Strong collection of early censuses, Incl the Massachusetts Direct Tax Record of 1798, actually a census of Maine and Massachusetts and more informative than the Federal decennial record of early national censuses. Earlier similarly useful records incl the Accounts of Pay for King Philip's War (1675-1676) kept by John Hull, War Treasurer.

MA —HISTORIC DEERFIELD-POCUMTUCK VALLEY MEMORIAL ASSOCIATION, Libraries, Memorial St, Box 53, Deerfield, 01342. David R Proper, Librn
Holdings: Vols (17,000) Cat Mss Maps Pix Microforms
Notes: Local and regional history, especially western Massachusetts. Also, remnants of several collection of books available to early Deerfield and Greenfield residents. Strong ms collection dealing with the region's families, businesses, etc. These consist of sermons, diaries, town and church records, voluntary societies' archives, etc. Extensive collection of photographs of the people and buildings of Deerfield and its environs, and travels in Maine, California, and England (1880s to 1920s). Also, large collection of glassplate negatives. Houses the Connecticut Valley Bibliography, a comprehensive card file on the history and culture of the Connecticut Valley of Massachusetts.

MA —SOCIETY FOR THE PRESERVATION OF COLONIAL CULTURE LIBRARY, 52 New Spalding St, Lowell, 01851. Vincent Lowell Kehoe, Cur
Holdings: Vols 1500 Cat

MA —BRANDEIS UNIVERSITY, Goldfarb Library, 415 South St, Waltham, 02154.
Bessie Hahn, Dir
Holdings: Vols
Notes: Perry Miller Collection on the Colonial Religious Experience in America: Consists of 18 linear ft of books dating from the 17th and 18th century relating to the religious experience in the American colonies. Access to the collection is through the Main Card Catalog and Special Collections Card Catalog.

MI —NORTHERN MICHIGAN UNIVERSITY, Lydia M Olson Library, Elizabeth L Harden Drive, Marquette, 49855. Stephen H Peters, Cataloger
Notes: A major section of the personal library of Moses Coit Tyler. Strong in the Colonial and Early National periods. Includes biographies and published letters and writings of such figures as Benjamin Franklin, John Adams, John Jay, Thomas Jefferson, Charles Sumner.

NH —NEW HAMPSHIRE HISTORICAL SOCIETY, Manuscripts Library, 30 Park St, Concord, 03301. Thomas E Camden, Cur
Holdings: Vols (500,000) Cat Mss
Budget: ($12,500)
Notes: Photocopying of individual items only. Consultation of original mss materials strongly encouraged. Mss and books related to New Hampshire history. Especially strong in politics, particularly during the post- Civil War 19th century and the early 20th century. Highlights: Mason Weare Tappan Papers, Austin Pike Papers, Charles Marseilles Papers, Jacob H Gallinger Papers, James O Lyfor Papers and George H Moses Papers. Also papers of many other New Hampshire people, among them, John Badger Bachelder, Josiah Bartlett, Moody Bedel, Timothy Bedel, Mary Baker Eddy, Joseph A Gilmore, John Hatch George, Isaac Hill, John Langdon, Jeremiah Mason, Charles Sanger Mellen, John Fabyan Parrott, Nathaniel Peabody, William Plumer, Lorenzo Sabine, Jean Joseph Marie Toscan, Robert W Upton, John Wentworth and Levi Woodbury. The records of the Dover (New Hampshire) Manufacturing Company; 650 account books, most of which were kept by general merchants in New Hampshire during the 18th and 19th centuries; town records, mostly before 1825, for approx 230 New Hampshire towns; and military records and orderly books relating to New Hampshire military units of the 18th and 19th centuries (French & Indian War through the Civil War). About 500,000 ms pieces, 4000 books, 1000 maps.

NJ —GLASSBORO STATE COLLEGE, Savitz Library, Stewart Room, Glassboro, 08028. Clara Kirner, Special Collection Librn
Holdings: Vols 100 Cat Mss Maps Pix

NY —NEW YORK HISTORICAL SOCIETY, Library, 170 Central Park W, New York, 10024. James Gregory, Librn
Holdings: Mss
Notes: Incl original mss, illustrative materials, etc.

NY —NEW YORK PUBLIC LIBRARY, Research Libraries, American History Div, Fifth Ave & 42 St, New York, 10018.
Holdings: Vols (25,000) Maps Microforms
Notes: See *Dictionary Catalog of the History of Americas Collection* (Boston: G K Hall, 1961), 28 vols.

PA —HISTORICAL SOCIETY OF PENNSYLVANIA, Library, 1300 Locust St, Philadelphia, 19107. David Fraser, Librn
Holdings: Vols (230,000) Mss Maps Pix Microforms
Notes: Incl over 14,000,000 ms pieces. The Library Company of Philadelphia mss are on deposit with the Historical Society of Pennsylvania. Many of the Society's rare books are on deposit with the Library Company. The Society maintains the collections of the Genealogical Society of Pennsylvania, incl some 20,000 printed genealogies, original mss, family, church, and civil records.

PA —INDEPENDENCE NATIONAL HISTORICAL PARK, Library, 313 Walnut St, Philadelphia, 19106. David C G Dutcher, Chief Historian; Shirley A Mays, Librn
Holdings: Vols 5000 Cat Mss Videotapes Films
Budget: ($25,000)
Notes: Emphasis on Pennsylvania and Philadelphia, incl arts and crafts to early 19th century. Incl some 2000 ms pieces; 25,000 pictures; 3000 slides; 600 microfilm reels. No photocopying.

PA —UNIVERSITY OF PITTSBURGH, Darlington Memorial Library, Special Collections, 601 Cathedral of Learning, Pittsburgh, 15260. Dennis Lambert, Darlington Librn
Holdings: Vols (17,000) Cat Mss Maps Pix
Notes: The Darlington Collection is especially rich in American history of the colonial period, the French and Indian War, the Revolution, and the War of 1812 with geographical emphasis on Western Pennsylvania and Ohio Valley history to 1870 and on Pittsburgh history to 1900. Indian treaties, captivity accounts, US and Pennsylvania travel and description, and early American fiction and prose are represented. A partial guide to the Darlington Manuscript Collections is available by writing for *Darlington Memorial Library: A Descriptive Checklist of its Manuscript Collections,* University of Pittsburgh Bibliographic Series 5, 1969. Noncirculating.

RI —BROWN UNIVERSITY, John Carter Brown Library, Providence, 02912. Norman Fiering, Librn; Everett C Wilkie Jr, Bibliographer; Susan Danforth, Cur Maps & Prints
Holdings: Vols (40,000) Cat Mss Maps Pix
Notes: History of the Americas during the Colonial Period.

RI —RHODE ISLAND STATE ARCHIVES, Library, Room 43, State House, Smith St, Providence, 02903. Phyllis Silva, Dir
Holdings: Cat Mss Maps Microforms
Notes: All original mss, 1638-1860. Colony Records, census. Petition to Gen Assembly, Letters to and from governors, Revolutionary War Records, etc. We are primarily a General Assembly Archives.

SC —FRANCIS MARION COLLEGE, James A Rogers Library, Florence, 29501. H Paul Dove, Dir; Roger K Hux, Special Collections Librn
Holdings: Vols (600) Cat Maps Audiotapes Microforms
Notes: The Pee Dee Region of South Carolina. Emphasis on Colonial and Revolutionary periods, rice and indigo culture, plantations. Includes old rural church library with children's books.

VA —RANDOLPH-MACON COLLEGE, Walter Hines Page Library, Ashland, 23005. Flavia Reed Owen, Librn
Holdings: Vols 5000 Serials
Budget: $6000
Notes: Bibliographical listing of collection in Intellectual Life in The Colonial South, 1585-1763/by Richard Beale Davis. (Knoxville: University of Tennessee Press, c 1978) 3 v.

VA —PORTSMOUTH PUBLIC LIBRARY, 601 Court St, Portsmouth, 23704. Dean Burgess, Library Dir
Holdings: Vols 500 Cat Mss Maps Pix Slides Microforms
Notes: Portsmouth was founded in 1752 and was the headquarters for the British army throughout the Revolution. It has the oldest and now the largest American Navy Shipyard dating to before the Revolution and called the Norfolk Naval Shipyard. It also was the site of the building of the Merimac (which battled the Monitor off Portsmouth's waterfront). Several pre-revolutionary houses remain in the historic downtown area although most are from the Federal period 1800-1830. Portsmouth is often neglected in American history books perhaps because it was a Tory town.

VA —VIRGINIA STATE LIBRARY, 12 & Capitol Sts, Richmond, 23219.
Holdings: Vols 5400 Cat Mss Maps Pix Microforms

VA —COLONIAL WILLIAMSBURG FOUNDATION, Research Center Library, PO Drawer C, Williamsburg, 23187. John E Ingram, Research Archivist
Holdings: Vols (30,000) Cat Mss Maps Pix

U.S.—HISTORY—COLONIAL PERIOD (cont.)

Microforms
Budget: ($20,000)
Notes: Virginia and the Chesapeake in the 17th-18th centuries. Particular strengths include social, economic, agricultural and architectural history. The collection encompasses over 6000 rare books, 18th Century music scores and 12,000 manuscripts, as well as a complete set of Virginia Colonial Records Project microfilm (1000 reels).

U.S.—HISTORY—FRENCH AND INDIAN WAR, 1755-1763

DC —LIBRARY OF CONGRESS, Geography and Map Division, Washington, 20540. John A Wolter, Chief
Notes: The William Faden Collection of ms and printed maps of the French and Indian and Revolutionary Wars.

MA —AMHERST COLLEGE, Library, Amherst, 01002. John Lancaster, Special Collections Librn
Holdings: Cat Mss Maps

MA —AMERICAN ANTIQUARIAN SOCIETY LIBRARY, 185 Salisbury St, Worcester, 01609. Marcus A McCorison, Dir & Librn
Holdings: Cat Mss
Notes: Incl considerable manuscript material.

PA —UNIVERSITY OF PITTSBURGH, Darlington Memorial Library, Special Collections, 601 Cathedral of Learning, Pittsburgh, 15260. Dennis Lambert, Darlington Librn
Holdings: Vols (17,000) Cat Mss Maps Pix
Notes: The Darlington Collection is especially rich in American history of the colonial period, the French and Indian War, the Revolution, and the War of 1812 with geographical emphasis on Western Pennsylvania and Ohio Valley history to 1870 and on Pittsburgh history to 1900. Indian treaties, captivity accounts, US and Pennsylvania travel and description, and early American fiction and prose are represented. A partial guide to the Darlington Manuscript Collections is available by writing for *Darlington Memorial Library: A Descriptive Checklist of its Manuscript Collections*, University of Pittsburgh Bibliographic Series 5, 1969. Noncirculating.

U.S.—HISTORY—1763-1820

CT —UNIVERSITY OF CONNECTICUT, Library, Storrs, 06268. R H Schimmelpfeng, Dir of Special Collections
Holdings: Vols 4600 // Uncat Mss Maps
Notes: The library of Pierce Welch Gaines of Federalist material, chiefly contemporary books and mss. Emphasis on Washington, Jefferson and Adams.

VA —COLONIAL WILLIAMSBURG FOUNDATION, Research Center Library, PO Drawer C, Williamsburg, 23187. John E Ingram, Research Archivist
Holdings: Vols (30,000) Cat Mss Maps Pix Microforms
Budget: ($20,000)
Notes: Virginia and the Chesapeake in the 17th-18th centuries. Particular strengths include social, economic, agricultural and architectural history. The collection encompasses over 6000 rare books, 18th Century music scores and 12,000 manuscripts, as well as a complete set of Virginia Colonial Records Project microfilm (1000 reels).

U.S.—HISTORY—REVOLUTION

CA —COPLEY NEWSPAPERS, James S Copley Library, 1134 Kline St, PO Box 1530, La Jolla, 92038. Richard Reilly, Cur; Suzanne Carnes, Librn
Holdings: Vols (1500) Cat
Notes: Collection incl materials on American Revolutionary period and California and western Americana, with autograph letters

and documents. Library open to graduate students who obtain reading privileges from curator or librarian.

CA —UNIVERSITY OF CALIFORNIA, SAN DIEGO, Central University Library, Mandeville Dept of Special Collections, La Jolla, 92093. Lynda Corey Claassen, Head
Notes: Manuscript collection incl family correspondence from the American Revolution and the Civil War.

CA —CALIFORNIA STATE UNIVERSITY, LONG BEACH, Library, Dept of Special Collections & Archives, 1250 Bellflower Blvd, Long Beach, 90840. John Ahouse, Special Collections Librn
Holdings: Vols 400 Cat
Notes: Incl pamphlets, tracts, memoirs, 1770-1790.

CT —YALE UNIVERSITY, Box 1603A, Yale Station, New Haven, 06520.

CT —CONNECTICUT COLLEGE, Library, Mohegan Ave, New London, 06320. Brian Rogers, College Librn
Holdings: Vols (382,000) Cat Mss Maps Pix
Notes: Collection includes material relating to New London and surrounding communities, including Groton, Norwich and Stonington. Includes pamphlets and broadsides printed in New London by the Greens during the Revolutionary period. Also "Atlantic Neptune" facsimiles.

DC —LIBRARY OF CONGRESS, Manuscript Division, Washington, 20540. John C Broderick, Chief
Notes: Papers and revolutionary war maps of the Comte de Rochambeau.

DC —SOCIETY OF THE CINCINNATI, Library, 2118 Massachusetts Ave NW, Washington, 20008. John D Kilbourne, Dir of Museum & Library
Holdings: Vols (12,000) Cat Mss Maps Pix Slides Microforms
Budget: ($65,000)
Notes: Because of the French connections of the Society of the Cincinnati, a particular effort is made to incl information about the French contribution to the American Revolution. The collection is also rich in biographical materials concerning the officer personnel of the American and French armies of the American Revolution. There are two significant sub-sections of this collection: The George Rogers Clark Collection concerning the history of the Old Northwest (to 1820); and the Member-Author collection, writings of members of the Society of the Cincinnati in various fields. The archival collection, formerly housed at the Library of Congress, has been returned to the Society. It is advisable to make an appointment for use of the collections.

IL —NEWBERRY LIBRARY, 60 W Walton St, Chicago, 60610. Diana Haskell, Cur of Modern Mss
Holdings: Cat Mss Maps
Notes: Incl the Frank Cutter Deering Collection of rare Colonial and Revolutionary Period works-over 2100 items.

IL —UNIVERSITY OF ILLINOIS, URBANA/CHAMPAIGN, Library, Illinois Historical Survey Library, 1408 W Gregory Dr, 1A Library, Urbana, 61801.
Holdings: Vols 500 Cat Mss Maps Microforms
Notes: Colonial and Revolutionary Period-- Midwest, particularly Illinois. Important ms collections (75 cubic feet) under this subject incl: Baynton, Wharton and Morgan, papers, 1757-1799, 6 reels of microfilm; British Archives, 1547-1858, 7000 items, 40 reels of microfilm; Cunningham Collection, 1600-1836, 40 cubic feet (typed copies from Archives in Spain and South America); French Archives, 1671-1796, 3500 items; Gage, Thomas, papers, 1759-1773, 1300 items; Morgan, George, papers, 1766-1826, 280 items, 5 reels of microfilm; Randolph County Records, 1720-1853, 91 items, 59 reels of microfilm; St Clair County Records, 1722-1809, 6 items, 5 reels of microfilm. Guide to the collections published: Maynard J Brichford, Robert M Sutton, Dennis F Walle, *Manuscripts Guide to Collections at the University of Illinois at*

Urbana-Champaign(Urbana, Chicago, London: University of Illinois Press, 1976).

IN —INDIANA UNIVERSITY, Lilly Library, Seventh St, Bloomington, 47405. William R Cagle, Librn
Holdings: Vols (1000) // Cat Mss
Notes: 1000 vols of contemporary printings (largely British) on Anglo-American relations leading to the American Revolution.

LA —TULANE UNIVERSITY, Howard-Tilton Memorial Library, Special Collections Div, 7001 Freret St, New Orleans, 70118. Wilbur E Meneray, Librn
Holdings: Vols 400 Cat
Notes: A collection of rare pamphlets and books pertaining to the American Revolution, known as the Americana Collection.

LA —NICHOLLS STATE UNIVERSITY, Ellender Memorial Library, Thibodaux, 70310. Randall A Detro, Dir; Philip D Uzee, Archivist
Holdings: Uncat Mss Maps Pix Microforms
Notes: Louisiana and local history; family papers of the period, etc.

ME —BOWDOIN COLLEGE, Library, Brunswick, 04011. Dianne M Gutscher, Cur of Special Collections
Holdings: Mss
Notes: The Mellen Papers contain approx 5000 printed and mss items relating to New England history from the 18th to the 20th centuries. Of primary importance are the Henry Sewall papers, which incl his Revolutionary War correspondence, addresses, genealogical notes, and other documents. The archive also incl papers from the Mellen, Hawkins, Manley, Harward, and other New England families.

MD —JOHNS HOPKINS UNIVERSITY, Milton S Eisenhower Library, Charles & 34 Sts, Baltimore, 21218. Ann S Gwyn, Assistant Dir for Special Collections
Holdings: Vols Cat Mss
Notes: Strong section on the Revolution includes the Herbert Friedenwald collection of the Journals of the American (Continental) Congress. Mss of colonial leaders.

MD —WASHINGTON COLLEGE, Clifton M Miller Library, Chestertown, 21620.
Notes: Archive-library of source material, incl primary sources in microform, on the Chesapeake Bay during the American Revolutinary period.

MA —BOSTON UNIVERSITY, Mugar Memorial Library, Special Collections Dept, 771 Commonwealth Ave, Boston, 02215. Howard B Gotlieb, Dir
Holdings: Cat Mss
Notes: Correspondence in Bortman, Stone, Massachusetts First Corps of Cadets and Military Historical Society of Massachusetts Collections.

MA —MASSACHUSETTS HISTORICAL SOCIETY LIBRARY, 1154 Boylston St, Boston, 02215. John D Cushing, Librn
Holdings: Mss Maps Micorforms
Notes: One of more than 5000 individual collections in the Library, this collection incl the Adams Family papers and materials relating to Massachusetts and New England. The Library's collection of mss has been cataloged and issued in nine folio vols by G K Hall & Co of Boston. It is widely distributed throughout the United States and Europe.

MA —CONCORD FREE PUBLIC LIBRARY, 129 Main St, Concord, 01742. Rose Marie Mitten, Dir
Holdings: Cat Mss Maps Pix Slides
Notes: Extensive collection.

MA —CARY MEMORIAL LIBRARY, 1874 Massachusetts Ave, Lexington, 02173. Robert C Hilton, Dir
Holdings: Uncat Maps Pix Slides Phonorecords Audiotapes Videotapes 16mm Films Microforms
Notes: Strong on the Battle of Lexington and Concord and the events surrounding the battle. Worthen Collection of material on Lexington.

MA —WILLIAMS COLLEGE, Sawyer Library, Williamstown, 01267. Phyllis L Cutler, Dir
Holdings: Vols 78 // Cat
Notes: The Arthur H Masten Collection on the Saratoga Campaign, 1777.

U.S.—HISTORY—REVOLUTION (cont.)

MA —AMERICAN ANTIQUARIAN
SOCIETY LIBRARY, 185 Salisbury St,
Worcester, 01609. Marcus A McCorison,
Dir & Librn
Holdings: Cat Mss
Notes: Incl considerable manuscript material.

†MA —CLARK UNIVERSITY, Robert
Hutchings Goddard Library, Worcester,
01610. Dorothy Mosa Kowski, Rare Books
Librn
Holdings: Cat Mss
Notes: Eight original vols comprising the
Orderly Books of the Revolutionary War
General Anthony Wayne.

MI —UNIVERSITY OF MICHIGAN, William
L Clements Library, Ann Arbor, 48109.
John C Dann, Dir
Notes: The William L. Clements Library of
Americana is a non-circulating rare book library of
original source material, printed and manuscript,
dealing with America, from the discovery period
into the late nineteenth century. The collection
includes approximately 55,000 books and
pamphlets, 550 linear feet of manuscripts, 4,100
volumes of newspapers, 36,000 maps, 40,000
pieces of sheet music, and 1,000 prints. The
collection is strongest for the period of the
American Revolution, and includes the papers of
Thomas Gage, Sir Henry Clinton, and the Earl
of Shelburne. Other areas of strength include
antislavery, cartography and geography, discovery
and exploration, American Indians, The Civil War,
tune-books, sermons and orations, and the War of
1812. There are selective research collections
dealing with Christopher Columbus, Thomas
Paine, Benjamin Franklin, George Washington,
Thomas Jefferson, and the Federalist Papers.
Publications describing the collections of the
library are: Author/Title catalog of Americana
1493-1860 in the William L. Clements Library...
7 volumes, Boston, G. K. Hall, 1970; Guide to the
manuscript collections of the William L. Clements
Library, by Arlene P. Shy 3d edition, Boston,
G. K. Hall, 1978; Guide to the manuscript maps in
the William L. Clements Library, compiled by
Christian Burn, Ann Arbor, U. of Michigan, 1959;
and Research catalog of maps of America, to 1860
in the William L. Clements Library...,edited by
Douglas W. Marshall, 4 volumes, Boston, G. K.
Hall, 1972.

NH —NEW HAMPSHIRE HISTORICAL
SOCIETY, Manuscripts Library, 30 Park St,
Concord, 03301. Thomas E Camden, Cur
Holdings: Vols (500,000) Cat Mss
Budget: ($12,500)
Notes: Photocopying of individual items
only. Consultation of original mss materials
strongly encouraged. Mss and books related
to New Hampshire history. Especially strong
in politics, particularly during the post- Civil
War 19th century and the early 20th
century. Highlights: Mason Weare Tappan
Papers, Austin Pike Papers, Charles
Marseilles Papers, Jacob H Gallinger Papers,
James O Lyfor Papers and George H Moses
Papers. Also papers of many other New
Hampshire people, among them, John
Badger Bachelder, Josiah Bartlett, Moody
Bedel, Timothy Bedel, Mary Baker Eddy,

Joseph A Gilmore, John Hatch George,
Isaac Hill, John Langdon, Jeremiah Mason,
Charles Sanger Mellen, John Fabyan Parrott,
Nathaniel Peabody, William Plumer,
Lorenzo Sabine, Jean Joseph Marie Toscan,
Robert W Upton, John Wentworth and Levi
Woodbury. The records of the Dover (New
Hampshire) Manufacturing Company; 650
account books,most of which were kept by
general merchants in New Hampshire during
the 18th and 19th centuries; town records,
mostly before 1825, for approx 230 New
Hampshire towns; and military records and
orderly books relating to New Hampshire
military units of the 18th and 19th centuries
(French & Indian War through the Civil
War). About 500,000 ms pieces, 4000 books,
1000 maps.

NJ —GLASSBORO STATE COLLEGE,
Savitz Library, Stewart Room, Glassboro,
08028. Clara Kirner, Special Collection
Librn
Holdings: Vols 202 Cat Mss Maps Pix
Notes: Incl biographies of Washington and
Franklin, general histories. Loyalists'
materials and Revolutionary figures in New
Jersey campaigns. Steven's facsimiles of mss
in European archives relating to America,
1773-1783.

NJ —TRENTON FREE PUBLIC LIBRARY,
120 Academy St, Trenton, 08608. Nan
Wright, Supervising Reference Librn
Holdings: Vols 100 Cat Mss Maps Pix Slides
Microforms
Notes: Incl mss, maps and prints. Also
cataloged pamphlets on Trentonia.

NJ —TRENTON STATE COLLEGE, Roscoe
L West Library, Pennington Rd, PO Box
940, Trenton, 08625. Paul A DuBois, Dir
Holdings: // Cat Mss
Notes: Although officially called "The Sol
Feinstone Collection of the American
Revolution" in honor of the donor, a resident
of Washington Crossing, Pennsylvania, the
collection includes several items dealing with
the War of 1812. The books and pamphlets
were published between 1764 and 1965; ms
material consists of legislative acts
originating both with Parliament and the
New Jersey Assembly, as well as several
letters and miscellaneous items.

NY —FORDHAM UNIVERSITY LIBRARY,
Bronx, 10458. Joseph A LoSchiavo,
Reference Librn
Holdings: Vols 151// Uncat Mss
Notes: Charles Allen Munn Collection of
Rare Americana. Incl 37 Trumbell sketches.
No photocopying.

NY —NEW YORK STATE OFFICE OF
PARKS & RECREATION, TACONIC
REGION, Clermont State Historic Park,
Library, RR 1, Box 215, Germantown,
12526. Bruce E Naramore, Historic Site
Manager
Holdings: Vols (5000) Cat Mss
Notes: This library may be considered
unique in that seven generations of the
Livingston family owned and added to it
throughout the years (1730-1962). Many of
these items belonged to the Chancellor
Robert R Livingston (1746-1813), prominent
early American statesman. Many volumes
concern Livingston family history, the
forming of the US and early history of the
Hudson River Valley (pre- and post-
American Revolutionary War). Many first
editions. Also concerns agriculture,
technology, poetry, politics, etc. Additions to
the collection are being considered if it can
be ascertained that the volume belonged to
the family or the estate. No photocopying.

NY —COLUMBIA UNIVERSITY
LIBRARIES, Rare Book & Manuscript
Library, 801 Butler Library, 535 W 114 St,
New York, 10027. Kenneth A Lohf, Librn
Holdings: Mss
Notes: Over 200 photocopies of American
Revolutionary documents and letters
(photocopies) and other historical
autographs. Major General William H
Donovan's papers on espionage during the
American Revolution. 15,000 items.

NY —NEW YORK HISTORICAL SOCIETY,
Library, 170 Central Park W, New York,
10024. James Gregory, Librn
Holdings: Mss
Notes: Incl original mss, illustrative
materials, etc.

NY —NEW YORK PUBLIC LIBRARY,
Research Libraries, American History Div,
Fifth Ave & 42 St, New York, 10018.
Holdings: Vols (25,000) Maps Microforms
Notes: See Dictionary Catalog of the History
of Americas Collection (Boston: G K Hall,
1961), 28 vols.

NY —HISTORICAL SOCIETY OF THE
TARRYTOWNS, Library, One Grove St,
Tarrytown, 10591. Adelaide R Smith, Cur
Holdings: Vols 95 Cat Mss Maps Pix VF
Notes: Since the capture of Major Andre
occurred in the Tarrytown area, 23 Sept
1780, we have comprehensive
documentation and a variety of artifacts
relating to this event. Our files cover the
lives of the 3 captors. John Paulding, Isaac
Van Wart and David Williams, as well as
Major Andre. Limited material on Benedict
Arnold.

NY —US MILITARY ACADEMY LIBRARY,
West Point, 10996. Marie T Capps, Maps &
Mss Librn
Holdings: Vols (2000) // Mss Maps
Notes: One descriptive catalog of a portion
of this collection is: Marie T Capps and
Theodore G Stroup, US Military Academy
Library Map Collection: The Period of the
American Revolution 1753-1800 (West
Point, NY: US Military Academy, 1971), 82
pp.

†NC —WAKE FOREST UNIVERSITY, Z
Smith Reynolds Library, Box 7777, Reynold
Sta, Winston-Salem, 27109. Richard J
Murdoch, Rare Book Librn
Holdings: Vols (1000) // Cat
Notes: Emphasis on the South and North
Carolina. Primarily rare books and high
spots.

OH —OHIO HISTORICAL SOCIETY,
Archives Library Division, 1982 Velma Ave,
Columbus, 43211. Dennis East, Division
Chief
Holdings: Vols 400 // Cat Mss
Notes: Based on the collection of Wilbur H
Siebert; incl manuscripts and notes.

PA —HISTORICAL SOCIETY OF
PENNSYLVANIA, Library, 1300 Locust St,
Philadelphia, 19107. David Fraser, Librn
Holdings: Vols (230,000) Mss Maps Pix
Microforms
Notes: Incl over 14,000,000 ms pieces. The
Library Company of Philadelphia mss are on
deposit with the Historical Society of
Pennsylvania. Many of the Society's rare
books are on deposit with the Library
Company. The Society maintains the
collections of the Genealogical Society of
Pennsylvania, incl some 20,000 printed
genealogies, original mss, family, church, and
civil records.

PA —INDEPENDENCE NATIONAL
HISTORICAL PARK, Library, 313 Walnut
St, Philadelphia, 19106. David C G Dutcher,
Chief Historian; Shirley A Mays, Librn
Holdings: Vols 5000 Cat Mss Videotapes
Films
Budget: ($25,000)
Notes: Emphasis on Pennsylvania and
Philadelphia, incl arts and crafts to early
19th century. Incl some 2000 ms pieces; 25,
000 pictures; 3000 slides; 600 microfilm
reels. No photocopying.

PA —LIBRARY COMPANY OF
PHILADELPHIA, 1314 Locust St,
Philadelphia, 19107. Edwin Wolf II, Librn;
Kenneth Finkel, Cur of Prints
Holdings: Vols 3000 Cat Mss
Budget: ($25,000)
Notes: Printed material relating to the rise,
progress and termination of the American
Revolutionary War. Incl political pamphlets
from the period 1763-1783, both American
and British. Among the largest collection of
this kind.

PA —UNIVERSITY OF PITTSBURGH,
Darlington Memorial Library, Special
Collections, 601 Cathedral of Learning,
Pittsburgh, 15260. Dennis Lambert,
Darlington Librn
Holdings: Vols (17,000) Cat Mss Maps Pix
Notes: The Darlington Collection is
especially rich in American history of the
colonial period, the French and Indian War,
the Revolution, and the War of 1812 with
geographical emphasis on Western

U.S.—HISTORY—REVOLUTION (cont.)

Pennsylvania and Ohio Valley history to 1870 and on Pittsburgh history to 1900. Indian treaties, captivity accounts, US and Pennsylvania travel and description, and early American fiction and prose are represented. A partial guide to the Darlington Manuscript Collections is available by writing for *Darlington Memorial Library: A Descriptive Checklist of its Manuscript Collections*, University of Pittsburgh Bibliographic Series 5, 1969. Noncirculating.

PA —WASHINGTON AND JEFFERSON COLLEGE, Library, Washington, 15301. Robert E Connell, Librn
Holdings: Vols 2100 Cat Mss Maps Pix
Notes: A general subject and author card catalog has been prepared for the ms collection. Published description of the collection appears in: Pennsylvania, Historical and Museum Commission, *Historical Manuscript Depositories in Pennsylvania* (Harrisburg, 1965), compiled by Irwin Richman. Incl are materials concerning the "Westward movement"-- letters, land grants, etc. Much on the Revolutionary War, the "Whiskey Rebellion" of 1794. Many other small collections of mss, some containing American Indian and Western Pennsylvania history.

RI —BROWN UNIVERSITY, John Hay Library, 20 Prospect St, Providence, 02912. Mark N Brown, Cur Mss
Holdings: Mss
Notes: Various miscellaneous items and a few colletions involve the American Revolutionary War. Incl the Solomon Drowne Collection (qv); the Charles Warren Lippit Collection (qv); the James Manning Collection (qv); the Sydney S Rider Collection (qv); the George Weedon Manuscript Collection; and the Isaac Backus Collection (qv).

RI —BROWN UNIVERSITY, John Carter Brown Library, Providence, 02912. Norman Fiering, Librn; Everett C Wilkie Jr, Bibliographer; Susan Danforth, Cur Maps & Prints
Notes: Extensive collections, both mss and printed, documenting rise of revolutionary spirit in British colonies and the War of Independence.

RI —RHODE ISLAND STATE ARCHIVES, Library, Room 43, State House, Smith St, Providence, 02903. Phyllis Silva, Dir
Holdings: Cat Mss Maps Microforms
Notes: All original mss, 1638-1860, Colony Records, census, Petition to Gen Assembly, Letters to and from governors, Revolutionary War Records, etc. We are primarily a General Assembly Archives.

SC —COLLEGE OF CHARLESTON LIBRARY, Special Collections Dept, Charleston, 29401.
Notes: Program booklet and guest list of the "Dinner given to the General Society of the Cincinnati by the ... Charleston, South Carolina," April 8, 1908. Includes colored engravings of the Revolutionary War attack upon Fort Moultrie, drawn by one of its defenders, Lieutenant Henry Gray.

SC —FRANCIS MARION COLLEGE, James A Rogers Library, Florence, 29501. H Paul Dove, Dir; Roger K Hux, Special Collections Librn
Holdings: Vols (600) Cat Maps Audiotapes Microforms
Notes: The Pee Dee Region of South Carolina. Emphasis on Colonial and Revolutionary periods, rice and indigo culture, plantations. Includes old rural church library with children's books.

VA —UNIVERSITY OF VIRGINIA, Alderman Library, Manuscripts Dept, Charlottesville, 22901. Edmund Berkeley Jr, Cur
Holdings: Cat Mss Maps Pix
Notes: Personal and official papers of Sir Andrew Snape Hamond and Graham Eden Hamond concern British naval operations during the American Revolution and in the Mediterranean during the Napoleonic Wars. Paul P Hoffman (ed) *Guide to the Naval*

Papers of Sir Andrew Snape Hamond . . . and Sir Graham Eden Hamond . . . (Charlottesville, Va: Microfilm Publications, University of Virginia, 1966). Papers of US and Confederate naval officer Samuel Barron; US fleet surgeon and Brooklyn Navy Yard surgeon Gustavus R B Horner; US naval surgeon John S Whittle on a scientific expedition to the Pacific, 1838-1841; and US naval officer William Conway Whittle on West Indies and Mediterranean cruises, 1823-1831.

VA —VIRGINIA STATE LIBRARY, 12 & Capitol Sts, Richmond, 23219.
Holdings: Vols 6540 Cat Mss Maps Pix Microforms

VA —COLONIAL WILLIAMSBURG FOUNDATION, Research Center Library, PO Drawer C, Williamsburg, 23187. John E Ingram, Research Archivist
Holdings: Vols (30,000) Cat Mss Maps Pix Microforms
Budget: ($20,000)
Notes: Virginia and the Chesapeake in the 17th-18th centuries. Particular strengths include social, economic, agricultural and architectural history. The collection encompasses over 6000 rare books, 18th Century music scores and 12,000 manuscripts, as well as a complete set of Virginia Colonial Records Project microfilm (1000 reels).

U.S. —HISTORY—REVOLUTION—NAVAL OPERATIONS

DC —LIBRARY OF CONGRESS, Geography and Map Division, Washington, 20540. John A Wolter, Chief
Notes: Pierre Ozanne Collection of maps and views of French naval operations during the American Revolution.

U.S.—HISTORY—WHISKEY INSURRECTION, 1794 see Whiskey Insurrection, 1794

U.S.—HISTORY—WAR WITH FRANCE, 1798-1800

NJ —GLOUCESTER COUNTY HISTORICAL SOCIETY LIBRARY, 17 Hunter St, PO Box 409, Woodbury, 08096. Edith E Hoelle, Librn
Holdings: Cat Mss
Notes: Richard Somers was in the US Navy during the War with France and the War with Tripoli. This collection incl lists of ships' stores, letters to and from Somers regarding his command, orders, lists of his crews, receipts for supplies, his Oath of Allegiance as Midshipman (May 8, 1798), memoranda, deeds, etc.

U.S.—HISTORY—TRIPOLITAN WAR, 1801-1805

IL —MILLIKIN UNIVERSITY, Staley Library, 1184 W Main St, Decatur, 62522. Charles E Hale, Librn
Holdings: Vols 50 Cat Mss Pix
Budget: $100
Notes: The Stephen Decatur Collection. The core of this collection was given by John Valentine (1895-1955) to the Millikin University Library in 1947. Also have realia of coins, busts, etc.

NJ —GLOUCESTER COUNTY HISTORICAL SOCIETY LIBRARY, 17 Hunter St, PO Box 409, Woodbury, 08096. Edith E Hoelle, Librn
Holdings: Cat Mss
Notes: Richard Somers was in the US Navy during the War with France and the War with Tripoli. This collection incl lists of ships' stores, letters to and from Somers regarding his command, orders, lists of his crews, receipts for supplies, his Oath of Allegiance as Midshipman (May 8, 1798), memoranda, deeds, etc.

U.S.—HISTORY—WAR OF 1812

GA —GEORGIA SOUTHERN COLLEGE, Library, Statesboro, 30458. Edna Earle

Brown, Acting Dir
Holdings: // Mss Pix
Notes: The Spencer Houghton Cone papers on the War of 1812.

IL —NEWBERRY LIBRARY, 60 W Walton St, Chicago, 60610. Diana Haskell, Cur of Modern Mss
Holdings: Cat

IN —INDIANA UNIVERSITY, Lilly Library, Seventh St, Bloomington, 47405. William R Cagle, Librn
Holdings: Vols (1300) Cat Mss Pix
Notes: Correspondence, log books, legal documents, diaries, speeches, letter copybooks, orderly books, and receipts. 3181 items. Incl prints.

MD —MARYLAND HISTORICAL SOCIETY, Library, 201 W Monument St, Baltimore, 21201. William B Keller, Head Librn
Holdings: Cat Mss Maps Pix
Notes: The Lester S Levy "Star Spangled Banner" Collection, probably the largest in the world--over 250 pieces.

MD —UNIVERSITY OF MARYLAND, BALTIMORE COUNTY, Albin O Kuhn Library and Gallery, 5401 Wilkens Ave, B•ltimore, 21228. Ann Copeland, Special Collections Librn
Holdings: Vols (1500) Uncat Maps
Notes: The Edward G Howard Collection includes many 18th and 19th century first editions of foreign visitors' accounts of their travels through Baltimore and Maryland. These accounts provide excellent descriptions of Maryland history and culture. In addition to local histories and magazines, the collection also includes Francis Scott Key's personal copy of *Maryland in Liberia* and a strong section on the War of 1812. The collection is also strong in 20th century material.

MD —CALVERT MARINE MUSEUM, Library, PO Box 97, Solomons, 20688.
Holdings: Uncat Mss Maps
Notes: Result of an ongoing project with the Nautical Archeological Associates to obtain information on the naval history of Patuxent River during the War of 1812.

MI —UNIVERSITY OF MICHIGAN, William L Clements Library, Ann Arbor, 48109. John C Dann, Dir

Notes: The William L. Clements Library of Americana is a non-circulating rare book library of original source material, printed and manuscript, dealing with America, from the discovery period into the late nineteenth century. The collection includes approximately 55,000 books and pamphlets, 550 linear feet of manuscripts, 4,100 volumes of newspapers, 36,000 maps, 40,000 pieces of sheet music, and 1,000 prints. The collection is strongest for the period of the American Revolution, and includes the papers of Thomas Gage, Sir Henry Clinton, and the Earl of Shelburne. Other areas of strength include antislavery, cartography and geography, discovery and exploration, American Indians, The Civil War, tune-books, sermons and orations, and the War of 1812. There are selective research collections dealing with Christopher Columbus, Thomas Paine, Benjamin Franklin, George Washington, Thomas Jefferson, and the Federalist Papers. Publications describing the collections of the library are: Author/Title catalog of Americana 1493-1860 in the William L. Clements Library . . . 7 volumes, Boston, G. K. Hall, 1970; Guide to the manuscript collections of the William L. Clements Library, by Arlene P. Shy 3d edition, Boston, G. K. Hall, 1978; Guide to the manuscript maps in the William L. Clements Library, compiled by Christian Burn, Ann Arbor, U. of Michigan, 1959; and Research catalog of maps of America, to 1860 in the William L. Clements Library . . . , edited by Douglas W. Marshall, 4 volumes, Boston, G. K. Hall, 1972.

U.S.—HISTORY—WAR OF 1812 (cont.)

MI —DETROIT PUBLIC LIBRARY, Burton
Historical Collection, 5201 Woodward Ave,
Detroit, 48202. Alice Dalligan, Chief

MI —MONROE COUNTY LIBRARY
SYSTEM, Ellis Reference and Information
Center, 3700 S Custer Rd, Monroe, 48161.
Marie D Chulski, Head of Reference
Services

NH —PORTSMOUTH ATHENAEUM, 9
Market Sq, Box 848, Portsmouth, 03801.
Joseph P Copley, Cur
Holdings: Vols Cat Mss
Notes: Incl Larkin Papers, 1758-1798 (235
items); papers of Daniel and John Peirce, ca
1730-1800 (115 items); and papers of NH
Fire and Marine Insurance Co, 1803-1823
(1800 items).

NJ —GLASSBORO STATE COLLEGE,
Savitz Library, Stewart Room, Glassboro,
08028. Clara Kirner, Special Collection
Librn
Holdings: Cat Mss
Notes: Mss collection emphasizes military
orders, letters, enlistment and discharge
papers, Fife and Drum Corps papers and
memorabilia. Also papers of the Gloucester
County, New Jersey military units.

NJ —TRENTON STATE COLLEGE, Roscoe
L West Library, Pennington Rd, PO Box
940, Trenton, 08625. Paul A DuBois, Dir
Holdings: // Cat Mss
Notes: Although officially called "The Sol
Feinstone Collection of the American
Revolution" in honor of the donor, a resident
of Washington Crossing, Pennsylvania, the
collection includes several items dealing with
the War of 1812. The books and pamphlets
were published between 1764 and 1965; ms
material consists of legislative acts
originating both with Parliament and the
New Jersey Assembly, as well as several
letters and miscellaneous items.

NY —BUFFALO & ERIE COUNTY
HISTORICAL SOCIETY, 25 Nottingham
Court, Buffalo, 14216. Herman Sass, Librn
Notes: Collection strong on War of 1812,
Civil War and the two World Wars. Material
on all phases of military history. In various
resource departments. No separate catalog.

NY —SAINT LAWRENCE UNIVERSITY,
Owen D Young Library, Canton, 13617.
Mahlon Peterson, Librn
Holdings: Cat Mss Maps Pix
Notes: The Parish-Rosseel Papers. The bulk
of the material falls within the period 1807-
1816 and consists of the correspondence of
David Parish and Joseph Rosseel. Very
valuable source of information on the
settlement of the North Country and the
War of 1812 as well as the general social and
economic conditions of the time. Approx
1600 items.

NY —NEW YORK PUBLIC LIBRARY,
Research Libraries, American History Div,
Fifth Ave & 42 St, New York, 10018.
Holdings: Vols (25,000) Maps Microforms
Notes: See *Dictionary Catalog of the History
of Americas Collection* (Boston: G K Hall,
1961), 28 vols.

NY —UNIVERSITY OF ROCHESTER, Rush
Rhees Library, Department of Rare Books
and Special Collections, Rochester, 14627.
Peter Dzwonkoski, Librn
Holdings: Mss
Notes: William Henry Seward papers, which
contain approximately 250,000 items, relate
to American political, social, and diplomatic
history, ca 1825-1872. Also a collection of
approx 4000 pamphlets of the same time
period and subjects, which were owned by

him. The latter are fully cataloged. Each
letter in the collection has been indexed by
name of letter writer. Unpublished register is
available in repository.

PA —UNIVERSITY OF PITTSBURGH,
Darlington Memorial Library, Special
Collections, 601 Cathedral of Learning,
Pittsburgh, 15260. Dennis Lambert,
Darlington Librn
Holdings: Vols (17,000) Cat Mss Maps Pix
Notes: The Darlington Collection is
especially rich in American history of the
colonial period, the French and Indian War,
the Revolution, and the War of 1812 with
geographical emphasis on Western
Pennsylvania and Ohio Valley history to
1870 and on Pittsburgh history to 1900.
Indian treaties, captivity accounts, US and
Pennsylvania travel and description, and
early American fiction and prose are
represented. A partial guide to the
Darlington Manuscript Collections is
available by writing for *Darlington Memorial
Library: A Descriptive Checklist of its
Manuscript Collections,* University of
Pittsburgh Bibliographic Series 5, 1969.
Noncirculating.

RI —BROWN UNIVERSITY, John Hay
Library, 20 Prospect St, Providence, 02912.
Mark N Brown, Cur Mss
Holdings: // Mss
Notes: Papers of Henry Wheaton, Jurist, US
Charge d'Affaires to Denmark, and Minister
to Prussia. Brown Class of 1802. A
collection of 275 letters and mss for the
period 1786-1899, chiefly correspondence of
Henry Wheaton and his family in Europe
and America concerning personal
diplomatic, legal, and political affairs,
especially during the War of 1812. Also
Wheaton's diaries, 1827-1835, an 1835 diary
kept by his daughter, Abby, and biographical
notes about Wheaton and his uncle, Dr Levi
Wheaton, Professor of Medicine at Brown.

VA —PORTSMOUTH PUBLIC LIBRARY,
601 Court St, Portsmouth, 23704. Dean
Burgess, Library Dir
Holdings: Vols 1300 Cat
Notes: Although particularly interested in
Tidewater and Lower Tidewater history, we
buy most books we can locate on Virginia as
well. In 1972 we were given the
distinguished collection of Judge White of
Lynnhaven.

ON —FORT MALDEN NATIONAL
HISTORIC PARK, Library, 100 Laird Ave,
Box 38, Amherstburg, N9V 2Z2, Can. Sally
E Snyder, Librn
Holdings: Vols (150) Cat Mss Maps Pix
Slides Microforms

ON —NIAGARA FALLS PUBLIC LIBRARY,
4848 Victoria Ave, Niagara Falls, L2E 4C5,
Can. D Van Slyke, Chief Librn

U.S.—HISTORY—1825-1872

DC —NATIONAL ARCHIVES AND
RECORDS SERVICE, National Archives
Library, Pennsylvania Ave & Eighth St NW,
Washington, 20408.
Notes: Journals kept by Commodore
Matthew C Perry (1794-1858) on his
expedition to Japan inn 1852-1854. The three
journals were kept by Perry as his personal
account of the trip, undertaken as a
diplomatic mission to establish trade
relations with Japan. Incl numerous
illustrations of rare birds, flowers, fish,
animals, and the life and ceremonies of trade
ports along Perry's route.

U.S.—HISTORY—BLACK HAWK WAR, 1832 see Black Hawk War, 1832

U.S.—HISTORY—WAR WITH MEXICO, 1845-1848

CA —CALIFORNIA HISTORICAL
SOCIETY, Schubert Hall Library, 2099
Pacific Ave, San Francisco, 94109. Bruce L
Johnson, Library Dir
Holdings: Vols (50,000) Cat Mss Maps Pix
See also entry under California - History.

CT —YALE UNIVERSITY, Box 1603A, Yale
Station, New Haven, 06520.
Notes: Large collection of Mexican tracts
and broadsides.

LA —TULANE UNIVERSITY, Howard-Tilton
Memorial Library, Special Collections Div,
7001 Freret St, New Orleans, 70118. Wilbur
E Meneray, Librn
Holdings: Cat Mss
Notes: Official, personal and family
correspondence of Albert Sidney Johnston
incl letter and order books. Incl the Mexican
War, the Utah Campaign and the Civil War.
Indexed.

MS —UNIVERSITY OF SOUTHERN
MISSISSIPPI, William David McCain
Graduate Library, Box 5148, Southern Sta,
Hattiesburg, 39406.
Holdings: Cat Mss
Notes: Correspondence and records (1847-
1892) relating to Alexander Melvorne
Jackson's participation in the Mexican War,
his service as Secretary of the State of the
New Mexico Territory (1857-1861), and his
participation in the Civil War on the side of
the Confederacy. Among his correspondents
were Albert Gallatin Brown, Reuben Davis,
Miguel A Otero, Jacob Thompson, and John
Ireland. Incl are photographs of Austin,
Texas, ca 1890. 1.1 cubic feet holdings.

NY —NEW YORK PUBLIC LIBRARY,
Research Libraries, American History Div,
Fifth Ave & 42 St, New York, 10018.
Holdings: Vols (25,000) Maps Microforms
Notes: See *Dictionary Catalog of the History
of Americas Collection* (Boston: G K Hall,
1961), 28 vols.

NY —US MILITARY ACADEMY LIBRARY,
West Point, 10996. Marie T Capps, Maps &
Mss Librn
Holdings: Vols (2000) // Mss Maps
Notes: One descriptive catalog of a portion
of this collection is: Marie T Capps and
Theodore G Stroup, *US Military Academy
Library Map Collection: The Period of the
American Revolution 1753-1800* (West
Point, NY: US Military Academy, 1971), 82
pp.

PA —US ARMY MILITARY HISTORY
INSTITUTE, Carlisle Barracks, 17013.
Richard J Sommers, Chief Archivist-
Historian
Holdings: Cat //
Notes: The James D Graham papers
(Mexican War Miscellaneous Collection), his
diary, 13-26 April 1848, recounting personal
observations on his mission to Mexico City
for President Polk.

TX —UNIVERSITY OF TEXAS,
ARLINGTON, Library, PO Box 19497,
Arlington, 76019. Chas Colley, Dir Special
Collections
Holdings: Vols (8000) Cat Mss Maps Pix
Microforms
Notes: Research collection documenting the
history and culture of Texas and the
American Southwest. Contains a wide range
of Texana, especially pre-statehood Texas.
Incl one of the most important collections
relating to the US-Mexcan War, incl all of
the items from the Eberstadt Collection
relevant to the war. Much rare 19th century
Texana. Library routinely acquires all
monographs and serial secondary
publications of research importance. Separate
catalog.

TX —UNIVERSITY OF TEXAS LIBRARIES,
General Libraries, Barker Texas History
Center, PO Box P, Austin, 78712. Don
Carleton, Dir
Holdings: Vols (132,000) Cat Mss Maps Pix
Slides Phonorecords Audiotapes Microforms
Notes: See description of collection under
Texas-History.

TX —EL PASO PUBLIC LIBRARY, Mexican
American Collection, 501 N Oregon, El
Paso, 79901. Iris Espino, Librn
Notes: History and culture of Mexico from
pre-Columbian times to the present.

TX —STAR OF THE REPUBLIC MUSEUM,
Library, PO Box 317, Washington, 77880. D
Ryan Smith Dir
Holdings: Vols Cat Mss Maps Slides
Notes: Books, maps, mss, etc dealing with
the Texas republic; scope incl Spanish
Colonial period and Mexican War (1690-
1848).

U.S.—HISTORY—UTAH CAMPAIGN, 1857

LA —TULANE UNIVERSITY, Howard-Tilton
Memorial Library, Special Collections Div,

U.S.—HISTORY—UTAH CAMPAIGN, 1857 (cont.)

7001 Freret St, New Orleans, 70118. Wilbur E Meneray, Librn
Holdings: Cat Mss
Notes: Official, personal and family correspondence of Albert Sidney Johnston incl letter and order books. Incl the Mexican War, the Utah Campaign and the Civil War. Indexed.

U.S.—HISTORY—CIVIL WAR

AL —BIRMINGHAM PUBLIC LIBRARY, Dept of Archives & Mss, 2020 Seventh Ave N, Birmingham, 35203. Marvin Y Whiting, Archivist & Cur
Holdings: Mss
Notes: Antebellum period, although some Civil War materials are also represented in the collection. 15,000 ms pieces.

AL —MOBILE PUBLIC LIBRARY, Special Collections Div, 701 Government St, Mobile, 36602.
Notes: Personal papers, documents, etc, of Daniel Geary, Director of Defenses of Mobile, 1861- .

†AL —MUSEUMS OF THE CITY OF MOBILE, Reference Library, 355 Government St, Mobile, 36602. Caldwell Delaney, Adminr
Notes: Confederate States of America Coll.

AL —TROY STATE UNIVERSITY, Library, Troy, 36081. Kenneth Croslin, Dir of University Libraries
Holdings: // Mss
Notes: Incl the John Horry Dent Papers, 1851-1892, 25 vols, mss, farm journals, account books, letters, legal documents, clippings and miscellaneous memorabilia of a planter, plantation owner, investor, who lived in Barbour County, Alabama from 1837 to 1867 and in Floyd County, Georgia from 1867 to 1892. Typescript from tape "Sharecropping farming in Pike County, Alabama in early 1900's" (56p). Typescript of tapes of "Source material extracted from Troy, Alabama newspapers, 1871-1935" indexed under 9 subjects by color code.

AZ —NORTHERN ARIZONA UNIVERSITY, Special Collection Library, CU Box 6022, Flagstaff, 86011. Peter M Whiteley, Coordr/Archivist; William Mullane, Librn
Notes: Joe Strachan Collection; copies of letters written by Captain Carl Kostmann, Company C, 3rd Iowa Infantry, during the Civil War. The letters are in German, 1860-1863.

CA —CLAREMONT COLLEGES, Honnold Library, Ninth & Dartmouth, Claremont, 91711. Tania Rizzo, Special Collections Dept Head
Holdings: Vols (70,000) Cat
Notes: Subject strength.

CA —UNIVERSITY OF CALIFORNIA, SAN DIEGO, Central University Library, Mandeville Dept of Special Collections, La Jolla, 92093. Lynda Corey Claassen, Head
Notes: Manuscript collection incl family correspondence from the American Revolution and the Civil War.

CA —OCCIDENTAL COLLEGE, Library, 1600 Campus Rd, Los Angeles, 90041. Michael C Sutherland, Special Collections Librn
Holdings: Uncat Mss Maps Pix
Notes: Books and pamphlets, arranged chronologically by subject. Access is by bibliography and inventory list.

CA —CALIFORNIA INSTITUTE OF TECHNOLOGY, Robert A Millikan Memorial Library, Archives, 1201 E California Blvd, Pasadena, 91125. Judith R Goodstein, Archivist
Holdings: Vols (3000) Uncat Mss Maps Pix Slides Phonorecords Audiotapes Videotapes 16mm Films Microforms
Notes: Family letters relating to 19th century American life before and during the Civil War (the Morley papers; the Amos G Throop papers).

CA —LINCOLN MEMORIAL SHRINE, A K Smiley Public Library, 125 W Vine St,

Redlands, 92373. Larry E Burgess, Archivist
Holdings: Vols (3000) Cat Mss Maps Pix Slides Phonorecords 16mm Films Microforms
Budget: ($18,000)
Notes: One of the larger collections on Lincoln and his times. Incl broadsides, letters, prints, campaign badges, stamps, coins, medals; bust, by George Grey Bernard. Endowment of Watchorn Lincoln Memorial Association. There is an additional pamphlet collection of more than 3000 pieces; an extensive philately collection incl first-day covers, commemorative and foreign issues, and Civil War

CA —SAN DIEGO PUBLIC LIBRARY, 820 E St, San Diego, 92101. Marion L Buckner, Supervising Librn
Holdings: Vols 2700 Cat Maps Pix

CA —SAN DIEGO STATE UNIVERSITY, Malcolm A Love Library, 5300 Campanile Dr, San Diego, 92182. D Dickinson, Univ Librn; Don L Bosseau, Dir
Notes: U S Civil War Collection. Includes original documents, letters, diaries, journals, maps, drawings, medals, pictures, tokens, scrapbooks of soldiers, Confederate money, stamps, special issue newspapers, sheet music and other artifacts from the period 1811-1869.

CA —UNIVERSITY OF CALIFORNIA, SANTA BARBARA, Library, Dept of Special Collections, Santa Barbara, 93106. Christian F Brun, Head
Holdings: Vols 31,000 Cat Mss Maps Pix Microforms
Budget: $7000
Notes: The William Wyles Collection of Americana. Incl American Civil War, Abraham Lincoln, Westward Movement, Americans for the Orient, slavery, abolition movement, etc.

CA —STANFORD UNIVERSITY LIBRARIES, Cecil H Green Library, Stanford, 94305. Michael T Ryan, Cur
Holdings: Mss
Notes: US Civil War and papers of General Frederick Steele, and Brigadier General William R Schafter.

CT —TRINITY COLLEGE LIBRARY, Watkinson Library, 300 Summit St, Hartford, 06106. Jeffrey Kaimowitz, Cur
Holdings: Cat

DE —HAGLEY MUSEUM AND LIBRARY, Eleutherian Mills-Hagley Foundation Inc, PO Box 3630, Greenville, 19807. Richmond D Williams, Dir; Heddy A Richter, Imprints Librn
Holdings: Mss
Notes: 1500 cubic feet of mss. The library holds the books and papers of Pierre Samuel du Pont de Nemours (173-1817), physiocrat and economic theorist; the papers of E I du Pont (1771-1834), powder company founder; and his brother Victor (1767-1827). The Admiral Samuel Francis du Pont (1803-1865) papers contain some 49,000 items documenting in detail his naval career and the papers of General Henry du Pont (1812-1889) illuminate Delaware's history during the Civil war. Also held are the papers of Colonel Henry A du Pont (1838-1926).

DC —AMERICAN NATIONAL RED CROSS, National Headquarters Library, 17th & D St NW, Washington, 20006. Roberta F Biles, Library Director
Holdings: Vols 180 Cat Mss
Notes: The Clara Barton Memorial Collection. Incl *The Rebellion Record*, 12 vols; *History of the US Sanitary Commission; Sanitary Commission* pamphlets (bound); *Annals of the United States Christian Commission; Our Women of the War; Hospital Transports*; camp and hospital manuals and recipes used in special diet kitchens. (Publication dates 1855-1888.)

DC —GEORGETOWN UNIVERSITY, Library, Special Collections Div, 37 & O Sts NW, Washington, 20057. George M Barringer, Special Collections Librn; Nicholas B Sheetz, Mss Librn
Holdings: Mss
Notes: Correspondnece of William Oswald Dundas. Outgoing letters addressed chiefly to Edward I Devitt, SJ (1841-1920),

archivist and professor of history at Georgetown College and Henry J Shandelle, SJ (1848-1925), librarian and professor of English and philosophy; extensive recollections of student life at Georgetown 1856-58 and of life in Washington during the 1850's. Incoming correspondence incl letters from James Edward Calhoun (1796-1889) of South Carolina, cousin and brother-in-law of John C Calhoun and a member of Long's expedition of 1819-1820; and official letters from various public officials, incl Sen James Vardaman of Mississippi, Gov William Hodges Mann of Virginia, and Robert Bacon, all in connection with Dundas' attempts to obtain a roster of Confederate troops for Fr Devitt. Family correspondence sundry family documents and personalreminiscences complete the collection.

DC —LIBRARY OF CONGRESS, Manuscript Division, Washington, 20540. John C Broderick, Chief
Notes: Papers of General William Tecumseh Sherman.

GA —EMORY UNIVERSITY, Robert W Woodruff Library, Special Collections Dept, Atlanta, 30322. Linda M Matthews, Head Special Collections; Virginia J H Cain, Processing Archivist; Richard H F Lindemann, Reference Archivist
Holdings: Vols (16,000) Cat Mss Maps Pix Microforms

GA —CARNEGIE LIBRARY, Henderson Room, 607 Broad St, Rome, 30161. Beatrice Millican, Librn
Holdings: Vols (450) Cat Maps
Budget: ($2700)

GA —GEORGIA SOUTHERN COLLEGE, Library, Statesboro, 30458. Edna Earle Brown, Acting Dir
Holdings: // Mss Pix
Notes: The Spencer Wallace Cone papers on the Civil War.

IL —McLEAN COUNTY HISTORICAL SOCIETY LIBRARY & MUSEUM, 201 E Grove, Bloomington, 61701. Barbara Dunbar, Dir; Greg Koos, Archivist
Holdings: Vols (3000) Cat Mss Maps Pix
Notes: Illinois history, emphasis on McLean County. Strong in military heritage of Illinois, particularly the 33rd and 94th regiments (III Vol Inf) in the Civil War. Incl 150 LF archives and 1000 pictures. Photocopying.

IL —CHICAGO HISTORICAL SOCIETY, Library, Clark St at North Ave, Chicago, 60614. Robert L Brubaker, Librn
Holdings: Vols (150,000) Cat Mss Maps Pix
Notes: Incl Meserve Americana (27 vols), mostly of Civil War era (8000 portraits).

IL —CHICAGO PUBLIC LIBRARY, Special Collections Div, Cultural Center, 78 E Washington St, Chicago, 60602. Laura Linard, Cur
Holdings: Vols (7000) Cat Mss Maps Pix
Notes: The Civil War and American History Research Collection at the Chicago Public Library is our largest collection. It spans the pre-war sectional crisis as well as Reconstruction. Scarce slavery pamphlets; large collection of regimental histories; manuscripts of US Grant, Sherman, Breckinridge; letters and diaries of soldiers and other officers; original photographs of individuals and field shots; Confederate Battle Plan for the Battle of Shiloh (original); swords, rifles, uniforms, flags and other military accessories. A substantial part of this collection has been cataloged. (The museum objects are inventoried (Grand Army Hall and Memorial Association of Illinois Collection).See *Treasures of The Chicago Public Library*, comp by Thomas A Oriando and Marie Gecik, 1977, pp 36-79.

IL —NEWBERRY LIBRARY, 60 W Walton St, Chicago, 60610. Diana Haskell, Cur of Modern Mss
Holdings: Cat
Notes: Extensive collection.

IL —GALESBURG PUBLIC LIBRARY, 40 E Simmons St, Galesburg, 61401. Jane M Willenborg, Special Collections Librn
Holdings: Vols (6113) Cat Mss Maps Pix Slides Phonorecords Audiotapes Microforms
Budget: ($10,500)
Notes: Incl extensive collection of Illinois

U.S.—HISTORY—CIVIL WAR (cont.)

histories--state, county, city, town, and village; Illinois laws and statutes, 1829-1977; state and county atlases and plat books (listed in *United States Atlases,* vol II, Library of Congress, 1953); Lincoln books; works of Illinois authors; Civil War Illinois regimental histories; photographs of local interest (incl numerous photos of Carl Sandburg); and local newspapers and city directories on microfilm. Incl mss (26 ft), 79 maps, 4371 pictures, 3515 slides. 3053 negatives (some are duplicates of the photographs). Separate catalog. Restricted use: noncirculating; limited photocopying.

IL —KNOX COLLEGE, Henry M Seymour Library, Galesburg, 61401. Douglas L Wilson, Dir
Holdings: Vols 4870 Cat Maps Pix

IL —ILLINOIS STATE UNIVERSITY, Milner Library, Dept of Special Collections, Normal, 61761. Robert Sokan, Librn
Holdings: Vols 1200 Cat
Notes: The Harold K Sage Lincoln Collection consists of approx 1200 book items, 1500 pamphlets which are uncataloged, and ephemera (ie newspaper clippings, correspondence). The collection incl biographies, collections of his speeches, commemoration ceremony speeches, juvenalia and books dealing with Lincoln's relationship to special subject areas such as religion and slavery. Many of the books are limited editions, persentation or autographed copies with correspondence from authors and/or editors inserted.

IL —ILLINOIS STATE HISTORICAL SOCIETY, Library, Old State Capitol, Springfield, 62706. Roger D Bridges, Head Librn
Holdings: Vols (160,000) Cat Mss Maps Pix Microforms
Notes: Downs 2192.

IN —INDIANA UNIVERSITY, Lilly Library, Seventh St, Bloomington, 47405. William R Cagle, Librn
Holdings: Vols 5000 Cat Mss
Notes: Emphasis on materials printed during Lincoln's lifetime. Mss incl papers and correspondence of Lincoln, members of his family, and members of his cabinet.

IN —WILLARD LIBRARY, 21 First Ave, Evansville, 47710. Joan Elliott, Special Collections Librn
Holdings: Vols 500 Cat Mss
Budget: ($4000)
Notes: Incl books and pamphlets (lives of generals, battle accounts, memoirs); some letters and diaries; *War of the Rebellion.*

IN —BUTLER UNIVERSITY, Irwin Library, Hugh Thomas Miller Rare Book Room, 4600 Sunset Ave, Indianapolis, 46208. Gisela Terrell, Rare Books Librn
Holdings: Vols Cat Mss Newspapers
Notes: Lincoln Collection. Assembled for the greater part by Charles W Moores, 1862-1923; accepted by Bulter U 1925; sorted and catalogued 1981-82. The newspapers, clippings, other memorabilia. Books and pamphlets include materials related to the Civil War in general. An annotated bibliography of the booklets, pamphlets and most mss was printed in 1983; it is available for $10. A related collection of materials about Lincoln statues and their sculptors remains to be sorted.

IN —MORRISSON-REEVES LIBRARY, 80 N Sixth St, Richmond, 47374. Harriet E Bard, Librn
Holdings: Vols 800 Cat
Notes: Clarence M Brown Memorial Collection emphasizing the Civil War and the life of Abraham Lincoln. Some vols are library use only.

IA —STATE HISTORICAL SOCIETY OF IOWA LIBRARY, 402 Iowa Ave, Iowa City, 52240. Darold J Brown, Librn
Holdings: Vols 2500 Cat Mss
Notes: General collection, plus specific Iowa materials incl regimental histories. Mss incl diaries, records of officers, regiments.

KY —WESTERN KENTUCKY UNIVERSITY, Kentucky Library, Bowling Green, 42101. Riley Handy, Head, Special

Collections; Connie Mills, Maps & Music Librn; Nancy Baird, Photographs Librn; Nancy Solley, Conservation Librn
Holdings: Vols (25,000) Cat Mss Maps Pix Microforms
Notes: Besides Kentucky history, other strengths are Mammoth Cave, South Union Shakers, Kentucky religion; and steamboat photos (3300 cataloged pictures); 8000 Kentucky postal cards, etc.

LA —LOUISIANA STATE UNIVERSITY, Troy H Middleton Library, Baton Rouge, 70803. Lance E Dickson, Acting Dir
Holdings: Vols 5000 Uncat Maps Pix
Notes: Core is composed of the Warren L Jones Lincoln Collection. Incl the major Lincoln biographies pamphlets, photographs, periodicals, broadsides, museum objects, special editions, and some items pertaining to the Civil War.

LA —TULANE UNIVERSITY, Howard-Tilton Memorial Library, Special Collections Div, 7001 Freret St, New Orleans, 70118. Wilbur E Meneray, Librn
Holdings: Cat Mss Maps Pix
Notes: An extensive collection of letters and diaries of Louisiana soldiers and officers in the Civil War. Also includes some correspondence of such Civil War Generals as P G T Beauregard, T J Jackson, A S Johnston, R E Lee, G G Shepley, J H Stibbs, R Taylor and M J Thompson.

ME —BOWDOIN COLLEGE, Library, Brunswick, 04011. Dianne M Gutscher, Cur of Special Collections
Holdings: Mss Pix
Notes: (1) The Chamberlain Papers consist of 1900 mss pieces of correspondence, addresses, lecture notes, diaries, and clippings relating to Chamberlain's career in the United States Army (1862-1865), as governor of Maine (1867-1870), and as president of Bowdoin College (1871-1883). (2) The Fessenden Family Papers contain 4000 mss for the period 1801-1908 and incl almost 1300 letters written by William Pitt Fessenden, US Senator from Maine, 1854-1869, and Secretary of the Treasury, 1864-65, and about 50 letters written by William Pitt's sons, James and Francis, during their service in the Union Army. (3) The Oliver Otis Howard Papers consist of more than 150,000 pieces of correspondence, articles, lectures, and ephemera for the period 1843-1908, covering his services as a Civil War officer, as founder of the Freedmen's Bureau, as president ofHoward University, and as superintendent of the US Military Academy at West Point. (4) The Charles Henry Howard Papers contain more than 400 pieces of correspondence, articles, and addresses, 1852-1907, of this Civil War officer and Secretary of the American Missionary Association. (5) The Hubbard Family Papers contain more than 12,000 pieces of correspondence and other mss materials relating to the Hubbard Family, for the period 1794-1915, and incl letters, journals, and military records of John Barrett Hubbard and Thomas Hamlin Hubbard, who served in the Union Army. (6) The McArthur Family Papers, containing ca 8000 ms items from this Limington, Maine, family, cover the years 1790-1890, and incl letters and documents for the Civil War and Reconstruction years, financial records, diaries and journals, and military records.

ME —MAINE HISTORICAL SOCIETY, Library, 485 Congress St, Portland, 04101.
Holdings: Vols (60,000) Cat Mss Maps Pix
Notes: The Society's holdings cover all of Maine in its scope, with special emphasis on the Portland region.

MD —HOOD COLLEGE, Joseph Henry Apple Library, Rosemont Ave, Frederick, 21701.
Holdings: Vols 500 Cat
Budget: $500
Notes: The Irving M Landauer Civil War Collection.

MD —SALISBURY STATE COLLEGE, Blackwell Library, Salisbury, 21801. James R Thrash, Dir
Holdings: Vols 1050 Cat
Notes: Millard G Les Callette Memorial Collection.

MD —ANTIETAM NATIONAL BATTLEFIELD SITE, Library, PO Box 158, Sharpsburg, 21782. Betty J Otto, Librn
Holdings: Vols 800 Cat Maps Slides Phonorecords Audiotapes 16mm Films Filmstrips Microforms
Notes: Civil War copies of limited letters and diaries, monographs of regiments and soldiers who fought in the Maryland Campaign of Sept 1862. Limited. Noncirculating.

MA —MEMORIAL HALL LIBRARY, Elm Sq, Andover, 01810. Nancy C Jacobson, Dir
Holdings: Vols 100 // Cat Mss Maps Pix
Notes: Incl original drawing of Lincoln by Charles Barry, Springfield, Ill, 1860.

MA —BOSTON UNIVERSITY, Mugar Memorial Library, Special Collections Dept, 771 Commonwealth Ave, Boston, 02215. Howard B Gotlieb, Dir
Holdings: Cat Mss Pix
Notes: Correspondence books.

MA —STATE LIBRARY OF MASSACHUSETTS, 341 State House, Boston, 02133. Gaspar Caso, State Librn
Holdings: Vols 5000 Cat Mss Maps Pix
Notes: Especially strong on New England contribution.

MA —HARVARD UNIVERSITY LIBRARY, Widener Library, American History Collection, Cambridge, 02138. F Nathaniel Bunker, Bibliographer; Charles Warren, Bibliographer
Holdings: Cat
Notes: For pamphlets, see *Harvard Library Notes,* 1 (1922); pp 160-162.

MA —CONCORD FREE PUBLIC LIBRARY, 129 Main St, Concord, 01742. Rose Marie Mitten, Dir
Holdings: Cat Mss Maps Pix Slides
Notes: Extensive collection.

MA —LYNN PUBLIC LIBRARY, 5 N Common St, Lynn, 01902. Barbara J Schaller, Dir
Holdings: Cat Maps

MI —UNIVERSITY OF MICHIGAN, William L Clements Library, Ann Arbor, 48109. John C Dann, Dir

Notes: The William L. Clements Library of Americana is a non-circulating rare book library of original source material, printed and manuscript, dealing with America, from the discovery period into the late nineteenth century. The collection includes approximately 55,000 books and pamphlets, 550 linear feet of manuscripts, 4,100 volumes of newspapers, 36,000 maps, 40,000 pieces of sheet music, and 1,000 prints. The collection is strongest for the period of the American Revolution, and includes the papers of Thomas Gage, Sir Henry Clinton, and the Earl of Shelburne. Other areas of strength include antislavery, cartography and geography, discovery and exploration, American Indians, The Civil War, tune-books, sermons and orations, and the War of 1812. There are selective research collections dealing with Christopher Columbus, Thomas Paine, Benjamin Franklin, George Washington, Thomas Jefferson, and the Federalist Papers. Publications describing the collections of the library are: Author/Title catalog of Americana 1493-1860 in the William L. Clements Library... 7 volumes, Boston, G. K. Hall, 1970; Guide to the manuscript collections of the William L. Clements Library, by Arlene P. Shy 3d edition, Boston, G. K. Hall, 1978; Guide to the manuscript maps in the William L. Clements Library, compiled by Christian Burn, Ann Arbor, U. of Michigan, 1959; and Research catalog of maps of America, to 1860 in the William L. Clements Library..., edited by Douglas W. Marshall, 4 volumes, Boston, G. K. Hall, 1972.

U.S.—HISTORY—CIVIL WAR (cont.)

MI —ANDREWS UNIVERSITY, James White Library, Berrien Springs, 49104. Marley H Soper, Dir
Holdings: // Cat Pix
Notes: The Courville Civil War Collection. Over 350 items; incl weapons and memorabilia.

MI —MONROE COUNTY LIBRARY SYSTEM, Ellis Reference and Information Center, 3700 S Custer Rd, Monroe, 48161. Marie D Chulski, Head of Reference Services
Holdings: Vols (35,000) Cat Mss Maps PixSlides Audiotapes 16mm Films Microms
Budget: ($15,000)
Notes: Historic Monroe County, tracing its beginnings to 1780, is a definite part of Michigan's history. Many events of the area and citizens are part of Michigan's heritage. The Michigan collection besides general works contains individual county histories, atlases, biographies, etc. The Monroe County history collection contains veteran records, plat books, oral history tapes, family histories, church records, cemetery index, atlases and census records. Genealogy emphasis is not only Monroe County but includes surrounding counties and the states with large migration to the area, such as Ohio, Kentucky, Tennessee and the New England states. Also incl paintings and memorabilia.

MS —UNIVERSITY OF SOUTHERN MISSISSIPPI, William David McCain Graduate Library, Box 5148, Southern Sta, Hattiesburg, 39406.
Holdings: Vols (5000) Mss
Notes: The Ernest A Walen Collection on the history of the Confederate States of America. Incl over 600 Confederate imprints. Various ms collections incl the experiences of individuals on both sides of the conflict. Catalog in progress.

MO —WASHINGTON UNIVERSITY, Libraries, Special Collections Dept, Campus Box 1061, St Louis, 63130.
Notes: Farmer Family correspondence, 1840-1870.

MO —CENTRAL MISSOURI STATE UNIVERSITY, Ward Edwards Library, Warrensburg, 64093. Nancy E Littlejohn, Social Sciences Librn
Holdings: Vols 2200 Cat Microforms
Notes: Incl 662 microforms.

MT —EASTERN MONTANA COLLEGE, Library, 1500 N 30 St, Billings, 59101. Edward Neroda, Dir
Holdings: Mss
Notes: Incl Custer's personal and military papers and those of his widow relating to his career. Also, imcomplete 7th Cavalry records and papers of the Battle of Little Big Horn. Many Civil War papers. Collection formerly at the Custer Battlefield National Monument.

NH —NEW HAMPSHIRE HISTORICAL SOCIETY, Manuscripts Library, 30 Park St, Concord, 03301. Thomas E Camden, Cur
Holdings: Vols (500,000) Cat Mss
Budget: ($12,500)
Notes: Photocopying of individual items only. Consultation of original mss materials strongly encouraged. Mss and books related to New Hampshire history. Especially strong in politics, particularly during the post- Civil War 19th century and the early 20th century. Highlights: Mason Weare Tappan Papers, Austin Pike Papers, Charles Marseilles Papers, Jacob H Gallinger Papers, James O Lyfor Papers and George H Moses Papers. Also papers of many other New Hampshire people, among them, John Badger Bacheldor, Josiah Bartlett, Moody Bedel, Timothy Bedel, Mary Baker Eddy, Joseph A Gilmore, John Hatch George, Isaac Hill, John Langdon, Jeremiah Mason, Charles Sanger Mellen, John Fabyan Parrott, Nathaniel Peabody, William Plumer, Lorenzo Sabine, Jean Joseph Marie Toscan, Robert W Upton, John Wentworth and Levi Woodbury. The records of the Dover (New Hampshire) Manufacturing Company; 650 account books,most of which were kept by general merchants in New Hampshire during the 18th and 19th centuries; town records, mostly before 1825, for approx 230 New Hampshire towns; and military records and orderly books relating to New Hampshire military units of the 18th and 19th centuries (French & Indian War through the Civil War). About 500,000 ms pieces, 4000 books, 1000 maps.

NJ —PRINCETON UNIVERSITY, Library, Manuscript Collection, Nassau St, Princeton, 08540. Jean F Preston, Cur
Notes: The James Perkins Walker manuscripts collection, which fills 6 ms boxes, is strong in Civil War materials. See *Manuscripts*, v 17 no 2, p 39-42. An unpublished typescript guide (7 p) is available in the Library.

NY —BUFFALO & ERIE COUNTY HISTORICAL SOCIETY, 25 Nottingham Court, Buffalo, 14216. Herman Sass, Librn
Notes: Collection strong on War of 1812, Civil War and the two World Wars. Material on all phases of military history. In various resource departments. No separate catalog.

NY —SAINT LAWRENCE UNIVERSITY, Owen D Young Library, Canton, 13617. Mahlon Peterson, Librn
Holdings: Mss Pix
Notes: This collection consists of letters written home by two soldiers in the Union Army between 1861 and 1864 (approx 100 items). Also the papers of Pryce Lewis, a spy for the Union Army during the Civil War who later served as bailiff of Old Capitol Prison for the Union Army (approx 200 items).

NY —FENTON HISTORICAL SOCIETY, Library, 67 South Washington, Jamestown, 14701. Ellen Fessenden, Co-Dir; Candy Larson, Co-Dir
Holdings: Vols 350 Mss
Notes: Incl muster rolls and histories of New York State Regiments, records of GAR James M Brown Post, Jamestown, letters and diaries of soldiers.

NY —COLUMBIA UNIVERSITY LIBRARIES, Rare Book & Manuscript Library, 801 Butler Library, 535 W 114 St, New York, 10027. Kenneth A Lohf, Librn
Holdings: Mss
Notes: Incl Professor Allan Nevin's files (40,000 items), US Civil War Collection (1300 items), Peter Wellington Alexander papers (7500 items), and Sydney Howard Gay papers (20,000 items). Restricted use.

NY —NEW YORK HISTORICAL SOCIETY, Library, 170 Central Park W, New York, 10024. James Gregory, Librn
Holdings: Mss
Notes: Incl original mss, illustrative materials, etc.

NY —NEW YORK PUBLIC LIBRARY, Research Libraries, American History Div, Fifth Ave & 42 St, New York, 10018.
Holdings: Vols (25,000) Maps Microforms
Notes: See *Dictionary Catalog of the History of Americas Collection* (Boston: G K Hall, 1961), 28 vols.

†NY —UNION LEAGUE CLUB, Library, 38 E 37th St, New York, 10016. Jane Reed, Librn
Holdings: Vols (30,000)
Notes: American biography, American history, Civil War.

NY —UNIVERSITY CLUB, Library, One W 54 St, New York, 10019. Guy St Clair, Library Dir
Holdings: Vols (100,000) Cat Mss Maps Pix
Notes: A private library for the members of the University Club, their guests, and serious scholars upon written application to the Library Director. Holds the Southern Society Collection of materials on the South, the Civil War and Reconstruction.

NY —SAINT JOHN FISHER COLLEGE, Library, Rochester, 14618.
Notes: Grand Army of the Republic. 1000 items, incl papers, records, Civil War records.

NY —UNIVERSITY OF ROCHESTER, Rush Rhees Library, Department of Rare Books and Special Collections, Rochester, 14627. Peter Dzwonkoski, Librn
Holdings: Mss
Notes: Thurlow Weed, 1797-1882. Papers of this American journalist; editor of the *Albany (NY) Evening Journal.* Influence in 19th century American politics. Each letter in the collection has been indexed by name of letter writer. Unpublished register available in the repository. Also, the William Henry Seward papers, which contain aproximately 150,000 items, relate to American political, social, and diplomatic history, ca 1825-1872. Also a collection of approx 4000 pamphlets of the same time period and subjects, which were owned by him. The latter are fully cataloged. Each letter in the collection has been indexed by name of letter writer. Unpublished register is available in repository.

NC —UNIVERSITY OF NORTH CAROLINA, CHAPEL HILL, Wilson Library, Rare Book Collection, Chapel Hill, 27514. Paul S Koda, Cur of Rare Books
Holdings: Vols 825 Cat
Notes: The Wilmer Collection of Civil War Novels consists of over 825 novels from 1861 to the present concerning the Civil War, as well as related bibliographical material.

NC —DUKE UNIVERSITY, William R Perkins Library, Manuscript Dept, Durham, 27706. Ellen Gartrell, Cur of Mss
Holdings: Cat Mss
Notes: Strong collection incl papers of many officers (R E Lee, P T G Beauregard, etc), Confederate governments, and leaders (Jefferson Davis, etc), thousands of letters and diaries from Union and Confederate soldiers and homefront.

OH —OHIO UNIVERSITY, Vernon R Alden Library, Department of Archives and Special Collections, Athens, 45701. Gary A Hunt, Head
Holdings: Mss
Notes: The Brown Family Papers, containing over 400 letters written by members of the Brown family, early settlers in Athens County, Ohio. Most of the letters deal with the Civil War, in particular activities of the Ohio 36th Regiment, the West Virginia 4th Regiment, and the Kentucky campaigns.

OH —OHIO UNIVERSITY, Vernon R Alden Library, Athens, 45701. Kent Mulliner, Africana Specialist
Notes: Civil War letters and mss of the Brown and Van Voorhis families, both among the earliest settlers in southeastern Ohio. Mostly written by three members of the family serving in the Union armies between 1861 and 1865.

OH —PUBLIC LIBRARY OF CINCINNATI & HAMILTON COUNTY, History Dept, 800 Vine St, Cincinnati, 45202. J Richard Abell, Head
Holdings: Vols 4470 Cat
Notes: Above count does not incl Civil War biographies unless they are classified within the Civil War numbers. Of the 4168 volumes 1033 are Civil War Military Unit Histories.

OH —WESTERN RESERVE HISTORICAL SOCIETY, History Library, William P Palmer Civil War Collection, 10825 East Blvd, Cleveland, 44106. Kermit J Pike, Dir
Notes: The William P Palmer Civil War Collection.

OH —OHIO HISTORICAL SOCIETY, Archives Library Division, 1982 Velma Ave, Columbus, 43211. Dennis East, Division Chief
Holdings: Vols (96,000) Cat Mss Maps Pix Slides Microforms
Budget: ($18,000)
Notes: This library is the primary collection for Ohio. Most purchases are on the rare and op market. Collecting area is early American history, esp relating to exploration into the Northwest Territory. Major subject areas are Ohio politics and government (8 presidents), military history (good collection of regimental histories and Ohio narratives of the Civil War), economic and social history, local history, esp county histories & atlases and city directories. Also, Ohio

U.S.—HISTORY—CIVIL WAR (cont.)

archaeology, natural history, artifacts. Major media collections are books (96,000), newspapers (25,000 vols and 22,000 microfilm), pictures (50,000), maps (500), manuscripts (1,500,000). Library is noncirculating except through interlibrary loan of microfilm.

OH —WILMINGTON COLLEGE, Watson Library, Quaker Collection, Pyle Center, Box #1227, Wilmington, 45177. Audrey Haines, Cur
Holdings: Vols (6000) Cat Mss Maps Pix Microforms
Notes: Collection houses Wilmington College archives, 1870-present, and serves as repository for the records of the Wilmington and Ohio Valley Yearly Meetings of the Religious Society of Friends (Quakers), ca 1800-present. Also incl 120 Quaker periodical and newsletter titles, ca 1828-present; several hundred pamphlets, tracts, and epistles; 220 genealogical works, primarily Quaker families; and 3900 vols on Quaker history, philosophy, thought, and practice, particularly peace, war, slavery, education, and biography, ca 1750-present. Incl some fiction, poetry and children's books. Rare or fragile materials, reference works, pamphlets, and genealogies do not circulate. Please notify prior to visiting.

PA —US ARMY MILITARY HISTORY INSTITUTE, Carlisle Barracks, 17013. Richard J Sommers, Chief Archivist-Historian
Holdings: Mss Cat
Notes: 950 folders and 50 boxes of mss. The Civil War Collection, personal letters, diaries, memoirs of Federal and Confederate officers and enlisted men serving on virtually every from, 1861-1865.

PA —ADAMS COUNTY HISTORICAL SOCIETY, Drawer A, Gettysburg, 17325. Charles H Glatfelter, Dir
Holdings: Vols 50 Cat Mss Maps Pix
Notes: Emphasis on Adams County and the Gettysburg area. Strength of collection in mss, maps, and pictorial items.

PA —GETTYSBURG COLLEGE, Musselman Library, Gettysburg, 17325. Willis M Hubbard, College Librn
Holdings: Vols (4000) Cat Mss Maps Pix Slides Microforms
Budget: ($1200)
Notes: Incl material on slavery.

PA —GETTYSBURG NATIONAL MILITARY PARK, Gettysburg, 17325. Thomas J Harrison, Cultural Resources Specialist
Holdings: Vols (3000) Cat Mss Maps Pix Slides Microforms
Budget: $400
Notes: Civil War, especially Campaign and Battle of Gettysburg, 1863. Incl pictures (18,000) and slides (3500).

PA —MILITARY ORDER OF THE LOYAL LEGION OF THE UNITED STATES, War Library and Museum, 1805 Pine St, Philadelphia, 19103. Karla M Steffen, Librn
Holdings: Vols (10,000) Cat Mss Maps Pix
Budget: $2000

PA —UNION LEAGUE OF PHILADELPHIA, Library, 140 S Broad St, Philadelphia, 19102. James G Mundy Jr, Librn
Holdings: Vols (23,000) Cat Mss Pix
Notes: Emphasis on Civil War, American social and political history, Philadelphia and Pennsylvania history.

PA —UNIVERSITY OF PITTSBURGH, Hillman Library, Pittsburgh, 15260.
Holdings: Vols (10,000)
Notes: The entire contents of the oldest used book ship in Pittsburgh, the John C Daub Book Store. The collection deals mainly in the areas of military history; works dealing with the Civil War, the World Wars and other military topics; and local history: county histories, city, state or regional histories. Also incl are military works containing colored plates; a large group of Americana, and many framed, colored prints on military subjects.

RI —BROWN UNIVERSITY, John Hay Library, 20 Prospect St, Providence, 02912.

Mark N Brown, Cur Mss
Notes: Several ms collections relating to the American Civil War, incl the Eli H Canfield, 1817-1898, Manuscript Collection (qv) (1500 items); the William Corliss Manuscript Collection (6 diaries); the Ephraim Elmer Ellsworth, 1837-1861, Manuscript Collection (225 items); the Rush Christopher Hawkins, 1831-1920, Manuscript Collection (7000 items); the John Hay, 1838-1905, Manuscript Collection (12,000 items); the Abraham Lincoln, 1809-1865, Manuscript Collection (part of the McLellan-Lincoln Collection, qv) (2600 items); and the Augustus Woodbury, 1835-1895, Manuscript Collection (100 items).

RI —BROWN UNIVERSITY, John Hay Library, McLellan Lincoln Collection, 20 Prospect St, Providence, 02912. Jennifer B Lee, Special Collections Librn
Holdings: Vols (15,000) Cat Mss Pix Phonorecords Microforms
Notes: The McLellan Lincoln Collection was originally the property of Charles Woodberry McLellan, one of 5 great Lincoln collectors at the turn of the century. It was acquired for Brown University in 1923 by John D Rockefeller and others. Increased steadily since that time, the book collection is especially strong in biographies and early editions of the campaign lives. About 85 percent of the titles in *Lincoln Bibliography, 1829-1939*, by Jay Monaghan, are in the collection. Of the 218 foreign titles listed in this bibliography, the collection has some 167 books and 16 films or photostats. In conjunction with The Harris Collection, the John Hay Library holds what is probably the largest number of poems on Lincoln in any one place. There is also a good selection of representative titles of the books which Lincoln read. The ms collection incl original letters, notes and documents, over 950 of which were written or signed by Lincoln; from 1838 on, there is something for every year of his life. The Lincoln mss appear in *The Collected Works of Abraham Lincoln* edited by Roy P Basler, and its supplement. Ms material of Lincoln's family and associates as well as ms facsimiles of holdings of Lincoln material in other libraries are in the collection. The broadsides incl many song sheets, contemporary political sheets, ballots, and posters; also 27 of the 52 printed editions of the "Emancipation Proclamation" listed by Charles Eberstadt in *Lincoln's Emancipation Proclamation*. There is a selection of newspapers for the war years, 1860-1865, and an index of over 11,300 entries for Lincoln items in all existing files of the Illinois newspapers down through the Civil War. The prints, arranged according to Meserve numbers, contains most of theknown photographs of Lincoln, rare engravings, caricatures, Currier and Ives prints, and original oil portraits done by artists of Lincoln's day, as well as original paintings of Lincoln's deathbed by Alonzo Chappel and Alexander Ritchie; some original drawings, as well as a scrapbook of Thomas Nast's Civil War sketches. Sheet music collection has almost every piece of Lincoln sheet music known to exist from minstrel songs to funeral marches, memorial songs and campaign songs. Statuary is well represented and incl two Rogers groups, an original Truman Bartlett plaster statuette of Lincoln, and replicas of Leonard Volk's work. The museum objects incl over 550 medals, mourning and campaign badges, coins, postage stamps and other miscellany. For a more detailed description of the collection, see Esther C Cushman: The McLellan Lincoln Collection at BrownUniversity (Brown University Library, 1928). The collection is housed in two separate rooms plus stack space. It has its own catalog and is restricted to reference use.
See also entry under Hay, John

RI —PROVIDENCE PUBLIC LIBRARY, 150 Empire St, Providence, 02903. Lance J Bauer, Special Collections Librn
Holdings: Vols 5000 Cat Mss Maps Pix
Notes: The Harris Collection on the

American Civil War and Slavery. Incl 18th and 19th century books, rare pamphlets, and periodicals concerning slavery and the slave trade, and origins, progress and results of the Civil Civil War; also regimental histories; military and naval tactics; personal narratives; women's accounts of the Civil War; works on abolition; sheet music; Union and Confederate broadside ballads; Confederate imprints; *The Liberator* from 1843 through the Civil War; and over 85 editions of *Uncle Tom's Cabin* in 14 languages. Excellent primary and secondary sources for the study of the Civil War and slavery. Material must be used in-house. Photocopying when condition of material allows.

SC —COLLEGE OF CHARLESTON LIBRARY, Special Collections Dept, Charleston, 29401.
Notes: Papers incl the Bank of Charleston, SC's ledgers for deposits, loans, bonds, stocks, real estate holdings, businesses' accounts, and accounts with the Bank of Liverpool and the Merchant's National Bank, 1837-1872; also contains a ledger of information regarding foreign investments; *Charleston Mercury* broadside, "The Union is Dissolved;" a request by two Charleston Women (Mrs Minis and Miss Rosalie Cohen) for a pass to travel to New York, approved by Generals Gillmore, Hazen, and Hatch (May 3-10, 1865); papers of numerous families and individuals which incl references to their experiences during the Civil War.

SC —SOUTH CAROLINA HISTORICAL SOCIETY LIBRARY, Fireproof Bldg, 100 Meeting St, Charleston, 29401. Gene Widdell, Dir
Holdings: Vols (50,000) Cat Mss Maps Pix Microforms
Notes: In addition to material dealing exclusively with South Carolina, the society also has holdings in the field of regional history which incl South Carolina, and books relating to other neighboring states.

SC —UNIVERSITY OF SOUTH CAROLINA, Thomas Cooper Library, Columbia, 29208. Kenneth E Toombs, Dir of Libraries; Roger Mortimer, Rare Book Librn
Holdings: Vols 5000 Cat
Notes: This collection is said to be the finest south of the Potomac River. Particularly strong in regimental histories of Northern Army.

TN —UNIVERSITY OF TENNESSEE, CHATTANOOGA, Library, Chattanooga, 37401. Joseph A Jackson, Dir of Libraries
Holdings: Vols 6000 Cat Maps
Notes: The Civil War Collection, a gift of about 3500 vols for The Charles R and Anne Bachman Hyde Collection from Mrs Hyde, who spent a lifetime collecting Southern Americana with particular emphasis on the Confederate viewpoint. Also incl the Wilder Collection, from the Federal point of view. Established as a memorial to Gen John T Wilder. Restricted use: reference only.

TN —LINCOLN MEMORIAL UNIVERSITY, Carnegie Library with Bert Vincent Memorial Wing, Harrogate, 37752. Edgar Archer, Dir
Holdings: Vols 18,000 Cat Maps Pix Phonorecords 16mm Films
Notes: The Abraham Lincoln Center for Lincoln studies located at Abraham Lincoln Museum on the campus of Lincoln University established to display one of the largest collections of Lincoln and Civil War materials in the United States. Described fully in the Lincoln Herald, summer, 1973 (entire issue). National Lincoln Civil War Council Center for study of military surgery and medicine from the Civil War. National headquarters for the Society of Civil War surgeons. Also the center for the study of military music. 7000 pieces of sheet music dating from the War of 1812.

TN —MEMPHIS PINK PALACE MUSEUM, Library, 3050 Central Ave, Memphis, 38111. Coralu D Buddenbahm, Librn
Holdings: Vols (3600) Cat Maps Pix Slides Phonorecords Audiotapes Videotapes 16mm Films Filmstrips
Budget: ($4000)
Notes: Museum specializes in the history

U.S.—HISTORY—CIVIL WAR (cont.)

and culture of the Mid-South. A number of books owned by The Shiloh Military Trail, Inc are on loan to the Museum and are available for reference.

TN —PUBLIC LIBRARY OF NASHVILLE & DAVIDSON COUNTY, Nashville Room, Eighth Ave N & Union St, Nashville, 37203. Mary Glenn Hearne, Head
Holdings: Vols (350) // Cat
Notes: Books and periodicals of the South, especially Tennessee, collected mainly during 1920s and 1930s, but also many earlier rare imprints. Named for former Nashville *Banner* publisher, James G Stahlman, and donated by the then-current publisher, Wayne Sargent. Cataloged. *The Stahlman Collection* (Nashville: Public Library of Nashville and Davidson County, 1975).

TX —UNIVERSITY OF TEXAS LIBRARIES, General Libraries, PO Box P, Austin, 78713. Carolyn Bucknell, Asst Dir for Collection Development
Holdings: Vols Cat Microforms
Notes: The Littlefield Collection of research materials, incl many rare items, on the history of the Old South.

TX —RICE UNIVERSITY, Fondren Library, Woodson Research Center, 6100 S Main St, PO Box 1892, Houston, 77251. Nancy Parker, Dir Woodson Research Center
Notes: Several collections of letters, papers, diaries and military records in ms form.

TX —SAM HOUSTON STATE UNIVERSITY, Library, PO Box 2179, Huntsville, 77340. Chas Dwyer, Librn
Holdings: Vols 2880 Cat Mss Pix Microforms
Notes: The Porter Confederate Collection is particularly rich in rare material relating to Texas in the Confederacy.

VA —UNIVERSITY OF VIRGINIA, Alderman Library, Manuscripts Dept, Charlottesville, 22901. Edmund Berkeley Jr, Cur
Holdings: Cat Mss Maps Pix
Notes: About 1500 collections have material pertaining to the Civil War and particularly to the Army of Northern Virginia and campaigns and battles in Virginia. There are letters, diaries, reminiscences, maps, and pictorial material of Confederate soldiers and civilians, as well as papers of Robert E Lee, J E B Stuart, Thomas L Rosser, Jubal A Early, John Daniel Imboden, William "Extra Billy" Smith, Henry Alexander Wise, Eppa Hunton, John S Mosby, and Samuel Barron.

VA —UNIVERSITY OF VIRGINIA, Alderman Library, Tracy W McGregor Collection, Charlottesville, 22901. William H Runge, Cur
Holdings: Vols 18,000 Cat Mss Maps Pix Microforms
Notes: Library spans 15th-20th century, concentrating on Southeastern American history. Rare collection of books on early exploration and travel; foundation of the Virginia Colony; Civil War. Books in foreign languages. Collection cataloged by date of publication. Special shellist. Published descritpions: William H Runge, "The Tracy W McGregor Library and Its Founder," *The University of Virginia News Letter* vol 39, no 11, July 15, 1963; *Description of the Tracy W McGregor Library, University of Virginia, With Rules for Its Use and a Biographical Sketch of Its Founder* (Charlottesville: Tracy W McGregor Library, 1951).

†VA —GEORGE C MARSHALL RESEARCH FOUNDATION AND LIBRARY, Drawer 920, Lexington, 24450. Royster Lyle Jr, Cur Collections
Holdings: Vols Uncat Mss
Notes: The William F. Friedman Collection. Separate catalog. Incl. papers and correspondence relating to William and Elizabeth S. Friedman's personal interests and U.S. government assignments: books, pamphlets, technical papers, periodicals, microfilm, slides and newspaper clippings dealing with cryptology. Items on secret writing and signaling, radar, telephony and telegraphy, and the study of the Shakespeare-

Bacon authorship controversy, Vols. of fiction relating to spies and codes, cryptographic game books for children, Civil War code items. Examples of ancient writings of Europe, Crete, and Easter Island, and material on the Aztecs, Incas, and particularly the Mayans. Also a copy of the Voynich mss., an undeciphered work, and other rare vols. on the subject dating from the 17th century. The library also has a separate collection of diaries kept by Gilbert Sandford Vernam, cryptographer and inventor. The diary is an almost day-by-day record, 1918-1926, of Vernam's inventions and development of his outstanding contributions to cryptography including techniques widely adopted by the armed forces for enciphering and deciphering coded messages. There is a typed index to this collection. No photocopying.

VA —PETERSBURG NATIONAL BATTLEFIELD, Library, Box 549, Petersburg, 23804. C M Calkins, Librn
Holdings: Vols 2000 Cat Mss Maps Pix Slides
Notes: Engagements during siege which we have information on: Battle for Petersburg, June 1864; Jerusalem Plank Road, June 1864; Battle of the Crater, July 1864; Weldon Railroad, August 1864; Reams Station, August 1864; Peebles Farm, Sept-Oct 1864; Boydton Plant Road, Oct 1864; Hatchers Run, Feb 1864; Fort Stedman, March 1865; Five Forks, April 1865; Assault on Petersburg, April 1865. Noncirculating.

VA —PORTSMOUTH PUBLIC LIBRARY, 601 Court St, Portsmouth, 23704. Dean Burgess, Library Dir
Holdings: Vols 1300 Cat
Notes: Although particularly interested in Tidewater and Lower Tidewater history, we buy most books we can locate on Virginia as well. In 1972 we were given the distinguished collection of Judge White of Lynnhaven.

VA —WASHINGTON AND LEE UNIVERSITY, Library, Lexington, 24450. Maurice Leach, Dir; Richard Oram, Asst Special Collections Librn
Holdings: Vols (25,000) Cat Mss Maps Pix
Notes: Incl over 10,000 ms pieces, the collection emphasizes the life of General Robert E Lee, Virginia, and the Civil War, etc. Pictures from 1870-1930; 8000 glass photographs by Miley.

VA —VIRGINIA STATE LIBRARY, 12 & Capitol Sts, Richmond, 23219.
Holdings: Vols 15,000 Cat Mss Maps Pix Microforms
Notes: Incl a vast collection of pictorial materials.

WV —UNIVERSITY OF CHARLESTON, Andrew S Thomas Memorial Library, 2300 MacCorkie Ave, SE, Charleston, 25304. Frank Badger, Librn
Holdings: Vols 405 // Cat

WI —STATE HISTORICAL SOCIETY OF WISCONSIN, Archives, 816 State St, Madison, 53706. Harold L Miller, Reference Archivist
Holdings: Mss Maps Pix Microforms
Notes: Records and papers of Wisconsin organizations, business and individuals documenting all facets of Wisconsin history and government. Topics covered incl discovery and exploration, native Americans, civil war, progressivism, and many others. Also incl are official records of state, county and local officials, offices and legislative bodies. Collections are described in the

Guide to Manuscripts of the State Historical Society of Wisconsin (3 vols, 1944, 1957, 1966), *Guide to the Wisconsin State Archives* (1966), inc current accession notes in the *Wisconsin Magazine of History*, and in other special Society publications. Major collections are also listed in Hamer, *Guide to Manuscripts and Archives in the United States* and the *National Union Catalog of Manuscripts Collections*, (1959-date). Also incl public records and tape recordings.

WI —UNIVERSITY OF WISCONSIN, MADISON, Memorial Library, Rare Books Collection, 728 State St, Madison, 53706. Gretchen Lagana, Cur
Notes: Extremely rare collection of manuscripts of a military brass band which marched with General Sherman's Union Army.
See also entry under US - History - Civil War - Regimental Histories.

WI —UNIVERSITY OF WISCONSIN, MILWAUKEE, Library, Box 604, Milwaukee, 53201. William C Roselle, Dir
Holdings: Vols 800 Cat Mss Maps
Notes: Allen M Slichter Collection, reflecting Confederate point of view. Restricted use. Noncirculating.

U.S.—HISTORY—CIVIL WAR—IMPRINTS

NY —CORNELL UNIVERSITY LIBRARIES, Collection of Regional History, Dept of Manuscripts and Univ Archives, Ithaca, 14853.
Notes: Incl 341 items, mounted in an unknown collector's scrapbook. See 1950-1954 *Report*.

TX —RICE UNIVERSITY, Fondren Library, Woodson Research Center, 6100 S Main St, PO Box 1892, Houston, 77251. Nancy Parker, Dir Woodson Research Center
Holdings: Vols 2500 Cat
Notes: Cataloged and shelved by Crandall and Harwell number. Incl some Confederate imprints not in Crandall and Harwell, plus other Civil War imprints.

U.S.—HISTORY—CIVIL WAR—MAPS

DC —LIBRARY OF CONGRESS, Manuscript Division, Washington, 20540. John C Broderick, Chief
Notes: The Jedediah Hotchkiss Collection of his papers and Civil War maps. Also, the papers of Geneeral William Tecumsah Sherman contain Civil War maps.

U.S.—HISTORY—CIVIL WAR—MUSIC

NC —DUKE UNIVERSITY, William R Perkins Library, Rare Book Room, Durham, 27706. John L Sharpe, III, Cur
Notes: Collection of more than 3500 titles of Confederate imprints. Possibly the largest such collection in the country, it includes broadsides, maps, music, newspapers, Union and Confederate regimental histories, and sheet music.

RI —BROWN UNIVERSITY, John Hay Library, 20 Prospect St, Providence, 02912. Mark N Brown, Cur Mss
Holdings: Uncat
Notes: The Sheet Music Collection concentrates on music of American imprint, incl 170,000 vocal pieces filed by title, plus 80,000 instrumental pieces filed by composer. Major strengths are in 19th century music, especially prior to 1830; Civil War music, both Union and Confederate; lithographic covers; World War I songs; political campaign music; and band music. An additional 100,000 pieces of American and European imprint remain unprocessed.
See also entry under US - History - Civil War

U.S.—HISTORY—CIVIL WAR—NAVAL OPERATIONS

MI —UNIVERSITY OF MICHIGAN, Engineering-Transportation Library, 312 Undergraduate Library, Ann Arbor, 48109. Sharon A Balius, Assoc Librn
Notes: Letters and papers of Charles Ellet,

U.S.—HISTORY—CIVIL WAR—NAVAL OPERATIONS (cont.)

Jr, and family, especially as related to construction of railroads, canals, and bridges and to the construction and command of the Union ram fleet in the Civil War.

U.S.—HISTORY—CIVIL WAR—PICTURES, ILLUSTRATIONS, ETC.

DC —LIBRARY OF CONGRESS, Prints & Photographs Div, Washington, 20540.
Notes: Civil War Photograph Collection incl photographs commissioned by Mathew Brady and others. Brady employed 20 photographers at the height of his operations. His staff incl Alexander and James Gardner, James F Gibson, and Thomas C Roche.

OH —RUTHERFORD B HAYES LIBRARY, 1337 Hayes Ave, Fremont, 43420. Watt P Marchman, Dir
Holdings: Cat Mss Maps Pix Microforms
Notes: In addition to the book collection, the Library has several individual ms collections containing diaries, letters and other ms materials pertaining to the Civil War. Also numerous items pertaining to Civil War prisons, particularly Johnson's Island Index. Listed under subject in *Guide to Manuscripts at the Ohio Historical Society*. 1300 items.

VA —VIRGINIA STATE LIBRARY, 12 & Capitol Sts, Richmond, 23219.
Holdings: Cat Pix
Notes: Incl 86,960 prints, photographs, etc, chiefly of Virginia, the Civil War, and the Confederacy.

U.S.—HISTORY—CIVIL WAR—REGIMENTAL HISTORIES

†AL —MUSEUMS OF THE CITY OF MOBILE, Reference Library, 355 Government St, Mobile, 36602. Caldwell Delaney, Adminr
Notes: Confederate States of America Collection.

CA —UNIVERSITY OF CALIFORNIA, SANTA BARBARA, Library, Dept of Special Collections, Santa Barbara, 93106. Christian F Brun, Head

NE —NEBRASKA STATE HISTORICAL SOCIETY, Library, 1500 R St, Box 82554, Lincoln, 68501. M Ann Reinert, Library Dept Head
Holdings: Vols (100,000) Cat Maps Pix Microforms
Budget: ($200,000)
Notes: Esp relating to Nebraska.
See also entry under Great Plains

NY —NEW YORK PUBLIC LIBRARY, Research Libraries, General Research Division, Fifth Ave & 42 St, New York, 10018. Rodney Phillips, Chief
Holdings: Vols (2,225,000) Cat Maps Pix Microforms
Budget: ($775,718)

NC —DUKE UNIVERSITY, William R Perkins Library, Rare Book Room, Durham, 27706. John L Sharpe, III, Cur
Notes: Collection of more than 3500 titles of Confederate imprints. Possibly the largest such collection in the country, it includes broadsides, maps, music, newspapers, Union and Confederate regimental histories, and sheet music.

OH —PUBLIC LIBRARY OF CINCINNATI & HAMILTON COUNTY, History Dept, 800 Vine St, Cincinnati, 45202. J Richard Abell, Head
Holdings: Vols 4470 Cat
Notes: Above count does not incl Civil War biographies unless they are classified within the Civil War numbers. Of the 4168 volumes 1033 are Civil War Military Unit Histories.

OH —OHIO HISTORICAL SOCIETY, Archives Library Division, 1982 Velma Ave, Columbus, 43211. Dennis East, Division Chief
Holdings: Vols (96,000) Cat Mss Maps Pix Slides Microforms
Budget: ($18,000)
Notes: This library is the primary collection for Ohio. Most purchases are on the rare and op market. Collecting area is early American history, esp relating to exploration into the Northwest Territory. Major subject areas are Ohio politics and government (8 presidents), military history (good collection of regimental histories and Ohio narratives of the Civil War), economic and social history, local history, esp county histories & atlases and city directories. Also, Ohio archaeology, natural history, artifacts. Major media collections are books (96,000), newspapers (25,000 vols and 22,000 microfilm), pictures (50,000), maps (2500), manuscripts (1,500,000). Library is noncirculating except through interlibrary loan of microfilm.

PA —PENNSYLVANIA STATE UNIVERSITY, Fred Lewis Pattee Library, Special Collections Dept, University Park, 16802. Charles Mann, Chief, Special Collections
Holdings: Vols (1976) Cat Mss Pix Slides
Budget: ($37,000)
Notes: Includes The Beaver Collection (576 vols) in honor of James Beaver, Governor of Pennsylvania, mostly county histories, atlases and Regimental Civil War histories; John M Read Pamphlets (1400 titles), 1830-1890, relating to canals, railroads and civil law. No photocopying.

RI —PROVIDENCE PUBLIC LIBRARY, 150 Empire St, Providence, 02903. Lance J Bauer, Special Collections Librn
Holdings: Vols 5000
Notes: The Harris Collection on the American Civil War and Slavery. Incl 18th and 19th century books, rare pamphlets, and periodicals concerning slavery and the slave trade, and origins, progress and results of the Civil War; also regimental histories; military and naval tactics; personal narratives; women's accounts of the Civil War; works on abolition; sheet music; Union and Confederate broadside ballads; Confederate imprints; *The Liberator* from 1843 through the Civil War; and over 85 editions of *Uncle Tom's Cabin* in 14 languages. Excellent primary and secondary sources for the study of the Civil War and slavery. Material must be used in-house. Photocopying when condition of material allows.

WI —UNIVERSITY OF WISCONSIN, MADISON, Memorial Library, Rare Books Collection, 728 State St, Madison, 53706. Gretchen Lagana, Cur
Holdings: Vols (12)// Mss Pix
Notes: Mss, part books, and photographs of the Brodhead Wisconsin Silver Cornet Band which during the latter parts of the Civil War, formed the band of the 1st Brigade, 3rd Division, 15th Army Corp, which marched across Georgia with General Sherman. Housed in the Dept of Rare Books and Special Collections.

U.S.—HISTORY—RECONSTRUCTION, 1863-1877 see Reconstruction (U.S., 1863-1877)

U.S.—HISTORY—REVOLUTION—MAPS

DC —LIBRARY OF CONGRESS, Geography and Map Division, Washington, 20540. John A Wolter, Chief
Notes: The William Faden Collection of ms and printed maps of the French and Indian and Revolutionary Wars.

U.S.—HISTORY—WAR OF 1898

CT —UNIVERSITY OF CONNECTICUT, Library, Storrs, 06268. R H Schimmelpfeng, Dir of Special Collections
Holdings: // Uncat Mss
Notes: Manuscript material relating to activities in the Philippines and Spain of Valeriano Weyler y Nicolau, Duque de Rubi ("Butcher Weyler").

NY —NEW YORK PUBLIC LIBRARY, Research Libraries, American History Div, Fifth Ave & 42 St, New York, 10018.
Holdings: Vols (25,000) Maps Microforms
Notes: See *Dictionary Catalog of the History of Americas Collection* (Boston G K Hall, 1961), 28 vols.

NY —US MILITARY ACADEMY LIBRARY, West Point, 10996. Marie T Capps, Maps & Mss Librn
Holdings: Vols (2000) // Mss Maps
Notes: One descriptive catalog of a portion of this collection is: Marie T Capps and Theodore G Stroup, *US Military Academy Library Map Collection: The Period of the American Revolution 1753-1800* (West Point, NY: US Military Academy, 1971), 82 pp.

PA —US ARMY MILITARY HISTORY INSTITUTE, Carlisle Barracks, 17013. Richard J Sommers, Chief Archivist-Historian
Holdings: Mss Cat
Notes: 2500 folders and 50 boxes. The Spanish-American War survey, personal letters, diaries, and recollections of American officers and enlisted men in Regular and Volunteer Army units as well as in the Navy, Marine Corps, and Revenue Service (Coast Guard) serving stateside and overseas during the Spanish-American War and Philippine Insurrection. This is the largest collection in the world of personal papers of American servicemen at the turn of the century.

U.S.—HISTORY—WORLD WAR I see World War, 1914-1918

U.S.—HISTORY—DEPRESSION, 1929 see Depressions—1929 — U.S.

U.S.—HISTORY—1933-1945

DC —LIBRARY OF CONGRESS, Prints & Photographs Div, Washington, 20540.
Notes: Farm Security Administration Collection of photographs of American life, 1935-1942. Approx 164,000 original FSA negatives, 2600 Kodachrome transparencies, 75,000 photoprints, and some photographers' notebooks.

†MA —JOHN F KENNEDY LIBRARY, Columbia Point, Boston, 02125. Dan H Fenn Jr, Dir
Holdings: // Cat
Notes: Louis Brownlow's papers relating to government reorganization during the Roosevelt administration and James P Warburg's personal papers and general files relating to the New Deal and his role as advisor to FDR. 23 linear ft of mss. Holdings are described in "Historical Materials in the John F Kennedy Library." Copies may be obtained by writing the Research Archivist.

OH —WILMINGTON COLLEGE, Peace Resource Center, Hiroshima/Nagasaki Memorial Collection, Pyle Center Box 1183, Wilmington, 45177. Helen Redding, Librn
Holdings: Vols Pix Slides Audiotapes Videotapes Film Art Reproductions VF
Notes: The Hiroshima/Nagasaki Memorial Collection is nationally known and respected as a major source of information, films, slides and audiotapes about the atomic bombings of Hiroshima and Nagasaki. An especially signifciant part of the Collection is a continually growing library in Japanese currently numbering more than 500 vols. Here are recorded eyewitness account of the atomic bombings, as well as details of what life has been like in the intervening years for the thousands of survivors (*hibakusha*). Also incl are books of poetry, photo books, juvenile literature, and books dealing with medical information, peace research, peace education, nuclear power, etc. All books in the Hiroshima/Nagasaki Memorial Collection are available for interlibrary loan. An *Annotated Bibliography of Japanese A-Bomb Literature* may be purchased or borrowed from the PRC. In it are briefsummaries in English of each book in the Collection.

U.S.—HISTORY—WORLD WAR II see World War, 1939-1945

U.S.—HISTORY, LOCAL

IL —NEWBERRY LIBRARY, 60 W Walton St, Chicago, 60610. Diana Haskell, Cur of Modern Mss
Holdings: Cat

U.S.—HISTORY, MILITARY

CA —LOS ANGELES PUBLIC LIBRARY, History Dept, 630 W Fifth St, Los Angeles, 90071. Frank Louch, Sr Librn
Holdings: Vols 18,500 Cat Maps
Budget: ($85,000)
Notes: A well-rounded collection with emphasis on unit histories of World War II.

CA —HOOVER INSTITUTION ON WAR, REVOLUTION & PEACE, Stanford University, Stanford, 94305. Milorad M Drachkovitch, Archivist
Holdings: Mss
Notes: Four collections. (1) Papers of Lt Gen Clovis E Byers, 1917-1961, incl correspondence, memoranda, diaries, speeches and writings, clippings, personnel records, and audiovisual matter, relating to his military career in the Pacific theater during World War II, in the army of occupation in Japan, in the Korean War, and in the North Atlantic Treaty Organization (NATO) command in Euripe, 40ms boxes. (2) Three handwritten diaries, July, 10, 1951-May 22, 1952, by Admiral Charles Turner Joy. Chief United Nations negotiator at the Korean military armistice negotiations at Panmunjom, 1951-1953, mainly concerning prison of war issues and repatriation questions, 3 vols in 1/2 ms box. (3) Papers of Victor H Krulak, Lt Gen, US Marine Corps, and vice-president of Copley News Service, incl writings, speeches, interviews, and newspaper clippings, 1958-1977, relating to MarineCorps activities in China in the 1930s and during World War II, the Korean War, and the Vietnamese Conflict. 1 ms box. (4) Typewritten documentation of events and conditions leading up to the Japanese attack on Pearl Harbor, December 7, 1941, assembled by Lt Gen W C Short, Commanding General, US Army, Hawaiian Department, for his defense before the "Roberts Commission," which investigated the attack. 1/2 ms box.

NY —FORT ONTARIO HISTORIC SITE, Oswego, 13126. Shelley B Weinreb, Historic Site Mgr
Holdings: Vols (400) Cat Mss Maps Pix Slides
Notes: Primary focus is upon military activities at the mouth of the Oswego River and the utilization of fortifications (Fort Ontario, Fort Oswego, and Fort George) at that point which served to control the outlet of the traditional Mohawk-Oneida-Oswego route to the Great Lakes. A limited number of sources on fortification design, weapons, uniforms, and military equipment are included. Also incl 4000 slides and 400 pictures.

NY —US MILITARY ACADEMY LIBRARY, West Point, 10996. Richard J Hellinger, Chief, USMA Archives
Holdings: Uncat Pix
Notes: National Archives and Records Service Group 404. Records of the US Military Academy. Collection is developed according to the Army records management system which coordinates retirement of official records. This extensive archival collection dating from 1801 to date includes virtually all formats by which information is recorded and transferred, the majority of which is typescript or manuscript. Inventory of this record group has been published by the National Archives and Records Service (A Preliminary Inventory of the Records of the United States Military Academy, compiled by Stanley P Tozeski, US National Archives and Records Survey, 1976 NARS pub #PI 185, LC listing CD 3026 .A32). The USMA Library's Rare Books Collection, separately administered by the Special Collection Librarian, also contains West Pointiana and military manuscripts numbering nearly5000 items. Cullum Biographical files are maintained by the Association of Graduates of the US Military Academy, the greater part dating from the 1840's to the 20th century. These files from classes of 1802-1905 have been transferred to the library and include letters, photographs, and clippings about the graduates.

NC —DUKE UNIVERSITY, William R Perkins Library, Manuscript Dept, Durham, 27706. Ellen Gartrell, Cur of Mss
Holdings: Cat Mss
Notes: Especially strong for Civil War; also material from most wars that involved US. Notable WW II collection is papers of General Robert L Eichelberger (20,000 items).

RI —PROVIDENCE PUBLIC LIBRARY, 150 Empire St, Providence, 02903. Lance J Bauer, Special Collections Librn
Holdings: Vols 5000
Notes: The Harris Collection on the American Civil War and Slavery. Incl 18th and 19th century books, rare pamphlets, and periodicals concerning slavery and the slave trade, and origins, progress and results of the Civil War; also regimental histories; military and naval tactics; personal narratives; women's accounts of the Civil War; works on abolition; sheet music; Union and Confederate broadside ballads; Confederate imprints; *The Liberator* from 1843 through the Civil War; and over 85 editions of *Uncle Tom's Cabin* in 14 languages. Excellent primary and secondary sources for the study of the Civil War and slavery. Material must be used in-house. Photocopying when condition of material allows.

U.S.—HISTORY, POLITICAL see U.S—Politics and Government

U.S.—IMMIGRATION see U.S.—Emigration and Immigration

U.S.—IMPRINTS

DC —LIBRARY OF CONGRESS, Rare Book & Special Collections Div, Washington, 20540. William Matheson, Chief
Holdings: Vols 14,000 Cat
Notes: The American Imprints Collection consists of items printed in the US from 1640 to 1800, and represents about 43 percent of the titles cited in Charles Evans' *American Bibliography.* Incl among its more notable items is an imperfect copy of the Bay Psalm Book. Card files in the Division exist for author/title, printer/publisher, place and date. Other collections such as the Bible Collection, Pamphlet Collections, Documents of the First Fourteen Congresses, the Broadside Collection and the Almanac Collection also contain American imprints before 1800.

ME —BOWDOIN COLLEGE, Library, Brunswick, 04011. Dianne M Gutscher, Cur of Special Collections
Holdings: Vols 2500 Cat
Notes: Books and pamphlets printed in the English colonies and the United States before 1821.

MD —MEDICAL & CHIRURGICAL FACULTY OF THE STATE OF MARYLAND, Library, 1211 Cathedral St, Baltimore, 21201. Joseph E Jensen, Librn
Holdings: Vols (10,000) // Cat Mss Maps Pix
Notes: The history of medicine and rare medical book collection incl early literature (some medical incunabula), texts, and periodicals (strong in Garrison & Morton items), histories, bibliographies, reprints, lecture notes, health department reports, hospital and physician records, medical society transactions, etc. Materials generally span the 16th through the 19th centuries. Very strong in Early American imprints relating to medicine (Austin items), European medical classics, and 18th and 19th century medical periodicals.

NY —NEW YORK HISTORICAL SOCIETY, Library, 170 Central Park W, New York, 10024. James Gregory, Librn
Holdings: Mss
Notes: Incl original mss, illustrative materials, etc.

U.S.—INTELLECTUAL LIFE

NC —SOUTHEASTERN BAPTIST THEOLOGICAL SEMINARY LIBRARY, PO Box 752, Wake Forest, 27587. H Eugene McLeod, Librn
Holdings: Cat Audiotapes Microforms
Notes: Incl early American sources in Readex Microprint edition of materials listed in Evan's *American Bibliography* and in Shaw and Shoemaker's *American Bibliography: a Preliminary Checklist.*

U.S.—JUDICIARY see Courts—U.S.

U.S.—MAPS

DC —LIBRARY OF CONGRESS, Geography and Map Division, Washington, 20540. John A Wolter, Chief
Holdings: Cat Mss Maps Pix Slides Microforms
Notes: *Cartographic Materials.* One of the largest cartographic collections in the world, all-inclusive in coverage. Early original manuscript maps, navigation charts by Italian, Portuguese, and Spanish 15th, 16th, and 17th-century cartographers; the Hummel & Warner Collections of rare manuscript and printed maps and atlases of China and Korea from the 17th, 18th, and 19th centuries; manuscript and printed maps of colonial America, the Revolutionary War, the War of 1812, the Civil War, and wars of the 20th century; individual sheets of large and medium-scale set maps and charts published in the 19th and 20th centuries, including official topographic, geologic, soil, mineral, and resource maps, and nautical and aeronautical charts for most countries of the world; special subject maps of the world and its various political entities; maps of the United States and the separateStates; county maps and plans of cities and towns, and the Sanborn Fire Insurance Maps, dating back to 1866 for some 13,000 cities in the United States. Atlases include earliest printed editions of Ptolemy's Geography (1482), and representative volumes of leading atlas publishers of the last five centuries covering individual continents, countries, states, counties, cities, and the world. Total: 3,800,000 maps, 49,000 atlases, 400 globes and 2000 relief models. See *The Geography and Map Division: A Guide to Its Collections and Services,* rev ed, 1975 (LC 5.2:SE6/975).

OK —SOCIETY FOR THE NORTH AMERICAN CULTURAL SURVEY, Dept of Geography, Oklahoma State University, Stillwater, 74078. John Rooney, Dir; Todd Zdorkowski, Asst
Notes: Has produced a cultural atlas of North America, 309 pages of maps and text gathered from the major geographical, historical, and cultural source-literatures.

U.S.—MERCHANT MARINE see Merchant Marine

U.S.—MILITARY POLICY

DC —GEORGETOWN UNIVERSITY, Library, Special Collections Div, 37 & O Sts NW, Washington, 20057. George M Barringer, Special Collections Librn; Nicholas B Sheetz, Mss Librn
Holdings: Mss Cat
Notes: The archives of the Commission on Security and Economic Assistance, chaired by Frank C Carlucci, consist of memberships correspondence files; papers generated or solicited by the Commission; minutes from Commission meetings and public hearings; and drafts of the Commission's final report.

PA —US ARMY WAR COLLEGE LIBRARY, Carlisle Barracks, 17013. Barbara E Stevens, Dir
Holdings: Vols (125,000) Cat Maps Microforms Audiotapes
Budget: ($251,000)
Notes: Physical access to the collection is limited. Individual items available on interlibrary loan. Older historical material is in the US Army Military History Institute, Carlisle Barracks, Pennsylvania, 17013.

U.S.—MORAL CONDITIONS

MA —BRANDEIS UNIVERSITY, Goldfarb Library, 415 South St, Waltham, 02154.

U.S.

U.S.—MORAL CONDITIONS (cont.)

Bessie Hahn, Dir
Notes: Hall-Hoag Archives on Extremism in the U.S. Approx 5000 pieces of Extremist literature, both Right and Left, dealing with various social, religious and political aspects of the US from the 1960s, 1970s and 1980s. A finding list is in Special Collections. Material is arranged by the name of the sponsoring organization in alphabetical order.

U.S.—PHILIPPINE COMMONWEALTH

DC —AMERICAN HISTORICAL COLLECTION, US Embassy, Manilla, Philippines, c/o US Dept of State, Washington, 20525. Aurora P Galvez, Librn; Lewis E Gleeck Jr, Cur
Notes: The American Historical Collection is located at 1201 Roxas Blvd, Metro Manila, Philippines. Incl the William Cameron Forbes, Eugene A Perkins Memorial Library, Leonard Dawson, and Sternberg Collections. Some Spanish Period materials and much on later history, espec Commonwealth Period (except 1942-45). Considerable on Japanese in World War II and the Japanese-supported "Philippine Republic" (approx 1946-53), incl political and trade relations, and on military bases. Strong on Philippines during the American period. Collections incl mss, documents, reports, theses. Library maintains special picture-file collections. Also incl bound periodicals published during the American period 1900-1930. Complete reports of the Philippine Commission (1900-1915); reportsof the Governor-General (1916-1930); High Commissioner Reports (1931-1935); original minutes and memoranda of the internees of the US Internment Camp. Mailing address: OB-442 US Embassy, Roxas Blvd, Manila.

U.S.—POLITICS AND GOVERNMENT

AL —MILES COLLEGE, C A Kirkendoll Library, Birmingham, 35208. Mattie Jackson, Librn
Holdings: Vols (3000) Cat
Notes: Books from the private library of Dr Clinton Rossiter, well-known political scientist, historian, lecturer, writer and one of the foremost authorities on American constitutional history and political theory.
CA —CLAREMONT COLLEGES, Honnold Library, Ninth & Dartmouth, Claremont, 91711. Tania Rizzo, Special Collections Dept Head
Holdings: Vols (200) Cat Mss Documents Pix Records
Notes: The papers of former Democratic Congressman Jerry Voorhis, from the 1930s to present, occupying nearly 100 document boxes. The papers reflect his life and career, incl biographical material, the history of the Voorhis School for Boys, his involvement in the Dies Committee, and his wide-ranging interests in American economic and social issues, such as cooperatives, monopolies and cartels, Latin American relations, consumers, and senior citizens. Books by and about him, with research files. Correspondence with political leaders. Inventory available. Restricted use.
CA —FRANCIS BACON LIBRARY, 655 N Dartmouth Ave, Claremont, 91711. Elizabeth S Wrigley, Dir
Holdings: Vols 300 Cat Pix Microforms
Notes: American political theory (Lee-Bernard Collection). Contains a significant part of "statesman's library," incl periodicals, that James Madison and Thomas Jefferson listed in 1783 and urged the Continental Congress to buy. Collection made by the late Dr Douglass Adair, professor of history at the Claremont Graduate School and was given by him to the Francis Bacon Library. Long-title catalog of the collection published by the Library in 1972.
CA —CALIFORNIA STATE UNIVERSITY, FULLERTON, Library, 800 N State College Blvd, Fullerton, 92634. Lynn M Coppel, Librn
Holdings: Pamphlets Serials Ephemera
Notes: Freedson Center of Polemic Political

Ephemera incl 8000 pamphlets and over periodical titles. Strongest in right wing American politics and British socialism. Separate card catalogs for the pamphlets and folders. Periodicals are listed in the CSUF periodicals printout and the *California State University and Colleges Union List of Periodicals*.
CA —UNIVERSITY OF CALIFORNIA, LOS ANGELES, Research Library, Dept of Special Collections, 405 Hilgard Ave, Los Angeles, 90024. Edward Shreeves, Chairman, Bibliographers Group; David S Zeidberg, Head
Holdings: Mss
Notes: 90 linear feet in various collections pertaining to political and social activities in the US, Europe, Latin America and the USSR. In addition, 14 linear feet of mss and printed materials of the Socialist Party (US), collected by Hyman Weintraub, William Goldberg, and others, incl Minutes of the National Executive Committee.
CA —UNIVERSITY OF CALIFORNIA, LOS ANGELES, Research Library, Public Affairs Service, 405 Hilgard Ave, Los Angeles, 90024. Edward Shreeves, Chairman, Bibliographers Group; Eugenia Eaton, Head, Public Affairs Service
Holdings: Uncat
Notes: Current non-governmental English-language pamphlets (192,819), broadsides, leaflets and other ephemera on public affairs, from 1960, representing a wide spectrum of political and social opinions. Social welfare and industrial relations are strong fields. Legal loose-leaf labor services, such as the *Daily Labor Report*, the *Government Employee Relations Report* and the *Labor Relations Reporter*, as well as labor pamphlets from the mid-1940s, reflect a long-standing responsibility to the University's Institute of Industrial Relations.
CA —COMMONWEALTH CLUB OF CALIFORNIA, Library, 681 Market St, San Francisco, 94105. Virginia Rees, Librn
Holdings: Vols (6500) Cat Maps Pix
Budget: ($2000)
CA —HOOVER INSTITUTION ON WAR, REVOLUTION & PEACE, Stanford University, Stanford, 94305. Milorad M Drachkovitch, Archivist
Holdings: Mss Pix
Notes: Papers of William Y Elliott, author, university professor, staff director of the House Select Committee on Foreign Affairs, 1947-49, member of the planning board of the National Security Council, 1958-1970, incl correspondnece, writings, speeches, research notes, clippings, government documents, and printed matter, 1930-1970, relating to his government service, teaching endeavors at Harvard University, US national security and defense, US politics and foreign relations, US military-industrial relations and the US national labor policy. 173 ms, boxes. Also, records of *National Republic* magazines,incl newspaper clippings, printed matter, pamphlets, reports, indices, notes, bulletins, lettergrams, weekly letters, and photographs, 1905-1960, relating to pacifist, communist, fascist, and other radical movements as well as political developments in the USand Soviet Russia. 826 ms boxes.
CA —STANFORD UNIVERSITY LIBRARIES, Cecil H Green Library, Stanford, 94305. Michael T Ryan, Cur
Holdings: Mss Pix
Notes: The Elmer E Robinson Collection of American History and Government. Incl correspondence of early American statesmen.
†CO —UNIVERSITY OF DENVER, Penrose Library, 2150 E Evans, Denver, 80208.
Notes: Papers of Congressman Wayne Aspinall and Senator Peter Dominick.
CT —TRINITY COLLEGE LIBRARY, 300 Summit St, Hartford, 06106. Peter J Knapp, Archivist
Holdings: Uncat // Mss Pix
Notes: Late 18th and 19th century mss, letter, diaries, etc of the Curtis Family of Connecticut and New York, with emphasis on: William Edmond (1755-1838), US Congressman from Conn; Holbrook Curtis (1787-1858); William Edmond Curtis (1823-

1880), Chief Justice of Superior Court of New York; Mary Ann Scovill Curtis (1831-1908); and William Edmond Curtis Jr, (1855-1923), US Asst Secy of the Treasury. Incl on basis of relation through marriage are late 18th and 19th century mss, letters and diaries of the Hiester, McLanahan and Muhlenberg Families of Pennsylvania, with emphasis on Joseph Hiester (1752-1832), US Congressman and Governor of Pennsylvania; and Andrew Gregg (1755-1835), US Congressman and Senator from Pennsylvania. 12 linear feet.
CT —YALE UNIVERSITY, Box 1603A, Yale Station, New Haven, 06520.
CT —UNIVERSITY OF CONNECTICUT, Library, Storrs, 06268. R H Schimmelpfeng, Dir of Special Collections
Notes: Congressman Robert N Giaimo's papers. Closed for research until 1986.
DE —UNIVERSITY OF DELAWARE, Hugh M Morris Library, S College Ave, Newark, 19711. T Stuart Dick, Special Collections
Holdings: // Cat Mss
Notes: Incl business, legal, personal and political papers of Willard Saulsbury, spanning 1850-1927. Saulsbury was a US Senator from Delaware. Incl letters and telegrams from Woodrow Wilson relating to the work of the Democratic National Committee, party politics, etc (1912-1918).
DC —DISTRICT OF COLUMBIA PUBLIC LIBRARY, Martin Luther King Memorial Library, Washingtoniana Div and Washington Star Collection, 901 G St NW, Washington, 20001. Roxanna Deane, Chief
Notes: *Washington Star* Collection was the working morgue and photo library of the *Washington Star* newspaper. There are an estimated one million photos dating from about 1930 to 1981. These are arranged by subject and personal name and cover international, national and local news. There are approx 13 million news clippings arranged by subject and personal name for the same period. Each *Star* article was clipped and placed in as many different files as was necessary to cover all topics or personal names mentioned in the article. Reproductions from the photo collection may be purchased.
DC —GEORGETOWN UNIVERSITY, Library, Special Collections Div, 37 & O Sts NW, Washington, 20057. George M Barringer, Special Collections Librn; Nicholas B Sheetz, Mss Librn
Holdings: Cat Mss Maps Pix Slides Phonorecords Audiotapes
Notes: Includes the papers (1912-49) of Sen Robert F Wagner; the archives (1903-) of the American Political Science Association and of its local Washington chapter; the archives of the Center for Public Financing of Elections; a collection of several hundred political cartoons by Eric Smith; and other smaller collections. The Division has received the complete collection of materials generated by Senator Eugene McCarthy's 1968 bid for the Presidency, ca 600 linear ft, incl photos, audiotapes, videotapes.
DC —GEORGETOWN UNIVERSITY, Library, Special Collections Div, 37 & O Sts NW, Washington, 20057. George M Barringer, Special Collections Librn; Nicholas B Sheetz, Mss Librn
Holdings: Mss Cat Pix
Notes: Papers and memorabilia of the Honorable Alfred E Smith (1873-1944) former Governor of New York and candidate for President in 1928. Among significant items in the collection are a series of scrapbooks containing newspaper clippings, letters, photographs, and related material documenting the political rise of the "Happy Warrior." The scrapbooks span Smith's political career from 1913, when he was elected Speaker of the New York Assembly, through the twenties, when he was the unsuccessful Democratic candidate for the Presidency. Photographs cover many aspects of his family life and political career. The collection incl a small quantity of correspondence with politicians such as Nelson A Rockefeller and Robert F Wagner.
DC —GEORGE WASHINGTON UNIVERSITY, Gelman Library, 2130 H St

U.S.—POLITICS AND GOVERNMENT (cont.)

NW, Washington, 20052.
Holdings: // Cat Mss
Notes: The Gilbert Gude Congressional papers cover his terms in the House of Representatives from the 90th to the 94th Congresses (1967-76). During his tenure in office as representative from the 8th District, Maryland, Mr Gude served on the Government Operations Committee and its Conservation, Energy, and Natural Resources Subcommittee; the House Environmental Study; the FDR Memorial Commission; the Select Committee on Aging; and the House District of Columbia Committee. Papers reflect the working files of a congressional office and include bills, voting records, correspondence, press materials, special projects, record statements, speeches, testimony, subject files, and case studies (restricted). Cataloged as a collection with unpublished inventory of access. Also, the Chauncey Mitchell Depew papers cover the period of ca 1872-1928 and include correspondence(primarily incoming), manuscript speeches and misc papers, photographs, and scrapbooks of his Senate campaigns, travels, and obituary notices. The collection primarily reflects Depew's career as a public speaker and is cataloged as a collection with an unpublished inventory for access. The inventory includes an index of correspondents.

DC —HOWARD UNIVERSITY, Moorland-Spingarn Research Center, 500 Howard Place NW, Washington, 20059. Clifford L Muse, Jr, Acting Dir
Holdings: Vols (106,086) Mss Maps Pix Slides Phonorecords Audiotapes 16mm Films Filmstrips Microforms
Budget: ($854,753)
See also entry under Blacks

DC —LIBRARY OF CONGRESS, Manuscript Division, Washington, 20540. John C Broderick, Chief
Notes: The papers of former Secretary of State Alexander M Haig. Access to the collection is restricted. Also, papers of Henry A Kissinger. Papers of Robert Taft, Jr, Emanuel Celler, Abraham Ribicoff, John Brademas, and other Senators and Representatives.

DC —LIBRARY OF CONGRESS, Washington, 20540.
Notes: Papers of Senator Abraham Ribicoff. His gubernatorial and some other papers are at the Connecticut State Library.

DC —LIBRARY OF CONGRESS, Law Library, 101 Independence Ave, SE, Washington, 20540. Carleton W Kenyon, Dir
Holdings: Cat Microforms
Notes: Collection incl a nearly complete set of House and Senate bills and resolutions.

DC —LIBRARY OF CONGRESS, Motion Pictures, Broadcasting and Recorded Sound Div, Washington, 20540.
Notes: The entire radio archive of the National Broadcasting Company. Incl 175,000 recordings of radio programs and events broadcast from 1933-70. Duplicated at the Museum of Broadcasting in New York City.

DC —NATIONAL ARCHIVES AND RECORDS SERVICE, Civil Archives Division, Washington, 20408.

DC —REPUBLICAN NATIONAL COMMITTEE LIBRARY, 310 First St SE, Washington, 20003. Joanna Evans, Librn
Holdings: Vols 5000 Cat Maps Microforms

DC —UNIVERSITY OF THE DISTRICT OF COLUMBIA, Mount Vernon Campus, Library & Media Services Div, 800 Mount Vernon Pl, NW, Washington, 20001. Lottie Wright, Librn
Holdings: Vols (2500) // Uncat
Notes: American history, incl literature, education, politics, and government.

FL —FLORIDA STATE UNIVERSITY, Robert Manning Strozier Library, Special Collections Dept, Tallahassee, 32306. Opal M Free, Head, Special Collections
Notes: The official papers, documents, photographs, recordings, and memorabilia of

US Representative Claude Pepper. Incl the papers, photographs, and memorabilia of his wife, Mildred Irene Webster Pepper (706, 536 items).

FL —UNIVERSITY OF SOUTH FLORIDA, Library, Tampa, 33620. J B Dobkin, Special Collections Librn
Notes: Public and private papers of Nelson Poynter, Chairman of the board of Times Publishing Company. Incl political correspondence, photographs, and Pulitzer Prize commendation records.

GA —UNIVERSITY OF GEORGIA, Libraries, Special Collections Division, Athens, 30602. Vesta Lee Gordon, Asst Dir for Special Collections
Notes: Collection contains 1394.8 linear feet of mss: papers of US Senator Richard B Russell; US Congressmen John W Davis, Maston O'Neal, Robert G Stephens Jr, John L Pilcher, Dudley M Hughes; Governors Hoke Smith, Lester Maddox, Carl Sanders.

IL —CHICAGO HISTORICAL SOCIETY, Library, Clark St at North Ave, Chicago, 60614. Archie Motley, Manuscript Librn
Notes: Papers of these Presidents and other officials of the executive branch of the federal government: John Cabell Breckinridge (Representative and Senator Vice President, Confederate Secretary of War); John C Calhoun (Representative and Senator, Secretary of War, Vice President and Secretary of State); Schuyler Colfax (Representative, Vice President); Henry Dearborn (Representative, Secretary of War, War of 1812 officer); Henry A S Dearborn (Representative, political leader); Zebina Eastman (journalist, abolitionist); Ulysses S Grant (US Army officer, US President); Andrew Jackson (Representative, Senator, US Army officer, President); Joseph R Jones (businessman, member of US Diplomatic Corps, associate of Ulysses S Grant); Abraham Lincoln (Representative, US President); Robert Todd Lincoln papers in the Library ofCongress; Henry Crittenden Morris (lawyer, US Consul at Ghent); George Washington (US President); All other Presidents and many other federal officers are represented in small quantities.

IL —CHICAGO HISTORICAL SOCIETY, Library, Clark St at North Ave, Chicago, 60614. Archie Motley, Manuscript Librn
Notes: Papers of these nineteenth century political figures: Mason Brayman (lawyer, editor, Civil War officer, Governor of Idaho Territory); William Butler (State Treasurer); Edward Coles (Governor, abolitionist); Joseph Gillespie (judge, member of state legislature); Madison Y Johnson (lawyer, railroad executive, Peace Democrat); Pierre Menard (fur trader, merchant, Indian agent, Lt Governor of Illinois); Menard family; William B Ogden (pioneer, railroad executive, realtor, mayor of Chicago); Logan Uriah Reavis (editor, author, political leader); other Illinois politicians are represented in small quantities.

IL —EVERETT M DIRKSEN CONGRESSIONAL LEADERSHIP RESEARCH CENTER, Fourth & Broadway, Pekin, 61554. William C McCully Jr, Dir
Holdings: Cat Mss Maps Pix Slides Phonorecords Audiotapes Videotapes 16mm Films
Notes: Especially on Congressional leadership.

†IL —ILLINOIS STATE HISTORICAL SOCIETY, Library, Old State Capitol, Springfield, 62706.
Notes: Papers, incl letters and mss of US Senator Lyman Trumball (1813-1896).

IL —UNIVERSITY OF ILLINOIS, URBANA/CHAMPAIGN, Library, Urbana, 61801.

IN —INDIANA UNIVERSITY, Lilly Library, Seventh St, Bloomington, 47405. William R Cagle, Librn
Holdings: // Mss Pix Phonorecords
Notes: Papers and correspondence of 1940 Republican presidential candidate Wendell Willkie. 500,000 items. Bulk of material is for 1934-44. Incl campaign-related correspondence, speeches, writings and publications, material on One World,

scrapbooks, clippings, photographs, election memorabilia, etc. Also, Willkie Clubs collection. Contains the presidential campaign files of the Associated Willkie Clubs of America, 1940. 64,417 items. Also, the papers of former US Senator Birch Evans Bayh (D-Ind), 1962-80. Closed until 1990.

IN —PURDUE UNIVERSITY LIBRARIES, Special Collections Dept, West Lafayette, 47907. Keith Dowden, Asst Dir, Special Collections
Notes: Papers of Earl L Butz relating to his service as Secretary of Agriculture under Presidents Nixon and Ford (1971-76).

IA —DRAKE UNIVERSITY, Cowles Library, 28 St & University Ave, Des Moines, 50311.
Holdings: Cat Mss Pix
Notes: Working papers of Walter R Mears, Asst Bureau Chief for the Associated Press, concerning the 1964 Presidential Campaign of Senator Barry Goldwater.

KS —EMPORIA STATE UNIVERSITY, William Allen White Library, Emporia, 66801. Mary E Bogan, Special Collections Librn
Holdings: Vols (277) // Cat Mss Pix Phonorecords Audiotapes
Notes: The William Allen White Collection contains books by and about Mr White as well as inscribed volumes from his personal library, manuscripts, photographs, newspaper and periodical articles, memorabilia, as well as letters and telegrams exchanged between Mr White and such national figures as Herbert Hoover, Calvin Coolidge, Theodore Roosevelt, Franklin D Roosevelt, William Dean Howells, William Howard Taft, Robert Taft and many others.

IA —UNIVERSITY OF IOWA, University Libraries, Iowa City, 52242. Robert A McCown, Mss Librn
Holdings: Mss Pix
Notes: Three collections concerning the Progressive Party: The Curtis D. MacDougall collection of Progressive Party Records, 1946-54, including speeches, reports, business records, articles, campaign materials, fact sheets, form letters, directives, telegrams, pamphlets, press releases, clippings, and other related materials concerning the party and the national election of 1948; the Fred W. Stover Progressive Party Papers, 1948-1954, including newsletters, news releases, speeches, reports, minutes, legislative bulletins, pamphlets, clippings and memoirs of the farm organization leader and official of the Progressive Party; and the Calvin Benham Baldwin Papers, 1933-1975, including correspondence, speeches, news releases, clippings, minutes, proceedings, broadsides, pamphlets, photographs, scrapbooks and tape recordings of a Progressive Party officer. See Marc J. Epstein, "The Progressive Party of 1948," Books at Iowa, no. 16 (April 1975). pp. 34-40. 60 ft. of mss.

KS —KANSAS STATE UNIVERSITY, Library, Special Collections & University Archives, Manhattan, 66506. Antonia Q Pigno, Coordr; John J Vander Velde, Librn; Anthony R Crawford, Univ Archivist
Holdings: Vols 25 // Cat Mss
Notes: Dan Casement, 1868-1953, was a wealthy Manhattan rancher. He graduated from Princeton in 1890. During the years 1897-1901 he helped his father, Jack, build a railroad across Costa Rica. Jack had built the Union Pacific across the US. Dan Casement opposed the New Deal, incl the Agricultural Adjustment Act; he wrote articles and made radio speeches against them. Most of the 2500 letters congratulate him on his stand.

U.S.—POLITICS AND GOVERNMENT
(cont.)

LA —NICHOLLS STATE UNIVERSITY, Ellender Memorial Library, Thibodaux, 70310. Randall A Detro, Dir; Philip D Uzee, Archivist
Notes: Official papers of Senator Allen J Ellender (1936-1972).

ME —BOWDOIN COLLEGE, Library, Brunswick, 04011. Dianne M Gutscher, Cur of Special Collections
Holdings: Mss
Notes: (1) The Charles S Daveis Papers consist of about 400 items of correspondence, addresses, and documents, 1808-1864, of this Portland, Maine, lawyer who was active in the settlement of the dispute with Great Britain over Maine's northeastern boundary. (2) The Fessenden Family Papers contain 4000 mss for the period 1801-1908 and incl almost 1300 letters written by William Pitt Fessenden, US Senator from Maine, 1854-1869, and Secretary of the Treasury, 1864-65. (3) The Robert Hale Papers contain more than 1000 items relating to this US Congressman, incl correspondence, speeches, addresses, articles, and newsclippings covering the period 1938-1975.

ME —MARGARET CHASE SMITH LIBRARY CENTER, Skowhegan, 04976. James C MacCampbell, Dir
Notes: Senator Margaret Chase Smith's papers, her home and property in Skowhegan, donated by her to Northwood Institute, a business education college headquartered in Midland, Michigan. Also information on Senator Joseph McCarthy.

MA —BOSTON UNIVERSITY, Mugar Memorial Library, Special Collections Dept, 771 Commonwealth Ave, Boston, 02215. Howard B Gotlieb, Dir
Holdings: Cat Mss
Notes: The John W McCormack Collection of papers, documents, memoranda, correspondence, background files and memorabilia covering Administrations from President Coolidge to President Nixon, primarily 1957-1970. About three to four million pieces. Papers of F Bradford Morse.

†MA —JOHN F KENNEDY LIBRARY, Columbia Point, Boston, 02125. Dan H Fenn Jr, Dir
Holdings: Cat Mss Pix Audiotapes Videotapes 16mm Films
Notes: 20,000,000 pages of papers of John F Kennedy and Robert Kennedy, their staffs, associates and families incl oral history interviews and audiovisual materials; the papers of the Democratic National Committee Records, 1952-1963; congressional, personal and official papers of Brooks Hays, 1934-1966; White House staff files of the Congressional Liaison Office, 1961-1963; and manuscripts of Theodore White, author of *The Making of the President* series. Holdings are described in "Historical Materials in the John F Kennedy Library." Copies may be obtained by writing the Research Archivist.

MA —JOHN F KENNEDY LIBRARY, Columbia Point, Boston, 02125. Henry J Gwiazda II, Cur
Notes: The Robert F Kennedy Papers cover the period from 1937-1968 and are divided into four subcollections: the Pre-Administration, Attorney General's, Senate, and 1968 Presidential Campaign Papers. In the Pre-Administration Papers, over 140 archives boxes or 70 percent of the materials are open to research. The Personal and Political Papers of this subcollection are almost entirely open. Most of the unprocessed mss are in the Working Files and involve investigative work on labor racketeering. Seventy five percent or 185 archives boxes of the Attorney General's Papers are open, incl the correspondence, the John F Kennedy Library File, the Speech and Trip Files for 1961-1964. For the Senate Papers, 200 boxes are open for the 1964 Senate Campaign, the Legislative Subject File, and the Speech and Trip Files for 1964-1968. The speeches and press

releases(incl in the Senate subcollection Speech File) and "The Black Books" (16 boxes) on state and delegate information are open for the 1968 campaign. Each subcollection has its own finding aid. The Library also has available for research about 100 audiotapes of Robert F Kennedy's public addresses from 1962-1966 and some 50 oral history interviews on RFK and one (1000 pages) by RFK. There are also available the major documentaries on RFK and a number of films donated by the major networks for research use in the Library.

MA —HARVARD UNIVERSITY LIBRARY, Law School Library, Langdell Hall, Cambridge, 02138. Harry S Martin III, Librn
Notes: Personal and legal papers of William Henry Hastic, Governor of the Virgin Islands, Judge of the US Court of Appeals, Third Circuit, who died in April 1976. Much on his involvement in civic and antidiscrimination cases.

MA —MASSACHUSETTS INSTITUTE OF TECHNOLOGY, Institute Archives, Special Collections, Cambridge, 02139.
Notes: Correspondence, newsletters, factsheets, newspaper and magazine articles, books and reports of the Citizens' League Against the Sonic Boom, established in 1967 by William Shurcliff to oppose the sonic boom, stop commercial supersonic transport production, and influence public opinion and policy decisions on the SST. Major correspondents incl Bo Lundberg, Richard Wiggs, several US congressmen, and CLASB members.

MA —RADCLIFFE COLLEGE, Arthur & Elizabeth Schlesinger Library on the History of Women in America, 3 James St, Cambridge, 02138. Patricia Miller King, Dir; Eva Moseley, Cur of Mss
Notes: Incl the audiotapes and transcripts of the Women in the Federal Government Oral History Project, also papers of Clara M Beyer, Martha May Eliot, MD, Elizabeth Holtzman, Jeannette Rankin, Edith Nourse Rogers, and Mary Elizabeth Switzer.

MA —BOSTON COLLEGE LIBRARIES, Chestnut Hill, 02167.
Notes: 5000 linear feet. Papers of US Representative, Rev Robert F Drinan, SJ (D-Mass) 1971-1980, the first and only Catholic priest to hold a seat in Congress. Collection incl general and legislative correspondence, committee hearings and reports, voting records, speeches, campaigns, testimonials, local office files. For reference use only, by arrangement with librarian.

MA —STONEHILL COLLEGE, Cushing-Martin Library, Washington St, North Easton, 02356. James J Kenneally, Cur
Holdings: Cat Mss Pix
Notes: About 12,000 letters, speeches and photographs; 104 scrapbooks, plus other memorabilia of Representative Martin, of Massachusetts, 1925-1965; Speaker of the House, 1947-1949, 1953-1955.

MA —BRANDEIS UNIVERSITY, Goldfarb Library, 415 South St, Waltham, 02154. Bessie Hahn, Dir
Notes: Daniel Webster Collection. Consists of 11 linear ft of correspondence mainly to Daniel Webster. A finding list to the collection is located in Special Collections.

MI —FERRIS STATE COLLEGE ARCHIVES, 901 S State St, Big Rapids, 49307. R Lawrence Martin, Coordr
Holdings: Vols 11,500 Cat Mss Pix Audiotapes
Notes: Incl 36 volumes of letters written by W N Ferris as well as numerous ms letters; also Ferris State College history. Ferris was founder of the college, Governor of Michigan (1913-1916), and a US Senator (1923-1928).

MI —NATIONAL HAMILTONIAN PARTY, Library, 3314 Dillon Rd, Flushing, 48433.
Holdings: Vols Cat Mss
Notes: The life and writings of Alexander Hamilton. The National Hamiltonian Library is a part of the offices of the Hamiltonian National Committee, the governing body of the National Hamiltonian Party, a Neo-Federalist political movement. Incl 4835 vols. Also the Kelly Collection, a group of over 10,000 pieces of American political

memorabilia covering presidents and presidential hopefuls of major and minor parties as well as special sectons on women, minorities and families in politics.

MN —UNIVERSITY OF MINNESOTA, Immigration History Research Center, 826 Berry St, Saint Paul, 55114. Susan Griegs, Cur
Holdings: Vols (35,000) Mss Maps Pix Phonorecords Audiotapes 16mm Films Microforms
Notes: The Archives contain both published and ms material. Presently the imprint collections consist of nearly 25,000 vols of monographs, 3000 periodical titles, and files of more than 900 ethnic newspapers (of which ca 140 are currently received). For the most part, the printed items were published by ethnic presses in North America. Many of the extensive runs of newspapers are to be found in the Archives' microfilm collection of approx 5000 reels. The Archives' ms holdings are made up of 450 individual collections of papers, amounting to 2400 linear ft, or approx 3,000, 000 items. Incl are the records of such societies, churches and publishing companies, as well as collections of personal papers of ethnic leaders, clergymen, journalists, labor leaders, writers, poets and politicians. Partially cataloged.

MS —UNIVERSITY OF SOUTHERN MISSISSIPPI, William David McCain Graduate Library, Box 5148, Southern Sta, Hattiesburg, 39406.
Holdings: Cat Mss Pix
Notes: 965 cubic feet. Papers (1915-47) of Mississippi Senator Theodore G Bilbo and papers (1933-73) of Mississippi Congressman William M Colmer. Each collection is primarily composed of official records, but each also incl personal papers and Mississippi political records. See entries under individual names.

MS —MISSISSIPPI STATE UNIVERSITY, Mitchell Memorial Library, Box 5408, Mississippi State, 39762. Frances N Coleman, Head, Special Collections
Holdings: Vols (15,000) Cat Mss Maps Pix Microforms
Notes: Social and political history of Mississippi, incl University Archives (now separate branch). Microfilms of Protestant Church records. There are strong collections on history of the Southern States, Mississippi authors (especially Faulkner, Williams, Carter, Welty, and Young); also the John C Stennis Collection of over 2 million items, his books, papers, photographs, etc. Incl 400 collections of mss; papers of US Rep David R Bowen 1973-1983; papers of US Rep G V Montgomery 1967-.

NE —NEBRASKA STATE HISTORICAL SOCIETY, Archives, 1500 R St, Box 82554, Lincoln, 68501. James E Potter, State Archivist
Holdings: Cat Mss Microforms
Budget: ($290,000)
Notes: Collection estimated 4,000 cu. ft. of personal papers, business records, church records, and organizational records relating to the history of Nebraska and the Great Plains, ca. 1854-present with a particularly strong emphasis in the subject areas of Indians of North America, agriculture, railroad history, 19th century agrarian political movements, irrigation, and settlement of the Great Plains. Public records holdings of an estimated 10,000 cu. ft. of Nebraska state, county and some municipal government agencies include the official files of Nebraska governors, the Nebraska Legislature, and many territorial and state agencies 1854-present; and numerous tax records, court records, marriage records, naturalization records,

U.S.—POLITICS AND GOVERNMENT (cont.)

and school census records for Nebraska counties. Newspaper collection of 20,000 rolls of microfilm, non-circulating but available for purchase, cataloged according to place published so specific titles must be requested. See A GUIDE TO THE NEWSPAPER COLLECTION OF THE STATE ARCHIVES (Lincoln: Nebraska State Historical Society, 1977), A GUIDE TO THE MANUSCRIPT DIVISION OF THE STATE ARCHIVES (Lincoln: Nebraska State Historical Society, 1974), and A GUIDE TO THE MANUSCRIPT DIVISION OF THE STATE ARCHIVES, a supplement (Lincoln: Nebraska State Historical Society, 1983). Microform holdings of manuscript and public records can also be purchased.

NJ —MACCULLOCH HALL HISTORICAL MUSEUM, Morristown, 07960. Alice A Caulkins, Curator
Notes: The W Parsons Todd Collection.

NJ —PRINCETON UNIVERSITY, Library, Manuscript Collection, Nassau St, Princeton, 08540. Jean F Preston, Cur
Holdings: // Cat Mss Pix
Notes: The Adlai Stevenson Collection of personal papers is contained in 1569 boxes. Terms of Access: The bulk of the personal papers may be read by qualified scholars. See Princeton University Library Chronicle, v 26, p 15. An unpublished typescript guide (456 p) is available in the Library. Also, 3 cartons of papers relating to the Bricker Amendment and the treaty-making power of the United States, 1952-57. Also, the Blair-Lee Families Collection, which deals in large part with American political and naval history of the period 1733 to 1916, fills 300 boxes. It incl the papers of Francis Preston Blair, Sr, Samuel Phillips Lee, Elizabeth Blair Lee, and Blair Lee. An unpublished partial typescript guide (75 p) is available in the Library.

NJ —PRINCETON UNIVERSITY, Seeley G Mudd Manuscript Library, Public Affairs Papers Collection, Princeton, 08544. Nancy Bressler, Cur
Notes: "Common Cause" archives, 1968-date. Incl 130 boxes.

NM —EASTERN NEW MEXICO UNIVERSITY, Golden Library, Special Collections, Portales, 88130. Mary Jo Walker, Special Collections Librn
Notes: Papers and files of the late Congressman Harold Runnels (D NMex).

NY —NEW YORK STATE LIBRARY, State Education Bldg Annex, Washington Ave, Albany, 12224.
Notes: The papers of former Senator Jacob Javits, covering his press releases, speeches, and campaign materials for the years 1957-1978. Incl 6 boxes materials.

NY —SAINT LAWRENCE UNIVERSITY, Owen D Young Library, Canton, 13617. Mahlon Peterson, Librn
Holdings: Cat Mss
Notes: Business and personal letters and documents dating from 1816-1847 written by Silas Wright, governor of New York. Also incl some papers of family and friends. Approx 100 items.

NY —CORNELL UNIVERSITY, New York State School of Industrial & Labor Relations, Martin P Catherwood Library, Ives Hall, Ithaca, 14853. Shirley F Harper, Dir
Holdings: Vols (150,000) Cat Mss Pix Phonorecords Microforms
Notes: Collection incl approx 1000 periodicals and union journals currently received, and ms collections of labor unions, arbitrators, and scholars. 6000 linear ft.

Library Catalog of the New York State School of Industrial and Labor Relations (Boston: G K Hall, 1967), 12 volumes; Cumulation of the Library Catalog Supplements of the New York State School of Industrial and Labor Relations (Boston: G K Hall, 1976), 8 volumes.

NY —INTERNATIONAL PAPER CO, Corporate Information Center, 77 W 45 St, New York, 10036. Elizabeth Skerritt, Corporate Librn
Holdings: Vols 600

NY —MUSEUM OF BROADCASTING, Library, 1 E 53rd St, New York, 10022. Douglas Gibbons, Dir
Notes: The entire radio archive of the National Broadcasting Company. Incl 175,000 recordings of radio programs and events broadcast from 1933-1970. Duplicated at the Library of Congress.

NY —STATE UNIVERSITY OF NEW YORK, COLLEGE AT OSWEGO, Penfield Library, Oswego, 13126. Anne Commerton, Dir
Holdings: Mss
Notes: About 10,000 Millard Fillmore letter (by and to him), incl about 80 from Dorothea Dix. See New York Times, 24 March 1969.

NY —UNIVERSITY OF ROCHESTER, Rush Rhees Library, Department of Rare Books and Special Collections, Rochester, 14627. Peter Dzwonkoski, Librn
Holdings: Cat Mss
Notes: Collections include (1) Thurlow Weed, 1797-1882. Papers of this American journalist; editor of the Albany (NY) Evening Journal. Influence in 19th century American politics. Each letter in the collection has been indexed by name of letter writer. Unpublished register available in the repository. (2) The William Henry Seward papers, which contain approximately 150,000 items, relate to American political, social, and diplomatic history, ca 1825-1872. (3) A collection of approximately 4000 pamphlets of the same time period and subjects, which were owned by him. The latter are fully cataloged. Each letter in the collection has been indexed by name of letter writer. Unpublished register is available in repository. (4) A beginning collection of letters from Vietnam veterans, their families, and friends, and individuals who opposed the war, expected to create a resource toward historical understanding of attitudes and reactions concerning war and the Vietnam Conflict.

NY —STATE UNIVERSITY OF NEW YORK, STONY BROOK, Melville Library, Dept of Special Collections, Stony Brook, 11794. Evert Volkersz, Head
Notes: The political papers of New York State Republican Jacob K Javits, who served in the US House of Representatives from 1948-54 and in the US Senate from 1956-81. The collection is expected to be open for research in 1985, when finding aids will be available.

NC —DUKE UNIVERSITY, William R Perkins Library, Durham, 27706. Elvin E Strowd, University Librn
Notes: The (Quasi)-Nazi collection consists of approximately 7000 items, primarily pamphlets published in the United States by and about Nazi sympathizers Gerald K Smith, Father Coughlin, etc and organizations with Nazi leanings.

NC —DUKE UNIVERSITY, William R Perkins Library, Manuscript Dept, Durham, 27706. Ellen Gartrell, Cur of Mss
Holdings: Cat Mss
Notes: Especially strong for Southern states, 19th-20th centuries. Major collections incl papers of US senators Furnifold M Simmons, Josiah W Bailey, Clyde R Hoey, B Everett Jordan; also Campbell Family, C C Clay, Henry Clay, Daniel C Roper, Harry A Slattery, Socialist Party of America Papers.

NC —DUKE UNIVERSITY, William R Perkins Library, Public Documents and Maps Department, Durham, 27706. Jaia Barrett, Head
Holdings: Vols Maps Pamphlets Microforms
Notes: A selective depository for US Government publications since 1890, the

Department currently holds well over 500,000 items, plus publications of the European Community (a depository collection), the League of Nations, the UN and UN-affiliated agencies. Other international organizations, publications are acquired also, as are state government publications, especially from the Southeast, California, New York and Illinois. The Documents Department holds services the major map collections of Perkins Library. These collections include topographic, geologic, and special subject maps which are worldwide in coverage. The department is a depository for the US Defense Mapping Agency and the US Geological Survey. In addition, there are many other maps of general and specific interest, including US and foreign road maps. As appropriate, maps are also held in the Perkins Library's Rare BookRoom and Manuscript Department. Atlases are shelved in the Reference Department and in the bookstacks of Perkins Library.

NC —UNIVERSITY OF NORTH CAROLINA, GREENSBORO, Walter Clinton Jackson Library, Special Collections Dept, 1000 Spring Garden St, Greensboro, 27412. Emilie W Mills, Librn
Holdings: Uncat
Notes: Time-Life News Science files of Bonnie Angelo, Washington correspondent; incl News Service Convention files of the Democratic National Conventions for 1968, 1972 and 1976; Republican National Conventions for 1968, 1972 and 1976; transcripts of Nixon Press Conferences, 1969-1973; files on Nixon finances, 1973; transcripts of Ford Press Conferences, 1974-1976. No photocopying.

OH —RUTHERFORD B HAYES LIBRARY, 1337 Hayes Ave, Fremont, 43420. Watt P Marchman, Dir
Holdings: Vols 10,000 Cat Mss Maps Pix Slides Microforms Audiotapes
Notes: The Rutherford B Hayes Family Collections. The collections comprise papers, books, correspondence, diaries, speeches, account books, financial and real estate records, law cases, ephemera, and memorabilia of members of the Rutherford B Hayes family; his wife, Lucy Webb Hayes; their children: Birchard Austin Hayes; Webb C Hayes I; Rutherford Platt Hayes; Scott Russell Hayes; Fanny Hayes; grandchildren: Dalton Hayes; Webb C Hayes, II; daughter-in-law, Mary Miller Hayes. Mss of the collection are described in Guide to Manuscripts of the Ohio Historical Society, 208, 209, 210, 211, 212, 214, 216, 217, 218, 219. Indexed, listed. The collections are housed in the mss division and newspapers division. Ms materials of 256 linear feet; 50,000 pictures; slides; tapes; moving pictures, maps. The papers of Rutherford Birchard Hayes available on 304 rolls of microfilm. The collection described in Guide to the Microfilm Edition of the Papers of Rutherford Birchard Hayes, the Nineteenth President of the United States. Fremont, Ohio: The Rutherford B Hayes Presidential Center, 1983. In addition, the Great Lakes Marine Collection, incl Capt Frank E Hamilton Collection; Great Lakes boats and shipping. Incl 300 charts, over 20,000 pictures (with 2500 negatives, 30 glass plates). Index and finding aids with the collection.

OK —UNIVERSITY OF OKLAHOMA, Bizzell Memorial Library, Western History Collections, 401 W Brooks, Norman, 73069. John Ezell, Cur
Notes: Subject scope covers all aspects of history and culture of American Trans-Mississippi West and the North American Indians with special emphasis on Oklahoma and adjacent states, the Southwest and Spanish borderlands. Printed and non-print holdings cover Indians, explorations and surveys, range cattle industry, fur-trade,

U.S.—POLITICS AND GOVERNMENT (cont.)

transportation, overland travels, emigration and immigration, frontier life, agriculture, mining, oil gas industry, conservation, literature, and the social-cultural history as well as the usual political and economic interests. The large holdings of U.S. Congressional papers also reflect other national and international affairs.

PA —BALCH INSTITUTE FOR ETHNIC STUDIES, Library, 18 S Seventh St, Philadelphia, 19106. R Joseph Anderson, Library Dir

PA —UNION LEAGUE OF PHILADELPHIA, Library, 140 S Broad St, Philadelphia, 19102. James G Mundy Jr, Librn
Holdings: Vols (23,000) Cat Mss Pix
Notes: Emphasis on Civil War, American social and political history, Philadelphia and Pensylvania history.

†SC —STROM THURMOND CENTER FOR EXCELLENCE IN GOVERNMENT AND PUBLIC SERVICE, Clemson University Library, Clemson, 29631.
Notes: Public papers and memorabilia of Senator Strom Thurmond (R, SC).

SD —NATIONAL COLLEGE OF BUSINESS, Thomas Jefferson Learning Resource Center, 321 Kansas City St, Rapid City, 57701. Linda Watson, Library Dir
Holdings: Vols (26,000) Cat
Notes: Analyses (Index) of national and international issues. Published at irregular, frequent intervals, produced by the American Enterprise Institute for Public Policy Research.

TX —ABILENE CHRISTIAN UNIVERSITY, Margaret & Herman Brown Library, ACU Sta, Abilene, 79601. Callie Faye Milliken, Assoc Dir
Holdings: Vols 5000 // Cat
Notes: Donner Library of Americanism Books, pamphlets, documents, and periodical materials dealing with American politics of the far right collected by Robert Donner during and after World War II. Also incl materials on Jews and Freemasonry.

†TX —UNIVERSITY OF TEXAS LIBRARIES, General Libraries, Humanities Research Center, PO Box 7219, Austin, 78712. John Chalmers, Librn
Notes: The John W F Dulles collection of correspondence, diaries, autographs, speeches, and paintings by famous historical figures from the 17th century to the present. Much of the material is related to Mr Dulles' three relatives who served as Secretaries of State: John Foster Dulles, Robert Lansing, and John W Foster.

TX —SAM RAYBURN FOUNDATION LIBRARY, 800 W Sam Rayburn Dr, Box 123, Bonham, 75418.
Holdings: Vols 8000 Cat Mss Pix Microforms
Notes: Historical research library-contains all of Speaker Rayburn's papers. Incl books on American history, biography, politics and government, and the Presidents and their writings.

TX —TEXAS A&M UNIVERSITY, Sterling C Evans Library, University Archives, College Station, 77843. Charles R Schultz, University Archivist
Holdings: Mss
Notes: The Archives of Modern Politics: the papers of Texas Congressman Olin E Teague, 1946-1975; Graham Purcell, 1961-1971; Robert R Casey, 1958-1976; and John Young, 1963-1976; Texas Legislators Will L Smith, 1962-1971; Tom Creighton, 1961-1980; Bill Presnal 1974-1983, and Bill Clayton, 1961-1983; Washington DC journalist Bascom N Timmons, ca 1920-1970; and political candidate and religious zealot Jonnie Mae Hackworth, ca 1945-1980.

VA —UNIVERSITY OF VIRGINIA, Alderman Library, Manuscripts Dept, Charlottesville, 22901. Edmund Berkeley Jr, Cur
Holdings: Cat Mss Pix Phonorecords Audiotapes Videotapes 16mm Films Microforms
Notes: Twentieth

WI —UNIVERSITY OF WISCONSIN, MILWAUKEE, Library, Box 604, Milwaukee, 53201. William C Roselle, Dir
Holdings: Vols 2500 Cat Mss Pix
Notes: Papers of FDR's Secretary of Commerce, Daniel C Roper.

U.S.—POPULATION

NC —CAROLINA POPULATION CENTER, Library, University Sq E, Chapel Hill, 27514. Patricia Shipman, Head Librn
Holdings: Vols (20,000) Cat
Budget: ($10,500)
Notes: Try to acquire everything published in English on population, with particular emphasis on the US and developing countries. Also acquire conference proceedings, seminar papers. These and journal articles are indexed and the analytics are incl in the catalog. Incl 13,000 reprints and other pieces of ephemera. Most extensive area files are on India, Africa, Thailand, Iran, Korea, and Latin America. Holdings are recorded on an automated data base. A microfiche catalog is available for use in the Library and for purchase. Access by subject & geographic area are available through the Library's own thesaurus-based indexing systems.

OK —SOCIETY FOR THE NORTH AMERICAN CULTURAL SURVEY, Dept of Geography, Oklahoma State University, Stillwater, 74078. John Rooney, Dir; Todd Zdorkowski, Asst
Notes: Has produced a cultural atlas of North America that describes the regional variations in North America's folk and popular sub populations.

U.S.—PRESIDENTS see Presidents—U.S.

U.S.—PUBLIC DOCUMENTS see U.S. —Government Publications

U.S.—RELIGIOUS LIFE AND CUSTOMS

GA —EMORY UNIVERSITY, Candler School of Theology, Pitts Theology Library, Atlanta, 30322. Channing Jeschke, Librn; Anita K Delaries, Curator
Notes: The Hartford Seminary Foundation Library (partial). About 205,000 vols, pamphlets, etc.

IL —NEWBERRY LIBRARY, 60 W Walton St, Chicago, 60610. Diana Haskell, Cur of Modern Mss
Holdings: Cat
Notes: Good collection.

IL —WHEATON COLLEGE, Billy Graham Center Library and Archives, Wheaton, 60187. Ferne Lauraine Weimer, Dir of Library; Robert Shuster, Dir of Archives
Notes: Archives of the Center.

MA —BRANDEIS UNIVERSITY, Goldfarb Library, 415 South St, Waltham, 02154. Bessie Hahn, Dir
Notes: Perry Miller Collection on the Colonial Religious Experience in America: 18 linear ft of books dating from the 17th and 18th century relating to the religious experience in the American colonies. Access to the collection is through the Main Card Catalog and Special Collections Card Catalog.

NJ —DREW UNIVERSITY, Library, Madison, 07940. Caroline Coughlin, Assoc Dir
Notes: The national archives of the United Methodist Church.

NY —GENERAL THEOLOGICAL SEMINARY, Saint Marks Library, 175 Ninth Ave, New York, 10011. David Green, Dir
Holdings: Vols (200,000) Cat Mss Maps Pix Slides Microforms

NC —BELMONT ABBEY COLLEGE, Abbot Vincent Taylor Library, Belmont, 28012. Marjorie McDermott, Dir
Holdings: Vols (1000) Cat
Notes: Consists of books dealing with the history of North and South Carolina from colonial times to be present. Incl are several county histories, some early newspapers, and a strong section on the history of religion (especially the Roman Catholic Church) in the two states.

NC —DUKE UNIVERSITY, William R Perkins Library, Manuscript Dept, Durham, 27706. Ellen Gartrell, Cur of Mss
Holdings: Cat Mss
Notes: Especially US South, Methodist Church Papers (records of local and regional units) also many personal and professional papers of clergy, missionaries, and laymen, 19th-20th centuries. Methodist John Lakin Brasher (holiness movement leader), Carlyle Marney (Southern Baptist minister), Methodist Bishop James Cannon, missionary Martha Foster Crawford.

NC —DUKE UNIVERSITY, Divinity School Library, Durham, 27706. Donn Michael Farris, Librn
Holdings: Vols (225,000)
Notes: Special collections and subject emphases in this library include: Archaeology, Egyptian; Archaeology, Middle Eastern; Art, Jewish; Bible; Bible-New Testament; Bible-Symbolism; Church Architecture; Egyptology; Fathers of the Church; Society of Friends; Great Britain-Religion-Methodism and Methodist Church; Hymns and Hymnals; Jansenists and Jansenism; Judaica; Mediaeval Christian Mysticism; Methodism and Methodist Church; Methodist Episcopal Church; Methodist Episcopal Church, South; Reformation; Religion-US-History; Rural Church; Theology-Great Britain-17th Century; Theology-Great Britain-18th Century; United Methodist Church; US-Church History; John Wesley.

NC —SOUTHEASTERN BAPTIST THEOLOGICAL SEMINARY LIBRARY, PO Box 752, Wake Forest, 27587. H Eugene McLeod, Librn
Holdings: Cat Slides Audiotapes Videotapes Microforms
Notes: Incl early American sources in Readex Microprint edition of materials listed in Evan's *American Bibliography* and in Shaw and Shoemaker's *American Bibliograpy: a Preliminary Checklist*.

OH —RUTHERFORD B HAYES LIBRARY, 1337 Hayes Ave, Fremont, 43420. Watt P Marchman, Dir
Holdings: Uncat Mss Pix Microforms
Notes: The Frank Ohlinger Family Collection: American religion: Chinese misssionary; education. (9 linear feet). Index in collections.

OH —KENT STATE UNIVERSITY, University Archives, Kent, 44242. Stephen C Morton, University Archivist
Holdings: Uncat Mss
Notes: Books and papers by A O Fuller, Cornelia Cowles Fuller, and Jeannette Fuller. Allen O Fuller was an ordained Baptist Minister in Northeastern, Ohio. The collection, in addition to periodical newspaper articles by A O Fuller, includes miscellaneous folders containing Fuller's religious and medical theories and other materials and two journals dated 1851-1854 and 1857.

PA —BALCH INSTITUTE FOR ETHNIC STUDIES, Library, 18 S Seventh St, Philadelphia, 19106. R Joseph Anderson, Library Dir

PA —FRIENDS HISTORICAL LIBRARY OF SWARTHMORE COLLEGE, Swarthmore, 19081. J William Frost, Dir
Holdings: Vols (35,000) Cat Mss Pix Microforms
Notes: Library's collection contain information on the history and doctrine of the Society of Friends, Quaker contributions to literature, science, business, education, and government, plus their reform efforts in peace, Indian rights, women's rights, and abolition of slavery. As an official depository of the records of the records of Philadelphia and Baltimore Yearly Meetings, the library holds, either in the original manuscript or on microfilm, the largest collection in the world of Quaker meeting archives, incl some records of Ohio and Illinois Yearly Meetings

U.S.—RELIGIOUS LIFE AND CUSTOMS (cont.)

(Hicksite), and microfilm copies of minutes and registers of many meetings in New England, New York, North Carolina, Indiana, and Great Britain. Among the more than 250 mss collections, described in *Guide to the Manuscript Collections of Friends Historical Library of Swarthmore College* (1982), are papers of individual Quaker leaders, families, and organizations.

TN —HISTORICAL COMMISSION-SUNDAY SCHOOL BOARD, Southern Baptist Convention, Dargan-Carver Library, 127 Ninth Ave N, Nashville, 37234. Howard Gallimore, Supvr
Holdings: Vols (10,000) Cat Mss Maps Pix Slides Phonorecords Audiotapes Videotapes 16mm Films Filmstrips Microforms
Budget: ($38,734)
Notes: Extensive holdings in proceedings and minutes of organized Baptist bodies; state conventions and associatons, Baptist journals, and documentation of major Southern Baptist controversies. Material on Black, Russian, and other Baptists. Much on religious education and American religion. Large collection of Sunday School literature. Includes photographs, slides, sound recordings, 12,000,000 pages of microforms, and 1200 linear feet of archival and manuscripts material.

U.S.—SOCIAL LIFE AND CUSTOMS

CA —HUNTINGTON BEACH PUBLIC LIBRARY, 7111 Talbert Ave, Huntington Beach, 92648. Walter Johnson, Library Dir
Holdings: Vols 19,000 // Cat Microforms
Notes: American civilization: literature, social life, customs, etc. See: *Microbook Library of American Civilization.*

CA —UNIVERSITY OF CALIFORNIA, LOS ANGELES, Research Library, Dept of Special Collections, 405 Hilgard Ave, Los Angeles, 90024. Edward Shreeves, Chairman, Bibliographers Group; David S Zeidberg, Head
Notes: Various collections, incl almanacs, comic books, commercial catalogs, fantasy fiction, pulp magazines, trade cards, and 19th century American paperbacks. Also, 90 linear feet in various collections pertaining to political and social activities in the US, Europe, Latin America, and the USSR.

CA —CALIFORNIA INSTITUTE OF TECHNOLOGY, Robert A Millikan Memorial Library, Archives, 1201 E California Blvd, Pasadena, 91125. Judith R Goodstein, Archivist
Holdings: Vols (3000) Uncat Mss Maps Pix Slides Phonorecords Audiotapes Videotapes 16mm Films Microforms
Notes: Over 70 collections (1830s-present) relating to history of 19th-20th centuries science and technology and the history of the Institute. Included are personal and professional papers of Caltech scientists and administrative officers; divisional records and faculty committees; over 5000 photographs of American and European scientists. Mss collections documents more than a century of American political, social, and intellectual history; the development of the physical sciences, aeronautics, molecular biology, and seismology in the US and abroad; and social and political conditions in Europe between the two World Wars. There are also family letters relating to 19th century American life before and during the Civil War (the Morley and A G Throop papers); to 19th century social conditions in Russia and Hungary (the Paul Epstein papers and Theodore von Karman papers); andto the development of 20th century Italian mathematics.

DC —HOWARD UNIVERSITY, Moorland-Spingarn Research Center, 500 Howard Place NW, Washington, 20059. Clifford L Muse, Jr, Acting Dir
Holdings: Vols (106,086) Cat Mss Maps Pix Slides Phonorecords Audiotapes 16mm Films Filmstrips Microforms
Budget: ($854,753)
Notes: *The Glenn Carrington Collection: A*

Guide to the Books, Manuscripts, Music and Recordings (DC MSRC, 1977). *Dictionary Catalog of the Jesse E Moorland Collection of Negro Life and History,* 9 vols and Supplement, 3 vols (Boston: G K Hall, 1970, 1977). *Dictionary Catalog of the Arthur Spingarn Collection of Negro Authors,* 2 vols (Boston: G K Hall, 1970). Guide to Processed Collections in the Manuscript Division of the Moorland-Spingarn Research Center (DC, MSRC, 1983). The Moorland-Spingran Research Center is recognized as one of the largest and most comprehensive repositories in the world for the collection, preservation and dissemination of historical materials documenting from antiquity to the present the history and culture of Black people in Africa, Europe, the Caribbean and the US. Since 1973, the Research Center has greatly expanded its facilitiesand resources and currently provides research services in all aspects of library and archival research, including manuscripts, oral history, music, prints and photographs and general library materials. The Research Center also maintains professional zerographic, micrographic, photographic and similar reproduction laboratories.

DC —LIBRARY OF CONGRESS, Prints & Photographs Div, Washington, 20540.
Notes: Effective October 1, the Library's Prints and Photographs Division has discontinued reproduction and reference service on its collection of photographs which appeared in *Look* magazine from 1937 to 1971. This limitation on service will remain in effect until questions of rights and permissions affecting these photographs can be clarified. The Library acquired the *Look* archive in 1971 as additional resources for research in American life by scholars and other investigators. It was anticipated that the photographs would serve as a study collection for researchers in many fields, but the major use of the collection has been by publishers, advertisers, and makers of documentary films. Such picture users require clear rights to reproduce the images. The Library has been unable to satisfy these requests because of the donor's stipulation precluding such use. Until some accommodation canbe made with the donor to free the collection for a wider range of public use, collection will remain in remote cold storage to retard deterioration of sensitive films, especially color films. This policy will remain in effect until further notice. LC Information Bulletin, 10 Oct 83.

DC —LIBRARY OF CONGRESS, Motion Pictures, Broadcasting and Recorded Sound Div, Washington, 20540.
Notes: The entire radio archive of the National Broadcasting Company. Incl 175, 000 recordings of radio programs and events broadcast from 1933-70. Duplicated at the Museum of Broadcasting in New York City.

MD —US DEPT OF AGRICULTURE, National Agricultural Library, 10301 Baltimore Blvd, Beltsville, 20705. Joseph H Howard, Director
Notes: Worldwide coverage of all aspects of agriculture and related fields. Crop ecology, agro-climatic analogs; air pollution effects. Agronomy: agricultural and tropical and desert agriculture. For use by the staff of the USDA. Incl in the former collections of American Institute of Crop Ecology.

MA —CHILDREN'S MUSEUM, Resource Center, Museum Wharf, 300 Congress St, Boston, 02210. Marie Ariel, Librn; Maria Russell, Resource Services Mgr
Holdings: Vols (400) Cat Mss Slides Audiotapes Phonorecords Filmstrips
Notes: Focus is on changes in US life over the past 100 years. Curriculum materials and materials for children and adults. Available for reference use by the public; borrowing privileges for Museum members; activity and curriculum kits available to public, schools and community groups for rental fee. Subject-related programs and services offered by Museum staff.

MA —PEABODY INSTITUTE LIBRARY, Danvers Public Library, 15 Sylvan St, Danvers, 01923. John Moak, Dir
Holdings: Vols 1000 Cat
Notes: American social history.

MI —MICHIGAN STATE UNIVERSITY, Libraries, Special Collections Div, East Lansing, 48824. Jannette Fiore, Librn
Holdings: Vols (55,000) Mss Pix
Notes: Collection of 19th century authors, including selected expatriate authors. Popular Culture Collections have four principal categories of materials: Comic Art, ca 23,500 items (comics, aprox 21,000 cataloged issues, big-little books, reprints and anthologies, etc); Popular Fiction, ca 24,000 items (dime novels, story magazines and pulps, juvenile series, detective, science fiction, western and romantic novels); Popular Information, ca 5000 items (over 2000 public school text books, along with almanacs, big and little blue books, "self-education" materials, etc); Popular Performing Arts, ca 2300 items (tent-show materials, including 250 scripts, photographs, handbills, records and correspondence; plays and entertainments for home and popular performance and print materials relating to radio-TV-film). Partially cataloged.

NY —NEW YORK STATE HISTORICAL ASSOCIATION, Library, Lake Rd, Cooperstown, 13326. Amy Barnum, Librn
Holdings: Vols (55,000) Cat Mss Maps Pix Slides Microforms Tapes
Notes: Emphasis on New York Stae in 19th century. Incl Cooperstown Graduate Program Archives and Swilte-Telfer Collection of 60,000 glass plate negative, Otsego County, about 1850-1950.

NY —MUSEUM OF BROADCASTING, Library, 1 E 53rd St, New York, 10022. Douglas Gibbons, Dir
Notes: The entire radio archive of the National Broadcasting Company. Incl 175, 000 recordings of radio programs and events broadcast from 1933-1970. Duplicated at the Library of Congress.

NC —DUKE UNIVERSITY, William R Perkins Library, Jay B Hubbell Center for American Literary Historiography, Durham, 27706. Erma Whittington, Librn
Notes: 77,312 items, including manuscripts, pictures, clippings, and correspondence. "The objective of the Center is to gather the papers and materials of significant scholars and critics in American literary history." The Center is a part of the Perkins Library Manuscripts Department.

OK —SOCIETY FOR THE NORTH AMERICAN CULTURAL SURVEY, Dept of Geography, Oklahoma State University, Stillwater, 74078. John Rooney, Dir; Todd Zdorkowski, Asst
Notes: Has produced a cultural atlas of North America. Contents incl sports and games, general cultural and popular regions, settlement patterns, land division patterns, folk and modern architecture, regional variations in social organization and behavior, language and place names, ethnicity, religion, politics, food ways, music and dance, and place perception.

PA —TEMPLE UNIVERSITY LIBRARIES, Special Collections Dept, Contemporary Culture Collection, Philadelphia, 19122. Patricia J Case, Cur
Notes: The Contemporary Culture Collection is devoted to underground and alternative press material dating from 1960. Acquisitions fall into two categories: social and political movement material and small press literature. Manuscripts relating to these areas are also being acquired. These include the archives of the Committee of Small Magazine Editors and Publishers (COSMEP), Youth Liberation, the Liberation News Service, *Dramaticka, Nola Express,* and personal papers of Lyn Lifshin. Particular strengths are underground newspapers, military and high school papers; papers of feminist, Third World and gay rights movements; publications from new communal and international societies and new religions; small press poetry and little magazines. Other collection areas are: radical approaches to education, ecology, alternative lifestyles, underground comics, anti-communist, white supremacist, anti-racist and anti-nationalist publications, libertarianism and prison reform. Collection holdings incl 5100 journals, newspapers,

U.S.—SOCIAL LIFE AND CUSTOMS (cont.)

newsletter titles; 6000 books and pamphlets; microfilm, audiotapes, posters and broadsides, ephemera and manuscript collections.

PA —UNION LEAGUE OF PHILADELPHIA, Library, 140 S Broad St, Philadelphia, 19102. James G Mundy Jr, Librn
Holdings: Vols (23,000) Cat Mss Pix
Notes: Emphasis on Civil War, American social and political history, Philadelphia and Pennsylvania history.

VA —GEORGE MASON UNIVERSITY, Fenwick Library, Special Collections Dept, 4400 University Drive, Fairfax, 22030. Ruth Kerns, Public Services Librn
Notes: The Ollie Atkins Photographic Collection. Atkins, award-winning photographer with the *Saturday Evening Post*, was also White House photographer under several administrations. The collection incl more than 15,000 prints, negatives, contact sheets, slides and 4000 images covering subjects of historical, artistic and social significance from 1948 to 1968.

U.S.—TREATIES see U.S.—Foreign Relations_Treaties

U.S. AIR FORCE—HISTORY

†DC —NATIONAL BUREAU OF STANDARDS, Library, Records Holding Area, Administration Bldg E120, Washington, 20234.
Notes: Papers of the mathematician William J Youden, dating mostly from about 1920-69, concerning his service as consultant to the US Army Air Force, 1942-45, as well as other aspects of his career.

NC —82ND AIRBORNE DIVISION, War Memorial Museum, Reference Library, Ardennes & Gela Sts, Fort Bragg, 28307. John S Duvall, Chief Cur
Holdings: Vols (300) Uncat Mss Maps Pix
Notes: The collection is intended to be a research tool for persons studying the history of the 82nd Airborne Division and the development of airborne warfare.

U.S. APPELLATE COURTS

DC —LIBRARY OF CONGRESS, Law Library, 101 Independence Ave, SE, Washington, 20540. Carleton W Kenyon, Dir
Holdings: Cat
Notes: All circuits from 1891 but holdings vary for each circuit.

U.S. ARCHIVES see Archives, U.S

U.S. ARMY

GA —US ARMY INFANTRY CENTER, National Infantry Museum, Fort Benning, 31905. Dick D Grube, Dir; Z Frank Hanner, Cur; Carol Sims, Librn
Holdings: Vols (6000) Cat Mss Maps Pix Slides
Notes: Published and unpublished works dealing with infantry history, equipment, and units, for research on the Museum's collections of artifacts. Items cannot be checked out except under unusual and compelling circumstances. The collection traces the two centuries of history of the US Infantry. Of special interest are: unpublished reports of tests conducted on US Army Infantry equipment; photographs showing the history of Fort Benning; books and periodical articles dealing with Infantry small arms, both American and foreign, especially Japanese, Soviet, Chinese, and British; US Army manuals, incl many from the early 20th and late 19th centuries; WWII battlefield maps; WWI and WWII posters; histories of WWI; US Army insignia and medals; WWII era German uniforms and insignia. Also, over 2500 weapons.

PA —US ARMY WAR COLLEGE LIBRARY, Carlisle Barracks, 17013. Barbara E Stevens,

Dir
Holdings: Vols (125,000) Cat Maps Microforms Audiotapes
Budget: ($251,000)
Notes: Physical access to the collection is limited. Individual items available on interlibrary loan. Older historical material is in the US Army Military History Institute, Carlisle Barracks, Pennsylvania, 17013.

VA —MACARTHUR MEMORIAL, Library & Archives, MacArthur Sq, Norfolk, 23510. Ellen E Folkama, Asst Archivist
Holdings: Vols (4000) Cat Maps Pix Slides Phonorecords Audiotapes 16mm Films Microforms
Notes: Everything relating to the life and related activities of MacArthur. The Archives of the collection consist of 600 shelf-feet of documents from Gen MacArthur's official headquarters files over the period 1941-1951. These papers pertain to all matters with which his various commands were involved: military, naval and air matters; international relations; political science; Japanese occupation, peace treaty and Constitution, etc. Each Record Group is indexed. The indexes are retained here since they are being expanded. They are available for researchers.

U.S. ARMY—ARTILLERY

KS —UNIVERSITY OF KANSAS, Kenneth Spencer Research Library, Kansas Collection, Lawrence, 66045. Sheryl K Williams, Cur
Holdings: Cat Pix
Notes: The JJ Pennell Collection. Joseph Judd Pennell (1866-1922) was a commercial photographer living and working in Junction City, Kansas from 1888 to 1922. This collection of more than 30,000 glass negatives and nearly 6000 prints is a pictorial record of Junction City, Kansas and nearby Ft Riley. The residents of Junction City have been photographed in their various business, professional, social, and cultural activities, while the army post, Fort Riley, has been documented as a cavalry and light artillery post, as well as an important military post during the First World War and after. The various ethnic groups which made up the population of Junction City, whites, blacks, and Mexican-Americans, are represented in the collection. Pennell's day books accompany the photographic collection.

OK —US ARMY FIELD ARTILLERY SCHOOL LIBRARY, Morris Swett Library, Snow Hall, Fort Sill, 73503. Lester L Miller Jr, Chief Librn
Holdings: Vols 265,958 Documents Pix Maps Slides Microforms
Notes: Field artillery; artillery; ordnance; military history; military science; weapons and weapons systems; ammunition; ballistics; missiles; Field Artillery unit histories; military periodicals analytical index file (VF). Incl US and foreign artillery; survey data; historical material on the army in Indian Territory and settlement of the southwest; photographs on army subjects, Indian Territory, Oklahoma history, Indians of the southwest.

U.S. ARMY—CAVALRY

KS —UNIVERSITY OF KANSAS, Kenneth Spencer Research Library, Kansas Collection, Lawrence, 66045. Sheryl K Williams, Cur
Holdings: Cat Pix
Notes: The J J Pennell Collection. Joseph Judd Pennell (1866-1922) was a commercial photographer living and working in Junction City, Kansas from 1888 to 1922. This collection of more than 30,000 glass negatives and nearly 6000 prints is a pictorial record of Junction City, Kansas and nearby Fort Riley. The residents of Junction City have been photographed in their various business, professional, social, and cultural activities, while the army post, Fort Riley, has been documented as a cavalry and light artillery post, as well as an important military post during the First World War

and after. The various ethnic groups which made up the population of Junction City (whites, blacks, and Mexican-Americans) are represented in the collection. Pennell's day books accompany the photographic collection.

KY —PATTON MUSEUM OF CAVALRY & ARMOR, Emert L Davis Memorial Library, PO Box 208, Fort Knox, 40121. Phyllis S Cassler, Librn
Holdings: Vols (6500) Cat Mss Maps Pix
Budget: ($1800)
Notes: Technical works, particularly technical and field manuals, concerning equipment used by US Army Mechanized Cavalry and Armour. Incl 10,000 pictures.

MI —MONROE COUNTY LIBRARY SYSTEM, Ellis Reference and Information Center, 3700 S Custer Rd, Monroe, 48161. Marie D Chulski, Head of Reference Services
Holdings: Vols 35,000 Cat Mss Maps Pix Slides 16mm Films Microforms Periodicals Sound Recordings Paintings Memorabilia
Budget: ($15,000)
Notes: Historic Monroe County, tracing its beginnings to 1780, is a definite part of Michigan's history. Many events of the area and citizens are part of Michigan's heritage. The Michigan collection besides general works contains individual county histories, atlases, biographies, etc. The Monroe County history collection contains veteran records, plat books, oral history tapes, family histories, church records, cemetery index, atlases and census records. Genealogy emphasis is not only Monroe County but includes surrounding counties and the states with large migration to the area, such as Ohio, Kentucky, Tennessee and the New England states.

OK —US ARMY FIELD ARTILLERY SCHOOL LIBRARY, Morris Swett Library, Snow Hall, Fort Sill, 73503. Lester L Miller Jr, Chief Librn
Notes: Incl data on Fort Sill, Indian Territory, settlement of Kiowa, Apache and Commanche tribes, imprisonment of Geronimo, Oklahoma territory, settlement of Lawton. Unit histories, incl 10th Cavalry (Buffalo Soldiers, a black unit that built Fort Sill); working papers of Sheridan, Grierson and other commanders; Field Artillery School. Photographs on army subjects, Fort Sill, Indians, Indian Territory, settlement of Southwest Oklahoma.

U.S. ARMY—HISTORY

DC —LIBRARY OF CONGRESS, Manuscript Division, Washington, 20540. John C Broderick, Chief
Notes: The papers of General John Joseph Pershing (14,000 items).

GA —US ARMY INFANTRY SCHOOL LIBRARY, Fort Benning, 31905. Vivian S Dodson, Chief Librn
Holdings: Vols 165,000 Microforms
Budget: $47,000
Notes: Military art and science, with emphasis on infantry. Each Army service school and branch school has an academic library. Incl books, classified and unclassified documents, periodicals (cat).

IL —NEWBERRY LIBRARY, 60 W Walton St, Chicago, 60610. Diana Haskell, Cur of Modern Mss
Holdings: Vols 4400 Cat
Notes: Incl Ephraim C Dawes collection of regimental histories. Restricted use: Noncirculating.

NC —82ND AIRBORNE DIVISION, War Memorial Museum, Reference Library, Ardennes & Gela Sts, Fort Bragg, 28307. John S Duvall, Chief Cur
Holdings: Vols (300) Uncat Mss Maps Pix
Notes: The collection is intended to be a research tool for persons studying the history of the 82nd Airborne Division and the development of airborne warfare.

PA —US ARMY MILITARY HISTORY INSTITUTE, Carlisle Barracks, 17013. Richard J Sommers, Chief Archivist-Historian
Notes: Books 350,000; bound periodicals 30,000; military publications 700,000; periodical

U.S. ARMY—HISTORY (cont.)

subscriptions 110; microform 12,000 incl fiche 6000, reels 6000; reports and studies 150,000; military unit histories 5000. The World War I survey: Personal correspondence, diaries, and memoirs of American officers and enlisted men of Regular, National Guard, and National Army units (also sailors, Marines, and Coast Guardsmen) serving in the United States, England, France, Italy, Germany, the Ottoman Empire, and Russia during and immediately after the First World War. This is the largest collection anywhere of personal papers of US forces in the Great War. (6500 folders and 100 boxes mss.) The World War II collection: Personal letters, daily logs, reminiscences, speeches, and official papers of American officers and soldiersserving in the European, Mediterranean, Middle Eastern, China-Burma-India, Southwest Pacific, and Central Pacific Theaters and in the Zone of the Interior during the Second World War. Most of these collections are mss of General officers, incl Omar Bradley, Stephen Chamberlin, Lewis Hershey, John Lucas, William Simpson, and Brehon Somervell. The Korean War collection: Personal correspondence, daily logs, recollections, and official papers of US officers and soldiers serving in the Korean War, incl Generals Edward Almond, George Barth, Bruce Clarke, Matthew Ridgway, and Arthur Trudeau. The Viet Nam War collection: Personal letters, daily logs, memoirs, speeches, and official paeprs of American officers and soldiers serving in Viet Nam or elsewhere in the world during the era. Almost all these paeprs are from Generals, incl William DePuy, Harold K Johnson, Bruce Palmer,Jonathan Seaman, and William Westmoreland. (2000 boxes mss.)

RI —BROWN UNIVERSITY, John Hay Library, 20 Prospect St, Providence, 02912. Mark N Brown, Cur Mss
Holdings: Mss
Notes: Several ms collections relating to the history of the US Army, incl the Ephraim Elmer Ellsworth, 1837-1861, Collection (225 items); the Benjamin Fry, 1755-1840. Collection (800 items); the Rush Christopher Hawkins, 1831-1920. Collection (130 items); and the Augustus Woodbury, 1825-1895. Collection (ca 100 items).

U.S. ARMY—INFANTRY

GA —US ARMY INFANTRY SCHOOL LIBRARY, Fort Benning, 31905. Vivian S Dodson, Chief Librn
Holdings: Vols 165,000 Cat Microforms
Notes: Military history; military art and science, with emphasis on infantry.

U.S. ARMY—REGIMENTAL HISTORIES

CA —LOS ANGELES PUBLIC LIBRARY, History Dept, 630 W Fifth St, Los Angeles, 90071. Frank Louch, Sr Librn
Holdings: Vols 1000 Cat Maps
Budget: ($85,000)
Notes: A well-rounded collection with emphasis on unit histories of World War II.

IL —NEWBERRY LIBRARY, 60 W Walton St, Chicago, 60610. Diana Haskell, Cur of Modern Mss
Holdings: Vols 4400 Cat
Notes: Incl Ephraim C Dawes collection of regimental histories. Restricted use: Noncirculating.

MT —EASTERN MONTANA COLLEGE, Library, 1500 N 30 St, Billings, 59101. Edward Neroda, Dir
Holdings: Mss
Notes: Incl Custer's personal and military papers and those of his widow relating to his career. Also, imcomplete 7th Cavalry records and papers of the Battle of Little Big Horn. Many Civil War papers. Collection formerly at the Custer Battlefield National Monument.

NY —NEW YORK PUBLIC LIBRARY, Research Libraries, General Research Division, Fifth Ave & 42 St, New York, 10018. Rodney Phillips, Chief
Holdings: Vols (2,225,000) Cat Maps Pix Microforms
Budget: ($775,718)
Notes: See *Subject Catalog of the World War II Collection, The Research Libraries of the New York Public Library*, 1977, 3 vols (47,671 cards). $240. Particular strengths incl military, naval and aerial history and operations; economic aspects of the wars; communication and propaganda; prisoners, prisons, concentration camps and war crimes; and the influence of the war of cultural institutions and art forms.

OK —US ARMY FIELD ARTILLERY SCHOOL LIBRARY, Morris Swett Library, Snow Hall, Fort Sill, 73503. Lester L Miller Jr, Chief Librn
Holdings: Vols (265,958) Documents Pix Maps Slides Microforms
Notes: Field artillery; artillery; ordnance; military history; military science; weapons and weapons systems; ammunition; ballistics; missiles; Field Artillery unit histories; military periodicals analytical index file (VF). Incl US and foreign artillery; survey data; historical material on the army in Indian Territory and settlement of the southwest; photographs on army subjects, Indian Territory, Oklahoma history, Indians of the southwest.

†VA —GEORGE C MARSHALL RESEARCH FOUNDATION AND LIBRARY, Drawer 920, Lexington, 24450. Royster Lyle Jr, Cur Collections
Holdings: Vols Cat Mss Maps Pix Phonorecords Audiotapes Films Filmstrips Microforms
Notes: About 400 posters-American, German, French; complete *Stars and Stripes* for WWII; approx 5000 cataloged photographs, over 5000 uncataloged Office of War information photos, and over 10,000 US Signal Corps photos (uncat). Approx 250 regimental histories, operation reports, and army manuals; published memoirs and letters of Marshall associates; official military histories (American, British); set of 40 books by "Remy" (G Renault-Roulier); over 1200 maps-approx 300 newsmaps, 800 daily situation maps (European Theatre), 37 bound vols of daily situation maps 1944-1945; seven of the *Why We Fight* series (films). Major ms collections incl the papers of generals George C Marshall, Marshall S Carter, William T Sexton, Lucian Truscott, William R Arnold, Paul M Robinett, Frank McCarthy; Forrest C Pogue; colonels Collas Harris, Francis P Miller, William F Friedman;officers of the Women's Army Corps. Hearings and government documents. Agency records copied from NARS. Vertical file arranged by subject.

U.S. ARMY—TANK CORPS

KY —PATTON MUSEUM OF CAVALRY & ARMOR, Emert L Davis Memorial Library, PO Box 208, Fort Knox, 40121. Phyllis S Cassler, Librn
Holdings: Vols (6500) Cat Mss Maps Pix
Budget: ($1800)
Notes: Technical works, particularly technical and field manuals, concerning equipment used by US Army Mechanized Cavalry and Armour. Incl 10,000 pictures.

U.S. ARMY—TRANSPORTATION

VA —US ARMY TRANSPORTATION MUSEUM, Library, Bldg 300, Fort Eustis, 23604. Dennis P Mroczkowski, Museum Cur
Holdings: Vols (1254) Uncat Maps Pix 16mm Films
Budget: ($150)
Notes: Mainly US Army transportation from WW II on.

U.S. ARMY—UNIT HISTORIES

MI —MONROE COUNTY LIBRARY SYSTEM, Ellis Reference and Information Center, 3700 S Custer Rd, Monroe, 48161. Marie D Chulski, Head of Reference Services
Holdings: Vols 35,000 Cat Mss Maps Pix Slides 16mm Films Microforms Periodicals Sound Recordings Paintings Memorabilia
Budget: ($15,000)
Notes: Historic Monroe County, tracing its beginnings to 1780, is a definite part of Michigan's history. Many events of the area and citizens are part of Michigan's heritage. The Michigan collection besides general works contains individual county histories, atlases, biographies, etc. The Monroe County history collection contains veteran records, plat books, oral history tapes, family histories, church records, cemetery index, atlases and census records. Genealogy emphasis is not only Monroe County but includes surrounding counties and the states with large migration to the area, such as Ohio, Kentucky, Tennessee and the New England states.

NC —82ND AIRBORNE DIVISION, War Memorial Museum, Reference Library, Ardennes & Gela Sts, Fort Bragg, 28307. John S Duvall, Chief Cur
Notes: The collection is intended to be a research tool for persons studying the history of the 82nd Airborne Division and the development of airborne warfare.

OK —US ARMY FIELD ARTILLERY SCHOOL LIBRARY, Morris Swett Library, Snow Hall, Fort Sill, 73503. Lester L Miller Jr, Chief Librn
Holdings: Vols (265,958) Documents Pix Maps Slides Microforms
Notes: Field artillery; artillery; ordnance; military history; military science; weapons and weapons systems; ammunition; ballistics; missiles; Field Artillery unit histories; military periodicals analytical index file (VF). Incl US and foreign artillery; survey data; historical material on the army in Indian Territory and settlement of the southwest; photographs on army subjects, Indian Territory, Oklahoma history, Indians of the southwest.

U.S. ARMY FORCES, PACIFIC (USAFPAC)

VA —MACARTHUR MEMORIAL, Library & Archives, MacArthur Sq, Norfolk, 23510. Ellen E Folkama, Asst Archivist
Holdings: Vols (4000) Cat Maps Pix Slides Phonorecords Audiotapes 16mm Films Microforms
Notes: Everything relating to the life and related activities of MacArthur. The Archives of the collection consist of 600 shelf-feet of documents from Gen MacArthur's official headquarters files over the period 1941-1951. These papers pertain to all matters with which his various commands were involved: military, naval and air matters; international relations; political science; Japanese occupation, peace treaty and Constitution, etc. Each Record Group is indexed. The indexes are retained here since they are being expanded. They are available for researchers.

U.S. ATOMIC ENERGY COMMISSION

DC —LIBRARY OF CONGRESS, Manuscript Division, Washington, 20540. John C Broderick, Chief
Holdings: Cat Mss Pix

IA —IOWA STATE UNIVERSITY, Library, Dept of Special Collections, Ames, 50011. Stanley M Yates, Head
Notes: US Atomic Energy Commission, Ames Laboratory records and research notebooks.

IA —HERBERT HOOVER PRESIDENTIAL LIBRARY, West Branch, 52358. Dale C Mayer, Archivist
Notes: Papers of Lewis L Strauss, former Chairman of the Atomic Energy Commission. These papers are being processed and opened for research as rapidly as possible, but certain sections remain closed for research. Correspondence with and about a large number of physicists and atomic scientists is contained in the collection.

MA —MASSACHUSETTS INSTITUTE OF TECHNOLOGY, Institute Archives, Special

U.S. ATOMIC ENERGY COMMISSION (cont.)

Collections, Cambridge, 02139.
Notes: Papers of Carroll Louis Wilson, an environmental energy analyst, educator, and first General Manager of the Atomic Energy Commission. Collection incl alphabetical subject files documenting Wilson's personal life and professional career, primarily from 1959 to 1983. Incl correspondence on energy and environmental issues reflecting his involvement in the Atomic Energy Commission, etc. Folder list available in the Institute Archives. Access partially restricted; consult the Institute Archivist for further information.

U.S. BICENTENNIAL, 1976 see Bicentennial of the U.S., 1776-1976

U.S. COMMISSION OF RAILWAY EXPERTS TO RUSSIA

CA —HOOVER INSTITUTION ON WAR, REVOLUTION & PEACE, Stanford University, Stanford, 94305. Milorad M Drachkovitch, Archivist
Holdings: // Mss
Notes: Records, 1917-1923, 1931-1936, on the US Commission of Railway Experts to Russia. Papers relating to activities of the commission, to the Russian railway Service Corps, the Inter-Allied Railway Committee, the Russian political scene, and events in Siberia during the Russian Revolution and civil war. Persons represented incl John Frank Stevens, chairman of the commission. Correspondents incl George H Emerson, HH Fisher, Benjamin O Johnson, and Charles H Smith. 2 boxes.

U.S. CONFERENCE OF MAYORS

DC —NATIONAL LEAGUE OF CITIES, Municipal Reference Service, 1301 Pennsylvania Ave NW, Washington, 20004. Olivia Kredel, Mgr
Holdings: Vols (20,000)
Notes: City reports and plans, financial reports, budgets, commission reports, plans, etc. Federal legislation on urban affairs, etc.

U.S. CONGRESS

DC —LIBRARY OF CONGRESS, Rare Book & Special Collections Div, Washington, 20540. William Matheson, Chief
Notes: Public documents of the first 14 Congresses (1789-1817). Contains over 3680 separate titles. Also, printed texts of 3570 speeches delivered by members of Congress between 1825 and 1940. See A W Greely's *Public Documents of the First Fourteen Congresses*, (New York: Johnson Reprint Corporation, 1973).
DC —LIBRARY OF CONGRESS, Law Library, 101 Independence Ave, SE, Washington, 20540. Carleton W Kenyon, Dir
Holdings: Cat Microforms
Notes: Collection incl a nearly complete set of House and Senate bills and resolutions.
IL —EVERETT M DIRKSEN CONGRESSIONAL LEADERSHIP RESEARCH CENTER, Fourth & Broadway, Pekin, 61554. William C McCully Jr, Dir
Holdings: Cat Mss Maps Pix Slides Phonorecords Audiotapes Videotapes 16mm Films
Notes: Especially on Congressional leadership.
†MA —BOSTON PUBLIC LIBRARY, Copley Sq, Boston, 02117.
Holdings: Cat Microforms
Notes: Microform Publication by Greenwood Press. US Congressional Hearings, 1869-1934, 1935-date. Also LC set of US House and Senate Bills, 1789-date.
†MA —JOHN F KENNEDY LIBRARY, Columbia Point, Boston, 02125. Dan H Fenn Jr, Dir
Holdings: // Cat Mss
Notes: Lawrence O'Brien's papers relating

to his position as Special Assistant to the President for Congressional Relations, 1961-1963. 13 linear ft of mss. Holdings are described in "Historical Materials in the John F Kennedy Library." Copies may be obtained by writing the Research Archivist.
MS —UNIVERSITY OF SOUTHERN MISSISSIPPI, William David McCain Graduate Library, Box 5148, Southern Sta, Hattiesburg, 39406.
Holdings: Cat Mss Pix
Notes: 965 cubic feet. Papers (1915-1947) of Mississippi Senator Theodore G Bilbo and papers (1933-1973) of Mississippi Congressman William M Colmer. Each collection is primarily composed of official records, but each also incl personal papers and Mississippi political records. See entries under individual names.
VA —UNIVERSITY OF VIRGINIA, Alderman Library, Manuscripts Dept, Charlottesville, 22901. Edmund Berkeley Jr, Cur
Holdings: Mss Pix Phonorecords Audiotapes Videotapes 16mm Films
Notes: Papers of Members of the US Congress. Predominantly composed of official papers, but personal papers are often included, and political material forms a large part of each set. Unless otherwise noted, persons named represented Virginia. All sets of papers have unpublished guides available, some of them available on interlibrary loan. Several sets are restricted. Collection incl: Harry F Byrd, Sr, senator, 1933-1969 (restricted); Harry F Byrd, Jr, senator, 1965-; John Warwick Daniel, representative, 1885-1886; and senator, 1887-1910; Herb Harris, representative, 1975-1981; Carter Glass, representative, 1902-1918, and senator, 1920-1946; Robert M T Hunter, representative, 1837-1843, 1845-1847, and senator, 1847-1861; William Atkinson Jones, representative, 1891-1918; Richard Harding Poff, representative, 1953-1972; Miles Poindexter, representative,1909-1910, and senator, Washington state, 1910-1923; John Randolph, representative 1799-1813, 1815-1817, 1819-1825, 1827-1829, 1833, and senator, 1825-1827; William Cabell Rives, representative, 1823-1829, and senator, 1832-1834, 1836-1845; Hugh Scott, representative, 1941-1945, 1947-1959, and senator, Pennsylvania, 1958-1976 (restricted); Campbell Bascom Slemp, representative, 1907-1923; Howard Worth Smith, representative, 1931-1967; Claude Swanson, representative, 1893-1906, senator, 1910-1933; John Warner, senator, 1979-.

U.S. CONSTITUTION

IN —INDIANA UNIVERSITY, Lilly Library, Seventh St, Bloomington, 47405. William R Cagle, Librn
Holdings: Cat Mss
Notes: Books and mss relative to the Constitution from the 18th century to the present.
PA —HISTORICAL SOCIETY OF PENNSYLVANIA, Library, 1300 Locust St, Philadelphia, 19107. David Fraser, Librn
Holdings: Vols (230,000) Mss Maps Pix Microforms
Notes: Incl over 14,000 ms pieces. The Library Company of Philadelphia mss are on deposit with the Historical Society of Pennsylvania. Many of the Society's rare books are on deposit with the Library Company. The Society maintains the collections of the Genealogical Society of Pennsylvania, incl some 20,000 printed genealogies, original mss, family church,, and civil records.

U.S. CONSULAR SERVICE see U.S. —Diplomatic and Consular Service

U.S. CONTINENTAL CONGRESS

DE —UNIVERSITY OF DELAWARE, Hugh M Morris Library, S College Ave, Newark, 19711. T Stuart Dick, Special Collections
Holdings: // Mss
Notes: Incl Samuel Meredith's household,

farming and business receipts, representing quite fully the day-to-day expenses of a wealthy Philadelphian of the 1780s and 1790s. Meredith was a member of the Continental Congress, 1787-1788 and first Treasurer of the United States, 1789-1801. The papers cover the years 1764-1814.

U.S. CUSTOMS HOUSE, PROVIDENCE

RI —RHODE ISLAND HISTORICAL SOCIETY, Library, 121 Hope St, Providence, 02906. Paul R Campbell, Library Dir
Budget: ($200,000)
Notes: 270 cubic feet of records, incl records of US Customs House in Providence, Rhode Island. Correspondence, crew lists, alien and passenger lists, manifests, entries and clearances (1790-1900).

U.S. DEPARTMENT OF AGRICULTURE

IA —IOWA STATE UNIVERSITY, Library, Dept of Special Collections, Ames, 50011. Stanley M Yates, Head
Holdings: // Mss
Notes: Nils A Olsen (1886-1940) Papers. Collection contains correspondence, diary (1925-1935), printed matter and newspaper clippings relating to his work as Chief of Bureau of Agricultural Economics of the USDA (1928-1935). 750 items. Finding aid available.

U.S. DEPARTMENT OF DEFENSE

IN —ANDERSON COLLEGE, Charles E Wilson Library, 1033 E Third St, Anderson, 46012. Richard Snyder, Dir
Holdings: Vols (120,000) Cat
Notes: The Charles E Wilson Archives (president of General Motors Corp, 1941-1953 and Secretary of Defense, 1953-1957). Incl 180 mss boxes of personal correspondence, 35 bound vols of speeches, press clippings, photographs.

U.S. DEPARTMENT OF ENERGY

TN —US DEPT OF ENERGY, Technical Information Center, PO Box 62, Oak Ridge, 37831. Joseph G Coyne, Manager
Notes: TIC manages the technical information program of the DOE through which the DOE scientific research and development information is disseminated for offical and public use. TIC is also responsible for producing the DOE Energy Data Base and a number of abstracting and indexing journals which provide worldwide coverage of the energy literature. Cataloged holdings incl 500,000 reports, 94,000 engineering drawings and 10,000 books. 800 journal titles are received, with most not being retained.
TX —RICE UNIVERSITY, Fondren Library, 6100 S Main St, PO Box 1892, Houston, 77251. Dr Samuel M Carrington, Jr, University Librn
Holdings: Microforms
Notes: Receives all depository DOE reports.

U.S. DIXIE MISSION

CA —HOOVER INSTITUTION ON WAR, REVOLUTION & PEACE, Stanford University, Stanford, 94305. Milorad M Drachkovitch, Archivist
Holdings: Mss Pix Phonorecords
Notes: Papers of David D Barrett, Colonel, US Army, chief of the US Dixie Mission to Chinese Communist forces, 1944, incl mss of writings, correspondence, printed matter, photographs and phonorecords, 1933-70, relating to the Dixie Mission and the military situation in China during World War II. 1/2 ms box, 4 envelopes, 2 phonorecords, 1 oversize box.

U.S. ENERGY DEPARTMENT see U.S. Department of Energy

U.S. EXECUTIVE BRANCH ORGANIZATION COMMISSIONS (HOOVER COMMISSIONS)

CA —HOOVER INSTITUTION ON WAR, REVOLUTION & PEACE, Stanford

U.S. EXECUTIVE BRANCH ORGANIZATION COMMISSIONS (HOOVER COMMISSIONS) (cont.)

University, Stanford, 94305. Milorad M Drachkovitch, Archivist
Holdings: Mss
Notes: Records of the US Executive Branch Organization Commissions (Hoover Commissions), 1947-1949 and 1953-1955, incl correspondence, reports, minutes, press releases, and printed matter, relating to the Commissions' efforts to rationalize the organization of the executive branch of the federal government and especially to the work of the Chairman Herbert Hoover. 27 ms boxes. Also, records of the National Citizens Committee for the Reorganization of the Executive Branch of the Government and the Citizens Committee for the Hoover Report, 1949-1958. 103 ms boxes.

U.S. FARM SECURITY PROGRAM

NY —COLUMBIA UNIVERSITY LIBRARIES, Rare Book & Manuscript Library, 801 Butler Library, 535 W 114 St, New York, 10027. Kenneth A Lohf, Librn
Holdings: Mss
Notes: The papers of Professor Frank Tannenbaum, approx 28,000 items of correspondence and mss relating to Latin American and Mexican history, also the US Farm Security Program, 1934-1937. Professor Tannenbaum also bequeathed his research library of more than 3000 vols on all phases on Latin American history and literature to Columbia. Restricted use.

U.S. FEDERAL AVIATION AGENCY

MA —MASSACHUSETTS INSTITUTE OF TECHNOLOGY, Institute Archives, Special Collections, Cambridge, 02139.
Notes: Correspondence, newsletters, factsheets, newspaper and magazine articles, books and reports of the Citizens' League Against the Sonic Boom, established in 1967 by William Shurcliff to oppose the sonic boom, stop commercial supersonic transport production, and influence public opinion and policy decisions on the SST. Major correspondents incl Bo Lundberg, Richard Wiggs, several US congressmen, and CLASB members.

U.S. FEDERAL POWER COMMISSION

DC —LIBRARY OF CONGRESS, Manuscript Division, Washington, 20540. John C Broderick, Chief
Notes: Papers of Joseph C Swidler, Chairman, Federal Power Commission, Kennedy Administration.

U.S. FOOD ADMINISTRATION, 1917-1919

CA —HOOVER INSTITUTION ON WAR, REVOLUTION & PEACE, Stanford University, Stanford, 94305. Milorad M Drachkovitch, Archivist
Holdings: // Mss
Notes: Records of the US Food Adminstration, 1917-1919. Correspondence, addresses, minutes, resolutions, surveys, regulations, legal documents, agreements, statistics, and memoranda relating to foodstuffs, clothing, livestock, home conservation, food conservation, imports, exports, prices, and administration. Areas covered incl central and eastern Europe. Persons represented incl Ben S Allen, Julius Barnes, Edgar M Flesh, Prentiss N Gray, George E Haskell, Herbert Hoover, Vernon L Kellogg, Edgar Rickard, Edwin P Shattuck, Frank M Surface, Alonzo E Taylor, and Theodore F Whitmarsh. Unpublished register is available in repository.

U.S. FORESTRY SERVICE

AZ —ARIZONA HERITAGE CENTER, Library, 949 E Second St, Tucson, 85719.

Michael Weber, Dir
Notes: Espec with reference to Arizona, the West, and the Southwest.

U.S. HISTORICAL RECORDS SURVEY

TX —UNIVERSITY OF TEXAS LIBRARIES, General Libraries, Barker Texas History Center, PO Box P, Austin, 78712. Don Carleton, Dir
Notes: Papers, etc, documenting the career of Luther H Evans.

U.S. LIBRARY OF CONGRESS see Library of Congress

U.S. LIFESAVING SERVICE

NC —NATIONAL PARK SERVICE, Cape Hatteras National Seashore, Reference Library, Rte 1, Box 675, Manteo, 27954.
Holdings: Cat Mss Maps Pix
Notes: US Lifesaving Service, records and annual reports.

U.S. MARINE BAND

DC —LIBRARY OF CONGRESS, Music Division, Washington, 20540.
Holdings: Pix
Notes: The Francis Maria Scala Collection. Scala led the US Marine Band, 1855-1871. Incl music, correspondence, clippings, programs, and photographs.

U.S. MARINE CORPS

CA —HOOVER INSTITUTION ON WAR, REVOLUTION & PEACE, Stanford University, Stanford, 94305. Milorad M Drachkovitch, Archivist
Notes: Two collections: (1) Papers of Victor H Krulak, Lt Gen US Marine Corps, and vice-president of Copley News Service, incl writings, speeches, interviews and newspaper clippings, 1958-1977, relating to Marine Corps activities in China in the 1930s and during World War II, the Korean War, and the Vietnamese Conflict. 1 ms box (2) Papers of David M Shoup, Gen US Marine Corps, commander of Marine forces at Tarawa, 1943, chief of staff, 2d Marine Division. 1944, and commandant of the Marine Corps, 1960-63, incl correspondence, memoranda, writings, printed matter, photographs, films and sound recordings, 1927-71, relating to the Tarawa campaign, other World War II campaigns in the Pacific Theater, postwar activities of the Marine Corps, and the Vietnam war 21 ms boxes, 9 linear ft.

†DC —US MARINE CORPS HISTORICAL CENTER, Library, Code HDS-5 Bldg 58, Washington Navy Yard, Washington, 20374. Evelyn Englander, Librn

U.S. MILITARY ACADEMY AT WEST POINT

DC —GEORGETOWN UNIVERSITY, Library, Special Collections Div, 37 & O Sts NW, Washington, 20057. George M Barringer, Special Collections Librn; Nicholas B Sheetz, Mss Librn
Holdings: Mss Cat
Notes: The papers of Rev James Clark, SJ (1809-1885), a graduate of West Point who converted to Catholicism and entered the Society of Jesus in 1844. He spent a number of years at Georgetown College where he acted as first prefect, professor of mathematics and then as treasurer of the College. He subsequently served as president of Holy Cross and Gonzaga Colleges. The papers incl correspondence conerning his family, his West Point and army carreers, and his life as a Jesuit. Also incl are mss of sermons and various documents such as his West Point diploma (1829) and registers of officers and cadets at West Point (1827-28).

ME —BOWDOIN COLLEGE, Library, Brunswick, 04011. Dianne M Gutscher, Cur of Special Collections
Holdings: Mss Pix
Notes: The Oliver Otis Howard Papers

consist of more than 150,000 pieces of correspondence, articles, lectures, and ephemera for the period 1843-1908, covering his services as a Civil War officer, as founder of the Freedmen's Bureau, as president of Howard University, and as superintendent of the US Military Academy at West Point.

NY —US MILITARY ACADEMY LIBRARY, West Point, 10996. Richard J Hellinger, Chief, USMA Archives
Holdings: Uncat Pix
Notes: National Archives and Records Service Group 404. Records of the US Military Academy. Collection is developed according to the Army records management system which coordinates retirement of official records. This extensive archival collection dating from 1801 to date includes virtually all formats by which information is recorded and transferred, the majority of which is typescript or manuscript. Inventory of this record group has been published by the National Archives and Records Service (A Preliminary Inventory of the Records of the United States Military Academy, compiled by Stanley P Tozeski, US National Archives and Records Survey, 1976 NARS pub #PI 185, LC listing CD 3026 .A32). The USMA Library's Rare Books Collection, separately administered by the Special Collection Librarian, also contains West Pointiana and military manuscripts numbering nearly5000 items. Also, in Special Collections are West Point Thayer Collection, the Schley Military Engineering and the Sinnott Chess Collections. Cullum Biographical files are maintained by the Association of Graduates of the US Military Academy, the greater part dating from the 1840's to the 20th century. These files from class of 1802-1905 have been transferred to the library and include letters, photographs, and clippings about the graduates.

U.S. MINT (PHILADELPHIA)

NJ —GLASSBORO STATE COLLEGE, Savitz Library, Stewart Room, Glassboro, 08028. Clara Kirner, Special Collection Librn
Holdings: Vols 50 Cat Mss Pix
Notes: Incl mss of Frank H Stewart's History of the First US Mint and mss of the Rush-Boudinot controversy, 1802. Also a small collection of coins found at the first US Mint building.

U.S. NASA see U.S. National Aeronautics and Space Administration

U.S. NATIONAL ADVISORY COMMITTEE FOR AERONAUTICS

FL —EMBRY-RIDDLE AERONAUTICAL UNIVERSITY, Regional Airport, Daytona Beach, 32014. M Judy Luther, Dir of Learning Resources

U.S. NATIONAL AERONAUTICS AND SPACE ADMINISTRATION

CA —HOOVER INSTITUTION ON WAR, REVOLUTION & PEACE, Stanford University, Stanford, 94305. Milorad M Drachkovitch, Archivist
Holdings: Mss
Notes: Papers of Charles E Weakley, Vice Admiral, US Navy, commander, Antisubmarine Warfare Force, Atlantic Fleet, 1963-67, and assistant administrator for management development, National Aeronautics and Space Administration, 1968-72, incl correspondence, orders, drafts of speeches, printed matter, photographs, and sound recordings, 1945-72, relating to post-World War II US antisubmarine force operations and to NASA activities. 4 ms boxes.

FL —EMBRY-RIDDLE AERONAUTICAL UNIVERSITY, Regional Airport, Daytona Beach, 32014. M Judy Luther, Dir of Learning Resources

NY —AMERICAN MUSEUM-HAYDEN PLANETARIUM, Richard S Perkin Library, 81 St & Central Park W, New York, 10024.

U.S. NATIONAL AERONAUTICS AND SPACE ADMINISTRATION (cont.)

Sandra Kitt, Librn
Notes: Unofficial depository of NASA reports and photographs.

TX —RICE UNIVERSITY, Fondren Library, 6100 S Main St, PO Box 1892, Houston, 77251. Dr Samuel M Carrington, Jr, University Librn
Notes: The Johnson Space Center History Archive, a manned flight collection transferred from NASA, originally housed at the Lyndon B Johnson Space Center. Contains documentation on the Mercury, Gemini, and Skylab programs; Soyuz Test Project. Incl 500 linear ft.

†UT —UNIVERSITY OF UTAH, Marriott Library, Salt Lake City, 84112.
Notes: The papers of James Chipman Fletcher, generated while director of the National Aeronautics and Space Administration, 1971-1977.

U.S. NATIONAL INDUSTRIAL CONFERENCE

CA —HOOVER INSTITUTION ON WAR, REVOLUTION & PEACE, Stanford University, Stanford, 94305. Milorad M Drachkovitch, Archivist
Holdings: Mss
Notes: Stenographic transcripts of the minutes of the First and Second National Industrial Conferences of 1919-1920. 15 ms boxes.

U.S. NATIONAL PARK SERVICE

AZ —NORTHERN ARIZONA UNIVERSITY, Special Collection Library, CU Box 6022, Flagstaff, 86011. Peter M Whiteley, Coordr/Archivist; William Mullane, Librn
Notes: Newsletters covering the period from 1969-1978.

CA —UNIVERSITY OF CALIFORNIA, LOS ANGELES, Research Library, Dept of Special Collections, 405 Hilgard Ave, Los Angeles, 90024. Edward Shreeves, Chairman, Bibliographers Group; David S Zeidberg, Head
Notes: Horace M Albright's correspondence and ephemera recording his activity as a conservationist and his directorship of the National Park Service.

VA —US NATIONAL PARK SERVICE, Harpers Ferry Center, Library, Harpers Ferry, 25425. David Nathanson, Chief Librn
Holdings: Vols (4000) Cat Mss Maps Pix Slides Phonorecords Audiotapes 16mm Films Microforoms
Budget: ($105,000)

†WA —WASHINGTON STATE UNIVERSITY, Library, Manuscripts, Archives & Special Collections, Pullman, 99164. John F Guido, Head
Holdings: Cat Mss Maps Pix
Notes: The Carl Parcher Russell papers, a vast resource (24,916 items; 45 linear feet) on American Indian and Western pioneer activities and artifacts. Much on the fur trade; pioneer; mountain men and trapping; wildlife; primitive life in detail. Also the National Park Service, parks, monuments, etc. Described in *Carl Parcher Russell: An Indexed Register of His Scholarly and Professional Papers, 1920-1967, in the Washington State University Library* (Pullman, 1970), 149 pp.

U.S. NATIONAL STUDENT ASSOCIATION

CA —HOOVER INSTITUTION ON WAR, REVOLUTION & PEACE, Stanford University, Stanford, 94305. Milorad M Drachkovitch, Archivist
Holdings: Mss Pix
Notes: Records of the International Commission of the US National Student Association, a confederation of student bodies at American colleges and universities, incl correspondence, reports, memoranda, minutes of meetings, bulletins, circulars, questionnaires, notes, lists, financial records, printed matter, and photographs, 1946-1967, relating to the international activities of the association, such as delegation and scholarship exchanges with other nations, American representation at annual International Student Conferences, and relatings with analogous student organizations abroad as well as to the effects of world politics on education. 313 ms boxes and 7 envelopes.

U.S. NAVAL ACADEMY AT ANNAPOLIS

MD —US NAVAL ACADEMY, Nimitz Library, Annapolis, 21402. Alice S Creighton, Assistant Librn for Special Collections
Holdings: Vols (22,000) Cat Mss Pix
Notes: Books and periodicals, with emphasis on seapower. Incl rare and historically significant works, naval and general history. US Naval Academy materials (histories, class albums, Lucky Bags, student publications, etc), and copies of transcripts of the Naval Institute's oral history interviews with US naval officers. Manuscripts incl 205 volumes of ships' logs, letterbooks, order books, and watch, station and quarter bills, 1796-1938; papers of various naval officers, incl. Vice Admiral Wilson Brown, Commander George M Bache, Admiral Harry S Knapp, Lieutenant Edwin J DeHaven, and others; family correspondence of Admiral David Dixon Porter; and several thousand World War II naval action reports. Approximately 15,000 pictures incl portraits of naval officers, pictures of US and some foreign ships, World War II naval news photos and USNA photographs.

RI —US NAVAL WAR COLLEGE, Historical Collection & Museum, Newport, 02841. Anthony S Nicolosi, Dir; Evelyn Cherpak, Cur
Holdings: Mss
Notes: Collections incl over 200,000 separate pieces; chiefly papers of naval officers and records of organizations associated with the US Navy, the Naval War College, the college's major study areas, and the Navy in the Narragansett Bay region; oral history collection; Naval War College Archives, 1884-present; records of conferences held at the College; newspaper collections treating with naval themes and military conflicts.

U.S. NAVAL STATION (NEWPORT)

RI —US NAVAL WAR COLLEGE, Historical Collection & Museum, Newport, 02841. Anthony S Nicolosi, Dir; Evelyn Cherpak, Cur
Holdings: Mss
Notes: Collections incl over 200,000 separate pieces; chiefly papers of naval officers and records of organizations associated with the US Navy, the Naval War College, the college's major study areas, and the Navy in the Narragansett Bay region; oral history collection; Naval War College Archives, 1884-present; records of conferences held at the College; newspaper collections dealing with naval themes and military conflicts.

U.S. NAVAL WAR COLLEGE

RI —US NAVAL WAR COLLEGE, Historical Collection & Museum, Newport, 02841. Anthony S Nicolosi, Dir; Evelyn Cherpak, Cur
Holdings: Mss
Notes: Collections incl over 200,000 separate pieces; chiefly papers of naval officers and records of organizations associated with the US Navy, the Naval War College, the college's major study areas, and the Navy in the Narragansett Bay region; oral history collection; Naval War College Archives, 1884-present; records of conferences held at the College; newspaper collections dealing with naval themes and military conflicts.

U.S. NAVY—HISTORY

CA —HOOVER INSTITUTION ON WAR, REVOLUTION & PEACE, Stanford University, Stanford, 94305. Milorad M Drachkovitch, Archivist
Holdings: Mss Pix
Notes: Four collections; (1) Papers of Lloyd M Bucher, Comander, US Navy, and Commander of the USS *Pueblo*, incl correspondence, newspaper clippings, reports, copies of court inquiries, photographs, plaques, memorabilia, and other materials, 1970-75, relating to the *Pueblo* incident and its aftermath. Incl is a typewritten manuscript of his memoirs, entitled "Bucher, My Story." 68 ms boxes. 1 oversize package. (2) Papers of Elton W Grenfell, Vice Admiral, US Navy; commander. Submarine Force, Pacific Fleet. 1956-59; and commander, Submarine Force, Atlantic Fleet, 1960-64; incl correspondence, orders, drafts of speeches and photographs, 1926-69, relating to US submarine operations during World War II and in the postwar period 11 1/2 ms boxes. 5 binders. (3) Typewritten documentation of events and conditions leading up the Japanese attack on Pearl Harbor, December7, 1941, assembled by Lt Gen WC Short, Commanding General, US Army Hawaiian Department, for his defense before the Roberts Commission, which investigated the attack 1/2 ms box (4) Papers of Robert A Theobald. Rear Admiral, US Navy; Destroyer Commander, Pacific Fleet, 1940-41; and Commander, Northern Pacific Force in Alaskan Operations, May 1942-January 1943; incl correspondence, speeches and writings, war diaries, dispatches, operations plans and orders, manuals, service lists, memoranda, reports, and war estimates, 1908-59, relating to his career in the US Navy; naval operations in Alaska, May 1942- January 1943, incl the Japanese invasion of the Aleutians, June 1942; and the Japanese attack on Pearl Harbor, 12 ms boxes.

DC —LIBRARY OF CONGRESS, Manuscript Division, Washington, 20540. John C Broderick, Chief
Notes: The Naval Historical Foundation Collection contains personal papers relating to American naval history.

DC —NATIONAL ARCHIVES AND RECORDS SERVICE, National Archives Library, Pennsylvania Ave & Eighth St NW, Washington, 20408.
Notes: Journals kept by Commodore Matthew C Perry (1794-1858) on his expedition to Japann in 1852-1854. The three journals were kept by Perry as his personal account of the trip, undertaken as a diplomatic mission to establish trade relations with Japan. Incl numerous illustrations of rare birds, flowers, fish, animals, and the life and ceremonies of trade ports along Perry's route.

MD —US NAVAL ACADEMY, Nimitz Library, Annapolis, 21402. Alice S Creighton, Assistant Librn for Special Collections
Holdings: Vols (22,000) Cat Mss Pix
Notes: Books and periodicals, with emphasis on seapower. Incl rare and historically significant works, naval and general history. US Naval Academy materials (histories, class albums, Lucky Bags, student publications, etc), and copies of transcripts of the Naval Institute's oral history interviews with US naval officers. Manuscripts incl 205 volumes of ships' logs, letterbooks, order books, and watch, station and quarter bills, 1796-1938; papers of various naval officers, incl. Vice Admiral Wilson Brown, Commander George M Bache, Admiral Harry S Knapp, Lieutenant Edwin J DeHaven, and others; family correspondence of Admiral David Dixon Porter; and several thousand World War II naval action reports. Approximately 15,000 pictures incl portraits of naval officers, pictures of US and some foreign ships, World War II naval news photos and USNA photographs.

U.S. NAVY—HISTORY (cont.)

MD —CALVERT MARINE MUSEUM,
Library, PO Box 97, Solomons, 20688.
Holdings: Uncat Mss Maps
Notes: Result of an ongoing project with the
Nautical Archeological Associates to obtain
information on the naval history of Patuxent
River during the War of 1812.

MI —UNIVERSITY OF MICHIGAN,
Engineering-Transportation Library, 312
Undergraduate Library, Ann Arbor, 48109.
Sharon A Balius, Assoc Librn
Notes: Letters and papers of Charles Ellet,
Jr, and family, especially as related to
construction of railroads, canals, and bridges
and to the construction and command of the
Union ram fleet in the Civil War.

NJ —PRINCETON UNIVERSITY, Library,
Manuscript Collection, Nassau St, Princeton,
08540. Jean F Preston, Cur
Holdings: // Cat Mss Pix
Notes: The James Vincent Forrestal
Collection, incl 134 boxes and 19 cartons of
papers, 1940-1949; and 19 volumes of
diaries. 1944-1949. Terms of Access: Diaries
are mostly open; personal papers require
permission of Forrestal estate, which Library
staff can process. An unpublished typescript
guide (362 p) is available in the Library.

RI —US NAVAL WAR COLLEGE, Historical
Collection & Museum, Newport, 02841.
Anthony S Nicolosi, Dir; Evelyn Cherpak,
Cur
Holdings: Mss
Notes: Collections incl over 200,000
separate pieces; chiefly papers of naval
officers and records of organizations
associated with the US Navy, the Naval War
College, the college's major study areas, and
the Navy in the Narragansett Bay region;
oral history collection; Naval War College
Archives, 1884-present; records of
conferences held at the College; newspaper
collections dealing with naval themes and
military conflicts.

TN —PT BOATS MUSEUM & LIBRARY, PO
Box 109, Memphis, 38101. J M "Boats"
Newberry, Librn
Holdings: Vols (2000) Uncat Maps Pix
Slides Phonorecords Audiotapes 16mm
Films Microforms Videotapes Biographies
Budget: ($25,000)
Notes: PT Boats, Inc is an 8000 man
organization of PT boat veterans, families,
modelers and history buffs who have
donated a sizable collection of artifacts and
records pertaining to their PT boat service.
The collection also contains an 80-foot Elco
PT boat and a 78-foot Higgins PT boat, both
restored. National headquarters and archives
are in Memphis, and the display collection is
located on board the USS Massachusetts at
Battleship Cove, Fall River, Mass, 02721. To
use the library, write PT Boat Coordinator,
William C Hindle and/or Don Rhoads, Chief
Administrative Officer in Memphis.
Memphis headquarters has some 10,000
photos and line drawings with specifications.

U.S. NAVY—SHIPYARDS

VA —PORTSMOUTH PUBLIC LIBRARY,
601 Court St, Portsmouth, 23704. Dean
Burgess, Library Dir
Holdings: Vols 500 Cat Mss Maps Pix Slides
Microforms
Notes: Although particularly interested in
Tidewater and Lower Tidewater history, we
buy most books we can locate on Virginia as
well. In 1972 we were given the
distinguished collection of Judge White of
Lynnhaven.

U.S. OFFICE OF STRATEGIC SERVICES

IL —NORTHWESTERN UNIVERSITY,
Library, Special Collections Dept, 1937
Sheridan Rd, Evanston, 60201. R Russell
Maylone, Cur
Holdings: Vols 300 Uncat
Notes: Propaganda-OSS, WW II materials
for both Europe and Asia.

U.S. OLYMPIC COMMITTEE

IL —UNIVERSITY OF ILLINOIS,
URBANA/CHAMPAIGN, Library,
University Archives, 19 Library, 1408 W
Gregory Drive, Urbana, 61801. Maynard
Brichford, University Archivist
Holdings: Vols (1663) // Cat Mss Pix
Notes: The Avery Brundage Collection. Incl
his papers and material on amateur athletics,
Olympic games, and sports. Published guide
is available: Avery Brundage Collection,
1908-1975 (Cologne: Karl Hofmann
Schorndorf, 1977). 517,000 ms pieces. There
is also a collection on Olympic sports and
other aspects of sports kept in the Brundage
Room.

U.S. POSTAL SERVICE see Postal Service

U.S. PRESIDENTS see Presidents—U.S.

U.S. PRESIDENT'S FAMINE EMERGENCY COMMITTEE, 1946-1947

CA —HOOVER INSTITUTION ON WAR,
REVOLUTION & PEACE, Stanford
University, Stanford, 94305. Milorad M
Drachkovitch, Archivist
Holdings: Mss
Notes: Records of the Famine Emergency
Committee, an organization for the
coordination of international famine relief
after World War II, incl correspondence,
reports, notes, and clippings, 1946-47,
relating to US food conservation and to
famine conditions throughout the world. Incl
Memoranda and diaries of Herbert Hoover,
Honorary Chairman of the Committee. 30
ms boxes, 2 envelopes.

U.S. PUBLIC HEALTH SERVICE

MI —UNIVERSITY OF MICHIGAN, Public
Health Library, Ann Arbor, 48109. Mary
Townsend, Head
Holdings: Vols (55,000) Cat Maps Pix
Budget: ($24,000)

U.S. SANITARY COMMISSION

DC —AMERICAN NATIONAL RED
CROSS, National Headquarters Library,
17th & D St NW, Washington, 20006.
Roberta F Biles, Library Director
Holdings: Vols 180 Cat Mss
Notes: The Clara Barton Memorial
Collection. Incl The Rebellion Record, 12
vols; History of the US Sanitary
Commission; Sanitary Commission
pamphlets (bound); Annals of the United
States Christian Commission; Our Women of
the War; Hospital Transports; camp and
hospital manuals and recipes used in special
diet kitchens. (Publication dates 1855-1888.)

U.S. SECURITIES AND EXCHANGE COMMISSION

DC —LIBRARY OF CONGRESS, Manuscript
Division, Washington, 20540. John C
Broderick, Chief
Notes: The papers of William O Douglas,
incl judicial case files from 1939 through
1952, correspondence, subject files relating
to the Securities and Exchange Commission,
and lecture notes he used as a law professor.

UNITED STATES SOARING HALL OF FAME

NY —NATIONAL SOARING MUSEUM,
Library, Harris Hill, RD #3, Elmira, 14903.
Holdings: Cat Pix
Notes: Biographies of soaring personalities.

U.S. STATE DEPARTMENT—HISTORY

†TX —UNIVERSITY OF TEXAS
LIBRARIES, General Libraries, Humanities
Rese•:ch Center, PO Box 7219, Austin,
78712. John Chalmers, Librn
Notes: The John W F Dulles collection of
correspondence, diaries, autographs,
speeches, and paintings by famous historical
figures from the 17th century to the present.
Much of the material is related to Mr
Dulles' three relatives who served as
Secretaries of State: John Foster Dulles,
Robert Lansing, and John W Foster.

U.S. SUBVERSIVE ACTIVITIES CONTROL BOARD, 1950-1972

CA —HOOVER INSTITUTION ON WAR,
REVOLUTION & PEACE, Stanford
University, Stanford, 94305. Milorad M
Drachkovitch, Archivist
Holdings: Mss
Notes: Reports and transcripts of hearing
(printed, memeographed and typewritten), of
the US Subversive Activities Control Board,
a quasi-judical US government agency, 1950-
72, relating to communist and communist-
front activities in the US. 70 ms boxes, 6 cu
ft boxes.

U.S. SUPREME COURT

DC —LIBRARY OF CONGRESS, Manuscript
Division, Washington, 20540. John C
Broderick, Chief
Holdings: 143,000 Items
Notes: The papers of Justice William Orville
Douglas.

DC —LIBRARY OF CONGRESS, Law
Library, 101 Independence Ave, SE,
Washington, 20540. Carleton W Kenyon,
Dir
Holdings: Vols 10,000 Uncat Microforms
Notes: US Supreme Court records and briefs.
Microfilm 1832-1915 (records from January
term 1832; briefs from January term 1854);
microfiche 1934-date.

ME —BOWDOIN COLLEGE, Library,
Brunswick, 04011. Dianne M Gutscher, Cur
of Special Collections
Holdings: Vols Mss Pix
Notes: The Harold Hitz Burton Supreme
Court Collection contains about 175
volumes, incl presentation copies from Felix
Frankfurter, Hugo Black, and others of that
stature, and Supreme Court procedural rules
and legal texts with the Justice's
annotations. Also part of the collection are
about 100 letters, many speeches, and
autographed presentation photographs of
fellow Justices.

MA —HARVARD UNIVERSITY LIBRARY,
Law School Library, Langdell Hall,
Cambridge, 02138. Erika S Chadbourn, Cur
of Mss
Notes: Incl papers of Felix Frankfurter,
Learned Hand, Oliver Wendell Holmes, etc.

MA —BRANDEIS UNIVERSITY, Goldfarb
Library, 415 South St, Waltham, 02154.
Bessie Hahn, Dir
Notes: Louis D Brandeis Collection. Approx
500 books and periodical articles by and
about Justice Louis D Brandeis. Incl also are
72 linear ft of correspondence to and from
Louis D Brandeis and his wife, Alice. A card
catalog to the books and pamphlets can be
found in Special Collections, as well as a
finding list to some of the correspondence.

RI —PROVIDENCE PUBLIC LIBRARY, 150
Empire St, Providence, 02903. Lance J
Bauer, Special Collections Librn
Holdings: Vols 500 // Uncat
Notes: A 1968 gift of the late Providence
lawyer William H Edwards, this collection
deals primarily with the history of the
Supreme Court of the United States. It incl
rare pamphlet material, as well as books
from the 18th century to the present.

U.S. SUPREME COURT—HISTORY

DC —SUPREME COURT HISTORICAL
SOCIETY, 1511 K St NW, Suite 612,
Washington, 20005. Gary Aichele, Exec Dir

U.S. TREASURY DEPARTMENT—HISTORY

CA —UNIVERSITY OF CALIFORNIA,
SANTA CRUZ, University Library, Special
Collections, Santa Cruz, 95064. Rita
Bottoms, Special Collections Librn; Margaret
Felts, South Pacific Collection Bibliographer
Notes: Monographs, rare books, serials,
documents and atlases which treat of the
Pacific areas of Polynesia, Melanesia,
Micronesia, Australia and New Zealand, but
excluding western New Guinea (Irian Jaya),

U.S. TREASURY DEPARTMENT—HISTORY (cont.)

the Phillippines and Southeast Asia. Approximately 10 per cent of the titles are multi-volume documents such as parliamentary papers, legislative journals, official yearbooks, statistical sourcebooks, laws and statutes. The collection includes an exhaustive selection of current journals and monographic series from and about the Pacific: early serials, South Pacific Commission publications. US Government and US Trust Territory publications, serials from museums, universities and scholarly societies. Chief emphasis has been placed on acquisition of the literature of history, description and travel, ethnology and anthropology, literature and literary criticism,political and constitutional histories. Other extensive holdings are in the fields of geography and maps, voyages, mission histories, mythology and folklore, art, linguistics, and science fields of natural history, environmental studies, biology, zoology, botany, geology and astronomy.

DE —UNIVERSITY OF DELAWARE, Hugh M Morris Library, S College Ave, Newark, 19711. T Stuart Dick, Special Collections
Holdings: // Mss
Notes: Incl Samuel Meredith's household, farming and business receipts, representing quite fully the day-to-day expenses of a wealthy Philadelphian of the 1780s and 1790s. Meredith was a member of the Continental Congress, 1787-1801. The papers cover the years 1764-1814.

DC —US TREASURY DEPT, Library, 15 & Pennsylvania Ave NW-Room 5030, Washington, 20220. Elisabeth S Knauff, Mgr Information Services Division
Holdings: Vols (10,000) Cat Microforms
Notes: Incl department publications.

IN —INDIANA UNIVERSITY, Lilly Library, Seventh St, Bloomington, 47405. William R Cagle, Librn
Holdings: Mss
Notes: Papers of Hugh McCulloch, US Comptroller of Currency, 1863-65, US Secretary of the Treasury, 1865-69, Oct 1884-March 1885. Incl business and family correspondence, scrapbooks, letterpress books, and some US Treasury related correspondence. 15,749 items.

U.S. WAR RELOCATION AUTHORITY

CA —UNIVERSITY OF CALIFORNIA, LOS ANGELES, Research Library, Dept of Special Collections, 405 Hilgard Ave, Los Angeles, 90024. Edward Shreeves, Chairman, Bibliographers Group; David S Zeidberg, Head
Holdings: Cat Mss
Notes: 63 linear feet of administrative records, reports, and camp newspapers of the US War Relocation Authority, Relocation Center, Manzanar, Calif. Incl records of Ralph Palmer Merritt, director of the Center.

CA —CALIFORNIA STATE UNIVERSITY, NORTHRIDGE, Delmar T Oviatt & South Libraries, 1811 Nordhoff St, Northridge, 91330. Donald L Read, Special Collections Dept
Holdings: Cat
Notes: Incl 4 boxes of newspapers published in war relocation camps, 6 boxes ephemera, either published in or relating to the camps.

U.S. WORK PROJECTS ADMINISTRATION

NE —UNIVERSITY OF NEBRASKA, OMAHA, Library, 60 & Dodge Sts, Omaha, 68132. Mel Bohn, Librn
Holdings: Mss
Notes: Omaha History - Works Progress Administration manuscripts. 24 linear ft of mss materials. WPA papers, newspaper clippings, radio scripts, and published volumes.

SC —COLLEGE OF CHARLESTON LIBRARY, Special Collections Dept, Charleston, 29401.
Notes: US Work Projects Administration,

State of South Carolina Papers, 1938-1941, contains work news, community improvement appraisal, monthly reports on unemployment, business and economic reports, monthly reports on employment and economic conditions, statistical summary of WPA operations, and a report of work on the Santee-Cooper Hydro-electric Development and Navigation Project.

UNITED STEEL WORKERS OF AMERICA (USWA)

PA —PENNSYLVANIA STATE UNIVERSITY, Fred Lewis Pattee Library, Labor History Collection, University Park, 16802. Peter Gottlieb, Archivist
Notes: Penn State is "provisional repository" for papers and records of the United Steel Workers of America, incl records from the USWA international headquarters in Pittsburgh and from 29 district offices. A comprehensive oral history program with union members is underway.

UNITED TRANSPORTATION UNION

NY —CORNELL UNIVERSITY, New York State School of Industrial & Labor Relations, Martin P Catherwood Library, Ives Hall, Ithaca, 14853. Shirley F Harper, Dir
Holdings: Cat Mss Pix
Notes: All nonoperating files and memorabilia of the United Transportation Union. A•o material on and from other railroad unions, and records of the New York, Ontario, and Western Railway, the New York and Pennsylvania Railway, and the American Shortline Railroad Association.

UNITED VERDE COPPER COMPANY

AZ —NORTHERN ARIZONA UNIVERSITY, Special Collection Library, CU Box 6022, Flagstaff, 86011. Peter M Whiteley, Coordr/Archivist; William Mullane, Librn
Notes: Correspondence, business correspondence, office files, ca 1900's-1940's of the United Verde Copper Company and United Verde Extension Copper Company, Jerome, Ariz. Incl records of the Verde Tunnes and Smelter Railroad, ca 1915-1930's and files on combined United Verde Extension Pollution and Environmental Study of the Verde Valley, 1920's-1930's (190 feet).
See also entry under Mines and Mining-History.

UNITED WORLD FEDERALISTS

TX —UNIVERSITY OF TEXAS LIBRARIES, General Libraries, Barker Texas History Center, PO Box P, Austin, 78712. Don Carleton, Dir
Notes: Papers, etc, documenting the career of Luther H Evans.

UNITY SCHOOL OF CHRISTIANTY

MO —UNITY LIBRARY, Unity School of Christianity, Unity Village, 64065. Alfreda Williams, Library Dir
Holdings: Vols (50,000) Cat Mss Maps Pix Slides Microforms
Notes: Incl Archives and Historical collections of the Unity School of Christianity, as well as the archives of the International New Thought Alliance.

UNITY THEATRE (GREAT BRITAIN)

IL —SOUTHERN ILLINOIS UNIVERSITY, CARBONDALE, Delyte W Morris Library, Special Collections Dept, Carbondale, 62901. David V Koch, Cur of Special Collections; Louisa Bowen, Cur of Manuscripts
Holdings: Cat Mss Pix
Notes: Papers, 1936-1950, 6 linear feet.

UNIVAC

DE —HAGLEY MUSEUM AND LIBRARY, Eleutherian Mills-Hagley Foundation Inc,

PO Box 3630, Greenville, 19807. Richmond D Williams, Dir; Heddy A Richter, Imprints Librn
Notes: Records of the Sperry-Univac Company (1940-1975; 400 cubic feet) document the early development and rapid growth of the computer industry. The collection incl technical and administrative documents relating to the ENIAC, BINAC and UNIVAC computers.

UNIVERSAL HISTORY see World History

UNIVERSAL MOVEMENT THEATRE REPERTORY

CA —UNIVERSITY OF CALIFORNIA, DAVIS, Shields Library, Dept of Special Collections, Davis, 95616. Donald Kunitz, Head; C Danial Elliott, Asst Head
Holdings: Vols (28,000) Mss Pix Slides Audiotapes Videotapes 16mm Films
Notes: Files of the Universal Movement Theatre Repertory, a booking agency in New York. 4750 items. Described in: Whalon, Marion D, "Avant-Garde and Radical Theater Holdings." Broadside, vol 3, no 3 (winter 1976).

UNIVERSAL PICTURES CORPORATION

CA —UNIVERSITY OF CALIFORNIA, LOS ANGELES, Research Library, Dept of Special Collections, 405 Hilgard Ave, Los Angeles, 90024. Edward Shreeves, Chairman, Bibliographers Group; David S Zeidberg, Head
Notes: 23 linear feet of correspondence, ephemera, slides, etc, concerning Walter Beyer's work as an engineer at Paramount Pictures, the development of VistaVision, the Motion Picture Research Council, and Universal Pictures.

CA —UNIVERSITY OF SOUTHERN CALIFORNIA, Edward L Doheny Memorial Library, Archives of Performing Arts, University Park, Los Angeles, 90089. Robert Knutson, Librn
Holdings: Mss
Notes: Universal Pictures Corporation Collection incl 600 boxes of production and publicity department records, incl 1,500 screenplays.

NY —NEW YORK PUBLIC LIBRARY, Performing Arts Research Center, Billy Rose Theatre Collection, 111 Amsterdam Ave, New York, 10023. Dorothy L Swerdlove, Cur
Holdings: Cat
Notes: See entry under Moving Picture Industry.

UNIVERSALIST CHURCH

MA —HARVARD UNIVERSITY, Harvard Divinity School, Andover-Harvard Theological Library, 45 Francis Ave, Cambridge, 02138. Maria Grossmann, Librn
Holdings: Vols (370,000) Cat
Notes: Collection formerly at Tufts University.

UNIVERSE see Cosmography; Cosmology

UNIVERSITIES AND COLLEGES

CT —SACRED HEART UNIVERSITY, Library, 5229 Park Ave, PO Box 6460, Bridgeport, 06606. Roch-Josef di Lisio, Actg Dir
Holdings: Vols 1200 Cat
Notes: The John A Rycenga Memorial Collection on American Catholic Higher Education.

DC —HOWARD UNIVERSITY, Moorland-Spingarn Research Center, 500 Howard Place NW, Washington, 20059. Clifford L Muse, Jr, Acting Dir
Holdings: Vols (106,086) Mss Maps Pix Slides Phonorecords Audiotapes 16mm Films Filmstrips Microforms
Budget: ($854,753)
See also entry under Blacks

UNIVERSITIES AND COLLEGES (cont.)

NY —COLUMBIA UNIVERSITY LIBRARIES, Teachers College, Milbank Memorial Library, 525 W 120 St, New York, 10027. Jane P Franck, Dir
Holdings: Mss
Notes: Collection consists of records of administrative offices, departments, faculty, students, and related materials.

WA —UNIVERSITY OF WASHINGTON LIBRARIES, Suzzallo Library, Manuscripts Section, FM-25, Seattle, 98195. Karyl Winn, Librn
Holdings: Mss
Notes: Personal papers and organizational records with emphasis on Pacific Northwest history and recent focus on twentieth century Western Washington. Holdings pertain to urban problems and policies, labor history, women's history, natural resource development, environmental politics, race relations, ethnic history, oral history, and the arts. Holdings are complemented by textual records in the University Archives (7045 linear feet) and by graphic and printed holdings in the Pacific Northwest Collection. Described in *Comprehensive Guide to the Manuscripts Collection and to Personal Papers in the University Archives,* 1980 and in *Historical Records of Washington State: Records and Papers Held at Repositories,* 1981 and in unpublished inventories to most accessions. 15,981 linear feet of manuscripts.

WA —UNIVERSITY OF WASHINGTON LIBRARIES, University Archives, HO-10, Seattle, 98195. Richard C Berner, University Archivist
Notes: University records and personal papers of university faculty and administrators, covering a spectrum of subjects as wide as the academic range of the university and higher education administration per se. 7000 linear feet.
See also entry under Manuscripts - Collections

UNIVERSITIES AND COLLEGES—BUILDINGS

CA —ESHERICK, HOMSEY, DODGE & DAVIS, Library, 2789 25th St, San Francisco, 94110. Elizabeth Walton, Librn
Holdings: Vols (2500) Cat Maps Pix Slides
Notes: General history of architecture; solar energy applications to architecture; residential architecture; zoo architecture; handbooks, codes, and standards; school and university architecture. Also incl is a large collection of product literature catalogs and samples (uncataloged).

NY —CORNELL UNIVERSITY LIBRARIES, Collection of Regional History, Dept of Manuscripts and Univ Archives, Ithaca, 14853.
Notes: Architectural reports (1928-30) concerning proposed construction at Cornell University, NY.

UNIVERSITIES AND COLLEGES—CANADA

ON —ASSOCIATION OF UNIVERSITIES & COLLEGES OF CANADA LIBRARY, 151 Slater St, Ottawa, K1P 5N1, Can. Hazel J Roberts, Head Librn
Holdings: Vols 8000 Cat
Budget: $5000
Notes: Provides documentation relating to higher education in Canada and elsewhere, for the use of the association and its member institutions. Subjects covered incl university administration, teaching effectiveness, financing, student activities, the role of universities, international education, collective bargaining, academic freedom, etc. Coverage primarily Canadian with some supporting documentation for other countries, particularly the US, Commonwealth nations and French-language countries. Items from Canadian universities and colleges incl calendars, presidents' reports, faculty handbooks, student newspapers, press releases, newspapers issued by Information Offices and faculties,

faculty bargaining agreements, published and unpublished reports from administrative units with the University. Extensive clipping file maintained.

UNIVERSITIES AND COLLEGES—CATALOGS see Catalogs, College

UNIVERSITIES AND COLLEGES—HISTORY

IL —NEWBERRY LIBRARY, 60 W Walton St, Chicago, 60610. Diana Haskell, Cur of Modern Mss
Holdings: Cat
Notes: Incl early learned periodicals, bio-bibliographies, encyclopedias. Strong in history of universities and libraries.

MO —SAINT LOUIS UNIVERSITY, Pius XII Memorial Library, 3655 W Pine Blvd, Saint Louis, 63108. William Cole, Dir
Holdings: Slides Microforms
Notes: Collection covers all areas of learning and European history from Classical Antiquity to early modern period. Researchers using collection receive assistance in paleography, bibliography and reference search. Approx 10,000 1000-foot reels of microfilm (not counting master negatives) reproducing Vatican Library's Latin, Greek, Hebrew, Arabic and Ethiopic mss. Some 8000 100-foot reels of microfilm (again not counting master negative) reproducing rare and out of print books relating to subject areas in the mss. Over 50,000 color slides of medieval and Renaissance mss illuminations. A reference collection of modern materials relating to ms research.

NY —UNIVERSITY CLUB, Library, One W 54 St, New York, 10019. Guy St Clair, Library Dir
Holdings: Vols (100,000) Cat Mss Pix
Notes: A private library for the members of the University Club, their guests, and serious scholars upon written application to the Library Director. Holds a large collection of collegiana, incl early materials about Yale, Harvard, Columbia, and especially Princeton. Also holds general histories of most other American and British universities.

RI —BROWN UNIVERSITY, John Carter Brown Library, Providence, 02912. Norman Fiering, Librn; Everett C Wilkie Jr, Bibliographer; Susan Danforth, Cur Maps & Prints
Notes: History of the Americas during the Colonial Period. See also *The John Carter Brown Library Catalogues; Opportunities for Research in the John Carter Brown Library; Reprint of the John Carter Brown Library Annual Reports and Index-1901-1966.*

SK —UNIVERSITY OF SASKATCHEWAN, Library, Saskatoon, S7N 0W0, Can. S Perkins, Librn
Notes: Extensive collection (in book form; some reprints) of matriculation records of English, Scottish, French, German, Italian, and other universities, dating from the Middle Ages and Renaissance.

UNIVERSITY CATALOGS see Catalogs, College

UNIVERSITY IN EXILE

NY —STATE UNIVERSITY OF NEW YORK AT ALBANY, Library, Special Collections Dept, 1400 Washington Ave, Albany, 12222. Marion P Munzer, Coordr
Holdings: Mss Maps Pix
Notes: Fred R Brown's correspondence, mss, photographs, and maps. He was as Methodist missionary to China from 1910-31 (6 linear feet). Part of the Library's German Exile Collection.

UNIVERSITY LIBRARIES see Libraries, University and College

UNIVERSITY OF PENNSYLVANIA

PA —UNIVERSITY OF PENNSYLVANIA, University Archives, North Arcade Franklin

Field E-6, Philadelphia, 19104. Francis James Dallett, University Archivist
Notes: The University of Pennsylvania Archives holds the papers of 125 individuals, all with a University affiliation (former faculty, trustees, alumni, etc), some 175,000 individual biographical files of University-connected persons in the same categories who are deceased, as well as the non-current records and files of the academic and administrative divisions of the University and its predecessors beginning in 1740 (an overall collection of 8000 cubic feet). It is one of the six largest University Archives (of purely institutionally-related records) in the country. Sporadic reporting of holdings to NUCMUC have not been kept up in recent years. Severe staff limitations prevent more than reporting of additions to the collection to subject surveys and bibliographies.

UNIVERSITY OF THE SOUTH

TN —UNIVERSITY OF THE SOUTH ARCHIVES, Jessie Ball DuPont Library, Sewanee, 37375. Gertrude French Mignery, Archivist
Holdings: Vols (3000) Cat Mss Maps Pix Slides Microforms
Notes: Collection is comprised almost entirely of materials relating to the Episcopal Church and the University and its relationship to the 24 owning Southern dioceses. This collection is not duplicated in the library of the School of Theology. The collection encompasses some 250 cubic feet of official University records, mss (ca 15,000 pieces), bound vols (ca 3000), pamphlets (ca 700), audiovisual resources (ca 100 tape recordings, 100 motion picture films, 5000 loose photographs, and 950 slides), microfilms (ca 90 reels), maps (ca 100 of Sewanee and Franklin County), scrapbooks (ca 100), and museum pieces (ca 300 objects). Almost all of the larger collections have been reported to the National Union Catalog of Manuscript Collections. Such collections incl the papers of Bishops Leonidas Polk, Charles Todd Quintard, James Hervey Otey, as well as extensive collections of all pastVice-Chancellors. A collection of letters of the American Episcopate, 1784-1953 (ca 1200 pieces) has recently been processed for the collection. A master name and subject for the entire holdings.

UNIVERSITY PRESSES

NY —GRADUATE CENTER OF THE CITY UNIVERSITY OF NEW YORK, William H and Gwynne K Crouse Library for Publishing Arts, 33 W 42 St, New York, 10036. Alfred H Lane, Dir
Notes: Expected to become the authoritative source of materials in the field, of particular value in research about the publishing industry. Open to staff members of publishing houses, students, scholars, authors, printers, and booksellers. Primarily 20th century materials, and particularly useful for research on technical, financial, and historical matters. Much on the history of individual houses, economics of authorship; marketing and distribution of books; etc.

UNKNOWN LANGUAGES see Languages, Unknown

UNO, EDISON

†CA —UNIVERSITY OF CALIFORNIA, Library, Los Angeles, 90024.
Notes: Personal papers of Edison Uno.

UNTERMEYER, LOUIS AND JEAN STARR

CT —YALE UNIVERSITY, Box 1603A, Yale Station, New Haven, 06520.
Notes: Incl first editions of their books.

DE —UNIVERSITY OF DELAWARE, Hugh M Morris Library, S College Ave, Newark, 19711. T Stuart Dick, Special Collections
Holdings: Mss
Notes: Incl letters and mss sent to Louis

UNTERMEYER, LOUIS AND JEAN STARR (cont.)

Untermeyer, 1906-1940, with the majority being from 1912-1925. Among others, important groups of letters from Leonie Adams, Conrad Aiken, WR Benet, WS Braithwaite, Floyd Dell, Jahn Gould Fletcher, Alfred Kreymborg, Carl Sandburg and John Hall Wheelock are included. Index available.

IN —INDIANA UNIVERSITY, Lilly Library, Seventh St, Bloomington, 47405. William R Cagle, Librn
Holdings: Vols 2000 // Cat Mss
Notes: Volumes from their library of 20th century American (with some British) poetry. Correspondence with various poets, incl mss of material for inclusion in anthologies; also ms for Untermeyer's *Lives of the Poets: The Story of One Thousand Years of English and American Poetry.* 1036 items, 1901-1959.

UPANISHADS

DE —UNIVERSITY OF DELAWARE, Hugh M Morris Library, S College Ave, Newark, 19711. T Stuart Dick, Special Collections
Notes: Extensive Yeats holdings, incl a collection of personal correspondence which features 67 unpublished letters and telegrams written in 1931-39 to Swami Shri Purohit, an Indian mystic, who with Yeats cotranslated the *Upanishads* into English.

UPDEGRAFF, CLARENCE MILTON

IA —UNIVERSITY OF IOWA, University Libraries, Iowa City, 52242. Robert A McCown, Mss Librn
Holdings: Mss
Notes: Two collections: labor arbitration case files, 1940-1970, of Clarence Milton Updegraff, consisting of briefs, decisions, correspondence, notes, transcripts of hearings, hearing statements, agreements, photographs and other material; and arbitration awards, 1963-1971, of the American Arbitration Association. 86 ft of mss.

UPDIKE, DANIEL BERKELEY

ME —BOWDOIN COLLEGE, Library, Brunswick, 04011. Dianne M Gutscher, Cur of Special Collections
Holdings: Vols
Notes: The Frederic Wilson Main Collection contains several hundred books, pamphlets, and clippings relating to the art of printing and bookmaking. Most major contemporary presses are represented, and it incl examples of the typographic work of Bruce Rogers, Frederic W Goudy, Daniel Berkeley Updike, and Rudolph Ruzicka, to mention only a few.

NY —ROCHESTER INSTITUTE OF TECHNOLOGY, Melbert B Cary Jr Graphic Arts Collection, School of Printing, One Lomb Memorial Drive, Rochester, 14623. David Pankow, Cur
Holdings: Vols (11,000) Cat Mss Pix

RI —PROVIDENCE PUBLIC LIBRARY, 150 Empire St, Providence, 02903. Lance J Bauer, Special Collections Librn
Holdings: Vols (6300) Cat Mss Pix
Notes: The

UPDIKE, JOHN

MO —WASHINGTON UNIVERSITY, Libraries, Campus Box 1061, Saint Louis, 63130.
Notes: A collection of primary material.

NV —UNIVERSITY OF NEVADA, RENO, University Library, Special Collections Dept, Reno, 89557. Robert E Blesse, Head
Holdings: Vols 170 Cat
Notes: Includes individual works by author in all editions including translations; also prefaces, introductions, published correspondence, appearances in anthologies, periodicals, etc. Bibliographical research collection, part of Modern Authors Collection.

UPHAM, THOMAS COGSWELL, 1799-1872

ME —BOWDOIN COLLEGE, Library, Brunswick, 04011. Dianne M Gutscher, Cur of Special Collections
Holdings: Vols Cat Mss
Notes: The Thomas C Upham Collection contains 65 volumes of his writings, as well as a few letters.

UPJOHN, RICHARD, 1802-1878

ME —BOWDOIN COLLEGE, Library, Brunswick, 04011. Dianne M Gutscher, Cur of Special Collections
Holdings: Mss
Notes: The Chapel Papers, part of the Bowdoin College Buildings Archive, contains ca 50 letters from or to Richard Upjohn, architect of the College chapel.

MA —SOCIETY FOR THE PRESERVATION OF NEW ENGLAND ANTIQUITIES, Library, 141 Cambridge St, Boston, 02114. Ellie Reichlin, Librn & Cur of Photographic Collections
Holdings: Vols (3000) // Cat Pix Microforms
Budget: ($75,000)
Notes: Architecture of the Northeast. Drawings (original designs, measured drawings, plot plans, etc). Over 7500 items, incl extensive collections of original designs by Ogden Codman, Jr (1890s-early 1900s); Arthur Little and Herbert Browne (1890s-1920s); Luther Briggs (1840s-1860s); Arland Dirlam (1930s-1960s), together with important examples of the work of Asher Benjamin, Richard Upjohn, and others. Measured drawings incl extensive holdings of work undertaken by HABS (Historic American Buildings Survey) in Massachusetts in the 1930s, 1940s under director Frank Chouteau Brown. Also represented are several residential and commercial commissions by F C Brown, not connected with HABS. Collection incl architectural pattern books, builders guides, 18th-19th century. Approx 350 volumes, English and American publications.

UPPER ATMOSPHERE see Atmosphere, Upper

UPPER VOLTA

DC —HOWARD UNIVERSITY, Moorland-Spingarn Research Center, 500 Howard Place NW, Washington, 20059. Clifford L Muse, Jr, Acting Dir

MI —MICHIGAN STATE UNIVERSITY, International Library, Sahel Documentation Center, East Lansing, 48824. Eugene deBenko, Librn; Learthen Dorsey, Librn
Holdings: Vols (5100) Cat Mss Maps Pix Slides Phonorecords Audiotapes Videotapes Microforms
Budget: ($8000)
Notes: See description under The Sahel.

UPTON, HARRIET TAYLOR

NY —UNIVERSITY OF ROCHESTER, Rush Rhees Library, Department of Rare Books and Special Collections, Rochester, 14627. Peter Dzwonkoski, Librn
Holdings: Cat Mss Pix
Notes: Approximately 300 letters including correspondence with Rachel Foster Avery (178 letters); Harriet Taylor Upton, Amy Post, Elizabeth Cady Stanton, and others. Also includes photographs, printed ephemera, and museum pieces.

URALIAN LANGUAGES see Finno-Ugrian Languages and Literatures; Hyperborean Languages and Literatures

URANIUM

OH —GOODYEAR ATOMIC CORP, Technical Library, PO Box 628, Piketon, 45661. Robert Holland, Supvr
Holdings: Vols (50,000) Cat Mss Microforms
Notes: Uranium enrichment; gas flow, heat transfer, isotope analyses, uranium-fluoride chemistry.

ON —RIO ALGOM LIMITED, Library, 120 Adelaide St W, Toronto, M5H 1W5, Can. Penny Lipman, Librn
Holdings: Vols (1500) Cat
Budget: ($7000)
Notes: Espec mining of uranium and copper; geology; mining methods; nuclear energy.

URARTAEAN LANGUAGE

NY —NEW YORK PUBLIC LIBRARY, Oriental Div, Fifth Ave & 42 St, New York, 10018. E Christian Filstrup, Chief
Holdings: Cat Mss Microforms
Budget: ($56,455)
Notes: Published catalog of holdings.

URBAN AFFAIRS

CT —YALE UNIVERSITY, Social Science Library, 140 Prospect St, New Haven, 06520. Billie I Salter, Librn
Holdings: Vols (40,000) Cat Microforms
See also entry under Social Sciences.

DC —NATIONAL LEAGUE OF CITIES, Municipal Reference Service, 1301 Pennsylvania Ave NW, Washington, 20004. Olivia Kredel, Mgr
Holdings: Vols (20,000)
Notes: Publications covering a wide variety of topics related to cities and local government.

DC —US DEPT OF HOUSING & URBAN DEVELOPMENT, HUD Library, 451 Seventh St SW Room 8141, Washington, 20410. Carol A Johnson, Project Manager
Holdings: Vols Cat Documents Microforms
Notes: 600,000 pieces. Strong in all phases of community planning. Extensive coverage of the production and financing of housing. Emphasis on federal legislation.

IL —INSTITUTE ON THE CHURCH IN URBAN-INDUSTRIAL SOCIETY, Library, 5700 S Woodlawn, Chicago, 60637.
Holdings: Vols 1000 Cat Microforms
Notes: Urban-industrial involvement of the churches world-wide, international urban literature, corporate responsibility, human factors of urbanization and industrialization. Library holdings are dorment at present.

MI —WAYNE STATE UNIVERSITY, Kresge Library (Education), Detroit, 48202. Theodore Manheim, Librn
Holdings: Vols (65,000) Cat Mss Microforms
Budget: ($2000)
Notes: The Eloise Ramsey Collection (10, 000 vols). See, *The Eloise Ramsey Collection of Literature for Young People: A Catalogue;* compiled by Joan Cusenza (Detroit: Wayne State University Libraries, 1967). Besides the Ramsey Collection, which is housed separately and does not circulate, the Education Library has approx 55,000 volumes of children's and young adults' literature, with a very large picture-book collection, a large poetry collection; all with special emphasis on urban and ethnic materials.

MI —WAYNE STATE UNIVERSITY, Walter P Reuther Library, Archives of Labor & Urban Affairs, Detroit, 48202. Philip Mason, Dir
Holdings: Vols (4000) Cat Mss Pix Slides Phonorecords Audiotapes Videotapes 16mm Films Filmstrips Micrforms
Budget: ($450,000)
Notes: See Warner Pflug, *A Guide to the Archives of Labor History and Urban Affairs* (Wayne State University Press, 1974).

MI —MICHIGAN STATE UNIVERSITY, Urban Policy & Planning Library, East Lansing, 48824. Dale E Casper, Librn
Holdings: Vols (4900) // Cat
Budget: ($35,000)
Notes: A reference collection in the Urban Policy and Planning Library consists of indexes, abstracts, bibliographies, directories and statistical handbooks. There is a 4000 volume pamphlet collection which covers topics incl: community development block grants, redlining, revenue sharing, municipal finance, land use and many other topics as well. A topically arranged newspaper

URBAN AFFAIRS (cont.)

clippings collection provides retrospective and current newsorthy information on urban problems, legislation and solutions. A periodical collection consists of the current issues of about 120 urban and ethnic studies journals.

MO —WASHINGTON UNIVERSITY, John M Olin Library, Lindell & Skinker Blvd, Saint Louis, 63130. Beryl H Manne, Archivist
Holdings: Mss Pix Audiotapes 16mm Films Filmstrips Microforms
Notes: The University Archives and Research Collection at the John M Olin Library of Washington University is a growing ms archives collecting original source material pertaining to 20th century political, business, and social welfare history of the St Louis metropolitan area. Incl the personal papers of prominent St Louis politicians, businessmen, engineers, educators, scientist, architects. Holdings especially strong in municipal and county governmental affairs.

NY —COLUMBIA UNIVERSITY LIBRARIES, Rare Book & Manuscript Library, 801 Butler Library, 535 W 114 St, New York, 10027. Kenneth A Lohf, Librn
Holdings: Mss
Notes: Papers of the Community Service Society of New York. Incl files, books, photographs (1000) and bound volumes of periodicals and conference proceedings. Among the papers are central and district administrative records, committee correspondence and minutes, and files of programs sponsored by the organization. Also more than 1000 photographs by Jessie Tarbox Beals and Lewis W Hine depicting conditions of the poor. 276,000 items. Restricted use.

NY —NEW YORK CITY HUMAN RESOURCES ADMINISTRATION, McMillan Library, 109 E 16 St, New York, 10003. Harold Benson, Librn
Holdings: Vols (13,000) Cat Mss
Budget: ($18,000)
Notes: Public welfare in all aspects; the poor in America, administration, management, child welfare, social services, social work in contemporary society, and urban affairs.

PA —TEMPLE UNIVERSITY, Samuel Paley Library, Berks & 13 Sts, Philadelphia, 19122.
Notes: 150 oral history interviews of individuals prominently associated with the Philadelphia Renaissance era from the 1940s to the early 1970s.

†PA —TEMPLE UNIVERSITY LIBRARIES, Special Collections Dept, Urban Archives Center, Philadelphia, 19122. Thomas Whitehead, Cur of Mss
Holdings: Cat
Notes: Incl the records of several separate collections which are deposited in the Urban Archives Center. Many collections contain photographs, maps and pamphlets, in addition to manuscripts. All collections in the Urban Archives are seperately cataloged.

PA —UNIVERSITY OF PITTSBURGH, Hillman Library, Pittsburgh, 15260. Glenora E Rossell, Head
Holdings: Vols (20,000) Cat
Notes: Especially strong in social theory, social history, social groups, criminology and urban sociology. Emphasis is currently being given to administration of justice, sociology of the child, sociology of the aged, sociology of education and sociology of religion. This collection is strengthened by the US government publications depository collection, the partial UN depository collection, the Canadian government publications collection, the collection of the Social Work Library, and the Graduate School of Public and International Affairs.

PA —UNIVERSITY OF PITTSBURGH, Economics/Center for Regional Economics Studies Library, 4956 Forbes Quad, Pittsburgh, 15260. Patricia Suozzi-Crehan, Librn
Holdings: Vols 20,000
Budget: ($25,724)
Notes: Card catalog for collection. Cards for

Economics Collection are in Hillman Library catalog. Collections are working collections reflecting the research and teaching interests of the Dept of Economics faculty and graduate students. The collection covers all aspects of the field of economics and demography.

WA —SEATTLE PUBLIC LIBRARY, Governmental Research Assistance Library, 307 Municipal Bldg, Seattle, 98104. Barbara J Guptill, Librn
Holdings: Vols (18,000) Cat Mss Maps
Budget: ($16,700)
Notes: Includes pamphlets and clippings on municipal affairs, especially Seattle. Emphasis on urban planning, criminal investigation, policy analysis, finance.

WA —UNIVERSITY OF WASHINGTON LIBRARIES, Suzzallo Library, Manuscripts Section, FM-25, Seattle, 98195. Karyl Winn, Librn
Holdings: Mss
Notes: Personal papers and organizational records with emphasis on Pacific Northwest history and recent focus on twentieth century Western Washington. Holdings pertain to urban problems and policies, labor history, women's history, natural resource development, environmental politics, race relations, ethnic history, oral hsitory, and the arts. Holdings are complemented by textual records in the University Archives (7045 linear feet) and by graphic and printed holdings in the Pacific Northwest Collection. Described in *Comprehensive Guide to the Manuscripts Collection and to Personal Papers in the University Archives,* 1980 and in *Historical Records of Washington State: Records and Papers Held at Repositories,* 1981 and in unpublished inventories to most accessions. 15,981 linear feet of manuscripts.

WI —LEGISLATIVE REFERENCE BUREAU LIBRARY, City of Milwaukee, City Hall Rm 404, 200 E Wells St, Milwaukee, 53202. Ronald Leonhardt, Dir
Holdings: Vols (50,000) Cat Mss Maps Pix Microforms
Budget: ($8000)
Notes: Administration, employment.

WI —UNIVERSITY OF WISCONSIN, MILWAUKEE, Library, Box 604, Milwaukee, 53201. William C Roselle, Dir
Holdings: Cat Microforms
Notes: Wisconsin Legislative Reference Bureau Clippings File. Special strength in a collection mostly of Wisconsin emphasis. 440 reels of 16mm microfilm. A subject-chronological arrangement (approximately 1200 subjects covering the years from the 1890s through 1970) of pamphlets and a variety of fugitive materials and of clippings from national and Wisconsin newspapers, popular magazines and scholarly journals, and federal, state, and local government documents.

MB —UNIVERSITY OF MANITOBA, Architecture & Fine Arts Library, Winnipeg, R3T 2N2, Can. Peter Anthony, Head
Holdings: Vols (50,000) Maps Microforms
Notes: Incl government publications.

MB —UNIVERSITY OF WINNIPEG, Library, 515 Portage Ave, Winnipeg, R3B 2E9, Can. W R Converse, Chief Librn
Holdings: Vols 3000 Cat

ON —METROPOLITAN TORONTO LIBRARY, Municipal Reference Library, City Hall, Toronto, M5H 2N1, Can. Margot Hewings, Head
Holdings: Vols (60,000) Cat Maps Pix Microforms Slides VF
Budget: ($112,600)
Notes: Community development; municipal finance; local municipal government; housing; urban pollution; urban transportation; urban affairs; urban geography.

URBAN DESIGN see Urban Renewal

URBAN DEVELOPMENT see Cities and Towns—Planning

URBAN EDUCATION see Education, Urban

URBAN PLANNING see Cities and Towns—Planning

URBAN REDEVELOPMENT see Urban Renewal

URBAN RENEWAL

AZ —ARIZONA STATE UNIVERSITY, Howe Architecture Library, Tempe, 85281.
Holdings: Vols 17,000 Cat Microforms

CA —UNIVERSITY OF CALIFORNIA, LOS ANGELES, Graduate School of Management Library, UCLA Campus, Los Angeles, 90024. Robert Bellanti, Head Librn
Holdings: Vols (128,000) Cat Mss Microforms
Notes: The collection is broad in scope covering all aspects of business and management; emphasis is placed on in-depth collecting in the Graduate School of Management's core curriculum areas: accounting, behavioral and organizational science, business economics, computers and information science, finance, management science/operations research, marketing, organization and strategic studies, production and operations managements, public/non-profit management and urban land economics.

CA —UNIVERSITY OF CALIFORNIA, LOS ANGELES, Architecture & Urban Planning Library, 1302 Architecture Bldg, Los Angeles, 90024. Jon S Greene, Librn
Holdings: Vols (18,000) Cat
Budget: ($30,000)

DC —NATIONAL ASSOCIATION OF HOUSING AND REDEVELOPMENT OFFICIALS, Resource Center, 2600 Virginia Ave NW, Washington, 20037. Mary L Pike, Librn
Holdings: Vols 1000
Notes: Public housing and community development, incl urban renewal and housing code enforcement.

DC —NATIONAL RESEARCH COUNCIL, Transportation Research Board Library, 2101 Constitution Ave NW, Washington, 20418. Lisbeth L Luke, Librn
Holdings: Vols (17,000) Cat Microforms VF
Notes: Photocopying available.

GA —EMORY UNIVERSITY, Robert W Woodruff Library, Special Collections Dept, Atlanta, 30322. Linda M Matthews, Head Special Collections; Virginia J H Cain, Processing Archivist; Richard H F Lindemann, Reference Archivist
Holdings: Vols 2000 Cat Mss Maps Pix Slides
Notes: Personal books, papers, diaries and printed materials of Charles Forrest Palmer of Atlanta. About 15,000 pieces.

IL —BARTON-ASCHMAN ASSOCIATES, Library, 820 Davis St, Evanston, 60204.
Holdings: Vols (9000) Cat Mss Microforms

IL —LAKE FOREST COLLEGE, Donnelley Library, Lake Forest, 60045. Arthur H Miller Jr, College Librn
Holdings: Vols (500) Cat Maps
Budget: ($1200)
Notes: Focus on development of suburban fringe areas, particularly Lake Co, Ill, and Chicago region: local documents (plans, transit, zoning maps, etc), US documents, and special studies of suburban issues, such as historic preservation and land use.

IL —UNIVERSITY OF ILLINOIS, URBANA/CHAMPAIGN, Library, City Planning & Landscape Architecture Library, 203 Mumford Hall, 1301 West Gregory Drive, Urbana, 61801. Mary D Ravenhall, Librn
Holdings: Vols (20,000) Cat
Budget: ($11,000)
Notes: Urban and regional planning; landscape architecture.

MD —MARYLAND-NATIONAL CAPITAL PARK & PLANNING COMMISSION, Montgomery County Planning Department Library, 8787 Georgia Ave, Silver Spring, 20907. Janice C Holt, Librn
Holdings: Vols (5000) Cat
Notes: Specific subject areas include: community facilities, conservation, economics, flood control, highways, housing, human and natural resources. landscape architecture, open space, parks, pollution, population, recreation, transportation, urban renewal, and zoning. Commission's publications are maintained by Records Management (not Library).

MA —HARVARD UNIVERSITY, Graduate School of Design, Frances Loeb Library, Gund Hall, Cambridge, 02138. James Hodgson, Librn
Holdings: Vols (225,000) Cat Mss Maps Pix Slides Microforms
Budget: ($500,000)
Notes: Covers architecture, landscape

URBAN RENEWAL (cont.)

architecture, city and regional planning, and
urban design. Catalog, in 44 volumes,
published in 1968, with 2-volume
supplement in 1970, 5-volume supplement in
1974, and 3-volume supplement in 1979. It
also analyzes periodical articles. Architecture
collection described in *Harvard Library
Bulletin*, VI (1952): pp 263-269. Noteworthy
holdings incl those on Abbey of Cluny, Le
Corbusier, amd Henry Hobson Richardson.
MI —UNIVERSITY OF MICHIGAN, Art and
Architecture Library, 2106 Art and
Architecture Bldg, Ann Arbor, 48109. Peggy
Ann Kusnerz, Librn; Dot Shields, Asst Librn
Holdings: Vols (45,000)
Budget:
Notes: Incl 200 maps, 35,000 slides, vertical
file, videocassettes, blueprints, Jens Jensen
Landscape drawings, oral history, and 400
serial titles.
MI —MICHIGAN STATE UNIVERSITY,
Urban Policy & Planning Library, East
Lansing, 48824. Dale E Casper, Librn
Holdings: Vols (12,800) Cat
Budget: ($35,000)
Notes: Serves the curricular and research
needs of faculty and students involved in
urban and regional policy analysis and
community planning.
MI —OAKLAND COUNTY REFERENCE
LIBRARY, 1200 N Telegraph Rd, Pontiac,
48053. Phyllis Jose, Library Dir
Holdings: Vols (11,000) Cat
Budget: ($34,000)
NJ —RUTGERS, THE STATE UNIVERSITY
OF NEW JERSEY, Center for Urban Policy
Research Library, Bldg 4051-Kilmer, New
Brunswick, 08903. Edward E Duensing, Jr
Holdings: Vols 3500 Cat Periodicals VF
Budget: ($4000)
Notes: Collection focuses on the subjects of
housing, municipal finance, and planning in
American cities. The emphasis is on current
material. Incl 5000 cataloged vertical files,
157 periodical subscriptions.
NY —CORNELL UNIVERSITY LIBRARIES,
Collection of Regional History, Dept of
Manuscripts and Univ Archives, Ithaca,
14853.
Notes: Records, ca 1908-(33-56)-69, of San
Francisco Planning and Urban Renewal
(SPUR); 4 ft.
NY —NEW YORK STATE DIVISION OF
HOUSING & COMMUNITY RENEWAL,
Library, 2 World Trade Center, New York,
10047. Carole Williams, Asst Librn, Special
Reference Room
Holdings: Vols 2100 Cat Pix
Budget: $1500
Notes: No photocopying.
NY —NEW YORK STATE DIVISION OF
HUMAN RIGHTS, Reference Library, Two
World Trade Center, Rm 5356, New York,
10047. Rosalind Spriggs, Librn
Holdings: Vols 1200 // Cat
Notes: Emphasis on materials which deal
with the problems of discrimination in
housing, the development of cities, and
urban unrest. See *Bibliography on Housing
and Urban Renewal* by Simon Fediuk.
Special Collection, No 1 of a Series. 2nd
printing, New York, 1972. 92 pp. This
special collection contains about 1200 items;
books, studies, journals, pamphlets, reports,
reprints, and research data.
OH —CLEVELAND PUBLIC LIBRARY,
Public Administration Library, City Hall,
601 Lakeside Ave NE Rm 100, Cleveland,
44114. Janice Ryan Novak, Head
Holdings: Vols 700 Cat
OH —KENT STATE UNIVERSITY,
Architecture Urban Studies Library, Kent,
44242.
Notes: Urban Renewal materials located in
main library.
†PA —TEMPLE UNIVERSITY LIBRARIES,
Special Collections Dept, Urban Archives
Center, Philadelphia, 19122. Thomas
Whitehead, Cur of Mss
Holdings: Mss
Notes: Ms collection focusing on urban life
and development and drawing on the
Philadelphia metropolitan area since the

Civil War. Incl the papers of several private
organizations, such as the Phildelphia
Housing Association (1909-1972); Delaware
Valley Regional Planning Commission
(1965-1972); Greater Philadelphia
Movement (1949-1976); YWCA of
Philadelphia (1870-1960); YMCA of
Philadelphia (1854-1970); Health and
Welfare Council of Philadelphia (1922-
1969); United Fund of Philadelphia and
Vicinity (1920-1975); Philadelphia Urban
League (1935-1967); ACLU-Philadelphia
Chapter (1948-1975); Legal Aid Society of
Philadelphia (1933-1976); etc.
WA —SEATTLE PUBLIC LIBRARY,
Governmental Research Assistance Library,
307 Municipal Bldg, Seattle, 98104. Barbara
J Guptill, Librn
Holdings: Vols (18,000) Cat Mss Maps
Budget: ($16,700)
Notes: Includes pamphlets and clippings on
municipal affairs, especially Seattle.
Emphasis on urban planning, criminal
investigation, policy analysis, finance.
WA —UNIVERSITY OF WASHINGTON
LIBRARIES, Architecture-Urban Planning
Library, 11, JO-30, Seattle, 98195. Betty L
Wagner, Librn
Holdings: Vols (26,085) Cat Microforms
Budget: ($33,127)
Notes: Incl microforms (5241), cataloged.
ON —CANADIAN HOUSING
INFORMATION CENTER, Canada
Mortgage and Housing Corp, CMHC Annex
Bldg Ground Floor, Montreal Rd, Ottawa,
K1A 0P7, Can. Leslie Jones, Mgr
Holdings: Cat
Notes: City and town planning, all aspects,
incl urban renewal, residential rehabilitation,
new towns, suburban development, etc.
Urban planning.

URBAN SOCIOLOGY see Sociology, Urban

URBAN STUDIES see Cities and Towns—Study and Teaching

URBAN TRAFFIC see Traffic Engineering

URBAN TRANSIT see Local Transit

URBANISM see Cities and Towns

URDANG, CONSTANCE

MO —WASHINGTON UNIVERSITY,
Libraries, Special Collections Dept, Campus
Box 1061, St Louis, 63130.
Notes: A major collection, incl books, mss,
correspondence, literary papers, photographs,
etc. Described in *Special Collections: an
Annotated Guide to the Holdings of the
Manuscript Division and the University
Archives and Research Collection.*

URDU LANGUAGE AND LITERATURE

AZ —UNIVERSITY OF ARIZONA, Library,
Oriental Studies Collection, Tucson, 85721.
Mary J McWhorter, Actg Head Librn
Holdings: Vols (95,000) Cat Microforms
Budget: ($30,000)
See also entry under Oriental Languages and
Literatures
DC —LIBRARY OF CONGRESS, African and
Middle Eastern Division, Washington,
20540.
Holdings: Cat Mss Microforms
Notes: Southern Asian: over 137,000 vols of
literature of the area from Pakistan to the
Philippines.
MA —HARVARD UNIVERSITY LIBRARY,
Widener Library, Cambridge, 02138.
Holdings: Cat Mss
MI —UNIVERSITY OF MICHIGAN,
Graduate Library, South Asian Dept, Ann
Arbor, 48109. Om P Sharma, Librn
Holdings: Vols (365,000) Cat Maps Slides
Microforms
Notes: The major emphasis is on social
sciences and humanities. Besides materials in
classical languages, South Asian vernaculars
being retained are Hindi, Bengali, Urdu,

Marathi and Tamil; strong in classical
languages, especially Sanskrit, Pali, and
Prakrit.
MI —MICHIGAN STATE UNIVERSITY,
International Library, South and Southeast
Asia Collection, East Lansing, 48824.
Clinton Lockert, Bibliographer
Holdings: Vols 55,700 // Cat Mss Maps
Audiotapes Microforms
Notes: Serials and monographs of South
Asia received on PL 480 for India, Pakistan,
Sri Lanka, and Nepal since 1968. Emphasis
is upon social sciences, humanities, and
science. Areas of strength are anthropology
and rural development. This subject has been
de-emphasized, additions are not being
made.
NY —NEW YORK PUBLIC LIBRARY,
Oriental Div, Fifth Ave & 42 St, New York,
10018. E Christian Filstrup, Chief
Holdings: Cat Mss Microforms
Budget: ($56,455)
Notes: Published catalog of holdings.
NY —NEW YORK PUBLIC LIBRARY,
Donnell Foreign Language Library, 20 W 53
St, New York, 10019. Bosiljka Stevanovic,
Supvr Librn
Holdings: Vols 341 Cat
Notes: Urdu collection incl Urdu authors of
Urdu expression. No separate catalog.
TX —UNIVERSITY OF TEXAS LIBRARIES,
Asian Collection, PO Box P, Austin, 78712.
Kevin Lin, Asian Librn; Merry Burlingham,
South Asian Librn
Holdings: Vols (56,000) Microforms
Notes: Materials in Hindi, Sanskrit, Urdu,
Prakrit, and Pali (acquired chiefly through
the Special Foreign Acquisitions Program)
and selected English-language materials,
including Indian censuses and district
gazetteers and Pakistani censuses.

UREY, HAROLD CLAYTON, 1893-1981

CA —UNIVERSITY OF CALIFORNIA, SAN
DIEGO, Central University Library,
Mandeville Dept of Special Collections, La
Jolla, 92093. Lynda Corey Claassen, Head
Notes: Papers of Harold Clayton Urey
(1893-1981), winner of the 1934 Nobel Prize
in chemistry for his discovery of Deuterium.
Incl files concerning the Emergency
Committee of Atomic Scientists, 1946-49;
also some material on the Rosenberg/Sobell
spy cases; also on his works as science
advisor to John F Kennedy (president-elect).

URIANKHAI LANGUAGE see Soyot Language

URIYA LANGUAGE see Oriya Language and Literature

UROLOGY—HISTORY

CA —UNIVERSITY OF CALIFORNIA, LOS
ANGELES, Biomedical Library, Center for
the Health Sciences, Los Angeles, 90024.
Alison Bunting, Acting Biomedical Librn;
Victoria Steele, Head, History & Special
Collections Div
Holdings: Vols 778 // Cat Mss
Notes: The John A Benjamin Collection.
Classics in the history of urology, 14th-20th
centuries; mss, incunabula and related
reference works. Landmarks in the history of
medicine and science. Printed catalog
available.
GA —MEDICAL COLLEGE OF GEORGIA,
Library, Laney Walker Blvd, Augusta,
30902. Dorothy H Mims, Librn for Special
Collections
Holdings: Vols (2500) // Cat
Notes: Special collection of late 18th and
early 19th century medical books; reflects
the strong emphases of this period on
lithotomy, and incl classics on the genito-
urinary system.
IL —UNIVERSITY OF ILLINOIS AT
CHICAGO, Library of the Health Sciences,
1750 W Polk St, PO Box 7509, Chicago,
60612. Robert J Adelsperger, Cur, Special
Collections
Holdings: Vols 1829 Cat
Notes: Published catalog. *The Joseph H*

UROLOGY—HISTORY (cont.)

Kiefer Catalog of History of Urology and Medicine. Chicago, Library of the Health Sciences, 1981.

TN —VANDERBILT UNIVERSITY, Medical Center Library, Nashville, 37232. Mary H Teloh, Special Collections Librn
Holdings: Vols 3000 Cat Mss Pix Slides
Notes: The rare books collection incl works by Auenbrugger, Beaumont, Elyot, Jenner, Laennec, Vesalius, and Vigo. The working collection for the history of medicine is particularly strong in American imprints of the late 18th and 19th century. These emphases are supported in the general collection by some notable runs of the 18th and 19th century European and American medical journals. Strong subject collections include: military medicine, nutrition, surgery and urology. There is also under development a collection of the scientific writings of medical educators connected with Vanderbilt.

URQUHART, SIR THOMAS

CT —YALE UNIVERSITY, Box 1603A, Yale Station, New Haven, 06520.

URSULINES

NY —COLLEGE OF NEW ROCHELLE, Gill Library, Castle Place, New Rochelle, 10801. Gloria T Greco, Librn
Holdings: Vols 242 Cat Mss Microforms
Notes: Ursuline Collection: mss and early editions of works pertaining to the history of the Order of St Ursula, founded by Angela Merici in 1535. Separate shelflist.

URUGUAY

CT —YALE UNIVERSITY, Sterling Memorial Library, Latin American Collections, New Haven, 06520. Lee H Williams Jr, Cur
Holdings: Vols (300,000) Cat Mss Pix Slides Phonorecords 16mm Films Filmstrips
Notes: See entry for Yale University under Latin America.

MO —WASHINGTON UNIVERSITY, John M Olin Library, Campus Box 1061, St Louis, 63130.
Holdings: Vols (50,000) Cat
Notes: Strong collection. Much unusual material.

TX —UNIVERSITY OF TEXAS LIBRARIES, Nettie Lee Benson Latin American Collection, Sid Richardson Hall 1.109, Austin, 78712. Laura Gutierrez-Witt, Head Librn
Holdings: Vols (450,000) Cat Microforms
Notes: Collection of Simon Luciux.
See also entry under Latin America.

USAGE AND CUSTOM (LAW) see Customary Law

USAGES see Etiquette

USEFUL ARTS see Industrial Arts; Technology

USES, CHARITABLE see Charitable Uses, Trusts, and Foundations

USTICK, THOMAS

RI —BROWN UNIVERSITY, John Hay Library, 20 Prospect St, Providence, 02912. Mark N Brown, Cur Mss
Holdings: Vols (2000) Cat Mss
Notes: Several collections of religious history strong in material on Baptist, Congregational, and Unitarian Churches in the 19th century, incl the ms records some Rhode Island congregations plus the papers of Isaac Backus, Brown University presidents and faculty, Jones Very, Mary Ann Atwood, Thomas Ustick, and Charles King Newcomb; incl numerous ephemeral and pamphlet publications that relate to Baptist Church history, creed, biography, Sunday School literature and missions.

UTAH

UT —UTAH STATE UNIVERSITY, Merrill Library, Department of Special Collections & Archives, Logan, 84322. A J Simmonds, Curator; Jeanie F Simmonds, Archivist; Bradford R Cole, Mss Librn
Holdings: Vols 1300 Cat Mss Pix Microforms
Notes: Collection tries to include everything on Utah-its history, government, education, agriculture, etc 1420 ft of mss. Ephemeral materials and publications (incl 10,000 pamphlets), cataloged or registered. 800 microfilm rolls; 400 maps; is a Utah State Documents depository. Considerable overlap with the Library's Mormon History Collection (qv)

UT —UNIVERSITY OF UTAH, Marriott Library, Special Collections, Salt Lake City, 84112. Gregory C Thompson, Cur

UTAH—DESCRIPTION AND TRAVEL—VIEWS

CA —POMONA PUBLIC LIBRARY, Special Collections, 625 S Garey Ave, PO Box 2271, Pomona, 91766. David Streeter, Librn
Holdings: Uncat Slides
Notes: Contains 550 lantern slides (mostly of California) and 4200 color 35mm transparencies of world travel, 1960s. Also, the Burton Frasher Postal Card Collection of 60,000 negatives and prints of California, Arizona, Colorado, New Mexico, Nevada, and Utah; 30,000 world views; 8000 California views. There are also world views in nearly 1000 stereophotographs.

UTAH—HISTORY

CA —AZUSA PACIFIC COLLEGE, Marshburn Memorial Library, Citrus & Alosta, Azusa, 91702. Edward Peterman, Librn
Holdings: Vols (6000) Uncat
Budget: ($30,000)
Notes: Significant holdings in the George E Fullerton Library of Californiana and Western Amricana.

LA —TULANE UNIVERSITY, Howard-Tilton Memorial Library, Special Collections Div, 7001 Freret St, New Orleans, 70118. Wilbur E Meneray, Librn
Holdings: Cat Mss
Notes: Official, personal and family correspondence of Albert Sidney Johnston incl letter and order books. Incl the Mexican War, the Utah Campaign and the Civil War. Indexed.

UT —PROVO CITY PUBLIC LIBRARY, 13 N 100 E, Provo, 84601. Larry Hortin, Dir
Holdings: Vols (600) Cat
Notes: Western states history with emphasis on Utah State and Utah County.

†UT —UNIVERSITY OF UTAH, Marriott Library, Salt Lake City, 84112.
Notes: Original drawings and personal papers of John Hudson, a gold rush Forty-Niner who helped chart the Great Salt Lake with Captain Howard Stansbury.

UT —UTAH STATE HISTORICAL SOCIETY, Library, 300 Rio Grande, Salt Lake City, 84101. Jay M Haymond, Coordr, Collections & Research Services
Holdings: Vols (80,000) Cat Mss Maps Pix Slides Phonorecords Audiotapes 16mm Films Filmstrips Microforms
Budget: ($111,000)

UT —ZION NATIONAL PARK, Library, Springdale, 84767. Roy Given, Asst Chief Park Naturalist; Marion Hilkey, Librn
Holdings: Vols (2700) Cat Mss Maps Pix Audiotapes
Budget: ($1000)
Notes: Emphasis on history and natural history of Zion National Park and vicinity and other information bearing on the management and operation of the Park. ILL permitted upon prior approval of the Park Superintendent.

UTAH—MAPS

OK —TULSA CITY-COUNTY LIBRARY, Business & Technology Dept, 400 Civic Center, Tulsa, 74103. Craig Buthod, Head
Notes: Original General Land Office survey maps for the states of Arizona, Arkansas, Colorado, Illinois, Indiana, Idaho, Kansas, Michigan, Missouri, Montana, Nebraska, Nevada, New Mexico, North Dakota, Ohio, Oklahoma, South Dakota, Utah and Wyoming. Incomplete coverage of each state.

UT —UNIVERSITY OF UTAH, Marriott Library, Special Collections, Salt Lake City, 84112. Gregory C Thompson, Cur
Notes: Approx 1000 historical maps of Utah, including Sanborn Maps.

UTAH AUTHORS see Authors, Utah

UTILIZATION OF WASTE see Salvage (Waste, Etc.); Waste Products

UTOPIAS

CA —CALIFORNIA STATE UNIVERSITY, FRESNO, Henry Madden Library, Dept of Special Collections, Fresno, 93740. Ronald J Mahoney, Head
Holdings: Vols 130 Cat Mss Maps Pix
Notes: Archives of Albert Kimsey Owen, founder of the utopian colony at Topolobampo, Sinaloa, Mexico. Over 10,000 letters, maps, documents, pictures, newspapers, pamphlets, and plans, relating to the colony and the Credit Foncier Company already to the colony and the Credit Foncier Company already represented in the Library by the Viola Gabriel Collection of about 800 simiar items and nearly 400 photographs. See Cat's Paw Utopia, by Ray Reynolds (El Cajon, Calif, 1971). Incl 20 linear feet of ms material. Particially cataloged.

CA —UNIVERSITY OF CALIFORNIA, SAN DIEGO, Central University Library, Mandeville Dept of Special Collections, La Jolla, 92093. Lynda Corey Claassen, Head
Notes: Largely manuscript materials, pamphlets, newspapers. Also, 300 volumes of utopian literature, including books and photographs about the Topolobampo Community established in 1866 on the west coast of Mexico.

CA —UNIVERSITY OF CALIFORNIA, RIVERSIDE, University Library, 4045 Canyon Crest Dr, Box 5900, Riverside, 92517.
Holdings: Vols 500 Cat Mss
Notes: Modern printed works and manuscript collections on utopias and utopian colonies, especially in North America.

CA —SAN DIEGO PUBLIC LIBRARY, 820 E St, San Diego, 92101. Rhoda E Kruse, Sr Librn
Notes: Records of the Little Landers colony, a 1910 Utopian group founded in the Tia Juana River Valley.

IL —NEWBERRY LIBRARY, 60 W Walton St, Chicago, 60610. Diana Haskell, Cur of Modern Mss
Holdings: Cat
Notes: American cooperative communities.

IL —UNIVERSITY OF ILLINOIS, URBANA/CHAMPAIGN, Library, Illinois Historical Survey Library, 1408 W Gregory Dr, 1A Library, Urbana, 61801.
Holdings: Vols 50 Cat Mss Maps Pix Microforms
Notes: Communitarianism in America. The ms material, contained in 30 separate collections (10 cubic feet), concentrates on the period 1840-70. It incl correspondence, records, minutes, ledgers and diaries. Communal societies such as Bishop Hill, Brook Farm, New Harmony, the North American Phalanx and the Sodus Bay Phalanx are represented. Among the correspondents are Albert Brisbane, Parke Godwin, Sarah Grimke, Richard Owen, Robert Owen, Robert Dale Owen, and Geogre Ripley. Numerous pictures. Guide to the collections published in 1976.

IN —INDIANA UNIVERSITY, Lilly Library, Seventh St, Bloomington, 47405. William R Cagle, Librn
Holdings: // Cat Mss
Notes: First and early printings of the Icarian communities (1840-1880) and of works by Rappites and the Owenites; also New Harmony, Indiana. Mss relating to the

UTOPIAS (cont.)

Shaker community in Kentucky (1826-1828) in the Charles Willing Byrd collection.

IN —PURDUE UNIVERSITY LIBRARIES, Graduate School of Management, Krannert Library, West Lafayette, 47907. Gordon Law, Librn
Notes: An important resource at the Krannert Library is its Special Collection of Business and Economics, consisting of some 8000 rare pre-20th century strengths in books, journals, tracts and pamphlets covering primarily the early literature of economic thought and business practices in America and abroad, 1500-1870. A catalog was issued in 1979.

MD —UNIVERSITY OF MARYLAND, BALTIMORE COUNTY, Albin O Kuhn Library and Gallery, 5401 Wilkens Ave, Baltimore, 21228. Ann Copeland, Special Collections Librn
Holdings: 2200 Cat //
Notes: Nineteenth century British and American Socialism is one theme of the 2200 volume Needle Collection. Explored are prison reform, Pennsylvania pietistic movements and ideal communities from 1800-1875.

MA —HARVARD UNIVERSITY LIBRARY, Cambridge, 02138.
Holdings: Cat
Notes: See *Harvard Library Notes, III* (1935): pp 46-50.

MA —FRUITLANDS MUSEUMS LIBRARY, Prospect Hill, RR 2 Box 87, Harvard, 01451. Richard S Reed, Dir; John L Crispen, Admin Secy
Budget: ($21,900)
Notes: Fruitlands (utopian community), books and manuscripts; New England Transcendentalism; and Shakers' books and mss, primarily the Harvard Shaker Society and Shirley Shaker Society. Secondary works, general utopia reference.

MO —UNIVERSITY OF MISSOURI-SAINT LOUIS, Thomas Jefferson Library, 8001 Natural Bridge Rd, Saint Louis, 63121.
Notes: American and British Utopian Literature: Approximately 1000 vols of Literary Utopias. Collection is partially described and listed in Sargent, Lyman Tower *British and American Utopian Literature, 1516-1975: An Annotated Bibliography*, (G K Hall, 1979); note: a second edition is in preparation. Collection also includes galley proofs of some of the titles.

NY —NEW YORK STATE LIBRARY, State Education Bldg Annex, Washington Ave, Albany, 12224.

NY —COLUMBIA UNIVERSITY LIBRARIES, Rare Book & Manuscript Library, 801 Butler Library, 535 W 114 St, New York, 10027. Kenneth A Lohf, Librn
Holdings: Mss
Notes: Consisting of music mss of the Ephrata Community, by the founder of the community, Conrad Beissel. Restricted use.

NY —SYRACUSE UNIVERSITY LIBRARIES, Ernest S Bird Library, George Arents Research Library for Special Collections, Syracuse, 13210. Carolyn A Davis, Manuscripts Librn; Amy S Doherty, University Archivist; Mark F Weimer, Rare Book Librn
Holdings: Vols 225 Cat Pix
Notes: A collection of publications by and about the Hopedale and Oneida communities and their forerunners; supplemented by reference works dealing with Communistic societies in general. Contains ephemeral handbooks, annual reports and periodicals; particularly relating to John Humphrey Noyes.

NC —DUKE UNIVERSITY, William R Perkins Library, Rare Book Room, Durham, 27706. John L Sharpe, III, Cur
Notes: The Glenn Negley Utopia collection. More than 500 titles, many of which were gifts of professors Glenn Negley and John Lievsay.

OH —MASSILLON PUBLIC LIBRARY, 208 Lincoln Way E, Massillon, 44646. Camille Leslie, Dir
Holdings: Vols 73 Cat Mss
Budget: $100
Notes: Collection is limited to historical studies; nothing on modern communes. Special emphasis on Shakers and Zoarites. No separate catalog.

OH —ANTIOCH COLLEGE, Olive Kettering Library, Livermore St, Yellow Springs, 45387. Nina Myatt, Cur
Holdings: Cat Mss Pix
Notes: Personal papers, corresondence, 1920-1975. Mss, film out-takes, diaries, materials from Tennessee Valley Authority (Morgan was first chairman), Antioch College (Morgan was president 1920-1936), materials on Edward Bellamy (Morgan wrote biography of Bellamy). About 175 file boxes.

PA —PENNSYLVANIA DIV OF ARCHIVES & MANUSCRIPTS, State Archives, PO Box 1026, Harris, 17108. Roland M Baumann, Chief, History & Museums
Holdings: Vols (3000) // Uncat Mss Maps Pix
Budget: ($40,000)
Notes: The Harmony Society (1785-1905), a German communistic and spiritual community, which immigrated to the US in 1805 and established their community in Harmony, Pennsylvania, moved to New Harmony, Indiana, and returned to Pennsylvania to set up the town of Economy, 20 miles north of Pittsburgh on the Ohio River. The Harmonists had a vast impact on the economy of the areas in which they lived. They were involved in agriculture, manufacturing and investing. 300,000 cu ft.

PA —BALCH INSTITUTE FOR ETHNIC STUDIES, Library, 18 S Seventh St, Philadelphia, 19106. R Joseph Anderson, Library Dir

RI —BROWN UNIVERSITY, John Carter Brown Library, Providence, 02912. Norman Fiering, Librn; Everett C Wilkie Jr, Bibliographer; Susan Danforth, Cur Maps & Prints
Notes: Spurious, imaginary, visionary, or utopian works dealing with the New World or set in the New World, published before 1835.

TX —UNIVERSITY OF TEXAS, ARLINGTON, Library, PO Box 19497, Arlington, 76019. Chas Colley, Dir Special Collections
Holdings: // Mss
Notes: Santerre Collection. This is the library of the Santerre family who emigrated from France, Belgium, and Switzerland in 1855 to join the Utopian Socialist colony of Victor Prosper Condiserant in what is now Dallas, Texas. Typical selection of books of a middle-class, well-educated family of the period. Some title deeds, legal papers, family letters, first Paris editions of works of Considerant, Charles Fourier; French translations of English classics, devotional works. See George H Santerre, *White Cliffs of Dallas* (Dallas, Texas: Book Craft, 1955).

WI —UNIVERSITY OF WISCONSIN, GREEN BAY, Library/Learning Center, Green Bay, 54301. Marian A Gould, Acting Dir, Special Collections/University Archives
Holdings: Vols 700 // Cat
Notes: This represents the collection of Leon Kramer, "idealist, philosophical anarchist and bookseller." Much of the material concerns radical literature and small socialist and communist parties in the US, although there is a considerable amount of books, booklets, and pamphlets published in Germany, Italy, and other parts of Europe. Incl uncounted pamphlets.

UZBEG LANGUAGE see Uzbek Language and Literature

UZBEK LANGUAGE (OLD) see Jagataic Language and Literature

UZBEK LANGUAGE AND LITERATURE

NY —NEW YORK PUBLIC LIBRARY, Oriental Div, Fifth Ave & 42 St, New York, 10018. E Christian Filstrup, Chief
Holdings: Cat Mss Microforms
Budget: ($56,455)
Notes: Published catalog of holdings.

V

VACATIONS

IL —UNIVERSITY OF ILLINOIS,
URBANA/CHAMPAIGN, Library, Applied
Life Studies Library, 1408 W Gregory Dr,
Urbana, 61801.
Holdings: Vols (38,000) Cat Microforms
Notes: Special emphasis on leisure studies,
recreation surveys and plans, outdoor
education, recreation programs, theories of
play, supervision, and therapeutic recreation.

IA —IOWA FALLS PUBLIC LIBRARY, 520
Rocksylvania, Iowa Falls, 50126. Deanne
Keller, Librn
Holdings: Vols 707 Maps Filmstrips
Notes: Regional collection includes modes of
travel, various kinds of vacations in the US
and world-wide. Information on hotels, as
well. An additional (150) travel books in the
Children's collection.

ON —SIRLS, Faculty of Human Kinetics &
Leisure Studies, University of Waterloo,
Waterloo, N2L 3G1, Can. Betty Smith,
Database Mgr
Notes: Information Retrieval System for the
Sociology of Leisure and Sport (SIRLS) is a
computerized online database of about 13,
000 entries (1983). Incl dance as a leisure
time activity.

VACCINATION—HISTORY

CT —YALE UNIVERSITY, Medical Historical
Library, Klebs Collection, 333 Cedar St,
New Haven, 06520. Ferenc A Gyorgyey,
Librn
Notes: The Arnold Carl Klebs Medical
Collection books, pamphlets, etc, incl the
library of his father, Edwin T A Klebs,
pathologist. Strong in bibliography of early
printed medical books, herbals, plague tracts,
inoculation, vaccination and tubercular
diseases.

MD —JOHNS HOPKINS UNIVERSITY,
Institute of the History of Medicine, 1900 E
Monument St, Baltimore, 21205. Doris
Thibodeau, Librn
Holdings: Vols 1053 Cat

VACUUM—INDUSTRIAL
APPLICATIONS see Vacuum Science and
Technology

VACUUM SCIENCE AND
TECHNOLOGY

PA —FRANKLIN INSTITUTE LIBRARY, 20
& The Parkway, Philadelphia, 19103.
Miriam Padusis, Dir; Charles Wilt, Readers
Servs Librn
Holdings: Vols (300,000) Cat maps Pix
Microforms

VAGIONIS, NICHOLAS

†PA —BALCH INSTITUTE FOR ETHNIC
STUDIES, Library, 18 S Seventh St,
Philadelphia, 19106.
Notes: Papers of Nicholas Vagionis,
president of the American Greek
Democratic Association.

VAILE, WILLIAM NEWELL

CO —DENVER PUBLIC LIBRARY, 1357
Broadway, Denver, 80203.
Notes: Correspondence, papers, pictures,
diaries, etc.

VALACHIAN LANGUAGE AND
LITERATURE

OH —OHIO STATE UNIVERSITY, William
Oxley Thompson Memorial Library, 1858
Neil Ave, Columbus, 43210. A Robert
Thorson, Head, Circulation Dept
Holdings: Cat Mss Microforms
Notes: This collection presently contains
films of 2000 mss from the Hilandar
Monastery, Mt Athos. Expansion will add
Byzantine, Bulgarian, Russian and Valachian
mss on film.

VALENTE, ALFREDO

NY —NEW YORK PUBLIC LIBRARY,
Performing Arts Research Center, Billy Rose
Theatre Collection, 111 Amsterdam Ave,
New York, 10023. Dorothy L Swerdlove,
Cur
Holdings: Cat Pix
Notes: Photo collection.

VALENTINES

CT —TRINITY COLLEGE LIBRARY,
Watkinson Library, 300 Summit St,
Hartford, 06106. Jeffrey Kaimowitz, Cur
Holdings: // Uncat
Notes: Early valentines.

MA —AMERICAN ANTIQUARIAN
SOCIETY LIBRARY, 185 Salisbury St,
Worcester, 01609. Marcus A McCorison,
Dir & Librn
Holdings: Cat Maps Pix
Notes: Over 6000 American prints, arranged
by lithographer. Incl political caricatures and
cartoons, maps, sheet music. Also
advertising cards, Valentines, etc.

VALENZUELA, EDWARD

CA —STANFORD UNIVERSITY
LIBRARIES, Cecil H Green Library,
Stanford, 94305. Michael T Ryan, Cur
Notes: Papers of Ernesto Galarza, Bert
Corona, Manuel Ruiz, Jr, Eduardo Queredo,
Edward Valenzuela.

VALLANCE, WILLIAM ROY

NY —UNIVERSITY OF ROCHESTER, Rush
Rhees Library, Department of Rare Books
and Special Collections, Rochester, 14627.
Peter Dzwonkoski, Librn
Holdings: Cat Mss
Notes: Correspondence, reports, printed
material regarding immigration laws,
prohibition violations (rum runners), radio
and telegraph laws between 1920 and 1940
when Vallance served as a member of the
State Department.

VALLEY FEVER

OH —MIAMI UNIVERSITY, Science Library,
Oxford, 45056.
Notes: Zoonoses and related diseases.
Collection partially transferred from Parker-
Davis Memorial Library, Hamilton, Mont.

VALUATION

IL —INTERNATIONAL ASSOCIATION OF
ASSESSING OFFICERS, Research &
Technical Services Dept, 1313 E 60 St,
Chicago, 60637. Stuart W Miller, Librn
Holdings: Vols 6000 Cat Documents
Microforms
Budget: ($3500)
Notes: Extensive collection of materials
relating to the property tax and its
administration, incl assessment studies,
reports of legislative and civic groups,
manuals, judicial decisions and other works.
Subscription information service available.
Library is an OCLC member and lends on
ILL. The Library is open to the public (at
least 24 hours notice required) and accepts
telephone inquiries.

VALVERDE, JUAN DE

CA —UNIVERSITY OF CALIFORNIA, LOS
ANGELES, Biomedical Library, Center for
Health Sciences, Los Angeles, 90024. Louise
Darling, Biomedical Librn
Notes: Incl a unique set of 42 anatomical
facsimile plants from Juan de Valverde's
Vivae Imagines...printed by the Plantin Press
in 1969. Described in *UCLA Librarian*, vol
25, no 3, March 1972.

VAMBERY, RUSZTEM, 1872-1948

CA —HOOVER INSTITUTION ON WAR,
REVOLUTION & PEACE, Stanford
University, Stanford, 94305. Milorad M
Drachkovitch, Archivist
Holdings: Mss
Notes: Papers of Rusztem Vambery,
Hungarian author lawyer, and Minister to
the US, 1947-48, incl correspondence,
speeches and writings, reports, printed
matter, and other material, 1905-48, relating
to his legal and political careers, to
criminology, and to Hungarian domestic and
foreign affairs. 9 ms boxes.

VAN ALLEN, JAMES

IA —HERBERT HOOVER PRESIDENTIAL
LIBRARY, West Branch, 52358. Dale C
Mayer, Archivist
Notes: Papers.

VANAUKEN, SHELDON

IL —WHEATON COLLEGE, Library, Marion
E Wade Collection, Irving & Franklin Sts,
Wheaton, 60187. Lyle Dorsett, Cur;
Marjorie Mead, Associate Cur
Holdings: Vols (6500) Mss
Notes: Extensive Marion E Wade Collection
contains materials relating to Vanauken's *A
Severe Mercy* and *Gateway tHeaven.*
See also entry under C S Lewis

VAN BIESBROECK, GEORGE

IL —UNIVERSITY OF CHICAGO
LIBRARY, Dept of Special Collections,
1100 E 57 St, Chicago, 60637.
Notes: Miscellaneous research files, incl
observation records of George Van
Biesbroeck.

VAN BUREN, MARTIN

DC —LIBRARY OF CONGRESS, Manuscript
Division, Washington, 20540. John C
Broderick, Chief
Notes: The Presidential Papers collection
incl the papers, etc, of numerous Presidents.

VAN BUREN, RAEBURN

MA —BOSTON UNIVERSITY, Mugar
Memorial Library, Special Collections Dept,
771 Commonwealth Ave, Boston, 02215.
Howard B Gotlieb, Dir
Holdings: Cat Pix
Notes: Original drawings and comic strips of
"Abbie and Slats".

VANCOUVER ISLAND, B.C.

BC —VANCOUVER ISLAND REGIONAL
LIBRARY, 10 Strickland St, Nanaimo, V9R
5G7, Can. R W Reeves, Librn
Holdings: Vols 2200 Cat Pix Microforms
Notes: Emphasis on British Columbia
history, especially Vancouver Island. Incl
pamphlets and 150 microforms.

VANDAMM STUDIO

NY —NEW YORK PUBLIC LIBRARY,
Performing Arts Research Center, Billy Rose
Theatre Collection, 111 Amsterdam Ave,
New York, 10023. Dorothy L Swerdlove,
Cur
Holdings: Cat Pix
Notes: Photo collection.

VAN DONGEN, HELEN

NY —MUSEUM OF MODERN ART, Dept of
Film, 11 W 53 St, New York, 10019. Eileen
Bowser, Cur
Holdings: Mss Pix
Notes: Papers, correspondence, scrapbooks,
pictures, etc. Partially cataloged.

VAN DOREN, MARK ALBERT

NY —COLUMBIA UNIVERSITY
LIBRARIES, Rare Book & Manuscript
Library, 801 Butler Library, 535 W 114 St,
New York, 10027. Kenneth A Lohf, Librn
Holdings: Mss
Notes: His papers. Restricted use.

VAN DOREN FAMILY

NY —COLUMBIA UNIVERSITY
LIBRARIES, Rare Book & Manuscript

VAN DOREN FAMILY (cont.)

Library, 801 Butler Library, 535 W 114 St, New York, 10027. Kenneth A Lohf, Librn
Holdings: Mss
Notes: Various papers of different members of the modern literary Van Doren family. Incl much other correspondence with important contemporary literary and other public figures. 15,000 items. Restricted use.

VAN DUSEN, HENRY PITNEY

NY —UNION THEOLOGICAL SEMINARY, Library, 3041 Broadway at Reinhold Niebuhr Place, New York, 10027. Richard D Spoor, Dir
Holdings: Vols (55,000) Cat Mss Microforms
Budget: ($350,000)

VAN DUYN, MONA

MO —WASHINGTON UNIVERSITY, John M Olin Library, Campus Box 1061, St Louis, 63130.
Notes: A major collection, incl mss, correspondence, literary papers, photographs, etc. Described in *Special Collections: an Annotated Guide to the Holdings of the Manuscript Division and the University Archives and Research Collection.*

VAN DYKE, HENRY

NY —SAINT JOHN'S UNIVERSITY, Special Collections Dept, Grand Central & Utopia Pkwys, Jamaica, 11439. Szilvia E Szmuk, Librn
Holdings: // Cat
Notes: No photocopying.

VAN HOBOKEN, ANTHONY

CA —UNIVERSITY OF CALIFORNIA, RIVERSIDE, University Library, 4045 Canyon Crest Dr, Box 5900, Riverside, 92517.
Notes: The Oswald Jonas Memorial Collection holds the musicological mss, letters, biographical materials, and notebooks of Heinrich Schenker and also the papers of the late Oswald Jonas, musicologist and leading authority on the life and work of Schenker. Incl Schenker's diary; correspondence with Anthony van Hoboken, Reinhard Oppel, Moriz Violin, Eugen d'Albert, and Oswald Jonas; the proofs and mss of his published works; printed editions from his library with notes, marginalia, and critical annotations; *Urlinie* tables; and miscellanea. A guide to the collection will be published by the library.

VANITY FAIR (MAGAZINE)

MN —MAYO MEDICAL LIBRARY, History of Medicine Collection, Rochester, 55905. Nancy R Hensel, Librn
Holdings: Pix
Notes: The Comfort Collection of caricatures of physicians and scientists from *Vanity Fair.* Description: Mann, Ruth J: "The unheroic representation of heroes." *Mayo Clin Proc.* 46:197-199, Mar 1971.

VAN ITALLIE, JEAN-CLAUDE see Itallie, Jean-Claude Van

VAN KLEECK, EDWIN ROBERT, 1906-1965

NY —STATE UNIVERSITY OF NEW YORK AT ALBANY, Library, Special Collections Dept, 1400 Washington Ave, Albany, 12222. Marion P Munzer, Coordr
Notes: Correspondence relating to Van Kleeck genealogy (2.5 linear feet); articles, speeches, pamphlets relating to New York historical societies and historic sites. *See also* entry under New York (State) - History

VAN LOON, HENDRIK WILLEM, 1882-1944

NY —CORNELL UNIVERSITY LIBRARIES, Collection of Regional History, Dept of Manuscripts and Univ Archives, Ithaca, 14853.
Notes: Author. Papers, ca 1895-(1919-44)-58; 36 ft., 3 map case drawers.

VAN NESS, WILLIAM P.

NY —NEW YORK HISTORICAL SOCIETY, Library, 170 Central Park W, New York, 10024. James Gregory, Librn
Holdings: Cat Mss
Notes: Papers of Aaron Burr's second in the duel with Alexander Hamilton.

VANNIC LANGUAGE

NY —NEW YORK PUBLIC LIBRARY, Oriental Div, Fifth Ave & 42 St, New York, 10018. E Christian Filstrup, Chief
Holdings: Cat Mss Microforms
Budget: ($56,455)
Notes: Published catalog of holdings.

VAN VECHTEN, CARL, 1880-1964

CT —YALE UNIVERSITY, Box 1603A, Yale Station, New Haven, 06520.
Holdings: Cat Mss Pix
Notes: Incl mss, correspondence, pictures.
MA —BRANDEIS UNIVERSITY, Goldfarb Library, 415 South St, Waltham, 02154. Bessie Hahn, Dir
Notes: Carl Van Vechten Photographic Collection. Consists of approx 8 linear ft of photographs of famous American personage taken by Carl Van Vechten. The collection is unprocessed.
NY —NEW YORK PUBLIC LIBRARY, Rare Books and Manuscripts Div, Fifth Ave & 42 St, New York, 10018. William L Joyce, Asst Dir; Susan E Davis, Cur of Mss
Holdings: Mss
Budget: ($7161)
Notes: Incl personal and literary mss, papers, etc.

VAN VLECK, JOHN HASBROUCK, 1899-1980

NY —AMERICAN INSTITUTE OF PHYSICS, Center for the History of Physics, Niels Bohr Library, 335 E 45 St, New York, 10017. John Aubry, Librn
Notes: Primarily professional correspondence from the 1920s to the 1970s of Prof John Hasbrouck Van Vleck, first American awarded a PhD in theoretical physics (1922). Won the Nobel Prize for his work in quantum physics theory and on solid state physics. Other of his papers are deposited in the Harvard University Archives.

VAN VOLKENBURG, ELLEN

MI —UNIVERSITY OF MICHIGAN, Library, Dept of Rare Books & Special Collections, Ann Arbor, 48109. Robert J Starring, Head
Holdings: Cat Mss Pix
Notes: Extensiveholdings of books on the theatre. Also, in the Charles Sanders Collection, about 14,000 British and American playbills and programs mostly of the 19th century, as well as scrapbooks, posters, and about 750 photographs and prints of actors and actresses. In the Ellen Van Volkenburg-Maurice Browne Collection, about 4000 photographs of stage productions and friends and associates, as well as programs, posters, scrapbooks of mounted clippings, about 200 original stage and costume designs, promptbooks, and play manuscripts, representing the American and British careers of this husband-wife team from 1912 to about 1940. The Chicago Little Theatre, 1912-1917, is well represented. Also contains more than 6000 items of correspondence with theatrical and literary figures. Another collection contains 143 Alfred Lunt letters, mainly from 1901-1915.

VAN VOORHIS FAMILY

OH —OHIO UNIVERSITY, Vernon R Alden Library, Athens, 45701. Kent Mulliner, Africana Specialist
Notes: Civil War letters and mss of the Brown and Van Voorhis families, both among the earliest settlers in southeastern Ohio. Mostly written by three members of the family serving in the Union armies between 1861 and 1865.

VANZETTI, BARTOLOMEO, 1888-1927

IN —INDIANA STATE UNIVERSITY, Cunningham Memorial Library, Dept of Rare Books & Special Collections, Terre Haute, 47809. Lawrence J McCrank, Head
Notes: The Debs Collection consists of aprox 7000 pieces of correspondence between Theodore Debs (brother of E V) and other persons, such as Sinclair Lewis, Upton Sinclair, Ethel Barrymore, Emma Goldman, Robert G Ingersoll, Carl Sandburg, Norman Thomas, Sacco and Vanzetti and many others. Many of the letters are from E V Debs to his brother; a good portion of these are from the federal penitentiary at Atlanta. Entire correspondence file has been microfilmed. 750 pamphlets cover all aspects of the labor movement, socialism and radical thought from the 19th century to appprox 1950. A collection ca 200 related books is also housed in the collection. See: J Robert Constantine and Gail Malmgreen, eds, *The Papers of Eugene V Debs, 1834-1945. A Guide to the Microfilm Edition.* NY: Microfilming Corp of America, 1983 (University Microfilms is the new distributer).
MA —HARVARD UNIVERSITY LIBRARY, Law School Library, Langdell Hall, Cambridge, 02138. Erika S Chadbourn, Cur of Mss
Notes: Legal documents, pictorial material, microfilms. Incl holograph letters of Sacco and Vanzetti, 1920-1928. Typed chronological list in repository.
MA —BRANDEIS UNIVERSITY, Goldfarb Library, 415 South St, Waltham, 02154. Bessie Hahn, Dir
Notes: Sacco and Vanzetti Case Collection. 23 linear ft of material collected by both Tom O'Connor and Francis Russell relating to this celebrated American trial. This collection is unprocessed.

VAQUEROS see Cowboys

VARIETY THEATRES see Music Halls (Variety Theatres, Cabarets, Night Clubs, Etc.); Vaudeville

VARLEY, JOHN

†PA —TEMPLE UNIVERSITY LIBRARY, Philadelphia, 19122. Thomas M Whitehead, Librn
Notes: More than 100 cubic ft of mss, incl papers of Michael Bishop, Ben Bova, Jack Dann, Gardner Dozois, Lloyd Eshback, Tom Purdom, Pamela Sargent, John Varley, and George Zebrowski.

VASCONCELOS, JOSE

PA —UNIVERSITY OF PITTSBURGH, Hillman Library, Pittsburgh, 15260. Glenora E Rossell, Head
Holdings: Cat Maps Pix
Notes: Incl the John M Malone Collection (300 vols) and the Cassasola collection of photographs of 20th century Mexico; virtually all the works of the Mexican philospher Jose Vasconelous.

VASCULAR HYPERTENSION see Hypertension

VASCULAR PLANTS see Botany

VASCULAR SYSTEM see Cardiovascular System

VASE PAINTING, GREEK

NY —COLUMBIA UNIVERSITY LIBRARIES, Avery Architectural and Fine

VASE PAINTING, GREEK (cont.)

Arts Library, 201 Avery Hall, New York,
10027. Angela Giral, Librn
Holdings: Vols 300 Cat
Notes: Restricted use: noncirculating.

VASEK, VLADIMIR

IN —INDIANA UNIVERSITY, Lilly Library,
Seventh St, Bloomington, 47405. William R
Cagle, Librn
Holdings: Vols (400) // Cat
Notes: First editions and later printings of
Karel H Macha (100 vols) and Vladimir
Vasek (300 vols).

VASSAR COLLEGE TRAINING CAMP FOR NURSES

MA —SIMMONS COLLEGE ARCHIVES,
300 The Fenway, Boston, 02115. Megan
Sniffin-Marinoff, College Archivist
Notes: Archives of the Simmons College
School of Public Health Nursing (later
reorganized into the School of Nursing)
cover the years 1902-1970. Important
correspondents in the collection incl M
Adelaide Nutting, Mary Beard, Isabel
Stewart, and Anne Hervey Strong, etc. Incl
Strong's records of activity with regard to
nursing education in the National
Organization for Public Health Nursing,
1918-22. 1000 linear feet in institution, incl
special collections nursing and photographs,
nursing.

VASSILIKOS, VASSILIS

MA —BOSTON UNIVERSITY, Mugar
Memorial Library, Special Collections Dept,
771 Commonwealth Ave, Boston, 02215.
Howard B Gotlieb, Dir
Holdings: Vols 50 Mss
Notes: Mss, correspondence, etc collected in
depth; incl publications by or about.

VATCHER, WILLIAM HENRY, JR.

CA —HOOVER INSTITUTION ON WAR,
REVOLUTION & PEACE, Stanford
University, Stanford, 94305. Milorad M
Drachkovitch, Archivist
Holdings: Mss Pix Slides
Notes: Papers of W H Vatcher, Jr, 1939-65,
incl correspondence, mss, pamphlets, leaflets,
slides, photographs, and other material,
relating to South African political parties;
Afrkaner and African nationalism; Afrkaner
Broederbond; US, Japanese, and Northern
Korean propaganda and psychological
warfare methods during World War II and
the Korean war. Incl "Siberian Sketchbook,"
a ms with photos by W H Vatcher. 18 ms
boxes, 1 box, 4 envelopes.

VATICAN ARCHIVES

CA —UNIVERSITY OF CALIFORNIA,
BERKELEY, School of Law, Library,
Berkeley, 94720. Stephan G Kuttner, Dir,
Canon Law Collection
Notes: Library is in process ofobtaining
complete microfilms of all canon and
medieval Roman law mss held by the
Vatican Library.

VATICAN COUNCIL, 1869-1870

GA —EMORY UNIVERSITY, Candler School
of Theology, Pitts Theology Library, Atlanta,
30322. Channing Jeschke, Librn; Anita K
Delaries, Curator
Notes: 10 linear feet of ms and printed
material (1822-92) documenting the life of
Cardinal Henry Edward Manning (1808-92).
The most notable items are his sermons,
sermon notes and speeches; items on
Archdiocese of Westminster. Finding aid
available.

OH —KENT STATE UNIVERSITY,
University Archives, Kent, 44242. Stephen C
Morton, University Archivist
Holdings: Uncat Mss Maps Pix
Phonorecords Filmstrips Microforms
Notes: Diocese of Youngstown Chancery

Office and Parish Files. Collection on
deposit. Some materials are restricted.
Contains materials on the second Vatican
Council and Council Review Days,
Cathedral records and plans, parochial
school photography collection, Canon Law
collection. The parish records are especially
valuable for researching births, marriages,
and deaths. A large amount of ethnic
material is also found in the files.

VATICAN LIBRARY—COLLECTIONS

DC —CATHOLIC UNIVERSITY OF
AMERICA, Canon Law Library, 300B
Mullen Library, Washington, 20064. R
Bruce Miller, Librn
Holdings: Vols (22,000)
Notes: The collection includes extensive
16th, 17th, and 18th century works in both
Latin and Italian. There are many printed
editions of pre-16th century sources. Both
the 19th and 20th century materials are well
represented. This collection is also rich in
materials relating to the Second Vatican
Council and its aftermath and is up-to-date
on the new (1983) Code of Canon Law.
Current periodical subscriptions to journals
in English, German, French, Italian, and
Spanish.

MO —SAINT LOUIS UNIVERSITY, Pius XII
Memorial Library, Vatican Film Library
Collection, 3655 W Pine Blvd, Saint Louis,
63108. Charles J Ermatinger, Librn
Holdings: Mss Slides Microforms
Notes: Vatican Film Library has 75 percent
of the Greek, Latin and western European
vernacular holdings in the Vatican Library,
plus all the Hebrew, Arabic and Ethiopic
holdings on film. Covers 5th-19th centuries.
Sizable collection of western European
books. In addition, has largest collection on
the work of the Jesuits in Latin America, the
US and the Philippines, filmed from
European Jesuit archives. Excellent catalogs
and guides to all collections. Also, 50,608
slides of illuminated mss; 26,470 reels of
microfilm.

NC —UNIVERSITY OF NORTH
CAROLINA, CHAPEL HILL, Music
Library, Hill Hall, Chapel Hill, 27514.
Holdings: Vols (90,000) Cat Mss Pix Slides
Phonorecords Audiotapes Microforms
Budget: ($60,000)
Notes: Microfilms of Vatican Library
holdings of mss containing hymns.

VATICAN II

DC —CATHOLIC UNIVERSITY OF
AMERICA, Canon Law Library, 300B
Mullen Library, Washington, 20064. R
Bruce Miller, Librn
Holdings: Vols (22,000)
Notes: The collection includes extensive
16th, 17th, and 18th century works in both
Latin and Italian. There are many printed
editions of pre-16th century sources. Both
the 19th and 20th century materials are well
represented. This collection is also rich in
materials relating to the Second Vatican
Council and its aftermath and is up-to-date
on the new (1983) Code of Canon Law.
Current periodical subscriptions to journals
in English, German, French, Italian, and
Spanish.

NY —GENERAL THEOLOGICAL
SEMINARY, Saint Marks Library, 175
Ninth Ave, New York, 10011. David Green,
Dir
Holdings: Vols (200,000) Cat Mss Maps Pix
Slides Microforms
Notes: Extensive collection.

VATJAN LANGUAGE see Votish Language and Literature

VAUDEVILLE

IL —CHICAGO PUBLIC LIBRARY, Music
Section, Fine Arts Division, 78 E
Washington St, Chicago, 60602. Rosalinda I
Hack, Fine Arts Division Chief; Richard C
Schwegel, Head, Music Section
Holdings: // Uncat
Notes: The Chicago Public Library received

the Sheet Music Archive (1700 cu ft) of the
Plitt Theatre Corporation, Chicago, in 1975.
This vast unprocessed collection contains
thousands of pieces of music played during
intemissions in the Plitt Theatre palaces in
Chicago during the 1920-40s. An inventory
of the collection is available, organized by
composer and form (e g "Fox Trots"); titles
are not yet compiled. The collection is
presently in storage at the Record Center
Corporation, The Chicago Public Library's
storage facility for little-used materials.

IL —ILLINOIS STATE UNIVERSITY, Milner
Library, Dept of Special Collections,
Normal, 61761. Robert Sokan, Librn
Holdings: Vols (6200) Cat Mss Pix Slides
Notes: Circus and related arts collection
consists of approx 6200 book items and
approx 250,000 nonbook items. The books
date from the 16th century to the present,
and incl vols specifically concerned with the
circus past and present, vaudeville, music
halls and variety theaters, theatrical and
animal history, biographies, autobiographies
and memoirs, novels, poetry, drama,
juvenalia and other subjects relating to the
circus. Many of the books are limited
editions, presentation copies or autographed
copies. Incl archives of the Dobritch
International Circus (20,000 items).

IN —INDIANA UNIVERSITY, Lilly Library,
Seventh St, Bloomington, 47405. William R
Cagle, Librn
Holdings: // Uncat
Notes: Theatre music in the Starr Collection
of American Sheet Music.

IA —UNIVERSITY OF IOWA, University
Libraries, Iowa City, 52242. Robert A
McCown, Mss Librn
Holdings: Mss
Notes: Keith/Albee Vaudeville Collection.
Records of a vaudeville, theatre, and
moving-pictures business established by
Benjamin Franklin Keith, 1846-1914, and
Edward Franklin Albee, 1857-1930. The
collection includes clipping books, report
books, cash books, subject files, signs and
posters. Theatres in the following cities are
represented in the collection: Providence,
RI, Pawtucket, RI, Woonsocket, RI, and
Webster, Mass. The business was later part
of RKO Pictures, Inc. Unpublished register
in the library. 50 ft of mss.

†NJ —PRINCETON UNIVERSITY, Library,
William Seymour Theatre Collection,
Princeton, 08540.

PA —FREE LIBRARY OF PHILADELPHIA,
Theatre Collection, Logan Sq, Philadelphia,
19103. Geraldine Duclow, Librn-in-Charge
Holdings: Vols (1,250,000) Uncat Pix
Notes: The Theatre Collection contains
books, magazines, playbills, broadsides,
posters, photographs, and other memorabilia
covering theatre, motion pictures, minstrels,
vaudeville, circus, radio and television. The
Library's Philadelphia Theatre Index lists
the major productions here since 1855, and
partially indexes the collection of local
playbills which date back to 1803. There are
also programs from many other cities, incl
New York; some from London date back to
1800. Early film companies as well as the
present movie industry are represented by
advertising materials and over 30,000 film
stills. The Lubin Film Co (1910-1916)
Archive has been established with over 600
photographs and related items. Circus
programs and route books date back to 1900.
There are minstrel programs as early as
1865. Most significant are the mss from
Philadelphia's Dumont Minstrels.
Variousfiles contain autographs, photographs,
newspaper articles and reviews in all
pertinent subject areas. Noncirculating.

PA —UNIVERSITY OF PITTSBURGH,
Special Collections Dept, Curtis Theatre
Collection, 363 Hillman Library, Pittsburgh,
15260. Jeanette Blanco, Cur
Holdings: Vols (4000) Cat Mss Documents
Microforms Pix Slides VF
Notes: The legitimate theatre of plays,
musicals and vaudeville, chiefly of New
York City and Pittsburgh, from 1865, and
other US, community, summer, college and
foreign theatre. Incl 500,000 programs, 12,
000 pictures, 300 posters, the Oliver P

VAUDEVILLE (cont.)

Merriman Scrapbooks and 300 other scrapbooks, clippings and other ephemera. Vols incl over 3000 acting editions and playscripts. Separate collections: Ralph G Allen Burlesque Skits Collection; Michael Ellis Papers; William P Halstead Theatre Collection; Kenyon Family Papers; Philip Dunning Playscripts Collection; Pittsburgh Playhouse Records; Pittsburgh Savoyards Records. Noncirculating.

SC —COLLEGE OF CHARLESTON LIBRARY, Special Collections Dept, Charleston, 29401.
Notes: The Kenneth Hanson Archives of Sound Recordings chronicling the growth of the recording industry through the 1940s. Over 400 cylinder records of marches, popular songs, vaudeville acts, and speeches.

VA —GEORGE MASON UNIVERSITY, Fenwick Library, Special Collections Dept, 4400 University Drive, Fairfax, 22030. Ruth Kerns, Public Services Librn
Notes: The Federal Theatre Project (FTP) was established in August 1935 as a part of the arts program of the Works Progress Administration (renamed Work Projects Administration in 1939). Supporting 150 separate units throughout the United States, the FTP produced over 830 major stage plays, 6000 radio programs, and innumerable marionette plays, vaudeville shows, outdoor pageants, and circuses. At the conclusion of the project in June 1939, the "product materials" generated by the FTP were sent to the Library of Congress, and the administrative records to the National Archives. The Library's Federal Theatre Project collection was placed on deposit at George Mason University in Fairfax, Virginia, in 1974.

ON —METROPOLITAN TORONTO LIBRARY, Theatre Dept, 789 Yonge St, Toronto, M4W 2G8, Can. Heather McCallum, Head
Notes: Collections of playbills, clippings and correspondence document the career of Charles Manny (1890-1962) in both England and the United States; interviews and reminiscences on tape are available for the first all-sister act in vaudeville, the Canadian born O'Conner Sisters.
See also entry under Theatre - Canada.

VAUGHAN, HENRY, 1845-1917

ME —BOWDOIN COLLEGE, Library, Brunswick, 04011. Dianne M Gutscher, Cur of Special Collections
Holdings: Mss
Notes: The Hubbard Family Papers contain letters from this architect who designed two buildings on the Bowdoin campus: Hubbard Hall and the Mary Frances Searles Science Building.

VAUGHAN FAMILY

ME —BOWDOIN COLLEGE, Library, Brunswick, 04011. Dianne M Gutscher, Cur of Special Collections
Holdings: Vols Mss
Notes: The Vaughan Collection comprises ca 1200 volumes, originally the private library of Samuel Vaughan (1762-1826). A collection of several hundred pamphlets of the French Revolution was also presented to the College by Samuel's brother, Benjamin Vaughan (1751-1835). The Abbott Memorial Collection contains two scrapbooks of Vaughan family material, incl letters from the elder Samuel Vaughan (1720-1802), a Vice President of the American Philosophical Society, and a letter book of transcripts of some 114 letters and documents by or related to Benjamin Vaughan during the period 1778-98 when he was private secretary to the Earl of Shelburne. The Parker Cleaveland Papers also contain 125 letters from Benjamin Vaughan, 1806-1835.

VAUGHAN WILLIAMS, RALPH

NY —CORNELL UNIVERSITY LIBRARIES, Music Library, 225 Lincoln Hall, Ithaca, 14853. Lenore Coral, Music Librn
Holdings: // Cat Microforms
Notes: Papers, 1909-1958. 15 reels of microfilm of mss (84 entries) owned by Ursula Vaughan Williams, now mostly in the British Museum: scores and sketches; printed proofs and unpublished scores with ms annotations; some correspondence relating to the works. Gift of Mrs Vaughan Williams, 1970. A guide to the collection is available from the Music Library (no charge).

BC —UNIVERSITY OF VICTORIA, McPherson Library, Victoria, V8W 3H5, Can.
Notes: Letters from Gustav Holst and R Vaughan Williams to Stanley Bulley.

VAUX, RICHARD

PA —FRIENDS HISTORICAL LIBRARY OF SWARTHMORE COLLEGE, Swarthmore, 19081. J William Frost, Dir
Holdings: Vols (31,340) Cat Mss Pix
Notes: Incl works on prison conditions, capital punishment, and works by and about Quaker prison reformers, Elizabeth Fry, John Howard, Richard Vaux, Roberts Vaux, American Friends Service Committee, and others.

VEDANTA

†CA —ATMANIKETAN ASHRAM LIBRARY, 1291 Weber St, Pomona, 91768.
Notes: Sri Aurobindo, Indian spirituality, Vedanta, Sanskrit studies, Vedic-Upanishadic texts, education.

VEDIC LITERATURE

†CA —ATMANIKETAN ASHRAM LIBRARY, 1291 Weber St, Pomona, 91768.
Notes: Sri Aurobindo, Indian spirituality, Vedanta, Sanskrit studies, Vedic-Upanishadic texts, education.

VEGA, FELIX LOPE DE

CA —UNIVERSITY OF CALIFORNIA, BERKELEY, University Library, Hispanic Collections, Berkeley, 94720. Gaston Somoshegyi-Szokol, Librn
See also entry under Spanish Language and Literature.

†CT —UNIVERSITY OF CONNECTICUT LIBRARY, Special Collections Dept, Storrs, 06268. Richard H Schimmelpfeng, Dir of Special Collections
Notes: Good and unusual collection.

VEGETABLE GARDENING

MA —OLD STURBRIDGE VILLAGE, Research Library, Sturbridge, 01566. Theresa Rini Percy, Librn
Holdings: Cat
Notes: Northeastern US, 1790-1850.

VEGETABLE KINGDOM see Botany; Plants

VEGETABLE MOLD see Soils

VEGETABLE OILS see Essences and Essential Oils; Oils and Fats

VEGETABLE PATHOLOGY see Plant Diseases

VEGETABLES

FL —RARE FRUIT COUNCIL INTERNATIONAL, 13609 Old Cutler Rd, Miami, 33158. Fred Frazer, Pres; Louise Garavatlia, Librn
Holdings: Vols (300)
Notes: Not open to the public.

IL —MORTON ARBORETUM, Sterling Morton Library, Lisle, 60532. Ian MacPhail, Librn
Holdings: Vols (20,000) Cat Maps Pix
Budget: ($10,000)
Notes: The library is especially concerned with the literature of woody plants (trees and shrubs) of north temperate zones but has substantial holdings in the taxonomy and systematics of plants in general, both wild and cultivated, flora of different parts of the world, and a growing collection on plant monographs. Also about 2000 pictures. Described in The Morton Arboretum Quarterly, vol 9 no 4 (Winter 1973), pp 56-61.

MA —HARVARD UNIVERSITY LIBRARY, Cambridge, 02138.
Holdings: Cat

PE —AGRICULTURE CANADA, Research Station Library, PO Box 1210, Charlottetown, C1A 7M8, Can. Barrie Stanfield, Librn
Holdings: Vols (2300) Cat
Budget: ($5000)

VEHICLE MOBILITY

AL —US DEPT OF AGRICULTURE, SCIENCE & EDUCATION ADMINISTRATION, National Tillage Machinery Laboratory, Library, PO Box 792, Auburn, 36830. William A Gill, Collaborator
Holdings: Vols (39,000) Cat Mss Maps Pix Slides 16mm Films Microforms
Budget: ($20,000)
Notes: The National Tillage Machinery Laboratory (NTML) has a special technical library comprised of highly selective engineering and physical science materials pertinent to soil-machine relations, such as tillage, earthmoving, mining, soil trafficability, and vehicle mobility. A high percentage of thc library material comes from sources outside the US and outside agriculture. Particularly strong in Russian-language literature.

VEHICLES

CA —BLACKHAWK LIBRARY, 1975 San Ramon Valley Blvd, San Ramon, 94583. Gene Babow, Librn
Holdings: Vols 6800 Cat Mss Maps Pix Slides Microforms
Notes: Consists of books, magazines, catalogs, advertisements, photos, original drawings, clippings, VFs, from antiquity to future concepts, worldwide. Incl engineering and styling information; current projects. A rich and unique source of history and biography for the vehicle industry.

MI —UNIVERSITY OF MICHIGAN, Transportation Research Institute, Library, 2901 Baxter Rd, Ann Arbor, 48109. Ann C Grimm, Librn
Holdings: Vols (57,000) Cat Mss Maps Pix Slides Microforms
Budget: ($25,000)
Notes: All aspects of highway safety. All items are cataloged and indexed using a thesaurus developed in-house. Incl engineering medical, biomechanical, psychological, legal, economic and social aspects of highway, vehicle and traffic safety.

NH —NEW HAMPSHIRE HISTORICAL SOCIETY, Manuscripts Library, 30 Park St, Concord, 03301. Thomas E Camden, Cur
Holdings: cAT mSS pIX
Notes: Abbot-Downing Truck and Body Co records 1813-1945. Incl correspondence, account book, journals, ledgers, order books, accounts receivable, records of sales, balance sheet for New York branch, records of material mortgaged to Josiah E Fernald, banker, of Concord, New Hampshire, other financial clippings, advertisements, and other papers of a firm based in Concord, New Hampshire, and manufacturing wagons, coaches, carriages, and motor-truck 33 linear feet, about 22,000 items.

PA —FREE LIBRARY OF PHILADELPHIA, Automobile Reference Collection, Logan Sq, Philadelphia, 19103. Louis G Helverson, Jr, Librn in Charge
Holdings: Vols (14,000) Cat Pix Slides
Notes: Collection is concerned with all aspects of automotive industry and its history. Includes shop manuals, instruction books, and periodicals dealing with all types of bicycles, tricycles and motor vehicles. Industry statistics, corporate annual reports, environmental problems, safety. Incl 18,000

VEHICLES (cont.)

pictures, 1700 slides, 648 microfilm reels, 23,000 sales catalogs, 5000 pieces of ephemera.

VEHICLES, ARMORED (MILITARY SCIENCE) see Armored Vehicles, Military

VEHICLES, MILITARY

MS —US ARMY ENGINEER WATERWAYS EXPERIMENT STATION, Library Branch, PO Box 631, Vicksburg, 39180. Bernice Black, Chief Librn
Holdings: Vols (350,000) Cat Mss Maps Microforms
VA —US ARMY TRANSPORTATION MUSEUM, Library, Bldg 300, Fort Eustis, 23604. Dennis P Mroczkowski, Museum Cur
Holdings: Vols (1254) Uncat Maps Pix 16mm Films
Budget: ($150)
Notes: Mainly US Army transportation from WW II on.
ON —NATIONAL MUSEUMS OF CANADA, Library Services Directorate, Ottawa, K1A 0M8, Can. Valerie Monkhouse, Director
Holdings: Vols 12,000 Cat
Budget: ($60,000)
Notes: Collection includes; arms and armour, military aeronautics, military and naval arts and sciences, military and naval equipment, general military and naval history, military and naval history of Canada. Research collection, interlibrary loans available, public may use on the premises.

VELDE, HAROLD HIMMEL, 1910-

IL —EVERETT M DIRKSEN CONGRESSIONAL LEADERSHIP RESEARCH CENTER, Fourth & Broadway, Pekin, 61554. William C McCully Jr, Dir
Holdings: Mss Pix Phonorecords Audiotapes
Notes: The Velde Papers are not comprehensive.

VELLUM CHARTS

DC —LIBRARY OF CONGRESS, Geography and Map Division, Washington, 20540. John A Wolter, Chief
Notes: Rare nautical charts on vellum.

VELOCIPEDES see Bicycles and Tricycles

VENDIG, IRVING

MA —BOSTON UNIVERSITY, Mugar Memorial Library, Special Collections Dept, 771 Commonwealth Ave, Boston, 02215. Howard B Gotlieb, Dir
Holdings: Mss Pix
Notes: Mss, correspondence, etc collected in depth.

VENEREAL DISEASES—HISTORY

CT —YALE UNIVERSITY, Medical Historical Library, Klebs Collection, 333 Cedar St, New Haven, 06520. Ferenc A Gyorgyey, Librn
Notes: The Arnold Carl Klebs Medical Collection books, pamphlets, etc, incl the library of his father, Edwin T A Klebs, pathologist. Strong in bibliography of early printed medical books, herbals, plague tracts, inoculation, vaccination and tubercular diseases.
MD —MEDICAL & CHIRURGICAL FACULTY OF THE STATE OF MARYLAND, Library, 1211 Cathedral St, Baltimore, 21201. Joseph E Jensen, Librn
Holdings: Vols (10,000) // Cat Mss Maps Pix
See also entry under Medicine - History and Historic
OH —CLEVELAND MEDICAL LIBRARY ASSOCIATION/CASE WESTERN RESERVE UNIVERSITY, Cleveland Health Sciences Library, Historical Division, Allen Memorial Medical Library, 11000 Euclid Ave, Cleveland, 44106. Glen Jenkins, Rare

Book Librarian & Archivist
Holdings: Vols 235 Cat
Notes: Described in "The Cole Collection of Venereals," *Bulletin of the Cleveland Medical Library*, 1954, vol 1, pp 4-6.

VENETIAN REPUBLIC—HISTORY see Venice—History

VENEZUELA

CT —YALE UNIVERSITY, Sterling Memorial Library, Latin American Collections, New Haven, 06520. Lee H Williams Jr, Cur
Holdings: Vols (300,000) Cat Maps Pix Slides Phonorecords 16mm Films Filmstrips
See also entry under Latin America
NY —STATE UNIVERSITY OF NEW YORK, COLLEGE AT BUFFALO, Poetry/Rare Books Collection, 420 Capen Hall, Buffalo, 14260. Robert J Bertholf, Cur
Holdings: Vols 4200 Cat Mss Maps Pix
Notes: Materials incl books, mss, official gazettes, and periodicals for research on the short-lived political entity known as Gran Colombia (the present-day countries of Colombia, Venezuela, and Ecuador); special emphasis is on the first half of the 19th century but earlier and later periods are incl.
TX —UNIVERSITY OF TEXAS LIBRARIES, Nettie Lee Benson Latin American Collection, Sid Richardson Hall 1.109, Austin, 78712. Laura Gutierrez-Witt, Head Librn
Holdings: Vols (450,000) Cat Mss Maps Pix Phonorecords Filmstrips Microforms
See also entry under Latin America.

VENICE—HISTORY

NY —UNIVERSITY OF ROCHESTER, Rush Rhees Library, Department of Rare Books and Special Collections, Rochester, 14627. Peter Dzwonkoski, Librn
NY —SYRACUSE UNIVERSITY LIBRARIES, Ernest S Bird Library, George Arents Research Library for Special Collections, Syracuse, 13210. Carolyn A Davis, Manuscripts Librn; Amy S Doherty, University Archivist; Mark F Weimer, Rare Book Librn
Notes: Private library of Leopold von Ranke, father of modern historical scholarship, acquired in 1886. More than 17,000 volumes, 4000 pamphlets, and 430 mss, and private papers and letters. A complete catalogue of the ms collection published in 1983. Incl more than 100 dispatches (Relazioni) from Venetian ambassadors, 1500-1800, etc. Much unpublished primary source material.

VENTILATION

KY —UNIVERSITY OF KENTUCKY, Robert E Shaver Library of Engineering, 355 Anderson Hall, Lexington, 40506. Russell H Powell, Engineering Librn
Holdings: Vols (48,000) Cat Microforms
†NY —TECHNICAL CAREER INSTITUTE LIBRARY, 320 W 31st Street, New York, 10001. Michael Brent, Librn
Holdings: Vols (3500)

VENTILATION—HISTORY

IN —PURDUE UNIVERSITY LIBRARIES, Graduate School of Management, Krannert Library, West Lafayette, 47907. Gordon Law, Librn
Notes: Business history. The collection consist of books, journals and pamphlets dating from the early 16th to late 19th century, covering to a large degree early literature in economic thought and business practices both here and abroad. No photocopying.

VERBARG, LEONARD

CA —SAINT MARY'S COLLEGE, Library, Moraga, 94575. Brother Casimir Reichlin, Dir of the Library; Brother Richard Lemberg FSC, Asst Librn
Notes: The Leonard Verbarg library of over

800 books on Western Americana, especially California. Incl vertical files containing over 1100 entries related to Californiana in the form of clippings and correspondence amassed during editorship of "The Knave" page of local history in the *Oakland Tribune*.

VERDI, GIUSEPPE, 1813-1901

NY —AMERICAN INSTITUTE FOR VERDI STUDIES, New York University, Bobst Library, Music Div, New York, 10023. Ruth B Hilton, Librn
Holdings: Mss Maps Pix Slides Microforms
Notes: Contains the archives for the Institute for Verdi Studies.

VERGIL

NJ —PRINCETON UNIVERSITY, Library, Rare Books Dept, Princeton, 08544. Stephen Ferguson, Cur
Holdings: Cat
Notes: Junius S Morgan Collection of Editions of Vergil. Because of the high esteem Vergil held since even before printing began, the collection covers not only early, unusual, or scholarly editions and translations but also outstanding examples in the history of fine printing, book illustration and book binding. The collection incl the only copy in the United States of the first edition of his *Opera* (Rome, Sweynheym and Pannarta, 1469), the first Vergil printed in France (Paris, 1470-1472), the important editions of Aldus Manutius, Giunta, Estienne, Plantin, Elzevir, Tonson, Baskerville, Foulis, Heyne, Bodoni and Didot, as well as a 1541 Aldine Vergil bound for Jean Grolier and the 1524-32 Estienne folio edition of the *Opera*, which belonged to Philip Melanchthon, with his notes (VRG) 2945.1532q. Today, the collection numbers about 900 vols and incl as well 13 manuscripts.
PA —UNIVERSITY OF PITTSBURGH, Hillman Library, Pittsburgh, 15260. Glenora E Rossell, Head
Holdings: Vols (11,550) Cat
Notes: The classics collection is particularly storng in Greek and Latin literature, Greek and Roman history, Greek philosophy, Greek and Latin language, and Greek epigraphy. In combination with the Frick Fine Arts collection it has a good collection in Greek and Roman art and archaeology. The collection of journals is also quite strong in these areas. There has been an emphasis in collecting books by and about Homer, Aristotles, Euripides, Vergil, Cicero and Petronius. It has a unique collection unpublished PhD dissertations and Master's theses on Petronius. It has a basic collection on Greek and Latin paleography and papyrology.

VERGIL, POLYDORE

OH —CLEVELAND PUBLIC LIBRARY, Fine Arts and Special Collections Department, 325 Superior Ave, Cleveland, 44114. Alice N Loranth, Head
Holdings: Vols 61 Cat
Notes: Special strength. Early and rare 15th-17th Century editions, translations and versions. Separate "edition" catalog is maintained.
See also entry under Rare Books.

VERLAINE, PAUL

MA —HARVARD UNIVERSITY LIBRARY, Houghton Library, Cambridge, 02138. Rodney G Dennis, Cur of Manuscripts
Holdings: Cat Mss

VERMANDEL, JANET GREGORY

MA —BOSTON UNIVERSITY, Mugar Memorial Library, Special Collections Dept, 771 Commonwealth Ave, Boston, 02215. Howard B Gotlieb, Dir
Holdings: Cat Mss
Notes: Mss, correspondence, etc collected in depth incl publications by or about.

VERMES see Worms

VERMIN see Pests and Pest Control

VERMONT

VT —MARTHA CANFIELD MEMORIAL FREE LIBRARY, Russell Vermontiana

VERMONT (cont.)

Collection, Arlington, 05250. D L Thomas, Cur; M L Thomas, Cur
Holdings: Vols 4500 Cat Mss Maps Pix
Budget: ($1800)
Notes: Russell Collection of Vermontiana. 260 pamphlet boxes (nonbook items). Special railroad collection (unindexed). Also 250 diaries, ledgers, account books and minute books, 1757-1940. Not all briefed. Incl 1000 mss, 100 maps, 300 pictures, Canfield family and Dorothy Canfield Fisher papers.

VT —UNIVERSITY OF VERMONT, Guy W Bailey/David W Howe Library, Burlington, 05405. John Buehler, Asst Dir for Special Collections

VT —LYNDON STATE COLLEGE LIBRARY, Lyndonville, 05851. Suzanne Gallagher, Head Librn
Holdings: Vols 1200 Cat Mss Maps Pix Microforms
Budget: ($45,000)
Notes: Collection incl any and all works on Vermont and Vermonters as well as reports from state and local government agencies. Particular attention is paid to Northeast Kingdom.

VT —VERMONT DEPARTMENT OF LIBRARIES, Law & Documents Unit, 111 State St, Montpelier, 05602. Vivian Bryan, Librn
Holdings: Vols (42,000) Cat Maps Microforms
Budget: ($3000)
Notes: Vermontiana. Incl largest known collection of Vermont newspapers, authors and imprints. The library prepares an annual *Checklist of Available Vermont State Publications*.

VERMONT—GENEALOGY

VT —BENNINGTON MUSEUM, Genealogical Library, W Main St, Bennington, 05201. Charles G Bennett, Librn
Holdings: Vols 1400 Uncat Maps Pix
Notes: Vermont regional history and genealogy emphasis.

VT —TRINITY COLLEGE LIBRARY, Colchester Ave, Burlington, 05401.
Holdings: Vols (650) Cat
Budget: ($500)
Notes: "Vermont Collection" is chiefly a collection of Vermontiana book titles, many of which are cataloged and in most cases are available for general circulation. A limited number of special (fine/rare) titles are designated for in-house use only. Emphasis is upon Vermont history, works by and about Vermont authors, with some titles related to genealogy.

VERMONT—HISTORY

MA —OLD STURBRIDGE VILLAGE, Research Library, Sturbridge, 01566. Theresa Rini Percy, Librn
Holdings: Cat Maps Microforms
Notes: To 1900.

NY —STATE UNIVERSITY OF NEW YORK, COLLEGE AT PLATTSBURGH, Feinberg Library, Special Collections, 153 Hawkins Hall, Plattsburgh, 12901. Joseph G Swinyer, Librn
Holdings: Vols (500) Cat Mss Maps Pix Phonorecords Microforms
See also entry under New York (State) - History

VT —MARTHA CANFIELD MEMORIAL FREE LIBRARY, Russell Vermontiana Collection, Arlington, 05250. D L Thomas, Cur; M L Thomas, Cur
Holdings: Vols 4500 Cat Mss Maps Pix
Budget: ($1800)
Notes: Russell Collection of Vermontiana. 260 pamphlet boxes (nonbook items). Special railroad collection (unindexed). Also 250 diaries, ledgers, account books and minute books, 1757-1940. Not all briefed. Incl 1000 mss, 100 maps, 300 pictures, Canfield family and Dorothy Canfield Fisher papers.

VT —BENNINGTON MUSEUM, Genealogical Library, W Main St, Bennington, 05201. Charles G Bennett, Librn
Holdings: Vols 1400 Uncat Maps Pix
Notes: Vermont regional history and genealogy emphasis.

VT —FLETCHER FREE LIBRARY, 235 College St, Burlington, 05401. Maxie Ewins, Librn
Holdings: Vols 1200 Cat Maps Pix
Notes: Concentration on Burlington, Vermont. Complete run of Burlington City Reports, from 1860. Limited genealogies.

VT —TRINITY COLLEGE LIBRARY, Colchester Ave, Burlington, 05401.
Holdings: Vols (650) Cat
Budget: ($500)
Notes: "Vermont Collection" is chiefly a collection of Vermontiana book titles, many of which are cataloged and in most cases are available for general circulation. A limited number of special (fine/rare) titles are designated for in-house use only. Emphasis is upon Vermont history, works by and about Vermont authors, with some titles related to genealogy.

VT —UNIVERSITY OF VERMONT, Guy W Bailey/David W Howe Library, Burlington, 05405. John Buehler, Asst Dir for Special Collections
Notes: The Windsor County (Vermont) Court Records (1780-1835). Incl papers of Paul Brigham (1746-1824), lieutenant governor of Vermont (1796-1813, 1815-1820); and the papers of John Johnson (1771-1842), surveyor general of Vermont (1813-23, 1832-38).

VT —MIDDLEBURY COLLEGE, Egbert Starr Library, Middlebury, 05753. Hans Raum, Cur
Holdings: Vols 2500
Budget: $2000
Notes: New England historical and literary materials, incl Vermontiana and Vermont estate documents.

VT —ORLEANS COUNTY HISTORICAL SOCIETY, Old Stone House, Orleans, 05860. Reed Cherington, Adminr
Holdings: Vols 2500 Mss Maps Pix Slides Audiotapes
Budget: $1000

VT —SHELBURNE MUSEUM, Library, Shelburne, 05482. Barbara Reenstierna, Librn
Holdings: Vols 600 Cat

VT —SAINT MICHAEL'S COLLEGE, Durick Library, Winooski, 05404. Joseph Popecki, Dir; Henry Nadeau, Head of Archives & Special Collections
Holdings: Vols 600 Cat
Budget: $500
Notes: Includes material on the Catholic Church in Vermont.

VERMONT AUTHORS see Authors, Vermont

VERNAM, GILBERT SANDFORD

†VA —GEORGE C MARSHALL RESEARCH FOUNDATION AND LIBRARY, Drawer 920, Lexington, 24450. Royster Lyle Jr, Cur Collections
Holdings: Vols Uncat Mss Slides Microforms
Notes: A collection of diaries kept by Gilbert Sanford Vernam, cryptographer and inventor. The diary is an almost day-by-day record, 1918-1926, of Vernam's inventions and development of his outstanding contributions to cryptography including techniques widely adopted by the armed forces for enciphering and deciphering coded messages. There is a typed index to this collection. No photocopying.

VERNE, JULES

CA —UNIVERSITY OF CALIFORNIA, RIVERSIDE, University Library, 4045 Canyon Crest Dr, Box 5900, Riverside, 92517.
Holdings: Vols (30,000)
Notes: The Eaton Collection of science fiction and fantasy materials, incl 5,600 pulp magazines; also horror, supernatural, and Gothic mystery fiction; boys' books; utopian and dystopian fiction, imaginary voyages, future war and lost race fiction; large holdings in French language science fiction and fantasy; critical and scholarly works pertaining to these genres; videotapes of science fiction/fantasy films and shooting scripts. Collection covers science fiction/fantasy literature from the 16th-17th centuries to the present. Strong individual author collections of Jules Verne, H Rider Haggard, H G Wells, Edgar Rice Burroughs, and Philip K Dick. For a complete description of the collection see: George Slusser, "The J Lloyd Eaton Collection," *Special Collections*, II, 1/2, 25-38 (1983), and *Dictionary Catalog of the J Lloyd Eaton Collection of Science Fiction and Fantasy Literature* (Boston: G K Hall) 1982.

DC —LIBRARY OF CONGRESS, Rare Book & Special Collections Div, Washington, 20540. William Matheson, Chief
Notes: Late 19th and early 20th century English and American editions of Jules Verne, many with distinctive illustrations and bindings.

IN —INDIANA UNIVERSITY, Lilly Library, Seventh St, Bloomington, 47405. William R Cagle, Librn
Holdings: Vols 230 // Cat
Notes: First and early English editions. Hetzel publications, etc.

VERTEBRATES

CA —UNIVERSITY OF CALIFORNIA, BERKELEY, Museum of Vertebrate Zoology, Grinnell-Miller Library, Berkeley, 94720.
Holdings: Vols (2000) Cat
Notes: Vertebrate zoology, with emphasis on birds and mammals of the Pacific States.

CA —UNIVERSITY OF CALIFORNIA, LOS ANGELES, Biomedical Library, Center for the Health Sciences, Los Angeles, 90024. Alison Bunting, Acting Biomedical Librn; Victoria Steele, Head, History & Special Collections Div
Holdings: Vols (400,000) Cat Slides Phonorecords Audiotapes Videotapes 16mm Films Microforms
Notes: The UCLA Biomedical Library serves primarily the Schools of Medicine, Dentistry, Nursing, and Public Health, the UCLA Medical Center, the Departments of Microbiology and Biology in the College of Letters and Science, and related institutes in biomedicine. The collections of the Library are broad in scope, designed not only to support the teaching and research needs of its many users, but also to function as a resource for the health sciences-biological field as a whole. The outstanding feature of the collection is the strength of its periodical holdings, both current and retrospective. The Library also has an excellent reference collection, a comprehensive historical section, and gives special emphasis to the fields of neuroscience, psychiatry, ophthalmology, radiation biology, molecular biology, and vertebrate zoology. Increased emphasis is being given to the acquisition of audiovisual materials.

CA —WESTERN FOUNDATION OF VERTEBRATE ZOOLOGY, Library, 1100 Glendon Ave, Los Angeles, 90024. Lloyd F Kiff, Dir
Holdings: Vols (4000) Uncat Mss Pix Slides 16mm Films
Budget: ($10,000)
Notes: This is probably the third largest collection on birds in the Western US. It incl

VERTEBRATES (cont.)

the combined resources of 10 former private libraries on this topic, plus additions made by us during the past 20 years. There is special emphasis on oology, or the study of bird eggs. The collection is freely available for use by any interested researcher.

DC —SMITHSONIAN INSTITUTION LIBRARIES, Natural History Branch, Washington, 20560. Sylvia Churgin, Chief Librn
Holdings: Vols (75,550) Cat Mss Maps Pix Slides Microforms
Notes: Incl vertebrate and invertebrate paleontology; vertebrate zoology: systematics and taxonomy.

FL —ARCHBOLD BIOLOGICAL STATION, Library, Rt 2, Box 180, Lake Placid, 33852. Fred E Lohrer, Librn
Holdings: Uncat VF
Notes: Physiological ecology of vertebrates. Incl 3 vertical files of reprints, etc. Extensive and growing cataloged collection on Florida mammals also. (Library is no longer enlarging reprint collection.)

HI —BERNICE P BISHOP MUSEUM, Library, PO Box 19000-A, Honolulu, 96819. Cynthia Timberlake, Librn
Holdings: Vols (90,000) Cat Mss Maps Pix Slides Microforms
Budget: ($30,000)
Notes: Only American library devoted exclusively to the Pacific region. Collection reflects historical and contemporary research emphases of Bishop Museum; ie the natural and cultural history of the Pacific. Areas of concentration incl archaeology, ethnology, linguistics, voyages and explorations, history, vertebrate and invertebrate zoology, botany and museology. Strong special collections incl photographs, mss and archives, maps and art. Publications: Quarterly "Additions to the Catalog," *Dictionary Catalog of the Library* (9 vols and 2 suppl; Boston: G K Hall, 1964-69).

IA —IOWA STATE UNIVERSITY, Library, Ames, 50011. Warren B Kuhn, Dean of Library Services
Holdings: Cat
Notes: Extensive serial holdings supplement this strong collection.

IA —IOWA STATE UNIVERSITY, Library, Dept of Special Collections, Ames, 50011. Stanley M Yates, Head
Holdings: // Mss Pix
Notes: The Paul Errington (1902-1962) Papers. Professor of zoology at ISU (1932-1962) and a leading authority of vertebrate ecology and animal population dynamics. Collection incl correspondence, mss and articles. Collection is 15 linear feet.

NY —NEW YORK ZOOLOGICAL SOCIETY LIBRARY, Bronx Zoo, Bronx, 10460. Steven P Johnson, Archivist and Librn
Holdings: Vols (6000) Cat Mss
Budget: ($50,000)
Notes: Collection consists primarily of journals in captive management of animals, vertebrate zoology, and veterinary medicine. Primarily intended for the scientific staff, the collection is open to the public on a noncirculating basis, by appointment, (212) 220-6874.

VERTEBRATES, FOSSIL

CA —UNIVERSITY OF CALIFORNIA, BERKELEY, Physical Sciences Libraries, Earth Sciences Library, 230 Earth Sciences Bldg, Berkeley, 94720. Julie F Rinaldi, Librn
Holdings: Vols (83,202) Cat Microforms
Budget: ($74,880)
Notes: A strong collection, giving particular emphasis to vertebrates and invertebrates. Especially rich in serials; approx (2850) current titles received on subscription, and in foreign-language publications.

CT —YALE UNIVERSITY, Geology Library, 210 Whitney Ave, PO Box 6666, New Haven, 06511. Harry Scammell, Librn
Holdings: Vols (100,000) Cat Maps Pix Microforms
Budget: ($115,000)
Notes: The O C Marsh Collection (vertebrate paleontoogy) is also here.

ID —IDAHO MUSEUM OF NATURAL HISTORY, Research Library, Campus Box 8096, Pocatello, 83209. Michael L Perry, Dir
Holdings: Vols 8300 Mss Maps Pix Slides

NY —AMERICAN MUSEUM OF NATURAL HISTORY, Library Services Dept, Central Park W & 79th St, New York, 10024. Nina J Root, Chairwoman; Mary Genett, Asst Librn for Reference Services
Holdings: Vols (385,000) Cat Mss Maps Pix Slides Microforms
Notes: Nearly all collections are outstanding for depth of coverage and international range. Early and historic works, rare books, colored illustrations, and relevant serial publications supplement the modern scientific publications necessary to the researches of the scientific staff and the work of the educational division. Open to the public.

PA —CARNEGIE LIBRARY OF PITTSBURGH, Science & Technology Dept, 4400 Forbes Ave, Pittsburgh, 15213. Catherine M Brosky, Dept Head
Notes: Subject of secondary interest with emphasis on North America. Covers paleobotany, vertebrates and invertebrates, foraminifera, mollusks, fish, reptiles, mammals. Abstracts, indexes, catalogs bibliographies, journals, continuations, federal, state and society publications available.

ON —NATIONAL MUSEUMS OF CANADA, Library Services Directorate, Ottawa, K1A 0M8, Can. Valerie Monkhouse, Director
Holdings: Vols (90,000) Cat Mss Microforms
Budget: ($81,000)
Notes: Emphasis on Canadian and circumpolar natural history. Collection incl botany, herpetology, ichthyology, invertebrate zoology, malacology, mammology, mineralogy, ornithology, paleobiology, zooarchaeology. Exceptional collections in lichenology, bryology, malacology, ornithology. Paleobiology, palynology, paleoclimatology. A library of reprints, consisting of approx 6000 items presented by C S Sternberg. The reprints are restricted to the subj of vertebrate paleontology, (and form a definitive collection for Canada); incl, many early papers. The National Museums Library is gradually binding the collection, and filling gaps whenever possible. Recently added; J F Grayson Collection. Approx 5000 reprints plus textbooks, catalogues, periodicals, and transparencies presented by him. Research collection, interlibrary loans available, public may use onthe premises.

VERY, JONES, 1813-1880

RI —BROWN UNIVERSITY, John Hay Library, 20 Prospect St, Providence, 02912. Mark N Brown, Cur Mss
Holdings: // Mss
Notes: Mss, etc of the American poet and Transcendentalist. About 150 mss for the period 1839-1886 incl sermons, poems, essays, and a biographical note by James Freeman Clarke. Incl some poems by Lydia Very (1823-1901), poet, teacher, and sister of Joes Very.

VESALIUS, ANDREAS, 1514-1564

CT —YALE UNIVERSITY, Medical Historical Library, 333 Cedar St, New Haven, 06510. Ferenc A Gyorgyey, Librn
Holdings: Vols 800 Cat Mss
Notes: Harvey Cushing, *A Bio-Bibliography of Andreas Vesalius*, 2d ed, Hamden, Conn: Archon Books 1962. (Based un gret part on the collection; YML holdings noted in it).

VESTIBULE SCHOOLS see Employees, Training of

VESTMENTS see Church Vestments

VETERANS, CONFEDERATE

MS —UNIVERSITY OF SOUTHERN MISSISSIPPI, William David McCain Graduate Library, Box 5148, Southern Sta, Hattiesburg, 39406.
Holdings: Cat Mss
Notes: Jefferson Davis' Home, Beauvoir, at Biloxi, Mississippi, was used as a confederate veterans home from 1902-1957. The Jefferson Davis Soldiers' Home Records document its operations between 1920 and 1954. 2.7 cubic feet of mss.

VETERANS OF FOREIGN WARS (VFW)

CO —DENVER PUBLIC LIBRARY, Western History Department, 1357 Broadway, Denver, 80203. Eleanor M Gehres, Head
Holdings: Vols (50,000) Cat Mss Maps Pix Audiotapes Microforms
Notes: Western US History. The department has a separate catalog, published in 1970 in 7 vols by G K Hall Co. First supplement published in 1975 in 1 vol. There is a subject index of some 3 million entries to newspapers and magazines of the Rocky Mountain region, added to daily. The Western Newspaper Microfilm Center contains approx 7000 reels of Western US newspapers. Collection has ca 275,000 negatives and prints of Western life; and ca 2500 maps, cataloged and classified.

VETERINARY MEDICINE

AL —AUBURN UNIVERSITY, Veterinary Medical Branch Library, Auburn, 36849. Robert J Veenstra, Veterinary Medical Librn
Holdings: Vols 28,000 Cat Slides Videotapes Microforms
Notes: Incl 81 videotapes and 160 microforms.

AL —UNIVERSITY OF ALABAMA, BIRMINGHAM, Lister Hill Library of the Health Sciences, University Sta, Birmingham, 35294. Richard B Fredericksen, Dir

CA —UNIVERSITY OF CALIFORNIA, DAVIS, Health Sciences Library, Davis, 95616. Marjan Merala, Health Sciences Librn
Holdings: Vols (164,000) Cat Microforms
Budget: ($509,737)
Notes: Human medicine: ca 82,000 vols; veterinary medicine: ca 19,700 vols; allied sciences (biochemistry, physiology, etc); reference works: ca 62,300 vols.

†CA —ZOOLOGICAL SOCIETY OF SAN DIEGO, Ernst Schwarz Library, San Diego Zoo, Box 551, San Diego, 92112.

CO —COLORADO STATE UNIVERSITY, Libraries, Fort Collins, 80523. K Suzanne Johnson, Biomedical Sciences, Librn
Holdings: Vols 150,000 Cat Mss
Budget: $120,000

CT —YALE MEDICAL LIBRARY, 333 Cedar St, New Haven, 06510.

DE —UNIVERSITY OF DELAWARE, Agriculture Library, 2 Townsend Hall, Newark, 19717. Frederick Getze, Assoc Librn
Holdings: Vols (32,500) Cat Pix Microforms
Notes: Strong in entomology and ornamental horticulture. Extensive collection of state agriculture documents for each US state and Puerto Rico. Library subscribes to 600 serials (English and foreign).

DC —SMITHSONIAN INSTITUTION LIBRARIES, National Zoological Park Branch, Washington, 20008. Kay Kenyon, Chief Librn
Holdings: Vols (5500) Cat
Notes: Collection incl animal nutrition, capture and care of animals in captivity, conservation and endangered species, pathology, veterinary medicine, zoology.

IL —UNIVERSITY OF ILLINOIS, URBANA/CHAMPAIGN, College of Veterinary Medicine, Library, 1257 VMBS Bldg, 2001 S Lincoln Ave, Urbana, 61801.
Holdings: Vols 27,478 Cat Maps Pix Slides Microforms
Notes: Separate card catalog for this collection.

IN —PURDUE UNIVERSITY LIBRARIES, Veterinary Medical Library, C J Lynn Hall of Veterinary Medicine, West Lafayette,

VETERINARY MEDICINE (cont.)

47907. Gretchen Stephens, Librn
Holdings: Vols (31,022) Cat
Budget: ($106,281)
Notes: The collection contains the outstanding books and serials in English that are germane to comparative and veterinary medicine. Foreign language materials are added selectively. Subjects of particular strength are laboratory animal medicine, pathology, comparative anatomy, animal behavior and clinical veterinary medicine.

IA —IOWA STATE UNIVERSITY, Library, Ames, 50011. Warren B Kuhn, Dean of Library Services
Holdings: Cat
Notes: Extensive serial holdings.

IA —IOWA STATE UNIVERSITY, College of Veterinary Medicine, Veterinary Medical Library, Ames, 50011. Sara R Peterson, Librn
Holdings: Vols (17,000) Cat Microforms
Notes: Incl comparative and veterinary medicine with emphasis in the fields of mammalian anatomy and physiology, laboraory animal medicine, pathology, toxicology, biomedical engineering and clinical veterinary medicine. Incl 2000 uncataloged German theses.

KS —KANSAS STATE UNIVERSITY, College of Veterinary Medicine, Veterinary Medical Library, Veterinary Medical Teaching Bldg, Rm 400, Manhattan, 66506. E Guy Coffee, Librn
Holdings: Vols (20,297) Cat Slides Audiotapes Videotapes Microforms
Notes: Veterinary medicine and comparative medicine.

KY —UNIVERSITY OF KENTUCKY, Agricultural Library, Agricultural Science Center North, Lexington, 40506. Antoinette Paris Powell, Librn
Holdings: Vols (90,000) Cat Microforms
Budget: ($110,385)

MD —US DEPT OF AGRICULTURE, National Agricultural Library, 10301 Baltimore Blvd, Beltsville, 20705. Joseph H Howard, Director
Notes: Worldwide coverage of all aspects of agriculture and related fields. Crop ecology, agro-climatic analogs; air pollution effects. Agronomy: agricultural and tropical and desert agriculture. For use by the staff of the USDA. Incl in the former collections of American Institute of Crop Ecology.

MD —US ARMED FORCES RADIOBIOLOGY RESEARCH INSTITUTE, Naval Medical Command, Bethesda, 20014. Nannette M Pope, Head, Library Division
Holdings: Vols (50,000)
Budget: ($150,000)
Notes: Collection consists of monographs, technical reports, serials, and microfiche related to radiation effects on human and animal biology.

MA —UNIVERSITY OF MASSACHUSETTS AT AMHERST, Library, Amherst, 01003. Siegfried Feller, Assoc Dir for Collection Development
Holdings: Cat
Notes: Veterinary medicine and animal sciences. Special emphasis: reproductive physiology, poultry genetics, animal nutrition.

MA —TUFTS UNIVERSITY, Health Sciences Library, 136 Harrison Ave, Boston, 02111. Elizabeth K Eaton, Dir
Holdings: Vols (91,252) Cat Slides Phonorecords Audiotapes Videotapes Microforms
Budget: $14,585
Notes: Incl 219 titles, 4 journal titles, 653 videotapes, 3104 microfilms, 7027 microcards, and 1051 serials.

MA —HARVARD MEDICAL SCHOOL, New England Primate Research Center Library, 1 Pine Hill Dr, Southborough, 01772. Sydney Fingold, Librn
Holdings: Vols (4000)

MI —WARNER-LAMBERT/PARKE-DAVIS, Research Library, 2800 Plymouth Rd, Ann Arbor, 48106. Katherine C Owen, Mgr, Library Services
Holdings: Vols (27,977) Cat

MI —MICHIGAN STATE UNIVERSITY, Science Library, East Lansing, 48824. Carole S Armstrong, Head
Holdings: Vols (36,000) Cat Mss
Notes: Current issues of most-used journals plus core reference collection in the Veterinary Clinical Center Library. Main collection in the Science Library. Rare books in Special Collections, includes mss and books from 15th-19th centuries

MN —MINNESOTA ZOOLOGICAL GARDEN, Apple Valley, 55124. Angela Norell, Librn
Notes: Classified card catalog; Journal reprints are fairly comprehensive for the animals in the collection, which are primarily Southeast Asian, Northern-dwelling, and native Minnesotan. Collection includes 2000 books, 60 periodical subscriptions and 3000 reprints of journal articles.

NE —UNIVERSITY OF NEBRASKA-LINCOLN, C Y Thompson Library, East Campus, Lincoln, 68583. Lyle Schreiner, Librn
Holdings: Vols (220,000) Cat
Notes: Agriculture, with major strength in entomology, agronomy, and animal science: medicine; veterinary medicine: and home economics.

NY —US DEPT OF AGRICULTURE, Agriculture Research Service, Plum Island Animal Disease Laboratory, PO Box 848, Greenport, 11944. Stephen Perlman, Librn
Holdings: Vols (15,000) Cat Pix Slides Microforms
Budget: ($37,000)

NY —CORNELL UNIVERSITY, New York State College of Veterinary Medicine, Flower Veterinary Library, Ithaca, 14853. Susanne Whitaker, Librn
Holdings: Vols (74,000) Cat Audiotapes Slides Videotapes
Notes: Veterinary college library; incl biomedical publications as well as purely veterinary titles.

OH —OHIO STATE UNIVERSITY, Veterinary Medicine Library, 229 Sisson Hall, 1900 Coffey Rd, Columbus, 43210. Bruce A Evans, Head
Holdings: Vols 36,000 Cat
Budget: $62,400

†OK —OKLAHOMA STATE UNIVERSITY, Veterinary Medicine Library, Stillwater, 74074.

PA —UNIVERSITY OF PENNSYLVANIA, Jean Austin duPont Libary, New Bolton Center, 382 W Street Rd, Kennett Square, 19348. Alice K Holton, Librn
Holdings: Vols 3200 Cat
Notes: Emphasis is on large animal medicine.

PA —COLLEGE OF PHYSICIANS OF PHILADELPHIA, Library, 19 S 22 St, Philadelphia, 19103. Anthony Aguirre, Libr Dir
Holdings: Vols (316,223) // Cat Mss Microforms
Budget: ($1,096,557)
Notes: Incl 13,515 pamphlets; 1435 mss; 326,367 reports, dissertations, and reprints. Strong historical and bibliographical collections, as well as current materials. Medical documentation service provides current alerting, incl abstracting, etc.

PA —UNIVERSITY OF PENNSYLVANIA, School of Veterinary Medicine, C J Marshall Memorial Library, 3800 Spruce St, Philadelphia, 19104. Lillian D Bryant, Librn
Holdings: Vols 31,000 Cat

PA —ZOOLOGICAL SOCIETY OF PHILADELPHIA, Library, 34 & Girard Ave, Philadelphia, 19104. Alyssa N Scheuermann, Librn
Holdings: Vols (500) Cat
Notes: Photocopying with permission.

TN —UNIVERSITY OF TENNESSEE, KNOXVILLE, Agriculture-Veterinary Medicine Library, A113 Vet Teach Hospital, Knoxville, 37916. Don W Jett, Librn
Holdings: Vols (100,000) Cat Microforms
Budget: ($50,500)
Notes: The Agriculture Library serves the Tennessee Agriculture Experiment Station, the Agriculture Extension Service and the Colleges of the Agriculture and Veterinary Medicine. Incl 2000 microforms. Separate

catalog; holdings also listed in public catalog in Main Library and in the Oak Ridge/Knoxville area.

†WA —WASHINGTON STATE UNIVERSITY, Library, Manuscripts, Archives & Special Collections, Pullman, 99164. John F Guido, Head
Notes: The J F Smithcors library of veterinary medicine. More than 1000 vols, incl mss, broadsides, and ephemera, ranges from 16th-20th centuries. Many important modern texts.

WA —WASHINGTON STATE UNIVERSITY, Veterinary Medical & Pharmacy Library, 701 Wegner Hall, Pullman, 99164. Vicki F Croft, Head
Holdings: Vols (42,000) Cat Mss Microforms
Budget: ($146,667)

WI —UNIVERSITY OF WISCONSIN, MADISON, College of Agricultural & Life Sciences, Steenbock Memorial Library, 550 Babcock Dr, Madison, 53706. Jan Kennedy, Dir
Holdings: Vols (186,312) Cat Docs Slides Videotapes
Notes: Supports programs in newly opened School of Veterinary Medicine.

ON —UNIVERSITY OF GUELPH, McLaughlin Library, Guelph, N1G 2W1, Can. Margaret Beckman, Head Librn; David Hull, Sciences Librn
Holdings: Vols 72,000 Cat
Budget: $100,000
Notes: 2000 government documents; 690 serial titles, A/V collection.
See also entry under Agriculture

ON —AGRICULTURE CANADA, Animal Dieases Research Institute, Library, PO Box 11300 Sta H, Ottawa, K2H 8P9, Can. John Miska, Area Coordinator; P A Atherton, Librn
Holdings: Vols (11,000) Cat Mss
Budget: ($45,500)

PQ —UNIVERSITY OF MONTREAL, Veterinary Medical Library, CP 5000, Saint-Hyacinthe, J2S 7C6, Can. Jean-Paul Jette, Librn
Holdings: Vols (11,500) Cat Microfilms

VETERINARY MEDICINE—EARLY WORKS TO 1850

MI —MICHIGAN STATE UNIVERSITY, Libraries, Special Collections Div, East Lansing, 48824. Jannette Fiore, Librn
Holdings: Vols 1600 Cat Mss
Notes: Works before 1850.

†WA —WASHINGTON STATE UNIVERSITY, Library, Manuscripts, Archives & Special Collections, Pullman, 99164. John F Guido, Head
Notes: The J F Smithcors library of veterinary medicine. More than 1000 vols, incl mss, broadsides, and ephemera, ranges from 16th-20th centuries. Many important modern texts.

VETERINARY MEDICINE—HISTORY

AZ —NORTHERN ARIZONA UNIVERSITY, Special Collection Library, CU Box 6022, Flagstaff, 86011. Peter M Whiteley, Coordr/Archivist; William Mullane, Librn
Notes: Handwritten recipe book containing many recipes for cures, often for farm animals, late 1800's.

†WA —WASHINGTON STATE UNIVERSITY, Library, Manuscripts, Archives & Special Collections, Pullman, 99164. John F Guido, Head
Holdings: Cat Mss Maps Pix
Notes: The J F Smithcors library of veterinary medicine. More than 1000 vols, incl mss, broadsides, and emphemera, ranges from 16th-20th centuries. Many important modern texts. Described in Selected Manuscript Resources in the Washington State University Library (Pullman, 1974); and other published and unpublished inventories and registers.

VETERINARY PATHOLOGY

DE —UNIVERSITY OF DELAWARE, Agriculture Library, 2 Townsend Hall,

VETERINARY PATHOLOGY (cont.)

Newark, 19717. Frederick Getze, Assoc Librn
Holdings: Vols (32,500) Cat Pix Microforms
Notes: Strong in entomology and ornamental horticulture. Extensive collection of state agriculture documents for each US state and Puerto Rico. Library subscribes to 600 serials (English and foreign).

IN —PURDUE UNIVERSITY LIBRARIES, Veterinary Medical Library, C J Lynn Hall of Veterinary Medicine, West Lafayette, 47907. Gretchen Stephens, Librn
Holdings: Vols (31,022) Cat
Budget: ($106,281)
Notes: The collection contains the outstanding books and serials in English that are germane to comparative and veterinary medicine. Foreign language materials are added selectively. Subjects of particular strength are laboratory animal medicine, pathology, comparative anatomy, animal behavior and clinical veterinary medicine.

IA —IOWA STATE UNIVERSITY, College of Veterinary Medicine, Veterinary Medical Library, Ames, 50011. Sara R Peterson, Librn
Holdings: Vols (17,000) Cat Microforms
Notes: Incl comparative and veterinary medicine with emphasis in the fields of mammalian anatomy and physiology, laboratory animal medicine, pathology, toxicology, biomedical engineering and clinical veterinary medicine. Incl 2000 uncataloged German theses.

NY —US DEPT OF AGRICULTURE, Agriculture Research Service, Plum Island Animal Disease Laboratory, PO Box 848, Greenport, 11944. Stephen Perlman, Librn
Holdings: Vols (15,000) Cat Pix Slides Microforms
Budget: ($37,000)

VETERINARY PHYSIOLOGY

MA —UNIVERSITY OF MASSACHUSETTS AT AMHERST, Library, Amherst, 01003. Siegfried Feller, Assoc Dir for Collection Development
Holdings: Cat
Notes: Veterinary medicine and animal sciences. Special emphasis: reproductive physiology, poultry genetics, animal nutrition.

ON —AGRICULTURE CANADA, Animal Dieases Research Institute, Library, PO Box 11300 Sta H, Ottawa, K2H 8P9, Can. John Miska, Area Coordinator; P A Atherton, Librn
Holdings: Vols (11,000) Cat Mss
Budget: ($45,500)

VETERINARY QUARANTINE see Quarantine, Veterinary

VETERINARY RESEARCH

NY —US DEPT OF AGRICULTURE, Agriculture Research Service, Plum Island Animal Disease Laboratory, PO Box 848, Greenport, 11944. Stephen Perlman, Librn
Holdings: Vols (15,000) Cat Pix Slides Micoforms
Budget: ($37,000)

VEXILLOLOGY see Flags (Vexillology)

VFW see Veterans of Foreign Wars (VFW)

VIBRATION

MN —MTS SYSTEMS CORP, Information Services, PO Box 24012, Minneapolis, 55424. Kathleen Werner, Technical Librn
Holdings: Cat Mss Pix Slides Phonorecords Audiotapes Videotapes 16mm Films Microforms
Notes: Material testing machines. Incl 2000 ms reports, 10,000 pictures, 6000 slides.

OH —PREFORMED LINE PRODUCTS CO, Research & Engineering Library, 660 Beta Drive, Mayfield Village, (Mailing add: PO Box 91129, Cleveland, 44101). Edwina T Barron, Librn
Holdings: Vols (11,500) Cat Mss Microfiche

Pix VF
Budget: ($30,500)
Notes: Library covering research and engineering fields emphasizing this subject. Aerodynamic characteristics and electrical characteristics of power cables, communication cables (including fiber optics), cable support systems, as well as associated fittings and hardware; in service behavior of manufactured products and materials as it relates to its static and dynamic forces and environmental conditions; oceanographic cable fittings and terminations.

VICE

IL —NATIONAL COUNCIL OF THE YMCAS, YMCA Historical Library, 6400 Shafer Ct, Rosemont, 60018. Eleanor R Murphy, Librn
Holdings: Vols (15,000) Cat
Notes: Early young men's societies. Incl very little primary material; mainly published material. Societies incl are very varied, such as the Young Men's Christian Union of Boston; the Society for Reformation of Manners, 1657-1690; Society for Suppression of Vice; and the Woman's Seamen's Friend Society. In addition, there are early bound periodicals, essays, etc, for the guidance and "betterment" of young men. Separate catalog.

VICTOR ANIMATOGRAPH CORPORATION

IA —UNIVERSITY OF IOWA, University Libraries, Iowa City, 52242. Robert A McCown, Mss Librn
Holdings: Mss Pix
Notes: The Victor Animatograph Corporation records, 1912-1966, including business correspondence, office records, photos, scrapbooks, and catalogs of a motion picture equipment manfacturer of Davenport, Iowa. See David H Shepard, "Victor Animatograph Company and the Beginnings of Non-Theatrical Film," *Books at Iowa,* no 24 (April, 1976) pp 40-55.

VICTOR TALKING MACHINE RECORDS

DC —LIBRARY OF CONGRESS, Motion Pictures, Broadcasting and Recorded Sound Div, Washington, 20540.
Holdings: Cat
Notes: 133 Berliner Gramophone Co records, 1896-1900; 31 Zonophone records, 1899-1904; 2 rare Vitaphone records, 1899; 67 Eldridge R Johnson records, 1900-1901; and 30 Victor Talking Machine Co records, 1902-1909.

VICTORIA, QUEEN

MA —BRANDEIS UNIVERSITY, Goldfarb Library, 415 South St, Waltham, 02154. Bessie Hahn, Dir
Notes: Benjamin Disraeli Correspondence. Contains approx 80 letters and other ephemeral items of Benjamin Disraeli, Lord Beaconsfield. A finding list is available in Special Collections.

NY —UNIVERSITY OF ROCHESTER, Rush Rhees Library, Department of Rare Books and Special Collections, Rochester, 14627. Peter Dzwonkoski, Librn
Holdings: Vols Cat Mss Pix
Notes: The Robert Metzdorf Collection about Queen Victoria, her family, and the court. With first editions by Benjamin Disraeli.

UT —BRIGHAM YOUNG UNIVERSITY, Harold B Lee Library, Unversity Hill, Provo, 84602. Sterling Albrecht, Dir
Holdings: Vols 2000 Cat
Notes: A large collection covering all phases of literature and life in the Age of Queen Victoria. Incl an unusual collection of "Yellow Backs" (1759 printer's proofs for yellow-back covers of original paperbacks of the 19th century).

VICTORIAN LITERATURE

CA —UNIVERSITY OF CALIFORNIA, LOS ANGELES, Research Library, Dept of

Special Collections, 405 Hilgard Ave, Los Angeles, 90024. Edward Shreeves, Chairman, Bibliographers Group; David S Zeidberg, Head
Holdings: Vols 15,000
Notes: 10,000 books (Michael Sadleir Collection of 19th Century Fiction); 5000 supplementary volumes; scattered letters and mss.

CA —UNIVERSITY OF THE PACIFIC, Library, Stockton, 95211. Hiram L Davis, Dir of Libraries
Holdings: Vols (350) Uncat Pix
Notes: A general collection of Victorian literature and life given to the University by James M Perrin in 1968-1970. The primary specialization is material by and about William Morris and the Kelmscott Press, but the collection also is rich in Victorian first editions, Pre-Raphaelites and Pre-Raphaelitism, and early colored illustrations and chromolithography.

CT —YALE UNIVERSITY, Box 1603A, Yale Station, New Haven, 06520.

IL —CHICAGO PUBLIC LIBRARY, Special Collections Div, Cultural Center, 78 E Washington St, Chicago, 60602. Laura Linard, Cur
Holdings: Cat
Notes: Since Thomas Hughes, MP and author of *Tom Brown's Schooldays,* was instrumental in the founding of The Chicago Public Library in 1871, the Library has begun to collect him in depth. The collection is small at present but several bookdealers in the US and Great Britain are searching for Hughes material and we purchase nearly 90 per cent of what is quoted. The Hughes Collection supplements the English Book Donation of 1871, originally about 7000 volumes (now only 500 are preserved), sponsored by Hughes. The Donation comprises primarily books donated by Oxford University and bears Oxford's gift-stamp and bookplate; the other extant books are late editions of Victorian literary and historical writers.

IL —NEWBERRY LIBRARY, 60 W Walton St, Chicago, 60610. Diana Haskell, Cur of Modern Mss
Holdings: Cat
Notes: Especially strong in periodicals and illustrated books of the period.

IN —INDIANA UNIVERSITY, Lilly Library, Seventh St, Bloomington, 47405. William R Cagle, Librn
Holdings: Cat Mss Pix
Notes: Extensive holdings of first editions. Mss incl illustrations for Victorian literature and letters of many authors.

KS —UNIVERSITY OF KANSAS, Kenneth Spencer Research Library, Special Collections Dept, Lawrence, 66045. Alexandra Mason, Librn
Holdings: Cat Mss
Notes: Strongest in 18th and 19th century. Old English (Clubb Collection); 18th-century plays, poems, sermons. English Poetical Miscellanies collection. Literary periodicals and newspapers (18th century). Noncirculating.

NJ —PRINCETON UNIVERSITY, Library, Morris L Parrish Collection, Princeton, 08540. Alexander D Wainwright, Cur
Holdings: Vols (6500) Cat Mss
Notes: The collection contains over 6500 vols, as well as many theatre programs, playbills, photographs, clippings and other miscellanea. Parrish's goal was to assemble in both the English and the American first editions, in the original condition as issued, everything that a given author published. He was also interested in a high standard of condition for his books. Many additions have been acquired since the Parrish collection came to the Library as a bequest in 1944. The collection is an assemblage of author collections, consisting of books by: William Harrison Ainsworth, James Matthew Barrie, William Black, The Brontes, William Wilkie Collins, Dinah Mulock Craik, Marie de la Ramee ("Ouida"), Benjamin Disraeli, Charles Dickens, Charles Dodgson, George du Maurier, George Eliot (ie Mary Ann Evans), Elizabeth Gaskell, Thomas Hardy, Thomas Hughes,Charles

VICTORIAN LITERATURE (cont.)

Kingsley, Charles Lever, Edward George Earle Bulwer-Lytton, Mary Maxwell, George Meredith, Charles Reade, Walter Scott, Robert Louis Stevenson, William Makepeace Thackeray, Trollope Family, Ellen Wood, and Charlotte Yonge.

†NY —COLUMBIA UNIVERSITY LIBRARIES, Butler Library, Rare Book and Manuscript Library, 535 W 114 St, New York, 10027.
Notes: The William B Liebmann Benjamin Disraeli Collection. Incl first editions, writings about him, letters, memorabilia, photographs, engravings, cartoons, sheet music and works about the Victorian era.

NY —SYRACUSE UNIVERSITY LIBRARIES, Ernest S Bird Library, George Arents Research Library for Special Collections, Syracuse, 13210. Carolyn A Davis, Manuscripts Librn; Amy S Doherty, University Archivist; Mark F Weimer, Rare Book Librn
Notes: Microfilm copies of Benjamin Disraeli's complete papers (200,000 frames) incl family, domestic and personal papers, copies of speeches, royal and general correspondence, papers on domestic and foreign affairs, correspondence on honors and titles, Mrs Disraeli's papers, mss of his novels and proofs and notices and correspondence about the novels. Also the papers of his father Isaac D'Israeli, of his grandfather Benjamin D'Israeli's biographers, Monypenny and Buckle.

RI —BROWN UNIVERSITY, John Hay Library, 20 Prospect St, Providence, 02912. Mark N Brown, Cur Mss
Holdings: // Mss
Notes: Papers of Harry Lyman Koopman, writer, librarian, and Professor of Bibliography at Brown University. 61 boxes of mss and typescript of prose and poetry for the period 1877 to 1937; and 29 portfolios containing account books, journals, essays, speeches, articles, translations, a novel, short stories, and poetry. 23 boxes contain articles, written for *The Providence Journal* 1926-1937. Also a vast correspondence by Koopman as Librarian. Incl Koopman's private collection of more than 2000 mss relating to Victorian writers.

TX —UNIVERSITY OF TEXAS LIBRARIES, General Libraries, PO Box P, Austin, 78713. Carolyn Bucknell, Asst Dir for Collection Development
Holdings: Cat Microforms

TX —BAYLOR UNIVERSITY, Armstrong Browning Library, 700 Speight, Box 6336, Waco, 76706. Jack W Herring, Dir
Holdings: Vols 10,000 Cat Mss Pix Slides Phonorecords 16mm Films Filmstrips Microforms
Notes: Largest Browning collection in the world. Contains books that belonged to the Brownings (300); letters written by Browning (1100); letters written by Elizabeth B Browning; letters written to the Brownings; furniture from the Brownings' homes; jewelry which belonged to the Brownings; 51 stained-glass windows depicting poems; music composed to accompany the poems (1500 pieces), etc. Noncirculating. Publish "Studies in Browning and His Circle" (semi-annual).

UT —BRIGHAM YOUNG UNIVERSITY, Harold B Lee Library, Unversity Hill, Provo, 84602. Sterling Albrecht, Dir
Holdings: Vols 3000 Mss
Notes: Victorian books, autographed letters, mss and original drawings.

ON —UNIVERSITY OF TORONTO, Thomas Fisher Rare Book Library, 120 Saint George St, Toronto, M5S 1A5, Can. Richard G Landon, Head
Holdings: Vols (1700) Uncat
Notes: Popular scientific books on English natural history written in the 19th century for the amateur observer and collector. Particularly notable for holdings of Philip Henry Gosse.

VICTORIANISM

CA —UNIVERSITY OF THE PACIFIC, Library, Stockton, 95211. Hiram L Davis, Dir of Libraries
Holdings: Vols (350) Uncat Pix
Notes: A general collection of Victorian literature and life given to the University by James M Perrin in 1968-1970. The primary specialization is material by and about William Morris and the Kelmscott Press, but the collection also is rich in Victorian first editions, Pre-Raphaelites and Pre-Raphaelitism, and early colored illustrations and chromolithography.

MA —BRANDEIS UNIVERSITY, Goldfarb Library, 415 South St, Waltham, 02154. Bessie Hahn, Dir
Notes: Victorian Printed Ephemera Collection. About 300 ephemeral items exemplifying the printing process from the Victorian period. No finding list or catalog present.

NJ —PRINCETON UNIVERSITY, Library, Morris L Parrish Collection, Princeton, 08540. Alexander D Wainwright, Cur
Holdings: Vols (6500) Cat Mss
Notes: The collection contains over 6500 vols, as well as many theatre programs, playbills, photographs, clippings and other miscellanea. Parrish's goal was to assemble in both the English and the American first editions, in the original condition as issued, everything that a given author published. He was also interested in a high standard of condition for his books. Many additions have been acquired since the Parrish collection came to the Library as a bequest in 1944. The collection is an assemblage of author collections, consisting of books by: William Harrison Ainsworth, James Matthew Barrie, William Black, The Brontes, William Wilkie Collins, Dinah Mulock Craik, Marie de la Ramee ("Ouida"), Benjamin Disraeli, Charles Dickens, Charles Dodgson, George du Maurier, George Eliot (ie Mary Ann Evans), Elizabeth Gaskell, Thomas Hardy, Thomas Hughes, Charles Kingsley, Charles Lever, Edward George Earle Bulwer-Lytton, Mary Maxwell, George Meredith, Charles Reade, Walter Scott, Robert Louis Stevenson, William Makepeace Thackeray, Trollope Family, Ellen Wood, and Charlotte Yonge.

†NY —COLUMBIA UNIVERSITY LIBRARIES, Butler Library, Rare Book and Manuscript Library, 535 W 114 St, New York, 10027.
Notes: The William B Liebmann Benjamin Disraeli Collection. Incl first editions, writings about him, letters, memorabilia, photographs, engravings, cartoons, sheet music and works about the Victorian era.

VIDEO see Television

VIDEO EDUCATION AND INSTRUCTION see Audiovisual Education and Instruction

VIDOR, KING, 1895-1982

CA —UNIVERSITY OF CALIFORNIA, LOS ANGELES, Research Library, Dept of Special Collections, 405 Hilgard Ave, Los Angeles, 90024. Edward Shreeves, Chairman, Bibliographers Group; David S Zeidberg, Head
Holdings: Mss Pix
Notes: 7 linear feet of moving picture scripts and related materials.

CA —UNIVERSITY OF SOUTHERN CALIFORNIA, Edward L Doheny Memorial Library, Archives of Performing Arts, University Park, Los Angeles, 90089. Robert Knutson, Librn
Holdings: Mss Pix
Notes: Personal collection of papers, pictures, etc.

VIENNA—HISTORY

TX —RICE UNIVERSITY, Fondren Library, 6100 S Main St, PO Box 1892, Houston, 77251. Dr Samuel M Carrington, Jr, University Librn
Holdings: //
Notes: The Stephen K Swift Collection, incl Austro-Hungarian and Austrian history (3600 items). Has complete British Intelligence Service reports on Austria, 1945-1955; original charter from the Austrian Empire to the Hungarian government (ca 1527), with signature of Charles V. Also a 360 vol history of the city of Vienna.

VIERECK, GEORGE SYLVESTER, 1884-1962

CA —HOOVER INSTITUTION ON WAR, REVOLUTION & PEACE, Stanford University, Stanford, 94305. Milorad M Drachkovitch, Archivist
Holdings: Mss
Notes: Collection of clippings, 1903-42, relating to the literary career of G S Viereck, his arrest and trial as a pro-German propagandist in the US during World War II, German-American relations, and US foreign policy during World War I. Many of the clippings are articles by G S Viereck. 32 scrapbooks.

CT —YALE UNIVERSITY, Box 1603A, Yale Station, New Haven, 06520.
Holdings: Cat Mss

IA —UNIVERSITY OF IOWA, University Libraries, Iowa City, 52242. Robert A McCown, Mss Librn
Holdings: Mss Pix
Notes: Collection includes about 1400 items of correspondence, drafts of magazine articles, photos, clippings, manuscripts of poems in German and in English, notebooks, pamphlets, legal documents, and related material. Described in *Books at Iowa*, 9 (Nov 1968), pp 22-24, 29-36, in an article entitled "George Sylvester Viereck: Poet and propagandist," by Niel M Johnson.

VIERTEL, PETER

MA —BOSTON UNIVERSITY, Mugar Memorial Library, Special Collections Dept, 771 Commonwealth Ave, Boston, 02215. Howard B Gotlieb, Dir
Holdings: Cat Mss
Notes: Mss, collected in depth; incl publications by or about.

VIET CONG see Vietnamese Conflict, 1961-1975

VIETNAM

HI —UNIVERSITY OF HAWAII, Library, 2550 The Mall, Honolulu, 96822. Joyce Wright, Head, Asia Collection; Masato Matsu, Head, East Asia Vernacular Collection
Holdings: Vols 331,620 Cat Microforms
Notes: The Asia Collection holds materials from and about Southeast Asia: Brunei, Burma, Cambodia (Kampuchea), Indonesia, Laos, Malaysia, Philippines, Singapore, Thailand. Large contemporary Indonesian language collection. Several thousand vols in Thai and in Vietnamese. Minimal holdings in Burmese, Khmer, Lao languages. Social sciences and humanities emphasis for the post-World War II period. Western language coverage supplemented by retrospective holdings in the main library collection.

IL —SOUTHERN ILLINOIS UNIVERSITY, CARBONDALE, Delyte W Morris Library, Carbondale, 62901.
Holdings: Vols (4100) Cat Maps Audiotapes Microforms
Notes: The Vietnamese collection has been transferred to the general library. It incl 1200 cataloged titles in the Vietnamese language, plus 56 Vietnamese language microfilms. A profile of the area emphasis on the collection appears from the following distribution of the 2987 titles entered in the holdings and accessions lists published by the Southern Illinois University Center for Vietnamese Studies: Vietnam, 1965; Cambodia and Laos, 63; Other Southeast Asia (incl Indonesia), 916; East Asia (mostly China), 246; General (reference works, bibliographies, etc), 197. Also over 1000 maps.

IL —CENTER FOR RESEARCH LIBRARIES, 6050 S Kenwood Ave,

VIETNAM (cont.)

Chicago, 60637. Donald B Simpson, Dir;
Esther Smith, Collection Development Libn
Holdings: Cat Microforms
Notes: Incl microfilm of about 1200 Viet
Cong documents collected by Douglas Pike;
collection of transcripts of interviews and
some other South Vietnamese material
collected by Jeffrey Race; and film of some
North Vietnamese newspapers and
periodicals, incomplete, from varying dates
in 1960s.

†MA —JOHN F KENNEDY LIBRARY,
Columbia Point, Boston, 02125. Dan H Fenn
Jr, Dir
Holdings: // Uncat Microforms
Notes: Microfilm (64 rolls) from the
Vietnamese-American Association of
Records of the Nguyen Dynasty, 1802-1860.
Holdings are described in "Historical
Materials in the John F Kennedy Library."
Copies may be obtained by writing the
Research Archivist.

MA —HARVARD UNIVERSITY LIBRARY,
Widener Library, Cambridge, 02138.
Holdings: Cat
Notes: Joseph Buttinger Collection. Vietnam
history. Primarily French and English
language publications, 19th and 20th
centuries.

MI —UNIVERSITY OF MICHIGAN, Harlan
Hatcher Graduate Library, Ann Arbor,
48109. Susan Go, Libn
Holdings: Vols (250,000) Cat Mss Maps Pix
Slides Microforms
Notes: Incl in the Michigan Historical
Collections (primarily archival material) are
papers of Michiganders in southeast Asia,
mostly the Philipines, eg papers of Joseph R
Hayden, Frank Murphy and G Mennen
Williams, also, on film, the selected papers
of Philippines president Manuel Quezon. All
aspects of the countries, cultures and peoples
of Brunei, Burma, Khymer, Indonesia, Laos,
Malaysia, Philippines, Singapore, Thailand,
Portuguese Timor and Vietnam. Also the
Malayo-Polynesian (Austronesian), Mon-
Khmer (Austroasiatic), and Sino-Tibetan
language groupings.

NY —CORNELL UNIVERSITY LIBRARIES,
Collection of Regional History, Dept of
Manuscripts and Univ Archives, Ithaca,
14853.
Notes: Records, 1972-74; Vietnam Veterans
Against the War, Inc; incl reel of movie film.
Also, records ca 1979-1981; Vietnam War
Veterans Archives and History Center; 2.2
ft. Restricted.

NY —CORNELL UNIVERSITY LIBRARIES,
John M Olin Library, John M Echols
Collection on Southeast Asia, Ithaca, 14853.
Giok Po Oey, Curator
Holdings: Vols (167,000) Cat Mss Maps Pix
Microforms
Budget: ($90,000)
Notes: Additions published in the
collection's monthly accessions list (Ithaca:
Cornell University, Southeast Asia Program,
1959-). Holdings through December 1980
listed in *Cornell University Libraries
Southeast Asia Catalog* (Boston: G K Hall,
1976, First supplement, 1983), 10 vols.

VIETNAM (SOUTH)

MI —MICHIGAN STATE UNIVERSITY,
International Library, South and Southeast
Asia Collection, East Lansing, 48824.
Clinton Lockert, Bibliographer
Holdings: Vols (6000) Cat Maps Microforms
Notes: Emphasis is upon South and South-
east Asia especially Bangladesh and Vietnam
(South). Attempt to collect extensively the
economic and social development plans of
the developing nations. Monographs and
serials received on PL 480 from India,
Pakistan, Sri Lanka and Nepal since 1968.
Extensive holdings of Academy for Rural
Development, Comilla, Bangladesh (1959-),
and of the Michigan State University
Vietnam Advisory Group (1955-1962).

NY —COLUMBIA UNIVERSITY
LIBRARIES, Rare Book & Manuscript
Library, 801 Butler Library, 535 W 114 St,

New York, 10027. Kenneth A Lohf, Librn
Holdings: Mss
Notes: The papers of Profesor Carter
Goodrich, economic historian, incl his
papers as chairman of the governing body of
the International Labor Office, 1939-1945;
chief of the United Nations economic
mission in Vietnam, 1955-1956; and special
representative to Bolivia for the Secretary-
General of the United Nations, 1952-1953.
About 28,000 items. Restricted use.

VIETNAM, AMERICAN FRIENDS OF
see American Friends of Vietnam

VIETNAMESE CONFLICT, 1961-1975

AL —BIRMINGHAM PUBLIC LIBRARY,
Dept of Archives & Mss, 2020 Seventh Ave
N, Birmingham, 35203. Marvin Y Whiting,
Archivist & Cur
Notes: Collected papers, 1963-1967 for
Albert Boutwell, first mayor of Birmingham,
Alabama under the mayor-council form of
government. His administration was
dominated by several concerns: the Civil
Rights Movement, the growth of police
surveillance powers within the community,
the effort to revitalize the inner city, and
stimulate economic growth. Correspondence,
memoranda, reports, and other documents
are organized by subject categories. Subjects
which may be of interest incl the "Big Red
One" (First Infantry Division), which
involved an attempt to build up community
support for the Vietnam War. "Civic Center",
"Operation New Birmingham", and "Festival
of Arts" files show the beginnings of
revitalization efforts to make the inner city a
cultural showpiece. "Negro Activities",
"School Desegregation", and "Civil Rights"
filesreflect racial turmoil and Boutwell's
efforts to implement national policies.

CA —UNIVERSITY OF CALIFORNIA, LOS
ANGELES, Research Library, Social
Sciences Collection, 405 Hilgard Ave, Los
Angeles, 90024. Edward Shreeves,
Chairman, Bibliographers Group; Oscar L
Sims, Social Sciences Bibliographer
Holdings: Microforms
Notes: A collection of over 200 underground
newspapers on 26 reels of microfilm. Among
the titles included are: *The Tribe, The
Berkeley Barb, New York Roach, Rat*, and
Win.

CA —HOOVER INSTITUTION ON WAR,
REVOLUTION & PEACE, Stanford
University, Stanford, 94305. Milorad M
Drachkovitch, Archivist
Notes: Reports (printed copies), 1965-1972,
prepared by the Rand Corporation, relating
to the organization, operations, motivation,
and morale of the Viet Cong and the North
Vietnamese, 1964-1968, and based on 2400
interviews with Vietnamese. 3 ms boxes.

CT —UNIVERSITY OF CONNECTICUT,
Library, Storrs, 06268. R H Schimmelpfeng,
Dir of Special Collections
Holdings: // Uncat Mss Pix
Notes: The archives consist of the business
records and mss, published and unpublished,
of the First Casualty Press, which was
deeply involved with Vietnam veterans'
experiences in Vietnam. Vols issued by the
press were *Winning Hearts and Mines* and
Free Fire Zone, both literary.

DC —GEORGETOWN UNIVERSITY,
Library, Special Collections Div, 37 & O Sts
NW, Washington, 20057. George M
Barringer, Special Collections Libro;
Nicholas B Sheetz, Mss Librn
Holdings: Mss Cat
Notes: The papers of Ambassador Martin F
Herz (1917-1983), containing
correspondence, reports, memoranda,
posters, propaganda leaflets, and other
ephemeral material relating to psychological
warfare in World War II and Vietnam; also
much material on the Cold War and
American foreign policy in the years
following World War II.

DC —HOWARD UNIVERSITY, Founders
Library, Bernard B Fall Collection
(Southeast Asia Collection), Washington,
20059. Steven Ilsang Yoon, Cur
Holdings: Vols (6000) Cat Microforms
Budget: ($15,000)
Notes: The Bernard B Fall Collection has

more than 6000 books, incl 1200 books
purchased from the Kendric N Marshall
Estate, 3000 items in vertical files, 300
pamphlets, and 800 microfilms, about
Southeast Asia and China. In addition, there
are nearly 100 current periodicals and
another 100 older periodicals about
Indochina in the Collection.

MI —MICHIGAN STATE UNIVERSITY,
International Library, South and Southeast
Asia Collection, East Lansing, 48824.
Clinton Lockert, Bibliographer
Holdings: Vols (3500) Cat Mss Maps Pix
Audiotapes Microforms
Notes: Emphasis is on South Vietnam (1955-
1962). The University had a Vietnam
Advisory Group headquartered in Saigon
during this period. Have complete holdings
of *Reports and Documents* Series of the
MSU Vietnam Advisory Group. Extensive
correspondence, documents and publications
of the American Friends of Vietnam, and of
the International Rescue Committee. Very
extensive clippings, correspondence,
documents, and photographs from the
Gilbert Jonas Collection, and the Wesley
Fishel Collection. Significant unique items.
Representative selection of Vietnamese
literature.

MO —NORTHEAST MISSOURI STATE
UNIVERSITY, Pickler Memorial Library,
Kirksville, 63501. George N Hartje, Libn
Holdings: Cat Mss Microforms
Notes: 350 microfiche cards of over 19,000
pages of documents on Vietnam-incl
government publications of both sides of the
conflict, and US government materials (a
tripartite view of social, political, and
military aspects of the war from 1960-1971).
Verbatim translations of prisoner
interrogations, broadcasts, etc (incl Radio
Hanoi and Liberation Radio, 1969-1971).

NY —UNIVERSITY OF ROCHESTER, Rush
Rhees Library, Department of Rare Books
and Special Collections, Rochester, 14627.
Peter Dzwonkoski, Librn
Holdings: Mss
Notes: A beginning collection of letters from
Vietnam veterans, their families, and friends,
and individuals who opposed the war,
expected to create a resource toward
historical understanding of attitudes and
reactions concerning war and the Vietnam
Conflict in particular.

NY —SYRACUSE UNIVERSITY
LIBRARIES, Ernest S Bird Library, George
Arents Research Library for Special
Collections, Syracuse, 13210. Carolyn A
Davis, Manuscripts Librn; Amy S Doherty,
University Archivist; Mark F Weimer, Rare
Book Librn
Notes: Incl correspondence of Dr Benjamin
Spock on medical subjects, Vietnam peace
movement, nuclear disarmament, state and
national politics, education and civil rights.

PA —US ARMY MILITARY HISTORY
INSTITUTE, Carlisle Barracks, 17013.
Richard J Sommers, Chief Archivist-
Historian
Holdings: Mss Cat
Notes: 2000 boxes mss. The Viet Nam War
collection, personal letters, daily logs,
memoirs, speeches, and official papers of
American officers and soldiers serving in
Viet Nam or elsewhere in the world during
the era. Almost all these papers are from
Generals, incl William DePuy, Harold K
Johnson, Bruce Palmer, Jonathan Seaman,
and William Westmoreland.

PA —GETTYSBURG COLLEGE, Musselman
Library, Gettysburg, 17325. Willis M
Hubbard, College Librn
Holdings: Vols 175 Cat Mss Pix
Notes: This collection contains photocopies
of original letters to parents, several hundred
Army newspapers, periodicals, press releases,
photographs and personal diaries of Stephen
Henry Warner, killed in the Vietnamese
conflict. Books on the subject are added as
published, from the funds of the Warner
Memorial.

TX —UNIVERSITY OF TEXAS, EL PASO,
Special Collections Dept, The S L A
Marshall Military History Collection, El
Paso, 79968. Thomas Burdett, Cur
Holdings: Vols 7000 Cat Periodicals Mss
Budget: $2000
Notes: The collection contains all of General

VIETNAMESE CONFLICT, 1961-1975 (cont.)

Samuel Lyman Atwood Marshall's published works, his personal library and his personal papers. General Marshall was a prolific military historian and journalist. The collection's strengths are in its coverage of the wars of the twentieth century, specifically the two world wars, the Korean conflict and the war in Vietnam. The Marshall Room where the collection is housed is opened to the public.

UT —UNIVERSITY OF UTAH, Marriott Library, Special Collections, Salt Lake City, 84112. Gregory C Thompson, Cur
Notes: Papers of George Latimer, attorney for Lt William Calley. Complete record of court-martial trial 1968-1973.

WI —STATE HISTORICAL SOCIETY OF WISCONSIN, Archives, 816 State St, Madison, 53706. Harold L Miller, Reference Archivist
Holdings: Mss Pix Audiotapes Microforms
Notes: Records and papers of organizations and individuals engages in social and political reform activities. Major focus areas are civil rights, 1950s to the present, and anti-Vietnam war and other protest movements of the 1960s to the present. Also covered are other reform movements, socialism, and communism from the 1930s to the present. Collections are described in *Social Action Collection at the State Historical Society of Wisconsin: A Guide*, (1983) and in current accession notes in the *Wisconsin Magazine of History*. Major collections are also listed in Hamer, *Guide to Manuscripts and Archives in the United States*, (1961) and in the *National Union Catalog of Manuscript Collections*, (1959-date).

VIETNAMESE CONFLICT FICTION

CO —COLORADO STATE UNIVERSITY, Libraries, Fort Collins, 80523. John Newman, Special Collections Librn
Holdings: Vols (1000)
Notes: The Vietnam War Literature collection is a comprehensive holding of novels, short stories, plays, poetry, sketches and other works of the imagination depicting Americans fighting in Vietnam. The collection incl unpublished manuscripts, but does not incl non-fiction material. For an annotated bibliography, see John Newman, *Vietnam War Fiction*, Scarecrow, 1982.

VIETNAMESE IN THE U.S.

CA —LOS ANGELES PUBLIC LIBRARY, Social Sciences Dept, 630 W Fifth St, Los Angeles, 90071. Marilyn C Wherley, Principal Librn
Holdings: Vols 4000 Microforms
Budget: ($150,000)
Notes: Emphasis on minorities: immigration policies, background and social problems of ethnic monorities in the US in particular. Incl periodicals, government publications and documents, popular and scholarly works on Blacks, Hispanics, and Asians predominantly.

†NY —STATE UNIVERSITY OF NEW YORK, COLLEGE AT BUFFALO, Vietnamese Immigration Collection, Buffalo, 14260.
Notes: Oral history, interviews, orientation materials, and refugee camp newspapers.

VIETNAMESE LANGUAGE AND LITERATURE

CA —LOS ANGELES PUBLIC LIBRARY, Foreign Languages Dept, 630 W Fifth St, Los Angeles, 90071. Sylva Manoogian, Principal Librn
Holdings: Vols 400 Cat
Budget: ($41,500)

CA —UNIVERSITY OF CALIFORNIA, LOS ANGELES, Research Library, Indo/Pacific Collection, 405 Hilgard Ave, Los Angeles, 90024. Edward Shreeves, Chairman, Bibliographers Group; Charlotte Spence,

Indo/Pacific Bibliographer
Holdings: Vols Cat Mss Maps Pix Microforms
Notes: The Southeast Asian collection has been developed on a combination of the research and teaching levels; it focuses on the cultural, economic, political and social history of the area from ancient times to the present day. Although all the individual countries of the region are represented, some priority is given to Malaysia, Singapore, Indonesia and the Philippines. The majority of the materials is in Western languages except for a collection of several thousand books in Thai, and a smaller collection of materials in Vietnamese, Indonesian, Malaysian, and the Philippine languages.

CA —SAN JOSE PUBLIC LIBRARY, 180 W San Carlos St, San Jose, 95113. Homer Fletcher, Dir
Holdings: Vols 7000

DC —LIBRARY OF CONGRESS, African and Middle Eastern Division, Washington, 20540.
Holdings: Cat Mss Microforms
Notes: Southern Asian: over 137,000 vols of literature of the area from Pakistan to the Philipines.

HI —UNIVERSITY OF HAWAII, Library, 2550 The Mall, Honolulu, 96822. Joyce Wright, Head, Asia Collection; Masato Matsu, Head, East Asia Vernacular Collection
Holdings: Vols 331,620 Cat Microforms
Notes: The Asia Collection holds materials from and about Southeast Asia: Brunei, Burma, Cambodia (Kampuchea), Indonesia, Laos, Malaysia, Philippines, Singapore, Thailand. Large contemporary Indonesian language collection. Several thousand vols in Thai and in Vietnamese. Minimal holdings in Burmese, Khmer, Lao languages. Social sciences and humanities emphasis for the post-World War II period. Western language coverage supplemented by retrospective holdings in the main library collection.

IL —SOUTHERN ILLINOIS UNIVERSITY, CARBONDALE, Delyte W Morris Library, Carbondale, 62901.
Holdings: Vols (4100) Cat Maps Audiotapes Microforms
Notes: The Vietnamese collection has been transferred to the general library. It incl 1200 cataloged titles in the Vietnamese language, plus 56 Vietnamese language microfilms. A profile of the area emphasis on the collection appears from the following distribution of the 2987 titles entered in the holdings and accessions lists published by the Southern Illinois University Center for Vietnamese Studies: Vietnam, 1965; Cambodia and Laos, 63; Other Southeast Asia (incl Indonesia), 916; East Asia (mostly China), 246; General (reference works, bibliographies, etc), 197. Also over 1000 maps.

MI —MICHIGAN STATE UNIVERSITY, International Library, South and Southeast Asia Collection, East Lansing, 48824. Clinton Lockert, Bibliographer
Holdings: Vols 55,700 // Cat Mss Maps Audiotapes Microforms
Notes: Emphasis is upon South and Southeast Asia, especially Bangladesh and Vietnam (South). Attempt to collect extensively the economic and social development plans of the developing nations. Monographs and serials received on PL 480 from India, Pakistan, Sri Lanka and Nepal since 1968. Extensive holdings of Academy for Rural Development, Comilla, Bangladesh (1959-1976), and of the Michigan State University Vietnam Advisory Group (1955-1962). No additions to collection since 1976.

NY —NEW YORK PUBLIC LIBRARY, Oriental Div, Fifth Ave & 42 St, New York, 10018. E Christian Filstrup, Chief
Holdings: // Cat Mss Microforms
Budget: ($56,455)
Notes: Published catalog of holdings. Currently collected in Western language materials only.

NY —NEW YORK PUBLIC LIBRARY, Donnell Foreign Language Library, 20 W 53 St, New York, 10019. Bosiljka Stevanovic, Supvr Librn
Holdings: Vols 816 Cat
Notes: Vietnamese collection incl

Vietnamese authors of Vietnamese expression. No separate catalog.

NY —INSTITUTE FOR ADVANCED STUDIES OF WORLD RELIGIONS (IASWR), Melville Memorial Library, State University of New York, Stony Brook, 11794. C T Shen, Dir
Holdings: Vols 400 Periodicals Maps
Notes: Incl works in Vietnamese, French, English, Chinese on history culture, systems of thought, ie, Buddhism, Confucianism, Cao Dai, etc.

NC —CUMBERLAND COUNTY PUBLIC LIBRARY, North Carolina Foreign Language Center, 328 Gillespie St, Fayetteville, 28301. Patrick M Valentine, Coordinator
Holdings: Vols 1000 Cat
Budget: $1250
Notes: The largest book collections are, in descending order of size, German Spanish, French, Japanese, Korean and Vietnamese, with fair sized collections in Italian, Russian, Chinese, Arabic, Greek, Hungarian, Polish, Hebrew, Thai, and Hindi. The Center has several shelves each of books in Bengali, Dutch, Marathi, Portuguese, Urdu, and Yiddish. Smaller collections of one to three shelves each incl Catalan, Croatian, Czech, Danish, Finnish, Gujarati, Icelandic, Kannada, Latin, Lithuanian, Malayalam, Norwegian, Panjabi, Persian (Farsi), Romanian, Slovak, Swedish, Tagalog, Tamil, Telegu, and Ukrianian. The Center has grammars, dictionaries and occasionally other readings in languages from Afrikaans and Albanian to Welsh, Yoruba and Zulu.

OH —CLEVELAND PUBLIC LIBRARY, Foreign Literature Dept, 325 Superior Ave, Cleveland, 44114. Natalia Bezugloff, Head
Holdings: Vols 1710 Cat
Notes: A popular circulating collection containing classics and the standard works with emphasis on belles lettres, history and biography. A variety of other subjects such as learning languages, how to do books, art, children's books, spoken phonodiscs and cassettes, periodicals, etc. Incl 80 ephemera. *See also* entry under Foreign Language Collections

VIETNAMESE REFUGEES see Refugees, Vietnamese

VIEW BOOKS

NY —COLUMBIA UNIVERSITY LIBRARIES, Avery Architectural and Fine Arts Library, 201 Avery Hall, New York, 10027. Angela Giral, Librn
Notes: Souvenir books of pictures of single American cities, towns, resorts, expositions, etc, places featuring buildings. They vary in size, are frequently in paper covers and the plates are usually photographic. Date from ca 1880-1940. Guidebooks to cities are also available.

VIEWS

CA —POMONA PUBLIC LIBRARY, Special Collections, 625 S Garey Ave, PO Box 2271, Pomona, 91766. David Streeter, Librn
Holdings: Uncat Slides
Notes: Contains 550 lantern slides (mostly of California) and 4200 color 35mm transparencies of world travel, 1960s. Also, the Burton Frasher Postal Card Collection of 60,000 negatives and prints of California, Arizona, Colorado, New Mexico, Nevada, and Utah; 30,000 world views; 8000 California views. There are also world views in nearly 1000 stereophotographs.

CT —YALE UNIVERSITY, Yale Center for British Art, Rare Book Dept, New Haven, 06520. Joan Friedman, Cur
Notes: One of the greatest assemblages of British Art of the 17th-19th centuries.

IL —LAKE COUNTY MUSEUM LIBRARY, Lakewood Forest Preserve, Wauconda, 60084. Rebecca Goldberg, Dir; Katherine Hamilton-Smith, Cur
Notes: "The world's largest postcard collection. The Curt Teich Industries assets, consisting of several million postcards and

VIEWS (cont.)

associated artwork depicting local communities around the world, cards donated by Regensteiner Enterprises Inc. Curt Teich is considered one of the originators of present day postcards. Project funded by the Curt Teich Foundation."

MA —AMERICAN ANTIQUARIAN SOCIETY LIBRARY, 185 Salisbury St, Worcester, 01609. Marcus A McCorison, Dir & Librn
Holdings: Cat Maps Pix Slides
Notes: About 90,000 postal cards and 60,000 stereophotographs. Arranged geographically or by subject. Postal cards date from 1893; steros 1860-1890. Also some rare copybook cover of views, 1794-1860. Extensive slide collection.

PA —PENNSYLVANIA STATE UNIVERSITY, Fred Lewis Pattee Library, Special Collections Dept, University Park, 16802. Charles Mann, Chief, Special Collections
Holdings: Pix
Budget: ($37,000)
Notes: City views of Pennsylvania.

TN —TENNESSEE STATE LIBRARY & ARCHIVES, 403 Seventh Ave N, Nashville, 37219. Olivia K Young, State Librn & Archivist
Holdings: Uncat Pix
Notes: Mainly picture postcards of Tennessee and southern scenes, but largest part of the collection is the Mrs Joseph H Thompson Collection incl cards from Europe, Africa, Asia and North and South America.

VIGILANCE COMMITTEES AND VIGILANTES

NY —NEW YORK PUBLIC LIBRARY, Research Libraries, American History Div, Fifth Ave & 42 St, New York, 10018.
Holdings: Vols (14,000) Cat
Notes: Outstanding collection of material on the Old West, incl early settlement, the lawless era, and the resulting vigilantism.

VIGNAUD, JEAN HENRY

CT —YALE UNIVERSITY, Box 1603A, Yale Station, New Haven, 06520.
Holdings: Cat Mss
Notes: 15 bound volumes of his mss (about 7100 leaves), apparently all unpublished; with 50 boxes of printed materials being his working library on discovery and exploration of the Western Hemisphere.

VIKINGS

NY —CORNELL UNIVERSITY LIBRARIES, John M Olin Library, Fiske Icelandic Collection, Ithaca, 14853. Louis A Pitschmann, Librn
Holdings: Vols (34,000) Cat Mss Maps Pix Microforms
Budget: ($3000)
Notes: Collection aims at comprehensive coverage of Iceland in all aspects with major emphasis on the literature and language (both old and modern). Such subjects as runology, Scandinavian and Germanic mythology, early Norwegian history and history of the Viking period and of the Norse explorations of Greenland and North America are also well represented. For printed catalogs of the Collection's holdings see Downs 3608, 3609. Records for approximately 40 percent of the collection have been entered into OCLC and RLIN.

VILLA-LOBOS, HEITOR

DC —LIBRARY OF CONGRESS, Music Division, Washington, 20540.
Notes: Mss in Koussevitzky Archives.

VILLARD, HENRY S.

MA —BOSTON UNIVERSITY, Mugar Memorial Library, Special Collections Dept, 771 Commonwealth Ave, Boston, 02215.

Howard B Gotlieb, Dir
Holdings: Cat Mss Pix
Notes: Mss, correspondence, etc collected in depth; incl publications by or about.

VILLARD, OSWALD G., AND FAMILY

MA —HARVARD UNIVERSITY LIBRARY, Houghton Library, Cambridge, 02138. Rodney G Dennis, Cur of Manuscripts
Holdings: Cat Mss
Notes: Incl 80 boxes of collected papers of Oswald Garrison Villard.

VILLAS see Architecture, Domestic

VINCENT, JOHN

CA —UNIVERSITY OF CALIFORNIA, LOS ANGELES, Music Library, Schonberg Hall, Los Angeles, 90024. Stephen M Fry, Music Librn
Notes: Mss.

VINER, JACOB, 1892-1970

NJ —PRINCETON UNIVERSITY, Seeley G Mudd Manuscript Library, Public Affairs Papers Collection, Princeton, 08544. Nancy Bressler, Cur
Notes: Incl 94 boxes. The papers cover the period 1923-70. An unpublished 44p guide is available in the Library.

VINEYARDS see Grapes; Viticulture

VINGE, JOAN

CA —SAN DIEGO STATE UNIVERSITY, Malcolm A Love Library, 5300 Campanile Dr, San Diego, 92182. D Dickinson, Univ Librn; Don L Bosseau, Dir
Holdings: Mss Cassettes
Notes: Elizabeth Chater Collection in Science Fiction. Includes Tolkien Collection, fantasy, folklore, Gothic novels, mostly autographed first editions, some rare and scarce, includes manuscripts, graphics, cassette tapes. Examples: authors included, Isaac Asimov, Ray Bradbury, Joan Vinge, Greg Baer, Frederick Pohl, Andre Norton, etc. Examples of periodicals, Amazing Stories, Famous Fantastic Mysteries of the 1940s, The Black Cat, 1895. (3000 items)

VINICULTURE see Viticulture

VINLAND—DISCOVERY AND EXPLORATION

NY —CORNELL UNIVERSITY LIBRARIES, John M Olin Library, Fiske Icelandic Collection, Ithaca, 14853. Louis A Pitschmann, Librn
Holdings: Vols (34,000) Cat Mss Maps Pix Microforms
Budget: ($3000)
Notes: Collection aims at comprehensive coverage of Iceland in all aspects with major emphasis on the literature and language (both old and modern). Such subjects as runology, Scandinavian and Germanic mythology, early Norwegian history and history of the Viking period and of the Norse explorations of Greenland and North America are also well represented. For printed catalogs of the Collection's holdings see Downs 3608, 3609. Records for approximately 40 percent of the collection have been entered into OCLC and RLIN.

VINSON, CARL

GA —GEORGIA COLLEGE, Ina Dillard Russell Library, Special Collections Dept, Milledgeville, 31061. Janice C Fennell, Dir of Libraries; Nancy Davis, Special Collections Assoc
Holdings: Uncat Mss
Notes: Personal and official correspondence of Judge U Erwin Sibley, 1912-1978. Incl personal correspondence between Judge Sibley and Congressman Carl Vinson for years 1932-1972 (34 folders).

VINSON, FREDERICK MOORE

KY —UNIVERSITY OF KENTUCKY, Margaret I King Library, Dept of Special

Collections, Lexington, 40506. William Marshall, Head
Holdings: Cat Mss Pix Audiotapes Films
Notes: Incl 302,462 pieces; papers relating to his Congressional career, US Circuit court of Appeals for the District of Columbia, the Bretton Woods Conference, Secretary of the Treasury files and the Supreme Court papers. Vinson became Chief Justice in 1946. Period covered: 1907-53. Unpublished inventory.

VINTAGE CARS

IN —INDIANAPOLIS MOTOR SPEEDWAY, Hall of Fame Museum, 4790 W 16th St, Indianapolis, 46222. Jack L Martin, Dir
Holdings: Uncat Mss Maps Pix Slides Phonorecords Audiotapes 16mm Films
Notes: No photocopying.

MI —EDISON INSTITUTE, Greenfield Village and Henry Ford Museum, Archives & Research Library, PO Box 1970, Dearborn, 48121. Steve Hamp, Dir; Joan W Gartland, Librn
Notes: Incl Dunbar collection of prints, broadsides and drawings documenting History of Travel in America, 1680-1910 (1741 items) and the Walker Locomotive collection, 1820-1931 (308 items). It also incl 19th century maps and travelers' guides and an antique automotive file.

MI —R E OLDS MUSEUM LIBRARY, 240 Museum Drive, Lansing, 48933.
Notes: Emphasizes the contributions that Lansing has made to transportation history; materials on Oldsmobile, Reo, Star, Durant, and Bates cars. Incl books, manuals, magazines, advertisements, photographs, films, slides, audiotapes, videotapes, VF, and art reproductions.

MI —HUDSON-ESSEX-TERRAPLANE CLUB LIBRARY, 5765 Munger Rd, Ypsilanti, 48197. Charles Liskow, Librn
Notes: Hudson-Essex-Terraplane car advertisements, parts books, owners' manuals, service procedure manuals, sales catalogs and brochures, color specifications, service bulletins, etc. Nominal charge is made for copies. No material will be loaned. About 13 feet shelf length holdings. Cataloged.

VINTON, WARREN J., 1889-1969

NY —CORNELL UNIVERSITY LIBRARIES, Collection of Regional History, Dept of Manuscripts and Univ Archives, Ithaca, 14853.
Notes: Economist, Assistant Commissioner of US Public Housing Authority. Papers, ca 1920-(35-69); 28 ft.

VIOLENCE, FAMILY see Family Violence

VIOLENCE RESEARCH

MD —UNIVERSITY OF MARYLAND, BALTIMORE COUNTY, Albin O Kuhn Library and Gallery, 5401 Wilkens Ave, Baltimore, 21228. Ann Copeland, Special Collections Librn
Holdings: Vols 1000 // Uncat
Notes: The Hugh Davis Graham papers relate to Dr Graham's work as Co-Director of the Task Force on the History of Violence in America (for the National Commission on the Causes and Prevention of Violence). The Collection consists of materials dealing with all aspects of violence as well as movements specifically related to the 1960s "(Ban the Bomb," etc). The collection is topically arranged and available for the research team.

VIOLIN

DC —LIBRARY OF CONGRESS, Music Division, Washington, 20540.
Holdings: Cat Mss Maps Pix Slides Microforms
Notes: Incl the Whittall Foundation of Stradivari instruments (3 violins, viola, cello).

VIOLIN, MORIZ

CA —UNIVERSITY OF CALIFORNIA, RIVERSIDE, University Library, 4045 Canyon Crest Dr, Box 5900, Riverside, 92517.
Notes: The Oswald Jonas Memorial Collection holds the musicological mss, letters, biographical materials, and notebooks of Heinrich Schenker and also the papers of the late Oswald Jonas, musicologist and leading authority on the life and work of Schenker. Incl Schenker's diary; correspondence with Anthony van Hoboken, Reinhard Oppel, Moriz Violin, Eugen d'Albert, and Oswald Jonas; the proofs and mss of his published works; printed editions from his library with notes, marginalia, and critical annotations; *Urlinie* tables; and miscellanea. A guide to the collection will be published by the library.

VIOLIN AND PIANO MUSIC—COLLECTIONS

IL —UNIVERSITY OF ILLINOIS, URBANA/CHAMPAIGN, Library, Music Library, Urbana, 61801. William M McClellan, Librn
Holdings: Vols (200,000) Cat Mss Slides Sound Recordings Microforms Books Scores
Budget: ($65,000)
Notes: Introductory, instructive, research and reference materials to support work at graduate level in ethnomusicology,, musicology, music education, performance areas. Special areas incl about 2500 pre-1800 music mss and editions of music on microfilm, 2400 graduate music theses on microfilm, a special collection of 30,000 titles of American vocal sheet music covering the period 1790-1970, the Rafael Joseffy Collection of about 2000 pieces of 19th century piano music (incl performer markings), the Joseph Szigeti Collection (700 items: published music, mss, recordings), mainly violin and piano music by various compposers. Also incl a special collection of 45,000 78 rpm sound recordings (uncat) of classical music and jazz; a collection of 2900 titles from Chicago radio station WGN. Incl orchestrations, a collection of 500,000 items (uncat) from stock of Hunleth Music Store, St Louis, Missouri, mainly early 20th century imprints of songs, wind music, string music, piano, sets of theatre orchestra parts, dance band orchestrations. A separate collection of choral octavos and instrumental parts is maintained, incl 135,000 pieces of choral music, 30,500 orchestral parts, and 5500 wind ensemble parts. Also, music publishers' catalogues (mainly European and American), ca 126 cubic feet, 1860s-1950s.

VIOLIN MUSIC—COLLECTIONS

OH —CLEVELAND PUBLIC LIBRARY, Fine Arts and Special Collections Department, 325 Superior Ave, Cleveland, 44114. Alice N Loranth, Head
Holdings: Vols (21,350) Cat
Notes: Part of the Instrumental Music Collection which incl part sets for chamber music and orchestral music indexed by instrumentation or form. Collected works editions of major composers or periods in music. Study scores, piano, violin, organ and other instrumental music.

VIOLINISTS, VIOLONCELLISTS, ETC.

NC —UNIVERSITY OF NORTH CAROLINA, GREENSBORO, Walter Clinton Jackson Library, Special Collections Dept, 1000 Spring Garden St, Greensboro, 27412. Emilie W Mills, Librn
Holdings: Vols (2000) Cat Mss Pix Phonorecords Microforms
Notes: The original collection of over 2000 books, mss, music scores, published and unpublished cello compositions, notes, programs, photographs and related items came from the library of Luigi Silva, cellist, teacher, and musicologist. Special strength is in recital pieces for the cello. The cello music dates from the 18th century and incl Silva's own transcriptions and arrangements for his projected editions of all the Boccherini sonatas, left incomplete at the time of his death in 1961. Silva's own history of cello techniques, also unfinished, is in the collection. Several 18th century cello sonatas were added to the collection by Silva's long-time friend and eminent cellist, Janos Scholz. A published catalog is available.

VIOLONCELLO MUSIC

NC —UNIVERSITY OF NORTH CAROLINA, GREENSBORO, Walter Clinton Jackson Library, Special Collections Dept, 1000 Spring Garden St, Greensboro, 27412. Emilie W Mills, Librn
Holdings: Vols (2000) Cat Mss Pix Phonorecords Microforms
Notes: The original collection of over 2000 books, mss, music scores, published and unpublished cello compositions, notes, programs, photographs and related items came from the library of Luigi Silva, cellist, teacher, and musicologist. Special strength is in recital pieces for the cello. The cello music dates from the 18th century and incl Silva's own transcriptions and arrangements for his projected editions of all the Boccherini sonatas, left incomplete at the time of his death in 1961. Silva's own history of cello techniques, also unfinished, is in the collection. Several 18th century cello sonatas were added to the collection by Silva's long-time friend and eminent cellist, Janos Scholz. A published catalog is available.

VIPERS see Snakes

VIRCHOW, RUDOLF LUDWIG KARL, 1821-1902

KS —UNIVERSITY OF KANSAS MEDICAL CENTER, College of Health Sciences & Hospital, Clendening History of Medicine Library, Rainbow Blvd at 39th, Kansas City, 66103. Robert P Hudson, Chmn/Cur
Holdings: Mss
Notes: Correspondence and mss, 1869-1900. Also, 2 ms boxes (1/2 linear ft). Approx 35 items. Handwritten letters by Virchow to Friedrich Alfred Krupp: Emperor Frederick III's Lord Chamberlain about the laryneal growth removed by Sir Morell Mackenzie from the Emperor: Luigi Palma Di Cesnola, Director of the Metropolitan Museum, New York, regarding gifts made to the museum, etc. Handwritten mss of journal articles which were later published; an autobiography handwritten by Virchow, probably required for his election to some scientific society. A collection of letters written to Virchow from vaious persons, some of great note, incl Curschman, Jaeger, Lancereaux, etc. An official letter to Virchow, from the Ambassador of France to Germany, notifying him that he has been made a Commander of the Legion of Honor. Bookplate: Thor Jager, MD.

VIRGIN BIRTH

OH —UNIVERSITY OF DAYTON, Marian Library, 300 College Park Ave, Dayton, 45469. Rev Theodore Koehler, SM, Dir/Cur
Holdings: Vols (65,000) Cat Mss Pix Slides Phonorecords Audiotapes Filmstrips Microforms
Budget: ($12,000)
Notes: Largest and most comprehensive collections of literature on Virgin Mary in the world. Covers all five centuries of printing. Some 50 languages represented. Incl doctrinal, polemical, popular works, children's books. Catholic and non-Catholic. Especially strong in publications on French shrines (Clugnet collection), on the Immaculate Conception, and materials after 1950. Has Vloberg collection of pictures, ms notes and offprints on Marian iconography. Complete files of major journals in Mariology and partial runs or more than 100 others. Files of 48,000 clippings from domestic and foreign periodicals. 10,000 holy cards from 19th and 20th centuries. 2600 postcard views of shrines. 3000 postcards of Marian art. Philatelic collection of 1000 stamps and 200 first-day cover. 1000 photographs. 300 medals. General reference collection strong inpatristic sources, biblical literature, religious inconography (especially of Eastern Churches), general bibliography, and bibliography of religious orders. Union catalog of Marian holdings in American and others libraries. Library publishes *Marian Library Studies* and *Marian Library* Newsletter. Has had scholors in residence since 1972. Since 1975 recognized as a Pontifical Institute in affiliation with the Marianum in Rome empowered to prepare candidates for pontifical degree with specialization in Marian studies. In 1976 began summer schools in Mariology. History of the Library and description of its holdings in Fackovec, William, S M, "The Marian Library of the University of Dayton," in *Marian Library Studies* (New Series) vol 1 (1969), pp 9-76.

VIRGIN ISLANDS

CT —YALE UNIVERSITY, Sterling Memorial Library, Latin American Collections, New Haven, 06520. Lee H Williams Jr, Cur
Holdings: Vols (300,000) Cat Maps Pix Slides Phonorecords 16mm Films Filmstrips
See also entry under Latin America
DC —GEORGETOWN UNIVERSITY, Library, Special Collections Div, 37 & O Sts NW, Washington, 20057. George M Barringer, Special Collections Librn; Nicholas B Sheetz, Mss Librn
Holdings: Cat
Notes: Papers of Chauncey Brewster Chapman, Jr (1919-1980), attorney, from his early legal career in private practice and his years in the Department of Interior where he served as solicitor for territories from 1967-1979. The bulk of the papers concerns judicial and legal matters in regard to territories outside the United States, as well as internal departmental affairs. Of particular interest is material concerning Samoa from 1969-1980.
MA —HARVARD UNIVERSITY LIBRARY, Law School Library, Langdell Hall, Cambridge, 02138. Harry S Martin III, Librn
Notes: Personal and legal papers of William Henry Hastic, Governor of the Virgin Islands, Judge of the US Court of Appeals, Third Circuit, who died in April 1976. Much on his involvement in civic and antidiscrimination cases.
VI —VIRGIN ISLANDS BUREAU OF LIBRARIES, MUSEUMS & ARCHAEOLOGICAL SERVICES, Enid M Baa Library & Archives, Von Scholten Collection, PO Box 390, Saint Thomas, 00801. June A V Lindqvist, Cur
Holdings: Vols (13,000) Cat Mss Maps Pix Microforms
Notes: Caribbeana, with emphasis on the Virgin Islands. Library collects in all aspects of Virgin Islands life, incl natural and cultural history. Collection is especially strong in Danish West Indian and Virgin Islards newspapers and in dissertations on Caribbean subjects. Library is a full depository for USVI documents. Auxiliary collections are located in the Bureau's libraries in St Croix and St John.

VIRGIN MARY see Mary, Virgin

VIRGINIA

NC —DUKE UNIVERSITY, William R Perkins Library, Durham, 27706. Elvin E Strowd, University Librn
Notes: The Flowers Collection of Southern Americana currently consists of 4,300,500 items. Additions are ongoing. Included in this collection are several types of materials, which are housed in appropriate sections of the library. The various types of materials are: manuscripts, books, pamphlets, maps,

VIRGINIA (cont.)

music, broadsides, newspapers, photographs, engravings, prints and memorabilia.

VIRGINIA—GENEALOGY

FL —ORLANDO PUBLIC LIBRARY, Local History & Genealogy Dept, 100 Block of Central Ave, Orlando, 32806. Eileen B Willis, Librn
Holdings: Vols 11,000 Cat Maps Microforms
Budget: $8000
Notes: Strong collection in local genealogy materials on Mass, NY, Va, Ga, and Florida. Contains exceptional holdings on all New England States, Penn, and NJ.
See also entry under Genealogy - Collections.

KY —BOWLING GREEN PUBLIC LIBRARY, 1225 State St, Bowling Green, 42101. Karen A Turner, Dir
Holdings: Vols 176 Cat

LA —R W NORTON ART GALLERY, Library, 4747 Creswell Ave, Shreveport, 71106. Jerry M Bloomer, Librn
Holdings: Vols 550 Cat
Notes: Incl the James M Owens memorial Collection of early American with emphasis on Virginia state and local histories, and genealogies.

VA —EASTERN SHORE PUBLIC LIBRARY, Accomac, 23301. Brooks M Barnes, Librn
Holdings: Vols 700 Cat Mss Maps Pix Slides Microforms
Notes: Separate author catalog. A selected, annotated bibliography for the colonial period has been prepared. An indexing project for local newspapers from 1881 is in progress.

VA —ALEXANDRIA LIBRARY, Lloyd House, 220 N Washington St, Alexandria, 22314. Allan Robbins, Librn
Holdings: Vols 5200 Cat Mss Maps Pix Slides Audiotapes Microforms
Budget: $500
Notes: Virginia history, especially local history of northern Virginia area, incl a number of rare pamphlets, etc, covering Alexandria City history. Newspaper clippings, slides, oral tapes and some primary source material.

VA —CHESAPEAKE PUBLIC LIBRARY, Jody C Treadway, William McGehee Wallace Memorial Collection, Civic Center, 300 Cedar Rd, Chesapeake, 23320.
Holdings: Vols (3400) Cat Mss Maps Pix Microforms
Notes: This collection is the property of the Norfolk County Historical Society. Partially cataloged.

VA —EASTERN MENNONITE COLLEGE, Menno Simons Historical Library & Archives, Harrisonburg, 22801. Grace Showalter, Librn
Holdings: Vols (15,318) Cat Mss Maps Pix Microforms VF
Budget: ($30,500)
Notes: Anabaptist, Mennonite, and local history and genealogy.

VA —NORFOLK PUBLIC LIBRARY, Sargeant Memorial Room, 301 E City Hall Ave, Norfolk, 23510. Lucile B Portlock, Cur
Holdings: Vols (12,500) Cat Mss Maps Pix Microforms
Budget: $1500
Notes: Incl microfilms (2128) of local newspapers, 1736-1962. Incl 3000 picutres, indexed; chronological index to maps. Separate catalog. Also incl published and unpublished genealogies; county records; indexes to family names; and census records on microfilm of all counties of Virginia and North Carolina, 1790-1880.

VA —VIRGINIA STATE LIBRARY, 12 & Capitol Sts, Richmond, 23219.
Holdings: Vols 6250 Cat Mss Pix

VA —ROANOKE CITY PUBLIC LIBRARY, Virginia Room, 706 S Jefferson St, Roanoke, 24011. Alice Carol Tuckwiller, Librn
Holdings: Vols 12,000 Cat
Notes: Collection contains pamphlets, newspapers, postcards, mss, maps, pix, microforms, vertical files. Strong in genealogical materials. There is a separate Virginia catalog.

VIRGINIA—HISTORY

DC —DISTRICT OF COLUMBIA PUBLIC LIBRARY, Martin Luther King Memorial Library, Washingtoniana Div and Washington Star Collection, 901 G St NW, Washington, 20001. Roxanna Deane, Chief
Holdings: Vols (50,000) Cat Maps Pix Slides
Budget: ($5500)
Notes: Washington Star Collection was the working morgue and photo library of the Washington Star newspaper. There are an estimated one million photos dating from about 1930 to 1981. These are arranged by subject and personal name and cover international, national and local news. There are approx 13 million news clippings arranged by subject and personal name for the same period. Each Star article was clipped and placed in as many different files as was necessary to cover all topics or personal names mentioned in the article. Reproductions from the photo collection may be purchased.

DC —GEORGETOWN UNIVERSITY, Library, Special Collections Div, 37 & O Sts NW, Washington, 20057. George M Barringer, Special Collections Librn; Nicholas B Sheetz, Mss Librn
Holdings: Mss Cat
Notes: Correspondence and documents constituting the papers of Col John Fitzgerald. Fitzgerald, a colonial merchant, served as a member of the Committee of Safety in Alexandria, Virginia, and received his military rank during the Revolution. After the war he became mayor and customs collector of Alexandria. In 1799, while serving in the latter capacity, Fitzgerald was held responsible for the sum of forty thousand dollars discovered missing from the treasury. Apart from miscellaneous correspondence and deeds, the papers primarily concern this incident. Incl is correspondence from Oliver Wolcott, Secretary of the Treasury.

DC —GEORGETOWN UNIVERSITY, Library, Special Collections Div, 37 & O Sts NW, Washington, 20057. George M Barringer, Special Collections Librn; Nicholas B Sheetz, Mss Librn
Holdings: Mss Cat Pix
Notes: The personal papers of Richard T Crane (1882-1938), private secretary to Robert Lansing, 1915-1919; first American ambassador to Czechoslovakia, 1919-1921; and owner of the Westover Plantation in Virginia, 1921-1938. The papers - divided into three series, State Department, Prague and Westover - contain correspondence, memoranda, reports, diaries, documents, mss, printed material, and newspaper clippings. Correspondence incl letters from Robert Lansing, Charles Crane, Woodrow Wilson, Franklin Roosevelt, T G Masaryk, Jan Masaryk, Eduard Benes, Edward House, Herbert Hoover, Hugh Gibson, Joseph C Grew, Allan Dulles, and John Foster Dulles, among others.

KY —BOWLING GREEN PUBLIC LIBRARY, 1225 State St, Bowling Green, 42101. Karen A Turner, Dir
Holdings: Vols 51 Cat

LA —R W NORTON ART GALLERY, Library, 4747 Creswell Ave, Shreveport, 71106. Jerry M Bloomer, Librn
Holdings: Vols 550 Cat
Notes: Incl the James M Owens memorial Collection of early American with emphasis on Virginia state & local histories, and genealogies.

NC —DUKE UNIVERSITY, William R Perkins Library, Manuscript Dept, Durham, 27706. Ellen Gartrell, Cur of Mss
Holdings: Cat Mss
Notes: Especially strong for North Carolina, South Carolina, Virginia, Georgia, and Alabama. 18th-20th centuries. See Guide to the Cataloged Collections of the Manuscript Department of the William R Perkins Library (1980, ed by Richard C Davis and Linda A Miller).

PA —FRIENDS HISTORICAL LIBRARY OF SWARTHMORE COLLEGE, Swarthmore, 19081. J William Frost, Dir
Holdings: Vols (35,000) Cat Mss Pix Microforms
Notes: Library's collection contain information on the history and doctrine of the Society of Friends, Quaker contributions to literature, science, business, education, and government, plus their reform efforts in peace, Indian rights, women's rights, and abolition of slavery. As an official depository of the records of the Baltimore Yearly Meetings, the library holds, either in the original manuscript or on microfilm, records of Friends meetings in Virginia. Among the over 250 mss collections are several which concern Virginia Quaker leaders and Quaker families.

RI —BROWN UNIVERSITY, John Hay Library, 20 Prospect St, Providence, 02912. Mark N Brown, Cur Mss
Holdings: // Mss
Notes: Solomon Drowne papers. He was a physician and Professor of Botany at Brown, Class of 1773. Mss incl accounts, invoices, receipts; originals and copies of prose and poetry; notes of Dr Drowne; sketches and valentines; political, legal, and military documents; and ships' papers. Subjects incl Colonial and Revolutionary history of Rhode Island and Brown University; medicine and botany 1770-1834; the early history of Morgantown, Virginia; Union, Pennsylvania; and Marietta, Ohio; business and trade in the Colonial period; and the Continental Congress. Correspondence with most persons of importance in his time.

TX —UNIVERSITY OF TEXAS LIBRARIES, General Libraries, Barker Texas History Center, PO Box P, Austin, 78712. Don Carleton, Dir

VA —EASTERN SHORE PUBLIC LIBRARY, Accomac, 23301. Brooks M Barnes, Librn
Holdings: Vols 700 Cat Mss Maps Pix Slides Microforms
Notes: Separate author catalog. A selected, annotated bibliography for the colonial period has been prepared. An indexing project for local newspapers from 1881 is in progress.

VA —ALEXANDRIA LIBRARY, Lloyd House, 220 N Washington St, Alexandria, 22314. Allan Robbins, Librn
Holdings: Vols 5200 Cat Mss Pix Slides Audiotapes Microforms
Budget: $5000
Notes: Virginia history, especially local history of northern Virginia area, incl a number of rare pamphlets, etc, covering Alexandria City history. Newspaper clippings, slides, oral tapes and some primary source material.

VA —ARLINGTON COUNTY LIBRARIES, Virginiana Collection, 1015 N Quincy St, Arlington, 22201. Sara Collins, Librn
Holdings: Vols (6800) Cat Mss Maps Pix Audiotapes Videotapes VF
Notes: Collection incl books, magazines, pamphlets, clippings and maps on Virginia history, especially local history of the northern Virginia area. Incl a number of rare pamphlets and leaflets concerning Arlington County history in the early part of the century, as well as county and state documents on matters of current concern. One feature is the Oral and Video History collection, aimed at collecting personal recollections and programs on Arlington's development and history from all members of the community, including Blacks. A special community archive project is collecting and organizing manuscripts of collections donated by individuals and community groups. Researchers should make an appointment for use of special materials.

VA —VIRGINIA POLYTECHNIC INSTITUTE AND STATE UNIVERSITY LIBRARY, Blacksburg, 24061. Glenn L McMullen, Special Collections Librn
Holdings: Vols (2000) Cat Mss Maps Pix Audiotapes
Notes: Primarily Southwest Virginia materials. Collection incl ca 200 mss, account books and other archival records of nineteenth century area businesses and other mining operations; the extant archival records of several Southwest Virginia railroads, incl the Virginia and Tennessee Railroad and the Norfolk and Western

VIRGINIA—HISTORY (cont.)

Railroad; and papers of historically prominent Southwest Virginians, incl John Apperson, Dr Harvy Black, James P Charlton, W Graham Claytor, Henley Fugate, Clement D Johnston, Germanicus Kent, William Preston, J Hoge Tyler, and William C Wampler. Several oral history collections incl material on Appalachian customs and folklore, particularly in Patrick County.

VA —UNIVERSITY OF VIRGINIA, Alderman Library, Manuscripts Dept, Charlottesville, 22901. Edmund Berkeley Jr, Cur
Holdings: Cat Mss Maps Pix Phonorecords
Notes: Virginia Political Collection (345 linear ft) incl the papers of Virginians who did not serve in elective offices of the United States government, but who were instrumental in the political and legal processes of the Commonwealth of Virginia during the 19th and 20th centuries either as elected or appointed officials, or in private capacities. Guides are available at the Library except as noted; the guides are unpublished. The collection incl papers of the following governors of Virginia: James Barbour, John Stewart Battle, Westmoreland Davis, James Lawson Kemper, William Hodges Mann, and Wilson Cary Nicholas. Members of the General Assembly whose papers are in the collection incl Lloyd Campbell Bird, Armistead Boothe, Edward L Breeden (restricted), John Warren Cooke, John Hannah Daniel, Joseph Hutcheson, Martin Hutchinson, James Harry Michael (restricted),G Fred Switzer. Other papers of note incl those of Allen Caperton Braxton, a delegate to the 1902 Constitutional Convention, Stuart E Brown, Jr, Virginia Democratic campaign worker, Everett Randolph Combs, clerk of the State Senate, Flora Crater, political and civic leader, and Francis Pickens Miller, gubernatorial-senatorial candidate. Also 19th Century Virginia Family Papers Collections, which enable a researcher to obtain an excellent picture of the economic and social interactions on large plantations in Virginia during the 19th century. They are invaluable as research sources in the study of slavery, women's history, economic history, agrarian and political history. Among the more notable collections are the papers of John Hartwell Cocke and the Cocke family, Berkeley family, Joseph Carrington Cabell, Carter family, Watson family, Pocket Plantation,Bruce family, Hubard family, and many others. 100 linear ft of mss.

VA —UNIVERSITY OF VIRGINIA, Alderman Library, Manuscripts Dept, Charlottesville, 22901. Edmund Berkeley Jr, Cur
Holdings: Cat Mss Pix
Notes: Material in over 420 collections documents the history and culture of Afro-Americans incl letters and narratives by slaves and masters, plantation accounts, letters from Liberian immigrants, folklore, literature, the desegregation movement in Virginia in the 1960s and 1970s and the "massive resistance" of Virginia political leaders. Michael F Plunkett (ed) *A Guide to Materials on the History, Literature, and Culture of Afro-Americans in the Manuscripts Department, University of Virginia Library.*

VA —UNIVERSITY OF VIRGINIA, Alderman Library, Tracy W McGregor Collection, Charlottesville, 22901. William H Runge, Cur
Holdings: Vols 18,000 Cat Mss Maps Pix Microforms
Notes: Library spans 15th-20th century, concentrating on Southeastern American history. Rare collection of books on early exploration and travel; foundation of the Virginia Colony; Civil War. Books in foreign languages. Collection cataloged by date of publication. Special shelflist. Published descriptions: William H Runge, "The Tracy W McGregor Library and Its Founder," *The University of Virginia News Letter* vol 39,

no 11, July 15 1963; *Descriptions of the Tracy W McGregor Library, University of Virginia, With Rules for Its Use and a Biographical Sketch of Its Founder.*

VA —CHESAPEAKE PUBLIC LIBRARY, Jody C Treadway, William McGehee Wallace Memorial Collection, Civic Center, 300 Cedar Rd, Chesapeake, 23320.
Holdings: Vols (3400) Cat Mss Maps Pix Microforms VF
Notes: This collection is the propety of the Norfolk County Historical Society. Partially cataloged.

VA —PAMUNKEY REGIONAL LIBRARY, PO Box 119, Hanover, 23069. Fran Freimarck, Dir
Holdings: Vols 690 Cat Maps

VA —EASTERN MENNONITE COLLEGE, Menno Simons Historical Library & Archives, Harrisonburg, 22801. Grace Showalter, Librn
Holdings: Vols (15,318) Cat Mss Maps Pix Microforms Audiotapes VF
Budget: ($30,500)
Notes: Anabaptist, Mennonite, and local history and genealogy.

VA —WASHINGTON AND LEE UNIVERSITY, Library, Lexington, 24450. Maurice Leach, Dir; Richard Oram, Asst Special Collections Librn
Holdings: Vols (25,000) Cat Mss Maps Pix
Notes: Incl over 10,000 ms pieces, the collection emphasizes the life of General Robert E Lee, Virginia, and the Civil War, etc. Pictures from 1870-1930; 8000 glass photographs by Miley.

VA —CENTRAL VIRGINIA COMMUNITY COLLEGE, Library, 3506 Wards Rd, Lynchburg, 24502. John B St Leger, Dir of Library Servs
Holdings: Vols (6000)

VA —BELLE GROVE, INC, Library, PO Box 137, Middletown, 22645. Wynn Lee, Exec Dir
Holdings: Vols (500) Mss
Notes: Belle Grove is a historic property of the National Trust. It maintains no library but has a small collection of manuscript and secondary source materials related to the construction of the house and the family who built it.

VA —NORFOLK PUBLIC LIBRARY, Sargeant Memorial Room, 301 E City Hall Ave, Norfolk, 23510. Lucile B Portlock, Cur
Holdings: Vols (12,500) Cat Mss Maps Pix Microforms
Budget: $1500
Notes: Incl microfilms (2128) of local newspapers. 1736-1962. Incl 3000 pictures, indexed; chronological index to maps. Separate catalog. Also incl published and unpublished genealogies county records; indexes to family names; and census records on microfilm of all counties of Virginia and North Carolina, 1790-1880.

VA —PORTSMOUTH PUBLIC LIBRARY, 601 Court St, Portsmouth, 23704. Dean Burgess, Library Dir
Holdings: Vols 1300 Cat
Notes: Virginia history, with emphasis on Tidewater and Lower Tidewater history. Incl collection of Judge White of Lynnhaven.

VA —RADFORD UNIVERSITY, John Preston McConnell Library, Radford, 24142. Ann Swain, Librn
Holdings: Vols 7500 Cat Mss Maps Pix Slides Audiotapes
Notes: Southwest Virginia, black history, Virginiana and Appalachian books. The collection is built around, and organized with, the University Archives. Incl scrapbooks, clippings, etc.

VA —VIRGINIA STATE LIBRARY, 12 & Capitol Sts, Richmond, 23219.
Holdings: Vols 60,700 Cat Mss Maps Pix Microforms
Notes: Incl archives of Virginia, mainly noncurrent public records, but incl other mss, relating to Virginia and the South. Contains 80,000 bound vols, 27,000,000 ms pieces and 85,000 maps. Partially cataloged.

VA —ROANOKE CITY PUBLIC LIBRARY, Virginia Room, 706 S Jefferson St, Roanoke, 24011. Alice Carol Tuckwiller, Librn
Holdings: Vols 12,000 Cat
Notes: Collection contains pamphlets,

newspapers, postcards, mss, maps, pix, microforms, vertical files. There is a separate Virginia catalog.

VA —VIRGINIA BEACH PUBLIC LIBRARY, Information Services Division, 936 Independence Blvd, Virginia Beach, 23455. Carolyn L Powell, Coordinator
Holdings: Vols 200 Cat Pix
Notes: Local history of Princess Anne County.

VA —WAYNESBORO PUBLIC LIBRARY, 600 S Wayne Ave, Waynesboro, 22980. Dorothy Anne Reinbold, Library Dir
Holdings: Vols 1200 Cat Maps Slides Audiotapes Microforms
Budget: $1600
Notes: Local history of Waynesboro and Augusta County. Partially cataloged. Also, we add about 30-50 vols a year on history with an additional $600-700 worth of materials from the Friends of the Library.

VA —COLLEGE OF WILLIAM AND MARY, Earl Gregg Swem Library, Williamsburg, 23185. Margaret C Cook, Cur of Manuscripts & Rare Books
Holdings: Vols 2000 Cat Mss Maps Pix
Notes: Virginia books and pamphlets through 1870. This collection incl files of 18th and 19th century Virginia newspapers.

VA —COLONIAL WILLIAMSBURG FOUNDATION, Research Center Library, PO Drawer C, Williamsburg, 23187. John E Ingram, Research Archivist
Holdings: Vols (15,000) Cat Mss Maps Pix Microforms
Budget: ($12,000)

VIRGINIA—INDUSTRIES

DE —HAGLEY MUSEUM AND LIBRARY, Eleutherian Mills-Hagley Foundation Inc, PO Box 3630, Greenville, 19807. Richmond D Williams, Dir; Heddy A Richter, Imprints Librn
Notes: Westmoreland Coal Company records (1854-1982; 350 cubic feet) document the history of the nation's oldest bituminous coal mining company which operated in the Connellsville, Pa area (1880-89) and southern West Virginia (1906-56). Penn Virginia Corporation records (1864-1970; 120 cubic feet) document the history of one of Virginia's most significant coal mining companies. Also, Saint Clair Coal Company (1895-1930; 15 cubic feet). Records document the history of an important Schuylkill County, Pa anthracite coal producer. The colleciton incl minute books, financial records and photographs.

VIRGINIA—MAPS

DC —LIBRARY OF CONGRESS, Geography and Map Division, Washington, 20540. John A Wolter, Chief
Notes: The American Map Collection incl 167 works produced between 1750 and 1790 incl copies of *A Map of the Most Inhabited Part of Virginia* by Joshua Fry and Peter Jefferson (1755 and 1775 editions), John Montresor's *A Map of the Province of New York* (1777), William Gerard De Brahm's *A Map of South Carolina and a Part of Georgia* (1757), and *A Plan of the City of Philadelphia* (1776) by Benjamin Easburn.

DC —METROPOLITAN WASHINGTON COUNCIL OF GOVERNMENTS, Map Library, 1875 Eye St NW, Suite 200, Washington, 20006. Susan Kalish, Librn
Holdings: Cat Maps
Notes: 3000 current and retrospective maps covering metropolitan Washington region, incl the District of Columbia; Mongomery and Prince George's counties in Maryland; and Arlington, Fairfax, Prince William and Loudoun counties and the City of Alexandria in Virginia Maps cover land use, community facilities, transportation, topography, statistical units, and socioeconomic information. Record of holdings on computer printout.

VA —GEORGE MASON UNIVERSITY, Fenwick Library, Special Collections Dept, 4400 University Drive, Fairfax, 22030. Ruth Kerns, Public Services Librn
Notes: C Harrison Mann Collection: 18

VIRGINIA—MAPS (cont.)

atlases and 76 single maps primarily from the late 1500s to the late 1800s, incl rare atlases and maps of early Virginia and Maryland, and several foreign regions of the world.

VA —VIRGINIA STATE LIBRARY, 12 & Capitol Sts, Richmond, 23219.
Notes: Incl 250 atlases, 85,000 maps, chiefly of Virginia, but incl Army map service and US Geological Survey maps.

VIRGINIA—PICTURES, ILLUSTRATIONS, ETC.

VA —VIRGINIA STATE LIBRARY, 12 & Capitol Sts, Richmond, 23219.
Holdings: Cat Pix
Notes: Incl 86,960 prints, photographs, etc, chiefly of Virginia, the Civil War, and the Confederacy.

VIRGINIA—POLITICS AND GOVERNMENT

VA —UNIVERSITY OF VIRGINIA, Alderman Library, Manuscripts Dept, Charlottesville, 22901. Edmund Berkeley Jr, Cur
Holdings: Cat Mss Maps Pix Phonorecords
Notes: The collection includes papers of persons prominent in the field of journalism chiefly in Virginia, but also nationally in some instances. The papers of the following persons are included: Walter Scott Copeland, editor and publisher of the Newport News *Daily Press and Times - Herald*; Virginia Dabney, editor of the Richmond *Times-Dispatch*; Douglas Southall Freeman, editor of the Richmond *News-Leader*; Thomas Andrew Hanes, editor of the Norfolk *Ledger-Star*; Louis I Jaffe, editor of the Norfolk *Virginia Pilot*; James J Kilpatrick, editor of the Richmond *News-Leader*, and currently a print and broadcast columist; Philip Lightfoot Scruggs, editor of the Lynchburg, Virginia, *Daily Advance*; and Louis Spilman, publisher of the Waynesboro, Virginia, *New-Virginian*. 130 linear ft. 19th Century Virginia Family Papers Collections enable a researcher toobtain an excellent picture of the economic and social interactions on large plantations in Virginia during the 19th century. They are invaluable as research sources in the study of slavery, women's history, economic history, agrarian and political history.
See also entries under Agriculture - History; Authors, Virginia

VA —UNIVERSITY OF VIRGINIA, Alderman Library, Manuscripts Dept, Charlottesville, 22901. Edmund Berkeley Jr, Cur
Holdings: Cat Mss Pix
Notes: Material in over 420 collections documents the history and culture of Afro-Americans incl letters and narratives by slaves and masters, plantation accounts, letters from Liberian immigrants, folklore, literature, the desegregation movement in Virginia in the 1960s and 1970s and the "massive resistance" of Virginia political leaders. Michael F Plunkett (ed) *A Guide to Materials on the History, Literature, and Culture of Afro-Americans in the Manuscripts Department, University of Virginia Library.*

VA —COLLEGE OF WILLIAM AND MARY, Earl Gregg Swem Library, Williamsburg, 23185. Margaret C Cook, Cur of Manuscripts & Rare Books
Holdings: Vols 1500 Cat Mss
Notes: Tucker-Coleman Papers (1675-1956); Family, literary, and business papers of the Tucker Family, particularly St George Tucker (1752-1827) and Nathaniel Beverley Tucker (1784-1851). This collection, which incl 600 Jefferson items, is particularly important for the study of Virginia social, economic, and political history during the period 1770-1850. Also, 30,000 ms items.

VIRGINIA—RELIGIOUS LIFE AND CUSTOMS

VA —UNIVERSITY OF VIRGINIA, Alderman Library, Manuscripts Dept,

Charlottesville, 22901. Edmund Berkeley Jr, Cur
Holdings: Cat Mss Pix
Notes: Virginia Folklore Collection (23,000 items) incl the following collection: Virginia WPA Folklore Files, compiled ca 1936-1943, under US Works Project Administration, ca 800 items. Black and white folklore and folk music collected by filed workers from informants throughout Virginia. Incl ms reports, phonorecords. Described in Rosenberg, Bruce A (comp), *The Folksongs of Virginia: A Checklist of the WPA Holdings in the Alderman Library, University of Virginia* (Charlottesville: University Press of Virginia, 1969); also, typescript and computer printed guides; Charles L Perdue, Jr, and others (comps), *The White Folklore of the Virginia WPA Files A Checklist...* (Charlottesville, 1973); Thomas Barden and others (comps), *Afro-American Folklore of the WPA Folklore Files in the Alderman Library...*(Charlottesville, 1973). The collections also incl church records and clergymen's papers from several denominations particularly those of Frederick W Neve, archdeacon of the Blue Ridge, an Episcopal mission organizer.

VA —VIRGINIA UNION UNIVERSITY, William J Clark Library, 1500 N Lombardy St, Richmond, 23220. Verdelle V Bradley, Librn
Holdings: Vols 9905 Cat Pix Slides Phonorecords Audiotapes Filmstrips Microforms
Notes: Incl 1369 microforms. Special collection on slavery is not cataloged; oral history tapes of Black Virginians, especially in religious contexts.

VIRGINIA—SOCIAL LIFE AND CUSTOMS

VA —UNIVERSITY OF VIRGINIA, Alderman Library, Manuscripts Dept, Charlottesville, 22901. Edmund Berkeley Jr, Cur
Holdings: Mss Pix Audiotapes
Notes: The collection includes papers of persons prominent in the field of journalism chiefly in Virginia, but also nationally in some instances. The papers of the following persons are included: Virginius Dabney, editor of the Richmond *Times-Dispatch* (access restricted, apply to the curator of manuscripts); Douglas Southall Freeman, editor of the Richmond *New-Leader;* Thomas Andrew Hanes, editor of the Norfolk *Ledger-Star;* Louis I Jaffe, editor of the Norfolk *Virginian-Pilot;* James J Kilpatirck, editor of the Richmond *News-Leader,* and currently a print and broadcast columnist; Philip Lightfoot Scruggs, editor of the Lynchburg, Virginia, *Daily Advance;* and Louis Spilman, publisher of the Waynesboro, Virginia, *News-Virginian.* 125 linear ft.

VIRGINIA AND TRUCKEE RAILROAD

NV —UNIVERSITY OF NEVADA, RENO, University Library, Special Collections Dept, Reno, 89557. Robert E Blesse, Head
Holdings: Vols (150) Cat Mss Pix Maps
Notes: Includes 370 cu ft manuscripts, 2000 photographs. Major collection include papers of Nevada railroad companies Virginia and Truckee, Carson and Colorado, Eureka and Palisade, and Nevada Copper Belt. Materials are collected which deal with the history and development of railroads within Nevada and those which have run through the state.

VIRGINIA AUTHORS see Authors, Virginia

VIRGINIA BLUE RIDGE RAILWAY

NY —CORNELL UNIVERSITY LIBRARIES, Collection of Regional History, Dept of Manuscripts and Univ Archives, Ithaca, 14853.
Notes: Incl records, 1913-61; extensive administrative, fiscal, and legal files, and business correspondence.

VIRGINIA COMPANY OF LONDON

DC —LIBRARY OF CONGRESS, Manuscript Division, Washington, 20540. John C Broderick, Chief
Holdings: Cat Mss Pix
Notes: Mss, papers, records, etc.

VIRGINIA MANUSCRIPTS see Manuscripts, Virginia

VIROLOGY

DC —AMERICAN SOCIETY FOR MICROBIOLOGY, Archives, 1913 I Street NW, Washington, 20006. Donald Shay, Archivist
Notes: Collection of American and foreign books (texts, monographs, laboratory manuals, etc) on microbiology. 10,000 reprints are mostly old or connected to a past officer or award recipient. 150 theses incl American and foreign. Reprint collection incl Pratt collection on antibiotics, and C W Dodge collection on medical mycology. Ownership of all titles resides with the Society; Special Collections of University of Maryland Baltimore County serves as repository. The Society address is in Washington.

IA —IOWA STATE UNIVERSITY, Library, Ames, 50011. Warren B Kuhn, Dean of Library Services
Holdings: Cat
Notes: Extensive serial holdings.

MA —UNIVERSITY OF MASSACHUSETTS AT AMHERST, Library, Amherst, 01003. Siegfried Feller, Assoc Dir for Collection Development
Holdings: Cat
Notes: Microbiology, incl bacteriology, immunology, virology, and pathology.

MI —WARNER-LAMBERT/PARKE-DAVIS, Research Library, 2800 Plymouth Rd, Ann Arbor, 48106. Katherine C Owen, Mgr, Library Services
Holdings: Vols (27,977) Cat

NJ —RUTGERS, THE STATE UNIVERSITY OF NEW JERSEY, Waksman Institute of Microbiology, Library, PO Box 759, Piscataway, 08854. Helen Hoffman, Librn
Holdings: Vols (17,000) Cat
Budget: ($40,000)
Notes: Primarily concerned with basic research and applied microbiology. Little emphasis on clinical microbiology.

NY —COLD SPRING HARBOR LABORATORY, Library, PO Box 100, Cold Spring Harbor, 11724. Susan Gensel, Library Dir; Genemary Falvey, Librn
Holdings: Vols (30,000)
Budget: ($103,500)
Notes: The highly technical collection is comprised of 20,000 serial vols and 10,000 monographs. The library receives 500 current serial titles. Subjects covered incl molecular and cellular biology, virology, biochemistry, microbiology, oncology, neurobiology, biological risk assessment and genetic engineering/biotechnology. Special collections in eugenics and genetics are primarily historical dealing with the development of genetics in the US which had its beginnings here.

NY —US DEPT OF AGRICULTURE, Agriculture Research Service, Plum Island Animal Disease Laboratory, PO Box 848, Greenport, 11944. Stephen Perlman, Librn
Holdings: Vols (15,000) Cat Pix Slides Microforms
Budget: ($37,000)

OH —CHRIST HOSPITAL INSTITUTE OF MEDICAL RESEARCH, Research Library, 2141 Auburn Ave, Cincinnati, 45219. Lisa L McCormick, Research Librn
Holdings: Vols 16,000
Budget: $36,000

ON —ONTARIO MINISTRY OF HEALTH, Laboratory Services Branch, Library, Box 9000, Terminal A, Toronto, M5W 1R5, Can. Doris A Standing, Librn
Holdings: Vols (4000) Cat
Budget: ($50,000)
Notes: Medical laboratory technology and

VIROLOGY (cont.)

related subjects: microbiology; environmental bacteriology (limited to testing of milk, food and water for bacterial quality, etc); biological chemistry (clinical); mycology; parasitology; virology; immunology; serology; automated laboratory techniques; biohazard control.

VIRUS DISEASES OF PLANTS

OH —OHIO AGRICULTURAL RESEARCH & DEVELOPMENT CENTER, Dept of Plant Pathology, Madison Ave, Wooster, 44691. Richard M Ritter
Holdings: Vols 2000 Papers Journal Reprints
Notes: Virus dieases of corn. "Maize Virue Information Service."

VIRUSES

MA —UNIVERSITY OF MASSACHUSETTS AT AMHERST, Library, Amherst, 01003. Siegfried Feller, Assoc Dir for Collection Development
Holdings: Cat
Notes: Microbiology, incl bacteriology, immunology, virology, and pathology.

MI —WARNER-LAMBERT/PARKE-DAVIS, Research Library, 2800 Plymouth Rd, Ann Arbor, 48106. Katherine C Owen, Mgr, Library Services
Holdings: Vols (27,977) Cat

VISCERAL LEARNING see Biofeedback Training

VISCHER, EDWARD, 1808-1878

CA —CLAREMONT COLLEGES, Honnold Library, Ninth & Dartmouth, Claremont, 91711. Tania Rizzo, Special Collections Dept Head
Holdings: Vols 20 Cat Mss Pix
Notes: Several versions of Vischer's *Pictorial of California;* his *Sketches of Washoe, The Mission Era,* etc. Also 2 document boxes containing 30 original sketches and watercolors, numerous mounted photographs of Vischer's drawings, and family photographs, some published in Jeanne Van Nostrand's, *Edward Vischer's Drawings of the California Missions 1861-1878* (San Francisco, 1982).

VISIBILITY

MI —UNIVERSITY OF MICHIGAN, Transportation Research Institute, Library, 2901 Baxter Rd, Ann Arbor, 48109. Ann C Grimm, Librn
Holdings: Vols (57,000) Cat Mss Maps
Budget: ($25,000)
Notes: Special emphasis on accident investigation and data analysis, vehicle dynamics, biomechanical aspects of trauma, vision and visibility, alcohol and driving.

VISION

CA —UNIVERSITY OF CALIFORNIA, BERKELEY, General Library, Optometry Library, 490 Minor Hall, Berkeley, 94720. Alison Howard, Librn
Holdings: Vols (8000) Cat Pix Microforms
Budget: ($13,500)
Notes: Incl 350 microfiches.

CA —SOUTHERN CALIFORNIA COLLEGE OF OPTOMETRY, 2001 Associated Rd, Fullerton, 92631. Pat Carlson, Librn
Holdings: Vols (10,000) Cat Mss Pix Slides Microforms
Notes: Collection deals with vision and all that pertains to training optomerists. Core of the collection leans heavily towards optometry rest of collection deals with ophthalmology and related fields.

CT —YALE MEDICAL LIBRARY, 333 Cedar St, New Haven, 06510.
Notes: A special subject emphasis.

FL —UNIVERSITY OF MIAMI, School of Medicine, Louis Calder Memorial Library, PO Box 520875, Miami, 33152. Henry L Lemkau, Jr, Dir
Holdings: Vols (127,843) Cat Mss Maps Pix Slides Phonorecords Audiotapes Videotapes 16mm Films Filmstrips Microforms
Budget: ($915,000)
Notes: Ophthalmology Branch Library of 5231 vols incl in total count; University of Miami School of Medicine dissertations; 209 medical medallions; physicians' bookplates; postage stamps with medical themes.

IL —ILLINOIS COLLEGE OF OPTOMETRY, Carl F Shepard Memorial Library, 3241 S Michigan Ave, Chicago, 60616. Kevin K Wah, Dir of Library and Instructional Services
Holdings: Vols (13,000) Cat Slides Phonorecords Audiotapes Videotapes 16mm Films Filmstrips Microforms
Budget: ($25,000)
Notes: Research and teaching collection on every aspect of the eye and vision and their disorders, excl surgery. Incl historical and current materials. Library participates in Midwest Health Sciences Library Network and ILLINET.

IN —INDIANA UNIVERSITY, Optometry Branch Library, Bloomington, 47405. Roger Deckman, Head; Elizabeth Egan, Branch Librn
Holdings: Vols (11,000) Cat Slides Microforms
Budget:
Notes: Incl all aspects of vision: anatomy, physiology, pathology of the eye, neurophysiology, perception, colorimetry, illlumination, safety, etc. Interlibrary loans through Main Library, Indiana University, Bloomington.

MA —NEW ENGLAND COLLEGE OF OPTOMETRY, Library, 420 Beacon St, Boston, 02115. F Eleanor Warner, Librn
Holdings: Vols (7500) Cat Mss Slides Phonorecords Audiotapes Videotapes 16mm Films Microforms
Budget: ($30,000)
Notes: Acquisitions in optometry and ophthalmology are comprehensive; they are selective in areas of surgery and the therapeutic use of drugs. Collection incl 75 slide/tape programs; 75 videotapes; 11 VF drawers of pamphlets and reprints; 16 units of realia; 275 periodical subscriptions. Publishes periodicals holdings list, audiovisual holdings list and an acquisitions list. Open to the public for reference use.

MI —UNIVERSITY OF MICHIGAN, Transportation Research Institute, Library, 2901 Baxter Rd, Ann Arbor, 48109. Ann C Grimm, Librn
Holdings: Vols (57,000) Cat Mss Maps
Budget: ($25,000)
Notes: Special emphasis on accident investigation and data analysis, vehicle dynamics, biomechanical aspects of trauma, vision and visibility, alcohol and driving.

MO —INTERNATIONAL LIBRARY, ARCHIVES AND MUSEUM OF OPTOMETRY, 243 N Lindbergh, Saint Louis, 63141. Maria Dablemont, Librn
Holdings: Vols (12,000) Cat Mss Pix Slides Phonorecords Audiotapes Videotapes 16mm Films Filmstrips
Notes: Established to collect, preserve, and make available for researchers materials related to optometry and the visual sciences; the oldest special library of vision science in this country, serving the public worldwide with reference services and materials. The archives contain documents pertaining to the history of optometry and the history of the American Optometric Association. In the museum are found antique eyeglasses and optical instruments as well as artifacts from the history of the optometric profession and items associated with its leaders.

NY —NATIONAL SOCIETY FOR THE PREVENTION OF BLINDNESS, Conrad Berens Library, 79 Madison Ave, New York, 10016. Dede Silverston, Librn
Holdings: Vols (3000) Cat
Notes: Includes complete and up-to-date ophthalmology collection. Current vertical file of 21 drawers on phases of eye care.

NY —STATE UNIVERSITY OF NEW YORK, State College of Optometry, Harold Kohn Vision Science Library, 100 E 24 St, New York, 10010. Margaret S Lewis, Librn
Holdings: Vols (23,000) Cat Audiotapes Microforms
Notes: All subjects related to visual disabilities; much on vision disorders among children.

NY —MASONIC MEDICAL RESEARCH LIBRARY, 2150 Bleecker St, Utica, 13501. Irma A Tuttle, Librn
Holdings: Vols (2000) Cat Slides Microforms
Notes: Biochemical gerontology collection represents 10 percent of total holdings in basic medical research fields of physiology, pharmacology, vision and circulation. Incl 16,000 periodicals.

OR —PACIFIC UNIVERSITY LIBRARY, Forest Grove, 97116. Laurel Gregory, Science/Optometry Librn
Holdings: Vols (133,000) Cat Slides Microforms
Budget: ($49,000)

OR —OREGON STATE SCHOOL FOR THE BLIND, Library, 700 Church St SE, Salem, 97310. Delphie Schuberg, Librn
Holdings: Vols 200 cat
Notes: Professional materials related to visually and multiply handicapped children.

VISIONS

RI —BROWN UNIVERSITY, John Hay Library, 20 Prospect St, Providence, 02912. Mark N Brown, Cur Mss
Holdings: Vols (900) // Mss
Notes: John William Graham Collection of Literature of Psychic Science--350 predominantly late 19th and early 20th century books dealing with alchemy, black magic, dreams, demonology, church history, mysticism, mediumship, physical and somatic types of psychic experience. Collection described in *Index to Psychic Science* compiled by S R Morgan (Swathmore, 1950). Also, the Damon Collection of Occult and Visionary Literature--550 vols devoted to the development of western mysticism with particular emphasis on American and British thought, incl texts on alchemy, black magic, esoteric church history, dream interpretations, mysticism, witchcraft, the Kabbalah, and visionary testaments and manifestations of all types printed during the 16th to 20th centuries; and the Samuel Wyllys Papers--125 mss, transcripts, and photocopies of legal and government papers relating to Indianaffairs, colonial wars, civil and criminal cases, and the witchcraft trials of 1692-1693. Partially cataloged.

VISITING CARDS

†NY —COLUMBIA UNIVERSITY LIBRARIES, Butler Library, Rare Book and Manuscript Library, 535 W 114 St, New York, 10027.

VISITING NURSE ASSOCIATION

MA —SIMMONS COLLEGE ARCHIVES, 300 The Fenway, Boston, 02115. Megan Sniffin-Marinoff, College Archivist
Notes: Archives of the Simmons College School of Public Health Nursing (later reorganized into the School of Nursing) cover the years 1902-1970. Important correspondents in the collection incl M Adelaide Nutting, Mary Beard, Isabel Stewart, and Anne Hervey Strong, etc. Incl Strong's records of activity with regard to nursing education in the National Organization for Public Health Nursing, 1918-22. 1000 linear feet in institution, incl special collections nursing and photographs, nursing.

VISSON, ANDRE

DC —GEORGETOWN UNIVERSITY, Library, Special Collections Div, 37 & O Sts NW, Washington, 20057. George M Barringer, Special Collections Librn; Nicholas B Sheetz, Mss Librn
Holdings: Mss Cat
Notes: The papers of Andre Visson, journalist and writer about American-European relations from the beginning of World War II through the Cold War years.

VISTA

DC —ACTION, Photo Library, 806
Connecticut Ave NW, Washington, 20525.
Holdings: Pix Slides
Notes: Volunteer photos for ACTION,
VISTA, and older Americans programs. 15,
000 photographs.

VISUAL ARTS

CA —CRAFT AND FOLK ART MUSEUM,
Library, 5814 Wilshire Blvd, Los Angeles,
90036. Joan M Benedetti, Museum Librn
Holdings: Vols (2000) Slides VF
Notes: Incl 2000 books; 70 journal
subscriptions; artists' biographical files: 6 file
drawers; clipping files: 8 file drawers; 20,000
slides. Representation of the material culture
of all people, traditional and contemporary
expressions. Incl visual and printed
information on ethnic, traditional, popular,
decorative, idiosyncratic, and contemporary
crafts as well as vernacular architecture,
handmade houses, and design. Information
about and for professional artists on health
hazards, conservation, and career
management. Anthropological and art
historical works; exhibition catalogues; slides,
photographs, audiocassettes; clipping and
pamphlet files. Contemporary Slide Registry
of Craftspeople and extensive biographical
files of contemporary craft artists.
Information and referral files of craft related
galleries, shops, festivals, organizations, etc.
CA —SAN FRANCISCO ART INSTITUTE,
Anne Bremer Memorial Library, 800
Chestnut St, San Francisco, 94133. Jeff
Gunderson, Librn
Holdings: Vols (23,114) Cat Pix Slides
Audiotapes 16mm Films Microforms
Budget: ($15,000)
CT —YALE UNIVERSITY, Beinecke Rare
Book & Manuscript Library, Osborn
Collection, New Haven, 06520. Stephen R
Parks, Cur
Holdings: Mss
DC —NATIONAL ENDOWMENT FOR
THE ARTS, Library, 1100 Pen Ave NW,
Rm 213, Washington, 20506. Christine
Morrison, Arts Librn
Holdings: Vols (6000) Cat
Notes: Incl arts and education and public
policy in the arts.
IL —CHICAGO PUBLIC LIBRARY, Art
Section, Fine Arts Division, 78 E
Washington St, Chicago, 60602. Rosalinda I
Hack, Fine Arts Division Chief; Yvonne S
Brown, Head, Art Section
Holdings: Vols 42,000
Notes: Reference and circulating collection
of books, periodicals, exhibition catalogs,
dissertations, picture collections, and
microforms on all aspects of the visual arts.
Major concentration of art history, especially
European, with concentration on 19th and
20th century art movements and artists. We
attempt to represent the works of recognized
artists past and present. The Decorative Arts
are well represented especially in the areas
of antiques, interior decoration, and
handicrafts. The collection is supplemented
by a strong periodical collection, consisting
of 330 current English and Foreign
subscriptions, the majority of these titles we
bind, as well as strong bound retrospective
collections. The visual arts is supported by a
clipping File on Chicago Artists, a current
exhibition catalogs collection, as well as by
the microfilm collections of the *Chicago Art
Institute Scrapbooks*, the *Scrapbook on Art,
Artists*, and the *Index of American Design*.
MI —MICHIGAN STATE UNIVERSITY, Art
Library, East Lansing, 48824. Shirlee A
Studt, Librn
Holdings: Vols (45,000) Cat
Notes: The Illuminated Manuscript
Facsimile Collection includes examples of
religious and secular works from the earliest
codex to the age of printing. It has particular
strengths in Carolingian, Ottonian, French
Gothic and works from the British Isles. The
facsimile collection is strengthened by
related research materials (biographical
material, critical studies, etc) The facsimile

collection and related materials are part of a
45,000 volume separately housed and staffed
collection on the visual and decorative arts
(including photography) serving the
curricular and research needs of the
University community. A guide to full
facsimiles in the collection is available in the
Art Library and in the Special Collections
division. A strong collection of architectural
history.
†NY —NEIGHBORHOOD PLAYHOUSE
SCHOOL OF THE THEATRE, Irene
Lewisohn Library, 340 E 54 St, New York,
10022. Alice G Owen, Librn
Holdings: Vols
NY —VISUAL STUDIES WORKSHOP,
Research Center, 31 Prince St, Rochester,
14607. Linn Underhill, Coordr; Robert
Bretz, Librn
Holdings: Vols (8000) Cat Pix Slides
Audiotapes Videotapes
Notes: Strong emphasis on photography
(over 1,000,000 pictures) and the
photograhic arts in many subject areas incl
in this volume. Heavy emphasis on early
photographic processes and collections of
examples of them. Also collections of
individual photographers' works.
TX —EL PASO PUBLIC LIBRARY,
Southwest Collection, 501 N Oregon, El
Paso, 79901. Mary A Sarber, Head
Holdings: Vols (7000) Cat Pix
Budget: ($6000)
Notes: Emphasis on art and artists on the
Southwest, particularly Tom Lea, Jr, and
Southwestern Indian arts and crafts 36
drawers of pictures. See Hinshaw, Glennis,
and Lisabeth Lovelace, *A Bibliography of
Writings and Illustrations by Tom Lea* (El
Paso Public Library Association, 1971).

VISUAL PERCEPTION

NY —STATE UNIVERSITY OF NEW
YORK, State College of Optometry, Harold
Kohn Vision Science Library, 100 E 24 St,
New York, 10010. Margaret S Lewis, Librn
Holdings: Vols (23,000) Cat Audiotapes
Microforms
Notes: All subjects related to visual
disabilities; much on vision disorders among
children.

VITAL RECORDS see Registers of Births, Etc.

VITAL STATISTICS

CA —UNIVERSITY OF CALIFORNIA,
BERKELEY, Life Sciences Libraries, Public
Health Library, 42 Earl Warren Hall,
Berkeley, 94720. Thomas J Alexander, Librn
Holdings: Vols (75,000) Cat Microforms
Notes: Research collection covering all
aspects of public health. Health Department
annual reports from all 50 states are
acquired, as well as such reports from all
California health units and from major US
cities. Serial publications issued by Health
Departments in the 13 western states are
being received.
CA —LOS ANGELES PUBLIC LIBRARY,
Social Sciences Dept, 630 W Fifth St, Los
Angeles, 90071. Marilyn C Wherley,
Principal Librn
Holdings: Vols 800 Cat Maps
Budget: ($150,000)
Notes: Nearly complete set of US Census,
mainly population and housing statistics,
current reports, from 1790. Depository
(selective) since separate catalog. Continuous
updating of standard sources.
DC —US BUREAU OF THE CENSUS,
Library, Federal Office Bldg 3, Rm 2451,
Washington, 20233. Betty Baxtresser, Chief,
ASD Library Branch
Holdings: Cat Mss Maps Microforms
Notes: Publications and related source
materials issued by the Bureau of the Census
and its predecessor organizations from 1790
to the present. Also, reports based upon
surveys conducted by the Bureau for other
governmental agencies. Papers by Census
staff members, providing a rich source of
material on statistical methods, population
and other Bureau-related matters are
important.

IL —NEWBERRY LIBRARY, 60 W Walton
St, Chicago, 60610. Diana Haskell, Cur of
Modern Mss
Notes: Incl many published vital records.
MA —OLD STURBRIDGE VILLAGE,
Research Library, Sturbridge, 01566.
Theresa Rini Percy, Librn
Holdings: Cat
Notes: New England, to 1860.
NJ —PRINCETON UNIVERSITY, Office of
Population Research, Library, 21 Prospect
Ave, Princeton, 08540. Thomas Holzmann,
Librn
Holdings: Vols (25,000) Cat Mss Maps
Microforms
Notes: The library is attached to the Office
of Population Reserch, which publishes the
Populaton Index. Library is particularly
strong in statistical materials, such as
worldwide population censuses and vital
statistics; it is less strong in the biomedical
aspects of population research. Incl 10,000
reprints, pamphlets, mss, etc. ILL requests
should be addressed to Princeton University
Library, Interlibrary Services.
TX —HOUSTON ACADEMY OF
MEDICINE-TEXAS MEDICAL CENTER,
Library, Jesse H Jones Library Bldg,
Houston, 77030. Elizabeth Borst White,
Special Collections Librn
Holdings: Vols (900) Cat
Notes: Mading Collection on Public Health.
English-language materials dealing with
American public health conditions before
1925. Emphasis is on epidemiology and
infectious diseases (excluding venereal
disease), incl material on sanitation and
climatology. Federal, state or municipal
reports on health, mortality and sanitation
are included. Also 500 pamphlets.

VITAMIN B1

DC —LIBRARY OF CONGRESS, Manuscript
Division, Washington, 20540. John C
Broderick, Chief
Notes: Papers of Robert Ramapatnam
Williams (1886-1965), a pioneer in the field
of nutrition and public health who
synthesized thiamin (vitamin B1), helped to
effect the widespread enrichment of
foodstuff grains, and developed the Williams-
Waterman Fund to combat diseases caused
by inadequate nutrition. 20,000 items, incl
correspondence, reports, photographs, and
glass spectographic plates, document
research on and production of vitamin B1,
enrichment of cereal products, and the
Williams-Waterman Fund.

VITAMINS

CT —YALE MEDICAL LIBRARY, 333 Cedar
St, New Haven, 06510.
Notes: A special subject emphasis.
DC —LIBRARY OF CONGRESS, Manuscript
Division, Washington, 20540. John C
Broderick, Chief
Notes: Papers of Robert Ramapatnam
Williams (1886-1965), a pioneer in the field
of nutrition and public health who
synthesized thiamin (vitamin B1), helped to
effect the widespread enrichment of
foodstuff grains, and developed the Williams-
-Waterman Fund to combat diseases caused
by inadequate nutrition. 20,000 items, incl
correspondence, reports, photographs, and
glass spectographic plates, document
research on and production of vitamin B1,
enrichment of cereal products, and the
Williams--Waterman Fund.

VITAPHONE see Moving Pictures, Talking

VITAPHONE RECORDS

DC —LIBRARY OF CONGRESS, Motion
Pictures, Broadcasting and Recorded Sound
Div, Washington, 20540.
Holdings: Cat
Notes: 133 Berliner Gramophone Co
records, 1896-1900; 31 Zonophone records,
1899; 67 Eldridge R Johnson records, 1900-
1901; and 30 Victor Talking Machine Co
records, 1902-1909.

VITICULTURE

CA —ANAHEIM PUBLIC LIBRARY, 500 W
Broadway, Anaheim, 92805.
Holdings: Vols (2000) Cat
Notes: Original minute books and reocrds of
the Los Angeles Vineyard Society.

**CA —UNIVERSITY OF CALIFORNIA,
DAVIS**, General Library, Davis, 95616.
Bernard Kreissman, University Librn; C
Danial Elliott, Asst Head, Dept Special
Collections
Holdings: Vols 3000 Cat
Notes: A collection incl classic treatises and
recent texts on grapes and grape growing of
worldwide scope, eg, US, Europe, South
Africa, South America, Australia, etc.
Holdings of ampelographic works (grape
variety classification) are especially
significant.

**CA —CALIFORNIA STATE UNIVERSITY,
FRESNO**, Henry Madden Library, Dept of
Special Collections, Fresno, 93740. Ronald J
Mahoney, Head
Holdings: Vols (3400) Cat Maps Pix
Notes: Books and pamphlets relating to the
history and development of viticulture and
enology. Emphasizes pre-1920 worldwide
imprints. Incl 900 merchants' catalogs, 1400
pamphlets, 200 wine lists, 750 periodical
issues, and ephemera. Partially cataloged.

CA —SAINT HELENA PUBLIC LIBRARY,
1492 Library Lane, Saint Helena, 94574.
Clayla Davis, Library Admin
Holdings: Vols 3000 Cat Mss 16mm Films
Budget: $7000
Notes: Incl Napa Valley Wine Library.
Bibliography of holdings available.

**CA —WINE MUSEUM OF SAN
FRANCISCO**, Alfred Fromm Rare Wine
Books Library, 633 Beach St, San Francisco,
94109. Barbara W Thompson, Cur
Holdings: Vols (700) Cat Maps Pix
Notes: The Library consists primarily of
volumes on aspects of wine history, enology,
and viticulture. All texts are completely
cross-referenced by subject/title/author.
Noncirculating. Chronological listing
available at cost.

VIVANTE, ARTURO

MA —BOSTON UNIVERSITY, Mugar
Memorial Library, Special Collections Dept,
771 Commonwealth Ave, Boston, 02215.
Howard B Gotlieb, Dir
Holdings: Cat Mss
Notes: Mss, correspondence, etc collected in
depth; incl publications by or about.

VIVISECTION AND ANTIVIVISECTION

RI —BROWN UNIVERSITY, John Hay
Library, 20 Prospect St, Providence, 02912.
Mark N Brown, Cur Mss
Holdings: // Mss
Notes: Papers of William Williams Keen,
American surgeon, Brown Class of 1859. Of
the 13,700 items in this collection, 13,200
consist of correspondence for the period
1858 to 1932 with noted scientists,
physicians, and public figures. Also diaries,
mss, and typescripts of articles, addresses,
and lectures. A source for the history of
medicine and surgery in the US, 1860-1930.
Register available.

VOADEN, HERMAN

ON —YORK UNIVERSITY, Scott Library,
Downsview, M3J 2R2, Can. Hartwell
Bowsfield, University Archivist
Notes: Literary and political papers of
Canadian playwright, theatre director, and
teacher Herman Voaden, leading exponent
of Canadian national drama, and the concept
of "Symphonic theatre," encompassing all the
living arts, collection covers 1897-1975, incl
personal papers, diaries, etc. Over 700
playbills, 1926-1945, etc.

VOCAL CULTURE see Singing; Voice
Culture

VOCAL MUSIC

**CA —CALIFORNIA STATE UNIVERSITY,
HAYWARD**, Library, Hayward, 94542.
Melissa Rose, Dir
Holdings: Vols (15,986) Cat Phonorecords
Budget: ($21,000)
Notes: The score collection covers the entire
range of instrumental and vocal concert
music, incl collected works of various
composers, and representative collections of
hymnals, folk music, musical comedy, and
some popular music. Sound recordings range
from ethnomusicological collections to
electronic music. Emphasis is on concert
music, but there is a large collection of jazz
and a selective collection of popular music.
Separate catalog.

**CA —UNIVERSITY OF CALIFORNIA, LOS
ANGELES**, Music Library, Schonberg Hall,
Los Angeles, 90024. Stephen M Fry, Music
Librn
Holdings: Vols Cat Mss Microforms
Notes: Approx 6000 scores for European
and American operas, ca 1700-present.
Published descriptions of collection:
University of California Music Libraries,
Berkeley, Los Angeles, *Catalog of the Opera
Collections*, (Boston: G K Hall, 1983).

**CA —UNIVERSITY OF CALIFORNIA,
SANTA BARBARA**, Arts Library, Music
Section, Santa Barbara, 93106. Susan Sonnet
Bower, Asst Music Librn
Holdings: Cat phonorecords
Notes: The Archival Sound Recordings
Collection: 15,000 78rpm discs, containing
representative performances by almost every
opera and lieder singer recorded.

CT —YALE UNIVERSITY, Music Library, 98
Wall St, New Haven, 06520. Harold E
Samuel, Librn
Holdings: Vols (118,000) Cat Mss Pix
Phonorecords Audiotapes
Notes: Manuscript and archive collection
comprising over 500 individual musical mss
as well as the personal papers and musical
mss of such American musicians and
composers as Charles Ives, Carl Ruggles,
Haratio Parker, Quincy Porter, Richard
Donovan and David Stanley Smith, Leo
Ornstein, Armin Loos, Duane Davidson,
Alonzo Elliott, John Rosamind Johnson,
Hope Leroy Baumgartner, Gustave Stoeckel,
Hershy Kay, Virgil Thomson, Kurt Weill,
Lotte Lenya, Lowell Mason, Parker Bailey,
Henry Gilbert, Seymour Shifrin, Lehman
Engel, Ernest Trow Carter, and Alec
Templeton. Extensive Paul Hindemith
Collection. Also ca 35,000 pieces of
American sheet music, both instrumental
and vocal as well as extensive holdings of
17th & 18th century American hymn books.

**†DC —CATHOLIC UNIVERSITY OF
AMERICA**, Music Library, Washington,
20064. Betty Libbey, Head Music Library
Holdings: Cat Microforms
Notes: A large collection to support
advanced degree study. Emphasis on church
music, musicology, history and criticism,
instrumental and vocal music, solo music for
all voices, instruments, and musical forms.

IL —AURORA PUBLIC LIBRARY, 1 Benton
St, Aurora, 60506. Mary E Clark, Head
Librn
Holdings: Vols (23,000) Cat
Notes: Plus 1000 pieces of early popular
sheet music (uncataloged). Collection espec
strong in vocal and piano music and in
chamber music.

IL —NEWBERRY LIBRARY, 60 W Walton
St, Chicago, 60610. Diana Haskell, Cur of
Modern Mss
Holdings: Cat Mss Microforms
Notes: Incl the library of Count Pio Resse
and a portion of Alfred Cortot library.
Particularly strong in Italian theoretical
treatises, vocal music and music for fretted
instruments. Restricted use: noncirculating.

NJ —WESTMINSTER CHOIR COLLEGE,
Talbott Library, Hamilton Ave at Walnut
Lane, Princeton, 08540. Sherry L Vellucci,
Acting Dir
Holdings: Vols (43,500) Cat Scores
Periodicals Phonorecords Audiotapes
Videotapes Microforms
Budget: ($30,000)
Notes: Talbott Library supports the
curriculum of a music college which grants
undergraduate and graduate degrees in
church music, music education and music
performance (voice, piano, organ and choral
conducting), with an emphasis on choral
music. Incl 7000 phonorecords, 3500 titles in
quantity of choral music, 30,000 single
copies of choral music.

NY —BROOKLYN PUBLIC LIBRARY, Art
& Music Div, Grand Army Plaza, Brooklyn,
11238. Sue H Sharma, Chief
Holdings: Vols (4500) Cat Mss
Notes: Over 50,000 items, most of which
circulate to the public. The collection
contains some reference materials, incl the
complete works of many composers; over
3500 popular song folios with our own in-
house index for locating individual songs;
some rare editions and mss of local
composers; and a small collection of rare
sheet music beginning with the 18th century.
The circulating collection incl standard vocal
scores, methods, piano music, etc, and is one
of the largest public library collections in the
country.

NY —NEW YORK PUBLIC LIBRARY, Music
Div, 111 Amsterdam Ave, New York,
10023. Frank C Campbell, Chief
Holdings: Vols (300,000) Cat Mss Pix
Microforms
Notes: Described in *Dictionary Catalog of
the Music Collection, The Research
Libraries of the New York Public Library*,
33 vols (532,000 cards), 1964, $2190;
Supplement 1, 1 vol (17,000 cards), 1966,
$100. Also, *Bibliographic Guide to Music*, 2
vols, 1975-1976, $70 ea. Literature
pertaining to virtually all musical subjects,
and scores covering the broadest range of
musical style and history are represented in
this catalog. Special strengths of the
collection incl folk songs, 18th and 19th-
century librettos, full scores of operas,
complete works, historical editions,
Beethoven, Americana, American music,
periodicals, vocal music, literature on the
voice, programs, record catalogs, and mss in
detail; sheet music, 355,414; sound
recordings, 400,000; clippings and programs,
2 million; broadsides, 1821; songsters, 375;
pictures, 51,002; ms, 29,877.

OH —CLEVELAND PUBLIC LIBRARY, Fine
Arts and Special Collections Department,
325 Superior Ave, Cleveland, 44114. Alice
N Loranth, Head
Holdings: Vols 10,550 Cat
Notes: Incl oratorios, masses, cantatas, etc,
with mostly single copies, piano-vocal scores
and about 200 orchestral scores.

PA —FREE LIBRARY OF PHILADELPHIA,
Sheet Music Collection, Logan Sq,
Philadelphia, 19103. Connie Jessum, Librn
Budget: ($2000)
Notes: Covers entire span of American
popular expression in song and instrumental
music (piano) from colonial times to the
present. Incl Newland-Zeuner and Edward I
Keffer Collections on loan from the Musical
Fund Society. Items printed before 1825
indexed in Sonneck-Upton and Wolfe.
Checklists for cover illustrations, musical
shows or films and special subjects. Songs
are filed by title; piano music by composer.
Examples of special materials not filed in
regular collection incl early Philadelphia
composers and publications, national
(centennial and state), patriotic ("Star-
Spangled Banner"), political (Presidents), and
war (1861; 1914; 1939) songs. Most of the
ms materials are anonymous. Collection
contains 138,360 pieces of sheet music.

RI —BROWN UNIVERSITY, John Hay
Library, 20 Prospect St, Providence, 02912.
Mark N Brown, Cur Mss
Notes: The Sheet Music Collection
concentrates on music of American imprint,
incl 170,000 vocal pieces filed by title, plus
80,000 instrumental pieces filed by
composer. Major strengths are in 19th
century music, especially prior to 1830; Civil
War music, both Union and Confederate;
lithographic covers; World War I songs;
political campaign music; and band music.
An additional 100,000 pieces of American
and European imprint remain unprocessed.
Holdings of World War I and II sheet music,
sheet music relating to Women's and Afro-
American History, and sheet music authored
by writers included in the Bibliography of

VOCAL MUSIC (cont.)

American Literature, have been fully cataloged on RLIN.

RI —BROWN UNIVERSITY, John Hay Library, Harris Collection, Prospect St, Providence, 02912. Rosemary L Cullen, Cur Holdings: Vols (200,000) Cat Mss Pix Phonorecords
Budget: ($15,000)
Notes: The Harris Collection of American poetry and Plays is principally composed of American and Canadian poetry and plays from the 17th century to the present. Extensive holdings in songsters and sheet music with lyrics (170,000 pieces). Incl large collection of Stephen Foster sheet music and music by Rhode Island composers and lyricists. See *Dictionary Catalog of the Harris Collection of American Poetry and Plays* (Boston: G K Hall, 1972), 13 vols; Supplement (1977), 3 vols. Separate catalog.

WI —UNIVERSITY OF WISCONSIN, MADISON, Mills Music Library, 728 State St, Madison, 53706. Arne Arneson, Music Librn
Holdings: // Uncat Mss
Notes: Tams-Witmark Collection formed part of the rental collection of the firm bearing that name. Includes piano-conductor scores (some in mss); ca 65 sets of orchestral parts for operas; 70 vocal scores of works by American composers including Herbert, Sousa, Edwards and De Koven; ca 4000 vocal scores of European operas. Restricted use.

VOCALISTS see Singers

VOCATION, CHOICE OF see Vocational Guidance

VOCATIONAL EDUCATION

CA —LANEY COLLEGE, Library, 900 Fallon St, Oakland, 94607. Marita Davila, Dir Holdings: Vols (70,000) Cat Maps Pix Slides Microforms

DC —INTERNATIONAL LABOR ORGANIZATION, International Labor Office, Washington Branch Library, 1750 New York Ave NW, Rm 330, Washington, 20006. Karen J Mark, Librn
Holdings: Vols (13,500) Cat Pix 16mm Films Monographs
Notes: Wide range of titles dealing with worldwide labor and social matters. The library contains ILO publications and documentation only, dating back to 1919. Also, a collection of ILO films and photos. See *Subject Guide to Publications of the ILO, 1919-1964* and *ILO Catalogue of Publications in Print, 1982* (ILO).

MA —HARVARD UNIVERSITY, Office of Career Services & Off-Campus Learning, Library, 54 Dunster St, Cambridge, 02138. Susan M Vacca, Librn
Holdings: Vols 7800 Cat Microforms VF
Budget: $24,000
Notes: Collection relates to career education. Not a public facility; for Harvard and Radcliffe students, staff and faculty only. Refer to *A Bibliography of Directories, Handbooks and Guides in the Office of Career Services and Off-Campus Learning (A Systematic Enumerative Shelflist of Harvard's Career Services Library)*, by C Kovacs (Cambridge: Harvard Univ, Office of Career Services and Off-Campus Learning, 1977), 286 pp.

WI —UNIVERSITY OF WISCONSIN-STOUT, Library Learning Center, Menomonie, 54751. Philip Sawin Jr, Coll Develop Librn
Notes: University has a national reputation for its program in Vocational Education. This program started in 1935 and is supported by an indepth vocational education collection. Including the papers of Verne C Fryklund (qv).

BC —VANCOUVER COMMUNITY COLLEGE, Vancouver Vocational Institute Library, 250 W Pender St, Vancouver, V6B 1S9, Can. Ross Henderson, Librn
Holdings: Vols (16,000) Cat Audiotapes

Videotapes Films Slides
Budget: ($211,000)
Notes: Curriculum support for technical programs, service programs, industrial programs, and business and health programs.

VOCATIONAL GUIDANCE

CA —SAN DIEGO PUBLIC LIBRARY, Social Sciences Section, 820 E St, San Diego, 92101. Margaret E Queen, Supvr
Budget: ($36,000)
Notes: Good collection of books, incl directories and bibliographies. Good collection of material in separate vocational pamphlet file. Also, loose-leaf occupational guide service published by the state of California and constantly revised and updated. Index of subject headings used in vocational pamphlet file.

IL —CHICAGO PUBLIC LIBRARY, Business/Science/Technology Div, Science/Technology Information Center, 425 North Michigan Ave, Chicago, 60611. Lynda Sanford, Head; John R Moore, Environment Collection Coordinator & Engineering Librn
Budget: $15,000
Notes: Books on careers complemented by Education/Philosophy Information Center's collection of college catalogs and guides and Business Information Center's collections. Over 500 titles; 3 VF cabinets pamphlet materials.
See also entry under Business.

IL —JEWISH VOCATIONAL SERVICE, Library, One S Franklin St, Chicago, 60606. Elisa Feiden, Dir of Information Services
Holdings: Vols 1,200 Cat

IL —WAUKEGAN PUBLIC LIBRARY, 128 N County St, Waukegan, 60085. Andrew W Stimson, Librn
Holdings: Vols 1000 Cat
Notes: Collection of career and school information.

NY —MANHASSET PUBLIC LIBRARY, 30 Onderdonk Ave, Manhasset, 11030. Sylvia Levin, Dir
Holdings: Vols 600
Notes: Career materials.

NY —BANK STREET COLLEGE OF EDUCATION LIBRARY, 610 W 112 St, New York, 10025. Eleanor Kule Seid, Library Dir
Holdings: Vols (90,000) Cat Microforms
Notes: Education, guidance, psychology, educational psychology, curricula, textbooks, Black Studies, etc. All subjects are integrated in one professional collection; in addition there are two separately cataloged and shelved collection: Children's and Elementary Curriculum Materials.

NY —CATALYST, Library, 14 E 60 St, New York, 10022. Gurley Turner, Dir of Information Services
Holdings: Vols (6000) Cat Mss VF
Notes: Working Women (current information); career and family issues plus career library.

NY —FEDERATION EMPLOYMENT & GUIDANCE SERVICE, Richard J Bernhard Memorial Library, 510 Sixth Ave, 4th Floor, New York, 10011. Otto Kanocz, Chief Librn
Holdings: Vols (4000) Cat Microforms Videotapes Audiotapes VF
Notes: Occupational information, guidance and counseling, vocational rehabilitation. Incl 30,000 pamphlets; 200 periodical titles. Also incl 50 vertical files and microfiche. Open to the public.

NY —NEW YORK PUBLIC LIBRARY, Mid-Manhattan Library, History and Social Sciences Dept, 455 Fifth Ave, New York, 10016. Robert Sheehan, Sr Principal Librn
Holdings: Vols 20,000 Cat Audiotapes Microforms
Budget: $16,700
Notes: Strong undergraduate level collection with duplicate reference and circulating copies of books in many instances. Good collection of college catalgs incl some foreign catalogs. 65 vertical file drawers; 250 periodicals. ERIC index and microfiche collection from 1966.

NY —NEW YORK PUBLIC LIBRARY, Mid-Manhattan Library, Education Collection, 455 Fifth Ave, New York, 10016.
Holdings: Vols (31,000) Cat Audiotapes

Microforms
Budget: ($22,550)
Notes: Strong undergraduate level collection of reference and circulating books. Good collection of current college catalogs incl some foreign catalogs. 32 vertical file drawers; 250 periodicals; ERIC index and microfiche collection from 1966.

NY —NEW YORK PUBLIC LIBRARY, Mid-Manhattan Library, Job Information Center, 455 Fifth Ave, New York, 10016. Barbara Shapiro, Principal Librn
Holdings: Vols 12,000
Notes: Collection of reference and circulating materials which cover all aspects of career planning and the job search process. The collection incl materials on specific careers, interviewing and resume writing. There are items geared for different interest groups, i e students, women, minorities, the disabled, and older job seekers. Information is available in the form of books, directories, periodicals, newspapers, and pamphlets.

NC —FORSYTH COUNTY PUBLIC LIBRARY, Adult Continuing Education (ACE) Div, 660 W Fifth St, Winston-Salem, 27101. Ann R Gehlen, Librn
Holdings: Vols 3500 Phonorecords Audiotapes Videotapes 16mm Films Filmstrips Microforms
Budget: $6900
Notes: Special emphasis on high school equivalency preparation, adult new readers, improvement in language and math, secretarial skills, job-hunting techniques, college alternatives, test preparation, and support to independent study in popular subject areas. Extensive pamphlet files of up-to-date career information, indexed. Some 600 bound college catalogs plus national microfiche collection. Current local job openings on microfiche. Information and referral files maintained to relevant local resources (courses, etc). Partially cataloged.

PA —CARLOW COLLEGE, Grace Library, Fifth Ave, Pittsburgh, 15213. Joan M Mitchell, Dir of Library Services
Holdings: Vols (252) Cat
Budget: ($300)
Notes: The Career Resources Center consists of career and counseling materials for college students with special emphasis on the career guidance needs of the Continuing Education student.

VOCATIONAL OPPORTUNITIES see Vocational Guidance

VOCATIONAL REHABILITATION

DC —INTERNATIONAL LABOR ORGANIZATION, International Labor Office, Washington Branch Library, 1750 New York Ave NW, Rm 330, Washington, 20006. Karen J Mark, Librn
Holdings: Vols (13,500) Cat Pix 16mm Film Monographs
Notes: Wide range of titles dealing with worldwide labor and social matters. The library contains ILO publications and documentation only, dating back to 1919. Also, a collection of ILO films and photos. See *Subject Guide to Publications of the ILO, 1919-1964* and *ILO Catalogue of Publications in Print, 1982* (ILO).

IL —JEWISH VOCATIONAL SERVICE, Library, One S Franklin St, Chicago, 60606. Elisa Feiden, Dir of Information Services
Holdings: Vols 1,200 Cat

MA —MASSACHUSETTS REHABILITATION COMMISSION, Library, 20 Park Plaza, Boston, 02116. June C Holt, Librn
Holdings: Vols (15,000) Cat Audiotapes 16mm Films Microforms
Budget: ($18,000)
Notes: For staff and community interested in rehabilitation literature, defined as publications which deal with impairments resulting in disabling conditions; mental and behavioral disorders; employment of the handicapped; counseling techniques with handicapped populations; sheltered workshops, rehabilitation facilities; halfway

VOCATIONAL REHABILITATION
(cont.)

houses and independent living arrangements; psychological aspects of disability; attitudes toward the handicapped; and other material on services for the handicapped. Library subscribes to 70 journals relating to disability and rehabilitation.

NY —FEDERATION EMPLOYMENT & GUIDANCE SERVICE, Richard J Bernhard Memorial Library, 510 Sixth Ave, 4th Floor, New York, 10011. Otto Kanocz, Chief Librn
Holdings: Vols (4000) Cat Microforms Videotapes Audiotapes VF
Notes: Occupational information, guidance and counseling, vocational rehabilitation. Incl 30,000 pamphlets; 200 periodical titles. Also incl 50 vertical files and microfiche. Open to the public.

WI —UNIVERSITY OF WISCONSIN-STOUT, Library Learning Center, Menomonie, 54751. Philip Sawin Jr, Coll Develop Librn
Notes: A strong collection. Materials in the area of work samples, vocational assessment, job placement, adjustment services and situational assessment are collected. This material supports a graduate program, which is the largest of five programs in the United States. This program was begun in 1967.

†ON —METROPOLITAN TORONTO LIBRARY, Social Sciences Dept, 789 Yonge St, Toronto, M4W 2G8, Can. Abdus Salam, Head
Holdings: Vols Cat Maps Phonorecords Audiotapes 16mm Films Microforms
Notes: Historical and contemporary Canadian material covering federal and provincial policies and programs in the fields of health care, geriatrics, child welfare, corrections, and care and rehabilitation of the physically and mentally handicapped.

VOEGELIN, ERIC

CA —HOOVER INSTITUTION ON WAR, REVOLUTION & PEACE, Stanford University, Stanford, 94305. Milorad M Drachkovitch, Archivist
Holdings: Mss
Notes: Papers of Eric Voegelin, philosopher, professor, and political scientist, incl correspondence, speeches and writings, reports, memoranda, and other material, 1930-1974, relating to his career as professor and author of numerous works dealing with philosophy and political science. 26 boxes.

VOICE CULTURE

NY —NEW YORK PUBLIC LIBRARY, Music Div, 111 Amsterdam Ave, New York, 10023. Frank C Campbell, Chief
Holdings: Vols (300,000) Cat Mss Pix Microforms
Notes: Described in Dictionary Catalog of the Music Collection, The Research Libraries of the New York Public Library, 33 vols (532,000 cards), 1964, $2190; Supplement 1, 1 vol (17,000 cards), 1966, $100. Also, Bibliographic Guide to Music, 2 vols, 1975-1976, $70 ea. Literature pertaining to virtually all musical subjects, and scores covering the broadest range of musical style and history are represented in this catalog. Special strengths of the collection incl folk songs, 18th and 19th-century librettos, full scores of operas, complete works, historical editions, Beethoven, Americana, American music, periodicals, vocal music, literature on the voice, programs, record catalogs, and mss in detail; sheet music, 355,414; sound recordings, 400,000; clippings and programs, 2 million; broadsides, 1821; songsters, 375; pictures, 51,002; ms, 29,877.

VOICE OF AMERICA (RADIO PROGRAM)

DC —LIBRARY OF CONGRESS, Motion Pictures, Broadcasting and Recorded Sound Div, Washington, 20540.
Notes: Broadcast recordings of Voice of America music programs.

IL —CENTER FOR RESEARCH LIBRARIES, 6050 S Kenwood Ave, Chicago, 60637. Donald B Simpson, Dir; Esther Smith, Collection Development Librn
Holdings: Microforms
Notes: Microfilm of Voice of America scripts, 1953-.

VOLATILE OILS see Essences and Essential Oils

VOLCANOES

IL —UNIVERSITY OF ILLINOIS, URBANA/CHAMPAIGN, Library, Geology Library, 223 Natural History Bldg, Urbana, 61801. Dederick Ward, Librn
Holdings: Vol (105,186) Cat Maps Microforms

NY —AMERICAN MUSEUM OF NATURAL HISTORY, Library Services Dept, Central Park W & 79th St, New York, 10024. Nina J Root, Chairwoman; Mary Genett, Asst Librn for Reference Services
Notes: Especially strong in periodical literature.

NY —COLUMBIA UNIVERSITY LIBRARIES, Geoscience Library, Lamont-Doherty Geological Observatory, Palisades, 10964. Susan Klimley, Librn
Holdings: Vols (20,000) Cat
Notes: Geosciences, incl geochemistry, marine geology, seismology and paleoclimatology.

ON —ENERGY, MINES & RESOURCES CANADA, Earth Physics Branch Library, Ottawa, K1A 0Y3, Can. W M Tsang, Chief Librn
Holdings: Vols (6000) Cat Maps Pix Slides Microforms
Notes: Incl an extensive collection of references called Seismological Pamphlet File incl reprints, private reports, seismograms, etc, all cataloged separately and being added to continuously.

VOLGA GERMANS see Russian Germans

VOLHYNIA, UKRAINE

IN —VOLHYNIAN BIBLIOGRAPHIC CENTER, 307 N Overhill Drive, Bloomington, 47401. Max Boyko, Mgr
Notes: Collect materials on Volhynia in Western Ukraine. Compile and publish bibliographies on the region.

VOLKHOVSKII, FELIKS VADIMOVICH

CA —HOOVER INSTITUTION ON WAR, REVOLUTION & PEACE, Stanford University, Stanford, 94305. Milorad M Drachkovitch, Archivist
Holdings: // Mss
Notes: Papers, 1875-1923, of Feliks Vadimovich Volkhovskii, Russian revolutionist. In part, transcripts. Personal correspondence, originals and copies of writings, photos, clippings and other printed material, relating to revolutionary movements in Imperial Russia. 24 boxes. Unpublished preliminary inventory in repository.

VOLKOFF, BORIS

ON —METROPOLITAN TORONTO LIBRARY, Theatre Dept, 789 Yonge St, Toronto, M4W 2G8, Can. Heather McCallum, Head
Notes: The Boris Volkoff Collection documents the Russian-born dancer's 45 year career in Canada and his important contribution to the development of Canadian ballet. The collection incl scrapbooks, costume and set designs (incl original stage designs by Mstislav Dobujinsky for the Canadian ballet Red Ear of Corn, produced by Volkoff in 1949), photographs, programs, correspondence, choreographic notebooks, and a portrait of Boris Volkloff painted by Yulia Biriukova.

VOLLEYBALL

IL —NATIONAL COUNCIL OF THE YMCAS, YMCA Historical Library, 6400

Shafer Ct, Rosemont, 60018. Eleanor R Murphy, Librn
Notes: Large collection, incl historical material, on basketball, wrestling, track and field, swimming, diving, scuba and volleyball.

MA —SPRINGFIELD COLLEGE LIBRARY, Babson Library, Springfield, 01109. Henry Dutcher, Reference Librn
Holdings: Vols (130,000) Cat
Budget: ($65,000)

VOLTAIRE, FRANCOIS MARIE AROUET

IN —INDIANA UNIVERSITY, Lilly Library, Seventh St, Bloomington, 47405. William R Cagle, Librn
Holdings: Cat
Notes: The Mary-Margaret Barr Koon Collection contains extensive holdings of works by and about Voltaire.

ON —UNIVERSITY OF TORONTO, Thomas Fisher Rare Book Library, 120 Saint George St, Toronto, M5S 1A5, Can. Richard G Landon, Head
Holdings: Vols 900 Cat
Notes: Harcourt Brown Voltaire Collection, named for donor. Chiefly 18th century editions of Voltaire's works, including rare piracies; also includes contemporary and later works relating to Voltaire.

VOLTERRA, VITO

MA —BRANDEIS UNIVERSITY, Goldfarb Library, 415 South St, Waltham, 02154. Bessie Hahn, Dir
Notes: Vito Volterra Collection on the History of Science and Mathematics. A collection of more than 5000 vols containing the major works in Volterra. Inclusive dates are the 16th through the 20th century. The collection also contains over 16,000 offprints and pamphlets, most of which are dedication copies from the author to Volterra. No catalog of the books extant, but an author-title finding list for the 16,000 offprintsand pamphlets is available in Special Collections.

VOLUNTEER WORKERS

DC —PEACE CORPS, Information Services Division, 806 Connecticut Ave NW, Room M407, Washington, 20526. Rita C Warpeha, Chief Librn
Holdings: Vols (35,000) Cat
Budget: ($10,000)
Notes: Voluntarism as it relates to basic human needs in Asia, Africa, and Latin America.

MA —RADCLIFFE COLLEGE, Arthur & Elizabeth Schlesinger Library on the History of Women in America, 3 James St, Cambridge, 02138. Patricia Miller King, Dir; Eva Moseley, Cur of Mss
Notes: Papers of individual women and organizations concerned with or using volunteer workers, dating from the 19th and 20th centuries.

VOLUNTEER WORKERS IN HOSPITALS

NY —UNITED HOSPITAL FUND OF NEW YORK, Library, 3 E 54th St, New York, 10022. Christine Bahr, Librn
Holdings: Vols (4000) Cat Mss Maps Pix
Notes: Incl 100 journal titles.

VOLUNTEERS IN SERVICE TO AMERICA see Vista

VON KARMAN, THEODORE see Karman, Theodore Von

VONDEL, JOOST VAN DEN, 1587-1679

MA —HARVARD UNIVERSITY LIBRARY, Cambridge, 02138.
Holdings: Cat

TX —RICE UNIVERSITY, Fondren Library, 6100 S Main St, PO Box 1892, Houston, 77251. Dr Samuel M Carrington, Jr, University Librn
Holdings: Vols 750 // Cat
Notes: Incl books by and about him.

VONNEGUT, KURT

AZ —UNIVERSITY OF ARIZONA,
University Library, Special Collections,
Tucson, 85721. Louis A Hieb, Head
Holdings: Vols (7000) Cat Mss Microforms
Budget: ($30,000)
Notes: In the 20th century, the major
emphasis is Bukowski, Wakoski, Wilder,
Reznikoff, Ginzberg, Ferlinghetti, Snyder,
Whalen, Everson, Joyce Carol Oates, and
Kurt Vonnegut.

DE —UNIVERSITY OF DELAWARE, Hugh
M Morris Library, S College Ave, Newark,
19711. T Stuart Dick, Special Collections
Holdings: Cat Mss Pix
Notes: Manuscripts, fact sheets, contract
informaton, royalty statements, foreign
movie and reprint rights: correspondence for
the period 1966-1982 with the publisher,
Seymour Lawrence.

NV —UNIVERSITY OF NEVADA, RENO,
University Library, Special Collections Dept,
Reno, 89557. Robert E Blesse, Head
Holdings: Vols 64 Cat
Notes: Includes individual works by author
in all editions including translations; also
prefaces, introductions, published
correspondence, appearances in anthologies,
periodicals, etc. Bibliographical research
collection, part of Modern Authors
Collection.

VOODOO

CT —LEE ASH, (personal collection), 66
Humiston Dr, Bethany, 06525.

VOORHIS, HORACE JEREMIAH, 1901-

CA —CLAREMONT COLLEGES, Honnold
Library, Ninth & Dartmouth, Claremont,
91711. Tania Rizzo, Special Collections
Dept Head
Holdings: Vols (200) Cat Mss Documents
Pix Records
Notes: The papers of former Democratic
Congressman Jerry Voorhis, from the 1930s
to present, occupying nearly 100 document
boxes. The papers reflect his life and career,
incl biographical material, the history of the
Voorhis School for Boys, his involvement in
the Dies Committee, and his wide-ranging
interests in American economic and social
issues, such as cooperatives, monopolies and
cartels, Latin American relations, consumers,
and senior citizens. Books by and about him,
with research files. Correspondence with
political leaders. Inventory available.
Restricted use.

VOROS, SANDOR

NY —ADELPHI UNIVERSITY, Library,
Garden City, 11530. Jerome Yavarkovsky,
Dean of Libraries
Holdings: Vols 10 // Cat Mss Maps Pix
Notes: Drawings, cartoons, military report
leaflets and photographs of Spanish Civil
War.

VORSE, MARY HEATON

MI —WAYNE STATE UNIVERSITY, Walter
P Reuther Library, Archives of Labor &
Urban Affairs, Detroit, 48202. Philip Mason,
Dir
Notes: Papers, etc of Mary Heaton Vorse,
author, labor journalist, and social critic,
have also placed their papers in the
Archives.

VORTICISM

CT —YALE UNIVERSITY, Beinecke Rare
Book & Manuscript Library, Osborn
Collection, New Haven, 06520. Stephen R
Parks, Cur
Holdings: Mss

VORYS, JOHN W.

OH —OHIO HISTORICAL SOCIETY,
Archives Library Division, 1982 Velma Ave,
Columbus, 43211. Dennis East, Division
Chief
Notes: Papers of the US congressman, 1939-
1959.

VOT LANGUAGE see Votish Language and Literature

VOTERS, REGISTRATION OF

†MA —JOHN F KENNEDY LIBRARY,
Columbia Point, Boston, 02125. Dan H Fenn
Jr, Dir
Holdings: // Cat Mss
Notes: Records of the President's
Commission on Registration and Voting
Participation, 1963-1964. 9 linear ft of mss.
Holdings are described in "Historical
Materials in the John F Kennedy Library."
Copies may be obtained by writing the
Research Archivist.

VOTIAK LANGUAGE AND LITERATURE

NY —NEW YORK PUBLIC LIBRARY,
Slavonic Div, Fifth Ave & 42 St, New York,
10018. Edward Kasinec, Chief
Holdings: Cat Microforms
Notes: See New York Public Library,
Dictionary Catalog of the Slavonic
Collection (Boston: G K Hall, 1974), 44
vols.

VOTIAN LANGUAGE see Votish Language and Literature

VOTISH LANGUAGE AND LITERATURE

NY —NEW YORK PUBLIC LIBRARY,
Slavonic Div, Fifth Ave & 42 St, New York,
10018. Edward Kasinec, Chief
Holdings: Cat Microforms
Notes: See New York Public Library,
Dictionary Catalog of the Slavonic
Collection (Boston: G K Hall, 1974), 44
vols.

VOYAGERS see Explorers; Travelers

VOYAGES, IMAGINARY see Imaginary Voyages

VOYAGES, SCIENTIFIC see Scientific Expeditions

VOYAGES AND TRAVELS

AL —SAMFORD UNIVERSITY, Special
Collections Library, 800 Lakeshore Dr,
Birmingham, 35229. Annie Ford Wheeler,
Acting Head Librn
Holdings: Uncat Mss Maps Pix Microforms
Notes: The William H Brantley Collection is
in superb condition, consisting of early
works on travels, Indians, and law in the
southeast, plus scarce imprints of Alabama.

AK —ALASKA STATE LIBRARY, Alaska
Historical Library Collection, Pouch G,
Juneau, 99811. Phyllis Demuth, Readers
Services Librn
Holdings: Vols (24,000) Cat Mss Maps Pix
Slides Phonorecords Audiotapes Videotapes
16mm Films Microforms

AZ —NORTHERN ARIZONA
UNIVERSITY, Special Collection Library,
CU Box 6022, Flagstaff, 86011. Peter M
Whiteley, Coordr/Archivist; William
Mullane, Librn
Holdings: Maps
Notes: Early Travel and Exploration of the
West collection incl Wheeler Atlas of Israel
C Russell, 1870's. One of the most
comprehensive collections of Wheeler
Survey Maps in existence. Also, Clarence
King Survey of the 40th Parallel, 1877.

CA —CLAREMONT COLLEGES, Honnold
Library, Ninth & Dartmouth, Claremont,
91711. Tania Rizzo, Special Collections
Dept Head
Holdings: Vols 561 // Cat Mss Maps
Notes: Henry Raup Wagner Collection:
cartography of the West Coast, voyages,
related history and geography, 15th century
and later. Most maps are photostats from
European and American archives and
libraries. Bound typescripts of sources
Wagner used in preparing his Evolution of
Maps of the Northwest Coast, some
facsimiles of mss, with transliteration or
translation. Original copy (bound) of
typescript of his "The Cartography of the
Northwest Coast of America to the Year
1800" with pencilled and typed corrections
and notes. Downs 2725. Mario C Schnitzler,
"Annotated Bibliography of the Henry Raup
Wagner Collection of Early Hispanic-
American History and Geography" (thesis,
1955).

CA —CALIFORNIA STATE UNIVERSITY,
HAYWARD, Library, Hayward, 94542.
Melissa Rose, Dir
Holdings: Vols (14,000) Cat Maps Pix
Budget: ($7408)
Notes: Editions in several languages of
writings in the field of early voyages and
travels, incl publications from the 16th
century to the present. Noncirculating.

CA —UNIVERSITY OF CALIFORNIA, SAN
DIEGO, Central University Library,
Mandeville Dept of Special Collections, La
Jolla, 92093. Lynda Corey Claassen, Head
Holdings: Vols (2400) Cat Mss Maps
Notes: The Hill Collection of Pacific
Voyages, including reports and
commentaries of important voyages in the
Pacific, from those of Magellan and Sir
Francis Drake to exploration through the
first half of the 19th century. Includes many
rare overland accounts to the Pacific across
North America, Mexico, and Panama.
Bibliography: Silveira de Braganza, Ronald,
The Hill Collection of Pacific Voyages (La
Jolla: Calif, 1974-1983).

CA —UNIVERSITY OF CALIFORNIA, LOS
ANGELES, Research Library, Dept of
Special Collections, 405 Hilgard Ave, Los
Angeles, 90024. Edward Shreeves,
Chairman, Bibliographers Group; David S
Zeidberg, Head
Notes: Various collections, incl the Baron
Charles Stuart de Rothesay Collection of
530 continental maps, 1715-1840; the
Richard C Rudolph Collection of 200
Japanese woodblock and ms maps, 1614-
1896; 1500 maps and atlases emphasizing
the southwest US and Pacific voyages and
travels; and 15 linear feet of pamphlet maps.

CA —UNIVERSITY OF CALIFORNIA, LOS
ANGELES, Research Library, Indo/Pacific
Collection, 405 Hilgard Ave, Los Angeles,
90024. Edward Shreeves, Chairman,
Bibliographers Group; Charlotte Spence,
Indo/Pacific Bibliographer
Holdings: Vols Cat Mss Maps Pix
Microforms
Notes: The Pacific area collection has been
developed on a combination of the research
and teaching levels. It focuses on the
cultural, economic, political and social
history of Australia, New Zealand and the
various island groups. The accounts of the
early European voyagers are well
represented, with the highlight being the
Captain Cook collection. An effort has also
been made to collect the novels, poetry,
drama, etc, of Australian and New Zealand
authors.

CA —UNIVERSITY OF SOUTHERN
CALIFORNIA, Allan Hancock Foundation,
Hancock Library of Biology and
Oceanography, Los Angeles, 90007.
Kimberly Douglas, Librn
Holdings: Vols (16,000) Cat Maps
Notes: Mostly marine, but incl some land
expeditions. Covers all geographical areas.
Also incl serial collection of 80,000 vols.

CA —PACIFIC GROVE PUBLIC LIBRARY,
550 Central Ave, Pacific Grove, 93950.
Margaret McBride, Library Dir
Holdings: Vols (1200) // Cat
Notes: Alvin Seale South Seas Collection,
incl rare and unusual items, accounts of early
voyages, ships' logs and artifacts. Separate
catalog. Gift of Alvin Seale, curator of
Steinhart Aquarium, San Francisco, 1937.

CA —CALIFORNIA HISTORICAL
SOCIETY, Schubert Hall Library, 2099
Pacific Ave, San Francisco, 94109. Bruce L
Johnson, Library Dir
Holdings: Vols (50,000) Cat Mss Maps Pix
See also entry under California - History.

VOYAGES AND TRAVELS (cont.)

CA —SOCIETY OF CALIFORNIA
PIONEERS, Library, 456 McAllister St, San
Francisco, 94102. Grace E Baker, Librn
Holdings: Vols (12,000) Cat Mss Maps Pix
Microforms
Notes: California history, especially the gold
rush and the San Francisco earthquake,
Sherman collection of early California music,
business letterheads of early California firms,
San Francisco City Directories 1850-1944,
records of California Battalion 1846-47, ms
material on overland diaries, ships' logs and
passenger lists. Also, large photograph
collection.

CA —UNIVERSITY OF CALIFORNIA,
SANTA CRUZ, University Library, Special
Collections, Santa Cruz, 95064. Rita
Bottoms, Special Collections Librn; Margaret
Felts, South Pacific Collection Bibliographer
Holdings: Vols (10,000) Cat
Notes: South Pacific Collection.
Monographs, rare books, serials, documents
and atlases which treat of the Pacific areas of
Polynesia, Melanesia, Micronesia, Australia
and New Zealand, but excluding western
New Guinea (Irian Jaya), the Philippines
and Southeast Asia. Approximately 10
percent of the titles are multi-volume
documents such as parliamentary papers,
legislative journals, official yearbooks,
statistical sourcebooks, laws and statutes.
The collection includes an exhaustive
selection of current journals and
monographic series from and about the
Pacific: early serials, South Pacific
Commission publications, US Government
and US Trust Territory publications, serials
from museums, universities and scholarly
societies. Chief emphasis has been placed on
acquisition of the literature of history,
description and travel, ethnology
andanthropology, literature and literary
criticism, political and constitutional
histories. Other extensive holdings are in the
fields of geography and maps, voyages,
mission histories, mythology and folklore,
art, linguistics, and science fields of natural
history, environmental studies, biology,
zoology, botany, geology and astronomy.
Printed catalog is available. This is an ongoing, growing collection.

CT —TRINITY COLLEGE LIBRARY,
Watkinson Library, 300 Summit St,
Hartford, 06106. Jeffrey Kaimowitz, Cur
Holdings: Cat

CT —YALE UNIVERSITY, Box 1603A, Yale
Station, New Haven, 06520.

CT —YALE UNIVERSITY, Beinecke Rare
Book & Manuscript Library, Henry C Taylor
Collection, New Haven, 06520.
Holdings: Vols 396 Cat Mss
Notes: Early navigation and Americana. See
Kebabian, John S. The Henry C Taylor
Collection (New Haven: Yale University
Library, 1971).

DC —LIBRARY OF CONGRESS, Rare Book
& Special Collections Div, Washington,
20540. William Matheson, Chief
Notes: The Hans P and Hanni Kraus
Collection of contemporary materials (maps,
books, mss, medals and portraits) designed
to present Sir Francis Drake as his
contemporaries would have learned about
him. See Kraus, Hans P, Sir Francis Drake, a
Pictorial Biography, (Amsterdam, N Israel,
1970).

DC —LIBRARY OF CONGRESS, Manuscript
Division, Washington, 20540. John C
Broderick, Chief
Notes: The Hans P Kraus Collection of
documents relating to colonial Spanish
America, 1492-1819. Focusing on colonial
Mexico, incl material on exploration,
government, activities of the Inquisition,
taxation and economic conditions, relations
with the Indians and the French, and the
impending loss of land to Anglo-American
settlers. Also contains items concerning the
history of Spanish Florida, Tezozomoc's
chronicle on the history of the Aztecs, and
mss describing the explorations of Amerigo
Vespucci, Giovanni da Verrazzano, Alvar
Nunez Cabeza de Vaca, Pedro de Ursua, and
Lope de Aguirre.

DC —NATIONAL GEOGRAPHIC
SOCIETY, Library, 1146 16th St NW,
Washington, 20036. Susan Fifer Canby, Dir
Holdings: Vols (63,000) Cat Mss Maps Pix
Notes: Material concerning land, sea, and
space exploration--past and present. All
fields of anthropology, natural history,
geography, etc.

DC —SMITHSONIAN INSTITUTION
LIBRARIES, General Library, Washington,
20560. Mary Claire Grey, Chief Cent Ref &
Loan Servs
Holdings: Vols (79,000) Cat Mss Maps Pix
Slides Microforms

HI —BERNICE P BISHOP MUSEUM,
Library, PO Box 19000-A, Honolulu, 96819.
Cynthia Timberlake, Librn
Holdings: Vols (90,000) Cat Mss Maps Pix
Slides Microforms
Budget: ($30,000)
Notes: Only American library devoted
exclusively to the Pacific region. Collection
reflects historical and contemporary research
emphases of Bishop Museum; ie the natural
and cultural history of the Pacific. Areas of
concentration incl archaeology, ethnology,
linguistics, voyages and explorations, history,
vertebrate and invertebrate zoology, botany
and museology. Strong special collections
incl photographs, mss and archives, maps
and art. Publications: Quarterly "Additions
to the Catalog," Dictionary Catalog of the
Library (9 vols and 2 suppl; Boston: G K
Hall, 1964-69).

HI —HAWAIIAN MISSION CHILDREN'S
SOCIETY LIBRARY, 553 S King St,
Honolulu, 96813. Mary Jane Knight, Librn
Holdings: Vols 15,000 Cat Mss Pix
Notes: Missionary period of Hawaiian
history, 1819-1880, incl a general collection
of Hawaiian history and travel, an
outstanding collection of early voyages to
the Pacific, and an almost complete
collection of early Hawaiian imprints, ie,
publications in the Hawaiian language during
the 19th century. Ms material incl letters,
journals and reports of the Protestant
missionaries who came to Hawaii (the
Sandwich Islands) under the auspices of the
American Board of Commissioners for
Foreign Missions. The material is for
research only; the stacks are closed.
Unpublished papers may be examined by
qualified researchers on application to the
librarian. Published material is cataloged.
Hawaiian imprints are cataloged, except for
the Dewey classification 300's which are
mainly governmentdocuments. Ms
collections are cataloged or in the process of
being completely arranged and cataloged.

HI —PACIFIC SCIENTIFIC INFORMATION
CENTER, Bernice P Bishop Library,
Geography and Map Division, PO Box
19000A, Honolulu, 96819. Lee S Motteler,
Geographer; Valerie T Higa, Asst
Geographer
Holdings: Vols (2000) Cat Mss Maps Pix
Notes: Incl 20,000 maps and 70,000 aerial
photos of Hawaii and the Pacific.

HI —UNIVERSITY OF HAWAII, Library,
2550 The Mall, Honolulu, 96822. David
Kittelson, Hawaiian Cur
Holdings: Vols (65,000) Cat Microforms
Budget: ($2000)
Notes: This is a comprehensive collection of
material published in and about Hawaii,
including especially 29th century
publications, and University of Hawaii
publications and theses. The Collection
publishes Current Hawaiiana, a quarterly
bibliography of recently available
publications. There is a separate Hawaiian
Collection card catalog; it was published in
1963 by G K Hall as a 4-volume set.

IL —NEWBERRY LIBRARY, 60 W Walton
St, Chicago, 60610. Diana Haskell, Cur of
Modern Mss
Holdings: Cat Mss Maps Pix
Notes: Strong general collection to 1900.

IN —INDIANA UNIVERSITY, Lilly Library,
Seventh St, Bloomington, 47405. William R
Cagle, Librn
Holdings: Cat
Notes: First and early printings of 15th
through 17th century European voyages to
the western hemisphere, incl such collections

as the Decades of Peter Matyr, the Grands
and Petits Voyages gathered by DeBry, and
Hakluyt's Principall Navigations; travels to
the Orient, incl first printed accounts of
Marco Polo; the Portuguese in India from
the time of the arrival of Vasco da Gama;
18th century voyages by Captain James
Cook, Le Comte de Laperouse, and others;
and the great scientific expeditions of the
18th and 19th centuries.

IN —BUTLER UNIVERSITY, Irwin Library,
Hugh Thomas Miller Rare Book Room,
4600 Sunset Ave, Indianapolis, 46208.
Gisela Terrell, Rare Books Librn
Holdings: Vols 2500 Cat Maps Pix
Notes: The William F Charters South Seas
Collection. With the additions made by
Butler University since the acceptance of
this collection in 1931, we are housing circa
2500 volumes pertaining to the Pacific
islands and their peoples; materials range
from the earliest explorers' and
circumnavigators' reports to detailed studies
in anthropology, history, religion, art, socio-
political structures, botany and zoology.

IN —INDIANA STATE UNIVERSITY,
Cunningham Memorial Library, Dept of
Rare Books & Special Collections, Terre
Haute, 47809. Lawrence J McCrank, Head
Holdings: Vols 400 Uncat Maps
Notes: Nature of this material essentially
that of the books listed in E G Cox, A
Reference Guide to the Literature of Travel.
Books range from the 16th century to early
1960s, in English, French, German, Latin,
Italian, and Dutch. Strong in Cook materials
(ie, original editions of first 3 voyages, in
English and French and some Dutch).

KS —UNIVERSITY OF KANSAS, Kenneth
Spencer Research Library, Special
Collections Dept, Lawrence, 66045.
Alexandra Mason, Librn
Holdings: Vols 3000 Cat Mss Maps
Notes: Principal areas covered are North
and South America; Europe, particularly the
British Isles and Eastern Europe. Many
scientific expeditions' reports.
Noncirculating.

MD —JOHNS HOPKINS UNIVERSITY,
Milton S Eisenhower Library, Special
Collections, John Work Garrett Library,
4545 N Charles St, Baltimore, 21210. Jane
Katz, Garrett Librn
Holdings: Vols Cat Mss Maps
Notes: Library incl early voyages and
travels. Downs (1961-70) 444.

MD —JOHNS HOPKINS UNIVERSITY,
Milton S Eisenhower Library, George
Peabody Collection, 17 E Mt Vernon Place,
Baltimore, 21201. Lyn Hart, Peabody Librn
Holdings: Vols (20,000) Cat Maps

MD —MARYLAND HISTORICAL
SOCIETY, Library, 201 W Monument St,
Baltimore, 21201. William B Keller, Head
Librn
Holdings: Maps Pix Films
Notes: Ships and shipping, description and
travel, yachts and yachting, sailing, marine
transport, Baltimore, and the Port of
Maryland. Incl books, periodicals, maps,
charts, pictures, ship plans, log books, films,
etc.

MA —BOSTON COLLEGE LIBRARIES,
Thomas P O'Neill Library, Nicholas M
Williams Ethnological Collection, Chestnut
Hill, 02167. Frank J Seegraber, Special
Collections Librn
Holdings: Vols 10,000 // Cat Mss Maps
Notes: Collection emphasizes Caribbeana,
especially Jamaica, to 1940. Incl discovery,
exploration and natural history of the
British, French and Spanish settlements; the
slave question; piracy. There are over 6000
mss, 5000 of which are Anansi folk tales
recorded by native school children. Also
small ancillary sections of Africana and
Judaica. For reference use only, by
arrangement with librarian.

MA —PEABODY MUSEUM OF SALEM,
Phillips Library, E India Sq, Salem, 01970.
Gregor Trinkaus-Randall, Librn
Holdings: Vols (100,000) Cat Mss Maps Pix
Notes: Pacific and Arctic voyages.

MA —BRANDEIS UNIVERSITY, Goldfarb
Library, 415 South St, Waltham, 02154.
Bessie Hahn, Dir
Notes: McKew-Parr Collection on Magellan

VOYAGES AND TRAVELS (cont.)

and the Age of Discovery. Approx 4000 books relating to Magellan and Columbus and other voyagers of the 15th and early 16th century. A card catalog to the collection is located in Special Collections.

MA —GORDON COLLEGE, Winn Library, Vining Collection, 255 Grapevine Rd, Wenham, 01984. John Beauregard, Dir
Holdings: Vols 800 Cat Mss
Notes: The Vining Collection (of rare books). Incl early circumnavigation of the globe.

MI —EDISON INSTITUTE, Greenfield Village and Henry Ford Museum, Archives & Research Library, PO Box 1970, Dearborn, 48121. Steve Hamp, Dir; Joan W Gartland, Librn
Notes: Incl Dunbar collection of prints, broadsides and drawings documenting *History of Travel in America*, 1680-1910 (1741 items) and the Walker Locomotive collection, 1820-1931 (308 items). It also incl 19th century maps and travelers guides and an antique automotive file.

MI —OLIVET COLLEGE, Burrage Library, Olivet, 49076. Chris Miko, Dir
Holdings: Vols (2000) Cat
Notes: The collection consists primarily of early printed voyages of the arctic and antarctic from the earliest times to the mid-20th century.

MN —MINNEAPOLIS PUBLIC LIBRARY & INFORMATION CENTER, History & Travel Dept, 300 Nicollet Mall, Minneapolis, 55401. Robert K Bruce, Head
Holdings: Vols (186,500) Cat Maps Phonorecords Audiotapes Microforms

MN —UNIVERSITY OF MINNESOTA, James Ford Bell Library, 309 19th Ave S, Minneapolis, 55455. John Parker, Cur
Holdings: Vols (11,000) Cat Mss Maps
Notes: Collection of original materials relating to European expansion, 1400-1800.

NV —FORESTA INSTITUTE FOR OCEAN AND MOUNTAIN STUDIES, Library, 6205 Franktown Rd, Carson City, 89701. Shannon Porter, Librn
Holdings: Vols 500 Cat Mss Maps Pix Slides
Notes: Collection incl historical and contemporary accounts of Antarctic voyages; special emphasis on ecology, plant and animal life, fish, and whales. Also, about 1500 pamphlets, etc. Bibliography of whales and whaling materials in library published in 1977.

NY —NEW YORK STATE LIBRARY, State Education Bldg Annex, Washington Ave, Albany, 12224.
Holdings: Vols 2200 Cat
Notes: Major emphasis on the New World.

NY —C W POST CENTER OF LONG ISLAND UNIVERSITY, B Davis Schwartz Memorial Library, Greenvale, 11548. Jean Goldberg, Special Collections Librn
Notes: Travel guide collection.

NY —AMERICAN MUSEUM OF NATURAL HISTORY, Library Services Dept, Central Park W & 79th St, New York, 10024. Nina J Root, Chairwoman; Mary Genett, Asst Librn for Reference Services
Holdings: Vols (385,000) Cat Mss Maps Pix Slides Microforms
Notes: Nearly all collections are outstanding for depth of coverage and international range. Early and historic works, rare books, colored illustrations, and relevant serial publications supplement the modern scientific publications necessary to the researches of the scientific staff and the work of the educational division. Open to the public.

NY —EXPLORERS CLUB, James B Ford Memorial Library, 46 E 70 St, New York, 10021. Janet Baldwin, Librn
Holdings: Vols (24,000) Cat Maps
Notes: Additions to the collection depend upon gifts. Access by appointment only. Collections incl the Ted Banks Collection; begun by Prof Harley H Bartlett, bequeathed to American Institute for Exploration, with additions by Prof Ted Bank II, and subsequently acquired by the Explorers Club. Incl field notes, diaries, and photographs of

Bank, who led more than 30 scientific expeditions to the Arctic, Aleutians, Sea of Okhotsk, Japan, Taiwan, Southeast Asia and Africa.

NY —HISPANIC SOCIETY OF AMERICA, Library, 613 W 155 St, New York, 10032. Martha M de Narvaez, Cur of Mss; Irene S Frye, Asst Librn
Holdings: Vols (150,000) Cat Mss Maps Pix Slides Phonorecords Microforms
Notes: History, art, literature and general culture of the Hispanic countries (where Spanish or Portuguese is spoken). Incl (18,000) vols printed before 1701, incl (250) incunabula; over (100,000) later vols, plus thousands of periodicals. About (200,000) mss incl ms maps. Printed atlases are in the Book Collection. Some microfilms, chiefly of our early books. Engraved and printed separate maps; reference collection of over 100,000 photographs; slides: all in Department of Iconography, not in library. Catalogs: *Catalogue of the Hispanic Society of America* (Boston: G K Hall, 1962), 10 vols; *First Supplement* (Boston, 1970), 4 vols. Early books: *Printed Books 1468-1700*; Mss: *Catalogo de los Manuscritos Poeticos Castellanos* (15th-17th centuries; 3 vols); *Medieval Manuscripts in the Library*; *Golden Age Drama Manuscripts* (the latter in press).

NY —NEW YORK PUBLIC LIBRARY, Research Libraries, General Research Division, Fifth Ave & 42 St, New York, 10018. Rodney Phillips, Chief
Holdings: Vols (2,225,000) Cat Maps Pix Microforms
Budget: ($775,718)

NY —NEW YORK PUBLIC LIBRARY, Rare Books and Manuscripts Div, Fifth Ave & 42 St, New York, 10018. William L Joyce, Asst Dir; Francis O Mattson, Curator
Holdings: Cat
Budget: ($7161)
Notes: Incl one of the most extensive collections of De Bry and Hulius and one of the finest sets of Canadian Jesuit Relations. Most editions of Columbus' "Letter."

NY —SEAMEN'S CHURCH INSTITUTE OF NEW YORK, Joseph Conrad Library, 15 State St, New York, 10004. Bonnie Golightly, Librn
Holdings: Vols (23,500)
Budget: ($8500)
Notes: Merchant seamen, merchant ships, voyages, navigation, marine engineering, shipbuilding. Large collection of ship registers: *Lloyd's Register of Shipping*, a partial coverage of the years 1764-1865 in reprints, complete coverage for the years 1877 to date; *American Bureau of Shipping*, 1916 to date; *Merchant Vessels of the US*, 1891 to date. *Society of Naval Architects and Marine Engineers Transactions*, vol 1, 1893 to date. The picture file consists mostly of photographs of merchant ships. This is supplemented by scrapbooks. The index to the pictures, scrapbooks, books and vertical file are in one subject catalog. We subscribe to and keep for several years numerous maritime periocals. The maritime history collection incl sailing ships as well as steamships.

NY —UNIVERSITY CLUB, Library, One W 54 St, New York, 10019. Guy St Clair, Library Dir
Holdings: Vols (100,000) Cat Mss Maps Pix
Notes: A private library for the members of the University Club, their guests, and serious scholars upon written application to the Library Director.

NY —UNIVERSITY OF ROCHESTER, Rush Rhees Library, Department of Rare Books and Special Collections, Rochester, 14627. Peter Dzwonkoski, Librn
Holdings: Vols 75 Cat
Notes: Collection includes accounts of voyages by Cook, Churchill, Pinkerton, Hawkesworth, and other accounts of 18th and 19th-century polar, continental, and oceanic explorations.

NC —DUKE UNIVERSITY, William R Perkins Library, Rare Book Room, Durham, 27706. John L Sharpe, III, Cur
Holdings: Vols 1000
Notes: Collection of various accounts of

voyages and scientific expeditions, primarily in the 18th and 19th centuries.

OH —CLEVELAND PUBLIC LIBRARY, Fine Arts and Special Collections Department, 325 Superior Ave, Cleveland, 44114. Alice N Loranth, Head
Holdings: Vols 7600 Cat Mss Maps
Notes: Part of Rare Books and Orientalia collection. Extensive holdings incl over 1100 rare Americana, Canadiana, Latin Americana; 19th Century European travelers; arctic and antarctic voyages and 6500 vols on early travel in Asia, Africa, South Pacific and Australia.
See also entries under Oriental Antiquities; Rare Books.

OH —CLEVELAND PUBLIC LIBRARY, History and Geography Department, 325 Superior Ave, Cleveland, 44114. JoAnn Petrello, Head
Holdings: Cat Maps
Notes: Collection incl rare books, especially Americana, Canadiana, Latin Americana; 19th century European travelers; Arctic and Antarctic voyages.

OH —OHIO HISTORICAL SOCIETY, Archives Library Division, 1982 Velma Ave, Columbus, 43211. Dennis East, Division Chief
Holdings: Vols 2000 // Cat Mss Pix
Notes: Collection is comprised of books by Grey, magazines in which his writings appeared, mss & typescripts, and 700 items from his personal library, incl scarce items on hunting, big-game fishing, and travel. Museum objects are at the Zane Grey Museum, Zanesville, Ohio, operated by the Ohio Historical Society.

OH —FLESH PUBLIC LIBRARY, 124 W Greene St, Piqua, 45356. Wallace White, Librn
Holdings: Vols (1400) // Cat Maps
Notes: The Jerome C Smiley Collection.

OR —UNIVERSITY OF OREGON LIBRARY, Special Collections Div, Eugene, 97403. Kenneth W Duckett, Curator
Holdings: Cat
Notes: Extensive holdings in 17th-19th century voyages in many languages, especially Northwest coast explorations and American overlands.

PA —ATHENAEUM OF PHILADELPHIA, 219 S Sixth St, Philadelphia, 19106. Roger W Moss Jr, Librn
Holdings: Vols 2000 Cat Mss Maps Pix
Notes: Separate catalog by date.

†PA —LIBRARY COMPANY OF PHILADELPHIA, 1314 Locust St, Philadelphia, 19107. Edwin Wolf II, Librn
Holdings: Vols (450,000)

PA —UNIVERSITY OF PENNSYLVANIA, Van Pelt Library, Rare Books Collection, 34 & Walnut Sts, Philadelphia, 19104. Daniel Traister, Special Collections Librn
Holdings: Vols 2500 //
Notes: Robert Dechert Collection: early exploration, 17th and 18th centuries; western Americana, 19th century; Canadiana, incl Jesuit relations.

PA —PENNSYLVANIA STATE UNIVERSITY, Fred Lewis Pattee Library, University Park, 16802. Stuart Forth, Dean of Libraries
Holdings: Vols Cat Maps
Notes: Based primarily on an interest in Australia and the Pacific Ocean, the Pennsylavania State University Libraries have developed a strong collection of voyages, including many 17th and 18th century editions of specific voyages, eg, Cook, La Perouse, Vancouver, collected editions both French and English, together with related publications, eg, De Brosses, Dalrymple. The collections include both exploration and scientific voyages in original editions and reprints.

RI —BROWN UNIVERSITY, John Hay Library, 20 Prospect St, Providence, 02912. Mark N Brown, Cur Mss
Notes: Two collections: (1) Eberstadt Collection of Narratives of California Pioneer's personal narratives written by pioneers who crossed the Plains to California after the discovery of gold in 1849. A large portion of the books were printed in late 19th and early 20th centuries and deal with:

VOYAGES AND TRAVELS (cont.)

Indian contacts, captivities, frontier lore, travel routes, topography, fauna and flora, outlaws, traders and trappers, and frontier army life (350 vols uncat). (2) George Earl Church Collection (3500 vols)--formed by a civil engineer, explorer and Fellow of the Royal Geographic Society, who specialized in railroad construction. Although part of the collection is devoted to American Revolutionary and Civil War history, the majority, over 2000 vols, pertains to Central and South America. The imprints, which arepredominantly 18th century, include Lima, Madrid, Rome, Mexico City, Seville, Barcelona, Lisbon, and Cadiz as well as *Nova orbis regionum ac insularum veteribus incognitarum* (Basle: 1537). Major subject areas are anthropology, commerce, economics, engineering, ethnology, geography, history, law, mineral resources, railroad surveys, voyages of exploration and dictionaries of the South American Indian languages. The most significant ms is an historical account of the Bolivian mining town of Potosi, 1545-1737.

RI —BROWN UNIVERSITY, John Carter Brown Library, Providence, 02912. Norman Fiering, Librn; Everett C Wilkie Jr, Bibliographer; Susan Danforth, Cur Maps & Prints
Holdings: Vols (40,000) Cat Mss Maps Pix
Notes: History of the Americas during the Colonial Period.
See also entry under Imaginary Voyages.

RI —PROVIDENCE ATHENAEUM, 251 Benefit St, Providence, 02903. Sally Duplaix, Dir
Holdings: Vols 12,500 Cat
Notes: Concentration is on the 18th and 19th centuries, worldwide in coverage. Incl many scientific expedition accounts. Approx 3000 may be categorized as rare books/special collections. The library projects a Short Title Catalogue of its rarer holdings in this area within the next few years.

SC —UNIVERSITY OF SOUTH CAROLINA, Thomas Cooper Library, Columbia, 29208. Kenneth E Toombs, Dir of Libraries; Roger Mortimer, Rare Book Librn
Holdings: Vols 500 Cat
Notes: Particularly strong in landmark titles published in the 18th and 19th centuries.

SC —WOFFORD COLLEGE, Sandor Teszler Library, N Church St, Spartanburg, 29301. Frank J Anderson, Librn
Holdings: Vols 300 Uncat Maps
Notes: Material from 16th-20th century atlases. A misc collection relating to voyages, travel and description of various parts of the world. Bulk of titles are 19th century imprints. Described in: *Geography and Travels*, compiled and edited by Frank J Anderson (Wofford College Library. Special Collections Checklist no 2), Spartanburg, SC: Wofford Library Press, 1970; 54 pp, mimeo with subject index.

TX —SOUTHERN METHODIST UNIVERSITY, DeGolyer Library, Box 396, SMU, Dallas, 75275. Clifton H Jones, Dir
Holdings: Vols 50,000 Cat Mss Maps Pix
Notes: History of the trans-Mississippi West and Mexico, from discovery to present. Original editions of most of the important early collections of travel.

VA —UNIVERSITY OF VIRGINIA, Alderman Library, Rare Book Dept, Charlottesville, 22901. Julius P Barclay, Cur
Holdings: Vols 180
Notes: The Mrs Charles T Neale Collection comprises mainly 18th and 19th century voyages and travels.

†WA —WASHINGTON STATE UNIVERSITY, Library, Manuscripts, Archives & Special Collections, Pullman, 99164. John F Guido, Head
Holdings: Cat Mss Maps Pix
Notes: The collection is especially rich in documents relating to the exploration, settlement and development of the Palouse Country, the Inland Empire, the Columbia Basin and the Pacific Northwest. Described in *Selected Manuscript Resources in the Washington State University Library* (Pullman, 1974); and other published and unpublished inventories and registers.

WA —UNIVERSITY OF WASHINGTON LIBRARIES, Suzzallo Library, Special Collections Division, Rare Book Collection, FM-25, Seattle, 98195. Gary Menges, Coordinator for Special Collections
Holdings: Vols (12,000) Cat Maps
Notes: American, British, French, German and Italian books printed before 1800, chiefly in the fields of history and literature. Fine bindings and illustrated works are represented. Incl incunabula, emblemata, voyages and travel, and poetry.

WI —UNIVERSITY OF WISCONSIN, MILWAUKEE, American Geographical Society Collection, 2311 E Hartford Ave, PO Box 399, Milwaukee, 53201. Roman Drazniowsky, Cur
Holdings: Vols (196,800)
Budget: ($270,000)
Notes: The largest special collection in the field of geography, cartography, and related fields in the Western Hemisphere. Incl 6469 atlases; 385,610 maps; 72 globes; 33,700 pamphlets; 79,000 photographs; 99,000 Landsat Images. Catalog published by G K Hall, Boston.

AB —GLENBOW-ALBERTA INSTITUTE, Historical Library & Archives, 130 9th Avenue SE, Calgary, T2G 0P3, Can. Leonard J Gottseleg, Chief Librn
Holdings: Vols (60,000) Cat Mss Maps Pix Microforms
Notes: Main emphasis is on Western Canadian history. Equally important emphasis is placed on the Canadian Arctic and Alaska, Northwest Coast explorations, aboriginal peoples of the North and Canadian West, and the fur trade in the US Northwest.

NS —NOVA SCOTIA MUSEUM, Library, 1747 Summer St, Halifax, B3H 3A6, Can. M S Whiteside, Librn
Notes: Emphasis is on social history.

ON —METROPOLITAN TORONTO LIBRARY, History Dept, 789 Yonge St, Toronto, M4W 2G8, Can. Michael Pearson, Head
Holdings: Vols (2500) Cat
Notes: The collection includes reports, diaries and personal narratives of travels and voyages of exploration and discovery from the Renaissance to the present day. Areas of emphasis are the exploration of the interior of North America, early oceanic voyages of discovery and accounts of travellers to Russia. The collection also includes a number of early editions, standard collected works such as the publications of the Hakluyt Society, accounts of shipwrecks as well as a representative collection of guide books from the 18th century to the present.

VOYAGES AND TRAVELS—VIEWS see Pictures—Collections; Views

VOYAGEURS

MN —UNIVERSITY OF MINNESOTA, DULUTH, Library & Learning Resources Service, Duluth, 55812. James V. Litha, Archivist
Holdings: Vols (1700) Cat Mss Maps Pix
Notes: The Voyageur Collection incl the Grace Lee Nute Papers. Books and materials relating to the Voyageur period (1650-1850) and the area of Northeastern Minnesota, Michigan, Wisconsin, Southern Canada. Emphasis on all subjects listed in this volume.

VOYEURISM AND VOYEURS

†CA —INSTITUTE FOR THE ADVANCED STUDY OF HUMAN SEXUALITY, 1523 Franklin St, San Francisco, 94109.
IN —INDIANA UNIVERSITY, Institute for Sex Research Library, 416 Morrison Hall, Bloomington, 47401. Douglas Freeman, Collections and Services Librn; Joan Brewer, Information Services Librn
Holdings: Vols (62,000) Cat Mss Pix Microforms
See also entry under Sex.

VOYNICH, ETHEL

CT —YALE UNIVERSITY, Box 1603A, Yale Station, New Haven, 06520.
Holdings: Cat Pix
Notes: Some 40 different editions and translations of her book, *The Gadfly*. Also 2 prints of the Russian 16mm color film (with music by Shostakovich) and a documentary film showing her viewing the earlier picture.

VOYNICH, WILFRED

NY —GROLIER CLUB OF NEW YORK LIBRARY, 47 E 60 St, New York, 10022. Robert Nikirk, Librn
Notes: Archive of the noted bookseller, covering the years of his US career.

VOYNICH MANUSCRIPT

†VA —GEORGE C MARSHALL RESEARCH FOUNDATION AND LIBRARY, Drawer 920, Lexington, 24450. Royster Lyle Jr, Cur Collections
Holdings: Vols Uncat Mss
Notes: A copy of the Voynich Mss, an undeciphered work, and other rare volumes on the subject dating from the 16th century.

VREELAND, FRANCIS WILLIAM

CA —LOS ANGELES PUBLIC LIBRARY, Frances Howard Goldwyn Hollywood Regional Library, 1623 Ivar Ave, Los Angeles, 90028. Sally Dumaux, Librn
Holdings: Vols (100,000) Cat Pix VF
Budget: ($60,000)
Notes: Special Collections: Francis William Vreeland, local artist, incl correspondence, working papers, scrapbooks, photographs; Gladys Littell Collection incl Hollywood Bowl Sunrise Services 1920s-1940s, Hollywood Conservatory of Music, 1920s, Hollywood Chamber of Commerce, incl correspondence, programs, working papers, and photographs; Holly Leaves, Hollywood, Calif, 1916-1930.

W

W. R. GRACE AND CO. see Grace and Co., W. R.

WACS see Women'S Army Corps (Wacs)

WADSWORTH FAMILY

NY —STATE UNIVERSITY OF NEW YORK, COLLEGE OF ARTS & SCIENCE AT GENESEO, Milne Library, Geneseo, 14454. William T Lane, Head of Information Services & Archivist
Holdings: Uncat Mss Maps Pix Microforms Notes: The Wadsworth Family Papers. 165 linear ft. Business and family correspondence, account books, maps, deeds, leases and business records of the Wadsworth Family, early landowners in the Genesee region of western New York. Major family members represented in the collection incl Jeremiah Wadsworth (1743-1804), William Wadsworth (1761-1833), Daniel Wadsworth (1771-1848), James Wadsworth (1768-1844), James Samuel Wadsworth (1807-1864), William Wolcott Wadsworth (1810-1852), Emmeline Austin Wadsworth (1808-1885), James Wolcott Wadsworth (1846-1926), William Austin Wadsworth (1847-1918), Herbert Wadsworth (1851-1930), Martha Blow Wadsworth (1864-1934), Craig W Wadsworth (1872-1960), Charles F Wadsworth (1835-1899), James Wolcott Wadsworth Jr (1877-1952), James Jeremiah Wadsworth (1905-), and William P Wadsworth (1906-1982). Inventory in repository. Open toqualified investigators with permission of archivist. Gift of William P Wadsworth and the Hon James J Wadsworth, Geneseo, NY, 1976- , and Michael Moukanoff, Ashantee, NY, 1976. The Wadsworth Family papers cover the years from 1790 to the early 20th century. See also entry under Photographs - Collections

WAGENKNECHT, EDWARD

MA —BOSTON UNIVERSITY, Mugar Memorial Library, Special Collections Dept, 771 Commonwealth Ave, Boston, 02215. Howard B Gotlieb, Dir
Holdings: Cat Mss Pix
Notes: Mss, correspondence, etc collected in depth; incl publications by or about.
NE —UNIVERSITY OF NEBRASKA-LINCOLN, Don L Love Library, University Archives and Special Collections, Lincoln, 68588. Joseph G Svoboda, University Archivist
Notes: Virginia Faulkner was recognized as one of Nebraska's most distinguished writers and scholars. The Virginia Faulkner Collection, containing over 2000 titles, is housed in the Special Collections Department of Love Library. It is especially strong in twentieth century writers and in University of Nebraska Press Publications. Of especial value to scholars are her extensive holdings of Willa Cather, Wright Morris and John Neihardt. Her correspondence with S N Behrman, E B White, Edward Wagenknecht, Donald Sutherland, Wright Morris, Louise Pound, Mari Sandoz, Hazel Barnes, Alfred A and Blanche Knopf, and others provide insight into the literary development of these figures, as well as chronicle the intellectual thought of the period. Amassed in a separate file, these letters are available to interested scholars.

WAGES AND SALARIES

DC —AMERICAN SOCIETY OF ASSOCIATION EXECUTIVES, Information Central, 1575 Eye St NW, Washington, 20005. Cathy L Lalush, Mgr of Research and Info
Notes: Information regarding association management. Resources are designed to provide the association executive with the background knowledge for management decisions through case studies, research and statistical reports, bibliographies, and articles.
DC —US DEPT OF LABOR, Library, 200 Constitution Ave NW, Washington, 20210.

Sabina Jacobson, Dir
Holdings: Vols (550,000) Cat
ON —CANADA DEPT OF LABOUR, Library, Ottawa, K1A 0J2, Can. Monique Marchand, Chief Librn
Holdings: Vols (100,000) Cat Microforms

WAGGAMAN AND RAY, ARCHITECTS

DC —LIBRARY OF CONGRESS, Prints & Photographs Div, Washington, 20540.
Notes: Drawings by the Washington, DC architectural firm, Waggaman and Ray, early 20th century. Contains presentation drawings, working sketches, renderings of structural and mechanical details, blueprints, and a small number of photographs and letters pertaining to 400 different projects. Incl 16,000 items.

WAGNER, GEOFFREY

MA —BOSTON UNIVERSITY, Mugar Memorial Library, Special Collections Dept, 771 Commonwealth Ave, Boston, 02215. Howard B Gotlieb, Dir
Holdings: Cat Mss
Notes: Mss, correspondence, etc collected in depth; incl publications by or about.

WAGNER, HENRY RAUP, 1862-1957

CA —CLAREMONT COLLEGES, Honnold Library, Ninth & Dartmouth, Claremont, 91711. Tania Rizzo, Special Collections Dept Head
Holdings: Vols 561 // Cat Mss Maps
Notes: Henry Raup Wagner Collection: cartography of the West Coast, voyages, related history and geography, 15th century and later. Most maps are photostats from European and American archives and libraries. Bound typescripts of sources Wagner used in preparing his Evolution of Maps of the Northwest Coast, some facsimiles of mss, with transliteration or translation. Original copy (bound) of typescript of his "The Cartography of the Northwest Coast of America to the Year 1800" with pencilled and typed corrections and notes. Downs 2725. Mario C Schnitzler, "Annotated Bibliography of the Henry Raup Wagner Collection of Early Hispanic-American History and Geography" (thesis, 1955).
CA —SAN DIEGO STATE UNIVERSITY, Malcolm A Love Library, 5300 Campanile Dr, San Diego, 92182. D Dickinson, Univ Librn; Don L Bosseau, Dir
Notes: Collected works in first edition of certain prominent authors, as H G Wells, Somerset Maugham, William Dean Howells, Gertrude Atherton, Tom Stoppard, James Clavell, G A Henty, Henry Raup Wagner.
DC —LIBRARY OF CONGRESS, Rare Book & Special Collections Div, Washington, 20540. William Matheson, Chief
Notes: See description of the collection under The West.

WAGNER, ROBERT F.

DC —GEORGETOWN UNIVERSITY, Library, Special Collections Div, 37 & O Sts NW, Washington, 20057. George M Barringer, Special Collections Librn; Nicholas B Sheetz, Mss Librn
Holdings: Cat Mss Maps Pix Slices Phonorecords Audiotapes
Notes: Includes the papers (1912-49) of Sen Robert F Wagner; the archives (1903-) of the American Political Science Association and of its local Washington chapter; the archives of the Center for Public Financing of Elections; a collection of several hundred political cartoons by Eric Smith; and other smaller collections.

WAGON MAKING see Carriage, Cart, and Wagon Making

WAGONER, DAVID

MO —WASHINGTON UNIVERSITY, Libraries, Special Collections Dept, Campus

Box 1061, St Louis, 63130.
Notes: A major collection, incl books, mss, correspondence, literary papers, photographs, etc. Described in Special Collections: an Annotated Guide to the Holdings of the Manuscript Division and the University Archives and Research Collection.

WAGONS

NH —NEW HAMPSHIRE HISTORICAL SOCIETY, Manuscripts Library, 30 Park St, Concord, 03301. Thomas E Camden, Cur
Holdings: Cat Mss Pix
Notes: Abbot-Downing Truck and Body Co records 1813-1945. Incl correspondence, account book, journals, ledgers, order books, accounts receivable, records of sales, balance sheet for New York branch, records of material mortgaged to Josiah E Fernald, banker, of Concord, New Hampshire, other financial papers, drawings, catalogs, and photos of vehicles, clippings, advertisments, and other papers of a firm based in Concord, New Hampshire, and manufacturing wagons, coaches, carriages, and motor-trucks. 33 linear feet, about 22,000 items.
OK —MUSEUM OF THE GREAT PLAINS, Research Center, 601 Ferris, PO Box 68, Lawton, 73502. Steve Wilson, Dir; Paula Williams, Special Collections
Notes: Large holdings of hardware and agricultural catalogs and trade periodicals dating 1869 to 1926. Collection incl over 2000 photographs of wagons and carriages from various manufacturer's catalogs and trade periodicals. Catalogs and periodicals are indexed. Collections are described in Vol 17 (1978) Great Plains Journal published by the Museum.
TX —PANHANDLE-PLAINS HISTORICAL MUSEUM, Research Center, Box 967, WT Sta, Canyon, 79016. Claire R Kuehn, Archivist-Librn
Holdings: Vols 85 Cat
Budget: $300
Notes: Supplements Museum's wagon and carriage collections. Incl periodicals and catalogs.
†WA —WASHINGTON STATE UNIVERSITY, Library, Manuscripts, Archives & Special Collections, Pullman, 99164. John F Guido, Head
Holdings: Cat Mss Maps Pix
Notes: The Carl Parcher Russell papers, a vast resource (24,916 items; 45 linear feet) on American Indian and Western pioneer activities and artifacts. Much on the fur trade; pioneer life; mountain men and trapping; wildlife; primitive life in detail. Also the National Park Service, parks, monuments, etc. Described in Carl Parcher Rusell: An Indexed Register of His Scholarly and Professional Papers, 1920-1967, in the Washington State University Library (Pullman, 1970), 149 pp.

WAGONS, ARMY see Vehicles, Military

WAHPAKOOTA SIOUX INDIANS see Dakota Indians

WAKEFIELD, DAN

MA —BOSTON UNIVERSITY, Mugar Memorial Library, Special Collections Dept, 771 Commonwealth Ave, Boston, 02215. Howard B Gotlieb, Dir
Holdings: Mss
Notes: Mss, correspondence, etc collected in depth; incl publications by or about.

WAKOSKI, DIANE, 1937-

AZ —UNIVERSITY OF ARIZONA, University Library, Special Collections, Tucson, 85721. Louis A Hieb, Head
Holdings: Vols (7000) Cat Mss Microforms Budget: ($30,000)
Notes: In the 20th century, the major emphasis is Bukowski, Wakoski, Wilder, Reznikoff, Ginzberg, Ferlinghetti, Snyder, Whalen, Everson, Joyce Carol Oates, and Kurt Vonnegut.

WAKOSKI, DIANE, 1937- (cont.)

FL —UNIVERSITY OF MIAMI, Otto G
Richter Library, PO Box 248214, Coral
Gables, 33124. Frank Rodgers, Dir of
Libraries
Notes: Innovative and experimental writing
of the 1960s and 1970s. Incl generous
proportion of press books: Black Sparrow,
Auerhahn, and many others; also other
private publications ranging from the best to
the least attractive. Format incl postcards
and broadsides as well as periodical and
book form. Writers incl Charles Bukowski,
Diane Wakoski, Jerome Rothenberg, Clayton
Eshleman, and many of their
contemporaries. 2400 items.
See also entry under Poetry, Modern.

VT —UNIVERSITY OF VERMONT, Guy W
Bailey/David W Howe Library, Burlington,
05405. John Buehler, Asst Dir for Special
Collections

WALCOTT, CHARLES DOOLITTLE

DC —SMITHSONIAN INSTITUTION,
Archives Div, Washington, 20560. William
W Moss, Archivist
Holdings: Cat Mss Pix
Notes: The Archives holds the official
records of Walcott's tenure as Secretary of
the Smithsonian, 1907-1927, and the bulk of
his personal papers, dated 1851-1940.
See also entry under Paleobiology

WALD, LILLIAN D.

NY —COLUMBIA UNIVERSITY
LIBRARIES, Rare Book & Manuscript
Library, 801 Butler Library, 535 W 114 St,
New York, 10027. Kenneth A Lohf, Librn
Holdings: Mss
Notes: Papers of Lillian D Wald, relating to
the founding and administration of the
Henry Street Settlement, and other
philanthropic and liberal causes in which she
was active. 30,000 items. Restricted use.

WALDIE, JOHN, 1781-1862

CA —UNIVERSITY OF CALIFORNIA, LOS
ANGELES, Research Library, Dept of
Special Collections, 405 Hilgard Ave, Los
Angeles, 90024. Edward Shreeves,
Chairman, Bibliographers Group; David S
Zeidberg, Head
Notes: 93 volumes of ms journals and letters,
1793-1862, incl an eyewitness narrative of
the Battle of Waterloo.

WALDMAN, ANNE

BC —SIMON FRASER UNIVERSITY,
Library, Burnaby, V5A 1S6, Can. Percilla
Groves, Special Collections Librn
Holdings: // Cat Mss
Notes: Letters from Anne Waldman to
Lewis Warsh, many concerned with *Silo* and
Angel Hair Press, 1965-1973; some mss
enclosed.

WALES, NYM (HELEN FOSTER SNOW), 1907-

CA —HOOVER INSTITUTION ON WAR,
REVOLUTION & PEACE, Stanford
University, Stanford, 94305. Milorad M
Drachkovitch, Archivist
Holdings: Mss
Notes: Papers of Nym Wales (Helen Foster
Snow), journalist and writer, incl personal
and collected correspondence, speeches and
writings, news dispatches, interviews,
reports, memoranda, organizational records,
and other material, 1931-1954, related
primarily to her experiences in China with
the Chinese communists, industrial
cooperative movement, Sian incident (1936),
Sino-Japanese conflict, and art and literature.
37 ms boxes; 30 photo envelopes.

WALEY, ARTHUR D.

NJ —RUTGERS, THE STATE UNIVERSITY
OF NEW JERSEY, Alexander Library,
Special Collections and Archives, College
Ave & Huntington St, New Brunswick,
08903. Ronald L Becker, Cur of Manuscripts
and Rare Books
Holdings: Mss
Notes: 14 boxes of mss; 154 vols from his
library. Partially cataloged.

WALKER, BARCLAY

IN —INDIANA UNIVERSITY, Lilly Library,
Seventh St, Bloomington, 47405. William R
Cagle, Librn
Notes: Extensive holdings of American sheet
music; first editions of works by great
composers (operas, symphonies, chamber
music, etc); sources annotated for
performances conducted by Fritz Busch. Ms
incl small collections of Hoagy Carmichael
materials, Paul Dresser memorabilia, and
Barclay Walker compositions.

WALKER, MADAM C. J., COMPANY

IN —INDIANA HISTORICAL SOCIETY,
Library, 315 W Ohio St, Indianapolis,
46202. Robert K O'Neill, Dir
Holdings: Vols Cat Mss Pix
Notes: Materials on blacks in Indiana, from
stathood to the present day. Incl books,
letters, church and organization records, and
photographs. Incl records of the Madam C J
Walker Company, a black cosmetics firm in
Indianapolis.

WALKER, ELKANAH

†WA —WASHINGTON STATE
UNIVERSITY, Library, Manuscripts,
Archives & Special Collections, Pullman,
99164. John F Guido, Head
Holdings: Vols Cat Mss Maps Pix
Microforms
Notes: Ms resources for the study of Pacific
Northwest Indians incl the papers of
historians William Compton Brown, Carl
Parcher Russell, and Lucullus Virgil
McWhorter; and missionaries Henry
Harmon Spalding, Elkanah Walker and
Marcus Whitman. A few of these resources
have been described in the following
publications: *William Compton Brown: A
Calendar of His Papers in the Washington
State University Library* (Pullman, 1966);
*Carl Parcher Russell: An Indexed Register of
His Scholarly and Professional Papers, 1920-
1967, in the Washington State University
Library* (Pullman, 1970); *The Papers of
Lucullus Virgil McWhorter*, compiled by
Nelson A Ault (Pullman, 1959).

WALKER, JAMES PERKINS, 1829-1868

NJ —PRINCETON UNIVERSITY, Library,
Manuscript Collection, Nassau St, Princeton,
08540. Jean F Preston, Cur
Notes: The James Perkins Walker
manuscripts collection, which fills 6 ms
boxes, is strong in Civil War materials. see
Manuscripts, v 17 no 2, p 39-42. An
unpublished typescript guide (7 p) is
available in the Library.

WALKER, JOHN H.

IL —UNIVERSITY OF ILLINOIS,
URBANA/CHAMPAIGN, Library, Illinois
Historical Survey Library, 1408 W Gregory
Dr, 1A Library, Urbana, 61801.
Holdings: Vols 50 Cat Mss Pix Microforms
Notes: Important ms collection on the labor
movement and radicalism incl: Adolph
Germer, papers, 1918, 1928, 1930-31, 44
folders; Thomas J Morgan, 1880-1910, 64
folders, 19 vols; John H Walker, papers,
1910-1955, 66 boxes. Guide to the
collections' published in 1976.

WALKER, MORT

MA —BOSTON UNIVERSITY, Mugar
Memorial Library, Special Collections Dept,
771 Commonwealth Ave, Boston, 02215.
Howard B Gotlieb, Dir
Holdings: Cat
Notes: Original cartoons of "Beetle Bailey"
350. Incl publications by.

WALKER, RALPH

NY —SYRACUSE UNIVERSITY
LIBRARIES, Ernest S Bird Library, George
Arents Research Library for Special
Collections, Syracuse, 13210. Carolyn A
Davis, Manuscripts Librn; Amy S Doherty,
University Archivist; Mark F Weimer, Rare
Book Librn
Notes: The George Arents Research Library
for Special Collections at Syracuse
University contains the papers of Harley
James McKee, Lorimer Rich, Frederick
Lear, Max Abramovitz, James I Arnold,
Pietro Bulluschi, Claude Bragdon, Marcel
Breuer, William Lescaze, Skidmore Owings
& Merrill, Ralph Walker, Eric Fisher Wood,
Minoru Yamasaki, Joseph Louis Young, and
Archimedes Russell.

WALKER, WILLIAM

CA —UNIVERSITY OF CALIFORNIA,
RIVERSIDE, University Library, 4045
Canyon Crest Dr, Box 5900, Riverside,
92517.
Holdings: Vols 75
Notes: Collection of printed contemporary
and modern sources relating especially to
William Walker, Nicaragua and the
Filibusters of 1855-60, as well as to
American Filibusters in Mexico.

WALKER-GORDON LABORATORY COMPANY

NY —CORNELL UNIVERSITY LIBRARIES,
Collection of Regional History, Dept of
Manuscripts and Univ Archives, Ithaca,
14853.
Notes: Records, 1920-71; 62 ft. Restricted in
part.

WALKING

NY —UNIVERSITY OF ROCHESTER,
School of Medicine and Dentistry, Edward
G Miner Library, 601 Elmwood Ave,
Rochester, 14642. Lucretia McClure,
Medical Librn; Janet Brady Berk, History of
Medicine Librn
Holdings: Slides
Notes: Very rare historical collection of
some 300 glass slides, most of which relate
to human gait, the foot, footwear, and
myodynamics.

WALL, EDWARD JOHN

NY —SYRACUSE UNIVERSITY
LIBRARIES, Ernest S Bird Library, George
Arents Research Library for Special
Collections, Syracuse, 13210. Carolyn A
Davis, Manuscripts Librn; Amy S Doherty,
University Archivist; Mark F Weimer, Rare
Book Librn
Notes: The George Arents Research Library
for Special Collections at Syracuse
University contains the papers of Margaret
Bourke-White, Clara Sipprell, Gerda
Peterich, Edward John Wall, Louis Fabian
Bachrach, Joseph Costa (National Press
Photographers Association), the University
Archives Photographic Collection, and other
misc photographs.

WALL DECORATION see Mural Painting and Decoration

WALL PAINTING see Mural Painting and Decoration

WALLACE, HENRY A.

IA —UNIVERSITY OF IOWA, University
Libraries, Iowa City, 52242. Frank Paluka,
Head, Special Collections Dept
Holdings: Vols 103 Cat Mss Pix
Notes: The Henry A Wallace Collection, incl
186 linear feet of ms material. Collection
available on microfilm: *Henry A Wallace:
Oral History, Diary and Papers* (Microfilm
Corp of America). See also *The Wallace
Papers: An Index to the Microfilm Editions*

WALLACE, HENRY A. (cont.)

of the Henry A Wallace Papers in the University of Iowa Libraries, the Library of Congress, and the Franklin D Roosevelt Library, Earl M Rogers. 2 vols. (Iowa City, 1975).

WALLACE, IRVING, 1916-

CA —CLAREMONT COLLEGES, Honnold Library, Ninth & Dartmouth, Claremont, 91711. Tania Rizzo, Special Collections Dept Head
Holdings: Vols 600 Cat Mss Pix Audiotapes Videotapes VF
Notes: The Irving Wallace Archive of papers documenting his entire writing career, from magazine articles and screenplays to non-fiction books, novels, and Wallace family writing projects. Currently incl 100 document boxes containing original drafts (some in photocopy) and corrected proofs of all his books, related correspondence, contracts, and publicity, notably from publishers Alfred A Knopf and Simon and Schuster, research files, and excerpts and serializations. Copies of all his books, in all editions and translations published, are included. The Archive similarly represents the literary work of Irving Wallace's wife, Sylvia.
MA —BRANDEIS UNIVERSITY, Goldfarb Library, 415 South St, Waltham, 02154. Bessie Hahn, Dir
Notes: Approx 270 books by Irving Wallace, incl first editions, foreign translations and books used by Wallace to research his novels. In addition, there are 57 linear ft of mss material relating to various novels. A separate card catalog to the books can be found in Special Collections.

WALLACE, LEW

IN —INDIANA HISTORICAL SOCIETY, Library, 315 W Ohio St, Indianapolis, 46202. Robert K O'Neill, Dir
Holdings: Vols 20 Cat Mss Pix
Notes: Wallace's personal papers, occupying 36 boxes. First editions of his works.

WALLACE, LORABEL

AZ —NORTHERN ARIZONA UNIVERSITY, Special Collection Library, CU Box 6022, Flagstaff, 86011. Peter M Whiteley, Coordr/Archivist; William Mullane, Librn
Notes: Sisters of Loretto Collection; correspondence, class records, photos, publications, 1912-1966. Sisters of Loretto operated the School of Nativity, Flagstaff, 1899-1966. Incl information on Sister Mary Imelda (Lorabel Wallace), Flagstaff native, educator and Pulitzer Prize winning children's author.

WALLACE, MARY LONGSTREET

PA —TEMPLE UNIVERSITY LIBRARIES, Special Collections Dept, Conwellana-Templana Collection, 13 & Berks St, Philadelphia, 19122. Miriam I Crawford, Cur
Holdings: Vols 5 Cat Mss
Budget: ($30,000)
Notes: Published novels, magazine writings, typescripts, galley and page proofs, and correspondence of Mary Wallace, popular contemporary novelist, including extended correspondence with her literary agent, Muriel Fuller, and examples of her detailed work and painstaking rewriting in her stories of the close-knit family lives of Irish-Americans.

WALLACE, PAUL A. W.

BC —UNIVERSITY OF VICTORIA, McPherson Library, Victoria, V8W 3H5, Can.

WALLCUT, THOMAS, 1758-1840

ME —BOWDOIN COLLEGE, Library, Brunswick, 04011. Dianne M Gutscher, Cur

of Special Collections
Holdings: Vols
Notes: The Thomas Wallcut Collection comprises 558 volumes presented to the College in 1820 by the Boston Book collector. It contains books printed in the 16th, 17th and 18th centuries, with emphasis on British imprints and religious works, incl a copy of the 1611 *King James Bible*.

WALLER, LESLIE

MA —BOSTON UNIVERSITY, Mugar Memorial Library, Special Collections Dept, 771 Commonwealth Ave, Boston, 02215. Howard B Gotlieb, Dir
Holdings: Cat Mss Pix Audiotapes
Notes: Mss, correspondence, etc collected in depth; incl publications by or about.

WALLIN, THEODORE B.

IL —WHEATON COLLEGE, Buswell Memorial Library, Wheaton, 60187. Paul Snezek, Library Dir
Holdings: Mss Cat
Notes: Material consists of word lists, a conversation manual, a dictionary and the translated New Testament. All of the material collected by Zaire Missionary pioneer, Theodore B Wallin. *Related Topics:* Radio.

WALLPAPER DESIGN

NY —FASHION INSTITUTE OF TECHNOLOGY, Edward C Blum Design Laboratory, 227 W 27 St, New York, 10001. Laura Sinderbrand, Dir
Holdings: Cat Pix Slides
Notes: The largest resource of it kind consisting of 4 million indexed swatches and 300 swatch books, jacquard point paper, croquis, quilts, rug samples, laces, embroideries, and color swatch cards. A collection of international scope incl antique and contemporary textiles; woven and printed patterns created for apparel and home furnishings which may be adapted to china, giftware, floor covering, wallpaper, and package design. A comprehensive research facility comprised of over one million articles of dress dating from the 17th Century to the present, incl men's, women's, children's clothes, furs, foundation garments and lingerie, as well as an outstanding grouping of 19th and 20th century designer clothing. Accessories as diverse as hats, handbags, gloves, hosiery, shoes, shawls, and costume jewelry offer an additonal resource to this international collection.

WALPOLE, HORACE

CT —LEWIS WALPOLE LIBRARY, 154 Main St, Farmington, 06032. Catherine Jestin, Librn
Holdings: Vols 24,000 Cat
Notes: Horace Walpole and his times. Collection is principal resource for the Yale Edition of the Correspondence and of the Memoirs of Horace Walpole. Considerable memorabilia. A research center for English eighteenth-century studies. A department of Yale University Library. Scholars may visit by appointment only.
CT —YALE UNIVERSITY, Box 1603A, Yale Station, New Haven, 06520.
Holdings: Cat Mss
Notes: Incl correspondence.
DE —UNIVERSITY OF DELAWARE, Hugh M Morris Library, S College Ave, Newark, 19711. T Stuart Dick, Special Collections
Holdings: Cat
MA —HARVARD UNIVERSITY LIBRARY, Houghton Library, Cambridge, 02138. F Thomas Noonan, Cur, Reading Room; Lawrence Dowler, Associate Librn
Holdings: Cat Mss
Notes: See *Harvard Library Notes*, II (1925): pp 23-29, and III (1935): pp 41-45.

WALPOLE, HUGH

DC —LIBRARY OF CONGRESS, Rare Book & Special Collections Div, Washington,

20540. William Matheson, Chief
Holdings: Vols 91 Cat
Notes: The Jean Hersholt Collection comprises first editions, presentation copies, association items, proofs, mss and letters of the author. Autograph mss incl those of *The Duchess of Wrexe, The Captives,* and *Wintersmoon* (of the last, corrected proofs as well).
IL —ILLINOIS STATE UNIVERSITY, Milner Library, Dept of Special Collections, Normal, 61761. Robert Sokan, Librn
Notes: First editions, limited editions, ephemera, etc.
NC —UNIVERSITY OF NORTH CAROLINA, CHAPEL HILL, Wilson Library, Rare Book Collection, Chapel Hill, 27514. Paul S Koda, Cur of Rare Books
Holdings: Cat
Notes: Fully representative collection.

WALPOLE, SIR ROBERT

†KS —UNIVERSITY OF KANSAS, Watson Library, Department of Special Collections, Lawrence, 66045. David W Heron, Dir
Holdings: Cat Mss Pix
Notes: The Really Collection, literary manuscripts of Mr & Mrs Joseph A Howells brother, and of his father, William Cooper Howells. The Howells Collection is housed in a special room, The Howells Room, in the Hayes Library.

WALSH, DAVID I., 1872-1947

MA —COLLEGE OF THE HOLY CROSS, Dinand Library, College St, Worcester, 01610. James M Mahoney, Cur of Special Collection
Holdings: Vols 1325 // Cat Mss Pix Microforms
Notes: Governor of Massachusetts and US Senator. Mss of speeches; journals; newspaper clippings; correspondence; personal library.

WALSH, REV. EDMUND A., S.J.

DC —GEORGETOWN UNIVERSITY, Library, Special Collections Div, 37 & O Sts NW, Washington, 20057. George M Barringer, Special Collections Librn; Nicholas B Sheetz, Mss Librn
Holdings: Cat Mss
Notes: His papers, etc.

WALSH, BISHOP EMMET W.

OH —KENT STATE UNIVERSITY, University Archives, Kent, 44242. Stephen C Morton, University Archivist
Holdings: Uncat Mss Pix
Notes: Diocesan and personal correspondence of Bishop Emmet W Walsh, late Bishop of Youngstown. The collection is on deposit and the materials are restricted.

WALSH, FRAN P.

NY —NEW YORK PUBLIC LIBRARY, Rare Books and Manuscripts Div, Fifth Ave & 42 St, New York, 10018. William L Joyce, Asst Dir; Susan E Davis, Cur of Mss
Holdings: Mss
Budget: ($7161)
Notes: Incl personal and literary mss, papers, etc.

WALTER, THOMAS USTICK

PA —ATHENAEUM OF PHILADELPHIA, 219 S Sixth St, Philadelphia, 19106. Roger W Moss Jr, Librn
Holdings: Mss
Notes: Incl 450 drawings of Thomas Ustick Walter from 1804-1887.

WALTHER, JOSEPHINE L.

IN —INDIANA UNIVERSITY, Lilly Library, Seventh St, Bloomington, 47405. William R Cagle, Librn
Holdings: // Mss Pix
Notes: Letters from Havelock Ellis to Josephine L Walther, a staff member of the

WALTHER, JOSEPHINE L. (cont.)

Detroit Institute of Arts, 1925-1935. 164 items, incl nine photographs of Ellis.

WALTON, IZAAK

CT —TRINITY COLLEGE LIBRARY, 300 Summit St, Hartford, 06106. Ralph S Emerick, Librn
Holdings: Cat
Notes: Incl Sherman Parker Collection of 175 editions of Izaak Walton.

CT —YALE UNIVERSITY, Box 1603A, Yale Station, New Haven, 06520.

IL —NEWBERRY LIBRARY, 60 W Walton St, Chicago, 60610. Diana Haskell, Cur of Modern Mss
Holdings: Cat

MA —HARVARD UNIVERSITY LIBRARY, Cambridge, 02138.
Holdings: Cat Mss

MO —CENTRAL MISSOURI STATE UNIVERSITY, Ward Edwards Library, Warrensburg, 64093. Nancy E Littlejohn, Social Sciences Librn
Holdings: Vols 200 Cat
Notes: Over 160 different editions of the *Compleat Angler* plus other related books by and about Walton.

NY —COLUMBIA UNIVERSITY LIBRARIES, Rare Book & Manuscript Library, 801 Butler Library, 535 W 114 St, New York, 10027. Kenneth A Lohf, Librn
Notes: The Elliot V Bell Collection of over 500 books on fishing and angling, from the 17th to 20th centuries; more than 20 early editions of Izaak Walton. Restricted use.

NC —UNIVERSITY OF NORTH CAROLINA, GREENSBORO, Walter Clinton Jackson Library, Special Collections Dept, 1000 Spring Garden St, Greensboro, 27412. Emilie W Mills, Librn
Holdings: Vols (100) Cat Pix Microforms
Notes: First, early and later editions of George Herbert, 17th to 20th centuries. Early manuscripts and documents relating to Nicolas Ferrar and the Herbert family (microfilm). Also incl are early works of Edward, Lord Herbert of Cherbury, Izaak Walton and Nicolas Ferrar; items issued by the Friends of Bemerton are added as published.

PA —LAFAYETTE COLLEGE, David Bishop Skillman Library, Easton, 18042. Dorothy Cieslicki, Librn
Holdings: Vols (825) Cat
Notes: Robert Tinsman Angling Collection. Incl 58 editions of Walton, *Compleat Angler*. Also, the Robert S Conahay Jr, Atlantic Salmon Collection, which incl over 1000 hand-tied salmon and trout flies, many mounted and framed.

PA —UNIVERSITY OF PITTSBURGH, Hillman Library, Special Collections Dept, Hervey Allen Collection, Pittsburgh, 15260. Charles E Aston, Jr, Coordr
Holdings: Vols 375 Cat
Notes: A collection of 231 editions of Izaak Walton's *Compleat Angler*, represented by 375 different issues and states, donated to the University of Pittsburgh Libraries as a memorial to the late Bernard S Horne. One of the largest collections of the *Angler* in existence, it begins with the second edition (London, 1655) and presently ends with the Buchan Reprint (London, 1967). The collection is described in full in Bernard S Horne's *Compleat Angler, 1653-1967: a New Bibliography* (Pittsburgh, 1970). Noncirculating.

WAMPLER, WILLIAM C.

VA —VIRGINIA POLYTECHNIC INSTITUTE AND STATE UNIVERSITY LIBRARY, Blacksburg, 24061. Glenn L McMullen, Special Collections Librn
Holdings: Vols (2000) Cat Mss Maps Pix Audiotapes
Notes: Primarily Southwest Virginia materials. Collection incl ca 200 mss, account books and other archival records of nineteenth century area businesses and other mining operations; the extant archival

records of several Southwest Virginia railroads, incl the Virginia and Tennessee Railroad and the Norfolk and Western Railroad; and papers of historically prominent Southwest Virginians, incl John Apperson, Dr Harvy Black, James P Charlton, W Graham Claytor, Henley Fugate, Clement D Johnston, Germanicus Kent, William Preston, J Hoge Tyler, and William C Wampler. Several oral history collections incl material on Appalachian customs and folklore, particularly in Patrick County.

WANDERING JEW

RI —BROWN UNIVERSITY, John Hay Library, 20 Prospect St, Providence, 02912. Mark N Brown, Cur Mss
Holdings: Vols 1500 Cat Mss
Notes: A virtually complete collection of the literature dealing with the Legend of the Wandering Jew printed from the 17th century to date. In addition to historical discussion of the legend, there are sections devoted to the appearance of Ahasuerus in drama, fiction, illustrations, poetry, song, and music.

WAPPO INDIANS

NY —HOFSTRA UNIVERSITY, Library, 1000 Fulton Ave, Hempstead, 11550. Charles R Andrews, Dean of Library Services
Notes: The personal library of Paul Radin. See description of the American Philosophical Society Library's collection of his anthropological papers under this entry (Pa).

PA —AMERICAN PHILOSOPHICAL SOCIETY, Library, 105 S Fifth St, Philadelphia, 19106. Edward C Carter II, Librn
Notes: The anthropological papers of Paul Radin in fields of ethnology, social organization, primitive religion, linguistics, and mythology. He worked mostly among the Winnebago, Ojibwa, Fox, Zapotec, Wappo, Wintun, and Huave Indian tribes; also Italian and other ethnic minorities of San Francisco.

WAR

CA —WESTERN COSTUME COMPANY, Research Library, 5335 Melrose Ave, Hollywood, 90038. Nancy S Kinney, Dir of Research
Holdings: Vols 3000
Notes: Incl 25 vertical file drawers of photographs, 30 bound periodical volumes, bound uniform regulations, insignia and decorations charts, 27 periodical subscriptions. Card file index on selected military uniform pictures from periodicals holdings. Collection can be used only by the customers of Western Costume Company. All other use is on a fee basis. Collection is non-circulating. Photocopying available.

CA —HOOVER INSTITUTION ON WAR, REVOLUTION & PEACE, Stanford University, Stanford, 94305. Milorad M Drachkovitch, Archivist
Holdings: Cat Mss Maps Pix Slides Microforms
Notes: One of the nation's most extensive collections in many specialized areas. Described in *Archival and Manuscript Materials at the Hoover Institution...A Checklist of Major Collections* (July 1977). $2.00.

CO —COLORADO STATE UNIVERSITY, Libraries, Fort Collins, 80523. John Newman, Special Collections Librn
Holdings: Vols (900) Cat
Notes: The Imaginary Wars Collection incl ficitonal accounts of future wars, imaginary wars in the past and the greatly altered outcomes of real wars. Stories must depict known societies on Earth or close parallels to known societies. At present, the collection consists primarily of monographs. Future plans call for the identification of appropriate short stories. for an annotated bibliography of American imprints in the collection see

John Newman, "America at War: Horror Stories for a Society," *Extrpolation*, XVI, No 1 and 2 (December 1974 and May 1975).

NY —UNIVERSITY OF ROCHESTER, Rush Rhees Library, Department of Rare Books and Special Collections, Rochester, 14627. Peter Dzwonkoski, Librn
Holdings: Mss
Notes: A beginning collection of letters from Vietnam veterans, their families, and friends, and individuals who opposed the war, expected to create a resource toward historical understanding of attitudes and reactions concerning war and the Vietnam Conflict in particular.

NY —US MILITARY ACADEMY LIBRARY, West Point, 10996. Egon A Weiss, Librn
Holdings: Vols (100,000) Cat Mss Maps Pix Slides Phonorecords Videotapes 16mm Films Filmstrips Microforms
Notes: Described in *Subject Catalog of the Military Art and Science Collection in the Library of the US Military Academy* (Greenwood Publishing Corp, 1969).

OH —WILMINGTON COLLEGE, Watson Library, Quaker Collection, Pyle Center, Box #1227, Wilmington, 45177. Audrey Haines, Cur
Holdings: Vols (6000) Cat Mss Maps Pix Microforms
Notes: Collection houses Wilmington College archives, 1870-present, and serves as repository for the records of the Wilmington and Ohio Valley Yearly Meetings of the Religious Society of Friends (Quakers), ca 1800-present. Also incl 120 Quaker periodical and newsletter titles, ca 1828-present; several hundred pamphlets, tracts, and epistles; 220 genealogical works, primarily Quaker families; and 3900 vols on Quaker history, philosophy, thought, and practice, particularly peace, war, slavery, education, and biography, ca 1750-present. Incl some fiction, poetry and children's books. Rare or fragile materials, reference works, pamphlets, and genealogies do not circulate. Please notify prior to visiting.

PA —SWARTHMORE COLLEGE, Peace Collection, Swarthmore, 19081. Jean R Soderlund, Cur of Peace Collection
Holdings: Vols (10,000) Cat Mss Pix Microforms
Notes: Books, pamphlets, posters, periodicals and other materials showing war in its economic, political and social aspects, past, present, and future. Recent acquisitions incl considerable material, both printed and pictorial, on the US-Vietnamese conflict, and the many forms of protest against it. Files on individual and group pacifist activities, documents of underground military publications, and records of antiwar actions and groups, incl Vietnam Summer (1967); A Quaker Action Group (1966-1971); War Resisters League.
See also entry under Pacifism - History.

RI —US NAVAL WAR COLLEGE, Historical Collection & Museum, Newport, 02841. Anthony S Nicolosi, Dir; Evelyn Cherpak, Cur
Holdings: Mss
Notes: Collections incl over 200,000 separate pieces; chiefly papers of naval officers and records of organizations associated with the US Navy, the Naval War College, the college's major study areas, and the Navy in the Narragansett Bay region; oral history collection; Naval War College Archives, 1884-present; records of conferences held at the College; newspaper collections dealing with naval themes and military conflicts.

RI —BROWN UNIVERSITY, John Hay Library, 20 Prospect St, Providence, 02912. Mary T Russo, Cur of Broadsides
Notes: The Broadside Collection consists of 35,000 separate, printed pieces, chiefly American, ranging in date from 1700 to the present. Its special area of strength lies in American poetry represented by about 28,000 items, ranging from anonymous 18th and 19th century ephemeral verse commemorating, admonishing, proclaiming or advertising to contemporary broadsides displaying the work of modern poets. Excellent collections of Carriers' Addresses

WAR (cont.)

and Slip Ballads are other areas of concentration, along with smaller collections of greeting cards, postcards, and posters. Historical material is represented by the Lincoln, John Hay, Rider and Drowne Collections. The Koopman Collection is especially strong in examples of fine printing. There is a general category which contains misc material. Separate catalog. Partially cataloged.

RI —BROWN UNIVERSITY, John Hay Library, Anne S K Brown Military Collection, 20 Prospect St, Providence, 02912. Richard B Harrington, Cur
Notes: The Anne S K Brown Military Collection has been formed over the past forty or more years by Mrs John Nicholas Brown, now of Newport, and contains approximately 40,000 volumes and 60,000 prints, drawings and watercolors as well as a number of oil paintings and about 5000 miniature model soldiers. At its beginning (and still today) the emphasis or focus of this collection has been upon the history of, and the accurate contemporary illustration of, military and naval uniforms of all nations from the early XVII century to the present. In the course of time, however, the collection has come to incl also a vast and related amount of material on military and naval history, military and naval arts and tactics, wars, campaigns, ceremonies, biography, portraits and caricatures of this and earlier periods. It has been probably the largest private collection of such a nature inthe world, and it contains much ms and graphic documentation which is unique. It has been useful to numerous scholars and historians, editors, filmmakers and publishers for research and for illustrative material and has also contributed to many museum exhibitions. In 1982 the entire collection, with its complete card catalog and subject index, has been presented to Brown University, where it is located in the John Hay Library. Special requests are taken care of by phone, mail and appointments with the curator.

WAR CONSERVATION OF CULTURAL RESOURCES see Conservation of Cultural Resources in Wartime

WAR—PICTURES, ILLUSTRATIONS, ETC.

DC —LIBRARY OF CONGRESS, Prints & Photographs Div, Washington, 20540.
Holdings: Cat Pix
Notes: Civil War Photograph Collection incl photographs commissioned by Mathew Brady and others. Brady employed 20 photographers at the height of his operations. His staff incl Alexander and James Gardner, James F Gibson, and Thomas C Roche.

PA —UNIVERSITY OF PITTSBURGH, Hillman Library, Pittsburgh, 15260.
Holdings: Vols (10,000)
Notes: The entire contents of the oldest used book shop in Pittsburgh, the John C Daub Book Store. The collection deals mainly in the areas of military history; works dealing with the Civil War, the World Wars and other military topics; and local history: county histories, city, state or regional histories. Also incl are military works containing colored plates; a large group of Americana; and many framed, colored prints on military subjects.

RI —BROWN UNIVERSITY, John Hay Library, Anne S K Brown Military Collection, 20 Prospect St, Providence, 02912. Richard B Harrington, Cur
Notes: The Anne S K Brown Military Collection has been formed over the past forty or more years by Mrs John Nicholas Brown, now of Newport, and contains approximately 40,000 volumes and 60,000 prints, drawings and watercolors as well as a number of oil paintings and about 5000 miniature model soldiers. At its beginning (and still today) the emphasis or focus of this collection has been upon the history of, and the accurate contemporary illustration of, military and naval uniforms of all nations from the early XVII century to the present. In the course of time, however, the collection has come to incl also a vast and related amount of material on military and naval history, military and naval arts and tactics, wars, campaigns, ceremonies, biography, portraits and caricatures of this and earlier periods. It has been probably the largest private collection of such a nature inthe world, and it contains much ms and graphic documentation which is unique. It has been useful to numerous scholars and historians, editors, filmmakers and publishers for research and for illustrative material and has also contributed to many museum exhibitions. In 1982 the entire collection, with its complete card catalog and subject index, has been presented to Brown University, where it is located in the John Hay Library. Special requests are taken care of by phone, mail and appointments with the curator.

WAR, MARITIME see Naval Art and Science

WAR ATROCITIES see European War Atrocities; World War, 1939-1945—Atrocities

WAR BONDS

CA —CLAREMONT COLLEGES, Honnold Library, Ninth & Dartmouth, Claremont, 91711. Tania Rizzo, Special Collections Dept Head
Holdings: Vols 250 Uncat Mss Maps Pix
Notes: Combined holdings of memorabilia of both world wars, primarily WWII. The Howard D Mills Collection on War Bonds occupies 33 linear ft of scrapbooks, documents, mss, and photographs, in addition to several dozen War Bond, Liberty Bond, and recruitment posters. Nazi propaganda and German medals. Soldiers' handbooks, maps, pamphlets, scrapbooks of clippings, photographs, and recordings. Restricted use.

WAR CRIME TRIALS

CA —PACIFIC UNION COLLEGE, Nelson Memorial Library, Angwin, 94508. Taylor D Ruhl, Dir
Holdings: Vols Cat Microfroms
Notes: Mimeographed copies of all the Japanese war crime trials.

CA —UNIVERSITY OF CALIFORNIA, DAVIS, Shields Library, Dept of Special Collections, Davis, 95616. Donald Kunitz, Head; C Danial Elliott, Asst Head

CA —HOOVER INSTITUTION ON WAR, REVOLUTION & PEACE, Stanford University, Stanford, 94305. Milorad M Drachkovitch, Archivist
Holdings: Mss
Notes: Documents dealing with the International Military Tribunal Nuremberg War Crimes Trials, 1946-1949. 395 ft. Records of the International Military Tribunal for the Far East, incl exhibits, transcripts and summaries of proceedings, summations of counsel, judgements of the tribunal, and indexes, 1946-1948, relating to the trials of Japanese officials accused of World War II war crimes. 81 linear ft.

CA —UNIVERSITY OF THE PACIFIC, Holt-Atherton Pacific Center for Western Studies, Stockton, 95211. Hiram L Davis, Dir of Libraries
Holdings: // Cat Mss
Notes: This collection contains transcripts and related documents of the Nuremberg trials, 1945-1946, gathered by an American staff officer for the court. 13 linear ft. (13 document boxes).

†CT —CONNECTICUT STATE LIBRARY, Hartford, 06106.
Notes: The papers of Sen Thomas J Dodd.

"In his early career Sen Dodd was counsel for the Nuremberg war crime trials and his papers incl the most complete record of htose trials."

IL —CENTER FOR RESEARCH LIBRARIES, 6050 S Kenwood Ave, Chicago, 60637. Donald B Simpson, Dir; Esther Smith, Collection Development Librn
Holdings: Vols Cat Microforms
Notes: Substantially complete set of records of Nuremberg trials and subsequent proceedings. Collection of judgements in war crimes trials in trials in West German courts. Fairly complete set of records of International Military Tribunal for the Far East. Some other materials. Microfilm holdings of newspapers, official gazette. Microfilm and reprint of Imperial and National Diet proceedings. Archival material, Tokugawa period forward. Microfilm of annual reports of over 2000 companies, 1872-1945. Meiji and Taisho prefectural statistics. Prange collection of censored periodicals, occupation period. Nearly complete collection of records of the International Military Tribunal for the Far East. 520 current periodical subscriptions. Descriptive pamphlet available.

WAR GAMES

RI —US NAVAL WAR COLLEGE, Historical Collection & Museum, Newport, 02841. Anthony S Nicolosi, Dir; Evelyn Cherpak, Cur
Holdings: Mss
Notes: Collections incl over 200,000 separate pieces; chiefly papers of naval officers and records of organizations associated with the US Navy, the Naval War College, the college's major study areas, and the Navy in the Narragansett Bay region; oral history collection; Naval War College Archives, 1884-present; records of conferences held at the College; newspaper collections dealing with naval themes and military conflicts.

RI —BROWN UNIVERSITY, John Hay Library, Anne S K Brown Military Collection, 20 Prospect St, Providence, 02912. Richard B Harrington, Cur
Notes: The Anne S K Brown Military Collection has been formed over the past forty or more years by Mrs John Nicholas Brown, now of Newport, and contains approximately 40,000 volumes and 60,000 prints, drawings and watercolors as well as a number of oil paintings and about 5000 miniature model soldiers. At its beginning (and still today) the emphasis or focus of this collection has been upon the history of, and the accurate contemporary illustration of, military and naval uniforms of all nations from the early XVII century to the present. In the course of time, however, the collection has come to incl also a vast and related amount of material on military and naval history, military and naval arts and tactics, wars, campaigns, ceremonies, biography, portraits and caricatures of this and earlier periods. It has been probably the largest private collection of such a nature inthe world, and it contains much ms and graphic documentation which is unique. It has been useful to numerous scholars and historians, editors, filmmakers and publisher for research and for illustrative material and has also contributed to many museum exhibitions. In 1982 the entire collection, with its complete card catalog and subject index, has been presented to Brown University, where it is located in the John Hay Library. Special requests are taken care of by phone, mail and appointments with the curator.

WAR OF 1914 see World War, 1914-1918

WAR OF SECESSION (U.S.) see U.S.—History—Civil War

WAR OF THE AMERICAN REVOLUTION see U.s.—History—Revolution

WAR ORPHANS

NY —HAMPDEN-BOOTH THEATRE LIBRARY AT THE PLAYERS, 16

WAR ORPHANS (cont.)

Gramercy Park, New York, 10003. Louis A
Rachow, Librn/Cur
Holdings: // Uncat Mss
Notes: The

WAR POSTERS see Posters—Collections

WAR PROTESTS

CA —UNIVERSITY OF CALIFORNIA, LOS
ANGELES, Research Library, Social
Sciences Collection, 405 Hilgard Ave, Los
Angeles, 90024. Edward Shreeves,
Chairman, Bibliographers Group; Oscar L
Sims, Social Sciences Bibliographer
Notes: A collection of over 200 underground
newspapers on 26 reels of microfilm. Among
the titles included are: *The Tribe, The
Berkeley Barb, New York Roach, Rat,* and
Win.

CT —UNIVERSITY OF CONNECTICUT,
Library, Storrs, 06268. Ellen Embardo, Cur
Special Collections
Holdings: Cat
Notes: Alternative Press Collection.
Primarily periodicals and newspapers from
the 1960s to today of an alternative or
underground nature. Books and pamphlets
are incl, representing both the left and the
right-wing viewpoints. A catalog is available.
Also have archives of the First Casualty
Press, which was deeply involved with
Vietnam veterans' experiences in Vietnam.

DC —LIBRARY OF CONGRESS,
Washington, 20540.
Notes: Some 4500 pamphlets and sheets
dealing primarily with subversive and radical
activities in the US from 1900 to 1950. Incl
tracts and campaign literture of the
Communist and Socialist Parties in the US
and works by party leaders; materials on the
economic, political, and human rights issues
of the pre-World War II, World War II, and
early civil rights campaign periods; and
pamphlets by various anti-war and anti-draft
organizations, material on Russia, and
materials on the communist movement in
other countries.

OH —KENT STATE UNIVERSITY,
University Archives, Kent, 44242. Stephen C
Morton, University Archivist
Holdings: Cat Mss Maps Pix Microforms
Notes: The May 4, 1970 incident; 50 linear
ft. Separate catalog. Partial description in
Cleveland State Law Review, Winter, 1973.

WI —STATE HISTORICAL SOCIETY OF
WISCONSIN, Archives, 816 State St,
Madison, 53706. Harold L Miller, Reference
Archivist
Holdings: Mss Pix Microforms Audiotapes
Notes: Records and papers of organizations
and individuals engages in social and
political reform activities. Major focus areas
are civil rights, 1950s to the present, and
anti-Vietnam war and other protest
movements of the 1960s to the present. Also
covered are other reform movements,
socialism, and communism from the 1930s
to the present. Collections are described in
*Social Action Collection at the State
Historical Society of Wisconsin: A Guide,*
(1983) and in current accession notes in the
Wisconsin Magazine of History. Major
collections are also listed in Hamer, *Guide
to Manuscripts and Archives in the United
States,* (1961) and in the *National Union
Catalog of Manuscript Collections,* (1959-
date).

WAR RELIEF

IL —NATIONAL COUNCIL OF THE
YMCAS, YMCA Historical Library, 6400
Shafer Ct, Rosemont, 60018. Eleanor R
Murphy, Librn
Holdings: Vols (15,000) Cat Mss Pix
Notes: World War I relief work, incl
material on the YMCA's work with US
troops, both here and abroad, with foreign
armies such as the French, with prisoners of
war of both the Allies and the German/
Austrian/Turkish Armies, and with civilians
employed in war industries or simply victims
of the War. Aspects of the work covered incl
education, physical education, entertainment,
and religious work. A collection of
interviews conducted by the YMCA's War
Historical Bureau in the period 1919-22 is
also available in transcript form.

WAR RELOCATION AUTHORITY see
U.s. War Relocation Authority

WAR RESISTERS

NY —UNIVERSITY OF ROCHESTER, Rush
Rhees Library, Department of Rare Books
and Special Collections, Rochester, 14627.
Peter Dzwonkoski, Librn
Holdings: Mss
Notes: A beginning collection of letters from
Vietnam veterans, their families, and friends,
and individuals who opposed the war,
expected to create a resource toward
historical understanding of attitudes and
reactions concerning war and the Vietnam
Conflict in particular.

WAR SONGS

CA —SAN DIEGO PUBLIC LIBRARY, Art,
Music & Recreation Sect, 820 E St, San
Diego, 92101. Barbara A Tuhill, Supvr
Holdings: Vols 132 Cat
Notes: A collection of gift sheet music has
been organized into bound vols by date of
copyright covering popular songs from the
1800s through the 1950s. Each vol is
arranged with a table of contents by title,
and is also indexed in a special Song Title
Index. Special vols also cover the hits of
World War I, ballads, religious songs and
other subjects. Reference use only.

IL —CHICAGO PUBLIC LIBRARY, Special
Collections Div, Cultural Center, 78 E
Washington St, Chicago, 60602. Laura
Linard, Cur
Holdings: Vols (7000) Cat Mss Maps Pix
Notes: The Civil War and American History
Research Collection at the Chicago Public
Library is our largest collection. It spans the
pre-war sectional crisis as well as
Reconstruction. Scarce slavery pamphlets;
large collection of regimental histories;
manuscripts of US Grant, Sherman,
Breckinridge; letters and diaries of soldiers
and other officers; original photographs of
individuals and field shots; Confederate
Battle Plan for the Battle of Shiloh (original);
swords, rifles, uniforms, flags and other
military accessories. A substantial part of
this collection has been cataloged. The
museum objects are inventoried (Grand
Army Hall and Memorial Association of
Illinois Collection).See *Treasures of The
Chicago Public Library,* comp by Thomas A
Oriando and Marie Gecik, 1977, pp 36-79.

PA —FREE LIBRARY OF PHILADELPHIA,
Sheet Music Collection, Logan Sq,
Philadelphia, 19103. Connie Jessum, Librn
Budget: ($2000)
Notes: Covers entire span of American
popular expression in song and instrumental
music (piano) from colonial times to the
present. Incl Newland-Zeuner and Edward I
Keffer Collections on loan from the Musical
Fund Society. Items printed before 1825
indexed in Sonneck-Upton and Wolfe.
Checklists for cover illustrations, musical
shows or films and special subjects. Songs
are filed by title; piano music by composer.
Examples of special materials not filed in
regular collection incl early Philadelphia
composers and publications, national
(centennial and state), patriotic ("Star-
Spangled Banner"), political (Presidents), and
war (1861; 1914; 1939) songs. Most of the
ms materials are anonymous. Collection
contains 138,360 pieces of sheet music.

RI —BROWN UNIVERSITY, John Hay
Library, 20 Prospect St, Providence, 02912.
Mark N Brown, Cur Mss
Holdings: Uncat Cat
Notes: The Sheet Music Collection
concentrates on music of American imprint,
incl 170,000 vocal pieces filed by title, plus
80,000 instrumental pieces filed by
composer. Major strengths are in 19th
century music, especially prior to 1830; Civil
War music, both Union and Confederate;
lithographic covers; World War I songs;
political campaign music; and band music.
An additional 100,000 pieces of American
and European imprint remain unprocessed.
The World War I and II sheet music
holdings have been fully catalogued on
RLIN.

WARBURG, JAMES P.

†MA —JOHN F KENNEDY LIBRARY,
Columbia Point, Boston, 02125. Dan H Fenn
Jr, Dir
Holdings: // Cat Mss
Notes: Personal papers and files relating to
his banking career, the New Deal, World
War II, and foreign policy, 1920-1969. 33
linear ft of mss. Holdings are described in
"Historical Materials in the John F Kennedy
Library." Copies may be obtained by writing
the Research Archivist.

WARD, BARBARA

MA —BOSTON UNIVERSITY, Mugar
Memorial Library, Special Collections Dept,
771 Commonwealth Ave, Boston, 02215.
Howard B Gotlieb, Dir
Holdings: Cat Mss

WARD, EDWARD

CA —UNIVERSITY OF CALIFORNIA, LOS
ANGELES, Music Library, Schonberg Hall,
Los Angeles, 90024. Stephen M Fry, Music
Librn
Notes: Mss.

WARD, HENRY AUGUSTUS

IL —UNIVERSITY OF ILLINOIS,
URBANA/CHAMPAIGN, Library,
University Archives, 19 Library, 1408 W
Gregory Drive, Urbana, 61801. Maynard
Brichford, University Archivist
Holdings: Cat Mss Maps Pix Slides
Microforms
Notes: Papers, archival records, etc.

NY —UNIVERSITY OF ROCHESTER, Rush
Rhees Library, Department of Rare Books
and Special Collections, Rochester, 14627.
Peter Dzwonkoski, Librn
Holdings: Vols Cat Mss Pix
Notes: Papers of Henry Augustus Ward,
includes correspondence, reports, diaries
related to Ward's work as a naturalist and
founder of Ward's Natural Science
Establishment.

WARD, JERRY W.

MS —TOUGALOO COLLEGE, L Zenobia
Coleman Library, Tougaloo, 39174. Virgia
Brocks-Shedd, Acting Dir
Budget: ($142,650)
Notes: Civil rights cases and legal papers;
lawsuits; Mississippi, 1960-1968. Local
attorneys have donated papers of cases they
have handled, espec attorneys of two
government-funded legal services offices.
Individual collections: Jerry W Ward, Lance
Jeffers, (Ret) Lt Col Jesse Johnson on Blacks
in the military. Incl VF holdings of articles
from 1930 and on.

WARD, JOSEPH

IL —CHICAGO HISTORICAL SOCIETY,
Library, Clark St at North Ave, Chicago,
60614. Archie Motley, Manuscript Librn
Notes: Joseph Ward papers (particularly
their John Fenno letters) and Van Schaack
papers being of particular importance as
regards the latter; along with smaller,
important lots of papers of Presidents
Andrew Jackson, Abraham Lincoln and
Ulysses S Grant, plus papers of John Brown
(the abolitionist).

WARD, LESLIE (SPY)

MN —MAYO MEDICAL LIBRARY, History
of Medicine Collection, Rochester, 55905.
Nancy R Hensel, Librn
Holdings: Pix
Notes: The Comfort Collection of caricatures

WARD, LESLIE (SPY) (cont.)

of physicians and scientists from *Vanity Fair*. Description: Mann, Ruth J: "The unheroic representation of heroes." *Mayo Clin Proc.* 46:197-199, Mar 1971.

WARD, LESTER FRANK

RI —BROWN UNIVERSITY, John Hay Library, 20 Prospect St, Providence, 02912. Mark N Brown, Cur Mss
Holdings: Vols 1200 // Cat Mss Pix
Notes: The Lester Frank Ward Collection is formed from the library and literary remains of Lester Frank Ward, a pioneer in the study of sociology. Books and pamphlets which reflect his interest in botany, geology, philosophy and sociology are supplemented by Ward's working scrapbooks and card indexes. The mss incl personal papers, notes, typescripts, proofs of published writings, diaries for 1860-1890, an unpublished autobiography and 5800 letters received by him.
See also entry under Sociology

WARD, LYND

DC —GEORGETOWN UNIVERSITY, Library, Special Collections Div, 37 & O Sts NW, Washington, 20057. George M Barringer, Special Collections Librn; Nicholas B Sheetz, Mss Librn
Notes: The papers, files, art work, etc of Lynd Ward and his wife, May McNeer.

WARD, MARY AUGUSTA (ARNOLD), MRS. HUMPHRY WARD

CA —CLAREMONT COLLEGES, Honnold Library, Ninth & Dartmouth, Claremont, 91711. Tania Rizzo, Special Collections Dept Head
Holdings: Vols 50 Cat Mss Pix
Notes: Ms notebooks and unbound leaves of 44 novels and other writings, usually incomplete, 1863-1916; 1600 items of in and out correspondence with her publishers, notably Smith, Elder & Co, 1885-1919; notebooks incl observations, travel diaries, preliminary drafts for novels; minute book, 1906-1913, for Jowett Lectureship Committee, Passmore Edwards Settlement; 6 letters from Benjamin Jowett. Restricted use.

WARD, WINIFRED

AZ —ARIZONA STATE UNIVERSITY, Library, Tempe, 85287. Marilyn Wurzburger, Special Collections Librn
Holdings: Vols (108) Pix
Notes: Collection covers various aspects of Children's Theatre from 1944 through the present. Areas of emphasis incl International and National Child Drama Associations, award-winning theatres, educational programs, regional groups and prominent figures in Children's Theatre incl: Irene Vickers Baker, Isabel Burger, Virginia Lee Comer, Rita Criste, Moses Goldberg, Kenneth Graham, Aurand Harris, Paul Kozelka, George Latshaw, Rosemary Musil, Sara Spencer, Winifred Ward, Susan Zeder and Lin Wright. Publications incl newsletters, research papers, bibliographies and records of the proceedings of the Children's Theatre Association of America. 80 linear feet of scripts, documents, publications, films, tapes (oral history) programs, correspondence, photographs, working papers and clippings. Partially indexed; finding guides available.

WARDE, FREDERIC

NY —GROLIER CLUB OF NEW YORK LIBRARY, 47 E 60 St, New York, 10022. Robert Nikirk, Librn
Notes: The Frederic Warde archive.

WARDLE, SIR THOMAS

NC —DUKE UNIVERSITY, William R Perkins Library, Manuscript Dept, Durham, 27706. Ellen Gartrell, Cur of Mss
Holdings: Cat Mss
Notes: Papers of various southern textile mills, especially North Carolina, 19th-20th century, incl material on unions and strikes; Sir Thomas Wardle Papers (93 letters of William Morris).

WARE, CHARLOTTE (BARRELL), 1862-1945

MA —BOSTON UNIVERSITY, Mugar Memorial Library, Special Collections Dept, 771 Commonwealth Ave, Boston, 02215. Howard B Gotlieb, Dir
Holdings: // Cat Mss
Notes: Mss relating to work in agriculture and public health.

WARE, WILLIAM ROBERT, 1832-1915

MA —MASSACHUSETTS INSTITUTE OF TECHNOLOGY, Institute Archives, Special Collections, Cambridge, 02139.
Notes: Papers of William Robert Ware, architect and founder of MIT's School of Architecture and Urban Planning, the first such architectural training program in the United States. Incl unfinished biography of Ware. Unpublished finding aid, incl a correspondent index, available in the Institute Archives.

WARFARE, AMPHIBIOUS see Amphibious Warfare

WARFARE, BIOLOGICAL see Biological Warfare

WARFARE, CHEMICAL see Chemical Warfare

WARFARE, INSHORE UNDERSEA see Undersea Warfare Inshore

WARFARE, PSYCHOLOGICAL see Psychological Warfare

WARFARE, SUBMARINE see Submarine Warfare

WARFIELD, DAVID

MA —AMHERST COLLEGE, Library, Amherst, 01002. John Lancaster, Special Collections Librn
Holdings: Vols (20,000) Uncat Mss
Notes: Contains a comprehensive collection of paperbound Samuel French acting editions (15,000) and many from other publishers; also Augustin Daly manuscripts, David Warfield acting scripts, and the library of Clyde Fitch. 200 mss.

WARING, GEORGE E.

MD —NATIONAL LIBRARY OF MEDICINE, 8600 Rockville Pike, Bethesda, 20209. Harold M Schoolman, Actg Dir
Budget: ($46,400)
Notes: Correspondence of George E Waring, pioneering American sanitary engineer of the 19th century.

WARING, JULIUS WAITES

SC —COLLEGE OF CHARLESTON LIBRARY, Special Collections Dept, Charleston, 29401.
Notes: Papers incl certificate of posthumous awarding of the annual Walter White Award by the National Association for the Advancement of Colored People, 1979.

WARNER, CHARLES DUDLEY, 1829-1900

CT —STOWE-DAY LIBRARY, 77 Forest St, Hartford, 06105. Diana J Royce, Librn
Holdings: Vols (15,000) Cat Mss Pix
Notes: 100,000 cataloged mss and publications concerning architecture, decorative arts, history and literature of the period 1840-1900, with emphasis on Nook Farm, Mark Twain, Harriet Beecher Stowe, Calvin E Stowe, Charles Dudley Warner, William Hooker Gillette, Isabella Beecher Hooker.
CT —TRINITY COLLEGE LIBRARY, Watkinson Library, 300 Summit St, Hartford, 06106. Jeffrey Kaimowitz, Cur
Holdings: Cat Mss
Notes: Extensive collection of letters written to Charles Dudley Warner along with Warner's travel notebooks and mss of books and articles.
CT —YALE UNIVERSITY, Box 1603A, Yale Station, New Haven, 06520.
Holdings: Cat Mss

WARNER, JOHN

VA —UNIVERSITY OF VIRGINIA, Alderman Library, Manuscripts Dept, Charlottesville, 22901. Edmund Berkeley Jr, Cur
Notes: Papers of John Warner, former Secretary of the Navy and US Senator, 1979-present.

WARNER, JOHN W.

VA —UNIVERSITY OF VIRGINIA, Alderman Library, Manuscripts Dept, Charlottesville, 22901. Edmund Berkeley Jr, Cur
Holdings: Cat Mss Microforms
Notes: Personal, political, and business papers.

WARNER, SUSAN AND ANNA B.

NY —CONSTITUTION ISLAND ASSOCIATION, Warner House Library, Box 41, West Point, 10996.
Holdings: Vols 500 Cat Mss
Notes: The writings of Susan and Anna B Warner have been listed and annotated in a bibliography *They Wrote for A Living*, by Dorothy Sanderson (Constitution Island Association, 1976). No photocopying.

WARNER, SYLVIA T.

IL —ILLINOIS STATE UNIVERSITY, Milner Library, Dept of Special Collections, Normal, 61761. Robert Sokan, Librn
Notes: First editions, limited edtitions, ephemera, etc.

WARNER BROTHERS FILMS

CA —UNIVERSITY OF SOUTHERN CALIFORNIA, Edward L Doheny Memorial Library, Archives of Performing Arts, University Park, Los Angeles, 90089. Robert Knutson, Librn
Holdings: Mss Pix
Notes: Warner Brothers Films Studio Collection (1920s-1968) incl 700,000 stills and negatives; 3,000 titles of feature, short subject and television screenplays, script materials, set designs, engineering drawings, production records, patent records, music and legal files. Over 1,000 bound vols describing the inventory and 100 bound vols of index to the inventory.
DC —LIBRARY OF CONGRESS, American Film Institute Collection, Washington, 20540.
Notes: Original master negatives of the entire pre-1949 Warner Brothers library of films.
†WI —STATE HISTORICAL SOCIETY OF WISCONSIN, Mass Communications History Center, 816 State Street, Madison, 53706.
Notes: 800 Warner Brothers films.

WARPING see Weaving

WARRANTS, AGRICULTURAL see Agricultural Credit

WARREN, L. D.

OH —OHIO STATE UNIVERSITY, Library for Communication and Graphic Arts, 242

WARREN, L. D. (cont.)

W 18th St, Columbus, 43210. Lucy S
Caswell, Curator
Notes: The original works of editorial
cartoonists Art Poinier, Scott Willis, Brian
Basset, Billy Ireland, Frank Williams,
Charles Werner, Ned Beard, L D Warren,
Edward D Kuekes, Ray Osrin, Mike Peters,
Draper Hill, Eugene Craig and Bert
Whitman.

WARREN, ROBERT PENN

CT —YALE UNIVERSITY, Box 1603A, Yale
Station, New Haven, 06520.
Holdings: Cat Mss
KY —UNIVERSITY OF KENTUCKY,
Margaret I King Library, Dept of Special
Collections, Lexington, 40506. William
Marshall, Head
Holdings: Vols 68 Cat Mss Audiotapes
Notes: Mss incl letters, copies of works
include rough drafts, galleys and tape
recordings.
NV —UNIVERSITY OF NEVADA, RENO,
University Library, Special Collections Dept,
Reno, 89557. Robert E Blesse, Head
Holdings: Vols 107 // Cat
Notes: Includes individual works by author
in all editions including translations; also
prefaces, introductions, published
correspondence, appearances in anthologies,
periodicals, etc. Bibliographical research
collection, part of Modern Authors
Collection.
TN —VANDERBILT UNIVERSITY, Library,
Nashville, 37240. Marice Wolfe, Special
Collections Librn
Holdings: Vols 1000 Cat Mss Pix
Notes: Collection relating to the Fugitive
poets of the 1920s, the Agrarian writers of
the 1930s and their subsequent careers, as a
complement to extensive mss collections in
this field. Chief figures incl Allen Tate, John
Crowe Ransom, Robert Penn Warren,
Andrew Lytle, Donald Davidson, Merrill
Moore, Laura Riding, et al.

WARS see Military History

WARS AND BATTLES, IMAGINARY
see Imaginary Wars and Battles

WARSH, LEWIS

BC —SIMON FRASER UNIVERSITY,
Library, Burnaby, V5A 1S6, Can. Percilla
Groves, Special Collections Librn
Holdings: // Cat Mss
Notes: Letters from Anne Waldman to
Lewis Warsh, many concerned with *Silo* and
Angel Hair Press, 1965-1973; some mss
enclosed.

WARSHIPS

MD —US NAVAL ACADEMY, Nimitz
Library, Annapolis, 21402. Alice S
Creighton, Assistant Librn for Special
Collections
Holdings: Vols (22,000) Cat Mss Pix
Notes: Books and periodicals, with emphasis
on seapower. Incl rare and historically
significant works, naval and general history.
US Naval Academy materials (histories,
class albums, Lucky Bags, student
publications, etc), and copies of transcripts
of the Naval Institute's oral history
interviews with US naval officers.
Manuscripts incl 205 volumes of ships' logs,
letterbooks, order books, and watch, station
and quarter bills, 1796-1938; papers of
various naval officers, incl. Vice Admiral
Wilson Brown, Commander George M
Bache, Admiral Harry S Knapp, Lieutenant
Edwin J DeHaven, and others; family
correspondence of Admiral David Dixon
Porter; and several thousand World War II
naval action reports. Approximately 15,000
pictures incl portraits of naval officers,
pictures of US and some foreign ships,
World War II naval news photos and USNA
photographs.

WASHINGTON (STATE)

WA —UNIVERSITY OF WASHINGTON
LIBRARIES, Pacific Northwest Collection,
Seattle, 98195. Andrew F Johnson, Librn
Holdings: Vols (50,000) Cat Mss Map
Budget: ($12,000)
Notes: The Pacific Northwest Collection
contains printed materials documenting the
historic and contemporary life and culture of
the region in a broad range of subject areas.
The Pacific Northwest is defined as the
geographic region including Washington,
Oregon, Idaho, Montana, British Columbia,
Yukon Territory, and Alaska. Printed
materials including books, periodicals,
government documents, maps, weekly and
local regional newspapers, theses and
dissertations, as well as photographs and
architectural drawings are included in the
Pacific Northwest Collection. Photographic
works of over 200 photographers active in
the Pacific Northwest, Alaska, and the
Yukon Territory (Canada) during the period
1860-1930, including Asahel and Edward S
Curtis, Eric Hegg, and Clark Kinsey, are
represented in a print collection of more
than 300,000 images. The
architecturaldrawings collection includes
over 19,000 original plans, drawings,
sketches, renderings and blue prints
pertaining to the history of architecture and
urban planning and landscape gardening in
the Pacific Northwest ca 1880-1940. Areas
of particular strength are the holdings of
over 1100 published journals of Pacific
Northwest exploration expeditions,
photographs of Northwest Coast Native
Americans and of historic Seattle,
newspapers issued within the Japanese-
American relocation camps, 1942-1945,
materials relating to the 1980 eruption of Mt
St Helens, and Sanborne fire insurance maps
for Washington. A unique feature of the
Collection is the subject index to regional
periodicals and local newspapers maintained
by the PNW Collection staff; over 100 titles
are currently indexed. G K Hall Company
published a books catalog of the Pacific
Northwest Collectionin 1973.
WA —UNIVERSITY OF WASHINGTON
LIBRARIES, Suzzallo Library, Manuscripts
Section, FM-25, Seattle, 98195. Karyl Winn,
Librn
Holdings: Mss
Notes: Personal papers and organizational
records with emphasis on Pacific Northwest
history and recent focus on twentieth
century Western Washington. Holdings
pertain to urban problems and policies, labor
history, women's history, natural resource
development, environmental politics, race
relations, ethnic history, oral hsitory, and the
arts. Holdings are complemented by textual
records in the University Archives (7045
linear feet) and by graphic and printed
holdings in the Pacific Northwest Collection.
Described in *Comprehensive Guide to the
Manuscripts Collection and to Personal
Papers in the University Archives*, 1980 and
in *Historical Records of Washington State:
Records and Papers Held at Repositories*,
1981 and in unpublished inventories to most
accessions. 15,981 linear feet of manuscripts.
WA —UNIVERSITY OF WASHINGTON
LIBRARIES, Suzzallo Library, Manuscripts
Section, FM-25, Seattle, 98195. Karyl Winn,
Librn
Holdings: Mss Audiotapes
Notes: Personal papers and organizational
records of the Jewish population of the
greater Seattle, Washington area and to a
lesser extent, Washington state. Holdings
includes synagogue records, philanthropic
and educational organization records, papers
of community leaders and families, and
recorded interviews. Photographs
administered by the Libraries' Pacific
Northwest Collection. Many interviews have
been transcribed. Inventories for all larger
accessions. Includes 260 linear feet of
manuscript and 250 audiotapes.

WASHINGTON (STATE)
—DESCRIPTION AND
TRAVEL—VIEWS

WA —UNIVERSITY OF WASHINGTON
LIBRARIES, Pacific Northwest Collection,
Seattle, 98195. Andrew F Johnson, Librn
Holdings: Vols (50,000) Cat Mss Map
Budget: ($12,000)
Notes: The Pacific Northwest Collection
contains printed materials documenting the
historic and contemporary life and culture of
the region in a broad range of subject areas.
The Pacific Northwest is defined as the
geographic region including Washington,
Oregon, Idaho, Montana, British Columbia,
Yukon Territory, and Alaska. Printed
materials including books, periodicals,
government documents, maps, weekly and
local regional newspapers, theses and
dissertations, as well as photographs and
architectural drawings are included in the
Pacific Northwest Collection. Photographic
works of over 200 photographers active in
the Pacific Northwest, Alaska, and the
Yukon Territory (Canada) during the period
1860-1930, including Asahel and Edward S
Curtis, Eric Hegg, and Clark Kinsey, are
represented in a print collection of more
than 300,000 images. The
architecturaldrawings collection includes
over 19,000 original plans, drawings,
sketches, renderings and blue prints
pertaining to the history of architecture and
urban planning and landscape gardening in
the Pacific Northwest ca 1880-1940. Areas
of particular strength are the holdings of
over 1100 published journals of Pacific
Northwest exploration expeditions,
photographs of Northwest Coast Native
Americans and of historic Seattle,
newspapers issued within the Japanese-
American relocation camps, 1942-1945,
materials relating to the 1980 eruption of Mt
St Helens, and Sanborne fire insurance maps
for Washington. A unique feature of the
Collection is the subject index to regional
periodicals and local newspapers maintained
by the PNW Collection staff; over 100 titles
are currently indexed. G K Hall Company
published a books catalog of the Pacific
Northwest Collectionin 1973.

WASHINGTON (STATE)
—GENEALOGY

WA —WASHINGTON STATE LIBRARY,
Washington/Northwest Rm, State Library
Bldg, Olympia, 98504. Nancy B Pryor,
Research Consultant
Holdings: Cat Mss Pix Microforms
Notes: Collection of material on Washington
territorical and state history contains
information useful for genealogical research--
census records, both original schedules and
on microfilm, donation land claim papers on
microfilm, indexes to biographical material
in books, newspapers, etc, interviews with
pioneers, and published works of local
history and genealogies of Washington state
families.
WA —TACOMA PUBLIC LIBRARY, 1102
Tacoma Ave S, Tacoma, 98402. Kevin
Hegarty, Dir
Holdings: Vols 1500 Cat Mss Microforms
Notes: Depository for Tacoma Genealogical
Society.

WASHINGTON (STATE)—POLITICS
AND GOVERNMENT

WA —WESTERN WASHINGTON
UNIVERSITY, Center for Pacific Northwest
Studies, High St, Bellingham, 98225. James
W Scott, Dir
Holdings: Uncat Mss Pix
Notes: Farmer and former member of the
Washington State House, Ernest W Lennart
died in office in the late 1960s, a member of
the State Senate. Papers are very largely
political in nature, incl letters, speeches and
documents.
WA —WESTERN WASHINGTON
UNIVERSITY, Center for Pacific Northwest
Studies, High St, Bellingham, 98225. James
W Scott, Dir
Holdings: Mss Maps Pix
Notes: The Vaughan Brown Collection.
Vaughan Brown, a retired attorney, is a
former Postmaster of Bellingham and a
former member of the house and senate of

WASHINGTON (STATE)—POLITICS AND GOVERNMENT (cont.)

Washington State, retiring from the latter in the 1950s. This voluminous collection consists of political papers and materials in large part, covering state and local matters. Rural electrification is one of the major topics covered, and there is much illustrative campaign literature, largely Democratic, but incl some Republican. Personal, financial and legal papers are also included. Mainly Pacific Northwest--especially Washington and in particular Whatcom County, but also some items on Arkansas, home of O P Brown, his father, some of whose papers are included. Partially cataloged. Also papers of Ernest W Lennart, farmer and former member of the Washington State Senate, (deceased in office late 1960s) are largelypolitical in nature, includes letters, speeches and documents.

WA —UNIVERSITY OF WASHINGTON LIBRARIES, Suzzallo Library, Manuscripts Section, FM-25, Seattle, 98195. Karyl Winn, Librn
Notes: Correspondence, legislation, and similar papers of the follwing legislators: Wesley L Jones, 1898-1932, 147 lin ft; Marion Zioncheck, 1932-1936, 1.75 lin ft; Warren G Magnuson, 1936-1944, 99 lin ft; Homer T Bone, 1932-1936, 1.75 lin ft; High B Mitchell, 1944-1946, 59 lin ft; Donald Magnuson, 1953-1963, 27 lin ft; Thor Tollefson, 1947-1964, 76 lin ft; Julia Butler Hansen, 1961-1974, 217 lin ft; Lloyd Meeds, 1966-1978, 371 lin ft; Brock Adams, 1965-1976, 350 lin ft. Described in preliminary or final inventories. Papers of Henry M Jackson, 1940-1983, and Senate papers of Warren G Magnuson, 1944-1980, not processed and not open for use as of 1984. Incl 1,547 linear feet of Congressional papers.

WASHINGTON (STATE)—HISTORY

CA —UNIVERSITY OF CALIFORNIA, BERKELEY, Bancroft Library, Manuscripts Division, Berkeley, 94720. James D Hart, Dir
Holdings: Vols Mss Maps Pix Slides Microforms
Notes: Approxi. twelve million pieces, with primary emphasis on California, with a lesser emphasis on the other Pacific States, incl. Alaska and the Province of British Columbia. In general, the Bancroft Library seeks to acquire historical and biographical works and primary source materials, documenting: the development of a geographic area or political unit; man and his activities, and his impact on the land and on his institutions. Methodological and theoretical work and texts in the physical and biological sciences are not collected, as a rule; exceptions here are publications essential to the study of an area's historical development and those providing general background information. Hubert Howe Bancroft's own distinguished holdings, assembled 1860-1880, constitute the core of the collection. The Bancroft Library's collections are noncirculating. A. G. K. Hall catalog has been published. The Bolton Collection (146,000 pages of archival material) contains ms. materials for the history of the Pacific Coast and the Southwest, gathered by Herbert Eugene Bolton. There is a comprehensive key to the arrangement of the collection.

DC —GEORGETOWN UNIVERSITY, Library, Special Collections Div, 37 & O Sts

NW, Washington, 20057. George M Barringer, Special Collections Librn; Nicholas B Sheetz, Mss Librn
Holdings: Mss Cat
Notes: The papers of the explorer John Mullan (1859-1940), containing correspondence, letter books, legal documents, photographs, and clippings; for the most part pertaining to Mullan's activities as claims agent for Washington Territory; the states of California, Oregon, Nevada, and Colorado; and a few individuals. Of interest for the study of mandamus and estoppel in contract law in the Progressive Era, as well as in the study of claims activities, and anti-lawyer sentiment in the West during the same period. There is also present a small amount of material on the Military Road from Fort Walla Walla to Fort Benton.

WA —WESTERN WASHINGTON UNIVERSITY, Center for Pacific Northwest Studies, High St, Bellingham, 98225. James W Scott, Dir
Holdings: Cat Mss Maps Pix
Notes: Two collections. (1) The Percival R Jeffcott Collection of Local History is particularly rich in photographic materials, incl about 1800 negatives and about 1100 photographs, which deal with pioneer settlement and economic and cultural developments in Whatcom County, Washington, and a few adjacent areas, such as the Lower Mainland of British Columbia to the north and neighboring counties of Washington to the south and west. Incl also ms versions of Jeffcott's published works: *Nonosack Tales and Trials, Chechaco and Sourdough* and *Blanket Bill Jarman* and numerous unpublished papers and workbooks. A small collection of Jeffcott materials is housed in the Washington State Historical Society, Tacoma, and for this there is an unpublished inventory. An inventory of the present collection is being prepared for publication by the Center for Pacific Northwest Studies. (2) TheHoward E Buswell Collection. Comprehensive in its coverage of economic activities, cultural interests, etc, of Whatcom County and its environs, incl some of the islands of Puget Sound and the Strait of Georgia. Partially cataloged.

WA —SKAGIT COUNTY HISTORICAL MUSUEM, Library, Po Box 818, La Conner, 98257. David J Van Meer, Cur & Librn
Holdings: Vols 240 Cat Mss Maps Pix Slides Audiotapes
Notes: History of Skagit County and the Pacific Northwest. Incl 179 mss, 109 maps, 8000 pictures, 100 slides and 235 audiotapes.

WA —WASHINGTON STATE LIBRARY, Washington/Northwest Rm, State Library Bldg, Olympia, 98504. Nancy B Pryor, Research Consultant
Holdings: Vols 8000 Cat Mss Maps Pix Microforms
Notes: Mss, photographs and microfilm largely limited to Washington territorial and state materials as is the file of pamphlets and newspaper clippings, which includes both historical and current material. The book collection incl works on the four Pacific Northwest States, Alaska, and British Columbia, and books by Washington authors.

†WA —WASHINGTON STATE UNIVERSITY, Library, Manuscripts, Archives & Special Collections, Pullman, 99164. John F Guido, Head
Holdings: Cat Mss Maps Pix
Notes: The ms collection incl business and financial records of banks, breweries, insurance, land, lumber and livestock companies, trade and commodity associations; as well as the personal and professional papers of authors, aviators, educators, engineers, farmers, historians, pioneers, politicians and scientists; especially rich in documents relating to the exploration, settlement and development of the Palouse Country, the Inland Empire, the Columbia Basin and the Pacific Northwest. Described in *Selected Manuscript Resources in the Washington State University Library* (Pullman, 1974); and other published and unpublished inventories and registers.

†WA —WASHINGTON STATE UNIVERSITY, Library, Manuscripts, Archives & Special Collections, Pullman, 99164. John F Guido, Head
Holdings: Vols Cat Mss Maps pix
Notes: The personal and political papers of Fred C Ashley, William Edward Carty, Knute Hill, Walter Franklin Horan, William Lon Johnson, Catherine May, and Austin Mires are among the holdings of the library. Most collections described in printed registers.

WA —HISTORICAL SOCIETY OF SEATTLE AND KING COUNTY, Sophie Frye Bass Library, 2161 E Hamlin, Seattle, 98112. Rick Caldwell, Librn
Holdings: Vols (20,000) Cat Mss Maps Pix Slides
Notes: Incl 15,000 pictures on Pacific Northwest.

WA —UNIVERSITY OF WASHINGTON LIBRARIES, Pacific Northwest Collection, Seattle, 98195. Andrew F Johnson, Librn
Holdings: Vols (50,000) Cat Maps Pix
Budget: ($12,000)
Notes: The Pacific Northwest Collection contains printed materials documenting the historic and contemporary life and culture of the region in a broad range of subject areas. The Pacific Northwest is defined as the geographic region including Washington, Oregon, Idaho, Montana, British Columbia, Yukon Territory, and Alaska. Printed materials including books, periodicals, government documents, maps, weekly and local regional newspapers, theses and dissertations, as well as photographs and architectural drawings are included in the Pacific Northwest Collection. Photographic works of over 200 photographers active in the Pacific Northwest, Alaska, and the Yukon Territory (Canada) during the period 1860-1930, including Asahel and Edward S Curtis, Eric Hegg, and Clark Kinsey, are represented in a print collection of more than 300,000 images. The architecturaldrawings collection includes over 19,000 original plans, drawings, sketches, renderings and blue prints pertaining to the history of architecture and urban planning and landscape gardening in the Pacific Northwest ca 1880-1940. Areas of particular strength are the holdings of over 1100 published journals of Pacific Northwest exploration expeditions, photographs of Northwest Coast Native Americans and of historic Seattle, newspapers issued within the Japanese-American relocation camps, 1942-1945, materials relating to the 1980 eruption of Mt St Helens, and Sanborne fire insurance maps for Washington. A unique feature of the Collection is the subject index to regional periodicals and local newspapers maintained by the PNW Collection staff; over 100 titles are currently indexed. G K Hall Company published a books catalog of the Pacific Northwest Collectionin 1973.

WA —UNIVERSITY OF WASHINGTON LIBRARIES, Suzzallo Library, Manuscripts Section, FM-25, Seattle, 98195. Karyl Winn, Librn
Holdings: Mss
Notes: Personal papers and organizational records with emphasis on Pacific Northwest history and recent focus on twentieth century Western Washington. Holdings pertain to urban problems and policies, labor history, women's history, natural resource development, environmental politics, race relations, ethnic history, oral hsitory, and the arts. Holdings are complemented by textual records in the University Archives (7045 linear feet) and by graphic and printed holdings in the Pacific Northwest Collection. Described in *Comprehensive Guide to the Manuscripts Collection and to Personal Papers in the University Archives*, 1980 and in *Historical Records of Washington State: Records and Papers Held at Repositories*, 1981 and in unpublished inventories to most accessions. 15,981 linear feet of manuscripts.

WA —UNIVERSITY OF WASHINGTON LIBRARIES, Suzzallo Library, Manuscripts Section, FM-25, Seattle, 98195. Karyl Winn, Librn
Holdings: Mss Audiotapes
Notes: Personal papers and organizational

WASHINGTON (STATE)—HISTORY (cont.)

records of the Jewish population of the greater Seattle, Washington area and to a lesser extent, Washington state. Holdings includes synagogue records, philanthropic and educational organization records, papers of community leaders and families, and recorded interviews. Photographs administered by the Libraries' Pacific Northwest Collection. Many interviews have been transcribed. Inventories for all larger accessions. Includes 260 linear feet of manuscript and 250 audiotapes.

WA —TACOMA PUBLIC LIBRARY, 1102 Tacoma Ave S, Tacoma, 98402. Kevin Hegarty, Dir
Holdings: Vols 10,000 Mss Maps Pix
Notes: Major emphasis on Pacific Northwest, incl mss, archives, 250 linear ft 175,000 photographic negatives from collections of Marvin D Boland and Chapin Bowen, etc 40 vertical file drawers of clippings (maintained since 1909) under 2600 subject headings. Genealogies, official records, etc. Picture collection also incl 20,000 mounted and 5000 unmounted items, with posters, postcards, matted reproductions, etc.

WA —WASHINGTON STATE HISTORICAL SOCIETY LIBRARY, 315 N Stadium Way, Tacoma, 98403. Frank L Green, Librn
Holdings: Vols 15,000 Cat Mss Maps Pix Microforms
Notes: Scope is entire Pacific Northwest, with emphasis on Washington.

WASHINGTON, BOOKER T., 1856-1915

DC —LIBRARY OF CONGRESS, Manuscript Division, Washington, 20540. John C Broderick, Chief
Notes: His papers.
MA —HARVARD UNIVERSITY LIBRARY, Houghton Library, Cambridge, 02138. Rodney G Dennis, Cur of Manuscripts
Holdings: Cat Mss

WASHINGTON, D.C. see District of Columbia

WASHINGTON, GEORGE, 1732-1799

CA —CLAREMONT COLLEGES, Honnold Library, Ninth & Dartmouth, Claremont, 91711. Tania Rizzo, Special Collections Dept Head
Holdings: // Cat Mss Pix
Notes: Photostats, typescripts, clippings, journal articles used by Rupert Hughes in preparation for publication of his 3-vol *George Washington*, 1926-1930. Scrapbook incl clippings Apr 30, May 1, 1889-- celebration of centenary of Washington's first inaugural. Seven boxes and scrapbook. Restricted use.
CT —UNIVERSITY OF CONNECTICUT, Library, Storrs, 06268. R H Schimmelpfeng, Dir of Special Collections
Holdings: Vols 4600 // Uncat Mss Maps
Notes: The library of Pierce Welch Gaines of Federalist material, chiefly contemporary books and mss. Emphasis on Washington, Jefferson and Adams.
DC —LIBRARY OF CONGRESS, Manuscript Division, Washington, 20540. John C Broderick, Chief
Notes: The Presidential Papers collection incl the papers, etc, of numerous Presidents.
KS —KANSAS STATE UNIVERSITY, Library, Special Collections & University Archives, Manhattan, 66506. Antonia Q Pigno, Coordr; John J Vander Velde, Librn; Anthony R Crawford, Univ Archivist
Holdings: Vols (3500)
Notes: General collection; also includes books on Abraham Lincoln and the US Civil War.
MA —HARVARD UNIVERSITY LIBRARY, Houghton Library, Cambridge, 02138. Rodney G Dennis, Cur of Manuscripts
Holdings: Cat
Notes: For calendar of 56 letters to Benjamin Lincoln, see *Harvard Library Bulletin*, X (1956): pp 39-72.

MI —UNIVERSITY OF MICHIGAN, William L Clements Library, Ann Arbor, 48109. John C Dann, Dir
Notes: The William L. Clements Library of Americana is a non-circulating rare book library of original source material, printed and manuscript, dealing with America, from the discovery period into the late nineteenth century. The collection includes approximately 55,000 books and pamphlets, 550 linear feet of manuscripts, 4,100 volumes of newspapers, 36,000 maps, 40,000 pieces of sheet music, and 1,000 prints. The collection is strongest for the period of the American Revolution, and includes the papers of Thomas Gage, Sir Henry Clinton, and the Earl of Shelburne. Other areas of strength include antislavery, cartography and geography, discovery and exploration, American Indians, The Civil War, tune-books, sermons and orations, and the War of 1812. There are selective research collections dealing with Christopher Columbus, Thomas Paine, Benjamin Franklin, George Washington, Thomas Jefferson, and the Federalist Papers. Publications describing the collections of the library are: Author/Title catalog of Americana 1493-1860 in the William L. Clements Library... 7 volumes, Boston, G. K. Hall, 1970; Guide to the manuscript collections of the William L. Clements Library, by Arlene P. Shy 3d edition, Boston, G. K. Hall, 1978; Guide to the manuscript maps in the William L. Clements Library, compiled by Christian Burn, Ann Arbor, U. of Michigan, 1959; and Research catalog of maps of America, to 1860 in the William L. Clements Library...,edited by Douglas W. Marshall, 4 volumes, Boston, G. K. Hall, 1972.

NJ —GLASSBORO STATE COLLEGE, Savitz Library, Stewart Room, Glassboro, 08028. Clara Kirner, Special Collection Librn
Holdings: Vols 90 Cat Mss Pix
Notes: Incl mss of letters of military campaign in New Jersey and portraits by Gilbert Stuart and Rembrant Peale (originals).

NJ —RUTGERS, THE STATE UNIVERSITY OF NEW JERSEY, Alexander Library, Special Collections and Archives, College Ave & Huntington St, New Brunswick, 08903. Ronald L Becker, Cur of Manuscripts and Rare Books
Holdings: Pix
Notes: The pictorial collection of Special Collections, dating from the 18th century to the present, incl foreign, US, and New Jersey material, portraits, local views, historical scenes. Special groups: George Washington and Benjamin Franklin engraved portraits; photos of New Jersey Dutch houses and New Jersey localities (among these about 10,000 postal cards).

NY —NEW YORK STATE LIBRARY, State Education Bldg Annex, Washington Ave, Albany, 12224.
Notes: Eulogies, memorabilia, etc, incl the first draft of the Farewell Address in Washington's own hand, and his surveying instruments.

NY —NEW YORK HISTORICAL SOCIETY, Library, 170 Central Park W, New York, 10024. James Gregory, Librn
Notes: Misc papers, correspondence, etc.

NY —NEW YORK PUBLIC LIBRARY, Research Libraries, General Research Division, Fifth Ave & 42 St, New York, 10018. Rodney Phillips, Chief
Holdings: Vols (2,225,000) Cat Maps Pix Microforms
Budget: ($775,718)
NY —NEW YORK PUBLIC LIBRARY, Rare Books and Manuscripts Div, Fifth Ave & 42 St, New York, 10018. William L Joyce, Asst Dir; Susan E Davis, Cur of Mss
Holdings: Cat Mss
Budget: ($7161)
Notes: Includes the only extant copy of Washington's Farewell Address written in his own hand; 236 letters written during the period 1792 to 1799, several vols of Washington's letterpress copybooks, and an orderly book, also a military journal written during his colonelcy in the Virginia militia, 1757.
PA —HARRY C TREXLER MASONIC LIBRARY, Masonic Temple, Allentown, 18102.
Holdings: Vols (5000) Mss Pix
PA —HISTORICAL SOCIETY OF PENNSYLVANIA, Library, 1300 Locust St, Philadelphia, 19107. David Fraser, Librn
Holdings: Vols (230,000) Mss Maps Pix Microforms
Notes: Incl over 14,000,000 ms pieces. The Library Company of Philadelphia mss are on deposit with the Historical Society of Pennsylvania. Mamy of the Society's rare books are on deposit with the Library Company. The Society maintains the collections of the Genealogical Society of Pennsylvania, incl some 20,000 printed genealogies, original mss, family, church, and civil records.
VA —MOUNT VERNON LADIES' ASSOCIATION OF THE UNION, Research & Reference Library, Mount Vernon, 22121. Ellen McCallister Clark, Librn; John Rhodehamel, Dir of Education
Holdings: Vols (12,000) Cat Mss Maps Pix Slides
Notes: The Washington family and Mount Vernon. The history of the Mount Vernon Ladies' Association and historic preservation.
VA —VIRGINIA STATE LIBRARY, 12 & Capitol Sts, Richmond, 23219.
Holdings: Vols 5600 Cat Mss Maps Pix

WASHINGTON, HAROLD

IL —CHICAGO HISTORICAL SOCIETY, Library, Clark St at North Ave, Chicago, 60614. Archie Motley, Manuscript Librn
Notes: Primary and general mayoral election campaign file records, 1982-1983.

WASHINGTON, LAWRENCE

IL —CHICAGO HISTORICAL SOCIETY, Library, Clark St at North Ave, Chicago, 60614. Archie Motley, Manuscript Librn
Notes: Lawrence Washington will, 1752, by which Mount Vernon came to possession of George Washington.

WASHINGTON LIGHT INFANTRY

SC —COLLEGE OF CHARLESTON LIBRARY, Special Collections Dept, Charleston, 29401.
Notes: Papers, 1807-1936 of Charleston, SC organization incl historical sketch (1807-1846).

WASHINGTON STAR (NEWSPAPER)

DC —DISTRICT OF COLUMBIA PUBLIC LIBRARY, Martin Luther King Memorial Library, Washingtoniana Div and Washington Star Collection, 901 G St NW, Washington, 20001. Roxanna Deane, Chief
Holdings: Vols (20,000) Cat Maps Pix Slides
Budget: ($5500)
Notes: *Washington Star* Collection was the working morgue and photo library of the *Washington Star* newspaper. There are an estimated one million photos dating from about 1930 to 1981. These are arranged by subject and personal name and cover

WASHINGTON STAR (NEWSPAPER) (cont.)

international, national and local news. There are approx 13 million news clippings arranged by subject and personal name for the same period. Each *Star* article was clipped and placed in as many different files as was necessary to cover all topics or personal names mentioned in the article. Reproductions from the photo collection may be purchased.

WASHO INDIANS

NV —UNIVERSITY OF NEVADA, RENO, University Library, Special Collections Dept, Reno, 89557. Robert E Blesse, Head
Holdings: Vols 1100 Mss Pix
Notes: Incl over 5000 photographs, government documents, periodicals, 80 cubic feet, mss, and audiotapes. The Great Basin Indian Collection contains materials on the anthropology, archaeology, and ethnohistory of the Great Basin region. Materials are collected for a defined group of 65 tribes incl Washo, Shoshone, Northern and Southern Paiute, the major tribes of the region. Collection of importance incl the Sven Liljeblad Collection, linguistics and ethnography; papers of US agent Lorenzo D Greel, 1902-22; Robert Leland Collection, Indian water rights.

WASPS

NY —AMERICAN MUSEUM OF NATURAL HISTORY, Library Services Dept, Central Park W & 79th St, New York, 10024. Nina J Root, Chairwoman; Mary Genett, Asst Librn for Reference Services
Notes: A major literature collection supplements the museum's entomology collections; perhaps the largest in the world.

WASTE, DISPOSAL OF see Refuse and Refuse Disposal; Waste Products

WASTE, RADIOACTIVE see Radioactive Waste

WASTE MANAGEMENT see Refuse and Refuse Disposal; Salvage (Waste, Etc.); Waste Products

WASTE PRODUCTS

CA —CALIFORNIA DEPT OF TRANSPORTATION, Transportation Library, 5900 Folsom Blvd, PO Box 19128, Sacramento, 95819. Eva Caro, Librn
Holdings: Vols (10,000) Cat Mss Maps Pix Slides Phonorecords Audiotapes Videotapes 16mm Films Filmstrips Micoforms
IL —GREELEY & HANSEN ENGINEERS, 222 S Riverside Plaza, Chicago, 60606. Marilyn Cichom, Librn
Holdings: Vols (6000) Cat Maps Slides Microforms
MA —CAMP, DRESSER & MCKEE, Herman G Dresser Library, One Center Plaza, Boston, 02108. Virginia L Carroll, Librn
Holdings: Vols (15,000) Cat Maps Slides Microforms
Notes: Air, land, and water pollution; environmental engineering; hazardous wastes; water resources; solid wastes; resource recycling.
MA —ABCOR, INC, Library, 850 Main St, Wilmington, 01887. Eileen Smith, Librn
Holdings: Vols (2000) Cat
Budget: ($10,000)
Notes: Environmental technology; untrafiltration; waste treatment processes. Incl technical reports. Extensive microfiche collection on air pollution.
PA —PENNSYLVANIA DEPT OF ENVIRONMENTAL RESOURCES, Office of Environmental Protection, Technical Reference Library, Fulton Bldg, 17th Floor, Box 2063, Harrisburg, 17120. Wanda R Bell, Librn
Holdings: Vols (2000) Cat Slides Microforms
Notes: 10,000 technical reports; water and

wastewater feasibility plans; *Pennsylvania Bulletin*, 1970-present; water pollution; solid waste; mining and reclamation; air quality; acid mine drainage.
UT —EIMCO TECHNOLOGY & RESEARCH CENTER, Process Machinery Div, Technical Library, 414 W 300 S, Salt Lake City, 84110.
Holdings: Vols (1450) Cat

WASTE RECLAMATION see Salvage (Waste, Etc.)

WASTE WATER RECLAMATION see Water Reuse

WATCHES see Clocks and Watches

WATCHORN FAMILY PAPERS

CA —LINCOLN MEMORIAL SHRINE, A K Smiley Public Library, 125 W Vine St, Redlands, 92373. Larry E Burgess, Archivist
Holdings: Vols (3000) Cat Mss Maps Pix Slides Phonorecords 16mm Films Microforms
Budget: ($18,000)
Notes: One of the larger collections on Lincoln and his times. Incl broadsides, letters, prints, campaign badges, stamps, coins, medals; bust, by George Grey Bernard. Endowment of Watchorn Lincoln Memorial Association. There is an additional pamphlet collection of more than 3000 pieces; en extensive philately collection incl first-day covers, commemorative and foreign issues, and Civil War envelopes.

WATER

CO —COLORADO HISTORICAL SOCIETY, Research Collections, 1300 Broadway, Denver, 80203. Catherine Kane, Head Public Service and Access
Holdings: Mss
Budget:
Notes: Strong ms holdings in western and Colorado business history in such areas as mining, water, transportation, sugar industry.
FL —SOUTH FLORIDA WATER MANAGEMENT DISTRICT, Library, PO Box V, West Palm Beach, 33402. Cynthia H Plockelman, Research Librn
Holdings: Cat Slides Microforms Periodicals
Budget: ($13,000)
Notes: A state agency dealing in all aspects of water management, flood control, hydrology, changing environmental conditions, etc. Emphasis is changing from flood control to general water management.
IL —ILLINOIS STATE WATER SURVEY, Library, 605 E Springfield, Champaign, 61820. Marcia E Nelson, Head Librn
Holdings: Vols (22,000) Cat Maps
Notes: Emphasis on Illinois and region. Materials on water resources development, water resources and atmospheric sciences.
MA —UNIVERSITY OF MASSACHUSETTS AT AMHERST, Physical Sciences Library, Amherst, 01003. Siegfried Feller, Assoc Dir for Collection Development
Holdings: Vols Cat Microforms
Notes: Environmental sciences. Extensive journal holdings; incl water resources engineering and management.
MA —MASSACHUSETTS AUDUBON SOCIETY, Hathaway Environmental Education Institute, Lincoln, 01773. Louise C Maglione, Librn
Notes: Largest and most comprehensive collection in the field of environmental education; especially good in the curriculum area. Extensive sections on animal, behavioral and environmental issues, and quality of environment.
NM —US GEOLOGICAL SURVEY, Water Resources Division Library, Western Bank, 505 Marquette, Rm 714, Albuquerque, 87102. Janie S Jones, Librn
Holdings: Vols (38,000) Mss Maps
Notes: Primarily hydrology and geology of New Mexico. Incl 20,000 maps.
OR —OREGON STATE UNIVERSITY, Library, Corvallis, 97331. Melvin George, Dir
Holdings: Vols (980,000) Cat

PA —FRANKLIN INSTITUTE LIBRARY, 20 & The Parkway, Philadelphia, 19103. Miriam Padusis, Dir; Charles Wilt, Readers Servs Librn
Holdings: Vols (300,000) Cat Maps Pix Microforms
TX —TEXAS A&M UNIVERSITY, Sterling C Evans Library, Documents Div, College Station, 77843. Lisa Abbott, Technical Reports Librn; Jan Swanbeck, Doc Librn
Holdings: Vols Cat Mss Microforms
Notes: Technical Reports Department incl 24,045 state and foreign government reports on water, transportation, and oceanography, as well as servicing the NTIS microfiche collection of 600,000 films.
UT —EIMCO TECHNOLOGY & RESEARCH CENTER, Process Machinery Div, Technical Library, 414 W 300 S, Salt Lake City, 84110.
Holdings: Vols (1450) Cat
WI —UNIVERSITY OF WISCONSIN, MADISON, Water Resources Reference Services, 1975 Willow Dr, Madison, 53706. Sarah L Calcese, Librn
Holdings: Vols 15,150 Cat Maps
Budget: $4000
Notes: Coordination point for campus resources relating to water; arranged in 30 categories which parallel those established by the Committee on Water Resources Research, Federal Council for Science and Technology. University of Wisconsin Indexing System generates keyword and author indexes. Keywords are taken from the Office of Water Resources Research Thesaurus. Report literature from the Environmental Protection Agency, state water resources centers and other agencies comprises a large portion of the collection.

WATER—ANALYSIS

PA —PENNSYLVANIA DEPT OF ENVIRONMENTAL RESOURCES, Office of Environmental Protection, Technical Reference Library, Fulton Bldg, 17th Floor, Box 2063, Harrisburg, 17120. Wanda R Bell, Librn
Holdings: Vols (2000) Cat Slides Microforms
Notes: 10,000 technical reports; water and wastewater feasibility plans; *Pennsylvania Bulletin*, 1970-present; water pollution; solid waste; mining and reclamation; air quality; acid mine drainage.

WATER—CONSERVATION see Water Conservation

WATER—LAWS AND LEGISLATION

TX —TEXAS DEPT OF WATER RESOURCES, Library, 1700 N Congress, PO Box 13087, Capitol Sta, Austin, 78711. Sylvia von Fange, Head Librn
Holdings: Vols (58,000) Cat Pix Microforms
Notes: A comprehensive technical collection which incl information on all aspects of water resources. Publications Catalog; Library Bulletin (monthly).

WATER—POLLUTION AND CONTROL

CA —CALIFORNIA DEPT OF TRANSPORTATION, Transportation Library, 5900 Folsom Blvd, PO Box 19128, Sacramento, 95819. Eva Caro, Librn
Holdings: Vols (10,000) Cat Mss Maps Pix Slides Phonorecords Audiotapes Videotapes 16mm Films Filmstrips Microforms
CO —COLORADO STATE UNIVERSITY, Libraries, Fort Collins, 80523. K Suzanne Johnson, Biomedical Sciences, Librn
Holdings: Vols (2000) Cat Microforms
Budget: ($2000)
FL —EVERGLADES NATIONAL PARK, South Florida Research Center, PO Box 279, Homestead, 33030. Gary Hendrix, Librn
Holdings: Vols (5500) Cat Microforms
Notes: Water management. Emphasis on South Florida, birds, water problems. This is a special reference collection maintained for the Park Staff only. Noncirculating. Estuaries. ILL available.

WATER—POLLUTION AND CONTROL (cont.)

IL —ILLINOIS STATE WATER SURVEY, Library, 605 E Springfield, Champaign, 61820. Marcia E Nelson, Head Librn
Holdings: Vols (22,000) Cat Maps
Notes: Emphasis on Illinois and region. Materials on water resources development, water resources and atmospheric sciences.

IL —GREELEY & HANSEN ENGINEERS, 222 S Riverside Plaza, Chicago, 60606. Marilyn Cichom, Librn
Holdings: Vols (6000) Cat Maps Slides Microforms

MD —CHARLES COUNTY COMMUNITY COLLEGE, Learning Resource Center, PO Box 910, La Plata, 20646. J Elaine Ryan, Dean
Holdings: Vols (1500) // Uncat 16mm Films Microforms
Notes: Primarily composed of government documents, this collection emphasizes the technical aspects of waste water treatment. Additional point of emphasis is desalination.

MA —CAMP, DRESSER & MCKEE, Herman G Dresser Library, One Center Plaza, Boston, 02108. Virginia L Carroll, Librn
Holdings: Vols (15,000) Cat Maps Slides Microforms
Notes: Air, land, and water pollution; environmental engineering; hazardous wastes; water resources; solid wastes; resource recycling.

MA —TUFTS UNIVERSITY, Engineering Library, Medford, 02155. Wayne Powell, Science-Engineering Librn
Holdings: Vols (20,000) Cat
Notes: Also 25,000 technical reports. Subject emphases: solid waste management, water pollution control, fluid mechanics.

MO —US FISH & WILDLIFE SERVICE, Columbia National Fisheries Research Laboratory, Rte One, Columbia, 65201. Axie Hindman, Librn
Holdings: Vols (2000) Cat Microforms
Budget: ($7000)
Notes: Pesticides in aquatic biota; fisheries research; fresh-water ecology. Also incl collection in water pollution, acid rain, aquatic invertebrets, environment and 10,000 reprints.

NY —NASSAU COUNTY DEPARTMENT OF HEALTH, Division of Laboratories & Research, 209 Main St, Hempstead, 11550. Madeline Burston, Librn; Beatrice R Sewald, Asst Librn
Holdings: Vols (4076) Cat Mss Slides Microforms

NY —BOYCE THOMPSON INSTITUTE FOR PLANT RESEARCH, Library, Cornell University, Tower Rd, Ithaca, 14853. Greta Colavito, Librn
Holdings: Vols (5300) Cat
Budget: ($46,000)
Notes: Mainly plant physiology, biochemistry, entomology, air and water pollution, pesticides, and plant pathology.

NY —UNIVERSITY OF ROCHESTER, Engineering Library, Gavett Hall, River Campus, Rochester, 14627. Isabel Kaplan, Librn
Holdings: Vols (22,465) Cat
Notes: Strong collection in the field and related areas.

OH —CASE WESTERN RESERVE UNIVERSITY LIBRARIES, Cleveland, 44106. Susie Hanson, Special Collections Librn
Holdings: Vols 1000 Cat
Notes: The collection was previously titled the Lake Erie Study Collection. As its scope has increased, it has been renamed the Environmental Sciences Collection and has been fully incorporated into the collection of the Sears Library,, which serves the University in the areas of science and technology, economics and management. The Environmental Sciences Collection incl government and nongovernment reports, monographs and serials.

OH —CLEVELAND PUBLIC LIBRARY, Science & Technology Dept, 325 Superior Ave, Cleveland, 44114. Jean Z Piety, Head
Holdings: Cat Pix
Notes: Special collection covers the environmental sciences concerned with the Great Lakes-St Lawrence drainage basins. Emphasis is on limnology, ecology, meteorology, hydraulics, biology, pollution of air and water, natural history and general research. Most of the material indexed has been donated by numerous agencies around the Great Lakes.

OH —ANTIOCH COLLEGE, Olive Kettering Library, Livermore St, Yellow Springs, 45387. Nina Myatt, Cur
Notes: Personal papers and correspondence (1920-1975) of Arthur E Morgan former President of Antioch (1920-1936), first director of Ohio's Miami Valley Conservancy District, and first Chairman of the Tennessee Valley Authority (TVA). Mss, film, out-takes, much on the engineering of over 50 water-control projects in this country, Africa, and India. Materials on Edward Bellamy (Morgan wrote biography of Bellamy). Incl family papers. About 175 file boxes.

PA —PENNSYLVANIA DEPT OF ENVIRONMENTAL RESOURCES, Office of Environmental Protection, Technical Reference Library, Fulton Bldg, 17th Floor, Box 2063, Harrisburg, 17120. Wanda R Bell, Librn
Holdings: Vols (2000) Cat Slides Microfilm Microfiche
Budget: 5
Notes: 10,000 technical reports; water and wastewater feasibility plans; PA Bulletin, 1970-Present; water pollution; solid waste; mining and reclamation; air quality; acid mine drainage.

PA —FRANKLIN INSTITUTE LIBRARY, 20 & The Parkway, Philadelphia, 19103. Miriam Padusis, Dir; Charles Wilt, Readers Servs Librn
Holdings: Vols (300,000) Cat Maps Pix Microforms

TX —TEXAS DEPT OF WATER RESOURCES, Library, 1700 N Congress, PO Box 13087, Capitol Sta, Austin, 78711. Sylvia von Fange, Head Librn
Holdings: Vols (58,000) Cat Pix Microforms
Notes: A comprehensive technical collection which incl information on all aspects of water resources. Publications Catalog: Library Bulletin (monthly).

VA —UNIVERSITY OF VIRGINIA, Alderman Library, Manuscripts Dept, Charlottesville, 22901. Edmund Berkeley Jr, Cur
Holdings: Cat Mss Maps Pix
Notes: Papers of the Conservation Council of Virginia, and its chairman, the Central Atlantic Environment Center, the Virginia Electric and Power Co, the US Atomic Energy Commission, State Water Control Board Chairman, and members of the Governor's Council on the Environment focus on a variety of environmental issues particularly the location of a nuclear power plant on an alleged geological fault, water pollution and the Potomac River cleanup of the 1970s and state environmental goals regarding water and air pollution, preservation, and development.

WA —URS ENGINEERS, Library, 2615 Fourth Ave, Seattle, 98121. Jill Phelps, Librn
Holdings: Vols (3100) Cat
Budget: ($5000)
Notes: Environmental impact assessment, hazardous materials disposal, oil spill cleanup and environmental effects of waterborn pollutants, especially with regard to California and the western environment.

WI —COLT INDUSTRIES, FM Engine Div, Library, 701 Lawton Ave, Beloit, 53511. Westley A Brill, Library Admin
Holdings: Vols 100 Cat Mss

AB —ALBERTA DEPT OF THE ENVIRONMENT, Library, Oxbridge Place, 9820 106th St, Edmonton, T5K 2J6, Can. Marilyn Corbett, Head, Library Services Branch
Holdings: Vols (20,000) Cat Microforms

ON —CANADA CENTRE FOR INLAND WATERS, Library, 867 Lakeshore Rd, Burlington, L7R 4A6, Can. Eve Dowie, Head Library Services
Holdings: Vols (20,000)
Budget: ($150,000)
Notes: A research collection oriented towards Canadian limnological research. Incl 312 subscriptions.

WATER—PURIFICATION

IL —GREELEY & HANSEN ENGINEERS, 222 S Riverside Plaza, Chicago, 60606. Marilyn Cichom, Librn
Holdings: Vols (6000) Cat Maps Slides Microforms

KY —UNIVERSITY OF KENTUCKY, Robert E Shaver Library of Engineering, 355 Anderson Hall, Lexington, 40506. Russell H Powell, Engineering Librn
Holdings: Vols (48,000) Cat Microforms

NY —US ENVIRONMENTAL PROTECTION AGENCY, Region II, Technical Library, 26 Federal Plaza, New York, 10278. Audrey Thomas, Regional Librn
Holdings: Vols 4200 Cat
Notes: Incl 16,000 reports, 170,000 microfiche, 275 current subscriptions.

WATER—QUALITY see Water Quality

WATER—REUSE see Water Reuse

WATER—THERAPEUTIC USE see Hydrotherapy

WATER, SUBTERRANEAN see Water, Underground

WATER, UNDERGROUND

IL —UNIVERSITY OF ILLINOIS, URBANA/CHAMPAIGN, Library, Geology Library, 223 Natural History Bldg, Urbana, 61801. Dederick Ward, Librn
Holdings: Vols (105,186) Cat Maps Microforms

WATER BIRDS

FL —EVERGLADES NATIONAL PARK, South Florida Research Center, PO Box 279, Homestead, 33030. Gary Hendrix, Librn
Holdings: Vols (5500) Cat Microforms
Notes: Emphasis on South Florida, birds, water problems. This is a special reference collection maintained for the Park Staff only. Noncirculating. Estuaries. ILL available.

IL —ILLINOIS NATURAL HISTORY SURVEY LIBRARY, 196 Natural Resources Bldg, Champaign, 61820. Carla G Heister, Librn
Holdings: Vols (36,000) Cat Microforms
Budget: ($25,500)
Notes: A Research and Science Branch of the State of Illinois, the Natural History Survey maintains a library of books, journals and reports on various aspects of natural history. Material is collected in all major languages. The library maintains its own exchange arrangements with some 600 worldwide institutions and organizations. Interlibrary loans and photocopy services are available through the University of Illinois Library. Publications issued regularly by the Survey incl Biological Notes, The Bulletin, and Circulars.

ND —NORTHERN PRAIRIE WILDLIFE RESEARCH CENTER, Library, PO Box 1747, Jamestown, 58401.
Holdings: Vols (2500) Cat Pix Slides
Budget: ($10,000)
Notes: Wildlife management and research, incl avian biology, plant and animal ecology as related to wetlands and prairies, waterfowl research, and effects of predators on waterfowl.

WATER CONSERVATION

TX —AMARILLO PUBLIC LIBRARY, 413 E Fourth, Amarillo, 79101. Mary Kay Snell, Librn
Notes: John L McCarty, newspaper editor, author, artist, and businessman in Amarillo and Dalhart, Texas. Papers incl 4030 notes, interviews, photographs unpublished theses, clippings, and historical editions. A wide variety of subjects incl buffalo hunting, Indian wars, cowboys and the open range,

WATER CONSERVATION (cont.)

the arrival of the farmers, fences, and and towns. His work begins around the turn of the century and ranges through the depression years, the Dust Bowl, and soil and water conservation studies.

WATER CONTROL see Water—Pollution and Control

WATER CURE

†NY —MEDICAL RESEARCH LIBRARY OF BROOKLYN, Academy of Medicine of Brooklyn & The State University of New York Downstate Medical Center, 450 Clarkson St, Brooklyn, 11203. Kenneth E Moody, Dir
Notes: Extensive collection of 18th-19th century material.
See also entry under Medicine.

WATER FLIES see Flies

WATER FOWL see Water Birds

WATER MILLS

IN —INDIANA HISTORICAL SOCIETY, Library, 315 W Ohio St, Indianapolis, 46202. Robert K O'Neill, Dir
Holdings: Cat Mss Maps Pix
Notes: Incl in *Directory of Special and Subject Collections in Indiana* (Indiana Library Studies, report number 12).

WATER POLLUTION see Water—Pollution and Control

WATER POWER

MA —MERRIMACK VALLEY TEXTILE MUSEUM, Library, 800 Massachusetts Ave, North Andover, 01845. Clare Sheridan, Librn; Laurence Gross, Cur
Holdings: Vols (35,000) Cat Mss Maps Pix Slides
Notes: See entry under Textile Industry and Fabrics-History.
MA —OLD STURBRIDGE VILLAGE, Research Library, Sturbridge, 01566. Theresa Rini Percy, Librn
Holdings: Vols (23,000) // Mss
Notes: Kinne Collection of trade catalogs of turbines and related machinery, material on water-power history, and turbine patents, 1790-1946. Also Clarence E Kinne papers, 1906-1949. 13 boxes (*Kinne Collection Checklist*, October 1977.)
NY —CARY ARBORETUM OF THE NEW YORK BOTANICAL GARDEN, Library, Box AB, Millbrook, 12545. Fred Strum, Librn
Notes: This collection of alternative energy sources consists of publications concerned with solar energy, wind power, biofuel, methanol, small hydroelectric projects, and wood power.
OH —ANTIOCH COLLEGE, Olive Kettering Library, Livermore St, Yellow Springs, 45387. Nina Myatt, Cur
Notes: Personal papers and correspondence (1920-1975) of Arthur E Morgan former President of Antioch (1920-1936), first director of Ohio's Miami Valley Conservancy District, and first Chairman of the Tennessee Valley Authority (TVA). Mss, film, out-takes, much on the engineering of over 50 water-control projects in this country, Africa, and India. Materials on Edward Bellamy (Morgan wrote biography of Bellamy). Incl family papers. About 175 file boxes.
WI —MILWAUKEE SCHOOL OF ENGINEERING, Library, 500 E Kilbourn Ave, PO Box 644, Milwaukee, 53201. Mary Ann Schmidt, Head Librn
Holdings: Vols (34,500) Cat
Budget: ($215,800)

WATER POWER—LAWS AND LEGISLATION see Water—Laws and Legislation

WATER PURIFICATION see Water—Purification

WATER PURIFICATION PLANTS see Water Treatment Plants

WATER QUALITY

TX —TEXAS DEPT OF WATER RESOURCES, Library, 1700 N Congress,

PO Box 13087, Capitol Sta, Austin, 78711. Sylvia von Fange, Head Librn
Holdings: Vols (58,000) Cat Pix Microforms
Notes: A comprehensive technical collection which incl information on all aspects of water resources. Publications Catalog; Library Bulletin (monthly).
ON —INTERNATIONAL JOINT COMMISSION LIBRARY, 100 Ouellette Ave, Seventh Floor, Windsor, N9A 6T3, Can. Pat Murrary, Librn
Notes: Emphasis on water resources, water quality, land use, coastal zones, Great Lakes. Library includes 40,000 government reports from federal, provincial and state governments; 5000 monographs to support Great Lakes Water Quality Agreement Community. Collection also includes 243 periodicals, 1700 microfiche, 800 slides & vertical files.

WATER QUALITY BIOASSAY

CA —CALIFORNIA STATE UNIVERSITY, FULLERTON, Library, Box 4150, Fullerton, 92634. Linda Herman, Special Collections Librn
Holdings: Cat
Notes: Dr Leonard B Schultz Ichthyology Collection of 13,000 pieces incl books, pamphlets, articles and ephemera. It is supplemented by the Ecology of Bay and Estuarine Fishes Collections.

WATER RECLAMATION see Water Reuse

WATER RESOURCES DEVELOPMENT

AZ —TUCSON PUBLIC LIBRARY, Governmental Reference Library, PO Box 27210, City Hall, Tucson, 85726. Ann Strickland, Librn
Holdings: Vols (4000) Cat Maps Audiotapes Microforms
Notes: Special emphasis on public administration, including public finance, public personnel management, social services, urban planning, public transportation, public works, water management, solid waste management, public recreation and government of growing southwestern US cities in 200,000 to 500, 000 population range.
CA —UNIVERSITY OF CALIFORNIA, BERKELEY, Water Resources Center Archives, 410 O'Brien Hall, Berkeley, 94720. Gerald J Giefer, Librn
Holdings: Vols (83,000) Cat Mss Maps
Notes: The engineering, economic, social and legal aspects of water; water as a natural resource and its utilization; irrigation and reclamation; flood control; municipal and industrial water uses and problems; water rights; and water development projects. Particular concentration is on California and the West. Much ephemeral material. See *Dictionary Catalog of the Water Resources Center Archives, University of California* (Boston: GK Hall, 5 vols; First Supp, 1971; Second Supp, 1972; Third Supp, 1973; Fourth Supp, 1974; Fifth Supp, 1976; and Sixth Supp, 1978).
CA —CLAREMONT COLLEGES, Honnold Library, Ninth & Dartmouth, Claremont, 91711. Tania Rizzo, Special Collections Dept Head
Holdings: Vols 1545 Cat Mss Maps Pix Periodicals VF
Notes: Concerning southern California water resources. Incl 250 document cases and 3 vertical file drawers of archival-type materials; water engineers' and consultants' reports; well-logs, etc, correspondence; pamphlets and related ephemeral items. Litigations of water companies and districts. Downs Suppl 1316. Card index for uncataloged items.
CA —UPDATA PUBLICATIONS INC, Library, 1756 Westwood Blvd, Los Angeles, 90024. Sara Ferguson, Dir; Judith Harrington, Librn
Holdings: Vols (300) Uncat Maps Microforms
Notes: Incl 800,000 microforms, 35 periodicals.

CA —ASSOCIATION OF BAY AREA GOVERNMENTS, MTC/ABAG Library, 101 Eighth St, Oakland, 94607. Diane Gillman, Information Coord
Notes: Concentrates heavily on the nine-county Bay Area region. About 10,000 monographs and serials. Title catalog, OCLC/ATS. Central collection of documents for six transit properties in Bay Area.
CO —COLORADO STATE UNIVERSITY, Libraries, Fort Collins, 80523. Marjorie Rhoades, Engineering Sciences Librn
Holdings: Vols (40,000) Cat Maps Microforms
Budget: ($30,000)
Notes: Water and Soil in Arid Regions (WASAR) is an index and guide to books, conference papers, journal articles, government documents and technical reports, mostly in English, within the appropriate subject areas and held by Colorado State University Libraries. The bibliographical citations are of selected items dealing with soils, water, arid lands, crops, foods and nutrition with certain economic, political, ecological and historical parameters also included. The information needs of developing countries and of those who serve them are the prime criteria for inclusion.
DC —CONSERVATION FOUNDATION, Library, 1717 Massachusetts Ave NW, Washington, 20036. Barbara K Rodes, Librn
Holdings: Vols (8000) Cat Maps
Notes: Collection incl natural resources, ecology, city and regional planning, land use, recreation, energy conservation, environmental economics, pollution control, water resources.
IL —ILLINOIS STATE WATER SURVEY, Library, 605 E Springfield, Champaign, 61820. Marcia E Nelson, Head Librn
Holdings: Vols (22,000) Cat Maps
Notes: Emphasis on Illinois and region. Materials on water resources development, water resources and atmospheric sciences.
IL —GREELEY & HANSEN ENGINEERS, 222 S Riverside Plaza, Chicago, 60606. Marilyn Cichom, Librn
Holdings: Vols (6000) Cat Maps Slides Microforms
KY —UNIVERSITY OF KENTUCKY, Robert E Shaver Library of Engineering, 355 Anderson Hall, Lexington, 40506. Russell H Powell, Engineering Librn
Holdings: Vols (48,000) Cat Microforms
MD —CHARLES COUNTY COMMUNITY COLLEGE, Learning Resource Center, PO Box 910, La Plata, 20646. J Elaine Ryan, Dean
Holdings: Vols (1500) // Uncat 16mm Films Microforms
Notes: Primarily composed of government documents, this collection emphasizes the techncial aspects of waste water treatment. Additional point of emphasis is desalination.
MA —UNIVERSITY OF MASSACHUSETTS AT AMHERST, Physical Sciences Library, Amherst, 01003. Siegfried Feller, Assoc Dir for Collection Development
Holdings: Vols Cat Microforms
Notes: Environmental sciences. Extensive journal holdings; incl water resources engineering and management.
MA —BOSTON COLLEGE LIBRARIES, Catherine B O'Connor Geophysics Library, Weston Observatory, Weston, 02193. F Clifford McElroy, Science Librn
Holdings: Vols (10,231) Cat Maps Microforms
Budget: ($10,000)
Notes: This collection is being absorbed into the general collection.
NV —UNIVERSITY OF NEVADA, RENO, Desert Research Institute, PO Box 60220, Reno, 89557. Roberta Kiefer Orcutt, Librn
Holdings: Vols 800 Cat Journals
Notes: Incl 5000 cataloged technical reports, 7000 government documents and journals.
NV —UNIVERSITY OF NEVADA, RENO, University Library, Special Collections Dept, Reno, 89557. Robert E Blesse, Head
Holdings: Vols (75) Cat Photogs Mss
Notes: 25 Manuscript collections (145 cu ft) containing papers, records, documents, notes of individuals, businesses, and organizations

WATER RESOURCES DEVELOPMENT (cont.)

that have been involved with the development of water resources in Nevada and the eastern Sierra Nevada mountains, including Lake Tahoe. Includes photographs of lakes and rivers of the area.

NM —US GEOLOGICAL SURVEY, Water Resources Division Library, Western Bank, 505 Marquette, Rm 714, Albuquerque, 87102. Janie S Jones, Librn
Holdings: Vols (38,000) Mss Maps
Notes: Primarily hydrology and geology of New Mexico. Incl 20,000 maps.

NC —NORTH CAROLINA STATE UNIVERSITY, D H Hill Library, Box 7111, Raleigh, 27695. I T Littleton, Dir
Holdings: Vols 3300 Cat
Notes: Library provides a computer-based literature searching service for water resources through its "Southern Water Resources Scientific Information Center." Data base incl over 40,000 items published in Selected Water Resources Abstracts.

PA —UNIVERSITY OF PENNSYLVANIA, Towne Scientific Library, 220 S 33 St, Philadelphia, 19104. Charles Meyers, Librn
Holdings: Vols (65,000) Cat

TX —TEXAS DEPT OF WATER RESOURCES, Library, 1700 N Congress, PO Box 13087, Capitol Sta, Austin, 78711. Sylvia von Fange, Head Librn
Holdings: Vols (58,000) Cat Pix Microforms
Notes: A comprehensive technical collection which incl information on all aspects of water resources. Publications Catalog; Library Bulletin (monthly).

†TX —UNIVERSITY OF TEXAS, EL PASO, Library, El Paso, 79968.
Notes: Significant collections of water resources information about Texas and California.

TX —TEXAS TECH UNIVERSITY, Library, Lubbock, 79409. David J Murrah, Assoc Dir for Special Collections

WI —UNIVERSITY OF WISCONSIN, MADISON, Water Resources Reference Services, 1975 Willow Dr, Madison, 53706. Sarah L Calcese, Librn
Holdings: Uncat
Notes: Over 700 reprints filed by author. University has been designated a center of competence in water resources economics by the Office of Water Resources Research of the US Dept of Interior. Reprints are abstracted in Selected Water Resources Abstracts, and the collection can be approached through a search of the GIPSY (General Informaton Processing System) data base centered at the University of Oklahoma.

WI —WISCONSIN DEPT OF NATURAL RESOURCES, Technical Library, 3911 Fish Hatchery Rd, Madison, 53711. Rose Smith, Librn
Holdings: Vols (1200) Cat
Budget: $2000

ON —INTERNATIONAL JOINT COMMISSION LIBRARY, 100 Ouellette Ave, Seventh Floor, Windsor, N9A 6T3, Can. Pat Murrary, Librn
Notes: Emphasis on water resources, water quality, land use, coastal zones, Great Lakes. Library includes 40,000 government reports from federal, provincial and state governments; 5000 monographs to support Great Lakes Water Quality Agreement Community. Collection also includes 243 periodicals, 1700 microfiche, 800 slides & vertical files.

SK —CANADA PRAIRIE FARM REHABILITATION ADMINISTRATION LIBRARY, Motherwell Bldg, Regina, S4P 0R5, Can. C Kosack, Head
Holdings: Vols (10,000) Cat
Budget: ($8000)
Notes: PFRA is a Canadian federal government agency initiated to alleviate the effects of drought and water shortages on the prairies. The collection covers engineering (dams), agricultural economics, hydrology, irrigation, community pastures, and soil and water conservation.

WATER RESOURCES DEVELOPMENT—HISTORY

AZ —NORTHERN ARIZONA UNIVERSITY, Special Collection Library, CU Box 6022, Flagstaff, 86011. Peter M Whiteley, Coordr/Archivist; William Mullane, Librn
Notes: Jay Price Collection; correspondence, files, and reports pertaining to Forestry Topics, 1950's. Incl information on watershed and forest management for the Salt River and Central Arizona Projects as part of the Arizona Water Resource Committee files, 1956-1960; and files of the Soil Conservation Society, Arizona Chapter, 1956-1957 (2 feet). Also, Williams Water Works Collection; articles of incorporation and minutes of meetings, 1899-1901, Williams, Ariz.

CA —UNIVERSITY OF CALIFORNIA, LOS ANGELES, Research Library, Dept of Special Collections, 405 Hilgard Ave, Los Angeles, 90024. Edward Shreeves, Chairman, Bibliographers Group; David S Zeidberg, Head
Holdings: // Uncat Mss
Notes: In various collections, incl the Henry Baker Lynch, John Randolph Haynes and Dora Haynes Foundation Collections, Charles Frank Stern, and Philip David Swing Collections.

CA —A K SMILEY PUBLIC LIBRARY, 125 W Vine St, Redlands, 92373. Larry E Burgess, Archivist
Holdings: Vols (3500) Mss Maps Pix Phonorecords Microforms
Budget: ($45,000)
Notes: Emphasis on San Bernadino County and the Redlands area. Especially prized in The Citrograph, 1887-1908 (bound vols and microfilm) edited by Scipio Craig, prominent in state, national, and newspaper circles. The ms collection (250,000 pieces) incl the Smiley Family papers, much on water development, and on the citrus industry. The photograph collection (over 5000) covers the history of the area; there are many stereographs and glass slides. The collection on Indians of California and the Southwest was begun from a special gift by Andrew Carnegie honoring his friend, Albert K Smiley.

WY —UNIVERSITY OF WYOMING, William Robertson Coe Library, Western History Research Center, Laramie, 82071. Gene M Gressley, Dir, Asst to Pres
Holdings: Vols 2000 Cat Mss Pix
Notes: One of the collecting areas at the Western History Research Center is "Water Resources and Reclamation History," a section consisting of perhaps 120 significant collections of water resource leaders of the 20th century, and lesser significant papers of another 60.

WATER REUSE

CO —AMERICAN WATER WORKS ASSOCIATION, Technical Information Center, 6666 W Quincy, Denver, 80235. Kurt M Keeley, Tech Librn
Holdings: Vols (2000) Cat Slides Audiotapes Videotapes 16mm Films Filmstrips Microforms
Budget: ($12,000)
Notes: Covers water works industry, primarily treated and potable water, incl potable reuse. Worldwide coverage of water treatment and supply.

MA —ABCOR, INC, Library, 850 Main St, Wilmington, 01887. Eileen Smith, Librn
Holdings: Vols (2000) Cat
Budget: ($10,000)
Notes: Environmental technology; ultrafiltration; waste treatment processes. Incl technical reports. Extensive microfiche collection on air pollution.

UT —EIMCO TECHNOLOGY & RESEARCH CENTER, Process Machinery Div, Technical Library, 414 W 300 S, Salt Lake City, 84110.
Holdings: Vols (1450) Cat

WATER RIGHTS

AZ —NORTHERN ARIZONA UNIVERSITY, Special Collection Library, CU Box 6022, Flagstaff, 86011. Peter M Whiteley, Coordr/Archivist; William Mullane, Librn
Notes: Newspaper articles, mainly from the Arizona Republic, about the Colorado River Commission which was involved with the rights of individual states in their use of the water in the Colorado River. Many of the articles are about W S Norviel, the Arizona State Water Commissioner at the time, 1921-1923.

CA —UNIVERSITY OF CALIFORNIA, BERKELEY, Water Resources Center Archives, 410 O'Brien Hall, Berkeley, 94720. Gerald J Giefer, Librn
Holdings: Vols (83,000) Cat Mss Maps
Notes: The engineering, economic, social and legal aspects of water; water as a natural resource and its utilization; irrigation and reclamation; flood control; municipal and industrial water uses and problems; water rights; and water development projects. Particual concentration is on Califonia and the West. Much ephemeral material. See Dictionary Catalog of the Water Resources Center Archives, University of California (Boston: GK Hall, 5 vols; First Supp, 1971; Second Supp, 1972; Third Supp, 1973; Fourth Supp, 1974; Fifth Supp, 1976; and Sixth Supp, 1978).

CA —CLAREMONT COLLEGES, Honnold Library, Ninth & Dartmouth, Claremont, 91711. Tania Rizzo, Special Collections Dept Head
Holdings: Vols 1545 Cat Mss Maps Pix Periodicals VF
Notes: Concerning southern California water resources. Incl 250 document cases and 3 vertical file drawers of archival-type materials; water engineers' and consultants' reports; well-logs, etc, correspondence; pamphlets and related ephemeral items. Litigations of water companies and districts. Downs Suppl 1316. Card index for uncataloged items.

CA —UNIVERSITY OF CALIFORNIA, LOS ANGELES, Research Library, Dept of Special Collections, 405 Hilgard Ave, Los Angeles, 90024. Edward Shreeves, Chairman, Bibliographers Group; David S Zeidberg, Head
Holdings: // Uncat Mss
Notes: In various collections, incl the John Randolph Haynes and Dora Haynes Foundation Collections, Charles Frank Stern, and Philip David Swing Collections.

NV —UNIVERSITY OF NEVADA, RENO, University Library, Special Collections Dept, Reno, 89557. Robert E Blesse, Head
Holdings: Vols (75) Cat Mss
Notes: Papers, reports, documents of individuals and organizations which have been involved with water rights cases and legislation in Nevada and California. Includes 19th and 20th centuries. Approximately 75 cu ft of ms material. Considerable on Indian's rights.

TX —TEXAS DEPT OF WATER RESOURCES, Library, 1700 N Congress, PO Box 13087, Capitol Sta, Austin, 78711. Sylvia von Fange, Head Librn
Holdings: Vols (58,000) Cat Pix Microforms
Notes: A comprehensive technical collection which incl information on all aspects of water resources. Publications Catalog; Library Bulletin (monthly).

WATER SALVAGE see Water Reuse

WATER SPORTS see Aquatic Sports

WATER SUPPLY

CA —AZUSA PACIFIC COLLEGE, Marshburn Memorial Library, Citrus & Alosta, Azusa, 91702. Edward Peterman, Librn
Holdings: Vols 5000 // Maps Pix
Notes: Azusa Foothill Citrus and Local History collection is related to the genesis of Azusa, the citrus industry, the Slauson and Macneil families, and such companies as the Azusa Land and Water Company, Azusa Electric Lighting and Power Company, Azusa Foothill Citrus Association, Azusa Agricultural Water Company, and the Azusa Foothill Citrus Company. Includes letters, ledgers, etc.

CA —UNIVERSITY OF CALIFORNIA, BERKELEY, Giannini Foundation of

WATER SUPPLY (cont.)

Agricultural Economics, Library, 248
Giannini Hall, Berkeley, 94720. Grace Dote,
Librn
Holdings: Vols (18,000) Cat Mss Maps
Microforms
Notes: Noncirculating collection. No
interlibrary loans. Also about 124,000
unbound vols. Open to graduate students
and faculties of universities and colleges,
research workers and interested public.
Mostly English language materials, primarily
1900 to date. Card catalog published by G K
Hall Co *Dictionary Catalog of the Giannini
Foundation of Agricultural Economics
Library, University of California,* 12 volumes
(holdings through 7/71).

CA —UNIVERSITY OF CALIFORNIA,
BERKELEY, Water Resources Center
Archives, 410 O'Brien Hall, Berkeley,
94720. Gerald J Giefer, Librn
Holdings: Vols (83,000) Cat Mss Maps
Notes: The engineering, economic, social
and legal aspects of water: water as a natural
resource and its utilization; irrigation and
reclamation; flood control; municipal and
industrial water uses and problems; water
rights; and water development projects.
Particular concentration is on California and
the West. Much ephemeral material. See
*Dictionary Catalog of the Water Resources
Center Archives, University of California*
(Boston: G K Hall, 5 volumes; supplements,
1971, 1972, 1973, 1974, 1976, 1978).

CA —POMONA PUBLIC LIBRARY, Special
Collections, 625 S Garey Ave, PO Box 2271,
Pomona, 91766. David Streeter, Librn
Holdings: // Uncat Mss Maps Pix
Notes: Contains 21 linear feet of 16 Pomona
Valley water companies, reports, archives,
etc.

CO —AMERICAN WATER WORKS
ASSOCIATION, Technical Information
Center, 6666 W Quincy, Denver, 80235.
Kurt M Keeley, Tech Librn
Holdings: Vols (2000) Cat Slides Audiotapes
Videotapes 16mm Films Filmstrips
Microforms
Budget: ($12,000)
Notes: Covers water works industry,
primarily treated and potable water, incl
potable reuse. Worldwide coverage of water
treatment and supply.

CO —COLORADO STATE UNIVERSITY,
Libraries, Fort Collins, 80523. Marjorie
Rhoades, Engineering Sciences Librn
Holdings: Vols (6000) Cat
Budget: ($5000)
Notes: Water and Soil in Arid Regions
(WASAR) is an index and guide to books,
conference papers, journal articles,
government documents and technical
reports, mostly in English, within the
appropriate subject areas and held by
Colorado State University Libraries. The
bibliographical citations are of selected items
dealing with soils, water, arid lands, crops,
foods and nutrition with certain economic,
political, ecological and historical parameters
also included. The information needs of
developing countries and of those who serve
them are the prime criteria for inclusion.

IL —ILLINOIS STATE WATER SURVEY,
Library, 605 E Springfield, Champaign,
61820. Marcia E Nelson, Head Librn
Holdings: Vols (22,000) Cat Maps
Notes: Emphasis on Illinois and region.
Materials on water resources development,
water resources and atmospheric sciences.

IL —GREELEY & HANSEN ENGINEERS,
222 S Riverside Plaza, Chicago, 60606.
Marilyn Cichom, Librn
Holdings: Vols (6000) Cat Maps Slides
Microforms

NY —JERVIS PUBLIC LIBRARY, 613 N
Washington St, Rome, 13440. William A
Dillon, Dir
Holdings: Vols (1500) // Cat Mss Maps
Slides
Notes: John Bloomfield Jervis Collection
contains personal library (1500 vols) and
papers (1300 items) of chief engineer of
Croton aqueduct and other waterworks,
canals, and railroads circa 1825-1860. Papers

available on microfilm; indexes to papers
available from Jervis Public Library.

OH —CLEVELAND PUBLIC LIBRARY, 325
Superior Ave, Cleveland, 44114.
Holdings: Cat Maps Pix
Notes: Library collection in the subject
departments incl. state and local history; city
directories; business and industry; canals and
waterworks; technoogy; local authors and
artists; tourist and travel information (only
advisory), vital statistics. Early Ohio pictures
and historic maps. See also Western Reserve.
Cleveland Public Library.

PA —DELAWARE COUNTY PLANNING
DEPT, Library, Third & Orange St, Media,
19063. Jane Taggart Quin, Librn
Holdings: Vols 4800 Cat
Budget: $1500

PA —FRANKLIN INSTITUTE LIBRARY, 20
& The Parkway, Philadelphia, 19103.
Miriam Padusis, Dir; Charles Wilt, Readers
Servs Librn
Holdings: Vols (300,000) Cat Maps Pix
Microforms

†TX —UNIVERSITY OF TEXAS, EL PASO,
Library, El Paso, 79968.
Notes: Significant collections of water
resources information about Texas and
California.

SK —CANADA PRAIRIE FARM
REHABILITATION ADMINISTRATION
LIBRARY, Motherwell Bldg, Regina, S4P
0R5, Can. C Kosack, Head
Holdings: Vols (10,000) Cat
Budget: ($8000)
Notes: PFRA is a Canadian federal
government agency initiated to alleviate the
effects of drought and water shortages on the
prairies. The collection covers engineering
(dams), agricultural economics, hydrology,
irrigation, community pastures, and soil and
water conservation.

WATER SUPPLY—LAWS AND LEGISLATION see Water—Laws and Legislation

WATER SUPPLY, INDUSTRIAL

CA —UNIVERSITY OF CALIFORNIA,
BERKELEY, Water Resources Center
Archives, 410 O'Brien Hall, Berkeley,
94720. Gerald J Giefer, Librn
Holdings: Vols (83,000) Cat Mss Maps
Notes: The engineering, economic, social
and legal aspects of water: water as a natural
resource and its utilization; irrigation and
reclamation; flood control; municipal and
industrial water uses and problems; water
rights; and water development projects.
Particular concentration is on California and
the West. Much ephemeral material. See
*Dictionary Catalog of the Water Resources
Center Archives, University of California*
(Boston: GK Hall, 5 vols; First Supp, 1971;
Second Supp, 1972; Third Supp, 1973;
Fourth Supp, 1974; Fifth Supp, 1976, and
Sixth Supp, 1978).

WATER SUPPLY ENGINEERING

CO —COLORADO STATE UNIVERSITY,
Libraries, Fort Collins, 80523. Marjorie
Rhoades, Engineering Sciences Librn
Holdings: Vols (40,000) Cat Maps
Microforms
Budget: ($30,000)
Notes: This is one of the most extensive
collections in the region on water resources
engineering and management.

NY —ENGINEERING SOCIETIES
LIBRARY, 345 E 47 St, New York, 10017.
S Kirk Cabeen, Dir
Holdings: Vols 250,000 Cat Maps 16mm
Films Microforms
Notes: One of the largest, most
comprehensive engineering libraries in the
world. Covers all engineering disciplines;
particularly strong in electrical and
electronic, mechanical, mining and
metallurgical, petroleum, chemical,
industrial, air conditioning and refrigeration
engineering. Incl Wheeler Collection of early
materials on magnetisn and electricity. 125,
000 bound periodical volumes; 10,000 maps;

5000 serial subscriptions (many foreign-
language). Virtually all materials abstracted
in *Engineering Index* (1884-date) are incl in
Library. Noncirculating, except to members
of professional engineering societies which
support the Library. See *Engineering
Societies Library, New York, Classed
Subject Catalog and Index* (Boston: G K
Hall, 1963); and *Supplements,* 1-10, 1964-
1973.

WATER TRANSPORTATION see Shipping

WATER TRANSPORTATION, INLAND see Inland Water Transportation

WATER TREATMENT PLANTS

CO —AMERICAN WATER WORKS
ASSOCIATION, Technical Information
Center, 6666 W Quincy, Denver, 80235.
Kurt M Keeley, Tech Librn
Holdings: Vols (2000) Cat Slides Audiotapes
Videotapes 16mm Films Filmstrips
Microforms
Budget: ($12,000)
Notes: Covers water works industry,
primarily treated and potable water, incl
potable reuse. Worldwide coverage of water
treatment and supply.

WATERCOLORS, FLORAL

†CO —DENVER BOTANIC GARDENS,
Helen Fowler Library, 909 York St, Denver,
80206. Solange G Gignac, Librn
Notes: Emphasis on Bromeliada Literature;
horticulture; Colorado, Oregon, and Rocky
Mountains Region botany; landscape
architecture; juvenile horticultural and
botanical literature. Incl over 5000
pamphlets on botany and horticulture; also,
197 watercolors of Colorado wildflowers by
Emma Irvine, and 250 of Oregon by Lillian
Hallock.

WATERFOWL X see Water Birds

WATERGATE AFFAIR, 1972-

†CA —RICHARD M NIXON
PRESIDENTIAL LIBRARY, San Clemente,
92672.
Notes: Library is planned (1984) to be built
with private funds raised by the Richard M
Nixon Archives Foundation. Not expected
to open prior to 1987.

IL —CHICAGO HISTORICAL SOCIETY,
Library, Clark St at North Ave, Chicago,
60614. Archie Motley, Manuscript Librn
Notes: Papers of Albert E Jemmer, Jr
(Chicago attorney, member of the Warren
Commission, minority counsel during the
Nixon impeachment hearings, 1968-74, 10
linear ft incl photocopies).

NC —UNIVERSITY OF NORTH
CAROLINA, CHAPEL HILL, Louis Round
Wilson Academic Affairs Library, Southern
Historical Collection, Chapel Hill, 27514.
Carolyn Wallace, Librn
Holdings: Mss
Notes: The papers of Senator Samuel J
Ervin, Jr.

WATERING PLACES see Health Resorts, Watering Places, Etc.

WATERLOO, BATTLE OF, 1815

CA —UNIVERSITY OF CALIFORNIA, LOS
ANGELES, Research Library, Dept of
Special Collections, 405 Hilgard Ave, Los
Angeles, 90024. Edward Shreeves,
Chairman, Bibliographers Group; David S
Zeidberg, Head
Notes: An eyewitness narrative is incl in the
John Waldie journals and letters.

WATERMARKS (PAPER)

CA —CLAREMONT COLLEGES, Ella Strong
Denison Library, Scripps College,
Claremont, 91711. Judy Harvey Sahak,
Librn
Holdings: Vols (200) Uncat
Notes: In addition to books, the Kimberly

WATERMARKS (PAPER) (cont.)

Stuart Collection on the history of paper and papermaking includes trade journals, examples of handmade papers and watermarks and a distinguished collection of Dard Hunter books and ephemera.

IL —NEWBERRY LIBRARY, 60 W Walton St, Chicago, 60610. Diana Haskell, Cur of Modern Mss
Holdings: Cat Mss Pix
Notes: Emphasis on hand-made paper, incl watermarks. A small working collection on modern papermaking, mainly for use of our conservation department. A few mss on early American papermaking machinery.

MA —AMERICAN ANTIQUARIAN SOCIETY LIBRARY, 185 Salisbury St, Worcester, 01609. Marcus A McCorison, Dir & Librn
Holdings: Cat
Notes: Some 800 examples of watermarks in early American paper, from 1699.

NY —HISPANIC SOCIETY OF AMERICA, Library, 613 W 155 St, New York, 10032. Martha M de Narvaez, Cur of Mss; Irene S Frye, Asst Librn
Holdings: Vols (150,000) Cat Mss Maps Pix Slides Phonorecords Microforms

WATERPROOFING

MI —CONSTRUCTION CONSULTANTS, 900 Pallister, Detroit, 48202. Joan M Boram, Librn
Holdings: Vols (500) Cat Microforms
Notes: The only library in the country devoted entirely to the subject of roofing and waterproofing. Incl books and vinyl binders' containing articles culled from various journals, papers from manufacturers and independent testing and laboratory facilities pertinent government documents, and in-house papers, arranged according to subject matter and indexed. When necessary, papers are cross-referenced. Also, an extensive collection of legal materials relating to roofing and waterproofing failures. Lawyers from all parts of the country avail themselves of these materials.

WATERS, MINERAL see Mineral Waters

WATERWAYS

MA —HARVARD UNIVERSITY, Baker Library of the Graduate School of Business Administration, Kress Library of Business and Economics, Soldiers Field, Boston, 02163. Ruth E Rogers, Cur
Notes: An extensive collection. Historical emphasis on railroads and canals.

WATERWORKS see Water Supply

WATKINS, ERNEST SHILSTON, 1902

AB —UNIVERSITY OF CALGARY, Libraries, Special Collections Div, 2500 University Dr, Calgary, T2N 1N4, Can.
Holdings: Mss
Notes: The papers reflect Ernest Watkins' activities as lawyer, politician and writer in Canada and Britian and include correspondence, speeches, broadcasts, as well as manuscripts of books, articles, plays, short stories and novels.

WATKINS, LEE H.

CA —UNIVERSITY OF CALIFORNIA, DAVIS, Shields Library, Dept of Special Collections, Davis, 95616. Donald Kunitz, Head; C Danial Elliott, Asst Head
Holdings: Vols (5200) Cat Mss Pix Slides
Notes: Books and periodicals on the bee industry of worldwide scope. More specialized materials in the collection incl the records, convention programs, and correspondence from the American Beekeeping Federation and the California State Beekeepers' Association; and collections centered in John E Eckert, John S Harbison, MC Richter, and Lee H Watkins, apiculturalists.

WATSON, ALFRED EDWARD THOMAS, 1849-1922

BC —UNIVERSITY OF VICTORIA, McPherson Library, Victoria, V8W 3H5, Can.

WATSON, EDWIN M.

VA —UNIVERSITY OF VIRGINIA, Alderman Library, Manuscripts Dept, Charlottesville, 22901. Edmund Berkeley Jr, Cur
Holdings: Cat Mss Pix
Notes: The papers of Maj Gen Edwin M Watson (Pres Franklin D Roosevelt's military aide in the years before and during World War II). Incl some 16,000 documents and other articles, reflect both the full scope of Watson's duties as an aide to Roosevelt and his personal associations with the president and other national leaders during his years of service.

WATSON, ELMO SCOTT

IL —NEWBERRY LIBRARY, 60 W Walton St, Chicago, 60610. Diana Haskell, Cur of Modern Mss
Holdings: // Mss Pix
Notes: The Elmo Scott Watson Clipping Collection consists of two file cabinets of newspaper clippings and pictures relating to the American West (Indians, frontiersmen, correspondents, the army) which originally appeared as syndicated newspaper columns. Much material cannot be found elsewhere, without research.

WATSON, JOHN BROWN

RI —BROWN UNIVERSITY, John Hay Library, 20 Prospect St, Providence, 02912. Mark N Brown, Cur Mss
Holdings: Mss
Notes: Papers of Black educator John Brown Watson (1872-1942), President of Leland College, Louisiana (1923-1928) and Arkansas Agricultural, Mechanical and Normal College (1928-1942). Correspondents incl Booker T Washington, John Hope, Mary M Bethune, Florence M Read, W E B DuBois, Benjamin E Mays, S H Archer, C G Woodson, Rufus Clement, Mordecai Johnson, Hale Woodruff, Trevor Arnett, Langston Hughes, Lucy H Tapley, Channing Tobias, and Joe Louis.

WATSON, SIR WILLIAM

CA —UNIVERSITY OF SAN FRANCISCO, Richard A Gleeson Library, The Countess Bernardine Murphy Donohue Rare Book Room, San Francisco, 94117. D Steven Corey, Special Collections Librn
Holdings: Vols 40
Notes: Large group of correspondence with John Lane and Francis Burdett Money-Coutts, group of mss poems, material concerning the Watson Testimonial Appeal Fund.

CT —YALE UNIVERSITY, Box 1603A, Yale Station, New Haven, 06520.
Holdings: Cat Mss

OH —OHIO UNIVERSITY, Vernon R Alden Library, Department of Archives and Special Collections, Athens, 45701. Gary A Hunt, Head
Holdings: Vols 59 Cat
Notes: A comprehensive collection of first and later editions.

WATSON, THOMAS E., 1856-1922

NC —UNIVERSITY OF NORTH CAROLINA, CHAPEL HILL, Wilson Library, Rare Book Collection, Chapel Hill, 27514. Paul S Koda, Cur of Rare Books
Holdings: Cat Mss
Notes: Political, personal and business papers of Watson (1856-1922), Georgian lawyer, planter, US Senator and Representative, Populist Party leader, author and editor.

WATSON FAMILY

VA —UNIVERSITY OF VIRGINIA, Alderman Library, Manuscripts Dept, Charlottesville, 22901. Edmund Berkeley Jr, Cur
Holdings: Cat Mss Maps Pix
Notes: 19th century Virginia Family Papers Collections enable a researcher to obtain an excellent picture of the economic and social interactions on large plantations in Virginia during the 19th century. They are invaluable as research sources in the study of slavery, women's history, economic history, agrarian and political history.

WAUD, ALFRED R.

DC —LIBRARY OF CONGRESS, Prints & Photographs Div, Washington, 20540.
Notes: The Civil War Drawings Collection consists of 1600 original eyewitness drawings by Alfred R Waud, William Waud, and Edwin Forbes.

WAUD, WILLIAM

DC —LIBRARY OF CONGRESS, Prints & Photographs Div, Washington, 20540.
Notes: The Civil War Drawings Collection consists of 1600 original eyewitness drawings by Alfred R Waud, William Waud, and Edwin Forbes.

WAUGH, EVELYN

DC —GEORGETOWN UNIVERSITY, Library, Special Collections Div, 37 & O Sts NW, Washington, 20057. George M Barringer, Special Collections Librn; Nicholas B Sheetz, Mss Librn
Holdings: Mss
Notes: Extensive collection of books, manuscripts, and correspondence by novelist Evelyn Waugh. Incl his letters to Graham Greene, Leonard Russell, Douglas Woodruff, Handasyde Buchanan, and Christopher Sykes. Also present are Syke's own papers containing research material about Waugh. Also in Archives of the Gallery of Living Catholic Authors.
See also entries under Sykes, Christopher; Catholic Literature

NV —UNIVERSITY OF NEVADA, RENO, University Library, Special Collections Dept, Reno, 89557. Robert E Blesse, Head
Holdings: Vols 117 Cat
Notes: Includes individual works by author in all editions including translations; also prefaces, introductions, published correspondence, appearances in anthologies, periodicals, etc. Bibliographical research collection, part of Modern Authors Collection.

†TX —UNIVERSITY OF TEXAS LIBRARIES, General Libraries, Humanities Research Center, PO Box 7219, Austin, 78712. John Chalmers, Librn

WAUGH, SIDNEY BIEHLER

MA —JONES LIBRARY, 43 Amity St, Amherst, 01002. Daniel J Lombardo, Cur of Special Collections
Holdings: Vols 30 Cat Mss Pix
Notes: Incl drawings, photographs, and models and many of Sidney Waugh's sculptures. Unpublished guide available.

WAXES

OH —BLAIR MUSEUM OF LITHOPHANES & CARVED WAXES, 2032 Robinwood Ave, Toledo, 43620. Laurel G Blain, Cur
Holdings: Mss Pix
Notes: Several books have been written about wax carvings, the latest of which was by Mr E J Pyke.

WAY AND WILLIAMS (PUBLISHERS)

IL —NORTHERN ILLINOIS UNIVERSITY, Founders Memorial Library, Rare Books and Special Collections Dept, De Kalb, 60115. William R DuBois, Dept Head
Holdings: Vols (450) Cat
Notes: Works on the history of books and

WAY AND WILLIAMS (PUBLISHERS) (cont.)

printing and representative examples of fine printing. Includes more than 50 titles published in Chicago by Way & Williams.
NC —UNIVERSITY OF NORTH CAROLINA, GREENSBORO, Walter Clinton Jackson Library, Special Collections Dept, 1000 Spring Garden St, Greensboro, 27412. Emilie W Mills, Librn
Notes: All but nine of the titles published by Way and Williams of Chicago, 1895-1898. First, variant editions, many autographed by authors or publisher. Many association items. Letters to Chauncey Williams from William Allen White, Maxfield Parrish, Charles Lummis, Opie Read, etc. Photographs of Williams and several authors. Original artwork by Parrish, Will Bradley and ephemeral printing incl in the scrapbook compiled by Chauncey L Williams, ca 1919. Major part of the collection the gift of John M Williams in memory of Chauncey L Williams.

WAYBURN, NED

NY —NEW YORK PUBLIC LIBRARY, Performing Arts Research Center, Billy Rose Theatre Collection, 111 Amsterdam Ave, New York, 10023. Dorothy L Swerdlove, Cur
Holdings: Cat
Notes: Incl many scrapbooks relating to his career in England and the US.

WAYLAND, FRANCIS, 1796-1865

RI —BROWN UNIVERSITY, John Hay Library, 20 Prospect St, Providence, 02912. Mark N Brown, Cur Mss
Holdings: Mss
Notes: 7 portfolios, a letterbook, and 16 ms boxes of letters and mss for the period 1819-1865 consisting of about 800 letters concerning Brown University, personal, business, and religious matters, his journal, reminiscences, sermons, lectures, notes, and essays.

WAYMACK, W. W.

IA —STATE HISTORICAL SOCIETY OF IOWA LIBRARY, 402 Iowa Ave, Iowa City, 52240. Darold J Brown, Librn
Holdings: Cat
Notes: Thousands of individual items and smaller collections. Two hundred larger collections incl the papers of Cyrus C Carpenter, Jonathan P Dolliver, Gilbert Haugen, W W Waymack, Ephraim Adams, A C Dodge, Dorothy Houghton, Jesse Macy, Agnes Samuelson, Donald Johnson, Jack Miller, Ruth Sayre, Samuel Kirkwood, Thomas McKnight, Robert Lucas, Dwight McCarty, William Larrabee. Includes church, school, company and organization records, Civil War materials.

WAYNE, GEN. ANTHONY

MD —JOHNS HOPKINS UNIVERSITY, Milton S Eisenhower Library, Charles & 34 Sts, Baltimore, 21218. Ann S Gwyn, Assistant Dir for Special Collections
†MA —CLARK UNIVERSITY, Robert Hutchings Goddard Library, Worcester, 01610. Dorothy Mosa Kowski, Rare Books Librn
Holdings: Cat Mss
Notes: Eight original vols comprising the Orderly Books of the Revolutionary War General Anthony Wayne.
PA —WEST CHESTER UNIVERSITY, Francis Harvey Green Library, West Chester, 19380. R Gerald Schoelkopf, Special Collections Librn
Holdings: Uncat Mss Pix
Notes: Historical Treasures Collection contains: all four Shakespeare Folios, *Biographies of the Signers of the Declaration of Independence* by John Sanderson, illustrated by Thomas Addis Emmet. Inset in the volumes are actual autographs of the signers. Also, Anthony Wayne Letters-15 original letters comprising correspondence between General Anthony Wayne and Generals Washington, Arnold, Gates, Putnam and Schuyler, as well as others.

WEAKLEY, CHARLES ENRIGHT, 1906-1972

CA —HOOVER INSTITUTION ON WAR, REVOLUTION & PEACE, Stanford University, Stanford, 94305. Milorad M Drachkovitch, Archivist
Holdings: Mss
Notes: Papers of Charles E Weakley, Vice Admiral, US Navy, commander, Antisubmarine Warfare Force, Atlantic Fleet, 1963-67, and assitant administrator for management development, National Aeronautics and Space Administration, 1968-72, incl correspondence, orders, drafts of speeches, printed matter, photographs, and sound recordings, 1945-72, relating to post-World War II US antisubmarine force operations and to NASA activities, 4 ms boxes.

WEAPONS see Arms and Armor; Firearms

WEAPONS, ATOMIC see Atomic Weapons

WEAPONS, THERMONUCLEAR see Thermonuclear Weapons

WEAPONS CONTROL see Arms Control

WEAPONS EFFECTS

MS —US ARMY ENGINEER WATERWAYS EXPERIMENT STATION, Library Branch, PO Box 631, Vicksburg, 39180. Bernice Black, Chief Librn
Holdings: Vols (350,000) Cat Mss Maps Microforms

WEAPONS SYSTEMS

CA —UNIVERSITY OF CALIFORNIA, LIVERMORE, Lawrence Livermore National Laboratory, Library, PO Box 5500, Livermore, 94550. John B Verity, Library Mgr
Holdings: Vols (160,000) Cat 16mm Films Microforms
Budget: ($2,323,000)
Notes: The LLL library system includes a central collection in physics, chemistry, engineering, geology, mathematics, and computer science; and branch holdings in bio-medicine, environmental science, nuclear chemistry, energy research, theoretical physics, materials science, and nuclear weapons. Collections include 160,000 books, 145,000 technical reports, 530,000 reports on microfiche, and 3000 periodical subscriptions. LLL libraries are not open to the public. Unclassified materials may be borrowed on interlibrary loan.
CA —AEROJET ORDNANCE & MANUFACTURING CO, Library, 2521 Michelle Dr, Tustin, 92680. Norman J Storrer, Database Manager
Holdings: Vols 7000 Cat
Notes: Ordnance and weapons systems. Also 150,000 documents; 80,000 microforms.
NM —UNIVERSITY OF CALIFORNIA, Los Alamos National Laboratory, Libraries, PO Box 1663, MSP 362, Los Alamos, 87545. J Arthur Freed, Head Librn
Holdings: Vols (800,000) Cat Films Microforms
Budget: ($700,000)
Notes: Incl 500,000 classified and unclassified reports. There are 25 branch libraries and a central collection. The Medical Library contains about 40,000 vols in the areas of biomedical research.

WEATHER

AZ —NORTHERN ARIZONA UNIVERSITY, Special Collection Library, CU Box 6022, Flagstaff, 86011. Peter M Whiteley, Coordr/Archivist; William Mullane, Librn
Notes: Notebook and weather report articles beloning to V W Abbott of Flagstaff, Ariz, 1900-1912. Also, (1) Flagstaff Weather Bureau Collection; weather records, 1898-1969. (2) Winslow, Ariz, Weather Bureau Collection; weather records, 1949-1969 (6 feet).
FL —UNIVERSITY OF MIAMI, Otto G Richter Library, PO Box 248214, Coral Gables, 33124. Frank Rodgers, Dir of Libraries
Holdings: Vols Microforms
Notes: The Rosenstiel School of Marine and Atmospheric Sciences Library is one of the major marine science collections in the United States and is especially strong in the literature of tropical oceanography. Special collections in the library incl 200 oceanographic atlases and more than 50 sets of the world's major expedition reports. The library also maintains a nautical chart collection. 3000 microforms; 1000 current subscriptions.
HI —INTERNATIONAL TSUNAMI INFORMATION CENTER, PO Box 50027, Honolulu, 96850. Bonnie Dong, Librn
Notes: Large collection on tsunamis, their causes, oceanographic organization and mareographic records, forecasting, mapping, etc.
IL —SOUTHERN ILLINOIS UNIVERSITY, CARBONDALE, Morris Library, Carbondale, 62901. Jean M Ray, Map Librn
Holdings: Cat Maps Pix
Budget: ($1070)
Notes: Emphasis of map collection is Southern Illinois and Mississippi Valley. Incl 158,000 maps; 47,000 aerial photographs of Southern Illinois; 2000 atlases, reference books, etc; 4000 issues of weather map series (historical, daily, monthly); and 360 Illinois county platbooks. Includes Sang Collection-- 60 early maps of North America, especially Mississippi Valley, 1584-1840.
NJ —MONMOUTH COLLEGE, Murry & Leonie Guggenheim Memorial Library, New Jersey Collection, West Long Branch, 07764. Audrey K Wilson, Librn
Holdings: Vols (3025) Cat Maps Pix Microforms
Budget: ($1000)
Notes: Espec Monmouth County region. Incl periodicals, pamphlets, clippings. New Jersey Documents Depository. Picture collection, incl pictures of theatre personalities who came to this popular summer resort. Weather records kept by William Martin and his father at Long Branch, 1909-1963. Collection noncirculating.
NY —AMERICAN MUSEUM OF NATURAL HISTORY, Library Services Dept, Central Park W & 79th St, New York, 10024. Nina J Root, Chairwoman; Mary Genett, Asst Librn for Reference Services
PA —CARNEGIE LIBRARY OF PITTSBURGH, Science & Technology Dept, 4400 Forbes Ave, Pittsburgh, 15213. Catherine M Brosky, Dept Head
Notes: Long runs of journals, reports of geological surveys and society publications. Incl abstracts, indexes, bibliographies, literature guides, dictionaries, handbooks, manuals, compilations of data, maps, history and biography. Complete sets of US topographic maps and geologic folios, climatological data, water supply papers and soil surveys available.
TN —W R GRACE & CO, Planning Services Library, 100 N Main, PO Box 277, Memphis, 38103. Carolyn A Wilhite, Librn
Holdings: Vols (6000) Cat Mss Maps Microforms
Budget: ($85,000)
Notes: Animal nutrition and production; fertilizers; weather; and agricultural statistics.
WI —MILWAUKEE PUBLIC LIBRARY, 814 W Wisconsin Ave, Milwaukee, 53233. Donald J Sager, City Librn
Holdings: Cat Maps
Notes: Of primary interest, subject area well developed with emphasis on Wisconsin geology, other states of secondary interest. Long runs of journals, reports of geological surveys and society publications. Incl

WEATHER (cont.)

abstracts, indexes, bibliographies, literature guides, dictionaries, handbooks, manuals, and climatological data. Strong general reference service.
See also entry under Geology

NS —ENVIRONMENT CANADA, Dept of Environment Regional Library, 1497 Bedford Hwy, Bedford, E4A 1E5, Can. Fraizer Macniel, Special Collections Librn
Holdings: Vols 500 Maps Microforms
Notes: Reference collection for a regional weather analysis and forecasting center and to a small staff of professionals involved in consultation and applications. Principal meteoroligical and related journals are purchased. Library also houses regional climatological data base. Partially cataloged.

WEATHER, DRY see Droughts

WEATHER CONTROL

IL —ILLINOIS STATE WATER SURVEY, Library, 605 E Springfield, Champaign, 61820. Marcia E Nelson, Head Librn
Holdings: Vols (3000) Cat Maps
Notes: Weather modification.
NV —UNIVERSITY OF NEVADA, RENO, Desert Research Institute, PO Box 60220, Reno, 89557. Roberta Kiefer Orcutt, Librn
Holdings: Vols (10,480) Cat Maps Microforms
Notes: Incl materials in atmospheric physics, meteorology, climatology, weather modification, antarctic studies and related materials in basic sciences. Over 3000 microforms; also 1300 technical reports and 18,000 government publications.
†SD —SOUTH DAKOTA SCHOOL OF MINES & TECHNOLOGY, Devereaux Library, Rapid City, 57701.
Holdings: Vols (3786) Cat Mss Maps Pix Audiotapes
Notes: This special collection, in general, relates to the Black Hills area of South Dakota and Wyoming, especially mining and exploration of the area; the West River area of South Dakota, primarily county histories; and South Dakota Territorial and State materials. There are also specialized areas of this collection: (1) *Marion N Bruce Collection.* Documents, correspondence, books and periodicals dealing with weather modification in South Dakota; (2) *Mildred Fielder Collection.* Mss, pictures, books and periodicals from an author whose special area was the Black Hills. Most of her work on railroads, mines, trails, etc, related to historical aspects. Collection incl research materials, galley proofs and final copies of her various publications; (3) *Cleophas C O'Harra Collection.* Mss, pictures, books and original source materials, primarily related to the Black Hills areaand expeditions therto. Much of the data was collected for a book on the Black Hills which was never published; and (4) *Craving Collection.* Maps of various caves in Black Hills area, being kept current and updated by members of the Paha Sapa Grotto. Also, some books and periodicals on caving in general.
TX —TEXAS DEPT OF WATER RESOURCES, Library, 1700 N Congress, PO Box 13087, Capitol Sta, Austin, 78711. Sylvia von Fange, Head Librn
Holdings: Vols (58,000) Cat Pix Microforms
Notes: A comprehensive technical collection which incl information on all aspects of water resources. Publications Catalog: Library Bulletin (monthly).
UT —NORTH AMERICAN WEATHER CONSULTANTS, Technical Library, 1141 E 3900 South, Suite A130, Salt Lake City, 84124. Eleanor Furnival, Librn
Holdings: Vols (7000) Cat Maps 16mm Films Microforms
Budget: ($5000)
Notes: Incl 500 maps and 3000 microforms.

WEATHER MODIFICATION see Weather Control

WEATHERWAX, PAUL, 1888-1976

IN —INDIANA UNIVERSITY, Lilly Library, Seventh St, Bloomington, 47405. William R

Cagle, Librn
Holdings: // Mss Pix
Notes: Collections incl papers of geneticists and biologists, most notably those of Nobel Prize winner Hermann Joseph Muller, 1890-1967 and Tracy Morton Sonneborn, 1905-1981. Also papers of plant geneticists Ralph Erskine Cleland, 1892-1971, and Paul Weatherwax, 1888-1976.

WEAVER, CLAUDE

OK —UNIVERSITY OF OKLAHOMA, Bizzell Memorial Library, Western History Collections, 401 W Brooks, Norman, 73069. John Ezell, Cur
Holdings: Mss Documents Pix
Notes: US Representative. His papers. Guide available.

WEAVER, GORDON

MA —BOSTON UNIVERSITY, Mugar Memorial Library, Special Collections Dept, 771 Commonwealth Ave, Boston, 02215. Howard B Gotlieb, Dir
Holdings: Cat Mss Pix
Notes: Mss, correspondence, etc collected in depth; incl publications by or about.

WEAVER, WILLIAM

CA —UNIVERSITY OF CALIFORNIA, LOS ANGELES, Research Library, Dept of Special Collections, 405 Hilgard Ave, Los Angeles, 90024. Edward Shreeves, Chairman, Bibliographers Group; David S Zeidberg, Head
Notes: 1 linear foot of ms translations and ephemera.

WEAVING

CA —CALIFORNIA COLLEGE OF ARTS & CRAFTS, Meyer Library, Broadway at College, Oakland, 94618. Robert L Harper, Head Librn
Holdings: Vols (29,000) Cat Pix
Budget: ($10,000)
Notes: All fields of arts and crafts.
IA —DES MOINES ART CENTER, Library, Greenwood Park, Des Moines, 50312. Georgeanne Kudron, Dir of Education
Holdings: Vols 175 // Uncat Mss
Notes: Pennington Collection. Primarily emphasis on Scandinavian weaving. *Seen by appointment only.* Inaccessable indefinitely due to building program.
MA —UNIVERSITY OF LOWELL, Library, One University Ave, Lowell, 01854. Martha Mayo, Special Collections Librn
Notes: The Olney Collections contain books and journals on all aspects of textile technology particularly textile chemistry and textile engineering. The Flather Collection of the Boott Mill company papers 1835-1954. Photographic collections with emphasis on Lowell's textile industry.
MA —OLD STURBRIDGE VILLAGE, Research Library, Sturbridge, 01566. Theresa Rini Percy, Librn
Holdings: Cat Mss Pix Microforms
Notes: Historical material on New England methods, to 1860.
MI —CRANBROOK ACADEMY OF ART, 500 Lone Pine Rd, Box 801, Bloomfield Hills, 48013. Diane Gunn, Librn
Holdings: Vols (25,000) Slides
MI —PORTAGE LAKE DISTRICT LIBRARY, 105 Huron, Houghton, 49931. Bethany Patterson, Dir
Holdings: Vols 100 Cat Pix
Notes: Weaving and related crafts, spinning, etc. Some foreign language materials.
NJ —PASSAIC COUNTY HISTORICAL SOCIETY, Lamhurt Castle, Valley Rd, Paterson, 07503. Helen D Hamilton, Dir
Holdings: Vols (5000) Cat Mss Maps Pix

NY —SUFFOLK COUNTY HISTORICAL SOCIETY, Library, 300 W Main St, Riverhead, 11901. Betty Carpenter, Librn
Holdings: Vols (15,000) Cat Mss Maps Pix
Notes: Talmage Weaving Collection of weaving and fiber arts.

NC —PUBLIC LIBRARY OF CHARLOTTE & MECKLENBURG COUNTY, 310 N Tyron St, Charlotte, 28202. Mae S Tucker, Asst Dir
Holdings: Vols (3950) Cat Slides 16mm Films Filmstrips
Notes: Weaving, chemistry, dyes and dyeing, and color are emphasized. Also, hosiery, knitting, machinery, manufacturing, directories and statistics. Have specialized dictionaries in the subject field in both English and other languages. 110 periodical titles.

VT —SHELBURNE MUSEUM, Library, Shelburne, 05482. Barbara Reenstierna, Librn
Holdings: Vols (275) Cat Slides

WA —UNIVERSITY OF WASHINGTON LIBRARIES, Costume and Textile Collection, FM-25, Seattle, 98195. Krista Jensen Turnbull, Cur
Holdings: Vols (1500) Cat Pix Slides
Notes: Incl the Elizabeth Bayley Willis Collection of more than 1000 textiles from India, and the Seattle Weavers' Guild Collection of Guatemalan textiles. Coptic textiles are on loan from Yale University, and the Boston Museum of Fine Arts gave the Choate Collection of lace. There are also good collections of ecclasiastical vestments and embroideries from many nations, ranging from 1500 BC to the present.
WI —MILWAUKEE PUBLIC LIBRARY, 814 W Wisconsin Ave, Milwaukee, 53233. Donald J Sager, City Librn
Holdings: Vols Cat
Notes: Special strength.
See also entry under Art, Decorative.
AB —SOUTHERN ALBERTA INSTITUTE OF TECHNOLOGY, Learning Resources Centre, 1301 16 Ave NW, Calgary, T2M 0L4, Can. Tom Skinner, Historian
Holdings: Vols (5000) Cat Pix Slides Films Audiotapes Filmstrips Videotapes
Notes: Serves Alberta College of Art (4-year professional course).

WEAVING—PATTERNS

CA —CARLSBAD CITY LIBRARY, 1250 Elm Ave, Carlsbad, 92008. Clifford E Lange, Library Dir
Holdings: Vols (2297) Cat
Notes: Collection of sewing patterns. Catalogs of the patterns have been made up with complete information on size, etc, and have been divided into subject areas, such as gift ideas, toys, dolls, women's clothes, men's clothes, children's clothes, etc. Also patterns for knitted and crocheted wearing apparel. Incl patterns for children's costumes, historical fashions and antique dolls.

WEBB, ARTHUR PATTERSON, 1889-1959

BC —UNIVERSITY OF VICTORIA, McPherson Library, Victoria, V8W 3H5, Can.
Notes: Presbyterian minister. Incl transcripts: 15 cm, 1918-35; personal papers: diary 1923, correspondence, biographical miscellany; professional papers: appreciations, music, copywriting, magazine publications, correspondence; papers collected by Webb: pamphlets, press clippings, ephemera.

WEBB, CHARLES HENRY

MD —JOHNS HOPKINS UNIVERSITY, Milton S Eisenhower Library, Charles & 34

WEBB, CHARLES HENRY (cont.)

Sts, Baltimore, 21218. Ann S Gwyn, Assistant Dir for Special Collections
Holdings: Cat Mss
MA —BOSTON UNIVERSITY, Mugar Memorial Library, Special Collections Dept, 771 Commonwealth Ave, Boston, 02215. Howard B Gotlieb, Dir
Holdings: Cat Mss Pix
Notes: Mss, correspondence, etc collected in depth; incl publications by or about.

WEBB, JACK

CA —UNIVERSITY OF CALIFORNIA, LOS ANGELES, Theater Arts Library, Los Angeles, 90024. Edward Shreeves, Chairman, Bibliographers Group; Audree Malkin, Head, Theater Arts Library
Notes: Jack Webb (television and radio actor/producer) Collection: scripts for 318 episodes of the *Dragnet* radio series (1949-1955) and 276 episodes of *Dragnet* television series (1951-1959). Also incl are the radio series *Pat Novak for Hire, Noah's Ark,* and *The DA's Man.* Bound in the volumes are production stills relating to particular scenes.

WEBB, MARY GLADYS MEREDITH

CA —UNIVERSITY OF SAN FRANCISCO, Richard A Gleeson Library, The Countess Bernardine Murphy Donohue Rare Book Room, San Francisco, 94117. D Steven Corey, Special Collections Librn
Holdings: Vols 56
Notes: Comprehensive collection.
TX —NORTH TEXAS STATE UNIVERSITY, Rare Book and Texana Collections, NT Station Box 5188, Denton, 76203. Kenneth Lavender, University Bibliographer
Notes: 47 editions; memorabilia. Separate card catalog. Part of a larger collection containing works influencing or owned by Mary Webb.

WEBB, PHYLLIS

ON —NATIONAL LIBRARY OF CANADA, 395 Wellington St, Ottawa, K1A 0N4, Can. Andre Preibish, Dir
Notes: Literary Manuscripts collection contains papers of several important Canadian authors writing in English and/or French eg Clare Bice (1909-1976), noted author and illustrator of children's books; Andre Giroux, novelist, writer for television and broadcaster; Roger Lemelin, well-known author of Au pied de la pente douce, Les Plouffe, and Pierre le magnifique; Gabrielle Roy (1909-1983), author of many novels, including Bonheur d'occasion, La Petite Poule d'Eau and Rue Deschambault; Laura Goodman Salverson (1890-1970), writer, public speaker and teacher; Phyllis Webb, poet.

WEBB, W.

TX —SAN ANTONIO COLLEGE, Library, 1001 Howard St, San Antonio, 78284. James O Wallace, Dir
Holdings: Vols 2500 Cat Microforms
Notes: The Morrison Collection of Eighteenth Century British Literature. Partially described in: Hennington, Betty M. "Lois G Morrison Collection of Eighteenth Century English Literature: a Checklist" (unpublished MLS theses), Texas Woman's University, 1968. Also see "The Morrison Collection." *Scriblerian,* vol 1 pp 32-33 (spring 1969). Especially strong in material relating to Eustace Budgell; A Moore, W Webb and Edmund Curll imprints. A seperate catalog is maintained for the collection with entries for author, title, personal subjects, printers and booksellers, date of publication, engravers and association copies.

WEBB, WALTER PRESCOTT

TX —UNIVERSITY OF TEXAS LIBRARIES, General Libraries, Barker Texas History

Center, PO Box P, Austin, 78712. Don Carleton, Dir
Holdings: Vols (132,000) Cat Mss Maps Pix Slides Phonorecords Audiotapes Microforms
Notes: See description of collection under Texas-History.

WEBERN, ANTON VON

DC —LIBRARY OF CONGRESS, Music Division, Washington, 20540.
Notes: Papers and recordings of composer Arnold Schoenberg. Extensive correspondence with other composers, writers, etc.

WEBSTER, DANIEL, 1782-1852

†MA —UNIVERSITY OF MASSACHUSETTS AT AMHERST, Library, Amherst, 01003.
Notes: Microform collections of materials in other American libraries.
MA —BRANDEIS UNIVERSITY, Goldfarb Library, 415 South St, Waltham, 02154. Bessie Hahn, Dir
Notes: Daniel Webster Collection. 11 linear ft of correspondence mainly to Daniel Webster. A finding list to the collection is located in Special Collections.
NH —NEW HAMPSHIRE HISTORICAL SOCIETY, Manuscripts Library, 30 Park St, Concord, 03301. Thomas E Camden, Cur
Holdings: Cat Mss
Notes: Daniel Webster Papers incl correspondence, addresses, memoranda, articles and misc material relating to Webster's political, social, business, and personal life. There is a typewritten index to the collection. 20 vols, 3 boxes; about 2500 items.
NH —DARTMOUTH COLLEGE, Baker Memorial Library, Hanover, 03755.
Holdings: Cat Mss Pix
Notes: His writings, mss, etc, incl memorabilia. Microfilm and letterpress editions of the papers and correspondence available.

WEBSTER, DAVID LOCKE

IA —HERBERT HOOVER PRESIDENTIAL LIBRARY, West Branch, 52358. Dale C Mayer, Archivist
Notes: Papers.

WEBSTER, FRANK V.

OH —OHIO UNIVERSITY, Vernon R Alden Library, Department of Archives and Special Collections, Athens, 45701. Gary A Hunt, Head
Holdings: Vols (1400) Uncat
Notes: A miscellaneous collection of children's books by American and English authors, with most imprint dates in the period 1870-1930; numerous series books. Authors incl Jacob Abbott (196 v), "Oliver Optic" (84 v), Horatio Alger (89 v), J H Ewing (53 v), Martha Finley (47 v), G A Henty (46 v), Frank V Webster (38 v), and many others.

WEBSTER, HENRY KITCHELL

IL —NEWBERRY LIBRARY, 60 W Walton St, Chicago, 60610. Diana Haskell, Cur of Modern Mss
Holdings: Cat Mss
Notes: Primary repository; some 5000 pieces. Cataloged mss. Restricted use: noncirculating.

WEBSTER, JOHN MCADAM

†WA —WASHINGTON STATE UNIVERSITY, Library, Manuscripts, Archives & Special Collections, Pullman, 99164. John F Guido, Head
Holdings: Vols Cat Mss Maps Pix Microforms
Notes: Ms resources in the Washington State University Library for the study of Pacific Northwest history incl the personal papers of Frank A Banks, William Compton Brown, Enoch Albert Bryan, Ernest Otto Holland,

William Lon Johnson, Catherine May, Lucullus Virgil McWhorter, Austin Mires, Carl Parcher Russell, Pierre Jean de Smet, Henry Harmon Spalding, Elkanah Walker, John McAdam Webster, Marcus Whitman, as well as many business records of banks, insurance firms and agencies, breweries, lumber mills, merchants, enterpreneurs and farmers. All ms collections are described in a catalog, a published register or an unpublished finding aid.

WEBSTER, MARGARET

DC —LIBRARY OF CONGRESS, Manuscript Division, Washington, 20540. John C Broderick, Chief
Notes: The Margaret Webster Papers, incl some 50 prompt books of her productions. Also correspondence, copybooks, scrapbooks, etc. Described in *LC Information Bulletin,* 29 February 1968.

WEBSTER, NOAH

MA —AMHERST COLLEGE, Library, Amherst, 01002. John Lancaster, Special Collections Librn
Holdings: Vols 65 Cat Mss
MA —JONES LIBRARY, 43 Amity St, Amherst, 01002. Daniel J Lombardo, Cur of Special Collections
Holdings: Vols 93 Cat Pix
Notes: Editions, letter, newspapers clippings. Does not circulate. Unpublished guide available.
NY —NEW YORK PUBLIC LIBRARY, Rare Books and Manuscripts Div, Fifth Ave & 42 St, New York, 10018. William L Joyce, Asst Dir; Susan E Davis, Cur of Mss
Holdings: Mss
Budget: ($7161)
Notes: Incl personal and literary mss, papers, etc.

WEDDING PUBLICATIONS see Festschriften

WEDDINGTON, SARAH

TX —TEXAS WOMAN'S UNIVERSITY, Bralley Memorial Library, Box 23715, TWU Sta, Denton, 76204. Metta Nicewarner, Spec Collections Librn
Holdings: Vols Uncat Mss Pix
Notes: The Sarah Weddington Collection concerns the Texas lawyer, politician, feminist. Includes correspondence, working notes, official publications, campaign memorabilia, scrapbooks, books, pamphlets, legal documents, and speeches.

WEED, THURLOW

NY —UNIVERSITY OF ROCHESTER, Rush Rhees Library, Department of Rare Books and Special Collections, Rochester, 14627. Peter Dzwonkoski, Librn
Holdings: Vols 10 Cat Mss
Notes: Thurlow Wee, 1797-1882. Papers of this American journalist; editor of the *Albany (NY) Evening Journal.* Influential in 19th century American politics. Each letter in the collection has been indexed by name of letter writer. Unpublished register available in the repository.

WEED CONTROL

IA —IOWA STATE UNIVERSITY, Library, Dept of Special Collections, Ames, 50011. Stanley M Yates, Head
Holdings: Mss
Notes: Papers of Weed Science Society of America. The Society consists of individuals and organizations engaged or interested in the study and control of weeds. 10 linear ft, finding aid available.
PE —AGRICULTURE CANADA, Research Station Library, PO Box 1210, Charlottetown, C1A 7M8, Can. Barrie Stanfield, Librn
Holdings: Vols (2300) Cat
Budget: ($5000)

WEED SCIENCE SOCIETY OF AMERICA

IA —IOWA STATE UNIVERSITY, Library, Dept of Special Collections, Ames, 50011.

WEED SCIENCE SOCIETY OF AMERICA (cont.)

Stanley M Yates, Head
Holdings: Mss
Notes: Papers of Weed Science Society of America. The Society consists of individuals and organizations engaged or interested in the study and control of weeds. 10 linear ft, finding aid available.

WEEDON, GEORGE, 1730?-1790

RI —BROWN UNIVERSITY, John Hay Library, 20 Prospect St, Providence, 02912. Mark N Brown, Cur Mss
Holdings: Mss
Notes: Materials relative to the history of the US Army.

WEEGEE

AZ —UNIVERSITY OF ARIZONA, Center for Creative Photography, 843 E University Blvd, Tucson, 85721. James Enyeart, Dir; Terence Pitts, Cur and Librn
Notes: Center has significant collections consisting of more than 25 photographs plus other archival material such as negatives, contact sheets, work prints, correspondence, financial records, diaries, project files, etc. Inventories of the collections are available to researchers. Published guides available for some collections.

WEEKS FAMILY

NH —DARTMOUTH COLLEGE, Baker Memorial Library, Hanover, 03755.
Holdings: Cat Mss
Notes: Lancaster, New Hampshire family. Personal papers. Microfilm available.

WEES, FRANCES SHELLEY

MA —BOSTON UNIVERSITY, Mugar Memorial Library, Special Collections Dept, 771 Commonwealth Ave, Boston, 02215. Howard B Gotlieb, Dir
Holdings: Cat Mss Pix
Notes: Mss correspondence, etc collected in depth; incl publications by or about.

WEESE, HARRY M., AND ASSOCIATES

IL —CHICAGO HISTORICAL SOCIETY, Library, Clark St at North Ave, Chicago, 60614. Archie Motley, Manuscript Librn
Notes: Chicago Architectural Archive contains the papers of Chicago architects Barry Byrne and Earl H Reed, the records of the Illinois Society of Architects, and the voluminous files of two leading Chicago architectural firms, Holabird & Root and Harry M Weese and Associates. Access to these collections is by arrangement with Frank Jewell, The Society's Curator of Architectural Collections.

WEEVILS see Beetles

WEGELIN, OSCAR

RI —BROWN UNIVERSITY, John Hay Library, 20 Prospect St, Providence, 02912. Mark N Brown, Cur Mss
Holdings: Mss
Notes: Papers of Oscar Wegelin (1876-1970). About 400 items incl correspondence relating to his bibliography of American poetry; original verse and other writings; printed programs and clippings.

WEI CHI (GAME) see Go (Game)

WEIDENBAUM, MURRAY LEW, 1927-

CA —HOOVER INSTITUTION ON WAR, REVOLUTION & PEACE, Stanford University, Stanford, 94305. Milorad M Drachkovitch, Archivist
Holdings: Mss
Notes: Papers of Murray L Weidenbaum, author professor of economics, economist at the US Bureau of the Budget, 1949-1957, and Assistant Secretary of the Treasury for Economic Policy, 1969-1971, incl speeches and writings, pamphlets, clippings, and other matter, 1960- 1971, incl speeches and writings, pamphlets, clippings, and other matter, 1960-1977, relating to his service in the US government, US federal credit programs, business and inflation, government regulation of business, utility regulation, and military-industrial relations. 2 ms boxes.

WEIDMAN, CHARLES

NY —NEW YORK PUBLIC LIBRARY, Performing Arts Research Center, Dance Collection, 111 Amsterdam Ave, New York, 10023. Genevieve Oswald, Cur
Notes: Extensive biographical and visual documentation. Includes photographs, clippings, programs, scrapbooks, original drawings, motion pictures, tape-recorder interviews, and manuscripts. Much material also relates to his association with the Denishawn Dancers and with Doris Humphrey.

WEIGEL, REV. GUSTAVE, S.J.

DC —GEORGETOWN UNIVERSITY, Library, Special Collections Div, 37 & O Sts NW, Washington, 20057. George M Barringer, Special Collections Librn; Nicholas B Sheetz, Mss Librn
Holdings: Cat Mss
Notes: His papers, etc.

WEIGHTLESSNESS

PA —ENSANIAN PHYSICOCHEMICAL INSTITUTE, Library, PO Box 98, Eldred, 16731. Elisabeth Anahid Ensanian, Chief Librn
Holdings: Vols 200 Cat Mss Slides Films Microforms
Budget: $3800
Notes: The institute has pioneered the field of Gravitation Chemistry (term coined at the institute) and has original data and reports on this phenomenon, generated from its own research, that cannot be found elsewhere in the world. Also publishes own technical journal. This special collection, which also incl the biological effects of weightlessness, is continually being increased.

WEIGHTS AND MEASURES

CT —YALE UNIVERSITY, Beinecke Rare Book & Manuscript Library, Osborn Collection, New Haven, 06520. Stephen R Parks, Cur
Holdings: Mss
NY —COLUMBIA UNIVERSITY LIBRARIES, Rare Book & Manuscript Library, 801 Butler Library, 535 W 114 St, New York, 10027. Kenneth A Lohf, Librn
Holdings: Vols 1000 // Cat Mss
Notes: Restricted use: noncirculating. Incl 10,000 items.

WEIGHTS AND MEASURES—HISTORY

CT —YALE UNIVERSITY, Medical Historical Library, 333 Cedar St, New Haven, 06510. Ferenc A Gyorgyey, Librn
Holdings: Vols 350
Notes: Museum collection (with supporting literature): The Edward Clark Streeter Collection of Weights and Measures.

WEIK, MARY HAYES

MI —UNIVERSITY OF MICHIGAN, Dept of Rare Books & Special Collections, Ann Arbor, 48109. Edward C Weber, Head, Labadie Collection
Notes: The Labadie Collection of radical materials, containing papers, tracts, handbills, and publications of minority political and social reform organizations from the mid-1800s to the present, incl 8000 serial titles and 20,000 uncataloged pamphlets. Also ms collections of the papers of Mary Hayes Weik.

WEIL FAMILY

NC —NORTH CAROLINA DIV OF ARCHIVES & HISTORY, 109 E Jones St, Raleigh, 27611.
Holdings: Mss
Notes: The papers of Gertrude Weil, correspondence, material about her activities in various organizations, particularly for women's interests. 51 cubic ft of mss.

WEILL, KURT

CT —YALE UNIVERSITY, Music Library, 98 Wall St, New Haven, 06520. Harold E Samuel, Librn
Notes: Personal papers and musical mss.
See also entry under Music, American.

WEINBERGER, JACOB

AZ —NORTHERN ARIZONA UNIVERSITY, Special Collection Library, CU Box 6022, Flagstaff, 86011. Peter M Whiteley, Coordr/Archivist; William Mullane, Librn
Notes: Globe Western Copper Company, records, 1906. Delegate to the Arizona Constitutional Convention, 1910. Resident of Globe, Ariz.

WEINREICH, MAX

NY —YIVO INSTITUTE FOR JEWISH RESEARCH, Library & Archives, 1048 Fifth Ave, New York, 10028. Dina Abramowicz, Librn; Marek Web, Archivist
Holdings: Vols 315,000 Mss Maps Pix Slides
Notes: The most extensive collection in existence of Yiddish books and periodicals. Covers American, European, Soviet, Israeli and other publications from 16th century to the present. Scholarship in the Yiddish field, as well as translations from Yiddish into other languages are incl. The archives Division contains unpublished mss, correspondence and pictures, incl the library and archives of Max Weinreich.
Publications: Guide to the YIVO Library, 1975; Guide to Major Collections in the YIVO Archives, 1973.

WEINSTEIN, RABBI JACOB J.

IL —CHICAGO HISTORICAL SOCIETY, Library, Clark St at North Ave, Chicago, 60614. Archie Motley, Manuscript Librn
Notes: Papers.

WEISELBERGER, KARL, 1900-1970

BC —UNIVERSITY OF VICTORIA, McPherson Library, Victoria, V8W 3H5, Can.
Notes: Journalist, writer. Incl transcripts, correspondence; mss of plays, short stories, novels and poetry; newspaper articles; essays in German and English.

WEISS, ADOLPH

†IL —NORTHWESTERN UNIVERSITY, Music Library, 1937 Sheridan Rd, Evanston, 60201.
Notes: 300 mss in the Moldenhauer Archive.

WEISS, THEODORE

MO —WASHINGTON UNIVERSITY, Libraries, Special Collections Dept, Campus Box 1061, St Louis, 63130.
Notes: A small but significant collection.

WEITZENKORN, LOUIS

PA —KING'S COLLEGE, D Leonard Corgan Library, 14 W Jackson St, Wilkes-Barre, 18711. Judith Tierney, Special Collections Librn
Holdings: Mss
Notes: Personal papers, 1931-1942, of Louis Weitzenkorn, playwright and journalist. Approximately 100 items. Photocopying limited.

WELCH, REV. EDWARD HOLKER, S.J., 1822-1904

DC —GEORGETOWN UNIVERSITY, Library, Special Collections Div, 37 & O Sts

WELCH, REV. EDWARD HOLKER, S.J., 1822-1904 (cont.)

NW, Washington, 20057. George M Barringer, Special Collections Librn; Nicholas B Sheetz, Mss Librn
Holdings: Mss
Notes: Correspondence (1841-45, 1898-1900), documents, mss sermons, themes for class (1860-61) and diaries (1888-1904). Welch (1822-1904) graduated from Harvard College in 1840 and subsequently taught at Georgetown College. Also, present is an extensive correspondence with Frederick William Faber (1814-1863), poet and founder of the London Oratory. 1.75 linear feet.

WELFARE see Public Welfare

WELCH, LEW

CA —UNIVERSITY OF CALIFORNIA, SAN DIEGO, Central University Library, Mandeville Dept of Special Collections, La Jolla, 92093. Lynda Corey Claassen, Head; Michael Davidson, Cur, Archive for New Poetry
Notes: An extensive collection of modern English-language poetry published since World War II, the Archive contains over 28,000 books, over 1000 magazine titles, and some 900 tapes and records. The Archive maintains substantial collections of papers from Paul Blackburn, Charles Reznikoff, Lew Welch, Jerome Rothenberg, Louis Zukofsky, and other major contemporary American poets.

WELDING

CA —COLLEGE OF SAN MATEO, Library, 1700 W Hillsdale Blvd, San Mateo, 94402. Gregg T Atkins, Coordinator of Library Services
Holdings: Vols 500 Cat
IL —CHICAGO BRIDGE & IRON CO, Technical Library, 800 Jorie Blvd, Oak Brook, 60521. Susan Beatty, Librn
Holdings: Vols (7500) Cat
Budget: ($39,300)
NY —ENGINEERING SOCIETIES LIBRARY, 345 E 47 St, New York, 10017. S Kirk Cabeen, Dir
Holdings: Vols (250,000) Cat Maps 16mm Films Microforms
Notes: One of the largest, most comprehensive engineering libraries in the world. Covers all engineering disciplines; particularly strong in electrical and electronic, mechanical, mining and metallurgical, petroleum, chemical, industrial, air conditioning and refrigeration engineering. Incl Wheeler Collection of early materials on magnetism and electricity, 125,000 bound periodical volumes; 10,000 maps; 5000 serial subscriptions (many foreign-language). Virtually all materials abstracted in *Engineering Index* (1884-date) are incl in Library. Noncirculating, except to members of professional engineering societies which support the Library. See *Engineering Societies Library*, New York, *Classed Subject Catalog and Index* (Boston: G K Hall, 1963); and *Supplements*, 1-10, 1964-1973.
NC —TECHNICAL INSTITUTE OF ALAMANCE, Learning Resources Center, Jimmy Kerr Rd, PO Box 623, Haw River, 27258. Ron Plummer, Coordr
Holdings: Vols 170 Cat Phonorecords Audiotapes Filmstrips Microforms
OH —OHIO STATE UNIVERSITY, Materials Engineering Library, Watts Hall, 2041 N College Road, Columbus, 43210. Mary Jo V Arnold, Librn
Holdings: Vols (132,000)
Budget: ($110,000)
Notes: Welding Engineering.
OH —HOBART BROTHERS TECHNICAL CENTER, John H Blankenbuehler Memorial Library, Trade Sq E, Plant WS1PL, Troy, 45373. Martha Baker, Librn
Holdings: Vols 2000 Cat
Notes: Reference collection on welding and allied subjects, incl handbooks and standards of US and foreign technical and engineering societies, eg, American Welding Society, American Society for Metals, The Welding Institute of Engineering; and about 125 journal titles.
PA —FRANKLIN INSTITUTE LIBRARY, 20 & The Parkway, Philadelphia, 19103. Miriam Padusis, Dir; Charles Wilt, Readers Servs Librn
Holdings: Vols (300,000) Cat Maps Pix Microforms
SC —HORRY GEORGETOWN TECHNICAL COLLEGE, Library, Hwy 501, Box 1966, Conway, 29526. Barbara Brittain, Librn
Holdings: Vols (20,000) Cat Slides Microforms
TN —COMBUSTION ENGINEERING, Metallurgical Materials Library, 911 W Main St, Chattanooga, 37402. Nell T Holder, Tech Librn
Holdings: Vols (10,000) Cat
Notes: Metallurgical research and development. 350 serials and periodicals, 800 translations of foreign articles. 250,000 US Government Reports. MF Collection C-E Technical reports ASME.
TX —ECTOR COUNTY LIBRARY, Department of Business and Technology, 321 W 5th St, Odessa, 79760. Pat Jones, Dept Head
Notes: Incl 100 vertical files, 25 periodicals, 250 Trade Standards. Collections concentrated on the Drilling and Production industries. Also included are Exploration methods Reservoir Development, Pipeline, Construction, Well Servicing, Well Logging, and Well Control. Complete collection of the API Specifications, and Complete Welding "library".
WI —MADISON AREA TECHNICAL COLLEGE, Technical Center Library, 2125 Commercial Ave, Madison, 53704. J B Jeffcott, Librn
Holdings: Vols 425 Cat Slides Phonorecords Audiotapes Videotapes 16mm Films Filmstrips Microforms

WELFARE FEDERATIONS see Federations, Financial (Social Service)

WELFARE WORK see Public Welfare

WELLES, ORSON

IN —INDIANA UNIVERSITY, Lilly Library, Seventh St, Bloomington, 47405. William R Cagle, Librn
Holdings: Mss Pix Recordings
Notes: Correspondence, papers, and memorabilia, 1930-1959, of actor, producer, writer, and director Orson Welles. Includes material on the Federal Theater Project, Mercury Theatre, radio programming, film-making, RKO studios, etc. Radio scripts, screen plays, movie stills, and tape recordings of the radio shows done by Welles are all present. 19,875 items.
NY —NEW YORK PUBLIC LIBRARY, Performing Arts Research Center, Billy Rose Theatre Collection, 111 Amsterdam Ave, New York, 10023. Dorothy L Swerdlove, Cur
Holdings: Cat Mss Pix
Notes: Papers, scrapbooks, mss, photographs, memorabilia, etc.

WELLESLEY COLLEGE

MA —WELLESLEY COLLEGE, Margaret Clapp Library, College Archives, Wellesley, 02181.
Notes: Archives of Wellesley College (2750 linear feet). Contact Wellesley College Archives for details on holdings.

WELLESZ, EGON

DC —LIBRARY OF CONGRESS, Music Division, Washington, 20540.
Notes: Papers and recordings of composer Arnold Schoenberg. Extensive correspondence with other composers, writers, etc.

WELLINGTON, DUKE OF

†TX —SAINT MARY'S UNIVERSITY, Library, San Antonio, 78284.
Notes: Napolean and Napoleonic period.

WELLINGTON, J. W. DUKE

†IL —NEWBERRY LIBRARY, 60 W Walton St, Chicago, 60610.
Notes: Collection of color slides of the early 1950s. Photographs by the eight-year Superintendent of the Fort Belknap Indian Reservation in Montana, J W "Duke" Wellington, who was allowed to take pictures of some of the most important rituals of the Assiniboine and Gros Ventres Indians, dances, renewals, etc. An annotated collection.

WELLMAN, PAUL ISELIN, 1898-1966

CA —UNIVERSITY OF CALIFORNIA, LOS ANGELES, Research Library, Dept of Special Collections, 405 Hilgard Ave, Los Angeles, 90024. Edward Shreeves, Chairman, Bibliographers Group; David S Zeidberg, Head
Holdings: Vols 15 Mss
Notes: Incl 14 linear feet of mss and papers.

WELLS, BELLA FROMM

MA —BOSTON UNIVERSITY, Mugar Memorial Library, Special Collections Dept, 771 Commonwealth Ave, Boston, 02215. Howard B Gotlieb, Dir
Notes: Diplomatic correspondent in Berlin for Ullstein and *The Times*. Her papers.

WELLS, HERBERT GEORGE (H. G.)

CA —UNIVERSITY OF CALIFORNIA, RIVERSIDE, University Library, 4045 Canyon Crest Dr, Box 5900, Riverside, 92517.
Holdings: Vols (30,000)
Notes: The Eaton Collection of science fiction and fantasy materials, incl 5,600 pulp magazines; also horror, supernatural, and Gothic mystery fiction; boys' books; utopian and dystopian fiction, imaginary voyages, future war and lost race fiction; large holdings in French language science fiction and fantasy; critical and scholarly works pertaining to these genres; videotapes of science fiction/fantasy films and shooting scripts. Collection covers science fiction/fantasy literature from the 16th-17th centuries to the present. Strong individual author collections of Jules Verne, H Rider Haggard, H G Wells, Edgar Rice Burroughs, and Philip K Dick. For a complete description of the collection see: George Slusser, "The J Lloyd Eaton Collection," *Special Collections*, II, 1/2, 25-38 (1983), and *Dictionary Catalog of the J Lloyd Eaton Collection of Science Fiction and Fantasy Literature* (Boston: G K Hall) 1982.
CA —SAN DIEGO STATE UNIVERSITY, Malcolm A Love Library, 5300 Campanile Dr, San Diego, 92182. D Dickinson, Univ Librn; Don L Bosseau, Dir
Notes: Collected works in first edition of certain prominent authors, as H G Wells, Somerset Maugham, William Dean Howells, Gertrude Atherton, Tom Stoppard, James Clavell, G A Henty, Henry Raup Wagner.
CA —UNIVERSITY OF CALIFORNIA, SANTA BARBARA, Library, Dept of Special Collections, Santa Barbara, 93106. Christian F Brun, Head
CT —YALE UNIVERSITY, Box 1603A, Yale Station, New Haven, 06520.
IL —NORTHWESTERN UNIVERSITY, Library, Special Collections Dept, 1937 Sheridan Rd, Evanston, 60201. R Russell Maylone, Cur
Holdings: Vols 200 Cat Mss
IL —ILLINOIS STATE UNIVERSITY, Milner Library, Dept of Special Collections, Normal, 61761. Robert Sokan, Librn
Notes: First editions, limited editions, ephemera, etc.
IL —UNIVERSITY OF ILLINOIS, URBANA/CHAMPAIGN, Library, Rare

WELLS, HERBERT GEORGE (H. G.) (cont.)

Book Room, 346 Library, Urbana, 61801. Norman B Brown, Asst Dir for Special Collections; N Frederick Nash, Librn
Holdings: Cat Mss Maps Pix Slides Microforms
Notes: Extensive collection, described in: *Catalog of the Rare Book Room*, (Boston: G K Hall, 1972). Supplement (1978).

MA —BOSTON UNIVERSITY, Mugar Memorial Library, Special Collections Dept, 771 Commonwealth Ave, Boston, 02215. Howard B Gotlieb, Dir
Holdings: Cat Mss Pix
Notes: Correspondence, incl publications by.

NY —HOFSTRA UNIVERSITY, Library, 1000 Fulton Ave, Hempstead, 11550. Charles R Andrews, Dean of Library Services
Notes: Strong collection. Incl some mss.

OH —OHIO UNIVERSITY, Vernon R Alden Library, Department of Archives and Special Collections, Athens, 45701. Gary A Hunt, Head
Holdings: Vols 277 Cat Mss
Notes: A comprehensive collection of first editions, with a number of American firsts and a few later editions included.

WI —MILWAUKEE PUBLIC LIBRARY, 814 W Wisconsin Ave, Milwaukee, 53233. Donald J Sager, City Librn
Holdings: Cat
Notes: First and subsequent editions of Wells' books, pamphlets, magazine articles, introduction, prefaces, a few letters.

ON —McMASTER UNIVERSITY, Mills Memorial Library, Div of Archives & Research Collections, Hamilton, L8S 4L6, Can. G R Hill, Univ Librn
Holdings: // Cat Mss
Notes: H G Wells' correspondence with Siegfried Sassoon, 1916-1942, incomplete ms drafts of "The Mind of the Race, " "Mr Britting Sees It Through," "The Two Ways." Annotated typescripts of "The Two Ways," "The Mind of the Race," "Scientific War," "Civilians in Warfare" and carbon typescript of "The Problem of the Troublesome Collaborator," as well as large book and serial collection of Wells' writings.

WELLS, HEWITT

NV —UNIVERSITY OF NEVADA, RENO, University Library, Special Collections Dept, Reno, 89557. Robert E Blesse, Head
Holdings: Cat Mss Pix
Notes: Approximately 15,000 drawings, along with papers and photographs of three major Nevada architects. Frederic DeLongchamps, 1882-1969, was Nevada's most important for the first half of the 20th century designing many major public buildings. Edward S Parsons, Nevada's most prolific architect, did over 725 jobs between 1935 and 1983. Hewitt Wells designed the Washoe County Library, an internationally known building. These collections constitute the major holdings of the Nevada Architectural Archives.

WELLS, KATE GANNETT

†NY —UNIVERSITY OF ROCHESTER, Rush Rhees Library, Rochester, 14627.

WELLS, SANFORD BADGLEY, 1908-1975

NY —CORNELL UNIVERSITY LIBRARIES, Collection of Regional History, Dept of Manuscripts and Univ Archives, Ithaca, 14853.
Notes: Architect. Papers, ca 1940-65; ca 5 ft. New York, New Jersey.

WELLS FARGO AND COMPANY AND AGENTS

CA —WELLS FARGO BANK, Library, 475 Sansome St, San Francisco, 94144. Alice Hunsacker, Asst VP and Mgr of Libr
Holdings: Vols (50,000) Cat

NY —WELLS COLLEGE LIBRARY, Aurora, 13026. Marie G Delaney, Head Librn
Holdings: Letters
Notes: Noncirculating.

WELSH AMERICAN NEWSPAPERS see Newspapers, Welsh American

WELSH IN CANADA

PA —BALCH INSTITUTE FOR ETHNIC STUDIES, Library, 18 S Seventh St, Philadelphia, 19106. R Joseph Anderson, Library Dir

WELSH IN THE U.S.

NY —UTICA COLLEGE OF SYRACUSE UNIVERSITY, Frank E Gannett Memorial Library, Burrstone Rd, Utica, 13502. Harry Tarlin, Dir
Holdings: Vols 208 Cat
Notes: Welsh language materials originating in New York State, and any materials about the Welsh in New York State.

PA —BALCH INSTITUTE FOR ETHNIC STUDIES, Library, 18 S Seventh St, Philadelphia, 19106. R Joseph Anderson, Library Dir
Holdings: Vols 75 Cat Microforms

WELSH LANGUAGE AND LITERATURE

CA —SONOMA STATE UNIVERSITY, Salazar Library, 1801 E Cotati Ave, Rohnert Park, 94928. Sandra Walton, Librn
Holdings: Vols (650)
Notes: The W W Lyman Collection of Celtic literature, consisting of Irish. Scottish and Welsh fiction, poetry and plays.

IL —NEWBERRY LIBRARY, 60 W Walton St, Chicago, 60610. Diana Haskell, Cur of Modern Mss
Holdings: Cat Maps
Notes: The bulk of the collection (about 15, 000 vols) is in the Prince Lucien Bonaparte group, which deals with western European linguistics. In this group the major rare categories are Etruscan and Basque linguistic studies, although the bulk of the group treats the major European languages and their dialects, ie French, German, English, Spanish, Italian and Russian. There is also strong representation in Gaelic linguistics, particularly Irish, Cornish, Welsh and Manx. In other collections of the library, there are major groups of books and mss dealing with American Indian languages and Philippine languages (about 4500 books and mss).

MA —HARVARD UNIVERSITY LIBRARY, Widener Library, Cambridge, 02138.
Holdings: Cat
Notes: *Widener Library Shelflist* No 25 (1970) lists 8147 titles in Celtic languages and literatures, of which some 4800 are Welsh and 2000 are Irish. See *Harvard Library Bulletin,* I (1947): pp 52-65. There is also a Celtic seminar room in Widener Library containing 1200 vols.

NY —UTICA COLLEGE OF SYRACUSE UNIVERSITY, Frank E Gannett Memorial Library, Burrstone Rd, Utica, 13502. Harry Tarlin, Dir
Holdings: Vols 208 Cat
Notes: Welsh language materials originating in New York State, and any materials about the Welsh in New York State.

OH —CLEVELAND PUBLIC LIBRARY, Fine Arts and Special Collections Department, 325 Superior Ave, Cleveland, 44114. Alice N Loranth, Head
Holdings: Vols (1000) Cat
Notes: Part of the Celtic Language and Literature Collection. Medieval texts, translations, folk songs, linguistics are emphasized. The important scholarly journals, and the serials and publications of the Cymmrodorian Society, Irish Texts Society, Ossianic Society, etc, are well represented.
See also entry under Celtic Language and Literature.

WELTY, EUDORA

MS —MILLSAPS COLLEGE, Millsaps-Wilson Library, Jackson, 39210. Kathy Holden,

College Archivist
Holdings: Vols 25
Notes: Complete autographed collection of books by Eudora Welty, with 20 signed photographs then in Mississippi whilst working for the WPA as a publicity agent. Includes letters from Weity to Lehman Engel.

MS —MISSISSIPPI STATE UNIVERSITY, Mitchell Memorial Library, Box 5408, Mississippi State, 39762. Frances N Coleman, Head, Special Collections
Holdings: Vols (15,000) Cat Mss Maps Pix Microforms
Notes: Social and political history of Mississippi, incl University Archives (now separate branch). Microfilms of Protestant Church records. There are strong collections on history of the Southern States, Mississippi authors (especially Faulkner, Williams, Carter, Welty, and Young); also the John C Stennis Collection of over 2 million items, his books, papers, photographs, etc. Incl 400 collections of mss; papers of US Rep David R Bowen 1973-1983; papers of US Rep G V Montgomery 1967-.

NV —UNIVERSITY OF NEVADA, RENO, University Library, Special Collections Dept, Reno, 89557. Robert E Blesse, Head
Holdings: Vols 65 Cat
Notes: Includes individual works by author in all editions including translations; also prefaces, introductions, published correspondence, appearances in anthologies, periodicals, etc. Bibliographical research collection, part of Modern Authors Collection.

NY —VASSAR COLLEGE, Library, Rare Books & Manuscripts Collection, Box 20, Poughkeepsie, 12601. Lisa Browar, Cur
Notes: An extensive collection of Elizabeth Bishop's papers, incl notebooks, mss, drafts, galleys, etc, as well as correspondence and business files, with files of letters from Cummings, Toklas, Dylan Thomas, and Eudora Welty.

PA —BRYN MAWR COLLEGE, Canaday Library, Bryn Mawr, 19010. James Tanis, Dir
Notes: Rare books and manuscripts.

WENDIC DIALECT (SLOVENIAN) see Slovenian Language and Literature

WENDIC LANGUAGE AND LITERATURE

CA —STANFORD UNIVERSITY LIBRARIES, Cecil H Green Library, Stanford, 94305. Wojciech Zalewski, Cur, Russian & East European Collection
Notes: Beginning research collection.

DC —LIBRARY OF CONGRESS, Washington, 20540.

MA —HARVARD UNIVERSITY LIBRARY, Cambridge, 02138.

NY —NEW YORK PUBLIC LIBRARY, Slavonic Div, Fifth Ave & 42 St, New York, 10018. Edward Kasinec, Chief
Holdings: Cat
Notes: Serbian language and literature. See New York Public Library, *Dictionary Catalog of the Slavonic Collection* (Boston: G K Hall, 1974), 44 vols.

WERFEL, FRANZ AND ALMA

CA —UNIVERSITY OF CALIFORNIA, LOS ANGELES, Research Library, Dept of Special Collections, 405 Hilgard Ave, Los Angeles, 90024. Edward Shreeves, Chairman, Bibliographers Group; David S Zeidberg, Head
Holdings: Vols 100
Notes: Incl 18 linear feet of correspondence, mss, notebooks, etc.

CT —YALE UNIVERSITY, Box 1603A, Yale Station, New Haven, 06520.
Holdings: Mss Pix

PA —UNIVERSITY OF PENNSYLVANIA, Van Pelt Library, Rare Books Collection, 34 & Walnut Sts, Philadelphia, 19104. Daniel Traister, Special Collections Librn
Holdings: Cat Mss
Notes: "Note on the Alma Mahler Werfel

WERFEL, FRANZ AND ALMA (cont.)

Collection," by Adolf Klarmann and Rudolf Hirsch, (University of Pennsylvania) *Library Chronicle*, vol 35, no 1 and 2, 1969. Also 24 holograph mss of Werfel's works, some in two versions.

WERLICH, MCCENEY

DC —GEORGETOWN UNIVERSITY, Library, Special Collections Div, 37 & O Sts NW, Washington, 20057. George M Barringer, Special Collections Librn; Nicholas B Sheetz, Mss Librn
Holdings: Mss Pix
Notes: Correspondence, documents, journals, diaries, financial accounts, mss, photographs, and art work comprising the personal and professional papers of McCeney Werlich, diplomat, as well as those of his wife, Gladys Hinckley Werlich; Thomas Hinckley, and Robert O'Donnel Hinckley, both diplomats; papers of Eleanor O'Donnell Hinckley, mother of Gladys Werlich, and her husband Robert Hinckley, noted portrait painter. The papers incl: State Department correspondence and other material relating to McCeney Werlich's posts in Latvia (1926-1927), Poland (1927-1931), Costa Rica (1931-1932), Liberia (1932-1933), and France (1934-1936); correspondence from Robert O'Donnell Hinckley from his travels in the Orient, 1919; correspondence from Thomas Hinckley, incl accounts of the Austro-Hungarian empire, 1914-1915; as well as numerous journalsand diaries kept by Gladys Werlich regarding her extensive travels and variety of experiences.

WERNER, CHARLES

OH —OHIO STATE UNIVERSITY, Library for Communication and Graphic Arts, 242 W 18th St, Columbus, 43210. Lucy S Caswell, Curator
Notes: The original works of editorial cartoonists Art Poinier, Scott Willis, Brian Basset, Billy Ireland, Frank Williams, Charles Werner, Ned Beard, L D Warren, Edward D Kuekes, Ray Osrin, Mike Peters, Draper Hill, Eugene Craig and Bert Whitman.

WERTENBAKER, LAEL TUCKER

MA —BOSTON UNIVERSITY, Mugar Memorial Library, Special Collections Dept, 771 Commonwealth Ave, Boston, 02215. Howard B Gotlieb, Dir
Holdings: Cat Mss Pix
Notes: Mss, correspondence, etc collected in depth; incl publications by or about.

WESCOTT, GLENWAY

CT —YALE UNIVERSITY, Box 1603A, Yale Station, New Haven, 06520.
Holdings: Cat Mss
NV —UNIVERSITY OF NEVADA, RENO, University Library, Special Collections Dept, Reno, 89557. Robert E Blesse, Head
Holdings: Vols 25 Cat
Notes: Includes individual works by author in all editions including translations; also prefaces, introductions, published correspondence, appearances in anthologies, periodicals, etc. Bibliographical research collection, part of Modern Authors Collection.

WESENBERG, ALICE BIDWELL, 1878-1967

IN —BUTLER UNIVERSITY, Irwin Library, Hugh Thomas Miller Rare Book Room, 4600 Sunset Ave, Indianapolis, 46208. Gisela Terrell, Rare Books Librn
Holdings: Vols Cat Mss
Notes: Wesenberg Collection of 20th-century American poetry (mostly pre-1950). It includes first editions, poetry magazines, author's photographs, and manuscripts from the library of Alice Bidwell Wesenberg, poet. Mss include the Irwin Library by Dr Allegra

Stewart, in 1981.
See also entry under American Poetry

WESLEY, JOHN AND CHARLES

DC —WESLEY THEOLOGICAL SEMINARY, 4400 Massachusetts Ave NW, Washington, 20016. Roland E Kircher, Librn
Holdings: Vols (106,000) Cat Mss Pix
Notes: Wesleyana. Extensive collection of the historical records and publications of the former Methodist Protestant Church.
GA —EMORY UNIVERSITY, Robert W Woodruff Library, Special Collections Dept, Atlanta, 30322. Linda M Matthews, Head Special Collections; Virginia J H Cain, Processing Archivist; Richard H F Lindemann, Reference Archivist
Notes: Letters and other writings of John Wesley, Charles Wesley and other members of the Wesley family. Description and index available in repository.
GA —EMORY UNIVERSITY, Candler School of Theology, Pitts Theology Library, Atlanta, 30322. Channing Jeschke, Librn; Anita K Delaries, Curator
Holdings: Vols 2749 Cat
Notes: Works by and about John Wesley, the Wesley family, and early Methodist history.
IN —MARION COLLEGE LIBRARY, 4201 S Washington St, Marion, 46952. Harold W Boyce, Dir of Library Services
Holdings: Vols 850 Cat
Notes: Wesleyan history.
IN —FREE METHODIST CHURCH OF NORTH AMERICA, Marston Memorial Historical Center Library, 901 College Ave, Winona Lake, 46590. Evelyn L Mottweiler, Librn
Holdings: Vols (6000) Cat Mss
Budget: ($16,000)
Notes: Denominational headquarters of the Free Methodist Church in North America. The John and Charles Wesley Collection. Of the approximately 400 volumes, about 75 of them were published during Wesley's lifetime, from about 1740 to 1791. A number of the items are rare, and the collection is superior to many of the major libraries in this and other countries. Methodist holdings (4500 vols) of the Library are included in the Methodist Union Catalog: *Pre-1976 Imprints*, ed by Kenneth E Rowe.
KY —ASBURY THEOLOGICAL SEMINARY, B L Fisher Library, Wilmore, 40390. D William Faupel, Dir of Library Services
Holdings: Vols 4500 Cat Pix Microforms
Budget: ($40,000)
MI —ADRIAN COLLEGE, Shipman Library, Adrian, 49221. Ronald A Brunger, Cur
Holdings: Vols (4500) Cat Mss
Budget: ($4600)
NJ —DREW UNIVERSITY, Library, Madison, 07940. Caroline Coughlin, Assoc Dir
Notes: Third largest collection in the world of early editions of the works of John and Charles Wesley.
NY —HOUGHTON COLLEGE, Willard J Houghton Library, Houghton, 14744. Joyce Moore, Librn
Notes: Methodism and the Wesleys; books related to Wesleyan Methodism comprise the greatest part of the collection. To be incl in the Methodist Union Catalog being prepared under the editorial supervision of Dr Kenneth E Rowe of Drew University.
NC —DUKE UNIVERSITY, William R Perkins Library, Durham, 27706. Elvin E Strowd, University Librn
Notes: The Frank Baker collection of Wesleyana and British Methodistica contains more than 13,500 volumes and 4000 manuscripts and documents. This material is housed in various locations within the Perkins Library System.
NC —DUKE UNIVERSITY, William R Perkins Library, Manuscript Dept, Durham, 27706. Ellen Gartrell, Cur of Mss
Holdings: Cat Mss
Notes: Methodist Church Papers (records of local and regional units) also many personal and professional papers of clergy, missionaries and laymen, 19th-20th centuries, eg Methodist John Lakin Brasher

(holiness movement leader), Carlyle Marney (Southern Baptist minister), Methodist Bishop James Cannon, missionary Martha Foster Crawford.
NC —DUKE UNIVERSITY, Divinity School Library, Durham, 27706. Donn Michael Farris, Librn
Holdings: Vols (225,000)
Notes: Special collections and subject emphases in this library include: Archaeology, Egyptian; Archaeology, Middle Eastern; Art, Jewish; Bible; Bible-New Testament; Bible-Symbolism; Church Architecture; Egyptology; Fathers of the Church; Society of Friends; Great Britain-Religion-Methodism and Methodist Church; Hymns and Hymnals; Jansenists and Jansenism; Judaica; Mediaeval Christian Mysticism; Methodism and Methodist Church; Methodist Episcopal Church; Methodist Episcopal Church, South; Reformation; Religion-US-History; Rural Church; Theology-Great Britain-17th Century; Theology-Great Britain-18th Century; United Methodist Church; US-Church History; John Wesley.
ON —TORONTO SCHOOL OF THEOLOGY, Consortium of Libraries, University of Toronto, Toronto, M5S 1A5, Can. R Grane Bracewell, Library Coordr
Holdings: Cat
Notes: The Richard Green Collection. A consortium of 7 theological college and faculty libraries at the University of Toronto.
ON —VICTORIA UNIVERSITY, Library, 71 Queen's Park Crescent, Toronto, M5S 1K7, Can. Robert C Brandeis, Chief Librn
Holdings: Vols (1300) Cat Mss
Notes: Wesleyana and Green Collections: works of John, Charles and Samuel Wesley incl the collection of Dr Richard Green upon which his *The Works of John and Charles Wesley: A Bibliography* (London, 1906, 2nd rev ed) was based. Likely the strongest collection of the Wesleys' publications in North America.

WESLEYANISM see Methodism and Methodist Church

THE WEST

AZ —ARIZONA HERITAGE CENTER, Library, 949 E Second St, Tucson, 85719. Michael Weber, Dir
Notes: Espec with reference to Arizona, the West, and the Southwest.
CA —ARCADIA PUBLIC LIBRARY, 20 W Duarte Rd, Arcadia, 91006. James M Domney, City Librn
Notes: California history.
CA —AZUSA PACIFIC COLLEGE, Marshburn Memorial Library, Citrus & Alosta, Azusa, 91702. Edward Peterman, Librn
Holdings: Vols (6000) Uncat
Budget: ($30,000)
Notes: Significant holdings in the George E Fullerton Library of Californiana and Western Americana.
CA —KERN COUNTY LIBRARY SYSTEM, 1315 Truxtun Ave, Bakersfield, 93301. Mary Hanel, Historical Librn
Holdings: Vols 5000 Microforms
Notes: Primarily Kern County history, but collection also covers California and the bordering western states. Microfilm collection consists chiefly of local newspapers, some dating back to 1866, indexed from 1936-present.
CA —UNIVERSITY OF CALIFORNIA, BERKELEY, Bancroft Library, Manuscripts Division, Berkeley, 94720. James D Hart, Dir
Holdings: Vols Mss Maps Pix Slides Microforms
Notes: Approxi. twelve million pieces, with primary emphasis on California, with a lesser emphasis on the other Pacific States, incl. Alaska and the Province of British Columbia. In general, the Bancroft Library seeks to acquire historical and biographical works and primary source materials, documenting: the development of a geographic area or political unit; man and his activities, and his impact on the land and on his institutions.

THE WEST (cont.)

Methodological and theoretical work and texts in the physical and biological sciences are not collected, as a rule; exceptions here are publications essential to the study of an area's historical development and those providing general background information. Hubert Howe Bancroft's own distinguished holdings, assembled 1860-1880, constitute the core of the collection. The Bancroft Library's collections are noncirculating. A. G. K. Hall catalog has been published. The Bolton Collection (146,000 pages of archival material) contains ms. materials for the history of the Pacific Coast and the Southwest, gathered by Herbert Eugene Bolton. There is a comprehensive key to the arrangement of the collection.

CA —UNIVERSITY OF CALIFORNIA, BERKELEY, Life Sciences Libraries, Forestry Library, 260 Mulford Hall, Berkeley, 94720. Esther Johnson, Librn; Pete Evans, Ref Librn
Holdings: Vols (28,000) Cat Microforms
Budget: ($15,800)
Notes: Areas of particular strength are forestry, conservation, and wildlife management. The collection is rich in pamphlet material and serials, especially foreign publications. Although holdings are world-wide in scope, coverage of the western USA is given the highest priority. Dissertation and theses collection also. Forestry Library holdings are complemented by a 8000-vol specialized collection at the Forest Products Laboratory in Richmond, California.

CA —BURBANK PUBLIC LIBRARY, 110 N Glenoaks Blvd, Burbank, 91502. Mary Ann Grasso, Coordr; Barbara Stones, Coordr, Media Project
Holdings: Vols 4000 Cat
Notes: Incl material on all states west of the Mississippi River. Many good runs of state historical journals and regional periodicals. About half the listings in J Frank Dobie's Guide to Life and Literature of the Southwest. See description in California Librarian, April 1965, "The Burbank Western History Collection", By Thomas F Parker.

CA —CLAREMONT COLLEGES, Honnold Library, Ninth & Dartmouth, Claremont, 91711. Tania Rizzo, Special Collections Dept Head
Holdings: Vols 21,000 Cat Mss Maps Pix Doc Periodicals Scrapbooks VF
Notes: Trans-Mississippi West.

CA —COPLEY NEWSPAPERS, James S Copley Library, 1134 Kline St, PO Box 1530, La Jolla, 92038. Richard Reilly, Cur; Suzanne Carnes, Librn
Holdings: Vols (2000) Cat
Notes: Collection incl materials on American Revolutionary period and California and western Americana. Library open to graduate students who obtain reading privileges from curator.

CA —OCCIDENTAL COLLEGE, Library, 1600 Campus Rd, Los Angeles, 90041. Michael C Sutherland, Special Collections Librn
Holdings: Vols 250 // Cat
Notes: Pauley-Voorhis Collection of Western Americana.

CA —UNIVERSITY OF CALIFORNIA, LOS ANGELES, William Andrews Clark Memorial Library, 2520 Cimarron St, Los Angeles, 90018.
Holdings: Vols 2000 Cat Mss Maps Pix Slides
Notes: The Charles Kessler Collection, incl also about 4000 pamphlets, documents, etc, with more than 60 volumes of the Book of Mormon in English and foreign languages.

CA —SAINT MARY'S COLLEGE, Library, Moraga, 94575. Brother Casimir Reichlin, Dir of the Library; Brother Richard Lemberg FSC, Asst Librn
Notes: The Leonard Verbarg library of over 800 books on Western Americana, especially California. Incl vertical files containing over 1100 entries related to Californiana in the form of clippings and correspondence amassed during editorship of "The Knave" page of local history in the Oakland Tribune.

CA —OAKLAND PUBLIC LIBRARY, Oakland History Room, 125 14th St, Oakland, 94612. William W Sturm, Librn
Holdings: Vols (20,000) Cat Mss Maps Pix Microforms
Notes: The Oakland History Room Collection is a reference collection of books, pamphlets, periodicals, pictures, and newspaper clippings. California items incl as much biographical material as possible clipped from the Oakland Tribune, Oakland Post, California Voice, the Montclarion, and Alameda Times-Star. (Library no longer clips San Francisco Chronicle or Examiner). These clippings are filed by subjects. An index of all the subjects with many cross references are made. An index of articles from about 75 magazines dealing with California subjects is kept up to date. The log books of the Coast Guard Cutter Bear from 1889 to 1932 are in the collection. The Jack London collection is listed separately. Ms pages and letters from Joaquin Miller and a fewmiscellaneous letters from other authors are also incl. A set of George Sterling, both inscribed and not inscribed, is owned by the Room.

CA —SAN BERNARDINO COUNTY LIBRARY, 104 W Fourth St, San Bernardino, 92415.
Holdings: Cat Mss Maps Pix
Budget: ($3000)

CA —HUNTINGTON LIBRARY, Art Gallery & Botanical Gardens, 1151 Oxford Rd, San Marino, 91108. Robert L Middlekauff, Dir; Daniel H Woodward, Librn
Holdings: Mss Maps Pix Slides Microforms
Notes: Approx 350,000 rare books, 250,000 reference books, manuscript collection of nearly 2,500,000 pieces and between 200,000 and 300,000 prints, rare photographs and other related materials. The fullest available survey is now Guide to Literary Manuscripts in the Huntington Library, a 539-page handlist published by the Library in 1979.

CA —UNIVERSITY OF CALIFORNIA, SANTA BARBARA, Library, Dept of Special Collections, Santa Barbara, 93106. Christian F Brun, Head
Holdings: Cat
Notes: William Wyles Collection.

CA —STANFORD UNIVERSITY LIBRARIES, Cecil H Green Library, Stanford, 94305. Michael T Ryan, Cur
Holdings: Vols Cat Mss Pix Audiotapes
Notes: Manuscript Collections incl papers of the Progressive period in California; papers of New Almaden quicksilver mines; papers of J Arthur Younger (office records); comprehensive collection of personal, business, and legal papers of Goodwin J Knight; and miscellaneous Californiana. Farm labor materials incl papers gathered by Ernesto Galarza, Fr Victor Salandini and Fr James L Vizzard. First editions, correspondence and literary mss of numerous British and American authors, incl John Steinbeck, Jack London, Ambrose Bierce, Bruce Bliven, John Galsworthy, Wallace Stegner, Janet Lewis, Somerset Maugham and D H Lawrence. Collections in such fields as western American history, railroad transportation, and the American Civil War (incl the papers of Frederick Steele).

CA —UNIVERSITY OF THE PACIFIC, Library, Stockton, 95211. Hiram L Davis, Dir of Libraries
Holdings: Vols (25,000) Cat Mss Maps Pix Slides Microforms
Budget: ($1000)
Notes: The Stuart Library of Western Americana accounts for the bulk of the special collections in the university library. Established to support the research activities of the California History Foundation under the leadership of Rockwell D Hunt in 1947 and named after Reginald R Stuart and his late wife Grace who directed the Foundation from 1956 to 1965 and contributed the nucleus of the collection. While the collection covers all of the Trans-Mississippi West, special emphasis is upon original documents and accounts of the California gold rush and subsequent development of the Central Valley of California. The most notable holdings are the John Muir papers. Research papers are published in the Pacific Historian, a quarterly journal.

CO —UNIVERSITY OF COLORADO, Libraries, Western Historical Collections, Boulder, 80309.
Holdings: // Cat Mss Maps
Notes: Papers of John F Campion (1849-1916), who mined in California and Nevada before striking it rich in the 1880s in Leadville, Colorado. He owned Reindeer, Caribou, and Ibex (better known as Little Johnny) mining companies. He was the vice-president of the Denver National Bank and the Denver, Northwestern and Pacific Railroad, and was a founder of Colorado's sugar beet industry. The collection focuses on his Leadville mining activities, covering the period from 1887 to 1922. A guide is available to the 14 boxes of material. Typescript inventory is available.

CO —COLORADO HISTORICAL SOCIETY, Research Collections, 1300 Broadway, Denver, 80203. Catherine Kane, Head Public Service and Access
Holdings: Cat Mss Maps Pix Slides Microforms
Budget:
Notes: Strong collection of Colorado and western history totaling over 8,000,000 pieces. Special emphases incl people, places, land and cattle, railroads, business history, minority cultures. Colorado newspaper collection, mss, photographs.

CO —DENVER PUBLIC LIBRARY, Western History Department, 1357 Broadway, Denver, 80203. Eleanor M Gehres, Head
Holdings: Vols (50,000) Cat Mss Maps Pix Audiotapes Microforms
Notes: Western US History. The department has a separate catalog, published in 1970 in 7 vols by G K Hall Co. First supplement published in 1975 in 1 vol. There is a subject index of some 3 million entries to newspapers and magazines of the Rocky Mountain region, added to daily. The Western Newspaper Microfilm Center contains approx 7000 reels of Western US newspapers. Collection has ca 275,000 negatives and prints of Western life; and ca 2500 maps, cataloged and classified.

CO —DURANGO PUBLIC LIBRARY, 1188 Second Ave, Durango, 81301. Daniel P Brassell, Dir
Holdings: Vols 3025 Cat Mss Maps
Budget: $1000
Notes: Especially southwest Colorado history. Collection cataloged separately.

CO —COLORADO STATE UNIVERSITY, Libraries, Fort Collins, 80523. John Newman, Special Collections Librn
Holdings: Vols (11,000) Cat Mss Pix
Budget: ($7000)
Notes: The Western American Literature Collection incl fiction, poetry, pictures, art, and other works of the imagination set in the American Frontier West and modern rural West, especially the Rocky Mountain Area. There is also a collection of some 500 pulp magazines. "Westerns" mostly.

CO —LOVELAND PUBLIC LIBRARY, 205 E Sixth, Loveland, 80537. Elaine A Puls, Library Dir
Holdings: Vols 800 Cat

CO —PUEBLO REGIONAL LIBRARY DISTRICT, 100 E Abriendo Ave, Pueblo, 81004. Charles E Bates, Library Dir
Holdings: Vols 12,552 Cat Mss Maps Pix

THE WEST (cont.)

Microforms VF
Notes: Materials are noncirculating.

CT —YALE UNIVERSITY, Box 1603A, Yale
Station, New Haven, 06520.
Holdings: Vols Cat Mss Pix

DC —LIBRARY OF CONGRESS, Rare Book
& Special Collections Div, Washington,
20540. William Matheson, Chief
Notes: The Wagner-Camp Collection of 451
vols of rare books.

DC —LIBRARY OF CONGRESS, Prints &
Photographs Div, Washington, 20540.
Notes: The Erwin E Smith Collection of
cowboy and ranch life. Gift of 1776 original
glass and nitrate film negatives of pictures
taken by him. Gift of his sister, Mrs L McC
Pettis in 1949.

IL —NEWBERRY LIBRARY, 60 W Walton
St, Chicago, 60610. Diana Haskell, Cur of
Modern Mss
Holdings: Vols 12,000 Cat Mss Maps Pix
Notes: Edward E Ayer and Everett D Graff
collections. Incl travel, overland journeys,
early imprints, local documents, biographies,
autobiographies, local and church history.
Emphasis is on pre-1915 period. Also the
Elmo Scott Watson Clipping Collection; two
file cabinets of newspaper clippings and
pictures relating to the American West
(Indians, frontiersmen, correspondence, the
US Army), which originally appeared as
syndicated newspaper columns. Much of this
material cannot be found elsewhere without
research.

IL —LAKE FOREST COLLEGE, Donnelley
Library, Lake Forest, 60045. Arthur H
Miller Jr, College Librn
Holdings: Vols (1000)
Notes: Mostly 20th century books, journals
pamphlets and ephemera relating to the
West, particularly Western fiction (Twain,
Wister, Haycox, etc), outlaws, and the
Western movement, and Western art. Incl
some late 19th century highspots. from the
collections of Mr and Mrs DeWitte
O'Kieffe.

IN —INDIANA UNIVERSITY, Lilly Library,
Seventh St, Bloomington, 47405. William R
Cagle, Librn
Holdings: // Cat Mss Maps
Notes: Description and travel of the US
Plains and Rockies; overland accounts; issues
of California newspapers of the gold rush
era, etc.

KS —FORT HAYS KANSAS STATE
UNIVERSITY, Forsyth Library, Western
Collection, 600 Park St, Hays, 67601. Esta
Lou Riley, Archivist/Special Collections
Librn
Holdings: Vols (5500) Cat VF
Budget: ($1000)
Notes: Kansas material, emphasizing
Western Kansas; the cattle industry of the
Great Plains area to pre-World War I.

KS —UNIVERSITY OF KANSAS, Kenneth
Spencer Research Library, Kansas
Collection, Lawrence, 66045. Sheryl K
Williams, Cur
Holdings: Vols (90,000) Cat Mss Maps Pix
Notes: All aspects of the American West
and trans-Mississippi history, especially
northern and central regions. Overland
diaries, cartographic, history, Indians,
emigration and immigration, printing history,
cattle industry, agriculture and farm life,
conservation are some special interests, in
addition to the usual political, economic,
military and social interests.

KS —KANSAS STATE HISTORICAL
SOCIETY LIBRARY, Memorial Bldg, 120
W Tenth, Topeka, 66612. Portia Allbert,
Library Dir
Holdings: Vols (3900) Cat Mss Maps
Microforms
Budget: ($15,000)

KY —UNIVERSITY OF KENTUCKY,
Margaret I King Library, Dept of Special
Collections, Lexington, 40506. William
Marshall, Head
Holdings: Vols 75 Uncat
Notes: Collection confined to novels with a
Kentucky background only (Indian fighting,
political intrigue, adventure in the "wilds" of

Kentucky); 30 other novels relating to
Western adventures.

MD —UNIVERSITY OF BALTIMORE,
Langsdale Library, 1420 Maryland Ave,
Baltimore, 21201. Gerry Watkins, Head of
Special Collections Dept
Holdings: Cat Mss Maps
Notes: Incl the entire stock (10,000 vols) of
Peter Decker, New York antiquarian
bookdealer (acquired in 1970); incl Peter
Decker's mss of his published works and his
records as a dealer in Americana.

MA —AMERICAN ANTIQUARIAN
SOCIETY LIBRARY, 185 Salisbury St,
Worcester, 01609. Marcus A McCorison,
Dir & Librn
Holdings: Vols 1500 Cat
Notes: Narratives especially. Incl the Donald
McKay Frost Collection.

MI —MONROE COUNTY LIBRARY
SYSTEM, Ellis Reference and Information
Center, 3700 S Custer Rd, Monroe, 48161.
Marie D Chulski, Head of Reference
Services
Holdings: Vols (35,000) Cat
Budget: ($15,000)
Notes: The George Armstrong Custer
Collection is a burgeoning archive of
materials on General Custer and the events
surrounding and shaping his life. This incl
the Lawrence A Frost Collection of
Custerana acquired by the library system in
1977. The Custer Monograph Series is
produced by the Monroe County Library
System. Publications are printed in limited
numbered editions, aimed at providing
insight into the life and times of General
George Armstrong Custer. The continuing
series consists of reprints of significant
publications and original items.

MO —UNIVERSITY OF MISSOURI-
KANSAS CITY, General Library, Snyder
Collection of Americana, 5100 Rockhill
Road, Kansas City, 64110. Kenneth J
LaBudde, Dir; Robert Paustian, Asst Dir
Notes: Snyder Collection of Americana,
especially 19th century western.
See also entry under Americana.

MO —MISSOURI HISTORICAL SOCIETY,
Library, Jefferson Memorial Bldg, Saint
Louis, 63112. Stephanie Klein, Librn-
Archivist; Peter Michel, Cur of Manuscripts
Holdings: Cat Mss Maps Pix
Notes: Extensive ms holdings relating to
Missouri, US history, etc. Also ms
collections of many noted persons (all but
subsequent additions listed in Hamer, 1961).
Library holdings described in Whitehall,
Walter Muir, *Independent Historical
Societies* (Boston, 1962).

MO —SAINT LOUIS PUBLIC LIBRARY,
Gardner Rare Book Room, 1301 Olive St,
Saint Louis, 63103. Julanne M Good,
Supervisor; Martha Riley, Rare Books Librn
Holdings: Vols 100 Cat Maps
Budget: ($5573)
Notes: Small growing collection of travels
incl St Louis or Missouri, largely transferred
from the general stacks, although an
occasional purchase is made. Incl early
business directories of St Louis, river pilots'
handbooks and maps. Noncirculating.

MO —SAINT LOUIS UNIVERSITY, Pius XII
Memorial Library, Saint Louis Room
Collection, 3655 W Pine Blvd, Saint Louis,
63108. Catherine E Weidle, Rare Books
Librn
Holdings: Vols Cat
Notes: Books on early education, Jesuitica
and Western Americana.

MT —EASTERN MONTANA COLLEGE,
Library, 1500 N 30 St, Billings, 59101.
Edward Neroda, Dir
Holdings: Vols 2186 Cat Maps Pix
Notes: The Dora White Collection of
Western History; emphasis on Pacific
Northwest and Montana.

MT —MONTANA HISTORICAL SOCIETY
LIBRARY, 225 N Roberts St, Helena,
59601. Robert M Clark, Librn; Brian
Cockhill, State Archivist
Holdings: Vols 3000 Cat
Budget: ($2500)
Notes: The Ames and Margaret Booth
Teakel Range Life Memorial Collection
(cowboy and cattle range subjects). The

scope of this collection includes the entire
West, not just Montana and contiguous
states. Also, L A Huffman Collection; incl
1100 photographs.

NE —NEBRASKA STATE HISTORICAL
SOCIETY, Fort Robinson Museum, Box
304, Crawford, 69339. Vance Nelson, Cur
Holdings: Vols (1500) Cat Mss Maps Pix
Slides Phonorecords Audiotapes 16mm
Films Microforms
Notes: Materials related to the history of
Fort Robinson, and incl the Post Medical
Library, reference books on state
government, etc, Western Americana: books
on ranching, homesteaders, Indian wars, etc;
microfilm records for Fort Robinson records,
Crawford and Chadron Nebraska
newspapers, diaries and interviews. Library
incl the E Kopac Collection of books dealing
with Western Americana; particularly Indian
wars, transportation, guns and railroads.

NE —KEARNEY STATE COLLEGE, Calvin
T Ryan Library, Kearney, 68847. John
Mayeski, Dir; Anita Norman, Reference
Librn
Holdings: Vols 1700 Cat Mss Maps Pix
Slides Microforms
Notes: Collection attempts to cover total
historical development of Nebraska. Special
strengths of the collection incl overland
journeys, Pony Express, sod houses, and the
Union Pacific. Special consideration has
been given to Indians of Nebraska and the
cattle industry. The collection is well
supported by the library's general strength of
Western Americana.

NE —NEBRASKA STATE HISTORICAL
SOCIETY, Archives, 1500 R St, Box 82554,
Lincoln, 68501. James E Potter, State
Archivist
Holdings: Uncat Mss
Notes: Collection and mss of Judge E S
Ricker of Dawes County, Nebraska,
concerning Indians of the Great Plains and
their final conflict with the white man.
Interviews with soldiers, cowboys, trappers
and Indians.

NE —UNIVERSITY OF NEBRASKA-
LINCOLN, Don L Love Library, Lincoln,
68588. Joseph G Svoboda, University
Archivist
Holdings: Vols (1000) // Uncat Mss Maps
Pix Slides Audiotapes 16mm Films
Notes: The

NE —JOSLYN ART REFERENCE
LIBRARY, Joslyn Art Museum, 2200
Dodge St, Omaha, 68102. Ann Birney,
Librn; Marie Sedlacek, Cataloger-Slide Librn
Holdings: Vols (17,000) Cat Slides
Notes: Incl catalogs of exhibitions and
western US materials, especially early
Omaha and Nebraska. Large collections of
vertical files on subjects and artists; also
mounted prints, reproductions, slides.
filmstrips.

NV —FORESTA INSTITUTE FOR OCEAN
AND MOUNTAIN STUDIES, Library,
6205 Franktown Rd, Carson City, 89701.
Shannon Porter, Librn
Holdings: Vols (3000) Cat Mss Maps Pix
Slides
Notes: Material on plant, animal, and human
ecology with special emphasis on far western
US and Nevada ecology and environmental
problems. Also hold about 2000 reprints,
pamphlets, reports, etc.

NV —UNIVERSITY OF NEVADA, RENO,
University Library, Special Collections Dept,
Reno, 89557. Robert E Blesse, Head
Holdings: Vols (800) Cat
Notes: The Women in the West Collection
contains materials which document
experience of women in the trans-Mississippi
West. Major emphasis is on first-hand
experience, diaries, letters and
autobiographies, but major biographies of
women who were prominent or greatly
influenced others are also collected.
Emphasis is the 19th and 20th centuries.

NM —NEW MEXICO HIGHLANDS
UNIVERSITY, Donnelly Library, National
Ave, Las Vegas, 87701. Karen Jaggers,
Assoc Librn
Holdings: Vols (5000) Cat Mss Maps Pix
Microforms
Notes: The outstanding collection is the

THE WEST (cont.)

Arrott Collection on Fort Union, New Mexico, 1851-1891. Other collection incl Spanish Archives, Mexican Archives, Archdiocese of Santa Fe, Archivo del Parral; New Mexico Land Grants.

NY —MUSEUM OF THE AMERICAN INDIAN, Library, 9 Westchester Square, Bronx, 10401. Mary B Davis, Librn
Holdings: Vols (40,000) Cat Mss Maps Pix Microforms VF
Notes: Collections cover all aspects of the Indians of the Western Hemisphere; some materials on Eskimos. For scholarly research only.

NY —AMERICAN MUSEUM OF NATURAL HISTORY, Library Services Dept, Central Park W & 79th St, New York, 10024. Nina J Root, Chairwoman; Mary Genett, Asst Librn for Reference Services
Holdings: Cat Mss Pix Microforms
Notes: The Ernest Thompson Seton diaries. Thousands of pages of an unpublished 67-year diary record of one of the world's most famous naturalists, the gift of Joseph F Cullman III, a Trustee of the Museum. Preserved in 35 protective cases, the gift incl unpublished diaries, notebooks, and some other writings. The diary begins 12 June 1879; the last entries were written in hospital, just a month before Seton's death in 1946. Literally hundreds of examples of flora and fauna are pictured in the diaries in original pencil, pen-and-ink, and watercolor sketches, on nearly every page. Research will reveal information on the Indian sign language, the Boy Scouts of America, the Woodcraft League of America, and the wilderness of Canada, Florida, Texas, the West and Southwest, etc.

NY —NEW YORK PUBLIC LIBRARY, Research Libraries, American History Div, Fifth Ave & 42 St, New York, 10018.
Holdings: Vols (14,000) Cat
Notes: Outstanding collection of material on the Old West, incl early settlement, the lawless era, and the resulting vigilantism.

ND —THEODORE ROOSEVELT NATIONAL PARK, Library, PO Box 7, Medora, 58645. Susan Snow, Librn; Miki Hellickson, Chief Naturalist
Holdings: Vols (1500) Cat Mss Maps Pix Slides Audiotapes 16mm Films
Budget: ($5000)
Notes: Theodore Roosevelt, cattle country history, natural history. Also 2400 pictures and 2200 slides.

OK —UNIVERSITY OF OKLAHOMA, Bizzell Memorial Library, Western History Collections, 401 W Brooks, Norman, 73069. John Ezell, Cur
Holdings: Cat Mss Maps Pix Microforms

OK —NATIONAL COWBOY HALL OF FAME AND WESTERN HERITAGE, Library, 1700 NE 63 St, Oklahoma City, 73111. Esther Long, Librn
Holdings: Vols (8000) Uncat
Notes: Art of the American West. Covers western art and artists; rodeo and its history; cowboys; the cattle industry; and biographies on prominent westerners. Personal collection of Walter Brennen; collections of artists, Carl Link and James Earl Frazier.

OK —OKLAHOMA HISTORICAL SOCIETY, Library, Historical Bldg, Oklahoma City, 73105. Andrea Clark, Dir, Library Resources Division
Holdings: Vols (43,000) Cat Mss Maps Pix Microforms
Notes: The Society also has the Indian Archives Collection of 2,500,000 pieces (Mary Lee Boyle, Archivist). This is an extensive collection of records, particularly of the Five Civilized Tribes. Incl tribal rolls, agency reports, manuscripts, etc.

OK —PHILBROOK ART CENTER, Library, 2727 S Rockford Rd, Tulsa, 74114. Thomas E Young, Librn
Holdings: Vols (1000) Uncat Pix
Notes: The Roberta C Lawson Collection is mainly books, with some serials, and an uncounted group of photographs. The books are organized and partially cataloged; photographs are not. They deal with Indians and western Americana.

OK —THOMAS GILCREASE INSTITUTE OF AMERICAN HISTORY & ART LIBRARY, 1400 North 25th West Ave, Tulsa, 74127. Sarah Hirsch, Librn
Holdings: Vols Cat Mss Maps Pix
Notes: Trans-Mississippi West, US, Indian and Hispanic history. The Gilcrease Library contains a total of about 40,000 mss; 10,000 imprints; 5000 photographs; 600 maps and 50,000 vols.

OK —TULSA CITY-COUNTY LIBRARY, Business & Technology Dept, 400 Civic Center, Tulsa, 74103. Craig Buthod, Head
Holdings: Vols (18,000) Uncat
Notes: Original General Land Office survey maps for the states of Arizona, Arkansas, Colorado, Illinois, Indiana, Idaho, Kansas, Michigan, Missouri, Montana, Nebraska, Nevada, New Mexico, North Dakota, Ohio, Oklahoma, South Dakota, Utah and Wyoming. Incomplete coverage of each state.

PA —ATHENAEUM OF PHILADELPHIA, 219 S Sixth St, Philadelphia, 19106. Roger W Moss Jr, Librn
Holdings: Vols 400 Cat
Notes: Western Americana. Separate catalog by date. Numerous examples cataloged as part of early travel and exploration collection.

PA —UNIVERSITY OF PENNSYLVANIA, Van Pelt Library, Rare Books Collection, 34 & Walnut Sts, Philadelphia, 19104. Daniel Traister, Special Collections Librn
Holdings: Vols 2500 //
Notes: Robert Dechert Collection: early exploration, 17th and 18th centuries; western Americana, 19th century; Canadiana, incl Jesuit relations.

TX —HARDIN-SIMMONS UNIVERSITY, Richardson Library, Abilene, 79601. Joe F Dahlstrom, Dir
Holdings: Vols (10,000) Cat Mss Maps Pix Microforms
Notes: Special collection name is Richardson Research Center, named in honor of Dr Rupert N Richardson. Collect in the areas of his own research interests, especially that portion of the US that was once a part of Mexico. Emphases on the history of ranching, railroads, discovery and exploration, Texas county histories, etc. Incl 350 items printed and/or designed by El Paso printer Carl Hertzog; the Judge R C Crane collection of Texana and a similar collection of Louise Kelley's; and the Research Publication's Western Americana collection (microfilm).

TX —UNIVERSITY OF TEXAS, ARLINGTON, Library, PO Box 19497, Arlington, 76019. Chas Colley, Dir Special Collections
Holdings: Vols (8000) Cat Mss Maps Pix Microforms
Notes: The Jenkins Garrett Library is an in-depth research collection documenting the history and culture of Texas and the American Southwest. Containing a wide range of basic Texana, the Library specializes in pre-statehood Texas, and it houses one of the nation's most important collections of materials relating to the US-Mexican War, including all of the items concerning the war from the Eberstadt Collection. The Library is composed of materials of every type and character, with heavy emphasis upon rare 19th century Texana. In addition, the Library routinely acquires all monographs and serial secondary publications of research importance. The Garrett Library maintains a separate catalog which is integrated into the general UTA Library catalog, and its items carry a unique designation in the OCLC system.

TX —UNIVERSITY OF TEXAS LIBRARIES, General Libraries, Barker Texas History Center, PO Box P, Austin, 78712. Don Carleton, Dir
Holdings: Vols (132,000) Cat Mss Maps Pix Slides Phonorecords Audiotapes Microforms
Notes: See description of collection under Texas-History.

TX —WEST TEXAS STATE UNIVERSITY, Cornette Library, PO Box 748 WT Sta, Canyon, 79016. Faye Hendrickson, Special Collections Asst
Holdings: Vols (1850) Uncat Microforms
Notes: Includes microform collection.

TX —TEXAS A&M UNIVERSITY, Sterling C Evans Library, Special Collections Div, College Station, 77843. Donald H Dyal, Librn
Holdings: Vols (16,000) Mss Pix
Notes: Jeff Dykes Range Livestock Collection (incl a 600-item collection of J Frank Dobie works). Part of the Dobie Collection is described in Dykes, Jeff C *My Dobie Collection* (College Station, Tex; Friends of the Texas A & M University Library).

TX —DALLAS PUBLIC LIBRARY, Texas/ Dallas History and Archives Division, 1515 Young St, Dallas, 75201. Richard L Waters, Acting Dir; Wayne Gray, Manager
Holdings: Vols (30,000) Cat Maps Pix Slides Microforms
Budget: ($8450)
Notes: Dallas and Texas history.

TX —SOUTHERN METHODIST UNIVERSITY, DeGolyer Library, Box 396, SMU, Dallas, 75275. Clifton H Jones, Dir
Holdings: Vols 50,000 Cat Mss Maps Pix
Notes: History of the trans-Mississippi West and Mexico, from discovery to present. Original editions of most of the important early collections of travels.

TX —EL PASO PUBLIC LIBRARY, Southwest Collection, 501 N Oregon, El Paso, 79901. Mary A Sarber, Head
Holdings: Vols 10,000 Cat Mss Maps Pix Microforms
Budget: $5000
Notes: Research collection includes rare books and mss journals, vertical files, index to El Paso newspapers, microfilmed newspapers, photographs, and architectural plans. Separate catalog. Limited to materials on Texas, New Mexico, Arizona and Mexico. Special collections of material by and about Tom Lea Jr, and Carl Hertzog. Aultman Collection of photographs includes 3500 on El Paso Southwest and 2500 on Mexican Revolution. Cited in Lovelace, Lisa, "The Southwest Collection of the El Paso Public Library". *Great Plains Journal*, vol 2, no 2, pp 161-166; Aultman, Otis A *Photographs from the Border: The Otis A Aultman Collection*, El Paso Public Library Association, 1977.

TX —AMON CARTER MUSEUM, Library, 3510 Camp Bowie Blvd, PO Box 2365, Fort Worth, 76113. Nancy G Wynne, Librn
Holdings: Vols (25,000) Cat Mss Pix
Notes: The book collection, microfilm and photo archives have been built toward the goal of the interpretation of American history through art. At present, the greatest strengths are in Americana, Western Canadiana, bibliography, American exhibition catalogs and history of photography. Substantial books and files on American artists of the 19th and early 20th century, and particularly of Charles M Russell and Frederic Remington. Incl 25,000 pictures; 13,000 slides.
See also entries under Newspapers, American; Pictures - Collections.

TX —UNIVERSITY OF HOUSTON, M D Anderson Memorial Library, University Park, Houston, 77004. David Farmer, Cur, Special Collections; Jean Jackson, Assistant Cur
Holdings: Vols 2000 Cat Mss Maps Pix
Notes: Bulk of the collection is printed vols and several hundred pamphlets incl some of the oldest Texas almanacs. Incl the collections of Major Richard Burgess of El Paso and the William B Bates Collection of Texas and Western Americana. The Bates Collection is described in 2 exhibit catalogs, *The William B Bates Collection*, by Lorene Pouncey, Houston, 1965, and *The William B Bates Collection* by Marian Orgain, Houston, 1971. Stress is upon the annexation of Texas and the Mexican War.

UT —UTAH STATE UNIVERSITY, Merrill Library, Department of Special Collections & Archives, Logan, 84322. A J Simmonds, Curator; Jeanie F Simmonds, Archivist; Bradford R Cole, Mss Librn
Holdings: Vols 1100 Uncat Mss Pix Slides
Notes: The Austin E and Alla S Fife folklore archive of western, cowboy, and folksong materials. Over 300 pictures; 4200 slides;

THE WEST (cont.)

800 field recordings; 75 ft of ms items. Complete card index to folklore themes in the collection. See Catalog of recordings in "A Bibiliography of the Archives of the Utah Humanities Research Foundation," *Bulletin of the University of Utah*, vol XXXVIII, no 9 (Dec 1947): pp 26-35; description of Fife Mormon collection in *Western Folklore Quarterly*, vol VII, no 3 (July 1948): pp 299-301; description of "Fife Collection of Western American Folksong and Folklore" in *The Folklore and Folk Music Archivist*, vol VII, no 2 (Spring 1964): pp 41-44. Also books and pamphlets on the history of western grazing (cattle and sheep). Incl manuscript of WPA produced history of grazing, 1540-1936. Supported by 800 photographs.

UT —BRIGHAM YOUNG UNIVERSITY, Harold B Lee Library, Unversity Hill, Provo, 84602. Sterling Albrecht, Dir
Holdings: Vols 15,000

UT —PROVO CITY PUBLIC LIBRARY, 13 N 100 E, Provo, 84601. Larry Hortin, Dir
Holdings: Vols (600) Cat
Notes: Western states history with emphasis on Utah State and Utah County.

UT —UNIVERSITY OF UTAH, Marriott Library, Special Collections, Salt Lake City, 84112. Gregory C Thompson, Cur
Notes: Exploration of the West.

UT —UTAH STATE HISTORICAL SOCIETY, Library, 300 Rio Grande, Salt Lake City, 84101. Jay M Haymond, Coordr, Collections & Research Services
Holdings: Vols (20,000) Cat Mss Maps Pix Slides Phonorecords Audiotapes 16mm Films Filmstrips Microforms
Budget: $37,000

VA —VIRGINIA POLYTECHNIC INSTITUTE AND STATE UNIVERSITY LIBRARY, Blacksburg, 24061. Glenn L McMullen, Special Collections Librn
Holdings: Vols (4000)
Notes: Collection largely consists of nineteenth century and early twentieth century imprints, emphasizing the role of native Virginians in the development of the trans-Mississippi West, particularly Texas; cowboys and the cattle industry; outlaws and lawlessness; and emigrants' guidebooks to states, cities, and regions in the West.

†WA —WASHINGTON STATE UNIVERSITY, Library, Manuscripts, Archives & Special Collections, Pullman, 99164. John F Guido, Head
Holdings: Cat Mss Maps Pix
Notes: The Carl Parcher Russell papers, a vast resource (24,916 items; 45 linear feet) on American Indian and Western pioneer activities and artifacts. Much on the fur trade; pioneer life, mountain men and trapping; wildlife; primitive life in detail. Also the National Park Service, parks, monuments, etc. Described in *Carl Parcher Russell: An Indexed Register of His Scholarly and Professional Papers, 1920-1967, in the Washington State University Library* (Pullman, 1970), 149 pp.

WY —LARAMIE COUNTY LIBRARY SYSTEM, 2800 Central Ave, Cheyenne, 82001. Ed Byers, County Librn
Holdings: Vols 700 Cat Maps
Notes: Carpenter Collection of Western Americana.

WY —WYOMING STATE ARCHIVES MUSEUMS, AND HISTORICAL DEPARTMENT, Barrett Bldg, Cheyenne, 82002. Philip J Roberts, Documents Supvr; Jean F Brainerd, Research Asst
Holdings: Vols (12,000) Cat Mss Maps Pix Audiotapes Microforms
Budget: ($430,000)
Notes: Extensive mss, map, pamphlet, and picture collection relative to Wyoming, regional, and western history. Publish *Annals of Wyoming*.

WY —UNIVERSITY OF WYOMING, William Robertson Coe Library, Performing Arts Collections, Laramie, 82071. Gene M Gressley, Dir
Holdings: Vols (15,000) Cat Mss Maps Pix Microforms
Notes: The Western History Research Center of the University of Wyoming's William Robertson Coe Library has sizable ms collections in several areas pertaining to the history and development of the American West. Principal ms collection areas incl; cattle industry history, western literature, mining and petroleum history, transportation history, conservation history, water resources history, and related western history topics. The collections are supplemented by a fine Western Americana book collection cataloged by the main library but located at the Western History Research Center.

AB —UNIVERSITY OF ALBERTA, Cameron Library, The Bruce Peel Special Collections Room, Edmonton, T6G 2J8, Can. John Charles, Special Collections Librn
Holdings: Vols 21,000
Notes: Western Americana, incl Woods and Powers Collections; incl Canadian West.

ON —VICTORIA UNIVERSITY, Library, 71 Queen's Park Crescent, Toronto, M5S 1K7, Can. Robert C Brandeis, Chief Librn
Holdings: Vols (1000) // Cat Mss Maps Pix
Notes: Collection consists of books, pamphlets, and government reports mainly dealing with North American Indians and western explorations and missionary enterprises among the Indian tribes in Canada. Incl Indian Bibles and hymnbooks, and mss and vols by Peter Jones (an Indian missionary) and James Evans (inventor of the Cree syllabic alphabet).

THE WEST—GENEALOGY

KS —WICHITA PUBLIC LIBRARY, 223 S Main, Wichita, 67202. Richard Rademacher, Librn
Holdings: Vols (6570) Cat Microfilms
Notes: Incl approximately 2500 rolls of microfilm, 400 microcards. Not loaned.

THE WEST—MAPS

†CA —UNIVERSITY OF CALIFORNIA, BERKELEY, General Library, Map Room, Berkeley, 94720.
Notes: Emphasis on US, particularly California and the West.

†CA —UNIVERSITY OF CALIFORNIA, DAVIS, Peter J Shields Memorial Library, Map Collection, Davis, 95616.

CA —US GEOLOGICAL SURVEY LIBRARY, 345 Middlefield Rd, Menlo Park, 94025.
Holdings: Vols (200,000)

†CA —CALIFORNIA ACADEMY OF SCIENCES LIBRARY, Golden State Park, San Francisco, 94118.

CA —UNIVERSITY OF CALIFORNIA, SANTA BARBARA, Map and Imagery Laboratory, Santa Barbara, 93106. Larry Carver, Dept Head
Notes: Worldwide coverage of Landsat imagery donated by US Dept of Agriculture Aerial Photography Field Office. Consists of 153,000 scenes, covering most of the earth's surface between the years 1975 and 1980. Incl 300,000 maps, 1800 atlases, 9 globes, 300 relief models, 1,500,000 satellite imagery and aerial photographs, 700 reference books and gazetteers, 25 serials (titles received), and 21,000 microforms.

THE WEST IN ART

TX —TEXAS A&M UNIVERSITY, Sterling C Evans Library, Special Collections Div, College Station, 77843. Donald H Dyal, Librn
Notes: The Western Illustrators Collection is comprised of approximately 3500 illustrated books, pamphlets, and other items. The collection incl illustrated works by Charles Marion Russell, Frederic Sackrider Remington, and other artists of the American West. Numerous other artists of the West and Southwest are represented, many of them contemporary moderns. Quite a lot of the books have additional unique original drawings by the artists.

WEST, BENJAMIN, 1738-1820

PA —FRIENDS HISTORICAL LIBRARY OF SWARTHMORE COLLEGE, Swarthmore, 19081. J William Frost, Dir
Holdings: Vols (35,000) Cat Mss Pix
Notes: Books by and about the Quaker-born artist. A few paintings and a collection of his drawings are housed in the library.

WEST, DOROTHY

MA —BOSTON UNIVERSITY, Mugar Memorial Library, Special Collections Dept, 771 Commonwealth Ave, Boston, 02215. Howard B Gotlieb, Dir
Holdings: Cat Pix
Notes: Correspondence incl publications by.

WEST, JESSAMYN

CA —WHITTIER COLLEGE, Wardman Library, Whittier, 90608. Christine Erdmann, Special Collections Librn
Holdings: Uncat Mss
Notes: All of her mss to date.

WEST, NATHANAEL

NV —UNIVERSITY OF NEVADA, RENO, University Library, Special Collections Dept, Reno, 89557. Robert E Blesse, Head
Holdings: Vols 21 // Cat
Notes: Includes individual works by author in all editions including translations; also prefaces, introductions, published correspondence, appearances in anthologies, periodicals, etc. Bibliographical research collection, part of Modern Authors Collection.

WEST, PAUL

MA —BOSTON UNIVERSITY, Mugar Memorial Library, Special Collections Dept, 771 Commonwealth Ave, Boston, 02215. Howard B Gotlieb, Dir
Holdings: Cat Mss
Notes: Mss, correspondence, etc collected in depth; incl publications by or about.

WEST, REBECCA

CT —YALE UNIVERSITY, Box 1603A, Yale Station, New Haven, 06520.
Holdings: Cat Mss

DC —GEORGETOWN UNIVERSITY, Library, Special Collections Div, 37 & O Sts NW, Washington, 20057. George M Barringer, Special Collections Librn; Nicholas B Sheetz, Mss Librn
Holdings: Cat Mss
Notes: The papers of the English author, journalist, and historian Douglas Woodruff (1897-1978), containing correspondence, mss, and photographs. Incl is considerable material concerning his years at Oxford University; his editorship for many years of The "Tablet"; English Catholic society in general and English Catholic literature in particular. Also present are research files on the Tichborne Claimant, one of the most famous cases of impersonation in English legal history. There is extensive correspondence from such figures as: Hilaire Belloc; Tom Burns; Rev Martin D'Arcy, SJ; Christopher Dawson; Sir Roy Harrod; Christopher Hollis; Msgr Ronald Knox; Sir Shane Leslie; Sir Arnold Lunn; Rebecca West; and Evelyn Waugh.

NV —UNIVERSITY OF NEVADA, RENO, University Library, Special Collections Dept, Reno, 89557. Robert E Blesse, Head
Holdings: Vols 77 Cat
Notes: Includes individual works by author in all editions including translations; also prefaces, introductions, published correspondence, appearances in anthologies, periodicals, etc. Bibliographical research collection, part of Modern Authors Collection.

NY —ALFRED UNIVERSITY, Herrick Memorial Library, Alfred, 14802. June E Brown, Head Librn
Notes: The Evelyn Tennyson Openhym Collection of modern British literature and social history. Correspondence addressed to Ursula Roberts ("Susan Miles"), many pieces concerning the British peace movement of the 1930s.

WEST, REBECCA (cont.)

†NC —WAKE FOREST UNIVERSITY, Z
Smith Reynolds Library, Box 7777, Reynold
Sta, Winston-Salem, 27109.
Notes: A significant collection.

WEST AND EAST see East and West

WEST ARMENIAN LANGUAGE see
Armenian Language and Literature

WEST GERMANY see Germany

WEST INDIAN AUTHORS see Authors,
West Indian

WEST INDIAN FOLK SONGS see Folk
Songs, West Indian

WEST INDIAN NEWSPAPERS see
Newspapers, West Indian

WEST INDIES

CA —UNIVERSITY OF CALIFORNIA,
BERKELEY, Bancroft Library, Manuscripts
Division, Berkeley, 94720. James D Hart,
Dir
Holdings: Vols Cat Mss Microforms
Notes: In addition to numerous mss relating
to the history of western North America
(western plains to the Pacific Coast, Alaska
to Panama), The Bancroft Library has many
ms collections of significance in other areas.
The following collections are large enough to
justify the attention of serious researchers;
most are analyzed in unpublished keys to
arrangement. History collections incl
Archives of California (1757-1822), Archives
of Mexico and Spain (microcopies); Herbert
Eugene Bolton; British West Indies
Documents, Danish West Indies Documents,
Dutch West Indies Documents; John Charles
Fremont; Japanese American Evacuation
and Resettlement. Scientific and
technological collections incl the papers of
many important modern scientists (some
individually listed in this volume).
CT —TRINITY COLLEGE LIBRARY, 300
Summit St, Hartford, 06106. Ralph S
Emerick, Librn
Holdings: // Cat
FL —UNIVERSITY OF CENTRAL
FLORIDA, Library, Box 25000, Orlando,
32816.
Holdings: Vols (3000)
Notes: The William L Bryant West Indies
Collection of books, documents, periodicals,
paintings and artifacts either about or
produced in the islands of the West Indies
and Florida.
†MA —BOSTON PUBLIC LIBRARY, Copley
Sq, Boston, 02117.
Holdings: Vols (700) Cat Mss Maps Pix
Notes: The Benjamin P Hunt Collection,
formed prior to the Civil War, with
particular reference to Haiti, to which
substantial additions have been made. Also
about 3000 mss. Use restricted to qualified
scholars.
MA —BOSTON COLLEGE LIBRARIES,
Thomas P O'Neill Library, Nicholas M
Williams Ethnological Collection, Chestnut
Hill, 02167. Frank J Seegraber, Special
Collections Librn
Holdings: Vols 10,000 // Cat Mss Maps
Notes: Collection emphasizes Caribbeana,
especially Jamaica, to 1940. Incl discovery,
exploration and natural history of the
British, French and Spanish settlements; the
slave question; piracy. There are over 6000
mss, 5000 of which are Anansi folk tales
recorded by native school children. Also
small ancillary sections of Africana and
Judaica. For reference use only, by
arrangement with librarian.
MA —AMERICAN ANTIQUARIAN
SOCIETY LIBRARY, 185 Salisbury St,
Worcester, 01609. Marcus A McCorison,
Dir & Librn
Holdings: Vols 18,000 Cat
Notes: Strongest for New York,
Pennsylvania, Massachusetts and

Connecticut. Incl Canada, Hawaii, Mexico,
the West Indies; also Pennsylvania German.
About 18,000 or 90 percent of the almanacs
and yearbooks known to have been printed
in the United States before 1850; The Latin
American and Canadian collections are the
most complete in this country.
NY —HAMILTON COLLEGE, Daniel Burke
Library, Special Collections Dept, Clinton,
13323. Frank K Lorenz, Cur
Holdings: Vols 1300 Cat Mss Maps Pix
Notes: The Beinecke Lesser Antilles
Collection. Specialized works on the smaller
islands of the West Indies, incl history,
travel literature, flora and fauna,
anthropology. Incl numerous rare items in
many languages.
NY —NEW YORK PUBLIC LIBRARY,
Research Libraries, American History Div,
Fifth Ave & 42 St, New York, 10018.
Holdings: Vols 3100 Cat Maps Microforms
Notes: Histories of the islands of the
Caribbean are collected comprehensively,
along with the publications of various
historical societies.
NY —RESEARCH INSTITUTE FOR THE
STUDY OF MAN, Library, 162 E 78 St,
New York, 10021. Judith Selakoff, Librn
Holdings: Vols (14,500) Cat Mss Maps VF
Notes: The non-Hispanic Caribbean. Incl
material on all aspects of life in non-
Hispanic Caribbean, with primary emphasis
on anthropology and the social sciences.
RI —BROWN UNIVERSITY, John Carter
Brown Library, Providence, 02912. Norman
Fiering, Librn; Everett C Wilkie Jr,
Bibliographer; Susan Danforth, Cur Maps &
Prints
Holdings: Vols (40,000)
Notes: Collections cover European
colonization and settlements in the area until
1830; also incl are good coverage of slavery
controversy.
TX —UNIVERSITY OF TEXAS LIBRARIES,
Nettie Lee Benson Latin American
Collection, Sid Richardson Hall 1.109,
Austin, 78712. Laura Gutierrez-Witt, Head
Librn
Holdings: Vols (450,000) Cat Mss Maps Pix
Phonorecords Filmstrips Microforms
See also entry under Latin America
VI —COLLEGE OF THE VIRGIN ISLANDS,
Ralph M Paiewonsky Library, Saint Thomas,
00802. Ernest C Wagner, Dir
Holdings: Vols 8500 Cat Maps Microforms
Budget: $5500
Notes: West Indies: history, literature,
economics and social conditions. Incl copies
of materials published in journals and
pamphlets from the late 19th century to the
present.
VI —VIRGIN ISLANDS BUREAU OF
LIBRARIES, MUSEUMS &
ARCHAEOLOGICAL SERVICES, Enid M
Baa Library & Archives, Von Scholten
Collection, PO Box 390, Saint Thomas,
00801. June A V Lindqvist, Cur
Holdings: Vols (13,000) Cat Mss Maps Pix
Microforms
Notes: Caribbeana, with emphasis on the
Virgin Islands. Library collects in all aspects
of Virgin Islands life, incl natural and
cultural history. Collection is especially
strong in Danish West Indian and Virgin
Islands newspapers and in dissertations on
Caribbean subjects. Library is a full
depository for USVI documents. Auxiliary
collections are located in the Bureau's
libraries in St Croix and St John.

WEST INDIES—CIVILIZATION AND
CULTURE

NY —NEW YORK PUBLIC LIBRARY,
Schomburg Center for Research in Black
Culture, 515 Lenox Ave, New York, 10037.
Catherine J Lenix Hooker, Interim
Administrator
Notes: A repository for 10,000 phonodiscs
and 2000 tapes covering African and West
Indian folk music, early blues, and jazz.

WEST INDIES—IMPRINTS

FL —UNIVERSITY OF CENTRAL
FLORIDA, Library, Box 25000, Orlando,

32816.
Holdings: Vols (3000)
Notes: The William L Bryant West Indies
Collection of books, documents, periodicals,
paintings and artifacts either about or
produced in the islands of the West Indies
and Florida.

WEST INDIES—SOCIAL LIFE AND
CUSTOMS

NY —NEW YORK PUBLIC LIBRARY,
Schomburg Center for Research in Black
Culture, 515 Lenox Ave, New York, 10037.
Catherine J Lenix Hooker, Interim
Administrator
Notes: A repository for 10,000 phonodiscs
and 2000 tapes covering African and West
Indian folk music, early blues, and jazz.

WEST NEW GUINEA see Indonesia

WEST POINT see U.S. Military Academy
at West Point

WEST POINT AND CHISOLM RICE
MILL COMPANIES

SC —COLLEGE OF CHARLESTON
LIBRARY, Special Collections Dept,
Charleston, 29401.
Notes: Papers, 1873-1925, incl
correspondence, ledgers, and other financial
papers of two Charleston-based rice mills.

WEST VIRGINIA—GENEALOGY

FL —ORLANDO PUBLIC LIBRARY, Local
History & Genealogy Dept, 100 Block of
Central Ave, Orlando, 32806. Eileen B
Willis, Librn
Holdings: Vols 11,000 Cat Maps Microforms
Budget: $8000
Notes: Genealogy collection on Md, Del, W
Va, NC, SC, Ala, Miss, La, Texas, Ark, Ky,
Ohio, Ill, Ind, and Mich are well
represented. Most other states are covered
by smaller collections.
See also entry under Genealogy -
Collections.
WV —MARTINSBURG-BERKELEY
COUNTY PUBLIC LIBRARY, Public Sq,
Martinsburg, 25401. Peggy Young Batten,
Dir
Holdings: Vols (1000) Cat Maps Pix
Budget: $1000
Notes: Eastern Panhandle Room collection,
covering Morgan, Berkeley and Jefferson
counties.

WEST VIRGINIA—HISTORY

NC —DUKE UNIVERSITY, William R
Perkins Library, Manuscript Dept, Durham,
27706. Ellen Gartrell, Cur of Mss
Holdings: Cat Mss
Notes: Especially strong for North Carolina,
South Carolina, Virginia, Georgia, and
Alabama. 18th-20th centuries. See Guide to
the Cataloged Collections of the Manuscript
Department of the William R Perkins
Library (1980, ed by Richard C Davis and
Linda A Miller).
WV —CABELL COUNTY PUBLIC
LIBRARY, 455 9th Street Plaza,
Huntington, 25701. Judy K Rule, Actg Dir
Holdings: Vols 2000 Cat Maps Pix
Microforms
Notes: Local newspapers are kept on
microfilm.
WV —MARTINSBURG-BERKELEY
COUNTY PUBLIC LIBRARY, Public Sq,
Martinsburg, 25401. Peggy Young Batten,
Dir
Holdings: Vols (1000) Cat Maps Pix
Budget: $1000
Notes: Eastern Panhandle Room collection,
covering Morgan, Berkeley and Jefferson
counties.
WV —WEST VIRGINIA UNIVERSITY,
Library, West Virginia and Regional History
Collection, Morgantown, 26506. George P
Parkinson Jr, Cur
Holdings: Vols 30,000 Cat Mss Maps Pix
Audiotapes 16mm Films Filmstrips

WEST VIRGINIA—HISTORY (cont.)

Microforms
Budget: ($20,000)
Notes: The West Virginia Collection contains over 10,000 linear ft of mss, broadsides, pictures, photographs, and other items relating to West Virginia and the Appalachian region. There are published guides to the collections.
WV —SALEM COLLEGE, Library, Salem, 26426. Myron J Smith, Jr, Librn

WEST VIRGINIA—INDUSTRIES

DE —HAGLEY MUSEUM AND LIBRARY, Eleutherian Mills-Hagley Foundation Inc, PO Box 3630, Greenville, 19807. Richmond D Williams, Dir; Heddy A Richter, Imprints Librn
Notes: Westmoreland Coal Company records (1854-1982; 350 cubic feet) document the history of the nation's oldest bituminous coal mining company which operated in the Connellsville, Pa area (1880-89) and southern West Virginia (1906-56). Penn Virginia Corporation records (1864-1970; 120 cubic feet) document the history of one of Virginia's most significant coal mining companies. Also, Saint Clair Coal Company (1895-1930; 15 cubic feet). Records document the history of an important Schuylkill County, Pa anthracite coal producer. The colleciton incl minute books, financial records and photographs.

WEST VIRGINIA PULP AND PAPER COMPANY

NY —CORNELL UNIVERSITY LIBRARIES, Collection of Regional History, Dept of Manuscripts and Univ Archives, Ithaca, 14853.
Notes: Incl papers, 1925-54; business correspondence, office records, deeds, annual reports, legal documents and many materials relating to stock issues. Also, Hinde and Dauch Division records 1897-1953; 104 ft. Restricted.

WESTCOTT, JAN

MA —BOSTON UNIVERSITY, Mugar Memorial Library, Special Collections Dept, 771 Commonwealth Ave, Boston, 02215. Howard B Gotlieb, Dir
Holdings: Cat Mss
Notes: Mss, correspondence, etc collected in depth; incl publications by or about.

WESTERN FAIRS ASSOCIATION

CA —CALIFORNIA POLYTECHNIC STATE UNIVERSITY LIBRARY, Special Collections and University Archives, San Luis Obispo, 93407. Nancy E Loe, Head Librn
Holdings: Vols 100 Cat Mss Pix Slides
Notes: The Fairs Collection incl 56,000 mss materials (correspondence, scrapbooks, legislative opinions, and memoranda), photographs and slides documenting the Western Fairs Association of Sacramento, California, and the management and growth of fairs in California and around the world (materials in rough sorting stage).

WESTERN FEDERATION OF MINERS

CO —UNIVERSITY OF COLORADO, Libraries, Western Historical Collections, Boulder, 80309.
Holdings: Mss Pix
Notes: The Western Federation of Miners was a radical hard-rock miners' union that began in Montana and spead to Idaho, Washington, Utah, Colorado, Arizona, New Mexico, Nevada, and California. Its successor, Mine-Mill, resurged during the New Deal years. It merged with the United Steelworkers in 1967. This collection consists of 700 boxes of files, correspondence, and publications; 500 bound vols of minutes, ledgers, magazines, and court proceedings; the library of the

Research Department, consisting of approx 360 linear feet of books, pamphlets, and periodicals; a number of artifacts and curios incl union banners and seals, convention delegates' ribbons, photographs and membership cards. Most of the materials are for the period 1936-1967. Finding aides are available.

WESTERN FICTION see Fiction, Western

WESTERN INSURRECTION, 1794 see Whiskey Insurrection, 1794

WESTERN RESERVE

OH —CLEVELAND PUBLIC LIBRARY, History and Geography Department, 325 Superior Ave, Cleveland, 44114. JoAnn Petrello, Head
Holdings: Cat Maps Pix
Notes: History and description, incl maps and atlases, of the Great Lakes region and the Western Reserve.
OH —HIRAM COLLEGE, Teachout-Price Memorial Library, Hiram, 44234. Joanne M Sawyer, Archivist; Marjorie M Adams, Music Librn
Holdings: Vols 90 Cat Mss Maps Microforms
Notes: Collection incl antiquarian items in this subject area; general collection also emphasizes this subject; incorporates previous subject headings Ohio History and Western Reserve; restricted hours: call or write in advance.
OH —KENT STATE UNIVERSITY, University Archives, Kent, 44242. Stephen C Morton, University Archivist
Holdings: Uncat Mss
Notes: The ms material contained in 6 boxes (5 1/2 cubic feet). The collection comprises correspondence, journals, account books, sermons and miscellaneous material. From 1811 to 1834 Rev Cowles' journals provide an almost unbroken account of his activities as minister and missionary in the Western Reserve region of Ohio. There is also a sizable collection of material on the Fuller Family of Austinburg, Ohio (qv).

WESTERN UNION TELEGRAPH EXPEDITION

DC —SMITHSONIAN INSTITUTION, Archives Div, Washington, 20560. William W Moss, Archivist
Holdings: Mss Maps Pix
Notes: The Archives holds correspondence and records of a number of scientific expeditions with which the Smithsonian was connected, incl the Western Union Telegraph Expedition, the Smithsonian Roosevelt African Expedition, and the United States Exploring Expedition.

WESTERN WRITERS OF AMERICA

CA —UNIVERSITY OF CALIFORNIA, LOS ANGELES, Research Library, Dept of Special Collections, 405 Hilgard Ave, Los Angeles, 90024. Edward Shreeves, Chairman, Bibliographers Group; David S Zeidberg, Head
Notes: 25 linear feet of books, mss, and ephemera by or relating to members.

WESTHEIMER, DAVID A.

TX —RICE UNIVERSITY, Fondren Library, Woodson Research Center, 6100 S Main St, PO Box 1892, Houston, 77251. Nancy Parker, Dir Woodson Research Center
Holdings: Mss Pix
Notes: Incl mss and proofs of 10 novels, plus correspondence, clippings, photos.

WESTINGHOUSE, GEORGE

NY —UNION COLLEGE, Schaffer Library, Archives of Science and Technology, Schenectady, 12308. Ellen Fladger, Archivist
Notes: Papers etc.

WESTLAKE, DONALD

MA —BOSTON UNIVERSITY, Mugar Memorial Library, Special Collections Dept,

771 Commonwealth Ave, Boston, 02215. Howard B Gotlieb, Dir
Holdings: Cat Mss Pix
Notes: Mss, correspondence, etc collected in depth; incl publications by or about.

WESTLAND, JACK

WA —UNIVERSITY OF WASHINGTON LIBRARIES, Suzzallo Library, Manuscripts Section, FM-25, Seattle, 98195. Karyl Winn, Librn
Notes: Incl 6 linear ft, circa 1953-1964.

WESTMORELAND, WILLIAM

PA —US ARMY MILITARY HISTORY INSTITUTE, Carlisle Barracks, 17013. Richard J Sommers, Chief Archivist-Historian
Holdings: Mss Cat
Notes: 2000 boxes mss. The Viet Nam War collection, personal letters, daily logs, memoirs, speeches, and official papers of American officers and soldiers serving in Viet Nam or elsewhere in the world during the era. Almost all these papers are from Generals, incl William DePuy, Harold K Johnson, Bruce Palmer, Jonathan Seaman, and William Westmoreland.

WESTMORELAND COAL COMPANY

DE —HAGLEY MUSEUM AND LIBRARY, Eleutherian Mills-Hagley Foundation Inc, PO Box 3630, Greenville, 19807. Richmond D Williams, Dir; Heddy A Richter, Imprints Librn
Notes: Westmoreland Coal Company records (1854-1982; 350 cubic feet) document the history of the nation's oldest bituminous coal mining company which operated in the Connellsville, Pa area (1880-89) and southern West Virginia (1906-56). Penn Virginia Corporation records (1864-1970; 120 cubic feet) document the history of one of Virginia's most significant coal mining companies. Also, Saint Clair Coal Company (1895-1930; 15 cubic feet). Records document the history of an important Schuylkill County, Pa anthracite coal producer. The colleciton incl minute books, financial records and photographs.

WESTON, EDWARD, 1886-1958

AZ —UNIVERSITY OF ARIZONA, Center for Creative Photography, 843 E University Blvd, Tucson, 85721. James Enyeart, Dir; Terence Pitts, Cur and Librn
Notes: Center has significant collections consisting of more than 25 photographs plus other archival material such as negatives, contact sheets, work prints, correspondence, financial records, diaries, project files, etc. Inventories of the collections are available to researchers. Published guides available for some collections.
CA —HARRISON MEMORIAL LIBRARY, Ocean & Lincoln Sts, Carmel, 93921. Keith Brehmer, Ref Librn
Holdings: // Uncat
Notes: 125 original Edward Weston photographs, which may be viewed in library under staff supervision. No photocopying.
CA —UNIVERSITY OF CALIFORNIA, LOS ANGELES, Research Library, Dept of Special Collections, 405 Hilgard Ave, Los Angeles, 90024. Edward Shreeves, Chairman, Bibliographers Group; David S Zeidberg, Head
Notes: 250 photographs, the majority printed by Weston for publication in *Westways* magazine; a small group of early portraits.

WESTON, PLOWDEN

SC —COLLEGE OF CHARLESTON LIBRARY, Special Collections Dept, Charleston, 29401.
Notes: Papers, 1764-1855, incl Plowden Weston's business ledger (1764-1769) and platation journal (1802-1820), and metrological records for Waccamaw (1829-1847). The ledger also contains the plantation accounts kept by his son Francis Weston, added at a later date.

WESTWARD MOVEMENT see Frontier and Pioneer Life

WETLANDS

ND —NORTHERN PRAIRIE WILDLIFE
RESEARCH CENTER, Library, PO Box
1747, Jamestown, 58401.
Holdings: Vols (2500) Cat Pix Slides
Budget: ($10,000)
Notes: Wildlife management and research,
incl avian biology, plant and animal ecology
as related to wetlands and prairies, waterfowl
research, and effects of predators on
waterfowl.

WETMORE, ALEXANDER

DC —SMITHSONIAN INSTITUTION,
Archives Div, Washington, 20560. William
W Moss, Archivist
Holdings: Cat Mss Pix
Notes: The Archives holds the official
records of Wetmore's tenure as sixth
secretary of the Smithsonian, 1944-1952, as
well as the bulk of his personal papers, dated
1898-1976, documenting his career in
ornithology.

WEYLER Y NICOLAU, VALERIANO, DUQUE DE RUBI

CT —UNIVERSITY OF CONNECTICUT,
Library, Storrs, 06268. R H Schimmelpfeng,
Dir of Special Collections
Holdings: // Uncat Mss
Notes: Manuscript material relating to
activities in the Philippines and Spain of
Valeriano Weyler y Nicolau, Duque de Rubi
("Butcher Weyler").

WEYMAN, STANLEY JOHN, 1855-1928

CA —UNIVERSITY OF CALIFORNIA, LOS
ANGELES, Research Library, Dept of
Special Collections, 405 Hilgard Ave, Los
Angeles, 90024. Edward Shreeves,
Chairman, Bibliographers Group; David S
Zeidberg, Head
Holdings: Vols 25 Mss
Notes: Incl 650 pieces of business and
personal correspondence, mss, etc.

WHALES AND WHALING

AK —ALASKA STATE LIBRARY, Alaska
Historical Library Collection, Pouch G,
Juneau, 99811. Phyllis Demuth, Readers
Services Librn
Notes: No special emphasis. Part of Alaska/
Arctic holdings.
CT —MYSTIC SEAPORT, MUSEUM, G W
Blunt White Library, Greenmanville Ave,
Mystic, 06355. Gerald E Morris, Librn
Holdings: Vols (40,000) Imprints
Microforms
Budget: ($100,000)
Notes: American maritime history. The
library is also a government depository for
maritime materials with a subscription to
184 line items. Incl 400,000 mss, 4000 maps
and charts, 30,000 ships' plans. Open to the
public.
CT —YALE UNIVERSITY, Box 1603A, Yale
Station, New Haven, 06520.
ME —MAINE MARITIME MUSEUM,
Library and Archives, 963 Washington St,
Bath, 04530. Nathan R Lipfert, Asst Cur
Holdings: Vols (5000) Cat Maps Pix Slides
Notes: The collection is limited primarily to
shipbuilding in Bath, Maine, and to a lesser
extent Maine as a whole. The unique aspects
of the collection are a large collection of
photographs of wooden shipbuilding and
related trades, photographs of the vessels
themselves, and a large collection of papers
of a shipbuilding company in Bath active
throughout the 19th century.
MA —BEDFORD FREE PUBLIC LIBRARY,
613 Pleasant St, Bedford, 02740. Paul A
Cyr, Cur of the Melville Room
Holdings: Vols 1020 Cat Mss Pix
Notes: One of the nation's most extensive
collections (72,000 pieces) on American

whaling. Incl all forms of documents used in
the industry, over 40,000 mss. Library has a
printed list of its logbooks and a seamen's
card file of men who sailed from New
Bedford Customs District contains 250,000
names. Library has published an addendum
to "Starbuck" and "Whaling Masters," and
"Birth of a Whaleship," 1964, both by
Reginald B Hegarty.
MA —HARVARD UNIVERSITY, Graduate
School of Business Administration, Baker
Library, Soldiers Field, Boston, 02163. Mary
V Chatfield, Librn; Florence Bartoshesky,
Cur of Manuscripts and Archives
Holdings: Cat Mss
Notes: New England whaling logbooks from
the 19th century.
MA —DUKES COUNTY HISTORICAL
SOCIETY, School & Cooke Sts, Edgartown,
02539. Thomas E Norton, Dir
Holdings: Cat Mss Maps Pix Audiotapes
Microforms
Notes: History and genealogy of
Massachusetts, especially Martha's
Vineyard. Also, materials on whaling and
Indians of the region.
MA —OLD DARTMOUTH HISTORICAL
SOCIETY, 18 Johnny Cake Hill, New
Bedford, 02740. Richard C Kugler, Dir
Holdings: Vols (15,000) Cat Mss Maps
Slides Phonorecords Audiotapes 16mm
Films Microforms
Budget: ($5000)
Notes: Whaling Museum Library contains
one of the most comprehensive collections of
printed and manuscript material ever
assembled on the history of the whaling
industry. Although primary emphasis is on
American participation in this industry,
foreign works are well-represented.
Particularly noteworthy are the 5000 rare
books and pamphlets assembled by the
distinguished whaling scholar, Charles F
Batchelder. Also, material on merchant ships
and the natural history of whales. Incl 750 ft
mss, 1070 log books, 650 maps, 25,000 pix,
and 1800 microforms.
MA —PEABODY MUSEUM OF SALEM,
Phillips Library, E India Sq, Salem, 01970.
Gregor Trinkaus-Randall, Librn
Holdings: Vols (100,000) Cat Mss Maps Pix
Notes: Maritime history of New England.
No published indexes; listed in Hamer's
Guide to Archives. . .
MA —KENDALL WHALING MUSEUM
LIBRARY, PO Box 297, 27 Everett St,
Sharon, 02067. Stuart M Frank, Dir
Holdings: Vols 5000 Cat Mss Maps Pix
Slides Phonorecords 16mm Films
Microforms
Notes: All languages. Mss are topically
indexed. No photocopying. Appointment
required in advance.
NV —FORESTA INSTITUTE FOR OCEAN
AND MOUNTAIN STUDIES, Library,
6205 Franktown Rd, Carson City, 89701.
Shannon Porter, Librn
Holdings: Vols 500 Cat Mss Maps Pix Slides
Notes: Collection incl historical and
contemporary accounts of Anarctic voyages;
special emphasis on ecology, plant and
animal life, fish, and whales. Also, about
1500 pamphlets, etc. Bibliography of whales
and whaling materials in library published in
1977.
NY —STATE UNIVERSITY OF NEW
YORK, Maritime College, Stephen B Luce
Library, Fort Schuyler, Bronx, 10465.
Richard H Corson, Librn
Holdings: Vols (68,000) Cat Maps Pix Slides
Phonorecords Audiotapes 16mm Films
Filmstrips
Budget: ($90,000)
Notes: Incl history of ships with special
emphasis on US Sailing ships of the 19th
century. Extensive holdings in periodical
literature with long and complete runs of
many titles. Approximately 3500 recent
research reports in paper and microfiche
format. Mainly English language.
NY —WHALING MUSEUM SOCIETY, Cold
Spring Harbor Whaling Museum, Main St,
Cold Spring Harbor, 11724. Robert D
Farwell, Dir
Holdings: Cat Mss Maps Pix
Notes: Library of bound and printed books

covers Cold Spring Harbor whaling industry,
in general, and maritime affairs. Archives
contain thousands of original documents
concerning whaling activities, the Cold
Spring Harbor Whaling Company, and the
extensive maritime coastal trade conducted
out of Cold Spring Harbor after the whaling
era (latter 1800s). Considerable material
deals with the Jones and Hewlett families,
important in both local commerce and Long
Island and New York affairs.
NY —AMERICAN MUSEUM OF
NATURAL HISTORY, Library Services
Dept, Central Park W & 79th St, New York,
10024. Nina J Root, Chairwoman; Mary
Genett, Asst Librn for Reference Services
RI —BROWN UNIVERSITY, John Hay
Library, 20 Prospect St, Providence, 02912.
Mark N Brown, Cur Mss
Holdings: Vols (1200) Cat Mss Pix
Notes: Morse Whaling Collection incl books,
monographs, pamphlets, mss, log books,
photographs, printed laws and statutes, blue
prints of whaling vessels, and serial
publications. Emphasis is on American
works of 19th and 20th centuries with some
works in Dutch, French, German and
Japanese dating from the 18th century.
Collection is strong in classics of whaling
literature, personal narratives, whaling town
histories, ships' registers, account books, and
photographs of whaling vessels and
processes; incl extensive files of the
Whaleman's Shipping List (New Bedford),
the Merchant's Transcript (New Bedford),
and the Friend (Honolulu).
RI —PROVIDENCE PUBLIC LIBRARY, 150
Empire St, Providence, 02903. Lance J
Bauer, Special Collections Librn
Holdings: Cat Mss Maps Pix Microforms
Notes: The Nicholson Whaling Collection is
one of the largest and certainly most
distinguished whaling collections in the
world, amassed in the early part of this
century and bequeathed to the Providence
Public Library in 1956. The logbooks,
journals and account books record over 1000
voyages from 1762-1922 and incl many
illustrated logs and a large number of
journals of whaling wives. These are
completely cataloged and microfilmed. Also
incl are 13 boxes of business
correspondence, bills of ladings, ships'
papers, crew records, etc, and over 300
printed books. Many of the printed books
are also quite rare, especially some first
editions of 19th century voyages such as of
the Essex. Contains material on Hawaiian
whaling and material printed in Hawaii.
Material must be used in-house.
Photocopying on a restricted basis only for
educational purposes when condition allows.
No complete photocopying of logbooks. The
microfilm of the mss is available for
interlibrary loans.
VA —MARINERS MUSEUM, Library,
Newport News, 23606. Ardie L Kelly, Librn
Holdings: Vols (60,000) Cat Mss Maps Pix
Slides
Notes: Incl collections of over 150,000
photographs of merchant ships, naval vessels,
sailing ships, lighthouses, portraits of naval
men, harbors, canals, etc, and maps, ships'
papers, and log books. Catalogs of various
parts of the collection published by G K
Hall, Boston.
†WA —WASHINGTON STATE
UNIVERSITY, Library, Manuscripts,
Archives & Special Collections, Pullman,
99164. John F Guido, Head
Holdings: Cat Mss Maps Pix
Notes: The manuscript collection incl
business and financial records of banks,
breweries, fisheries, insurance, land lumber
and livestock companies, trade and
commodity associations; as well as the
personal and professional papers of authors,
aviators, educators, engineers, farmers,
historians, pioneers, politicans and scientists;
especially rich in documents relating to the
exploration, settlement and development of
the Palouse Country, the Inland Empire, the
Columbia Basin and the Pacific Northwest.
Described in Selected Manuscript Resources
in the Washington State University Library
(Pullman, 1974); and other published and
unpublished inventories and registers.

WHALEY, WILLIAM EDINGS

SC —COLLEGE OF CHARLESTON
LIBRARY, Special Collections Dept,
Charleston, 29401.
Notes: Small-Whaley papers concern
Thomas Whaley of Edisto Island, South
Carolina and some of his descendants, circa
1750 to 1970.

WHARTON, EDITH

CT —YALE UNIVERSITY, Box 1603A, Yale
Station, New Haven, 06520.
Holdings: Cat Mss Pix
IN —INDIANA UNIVERSITY, Lilly Library,
Seventh St, Bloomington, 47405. William R
Cagle, Librn
Holdings: Cat Mss Pix
Notes: First editions, etc. Mss incl the
William Royall Tyler collection of Wharton
correspondence and mss.
NY —SAINT JOHN'S UNIVERSITY, Special
Collections Dept, Grand Central & Utopia
Pkwys, Jamaica, 11439. Szilvia E Szmuk,
Librn
Holdings: // Cat
Notes: No photocopying.
OH —OHIO STATE UNIVERSITY, William
Oxley Thompson Memorial Library, 1858
Neil Ave Mall, Columbus, 43210. Robert A
Tibbetts, Cur of Special Collections
Holdings: Vols 60 Cat
SC —UNIVERSITY OF SOUTH CAROLINA,
Thomas Cooper Library, Columbia, 29208.
Kenneth E Toombs, Dir of Libraries; Roger
Mortimer, Rare Book Librn
Holdings: Vols 125 Cat
Notes: A good collection of first and variant
editions.
VA —UNIVERSITY OF VIRGINIA,
Alderman Library, Clifton Waller Barrett
Collection, Charlottesville, 22901. Joan St C
Crane, Cur of American Literature
Collections
Notes: Papers.

WHARTON, JOSEPH, 1826-1909

PA —FRIENDS HISTORICAL LIBRARY OF
SWARTHMORE COLLEGE, Swarthmore,
19081. J William Frost, Dir
Holdings: Mss
Notes: Personal papers of Joseph Wharton,
Philadelphia Quaker merchant, industrialist
and educational philanthropist, who was
active in the manufacture of iron, zinc, and
nickel.

WHEAT FARMING

KS —HARVEY COUNTY HISTORICAL
SOCIETY, Historical Library & Museum,
203 Main St, Newton, 67114. Mike Smurr,
Dir
Holdings: Maps Pix
Notes: Our Library-Museum is limited to
literature, pictures and artifacts of interest to
the locality, Harvey County, KS. Newton
has been a railroad point since the Santa Fe
built here in 1871, so we have an unusually
good collection of railroad items. Hundreds
of pictures, many timetables, passes, and
items small enough to be housed in our
building. Attention is also given to early-day
agriculture in mid-Kansas, especially wheat-
raising by early settlers in central Kansas.

WHEATLEY, PHYLLIS

RI —BROWN UNIVERSITY, John Hay
Library, Harris Collection, Prospect St,
Providence, 02912. Rosemary L Cullen, Cur
Holdings: Vols (200,000) Cat Mss Pix
Phonorecords Microforms
Budget: ($15,000)
Notes: The Harris Collection of American
Poetry and Plays is principally composed of
American and Canadian poetry and plays,
17th century-date. Extensive holdings in
songsters, gift books and annuals, hymnals,
pageants, broadside verse, carriers'
addresses, women poets, juvenile poetry,
(incl Mother Goose and *The Night Before
Christmas*), sheet music with lyrics, small
press publications, fine printing, black poets,
"little magazines," Yiddish-American
literature. All movements or schools of
American poetry are represented. Incl first
editions of most American poets and
playwrights, notably Whitman, Poe, Wallace
Stevens, Eugene O'Neill, Edward Albee,
Ezra Pound, T S Eliot, William Carlos
Williams, Amy Lowell, Phyllis Wheatley,
Robert Frost, Allen Ginsberg, Bliss Carman,
and Stephen Foster sheet music. Also incl
the Saunders Walt Whitman Collection
(1300 vols); the LangdonCollection of
Pageants (250 vols); the Asa Cushman
Collection of plays in ms and prompt copies;
the MacDougall Collection of Psalters and
Hymnals; 4000 plays issued by Walter H
Baker Co, Boston (1890-1957); the Vaxer
Collection of Yiddish Poetry, Plays and
Music (1700 vols). Collections incl 200,000
vols, 30,000 broadsides, 55,000 mss, 170,000
pieces of sheet music, 450 phonorecords, and
375 microfilm reels. See *Dictionary Catalog
of the Harris Collection of American Poetry
and Plays* (Boston: G K Hall, 1972), 13 vols;
Supplement (1977), 3 vols. See also,
*American Poetry, 1609-1900, A Collection
on Microfilm, Segment I* (1609-1820);
Segment II (1821-1850); *Segment III* (1851-
1870) (Woodbridge, Conn: Research
Publications). Separate catalog.

WHEATON, HENRY, 1785-1848

RI —BROWN UNIVERSITY, John Hay
Library, 20 Prospect St, Providence, 02912.
Mark N Brown, Cur Mss
Holdings: // Mss
Notes: Papers of Henry Wheaton, Jurist, US
Charge d'Affaires to Denmark, and Minister
to Prussia. Brown Class of 1802. A
collection of 275 letters and mss for the
period 1786-1899, chiefly correspondence of
Henry Wheaton and his family in Europe
and America concerning personal,
diplomatic, legal, and political affairs,
especially during the War of 1812. Also
Wheaton's diaries, 1827-1835, and 1835
diary kept by his daughter, Abby, and
biographical notes about Wheaton and his
uncle, Dr Levi Wheaton, Professor of
Medicine at Brown.

WHEATON FEMALE SEMINARY

MA —WHEATON COLLEGE, Library,
Norton, 02766. Sherrie S Bergman, College
Librn
Holdings: Vols 960 // Cat
Notes: The Wheaton Seminary Library
Collection. The library of Wheaton Female
Seminary, as it existed in 1912.
MA —WHEATON COLLEGE, Library,
Norton, 02766. Sherrie S Bergman, College
Librn
Holdings: Vols 960 // Cat
Notes: The Wheaton Seminary Library
Collection. The library of Wheaton Female
Seminary, as it existed in 1912.

WHEELER, CHARLES B., JR.

MO —UNIVERSITY OF MISSOURI-
KANSAS CITY, General Library, State
Historical Society of Missouri Manuscripts,
5100 Rockhill Road, Kansas City, 64110.
Kenneth J LaBudde, Dir; Gordon
Hendrickson, Assoc Dir
Holdings: Mss
Notes: Western Historical Manuscript
Collection incl papers of Charles B Wheeler,
Jr, Charles N Kimball, Arthur Mag, Oscar D
Nelson, Lou B Holland, J C Nichols, Perry
Cookingham, Blevins Davis, Daniel
MacMorris, and the records of the Kansas
City Board of Trade.

WHEELER, EVERETT

NY —CITY UNIVERSITY OF NEW YORK,
City College, Morris R Cohen Library,
North Academic Center, Convent Ave &
137th St, New York, 10031. Barbara J
Dunlap, Archivist
Holdings: Cat Mss Pix
Notes: Incl personal papers.

WHEELER, GERVASE

ME —BOWDOIN COLLEGE, Library,
Brunswick, 04011. Dianne M Gutscher, Cur
of Special Collections
Holdings: Mss
Notes: The Chapel Papers, part of the
Bowdoin College Buildings Archive, contains
ca 30 letters and designs of Gervase
Wheeler, who provided designs for the
interior decoration of the College chapel.

WHEELER, JOHN

PA —AMERICAN PHILOSOPHICAL
SOCIETY, Library, 105 S Fifth St,
Philadelphia, 19106. Edward C Carter II,
Librn
Holdings: Mss
Notes: Research notebooks, 1946-1976 (16.5
linear ft).

WHEELER, JOSEPH L.

VT —VERMONT DEPARTMENT OF
LIBRARIES, Law & Documents Unit, 111
State St, Montpelier, 05602. Vivian Bryan,
Librn
Holdings: Vols 2500 Cat
Notes: Incl a large portion of the library of
the late Joseph L Wheeler, former head of
Enoch Pratt and for many years a busy
library consultant. This addition provided
the impetus to pull together all library
science materials, and they are now housed
in the Wheeler Memorial Room, open to the
public for research and circulation. This
represents the most complete collection of
this kind of information in northern New
England. Emphasis in on librarianship and
library science as they pertain to Vermont.
Extensive periodical runs (150 titles).

WHEELOCK, ELEAZAR

NH —DARTMOUTH COLLEGE, Baker
Memorial Library, Hanover, 03755.
Holdings: Cat Mss
Notes: Personal papers. Microfilm available.

WHEELOCK, JOHN HALL

CT —YALE UNIVERSITY, Box 1603A, Yale
Station, New Haven, 06520.
Holdings: Cat Mss
MO —WASHINGTON UNIVERSITY,
Libraries, Special Collections Dept, Campus
Box 1061, St Louis, 63130.
Notes: A small but significant collection.
NC —DUKE UNIVERSITY, William R
Perkins Library, Jay B Hubbell Center for
American Literary Historiography, Durham,
27706. Erma Whittington, Librn
Notes: 77,312 items, including manuscripts,
pictures, clippings, and correspondence. "The
objective of the Center is to gather the
papers and materials of significant scholars
and critics in American literary history." The
Center is a part of the Perkins Library
Manuscripts Department.

WHEELWRIGHT, JOHN BROOKS, 1897-1940

RI —BROWN UNIVERSITY, John Hay
Library, 20 Prospect St, Providence, 02912.
Mark N Brown, Cur Mss
Holdings: // Cat Mss
Notes: More than 3000 pieces of
correspondence of John Brooks
Wheelwright, American poet and socialist,
dealing with political, social, literary, and
personal matters in 45 ms boxes and 3
scrapbooks for the period 1915-1940. Incl
architectural notes; literary mss incl a diary,
unpublished verse, reviews, early drafts of
books, and notes for *A Novel about Ideas;*
and several hundred mss dealing with
socialist theory, ethics and practice, and
politics related to his association with the
Socialist Workers Party.

WHIDDINGTON, H. M. (fl. 1906-1920)

AB —UNIVERSITY OF CALGARY,
Libraries, Special Collections Div, 2500

WHIDDINGTON, H. M. (fl. 1906-1920) (cont.)

University Dr, Calgary, T2N 1N4, Can.
Holdings: Cat // Pix
Notes: Architectural drawings (136), mostly undated, of Alberta architect H M Whiddington, also W A Whiddington, and Whiddington & Fry, of Lethbridge. Projects include churches, schools, stores, banks, etc. An inventory is on hand.

WHIPPLE, GEORGE H.

NY —UNIVERSITY OF ROCHESTER, School of Medicine and Dentistry, Edward G Miner Library, 601 Elmwood Ave, Rochester, 14642. Lucretia McClure, Medical Librn; Janet Brady Berk, History of Medicine Librn
Holdings: Mss Pix Audiotapes Films
Notes: Manuscripts, scrapbooks, tapes and films illustrating the life and work of the Nobel Laureate.

WHIRLWIND COMPUTER

MA —MASSACHUSETTS INSTITUTE OF TECHNOLOGY, Institute Archives, Special Collections, Cambridge, 02139.
Notes: The materials in the Magnetic Core Memory collection assembled in support of MIT during the patent litigation over the magnetic core memory. Invented in 1947 by Jay Forrester during the development of the Whirlwind Computer, magnetic core memory set the stage for the development of high-speed digital computers. Though Whirlwind was originally begun as an aircraft simulator project during World War II, the computer which resulted became the prototype for most large scale general purpose computers. The collection dates mostly from the 1940s and 1950s.

WHISKEY INSURRECTION, 1794

DE —UNIVERSITY OF DELAWARE, Hugh M Morris Library, S College Ave, Newark, 19711. T Stuart Dick, Special Collections
Holdings: // Mss
Notes: Correspondence (1782-1832) relating to all phases of David Lenox's career subsequent to the Revolution, ie, land speculation, duties in the Whiskey Rebellion, executorship of the estate of John Lukens, his banking career, household receipts and settlement of his estate. Photocopying may be arranged.
PA —WASHINGTON AND JEFFERSON COLLEGE, Library, Washington, 15301. Robert E Connell, Librn
Holdings: Vols 2100 Cat Mss Maps Pix
Notes: A general subject and author card catalog has been prepared for the ms collection. Published description of the collection appears in: Pennsylvania, Historical and Museum Commission, *Historical Manuscript Depositories in Pennsylvania* (Harrisburg, 1965), compiled by Irwin Richman. Incl materials concerning the "Westward movement"-- letters, land grants, etc. Much on the Revolutionary War, the "Whiskey Rebellion" of 1794. Many other small collections of mss, some containing American Indian and Western Pennsylvania history.

WHISTLER, JAMES ABBOTT MCNEILL, 1834-1903

CA —UNIVERSITY OF SAN FRANCISCO, Richard A Gleeson Library, The Countess Bernardine Murphy Donohue Rare Book Room, San Francisco, 94117. D Steven Corey, Special Collections Librn
Holdings: Vols 55
Notes: Comprehensive collection of his books, particularly editions of the *Ten O'Clock*, catalogues of exhibits of his work.
DC —LIBRARY OF CONGRESS, Manuscript Division, Washington, 20540. John C Broderick, Chief
Notes: The Joseph and Elizabeth Robbins Pennell Collection of Whistleriana contains graphic art and papers of Whistler, and photographs, publications, and research materials relating to his life.
FL —UNIVERSITY OF MIAMI, Otto G Richter Library, PO Box 248214, Coral Gables, 33124. Frank Rodgers, Dir of Libraries
Holdings: Vols 200 Cat Mss Microforms
Notes: Critical works, exhibition catalogs, microfilm copies from substantial ms collections.
MA —BRANDEIS UNIVERSITY, Goldfarb Library, 415 South St, Waltham, 02154. Bessie Hahn, Dir
Notes: James M Whistler Collection. 3 linear ft of correspondence to and from James McNeill Whistler, as well as newspaper clippings and other ephemera. A finding list to the collection can be found in Special Collections.

WHISTLER, REX, 1905-1944

CA —UNIVERSITY OF CALIFORNIA, LOS ANGELES, Research Library, Dept of Special Collections, 405 Hilgard Ave, Los Angeles, 90024. Edward Shreeves, Chairman, Bibliographers Group; David S Zeidberg, Head
Notes: Incl 9 unpublished illustrations for *Perronik the Fool* (1926), with an extract from Whistler's diary and a letter from Moore discussing the project.

WHITE, ANDREW DICKSON, 1832-1918

MD —JOHNS HOPKINS UNIVERSITY, Milton S Eisenhower Library, Charles & 34 Sts, Baltimore, 21218. Ann S Gwyn, Assistant Dir for Special Collections
Holdings: Cat Mss
Notes: 347 letters; cataloged in manuscript room.
NY —CORNELL UNIVERSITY LIBRARIES, Collection of Regional History, Dept of Manuscripts and Univ Archives, Ithaca, 14853.
Notes: Historian, diplomat, President of Cornell University. Incl papers, 1850-(1879-1918); letters and microfilms of personal and professional correspondence.

WHITE, ANTHONY WALTON, 1750-1803

NJ —RUTGERS, THE STATE UNIVERSITY OF NEW JERSEY, Alexander Library, Special Collections and Archives, College Ave & Huntington St, New Brunswick, 08903. Ronald L Becker, Cur of Manuscripts and Rare Books
Holdings: Mss
Notes: Papers, etc.

WHITE, E. B.

NE —UNIVERSITY OF NEBRASKA-LINCOLN, Don L Love Library, University Archives and Special Collections, Lincoln, 68588. Joseph G Svoboda, University Archivist
Notes: Virginia Faulkner was recognized as one of Nebraska's most distinguished writers and scholars. The Virginia Faulkner Collection, containing over 2000 titles, is housed in the Special Collections Department of Love Library. It is especially strong in twentieth century writers and in University of Nebraska Press publications. Of especial value to scholars are her extensive holdings of Willa Cather, Wright Morris, and John Neihardt. Her correspondence with S N Behrman, E B White, Edward Wagenknecht, Donald Sutherland, Wright Morris, Louise Pound, Mari Sandoz, Hazel Barnes, Alfred A and Blanche Knopf, and others provide insight into the literary development of these figures, as well as chronicle the intellectual thought of the period. Amassed in a separate file, these letters are available to interested scholars.
NY —CORNELL UNIVERSITY LIBRARIES, John M Olin Library, Dept of Rare Books, Ithaca, 14853. Donald D Eddy, Librn
Holdings: Vols 2350 Cat Mss Pix

WHITE, EDWARD LUCAS

MD —JOHNS HOPKINS UNIVERSITY, Milton S Eisenhower Library, Charles & 34 Sts, Baltimore, 21218. Ann S Gwyn, Assistant Dir for Special Collections
Holdings: Vols Uncat Mss
Notes: 38 linear feet of letters and mss of prose and poetry, published and unpublished.

WHITE, ELLEN G.

CA —PACIFIC UNION COLLEGE, Nelson Memorial Library, Angwin, 94508. Taylor D Ruhl, Dir

WHITE, EMMA EDMUNDS

VA —RANDOLPH-MACON WOMAN'S COLLEGE, Lipscomb Library, Lynchburg, 24503. Frances White, Ref Librn
Notes: Life-long correspondence from Pearl S Buck to Randolph-Macon Woman's College class mate Emma Edmunds White.

WHITE, GEORGE LEONARD

NY —CORNELL UNIVERSITY LIBRARIES, Collection of Regional History, Dept of Manuscripts and Univ Archives, Ithaca, 14853.
Notes: One letter, dated July 8, 1891, to Miss Rhoda E Mead of Waterbury, CT.
OH —OHIO HISTORICAL SOCIETY, Archives Library Division, 1982 Velma Ave, Columbus, 43211. Dennis East, Division Chief
Notes: Papers of the governor, 1931-1935.

WHITE, GILBERT

MA —HARVARD UNIVERSITY LIBRARY, Houghton Library, Cambridge, 02138. Rodney G Dennis, Cur of Manuscripts
Holdings: Cat Mss

WHITE, HARRY DEXTER, 1892-1948

NJ —PRINCETON UNIVERSITY, Library, Manuscript Collection, Nassau St, Princeton, 08540. Jean F Preston, Cur
Holdings: // Cat Mss
Notes: Incl 13 boxes; 2 ring binders of papers. An unpublished typescript guide (14 p) is available in the Library.

WHITE, IGNATIUS, MARQUIS D'ALBEVILLE

IN —INDIANA UNIVERSITY, Lilly Library, Seventh St, Bloomington, 47405. William R Cagle, Librn
Holdings: Vols (570) // Cat Mss
Notes: Incl contemporary printings of government publications. Mss incl papers of Ignatius White, Marquis d'Albeville. 1653-1690, 335 items.

WHITE, LEE

†MA —JOHN F KENNEDY LIBRARY, Columbia Point, Boston, 02125. Dan H Fenn Jr, Dir
Holdings: Cat Mss
Notes: Papers of JFK and White House aides Lee White and Harris Wofford and RFK and Justice Department aide Burke Marshall, dealing with civil rights, 1961-1964. 42 linear ft of mss. Holdings are described in "Historical Materials in the John F Kennedy Library." Copies may be obtained by writing the Research Archivist.

WHITE, LESLIE TURNER

MA —BOSTON UNIVERSITY, Mugar Memorial Library, Special Collections Dept, 771 Commonwealth Ave, Boston, 02215. Howard B Gotlieb, Dir
Holdings: // Cat Mss Pix
Notes: Mss, correspondence, etc collected in depth; incl publications by or about.

WHITE, NED

OH —OHIO STATE UNIVERSITY, Library
for Communication and Graphic Arts, 242
W 18th St, Columbus, 43210. Lucy S
Caswell, Curator
Notes: Original cartoons by Winsor McCay,
John T McCutcheon, Dick Moores, Ned
White, Walter Berndt, Jim Larrick, Carl
Rose and Bill Crawford.

WHITE, PAUL DUDLEY, M.D.

†NY —NEW YORK ACADEMY OF
MEDICINE, Library, 2 E 103 ST, New
York, 10029.
Notes: Papers of Walter Timme, MD (1874-
1956). Timme was a pioneer endocrinologist;
described pluriglandular disease, "Timme's
Syndrome." Incl correspondence from
Harvey Cushing, Paul Dudley White,
Charles A Elsberg, Louis I Dublin, Ely
Smith Jelliffe, John F Fulton, Edna St
Vincent Millay, Eva Le Gallienne, and
Irving Ramsey Wiles.

WHITE, RICHARD GRANT AND STANFORD

NY —NEW YORK HISTORICAL SOCIETY,
Library, 170 Central Park W, New York,
10024. James Gregory, Librn
Holdings: Mss
Notes: 4 linear ft of correspondence and
papers, 1842-1920, of Richard Grant White
(author) and of his son, Stanford White
(architect). Incl in the papers are literary
mss, ms music, 26 letters from James Russell
Lowell and 11 letters from Thomas Bailey
Aldrich.

WHITE, RICHARDSON

†MA —JOHN F KENNEDY LIBRARY,
Columbia Point, Boston, 02125. Dan H Fenn
Jr, Dir
Holdings: // Cat Mss
Notes: Background papers of Richardson
White for his study "Youth and Opportunity;
The Federal Anti-Delinquency Program" and
Daniel Knapp's papers relating to the
President's Commission on Juvenile
Delinquency, late 1950s-late 1960s. 21 linear
ft of mss . Holdings are described in
"Historical Materials in the John F Kennedy
Library." Copies may be obtained by writing
the Research Archivist.

WHITE, STANFORD see White, Richard Grant and Stanford

WHITE, THEODORE

†MA —JOHN F KENNEDY LIBRARY,
Columbia Point, Boston, 02125. Dan H Fenn
Jr, Dir
Holdings: // Cat Mss
Notes: Draft mss of the writings of Theodore
White, especially *The Making of the
President, 1960, 1964* and *1968.* 12 linear ft
of mss. Holdings are described in "Historical
Materials in the John F Kennedy Library."
Copies may be obtained by writing the
Research Archivist.

WHITE, WALTER

TX —NORTH TEXAS STATE UNIVERSITY,
Archives, NT Station Box 5188, Denton,
76203. Robert LaForte, University Archivist
Notes: The NTSU Archives houses the
patron's copy of oral history interviews that
are part of the Oral History Collection, an
independent project not part of the Archives.
This collection of interviews covers, in part,
the following subject areas: World War II
Pearl Harbor survivors, World War II
prisoners of war, Texas legislators, ex-
governors of Texas, Texans employed by the
administrations of FDR, Texas businessmen
and businesswomen, development of the
Coastal Bend area of south Texas, and
Mexican-American social action activities.
Cataloged. Transcriptions available. See *Oral*

*History Collection, North Texas State
University Bulletin*, April 1981.

WHITE, WILLIAM ALLEN

KS —BUTLER COUNTY HISTORICAL
SOCIETY, 383 E Central, El Dorado,
67042.
Holdings: Vols 300
Notes: Books by and owned by William
Allen White, Emporia newspaperman.
KS —EMPORIA STATE UNIVERSITY,
William Allen White Library, Emporia,
66801. Mary E Bogan, Special Collections
Librn
Holdings: Vols (277)// Mss Pix
Phonorecords Audiotapes
Notes: The William Allen White Collection
contains letters and telegrams exchanged
between Mr White and such national figures
as Herbert Hoover, Calvin Coolidge,
Theodore Roosevelt, Franklin D Roosevelt,
William Dean Howells, William Howard
Taft, Robert Taft, and many others. The text
of approximately 835 articles appearing in
the nation's leading magazines written by
and about Mr White are preserved in the
collection as well as hundreds of newspaper
editorials, stories, and features by and about
him. The manuscripts of 20 of Mr White's
published books and one of his unpublished
works are housed here. The manuscripts of
many speeches, editorials, poems, songs (by
others), and part of his personal diary,
written during his college years, are
included. Therealia section of the collection
includes original illustrations from the White
books, scrapbooks, and materials from
worldwide travels. The collection's
photograph section contains numerous
photos of Mr White and his family and the
many national figures with whom he
associated and corresponded. In
commemoration of the 1968 centennial
anniversary of Mr White's birth, Emporia
State University published a two volume
annotated and illustrated bibliography of
William Allen White materials in the
collection. Copies of the bibliography may be
purchased from the William Allen White
Library. *A Bibliography of William Allen
White* prepared by Kansas State Teachers
College from the William Allen White
Collection, William Allen White Library
(Emporia: Teachers College Press, 1969).

WHITE, WILLIAM ANTHONY PARKER (TONY BOUCHER)

IN —INDIANA UNIVERSITY, Lilly Library,
Seventh St, Bloomington, 47405. William R
Cagle, Librn
Holdings: Cat Mss
Notes: Correspondence, writings and
memorabilia, 1932-1969, of critic and author
W A P White, known as Tony Boucher,
1911-1968. Includes correspondence with
many prominent mystery and fantastic
fiction authors and numerous radio scripts
for mystery shows.

WHITE, WILLIAM COMINGS

NY —UNION COLLEGE, Schaffer Library,
Archives of Science and Technology,
Schenectady, 12308. Ellen Fladger, Archivist
Notes: Papers etc.

WHITE, WILLIAM JOHN, 1886-1934

BC —UNIVERSITY OF VICTORIA,
McPherson Library, Victoria, V8W 3H5,
Can.
Notes: Barrister. Incl 70 leaves; privately
leatherbound vol containing 13 articles and
addresses on 70 typed carbon leaves.

WHITE ANTS see Termites

WHITE HOUSE CONFERENCES

CA —HOOVER INSTITUTION ON WAR,
REVOLUTION & PEACE, Stanford
University, Stanford, 94305. Milorad M
Drachkovitch, Archivist
Holdings: Mss
Notes: Records of the White House

Conference on Child Health and Protection,
established in 1930 by President Herbert
Hoover to investigate child welfare in the
US, incl correspondence, reports,
memoranda, expense statements and
pamphlets, 1909-1950, relating to the
physical and social conditions of children in
the US, the status of school health education
and health service programs, and proposals
for the promotion of child welfare. Incl
reports of the American Child Welfare
Association. 143 ms boxes. 5 posters.

WHITE MOUNTAINS, NEW HAMPSHIRE

MA —APPALACHIAN MOUNTAIN CLUB,
5 Joy St, Boston, 02108. Fran Belcher, Librn
Holdings: Vols (6500) Cat Maps Pix Slides
Budget: ($1000)
Notes: Mountaineering, espec the White
Mountains.
NH —DARTMOUTH COLLEGE, Baker
Memorial Library, Hanover, 03755.
Holdings: Cat Mss Maps Pix Slides
Notes: Strong collection of books, mss,
pictures, etc. Microfilm of "Among the
Clouds" available.

WHITE RIVER BADLANDS

†SD —SOUTH DAKOTA SCHOOL OF
MINES & TECHNOLOGY, Devereaux
Library, Rapid City, 57701.
Holdings: Vols (166,200) Cat Mss Maps Pix
Microforms
Notes: Emphasis on the White River
Badlands. The Museum has an extensive
collection of reprint materials in this specific
area (which is supportive of, and
complementary to, the resources of the
Library).

WHITE RIVER SHEEP COMPANY

AZ —NORTHERN ARIZONA
UNIVERSITY, Special Collection Library,
CU Box 6022, Flagstaff, 86011. Peter M
Whiteley, Coordr/Archivist; William
Mullane, Librn
Notes: Account journal, 1916-1934, Ariz, of
the White River Sheep Company. This
company appears to have been connected
with T E Pollock, Flagstaff, Ariz.

WHITE RUSSIA—HISTORY

CA —HOOVER INSTITUTION ON WAR,
REVOLUTION & PEACE, Stanford
University, Stanford, 94305. Milorad M
Drachkovitch, Archivist
Holdings: // Mss
Notes: Two collections: (1) Papers, 1919-
1920, of Nikolai Nikolaevich Yudenich,
commander of White Russian military forces
in Northwest Russia. Correspondence, battle
orders, memoranda and reports relating to
the anit-Bolshevik activities of the White
Russian forces in Northwest Russia. Papers
chiefly in Russian, also some in English,
French, German, Estonian, and Finnish. 8 ft.
(2) Papers, 1917-1923, of Vasilii Alekseevich
Maklakov, ambassador to France, appointed
by the Russian Political Conference, Paris
1919. Diplomatic correspondence, reports,
memoranda and notes relating to the
activities of White Russian groups before the
Paris Peace Conference and to events and
conditions during the period of civil war in
Russia. The records are from the Russian
embassy archives in Paris. 9 ft.
IL —UNIVERSITY OF ILLINOIS,
URBANA/CHAMPAIGN, Slavic and East
European Library, Urbana, 61801. Marianna
Tax Choldin, Head
Holdings: Vols (420,000) Cat
Notes: One of the largest Slavic and East
European collections. Strong in Russian and
Soviet materials-humanities, sciences, and
social sciences; languages and literatures;
periodicals, newspapers, and microforms. Ca
260,000 volumes in languages of the Soviet
Union plus 20,000 Russian and Ukrainian
titles on microform. Extensive coverage of
Czechoslovakia (35,000 vols); Yugoslavia

WHITE RUSSIA—HISTORY (cont.)

(31,000 vols); Bulgaria (9200 vols); Poland (34,600 vols); Romania (13,000 vols); and Hungary (18,000 vols) and the languages, literatures, and history of these countries.

NY —NEW YORK PUBLIC LIBRARY, Slavonic Div, Fifth Ave & 42 St, New York, 10018. Edward Kasinec, Chief
Holdings: Vols 2200 Cat Microforms
Notes: Subject strength is in literature, incl the literature of the early 20th century. Linguistics and folklore are also well represented. The collection of early White Russian newspapers is quite strong. See New York Public Library, *Dictionary Catalog of the Slavonic Collection* (Boston: G K hall, 1974), 44 vols.

WHITE RUSSIAN LANGUAGE AND LITERATURE

NY —NEW YORK PUBLIC LIBRARY, Slavonic Div, Fifth Ave & 42 St, New York, 10018. Edward Kasinec, Chief
Holdings: Vols 2200 Cat Microforms
Notes: Subject strength is in literature, incl the literature of the early 20th century. Linguistics and folklore are also well represented. The collection of early White Russian newspapers is quite strong. See New York Public Library, *Dictionary Catalog of the Slavonic Collection* (Boston: G K Hall, 1974), 44 vols.

WHITE RUSSIAN NEWSPAPERS see Newspapers, White Russian

WHITE RUSSIANS IN THE U.S.

NY —NEW YORK PUBLIC LIBRARY, Slavonic Div, Fifth Ave & 42 St, New York, 10018. Edward Kasinec, Chief
Holdings: Cat Microforms
Notes: See: New York Public Library, Slavonic Div, *Dictionary Catalog of the Slavonic Collection*, 2nd ed, rev and enl (Boston: G K Hall, 1974), 44 vols; and New York Public Library, *Dictionary Catalog of the Research Libraries* (New York, 1972-).

WHITE SLAVE TRAFFIC see Prostitution

WHITE STUDIO

NY —NEW YORK PUBLIC LIBRARY, Performing Arts Research Center, Billy Rose Theatre Collection, 111 Amsterdam Ave, New York, 10023. Dorothy L Swerdlove, Cur
Holdings: Cat Pix
Notes: Photo collection.

WHITEAKER, JOHN

OR —LANE COUNTY MUSEUM, Library, 740 W 13 Ave, Eugene, 94701. Margret West, Cur of Special Collections
Holdings: Vols 250 Cat Mss Maps Pix Slides Audiotapes 16mm Films Microforms
Budget: $2000
Notes: Emphasis on Oregon and Lane County history. Collection of 10,000 photographs of Lane County; Kennell-Ellis photographers, 3500 commercial photographs of Eugene area, 1927-42. Also papers of John Whiteaker 1858-1944.

WHITEHEAD, ALFRED NORTH

†IL —SOUTHERN ILLINOIS UNIVERSITY, CARBONDALE, Library, Special Collections Dept, Carbondale, 62901.
Notes: Archives of the Library of Living Philosophers, a publishing project founded by Paul Arthur Schilpp in 1938 to provide a forum for contemporary philosophers to reply to their critics. Incl correspondence from John Dewey, George Santayana, Alfred North Whitehead, G E Moore, and Albert Einstein.

WHITEMAN, PAUL

MA —WILLIAMS COLLEGE, Sawyer Library, Williamstown, 01267. Phyllis L

Cutler, Dir
Holdings: Vols 4100 Cat Mss Pix
Notes: Incl recordings, memorabilia, etc.

WHITFORD, A. E.

NY —AMERICAN INSTITUTE OF PHYSICS, Center for the History of Physics, Niels Bohr Library, 335 E 45 St, New York, 10017. John Aubry, Librn
Notes: The Sources for History of Modern Astrophysics documents the history of 20th-century astrophysics. Incl some 400 hours of oral history interviews with astronomers, such as Bart Bok, S Chandrasekhar, Martin Schwarzschild, and A E Whitford. The project also organized and cataloged the papers of Henry Norris Russell, Frank Schlesinger, Otto Struve, Ejnar Hertzsprung, Harlow Shapley, Charles Young, Robert Atkinson, Seth Chandler, Theodore Dunham, Jr, and G C McVittie.

WHITING, SARAH FRANCES

MA —WELLESLEY COLLEGE, Margaret Clapp Library, College Archives, Wellesley, 02181.
Notes: Records of the Department of Astronomy of Wellesley College (1882-1955), 3 linear feet; also papers of Sarah Frances Whiting.

WHITLOCK, BRAND, 1869-1934

CA —HOOVER INSTITUTION ON WAR, REVOLUTION & PEACE, Stanford University, Stanford, 94305. Milorad M Drachkovitch, Archivist
Holdings: Mss Pix
Notes: Papers of Brand Whitlock, author and US Ambassador to Belguim, 1913-22, incl writings, diaries, printed matter and photographs, 1913-34, relating to US-Belgian relations during World War I, work of the Commission for Relief in Belgium, and fictional writings of Brand Whitlock. 7 ms boxes, 1 oversize folder.

WHITMAN, BERT

OH —OHIO STATE UNIVERSITY, Library for Communication and Graphic Arts, 242 W 18th St, Columbus, 43210. Lucy S Caswell, Curator
Notes: The original works of editorial cartoonists Art Poinier, Scott Willis, Brian Basset, Billy Ireland, Frank Williams, Charles Werner, Ned Beard, L D Warren, Edward D Kuekes, Ray Osrin, Mike Peters, Draper Hill, Eugene Craig and Bert Whitman.

WHITMAN, MARCUS

†WA —WASHINGTON STATE UNIVERSITY, Library, Manuscripts, Archives & Special Collections, Pullman, 99164. John F Guido, Head
Holdings: Vols Cat Mss Maps Pix Microforms
Notes: Ms resources of the study of Pacific Northwest Indians incl the papers of historians William Compton Brown, Carl Parcher Russell, and Lucullus Virgil McWhorter; and missionaries Henry Harmon Spalding, Elkanah Walker and Marcus Whitman. A few of these resources have been described in the following publications: *William Compton Brown: A Calendar of His Papers in the Washington State University Library* (Pullman, 1966); *Carl Parcher Russell: An Indexed Register of His Scholarly and Professional Papers, 1920-1967, in the Washington State University Library* (Pullman, 1970); *The Papers of Lucullus Virgil McWhorter*, compiled by Nelson A Ault (Pullman, 1959).

WHITMAN, SARAH HELEN, 1803-1898

IN —INDIANA UNIVERSITY, Lilly Library, Seventh St, Bloomington, 47405. William R Cagle, Librn
Holdings: Mss Pix
Notes: Correspondence of Sarah Helen

Whitman concerning her friendship with Poe, 1846-1878. 311 items.

RI —BROWN UNIVERSITY, John Hay Library, 20 Prospect St, Providence, 02912. Mark N Brown, Cur Mss
Holdings: // Mss
Notes: Sarah Helen Whitman, 1803-1898, an American poet and friend of Edgar Allan Poe. A group of about 500 mss for the period 1835-1922, chiefly correspondence, notes, and articles by Mrs Whitman. Subjects include: Poe, English and American literature, spiritualism, and personal matters. Also incl correspondence and copies of letters, mss, and reminiscences of Mrs Whitman gathered by her literary heirs; letters to and from James Albert Harrison (1848-1911) regarding his books on Poe; and letters from Maria Clemm Poe to Mrs Whitman about Poe.

WHITMAN, WALT, 1819-1892

CT —YALE UNIVERSITY, Box 1603A, Yale Station, New Haven, 06520.
Holdings: Cat Mss Pix

DC —LIBRARY OF CONGRESS, Rare Book & Special Collections Div, Washington, 20540. William Matheson, Chief
Holdings: Vols 480 Cat Mss Pix
Notes: The Carolyn Wells Houghton Collection, noted for both its extent and the rarity of a number of its items; incl nearly 100 copies of *Leaves of Grass*, many presentation and association copies, a number of mss, letters, photographs and other memorabilia. Other Whitman items, such as a presentation copy of the rare second edition of *Leaves* to Thoreau and one of the four known copies of his first work *(Franklin Evans)* in paper covers, are found in the Charles E Feinberg Collection of more than 1300 of Whitman's mss, nearly 1200 of his letters, notes and memoranda, over 1700 letters addressed to him, 125 vols from the poet's library, first editions of Whitman's books, revised editions, association copies, and some 3000 books about him. The ms portions of theFeinberg Collection are in the custody of the Manuscript Division.

†DC —LIBRARY OF CONGRESS, Manuscript Division, Washington, 20540.
Notes: The Horace and Anne Montgomerie Traubel Papers. Horace Traubel was Walt Whitman's friend and disciple, and one of his three literary executors.

FL —ROLLINS COLLEGE, Mills Memorial Library, Winter Park, 32789. Patricia J Delks, Dir of Libraries
Holdings: Vols 1000 Cat Mss
Notes: Incl letters. Noncirculating.

GA —OGLETHORPE UNIVERSITY, Library, 4484 Peachtree RD, NE, Atlanta, 30319. Thomas W Chandler, Librn
Holdings: Vols 300 Cat Pix Recordings
Notes: Collection contains contemporary and later editions of his writings, incl several original editions of *Leaves of Grass*; also critical and biographical materials, special editions.

IL —SOUTHERN ILLINOIS UNIVERSITY, CARBONDALE, Delyte W Morris Library, Special Collections Dept, Carbondale, 62901. David V Koch, Cur of Special Collections; Louisa Bowen, Cur of Manuscripts
Holdings: Vols 175 Cat
Notes: A collection of most of the contemporary editions of *Leaves of Grass* incl the first; plate proofs with autograph corrections of *Passage to India, Specimen Days* and *Leaves of Grass*. Also about 275 pieces of ephemera.

IL —NORTHERN ILLINOIS UNIVERSITY, Founders Memorial Library, Rare Books and Special Collections Dept, De Kalb, 60115. William R DuBois, Dept Head
Holdings: Vols 200 Cat Pix
Notes: Noncirculating.

IL —NORTHWESTERN UNIVERSITY, Library, Special Collections Dept, 1937 Sheridan Rd, Evanston, 60201. R Russell Maylone, Cur
Holdings: Vols 228 Cat Mss Pix
Notes: First editions of Walt Whitman with serials and a small group of secondary materials. Additional material in general collection.

WHITMAN, WALT, 1819-1892 (cont.)

KS —UNIVERSITY OF KANSAS, Kenneth Spencer Research Library, Special Collections Dept, Lawrence, 66045. Alexandra Mason, Librn
Holdings: Cat Mss
Notes: Whitman, Mencken, Mark Twain, nonacademic poetry after 1960, science fiction, miscellaneous 19th and 20th century authors, 19th and 20th century children's literature. Noncirculating.

MD —JOHNS HOPKINS UNIVERSITY, Milton S Eisenhower Library, Charles & 34 Sts, Baltimore, 21218. Ann S Gwyn, Assistant Dir for Special Collections
Holdings: Vols Cat Mss Microforms
Notes: The Osler Collection (Tudor and Stuart Club) contains original editions of Shelley, Milton, Keats, Donne, Defoe, Thomas Fuller, Golden Book of Marcus Aurelius (1559). A collection of his articles made by Walt Whitman. 17th and 18th century commonplace books in English and French, in ms. Most English translations of Jakob Boehme. Cards in main catalog. Also, not included in the above figure, Pollard and Redgrave's, and Wing's Early English Books on microfilm.

MA —AMHERST COLLEGE, Library, Amherst, 01002. John Lancaster, Special Collections Librn
Holdings: Vols 100 Cat Mss Pix

MA —BOSTON UNIVERSITY, Mugar Memorial Library, Special Collections Dept, 771 Commonwealth Ave, Boston, 02215. Howard B Gotlieb, Dir
Holdings: Cat Mss Pix
Notes: Incl the Alice & Rollo Silver Collection of books, letters, pictures, etc. Extensive research collection.

MA —MOUNT HOLYOKE COLLEGE, Williston Memorial Library, South Hadley, 01075. Anne C Edmonds, Librn
Holdings: Vols 71 Cat
Notes: Small collection of books by and about him; incl some miscellaneous periodical articles and reviews.

MA —BRANDEIS UNIVERSITY, Goldfarb Library, 415 South St, Waltham, 02154. Bessie Hahn, Dir
Notes: 21 linear ft of books by and about Walt Whitman. Access to the collection is through the Main Card Catalog and the Special Collections Catalog.

†MA —WILLIAMS COLLEGE, Chapin Library of Rare Books, PO Box 426, Williamstown, 01267. Robert L Volz, Custodian
Holdings: Vols 650 Cat
Notes: No material available on interlibrary loan.

MI —UNIVERSITY OF MICHIGAN, Library, Dept of Rare Books & Special Collections, Ann Arbor, 48109. Robert J Starring, Head
Holdings: Vols 140 Cat
Notes: Includes many first editions.

NJ —RUTGERS, THE STATE UNIVERSITY OF NEW JERSEY, Alexander Library, Special Collections and Archives, College Ave & Huntington St, New Brunswick, 08903. Ronald L Becker, Cur of Manuscripts and Rare Books
Holdings: Mss
Notes: Papers, etc.

NY —BROOKLYN PUBLIC LIBRARY, Literature, Languages, Fiction Collection, Grand Army Plaza, Brooklyn, 11238. Monte Olenick, Dept Chief
Holdings: Vols 400 Cat Mss
Notes: Walt Whitman Collection: books by and about Whitman, incl some rare items, among them a first edition of Leaves of Grass.

NY —HEMPSTEAD PUBLIC LIBRARY, 115 Nichols Court, Hempstead, 11550. Irene A Duszkiewicz, Dir
Holdings: Vols 275 Cat Mss Pix
Notes: Walt Whitman Collection. New and out-of-print materials added as they become available. Incl editions of Whitman's work as well as critical and biographical materials. A bibliography of this collection has been compiled as a master's thesis.

NY —NEW YORK PUBLIC LIBRARY, Rare Books and Manuscripts Div, Fifth Ave & 42 St, New York, 10018. William L Joyce, Asst Dir; Francis O Mattson, Curator
Holdings: Cat
Budget: ($7161)
Notes: Literary first editions. Incl notable collections of Shakespeare, Milton, Walton, Bunyan and Whitman (The Oscar Lion Collection).

NY —YESHIVA UNIVERSITY, Library, 500 West 185th Street, New York, 10033. Pearl Berger
Holdings: Cat

NY —SYRACUSE UNIVERSITY LIBRARIES, Ernest S Bird Library, George Arents Research Library for Special Collections, Syracuse, 13210. Carolyn A Davis, Manuscripts Librn; Amy S Doherty, University Archivist; Mark F Weimer, Rare Book Librn
Holdings: Vols 450 Cat
Notes: First and variant editions; large collection of books, etc about the poet.

NC —WESTERN CAROLINA UNIVERSITY, Hunter Memorial Library, Cullowhee, 28723. James B Lloyd, Cur
Notes: Correspondence, photographs, and clippings relating to Walt Whitman (1819-92) and his family.

NC —DUKE UNIVERSITY, William R Perkins Library, Rare Book Room, Durham, 27706. John L Sharpe, III, Cur
Notes: Trent collection of Walt Whitman material. Consists of books, manuscripts, pictures, and a variety of other items relating to the American poet. "By far the most important special collection in the literary Americana" on the Perkins Library shelves, "outranked only by the possessions of the Library of Congress and the New York Public Library."

OH —BOWLING GREEN STATE UNIVERSITY, Jerome Library, Center for Archival Collections, Bowling Green, 43403. Paul D Yon, Dir; Elaine R Ezell, Reference Archivist; Nancy Steen, Rare Books Librn
Holdings: Vols 400 Cat Periodicals Pix
Budget: ($3000)
Notes: The Robert R Hubach Whitman Collection of many of the poet's works as well as many secondary sources. Descriptive catalog available.

PA —BRYN MAWR COLLEGE, Canaday Library, Bryn Mawr, 19010. James Tanis, Dir
Notes: Rare books and manuscripts.

RI —BROWN UNIVERSITY, John Hay Library, 20 Prospect St, Providence, 02912. Mark N Brown, Cur Mss
Notes: The Henry Scholey Saunders Collection of Whitman and Whitmaniana, collected 1915-1940, which contains very few original items by Whitman and consists mainly of about 15,000 of Saunders' bibliographical and topical notes, as well as essays and lectures by himself and other Whitmanites.

RI —BROWN UNIVERSITY, John Hay Library, Harris Collection, Prospect St, Providence, 02912. Rosemary L Cullen, Cur
Holdings: Vols (200,000) Cat Mss Pix Phonorecords Microforms
Budget: ($15,000)
Notes: Extensive collection of first editions, biographical and critical material, ephemera, portraits, association items, mss, and sheet music. Incl the Henry S Saunders Walt Whitman Collection (1300 vols). See Dictionary Catalog of The Harris Collection of American Poetry and Plays (Boston: G K Hall, 1972), 13 vols; Supplement (1977), 3 vols. See also, American Poetry, 1609-1900, A Collection on Microfilm, Segment I (1609-1820); Segment II (1821-1850); Segment III (1851-1870) (Woodbridge, Conn: Research Publications). Separate catalog.

SC —UNIVERSITY OF SOUTH CAROLINA, Thomas Cooper Library, Columbia, 29208. Kenneth E Toombs, Dir of Libraries; Roger Mortimer, Rare Book Librn
Holdings: Vols 175 Cat
Notes: A strong collection of first and variant editions.

VA —UNIVERSITY OF VIRGINIA, Alderman Library, Clifton Waller Barrett Collection, Charlottesville, 22901. Joan St C Crane, Cur of American Literature Collections
Holdings: Vols 550 Cat Mss Pix
Notes: First editions. Extremely important mss collection, including Leaves of Grass; letters. Critical works. Bibliography: Marjorie D Carver, Fannie Mae Elliott and Lucy T Clark, comps, The Barrett Library Walt Whitmans: A Checklist of Printed and Manuscript Works of Walt Whitman in the Library of the University of Virginia (Charlottesville: University of Virginia Press, 1961).

WA —UNIVERSITY OF WASHINGTON LIBRARIES, Suzzallo Library, Special Collections Division, Rare Book Collection, FM-25, Seattle, 98195. Gary Menges, Coordinator for Special Collections
Notes: Extensive collection; includes first editions.

WHITNEY, GEN. COURTNEY

VA —MACARTHUR MEMORIAL, Library & Archives, MacArthur Sq, Norfolk, 23510. Ellen E Folkama, Asst Archivist
Holdings: Vols (4000) Cat Maps Pix Slides Phonorecords Audiotapes 16mm Films Microforms
Notes: Everything relating to the life and related activities of MacArthur. The Archives of the collection consist of 600 shelf-feet of documents from Gen MacArthur's official headquarters files over the period 1941-1951. These papers pertain to all matters with which his various commands were involved: military, naval and air matters; international relations; political science; Japanese occupation, peace treaty and Constitution, etc. Each Record Group is indexed. The indexes are retained here since they are being expanded. They are available for researchers.

WHITNEY, PHYLLIS

MA —BOSTON UNIVERSITY, Mugar Memorial Library, Special Collections Dept, 771 Commonwealth Ave, Boston, 02215. Howard B Gotlieb, Dir
Holdings: Cat Mss
Notes: Mss, correspondence, etc collected in depth; incl publications by or about.

WHITTIER, JOHN GREENLEAF, 1807-1882

CA —WHITTIER COLLEGE, Wardman Library, Whittier, 90608. Christine Erdmann, Special Collections Librn
Holdings: Vols 5000 Uncat Pix
Notes: The Frederick M Meek Collection of 7000 items by and about Whittier, incl copies of limited editions and association copies, virtually all of his published works in all states, issues and editions, runs of newspapers to which Whittier contributed, magazine articles, broadsides, handbills, pamphlets, and correspondence, incl much with Mass Gov Claflin on contemporary politics. Also, autograph letters signed. Title card file.

CT —YALE UNIVERSITY, Box 1603A, Yale Station, New Haven, 06520.
Holdings: Cat Mss

MA —JOHN GREENLEAF WHITTIER HOME, Library, 86 Friend, Amesbury, 01913. Debra Martz Moore, Cur
Holdings: Cat Mss Pix
Notes: Original books of his collection. Maintain comprehensive genealogy of Whittiers in America.

MA —AMHERST COLLEGE, Library, Amherst, 01002. John Lancaster, Special Collections Librn
Holdings: Vols 125 Cat

MA —HARVARD UNIVERSITY LIBRARY, Houghton Library, Cambridge, 02138. Rodney G Dennis, Cur of Manuscripts
Holdings: Cat Mss

MA —WHEATON COLLEGE, Library, Norton, 02766. Sherrie S Bergman, College Librn
Holdings: Vols (280) Cat
Notes: The Larcom Collection, books by and

WHITTIER, JOHN GREENLEAF, 1807-1882 (cont.)

about Lucy Larcom, and her personal library. Mss, poetry, correspondence with John Greenleaf Whittier and others, diaries, watercolors.

NC —DUKE UNIVERSITY, William R Perkins Library, Durham, 27706. Elvin E Strowd, University Librn
Notes: The Ethel Carr Peacock collection of 7000 volumes is strong in holdings of 19th century American literature.

PA —FRIENDS HISTORICAL LIBRARY OF SWARTHMORE COLLEGE, Swarthmore, 19081. J William Frost, Dir
Holdings: Vols (35,000) Cat Mss Pix
Notes: 2000 vols, 750 mss. Printed items incl most editions and variants, poems published in newspapers and magazines; books from the poet and abolitionist's personal library. Ms collection incl poems and correspondence, some of the latter being copies.

VA —UNIVERSITY OF VIRGINIA, Alderman Library, Clifton Waller Barrett Collection, Charlottesville, 22901. Joan St C Crane, Cur of American Literature Collections
Notes: Papers.

WHITTINGHAM, CHARLES

VT —UNIVERSITY OF VERMONT, Guy W Bailey/David W Howe Library, Burlington, 05405. John Buehler, Asst Dir for Special Collections

WHITTLE, JOHN S.

VA —UNIVERSITY OF VIRGINIA, Alderman Library, Manuscripts Dept, Charlottesville, 22901. Edmund Berkeley Jr, Cur
Holdings: Cat Mss Maps Pix
Notes: Personal and official papers of Sir Andrew Snape Hamond and Graham Eden Hamond concern British naval operations during the American Revolution and in the Mediterranean during the Napoleonic Wars. Paul P Hoffman (ed) *Guide to the Naval Papers of Sir Andrew Snape Hamond . . . and Sir Graham Eden Hamond . . .* (Charlottesville, Va: Microfilm Publications, University of Virginia, 1966). Papers of US and Confederate naval officer Samuel Barron; US fleet surgeon and Brooklyn Navy Yard surgeon Gustavus R B Horner; US naval surgeon John S Whittle on a scientific expedition to the Pacific, 1838-1841; and US naval officer William Conway Whittle on West Indies and Mediterranean cruises, 1823-1831.

WHITTLE, WILLIAM CONWAY

VA —UNIVERSITY OF VIRGINIA, Alderman Library, Manuscripts Dept, Charlottesville, 22901. Edmund Berkeley Jr, Cur
Holdings: Cat Mss Maps Pix
Notes: Personal and official papers of Sir Andrew Snape Hamond and Graham Eden Hamond concern British naval operations during the American Revolution and in the Mediterranean during the Napoleonic Wars. Paul P Hoffman (ed) *Guide to the Naval Papers of Sir Andrew Snape Hamond . . . and Sir Graham Eden Hamond . . .* (Charlottesville, Va: Microfilm Publications, University of Virginia, 1966). Papers of US and Confederate naval officer Samuel Barron; US fleet surgeon and Brooklyn Navy Yard surgeon Gustavus R B Horner; US naval surgeon John S Whittle on a scientific expedition to the Pacific, 1838-1841; and US naval officer William Conway Whittle on West Indies and Mediterranean cruises, 1823-1831.

WHITTLING see Wood Carving

WHITTEMORE, REED

MO —WASHINGTON UNIVERSITY, Libraries, Special Collections Dept, Campus Box 1061, St Louis, 63130.
Notes: A small but significant collection.

WHYTE, LANCELOT LAW

MA —BOSTON UNIVERSITY, Mugar Memorial Library, Special Collections Dept, 771 Commonwealth Ave, Boston, 02215. Howard B Gotlieb, Dir
Holdings: Vols 500 Cat Mss Pix
Notes: Mss, correspondence, etc collected in depth; incl publications by or about.

WICKERSHAM, VICTOR EUGENE

OK —UNIVERSITY OF OKLAHOMA, Bizzell Memorial Library, Western History Collections, 401 W Brooks, Norman, 73069. John Ezell, Cur
Holdings: Mss Documents Pix Maps
Notes: US Representative. His papers. Guide available.

WICKES, ELBERT A.

CA —CLAREMONT COLLEGES, Honnold Library, Ninth & Dartmouth, Claremont, 91711. Tania Rizzo, Special Collections Dept Head
Holdings: Vols 250// Uncat Mss Documents Photographs Scrapbooks
Notes: Papers of Elbert A Wickes, 1884-1975, theatrical and lecture tour manager. Among his clients were Winston Churchill, William Butler Yeats, Houdini, Lowell Thomas, Vilhjalmur Stefansson, and Roy Chapman Andrews.

WICKSON, E. J.

CA —UNIVERSITY OF CALIFORNIA, DAVIS, Shields Library, Dept of Special Collections, Davis, 95616. Donald Kunitz, Head; C Danial Elliott, Asst Head
Holdings: Cat Mss
Notes: Correspondence between Luther Burbank and E J Wickson, regarding Burbank's developments and Wickson's writing about him. Also extracts from Burbank's scrapbooks (Wickson's copies), articles on Burbank. 287 items.

WIDENMANN, HANS A., 1897-1976

NJ —PRINCETON UNIVERSITY, Seeley G Mudd Manuscript Library, Public Affairs Papers Collection, Princeton, 08544. Nancy Bressler, Cur
Notes: Incl 72 boxes. The papers cover the period 1915-77. An unpublished 114p guide is available in the Library.

WIDERSTAND

NY —STATE UNIVERSITY OF NEW YORK AT ALBANY, Library, Special Collections Dept, 1400 Washington Ave, Albany, 12222. Marion P Munzer, Coordr
Notes: Primarily newspaper clippings concerning the German Resistance Movement against Hitler, assembled by Karl Otto Paetel (2 linear feet). Part of the German Exile Collection.
See also entries under World War, 1939-1945 - Underground Movements and Publications; Karl Otto Paetel.

WIDMER WINE CELLARS INCORPORATED

NY —CORNELL UNIVERSITY LIBRARIES, Collection of Regional History, Dept of Manuscripts and Univ Archives, Ithaca, 14853.
Notes: Records, 1918-60; 17 ft.

WIDOWHOOD

MA —NATIONAL CENTER FOR DEATH EDUCATION, New England Resource Center for Thanatology & Funeral Service, 656 Beacon St, Boston, 02215. Gail Gruner, Librn

WIEBE, RUDY, 1934-

AB —UNIVERSITY OF CALGARY, Libraries, Special Collections Div, 2500 University Dr, Calgary, T2N 1N4, Can.
Holdings: Cat Mss
Notes: The papers cover the period 1955-1975 and incl complete and dated draft manuscripts of Rudy Wiebe's published novels, short stories, poems and articles, files of research notes relating to his historical fiction, correspondence, publishers' files, interviews, and reviews.

WIEGAND, KARL HENRY VON, 1874-1961

CA —HOOVER INSTITUTION ON WAR, REVOLUTION & PEACE, Stanford University, Stanford, 94305. Milorad M Drachkovitch, Archivist
Holdings: Mss Pix
Notes: Papers of Karl H von Wiegand, Hearst newspaper foreign correspondent, 1917-61, incl correspondence, dispatches, mss of writings, photos, clippings, and printed matter, 1911-61, relating to European diplomacy and German politics between the world war, the Sino-Japanese War, the European theater in World War II, the Cold War, the postwar Middle Eastern situation, and US foreign policy. In English and German. 88 ms boxes, 6 binders, 1 stack of oversize mounted clippings, 2 swords, 1 shield.

WIELAND, CHRISTOPH MARTIN

MD —JOHNS HOPKINS UNIVERSITY, Milton S Eisenhower Library, Charles & 34 Sts, Baltimore, 21218. Ann S Gwyn, Assistant Dir for Special Collections
Holdings: Vols 300 Cat Mss
Notes: Very complete collection. First editions. Ms letters 1769-1812, cataloged.

WIEMAN, HENRY NELSON

IL —SOUTHERN ILLINOIS UNIVERSITY, CARBONDALE, Delyte W Morris Library, Special Collections Dept, Carbondale, 62901. David V Koch, Cur of Special Collections; Louisa Bowen, Cur of Manuscripts
Holdings: Vols 30 Cat Mss Pix
Notes: Twenty Collections relating to 20th century American philosophy incl the archives of Henry Nelson Wieman, American theologian and philosopher consist of some 30 vols which Wieman authored or co-authored, together with mss (published and unpublished), autobiographical materials, letters, lecture notes, and other papers. See Martin Luther King, *A Comparison of the Conception of God in the Thinking of Paul Tillich and Henry Nelson Wieman*, 1955. Inventory and name index available at the library.

WIENER, NORBERT, 1894-1964

MA —MASSACHUSETTS INSTITUTE OF TECHNOLOGY, Institute Archives, Special Collections, Cambridge, 02139.
Notes: Papers of Norbert Wiener, renowned mathematician, was instrumental in the development of communication and control theories. He coined the word "cybernetics" to describe this new science. Professional papers document the development of this theory, his development as a mathematician, and his effective collaboration with students and colleagues including Vannevar Bush and John von Neumann. Unpublished finding aid with correspondent index is available in the Institute Archives.

WIENER, SAMUEL G., SR.

LA —LOUISIANA STATE UNIVERSITY, SHREVEPORT, Library-Archives, 8515 Youree Dr, Shreveport, 71129. Patricia L Meador, Archivist & Asst Librn
Notes: Archives incl catalogued manuscripts and records, 500 maps, more than 5000 photographs, 1000 architectural drawings, slides. The collection's primary emphasis is the history of North Louisiana, particularly Northwest Louisiana. The 1500 linear ft incl area plantation records and ledgers; personal

WIENER, SAMUEL G., SR. (cont.)

papers of area pioneers, planters, legislators, politicians, educators, businessmen, and architects; papers and records of longtime (1919-1961) Caddo Parish Coroner, Willis P Butler; the Samuel G Wiener, Sr architectual records (1921-1976) with drawings and photographs; the Ted Flaxman architectual records (1919-1968); the papers (1860-1921) of architect Nathaniel S Allen; the collection of Dewey A Somdal, Shreveport architect, historian and collector, with emphasis on steamboats, travel on the Red River and Louisiana history, 1780-1972.

WIFE AND HUSBAND see Husband and Wife

WIFE BEATING

NY —YWCA NATIONAL BOARD, Library, 726-730 Broadway, New York, 10012. Elizabeth Norris, Librn
Holdings: Vols (3000) Cat Mss
Budget: ($2400)
Notes: Women and their contemporary concerns.

WIGGIN, KATE DOUGLAS (SMITH), 1856-1923

ME —BOWDOIN COLLEGE, Library, Brunswick, 04011. Dianne M Gutscher, Cur of Special Collections
Holdings: Vols 425 // Cat Mss
Notes: Incl 115 first and later editions (several in Braille); 310 volumes from her library, chiefly presentation copies; 2 albums of periodical and newspaper appearances (some anonymous); 16 scrapbooks of clippings and notices; 4 boxes of mss, and about 100 letters of this author and pioneer kindergarten worker.

WIGGS, RICHARD

MA —MASSACHUSETTS INSTITUTE OF TECHNOLOGY, Institute Archives, Special Collections, Cambridge, 02139.
Notes: Correspondence, newsletters, factsheets, newspaper and magazine articles, books and reports of the Citizens' League Against the Sonic Boom, established in 1967 by William Shurcliff to oppose the sonic boom, stop commercial supersonic transport production, and influence public opinion and policy decisions on the SST. Major correspondents incl Bo Lundberg, Richard Wiggs, several US congressmen, and CLASB members.

WIGHTMAN FAMILY

SC —COLLEGE OF CHARLESTON LIBRARY, Special Collections Dept, Charleston, 29401.
Notes: Papers incl correspondence between members of the Wightman family of Canada, New England, and Charleston, SC, regarding family history; incl a photograph of the family coat of arms.

WIGMAN, MARY

ON —METROPOLITAN TORONTO LIBRARY, Theatre Dept, 789 Yonge St, Toronto, M4W 2G8, Can. Heather McCallum, Head
Notes: Theatre Department is one of eleven subject departments of the Metropolitan Toronto Library, which is generally acknowledged to be the most comprehensive of Canadian public library collections. The collection balances book and nonbook material in all areas of the performing arts. Production history is the special emphasis of the dance collection, as it is for all the material in the Theatre Department. This is supported by the department's extensive holdings of programs, posters, photographs and press clippings for Canadian productions and dancers, as well as a representative selection of material for non-Canadian dance. Important original stage designs in

the collection incl work by Mstislav Dobujinsky for the Canadian ballet *Red Ear of Corn*, which was produced by Boris Volkoff in 1949; Maurice Strike's work for the National Ballet of Canada's production of *Coppelia*, and Desmond Heeley's designs for that company's *Swan Lake*. Ms collections incl: The Boris Volkoff Collection (qv); papers of the Toronto dance teacher Bettina Byers; the papers of two Canadian dance critics, Ralph Hicklin and John Fraser; and the Mary Wigman Collection, consisting of xerox copies of letters exchanged between Miss Wigman and her Canadian pupil Judy Jarvis, and a taped conversation with Miss Wigman.

WILBERFORCE, HENRY

DC —GEORGETOWN UNIVERSITY, Library, Special Collections Div, 37 & O Sts NW, Washington, 20057. George M Barringer, Special Collections Librn; Nicholas B Sheetz, Mss Librn
Holdings: Vols 150 Cat Mss Pix
Notes: Mss incl over 375 letters, principally to Henry Wilberforce.

WILBERFORCE, WILLIAM

NC —DUKE UNIVERSITY, William R Perkins Library, Manuscript Dept, Durham, 27706. Ellen Gartrell, Cur of Mss
Holdings: Cat Mss
Notes: Incl 50,000 items, 18th-20th centuries, representing the political, diplomatic, military, ecclesiastical, and economic affairs of Great Britain and the British Empire. Incl papers of William Wilberforce, William Smith, John Wilson Croker, John Backhouse, Malet Family, etc. *See also* entry under Slavery and Antislavery.

WILBUR, RAY LYMAN

CA —HOOVER INSTITUTION ON WAR, REVOLUTION & PEACE, Stanford University, Stanford, 94305. Milorad M Drachkovitch, Archivist
Holdings: // Mss Pix
Notes: Two collections: (1) Papers, 1917-1949, of Ray Lyman Wilbur, president and chancellor of Stanford University and US Secretary of the Interior. Personal files as Secretary of the Interior and correspondence and records of the several social studies conducted under the Hoover administration. Incl papers relating to child health and better homes. Ca 80 ft. Finding aid in repository. (2) Collection of correspondence, reports, memoranda, study papers, press releases, printed matter and photographs, 1925-1960, relating to the study of political, social and economic conditions in the Far East and of US foreign policy in the Far East by the American Council of the Institute of Pacific Relations, collected by Ray Lyman Wilbur. 21 ms boxes, 1 album, 1 envelope.
CA —STANFORD UNIVERSITY LIBRARIES, Lane Medical Library, Stanford University, Medical Center, Stanford, 94305. Peter Stangl, Librn
Holdings: Mss Cat
Notes: Correspondence and assorted materials from 1913 - 54 including work on Baruch Committee on Physical Medicine, Commission on Graduate Medical Education, Committee on Cost of Medical Care, Commission on Medical Education, Commission on Hospital Care, etc.

WILBUR, RICHARD

MA —AMHERST COLLEGE, Library, Amherst, 01002. John Lancaster, Special Collections Librn
Holdings: Vols 23 Cat Mss
NV —UNIVERSITY OF NEVADA, RENO, University Library, Special Collections Dept, Reno, 89557. Robert E Blesse, Head
Holdings: Vols 62 Cat
Notes: Includes individual works by author in all editions including translations; also prefaces, introductions, published correspondence, appearances in anthologies,

periodicals, etc. Bibliographical research collection, part of Modern Authors Collection.

WILBUR, MR. AND MRS. ROBERT L.

†NY —COLUMBIA UNIVERSITY LIBRARIES, Butler Library, Rare Book and Manuscript Library, 535 W 114 St, New York, 10027.
Notes: Papers, etc. Also, the files of Gramercy Bookshop in New York, 1940-1979.

WILCHEK, STELLA

MA —BOSTON UNIVERSITY, Mugar Memorial Library, Special Collections Dept, 771 Commonwealth Ave, Boston, 02215. Howard B Gotlieb, Dir
Holdings: Cat Mss Pix
Notes: Mss, correspondence, etc collected in depth; incl publications by or about.

WILCOX FAMILY

CA —AZUSA PACIFIC COLLEGE, Marshburn Memorial Library, Citrus & Alosta, Azusa, 91702. Edward Peterman, Librn
Holdings: Vols (1000) // Uncat Maps Pix
Notes: Macneil Family Collection on Local History. These items relate to the Slauson, Macneil and Wilcox families, incl photographs, diaries, letters, maps, books, and financial and legal documents.

WILD ANIMALS, CAPTIVE

†CA —ZOOLOGICAL SOCIETY OF SAN DIEGO, Ernst Schwarz Library, San Diego Zoo, Box 551, San Diego, 92112.
DC —SMITHSONIAN INSTITUTION LIBRARIES, National Zoological Park Branch, Washington, 20008. Kay Kenyon, Chief Librn
Holdings: Vols (5500) Cat
Notes: Collection incl animal nutrition, capture and care of animals in captivity, conservation and endangered species, pathology, veterinary medicine, zoology.
MN —MINNESOTA ZOOLOGICAL GARDEN, Apple Valley, 55124. Angela Norell, Librn
Notes: Classified card catalog; Journal reprints are fairly comprehensive for the animals in the collection, which are primarily Southeast Asian, Northern-dwelling, and native Minnesotan. Collection includes 2000 books, 60 periodical subscriptions and 3000 reprints of journal articles.
NY —NEW YORK ZOOLOGICAL SOCIETY LIBRARY, Bronx Zoo, Bronx, 10460. Steven P Johnson, Archivist and Librn
Holdings: Vols (6000) Cat Mss
Budget: ($50,000)
Notes: Collection consists primarily of journals in captive management of animals, vertebrate zoology, and veterinary medicine. Primarily intended for the scientific staff, the collection is open to the public on a noncirculating basis, by appointment, (212) 220-6874.

WILD DOG (MAGAZINE)

TX —SAM HOUSTON STATE UNIVERSITY, Library, PO Box 2179, Huntsville, 77340. Chas Dwyer, Librn
Holdings: Cat Mss
Notes: The *Wild Dog* was a little magazine which published 20 issues from April 1963 to January 1964. The *Wild Dog* Collection consists of the typescripts for the published issues; correspondence with contributors, would-be contributors, bookshops, and individual subscribers; and the original cover art work with correspondence with the artists. There are approximately 600 letters and cards from the above mentioned sources; approximately 450 typescripts, some signed and corrected, by the authors who were published in the *Wild Dog*; and approximately 25 letters from artists accompanying the original cover art work. In connection with this archival material,

WILD DOG (MAGAZINE) (cont.)

additional separately published works by the contributing authors (approximately 120 volumes). No photocopying.

WILD FLOWERS

MN —UNIVERSITY OF MINNESOTA, Landscape Arboretum, Andersen Horticultural Library, 3675 Arboretum Drive, Box 39, Chanhassen, 55317. June Rogier, Head
Holdings: Vols (8000)

WILD FOWL see Game and Game Birds

WILD LIFE, CONSERVATION OF see Wildlife Conservation

WILDE, OSCAR

CA —UNIVERSITY OF CALIFORNIA, LOS ANGELES, William Andrews Clark Memorial Library, 2520 Cimarron St, Los Angeles, 90018.
Holdings: Vols 1500 Cat Mss Pix Slides
Notes: One of the greatest collections of Wilde, incl about 1500 printed books, practically all of the various editions in the original and in foreign translations, and most of the critical and biographical studies that have been published during the last 70 years. Also some 3000 original mss, typescripts, holograph letters and association items, a guide to which has been published.

CA —UNIVERSITY OF SAN FRANCISCO, Richard A Gleeson Library, The Countess Bernardine Murphy Donohue Rare Book Room, San Francisco, 94117. D Steven Corey, Special Collections Librn
Holdings: Vols 156
Notes: Nearly complete collection of the major first editions with editions in depth for certain titles.

NC —DUKE UNIVERSITY, William R Perkins Library, Rare Book Room, Durham, 27706. John L Sharpe, III, Cur
Notes: The Oscar Wilde collection. Collection of first and early editions, several autographed copies, includes a unique copy of The Duchess of Padua.

OH —BOWLING GREEN STATE UNIVERSITY, Jerome Library, Center for Archival Collections, Bowling Green, 43403. Paul D Yon, Dir; Elaine R Ezell, Reference Archivist; Nancy Steen, Rare Books Librn
Holdings: Vols 1600 Cat Mss Letters Pix
Budget: ($3000)
Notes: The Robert Aickman Collection contains about 40 of Aickman's manuscripts of both published and unpublished works as well as the late author's personal library which is strong in the areas of English literature and theatre of the 19th and 20th centuries and in the area of the supernatural.

NS —DALHOUSIE UNIVERSITY LIBRARY, Halifax, B3H 4H8, Can.
Holdings: Vols 305 Cat
Notes: Strong holdings of first and limited editions of Wilde's work are contained in the collection. Later editions, biographies and critical studies, as well as first editions of contemporaries associated with Wilde, such as Lord Alfred Douglas, Frank Harris, Aubrey Beardsley and Max Beerbohm are well represented. Highlights incl: Ravenna (Oxford, 1878), and autogrpahed first editions of Poems, An Ideal Husband, Importance of Being Earnest, and The Picture of Dorian Gray.
See also entries under Beardsley, Aubrey Vincent, 1872-1898; Douglas, Lord Alfred; Harris, Frank.

WILDER, LAURA INGALLS

CA —POMONA PUBLIC LIBRARY, Special Collections, 625 S Garey Ave, PO Box 2271, Pomona, 91766. David Streeter, Librn
Holdings: Uncat Mss
Notes: Original mss of Little House on the Prairie, galley proofs, TV series scripts, photographs, Wilder books in English and foreign translations. Published works (ca 200 items). Also, memorabilia, dolls, letters.

WILDER, ROBERT, 1901-1974

MA —BOSTON UNIVERSITY, Mugar Memorial Library, Special Collections Dept, 771 Commonwealth Ave, Boston, 02215. Howard B Gotlieb, Dir
Holdings: // Cat Mss
Notes: Mss, correspondence, etc collected in depth; incl publications by or about.

WILDER, THORNTON

AZ —UNIVERSITY OF ARIZONA, University Library, Special Collections, Tucson, 85721. Louis A Hieb, Head
Holdings: Vols (7000) Cat Mss Microforms
Budget: ($30,000)
Notes: In the 20th century, the major emphasis is Bukowski, Wakoski, Wilder, Reznikoff, Ginzberg, Ferlinghetti, Snyder, Whalen, Everson, Joyce Carol Oates, and Kurt Vonnegut.

CT —YALE UNIVERSITY, Box 1603A, Yale Station, New Haven, 06520.
Holdings: Cat Mss Pix

NV —UNIVERSITY OF NEVADA, RENO, University Library, Special Collections Dept, Reno, 89557. Robert E Blesse, Head
Holdings: Vols 78 // Cat
Notes: Includes individual works by author in all editions including translations; also prefaces, introductions, published correspondence, appearances in anthologies, periodicals, etc. Bibliographical research collection, part of Modern Authors Collection.

OH —KENT STATE UNIVERSITY, Libraries, Dept of Special Collections, Kent, 44242. Dean H Keller, Cur
Holdings: Vols 53 Cat Mss

VA —UNIVERSITY OF VIRGINIA, Alderman Library, Manuscripts Dept, Charlottesville, 22901. Edmund Berkeley Jr, Cur
Holdings: Cat Mss
Notes: First editions, mss, papers, etc.

WILDFLOWERS see Wild Flowers

WILDLIFE AND OIL SPILLS see Oil Spills and Wildlife

WILDLIFE CONSERVATION

CA —UNIVERSITY OF CALIFORNIA, BERKELEY, Life Sciences Libraries, Forestry Library, 260 Mulford Hall, Berkeley, 94720. Esther Johnson, Librn; Pete Evans, Ref Librn
Holdings: Vols (28,000) Cat Microforms
Budget: ($15,800)
Notes: Areas of particular strength are forestry, conservation, and wildlife management. The collection is rich in pamphlet material and serials, especially foreign publications. Although holdings are world-wide in scope, coverage of the western USA is given the highest priority. Dissertation and theses collection also. Forestry Library holdings are complemented by a 8000-vol specialized collection at the Forest Products Laboratory in Richmond, California.

†CA —ZOOLOGICAL SOCIETY OF SAN DIEGO, Ernst Schwarz Library, San Diego Zoo, Box 551, San Diego, 92112.

CO —DENVER PUBLIC LIBRARY, Conservation Library Center, 1357 Broadway, Denver, 80203.
Holdings: Vols (10,330) Cat
Notes: Historical, sociological, and economic aspects, but not scientific, except for Colorado research reports. Also, fish and wildlife reports of all states.

CO —COLORADO STATE UNIVERSITY, Libraries, Fort Collins, 80523. Curtis L Gifford, Forestry & Agricultural Sciences Librn
Holdings: Vols (24,444) Cat Maps Microforms
Budget: ($9000)
Notes: The 9300 microforms are primarily on wildlife management and behavior.

DC —SMITHSONIAN INSTITUTION LIBRARIES, National Zoological Park Branch, Washington, 20008. Kay Kenyon, Chief Librn
Holdings: Vols (5500) Cat
Notes: Collection incl animal nutrition, capture and care of animals in captivity, conservation and endangered species, pathology, veterinary medicine, zoology.

IL —ILLINOIS NATURAL HISTORY SURVEY LIBRARY, 196 Natural Resources Bldg, Champaign, 61820. Carla G Heister, Librn
Holdings: Vols (36,000) Cat Microforms
Budget: ($25,500)
Notes: A Research and Science Branch of the State of Illinois, the Natural History Survey maintains a library of books, journals and reports on various aspects of natural history. Material is collected in all major languages. The library maintains its own exchange arrangements with some 600 worldwide institutions and organizations. Interlibrary loans and photocopy services are available through the University of Illinois Library. Publications issued regularly by the Survey incl Biological Notes, The Bulletin, and Circulars.

IL —CHICAGO PUBLIC LIBRARY, Business/Science/Technology Div, Science/ Technology Information Center, 425 North Michigan Ave, Chicago, 60611. Lynda Sanford, Head; John R Moore, Environment Collection Coordinator & Engineering Librn
Holdings: Vols 400 Cat Maps Films Slides Phonorecords Audiotapes Microforms
Budget: $1400
Notes: Incl Aaron Montgomery Ward Collection.

IA —IOWA STATE UNIVERSITY, Library, Ames, 50011. Warren B Kuhn, Dean of Library Services
Holdings: Cat Mss
Notes: Incl wildlife biology and management.

IA —IOWA STATE UNIVERSITY, Library, Dept of Special Collections, Ames, 50011. Stanley M Yates, Head
Holdings: // Mss
Notes: American School of Wildlife Protection existed from 1919-1941. One box, finding aid available.

MO —US FISH & WILDLIFE SERVICE, Columbia National Fisheries Research Laboratory, Rte One, Columbia, 65201. Axie Hindman, Librn
Holdings: Vols (2000) Cat Microforms
Budget: ($7000)
Notes: Pesticides in aquatic biota; fisheries research; fresh-water ecology. Also incl collection in water pollution, acid rain, aquatic invertebrets, environment and 10,000 reprints.

NY —STATE UNIVERSITY OF NEW YORK AT ALBANY, Library, Special Collections Dept, 1400 Washington Ave, Albany, 12222. Marion P Munzer, Coordr
Notes: Correspondence, lecture notes, speeches, mss, clippings dealing with work by Robert Rienow and his wofe, Leona Train, on wildlife conservation, anti-nuclear movement, and population control (15 linear feet).

NY —ADIRONDACK HISTORICAL ASSOCIATION, Museum Library, Blue Mountain Lake, 12812. Jerold Pepper, Librn
Holdings: Vols (7500) Cat Mss Maps Pix Phonorecords Audiotapes 16mm Films Microforms
Notes: Anything about the Adirondacks-- history, people, economics, places, things. Strong in Adirondack art, outdoor recreation, logging, small boats. Resources incl more than 1000 maps, 40,000 pictures, 1600 microfilm reels, 576 linear ft of ms material, and 12 cabinets of VF ephemera, etc.

NY —NEW YORK BOTANICAL GARDEN LIBRARY, Bronx, 10458. Charles R Long, Asst Vice Pres & Dir
Holdings: Vols 2000 Cat VF
Budget: ($356,000)
Notes: Over 900,000 items, incl books, serials, pamphlets, archives and manuscripts, vertical files, microfiche and microfilm, nursery and seed catalogs, photographs, paintings, prints, drawings and engravings. Covering all areas of botanical sciences.

WILDLIFE CONSERVATION (cont.)

NY —NEW YORK ZOOLOGICAL SOCIETY
LIBRARY, Bronx Zoo, Bronx, 10460.
Steven P Johnson, Archivist and Librn
Holdings: Vols (6000) Cat Mss
Budget: ($50,000)
Notes: Collection consists primarily of
journals in captive management of animals,
vertebrate zoology, and veterinary medicine.
Primarily intended for the scientific staff, the
collection is open to the public on a
noncirculating basis, by appointment, (212)
220-6874.

NY —AMERICAN MUSEUM OF
NATURAL HISTORY, Library Services
Dept, Central Park W & 79th St, New York,
10024. Nina J Root, Chairwoman; Mary
Genett, Asst Librn for Reference Services

NY —SAGAMORE HILL NATIONAL
HISTORIC SITE, Library, 304 Cove Neck
Rd, Oyster Bay, 11771.
Holdings: Cat

NY —STATE UNIVERSITY OF NEW
YORK, COLLEGE OF
ENVIRONMENTAL SCIENCE AND
FORESTRY, F Franklin Moon Library,
Syracuse, 13210. Donald F Webster, Librn
Holdings: Vols (86,430) Cat
Budget: ($120,000)

NC —NORTH CAROLINA STATE
UNIVERSITY, Forest Resources Library,
4012 Biltmore Hall, Raleigh, 27650. Pamela
E Puryear, Head
Holdings: Vols (9000) Cat Microforms
Notes: Forestry, wood and paper sciences;
recreation; remote sensing; FAO and forest
service and forest products labs. Publications
and audiovisual materials.

ND —NORTHERN PRAIRIE WILDLIFE
RESEARCH CENTER, Library, PO Box
1747, Jamestown, 58401.
Holdings: Vols (2500) Cat Pix Slides
Budget: ($10,000)
Notes: Wildlife management and research,
incl avian biology, plant and animal ecology
as related to wetlands and prairies, waterfowl
research, and effects of predators on
waterfowl.

†PA —PENNSYLVANIA STATE
UNIVERSITY, Du Bois Campus Library,
College Place, Du Bois, 15801.
Notes: The Paul A Handwerk Collection and
the David D Wanless Collection of materials
in fisheries and wildlife.

TN —TENNESSEE VALLEY AUTHORITY
(TVA), Technical Library, 400 W Summit
Hill Dr, E2 B7, Knoxville, 37902. Jesse C
Mills, Chief Librn
Holdings: Vols (106,900) Cat Mss Maps Pix
Audiotapes Microforms
Budget: ($2,025,000)
Notes: The Technical Library Headquarters
Staff (order, cataloging, information, and
administration) is located in Knoxville,
Tenn. In addition there are branch libraries
in Knoxville, Norris, and Chattanooga,
Tennessee, and Muscle Shoals, Alabama.

TN —TENNESSEE VALLEY AUTHORITY
(TVA), Norris Branch Library, Norris,
37828. Debra D Mills, Librn
Holdings: Vols (8000) Cat Microforms
Budget: ($35,000)

WA —UNIVERSITY OF WASHINGTON
LIBRARIES, Forest Resources Library, AQ-
15, Seattle, 98195. Barbara B Gordon, Head
Holdings: Vols (43,248) Cat Microforms
Budget: ($41,103)
Notes: Modern imprints only. Mostly in
English, some geographical limits with
emphasis on Pacific Northwest.

WA —URS ENGINEERS, Library, 2615
Fourth Ave, Seattle, 98121. Jill Phelps,
Librn
Holdings: Vols (3100) Cat
Budget: ($5000)
Notes: Environmental impact assessment,
hazardous materials disposal, oil spill
cleanup and environmental effects of
waterborne pollutants, especially with regard
to California and the western environment.

WI —UNIVERSITY OF WISCONSIN,
MADISON, College of Agricultural & Life
Sciences, Steenbock Memorial Library, 550
Babcock Dr, Madison, 53706. Jan Kennedy,
Dir
Holdings: Vols (186,312) Cat Docs Maps
Microforms

MB —UNIVERSITY OF MANITOBA,
Elizabeth Dafoe Library, Government
Publications Section, Winnipeg, R3T 2N2,
Can. June Dutka, Head
Holdings: Vols 1300 // Uncat Maps Pix
Notes: The collection, which dates from
1975, consists of written direct testimonies
and responses with supporting exhibits from
over 100 oil and gas companies, Indian and
native associations and concerned citizen
groups. The content of these documents incl
construction plans, financial statements,
alternate corridors, and describes the social
and economic impact of the Arctic Gas
Pipline in northern Canada. The *Biological
Report Series* offers vital information on
soils and vegetation, movements of
porcupine, caribou herds, bird distribution
and fisheries research. An index listing the
various company exhibits accompanies this
collection.

ON —ONTARIO MINISTRY OF NATURAL
RESOURCES, Natural Resources Library,
Whitney Block 4540, Toronto, M5S 1B3,
Can. Sandra Louet, Librn
Holdings: Cat

WILDLIFE MANAGEMENT

MA —HARVARD UNIVERSITY, Harvard
Forest Library, Petersham, 01366. Catherine
M Danahar, Librn

NY —CARY ARBORETUM OF THE NEW
YORK BOTANICAL GARDEN, Institute
of Ecosystem Studies, Library, Box AB,
Millbrook, 12545. Betsy Calvin, Librn
Holdings: Vols 10,,000

NC —NORTH CAROLINA STATE
UNIVERSITY, Forest Resources Library,
4012 Biltmore Hall, Raleigh, 27650. Pamela
E Puryear, Head
Holdings: Vols (9000) Cat Microforms
Notes: Forestry, wood and paper sciences;
recreation; remote sensing; FAO and forest
service and forest products labs. Publications
and audiovisual materials.

†PA —PENNSYLVANIA STATE
UNIVERSITY, Du Bois Campus Library,
College Place, Du Bois, 15801.
Notes: The Paul A Handwerk Collection and
the David D Wanless Collection of materials
in fisheries and wildlife.

WI —WISCONSIN DEPT OF NATURAL
RESOURCES, Technical Library, 3911 Fish
Hatchery Rd, Madison, 53711. Rose Smith,
Librn
Holdings: Vols (1200) Cat
Budget: $2000

WILDT, RUPERT

CT —YALE UNIVERSITY, Box 1603A, Yale
Station, New Haven, 06520.
Holdings: Mss
Notes: Papers of Rupert Wildt, professor of
astrophysics.

WILE, IRA SOLOMON

NY —UNIVERSITY OF ROCHESTER, Rush
Rhees Library, Department of Rare Books
and Special Collections, Rochester, 14627.
Peter Dzwonkoski, Librn
Holdings: Cat Mss
Notes: Correspondence, reports, articles
written by Wile on birth control (including
many letters from Margaret Sanger), left and
right handedness, sex education, child
development, and mental hygiene.

WILES, IRVING RAMSEY

†NY —NEW YORK ACADEMY OF
MEDICINE, Library, 2 E 103 ST, New
York, 10029.
Notes: Papers of Walter Timme, MD (1874-
1956). Timme was a pioneer endocrinologist;
described pluriglandular disease, "Timme's
Syndrome." Incl correspondence from
Harvey Cushing, Paul Dudley White,
Charles A Elsberg, Louis I Dublin, Ely
Smith Jelliffe, John F Fulton, Edna St
Vincent Millay, Eva Le Gallienne, and
Irving Ramsey Wiles.

WILGUS, WILLIAM JOHN

NY —NEW YORK PUBLIC LIBRARY, Rare
Books and Manuscripts Div, Fifth Ave & 42
St, New York, 10018. William L Joyce, Asst
Dir; Susan E Davis, Cur of Mss
Holdings: Mss
Budget: ($7161)
Notes: Incl personal and literary mss, papers,
etc.

WILKE, WILLIAM

CA —UNIVERSITY OF CALIFORNIA,
SANTA BARBARA, Library, Dept of
Special Collections, Santa Barbara, 93106.
Christian F Brun, Head
Holdings: Uncat Mss Pix
Notes: Important collection of drawings,
plates, imprints, etc, of this San Francisco
designer who worked for John Henry Nash,
etc. 2 typescript vols, 1935-1936, 1936-1937.
Words and music to ca 300 songs, with
informants, dates, locations where collected.
Title indexes.

WILKINS, ROY, 1901-1981

DC —LIBRARY OF CONGRESS, Manuscript
Division, Washington, 20540. John C
Broderick, Chief
Notes: The papers of Roy Wilkins, former
Executive Director, NAACP.

WILLAN, HEALY

ON —NATIONAL LIBRARY OF CANADA,
395 Wellington St, Ottawa, K1A 0N4, Can.
Andre Preibish, Dir
Holdings: Vols 35,000
Notes: Includes 2000 pieces of Canadian
sheet music (mostly 19th century imprints),
40,000 cylinders, discs, tapes; over 600
serials titles devoted to music; 200 archival
collections of composers, musicians and
conductors, eg papers of Healy Willan,
eminent composer; Glen Gould, well-known
pianist; Sir Ernest MacMillan, conductor,
director and composer. Since 1950 the
Canadian imprints have been received on
legal deposit. Intensive purchases aim at a
comprehensive collection of Canadian music.

WILLARD, ARTHUR

IL —UNIVERSITY OF ILLINOIS,
URBANA/CHAMPAIGN, Library,
University Archives, 19 Library, 1408 W
Gregory Drive, Urbana, 61801. Maynard
Brichford, University Archivist
Holdings: Cat Mss Maps Pix Slides
Microforms
Notes: Papers, archival records, etc.

WILLAUER, WHITING, 1906-1962

NJ —PRINCETON UNIVERSITY, Library,
Manuscript Collection, Nassau St, Princeton,
08540. Jean F Preston, Cur
Holdings: Mss Pix
Notes: Incl 5 cartons of papers.

WILLEBRANDT, MABEL WALKER, 1889-1963

†DC —LIBRARY OF CONGRESS,
Manuscript Division, Washington, 20540.
Notes: The papers, etc, of Mabel Walker
Willebrandt.

WILLETT, JOSEPH J.

AL —SAMFORD UNIVERSITY, Special
Collections Library, 800 Lakeshore Dr,
Birmingham, 35229. Annie Ford Wheeler,
Acting Head Librn
Holdings: Vols 3000 Uncat Mss Maps Pix
Notes: Alabama literature and history; ms
collection exceeds 200,000 pieces, chiefly of
Joseph J Willett papers and Bledsoe-Kelly
Collection. Representative collection of
maps, some pictures.

WILLETT-PASHLEY ARCHITECTURAL CORPORATION

KS —UNIVERSITY OF KANSAS, Kenneth
Spencer Research Library, Special

WILLETT-PASHLEY ARCHITECTURAL CORPORATION (cont.)

Collections Dept, Lawrence, 66045.
Alexandra Mason, Librn
Holdings: Cat Mss Pix Slides
Notes: Two main groups: Willett-Pashley collection (working library of 19th century Chicago architectural firm)--ca 800 volumes; cataloged. Frank Lloyd Wright collection (mss, photographs, slides, books, clippings)-- ca 6 Hollinger boxes, photos & mss & ca. 447 magazines and books; uncataloged. Noncirculating.

WILLIAMS, ANNIE LAURIE

NY —COLUMBIA UNIVERSITY LIBRARIES, Rare Book & Manuscript Library, 801 Butler Library, 535 W 114 St, New York, 10027. Kenneth A Lohf, Librn
Holdings: Mss
Notes: Publications and papers, by and about. 35,000 items. Restricted use.

WILLIAMS, C. MILO

LA —NEW ORLEANS PUBLIC LIBRARY, Louisiana Div, 219 Loyola Ave, New Orleans, 70140. Collin B Hamer Jr, Head; Brenda M Osbey, Library Associate
Holdings: Cat Maps Pix
Notes: Louisiana and New Orleans Picture File Collection ranges from the late 19th century-date and incl the following separate collections: Alexander Allison (ca 1898-1951, 337 pieces); Charles Franck (ca 1920-50, 170 pieces); Leda Plauche (ca 1935-53, 220 pieces); C Milo Williams (ca 1910, 85 pieces); Wilson S Howell (ca 1890, 49 pieces); Grauman Marks (ca 1960, 268 pieces); Robert Tallant (ca 1940-50, 70 pieces); Robert E Tracy (1959, 87 pieces); Anthony J Flaherty (ca 1970-84, 83 pieces); George F Mugnier (1880-1920, 186 pieces); Color Slides (ca 1945-date, 500 pieces); 30,000 photographs incl 500 color slides and 104 negatives. Use of the material is restricted to on-site research. Publication must be accompanied by credit cut line.

WILLIAMS, CHARLES

IL —WHEATON COLLEGE, Library, Marion E Wade Collection, Irving & Franklin Sts, Wheaton, 60187. Lyle Dorsett, Cur; Marjorie Mead, Associate Cur
Holdings: Vols (6500) Mss Pix Audiotapes Videotapes
Notes: Extensive Marion E Wade Collection of seven British authors incl over 800 Williams letters, nearly all of Williams published and unpublished manuscripts, and a wide variety of secondary source materials, incl works on Arthurian literature.

NV —UNIVERSITY OF NEVADA, RENO, University Library, Special Collections Dept, Reno, 89557. Robert E Blesse, Head
Holdings: Vols 45 // Cat
Notes: Includes individual works by author in all editions including translations; also prefaces, introductions, published correspondence, appearances in anthologies, periodicals, etc. Bibliographical research collection, part of Modern Authors Collection.

WILLIAMS, DAVID RHYS, 1890-1970

NY —UNIVERSITY OF ROCHESTER, Rush Rhees Library, Department of Rare Books and Special Collections, Rochester, 14627. Peter Dzwonkoski, Librn
Holdings: Cat Mss
Notes: Correspondence, annual reports, financial records and ephemera of congregation, 1829-1960. Church attended by Susan B Anthony and other active social reformers. Papers of ministers William Channing Gannett (1840-1923) and David Rhys Williams (1890-1970).

WILLIAMS, FRANK

OH —OHIO STATE UNIVERSITY, Library for Communication and Graphic Arts, 242 W 18th St, Columbus, 43210. Lucy S Caswell, Curator
Notes: The original works of editorial cartoonists Art Poinier, Scott Willis, Brian Basset, Billy Ireland, Frank Williams, Charles Werner, Ned Beard, L D Warren, Edward D Kuekes, Ray Osrin, Mike Peters, Draper Hill, Eugene Craig and Bert Whitman.

WILLIAMS, FRANKWOOD E., 1883-1936

KS —MENNINGER FOUNDATION, Archives, 5600 W Sixth St, Box 829, Topeka, 66601. Alice Brand, Librn; Mark West, Archivist
Notes: 2 boxes, 1906-36. Consists of mss and correspondence.

WILLIAMS, GAAR

IN —BUTLER UNIVERSITY, Irwin Library, Hugh Thomas Miller Rare Book Room, 4600 Sunset Ave, Indianapolis, 46208. Gisela Terrell, Rare Books Librn
Holdings: Cat Mss Pix
Notes: *Gaar Williams/Kin Hubbard* Collection. This collection was presented to the library by Blanche Stillson in 1964. It contains original cartoons and other drawings, books (many of them inscribed), magazines, letters and other manuscripts, photographs, and memorabilia by both Hoosier cartoonists and humorists. A catalogue of the Gaar Williams ("Abe Martin") items was printed in 1981. It is available upon request.

WILLIAMS, HOWARD S.

MS —UNIVERSITY OF SOUTHERN MISSISSIPPI, William David McCain Graduate Library, Box 5148, Southern Sta, Hattiesburg, 39406.
Holdings: Cat Mss Pix
Notes: The Howard S Williams Papers (1916-1960; 1.8 cubic feet) contain correspondence, newspaper clippings, sermons, promotional material, broadsides, and photographs which document Williams' life as a traveling evangelist in the Southeastern and United States.

WILLIAMS, JAY

MA —BOSTON UNIVERSITY, Mugar Memorial Library, Special Collections Dept, 771 Commonwealth Ave, Boston, 02215. Howard B Gotlieb, Dir
Holdings: // Cat Mss Pix Audiotapes
Notes: Mss, correspondence, etc collected in depth; incl publications by or about.

WILLIAMS, JOHN SKELTON

VA —UNIVERSITY OF VIRGINIA, Alderman Library, Manuscripts Dept, Charlottesville, 22901. Edmund Berkeley Jr, Cur
Holdings: Cat Mss Pix
Notes: Personal, political, and business papers.

WILLIAMS, JONATHAN

MO —WASHINGTON UNIVERSITY, Libraries, Special Collections Dept, Campus Box 1061, St Louis, 63130.
Notes: A small but significant collection.

VA —UNIVERSITY OF VIRGINIA, Alderman Library, Clifton Waller Barrett Collection, Charlottesville, 22901. Joan St C Crane, Cur of American Literature Collections
Notes: Papers.

WILLIAMS, REV. JOSEPH J., S.J.

MA —COLLEGE OF THE HOLY CROSS, Dinand Library, College St, Worcester, 01610. James M Mahoney, Cur of Special Collection
Holdings: // Mss
Notes: The Joseph J Williams, SJ Collection contains 107 mss and 865 letters concerning religious practices of tribes in Africa. Collection is indexed, restricted use.

WILLIAMS, ORLO

IN —INDIANA UNIVERSITY, Lilly Library, Seventh St, Bloomington, 47405. William R Cagle, Librn
Holdings: // Mss
Notes: A small collection of letters, 1924-1952, to author Orlo Williams from T S Eliot, 19 items.

WILLIAMS, OSCAR

IN —INDIANA UNIVERSITY, Lilly Library, Seventh St, Bloomington, 47405. William R Cagle, Librn
Holdings: // Cat Mss Pix
Notes: Poetry anthologies and books from his library. Extensive mss.

WILLIAMS, RICHARD D'ALTON

LA —NICHOLLS STATE UNIVERSITY, Ellender Memorial Library, Thibodaux, 70310. Randall A Detro, Dir; Philip D Uzee, Archivist
Holdings: Uncat Mss Maps Pix Microforms
Notes: Louisiana and local history; family paprs of the period, etc.

WILLIAMS, ROBERT RAMAPATNAM

DC —LIBRARY OF CONGRESS, Manuscript Division, Washington, 20540. John C Broderick, Chief
Notes: Papers of Robert Ramapatnam Williams (1886-1965), a pioneer in the field of nutrition and public health who synthesized thiamin (vitamin B1), helped to effect the widespread enrichment of foodstuff grains, and developed the Williams--Waterman Fund to combat diseases caused by inadequate nutrition. 20,000 items, incl correspondence, reports, photographs, and glass spectographic plates, document research on and production of vitamin B1, enrichment of cereal products, and the Williams--Waterman Fund.

WILLIAMS, ROGER

RI —BROWN UNIVERSITY, John Hay Library, 20 Prospect St, Providence, 02912. Mark N Brown, Cur Mss
Holdings: // Mss
Notes: 8 mss in the hand of Roger Williams incl his copy of Chief Ousamaquin's Massasoit's deed of land (1646), letters to the Plymouth Colony, a copy of *Proceedings of the General Assembly* (1655), and his proposals to resolve the Pawtuxet-Providence boundary dispute.

WILLIAMS, SAMUEL MAY

TX —ROSENBERG LIBRARY, Galveston and Texas History Center, 2310 Sealy Ave, Galveston, 77550. Jane Kenamore, Archivist
Holdings: Cat Mss
Notes: Papers of Samuel May Williams, secretary of Stephen F Austin's Colony, the earliest banker in Texas. Incl are correspondence with leading public figures in Texas and Mexico (in English and Spanish). Incl 57 S F Austin letters among the 4000 ms papers. See *Samuel May Williams, 1795-1858; Biography*. Calendar to Samuel May Williams papers compiled by Ruth G Nichols and S E Lifflander (Galveston, Tex; Rosenberg Library Press, 1956).

WILLIAMS, TENNESSEE, 1911-1983

CA —UNIVERSITY OF CALIFORNIA, LOS ANGELES, Research Library, Dept of Special Collections, 405 Hilgard Ave, Los Angeles, 90024. Edward Shreeves, Chairman, Bibliographers Group; David S Zeidberg, Head
Holdings: Vols 25 Mss
Notes: 25 first and other editions of his work; 1 linear foot of papers, primarily literary mss.

WILLIAMS, TENNESSEE, 1911-1983 (cont.)

GA —UNIVERSITY OF GEORGIA,
Libraries, Special Collections Division,
Athens, 30602. Vesta Lee Gordon, Asst Dir
for Special Collections
Notes: Theater Collection contains the Paris
Music Hall set and costume designs with
original drawings by Erte, Barbier, Zig and
others; British Music Hall Papers; European
toy theater collection; Charles Coburn
papers; television script collection; Tennessee
Williams papers. Collection contains 16,000
pieces.

MS —MISSISSIPPI STATE UNIVERSITY,
Mitchell Memorial Library, Box 5408,
Mississippi State, 39762. Frances N
Coleman, Head, Special Collections
Holdings: Vols (15,000) Cat Mss Maps Pix
Microforms
Notes: Social and political history of
Mississippi, incl University Archives (now
separate branch). Microfilms of Protestant
Church records. There are strong collections
on history of the Southern States, Mississippi
authors (especially Faulkner, Williams,
Carter, Welty, and Young); also the John C
Stennis Collection of over 2 million items,
his books, papers, photographs, etc. Incl 400
collections of mss; papers of US Rep David
R Bowen 1973-1983; papers of US Rep G V
Montgomery 1967-.

MO —SAINT LOUIS PUBLIC LIBRARY,
Gardner Rare Book Room, 1301 Olive St,
Saint Louis, 63103. Julanne M Good,
Supervisor; Martha Riley, Rare Books Librn
Holdings: Vols (2300) Cat
Budget: ($5573)
Notes: First editions of authors having some
association with William Marion Reedy and
Reedy's Mirror, such as Sara Teasdale, Zoe
Akins, Fannie Hurst, Edgar Lee Masters,
Babette Deutsch, Richard LeGallienne, etc.
Also first editions of selected St Louis and/
or Missouri authors such as T S Eliot,
Samuel L Clemens, Theodore Dreiser and
Tennessee Williams. Noncirculating.

NY —COLUMBIA UNIVERSITY
LIBRARIES, Rare Book & Manuscript
Library, 801 Butler Library, 535 W 114 St,
New York, 10027. Kenneth A Lohf, Librn
Holdings: Mss Pix
Notes: Papers, incl mss, letters, reviews, etc.
150 items. Restricted use.

WILLIAMS, VAN ZANDT

NY —AMERICAN INSTITUTE OF
PHYSICS, Center for the History of Physics,
Niels Bohr Library, 335 E 45 St, New York,
10017. John Aubry, Librn
Notes: Papers and records.

WILLIAMS, WILLIAM CARLOS

CA —FRANCIS BACON LIBRARY, 655 N
Dartmouth Ave, Claremont, 91711.
Elizabeth S Wrigley, Dir
Holdings: Mss Pix
Notes: Arensberg's miscellaneous
correspondence with American literary
figures (1920's-50's) including Bruce Bliven,
Catherine Drinker Bowen, Kay Boyle, Witter
Bynner, Edwin Corle, Helen A Keller,
Lysander Kemp, Kenneth Macgowan, John
Macy, Henry Miller, Lewis Mumford,
Clifford Odets, Kenneth Patchen, Irving
Stone, and William Carlos Williams.

CT —YALE UNIVERSITY, Box 1603A, Yale
Station, New Haven, 06520.
Holdings: Cat Mss

DE —UNIVERSITY OF DELAWARE, Hugh
M Morris Library, S College Ave, Newark,
19711. T Stuart Dick, Special Collections
Holdings: Cat Mss Pix
Notes: Manuscripts, etc, incl literary
correspondence.

FL —UNIVERSITY OF MIAMI, Otto G
Richter Library, PO Box 248214, Coral
Gables, 33124. Frank Rodgers, Dir of
Libraries

IN —INDIANA UNIVERSITY, Lilly Library,
Seventh St, Bloomington, 47405. William R
Cagle, Librn
Holdings: Cat Mss
Notes: First editions, etc. Mss incl

significant correspondence files with Ezra
Pound, Nicolas Calas, William Bird, et al.
Holdings are described in William Carlos
Williams Newsletter, June 1977.

MO —WASHINGTON UNIVERSITY, John
M Olin Library, Campus Box 1061, St Louis,
63130.
Notes: Extensive collection.

NV —UNIVERSITY OF NEVADA, RENO,
University Library, Special Collections Dept,
Reno, 89557. Robert E Blesse, Head
Holdings: Vols 104 // Cat
Notes: Includes individual works by author
in all editions including translations; also
prefaces, introductions, published
correspondence, appearances in anthologies,
periodicals, etc. Bibliographical research
collection, part of Modern Authors
Collection.

NJ —FAIRLEIGH DICKINSON
UNIVERSITY, Messler Library, 207
Montross Ave, Rutherford, 07070.
Holdings: Vols 300 Cat Pix Phonorecords
Notes: Books by and about William Carlos
Williams. Also, 700 vols from Dr William's
private collection.

NY —NEW YORK UNIVERSITY, Elmer
Holmes Bobst Library, Div of Special
Collections, Washington Sq S, New York,
10012. Frank Walker, Librn; Patrick
McGuire, Asst Librn
Holdings: Vols (100,000) Cat Mss Pix
Notes: The Fales Collection of first (and
other) editions of English and American
novels from about 1750 to date (about 70,
000 titles). Mss (30,000) pieces.

OH —KENT STATE UNIVERSITY, Libraries,
Dept of Special Collections, Kent, 44242.
Dean H Keller, Cur
Holdings: Vols 130 Cat Mss
Notes: Incl books by and about Williams,
mss (incl letters) and contributions by him to
books and periodicals.

RI —BROWN UNIVERSITY, John Hay
Library, Harris Collection, Prospect St,
Providence, 02912. Rosemary L Cullen, Cur
Holdings: Vols (200,000) Cat Mss Pix
Phonorecords Microforms
Budget: ($15,000)
Notes: The Harris Collection of American
Poetry and Plays is principally composed of
American and Canadian poetry and plays,
17th century-date. Extensive holdings in
songsters, gift books and annuals, hymnals,
pageants, broadside verse, carriers'
addresses, women poets, juvenile poetry,
(incl Mother Goose and The Night Before
Christmas), sheet music with lyrics, small
press publications, fine printing, black poets,
"little magazines," Yiddish-American
literature. All movements or schools of
American poetry are represented. Incl first
editions of most American poets and
playwrights, notably Whitman, Poe, Wallace
Stevens, Eugene O'Neill, Edward Albee,
Ezra Pound, T S Eliot, William Carlos
Williams, Amy Lowell, Phyllis Wheatley,
Robert Frost, Allen Ginsberg, Bliss Carman,
and Stephen Foster sheet music. Also incl
the Saunders Walt Whitman Collection
(1300 vols); the LangdonCollection of
Pageants (250 vols); the Asa Cushman
Collection of plays in ms and prompt copies;
the MacDougall Collection of Psalters and
Hymnals; 4000 plays issued by Walter H
Baker Co, Boston (1890-1957); the Vaxer
Collection of Yiddish Poetry, Plays and
Music (1700 vols). Collections incl 200,000
vols, 30,000 broadsides, 55,000 mss, 170,000
pieces of sheet music, 450 phonorecords, and
375 microfilm reels. See Dictionary Catalog
of the Harris Collection of American Poetry
and Plays (Boston: G K Hall, 1972), 13 vols;
Supplement (1977), 3 vols. See also,
American Poetry, 1609-1900, A Collection
on Microfilm, Segment I (1609-1820);
Segment II (1821-1850); Segment III (1851-
1870) (Woodbridge, Conn: Research
Publications). Separate catalog.

BC —SIMON FRASER UNIVERSITY,
Library, Burnaby, V5A 1S6, Can. Percilla
Groves, Special Collections Librn
Holdings: Vols (12,000) Cat Mss
Notes: This collection concentrates on
avant-garde American poetry since World
War II. Incl some Canadian poetry

(particularly West Coast poets), some British
and certain of the International Concrete
school. It particularly features the Black
Mountain and San Francisco schools and
those American and Canadian poets
influenced by them. There is a relatively
complete collection of works. There is a
relatively complete collection of books by
Ezra Pound (qv) and William Carlos
Williams together with considerable criticism
on both. Also incl certain underground
newspapers and 1600 little magazines.

WILLIAMS, WIRT

MA —BOSTON UNIVERSITY, Mugar
Memorial Library, Special Collections Dept,
771 Commonwealth Ave, Boston, 02215.
Howard B Gotlieb, Dir
Holdings: Cat Mss
Notes: Mss, correspondence, etc collected in
depth; incl publications by or about.

WILLIAMS-DAMERON FAMILY

NC —NORTH CAROLINA DIV OF
ARCHIVES & HISTORY, 109 E Jones St,
Raleigh, 27611.
Notes: Papers, 1804-1968; 400 items.

WILLIAMS-WATERMAN FUND

DC —LIBRARY OF CONGRESS, Manuscript
Division, Washington, 20540. John C
Broderick, Chief
Notes: Papers of Robert Ramapatnam
Williams (1886-1965), a pioneer in the field
of nutrition and public health who
synthesized thiamin (vitamin B1), helped to
effect the widespread enrichment of
foodstuff grains, and developed the Williams-
Waterman Fund to combat diseases caused
by inadequate nutrition. 20,000 items, incl
correspondence, reports, photographs, and
glass spectographic plates, document
research on and production of vitamin B1,
enrichment of cereal products, and the
Williams-Waterman Fund.

WILLIAMSBURG (COLONIAL), VIRGINIA see Colonial Williamsburg (1926-1961)

WILLIAMSBURGH GAZETTE

NY —LONG ISLAND HISTORICAL
SOCIETY, 128 Pierrepont St, at Clinton St,
Brooklyn, 11201.
Notes: Books and pamphlets relating to the
history of Brooklyn. Over 350 newspapers
and periodical resources, incl The Long
Island Star (1809-1863) and Williamsburgh
Gazette (1835-1853). 10,000 photographs.
Paintings, prints, and broadsides. More than
1400 mss collections relating primarily to
Brooklyn, dating from 1650 to 1980s. 750
maps and atlases, artifacts, archives, and
Decorative Arts collections. Two published
guides to Manuscripts: Calendar of
Manuscripts: 1783-1783, LIHS by Karin N
Mango, 1980. Also, A Guide to Brooklyn
Manuscripts in the Long Island Historical
Society. Prepared by Brooklyn Rediscovery,
a program of the Brooklyn Educational and
Cultural Alliance, 1980. Also, guide to
Museum Exhibit, Brooklyn Before the
Bridge - American paintings from the Long
Island Historical Society. Published by
Brooklyn Museum, 1982.

WILLIAMSON, CHARLES C.

NY —COLUMBIA UNIVERSITY
LIBRARIES, Rare Book & Manuscript
Library, 801 Butler Library, 535 W 114 St,
New York, 10027. Kenneth A Lohf, Librn
Holdings: Mss
Notes: Papers of the former director of the
libraries and dean of the School of Library
Service, Columbia University. 11,000 items.
Restricted use.

WILLIAMSON, HENRY

IL —ILLINOIS STATE UNIVERSITY, Milner
Library, Dept of Special Collections,

WILLIAMSON, HENRY (cont.)

Normal, 61761. Robert Sokan, Librn
Notes: First editions, limited editions, ephemera, etc.

WILLIAMSON, JACK

NM —EASTERN NEW MEXICO UNIVERSITY, Golden Library, Special Collections, Portales, 88130. Mary Jo Walker, Special Collections Librn
Holdings: Vols 11,940 Cat Mss Pix Audiotapes
Notes: Incl 700 magazine titles (10,318 issues), 11,940 vols, mss and correspondences of the following science fiction writers: Jack Williamson, Edmond Hamilton, Leigh Brackett, Forrest J Ackerman and Piers Anthony (Jacob), plus *Astounding/Analog* ms files (1954-1975). Also serves as a depository for Science Fiction Writers of America. Incl separate catalog for published books and unpublished registers to personal papers. The Williamson Register is being prepared for publication. Collection is described in *Anatomy of Wonder*, by Neil Barron (NY: Bowker, 1981); and *Special Collections, II* (winter, 1982), pp 49-57.

WILLIAMSON, JOSEPH

ME —BOWDOIN COLLEGE, Library, Brunswick, 04011. Dianne M Gutscher, Cur of Special Collections
Notes: Besides a general collection of 13,000 volumes relating to the State of Maine, there are also many ms collections touching on the political, economic and social history of Maine. These incl Joseph Williamson Papers, 125 letters of this Maine bibliographer.

WILLIS, J. FRANK

PQ —CONCORDIA UNIVERSITY LIBRARIES, Norris Library, 1435 Drummond, Montreal, H3G 1M8, Can. N Robins, Special Collections Librn
Holdings: Cat Mss
Notes: Collection of 14,000 English language radio drama scripts broadcast over the Canadian Broadcasting Corp from 1930s to date. Presently being accessed by computer. Contains two sections; the main section is the Esse W Ljungh Collection: besides plays, incl CBC memos, correspondence, etc; the second is the T Frank Willis Collection and consists of the scripts, letters and memos of the late producer.

WILLIS, SCOTT

OH —OHIO STATE UNIVERSITY, Library for Communication and Graphic Arts, 242 W 18th St, Columbus, 43210. Lucy S Caswell, Curator
Notes: The original works of editorial cartoonists Art Poinier, Scott Willis, Brian Basset, Billy Ireland, Frank Williams, Charles Werner, Ned Beard, L D Warren, Edward D Kuekes, Ray Osrin, Mike Peters, Draper Hill, Eugene Craig and Bert Whitman.

WILLIS, WILLIAM

ME —BOWDOIN COLLEGE, Library, Brunswick, 04011. Dianne M Gutscher, Cur of Special Collections
Holdings: Vols (13,000)
Notes: Besides a general collection of 13,000 volumes relating to the State of Maine, there are also many mss collections touching on the political, economic and social history of Maine. These incl William Willis Papers, 350 items, 1862-1869, of a president of the Maine Historical Society.
ME —PORTLAND PUBLIC LIBRARY, 5 Monument Sq, Portland, 04101. Edward V Chenevert, Library Dir
Holdings: Vols 2600 // Cat
Notes: Library of William Willis, 1794-1870, a noted Portland historian. The library, with the addition of a number of titles added by

his immediate heirs, has been kept intact. Contains books, pamphlets and periodicals printed in the 18th and 19th centuries, many autographed by the authors. Its subject matter is general is scope though it is strong in Maine material.

WILLKIE, WENDELL LEWIS, 1892-1944

IN —INDIANA UNIVERSITY, Lilly Library, Seventh St, Bloomington, 47405. William R Cagle, Librn
Holdings: // Mss Pix Phonorecords
Notes: Papers and correspondence of 1940 Republican presidential candidate Willkie. 500,000 items. Bulk of material is for 1939-1944. Incl campaign-related correspondence, speeches, writings and publications, material on *One World*, scrapbooks, clippings, photographs, election memorabilia, etc. Correspondence, research notes, and ms of Willkie biography prepared by Ellsworth Barnard, 1907- Collection relates to Professor Barnard's book *Wendell Willkie: Fighter for Freedon* (Northern Michigan University Press, 1966). 462 items. Also Willkie Clubs collection. Contains the presidential campaign files of the Associated Willkie Clubs of America, 1940. 64,417 items.

WILLOUGHBY, GEN. CHARLES A.

VA —MACARTHUR MEMORIAL, Library & Archives, MacArthur Sq, Norfolk, 23510. Ellen E Folkama, Asst Archivist
Holdings: Vols (4000) Cat Maps Pix Slides Phonorecords Audiotapes 16mm Films Microforms
Notes: Everything relating to the life and related activities of MacArthur. The Archives of the collection consist of 600 shelf-feet of documents from Gen MacArthur's official headquarters files over the period 1941-1951. These papers pertain to all matters with which his various commands were involved: military, naval and air matters; international relations; political science; Japanese occupation, peace treaty and Constitution, etc. Each Record Group is indexed. The indexes are retained here since they are being expanded. They are available for researchers.

WILMINGTON TEN

NC —UNIVERSITY OF NORTH CAROLINA, CHARLOTTE, J Murrey Atkins Library, UNCC Station, Charlotte, 28223. Robert F Brabham Jr, Special Collections Librn
Holdings: Mss Pix Cat
Notes: Incl pamphlets, newspapers, and ephemera published by various radical groups, 1960s and 1970s, based largely in the Midwest; also papers of T J Reddy, a member of the Charlotte 3, concerning civil rights, the Wilmington 10, and prison reforms.

WILSHIRE, HENRY GAYLORD

CA —UNIVERSITY OF CALIFORNIA, LOS ANGELES, Research Library, Dept of Special Collections, 405 Hilgard Ave, Los Angeles, 90024. Edward Shreeves, Chairman, Bibliographers Group; David S Zeidberg, Head
Holdings: Mss
Notes: 11 linear feet of correspondence, mss, personal papers, etc, of Henry Gaylord Wilshire, his wife, Mary (MacReynolds), and their son, Logan Gaylord. Additional material in the Maude Emily Glass papers.
IA —UNIVERSITY OF IOWA, University Libraries, Iowa City, 52242. Frank Paluka, Head, Special Collections Dept

WILSON, ANGUS

IL —NORTHERN ILLINOIS UNIVERSITY, Founders Memorial Library, Rare Books and Special Collections Dept, De Kalb, 60115. William R DuBois, Dept Head
Holdings: Vols 50 // Cat
Notes: Incl mss.

NV —UNIVERSITY OF NEVADA, RENO, University Library, Special Collections Dept, Reno, 89557. Robert E Blesse, Head
Holdings: Vols 83 Cat
Notes: Includes individual works by author in all editions including translations; also prefaces, introductions, published correspondence, appearances in anthologies, periodicals, etc. Bibliographical research collection, part of Modern Authors Collection.

WILSON, CARROLL LOUIS, 1910-1983

MA —MASSACHUSETTS INSTITUTE OF TECHNOLOGY, Institute Archives, Special Collections, Cambridge, 02139.
Notes: Papers of Carroll Louis Wilson, an environmental energy analyst, educator, and first General Manager of the Atomic Energy Commission. Collection incl alphabetical subject files documenting Wilson's personal life and professional career, primarily from 1959 to 1983. Incl correspondence on energy and environmental issues reflecting his involvement in the Atomic Energy Commission, etc. Folder list available in the Institute Archives. Access partially restricted; consult the Institute Archivist for further information.

WILSON, CARTER

MA —BOSTON UNIVERSITY, Mugar Memorial Library, Special Collections Dept, 771 Commonwealth Ave, Boston, 02215. Howard B Gotlieb, Dir
Holdings: Cat Mss
Notes: Mss, correspondence, etc collected in depth; incl publications by or about.

WILSON, CHARLES E.

IN —ANDERSON COLLEGE, Charles E Wilson Library, 1033 E Third St, Anderson, 46012. Richard Snyder, Dir
Holdings: Vols (120,000) Cat
Notes: The Charles E Wilson Archives (president of General Motors Corp, 1941-1953 and Secretary of Defense, 1953-1957). Incl 180 mss boxes of personal correspondence, 35 bound vols of speeches, press clippings, photographs.

WILSON, COLIN

BC —UNIVERSITY OF VICTORIA, McPherson Library, Victoria, V8W 3H5, Can.

WILSON, EDMUND

CT —YALE UNIVERSITY, Box 1603A, Yale Station, New Haven, 06520.
Holdings: Cat Mss
DE —UNIVERSITY OF DELAWARE, Hugh M Morris Library, S College Ave, Newark, 19711. T Stuart Dick, Special Collections
Holdings: Cat Mss Pix
Notes: Early typescript draft of Arthur Mizener's biography of F Scott Fitzgerald with extensive critical comment and correspondence from Edmund Wilson.
NY —SAINT LAWRENCE UNIVERSITY, Owen D Young Library, Canton, 13617. Mahlon Peterson, Librn
Holdings: Mss
Notes: Correspondence between Edmund Wilson and William Fenton during the years 1857-1872. The letters are concerned primarily with New York State Indians and Wilson's book *Apologies to the Iroquois*. Approx 60 items.
OK —UNIVERSITY OF TULSA, McFarlin Library, Dept of Rare Books and Special Collections, 600 S College, Tulsa, 74104. David Farmer, Dir; Toby Murray, Archivist; Caroline Swinson, Cur of Manuscripts & Art
Holdings: Vols 10,000 //
Notes: His library collection.

WILSON, FRANCIS

NY —NEW YORK PUBLIC LIBRARY, Performing Arts Research Center, Billy Rose Theatre Collection, 111 Amsterdam Ave,

WILSON, FRANCIS (cont.)

New York, 10023. Dorothy L Swerdlove, Cur
Holdings: Cat Mss Pix
Notes: Papers, scrapbooks, mss, photographs, memorabilia, etc.

WILSON, GEORGE HOWARD

OK —UNIVERSITY OF OKLAHOMA, Bizzell Memorial Library, Western History Collections, 401 W Brooks, Norman, 73069. John Ezell, Cur
Holdings: Mss Maps Pix Documents
Notes: US Representative. His papers. Guide available (1985).

WILSON, H. HUBERT, 1909-1977

NJ —PRINCETON UNIVERSITY, Seeley G Mudd Manuscript Library, Public Affairs Papers Collection, Princeton, 08544. Nancy Bressler, Cur
Notes: Incl 22 cartons. The papers cover the period 1947-75. An unpublished 6p checklist is available in the Library.

WILSON, HENRY, 1812-1875

OH —RUTHERFORD B HAYES LIBRARY, 1337 Hayes Ave, Fremont, 43420. Watt P Marchman, Dir
Holdings: Cat Mss Pix
Notes: Henry Wilson and William and Mary B Claflin of Massachusetts. Mainly correspondence. Index to about 9000 items in the collection. 12 linear ft. Listed in *Guide to Manuscripts of the Ohio Historical Society*, 71.

WILSON, JAMES

PA —FREE LIBRARY OF PHILADELPHIA, Rare Book Dept, Logan Sq, Philadelphia, 19103. Marie E Korey, Rare Book Librn
Holdings: Mss
Notes: 36 notebooks of the signer of the Declaration of Independence.

WILSON, JOHN G.

MO —WASHINGTON UNIVERSITY, Libraries, Special Collections Dept, Campus Box 1061, St Louis, 63130.
Notes: Family and business correspondence.

WILSON, LOIS

OH —KENT STATE UNIVERSITY, Libraries, Dept of Special Collections, Kent, 44242. Dean H Keller, Cur
Holdings: Vols 10 Cat Mss Pix

WILSON, MITCHELL

MA —BOSTON UNIVERSITY, Mugar Memorial Library, Special Collections Dept, 771 Commonwealth Ave, Boston, 02215. Howard B Gotlieb, Dir
Holdings: Cat Mss
Notes: Mss, correspondence, etc collected in depth; incl publications by or about.

WILSON, MORTIMER

CA —UNIVERSITY OF CALIFORNIA, LOS ANGELES, Music Library, Schonberg Hall, Los Angeles, 90024. Stephen M Fry, Music Librn
Notes: Mss.

WILSON, SAMUEL M.

KY —UNIVERSITY OF KENTUCKY, Margaret I King Library, Dept of Special Collections, Lexington, 40506. William Marshall, Head
Holdings: Cat Mss Maps Pix
Notes: History of Kentucky, Ohio Valley and Presbyterian Church. Consists of books, letters, maps, etc; about 10,000 pieces.

WILSON, SLOAN

MA —BOSTON UNIVERSITY, Mugar Memorial Library, Special Collections Dept,

771 Commonwealth Ave, Boston, 02215. Howard B Gotlieb, Dir
Holdings: Cat Mss Pix
Notes: Mss, correspondence, etc collected in depth; incl publications by or about.

WILSON, WOODROW

CA —HOOVER INSTITUTION ON WAR, REVOLUTION & PEACE, Stanford University, Stanford, 94305. Milorad M Drachkovitch, Archivist
Holdings: Mss
Notes: Correspondence between Herbert Hoover and Woodrow Wilson, 1915-1920. 152 items. Also the Paul A Hill Collection of some 300 letters from famous people concerning their opinions of Wilson.

CT —YALE UNIVERSITY, Box 1603A, Yale Station, New Haven, 06520.
Holdings: Cat Mss
Notes: The Edward M House Papers.

DE —UNIVERSITY OF DELAWARE, Hugh M Morris Library, S College Ave, Newark, 19711. T Stuart Dick, Special Collections
Holdings: // Cat Mss
Notes: Incl business, legal, personal and political papers of Willard Saulsbury, spanning 1850-1927. Saulsbury was a US Senator from Delaware. Incl letters and telegrams from Woodrow Wilson relating to the work of the Democratic National Committee, party politics, etc (1912-1918).

DC —LIBRARY OF CONGRESS, Rare Book & Special Collections Div, Washington, 20540. William Matheson, Chief
Notes: Books and personal mementos of President Woodrow Wilson, incl his personal library.

DC —LIBRARY OF CONGRESS, Manuscript Division, Washington, 20540. John C Broderick, Chief
Notes: The Presidential Papers collection incl the papers, etc, of numerous Presidents.

IL —NORTHWESTERN UNIVERSITY, Library, Special Collections Dept, 1937 Sheridan Rd, Evanston, 60201. R Russell Maylone, Cur
Holdings: Vols 324 Cat Pix
Notes: The Woodrow Wilson Collection. Incl pamphlets, etc. Additional material in general collections.

MD —JOHNS HOPKINS UNIVERSITY, Milton S Eisenhower Library, Charles & 34 Sts, Baltimore, 21218. Ann S Gwyn, Assistant Dir for Special Collections
Holdings: Vols 200 Cat Mss

NJ —PRINCETON UNIVERSITY, Library, Manuscript Collection, Nassau St, Princeton, 08540. Jean F Preston, Cur
Holdings: Cat Mss
Notes: The Woodrow Wilson Collection. Incl 63 boxes. Terms of Access: A large part of the collection may be read by qualified scholars but certain sections have been restricted by various donors and access to them usually requires special permission from the Librarian of Princeton University. Reproduction: Certain parts of the collection may not be reproduced and in several instances reproduction is permitted only to those readers who have been granted access to specific papers in the collection. See *Princeton University Library Chronicle*, v 7, p 7-18; v 17, p 113-62; v 17, p 173-82.

NC —DAVIDSON COLLEGE, E H Little Library, Davidson, 28036. Leland M Park, Dir; Chalmers G Davidson, Dir
Holdings: Vols 200 Cat Mss Pix Films

VA —WOODROW WILSON BIRTHPLACE, PO Box 24, Staunton, 24401. Gertrude Davis, Librn
Holdings: Vols 3500 Cat Mss Pix
Budget: $500

WI —BELOIT COLLEGE LIBRARIES, Beloit, 53511. Dennis W Dickinson, Dir
Holdings: Vols 200 Cat
Notes: The Irving S Kull Collection. Covers roughly the period 1900-1920. Books by and about Wilson. Incl books written about the Wilson era.

WILTSIE, CHARLES H.

NY —UNIVERSITY OF ROCHESTER, Rush Rhees Library, Department of Rare Books

and Special Collections, Rochester, 14627. Peter Dzwonkoski, Librn
Holdings: Mss
Notes: His papers and memorabilia. Prominent in Rochester civic activities.

WIND, SOLAR see Solar Wind

WIND ENSEMBLES—COLLECTIONS

IL —UNIVERSITY OF ILLINOIS, URBANA/CHAMPAIGN, Library, Music Library, Urbana, 61801. William M McClellan, Librn
Holdings: Vols (200,000) Cat Mss Slides Sound Recordings Microforms Books Scores
Budget: ($65,000)
Notes: Introductory, instructive, research and reference materials to support work at graduate level in ethnomusicology,, musicology, music education, performance areas. Special areas incl about 2500 pre-1800 music mss and editions of music on microfilm, 2400 graduate music theses on microfilm, a special collection of 30,000 titles of American vocal sheet music covering the period 1790-1970, the Rafael Joseffy Collection of about 2000 pieces of 19th century piano music (incl performer markings), the Joseph Szigeti Collection (700 items: published music, mss, recordings), mainly violin and piano music by various commposers. Also incl a special collection of 45,000 78 rpm sound recordings (uncat) of classical music and jazz; a collection of 2900 titles from Chicago radio station WGN. Incl orchestrations, a collection of 500,000 items (uncat) from stock of Hunleth Music Store, St Louis, Missouri, mainly early 20th century imprints of songs, wind music, string music, piano, sets of theatre orchestra parts, dance band orchestrations. A separate collection of choral octavos and instrumental parts is maintained, incl 135,000 pieces of choral music, 30,500 orchestral parts, and 5500 wind ensemble parts. Also, music publishers' catalogues (mainly European and American), ca 126 cubic feet, 1860s-1950s.

SD —UNIVERSITY OF SOUTH DAKOTA, Shrine to Music Museum, USD Box 194, Vermillion, 57069. Andre P Larson, Dir
Budget: ($205,036)
Notes: The Shrine to Music Museum is one of America's major collections of musical resource materials, incl more than 4000 antique musical instruments from all over the world, plus an extensive supporting library of several thousand books, music, periodicals, recordings, photographs, and related musical memorabilia. The collection of 19th and early 20th-century sheet music and music for wind instruments is probably the most extensive in the country. Inquiries and visits are welcomed.

WIND INSTRUMENTS

DC —LIBRARY OF CONGRESS, Music Division, Washington, 20540.
Holdings: Cat Mss Maps Pix Slides Microforms
Notes: The Dayton C Miller Flute Collection, incl nearly 1600 instruments, plus music and books.

IL —UNIVERSITY OF ILLINOIS, URBANA/CHAMPAIGN, Library, Bands & Busch Instrument Collection, 1103 S Sixth St, Champaign, 61820. John Cranford, Librn
Notes: This collection of 212 old and unusual wind and percussion instruments comes from two sources: The Carl Busch collection, and instruments collected by the late Director of University Bands Emeritus, Dr A A Harding. The museum is open from 8 to 5 Monday through Friday, by appointment only.

†MD —UNIVERSITY OF MARYLAND, Library, The National Association of College Wind & Percussion Instructors Library, College Park, 20742. Pearl Z Tubiash, Supvr
Holdings: Cat
Notes: Primarily scores, along with some organizational papers and publications.

SD —UNIVERSITY OF SOUTH DAKOTA, Shrine to Music Museum, USD Box 194, Vermillion, 57069. Andre P Larson, Dir
Budget: ($205,036)
Notes: The Shrine to Music Museum is one

WIND INSTRUMENTS (cont.)

of America's major collections of musical resource materials, incl more than 4000 antique musical instruments from all over the world, plus an extensive supporting library of several thousand books, music, periodicals, recordings, photographs, and related musical memorabilia. The collection of 19th and early 20th-century sheet music and music for wind instruments is probably the most extensive in the country. Inquiries and visits are welcomed.

WA —UNIVERSITY OF WASHINGTON LIBRARIES, Music Library, DN-10, Seattle, 98195. David A Wood, Music Librn
Budget: ($7373)
Notes: The Melvin Harris Collection of pre-LP recordings of brass and woodwind music, 1,700 items.

WIND POWER

NY —CARY ARBORETUM OF THE NEW YORK BOTANICAL GARDEN, Library, Box AB, Millbrook, 12545. Fred Strum, Librn
Notes: This collection of alternative energy sources consists of publications concerned with solar energy, wind power, biofuel, methanol, small hydroelectric projects, and wood power.

WIND TUNNELS

†MA —MASSACHUSETTS INSTITUTE OF TECHNOLOGY, Cambridge, 02139.
Notes: Archival collections and papers at MIT.

ON —NATIONAL RESEARCH COUNCIL OF CANADA, Aeronautical/Mechanical Engineering Branch Library, Montreal Rd, Ottawa, K1A 0R6, Can. Louise Fletcher, Head
Notes: This branch library of the Canada Institute for Scientific and Technical Information (CISTI) of the National Research Council of Canada, Ottawa, has a collection strong in aeronautical engineering, automatic control, CAD/CAM, robotics, ocean, wind, and solar energy power, hydraulic and coastal engineering, icing, low temperature research, naval engineering, metals and metallurgy, incl composites, tribology, and air, railroad, marine transportation. Library supported the Council contribution to the development of the remote manipular Canadarm for NASA's Space Shuttle Orbiters and more recently, the Canadian Astronaut Program which will contribute payload specialists to NASA's Space Shuttle Program in 1984. 35,000 monographs, 1200 serials. Report collection: over 500,000 items.

WINDBREAKS, SHELTERBELTS, ETC.

SK —CANADA PRAIRIE FARM REHABILITATION ADMINISTRATION LIBRARY, Motherwell Bldg, Regina, S4P 0R5, Can. C Kosack, Head
Notes: PFRA is a Canadian federal government agency initiated to alleviate the effects of drought and water shortages on the prairies.
See also entry under Soil Conservation

WINDIC DIALECT (SLOVENIAN) see Slovenian Language and Literature

WINDMILLS

NY —CARY ARBORETUM OF THE NEW YORK BOTANICAL GARDEN, Library, Box AB, Millbrook, 12545. Fred Strum, Librn
Notes: This collection of alternative energy sources consists of publications concerned with solar energy, wind power, biofuel, methanol, small hydroelectric projects, and wood power.

TX —PANHANDLE-PLAINS HISTORICAL MUSEUM, Research Center, Box 967, WT Sta, Canyon, 79016. Claire R Kuehn, Archivist-Librn
Holdings: Mss
Budget: $200
Notes: "This in the finest collection of

literature on windmills and water supply equipment in a public repository." Covers the period 1880-1930. Incl manufacturers' catalogs (75), pamphlets, brochures, and advertisements (200), and other ms items. Supplements the Museum's windmill artifact collection.

WINDOWS, STAINED GLASS see Glass Painting and Staining

WINDS—ENERGY

KS —WICHITA PUBLIC LIBRARY, 223 S Main, Wichita, 67202. Larry DePiesse, Head, Business & Technology Dept; Jayne F Young, Business & Technology Dept
Holdings: Vols 800 Cat
Budget: $700
Notes: 456 of our holdings are circulating books. The remaining 344 books are in a special non-circulating collection, the "Energy Collection." Includes solar, wind, nuclear, etc.

WINDS ALOFT

CA —UNIVERSITY OF CALIFORNIA, LOS ANGELES, Engineering & Mathematical Sciences Library, 405 Hilgard, Los Angeles, 90024. Rosalee I Wright, Librn
Notes: Collection includes WMO publications (comprehensive); IGY data series on surface observations, radiosonde and rawinsonde observations, upper wind observations, and radiation data (mostly in microform); selected government report or data series, eg from NOAA, NCC and AF Geophysics Laboratory.

ON —NATIONAL RESEARCH COUNCIL OF CANADA, Aeronautical/Mechanical Engineering Branch Library, Montreal Rd, Ottawa, K1A 0R6, Can. Louise Fletcher, Head
Notes: This branch library of the Canada Institute for Scientific and Technical Information (CISTI) of the National Research Council of Canada, Ottawa, has a collection strong in aeronautical engineering, automatic control, CAD/CAM, robotics, ocean, wind, and solar energy power, hydraulic and coastal engineering, icing, low temperature research, naval engineering, metals and metallurgy, incl composites, tribology, and air, railroad, marine transportation. Library supported the Council contribution to the development of the remote manipular Canadarm for NASA's Space Shuttle Orbiters and more recently, the Canadian Astronaut Program which will contribute payload specialists to NASA's Space Shuttle Program in 1984. 35,000 monographs, 1200 serials. Report collection: over 500,000 items.

WINDSOR, CLAIRE

CA —UNIVERSITY OF SOUTHERN CALIFORNIA, Edward L Doheny Memorial Library, Archives of Performing Arts, University Park, Los Angeles, 90089. Robert Knutson, Librn
Holdings: Mss Pix
Notes: Personal collection of papers, pictures, etc.

WINDWARD ISLANDS see Dominica; Grenada; Martinique

WINE AND WINE MAKING

CA —UNIVERSITY OF CALIFORNIA, DAVIS, Shields Library, Dept of Special Collections, Davis, 95616. Donald Kunitz, Head; C Danial Elliott, Asst Head
Holdings: Uncat Mss Pix Pamphlets
Notes: The Cebis Wine Collection (2500 items) incl brochures, wine lists and labels from Eastern Europe, clippings and brochures on wine by subject. The California Wineries Records (24,000 items) incl correspondence, inspection reports with emphasis on wine production, the physical nature of specific wineries, import/export involvement. These records, filed with the

Federal Bureau of Alcohol, Tobacco and Firearms, cover 1922-53. Wine bottle labels for wines and liquors imported into the United States or bottled here which were submitted of the Alcohol and Tobacco Tax Division of the Internal Revenue Service for approval, 1963-68, are held in the Wine Bottle Label Collection (21,000 items).

CA —UNIVERSITY OF CALIFORNIA, DAVIS, General Library, Davis, 95616. Bernard Kreissman, University Librn; C Danial Elliott, Asst Head, Dept Special Collections
Holdings: Vols 6000 Cat
Notes: A collection of books and journals concerned with wines and wine making from nearly all of the grape growing and wine producing areas of the world, eg, US, France, Germany and Central Europe, Soviet Russia, South Africa, South America, Australia, etc. Books from nonwine producing areas, such as the Scandinavian countries and Holland, are represented in the collection. Uncataloged. Pamphlets (3000) also available.

CA —CALIFORNIA STATE UNIVERSITY, FRESNO, Henry Madden Library, Dept of Special Collections, Fresno, 93740. Ronald J Mahoney, Head
Holdings: Vols (3400) Cat Maps Pix
Notes: Books and pamphlets relating to the history and development of viticulture and enology. Emphasizes pre-1920 worldwide imprints. Incl 900 merchants' catalogs, 1400 pamphlets, 200 wine lists, 750 periodical issues, and ephemera. Partially cataloged.

CA —LOS ANGELES PUBLIC LIBRARY, Science & Technology Dept, 630 W Fifth St, Los Angeles, 90071. Billie M Connor, Dept Head
Holdings: Vols (14,000) Cat Mss
Notes: Includes agricultural publications of the US Department of Agriculture, California and other state experiment station publications on all aspects of plant and animal husbandry, soil science and analysis, including Soil Surveys. Emphasis is on the Western states and semi-tropical areas.
See also entries under Agriculture; Cookery and Cook Books.

CA —UNIVERSITY OF CALIFORNIA, LOS ANGELES, Research Library, Dept of Special Collections, 405 Hilgard Ave, Los Angeles, 90024. Edward Shreeves, Chairman, Bibliographers Group; David S Zeidberg, Head
Holdings: Vols 350 Periodicals
Notes: Incl 4 linear feet of magazines and ephemera.

CA —E & J GALLO WINERY LIBRARY, PO Box 1130, Modesto, 95353. Jill Elliott, Librn
Holdings: Vols 8000 Cat
Notes: Will photocopy up to 30 pages at no charge.

CA —POMONA PUBLIC LIBRARY, Special Collections, 625 S Garey Ave, PO Box 2271, Pomona, 91766. David Streeter, Librn
Holdings: Cat
Notes: Incl labels (6000) from California wineries. Expansion anticipated.

CA —SAINT HELENA PUBLIC LIBRARY, 1492 Library Lane, Saint Helena, 94574. Clayla Davis, Library Admin
Holdings: Vols 3000 Cat Mss 16mm Films
Budget: $7000
Notes: Incl Napa Valley Wine Library. Bibliography of holdings available.

CA —CITY COLLEGE OF SAN FRANCISCO, Alice Statler Library, Hotel & Restaurant Dept, 50 Phelan Ave, San Francisco, 94112. Mary B Smyth, Librn
Holdings: Vols (7300) Cat Slides 16mm Films Filmstrips Microforms
Budget: ($5000)
Notes: The collection covers all aspects of the public hospitality industry. In addition to the book collection, it has 6000 cataloged pamphlets, 1500 menus. It also has bound hotel and restaurant magazines dating back to the 19th century. Receives 85 current periodicals in hospitality industry.

CA —WINE MUSEUM OF SAN FRANCISCO, Alfred Fromm Rare Wine Books Library, 633 Beach St, San Francisco, 94109. Barbara W Thompson, Cur
Holdings: Vols (700) Cat Maps Pix
Notes: The Library consists primarily of

WINE AND WINE MAKING (cont.)

volumes on aspects of wine history, enology, and viticulture. All texts are completely cross-referenced by subject/title/author. Noncirculating. Chronological listing available at cost.

CA —THE HAGGIN MUSEUM, Petzinger Library of Californiana, 1201 N Pershing Ave, Stockton, 95203. Diane Freggiaro, Librn/Archivist
Holdings: Vols (7000) Cat Mss Maps Pix Slides Audiotapes 16mm Films
Notes: The Petzinger Library is open by appointment only. Special emphasis on Stockton and San Joaquin County and Valley area, local biography, agriculture, agricultural history, industrial history, farm machinery (especially Holt Manufacturing Co, Stockton). There is a photograph collection of 8500 pictures, and extensive manuscript holdings (about 17,000 pieces).

IN —HURTY-PECK LIBRARY OF BEVERAGE LITERATURE, 5650 W Raymond Street, PO Box 41167, Indianapolis, 46208. Ben Wilson, Librn
Holdings: Vols (6000) Cat //
Notes: The most comprehensive collection, in English, in the world on beverages of all types. History, manufacture, formulae, customs. Books on beer and brewing; cocoa and chocolate; coffee; liquors and spirits; soft drinks; tea; and wine.

NY —CULINARY INSTITUTE OF AMERICA, Katharine Angell Library, North Rd, Hyde Park, 12538. Eileen deVries, Librn
Notes: The Tastevin Collection, one of the most complete collections on wine and spirits in the eastern US.

OH —CASE WESTERN RESERVE UNIVERSITY LIBRARIES, Cleveland, 44106. Susie Hanson, Special Collections Librn
Holdings: Vols 340 Cat
Notes: The Frank Hadley Ginn Collection, a gift of Dr and Mrs W Powell Jones.

WING, STC BOOKS

CA —CLAREMONT COLLEGES, Honnold Library, Ninth & Dartmouth, Claremont, 91711. Tania Rizzo, Special Collections Dept Head
Holdings: Vols (70,000) Cat
Notes: Several collections particularly strong in 17th century English imprints: Burton, Dryden, Milton, Oxford, and Crispin (rare books). Also 784 pamphlets arranged by Wing number; inventory available.

CA —FRANCIS BACON LIBRARY, 655 N Dartmouth Ave, Claremont, 91711. Elizabeth S Wrigley, Dir
Notes: Over 1000 titles in the STC and Wing periods; detailed collations of these vols published.

CA —UNIVERSITY OF CALIFORNIA, LOS ANGELES, William Andrews Clark Memorial Library, 2520 Cimarron St, Los Angeles, 90018.
Holdings: Cat
Notes: Extensive collection, first editions, etc.

IL —NEWBERRY LIBRARY, 60 W Walton St, Chicago, 60610. Diana Haskell, Cur of Modern Mss
Holdings: Cat
Notes: Very strong collection.

IN —INDIANA UNIVERSITY, Lilly Library, Seventh St, Bloomington, 47405. William R Cagle, Librn
Holdings: Vols 5800 Cat

MN —UNIVERSITY OF MINNESOTA, O Meredith Wilson Library, 309 19 Ave S, Minneapolis, 55455. Austin J McLean, Chief, Special Collections
Holdings: Vols (9000) Cat
Notes: Special concentration on volumes from the Stuart Period. Holdings are cited in the new revisions of the STC and Wing.

NY —NEW YORK STATE LIBRARY, State Education Bldg Annex, Washington Ave, Albany, 12224.
Holdings: Microforms
Notes: English books, 1475-1640. University

Microfilms collection. Access thru Pollard and Redgrave, *Short-title Catalogue,* English books, 1641-1700. University Microfilms collections. Access thru *Wing, Short-title Catalogue.*

NY —BUFFALO & ERIE COUNTY PUBLIC LIBRARY, Rare Book Room, Lafayette Sq, Buffalo, 14203. William H Loos, Cur
Holdings: Vols 900 Cat
Notes: Holdings described in *Pollard and Redgrave Titles; A Checklist of Items in the Rare Book Room of the Buffalo and Erie County Public Library* (Buffalo, 1968); and *Wing Titles; A Checklist of Items in the Rare Book Room, Buffalo and Erie County Public Library* (Buffalo, 1968).

PA —FREE LIBRARY OF PHILADELPHIA, Rare Book Dept, Logan Sq, Philadelphia, 19103. Marie E Korey, Rare Book Librn
Holdings: Vols (1000) // Uncat
Notes: Wing and Short Title Catalogue Books: books and pamphlets printed in Great Britain between 1475 and 1700.

PA —UNIVERSITY OF PENNSYLVANIA, Van Pelt Library, Rare Books Collection, 34 & Walnut Sts, Philadelphia, 19104. Daniel Traister, Special Collections Librn
Holdings: Vols 7500 Cat
Notes: A printed catalog is in press (Feb 1978).

†WA —WASHINGTON STATE UNIVERSITY, Library, Manuscripts, Archives & Special Collections, Pullman, 99164. John F Guido, Head
Holdings: Vols Cat Mss
Notes: Among the significant holdings are the William George Fretton papers relating to Convertry, England; the Thomas Balston collection of Sitwelliana, which incl correspondence, monographs and first editions, as well as holograph poems of Edith, Osbert and Sacheverell Sitwell; and first editions and correspondence of Elizabeth Robins. A short-title catalog of English books prior to 1700 is cited in Down's *American Literary Resources:* p 664.

ON —QUEEN'S UNIVERSITY, Douglas Library, Kingston, K7L 5C4, Can. William F E Morley, Cur, Special Collections
Holdings: Vols 925 Cat Mss
Notes: Dated collection (books printed before 1700).

WINNEBAGO INDIANS

NY —HOFSTRA UNIVERSITY, Library, 1000 Fulton Ave, Hempstead, 11550. Charles R Andrews, Dean of Library Services
Notes: The personal library of Paul Radin. See description of the American Philosophical Society Library's collection of his anthropological papers under this entry (Pa).

PA —AMERICAN PHILOSOPHICAL SOCIETY, Library, 105 S Fifth St, Philadelphia, 19106. Edward C Carter II, Librn
Notes: The anthropological papers of Paul Radin in fields of ethnology, social organization, primitive religion, linquistics, and mythology. He worked mostly among the Winnebago, Ojibwa, Fox, Zapotec, Wappo, Wintun, and Huave Indian tribes; also Italian and other ethnic minorities of San Francisco.

WINNIPEG—HISTORY

MB —UNIVERSITY OF MANITOBA, Elizabeth Dafoe Library, Archives and Special Collections Dept, Winnipeg, R3T 2N2, Can. Richard E Bennett, Dept Head; Corrado A Santoro, Reference Archivist
Holdings: Mss
Notes: Unpublished work by Rev George Bryce on the history of Winnipeg circa 1905. History of Fort Garry from Gov Simpson to incorporation of Winnipeg in 1873.

†MB —UNIVERSITY OF MANITOBA, Library, Winnipeg, R3T 2N2, Can.
Notes: Complete research archive of ninety years of the Winnipeg *Times,* defunct in 1980. Millions of newspaper clippings, indexed and in chronological order; about

one million photographs, identified and dated; 10,000 books, etc.

WINNIPEG FREE PRESS

MB —UNIVERSITY OF MANITOBA, Elizabeth Dafoe Library, Archives and Special Collections Dept, Winnipeg, R3T 2N2, Can. Richard E Bennett, Dept Head; Corrado A Santoro, Reference Archivist
Notes: Papers relating to Miss Hind's career in journalism as Commercial and Agricultural Editor of the Winnipeg *Free Press.* Includes materials on her two world tours (1935-37) sponsored by the *Free Press.* Also, published editorials of Frederick Simha Manor, which appeared in the Winnipeg *Free Press* from 1964-1978.

WINNIPEG TIMES

†MB —UNIVERSITY OF MANITOBA, Library, Winnipeg, R3T 2N2, Can.
Notes: Complete research archive of ninety years of the Winnipeg *Times,* defunct in 1980. Millions of newspaper clippings, indexed and in chronological order; about one million photographs, identified and dated; 10,000 books, etc.

WINNIPEG TRIBUNE

MB —UNIVERSITY OF MANITOBA, Elizabeth Dafoe Library, Archives and Special Collections Dept, Winnipeg, R3T 2N2, Can. Richard E Bennett, Dept Head; Corrado A Santoro, Reference Archivist
Notes: Newsclippings from the *Tribune* dating from the mid-1920's to 1980. Index in Reading Room and also Unpublished Register.

WINOGRAND, GARRY

AZ —UNIVERSITY OF ARIZONA, Center for Creative Photography, 843 E University Blvd, Tucson, 85721. James Enyeart, Dir; Terence Pitts, Cur and Librn
Notes: Center has significant collections consisting of more than 25 photographs plus other archival material such as negatives, contact sheets, work prints, correspondence, financial records, diaries, project files, etc. Inventories of the collections are available to researchers. Published guides available for some collections.

WINSLOW, C. E. A.

CT —YALE UNIVERSITY, Box 1603A, Yale Station, New Haven, 06520.
Holdings: Mss Pix
Notes: The Contemporary Medical Care and Health Policy Collection. Letters, memos, records, photographs, etc of the principal strategists of the social medical movement in the US.

WINSOR, JUSTIN

MD —JOHNS HOPKINS UNIVERSITY, Milton S Eisenhower Library, Charles & 34 Sts, Baltimore, 21218. Ann S Gwyn, Assistant Dir for Special Collections
Holdings: Cat Mss

WINSTON, ELLEN BLACK

NC —UNIVERSITY OF NORTH CAROLINA, GREENSBORO, Walter Clinton Jackson Library, Special Collections Dept, 1000 Spring Garden St, Greensboro, 27412. Emilie W Mills, Librn
Holdings: Mss Pix
Notes: Papers of the Commissioner of Public Welfare in North Carolina and later (1963-67) the first US Commissioner of Welfare in the Department of Health, Education, and Welfare. Speeches, general correspondence, news items, clippings, photographs, memorabilia, tape recorded interviews.

WINTER, ELLA

†NY —COLUMBIA UNIVERSITY LIBRARIES, Butler Library, Rare Book and

WINTER, ELLA (cont.)

Manuscript Library, 535 W 114 St, New York, 10027.
Notes: Papers, correspondence, and photographs.

WINTER, JACK

ON —MCMASTER UNIVERSITY, Mills Memorial Library, Div of Archives & Research Collections, Hamilton, L8S 4L6, Can. G R Hill, Univ Librn
Holdings: Mss
Notes: Typescripts and mss of poems, articles, plays, adaptations of plays, and correspondence, 1958-1977.

WINTERS, YVOR

CA —STANFORD UNIVERSITY LIBRARIES, Cecil H Green Library, Stanford, 94305. Michael T Ryan, Cur
Holdings: Vols Cat
Notes: Also incl correspondence and literary mss.

WINTERTON, PAUL

MA —BOSTON UNIVERSITY, Mugar Memorial Library, Special Collections Dept, 771 Commonwealth Ave, Boston, 02215. Howard B Gotlieb, Dir
Holdings: Cat Mss

WINTHROP, JAMES

PA —ALLEGHENY COLLEGE, Lawrence Lee Pelletier Library, Meadville, 16335. Margaret L Moser, Librn
Holdings: Vols (3000) Cat
Notes: Part of the original gift to this library, listed in *Catalogus Bibliothecae Collegii Alleghaniensis*, by Timothy Alden, 1823. Downs 180.

WINTHROP, GOV. JOHN

NY —NEW YORK ACADEMY OF MEDICINE, Library, 2 E 103 St, New York, 10029. Brett A Kirkpatrick, Librn
Holdings: Vols // Cat
Notes: Incl over 100 vols held in the John Winthrop (The Younger) private library.
NY —NEW YORK SOCIETY LIBRARY, 53 E 79 St, New York, 10021. Mark Piel, Librn
Notes: Incl Governor John Winthrop's Collection on chemistry and alchemy (part of which is at the New York Academy of Medicine Library).

WINTHROP, ROBERT CHARLES

MD —JOHNS HOPKINS UNIVERSITY, Milton S Eisenhower Library, Charles & 34 Sts, Baltimore, 21218. Ann S Gwyn, Assistant Dir for Special Collections
Holdings: Cat Mss

WINTUN INDIANS

NY —HOFSTRA UNIVERSITY, Library, 1000 Fulton Ave, Hempstead, 11550. Charles R Andrews, Dean of Library Services
Notes: The personal library of Paul Radin. See description of the American Philosophical Society Library's collection of his anthropological papers under this entry (Pa).
PA —AMERICAN PHILOSOPHICAL SOCIETY, Library, 105 S Fifth St, Philadelphia, 19106. Edward C Carter II, Librn
Notes: The anthropological papers of Paul Radin in fields of ethnology, social organization, primitive religion, linguistics, and mythology. He worked mostly among the Winnebago, Ojibwa, Fox, Zapotec, Wappo, Wintun, and Huave Indian tribes; also Italian and other ethnic minorities of San Francisco.

WINWAR, FRANCES

MA —BOSTON UNIVERSITY, Mugar Memorial Library, Special Collections Dept, 771 Commonwealth Ave, Boston, 02215. Howard B Gotlieb, Dir
Holdings: Cat Mss
Notes: Mss, correspondence, etc collected in depth; incl publications by or about.

WIRE ROPE AND WIRE

OH —PREFORMED LINE PRODUCTS CO, Research & Engineering Library, 660 Beta Drive, Mayfield Village, (Mailing add: PO Box 91129, Cleveland, 44101). Edwina T Barron, Librn
Holdings: Vols (11,500) Cat Mss Microfiche Pix VF
Budget: ($30,500)
Notes: Library covering research and engineering fields emphasizing this subject. Aerodynamic characteristics and electrical characteristics of power cables, communication cables (including fiber optics), cable support systems, as well as associated fittings and hardware; in service behavior of manufactured products and materials as it relates to its static and dynamic forces and environmental conditions; oceanographic cable fittings and terminations.

WIREGRASS REGION

DC —LIBRARY OF CONGRESS, American Folklife Center, Archive of Folk Culture, Washington, 20540.
Notes: Georgia vernacular architecture, food customs, storytelling, and gospel singing traditions, in local black and white communities. Thousands of color transparencies, etc.

WIRELESS TELEGRAPH see Telegraph, Wireless

WIRELESS TELEPHONE see Telephone, Wireless

WIRT, WILLIAM

IN —INDIANA UNIVERSITY, Lilly Library, Seventh St, Bloomington, 47405. William R Cagle, Librn
Holdings: // Mss Pix
Notes: The papers of William Wirt, educator, relate entirely to his work as superintendent of schools in Gary, Indiana, 1907-1938, where he developed the so-called "Gary system" of education. 22,232 items.

WISCONSIN

WI —STATE HISTORICAL SOCIETY OF WISCONSIN, Archives, 816 State St, Madison, 53706. Harold L Miller, Reference Archivist
Holdings: Cat Mss Microforms
Notes: About 22 million pieces. Major ms emphasis is American, with special collections in the history of agriculture, industry, labor, mass communications, and Wisconsin. There is a separate card catalog to mss. Collections are described in the *Guide to Manscripts of the State Historical Society of Wisconsin* (3 vols, 1944, 1957, 1966), in current accession notes in the *Wisconsin Magazine of History*, and in other special Society publications. Major collections are also listed in Hamer, *Guide to Manuscripts and Archives in the United States* (1961) and in the *National Union Catalog of Manuscript Collections* (1959-date). Original mss are non circulating. Collections available in microfilm form may be used through interlibrary loan.

WISCONSIN—DESCRIPTION AND TRAVEL—VIEWS

WI —STATE HISTORICAL SOCIETY OF WISCONSIN, Archives, 816 State St, Madison, 53706. Harold L Miller, Reference Archivist
Holdings: Vols 2500 Cat Maps
Notes: Incl 25,000 sheet maps and 2500 atlases. Collection specializes in maps of Wisconsin, its counties, and its cities, but also is strong in coverage of adjacent states of Middle West and North America as a whole. We also have a collection of European atlases from the 16th through 18th centuries, and many maps of North American areas prior to 1800. There is a separate card catalog of the map collection, and a descriptive brochure is available upon request. Maps and atlases are noncirculating.
WI —MILWAUKEE PUBLIC LIBRARY, 814 W Wisconsin Ave, Milwaukee, 53233. Donald J Sager, City Librn
Budget: ($10,661)
Notes: Collection incl local history and archival photographs of the greater Milwaukee area, instruction manuals and history of photography.

WISCONSIN—GENEALOGY

WI —STATE HISTORICAL SOCIETY OF WISCONSIN, Archives, 816 State St, Madison, 53706. Harold L Miller, Reference Archivist
Holdings: Mss Maps Public Records Microforms
Notes: Incl are unpublished genealogies, records of Wisconsin cemeteries and churches, and mss, incl the Lyman C Draper Manuscripts. Also incl are Wisconsin state, county and local governmental records, incl 19th century state census records, civil war service records and some naturalization records. Collections described in *Genealogical Research: An Introduction to the Resources of the State Historical Society of Wisconsin*, (1980).
WI —STATE HISTORICAL SOCIETY OF WISCONSIN, Library, 816 State St, Madison, 53706. James L Hansen, Reference Librn
Holdings: Vols (1,600,000) Cat Mss Maps Pix Microforms
Notes: Includes individual family histories and town and county histories. Special indices to Wisconsin holdings including censuses of 1820-1870 and biographical sketches in Wisconsin county histories and selected obituaries. Microfilm of pre-1907 vital statistics recorded in Wisconsin. Restricted use: most noncirculating, except Wisconsin census, 1820-1900 and indexes 1820-1870.
WI —MILWAUKEE PUBLIC LIBRARY, 814 W Wisconsin Ave, Milwaukee, 53233. Donald J Sager, City Librn
Holdings: Vols 5000 Cat
Notes: The largest genealogy collection in Wisconsin, excepting the State Historical Society at Madison.

WISCONSIN—HISTORY

MN —UNIVERSITY OF MINNESOTA, DULUTH, Library & Learning Resources Service, Duluth, 55812. James V. Litha, Archivist
Holdings: Vols (1700) Cat Mss Maps Pix
Notes: The Voyageur Collection incl the Grace Lee Nute Papers. Books and materials relating to the Voyageur period (1650-1850) and the area of Northeastern Minnesota, Michigan, Wisconsin, Southern Canada. Emphasis on all subjects listed in this volume.
WI —BARABOO PUBLIC LIBRARY, 230 Fourth Ave, Baraboo, 53913. Josephine H Zipsie, Dir
Holdings: // Mss
Notes: Baraboo and Sauk County history. Incl indexes to county histories and local newspaper.
WI —HOARD HISTORICAL MUSEUM, Fort Atkinson Historical Society, 407 Merchant Ave, Fort Atkinson, 53538. Hannah Werwath Swart, Cur
Holdings: Vols (4663) Cat Mss Maps Pix Slides
Notes: Entirely devoted to books, mss, etc, concerning the local history of Fort Atkinson and Jefferson County, with particular emphasis on the Black Hawk War.
WI —UNIVERSITY OF WISCONSIN, GREEN BAY, Library/Learning Center, Green Bay, 54301. Marian A Gould, Acting Dir, Special Collections/University Archives

WISCONSIN—HISTORY (cont.)

Holdings: Vols 4200 Cat Mss Maps Pix
Notes: Area research collection belonging to the State Historical Society of Wisconsin consisting of county and municipal records, private papers of individuals, and company records of business firms and industries located in the counties of northeastern Wisconsin.

WI —JANESVILLE PUBLIC LIBRARY, Janesville Room of Local History, Janesville, 53545. Carol Liddle, Public Services Librn
Holdings: Vols 500 Cat Pix
Budget: $100
Notes: History of Janesville and Rock County Wisconsin.

WI —UNIVERSITY OF WISCONSIN, LA CROSSE, Murphy Library, 1631 Pine St, La Crosse, 54601. Edwin L Hill, Special Collections Librn
Holdings: Vols 5000 Cat Mss Maps Pix Microforms
Notes: Local and regional history of La Crosse area. Collection incl the Area Research Center, which is under the jurisdiction of the State Historical Society of Wisconsin. This is largely a ms and document collection and is supplemented by books, photos, documents, clippings, tapes pertinent to regional history. Incl approx 20,000 photos of Mississippi River steamboats, with data files. Holdings approx 5000 vols, 1000 mss, 400 maps, 50,000 pictures, oral history tapes, clippings, reports, etc.

WI —STATE HISTORICAL SOCIETY OF WISCONSIN, Archives, 816 State St, Madison, 53706. Harold L Miller, Reference Archivist
Holdings: Mss Maps Pix Microforms
Notes: Records and papers of Wisconsin organizations, business and individuals documenting all facets of Wisconsin history and government. Topics covered incl discovery and exploration, native Americans, civil war, progressivism, and many others. Also incl are official records of state, county and local officials, offices and legislative bodies. Collections are described in the *Guide to Manuscripts of the State Historical Society of Wisconsin* (3 vols, 1944, 1957, 1966), *Guide to the Wisconsin State Archives* (1966), in current accession notes in the *Wisconsin Magazine of History*, and in other special Society publications. Major collections are also listed in Hamer, *Guide to Manuscripts and Archives in the United States* and the *National Union Catalog of Manuscripts Collections*, (1959-date). Also incl public records and tape recordings.

WI —STATE HISTORICAL SOCIETY OF WISCONSIN, Library, 816 State St, Madison, 53706. James L Hansen, Reference Librn
Holdings: Vols (1,600,000) Cat Mss Maps Pix Microforms
Notes: Comprehensive collection of published material relating to Wisconsin history from earliest times to the present, including local history and genealogy, archeology, and allied disciplines. Includes pamphlets, newspapers, microfilms amd government documents.

WI —LEGISLATIVE REFERENCE BUREAU LIBRARY, City of Milwaukee, City Hall Rm 404, 200 E Wells St, Milwaukee, 53202. Ronald Leonhardt, Dir
Holdings: Vols (50,000) Cat Mss Maps Pix Microforms
Budget: ($8000)

WI —MILWAUKEE PUBLIC LIBRARY, 814 W Wisconsin Ave, Milwaukee, 53233. Donald J Sager, City Librn
Notes: Incl extensive collection of county and city histories, rare books, and pamphlets.

WI —UNIVERSITY OF WISCONSIN, MILWAUKEE, Library, Box 604, Milwaukee, 53201. William C Roselle, Dir
Holdings: Cat Microforms
Notes: Wisconsin Legislative Reference Bureau Clippings File. Special strength in a collection mostly of Wisconsic emphasis. 440 reels of 16mm microfilm. A subject-chronological arrangment (approximately 1200 subjects covering the years from the 1890s through 1970) of pamphlets and a variety of fugitive materials and of clippings from national and Wisconsin newspapers, popular magazines and scholarly journals, and federal, state, and local government documents.

WI —NEENAH PUBLIC LIBRARY, 240 E Wisconsin Ave, Neenah, 54956. Mary Ellen Elliott, Librn
Holdings: Vols 540 Cat Mss Maps Pix Slides Audiotapes Films Microforms
Notes: Wisconsin history; emphasis on Neenah area. Incl a nearly complete set of local newspapers on microfilm from 1856 to the present. Collection also incl a bound set of the *Wisconsin Magazine of History* with all indexes. A clipping file is being established.

WI —OSHKOSH PUBLIC MUSEUM, Library, 1331 Algoma Blvd, Oshkosh, 54901. Kitty A Hobson, Archivist
Holdings: Cat Mss Maps Pix Slides Audiotapes 16mm Films
Notes: Books, mss, photographs, etc, dealing with the history of Oshkosh and Winnebago County Wisconsin, with special emphasis on lumbering and steamboating.

WI —WAUKESHA COUNTY HISTORICAL MUSEUM, Research Center, 101 W Main St, Waukesha, 53186. Terry Becker, Research Tech
Holdings: Vols 2500 Cat Mss Maps Pix Slides Audiotapes
Budget: $500
Notes: Incl books, pamphlets, ephermera, news clippings and ms, and diaries, papers and documents relating to Waukesha County history, 1834 to the present. Partial description of the collection is available in *Primary Bibliography for Research in Waukesha History*, by Jean Penn Loerke (Waukesha, 1973).

WISCONSIN—MAPS

WI —STATE HISTORICAL SOCIETY OF WISCONSIN, Archives, 816 State St, Madison, 53706. Harold L Miller, Reference Archivist
Notes: Incl 25,000 sheet maps and 2500 atlases. Collection specializes in maps of Wisconsin, its counties, and its cities, but also is strong in coverage of adjacent states of Middle West and North America as a whole. We also have a collection of European atlases from the 16th through 18th centuries, and many maps of North American areas prior to 1800. There is a separate card catalog of the map collection, and a descriptive brochure is available upon request. Maps and atlases are noncirculating.

WI —MILWAUKEE PUBLIC LIBRARY, 814 W Wisconsin Ave, Milwaukee, 53233. Donald J Sager, City Librn
Notes: Comprehensive collection of every type map of Milwaukee metropolitan area (2500). Incl fire insurance atlases, street car and bus maps and other specialized maps. Historical and contemporary. Goverment and commerical publishers and unpublished maps. Listed in library's main card catalog.

WISCONSIN—POLITICS AND GOVERNMENT

WI —STATE HISTORICAL SOCIETY OF WISCONSIN, Archives, 816 State St, Madison, 53706. Harold L Miller, Reference Archivist
Holdings: Mss Maps Pix Microforms
Notes: Records and papers of Wisconsin organizations, business and individuals documenting all facets of Wisconsin history and government. Topics covered incl discovery and exploration, native Americans, civil war, progressivism, and many others. Also incl are official records of state, county and local officials, offices and legislative bodies. Collections are described in the *Guide to Manuscripts of the State Historical Society of Wisconsin* (3 vols, 1944, 1957, 1966), *Guide to the Wisconsin State Archives* (1966), in current accession notes in the *Wisconsin Magazine of History*, and in other special Society publications. Major collections are also listed in Hamer, *Guide to Manuscripts and Archives in the United States* and the *National Union Catalog of Manuscripts Collections*, (1959-date). Also incl public records and tape recordings. Collections of note include papers of Eugene and Peggy Dennis, Communist Party activists, 1926 to date. Dennis was national head of Communist Party, USA. Other papers trace development of CIO in 1930s, Farmer-Labor-Progressive Federation, and other Wisconsin and national political groups. Much on Senator Joseph McCarthy.

WI —UNIVERSITY OF WISCONSIN, MILWAUKEE, Library, Box 604, Milwaukee, 53201. William C Roselle, Dir
Holdings: Cat Microforms
Notes: Wisconsin Legislative Rederence Bureau Clippings File. Special strength in a collection mostly of Wisconsin emphasis. 440 reels of 16mm microfilm. A subject-chronological arrangement (approximately 1200 subjects covering the years from the 1890s through 1970) of pamphlets and a variety of fugitive materials and of clippings from national and Wisconsin newspapers, popular magazines and scholarly journals, and federal, state, and local government documents.

WISCONSIN NEWSPAPERS see
Newspapers, Wisconsin

WISE, HENRY ALEXANDER

VA —UNIVERSITY OF VIRGINIA, Alderman Library, Manuscripts Dept, Charlottesville, 22901. Edmund Berkeley Jr, Cur
Holdings: Cat Mss Maps Pix
Notes: About 1500 collections have material pertaining to the Civil War and particularly to the Army of Northern Virginia and campaigns and battles in Virginia. There are letters, diaries, reminiscences, maps, and pictorial material of Confederate soldiers and civilians, as well as papers of Robert E Lee, J E B Stuart, Thomas L Rosser, Jubal A Early, John Daniel Imboden, William "Extra Billy" Smith, Henry Alexander Wise, Eppa Hunton, and John S Mosby.

WISE, ROBERT

CA —UNIVERSITY OF SOUTHERN CALIFORNIA, Edward L Doheny Memorial Library, Archives of Performing Arts, University Park, Los Angeles, 90089. Robert Knutson, Librn
Holdings: Mss Pix
Notes: Personal collection of papers, pictures, etc.

WISE, THOMAS JAMES

CA —HUNTINGTON LIBRARY, Art Gallery & Botanical Gardens, 1151 Oxford Rd, San Marino, 91108. Robert L Middlekauff, Dir; Daniel H Woodward, Librn
Holdings: Cat
Notes: Material by and about TJ Wise, incl the forgeries.

CT —YALE UNIVERSITY, Box 1603A, Yale Station, New Haven, 06520.
Notes: Books about Wise and copies of his forgeries.

IN —INDIANA UNIVERSITY, Lilly Library, Seventh St, Bloomington, 47405. William R Cagle, Librn
Holdings: Vols 93 Cat Mss
Notes: Mss incl a collection of William Henry Ireland fabrications of Shakespeare. 69 items, 1805. Also, forgeries of Edgar Allan Poe by Joseph Cosey (4 items) and James Whitcomb Riley's Poe forgery of "Leonainie." Much on the forgeries of T J Wise.

MA —HARVARD UNIVERSITY LIBRARY, Cambridge, 02138.
Holdings: Cat
Notes: Materials by and about T J Wise, incl the forgeries.

NY —COLUMBIA UNIVERSITY LIBRARIES, Rare Book & Manuscript Library, 801 Butler Library, 535 W 114 St,

WISE, THOMAS JAMES (cont.)

New York, 10027. Kenneth A Lohf, Librn
Holdings: Vols 50
Notes: 19th century English literary
forgeries by Thomas J Wise.
NY —SYRACUSE UNIVERSITY
LIBRARIES, Ernest S Bird Library, George
Arents Research Library for Special
Collections, Syracuse, 13210. Carolyn A
Davis, Manuscripts Librn; Amy S Doherty,
University Archivist; Mark F Weimer, Rare
Book Librn
Holdings: Cat
Notes: Materials by and about TJ Wise, incl
the forgeries.

WISELL, RICHARD, 1952-

CT —LEE ASH, (personal collection), 66
Humiston Dr, Bethany, 06525.
Holdings: Mss Pix
Notes: Letters and pictures of the Sharon,
Conn, writer.

WISEMAN, THOMAS

MA —BOSTON UNIVERSITY, Mugar
Memorial Library, Special Collections Dept,
771 Commonwealth Ave, Boston, 02215.
Howard B Gotlieb, Dir
Holdings: Cat Mss Pix
Notes: Mss, correspondence, etc collected in
depth; incl publications by or about.

WISEMAN, NICHOLAS CARDINAL, 1802-1865

DC —GEORGETOWN UNIVERSITY,
Library, Special Collections Div, 37 & O Sts
NW, Washington, 20057. George M
Barringer, Special Collections Librn;
Nicholas B Sheetz, Mss Librn
Holdings: Mss Cat
Notes: A portion of the papers of Bishop
William Bernard Ullathorne (1806-1889),
incl correspondence to and from other
English prelates such as Nicholas Cardinal
Wiseman (1802-1865) and Henry Edeward
Cardinal Manning (1808-1892).

WISSON, GORDON AND TINA

MA —HARVARD UNIVERSITY LIBRARY,
Botanical Museum Library, Cambridge,
02138.
Holdings: Vols (2400) Mss Pix
Notes: The Tina and Gordon Wisson
Ethnomycological Collection, one of the
most important modern collections, acquired
as an adjunct to the Museum's Economic
Botany Library of Oakes Ames. From 15th
to 20th century, it deals with hallucinogenic
mushrooms in art, religion, and folklore;
chemistry, pharmacology, linguistics,
archaeological artifacts of Mexico,
Guatemala, India, Japan, China, etc.
Personal papers, etc.

WISTER, OWEN

VA —UNIVERSITY OF VIRGINIA,
Alderman Library, Clifton Waller Barrett
Collection, Charlottesville, 22901. Joan St C
Crane, Cur of American Literature
Collections
Notes: Papers.

WISWESSER LINE NOTATION (CHEMISTRY)

PA —LEHIGH UNIVERSITY LIBRARIES,
Mart Science & Engineering Library,
Bethlehem, 18015.
Holdings: Mss
Notes: Papers of Dr William J Wiswesser on
his system for encoding all possible chemical
compounds.

WIT AND HUMOR

CA —HUNTINGTON LIBRARY, Art Gallery
& Botanical Gardens, 1151 Oxford Rd, San
Marino, 91108. Robert L Middlekauff, Dir;
Daniel H Woodward, Librn
Holdings: Vols 100 Cat
Notes: Refer to: Zall, P M "English Prose
Jest Books in the Huntington Library: A
Chronological Checklist (1535?-1799)," in
Shakespearean Research Opportunities, no 4,
1968/69, pp 78-91, revised, 1983.
Collections of prose anecdotes or tales with
humorous intent incl apothegms and books
that mix prose and verse, conventionally, in
the 18th century.
DC —LIBRARY OF CONGRESS, Prints &
Photographs Div, Washington, 20540.
Notes: Incl the Caroline and Erwin Swann
Collection of caricatures and cartoons.
Strong in the work of modern artists from
the middle of the 19th century. *The New
Yorker* Collection contains original cartoons
and cover illustrations from the magazine,
mid-20th century.
IL —UNIVERSITY OF ILLINOIS,
URBANA/CHAMPAIGN, Library, Rare
Book Room, 346 Library, Urbana, 61801.
Norman B Brown, Asst Dir for Special
Collections; N Frederick Nash, Librn
Holdings: Cat Mss Maps Pix Slides
Microforms
Notes: American Wit and Humor. Meine
Collection, described in: *Catalog of the Rare
Book Room,* (Boston: G K Hall, 1972).
Supplement (1978).
IN —INDIANA UNIVERSITY, Institute for
Sex Research Library, 416 Morrison Hall,
Bloomington, 47401. Douglas Freeman,
Collections and Services Librn; Joan Brewer,
Information Services Librn
Holdings: Vols (62,000) Cat Mss Pix
Phonorecords Audiotapes Slides Films
Microforms
Budget: ($20,000)
Notes: One of the greatest and most
extensive collection on sexual behavior, the
library collects materials on all aspects of sex
activity, with special emphasis on behavioral
and social aspects. Also collects erotic
literature and sexual ephemera. Incl 105
audiotapes, 23 vertical file drawers, 108
phonorecords, 55,000 pictures, 5000 slides,
and 1700 films. Rich in French, German and
American sources; also much Oriental.
Semitradional erotic poetry and song of
17th-18th century England. Bawdy
limericks, douuble-entendre, puns, slang,
erotic literature, graffiti, slang and special
dictionaries, proverbs and sayings, epigrams
and research materials of the Kinsey Studies,
etc. Contact Information Service for:
literature searching, preparation of
bibliographies, permission to use collection.
Limited photocopying.
IN —BUTLER UNIVERSITY, Irwin Library,
Hugh Thomas Miller Rare Book Room,
4600 Sunset Ave, Indianapolis, 46208.
Gisela Terrell, Rare Books Librn
Holdings: Cat Mss Pix
Notes: *Gaar Williams/Kin Hubbard*
Collection. This collection was presented to
the library by Blanche Stillson in 1964. It
contains original cartoons and other
drawings, books (many of them inscribed),
magazines, letters and other manuscripts,
photographs, and memorabilia by both
Hoosier cartoonists and humorists. A
catalogue of the Gaar Williams ("Abe
Martin") items was printed in 1981. It is
available upon request.
KS —WICHITA PUBLIC LIBRARY, Art &
Music Division, 223 S Main, Wichita,
67202. Leonard Messineo, Jr, Head, Art &
Music Division; Deborah Hamilton, Special
Collections Librn
Notes: Joan O'Bryant Kansas Folklore
Collection. Contains approximately 200
hours of folkmusic and oral histories on tape;
over 27,000 note cards covering topics such
as anecdotes, beliefs, customs, games, jokes,
medicines and cures, proverbs, recipes,
rhymes, riddles, sayings, songs, speech and
dialect, etc; 102 research papers covering
family histories, town and area histories,
biographies, tales, recipes, etc; and well over
70 mounted quilt blocks-covering the folk
history of Kansas. This material was
collected by Joan O'Bryant and her students
from 1947-1964, the period in which she
taught Folklore and English at Wichita State
University.
KY —UNIVERSITY OF LOUISVILLE,
Ekstrom Library, Rare Books & Special
Collections, 2301 S Third St, Louisville,
40208. George T McWhorter, Cur; Delinda
Stephens Buie, Asst Cur
Holdings: Vols 1200 Cat
Budget: ($1500)
Notes: Over 1200 works of 19th and 20th
century American humorists: sketches, short
stories, novels, poetry and graphics.
MA —BOSTON PUBLIC LIBRARY, Print
Collection, Dartmouth St at Copley Sq,
Boston, 02117. Sinclair H Hitchings, Keeper
of Prints
Holdings: Cat
Notes: The caricature collection incl 300
American prints (colonial period to 1900),
65 of these are by Thomas Nast; 400 English
prints (mostly 18th century), many by
Thomas Rowlandson and James Gillray; and
several thousand 19th century French items,
large numbers of them by Daumier. Items
are cataloged by artist when known; or else
by publisher or country. In addition, the
American caricatures are arranged
chronologically.
NY —HAMPDEN-BOOTH THEATRE
LIBRARY AT THE PLAYERS, 16
Gramercy Park, New York, 10003. Louis A
Rachow, Librn/Cur
Holdings: Mss Pix
Notes: Nearly 300 burlesque scripts and
vaudeville skits, music in ms, 25 photographs
in character, two song books of the period, a
notebook of stage gags and repartee,
typescript of biography of Chuck Callahan
(30 pages), and a number of ephemeral
pieces, stage money, programs, etc. 4 boxes
of indexed material. Described in *The
Players Bulletin*, Spring 1966, pp 20-21; and
Performing Arts Resources vol 3 (New
York: Theatre Library Association, 1976), pp
143-150. Described in *Theatre & Performing
Arts Collections* (New York: Haworth Press,
1981).
NY —UNION COLLEGE, Schaffer Library,
Schenectady, 12308. Ann Seemann, Librn;
Ellen Fladger, Archivist
Holdings: Vols 2200 Cat
Notes: The Bailey Collection of 19th century
North American Wit and Humor.
OK —WILL ROGERS MEMORIAL
LIBRARY, W Will Rogers Blvd, Box 157,
Claremore, 74017. Reba N Collins, Dir
Holdings: Vols (2800) Cat Slides
Phonorecords Audiotapes Videotapes 16mm
Films Microforms
Notes: Thousands of original manuscripts,
letters, photographs, plus many other
personal items, all by or about Will Rogers.
Library is available by appointment or
special permission.
TX —SOUTHERN METHODIST
UNIVERSITY, DeGolyer Library, Box 396,
SMU, Dallas, 75275. Clifton H Jones, Dir
Holdings: Vols (80,000) Cat Mss Maps Pix
Slides Microforms
Notes: First editions of prominent authors;
also of books in subject emphasis collections.
All subjects listed in this vol are strong.
Numerous collections of personal papers
relating to subjects also.
WY —UNIVERSITY OF WYOMING,
William Robertson Coe Library, 13 &
Ivinson, Laramie, 82071.
Notes: 2000 volumes of popular humor, incl
books of cartoons, humorous novels, and the
like.

WIT AND HUMOR, AMERICAN see
American Wit and Humor

WITCHCRAFT

CA —GRADUATE THEOLOGICAL UNION
LIBRARY, New Religious Movements
Research Collection, Public Services and
Special Collections Dept, 2400 Ridge Road,
Berkeley, 94709. Diane Choquette, Dept
Head
Holdings: Vols (3000) Mss Pix
Notes: Begun in 1977, the collection focuses
on religious movements new to America
since 1960, and unorthodox religious
movements resurgent since 1960. American
forms of Hinduism, Buddhism, Sikhism, and
Sufism are included along with occultism,

WITCHCRAFT (cont.)

Neo-Paganism, esoteric and alternative forms of Christianity, feminist spirituality, and human potential movements having a spiritual aspect. Legal issues, such as deprogramming, and the question of church/state relations are an important part of the collection. The Library is a depository for publications of the Unification Church in America, the Church of Scientology, and the International Society for Krishna Consciousness (America). The responses of mainstream religions and concerned citizens groups are also included. Besides 3000 monographs, the library has 400 periodical titles, 200 posters from the San FranciscoBay Area, 1965-77, 300 research papers, and 31 linear feet of ephemera.

CA —FRANCIS BACON LIBRARY, 655 N Dartmouth Ave, Claremont, 91711. Elizabeth S Wrigley, Dir
Notes: Collection incl witchcraft and magic from early times to the 20th century. Many 17th century volumes.

CA —LOS ANGELES PUBLIC LIBRARY, Philosophy & Religion Dept, 630 W Fifth St, Los Angeles, 90071. Marilyn C Wherley, Librn
Holdings: Vols 300 Cat
Budget: ($60,000)
Notes: Scholarly and popular works as part of the comprehensive occult collection. Includes some special indexes.

CA —SAN DIEGO PUBLIC LIBRARY, Literature & Language Sect, 820 E St, San Diego, 92101. Alyce Archuleta, Senior Librn
Holdings: Cat
Notes: Old and current reference and circulating works on the subject. Incl complete works by Blavatsky, much by Rudolf Steiner, and C Zain. Strong in astrology, witchcraft, parapsychology.

CT —LEE ASH, (personal collection), 66 Humiston Dr, Bethany, 06525.
Holdings: Mss Maps Pix

CT —TRINITY COLLEGE LIBRARY, Watkinson Library, 300 Summit St, Hartford, 06106. Jeffrey Kaimowitz, Cur
Holdings: Cat

CT —YALE UNIVERSITY, Box 1603A, Yale Station, New Haven, 06520.

CT —YALE UNIVERSITY, Medical Historical Library, Klebs Collection, 333 Cedar St, New Haven, 06520. Ferenc A Gyorgyey, Librn
Holdings: Cat Mss Pix

DC —LIBRARY OF CONGRESS, Rare Book & Special Collections Div, Washington, 20540. William Matheson, Chief
Holdings: Cat
Notes: The Houdini Collection of Magic and Spiritism consists of over 4000 vols of printed works and a large number of scrapbooks containing clippings, programs, catalogs, posters, etc. The McManus-Young collection of 1076 vols, as well as mss, prints, and organized scrapbooks on Houdini, the history of magic, and related fields.

DC —LIBRARY OF CONGRESS, Washington, 20540.
Notes: Incl materials in the Houdini Collection as examined by John Mulholland.

IL —NEWBERRY LIBRARY, 60 W Walton St, Chicago, 60610. Diana Haskell, Cur of Modern Mss
Holdings: Cat
Notes: Several hundred European titles, 15th-17th centuries.

IL —UNIVERSITY OF ILLINOIS, URBANA/CHAMPAIGN, Library, University Archives, 19 Library, 1408 W Gregory Drive, Urbana, 61801. Maynard Brichford, University Archivist
Holdings: Vols (5000) Cat
Budget: ($7000)
Notes: The Mandeville Collection in Parapsychology and Occult Sciences. Titles in the Merten J Mandeville Collection are purchased by funds from an endowment provided specifically for the collection on its establishment in 1966 by Merten J Mandeville, Professor Emeritus of Management, who donated 400 vols from his personal library as the nucleus of the collection. There are currently about 5000 titles in the collection, supplemented by related materials in the general collection. Topics include astrology, extrasensory perception, yoga, magic, satanism, faith healing, hypnosis, Eastern religions, witchcraft, fortune telling, reincarnation, flying saucers, ghosts, dreams, numerology, graphology, and mysticism. Biographies and reference books are a part of the collection as are journals devoted to the scientific study of parapsychology.

IN —INDIANAPOLIS-MARION COUNTY PUBLIC LIBRARY, Social Sciences Div, PO Box 211, Indianapolis, 46206. Lois R Laube, Head
Holdings: Vols 358 Cat
Notes: Restricted use. No photocopying.

MD —JOHNS HOPKINS UNIVERSITY, Milton S Eisenhower Library, George Peabody Collection, 17 E Mt Vernon Place, Baltimore, 21201. Lyn Hart, Peabody Librn
Notes: Noncirculating.

MA —FRANCIS A COUNTWAY LIBRARY OF MEDICINE, Boston Medical Library/Harvard Medical Library, 10 Shattuck St, Boston, 02115. C Robin LeSueur, Librn; Richard J Wolfe, Cur, Rare Books & Manuscripts
Holdings: Vols (500,000) Cat Mss Maps Pix Microforms
Notes: Combines resources of the Harvard Medical School and the Boston Medical Library. Strong in serials and medical history in all fields of medicine, incl incunabula, non-medical books by doctors, travel books by doctors. 500,000 medical dissertations and theses. Special strength in all medical subjects listed in this volume.

MA —HARVARD UNIVERSITY LIBRARY, Widener Library, Cambridge, 02138.
Holdings: Cat

MA —PEABODY INSTITUTE LIBRARY, Danvers Archival Center, 15 Sylvan St, Danvers, 01923. Richard B Trask, Archivist, Rare Books & Special Collections
Holdings: Vols 1200 Cat Mss Maps Pix Microforms
Notes: The Ellerton J Brehaut Collection on New England witchcraft, especially Salem witchcraft. (Danvers, where the library is located, was part of Salem at the time of the witchcraft trials.) 17th and 18th century English and American books on witchcraft; transcripts of all known trial records. Manuscript records of the First Church of Salem Village. Special catalog to collection. Danvers History Collection consists of 5000 volumes, 250,000 mss, numerous photos, newspaper clippings, maps, audiotapes, and visual tapes.

MA —ESSEX INSTITUTE, James Duncan Phillips Library, 132-34 Essex St, Salem, 01970. Prudence K Backman, Manuscript Librn
Holdings: Vols Mss
Notes: Original legal documents and supporting monographs of Salem witchcraft trials of 1692. Finding aid for manuscripts available.

†MA —OLD STURBRIDGE VILLAGE, Research Library, Sturbridge, 01566.

MI —MICHIGAN STATE UNIVERSITY, Libraries, Special Collections Div, East Lansing, 48824. Jannette Fiore, Librn
Holdings: Vols 1440 // Uncat Mss
Notes: Works from 15th to 19th centuries on criminolgy, criminal law and jurisprudence, including witchcraft, demonolgy, et al, chiefly in German and Latin.

NY —CORNELL UNIVERSITY LIBRARIES, John M Olin Library, Dept of Rare Books, Ithaca, 14853. Donald D Eddy, Librn
Holdings: Vols 2847 Cat Mss Pix
Notes: Also holdings in other parts of the library which has a very extensive collection. See Catalogue of the Witchcraft Collection in Cornell University Library, ed by Martha J Crowe (Millwood, NY: KTO Press, 1977).

NY —NEW YORK PUBLIC LIBRARY, Research Libraries, General Research Division, Fifth Ave & 42 St, New York, 10018. Rodney Phillips, Chief
Holdings: Vols (2,225,000) Cat Maps Pix Microforms
Budget: ($775,718)

OH —CLEVELAND PUBLIC LIBRARY, Fine Arts and Special Collections Department, 325 Superior Ave, Cleveland, 44114. Alice N Loranth, Head
Holdings: Vols 1600 Cat Mss
Notes: Witchcraft, magic, sorcery, magical manuals, devil worship, incantations, charms, talismans, amulets and spells are incl. Contemporary urban practices are almost entirely omitted.
See also entries under Folklore; Occult Sciences.

PA —UNIVERSITY OF PENNSYLVANIA, Lea Library, 3420 Walnut St, Philadelphia, 19104. Daniel Traister, Special Collections Librn
Holdings: Vols (20,000) Cat Mss
Notes: An outstanding collection. See Downs 4241, 4234.

RI —BROWN UNIVERSITY, John Hay Library, 20 Prospect St, Providence, 02912. Mark N Brown, Cur Mss
Holdings: Vols (900) // Mss
Notes: John William Graham Collection of Literature of Psychic Science--350 predominantly late 19th and early 20th century books dealing with alchemy, black magic, dreams, demonology, church history, mysticism, mediumship, physical and somatic types of psychic experience. Collection described in Index to Psychic Science compiled by S R Morgan (Swarthmore, 1950). Also, the Damon Collection of Occult and Visionary Literature--550 vols devoted to the development of western mysticism with particular emphasis on American and British thought; incl texts on alchemy, black magic, esoteric church history, dream interpretation, mysticism, witchcraft, the Kabbalah, and visionary testaments and manifestations of all types printed during the 16th to 20th centuries. Also, papers of Samuel Wyllys, 1632-1709, Colonial magistrate of Connecticut. A collection of 125 mss, transcripts, andphotocopies of legal and government papers relating to Indian affairs, colonial wars, civil and criminal cases, and trails for witchcraft. The witchcraft trials of 1692-1693 are of particular interest as revealed in the Oyer and Terminer Court Records of the witnesses. The Library has one-half (1622-1693) of the original collection which Annmary Brown inherited from her father; the other half (1694-1696) is in the Connecticut State Library.

VA —UNIVERSITY OF VIRGINIA, Alderman Library, Tracy W McGregor Collection, Charlottesville, 22901. William H Runge, Cur
Holdings: Vols 2500 Cat Mss
Notes: This collection was gathered by William Gwinn Mather, a direct descendant of the New England Mathers. It is one of the 3 important Mather collections in the world. Excellent collection on magic and witchcraft in America. Collection incl 20th century imprints. Thomas J Holmes used this collection as a basis for his monumental biographies of Increase Mather, Cotton Mather and the Minor Mathers.

WITHERSPOON, JOHN

NJ —PRINCETON UNIVERSITY, Library, Rare Books Dept, Princeton, 08544. Stephen Ferguson, Cur
Holdings: Cat
Notes: John Witherspoon's Library. About 950 vols.

WITTKOWER, RUDOLPH

†NY —COLUMBIA UNIVERSITY LIBRARIES, Butler Library, Rare Book and Manuscript Library, 535 W 114 St, New York, 10027.
Notes: Papers, etc.

WODEHOUSE, PELHAM GRANVILLE (P. G.)

NY —HOFSTRA UNIVERSITY, Library, 1000 Fulton Ave, Hempstead, 11550. Charles R Andrews, Dean of Library Services

WOFFORD, HARRIS

†MA —JOHN F KENNEDY LIBRARY,
Columbia Point, Boston, 02125. Dan H Fenn
Jr, Dir
Holdings: Cat Mss
Notes: Papers of JFK and White House
aides Lee White and Harris Wofford and
RFK and Justice Department aide Burke
Marshall, dealing with civil rights, 1961-
1964. 42 linear ft of mss. Holdings are
described in "Historical Materials in the
John F Kennedy Library." Copies may be
obtained by writing the Research Archivist.

WOLCOT, JOHN, 1738-1819

NC —UNIVERSITY OF NORTH
CAROLINA, CHARLOTTE, J Murrey
Atkins Library, UNCC Station, Charlotte,
28223. Robert F Brabham Jr, Special
Collections Librn
Holdings: Vols Cat
Notes: Incl several collected editions as well
as about two-thirds of the poems which were
published separately. 52 titles in 17 vols.

WOLCOTT, OLIVER

DC —GEORGETOWN UNIVERSITY,
Library, Special Collections Div, 37 & O Sts
NW, Washington, 20057. George M
Barringer, Special Collections Librn;
Nicholas B Sheetz, Mss Librn
Holdings: Mss Cat
Notes: Correspondence and documents
constituting the papers of Col John
Fitzgerald. Fitzgerald, a colonial merchant,
served as a member of the Committee of
Safety in Alexandria, Virginia, and received
his military rank during the Revolution.
After the war he became mayor and customs
collector of Alexandria. In 1799, while
serving in the latter capacity, Fitzgerald was
held responsible for the sum of forty
thousand dollars discovered missing from the
treasury. Apart from miscellaneous
correspondence and deeds, the papers
primarily concern this incident. Incl is
correspondence from Oliver Wolcott,
Secretary of the Treasury.

WOLF, HERMAN

MI —WAYNE STATE UNIVERSITY, Walter
P Reuther Library, Archives of Labor &
Urban Affairs, Detroit, 48202. Philip Mason,
Dir
Notes: Papers, etc of Herman Wolf, labor
publicist and editor for various unions and
labor departments.

WOLF, JOSEPH

NY —AMERICAN MUSEUM OF
NATURAL HISTORY, Library Services
Dept, Central Park W & 79th St, New York,
10024. Nina J Root, Chairwoman; Mary
Genett, Asst Librn for Reference Services
Holdings: Cat Mss Maps Pix Slides 16mm
Films
Notes: Original artwork for D G Eliot
monographs.

WOLFE, BERTRAM DAVID, 1896-1977

CA —HOOVER INSTITUTION ON WAR,
REVOLUTION & PEACE, Stanford
University, Stanford, 94305. Milorad M
Drachkovitch, Archivist
Holdings: Mss
Notes: Papers of Bertram D Wolfe,
American historian and author, Hoover
Institution Senior Fellow, 1949-1950 and
1965-1968, and Senior Research Fellow,
1969-1977, incl writings, correspondence,
clippings, printed matter and photographs,
1913-1977, relating primarily to international
communism and communism in the Soviet
Union.

WOLFE, HUMBERT

IL —ILLINOIS STATE UNIVERSITY, Milner
Library, Dept of Special Collections,
Normal, 61761. Robert Sokan, Librn
Notes: First editions, limited editions,
ephemera, etc.

OH —OHIO UNIVERSITY, Vernon R Alden
Library, Department of Archives and Special
Collections, Athens, 45701. Gary A Hunt,
Head
Holdings: Vols 56 Cat
Notes: Incl both trade and limited editions
of most of Wolfe's books.

WOLFE, THOMAS

IL —ILLINOIS STATE UNIVERSITY, Milner
Library, Dept of Special Collections,
Normal, 61761. Robert Sokan, Librn
Holdings: Vols 260 Cat
Notes: Contains many foreign translations of
his works--20 languages represented.

MA —HARVARD UNIVERSITY LIBRARY,
Houghton Library, Cambridge, 02138.
Rodney G Dennis, Cur of Manuscripts
Holdings: Cat Mss
Notes: See *Harvard Library Bulletin,* I
(1947): pp 280-287.

MN —UNIVERSITY OF MINNESOTA, O
Meredith Wilson Library, 309 19 Ave S,
Minneapolis, 55455. Austin J McLean,
Chief, Special Collections
Holdings: Vols 496 Uncat
Notes: First and later editions of all
published works, incl periodical contributions
and critical and biographical works about
him. Complete listing available in the
Division.

NV —UNIVERSITY OF NEVADA, RENO,
University Library, Special Collections Dept,
Reno, 89557. Robert E Blesse, Head
Holdings: Vols 73 // Cat
Notes: Includes individual works by author
in all editions including translations; also
prefaces, introductions, published
correspondence, appearances in anthologies,
periodicals, etc. Bibliographical research
collection, part of Modern Authors
Collection.

NY —HAMPDEN-BOOTH THEATRE
LIBRARY AT THE PLAYERS, 16
Gramercy Park, New York, 10003. Louis A
Rachow, Librn/Cur
Holdings: Mss Pix
Notes: The Franklin Heller Collection, incl
correspondence, photographs; playscripts by
Moss Hart and George S Kaufman, John
Steinbeck, Thomas Wolfe, and others. (110
items). Described in *Theatre & Performing
Arts Collections* (New York: Haworth Press,
1981).

NY —NEW YORK UNIVERSITY, Elmer
Holmes Bobst Library, Div of Special
Collections, Washington Sq S, New York,
10012. Frank Walker, Librn; Patrick
McGuire, Asst Librn
Holdings: Vols (100,000) Cat Mss Pix
Notes: The Fales Collection of first (and
other) editions of English and American
novels from about 1750 to date (about 70,
000 titles). Mss (30,000) pieces.

NC —PACK MEMORIAL PUBLIC
LIBRARY, North Carolina Collection, 67
Haywood St, Asheville, 28801. John Toms,
Dept Head
Notes: Collection incl early ms accounts of
western North Carolina; Civil War letters;
letters, diary, and mss of Horace Kephart;
mss of Thomas Dixon; Thomas Wolfe
Collection; contemporary North Carolina
authors; North Carolina censuses, 1790-
1910; rare newspapers and runs of local
newspapers, and clippings from Asheville
newspapers, from 1920s; early maps;
information on Cherokee Indians; approx
400 vols of North Carolina genealogy and
file of unpublished genealogies. Collection
concentrates on western North Carolina,
with some general Appalachian materials.
Incl 4000 local and state photographs,
separate catalog.

NC —SAINT MARY'S COLLEGE, Sarah
Graham Kenan Library, 900 Hillsborough St,
Raleigh, 27611.
Holdings: Vols Cat Mss Pix Slides
Phonorecords Audiotapes Filmstrips
Periodicals Art Reproductions VF

VA —UNIVERSITY OF VIRGINIA,
Alderman Library, Clifton Waller Barrett
Collection, Charlottesville, 22901. Joan St C
Crane, Cur of American Literature
Collections
Notes: Papers.

WOLFF, KURT

CT —YALE UNIVERSITY, Beinecke Rare
Book & Manuscript Library, German
Literature Collection, Box 1603A, Yale Sta,
New Haven, 06520. Christa Sammons, Cur
Holdings: // Cat Mss
Notes: Kurt Wolff Verlag. An archive of
Kurt Wolff's business correspondence,
chiefly from the German Expressionist
period. 4000 ms pieces. Many of the items
from this collection are printed in: Kurt
Wolff, *Briefwechsel eines Verlegers,*
1911-1963, ed Bernhard Zeller and Ellen
Otten (Frankfurt aM: Scheffler, 1966).

WOLFSKILL, JOHN R.

CA —UNIVERSITY OF CALIFORNIA,
DAVIS, Shields Library, Dept of Special
Collections, Davis, 95616. Donald Kunitz,
Head; C Danial Elliott, Asst Head
Holdings: Cat Mss Pix
Notes: The Wolfskill Collection of
scrapbooks, memorabilia and family papers,
relate to John R Wolfskill, early settler in
Solano County, (1842). 1150 items.

WOLFSON, VICTOR

MA —BOSTON UNIVERSITY, Mugar
Memorial Library, Special Collections Dept,
771 Commonwealth Ave, Boston, 02215.
Howard B Gotlieb, Dir
Holdings: Cat Mss
Notes: Mss, correspondence, etc collected in
depth; incl publications by or about.

WOLLSTONECRAFT, MARY

NY —CARL H PFORZHEIMER LIBRARY,
41 E 42 St, New York, 10017. Mihai H
Handrea, Librn
Holdings: Cat Mss Pix
Notes: English Literature from Caxton to
1700; first editions of 18th and 19th
centuries, incl mss material on Shelley and
his circle; fine presses (Bruce Rogers);
George Gissing; women writers 1790-1840,
(Mary Wollstonecraft, Mary Hays, Lady
Blessington).

WOLMAN, LEO

DC —LIBRARY OF CONGRESS, Manuscript
Division, Washington, 20540. John C
Broderick, Chief
Notes: Papers.

WOLPER, DAVID L.

CA —UNIVERSITY OF CALIFORNIA, LOS
ANGELES, Research Library, Dept of
Special Collections, 405 Hilgard Ave, Los
Angeles, 90024. Edward Shreeves,
Chairman, Bibliographers Group; David S
Zeidberg, Head
Notes: 5 linear feet of scripts, etc, for his
television series, *Biography,* produced by
Wolper Productions, Inc.

CA —UNIVERSITY OF SOUTHERN
CALIFORNIA, Edward L Doheny
Memorial Library, Archives of Performing
Arts, University Park, Los Angeles, 90089.
Robert Knutson, Librn
Holdings: Videotapes
Notes: Incl 400 videotapes.

WOLPER PRODUCTIONS, INC.

CA —UNIVERSITY OF CALIFORNIA, LOS
ANGELES, Research Library, Dept of
Special Collections, 405 Hilgard Ave, Los
Angeles, 90024. Edward Shreeves,
Chairman, Bibliographers Group; David S
Zeidberg, Head
Notes: 5 linear feet of scripts, etc, for his
television series, *Biography,* produced by
Wolper Productions, Inc.

WOMAN'S EDUCATION
ASSOCIATION (BOSTON)

MA —SIMMONS COLLEGE ARCHIVES,
300 The Fenway, Boston, 02115. Megan

WOMAN'S EDUCATION ASSOCIATION (BOSTON) (cont.)

Sniffin-Marinoff, College Archivist
Notes: (I) Minutes of the Industrial
Committee of the Woman's Education
Association (1873-1929) from Feb 15, 1872
to Dec 5, 1882. Primarily concerned with
the Committee's development of the Boston
Cooking School. Figuring prominently in the
minutes are Maria Parloa (1843-1909), one
of the first instructors at the school, and
Mary Johnson Bailey Lincoln (1844-1921),
under whose leadership the Boston Cooking
School began to attain a national reputation.
For further information on these women, see
Notable American Women. The
Committee's relationship with the NY Diet
Kitchen, the North Bennett St Industrial
School (Boston), and the Massachusetts
Institute of Technology also are discussed in
the minutes. In addition to organizing a
school for cooking, the Committee
concerned itself with the education for
women in dressmaking, nursing,
phonography, andwoodcarving (based on the
Cincinnati carving school). (II) Account
books of the Household Aid Co (The
Domestic Economy Committee) of the
Woman's Education Association from
August, 1903 to May, 1905. Organized by
the Association of Collegiate Alumnae and
the Woman's Education Association, the
company was a cooperative residence for 20
servants with a training and placement
program and a mediation service to deal
with employers.

WOMAN'S UNION MISSIONARY SOCIETY

†IL —WHEATON COLLEGE, Billy Graham
Center, Wheaton, 60187.
Notes: Papers of the Woman's Union
Missionary Society, an evangelical group
founded in New York in 1861. Records
document their missionary work in India,
China, Japan, Burma, Pakistan, Greece, and
Cyprus.

WOMEN

AL —BIRMINGHAM PUBLIC LIBRARY,
Dept of Archives & Mss, 2020 Seventh Ave
N, Birmingham, 35203. Marvin Y Whiting,
Archivist & Cur
Holdings: Mss Pix
Notes: Main collections to date are the
League of Women Voters of Birmingham
Papers and the YWCA Papers. 19,600 ms
pieces.

CA —CLAREMONT COLLEGES, Ella Strong
Denison Library, Scripps College,
Claremont, 91711. Judy Harvey Sahak,
Librn
Holdings: Vols (2000) Cat Mss Pix
Notes: Ida Rust Macpherson Collection
centers on the humanistic accomplishments
of women, suffrage and emancipation,
domestic economy, and women in the
Westward movement. Provides historical
materials for the contemporary women's
movement.

CA —LOS ANGELES PUBLIC LIBRARY,
Social Sciences Dept, 630 W Fifth St, Los
Angeles, 90071. Marilyn C Wherley,
Principal Librn
Holdings: Vols 10,000 Microforms
Budget: ($150,000)
Notes: Clippings, pamphlets, periodicals,
government publications, bibliographies,
popular and scholarly works on women and
their role and place in society with particular
emphasis on the suffrage and liberation
movements.

CA —UNIVERSITY OF CALIFORNIA, LOS
ANGELES, Research Library, Social
Sciences Collection, 405 Hilgard Ave, Los
Angeles, 90024. Edward Shreeves,
Chairman, Bibliographers Group; Oscar L
Sims, Social Sciences Bibliographer
Holdings: Mss Pix Microforms
Notes: A comprehensive microfilm
collection of literature by and about women
on 1247 reels of film. The collection is

arranged chronologically through the year
1920, and is divided into five sections:
Monographs; Pamphlets; Periodicals;
Manuscripts; and Selected Photographs.
Published by Research Publications, Inc,
New Haven, CT, 1976-79. A printed guide,
*History of Women: Guide to the Microfilm
Collection*, provides access to this material.

CA —UNIVERSITY OF CALIFORNIA,
RIVERSIDE, University Library, 4045
Canyon Crest Dr, Box 5900, Riverside,
92517.
Holdings: Vols 5,000
Notes: Extensive collection of modern works
on history and biography of women,
sociological studies, political and professional
aspects, with special emphasis on women in
Latin America. Significant holdings of
literary works by and about Latin American
and Portuguese (late 19th century to
present) women authors.

CA —CALIFORNIA HISTORICAL
SOCIETY, Schubert Hall Library, 2099
Pacific Ave, San Francisco, 94109. Bruce L
Johnson, Library Dir
Holdings: Vols (50,000) Cat Mss Maps Pix
See also entry under California - History.

CA —COLLEGE OF SAN MATEO, Library,
1700 W Hillsdale Blvd, San Mateo, 94402.
Gregg T Atkins, Coordinator of Library
Services
Holdings: Vols 3000 Cat

CA —UNIVERSITY OF CALIFORNIA,
SANTA BARBARA, Library, Dept of
Special Collections, Santa Barbara, 93106.
Christian F Brun, Head

CT —CONNECTICUT COLLEGE, Library,
Mohegan Ave, New London, 06320. Brian
Rogers, College Librn
Holdings: Vols (382,000) Cat
Notes: Papers of women.

DC —BUSINESS & PROFESSIONAL
WOMEN'S FOUNDATION, Marguerite
Rawalt Resource Center, 2012
Massachusetts Ave NW, Washington, 20036.
Cheryl A Sloan, Librn
Holdings: Vols (20,000) Cat Documents
Microforms VF
Budget: ($10,000)
Notes: VF, containing about 13,000 items
(studies, periodical articles, newspaper
clippings, documents) current. All items are
filed by subject and indexed in our card
catalog by author, title and subject. 200 tape
recordings in Oral History Collection. The
Resource Center is currently being
automated starting with thesaurus
construction, then data base design, and
finally the implementaion phase which incl
cataloging, abstracting, and indexing each
item. Microfilms are mainly of doctoral
theses. Our emphasis is on the working
woman and encompasses economic issues of
concern to women such as education for
women, working mothers, sex roles, women
executives, counseling for women, and work
force entry by mature women. Most of the
material is about women in the United
States. Collection incl 500 microfilms.
Publish a bimonthly selected acquisitions list.

DC —LIBRARY OF CONGRESS, Manuscript
Division, Washington, 20540. John C
Broderick, Chief
Notes: Records of ERAmerica; 120,000
pieces. Also, papers of National Women's
Trade Union League of America.

DC —US DEPT OF LABOR, Library, 200
Constitution Ave NW, Washington, 20210.
Sabina Jacobson, Dir
Holdings: Vols (550,000) Cat

IL —CHICAGO HISTORICAL SOCIETY,
Library, Clark St at North Ave, Chicago,
60614. Archie Motley, Manuscript Librn
Notes: Women's organizations collections
incl these papers: Chicago Women's Club;
Chicago Women's Liberation Union; Hyde
Park Travel Club, Chicago; Illinois Home
Economics Association; National Council of
Jewish Women-Chicago Section; National
Woman Suffrage Association, 1880 Chicago
national convention; City Club of Chicago
(civic improvement organization).

IL —NORTHWESTERN UNIVERSITY,
Library, Special Collections Dept, 1937
Sheridan Rd, Evanston, 60201. R Russell
Maylone, Cur
Holdings: Vols 5001
Notes: Books, newsletters, newspapers,

pamphlets, posters, ephemera written and
distributed by women active in the Women's
Liberation Movement from the early 1960s
to the present. Countries currently
represented are the US, Canada, Great
Britain, Australia, Sweden, Denmark,
Germany, France, Italy, and the
Netherlands. Emphasis is on current
literature, but some historical material is incl.
Literature: *Women's Collection Newsletter*,
Sarah Sherman, ed. (Evanston, 1974). Incl
2500 periodicals, 2700 folders ephemeral
materials.

IA —IOWA FALLS PUBLIC LIBRARY, 520
Rocksylvania, Iowa Falls, 50126. Deanne
Keller, Librn
Holdings: Vols (75) Cat
Notes: History of the women's movement
biographies, employment studies, records of
achievements, etc.

KS —UNIVERSITY OF KANSAS, Kenneth
Spencer Research Library, Kansas
Collection, Lawrence, 66045. Sheryl K
Williams, Cur
Holdings: Vols (92,000) Cat Mss Pix
Audiotapes
Notes: All aspects of women's history in
Kansas and the region. The collection incl
personal papers, such as those of Peggy Hull
Deuell (first accredited woman war
correspondent), and Mary Huntoon (art
therapist); diaries; and organizational records
of many women's organizations, such as the
Kansas League of Women Voters, the
Missouri State Association of
Parliamentarians and women's literary and
service clubs.

KS —UNIVERSITY OF KANSAS, Kenneth
Spencer Research Library, Special
Collections Dept, Lawrence, 66045.
Alexandra Mason, Librn
Holdings: Vols 4000 // Cat
Notes: Gerritsen Collection "La Femme et la
Feminisme," especially strong in late 19th
and early 20th century European women's
periodicals and newspapers. Formerly at
John Crerar Library. Noncirculating.

MA —BOSTON UNIVERSITY, Mugar
Memorial Library, Special Collections Dept,
771 Commonwealth Ave, Boston, 02215.
Howard B Gotlieb, Dir
Holdings: // Cat Mss Pix
Notes: Papers of ca 320 women, and of ca
30 primarily women's institutions and
organizations primarily in the History of
Nursing Archives.

†MA —JOHN F KENNEDY LIBRARY,
Columbia Point, Boston, 02125. Dan H Fenn
Jr, Dir
Holdings: // Cat Mss
Notes: Records of the President's
Commission on the Status of Women, 1961-
1963. 8 linear ft of mss. Holdings are
described in "Historical Materials in the
John F Kennedy Library." Copies may be
obtained by writing the Research Archivist.

MA —RADCLIFFE COLLEGE, Arthur &
Elizabeth Schlesinger Library on the History
of Women in America, 3 James St,
Cambridge, 02138. Patricia Miller King, Dir;
Eva Moseley, Cur of Mss
Holdings: Vols (22,000) Cat Mss Pix
Microforms
Budget: ($300,000)
Notes: Emphasis on women in the US;
subject areas incl woman's rights, suffrage,
feminism, and the women's movement; the
family; women in government and politics,
social welfare and reform, and the trade
unions; women's education, employment,
and health; mss collections incl those of the
Blackwell family, the Beecher-Stowe family,
Betty Friedan, Charlotte Perkins Gilman,
Emma Goldman, Dr Alice Hamilton and the
Hamilton family, the National Abortion
Rights Action League, the National
Organization for Women, Leonora O'Reilly,
and the Women's Equity Action League.
For description see *Harvard Library Bulletin
XVI* (1968), pp 385-99; *Wilson Library
Bulletin LV, 10* (1981), pp 750-55; *Special
Collections* (forthcoming 1984); also the
Library's *40th Anniversary Report* (1983).
Formerly the Women's Archives. Incl 463
personal and family collections and
103organizational collections; also incl 40,

WOMEN (cont.)

000 pictures, 10,000 microforms; oral history tapes and transcripts.

MA —WHEATON COLLEGE, Library, Norton, 02766. Sherrie S Bergman, College Librn
Notes: Partially cataloged.

MI —WAYNE STATE UNIVERSITY, Walter P Reuther Library, Archives of Labor & Urban Affairs, Detroit, 48202. Philip Mason, Dir
Holdings: Vols 2000 Journals Pamphlets
Notes: See Warner Pflug, *A Guide to the Archives of Labor History and Urban Affairs*, Wayne State University Press, Detroit, 1974. Philip P Mason, "The Archives of Labor and Urban Affairs, Walter P Reuther Library, Wayne State University," *Labor History*, Number 4, Vol 23, Fall 1982.

MI —OAKLAND UNIVERSITY, Kresge Library, Rochester, 48063. Suzanne O Frankie, Dean; Elizabeth Titus, Special Collections Librn
Notes: Hicks Collection on Women in Literature. 900 vols by or about women from 17th century to date. English books about or by women before 1901.

MN —COLLEGE OF SAINT CATHERINE, Library, 2004 Randolph Ave, Saint Paul, 55105. Sister Elizabeth Delmore, Library Dir
Holdings: Vols 4100 Cat Mss Phonorecords Audiotapes Microforms
Budget: $3000
Notes: Special emphasis on the psychological emancipation of woman and a growing emphasis on women in ministry. Vertical file of fugitive materials. Separate classified catalog.

MO —MISSOURI HISTORICAL SOCIETY, Library, Jefferson Memorial Bldg, Saint Louis, 63112. Stephanie Klein, Librn-Archivist; Peter Michel, Cur of Manuscripts
Notes: A collection of material on 119 women who lived or worked in St Louis and Missouri as educators, artists, and homemakers, or played significant roles in US politics and social reform. Incl Sacajawea, Susan B Anthony, Fannie Hurst, Carry Nation, Patience Worth, etc.

NV —UNIVERSITY OF NEVADA, RENO, University Library, Special Collections Dept, Reno, 89557. Robert E Blesse, Head
Holdings: Vols (800) Cat
Notes: The Women in the West Collection contains materials which document experience of women in the trans-Mississippi West. Major emphasis is on first-hand experience, diaries, letters and autobiographies, but major biographies of women who were prominent or greatly influenced others are also collected. Emphasis is the 19th and 20th centuries.

NJ —NEW JERSEY HISTORICAL SOCIETY, Library and Museum, 230 Broadway, Newark, 07104. Joan C Hull, Exec Dir; Barbara S Irwin, Library Dir; Alan R Fraser, Cur
Holdings: Mss
Budget: ($100,000)
Notes: For mss materials, see Morris & Skemer, *Guide to the Manuscript Collections of the New Jersey Historical Society*, 1979. Incl printed and manuscript collections.

NY —ELMIRA COLLEGE, Gannett-Tripp Learning Center, Elmira, 14901. James D Gray, Dir
Holdings: Cat Pix
Notes: Collection on the history and condition of women to 1900. Also, archives of the New York State Federation of Women's Clubs.

NY —CATALYST, Library, 14 E 60 St, New York, 10022. Gurley Turner, Dir of Information Services
Holdings: Vols (6000) Cat Mss VF
Notes: Working Women (current information); career and family issues plus career library.

NY —NEW YORK PUBLIC LIBRARY, Research Libraries, Economic & Public Affairs Div, Fifth Ave & 42 St, New York, 10018. Edward DiRoma, Chief
Holdings: Vols (1,500,000) Cat Microforms

NY —PLANNED PARENTHOOD FEDERATION OF AMERICA, Katharine Dexter McCormick Library, 810 Seventh Ave, New York, 10019. Gloria A Roberts, Head Librn
Holdings: Vols (4000) Cat
Notes: Birth control, teenagers, contraception and contraceptive research, family planning, religion and birth control.

NY —STATE UNIVERSITY OF NEW YORK, STONY BROOK, Melville Library, Dept of Special Collections, Stony Brook, 11794. Evert Volkersz, Head
Holdings: Cat Mss
Notes: Printed and ms materials relating to local and regional Long Island history. Ms collections focus on women, environment, social welfare, and politics.

NC —UNIVERSITY OF NORTH CAROLINA, CHARLOTTE, J Murrey Atkins Library, UNCC Station, Charlotte, 28223. Robert F Brabham Jr, Special Collections Librn
Holdings: Cat Vols Mss Pix
Notes: Files of Bonnie Ethel Cone as first president of Charlotte College and vice chancellor of the University of North Carolina at Charlotte; papers of Charlotte area women's organizations, eg AAUW and DAR; archives of Charlotte Unitarian Church; papers of novelist and short story writer Marian Sims; collections of family papers from North and South Carolina; and first editions of 18th and early 20th century American women novelists.

ND —UNIVERSITY OF NORTH DAKOTA, Chester Fritz Library, Dept of Special Collections, Grand Forks, 58202. Daniel F Rylance, Special Collections Coordr
Holdings: Vols (5500) Uncat Mss Maps Pix Microforms
Budget: ($2500)
Notes: Also the Orin G Libby Manuscript Collection (900 collections), and the Aandahl Collection of Western History on North Dakota and the Northern Great Plains. Emphasis on agriculture, politics, pioneering, Germans from Russia, etc. Guides to the collections available from the Coordinator of Special Collections.

PA —HAVERFORD COLLEGE, Magill Library, Quaker Collection, Haverford, 19041. Edwin B Bonner, Librn & Cur
Holdings: Vols (32,000) Cat Mss Maps Pix Phonorecords Audiotapes Microforms
Notes: Incl material about Society of Friends from inception in England, 1650, to the present. Formats incl periodicals, diaries, documents of individual Friends, families, Quaker Meetings and institutions, incl archives of Haverford College. Emphases on American Indians, antislavery, women, minorities, the Rufus M Jones Mysticism collection, Quaker fiction, and Delaware Valley, Pennsylvania.

PA —CARLOW COLLEGE, Grace Library, Fifth Ave, Pittsburgh, 15213. Joan M Mitchell, Dir of Library Services
Holdings: Vols (2100) Cat 16mm Films
Budget: ($1000)
Notes: The holdings in Women's Studies are not housed together in a special collection, but are part of the main collection. The particular strengths are in the areas of women in literature and the history and condition of women.

PA —UNIVERSITY OF PITTSBURGH, Hillman Library, Pittsburgh, 15260. Glenora E Rossell, Head
Holdings: Cat Microforms
Notes: The collection supports the Women Studies Program for research and the curriculum.

PA —FRIENDS HISTORICAL LIBRARY OF SWARTHMORE COLLEGE, Swarthmore, 19081. J William Frost, Dir
Holdings: Vols (35,000) Cat Mss Pix Microforms
Notes: Library's collections contain information on the history and doctrine of the Society of Friends, Quaker contributions to literature, science, business, education, and government, plus their reform efforts in peace, Indian rights, women's rights, and abolition of slavery. As an official depository of the records of women's meetings of

Philadelphia and Baltimore Yearly Meetings, the library holds either in the original or on microfilm the largest collection in the world of Quaker meeting archives, incl some records of Ohio and Illinois Yearly Meetings (Hicksite), and microfilm copies of women's minutes and registers of many meetings in New England, New York, North Carolina, Indiana, and Great Britain. Incl in the more than 250 mss collections are diaries and religious journals written by women, family correspondence, papers of women educators andreformers, and records of numerous charities managed by Quaker women.

SC —WINTHROP COLLEGE, Ida Jane Dacus Library, Rock Hill, 29733. Ron J Chepesiuk, Special Collections Librn
Holdings: Cat Mss Maps Slides Videotapes 16mm Films Microforms
Budget: ($30,000)
Notes: Concentrates on women's history in South Carolina; local history; Winthrop College archives and records. 200,000 ms pieces.

TX —TEXAS WOMAN'S UNIVERSITY, Bralley Memorial Library, Box 23715, TWU Sta, Denton, 76204. Metta Nicewarner, Spec Collections Libn
Holdings: Vols 10,000 Cat Mss Pix Phonorecords Audiotapes 16mm Films Filmstrips Microforms
Budget: $5000

UT —UNIVERSITY OF UTAH, Marriott Library, Special Collections, Salt Lake City, 84112. Gregory C Thompson, Cur
Holdings: Cat Mss Oral History
Notes: Variety of sources concerning women in Utah history, politics, religion, organizations.

WI —STATE HISTORICAL SOCIETY OF WISCONSIN, Library, Newspaper and Periodicals Section, 816 State St, Madison, 53706. James P Danky, Librn
Notes: The largest collection of women's periodicals and newspapers in the US. The library's resources as well as those in other areas of the Society are described in *Women's History: Resources at the State Historical Society of Wisconsin*. Madison, The Society. 4th edition, 1982. (ERIC Report ED 225922). Holdings described in: *Women's Periodicals and Newspapers from the 18th Century to 1981: A Union List...* Boston, G K Hall, 1982.

WI —ALVERNO COLLEGE, Research Center on Women, 3401 S 39 St, Milwaukee, 53215. Lola Stuller, Coordr
Holdings: Vols 2400 Cat Mss Pix Slides Phonorecords Audiotapes Videotapes Filmstrips
Budget: $2350
Notes: The Research Center on Women is both a research and resource center. In addition to the library materials listed above, there are approximately 200 periodicals and newsletters and a vertical file of clippings from three metropolitan newspapers, pamphlets, conference proceedings, unpublished papers, etc. Use of the Center and resources is available to anyone who comes in and reference service is available at all times. Response is given to telephone and written requests for information.

NS —MOUNT SAINT VINCENT UNIVERSITY, Library, 166 Bedford Hwy, Halifax, B3M 2J6, Can. Lucian Bianchini, University Librn
Holdings: Vols 18,000 Cat Mss Maps Pix Slides Microforms
Budget: ($125,000)
Notes: New acquisitions have been put into the general collection, rather than keeping them separate. Emphasis has been on cultural, ethnic, sociological, historical, political, and professional aspects of womanhood, international in scope. The collection circulates.

ON —CANADA DEPT OF LABOUR, Library, Ottawa, K1A 0J2, Can. Monique Marchand, Chief Librn
Holdings: Vols (100,000) Cat Microforms

WOMEN—CIVIL RIGHTS

AL —BIRMINGHAM PUBLIC LIBRARY, Southern Women's Archives, 2020 Park

WOMEN—CIVIL RIGHTS (cont.)

Place, Birmingham, 35203. Theresa A
Ceravolo, Archivist
Holdings: Cat Docs Mss
Notes: Collected records, 1974-1980, of
Alabama Women's Commission consist of
correspondence, 1975-1979 and transcripts
of testimony given at public hearings held in
Alabama's congressional districts, 1974-
1980. The testimonies encompass such topics
as abortion, the Equal Rights Amendment,
pay equity, health, and educational
opportunities for women.

CA —CLAREMONT COLLEGES, Ella Strong
Denison Library, Scripps College,
Claremont, 91711. Judy Harvey Sahak,
Librn
Holdings: Vols (2000) Cat Mss Pix
Notes: Ida Rust Macpherson Collection
centers on the humanistic accomplishments
of women, suffrage and emancipation,
domestic economy, and women in the
Westward movement. Provides historical
materials for the contemporary women's
movement.

CA —LOS ANGELES PUBLIC LIBRARY,
Social Sciences Dept, 630 W Fifth St, Los
Angeles, 90071. Marilyn C Wherley,
Principal Librn
Holdings: Vols 600 Cat Microforms
Budget: ($150,000)
Notes: Books, pamphlets, bibliographies,
periodicals, legislation, popular and scholarly
works on history and significance of suffrage
and liberation movements. No separate
catalog.

CA —HOOVER INSTITUTION ON WAR,
REVOLUTION & PEACE, Stanford
University, Stanford, 94305. Milorad M
Drachkovitch, Archivist
Holdings: Mss
Notes: Papers of Alice Park, 1883-1957, incl
diaries, correspondence, pamphlets,
clippings, and leaflets, relating to Pacifism
and the peace movement, the Ford Peace
Ship Expedition of 1915-1916, feminism,
socialism, the labor movement, prison
reform, child labor legislation, civil liberties,
and a variety of other reform movements in
the US. 30 ms boxes, 3 envelopes.

CO —UNIVERSITY OF COLORADO,
Libraries, Western Historical Collections,
Boulder, 80309.
Holdings: Cat Mss
Notes: The Women's International League
for Peace and Freedom Papers consist
mostly of correspondence and reports
between its Geneva headquarters and its
national affiliates in Europe and the
Americas. While the letters in this collection
come from many countries, most are written
in English. The WILPF, an activist women's
group founded in 1915 by America's Jane
Addams and European leaders, is concerned
with modifying public policy and attitudes
toward war and other conditions which are
detrimental to human welfare. 115 boxes. A
printed guide is available.

DC —GEORGETOWN UNIVERSITY,
Library, Special Collections Div, 37 & O Sts
NW, Washington, 20057. George M
Barringer, Special Collections Librn;
Nicholas B Sheetz, Mss Librn
Holdings: Mss Cat Pix
Notes: The papers of James Brown Scott
(1866-1945), internationalist and authority in
international law, consisting of
correspondence, memoranda, documents,
minutes, printed material, manuscripts of
articles and addresses, photographs, and
newspaper clippings. Incl is material from
Scott's activities as Solicitor (1906-1910)
and Special Advisor (1914-1917) for the
State Department, as delegate to the Second
Hague Conference (1907) and the Paris
Peace Conference (1919), his membership
and offices in the Carnegie Endowment for
International Peace, the American Society of
International Law, and the Institut de Droit
International, as well as Scott's involvement
in numerous courts of international
arbitration. Also incl is material relating to
Pan-American law. Correspondence incl
letters from Charles Evans Hughes, Robert

Bacon, William Jennings Bryam,James
Bryce, Nicholas Murray Bulter, Andrew
Carnegie, Charles Francis Adams, Frank B
Kellogg, Robert Lansing, Franklin Roosevelt,
Elihu Root, and Woodrow Wilson, among
many others.

DC —HOWARD UNIVERSITY, Moorland-
Spingarn Research Center, 500 Howard
Place NW, Washington, 20059. Clifford L
Muse, Jr, Acting Dir
Holdings: Vols (106,086) Mss Maps Pix
Slides Phonorecords Audiotapes 16mm
Films Filmstrips Microforms
Budget: ($854,753)
See also entry under Blacks

DC —LIBRARY OF CONGRESS, Manuscript
Division, Washington, 20540. John C
Broderick, Chief
Notes: Papers of Maud Wood Park (1871-
1955), first president of the League of
Women Voters. 3500 items, incl personal
and professional correspondence, family
papers, speeches and lectures, reports,
photographs, and an autograph collection,
documenting the women's rights movement
in the US, particularly in the first half of the
20th century.

IL —NORTHWESTERN UNIVERSITY,
Library, Special Collections Dept, 1937
Sheridan Rd, Evanston, 60201. R Russell
Maylone, Cur
Holdings: Vols 500
Notes: Books, newsletters, newspapers,
pamphlets, posters, ephemera written and
distributed by women active in the Women's
Liberation Movement from the early 1960s
to the present. Countries currently
represented are the US, Canada, Great
Britain, Australia, Sweden, Denmark,
Germany, France, Italy, and the
Netherlands. Emphasis is on current
literature, but some historical material is incl.
Literature: *Women's Collection Newsletter*,
Sarah Sherman, ed. (Evanston, 1974). Incl
2500 periodicals, 2700 folders ephemeral
materials.

IA —IOWA STATE UNIVERSITY, Library,
Dept of Special Collections, Ames, 50011.
Stanley M Yates, Head
Holdings: // Mss
Notes: Austin Adams Family Papers.
Collection contains correspondence, diaries
(1872-1874, 1900) notes, and lectures and
essays of Mary Newbury Adams (1837-
1901) and her husband, Austin Adams
(1827-1890), lawyer and Iowa Supreme
Court Justice, of Dubuque, Iowa. Contains
references to Ralph Waldo Emerson and A
Bronson Alcott (including letters from him).
2 linear feet. Finding aid available.

†MA —JOHN F KENNEDY LIBRARY,
Columbia Point, Boston, 02125. Dan H Fenn
Jr, Dir
Holdings: // Cat Mss
Notes: Records of the President's
Commission on the Status of Women, 1961-
1963. 8 linear ft of mss. Holdings are
described in "Historical Materials in the
John F Kennedy Library." Copies may be
obtained by writing the Research Archivist.

MA —RADCLIFFE COLLEGE, Arthur &
Elizabeth Schlesinger Library on the History
of Women in America, 3 James St,
Cambridge, 02138. Patricia Miller King, Dir;
Eva Moseley, Cur of Mss
Holdings: Vols (15,000) Cat Mss Pix
Phonorecords Audiotapes Videotapes
Notes: Many mss collections of individuals
and organizations document the Women's
Suffrage Movement or the Women's
Liberation Movement, as well as feminist
activities between 1920 and 1966. Suffrage
collections incl the Woman's Rights
Collection, papers collected by Mary Earhart
Dillon, papers of Susan Brownell Anthony
(1820-1906), Lydia Maria (Francis) Child
(1802-1880), Lucy Stone (1818-1893), and
many others. Recent collections incl the
papers of Betty (Goldstein) Friedan (1921-),
records of the National Abortion Rights
Action League, National Organization for
Women, and Women's Equity Action
League (all four partly restricted), and
photographs of women's movement activities
by Diana Mara Henry, Bettye Lane, et al.
Also papers of several leaders of the

National Women's Party and some records
of the President's Commission on the Status
of Women (1961-63) and papersof
commission member Esther (Eggertsen)
Peterson (1906-).

NY —YWCA NATIONAL BOARD, Library,
726-730 Broadway, New York, 10012.
Elizabeth Norris, Librn
Holdings: Vols (3000) Cat Mss
Budget: ($2400)
Notes: Women and their contemporary
interests.

NY —VASSAR COLLEGE, Library, Rare
Books & Manuscripts Collection, Box 20,
Poughkeepsie, 12601. Lisa Browar, Cur
Holdings: Mss Pix
Notes: Emphasis is on women in the US,
women's rights, suffrage and Equal Rights
Amendment. Manuscript collections incl
papers of Elizabeth Cady Stanton, Paulina
Wright Davis, Maria Mitchell and Alma
Lutz.

NY —UNIVERSITY OF ROCHESTER, Rush
Rhees Library, Department of Rare Books
and Special Collections, Rochester, 14627.
Peter Dzwonkoski, Librn
Holdings: Mss Pix
Notes: Incl manuscript collections related to
the National, New York State, and
Rochester women's suffrage organizations,
1880-1920. Also incl numerous pamphlets,
broadsides, and memorabilia of the Suffrage
Movement.
See also entry under Anthony, Susan
Brownell, 1820-1906

OH —KENT STATE UNIVERSITY,
University Archives, Kent, 44242. Stephen C
Morton, University Archivist
Holdings: Uncat Mss
Notes: One cubic foot of manuscripts and
printed materials of Betsy Mix Cowles,
abolitionist, educator and women's rights
advocate. Ms Cowles chaired the Women's
Rights Convention at Salem, Ohio in 1850.
The collection contains correspondence
dating from 1832, diaries, financial records,
anti-slavery tracts, addresses, poems,
pamphlets, and materials about Ms Cowles.

RI —BROWN UNIVERSITY, John Hay
Library, 20 Prospect St, Providence, 02912.
Mark N Brown, Cur Mss
Holdings: // Mss
Notes: Three ms boxes and 29 notebooks of
George S Burleigh, containing letters for the
period 1839 to 1903 reflecting his interests
in Transcendentalism; the anti-slavery,
temperance, and women's liberation
movements; the Sabbath Question; and the
publication of his writing in reform
periodicals. Two manuscript boxes and 29
notebooks contain poems by Burleigh.

TX —TEXAS WOMAN'S UNIVERSITY,
Bralley Memorial Library, Box 23715, TWU
Sta, Denton, 76204. Metta Nicewarner, Spec
Collections Libn
Holdings: Vols Uncat Mss Audiotapes
Notes: The Hermine Tobolowsky Collection
includes material on the Texas lawyer called
the "Mother of the Equal Legal Rights
Amendment in Texas". Items include
correspondence, congressional bills and
resolutions, court cases, campaign and
platform congressional pledges of support.

WOMEN—DISEASES see Gynecology

WOMEN—EDUCATION see Education of Women

WOMEN—EMANCIPATION see Women—Civil Rights

WOMEN—EMPLOYMENT

CA —WOMEN'S HISTORY RESEARCH
CENTER, Microfilm Library, 2325 Oak St,
Berkeley, 94708. Laura X, Librn
Holdings: Microforms
Notes: Incl 500 subject files of material on
Women and Law (General); Politics;
Employment; Education; Rape/Prison/
Prostitution; Black and Third World women.
Collection at University of Wyoming,
Archive of Contemporary History, PO Box
3334, Laramie, Wyoming 82071, c/o David

WOMEN—EMPLOYMENT (cont.)

Crosson. Reasearch inquiries accepted. Microfilm of collection (40 reels & reel guides) available through Women's History Research Center, 2325 Oak St, Berkeley, CA 94708. No collections housed at this address.

DC —INTERNATIONAL LABOR ORGANIZATION, International Labor Office, Washington Branch Library, 1750 New York Ave NW, Rm 330, Washington, 20006. Karen J Mark, Librn
Holdings: Vols (13,500) Cat Pix 16mm Films Monographs
Notes: Wide range of titles dealing with worldwide labor and social matters. The library contains ILO publications and documentation only, dating back to 1919. Also, a collection of ILO films and photos. See *Subject Guide to Publications of the ILO, 1919-1964* and *ILO Catalogue of Publications in Print, 1982* (ILO).

IL —INSTITUTE ON THE CHURCH IN URBAN-INDUSTRIAL SOCIETY, Library, 5700 S Woodlawn, Chicago, 60637.
Holdings: Vols 1000 Cat Microforms
Notes: Urban-industrial involvement of the churches world-wide, international urban literature, corporate responsibility, human factors of urbanization and industrialization. Library holdings are dorment at present.

NY —CENTER FOR LABOR STUDIES, SUNY, Empire State College, Labor College Library, 330 W 42nd St, New York, 10036. Jayne Adler, Librn
Holdings: Vols (3000) Cat Videotapes VF
Budget: ($4000)
Notes: Areas being emphasized in development of the library are: Women and Labor, Occupational Health and Safety, and Trade Union Leadership.

NC —DUKE UNIVERSITY, William R Perkins Library, Manuscript Dept, Durham, 27706. Ellen Gartrell, Cur of Mss
Holdings: Cat Mss
Notes: Numerous collection contain personal or professional papers of women, especially in southern US, eg Lucy Randolph Mason, Alliance for Guidance of Rural Youth, Amy Morris Bradley, Carson McCullers, Campbell Family.

PA —CARLOW COLLEGE, Grace Library, Fifth Ave, Pittsburgh, 15213. Joan M Mitchell, Dir of Library Services
Holdings: Vols (252) Cat
Budget: ($300)
Notes: The Career Resources Center consists of career and counseling materials for college students with special emphasis on the career guidance needs of the Continuing Education student. The holdings in Women's Studies are not housed together in a special collection, but are part of the main collection. The particular strengths are in the areas of women in literature and the history and condition of women.

ON —ONTARIO MINISTRY OF LABOUR, Library, 400 University Ave, Toronto, M7A 1T7, Can. Jean Collins-Williams, Librn
Holdings: Vols (80,000) Microforms Films

WOMEN—HISTORY

CA —WOMEN'S HISTORY RESEARCH CENTER, Microfilm Library, 2325 Oak St, Berkeley, 94708. Laura X, Librn
Holdings: Microforms
Notes: Microfilm (90 reels; reel guides) of collection on women's periodicals, 1956-1974, "Herstory," housed at Northwestern University Library, Special Collections Dept, Evanston, Ill 60201, c/o Sarah Sherman. Available at many universities and for purchase at the Women's History Research Center, 2325 Oak St, Berkeley, Ca 94708.

CA —UNIVERSITY OF CALIFORNIA, LOS ANGELES, Research Library, Social Sciences Collection, 405 Hilgard Ave, Los Angeles, 90024. Edward Shreeves, Chairman, Bibliographers Group; Oscar L Sims, Social Sciences Bibliographer
Holdings: Mss Pix Microforms
Notes: A comprehensive microfilm collection of literature by and about women on 1247 reels of film. The collection is arranged chronologically through the year 1920, and is divided into five sections: Monographs; Pamphlets; Periodicals; Manuscripts; and Selected Photographs. Published by Research Publications, Inc, New Haven, CT, 1976-79. A printed guide, *History of Women: Guide to the Microfilm Collection*, provides access to this material.

CA —MILLS COLLEGE LIBRARY, Oakland, 94613. Steven P Pandolfo, Librn
Holdings: Vols 300 Cat
Notes: Books printed from 17th-20th centuries; primarily 19th century with emphasis on education, women's suffrage, domestic economy and etiquette.

CT —YALE UNIVERSITY, Box 1603A, Yale Station, New Haven, 06520.

IL —MCLEAN COUNTY HISTORICAL SOCIETY LIBRARY & MUSEUM, 201 E Grove, Bloomington, 61701. Barbara Dunbar, Dir; Greg Koos, Archivist
Holdings: Vols (3000) Cat Mss Maps Pix
Notes: Illinois history, emphasis on McLean County. Strong in military heritage of Illinois, particularly the 33rd and 94th regiments (III Vol Inf) in the Civil War. Incl 150 LF archives and 1000 pictures. Photocopying.

IN —PURDUE UNIVERSITY LIBRARIES, Graduate School of Management, Krannert Library, West Lafayette, 47907. Gordon Law, Librn
Notes: An important resource at the Krannert Library is its Special Collection of Business and Economics, consisting of some 8000 rare pre-20th century strengths in books, journals, tracts and pamphlets covering primarily the early literature of economic thought and business practices in America and abroad, 1500-1870. A catalog was issued in 1979.

MO —MISSOURI HISTORICAL SOCIETY, Library, Jefferson Memorial Bldg, Saint Louis, 63112. Stephanie Klein, Librn-Archivist; Peter Michel, Cur of Manuscripts
Notes: A collection of material on 119 women who lived or worked in St Louis and Missouri as educators, artists, and homemakers, or played significant roles in US politics and social reform. Incl Sacajawea, Susan B Anthony, Fannie Hurst, Carry Nation, Patience Worth, etc.

MO —UNIVERSITY OF MISSOURI-SAINT LOUIS, Thomas Jefferson Library, Manuscript and Historical Society Collection, 8001 Natural Bridge Rd, Saint Louis, 63121.
Holdings: Mss Pix Tapes
Notes: ca

NC —UNIVERSITY OF NORTH CAROLINA, GREENSBORO, Walter Clinton Jackson Library, Special Collections Dept, 1000 Spring Garden St, Greensboro, 27412. Emilie W Mills, Librn
Holdings: Vols (3500) Cat Mss Pix
Notes: Incl books printed from 16th century to early 20th century. Major authors incl Mary Wollstonecraft, Aphra Behn, Mary Astell; North Carolina 19th century authors. The collection is primarily 19th and 20th century with emphasis on non-fiction. Subjects incl education, hygiene, physical education, household economy, women's rights. Organization and private papers of state/regional groups and eminent women incl Harriet Wisemen Elliot Papers, Ellen Black Winston Papers, North Carolina Council of Women's Organizations, Southern Association of Physical Education for College Women (see entries for more information about each collection). The University Archives houses 80 years of the history of the school, once the largest state-supported residential college for women in the US, whichbecame coeducational in 1963.

NC —NORTH CAROLINA DIV OF ARCHIVES & HISTORY, 109 E Jones St, Raleigh, 27611.
Holdings: Mss
Notes: The papers of Gertrude Weil, correspondence, material about her activities in various organizations, particularly for women's interests. 51 cubic ft of mss.

OH —BOWLING GREEN STATE UNIVERSITY, Jerome Library, Center for Archival Collections, Bowling Green, 43403. Paul D Yon, Dir; Elaine R Ezell, Reference Archivist; Nancy Steen, Rare Books Librn
Holdings: Vols (4000) Cat Mss Pix Slides Maps Microforms
Budget: ($25,000)
Notes: The Women's Studies Archives (WSA) incl pamphlets and over 100 ms collections documenting women predominately from the northwest Ohio region. Diaries and correspondence of individual women date primarily from the 1840's through the 1970's. They document the daily lives of farm women, schoolteachers, and women who are involved in the political arena and social reform activities. Women's involvement in organizations also is heavily documented in these collections. The records of literary clubs, women's federated clubs, professional and educational associations, dating from the 1880's through the present are located within the WSA. All collections are open for research use.

PA —CARLOW COLLEGE, Grace Library, Fifth Ave, Pittsburgh, 15213. Joan M Mitchell, Dir of Library Services
Holdings: Vols (2100) Cat 16mm Films
Budget: ($1000)
Notes: The holdings in Women's Studies are not housed together in a special collection, but are part of the main collection. The particular strengths are in the areas of women in literature and the history and condition of women.

TX —TEXAS WOMAN'S UNIVERSITY, Bralley Memorial Library, Box 23715, TWU Sta, Denton, 76204. Metta Nicewarner, Spec Collections Libn
Holdings: Vols Uncat Mss Pix
Notes: The exhibit, "Texas Women: A Celebration of History," prepared by Texas Foundation for Women's Resources, for the Texas Women's History Project, and all resource material used in its completion. Includes books, pamphlets, oral histories, photographs, correspondence and manuscripts.

WA —UNIVERSITY OF WASHINGTON LIBRARIES, Suzzallo Library, Manuscripts Section, FM-25, Seattle, 98195. Karyl Winn, Librn
Holdings: Mss
Notes: Personal papers and organizational records with emphasis on Pacific Northwest history and recent focus on twentieth century Western Washington. Holdings pertain to urban problems and policies, labor history, women's history, natural resource development, environmental politics, race relations, ethnic history, oral hsitory, and the arts. Holdings are complemented by textual records in the University Archives (7045 linear feet) and by graphic and printed holdings in the Pacific Northwest Collection. Described in *Comprehensive Guide to the Manuscripts Collection and to Personal Papers in the University Archives*, 1980 and in *Historical Records of Washington State: Records and Papers Held at Repositories*, 1981 and in unpublished inventories to most accessions. 15,981 linear feet of manuscripts.

WOMEN—LITERARY COLLECTIONS

MI —OAKLAND UNIVERSITY, Kresge Library, Rochester, 48063. Suzanne O Frankie, Dean; Elizabeth Titus, Special Collections Libn
Holdings: Vols 1000 Cat
Notes: The Hicks Collection of approx 1000 English-language volumes written by and about women in the 17th, 18th and 19th centuries.

WOMEN—SOCIAL AND MORAL QUESTIONS

CA —UNIVERSITY OF CALIFORNIA, LOS ANGELES, Research Library, Social Sciences Collection, 405 Hilgard Ave, Los Angeles, 90024. Edward Shreeves, Chairman, Bibliographers Group; Oscar L Sims, Social Sciences Bibliographer
Holdings: Mss Pix Microforms
Notes: A comprehensive microfilm

WOMEN—SOCIAL AND MORAL QUESTIONS (cont.)

collection of literature by and about women on 1247 reels of film. The collection is arranged chronologically through the year 1920, and is divided into five sections: Monographs; Pamphlets; Periodicals; Manuscripts; and Selected Photographs. Published by Research Publications, Inc, New Haven, CT, 1976-79. A printed guide, *History of Women: Guide to the Microfilm Collection*, provides access to this material.

IL —LAKE FOREST COLLEGE, Donnelley Library, Lake Forest, 60045. Arthur H Miller Jr, College Librn
Holdings: Vols (500) Cat
Notes: Developed in the mid 1970s, the collection reflects current women's issues, along with relevant historical and scholarly treatments. Includes ephemera (pamphlets and periodicals). Kathi Amato, compiler, *Womenstudy: A series of Research Guides* (1980) is based on 170 titles from the collection.

KS —UNIVERSITY OF KANSAS, Kenneth Spencer Research Library, Special Collections Dept, Lawrence, 66045. Alexandra Mason, Librn
Holdings: Vols 4000 // Cat
Notes: Gerritsen Collection "La Femme et la Feminisme," especially strong in late 19th and early 20th century European women's periodicals and newspapers. Formerly at John Crerar Library. Noncirculating.

MA —UNIVERSITY OF LOWELL, Library, One University Ave, Lowell, 01854. Martha Mayo, Special Collections Librn
Holdings: Vols 15,000 Cat Pix
Notes: Lowell History Collection contains photographs, lithographs, post cards, stereoviews, and lanternslides pertaining to the history of the area with special focus on the textile industry and the men and women who worked in the mills from New England Yankee farm girls to the Irish, French-Canadian, and Greek immigrants. The Locks and Canals Collection contains photographs taken from 1875-1947 showing the day to day operations of the company.

NY —LESBIAN HERSTORY EDUCATIONAL FOUNDATION INC, Lesbian Herstory Archives, PO Box 1258, New York, 10116. Deborah Edel, Treasurer
Notes: Lesbian, feminist, and Gay books and periodicals on all aspects of Lesbian culture, photographs and slides of Lesbians and Lesbian art, records, tapes, graphics and crafts. Also, unpublished materials such as first drafts, term papers from Lesbian and Gay studies courses, diaries, letters, poetry, and conference notes.

NY —YWCA NATIONAL BOARD, Library, 726-730 Broadway, New York, 10012. Elizabeth Norris, Librn
Holdings: Vols (3000) Cat Mss
Budget: ($2400)
Notes: Women and their contemporary interests.

RI —PROVIDENCE PUBLIC LIBRARY, 150 Empire St, Providence, 02903. Lance J Bauer, Special Collections Librn
Holdings: Vols 5000 Cat Mss Maps Pix
Notes: The Harris Collection on the American Civil War and Slavery. Incl 18th and 19th century books, rare pamphlets, and periodicals concerning slavery and the slave trade, and origins, progress and results of the Civil Civil War; also regimental histories; military and naval tactics; personal narratives; women's accounts of the Civil War; works on abolition; sheet music; Union and Confederate broadside ballads; Confederate imprints; *The Liberator* from 1843 through the Civil War; and over 85 editions of *Uncle Tom's Cabin* in 14 languages. Excellent primary and secondary sources for the study of the Civil War and slavery. Material must be used in-house. Photocopying when condition of material allows.

WI —UNIVERSITY OF WISCONSIN, MADISON, Memorial Library, 728 State St, Madison, 53706. Erwin K Welsch, Social Studies Bibliographer
Holdings: Vols (15,000) Cat Mss Microforms

Notes: A collection of pamphlets, books, and periodicals relating to the rise and dominance of National Socialism in Germany. There is particular strength in the periodicals collection with many titles unusually complete. Among the manuscripts are those of a soldier on the eastern front and of a Nazi school for girls.

WOMEN—SUFFRAGE

CA —CLAREMONT COLLEGES, Ella Strong Denison Library, Scripps College, Claremont, 91711. Judy Harvey Sahak, Librn
Holdings: Vols (2000) Cat Mss Pix
Notes: Ida Rust Macpherson Collection centers on the humanistic accomplishments of women, suffrage and emancipation, domestic economy, and women in the Westward movement. Provides historical materials for the contemporary women's movement.

CA —LOS ANGELES PUBLIC LIBRARY, Social Sciences Dept, 630 W Fifth St, Los Angeles, 90071. Marilyn C Wherley, Principal Librn
Holdings: Vols 200 Microforms
Budget: ($150,000)
Notes: Books, pamphlets, bibliographies, periodicals, legislation, popular and scholarly works on history and significance of suffrage and liberation movements. No separate catalog.

CA —UNIVERSITY OF CALIFORNIA, LOS ANGELES, Research Library, Dept of Special Collections, 405 Hilgard Ave, Los Angeles, 90024. Edward Shreeves, Chairman, Bibliographers Group; David S Zeidberg, Head
Holdings: // Uncat Mss
Notes: In various collections, incl the Katherine Philipps Edson, John Randolph Haynes and Dora Haynes Foundation, and Frances Noel Collections.

CA —MILLS COLLEGE LIBRARY, Oakland, 94613. Steven P Pandolfo, Librn
Holdings: Vols (300) Cat
Notes: Books printed from 17th-20th centuries; primarily 19th century with emphasis on education, women's suffrage, domestic economy and etiquette.

†CA —UNIVERSITY OF SAN FRANCISCO, Richard A Gleeson Library, The Countess Bernardine Murphy Donohue Rare Book Room, San Francisco, 94117. D Steven Corey, Special Collections Librn
Holdings: // Uncat Mss
Notes: Papers and correspondence of Mary MacNaughton (Mrs Arthur Powell Davis) and Clara W MacNaughton ca 1890-1910.

CO —UNIVERSITY OF COLORADO, Libraries, Western Historical Collections, Boulder, 80309.
Holdings: Mss
Notes: The Colorado WCTU was organized in Longmont in 1880, two years after the formation of the first three locals in Greeley, Evans and Longmont. The Colorado WCTU was active in woman's suffrage, prison reform, homes for unwed mothers, day nurseries, 8-hour laws, and other reforms in addition to their primary concern of prohibition. The collection contains minutes of the Boulder Chapter (1881-1950) plus minutes of other Colorado local chapters for shorter periods of time. In addition there are state convention proceedings (1882-1969), state officers' minutes and reports, and many pamphlets and publications. 13 boxes and 12oversize folders, 1878-1975. A published guide is available.

CT —STOWE-DAY LIBRARY, 77 Forest St, Hartford, 06105. Diana J Royce, Librn
Holdings: Vols (15,000) Cat Mss
Notes: Incl (6000) additional pamphlets. The entire collection covers architecture, decorative arts, history, literature, woman suffrage, and Harriet Beecher Stowe, through the 19th century.

DC —GEORGETOWN UNIVERSITY, Library, Special Collections Div, 37 & O Sts NW, Washington, 20057. George M Barringer, Special Collections Librn; Nicholas B Sheetz, Mss Librn
Holdings: Mss
Notes: The papers of Miss Janet E Richards,

lecturer and columnist, consisting of correspondence, family records, and photographs; incl material on women's suffrage and the Oberammergau Passion Play.

DC —LIBRARY OF CONGRESS, Rare Book & Special Collections Div, Washington, 20540. William Matheson, Chief
Holdings: Vols 709 Cat
Notes: A collection of books on the women's movement and kindred subjects presented to the library by the National American Woman Suffrage Association and its president, Mrs Carrie Chapman Catt. It consists of the feminist library of Mrs Catt, collected since 1890, and various older books contributed from the libraries of Elizabeth Cady Stanton, Susan B Anthony (qv), Lucy Stone, Alice Stone Blackwell, Julia Ward Howe, Mary A Livermore and others, together with bound sets of periodicals relating to woman suffrage. The Susan B Anthony Collection represents her personal library, presented to the Library in 1903. Incl, apart from Miss Anthony's own books, are a large number of inscribed copies given to the reformer by authors and friends, nearly all of which are relevant to the rights of women, enfranchisement, etc. Supplementary are files ofsuch materials as official reports of the National Suffrage Conventions, addresses made at Congressional hearings, scrapbooks containing clippings from newspapers and periodicals, handbills, and other memorabilia.

DC —LIBRARY OF CONGRESS, Manuscript Division, Washington, 20540. John C Broderick, Chief
Notes: Papers of Maud Wood Park (1871-1955), first president of the League of Women Voters. 3500 items, incl personal and professional correspondence, family papers, speeches and lectures, reports, photographs, and an autograph collection, documenting the women's rights movement in the US, particularly in the first half of the 20th century. The papers of Carrie Chapman Catt date chiefly from 1890-1920 and pertain to her efforts to secure voting rights for women. Material from after 1920 relates to her world peace movement activities. Also, many materials related to Susan B Anthony.

KY —UNIVERSITY OF KENTUCKY, Margaret I King Library, Dept of Special Collections, Lexington, 40506. William Marshall, Head
Holdings: // Cat Mss
Notes: Woman suffrage. About 6000 pieces; correspondence, etc.

MA —RADCLIFFE COLLEGE, Arthur & Elizabeth Schlesinger Library on the History of Women in America, 3 James St, Cambridge, 02138. Patricia Miller King, Dir; Eva Moseley, Cur of Mss
Notes: Numerous mss collections of suffragists incl records of suffrage organizations. The two largest are the Woman's Rights Collection, assembled by Maud Wood Park (1871-1955) and forming the original nucleus of the Schlesinger Library, and the Mary Earhart Dillon collection, which consists of papers of Anna Howard Shaw (1874-1919) and several Illinois suffragists.

NY —UNIVERSITY OF ROCHESTER, Rush Rhees Library, Department of Rare Books and Special Collections, Rochester, 14627. Peter Dzwonkoski, Librn
Holdings: Mss Pix
Notes: Incl manuscript collections related to the National, New York State, and Rochester women's suffrage organizations, 1880-1920. Also incl numerous pamphlets, broadsides, and memorabilia of the Suffrage Movement.
See also entry under Anthony, Susan Brownell, 1820-1906.

NC —UNIVERSITY OF NORTH CAROLINA, GREENSBORO, Walter Clinton Jackson Library, Special Collections Dept, 1000 Spring Garden St, Greensboro, 27412. Emilie W Mills, Librn
Holdings: Cat Mss
Notes: 78 letters by the English composer

WOMEN—SUFFRAGE (cont.)

Dame Ethel Mary Smyth, chiefly to Emmeline Pankhurst, written from Helouan, Egypt, 1913-1914. Other letters incl several from Empress Eugenie and members of her circle, and several letters to Lady Ponsonby. This group of letters mainly traces the composer's interest in the suffrage movement and the development of her musical career. No photocopying.

WOMEN, AFRICAN

DC —HOWARD UNIVERSITY, Moorland-Spingarn Research Center, 500 Howard Place NW, Washington, 20059. Clifford L Muse, Jr, Acting Dir

WOMEN, AMERICAN

CA —UNIVERSITY OF CALIFORNIA, LOS ANGELES, Research Library, Social Sciences Collection, 405 Hilgard Ave, Los Angeles, 90024. Edward Shreeves, Chairman, Bibliographers Group; Oscar L Sims, Social Sciences Bibliographer
Holdings: Mss Pix Microforms
Notes: A comprehensive microfilm collection of literature by and about women on 1247 reels of film. The collection is arranged chronologically through the year 1920, and is divided into five sections: Monographs; Pamphlets; Periodicals; Manuscripts; and Selected Photographs. Published by Research Publications, Inc, New Haven, CT, 1976-79. A printed guide, *History of Women: Guide to the Microfilm Collection*, provides access to this material.
CA —CALIFORNIA HISTORICAL SOCIETY, Schubert Hall Library, 2099 Pacific Ave, San Francisco, 94109. Bruce L Johnson, Library Dir
Holdings: Vols (50,000) Cat Mss Maps Pix
See also entry under California - History.
CO —UNIVERSITY OF COLORADO, Libraries, Western Historical Collections, Boulder, 80309.
Holdings: Mss
Notes: The Colorado WCTU was organized in Longmont in 1880, two years after the formation of the first three locals in Greeley, Evans and Longmont. The Colorado WCTU was active in woman's suffrage, prison reform, homes for unwed mothers, day nurseries, 8-hour laws, and other reforms in addition to their primary concern of prohibition. The collection contains minutes of the Boulder Chapter (1881-1950) plus minutes of other Colorado local chapters for shorter periods of time. In addition there are state convention proceedings (1882-1969), state officers' minutes and reports, and many pamphlets and publications. 13 boxes and 12 oversize folders, 1878-1975. A published guide is available.
DC —HOWARD UNIVERSITY, Moorland-Spingarn Research Center, 500 Howard Place NW, Washington, 20059. Clifford L Muse, Jr, Acting Dir
Holdings: Vols (106,086) Mss Maps Pix Slides Phonorecords Audiotapes 16mm Films Filmstrips Microforms
Budget: ($854,753)
See also entry under Blacks
MA —RADCLIFFE COLLEGE, Arthur & Elizabeth Schlesinger Library on the History of Women in America, 3 James St, Cambridge, 02138. Patricia Miller King, Dir; Eva Moseley, Cur of Mss
Holdings: Vols (22,000) Cat Mss Pix Audiotapes Microforms
Notes: Formerly the Women's Archives, but the name of the library has been changed. 463 personal collections; 103 organization collections. Collections on the current Women's Movement both in mss and printed materials.
NE —UNIVERSITY OF NEBRASKA-LINCOLN, Don L Love Library, University Archives and Special Collections, Lincoln, 68588. Joseph G Svoboda, University Archivist
Holdings: Vols (1000) // Cat Mss Maps Pix Audiotapes 16mm Films
Notes: THE *MARI *SANDOZ

Notes: The Mari Sandoz Collection consists of four basic parts. The first contains correspondence files, 25,000 letters in all, including letters received from 1925 on and carbon copies of letters sent. The correspondence files are a rich source of information about the author's life and career, creative writing, and Plains Indian and western American history. The second portion of the collection is the author's personal library of books and periodicals, many annotated. Part three contains the author's published works, including most of the editions, foreign and domestic and some unpublished manuscripts as well. Many of the early drafts of books, copy-edited manuscripts, and galley and proofs are also contained in this portion of the collection. The final part of the collections consists of the author's resource files, research and reading notes, clippings, and related materials. These materials fill over fifty standard letter boxes. In addition, the prepared 45,000 index cards refering to information contained both in and out of the collection.

NV —UNIVERSITY OF NEVADA, RENO, University Library, Special Collections Dept, Reno, 89557. Robert E Blesse, Head
Holdings: Vols 800 Cat
Notes: The Women in the West Collection contains materials which document experience of women in the trans-Mississippi West. Major emphasis is on first-hand experience, diaries, letters and autobiographies, but major biographies of women who were prominent or greatly influenced others are also collected. Emphasis is the 19th and 20th centuries.

NY —BARNARD COLLEGE LIBRARY, Broadway & 117 St, New York, 10027. Patricia K Ballou, Archivist and Tech Services Librn
Holdings: Vols (2300) Cat Mss
Notes: Overbury Collection. Books by and about American women authors. Incl first editions, critical and biographical works, letters, and nearly a thousand literary mss.

NY —CATALYST, Library, 14 E 60 St, New York, 10022. Gurley Turner, Dir of Information Services
Holdings: Vols (6000) Cat Mss VF
Notes: Working Women (current information); career and family issues plus career library.

NY —YWCA NATIONAL BOARD, Library, 726-730 Broadway, New York, 10012. Elizabeth Norris, Librn
Holdings: Vols (3000) Cat Mss
Budget: ($2400)
Notes: Women and their contemporary interests.

NY —VASSAR COLLEGE, Library, Rare Books & Manuscripts Collection, Box 20, Poughkeepsie, 12601. Lisa Browar, Cur
Holdings: Mss Pix
Notes: Emphasis is on women in the US, women's rights, suffrage and Equal Rights Amendment. Manuscript collections incl papers of Elizabeth Cady Stanton, Paulina Wright Davis, Maria Mitchell and Alma Lutz.

NC —DUKE UNIVERSITY, William R Perkins Library, Manuscript Dept, Durham, 27706. Ellen Gartrell, Cur of Mss
Holdings: Cat Mss
Notes: Numerous collections contain personal or professional papers of women, especially in southern US, incl Lucy Randolph Mason, Alliance for Guidance of Rural Youth, Amy Morris Bradley, Carson McCullers, Campbell Family.

SC —WINTHROP COLLEGE, Ida Jane Dacus Library, Rock Hill, 29733. Ron J Chepesiuk,

Special Collections Librn
Holdings: Cat Mss Maps Slides Videotapes 16mm Films Microforms
Budget: ($30,000)
Notes: Concentrates on women's history in South Carolina; local history; Winthrop College archives and records. 200,000 ms pieces.

WOMEN, BLACK

CA —WOMEN'S HISTORY RESEARCH CENTER, Microfilm Library, 2325 Oak St, Berkeley, 94708. Laura X, Librn
Holdings: Mss Pix Microforms
Notes: Incl material (150 subject files) on physical and mental health and illnesses; sex roles; biology; women and the life cycle; birth/population control; sex and sexuality; black and Third World women. Collection at University of Wyoming. Archive of Contemporary History, PO Box 3334, Laramie, Wyoming 82701, c/o David Crosson. Research inquiries accepted. Microfilm of collection (14 reels and reel guides) available at many universities and through Women's History Research Center, 2325 Oak St, Berkeley, CA 94708. No collections housed at this address.
DC —HOWARD UNIVERSITY, Moorland-Spingarn Research Center, 500 Howard Place NW, Washington, 20059. Clifford L Muse, Jr, Acting Dir
IN —INDIANA HISTORICAL SOCIETY, Library, 315 W Ohio St, Indianapolis, 46202. Robert K O'Neill, Dir
Holdings: Vols Cat Mss Pix
Notes: Materials on blacks in Indiana, from statehood to the present day. Incl books; letters; church and organization records; photographs. Incl records of the Madam C J Walker Company, a black cosmetics firm in Indianapolis.
MA —RADCLIFFE COLLEGE, Arthur & Elizabeth Schlesinger Library on the History of Women in America, 3 James St, Cambridge, 02138. Patricia Miller King, Dir; Eva Moseley, Cur of Mss
Notes: Black Women Oral History Project (1976-). Interviews (tapes and transcripts) with 72 American black women who have made significant contributions toward the improvement of the lives of black people and to US society. Sponsored by the Schlesinger Library.

WOMEN, CANADIAN

†ON —METROPOLITAN TORONTO LIBRARY, Social Sciences Dept, 789 Yonge St, Toronto, M4W 2G8, Can. Abdus Salam, Head
Holdings: Vols Cat Maps Phonorecords Audiotapes 16mm Films Microforms
Notes: This collection, contemporary and historical in scope, includes material on the social and legal status of women, particularly rights, education, and health care. Also included are biographies and directories. Special emphasis is the feminist movement in Canada.
ON —UNIVERSITY OF WATERLOO, Library, Waterloo, N2L 3G1, Can. Susan Bellingham, Special Collections Librn
Holdings: Vols 1200
Notes: Nucleus of collections is the "Lady Aberdeen Library on the History of Women" donated by the National Council of Women of Canada. Collection contains rare books and manuscripts of notable Canadian women (ie Dr Elizabeth Shortt, Emily Murphy). Collection listed in *A Catalogue of the Lady Aberdeen Library on the History of Women in the University of Waterloo Library*. University of Waterloo Library Bibliography #7.

WOMEN, CATHOLIC

DC —GEORGETOWN UNIVERSITY, Library, Special Collections Div, 37 & O Sts NW, Washington, 20057. George M Barringer, Special Collections Librn; Nicholas B Sheetz, Mss Librn
Holdings: Mss
Notes: Transcripts and other material

WOMEN, CATHOLIC (cont.)

concerning the National Council of Catholic Women. Incl are transcripts from the "Catholic Hour," a program sponsored by the Council from 1960-1968; published proceedings of the NCCW conventions from 1932-1962; and printed material on the "Parish Program," a service offered by the Council.

WOMEN, LATIN AMERICAN

CA —UNIVERSITY OF CALIFORNIA, RIVERSIDE, University Library, 4045 Canyon Crest Dr, Box 5900, Riverside, 92517.
Holdings: Vols 5,000
Notes: Extensive collection of modern works on history and biography of women, sociological studies, political and professional aspects, with special emphasis on women in Latin America. Significant holdings of literary works by and about Latin American and Portuguese (late 19th century to present) women authors.

WOMEN, NATIONAL ORGANIZATION FOR see National Organization for Women (NOW)

WOMEN, ORDINATION OF see Women Ministers

WOMEN, POLISH

IL —POLISH WOMEN'S ALLIANCE OF AMERICA, 205 S Northwest Highway, Park Ridge, 60068.
Holdings: 1500 Vols

WOMEN ACTORS see Actors and Actresses

WOMEN AND HEALTH

AL —BIRMINGHAM PUBLIC LIBRARY, Southern Women's Archives, 2020 Park Place, Birmingham, 35203. Theresa A Ceravolo, Archivist
Holdings: Cat Mss
Notes: Monthly legislative reports, 1981-1983, which discuss Alabama legislative and, to some extent, US Congress activities regarding abortion, domestic violence, child support, and other related issues. Collected records, 1974-1980, of Alabama Women's Commission consist of correspondence, 1975-1979 and transcripts of testimony given at public hearings held in Alabama's congressional districts, 1974-1980. The testimonies encompass such topics as abortion, the Equal Rights Amendment, pay equity, health, and educational opportunities for women.

CA —WOMEN'S HISTORY RESEARCH CENTER, Microfilm Library, 2325 Oak St, Berkeley, 94708. Laura X, Librn
Holdings: Mss Pix Microforms
Notes: Incl material (150 subject files) on physical and mental health and illnesses; sex roles; biology; women and the life cycle; birth/population control; sex and sexuality; black and Third World women. Collection at University of Wyoming. Archive of Contemporary History, PO Box 3334, Laramie, Wyoming 82701, c/o David Crosson. Research inquiries accepted. Microfilm of collection (14 reels and reel guides) available at many universities and through Women's History Research Center, 2325 Oak St, Berkeley, CA 94708. No collections housed at this address.

WOMEN AND LAW

AL —BIRMINGHAM PUBLIC LIBRARY, Southern Women's Archives, 2020 Park Place, Birmingham, 35203. Theresa A Ceravolo, Archivist
Holdings: Cat Mss
Notes: Monthly legislative reports, 1981-1983, which discuss Alabama legislative and, to some extent, US Congress activities regarding abortion, domestic violence, child support, and other related issues. Collected records, 1974-1980, of Alabama Women's Commission consist of correspondence, 1975-1979 and transcripts of testimony given at public hearings held in Alabama's congressional districts, 1974-1980. The testimonies encompass such topics as abortion, the Equal Rights Amendment, pay equity, health, and educational opportunities for women.

CA —WOMEN'S HISTORY RESEARCH CENTER, Microfilm Library, 2325 Oak St, Berkeley, 94708. Laura X, Librn
Holdings: Microforms
Notes: Incl 500 subject files of material on Women and Law (General); Politics; Employment; Education; Rape/Prison/ Prostitution; Black and Third World women. Collection at University of Wyoming, Archive of Contemporary History, PO Box 3334, Laramie, Wyoming 82071, c/o David Crosson. Reasearch inquiries accepted. Microfilm of collection (40 reels & reel guides) available through Women's History Research Center, 2325 Oak St, Berkeley, CA 94708. No collections housed at this address.

WOMEN ARCHITECTS

MA —MASSACHUSETTS INSTITUTE OF TECHNOLOGY, Institute Archives, Special Collections, Cambridge, 02139.
Notes: Papers of Howe, Manning and Almy, an architectural firm that started in 1913 as Lois Lilley Howe and Manning, was an unusual and successful partnership of women architects. The collection incl correspondence, financial data, reports, specifications, photographs, blueprints, drawings, and research material from the firm. Housing projects incl Mariemont, Ohio, as well as designs and renovations for New England especially in the Colonial Revival style.

WOMEN AS COMPOSERS see Women Composers

WOMEN AS POETS see Women Poets

WOMEN AUTHORS

CA —UNIVERSITY OF CALIFORNIA, RIVERSIDE, University Library, 4045 Canyon Crest Dr, Box 5900, Riverside, 92517.
Holdings: Vols 5,000
Notes: Extensive collection of modern works on history and biography of women, sociological studies, political and professional aspects, with special emphasis on women in Latin America. Significant holdings of literary works by and about Latin American and Portuguese (late 19th century to present) women authors.

CA —STANFORD UNIVERSITY LIBRARIES, Cecil H Green Library, Stanford, 94305. Peter R Frank, Cur, CDP-Germanic Collection
Notes: Library of Prof Rudolf Hildebran, Leipzig, the first large collection acquired by Stanford in 1895/1896, laid the foundation for an extensive German collection. Hildebrand's library is especially strong in German and Austrian philology (rare dictionaries, etc.), but also in literary works. The collection is now especially strong for the period of the Reformation and Baroque, up to the present, with many rare editions, journals, almanacs, and the like. Sizable collections of women's working class and popular literature, dissertations and Schulschriften. Rare and valuable items in the Stanford Collection of German, Austrian and Swiss Culture, Special Collections. Catalog: *Katalog der Bibliothek des Herrn Prof Dr Rudolf Hildebrand*. Description: *The German Area Collection: A Stanford Tradition* by Peter R Frank.

ME —WESTBROOK COLLEGE, Library, 716 Stevens Ave, Portland, 04103. Dorothy M Healy, Special Collections Librn
Holdings: Vols (3000) Cat Mss Pix
Notes: Collection incl work of Maine women writers. Many mss and scrapbooks are incl. Memorabilia of Mrs Robert E Peary, Mary Ellen Chase, Florence B Jacobs, Celia Thaxter, and Edna St Vincent Millay are notable items. Some rare books, ie Madame Wood novels, are part of the collection.

MI —OAKLAND UNIVERSITY, Kresge Library, Rochester, 48063. Suzanne O Frankie, Dean; Elizabeth Titus, Special Collections Librn
Holdings: Vols 1000 Cat
Notes: The Hicks Collection of approx 1000 English-language volumes written by and about women in the 17th, 18th and 19th centuries.

NY —BARNARD COLLEGE LIBRARY, Broadway & 117 St, New York, 10027. Patricia K Ballou, Archivist and Tech Services Librn
Holdings: Vols (2300) Cat Mss
Notes: Overbury Collection. Books by and about American women authors. Incl first editions, critical and biographical works, letters, and nearly a thousand literary mss.

NY —CARL H PFORZHEIMER LIBRARY, 41 E 42 St, New York, 10017. Mihai H Handrea, Librn
Holdings: Cat Mss Pix
Notes: English Literature from Caxton to 1700; first editions of 18th and 19th centuries, incl mss material on Shelley and his circle; fine presses (Bruce Rogers); George Gissing; women writers 1790-1840, (Mary Wollstonecraft, Mary Hays, Lady Blessington).

†NY —COLUMBIA UNIVERSITY LIBRARIES, Butler Library, Rare Book and Manuscript Library, 535 W 114 St, New York, 10027.
Notes: Archives of the Women's National Book Association, Inc.

NC —UNIVERSITY OF NORTH CAROLINA, CHARLOTTE, J Murrey Atkins Library, UNCC Station, Charlotte, 28223. Robert F Brabham Jr, Special Collections Librn
Holdings: Vols Cat Mss Pix
Notes: Files of Bonnie Ethel Cone as first president of Charlotte College and vice chancellor of the University of North Carolina at Charlotte; papers of Charlotte area women's organizations, eg AAUW and DAR; archives of Charlotte Unitarian Church; papers of novelist and short story writer Marian Sims; collections of family papers from North and South Carolina; and first editions of 18th and early 20th century American women novelists.

†OH —OHIO NORTHERN UNIVERSITY, Heterick Memorial Library, 525 S Main St, Ada, 45810.
Notes: Ohio women authors.

RI —BROWN UNIVERSITY, John Hay Library, Harris Collection, Prospect St, Providence, 02912. Rosemary L Cullen, Cur
Holdings: Vols (200,000) Cat Mss Phonorecords Microforms
Budget: ($15,000)
Notes: The Harris Collection of American Poetry and Plays is principally composed of American and Canadian poetry and plays, 17th century-date. Extensive holdings in songsters, gift books and annuals, hymnals, pageants, broadside verse, carriers' addresses, women poets, juvenile poetry, (incl Mother Goose and *The Night Before Christmas*), sheet music with lyrics, small press publications, fine printing, black poets, "little magazines," Yiddish-American literature. All movements or schools of American poetry are represented. Incl first editions of most American poets and playwrights, notably Whitman, Poe, Wallace Stevens, Eugene O'Neill, Edward Albee, Ezra Pound, T S Eliot, William Carlos Williams, Amy Lowell, Phyllis Wheatley, Robert Frost, Allen Ginsberg, Bliss Carman, and Stephen Foster sheet music. Also incl the Saunders Walt Whitman Collection (1300 vols); the LangdonCollection of Pageants (250 vols); the Asa Cushman Collection of plays in ms and prompt copies; the MacDougall Collection of Psalters and Hymnals; 4000 plays issued by Walter H Baker Co, Boston (1890-1957); the Vaxer Collection of Yiddish Poetry, Plays and

WOMEN AUTHORS (cont.)

Music (1700 vols). Collections incl 200,000 vols, 30,000 broadsides, 55,000 mss, 170,000 pieces of sheet music, 450 phonorecords, and 375 microfilm reels. See *Dictionary Catalog of the Harris Collection of American Poetry and Plays* (Boston: G K Hall, 1972), 13 vols; *Supplement* (1977), 3 vols. See also, *American Poetry, 1609-1900, A Collection on Microfilm, Segment I* (1609-1820); *Segment II* (1821-1850); *Segment III* (1851-1870) (Woodbridge, Conn: Research Publications). Separate catalog.

TX —TEXAS WOMAN'S UNIVERSITY, Bralley Memorial Library, Box 23715, TWU Sta, Denton, 76204. Metta Nicewarner, Spec Collections Libn
Holdings: Uncat Mss Pix
Notes: The Claire Myers Owens Papers belong to the Texas author, religious philosopher, Zen Buddhist. Includes correspondence, edited mss, galleys and personal items.

VA —RANDOLPH-MACON WOMAN'S COLLEGE, Lipscomb Library, Lynchburg, 24503. Frances White, Ref Libn
Holdings: Vols 1704 Cat Mss
Notes: Published writings by Virginia women.

†WA —WASHINGTON STATE UNIVERSITY, Library, Manuscripts, Archives & Special Collections, Pullman, 99164. John F Guido, Head
Holdings: Vols Mss Pix
Notes: The library of Virginia and Leonard Woolf (from Monk's House and Victoria Sq) forms the nucleus of the collection, which incorporates the library of Sir Leslie Stephen, Virginia's father. Leonard's interests are reflected by works concerning the Labour Party, the Fabian Society, as well as Ceylon. Their interest in printing and publishing works of significance is reflected by the collection of Hogarth Press publications (1917-1941). Incl works by Virginia and Leonard Woolf, the Bloomsbury Group, as well as by other friends--eg, Elizabeth Robins, Victoria Sackville-West, Harold Nicholson, etc. Many of these are unique copies, ie, association and textual interest. Other 20th century English authors incl: the Sitwells, Margaret Sackville, Rose Macaulay, D H Lawrence, John Masefield, Rupert Croft-Cooke, & Charles Williams. Partially cataloged.

WI —UNIVERSITY OF WISCONSIN, MADISON, Memorial Library, British & American Language & Literature Collection, 728 State St, Madison, 53706. Yvonne Schofer, Bibliographer
Holdings: Vols 2200 Mss Microforms Documents Periodicals
Notes: A collection of primary and secondary materials for nine major American women writers: Anne Bradstreet; Louisa May Alcott, Emily Dickinson, Kate Chopin, Mary Williams Freeman, Margaret Fuller, Sarah Orne Jewett, Charlotte Perkins Gilman, Harriet Beecher Stowe. Primary materials also collected for a list of less well known authors together with manuscripts and archives of letters of special research interest. Variety of holdings: fiction, poetry, drama, biography and autobiography, letters, memoirs, diaries, travel, domestic economy and other kinds of writings by women mostly of the 19th century. Held in Dept of Rare Books and Special Collections.

WOMEN COMPOSERS

MA —WELLESLEY COLLEGE, Music Library, Wellesley, 02181. Mary Wallace Davidson, Music Libn
Notes: Incl 12,500 bound vols of music scores and 12,000 phonorecords and tapes.

MI —UNIVERSITY OF MICHIGAN, School of Music, Music Library, Moore Bldg, Ann Arbor, 48109. Peggy Daub, Head
Holdings: Vols 2000 Cat Mss
Notes: Women's Music Collection. Unusual collection of music by women composers published from 1750-1950. Includes some material closely associated with Dame Ethel

Smyth and a small collection of letters by women musicians in Hatcher Graduate Library. Catalog to be published late in 1984.

WOMEN ENGINEERS see Women in Engineering

WOMEN IN AERONAUTICS

CA —CLAREMONT COLLEGES, Norman F Sprague Memorial Library, 12 & Dartmouth, Claremont, 91711. David Kuhner, Libn
Holdings: Vols 3500 Cat Mss Maps Pix Phonorecords
Notes: Gift of Rev and Mrs John F B Carruthers of Pasadena, 1950. Emphasis on history of ballooning, early aviation, World War I and World War II military aviation, pioneer flyers and flights, women in aviation, cartoons, songs, memorabilia, some diaries and journals. Restricted use. Collections transferred here from Honnold Library.

DC —SMITHSONIAN INSTITUTION LIBRARIES, National Air & Space Museum Branch, NASM Bldg, Sixth & Independence Ave SW, Washington, 20560. Frank A Pietropaoli, Branch Chief
Holdings: Vols (39,000) Cat Mss Maps Pix Slides Microforms
Notes: History of flight and aerospace development, incl biographical material on aviation pioneers, balloons and ballooning. Extensive photographic collection (600,000 pictures). Incl the Sherman Fairchild Collection of aeronautical photographs (transferred from the American Institute of Aeronautics and Astronautics). Also incl the Bella Landauer Aeronautical Sheet Music Collection (1500 pieces). 2000 films; 800,000 microforms; 9000 volumes bound.

IN —PURDUE UNIVERSITY LIBRARIES, Special Collections Dept, West Lafayette, 47907. Keith Dowden, Asst Dir, Special Collections
Holdings: Mss Maps Pix
Notes: Amelia Earhart Collection. Incl charts, maps, medals, certificates, letters and telegrams and other memorabilia.

MA —RADCLIFFE COLLEGE, Arthur & Elizabeth Schlesinger Library on the History of Women in America, 3 James St, Cambridge, 02138. Patricia Miller King, Dir; Eva Moseley, Cur of Mss
Notes: Cache of correspondence, largely made up of letters to and from Amelia Earhart, her mother, Amy Otis Earhart, sister, and her husband George Palmer Putnam.

OK —NINETY-NINES, Library, PO Box 59964, Will Rogers World Airport, Oklahoma City, 73159. Lorretta Craig, Libn
Holdings: Vols 350 Cat Pix
Budget: $700
Notes: 10,000 books, periodicals, catalogs on history of aviation. Women's aviation resource center. Collection from the first women aviatrix, Harriet Quinley, 1905-, Matilda Morant, 1925-. 7000 bound periodicals from 1929, 10 issues a year, from the magazine first called "Airwomen" to the "Ninety-Nines". Members of the "Ninety-Nines" incl 7 women astronauts (Betty Smith).

WOMEN IN BUSINESS

DC —BUSINESS & PROFESSIONAL WOMEN'S FOUNDATION, Marguerite Rawalt Resource Center, 2012 Massachusetts Ave NW, Washington, 20036. Cheryl A Sloan, Libn
Holdings: Vols (20,000) Cat Microforms VF
Budget: ($10,000)
Notes: Vertical files, containing ca 13,000 items (studies, periodical articles, newspaper clippings, documents) current. All items are filed by subject and indexed in our card catalog by author, title and subject. 200 tape recordings in Oral History Collection. The Resource Center is currently being automated, starting with thesaurus construction, then data base design, and finally the implementation phase, which incl cataloging, abstracting, and indexing each

item. Microfilms are mainly of doctoral theses. Our emphasis is on the working woman and encompasses economic issues of concern to women such as education for women, working mothers, sex roles, women executives, counseling for women, and work force entry by mature women. Most of the material is about women in the US. Collection incl 500 microfilms.Publish a bimonthly selected acquisitions list.

NY —YWCA NATIONAL BOARD, Library, 726-730 Broadway, New York, 10012. Elizabeth Norris, Libn
Holdings: Vols (3000) Cat Mss
Budget: ($2400)
Notes: Women and their contemporary interests.

PA —CARLOW COLLEGE, Grace Library, Fifth Ave, Pittsburgh, 15213. Joan M Mitchell, Dir of Library Services
Holdings: Vols (252) Cat
Budget: ($300)
Notes: The Career Resources Center consists of career and counseling materials for college students with special emphasis on the career guidance needs of the Continuing Education Student.

TX —NORTH TEXAS STATE UNIVERSITY, Archives, NT Station Box 5188, Denton, 76203. Robert LaForte, University Archivist
Notes: Part of Business Archive Project. Interviews with cometics entrepreneur Mary K Ash (Mary K Cosmetics) and Bettie C Graham (Liquid Paper Corporation).

WOMEN IN CANADA

†ON —METROPOLITAN TORONTO LIBRARY, Social Sciences Dept, 789 Yonge St, Toronto, M4W 2G8, Can. Abdus Salam, Head
Holdings: Vols Cat Maps Phonorecords Audiotapes 16mm Films Microforms
Notes: This collection, contemporary and historical in scope, includes material on the social and legal status of women, particularly rights, education, and health care. Also included are biographies and directories. Special emphasis is the feminist movement in Canada.

WOMEN IN DRAMA see Women in Literature

WOMEN IN ECONOMIC DEVELOPMENT

CA —UNIVERSITY OF CALIFORNIA, LOS ANGELES, Research Library, Social Sciences Collection, 405 Hilgard Ave, Los Angeles, 90024. Edward Shreeves, Chairman, Bibliographers Group; Oscar L Sims, Social Sciences Bibliographer
Holdings: Mss Pix Microforms
Notes: A comprehensive microfilm collection of literature by and about women on 1247 reels of film. The collection is arranged chronologically through the year 1920, and is divided into five sections: Monographs; Pamphlets; Periodicals; Manuscripts; and Selected Photographs. Published by Research Publications, Inc, New Haven, CT, 1976-79. A printed guide, *History of Women: Guide to the Microfilm Collection*, provides access to this material.

MA —HARVARD UNIVERSITY, Institute for International Development, Library, Coolidge Hall, 1737 Cambridge St, Cambridge, 02138. Barbara Mitchell, Libn
Holdings: Vols (17,000) Periodicals
Notes: Economic development, rural development, statistical material on selected underdeveloped countries. Incl 75 periodical titles.

WI —UNIVERSITY OF WISCONSIN, MADISON, Land Tenure Center Library, 434 Steenbock Memorial Library, 550 Babcock Dr, Madison, 53706. Teresa J Anderson, Libn
Holdings: Vols (60,000) Cat Mss Maps Microforms
Budget: ($65,000)
Notes: Socio-economic aspects of agricultural development in the Third World. All materials in the collection are cataloged and classified. The library has its own catalog.

WOMEN IN EDUCATION

NY —YWCA NATIONAL BOARD, Library, 726-730 Broadway, New York, 10012. Elizabeth Norris, Librn
Holdings: Vols (3000) Cat Mss
Budget: ($2400)
Notes: Women and their contemporary interests.

NC —UNIVERSITY OF NORTH CAROLINA, CHARLOTTE, J Murrey Atkins Library, UNCC Station, Charlotte, 28223. Robert F Brabham Jr, Special Collections Librn
Holdings: Vols Cat Mss Pix
Notes: Files of Bonnie Ethel Cone as first president of Charlotte College and vice chancellor of the University of North Carolina at Charlotte; papers of Charlotte area women's organizations, eg AAUW and DAR; archives of Charlotte Unitarian Church; papers of novelist and short story writer Marian Sims; collections of family papers from North and South Carolina; and first editions of 18th and early 20th century American women novelists.

WOMEN IN ENGINEERING

NY —ENGINEERING SOCIETIES LIBRARY, 345 E 47 St, New York, 10017. S Kirk Cabeen, Dir
Holdings: Vols 250,000 Cat Maps 16mm Films Microforms
Notes: One of the largest, most comprehensive engineering libraries in the world. Covers all engineering disciplines; particularly strong in electrical and electronic, mechanical, mining and metallurgical, petroleum, chemical, industrial, air conditioning and refrigeration engineering. Incl Wheeler Collection of early materials on magnetism and electricity. 125,000 bound periodical volumes; 10,000 maps; 5000 serial subscriptions (many foreign-language). Virtually all materials abstracted in *Engineering Index* (1884-date) are incl in Library. Noncirculating, except to members of professional engineering societies which support the Library. See *Engineering Societies Library, New York, Classed Subject Catalog and Index* (Boston: G K Hall, 1963); and *Supplements*, 1-10, 1964-1973.

WOMEN IN LABOR FORCE see Women Laborers

WOMEN IN LITERATURE

MI —OAKLAND UNIVERSITY, Kresge Library, Rochester, 48063. Suzanne O Frankie, Dean; Elizabeth Titus, Special Collections Librn
Holdings: Vols 1000 Cat
Notes: The Hicks Collection of approx 1000 English-language volumes written by and about women in the 17th, 18th and 19th centuries.

PA —CARLOW COLLEGE, Grace Library, Fifth Ave, Pittsburgh, 15213. Joan M Mitchell, Dir of Library Services
Holdings: Vols (2100) Cat 16mm Films
Budget: ($1000)
Notes: The holdings in Women's Studies are not housed together in a special collection, but are part of the main collection. The particular strengths are in the areas of women in literature and the history and condition of women.

WOMEN IN MANAGEMENT

NY —YWCA NATIONAL BOARD, Library, 726-730 Broadway, New York, 10012. Elizabeth Norris, Librn
Holdings: Vols (3000) Cat Mss
Notes: Women and their contemporary interests.

WOMEN IN MEDICINE

CA —STANFORD UNIVERSITY LIBRARIES, Lane Medical Library, Stanford University, Medical Center, Stanford, 94305. Peter Stangl, Librn
Holdings: Vols 10,000 Mss Pix
Notes: Mss Lane Hospital School of Nursing and Stanford University School of Nursing, experiences of nurses who were captured on Bataan, Phillipine Islands.

LA —TULANE UNIVERSITY, Rudolph Matas Medical Library, 1430 Tulane Ave, New Orleans, 70112. W D Postell Jr, Librn
Holdings: Cat Mss Pix
Notes: Incl the Elizabeth Bass Collection of personalized material on women doctors (3640 vols).

MA —RADCLIFFE COLLEGE, Arthur & Elizabeth Schlesinger Library on the History of Women in America, 3 James St, Cambridge, 02138. Patricia Miller King, Dir; Eva Moseley, Cur of Mss
Notes: Mss collections of or about women physicians, incl Elizabeth (1821-1910) and Emily (1826-1910) Blackwell, founders of New York Infirmary; Martha May Eliot (1891-1978), a pediatrician who was head of the US Children's Bureau and Asst Dir-General of WHO; industrial toxicologist Alice Hamilton (1869-1970); Yale Pediatrician and psychiatrist Edith Banfield Jackson (1895-1977); New York physician Mary (Putnam) Jacobi (1842-1906); and Ida Sophia Scudder (1870-1960), medical missionary in India. Also several collections concerning New England Hospital for Women and Children, and oral history interviews in the Family Planning Oral History Project.

PA —MEDICAL COLLEGE OF PENNSYLVANIA, Florence A Moore Library of Medicine, Archives & Special Collections on Women in Medicine, 3300 Henry Ave, Philadelphia, 19129. Sandra L Chaff, Archivist
Holdings: Vols 700 Cat Mss Pix Slides Phonorecords Audiotapes 16mm Films
Notes: "One of the most comprehensive US collections of historical material on women physicians." Incl personal papers of women physicians; audiotapes and transcripts of interviews conducted by the Oral History Project on Women Physicians; the American Medical Women's Associationhistorical collection; the American Women's Hospitals Service collection; the Kate Campbell Hurd-Mead collection; a file of 10,000 photos relating to women physicians; and 5100 reprints of which 4000 citations appear in *Women in Medicine: A Bibliography of the Literature on Women Physicians*, by Sandra L Chaff et al. (Metuchen, NJ: Scarecrow Press, 1977).

WOMEN IN POETRY see Women in Literature

WOMEN IN POLITICS

MI —NATIONAL HAMILTONIAN PARTY, Library, 3314 Dillon Rd, Flushing, 48433.
Holdings: Vols Cat Mss
Notes: The life and writings of Alexander Hamilton. The National Hamiltonian Library is a part of the offices of the Hamiltonian National Committee, the governing body of the National Hamiltonian Party, a Neo-Federalist political movement. Incl 4835 vols. Also the Kelly Collection, a group of over 10,000 pieces of American political memorabilia covering presidents and presidential hopefuls of major and minor parties as well as special sectons on women, minorities and families in politics.

NY —YWCA NATIONAL BOARD, Library, 726-730 Broadway, New York, 10012. Elizabeth Norris, Librn
Holdings: Vols (3000) Cat Mss
Budget: ($2400)
Notes: Women and their contemporary interests.

TX —NORTH TEXAS STATE UNIVERSITY, Archives, NT Station Box 5188, Denton, 76203. Robert LaForte, University Archivist
Notes: The NTSU Archives houses the patron's copy of oral history interviews that are part of the Oral History Collection, an independent project not part of the Archives. This collection of interviews covers, in part, the following subject areas: World War II Pearl Harbor survivors, World War II prisoners of war, Texas legislators, ex-governors of Texas, Texans employed by the administrations of FDR, Texas businessmen and businesswomen, development of the Coastal Bend area of south Texas, and Mexican-American social action activities. Cataloged. Transcriptions available. See *Oral History Collection*, North Texas State University Bulletin, April 1981.

WOMEN IN PROFESSIONS

AL —BIRMINGHAM PUBLIC LIBRARY, Southern Women's Archives, 2020 Park Place, Birmingham, 35203. Theresa A Ceravolo, Archivist
Holdings: Cat Mss
Notes: Collected records, 1919-1969, of Alabama Federation of Business and Professional Women. By-laws, constitution, convention files, minutes of meetings, and presidents' correspondence files, 1919-1969; lists of new clubs and members, 1923-1969; and the following publications: *Can Happen, The Alabama Businesswoman, B. P. W. Bulletin, The Pepper Pot, The Independent Woman*, and *The National Businesswoman*. Also, collected records, 1974-1980, of Alabama Women's Commission, incl testimony given at public hearings held in Alabama's congressional districts, 1974-1980. The testimonies encompass such topics as pay equity and educational opportunities for women.

CA —STANFORD UNIVERSITY LIBRARIES, Lane Medical Library, Stanford University, Medical Center, Stanford, 94305. Peter Stangl, Librn
Notes: Mss Lane Hospital School of Nursing and Stanford University School of Nursing, experiences of nurses who were captured on Bataan, Phillipine Islands.

DC —BUSINESS & PROFESSIONAL WOMEN'S FOUNDATION, Marguerite Rawalt Resource Center, 2012 Massachusetts Ave NW, Washington, 20036. Cheryl A Sloan, Librn
Holdings: Vols (20,000) Cat Documents MicroformsVF
Budget: ($10,000)
Notes: VF, containing about 13,000 items (studies, periodical articles, newspaper clippings, documents) current. All items are filed by subject and indexed in our card catalog by author, title and subject. 200 tape recordings in Oral History Collection. The Resource Center is currently being automated starting with thesaurus construction, then data base design, and finally the implementaion phase which incl cataloging, abstracting, and indexing each item. Microfilms are mainly of doctoral theses. Our emphasis is on the working woman and encompasses economic issues of concern to women such as education for women, working mothers, sex roles, women executives, counseling for women, and work force entry by mature women. Most of the material is about women in the United States. Collection incl 500 microfilms. Publish a bimonthly selected acquisitions list.

MO —UNIVERSITY OF MISSOURI-SAINT LOUIS, Thomas Jefferson Library, Manuscript and Historical Society Collection, 8001 Natural Bridge Rd, Saint Louis, 63121.
Holdings: Mss
Notes: Margaret Hickey's papers.

†NJ —ADELPHI UNIVERSITY, Library, Garden City, 11530.
Notes: Marie Beynon (Lyons) Ray Collection incl mss, correspondence with prominent psychiatrists and others during the years 1937-1958.

WOMEN IN PUBLISHING

†NY —COLUMBIA UNIVERSITY LIBRARIES, Butler Library, Rare Book and Manuscript Library, 535 W 114 St, New York, 10027.
Notes: Archives of the Women's National Book Association, Inc.

WOMEN IN RELIGION

†PA —TEMPLE UNIVERSITY LIBRARIES, Special Collections Dept, Contemporary Culture Collection, Philadelphia, 19122. Patricia J Case, Cur
Holdings: Uncat
Notes: Extensive collection (2 file drawers) of ephemeral material relating to the position of women in the hierarchy of the established church; newsletters, clippings, programs, articles, press releases, etc.

WOMEN IN RURAL DEVELOPMENT

MA —HARVARD UNIVERSITY, Institute for International Development, Library, Coolidge Hall, 1737 Cambridge St, Cambridge, 02138. Barbara Mitchell, Librn
Holdings: Vols (17,000) Periodicals
Notes: Economic development, rural development, statistical material on selected underdeveloped countries. Incl 75 periodical titles.

ON —UNIVERSITY OF GUELPH, Library, Guelph, N1G 2W1, Can. Margaret Beckman, Chief Librn; Ellen Pearson, Ref Librn
Holdings: Vols 30,000 Cat Audiotapes Videotapes 16mm Films Microforms
Notes: 320 periodical titles. Special cats can be produced for any part of the collection. Additional historical material in archives on early rural movements, such as the women's institutes.
See also entry under Rural Sociology

WOMEN IN SPORTS

OK —SOCIETY FOR THE NORTH AMERICAN CULTURAL SURVEY, Dept of Geography, Oklahoma State University, Stillwater, 74078. John Rooney, Dir; Todd Zdorkowski, Asst
Notes: Producing a cultural survey of North American sports and games. John Rooney has published several books on the geography of sports. SWAC's current project involves mapping the continent-wide distributions and the participation patterns for the major and minor professional, college and high school sports.

PA —PENNSYLVANIA STATE UNIVERSITY, Fred Lewis Pattee Library, University Park, 16802.
Notes: Numerous and large collections on many sports. Also, materials supporting every aspect of the program of the Center for Women and Sport, incl research into kinetics, endocrinology, physiology, psychology, etc.

WOMEN IN THE FEDERAL GOVERNMENT

MA —RADCLIFFE COLLEGE, Arthur & Elizabeth Schlesinger Library on the History of Women in America, 3 James St, Cambridge, 02138. Patricia Miller King, Dir; Eva Moseley, Cur of Mss
Notes: Oral history interviews (tapes and mss) of about 45 women who have held appointive positions in various federal agencies. This is the "Women in the Federal Government Oral History Project" (in progress, 1984).

WOMEN IN THE LABOR FORCE see Women Laborers

WOMEN IN THE MILITARY

TX —NORTH TEXAS STATE UNIVERSITY, Archives, NT Station Box 5188, Denton, 76203. Robert LaForte, University Archivist
Notes: Oral History Collection. Incl interviews with survivors of attack on Pearl Harbor, incl soldiers, sailors, nurses, civilians, family members present during the attack. Cataloged. Transcriptions available.

†VA —GEORGE C MARSHALL RESEARCH FOUNDATION AND LIBRARY, Drawer 920, Lexington, 24450. Royster Lyle Jr, Cur Collections
Holdings: Vols Cat Mss Pix
Notes: Personal papers, scrapbooks,

photographs, mementos of Mary Fry Fritch, Lelia Cocke Bagbey, Martha Rector McGee, Margaret Craighill Wotherspoon, and Rebecca L Brockenbrough. Inventories to mss collections are available.

WOMEN IN TRADE UNIONS see Trade Unions

WOMEN JOURNALISTS

GA —EMORY UNIVERSITY, Robert W Woodruff Library, Special Collections Dept, Atlanta, 30322. Linda M Matthews, Head Special Collections; Virginia J H Cain, Processing Archivist; Richard H F Lindemann, Reference Archivist
Notes: Extensive collections of papers of Henry W Grady, Corra Harris, Joel Chandler Harris, Julian LaRose Harris, Julia Collier Harris, Clark Howell, Ralph E McGilll, Harold H Martin, Mildred Seydell, and Claude Sitton, among others, most associated with the Atlanta *Constitution*. Descriptions and index are availalbe in repository.

OH —RUTHERFORD B HAYES LIBRARY, 1337 Hayes Ave, Fremont, 43420. Watt P Marchman, Dir
Holdings: Mss
Notes: A collection of newspaper clippings, poems and some ms materials written by somen journalists in the latter half of the 19th century, eg, Mary Clemmer Ames, Austine and Fayette Snead, C H Mohun, who wrote as "Raymonde." The Ames papers are listed in Guide to manuscripts at the Ohio Historical Society.

WOMEN LABORERS

DC —HOWARD UNIVERSITY, Moorland-Spingarn Research Center, 500 Howard Place NW, Washington, 20059. Clifford L Muse, Jr, Acting Dir
Holdings: Vols (106,086) Mss Maps Pix Slides Phonorecords Audiotapes 16mm Films Filmstrips Microforms
Budget: ($854,753)
See also entry under Blacks

DC —INTERNATIONAL LABOR ORGANIZATION, International Labor Office, Washington Branch Library, 1750 New York Ave NW, Rm 330, Washington, 20006. Karen J Mark, Librn
Holdings: Vols (13,500) Cat Pix 16mm Films Monographs
Notes: Wide range of titles dealing with worldwide labor and social matters. The library contains ILO publications and documentation only, dating back to 1919. Also, a collection of ILO films and photos. See *Subject Guide to Publications of the ILO, 1919-1964* and *ILO Catalogue of Publcations in Print, 1982* (ILO).

MA —UNIVERSITY OF LOWELL, Library, One University Ave, Lowell, 01854. Martha Mayo, Special Collections Librn
Holdings: Vols 15,000 Cat Pix
Notes: Lowell History Collection contains photographs, lithographs, post cards, stereoviews, and lanternslides pertaining to the history of the area with special focus on the textile industry and the men and women who worked in the mills from New England Yankee farm girls to the Irish, French-Canadian, and Greek immigrants. The Locks and Canals Collection contains photographs taken from 1875-1947 showing the day to day operations of the company.

NY —CENTER FOR LABOR STUDIES, SUNY, Empire State College, Labor College Library, 330 W 42nd St, New York, 10036. Jayne Adler, Librn
Holdings: Vols (3000) Cat Videotapes VF
Budget: ($4000)
Notes: Areas being emphasized in development of the library are: Women and Labor, Occupational Health and Safety, and Trade Union Leadership.

ON —ONTARIO MINISTRY OF LABOUR, Library, 400 University Ave, Toronto, M7A 1T7, Can. Jean Collins-Williams, Librn
Holdings: Vols (80,000) Microforms Films

WOMEN MINISTERS

MN —COLLEGE OF SAINT CATHERINE, Library, 2004 Randolph Ave, Saint Paul,

55105. Sister Elizabeth Delmore, Library Dir
Holdings: Vols 4100 Cat Mss Phonorecords Audiotapes
Budget: $3000
Notes: Special emphasis on the psychological emancipation of woman and a growing emphasis on women in ministry. Vertical file of fugitive materials. Separate classified catalog.

†PA —TEMPLE UNIVERSITY LIBRARIES, Special Collections Dept, Contemporary Culture Collection, Philadelphia, 19122. Patricia J Case, Cur
Holdings: Uncat
Notes: Extensive collection (2 file drawers) of ephemeral material relating to the position of women in the hierarchy of the established church; newsletters, clippings, programs, articles, press releases, etc.

WOMEN PHOTOGRAPHERS

KY —UNIVERSITY OF LOUISVILLE, Ekstrom Library, Photographic Archives, Louisville, 40292. J C Anderson, Cur; David G Horvath, Asst Cur
Holdings: Vols (750,000) Cat Pix Slides
Budget: ($60,000)
Notes: Photographs in three broad areas: works of outstanding photographers; examples of major developments in the art and technology of photography; photographs important as sociological, historical, or behavioral documents. Actors and actresses, Louisville's Macauley Theatre. Standard Oil of New Jersey Collection, 85,000 pictures of oil industry's effect on life in the 20th century (1943-1950, directed by Roy Stryker); Stryker's collection from Farm Security Administration series on rural conditions, 1935-1942; Jones and Laughlin Steel Corp. Picture Library, by Stryker. Stryker manuscripts, 1934-1973. Caufield and Shook commercial photographs, Louisville area, 1920-1949. Jean Thomas "The Traipsin' Woman" photographs of Kentucky mountain folkways. Kate Matthews' (1870-1956) photographs incl prototypes for "Little Colonel" Series. Other collections describedin unpublished brochure. Print duplication service.

WOMEN PHYSICIANS

NY —CORNELL UNIVERSITY LIBRARIES, Collection of Regional History, Dept of Manuscripts and Univ Archives, Ithaca, 14853.
Notes: *Women Physicians of the World* (manuscript copy), 1978; Medical Women's International Association; .5 ft.

PA —MEDICAL COLLEGE OF PENNSYLVANIA, Florence A Moore Library of Medicine, Archives & Special Collections on Women in Medicine, 3300 Henry Ave, Philadelphia, 19129. Sandra L Chaff, Archivist
Holdings: Vols 700 Cat Mss Pix Slides Phonorecords Audiotapes 16mm Films
Notes: "One of the most comprehensive US collections of historical material on women physicians." Incl personal papers of women physicians; audiotapes and transcripts of interviews conducted by the Oral History Project on Women Physicians; the American Medical Women's Association historical collection; the American Women's Hospitals Service collection; the Kate Campbell Hurd-Mead collection; a file of 10,000 photos relating to women physicians; and 5100 reprints of which 4000 citations appear in *Women in Medicine: A Bibliography of the Literature on Women Physicians,* by Sandra L Chaff et al. (Metuchen, NJ: Scarecrow Press, 1977).

WOMEN PLAYWRIGHTS

NY —MOUNT PLEASANT PUBLIC LIBRARY, 350 Bedford Rd, Pleasantville, 10570. Charlotte Miller, Dir
Holdings: Vols 175 Cat
Notes: The John W Frost collection consists almost exclusively of 17th and 18th century British drama. An interesting selection of

WOMEN PLAYWRIGHTS (cont.)

women playwrights: a 2-vol set of works of Aphra Behn (Astrea) (1682), *Plays Never Before Printed* by Margaret Cavendish, Duchess of Newcastle (1668), Mrs Hannah Cowley's *The Belle's Stratagem* (1782), Lady Wallace's *The Ton: or Follies of the Fashion* (1783) and the actress Fanny Kemble's *Star of Seville* printed in New York (1837).

WOMEN POETS

RI —BROWN UNIVERSITY, John Hay Library, Harris Collection, Prospect St, Providence, 02912. Rosemary L Cullen, Cur
Holdings: Vols (200,000) Cat Mss Pix Phonorecords Microforms
Budget: ($15,000)
Notes: The Harris Collection of American Poetry and Plays is principally composed of American and Canadian poetry and plays, 17th century-date. Extensive holdings in songsters, gift books and annuals, hymnals, pageants, broadside verse, carriers' addresses, women poets, juvenile poetry, (incl Mother Goose and *The Night Before Christmas*), sheet music with lyrics, small press publications, fine printing, black poets, "little magazines," Yiddish-American literature. All movements or schools of American poetry are represented. Incl first editions of most American poets and playwrights, notably Whitman, Poe, Wallace Stevens, Eugene O'Neill, Edward Albee, Ezra Pound, T S Eliot, William Carlos Williams, Amy Lowell, Phyllis Wheatley, Robert Frost, Allen Ginsberg, Bliss Carman, and Stephen Foster sheet music. Also incl the Saunders Walt Whitman Collection (1300 vols); the LangdonCollection of Pageants (250 vols); the Asa Cushman Collection of plays in ms and prompt copies; the MacDougall Collection of Psalters and Hymnals; 4000 plays issued by Walter H Baker Co, Boston (1890-1957); the Vaxer Collection of Yiddish Poetry, Plays and Music (1700 vols). Collections incl 200,000 vols, 30,000 broadsides, 55,000 mss, 170,000 pieces of sheet music, 450 phonorecords, and 375 microfilm reels. See *Dictionary Catalog of the Harris Collection of American Poetry and Plays* (Boston: G K Hall, 1972), 13 vols; *Supplement* (1977), 3 vols. See also, *American Poetry, 1609-1900, A Collection on Microfilm, Segment I* (1609-1820); *Segment II* (1821-1850); *Segment III* (1851-1870) (Woodbridge, Conn: Research Publications). Separate catalog.

WOMEN STUDIES see Women's Studies

WOMEN'S ARMY CORPS (WACS)

DC —LIBRARY OF CONGRESS, Manuscript Division, Washington, 20540. John C Broderick, Chief
Notes: Papers of Oveta Culp Hobby, incl correspondence, contracts, memos, programs, play typescripts, notes and photographs; much on the WACS.
†VA —GEORGE C MARSHALL RESEARCH FOUNDATION AND LIBRARY, Drawer 920, Lexington, 24450. Royster Lyle Jr, Cur Collections
Holdings: Vols Cat Mss Pix
Notes: Personal papers, scrapbooks, photographs, mementos of Mary Fry Fritch, Lelia Cocke Bagbey, Martha Rector McGee, Margaret Craighill Wotherspoon, and Rebecca L Brockenbrough. Inventories to mss collections are available.

WOMEN'S ASSOCIATIONS AND CLUBS

AZ —NORTHERN ARIZONA UNIVERSITY, Special Collection Library, CU Box 6022, Flagstaff, 86011. Peter M Whiteley, Coordr/Archivist; William Mullane, Librn
Notes: Arizona Federation of Women's Clubs Collection; directories, yearbooks, programs, scrapbooks, 1903-1965 (scattered years). Incl files on the Flagstaff Women's Club and the Northern District Clubs of Arizona.
IL —CHICAGO HISTORICAL SOCIETY, Library, Clark St at North Ave, Chicago, 60614. Archie Motley, Manuscript Librn
Notes: Women's organizations collections incl these papers: Chicago Women's Club; Chicago Women's Liberation Union; Hyde Park Travel Club, Chicago; Illinois Home Economics Association; National Council of Jewish Women-Chicago Section; National Woman Suffrage Association, 1880 Chicago national convention; City Club of Chicago (civic improvement organization).
TX —TEXAS WOMAN'S UNIVERSITY, Bralley Memorial Library, Box 23715, TWU Sta, Denton, 76204. Metta Nicewarner, Spec Collections Libn
Holdings: Uncat Mss Pix
Notes: TWU is the official repository of AAUW archives for the state of Texas. Includes correspondenc, legal documents, yearbooks, financial documents, minutes and reports. Also have the Women's Shakespeare Club of Denton Collection (1899-), and the Ariel Club Collection (1891-), which includes correspondence, yearbooks, minutes, treasurer's reports and membership listings.

WOMEN'S EQUITY ACTION LEAGUE

MA —RADCLIFFE COLLEGE, Arthur & Elizabeth Schlesinger Library on the History of Women in America, 3 James St, Cambridge, 02138. Patricia Miller King, Dir; Eva Moseley, Cur of Mss
Holdings: Vols (23,000) Cat Mss Pix Microforms
Budget: ($300,000)
Notes: Ms collection incl Blackwell family, Beecher-Stowe family, Betty Friedan, Charlotte Perkins Gilman, Emma Goldman, Dr Alice Hamilton and the Hamilton family, the National Abortion Rights Action League, the National Organization for Women, Leonora O'Reilly, and the Women's Equity Action League.

WOMEN'S FICTION see Fiction, Women's

WOMEN'S INTERNATIONAL LEAGUE FOR PEACE AND FREEDOM

CO —UNIVERSITY OF COLORADO, Libraries, Western Historical Collections, Boulder, 80309.
Holdings: Cat Mss
Notes: The Women's International League for Peace and Freedom Papers consist mostly of correspondence and reports between its Geneva headquarters and its national affiliates in Europe and the Americas. While the letters in this collection come from many countries, most are written in English. The WILPF, an activist women's group founded in 1915 by America's Jane Addams and European leaders, is concerned with modifying public policy and attitudes toward war and other conditions which are detrimental to human welfare. 115 boxes. A printed guide is available.
MN —MINNESOTA HISTORICAL SOCIETY LIBRARY, 690 Cedar St, Saint Paul, 55101. Patricia C Harpole, Chief of Reference Library; Bonnie G Wilson, Head of Special Libraries
Notes: The Oral History Collection. Activities of such groups as the Women's International League for Peace and Freedom, labor organizations, and the Izaak Walton League are discussed in interviews.
PA —SWARTHMORE COLLEGE, Peace Collection, Swarthmore, 19081. Jean R Soderlund, Cur of Peace Collection
Holdings: Vols (10,000) Cat Mss Pix Microforms
Notes: International arbitration has been one of the central subject emphases of the Peace Collection since its inception in 1930. A large proportion of the total book collection deals with international arbitration. In addition, major records and document collections in this area incl those of the Women's Peace Party (1915-1919), and its successor, the Women's International League for Peace and Freedom (1919-); the Lake Mohonk (New York) Arbitration Conferences (1895-1917); the American Peace Society and its branches (1828-1947); the World Peace Foundation (1911-); the Post War World Council (1942-1967); also, books and other materials on the Hague Peace Conferences of 1899 and 1907, and other peace congresses and conventions. The Peace Collection has been described in Downs 972, 978, 4633, and in Downs 1950-1961 Supplement 507 and 916. Fordescriptions of major document groups, see the *Guide to the Swarthmore College Peace Collection,* 2nd ed (1981).
See also entry under Pacifism - History.

WOMEN'S LIBERATION MOVEMENT

CA —GRADUATE THEOLOGICAL UNION LIBRARY, New Religious Movements Research Collection, Public Services and Special Collections Dept, 2400 Ridge Road, Berkeley, 94709. Diane Choquette, Dept Head
Holdings: Vols (3000) Mss Pix
Notes: Begun in 1977, the collection focuses on religious movements new to America since 1960, and unorthodox religious movements resurgent since 1960. American forms of Hinduism, Buddhism, Sikhism, and Sufism are included along with occultism, Neo-Paganism, esoteric and alternative forms of Christianity, feminist spirituality, and human potential movements having a spiritual aspect. Legal issues, such as deprogramming, and the question of church/state relations are an important part of the collection. The Library is a depository for publications of the Unification Church in America, the Church of Scientology, and the International Society for Krishna Consciousness (America). The responses of mainstream religions and concerned citizens groups are also included. Besides 3000 monographs, the library has 400 periodical titles, 200 posters from the San FranciscoBay Area, 1965-77, 300 research papers, and 31 linear feet of ephemera.
CA —UNIVERSITY OF CALIFORNIA, DAVIS, Shields Library, Dept of Special Collections, Davis, 95616. Donald Kunitz, Head; C Danial Elliott, Asst Head
Notes: Overview of American political movements from the 1890s to the present: socialism, communism, labor, to ecology and women's liberation.
CA —LOS ANGELES PUBLIC LIBRARY, Social Sciences Dept, 630 W Fifth St, Los Angeles, 90071. Marilyn C Wherley, Principal Librn
Holdings: Vols 250 Cat
Budget: ($150,000)
Notes: Clippings, pamphlets, periodicals, government publications, bibliographies on the current Women's Movement, incl sexual freedom. Popular and scholarly works on history and significance of this and suffrage movements. No separate catalog.
CA —SOUTHERN CALIFORNIA LIBRARY FOR SOCIAL STUDIES & RESEARCH, 6120 S Vermont Ave, Los Angeles, 90044. Sarah Cooper, Dir
Holdings: Vols (15,000) Mss Maps Pix Slides Phonorecords Audiotapes 16mm Films
Budget: ($30,000)
Notes: Marxist, non-Marxist and anti-Marxist approaches to social change. Other important functions of the library: to make available source materials to those engaged in the Marxist vs no-Marxist dialog; to aid historians, economists, sociologists, writers, students and labor organizations researching the history of grassroots social movements; and to preserve primary and secondary sources on labor, minorities, women and radicalism. Collection incl 50 mss, 75 maps, 500 pictures, 1000 slides, 100 phonorecords, 2000 audiotapes, 50 16mm films and 150, 000 newspaper clippings.
CT —UNIVERSITY OF CONNECTICUT, Library, Storrs, 06268. Ellen Embardo, Cur Special Collections
Holdings: Cat
Notes: Alternative Press Collection.

WOMEN'S LIBERATION MOVEMENT (cont.)

Primarily periodicals and newspapers from the 1960s to today of an alternative or underground nature. Books and pamphlets are incl, representing both the left and the right-wing viewpoints. A catalog is available. Also have archives of the First Casualty Press, which was deeply involved with Vietnam veterans' experiences in Vietnam.

DC —HOWARD UNIVERSITY, Moorland-Spingarn Research Center, 500 Howard Place NW, Washington, 20059. Clifford L Muse, Jr, Acting Dir
Holdings: Vols (106,086) Mss Maps Pix Slides Phonorecords Audiotapes 16mm Films Filmstrips Microforms
Budget: ($854,753)
See also entry under Blacks

IL —NORTHWESTERN UNIVERSITY, Library, Special Collections Dept, 1937 Sheridan Rd, Evanston, 60201. R Russell Maylone, Cur
Holdings: Vols 500 Cat
Notes: Books, newsletters, newspapers, pamphlets, posters, ephemera written and distributed by women active in the Women's Liberation Movement from the early 1960s to the present. Countries currently represented are the US, Canada, Great Britain, Australia, Sweden, Denmark, Germany, France, Italy, and the Netherlands. Emphasis is on current literature, but some historical material is incl. Literature: *Women's Collection Newsletter*, Sarah Sherman, ed. (Evanston, 1974). Incl 2500 periodicals, 2700 folders ephemeral materials.

IL —LAKE FOREST COLLEGE, Donnelley Library, Lake Forest, 60045. Arthur H Miller Jr, College Librn
Holdings: Vols (500) Cat
Notes: Developed in the mid 1970s, the collection reflects current women's issues, along with relevant historical and scholarly treatments. Includes ephemera (pamphlets and periodicals). Kathi Amato, compiler, *Womenstudy: A series of Research Guides* (1980) is based on 170 titles from the collection.

MA —RADCLIFFE COLLEGE, Arthur & Elizabeth Schlesinger Library on the History of Women in America, 3 James St, Cambridge, 02138. Patricia Miller King, Dir; Eva Moseley, Cur of Mss
Holdings: Vols (15,000) Cat Mss Pix Phonorecords Audiotapes Videotapes
Notes: Papers of Betty (Goldstein) Friedan (1921-), Wilma Scott Heide, and other leaders; records of the National Abortion Rights Action League, National Organization for Women, Women's Equity League, 9 to 5: Organization for Women Office Workers, and other organizations; letters from readers to *Ms Magazine*. All partly restricted.

MA —NEW ENGLAND QUAKER RESEARCH LIBRARY, PO Box 655, North Amherst, 01059. Francis W Holmes, Librn
Holdings: Vols (6000) Cat Mss Pix Slides Phonorecords Audiotapes Microforms
Budget: ($300)
Notes: No photocopying on premises. Subject emphases: Quakers and Quaker concerns; Pacifism; Racism; Feminism; Religion; Bible; Poverty.

MI —UNIVERSITY OF MICHIGAN, Dept of Rare Books & Special Collections, Ann Arbor, 48109. Edward C Weber, Head, Labadie Collection
Holdings: Vols (40,000) Cat Phonorecords Audiotapes

MI —MICHIGAN STATE UNIVERSITY, Libraries, Special Collections Div, East Lansing, 48824. Jannette Fiore, Librn
Holdings: Vols (10,500) Cat Mss
Notes: Published and unpublished material generated by (1) American left and right, 1900, (2) the New Left, 1969-1970, and (3) current left, right, and alternate life-style groups. (Supported by appropriate secondary material in the Research Library). Also have in microform radical pamphlet literature

from the Tamiment Library (New York University), the Right Wing Collection of the University of Iowa, et al.

PA —TEMPLE UNIVERSITY LIBRARIES, Special Collections Dept, Contemporary Culture Collection, Philadelphia, 19122. Patricia J Case, Cur
Notes: The Contemporary Culture Collection. See full entry under US-Social Life and Customs.

PA —CARLOW COLLEGE, Grace Library, Fifth Ave, Pittsburgh, 15213. Joan M Mitchell, Dir of Library Services
Holdings: Vols (2100) Cat 16mm Films
Budget: ($1000)
Notes: The holdings in Women's Studies are not housed together in a special collection, but are part of the main collection. The particular strengths are in the areas of women in literature and the history and condition of women.

WI —ALVERNO COLLEGE, Research Center on Women, 3401 S 39 St, Milwaukee, 53215. Lola Stuller, Coordr
Holdings: Vols 2400 Cat Mss Pix Slides Phonorecords Audiotapes Videotapes Filmstrips
Budget: $2350
Notes: The Research Center on Women is both a research and resource center. In addition to the library materials listed above, there are approximately 200 periodicals and newsletters and a vertical file of clippings from three metropolitan newspapers, pamphlets, conference proceedings, unpublished papers, etc. Use of the Center and resources is available to anyone who comes in and reference service is available at all times. Response is given to telephone and written requests for information.

†ON —METROPOLITAN TORONTO LIBRARY, Social Sciences Dept, 789 Yonge St, Toronto, M4W 2G8, Can. Abdus Salam, Head
Holdings: Vols Cat Maps Phonorecords Audiotapes 16mm Films Microforms
Notes: This collection, contemporary and historical in scope, includes material on the social and legal status of women, particularly rights, education, and health care. Also included are biographies and directories. Special emphasis is the feminist movement in Canada.

ON —WOMEN'S MOVEMENT ARCHIVES, PO Box 928, Station Q, Toronto, M5W 1G2, Can.
Holdings: Vols (250) Pix

WOMEN'S NATIONAL BOOK ASSOCIATION, INC.

†NY —COLUMBIA UNIVERSITY LIBRARIES, Butler Library, Rare Book and Manuscript Library, 535 W 114 St, New York, 10027.
Notes: Archives of the Women's National Book Association, Inc.

WOMEN'S NEWSPAPERS see Newspapers, Women'S

WOMEN'S ORGANIZATIONS, NORTH CAROLINA COUNCIL OF see North Carolina Council of Women'S Organizations

WOMEN'S PERIODICALS see Periodicals, Women'S

WOMEN'S STUDIES

PA —BRYN MAWR COLLEGE, Canaday Library, Bryn Mawr, 19010. James Tanis, Dir
Notes: College Archives, incl M Carey Thomas papers; Research Publications' microfilm collection on women's history.

PA —CARLOW COLLEGE, Grace Library, Fifth Ave, Pittsburgh, 15213. Joan M Mitchell, Dir of Library Services
Holdings: Vols (2100) Cat 16mm Films
Budget: ($1000)
Notes: The holdings in Women's Studies are not housed together in a special collection,

but are part of the main collection. The particular strengths are in the areas of women in literature and the history and condition of women.

ON —ONTARIO MINISTRY OF COMMUNITY & SOCIAL SERVICES, Library, 880 Bay St, Rm 663, Toronto, M7A 1E9, Can. Sandra Walsh, Chief Librn
Holdings: Vols (30,000) Cat Slides Videotapes 16mm Films Microforms

WOMEN'S SUFFRAGE see Women—Suffrage

WOMEN'S TRADE UNION LEAGUE

MA —RADCLIFFE COLLEGE, Arthur & Elizabeth Schlesinger Library on the History of Women in America, 3 James St, Cambridge, 02138. Patricia Miller King, Dir; Eva Moseley, Cur of Mss
Notes: Several mss collections incl in *Papers of the Women's Trade Union League and Its Principal Leaders* (New Haven: Research Publications, Inc, 1981); also papers of Mary Elisabeth Dreier (1875-1963) and others active in the League.

WOOD

CA —UNIVERSITY OF CALIFORNIA, RICHMOND, Forest Products Library, 1301 S 46th St, Richmond, 94804. Peter A Evans, Librn
Holdings: Vols (8000) Cat Maps Audiotapes Microforms
Notes: Areas of strength are pulp and paper, physical properties of wood, seasoning, wood preservation, wood extractives chemistry, adhesion and adhesives.

CT —YALE UNIVERSITY, Forestry Library, 205 Prospect St, New Haven, 06511. Joseph A Miller, Librn
Holdings: Vols (115,000) Cat Microforms
Notes: The Forestry Library is a unit of the Yale University Library, housed in and serving primarily the School of Forestry and Environmental Studies. Founded in 1900, it has become one of the largest forestry libraries in the world. Forestry is construed broadly to incl underlying or closely related social, physical, and biological sciences. The literature of North American forestry and forest products is most completely covered, though other countries and foreign languages are well represented. Environmental studies and allied fields of natural resources management have been emphasized during the past 10 years. See *Dictionary Catalog of the Yale Forestry Library*, 12 vols (Boston: G K Hall, 1962).

MA —UNIVERSITY OF MASSACHUSETTS AT AMHERST, Physical Sciences Library, Amherst, 01003. Siegfried Feller, Assoc Dir for Collection Development
Holdings: Cat
Notes: Wood technology.

NC —NORTH CAROLINA STATE UNIVERSITY, Forest Resources Library, 4012 Biltmore Hall, Raleigh, 27650. Pamela E Puryear, Head
Holdings: Vols (9000) Cat Microforms
Notes: Forestry, wood and paper sciences; recreation; remote sensing; FAO and forest service and forest products labs. Publications and audiovisual materials.

WA —TACOMA PUBLIC LIBRARY, 1102 Tacoma Ave S, Tacoma, 98402. Kevin Hegarty, Dir
Holdings: Vols 650 Cat

WI —US FOREST SERVICE, Forest Products Laboratory Library, Box 5130, Madison, 53705. Roger Schurmer, Librn; Dr Regis Miller, Librn; Dr Harold H Burdsall, Jr, Librn
Notes: Collection include 2500 genera and many more species. 45,000 wood specimens in the Madison (MADw) collection; 55,000 specimens in the record (SJRw) collection.

WOOD—ANALYSIS see Wood—Chemistry

WOOD—CHEMISTRY

CA —UNIVERSITY OF CALIFORNIA, RICHMOND, Forest Products Library,

WOOD—CHEMISTRY (cont.)

1301 S 46th St, Richmond, 94804. Peter A Evans, Librn
Holdings: Vols (8000) Cat Maps Audiotapes Microforms
Notes: Areas of strength are pulp and paper, physical properties of wood, seasoning, wood preservation, wood extractives chemistry, adhesion and adhesives.

NY —STATE UNIVERSITY OF NEW YORK, COLLEGE OF ENVIRONMENTAL SCIENCE AND FORESTRY, F Franklin Moon Library, Syracuse, 13210. Donald F Webster, Librn
Holdings: Vols (86,430) Cat
Budget: ($120,000)

WOOD, ALAN, STEEL COMPANY

DE —HAGLEY MUSEUM AND LIBRARY, Eleutherian Mills-Hagley Foundation Inc, PO Box 3630, Greenville, 19807. Richmond D Williams, Dir; Heddy A Richter, Imprints Librn
Notes: Records of the Lukens Steel Co of Coatsville, Pa (1798-1944; 750 cubic feet) incl administrative, accounting, payroll, production and sales records documenting the history of one of America's oldest iron and steel companies. Records of the Phoenix Steel Corporation (1827-1962; 335 cubic feet) incl minute books, financial records, payroll and production records documenting the history of this important Delaware Valley steel producer. Also, Alan Wood Steel Company of Conshohocken, Pa (1728-1937; 250 cubic feet).

WOOD, ART

†VA —UNIVERSITY OF VIRGINIA, Library, Charlottesville, 22901.
Notes: Bernard Meeks original cartoons and drawings collection, 326 items incl some original comic strip art. Fred O Seibel collection of ca 6000 original drawings, and cartoonists' working papers and files. Additional collection of editorial cartoons by Oscar Cesare, Jeff MacNelly, Art Wood, etc. Examples of almost all political and many comic artists working in he mid-20th century.

WOOD, ERIC FISHER

NY —SYRACUSE UNIVERSITY LIBRARIES, Ernest S Bird Library, George Arents Research Library for Special Collections, Syracuse, 13210. Carolyn A Davis, Manuscripts Librn; Amy S Doherty, University Archivist; Mark F Weimer, Rare Book Librn
Notes: The George Arents Research Library for Special Collections at Syracuse University contains the papers of Harley James McKee, Lorimer Rich, Frederick Lear, Max Abramovitz, James I Arnold, Pietro Bulluschi, Claude Bragdon, Marcel Breuer, William Lescaze, Skidmore Owings & Merrill, Ralph Walker, Eric Fisher Wood, Minoru Yamasaki, Joseph Louis Young, and Archimedes Russell.

WOOD, EDITH ELMER

NY —COLUMBIA UNIVERSITY LIBRARIES, Avery Architectural and Fine Arts Library, 201 Avery Hall, New York, 10027. Angela Giral, Librn
Notes: 100 boxes of correspondence, mss, working files.

WOOD, ELLEN PRICE, 1814-1887

CA —UNIVERSITY OF CALIFORNIA, LOS ANGELES, Research Library, Dept of Special Collections, 405 Hilgard Ave, Los Angeles, 90024. Edward Shreeves, Chairman, Bibliographers Group; David S Zeidberg, Head
Holdings: Vols 140 Cat Mss
Notes: 75 first and other editions of the books of Mrs Henry Wood (Ellen Price Wood), 1814-1887; also 15 letters.

CT —YALE UNIVERSITY, Box 1603A, Yale Station, New Haven, 06520.

NJ —PRINCETON UNIVERSITY, Library, Morris L Parrish Collection, Princeton, 08540. Alexander D Wainwright, Cur
Holdings: Vols 11
Notes: The collection contains over 6500 vols, as well as many theatre programs, playbills, photographs, clippings and other miscellanea. Parrish's goal was to assemble in both the English and the American first editions, in the original condition as issued, everything that a given author published. He was also interested in a high standard of condition for his books. Many additions have been acquired since the Parrish collection came to the Library as a bequest in 1944. The collection is an assemblage of author collections, consisting of books by: William Harrison Ainsworth, James Matthew Barrie, William Black, The Brontes, William Wilkie Collins, Dinah Mulock Craik, Marie de la Ramee ("Ouida"), Benjamin Disraeli, Charles Dickens, Charles Dodgson, George du Maurier, George Eliot (ie Mary Ann Evans), Elizabeth Gaskell, Thomas Hardy, Thomas Hughes,Charles Kingsley, Charles Lever, Edward George Earle Bulwer-Lytton, Mary Maxwell, George Meredith, Charles Reade, Walter Scott, Robert Louis Stevenson, William Makepeace Thackeray, Trollope Family, Ellen Wood, and Charlotte Yonge.

WOOD, GEORGE BACON

PA —LIBRARY COMPANY OF PHILADELPHIA, 1314 Locust St, Philadelphia, 19107. Edwin Wolf II, Librn; Kenneth Finkel, Cur of Prints
Holdings: 541 Platinum Prints
Notes: Genre photographs by the 19th-century Germantown photographer, George Bacon Wood. Incl numerous photographs of earlier members of the Wood Family.

WOOD, HARRY OSCAR, 1879-1958

CA —CALIFORNIA INSTITUTE OF TECHNOLOGY, Robert A Millikan Memorial Library, Archives, 1201 E California Blvd, Pasadena, 91125. Judith R Goodstein, Archivist
Notes: 22 boxes. Seismologist. Chiefly correspondence; together with mss of writings, reprints, notes, reports, records of earthquakes and epicenters, and copies of the publication, Volcano Letter (1934-40). Incl large groups of correspondence with Carnegie Institution of Washington (relating to the establishment of a central station for seismological investigation), with Seismological Society of America (relating to mapping earthquake faults in the US, recording earthquakes, and establishing safe building codes), and with US Coast and Geodetic Survey (exchanging seismological data). Incl material relating to the earthquake situation in southern California and correspondence with George Louderback relating to the 1857 earthquake. Other correspondents incl various seismological observatories and manufacturers of instruments and equipment for seismologicallaboratories. Unpublished finding aid in the repository.

WOOD, MRS. HENRY see Wood, Ellen Price, 1814-1887

WOOD, L. HOLLINGWORTH

PA —HAVERFORD COLLEGE, Magill Library, Quaker Collection, Haverford, 19041. Edwin B Bonner, Librn & Cur
Notes: Papers.

WOOD, PEGGY

NY —NEW YORK PUBLIC LIBRARY, Performing Arts Research Center, Billy Rose Theatre Collection, 111 Amsterdam Ave, New York, 10023. Dorothy L Swerdlove, Cur
Holdings: Cat Mss Pix
Notes: Papers, scrapbooks, mss, photographs, memorabilia, etc.

WOOD, ROBERT W.

NY —AMERICAN INSTITUTE OF PHYSICS, Center for the History of Physics, Niels Bohr Library, 335 E 45 St, New York, 10017. John Aubry, Librn
Notes: Papers and records.

WOOD, WILLIAM

BC —UNIVERSITY OF VICTORIA, McPherson Library, Victoria, V8W 3H5, Can.
Notes: Incl diaries and correspondence.

WOOD AS FUEL

NY —CARY ARBORETUM OF THE NEW YORK BOTANICAL GARDEN, Library, Box AB, Millbrook, 12545. Fred Strum, Librn
Notes: This collection of alternative energy sources consists of publications concerned with solar energy, wind power, biofuel, methanol, small hydroelectric projects, and wood power.

WOOD CARVING

OH —CLEVELAND PUBLIC LIBRARY, Fine Arts and Special Collections Department, 325 Superior Ave, Cleveland, 44114. Alice N Loranth, Head
Holdings: Vols (16,000) Cat
Notes: Part of the Handicrafts Collection, which incl many ethnic groups in Cleveland.

WI —UNIVERSITY OF WISCONSIN-STOUT, Library Learning Center, Menomonie, 54751. Philip Sawin Jr, Coll Develop Librn
Notes: This collection is a major one, including the Verne C Fryklund Papers. The program was begun in 1883 as an original purpose of the University. The collection contains original editions on sloyd, a 19th century Swedish system of manual training based on wood carving and carpentry.

WOOD ENGRAVINGS

CA —UNIVERSITY OF CALIFORNIA, LOS ANGELES, Research Library, Dept of Special Collections, 405 Hilgard Ave, Los Angeles, 90024. Edward Shreeves, Chairman, Bibliographers Group; David S Zeidberg, Head
Holdings: Vols 125 Cat
Notes: 125 books by and illustrated by Bewick; 16 original woodblocks.

DC —GEORGETOWN UNIVERSITY, Library, Special Collections Div, 37 & O Sts NW, Washington, 20057. George M Barringer, Special Collections Librn; Nicholas B Sheetz, Mss Librn
Notes: The papers, files, art work, etc of Lynd Ward and his wife, May McNeer.

MA —AMERICAN ANTIQUARIAN SOCIETY LIBRARY, 185 Salisbury St, Worcester, 01609. Marcus A McCorison, Dir & Librn
Holdings: Cat Maps Pix
Notes: Over 6000 American prints, arranged by lithographer. Incl political caricatures and cartoons, maps, sheet music. Also advertising cards, Valentines, etc.

MO —SAINT LOUIS PUBLIC LIBRARY, Gardner Rare Book Room, 1301 Olive St, Saint Louis, 63103. Julanne M Good, Supervisor; Martha Riley, Rare Books Librn
Holdings: Vols 50 Cat Mss
Budget: ($5573)
Notes: Collection of books on wood engraving and book illustration in that medium, including some notable books illustrated by Thomas Bewick, the famous nineteenth century wood engraver. Largely the gift of Leonard Blake, a private collector, although an occasional purchase is made. Noncirculating.

VA —UNIVERSITY OF VIRGINIA, Alderman Library, Rare Book Dept, Charlottesville, 22901. Julius P Barclay, Cur
Holdings: Vols (6500) // Mss
Notes: The Oscar Ogg Collection of Book Arts covers calligraphy, letterforms,

WOOD ENGRAVINGS (cont.)

typography, printing, and graphic arts. Contains early writing books and printed works, as well as modern manuals and other works on printing, publishing, and promotion through graphic arts. The Dept also has the Edward L Stone Collection of Printing Specimens, 3000 items. Contains materials tracing the history of printing, inks, binding styles and materials, types. Also the Tompkins Collection (2000 vols), and the Stevens Watts collection (900 vols).

PQ —MCGILL UNIVERSITY, McLennan Library, Rare Books and Special Collections Dept, 3459 McTavish St, Montreal, H3A 1Y1, Can.
Notes: 12,680 original prints and posters dating from the 16th century to the present. Prints representing many graphic techniques; special subject areas such as: early railways, Japanese woodblocks, Napoleon, early Canadian portraits.

WOOD ENGRAVINGS, COLOR see Color Prints

WOOD POWER see Wood As Fuel

WOOD PRODUCTS

CA —FOREST HISTORY SOCIETY INC, Library, 109 Coral St, Santa Cruz, 95060. Mary E Johnson, Librn
Holdings: Vols (4000) Cat Mss Maps Pix Slides Audiotapes Microforms Serials Films VF
Budget: ($2000)
Notes: Incl archives of the Society of American Foresters, the American Forestry Association, the National Lumber Manufacturers Association, and the American Forest Institute.
DC —NATIONAL FOREST PRODUCTS ASSOCIATION, Bemis Information Center, 1619 Massachusetts Ave NW, Washington, 20036. Barbara A Beall, Mgr
Holdings: Vols (5000) Cat Maps Pix
Notes: Plus 25,000 pamphlets.
NY —STATE UNIVERSITY OF NEW YORK, COLLEGE OF ENVIRONMENTAL SCIENCE AND FORESTRY, F Franklin Moon Library, Syracuse, 13210. Donald F Webster, Librn
Holdings: Vols (86,430) Cat
Budget: ($120,000)
NC —NORTH CAROLINA STATE UNIVERSITY, Forest Resources Library, 4012 Biltmore Hall, Raleigh, 27650. Pamela E Puryear, Head
WA —TACOMA PUBLIC LIBRARY, 1102 Tacoma Ave S, Tacoma, 98402. Kevin Hegarty, Dir

WOOD SECTIONS

ON —LAURENTIAN UNIVERSITY LIBRARY, Ramsey Lake Rd, Sudbury, P3E 2C6, Can. Suzanne Brunette, Special Collection Librn; Sue Vongpeisal, Head Librn
Notes: Materials on northern Canada, incl 2200 books and pamphlets, 60,000 press clippings on northern topics 75 series of periodicals and over 1500 maps, plus photographs and thousands of samples of arctic and subarctic plants incl mosses, lichens, algae and wood sections. Much of the material is in French.

WOOD TECHNOLOGY see Wood Products

WOOD-USING INDUSTRIES

GA —EMORY UNIVERSITY, Robert W Woodruff Library, Special Collections Dept, Atlanta, 30322. Linda M Matthews, Head Special Collections; Virginia J H Cain, Processing Archivist; Richard H F Lindemann, Reference Archivist
Notes: Correspondence and other materials of Charles Holmes Herty (1867-1937), who was known for his work in applying chemistry to the improvement of industry and who served as president of the American Chemical Association; items reflect Herty's naval stores and other forestry products. 300,000 items.
WI —US FOREST SERVICE, Forest Products Laboratory Library, Box 5130, Madison, 53705. Roger Schurmer, Librn; Dr Regis Miller, Librn; Dr Harold H Burdsall, Jr, Librn
Holdings: Vols (136,240) Cat Microforms //
Budget: ($122,083)
Notes: Forest products utilization research. KWIC index of FPL reports; centralized title service from Forestry Bureau, Oxford, England (card and microfilm).

WOODBLOCK PRINTS

ON —METROPOLITAN TORONTO LIBRARY, Theatre Dept, 789 Yonge St, Toronto, M4W 2G8, Can. Heather McCallum, Head
Notes: A representative collection of 19th century Japanese woodblock prints depicts theatres, scenes and actors from the Kabuki and Noh theatres in Edo and Osaka.
See also entry under Theatre - Canada.

WOODBURY, AUGUSTUS, 1825-1895

RI —BROWN UNIVERSITY, John Hay Library, 20 Prospect St, Providence, 02912. Mark N Brown, Cur Mss
Holdings: Mss
Notes: Materials relative to the history of the US Army.

WOODBURY, LEVI, HON., 1789-1851

NH —PORTSMOUTH ATHENAEUM, 9 Market Sq, Box 848, Portsmouth, 03801. Joseph P Copley, Cur
Holdings: Uncat Mss

WOODCRAFT LEAGUE OF AMERICA

NY —AMERICAN MUSEUM OF NATURAL HISTORY, Library Services Dept, Central Park W & 79th St, New York, 10024. Nina J Root, Chairwoman; Mary Genett, Asst Librn for Reference Services
Holdings: Cat Mss Pix Microforms
Notes: The Ernest Thompson Seton diaries. Thousands of pages of an unpublished 67-year diary record of one of the world's most famous naturalists, the gift of Joseph F Cullman III, a Trustee of the Museum. Preserved in 35 protective cases, the gift incl unpublished diaries, notebooks, and some other writings. The diary begins 12 June 1879; the last entries were written in hospital, just a month before Seton's death in 1946. Literally hundreds of examples of flora and fauna are pictured in the diaries in original pencil, pen-and-ink, and watercolor sketches, on nearly every page. Research will reveal information on the Indian sign language, the Boy Scouts of America, the Woodcraft League of America, and the wilderness of Canada, Florida, Texas, the West and Southwest, etc.

WOODCUTS see Wood Engravings

WOODFIELD, WILLIAM READ

CA —UNIVERSITY OF CALIFORNIA, LOS ANGELES, Research Library, Dept of Special Collections, 405 Hilgard Ave, Los Angeles, 90024. Edward Shreeves, Chairman, Bibliographers Group; David S Zeidberg, Head
Notes: 2 linear feet of television scripts, production material, and photographs.

WOODHOUSE, MARTIN

MA —BOSTON UNIVERSITY, Mugar Memorial Library, Special Collections Dept, 771 Commonwealth Ave, Boston, 02215. Howard B Gotlieb, Dir
Holdings: Cat Mss
Notes: Incl publications by.

WOODPULP AND WOODPULP INDUSTRY

CA —UNIVERSITY OF CALIFORNIA, RICHMOND, Forest Products Library, 1301 S 46th St, Richmond, 94804. Peter A Evans, Librn
Holdings: Vols (8000) Cat Maps Audiotapes Microforms
Notes: Areas of strength are pulp and paper, physical properties of wood, seasoning, wood preservation, wood extractives chemistry, adhesion and adhesives.
GA —TECHNICAL ASSOCIATION OF THE PULP & PAPER INDUSTRY, James d'A Clark Library, PO Box 105113, Atlanta, 30348. Elizabeth A Bibby, Information Services Adminr
Holdings: Vols 2500 Cat Audiotapes Slides Microforms
Budget: $3500
Notes: Collection open to public, call for times/hours. FEC-Based reference service available.
NC —NORTH CAROLINA STATE UNIVERSITY, Forest Resources Library, 4012 Biltmore Hall, Raleigh, 27650. Pamela E Puryear, Head
Holdings: Vols (9000) Cat Microforms
Notes: Forestry, wood and paper sciences; recreation; remote sensing; FAO and forest service and forest products labs. Publications and audiovisual materials.
PA —CARNEGIE LIBRARY OF PITTSBURGH, Science & Technology Dept, 4400 Forbes Ave, Pittsburgh, 15213. Catherine M Brosky, Dept Head
Notes: General information acquired in various subject areas especially those relating to iron and steel and other metals, rubber, leather, pulp and paper, textiles, glass, petroleum and coal tar by-products, lumber, plastics, etc. Manufacturers directories, including old editions, standards and specifications, trade catalogs, basic periodicals, indexes, and bibliographies.
See also entry under Science.
PA —P H GLATFELTER CO, Research Library, Dept of Research, Spring Grove, 17362. Jean M Bailey, Librn
Holdings: Vols (2000) Cat Microfilms
Notes: Pulp and paper technology.
SC —SONOCO PRODUCTS CO, Research Laboratory, Technical Information Center, One N Second St, Hartsville, 29550. Ken Chavis, Dir
Holdings: Vols (4000) Cat Mss Slides Microforms
Notes: Restricted to Sonoco employees. No photocopying.
WA —UNIVERSITY OF WASHINGTON LIBRARIES, Forest Resources Library, AQ-15, Seattle, 98195. Barbara B Gordon, Head
Holdings: Vols (43,248) Cat Microforms
Budget: ($41,103)
Notes: Modern imprints only. Mostly in English. Emphasis is on Pacific Northwest.
WI —US FOREST SERVICE, Forest Products Laboratory Library, Box 5130, Madison, 53705. Roger Schurmer, Librn; Dr Regis Miller, Librn; Dr Harold H Burdsall, Jr, Librn
Holdings: Vols (136,240) Cat Microforms //
Budget: ($122,083)
Notes: Forest products utilization research. KWIC index of FPL reports; centralized title service from Forestry Bureau, Oxford, England (card and microfilm).
ON —CIP RESEARCH, Library, 179 Main St W, Hawkesbury, K6A 2H4, Can. Margaret Higginson, Librn
Holdings: Vols (12,000) Cat
Budget: ($40,000)
Notes: Pulp and paper technology.
PQ —PULP AND PAPER RESEARCH INSTITUTE OF CANADA, Library, Saint John's Rd, Pointe-Claire, H9R 3J9, Can. Alison Finnemore, Librn
Holdings: Vols (14,000) Cat Microforms
Budget: ($16,000)
Notes: Book catalog.
PQ —TROIS-RIVIERES COLLEGE LIBRARY, CEGEP de Trois-Rivieres-Bibliotheque, 3500 de Courval, Trois-Rivieres, G9A 5E6, Can. Denis Simard, Librn
Holdings: Vols 4000
Budget: ($80,000)
Notes: 4000 volumes to support the curriculum.

WOODRESS, JAMES LESLIE, 1916-

NC —DUKE UNIVERSITY, William R Perkins Library, Jay B Hubbell Center for

WOODRESS, JAMES LESLIE, 1916- (cont.)

American Literary Historiography, Durham, 27706. Erma Whittington, Librn
Notes: 77,312 items, including manuscripts, pictures, clippings, and correspondence. "The objective of the Center is to gather the papers and materials of significant scholars and critics in American literary history." The Center is a part of the Perkins Library Manuscripts Department.

WOODRUFF, DOUGLAS

DC —GEORGETOWN UNIVERSITY, Library, Special Collections Div, 37 & O Sts NW, Washington, 20057. George M Barringer, Special Collections Librn; Nicholas B Sheetz, Mss Librn
Holdings: Cat Mss
Notes: The papers of the English author, journalist, and historian Douglas Woodruff (1897-1978), containing correspondence, mss, and photographs. Incl is considerable material concerning his years at Oxford University; his editorship for many years of The "Tablet"; English Catholic society in general and English Catholic literature in particular. Also present are research files on the Tichborne Claimant, one of the most famous cases of impersonation in English legal history. There is extensive correspondence from such figures as: Hilaire Belloc; Tom Burns; Rev Martin D'Arcy, SJ; Christopher Dawson; Sir Roy Harrod; Christopher Hollis; Msgr Ronald Knox; Sir Shane Leslie; Sir Arnold Lunn; Rebecca West; and Evelyn Waugh.

WOODS, HARRIETT

MO —UNIVERSITY OF MISSOURI-SAINT LOUIS, Thomas Jefferson Library, Manuscript and Historical Society Collection, 8001 Natural Bridge Rd, Saint Louis, 63121.

WOODS, VENA

CA —UNIVERSITY OF THE PACIFIC, Library, Stockton, 95211. Hiram L Davis, Dir of Libraries
Holdings: // Uncat Mss Pix
Notes: Papers of Vena Woods, 1880-1925, dramatic actress and author. Incl drafts of novels and plays, notes and photos relating to the California theatre. Twelve document boxes.

WOODSTOCK COLLEGE ARCHIVES

DC —GEORGETOWN UNIVERSITY, Library, Special Collections Div, 37 & O Sts NW, Washington, 20057. George M Barringer, Special Collections Librn; Nicholas B Sheetz, Mss Librn
Holdings: Vols (500) Cat Mss Maps Pix Slides
Notes: Includes the archives of Woodstock College (1866-); seminary of the Maryland Province, on deposit; the archives (1640-) of the Maryland Province of the Society of Jesus, on deposit; personal papers of Revs John LaFarge, SJ, Wilfrid Parsons, SJ, Edmund A Walsh, SJ, and Gustave Weigel, SJ. Also present are editorial files (1900-1920, incomplete later) of America magazine.

WOODWARD, GEORGE

RI —BROWN UNIVERSITY, John Hay Library, 20 Prospect St, Providence, 02912. Mark N Brown, Cur Mss
Holdings: Vols Uncat Mss Pix
Notes: Paul Revere Bullard Collection of 185 19th century caricatures by English, French, German, Russian, and Spanish cartoonists who lampooned Napoleon throughout his career plus 220 similar caricatures from other sources. The major English artists represented are: James Gillray, George and Isaac Cruikshank, Thomas Rowlandson, and George

Woodward. Some items also part of the Anne S. K. Brown Military Collection at Brown Univ.

WOODWARD, SIDNEY C.

IN —INDIANA UNIVERSITY, Lilly Library, Seventh St, Bloomington, 47405. William R Cagle, Librn
Holdings: // Mss Pix
Notes: Photographs, etc, of actors and actresses are located in 3 ms collections: (1) Johnson, William Spencer, 1813-1897, printer. Correspondence and photographs from actors and actresses, 1846-1894. 129 items; (2) Stock, Keith Lievesley, 1911- , professor. Autographs, etc of people associated with 19th-early 20th century theatre in England. 279 items; and (3) Woodward, Sidney C, journalist. Correspondence, autographs, and pictures, 1769-1961, of actors and actresses, and other theatre people, mostly American and British. 1235 items. Also, in Printed Books Division: small pictures (largely engravings excerpted from books) of Shakespearean actors and actresses, 18th into 20th century.

WOODWORK

MA —OLD STURBRIDGE VILLAGE, Research Library, Sturbridge, 01566. Theresa Rini Percy, Librn
Holdings: Cat Mss Pix Slides
Notes: New England, 1790-1850.
PA —CARNEGIE LIBRARY OF PITTSBURGH, Science & Technology Dept, 4400 Forbes Ave, Pittsburgh, 15213. Catherine M Brosky, Dept Head
Notes: Incl much of the material in Index to Handicrafts. Books for the home owner, repairman and craftsman and the general builder and mechanics are emphasized. Information of the use of tools and materials especially for woodworking and metal crafts; alsl optical instruments, clocks, guns, and other mechanic trades.
See also entry under Science.
WI —MADISON AREA TECHNICAL COLLEGE, Technical Center Library, 2125 Commercial Ave, Madison, 53704. J B Jeffcott, Librn
Holdings: Vols 500 Cat Slides Microforms
Notes: Wood technics.

WOODWORKING MACHINERY

WI —MADISON AREA TECHNICAL COLLEGE, Technical Center Library, 2125 Commercial Ave, Madison, 53704. J B Jeffcott, Librn
Holdings: Vols 300 Cat Slides Microforms
Notes: Wood technics.

WOODY PLANTS

CA —LOS ANGELES STATE & COUNTY ARBORETUM, Plant Science Library, 301 N Baldwin Ave, Arcadia, 91006. Joan DeFato, Librn
Holdings: Vols (24,000) Cat 16mm Films
Budget: ($6000)
Notes: Emphasis on woody plants, particularly of Australia and South Africa. Botany is weighted toward taxonomy rather than plant physiology.
DC —US NATIONAL ARBORETUM, Library, 3501 New York Ave NE, Washington, 20002. Judi Ho, Librn
Holdings: Vols (6000) Cat Microforms
Notes: Separate catalog. Botany and horticulture, especially of woody plants. Library is a branch of the National Agricultural Library. No photocopying.

WOOL

MA —MERRIMACK VALLEY TEXTILE MUSEUM, Library, 800 Massachusetts Ave, North Andover, 01845. Clare Sheridan, Librn; Laurence Gross, Cur
Holdings: Vols (35,000) Cat Mss Maps Pix Slides
Notes: Checklist of Prints, Drawings and Painting in the Merrimack Valley Textile Museum, Helena E Wright, 1972; Checklist

of Finished Textiles, Katherine R Koob, 1980; New City on the Merrimack: Prints of Lawrence 1845-1876, Helena Wright, 1974; Homespun to Factory Made: Woolen Textiles in America 1776-1876 (exhibit catalog) 1978; Textile Technology Prints: A Checklist of Prints, Drawings and Paintings in the Merrimack Valley Textile Museum, Helena E Wright, 1980; All Sorts of Good Sufficient Cloth: Linen-making in New England, 1640-1860, (exhibit catalogue) 1980; The Merrimack Valley Textile Museum: A Guide to the Manuscript Collections Helena E Wright, Garland Press 1983.

WOOLF, DOUGLAS

MO —WASHINGTON UNIVERSITY, Libraries, Special Collections Dept, Campus Box 1061, St Louis, 63130.
Notes: A small but significant collection.

WOOLF, VIRGINIA AND LEONARD

CA —UNIVERSITY OF CALIFORNIA, SAN DIEGO, Central University Library, Mandeville Dept of Special Collections, La Jolla, 92093. Lynda Corey Claassen, Head
Holdings: Vols 40 Cat
CA —UNIVERSITY OF CALIFORNIA, LOS ANGELES, Research Library, Dept of Special Collections, 405 Hilgard Ave, Los Angeles, 90024. Edward Shreeves, Chairman, Bibliographers Group; David S Zeidberg, Head
Holdings: Vols 100 Cat
Notes: 100 books; 6 letters; several mss edited by Virginia Woolf.
DE —UNIVERSITY OF DELAWARE, Hugh M Morris Library, S College Ave, Newark, 19711. T Stuart Dick, Special Collections
Holdings: Cat
Notes: Incl first and variant editions of publications issued by the Hogarth Press, founded by Leonard and Virginia Woolf.
IL —NORTHWESTERN UNIVERSITY, Library, Special Collections Dept, 1937 Sheridan Rd, Evanston, 60201. R Russell Maylone, Cur
Holdings: Vols 230 Cat
IL —ILLINOIS STATE UNIVERSITY, Milner Library, Dept of Special Collections, Normal, 61761. Robert Sokan, Librn
Notes: First editions, limited editions, ephemera, etc.
MA —HARVARD UNIVERSITY LIBRARY, Houghton Library, Cambridge, 02138. Rodney G Dennis, Cur of Manuscripts
Holdings: Cat Mss
NV —UNIVERSITY OF NEVADA, RENO, University Library, Special Collections Dept, Reno, 89557. Robert E Blesse, Head
Holdings: Vols 149 // Cat
Notes: Includes individual works by author in all editions including translations; also prefaces, introductions, published correspondence, appearances in anthologies, periodicals, etc. Bibliographical research collection, part of Modern Authors Collection.
NY —ALFRED UNIVERSITY, Herrick Memorial Library, Alfred, 14802. June E Brown, Head Librn
Notes: The Evelyn Tennyson Openhym Collection of modern British literature and social history.
NY —HOFSTRA UNIVERSITY, Library, 1000 Fulton Ave, Hempstead, 11550. Charles R Andrews, Dean of Library Services
Notes: Strong collection. Incl some mss.
NY —NEW YORK PUBLIC LIBRARY, Berg Collection of English & American Literature, Fifth Ave & 42 St, New York, 10018. Lola L Szladits, Cur
Notes: Largest collection of Woolf mss, etc. Incl her diaries.
OH —OHIO UNIVERSITY, Vernon R Alden Library, Department of Archives and Special Collections, Athens, 45701. Gary A Hunt, Head
Holdings: Vols 100 Cat
Notes: A small collection of the publications of Virginia and Leonard Woolf's Hogarth Press, mostly 1920s and 1930s.

WOOLF, VIRGINIA AND LEONARD (cont.)

PA —BRYN MAWR COLLEGE, Canaday Library, Bryn Mawr, 19010. James Tanis, Dir
Notes: Rare books in the Adelman Collection.

VA —SWEET BRIAR COLLEGE, Library, Sweet Briar, 24595. John Jaffe, Librn
Holdings: Vols 96 Cat
Budget: $500

†WA —WASHINGTON STATE UNIVERSITY, Library, Manuscripts, Archives & Special Collections, Pullman, 99164. John F Guido, Head
Holdings: Vols Mss Pix
Notes: The library of Virginia and Leonard Woolf (from Monk's House and Victoria Sq) forms the nucleus of the collection, which incorporates the library of Sir Leslie Stephen, Virginia's father. Leonard's interests are reflected by works concerning the Labour Party, the Fabian Society, as well as Ceylon. Their interest in printing and publishing works of significance is reflected by the collection of Hogarth Press publications (1917-1941). Incl works by Virginia and Leonard Woolf, the Bloomsbury Group, as well as by other friends--eg, Elizabeth Robins, Victoria Sackville-West, Harold Nicholson, etc. Many of these are unique copies, ie, association and textual interest. Other 20th century English authors incl: the Sitwells, Margaret Sackville, Rose Macaulay, D H Lawrence, John Masefield, Rupert Croft-Cooke, & Charles Williams. Partially cataloged.

ON —VICTORIA UNIVERSITY, Library, 71 Queen's Park Crescent, Toronto, M5S 1K7, Can. Robert C Brandeis, Chief Librn
Holdings: Vols Cat
Notes: A collection of first editions and others of Virginia Woolf and Bloomsbury writers: Clive Bell, Roger Fry, E M Forster, V Sackville-West, K Mansfield, etc. Contains a significant collection of Hogarth Press books, and many of those handprinted by the Woolfs.

WOOLLCOTT, ALEXANDER

MA —BOSTON UNIVERSITY, Mugar Memorial Library, Special Collections Dept, 771 Commonwealth Ave, Boston, 02215. Howard B Gotlieb, Dir
Holdings: Vols Cat Mss
Notes: Correspondence.

WOOLMAN, JOHN, 1720-1772

PA —FRIENDS HISTORICAL LIBRARY OF SWARTHMORE COLLEGE, Swarthmore, 19081. J William Frost, Dir
Holdings: Vols (35,000) Cat Mss Microforms
Notes: Books by and about the Quaker minister, social reformer, and antislavery advocate of Mount Holly, New Jersey. Mss of his Journal, some other writings, and a few of his letters.

WORCESTER, DEAN CONANT

MI —UNIVERSITY OF MICHIGAN, Library, Dept of Rare Books & Special Collections, Ann Arbor, 48109. Robert J Starring, Head
Holdings: Vols 1718 Cat Mss Pix
Notes: The Worcester Philippine Collection contains much of Dean Conant Worcester's official and personal correspondence as a Philippine Commissioner and later as Secretary of the Interior of the Islands. Between three and four thousand mss and printed items on government, history, politics, ethnology and archaeology. 12 photo albums. Covers chiefly the period 1899-1915. Ms collection partially described in *Balita mula Maynila* (1971) by Thomas Powers (Bulletin Special Publication No 1 of the Center for South and Southeast Asia Studies).

WORD-BLINDNESS see Learning Ability

WORDS

BC —VANCOUVER PUBLIC LIBRARY, Language & Literature Div, 750 Burrard St, Vancouver, V6Z 1X5, Can. B Kinnear, Head
Notes: A good general collection of language dictionaries, supplemented by clippings and a word file compiled by the staff. Incl books and pamphlets.

WORDSWORTH, WILLIAM

AZ —UNIVERSITY OF ARIZONA, University Library, Special Collections, Tucson, 85721. Louis A Hieb, Head
Holdings: Vols (7000) Cat Mss Microforms
Budget: ($30,000)
Notes: The major collection of 19th century authors are Byron, Dickens, Scott, Thackeray, Trollope, the Brownings, Stevens, Tennyson, and Wordsworth.

CA —UNIVERSITY OF CALIFORNIA, DAVIS, Shields Library, Dept of Special Collections, Davis, 95616. Donald Kunitz, Head; C Danial Elliott, Asst Head
Holdings: Vols 400 Cat Mss

CT —YALE UNIVERSITY, Box 1603A, Yale Station, New Haven, 06520.
Holdings: Cat Mss

IN —INDIANA UNIVERSITY, Lilly Library, Seventh St, Bloomington, 47405. William R Cagle, Librn
Holdings: Vols 2000 Cat Mss
Notes: First and later editions; works about Wordsworth; books on the Lake Country and on other writers of the Romantic period.

KY —UNIVERSITY OF KENTUCKY, Margaret I King Library, Dept of Special Collections, Lexington, 40506. William Marshall, Head
Holdings: Vols (8000) Cat Mss
Notes: W Hugh Peal Collection of mss and books chiefly relating to British and American literature. Particularly strong in Lamb, Wordsworth, Coleridge and Southey. Incl 4 cubic feet of mss. Incl 16th-20th centuries.

MA —AMHERST COLLEGE, Library, Amherst, 01002. John Lancaster, Special Collections Librn
Holdings: Vols 1256 Cat Mss Slides

MA —HARVARD UNIVERSITY LIBRARY, Houghton Library, Cambridge, 02138. F Thomas Noonan, Cur, Reading Room; Lawrence Dowler, Associate Librn
Holdings: Cat
Notes: See *Harvard Library Notes*, II (1925): pp 33-37.

NY —CORNELL UNIVERSITY LIBRARIES, John M Olin Library, Dept of Rare Books, Ithaca, 14853. Donald D Eddy, Librn
Holdings: Vols 3469 Cat Mss
Notes: Downs 2233; 3571. *The Cornell Wordsworth Collection: A Catalogue of Books and Manuscripts Presented to the University by Victor Emanuel, Cornell, 1919*, comp by George Harris Healey (Ithaca, 1957).

OH —OHIO UNIVERSITY, Vernon R Alden Library, Department of Archives and Special Collections, Athens, 45701. Gary A Hunt, Head
Holdings: Vols (10,191) Uncat Mss
Notes: The Edmund Blunden Collection of Romantic and Modern Literature, being the private library assembled by Blunden during 6 decades of active collecting. The bulk of the collection (6,264 titles) consists of English imprints from the period 1750-1850, concentrating on literature but also incl contemporary works on art, natural history, philosophy and other subjects important for understanding the background of English Romanticism. Among the authors most heavily represented by first and other early editions are: Allington, Barnes, Bloomfield, Byron, Clare, Coleridge, Cowper, Dyer, Edgeworth, Goldsmith, Hazlitt, Hunt, Lamb, Landor, Scott, Thompson and Wordsworth. Books written by Blunden himself, together with his Georgian contemporaries (particularly W H Davies, Walter De la Mare, and Sigfried Sassoon) form a second major area of strength. Many ofthe modern books are inscribed to Blunden, and nearly all the volumes in the collection bear his annotations.

PA —SWARTHMORE COLLEGE, Library, Swarthmore, 19081. Michael J Durkan, Librn
Notes: The Collection fromed by John Edwin Wells. Described in the artible: *"Wordsworth in Philadelphia Area Libraries, 1787-1850,"* by James A Butler, in *The Wordsworth Circle*, vol 4, no 2, Spring 1973.

WI —UNIVERSITY OF WISCONSIN, MADISON, Memorial Library, British & American Language & Literature Collection, 728 State St, Madison, 53706. Yvonne Schofer, Bibliographer
Holdings: Vols 200 // Mss Pix
Notes: Arthur Beatty Collection. Consists of over 1000 volumes, principally in the English poetry of the Romantic period, strong in Coleridge, Tennyson, Swinburne, the prose of De Quincy and the folk poetry and balladry of Great Britain and Europe. Outstanding for its first and other editions of Wordsworth. About 200 titles in the Department of Rare Books and Special Collections; the rest is in stacks.

AB —UNIVERSITY OF ALBERTA, Cameron Library, The Bruce Peel Special Collections Room, Edmonton, T6G 2J8, Can. John Charles, Special Collections Librn
Notes: Photocopies of Dove Cottage papers in Special Collections. Catalog by Dr R Siemens published 1971. Supporting texts and criticism in Special Collections and main stacks.

ON —VICTORIA UNIVERSITY, Library, 71 Queen's Park Crescent, Toronto, M5S 1K7, Can. Robert C Brandeis, Chief Librn
Holdings: Vols 1100 Cat Mss
Notes: A significant collection (second only to the British Museum) of books, mss, notebooks, correspondence, etc of Samuel Taylor Coleridge and his circle and family, including letters and mss of Wordsworth, Lamb and Southey. Catalog of collection by H O Dendurent in *The Wordsworth Circle* (Temple University, Philadelphia, Pa) 5: 4 (Autumn 1974).

WORK

DC —US DEPT OF LABOR, Library, 200 Constitution Ave NW, Washington, 20210. Sabina Jacobson, Dir
Holdings: Vols (550,000) Cat

ON —CANADA DEPT OF LABOUR, Library, Ottawa, K1A 0J2, Can. Monique Marchand, Chief Librn
Holdings: Vols (100,000) Cat Microforms

WORK, THERAPEUTIC EFFECT OF see Occupational Therapy

WORK EXPERIENCE see Vocational Education

WORKERS MUSIC LEAGUE (WML)

DC —LIBRARY OF CONGRESS, Music Division, Washington, 20540.
Notes: Musical aspects of the revolutionary workers' movement represented in the Workers Music League's publications and activities; also, the Composers' Collective, etc.

WORKING CONDITIONS

DC —INTERNATIONAL LABOR ORGANIZATION, International Labor Office, Washington Branch Library, 1750 New York Ave NW, Rm 330, Washington, 20006. Karen J Mark, Librn
Holdings: Vols (13,500) Cat Pix 16mm Films Monographs
Notes: Wide range of titles dealing with worldwide labor and social matters. The library contains ILO publications and documentation only, dating back to 1919. Also, a collection of ILO films and photos. See *Subject Guide to Publications of the ILO, 1919-1964* and *ILO Catalogue of Publications in Print, 1982* (ILO).

DC —US DEPT OF LABOR, Library, 200 Constitution Ave NW, Washington, 20210. Sabina Jacobson, Dir
Holdings: Vols (550,000) Cat

ON —CANADA DEPT OF LABOUR, Library, Ottawa, K1A 0J2, Can. Monique Marchand, Chief Librn
Holdings: Vols (100,000) Cat Microforms

WORKING CONDITIONS (cont.)

ON —ONTARIO MINISTRY OF LABOUR, Library, 400 University Ave, Toronto, M7A 1T7, Can. Jean Collins-Williams, Librn
Holdings: Vols (80,000) Microforms Films

WORKINGMEN'S ASSOCIATIONS see Trade Unions

WORKMEN'S CIRCLE (PHILADELPHIA)

PA —BALCH INSTITUTE FOR ETHNIC STUDIES, Library, 18 S Seventh St, Philadelphia, 19106. R Joseph Anderson, Library Dir
Holdings: Mss
Notes: The Balch Institute's current holdings span the years (1931-1968). They incl minutes, correspondence, financial records, and membership records from the City and District Committee, its predecessor the Joint Committee, and the District Organization Committee, the Cemetery Department, the Medical Department and the Educational Department. The records document the Workmen's Circle organizational concerns and benefit programs; there is little direct documentation of branch activities. The City and District Committee series, incl the District Organization Committee records, contains a long run of minutes and much correspondence. The records of the Cemetery and Medical Departments describe the services offered and the departments' administrative methods, through correspondence, financial records, and administrative files. Teachers' grade books from Shul 6 and the NorthPhiladelphia Mitelshule, extensive school financial records, and administrative records from Camp Hofnung's last three seasons comprise the Educational Department series. The minutes, department correspondence, and teacher's grade books are written mostly in Yiddish.

WORKSHOPS FOR THE HANDICAPPED see Vocational Rehabilitation

WORLD COUNCIL OF CHURCHES

KY —ASBURY THEOLOGICAL SEMINARY, B L Fisher Library, Wilmore, 40390. D William Faupel, Dir of Library Services
Holdings: Uncat
Notes: Official Numbered Documents, 1910-date. See Index, 1910-1948 and Check List, 1910-1970, Faith and Order Commission, World Council of Churches, Official Numbered Publications, A T DeGroot (Geneva, Switzerland: WCC, 1977), 258 pp.
NY —UNION THEOLOGICAL SEMINARY, Library, 3041 Broadway at Reinhold Niebuhr Place, New York, 10027. Richard D Spoor, Dir
Holdings: Vols (580,000) Cat Mss Microforms
Budget: ($750,000)
NC —SOUTHEASTERN BAPTIST THEOLOGICAL SEMINARY LIBRARY, PO Box 752, Wake Forest, 27587. H Eugene McLeod, Librn
Holdings: Cat Microforms
Notes: Incl official publications of the Faith and Order Commission of the World Council of Churches from 1910 to 1970, periodicals from many countries and religious bodies, and publications of the evangelical academies and lay training centers of Europe and Great Britain.

WORLD ECONOMICS see Economic Policy

WORLD FAIRS, EXPOSITIONS, ETC. see Exhibitions and Expositions

WORLD FEDERATION see International Organization

WORLD GOVERNMENT see International Organization

WORLD HEALTH ORGANIZATION (WHO)

MI —UNIVERSITY OF MICHIGAN, Public Health Library, Ann Arbor, 48109. Mary Townsend, Head
Holdings: Vols (55,000) Cat Maps Pix
Budget: ($24,000)

WORLD HISTORY

NY —NEW YORK PUBLIC LIBRARY, Research Libraries, General Research Division, Fifth Ave & 42 St, New York, 10018. Rodney Phillips, Chief
Holdings: Vols (2,225,000) Cat Maps Pix Microforms
Budget: ($775,718)

WORLD LITERATURE see Literature

WORLD MEDICINE see Medicine, World

WORLD ORGANIZATION see International Organization

WORLD POLITICS

CA —WORLD AFFAIRS COUNCIL OF NORTH CALIFORNIA, Library, 312 Sutter St, San Francisco, 94108. Lone C Beeson, Head Librn; Edith Malamud, Circulation Librn
Holdings: Vols 6500 Cat Maps
CA —ABC-CLIO, Inge Boehm Library, 2040 Alameda Padre Serra, PO Box 4397, Santa Barbara, 93103. Hope Smith, Librn
Holdings: Vols (2000) Uncat
Budget: ($10,000)
Notes: Current serials (2000) and reference works on histroy: world history, history, 1450-present; US and Canadian history, prehistory-present; and history-related social science and humanities. Library serves as support unit in the publication of Historical Abstracts and America: History and Life.
MA —HARVARD UNIVERSITY, Center for International Affairs, Library, Coolidge Hall, 1737 Cambridge St, Cambridge, 02138. Barbara Mitchell, Librn
Holdings: Vols (13,000) Periodicals
Notes: Collection emphasizes international politics and also contains considerable statistical material on individual countries. Library currently receives 115 periodical titles.
PA —CARLOW COLLEGE, Grace Library, Fifth Ave, Pittsburgh, 15213. Joan M Mitchell, Dir of Library Services
Holdings: Vols (977) Cat Pamphlets
Budget: ($300)
Notes: The Peace Studies Collection is a collection of books which deals with the search for peace in the modern world from the perspective of the Judeo-Christian tradition. It is especially strong in the area of social justice, civil rights and world politics.

WORLD TELEGRAM (NEWSPAPER)

DC —LIBRARY OF CONGRESS, Manuscript Division, Washington, 20540. John C Broderick, Chief
Notes: Papers of Roy W Howard (1883-1964), past president and chairman of the board of Scripps-Howard Newspapers. Some 85,000 items for the years 1923-64, incl business and personal correspondence, maintained under state and city of origin, with separate files in each year for the various Scripps-Howard newspapers, especially for the World Telegram (New York City).

WORLD TRADE LIBRARIES

CA —GOLDEN GATE UNIVERSITY, One Embarcadero Center, No 216, San Francisco, 94111. Jeanne Nichols, Librn
Notes: World Trade Libraries and archives.

WORLD WAR, 1914-1918

AZ —NORTHERN ARIZONA UNIVERSITY, Special Collection Library, CU Box 6022, Flagstaff, 86011. Peter M Whiteley, Coordr/Archivist; William Mullane, Librn
Notes: Various collections, incl (1) Bisbee Deportation Collection; photocopies of government publications and published articles concerning World War I and the Bisbee Deportation, 1917. Covers period 1917-1920, 1950's-1970's.
CA —CLAREMONT COLLEGES, Norman F Sprague Memorial Library, 12 & Dartmouth, Claremont, 91711. David Kuhner, Librn
Holdings: Vols (3500) Cat Mss Pix
Notes: Gift of Mr and Mrs John F B Carruthers. Major concentrations are European and American World War I aeronautical history; strong emphasis on ballooning, and early experiments with real or imaginary flight. Restricted use.
CA —CLAREMONT COLLEGES, Honnold Library, Ninth & Dartmouth, Claremont, 91711. Tania Rizzo, Special Collections Dept Head
Holdings: Vols (250) Uncat Maps Pix Doc Records Posters Scrapbooks
Notes: Several collections containing memorabilia from both world wars. WWI represented mainly in pamphlets, Liberty Bond posters, clippings, and photographs. Restricted use.
CA —LOS ANGELES PUBLIC LIBRARY, History Dept, 630 W Fifth St, Los Angeles, 90071. Frank Louch, Sr Librn
Holdings: Vols 5500 Cat Maps
Budget: ($85,000)
Notes: A well-rounded collection of World War I, with emphasis on unit histories.
CA —UNIVERSITY OF CALIFORNIA, LOS ANGELES, Research Library, Dept of Special Collections, 405 Hilgard Ave, Los Angeles, 90024. Edward Shreeves, Chairman, Bibliographers Group; David S Zeidberg, Head
Holdings: Pix
Notes: 3 linear feet of correspondence, photographs, and ephemera relating to pioneer men and women aviators, balloons, clippers, and the role of aviation in World Wars I and II, collected by Gregory.
CA —SAN DIEGO PUBLIC LIBRARY, 820 E St, San Diego, 92101. Marion L Buckner, Supervising Librn
Holdings: Vols 1700 Cat Maps Pix
CA —UNIVERSITY OF SAN FRANCISCO, Richard A Gleeson Library, The Countess Bernardine Murphy Donohue Rare Book Room, San Francisco, 94117. D Steven Corey, Special Collections Librn
Notes: The R T Clark Collection with an emphasis on Germany and the Balkan Peninsual, 1900-1920. 1000 items.
CA —HOOVER INSTITUTION ON WAR, REVOLUTION & PEACE, Stanford University, Stanford, 94305. Milorad M Drachkovitch, Archivist
Holdings: Mss Pix
Notes: Three collections; (1) Records of the Commission for Relief in Belgium, organized in 1914 under the chairmanship of Herbert Hoover, incl correspondence, reports, memoranda, accounts, pamphlets, bulletins and photographs, 1914-1924, relating to procurement of food and other supplies in the US and their distribution in German-occupied Belgium and nothern France during and immediately after World War I. 265 ft (2) Papers of William A Drayton, 1913-1946, incl correspondence, reports, memornada, speeches and writings, photographs, and other materials, relating to Serbia, during and after World War I, and WA Drayton's activities as an American volunteer in the Serbian Army, member of the Serbian Delegation to Paris Peace Conference, and Inter-Allied Commissioner of Bulgarian Atrocities Commission. 2 ms boxes. (3) The collection on the European War(World War I) forms the foundation of the Hoover Institution. Books, pamphlets, posters, periodicals, and newspapers are incl with emphasis on the original language of the publications. Of special interest and importance is the Paris Peace Treaty documentation.
CT —TRINITY COLLEGE LIBRARY, Watkinson Library, 300 Summit St, Hartford, 06106. Jeffrey Kaimowitz, Cur
Holdings: Cat
Notes: Collection of ephermeral material incl posters and pamphlets, particularly German and French, and other minor works.

WORLD WAR, 1914-1918 (cont.)

CT —YALE UNIVERSITY, Beinecke Rare Book & Manuscript Library, Osborn Collection, New Haven, 06520. Stephen R Parks, Cur
Holdings: Mss

DC —LIBRARY OF CONGRESS, Manuscript Division, Washington, 20540. John C Broderick, Chief
Holdings: 14,000 Items
Notes: The papers of General John Joseph Pershing.

†DC —LIBRARY OF CONGRESS, Washington, 20540.
Notes: One of the strongest collections in the country.

GA —US ARMY INFANTRY CENTER, National Infantry Museum, Fort Benning, 31905. Dick D Grube, Dir; Z Frank Hanner, Cur; Carol Sims, Librn
Holdings: Vols (6000) Cat Mss Maps Pix Slides
Notes: Published and unpublished works dealing with infantry history, equipment, and units, for research on the Museum's collections of artifacts. Items cannot be checked out except under unusual and compelling circumstances. The collection traces the two centuries of history of the US Infantry. Of special interest are: unpublished reports of tests conducted on US Army Infantry equipment; photographs showing the history of Fort Benning; books and periodical articles dealing with Infantry small arms, both American and foreign, especially Japanese, Soviet, Chinese, and British; US Army manuals, incl many from the early 20th and late 19th centuries; WWII battlefield maps; WWI and WWII posters; histories of WWI; US Army insignia and medals; WWII era German uniforms and insignia. Also, over 2500 weapons.

IL —LOYOLA UNIVERSITY OF CHICAGO, E M Cudahy Memorial Library, 6525 N Sheridan Rd, Chicago, 60626.
Notes: Dorr E Felt Pamphlet and Clipping Collection. Emphasizes political and economic issues, 1902-35, and documents Illinois Manufacturers Association Conference, September 8-9, 1919; Air Board of Chicago, April 16, 1921-August 1, 1930; Allied Debts to the US, May 15, 1923-September 30, 1926; Bolshevism, Communism, "Red" Russia, 1924-27; Child Labor Bill, March 30, 1915, 1914-20; Labor, March, 1902-March, 1932; Railroad Strike, August 25, 1916-August 7, 1920; The War, August, 1914-October 23, 1930; War Industries Commission, June, 1918-November 23, 1928. A pamphlet list is available for each topic.

NY —STATE UNIVERSITY OF NEW YORK AT ALBANY, Library, Special Collections Dept, 1400 Washington Ave, Albany, 12222. Marion P Munzer, Coordr
Notes: Correspondence, music mss, programs, and articles of Erwin Bodky. Letters to his fiancee during his service in the German army during World War I are of interest (4 linear feet).

NY —CORNELL UNIVERSITY LIBRARIES, Collection of Regional History, Dept of Manuscripts and Univ Archives, Ithaca, 14853.
Notes: Photographs; .3 ft.

NY —NEW YORK PUBLIC LIBRARY, Research Libraries, General Research Division, Fifth Ave & 42 St, New York, 10018. Rodney Phillips, Chief
Holdings: Vols (2,225,000) Cat Maps Pix Microforms
Budget: ($775,718)
Notes: See *Subject Catalog of the World War I Collection,* The Research Libraries of The New York Public Library, 1961. 10 x 14, 61,300 cards, 2772 pages, 4 vols. Price, $210. The Subject Catalog of The New York Public Library's World War I Collection forms an outstanding bibliography of the subject, incl as it does works in many languages, analytical entries for important articles in scholarly journals and thousands of pamphlets. Under the main heading "European War, 1914-1918," there are over

one thousand subdivisions running from "Addresses, sermons, etc," through "Women's work."

NY —UNIVERSITY CLUB, Library, One W 54 St, New York, 10019. Guy St Clair, Library Dir
Holdings: Vols (100,000) Cat Mss Maps Pix
Notes: A private library for the members of the University Club, their guests, and serious scholars upon written application to the Library Director.

NY —US MILITARY ACADEMY LIBRARY, West Point, 10996. Marie T Capps, Maps & Mss Librn
Holdings: Vols (2000) // Mss Maps
Notes: One descriptive catalog of a portion of this collection is: Marie T Capps and Theodore G Stroup, *US Military Academy Library Map Collection: The Period of the American Revolution 1753-1800* (West Point, NY: US Military Academy, 1971), 82 pp.

OK —UNIVERSITY OF TULSA, McFarlin Library, Dept of Rare Books and Special Collections, 600 S College, Tulsa, 74104. David Farmer, Dir; Toby Murray, Archivist; Caroline Swinson, Cur of Manuscripts & Art
Holdings: Vols 1500
Notes: Training manuals, pamphlets, history, memoirs, and literature of the First World War.

PA —US ARMY MILITARY HISTORY INSTITUTE, Carlisle Barracks, 17013. Richard J Sommers, Chief Archivist-Historian
Holdings: Mss Cat
Notes: 6500 folders and 100 boxes mss. The World War I survey, personal correspondence, diaries, and memoirs of American officers and enlisted men of Regular, National Guard, and National Army units (also sailors, Marines, and Coast Guardsmen) serving in the United States, England, France, Italy, Germany, the Ottoman Empire, and Russia during and immediately after the First World War. This is the largest collection anywhere of personal papers on US forces in the Great War.

PA —TEMPLE UNIVERSITY LIBRARIES, Special Collections Dept, Conwellana-Templana Collection, 13 & Berks St, Philadelphia, 19122. Miriam I Crawford, Cur
Holdings: // Mss
Budget: ($30,000)
Notes: The University archives contains two groups of letters written by former students in the armed forces to the University President and to the Dean, during World War I, recounting their experiences, another larger group of letters written by such students in World War II to the Director of Athletics, the letters of condolence written by the University President in the latter war to bereaved parents, and a file of brief autobiographical accounts of their war experiences written by the student soldiers after World War I.

PA —UNIVERSITY OF PITTSBURGH, Hillman Library, Pittsburgh, 15260.
Holdings: Vols (10,000)
Notes: The entire contents of the oldest used book shop in Pittsburgh, the John C Daub Book Store. The collection deals mainly in the areas of military history; works dealing with the Civil War, the World Wars and other military topics; and local histories. Also incl are military works containing colored plates; a large group of Americana; and many framed, colored prints on military subjects.

TX —UNIVERSITY OF TEXAS, EL PASO, Special Collections Dept, The S L A Marshall Military History Collection, El Paso, 79968. Thomas Burdett, Cur
Holdings: Vols 7000 Cat Periodicals Mss
Budget: $2000
Notes: The collection contains all of General Samuel Lyman Atwood Marshall's published works, his personal library and his personal papers. General Marshall was a prolific military historian and journalist. The collection's strengths are in its coverage of the wars of the twentieth century, specifically the two world wars, the Korean conflict and the war in Vietnam. The Marshall Room where the collection is housed is opened to the public.

†VA —GEORGE C MARSHALL RESEARCH FOUNDATION AND LIBRARY, Drawer 920, Lexington, 24450. Royster Lyle Jr, Cur Collections
Holdings: Vols Cat Mss Maps Pix Microforms
Notes: Regimental histories, operation reports and army manuals, government documents, personal narratives: 10 major collections of personal papers; 250 American, British, and French war posters; over 700 operational maps; photographs of military leaders and events; vertical file arranged by subject.
See also entry under World War, 1939-1945.

WA —TACOMA PUBLIC LIBRARY, 1102 Tacoma Ave S, Tacoma, 98402. Kevin Hegarty, Dir
Holdings: Vols 1300 Mss Maps
Notes: Collection of World War I propaganda pamphlets and posters, 1000 posters, mostly US, but some French.

BC —UNIVERSITY OF VICTORIA, McPherson Library, Victoria, V8W 3H5, Can.
Notes: Businessman. Transcripts of collection of letters home by a Canadian soldier in the First World War.

ON —MCMASTER UNIVERSITY, Mills Memorial Library, Div of Archives & Research Collections, Hamilton, L8S 4L6, Can. G R Hill, Univ Librn
Holdings: Vols 900 Uncat Mss Maps Pix
Notes: Contains a large book collection, as well as ms accounts of World War I. Incl scrapbooks, photograph albums, and maps, incl Luftwaffe target maps of British installations.

ON —METROPOLITAN TORONTO LIBRARY, History Dept, 789 Yonge St, Toronto, M4W 2G8, Can. Michael Pearson, Head
Holdings: Vols (11,000) Cat Phonorecords Audiotapes Microforms
Notes: Includes British army and navy lists and Prussian and French army lists from 18th century on; British regimental histories; works on military uniforms and insignia, especially European; Napoleonic and First and Second World Wars well represented.

WORLD WAR, 1914-1918—AMERICAN PROPAGANDA see Propaganda, American

WORLD WAR, 1914-1918—CAMPAIGNS—SERBIA

CA —HOOVER INSTITUTION ON WAR, REVOLUTION & PEACE, Stanford University, Stanford, 94305. Milorad M Drachkovitch, Archivist
Holdings: Mss Pix
Notes: Papers of William A Drayton, 1913-1946, incl correspondence, reports, memoranda, speeches and writings, photographs, and other materials, relating to Serbia, during and after World War I, and WA Drayton's activities as an American volunteer in the Serbian Army, member of the Serbian Army, member of the Serbian Delegation to Paris Peace Conference, and Inter-Allied Commissioner of Bulgarian Atrocities Commission. 2 ms boxes.

WORLD WAR, 1914-1918—CHARITIES see Red Cross

WORLD WAR, 1914-1918—GERMAN PROPAGANDA see Propaganda, German

WORLD WAR, 1914-1918—PICTURES, ILLUSTRATIONS, ETC.

AZ —UNIVERSITY OF ARIZONA, University Library, Special Collections, Tucson, 85721. Louis A Hieb, Head
Notes: Contains posters and stereographs.

DC —LIBRARY OF CONGRESS, Prints & Photographs Div, Washington, 20540.
Notes: Poster collection numbers about 70,000 American and foreign items from the 1850s to the present. Incl *Art Nouveau* of World War I and World War II, WPA,

WORLD WAR, 1914-1918—PICTURES, ILLUSTRATIONS, ETC. (cont.)

propaganda, performing arts, and psychedelic posters.

NY —BUFFALO & ERIE COUNTY PUBLIC LIBRARY, Rare Book Room, Lafayette Sq, Buffalo, 14203. William H Loos, Cur
Holdings: // Uncat
Notes: The collection of 3000 posters consists primarily of World War I posters with a few from World War II, as well as some modern posters.

WORLD WAR, 1914-1918—RECONSTRUCTION see Reconstruction (Europe, 1919-1923)

WORLD WAR, 1914-1918—REGIMENTAL HISTORIES

CA —LOS ANGELES PUBLIC LIBRARY, History Dept, 630 W Fifth St, Los Angeles, 90071. Frank Louch, Sr Librn
Holdings: Vols (5500) Cat Maps
Budget: ($85,000)
Notes: A well-rounded collection of World War I, with emphasis on unit histories.

DC —GEORGETOWN UNIVERSITY, Library, Special Collections Div, 37 & O Sts NW, Washington, 20057. George M Barringer, Special Collections Librn; Nicholas B Sheetz, Mss Librn
Holdings: Vols 2000 Cat Maps Pix
Notes: Strong in British regimental histories and personal narratives.

NC —82ND AIRBORNE DIVISION, War Memorial Museum, Reference Library, Ardennes & Gela Sts, Fort Bragg, 28307. John S Duvall, Chief Cur
Holdings: Vols (300) Uncat Mss Maps Pix
Notes: The collection is intended to be a research tool for persons studying the history of the 82nd Airborne Division and the development of airborne warfare.

†VA —GEORGE C MARSHALL RESEARCH FOUNDATION AND LIBRARY, Drawer 920, Lexington, 24450. Royster Lyle Jr, Cur Collections
Holdings: Vols Cat Mss Maps Pix Microforms
Notes: Regimental histories, operation reports and army manuals, government documents, personal narratives; 10 major collections of personal papers; 250 American, British, and French war posters; over 700 operational maps; photographs of military leaders and events; vertical file arranged by subject.
See also entry under World War, 1939-1945.

WORLD WAR, 1914-1918—WAR WORK—YMCA

IL —NATIONAL COUNCIL OF THE YMCA, YMCA Historical Library, 6400 Shafer Ct, Rosemont, 60018. Eleanor R Murphy, Librn
Holdings: Vols (15,000) Cat Mss Pix
Notes: World War I relief work, incl material on the YMCA's work with US troops, both here and abroad, with foreign armies such as the French, with prisoners of war of both the Allies and the German/Austrian/Turkish Armies, and with civilians employed in war industries or simply victims of the War. Aspects of the work covered incl education, physical education, entertainment, and religious work. A collection of interviews conducted by the YMCA's War Historical Bureau in the period 1919-22 is also available in transcript form.

PA —FRIENDS HISTORICAL LIBRARY OF SWARTHMORE COLLEGE, Swarthmore, 19081. J William Frost, Dir
Holdings: Vols (35,000) Cat Mss Pix Microforms
Notes: Library's collection contain information on the history and doctrine of the Society of Friends, Quaker contributions to literature, science, business, education, and government, plus their reform efforts in peace, Indian rights, women's rights, and abolition of slavery. Among the over 250

mss collections are several which have personal papers of Quaker relief and reconstruction workers in Europe following World War I, most of whom worked with the American Friends Service Committee.

WORLD WAR, 1939-1945

AZ —NORTHERN ARIZONA UNIVERSITY, Special Collection Library, CU Box 6022, Flagstaff, 86011. Peter M Whiteley, Coordr/Archivist; William Mullane, Librn
Notes: Collection of Robert Eunson, journalist, vice president, and assistant general manager of United Press International. NAU graduate. Incl correspondence, scrapbooks, subject files, photos, 1930's-1975. Eunson was a World War II correspondent. Also incl information on the Pacific and European theatres, Generals MacArthur and Eisenhower, and Arizona AP news articles from the Korean War era. Inventory available.

AZ —ARIZONA STATE UNIVERSITY, Library, Tempe, 85287. Marilyn Wurzburger, Special Collections Librn
Notes: The A T Steele Collection is a unique compilation of articles and documents dealing with events in China from 1932-1949. The collection is divided into five parts: dispatches, newspaper clippings, pamphlets and books, original documents of the Communist Party (circa 1945) and memorabilia, written and/or collected by American journalist A T Steele. Dispatches cover events in China from 1940-1949 and are mostly first-hand experiences of Steele. These dispatches, not all of which were published, often contain details absent in the final copy. Post-war topics incl truce negotiations between the Nationalists and Chinese Communists and the "Manchurian Question." Incl 12 linear feet of materials. Index available.

CA —CLAREMONT COLLEGES, Honnold Library, Ninth & Dartmouth, Claremont, 91711. Tania Rizzo, Special Collections Dept Head
Holdings: Vols (250) Uncat Mss Maps Doc Pix Rec Posters Scrapbooks
Notes: Combined holdings of memorabilia of both world wars, primarily WWII. The Howard D Mills Collection on War Bonds occupies 33 linear ft of scrapbooks, documents, mss, and photographs, in addition to several dozen War Bond, Liberty Bond, and recruitment posters. Nazi propaganda and German medals. Soldiers' handbooks, maps, pamphlets, scrapbooks of clippings, photographs, and recordings. Restricted use.

CA —UNIVERSITY OF CALIFORNIA, DAVIS, Shields Library, Dept of Special Collections, Davis, 95616. Donald Kunitz, Head; C Danial Elliott, Asst Head

CA —CALIFORNIA STATE UNIVERSITY, FRESNO, Henry Madden Library, Dept of Special Collections, Fresno, 93740. Ronald J Mahoney, Head
Holdings: Vols 6 Uncat
Notes: The Joseph A Lowande Collection of Worldwide Rationing contains 20th century ration material from Germany and the United States. Especially strong on local rationing from Stadtamhof, Bavaria, 1915-1923.

CA —CALIFORNIA STATE UNIVERSITY, FULLERTON, Library, Box 4150, Fullerton, 92634. Linda Herman, Special Collections Librn
Holdings: Vols (4000) Cat
Notes: Nearly complete papers of the League of Nations, an archive of the Holocaust as well as captured enemy records. Also incl approx 110 oral interviews with Japanese-Americans concerning relocation centers.

†CA —LOS ANGELES COUNTY PUBLIC LIBRARY, Gardena Library, 1731 W Gardena Blvd, Gardena, 90247.
Notes: Japanese language materials, incl World War II period Japanese-American newspapers; Japanese-American monographs on microfilm; Japanese-American newspapers.

CA —LOS ANGELES PUBLIC LIBRARY, History Dept, 630 W Fifth St, Los Angeles, 90071. Frank Louch, Sr Librn
Holdings: Vols (9000) Cat Maps
Budget: ($85,000)
Notes: Includes personal narratives, campaigns, diplomatic histories and peace treaties, memoirs of generals and statesmen, official reports and archives of participating countries. Collection of unit histories is particularly strong. There is an emphasis on personal accounts by combatants and noncombatants from all countries. Established as a memorial to Tom Treanor, correspondent for the Los Angeles Times, and includes his World War II writings. See also entry under Military History.

CA —UNIVERSITY OF CALIFORNIA, LOS ANGELES, Research Library, Dept of Special Collections, 405 Hilgard Ave, Los Angeles, 90024. Edward Shreeves, Chairman, Bibliographers Group; David S Zeidberg, Head
Holdings: Cat Mss Maps Pix Audiotapes
Notes: The Japanese American Research Project (JARP) Collection: 350 linear feet of books, pamphlets, audiotapes of interviews conducted with Japanese Americans; files of personal papers of Japanese families; materials relating to the Japanese consulates in the US; materials concerning Japanese social, cultural, and economic organizations, and war relocation and camp internment.

CA —CALIFORNIA STATE UNIVERSITY, NORTHRIDGE, Delmar T Oviatt & South Libraries, 1811 Nordhoff St, Northridge, 91330. Donald L Read, Special Collections Dept
Holdings: Cat
Notes: Incl 4 boxes of newspapers published in war relocation camps, 6 boxes ephemera, either published in or relating to the camps.

CA —HOOVER INSTITUTION ON WAR, REVOLUTION & PEACE, Stanford University, Stanford, 94305. Milorad M Drachkovitch, Archivist
Notes: Several important military collections incl the papers of Adm Charles M Cooke, Major Gen Robert T Frederick, Gen Robert C Richardson, Col M Preston Goodfellow, Vice Adm Milton E Miles, Col Lee V Harris, Brig Gen L R Boyd.

CA —STANFORD UNIVERSITY LIBRARIES, Lane Medical Library, Stanford University, Medical Center, Stanford, 94305. Peter Stangl, Librn
Holdings: Vols (10,000) Mss Pix
Budget: ($2785)
Notes: Mss of Lane Hospital School of Nursing and Stanford University School of Nursing; experiences of nurses who were captured on Bataan, Phillipine Islands.

CT —YALE UNIVERSITY, Beinecke Rare Book & Manuscript Library, Osborn Collection, New Haven, 06520. Stephen R Parks, Cur
Holdings: Mss

DC —GEORGETOWN UNIVERSITY, Library, Special Collections Div, 37 & O Sts NW, Washington, 20057. George M Barringer, Special Collections Librn; Nicholas B Sheetz, Mss Librn
Holdings: Mss Cat
Notes: The papers of Ambassador Martin F Herz (1917-1983), containing correspondence, reports, memoranda, posters, propaganda leaflets, and other ephemeral material relating to psychological warfare in World War II and Vietnam; also much material on the Cold War and American foreign policy in the years following World War II.

DC —LIBRARY OF CONGRESS, Rare Book & Special Collections Div, Washington, 20540. William Matheson, Chief
Notes: The Third Reich Collection comprises books and miscellaneous materials that originally belonged to the Reichskanzlei in Berlin or were in the Berghof, Hitler's mountain retreat. It contains some books specially printed or designed for Adolf Hitler, but principally regular trade books; periodicals; and books owned by or bearing autographs of Hitler's associates. Incl materials from the libraries of Hermann Goering, Heinrich Himmler, and Franz Xaver Schwarz.

WORLD WAR, 1939-1945 (cont.)

IL —NORTHWESTERN UNIVERSITY, Library, Special Collections Dept, 1937 Sheridan Rd, Evanston, 60201. R Russell Maylone, Cur
Holdings: Vols 300 Uncat
Notes: Propaganda-OSS, WW II materials for both Europe and Asia.

KY —UNIVERSITY OF LOUISVILLE, Ekstrom Library, Rare Books & Special Collections, 2301 S Third St, Louisville, 40208. George T McWhorter, Cur; Delinda Stephens Buie, Asst Cur
Holdings: Vols 2500 // Uncat Maps Pix
Notes: Maps, books (incl personal and historical accounts and humor), official documents, original art in prints, etchings, cartoons, and posters. The collection incl works in English, French, German, and Italian and documents of World Wars I and II.

MA —HARVARD UNIVERSITY LIBRARY, Widener Library, Cambridge, 02138.
Holdings: Cat Mss Maps Microforms
Notes: See Downs 5500, 5537, 5538. Some 12,000 volumes on the war are listed in *Widener Library Shelflist* No 32 (1970).

MN —MINNEAPOLIS PUBLIC LIBRARY & INFORMATION CENTER, 300 Nicollet Mall, Minneapolis, 55401. Richard J Hofstad, Athenaeum Librn
Holdings: Vols (8000) Cat Maps Pix
Notes: Incl 2000 posters of World War II era.

NE —UNIVERSITY OF NEBRASKA-LINCOLN, Don L Love Library, University Archives and Special Collections, Lincoln, 68588. Joseph G Svoboda, University Archivist
Holdings: // Uncat
Notes: Collection consists mainly of pamphlets, clippings, posters, and other World War II ephemera; 2000 items.

NJ —PRINCETON UNIVERSITY, Library, Manuscript Collection, Nassau St, Princeton, 08540. Jean F Preston, Cur
Holdings: // Cat Mss
Notes: Incl 200 boxes: The Fight for Freedom archives cover the period April to December, 1941.

NY —CORNELL UNIVERSITY LIBRARIES, Collection of Regional History, Dept of Manuscripts and Univ Archives, Ithaca, 14853.
Notes: Photographs; .3 ft.

NY —SAINT JOHN'S UNIVERSITY, Special Collections Dept, Grand Central & Utopia Pkwys, Jamaica, 11439. Szilvia E Szmuk, Librn
Holdings: // Uncat Mss
Notes: O'Dwyer Collections: papers dealing with Northern Ireland, 1973-1977; American Friends of Irish Neutrality, World War II a) The Paul O'Dwyer Papers deal with conditions in Northern Ireland, incl correspondence, speeches, press releases, and periodical articles contained in 18 labled manila envelopes and roughly indexed. b) American Friends of Irish Neutrality collection consists of 109 letters, membership and donation cards, minutes, press clippings, post cards, speeches, pamphlets, in 6 manila envelopes. No photocopying.

NY —COLUMBIA UNIVERSITY LIBRARIES, Rare Book & Manuscript Library, 801 Butler Library, 535 W 114 St, New York, 10027. Kenneth A Lohf, Librn
Notes: More than 2 million pieces.

NY —UNIVERSITY CLUB, Library, One W 54 St, New York, 10019. Guy St Clair, Library Dir
Holdings: Vols (100,000) Cat Mss Maps Pix
Notes: A private library for the members of the University Club, their guests, and serious scholars upon written application to the Library Director.

NY —STATE UNIVERSITY OF NEW YORK, STONY BROOK, Melville Library, Stony Brook, 11794. John B Smith, Dir
Holdings: Cat
Notes: Modern German history. Part of the Library's general research collections.

NY —US MILITARY ACADEMY LIBRARY, West Point, 10996. Marie T Capps, Maps & Mss Librn
Holdings: Vols (2000) // Mss Maps
Notes: One descriptive catalog of a portion of this collection is: Marie T Capps and Theodore G Stroup, *US Military Academy Library Map Collection: The Period of the American Revolution 1753-1800* (West Point, NY: US Military Academy, 1971), 82 pp.

NC —DUKE UNIVERSITY, William R Perkins Library, Manuscript Dept, Durham, 27706. Ellen Gartrell, Cur of Mss
Holdings: Cat Mss
Notes: Especially strong for Civil War; also material from most wars that involved US. Notable World War II collection is papers of Gen Robert L Eichelberger (over 20,000 items).

OH —OHIO UNIVERSITY, Vernon R Alden Library, Department of Archives and Special Collections, Athens, 45701. Gary A Hunt, Head
Holdings: Vols 674 Cat Mss Maps Pix Audiotapes
Notes: The Cornelius Ryan Memorial Collection of World War II Papers, containing the research files, correspondence and working library assembled by Ryan in the course of writing his three major books on World War II. The research papers incl some 3,072 files for individual participants in the Normandy invasion, the battle for Berlin, and the Market-Garden operation. Also incl are 166 audio recordings of interviews conducted by Ryan,many with leading figures associated with the war, such as Eisenhower, Chuikov, Gavin, Montgomery, and Prince Bernhard of the Netherlands.

OH —WILMINGTON COLLEGE, Peace Resource Center, Hiroshima/Nagasaki Memorial Collection, Pyle Center Box 1183, Wilmington, 45177. Helen Redding, Librn
Holdings: Vols Pix Slides Audiotapes Videotapes Film Art Reproductions VF
Notes: The Hiroshima/Nagasaki Memorial Collection is nationally known and respected as a major source of information, films, slides and audiotapes about the atomic bombings of Hiroshima and Nagasaki. An especially signifciant part of the Collection is a continually growing library in Japanese currently numbering more than 500 vols. Here are recorded eyewitness account of the atomic bombings, as well as details of what life has been like in the intervening years for the thousands of survivors (*hibakusha*). Also incl are books of poetry, photo books, juvenile literature, and books dealing with medical information, peace research, peace education, nuclear power, etc. All books in the Hiroshima/Nagasaki Memorial Collection are available for interlibrary loan. An *Annotated Bibliography of Japanese A-Bomb Literature* may be purchased or borrowed from the PRC. In it are briefsummaries in English of each book in the Collection.

OR —UNIVERSITY OF OREGON LIBRARY, Special Collections Div, Eugene, 97403. Kenneth W Duckett, Curator
Holdings: Cat and Uncat Mss Pix
Notes: Research material, incl correspondence, documents, and tapes of oral interviews, and ms of *The Thousand-Mile War: World War II in Alaska and the Aleutians* (1969) by Brian Garfield. Also, correspondence, reminiscences, documents, published articles, and photographs relating to the Aleutian campaign, compiled by Lawrence Reineke.

PA —US ARMY MILITARY HISTORY INSTITUTE, Carlisle Barracks, 17013. Richard J Sommers, Chief Archivist-Historian
Holdings: Mss Cat
Notes: The World War II collection, personal letters, daily logs, reminiscences, speeches, and official papers of American officers and soldiers serving in the European, Mediterranean, Middle Eastern, China-Burma-India, Southwest Pacific, and Central Pacific Theaters and in the Zone of the Interior during the Second World War. Most of these collections are manuscripts of General officers, incl Omar Bradley, Stephen Chamberlin, Lewis Hershey, John Lucas, William Simpson, and Brehon Somervell.

PA —ERIE COUNTY HISTORICAL SOCIETY LIBRARY, 417 State St, Erie, 16501. Helen Andrews, Librn
Notes: World War II and Korean War Veterans. 66 vertical file drawers containing mostly newspaper clippings.

PA —TEMPLE UNIVERSITY LIBRARIES, Special Collections Dept, Conwellana-Templana Collection, 13 & Berks St, Philadelphia, 19122. Miriam I Crawford, Cur
Holdings: // Mss
Budget: ($30,000)
Notes: The University archives contains two groups of letters written by former students in the armed forces to the University President and to the Dean, during World War I, recounting their experiences, another larger group of letters written by such students in World War II to the Director of Athletics, the letters of condolence written by the University President in the latter war to bereaved parents, and a file of brief autobiographical accounts of their war experiences written by the student soldiers after World War I.

PA —UNIVERSITY OF PITTSBURGH, Hillman Library, Pittsburgh, 15260.
Holdings: Vols (10,000)
Notes: The entire contents of the oldest used book shop in Pittsburgh, the John C Daub Book Store. The collection deals mainly in the areas of military history; works dealing with the Civil War, the World Wars and other military topics; and local history; county histories, city, state or regional histories. Also incl are military works containing colored plates; a large group of Americana; and many framed, colored prints on military subjects.

TX —NORTH TEXAS STATE UNIVERSITY, Archives, NT Station Box 5188, Denton, 76203. Robert LaForte, University Archivist
Notes: Oral History Collection. Incl interviews with survivors of attack on Pearl Harbor, on Corregidor, the Bataan Death March, the "Lost Battalion," prisoner of war camps. Also material on guerilla fighting in the Philippines. Cataloged. Transcriptions available.

TX —UNIVERSITY OF TEXAS, EL PASO, Special Collections Dept, The S L A Marshall Military History Collection, El Paso, 79968. Thomas Burdett, Cur
Holdings: Vols 7000 Cat Periodicals Mss
Budget: $2000
Notes: The collection contains all of General Samuel Lyman Atwood Marshall's published works, his personal library and his personal papers. General Marshall was a prolific military historian and journalist. The collection's strengths are in its coverage of the wars of the twentieth century, specifically the two world wars, the Korean conflict and the war in Vietnam. The Marshall Room where the collection is housed is opened to the public.

†VA —GEORGE C MARSHALL RESEARCH FOUNDATION AND LIBRARY, Drawer 920, Lexington, 24450. Royster Lyle Jr, Cur Collections
Holdings: Vols Cat Mss Pix Phonorecords Audiotapes Films Filmstrips Microforms
Notes: About 400 posters, American, German, French; complete *Stars and Stripes* for WWII; approx 5000 cataloged photographs, over 5000 uncataloged Office of War information photos, and over 10,000 US Signal Corps photos (uncat). Approx 250 regimental histories, operation reports, and army manuals; published memoirs and letters of Marshall associates; official military histories (American, British); set of 40 books by "Remy" (G Renault-Roulier); over 1200 maps, approx 300 newsmaps, 800 daily situation maps (European Theatre), 37 bound vols of daily situation maps 1944-1945; seven of the *Why We Fight* series (films). Major ms collections incl the papers of generals George C Marshall, Marshall S Carter, William T Sexton, Lucian Truscott, William R Arnold, Paul M Roninett, Frank McCarthy; Forrest C Pogue; colonels Collas Harris, Francis P Miller, William F Friedman;officers of the Women's Army Corps. Hearings and government documents. Agency records copied from NARS. Vertical file arranged by subject.

WORLD WAR, 1939-1945 (cont.)

BC —ROYAL ROADS MILITARY
COLLEGE, Coronel Memorial Library,
Victoria, V0S 1B0, Can. Susan Day, Librn
Holdings: Vols (7500) Cat
Budget: ($3000)
Notes: A collection of world military history
in the English language with a particular
emphasis on British military history in
World War II and Canadian military history
of the two world wars.

MB —UNIVERSITY OF MANITOBA,
Elizabeth Dafoe Library, Archives and
Special Collections Dept, Winnipeg, R3T
2N2, Can. Richard E Bennett, Dept Head;
Corrado A Santoro, Reference Archivist
Holdings: Pix
Notes: Postcards and photographs showing
details of Nazi Germany's bombings and
occupation of Holland in 1940. 37 items.

ON —MCMASTER UNIVERSITY, Mills
Memorial Library, Div of Archives &
Research Collections, Hamilton, L8S 4L6,
Can. G R Hill, Univ Librn
Holdings: // Mss Maps Pix
Notes: Colonel Steer-Webster played a
leading part in the invention, design, and
development of the "Mulberry" artificial
harbor installations used for the invasion of
Europe in World War II. The collection
comprises memoranda, drawings,
photographs, and maps.

ON —METROPOLITAN TORONTO
LIBRARY, History Dept, 789 Yonge St,
Toronto, M4W 2G8, Can. Michael Pearson,
Head
Holdings: Vols (11,000) Cat Phonorecords
Audiotapes Microforms
Notes: Includes British army and navy lists
and Prussian and French army lists from
18th century on; British regimental histories;
works on military uniforms and insignia,
especially European; Napoleonic and First
and Second World Wars well represented.

WORLD WAR, 1939-1945—ATROCITIES

CA —HOOVER INSTITUTION ON WAR,
REVOLUTION & PEACE, Stanford
University, Stanford, 94305. Milorad M
Drachkovitch, Archivist
Holdings: Mss Pix
Notes: Papers of Julius Epstein, journalist,
research associate at the Hoover Institution,
and author of *Operation Keelhaul: The Story
of Forced Repatriation*, incl correspondence,
speeches and writings, clippings,
photographs, and printed matter, 1939-72,
relating to his research on the events of
World War II, communism, forced
repatriation of Russian prisoners of the
Soviet Union following World War II, Katyn
forest massacres, and unreported deaths of
Soviet Cosmonauts, as well as his efforts to
obtain restricted government documents on
these subjects. 180 ms boxes.

IL —HEBREW THEOLOGICAL COLLEGE,
Saul Silber Memorial Library, 7135 N
Carpenter Rd, Skokie, 60077. Leah Mishkin,
Head Librn/Cur
Holdings: Vols (58,000) Cat Mss Microforms
Notes: Main subject is rabbinics (Halachic
literature). We also have a very large and
important Holocaust Collection.

MA —BRANDEIS UNIVERSITY, Goldfarb
Library, 415 South St, Waltham, 02154.
Bessie Hahn, Dir
Notes: Holocaust Survivors Collection.
Consists of 20 linear ft of recorded
interviews with survivors of the Holocaust,
now living in the US. The tapes are not
transcribed and the collection is
unprocessed, but the tapes are arranged
alphabetically by interviewee.

OH —HEBREW UNION COLLEGE-JEWISH
INSTITUTE OF RELIGION, Klau Library,
3101 Clifton Ave, Cincinnati, 45220. David
J Gilner, Reference Librn
Holdings: Cat
Notes: The Jewish Holocaust (1939-1945)
collection. Incl large collections of memorial
books, curricula and juvenile fiction.

OH —WILMINGTON COLLEGE, Peace
Resource Center, Hiroshima/Nagasaki
Memorial Collection, Pyle Center Box 1183,
Wilmington, 45177. Helen Redding, Librn
Holdings: Vols Pix Slides Audiotapes
Videotapes Film Art Reproductions VF
Notes: The Hiroshima/Nagasaki Memorial
Collection is nationally known and respected
as a major source of information, films, slides
and audiotapes about the atomic bombings of
Hiroshima and Nagasaki. An especially
signifcant part of the Collection is a
continually growing library in Japanese
currently numbering more than 500 vols.
Here are recorded eyewitness account of the
atomic bombings, as well as details of what
life has been like in the intervening years for
the thousands of survivors (*hibakusha*). Also
incl are books of poetry, photo books,
juvenile literature, and books dealing with
medical information, peace research, peace
education, nuclear power, etc. All books in
the Hiroshima/Nagasaki Memorial
Collection are available for interlibrary loan.
An *Annotated Bibliography of Japanese A-
Bomb Literature* may be purchased or
borrowed from the PRC. In it are
briefsummaries in English of each book in
the Collection.

WORLD WAR, 1939-1945—CAMPAIGNS—CHINA-BURMA-INDIA THEATRE

CA —HOOVER INSTITUTION ON WAR,
REVOLUTION & PEACE, Stanford
University, Stanford, 94305. Milorad M
Drachkovitch, Archivist
Holdings: Mss
Notes: Papers of Maj Gen Haydon L
Boatner, USA, 1941-1974, incl
correspondence, memoranda, reports,
studies, orders, maps, notes, and printed
matter relating to military policy and
operations in the China-Burma-Indian
Theatre during World War II. 5 ms boxes.
Also, papers, 1941-1945, of Joseph Warren
Stilwell, Army officer who commanded US
forces in the China-Burma-India Theatre,
1942-1944, and the 10th Army, Pacific
Theatre, 1945. Diary (1941-1944), "black-
book" (reflections and analyses of the day's
events, 1943-1944), other personal papers
and miscellaneous documents on military
operations. 6 ft.

WORLD WAR, 1939-1945—CHILDREN

NY —HAMPDEN-BOOTH THEATRE
LIBRARY AT THE PLAYERS, 16
Gramercy Park, New York, 10003. Louis A
Rachow, Librn/Cur
Holdings: // Uncat Mss
Notes: The British Actors Orphanage Fund was
incorporated in Los Angeles, California, in July
1940 "To promote and effect the transfer of male
and female minor orphans of deceased British
actors and actresses from their present home or
homes in Great Britain to America...and to
provide and pay for their complete maintenance,
housing and schooling therein, during the
pendency of the present war between Great Britain
and Germany, to the end that these orphans may be
removed from the horrors and perils of such war.
"The duties and activities of the Fund came to a
successful conclusion in 1946 when forty-eight of
the original fifty-four orphans returned to
England and the remaining six either became self-
supporting or their care was assumed by others.
The collection consists of copies of the charter and
by-laws, minutes, journals and ledgers, children's
travel arrangements, working files and preliminary
and general correspondence for the years
1940–1946 featuring such luminaries as Noel
Coward, Dame May Whitty, Boris Karloff,
Maurice Evans, Cole Porter, Peggy Wood and
Margaret Webster.

WORLD WAR, 1939-1945—ECONOMIC ASPECTS

CA —HOOVER INSTITUTION ON WAR,
REVOLUTION & PEACE, Stanford
University, Stanford, 94305. Milorad M
Drachkovitch, Archivist
Holdings: Mss
Notes: Two collections: (1) Records of the
European Technical Advisers, a private
American advisory organization created to
assist in European reconstruction after
World War I, incl correspondence, reports,
statistics, and financial records, 1919-1923,
relating to railway operation, fuel
production, and other aspects of economic
reconstruction in Austia, Poland,
Czechoslavakia and Yugoslavia. 72 ms
boxes. (2) Papers of John D Montgomery,
political scientist and author, incl mss of
writings, reports, notes, interview sumaries,
and printed matter, 1946-1959, relating to
US aid to South Vietnam and other
southeast Asian countries, economic
conditions in these countries, Japanese and
German public opinion regarding the purge
of wartime leaders after World War II, and
political, social, and economic effects of the
purge on Japan and Germany. 15 ms boxes.

MS —UNIVERSITY OF SOUTHERN
MISSISSIPPI, William David McCain
Graduate Library, Box 5148, Southern Sta,
Hattiesburg, 39406.
Holdings: Cat Mss
Notes: The William M Colmer Papers (1933-
1973) contain records (1944-1946) of the US
House of Representatives' Special
Committee of Postwar Economic Policy and
Planning of which Colmer was chairman.
See also entry under Colmer, William M

NJ —PRINCETON UNIVERSITY, Library,
Manuscript Collection, Nassau St, Princeton,
08540. Jean F Preston, Cur
Holdings: // Cat Mss
Notes: Incl 96 cartons, 30 card-tray files.
The archive of the Committee of Defend
America by Aiding the Allies covers the
period May 1940 to January 1942.

NY —COLUMBIA UNIVERSITY
LIBRARIES, Rare Book & Manuscript
Library, 801 Butler Library, 535 W 114 St,
New York, 10027. Kenneth A Lohf, Librn
Holdings: Mss
Notes: The papers of Professor Carter
Goodrich, economic historian, incl his
papers as chairman of the governing body of
the International Labor Office, 1939-1945;
chief of the United Nations economic
mission in Vietnam, 1955-1956; and special
representative to Bolivia for the Secretary-
General of the United Nations, 1952-1953.
About 28,000 items. Restricted use.

WORLD WAR, 1939-1945—FORCED REPATRIATION

CA —HOOVER INSTITUTION ON WAR,
REVOLUTION & PEACE, Stanford
University, Stanford, 94305. Milorad M
Drachkovitch, Archivist
Holdings: Mss Pix
Notes: Papers of Julius Epstein, journalist,
research associate at the Hoover Institution,
and author of *Operation Keelhaul: The Story
of Forced Repatriation*, incl correspondence,
speeches and writings, clippings,
photographs, and printed matter, 1939-72,
relating to his research on the events of
World War II, communism, forced
repatriation of Russian prisoners of the
Soviet Union followed World War II, Katyn
forest massacres, and unreported deaths of
Soviet Cosmonauts, as well as his efforts to
obtain restricted government documents on
these subjects. 180 ms boxes.

WORLD WAR, 1939-1945—GUERRILLAS see World War, 1939-1945—Underground Movements and Publications

WORLD WAR, 1939-1945—JEWS

MA —BRANDEIS UNIVERSITY, Goldfarb
Library, 415 South St, Waltham, 02154.

WORLD WAR, 1939-1945—JEWS (cont.)

Bessie Hahn, Dir
Notes: JewishResistance Collection:
Contains 21 linear ft of books, periodical
articles and contemporary ephemera
emphasizing the role Jews played in armed
resistance to the Nazi regime. A catalog of
the books is in the Special Colections
Catalog and Main Card Catalog.
Theresienstadt Concentration Camp
Documents: Consists of over 200 "daily
order" bulletins issued by the German
command. Many of them contain lists of
arrival and departure of internees. A finding
list to the documents is located in Special
Collections. No photocopying of the
documents is permitted. Holocaust Survivors
Collection: Consists of 20 linear ft of
recorded interviews with survivors of the
Holocaust, now living in the US. The tapes
are not transcribed and the collection is
unprocessed, but the tapes are arranged
alphabetically by interviewee.

NY —YIVO INSTITUTE FOR JEWISH
RESEARCH, Library & Archives, 1048
Fifth Ave, New York, 10028. Dina
Abramowicz, Librn; Marek Web, Archivist
Holdings: Cat Mss Pix Slides
Notes: Special collection of books and
periodicals, incl goverment publications,
which appeared in Germany between the
years 1933-1945. Extensive library and
archives collections on history of Jews under
Nazi rule in Europe, 1933-1945, in all
languages. Hundreds of memorial volumes
for towns destroyed by Nazis.

WORLD WAR, 1939-1945—LEND-LEASE OPERATIONS see Lend-Lease Operations, 1941-1945

WORLD WAR, 1939-1945—NAVAL OPERATIONS, AMERICAN

HI —PACIFIC SUBMARINE MUSEUM,
Library, Naval Submarine Base, Pearl
Harbor, 96860. Ray W de Yarmin, Cur
Holdings: Vols (1500) Cat Mss Maps Pix
Slides Phonorecords 16mm Films
Budget: ($600)
Notes: Incl 3000 pictures. Extensive missile
and torpedo collection; submarine models;
salvage/deep-sea diver exhibit; Arctic
exploration by submarines Worl War II
submarine components. Research program
for students, authors, lecturers, etc.

MD —US NAVAL ACADEMY, Nimitz
Library, Annapolis, 21402. Alice S
Creighton, Assistant Librn for Special
Collections
Holdings: Vols (22,000) Cat Mss Pix
Notes: Books and periodicals, with emphasis
on seapower. Incl rare and historically
significant works, naval and general history.
US Naval Academy materials (histories,
class albums, Lucky Bags, student
publications, etc), and copies of transcripts
of the Naval Institute's oral history
interviews with US naval officers.
Manuscripts incl 205 volumes of ships' logs,
letterbooks, order books, and watch, station
and quarter bills, 1796-1938; papers of
various naval officers, incl. Vice Admiral
Wilson Brown, Commander George M
Bache, Admiral Harry S Knapp, Lieutenant
Edwin J DeHaven, and others; family
correspondence of Admiral David Dixon
Porter; and several thousand World War II
naval action reports. Approximately 15,000
pictures incl portraits of naval officers,
pictures of US and some foreign ships,
World War II naval news photos and USNA
photographs.

WORLD WAR, 1939-1945—PACIFIC REGION

NE —UNIVERSITY OF NEBRASKA-
LINCOLN, Don L Love Library, Lincoln,
68588. Joseph G Svoboda, University
Archivist
Notes: World War II - Pacific Theater -
Psychological Warfare Collection, 1944-45,

ca 1000 item. Leaflets dropped from US
airplanes, scrapbooks, Japanese propaganda
materials, newspapers published by US
armed forces in the Philippines. Collection
assembled by J Robert Sandberg and Frank
M Hallgren who served in Psychological
Warfare Branch.

RI —US NAVAL WAR COLLEGE, Historical
Collection & Museum, Newport, 02841.
Anthony S Nicolosi, Dir; Evelyn Cherpak,
Cur
Notes: Collections incl over 200,000
separate pieces; chiefly papers of naval
officers and records of organizations
associated with the US Navy, the Naval War
College, the college's major study areas, and
the Navy in the Narragansett Bay region;
oral history collection; Naval War College
Archives, 1884-present; records of
conferences held at the College; newspaper
collections dealing with naval themes and
military conflicts.

WORLD WAR, 1939-1945—PHILIPPINES

DC —AMERICAN HISTORICAL
COLLECTION, US Embassy, Manilla,
Philippines, c/o US Dept of State,
Washington, 20525. Aurora P Galvez, Librn;
Lewis E Gleeck Jr, Cur
Notes: The American Historical Collection is
located at 1201 Roxas Blvd, Metro Manila,
Philippines. Incl the William Cameron
Forbes, Eugene A Perkins Memorial Library,
Leonard Dawson, and Sternberg Collections.
Some Spanish Period materials and much on
later history, espec Commonwealth Period
(except 1942-45). Considerable on Japanese
in World War II and the Japanese-supported
"Philippine Republic" (approx 1946-53), incl
political and trade relations, and on military
bases. Strong on Philippines during the
American period. Collections incl mss,
documents, reports, theses. Library
maintains special picture-file collections.
Also incl bound periodicals published during
the American period 1900-1930. Complete
reports of the Philippine Commission (1900-
1915); reportsof the Governor-General
(1916-1930); High Commissioner Reports
(1931-1935); original minutes and
memoranda of the internees of the US
Internment Camp. Mailing address: OB-442
US Embassy, Roxas Blvd, Manila.

TX —NORTH TEXAS STATE UNIVERSITY,
Archives, NT Station Box 5188, Denton,
76203. Robert LaForte, University Archivist
Notes: Oral History Collection. Incl
interviews with survivors of attack on
Corregidor, Bataan Death March, the "Lost
Battalion", prisoner of war camps. Also
material on guerilla fighting in the
Philippines. Cataloged. Transcriptions
available.

WORLD WAR, 1939-1945—PICTURES, ILLUSTRATIONS, ETC.

CA —HOOVER INSTITUTION ON WAR,
REVOLUTION & PEACE, Stanford
University, Stanford, 94305. Milorad M
Drachkovitch, Archivist
Holdings: Mss
Notes: Newsreels, 1939-1942, produced by
Universum-Film-Aktiengesellschaft (UFA), a
German motion picture company, and
distributed in Spain, relating to military
campaigns and conditions in Germany
during World War II. Incl a few
photographs. In German and Spanish. ca 460
reels.

DC —LIBRARY OF CONGRESS, Prints &
Photographs Div, Washington, 20540.
Notes: 70 photo albums in the Third Reich
Collection. Also, poster collection numbers
about 70,000 American and foreign items
from the 1850s to the present. Incl *Art
Nouveau* of World War I and World War II,
WPA, propaganda, performing arts, and
psychedelic posters.

IL —CHICAGO PUBLIC LIBRARY, Special
Collections Div, Cultural Center, 78 E
Washington St, Chicago, 60602. Laura
Linard, Cur
Holdings: // Cat
Notes: A mint collection of 500 World War

I posters, the greater part of which are from
Great Britain. Several of the posters were
only recently removed from their original
packages, dated 1919, and distributed to
public libraries by the British Information
Service. See *Take Up the Sword of Justice:
An Exhibition of British World War I
Posters from the Special Collections of The
Chicago Public Library*, compiled by Marie
Gecik and Thomas A Orlando, 1976. A
similar collection of World War II posters
(500) is almost exclusively American in
origin.

MN —UNIVERSITY OF MINNESOTA, O
Meredith Wilson Library, 309 19 Ave S,
Minneapolis, 55455. Austin J McLean,
Chief, Special Collections
Holdings: Vols (6000) // Uncat
Notes: Extensive collection of multi-lingual
propaganda pamphlets, political cartoons and
posters. Complete listing available in the
Division.

NY —BUFFALO & ERIE COUNTY PUBLIC
LIBRARY, Rare Book Room, Lafayette Sq,
Buffalo, 14203. William H Loos, Cur
Holdings: // Uncat
Notes: The collection of 3000 posters
consists primarily of World War I posters
with a few from World War II, as well as
some modern posters.

PA —TEMPLE UNIVERSITY LIBRARIES,
Special Collections Dept, Rare Books & Mss
Section, Philadelphia, 19122. Thomas M
Whitehead, Cur
Notes: 3000 posters of World Wars I and II,
and the Vietnam Conflict; US and foreign.
Card guide to World War I posters.

WI —MILWAUKEE PUBLIC LIBRARY, 814
W Wisconsin Ave, Milwaukee, 53233.
Donald J Sager, City Librn
Holdings: Vols 15,000
Notes: Emphsis on historical posters (World
Wars I and II).

WORLD WAR, 1939-1945—REGIMENTAL HISTORIES see World War, 1939-1945—Unit Histories

WORLD WAR, 1939-1945—RESISTANCE MOVEMENTS see World War, 1939-1945—Underground Movements and

WORLD WAR, 1939-1945—UNDERGROUND MOVEMENTS AND PUBLICATIONS

CA —UNIVERSITY OF CALIFORNIA, LOS
ANGELES, Research Library, Western
European Collection, Los Angeles, 90024.
Edward Shreeves, Chairman, Bibliographers
Group; Mary E Greco, Western European
Bibliographer
Holdings: Microforms
Notes: Microfilm records (8 reels) of 51
newspapers and periodicals of the French
Resistance, from 1940 to 1944.

IL —NORTHWESTERN UNIVERSITY,
Library, Special Collections Dept, 1937
Sheridan Rd, Evanston, 60201. R Russell
Maylone, Cur
Holdings: Vols 1100 Cat
Notes: World War II underground
publications especially from the Netherlands,
Denmark and Norway. Other countries
represented: Belgium, Czechoslovakia,
France, Germany, Greece, Italy, Poland,
Remania, Yugoslavia, etc.

MA —BRANDEIS UNIVERSITY, Goldfarb
Library, 415 South St, Waltham, 02154.
Bessie Hahn, Dir
Notes: JewishResistance Collection:
Contains 21 linear ft of books, periodical
articles and contemporary ephemera
emphasizing the role Jews played in armed
resistance to the Nazi regime. A catalog of
the books is in the Special Colections
Catalog and Main Card Catalog.
Theresienstadt Concentration Camp
Documents: Consists of over 200 "daily
order" bulletins issued by the German
command. Many of them contain lists of
arrival and departure of internees. A finding
list to the documents is located in Special

WORLD WAR, 1939-1945—UNDERGROUND MOVEMENTS AND PUBLICATIONS (cont.)

Collections. No photocopying of the documents is permitted. Holocaust Survivors Collection: Consists of 20 linear ft of recorded interviews with survivors of the Holocaust, now living in the US. The tapes are not transcribed and the collection is unprocessed, but the tapes are arranged alphabetically by interviewee.

NY —STATE UNIVERSITY OF NEW YORK AT ALBANY, Library, Special Collections Dept, 1400 Washington Ave, Albany, 12222. Marion P Munzer, Coordr
Notes: Primarily newspaper clippings concerning the German Resistance Movement against Hitler, assembled by Karl Otto Paetel (2 linear feet). Part of the German Exile Collection.
See also entry under Paetel, Karl Otto

NY —NEW YORK PUBLIC LIBRARY, Research Libraries, General Research Division, Fifth Ave & 42 St, New York, 10018. Rodney Phillips, Chief
Holdings: Vols (2,225,000) Cat Maps Pix Microforms
Budget: ($775,718)

WORLD WAR, 1939-1945—UNIT HISTORIES

CA —LOS ANGELES PUBLIC LIBRARY, History Dept, 630 W Fifth St, Los Angeles, 90071. Frank Louch, Sr Librn
Holdings: Vols (9000) Cat Maps
Budget: ($85,000)
Notes: Includes personal narratives, campaigns, diplomatic histories and peace treaties, memoirs of generals and statesmen, official reports and archives of participating countries. Collection of unit histories is particularly strong. There is an emphasis on personal accounts by combatants and noncombatants from all countries. Established as a memorial to Tom Treanor, correspondent for the Los Angeles Times, and includes his World War II writings.
See also entry under Military History.

NY —NEW YORK PUBLIC LIBRARY, Research Libraries, General Research Division, Fifth Ave & 42 St, New York, 10018. Rodney Phillips, Chief
Holdings: Vols (2,225,000) Cat Maps Pix Microforms
Budget: ($775,718)

NC —82ND AIRBORNE DIVISION, War Memorial Museum, Reference Library, Ardennes & Gela Sts, Fort Bragg, 28307. John S Duvall, Chief Cur
Holdings: Vols (300) Uncat Mss Maps Pix
Notes: The collection is intended to be a research tool for persons studying the history of the 82nd Airborne Division and the development of airborne warfare.

†VA —GEORGE C MARSHALL RESEARCH FOUNDATION AND LIBRARY, Drawer 920, Lexington, 24450. Royster Lyle Jr, Cur Collections
Holdings: Vols Cat Mss Maps Pix Phonorecords Audiotapes Films Filmstrips Microforms
Notes: About 400 posters, American, German, French; complete Stars and Stripes for WWII; approx 5000 cataloged photographs, over 5000 uncataloged Office of War information photos, and over 10,000 US Signal Corps photos (uncat). Approx 250 regimental histories, operation reports, and army manuals; published memoirs and letters of Marshall associates; official military histories (American, British); set of 40 books by "Remy" (G Renault-Roulier); over 1200 maps-approx 300 newsmaps, 800 daily situation maps (European Theatre), 37 bound vols of daily situation maps 1944-1945; seven of the Why We Fight series (films). Major ms collections incl the papers of generals George C Marshall, Marshall S Carter, William T Sexton, Lucian Truscott, William R Arnold, Paul M Robinett, Frank McCarthy; Forrest C Pogue; colonels Collas Harris, Francis P Miller, Willilam F Friedman; officers of the Women's Army

Corps. Hearings and government documents. Agency records copied from NARS. Vertical file arranged by subject.

WORLD WAR I see World War, 1914-1918

WORLD WAR II see World War, 1939-1945

WORLD'S COLUMBIAN EXPOSITION, CHICAGO, 1893

IL —CHICAGO HISTORICAL SOCIETY, Library, Clark St at North Ave, Chicago, 60614. Robert L Brubaker, Librn
Holdings: Vols (150,000) Cat Mss Maps Pix Slides
Notes: The Society has nearly everything published concerning the exposition.

IL —CHICAGO PUBLIC LIBRARY, Special Collections Div, Cultural Center, 78 E Washington St, Chicago, 60602. Laura Linard, Cur
Holdings: Vols (300) Cat Mss Pix Slides
Notes: The Chicago Public Library received deposit copies of World's Columbian Exposition publications from the Department of Publicity and Promotion, several of which are still uncataloged and not included in the NUC-Pre 1956 Imprints. The Papers of James W Wellsworth, prominent Chicago financier and member of the Board of Directors of the Exposition, are here; a finding aid to these papers has been prepared. Outstanding items in the World's Columbian collections are described in Treasures of the Chicago Public Library, compiled by Thomas A Orlando and Marie Gecik, 1977, pp 111-20.

IL —MUSEUM OF SCIENCE AND INDUSTRY, Library, 57th St and Lake Shore Dr, Chicago, 60637. Carla Hayden, Coordinator
Holdings: Vols (15,000) Cat Maps Pix Slides
Budget: ($10,000)
Notes: Occupying the site of the Fine Arts Building of Chicago's Columbian Exposition of 1893, the Museum Library has been the recipient of numerous gifts in this field, not only of materials from Chicago's Columbian Expositions, Century of Progress and Railroad Fairs but also from the New York World's Fair, St Louis, Paris Exposition Universelle, San Francisco's Panama-Pacific etc. Incl blueprints of some buildings and areas. No separate catalog or index to this extensive collection.

RI —US NAVAL WAR COLLEGE, Historical Collection & Museum, Newport, 02841. Anthony S Nicolosi, Dir; Evelyn Cherpak, Cur
Holdings: Mss
Notes: Collections incl over 200,000 separate pieces; chiefly papers of naval officers and records of organizations associated with the US Navy, the Naval War College, the college's major study areas, and the Navy in the Narragansett Bay region; oral history collection; Naval War College Archives, 1884-present; records of conferences held at the College; newspaper collections treating with naval themes and military conflicts.

WORLD'S FAIRS see Exhibitions and Expositions

WORLD'S STUDENT CHRISTIAN FEDERATION ARCHIVES

CT —YALE UNIVERSITY, Divinity School Library, 409 Prospect St, New Haven, 06520. John Bollier, Librarian
Holdings: Vols (340,000)
Notes: Collection incl 340,000 vols, 1452 periodical subscriptions, 8500 microforms and 3500 films.

WORM, A. TOXEN

†NY —SHUBERT ARCHIVE, Lyceum Theatre, 149 W 45th St, New York, 10036. Brigitte Kueppers, Archivist
Notes: The vast Shubert Archive, mostly

unexplored is the largest collection in the world representative of the "business" of the theatre. It includes almost all of the Shubert empire's correspondence from the turn of the century to the 1950s, road company records, thousands of playscripts (American and European), set and costume designs, music scores for Shubert productions, business, financial, and legal records, actors' contracts, etc.

WORMS

DC —SMITHSONIAN INSTITUTION LIBRARIES, Natural History Branch, Washington, 20560. Sylvia Churgin, Chief Librn
Holdings: Cat Mss Maps Pix Slides Microforms
Notes: Invertebrate zoology, Systematics. Incl crustacea, echinoderms, mollusks, worms, Cushman collection of foraminifera; Springer collection on crinoids; Wilson collection on copepoda.

IA —IOWA STATE UNIVERSITY, Library, Ames, 50011. Warren B Kuhn, Dean of Library Services
Holdings: Cat
Notes: Extensive serial holdings supplement this strong collection.

PE —AGRICULTURE CANADA, Research Station Library, PO Box 1210, Charlottetown, C1A 7M8, Can. Barrie Stanfield, Librn
Holdings: Vols (2300) Cat
Budget: ($5000)

WORSHIP

†NY —COLGATE ROCHESTER DIVINITY SCHOOL, Ambrose Swasey Library, 1100 S Goodman St, Rochester, 14620.
Notes: Incl general works about worship, its history and practice and contains manuals of worship, liturgies of primarily Protestant denomination, a sizeable collection of hymn books, with particular emphasis upon the Anglican tradition.

NC —SOUTHEASTERN BAPTIST THEOLOGICAL SEMINARY LIBRARY, PO Box 752, Wake Forest, 27587. H Eugene McLeod, Librn
Holdings: Cat Slides Audiotapes Videotapes Microforms

WORSLEY, EDWARD

†CA —UNIVERSITY OF SAN FRANCISCO, Richard A Gleeson Library, The Countess Bernardine Murphy Donohue Rare Book Room, San Francisco, 94117. D Steven Corey, Special Collections Librn
Holdings: Vols (300) Cat
Notes: Largely from the Virtue-Cahill library in England, and the collection of Charles A Fraccihia. Incl important works of Bayly, Cressy, Sergeant, and Worsley. Incl a contemporary manuscript of the trial of Father Garnet, accused of complicity in the Gunpowder Plot.

WORTH, PATIENCE

MO —MISSOURI HISTORICAL SOCIETY, Library, Jefferson Memorial Bldg, Saint Louis, 63112. Stephanie Klein, Librn-Archivist; Peter Michel, Cur of Manuscripts
Notes: A collection of material on 119 women who lived or worked in St Louis and Missouri as educators, artists, and homemakers, or played significant roles in US politics and social reform. Incl Sacajawea, Susan B Anthony, Fannie Hurst, Carry Nation, Patience Worth, etc.

WORTH, WILLIAM

IN —INDIANA UNIVERSITY, Lilly Library, Seventh St, Bloomington, 47405. William R Cagle, Librn
Notes: Ms collections incl editorial and correspondence files of Northwest Review, 1961-67.

WORTIS, JOSEPH, M.D.

NY —NEW YORK ACADEMY OF MEDICINE, Library, 2 E 103 St, New

WORTIS, JOSEPH, M.D. (cont.)

York, 10029. Brett A Kirkpatrick, Librn
Holdings: Uncat
Notes: Over 1000 monographs, pamphlets, journals, correspondence and personal files donated by Dr Joseph Wortis. Represents nearly the entire volume of literature on Russian psychiatry published between 1950 and 1965 in the Russian, German, and English languages.

WOUNDED, FIRST AID TO see First Aid

WOYTINSKY, WLADIMIR S.

MI —UNIVERSITY OF MICHIGAN, Library, Dept of Rare Books & Special Collections, Ann Arbor, 48109. Robert J Starring, Head
Holdings: Vols 69 Uncat Mss Microforms
Notes: Mss, books, pamphlets, reprints, extracts of articles in original editions or photocopies, in various languages, written by Woytinsky between 1905 and 1960. 69 vols, 16 pamphlets boxes and 36 reels of microfilm. Listed in *Bibliography of the Writings of WS Woytinsky*, prepared by Emma S Woytinsky, Washington, DC, 1961.

WPA FEDERAL THEATRE PROJECT see Federal Theatre Project (WPA)

WRANGEL, GEN. PETER

CA —HOOVER INSTITUTION ON WAR, REVOLUTION & PEACE, Stanford University, Stanford, 94305. Milorad M Drachkovitch, Archivist
Holdings: // Mss
Notes: Papers, 1917-1924, of Evgenii Karlovich Miller, chief military representative in Paris of Gen Peter Wrangel, commander-in-chief of the White Russian Forces. Documents relating to the activities of the White Russian forces, consisting chiefly of correspondence of Gen Miller with Wrangle's military representative in various countries. 6 ft.

WRAY, FAY

CA —UNIVERSITY OF SOUTHERN CALIFORNIA, Edward L Doheny Memorial Library, Archives of Performing Arts, University Park, Los Angeles, 90089. Robert Knutson, Librn
Holdings: Mss Pix
Notes: Personal collection of papers, pictures, etc.

WRECKS see Shipwrecks

WRESTLERS see Wrestling and Wrestlers

WRESTLING AND WRESTLERS

IL —NATIONAL COUNCIL OF THE YMCAS, YMCA Historical Library, 6400 Shafer Ct, Rosemont, 60018. Eleanor R Murphy, Librn
Notes: Large collection, incl historical material, on basketball, wrestling, track and field, swimming, diving, scuba and volleyball.
NY —RACQUET & TENNIS CLUB, Library, 370 Park Ave, New York, 10022. Gerald Belliveau, Jr, Librn
Holdings: Vols (14,800) Cat
Notes: Specializes in court tennis, lawn tennis, early American sport. See *Dictionary Catalogue of the Library of Sports in the Racquet and Tennis Club* (Boston: G K Hall, 1971). Also, Robert W Henderson, *Early American Sport*, 3rd ed. (Cranbury, NJ: Fairleigh Dickinson University Press, 1977).
OK —NATIONAL WRESTLING HALL OF FAME, 405 West Hall of Fame Ave, Stillwater, 74075.
Notes: Collection built around collegiate and amateur wrestling, incl Olympic competition, from the late 1890s to the present.

WRIGHT, CARROLL DAVIDSON

†MA —CLARK UNIVERSITY, Robert Hutchings Goddard Library, Worcester,

01610. Dorothy Mosa Kowski, Rare Books Librn
Holdings: Cat Mss Pix
Notes: The papers of Carroll Davidson Wright, first US Commissioner of Labor, establisher of the Bureau of Labor Statistics, distinguished economist and socialist.

WRIGHT, FRANK LLOYD

CA —STANFORD UNIVERSITY LIBRARIES, Cecil H Green Library, Stanford, 94305. Michael T Ryan, Cur
Holdings: Mss
Notes: Manuscript collections pertaining to the architect Frank Lloyd Wright.
IL —NORTHWESTERN UNIVERSITY, Library, Special Collections Dept, 1937 Sheridan Rd, Evanston, 60201. R Russell Maylone, Cur
Holdings: Vols 150 Cat Mss Pix
Notes: Works by and about Frank Lloyd Wright, with blueprints, drawings, letters, mss, photographs, clippings, ephemra.
IL —OAK PARK PUBLIC LIBRARY, 834 Lake St, Oak Park, 60301. Barbara Ballinger, Librn
Notes: Part of Local Authors Collection. Incl books, photographs, correspondence, prints and drawings cataloged.
KS —UNIVERSITY OF KANSAS, Kenneth Spencer Research Library, Special Collections Dept, Lawrence, 66045. Alexandra Mason, Librn
Holdings: Vols 447 Cat Mss Pix Slides
Notes: Two main groups: Willett-Pashley collection (working library of 19th century Chicago architectural firm) ca 800 volumes, cataloged. Frank Lloyd Wright collection (mss, photographs, slides, books, clippings) ca 6 Hollinger boxes, photos, mss and ca 100 magazines and books, uncataloged. Noncirculating.
NY —COLUMBIA UNIVERSITY LIBRARIES, Avery Architectural and Fine Arts Library, 201 Avery Hall, New York, 10027. Angela Giral, Librn
Holdings: Cat Mss Pix
Notes: Incl large collection of his drawings.
WI —MILWAUKEE PUBLIC LIBRARY, 814 W Wisconsin Ave, Milwaukee, 53233. Donald J Sager, City Librn
Holdings: Vols Cat
Notes: Strength in Frank Lloyd Wright material and Prairie School architects. *See also* entry under Architecture.

WRIGHT, JAMES ARLINGTON

NV —UNIVERSITY OF NEVADA, RENO, University Library, Special Collections Dept, Reno, 89557. Robert E Blesse, Head
Holdings: Vols 30 Cat
Notes: Includes individual works by author in all editions including translations; also prefaces, introductions, published correspondence, appearances in anthologies, periodicals, etc. Bibliographical research collection, part of Modern Authors Collection.

WRIGHT, LIN

AZ —ARIZONA STATE UNIVERSITY, Library, Tempe, 85287. Marilyn Wurzburger, Special Collections Librn
Holdings: Vols (108) Pix
Notes: Collection covers various aspects of Children's Theatre from 1944 through the present. Areas of emphasis incl International and National Child Drama Associations, award-winning theatres, educational programs, regional groups and prominent figures in Children's Theatre incl: Irene Vickers Baker, Isabel Burger, Virginia Lee Comer, Rita Criste, Moses Goldberg, Kenneth Graham, Aurand Harris, Paul Kozelka, George Latshaw, Rosemary Musil, Sara Spencer, Winifred Ward, Susan Zeder and Lin Wright. Publications incl newsletters, research papers, bibliographies and records of the proceedings of the Children's Theatre Association of America. 80 linear feet of scripts, documents, publications, films, tapes (oral history) programs, correspondence, photographs,

working papers and clippings. Partially indexed; finding guides available.

WRIGHT, ORVILLE see Wright, Wilbur and Orville

WRIGHT, RICHARD

CT —YALE UNIVERSITY, Beinecke Rare Book & Manuscripts Library, Wall & High St, New Haven, 06520. Louis A Martz, Dir
Holdings: Mss
Notes: The Richard Wright Archive. His papers, etc.
IL —CHICAGO PUBLIC LIBRARY, G Woodson Regional Library, George C Hall Branch, 9525 S Halsted, Chicago, 60628. Steven C Newsome, Cur; Hattie L Power, Regional Library Dir
Holdings: Vols 8000 Cat Mss Audiotapes Microforms
Notes: The Vivian G Harsh Collection on Afro-American History and Literature, in the George Cleveland Hall Branch of the Chicago Public Library, contains books, in print and on microfilm, periodicals, recordings, tapes, pamphlets and mss. Specializes in Afro-Americana, but contains a sizeable number of books on Africa. Also contains these noteworthy items: *The Negro in Illinois: the Illinois Writers Project Files; The Chicago Afro-American Union Analytic Catalog; Big Boy Leaves Home*, by Richard Wright (an original typewritten ms); *The Big Sea*, by Langston Hughes (3 original typewritten mss of this work). 7800 vols on microfilm.
NV —UNIVERSITY OF NEVADA, RENO, University Library, Special Collections Dept, Reno, 89557. Robert E Blesse, Head
Holdings: Vols 53 Cat
Notes: Includes individual works by author in all editions including translations; also prefaces, introductions, published correspondence, appearances in anthologies, periodicals, etc. Bibliographical research collection, part of Modern Authors Collection.
NY —NEW YORK PUBLIC LIBRARY, Schomburg Center for Research in Black Culture, 515 Lenox Ave, New York, 10037. Catherine J Lenix Hooker, Interim Administrator
Holdings: Cat Mss
Notes: Typescripts and mss of his novels and some personal papers.
NC —DUKE UNIVERSITY, William R Perkins Library, Manuscript Dept, Durham, 27706. Ellen Gartrell, Cur of Mss
Holdings: Cat Mss
Notes: Tobacco culture, marketing, trade, especially US South, 19th-20th century, incl papers of Duke Family, Richard H Wright, British-American Tobacco Co, James A Thomas, Edward J Parrish, United Cigarette Machine Co; also tobacco advertising (trade cards, etc).

WRIGHT, SILAS, JR., 1795-1847

NY —SAINT LAWRENCE COUNTY HISTORICAL ASSOCIATION, 3 1/2 E Main St, PO Box 8, Canton, 13617. John A Baule, Dir
Holdings: Vols 500 Uncat Mss
Notes: Papers of Silas Wright, a US Senator, 1833-44, Governor of New York State, 1844-46, and personal friend of Martin Van Buren. Incl personal letters and documents pertaining to his political career as well as his personal life during the 1830s and 1840s.
NY —SAINT LAWRENCE UNIVERSITY, Owen D Young Library, Canton, 13617. Mahlon Peterson, Librn
Holdings: Cat Mss
Notes: Business and personal letters and documents dating from 1816-1847 written by Silas Wright, governor of New York. Also incl some papers of family and friends. Approx 100 items.
NY —CORNELL UNIVERSITY LIBRARIES, Collection of Regional History, Dept of Manuscripts and Univ Archives, Ithaca, 14853.
Notes: Letter, June 17, 1840; 1 item.

WRIGHT, WILBUR AND ORVILLE

DC —LIBRARY OF CONGRESS, Manuscript
Division, Washington, 20540. John C
Broderick, Chief
Notes: Papers; additions, 1977- . Also
photographs.
DC —SMITHSONIAN INSTITUTION,
Archives Div, Washington, 20560. William
W Moss, Archivist
Holdings: Cat Mss Pix
Notes: The Archives holds records of the
Office of the Secretary and of third
Smithsonian Secretary Samuel Pierpont
Langley, documenting his construction of a
flying machine. Other Secretaries' records
incl materialon the Langley-Wright Brothers
controversy, and the National Advisory
Committee for Aeronautics. The Archives
also has records of the National Air and
Space Museum.
†MA —MASSACHUSETTS INSTITUTE OF
TECHNOLOGY, Cambridge, 02139.
Notes: Archival collections and papers at
MIT.
OH —WRIGHT STATE UNIVERSITY,
Greater Miami Valley Research Center,
University Library, Dayton, 45431. Patrick
B Nolan, Head of Archives
Holdings: Vols 75 Pix
Notes: Private papers of the Wright
Brothers. Incl 25 linear ft of private papers
and 3000 photographs.

WRINCH, DOROTHY

MA —SMITH COLLEGE, Sophia Smith
Collection, Women's History Archive,
Northampton, 01063. M E Murdock, Dir
Holdings: Mss
Notes: Papers of Dorothy Wrinch,
crystallographer.

WRITERS see Authors

WPA NEW YORK (CITY) DANCE INDEX see Dance Index

WRITERS, AGRARIAN see Agrarian Writers

WRITING

IL —NEWBERRY LIBRARY, 60 W Walton
St, Chicago, 60610. Diana Haskell, Cur of
Modern Mss
Holdings: Vols (2000) Cat Mss Pix
Notes: Printed writing-books and calligraphic
mss chosen to show the evolution of letter-
forms and their relationship to printing
types. Over 1000 writing-books, probably the
largest collection extant, incl about 200 from
the 16th and 17th centuries. John M Wing
Collection. Also materials on Platt R
Spencer, incl writing specimen books and
about 7000 ms pieces on American
handwriting, espec the Spencerian hand.
IL —NEWBERRY LIBRARY, John M Wing
Foundation on the History of Printing, 60 W
Walton St, Chicago, 60610. Diana Haskell,
Cur of Modern Mss
Holdings: Vols (30,000) Cat Mss
Budget: ($50,000)
Notes: The collection covers printing and
printing history of Western Europe and the
Americas from its invention to the present,
as well as calligraphy. It is particularly rich
in incunabula (about 2000); the works of the
great printers, among others Aldus, Bodoni,
Baskerville, and Rogers. Printed catalog: *A
Dictionary Catalogue.* (Boston G K Hall,
1961); *Supplemented* (1971). Brief
descriptions: James M Wells, "The John M
Wing Foundation of The Newberry Library,"
The Book Collector, VIII, 2 (Summer 1959),
pp 157-162; Lawrence W Towner, *An
Uncommon Collection of Uncommon
Collections* (Chicago: The Newberry Library,
1977). pp 25-26.
PA —FREE LIBRARY OF PHILADELPHIA,
Rare Book Dept, Logan Sq, Philadelphia,
19103. Marie E Korey, Rare Book Librn
Holdings: Vols (5600) Uncat Mss
Notes: A collection of printed writing books

(200), as well as the David N Carvalho
Collection of examples of handwriting from
the 9th to the 20th century.
†VA —GEORGE C MARSHALL
RESEARCH FOUNDATION AND
LIBRARY, Drawer 920, Lexington, 24450.
Royster Lyle Jr, Cur Collections
Holdings: Vols Uncat Maps
Notes: Items on secret writing and signaling,
radar, telephony and telegraphy, and the
study of the Shakespeare-Bacon authorship
controversy.

WRITING (AUTHORSHIP) see Authorship

WRITING—MATERIALS AND INSTRUMENTS

IL —NEWBERRY LIBRARY, John M Wing
Foundation on the History of Printing, 60 W
Walton St, Chicago, 60610. Diana Haskell,
Cur of Modern Mss
Holdings: Vols (26,500) Cat Mss
Budget: ($50,000)
Notes: The collection covers printing and
printing history of Western Europe and the
Americas from its invention to the present.
It is particularly rich in incunabula (about
2000); the works of the great printers,
among others Aldus, Bodoni, Baskerville,
and Rogers. Printed catalog: *A Dictionary
Catalogue...* (Boston: G K Hall, 1961);
Supplements (1981). Brief descriptions:
James M Wells, "The John M Wing
Foundation of the Newberry Library," *The
Book Collector, VIII,* 2 (Summer 1959), pp
157-162; Lawrece W Towner, *An
Uncommon Collection of Uncommon
Collections* (Chicago: The Newberry Library,
1977), pp 25-26.
IL —ORIENTAL INSTITUTE, 1155 E 58th
St, Chicago, 60637. John Larsen, Archivist
Notes: The Bernhard Moritz Collection.
Fine examples of bindings as well as of
Islamic calligraphy and writing materials--
papyrus, parchment, papers, etc. Extensive
collection is also in the Beatty Library in
Dublin, Ireland; Victoria and Albert
Museum in London; Libraries in East and
West Germany.
NY —BUFFALO MUSEUM OF SCIENCE,
Buffalo Society of Natural Sciences,
Research Library, Humboldt Park, Buffalo,
14211. Marcia T Morrison, Chief Librn
Holdings: Vols 900 Cat Mss Pix
Notes: The Elizabeth W Hamlin Oriental
Library of Art and Archaeology. Incl 75
scrolls.
RI —BROWN UNIVERSITY, John Hay
Library, 20 Prospect St, Providence, 02912.
Mark N Brown, Cur Mss
Holdings: Vols (53) //
Notes: Indic Manuscripts Collection--codices
written in Burmese, Cambodian, Telugu
Skandhas, Bengali, and Sinhalese script on
palm leaves, encased within wood covers,
some lacquered. Subjects include: Buddhist
canon, Pali grammar and lexicons, epics,
dance drama, and a treatise on midwifery.
Recorded in *A Census of Indic Manuscripts
in the United States and Canada* compiled
by Horace I Poleman (New Haven:
American Oriental Society, 1938).

WRITING—STUDY AND TEACHING see Penmanship

WRITING AS A PROFESSION see Authorship

WROTH, LAWRENCE C., 1884-1970

†ON —UNIVERSITY OF WESTERN
ONTARIO, School of Library and
Information Science, Special Collections
Room, London, N6A 5B9, Can.
Holdings: Vols 471 Cat
Notes: Books and pamphlets from L Wroth's
personal library.

WUPATKI NATIONAL MONUMENT

AZ —NORTHERN ARIZONA
UNIVERSITY, Special Collection Library,

CU Box 6022, Flagstaff, 86011. Peter M
Whiteley, Coordr/Archivist; William
Mullane, Librn
Notes: J C Clarke Collection;
correspondence between the Department of
the Interior and Clarke when he was
custodian of Wupatki National Monument
near Flagstaff, Ariz. Incl letters from Frank
Pinkley, who was the Superintendent of
Southwestern Monuments, National Park
Service, 1924-1926, 1932.

WURF, JERRY

MI —WAYNE STATE UNIVERSITY, Walter
P Reuther Library, Archives of Labor &
Urban Affairs, Detroit, 48202. Philip Mason,
Dir
Notes: Papers, etc of labor leader Jerry
Wurf.

WYANDOT INDIANS see Huron Indians

WYANT, ALEXANDER

AZ —NORTHERN ARIZONA
UNIVERSITY, Special Collection Library,
CU Box 6022, Flagstaff, 86011. Peter M
Whiteley, Coordr/Archivist; William
Mullane, Librn
Notes: Diary of Alexander Wyant's journey
with photographer Tim O'Sullivan as part of
the Wheeler Expedition through
Northeastern Arizona and Southern Utah
and New Mexico, 1873. Wyant was an
artist.

WYCLIFFE, JOHN

ON —WYCLIFFE COLLEGE, Leonard
Library, 5 Hoskin Ave, Toronto, M5S 1H7,
Can. Adrienne Taylor, Librn; Gayle Ford,
Library Technician
Holdings: Vols (47,000) Cat Microforms
Budget: ($11,000)
Notes: Collection of early and rare books of
prayer books, sermons, Bibles. Basic
reference collection of standard theological
dictionaries, encylopedias, commentaries.
Homiletics collection including 19th century
works. Strong in church history. Evangelical
Anglicanism, English Reformation, Wycliffe
studies.

WYCLYF, JOHN

†IL —UNIVERSITY OF CHICAGO
LIBRARIES, Joseph Regenstein Library,
Dept of Special Collections, 1100 E 57th St,
Chicago, 60637.
Notes: A collection of photostats and
microfilms of 383 medieval mss gathered by
Prof S Harrison Thomson in the course of
his research on Robert Grosseteste and John
Wyclyf. Inventory index of the collection
available.

WYETH, N. C.

DE —DELAWARE ART MUSEUM, Library,
2301 Kentmere Pkwy, Wilmington, 19806.
Anne Hoslam, Librn
Holdings: Vols 150 Cat
Notes: Incl clippings, periodicals,
scrapbooks, etc.
IN —INDIANA UNIVERSITY, Lilly Library,
Seventh St, Bloomington, 47405. William R
Cagle, Librn
Holdings: // Cat
Notes: Children's books, periodicals, etc
illustrated by him and miscellaneous
pictures. Partially cataloged.
MA —NEEDHAM FREE PUBLIC
LIBRARY, 1139 Highland Ave, Needham
Heights, 02194. Vivian D McIver, Dir
Holdings: Vols 114 Cat Pix
Notes: The library has a special NC Wyeth
Room, which displays 9 original oil paintings
and the book and picture collection. Also
incl 12 magazines with illustrations by NC
Wyeth and 7 catalogs of NC Wyeth exhibits.
PA —FREE LIBRARY OF PHILADELPHIA,
Rare Book Dept, Logan Sq, Philadelphia,
19103. Marie E Korey, Rare Book Librn
Holdings: Vols (1000) Cat Mss Pix
Notes: The Thornton Oakley Collection

WYETH, N. C. (cont.)

containing 1000 pieces of original art, autograph letters, and books and periodicals, illustrated by Howard Pyle and his students, incl Maxfield Parish, Frank Schoonover, Jessie Wilcox Smith, and N C Wyeth.

WYLER, WILLIAM

CA —UNIVERSITY OF CALIFORNIA, LOS ANGELES, Theater Arts Library, Los Angeles, 90024. Edward Shreeves, Chairman, Bibliographers Group; Audree Malkin, Head, Theater Arts Library
Notes: William Wyler (director) Collection: scripts in various drafts and versions, photographs, production material, press clippings and correspondence representing his career from the early 1930's through the 1960's. Over thirty 35mm prints.

WYLIE, ELINOR

CT —YALE UNIVERSITY, Box 1603A, Yale Station, New Haven, 06520.
Holdings: Cat Mss Pix
Notes: Incl mss, memoribilia, pictures.
VA —UNIVERSITY OF VIRGINIA, Alderman Library, Clifton Waller Barrett Collection, Charlottesville, 22901. Joan St C Crane, Cur of American Literature Collections
Notes: Papers.

WYLIE, MAX

MA —BOSTON UNIVERSITY, Mugar Memorial Library, Special Collections Dept, 771 Commonwealth Ave, Boston, 02215. Howard B Gotlieb, Dir
Holdings: Cat Mss Pix
Notes: Mss, correspondence, etc collected in depth; incl publications by or about.

WYLLYS, SAMUEL, 1632-1709

RI —BROWN UNIVERSITY, John Hay Library, 20 Prospect St, Providence, 02912. Mark N Brown, Cur Mss
Holdings: // Mss
Notes: Papers of Samuel Wyllys, 1632-1709, Colonial magistrate of Connecticut. A collection of 125 mss, transcripts, and photocopies of legal and government papers relating to Indian affairs, colonial wars, civil and criminal cases, and trials for witchcraft. The witchcraft trails of 1692-1693 are of particular interest as revealed in the Oyer and Terminer Court Records of the witnesses. The Library has one-half (1622-1693) of the original collection which Annmary Brown inherited from her father; the other half (1694-1696) is in the Connecticut State Library.

WYND, OSWALD

MA —BOSTON UNIVERSITY, Mugar Memorial Library, Special Collections Dept, 771 Commonwealth Ave, Boston, 02215. Howard B Gotlieb, Dir
Holdings: Cat Mss
Notes: Mss, correspondence, incl publications by or about.

WYNNE, JUSTIENNE

VA —RANDOLPH-MACON COLLEGE, Walter Hines Page Library, Ashland, 23005. Flavia Reed Owen, Librn
Holdings: Vols 3000
Notes: Collection incl books of Casanova and other minor 18th-century European authors-Ange Goudar, Sara Goudar, Justienne Wynne. Descriptions of collection in *Cassanoviana: An Annotated Bibliography of Jacques Casanova de Seingalt and of Works Concerning Him,* by J Rives Childs (Vienna: C M Nebehay, 1956, for the Casanova Society of Virginia) and in *Casanova Gleanings,* ed by J Rives Childs (Horn, Austria: Ferdinand Berger, 1958-).

WYOMING

UT —UNIVERSITY OF UTAH, Marriott Library, Special Collections, Salt Lake City, 84112. Gregory C Thompson, Cur

WYOMING—GENEALOGY

WY —LARAMIE COUNTY LIBRARY SYSTEM, 2800 Central Ave, Cheyenne, 82001. Ed Byers, County Librn
Holdings: Vols 6000 Cat Microforms
Budget: $1000
Notes: Joint Genealogy Collection (Laramie County Library System and Wyoming State Library).

WYOMING—HISTORY

DC —LIBRARY OF CONGRESS, Prints & Photographs Div, Washington, 20540.
Notes: The John C H Grabill collection of photographs of frontier life in Colorado, South Dakota, and Wyoming, late 19th century, incl views of hunters, prospectors, cowboys, Chinese immigrants, and US Army personnel.
†SD —SOUTH DAKOTA SCHOOL OF MINES & TECHNOLOGY, Devereaux Library, Rapid City, 57701.
Holdings: Vols (3786) Cat Mss Maps Pix Audiotapes Microforms
Notes: This special collection, in general, relates to the Black Hills area of South Dakota and Wyoming, especially mining and exploration of the area; the West River area of South Dakota, primarily county histories; and South Dakota Territorial and State materials. There are also specialized areas of this collection: (1) *Marion N Bruce* Collection. Documents, correspondence, books and periodicals dealing with weather modification in South Dakota; (2) *Mildred Fielder Collection.* Mss, pictures, books and peridocials from an author whose special area was the Black Hills. Most of her work on railroads, mines, trails, etc, related to historical aspects. Collection incl research materials, galley proofs and final copies of her various publications; (3) *Cleophas C O'Harra Collection.* Mss, pictures, books and original source materials, primarily related to the Black Hills area andexpeditions thereto. Much of the data collected for a book on the Black Hills which was never published; and (4) *Caving* Collection. Maps of various caves in Black Hills area, being kept current and updated by members of the Paha Sapa Grotto. Also, some books and periodicals on caving in general.
WY —NATRONA COUNTY PUBLIC LIBRARY, 307 E Second St, Casper, 82601. Jo W Wilbert, Documents/Reference Librn
Holdings: Vols (2048) Cat Mss Maps Pix
Notes: The Wyoming Room houses a collection of materials about Wyoming and/ or by Wyoming authors. The intent is to collect all possible material that relates to Wyoming. Incl city, county, and state documents.
WY —WYOMING STATE ARCHIVES MUSEUMS, AND HISTORICAL DEPARTMENT, Barrett Bldg, Cheyenne, 82002. Philip J Roberts, Documents Supvr; Jean F Brainerd, Research Asst
Holdings: Vols (12,000) Cat Mss Maps
Budget: ($430,000)
Notes: Extensive mss, map, pamphlet, and picture collection relative to Wyoming, regional, and western history. Publish *Annals of Wyoming.*
WY —FREMONT COUNTY LIBRARY, 451 N Second St, Lander, 82520. William J Heuer, Dir
Holdings: Vols 750 Cat Maps
Notes: One of the most extensive Wyoming/ Western Americana collections in the state.
WY —ANNA MILLER MUSEUM LIBRARY, PO Box 698, Newcastle, 82701. Mabel E Brown, Museum Dir
Holdings: Vols (1000) Cat
Notes: The Frank W Mondell Collection (Wyoming Congressman 1892-1922) incl congressional and senate records and reports, reports of government agencies, bound periodicals, law, special subject vols. Supporting materials, local history collection contains materials on Newcastle phase of Mondell career.

WYOMING—MAPS

OK —TULSA CITY-COUNTY LIBRARY, Business & Technology Dept, 400 Civic Center, Tulsa, 74103. Craig Buthod, Head
Notes: Original General Land Office survey maps for the states of Arizona, Arkansas, Colorado, Illinois, Indiana, Idaho, Kansas, Michigan, Missouri, Montana, Nebraska, Nevada, New Mexico, North Dakota, Ohio, Oklahoma, South Dakota, Utah and Wyoming. Incomplete coverage of each state.
WY —WYOMING STATE ARCHIVES MUSEUMS, AND HISTORICAL DEPARTMENT, Barrett Bldg, Cheyenne, 82002. Philip J Roberts, Documents Supvr; Jean F Brainerd, Research Asst
Notes: Extensive ms, map, pamphlet, and picture collection relative to Wyoming, regional, and western history. Publish *Annals of Wyoming.*

WYOMING NEWSPAPERS see
Newspapers, Wyoming

WYZANSKI, CHARLES EDWARD, JR., 1906-

MA —HARVARD UNIVERSITY LIBRARY, Law School Library, Langdell Hall, Cambridge, 02138. Erika S Chadbourn, Cur of Mss
Holdings: Cat Mss
Notes: Personal-professional papers. Typed inventory in repository. Inclusive dates: 1930-1968.

WZLESA, LECH

DC —LIBRARY OF CONGRESS, European Division, Washington, 20540.
Notes: The Library of Congress collection of "Solidarity" and other uncensored Polish materials incl books, periodicals, documents, bulletins, cartoons, and posters, most of which are photocopies of originals held by other libraries.

X

XENAKIS, IANNIS

DC —LIBRARY OF CONGRESS, Music Division, Washington, 20540. Notes: Mss in Koussevitzky Archives.

X-RAY METALLOGRAPHY

KY —UNIVERSITY OF KENTUCKY, Robert E Shaver Library of Engineering, 355 Anderson Hall, Lexington, 40506. Russell H Powell, Engineering Librn
Holdings: Vols (48,000) Cat Microforms

X-RAY PHOTOGRAPHY, MEDICAL see Tomography

X-RAY TECHNICIANS

NH —NEW HAMPSHIRE TECHNICAL INSTITUTE, Paul E Farnum Library, 5 Fan Rd, Concord, 03301. Wm John Hare, Librn
Holdings: Vols 950 Cat Slides Audiotapes
Budget: $1000

X-RAYS—COLLECTIONS

CT —YALE UNIVERSITY, School of Medicine, Dept of Obstetrics & Gynecology Library, Farnam Memorial Bldg, New Haven, 06510.
Holdings: Cat Mss Pix Slides
Notes: X-ray plates, 10,000 slides of monkey and human tissue and about 1000 slides of gynecological and obstetrical pathology, used as teaching and research materials. Other large collections of X-rays and radiotherapy photographs are in the Hunter Radiation Therapy Center.

X-RAYS—HISTORY

MD —MEDICAL & CHIRURGICAL FACULTY OF THE STATE OF MARYLAND, Library, 1211 Cathedral St, Baltimore, 21201. Joseph E Jensen, Librn
Holdings: Vols (10,000) // Cat Mss Maps Pix
See also entry under Medicine - History and Historic

MN —BAKKEN LIBRARY OF ELECTRICITY IN LIFE, 3537 Zenith Ave S, Minneapolis, 55416. John Edward Senior, Dir
Notes: Books (including periodicals, manuscripts, and archival materials) and instrument collection. 1500 instruments (focus-18th and 19th centuries). Relating to the history of electricity.

†NY —MEDICAL RESEARCH LIBRARY OF BROOKLYN, Academy of Medicine of Brooklyn & The State University of New York Downstate Medical Center, 450 Clarkson St, Brooklyn, 11203. Kenneth E Moody, Dir
See also entry under Medicine.

X-RAYS—THERAPEUTIC USE

OH —KETTERING COLLEGE OF MEDICAL ARTS, Learning Resources Center, 3737 Southern Blvd, Kettering, 45429. Edward Collins, Librn
Holdings: Vols 225 Cat Audiotapes Videotapes

XANTHAN GUM

CA —KELCO DIV OF MERCK, Library, 8355 Aero Dr, San Diego, 92123. Ann A Jenkins, Librn
Holdings: Cat Mss Maps Pix Slides Microforms
Notes: Kelco, as the largest producer of algin and xanthan gum in the world, supports a library specialized in the subject of natural gums and polysaccharies, incl all aspects of the suject: chemistry, biology, microbiology, applications (food, industrial, petroleum), etc.

XENIA, OHIO—TORNADO, 1974

OH —GREENE COUNTY DISTRICT LIBRARY, 76 E Market St, PO Box 520, Xenia, 45385. Julie M Overton, Local History Coordr
Holdings: Uncat
Notes: 8 notebooks concerning the killer tornado which hit Xenia, Ohio on April 3, 1974, which is said to be the worst in US history. This material consists of 2 vols of photos, 2 of personal stories, 3 of newspaper clippings arranged according to subject matter, 1 of miscellaneous material from other publications, some national. Also, 10 notebooks called Xenia Rebuilds, clippings concerning all facets of rebuilding from June 1, 1974 to the present, arranged by subject.

XEROGRAPHY

NY —NEW YORK PUBLIC LIBRARY, Rare Books and Manuscripts Div, Fifth Ave & 42 St, New York, 10018. William L Joyce, Asst Dir; Susan E Davis, Cur of Mss
Holdings: Cat Mss Pix
Notes: The personal and scientific papers of Chester F Carlson, inventor of xerography.

NY —XEROX CORP, Technical Information Center, PO Box 305, Webster, 14580. Michael D Majcher, Mgr
Holdings: Vols (30,000) Cat Microforms

XUMA, ALFRED B.

CA —HOOVER INSTITUTION ON WAR, REVOLUTION & PEACE, Stanford University, Stanford, 94305. Peter Duignan, Cur; Karen Fung, Deputy Cur
Holdings: Vols (60,000) Cat Mss Maps Pix Slides Microforms
Notes: Politics, economics, and history from 1870 to the present. About 500 current periodicals titles, about 90 current newspaper titles. Legislative debates, political ephemera. Have microfilm of Portuguese African nationalist material, confidential prints of Great Britian's foreign and colonial offices 1870 through 1922. Nigerian pamphlets (market literature, political and historical tracts), collection of the correspondence pamphlets and ephemera of Alfred B Xuma, collections on Zaire (1955-1963), South African nationalist publications on microfilm. Descriptions of the Collection: African and Middle East Collections pub by Hoover Institute, Handbook of American Resources for African Studies pub by Hoover. Holdings of the Collection in Hoover Institute on War, Revolution, and Peace Library Catalog pub by G K Hall, Emerging Nationalism in Portuguese Africa: A Bibliography pub by Hoover, German Africa pub by Hoover. The Treason Trail in South Africa: A Guide to the Microfilm Record of the Trial pub by Hoover. History of the Library and Archives of the Hoover Institution on War, Revolution and Peace, edited by Peter Duignan (Hoover Institution Press), Guide to Non-federal Archives and Manuscripts in the United States Relating to Africa, compiled Aloha P Smith (East Ardsley, Eng, Microform Ltd).

XYLOGRAPHY see Blockbooks

XYLOPHONE

MD —TOWSON STATE UNIVERSITY, Fine Arts Bldg, Room 457, Towson, 21204. Edwin L Gerhardt, Curator
Notes: The Gerhardt Marimba Xylophone Collection is a unique and comprehensive accumulation of marimba and xylophone lore. It incl literature, phonograph and tape recordings, catalogs, music, methods, pictures, correspondence, personal reminiscences and miscellaneous information. It is not a collection of instruments. A detailed outline is available upon request. Direct all correspondence to the curator, Edwin L Gerhardt, 4926 Leeds Ave, Baltimore, MD 21227, (301) 242-0328.

Y

YACHTS AND YACHTING

CT —YALE UNIVERSITY, Box 1603A, Yale Station, New Haven, 06520.
Notes: Papers of Walter Camp, father of American football and foremost authority on sports and physical fitness. 48 microfilm reels; incl also over 20,000 clippings, etc on sports, providing virtual history, 1866-1925. Published guide to the collection for sale.

FL —MARTIN COUNTY PUBLIC LIBRARY, 701 E Ocean Blvd, Stuart, 33494. LeRoy Hennings Jr, Dir
Holdings: Vols 173 Cat
Notes: Selim Walker McAuthur collection on sailing. The heart of the collection deals with the building of sailing ship models and dates from the 1920s. This material is unique.

MD —MARYLAND HISTORICAL SOCIETY, Library, 201 W Monument St, Baltimore, 21201. William B Keller, Head Librn
Holdings: Maps Pix Films
Notes: Ships and shipping, description and travel, yachts and yachting, sailing, marine transport, Baltimore, and the Port of Maryland. Incl books, periodicals, maps, charts, pictures, ship plans, log books, films, etc.

MA —MASSACHUSETTS INSTITUTE OF TECHNOLOGY MUSEUM, Hart Nautical Collections, 77 Massachusetts Ave, Rm 5-329, Cambridge, 02139. John W Waterhouse, Cur
Holdings: Vols (800) Cat Maps Pix
Notes: Ship and marine engineering development. Museum is under jurisdiction of MIT's Dept of Ocean Engineering. Collection incl various collections of prints and photographs of ships and yachts; working drawings from the Herreshoff Manufacturing Co, 1870-1945, and of the George Lawley and Son Corp; working drawings and models from the Munro, Owen, and Paine Collections.

MA —ABBOT PUBLIC LIBRARY, 235 Pleasant St, Marblehead, 01945. Genevieve A Moloney, Dir
Holdings: Vols 762 Cat

NY —RACQUET & TENNIS CLUB, Library, 370 Park Ave, New York, 10022. Gerald Belliveau, Jr, Librn
Holdings: Vols (17,500) Cat
Budget: ($6000)
Notes: Specializes in court tennis, lawn tennis, early American sport. See *Dictionary Catalogue of the Library of Sports in the Racquet and Tennis Club* (Boston: G K Hall, 1971). Also, Robert W Henderson, *Early American Sport*, 3rd ed. (Cranbury, NJ: Fairleigh Dickinson University Press, 1977).

MB —AQUATIC HALL OF FAME & MUSEUM OF CANADA, Library, 25 Poseidon Bay, Winnipeg, R3M 3E4, Can.
Notes: Aquatic sports, incl swimming, diving, water polo and synchronized swimming. Aquatic memorabilia: records covering Olympics, World Games, Pan-American Games, Commonwealth Games and Canadian Championships; coaching; record books. Collections on sailing and sailing ships, and yachts and yachting, incl books from the Cutty Sark Club of Winnipeg, covering sailing of the past.

YAGATAI LANGUAGE see Jagataic Language and Literature

YAKAMA INDIANS see Yakima Indians

YAKIMA INDIANS

†WA —WASHINGTON STATE UNIVERSITY, Library, Manuscripts, Archives & Special Collections, Pullman, 99164. John F Guido, Head
Holdings: Cat Mss Maps Pix
Notes: The collection is especially rich in documents relating to the exploration, settlement and development of the Palouse County, the Inland Empire, the Columbia Basin and the Pacific Northwest. Described in *Selected Manuscript Resources in the Washington State University Library* (Pullman, 1974); and other published and unpublished inventories and registers.

YAKUT LANGUAGE AND LITERATURE

NY —NEW YORK PUBLIC LIBRARY, Oriental Div, Fifth Ave & 42 St, New York, 10018. E Christian Filstrup, Chief
Holdings: Cat Mss Microforms
Budget: ($56,455)
Notes: Published catalog of holdings.

YALE, WILLIAM

MA —BOSTON UNIVERSITY, Mugar Memorial Library, Special Collections Dept, 771 Commonwealth Ave, Boston, 02215. Howard B Gotlieb, Dir
Holdings: Cat Mss Maps Pix
Notes: Mss, correspondence, etc collected in depth; incl publications by or about.

YAMACRAW INDIANS see Creek Indians

YAMASAKI, MINORU

NY —SYRACUSE UNIVERSITY LIBRARIES, Ernest S Bird Library, George Arents Research Library for Special Collections, Syracuse, 13210. Carolyn A Davis, Manuscripts Librn; Amy S Doherty, University Archivist; Mark F Weimer, Rare Book Librn
Notes: The George Arents Research Library for Special Collections at Syracuse University contains the papers of Harley James McKee, Lorimer Rich, Frederick Lear, Max Abramovitz, James I Arnold, Pietro Bulluschi, Claude Bragdon, Marcel Breuer, William Lescaze, Skidmore Owings & Merrill, Ralph Walker, Eric Fisher Wood, Minoru Yamasaki, Joseph Louis Young, and Archimedes Russell.

YARBOROUGH, WILLIAM

MA —BOSTON UNIVERSITY, Mugar Memorial Library, Special Collections Dept, 771 Commonwealth Ave, Boston, 02215. Howard B Gotlieb, Dir
Holdings: Cat Mss Maps Pix Slides
Notes: Mss, correspondence, etc collected in depth; incl publications by or about.

YATES, EDMUND HODGSON

CA —UNIVERSITY OF CALIFORNIA, LOS ANGELES, Research Library, Dept of Special Collections, 405 Hilgard Ave, Los Angeles, 90024. Edward Shreeves, Chairman, Bibliographers Group; David S Zeidberg, Head
Holdings: Vols 15
Notes: Incl diary and correspondence.

YATES, ELIZABETH

KS —EMPORIA STATE UNIVERSITY, William Allen White Library, Emporia, 66801. Mary E Bogan, Special Collections Librn
Holdings: Uncat Mss Pix Audiotapes
Notes: This collection honors Elizabeth Yates, the distinguished author, who was the recipient of the first William Allen White Children's Book Award. The galley proofs, page proofs and manuscript for *Amos Fortune, Free Man,* for which the first White Award in 1953 was given. Manuscript, page proofs and research materials as well as original art work by Nora S Unwin for *Prudence Crandall, Woman of Courage.* Photographs, articles and sound recordings are also part of this collection which commemorates Elizabeth Yates' visits to Emporia in 1953 as the first recipient of the William Allen White Children's Book Award and in 1977 on the occasion of the 25th anniversary of the White Award. Not cataloged but an inventory has been prepared. Two volumes.

MA —BOSTON UNIVERSITY, Mugar Memorial Library, Special Collections Dept, 771 Commonwealth Ave, Boston, 02215. Howard B Gotlieb, Dir
Holdings: Cat Mss Pix
Notes: Mss, correspondence, etc collected in depth; incl publications by or about.

YATES, PETER

CA —UNIVERSITY OF CALIFORNIA, SAN DIEGO, Central University Library, Mandeville Dept of Special Collections, La Jolla, 92093. Lynda Corey Claassen, Head
Notes: Manuscript Collection incl the correspondence and writings of composer Ernst Krenek and musicologist Peter Yates.

YAWS

RI —BROWN UNIVERSITY, John Carter Brown Library, Providence, 02912. Norman Fiering, Librn; Everett C Wilkie Jr, Bibliographer; Susan Danforth, Cur Maps & Prints

YEARBOOKS

CA —FIRST INTERSTATE BANK, Athletic Foundation, 2141 W Adams, Los Angeles, 90018. W R Schroeder, Managing Dir
Notes: One of the most extensive library and museum collections relating to sports, the Olympic Games, etc. Bound vols of sports sections from several newspapers. Large collection of college and university annuals and yearbooks; souvenir publications from amateur, college, and professional sporting events. Also, large museum collection of sports memorabilia, ledger of halls of fame with thousands of names of outstanding athletes in all sports. Repository for the Association of Sports Museums and Halls of Fame. Noncirculating.

YEAST

NY —ROCKEFELLER UNIVERSITY, Rockefeller Archive Center, Hillcrest, Pocantico Hills, North Tarrytown, 10591. Joseph W Ernst, Dir; J William Hess, Assoc Dir
Notes: Papers of Edward L Tatum, Rockefeller University professor. Conducted research in the genetics and metabolism of bacteria, yeasts, and molds. In 1958, he was joint recipient, with Joshua Lederberg and George Beadle, of the Nobel Prize in medicine and physiology.

YEASTS see Yeast

YEATON, IVAN D., 1906-

CA —HOOVER INSTITUTION ON WAR, REVOLUTION & PEACE, Stanford University, Stanford, 94305. Milorad M Drachkovitch, Archivist
Notes: Papers of Ivan D Yeaton, Colonel, US Army; Military Attache in Moscow, 1939-41; Commanding Officer of the Yenan Observer Group in China, 1945-1946; incl drafts and final copy of his memoirs, reports, memoranda, correspondence, orders and citations, charts, photographs, and other material, 1919-76, relating to Soviet military strength in 1941; US-Soviet relations, 1941-49; organization of US military intelligence during World War II; lend-lease operations; US relations with the Chinese communists, 1944-46; and the inspection of US Army procurement contracts, 1952-53. 2 ms boxes, 7 envelopes.

YEATS, ELIZABETH

CA —UNIVERSITY OF CALIFORNIA, SAN DIEGO, Central University Library, Mandeville Dept of Special Collections, La Jolla, 92093. Lynda Corey Claassen, Head
Holdings: Cat Mss
Notes: Complete set of Cuala Press books. Many manuscript letters between Elizabeth Yeats and R Ellis Roberts.

YEATS, JACK BUTLER

†NC —WAKE FOREST UNIVERSITY, Z
Smith Reynolds Library, Box 7777, Reynold
Sta, Winston-Salem, 27109. Richard J
Murdoch, Rare Book Librn
Holdings: Cat
PA —BUCKNELL UNIVERSITY, Ellen
Clarke Bertrand Library, Lewisburg, 17837.
Ann de Klerk, Librn
Holdings: Cat Mss
BC —UNIVERSITY OF VICTORIA,
McPherson Library, Victoria, V8W 3H5,
Can.
Notes: 1871-1957. Incl 52 pages;
photocopies: 19 pages, 1888-1942; menu
cards (1888); letters to Sarah Purser (1888-
89); miscellaneous humorous sketches;
sketchbook for *La La Noo* (1942).
Photocopied letters to Mr Quinn.

YEATS, JOHN BUTLER, 1839-1922

BC —UNIVERSITY OF VICTORIA,
McPherson Library, Victoria, V8W 3H5,
Can.
Notes: Incl 26 pages, 1844-1922; pencil and
ink sketches (1884-85); letters to Jack Butler
Yeats (1918-1922).

YEATS, WILLIAM BUTLER, 1865-1939

CA —CLAREMONT COLLEGES, Honnold
Library, Ninth & Dartmouth, Claremont,
91711. Tania Rizzo, Special Collections
Dept Head
Holdings: Vols (1300) // Uncat
Notes: The William W Clary Collection.
First, limited, and special editions of books,
pamphlets. offprints by or about him.
Restricted use.
CA —UNIVERSITY OF CALIFORNIA,
DAVIS, Shields Library, Dept of Special
Collections, Davis, 95616. Donald Kunitz,
Head; C Danial Elliott, Asst Head
Holdings: Vols 75 Cat
Notes: A representative collection of rare
and first editions.
CA —UNIVERSITY OF CALIFORNIA, SAN
DIEGO, Central University Library,
Mandeville Dept of Special Collections, La
Jolla, 92093. Lynda Corey Claassen, Head
Holdings: Vols 375 Cat
Notes: His first editions and press books.
CA —UNIVERSITY OF CALIFORNIA, LOS
ANGELES, William Andrews Clark
Memorial Library, 2520 Cimarron St, Los
Angeles, 90018.
Holdings: Cat Mss
Notes: Extensive collection, first editions,
etc.
CA —UNIVERSITY OF CALIFORNIA,
SANTA BARBARA, Library, Dept of
Special Collections, Santa Barbara, 93106.
Christian F Brun, Head
CT —CONNECTICUT COLLEGE, Library,
Mohegan Ave, New London, 06320. Brian
Rogers, College Librn
Holdings: Cat
Notes: Cuala Press and first editions.
DE —UNIVERSITY OF DELAWARE, Hugh
M Morris Library, S College Ave, Newark,
19711. T Stuart Dick, Special Collections
Notes: Extensive Yeats holdings, incl a
collection of personal correspondence which
features 67 unpublished letters and telegrams
written in 1931-39 to Swami Shri Purohit, an
Indian mystic, who with Yeats cotranslated
the *Upanishads* into English.
GA —EMORY UNIVERSITY, Robert W
Woodruff Library, Special Collections Dept,
Atlanta, 30322. Linda M Matthews, Head
Special Collections; Virginia J H Cain,
Processing Archivist; Richard H F
Lindemann, Reference Archivist
Holdings: Vols Cat Mss Pix
Notes: A collection of mss, letters, and
books of William Butler Yeats, most from
the library of Lady Gregory. Incl the play
The Unicorn From the Stars and an
autographed ms of the poem "On a Child's
Death."
See also entry under Gregory Family
IL —SOUTHERN ILLINOIS UNIVERSITY,
CARBONDALE, Delyte W Morris Library,

Special Collections Dept, Carbondale, 62901.
David V Koch, Cur of Special Collections;
Louisa Bowen, Cur of Manuscripts
Holdings: Vols 400 Cat Mss Pix
Notes: Collected papers, 1894-1935, incl 32
letters and mss of essays, speeches, plays,
and poetry. One linear foot. Inventory
available at library. There are 99 additional
letters in the collection of personal papers of
Lennox Robinson at the Library.
IL —NEWBERRY LIBRARY, 60 W Walton
St, Chicago, 60610. Diana Haskell, Cur of
Modern Mss
Holdings: Cat Mss
Notes: Almost all first editions and many
later ones.
IL —NORTHWESTERN UNIVERSITY,
Library, Special Collections Dept, 1937
Sheridan Rd, Evanston, 60201. R Russell
Maylone, Cur
Holdings: Vols 258 Cat Mss
Notes: First editions, works about. Incl
letters to Lady Gregory and 79 vols from the
personal library of Joseph Hone, one of
Yeat's earliest biographers. Complete
collection of Cuala Press books.
IN —INDIANA UNIVERSITY, Lilly Library,
Seventh St, Bloomington, 47405. William R
Cagle, Librn
Holdings: Vols 400 Cat Mss
Notes: First editions, etc.
KS —UNIVERSITY OF KANSAS, Kenneth
Spencer Research Library, Special
Collections Dept, Lawrence, 66045.
Alexandra Mason, Librn
Holdings: Vols 500 Cat Mss
Notes: Based on P S O'Hegarty's collection.
All first editions save *Mosada*; later editions,
periodicals, association material; Yeats-
Bullen correspondence and Yeats family
correspondence. Noncirculating. Described
in Black, Hester M, *William Butler Yeats, a
Catalogue of an Exhibition from the P S
O'Hegarty Collection in the Univeristy of
Kansas Library,* Lawrence, 1966.
KY —UNIVERSITY OF LOUISVILLE,
Ekstrom Library, Rare Books & Special
Collections, 2301 S Third St, Louisville,
40208. George T McWhorter, Cur; Delinda
Stephens Buie, Asst Cur
Holdings: Vols 3000 Cat
Budget: $1000
Notes: The Richard M Kain Collection.
Literary first editions of Joyce, Yeats, A E,
Lady Gregory and others; cultural and
political documents; mss; periodical runs;
clippings and related materials. Catalog in
progress.
MA —UNIVERSITY OF MASSACHUSETTS
AT AMHERST, Library, Amherst, 01003.
Siegfried Feller, Assoc Dir for Collection
Development
Holdings: Cat
Notes: The Russell K Alspach Collection of
first editions, etc, comprising 375 vols and
200 pamphlets, photocopies, etc. Cataloged
(except magazine appearances, which are
noted in a copy of Wade, third ed).
MA —HARVARD UNIVERSITY LIBRARY,
Houghton Library, Cambridge, 02138.
Rodney G Dennis, Cur of Manuscripts
Holdings: Cat Mss
MI —UNIVERSITY OF MICHIGAN, Library,
Dept of Rare Books & Special Collections,
Ann Arbor, 48109. Robert J Starring, Head
Holdings: Cat Mss
NY —CITY UNIVERSITY OF NEW YORK,
City College, Morris R Cohen Library,
North Academic Center, Convent Ave &
137th St, New York, 10031. Barbara J
Dunlap, Archivist
Holdings: // Cat
Notes: First editions. Restricted use.
NY —STATE UNIVERSITY OF NEW
YORK, STONY BROOK, Center for
Contemporary Arts & Letters, Yeats
Archives, Stony Brook, 11794. Lewis
Lusardi, Archives Administrator; Narayan
Hedge, Cur
Holdings: Vols 33 Microforms
Notes: The William Butler Yeats Archives.
The official archives, approved by the Estate
of W B Yeats. Partially cataloged.
†NC —WAKE FOREST UNIVERSITY, Z
Smith Reynolds Library, Box 7777, Reynold
Sta, Winston-Salem, 27109. Richard J
Murdoch, Rare Book Librn
Holdings: Vols 343 Cat

PA —BRYN MAWR COLLEGE, Canaday
Library, Bryn Mawr, 19010. James Tanis,
Dir
Notes: Rare books in the Adelman
Collection.
PA —BUCKNELL UNIVERSITY, Ellen
Clarke Bertrand Library, Lewisburg, 17837.
Ann de Klerk, Librn
Holdings: Cat Mss
Notes: Includes books and letters.
PA —CARLOW COLLEGE, Grace Library,
Fifth Ave, Pittsburgh, 15213. Joan M
Mitchell, Dir of Library Services
Holdings: Vols 543 // Cat Phonorecords
Audiotapes
Notes: The Gladys Wholey Curran
Collection, which consists primarily of titles
in the area of Irish Literature, specifically
those titles concerned with the study of the
Irish playwrights and poets. The collection is
particularly strong in volumes related to the
study of Jonathan Swift, John M Synge, and
William B Yeats. In addition, there is
notable focus upon Irish history of the 17th
and 18th centuries. No photocopying.
WA —UNIVERSITY OF WASHINGTON
LIBRARIES, Suzzallo Library, Special
Collections Division, Rare Book Collection,
FM-25, Seattle, 98195. Gary Menges,
Coordinator for Special Collections
Notes: Extensive collection; includes first
editions.
BC —UNIVERSITY OF VICTORIA,
McPherson Library, Victoria, V8W 3H5,
Can.
ON —QUEEN'S UNIVERSITY, Douglas
Library, Kingston, K7L 5C4, Can. William F
E Morley, Cur, Special Collections
Holdings: Vols 6980 Cat Mss Pix
Notes: Subject strength of the collections.
Incl all the original volumes in the Cuala
Press series and a facsimile reprint of each
plus about 170 other works by and about W
B Yeats, 200 by and about James Joyce, 240
by and about G B Shaw.
ON —UNIVERSITY OF TORONTO, Thomas
Fisher Rare Book Library, 120 Saint George
St, Toronto, M5S 1A5, Can. Richard G
Landon, Head
Holdings: Vols (5200) Cat
Notes: DeLury Collection named for original
donor, Alfred DeLury, Dean of Arts,
University of Toronto. Centered on works of
W B Yeats and his circle. Especially good
holdings of the Yeats family. A E, Lady
Gregory, and J M Synge. Incl extensive
holdings of many of the minor writers.

YEATS FAMILY

CA —MILLS COLLEGE LIBRARY, Oakland,
94613. Steven P Pandolfo, Librn
Holdings: Vols (65) Cat Mss
Notes: Books and ephemera from the Cuala
Press; ms correspondence between Albert M
Bender and the Yeats family.

YELLOW FEVER

CT —YALE UNIVERSITY, Medical Historical
Library, Klebs Collection, 333 Cedar St,
New Haven, 06520. Ferenc A Gyorgyey,
Librn
Notes: The Arnold Carl Klebs Medical
Collection books, pamphlets, etc, incl the
library of his father, Edwin T A Klebs,
pathologist. Strong in bibliography of early
printed medical books, herbals, plague tracts,
inoculation, vaccination and tubercular
diseases.
LA —LOUISIANA STATE UNIVERSITY,
Medical Center Library, 1542 Tulane Ave,
New Orleans, 70112. John P Ische, Dir, Div
of Libraries
Holdings: Vols 300 Cat
Notes: Incl the Yellow Fever Collection.
NY —UNIVERSITY OF ROCHESTER,
School of Medicine and Dentistry, Edward
G Miner Library, 601 Elmwood Ave,
Rochester, 14642. Lucretia McClure,
Medical Librn; Janet Brady Berk, History of
Medicine Librn
Notes: Strong in yellow fever, cholera,
orthopaedics, anatomy and original historic
medical photographs.
OH —CLEVELAND MEDICAL LIBRARY
ASSOCIATION/CASE WESTERN

YELLOW FEVER (cont.)

RESERVE UNIVERSITY, Cleveland Health Sciences Library, Historical Division, Allen Memorial Medical Library, 11000 Euclid Ave, Cleveland, 44106. Glen Jenkins, Rare Book Librarian & Archivist
Notes: Incl 15,000 historical vols, 6000 in the supporting collection. Incl about 1000 16th-18th century titles. Strength of collection: diseases, epidemiology, anatomy, surgery, medicine, obstetrics, gynecology, pediatrics and yellow fever. Incl also medical Americana, listed in Robert B Austin *Early American Medical Imprints,* 1668-1820 (Washington, DC, HEW, Public Health Service, 1961) and ca 7000 19th century works. Our total medical Americana collection also incl journals (not counted), mss and archives (900 linear ft) and 5000 pictures, especially of the Western Reserve. Anatomical works discussed in I Ebner and G Jenkins *Skeletons in Our Closet* (Cleveland, Cleveland Health Sciences Library, 1983)

PA —COLLEGE OF PHYSICIANS OF PHILADELPHIA, Library, 19 S 22 St, Philadelphia, 19103. Christine Ruggere, Cur, Historical Collections
Holdings: Vols (316,223) Cat Mss
Budget: ($1,096,557)
Notes: Very strong collection.
See also entry under Medicine

RI —BROWN UNIVERSITY, John Carter Brown Library, Providence, 02912. Norman Fiering, Librn; Everett C Wilkie Jr, Bibliographer; Susan Danforth, Cur Maps & Prints
Notes: Works by European and American physicians or scientists before 1835 dealing with diseases of warm climates or the tropics (ie, yellow feaver, yaws, dry belly-ache, etc).

TX —UNIVERSITY OF TEXAS, DALLAS, Health Science Center, Reference Dept & History of Health Sciences Dept, 5323 Harry Hines Blvd, Dallas, 75235. Helen Mayo, Head
Holdings: Vols (10,000) Cat Pix Slides Audiotapes Videotapes Microforms
Notes: History of Medicine collection contains ca 10,000 vols. This total is comprised of pre-1900 journals, primary materials in the History of Medicine and the History of Science, and secondary studies in these two areas. The major strengths of this collection are in the areas of epidemics and plagues, military medicine, and collected works of famous medical pioneers. Incl in this collection are the medical journals published by the county medical societies in Texas, local publications by Dallas County medical organizations, and ephemeral material in a similar vein. The university archives contain all theses and dissertations form UTHSCD and miscellaneous institutional documents circulated by the school's administration.

VA —UNIVERSITY OF VIRGINIA, Claude Moore Health Sciences Library, Charlottesville, 22901.
Holdings: // Mss
Notes: The Philip S and Mary K Hench Collection.

YELLOWBACKS (FICTION)

GA —EMORY UNIVERSITY, Robert W Woodruff Library, Atlanta, 30322. Herbert Johnson, Dir
Holdings: Vols (650,000) Cat Mss Microforms
Notes: Strong in 18th and 19th century literature, especially 19th century prose fiction, incl first editions and "yellow backs." Also incl the Kemp Malone collection of Old English, Middle English, Anglo-Norman and supporting materials.

KS —UNIVERSITY OF KANSAS, Kenneth Spencer Research Library, Special Collections Dept, Lawrence, 66045. Alexandra Mason, Librn
Holdings: Cat Mss
Notes: Strongest in 18th and 19th century. Old English (Clubb Collection); 18th-century plays, poems, sermons. English Poetical

Miscellanies collection. Literary periodicals and newspapers (18th century). Noncirculating.

UT —BRIGHAM YOUNG UNIVERSITY, Harold B Lee Library, Unversity Hill, Provo, 84602. Sterling Albrecht, Dir
Holdings: Vols 9000 Mss
Notes: A large collection covering all phases of literature and life in the Age of Queen Victoria. Incl an unusual collection of "Yellow Backs" (1759 printer's proofs for yellow-back covers of original paperbacks of the 19th century).

YELLOWSTONE NATIONAL PARK—HISTORY

MT —MONTANA STATE UNIVERSITY, Library, Bozeman, 59717. Minnie Ellen Paugh, Special Collections Libm
Holdings: Vols 7000
Notes: The bulk of the collection belonged to Jack Ellis Haynes, official Yellowstone Natl Park Historian. Supplemented by collection of James G Hamilton, who wrote an early history of the Park and was President of Montana State University. 7000 vols, restricted.

†WA —WASHINGTON STATE UNIVERSITY, Library, Manuscripts, Archives & Special Collections, Pullman, 99164. John F Guido, Head
Holdings: Cat Mss Maps Pix
Notes: The Carl Parcher Russell papers, a vast resource (24,916 items; 45 linear feet) on American Indian and Western pioneer activities and artifacts. Much on the fur trade; pioneer life; mountain men and trapping; wildlife; primitive life in detail. Also the National Park Service, parks, monuments, etc. Described in *Carl Parcher Russell: An Indexed Register of His Scholarly and Professional Papers, 1920-1967, in the Washington State University* Library (Pullman, 1970), 149 pp.

YEMEN, NORTH see Yemen Arab Republic (North Yemen)

YEMEN, SOUTH

CA —HOOVER INSTITUTION ON WAR, REVOLUTION & PEACE, Stanford University, Stanford, 94305. Peter Duignan, Cur; Karen Fung, Deputy Cur
Holdings: Vols (100,000)
Notes: For full description of collection, see Hoover Institution entry under Near East.

VA —UNIVERSITY OF VIRGINIA, Alderman Library, Manuscripts Dept, Charlottesville, 22901. Edmund Berkeley Jr, Cur
Holdings: Cat Mss Pix
Notes: Papers of J Rives Childs, foreign sevice officer in Saudi Arabia, Yemen, Ethiopia, and Morocco, and Casanova scholar.

YEMEN ARAB REPUBLIC (NORTH YEMEN)

CA —HOOVER INSTITUTION ON WAR, REVOLUTION & PEACE, Stanford University, Stanford, 94305. Peter Duignan, Cur; Karen Fung, Deputy Cur
Holdings: Vols (100,000)
Notes: For full description of collection, see Hoover Institution entry under Near East.

YERBY, FRANK

MA —BOSTON UNIVERSITY, Mugar Memorial Library, Special Collections Dept, 771 Commonwealth Ave, Boston, 02215. Howard B Gotlieb, Dir
Holdings: Cat Mss Pix
Notes: Mss, correspondence, etc collected in depth; incl publications by or about.

YERKES, ROBERT MEARNS, 1876-1956

CT —YALE UNIVERSITY, Box 1603A, Yale Station, New Haven, 06520.
Holdings: Cat Mss Pix
Notes: Materials by and about; 28 filing drawers.

YEZIERSKA, ANZIA, 1885-1970

MA —BOSTON UNIVERSITY, Mugar Memorial Library, Special Collections Dept, 771 Commonwealth Ave, Boston, 02215. Howard B Gotlieb, Dir
Holdings: // Cat Mss
Notes: Mss, correspondence, etc collected in depth; incl publications by or about.

YGLESIAS, JOSE

MA —BOSTON UNIVERSITY, Mugar Memorial Library, Special Collections Dept, 771 Commonwealth Ave, Boston, 02215. Howard B Gotlieb, Dir
Holdings: Cat Mss
Notes: Mss, correspondence, etc collected in depth; incl publications by or about.

YIDDISH AMERICAN NEWSPAPERS see Newspapers, Yiddish American

YIDDISH LANGUAGE AND LITERATURE

CA —JUDAH L MAGNES MEMORIAL MUSEUM, Morris Goldstein Library, 2911 Russell St, Berkeley, 94705. Jane Levy, Archivist
Holdings: Vols 7000 Cat Mss Maps 16mm Films
Notes: Judaica, incl Hebrew manuscripts, Yiddish literature, and Jewish music and art.

CA —LOS ANGELES PUBLIC LIBRARY, Foreign Languages Dept, 630 W Fifth St, Los Angeles, 90071. Sylva Manoogian, Principal Librn
Holdings: Vols 5299 Cat
Budget: ($41,500)

CA —UNIVERSITY OF CALIFORNIA, LOS ANGELES, Research Library, Jewish Studies Collection, 405 Hilgard Ave, Los Angeles, 90024. Edward Shreeves, Chairman, Bibliographers Group; Shimeon Brisman, Jewish Studies Bibliographer
Holdings: Vols (100,000) Cat Mss Microforms

DC —LIBRARY OF CONGRESS, African and Middle Eastern Division, Washington, 20540.
Holdings: Cat Mss Microforms
Notes: Hebraica: about 109,000 vols in Hebrew, Yiddish, Judeo-Arabic, Judeo-Persian, Ladino, Syriac, Ethiopic; espec strong in Biblical subjects, responsa literature, and socio-political aspects.

FL —UNIVERSITY OF FLORIDA LIBRARY, Isser and Rae Price Library of Judaica, 18 Libr East, Gainesville, 32611. Robert Singerman, Head Librn
Budget: ($30,000)
Notes: Total holdings estimated at 55,000 vols dealing with the political, social, economic and intellectual history of the Jews in the ancient, medieval and modern periods and in all geographic areas. The following areas are especially well represented by printed matter in all relevant languages: Bibliography, Festschriften, History, Bible, Judaism and Jewish theology, liturgy, responsa, rabbinical literature, Jewish law, Hebrew language and literature, Yiddish language and literature, anti-semitism, Zionism, Palestine and the *Yishuv,* and the State of Israel. German and American Judaica form a collecting emphasis with holdings for all the standard histories as well as histories of individual synagogues, institutions and local communities. Works in Hebrew and Yiddish comprise about 60 percent of the collection (estimated 30,000 vols). With few exceptions, holdingsare limited to nineteenth and twentieth century imprints, with complete sets of journals and thousands of ephemeral pamphlets, many of them commemorating anniversaries, enhancing the research value of the collection, the largest Judaica research library in the southeastern United States. Only about half of the collection is cataloged; the collection is a circulating one and vols may be borrowed on interlibrary loan. Incl the Leonard C Mishkin Collection

YIDDISH LANGUAGE AND LITERATURE (cont.)

(40,000 vols), the largest personal Judaica collection in the United States, the Shlomo Marenof Collection (3500 vols), and the inventory of Bernard Morgenstern's Lower East Side Book Store (8000 vols). Scholars should inquire in advance of their visit. *The Isser and Rae Price Library of Judaica* Report (circulation 2900 copies) is mailed gratis twice a year to all interested parties. Special catalogs:Pre-1881 Hebrew imprints recorded in a chronological card file.

†MA —HARVARD UNIVERSITY LIBRARY, Widener Library, Judaica Collection, Room M, Cambridge, 02138. Charles Berlin, Bibliographer
Holdings: Vols 12,000 Cat
Notes: Incl 12,000 vols in Yiddish, plus related items. *Catalogue of Hebrew Books* (6 vols) published by Library in 1968, with 3-vol supplement in 1972. See also *Jewish Book Annual*, XXVI (1968/9); pp 58-63, and *Harvard Alumni Bulletin*, XXXI (1929): pp 843-853.

MA —BRANDEIS UNIVERSITY, Goldfarb Library, 415 South St, Waltham, 02154. Bessie Hahn, Dir
Holdings: Microforms
Budget: ($20,000)
Notes: The library maintains a title catalog for materials in Hebrew and Yiddish. At present there are about 100,000 volumes of Judaica (incl Hebrew and Yiddish).

NY —HEMPSTEAD PUBLIC LIBRARY, Foreign Language Collection, 115 Nichols Court, Hempstead, 11550. Irene A Duszkiewicz, Dir
Notes: Mainly French, German, Italian, Spanish, Polish, Yiddish, Hebrew. Holdings in other languages, including Asian.

NY —JEWISH BRAILLE INSTITUTE OF AMERICA, 110 E 30St, New York, 10016. Richard Borgersen, Library Dir
Holdings: Vols (50,000) Cat Audiotapes
Budget: ($75,000)
Notes: A worldwide circulating library of English and Hebrew Braille, English, Hebrew and Yiddish tape talking books and English, Hebrew large type books. All books sent free of charge. Loan period 90 days.

†NY —JEWISH THEOLOGICAL SEMINARY OF AMERICA LIBRARY, 3080 Broadway, New York, 10027.

NY —NEW YORK PUBLIC LIBRARY, Donnell Foreign Language Library, 20 W 53 St, New York, 10019. Bosiljka Stevanovic, Supvr Librn
Holdings: Vols 698 Cat
Notes: Yiddish collection incl Yiddish authors of Yiddish expression. No separate catalog.

NY —NEW YORK PUBLIC LIBRARY, Jewish Division, Fifth Ave & 42 St, New York, 10018. Leonard S Gold, Chief
Holdings: Vols (200,000) Cat Mss Microforms
Budget: ($33,383)
Notes: A collection of material in all languages on Judaism, Jewish history, literature and traditions from the earliest times to date and works in the Hebrew alphabet (mainly Hebrew and Yiddish) on a variety of subjects. The division has extensive files of Jewish periodicals and newspapers. The collection of rare Hebraica incl medieval texts, cabalistic works, ethical and philosophical tracts in book form. See *Dictionary Catalog of the Jewish Collection* (Boston: G K Hall, 1960), 14 vols. First Supplement (Boston: G K Hall, 1975), 8 vols.

NY —YIVO INSTITUTE FOR JEWISH RESEARCH, Library & Archives, 1048 Fifth Ave, New York, 10028. Dina Abramowicz, Librn; Marek Web, Archivist
Holdings: Vols 315,000 Mss Maps Pix Slides
Notes: The most extensive collection in existence of Yiddish books and periodicals. Covers American, European, Soviet, Israeli and other publications from 16th century to the present. Scholarship in the Yiddish field, as well as translations from Yiddish into other languages are incl. The archives

Division contains unpublished mss, correspondence and pictures, incl the library and archives of Max Weinreich.
Publications: *Guide to the YIVO Library*, 1975; *Guide to Major Collections in the YIVO Archives*, 1973.

OH —HEBREW UNION COLLEGE-JEWISH INSTITUTE OF RELIGION, Klau Library, 3101 Clifton Ave, Cincinnati, 45220. David J Gilner, Reference Librn
Holdings: Cat
Notes: Incl most of the early Yiddish editions.

OH —CLEVELAND PUBLIC LIBRARY, Foreign Literature Dept, 325 Superior Ave, Cleveland, 44114. Natalia Bezugloff, Head
Holdings: Vols 3640 Cat
Notes: A popular circulating collection containing classics and the standard works with emphasis on belles lettres, history and biography. A variety of other subjects such as learning languages, how to do books, art, children's books, spoken phonodiscs and cassettes, periodicals, etc.
See also entry under Foreign Language Collections

OH —OHIO STATE UNIVERSITY, William Oxley Thompson Memorial Library, 1858 Neil Ave, Columbus, 43210. Amnon Zipin, Jewish Studies Bibliographer
Holdings: Vols (43,000) Cat Maps Microfilms
Budget: ($35,000)
Notes: Collection emphasis is materials on Jewish history (especially US, Israel and Europe) and Hebrew language and literature. Small collection of Yiddish materials.

PA —BALCH INSTITUTE FOR ETHNIC STUDIES, Library, 18 S Seventh St, Philadelphia, 19106. R Joseph Anderson, Library Dir
Holdings: Vols Uncat
Notes: Incl 6000 vols on Yiddish literature and 6500 vols on Yiddish language.

RI —BROWN UNIVERSITY, John Hay Library, Harris Collection, Prospect St, Providence, 02912. Rosemary L Cullen, Cur
Holdings: Vols (200,000) Cat Mss Pix Phonorecords Microforms
Budget: ($15,000)
Notes: The Harris Collection of American Poetry and Plays is principally composed of American and Canadian poetry and plays from the 17th century to the present. Extensive holdings in Yiddish-American literature, particularly of the late 19th and early 20th centuries. Incl the Vaxer Collection of Yiddish Poetry, Plays and Music (1700 vols). See *Dictionary Catalog of the Harris Collection of American Poetry and Plays* (Boston: G K Hall, 1972), 13 vols; Supplement (1977), 3 vols. Separate catalog.

TX —TEXAS TECH UNIVERSITY, Library, Lubbock, 79409. David J Murrah, Assoc Dir for Special Collections

UT —UNIVERSITY OF UTAH, Middle East Library, Salt Lake City, 84112. Ragai N Makar, Librn
Holdings: Vols 4000 Cat
Budget: ($40,000)
Notes: From the library of Samuel Mendelson.

PQ —MCGILL UNIVERSITY, McLennan Library, Rare Books and Special Collections Dept, 3459 McTavish St, Montreal, H3A 1Y1, Can.
Holdings: Vols 2275
Notes: Yiddish poetry of the 20th century of worldwide publication, incl rare Soviet Union imprints, in the Fishstein Collection.

YIDDISH LANGUAGE AND LITERATURE IN TRANSLATION

NY —YIVO INSTITUTE FOR JEWISH RESEARCH, Library & Archives, 1048 Fifth Ave, New York, 10028. Dina Abramowicz, Librn; Marek Web, Archivist
Holdings: Vols 315,000 Mss Maps Pix Slides
Notes: The most extensive collection in existence of Yiddish books and periodicals. Covers American, European, Soviet, Israeli and other publications from 16th century to the present. Scholarship in the Yiddish field as well as translations from Yiddish into

other languages are incl. The archives Division contains unpublished mss, correspondence and pictures, incl the library and archives of Max Weinreich.
Publications: *Guide to the YIVO Library*, 1975; *Guide to Major Collections in the YIVO Archives*, 1973.

YIDDISH THEATRE see Theatre—Jews

YIPPIES see Youth Movement

YISHUV

FL —UNIVERSITY OF FLORIDA LIBRARY, Isser and Rae Price Library of Judaica, 18 Libr East, Gainesville, 32611. Robert Singerman, Head Librn
Notes: Total holdings estimated at 55,000 vols dealing with the political, social, economic and intellectual history of the Jews in the ancient, medieval and modern periods and in all geographic areas. The following areas are especially well represented by printed matter in all relevant languages: Bibliography, Festschriften, History, Bible, Judaism and Jewish theology, liturgy, responsa, rabbinical literature, Jewish law, Hebrew language and literature, Yiddish language and literature, anti-semitism, Zionism, Palestine and the *Yishuv*, and the State of Israel. German and American Judaica form a collecting emphasis with holdings for all the standard histories as well as histories of individual synagogues, institutions and local communities. Works in Hebrew and Yiddish comprise about 60 percent of the collection (estimated 30,000 vols). With few exceptions, holdings are limited to nineteenth and twentieth century imprints, with complete sets of journals and thousands of ephemeral pamphlets, many of them commemorating anniversaries, enhancing the research value of the collection, the largest Judaica research library in the southeastern United States. Only about half of the collection is cataloged; the collection is a circulating one and vols may be borrowed on interlibrary loan. Incl the Leonard C Mishkin Collection (40,000 vols), the largest personal Judaica collection in the United States, the Shlomo Marenof Collection (3500 vols), and the inventory of Bernard Morgenstern's Lower East Side Book Store (8000 vols). Scholars should inquire in advance of their visit. *The Isser and Rae Price Library of Judaica* Report (circulation 2900 copies) is mailed gratis twice a year to all interested parties. Special catalogs:Pre-1881 Hebrew imprints recorded in a chronological card file.

YMCA see Young Men'S Christian Association (YMCA)

YODER, PAUL

AL —TROY STATE UNIVERSITY, Library, Troy, 36081. Kenneth Croslin, Dir of University Libraries
Holdings: Cat Phonorecords
Notes: Recordings of band music and original compositions of Paul Yoder performed at festivals in this country and abroad are gifts to the library. Also incl a collection of publishers' samples of band scores.

MS —UNIVERSITY OF SOUTHERN MISSISSIPPI, William David McCain Graduate Library, Box 5148, Southern Sta, Hattiesburg, 39406.
Holdings: Mss
Notes: The Paul Yoder Collection (1940-1980; 30 cubic feet) contains original musical scores and published copies of band music which Yoder composed or arranged. Some of the band music was written for foreign bands, especially Japanese. Catalog in progress.

YOGA

AZ —WORLD UNIVERSITY, Library, 711 E Blacklidge Dr, Tucson, 85719. Howard John Zitko, Cur
Holdings: Vols (15,000) Cat Mss Maps

YOGA (cont.)

Audiotapes
Notes: Collection concerns what are generally called the "frontier sciences." No interlibrary loan.

IL —UNIVERSITY OF ILLINOIS, URBANA/CHAMPAIGN, Library, University Archives, 19 Library, 1408 W Gregory Drive, Urbana, 61801. Maynard Brichford, University Archivist
Holdings: Vols (5000) Cat
Budget: ($7000)
Notes: The Mandeville Collection in Parapsychology and Occult Sciences. Titles in the Merten J Mandeville Collection are purchased by funds from an endowment provided specifically for the collection on its establishment in 1966 by Merten J Mandeville, Professor Emeritus of Management, who donated 400 vols from his personal library as the nucleus of the collection. There are currently about 5000 titles in the collection, supplemented by related materials in the general collection. Topics include astrology, extrasensory perception, yoga, magic, satanism, faith healing, hypnosis, Eastern religions, witchcraft, fortune telling, reincarnation, flying saucers, ghosts, dreams, numerology, graphology, and mysticism. Biographies and reference books are a part of the collection as are journals devoted to the scientific study of parapsychology.

YONGE, CHARLOTTE, 1823-1901

CA —UNIVERSITY OF CALIFORNIA, LOS ANGELES, Research Library, Dept of Special Collections, 405 Hilgard Ave, Los Angeles, 90024. Edward Shreeves, Chairman, Bibliographers Group; David S Zeidberg, Head
Holdings: Vols 100
Notes: 100 first and other editions of her books; 73 letters.

MA —HARVARD UNIVERSITY LIBRARY, Cambridge, 02138.
Holdings: Cat

NJ —PRINCETON UNIVERSITY, Library, Morris L Parrish Collection, Princeton, 08540. Alexander D Wainwright, Cur
Holdings: Vols 12
Notes: The collection contains over 6500 vols, as well as many theatre programs, playbills, photographs, clippings and other miscellanea. Parrish's goal was to assemble in both the English and the American first editions, in the original condition as issued, everything that a given author published. He was also interested in a high standard of condition for his books. Many additions have been acquired since the Parrish collection came to the Library as a bequest in 1944. The collection is an assemblage of author collections, consisting of books by: William Harrison Ainsworth, James Matthew Barrie, William Black, The Brontes, William Wilkie Collins, Dinah Mulock Craik, Marie de la Ramee ("Ouida"), Benjamin Disraeli, Charles Dickens, Charles Dodgson, George du Maurier, George Eliot (ie Mary Ann Evans), Elizabeth Gaskell, Thomas Hardy, Thomas Hughes,Charles Kingsley, Charles Lever, Edward George Earle Bulwer-Lytton, Mary Maxwell, George Meredith, Charles Reade, Walter Scott, Robert Louis Stevenson, William Makepeace Thackeray, Trollope Family, Ellen Wood, and Charlotte Yonge.

YONKERS, NEW YORK—HISTORY

NY —YONKERS PUBLIC LIBRARY, Information Services, 7 Main St, Yonkers, 10701. Martita Schwarz, Dept Head
Notes: Hudson River Museum branch has closed. Materials on history of Yonkers, with some materials on Hudson River history have been distributed to several other branches in the library system.

YORCK, RUTH

MA —BOSTON UNIVERSITY, Mugar Memorial Library, Special Collections Dept, 771 Commonwealth Ave, Boston, 02215. Howard B Gotlieb, Dir
Holdings: // Cat Mss Pix
Notes: Mss, correspondence, etc collected in depth; incl publications by or about.

YOSEMITE NATIONAL PARK

†WA —WASHINGTON STATE UNIVERSITY, Library, Manuscripts, Archives & Special Collections, Pullman, 99164. John F Guido, Head
Holdings: Cat Mss Maps Pix
Notes: The Carl Parcher Russell papers, a vast resource (24,916 items; 45 linear feet) on American Indian and Western pioneer activities and artifacts. Much on the fur trade; pioneer life in detail. Also the National Park Service, parks, monuments, etc. Described in *Carl Parcher Russell: An Indexed Register of His Scholarly and Professional Papers, 1920-1967*, in the *Washington State University Library* (Pullman, 1970), 149 pp.

YOSHIDA, SHIGERU

VA —MACARTHUR MEMORIAL, Library & Archives, MacArthur Sq, Norfolk, 23510. Ellen E Folkama, Asst Archivist
Holdings: Vols (4000) Cat Maps Pix Slides Phonorecords Audiotapes 16mm Films Microforms
Notes: Everything relating to the life and related activities of MacArthur. The Archives of the collection consist of 600 shelf-feet of documents from Gen MacArthur's official headquarters files over the period 1941-1951. These papers pertain to all matters with which his various commands were involved: military, naval and air matters; international relations; political science; Japanese occupation, peace treaty and Constitution, etc. Each Record Group is indexed. The indexes are retained here since they are being expanded. They are available for researchers.

YOUDEN, WILLIAM J., 1900-1971

†DC —NATIONAL BUREAU OF STANDARDS, Library, Records Holding Area, Administration Bldg E120, Washington, 20234.
Notes: Papers of the mathematician William J Youden, dating mostly from about 1920-69, concerning his service as consultant to the U.S. Army Air Force, 1942-45, as well as other aspects of his career.

YOUMANS, JOHN B., M.D.

TN —VANDERBILT UNIVERSITY, Medical Center Library, Nashville, 37232. Mary H Teloh, Special Collections Librn
Holdings: Uncat Mss Pix Videotapes
Notes: The nucleus of the developing nutrition collection at Vanderbilt is the papers of medical researcher Joseph Goldberger, MD, and his associate W Henry Sebrell, Jr, MD. The collection consists of first editions and translations of classic books on pellagra, and the letters, mss, and notebooks compiled by Dr Goldberger and Dr Sebrell during their years of research on pellagra. See *Nutrition Reviews*, 33(10):310-312, Oct 1975. 10 linear ft of mss. Library also has the archives of the American Institute of Nutrition and manuscripts representing the work of Karl Mason, PhD, Helen S Mitchell, PhD, Lydia J Roberts, PhD, and John B Youmans, MD.

YOUNG, ALEXANDER BELL FILSON, 1876-1938

BC —UNIVERSITY OF VICTORIA, McPherson Library, Victoria, V8W 3H5, Can.

YOUNG, ARTHUR N.

CA —HOOVER INSTITUTION ON WAR, REVOLUTION & PEACE, Stanford University, Stanford, 94305. Milorad M Drachkovitch, Archivist
Holdings: // Mss
Notes: Papers of Arthur N Young, incl a diary, correspondence, reports, studies, statistical summaries, financial statements, press releases, news clippings, and ephemeral publications, relating to the European financial crisis following World War I and to the economic and financial situation in China, 1929-1946. 110 ms boxes. Unpublished register is available in repository.

YOUNG, BRIGHAM

IL —CHICAGO HISTORICAL SOCIETY, Library, Clark St at North Ave, Chicago, 60614. Archie Motley, Manuscript Librn
Notes: Brigham Young's September 23, 1845 letter from Nauvoo, Illinois, giving the terms of the Mormon's departure from Hancock County, Illinois, on their westward course.

UT —UTAH STATE UNIVERSITY, Merrill Library, Department of Special Collections & Archives, Logan, 84322. A J Simmonds, Curator; Jeanie F Simmonds, Archivist; Bradford R Cole, Mss Librn
Notes: Incl all LDS Churches, though major emphasis is on the Salt Lake based Church of Jesus Christ of Latter-Day Saints and on the Mormon fundamentalists (polygamists). Additional material in the Library's Utah Collection. 800 rolls microform, 1000 linear feet Mss.

YOUNG, CHARLES

NY —AMERICAN INSTITUTE OF PHYSICS, Center for the History of Physics, Niels Bohr Library, 335 E 45 St, New York, 10017. John Aubry, Librn
Notes: The Sources for History of Modern Astrophysics documents the history of 20th-century astrophysics. Incl some 400 hours of oral history interviews with astronomers, such as Bart Bok, S Chandrasekhar, Martin Schwarzschild, and A E Whitford. The project also organized and cataloged the papers of Henry Norris Russell, Frank Schlesinger, Otto Struve, Ejnar Hertzsprung, Harlow Shapley, Charles Young, Robert Atkinson, Seth Chandler, Theodore Dunham, Jr, and G C McVittie.

YOUNG, EDWARD, 1683-1765

CO —UNIVERSITY OF COLORADO, Libraries, Special Collections, Boulder, 80309. Nora J Quinlan, Head
Holdings: Vols 213 Uncat
Notes: The Henry Petit Collection.

YOUNG, FRANCIS BRETT

NY —HOFSTRA UNIVERSITY, Library, 1000 Fulton Ave, Hempstead, 11550. Charles R Andrews, Dean of Library Services
Notes: Strong collection. Incl some mss.

YOUNG, JOHN

TX —TEXAS A&M UNIVERSITY, Sterling C Evans Library, University Archives, College Station, 77843. Charles R Schultz, University Archivist
Notes: The Archives of Modern Politics: the papers of John Young, 1963-1976.

YOUNG, JOSEPH LOUIS

NY —SYRACUSE UNIVERSITY LIBRARIES, Ernest S Bird Library, George Arents Research Library for Special Collections, Syracuse, 13210. Carolyn A Davis, Manuscripts Librn; Amy S Doherty, University Archivist; Mark F Weimer, Rare Book Librn
Notes: The George Arents Research Library for Special Collections at Syracuse University contains the papers of Harley James McKee, Lorimer Rich, Frederick Lear, Max Abramovitz, James I Arnold, Pietro Bulluschi, Claude Bragdon, Marcel Breuer, William Lescaze, Skidmore Owings

YOUNG, JOSEPH LOUIS (cont.)

& Merrill, Ralph Walker, Eric Fisher Wood, Minoru Yamasaki, Joseph Louis Young, and Archimedes Russell.

YOUNG, MORRIS N.

DC —LIBRARY OF CONGRESS, Rare Book & Special Collections Div, Washington, 20540. William Matheson, Chief
Notes: See description of McManus-Young Collection under Houdini, Harry.

YOUNG, NOEL

IN —INDIANA UNIVERSITY, Lilly Library, Seventh St, Bloomington, 47405. William R Cagle, Librn
Notes: Extensive holdings. Mss include Black Sparrow Press printing records Noel Young, printer, 1968-1974.

YOUNG, PHYLLIS BRETT

MA —BOSTON UNIVERSITY, Mugar Memorial Library, Special Collections Dept, 771 Commonwealth Ave, Boston, 02215. Howard B Gotlieb, Dir
Holdings: Cat Mss Pix
Notes: Mss, correspondence, etc collected in depth; incl publications by or about.

YOUNG, STARK

MS —MISSISSIPPI STATE UNIVERSITY, Mitchell Memorial Library, Box 5408, Mississippi State, 39762. Frances N Coleman, Head, Special Collections
Holdings: Vols (15,000) Cat Mss Maps Pix Microforms
Notes: Social and political history of Mississippi, incl University Archives (now separate branch). Microfilms of Protestant Church records. There are strong collections on history of the Southern States, Mississippi authors (especially Faulkner, Williams, Carter, Welty, and Young); also the John C Stennis Collection of over 2 million items, his books, papers, photographs, etc. Incl 400 collections of mss; papers of US Rep David R Bowen 1973-1983; papers of US Rep G V Montgomery 1967-.

YOUNG, STUART M.

AZ —NORTHERN ARIZONA UNIVERSITY, Special Collection Library, CU Box 6022, Flagstaff, 86011. Peter M Whiteley, Coordr/Archivist; William Mullane, Librn
Notes: Newspaper and magazine articles on Young and a number of material items (camera, pots, etc).

YOUNG, VICTOR, 1900-1956

MA —BOSTON PUBLIC LIBRARY, Music Division, 666 Boylston St, Box 286, Boston, 02117. Ruth Bleecker, Cur of Music
Holdings: Vols (100,000) Cat Mss Pix Microforms
Notes: Incl film scores, orchestral arrangements, radio music and original compositions.
MA —BRANDEIS UNIVERSITY, Goldfarb Library, 415 South St, Waltham, 02154. Bessie Hahn, Dir
Notes: Victor Young Collection. 39 linear ft of musical mss, phonodiscs and memorabilia. A finding list to the collection is located in Special Collections.

YOUNG, WHITNEY M.

NY —COLUMBIA UNIVERSITY LIBRARIES, Rare Book & Manuscript Library, 801 Butler Library, 535 W 114 St, New York, 10027. Kenneth A Lohf, Librn
Holdings: Mss
Notes: Papers of Whitney M Young, civil rights leader. 106,000 items. Restricted use.

YOUNG ADULT LITERATURE

CA —UNIVERSITY OF CALIFORNIA, BERKELEY, Humanities-Social Sciences Libraries, Education-Psychology Library, 2600 Tolman Hall, Berkeley, 94720. Sonya Kaufman, Acting Head
Holdings: Vols (110,000)
Notes: General research collection in fields of education and psycology. Education collection's emphases are in the areas of administration, policy planning, higher education, science and math education, language and literacy. Serial holdings are strong. The library receives approx 2200 current serial titles in education and psychology.
CA —SAN FRANCISCO STATE UNIVERSITY, J Paul Leonard Library, 1630 Holloway Ave, San Francisco, 94132. Susan Quinlan, Curriculum Librn
Holdings: Vols (49,246) Cat Phonorecords Audiotapes 8mm Films Microforms
Budget: ($8500)
Notes: The young people's collection or children's literature collection of 17,843 vols incl books with reading and interest levels ranging from preschool through senior high school. The Marguerite Archer collection of historical children's books contains an additional 3000 vols. Have 19,755 textbooks, 5150 curriculum guides, 1970 pamphlets. Collection emphasizes instructional materials that can be utitlized in the school classroom. Professional books and journals and other media relating to educational history, philosophy, research, theories of teaching, etc are in the main collection.

YOUNG MEN'S CHRISTIAN ASSOCIATION (YMCA)

CA —HOOVER INSTITUTION ON WAR, REVOLUTION & PEACE, Stanford University, Stanford, 94305. Milorad M Drachkovitch, Archivist
Holdings: // Mss
Notes: Papers, 1916-1932, of Hugh Anderson Moran, clergyman. Correspondence, photos, memoranda, ms articles and other papers relating to Moran's work as director of prisoner-of-war relief in Siberia, 1916-1917, as special aid to the Elihu Root diplomatic mission to Russia, 1917, and as secretary to the Young Men's Christian Association in Manchuria, 1918, and to his later interests in Russian affairs. 2 ft.
CA —WHITTIER COLLEGE, Wardman Library, Whittier, 90608. Christine Erdmann, Special Collections Librn
Holdings: Vols 600 Cat
IL —GEORGE WILLIAMS COLLEGE LIBRARY, 555 31 St, Downers Grove, 60515. Marilyn T Thompson, Dir of Library Services
Holdings: Vols 606 Cat Mss Pix
Notes: YMCA history.
IL —NATIONAL COUNCIL OF THE YMCAS, YMCA Historical Library, 6400 Shafer Ct, Rosemont, 60018. Eleanor R Murphy, Librn
Holdings: Vols (15,000) Cat Mss Pix Microforms
Notes: YMCA history and policy, local, national and international. Much correspondence and other primary source material not cataloged. Large collection on YMCA work in Russia and with Russian emigres in Europe; also YMCA work in China, 1895-1950. Considerable on early young men's societies. Large collection on YMCA World War relief work with the military, prisoners of war, and civilians. Large collection, incl historical material, on basketball, wrestling, track and field, swimming, diving, scuba and volleyball. Repository for the US Volleyball Association.
MA —SPRINGFIELD COLLEGE LIBRARY, Babson Library, Springfield, 01109. Henry Dutcher, Reference Librn
Holdings: Vols (130,000) Cat
Budget: ($65,000)
NY —ROCKEFELLER UNIVERSITY, Rockefeller Archive Center, Hillcrest, Pocantico Hills, North Tarrytown, 10591. Joseph W Ernst, Dir; J William Hess, Assoc Dir
Notes: Papers relative to the Rockefeller Family, Foundations, University, and other specific enterprises and contributions to particular areas of social, physical, educational, and historic reform, preservation, conservation, or development. Extensive records of administrative, financial, physical, or intellectual relationships.
†PA —TEMPLE UNIVERSITY LIBRARIES, Special Collections Dept, Urban Archives Center, Philadelphia, 19122. Thomas Whitehead, Cur of Mss
Holdings: Mss
Notes: Ms collection focusing on urban life and development and drawing on the Philadelphia metropolitan area since the Civil War. Incl the papers of several private organizations, such as the Philadelphia Housing Association (1909-1972); Delaware Valley Regional Planning Commission (1965-1972); Greater Philadelphia Movement (1949-1976); YWCA of Philadelphia (1870-1960); YMCA of Philadelphia (1854-1970); Health and Welfare Council of Philadelphia (1922-1969); United Fund of Philadelphia and Vicinity (1920-1975); Philadelphia Urban League (1935-1967); ACLU-Philadelphia Chapter (1948-1975); Legal Aid Society of Philadelphia (1933-1976); etc.

YOUNG MEN'S CHRISTIAN ASSOCIATION (YMCA)—WAR WORK
see World War, 1914-1918—War Work—Y M CA

YOUNG MEN'S SOCIETIES

IL —NATIONAL COUNCIL OF THE YMCAS, YMCA Historical Library, 6400 Shafer Ct, Rosemont, 60018. Eleanor R Murphy, Librn
Holdings: Vols (15,000) Cat
Notes: Early young men's societies. Incl very little primary material; mainly published material. Societies incl are very varied, such as the Young Men's Christian Union of Boston; the Society for Reformation of Manners, 1657-1690; Society for Suppression of Vice; and the Woman's Seamen's Friend Society. In addition, there are early bound periodicals, essays, etc, for the guidance and "betterment" of young men. Separate catalog.

YOUNG PEOPLE'S SOCIALIST LEAGUE

CA —UNIVERSITY OF CALIFORNIA, LOS ANGELES, Research Library, Dept of Special Collections, 405 Hilgard Ave, Los Angeles, 90024. Edward Shreeves, Chairman, Bibliographers Group; David S Zeidberg, Head
Holdings: Mss
Notes: 14 linear feet of mss and printed material collected by Hyman Weintraub, William Goldberg and others, incl minutes of the League's National Executive Committee.

YOUNG WOMEN'S CHRISTIAN ASSOCIATION (YWCA)

AL —BIRMINGHAM PUBLIC LIBRARY, Dept of Archives & Mss, 2020 Seventh Ave N, Birmingham, 35203. Marvin Y Whiting, Archivist & Cur
Holdings: Mss Pix
Notes: Main collections to date are the League of Women Voters of Birmingham Papers and the YWCA Papers. 19,600 ms pieces.
DC —HOWARD UNIVERSITY, Moorland-Spingarn Research Center, 500 Howard Place NW, Washington, 20059. Clifford L Muse, Jr, Acting Dir
Holdings: Vols (106,086) Mss Maps Pix Slides Phonorecords Audiotapes 16mm Films Filmstrips Microforms
Budget: ($854,753)
See also entry under Blacks
MO —UNIVERSITY OF MISSOURI-SAINT LOUIS, Thomas Jefferson Library, Manuscript and Historical Society

YOUNG WOMEN'S CHRISTIAN ASSOCIATION (YWCA) (cont.)

Collection, 8001 Natural Bridge Rd, Saint Louis, 63121.
Holdings: Mss Pix Tapes
Notes: ca

NY —YWCA NATIONAL BOARD, Library, 726-730 Broadway, New York, 10012. Elizabeth Norris, Librn
Holdings: Vols (6000) Uncat Mss Maps Pix Slides Phonorecords Audiotapes Filmstrips Microforms
Notes: Includes the history of the organization from 1858; published and unpublished works; the official records of the National Board YWCA from 1906 to the present.

NY —ROCKEFELLER UNIVERSITY, Rockefeller Archive Center, Hillcrest, Pocantico Hills, North Tarrytown, 10591. Joseph W Ernst, Dir; J William Hess, Assoc Dir
Notes: Papers relative to the Rockefeller Family, Foundations, University, and other specific enterprises and contributions to particular areas of social, physical, educational, and historic reform, preservation, conservation, or development. Extensive records of administrative, financial, physical, or intellectual relationships.

†PA —TEMPLE UNIVERSITY LIBRARIES, Special Collections Dept, Urban Archives Center, Philadelphia, 19122. Thomas Whitehead, Cur of Mss
Holdings: Mss
Notes: Ms collection focusing on urban life and development and drawing on the Philadelphia metropolitan area since the Civil War. Incl the papers of several private organizations, such as the Philadelphia Housing Association (1909-1972); Delaware Valley Regional Planning Commission (1965-1972); Greater Philadelphia Movement (1949-1976); YWCA of Philadelphia (1870-1960); YMCA of Philadelphia (1854-1970); Health and Welfare Council of Philadelphia (1922-1969); United Fund of Philadelphia and Vicinity (1920-1975); Philadelphia Urban League (1935-1967); ACLU-Philadelphia Chapter (1948-1975); Legal Aid Society of Philadelphia (1933-1976); etc.

YOUNGER, J. ARTHUR

CA —STANFORD UNIVERSITY LIBRARIES, Cecil H Green Library, Stanford, 94305. Michael T Ryan, Cur
Notes: Research collection.

YOURCENAR, MARGUERITE, 1903-

ME —BOWDOIN COLLEGE, Library, Brunswick, 04011. Dianne M Gutscher, Cur of Special Collections
Holdings: Vols 150 Cat Mss
Notes: The Marguerite Yourcenar Collection contains heavily annotated and presentation copies of more than 150 novels, essays, plays, poems, and translations, as well as mss and correspondence of this noted French author and first woman to be elected to the French Academy.

YOUTH

NY —BANK STREET COLLEGE OF EDUCATION LIBRARY, 610 W 112 St, New York, 10025. Eleanor Kule Seid, Library Dir
Holdings: Vols (90,000) Cat Microforms
Notes: Education, guidance, psychology, educational psychology, curricula, textbooks, Black Studies, etc. All subjects are integrated in one professional collection; in addition there are two separately cataloged and shelved collections: Children's and Elementary Curriculum Materials.

NY —ROCKEFELLER UNIVERSITY, Rockefeller Archive Center, Hillcrest, Pocantico Hills, North Tarrytown, 10591. Joseph W Ernst, Dir; J William Hess, Assoc Dir
Notes: Papers relative to the Rockefeller Family, Foundations, University, and other specific enterprises and contributions to particular areas of social, physical, educational, and historic reform, preservation, conservation, or development. Extensive records of administrative, financial, physical, or intellectual relationships.

NC —NORTH AMERICAN YOUTH SPORT INSTITUTE, 4985 Oak Garden Drive, Kernersville, 27284. Jack Hutslar, Exec Dir
Notes: A private management consulting and training firm for adults who are involved with school age youngsters in community sport, recreation and physical education.

TX —WEST TEXAS STATE UNIVERSITY, Cornette Library, PO Box 748 WT Sta, Canyon, 79016. Faye Hendrickson, Special Collections Asst
Holdings: Vols (451,253) Uncat Microforms
Notes: Includes microfilm collection.

†ON —MCMASTER UNIVERSITY, Library, Hamilton, L8S 4L6, Can.
Notes: Administrative files, correspondence, and printed material used by the Director of the Company of Young Canadians, 1966-1972.

YOUTH—EMPLOYMENT

DC —INTERNATIONAL LABOR ORGANIZATION, International Labor Office, Washington Branch Library, 1750 New York Ave NW, Rm 330, Washington, 20006. Karen J Mark, Librn
Holdings: Vols (13,500) Cat Pix 16mm Films Monographs
Notes: Wide range of titles dealing with worldwide labor and social matters. The library contains ILO publications and documentation only, dating back to 1919. Also, a collection of ILO films and photos. See *Subject Guide to Publications of the ILO, 1919-1964* and *ILO Catalogue of Publications in Print, 1982* (ILO).

DC —LIBRARY OF CONGRESS, Manuscript Division, Washington, 20540. John C Broderick, Chief
Notes: Records and photographs of the National Child Labor Committee, 1904-53.

YOUTH HOSTELS

NY —ROCKEFELLER UNIVERSITY, Rockefeller Archive Center, Hillcrest, Pocantico Hills, North Tarrytown, 10591. Joseph W Ernst, Dir; J William Hess, Assoc Dir
Notes: Papers relative to the Rockefeller Family, Foundations, University, and other specific enterprises and contributions to particular areas of social, physical, educational, and historic reform, preservation, conservation, or development. Extensive records of administrative, financial, physical, or intellectual relationships.

YOUTH MOVEMENT

CA —GRADUATE THEOLOGICAL UNION LIBRARY, New Religious Movements Research Collection, Public Services and Special Collections Dept, 2400 Ridge Road, Berkeley, 94709. Diane Choquette, Dept Head
Holdings: Vols (3000) Mss Pix
Notes: Begun in 1977, the collection focuses on religious movements new to America since 1960, and unorthodox religious movements resurgent since 1960. American forms of Hinduism, Buddhism, Sikhism, and Sufism are included along with occultism, Neo-Paganism, esoteric and alternative forms of Christianity, feminist spirituality, and human potential movements having a spiritual aspect. Legal issues, such as deprogramming, and the question of church/state relations are an important part of the collection. The Library is a depository for publications of the Unification Church in America, the Church of Scientology, and the International Society for Krishna Consciousness (America). The responses of mainstream religions and concerned citizens groups are also included. Besides 3000 monographs, the library has 400 periodical titles, 200 posters from the San FranciscoBay Area, 1965-77, 300 research papers, and 31 linear feet of ephemera.

CA —SOUTHERN CALIFORNIA LIBRARY FOR SOCIAL STUDIES & RESEARCH, 6120 S Vermont Ave, Los Angeles, 90044. Sarah Cooper, Dir
Holdings: Vols (15,000) Mss Maps Pix Slides Phonorecords Audiotapes 16mm Films
Budget: ($30,000)
Notes: Marxist, non-Marxist and anti-Marxist approaches to social change. Other important functions of the library: to make available source materials to those engaged in the Marxist vs no-Marxist dialog; to aid historians, economists, sociologists, writers, students and labor organizations researching the history of grassroots social movements; and to preserve primary and secondary sources on labor, minorities, women and radicalism. Collection incl 50 mss, 75 maps, 500 pictures, 1000 slides, 100 phonorecords, 2000 audiotapes, 50 16mm films and 150,000 newspaper clippings.

CA —UNIVERSITY OF CALIFORNIA, LOS ANGELES, Research Library, Dept of Special Collections, 405 Hilgard Ave, Los Angeles, 90024. Edward Shreeves, Chairman, Bibliographers Group; David S Zeidberg, Head
Holdings: Cat
Notes: Various collections, incl Italian Broadsides (ca 1676-1821); French Political Broadsides (1793-1871); American and British broadside ballads; Victorial broadsides; posters (World War I and II, travel, film); political broadsides (Californian, Mexican, student protest of the 60s).

CA —FITZ HUGH LUDLOW MEMORIAL LIBRARY, PO Box 99346, San Francisco, 94109. Michael R Aldrich, Exec Cur
Holdings: Mss Maps Pix Slides Phonorecords Audiotapes Videotapes
Notes: Collection stored. Important mail inquiries only. No interlibrary lending or telephone queries. The heart of this special collection of psychoactive drug literature is about 400 vols of memoirs or lightly-disguised fiction concerning psychoactive drugs, plus about 600 vols related to Beat writers of the 1950s-60s, plus about 300 vols related to the "Hippie" movement of the 1960s, plus 600 vols (mostly paperback) of drug-related pornography, and several hundred vols related to drug slang, drugs and music, drug art, drug cuisine, etc. In addition we have many boxes of offprints, files of newspaper clippings, complete runs to underground newspapers, and many artifacts related to this area. Much of the 1950s-60s-70s literature is autographed or inscribed.

CA —HOOVER INSTITUTION ON WAR, REVOLUTION & PEACE, Stanford University, Stanford, 94305. Milorad M Drachkovitch, Archivist
Notes: The New Left Politics Collection consists of monographs and serials on the New Left that are cataloged. In addition, the collection subscribes to numerous underground newspapers and has obtained special subject collections such as the Free Speech Movement at Berkeley 1964-1965, SNCC and Mississippi Summer 1964, and the insurrection at San Francisco State College in 1968-1969. There is also a good collection on the French Student revolts of 1968. The collection is a supervised one and not open to browsers. Interested students and scholars are welcome. Only limited photocopying is permitted.

CT —UNIVERSITY OF CONNECTICUT, Library, Storrs, 06268. Ellen Embardo, Cur Special Collections
Holdings: Cat
Notes: Alternative Press Collection. Primarily periodicals and newspapers from the 1960s to today of an alternative or underground nature. Books and pamphlets are incl, representing both the left and the right-wing viewpoints. A catalog is available. Also have archives of the First Casualty Press, which was deeply involved with Vietnam veterans' experiences in Vietnam.

IL —NORTHWESTERN UNIVERSITY, Library, Special Collections Dept, 1937

YOUTH MOVEMENT (cont.)

Sheridan Rd, Evanston, 60201. R Russell
Maylone, Cur
Holdings: Vols 1000 Cat
Notes: Very large collection of original
journals from the 1960s and 1970s, mostly
American and Canadian, but also several
English and French. Also high school
papers. Subjects incl left-wing politics,
American Indian ecology, drug culture, anti-
war and environmental issues. Women's
collection of serial holdings largest in
country. All hard copy with exception of
some of the Women's collection.

MI —UNIVERSITY OF MICHIGAN, Dept of
Rare Books & Special Collections, Ann
Arbor, 48109. Edward C Weber, Head,
Labadie Collection
Holdings: Vols (40,000) Cat Phonorecords
Audiotapes Microforms
Notes: Strongest in the youth and student
protest of the 1960s and 1970s, but there is
earlier US material.

MI —MICHIGAN STATE UNIVERSITY,
Libraries, Special Collections Div, East
Lansing, 48824. Jannette Fiore, Librn
Holdings: Vols (10,500) Cat Mss
Notes: Published and unpublished material
generated by (1) American left and right,
1900, (2) the New Left, 1969-1970, and (3)
current left, right, and alternate life-style
groups. (Supported by appropriate secondary
material in the Research Library). Also have
in microform radical pamphlet literature
from the Tamiment Library (New York
University), the Right Wing Collection of
the University of Iowa, et al.

NY —ROCKEFELLER UNIVERSITY,
Rockefeller Archive Center, Hillcrest,
Pocantico Hills, North Tarrytown, 10591.
Joseph W Ernst, Dir; J William Hess, Assoc
Dir
Notes: The Rockefeller Archive Center, a
division of The Rockefeller University,
preserves and makes available to scholars the
records of the University, the Rockefeller
Foundation, the Rockefeller Brothers Fund,
members of the family, and those of other
individuals and organizations associated with
their endeavors. Collections at the Center
document a century of philanthropy by
legions of associated social and scientific
pioneers, providing a unique window into the
past.

PA —TEMPLE UNIVERSITY LIBRARIES,
Special Collections Dept, Contemporary
Culture Collection, Philadelphia, 19122.
Patricia J Case, Cur
Notes: The Contemporary Culture
Collection. See full entry under US-Social
Life and Customs.

YOUTH PERIODICALS see Periodicals, Youth

YUCATAN

†AL —UNIVERSITY OF ALABAMA, Amelia
Gayle Gorgas Library, PO Box S,
University, 35486.
Notes: This collection consists of 119 reels
of microfilm. Separately published
bibliography: A Catalog of the Yucatan
Collection on Microfilm in the University of
Alabama Libraries (University: University of
Alabama Press), 1972.

TX —UNIVERSITY OF TEXAS,
ARLINGTON, Library, PO Box 19497,
Arlington, 76019. Chas Colley, Dir Special
Collections
Holdings: // Uncat Microforms
Notes: The Yucatan Archives. The
University of Texas at Arlington Library has
microfilmed the pre-1900 holdings of the
Archivo Notarial de Yucatan, a small part of
the Archivo General del Estado (the
Documentos Coloniales and Sesiones del
Congreso, 1823-1933), about half of the
Archivo del Arzobipado (Archivo de la
Secretaria del Arzobispado), and most of the
newspapers held by the Hemeroteca del
Estado de Yucatan. The collection contains
1052 rolls of 35mm microfilm copies. A
preliminary guide is available upon request.

TX —UNIVERSITY OF TEXAS LIBRARIES,
Nettie Lee Benson Latin American
Collection, Sid Richardson Hall 1.109,
Austin, 78712. Laura Gutierrez-Witt, Head
Librn
Holdings: Vols (450,000) Cat Mss Maps Pix
Phonorecords Filmstrips Microforms
See also entry under Latin America

YUDENICH, NICOLAI NICOLAEVICH

CA —HOOVER INSTITUTION ON WAR,
REVOLUTION & PEACE, Stanford
University, Stanford, 94305. Milorad M
Drachkovitch, Archivist
Holdings: // Mss
Notes: Papers, 1919-1920, of Nikolai
Nicolaevich Yudenich, commander of White
Russian military forces in Northwest Russia.
Correspondence, battle orders, memoranda
and reports relating to the anti-Bolshevik
activities of the White Russian forces in
Northwest Russia. Papers chiefly in Russian,
also some in English, French, German,
Estonian, and Finnish. 8 ft.

YUGOSLAV ACADEMY PUBLICATIONS

IL —UNIVERSITY OF ILLINOIS,
URBANA/CHAMPAIGN, Slavic and East
European Library, Urbana, 61801. Marianna
Tax Choldin, Head
Holdings: Vols (31,000) Cat
Notes: Extensive coverage.

YUGOSLAV LAW see Law, Yugoslav

YUGOSLAV LITERATURE see Yugoslavian Language and Literature

YUGOSLAV NEWSPAPERS see Newspapers, Yugoslavian

YUGOSLAV PERIODICALS see Periodicals, Yugoslav

YUGOSLAVIA

CA —UNIVERSITY OF CALIFORNIA,
BERKELEY, University Library, Slavic
Collections, Berkeley, 94720. Edward
Kasinec, Librn
Holdings: Vols (210,000) Cat Maps
Microforms
Budget: ($40,000)
Notes: Strong research collections for
Bulgaria, Czechoslovakia, Poland, Russia-
USSR, and Yugoslavia. Holdings are
excellent in economics, folklore, history,
linguistics, and literature. Publications issued
by academies, major universities, and
principal scholarly institutions are well
represented. Extensive periodical holdings
have been built up, largely as a result of
early exchange arrangements. More than
4000 Slavic-language serials are currently
being received. Farmington Plan and PL480
commitments have augmented Yugoslav
resources. Sizable Slavic-language collections
are to be found in Branch Libraries as well,
in such subjects as agriculture, biology, earth
sciences, forestry, and mathematics.

IL —UNIVERSITY OF ILLINOIS,
URBANA/CHAMPAIGN, Slavic and East
European Library, Urbana, 61801. Marianna
Tax Choldin, Head
Holdings: Vols (31,000) Cat
Notes: Extensive coverage.

NY —NEW YORK PUBLIC LIBRARY,
Slavonic Div, Fifth Ave & 42 St, New York,
10018. Edward Kasinec, Chief
Holdings: Vols 25,000 Cat Microforms
Notes: Subject strength is on languages,
literatures, folklore, ethnology, and history.
Texts in all Slavic languages of Yugoslavia,
ie, Serbo-Croatian, Slovenian, and
Macedonian are represented. See New York
Public Library, Dictionary Catalog of the
Slavonic Collection (Boston: G K Hall,
1974), 44 vols.

WI —UNIVERSITY OF WISCONSIN,
MADISON, Memorial Library, Slavic
Studies Collection, 728 State St, Madison,
53706. Aleksander Rolich, Bibliographer for
Slavic Studies; Robert P Gakovich, Slavic
Cataloger; Valdis J Zeps, Baltic Studies
Center
Holdings: Vols (25,000) Cat
Notes: The Balcanica collection in Memorial
Library exceeds 25,000 volumes and active
collecting continues at over 2000 titles per
year in Bulgarian, Rumanian, Turkish and
the languages of Yugoslavia. Many rare and
unique titles are to be found in this
collection, including serial titles, such as
Nova Vreme (1897-1923, 1947-to date),
Nova Europa (1920-1939), and unique
Turkish Salnameh. The emphasis is on
historical materials, but there is considerable
strength in South Slavic literatures and
linguistics. The Rumanian materials are of
more recent vintage.

YUGOSLAVIA—CURRENT EVENTS

DC —LIBRARY OF CONGRESS, General
Reading Rooms Division, Microform
Reading Room, Washington, 20540.
Holdings: Cat Mss Maps Pix Microforms
Notes: Microform materials only in this LC
Division. Works of individual authors;
holdings of collections; archival records, etc,
press releases and translations, etc.

YUGOSLAVIA—HISTORY

CA —UNIVERSITY OF CALIFORNIA, LOS
ANGELES, Library, Slavic Collection, 405
Hilgard Ave, Los Angeles, 90024. Edward
Shreeves, Chairman, Bibliographers Group;
Leon Ferder, Slavic Bibliographer
Holdings: Vols (250,000) Cat Maps
Microforms
Notes: The entire range of humanities, social
sciences, and the arts. One of the most
comprehensive US collections for material
not only on Russia and the Soviet Union,
but also on Bulgaria, Czechoslovakia,
Poland, Yugoslavia, the non-Slavic countries
of Eastern Europe (Romania, Hungary,
Albania) and Soviet Central Asia. Holdings
in Russian and Slavic linguistics, Russian
literature, and Russian history are
particularly strong, covering all periods. The
collections are described in some detail in
Paul Horecky's book on US Slavic
collections.

CA —STANFORD UNIVERSITY
LIBRARIES, Cecil H Green Library,
Stanford, 94305. Wojciech Zalewski, Cur,
Russian & East European Collection
Holdings: Vols (200,000) Cat Maps
Microforms
Budget: ($90,000)
Notes: Strong collection prior to 20th
century, but Stanford University Libraries'
collecting effort is coordinated with Hoover
Institution, Stanford, and holdings are not
duplicated. Collection descriptions: Wojciech
Zalewski, Russian Materials in the Main
Library of Stanford University, A Collection
Survey (Stanford: Stanford University
Libraries, 1974). Wojciech Zalerski,
"Stanford University" in P L Horecky, ed,
East Central and Southeast Europe, A
Handbook of Library and Archival
Resources in North America (Santa Barbara:
Clio Press, 1976).

CO —UNIVERSITY OF SOUTHERN
COLORADO, Library, 2200 Bonforte Blvd,
Pueblo, 81001.
Holdings: Vols (4000) Cat Mss Maps Pix
Phonorecords Audiotapes
Budget: ($10,000)
Notes: Yugoslavian; especially Slovenian
history and culture. The collection was
inaugurated in 1969. Besides published titles,
2800 in English, and 900 in Slavic languages,
there are memorabilia, organizational
records, and newspapers, magazines, and
music. There is a separate card catalog of
items in the collection. Colorado has had a
number of Slavic colonies and this collection
attempts to recapture the history of these
early settlers. Incl sheet music and
phonorecords.

IL —CENTER FOR RESEARCH
LIBRARIES, 6050 S Kenwood Ave,
Chicago, 60637. Donald B Simpson, Dir;
Esther Smith, Collection Development Librn

YUGOSLAVIA—HISTORY (cont.)

IN —INDIANA UNIVERSITY, University Libraries, Bloomington, 47401. Murlin Croucher, Librn for Slavic Studies
Holdings: Vols (250,000) Cat Maps Microforms
Budget: $55,000
Notes: The collection, established after World War II, covers material of, and on, the Soviet Union (55 percent) and Eastern Europe (45 percent) in the languages of the area and in western European languages as well. Material is chiefly in the fields of humanities and social sciences. Many other Slavic and East European books are located in the Lilly Library (rare book library).

MA —HARVARD UNIVERSITY LIBRARY, Widener Library, Slavic Collections, Cambridge, 02138. Hugh M Olmsted, Slavic Dept Head
Holdings: Cat Microforms
Notes: Yugoslavian history shelflist through June, 1976 lists 6085 titles (earlier version was incl in *Widener Library Shelflist,* volumes 28-31, 1971). The collections continue to be developed actively, and are strong both in current and in antiquarian materials. See also *East Central and Southeast Europe; A Handbook of Library and Archival Resources in North America,* edited by P L Horecky and D H Kraus, 1976, pp 149-154.

NY —NEW YORK PUBLIC LIBRARY, Slavonic Div, Fifth Ave & 42 St, New York, 10018. Edward Kasinec, Chief
Holdings: Vols 25,000 Cat Microforms
Notes: Subject strength is on languages, literaturess, folklore, ethnology, and history. Texts in all Slavic languages of Yugoslavia, ie, Serbo-Croatian, Slovenian, and Macedonian are represented. See New York Public Library, *Dictionary Catalog of the Slavonic Collection* (Boston: G K Hall, 1974), 44 vols.

OH —OHIO STATE UNIVERSITY, William Oxley Thompson Memorial Library, Hilander Room, 1858 Neil Ave Mall, Columbus, 43210. Predrag Matejic, Cur; G Koolemans Beynen, Slavic Bibliographer
Holdings: Vols (200,000) Cat Maps Microforms
Budget: ($45,000)
Notes: Area studies of Central, Southeastern and Eastern Europe. Emphasis on on Slavic literatures, languages and history. At present economics, sociology, law (Russian only) have been added. Within this framework the following priorities have been established: Material in Russian problems; then Medieval Slavic (Cyrillic); then Polish, then Serbo-Croatian, then Bulgarian, and now Romanian. Special attention is paid to serials, bibliographies, ms descriptions and dictionaries (incl biographical and encyclopedias). Apart from materials in native languages, materials in the following languages are acquired: Old Church Slavonic, Greek, English, French, German, Italian, a few in Scandinavian languages, incl Finnish, and a few in Baltic languages. The Hillandar Room holds approx 2000 Slavic mss, 1050 from Hilandar Monastery, Mount Athos, on microform and a related referencecollection.

WA —UNIVERSITY OF WASHINGTON LIBRARIES, Suzzallo Library, Slavic & East European Section, FM-25, Seattle, 98195. Barbara A Galik, Head
Holdings: Vols (250,000) Cat Mss Maps Pix Phonorecords Audiotapes Microforms
Budget: ($85,000)
Notes: Strong research collections for the history of all the republics of Yugoslavia. Holdings are excellent in historical source materials. There are extensive holdings of the publications of academies, major univeristies, and principal scholarly institutions, especially of long serial runs.

WI —UNIVERSITY OF WISCONSIN, MADISON, Memorial Library, Slavic Studies Collection, 728 State St, Madison, 53706. Aleksander Rolich, Bibliographer for Slavic Studies; Robert P Gakovich, Slavic Cataloger; Valdis J Zeps, Baltic Studies Center
Holdings: Vols (1000) Cat
Notes: The Komadinish Collection in Serbian and Yugoslav social and political history embraces publications and pamphlets of peasant, socialist and other radical movements of the last half of the nineteenth century up to World War II. It consists of some 1000 items, mostly in Serbo-Croatian, and represents only part of the private library acquired from the survivors of Milan Komadinic (1882-1944).

YUGOSLAVIAN LANGUAGE AND LITERATURE

CA —UNIVERSITY OF CALIFORNIA, LOS ANGELES, Library, Slavic Collection, 405 Hilgard Ave, Los Angeles, 90024. Edward Shreeves, Chairman, Bibliographers Group; Leon Ferder, Slavic Bibliographer
Holdings: Vols (250,000) Cat Mss Maps
Notes: The entire range of humanities, social sciences, and the arts. One of the most comprehensive US collections for material not only on Russia and the Soviet Union, but also on Bulgaria, Czechoslovakia, Poland, Yugoslavia, the non-Slavic countries of Eastern Europe (Romania, Hungary, Albania) and Soviet Central Asia. Holdings in Russian and Slavic linguistics, Russian literature, and Russian history are particularly strong, covering all periods. The collections are described in some detail in Paul Horecky's book on US Slavic collections.

CA —STANFORD UNIVERSITY LIBRARIES, Cecil H Green Library, Stanford, 94305. Wojciech Zalewski, Cur, Russian & East European Collection
Holdings: Vols (200,000) Cat Maps Microforms
Budget: ($90,000)
Notes: Strong collection prior to 20th century, but Stanford University Libraries' collecting effort is coordinated with Hoover Institution, Stanford, and holdings are not duplicated. Collection descriptions: Wojciech Zalewski, *Russian Materials in the Main Library of Stanford University, A Collection Survey* (Stanford: Stanford University Libraries, 1974). Wojciech Zalerski, "Stanford University" in P L Horecky, ed, *East Central and Southeast Europe, A Handbook of Library and Archival Resources in North America* (Santa Barbara: Clio Press, 1976).

IL —UNIVERSITY OF ILLINOIS, URBANA/CHAMPAIGN, Slavic and East European Library, Urbana, 61801. Marianna Tax Choldin, Head
Holdings: Vols (31,000) Cat
Notes: Extensive coverage.

MA —HARVARD UNIVERSITY LIBRARY, Cambridge, 02138.
NY —NEW YORK PUBLIC LIBRARY, Slavonic Div, Fifth Ave & 42 St, New York, 10018. Edward Kasinec, Chief
Holdings: Vols 25,000 Cat Microforms
Notes: Subject strength is on languages, literatures, folklore, enthnology, and history. Texts in all Slavic languages of Yugoslavia, ie, Serbo-Croatian, Slovenian, and Macedonian are represented. See New York Public Library, *Dictionary Catalog of the Slavonic Collection* (Boston: G K Hall, 1974), 44 vols.

YUKON TERRITORY

WA —UNIVERSITY OF WASHINGTON LIBRARIES, Pacific Northwest Collection, Seattle, 98195. Andrew F Johnson, Librn
Holdings: Vols (50,000) Cat Mss Maps Pix
Budget: ($12,000)
Notes: The Pacific Northwest Collection contains printed materials documenting the historic and contemporary life and culture of the region in a broad range of subject areas. The Pacific Northwest is defined as the geographic region including Washington, Oregon, Idaho, Montana, British Columbia, Yukon Territory, and Alaska. Printed materials including books, periodicals, government documents, maps, weekly and local regional newspapers, theses and dissertations, as well as photographs and architectural drawings are included in the Pacific Northwest Collection. Photographic works of over 200 photographers active in the Pacific Northwest, Alaska, and the Yukon Territory (Canada) during the period 1860-1930, including Asahel and Edward S Curtis, Eric Hegg, and Clark Kinsey, are represented in a print collection of more than 300,000 images. The architecturaldrawings collection includes over 19,000 original plans, drawings, sketches, renderings and blue prints pertaining to the history of architecture and urban planning and landscape gardening in the Pacific Northwest ca 1880-1940. Areas of particular strength are the holdings of over 1100 published journals of Pacific Northwest exploration expeditions, photographs of Northwest Coast Native Americans and of historic Seattle, newspapers issued within the Japanese-American relocation camps, 1942-1945, materials relating to the 1980 eruption of Mt St Helens, and Sanborne fire insurance maps for Washington. A unique feature of the Collection is the subject index to regional periodicals and local newspapers maintained by the PNW Collection staff; over 100 titles are currently indexed. G K Hall Company published a books catalog of the Pacific Northwest Collectionin 1973.

AB —GLENBOW-ALBERTA INSTITUTE, Historical Library & Archives, 130 9th Avenue SE, Calgary, T2G 0P3, Can. Leonard J Gottseleg, Chief Librn
Holdings: Vols (60,000) Cat Mss Maps Pix Microforms
Notes: Main emphasis is on Western Canadian history. Equally important emphasis is placed on the Canadian Arctic and Alaska, Northwest Coast explorations, Aboriginal peoples of the North and Canadian West, and the fur trade in the US Northwest.

YT —YUKON ARCHIVES, Box 2703, Whitehorse, Y1A 3C6, Can. Miriam

YUKON TERRITORY (cont.)

McTiernan, Territorial Archivist
Holdings: Vols (8000) Cat Mss Maps Pix
Phonorecords Audiotapes Videotapes 16mm
Films Microforms
Budget: $15,000
Notes: Yukon and regional history and
development. Incl also 500 mss; 10,000
maps; 30,000 pictures; 1200 microfilm rolls;
1115 oral history tapes, etc; Yukon
newspapers.

YUMAN LANGUAGES

MO —UNIVERSITY OF MISSOURI-
COLUMBIA, Museum of Anthropology
Archives, 104 Swallow Hall, Columbia,
65201. Lawrence H Feldman, Museum Dir
Holdings: Vols (30) Cat Mss Maps Slides
Microforms
Notes: Copies of Latin American and
colonial mss. Many of the ms copies are of
census, or census-like, documents of late
colonial Verapaz; a few are from Sonsonate,
El Salvador or Chiapas, Mexico. Additional
material in the archives incl an original
Eskimo manuscript (ca 1930) and an original
Diegueno Yuman card vocabulary (ca 1964)
and the Museum archives (papers on old
accession systems, etc). Uncataloged
microfilm copies of colonial Otomi and other
vocabularies are also part of the collection.
A catalog of material in this collection will
appear in the Annual Report of the Museum
of Anthropology, beginning with the 1976-
77 volume.

**YWCA see Young Women'S Christian
Association (Ywca)**

Z

ZABEL, MORTON DAUWEN

IL —NEWBERRY LIBRARY, 60 W Walton
St, Chicago, 60610. Diana Haskell, Cur of
Modern Mss
Holdings: // Uncat Mss Pix
Notes: Primary repository; ca 15,000 mss.
Noncirculating.

ZAIN, C.

CA —SAN DIEGO PUBLIC LIBRARY,
Literature & Language Sect, 820 E St, San
Diego, 92101. Alyce Archuleta, Senior Librn
Holdings: Cat
Notes: Old and current reference and
circulating works on the subject. Incl
complete works by Blavatsky, much by
Rudolf Steiner, and C Zain. Strong in
astrology, witchcraft, parapsychology.

ZAIRE

CA —HOOVER INSTITUTION ON WAR,
REVOLUTION & PEACE, Stanford
University, Stanford, 94305. Milorad M
Drachkovitch, Archivist
Holdings: Mss
Notes: Papers of Ernest W Lefever, 1956-
1969, incl ms drafts, correspondence,
reports, interviews, notes, pamphlets,
newspaper clippings, and printed matter,
relating to modern politics in Zaire (Republic
of the Congo), Ethiopia, and other African
nations. 3 ms boxes.
CA —HOOVER INSTITUTION ON WAR,
REVOLUTION & PEACE, Stanford
University, Stanford, 94305. Peter Duignan,
Cur; Karen Fung, Deputy Cur
Holdings: Vols (60,000) Cat Mss Maps Pix
Slides Microforms
Notes: Politics, economics, and history from
1870 to the present. About 500 current
periodicals titles, about 90 current newspaper
titles. Legislative debates, political ephemera.
Have microfilm of Portuguese African
nationalist material, confidential prints of
Great Britian's foreign and colonial offices
1870 through 1922. Nigerian pamphlets
(market literature, political and historical
tracts), collection of the correspondence
pamphlets and ephemera of Alfred B Xuma,
collections on Zaire (1955-1963), South
African nationalist publications on microfilm.
Descriptions of the Collection: *African and
Middle East Collections* pub by Hoover
Institute, *Handbook of American Resources
for African Studies* pub by Hoover. Holdings
of the Collection in *Hoover Institute on
War, Revolution, and Peace Library Catalog*
pub by G K Hall, *Emerging Nationalism in
Portuguese Africa: A Bibliography* pub by
Hoover, *German Africa* pub by Hoover. *The
Treason Trail in South Africa: A Guide to
the Microfilm Record of the Trial* pub by
Hoover. *History of the Library and Archives
of the Hoover Institution on War,
Revolution and Peace*, edited by Peter
Duignan (Hoover Institution Press), *Guide
to Non-federal Archives and Manuscripts in
the United States Relating to Africa*,
compiled Aloha P Smith (East Ardsley, Eng,
Microform Ltd).
DC —HOWARD UNIVERSITY, Moorland-
Spingarn Research Center, 500 Howard
Place NW, Washington, 20059. Clifford L
Muse, Jr, Acting Dir
IL —WHEATON COLLEGE, Buswell
Memorial Library, Wheaton, 60187. Paul
Snezek, Library Dir
Holdings: Mss Cat
Notes: Material consists of word lists, a
conversation manual, a dictionary and the
translated New Testament. All of the
material collected by Zaire Missionary
pioneer, Theodore B Wallin. *Related Topics:*
Radio.
MI —MICHIGAN STATE UNIVERSITY,
International Library, Africana Collection,
East Lansing, 48824. Eugene de Benko,
Librn; Onuma Ezera, Bibliographer for

Africana
Holdings: Vols (82,700) Cat Mss Maps Pix
Slides Phonorecords Audiotapes Videotapes
Filmstrips Microforms
Budget: ($78,000)
See also entry under Africa for full
description.
WI —UNIVERSITY OF WISCONSIN,
MADISON, Memorial Library, 728 State St,
Madison, 53706. David Henige, Librn
Holdings: // Cat Mss Maps Microforms
Notes: Congo Collection: Books, pamphlets,
colonial documents and ephemera concerned
with the colonial period in the history of the
Congo. Available in both the original and on
microfilm. Incl archival materials (5 reels)
relating to the career of Maurice Martin de
Ryck, who served as Governor of Equateur
Province, Belgian Congo, as well as other
misc data relating to Equateur Province. The
originals of these microforms are housed in
the Rare Book Dept.

ZAIRE—HISTORY

DC —LIBRARY OF CONGRESS,
Washington, 20540.
Notes: Project of a consortium to microfilm
about 200,000 pp of material on Great
Britain, France, Russian and Prussia, for the
period 1848-1918 in the ms and
documentary collections of the Austrian
State Archives. The collection will incl,
among others, documents on the Austro-
Prussian War of 1866, the treaty
negotiations between France and Italy in
1868-1870, the Orient Question of 1877-
1878, the persecution of Jews in Russia in
1882, the Congo Conference in Berlin, 1884-
1887 and the British-Portuguese conflict in
East Africa, 1889-1891. Copies are available
at LC, the Center for Research Libraries, the
Hampshire Inter-Library Center, and the
libraries of Boston College, Yale, Harvard,
Duke, Stanford and the University of
Virginia.

ZAMBIA

DC —HOWARD UNIVERSITY, Moorland-
Spingarn Research Center, 500 Howard
Place NW, Washington, 20059. Clifford L
Muse, Jr, Acting Dir

ZANG ZUNG LANGUAGE AND LITERATURE

†NY —INSTITUTE FOR ADVANCED
STUDIES OF WORLD RELIGIONS
(IASWR), Library, State University of New
York at Stony Brook, Stony Brook, 11794. C
T Shen, Librn
Holdings: Vols 4400 Mss Microforms

ZANGWILL, ISRAEL, 1864-1926

CA —UNIVERSITY OF CALIFORNIA, LOS
ANGELES, Research Library, Dept of
Special Collections, 405 Hilgard Ave, Los
Angeles, 90024. Edward Shreeves,
Chairman, Bibliographers Group; David S
Zeidberg, Head
Holdings: Vols 100
Notes: 100 first and other editions of his
books; 75 letters; clippings, etc.

ZANZIBAR see Tanzania

ZAPLITNY, FREDERICK SAMUEL, 1913-1964

MB —UNIVERSITY OF MANITOBA,
Elizabeth Dafoe Library, Archives and
Special Collections Dept, Winnipeg, R3T
2N2, Can. Richard E Bennett, Dept Head;
Corrado A Santoro, Reference Archivist
Notes: Papers of Frederick Samuel Zaplitny,
Member of Parliament from Dauphin,
Manitoba (1945-1957). One packet.

ZAPOTEC INDIANS

NY —HOFSTRA UNIVERSITY, Library,
1000 Fulton Ave, Hempstead, 11550.
Charles R Andrews, Dean of Library

Services
Notes: The personal library of Paul Radin.
See description of the American
Philosophical Society Library's collection of
his anthropological papers under this entry
(Pa).
PA —AMERICAN PHILOSOPHICAL
SOCIETY, Library, 105 S Fifth St,
Philadelphia, 19106. Edward C Carter II,
Librn
Notes: The anthropological papers of Paul
Radin in fields of ethnology, social
organization, primitive religion, linguistics,
and mythology. He worked mostly among
the Winnebago, Ojibwa, Fox, Zapotec,
Wappo, Wintun, and Huave Indian tribes;
also Italian and other ethnic minorities of
San Francisco.

ZEBROWSKI, GEORGE

†PA —TEMPLE UNIVERSITY LIBRARY,
Philadelphia, 19122. Thomas M Whitehead,
Librn
Notes: More than 100 cubic ft of mss, incl
papers of Michael Bishop, Ben Bova, Jack
Dann, Gardner Dozois, Lloyd Eshback, Tom
Purdom, Pamela Sargent, John Varley, and
George Zebrowski.

ZEDER, SUSAN

AZ —ARIZONA STATE UNIVERSITY,
Library, Tempe, 85287. Marilyn
Wurzburger, Special Collections Librn
Holdings: Vols (108) Pix
Notes: Collection covers various aspects of
Children's Theatre from 1944 through the
present. Areas of emphasis incl International
and National Child Drama Associations,
award-winning theatres, educational
programs, regional groups and prominent
figures in Children's Theatre incl: Irene
Vickers Baker, Isabel Burger, Virginia Lee
Comer, Rita Criste, Moses Goldberg,
Kenneth Graham, Aurand Harris, Paul
Kozelka, George Latshaw, Rosemary Musil,
Sara Spencer, Winifred Ward, Susan Zeder
and Lin Wright. Publications incl
newsletters, research papers, bibliographies
and records of the proceedings of the
Children's Theatre Association of America.
80 linear feet of scripts, documents,
publications, films, tapes (oral history)
programs, correspondence, photographs,
working papers and clippings. Partially
indexed; finding guides available.

ZEISL, ERIC

CA —UNIVERSITY OF CALIFORNIA, LOS
ANGELES, Music Library, Schonberg Hall,
Los Angeles, 90024. Stephen M Fry, Music
Librn
Notes: Mss.

ZEITLIN AND VER BRUGGE (BOOKSELLERS)

CA —UNIVERSITY OF CALIFORNIA, LOS
ANGELES, Research Library, Dept of
Special Collections, 405 Hilgard Ave, Los
Angeles, 90024. Edward Shreeves,
Chairman, Bibliographers Group; David S
Zeidberg, Head
Notes: 140 linear feet of correspondence,
business records, and ephemera, of this Los
Angeles bookseller.

ZELAZNY, ROGER

†MD —UNIVERSITY OF MARYLAND,
BALTIMORE COUNTY, Library,
Baltimore, 21228. Maureen Dwyer-Hirten,
Librn
Notes: Mss incl Harry Harrison and Roger
Zelazny.

ZELENY, CHARLES

IL —UNIVERSITY OF ILLINOIS,
URBANA/CHAMPAIGN, Library,
University Archives, 19 Library, 1408 W
Gregory Drive, Urbana, 61801. Maynard
Brichford, University Archivist
Holdings: Cat Mss Maps Pix Slides
Microforms
Notes: Papers, archival records, etc.

ZELIGS, MEYER AARON, 1909-1978

MA —HARVARD UNIVERSITY LIBRARY, Law School Library, Langdell Hall, Cambridge, 02138. Erika S Chadbourn, Cur of Mss
Holdings: Cat Mss
Notes: Papers relating to his research, writing, and publication of *Friendship and Fratricide*. Typed inventory in repository. Inclusive dates: 1923-1978.

ZEMLINSKY, ALEXANDER

DC —LIBRARY OF CONGRESS, Music Division, Washington, 20540.
Notes: Papers and recordings of composer Arnold Schoenberg. Extensive correspondence with other composers, writers, etc.

ZEMSTVO

IL —UNIVERSITY OF ILLINOIS, URBANA/CHAMPAIGN, Slavic and East European Library, Urbana, 61801. Marianna Tax Choldin, Head
Holdings: Cat Microforms
Notes: IDC microfiche collection. (959) titles of symbolism, futurism, constructivism, acmeism, imagism, and zemstvo publications.
MA —HARVARD UNIVERSITY LIBRARY, Houghton Library, Cambridge, 02138. Rodney G Dennis, Cur of Manuscripts
Holdings: Mss
Notes: Archives dealing with the Zemstvo and Russian Social Democratic Workers' party.

ZEN

†CA —CALIFORNIA INSTITUTE OF ASIAN STUDIES LIBRARY, 3494 21 St, San Francisco, 94110.
Notes: Philosophy, psychology, religion, Hindu and Buddhist literature, Yoga and Zen discipline, art, Asian languages.

ZEND LANGUAGE see Avesta Language and Literature

ZEPPELINS

OH —AKRON-SUMMIT COUNTY PUBLIC LIBRARY, Science & Technology Div, 55 S Main St, Akron, 44326. Joyce McKnight, Head
Holdings: Vols 820 Cat Pix
Notes: The Ligher-Than-Air Society book collection is in the Akron Public Library.

ZERO-GRAVITY STATE—PHYSIOLOGICAL EFFECT see Weightlessness

ZILAHY, LAJOS

MA —BOSTON UNIVERSITY, Mugar Memorial Library, Special Collections Dept, 771 Commonwealth Ave, Boston, 02215. Howard B Gotlieb, Dir
Holdings: Cat Mss Pix Audiotapes
Notes: Mss, correspondence, etc collected in depth; incl publications by or about.

ZIMBABWE see Rhodesia

ZIMMERMAN, WILLIAM

NM —UNIVERSITY OF NEW MEXICO, School of Law Library, 1117 Stanford Dr NE, Albuquerque, 87131. Myron Fink, Law Librn
Holdings: Vols (3000) Cat Mss
Notes: Collection supports the work of the American Indian Law Center, established by the law school. Has separate catalog with extensive subject analysis. Incl papers of William Zimmerman, Asst Commissioner of Indian Affairs, 1934-1950. Emphasis is on government relations, tribal government (especially tribal codes for all Indian tribes in US). Incl materials on indigenous peoples world-wide. Periodical literature is subject

indexed. Bibliography: Sabatini, Joseph D, *American Indian Law: A Bibliography of Books, Law Review Articles and Indian Periodicals*. (Albuquerque, 1973), Supplement, 1975.

ZINC

NY —ZINC INSTITUTE LEAD INDUSTRIES ASSOCIATION, 292 Madison Ave, New York, 10017. Mary W Covington, Mgr Information Servs
Notes: Technical information on lead and zinc.

ZINC TOXICOLOGY

MD —NATIONAL LIBRARY OF MEDICINE, 8600 Rockville Pike, Bethesda, 20209. Harold M Schoolinam, Actg Dir
Budget: ($46,400)

ZINN, EARL F.

RI —BROWN UNIVERSITY, John Hay Library, 20 Prospect St, Providence, 02912. Mark N Brown, Cur Mss
Holdings: Mss
Notes: Papers of Earl F Zinn, American psychiatrist, comprising medical records of 350 hours of analytical interviews with a schizophrenic patient for a period of about four years in the 1930s; also a portfolio of art work by the same patient and a letter from Freud.

ZION NATIONAL PARK

UT —ZION NATIONAL PARK, Library, Springdale, 84767. Roy Given, Asst Chief Park Naturalist; Marion Hilkey, Librn
Holdings: Vols (2700) Cat Mss Maps Pix Audiotapes
Budget: ($1000)
Notes: Emphasis on history and natural history of Zion National Park and vicinity and other information bearing on the management and operation of the Park. ILL permitted upon prior approval of the Park Superintendent.

ZIONCHECK, REP. MARION

WA —UNIVERSITY OF WASHINGTON LIBRARIES, Suzzallo Library, Manuscripts Section, FM-25, Seattle, 98195. Karyl Winn, Librn
Notes: Papers from 1932-36, 1.75 linear ft.

ZIONISM

†CA —HEBREW UNION COLLEGE, Jewish Institute of Religion, 3077 University Ave, Los Angeles, 90007.
Notes: Bible, Talmud, Rabbinics, Jewish history, philosophy, art and communal science, Hebrew literature, religion, Zionism.
CA —HOOVER INSTITUTION ON WAR, REVOLUTION & PEACE, Stanford University, Stanford, 94305. Milorad M Drachkovitch, Archivist
Holdings: Mss
Notes: Papers of Herbert Solow, American journalist, and editor of *Fortune*, 1945-1964, incl correspondence, speeches, drafts of writings, memoranda, depositions, clippings and other printed matter, 1924-76, relating to the communist movement in the US, the Non-Partisan Defense League, the Commission of Inquiry into the Charges Made Against Leon Trotsky in the Moscow Trials, Soviet espionage in the US, Zionism, and post-World War II international business enterprises. Incl some papers of Mrs Herbert Solow, 1964-76. 8 ms boxes.
FL —UNIVERSITY OF FLORIDA LIBRARY, Isser and Rae Price Library of Judaica, 18 Libr East, Gainesville, 32611. Robert Singerman, Head Librn
Budget: ($30,000)
Notes: Total holdings estimated at 55,000 vols dealing with the political, social, economic and intellectual history of the Jews in the ancient, medieval and modern periods and in all geographic areas. The following areas are especially well represented by

printed matter in all relevant languages: Bibliography, Festschriften, History, Bible, Judaism and Jewish theology, liturgy, responsa, rabbinical literature, Jewish law, Hebrew language and literature, Yiddish language and literature, anti-semitism, Zionism, Palestine and the *Yishuv*, and the State of Israel. German and American Judaica form a collecting emphasis with holdings for all the standard histories as well as histories of individual synagogues, institutions and local communities. Works in Hebrew and Yiddish comprise about 60 percent of the collection (estimated 30,000 vols). With few exceptions, holdingsare limited to nineteenth and twentieth century imprints, with complete sets of journals and thousands of ephemeral pamphlets, many of them commemorating anniversaries, enhancing the research value of the collection, the largest Judaica research library in the southeastern United States. Only about half of the collection is cataloged; the collection is a circulating one and vols may be borrowed on interlibrary loan. Incl the Leonard C Mishkin Collection (40,000 vols), the largest personal Judaica collection in the United States, the Shlomo Marenof Collection (3500 vols), and the inventory of Bernard Morgenstern's Lower East Side Book Store (8000 vols). Scholars should inquire in advance of their visit. *The Isser and Rae Price Library of Judaica* Report (circulation 2900 copies) is mailed gratis twice a year to all interested parties. Special catalogs:Pre-1881 Hebrew imprints recorded in a chronological card file.
†MA —HARVARD UNIVERSITY LIBRARY, Widener Library, Judaica Collection, Room M, Cambridge, 02138. Charles Berlin, Bibliographer
Holdings: Cat
Notes: For holdings, see *Widener Library Shelflist No 39* (1971) and the Library's *Catalogue of Hebrew Books* (1968), with *Supplement* (1972).
NY —NEW YORK PUBLIC LIBRARY, Jewish Division, Fifth Ave & 42 St, New York, 10018. Leonard S Gold, Chief
Holdings: Vols (200,000) Cat Mss Microforms
Budget: ($33,383)
Notes: A collection of material in all languages on Judaism, Jewish history, literature and traditions from the earliest times to date and works in the Hebrew alphabet (mainly Hebrew and Yiddish) on a variety of subjects. The division has extensive files of Jewish periodicals and newspapers. The collection of rare Hebraica incl medieval texts, cabalistic works, ethical and philosophical tracts in book form. See *Dictionary Catalog of the Jewish Collection* (Boston: G K Hall, 1960), 14 vols. First Supplement (Boston: G K Hall, 1975), 8 vols.
†NY —WORLD ZIONIST ORGANIZATION - AMERICAN SECTION, Zionist Archives and Library, 515 Park Ave, New York, 10022.
Notes: Israel, Zionism, Middle East, history of the Jews and Jewish life.
OH —HEBREW UNION COLLEGE-JEWISH INSTITUTE OF RELIGION, Klau Library, 3101 Clifton Ave, Cincinnati, 45220. David J Gilner, Reference Librn
Holdings: Cat
OH —OHIO STATE UNIVERSITY, William Oxley Thompson Memorial Library, 1858 Neil Ave, Columbus, 43210. Amnon Zipin, Jewish Studies Bibliographer
Holdings: Vols (43,000) Cat Maps Microfilms
Budget: ($35,000)
Notes: Collection emphasis is materials on Jewish history (especially US, Israel and Europe) and Hebrew language and literature. Small collection of Yiddish materials.

ZIONIST MOVEMENT see Zionism

ZIRIAN LANGUAGE see Syryenian Language and Literature

ZITTERBART, FIDELIS

PA —UNIVERSITY OF PITTSBURGH, Music Library, B-31 Music Bldg, Pittsburgh, 15260.

ZITTERBART, FIDELIS (cont.)

Norris L Stephens, Music Librn
Holdings: // Uncat Mss
Notes: Incl 1000 ms pieces of music, etc. A catalog is in preparation. No photocopying.

ZIV TELEVISION FILMS

†WI —STATE HISTORICAL SOCIETY OF WISCONSIN, Mass Communications History Center, 816 State Street, Madison, 53706.
Notes: 2000 Ziv television filsm

ZOARITES

OH —MASSILLON PUBLIC LIBRARY, 208 Lincoln Way E, Massillon, 44646. Camille Leslie, Dir
Holdings: Vols 73 Cat Mss
Budget: $100
Notes: Collection is limited to historical studies; nothing on modern communes. Special emphasis on Shakers and Zoarites. No separate catalog.

ZODOR, EUGENE

CA —UNIVERSITY OF CALIFORNIA, LOS ANGELES, Music Library, Schonberg Hall, Los Angeles, 90024. Stephen M Fry, Music Librn
Holdings: Mss

ZOLA, EMILE

MA —HARVARD UNIVERSITY LIBRARY, Houghton Library, Cambridge, 02138. Rodney G Dennis, Cur of Manuscripts
Holdings: Cat Mss
NY —SYRACUSE UNIVERSITY LIBRARIES, Ernest S Bird Library, George Arents Research Library for Special Collections, Syracuse, 13210. Carolyn A Davis, Manuscripts Librn; Amy S Doherty, University Archivist; Mark F Weimer, Rare Book Librn
Holdings: Cat Mss
Notes: 31 letters.
RI —BROWN UNIVERSITY, John Hay Library, 20 Prospect St, Providence, 02912. Mark N Brown, Cur Mss
Holdings: Mss
Notes: ALS by Zola, 1864-1901, 77 of which were addressed to Henri Ceard, novelist and playwright.

ZONING

MD —MARYLAND-NATIONAL CAPITAL PARK & PLANNING COMMISSION, Montgomery County Planning Department Library, 8787 Georgia Ave, Silver Spring, 20907. Janice C Holt, Librn
Holdings: Vols (5000) Cat
Notes: Specific subject areas include: community facilities, conservation, economics, flood control, highways, housing, human and natural resources. landscape architecture, open space, parks, pollution, population, recreation, transportation, urban renewal, and zoning. Commission's publications are maintained by Records Management (not Library).
PA —DELAWARE COUNTY PLANNING DEPT, Library, Third & Orange St, Media, 19063. Jane Taggart Quin, Librn
Holdings: Vols 4800 Cat
Budget: $1500

ZONOPHONE RECORDS

DC —LIBRARY OF CONGRESS, Motion Pictures, Broadcasting and Recorded Sound Div, Washington, 20540.
Holdings: Cat
Notes: 133 Berliner Gramophone Co records, 1896-1900; 31 Zonophone records, 1899-1904; 2 rare Vitaphone records, 1899; 67 Eldridge R Johnson records, 1900-1901; and 30 Victor Talking Machine Co records, 1902-1909.

ZOOARCHAEOLOGY

ON —NATIONAL MUSEUMS OF CANADA, Library Services Directorate, Ottawa, K1A 0M8, Can. Valerie Monkhouse, Director
Holdings: Vols (90,000) Cat Mss Microforms
Budget: ($81,000)
Notes: Emphasis on Canadian and circumpolar natural history. Collection incl botany, herpetology, ichthyology, invertebrate zoology, malacology, mammology, mineralogy, ornithology, paleobiology, zooarchaeology. Exceptional collections in lichenology, bryology, malacology, ornithology. Research collection, interlibrary loans available, public may use on the premises.

ZOOGEOGRAPHY

PA —CARNEGIE LIBRARY OF PITTSBURGH, Science & Technology Dept, 4400 Forbes Ave, Pittsburgh, 15213. Catherine M Brosky, Dept Head
Notes: Except for certain special areas, such as entomology and ornithology and a few others that are emphasized, this general subject is of secondary interest. Incl both modern and classic works. Kept up to date in cooperation with the Library in Carnegie Museum of Natural History. Materials available on the various phyla, classes, orders and species. Abstracts, indexes, bibliographies, taxomin manuals and standard reference books. Many journals and society publications complete from the beginning.

ZOOLOGICAL GARDENS

CA —ESHERICK, HOMSEY, DODGE & DAVIS, Library, 2789 25th St, San Francisco, 94110. Elizabeth Walton, Librn
Holdings: Vols (2500) Cat Maps Pix Slides
Notes: General history of architecture; solar energy applications to architecture; residential architecture; zoo architecture; handbooks, codes, and standards; school and university architecture. Also incl is a large collection of product literature catalogs and samples (uncataloged).
DC —SMITHSONIAN INSTITUTION LIBRARIES, National Zoological Park Branch, Washington, 20008. Kay Kenyon, Chief Librn
Holdings: Vols (5500) Cat
Notes: Collection incl animal nutrition, capture and care of animals in captivity, conservation and endangered species, pathology, veterinary medicine, zoology.
KS —TOPEKA ZOOLOGICAL PARK, Topeka Zoo Library, 635 Gage Blvd, Topeka, 66606. Ron Kaufman, Education Coordinator
Holdings: Vols (800) Cat Mss Maps Pix Slides Audiotapes 16mm Films Filmstrips Microforms
Budget: ($500)
NY —NEW YORK ZOOLOGICAL SOCIETY LIBRARY, Bronx Zoo, Bronx, 10460. Steven P Johnson, Archivist and Librn
Holdings: Vols (6000) Cat Mss
Budget: ($50,000)
Notes: Collection consists primarily of journals in captive management of animals, vertebrate zoology, and veterinary medicine. Primarily intended for the scientific staff, the collection is open to the public on a noncirculating basis, by appointment, (212) 220-6874.
PA —ZOOLOGICAL SOCIETY OF PHILADELPHIA, Library, 34 & Girard Ave, Philadelphia, 19104. Alyssa N Scheuermann, Librn
Holdings: Vols (500) Cat
Notes: Photocopying with permission. Collection includes history of zoos, zoo planning, maps of zoos, etc. Incl contracts, blueprints, artifacts.
WI —CIRCUS WORLD MUSEUM LIBRARY, 415 Lynn St, Baraboo, 53913. Robert L Parkinson, Research Center Dir
Holdings: Vols (1800) Cat Mss Pix Slides Phonorecords 16mm Films
Notes: Circus and "Wild West" shows. Owned by State Historical Society of Wisconsin. Incl 1800 books on circus subject; 400 route books; 9500 programs, 8000 circus lithographs, 15,000 photo negatives, 25,000 photo prints, heralds, couriers, tickets, letterheads, route cards, original circus artwork, records and documents of circus business, movies, newspaper ads, circus band music and periodicals of show business such as *Billboard, New York Clipper, White Tops,* Bandwagon, etc. Partially cataloged.

ZOOLOGICAL ILLUSTRATION

IN —BUTLER UNIVERSITY, Irwin Library, Hugh Thomas Miller Rare Book Room, 4600 Sunset Ave, Indianapolis, 46208. Gisela Terrell, Rare Books Librn
Holdings: Uncat
Notes: Zoological print collection tracing the history and development of zoological illustration from the 15th through the mid-19th centuries.

ZOOLOGICAL MYTHOLOGY see Animal Lore

ZOOLOGY

CA —UNIVERSITY OF CALIFORNIA, DAVIS, General Library, Davis, 95616. Bernard Kreissman, University Librn; C Danial Elliott, Asst Head, Dept Special Collections
Holdings: Vols 20,000 Cat Microforms
Notes: All fields of the zoological sciences are emphasized.
CA —UNIVERSITY OF CALIFORNIA, SAN DIEGO, Central University Library, Mandeville Dept of Special Collections, La Jolla, 92093. Lynda Corey Claassen, Head
Notes: Hill Collection: One of the most distinguished collections on early voyages to all parts of the Pacific Ocean, these materials include more than 2000 accounts of and commentaries on important voyages from the 16th to the mid 19th century, plus extensive anthropological, botanical, and zoological reports made by scientists who accompanied the explorers.
CA —UNIVERSITY OF CALIFORNIA, LOS ANGELES, Biomedical Library, Center for the Health Sciences, Los Angeles, 90024. Alison Bunting, Acting Biomedical Librn; Victoria Steele, Head, History & Special Collections Div
Holdings: Vols (400,000) Cat Slides Phonorecords Audiotapes Videotapes 16mm Films Microforms
Notes: The UCLA Biomedical Library serves primarily the Schools of Medicine, Dentistry, Nursing, and Public Health, the UCLA Medical Center, the Departments of Microbiology and Biology in the College of Letters and Science, and related institutes in biomedicine. The collections of the Library are broad in scope, designed not only to support the teaching and research needs of its many users, but also to function as a resource for the health sciences-biological field as a whole. The outstanding feature of the collection is the strength of its periodical holdings, both current and retrospective. The Library also has an excellent reference collection, a comprehensive historical section, and gives special emphasis to the fields of neuroscience, psychiatry, ophthalmology, radiation biology, molecular biology, and vertebrate zoology. Increased emphasis is being given to the acquisition of audiovisual materials.

CA —WESTERN FOUNDATION OF VERTEBRATE ZOOLOGY, Library, 1100 Glendon Ave, Los Angeles, 90024. Lloyd F Kiff, Dir
Holdings: Vols (4000) Uncat Mss Pix Slides

ZOOLOGY (cont.)

16mm Films
Budget: ($10,000)
Notes: This is probably the third largest collection on birds in the Western US. It incl the combined resources of 10 former private libraries on this topic, plus additions made by us during the past 20 years. There is special emphasis on oology, or the study of bird eggs. The collection is freely available for use by any interested researcher.

CA —CONTRA COSTA COUNTY LIBRARY, 1750 Oak Park Blvd, Pleasant Hill, 94523. Barbara Potter, Librn
Holdings: Vols (18,000)

CA —CALIFORNIA STATE POLYTECHNIC UNIVERSITY, POMONA, University Library, 3801 W Temple Ave, Pomona, 91768. Harold Schleiser, Actg Dir
Notes: General reference materials on agricultural business management, agricultural engineering, animal science, horticulture and plant and soil science.

†CA —ZOOLOGICAL SOCIETY OF SAN DIEGO, Ernst Schwarz Library, San Diego Zoo, Box 551, San Diego, 92112.

CA —CALIFORNIA ACADEMY OF SCIENCES, J W Mailliard Jr Library, Golden Gate Park, San Francisco, 94118. Ray Brian, Librn
Notes: Downs No 2160.

CO —COLORADO STATE UNIVERSITY, Libraries, Fort Collins, 80523. Curtis L Gifford, Forestry & Agricultural Sciences Librn
Holdings: Vols (24,444) Cat Maps Microforms
Budget: ($9000)
Notes: The 9300 microforms are primarily on wildlife management and behavior.

CT —YALE UNIVERSITY, Medical Historical Library, 333 Cedar St, New Haven, 06510. Ferenc A Gyorgyey, Librn
Holdings: Vols 600 Cat
Notes: The George Milton Smith Collection of early ichthyology.

CT —YALE UNIVERSITY, Kline Science Library, Kline Biology Tower Rm C-8, PO Box 6666, New Haven, 06511. Richard J Dionne, Head
Holdings: Vols (175,480) Cat 16mm Films Microforms
Budget: ($340,000)
Notes: Comprehensive collection on biological sciences, physics, and chemistry. Incl Evans Collection of Bryology and Lichenology (with catalog cards in both Kline Science Library and Sterling Memorial Library). Also incl AEC reports (hardcopy and microform) to 1970.

DC —NATIONAL GEOGRAPHIC SOCIETY, Library, 1146 16th St NW, Washington, 20036. Susan Fifer Canby, Dir
Holdings: Vols (63,000) Cat Mss Maps Pix
Notes: Material concerning land, sea, and space exploration--past and present. All fields of anthropology, natural history, geography, etc.

DC —SMITHSONIAN INSTITUTION, Archives Div, Washington, 20560. William W Moss, Archivist
Holdings: Cat Mss Maps Pix Slides
Notes: The Archives holds the records of the National Museum of Natural History's Dept of Invertebrate Zoology, Division of Echinoderms, Division of Marine Invertebrates, and Division of Mollusks, ca 1853-1975, as well as the personal papers of William H Dall, Paul Bartsch, Austin H Clark, and Waldo LaSalle Schmitt.

DC —SMITHSONIAN INSTITUTION, Smithsonian Tropical Research Institute, Washington, 20560. Carol Jopling, Chief Librn
Holdings: Vols (22,000) Cat Mss Maps Pix Slides 16mm Films Microforms
Budget: ($70,000)
Notes: Smithsonian Institution, Smithsonian Tropical Research Institute is located in Balboa, Panama.

DC —SMITHSONIAN INSTITUTION LIBRARIES, National Zoological Park Branch, Washington, 20008. Kay Kenyon, Chief Librn
Holdings: Vols (5500) Cat
Notes: Collection incl animal nutrition, capture and care of animals in captivity, conservation and endangered species, pathology, veterinary medicine, zoology.

DC —SMITHSONIAN INSTITUTION LIBRARIES, Natural History Branch, Washington, 20560. Sylvia Churgin, Chief Librn
Holdings: Vols (75,500) Cat Mss Maps Pix Slides Microforms
Notes: Incl vertebrate and invertebrate paleontology; vertebrate zoology: systematics and taxonomy.

FL —ARCHBOLD BIOLOGICAL STATION, Library, Rt 2, Box 180, Lake Placid, 33852. Fred E Lohrer, Librn
Holdings: Uncat VF
Notes: Physiological ecology of vertebrates. Incl 3 vertical files of reprints, etc. Extensive and growing cataloged collection on Florida mammals also. (Library is no longer enlarging reprint collection.)

HI —BERNICE P BISHOP MUSEUM, Library, PO Box 19000-A, Honolulu, 96819. Cynthia Timberlake, Librn
Holdings: Vols (90,000) Cat Mss Maps Pix Slides Microforms
Budget: ($30,000)
Notes: Only American library devoted exclusively to the Pacific region. Collection reflects historical and contemporary research emphases of Bishop Museum; ie the natural and cultural history of the Pacific. Areas of concentration incl archaeology, ethnology, linguistics, voyages and explorations, history, vertebrate and invertebrate zoology, botany and museology. Strong special collections incl photographs, mss and archives, maps and art. Publications: Quarterly "Additions to the Catalog," *Dictionary Catalog of the Library* (9 vols and 2 suppl; Boston: G K Hall, 1964-69).

IL —ILLINOIS NATURAL HISTORY SURVEY LIBRARY, 196 Natural Resources Bldg, Champaign, 61820. Carla G Heister, Librn
Holdings: Vols (36,000) Cat Microforms
Budget: ($25,500)
Notes: A Research and Science Branch of the State of Illinois, the Natural History Survey maintains a library of books, journals and reports on various aspects of natural history. Material is collected in all major languages. The library maintains its own exchange arrangements with some 600 worldwide institutions and organizations. Interlibrary loans and photocopy services are available through the University of Illinois Library. Publications issued regularly by the Survey incl *Biological Notes, The Bulletin, and Circulars.*

IL —FIELD MUSEUM OF NATURAL HISTORY, Library, Roosevelt Rd & Lake Shore Dr, Chicago, 60605. W Peyton Fawcett, Librn; Benjamin W Williams, Assoc Librn
Holdings: Vols (210,000) Cat
Budget: ($100,000)
Notes: Extensive collections--publications of learned societies and institutions and monographic works--in all fields of natural history, with emphasis on taxonomy and evolutionary biology; and on museum publications, American and foreign: anthropology, especially archaeology and ethnology of the Americas, Africa, East Asia, and Oceania; botany, particularly strong for the Americas; geology, chiefly paleontology and meteoritic studies; and zoology, worldwide (birds, fishes, insects, mammals, mollusks, reptiles and amphibians).

IL —UNIVERSITY OF CHICAGO LIBRARIES, John Crerar Library Collections, 1100 E 57th St, Chicago, 60637. Robert Rosenthal, Special Collections Librn
Notes: The John Crerar Library's extensive science, medicine, and engineering collections have been transferred in trust to the University of Chicago Libraries. Incl rare books and special collections as listed here.

IL —UNIVERSITY OF ILLINOIS, URBANA/CHAMPAIGN, Library, Biology Library, 101 Burrill Hall, 407 S Goodwin, Urbana, 61801. Elisabeth B Davis, Librn
Holdings: Vols (115,000) Cat Microforms
Budget: ($200,000)
Notes: The Biology Library incl books, periodicals, and reference works that cover the fields of anatomy, biophysics, botany, ecology, entomology, genetics, immunology, microbiology, physiology and zoology. About three-quarters of the total collection is made up of journals and other serials representing 2000 distinctive titles. The serial list is comprehensive for the biological sciences, contains most of the major international titles and consists of complete runs for almost all titles. Additional materials (approx 90,000 vols) in the biological sciences are available in the Natural History Survey Library and the bookstacks at the Main Library on the Urbana campus. Professional assistance is available for reference service, online searching, and library instruction. Interlibrary loan service is provided. Photocopying.

IN —INDIANA UNIVERSITY, Biology Library, Jordan Hall, Bloomington, 47405. Steven Sowell, Head
Holdings: Vols (105,461) Cat

IN —PURDUE UNIVERSITY LIBRARIES, Life Sciences Library, Lilly Hall of Life Sciences, West Lafayette, 47907. Martha J Bailey, Librn
Holdings: Vols (73,404) Cat Microforms
Budget: ($223,445)
Notes: Incl materials in agronomy, animal sciences, botany, entomology, forestry, horticulture, and biological sciences.

IA —IOWA STATE UNIVERSITY, Library, Ames, 50011. Warren B Kuhn, Dean of Library Services
Holdings: Cat
Notes: Extensive serial holdings supplemented this strong collection.

IA —IOWA STATE UNIVERSITY, Library, Dept of Special Collections, Ames, 50011. Stanley M Yates, Head
Holdings: // Mss Pix
Notes: The Paul Errington (1902-1962) Papers. Professor of zoology at ISU (1932-1962) and a leading authority on vertebrate ecology and animal population dynamics. Collection incl correspondence, mss and articles. Collection is 15 linear feet.

IA —UNIVERSITY OF IOWA, Zoology Library, Zoology Bldg, Iowa City, 52242. Jack W Dickey, Zoology Librn
Holdings: Vols 33,800 Cat
Budget: $69,000

KS —UNIVERSITY OF KANSAS, Kenneth Spencer Research Library, Special Collections Dept, Lawrence, 66045. Alexandra Mason, Librn
Holdings: Cat Mss
Notes: Ellis Collection of Ornithology, Natural History, and Voyages and Travels; De Beer Collection of offprints; Herrick-Coghill-Roofe collection of neurology; D'Arcy Wentworth Thompson offprints and separates. Noncirculating.

MD —NATIONAL LIBRARY OF MEDICINE, 8600 Rockville Pike, Bethesda, 20209. Harold M Schoolinam, Actg Dir
Holdings: Vols (3,150,000) Cat Mss Audiotapes Videotapes 16mm Films Filmstrips Microforms
Budget: ($46,400)
Notes: The world's largest medical library. Materials are collected exhaustively in some 40 biomedical areas and, to a lesser degree, in related subject areas such as general chemistry, physics, zoology, botany, and instrumentation. Holdings include 82,000 monographic volumes, pre-1871; 438,000 monographic volumes, 1871-present; 714,000 bound serial volumes; 281,000 theses; 172,000 pamphlets; 1,207,000 manuscripts; 156,000 microforms; 12,000 audiovisuals; and 75,000 prints and photographs. Pre-1871 material is in a separate historical collection. Approximately 24,000 serial titles are currenlty received.

MA —UNIVERSITY OF MASSACHUSETTS AT AMHERST, Library, Amherst, 01003. Siegfried Feller, Assoc Dir for Collection Development
Holdings: Cat Microforms
Notes: Special emphasis on cellular, developmental and physiological zoology.

MA —FRANCIS A COUNTWAY LIBRARY OF MEDICINE, Boston Medical Library/

ZOOLOGY (cont.)

Harvard Medical Library, 10 Shattuck St, Boston, 02115. C Robin LeSueur, Librn; Richard J Wolfe, Cur, Rare Books & Manuscripts
Holdings: Vols (500,000) Cat Mss Maps Pix Microforms
Notes: Combines resources of the Harvard School and the Boston Medical Library. Strong in serials and medical history in all fields of medicine, incl incunabula, non-medical books by doctors, travel books by doctors. 500,000 medical dissertations and theses. Special strength in all medical subjects listed in this volume.

MA —HARVARD UNIVERSITY, Museum of Comparative Zoology, Library, 26 Oxford St, Cambridge, 02138. Eva S Jonas, Librn
Holdings: Vols (225,000) Cat mss Microforms
Budget: ($336,000)
Notes: Catalog, in 8 vols, published in 1968. For description, see *Harvard Library Bulletin*, VI (1952): pp 202-218. Strong collections on ornithology and entomology, Linneana, and personal papers and archives of Louis Agassiz.

MA —WELLESLEY COLLEGE, Margaret Clapp Library, College Archives, Wellesley, 02181.
Notes: Records of the Departments of Astronomy, Biological Sciences, Botany, Chemistry, Geology, Physics, Zoology, and individuals connected with these departments at Wellesley College (27 linear feet).

NH —DARTMOUTH COLLEGE, Dartmouth-Hitchcock Medical Center, Dana Biomedical Library, Hanover, 03756. Shirley J Grainger, Librn
Holdings: Vols (143,611) Cat Mss Phonorecords Audiotapes Videotapes Microforms
Budget: ($280,000)

NY —NEW YORK ZOOLOGICAL SOCIETY LIBRARY, Bronx Zoo, Bronx, 10460. Steven P Johnson, Archivist and Librn
Holdings: Vols (6000) Cat Mss
Budget: ($50,000)
Notes: Collection consists primarily of journals in captive management of animals, vertebrate zoology, and veterinary medicine. Primarily intended for the scientific staff, the collection is open to the public on a noncirculating basis, by appointment. (212) 220-6874.

NY —CORNELL UNIVERSITY LIBRARIES, Collection of Regional History, Dept of Manuscripts and Univ Archives, Ithaca, 14853.
Notes: Incl records, 1941; letters, photos, grade transcripts, biographical information, recommendations, and dossiers on 22 applicants for an instructorship in the Cornell University Department of Zoology.

NY —AMERICAN MUSEUM OF NATURAL HISTORY, Library Services Dept, Central Park W & 79th St, New York, 10024. Nina J Root, Chairwoman; Mary Genett, Asst Librn for Reference Services
Holdings: Vols (385,000) Cat Mss Maps Pix Slides Microforms
Notes: Nearly all collections are outstanding for depth of coverage and international range. Early and historic works, rare books, colored illustrations, and relevant serial publicatons supplement the modern scientific publications necessary to the researches of the sceintific staff and the work of the educational division. Open to the public.

NY —COLUMBIA UNIVERSITY LIBRARIES, Rare Book & Manuscript Library, 801 Butler Library, 535 W 114 St, New York, 10027. Kenneth A Lohf, Librn
Holdings: Vols (34,000)

NY —STATE UNIVERSITY OF NEW YORK, COLLEGE OF ENVIRONMENTAL SCIENCE AND FORESTRY, F Franklin Moon Library, Syracuse, 13210. Donald F Webster, Librn
Holdings: Vols (86,430) Cat
Budget: ($120,000)

NC —UNIVERSITY OF NORTH CAROLINA, CHAPEL HILL, Zoology Dept Library, Wilson Hall 046A, Chapel Hill, 27514. John B Darling, Librn
Holdings: Vols (31,000) Cat
Notes: Collection incl theses and dissertations.

OH —OHIO STATE UNIVERSITY, Biological Sciences Library, 1735 Neil Ave, Columbus, 43210. Victoria Welborn, Librn
Holdings: Vols (85,000) Cat Mss Maps Microforms

OR —OREGON STATE UNIVERSITY, Library, Corvallis, 97331. Melvin George, Dir
Holdings: Vols 19,000 Cat Maps Pix

PA —ZOOLOGICAL SOCIETY OF PHILADELPHIA, Library, 34 & Girard Ave, Philadelphia, 19104. Alyssa N Scheuermann, Librn
Holdings: Vols (500) Cat
Notes: Photocopying with permission.

PA —CARNEGIE LIBRARY OF PITTSBURGH, Science & Technology Dept, 4400 Forbes Ave, Pittsburgh, 15213. Catherine M Brosky, Dept Head
Notes: Except for certain special areas, such as entomology and ornithology and a few others that are emphasized, this general subject is of secondary interst. Incl both modern and classic works. Kept up to date in cooperations with the Library in Carnegie Museum of Natural History. Materials available on the various phyla, classes, orders and species. Abstracts, indexes, bibliographies, taxonomic manuals and standard reference books. Many journals and society publications complete from the beginning.

PA —PENNSYLVANIA STATE UNIVERSITY, Fred Lewis Pattee Library, Life Sciences Library, University Park, 16802. Keith Roe, Head
Notes: This collection is strong in periodical runs, particularly European learned societies and agriculture. It contains extensive collections of Experiment Station publications and has developed specialties in Mycology and Fusaria. There is also a special collection of 1105 glass glides on early Pennsylvania lumbering.

TX —UNIVERSITY OF TEXAS LIBRARIES, Science Library, PO Box P, Austin, 78712. Betty White, Librn
Holdings: Vols (103,000) Cat Microforms

TX —UNIVERSITY OF TEXAS, Marine Science Institute Library, Port Aransas, 78373. Ruth Grundy, Librn
Holdings: Vols (45,000) Cat Maps Pix
Budget: ($70,000)
Notes: Current researches in marine science, especially concerning the Gulf of Mexico, the Texas Coastal Zone, and the Continental Shelf. Incl journals.

WA —UNIVERSITY OF WASHINGTON LIBRARIES, Suzzallo Library, Natural Sciences Library, FM-25, Seattle, 98195. Nancy G Blase, Head
Holdings: Vols (192,353) Cat
Budget: ($219,809)

WI —MILWAUKEE PUBLIC MUSEUM, Reference Library, 800 W Wells St, Milwaukee, 53233. Judith Campbell Turner, Museum Librn
Holdings: Vols (90,000) Cat Maps Microforms

MB —MANITOBA MUSEUM OF MAN & NATURE, Library, 190 Rupert Ave, Winnipeg, R3B 0N2, Can. V Hatten, Librn
Holdings: Vols (20,000) Cat

MB —UNIVERSITY OF MANITOBA, Science Library, Machray Hall, Winnipeg, R3T 2N2, Can. V Simosko, Head
Holdings: Vols (90,000) Cat Microforms

ON —NATIONAL MUSEUMS OF CANADA, Library Services Directorate, Ottawa, K1A 0M8, Can. Valerie Monkhouse, Director
Holdings: Vols (90,000) Cat Mss Microforms
Budget: ($81,000)
Notes: Emphasis on Canadian and circumpolar natural history. Collection incl botany, herpetology, ichthyology, invertebrate zoology, malacology, mammology, mineralogy, ornithology, paleobiology, zooarchaeology. Exceptional collections in lichenology, bryology, malacology, ornithology. Research collection, interlibrary loans available, public may use on the premises.

ON —ROYAL ONTARIO MUSEUM, Main Library and Archives, 100 Queen's Park, Toronto, M5S 2C6, Can. Julia Matthews, Head Librn
Holdings: Vols (85,000) Cat
Notes: Since January 1977, acquisitions have been entered in UTLAS.

PQ —MCGILL UNIVERSITY, Blacker-Wood Library of Zoology & Ornithology, 3459 McTavish St, Montreal, H3A 1Y1, Can. Eleanor MacLean, Librn
Holdings: Vols (77,600) Cat Mss
Notes: Special features of collection incl: Robert Gurney Collection of reprints on Crustaceana (//); 3000 folders of letters from naturalists (//); over 9000 original paintings of wildlife; a small collection of falconry equipment (//); the archives of the Montreal Natural History Society (//); the archives of the North American Falconry Association; 156 17th-century feather pictures of birds and people (//). Does not incl entomology collection.

ZOOLOGY—EMBRYOLOGY see Embryology

ZOOLOGY—HISTORY

MI —UNIVERSITY OF MICHIGAN, Library, Dept of Rare Books & Special Collections, Ann Arbor, 48109. Robert J Starring, Head
Holdings: Cat Mss Pix
Notes: Chiefly pre-1800 imprints.

NY —CORNELL UNIVERSITY LIBRARIES, John M Olin Library, History of Science Collections, Ithaca, 14853. Lillian A Clark, Administrative Supervisor; David W Corson, History of Science Librn
Notes: Very extensive collection of history, biography and bibliography.
See also entry under Science - History

ZOOLOGY—MORPHOLOGY see Anatomy, Comparative

ZOOLOGY—NOMENCLATURES

NY —CORNELL UNIVERSITY LIBRARIES, Comstock Memorial Library of Entomology, Ithaca, 14853. Edwin Spragg, Librn
Holdings: Vols (30,000) Cat Maps Pix Audiotapes Microforms
Budget: ($13,500)
Notes: Major topics: general and applied entomology. Minor topics: parasitology, medical entomology, ecology, zoological nomenclature and allied orders of arthropods. Separate catalog to the collection, also extensive collection of reprints. Apiculture material kept at nearby A R Mann Library.

ZOONOSES

MT —PARKER-DAVIS MEMORIAL LIBRARY, 504 S Third St, Hamilton, 59840. William L Jellison, Dir
Notes: Most of material for this library has been transferred to Science Library at Miami University, Oxford, Ohio.

OH —MIAMI UNIVERSITY, Science Library, Oxford, 45056.
Notes: Zoonoses and related diseases. Collection partially transferred from Parker-Davis Memorial Library, Hamilton, Mont.

ZOOPHYTA see Echinodermata

ZOOS see Zoological Gardens

ZOOTOMY see Anatomy, Comparative

ZOOT-SUIT RIOTS, 1944

CA —UNIVERSITY OF CALIFORNIA, LOS ANGELES, Research Library, Dept of Special Collections, 405 Hilgard Ave, Los Angeles, 90024. Edward Shreeves, Chairman, Bibliographers Group; David S Zeidberg, Head
Holdings: // Uncat Mss
Notes: The Carey McWilliams Collection of

ZOOT-SUIT RIOTS, 1944 (cont.)

personal papers, clippings and reports incl material on the Zoot-Suit Riots.

ZOROASTRIANISM

NY —NEW YORK PUBLIC LIBRARY, Oriental Div, Fifth Ave & 42 St, New York, 10018. E Christian Filstrup, Chief
Holdings: Cat Mss Microforms
Budget: ($56,455)
Notes: Described in *Dictionary Catalog of the Oriental Collection*, The Research Libraries of the New York Public Library, 1960, 16 vols, and *First Supplement*, 1976, 8 vols (144,000 cards). This catalog incl 318,000 entries for works in about 100 languages of the East, and all works in Western languages on Oriental subjects. The Oriental Collection numbers about 120,000 vols; its Arabic and Indic holdings and those on ancient Egypt and the ancient Near East are among the largest in the US. There is also a collection of 30,000 vols of PL 480 material from Egypt, Pakistan, and India to which there is main entry access, but which is not incorporated into the dictionary catalog. Other outstanding features of the Oriental Collection incl extensive holdings of Japanese technical and scientific periodicals; a unique collection of linguistic works, grammars, anddictionaries; and unusually good coverage of the field of Oriental religions and philosophies. The catalog contains numerous subject references to periodical articles in all languages. All entries are arranged alphabetically according to the Roman alphabet.

OH —CLEVELAND PUBLIC LIBRARY, Fine Arts and Special Collections Department, 325 Superior Ave, Cleveland, 44114. Alice N Loranth, Head
Holdings: Vols (7000) Cat Mss Pix
Notes: Part of the Oriental Religion Collection. Emphasis is on religion texts in their original languages and Western translations. Treatises on religious beliefs and practices are also incl. Strong holdings in Buddhism, Egyptian religion, Hinduism, Judaica, Lamaistic texts, Islam, Sikhism and Zoroastrianism.
See also entry under Religion, Oriental.

ZUKOFSKY, LOUIS

CA —UNIVERSITY OF CALIFORNIA, SAN DIEGO, Central University Library, Mandeville Dept of Special Collections, La Jolla, 92093. Lynda Corey Claassen, Head; Michael Davidson, Cur, Archive for New Poetry
Notes: An extensive collection of modern English-language poetry published since World War II, the Archive contains over 28,000 books, over 1000 magazine titles, and some 900 tapes and records. The Archive maintains substantial collections of papers from Paul Blackburn, Charles Reznikoff, Lew Welch, Jerome Rothenberg, Louis Zukofsky, and other major contemporary American poets.

DE —UNIVERSITY OF DELAWARE, Hugh M Morris Library, S College Ave, Newark, 19711. T Stuart Dick, Special Collections
Holdings: Cat Mss Pix
Notes: Manuscripts, etc, incl literary correspondence.

MD —JOHNS HOPKINS UNIVERSITY, Milton S Eisenhower Library, Charles & 34 Sts, Baltimore, 21218. Ann S Gwyn, Assistant Dir for Special Collections

MO —WASHINGTON UNIVERSITY, John M Olin Library, Campus Box 1061, St Louis, 63130.
Notes: Extensive collection.

NY —NEW YORK UNIVERSITY, Elmer Holmes Bobst Library, Div of Special Collections, Washington Sq S, New York, 10012. Frank Walker, Librn; Patrick McGuire, Asst Librn
Holdings: Vols (100,000) Cat Mss Pix
Notes: The Fales Collection of first (and other) editions of English and American novels from about 1750 to date (about 70,000 titles). Mss (30,000) pieces.

BC —SIMON FRASER UNIVERSITY, Library, Burnaby, V5A 1S6, Can. Percilla Groves, Special Collections Librn
Holdings: Cat Mss
Notes: Letters to Walter Lowenfels, 10 pp ALS and TLS, plus 83 letters and 58 postcards (141 items) from Zukofsky to poet and editor Cid Corman, with Corman's marginal notes on some pieces. Also, letters (8 pp) to Clayton Eshleman.

ZUKOR, ADOLPH

CA —ACADEMY OF MOTION PICTURE ARTS & SCIENCES, Margaret Herrick Library, 8949 Wilshire Blvd, Beverly Hills, 90211. Linda Harris Mehr, Library Administrator
Notes: Papers.
See also entry under Moving Pictures.

ZUNI INDIANS

AZ —NORTHERN ARIZONA UNIVERSITY, Special Collection Library, CU Box 6022, Flagstaff, 86011. Peter M Whiteley, Coordr/Archivist; William Mullane, Librn
Notes: H C Whitener Collection: Zuni language research notes and religious and Biblical translations in the Zuni language. Incl one folder on the Havasupai language. Inventory available.

NM —GALLUP PUBLIC LIBRARY, 115 W Hill Ave, Gallup, 87301. Octavia Fellin, Dir
Holdings: Vols (8000) Cat Maps Pix

ZUPPKE, ROBERT

IL —UNIVERSITY OF ILLINOIS, URBANA/CHAMPAIGN, Library, University Archives, 19 Library, 1408 W Gregory Drive, Urbana, 61801. Maynard Brichford, University Archivist
Holdings: Cat Mss Maps Pix Slides Microforms
Notes: Papers, archival records, etc.

ZWEIG, STEFAN AND FRIDERIKE

CA —CLAREMONT COLLEGES, Honnold Library, Ninth & Dartmouth, Claremont, 91711. Tania Rizzo, Special Collections Dept Head
Holdings: Vols 33 Cat Mss
Notes: First and special British and American editions. One TV script, and one inscribed presentation copy.

MA —HARVARD UNIVERSITY LIBRARY, Houghton Library, Cambridge, 02138. Rodney G Dennis, Cur of Manuscripts
Holdings: Cat Mss

NY —STATE UNIVERSITY OF NEW YORK, COLLEGE AT FREDONIA, Daniel A Reed Library, Fredonia, 14063. John P Saulitis, Dir of Library Services; Joanne L Schweik, Supv of Special Collections; Joseph Chouinard, Music Librn
Holdings: Vols 590 Cat Pix Audiotapes
Budget: $150
Notes: The Zweig Collection incl books and correspondence relating to the Zweigs and their circle. Books incl those from Friderike's personal library, plus new additions, many of which were published during the Zweig centennial in 1981. There are copies of Stefan Zweig's works in several languages. The correspondence incl entire correspondence between Stefan and Friderike, plus more than 6440 separate pieces of correspondence to Zweig from 332 separate individuals, most of them members of European artistic and intellectual circles between 1900 and 1940. There are also photocopies of Zweig correspondence held in the State Library in Vienna, Austria, and in the Archives of the Jewish National and University Library in Jerusalem, Israel.

ZWEMER, RAYMUND LULL

DC —LIBRARY OF CONGRESS, Manuscript Division, Washington, 20540. John C Broderick, Chief
Notes: Papers. Incl 12,000 items.

ZWILLINGER, FRANK, 1909-

MA —BRANDEIS UNIVERSITY, Goldfarb Library, 415 South St, Waltham, 02154.

Bessie Hahn, Dir
Notes: Frank Zwillinger Collection: 12 linear ft of drafts, revised drafts and final drafts of poetry and dramatic presentations in German by this Austrian literary figure. Incl in the collection are 3 linear ft of tape recordings of poetry readings by this author. A finding list to the collection is located in Special Collections.